PR R

Stanley Gibbons
Simplified Catalogue

Stamps of the World

Stanley Gibbons Simplified Catalogue

Stamps of the World

2014 Edition

Countries **Abu Dhabi – Charkhari**

1

Stanley Gibbons Ltd
London and Ringwood

By Appointment to
Her Majesty The Queen
Stanley Gibbons Limited
London
Philatelists

79th Edition
Published in Great Britain by
Stanley Gibbons Ltd
Publications Editorial, Sales Offices and Distribution Centre
7, Parkside, Christchurch Road,
Ringwood, Hampshire BH24 3SH
Telephone +44 (0) 1425 472363

British Library Cataloguing in
Publication Data.
A catalogue record for this book is available
from the British Library.

Volume 1
ISBN 10: 0-85259-882-3
ISBN 13: 978-0-85259-882-5

Published as Stanley Gibbons Simplified Catalogue from 1934 to 1970, renamed Stamps of the World in 1971, and produced in two (1982-88), three (1989-2001), four (2002-2005) five (2006-2010) and six from 2011 volumes as Stanley Gibbons Simplified Catalogue of Stamps of the World.

© Stanley Gibbons Ltd 2013

Item No. 2881– Set14

Printed and bound in Wales by Stephens & George

Contents – Volume 1

Gibbons Stamp Monthly

The first choice for stamp collectors since 1890

Subscribe TODAY!

Gibbons Stamp Monthly offers you:

- Great value, usually 20-30% more pages than other stamp magazines
- More news
- More articles
- More on Great Britain and Commonwealth
- A magazine written by stamp collectors for stamp collectors
- Comprehensive catalogue supplement every month

By subscribing you will also receive:

- Monthly subscriber letters offering big discounts off Stanley Gibbons products
- Savings on the latest Stanley Gibbons catalogues
- Free access to GSM online with postal subscription

The UK's **No.1** stamp magazine

3 easy ways to subscribe

 Subscription Hotline **0800 611 622** (UK)
+44 1425 472 363 (Overseas)

 subscriptions@stanleygibbons.com

 Complete the form facing this page and return to:
Gibbons Stamp Monthly, Stanley Gibbons Publications,
FREEPOST (BH252), Ringwood, Hampshire, BH24 3BR, UK

www.stanleygibbons.com

Est 1856
STANLEY GIBBONS
A Stanley Gibbons Publication

Introduction

The ultimate reference work for all stamps issued around the world since the very first Penny Black of 1840, now with an improved layout.

Stamps of the World provides a comprehensive, illustrated, priced guide to postage stamps, and is the standard reference tool for every collector. It will help you to identify those elusive stamps, to value your collection, and to learn more about the background to issues. *Stamps of the World* was first published in 1934 and has been updated every year since 1950.

Included is a guide to stamp identification so that you can easily discover which country issued your stamp.

Re-designed to provide more colourful, clearer, and easy-to-navigate listings, these volumes continue to present you with a wealth of information to enhance your enjoyment of stamp collecting.

Features:

▶ Current values for every stamp in the world

▶ Easy-to-use simplified listings

▶ World-recognised Stanley Gibbons catalogue numbers

▶ A wealth of historical, geographical and currency information

▶ Indexing and cross-referencing throughout the volumes

▶ Worldwide miniature sheets listed and priced

▶ Thousands of new issues since the last edition

For this edition, prices have been thoroughly reviewed for Great Britain up to date, and all Commonwealth countries up to 1970, with further updates for Commonwealth countries which have appeared in our recently-published or forthcoming comprehensive catalogues under the titles *West Africa, Windward Islands and Barbados, Hong Kong, Australia, India, Northern Caribbean, Belize, Guyana and Trinidad & Tobago*. Other countries with complete price updates from the following comprehensive catalogues are: *Germany, Antarctica, South-East Asia, Scandinavia and North-East Africa*. New issues received from all other countries have been listed and priced. The first *Gibbons Stamp Monthly* Catalogue Supplement to this edition is September 2013.

Information for users

Scope of the Catalogue

Stamps of the World contains listings of postage stamps only. Apart from the ordinary definitive, commemorative and air-mail stamps of each country there are sections for the following, where appropriate. Noted below are the Prefixes used for each section (see Guide to Entries for further information):

▶ postage due stamps –	Prefix in listing D
▶ parcel post or postcard stamps –	Prefix P
▶ official stamps –	Prefix O
▶ express and special delivery stamps -	Prefix E
▶ frank stamps –	Prefix F
▶ charity tax stamps –	Prefix J
▶ newspaper and journal stamps –	Prefix N
▶ printed matter stamps –	Prefix
▶ registration stamps -	Prefix R
▶ acknowledgement of receipt stamps –	Prefix AR
▶ late fee and too late stamps –	Prefix L
▶ military post stamps-	Prefix M
▶ recorded message stamps –	Prefix RM
▶ personal delivery stamps –	Prefix P
▶ concessional letter post –	Prefix CL
▶ concessional parcel post –	Prefix CP
▶ pneumatic post stamps –	Prefix PE
▶ publicity envelope stamps –	Prefix B
▶ bulk mail stamps –	Prefix BP
▶ telegraph stamps used for postage –	Prefix PT
▶ telegraph stamps (Commonwealth Countries) –	Prefix T
▶ obligatory tax –	Prefix T

As this is a simplified listing, the following are NOT included:

Fiscal or revenue stamps: stamps used solely in collecting taxes or fees for non-postal purposes. For example, stamps which pay a tax on a receipt, represent the stamp duty on a contract, or frank a customs document. Common inscriptions found include: Documentary, Proprietary, Internal Revenue and Contract Note.

Local stamps: postage stamps whose validity and use are limited in area to a prescribed district, town or country, or on certain routes where there is no government postal service. They may be issued by private carriers and freight companies, municipal authorities or private individuals.

Local carriage labels and Private local issues: many labels exist ostensibly to cover the cost of ferrying mail from one of Great Britain's offshore islands to the nearest mainland post office. They are not recognised as valid for national or international mail. Examples: Calf of Man, Davaar, Herm, Lundy, Pabay, Stroma.

Telegraph stamps: stamps intended solely for the prepayment of telegraphic communication.

Bogus or "phantom" stamps: labels from mythical places or non-existent administrations. Examples in the classical period were Sedang, Counani, Clipperton Island and in modern times Thomond and Monte Bello Islands. Numerous labels have also appeared since the War from dissident groups as propaganda for their claims and without authority from the home governments. Common examples are the numerous issues for Nagaland.

Railway letter fee stamps: special stamps issued by railway companies for the conveyance of letters by rail. Example: Talyllyn Railway. Similar services are now offered by some bus companies and the labels they issue likewise do not qualify for inclusion in the catalogue.

Perfins ("perforated initials"): stamps perforated with the initials or emblems of firms as a security measure to prevent pilferage by office staff.

Labels: Slips of paper with an adhesive backing. Collectors tend to make a distinction between stamps, which have postal validity and anything else, which has not.

Cut-outs: Embossed or impressed stamps found on postal stationery, which are cut out if the stationery has been ruined and re-used as adhesives.

Further information on a wealth of terms is in *Philatelic Terms Illustrated*, published by Stanley Gibbons, details are listed under Stanley Gibbons Publications. There is also a priced listing of the postal fiscals of Great Britain in our *Commonwealth & British Empire Stamps 1840-1970* Catalogue and in Volume 1 of the *Great Britain Specialised Catalogue* (5th and later editions). A full list of our current publications is given on page li

Organisation of the Catalogue

The catalogue lists countries in alphabetical order with country headers on each page and extra introductory information such as philatelic historical background at the beginning of each section. The Contents list provides a detailed guide to each volume, and the Index has full cross-referencing to locate each country in each volume.

Each country lists postage stamps in order of date of issue, from earliest to most recent, followed by separate sections for categories such as postage due stamps, express stamps, official stamps, and so on (see above for a complete listing).

"Appendix" Countries

Since 1968 Stanley Gibbons has listed in an appendix stamps which are judged to be in excess of true postal needs. The appendix also contains stamps which have not fulfilled all the

normal conditions for full catalogue listing. Full catalogue listing requires a stamp to be:

- ▶ issued by a legitimate postal authority
- ▶ recognised by the government concerned
- ▶ adhesive
- ▶ valid for proper postal use in the class of service for which they are inscribed
- ▶ available to the general public at face value with no artificial restrictions being imposed on their distribution (with the exception of categories such as postage dues and officials)

Only stamps issued from component parts of otherwise united territories which represent a genuine political, historical or postal division within the country concerned have a full catalogue listing. Any such issues which do not fulfil this stipulation will be recorded in the Catalogue Appendix only.

Stamps listed in the Appendix are constantly under review in light of newly acquired information about them. If we are satisfied that a stamp qualifies for proper listing in the body of the catalogue it will be moved in the next edition.

"Undesirable Issues"

The rules governing many competitive exhibitions are set by the Federation Internationale de Philatelie and stipulate a downgrading of marks for stamps classed as "undesirable issues".

This catalogue can be taken as a guide to status. All stamps in the main listings are acceptable. Stamps in the Appendix are considered, "undesirable issues" and should not be entered for competition.

Correspondence

We welcome information and suggestions but we must ask correspondents to include the cost of postage for the return of any materials, plus registration where appropriate. Letters and emails should be addressed to Lorraine Holcombe, 7 Parkside, Christchurch Road, Ringwood, Hampshire BH24 3SH, UK. lholcombe@stanleygibbons.co.uk. Where information is solicited purely for the benefit of the enquirer we regret we are seldom able to reply.

Identification of Stamps

We regret we do not give opinion on the authenticity of stamps, nor do we identify stamps or number them by our Catalogue.

Thematic Collectors

Stanley Gibbons publishes a range of thematic catalogues (see page li for details) and *Stamps of the World* is ideal to use with these titles, as it supplements those listings with extra information.

Type numbers

Type numbers (in bold) refer to illustrations, and are not the Stanley Gibbons Catalogue numbers.

A brief description of the stamp design subject is given below or beside the illustrations, or close by in the entry, where needed. Where a design is not illustrated, it is usually the same shape and size as a related design, unless otherwise indicated.

Watermarks

Watermarks are not covered in this catalogue. Stamps of the same issue with differing watermarks are not listed separately.

Perforations

Perforations – all stamps are perforated unless otherwise stated. No distinction is made between the various gauges of perforation but early stamp issues which exist both imperforate and perforated are usually listed separately. Where a heading states, "Imperf or perf" or "Perf. or rouletted" this does not necessarily mean that all values of the issue are found in both conditions

Se-tenant Pairs

Se-tenant Pairs – Many modern issues are printed in sheets containing different designs or face values. Such pairs, blocks, strips or sheets are described as being "*se-tenant*" and they are outside the scope of this catalogue, although reference to them may occur in instances where they form a composite design.

Miniature Sheets are now fully listed.

Guide to Entries

x

A **Country of Issue**

B **Part Number** – shows where to find more detailed listings in the Stanley Gibbons Comprehensive Catalogue. Part 6 refers to France and so on – see p. li for further information on the breakdown of the Catalogue.

C **Country Information** – Brief geographical and historical details for the issuing country.

D **Currency** – Details of the currency, and dates of earliest use where applicable, on the face value of the stamps. Where a Colony has the same currency as the Mother Country, see the details given in that country.

E **Year Date** – When a set of definitive stamps has been issued over several years the Year Date given is for the earliest issue, commemorative sets are listed in chronological order. As stamps of the same design or issue are usually grouped together, a list of King George VI stamps, for example, headed "1938" may include stamps issued from 1938 to the end of the reign.

F **Stanley Gibbons Catalogue number** – This is a unique number for each stamp to help the collector identify stamps in the listing. The Stanley Gibbons numbering system is universally recognized as definitive. The majority of listings are in chronological order, but where a definitive set of stamps has been re-issued with a new watermark, perforation change or imprint date, the cheapest example is given; in such cases catalogue numbers may not be in numerical order.

Where insufficient numbers have been left to provide for additional stamps to a listing, some stamps will have a suffix letter after the catalogue number. If numbers have been left for additions to a set and not used they will be left vacant.

The separate type numbers (in bold) refer to illustrations (see **M**).

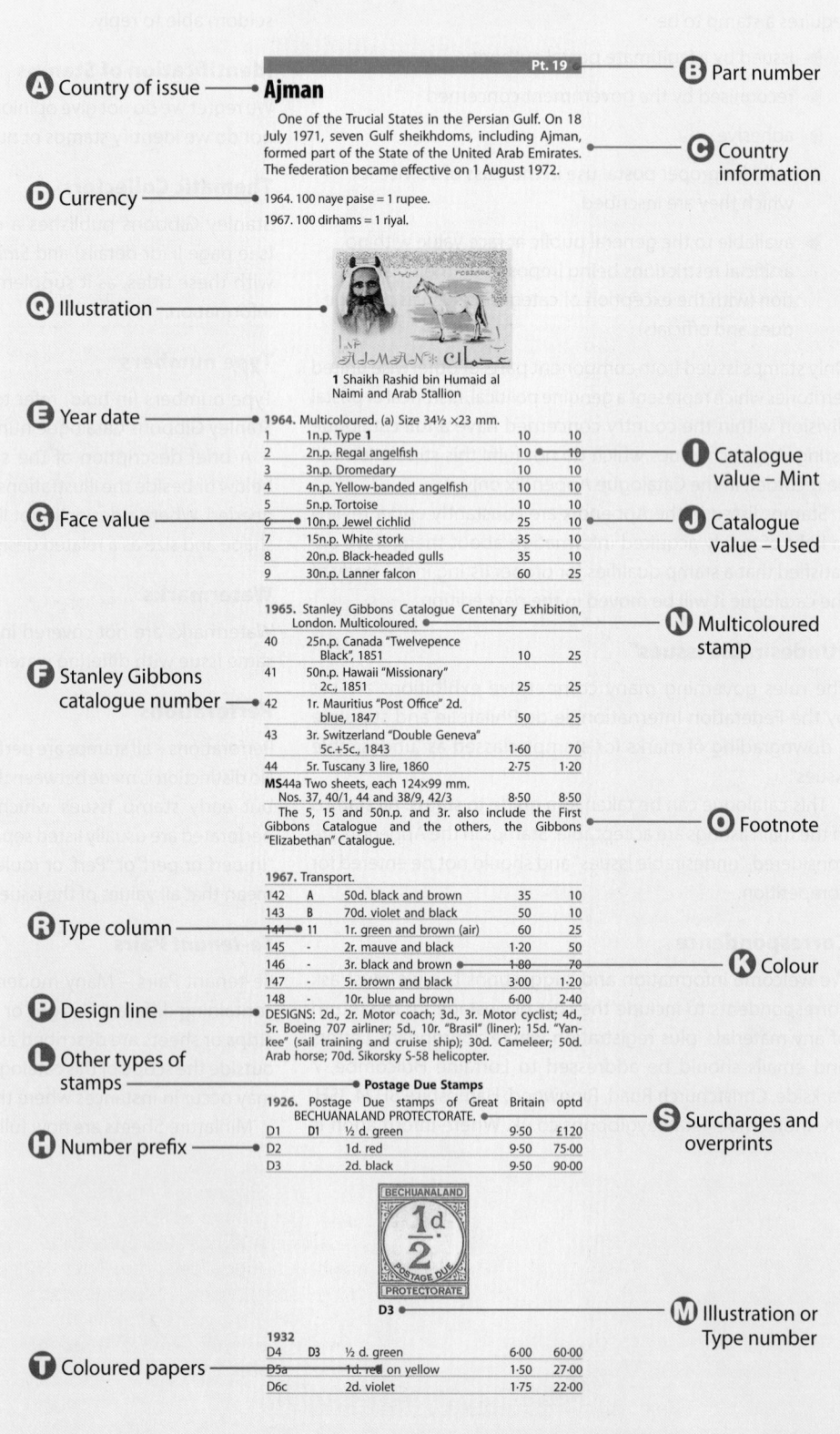

A Country of issue ⟶ **Ajman** ⟵ **B** Part number / Pt. 19

One of the Trucial States in the Persian Gulf. On 18 July 1971, seven Gulf sheikhdoms, including Ajman, formed part of the State of the United Arab Emirates. The federation became effective on 1 August 1972. ⟵ **C** Country information

D Currency ⟶ 1964. 100 naye paise = 1 rupee.
1967. 100 dirhams = 1 riyal.

Q Illustration

1 Shaikh Rashid bin Humaid al Naimi and Arab Stallion

E Year date ⟶ 1964. Multicoloured. (a) Size 34½ ×23 mm.

			Mint	Used
1		1n.p. Type **1**	10	10
2		2n.p. Regal angelfish	10	10
3		3n.p. Dromedary	10	10
4		4n.p. Yellow-banded angelfish	10	10
5		5n.p. Tortoise	10	10
6		10n.p. Jewel cichlid	25	10
7		15n.p. White stork	35	10
8		20n.p. Black-headed gulls	35	10
9		30n.p. Lanner falcon	60	25

G Face value
I Catalogue value – Mint
J Catalogue value – Used

1965. Stanley Gibbons Catalogue Centenary Exhibition, London. Multicoloured. ⟵ **N** Multicoloured stamp

40		25n.p. Canada "Twelvepence Black", 1851	10	25
41		50n.p. Hawaii "Missionary" 2c., 1851	25	25
42		1r. Mauritius "Post Office" 2d. blue, 1847	50	25
43		3r. Switzerland "Double Geneva" 5c.+5c., 1843	1·60	70
44		5r. Tuscany 3 lire, 1860	2·75	1·20

MS44a Two sheets, each 124×99 mm. Nos. 37, 40/1, 44 and 38/9, 42/3 | 8·50 | 8·50

The 5, 15 and 50n.p. and 3r. also include the First Gibbons Catalogue and the others, the Gibbons "Elizabethan" Catalogue. ⟵ **O** Footnote

1967. Transport.

					Mint	Used
142	A		50d. black and brown		35	10
143	B		70d. violet and black		50	10
144	11		1r. green and brown (air)		60	25
145	-		2r. mauve and black		1·20	50
146	-		3r. black and brown		1·80	70
147	-		5r. brown and black		3·00	1·20
148	-		10r. blue and brown		6·00	2·40

R Type column
K Colour

P Design line ⟶ DESIGNS: 2d., 2r. Motor coach; 3d., 3r. Motor cyclist; 4d., 5r. Boeing 707 airliner; 5d., 1r. "Brasil" (liner); 15d. "Yankee" (sail training and cruise ship); 30d. Cameleer; 50d. Arab horse; 70d. Sikorsky S-58 helicopter.

L Other types of stamps ⟶ **Postage Due Stamps**

1926. Postage Due stamps of Great Britain optd BECHUANALAND PROTECTORATE. ⟵ **S** Surcharges and overprints

				Mint	Used
D1	D1	½d. green		9·50	£120
D2		1d. red		9·50	75·00
D3		2d. black		9·50	90·00

H Number prefix

BECHUANALAND
1d.
½
POSTAGE DUE
PROTECTORATE

D3 ⟵ **M** Illustration or Type number

1932

				Mint	Used
D4	D3	½d. green		6·00	60·00
D5a		1d. red on yellow		1·50	27·00
D6c		2d. violet		1·75	22·00

T Coloured papers

462 Canadian
Maple Leaf
Emblem

1981
1030a **462** A (30c.) red 20 40
No. 1030a was printed before a new first class domes-
tic letter rate had been agreed, "A" representing the face
value of the stamp, later decided to be 30c.

G Face value – This refers to the value of
each stamp and is the price it was sold
for at the Post Office when issued. Some
modern stamps do not have their values in
figures but instead shown as a letter, see
for example the entry above for Canada
1030a/Illustration 462.

H Number Prefix – Stamps other than
definitives and commemoratives have a
prefix letter before the catalogue number.
Such stamps may be found at the end of
the normal listing for each country. (See
Scope of the Catalogue p.viii for a list of
other types of stamps covered, together
with the list of the main abbreviations used
in the Catalogue).

Other prefixes are also used in the
Catalogue. Their use is explained in the
text: some examples are A for airmail, E for
East Germany or Express Delivery stamps.

I Catalogue Value – Mint/Unused. Prices
quoted for pre-1945 stamps are for lightly
hinged examples. Prices quoted of unused
King Edward VIII to Queen Elizabeth II
issues are for unmounted mint.

J Catalogue Value – Used. Prices generally
refer to fine postally used examples. For
certain issues they are for cancelled-to-
order.

Prices
Prices are given in pence and pounds.
Stamps worth £100 and over are shown in
whole pounds:

Shown in Catalogue as	Explanation
10	10 pence
1.75	£1.75
15.00	£15
£150	£150
£2300	£2300

Prices assume stamps are in 'fine condition';
we may ask more for superb and less
for those of lower quality. The minimum

catalogue price quoted is 10p and is
intended as a guide for catalogue users.
The lowest price for individual stamps
purchased from Stanley Gibbons is £1.

Prices quoted are for the cheapest
variety of that particular stamp. Differences
of watermark, perforation, or other details,
outside the scope of this catalogue, often
increase the value. Prices quoted for mint
issues are for single examples. Those in
se-tenant pairs, strips, blocks or sheets
may be worth more. Where no prices
are listed it is either because the stamps
are not known to exist in that particular
condition, or, more usually, because there
is no reliable information on which to base
their value.

All prices are subject to change without
prior notice and we cannot guarantee
to supply all stamps as priced. Prices
quoted in advertisements are also subject
to change without prior notice. Due to
differing production schedules it is possible
that new editions of Parts 2 to 22 will show
revised prices which are not included in
that year's Stamps of the World.

K Colour – Colour of stamp (if fewer
than four colours, otherwise noted as
"multicoloured"– see N below). Colour
descriptions are simple in this catalogue,
and only expanded to aid identification
– see other more comprehensive Stanley
Gibbons catalogues for more detailed
colour descriptions (see p.xxxix).
Where stamps are printed in two or more
colours, the central portion of the design
is the first colour given, unless otherwise
stated.

L Other Types of Stamps – See Scope of
the Catalogue p.viii for a list of the types of
stamps included.

M Illustration or Type Number – These
numbers are used to help identify stamps,
either in the listing, type column, design line
or footnote, usually the first value in a set.
These type numbers are in a bold type face
– **123**; when bracketed (**123**) an overprint
or a surcharge is indicated. Some type
numbers include a lower-case letter – **123a**,
this indicates they have been added to an
existing set. New cross references are also
normally shown in bold, as in the example
below.

1990. Small Craft of Canada (2nd series). Early Work
Boats. As T **563**. Multicoloured.

N Multicoloured – Nearly all modern stamps
are multicoloured; this is indicated in the
heading, with a description of the stamp
given in the listing.

O Footnote – further information on
background or key facts on issues

P Design line – Further details on design
variations

Q Illustration – Generally, the first stamp in
the set. Stamp illustrations are reduced to
75%, with overprints and surcharges shown
actual size.

R Key Type – indicates a design type (see p.
xii for further details) on which the stamp
is based. These are the bold figures found
below each illustration. The type numbers
are also given in bold in the second column
of figures alongside the stamp description
to indicate the design of each stamp.
Where an issue comprises stamps of similar
design, the corresponding type number
should be taken as indicating the general
design. Where there are blanks in the type
number column it means that the type of
the corresponding stamp is that shown
by the number in the type column of the
same issue. A dash (–) in the type column
means that the stamp is not illustrated.
Where type numbers refer to stamps of
another country, e.g. where stamps of one
country are overprinted for use in another,
this is always made clear in the text.

S Surcharges and Overprints – usually
described in the headings. Any actual
wordings are shown in bold type.
Descriptions clarify words and figures used
in the overprint. Stamps with the same
overprints in different colours are not listed
separately. Numbers in brackets after the
descriptions are the catalogue numbers of
the non-overprinted stamps. The words
"inscribed" or "inscription" refer to the
wording incorporated in the design of a
stamp and not surcharges or overprints.

T Coloured Papers – stamps printed on
coloured paper are shown – e.g. "brn on
yell" indicates brown printed on yellow
paper. No information on the texture of
paper, e.g. laid or wove, is provided in this
catalogue.

Key-Types

Standard designs frequently occuring on the stamps of the French, German, Portuguese and Spanish colonies are illustrated below together with the descriptive names and letters by which they are referred to in the lists to avoid repetition. Please see the Guide to Entries for further information.

French Group

A "Blanc" B "Mouchon" C "Merson" D "Tablet"

INTERNATIONAL COLONIAL EXHIBITION

E F " G H

I "Faidherbe" J "Palms" K "Balay" L "Natives" M "Figure"

German Group

N "Yacht" O "Yacht"

Spanish Group

X "Alfonso XII" Y "Baby" Z "Curly Head"

Portuguese Group

P "Crown" Q "Embossed" R "Figures" S "Carlos" T "Manoel" U Ceres V "Newspaper" W "Due"

Selling Your Stamps?

Summary Tip #18: When it comes to Selling - all collections are Not created Equal.

Dear Collector,

I will return to the surprisingly large subject of 'certificates' in another article - but this article is prompted by developments we have observed over the past few years when purchasing private stamp collections.

Traditionally there are 5 different ways to sell your stamps:

1. The Stamp Dealer or Stamp Auction buying on their own account.
2. Dealers 'runners'.
3. Private Treaty - the idea of Private Treaty is that collectors 'place' their collection with a dealer or auction that charges a small commission (or the buyer a commission) to purchase the collection outright. Historically 'Private Treaty' has acquired notoriety as an excuse for the company handling the transaction to 'buy-in' the collection for themselves. Fortunately things are more transparent now.
4. Selling through auction on your own account - the auction house charges you a commission and handling costs.
5. Finally - the internet now permits you to sell your stamps on-line upon your own account via internet giants such as 'eBay'.

In selling your stamps there are two principles to understand. Collectors want to buy stamps that are missing in their collections: this is why Dealers exist. Dealers buy collections to 'break-down' into usually smaller units that collectors need for their collections: generally speaking breaking down for sale into small/smaller units adds 'value' and profit for the dealer.

Some collectors are 'hoarders' and will buy general lots - other collectors will buy intermediate sized collections in order to 'extract' the stamps they want ... and then 'turn' the balance back for resale to dealer or auction. The idea that collectors will buy large complete intact collections at retail prices is quaint and outmoded. In almost 40 years of dealing I have seen few intact collections purchased by collectors and continued by new collectors. Collectors enjoy creating their own collections. Few collectors have the budget to purchase a substantial intact collection and develop it still further.

Know your 'strengths' - (know the strength of your collection).

Choosing who is best to approach to sell your stamps or handle them depends upon your knowing the 'strength' and merits of your collection. For example ... on a basic level - if your collection consists of all different modern British sets that you have bought from the Post Offi ce at 'face value' ... the last thing you want to do is send this collection to auction. All you will be doing is paying an auction's commissions - up to 35% for them to sell your stamps, most probably, to a dealer below 'face value' - who will use a fair percentage of them upon commercial correspondence.

A few phone calls to dealers will elicit the percentage of 'face value' that the trade is paying for stamps that there are too many of - because the Post Office has recently printed and sold them.

Just don't forget to ask if there is anything 'better' in the period that you are selling - that may command a higher price.

In our next article (Volume 2) we'll focus on the merits of the 5 different ways to sell your stamps ... and which may be best for you.

Happy collecting from us all,

Andrew

PS. If you find this 'tip' interesting please forward it to a philatelic friend.

Andrew McGavin
Managing Director: Universal Philatelic Auctions, Omniphil & Avon Approvals, Avon Mixtures, UniversalPhilatelic (Ebay)

To read the rest of this series 'SELLING YOUR STAMPS?' see the relevant pages in each volume:

Summary Tip 18 – Volume 1 (opposite Key Types)
Summary Tip 19 – Volume 2 (opposite Key Types)
Summary Tip 20 – Volume 3 (opposite Key Types)
Summary Tip 21 – Volume 4 (opposite Key Types)
Summary Tip 22 – Volume 5 (opposite Key Types)

Please go to Volume 6 (opposite Key Types) to see how UPA can pay you up to 36% more for your collection.

Stanley Gibbons
Great Britain Department

World renowned specialist dealers in all aspects of Great Britain philatelic material and producer of the classic specialist reference catalogues. We are conveniently based in central London.

We have a team of specialist sales professionals who are always willing to help you find that elusive item for your collection. We produce a monthly catalogue of over 500 items of specialist stock and would be delighted to add your name to our database to receive this. Our catalogues and price lists are recognised throughout the industry as essential reference material and we offer you a lifetime guarantee of authenticity for your complete reassurance.
We have a worldwide client database that appreciates our range and depth of stock. We always hold in excess of £5 million of specialist material in stock alone and are recognised worldwide as leaders in the Great Britain philatelic field.

With our offices open from 09.00 to 17.30 we are here to help you with all your GB philatelic requirements, Please feel free to contact us.

Our services include:

- Over 3000 specialist items always in stock
- Monthly sales catalogue of over 500 items
- Production of World renowned specialist catalogues
- Industry standard price catalogues
- Respected for quality material throughout the trade
- Online shop -
 visit www.stanleygibbons.com for a full stocklisting
- Monitoring of clients wants list
- Lifetime guarantee of authenticity

Simply contact Mark Facey on **020 7557 4424** email **mfacey@stanleygibbons.com**
or Michael Barrell on **020 7557 4448** email **mbarrell@stanleygibbons.com** to register

Est 1856
STANLEY GIBBONS

Stanley Gibbons Limited
399 Strand, London, WC2R 0LX
+44 (0)20 7836 8444
www.stanleygibbons.com

Glossary of terms

English	French	German	Spanish	Italian	Arabic	English
Agate	Agate	Achat	Agata	Agata	عقيقي	Agate
Air stamp	Timbre de la poste aérienne	Flugpostmarke	Sello de correo aéreo	Francobollo per posta aerea	طابع بريد جوي	Air stamp
Apple Green	Vert-pomme	Apfelgrün	Verde manzana	Verde mela	أخضر تفاحي	Apple Green
Barred	Annulé par barres	Balkenentwertung	Anulado con barras	Sbarrato		Barred
Bisected	Timbre coupé	Halbiert	Partido en dos	Frazionato	مقسوم الى شطرين	Bisected
Bistre	Bistre	Bister	Bistre	Bistro	الذهبي المطفي - بيج	Bistre
Bistre-brown	Brun-bistre	Bisterbraun	Castaño bistre	Bruno-bistro	بيج غامق	Bistre-brown
Black	Noir	Schwarz	Negro	Nero	أسود	Black
Blackish Brown	Brun-noir	Schwärzlichbraun	Castaño negruzco	Bruno nerastro	بني مسود	Blackish Brown
Blackish Green	Vert foncé	Schwärzlichgrün	Verde negruzco	Verde nerastro	أخضر مسود	Blackish Green
Blackish Olive	Olive foncé	Schwärzlicholiv	Oliva negruzco	Oliva nerastro	زيتي مسود	Blackish Olive
Block of four	Bloc de quatre	Viererblock	Bloque de cuatro	Bloco di quattro	أربعة قطعة واحدة	Block of four
Blue	Bleu	Blau	Azul	Azzurro	أزرق	Blue
Blue-green	Vert-bleu	Blaugrün	Verde azul	Verde azzuro	أخضر مزرق	Blue-green
Bluish Violet	Violet bleuâtre	Bläulichviolett	Violeta azulado	Violtto azzurrastro	بنفسجي مزرق	Bluish Violet
Booklet	Carnet	Heft	Cuadernillo	Libretto	دفتر طوابع	Booklet
Bright Blue	Bleu vif	Lebhaftblau	Azul vivo	Azzurro vivo	أزرق فاتح	Bright Blue
Bright Green	Vert vif	Lebhaftgrün	Verde vivo	Verde vivo	أخضر فاتح	Bright Green
Bright Purple	Mauve vif	Lebhaftpurpur	Púrpura vivo	Porpora vivo	بنفسجي فاتح	Bright Purple
Bronze Green	Vert-bronze	Bronzegrün	Verde bronce	Verde bronzo	أخضر برونزي	Bronze Green
Brown	Brun	Braun	Castaño	Bruno	بني	Brown
Brown-lake	Carmin-brun	Braunlack	Laca castaño	Lacca bruno	بني قرميدي	Brown-lake
Brown-purple	Pourpre-brun	Braunpurpur	Púrpura castaño	Porpora bruno	البنفسجي الغامق	Brown-purple
Brown-red	Rouge-brun	Braunrot	Rojo castaño	Rosso bruno	أحمر غامق	Brown-red
Buff	Chamois	Sämisch	Anteado	Camoscio	أصفر داكن	Buff
Cancellation	Oblitération	Entwertung	Cancelación	Annullamento	الإلغاء	Cancellation
Cancelled	Annulé	Gestempelt	Cancelado	Annullato	ملغى	Cancelled
Carmine	Carmin	Karmin	Carmín	Carminio	قرمزي	Carmine
Carmine-red	Rouge-carmin	Karminrot	Rojo carmín	Rosso carminio	أحمر قرمزي	Carmine-red
Centred	Centré	Zentriert	Centrado	Centrato	متوسط	Centred
Cerise	Rouge-cerise	Kirschrot	Color de ceresa	Color Ciliegia	أحمر فاتح	Cerise
Chalk-surfaced paper	Papier couché	Kreidepapier	Papel estucado	Carta gessata	ورق سطحه طباشيري	Chalk-surfaced paper
Chalky Blue	Bleu terne	Kreideblau	Azul turbio	Azzurro smorto	أزرق طباشيري	Chalky Blue
Charity stamp	Timbre de bienfaisance	Wohltätigkeitsmarke	Sello de beneficenza	Francobollo di beneficenza	طابع خيري	Charity stamp
Chestnut	Marron	Kastanienbraun	Castaño rojo	Marrone	بني فاتح - كستناوي	Chestnut
Chocolate	Chocolat	Schokolade	Chocolate	Cioccolato	شوكولا	Chocolate
Cinnamon	Cannelle	Zimtbraun	Canela	Cannella	بني فاتح جدا - بيج	Cinnamon
Claret	Grenat	Weinrot	Rojo vinoso	Vinaccia	أحمر داكن	Claret
Cobalt	Cobalt	Kobalt	Cobalto	Cobalto	أزرق سماوي	Cobalt
Colour	Couleur	Farbe	Color	Colore	لون	Colour
Comb-perforation	Dentelure en peigne	Kammzähnung, Reihenzähnung	Dentado de peine	Dentellatura e pettine	تخريم مشطي	Comb-perforation
Commemorative stamp	Timbre commémoratif	Gedenkmarke	Sello conmemorativo	Francobollo commemorativo	طابع تذكاري	Commemorative stamp
Crimson	Cramoisi	Karmesin	Carmesí	Cremisi	أحمر داكن ـ قرزي	Crimson

English	French	German	Spanish	Italian	Arabic	English
Deep Blue	Blue foncé	Dunkelblau	Azul oscuro	Azzurro scuro	كحلي ـ أزرق غامق	Deep Blue
Deep bluish Green	Vert-bleu foncé	Dunkelbläulichgrün	Verde azulado oscuro	Verde azzurro scuro	أخضر غامق	Deep bluish Green
Design	Dessin	Markenbild	Diseño	Disegno	التصميم	Design
Die	Matrice	Urstempel. Type Platte,	Cuño	Conio, Matrice	قالب حديد يستخدم للصك	Die
Double	Double	Doppelt	Doble	Doppio	ضعف الكمية	Double
Drab	Olive terne	Trüboliv	Oliva turbio	Oliva smorto	لون كاكي	Drab
Dull Green	Vert terne	Trübgrün	Verde turbio	Verde smorto	أخضر باهت	Dull Green
Dull purple	Mauve terne	Trübpurpur	Púrpura turbio	Porpora smorto	بنفسجي باهت	Dull purple
Embossing	Impression en relief	Prägedruck	Impresión en relieve	Impressione a relievo	نافر ـ بارز	Embossing
Emerald	Vert-eméraude	Smaragdgrün	Esmeralda	Smeraldo	الزمرد	Emerald
Engraved	Gravé	Graviert	Grabado	Inciso	منقوش ـ طباعة بالحفر	Engraved
Error	Erreur	Fehler, Fehldruck	Error	Errore	خطأ	Error
Essay	Essai	Probedruck	Ensayo	Saggio	تجارب طباعية	Essay
Express letter stamp	Timbre pour lettres par exprès	Eilmarke	Sello de urgencia	Francobollo per espresso	طابع رسالة سريعه	Express letter stamp
Fiscal stamp	Timbre fiscal	Stempelmarke	Sello fiscal	Francobollo fiscale	طابع مالي	Fiscal stamp
Flesh	Chair	Fleischfarben	Carne	Carnicino	زهري غامق	Flesh
Forgery	Faux, Falsification	Fälschung	Falsificación	Falso, Falsificazione	تزييف	Forgery
Frame	Cadre	Rahmen	Marco	Cornice	إطار	Frame
Granite paper	Papier avec fragments de fils de soie	Faserpapier	Papel con filamentos	Carto con fili di seta	ورق الجرانيت	Granite paper
Green	Vert	Grün	Verde	Verde	أخضر	Green
Greenish Blue	Bleu verdâtre	Grünlichblau	Azul verdoso	Azzurro verdastro	أخضر مزرق	Greenish Blue
Greenish Yellow	Jaune-vert	Grünlichgelb	Amarillo verdoso	Giallo verdastro	أخضر مصفر	Greenish Yellow
Grey	Gris	Grau	Gris	Grigio	رمادي	Grey
Grey-blue	Bleu-gris	Graublau	Azul gris	Azzurro grigio	رمادي مزرق	Grey-blue
Grey-green	Vert gris	Graugrün	Verde gris	Verde grigio	رمادي مخضر	Grey-green
Gum	Gomme	Gummi	Goma	Gomma	صمغ	Gum
Gutter	Interpanneau	Zwischensteg	Espacio blanco entre dos grupos	Ponte	فراغ أبيض يفصل بين طابعين	Gutter
Imperforate	Non-dentelé	Geschnitten	Sin dentar	Non dentellato	غير مثقب ـ بدون تخريم	Imperforate
Indigo	Indigo	Indigo	Azul indigo	Indaco	نيلي ـ أزرق غامق	Indigo
Inscription	Inscription	Inschrift	Inscripción	Dicitura	النقش	Inscription
Inverted	Renversé	Kopfstehend	Invertido	Capovolto	معكوس ـ مقلوب	Inverted
Issue	Émission	Ausgabe	Emisión	Emissione	اصدار	Issue
Laid	Vergé	Gestreift	Listado	Vergato		Laid
Lake	Lie de vin	Lackfarbe	Laca	Lacca	أحمر غامق جداً ـ أحمر دموي	Lake
Lake-brown	Brun-carmin	Lackbraun	Castaño laca	Bruno lacca	أحمر أجري	Lake-brown
Lavender	Bleu-lavande	Lavendel	Color de alhucema	Lavanda	لون الموف	Lavender
Lemon	Jaune-citron	Zitrongelb	Limón	Limone	ليموني	Lemon
Light Blue	Bleu clair	Hellblau	Azul claro	Azzurro chiaro	أزرق فاتح	Light Blue
Lilac	Lilas	Lila	Lila	Lilla	لون نهدي	Lilac
Line perforation	Dentelure en lignes	Linienzähnung	Dentado en linea	Dentellatura lineare	ثقب الخط	Line perforation
Lithography	Lithographie	Steindruck	Litografía	Litografia	طباعة حجرية	Lithography
Local	Timbre de poste locale	Lokalpostmarke	Emisión local	Emissione locale	محلي	Local
Lozenge roulette	Percé en losanges	Rautenförmiger Durchstich	Picadura en rombos	Perforazione a losanghe	تخريم ناعم	Lozenge roulette
Magenta	Magenta	Magentarot	Magenta	Magenta	قرمزي	Magenta
Margin	Marge	Rand	Borde	Margine	هامش	Margin
Maroon	Marron pourpré	Dunkelrotpurpur	Púrpura rojo oscuro	Marrone rossastro	بنفسجي غامق	Maroon
Mauve	Mauve	Malvenfarbe	Malva	Malva	بنفسجي	Mauve
Multicoloured	Polychrome	Mehrfarbig	Multicolores	Policromo	متعدد الألوان	Multicoloured
Myrtle Green	Vert myrte	Myrtengrün	Verde mirto	Verde mirto	أخضر غامق	Myrtle Green

English	French	German	Spanish	Italian	Arabic	English
New Blue	Bleu ciel vif	Neublau	Azul nuevo	Azzurro nuovo	أزرق جديد	New Blue
Newspaper stamp	Timbre pour journaux	Zeitungsmarke	Sello para periódicos	Francobollo per giornali	طابع جريدة	Newspaper stamp
Obliteration	Oblitération	Abstempelung	Matasello	Annullamento	طمس	Obliteration
Obsolete	Hors (de) cours	Ausser Kurs	Fuera de curso	Fuori corso	لايستخدم	Obsolete
Ochre	Ocre	Ocker	Ocre	Ocra	بيج	Ochre
Official stamp	Timbre de service	Dienstmarke	Sello de servicio	Francobollo di	طابع حكومي	Official stamp
Olive-brown	Brun-olive	Olivbraun	Castaño oliva	Bruno oliva	بني زيتوني	Olive-brown
Olive-green	Vert-olive	Olivgrün	Verde oliva	Verde oliva	أخضر زيتوني	Olive-green
Olive-grey	Gris-olive	Olivgrau	Gris oliva	Grigio oliva	رمادي زيتوني	Olive-grey
Olive-yellow	Jaune-olive	Olivgelb	Amarillo oliva	Giallo oliva	أصفر زيتوني	Olive-yellow
Orange	Orange	Orange	Naranja	Arancio	برتقالي	Orange
Orange-brown	Brun-orange	Orangebraun	Castaño naranja	Bruno arancio	بني برتقالي	Orange-brown
Orange-red	Rouge-orange	Orangerot	Rojo naranja	Rosso arancio	أحمر برتقالي	Orange-red
Orange-yellow	Jaune-orange	Orangegelb	Amarillo naranja	Giallo arancio	أصفر برتقالي	Orange-yellow
Overprint	Surcharge	Aufdruck	Sobrecarga	Soprastampa	توشيح	Overprint
Pair	Paire	Paar	Pareja	Coppia	زوج	Pair
Pale	Pâle	Blass	Pálido	Pallido	شطب على القيمة أو	Pale
Pane	Panneau	Gruppe	Grupo	Gruppo	لوح	Pane
Paper	Papier	Papier	Papel	Carta	ورقة	Paper
Parcel post stamp	Timbre pour colis postaux	Paketmarke	Sello para paquete postal	Francobollo per pacchi postali	رزمة طوابع البريد	Parcel post stamp
Pen-cancelled	Oblitéré à plume	Federzugentwertung	Cancelado a pluma	Annullato a penna	ملغي بالقلم ـ مشطوب بالقلم	Pen-cancelled
Percé en arc	Percé en arc	Bogenförmiger Durchstich	Picadura en forma de arco	Perforazione ad arco	ثقب	Percé en arc
Percé en scie	Percé en scie	Bogenförmiger Durchstich	Picado en sierra	Foratura a sega	تخريم	Percé en scie
Perforated	Dentelé	Gezähnt	Dentado	Dentellato	صوة أبيض واسود	Perforated
Perforation	Dentelure	Zähnung	Dentar	Dentellatura	ثقب دبوس	Perforation
Photogravure	Photogravure, Heliogravure	Rastertiefdruck	Fotograbado	Rotocalco	صفحة لتحديد مكان الطبع	Photogravure
Pin perforation	Percé en points	In Punkten durchstochen	Horadado con alfileres	Perforato a punti	لون خوخي	Pin perforation
Plate	Planche	Platte	Plancha	Lastra, Tavola	طابع أجرة بريد مستحق	Plate
Plum	Prune	Pflaumenfarbe	Color de ciruela	Prugna	لون خوخي	Plum
Postage Due stamp	Timbre-taxe	Portomarke	Sello de tasa	Segnatasse	طابع مالي بريدي	Postage Due stamp
Postage stamp	Timbre-poste	Briefmarke, Freimarke, Postmarke	Sello de correos	Francobollo postale	طابع بريدي	Postage stamp
Postal fiscal stamp	Timbre fiscal-postal	Stempelmarke als Postmarke verwendet	Sello fiscal-postal	Fiscale postale	طابع مالي بريدي	Postal fiscal stamp
Postmark	Oblitération postale	Poststempel	Matasello	Bollo	ختم البريد	Postmark
Printing	Impression, Tirage	Druck	Impresión	Stampa, Tiratura	طباعة	Printing
Proof	Épreuve	Druckprobe	Prueba de impresión	Prova	بروفا	Proof
Provisionals	Timbres provisoires	Provisorische Marken. Provisorien	Provisionales	Provvisori	مؤقت ـ طابع محلي	Provisionals
Prussian Blue	Bleu de Prusse	Preussischblau	Azul de Prusia	Azzurro di Prussia	أزرق مسود	Prussian Blue
Purple	Pourpre	Purpur	Púrpura	Porpora	أرجواني	Purple
Purple-brown	Brun-pourpre	Purpurbraun	Castaño púrpura	Bruno porpora	بني ارجواني	Purple-brown
Recess-printing	Impression en taille douce	Tiefdruck	Grabado	Incisione	طباعة زاحفة	Recess-printing
Red	Rouge	Rot	Rojo	Rosso	أحم	Red
Red-brown	Brun-rouge	Rotbraun	Castaño rojizo	Bruno rosso	بني محمر	Red-brown
Reddish Lilac	Lilas rougeâtre	Rötlichlila	Lila rojizo	Lilla rossastro	أحمر زهري	Reddish Lilac
Reddish Purple	Poupre-rouge	Rötlichpurpur	Púrpura rojizo	Porpora rossastro	أرجواني محمر	Reddish Purple
Reddish Violet	Violet rougeâtre	Rötlichviolett	Violeta rojizo	Violetto rossastro	بنفسجي محمر	Reddish Violet
Red-orange	Orange rougeâtre	Rotorange	Naranja rojizo	Arancio rosso	برتقالي محمر	Red-orange
Registration stamp	Timbre pour lettre chargée (recommandée)	Einschreibemarke	Sello de certificado lettere	Francobollo per raccomandate	طابع تسجيل ـ مسجل	Registration stamp
Reprint	Réimpression	Neudruck	Reimpresión	Ristampa	إعادة طبع	Reprint

English	French	German	Spanish	Italian	Arabic	English
Reversed	Retourné	Umgekehrt	Invertido	Rovesciato	معكوس ـ مقلوب	Reversed
Rose	Rose	Rosa	Rosa	Rosa	وردي	Rose
Rose-red	Rouge rosé	Rosarot	Rojo rosado	Rosso rosa	أحمر وردي	Rose-red
Rosine	Rose vif	Lebhaftrosa	Rosa vivo	Rosa vivo	وردي غامق	Rosine
Roulette	Percage	Durchstich	Picadura	Foratura	تخريم ناعم	Roulette
Rouletted	Percé	Durchstochen	Picado	Forato	تخريم ناعم	Rouletted
Royal Blue	Bleu-roi	Königblau	Azul real	Azzurro reale	أزرق ملكي	Royal Blue
Sage green	Vert-sauge	Salbeigrün	Verde salvia	Verde salvia	أخضر معتدل	Sage green
Salmon	Saumon	Lachs	Salmón	Salmone	برتقالي فاتح قريب للزهري	Salmon
Scarlet	Écarlate	Scharlach	Escarlata	Scarlatto	قرمزي	Scarlet
Sepia	Sépia	Sepia	Sepia	Seppia	بني داكن	Sepia
Serpentine roulette	Percé en serpentin	Schlangenliniger Durchstich	Picado a serpentina	Perforazione a serpentina		Serpentine roulette
Shade	Nuance	Tönung	Tono	Gradazione de colore		Shade
Sheet	Feuille	Bogen	Hoja	Foglio	صفحة	Sheet
Slate	Ardoise	Schiefer	Pizarra	Ardesia	لون رصاصي	Slate
Slate-blue	Bleu-ardoise	Schieferblau	Azul pizarra	Azzurro ardesia	أزرق رمادي	Slate-blue
Slate-green	Vert-ardoise	Schiefergrün	Verde pizarra	Verde ardesia	أخضر مسود	Slate-green
Slate-lilac	Lilas-gris	Schierferlila	Lila pizarra	Lilla ardesia	نهدي مزرق	Slate-lilac
Slate-purple	Mauve-gris	Schieferpurpur	Púrpura pizarra	Porpora ardesia		Slate-purple
Slate-violet	Violet-gris	Schieferviolett	Violeta pizarra	Violetto ardesia		Slate-violet
Special delivery stamp	Timbre pour exprès	Eilmarke	Sello de urgencia	Francobollo per espressi	خدمة البريد السريعة	Special delivery stamp
Specimen	Spécimen	Muster	Muestra	Saggio	نموذج ـ عينة	Specimen
Steel Blue	Bleu acier	Stahlblau	Azul acero	Azzurro acciaio	أزرق فولاذي	Steel Blue
Strip	Bande	Streifen	Tira	Striscia	شريط	Strip
Surcharge	Surcharge	Aufdruck	Sobrecarga	Soprastampa	الضريبة الاضافية	Surcharge
Tête-bêche	Tête-bêche	Kehrdruck	Tête-bêche	Tête-bêche		Tête-bêche
Tinted paper	Papier teinté	Getöntes Papier	Papel coloreado	Carta tinta	ورق لون خفيف	Tinted paper
Too-late stamp	Timbre pour lettres en retard	Verspätungsmarke	Sello para cartas retardadas	Francobollo per le lettere in ritardo	طابع متأخر جداً	Too-late stamp
Turquoise-blue	Bleu-turquoise	Türkisblau	Azul turquesa	Azzurro turchese	أزرق تركوازي	Turquoise-blue
Turquoise-green	Vert-turquoise	Türkisgrün	Verde turquesa	Verde turchese	أخضر تركوازي	Turquoise-green
Typography	Typographie	Buchdruck	Tipografia	Tipografia	نوع من الطباعة	Typography
Ultramarine	Outremer	Ultramarin	Ultramar	Oltremare	أزرق لازوردي	Ultramarine
Unused	Neuf	Ungebraucht	Nuevo	Nuovo	غير مستخدم	Unused
Used	Oblitéré, Usé	Gebraucht	Usado	Usato	مستخدم	Used
Venetian Red	Rouge-brun terne	Venezianischrot	Rojo veneciano	Rosso veneziano	لون بندقي ـ بني محمر	Venetian Red
Vermilion	Vermillon	Zinnober	Cinabrio	Vermiglione	لون برتقالي محمر (قمرديني)	Vermilion
Violet	Violet	Violett	Violeta	Violetto	بنفسج	Violet
Violet-blue	Bleu-violet	Violettblau	Azul violeta	Azzurro violetto	أزرق بنفسجي	Violet-blue
Watermark	Filigrane	Wasserzeichen	Filigrana	Filigrana	علامة مائية	Watermark
Watermark sideways	Filigrane couché liegend	Wasserzeichen	Filigrana acostado	Filigrana coricata		Watermark sideways
Wove paper	Papier ordinaire, Papier uni	Einfaches Papier	Papel avitelado	Carta unita	ورقة منسوجه	Wove paper
Yellow	Jaune	Gelb	Amarillo	Giallo	أصفر	Yellow
Yellow-brown	Brun-jaune	Gelbbraun	Castaño amarillo	Bruno giallo	بني مصفر	Yellow-brown
Yellow-green	Vert-jaune	Gelbgrün	Verde amarillo	Verde giallo	أخضر مصفر	Yellow-green
Yellow-olive	Olive-jaunâtre	Gelboliv	Oliva amarillo	Oliva giallastro	زيتوني مصفر	Yellow-olive
Yellow-orange	Orange jaunâtre	Gelborange	Naranja amarillo	Arancio giallastro	برتقالي مصفر	Yellow-orange
Zig-zag roulette	Percé en zigzag	Sägezahnartiger Durchstich	Picado en zigzag	Perforazione a zigzag	تخريم ناعم متعرج	Zig-zag roulette

Abbreviations

Printers

A.B.N. Co.	American Bank Note Co, New York.
B.A.B.N.	British American Bank Note Co. Ottawa
B.W.	Bradbury Wilkinson & Co, Ltd.
C.B.N.	Canadian Bank Note Co, Ottawa.
Continental B.N. Co.	Continental Bank Note Co.
Courvoisier	Imprimerie Courvoisier S.A., La-Chaux-de-Fonds, Switzerland.
D.L.R.	De La Rue & Co, Ltd, London.
Enschedé	Joh. Enschedé en Zonen, Haarlem, Netherlands.
Harrison	Harrison & Sons, Ltd. London
P.B.	Perkins Bacon Ltd, London.
Waterlow	Waterlow & Sons, Ltd, London.

General Abbreviations

Alph	Alphabet
Anniv	Anniversary
Comp	Compound (perforation)
Des	Designer; designed
Diag	Diagonal; diagonally
Eng	Engraver; engraved
F.C.	Fiscal Cancellation
H/S	Handstamped
Horiz	Horizontal; horizontally
Imp, Imperf	Imperforate
Inscr	Inscribed
L	Left
Litho	Lithographed
mm	Millimetres
MS	Miniature sheet
N.Y.	New York
Opt(d)	Overprint(ed)
P or P-c	Pen-cancelled
P, Pf or Perf	Perforated
Photo	Photogravure
Pl	Plate
Pr	Pair
Ptd	Printed
Ptg	Printing
R	Right
R.	Row
Recess	Recess-printed
Roto	Rotogravure
Roul	Rouletted
S	Specimen (overprint)
Surch	Surcharge(d)
T.C.	Telegraph Cancellation
T	Type
Typo	Typographed
Un	Unused
Us	Used
Vert	Vertical; vertically

W or wmk	Watermark
Wmk s	Watermark sideways

(†) = Does not exist

(–) (or blank price column) = Exists, or may exist, but no market price is known.

/ between colours means "on" and the colour following is that of the paper on which the stamp is printed.

Colours of Stamps

Bl	(blue)
blk	(black)
brn	(brown)
car, carm	(carmine)
choc	(chocolate)
clar	(claret);
emer	(emerald)
grn	(green)
ind	(indigo)
mag	(magenta)
mar	(maroon)
mult	(multicoloured)
mve	(mauve)
ol	(olive)
orge	(orange)
pk	(pink)
pur	(purple)
scar	(scarlet)
sep	(sepia)
turq	(turquoise)
ultram	(ultramarine)
verm	(vermilion)
vio	(violet)
yell	(yellow).

Colour of Overprints and Surcharges

(B.)	= blue
(Blk.)	= black
(Br.)	= brown,
(C.)	= carmine
(G.)	= green
(Mag.)	= magenta
(Mve.)	= mauve
(Ol.)	= olive
(O.)	= orange,
(P.)	= purple
(Pk.)	= pink,
(R.)	= red,
(Sil.)	= silver
(V.)	= violet
(Vm.) or (Verm.)	= vermilion,
(W.)	= white
(Y.)	= yellow.

Arabic Numerals

As in the case of European figures, the details of the Arabic numerals vary in different stamp designs, but they should be readily recognised wit-h the aid of this illustration:

·	١	٢	٣	٤	٥	٦	٧	٨	٩
0	1	2	3	4	5	6	7	8	9

Features listing

Area	Feature	Collect British Stamps	Stamps of the World	Thematic Catalogues	Commonwealth and British Empire Stamps and one country catalogues	Comprehensive Catalogue, Parts 1-22 (including Commonwealth)	Great Britain Concise	Specialised catalogues
General	SG number	√	√	√		√	√	√
General	Specialised Catalogue number							√
General	Year of issue of first stamp in design	√	√	√		√	√	√
General	Exact date of issue of each design					√	√	√
General	Face value information	√	√	√		√	√	√
General	Historical and geographical information	√	√	√		√	√	√
General	General currency information, including dates used	√	√	√		√	√	√
General	Country name	√	√	√		√	√	√
General	Booklet panes					√	√	√
General	Coil stamps					√		
General	First Day Covers	√				√	√	√
General	Brief footnotes on key areas of note	√	√	√		√	√	
General	Detailed footnotes on key areas of note					√	√	√
General	Extra background information					√	√	√
General	Miniature sheet information (including size in mm)	√	√	√		√	√	√
General	Sheetlets					√		
General	Stamp booklets					√	√	√
General	Perkins Bacon "Cancelled"					√		
General	PHQ Cards	√					√	√
General	Post Office Label Sheets					√		
General	Post Office Yearbooks	√					√	√
General	Presentation and Souvenir Packs	√					√	√
General	Se-tenant pairs	√				√	√	√
General	Watermark details - errors, varieties, positions					√	√	√
General	Watermark illustrations	√				√	√	√
General	Watermark types	√				√	√	√
General	Forgeries noted					√		√
General	Surcharges and overprint information	√	√	√		√	√	√
Design and Description	Colour description, simplified		√	√				
Design and Description	Colour description, extended	√				√	√	√
Design and Description	Set design summary information	√	√	√		√	√	√
Design and Description	Designer name					√	√	√
Design and Description	Short design description	√	√	√		√	√	√
Design and Description	Shade varieties					√	√	√
Design and Description	Type number	√	√			√		
Illustrations	Multiple stamps from set illustrated	√				√	√	√
Illustrations	A Stamp from each set illustrated in full colour (where possible, otherwise mono)	√	√	√		√	√	√
Price	Catalogue used price	√	√	√		√	√	√
Price	Catalogue unused price	√	√	√		√	√	√
Price	Price - booklet panes					√	√	√
Price	Price - shade varieties					√	√	√
Price	On cover and on piece price					√	√	√
Price	Detailed GB pricing breakdown	√				√	√	√
Print and Paper	Basic printing process information	√	√	√		√	√	√
Print and Paper	Detailed printing process information, e.g. Mill sheets					√		√
Print and Paper	Paper information					√		√
Print and Paper	Detailed perforation information	√				√	√	√
Print and Paper	Details of research findings relating to printing processes and history							√
Print and Paper	Paper colour	√	√			√	√	√
Print and Paper	Paper description to aid identification					√	√	√
Print and Paper	Paper type					√	√	√
Print and Paper	Ordinary or chalk-surfaced paper					√	√	√
Print and Paper	Embossing omitted note							√
Print and Paper	Essays, Die Proofs, Plate Descriptions and Proofs, Colour Trials information							√
Print and Paper	Glazed paper					√	√	√
Print and Paper	Gum details					√		√
Print and Paper	Luminescence/Phosphor bands - general coverage	√				√	√	√
Print and Paper	Luminescence/Phosphor bands - specialised coverage							√
Print and Paper	Overprints and surcharges - including colour information	√	√	√		√	√	√
Print and Paper	Perforation/Imperforate information	√	√			√	√	√
Print and Paper	Perforation errors and varieties					√	√	√
Print and Paper	Print quantities					√		√
Print and Paper	Printing errors					√	√	√
Print and Paper	Printing flaws							√
Print and Paper	Printing varieties					√	√	√
Print and Paper	Punctured stamps - where official					√		
Print and Paper	Sheet positions					√	√	√
Print and Paper	Specialised plate number information							√
Print and Paper	Specimen overprints (only for Commonwealth & GB)					√		√
Print and Paper	Underprints						√	√
Print and Paper	Visible Plate numbers	√				√	√	√
Print and Paper	Yellow and Green paper listings					√		√
Index	Design index	√					√	

Stanley Gibbons Stamp Catalogue Complete list of parts

1 Commonwealth & British Empire Stamps 1840–1970
(114th edition, 2012)

Commonwealth Country Catalogues

Australia and Dependencies
(8th edition, 2013)

Bangladesh, Pakistan & Sri Lanka
(2nd edition, 2010)

Belize, Guyana, Trinidad & Tobago
(2nd edition, 2013)

Brunei, Malaysia & Singapore
(4th edition, 2013)

Canada (4th edition, 2011)

Central Africa (2nd edition, 2008)

Cyprus, Gibraltar & Malta
(3rd edition, 2011)

East Africa with Egypt and Sudan
(2nd edition, 2010)

Eastern Pacific (2nd edition, 2011)

Falkland Islands (5th edition, 2012)

Hong Kong (4th edition, 2013)

India (including Convention and Feudatory States)
(4th edition, 2013)

Indian Ocean (1st edition, 2006)

Ireland (4th edition, 2011)

Leeward Islands (2nd edition, 2012)

New Zealand (4th edition, 2011)

Northern Caribbean, Bahamas & Bermuda
(3rd edition, 2013)

St. Helena & Dependencies
(4th edition, 2011)

Southern & Central Africa
(1st edition, 2011)

West Africa (2nd edition, 2012)

Western Pacific (2nd edition, 2009)

Windward Islands and Barbados
(2nd edition, 2012)

Stamps of the World 2014

Volume 1 **Abu Dhabi – Charkhari**
Volume 2 **Chile – Georgia**
Volume 3 **German Commands – Jasdan**
Volume 4 **Jersey – New Republic**
Volume 5 **New South Wales – Singapore**
Volume 6 **Sirmoor – Zululand**

Foreign Countries

2 **Austria & Hungary**
(7th edition, 2009)

3 **Balkans** (5th edition, 2009)

4 **Benelux** (6th edition, 2010)

5 **Czechoslovakia & Poland**
(7th edition, 2012)

6 **France** (7th edition, 2010)

7 **Germany** (10th edition, 2012)

8 **Italy & Switzerland**
(8th edition, 2013)

9 **Portugal & Spain** (6th edition, 2011)

10 **Russia** (6th edition, 2008)

11 **Scandinavia** (7th edition, 2013)

12 **Africa since Independence A-E**
(2nd edition, 1983)

13 **Africa since Independence F-M**
(1st edition, 1981)

14 **Africa since Independence N-Z**
(1st edition, 1981)

15 **Central America** (3rd edition, 2007)

16 **Central Asia** (4th edition, 2006)

17 **China** (9th edition, 2012)

18 **Japan & Korea** (5th edition, 2008)

19 **Middle East** (7th edition, 2009)

20 **South America** (4th edition, 2008)

21 **South-East Asia** (5th edition, 2012)

22 **United States of America**
(7th edition, 2010)

Great Britain Catalogues

Collect British Stamps
(64th edition, 2013)

Great Britain Concise Stamp Catalogue (28th edition, 2013)

SPECIALISED CATALOGUES

Volume 1 **Queen Victoria**
(16th edition, 2011)

Volume 2 **King Edward VII to King George VI**
(13th edition, 2009)

Volume 3 **Queen Elizabeth II Pre-decimal issues**
(12th edition, 2011)

Volume 4 **Queen Elizabeth II Decimal Definitive Issues – Part 1**
(10th edition, 2008)

Queen Elizabeth II Decimal Definitive Issues – Part 2
(10th edition, 2010)

Volume 5 **Queen Elizabeth II Decimal Special Issues** (3rd edition, 1998 with 1998-99 and 2000/1 Supplements)

Thematic Catalogues

Stanley Gibbons Catalogues for use with **Stamps of the World.**

Collect Aircraft on Stamps
(2nd edition, 2009)

Collect Birds on Stamps
(5th edition, 2003)

Collect Chess on Stamps
(2nd edition, 1999)

Collect Fish on Stamps
(1st edition, 1999)

Collect Motor Vehicles on Stamps
(1st edition 2004)

Other publications

Africa Simplified (1st edition, 2011)

Asia Simplified (1st edition, 2010)

Antarctica (including Australian and British Antarctic Territories, French Southern and Antarctic Territories and Ross Dependency)
(2nd edition, 2012)

Collect Channel Islands and Isle of Man Stamps
(28th edition, 2013)

Commonwealth Simplified
(4th edition, 2010)

Enjoy Stamp Collecting
(7th edition, 2006)

Great Britain Numbers Issued
(3rd edition, 2008)

How to Identify Stamps
(5th edition, 2011)

North America Combined
(1st edition, 2010)

North-East Africa (1st edition 2013)

Philatelic Terms Illustrated
(4th edition, 2003)

United Nations (also including International Organizations based in Switzerland and UNESCO)
(1st edition, 2010)

Western Europe Simplified
(2nd edition 2012)

For other titles, and further details on the above, please see *www.stanleygibbons.com*

The Stanley Gibbons Group plc - About us

Our History

Edward Stanley Gibbons started trading postage stamps in his father's chemist shop in Plymouth in 1856; we have been at the forefront of stamp collecting for more than 150 years, making us the world's oldest philatelic company.

As Royal Warrant holders since 1914 we offer unsurpassed expertise and provide collectors worldwide with peace of mind that all stamps purchased from us come with our certified lifetime guarantee of authenticity*.

If you think of stamp collecting, you think of Stanley Gibbons and we are proud to uphold that tradition for you.

399 Strand

Our world famous stamp shop is a collector's paradise, with all of our latest catalogues, albums and accessories and of course, our unrivalled stockholding of postage stamps.

www.stanleygibbons.com
shop@stanleygibbons.co.uk
+44 (0)20 7836 8444

Specialist Stamp Sales

For the collector that appreciates the value of collecting the highest quality examples, Stanley Gibbons is the only choice. Our extensive range is unrivalled in terms of quality and quantity, with specialist stamps available from all over the world.

www.stanleygibbons.com/stamps
shop@stanleygibbons.co.uk
+44 (0)20 7836 8444

Mail order

Stamp collecting made easy! Order anything you need to enhance your collection, from our world famous catalogues to brand new supplements, from our long-running range of albums to cutting edge accessories, all available via telephone, email or post.

orders@stanleygibbons.com
FREEPHONE (UK only) 0800 611 622
+44 (0) 1425 472363

Stanley Gibbons Auctions and Valuations

Sell your collection or individual rare items through our prestigious public auctions and regular postal auctions. You too can benefit from the excellent prices being realised at auction currently.

We also provide an unparalleled valuation service-drop your collection or rare items into us at 399 Strand, call us about our collection service or make an appointment at one of our valuation days held at venues across the UK.

www.stanleygibbons.com/auctions
auctions@stanleygibbons.co.uk
+44 (0)20 7836 8444

Stanley Gibbons Investments

The Stanley Gibbons Investment Department offers a unique range of investment propositions that have consistently outperformed more traditional forms of investment, from guaranteed minimum return products with unlimited upside to portfolios made up of the world's rarest stamps and autographs.

www.stanleygibbons.com/investment
investment@stanleygibbons.co.uk
+44 (0)1481 708 270

Stanley Gibbons Publications

The world's first stamp catalogue was printed by Stanley Gibbons in 1865 and we haven't looked back since! Our catalogues are trusted worldwide as the industry standard and we print countless titles each year. We also publish the consumer and trade magazines, Gibbons Stamp Monthly and Philatelic Exporter; bringing you news, views and insights into all things philatelic. For more information see 'Stanley Gibbons Publications Information.'

www.stanleygibbons.com/shop
orders@stanleygibbons.co.uk
+44 (0)1425 472 363

stanleygibbons.com

Our website offers the complete philatelic service. Whether you are looking to buy stamps, invest, read news articles, browse our online stamp catalogue or find new issues, you are just one click away from anything you desire in the world of stamp collecting at stanleygibbons.com. Happy browsing!

www.stanleygibbons.com

Fraser's Autographs

Autographs, manuscripts and memorabilia from Henry VIII to current day. We have over 60,000 items in stock, including movie stars, musicians, sport stars, historical figures and royalty. Fraser's is the UK's market leading autograph dealer and has been dealing in high quality autographed material since 1978.

www.frasersautographs.com
sales@frasersautographs.co.uk
+44 (0)20 7557 4404

The Stanley Gibbons Lifetime Guarantee of Authenticity

Stanley Gibbons sells stamps and philatelic items on the basis that they are genuine originals; if they are proved not to fit the description as represented by us, you may return them at any time and we will refund you the original purchase price.

All stamps supplied by Stanley Gibbons are guaranteed originals under the following terms:

If not as described, and returned by the purchaser, we undertake to refund the price paid in the original transaction.

If any stamp is certified as genuine by the Expert Committee of the Royal Philatelic Society, London, or by B.P.A. Expertising Ltd., the purchaser shall not be entitled to make any claim against us for any error, omission or mistake in such certificate.

Consumers' statutory rights are not affected by the above guarantee.

Stanley Gibbons Group plc- Contact us

The Stanley Gibbons Group plc

Stanley Gibbons Auctions

399 Strand, London WC2R OLX
Telephone + 44 (0)20 7836 8444
Fax + 44 (0) 20 7836 7342
enquires@stanleygibbons.co.uk
www.stanleygibbons.com for all departments

Auction and Specialist Stamp Departments

Open Monday–Friday 9.30am to 5pm
Shop open Monday–Friday 9am to 5.30pm and Saturday 9.30am to 5.30pm

Fraser's

(a division of Stanley Gibbons Group plc)
399 Strand, London WC2R OLX
Autographs, photographs, letters and documents
Telephone + 44 (0) 20 7836 8444
Fax +44 (0) 20 7836 7342,
info@frasersautographs.co.uk
www.frasersautographs.com
Monday–Friday 9 a.m. to 5.30 p.m. and Saturday 10 a.m. to 4 p.m.

Stanley Gibbons Publications

7 Parkside, Christchurch Road, Ringwood, Hampshire BH24 3SH.
Telephone + 44 (0)1425 472363 (24 hour answer phone service)
UK FREEPHONE 0800 611 622
Fax +44 (0) 1425 470247
info@stanleygibbons.co.uk

Publications Mail Order

FREEPHONE 0800 611622
Monday–Friday 8.30 am to 5pm

Stanley Gibbons (Guernsey) Limited

Investments

18-20 Le Bordage, St Peter Port, Guernsey, Channel Islands, GY1 1DE
+44 (0) 1481 708 270
Toll free from USA +1 866 644 6146
investment@stanleygibbons.co.uk
www.stanleygibbons.com/investment

Gibbons Stamp Monthly and Philatelic Exporter

7 Parkside, Christchurch Road, Ringwood, Hampshire BH24 3SH.
Subscriptions. 01425 472363
Fax 01425 470247
gsm@stanleygibbons.co.uk

ABU DHABI

Pt. 1, Pt. 19

The largest of the Trucial States in the Persian Gulf. Treaty relations with Great Britain expired on 31 December 1966, when Abu Dhabi took over the postal services. On 18 July 1971, seven of the Gulf sheikhdoms, including Abu Dhabi, agreed to form the State of the United Arab Emirates. The federation came into being on 1 August 1972.

1964. 100 naye paise = 1 rupee.
1966. 1,000 fils = 1 dinar.

1 Shaikh Shakhbut bin Sultan

3 Ruler's Palace

1964

1	1	5n.p. green	4·50	4·50
2	1	15n.p. brown	4·25	2·50
3	1	20n.p. blue	4·25	2·00
4	1	30n.p. orange	4·25	1·75
5	-	40n.p. violet	6·50	1·50
6	-	50n.p. bistre	7·50	3·00
7	-	75n.p. black	10·00	6·50
8	3	1r. green	4·75	3·25
9	3	2r. black	9·00	4·75
10	-	5r. red	23·00	14·00
11	-	10r. blue	28·00	16·00

DESIGNS: As Type **1**: 40 to 75n.p. Mountain gazelle; As Type **3**: 5, 10r. Oil rig and camels.

5 Saker Falcon

1965. Falcony.

12	5	20n.p. brown and blue	15·00	2·75
13	-	40n.p. brown and blue	18·00	3·00
14	-	2r. sepia and turquoise	32·00	16·00

DESIGNS: 40n.p., 2r. Other types of Saker falcon on gloved hand.

1966. Nos. 1/11 surch in new currency ("Fils" only on Nos. 5/7) and ruler's portrait obliterated with bars.

15	1	5f. on 5n.p. green	13·00	6·50
16	1	15f. on 15n.p. brown	19·00	11·00
17	1	20f. on 20n.p. blue	19·00	8·50
18	1	30f. on 30n.p. orange	17·00	21·00
19	-	40f. on 40n.p. violet	14·00	1·00
20	-	50f. on 50n.p. bistre	55·00	55·00
21	-	75f. on 75n.p. black	55·00	55·00
22	3	100f. on 1r. green	18·00	4·75
23	3	200f. on 2r. black	18·00	13·00
24	-	500f. on 5r. red	30·00	38·00
25	-	1d. on 10r. blue	55·00	65·00

9 Shaikh Zaid bin Sultan al Nahayyan **10**

1967

26		5f. red and green	55	20
27		15f. red and brown	65	20
28		20f. red and blue	1·00	20
29		35f. red and violet	1·10	35
30	9	40f. green	1·60	35
38	10	40f. brown	4·75	2·40
31	9	50f. brown	1·90	55
39	10	50f. brown	5·75	1·70
32	9	60f. blue	2·20	55
40	10	60f. blue	21·00	4·00
33	9	100f. red	3·25	80
41	10	100f. red	30·00	10·50
34	-	125f. brown and green	6·75	2·50
35	-	200f. brown and blue	36·00	11·00
36	-	500f. violet and orange	17·00	7·75
37	-	1d. blue and green	40·00	22·00

DESIGNS—As Types **9**&**10**—VERT: 5f. to 35f. National flag. HORIZ: (47×27 mm); 125f. Mountain gazelle; 200f. Lanner falcon; 500f., 1d. Palace. Each with portrait of Ruler.

11 Human Rights Emblem and Shaikh Zaid

1968. Human Rights Year.

42	11	35f. multicoloured	2·20	90
43	11	60f. multicoloured	3·50	1·30
44	11	150f. multicoloured	9·00	3·25

12 Arms and Shaikh Zaid

1968. Anniv of Shaikh Zaid's Accession.

45	12	5f. multicoloured	3·25	65
46	12	10f. multicoloured	3·25	90
47	12	100f. multicoloured	8·75	2·20
48	12	125f. multicoloured	13·00	4·00

13 New Construction

1968. Second Anniv of Shaikh's Accession. "Progress in Abu Dhabi". Multicoloured.

49		5f. Type **13**	2·75	55
50		10f. Airport buildings (46½×34 mm)	5·25	1·20
51		35f. Shaikh Zaid, bridge and Northern goshawk (59×34 mm)	24·00	9·50

14 Petroleum Installations

1969. Third Anniv of Shaikh's Accession. Petroleum Industry. Multicoloured.

52		35f. Type **14**	2·00	70
53		60f. Marine drilling platform	5·25	1·60
54		125f. Separator platform, Zakum field	8·75	3·25
55		200f. Tank farm	14·50	7·75

15 Shaikh Zaid

1970

56	-	5f. multicoloured	70	20
57	15	10f. multicoloured	1·00	20
58	-	25f. multicoloured	1·90	20
59	15	35f. multicoloured	2·50	35
60	15	50f. multicoloured	3·50	55
61	-	60f. multicoloured	4·00	65
62	15	70f. multicoloured	6·75	80
63	-	90f. multicoloured	8·50	1·50
64	-	125f. multicoloured	12·50	2·00
65	-	150f. multicoloured	12·50	2·50
66	-	500f. multicoloured	38·00	13·50
67	-	1d. multicoloured	65·00	22·00

DESIGNS: Nos. 56, 58, 61 and 63 as Type **15**, but frames changed, and smaller country name; 125f. Arab stallion; 150f. Mountain gazelle; 500f. Fort Jahili; 1d. Great Mosque.

No. 67 has face value in Arabic only.

17 Shaikh Zaid and "Mt. Fuji" (T. Hayashi)

1970. "Expo 70" World Fair, Osaka, Japan.

68	17	25f. multicoloured	3·25	1·20
69	17	35f. multicoloured	4·75	1·90
70	17	60f. multicoloured	8·75	2·75

18 Abu Dhabi Airport

1970. 40th Anniv of Shaikh's Accession. Completion of Abu Dhabi Airport. Mult.

71		25f. Type **18**	3·25	90
72		60f. Airport entrance	7·25	2·10
73		150f. Aerial view of Abu Dhabi (vert)	17·00	5·25

19 Pres. G. A. Nasser

1971. Gamal Nasser (President of Egypt) Commemoration.

74	19	25f. black on pink	6·00	3·75
75	19	35f. black on lilac	8·25	5·50

20 Military Land Rover Series II 88

1971. Fifth Anniv of Shaikh's Accession. Defence Force. Multicoloured.

76		35f. Type **20**	6·00	1·60
77		60f. Patrol-boat "Baniyas"	8·00	2·20
78		125f. Armoured car	17·00	3·50
79		150f. Hawker Hunter FGA.76 jet fighters	22·00	6·75

1971. No. 60 surch.

80	15	5f. on 50f. multicoloured	95·00	80·00

22 Dome of the Rock

1972. Dome of the Rock, Jerusalem. Multicoloured.

81		35f. Type **22**	25·00	5·00
82		60f. Mosque entrance	43·00	9·00
83		125f. Mosque dome	80·00	22·00

1972. Provisional Issue. Nos. 56/67 optd **UAE** and arabic inscr.

84	-	5f. multicoloured	2·50	2·50
85	15	10f. multicoloured	2·50	1·50
86	-	25f. multicoloured	3·25	3·25
87	15	35f. multicoloured	5·00	4·50
88	15	50f. multicoloured	7·75	7·75
89	-	60f. multicoloured	9·00	9·00
90	15	70f. multicoloured	11·00	11·00
91	-	90f. multicoloured	17·00	17·00
92	-	125f. multicoloured	55·00	55·00
93	-	150f. multicoloured	65·00	65·00
94	-	500f. multicoloured	£150	£150
95	-	1d. multicoloured	£300	£300

For later issues see **UNITED ARAB EMIRATES**.

Pt. 1

ADEN

Peninsula on southern coast of Arabia. Formerly part of the Indian Empire. A Crown Colony from 1 April 1937 to 18 January 1963, when Aden joined the South Arabian Federation, whose stamps it then used.

1937. 16 annas = 1 rupee.
1951. 100 cents = 1 shilling.

1 Dhow

1937

1	1	½a. green	4·00	2·75
2	1	9p. green	3·75	3·50
3	1	1a. brown	3·75	2·00
4	1	2a. red	5·00	3·00
5	1	2½a. blue	7·00	2·00
6	1	3a. red	10·00	8·50
7	1	3½a. blue	7·50	6·00
8	1	8a. purple	26·00	11·00
9	1	1r. brown	60·00	13·00
10	1	2r. yellow	£110	38·00
11	1	5r. purple	£250	£140
12	1	10r. olive	£650	£600

2 King George VI and Queen Elizabeth

1937. Coronation.

13	2	1a. brown	65	1·25
14	2	2½a. blue	75	1·40
15	2	3½a. blue	1·00	3·00

3 Aidrus Mosque, Crater

1939

16	3	½a. green	2·00	60
17	-	¾a. brown	3·00	1·25
18	-	1a. blue	1·00	40
19	-	1½a. red	3·00	60
20	3	2a. brown	1·25	25
21	-	2½a. blue	2·00	30
22	-	3a. brown and red	2·00	25
23	-	8a. orange	2·25	40
23a	-	14a. brown and blue	4·50	1·00
24	-	1r. green	5·50	2·50
25	-	2r. blue and mauve	10·00	3·00
26	-	5r. brown and olive	32·00	16·00
27	-	10r. brown and violet	45·00	17·00

DESIGNS: ¾a., 5r. Adenese Camel Corps; 1a., 2r. The Harbour; 1½a., 1r. Adenese dhow; 2½, 8a. Mukalla; 3, 14a., 10r. "Capture of Aden, 1839" (Capt. Rundle).

9 Houses of Parliament, London

1946. Victory.

28	9	1½a. red	20	1·75
29	9	2½a. blue	80	1·00

10 **11** King George VI and Queen Elizabeth

1949. Royal Silver Wedding.

30	10	1½a. red	40	2·25
31	11	10r. purple	40·00	55·00

1949. 75th Anniv of U.P.U. As T **20/23** of Antigua surch with new values.

32		2½a. on 20c. blue	60	1·50
33		3a. on 30c. red	2·00	1·50
34		8a. on 50c. orange	1·75	2·00
35		1r. on 1s. blue	1·60	5·50

1951. Stamps of 1939 surch in cents or shillings.

36		5c. on 1a. blue	25	40
37		10c. on 2a. brown	15	45
38		15c. on 2½a. blue	30	1·25
39		20c. on 3a. brown and red	30	40
40		30c. on 8a. orange	50	65
41		50c. on 14a. brown and blue	1·50	35
42		70c. on 14a. brown and blue	2·25	1·50
43		1s. on 1r. green	3·00	30
44		2s. on 2r. blue and mauve	16·00	3·75
45		5s. on 5r. brown and olive	27·00	15·00
46		10s. on 10r. brown and violet	40·00	16·00

13 Queen Elizabeth II

1953. Coronation.

47	**13**	15c. black and green	1·50	1·25

14 Minaret **15** Camel Transport

1953

48	**14**	5c. green	20	10
49a	**14**	5c. turquoise	15	1·25
50	**15**	10c. orange	40	10
51	**15**	10c. red	30	30
52	-	15c. turquoise	1·25	60
79	-	15c. grey	1·00	5·50
80	-	25c. red	3·00	40
56	-	35c. blue	2·50	1·50
58	-	50c. blue	30	10
60	-	70c. grey	30	10
61	-	70c. black	1·75	35
62	-	1s. brown and violet	40	10
63	-	1s. black and violet	1·50	10
64	-	1s.25 blue and black	11·00	60
65	-	2s. brown and red	1·50	50
66	-	2s. black and red	13·00	50
67	-	5s. brown and blue	1·75	1·00
68	-	5s. black and blue	14·00	1·25
69	-	10s. brown and green	1·75	8·00
70	-	10s. black and bronze	17·00	1·75
71	-	20s. brown and lilac	6·50	10·00
72	-	20s. black and lilac	65·00	20·00

DESIGNS—HORIZ: 15c. Crater; 25c. Mosque; 1s. Dhow building; 20s. (38×27 mm); Aden in 1572. VERT: 35c. Dhow; 50c. Map; 70c. Salt works; 1s.25, Colony's badge; 2s. Aden Protectorate Levy; 5s. Crater Pass; 10s. Tribesmen.

1954. Royal Visit. As No. 62 but inscr "ROYAL VISIT 1954".

73		1s. sepia and violet	75	75

1959. Revised Constitution. Optd REVISED CONSTITUTION 1959 (in Arabic on No. 74).

74		15c. green (No. 53)	60	2·25
75		1s.25 blue and black (No. 64)	1·00	1·00

28 Protein Foods

1963. Freedom from Hunger.

76	**28**	1s.25 green	1·25	2·00

For later issues see **SOUTH ARABIAN FEDERATION.**

Pt. 16

AFGHANISTAN

An independent country in Asia, to N.W. of Pakistan. Now a republic, the country was formerly ruled by monarchs from 1747 to 1973.

1871. 60 paisa = 12 shahi = 6 sanar = 3 abasi = 2 kran = 1 rupee.
1920. 60 paisa = 2 kran = 1 rupee.
1926. 100 poul (pul) = 1 afghani (rupee).

The issues from 1860 to 1892 (Types **1** to **16**) are difficult to classify because the values of each set are expressed in native script and are generally all printed in the same colour. As it is not possible to list these in an intelligible simplified form we would refer users to the detailed list in the Stanley Gibbons Part 16 (Central Asia) Catalogue.

1 **4**

5 **6**

8 **10**

12 **16**

17 National Coat of Arms

1893. Dated "1310".

147	**17**	1a. black on green	3·25	3·25
148	**17**	1a. black on red	3·75	3·25
149a	**17**	1a. black on purple	3·75	3·50
150	**17**	1a. black on yellow	3·50	3·25
151	**17**	1a. black on orange	4·00	4·00
152	**17**	1a. black on blue	6·25	5·25

18 2 Abasi

1894. Undated

153	**18**	2a. black on green	12·50	8·25
154	**18**	1r. black on green	15·00	13·00

20 1 Abasi

1907. Imperf, roul or perf.

156a	**20**	1a. green	17·00	21·00
157	-	2a. blue	6·50	8·25
158	-	1r. green	45·00	23·00

The 2a. and 1r. are in similar designs.

23 **24** 1 Abasi

1909. Perf.

165	**23**	2 paisa brown	13·00	4·50
166	**24**	1a. blue	5·25	2·10
168	**24**	1a. red	1·20	1·00
169	-	2a. green	3·00	2·50
170a	-	2a. bistre	2·75	3·00
171	-	1r. brown	5·00	5·25
172	-	1r. olive	7·75	7·75

The frames of the 2a. and 1r. differ from Type **24**.

27 Royal Star of Order of Independence

1920. First Anniv of End of War of Independence. Size 39×47 mm.

173	**27**	10p. red	49·00	33·00
174	**27**	20p. purple	80·00	55·00
175	**27**	30p. green	£160	£160

1921. Size 23×29 mm.

177		10p. red	2·10	95
178		20p. purple	4·50	2·75
180b		30p. green	6·50	3·00

(28)

1923. Fifth Independence Day. Optd with T 28.

181		10p. red	41·00	41·00
181a		20p. brown	49·00	49·00
182		30p. green	60·00	60·00

29 Crest of King Amanullah

1924. Sixth Independence Day.

183	**29**	10p. brown (24×32 mm)	37·00	37·00

29a

1924

183b	**29a**	5k. blue	41·00	41·00
183c	**29a**	5r. mauve	16·00	25·00

1925. Seventh Independence Day.

184	**29**	10p. brown (29×37 mm)	60·00	45·00

1926. Seventh Anniv of Independence.

185		10p. blue (26×33 mm)	6·50	8·25

30 Crest of King Amanullah

1927. Eighth Anniv of Independence.

186	**30**	10p. mauve	18·00	13·00

Types **31/3**, **36/37** and **41**, National Seal.

31 **32**

33

1927. Perf or imperf.

188A	**31**	15p. red	1·30	1·30
189A	**32**	30p. green	2·75	1·20
190B	**33**	60p. blue	3·00	2·10

See also Nos. 207A/13A.

34 Crest of King Amanullah

1928. Ninth Anniv of Independence.

191	**34**	15p. red	5·00	5·00

36 **37**

1928

193	**36**	10p. green	1·10	40
194	**37**	25p. red	1·20	80
195	-	40p. blue	1·20	80
196	-	50p. red	1·50	1·00

The frames of the 40 and 50p. differ from Type **37**.
See also Nos. 207A/13A.

41

1929

207A	**36**	10p. brown	1·50	1·30
208A	**31**	15p. blue	1·30	1·30
209A	**37**	25p. blue	1·30	1·20
210A	**41**	30p. green	1·30	1·00
211A	-	40p. red	1·60	1·50
212A	-	50p. blue	2·10	1·50
213A	**33**	60p. black	3·25	2·30

42 Independence Memorial

1931. 13th Independence Day.

214	**42**	20p. red	2·50	1·20

46 National Assembly Building

1932. Inauguration of National Council.

215	-	40p. brown (31×24 mm)	65	40
216	-	60p. violet (29×26 mm)	1·10	80
217	**46**	80p. red (29×26 mm)	1·50	1·20
218	-	1a. black (24×27 mm)	10·50	7·75
219	-	2a. blue (36×25 mm)	5·25	4·00
220	-	3a. green (36×24 mm)	5·25	3·75

DESIGNS: Nos. 215/16, 218/19, Council Chamber; 3a. National Assembly Building (different).

50 Mosque at Balkh

1932

221	**50**	10p. brown	60	25
222	-	15p. brown	40	35
223	-	20p. red	65	25
224	-	25p. green	80	25
225	-	30p. red	80	25
226	-	40p. orange	1·00	50
227	-	50p. blue	1·50	1·30
228	-	60p. blue	1·30	90
229	-	80p. violet	2·50	2·10
230	-	1a. blue	4·50	80
231	-	2a. purple	5·00	2·30
232	-	3a. red	5·75	3·00

DESIGNS—32×23 mm: 15p. Kabul Fortress; 20, 25p. Parliament House, Darul Funun, Kabul; 40p. Memorial Pillar of Knowledge and Ignorance, Kabul; 1a. Ruins at Balkh; 2a. Minarets at Herat. 32×16 mm: 30p. Arch of Paghman. 23×32 mm: 60p. Minaret at Herat. 23×25 mm: 30p. Arch at Qalai Bust, near Kandahar; 50p. Independence Memorial, Kabul. 16×32 mm: 3a. Great Buddha at Bamian.

See also Nos. 237/51.

62 Independence Memorial

1932. 14th Independence Day.

233	**62**	1a. red	5·00	3·25

63 National Liberation Monument, Kabul

1932. Commemorative Issue.

234	**63**	80p. red	2·10	1·50

64 Arch of Paghman

1933. 15th Independence Day.
235 64 50p. blue 2·10 1·50

65 Independence Memorial

1934. 16th Independence Day.
236 65 50p. green 3·25 2·75

1934. As Nos. 219/20 and 221/30, but colours changed and new values.

237	50	10p. violet	25	15
238	-	15p. green	40	15
239	-	20p. mauve	40	15
240	-	25p. red	50	25
241	-	30p. orange	60	35
242	-	40p. black	65	35
243	-	45p. blue	2·10	1·60
244	-	45p. red	40	15
245	-	50p. red	75	25
246	-	60p. violet	80	40
247	-	75p. red	3·00	2·10
248	-	75p. blue	80	65
248b	-	80p. brown	1·30	80
249	-	1a. mauve	2·10	1·60
250	-	2a. grey	4·00	2·00
251	-	3a. blue	4·50	3·00

DESIGNS (new values)—34×23 mm: 45p. Royal Palace, Kabul. 20×34 mm: 75p. Hunters Canyon Pass, Hindu Kush.

68 Independence Memorial

1935. 17th Independence Day.
252 68 50p. blue 3·00 2·50

69 Firework Display

1936. 18th Independence Day.
253 69 50p. mauve 3·25 2·75

70 Independence Memorial and Mohamed Nadir Shah

1937. 19th Independence Day. Perf or imperf.
254 70 50p. brown and violet 7·25 2·20

71 Mohamed Nadir Shah

1938. 20th Independence Day. Perf or imperf.
255 71 50p. brown and blue 2·50 2·50

72 Aliabad Hospital

1938. Obligatory Tax. International Anti-cancer Fund.
256 72 10p. green 3·25 5·00
257 - 15p. blue 3·25 5·00
DESIGN—44×28 mm: 15p. Pierre and Marie Curie.

74 Mohamed Nadir Shah

1939. 21st Independence Day.
258 74 50p. red 2·30 1·50

76 Darul Funun Parliament House, Kabul

79 Independence Memorial

82 Mohamed Zahir Shah **83** Sugar Mill, Baghlan

1939

259	76	10p. purple (36½×24 mm)	25	20
260	76	15p. green (34×21 mm)	35	20
261	76	20p. purple (34×22½ mm)	40	25
262	-	25p. red	50	35
263	-	25p. green	35	25
264	-	30p. orange	40	25
265	-	35p. orange	1·50	1·00
266	-	40p. grey	80	50
267	79	45p. red	80	40
268	79	50p. orange	65	25
269	79	60p. violet	80	25
270	-	70p. violet	2·10	1·00
271	-	70p. purple	2·10	1·00
272	-	75p. blue	2·30	80
273	-	75p. purple	1·80	1·60
274	-	75p. red	3·00	3·00
275	-	80p. brown	1·50	1·00
276	82	1a. purple	1·60	80
277	-	1a. purple	1·60	1·00
278d	83	1a.25 blue	2·10	70
279a	-	2a. red	2·50	1·20
280	-	3a. blue	3·75	2·50

DESIGNS—31×19 mm: 25, 30p. Royal Palace, Kabul. 30×18 mm: 40p. Royal Palace, Kabul. 30×21 mm: 70p. Ruins at Qalai Bust, near Kandahar. 35½×21½ mm: 75p. Independence Memorial and Mohamed Nadir Shah. 34½×21 mm: 80p. As 75p. 35×20 mm: 1a. (No. 277), 2a. Mohamed Zahir Shah; 3a. As Type 82 but head turned more to left. 19×31 mm: 35p. Minarets at Herat.

85 Potez 25A2 over Kabul

1939. Air.
280a 85 5a. orange 5·75 4·50
280b 85 10a. blue 5·75 4·50
280c 85 20a. green 11·50 7·75
See also Nos. 300/2.

86 Mohamed Nadir Shah

1940. 22nd Independence Day.
281 86 50p. green 2·10 1·50

87 Arch of Paghman

1941. 23rd Independence Day.
282 - 15p. green 9·00 5·75
283 87 50p. brown 2·50 2·10
DESIGN: (19×29½ mm): 15p. Independence Memorial.

87b Mohamed Nadir Shah and Arch of Paghman

1942. 24th Independence Day.
284 - 35p. green 3·75 3·75
285 87b 125p. blue 3·00 2·10
DESIGN—VERT: 35p. Independence Memorial in medallion.

88 Independence Memorial and Mohamed Nadir Shah

1943. 25th Independence Day.
286 - 35p. red 14·00 12·50
287 88 1a.25 blue 3·25 2·50
DESIGN—HORIZ: 35p. Independence Memorial seen through archway and Mohamed Nadir Shah in oval frame.

89 Arch of Paghman

90 Independence Memorial and Mohamed Nadir Shah

1944. 26th Independence Day.
288 89 35p. red 1·30 75
289 90 1a.25 blue 2·30 2·00

91 Mohamed Nadir Shah and Independence Memorial

92 Arch of Paghman and Mohamed Nadir Shah

1945. 27th Independence Day.
290 91 35p. red 2·30 80
291 92 1a.25 blue 3·75 2·10

93 Independence Memorial

1946. 28th Independence Day. Dated "1946".
292 - 15p. green 1·20 75
293 93 20p. mauve 2·10 90
294 - 125p. blue 3·25 2·10
DESIGNS—HORIZ: 15p. Mohamed Zahir Shah. VERT: 125p. Mohamed Nadir Shah.

94 Mohamed Nadir Shah and Independence Memorial

1947. 29th Independence Day. Dated "1947".
295 - 15p. green 1·20 60
296 - 35p. mauve 1·30 80
297 94 125p. blue 3·25 2·00
DESIGNS—HORIZ: 15p. Mohamed Zahir Shah and ruins of Kandahar Fort; 35p. Mohamed Zahir Shah and Arch of Paghman.

95 Hungry Boy

1948. Child Welfare Fund.
298 95 35p. green 5·00 4·00
299 - 125p. blue 5·00 4·00
DESIGN—26×33½ mm: 125p. Hungry boy in vert frame. See also No. 307.

1948. Air. As T 85 but colours changed.
300 85 5a. green 23·00 23·00
301 85 10a. orange 23·00 23·00
302 85 20a. blue 23·00 23·00

96 Independence Memorial

1948. 30th Independence Day. Dated "1948".
303 - 15p. green 80 35
304 96 20p. mauve 1·00 40
305 - 125p. blue 2·20 1·10
DESIGNS—VERT: 15p. Arch of Paghman. HORIZ: 125p. Mohamed Nadir Shah.

97 U.N. Symbol

1948. Third Anniv of U.N.O.
306 97 1a.25 blue 11·00 9·00

98 Hungry Boy

1949. Obligatory Tax. Child Welfare Fund.
307 - 35p. orange 3·25 2·10
308 98 125p. blue 4·00 2·10
DESIGN—HORIZ: 35p. As Type 98 but 29×22½ mm.

99 Victory Monument

1949. 31st Independence Day. Dated "1949" (Nos. 310/11).
309 99 25p. green 1·00 50
310 - 35p. mauve 1·20 65
311 - 1a.25 blue 2·30 1·30
DESIGNS—HORIZ: 35p. Mohamed Zahir Shah and ruins of Kandahar Fort; 1a.25, Independence Memorial and Mohamed Nadir Shah.

100 Arch of Paghman

1949. Obligatory Tax. Fourth Anniv of U.N.O.
312 100 125p. green 15·00 9·00

101 King Mohamed Zahir Shah and Map of Afghanistan

1950. Obligatory Tax. Return of King Mohamed Zahir Shah from Visit to Europe.
313 101 125p. green 3·25 1·50

102 Hungry Boy

1950. Obligatory Tax. Child Welfare Fund.

314	**102**	125p. green	4·50	2·50

103 Mohamed
Nadir Shah

1950. 32nd Independence Day.

315	**103**	35p. brown	65	40
316	**103**	125p. blue	1·80	60

104

1950. Obligatory Tax. Fifth Anniv of U.N.O.

317	**104**	1a.25 blue	9·00	3·00

106

1950. 19th Anniv of Faculty of Medicine, Kabul.

318	**106**	35p. green (postage)	1·20	75
319	-	1a.25 blue	4·25	2·30
320	**106**	35p. red (obligatory tax)	1·00	50
321	-	1a.25 black	7·00	2·30

DESIGN: Nos. 319 and 321, Sanatorium. Nos. 318 and 320 measure 38½×25½ mm and Nos. 319 and 321, 45×30 mm.

107 Minaret
at Herat

109 Mohamed
Zahir Shah

110 Mosque at
Balkh

118

1951

322	**107**	10p. brown and yellow	50	15
323	**107**	15p. brown and blue	50	15
324	-	20p. black	9·75	5·25
325	**109**	25p. green	50	15
326	**110**	30p. red	60	15
327	**109**	35p. violet	65	15
328	-	40p. brown	65	15
329	-	45p. blue	65	15
330	-	50p. black	1·90	25
331	-	60p. black	1·50	25
332	-	70p. black, red and green	80	25
333	-	75p. red	1·20	50
334	-	80p. black and red	2·10	90
336	**118**	125p. black and purple	1·80	1·00
335	-	1a. violet and green	1·50	65
337	**118**	2a. blue	2·75	80
338	**118**	3a. blue and black	5·75	1·20

DESIGNS—19×29 mm: 20p. Buddha of Bamian; 45p. Maiwand Victory Monument; 60p. Victory Towers, Ghazni. 22×28 mm: 75, 80p., 1a. Mohamed Zahir Shah. 28×19 mm: 40p. Ruins at Qalai Bust; 70p. Flag. 30×19 mm: 50p. View of Kandahar.
See also Nos. 425/425k.

119 Douglas DC-3 over
Kabul

1951. Air.

339	**119**	5a. red	3·25	65
339a	**119**	5a. green	1·80	40
340	**119**	10a. grey	7·50	1·80
341	**119**	20a. blue	10·50	3·00

See also Nos. 415a/b.

120 Shepherdess

1951. Obligatory Tax. Child Welfare Fund.

342	**120**	35p. green	1·50	90
343	-	125p. blue	1·50	90

DESIGN—34½×44 mm: 125p. Young shepherd.

121 Arch of Paghman (122)

1951. 33rd Independence Day. Optd with T 122.

344	**121**	35p. black and green	1·20	65
345	-	125p. blue	3·00	1·40

DESIGN (34×18½ mm): 125p. Mohamed Nadir Shah and Independence Memorial.
See also Nos. 360/1b and 418/19.

IMPERF STAMPS. From 1951 many issues were made available imperf from limited printings.

124 Flag of Pashtunistan

1951. Obligatory Tax. Pashtunistan Day.

346	**124**	35p. brown	1·50	80
347	-	125p. blue	3·00	2·10

DESIGN—42½×21½ mm: 125p. Afridi tribesman.

125 Dove and Globe

1951. Obligatory Tax. United Nations Day.

348	**125**	35p. mauve	80	40
349	-	125p. blue	2·10	1·60

DESIGN—VERT: 125p. Dove and globe.

126 Avicenna
(physician)

1951. Obligatory Tax. 20th Anniv of Faculty of Medicine.

350	**126**	35p. mauve	7·75	1·50
351	**126**	125p. blue	3·00	4·00

127 Amir Sher Ali and
First Stamp

1951. Obligatory Tax. 76th Anniv of U.P.U.

352	**127**	35p. brown	65	40
353	-	35p. mauve	65	40
354	**127**	125p. blue	1·20	80
355	-	125p. blue	1·20	80

DESIGN: Nos. 353 and 355, Mohamed Zahir Shah and first stamp.

128 Children and
Postman

1952. Obligatory Tax. Child Welfare Fund.

356	**128**	35p. brown	80	65
357	-	125p. violet	1·60	1·00

DESIGN—HORIZ: 125p. Girl dancing (33×23 mm).

(129)

1952. Obligatory Tax. Birth Millenary of Avicenna (physician and philosopher). (a) Surch with T **129**.

358	**110**	40p. on 30p. red	5·25	3·00

(b) Surch **MILLIEME ANNIVERSAIRE DE BOALI SINAI BALKI 125 POULS** in frame.

359	125p. on 30p. red	7·50	3·50

(123)

1952. 34th Independence Day. As Nos. 344/5. (a) Optd with T 123.

360	**123**	35p. black and green	3·25	2·30
361	**123**	125p. blue	3·25	2·30

(b) Without opt.

361a	35p. black and green	1·40	60
361b	125p. blue	3·00	1·20

131 Soldier and
Flag of
Pashtunistan

1952. Obligatory Tax. Pashtunistan Day.

362	**131**	35p. red	80	80
363	**131**	125p. blue	1·20	1·20

132 Orderly and
Wounded Soldier

1952. Obligatory Tax. Red Crescent Day.

364	**132**	10p. green	80	65

133

1952. Obligatory Tax. United Nations Day.

365	**133**	35p. red	80	65
366	**133**	125p. turquoise	1·60	1·20

134 Staff of
Aesculapius

1952. Obligatory Tax. 21st Anniv of Faculty of Medicine.

367	**134**	35p. brown	75	50
368	**134**	125p. blue	2·00	1·30

135 Stretcher Bearers and
Wounded

1953. Obligatory Tax. Red Crescent Day.

369	**135**	10p. green and brown	80	80
370	-	10p. brown and orange	80	80

DESIGN: No. 370, Wounded soldier, orderly and eagle.

136 Prince
Mohamed Nadir

1953. Obligatory Tax. Children's Day.

371	**136**	35p. orange	40	25
372	**136**	125p. blue	80	60

137 Mohamed Nadir
Shah and Flag-bearer

1953. 35th Year of Independence. Inscr "1953".

373	**137**	35p. green	40	25
374	**137**	125p. violet	80	60

DESIGN—VERT: 125p. Independence Memorial and Mohamed Nadir Shah.

138 Flags of
Afghanistan
and
Pashtunistan

1953. Obligatory Tax. Pashtunistan Day. Inscr "1953".

375	**138**	35p. red	40	15
376	-	125p. blue	80	65

DESIGN—HORIZ: 125p. Badge of Pashtunistan (26×20 mm).

139 U.N.
Emblem

1953. Obligatory Tax. United Nations Day.

377	**139**	35p. mauve	1·00	80
378	**139**	125p. blue	2·10	1·50

140 Mohamed
Nadir Shah

1953. Obligatory Tax. 22nd Anniv of Faculty of Medicine.

379	**140**	35p. orange	1·50	1·50
380	-	125p. blue	3·00	3·00

DESIGN: 125p. As Type **140** but inscribed "1953" and with French inscription.
No. 379 was wrongly inscribed "23rd" in Arabic (the extreme right-hand figure in the second row of the inscription) and No. 380 was wrongly inscr "XXIII" and had the words "ANNIVERSAIRE" and "MEDECINE" wrongly spelt "ANNIVERAIRE" and "MADECINE". These mistakes were subsequently corrected but the corrected stamps are much rarer than the original issue.

141 Children's Band
and Map of Afghanistan

1954. Obligatory Tax. Child Welfare Fund.

381	**141**	35p. violet	65	40
382	**141**	125p. blue	1·80	80

142 Mohamed Nadir
Shah and Cannon

1954. 36th Independence Day.

383	**142**	35p. red	65	40
384	**142**	125p. blue	1·80	80

143 Hoisting the Flag

1954. Obligatory Tax. Pashtunistan Day.
385	**143**	35p. orange	65	40
386	**143**	125p. blue	1·80	80

144

1954. Red Crescent Day.
387	**144**	20p. red and blue	60	35

145 U.N. Flag and Map

1954. United Nations Day and Ninth Anniv of U.N.O.
388	**145**	35p. red	1·20	1·20
389	**145**	125p. blue	3·25	2·20

146 Globe and Clasped Hands

1955. Tenth Anniv of Signing of U.N. Charter.
390	**146**	35p. green	1·00	60
391	-	125p. blue	1·80	1·10

DESIGN—28½×36 mm. 125p. U.N. emblem and flags. See also Nos. 403/4.

147 Amir Sher Ali and Mohamed Zahir Shah

1955. 85th Anniv of Postal Service.
392	**147**	35p.+15p. red	1·00	60
393	**147**	125p.+25p. grey	1·90	1·10

148 Children on Swing

1955. Child Welfare Fund.
394	**148**	35p.+15p. green	1·20	75
395	**148**	125p.+25p. violet	2·50	1·20

149 Mohamed Nadir Shah (centre) and brothers

1955. 37th Year of Independence.
396	**149**	35p. blue	65	40
397	**149**	35p. mauve	65	40
398	-	125p. violet	1·40	90
399	-	125p. purple	1·40	90

DESIGN: 125p. Mohamed Zahir Shah and battle scene.

150

1955. Obligatory Tax. Pashtunistan Day.
400	**150**	35p. brown	60	25
401	**150**	125p. green	1·90	60

151 Red Crescent

1955. Obligatory Tax. Red Crescent Day.
402	**151**	20p. red and grey	60	35

152 U.N. Flag

1955. Obligatory Tax. Tenth Anniv of United Nations.
403	**152**	35p. brown	90	60
404	**152**	125p. blue	1·80	1·10

153 Child on Slide

1956. Children's Day.
405	**153**	35p.+15p. blue	90	40
406	**153**	140p.+15p. brown	2·30	80

154 Independence Memorial and Mohamed Nadir Shah

1956. 38th Year of Independence.
407	**154**	35p. green	60	35
408	**154**	140p. blue	2·30	90

155 Exhibition Building

1956. International Exhibition, Kabul.
409	**155**	35p. brown	80	40
410	**155**	50p. blue	80	40

156 Pashtun Square, Kabul

1956. Pashtunistan Day.
411	**156**	35p.+15p. violet	40	25
412	**156**	140p.+15p. brown	1·10	75

157 Mohamed Zahir Shah and Crescent

1956. Obligatory Tax. Red Crescent Day.
413	**157**	20p. green and red	40	25

158 Globe and Sun

1956. U.N. Day and Tenth Anniv of Admission of Afghanistan into U.N.O.
414	**158**	35p.+15p. blue	1·20	1·10
415	**158**	140p.+15p. brown	2·10	1·80

1957. Air. As Nos. 339/40, but colours changed.
415a	**119**	5a. blue	2·10	60
415b	**119**	10a. violet	3·00	1·10

159 Children on See-saw

1957. Child Welfare Fund.
416	**159**	35p.+15p. red	80	60
417	**159**	140p.+15p. blue	1·60	1·50

1957. 39th Independence Day. As Nos. 344/5 but 35p. has longer Arabic opt (19 mm) and 125p. optd **39 em Anv.**
418	**121**	35p. black and green	65	35
419	**121**	125p. blue	1·00	75

162 Pashtu Flag

1957. Pashtunistan Day.
420	**162**	50p. red	1·00	60
421	**162**	155p. violet	1·50	1·10

No. 421 is inscr "JOURNEE DU PASHTUNISTAN" beneath flag instead of Pushtu characters.

163 Red Crescent Headquarters, Kabul

1957. Obligatory Tax. Red Crescent Day.
422	**163**	20p. blue and red	90	60

164 U.N. Headquarters, New York

1957. U.N. Day.
423	**164**	35p.+15p. brown	60	40
424	**164**	140p.+15p. blue	1·10	1·10

165 Buzkashi Game

1957. As stamps of 1951, but colours changed and new value.
425	**110**	30p. brown	40	15
425a	-	40p. red	60	15
425b	-	50p. yellow	65	15
425c	-	60p. blue	80	15
425d	-	75p. violet	1·00	15
425e	-	80p. brown and violet	1·10	15
425g	**165**	140p. purple and green	2·75	65
425f	-	1a. blue and red	1·80	15
425k	**118**	2a. blue	5·75	80
425h	**118**	3a. black and orange	2·75	90

166 Children Bathing

1958. Child Welfare Fund.
426	**166**	35p.+15p. red	65	40
427	**166**	140p.+15p. brown	80	65

167 Mohamed Nadir Shah and Old Soldier

1958. 40th Independence Day.
428	**167**	35p. green	40	25
429	**167**	140p. brown	1·20	1·00

168 Exhibition Buildings

1958. International Exhibition, Kabul.
430	**168**	35p. green	50	25
431	**168**	140p. red	1·20	1·00

169

1958. Pashtunistan Day.
432	**169**	35p.+15p. turquoise	40	25
433	**169**	140p.+15p. brown	1·00	65

170 President Bayar

1958. Visit of Turkish President.
434	**170**	50p. blue	35	15
435	**170**	100p. brown	65	35

171 Red Crescent and Map of Afghanistan

1958. Obligatory Tax. Red Crescent Day.
436	**171**	25p. red and green	40	15

172

1958. 'Atoms for Peace'.
437	**172**	50p. blue	60	50
438	**172**	100p. purple	90	65

173 Flags of U.N. and Afghanistan

1958. U.N. Day.
439	**173**	50p. multicoloured	65	65
440	**173**	100p. multicoloured	1·40	1·20

174 UNESCO Headquarters, Paris

1958. Inauguration of UNESCO Headquarters Building, Paris.
441	**174**	50p. green	80	65
442	**174**	100p. brown	80	80

175 Globe and Torch

1958. Tenth Anniv of Declaration of Human Rights.
443	**175**	50p. mauve	50	50
444	**175**	100p. purple	1·00	1·20

176 Tug-of-War

1959. Child Welfare Fund.
445	**176**	35p.+15p. purple	60	35
446	**176**	165p.+15p. mauve	1·20	50

177 Mohamed Nadir
Shah and Flags

1959. 41st Independence Day.
447	**177**	35p. red	60	50
448	**177**	165p. violet	1·50	65

178 Tribal Dance

1959. Pashtunistan Day.
449	**178**	35p.+15p. green	60	35
450	**178**	165p.+15p. orange	1·20	75

179 Badge-sellers

1959. Obligatory Tax. Red Crescent Day.
451	**179**	25p. red and violet	40	15

180 Horseman

1959. United Nations Day.
452	**180**	35p.+15p. orange	35	25
453	**180**	165p.+15p. green	65	40

181 "Uprooted
Tree"

1960. World Refugee Year.
454	**181**	50p. orange	25	25
455	**181**	165p. blue	35	25
MS455a 108×80 mm. Nos. 454/5. Imperf			5·75	7·75
MS455b As last, colours transposed			7·50	9·00

182 Buzkashi Game **183** Buzkashi Game

1960. Buzkashi Game.
456	**182**	25p. pink	60	25
457	**182**	25p. violet	1·00	25
458	**182**	25p. olive	2·75	25
459	**182**	50p. turquoise	1·40	60
460	**182**	50p. blue	50	35
460a	**182**	50p. orange	50	35
461	**183**	100p. olive	80	25
462	**183**	150p. orange	65	35
463	**183**	175p. brown	2·50	50
464	**183**	2a. green	1·50	1·10

184 Children receiving
Ball

1960. Child Welfare Fund.
465	**184**	75p.+25p. blue	90	35
466	**184**	175p.+25p. green	1·80	50

185 Douglas DC-6 over
Mountains

1960. Air.
467	**185**	75p. violet	65	25
468	**185**	125p. blue	80	40
469	**185**	5a. olive	1·50	90

186
Independence
Monument,
Kabul

1960. 42nd Independence Day.
470	**186**	50p. blue	40	25
471	**186**	175p. mauve	1·10	40

187

1960. Pashtunistan Day.
472	**187**	50p.+50p. red	60	30
473	**187**	175p.+50p. blue	1·40	1·10

188 Insecticide Sprayer

1960. Anti-Malaria Campaign Day.
474	**188**	50p.+50p. orange	1·30	1·20
475	**188**	175p.+50p. brown	3·50	2·75

189 Mohamed Zahir Shah

1960. King's 46th Birthday.
476	**189**	50p. brown	65	25
477	**189**	150p. red	1·60	60

190 Ambulance

1960. Red Crescent Day.
478	**190**	50p.+50p. violet & red	65	50
479	**190**	175p.+50p. blue & red	1·60	1·00

191 Teacher with Globe
and Children

1960. Literacy Campaign.
480	**191**	50p. mauve	40	35
481	**191**	100p. green	1·10	50

192 Globe and Flags

1960. U.N. Day.
482	**192**	50p. purple	25	15
483	**192**	175p. blue	1·00	65
MS483a 128×86 mm. Nos. 482/3. Imperf			6·25	4·50

1960. Olympic Games, Rome. Optd **1960** in figures and
in Arabic and Olympic Rings.
484	**183**	175p. brown	1·80	2·10
MS484a 86×62 mm. No. 484. Imperf			6·25	8·25

1960. World Refugee Year. Nos. 454/5 surch **+25 Ps.**
485	**181**	50p.+25p. orange	1·80	1·80
486	**181**	165p.+25p. blue	1·80	1·80
MS486a 108×80 mm. Nos. 485/6. Imperf			6·25	6·50

195 Mir Wais
Nika (patriot)

1960. Mir Wais Nika Commemoration.
487	**195**	50p. mauve	65	40
488	**195**	175p. blue	1·20	50
MS488a 108×78 mm. Nos. 487/8. Imperf			3·75	3·75

The very numerous issues of Afghanistan which we do
not list appeared between 21 April 1961 and 15 March
1964 (both dates inclusive), and were made available to
the philatelic trade by an agency acting under the au-
thority of a contract granted by the Afghanistan Govern-
ment.

It later became evident that token supplies were only
placed on sale in Kabul for a few hours and some of
these sets contained stamps of very low denominations
for which there was no possible postal use.

When the contract for the production of these stamps
expired in 1963 it was not renewed and the Afghanistan
Government set up a Philatelic Advisory Board to formu-
late stamp policy. The issues from No. 489 onwards were
made in usable denominations and placed on sale with-
out restriction in Afghanistan and distributed to the trade
by the Philatelic Department of the G.P.O. in Kabul.

Issues not listed here will be found recorded in the
Appendix at the end of this country. It is believed that
some of the higher values from the agency sets were uti-
lised for postage in late 1979.

196 Band Amir Lake

1961. Band Amir Lake.
489	**196**	3a. blue	50	25
490	**196**	10a. purple	1·30	1·20

197 Independence
Memorial

1963. 45th Independence Day.
491	**197**	25p. green	15	15
492	**197**	50p. orange	35	25
493	**197**	150p. mauve	50	35

198 Tribesmen

1963. Pashtunistan Day.
494	**198**	25p. violet	15	15
495	**198**	50p. blue	25	25
496	**198**	150p. brown	65	40

199 Assembly Building

1963. National Assembly.
497	**199**	25p. brown	15	15
498	**199**	50p. red	15	15
499	**199**	75p. brown	25	15
500	**199**	100p. olive	25	15
501	**199**	125p. lilac	40	15

200 Balkh Gate

1963. Balkh Gate.
502	**200**	3a. brown	1·00	25

201 Kemal Ataturk

1963. 25th Death Anniv of Kemal Ataturk.
503	**201**	1a. blue	15	15
504	**201**	3a. violet	65	50

202 Mohamed
Zahir Shah

1963. King's 49th Birthday.
505	**202**	25p. green	15	15
506	**202**	50p. grey	25	15
507	**202**	75p. red	35	25
508	**202**	100p. brown	50	25

203 Afghan Stamp
of 1878

1964. Stamp Day.
509	**203**	1a.25 black, green & gold	25	15
510	**203**	5a. black, red and gold	60	40

204 Kabul International
Airport

1964. Air. Inauguration of Kabul Int Airport.
511	**204**	10a. green and purple	80	25
512	**204**	20a. purple and green	1·00	40
513	**204**	50a. turquoise and blue	2·75	1·20

205 Kandahar
International Airport

1964. Air. Inauguration of Kandahar International Airport.
514	**205**	7a.75 brown	65	40
515	**205**	9a.25 blue	90	80
516	**205**	10a.50 green	1·20	1·00
517	**205**	13a.75 red	1·40	1·10

206 Unisphere and Flags

1964. New York World's Fair.
518	**206**	6a. black, red and green	25	15

207 "Flame of
Freedom"

1964. First U.N. Human Rights Seminar, Kabul.
519	**207**	3a.75 multicoloured	25	15

208 Snow Leopard

1964. Afghan Wildlife.
520	**208**	25p. blue and yellow	1·80	25

521	–	50p. green and red	2·10	25
522	–	75p. purple and blue	2·50	25
523	–	5a. brown and green	2·75	90

ANIMALS—VERT: 50p. Ibex. HORIZ: 75p. Argali; 5a. Yak.

209 Herat

1964. Tourist Publicity. Inscr "1964".

524	**209**	25p. brown and blue	15	15
525	–	75p. blue and ochre	25	15
526	–	3a. black, red and green	50	25

DESIGNS—VERT: 75p. Tomb of Gowhar Shad, Herat. HORIZ: 3a. Map and flag.

210 Hurdling

1964. Olympic Games, Tokyo.

527	**210**	25p. sepia, red and bistre	15	10
528	–	1a. sepia, red and blue	15	15
529	–	3a.75 sepia, red and green	40	25
530	–	5a. sepia, red and brown	50	35
MS530a	95×95 mm. Nos. 527/30. Imperf. (sold at 15a.)		1·20	1·20

DESIGNS—VERT: 1a. Diving. HORIZ: 3a.75, Wrestling; 5a. Football.

211 Afghan Flag

1964. 46th Independence Day.

531	**211**	25p. multicoloured	15	15
532	**211**	75p. multicoloured	35	15

On the above the Pushtu inscription "33rd Anniversary" is blocked out in gold.

212 Pashtu Flag

1964. Pashtunistan Day.

533	**212**	100p. multicoloured	25	15

213 Mohamed Zahir Shah

1964. King's 50th Birthday.

534	**213**	1a.25 green and gold	25	15
535	**213**	3a.75 red and gold	40	40
536	**213**	50a. black and gold	3·50	2·30

214 "Blood Transfusion"

1964. Red Crescent Day.

537	**214**	1a.+50p. red and black	35	25

215 Badges of Afghanistan and U.N.

1964. U.N. Day.

538	**215**	5a. blue, black and gold	25	15

216 Doves with Necklace

1964. Women's Day.

539	**216**	25p. blue, green and pink	60	35
540	**216**	75p. blue, green & lt blue	90	40
541	**216**	1a. blue, green and silver	1·20	60

217 M. Jami

1964. 550th Birth Anniv of Mowlana Jami (poet).

542	**217**	1a.50 cream, green & blk	1·00	80

218 Scaly-bellied Woodpecker

1965. Birds. Multicoloured.

543	1a.25 Type **218**		3·00	40
544	3a.75 Lanceolated jay (vert)		5·25	90
545	5a. Himalayan monal pheasant (vert)		6·25	2·00

219 I.T.U. Emblem and Symbols

1965. Centenary of I.T.U.

546	**219**	5a. black, red and blue	50	35

220 "The Red City"

1965. Tourist Publicity. Inscr "1965". Multicoloured.

547	1a. Type **220**		25	10
548	3a.75 Bami Yan (valley and mountains)		40	15
549	5a. Band-E-Amir (lake and mountains)		60	25

221 I.C.Y. Emblem

1965. International Co-operation Year.

550	**221**	5a. multicoloured	50	35

222 Douglas DC-3 and Emblem

1965. Tenth Anniv of Afghan Airlines (ARIANA).

551	**222**	1a.25 multicoloured	35	10
552	–	5a. black, blue & purple	90	15
553	–	10a. multicoloured	1·60	60
MS553a	90×90 mm. Nos. 551/3. Imperf		3·00	3·00

DESIGNS: 5a. Convair CV 240; 10a. Douglas DC-6A.

223 Mohamed Nadir Shah

1965. 47th Independence Day.

554	**223**	1a. brown, black & green	40	15

224 Pashtu Flag

1965. Pashtunistan Day.

555	**224**	1a. multicoloured	40	15

225 Promulgation of New Constitution

1965. New Constitution.

556	**225**	1a.50 black and green	40	15

226 Mohamed Zahir Shah

1965. King's 51st Birthday.

557	**226**	1a.25 brown, blue & pink	25	15
558	**226**	6a. indigo, purple & blue	40	35

See also Nos. 579/80, 606/7 and 637/8.

227 First Aid Post

1965. Red Crescent Day.

559	**227**	1a.50+50 brn, grn & red	35	25

228 U.N. and Afghan Flags

1965. U.N. Day.

560	**228**	5a. multicoloured	25	15

229 Fat-tailed Gecko

1966. Reptiles. Multicoloured.

561	3a. Type **229**		1·00	25
562	4a. "Agama caucasica" (lizard)		1·20	35
563	8a. "Testudo horsfieldi" (tortoise)		2·00	65

230 Cotton

1966. Agriculture Day. Multicoloured.

564	1a. Type **230**		90	25
565	5a. Silkworm moth (caterpillar)		1·80	35
566	7a. Oxen		2·75	50

231 Footballer

1966. World Cup Football Championship, England.

567	**231**	2a. black and red	75	25
568	**231**	6a. black and blue	1·30	35
569	**231**	12a. black and brown	2·75	75

232 Independence Memorial

1966. Independence Day.

570	**232**	1a. multicoloured	35	25
571	**232**	3a. multicoloured	90	35

233 Pashtu Flag

1966. Pashtunistan Day.

572	**233**	1a. blue	60	25

234 Founding Members

1966. Red Crescent Day.

573	**234**	2a.+1a. green and red	35	25
574	**234**	5a.+1a. brown & mve	75	35

235 Map of Afghanistan

1966. Tourist Publicity. Multicoloured.

575	2a. Type **235**		25	25
576	4a. Bagh-i-Bala, former Palace of Abdur Rahman		50	35
577	8a. Tomb of Abdur Rahman, Kabul		75	75
MS578	111×80 mm. Nos. 575/7. Imperf		2·10	2·10

DESIGN: 6a. I.T.Y. emblem on map of Afghanistan.

1966. King's 52nd Birthday. Portrait similar to T **226** but with position of inscr changed. Dated "1966".

579	1a. green		25	25
580	5a. brown		60	35

236 Mohamed Zahir Shah and U.N. Emblem

1966. U.N. Day. Inscr "20TH ANNIVERSAIRE DES REFUGIES".

581	**236**	5a. green, brown & emer	40	15
582	**236**	10a. red, green & yellow	80	15

237 Children Dancing

1966. Child Welfare Day.

583	**237**	1a.+1a. red and green	15	10
584	**237**	3a.+2a. brown & yell	35	15
585	**237**	7a.+3a. green & purple	55	35

238 Construction of Power Station

1967. Afghan Industrial Development. Multicoloured
586	2a. Type **238**	25	25
587	5a. Handwoven carpet (vert)	25	25
588	8a. Cement works	50	35

239 UNESCO Emblem

1967. 20th Anniv (1966) of UNESCO.
589	**239**	2a. multicoloured	25	15
590	**239**	6a. multicoloured	40	15
591	**239**	12a. multicoloured	1·00	25

240 I.T.Y. Emblem

1967. International Tourist Year.
592	**240**	2a. black, blue and yellow	25	25
593	–	6a. black, blue and brown	50	25
MS594 110×70 mm. Nos. 592/3. Imperf. (sold at 10a.)			1·20	1·20

DESIGN: 6a. I.T.Y. emblem on map of Afghanistan.

241 Inoculation

1967. Anti-Tuberculosis Campaign.
595	**241**	2a.+1a. black & yellow	25	25
596	**241**	5a.+2a. brown & pink	65	35

242 Hydroelectric Power Station, Dorunta

1967. Development of Electricity for Agriculture.
597	**242**	1a. lilac and green	15	15
598	–	6a. turquoise and brown	40	25
599	–	8a. blue and purple	60	40

DESIGNS—VERT: 6a. Dam. HORIZ: 8a. Reservoir, Jalalabad.

243 Rhesus Macaque

1967. Wildlife.
600	**243**	2a. blue and buff	75	25
601	–	6a. sepia and green	1·30	35
602	–	12a. brown and blue	2·10	80

ANIMALS—HORIZ: 6a. Striped hyena; 12a. Goitred gazelles.

244 *Saving the Guns at Maiwand* (after R. Caton Woodville)

1967. Independence Day.
603	**244**	1a. brown and red	35	25
604	**244**	2a. brown and mauve	60	25

245 Pashtu Dancers

1967. Pashtunistan Day.
605	**245**	2a. violet and purple	60	25

1967. King's 53rd Birthday. Portrait similar to T **226** but with position of inscr changed. Dated "1967".
606	2a. brown	15	15
607	8a. blue	65	35

246 Red Crescent

1967. Red Crescent Day.
608	**246**	3a.+1a. red, blk & ol	25	25
609	**246**	5a.+1a. red, blk & blue	40	25

247 U.N. Emblem and Fireworks

1967. U.N. Day.
610	**247**	10a. multicoloured	75	35

248 Wrestling

1967. Olympic Games, Mexico City.
611	**248**	4a. purple and green	50	25
612	–	6a. brown and red	1·00	25
MS613 100×65 mm. Nos. 611/12			2·10	2·10

DESIGN: 6a. Wrestling throw.

249 Said Jamal-ud-Din Afghan

1967. 70th Death Anniv of Said Afghan.
614	**249**	1a. purple	25	25
615	**249**	5a. brown	40	25

250 Bronze Vase

1967. Archaeological Treasures (11th–12th century Ghasnavide era).
616	**250**	3a. brown and green	35	15
617	–	7a. green and yellow	65	25
MS618 65×100 mm. Nos. 616/17. Imperf			3·00	3·00

DESIGN: 7a. Bronze jar.

251 W.H.O. Emblem

1968. 20th Anniv of W.H.O.
619	**251**	2a. blue and bistre	25	25
620	**251**	7a. blue and red	50	35

252 Karakul Sheep

1968. Agricultural Day.
621	**252**	1a. black and yellow	25	25
622	**252**	6a. brown, black and blue	1·00	35
623	**252**	12a. brown, sepia & blue	1·60	50

253 Road Map of Afghanistan

1968. Tourist Publicity. Multicoloured.
624	2a. Type **253**	25	25

625	3a. Victory Tower, Ghazni (21×31 mm)	35	25
626	16a. Mausoleum, Ghazni (21×31 mm)	1·20	60

254 Queen Humaira

1968. Mothers' Day.
627	**254**	2a.+2a. brown	35	25
628	**254**	7a.+2a. green	90	60

255 Cinereous Vulture

1968. Wild Birds. Multicoloured.
629	1a. Type **255**	1·80	65	
630	6a. Eagle owl	4·25	2·00	
631	7a. Greater flamingos	6·25	2·30	

256 "Pig-sticking"

1968. Olympic Games, Mexico. Multicoloured.
632	2a. Olympic flame and rings (21×31 mm)	35	15
633	8a. Type **256**	65	40
634	12a. Buzkashi game	1·10	65

257 Flowers on Army Truck

1968. Independence Day.
635	**257**	6a. multicoloured	50	25

258 Pashtu Flag

1968. Pashtunistan Day.
636	**258**	3a. multicoloured	45	25

1968. King's 54th Birthday. Portrait similar to T **226** but differently arranged and in smaller size (21×31 mm).
637	2a. blue	25	25
638	8a. brown	60	35

259 Red Crescent

1968. Red Crescent Day.
639	**259**	4a.+1a. multicoloured	60	25

260 Human Rights Emblem

1968. U.N. Day and Human Rights Year.
640	**260**	1a. brown, bistre & green	25	25
641	**260**	2a. black, bistre & violet	25	25
642	**260**	6a. violet, bistre & purple	50	25
MS643 101×65 mm. **260** 10a. orange, bistre and purple. Imperf			1·80	1·80

261 Maolala Djalalodine Balkhi

1968. 695th Death Anniv of Maolala Djalalodine Balkhi (Rumi)
644	**261**	4a. mauve and green	35	25

262 Temple Painting

1969. Archaeological Treasures (Bagram era).
645	**262**	1a. red, yellow and green	35	25
646	–	3a. purple and violet	90	25
MS647 101×66 mm. Nos. 645/6. Imperf. (sold at 10a.)			1·60	1·60

DESIGN: 3a. Carved vessel.

263 I.L.O. Emblem

1969. 50th Anniv of I.L.O.
648	**263**	5a. black and yellow	35	25
649	**263**	8a. black and blue	60	35

264 Red Cross Emblems

1969. 50th Anniv of League of Red Cross Societies.
650	**264**	3a.+1a. multicoloured	65	35
651	**264**	5a.+1a. multicoloured	80	35

On Nos. 650/1 the commemorative inscr in English and Pushtu for the 50th Anniv of the League of Red Cross Societies has been obliterated by gold bars.

266 Mother and Child

1969. Mothers' Day.
654	**266**	1a.+1a. brown & yell	25	25
655	**266**	4a.+1a. violet & mve	40	35
MS656 121×81 mm. Nos. 654/5. Imperf. (sold at 10a.)			2·10	2·10

267 Road Map of Afghanistan

1969. Tourist Publicity. Badakshan and Pamir Region. Multicoloured.
657	**266**	2a. Type **267**	60	25
658	**266**	4a. Pamir landscape	65	35
659	**266**	7a. Mountain mule transport	1·10	65
MS660 136×90 mm. Nos. 657/9. Imperf (sold at 15a.)			2·50	2·50

268 Bust (Hadda era)

1969. Archaeological Discoveries. Multicoloured.

661	1a. Type **268**	15	10
662	5a. Vase and jug (Bagram period)	40	15
663	10a. Statuette (Bagram period)	65	35

269 Mohamed Zahir Shah and Queen Humaira

1969. Independence Day.

664	**269**	5a. red, blue and gold	40	25
665	**269**	10a. green, purple & gold	75	40

270 Map and Rising Sun

1969. Pashtunistan Day.

666	**270**	2a. red and blue	25	15

271 Mohamed Zahir Shah

1969. King's 55th Birthday.

667	**271**	2a. multicoloured	25	10
668	**271**	6a. multicoloured	60	25

272 Red Crescent

1969. Red Crescent Day.

669	**272**	6a.+1a. multicoloured	80	25

273 U.N. Emblem, Afghan Arms and Flag

1969. United Nations Day.

670	**273**	5a. multicoloured	80	25

274 I.T.U. Emblem

1969. World Telecommunications Day.

671	**274**	6a. multicoloured	35	25
672	**274**	12a. multicoloured	75	40

275 Indian Crested Porcupine

1969. Wild Animals. Multicoloured.

673	**274**	1a. Type **275**	50	35
674	**274**	3a. Wild boar	1·20	40
675	**274**	8a. Bactrian red deer	1·60	50

276 Footprint on the Moon

1969. First Man on the Moon.

676	**276**	1a. multicoloured	25	25
677	**276**	3a. multicoloured	35	25
678	**276**	6a. multicoloured	50	25
679	**276**	10a. multicoloured	75	40

277 "Cancer the Crab"

1970. W.H.O. 'Fight Cancer' Day.

680	**277**	2a. red, dp green & green	25	25
681	**277**	6a. red, deep blue & blue	50	25

278 Mirza Bedel

1970. 250th Death Anniv of Mirza Abdul Quader Bedel (poet).

682	**278**	5a. multicoloured	40	15

279 I.E.Y. Emblem

1970. International Education Year.

683	**279**	1a. black	25	25
684	**279**	6a. red	40	25
685	**279**	12a. green	90	40

280 Mother and Child

1970. Mothers' Day.

686	**280**	6a. multicoloured	35	25

281 U.N. Emblem, Scales and Satellite

1970. 25th Anniv of United Nations.

687	**281**	4a. blue, dp blue & yellow	25	25
688	**281**	6a. blue, deep blue & red	40	25

282 Road Map of Afghanistan with Location of Sites

1970. Tourist Publicity. Inscr "1970". Multicoloured.

689	**282**	2a. black, green and blue	15	15
690	-	3a. multicoloured	25	15

691	-	7a. multicoloured	60	25

DESIGNS: 36×26 mm: 3a. Lakeside mosque, Kabul; 7a. Arch of Paghman.

283 Common Quail

1970. Wild Birds. Multicoloured.

692	2a. Type **283**	2·10	65
693	4a. Golden eagle	4·00	1·00
694	6a. Common pheasant	5·25	1·60

284 Shah Reviewing Troops

1970. Independence Day.

695	**284**	8a. multicoloured	40	25

285 Group of Pashtus

1970. Pashtunistan Day.

696	**285**	2a. blue and red	40	25

286 Mohamed Zahir Shah

1970. King's 56th Birthday.

697	**286**	3a. violet and green	25	25
698	**286**	7a. purple and blue	75	35

287 Red Crescent Emblems

1970. Red Crescent Day.

699	**287**	2a. black, red and gold	25	15

288 U.N. Emblem and Plaque

1970. United Nations Day.

700	**288**	1a. multicoloured	25	25
701	**288**	5a. multicoloured	25	25

289 Afghan Stamps of 1871

1970. Centenary of First Afghan Stamps.

702	**289**	1a. black, blue & orange	35	25
703	**289**	4a. black, yellow & blue	60	25
704	**289**	12a. black, blue and lilac	1·00	40

290 Global Emblem

1971. World Telecommunications Day.

705	**290**	12a. multicoloured	65	40

291 *Callimorpha principalis*

1971. Butterflies and Moths. Multicoloured.

706	1a. Type **291**	1·30	60
707	3a. *Epizygaenella afghana*	2·75	1·20
708	5a. *Parnassius autocrator*	4·00	1·80

292 Lower half of old Kushan Statue

1971. UNESCO Kushan Seminar.

709	**292**	6a. violet and yellow	50	25
710	**292**	10a. purple and blue	80	35

293 Independence Memorial

1971. Independence Day.

711	**293**	7a. multicoloured	60	25
712	**293**	9a. multicoloured	90	35

294 Pashtunistan Square, Kabul

1971. Pashtunistan Day.

713	**294**	5a. purple	50	25

295 Mohamed Zahir Shah and Kabul Airport

1971. Air. Multicoloured.

714	50a. Type **295**	4·50	4·50
715	100a. King, airline emblem and Boeing 727 airplane	5·75	3·50

296 Mohamed Zahir Shah

1971. King's 57th Birthday.

716	**296**	9a. multicoloured	60	35
717	**296**	17a. multicoloured	1·20	65

297 Map, Nurse and Patients

1971. Red Crescent Day.
718	**297**	8a. multicoloured	50	35

298 Emblem of Racial Equality Year

1971. United Nations Day.
719	**298**	24a. blue	1·50	80

299 Human Heart

1972. World Health Day and World Heart Month.
720	**299**	9a. multicoloured	90	35
721	**299**	12a. multicoloured	1·80	40

300 *Tulipa lanata*

1972. Afghan Flora and Fauna. Multicoloured.
722	**300**	7a. Type 300	1·30	75
723		10a. Chukar partridge (horiz)	7·75	1·60
724		12a. Lynx (horiz)	2·50	1·20
725		18a. *Allium stipitatum*	2·50	1·30

301 Buddha of Hadda

1972. Tourist Publicity.
726	**301**	3a. blue and brown	60	25
727	-	7a. green and red	90	35
728	-	9a. purple and green	1·30	40

DESIGNS: 7a. Greco-Bactrian seal, 250 B.C.; 9a. Greek temple, Ai-Khanum, 3rd–2nd century B.C.

302 King with Queen Humaira at Independence Parade

1972. Independence Day.
729	**302**	25a. multicoloured	4·50	1·20

303 Wrestling

1972. Olympic Games, Munich. Various Wrestling Holds as T 303.
730	4a. multicoloured	35	15
731	8a. multicoloured	60	25
732	10a. multicoloured	65	35
733	19a. multicoloured	1·50	50
734	21a. multicoloured	1·60	60

MS735 160×110 mm. Nos. 730/4. Imperf (sold at 60a.) 3·25 3·25

304 Pathan and Mountain View

1972. Pashtunistan Day.
736	**304**	5a. multicoloured	60	25

305 Mohamed Zahir Shah

1972. King's 58th Birthday.
737	**305**	7a. blue, black and gold	75	25
738	**305**	14a. brown, black & gold	1·20	40

306 Ruined Town and Refugees

1972. Red Crescent Day.
739	**306**	7a. black, red and blue	65	25

307 E.C.A.F.E. Emblem

1972. U.N. Day. 25th Anniv of U.N. Economic Commission for Asia and the Far East.
740	**307**	12a. black and blue	60	35

308 Ceramics

1973. Afghan Handicrafts. Multicoloured.
741	**308**	7a. Type 308	40	25
742		9a. Embroidered coat (vert)	50	35
743		12a. Coffee set (vert)	75	40
744		16a. Decorated boxes	1·10	50

MS745 110×110 mm. Nos. 741/4. Imperf (sold at 45a.) 3·75 3·75

309 W.M.O. and Afghan Emblems

1973. Cent of World Meteorological Organization.
746	**309**	7a. green and mauve	60	25
747	**309**	14a. red and blue	1·40	40

310 Emblems and Harvester

1973. Tenth Anniv of World Food Programme.
748	**310**	14a.+7a. purple & blue	1·40	90

311 Al-Biruni

1973. Birth Millenary of Abu-al Rayhan al-Biruni (mathematician and philosopher).
749	**311**	10a. multicoloured	65	40

312 Association Emblem

1973. Family Planning Week.
750	**312**	9a. purple and orange	65	25

313 Himalayan Monal Pheasant

1973. Birds. Multicoloured.
751	8a. Type 313	3·00	2·10
752	9a. Great crested grebe	3·75	2·50
753	12a. Himalayan snowcock	4·50	3·25

314 Buzkashi Game

1973. Tourism.
754	**314**	8a. black	60	35

315 Firework Display

1973. Independence Day.
755	**315**	12a. multicoloured	65	35

316 Landscape and Flag

1973. Pashtunistan Day.
756	**316**	9a. multicoloured	65	15

317 Red Crescent

1973. Red Crescent.
757	**317**	10a. multicoloured	1·00	25

318 Kemal Ataturk

1973. 50th Anniv of Turkish Republic.
758	**318**	1a. blue	25	25
759	**318**	7a. brown	1·20	25

319 Human Rights Flame

1973. 25th Anniv of Declaration of Human Rights.
760	**319**	12a. blue, black and silver	60	40

320 Asiatic Black Bears

1974. Wild Animals. Multicoloured.
761	5a. Type 320	65	15
762	7a. Afghan hound	1·10	40
763	10a. Goitred gazelle	1·40	50
764	12a. Leopard	1·80	60

MS765 120×100 mm. Nos. 761/4. Imperf 10·50 10·50

321 "Workers"

1974. Labour Day.
766	**321**	9a. multicoloured	50	35

322 Arch of Paghman and Independence Memorial

1974. Independence Day.
767	**322**	4a. multicoloured	40	10
768	**322**	11a. multicoloured	60	25

323 Arms of Afghanistan and Hands clasping Seedling

1974. First Anniv of Republic. Multicoloured.
769	4a. Type 323	40	10
770	5a. Republican flag (36×26 mm)	60	15
771	7a. Gen. Mohammed Daoud (26×36 mm)	65	25
772	15a. Soldiers and arms	1·20	35

MS773 Two sheets. Imperf (a) 120×80 mm. Nos. 769 and 772. (b) 100×100 mm. Nos. 770/1. 3·75 3·75

324 Lesser Spotted Eagle

1974. Afghan Birds. Multicoloured.
774	1a. Type 324	2·10	50
775	6a. White-fronted goose, ruddy shelduck and greylag goose	4·50	80
776	11a. Black crane and common coots	7·50	1·30

325 Flags of Pashtunistan and Afghanistan

1974. Pashtunistan Day.
777	**325**	5a. multicoloured	35	25

326 Republic's Coat of Arms

1974. Coat of Arms
778	**326**	100p. green	80	25

327 Pres. Daoud

1974. Pres. Daoud

779	**327**	10a. multicoloured	65	25
780	**327**	16a. multicoloured	2·50	90
781	**327**	19a. multicoloured	90	50
782	**327**	21a. multicoloured	1·40	60
783	**327**	22a. multicoloured	3·75	2·00
784	**327**	30a. multicoloured	5·00	2·75

328 Arms and Centenary
Years

1974. Centenary of U.P.U.

785	**328**	7a. green, black and gold	35	25

329 "UN" and U.N.
Emblem

1974. United Nations Day.

786	**329**	5a. blue and ultramarine	40	15

330 Pres. Daoud

1975. Pres. Daoud

787	**330**	50a. multicoloured	2·75	1·40
788	**330**	100a. multicoloured	5·75	2·50

331 Minaret, Jam

1975. South Asia Tourist Year. Multicoloured.

789		7a. Type **331**	35	15
790		14a. "Griffon and Lady" (2nd century)	65	40
791		15a. Head of Buddha (4th–5th century)	80	40
MS792	130×90 mm. Nos. 789/91. Imperf		3·75	3·75

332 Afghan Flag

1975. Independence Day.

793	**332**	16a. multicoloured	80	25

333 Rejoicing Crowd

1975. Second Anniv of Revolution.

794	**333**	9a. multicoloured	50	15
795	**333**	12a. multicoloured	65	25

334 I.W.Y. Emblem

1975. International Women's Year.

796	**334**	9a. black, blue and purple	50	15

335 Rising Sun
and Flag

1975. Pashtunistan Day.

797	**335**	10a. multicoloured	40	15

336 Wazir M. Akbar
Khan

1976. 130th Death Anniv of Akbar Khan (resistance leader).

798	**336**	15a. multicoloured	60	40

337 Independence
Monument and Arms

1976. Independence Day.

799	**337**	22a. multicoloured	75	50

338 Pres. Daoud
raising Flag

1976. Third Anniv of Republic.

800	**338**	30a. multicoloured	80	60

339 Mountain

1976. Pashtunistan Day.

801	**339**	16a. multicoloured	65	50

340 Arms **340a**

1976. Arms.

802	–	25p. salmon	50	35
803	**340**	50p. green	60	25
803a	**340a**	50p. rosine	60	25
804	**340**	1a. blue	65	10

DESIGN: 25p. As Type **340** but with Arms on left and inscription differently arranged.

341 Flag and Monuments
on Open Book

1977. Independence Day.

805	**341**	20a. multicoloured	75	65

342 Presidential Address

1977. Election of First President and New Constitution. Multicoloured.

806		7a. President Daoud and Election (45×27 mm)	80	60
807		8a. Type **342**	90	75
808		10a. Inaugural ceremony	1·20	90
809		18a. Promulgation of new constitution (45×27 mm)	2·00	1·60
MS810	136×106 mm. Nos. 806/9. Imperf		3·75	3·75

343 Medal

1977. 80th Death Anniv of Sayed Jamaluddin (Afghan reformer).

811	**343**	12a. black, blue & gold	40	15

344 Crowd with
Afghan Flag

1977. Republic Day.

812	**344**	22a. multicoloured	75	40

345 Dancers around
Fountain

1977. Pashtunistan Day.

813	**345**	30a. multicoloured	1·20	90

346 Dome of the
Rock

1977. Palestinian Welfare.

814	**346**	12a.+3a. black, gold and pink	2·10	60

347 Arms and Carrier
Pigeon

1977. Arms and Carrier Pigeon.

815	**347**	1a. blue and black	40	15

348 President Daoud
acknowledging Crowd

1978. First Anniv of Presidential Election.

816	**348**	20a. multicoloured	2·10	1·20

349 U.P.U. Emblem on
Map of Afghanistan

1978. 50th Anniv of Admission to U.P.U.

817	**349**	10a. gold, green & black	40	15

350 Transmitting Aerial
and Early Telephone

1978. 50th Anniv of Admission to I.T.U.

818	**350**	8a. multicoloured	40	15

351 Red Crescent, Red
Cross and Red Lion
Emblems

1978. Red Crescent.

819	**351**	3a. black	1·20	65

352 Arms

1978. Arms

820	**352**	1a. red and gold	1·60	65
821	**352**	4a. red and gold	2·10	90

353 Ruin, Qalai Bust

1978. Independence Day. Multicoloured.

822		16a. Buddha, Bamian	1·20	50
823		22a. Type **353**	1·60	75
824		30a. Women in national costume	2·10	1·20

354 Afghans with
Flag

1978. Pashtunistan Day.

825	**354**	7a. red and blue	50	15

355 Crest and
Symbols of the Five
Senses

1978. International Literacy Day.

826	**355**	20a. red	90	40

356 Flag

1978. 'The Mail is in the Service of the People'.

827	**356**	8a. red, gold and brown	65	15
828	**356**	9a. red, gold and brown	1·00	15

357 Martyr

1978. 'The People's Democratic Party Honours its Martyrs'.
829 **357** 18a. green 1·00 40

358 President Mohammed Taraki

1978. 14th Anniv of People's Democratic Party.
830 **358** 12a. multicoloured 75 25

359 Emancipated Woman

1979. Women's Day.
831 **359** 14a. blue and red 1·20 50

360 Farmers planting Tree

1979. Farmers' Day.
832 **360** 1a. multicoloured 65 35

361 Map and Census Taking

1979. First Complete Population Census.
833 **361** 3a. black, blue and red 90 65

362 Pres. Taraki reading *Khalq*

1979. First Publication of *Khalq* (party newspaper).
834 **362** 2a. multicoloured 65 15

363 Pres. Taraki and Tank

1979. First Anniv of Sawr Revolution (1st issue).
835 **363** 50p. multicoloured 65 15

364 Pres. Taraki

1979. First Anniv of Sawr Revolution (2nd issue). Multicoloured.
836 **364** 4a. Type **364** 40 10

837 5a. Revolutionary H.Q. and
 Tank Monument, Kabul
 (47×32 mm) 60 15
838 6a. Command room, Revolu-
 tionary H.Q. (vert) 65 15
839 12a. House where first Khalq
 Party Congress was held
 (vert) 80 25

365 Carpenter and Blacksmith

1979. Workers' Solidarity.
840 **365** 10a. multicoloured 90 15

366 Children on Map of Afghanistan

1979. International Year of the Child.
841 **366** 16a. multicoloured 1·80 90

367 Revolutionaries and Kabul Monuments

1979. Independence Day.
842 **367** 30a. multicoloured 1·60 90

368 Afghans and Flag

1979. Pashtunistan Day.
843 **368** 9a. multicoloured 75 15

369 U.P.U. Emblem and Arms on Map

1979. Stamp Day.
844 **369** 15a. multicoloured 65 25

370 Headstone and Tomb

1979. Martyrs' Day.
845 **370** 22a. multicoloured 2·50 1·20

371 Doves around Globe

1979
845a **371** 2a. blue and red 1·20 25

372 Woman with Baby, Dove and Rifle

1980. International Women's Day.
846 **372** 8a. multicoloured 1·60 50

373 Farmers receiving Land Grants

1980. Farmers' Day.
847 **373** 2a. multicoloured 2·10 65

374 Healthy Non-smoker and Prematurely Aged Smoker

1980. World Health Day. Anti-smoking Campaign.
848 **374** 5a. multicoloured 1·60 65

375 "Lenin speaking from Tribune"

1980. 110th Birth Anniv of Lenin.
849 **375** 12a. multicoloured 2·50 80

376 Crowd and Clenched Fist

1980. Second Anniv of Sawr Revolution.
850 **376** 1a. multicoloured 65 15

377 Quarry Worker and Blacksmith

1980. Workers' Solidarity.
851 **377** 9a. multicoloured 50 15

378 Football

1980. Olympic Games, Moscow. Multicoloured
852 3a. Type **378** 60 15
853 6a. Wrestling 65 15
854 9a. Pigsticking 75 25
855 10a. Buzkashi 90 25

379 Soldiers attacking Fortress

1980. Independence Day.
856 **379** 3a. multicoloured 65 15

380 Pashtus with Flag

1980. Pashtunistan Day.
857 **380** 25a. multicoloured 1·00 40

381 Post Office

1980. World U.P.U. Day.
858 **381** 20a. multicoloured 1·00 40

382 Buzkashi

1980. Buzkashi.
859 **382** 50a. multicoloured 2·10 1·50
860 **382** 100a. multicoloured 4·00 1·60

383 Arabic "H", Medina Mosque and Kaaba

1981. 1400th Anniv of Hegira.
861 **383** 13a.+2a. multicoloured 1·80 35

384 Mother and Child with Dove and Globe

1981. International Women's Day.
862 **384** 15a. multicoloured 1·20 35

385 Ox Plough, Tractor and Planting Trees

1981. Farmers' Day.
863 **385** 1a. multicoloured 1·00 25

386 Urial

1981. Protected Wildlife.
864 **386** 12a. multicoloured 2·30 65

387 Crowd and Afghan Arms

1981. Third Anniv of Sawr Revolution.
865 **387** 50p. brown 65 15

388 Road Workers in Ravine

1981. Workers' Day.
866 **388** 10a. multicoloured 90 35

389 Red Crescent enclosing Scenes of Disaster and Medical Aid

1981. Red Crescent Day.
867 **389** 1a.+4a. multicoloured 65 80

390 Satellite Receiving Station

1981. World Telecommunications Day.
868 **390** 9a. multicoloured 65 15

391 Map enclosing playing Children

1981. International Children's Day.
869 **391** 15a. multicoloured 90 40

392 Afghans and Monument

1981. Independence Day.
870 **392** 4a. multicoloured 90 15

393 Pashtus around Flag

1981. Pashtunistan Day.
871 **393** 2a. multicoloured 65 15

394 Terracotta Horseman

1981. World Tourism Day.
872 **394** 5a. multicoloured 65 15

395 Siamese Twins and I.Y.D.P. Emblem

1981. International Year of Disabled Persons.
873 **395** 6a.+1a. multicoloured 90 50

396 Harvesting

1981. World Food Day.
874 **396** 7a. multicoloured 80 15

397 Peace, Solidarity and Friendship Organization Emblem

1981. Afro-Asian Peoples' Solidarity Meeting.
875 **397** 8a. blue 75 15

398 Heads and Clenched Fist on Globe and Emblem

1981. International Anti-apartheid Year.
876 **398** 4a. multicoloured 1·00 25

399 Lion (bas-relief at Stara Zagora)

1981. 1300th Anniv of Bulgarian State.
877 **399** 20a. stone, purple and red 1·50 50

400 Mother rocking Cradle

1982. Women's Day.
878 **400** 6a. multicoloured 60 15

401 Farmers

1982. Farmers' Day.
879 **401** 4a. multicoloured 65 15

402 Judas Tree

1982. Plants. Multicoloured.
880 3a. Type **402** 35 15
881 4a. Hollyhock 60 15
882 16a. Rhubarb 1·20 35

403 Hands holding Flags and Tulip

1982. Fourth Anniv of Sawr Revolution.
883 **403** 1a. multicoloured 1·20 15

404 Dimitrov

1982. Birth Centenary of Georgi Dimitrov (Bulgarian statesman).
884 **404** 30a. multicoloured 2·30 80

405 Blacksmith, Factory Workers, Weaver and Labourer

1982. Workers' Day.
885 **405** 10a. multicoloured 75 25

406 White Storks

1982. Birds. Multicoloured.
886 6a. Type **406** 1·60 50
887 11a. Eurasian goldfinches 2·10 60

407 Brandt's Hedgehog

1982. Animals. Multicoloured.
888 3a. Type **407** 60 15
889 14a. Cobra 1·50 25

408 National Monuments

1982. Independence Day.
890 **408** 20a. multicoloured 1·20 50

409 Pashtus and Flag

1982. Pashtunistan Day.
891 **409** 32a. multicoloured 2·50 75

410 Tourists

1982. World Tourism Day.
892 **410** 9a. multicoloured 80 35

411 Postman delivering Letter, Post Office and U.P.U. Emblem

1982. World UPU Day.
893 **411** 4a. multicoloured 90 25

412 Family eating Meal

1982. World Food Day.
894 **412** 9a. multicoloured 1·40 35

413 U.N. Emblem illuminating Globe

1982. 37th Anniv of United Nations.
895 **413** 15a. multicoloured 1·00 40

414 Earth Satellite Station

1982. I.T.U. Delegates' Conference, Nairobi.
896 **414** 8a. multicoloured 75 15

415 Dr. Robert Koch

1982. Centenary of Discovery of Tubercle Bacillus.
897 **415** 7a. black, brown & pink 50 25

416 Hand holding Torch, Globe and Scales

1982. 34th Anniv of Declaration of Human Rights.
898 **416** 5a. multicoloured 40 15

417 Lions

1982. Wild Animals. Multicoloured.
899 2a. Type **417** 40 15
900 7a. Asiatic wild asses 90 35
901 12a. Sable (vert) 2·00 50

418 Woman releasing Dove

1983. International Women's Day.
902 **418** 3a. multicoloured 25 15

419 Mir
Alicher-e-Nawai
(poet)

1983. 'Mir Alicher-e-Nawai and his Times' Study Decade.
903 **419** 22a. multicoloured 90 35

420 Distributing Land
Ownership Documents

1983. Farmers' Day.
904 **420** 10a. multicoloured 65 25

421 Revolution Monument

1983. Fifth Anniv of Sawr Revolution.
905 **421** 15a. multicoloured 65 25

422 World Map and
Hands holding
Cogwheel

1983. Labour Day.
906 **422** 20a. multicoloured 65 25

423 Broadcasting Studio,
Dish Aerial, Satellites and
Television

1983. World Communications Year. Multicoloured.
907 4a. Type **423** 35 10
908 11a. Telecommunications
headquarters 60 15

424 Hands holding Child

1983. International Children's Day.
909 **424** 25a. multicoloured 50 20

425 Arms and
Map of
Afghanistan

1983. Second Anniv of Nat Fatherland Front.
910 **425** 1a. multicoloured 35 15

426 Apollo

1983. Butterflies. Multicoloured.
911 9a. Type **426** 1·00 75
912 13a. Swallowtail 2·30 1·30
913 21a. Small tortoiseshell (horiz) 3·00 1·60

427 Racial
Segregation

1983. Anti-apartheid Campaign.
914 **427** 10a. multicoloured 50 15

428 National Monuments

1983. Independence Day.
915 **428** 6a. multicoloured 40 15

429 Pashtus with
Flag

1983. Pashtunistan Day.
916 **429** 3a. multicoloured 40 15

430 Afghan riding Camel

1983. World Tourism Day.
917 **430** 5a. multicoloured 40 25
918 - 7a. brown and black 60 25
919 - 12a. multicoloured 90 25
920 - 16a. multicoloured 1·20 25
DESIGNS—VERT: 7a. Stone carving. 16a. Carved stele.
HORIZ: 12a. Three statuettes.

431 Winter Landscape

1983. . Multicoloured.
921 50a. Type **431** 1·60 35
922 100a. Woman with camel 3·75 40

432 "Communications"

1983. World Communications Year. Multicoloured.
923 14a. Type **432** 65 15
924 15a. Ministry of Communica-
tions, Kabul 65 15

433 Fish Breeding

1983. World Food Day.
925 **433** 14a. multicoloured 80 15

434 Football

1983. Sports. Multicoloured.
926 1a. Type **434** 25 25
927 18a. Boxing 1·00 35
928 21a. Wrestling 1·20 35

435 Jewellery

1983. Handicrafts. Multicoloured.
929 2a. Type **435** 15 10
930 8a. Polished stoneware 35 15
931 19a. Furniture 60 15
932 30a. Leather goods 1·40 15

436 Map, Sun, Scales and
Torch

1983. 35th Anniv of Declaration of Human Rights.
933 **436** 20a. multicoloured 90 15

437 Polytechnic Buildings and
Emblem

1983. 20th Anniv of Kabul Polytechnic.
934 **437** 30a. multicoloured 1·20 25

438 Ice Skating

1984. Winter Olympic Games, Sarajevo. Multicoloured.
935 5a. Type **438** 25 10
936 9a. Skiing 35 10
937 11a. Speed skating 50 10
938 15a. Ice hockey 60 10
939 18a. Biathlon 65 15
940 20a. Ski jumping 80 15
941 22a. Bobsleigh 1·00 15

439 Dove,
Woman and
Globe

1984. International Women's Day.
942 **439** 4a. multicoloured 50 30

440 Ploughing with
Tractor

1984. Farmers' Day. Multicoloured.
943 2a. Type **440** 15 10
944 4a. Digging irrigation channel 15 10
945 7a. Saddling donkey by
water-mill 15 10
946 9a. Harvesting wheat 25 10
947 15a. Building haystack 40 15
948 18a. Showing cattle 60 15
949 20a. Ploughing with oxen and
sowing seed 75 15

441 "Luna I"

1984. World Aviation and Space Navigation Day.
Multicoloured.
950 5a. Type **441** 35 25
951 8a. "Luna II" 40 25
952 11a. "Luna III" 50 25
953 17a. "Apollo XI" 65 25
954 22a. "Soyuz VI" 80 35
955 28a. "Soyuz VII" 80 35

956 34a. "Soyuz VI", "VII" and "VIII" 1·00 40
MS957 66×87 mm. 25a. Sergei Korolev
(rocket designer) and rocket (29×41
mm) 1·40 80

442 Flags, Soldier and
Workers

1984. Sixth Anniv of Sawr Revolution.
958 **442** 3a. multicoloured 40 15

443 Hunting Dog

1984. Animals. Multicoloured.
959 1a. Type **443** 10 10
960 2a. Argali 25 15
961 6a. Przewalski's horse (horiz) 60 15
962 8a. Wild boar 80 25
963 17a. Snow leopard (horiz) 1·60 25
964 19a. Tiger (horiz) 2·75 25
965 22a. Indian elephant 3·00 35

444 Postal Messenger

1984. 19th U.P.U. Congress, Hamburg. Multicoloured.
966 25a. Type **444** 90 15
967 35a. Post rider 1·40 35
968 40a. Bird with letter 1·80 35
MS969 97×66 mm. 50a. black 3·00 1·80
DESIGNS: As T **444**—35a. Post rider; 40a. Bird with letter;
25×37 mm—50a. Hamburg 1859 2s. stamp.

445 Antonov AN-2

1984. 40th Anniv of Ariana Airline. Multicoloured.
970 1a. Type **445** 10 10
971 4a. Ilyushin Il-12 15 10
972 9a. Tupolev Tu-104A 60 15
973 10a. Ilyushin Il-18 80 15
974 13a. Yakovlev Yak-42 1·10 15
975 17a. Tupolev Tu-154 1·40 15
976 21a. Ilyushin Il-86 1·60 15

446 Ettore Bugatti (motor
manufacturer) and Bugatti
Type 43 Sports car, 1927

1984. Motor Cars. Multicoloured.
977 2a. Type **446** 15 10
978 5a. Henry Ford and Ford Model
A two-seater, 1903 35 10
979 8a. Rene Panhard (engineer)
and Panhard Limosine, 1899 60 10
980 11a. Gottlieb Daimler (engineer)
and Daimler DB 18 saloon,
1935 75 10
981 12a. Karl Benz and Benz
Viktoria two-seater (inscr
"Victoris"), 1893 1·00 15
982 15a. Armand Peugeot (motor
manufacturer) and Peugeot
vis-a-vis, 1892 1·10 15
983 22a. Louis Chevrolet (car
designer) and Chevrolet
Superior sedan, 1925 1·50 15

447 Open Book showing
Monuments and Fortress

1984. Independence Day.
984 **447** 6a. multicoloured 40 15

448 Truck on Mountain Road and Pashtunistan Badge

1984. Pashtunistan Day.
985	**448**	3a. multicoloured	40	15

449 Arch at Qalai Bust

1984. World Tourism Day. Multicoloured.
986	1a. Type **449**		10	10
987	2a. Ornamented belt		15	10
988	5a. Kabul monuments		15	15
989	9a. Statuette (vert)		25	15
990	15a. Buffalo riders in snow		40	25
991	19a. Camel in ornate caparison		80	25
992	21a. Buzkashi players		1·00	25

450 Pine Cone

1984. World Food Day. Multicoloured.
993	2a. Type **450**		15	10
994	4a. Walnuts		25	10
995	6a. Pomegranate		35	10
996	9a. Apples		50	10
997	13a. Cherries		60	15
998	15a. Grapes		75	15
999	26a. Pears		1·20	15

451 Globe and Emblem

1985. 20th Anniv (1984) of Peoples' Democratic Party.
1000	**451**	25a. multicoloured	1·20	40

452 Cattle

1985. Farmers' Day. Multicoloured.
1001	1a. Type **452**		35	15
1002	3a. Mare and foal		35	15
1003	7a. Galloping horse		35	15
1004	8a. Grey horse (vert)		60	25
1005	15a. Karakul sheep and sheepskins		90	25
1006	16a. Herder watching over cattle and sheep		1·10	35
1007	25a. Family with pack camels		1·50	40

453 Map and Geologist

1985. Geologists' Day.
1008	**453**	4a. multicoloured	35	15

454 Satellite

1985. 20th Anniv of 'Intelsat' Communications Satellite. Multicoloured.
1009	6a. Type **454**		50	15
1010	9a. "Intelsat III"		65	15
1011	10a. Rocket launch (vert)		90	15

455 *Visitors for Lenin* (V. Serov)

1985. 115th Birth Anniv of Lenin. Multicoloured.
1012	10a. Type **455**		65	25
1013	15a. "With Lenin" (detail, V. Serov)		80	25
1014	25a. Lenin and Red Army fighters		1·40	40
MS1015	90×21 mm. 50a. Lenin		2·30	1·40

456 Revolutionaries with Flags

1985. Seventh Anniv of Sawr Revolution.
1016	**456**	21a. multicoloured	1·00	15

457 Olympic Stadium and Moscow Skyline

1985. 12th World Youth and Students' Festival, Moscow. Multicoloured.
1017	7a. Type **457**		25	10
1018	12a. Festival emblem		40	25
1019	13a. Moscow Kremlin		50	35
1020	18a. Doll		65	60

458 Soviet Memorial, Berlin-Treptow, and Tank before Reichstag

1985. 40th Anniv of End of World War II. Multicoloured.
1021	6a. Type **458**		60	15
1022	9a. "Mother Homeland" war memorial, Volgograd, and fireworks over Moscow Kremlin		80	15
1023	10a. Cecilienhof Castle, Potsdam, and flags of United Kingdom, U.S.S.R. and U.S.A.		1·10	15

459 Weighing Baby

1985. UNICEF Child Survival Campaign. Multicoloured
1024	1a. Type **459**		10	15
1025	2a. Vaccinating child		15	15
1026	4a. Breast-feeding baby		35	15
1027	5a. Mother and child		40	15

460 Purple Blewit

1985. Fungi. Multicoloured.
1028	3a. Type **460**		15	10
1029	4a. Flaky-stemmed witches' mushroom		40	25

1030	7a. The blusher		60	35
1031	11a. Brown birch bolete		80	60
1032	12a. Common ink cap		1·10	60
1033	18a. *Hypholoma*		1·50	75
1034	20a. *Boletus aurantiacus*		1·60	75

461 Emblems

1985. United Nations Decade for Women.
1035	**461**	10a. multicoloured	65	25

462 Evening Primrose

1985. Argentina '85 International Stamp Exhibition, Buenos Aires. Flowers. Multicoloured.
1036	2a. Type **462**		15	10
1037	4a. Cockspur coral tree		35	15
1038	8a. *Tillandsia aeranthos*		60	15
1039	13a. Periwinkle		90	25
1040	18a. Marvel-of-Peru		1·30	35
1041	25a. *Cypella herbertii*		1·80	35
1042	30a. *Clytostoma callistegioides*		2·30	35
MS1043	80×100 mm. 75a. *Sesbania punicea* (51×36 mm)		5·75	80

463 Building

1985. Independence Day.
1044	**463**	33a. multicoloured	1·50	15

464 Dancers in Pashtunistan Square, Kabul

1985. Pashtunistan Day.
1045	**464**	25a. multicoloured	1·50	15

465 Guldara Stupa

1985. Tenth Anniv of World Tourism Organization. Multicoloured.
1046	1a. Type **465**		15	10
1047	2a. Mirwais tomb (vert)		15	10
1048	10a. Buddha of Bamian (vert)		60	10
1049	13a. No Gumbad mosque (vert)		80	10
1050	14a. Pule Kheshti mosque		90	15
1051	15a. Arch at Qalai Bust		1·00	15
1052	20a. Ghazni minaret (vert)		1·30	15

466 Boxing

1985. Sport. Multicoloured.
1053	1a. Type **466**		10	15
1054	2a. Volleyball		15	10
1055	3a. Football (vert)		50	10
1056	12a. Buzkashi		60	10
1057	14a. Weightlifting		65	15
1058	18a. Wrestling		75	15
1059	25a. Pigsticking		1·00	15

467 Fruit Stall

1985. World Food Day.
1060	**467**	25a. multicoloured	90	15

468 Flags and U.N. Building, New York

1985. 40th Anniv of United Nations Organization.
1061	**468**	22a. multicoloured	90	15

469 Black-billed Magpie

1985. Birds. Multicoloured.
1062	2a. Type **469**		25	10
1063	4a. Green woodpecker		1·00	50
1064	8a. Common pheasants		1·10	50
1065	13a. Bluethroat, Eurasian goldfinch and hoopoe		1·60	90
1066	18a. Peregrine falcons		2·00	1·00
1067	25a. Red-legged partridge		2·75	1·50
1068	30a. Eastern white pelicans (horiz)		3·50	1·70
MS1069	90×20 mm. 75a. Rose-ringed parakeets (29×41 mm)		7·50	80

470 Leopard and Cubs

1985. World Wildlife Fund. The Leopard. Multicoloured
1070	2a. Type **470**		40	25
1071	9a. Head of leopard		1·50	50
1072	11a. Leopard		2·50	80
1073	15a. Leopard cub		3·75	1·20

471 Triumph 650 and Big Ben Tower

1985. Motorcycles. Multicoloured.
1074	2a. Type **471**		15	10
1075	4a. Motobecane and Eiffel Tower, Paris		35	10
1076	8a. Bultaco motorcycles and Don Quixote monument, Madrid		60	15
1077	13a. Honda and Mt. Fuji, Japan		90	15
1078	18a. Jawa and Old Town Hall clock, Prague		1·10	15
1079	25a. MZ motorcycle and T.V. Tower, Berlin		1·60	25
1080	30a. Motorcycle and Colos-seum, Rome		2·00	25
MS1081	100×80 mm. 75a. Moskva Dnieper motorcycle and Red Square, Moscow		6·50	80

472 Crowd with Flags

1986. 21st Anniv of Peoples' Democratic Party.
1082	**472**	2a. multicoloured	35	25

473 Lenin writing

1986. 27th Soviet Communist Party Congress, Moscow.
1083 **473** 25a. multicoloured 80 40

474 "Vostok 1"

1986. 25th Anniv of First Manned Space Flight. Multicoloured.
1084 3a. Type **474** 25 15
1085 7a. Russian Cosmonaut Medal (vert) 25 15
1086 9a. Launch of "Vostok 1" (vert) 40 15
1087 11a. Yuri Gagarin (first man in space) (vert) 50 15
1088 13a. Cosmonauts reading newspaper 60 25
1089 15a. Yuri Gagarin and Sergei Pavlovich Korolev (rocket designer) 60 25
1090 17a. Valentina Tereshkova (first woman in space) (vert) 75 25

475 Footballers

1986. World Cup Football Championship, Mexico.
1091 **475** 3a. multicoloured 25 15
1092 - 4a. multicoloured (horiz) 35 15
1093 - 7a. multicoloured (horiz) 40 15
1094 - 11a. multicoloured 65 15
1095 - 12a. mult (horiz) 80 25
1096 - 18a. multicoloured 1·20 25
1097 - 20a. multicoloured 1·40 25
MS1098 120×90 mm. 75a. multicoloured (39×26 mm) 4·50 80
DESIGNS: 4a. to 75a. Various footballing scenes.

476 Lenin

1986. 116th Birth Anniv of Lenin.
1099 **476** 16a. multicoloured 75 40

477 Delegates voting

1986. First Anniv of Supreme Council Meeting of Tribal Leaders.
1100 **477** 3a. brown, red and blue 25 15

478 Flags and Crowd

1986. Eighth Anniv of Sawr Revolution.
1101 **478** 8a. multicoloured 40 15

479 Worker with Cogwheel and Globe

1986. Labour Day.
1102 **479** 5a. multicoloured 25 15

480 Patient receiving Blood Transfusion

1986. International Red Cross and Red Crescent Day.
1103 **480** 7a. multicoloured 50 25

481 St. Bernard

1986. Pedigree Dogs. Multicoloured.
1104 5a. Type **481** 25 10
1105 7a. Rough collie 40 10
1106 8a. Spaniel 50 15
1107 9a. Long-haired dachshund 60 15
1108 11a. German shepherd 65 25
1109 15a. Bulldog 90 25
1110 20a. Afghan hound 1·20 25

482 Tiger Barb

1986. Fish. Multicoloured.
1111 5a. Type **482** 25 15
1112 7a. Mbuna 40 15
1113 8a. Clown loach 50 15
1114 9a. Lisa 60 15
1115 11a. Figure-eight pufferfish 80 15
1116 15a. Six-barred distichodus 1·10 35
1117 20a. Sail-finned molly 1·40 35

483 Mother and Children

1986. World Children's Day. Multicoloured.
1118 1a. Type **483** 15 15
1119 3a. Woman holding boy and emblem 15 15
1120 9a. Circle of children on map (horiz) 40 15

484 Italian Birkenhead Locomotive

1986. 19th-century Railway Locomotives. Multicoloured
1121 4a. Type **484** 25 10
1122 5a. Norris locomotive 35 10
1123 6a. Stephenson "Patentee" type locomotive 40 15
1124 7a. Bridges Adams locomotive 50 15
1125 8a. Ansoldo locomotive 65 25
1126 9a. Locomotive "St. David" 80 25
1127 11a. Jones & Potts locomotive 90 25

485 Cobra

1986. Animals. Multicoloured.
1128 3a. Type **485** 15 10
1129 4a. Lizards (vert) 25 15
1130 5a. Praying mantis 35 15
1131 8a. Beetle (vert) 50 25
1132 9a. Spider 60 35
1133 10a. Snake 65 35
1134 11a. Scorpions 80 35
Nos. 1130/2 and 1134 are wrongly inscr "Les Reptiles".

486 Profiles on Globe

1986. World Youth Day.
1135 **486** 15a. multicoloured 65 25

487 National Monuments

1986. Independence Day.
1136 **487** 10a. multicoloured 50 25

488 11th-century Ship

1986. Stockholmia 86 International Stamp Exhibition. Sailing Ships. Multicoloured.
1137 4a. Type **488** 40 15
1138 5a. Roman galley 50 25
1139 6a. English royal kogge 65 25
1140 7a. Early dhow 80 25
1141 8a. Nao 1·00 25
1142 9a. Ancient Egyptian ship 1·10 25
1143 11a. Medieval galeasse 1·30 25
MS1144 86×64 mm. 50a. Early dhow (as 7a.) (41×29 mm) 4·00 80

489 Tribesmen

1986. Pashtunistan Day.
1145 **489** 4a. multicoloured 25 15

490 State Arms

1986. Supreme Council Meeting of Tribal Leaders.
1146 **490** 3a. gold, blue and black 40 25

491 Labourer reading

1986. World Literacy Day.
1147 **491** 2a. multicoloured 25 15

492 Dove and U.N. Emblem

1986. International Peace Year.
1148 **492** 12a. black and blue 60 25

493 Tulips, Flame and Man with Rifle

1986. Afghanistan Youth Day.
1149 **493** 3a. red and black 40 25

494 Crowd and Flags

1987. Ninth Anniv of Sawr Revolution.
1150 **494** 3a. multicoloured 25 15

495 Map and Dove

1987. National Reconciliation.
1151 **495** 3a. multicoloured 25 15

496 Oral Rehydration

1987. International Children's Day. Multicoloured.
1152 1a. Type **496** 15 10
1153 5a. Weighing babies 15 10
1154 9a. Vaccinating babies 35 15

497 Conference Delegates

1987. First Anniv of Tribal Conference.
1155 **497** 5a. multicoloured 35 25

498 *Pieris* sp.

1987. Butterflies and Moths. Multicoloured.
1156 7a. Type **498** 60 35
1157 9a. Brimstone and unidentified butterfly 75 35
1158 10a. Garden tiger moth (horiz) 1·00 50
1159 12a. *Parnassius* sp. 1·40 50
1160 15a. Butterfly (unidentified) (horiz) 1·50 65
1161 22a. Butterfly (unidentified) (horiz) 2·10 90
1162 25a. Butterfly (unidentified) 2·50 90

499 People on Hand

1987. First Local Government Elections.
1163	**499**	1a. multicoloured	25	15

500 Khan Abdul Ghaffar Khan

1987. Pashtun and Baluch Day.
1164	**500**	4a. multicoloured	25	15

501 "Sputnik 1"

1987. 30th Anniv of Launch of *Sputnik* (first artificial satellite). Multicoloured.
1165	10a. Type **501**		40	15
1166	15a. Rocket launch		60	15
1167	25a. "Soyuz"–"Salyut" space complex		80	15

502 Old and Modern Post Offices

1987. World U.P.U. Day.
1168	**502**	22a. multicoloured	1·10	60

503 Monument and Arch of Paghman

1987. Independence Day.
1169	**503**	3a. multicoloured	25	15

504 "Communications"

1987. United Nations Day.
1170	**504**	42a. multicoloured	4·50	1·00

505 Lenin

1987. 70th Anniv of Russian Revolution.
1171	**505**	25a. multicoloured	1·20	65

506 Castor Oil Plant

1987. Plants. Multicoloured.
1172	3a. Type **506**	15	15
1173	6a. Liquorice	35	15
1174	9a. Camomile	60	15
1175	14a. Thorn apple	80	15
1176	18a. Chicory	1·00	15

507 Field Mice

1987. Mice. Multicoloured.
1177	2a. Type **507**	40	15
1178	4a. Brown and white mice (horiz)	50	15
1179	8a. Ginger mice (horiz)	60	15
1180	16a. Black mice (horiz)	1·00	15
1181	20a. Spotted and ginger mice (horiz)	1·20	15

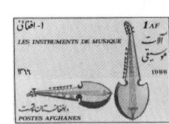

508 Four-stringed Instrument

1988. Musical Instruments. Multicoloured.
1182	1a. Type **508**	15	15
1183	3a. Drums	15	15
1184	5a. Two-stringed instruments with two pegs	25	15
1185	15a. Two-stringed instrument with ten pegs	60	15
1186	18a. Two-stringed instruments with fourteen or ten pegs	80	25
1187	25a. Four-stringed bowed instruments	1·20	25
1188	33a. Two-stringed bowed instruments	1·60	25

509 Mixed Arrangement

1988. Flowers. Multicoloured.
1189	3a. Type **509**	25	15
1190	5a. Tulips (horiz)	35	15
1191	7a. Mallows	50	25
1192	9a. Small mauve flowers	65	25
1193	12a. Marguerites	1·20	35
1194	15a. White flowers	1·50	35
1195	24a. Red and blue flowers (horiz)	2·10	35

510 Emblems and Means of Communication

1988. 60th Anniv of Membership of U.P.U. and I.T.U.
1196	**510**	20a. multicoloured	80	50

511 Tank Monument, Kabul, and Flags

1988. Tenth Anniv of Sawr Revolution.
1197	**511**	10a. multicoloured	80	50

512 Mesosaurus

1988. Prehistoric Animals. Multicoloured.
1198	3a. Type **512**	15	10
1199	5a. Styracosaurus (horiz)	25	10
1200	10a. Uintatherium (horiz)	50	15
1201	15a. Protoceratops (horiz)	75	15
1202	20a. Stegosaurus (horiz)	1·00	25
1203	25a. Ceratosaurus	1·30	25
1204	30a. Moa ("Dinornis maximus")	1·80	25

513 Baskets and Bowl of Fruit

1988. Fruit. Multicoloured.
1205	2a. Type **513**	25	15
1206	4a. Baskets of fruit	35	15
1207	7a. Large basket of fruit	35	25
1208	8a. Bunch of grapes on branch (vert)	50	25
1209	16a. Buying fruit from market stall	80	35
1210	22a. Arranging fruit on market stall	1·20	35
1211	25a. Stallholder weighing fruit (vert)	1·80	35

514 Memorial Pillar of Knowledge and Ignorance, Kabul

1988. Independence Day.
1212	**514**	24a. multicoloured	1·20	65

515 Heads encircled with Rope

1988. Pashtunistan Day.
1213	**515**	23a. multicoloured	90	60

516 Flags and Globe

1988. Afghan–Soviet Space Flight.
1214	**516**	32a. multicoloured	1·20	50

517 Anniversary Emblem

1988. 125th Anniv of International Red Cross.
1215	**517**	10a. multicoloured	80	50

518 Rocket and V. Tereshkova

1988. 25th Anniv of First Woman Cosmonaut Valentina Tereshkova's Space Flight. Multicoloured
1216	10a. Type **518**	80	35

1217	15a. Bird, globe and rocket (vert)		65	15
1218	25a. "Vostok 6" and globe		1·00	15

519 Decorated Metal Vessels

1988. Traditional Crafts. Multicoloured.
1219	2a. Type **519**	10	10
1220	4a. Pottery	15	10
1221	5a. Clothing (vert)	25	15
1222	9a. Carpets	35	15
1223	15a. Bags	35	25
1224	23a. Jewellery	90	25
1225	50a. Furniture	1·80	25

520 Indian Flag and Nehru

1988. Birth Centenary of Jawaharlal Nehru (Indian statesman).
1226	**520**	40a. multicoloured	2·10	80

521 Emeralds

1988. Gemstones. Multicoloured.
1227	13a. Type **521**	80	15
1228	37a. Lapis lazuli	1·80	35
1229	40a. Rubies	2·30	35

522 Ice Skating

1988. Winter Olympic Games, Calgary. Multicoloured
1230	2a. Type **522**	15	15
1231	5a. Slalom	25	15
1232	9a. Two-man bobsleigh	50	15
1233	22a. Biathlon	90	15
1234	37a. Speed skating	1·90	15
MS1235	80×60 mm. 75a. Ice hockey	4·00	80

523 Old City

1988. International Campaign for Preservation of Old Sana'a, Yemen.
1236	**523**	32a. multicoloured	1·50	1·10

524 Emblem

1989. Second Anniv of Move for National Reconciliation.
1237	**524**	4a. multicoloured	25	15

525 Bishop and Game from "The Three Ages of Man" (attr. Estienne Porchier)

1989. Chess. Multicoloured.

1238	1a. Type **525**	25	15
1239	3a. Faience queen and 14th century drawing of Margrave Otto IV of Brandenburg and his wife playing chess	35	15
1240	4a. French king and game	40	15
1241	7a. King and game	65	25
1242	16a. Knight and game	1·10	25
1243	24a. Arabian knight and "Great Chess"	1·50	35
1244	45a. Bishop and teaching of game	2·75	40

Nos. 1240/4 show illustrations from King Alfonso X's *Book of Chess, Dice and Tablings*.

526 *The Old Jew*

1989. Picasso Paintings. Multicoloured.

1245	4a. Type **526**	35	25
1246	6a. *The Two Harlequins*	40	25
1247	8a. *Portrait of Ambrouse Vollar*	50	25
1248	22a. *Majorcan Woman*	1·20	25
1249	35a. *Acrobat on Ball*	2·30	25
MS1250	70×90 mm. 75a. *Horta de Ebro Factory*. Imperf	4·00	80

527 Euphrates Jerboa

1989. Animals. Multicoloured.

1251	3a. Type **527**	35	25
1252	4a. Asiatic wild ass	35	25
1253	14a. Lynx	1·00	35
1254	35a. Lammergeier	3·50	1·50
1255	44a. Markhor	2·30	1·20
MS1256	70×90 mm. 100a. Oxus cobra	4·50	1·20

528 Bomb breaking, Dove and Woman holding Wheat

1989. International Women's Day (1988).

1257	**528**	8a. multicoloured	40	15

529 Cattle

1989. Farmers' Day. Multicoloured.

1258	1a. Type **529**	25	15
1259	2a. Ploughing with oxen and tractors	25	15
1260	3a. Picking cotton	25	15

530 Dish Aerial

1989. World Meteorology Day. Multicoloured.

1261	27a. Type **530**	1·20	25
1262	32a. World Meteorological Organization emblem and state arms	1·60	25
1263	40a. Data-collecting equipment (vert)	2·10	25

531 Rejoicing Crowd

1989. 11th Anniv of Sawr Revolution.

1264	**531**	20a. multicoloured	1·10	25

532 Outdoor Class

1989. Teachers' Day.

1265	**532**	42a. multicoloured	2·10	35

533 Eiffel Tower and Arc de Triomphe

1989. Bicentenary of French Revolution.

1266	**533**	25a. multicoloured	1·50	90

534 Transmission Mast

1989. Tenth Anniv of Asia-Pacific Telecommunity.

1267	3a. Type **534**	15	15
1268	27a. Dish aerial	1·10	25

535 National Monuments

1989. Independence Day.

1269	**535**	25a. multicoloured	1·20	35

536 Pashtu

1989. Pashtunistan Day.

1270	**536**	3a. multicoloured	35	25

537 White Spoonbill

1989. Birds. Multicoloured.

1271	3a. Type **537**	25	15
1272	5a. Purple swamphen	50	25
1273	10a. Eurasian bittern (horiz)	90	40
1274	15a. Eastern white pelican	1·20	50
1275	20a. Red-crested pochard	1·50	60
1276	25a. Mute swan	2·10	65
1277	30a. Great cormorant (horiz)	2·30	90

538 Duchs Tourer, 1910

1989. Vintage Cars. Multicoloured.

1278	5a. Type **538**	40	25
1279	10a. Ford Model T touring car, 1911	75	25
1280	20a. Renault Type AX two-seater, 1911	1·20	25
1281	25a. Russo-Balte tourer, 1911	1·50	35
1282	30a. Fiat 509 tourer, 1926	1·80	35

It is reported no stamps were issued by the Post Office from 1990—2001 inclusive. Any in circulation for these years are considered spurious.

Nos. 1986/8 and Types **540/2** are left for the issues of 2002, not yet received.

543 Scales

2002. 55th (2003) Anniv of Universal Declaration of Human Rights

1989	4a. multicoloured	1·70	1·70

544 Tractor ploughing

2003. Farmers' Day. Multicoloured.

1990	3a. Type **544**	15·00	15·00
1991	6a. Ploughing with oxen	30·00	20·00

545 *Calanthe veitchii*

2003. Orchids. Multicoloured.

1992	9a. Type **545**	85	85
1993	13a. *Euanthe sanderiana* (inscr 'Eulanthe')	1·20	1·20
1994	17a. *Ordontoglossum vuyl-stekeae* (inscr 'Ordontioda')	1·40	1·40
1995	20a. *Dendrobium infundibulum*	1·50	1·50
1996	30a. *Miltoniopsis roezlii* (inscr 'Miltonsiopsis')	1·70	1·70
1997	40a. *Cattleya labiata*	2·40	2·40
1998	100a *Vanda coerulea*	5·25	5·25

546 Minaret, Mosque and Kaaba,

2003. Birthday of Prophet Mohammed.

1999	**546**	10a. multicoloured	70·00	30·00

547 Children and 'STOP TB'

2003. International Tuberculosis Awareness Day. Multicoloured.

2000	1a. Type **547**	10	10
2001	4a. Treatment (horiz)		
2002	9a. Infection (horiz)	60	25

548 Assembly

2003. First Anniv of Loya Jirga to elect President Hamid Karzai

2003	**548**	20a. multicoloured	1·90	1·90

549 Map enclosing Poppy Head overlaid with Ears of Corn

2003. Struggle Against Narcotics Day. Multicoloured.

2004	1a. Type **549**	25	25
2005	2a. Poppy head, resin and skulls (vert)	55	55
2006	5a. Tractor ploughing in poppies	95	95
MS2006a	106×82 mm. 10a. Poppy head, resin and skulls (different)	1·90	1·90

550 Rottweiler

2003. Dogs. Multicoloured.

2007	10a. Type **550**	95	95
2008	20a. Cocker spaniel	1·70	1·70
2009	30a. Doberman	1·90	1·90
2010	40a. Afghan hound	2·10	2·10
2011	50a. Giant schnauzer	2·50	2·50
2012	60a. Boxer	2·75	2·75
MS2013	106×82 mm. 150a. Afghan hound (different)	9·00	9·00

551 Bird Island, South Africa

2003. Lighthouses. Multicoloured.

2014	10a. Type **551**	95	95
2015	20a Cordoun, France	1·90	1·90
2016	30a. Mahota Pagoda, China	2·30	2·30
2017	50a Bay Canh, Vietnam	2·75	2·75
2018	60a. Cap Roman Rock, South Africa	3·00	3·00
2019	100a Mikomoto Shima, Japan	4·75	4·75
MS2020	75×106 mm. 150a. Bell Rock, UK (inscr 'British Islands')	9·00	9·00

552 Monument and Arch

2003. Independence Day.

2021	**552**	15a. multicoloured	80·00	35·00

553 Dove Outline enclosing Students

2003. International Literacy Day

2022	**553**	2a. multicoloured	15·00	15·00

554 Globe and Dove holding Envelope

2003. World Post Day

2023	**554**	8a. multicoloured	45·00	20·00

555 Fragment of Woman's Face (fresco), Bamiyan

2003. Cultural Heritage. Multicoloured.
MS2024 20a. Type **555**; 40a. Buddha's head, Gandhara; 60a. Buddha (statue), Takht-i-Bahi Monastery, Gandhara; 100a. Buddha's hand, Bamiyan 6·50 6·50
Nos. 2025/7 are vacant.

556 Quran

2003. Transmission of the Quran
2028 **556** 9a. multicoloured 3·25 3·25

557 Statue

2003. World Tourism Day. Historical Artefacts. Multicoloured.
2029 4a. Type **557** 25·00 10·00
2030 8a. Hill fort 45·00 20·00
2030a 12a. Pot, coins and inscribed tablets 70·00 30·00
MS2030b 108×82 mm. 25a. Hill fort (detail) 1·20 1·20

557a Leopard

2003. Animals. Multicoloured.
2030c 6c. Type **557a** 10·00 10·00
2030d 11a. Jackal 65·00 30·00
2030e 15a. Asiatic ibex 80·00 35·00
MS2030f 107×83 mm. 40s. Leopard (different) 6·25 6·25

558 Woman holding Book and Flame

2004. International Women's Day.
2031 **558** 6a. multicoloured 35·00 20·00

559 Woman, Pills and Blood-stained Hankerchief

2004. World TB Awareness Day. Multicoloured.
2032 1a. Type **559** 35 35
2033 4a. Woman wearing mask and child 50 50
2034 9a. Raising awareness 85 85
2035 12a. TB sufferer and pills (vert) 1·20 1·20
2036 15a. Doctor examining patient (vert) 1·40 1·40

560 President Karzai

2004. Inauguration of President Hamid Karzai. Multicoloured.
2037 12a. Type **560** 1·50 1·50
MS2038 150×82 mm. 100a. As Type **560** (50×50 mm) 9·25 9·25

561 Voters

2004. First Direct Presidential Elections.
2039 **561** 15a. multicoloured 85·00 40·00
2040 - 25a. multicoloured 1·20 55·00
No. 2041 and Type **562** are left for Inauguration of President, Issued on 7 December 2004, not yet received.

563 Clasped Hands and Symbols of Afghanistan and China

2005. 50th Anniv of Afghanistan–China Diplomatic Relations.
2042 **563** 25a. multicoloured 1·20 55·00
MS2042a 134×93 mm. Size 60×40 mm.
150a. As Type **563** 6·50 6·50
No. MS2042 was printed on silk coated paper.

565 Crowd

2006. 87th Anniv of Independence Day.
2046 **565** 45a. multicoloured 2·20 95·00

566 Classroom

2006. World Literacy Day.
2047 **566** 12a. multicoloured 70·00 30·00

567 Dove enclosing Globe

2006. World Post Day. Multicoloured.
2048 15a. Type **567** 85·00 40·00
2049 15a. As Type **567** but with inscription and colour of date changed 85·00 40·00

567a Flags of Members

2006. Third Meeting of ECO Postal Authorities.
2049a **567a** 8a. multicoloured 45·00 20·00

569 Rumi, Dancers and Rûm (image scaled to 41% of original size)

2007. 800th Birth Anniv Mawlana Jalaluddin Mohammad al-Balkhi al-Rum (spiritual master and mystic poet). Sheet 116×78 mm
MS2053 **569** 150a. multicoloured

570 Dancers

2007. Aten Milli, National Dance
2054 **570** 38a. multicoloured 3·00 3·00
No. 2054 carries the imprint date '2006'.

571 Ustad Awal Mir (master singer)

2007. National Day of Fine Arts. Multicoloured.
2055 20a. Type **571** 1·00 50·00
2056 22a. Mirmum Parwin (first female singer of Afghanistan) 1·10 50·00

NEWSPAPER STAMPS

N35

1928. Newspaper Stamps
N192 **N35** 2p. blue 4·00 4·50

1929. Newspaper Stamps
N205A 2p. red 30 50

N43

1932. Newspaper Stamps
N215 **N43** 2p. red 40 50
N216 **N43** 2p. black 35 80
N217 **N43** 2p. green 40 75
N219 **N43** 2p. red 50 75

N75 Coat-of-Arms

1939. Arms
N259 **N75** 2p. green 25 65
N260 **N75** 2p. mauve (no gum) 15 1·00

1969. As Type N **75**, but larger and with different Pushtu inscr.
N652 100p. green 25 25
N653 150p. brown 35 25

OFFICIAL STAMPS

O27

1909
O173 **O27** (−) red 1·20 1·20

1939. Design 22¼×28 mm.
O281 **O86** 15p. green 1·10 80
O282 **O86** 30p. brown 1·50 1·50
O283 **O86** 45p. red 1·20 1·20
O284 **O86** 1a. mauve 2·00 1·80

O86

1954. Design 24½×31 mm.
O285b 50p. red 1·00 50

1965. Design 24×30½ mm.
O287 50p. pink 1·20 50

PARCEL POST STAMPS

P27

1909
P173 **P27** 3s. brown 1·20 2·10
P174 **P27** 3s. green 1·80 3·50
P175 **P27** 1k. green 2·10 3·50
P176 **P27** 1k. red 3·00 1·50
P177 **P27** 1r. orange 6·50 2·00
P178 **P27** 1r. grey 30·00
P179 **P27** 2r. green 3·50 3·50
P180 **P27** 2r. red 4·00 4·00
P181 **P27** 2r. blue 6·25 6·50

P28 Old Habibia College, Kabul

1921
P182 **P28** 10p. brown 4·00 5·75
P183 **P28** 15p. brown 5·75 6·50
P184 **P28** 30p. purple 10·50 6·50
P185 **P28** 1r. blue 12·50 12·50

1923. Fifth Independence Day. Optd with T **28**.
P186 10p. brown 90·00
P187 15p. brown £100
P188 30p. purple £200

P35 **P36**

1928
P192 **P35** 2a. orange 6·50 5·00
P193 **P36** 3a. green 10·50 10·50

1930
P214 **P35** 2a. green 7·50 7·50
P215 **P36** 3a. brown 9·00 10·50

REGISTRATION STAMP

R19

1894. Undated.
R155 **R19** 2a. black on green 9·75 11·50

APPENDIX

The following stamps have either been issued in excess of postal needs or have not been available to the public in reasonable quantities at face value. Such stamps may later be given full listing if there is evidence of regular postal use. Sheets, imperforate stamps etc, are excluded from this section.

1961

Agriculture Day. Fauna and Flora. 2, 2, 5, 10, 15, 25, 50, 100, 150, 175p.
Child Welfare. Sports and Games. 2, 2, 5, 10, 15, 25, 50, 100, 150, 175p.
UNICEF Surch on 1961 Child Welfare issue. 2+25, 2+25, 5+25, 10+25, 15p.+25p.
Women's Day. 50, 175p.
Independence Day. Mohamed Nadir Shah. 50, 175p.
International Exhibition, Kabul. 50, 175p.
Pashtunistan Day. 50, 175p.
National Assembly. 50, 175p.
Anti-malaria Campaign. 50, 175p.

King's 47th Birthday. 50, 175p.
Red Crescent Day. Fruits. 2, 2, 5, 10, 15, 25, 50, 100, 150, 175p.
Afghan Red Crescent Fund. 1961 Red Crescent Day issue surch 2+25, 2+25, 5+25, 10+25, 15p.+25p.
United Nations Day. 1, 2, 3, 4, 50, 75, 175p.
Teachers' Day. Flowers and Educational Scenes. 2, 2, 5, 10, 15, 25, 50, 100, 150, 175p.
UNESCO 1961 Teachers' Day issue surch 2+25, 2+25, 5+25, 10+25, 15p.+25p.

1962

15th Anniv (1961) of UNESCO 2, 2, 5, 10, 15, 25, 50, 75, 100p.
Ahmed Shah Baba. 50, 75, 100p.
Agriculture Day. Animals and Products. 2, 2, 5, 10, 15, 25, 50, 75, 100, 125p.
Independence Day. Marching Athletes. 25, 50, 150p.
Women's Day. Postage 25, 50p.; Air 100, 175p.
Pashtunistan Day. 25, 50, 150p.
Malaria Eradication. 2, 2, 5, 10, 15, 25, 50, 75, 100, 150, 175p.
National Assembly. 25, 50, 75, 100, 125p.
4th Asian Games, Djakarta, Indonesia. Postage 1, 2, 3, 4, 5p.; Air 25, 50, 75, 100, 150, 175p.
Children's Day. Sports and Produce. Postage 1, 2, 3, 4, 5p.; Air 75, 150, 200p.
King's 48th Birthday. 25, 50, 75, 100p.
Red Crescent Day. Fruits and Flowers. Postage 1, 2, 3, 4, 5p.; Air 25, 50, 100p.
Boy Scouts' Day. Postage 1, 2, 3, 4p.; Air 25, 50, 75, 100p.
1st Anniv of Hammarskjold's Death. Surch on 1961 UNESCO issue. 2+20, 2+20, 5+20, 10+20, 15+20, 25+20, 50+20, 75+20, 100p.+20p.
United Nations Day. Postage 1, 2, 3, 4, 5p.; Air 75, 100, 125p.
Teachers' Day. Sport and Flowers. Postage 1, 2, 3, 4, 5p.; Air 100, 150p.
World Meteorological Day. 50, 100p.

1963

Famous Afghans Pantheon, Kabul. 50, 75, 100p.
Agriculture Day. Sheep and Silkworms. Postage 1, 2, 3, 4, 5p.; Air 100, 150, 200p.
Freedom from Hunger. Postage 2, 3, 300p.; Air 500p.
Malaria Eradication Fund. 1962 Malaria Eradication issue surch 2+15, 2+15, 5+15, 10+15, 15+15, 25+15, 50+15, 75+15, 100+15, 150+15, 175p.+15p.
World Meteorological Day. Postage 1, 2, 3, 4, 5p.; Air 200, 300, 400, 500p.
"GANEFO" Athletic Games, Djakarta, Indonesia. Postage 2, 3, 4, 5, 10p., 9a.; Air 300, 500p.
Red Cross Centenary Postage 2, 3, 4, 5, 10p.; Air 100, 200p.; 4, 6a.
Nubian Monuments Preservation. Postage 100, 200, 500p.; Air 5a., 7a.50.

1964

Women's Day (1963). 2, 3, 4, 5, 10p.
Afghan Boy Scouts and Girl Guides. Postage 2, 3, 4, 5, 10p.; Air 2, 2, 2a.50, 3, 4, 5, 12a.
Child Welfare Day (1963). Sports and Games. Postage 2, 3, 4, 5, 10p.; Air 200, 300p.
Afghan Red Crescent Society. Postage 100, 200p.; Air 5a., 7a.50.
Teachers' Day (1963). Flowers. Postage 2, 3, 4, 5, 10p.; Air 3a., 3a.50.
United Nations Day (1963). Postage 2, 3, 4, 5, 10p.; Air 100p., 2, 3a.
15th Anniv of Human Rights Declaration. Surch on 1964 United Nations Day issue. Postage 2+50, 3+50, 4+50, 5+50, 10p.+50p.; Air 100p.+50p., 2a.+50p., 3a.+50p.
UNICEF (dated 1963). Postage 100, 200p.; Air 5a. 7a.50.
Malaria Eradication (dated 1963). Postage 2, 3, 4, 5p., 10p. on 4p.; Air 2, 10a.

2004

Deer. 80a.; 115a; 100a.

Pt. 1

AITUTAKI

Island in the South Pacific.

1903. 12 pence = 1 shilling; 20 shillings = 1 pound.
1967. 100 cents = 1 dollar.

A. NEW ZEALAND DEPENDENCY

The British Government, who had exercised a protectorate over the Cook Islands group since the 1880s, handed the islands, including Aitutaki, to New Zealand administration in 1901. Cook Islands stamps were used from 1932 to 1972.

1903. Pictorial stamps of New Zealand surch **AITUTAKI** and value in native language.

1	**23**	½d. green	4·75	6·50
2	**42**	1d. red	5·00	5·50
4	**26**	2½d. blue	17·00	12·00
5	**28**	3d. brown	18·00	15·00
6	**31**	6d. red	30·00	25·00
7	**34**	1s. orange	55·00	85·00

1911. King Edward VII stamps of New Zealand surch **AITUTAKI** and value in native language.

9	**51**	½d. green	1·00	7·50
10	**53**	1d. red	3·00	13·00
11	**51**	6d. red	50·00	£140
12	**51**	1s. orange	60·00	£150

1916. King George V stamps of New Zealand surch **AITUTAKI** and value in native language.

13a	**62**	6d. red	7·50	27·00
14	**62**	1s. orange	10·00	90·00

1917. King George V stamps of New Zealand optd **AITUTAKI**.

19		½d. green	1·00	6·00

20	**53**	1d. red	4·25	32·00
21	**62**	1½d. grey	3·75	30·00
22	**62**	1½d. brown	80	7·00
15a		2½d. blue	1·75	16·00
16a		3d. brown	1·50	28·00
17a		6d. red	4·75	21·00
18a		1s. orange	12·00	32·00

1920. As 1920 pictorial stamps of Cook Islands but inscr "AITUTAKI".

30		½d. black and green	2·00	22·00
31		1d. black and red	6·00	10·00
26		1½d. black and brown	6·00	12·00
32		2½d. black and blue	7·50	75·00
27		3d. black and blue	2·50	14·00
28		6d. brown and grey	5·50	14·00
29		1s. black and purple	9·50	16·00

B. PART OF COOK ISLANDS

On 9 August 1972 Aitutaki became a Port of Entry into the Cook Islands. Whilst remaining part of the Cook Islands, Aitutaki has a separate postal service.

1972. Nos. 227/8, 230, 233/4, 238, 240/1, 243 and 244 of Cook Islands optd **Aitutaki**.

33	**79**	½c. multicoloured	30	80
34	-	1c. multicoloured	70	1·40
35	-	2½c. multicoloured	2·25	7·00
36	-	4c. multicoloured	70	85
37	-	5c. multicoloured	2·50	7·50
38	-	10c. multicoloured	2·50	5·50
39	-	20c. multicoloured	3·75	1·00
40	-	25c. multicoloured	70	1·00
41	-	50c. multicoloured	2·75	2·75
42	-	$1 multicoloured	4·00	5·50

1972. Christmas. Nos. 406/8 of Cook Islands optd **Aitutaki**.

43	**130**	1c. multicoloured	10	15
44	-	5c. multicoloured	15	15
45	-	10c. multicoloured	15	25

1972. Royal Silver Wedding. As Nos. 413 and 415 of Cook Islands, but inscr "COOK ISLANDS Aitutaki".

46	**131**	5c. black and silver	2·75	2·25
47	-	15c. black and silver	1·25	1·25

1972. No. 245 of Cook Islands optd **AITUTAKI**.

48		$2 multicoloured	50	75

1972. Nos. 227/8, 230, 233, 234, 238, 240, 241, 243 and 244 of Cook Islands optd **AITUTAKI** within ornamental oval.

49	**79**	½c. multicoloured	15	10
50	-	1c. multicoloured	15	10
51	-	2½c. multicoloured	20	10
52	-	4c. multicoloured	25	15
53	-	5c. multicoloured	25	15
54	-	10c. multicoloured	35	25
55	-	20c. multicoloured	1·25	50
56	-	25c. multicoloured	50	55
57	-	50c. multicoloured	75	90
58	-	$1 multicoloured	1·25	1·75

13 Christ
Mocked
(Grunewald)

1973. Easter. Multicoloured.

59		1c. Type **13**	15	10
60		1c. St. Veronica (Van der Weyden)	15	10
61		1c. The Crucified Christ with Virgin Mary, Saints and Angels (Raphael)	15	10
62		1c. Resurrection (Piero della Francesca)	15	10
63		5c. The Last Supper (Master of Amiens)	20	15
64		5c. Condemnation (Holbein)	20	15
65		5c. Christ on the Cross (Rubens)	20	15
66		5c. Resurrection (El Greco)	20	15
67		10c. Disrobing of Christ (El Greco)	25	15
68		10c. St. Veronica (Van Oostsanen)	25	15
69		10c. Christ on the Cross (Rubens)	25	15
70		10c. Resurrection (Bouts)	25	15

1973. Silver Wedding Coinage. Nos. 417/23 of Cook Islands optd **AITUTAKI**.

71	**132**	1c. black, red and gold	10	10
72	-	2c. black, blue and gold	10	10
73	-	5c. black, green and silver	15	10

74	-	10c. black, blue and silver	20	10
75	-	20c. black, green and silver	30	15
76	-	50c. black, red and silver	50	30
77	-	$1 black, blue and silver	70	45

1973. Tenth Anniv of Treaty Banning Nuclear Testing. Nos. 236, 238, 240 and 243 of Cook Islands optd **AITUTAKI** within ornamental oval and **TENTH ANNIVERSARY CESSATION OF NUCLEAR TESTING TREATY**.

78		8c. multicoloured	15	15
79		10c. multicoloured	15	15
80		20c. multicoloured	30	20
81		50c. multicoloured	70	50

16 Red Hibiscus and Princess Anne

1973. Royal Wedding. Multicoloured.

82		25c. Type **16**	25	10
83		30c. Capt. Mark Phillips and blue hibiscus	25	10
MS84		114×65 mm. Nos. 82/3	50	40

17 "Virgin and Child"
(Montagna)

1973. Christmas. "Virgin and Child" paintings by artists listed below. Multicoloured.

85		1c. Type **17**	10	10
86		1c. Crivelli	10	10
87		1c. Van Dyck	10	10
88		1c. Perugino	10	10
89		5c. Veronese (child at shoulder)	25	10
90		5c. Veronese (child on lap)	25	10
91		5c. Cima	25	10
92		5c. Memling	25	10
93		10c. Memling	25	10
94		10c. Del Colle	25	10
95		10c. Raphael	25	10
96		10c. Lotto	25	10

18 Rose-branch Murex

1974. Sea Shells. Multicoloured.

97		½c. Type **18**	90	1·00
98		1c. New Caledonia nautilus	90	1·00
99		2c. Common or major harp	90	1·00
100		3c. Striped bonnet	90	1·00
101		4c. Mole cowrie	90	1·00
102		5c. Pontifical mitre	90	1·00
103		8c. Trumpet triton	90	1·00
104		10c. Venus comb murex	90	80
105		20c. Red-mouth olive	1·25	80
106		25c. Ruddy frog shell	1·25	80
107		60c. Widest pacific conch	4·00	1·25
108		$1 Maple-leaf triton or winged frog shell	2·50	1·40
109		$2 Queen Elizabeth II and Marlin-spike auger	6·00	9·00
110		$5 Queen Elizabeth II and Tiger cowrie	32·00	10·00

The $2 and $5 are larger, 53×25 mm.

19 Bligh and H.M.S. Bounty

1974. William Bligh's Discovery of Aitutaki. Multicoloured.

114		1c. Type **19**	60	60
115		1c. H.M.S. Bounty	60	60
116		5c. Bligh, and H.M.S. Bounty at Aitutaki	1·00	1·00
117		5c. Aitutaki chart of 1856	1·00	1·00
118		8c. Captain Cook and H.M.S. Resolution	1·40	1·40
119		8c. Map of Aitutaki and inset location map	1·40	1·40

See also Nos. 123/8.

20 Aitutaki Stamps of 1903, Sand Map

1974. Centenary of U.P.U. Multicoloured.

120		25c. Type **20**	75	50
121		50c. Stamps of 1903 and 1920, and map	1·00	75
MS122		66×75 mm. Nos. 120/1	1·25	2·75

1974. Air. As Nos. 114/119 in larger size (46×26 mm), additionally inscr "AIR MAIL".

123		10c. Type **19**	70	65
124		10c. H.M.S. Bounty	70	65
125		25c. Bligh, and H.M.S. Bounty at Aitutaki	80	75
126		25c. Aitutaki chart of 1856	80	75
127		30c. Captain Cook and H.M.S. Resolution	90	85
128		30c. Map of Aitutaki and inset location map	90	85

21 Virgin and Child
(Hugo van der Goes)

1974. Christmas. "Virgin and Child" paintings by artists named. Multicoloured.

129		1c. Type **21**	10	15
130		5c. Bellini	10	20
131		8c. Gerard David	10	20
132		10c. Antonello da Messina	10	15
133		25c. Joos van Cleve	20	30
134		30c. Master of the Life of St. Catherine	20	30
MS135		127×134 mm. Nos. 129/34	1·40	1·75

22 Churchill as Schoolboy

1974. Birth Centenary of Sir Winston Churchill. Multicoloured.

136		10c. Type **22**	20	25
137		25c. Churchill as young man	25	40
138		30c. Churchill with troops	25	45
139		50c. Churchill painting	30	60
140		$1 Giving "V" sign	40	75
MS141		115×108 mm. Nos. 136/40	1·25	1·50

1974. Children's Christmas Fund. Nos. 129/34 surch.

142	**21**	1c. +1c. multicoloured	10	10
143	-	5c. +1c. multicoloured	10	10
144	-	8c. +1c. multicoloured	10	10
145	-	10c. +1c. multicoloured	10	10
146	-	25c. +1c. multicoloured	20	20
147	-	30c. +1c. multicoloured	20	20

24 Soviet and U.S. Flags

1975. "Apollo–Soyuz" Space Project. Multicoloured.

148		25c. Type **24**	30	20
149		50c. Daedalus with space capsule	40	30
MS150		123×61 mm. Nos. 148/9	1·25	1·10

25 St. Francis

1975. Christmas. Multicoloured.

151	6c. Type **25**	10	10
152	6c. Madonna and Child	10	10
153	6c. St. John	10	10
154	7c. King and donkey	10	10
155	7c. Madonna, Child and King	10	10
156	7c. Kings with gifts	10	10
157	15c. Madonna and Child	15	15
158	15c. St. Onufrius	15	15
159	15c. John the Baptist	15	15
160	20c. Shepherd and cattle	20	15
161	20c. Madonna and Child	20	15
162	20c. Shepherds	20	15
MS163	104×201 mm. Nos. 151/62	2·25	2·50

Stamps of the same value were printed together, se-tenant, each strip forming a composite design of a complete painting as follows: Nos. 151/3, Madonna and Child with Saints Francis and John (Lorenzetti); 154/6, Adoration of the Kings (Van der Weyden); 157/9, Madonna and Child Enthroneth with Saints Onufrius and John the Baptist (Montagna); 160/2, Adoration of the Shepherds (Reni).

1975. Children's Christmas Fund. Nos. 151/62 surch.

164	**25** 6c. +1c. multicoloured	10	10
165	- 6c. +1c. multicoloured	10	10
166	- 6c. +1c. multicoloured	10	10
167	- 7c. +1c. multicoloured	10	10
168	- 7c. +1c. multicoloured	10	10
169	- 7c. +1c. multicoloured	10	10
170	- 15c. +1c. multicoloured	15	15
171	- 15c. +1c. multicoloured	15	15
172	- 15c. +1c. multicoloured	15	15
173	- 20c. +1c. multicoloured	20	20
174	- 20c. +1c. multicoloured	20	20
175	- 20c. +1c. multicoloured	20	20

26 The Descent
(detail,
15th-century
Flemish School)

1976. Easter. Multicoloured.

176	15c. Type **26**	15	10
177	30c. "The Descent" (detail)	20	15
178	35c. "The Descent" (detail)	25	20
MS179	87×67 mm. Nos. 176/8 forming a complete picture of "The Descent"	1·00	1·25

27 Left Detail

1976. Bicentenary of American Revolution. Paintings by John Turnball.

180	**27** 30c. multicoloured	20	10
181	- 30c. multicoloured	20	10
182	- 30c. multicoloured	20	10
183	- 35c. multicoloured	20	15
184	- 35c. multicoloured	20	15
185	- 35c. multicoloured	20	15
186	- 50c. multicoloured	20	15
187	- 50c. multicoloured	20	15
188	- 50c. multicoloured	20	15
MS189	132×120 mm. Nos. 180/8	1·75	1·10

PAINTINGS: Nos. 180/2, The Declaration of Independence; 183/5, The Surrender of Lord Cornwallis at Yorktown; 186/8, The Resignation of General Washington.

Stamps of the same value were printed together, se-tenant, each strip forming a composite design of the whole painting.

28 Cycling

1976. Olympic Games, Montreal. Multicoloured.

190	15c. Type **28**	80	15
191	35c. Sailing	45	20
192	60c. Hockey	1·00	25
193	70c. Sprinting	70	30
MS194	107×97 mm. Nos. 190/3	2·50	1·25

1976. Royal Visit to the U.S.A. Nos. 190/3 optd **VISIT ROYAL JULY 1976**.

195	**28** 15c. multicoloured	50	15

196	- 35c. multicoloured	45	25
197	- 60c. multicoloured	80	40
198	- 70c. multicoloured	70	45
MS199	107×97 mm. Nos. 195/8	2·00	1·25

30 "The
Visitation"

1976. Christmas.

200	**30** 6c. gold and green	10	10
201	- 6c. gold and green	10	10
202	- 7c. gold and purple	10	10
203	- 7c. gold and purple	10	10
204	- 15c. gold and blue	10	10
205	- 15c. gold and blue	10	10
206	- 20c. gold and violet	15	15
207	- 20c. gold and violet	15	15
MS208	128×96 mm. As Nos. 200/7 but with borders on three sides	1·00	1·40

DESIGNS: No. 201, Angel; 202, Angel; 203, Shepherds; 204, Joseph; 205, Mary and the Child; 206, Wise Man; 207, Two Wise Men.

Stamps of the same value were printed together, se-tenant, each pair forming a composite design.

1976. Children's Christmas Fund. Nos. 200/7 surch.

209	**30** 6c. +1c. gold and green	10	10
210	- 6c. +1c. gold and green	10	10
211	- 7c. +1c. gold and purple	10	10
212	- 7c. +1c. gold and purple	10	10
213	- 15c. +1c. gold and blue	15	15
214	- 15c. +1c. gold and blue	15	15
215	- 20c. +1c. gold and violet	15	15
216	- 20c. +1c. gold and violet	15	15
MS217	128×96 mm. As Nos. 209/16 but with a premium of "+2c." and borders on three sides	80	1·40

32 Alexander Graham Bell and First Telephone

1977. Centenary (1976) of Telephone.

218	**32** 25c. black, gold and red	20	15
219	70c. black, gold and lilac	40	40
MS220	116×59 mm. As Nos. 218/19 but with different colours	70	1·00

DESIGN: 70c. Satellite and Earth station.

33 Christ on the Cross (detail)

1977. Easter. 400th Birth Anniv of Rubens. Multicoloured.

221	15c. Type **33**	45	15
222	20c. Lamentation for Christ	60	20
223	35c. Christ with Straw	75	25
MS224	115×57 mm. Nos. 221/3	1·60	1·60

34 Captain Bligh, George III and H.M.S. Bounty

1977. Silver Jubilee. Multicoloured.

225	25c. Type **34**	35	35
226	35c. Rev. Williams, George IV and Aitutaki Church	40	40
227	50c. Union Jack, Queen Victoria and island map	45	45
228	$1 Balcony scene, 1953	50	50
MS229	130×87 mm. As Nos. 225/8 but with gold borders	1·25	1·25

35 The
Shepherds

1977. Christmas. Multicoloured.

230	6c. Type **35**	10	10
231	6c. Angel	10	10
232	7c. Mary, Jesus and ox	10	10
233	7c. Joseph and donkey	10	10
234	15c. Three Kings	10	10
235	15c. Virgin and Child	10	10
236	20c. Joseph	10	10
237	20c. Mary and Jesus on donkey	10	10
MS238	130×95 mm. Nos. 230/7	70	1·25

Stamps of the same value were printed together, se-tenant, forming composite designs.

1977. Children's Christmas Fund. Nos. 230/7 surch **+1c**.

239	6c. +1c. Type **35**	10	10
240	6c. +1c. Angel	10	10
241	7c. +1c. Mary, Jesus and ox	10	10
242	7c. +1c. Joseph and donkey	10	10
243	15c. +1c. Three Kings	15	10
244	15c. +1c. Virgin and Child	15	10
245	20c. +1c. Joseph	15	10
246	20c. +1c. Mary and Jesus on donkey	15	10
MS247	130×95 mm. As Nos. 239/46 but each with premium of "+2c."	70	85

37 Hawaiian Goddess

1978. Bicentenary of Discovery of Hawaii. Multicoloured.

248	35c. Type **37**	35	25
249	50c. Figurehead of H.M.S. "Resolution" (horiz)	60	40
250	$1 Hawaiian temple figure	70	70
MS251	168×75 mm. Nos. 248/50	1·50	1·75

38 Christ on the Way to Calvary (Martini)

1978. Easter. Paintings from the Louvre, Paris. Multicoloured.

252	15c. Type **38**	15	10
253	20c. Pieta of Avignon (E. Quarton)	20	10
254	35c. The Pilgrims at Emmaus (Rembrandt)	25	10
MS255	108×83 mm. Nos. 252/4	75	75

1978. Easter. Children's Charity. Designs as Nos. 252/4, but smaller (34×26 mm) and without margins, in separate miniature sheets 75×58 mm, each with a face value of 50c. + 5c.

MS256	As Nos. 252/4 Set of 3 sheets	1·00	1·00

39 The Yale of Beaufort

1978. 25th Anniv of Coronation. Multicoloured.

257	$1 Type **39**	30	50
258	$1 Queen Elizabeth II	30	50
259	$1 Aitutaki ancestral statue	30	50
MS260	98×127 mm. Nos 257/9×2	75	75

Stamps from No. MS260 have coloured borders, the upper row in lavender and the lower in green.

40 Adoration of the Infant Jesus

1978. Christmas. 450th Death Anniv of Durer. Multicoloured.

261	15c. Type **40**	25	15
262	17c. The Madonna with Child	30	15

263	30c. The Madonna with the Iris	45	20
264	35c. The Madonna of the Siskin	60	45
MS265	101×109 mm. As Nos. 261/4 but each with a premium of "+2c."	1·10	1·00

41 Captain Cook
(Nathaniel Dance)

1979. Death Bicent of Captain Cook. Multicoloured.

266	50c. Type **41**	1·00	80
267	75c. H.M.S. 'Resolution' and 'Adventure' at Matavai Bay, Tahiti (W. Hodges)	1·75	95
MS268	94×58 mm. Nos. 266/7	2·00	2·25

42 Girl with
Flowers

1979. International Year of the Child. Multicoloured.

269	30c. Type **42**	20	15
270	35c. Boy playing guitar	30	20
271	65c. Children in canoe	40	30
MS272	104×80 mm. As Nos. 269/71, but each with a premium of "+3c."	70	1·00

43 Man writing a Letter
(painting by Gabriel Metsu)

1979. Death Centenary of Sir Rowland Hill. Multicoloured.

273	50c. Type **43**	45	45
274	50c. Sir Rowland Hill with Penny Black, 1903 ½d. and 1911 1d. stamps	45	45
275	50c. Girl in Blue reading a Letter (Jan Vermeer)	45	45
276	65c. Woman writing a Letter (Gerard Terborch)	50	50
277	65c. Sir Rowland Hill, with Penny Black, 1903 3d. and 1920 ½d. stamps	50	50
278	65c. Lady reading a Letter (Jan Vermeer)	50	50
MS279	151×85 mm. 30c.×6. As Nos. 273/8	1·75	1·75

44 The Burial of
Christ (left detail)
(Quentin Metsys)

1980. Easter. Multicoloured.

280	20c. Type **44**	40	25
281	30c. The Burial of Christ (centre detail)	50	35
282	35c. The Burial of Christ (right detail)	65	45
MS283	93×71 mm. As Nos. 280/2, but each with premium of "+2c."	75	75

45 Einstein as a
Young Man

1980. 25th Death Anniv of Albert Einstein (physicist). Multicoloured.

284	12c. Type **45**	60	60

285	12c. Atom and "E=mc^{2n}" equation	60	60
286	15c. Einstein in middle-age	65	65
287	15c. Cross over nuclear explosion (Test Ban Treaty, 1963)	65	65
288	20c. Einstein as an old man	75	75
289	20c. Hand preventing atomic explosion	75	75
MS290	113×118 mm. Nos 284/9	3·00	3·00

46 Ancestor Figure, Aitutaki

1980. Third South Pacific Festival of Arts. Multicoloured.

291	6c. Type **46**	10	10
292	6c. Staff god image, Rarotonga	10	10
293	6c. Trade adze, Mangaia	10	10
294	6c. Carved image of Tangaroa, Rarotonga	10	10
295	12c. Wooden image Aitutaki	10	10
296	12c. Hand club, Rarotonga	10	10
297	12c. Carved mace "god", Mangaia	10	10
298	12c. Fisherman's god, Rarotonga	10	10
299	15c. Ti'i image, Aitutaki	15	15
300	15c. Fisherman's god, Rarotonga (different)	15	15
301	15c. Carved mace "god", Cook Islands	15	15
302	15c. Carved image of Tangaroa, Rarotonga (different)	15	15
303	20c. Chief's headdress, Aitutaki	15	15
304	20c. Carved mace "god", Cook Islands (different)	15	15
305	20c. Staff god image, Rarotonga (different)	15	15
306	20c. Carved image of Tangaroa, Rarotonga (different)	15	15
MS307	134×194 mm. Nos. 291/306	1·60	1·75

47 "Virgin and Child" (13th century)

1980. Christmas. Sculptures of "The Virgin and Child". Multicoloured.

308	15c. Type **47**	20	15
309	20c. 14th century	20	15
310	25c. 15th century	20	15
311	35c. 15th century (different)	30	20
MS312	82×120 mm. As Nos. 306/11 but each with premium of 2c.	70	80

48 "Mourning Virgin"

1981. Easter. Details of Sculpture "Burial of Christ" by Pedro Roldan.

313	**48** 30c. gold and green	25	25
314	– 40c. gold and lilac	30	30
315	– 50c. gold and blue	30	30
MS316	107×60 mm. As Nos. 313/15 but each with premium of 2c.	75	85

DESIGNS: 40c. "Christ"; 50c. "Saint John".

49 Gouldian Finch

1981. Birds (1st series). Multicoloured.

317	1c. Type **49**	45	30
318	1c. Common starling	45	30

319	2c. Golden whistler	50	30
320	2c. Scarlet robin	50	30
321	3c. Rufous fantail	60	30
322	3c. Peregrine falcon	60	30
323	4c. Java sparrow	70	30
324	4c. Barn owl	70	30
325	5c. Tahitian lory	70	30
326	5c. White-breasted wood swallow	70	30
327	6c. Purple swamphen	70	30
328	6c. Feral rock pigeon	70	30
329	10c. Chestnut-breasted mannikin	90	30
330	10c. Zebra dove	90	30
331	12c. Reef heron	1·00	40
332	12c. Common mynah	1·00	40
333	15c. Whimbrel (horiz)	1·25	40
334	15c. Black-browed albatross (horiz)	1·25	40
335	20c. Pacific golden plover (horiz)	1·50	55
336	20c. White tern (horiz)	1·50	55
337	25c. Pacific black duck (horiz)	1·75	70
338	25c. Brown booby (horiz)	1·75	70
339	30c. Great frigate bird (horiz)	2·00	85
340	30c. Pintail (horiz)	2·00	85
341	35c. Long-billed reed warbler	2·00	1·00
342	35c. Pomarine skua	2·00	1·00
343	40c. Buff-banded rail	2·25	1·25
344	40c. Spotted triller	2·25	1·25
345	50c. Royal albatross	3·00	1·50
346	50c. Stephen's lory	2·25	1·50
347	70c. Red-headed parrot-finch	5·50	3·00
348	70c. Orange dove	5·50	3·00
349	$1 Blue-headed flycatcher	4·50	3·75
350	$2 Red-bellied flycatcher	5·00	8·00
351	$4 Red munia	9·00	14·00
352	$5 Flat-billed kingfisher	12·00	16·00

See also Nos. 475/94.

50 Prince Charles

1981. Royal Wedding. Multicoloured.

391	60c. Type **50**	30	40
392	80c. Lady Diana Spencer	40	55
393	$1.40 Prince Charles and Lady Diana (87×70 mm)	60	80

1981. International Year for Disabled Persons. Nos. 391/3 surch **+5c.**

394	60c. +5c. Type **50**	50	90
395	80c. +5c. Lady Diana Spencer	60	1·10
396	$1.40 +5c. Prince Charles and Lady Diana	70	1·40

52 Footballers

1981. World Cup Football Championship, Spain (1982). Football Scenes. Multicoloured.

397	12c. Ball to left of stamp	50	35
398	12c. Ball to right	50	35
399	15c. Ball to right	55	40
400	15c. Ball to left	55	40
401	20c. Ball to left	55	50
402	20c. Ball to right	55	50
403	25c. Type **52**	60	55
404	25c. "ESPANA 82" inscription	60	55
MS405	100×137 mm. 12c.+2c., 15c.+2c., 20c.+2c., 25c.+2c., each × 2. As Nos. 397/404	3·50	3·00

53 The Holy Family

1981. Christmas. Etchings by Rembrandt. Each brown and gold.

406	15c. Type **53**	45	45
407	30c. Virgin with Child	70	70
408	40c. Adoration of the Shepherds (horiz)	95	95
409	50c. The Holy Family (horiz)	1·25	1·25

MS410	Designs as Nos. 406/9 in separate miniature sheets, 65×82 mm or 82×65 mm, each with a face value of 80c.+5c. Set of 4 sheets	4·00	3·00

54 Princess of Wales

1982. 21st Birthday of Princess of Wales. Multicoloured.

411	70c. Type **54**	2·00	60
412	$1 Prince and Princess of Wales	2·00	75
413	$2 Princess Diana (different)	3·25	1·50
MS414	82×91 mm. Nos. 411/13	6·00	2·75

1982. Birth of Prince William of Wales (1st issue). Nos. 391/3 optd.

415	60c. Type **50**	90	70
416	60c. Type **50**	90	70
417	80c. Lady Diana Spencer	1·10	80
418	80c. Lady Diana Spencer	1·10	80
419	$1.40 Prince Charles and Lady Diana	1·25	1·00
420	$1.40 Prince Charles and Lady Diana	1·25	1·00

OPTS: Nos. 415, 417 and 419, **21 JUNE 1982. PRINCE WILLIAM OF WALES.** Nos. 416, 418 and 420, **COMMEMORATING THE ROYAL BIRTH.**

1982. Birth of Prince William of Wales (2nd issue). As Nos. 411/13 but inscr "ROYAL BIRTH 21 JUNE 1982 PRINCE WILLIAM OF WALES".

421	70c. Type **54**	70	60
422	$1 Prince and Princess of Wales	80	75
423	$2 Princess Diana (different)	1·60	1·50
MS424	81×91 mm. Nos. 421/3	5·50	3·00

56 "Virgin and Child" (12th-century sculpture)

1982. Christmas. Religious Sculptures. Multicoloured.

425	18c. Type **56**	70	70
426	36c. Virgin and Child (12th-century)	85	85
427	48c. Virgin and Child (13th-century)	1·00	1·00
428	60c. Virgin and Child (15th-century)	1·40	1·40
MS429	99×115 mm. As Nos. 425/8 but each with 2c. charity premium	2·50	2·75

57 Aitutaki Bananas

1983. Commonwealth Day. Multicoloured.

430	48c. Type **57**	75	50
431	48c. Ancient Ti'i image	75	50
432	48c. Tourist canoeing	75	50
433	48c. Captain William Bligh and chart	75	50

58 Scouts around Campfire

1983. 75th Anniv of Boy Scout Movement. Multicoloured.

434	36c. Type **58**	65	65
435	48c. Scout saluting	75	75
436	60c. Scouts hiking	80	80
MS437	78×107 mm. As Nos. 434/6 but each with premium of 3c.	1·50	1·75

1983. 15th World Scout Jamboree, Alberta, Canada. Nos. 434/6 optd **15TH WORLD SCOUT JAMBOREE.**

438	36c. Type **58**	80	45
439	48c. Scout saluting	1·00	55
440	60c. Scouts hiking	1·25	75
MS441	78×107 mm. As Nos. 438/40 but each with premium of 3c.	1·50	2·00

60 Modern Sport Balloon

1983. Bicentenary of Manned Flight.

442	**60** 18c. multicoloured	55	30
443	– 36c. multicoloured	75	50
444	– 48c. multicoloured	90	60
445	– 60c. multicoloured	1·00	80
MS446	– 64×80 mm. $2.50, mult (48½×28½ mm)	1·50	2·00

DESIGNS: 36c. to $2.50, showing different modern sports balloons.

1983. Various stamps surch

Nos. 335/48 and 352

447	18c. on 20c. Pacific golden plover	2·75	1·25
448	18c. on 20c. White tern	2·75	1·25
449	36c. on 25c. Pacific black duck	3·75	1·50
450	36c. on 25c. Brown booby	3·75	1·50
451	36c. on 30c. Great frigate bird	3·75	1·50
452	36c. on 30c. Pintail	3·75	1·50
453	36c. on 35c. Long-billed reed warbler	3·75	1·50
454	36c. on 35c. Pomarine skua	3·75	1·50
455	48c. on 40c. Buff-banded rail	4·25	1·50
456	48c. on 40c. Spotted triller	4·25	1·50
457	48c. on 50c. Royal albatross	4·25	1·50
458	48c. on 50c. Stephen's lory	4·25	1·50
459	72c. on 70c. Red-headed parrot finch	7·50	3·00
460	72c. on 70c. Orange dove	7·50	3·00
461	$5.60 on $5 Flat-billed kingfisher (vert)	21·00	10·00

63 International Mail

1983. World Communications Year. Multicoloured.

466	48c. Type **63**	65	50
467	60c. Telecommunications	95	70
468	96c. Space satellite	1·40	1·00
MS469	126×53 mm. Nos. 466/8	2·50	2·50

64 Madonna of the Chair

1983. Christmas. 500th Birth Anniv of Raphael. Multicoloured.

470	36c. Type **64**	75	40
471	48c. The Alba Madonna	90	50
472	60c. Conestabile Madonna	1·25	70
MS473	95×116 mm. Nos. 470/2, but each with a premium of 3c.	2·50	1·40

1983. Christmas. 500th Birth Anniv of Raphael. Children's Charity. Designs as Nos. 470/2 in separate miniature sheets 46×47 mm, but with different frames and a face value of 85c.+5c. Imperf.

MS474	As Nos. 470/2 Set of 3 sheets	3·75	2·75

65 Gouldian Finch

1984. Birds (2nd series). Multicoloured.

475	2c. Type **65**	1·75	1·25
476	3c. Common starling	1·75	1·25
477	5c. Scarlet robin	1·75	1·40
478	10c. Golden whistler	2·25	1·40
479	12c. Rufous fantail	2·25	1·40
480	18c. Peregrine falcon	2·25	1·75
481	24c. Barn owl	2·25	1·75
482	30c. Java sparrow	2·25	1·50

483	36c. White-breasted wood swallow	2·25	1·50
484	48c. Tahitian lory	2·25	1·50
485	50c. Feral rock pigeon	2·50	2·50
486	60c. Purple swamphen	2·50	2·00
487	72c. Zebra dove	3·00	2·50
488	96c. Chestnut-breasted mannikin	3·00	2·50
489	$1.20 Common mynah	3·50	2·75
490	$2.10 Reef heron	7·00	3·75
491	$3 Blue-headed flycatcher	7·50	6·00
492	$4.20 Red-bellied flycatcher	3·50	6·00
493	$5.60 Red munia	3·50	9·50
494	$9.60 Flat-billed kingfisher	7·50	12·00

66 Javelin throwing

1984. Olympic Games. Los Angeles. Multicoloured.

495	36c. Type **66**	35	35
496	48c. Shot-putting	40	45
497	60c. Hurdling	45	55
498	$2 Basketball	1·75	1·50
MS499 88×117 mm. As Nos. 495/8, but each with a charity premium of 5c.		3·00	3·50

DESIGNS: 48c. to $2, show Memorial Coliseum and various events.

1984. Olympic Gold Medal Winners. Nos. 495/8 optd.

500	36c. Type **66** (optd **Javelin Throw Tessa Sanderson Great Britain**)	35	35
501	48c. Shot-putting (optd **Shot Put Claudia Losch Germany**)	40	45
502	60c. Hurdling (optd **Heptathlon Glynis Nunn Australia**)	45	55
503	$2 Basketball (optd **Team Basketball United States**)	1·10	1·50

67 Captain William Bligh and Chart

1984. "Ausipex" International Stamp Exhibition, Melbourne. Multicoloured.

504	60c. Type **67**	4·00	3·75
505	96c. H.M.S. *Bounty* and map	4·00	4·00
506	$1.40 Aitutaki stamps of 1974, 1979 and 1981 with map	4·00	4·25
MS507 85×113 mm. As Nos. 504/6, but each with a premium of 5c.		7·50	4·00

1984. Birth of Prince Henry (1st issue). No. 391 optd **15-9-84 Birth Prince Henry** and surch also.

508	$3 on 60c. Type **50**	2·00	3·25

69 The Annunciation

1984. Christmas. Details from Altarpiece, St Paul's Church, Palencia, Spain. Multicoloured.

509	36c. Type **69**	30	35
510	48c. The Nativity	40	45
511	60c. The Epiphany	45	50
512	96c. The Flight into Egypt	75	80
MS513 Designs as Nos. 509/12 in separate miniature sheets, each 45×53 mm and with a face value of 90c.+7c. Imperf. Set of 4 sheets		2·50	3·25

70 Princess Diana with Prince Henry

1984. Birth of Prince Henry (2nd issue). Multicoloured.

514	48c. Type **70**	2·75	2·25

515	60c. Prince William with Prince Henry	2·75	2·25
516	$2.10 Prince and Princess of Wales with children	3·50	4·50
MS517 113×65 mm. As Nos. 514/16, but each with a face value of 96c.+7c.		7·00	4·50

71 Grey Kingbird ("Gray Kingbird")

1985. Birth Bicentenary of John J. Audubon (ornithologist). Designs showing original paintings. Multicoloured.

518	55c. Type **71**	1·10	1·10
519	65c. Bohemian waxwing	1·25	1·25
520	75c. Summer tanager	1·40	1·40
521	95c. Common cardinal ("Cardinal")	1·50	1·50
522	$1.15 White-winged crossbill	1·90	1·90

72 The Queen Mother, aged Seven

1985. Life and Times of Queen Elizabeth the Queen Mother. Multicoloured.

523	55c. Type **72**	45	50
524	65c. Engagement photograph, 1922	50	55
525	75c. With young Princess Elizabeth	60	65
526	$1.30 With baby Prince Charles	1·00	1·10
MS527 75×49 mm. $3 Queen Mother on her 63rd birthday		2·25	2·40

73 *The Calmady Children* (T. Lawrence)

1985. International Youth Year. Multicoloured.

528	75c. Type **73**	3·00	2·75
529	90c. *Madame Charpentier's Children* (Renoir)	3·00	3·00
530	$1.40 *Young Girls at Piano* (Renoir)	3·75	4·00
MS531 103×104 mm. As Nos. 528/30, but each with a premium of 10c.		4·75	3·75

74 *Adoration of the Magi* (Giotto) and "Giotto" Spacecraft

1985. Christmas. Appearance of Halley's Comet (1st issue). Multicoloured.

532	95c. Type **74**	2·00	1·75
533	95c. As Type **74** but showing "Planet A" spacecraft	2·00	1·75
534	$1.15 Type **74**	2·00	1·75
535	$1.15 As No. 533	2·00	1·75
MS536 52×55 mm. $6.40. As Type **74** but without spacecraft (30×31 mm). Imperf		14·00	8·50

75 Halley's Comet A.D. 684 (from *Nuremberg Chronicle*)

1986. Appearance of Halley's Comet (2nd issue). Multicoloured.

537	90c. Type **75**	1·40	90
538	$1.25 Halley's Comet, 1066 (from Bayeux Tapestry)	1·75	1·10
539	$1.75 Halley's Comet, 1456 (from *Lucerne Chronicles*)	2·00	1·50

MS540 107×82 mm. As Nos. 537/9, but each with a face value of 95c.		6·50	6·50
MS541 65×80 mm. $4.20, *Melencolia I* (Albrecht Dürer woodcut) (61×76 mm). Imperf		6·00	3·50

76 Queen Elizabeth II on Coronation Day (from photo by Cecil Beaton)

1986. 60th Birthday of Queen Elizabeth II.

542	**76** 95c. multicoloured	2·00	2·25
MS543 58×68 mm. $4.20, As T **76**, but showing more of the portrait without oval frame		5·50	5·50

77 Head of Statue of Liberty

1986. Centenary of Statue of Liberty. Multicoloured.

544	$1 Type **77**	1·25	1·25
545	$2.75 Statue of Liberty at sunset	2·75	2·75
MS546 91×79 mm. As Nos. 544/5, but each with a face value of $1.25		3·25	2·50

78 Prince Andrew and Miss Sarah Ferguson

1986. Royal Wedding.

547	**78** $2 multicoloured	2·00	2·00
MS548 85×70 mm. Type **78** multicoloured		6·50	8·00

1986. "Stampex '86" Stamp Exhibition, Adelaide. No. MS507 with "Ausipex" emblems obliterated in gold.

MS549 As Nos. 504/6, but each with a premium of 5c.		13·00	14·00

The "Stampex '86" exhibition emblem is overprinted on the sheet margin.

1986. 86th Birthday of Queen Elizabeth the Queen Mother. Nos. 523/6 in miniature sheet, 132×82 mm.

MS550 Nos. 523/6		13·00	13·00

79 St. Anne with Virgin and Child

1986. Christmas. Paintings by Dürer. Multicoloured.

551	75c. Type **79**	1·25	1·25
552	$1.35 *Virgin and Child*	1·75	1·75
553	$1.95 *The Adoration of the Magi*	2·25	2·25
554	$2.75 *Madonna of the Rosary*	3·00	3·00
MS555 88×125 mm. As Nos. 551/4, but each with a face value of $1.65		13·00	14·00

1986. Visit of Pope John Paul II to South Pacific. Nos. 551/4 optd **NOVEMBER 21-24 1986 FIRST VISIT TO SOUTH PACIFIC** and surch also.

556	75c. +10c. Type **79**	3·00	2·50
557	$1.35 +10c. "Virgin and Child"	3·50	3·00
558	$1.95 +10c. "The Adoration of the Magi"	4·25	3·50
559	$2.75 +10c. "Madonna of the Rosary"	5·50	5·00
MS560 88×125 mm. As Nos. 556/9, but each with a face value of $1.65+10c.		17·00	15·00

1987. Hurricane Relief Fund. Nos. 544/5, 547, 551/4 and 556/9 surch **HURRICANE RELIEF +50c.**

561	75c. +50c. Type **79**	3·25	2·75
562	75c. +10c.+50c. Type **79**	4·00	3·50
563	$1 +50c. Type **77**	3·50	3·00

564	$1.35 +50c. *Virgin and Child*	3·75	3·25
565	$1.35 +10c.+50c. *Virgin and Child* (Dürer)	4·50	4·00
566	$1.95 +50c. *The Adoration of the Magi* (Dürer)	4·50	4·00
567	$1.95 +10c.+50c. *The Adoration of the Magi* (Dürer)	5·00	4·00
568	$2 +50c. Type **78**	4·50	4·00
569	$2.75 +50c. Statue of Liberty at sunset	5·00	4·50
570	$2.75 +50c. "Madonna of the Rosary" (Dürer)	5·00	4·50
571	$2.75 +10c.+50c. *Madonna of the Rosary* (Dürer)	6·50	5·50

1987. Royal Ruby Wedding. Nos. 391/3 surch **2.50 Royal Wedding 40th Anniv**.

572	$2.50 on 60c. Type **50**	2·25	2·50
573	$2.50 on 80c. Lady Diana Spencer	2·25	2·50
574	$2.50 on $1.40 Prince Charles and Lady Diana (87×70 mm)	2·25	2·50

83 Angels

1987. Christmas. Details of angels from *Virgin with Garland* by Rubens.

575	**83** 70c. multicoloured	2·00	2·00
576	– 85c. multicoloured	2·25	2·25
577	– $1.50 multicoloured	2·50	2·50
578	– $1.85 multicoloured	3·25	3·25
MS579 92×120 mm. As Nos. 575/8, but each with a face value of 95c.		13·00	14·00
MS580 96×85 mm. $6 "Virgin with Garland" (diamond, 56×56 mm)		13·00	14·00

84 Chariot Racing and Athletics

1988. Olympic Games, Seoul. Ancient and modern Olympic sports. Multicoloured.

581	70c. Type **84**	2·25	2·00
582	85c. Greek runners and football	2·50	2·25
583	95c. Greek wrestling and handball	2·50	2·25
584	$1.40 Greek hoplites and tennis	3·25	3·00
MS585 103×101 mm. As Nos. 581 and 584, but each with face value of $2		8·00	8·50

1988. Olympic Medal Winners, Los Angeles. Nos. 581/4 optd.

586	70c. Type **84** (optd **FLORENCE GRIFFITH JOYNER UNITED STATES 100 M AND 200 M**)	2·50	2·40
587	85c. Greek runners and football (optd **GELINDO BORDIN ITALY MARATHON**)	2·50	2·40
588	95c. Greek wrestling and handball (optd **HITOSHI SAITO JAPAN JUDO**)	2·75	2·50
589	$1.40 Greek hoplites and tennis (optd **STEFFI GRAF WEST GERMANY WOMEN'S TENNIS**)	2·75	2·50

85 *Adoration of the Shepherds* (detail)

1988. Christmas. Paintings by Rembrandt. Multicoloured.

590	55c. Type **85**	2·00	1·75
591	70c. *The Holy Family*	2·25	2·00
592	85c. *Presentation in the Temple*	2·50	2·25
593	95c. *The Holy Family* (different)	2·50	2·25
594	$1.15 *Presentation in the Temple* (different)	2·75	2·50
MS595 85×101 mm. $4.50, As Type **85** but 52×34 mm.		5·50	6·50

86 H.M.S. *Bounty* leaving Spithead and King George III

1989. Bicentenary of Discovery of Aitutaki by Captain Bligh. Multicoloured.

596	55c. Type **86**	2·25	2·00
597	65c. Breadfruit plants	2·50	2·25
598	75c. Old chart showing Aitutaki and Captain Bligh	2·75	2·50
599	95c. Native outrigger and H.M.S. *Bounty* off Aitutaki	3·00	2·75
600	$1.65 Fletcher Christian confronting Bligh	4·00	3·50
MS601 94×72 mm. $4.20 *Mutineers casting Bligh adrift* (Robert Dodd) (60×45 mm)		8·50	10·00

87 "Apollo 11" Astronaut on Moon

1989. 20th Anniv of First Manned Landing on Moon. Multicoloured.

602	75c. Type **87**	2·75	2·00
603	$1.15 Conducting experiment on Moon	3·25	2·50
604	$1.80 Astronaut on Moon carrying equipment	4·00	3·50
MS605 105×86 mm. $6.40 Astronaut on Moon with U.S. flag (40×27 mm)		8·00	9·50

88 Virgin Mary

1989. Christmas. Details from *Virgin in the Glory* by Titian. Multicoloured.

606	70c. Type **88**	2·50	2·00
607	85c. Christ Child	3·00	2·50
608	95c. Angel	3·25	2·75
609	$1.25 Cherubs	3·75	3·25
MS610 80×100 mm. $6 *Virgin in the Glory* (45×60 mm)		8·50	10·00

89 Human Comet striking Earth

1990. Protection of the Environment. Multicoloured.

611	$1.75 Type **89**	1·90	2·25
612	$1.75 Comet's tail	1·90	2·25
MS613 108×43 mm. Nos. 611/12		3·50	4·50

Nos. 611/12 were printed together, *se-tenant*, forming a composite design.

1990. 90th Birthday of Queen Elizabeth the Queen Mother. No. MS550 optd **Ninetieth Birthday**.

MS614 132×82 mm. Nos. 523/6		13·00	12·00

91 *Madonna of the Basket* (Correggio)

1990. Christmas. Religious Paintings. Multicoloured.

615	70c. Type **91**	1·50	1·50
616	85c. *Virgin and Child* (Morando)	1·60	1·60
617	95c. *Adoration of the Child* (Tiepolo)	1·75	1·75
618	$1.75 *Mystic Marriage of St. Catherine* (Memling)	2·50	2·75
MS619 165×93 mm. $6 *Donne Triptych* (Memling) (horiz)		12·00	13·00

1990. "Birdpex '90" Stamp Exhibition, Christchurch, New Zealand. Nos. 349/50 optd **Birdpex '90** and bird's head.

620	$1 Blue-headed flycatcher	4·50	4·50
621	$2 Red-bellied flycatcher	6·00	6·00

1991. 65th Birthday of Queen Elizabeth II. No. 352 optd **COMMEMORATING 65th BIRTHDAY OF H.M. QUEEN ELIZABETH II.**

622	$5 Flat-billed kingfisher	12·00	12·00

93 "The Holy Family" (A. Mengs)

1991. Christmas. Religious Paintings. Multicoloured.

623	80c. Type **93**	1·75	1·75
624	90c. *Virgin and the Child* (Lippi)	1·75	1·75
625	$1.05 *Virgin and Child* (A. Durer)	2·00	2·00
626	$1.75 *Adoration of the Shepherds* (G. de la Tour)	2·75	3·25
MS627 79×103 mm. *The Holy Family* (Michelangelo)		13·00	14·00

94 Hurdling

1992. Olympic Games, Barcelona. Multicoloured.

628	95c. Type **94**	1·75	1·50
629	$1.25 Weightlifting	2·00	1·75
630	$1.50 Judo	2·50	2·25
631	$1.95 Football	2·75	2·75

95 Vaka Motu Canoe

1992. Sixth Festival of Pacific Arts, Rarotonga. Sailing Canoes. Multicoloured.

632	30c. Type **95**	65	65
633	50c. Hamatafua	80	80
634	95c. Alia Kalia Ndrua	1·50	1·50
635	$1.75 Hokule'a Hawaiian	2·25	2·75
636	$1.95 Tuamotu Pahi	2·50	3·00

1992. Royal Visit by Prince Edward. Nos. 632/6 optd **ROYAL VISIT.**

637	30c. Type **95**	1·50	1·25
638	50c. Hamatafua	2·00	1·75
639	95c. Alia Kalia Ndrua	3·00	2·50
640	$1.75 Hokule'a Hawaiian	4·50	4·25
641	$1.95 Tuamotu Pahi	4·50	4·25

96 *Virgin's Nativity* (detail) (Reni)

1992. Christmas. Different details from *Virgin's Nativity* by Guido Reni.

642	**96**	80c. multicoloured	1·40	1·40
643	–	90c. multicoloured	1·60	1·60
644	–	$1.05 multicoloured	1·75	1·75
645	–	$1.75 multicoloured	2·50	3·00
MS646 – 101×86 mm. $6 multicoloured (as $1.05, but larger (36×46 mm))			6·50	8·00

97 The Departure from Palos

1992. 500th Anniv of Discovery of America by Columbus. Multicoloured.

647	$1.25 Type **97**	2·25	2·50
648	$1.75 Map of voyages	2·75	3·00
649	$1.95 Columbus and crew in New World	3·25	3·50

98 Queen Victoria and King Edward VII

1993. 40th Anniv of Coronation. Multicoloured.

650	$1.75 Type **98**	3·50	3·00
651	$1.75 King George V and King George VI	3·50	3·00
652	$1.75 Queen Elizabeth II in 1953 and 1986	3·50	3·00

99 *Madonna and Child* (Nino Pisano)

1993. Christmas. Religious Sculptures. Multicoloured.

653	80c. Type **99**	90	90
654	90c. *Virgin on Rosebush* (Luca della Robbia)	1·00	1·00
655	$1.15 *Virgin with Child and St. John* (Juan Francisco Rustici)	1·40	1·40
656	$1.95 *Virgin with Child* (Miguel Angel)	2·25	2·25
657	$3 *Madonna and Child* (Jacopo della Quercia) (32×47 mm)	3·25	4·00

100 Ice Hockey

1994. Winter Olympic Games, Lillehammer. Multicoloured.

658	$1.15 Type **100**	4·00	3·25
659	$1.15 Ski-jumping	4·00	3·25
660	$1.15 Cross-country skiing	4·00	3·25

101 *Ipomoea pes–caprae*

1994. Flowers. Multicoloured.

661	5c. Type **101**	30	30
662	10c. *Plumeria alba*	35	35
663	15c. *Hibiscus rosa-sinensis*	45	45
664	20c. *Allamanda cathartica*	50	50
665	25c. *Delonix regia*	50	50
666	30c. *Gardenia taitensis*	50	50
667	50c. *Plumeria rubra*	70	70
668	80c. *Ipomoea littoralis*	1·00	1·00
669	85c. *Hibiscus tiliaceus*	1·00	1·00
670	90c. *Erythrina variegata*	1·00	1·00
671	$1 *Solandra nitida*	1·00	1·10
672	$1.50 *Cordia subcordata*	1·50	1·75
673	$3 *Hibiscus rosa-sinensis* (different) (34×47 mm)	4·50	4·50
674	$5 As $3 (34×47 mm)	6·00	6·50
675	$8 As $3 (34×47 mm)	5·00	6·50

Nos. 671/5 include a portrait of Queen Elizabeth II at top right.

102 Cook Islands and U.S.A. Flags with Astronauts Collins, Armstrong and Aldrin

1994. 25th Anniv of First Manned Moon Landing. Multicoloured.

676	$2 Type **102**	7·50	7·50
677	$2 "Apollo 11" re-entering atmosphere and landing in sea	7·50	7·50

103 "The Madonna of the Basket" (Correggio)

1994. Christmas. Religious Paintings. Multicoloured.

678	85c. Type **103**	1·10	1·40
679	85c. *The Virgin and Child with Saints* (Memling)	1·10	1·40
680	85c. *The Virgin and Child with Flowers* (Dolci)	1·10	1·40
681	85c. *The Virgin and Child with Angels* (Bergognone)	1·10	1·40
682	90c. *Adoration of the Kings* (Dosso)	1·10	1·40
683	90c. *The Virgin and Child* (Bellini)	1·10	1·40
684	90c. *The Virgin and Child* (Schiavone)	1·10	1·40
685	90c. *Adoration of the Kings* (Dolci)	1·10	1·40

No. 678 is inscribed "Corregio" in error.

104 Battle of Britain

1995. 50th Anniv of End of Second World War. Multicoloured.

686	$4 Type **104**	9·50	8·50
687	$4 Battle of Midway	9·50	8·50

105 Queen Elizabeth the Queen Mother

1995. 95th Birthday of Queen Elizabeth the Queen Mother.

688	**105**	$4 multicoloured	7·50	8·00

106 Globe, Doves, United Nations Emblem and Headquarters

1995. 50th Anniv of United Nations.

689	**106**	$4.25 multicoloured	5·50	7·00

107 Green Turtle

1995. Year of the Sea Turtle. Multicoloured.

690	95c. Type **107**	1·75	1·75
691	$1.15 Leatherback turtle	2·00	2·00
692	$1.50 Olive Ridley turtle	2·25	2·25
693	$1.75 Loggerhead turtle	2·50	2·50

108 Queen Elizabeth II

1996. 70th Birthday of Queen Elizabeth II.

694	**108**	$4.50 multicoloured	8·50	8·00

109 Baron Pierre de Coubertin, Torch and Opening of 1896 Olympic Games

1996. Centenary of Modern Olympic Games. Multicoloured.
695	$2 Type **109**	5·00	5·00
696	$2 Athletes and American flag, 1996	5·00	5·00

110 Princess Elizabeth and Lieut. Philip Mountbatten with King George VI and Queen Elizabeth, 1947

1997. Golden Wedding of Queen Elizabeth and Prince Philip.
697	**110**	$2.50 multicoloured	4·50	3·50
MS698	78×102 mm. **110** $6 multicoloured	8·50	9·50	

111 Diana, Princess of Wales

1998. Diana, Princess of Wales Commemoration.
699	**111**	$1 multicoloured	1·00	1·00
MS700	70×100 mm. $4 Diana, Princess of Wales	2·50	3·75	

1998. Children's Charities. No. **MS**1427 surch **+$1 CHILDREN'S CHARITIES**.
MS701	70×100 mm. $4 + $1 Diana, Princess of Wales	2·75	4·50

1999. New Millennium. Nos. 632/6 optd **KIA ORANA THIRD MILLENNIUM**.
702	30c. Type **95**	50	50
703	50c. Hamatafua	60	60
704	95c. Alia Kalia Ndrua	85	85
705	$1.75 Hokule'a Hawaiian	1·40	1·60
706	$1.95 Tuamotu Pahi	1·60	1·75

2000. Queen Elizabeth the Queen Mother's 100th Birthday. As T **277** of Cook Islands.
707	$3 blue and brown	3·50	3·50
708	$3 multicoloured	3·50	3·50
709	$3 multicoloured	3·50	3·50
710	$3 green and brown	3·50	3·50
MS711	73×100 mm. $7.50 multicoloured	7·00	8·00

DESIGNS: No. 707, Queen Mother in evening dress and tiara; 708, Queen Mother in evening dress standing by table; 709, Queen Mother in Garter robes; 710, King George VI and Queen Elizabeth; MS711 Queen Mother holding lilies.

2000. Olympic Games, Sydney. As T **278** of Cook Islands. Multicoloured.
712	$2 Ancient Greek wrestlers	2·00	2·25
713	$2 Modern wrestlers	2·00	2·25
714	$2 Ancient Greek boxer	2·00	2·25
715	$2 Modern boxers	2·00	2·25
MS716	99×90 mm. $2.75 Olympic torch and Cook Island canoes	2·25	2·75

113 Blue Lorikeets and Flowers

2002. Endangered Species. Blue Lorikeet. Multicoloured.
717	80c. Type **113**	1·10	1·25
718	90c. Lorikeets and bananas	1·25	1·40
719	$1.15 Lorikeets on palm leaf	1·40	1·60
720	$1.95 Lorikeets in tree trunk	1·90	2·10

2003. "United We Stand". Support for Victims of 11 September 2001 Terrorist Attacks. Design as T **282** of Cook Islands. Multicoloured.
MS721	75×109 mm. $1.15×4 Twin Towers and flags of U.S.A. and Cook Islands	4·75	5·50

2005. Pope John Paul II Commemoration. As T **285** of Cook Islands. Multicoloured.
722	$1.95 Pope praying	3·50	3·50

114 Caterpillar and Chrysalis

2008. Endangered Species. Blue Moon Butterfly (*Hypolimna bolinas*). Multicoloured.
723	80c. Type **114**	2·00	2·25
724	90c. Female butterfly	2·00	2·25
725	$1.15 Male butterfly (wings closed)	2·25	2·50
726	$1.95 Male butterfly (wings open)	2·75	3·00

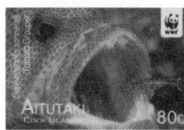

115 Tomato Grouper swallowing Shrimp

2010. Endangered Species. Tomato Grouper (*Cephalopholis sonnerati*) and Peacock Grouper (*Cephalopholis argus*). Multicoloured.
727	80c. Type **115**	1·10	1·25
728	90c. Peacock grouper on reef	1·25	1·40
729	$1.10 Three tomato groupers on reef	1·50	1·60
730	$1.20 Peacock grouper (close up)	1·60	1·75

116 Atoll and Saab 340 Airplane

2010. Tourism. Island Views. Multicoloured.
731	10c. Type **116**	20	25
732	20c. Palm trees and sunset over ocean	35	40
733	30c. Turquoise sea and atoll with sandy beach	45	50
734	40c. Two small islands, ocean, cloudy sky and *Southern Express* (freighter)	50	55
735	50c. Tree lined road	55	60
736	60c. Two islands under dark stormy sky	85	80
737	70c. Islanders fishing from causeway	90	95
738	80c. Sandy beach with leaning palm tree and island	1·00	1·10
739	90c. Overwater bungalows, Aitutaki Lagoon Resort	1·10	1·25
740	$1 Two peninsulas with palm trees and sandy beaches	1·25	1·40
741	$1.10 Looking over fence to sandy beach with two deckchairs	1·25	1·40
742	$1.20 Sun and clouds reflecting in ocean	1·40	1·50
743	$1.50 Half moon over two islands, reflecting in water	1·60	1·75
744	$2 Dusk with waves lapping sandy beach, island in background	2·10	2·25
745	$3 Church	3·25	3·50
MS746	240×180 mm. Nos. 731/45	17·00	17·00

117 Miss Kate Middleton on Gold Cup Day, Cheltenham

2011. Royal Engagement. Multicoloured.
747	50c. Type **117**	55	60
748	$1 Prince William laying wreath at the Cenotaph, London, 2009 (horiz)	1·25	1·40
749	$1 Prince William competing in Chakravarty Cup, Beaufort Polo Club (horiz)	1·25	1·40
750	$1 Kate Middleton, Prince William in background (horiz)	1·25	1·40
751	$1 Prince William (horiz)	1·25	1·40
752	$1 Kate Middleton (horiz)	1·25	1·40
753	$1 Prince William and Kate Middleton (horiz)	1·25	1·40
754	$1 Kate Middleton wearing black hat (horiz)	1·25	1·40
755	$1 Prince William (head and shoulders) (horiz)	1·25	1·40
756	$1 Prince William and Kate Middleton (facing each other) (horiz)	1·25	1·40
757	$1 Engagement ring on Kate Middleton's hand (horiz)	1·25	1·40
758	$5 Prince William competing in Chakravarty Cup, Beaufort Polo Club	5·25	5·00
MS759	108×70 mm. Nos. 747 and 758. P 13½	1·90	1·90
MS760	144×93 mm. $8.10 Prince William and Kate Middleton (38×50 mm)	9·00	9·00
MS761	58×95 mm. $11 As No. 747 (38×50 mm)	13·75	13·75
MS762	58×95 mm. $11 As No. 758 (38×50 mm)		

118 Duke and Duchess of Cambridge

2011. Royal Wedding. Sheet 108×73 mm containing T **118** and similar vert designs. Multicoloured.
MS763	$1.10 Type **118**; $1.20 Duke and Duchess of Cambridge during wedding ceremony (back view, kneeling)	2·75	2·75

119 Suspended Cages

2011. Aitutaki Marine Research Center. Clams. Multicoloured.
764	10c. Type **119**	20	25
765	20c. Station Manager Richard Story	35	40
766	80c. *Tridacna maxima* (two clams and sea urchin)	1·00	1·10
767	90c. *Tridacna maxima* (clams and sea bed)	1·10	1·25
768	$1.10 *Tridacna derasa* (close-up of clam)	1·10	1·25
769	$1.20 *Tridacna derasa* (clam, fish and corals on sea bed)	1·25	1·40
MS770	127×76 mm. $2 Diver (30×38 mm); $3 Boat loaded with clam cages (30×38 mm)	5·50	5·50

120 Nine Ladies Dancing

2011. Christmas. The Twelve Days of Christmas (carol). Multicoloured.
771	90c. Type **120**	1·10	1·25
772	$1 Ten Lords a Leaping	1·10	1·25
773	$1.20 Eleven Pipers Piping	1·25	1·40
774	$2 Twelve Drummers Drumming	2·10	2·25
MS775	203×138 mm. Nos. 771/4 and eight imperforate labels	5·50	6·00

121 Pope Benedict XVI

2012. Beatification of Pope John Paul II. Multicoloured.
776	$1.10 Type **121**	1·10	1·25
777	$5.10 Pope John Paul II	5·25	5·25

122 Humpback Whale (*Megaptera novaeangliae*)

2012. Whales and Dolphins. Multicoloured.
778	20c. Type **122**	20	20
779	30c. Tail of Humpback Whale (underside of tail flukes)	35	35
780	50c. Humpback Whale leaping above water (facing left)	55	55
781	80c. Two Striped Dolphins (seen from above)	90	90
782	90c. Striped Dolphin (swimming left)	1·10	1·25
783	$1 Two Striped Dolphins (leaping above water)	1·10	1·25
784	$1.10 Striped Dolphin (swimming to right)	1·10	1·25
785	$1.20 Five Striped Dolphins	1·25	1·40
786	$5 Pod of Striped Dolphins	5·25	5·25
787	$6 Tail of Humpback Whale (upperside)	6·50	6·50
788	$7.50 Humpback Whale leaping backwards	8·25	8·25
789	$10 Humpback Whales feeding	11·00	11·00
MS790	144×130 mm. Nos. 778/89	45·00	45·00

OFFICIAL STAMPS

1978. Nos. 98/105, 107/10 and 227/8 optd **O.H.M.S.** or surch also.
O1	1c. multicoloured	90	10
O2	2c. multicoloured	1·00	10
O3	3c. multicoloured	1·00	10
O4	4c. multicoloured	1·00	10
O5	5c. multicoloured	1·00	10
O6	8c. multicoloured	1·25	10
O7	10c. multicoloured	1·50	15
O8	15c. on 60c. multicoloured	2·75	20
O9	18c. on 60c. multicoloured	2·75	20
O10	20c. multicoloured	2·75	20
O11	50c. multicoloured	1·00	55
O12	60c. multicoloured	10·00	70
O13	$1 multicoloured (No. 108)	10·00	80
O14	$2 multicoloured	9·00	75
O15	$4 on $1 on $1 mult (No. 228)	1·75	75
O16	$5 multicoloured	11·00	1·25

1985. Nos. 351/2, 430/3, 475 and 477/94 optd **O.H.M.S.** or surch also.
O17	2c. Type **65**	1·75	2·00
O18	5c. Scarlet robin	2·00	2·00
O19	10c. Golden whistler	2·25	2·25
O20	12c. Rufous fantail	2·50	2·50
O21	18c. Peregrine falcon	3·50	2·50
O22	20c. on 24 c Barn owl	3·25	2·50
O23	30c. Java sparrow	2·25	1·50
O24	40c. on 36c. White-breasted wood swallow	2·25	1·50
O25	50c. Feral rock pigeon	2·25	1·50
O26	55c. on 48c. Tahitian lory	3·50	1·75
O27	60c. Purple swamphen	2·50	1·75
O28	65c. on 72c. Zebra dove	2·50	1·75
O38	75c. on 48c. on 48c. Type **57**	1·25	1·40
O39	75c. on 48c. on 48c. Ancient Ti'i image	1·25	1·40
O40	75c. on 48c. on 48c. Tourist canoeing	1·25	1·40
O41	75c. on 48c. on 48c. Captain William Bligh and chart	1·25	1·40
O29	80c. on 96c. Chestnut-breasted mannikin	2·50	1·75
O30	$1.20 Common mynah	3·25	2·50
O31	$2.10 Reef heron	4·75	3·75
O32	$3 Blue-headed flycatcher	7·00	7·00
O33	$4.20 Red-bellied flycatcher	8·00	8·00
O34	$5.60 Red munia	9·00	9·00
O35	$9.60 Flat-billed kingfisher	14·00	14·00
O36	$14 on $4 Red munia (35×48 mm)	16·00	16·00
O37	$18 on $5 Flat-billed kingfisher (35×48 mm)	18·00	18·00

Pt. 19

AJMAN

One of the Trucial States in the Persian Gulf. On 18 July 1971, seven Gulf sheikhdoms, including Ajman, formed part of the State of the United Arab Emirates. The federation became effective on 1 August 1972.

1964. 100 naye paise = 1 rupee.
1967. 100 dirhams = 1 riyal.

1 Shaikh Rashid bin Humaid al Naimi and Arab Stallion

1964. Multicoloured. (a) Size 34½×23 mm.
1	1n.p. Type **1**	10	10
2	2n.p. Regal angelfish	10	10
3	3n.p. Dromedary	10	10
4	4n.p. Yellow-banded angelfish	10	10
5	5n.p. Tortoise	10	10
6	10n.p. Jewel cichlid	25	10

7		15n.p. White stork	35	10
8		20n.p. Black-headed gulls	35	10
9		30n.p. Lanner falcon	60	25

(b) Size 42½×27 mm.

10		40n.p. Type **1**	25	25
11		50n.p. Regal angelfish	25	25
12		70n.p. Dromedary	35	25
13		1r. Yellow-banded angelfish	35	35
14		1r.50 Tortoise	70	60
15		2r. Jewel cichlid	95	85

(c) Size 53×34 mm.

16		3r. White stork	1·60	1·20
17		5r. Black-headed gulls	4·25	3·00
18		10r. Lanner falcon	7·25	5·50

2 Kennedy in Football Kit

1964. Pres. Kennedy Commem. Perf or imperf.

19	**2**	10n.p. purple and green	10	10
20	-	15n.p. violet and turquoise	10	10
21	-	50n.p. blue and brown	25	10
22	-	1r. turquoise and sepia	60	35
23	-	2r. olive and purple	95	60
24	-	3r. brown and green	1·40	95
25	-	5r. brown and violet	2·40	2·10
26	-	10r. brown and blue	4·75	3·50
MS26a	105×140 mm. Nos. 23/6 in new colours		24·00	12·00

DESIGNS—Various pictures of Kennedy: 15n.p. Diving; 50n.p. As naval officer; 1r. Sailing with Mrs. Kennedy; 2r. With Mrs. Eleanor Roosevelt; 3r. With wife and child; 5r. With colleagues; 10r. Full-face portrait.

3 Start of Race

1965. Olympic Games, Tokyo. Perf or imperf.

27	**3**	5n.p. slate, brown & mauve	10	10
28	-	10n.p. red, bronze and blue	10	10
29	**3**	15n.p. brown, violet & green	10	10
30	-	25n.p. black, blue and red	25	10
31	-	50n.p. slate, purple and blue	35	25
32	-	1r. blue, green and purple	60	35
33	-	1r.50 purple, violet and green	95	60
34	-	2r. blue, purple and ochre	1·20	85
35	-	3r. violet, brown and blue	1·80	1·10
36	-	5r. purple, green and yellow	3·25	1·90
MS36a	120×100 mm. Nos. 33/6 in new colours		12·00	8·50

DESIGNS: 10n.p., 1r.50, Boxing; 25n.p., 2r. Judo; 50n.p., 5r. Gymnastics; 1, 3r. Sailing.

4 First Gibbons Catalogue and Alexandria (U.S.) 5c. Postmaster's Stamp

1965. Stanley Gibbons Catalogue Centenary Exhibition, London. Multicoloured.

37		5n.p. Type **4**	10	10
38		10n.p. Austria (6k.) scarlet "Mercury" newspaper stamp	10	10
39		15n.p. British Guiana "One Cent", 1856	10	10
40		25n.p. Canada "Twelvepence Black", 1851	10	25
41		50n.p. Hawaii "Missionary" 2c., 1851	25	25
42		1r. Mauritius "Post Office" 2d. blue, 1847	50	20
43		3r. Switzerland "Double Geneva" 5c.+5c., 1843	1·60	70
44		5r. Tuscany 3 lire, 1860	2·75	1·20
MS44a	Two sheets, each 124×99 mm. Nos. 37, 40/1, 44 and 38/9, 42/3		8·50	8·50

The 5, 15 and 50n.p. and 3r. also include the First Gibbons Catalogue and the others, the Gibbons "Elizabethan" Catalogue.

1965. Pan Arab Games, Cairo. Perf or imperf. Nos. 29, 31 and 33/5 optd. (a) Optd **PAN ARAB GAMES CAIRO 1965.**

45	**3**	15n.p. brown, violet & green	10	10
46	-	50n.p. slate, purple and blue	50	50
47	-	1r.50 purple, violet & green	1·40	1·40
48	-	2r. blue, red and ochre	2·10	2·10
49	-	3r. violet, brown and blue	3·25	3·25

(b) Optd as Nos. 45/9 but equivalent in Arabic.

50	**3**	15n.p. brown, violet & green	10	10
51	-	50n.p. slate, purple and blue	50	50
52	-	1r.50 purple, violet and green	1·40	1·40
53	-	2r. blue, red and ochre	2·10	2·10
54	-	3r. violet, brown and blue	3·25	3·25

1965. Air. Designs similar to Nos. 1/9, but inscr "AIR MAIL". Mult. (a) Size 42½×25½ mm.

55		5n.p. Type **1**	10	10
56		25n.p. Regal angelfish	25	25
57		35n.p. Dromedary	25	25
58		50n.p. Yellow-banded angelfish	35	35
59		75n.p. Tortoise	60	60
60		1r. Jewel cichlid	85	85

(b) Size 53×34 mm.

61		2r. White stork	1·80	1·80
62		3r. Black-headed gull	2·40	2·40
63		5r. Lanner falcon	4·25	4·25

1966. Stamp Cent Exn, Cairo. Nos. 38/9 and 41/3 optd **STAMP CENTENARY EXHIBITION CAIRO, JANUARY 1966** and pyramid motif.

73		10n.p. multicoloured	10	10
74		15n.p. multicoloured	25	25
75		50n.p. multicoloured	55	55
76		1r. multicoloured	1·00	1·00
77		3r. multicoloured	3·00	3·00
MS78	Two sheets, each 124×99 mm. as MS44a		7·75	4·25

8 Sir Winston Churchill and Tower Bridge

1966. Churchill Commemoration. Each design includes portrait of Churchill. Multicoloured.

79		25n.p. Type **8**	10	10
80		50n.p. Buckingham Palace	25	10
81		75n.p. Blenheim Palace	35	25
82		1r. British Museum	60	25
83		2r. St. Paul's Cathedral in wartime	1·10	60
84		3r. National Gallery and St. Martin in the Fields Church	1·70	85
85		5r. Westminster Abbey	2·75	1·40
86		7r.50 Houses of Parliament at night	4·00	2·10
MS87	101×120 mm. Nos. 85/6		16·00	8·50

9 Rocket

1966. Space Achievements. Multicoloured. (a) Postage. Size as T **9.**

88		1n.p. Type **9**	10	10
89		3n.p. Capsule	10	10
90		5n.p. Astronaut entering capsule in space	10	10
91		10n.p. Astronaut outside capsule in space	10	10
92		15n.p. Astronauts and globe	10	10
93		25n.p. Astronaut in space	10	10
MS94	98×88 mm. 1r. and 3r. in designs of 15n.p. and 10n.p.		3·50	3·50

(b) Air. Size 38×38 mm.

95		50n.p. As Type **9**	35	10
96		1r. Astronauts and globe	60	25
97		3r. Astronaut outside capsule in space	1·80	60
98		5r. Capsule	3·25	1·10

1967. Various issues with currency names changed by overprinting in **Dh.** or **Riyals.** (a) Postage. Nos. 1/18 (1964 Definitives).

99		1d. on 1n.p.	10	10
100		2d. on 2n.p.	10	10
101		3d. on 3n.p.	10	10
102		4d. on 4n.p.	10	10
103		5d. on 5n.p.	10	10
104		10d. on 10n.p.	25	25
105		15d. on 15n.p.	25	25
106		20d. on 20n.p.	35	35
107		30d. on 30n.p.	60	60
108		40d. on 40n.p.	85	85
109		50d. on 50n.p.	1·10	1·10
110		70d. on 70n.p.	1·40	1·40
111		1r. on 1r.	1·90	1·90
112		1r.50 on 1r.50	3·00	3·00
113		2r. on 2r.	4·00	4·00
114		3r. on 3r.	2·40	2·40
115		5r. on 5r.	4·00	4·00
116		10r. on 10r.	7·75	7·75

(b) Air. Nos. 55/63 (Airmails).

117		15d. on 15n.p.	10	10
118		25d. on 25n.p.	25	25
119		35d. on 35n.p.	35	35
120		50d. on 50n.p.	50	50
121		75d. on 75n.p.	70	70
122		1r. on 1r.	95	95
123		2r. on 2r.	1·80	1·80
124		3r. on 3r.	3·00	3·00
125		5r. on 5r.	4·50	4·50

NEW CURRENCY SURCHARGES. Nos. 19/44 and 79/98 are known surch in new currency (dirhams and riyals), in limited quantities, but there is some doubt as to whether they were in use locally.

11 Fiat 1500 Saloon, 1962

1967. Transport.

135	**11**	1d. brown & blk (postage)	10	10
136	-	2d. blue and brown	10	10
137	-	3d. mauve and black	10	10
138	-	4d. blue and brown	10	10
139	-	5d. green and black	10	10
140	-	15d. blue and brown	10	10
141	-	30d. brown and black	25	10
142	-	50d. black and brown	35	10
143	-	70d. violet and black	50	10
144	**11**	1r. green and brown (air)	60	25
145	-	2r. mauve and brown	1·20	50
146	-	3r. black and brown	1·80	70
147	-	5r. brown and black	3·00	1·20
148	-	10r. blue and brown	6·00	2·40

DESIGNS: 2d., 2r. Motor coach; 3d., 3r. Motor cyclist; 4d., 5r. Boeing 707 airliner; 5d., 10r. "Brasil" (liner); 15d. "Yankee" (sail training and cruise ship); 30d. Cameleer; 50d. Arab horse; 70d. Sikorsky S-58 helicopter.

OFFICIAL STAMPS

1965. Designs similar to Nos. 1/9, additionally inscr "ON STATE'S SERVICE". Multicoloured. (i) Postage. Size 43×26 mm.

O64		25n.p. Type **1**	25	10
O65		40n.p. Regal angelfish	35	25
O66		50n.p. Dromedary	50	35
O67		75n.p. Yellow-banded angelfish	60	50
O68		1r. Tortoise	95	60

(ii) Air. (a) Size 43×26 mm.

O69		75n.p. Jewel cichlid	60	25

(b) Size 53×34 mm.

O70		2r. White stork	1·90	70
O71		3r. Black-headed gulls	3·00	1·10
O72		5r. Lanner falcon	4·75	1·80

1967. Nos. O64/72 with currency names changed by overprinting in **Dh.** or **Riyals.**

O126		25d. on 25n.p.	25	25
O127		40d. on 40n.p.	35	25
O128		50d. on 50n.p.	50	25
O129		75d. on 75n.p. (No. O67)	60	60
O130		75d. on 75n.p. (No. O69)	95	60
O131		1r. on 1r.	70	85
O132		2r. on 2r.	3·50	2·10
O133		3r. on 3r.	7·25	3·00
O134		5r. on 5r.	13·50	6·25

For later issues see **UNITED ARAB EMIRATES.**

APPENDIX

From June 1967 very many stamp issues were made by a succession of agencies which have been awarded contracts by the Ruler, sometimes two agencies operating at the same time. Several contradictory statements were made as to the validity of some of these issues which appeared 1967-72 and for this reason they are only listed in abbreviated form.

1967

50th Birth Anniv of President J. F. Kennedy. Air 10, 20, 40, 70d., 1r.50, 2, 3, 5r.

Paintings. Postage. Arab Paintings 1, 2, 3, 4, 5, 30, 70d.; Air. Asian Paintings 1, 2, 3, 5r.; Indian Painting 10r.

Tales from "The Arabian Nights". Postage 1, 2, 3, 10, 30, 50, 70d.; Air 90d., 1, 2, 3r.

World Scout Jamboree, Idaho. Postage 30, 70d., 1r.; Air 2, 3, 4r.

Olympic Games, Mexico (1968). Postage 35, 65, 75d., 1r.; Air 1r.25, 2, 3, 4r.

Winter Olympic Games, Grenoble (1968). Postage 5, 35, 60, 75d.; Air 1, 1r.25, 2, 3r.

Pres. J. F. Kennedy Memorial. Die-stamped on gold foil. Air 10r.

Paintings by Renoir and Terbrugghen. Air 35, 65d., 1, 2r.×3.

1968

Paintings by Velasquez. Air 1r.×2, 2r.×2.

Winter Olympic Games, Grenoble. Die-stamped on gold foil. Air 7r.

Paintings from Famous Galleries. Air 1r.×4, 2r.×6.

Costumes. Air 30d.×2, 70d.×2, 1r.×2, 2r.×2.

Olympic Games, Mexico. Postage 1r.×4; Air 2r.×4.

Satellites and Spacecraft. Air 30d.×2, 70d.×2, 1r.×2, 2r.×2, 3r.×2.

Paintings. Hunting Dogs. Air 2r.×6.

Paintings. Adam and Eve. Air 2r.×4.

Human Rights Year. Kennedy Brothers and Martin Luther King. Air 1r.×3, 2r.×3.

Kennedy Brothers Memorial. Postage 2r.; Air 5r.

Sports Champions. Inter-Milano Football Club. Postage 5, 10, 15, 20, 25d.; Air 10r.

Sports Champions. Famous Footballers. Postage 15, 20, 50, 75d., 1r.; Air 10r.

Cats. Postage 1, 2, 3d.; Air 2, 3r.

Olympic Games, Mexico. Die-stamped on gold foil. 5r.

5th Death Anniv of Pres. J. F. Kennedy. On gold foil. Air 10r.

Paintings of the Madonna. Air 30, 70d., 1, 2r.

Space Exploration. Postage 5, 10, 15, 20, 25d.; Air 15r.

Olympic Games, Mexico. Gold Medals. Postage 2r.×4; Air 5r.×4.

Christmas. Air 5r.

1969

Sports Champions. Cyclists. Postage 1, 2, 5, 10, 15, 20d.; Air 12r.

Sports Champions. German Footballers. Postage 5, 10, 15, 20, 25d.; Air 10r.

Sports Champions. Motor-racing Drivers. Postage 1, 5, 10, 15, 25d.; Air 10r.

Motor-racing Cars. Postage 1, 5, 10, 15, 25d.; Air 10r.

Sports Champions. Boxers. Postage 5, 10, 15, 20d.; Air 10r.

Sports Champions. Baseball Players. Postage 1, 2, 5, 10, 15d.; Air 10r.

Birds. Air 1r.×11.

Roses. 1r.×6.

Wild Animals. Air 1r.×6.

Paintings. Italian Old Masters. 5, 10, 15, 20d., 10r.

Paintings. Famous Composers. Air 5, 10, 25d., 10r.

Paintings. French Artists. 1r.×4.

Paintings. Nudes. Air 2r.×4.

Three Kings Mosaic. Air 1r.×2, 3r.×2.

Kennedy Brothers. Air 2, 3, 10r.

Olympic Games, Mexico. Gold Medal Winners. Postage 1, 2d., 10r.; Air 10d., 5, 10r.

Paintings of the Madonna. Postage 10d.; Air 10r.

Space Flight of "Apollo 9". Optd on 1968 Space Exploration issue. Air 10r.

Space Flight of "Apollo 10". Optd on 1968 Space Exploration issue. Air 15r.

1st Death Anniv of Gagarin. Optd on 1968 Space Exploration issue. 5d.

2nd Death Anniv of Edward White. Optd on 1968 Space Exploration issue. 10d.

1st Death Anniv of Robert Kennedy. Optd on 1969 Kennedy Brothers issue. Air 2r.

European Football Championship. Optd on 1968 Famous Footballers issue. Air 10r.

Olympic Games, Munich (1972). Optd on 1969 Mexico Gold Medal Winners issue. Air 10d., 5, 10r.

Moon Landing of "Apollo 11". Air 1, 2, 5r.

Moon Landing of "Apollo 11". Circular designs on gold or silver foil. Air 3r.×3, 5r.×3, 10r.×14.

Paintings. Christmas. Postage 1, 2, 3, 4, 5, 15d.; Air 2, 3r.

1970

"Apollo" Space Flights. Postage 1, 2, 4, 5, 10d.; Air 3, 5r.

Birth Bicentenary of Napoleon Bonaparte. Die-stamped on gold foil. Air 20r.

Paintings. Easter. Postage 5, 10, 12, 30, 50, 70d.; Air 1, 2r.

Moon Landing. Die-stamped on gold foil. Air 20r.

Paintings by Michelangelo. Postage 1, 2, 4, 5, 8, 10d.; Air 3, 5r.

World Cup Football Championship, Mexico. Air 25, 50, 75d., 1, 2, 3r.

"Expo 70" World Fair, Osaka, Japan. Japanese Paintings. Postage 1, 2, 3, 4, 5, 10, 15d.; Air 1, 5r.

Birth Bicent Napoleon Bonaparte. Postage 1, 2, 4, 5, 10d.; Air 3, 5r.

Paintings. Old Masters. Postage 1, 2, 5, 6, 10d.; Air 1, 2, 3r.

Space Flight of "Apollo 13". Air 50, 75, 80d., 1, 2, 3r.

World Cup Football Championship, Mexico. Die-stamped on gold foil. Air 20r.

Olympic Games, 1960–1972. Postage 15, 30, 50, 70d.; Air 2, 5r.

"Expo 70" World Fair, Osaka, Japan. Pavilions. Postage 1, 2, 3, 4, 10, 15d.; Air 1, 5r.

Brazil's Victory in World Cup Football Championship. Optd on 1970 World Cup issue. Air 25, 50, 75d., 1, 2, 3r.

"Gemini" and "Apollo" Space Flights. Postage 1, 2, 3, 4, 5, 6, 8, 10, 12, 15, 20, 25, 30, 35, 40, 50d.; Air 1, 1r.50, 2, 3r.

Vintage and Veteran Cars. Postage 1, 2, 4, 5, 8, 10d.; Air 2, 3r.

Pres. D. Eisenhower Commem. Postage 30, 50, 70d.; Air 1, 2, 3r.

Paintings by Ingres. Air 25, 30, 35, 50, 70, 85d., 1, 2r.

500th Birth Anniv (1971) of Albrecht Durer. Air 25, 30, 35, 50, 70, 85d., 1, 2r.

Christmas Paintings. Air 25, 30, 35, 50, 70, 85d., 1, 2r.

Winter Olympic Games, Sapporo, Japan (1972). Die-stamped on gold foil. Air 20r.

Meeting of Eisenhower and De Gaulle, 1942. Die-stamped on gold foil. Air 20r.

General De Gaulle Commem. Air 25, 50, 75d., 1, 2, 3r.

Winter Olympic Games, Sapporo, Japan (1972). Sports. Postage 1, 2, 5, 10d.; Air 3, 5r.

J. Rindt, World Formula 1 Motor-racing Champion. Die-stamped on gold foil. Air 20r.

1971

"Philatokyo" Stamp Exhibition, Tokyo. Japanese Paintings. Air 25, 30, 35, 50, 70, 85d., 1, 2r.
Mars Space Project. Air 50, 75, 80d., 1, 2, 3r.
Napoleonic Military Uniforms. Postage 5, 10, 15, 20, 25, 30d.; Air 2, 3r.
Olympic Games, Munich (1972). Sports. Postage 10, 15, 25, 30, 40d.; Air 1, 2, 3r.
Paintings by Modern Artists. Air 25, 30, 35, 50, 70, 85d.; 1, 2r.
Paintings by Famous Artists. Air 25, 30, 35, 50, 70, 85d.; 1, 2r.
25th Anniv of United Nations. Optd on 1971 Modern Artists issue. Air 25, 30, 35, 50, 70, 85d.; 1, 2r.
Olympic Games, Munich (1972). Sports. Postage 1, 2, 3, 4, 5, 6, 8, 10, 12, 15, 20, 25, 30, 35, 40, 50d.; Air 1, 1r.50, 2, 3r.
Butterflies. Air 25, 30, 35, 50, 70, 85d., 1, 2r.
Space Flight of "Apollo 14". Postage 5, 15, 25, 50, 60, 70d.; Air 5r.
Winter Olympic Games, 1924–1968. Postage 30, 40, 50, 75d., 1r.; Air 2r.
Signs of the Zodiac. 1, 2, 5, 10, 12, 15, 25, 30, 35, 45, 50, 60d.
Famous Men. Air 65, 70, 75, 80, 85, 90d., 1, 1r.25, 1r.50, 2, 2r.50, 3r.
Death Bicent of Beethoven. 20, 30, 40, 60d., 1r.50, 2r.
Dr. Albert Schweitzer Commem. 20, 30, 40, 60d., 1r.50, 2r.
Tropical Birds. Postage 1, 2, 3, 4, 5, 10d.; Air 2, 3r.
Paintings by French Artists. Postage 1, 2, 3, 4, 5, 10d.; Air 2, 3r.
Paintings by Modern Artists. Postage 1, 2, 3, 4, 5, 10d.; Air 2, 3r.
Paintings by Degas. Postage 1, 2, 3, 4, 5, 10d.; Air 2, 3r.
Paintings by Titian. Postage 1, 2, 3, 4, 5, 10d.; Air 2, 3r.
Paintings by Renoir. Postage 1, 2, 3, 4, 5, 10d.; Air 2, 3r.
Space Flight of "Apollo 15". Postage 25, 40, 50, 60d., 1r.; Air 6r.
"Philatokyo" Stamp Exhibition, Tokyo. Stamps. Postage 10, 15, 20, 30, 35, 50, 80d.; Air 1, 2r.
Tropical Birds. Postage 1, 2, 3, 5, 7, 10, 12, 15, 20, 25, 30, 40d.; Air 50, 80d.; 1, 3r.
Paintings depicting Venus. Postage 1, 2, 3, 4, 5, 10d.; Air 2, 3r.
13th World Scout Jamboree, Asagiri, Japan. Scouts. Postage 1, 2, 3, 5, 7, 10, 12, 15, 20, 25, 30, 35, 40, 50, 65, 80d.; Air 1, 1r.25, 1r.50, 2r.
Lions International Clubs. Optd on 1971 Famous Paintings issue. Air 25, 30, 35, 50, 70, 85d., 1, 2r.
13th World Scout Jamboree, Asagiri, Japan. Japanese Paintings. Postage 20, 30, 40, 60, 75d.; Air 3r.
25th Anniv of UNICEF Optd on 1971 Scout Jamboree (paintings) issue. Postage 20, 30, 40, 60, 75d.; Air 3r.
Christmas 1971. (1st series. Plain frames). Portraits of Popes. Postage 1, 2, 3, 4, 5, 10d.; Air 2, 3r.
Modern Cars. Postage 10, 15, 25, 50, 60d.; Air 2, 3r.
Olympic Games, Munich (1972). Show-jumping. Embossed on gold foil. Air 20r.
Exploration of Outer Space. Postage 15, 25, 50, 60, 70d.; Air 5r.
Royal Visit of Queen Elizabeth II to Japan. Postage 1, 2, 3, 4, 5, 10d.; Air 2, 3r.
Meeting of Pres. Nixon and Emperor Hirohito of Japan in Alaska. Design as 3r. value of 1970 Eisenhower issue but value changed and optd with commemorative inscr. Air 5r. (silver opt), 5r. (gold opt).
"Apollo" Astronauts. Postage 5, 20, 35, 40, 50d.; Air 1, 2, 3r.
Discoverers of the Universe. Astronomers and Space Scientists. Postage 5, 10, 15, 20, 25, 30d.; Air 2, 5r.
"ANPHILEX 71" Stamp Exn, New York. Air 2r.50.
Christmas 1971. Portraits of Popes (2nd series. Ornamental frames). Postage 1, 2, 3, 4, 5, 10d.; Air 2, 3r.
Royal Silver Wedding of Queen Elizabeth II and Prince Philip (1972). Air 1, 2, 3r.
Space Flight of "Apollo 16". Postage 20, 30, 40, 50, 60d.; Air 3, 4r.
Fairy Tales. "Baron Munchhausen" Stories. Postage 1, 2, 4, 5, 10d.; Air 3r.
World Fair, Philadelphia (1976). Paintings. Postage 25, 50, 75d.; Air 5r.
Fairy Tales. Stories of the Brothers Grimm. Postage 1, 2, 4, 5, 10d.; Air 3r.
European Tour of Emperor Hirohito of Japan. Postage 1, 2, 4, 5, 10d.; Air 6r.
13th World Scout Jamboree, Asagiri, Japan. Postage 5, 10, 15, 20, 25d.; Air 5r.
Winter Olympic Games, Sapporo, Japan (1972). Postage 5, 10, 15, 20, 25d.; Air 5r.
Olympic Games, Munich (1972). Postage 5, 10, 15, 20, 25d.; Air 5r.
"Japanese Life". Postage 10d.×4, 20d.×4, 30d.×4, 40d.×4, 50d.×4; Air 3r.×4.
Space Flight of "Apollo 15". Postage 5, 10, 15, 20, 25, 50d.; Air 1, 2, 3, 5r.
"Soyuz 11" Disaster. Air 50d., 1r., 1r.50.
"The Future in Space". Postage 5, 10, 15, 20, 25, 50d.
2500th Anniv of Persian Empire. Postage 10, 20, 30, 40, 50d., Air 3r.
Cats. Postage 10, 15, 20, 25d.; Air 50d., 1r.
50th Anniv of Tutankhamun Tomb Discovery. Postage 1, 2, 3, 4, 5, 6, 7, 8, 9, 10, 11, 12, 13, 14, 15, 16d.; Air 1r.×4.
400th Birth Anniv of Johannes Kepler (astronomer). Postage 50d.; Air 5r.
Famous Men. Air 1r.×5.

1972

150th Death Anniv of Napoleon Bonaparte (1971). Postage 10, 20, 30, 40d.; Air 1, 2, 3, 4r.
1st Death Anniv of General de Gaulle. Postage 10, 20, 30, 40d.; Air 1, 2, 3, 4r.
Wild Animals (1st series). Postage 5, 10, 15, 20, 25, 30, 35, 40d.
Tropical Fishes. Postage 5, 10, 15, 20, 25d.; Air 50, 75d., 1r.
Famous Musicians. Postage 5d.×3, 10d.×3, 15d.×3, 20d.×3, 25d.×3, 30d.×3, 35d.×3, 40d.×3.
Easter. Postage 5, 10, 15, 20, 25d.; Air 5r.
Wild Animals (2nd series). Postage 5, 10, 15, 20, 25d.; Air 5r.
"Tour de France" Cycle Race. Postage 5, 10, 15, 20, 25, 30, 35, 40, 45, 50, 55d.; Air 60, 65, 70, 75, 80, 85, 90, 95d., 1r.

Many other issues were released between 1 September 1971 and 1 August 1972, but their authenticity has been denied by the Ajman Postmaster-General. Certain issues of 1967-69 exist overprinted to commemorate other events but the Postmaster General states that these are unofficial. Ajman joined the United Arab Emirates on 1 August 1972 and the Ministry of Communications assumed responsibility for the postal services. Further stamps inscribed "Ajman" issued after that date were released without authority and had no validity.

Pt. 11

ALAND ISLANDS

Aland is an autonomous province of Finland. From 1984 separate stamps were issued for the area although stamps of Finland could also still be used there. On 1 January 1993 Aland assumed control of its own postal service and Finnish stamps ceased to be valid there.

1984. 100 pennia = 1 markka.
2002. 100 cents = 1 euro.

1 Fishing Boat

1984

1	**1**	10p. mauve	20	25
2	**1**	20p. green	35	25
3	**1**	50p. green	35	25
4	–	1m. green	70	60
5	**1**	1m.10 blue	70	60
6	**1**	1m.20 black	70	65
7	**1**	1m.30 green	80	80
8	–	1m.40 multicoloured	1·60	1·00
9a	–	1m.50 multicoloured	1·70	1·00
10	–	1m.90 multicoloured	1·30	1·20
12	–	3m. blue, green and black	2·00	1·40
14	–	10m. black, chestnut & brn	5·50	4·00
15	–	13m. multicoloured	7·75	7·25

DESIGNS—20×29 mm: 1m.50, Midsummer pole, Storby village. 21×31 mm: 13m. Rug, 1793. 26×32 mm: 3m. Map of Aland Islands. 30×20 mm: 1m. Farjsund Bridge. 31×21 mm: 1m.40, Aland flag; 1m.90, Mariehamn Town Hall. 32×26 mm: 10m. Seal of Aland showing St. Olaf (patron saint).

2 *Pommern* (barque) and Car Ferries, Mariehamn West Harbour

1984. 50th Anniv of Society of Shipowners.

16	**2**	2m. multicoloured	5·75	4·00

3 Grove of Ashes and Hazels

1985. Aland Scenes. Multicoloured.

17	**3**	2m. Type 3	2·50	1·30
18		5m. Kokar Church and shore (horiz)	3·25	2·50
19		8m. Windmill and farm (horiz)	5·25	4·50

4 Map, Compass and Measuring Instrument

1986. Nordic Orienteering Championships, Aland.

20	**4**	1m.60 multicoloured	4·00	2·50

5 Clay Hands and Burial Mounds, Skamkulla

1986. Archaeology. Multicoloured.

21		1m.60 Type **5**	2·50	1·00
22		2m.20 Bronze staff from Finby and Apostles	1·30	1·20
23		20m. Monument at ancient court site, Saltvik, and court in session (horiz)	10·50	9·75

6 "Onnigeby" (drawing, Victor Westerholm)

1986. Centenary of Onnigeby Artists' Colony.

24	**6**	3m.70 multicoloured	5·25	4·00

7 Eiders

1987. Birds. Multicoloured.

25		1m.70 Type **7**	10·00	9·50
26		2m.30 Tufted ducks	5·00	3·50
27		12m. Velvet scoters	7·75	6·50

8 Firemen in Horse-drawn Cart

1987. Centenary of Mariehamn Fire Brigade.

28	**8**	7m. multicoloured	7·75	7·75

9 Meeting and Item 3 of Report

1987. 70th Anniv of Aland Municipalities Meeting, Finstrom.

29	**9**	1m.70 multicoloured	2·20	1·60

10 Loading Mail Barrels at Eckero

1988. 350th Anniv of Postal Service in Aland.

30	**10**	1m.80 multicoloured	3·00	2·50

11 Ploughing with Horses

1988. Centenary of Agricultural Education in Aland.

31	**11**	2m.20 multicoloured	2·75	3·00

12 Baltic Galleass *Albanus*

1988. Sailing Ships. Multicoloured.

32		1m.80 Type **12**	3·25	2·50
33		2m.40 Schooner *Ingrid* (horiz)	5·00	4·25
34		11m. Barque *Pamir* (horiz)	13·00	11·00

13 St. Olaf's Church, Jomala

1988

35	**13**	1m.40 multicoloured	2·50	2·00

14 Elder-flowered Orchid

1989. Orchids. Multicoloured.

36		1m.50 Type **14**	3·25	2·10
37		2m.50 Narrow-leaved helleborine	4·00	2·75
38		14m. Lady's slipper	13·00	11·50

15 Teacher and Pupils

1989. 350th Anniv of First Aland School, Saltvik.

39	**15**	1m.90 multicoloured	2·00	1·70

16 St. Michael's Church, Finstrom

1989

40	**16**	1m.50 multicoloured	2·00	1·80

17 Baltic Herring

1990. Fish. Multicoloured.

41		1m.50 Type **17**	1·70	1·30
42		2m. Northern pike	1·80	1·60
43		2m.70 European flounder	2·00	1·80

18 St. Andrew's Church, Lumparland

1990

44	**18**	1m.70 multicoloured	2·20	2·00

19 *St. Catherine* (fresco, St. Anna's Church, Kumlinge)

1990

45	**19**	2m. multicoloured	1·70	1·60

20 West European Hedgehog

1991. Mammals. Multicoloured.

46		1m.60 Type **20**	1·30	1·00
47		2m.10 Eurasian red squirrel	1·70	1·40
48		2m.90 Roe deer	2·00	2·10

21 Volleyball

1991. Small Island Games, Mariehamn. Sheet 117×81 mm containing T **21** and similar vert designs. Multicoloured.

MS49	2m.10; Type **21**; 2m.10; Shooting; 2m.10; Football; 2m.10, Running	6·75	6·50

22 Canoeing

1991. Nordic Countries' Postal Co-operation. Tourism. Multicoloured.

50	2m.10 Type **22**	1·40	1·30
51	2m.90 Cycling	2·10	2·00

23 League of Nations Meeting, Geneva, 1921 (print by F. Rackwitz)

1991. 70th Anniv of Aland Autonomy.

52	**23**	16m. multicoloured	9·75	9·00

24 St. Mathias's Church, Vardo

1991

53	**24**	1m.80 multicoloured	2·10	1·60

25 Von Knorring (after Karl Jansson)

1992. Birth Bicentenary of Rev. Frans Peter von Knorring (social reformer).

54	**25**	2 klass (1m.60) mult	1·70	1·30

26 Barque Herzogen Cecilie and Wheat Transport Route Map

1992. 48th International Association of Cape Horners Congress, Mariehamn.

55	**26**	1 klass (2m.10) mult	2·50	2·00

27 Ranno Lighthouse

1992. Lighthouses. Multicoloured.

56	2m.10 Type **27**	6·75	5·75
57	2m.10 Salskar	6·75	5·75
58	2m.10 Lagskar	6·75	5·75
59	2m.10 Market	6·75	5·75

28 Lemland Landscape

1992. Birth Cent of Joel Pettersson (painter). Multicoloured.

60	2m.90 Type **28**	2·00	1·80
61	16m. Self-portrait	8·50	8·25

29 Delegates processing to Church Service

1992. 70th Anniv of First Aland Provincial Parliament.

62	**29**	3m.40 multicoloured	2·50	2·20

30 St. Catherine's Church, Hammarland

1992

63	**30**	1m.80 multicoloured	2·00	1·60

31 Arms

1993. Postal Autonomy. Multicoloured.

64		1m.60 Type **31**	1·70	1·30
MS65	129×80 mm. 1m.90 Cover with Kastelholm single-line postmark (26×35 mm); 1m.90 Mareinhamm Post Office; 1m.90 Post van leaving Alfägeln (ferry); 1m.90 Postal emblem (26×31 mm)		5·50	5·25

32 Fiddler

1993. Nordic Countries' Postal Co-operation. Tourism. Exhibits from Jan Karlsgarden Open-air Museum.

66	**32**	2m. red, pink and black	1·40	1·30
67	–	2m.30 blue, black and azure	1·60	1·40

DESIGN—HORIZ: 2m.30, Boat-house.

33 Saltvik Woman

1993. Costumes. Multicoloured.

68	1m.90 Type **33**	1·70	1·60
69	3m.50 Eckero and Brando women and Mariehamn couple	2·10	2·30
70	17m. Finstrom couple	10·50	9·50

34 Diabase Dyke, Sottunga

1993. Aland Geology. Multicoloured.

71	10p. Boulder field, Dano Gamlan	25	20
72	1m.60 Drumlin (hillock), Markusbole	90	1·00
73	2m. Type **34**	1·20	1·00
74	2m.30 Pitcher of Kallskar	1·30	1·20
75	2m.70 Pillow lava, Kumlinge	1·60	1·30
76	2m.90 Red Cow (islet), Lumpurn	1·80	1·70
77	3m.40 Erratic boulder, Torsskar, Kokar Osterbygge (horiz)	2·00	1·80
78	6m. Folded gneiss	3·25	3·00
79	7m. Pothole, Bano Foglo (horiz)	3·50	3·25

35 Mary Magdalene Church, Sottunga

1993

80	**35**	1m.80 multicoloured	1·70	1·60

37 Glanville's Fritillary (Melitaea cinxia)

1994. Butterflies. Multicoloured.

81	2m.30 Type **37**	1·70	1·60
82	2m.30 Quercusia querqus	1·70	1·60
83	2m.30 Clouded apollo (Parnassius mnemosyne)	1·70	1·60
84	2m.30 Hesperia comma	1·70	1·60

38 Genetic Diagram

1994. Europa. Medical Discoveries. Multicoloured.

85	2m.30 Type **38** (discovery of Von Willebrand's disease (hereditary blood disorder))	3·25	3·00
86	2m.90 Molecular diagram (purification of heparin by Erik Jorpes)	3·50	3·25

39 Comb Ceramic and Pitted Ware Pottery

1994. The Stone Age.

87	**39**	2m.40 brown	1·30	1·60
88	–	2m.80 blue	1·60	1·70
89	–	18m. green	10·00	9·75

DESIGNS—VERT: 2m.80, Stone tools. HORIZ: 18m. Canoe and tent by river (reconstruction of Stone-age village, Langbergsoda).

40 St. John the Baptist's Church, Sund

1994

90	**40**	2m. multicoloured	2·00	1·40

42 Skuta (Cargo Sailing Boat)

1995. Cargo Sailing Ships. Multicoloured.

91	2m.30 Type **42**	1·70	1·60
92	2m.30 Sump (well-boat)	1·70	1·60
93	2m.30 Storbat (farm boat)	1·70	1·60
94	2m.30 Jakt	1·70	1·60

43 National Colours and E.U. Emblem

1995. Admission of Aland Islands to European Union.

95	**43**	2m.90 multicoloured	2·30	2·10

44 Doves and Cliffs

1995. Europa. Peace and Freedom. Multicoloured.

96	2m.80 Type **44**	1·70	1·80
97	2m.90 Dove, night sky and island	1·80	2·00

45 Golf

1995. Nordic Countries' Postal Co-operation. Tourism. With service indicator. Multicoloured.

98	2 klass (2m.) Type **45**	1·70	1·60
99	1 klass (2m.30) Sport fishing	2·00	1·60

46 Racing Dinghies

1995. Optimist World Dinghy Championships, Mariehamn.

100	**46**	3m.40 multicoloured	2·50	2·20

47 St. George's Church, Geta

1995

101	**47**	2m. multicoloured	1·70	1·30

48 St. Olaf (Wooden Carving from Sund Church)

1995. Birth Millenary of St. Olaf.

102	**48**	4m.30 multicoloured	2·75	3·00

49 Fish holding Flag in Mouth ("Greetings from Aland")

1996. Greetings Stamps. With service indicator. Multicoloured.

103	1 klass Type **49**	2·00	1·60
104	1 klass Bird holding flower in beak ("Congratulations")	2·00	1·60

50 Landing on Branch

1996. Endangered Species. The Eagle Owl. Multicoloured.

105	2m.40 Type **50**	1·80	1·60
106	2m.40 Perched on branch	1·80	1·60
107	2m.40 Adult owl	1·80	1·60
108	2m.40 Juvenile owl	1·80	1·60

Nos. 105/6 form a composite design.

51 Sally Salminen
(novelist)

1996. Europa. Famous Women. Multicoloured.
109 2m.80 Type **51** 1·80 1·70
110 2m.90 Fanny Sundstrom
 (politician) 2·00 1·80

52 Choir

1996. Aland '96 Song and Music Festival, Mariehamn.
111 **52** 2m.40 multicoloured 1·70 1·60

53 "Haircut"

1996. 150th Birth Anniv of Karl Jansson (painter).
112 **53** 18m. multicoloured 11·00 10·50

54 *Trilobita
asaphus*

1996. Fossils. Multicoloured.
113 40p. Type **54** 25 45
114 9m. *Gastropoda euomophalus* 4·50 4·25

55 Brando
Church

1996
115 **55** 2m. multicoloured 1·70 1·40

56 Giant Isopod
(*Saduria entomon*)
and Opossum
Shrimp (*Mysis relicta*)

1997. Marine Survivors from the Ice Age. Multicoloured.
116 30p. Type **56** 25 25
117 2m.40 Four-horned sculpin
 (*Myotocephalus quadricornis*) 1·80 1·70
118 4m.30 Ringed seal (*Phoca
 hispida botrica*) 3·00 2·75

57 Coltsfoot (*Tussilago
farfara*)

1997. Spring Flowers. Multicoloured.
119 2m.40 Type **57** 1·40 1·60
120 2m.40 Blue anemone (*Hepatica
 nobilis*) 1·40 1·60
121 2m.40 Wood anemone
 (*Anemone nemorosa*) 1·40 1·60
122 2m.40 Yellow anemone
 (*Anemone ranunculoides*) 1·40 1·60

58 Floorball

1997. First Women's Floorball World Championship,
Mariehamn and Godby.
123 **58** 3m.40 multicoloured 2·50 2·10

59 The Devil's
Dance

1997. Europa. Tales and Legends.
124 **59** 2m.90 multicoloured 3·25 3·00

60 Kastelholm Castle
and Arms

1997. 600th Anniv of Kalmar Union between Sweden,
Denmark and Norway.
125 **60** 2m.40 multicoloured 1·80 2·00

61 Hologram of Schooner
Linden and "75 Years"

1997. 75th Anniv of Aland Autonomy. Sheet 128×80 mm.
MS126 **61** 20m. multicoloured 13·00 16·00

62 *Thornbury*
(freighter)

1997. Steam Freighters. Multicoloured.
127 2m.80 Type **62** 1·70 1·60
128 3m.50 *Osmo* (freighter) 1·80 1·70

63 St George's
Church,
Mariehamn

1997. 70th Anniv of Mariehamn Church.
129 **63** 1m.90 multicoloured 1·70 1·30

64 Man harvesting
Apples

1998. Horticulture. Multicoloured.
130 2m. Type **64** 1·30 1·40
131 2m.40 Woman harvesting
 cucumbers 2·00 1·80

65 Boy on Moped

1998. Youth Activities. Multicoloured.
132 2m.40 Type **65** 1·40 1·60
133 2m.40 Laptop computer 1·40 1·60
134 2m.40 CD disk and headphones 1·40 1·60
135 2m.40 Step aerobics 1·40 1·60

66 Midsummer
Celebrations

1998. Europa. National Festivals.
136 **66** 4m.20 multicoloured 3·50 3·25

67 *Isabella* (car ferry)

1998. Nordic Countries' Postal Co-operation. Shipping.
137 **67** 2m.40 multicoloured 2·00 1·80

68 Waves breaking

1998. International Year of the Ocean.
138 **68** 6m.30 multicoloured 4·00 3·50

69 Players

1998. Association of Tennis Professionals Senior Tour,
Mariehamn. Self-adhesive.
139 **69** 2m.40 multicoloured 1·70 1·60

70 Schooner,
Compass Rose and
Knots

1998. Ninth International Sea Scout Camp, Bomarsund
Fortress, Aland.
140 **70** 2m.80 multicoloured 2·00 1·70

71 Seffers Homestead,
Onningeby

1998. Traditional Porches. Multicoloured.
141 1m.60 Type **71** 1·20 1·00
142 2m. Labbas homestead, Storby 1·40 1·30
143 2m.90 Abras homestead, Bjorko 1·70 1·60

72 Eckero
Church

1998
144 **72** 1m.90 multicoloured 1·80 1·40

73 Sword and Dagger

1999. Bronze Age Relics. Multicoloured.
145 2m. Type **73** 1·00 1·20
146 2m.20 "Ship" tumulus (vert) 1·60 1·70

74 Wardrobe

1999. Folk Art. Decorated Furniture. Multicoloured.
147 2m.40 Type **74** 1·30 1·40
148 2m.40 Distaff 1·30 1·40
149 2m.40 Chest 1·30 1·40
150 2m.40 Spinning wheel 1·30 1·40

75 '*Pamir*' and '*Passat*'
(barques) off Port Victoria
(R. Castor)

1999. 50th Anniv of Rounding of Cape Horn by *Pamir* on
Last Wheat-carrying Voyage.
151 **75** 3m.40 multicoloured 2·20 2·10

76 Cowslip

1999. Provincial Plant of Aland. Self-adhesive.
152 **76** 2m.40 multicoloured 1·60 1·40

77 Ido Island, Kokar

1999. Europa. Parks and Gardens.
153 **77** 2m.90 multicoloured 2·75 2·50
No. 153 is denominated both in markkas and in euros.

78 Racing Yachts

1999. Sailing.
154 **78** 2m.70 multicoloured 1·80 1·60

79 Puffed Shield
Lichen
(*Hypogymnia
physodes*)

1999. Lichens. With service indicator. Multicoloured.
155 2 klass (2m.) Type **79** 1·70 1·60
156 1 klass (2m.40) Common
 orange lichen (*Xanthoria
 parietina*) 2·00 1·80

80 Loading Avions de
Transport Reginal ATR72

1999. 125th Anniv of Universal Postal Union.
157 **80** 2m.90 multicoloured 1·80 2·00

81 St. Bridget's
Church,
Lemland

1999
158 **81** 1m.90 multicoloured 1·60 1·30

82 Runners

1999. Finnish Cross-country Championships, Mariehamn.
159 **82** 3m.50 multicoloured 2·10 2·00

DENOMINATION. From No. 162 to 207 Aland Islands stamps are denominated both in markkas and in euros. As no cash for the latter is in circulation, the catalogue continues to use the markka value.

83 Arctic Tern (*Sterna
paradisaea*)

2000. Sea Birds. Multicoloured.
162	1m.80 Type **83**	1·20	1·00
164	2m.20 Mew gull (*Larus canus*) (vert)	1·40	1·30
166	2m.60 Great black-backed gull (*Larus marinus*)	1·70	1·60

84 International Peace Symbol and State Flag

2000. New Millennium Sheet. 100×80 mm. Multicoloured.
MS171	**84** 3m.40, yellow; 3m.40, red; 3m.40, blue; 3m.40, white	10·50	9·00

85 Elk

2000. The Elk (*Alces alces*). Multicoloured.
172	2m.60 Type **85**	1·60	1·70
173	2m.60 With young	1·60	1·70
174	2m.60 Beside lake	1·60	1·70
175	2m.60 In snow	1·60	1·70

86 "Building Europe"

2000. Europa.
176	**86** 3m. multicoloured	2·75	2·50

87 Gymnast

2000. Finno-Swedish Gymnastics Association Exhibition, Mariehamn. Self-adhesive.
177	**87** 2m.60 multicoloured	1·70	1·30

88 Crew and *Linden* (schooner)

2000. Visit by *Cutty Sark* Tall Ships' Race Competitors to Mariehamn.
178	**88** 3m.40 multicoloured	2·10	2·00

89 Lange on prow of Longship

2000. Death Millenary of Hlodver Lange the Viking.
179	**89** 4m.50 multicoloured	3·00	2·75

90 Wooden Ornamented Swiss-style House, Mariehamn

2000. 48th Death Anniv of Hilda Hongell (architect). Multicoloured.
180	3m.80 Type **90**	2·10	2·00
181	10m. House with central front entrance, Mariehamn	5·25	5·00

91 The Nativity

2000. 2000 Years of Christianity.
182	**91** 3m. multicoloured	2·00	1·80

92 Kokar Church

2000.
183	**92** 2m. multicoloured	1·60	1·30

93 Steller's Eider in Flight

2001. Endangered Species. The Steller's Eider (*Polysticta stelleri*). Multicoloured.
184	2m.70 Type **93**	1·60	1·60
185	2m.70 Duck and drake	1·60	1·60
186	2m.70 Duck and drake swimming	1·60	1·60
187	2m.70 Drake swimming	1·60	1·60

94 Swamp Horsetail (*Equisetum fluviatile*)

2001. Plants. Multicoloured.
188	1m.90 Type **94**	1·30	1·20
189	2m.80 Stiff clubmoss (*Lycopodium annotinum*)	1·80	1·70
190	3m.50 Polypody (*Polybodium vulgare*)	2·10	2·00

95 Heart and Graffiti on Brick Wall

2001. St. Valentine's Day.
200	**95** 3m.20 multicoloured	2·00	1·80

96 Fisherman and Fish

2001. Europa. Water Resources.
201	**96** 3m.20 multicoloured	2·75	2·50

97 Archipelago Windmill

2001. Windmills. Multicoloured.
202	3m. Type **97**	1·60	1·40
203	7m. Timbered windmill (horiz)	3·50	3·25
204	20m. Nest windmill (horiz)	10·50	10·00

98 Golden Retriever

2001. Puppies. Multicoloured.
205	2 klass (2m.30) Type **98**	1·60	1·40
206	1 klass (2m.70) Wire-haired dachshund	1·80	1·70

99 Foglo Church

2001
207	**99** 2m. multicoloured	1·30	1·00

100 Smooth Snake (*Coronella Austriaca*)

2002. Endangered Animals. Multicoloured.
208	5c. Type **100**	25	20
209	70c. Great crested newt (*Triturus cristatus*)	2·10	2·00

101 Woman pushing Shopping Trolley

2002. Euro Currency.
210	**101** 60c. multicoloured	2·20	2·00

102 Tidying up Christmas

2002. St. Canute's Day.
211	**102** €2 multicoloured	6·50	6·25

103 Spiced Salmon and New Potatoes

2002. Traditional Dishes. Multicoloured.
212	1 klass (55c.) Type **103**	1·80	1·70
213	1 klass (55c.) Fried herring, mashed potatoes and beetroot	1·80	1·70
214	1 klass (55c.) Black bread and butter	1·80	1·70
215	1 klass (55c.) Aland pancake with stewed prune sauce and whipped cream	1·80	1·70

104 Building

2002. Inauguration of New Post Terminal, Sviby.
216	**104** €1 multicoloured	3·25	2·75

105 Circus Elephant and Rider

2002. Europa. Circus.
217	**105** 40c. multicoloured	2·00	1·70

106 "Radar II" (sculpture, Stefan Lindfors)

2002. Nordic Countries' Postal Co-operation. Modern Art.
218	**106** €3 multicoloured	9·75	9·00

107 Kayaking

2002
219	**107** 90c. multicoloured	3·25	3·25

108 8th-century Buckle, Persby, Sud

2002. Iron Age Jewellery found on Aland. Multicoloured.
220	2 klass. (45c.) Type **108**	1·60	1·30
221	1 klass. (55c.) 8th-century pin, Sylloda, Saltvik	1·80	1·60

109 Saltvik Church

2002
222	**109** 35c. multicoloured	1·30	1·20

110 Holmen

2002. Janne Holmen (Olympic gold medallist, men's marathon).
223	**110** 1 klass. (55c.) mult	1·80	1·60

111 *Cantharellus cibarius*

2003. Fungi. Multicoloured.
224	10c. Type **111**	35	40
225	50c. *Boletus edulis*	1·70	1·20
226	€2.50 *Macrolepiota procera*	8·50	7·50

112 Tovis (kitten)

2003. Cat Photograph Competition Winners. Multicoloured.
227	2 klass (45c.) Type **112**	1·60	1·40
228	1 klass (55c.) Randi (cat) (horiz)	1·80	1·70

113 *Landscape in Summer* (detail) (Elin Danielson-Gambogi)

2003. Designs showing details of the painting. Multicoloured.

229	1 klass (55c.) Type **113**		1·80	1·70
230	1 klass (55c.) Trees and flowers		1·80	1·70
231	1 klass (55c.) Sunset over sea		1·80	1·70
232	1 klass (55c.) Shoreline and boats		1·80	1·70

114 *Freedom of Speech and Press* (Kurt Simons)

2003. Europa. Poster Art.

233	**114**	45c. multicoloured	2·20	1·70

115 *Pommern* (Arthur Victor Gregory)

2003. Centenary of *Pommern* (four mast steel barque, now museum). Self-adhesive.

234	**115**	55c. multicoloured	2·75	2·00

116 Two Boys

2003. 'My Aland'. Mark Levengood.

235	**116**	55c. multicoloured	1·80	1·70

117 Fiddle Player

2003. 50th Anniv of Aland Folk Music Association.

236	**117**	€1.10 multicoloured	3·25	2·75

118 Kumlinge Church

2003.

237	**118**	40c. multicoloured	1·30	1·20

119 Children dressed as St. Lucia and her Attendants

2003. St. Lucia Celebrations.

238	**119**	60c. multicoloured	2·00	1·70

120 Ermine (*Mustela erminea*)

2004. Predators. Multicoloured.

239	20c. Type **120**		85	65
240	60c. Fox (*Vulpes vulpes*)		2·00	2·00
241	€3 Pine martin (*Martes martes*)		10·00	9·00

121 Fenja and Menja (giantesses)

2004. Nordic Mythology. Sheet 105×70 mm.

MS250	**121**	55c. multicoloured	2·10	2·00

Stamps of a similar theme were issued by Denmark, Faroe Islands, Finland, Greenland, Iceland, Norway and Sweden.

122 Flag

2004. 50th Anniv of Aland Flag. Self-adhesive.

251	**122**	1klass (60c.) multicoloured	2·00	1·80

123 *Cajsa* (longboat) and Passengers, 1986

2004. 'My Aland'. Mauno Koivisto (Finnish president 1982–94).

252	**123**	90c. multicoloured	2·75	2·50

124 Yacht moored in Inlet

2004. Europa. Holidays.

253	**124**	75c. multicoloured	2·30	2·10

125 Bomarsund Fortress

2004. 150th Anniv of Fall of Bomarsund Fortress. Sheet 170×95 mm containing T **125** and similar vert designs.

MS254	75c.×4, Type **125**; Bomarsund (different); Three soldiers; Six soldiers	9·50	9·00

The stamps and margin of No. **MS254** form a composite design of painting by A. Lourde-Laplace.

126 Storklyndan, Brando

2004. Landscapes. Multicoloured.

255	2 klass (50c.) Type **126**		1·60	1·40
256	1 klass (60c.) Prästgardsnaset, Findstrom		1·80	1·70

127 Panathenaic Stadium, Athens

2004. Olympic Games, Athens.

257	**127**	80c. multicoloured	2·30	2·20

128 Father Christmas delivering Mail

2004. Christmas.

258	**128**	45c. multicoloured	1·60	1·40

129 Great Cormorant (*Phalacrocorax carbo sinensis*)

2005. Birds. Multicoloured.

259	15c. Type **129**		70	65
260	65c. Whooper swan (*Cygnus Cygnus*)		2·50	2·20
261	€4 Grey heron (*Ardea cinerea*)		12·50	11·50

130 Oakland Sport Chevrolet (1928) (⅔-size illustration)

2005. Vintage Cars. Multicoloured.

262	(60c.) Type **130**	2·20	2·00
263	(60c.) Ford V8 (1939)	2·20	2·00
264	(60c.) Buick Super 4D HT (1957)	2·20	2·00
265	(60c.) Volkswagen 1200 (1964)	2·20	2·00

131 Family and Bonfire

2005. Walpurgis Night. Self-adhesive.

266	**131**	(50c.) multicoloured	2·00	1·60

132 Fish

2005. Europa. Gastronomy.

267	**132**	90c. multicoloured	3·00	2·75

133 Bjorn Borg

2005. 'My Aland'. Bjorn Borg (tennis player).

268	**133**	55c. multicoloured	1·70	1·60

134 "A Visit to Bomarsund Fortress" (Fritz von Dardel)

2005. 150th Anniv of Fall of Bomarsund Fortress (2004) (2nd series).

269	**134**	€1.30 multicoloured	4·25	4·00

135 *Linden* (schooner)

2005

270	**135**	60c. multicoloured	2·20	2·00

136 Sando, Vardo

2005. Landscapes. Multicoloured.

271	70c. Type **136**	2·50	1·80
272	80c. Grondal, Geta	2·75	2·50

137 Boy and Girl Brownies

2005. Christmas.

273	**137**	45c. multicoloured	1·40	1·20

138 *Potosia cuprea*

2006. Beetles.

274	40c. Type **138**	1·00	90
275	65c. *Coccinella septempunctata*	1·70	1·60
276	€2 *Oryctes nasicornis*	5·75	5·25

139 Face

2006. Centenary of Women's Suffrage.

277	**139**	85c. multicoloured	3·00	2·75

140 Letesgubbe

2006. Nordic Mythology. Sheet 105×70 mm.

MS278	**140**	85c. multicoloured	3·25	3·00

Stamps of a similar theme were issued by Denmark, Greenland, Faroe Islands, Finland, Iceland, Norway and Sweden.

141 Bomarsund Fortress

2006. 150th Anniv of Demilitarization.

279	**141**	€1.50 multicoloured	5·50	5·25

142 Boy as King

2006. Europa. Integration.

280	**142**	€1.30 multicoloured	5·00	4·50

143 Girl posting Letter

2006. My Stamp. Self-adhesive.
281 **143** 1 klass multicoloured 2·50 2·30

144 Sail Boat

2006. 'My Aland'. Ake Lindman (actor and filmmaker).
282 **144** 75c. multicoloured 2·75 2·50

145 Soderby, Lemland

2006. Landscapes. Multicoloured.
283 55c. Type **145** 2·00 2·00
284 €1.20 Norra Essvik, Sottunga 4·50 4·25

146 Tribal-style Tattoo (Thomas Dahlgren)

2006. Tattoos. Multicoloured.
285 65c. Type **146** 2·50 2·30
286 65c. Seaman style (Mikael Sandholm) 2·50 2·30
287 65c. Floral (in memory of Tsunami disaster) (Linda Aberg) 2·50 2·30

147 Horse-drawn Sleigh

2006. Christmas. Inscribed 'JULPOST 06'.
288 **147** (50c.) multicoloured 1·80 1·70

148 *Tripolium vulgare*

2007. Waterside Plants. Multicoloured.
289 80c. Type **148** 2·75 2·50
290 90c. *Lythrum salicaria* 3·50 3·25
291 €5 *Angelica archangelica* 16·00 15·00

149 Junkers F13 flying boat

2007. Postal Transport. Multicoloured.
292 2 klass Type **149** 2·20 2·10
293 1 klass SAAB 340 2·50 2·30

150 Skaftö, Kumlinge

2007. Landscape.
294 **150** 2 klass multicoloured 2·10 2·00

151 *Fillyjonks, Sea Monster and Cliffs* (painting by Tove Janson)

2007. Art.
295 **151** 85c. multicoloured 3·25 3·00

152 Scout Emblem and Window

2007. Europa. Centenary of Scouting.
296 **152** 70c. multicoloured 2·75 2·50

153 Bridal Crown (Titti Sundblom)

2007. Arts and Crafts. Multicoloured.
297 1 klass Type **153** 2·75 2·50
298 1 klass Flower print (Maria Korpi-Gordon and Adam Gordon) 2·75 2·50
299 1 klass Ceramics (Judy Kuitunen) 2·75 2·50

154 Two Players

2007. My Stamp. Girls' Football in Aland. Self-adhesive.
300 **154** 1 klass multicoloured 2·50 2·30

155 *Windmills* (Ture Bengtz)

2007. Birth Centenary of Ture Bengtz (artist and emigrant to USA). Emigration.
301 **155** 75c. multicoloured 2·75 2·50

156 Landscape, Kjusan, Hammarland

2007. SEPAC (Ssmall European Postal Administration Co-operation).
302 **156** 1 klass multicoloured 2·50 2·30

157 Santa Claus (poster by Haddon Sundblom)

2007. Christmas. Inscr 'Julpost 07'.
303 **157** (50c.) multicoloured 2·00 1·80

158 *Perca fluviatilis*

2008. Fish. Paintings by Gosta Sundman. Multicoloured.
304 45c. Type **158** 1·70 1·60
305 €4.50 *Zander lucioperca* 15·00 14·50

159 Signhild at Drottningkleven

2008. Nordic Mythology. Mythical Places. Sheet 105×70 mm. Inscr 'VARLDEN'.
MS306 **159** multicoloured 3·50 3·25
Stamps of a similar theme were issued by Denmark, Faroe Islands, Finland, Greenland, Iceland, Norway and Sweden.
The stamp and margin of No. **MS**306 form a composite design.
MS306 was for use on international mail and was originally on sale for 85c.

160 Langvikshagen, Lumparland

2008. Landscapes. Inscr 'INRIKES'. Multicoloured.
307 (70c.) Type **160** 2·75 2·50
308 (70c.) Badhusberget, Mariehamn 2·75 2·50
Nos. 307/8 were for use on domestic mail and were originally on sale for 70c.

161 Emblem

2008. Olympic Games, Beijing. Inscr 'VARLDEN'.
309 **161** (90c.) multicoloured 3·50 3·25
No. 309 was for use on international mail and was originally on sale for 90c.

162 Letter, Ship and Sailor's Wife

2008. Europa. The Letter.
310 **162** €1 multicoloured 4·00 3·75

163 Marhallan

2008. Lighthouses. Inscr 'EUROPA'. Multicoloured.
311 (75c.) Type **163** 3·00 2·75
312 (75c.) Gustaf Dalen 3·00 2·75
313 (75c.) Bogskar 3·00 2·75
314 (75c.) Kokarsoren 3·00 2·75
Nos. 311/14 were for use on mail within Europe and were originally on sale for 75c.

164 Gravel Road and Profiles of Marcus Gronholm and Christoph Treier (trainer)

2008. My Aland. Marcus Gronholm (rally driver). Inscr 'VARLDEN'.
315 **164** (90c.) multicoloured 3·50 3·25
No. 315 was for use on international mail and was originally on sale for 90c.

165 *Aland Peasant Bride* (Karl Emanuel Jansson)

2008. Art.
316 **165** €1.50 multicoloured 6·00 5·75

166 Angel

2008. Christmas. Inscr 'JULPOST'.
317 **166** (55c.) multicoloured 2·20 2·10
No. 317 was on sale for 55c.

167 Horse Rider

2008. My Stamp. Inscr 'EUROPA'. Self-adhesive.
318 **167** (75c.) multicoloured 3·00 2·75
No. 318 was for use on mail within Europe and was originally on sale for 75c.

168 Boundary Post, Flojtan

2009. New Borders (bicentenary of Aland's integration into Russia). Inscr 'EUROPA'.
319 **168** (80c.) multicoloured 3·25 3·00
No. 319 was for use on mail within Europe and was originally on sale for 80c.

169 Wind Turbine

2009. Preserve Polar Regions and Glaciers. Centenary of Electricity Supply. Sheet 120×80 mm.
MS320 **169** €2 multicoloured 8·00 7·50

170 Ulla-Lena Lundberg

2009. Authors. Inscr 'EUROPA'. Multicoloured.
321 (80c.) Type **170** 3·25 3·00
322 (80c.) Anni Blomqvist 3·25 3·00
323 (80c.) Valdemar Nyman 3·25 3·00
Nos. 321/3, were issued for use on mail within Europe and were originally on sale for 80c.

171 May Irwin and
John Rice

2009. Centenary of Cinema in Aland.
324 **171** €1.60 multicoloured 6·50 6·00

172 Divers and *Plus*
(wreck)

2009. Diving. Inscr 'INRIKES'.
325 **172** (75c.) multicoloured 3·00 2·75
No. 325 was for use on mail within Aland and Finland
and was originally on sale for 75c.

173 The Plough
(constellation)

2009. Europa. Astronomy. Inscr 'EUROPA'.
326 **173** (80c.) multicoloured 3·25 3·00
No. 326 was for use on mail within Europe and was
originally on sale for 80c.

174 *Viking*

2009. Ferries. Inscr 'INRIKES' (327) or 'EUROPA' (328).
Multicoloured.
327 (75c.) Type **174** 3·00 2·75
328 (80c.) *Newbuilding* 3·25 3·00
No. 327 was for use on mail within Aland and Finland
and was originally on sale for 75c.
No. 328 was for use on mail within Europe and was
originally on sale for 80c.

175 Athlete

2009. My Stamp. Island Games XIII, Aland. Inscr
'VARLDEN'. Self-adhesive.
329 **175** (90c.) multicoloured 3·50 3·25
No. 329 was for use on international mail and was
originally on sale for 90c.

2009. Aland Flag. Multicoloured.
329a (65c.) As Type **122** 3·00 2·75

176 Algerso, Foglo

2009. Landscapes. SEPAC (small european mail services)
(331). Inscr 'INRIKES' (330) or 'EUROPA' (331).
Multicoloured.
330 (75c.) Type **176** 3·00 2·75
331 (80c.) Orrdalsklint, Saltvik 3·25 3·00
No. 330 was for use on mail within Aland and Finland
and was originally on sale for 75c.
No. 331 was for use on mail within Europe and was
originally on sale for 80c.

177 Cabin by Water

2009. My Aland. Martti Ahtisaari (President of Finland
1994–2000). Inscr 'VARLDEN'.
332 **177** (90c.) multicoloured 3·50 3·25
No. 332 was for use on international mail and was
originally on sale for 90c.

178 Santa's Helpers

2009. Christmas. Inscr 'JULPOST' (333) or 'VARLDEN' (334).
Multicoloured.
333 (60c.) Type **178** 2·40 2·30
334 (90c.) Girl 3·50 3·25
No. 333 was for use on Christmas mail within Aland
and Finland and was originally on sale for 60c.
No. 334 was for use on international mail and was
originally on sale for 90c.

179 Mail Jetty at Eckero

2010. 150th Birth Anniv of Victor Westerholm (artist).
Inscr 'EUROPA'.
335 **179** (80c.) multicoloured 3·25 3·00
No. 335 was for use on mail within Europe and was
originally on sale for 80c.

180 Head of Christ
(Walter Sallman)

2010. Religious Art. Inscr 'VARLDEN'.
336 **180** (90c.) multicoloured 3·50 3·25
No. 336 was for use on international mail and was
originally on sale for 90c.

181 Boats and Kobba Klintar

2010. Life at the Coast. Kobba Klintar (heritage pilot
station). Inscr 'VARLDEN'. Sheet 105×70 mm.
MS337 **181** (90c.) multicoloured 4·00 3·75
No. MS337 was for use on international mail and was
originally on sale for 90c.
Stamps of a similar theme were issued by Denmark,
Greenland, Faroe Islands, Finland, Iceland, Norway and
Sweden.

182 Sandwolf and
Zackarina (*Sandvargen*
by Åsa Lind)

2010. Europa. Children's Books. Inscr 'EUROPA'
338 **182** (85c.) multicoloured 3·50 3·25
No. 338 was for use on European mail and was origi-
nally on sale for 85c.

183 Skandia

2010. Ferries. Multicoloured.
339 75c. Type **183** 3·00 2·75
340 €3.50 *Prinsessan* 14·00 13·50

184 Moon Creature, c. 1960

2010. Plastic Toys by Plasto. Booklet stamps. Inscr
'EUROPA'. Multicoloured.
341 (85c.) Type **184** 3·50 3·25
342 (85c.) Tipper lorry 3·50 3·25
343 (85c.) Ducks 3·50 3·25
No. 341/3 were for use on European mail and were
originally on sale for 85c.

185 Farm Hand
delivering Mail

2010. Early Mail Delivery. Inscr 'INRIKES'
344 **185** (75c.) multicoloured 3·00 2·75

186 Boy sailing Laser Radial

2010. My Stamp. Inscr 'EUROPA'
345 **186** (85c.) multicoloured 3·50 3·25
No. 345 was for use on mail within Europe and was
originally on sale for 85c.

187 Stained Glass
Window (detail)
(Ture Bengtz),
Jomala Church

2010. Church Interiors. Multicoloured.
346 80c. Type **187** 3·25 3·00
MS347 105×70 mm. €1.60 Stained
glass window (horiz) 6·50 6·00
Stamps of a similar design were issued by Macau.
No. MS347 also contains a representation of the stamp
issued by Macau.

188 Degersand Beach,
Eckerö

2010. Aland Scenery. Multicoloured.
348 80c. Type **188** 3·25 3·00
349 (85c.) Lillnäsberget, Sund 3·50 3·25

189 Grannies bring
Home the Christmas
Tree

2010. Christmas. Inscr 'JULPOST'
350 **189** (60c.) multicoloured 2·50 2·30

190 Alandia

2011. Ferries. Multicoloured.
350a 80c. Type **190** 3·25 3·00
351 €1.50 *Apollo* 6·00 5·75

191 *Empress Maria
Alexandrovna* (F.
Winterhalter)

2011. 150th Anniv of Foundation of Mariehamn. Sheet
105×70 mm
MS352 **191** €1 multicoloured 4·00 3·75

192 *Georg August
Wallin* (Robert
Wilhelm Ekman)

2011. Birth Bicentenary of Georg August Wallin (Aland
born Finnish orientalist, explorer and professor)
353 **192** (90c.) Varlden multicol-
oured 3·50 3·25

193 Forest

2011. Europa. Forests
354 **193** Europa (85c.) multicol-
oured 3·50 3·25

194 The Arrow

2011. Superheroes. Multicoloured.
355 (90c.) Världen Type **194** 3·50 3·25
356 (90c.) Världen *Fantom of the Fair* 3·50 3·25
357 (90c.) Världen *Alias the Spider* 3·50 3·25

195 Champagne Bottle
and Glass

2011. Champagne Find (145 bottles of champagne from
1840 found by divers in July 2010). Multicoloured.
358 **195** (65c.) Lokalpost multi-
coloured 2·50 2·30

196 Strömma
Apple

2011. Apples. Multicoloured.
359 5c. Type **196** 20 10
360 €4 Stromma (yellow) 16·00 15·00

197 Crisps

2011. Chips Ab (potato crisp manufacturer)
361 **197** 85c. multicoloured 3·50 3·25

198 Women Players

2011. My Stamp. Beach Volleyball
362 **198** (90c.) Världen multicol-
oured 3·75 3·50

199 Kökar

2011. Aland Scenery. SEPAC (small European mail services) (No. 368). Multicoloured.

363	(85c.)	Inrikes Type **199**	3·50	3·25
364	(90c.)	Europa Jomala	3·50	3·25

200 White Hyacinth Blossom

2011. Christmas

365	**200**	(55c.) Julpost multicoloured	2·20	2·10

201 Birger Jarl

2012. Ferries. Multicoloured.

366	55c. Type **201**		2·20	2·10
367	(75c.) Sally Albatross		2·50	2·30

202 Fishermen

2012

MS368	**202**	(€1) multicoloured	4·00	3·75

203 Titanic Advertising Poster

2012. Centenary of Sinking of Titanic

369	**203**	€1.80 multicoloured	7·25	6·75

204 The Man at the Wheel

2012. 76th Anniv of The Man at the Wheel (statue), Mariehamn (memorial to those who perished at sea)

370	**204**	€3 multicoloured	12·00	11·50

205 Paddling

2012. Europa. Visit Aland

371	**205**	95c. multicoloured	3·75	3·50

206 Fish

2012. My Stamp. 'My Aland'. Carolina af Ugglas (artist). Inscr 'Inrikes'

372	**206**	Inrikes (95c.) multicoloured	3·75	3·50

207 Aeshna cyanaea (Southern Hawker)

2012. Dragonflies. Multicoloured.

373	(75c.) Type **207**		3·00	2·75

374	(95c.) Sympetrum sanguineum (Southern Hawker)		3·75	3·50

208 Miramar Guest House

2012. Architectural Heritage. Booklet Stamps. Inscr 'VARLDEN'. Multicoloured.

375	(€1) Type **208**		4·00	4·00
376	(€1) Societetshuset		4·00	4·00
377	(€1) Badhotellet		4·00	4·00

209 Volvo L224

2012. Buses. Inscr 'INRIKES' (No. 378) or 'EUROPA' (No. 379)

378	(95c.) Type **209**		3·50	3·50
379	(95c.) Ford TT		3·50	3·50

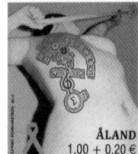

210 Tattooed Woman

2012. Charity Stamp. Breast Cancer Awareness Campaign

380	**210**	€1 +20c. multicoloured	4·20	4·20

211 Girl and Boat

2012. Christmas. Inscr 'JULPOST'

381	**211**	(60c.) multicoloured	3·25	3·25

212 Yearning (Guy Frisk)

2013. 50th Anniv of Art Museum

370	**212**	(€1.10) multicoloured	4·50	4·50

213 Ålandsfärjan

2013. Ferries

383	**213**	(80c.) multicoloured	3·75	3·75

<div style="text-align:right">Pt. 19</div>

ALAOUITES

A coastal district of Syria, placed under French mandate in 1920. Became the Republic of Latakia in 1930. Incorporated with Syria in 1937.

100 centimes = 1 piastre

1925. Stamps of France surch **ALAOUITES** and value in French and Arabic.

1	**11**	0p.10 on 2c. purple	2·00	10·50
2	**18**	0p.25 on 5c. orange	2·50	9·00
3	**15**	0p.75 on 15c. green	3·25	11·50
4	**18**	1p. on 20c. brown	2·30	9·00
5	**18**	1p.25 on 25c. blue	2·75	11·50
6	**18**	1p.50 on 30c. red	9·25	32·00
7	**18**	2p. on 35c. violet	1·00	9·75
8	**13**	2p. on 40c. red and blue	4·00	12·50
9	**13**	2p. on 45c. green and blue	10·00	32·00
10	**13**	3p. on 60c. violet and blue	2·30	17·00
11	**15**	3p. on 60c. violet	19·00	30·00
12	**15**	4p. on 85c. red	2·00	8·25
13	**13**	5p. on 1f. red and yellow	3·00	22·00
14	**13**	10p. on 2f. orange & grn	5·50	25·00
15	**13**	25p. on 5f. blue and buff	10·00	36·00

1925. "Pasteur" issue of France surch **ALAOUITES** and value in French and Arabic.

16	**30**	0p.50 on 10c. green	2·30	9·00

17	**30**	0p.75 on 15c. green	1·70	9·25
18	**30**	1p.50 on 30c. red	1·50	10·00
19	**30**	2p. on 45c. red	10·50	10·50
20	**30**	2p.50 on 50c. blue	3·25	11·50
21	**30**	4p. on 75c. blue	2·50	13·50

1925. Air. Stamps of France optd **ALAOUITES Avion** and value in French and Arabic.

22	**13**	2p. on 40c. red and blue	6·00	27·00
23	**13**	3p. on 60c. violet and blue	6·75	42·00
24	**13**	5p. on 1f. red and yellow	6·00	24·00
25	**13**	10p. on 2f. orange & green	6·00	28·00

1925. Pictorial stamps of Syria (1925) optd **ALAOUITES** in French and Arabic.

26	0p.10 violet	20	4·25
27	0p.25 black	1·10	7·75
28	0p.50 green	1·40	2·00
29	0p.75 red	2·10	6·75
30	1p. purple	90	2·30
31	1p.25 green	2·75	8·00
32	1p.50 pink	2·00	5·00
33	2p. brown	1·40	3·00
34	2p.50 blue	2·40	7·75
35	3p. brown	1·60	3·75
36	5p. violet	1·90	3·25
37	10p. purple	2·20	5·00
38	25p. blue	2·75	13·00

1925. Air. Nos. 33 and 35/37 optd **AVION** in French and Arabic.

40	2p. brown	2·30	10·50
41	3p. brown	1·10	9·25
42	5p. violet	1·20	7·75
43	10p. purple	1·10	7·00

1926. Air. Air stamps of Syria with airplane overprint optd **ALAOUITES** in French and Arabic.

44	2p. brown	2·00	12·00
45	3p. brown	2·00	12·00
46	5p. violet	2·00	12·00
47	10p. purple	2·00	12·00

See also Nos. 59/60 and 63.

1926. Pictorial stamps of 1925 surcharged.

53	05 on 0p.10 violet	20	5·00
54	2p. on 1p.25 green	14·50	9·75
48	3p.50 on 0p.75 red	90	5·25
49	4p. on 0p.25 black	2·30	5·50
56	4p.50 on 0p.75 red	2·50	7·00
50	6p. on 2p.50 blue	1·40	6·00
57	7p.50 on 2p.50 blue	2·30	2·50
51	12p. on 1p.25 green	3·00	8·25
58	15p. on 25p. blue	7·50	12·00
52	20p. on 1p.25 green	3·50	11·00

1929. Air. (a) Pictorial stamps of Syria optd with airplane and **ALAOUITES** in French and Arabic.

59	0p.50 green	2·30	9·50
60	1p. purple	3·50	16·00
61	25p. blue	20·00	60·00

(b) Nos. 54 and 58 of ALAOUITES optd with airplane.

62	2p. on 1p.25 green	3·00	12·00
63	15p. on 25p. blue	17·00	42·00

POSTAGE DUE STAMPS

1925. Postage Due stamps of France surch **ALAOUITES** and value in French and Arabic.

D26	**D11**	0p.50 on 10c. brown	1·30	12·50
D27	**D11**	1p. on 20c. green	1·10	12·50
D28	**D11**	2p. on 30c. red	1·00	13·00
D29	**D11**	3p. on 50c. purple	1·20	13·00
D30	**D11**	5p. on 1f. pur on yell	1·60	13·00

1925. Postage Due stamps of Syria (Nos. D192/6) optd **ALAOUITES** in French and Arabic.

D44	0p.50 brown on yellow	45	8·00
D45	1p. red on red	65	8·50
D46	2p. black on blue	90	9·75
D47	3p. brown on red	1·00	12·50
D48	5p. black on green	1·30	15·00

For later issues see **LATAKIA**.

<div style="text-align:right">Pt. 3</div>

ALBANIA

Albania, formerly part of the Turkish Empire, was declared independent on 28 November 1912, and this was recognized by Turkey in the treaty of 30 May 1913. After chaotic conditions during and after the First World War a republic was established in 1925. Three years later the country became a kingdom. From 7 April 1939 until December 1944, Albania was occupied, firstly by the Italians and then by the Germans. Following liberation a republic was set up in 1946.

1913. 40 paras = 1 piastre or grosch.
1913. 100 qint = 1 franc.
1947. 100 qint = 1 lek.

1913. Various types of Turkey optd with double-headed eagle and **SHQIPENIA**.

3	**28**	2pa. green (No. 271)	£425	£425

4	**28**	5pa. brown (No. 261)	£425	£425
2	**25**	10pa. green (No. 252)	£450	£350
5	**28**	10pa. green (No. 262)	£400	£250
12	**28**	10pa. green (No. 289)	£900	£850
11	**28**	10pa. on 20pa. red	£1300	£1300
6	**28**	20pa. red (No. 263)	£375	£250
13	**28**	20pa. red (No. 290)	£800	£850
7	**28**	1pi. blue (No. 264)	£325	£250
14a	**28**	1pi. blue (No. 291)	£2000	£1800
15	**28**	1pi. blk on red (No. D288)	£3250	£2750
8	**28**	2pi. black (No. 265)	£550	£475
14b	**28**	2pi. black (No. 292)	£3500	£3250
1	**25**	2½pi. brown (No. 239)	£750	£650
9	**28**	5pi. purple (No. 267)	£1400	£1200
10	**28**	10pi. red (No. 268)	£5000	£4750

2

1913

16	**2**	10pa. violet	16·00	16·00
17	**2**	20pa. red and grey	22·00	18·00
18	**2**	1g. grey	22·00	21·00
19	**2**	2g. blue and violet	27·00	21·00
20	**2**	5g. violet and blue	33·00	27·00
21	**2**	10g. blue and violet	33·00	27·00

3

1913. Independence Anniversaries.

22	**3**	10pa. black and green	5·50	4·25
23	**3**	20pa. black and red	8·25	6·25
24	**3**	30pa. black and violet	8·25	6·25
25	**3**	1g. black and blue	11·00	9·50
26	**3**	2g. black	16·00	10·50

4 Skanderbeg (after Heinz Kautsch)

1913

27	**4**	2q. brown and yellow	5·50	2·50
28	**4**	5q. green and yellow	5·50	2·50
29	**4**	10q. red	5·50	2·50
30	**4**	25q. blue	5·50	2·50
31	**4**	50q. mauve and red	13·00	5·25
32	**4**	1f. brown	30·00	16·00

1914. Arrival of Prince William of Wied. Optd **7 Mars 1461 RROFTE MBRETI 1914**.

33	2q. brown and yellow	75·00	85·00
34	5q. green and yellow	75·00	85·00
35	10q. red and rose	75·00	85·00
36	25q. blue	75·00	85·00
37	50q. mauve and rose	75·00	85·00
38	1f. brown	75·00	85·00

1914. Surch.

40	5pa. on 2q. brown & yellow	3·25	3·25
41	10pa. on 5q. green & yellow	3·25	3·25
42	20pa. on 10q. red	5·50	4·25
43	1g. on 25q. blue	5·50	4·25
44	2g. on 50q. mauve & red	5·50	5·25
45	5g. on 1f. brown	22·00	16·00

1914. Valona Provisional Issue. Optd **POSTE D'ALBANIE** and Turkish inscr in circle with star in centre.

45g	2q. brown & yellow	75·00	75·00
45h	10pa. on 5q. green & yellow	£110	£100
45i	20pa. on 10q. red and rose	55·00	50·00
45j	1gr. on 25q. blue	33·00	31·00
45k	2gr. on 50q. mauve and red	38·00	37·00
45l	5gr. on 1f. brown	55·00	50·00
45a	2q. brown and yellow	£325	£325
45b	5q. green and yellow	£425	£425
45c	10q. red and rose	43·00	42·00
45d	25q. blue	43·00	42·00
45e	50q. mauve and red	43·00	42·00
45f	1f. brown	£800	£800

11

1917. Inscribed "SHQIPERIE KORCE VETQEVERITARE" or "REPUBLIKA KORCE SHQIPTARE" or "QARKU-POSTES-I-KORCES".

75	11	1c. brown and green	3·75	3·25
76	11	2c. brown and green	3·75	3·25
77	11	3c. grey and green	3·75	3·25
78	11	5c. green and black	5·50	5·25
79	11	10c. red and black	5·50	5·25
72	11	25c. blue and black	22·00	10·50
80	11	50c. purple and black	9·75	8·25
81	11	1f. brown and black	27·00	23·00

1918. No. 78 surch **QARKUI KORCES 25 CTS.**

81a		25c. on 5c. green and black	£275	£325

12

1919. Fiscal stamps used by the Austrians in Albania. Handstamped with control.

83	12	(2)q. on 2h. brown	11·50	11·00
84	12	05q. on 16h. green	11·50	11·00
85	12	10q. on 8h. red	11·50	11·00
86	12	25q. on 64h. blue	13·00	12·50
87a	12	50q. on 32h. violet	5·50	5·50
88	12	1f. on 1.28h. brown on blue	14·00	13·50

Three sets may be made of this issue according to whether the handstamped control is a date, a curved comet or a comet with straight tail.

1919. No. 43 optd **SHKODER 1919**.

103	4	1g. on 25q. blue	26·00	17·00

1919. Fiscal stamps surch **POSTAT SHQIPTARE** and new value.

104	12	10q. on 2h. brown	11·00	7·75
111	12	10q. on 8h. red	11·00	7·75
112	12	15q. on 8h. red	11·00	7·75
113	12	20q. on 16h. green	11·00	7·75
113b	12	25q. on 32h. violet	11·00	7·75
107	12	25q. on 64h. blue	11·00	7·75
108	12	50q. on 32h. violet	11·00	7·75
113c	12	50q. on 64h. blue	30·00	21·00
113d	12	1f. on 96h. orange	13·00	10·50
113e	12	2f. on 160h. violet	22·00	16·00

17 Prince
William I

1920. Optd with double-headed eagle and **SHKORDA** or surch also.

114	17	1q. grey	80·00	£130
115	17	2q. on 10q. red	12·50	31·00
116	17	5q. on 10q. red	12·50	26·00
117	17	10q. red	12·50	26·00
118	17	20q. brown	35·00	50·00
119	17	25q. blue	£425	£750
120	17	25q. on 10q. red	12·50	21·00
121	17	50q. violet	47·00	95·00
122	17	50q. on 10q. red	12·50	42·00

19 Skanderbeg

1920. Optd with posthorn.

123	19	2q. orange	9·50	12·50
124	19	5q. green	17·00	21·00
125	19	10q. red	28·00	47·00
126	19	25q. blue	50·00	44·00
127	19	50q. green	11·50	16·00
128	19	1f. mauve	11·50	16·00

Stamps as Type **19** also exist optd **BESA** meaning 'Loyalty'.

1922. No. 123 surch with value in frame.

143		1q. on 2q. orange	11·00	10·50

24

1922. Views.

144	24	2q. orange (Gjinokaster)	1·10	2·10
145	24	5q. green (Kanina)	1·10	1·60
146	24	10q. red (Berat)	1·10	1·60
147	24	25q. blue (Veziri Bridge)	1·10	1·60
148	24	50q. green (Rozafat Fortress, Shkoder)	1·10	1·60
149	24	1f. lilac (Korce)	1·10	1·60
150	24	2f. green (Durres)	6·50	8·25

1924. Opening of National Assembly. Optd **TIRANE KALLNUER** 1924 in frame with **Mbledhje Kushtetuese** above.

151		2q. orange	27·00	26·00
152		5q. green	27·00	26·00
153		10q. red	20·00	19·00
154		25q. blue	20·00	19·00
155		50q. green	27·00	26·00

1924. No. 144 surch with value and bars.

156		1 on 2q. orange	8·25	10·50

1924. Red Cross. (a) Surch with small red cross and premium.

157		5q.+5q. green	27·00	36·00
158		10q.+5q. red	27·00	36·00
159		25q.+5q. blue	27·00	36·00
160		50q.+5q. green	26·00	36·00

(b) Nos. 157/60 with further surch of large red cross and premium.

161		5q.+5q.+5q. green	27·00	31·00
162		10q.+5q.+5q. red	27·00	31·00
163		25q.+5q.+5q. blue	27·00	31·00
164		50q.+5q.+5q. green	27·00	31·00

1925. Return of Government to Capital in 1924. Optd **Triumf' i legalitetit 24 Dhetuer 1924**.

164a	1	on 2q. orange (No. 156)	8·25	9·50
165		2q. orange	8·25	9·50
166		5q. green	8·25	9·50
167		10q. red	8·25	9·50
168		25q. blue	8·25	9·50
169		50q. green	16·00	18·00
170		1f. lilac	16·00	23·00

1925. Proclamation of Republic. Optd **Republika Shqiptare 21 Kallnduer 1925**.

171	1	on 2q. orange (No. 156)	7·00	10·50
172		2q. orange	7·00	10·50
173		5q. green	7·00	10·50
174		10q. red	7·00	10·50
175		25q. blue	7·00	10·50
176		50q. green	7·00	10·50
177		1f. lilac	7·00	10·50

1925. Optd **Republika Shqiptare**.

178	1	on 2q. orange (No. 156)	2·20	2·10
179		2q. orange	2·20	2·10
180		5q. green	2·20	2·10
181		10q. red	2·20	2·10
182		25q. blue	2·20	2·10
183		50q. green	2·20	2·10
184		1f. lilac	9·75	5·25
185		2f. green	15·00	5·25

32

1925. Air.

186	32	5q. green	4·25	4·25
187	32	10q. red	4·25	4·25
188	32	25q. blue	4·25	4·25
189	32	50q. green	7·50	7·25
190	32	1f. black and violet	13·00	12·50
191	32	2f. violet and olive	22·00	21·00
192	32	3f. green and brown	27·00	21·00

33 Pres.
Ahmed
Zogu, later
King Zog I

34

1925

193	33	1q. yellow	45	30
194	33	2q. brown	50	90
195	33	5q. green	35	30
196	33	10q. red	35	30
197	33	15q. brown	2·20	2·50
198	33	25q. blue	55	30
199	33	25q. blue	2·20	1·90
200	34	1f. blue and red	4·25	2·50
201	34	2f. orange and green	5·50	2·50
202	34	3f. violet	11·00	6·25
203	34	5f. black and violet	13·00	9·00

1927. Air. Optd **Rep. Shqiptare**.

204	32	5q. green	13·00	12·50
205	32	10q. red	13·00	12·50
206	32	25q. blue	11·00	12·50
207	32	50q. green	8·25	7·75
208	32	1f. black and violet	16·00	16·00
209	32	2f. violet and olive	16·00	12·50
210	32	3f. green and brown	22·00	18·00

1927. Optd **A.Z.** and wreath.

211	33	1q. yellow	1·60	1·30
212	33	2q. brown	85	50
213	33	5q. green	3·50	75
214	33	10q. red	75	50
215	33	15q. brown	20·00	19·00
216	33	25q. blue	1·60	50
217	33	50q. green	1·60	50
218	34	1f. blue and red	3·75	75
219	34	2f. orange and green	3·75	1·00
220	34	3f. violet and brown	6·50	2·10
221	34	5f. black and violet	11·00	3·75

1928. Inauguration of Vlore (Valona)-Brindisi Air Service. Optd **REP. SHQYPTARE Fluturim' i I-ar Vlone-Brindisi 21.IV.1928**.

222	32	5q. green	13·00	12·50
223	32	10q. red	13·00	12·50
224	32	25q. blue	13·00	12·50
225	32	50q. green	27·00	26·00
226	32	1f. black and violet	£140	£140
227	32	2f. violet and olive	£140	£140
228	32	3f. green and brown	£140	£140

1928. Surch in figures and bars.

229	33	1 on 10q. red (No. 214)	1·60	75
230	33	5 on 25q. blue (No. 216)	1·60	75

39 Pres.
Ahmed Zogu,
later King
Zog I

40

1928. National Assembly. Optd **Kujtim i Mbledhjes Kushtetuese 25.8.28**.

231	39	1q. brown	11·00	12·50
232	39	2q. grey	11·00	12·50
233	39	5q. green	11·00	16·00
234	39	10q. red	11·00	16·00
235	39	15q. brown	33·00	65·00
236	39	25q. blue	13·00	16·00
237	39	50q. lilac	22·00	21·00
238	40	1f. black and blue	13·00	16·00

1928. Accession of King Zog I. Optd **Mbretnia-Shqiptare Zog I 1.IX.1928**.

239	39	1q. brown	27·00	31·00
240	39	2q. grey	27·00	31·00
241	39	5q. green	22·00	26·00
242	39	10q. red	22·00	21·00
243	39	15q. brown	33·00	37·00
244	39	25q. blue	22·00	21·00
245	39	50q. lilac	22·00	21·00
246	40	1f. black and blue	27·00	26·00
247	40	2f. black and green	27·00	26·00

1928. Optd **Mbretnia-Shqiptare** only.

248	39	1q. brown	1·10	1·60
249	39	2q. grey	1·10	1·60
250	39	5q. green	7·50	4·75
251	39	10q. red	1·10	1·60
252	39	15q. brown	27·00	31·00
253	39	25q. blue	1·10	1·60
254	39	50q. lilac	2·20	2·50
255	40	1f. black and blue	4·25	3·25
256	40	2f. black and green	4·25	5·25
257	40	3f. olive and red	15·00	16·00
258	40	5f. black and violet	16·00	21·00

1929. Surch **Mbr. Shqiptare** and new value.

259	33	1 on 50q. green	75	1·00
260	33	5 on 25q. blue	75	1·00
261	33	15 on 10q. red	1·30	1·60

1929. King Zog's 35th Birthday. Optd **RROFT-MBRETI 8.X.1929**.

262		1q. yellow	16·00	26·00
263		2q. brown	16·00	26·00
264		5q. green	16·00	26·00
265		10q. red	16·00	26·00
266		25q. blue	16·00	26·00
267		50q. green	22·00	31·00
268	34	1f. blue and red	30·00	47·00
269	34	2f. orange and green	30·00	47·00

1929. Air. Optd **Mbr. Shqiptare**.

270	32	5q. green	11·00	16·00
271	32	10q. red	11·00	16·00
272	32	25q. blue	11·00	16·00
273	32	50q. green	£225	£300
274	32	1f. black and violet	£425	£500
275	32	2f. violet and olive	£500	£550
276	32	3f. green and brown	£600	£650

49 Lake
Butrinto

50 King
Zog I

1930. Second Anniv of Accession of King Zog I.

277	49	1q. grey	55	30
278	49	2q. red	55	30
279	49	5q. green	55	30
280	50	10q. red	55	50
281	50	15q. brown	55	50
282	50	25q. blue	55	50
283	49	50q. green	1·10	75
284		1f. violet	2·20	1·30
285	-	2f. blue	2·75	1·30
286	-	3f. green	8·25	2·10
287	-	5f. brown	11·00	5·25

DESIGNS—VERT: 1, 2f. Ahmed Zog Bridge, River Mati. HORIZ: 3, 5f. Ruins of Zogu Castle.

53 Junkers F-13 (over Tirana)

1930. Air. T **53** and similar view.

288	53	5q. green	2·20	2·50
289	53	15q. red	2·20	2·50
290	53	20q. blue	2·20	2·50
291	53	50q. olive	5·50	5·25
292	-	1f. blue	8·25	7·75
293	-	2f. brown	27·00	26·00
294	-	3f. violet	33·00	31·00

1931. Air. Optd **TIRANE-ROME 6 KORRIK 1931**.

295	53	5q. green	13·00	13·00
296	53	15q. red	13·00	13·00
297	53	20q. blue	13·00	13·00
298	53	50q. olive	13·00	13·00
299	-	1f. blue	75·00	75·00
300	-	2f. brown	75·00	75·00
301	-	3f. violet	75·00	75·00

1934. Tenth Anniv of Revolution. Optd **1924-24 Dhetuer-1934**.

302	49	1q. grey	13·00	16·00
303	49	2q. orange	13·00	16·00
304	50	5q. green	13·00	16·00
305	50	10q. red	13·00	16·00
306	50	15q. brown	13·00	16·00
307	50	25q. blue	16·00	17·00
308	49	50q. turquoise	22·00	21·00
309	-	1f. violet (No. 284)	22·00	26·00
310	-	2f. blue (No. 285)	33·00	40·00
311	-	3f. green (No. 286)	49·00	50·00

56 Horse and
Flag of
Skanderbeg

57 Albania in
Chains

1937. 25th Anniv of Independence.

312	56	1q. violet	55	50
313	57	2q. brown	80	75
314	-	5q. green	1·10	75
315	56	10q. olive	1·10	1·00
316	57	15q. red	1·60	1·30
317	-	25q. blue	3·25	2·50
318	56	50q. green	8·25	4·50
319	57	1f. violet	22·00	7·75
320	-	2f. green	27·00	12·50

MS320a 140×140 mm. 20q. purple (T **56**) | 33·00 | £190

DESIGN: 5, 25q., 2f. As Type **57**, but eagle with opened wings (Liberated Albania).

58 Countess Geraldine
Apponyi and King Zog

1938. Royal Wedding.

321	58	1q. purple	55	50
322	58	2q. brown	55	50
323	58	5q. green	55	50
324	58	10q. olive	2·20	1·00
325	58	15q. red	2·20	1·00
326	58	25q. blue	5·50	2·50
327	58	50q. green	11·00	5·25
328	58	1f. violet	22·00	10·50

MS328a 110×140 mm. 2 each 20q.
purple, 30q. brown　　65·00　£200

59 National　　　**60** King Zog
Emblems

1938. Tenth Anniv of Accession.

329	-	1q. purple	45	75
330	59	2q. red	55	75
331	-	5q. green	1·10	80
332	60	10q. brown	1·10	1·30
333	-	15q. red	2·20	1·60
334	60	25q. blue	2·40	1·80
335	59	50q. black	20·00	7·75
336	60	1f. green	27·00	11·50

MS336a 110×65 mm. 15q. red (333),
20q. green (**59**), 30q. violet (**60**)　　49·00　£140
DESIGN: 1, 5, 15q. As Type **60**, but Queen Geraldine's
portrait.

ITALIAN OCCUPATION

1939. Optd Mbledhja Kushtetuese 12-IV-1939 XVII. (a)
Postage.

337	49	1q. grey	1·60	1·60
338	49	2q. red	1·60	1·60
339	50	5q. green	1·10	1·00
340	50	10q. red	1·10	1·00
341	50	15q. brown	2·75	2·50
342	50	25q. blue	3·25	3·25
343	49	50q. turquoise	4·25	3·75
344	-	1f. violet (No. 284)	6·50	4·75
345	-	2f. blue (No. 285)	7·50	6·25
346	-	3f. green	16·00	14·50
347	-	5f. brown	22·00	25·00

(b) Air. Optd as Nos. 337/47 or surch also.

348	53	5q. green	7·50	6·75
349	53	15q. red	7·00	7·25
350	53	20q. on 50q. olive	12·00	11·50

62 Gheg　　**64** Broken Columns,　**63** King
　　　　　Botrint　　　　Victor
　　　　　　　　　　　Emmanuel

65 King and Fiat G18V on
Tirana–Rome Service

1939

351	62	1q. blue (postage)	1·10	50
352	-	2q. brown	1·10	50
353	-	3q. brown	1·10	50
354	-	5q. green	1·60	20
355	63	10q. brown	1·60	30
356	63	15q. red	1·70	30
357	63	25q. blue	1·70	1·00
358	63	30q. violet	2·75	2·10
359	-	50q. violet	4·25	1·80
360	-	65q. red	12·00	8·25
361	-	1f. green	12·00	5·75
362	-	2f. red	27·00	18·00
363	64	3f. black	46·00	33·00
364	-	5f. purple	55·00	46·00
365	65	20q. brown (air)	£110	18·00

DESIGNS—SMALL: 2q. Tosk man; 3q. Gheg woman; 5,
65q. Profile of King Victor Emmanuel; 50q. Tosk woman.
LARGE: 1f. Kruje Fortress; 2f. Bridge over River Kiri at Mes;
5f. Amphitheatre ruins, Berat.

66 Sheep Farming

1940. Air.

366	66	5q. green	2·50	1·60
367	-	15q. red	2·75	2·10
368	-	20q. blue	5·50	3·25
369	-	50q. brown	7·75	7·75
370	-	1f. green	8·25	9·50
371	-	2f. black	18·00	18·00
372	-	3f. purple	35·00	31·00

DESIGNS: Savoia Marchetti S.M.75 airplane and—HORIZ:
20q. King of Italy and Durres harbour; 1f. Bridge over Riv-
er Kiri at Mes. VERT: 15q. Aerial map; 50q. Girl and valley;
2f. Archway and wall, Durres; 3f. Women in North Epirus.

67 King
Victor
Emmanuel

1942. Third Anniv of Italian Occupation.

373	67	5q. green	2·40	2·50
374	67	10q. brown	2·40	2·50
375	67	15q. red	2·40	2·50
376	67	25q. blue	2·40	2·50
377	67	65q. brown	7·50	7·75
378	67	1f. green	7·50	7·75
379	67	2f. purple	7·50	7·75

1942. No. 352 surch 1 QIND.

380		1q. on 2q. brown	4·25	5·25

69

1943. Anti-tuberculosis Fund.

381	69	5q.+5q. green	1·80	2·10
382	69	10q.+10q. brown	1·80	2·10
383	69	15q.+10q. red	1·80	2·10
384	69	25q.+15q. blue	2·20	3·25
385	69	30q.+20q. violet	2·20	3·25
386	69	50q.+25q. orange	2·20	3·25
387	69	65q.+30q. grey	3·25	4·50
388	69	1f.+40q. brown	5·50	6·25

GERMAN OCCUPATION

1943. Postage stamps of 1939 optd 14 Shtator 1943 or
surch also.

389	-	1q. on 3q. brn (No. 353)	1·90	10·50
390	-	2q. brown (No. 352)	1·90	10·50
391	-	3q. brown (No. 353)	1·90	10·50
392	-	5q. green (No. 354)	1·90	10·50
393	63	10q. brown	1·90	10·50
394	-	15q. red (No. 356)	1·90	10·50
395	-	25q. blue (No. 357)	1·90	10·50
396	-	30q. violet (No. 358)	1·90	10·50
397	-	50q. on 65q. brn (No. 360)	2·75	16·00
398	-	65q. red (No. 360)	2·75	16·00
399	-	1f. green (No. 361)	18·00	32·00
400	-	2f. red (No. 362)	21·00	£110
401	64	3f. black	£110	£275

71 War Refugees

1944. War Refugees' Relief Fund.

402	71	5q.+5q. green	5·25	20·00
403	71	10q.+5q. brown	5·25	20·00
404	71	15q.+5q. red	5·25	20·00
405	71	25q.+10q. blue	5·25	20·00
406	71	1f.+50q. green	5·25	20·00
407	71	2f.+1f. violet	5·25	20·00
408	71	3f.+1f.50 orange	5·25	20·00

INDEPENDENT STATE

1945. Nos. 353/8 and 360/2 surch **QEVERIJA**
DEMOKRAT. E SHQIPERISE 22-X-1944 and value.

409	-	30q. on 3q. brown	8·25	16·00
410	-	40q. on 5q. green	8·25	16·00
411	-	50q. on 10q. brown	8·25	16·00
412	-	60q. on 15q. red	8·25	16·00
413	-	80q. on 25q. blue	8·25	16·00
414	-	1f. on 30q. violet	8·25	16·00
415	-	2f. on 65q. brown	8·25	16·00
416	-	3f. on 1f. green	8·25	16·00
417	-	5f. on 2f. red	8·25	16·00

73

1945. Second Anniv of Formation of People's Army. Surch
as T **73**.

418	49	30q. on 1q. grey	5·50	7·75
419	49	60q. on 1q. grey	5·50	7·75
420	49	80q. on 1q. grey	5·50	7·75
421	49	1f. on 1q. grey	11·00	16·00
422	49	2f. on 2q. red	13·00	18·00
423	49	3f. on 50q. green	27·00	33·00
424	-	5f. on 2f. blue (No. 285)	33·00	50·00

1945. Red Cross Fund. Surch with Red Cross, **JAVA E K.K.**
SHQIPTAR 4-11 MAJ 1945 and value.

425	69	30q.+15q. on 5q.+5q. green	11·00	16·00
426	69	50q.+25q. on 10q.+10q. brown	11·00	16·00
427	69	1f.+50q. on 15q.+10q. red	27·00	33·00
428	69	2f.+1f. on 25q.+15q. blue	38·00	47·00

75 Permet
Landscape

1945

429	-	20q. green	75	1·80
430	-	30q. orange	1·10	2·50
431	-	40q. brown	1·10	2·50
432	-	60q. red	1·60	3·75
433	-	1f. red	3·75	7·75
434	75	3f. blue	27·00	31·00

DESIGNS: 20q. Latinot; 40, 60q. Bridge at Berat; 1f. Permet
landscape.

1946. Constitutional Assembly. Optd **ASAMBLEJA**
KUSHTETEUSE 10 KALLNUER 1946.

435	-	20q. green	1·60	2·10
436	-	30q. orange	2·20	2·50
437	-	40q. brown (No. 431)	2·75	3·25
438	-	60q. red (No. 432)	4·25	5·25
439	-	1f. red (No. 433)	16·00	19·00
440	-	3f. blue (No. 434)	27·00	31·00

PEOPLE'S REPUBLIC

77 Globe, Dove and
Olive Branch

1946. International Women's Congress. Perf or imperf.

441A	77	20q. mauve and red	55	1·60
442A	77	40q. lilac and red	1·10	2·10
443A	77	50q. violet and red	2·20	3·25
444A	77	1f. blue and red	4·25	6·25
445A	77	2f. blue and red	5·50	10·50

1946. Proclamation of Albanian People's Republic. Optd
REPUBLIKA POPULLORE E SHQIPERISE.

446	75	20q. green	1·50	1·60
447	75	30q. orange	1·70	2·10
448	-	40q. brown (No. 431)	3·00	4·25
449	-	60q. red (No. 432)	6·00	7·75
450	-	1f. red (No. 433)	16·00	21·00
451	-	3f. blue (No. 434)	27·00	31·00

1946. Albanian Red Cross Congress. Surch **KONGRESI**
K.K.SH. 24-25-11-46 and premium.

452	75	20q.+10q. green	24·00	37·00
453	75	30q.+15q. orange	24·00	37·00
454	-	40q.+20q. brown	24·00	37·00
455	-	60q.+30q. red	24·00	37·00
456	-	1f.+50q. red	24·00	37·00
457	-	3f.+1f.50 blue	24·00	37·00

79 Athletes

1946. Balkan Games.

458	79	1q. black	16·00	12·50
459	79	2q. green	16·00	12·50
460	79	5q. brown	16·00	12·50
461	79	10q. red	16·00	12·50
462	79	20q. blue	16·00	12·50
463	79	40q. lilac	16·00	12·50
464	79	1f. orange	38·00	37·00

80 Qemal Stafa

1947. Fifth Death Anniv of Qemal Stafa (Communist
activist).

465	80	20q. dp brown & brown	13·00	16·00
466	80	28q. deep blue and blue	13·00	16·00
467	80	40q. dp brown & brown	13·00	16·00

81 Railway Construction

1947. Construction of Durres–Elbasan Railway.

468	81	1q. black and drab	5·50	1·80
469	81	4q. deep green and green	5·50	1·80
470	81	10q. dp brown & brown	5·75	1·80
471	81	15q. red and rose	5·75	2·10
472	81	20q. black and blue	13·00	2·50
473	81	28q. deep blue and blue	18·00	3·25
474	81	40q. red and purple	35·00	19·00
475	81	68q. dp brown & brown	43·00	31·00

82 Partisans　　**83** Enver Hoxha
　　　　　　　and Vasil Shanto

1947. Fourth Anniv of Formation of People's Army. Inscr
"1943–1947".

476	82	16q. brown	9·75	10·50
477	83	20q. brown	9·75	10·50
478	-	28q. blue	9·75	10·50
479	-	40q. brown and mauve	9·75	10·50

DESIGNS—HORIZ: 28q. Infantry column. VERT: 40q. Por-
trait of Vojo Kushi.

84 Ruined
Conference Building

1947. Fifth Anniv of Peza Conference.

480	84	2l. purple and mauve	7·00	7·75
481	84	2l.50 deep blue and blue	7·00	7·75

85 War Invalids

1947. First Congress of War Invalids.

482	85	1l. red	16·00	16·00

86 Peasants

1947. Agrarian Reform. Inscr "REFORMA AGRARE".

483	86	1l.50 purple	9·75	10·50
484	-	2l. brown	9·75	10·50
485	-	2l.50 blue	9·75	10·50
486	-	3l. red	9·75	10·50

DESIGNS—HORIZ: 2l. Banquet; 2l.50, Peasants rejoicing.
VERT: 3l. Soldier being chaired.

87 Burning Village

1947. Third Anniv of Liberation. Inscr "29-XI-1944–1947".

487	87	1l.50 red	5·50	5·25
488	-	2l.50 purple	5·50	5·25
489	-	5l. blue	11·00	8·25
490	-	8l. mauve	16·00	12·50
491	-	12l. brown	27·00	21·00

DESIGNS: 2l.50, Riflemen; 5l. Machine-gunners; 8l. Mounted soldier; 12l. Infantry column.

1948. Nos. 429/34 surch Lek and value.

492	75	0l.50 on 30q. orange	55	75
493	75	1l. on 20q. green	1·10	1·30
494	-	2l.50 on 60q. red	2·75	3·75
495	-	3l. on 1f. red	3·75	4·75
496	-	5l. on 3f. blue	8·25	7·75
497	-	12l. on 40q. brown	22·00	21·00

88 Railway Construction

1948. Construction of Durres–Tirana Railway.

498	88	0l.50 red	2·75	1·60
499	88	1l. green	3·00	1·80
500	88	1l.50 red	4·50	2·50
501	88	2l.50 brown	6·50	3·25
502	88	5l. blue	11·00	6·25
503	88	8l. orange	18·00	10·50
504	88	12l. purple	22·00	12·50
505	88	20l. black	43·00	26·00

89 Parade of Infantrymen

1948. Fifth Anniv of People's Army.

506	89	2l.50 brown	5·50	5·25
507	89	5l. blue	7·50	7·25
508	-	8l. slate (Troops in action)	14·00	10·50

90 Labourer, Globe and Flag

1949. Labour Day.

509	90	2l.50 brown	1·60	2·50
510	90	5l. blue	3·25	4·25
511	90	8l. purple	6·00	6·75

91 Soldier and Map

1949. Sixth Anniv of People's Army.

512	91	2l.50 brown	1·60	2·50
513	91	5l. blue	3·25	4·25
514	91	8l. orange	6·00	7·75

92 Albanian and Kremlin Tower

1949. Albanian–Soviet Amity.

515	92	2l.50 brown	1·60	2·50
516	92	5l. blue	3·75	5·25

93 Gen. Enver Hoxha

1949

517	93	0l.50 purple	35	10
518	93	1l. green	40	10
519	93	1l.50 red	55	10
520	93	2l.50 brown	1·10	15
521	93	5l. blue	2·20	1·00
522	93	8l. purple	4·25	3·25
523	93	12l. purple	11·50	5·75
524	93	20l. slate	13·50	7·25

94 Soldier and Flag

1949. Fifth Anniv of Liberation.

525	94	2l.50 brown	1·10	1·60
526	-	3l. red	1·10	3·25
527	94	5l. violet	3·25	4·25
528	-	8l. black	6·50	7·75

DESIGN—HORIZ: 3, 8l. Street fighting.

96 Joseph Stalin

1949. Stalin's 70th Birthday.

529	96	2l.50 brown	1·10	2·10
530	96	5l. blue	2·75	3·75
531	96	8l. lake	7·00	9·00

97 Symbols of Transport and 'UPU'

1950. 75th Anniv of U.P.U.

532	97	5l. blue	3·00	6·75
533	97	8l. purple	5·50	9·50
534	97	12l. black	11·00	18·00

98 Sami Frasheri

1950. Literary Jubilee. Inscr "1950-JUBILEU I SHKRIMTAREVE TE RILINDJES".

535	98	2l. green	1·60	1·60
536	-	2l.50 brown	2·20	2·50
537	-	3l. red	4·25	5·25
538	-	5l. blue	5·50	6·25

PORTRAITS: 2l.50, A. Zako (Cajupi); 3l. Naim Frasheri; 5l. K. Kristoforidhi.

99 Vuno-Himare

1950. Air.

539	99	0l.50 black	1·00	1·00
540	-	1l. purple	1·00	1·00
541	-	2l. blue	1·70	2·10
542	99	5l. green	6·00	5·75
543	-	10l. blue	14·00	10·50
544	-	20l. violet	27·00	16·00

DESIGNS: Douglas DC-3 airplane over—1, 10l. Rozafat Shkodor; 2, 20l. Keshtjelle-Butrinto.

100 Stafa and Shanto

1950. Albanian Patriots.

545	-	2l. green	1·40	1·30
546	-	2l.50 violet	1·60	1·60
547	-	3l. red	3·25	3·25
548	-	5l. blue	5·50	5·25
549	100	8l. brown	11·00	10·50

PORTRAITS: 2l. Ahmet Haxhia, Hydajet Lezha, Naim Gjylbegu, Ndoc Mazi and Ndoc Deda; 2l.50, Asim Zeneli, Ali Demi, Kajo Karafili, Dervish Hakali and Asim Vokshi; 3l. Ataz Shehu, Baba Faja, Zoja Cure, Mustafa Matohiti and Gjok Doci; 5l. Perlat Rexhepi, Bako, Vojo Kushi, Reshit Collaku and Misto Mame.

101 Arms and Flags

1951. Fifth Anniv of Republic.

550	101	2l.50 red	2·20	3·25
551	101	5l. blue	4·25	6·25
552	101	8l. black	7·00	9·50

102 Skanderbeg

1951. 483rd Death Anniv of Skanderbeg (patriot).

553	102	2l.50 brown	2·20	2·50
554	102	5l. violet	4·25	5·25
555	102	8l. bistre	7·00	7·75

103 Gen. Enver Hoxha and Assembly

1951. Seventh Anniv of Permet Congress.

556	103	2l.50 brown	1·10	1·60
557	103	3l. red	1·20	2·10
558	103	5l. blue	2·75	3·75
559	103	8l. mauve	5·00	6·25

104 Child and Globe

1951. International Children's Day.

560	104	2l. green	2·75	2·10
561	-	2l.50 brown	3·75	2·50
562	-	3l. red	5·00	3·25
563	104	5l. blue	7·50	3·75

DESIGN—HORIZ: 2l.50, 3l. Nurse weighing baby.

105 Enver Hoxha and Meeting-house

1951. Tenth Anniv of Albanian Communists.

564	105	2l.50 brown	65	1·00
565	105	3l. red	75	1·40
566	105	5l. blue	1·70	2·10
567	105	8l. black	3·25	3·50

106 Young Partisans

1951. Tenth Anniv of Albanian Young Communists' Union. Inscr "1941–1951".

568	106	2l.50 brown	1·10	1·60
569	-	5l. blue	2·20	2·50
570	-	8l. red	5·00	5·25

DESIGNS: Schoolgirl, railway, tractor and factories; 8l. Miniature portraits of Stafa, Spiru, Mame and Kondi.

1952. Air. Surch in figures.

571		0.50l. on 2l. blue (No. 541)	£250	£190
572	99	0.50l. on 5l. green	49·00	36·00

573	99	2l.50 on 5l. green	£375	£200
574	-	2l.50 on 10l. blue (No. 543)	60·00	44·00

108 Factory

1953

575	108	0l.50 brown	80	10
576	-	1l. green	1·10	20
577	-	2l.50 sepia	1·50	50
578	-	3l. red	1·90	75
579	-	5l. blue	3·25	1·30
580	-	8l. olive	3·75	1·60
581	-	12l. purple	5·75	4·75
582	-	20l. blue	11·00	4·75

DESIGNS—HORIZ: 1l. Canal; 2l.50, Girl and cotton mill; 3l. Girl and sugar factory; 5l. Film studio; 8l. Girl and textile machinery; 20l. Dam. VERT: 12l. Pylon and hydroelectric station.

109 Soldiers and Flags

1954. Tenth Anniv of Liberation.

583	109	0l.50 lilac	20	15
584	109	1l. green	70	50
585	109	2l.50 brown	1·10	1·00
586	109	3l. red	2·20	2·50
587	109	5l. blue	3·25	3·25
588	109	8l. purple	6·50	6·25

110 First Albanian School

1956. 70th Anniv of Albanian Schools.

589	110	2l. purple	55	50
590	-	2l.50 green	90	1·00
591	-	5l. blue	2·00	2·10
592	110	10l. turquoise	6·50	3·75

DESIGN: 2l.50, 5l. Portraits of P. Sotiri, P. N. Luarasi and N. Naci.

111

1957. 15th Anniv of Albanian Workers' Party.

593	111	2l.50 brown	80	50
594	-	5l. blue	1·70	75
595	-	8l. purple	3·00	3·00

DESIGNS: 5l. Party headquarters, Tirana; 8l. Marx and Lenin.

112 Congress Emblem

1957. Fourth World Trade Unions Congress, Leipzig.

596	112	2l.50 purple	60	20
597	112	3l. red	65	50
598	112	5l. blue	75	75
599	112	8l. green	2·75	2·40

113 Lenin and Cruiser Aurora

1957. 40th Anniv of Russian Revolution.

600	113	2l.50 brown	85	50
601	113	5l. blue	1·60	1·60
602	113	8l. black	2·10	1·80

114 Raising the
Flag

1957. 45th Anniv of Proclamation of Independence.
603	**114**	1l.50 purple	80	30
604	**114**	2l.50 brown	1·40	50
605	**114**	5l. blue	1·80	1·60
606	**114**	8l. green	4·25	2·10

115 N.
Veqilharxhi

1958. 160th Birth Anniv of Veqilharxhi (patriot).
607	**115**	2l.50 brown	80	30
608	**115**	5l. blue	1·60	50
609	**115**	8l. purple	3·25	1·60

116 L.
Gurakuqi

1958. Removal of Ashes of Gurakuqi (patriot).
610	**116**	1l.50 green	35	20
611	**116**	2l.50 brown	55	40
612	**116**	5l. blue	70	50
613	**116**	8l. sepia	3·25	1·40

117 Freedom
Fighters

1958. 50th Anniv of Battle of Mashkullore.
614	**117**	2l.50 ochre	70	20
615	-	3l. green	70	20
616	**117**	5l. blue	1·60	80
617	-	8l. brown	2·75	1·60
DESIGN: 3, 8l. Tree and buildings.

118 Soldiers in
Action

1958. 15th Anniv of Albanian People's Army.
618	**118**	1l.50 green	45	20
619	-	2l.50 brown	65	25
620	**118**	8l. red	1·60	1·40
621	-	11l. blue	2·50	2·30
DESIGN: 2l.50, 11l. Tank-driver, sailor, infantryman and
tanks.

119 Bust of Apollo and
Butrinto Amphitheatre

1959. Cultural Monuments Week.
622	**119**	2l.50 brown	80	30
623	**119**	6l.50 green	3·25	1·30
624	**119**	11l. blue	4·25	2·10

120 F. Joliot-Curie
and Council Emblem

1959. Tenth Anniv of World Peace Council.
625	**120**	1l.50 red	2·20	50
626	**120**	2l.50 violet	5·00	1·60
627	**120**	11l. blue	11·50	5·25

121 Basketball

1959. First National Spartacist Games.
628	**121**	1l.50 violet	1·10	25
629	-	2l.50 green	1·20	30
630	-	5l. red	2·20	1·00
631	-	11l. blue	6·50	3·75
DESIGNS: 2l.50, Football; 5l. Running; 11l. Runners with
torches.

122 Soldier

1959. 15th Anniv of Liberation.
632	**122**	1l.50 red	1·20	25
633	-	2l.50 brown	1·60	35
634	-	3l. green	2·20	45
635	-	6l.50 red	4·75	4·00
MS635a 141×96 mm. Nos. 632/5 but
in red. Imperf | 11·00 | 16·00 |
DESIGNS: 2l.50, Security guard. 3l. Harvester; 6l.50, Labo-
ratory workers.

123 Mother and Child

1959. Tenth Anniv of Declaration of Human Rights.
| 636 | **123** | 5l. blue | 6·25 | 3·25 |
MS636a 72×65 mm. No. 636. Imperf | 7·50 | 11·50 |

124 Woman
with Arm
Raised

1960. 50th Anniv of International Women's Day.
| 637 | **124** | 2l.50 brown | 1·10 | 50 |
| 638 | **124** | 11l. red | 4·25 | 1·60 |

125 Congress
Building

1960. 40th Anniv of Lushnje Congress.
| 639 | **125** | 2l.50 brown | 55 | 30 |
| 640 | **125** | 7l.50 blue | 1·60 | 1·00 |

126 A.
Moisiu

1960. 80th Birth Anniv of Alexandre Moisiu (actor).
| 641 | **126** | 3l. brown | 70 | 50 |
| 642 | **126** | 11l. green | 2·40 | 1·00 |

127 Lenin

1960. 90th Birth Anniv of Lenin.
| 643 | **127** | 4l. turquoise | 1·90 | 1·00 |
| 644 | **127** | 11l. red | 6·00 | 5·25 |

128 Vaso
Pasha

1960. 80th Anniv of Albanian Alphabet Study
Association.
645	**128**	1l. olive	55	20
646	-	1l.50 brown	1·00	20
647	-	6l.50 blue	2·10	85
648	-	11l. red	5·50	2·10
DESIGNS: 1l.50, Jani Vreto; 6l.50, Sami Frasheri; 11l. Asso-
ciation statutes.

129 Frontier
Guard

1960. 15th Anniv of Frontier Force.
| 649 | **129** | 1l.50 red | 55 | 30 |
| 650 | **129** | 11l. blue | 3·25 | 1·50 |

130 Family
with Policeman

1960. 15th Anniv of People's Police.
| 651 | **130** | 1l.50 green | 55 | 25 |
| 652 | **130** | 8l.50 brown | 3·25 | 1·60 |

131 Normal School,
Elbasan

1960. 50th Anniv of Normal School, Elbasan.
| 653 | **131** | 5l. green | 2·75 | 1·60 |
| 654 | **131** | 6l.50 purple | 2·75 | 1·60 |

132 Soldier
and Cannon

1960. 40th Anniv of Battle of Vlore.
655	**132**	1l.50 brown	75	50
656	**132**	2l.50 purple	1·20	75
657	**132**	5l. blue	2·75	1·00

133 Tirana Clock
Tower, Kremlin and
Tupolev Tu-104A
Jetliner

1960. Second Anniv of Tirana–Moscow Jet Air Service.
658	**133**	1l. brown	1·10	80
659	**133**	7l.50 blue	4·00	4·25
660	**133**	11l.50 grey	6·50	7·25

134 Federation
Emblem

1960. 15th Anniv of World Democratic Youth Federation.
| 661 | **134** | 1l.50 blue | 65 | 30 |
| 662 | **134** | 8l.50 red | 2·20 | 1·00 |

135 Ali
Kelmendi

1960. 60th Birth Anniv of Kelmendi (Communist).
| 663 | **135** | 1l.50 olive | 55 | 30 |
| 664 | **135** | 11l. purple | 2·20 | 1·00 |

136 Flags of
Albania and
Russia, and
Clasped Hands

1961. 15th Anniv of Albanian-Soviet Friendship Society.
| 665 | **136** | 2l. violet | 55 | 30 |
| 666 | **136** | 8l. purple | 2·20 | 1·00 |

137 Marx and
Lenin

1961. Fourth Albanian Workers' Party Congress.
| 667 | **137** | 2l. red | 55 | 30 |
| 668 | **137** | 8l. blue | 2·20 | 1·00 |

138 Malsi e
Madhe
(Shkoder)
Costume

1961. Provincial Costumes.
669	**138**	1l. black	1·10	50
670	-	1l.50 purple	1·40	75
671	-	6l.50 blue	4·25	1·90
672	-	11l. red	6·50	4·75
COSTUMES: 1l.50, Malsi e Madhe (Shkoder) (female); 6l.50,
Lume; 11l. Mirdite.

139 European Otter

1961. Albanian Fauna.
673	**139**	2l.50 blue	4·00	1·00
674	-	6l.50 green	8·00	2·40
675	-	11l. brown	16·00	8·25
DESIGNS: 6l.50, Eurasian badger; 11l. Brown bear.

140 Dalmatian
Pelicans

1961. Albanian Birds.
676	**140**	1l.50 red on pink	5·75	1·00
677	-	7l.50 violet on blue	7·00	3·25
678	-	11l. brown on pink	9·75	3·75
BIRDS: 7l.50, Grey heron; 11l. Little egret.

141 Cyclamen

1961. Albanian Flowers.
679	**141**	1l.50 purple and blue	2·20	50
680	-	8l. orange and purple	6·00	2·50
681	-	11l. red and green	7·50	3·25
FLOWERS: 8l. Forsythia; 11l. Lily.

142 M. G.
Nikolla

1961. 50th Birth Anniv of Nikolla (poet).

682	**142**	0l.50 brown	65	30
683	**142**	8l.50 green	2·20	1·60

143 Lenin and Marx on Flag

1961. 20th Anniv of Albanian Workers' Party.

684	**143**	2l.50 red	65	30
685	**143**	7l.50 purple	2·00	1·30

144 Anniversary Emblem

1961. 20th Anniv of Albanian Young Communists' Union.

686	**144**	2l.50 blue	65	30
687	**144**	7l.50 mauve	2·20	1·30

145 Yuri Gagarin and Vostok 1

1962. World's First Manned Space Flight. (a) Postage.

688	**145**	0l.50 blue	1·10	1·60
689	**145**	4l. purple	4·25	4·75
690	**145**	11l. green	11·00	11·50

(b) Air. Optd **POSTA AJRORE**.

691	0l.50 blue on cream	38·00	50·00
692	4l. purple on cream	38·00	50·00
693	11l. green on cream	38·00	50·00

147 P. N. Luarasi

1962. 50th Death Anniv of Petro N. Luarasi (patriot).

694	**147**	0l.50 blue	55	30
695	**147**	8l.50 brown	4·25	1·60

IMPERF STAMPS. Many Albanian stamps from No. 696 onwards exist imperf and/or in different colours from limited printings.

148 Campaign Emblem

1962. Malaria Eradication.

696	**148**	1l.50 brown	35	15
697	**148**	2l.50 red	55	30
698	**148**	10l. purple	1·10	80
699	**148**	11l. blue	1·40	1·00
MS699a 90×106 mm. Nos. 696/9			38·00	38·00

149 Camomile

1962. Medicinal Plants.

700	**149**	0l.50 yellow, green & blue	55	30
701	-	8l. green, yellow and grey	2·20	1·20
702	-	11l.50 violet, grn & ochre	3·75	1·60

PLANTS: 8l. Silver linden; 11l.50, Sage.

150 Throwing the Javelin

1962. Olympic Games, Tokyo, 1964 (1st issue). Inscr as in T **102**.

703		0l.50 black and blue	20	10
704		2l.50 sepia and brown	40	15
705		3l. black and blue	55	20
706	**150**	9l. purple and red	2·20	1·00
707	-	10l. black and olive	2·40	1·00
MS707a 81×63 mm. 15l. (as 3l.)			38·00	50·00

DESIGNS—VERT: 0l.50, Diving; 2l.50, Pole-vaulting; 10l. Putting the shot. HORIZ: 3l. Olympic flame.

See also Nos. 754/MS758a, 818/MS821a and 842/MS851a.

151 Sputnik 1 in Orbit

1962. Cosmic Flights.

708	**151**	0l.50 yellow and violet	65	50
709	-	1l. sepia and green	1·10	85
710	-	1l.50 yellow and red	1·60	1·00
711	-	20l. blue and purple	11·00	4·25
MS711a 101×76 mm. 14l. (+ 6l.) brown and blue (rocket)			65·00	80·00

DESIGNS: 1l. Laika (dog) and Sputnik 2; 1l.50, Artificial satellite and Sun; 20l. Lunik 3 photographing Moon.

152 Footballer and Ball in Net

1962. World Cup Football Championship, Chile.

712	**152**	1l. violet and orange	55	30
713	-	2l.50 blue and green	1·60	85
714	**152**	6l.50 purple and brown	2·20	1·00
715	-	15l. purple and green	3·25	2·10
MS715a 82×66 mm. 20l. brown and green (as 713 but larger)			50·00	80·00

DESIGN: 2l.50, 15l. As Type **152** but globe in place of ball in net.

153 'Europa' and Albanian Maps

1962. Tourist Publicity.

716	**153**	0l.50 red, yellow & green	55	1·00
717	-	1l. red, purple and blue	1·10	2·50
718	-	2l.50 red, purple and blue	8·75	14·50
719	**153**	11l. red, yellow and grey	16·00	18·00
MS719a 82×63 mm. 7l. red, yellow and grey (**153**), 8l. red and grey (as 717)			50·00	80·00

DESIGN: 1, 2l.50, Statue and map.

154 Dardhe Woman

1962. Costumes of Albania's Southern Region.

720	**154**	0l.50 red, purple and blue	45	20
721	-	1l. brown and buff	55	40
722	-	2l.50 black, violet & grn	1·60	1·30
723	-	14l. red, brown and green	7·00	3·75

COSTUMES: 1l. Devoll man; 2l.50, Lunxheri woman; 14l. Gjirokaster man.

155 Chamois

1962. Albanian Animals.

724	**155**	0l.50 purple and green	55	40
725	-	1l. black and yellow	2·20	1·00
726	-	1l.50 black and brown	2·75	1·60
727	-	15l. brown and green	22·00	5·25
MS727a 72×89 mm. 20l. brown and green (as 727 but larger)			£140	£180

ANIMALS—HORIZ: 1l. Lynx; 1l.50, Wild boar. VERT: 15l. Roe deer.

156 Golden Eagle

1962. 50th Anniv of Independence.

728	**156**	1l. brown and red	80	30
729	-	3l. black and brown	3·75	1·00
730	-	16l. black and mauve	7·50	3·75

DESIGNS: 3l. I. Qemali; 16l. "RPSH" and golden eagle.

157 Revolutionaries

1963. 45th Anniv of October Revolution.

731	**157**	5l. violet and yellow	1·30	75
732	-	10l. black and red	3·00	1·90

DESIGN: 10l. Statue of Lenin.

158 Henri Dunant and Globe

1963. Red Cross Centenary. Cross in red.

733	**158**	1l.50 black and red	70	30
734	**158**	2l.50 black and blue	1·10	50
735	**158**	6l. black, red and green	2·20	1·00
736	**158**	10l. black, red and yellow	3·75	2·50

159 Stalin and Battle

1963. 20th Anniv of Battle of Stalingrad.

737	**159**	8l. black & grn (postage)	11·00	4·25
738	-	7l. red and green (air)	11·00	4·25

DESIGN: 7l. 'Lenin' flag, map, tanks, etc.

160 Nikolaev and Vostok 3

1963. First 'Team' Manned Space Flights.

739	**160**	2l.50 brown and blue	65	40
740	-	7l.50 black and blue	1·60	1·00
741	-	20l. brown and violet	4·25	3·75
MS741a 88×73 mm. 25l. blue and brown (Popovich and Nikolaev)			45·00	45·00

DESIGNS—HORIZ: 7l.50, Globe, Vostok 3 and Vostok 4. VERT: 20l. P. Popovic and Vostok 4.

161 Cockchafer Beetle

1963. Insects.

742	**161**	0l.50 brown and green	1·30	50
743	-	1l. brown and blue	2·20	1·00
744	-	8l. purple and red	9·25	2·50
745	-	10l. black and yellow	12·00	3·75

INSECTS: 1l.50, Stagbeetle; 8l. *Procerus gigas* (ground beetle); 10l. *Cicindela albanica* (tiger beetle).

162 Policeman and Allegorical Figure

1963. 20th Anniv of Albanian Security Police.

746	**162**	2l.50 black, purple & red	1·10	80
747	**162**	7l.50 black, lake and red	3·75	2·50

163 Great Crested Grebe

1963. Birds. Multicoloured.

748		0l.50 Type **163**	1·60	40
749		3l. Golden eagle	3·25	1·00
750		6l.50 Grey partridge	8·25	1·70
751		11l. Western capercaillie	11·00	2·50

164 Official Insignia and Postmark of 1913

1963. 50th Anniv of First Albanian Stamps.

752	**164**	5l. multicoloured	2·20	95
753	-	10l. green, black and red	3·75	2·10

DESIGN: 10l. Albanian stamps of 1913, 1937 and 1962.

165 Boxing

1963. Olympic Games, Tokyo (1964) (2nd issue).

754	**165**	2l. green, red and yellow	70	1·00
755	-	3l. brown, blue & orange	90	2·10
756	-	5l. purple, brown and blue	1·40	30
757	-	6l. black, grey and green	1·90	30
758	-	9l. blue and brown	3·75	8·25
MS758a 61×82 mm. 15l. mult (Torch, rings and map)			20·00	27·00

SPORTS: 3l. Basketball; 5l. Volleyball; 6l. Cycling; 9l. Gymnastics.

166 Gen. Enver Hoxha and Labinoti Council Building

1963. 20th Anniv of Albanian People's Army.

759	**166**	1l.50 yellow, black & red	55	30
760	-	2l.50 bistre, brown & blue	1·10	65
761	-	5l. black, drab & turq	1·60	1·00
762	-	6l. blue, buff and brown	2·20	1·50

DESIGNS: 2l.50, Soldier with weapons; 5l. Soldier attacking; 6l. Peacetime soldier.

167 Gagarin

1963. Soviet Cosmonauts. Portraits in yellow and brown.

763	**167**	3l. violet	1·10	40
764	-	5l. blue	1·30	50
765	-	7l. violet and grey	1·60	65
766	-	11l. blue and purple	3·25	1·00
767	-	14l. blue and turquoise	5·00	1·60
768	-	20l. blue	7·50	3·75

COSMONAUTS: 5l. Titov; 7l. Nikolaev; 11l. Popovich; 14l. Bykovsky; 20l. Valentina Tereshkova.

168 Volleyball
(Rumania)

1963. European Sports Events, 1963.
769	**168**	2l. red, black and olive	55	30
770	-	3l. bistre, black and red	85	50
771	-	5l. orange, black & green	1·10	85
772	-	7l. green, black and pink	1·60	1·30
773	-	8l. red, black and blue	3·75	1·60

SPORTS: 3l. Weightlifting (Sweden); 5l. Football (European Cup); 7l. Boxing (Russia); 8l. Ladies' Rowing (Russia).

169 Celadon
Swallowtail

1963. Butterflies and Moths.
774	**169**	1l. black, yellow and red	65	25
775	-	2l. black, red and blue	1·10	30
776	-	4l. black, yellow & purple	2·20	1·00
777	-	5l. multicoloured	3·25	95
778	-	8l. black, red and brown	5·50	2·10
779	-	10l. orange, brown & blue	7·00	3·25

DESIGNS: 2l. Jersey tiger moth; 4l. Brimstone; 5l. Death's-head hawk moth; 8l. Orange tip; 10l. Peacock.

170 Lunik 1

1963. Air. Cosmic Flights.
780	**170**	2l. olive, yellow & orange	55	30
781	-	3l. multicoloured	1·10	40
782	-	5l. olive, yellow & purple	1·60	65
783	-	8l. red, yellow and violet	2·75	1·20
784	-	12l. red, orange and blue	5·50	3·75

DESIGNS: 3l. Lunik 2; 5l. Lunik 3; 8l. Venus 1; 12l. Mars 1.

171 Food Processing
Works

1963. Industrial Buildings.
785	**171**	2l.50 red on pink	1·10	50
786	-	20l. green on green	4·25	2·10
787	-	30l. purple on blue	9·75	4·25
788	-	50l. bistre on cream	11·00	5·25

DESIGNS—VERT: 20l. Naphtha refinery; 30l. Fruit-bottling plant. HORIZ: 50l. Copper-processing works.

172 Shield and
Banner

1963. First Army and Defence Aid Assn Congress.
789	**172**	2l. multicoloured	75	30
790	**172**	8l. multicoloured	2·20	1·60

173 Young Men of Three
Races

1963. 15th Anniv of Declaration of Human Rights.
791	**173**	3l. black and ochre	65	50
792	**173**	5l. blue and ochre	1·30	1·00
793	**173**	7l. violet and ochre	2·75	2·10

174 Bobsleighing

1963. Winter Olympic Games, Innsbruck. Inscr '1964'.
794	**174**	0l.50 black and blue	55	30
795	-	2l.50 black, red and grey	1·00	50
796	-	6l.50 black, yellow & grey	1·40	75
797	-	12l.50 red, black & green	2·75	2·10

MS797a 56×75 mm. 12l.50 black, green and blue (Ski jumper) (49×31 mm) 35·00 50·00

DESIGNS—VERT: 2l.50, Skiing; 12l.50, Figure-skating. HORIZ: 6l.50, Ice-hockey.

175 Lenin

1964. 40th Death Anniv of Lenin.
798	**175**	5l. olive and bistre	1·20	75
799	**175**	10l. olive and bistre	2·40	1·40

176 Hurdling

1964. GANEFO Games, Djakarta (1963).
800	**176**	2l.50 blue and lilac	55	30
801	-	3l. brown and green	1·10	50
802	-	6l.50 red and blue	1·60	90
803	-	8l. ochre and blue	2·75	2·10

SPORTS—HORIZ. 3l. Running; 6l.50, Rifle-shooting. VERT: 8l. Basketball.

177 Common
Sturgeon

1964. Fish. Multicoloured.
804	**177**	0l.50 Type **177**	55	30
805	-	1l. Gilthead seabream	1·10	40
806	-	1l.50 Flat-headed grey mullet	1·60	50
807	-	2l.50 Common carp	2·20	1·00
808	-	6l.50 Atlantic mackerel	3·25	2·10
809	-	10l. Lake Ochrid salmon	5·50	3·25

178 Eurasian Red Squirrel

1964. Forest Animals. Multicoloured.
810	**178**	1l. Type **178**	55	25
811	-	1l.50 Beech marten	85	30
812	-	2l. Red fox	1·10	40
813	-	2l.50 East European hedgehog	1·60	50
814	-	3l. Brown hare	2·20	75
815	-	5l. Golden jackal	2·75	85
816	-	7l. Wild cat	4·25	95
817	-	8l. Wolf	5·50	1·30

179 Lighting Olympic
Torch

1964. Olympic Games, Tokyo (3rd issue). Inscr "DREJT TOKIOS".
818	**179**	3l. yellow, buff and green	55	75
819	-	5l. blue, violet and red	75	1·00
820	-	7l. lt blue, blue & yellow	1·10	1·60
821	-	10l. multicoloured	1·60	2·50

MS821a 81×91 mm. 15l. buff, blue and violet (as 820) (49×62 mm) 30·00 40·00

DESIGNS: 5l. Torch and globes; 7l. Olympic flag and Mt. Fuji; 10l. Olympic Stadium, Tokyo.

180 Soldiers, Hand clutching Rifle, and Inscription

1964. 20th Anniv of Permet Congress.
822	**180**	2l. sepia, red and orange	1·60	1·00
823	-	5l. multicoloured	3·75	2·10
824	-	8l. sepia, red and brown	8·25	6·25

DESIGNS (each with different inscription at right): 5l. Albanian Arms; 8l. Gen. Enver Hoxha.

181 Revolutionaries with Flag

1964. 40th Anniv of Revolution.
825	**181**	2l.50 black and red	55	30
826	**181**	7l.50 black and mauve	1·60	1·00

1964. Verso Tokyo Stamp Exhibition, Rimini (Italy). Optd **Rimini 25-VI-64**.
827		10l. blue, violet, orange and black (No. 821)	8·75	8·75

183 Full Moon

1964. Moon's Phases.
828	**183**	1l. yellow and violet	55	20
829	-	5l. yellow and blue	1·10	85
830	-	8l. yellow and blue	1·60	1·00
831	-	11l. yellow and green	5·50	2·10

MS831a 67×78 mm. 15l. yellow and blue (New Moon) (34×39 mm). Imperf 27·00 35·00

PHASES: 5l. Waxing Moon; 8l. Half-Moon; 11l. Waning Moon.

184 Winter Wren

1964. Albanian Birds. Multicoloured.
832	**184**	0l.50 Type **184**	55	25
833	-	1l. Penduline tit	1·10	30
834	-	2l.50 Green woodpecker	1·60	40
835	-	3l. Common treecreeper	2·20	50
836	-	4l. Eurasian nuthatch	2·75	1·00
837	-	5l. Great tit	3·25	1·30
838	-	6l. Eurasian goldfinch	3·75	1·60
839	-	18l. Golden oriole	8·25	3·75

1964. Air. Riccione 'Space' Exhibition. Optd **Riccione 23-8-1964**.
840	**170**	2l. olive, yellow & orange	12·00	21·00
841	-	8l. red, yellow and violet (No. 783)	27·00	31·00

186 Running and Gymnastics

1964. Olympic Games, Tokyo.
842	**186**	1l. red, blue and green	20	15
843	-	2l. brown, blue and violet	25	20
844	-	3l. brown, violet and olive	35	20
845	-	4l. olive, turquoise & blue	55	30
846	-	5l. turquoise, purple & red	85	50
847	-	6l. ultram, lt blue & orge	1·10	80
848	-	7l. green, orange and blue	1·30	85

849	-	8l. grey, green and yellow	1·40	95
850	-	9l. lt blue, yellow & purple	1·50	1·00
851	-	10l. brown, green & turq	1·70	1·60

MS851a 70×96 mm. 20l. violet and bistre (Winners on Dais) (40×67 mm) 25·00 30·00

SPORTS: 2l. Weightlifting and judo; 3l. Horse-jumping and cycling; 4l. Football and water-polo; 5l. Wrestling and boxing; 6l. Various sports and cycling; 7l. Swimming and yachting; 8l. Basketball and volleyball; 9l. Rowing and canoeing; 10l. Fencing and pistol-shooting.

187 Chinese
Republican
Emblem

1964. 15th Anniv of Chinese People's Republic. Inscr 'I TETOR 1949 1964'.
852	**187**	7l. red, black and yellow	7·75	3·50
853	**187**	8l. black, red and yellow	7·75	4·75

DESIGN—HORIZ: 8l. Mao Tse-tung.

188 Karl Marx

1964. Centenary of 'First International'.
854	**188**	2l. black, red and lavender	1·10	50
855	-	5l. slate	2·75	1·60
856	-	8l. black, red and buff	5·50	2·10

DESIGNS: 5l. St. Martin's Hall, London; 8l. F. Engels.

189 J. de
Rada

1964. 150th Birth Anniv of Jeronim de Rada (poet).
857	**189**	7l. green	1·60	1·00
858	**189**	8l. violet	2·75	1·60

190 Arms and
Flag

1964. 20th Anniv of Liberation.
859	**190**	1l. multicoloured	55	40
860	-	2l. blue, red and yellow	1·10	85
861	-	3l. brown, red and yellow	1·60	1·30
862	-	4l. green, red and yellow	2·20	1·70
863	-	10l. black, red and blue	5·50	4·25

DESIGNS—HORIZ: 2l. Industrial scene; 3l. Agricultural scene. 4l. Laboratory worker. VERT: 10l. Hands holding Constitution, hammer and sickle.

191 Mercury

1964. Solar System Planets. Multicoloured.
864	**191**	1l. Type **191**	25	20
865	-	2l. Venus	55	30
866	-	3l. Earth	75	40
867	-	4l. Mars	80	45
868	-	5l. Jupiter	1·10	90
869	-	6l. Saturn	1·60	1·00
870	-	7l. Uranus	1·80	1·30
871	-	8l. Neptune	2·20	1·50
872	-	9l. Pluto	2·40	1·70

MS872a 88×72 mm. 15l. Solar system and rocket (61×51 mm). Imperf 35·00 47·00

192 Chestnut

1965. Winter Fruits. Multicoloured.
873	1l. Type **192**		35	20
874	2l. Medlars		55	30
875	3l. Persimmon		75	35
876	4l. Pomegranate		1·10	50
877	5l. Quince		2·20	75
878	10l. Orange		4·25	1·30

193 'Industry'

1965. 20th Anniv of Albanian Trade Unions. Inscr 'B.P.S.H. 1945–1965'.
879	**193**	2l. red, pink and black	7·50	7·25
880	-	5l. black, grey and ochre	11·50	11·00
881	-	8l. blue, lt blue & black	14·00	13·50

DESIGNS: 5l. Set square, book and dividers (Technocracy); 8l. Hotel, trees and sunshade (Tourism).

194 Buffalo Grazing

1965. Water Buffaloes.
882	**194**	1l. multicoloured	1·10	50
883	-	2l. multicoloured	2·20	1·00
884	-	3l. multicoloured	3·25	1·60
885	-	7l. multicoloured	7·50	2·10
886	-	12l. multicoloured	13·00	2·50

DESIGNS: 2l. to 12l. As Type **194**, showing different views of buffalo.

195 Coastal View

1965. Albanian Scenery. Multicoloured.
887	1l.50 Type **195**		1·60	50
888	2l.50 Mountain forest		3·50	1·00
889	3l. Lugina Peak (vert)		3·75	1·30
890	4l. White River, Thethi (vert)		5·00	1·60
891	5l. Dry Mountain		6·00	2·10
892	9l. Lake of Flowers, Lure		16·00	4·25

196 Frontier Guard

1965. 20th Anniv of Frontier Force.
893	**196**	2l.50 multicoloured	1·60	1·00
894	**196**	12l.50 multicoloured	9·25	4·25

197 Rifleman

1965. European Shooting Championships, Bucharest.
895	**197**	1l. purple, red and violet	35	20
896	-	2l. purple, ultram & blue	55	30
897	-	3l. red and pink	1·10	50
898	-	4l. multicoloured	2·20	40
899	-	15l. multicoloured	6·50	2·50

DESIGNS: 2, 15l. Rifle-shooting (different); 3l. Target map; 4l. Pistol-shooting.

198 I.T.U. Emblem and Symbols

1965. Centenary of I.T.U.
900	**198**	2l.50 mauve, black & grn	1·10	50
901	**198**	12l.50 blue, black & violet	6·50	1·80

199 Belyaev

1965. Space Flight of Vostod 2.
902	**199**	1l.50 brown and blue	20	10
903	-	2l. blue, ultram & lilac	35	20
904	-	6l.50 brown and mauve	1·10	50
905	-	20l. yellow, black & blue	4·25	2·10

MS906 71×86 mm. 20l. yellow, black and blue (as 905 but larger, 59×51 mm). Imperf 20·00 31·00
DESIGNS: 2l. Vostod 2; 6l.50, Leonov; 20l. Leonov in space.

200 Marx and Lenin

1965. Postal Ministers' Congress, Peking.
907	**200**	2l.50 sepia, red & yellow	85	50
908	**200**	7l.50 green, red & yellow	3·50	2·10

201 Mother and Child

1965. International Children's Day. Multicoloured.
909	1l. Type **201**		25	15
910	2l. Children planting tree		60	30
911	3l. Children and construction toy (horiz)		80	50
912	4l. Child on beach		1·10	85
913	15l. Child reading book		4·25	3·25

202 Wine Vessel

1965. Albanian Antiquities. Multicoloured.
914	1l. Type **202**		25	10
915	2l. Helmet and shield		55	30
916	3l. Mosaic of animal (horiz)		75	50
917	4l. Statuette of man		1·60	1·00
918	15l. Statuette of headless and limbless man		4·00	2·10

203 Fuchsia

1965. Albanian Flowers. Multicoloured.
919	1l. Type **203**		25	15
920	2l. Cyclamen		75	30
921	3l. Lilies		1·30	65
922	3l.50 Iris		1·60	75
923	4l. Dahlia		1·80	85
924	4l.50 Hydrangea		2·20	95
925	5l. Rose		2·40	1·00
926	7l. Tulips		3·25	1·30

1965. Surch.
927	5q. on 30l. (No. 787)		85	85
928	15q. on 30l. (No. 787)		1·10	1·00
929	25q. on 50l. (No. 788)		1·60	1·60
930	80q. on 50l. (No. 788)		3·75	3·75
931	1l.10 on 20l. (No. 786)		5·50	5·25
932	2l. on 20l. (No. 786)		8·75	8·25

205 White Stork

1965. Migratory Birds. Multicoloured.
933	10q. Type **205**		55	30
934	20q. European cuckoo		1·10	50
935	30q. Hoopoe		1·60	85
936	40q. European bee-eater		2·20	1·00
937	50q. European nightjar		2·75	1·30
938	1l.50 Common quail		8·25	3·75

206 War Veterans (after painting by B. Sejdini)

1965. War Veterans Conference.
939	**206**	25q. brown and black	3·25	85
940	**206**	65q. blue and black	8·25	2·10
941	**206**	1l.10 black	11·00	4·25

207 Hunter stalking Western Capercaillie

1965. Hunting.
942	**207**	10q. multicoloured	55	20
943	-	20q. brown, sepia & grn	1·10	20
944	-	30q. multicoloured	1·60	30
945	-	40q. purple and green	2·20	50
946	-	50q. brown, blue & black	2·75	1·00
947	-	1l. brown, bistre & green	5·50	1·60

DESIGNS: 20q. Shooting roe deer; 30q. Common pheasant; 40q. Shooting mallard; 50q. Dogs chasing wild boar; 1l. Hunter and brown hare.

208 Nerium oleander

1965. Mountain Flowers. Multicoloured.
948	10q. Type **208**		25	20
949	20q. *Myosotis alpestris*		55	25
950	30q. *Dianthus glacialis*		75	30
951	40q. *Nymphaea alba*		1·30	50
952	50q. *Lotus corniculatus*		1·60	75
953	1l. *Papaver rhoeas*		4·25	2·10

209 Tourist Hotel, Fier

1965. Public Buildings.
954	**209**	5q. black and blue	10	10
955	-	10q. black and buff	15	10
956	-	15q. black and green	20	10
957	-	25q. black and violet	75	20
958	-	65q. black and brown	1·60	40
959	-	80q. black and green	2·20	50
960	-	1l.10 black and purple	2·75	75
961	-	1l.60 black and blue	4·25	1·60
962	-	2l. black and pink	5·50	2·10
963	-	3l. black and grey	11·00	3·75

BUILDINGS: 10q. Peshkopi Hotel; 15q. Sanatorium, Tirana; 25q. 'House of Rest', Pogradec; 65q. Partisans Sports Palace, Tirana; 80q. 'House of Rest', Dajti Mountain; 1l.10. Palace of Culture, Tirana; 1l.60, Adriatic Hotel, Durres; 2l. Migjeni Theatre, Shkoder; 3l. 'A. Moisiu' Cultural Palace, Durres.

210 Freighter *Teuta*

1965. Evolution of Albanian Ships.
964	**210**	10q. green and light green	35	20
965	-	20q. bistre and green	45	20
966	-	30q. ultramarine and blue	55	30
967	-	40q. violet and light violet	75	50
968	-	50q. red and rose	1·60	75
969	-	1l. brown and ochre	3·75	1·30

DESIGNS: 20q. Punt; 30q. 19th-century sailing ship; 40q. 18th-century brig; 50q. Freighter *Vlora*; 1l. Illyrian galliots.

211 Head of Brown Bear

1965. Brown Bears. Different bear designs as T **211**.
970	10q. brown and buff		45	15
971	20q. brown and buff		55	20
972	30q. brown, red and buff		1·10	35
973	35q. brown and buff		1·30	40
974	40q. brown and buff		1·60	45
975	**211**	50q. brown and buff	2·75	50
976	-	55q. brown and buff	3·25	75
977	-	60q. brown, red and buff	6·00	2·75

The 10q. to 40q. are vert.

212 Championships Emblem

1965. Seventh Balkan Basketball Championships, Tirana. Multicoloured.
978	10q. Type **212**		35	10
979	20q. Competing players		45	15
980	30q. Clearing ball		75	20
981	50q. Attempted goal		1·60	50
982	1l.40 Medal and ribbon		3·25	1·30

213 Arms on Book

1966. 20th Anniv of Albanian People's Republic.
983	**213**	10q. gold, red and brown	20	10
984	-	20q. gold, blue & ultram	35	20
985	-	30q. gold, yellow and brown	75	50
986	-	60q. gold, lt grn & green	1·80	1·00
987	-	80q. gold, red and brown	2·30	1·60

DESIGNS (Arms and): 20q. Chimney stacks; 30q. Ear of corn; 60q. Hammer, sickle and open book; 80q. Industrial plant.

214 Cow

1966. Domestic Animals. Animals in natural colours; inscr in black: frame colours given.
988	**214**	10q. turquoise	20	20
989	-	20q. green	55	30
990	-	30q. blue	1·30	40
991	-	35q. lavender	1·60	50
992	-	40q. pink	2·20	50
993	-	50q. yellow	2·75	65
994	-	55q. blue	3·00	75
995	-	60q. yellow	5·50	1·00

ANIMALS—HORIZ. 20q. Pig; 30q. Sheep; 35q. Goat; 40q. Dog. VERT: 50q. Cat; 55q. Horse; 60q. Ass.

215 Football

1966. World Cup Football Championship (1st series).

996	215	5q. orange grey & buff	15	10
997	-	10q. multicoloured	20	10
998	-	15q. blue, yellow & buff	25	15
999	-	20q. multicoloured	35	20
1000	-	25q. sepia, red and buff	45	20
1001	-	30q. brown, green & buff	55	30
1002	-	35q. green, blue and buff	85	40
1003	-	40q. brown red and buff	90	50
1004	-	50q. multicoloured	1·10	75
1005	-	70q. multicoloured	1·60	1·00

DESIGNS—Footballer and map showing: 10q. Montevideo (1930); 15q. Rome (1934); 20q. Paris (1938); 25q. Rio de Janeiro (1950); 30q. Berne (1954); 35q. Stockholm (1958); 40q. Santiago (1962); 50q. London (1966); 70q. World Cup and football.
See also Nos. 1035/42.

216 A. Z. Cajupi

1966. Birth Centenary of Andon Cajupi (poet).

1006	216	40q. indigo and blue	1·10	60
1007	216	1l.10 bronze and green	3·25	2·10

217 Painted Lady

1966. Butterflies and Dragonflies. Multicoloured.

1008	217	10q. Type 217	45	20
1009		20q. *Calopteryx virgo*	55	25
1010		30q. Pale clouded yellow	75	30
1011		35q. Banded agrion	1·10	35
1012		40q. Banded agrion (different)	1·60	40
1013		50q. Swallowtail	2·20	50
1014		55q. Danube clouded yellow	2·75	75
1015		60q. Hungarian glider	7·00	1·30

The 20, 35 and 40q. are dragonflies, remainder are butterflies.

218 W.H.O. Building

1966. Inauguration of W.H.O. Headquarters, Geneva.

1016	218	25q. black and blue	55	20
1017	-	35q. blue and orange	1·10	30
1018	-	60q. red, blue and green	1·60	75
1019	-	80q. blue, yellow & brn	2·20	1·30

DESIGNS—VERT: 35q. Ambulance and patient; 60q. Nurse and mother weighing baby. HORIZ: 80q. Medical equipment.

219 Leaf Star

1966. Starfish. Multicoloured.

1020	219	15q. Type 219	45	30
1021		25q. Spiny Star	75	40
1022		35q. Brittle Star	1·30	45
1023		45q. Sea Star	1·60	65
1024		50q. Blood Star	1·80	75
1025		60q. Sea Cucumber	2·75	1·00
1026		70q. Sea Urchin	3·25	2·50

220 Luna 10

1966. Luna 10. Launching.

1027	220	20q. multicoloured	55	30
1028	-	30q. multicoloured	1·10	50
1029	220	70q. multicoloured	2·20	1·00
1030	-	80q. multicoloured	3·75	2·30

DESIGN: 30, 80q. Earth, Moon and trajectory of Luna 10.

221 Water-level Map of Albania

1966. International Hydrological Decade.

1031	221	20q. black, orge & red	55	30
1032	-	30q. multicoloured	85	50
1033	-	70q. black and violet	1·60	1·30
1034	-	80q. multicoloured	2·75	2·10

DESIGNS: 30q. Water scale and fields; 70q. Turbine and electricity pylon; 80q. Hydrological decade emblem.

222 Footballers (Uruguay, 1930)

1966. World Cup Football Championship (2nd series). Inscriptions and values in black.

1035	222	10q. purple and ochre	45	10
1036	-	20q. olive and blue	55	15
1037	-	30q. slate and red	75	20
1038	-	35q. red and blue	1·00	25
1039	-	40q. brown and green	1·10	30
1040	-	50q. green and brown	1·30	50
1041	-	55q. green and mauve	1·40	1·00
1042	-	60q. ochre and red	2·75	1·60

DESIGNS—Various footballers representing World Cup winners: 20q. Italy, 1934; 30q. Italy, 1938; 35q. Uruguay, 1950; 40q. West Germany, 1954; 50q. Brazil, 1958; 55q. Brazil, 1962; 60q. Football and names of 16 finalists in 1966 Championship.

223 Tortoise

1966. Reptiles. Multicoloured.

1043	223	10q. Type 223	35	20
1044		15q. Grass snake	45	25
1045		25q. Swamp tortoise	55	30
1046		30q. Lizard	65	40
1047		35q. Salamander	1·10	50
1048		45q. Green lizard	1·30	60
1049		50q. Slow-worm	1·40	75
1050		90q. Sand viper	2·75	1·60

224 Siamese Cat

1966. Cats. Multicoloured.

1051	224	10q. Type 224	45	20
1052		15q. Tabby	55	25
1053		25q. Kitten	1·10	30
1054		45q. Persian	1·70	75
1055		60q. Persian	2·75	1·00
1056		65q. Persian	3·00	1·20
1057		80q. Persian	3·75	1·40

Nos. 1053/7 are horiz.

225 P. Budi (writer)

1966. 400th Birth Anniv of P. Budi.

1058	225	25q. bronze and flesh	1·10	50
1059	225	1l.75 purple and green	3·25	2·50

226 UNESCO Emblem

1966. 20th Anniv of UNESCO. Multicoloured.

1060	226	5q. Type 226	35	15
1061		15q. Tulip and open book	35	20
1062		25q. Albanian dancers	75	40
1063		1l.55 Jug and base of column	3·25	2·10

227 Borzoi

1966. Dogs. Multicoloured.

1064	227	10q. Type 227	55	20
1065		15q. Kuvasz	75	25
1066		25q. Setter	1·30	50
1067		45q. Cocker spaniel	2·00	1·00
1068		60q. Bulldog	2·20	1·30
1069		65q. St. Bernard	3·00	1·60
1070		80q. Dachshund	4·25	2·10

228 Hand holding Book

1966. Fifth Workers Party Congress, Tirana. Multicoloured.

1071	228	15q. Type 228	35	15
1072		25q. Emblems of agriculture and industry	60	15
1073		65q. Hammer and sickle, wheat and industrial skyline	1·60	85
1074		95q. Hands holding banner on bayonet and implements	2·20	1·30

229 Ndre Mjeda (poet)

1966. Birth Centenary of Ndre Mjeda.

1075	229	25q. brown and blue	65	50
1076	229	1l.75 brown and green	3·75	1·80

230 Hammer and Sickle

1966. 25th Anniv of Albanian Young Communists' Union. Multicoloured.

1077	230	15q. Type 230	55	10
1078		25q. Soldier leading attack	75	20
1079		65q. Industrial worker	1·60	85
1080		95q. Agricultural and industrial vista	2·20	1·30

231 Young Communists and Banner

1966. 25th Anniv of Young Communists' Union. Multicoloured.

1081	231	5q. Manifesto (vert)	35	10
1082		10q. Type 231	55	20
1083		1l.85 Partisans and banner (vert)	3·50	2·30

232 Golden Eagle

1966. Birds of Prey. Multicoloured.

1084	232	10q. Type 232	55	20
1085		15q. White-tailed sea eagle	75	30
1086		25q. Griffon vulture	1·10	50
1087		40q. Northern sparrow hawk	1·30	65
1088		50q. Osprey	1·80	75
1089		70q. Egyptian vulture	2·75	1·30
1090		90q. Common kestrel	3·75	1·60

233 European Hake

1967. Fish. Multicoloured.

1091	233	10q. Type 233	45	20
1092		15q. Striped red mullet	55	30
1093		25q. Opali	1·10	50
1094		40q. Atlantic wolffish	1·30	65
1095		65q. Lumpsucker	1·60	75
1096		80q. Swordfish	2·75	1·30
1097		1l.15 Short-spined sea-scorpion	3·25	1·60

234 Dalmatian Pelicans

1967. Dalmatian Pelicans. Multicoloured.

1098	234	10q. Type 234	25	30
1099		15q. Three pelicans	55	40
1100		25q. Pelican and chicks at nest	1·60	50
1101		50q. Pelicans "taking off" and airborne	3·25	75
1102		2l. Pelican "yawning"	8·25	3·75

235 *Camellia williamsi*

1967. Flowers. Multicoloured.

1103	235	5q. Type 235	20	10
1104		10q. *Chrysanthemum indicum*	25	15
1105		15q. *Althaea rosea*	35	20
1106		25q. *Abutilon striatum*	1·10	30
1107		35q. *Paeonia chinensis*	1·30	50
1108		65q. *Gladiolus gandavensis*	2·20	1·00
1109		80q. *Freesia hybrida*	2·75	1·60
1110		1l.15 *Dianthus caryophyllus*	3·25	1·80

236 Congress Emblem

1967. Sixth Trade Unions Congress, Tirana.

1111	236	25q. red, sepia and lilac	1·10	50
1112	236	1l.75 red, green and grey	3·25	2·10

237 Rose

1967. Roses.

1113	**237**	5q. multicoloured	45	20
1114	-	10q. multicoloured	55	30
1115	-	15q. multicoloured	65	40
1116	-	25q. multicoloured	75	50
1117	-	35q. multicoloured	1·10	65
1118	-	65q. multicoloured	1·40	75
1119	-	80q. multicoloured	1·60	1·00
1120	-	1l.65 multicoloured	3·25	1·60

DESIGNS: 10q. to 1l.65 Various roses as Type **237**.

238 Borsh Coast

1967. Albanian Riviera. Multicoloured.

1121		15q. Butrinti (vert)	45	20
1122		20q. Type **238**	55	25
1123		25q. Piqeras village	1·10	30
1124		45q. Coastal view	1·30	40
1125		50q. Himara coast	1·50	50
1126		65q. Fishing boat, Saranda	2·20	75
1127		80q. Dhermi	2·40	1·00
1128		1l. Sunset at sea (vert)	3·25	1·60

239 Fawn

1967. Roe Deer. Multicoloured.

1129		15q. Type **239**	55	20
1130		20q. Head of buck (vert)	55	30
1131		25q. Head of doe (vert)	1·10	50
1132		30q. Doe and fawn	1·10	50
1133		35q. Doe and new-born fawn	1·60	75
1134		40q. Young buck (vert)	1·60	75
1135		65q. Buck and doe (vert)	3·25	1·00
1136		70q. Running deer	4·25	1·60

240 Costumes of Malesia e Madhe Region

1967. National Costumes. Multicoloured.

1137		15q. Type **240**	45	15
1138		20q. Zadrima	50	20
1139		25q. Kukesi	55	30
1140		45q. Dardhe	85	50
1141		50q. Myzeqe	1·00	75
1142		65q. Tirana	1·30	85
1143		80q. Dropulli	2·20	1·00
1144		1l. Laberise	2·30	1·30

241 Battle Scene and Newspaper

1967. 25 Years of the Albanian Popular Press. Multicoloured

1145		25q. Type **241**	65	30
1146		75q. Newspapers and printery	1·70	75
1147		2l. Workers with newspaper	4·25	2·10

242 University, Torch and Open Book

1967. Tenth Anniv of Tirana University.

1148	**242**	25q. multicoloured	55	40
1149	**242**	1l.75 multicoloured	3·50	1·80

243 Soldiers and Flag

1967. 25th Anniv of Albanian Democratic Front. Multicoloured.

1150		15q. Type **243**	35	20
1151		65q. Pick, rifle and flag	1·10	50
1152		1l.20 Torch and open book	2·40	1·30

244 Grey Rabbits

1967. Rabbit-breeding. Multicoloured.

1153		15q. Type **244**	35	15
1154		20q. Black and white rabbit (vert)	45	20
1155		25q. Brown hare	65	30
1156		35q. Brown rabbits	1·10	40
1157		40q. Common rabbits	1·30	50
1158		50q. Grey rabbit (vert)	2·20	75
1159		65q. Head of white rabbit (vert)	2·40	85
1160		1l. White rabbit	3·50	1·60

245 *Shkoder Wedding* (detail, Kole Idromeno)

1967. Albanian Paintings.

1161	**245**	15q. multicoloured	55	20
1162	-	20q. multicoloured	75	30
1163	-	25q. multicoloured	1·10	40
1164	-	45q. multicoloured	1·30	50
1165	-	50q. multicoloured	1·60	75
1166	-	65q. multicoloured	2·20	85
1167	-	80q. multicoloured	2·40	1·00
1168	-	1l. multicoloured	4·25	1·30

DESIGNS—VERT: 20q. *Head of the Prophet David* (detail, 16th-century fresco); 45q. Ancient mosaic head (from Durres); 50q. Detail, 16th-century icon (30×51 mm); 1l. *Our Sister* (K. Idromeno). HORIZ (51×30 mm): 25q. *Commandos of the Hakmarrja Battalion* (S. Shijaku); 65q. *Co-operative* (farm women, Z. Shoshi); 80q. *Street in Korce* (V. Mio).

246 Lenin and Stalin

1967. 50th Anniv of October Revolution. Multicoloured.

1169		15q. Type **246**	35	20
1170		25q. Lenin with soldiers (vert)	75	50
1171		50q. Lenin addressing meeting (vert)	1·10	75
1172		1l.10 Revolutionaries	2·40	1·00

247 Common Turkey

1967. Domestic Fowl. Multicoloured.

1173		15q. Type **247**	20	10
1174		20q. Goose	35	20
1175		25q. Hen	55	30
1176		45q. Cockerel	1·10	50
1177		50q. Helmeted guineafowl	1·30	65

1178		65q. Greylag goose (horiz)	1·60	75
1179		80q. Mallard (horiz)	2·20	1·00
1180		1l. Chicks (horiz)	3·25	1·30

248 First Aid

1967. Sixth Red Cross Congress, Tirana. Multicoloured.

1181		15q.+5q. Type **248**	1·10	65
1182		25q.+5q. Stretcher case	2·20	1·00
1183		65q.+25q. Heart patient	7·50	3·75
1184		80q.+40q. Nurse holding child	11·00	5·25

249 Arms of Skanderbeg

1967. 500th Death Anniv of Castriota Skanderbeg (patriot) (1st issue). Multicoloured.

1185		10q. Type **249**	20	10
1186		15q. Skanderbeg	35	15
1187		25q. Helmet and sword	55	20
1188		30q. Kruja Castle	65	30
1189		35q. Petrela Castle	75	40
1190		65q. Berati Castle	1·10	50
1191		80q. Meeting of chiefs	2·20	75
1192		90q. Battle of Albulena	2·30	1·00

See also Nos. 1200/7.

250 Winter Olympic Emblem

1967. Winter Olympic Games, Grenoble. Multicoloured

1193		15q. Type **250**	20	10
1194		25q. Ice hockey	25	15
1195		30q. Figure skating	35	20
1196		50q. Skiing (slalom)	55	30
1197		80q. Skiing (downhill)	1·10	50
1198		1l. Ski jumping	2·40	1·30

MS1199 58×67 mm. 2l. As Type **250** but larger. Imperf 9·25 10·50

251 Skanderbeg Memorial, Tirana

1968. 500th Death Anniv of Castriota Skanderbeg (2nd issue). Multicoloured.

1200		10q. Type **251**	35	20
1201		15q. Skanderbeg portrait	55	30
1202		25q. Skanderbeg portrait (different)	1·00	40
1203		30q. Equestrian statue, Kruja (vert)	1·10	45
1204		35q. Skanderbeg and mountains	1·30	50
1205		65q. Bust of Skanderbeg	2·20	75
1206		80q. Title page of biography	3·00	1·60
1207		90q. "Skanderbeg battling with the Turks" (painting) (vert)	3·50	2·10

252 Alpine Dianthus

1968. Flowers. Multicoloured.

1208		15q. Type **252**	20	10
1209		20q. Chinese dianthus	25	15
1210		25q. Pink carnation	35	20
1211		50q. Red carnation and bud	1·10	30
1212		80q. Two red carnations	1·60	50
1213		1l.10 Yellow carnations	2·20	1·00

253 Ear of Wheat and Electricity Pylon

1968. Fifth Agricultural Co-operative Congress. Multicoloured

1214		25q. Type **253**	55	30
1215		65q. Tractor (horiz)	1·60	85
1216		1l.10 Cow	2·20	1·30

254 Long-horned Goat

1968. Goats. Multicoloured.

1217		15q. Zane female	20	10
1218		20q. Kid	35	15
1219		25q. Long-haired capore	45	20
1220		30q. Black goat at rest	55	25
1221		40q. Kids dancing	65	30
1222		50q. Red and piebald goats	75	50
1223		80q. Long-haired ankara	1·60	65
1224		1l.40 Type **254**	3·25	1·60

The 15q., 20q. and 25q. are vert.

255 Zef Jubani

1968. 150th Birth Anniv of Zef Jubani (patriot).

1225	**255**	25q. brown and yellow	55	30
1226	**255**	1l.75 blue, black & vio	2·75	1·60

256 Doctor using Stethoscope

1968. 20th Anniv of W.H.O.

1227	**256**	25q. red and green	35	15
1228	-	65q. black, blue & yellow	1·30	85
1229	-	1l.10 brown and black	1·60	1·00

DESIGNS—HORIZ: 65q. Hospital and microscope. VERT: 1l.10, Mother feeding child.

257 Servicewoman

1968. 25th Anniv of Albanian Women's Union.

1230	**257**	15q. red and orange	45	20
1231	-	25q. turquoise and green	55	30
1232	-	60q. brown and ochre	1·60	75
1233	-	1l. violet and light violet	2·75	1·30

DESIGNS: 25q. Teacher; 60q. Farm-girl; 1l. Factory-worker.

258 Karl Marx

1968. 150th Birth Anniv of Karl Marx. Multicoloured.
1234	15q.	Type **258**	1·10	50
1235	25q.	Marx addressing students	1·60	75
1236	65q.	"Das Kapital", "Communist Manifesto" and marchers	2·75	1·60
1237	95q.	Karl Marx	4·25	3·75

259 Heliopsis

1968. Flowers. Multicoloured.
1238	15q.	Type **259**	20	10
1239	20q.	Red flax	35	15
1240	25q.	Orchid	45	20
1241	30q.	Gloxinia	50	30
1242	40q.	Orange lily	55	40
1243	80q.	Hippeastrum	1·60	1·00
1244	1l.40	Purple magnolia	2·75	1·60

260 A. Frasheri and Torch

1968. 90th Anniv of Prizren Defence League.
1245	**260**	25q. black and green	55	20
1246	-	40q. multicoloured	1·10	50
1247	-	85q. multicoloured	1·60	1·00

DESIGNS: 40q. League headquarters; 85q. Frasheri's manifesto and partisans.

261 *Shepherd* (A. Kushi)

1968. Paintings in Tirana Gallery. Multicoloured.
1248	15q.	Type **261**	15	10
1249	20q.	*Tirana* (V. Mio) (horiz)	20	10
1250	25q.	*Highlander* (G. Madhi)	20	10
1251	40q.	*Refugees* (A. Buza)	55	20
1252	80q.	*Partisans at Shahin Matrakut* (S. Xega)	1·10	30
1253	1l.50	*Old Man* (S. Papadhimitri)	2·75	85
1254	1l.70	*Shkoder Gate* (S. Rrota)	3·25	1·00
MS1255	90×114 mm. 2l.50 *Shkoder Costume* (Z. Colombi) (51×71 mm)		4·00	2·50

262 Soldiers and Armoured Vehicles

1968. 25th Anniv of People's Army. Multicoloured.
1256	15q.	Type **262**	55	20
1257	25q.	Sailor and naval craft	65	25
1258	65q.	Pilot and Ilyushin Il-28 and Mikoyan Gurevich MiG-17 aircraft (vert)	2·20	1·00
1259	95q.	Soldier and patriots	3·25	1·60

263 Common Squid

1968. Marine Fauna. Multicoloured.
1260	15q.	Type **263**	35	20
1261	20q.	Common lobster	40	30
1262	25q.	Common northern whelk	55	40
1263	50q.	Edible crab	70	50
1264	70q.	Spiny lobster	1·10	85

1265	80q.	Common green crab	1·90	1·00
1266	90q.	Norwegian lobster	2·20	1·60

264 Relay-racing

1968. Olympic Games, Mexico. Multicoloured.
1267	15q.	Type **264**	15	10
1268	20q.	Running	20	10
1269	25q.	Throwing the discus	25	10
1270	30q.	Horse-jumping	35	20
1271	40q.	High-jumping	45	30
1272	50q.	Hurdling	55	40
1273	80q.	Football	1·10	50
1274	1l.40	High diving	2·20	1·30
MS1275	90×81 mm. 2l. Olympic Stadium (64×54 mm.)		4·00	2·50

265 Enver Hoxha (Party Secretary)

1968. Enver Hoxha's 60th Birthday.
1276	**265**	25q. blue	45	30
1277	**265**	35q. purple	65	50
1278	**265**	80q. violet	1·40	1·00
1279	**265**	1l.10 brown	1·70	1·30
MS1280	80½×91 mm. **265** 1l.50 violet, red and gold. Imperf		£160	£180

266 Alphabet Book

1968. 60th Anniv of Monastir Language Congress.
1281	**266**	15q. lake and green	65	40
1282	**266**	85q. brown and green	3·25	2·10

267 Bohemian Waxwing

1968. Birds. Multicoloured.
1283	15q.	Type **267**	35	10
1284	20q.	Rose-coloured starling	55	20
1285	25q.	River kingfishers	75	30
1286	50q.	Long-tailed tit	1·10	50
1287	80q.	Wallcreeper	2·20	1·00
1288	1l.10	Bearded reedling	3·25	1·60

268 Mao Tse-tung

1968. Mao Tse-tung's 75th Birthday.
1289	**268**	25q. black, red and gold	1·10	50
1290	**268**	1l.75 black, red and gold	7·00	4·75

269 Adem Reka (dock foreman)

1969. Contemporary Heroes. Multicoloured.
1291	5q.	Type **269**	45	30
1292	10q.	Pjeter Lleshi (telegraph linesman)	55	40
1293	15q.	M. Shehu and M. Kepi (fire victims)	1·10	85
1294	25q.	Shkurte Vata (railway worker)	1·60	1·30
1295	65q.	Agron Elezi (earthquake victim)	1·90	1·40
1296	80q.	Ismet Bruca (school-teacher)	2·20	1·60
1297	1l.30	Fuat Cela (blind Co-op leader)	3·25	2·10

270 Meteorological Equipment

1969. 20th Anniv of Albanian Hydro-meteorology. Multicoloured.
1298	15q.	Type **270**	55	30
1299	25q.	"Arrow" indicator	85	50
1300	1l.60	Meteorological balloon and isobar map	4·25	2·30

271 *Student Revolutionaries* (P. Mele)

1969. Albanian Paintings since 1944. Multicoloured
1301	5q.	Type **271**	20	10
1302	25q.	*Partisans 1914* (F. Haxhiu) (horiz)	35	10
1303	65q.	*Steel Mill* (C. Ceka) (horiz)	55	20
1304	80q.	*Reconstruction* (V. Kilica) (horiz)	65	40
1305	1l.10	*Harvest* (N. Jonuzi) (horiz)	1·30	75
1306	1l.15	*Seaside Terraces* (S. Kaceli) (horiz)	1·60	1·30
MS1307	111×91 mm. 2l. *Partisans' Meeting* (N. Zajmi). Imperf		2·75	2·10

SIZES: The 25q., 80q., 1l.10 and 1l.15 are 50×30 mm.

272 Self-portrait

1969. 450th Death Anniv of Leonardo da Vinci.
1308	**272**	25q. agate, brown & gold	35	15
1309	-	35q. agate, brown & gold	65	20
1310	-	40q. agate, brown & gold	85	50
1311	-	1l. multicoloured	2·20	1·00
1312	-	2l. agate, brown & gold	4·25	1·80
MS1313	65×95 mm. 2l. multicoloured. Imperf		7·00	4·50

DESIGNS—VERT: 35q. *Lilies*; 1l. *Portrait of Beatrice*; 2l. *Portrait of a Lady*. HORIZ: 40q. *Design for Helicopter*.

273 Congress Building

1969. 25th Anniv of Permet Congress. Multicoloured.
1314	25q.	Type **273**	55	30
1315	2l.25	Two partisans	4·25	3·25
MS1316	95×101 mm. 1l. Albanian arms. Imperf		50·00	65·00

274 *Viola albanica*

1969. Flowers. Viola Family. Multicoloured.
1317	5q.	Type **274**	15	10
1318	10q.	*Viola hortensis*	20	10
1319	15q.	*Viola heterophylla*	35	15
1320	20q.	*Viola hortensis* (different)	45	20
1321	25q.	*Viola odorata*	55	20
1322	80q.	*Viola hortensis* (different)	1·60	85
1323	1l.95	*Viola hortensis* (different)	2·75	2·10

275 Plum

1969. Fruit Trees. Blossom and Fruit. Multicoloured.
1324	10q.	Type **275**	20	10
1325	15q.	Lemon	35	15
1326	25q.	Pomegranate	55	20
1327	50q.	Cherry	1·10	50
1328	80q.	Apricot	1·80	1·00
1329	1l.20	Apple	2·75	1·60

276 Throwing the Ball

1969. 16th European Basketball Championships, Naples. Multicoloured.
1330	10q.	Type **276**	35	10
1331	15q.	Trying for goal	45	15
1332	25q.	Ball and net (horiz)	55	20
1333	80q.	Scoring a goal	1·60	30
1334	2l.20	Intercepting a pass	3·25	1·60

277 Gymnastics

1969. National Spartakiad. Multicoloured.
1335	5q.	Pickaxe, rifle, flag and stadium	15	10
1336	10q.	Type **277**	20	10
1337	15q.	Running	35	10
1338	20q.	Pistol-shooting	45	15
1339	25q.	Swimmer on starting block	55	20
1340	80q.	Cycling	1·60	75
1341	95q.	Football	2·20	1·30

278 Mao Tse-tung

1969. 20th Anniv of Chinese People's Republic. Multicoloured.

1342	25q. Type **278**	1·60	50
1343	85q. Steel ladle and control room (horiz)	5·50	2·10
1344	1l.40 Rejoicing crowd	9·25	3·75

279 Enver Hoxha

1969. 25th Anniv of Second National Liberation Council Meeting, Berat. Multicoloured.

1345	25q. Type **279**	35	20
1346	80q. Star and Constitution	85	50
1347	1l.45 Freedom-fighters	2·20	1·30

280 Entry of Provisional Government, Tirana

1969. 25th Anniv of Liberation. Multicoloured.

1348	25q. Type **280**	45	20
1349	30q. Oil refinery	55	25
1350	35q. Combine harvester	75	30
1351	45q. Hydroelectric power station	1·30	50
1352	55q. Soldier and partisans	1·80	75
1353	1l.10 People rejoicing	3·25	1·30

281 Stalin

1969. 90th Birth Anniv of Joseph Stalin.

1354	**281**	15q. lilac	20	10
1355	**281**	25q. blue	55	20
1356	**281**	1l. brown	1·80	75
1357	**281**	1l.10 blue	2·20	1·00

282 Head of Woman

1969. Mosaics. (1st series). Multicoloured.

1358	15q. Type **282**	20	10
1359	25q. Floor pattern	35	20
1360	80q. Bird and tree	1·10	50
1361	1l.10 Diamond floor pattern	1·60	65
1362	1l.20 Corn in oval pattern	2·20	75

Nos. 1359/61 are horiz.
See also Nos. 1391/6, 1564/70 and 1657/62.

283 Manifesto and Congress Building

1970. 50th Anniv of Lushnje Congress.

1363	**283**	25q. black, red and grey	55	30
1364	–	1l.25 black, yell & grn	3·25	2·10

DESIGN: 1l.25, Lushnje postmark of 1920.

284 '25' and Workers

1970. 25th Anniv of Albanian Trade Unions.

1365	**284**	25q. multicoloured	55	30
1366	**284**	1l.75 multicoloured	3·25	2·10

285 Lilium cernum

1970. Lilies. Multicoloured.

1367	5q. Type **285**	25	15
1368	15q. Lilium candidum	35	20
1369	25q. Lilium regale	55	30
1370	80q. Lilium martagon	1·60	1·00
1371	1l.10 Lilium tigrinum	2·20	1·40
1372	1l.15 Lilium albanicum	2·75	1·80

Nos. 1370/2 are horiz.

286 Lenin

1970. Birth Cent of Lenin. Each blk, silver & red.

1373	5q. Type **286**	20	10
1374	15q. Lenin making speech	45	20
1375	25q. As worker	55	30
1376	95q. As revolutionary	1·30	75
1377	1l.10 Saluting	2·40	1·00

Nos. 1374/6 are horiz.

287 Frontier Guard

1970. 25th Anniv of Frontier Force.

1378	**287**	25q. multicoloured	55	30
1379	**287**	1l.25 multicoloured	2·75	1·80

288 Jules Rimet Cup

1970. World Cup Football Championship, Mexico. Multicoloured.

1380	5q. Type **288**	10	10
1381	10q. Aztec Stadium	15	10
1382	15q. Three footballers	20	10
1383	25q. Heading goal	25	15
1384	65q. Two footballers	55	20
1385	80q. Two footballers	1·10	50
1386	2l. Two footballers	2·75	1·40

MS1387 81×74 mm. 2l. Mexican horseman and Mt. Popocatepetil | 4·00 | 3·00

The design of **MS**1387 is larger, 56×45 mm.

289 New U.P.U. Headquarters Building

1970. New U.P.U. Headquarters Building, Berne.

1388	**289**	25q. blue, black and light blue	35	15
1389	**289**	1l.10 pink, black & orge	1·60	65
1390	**289**	1l.15 turq, blk & grn	1·80	1·00

290 Birds and Grapes

1970. Mosaics (2nd series). Multicoloured.

1391	5q. Type **290**	20	10
1392	10q. Waterfowl	35	10
1393	20q. Pheasant and tree stump	45	15
1394	25q. Bird and leaves	55	20
1395	65q. Fish	1·10	50
1396	2l.25 Peacock (vert)	3·75	2·10

291 Harvesters and Dancers

1970. 25th Anniv of Agrarian Reform.

1397	**291**	15q. lilac and black	45	20
1398	–	25q. blue and black	55	30
1399	–	80q. brown and black	1·60	50
1400	–	1l.30 brown and black	2·20	1·00

DESIGNS: 25q. Ploughed fields and open-air conference; 80q. Cattle and newspapers; 1l.30, Combine-harvester and official visit.

292 Partisans going into Battle

1970. 50th Anniv of Battle of Vlore.

1401	**292**	15q. brown, orge & black	35	20
1402	–	25q. brown, yell & black	75	30
1403	–	1l.60 myrtle, grn & blk	2·40	1·60

DESIGNS: 25q. Victory parade; 1l.60, Partisans.

293 The Harvesters (I. Sulovari)

1970. 25th Anniv of Liberation. Prize-winning Paintings. Multicoloured.

1404	5q. Type **293**	10	10
1405	15q. Return of the Partisan (D. Trebicka) (horiz)	20	10
1406	25q. The Miners (N. Zajmi) (horiz)	25	15
1407	65q. Instructing the Partisans (H. Nallbani) (horiz)	55	30
1408	95q. Making Plans (V. Kilica) (horiz)	1·10	75
1409	2l. The Machinist (Z. Shoshi)	3·25	2·10

MS1410 67×96 mm. 2l. The Guerrilla (S. Shijaku). (54×75 mm). Imperf | 3·75 | 2·50

294 Electrification Map

1970. Rural Electrification Completion. Multicoloured.

1411	15q. Type **294**	35	20
1412	25q. Lamp and graph	55	30
1413	80q. Erecting power lines	1·60	50
1414	1l.10 Uses of electricity	1·80	1·00

295 Engels

1970. 150th Birth Anniv of Friedrich Engels.

1415	**295**	25q. blue and bistre	55	20
1416	–	1l.10 purple and bistre	1·60	75
1417	–	1l.15 olive and bistre	1·80	85

DESIGNS: 1l.10, Engels as a young man; 1l.15, Engels making speech.

295a Tractor Factory, Tirana

1971. Industry. Multicoloured.

1417a	10q. Type **295a**	£275	£160
1417b	15q. Fertiliser factory, Fier	£275	£160
1417c	20q. Superphosphate factory, Lac (vert)	£275	£160
1417d	25q. Cement factory, Elbasan	£275	£160
1417e	80q. Factory, Oytreki Stalin	£275	£160

296 Beethoven's Birthplace

1970. Birth Bicentenary of Beethoven.

1418	**296**	5q. violet and gold	20	10
1419	–	15q. purple and silver	35	20
1420	–	25q. green and gold	55	30
1421	–	65q. purple and silver	1·30	85
1422	–	1l.10 blue and gold	2·40	1·00
1423	–	1l.80 black and silver	4·25	1·90

DESIGNS—VERT: Beethoven: 15q. In silhouette; 25q. As young man; 65q. Full-face; 1l.10, Profile. HORIZ: 1l.80, Stage performance of Fidelio.

297 Republican Emblem

1971. 25th Anniv of Republic.

1424	**297**	15q. multicoloured	35	20
1425	–	25q. multicoloured	45	30
1426	–	80q. black, gold & green	1·30	1·00
1427	–	1l.30 black, gold & brn	1·80	1·40

DESIGNS: 25q. Proclamation; 80q. Enver Hoxha; 1l.30, Patriots.

298 Storming the Barricades

1971. Centenary of Paris Commune.

1428	25q. blue and deep blue	55	20	
1429	50q. green and grey	75	40	
1430	**298**	65q. chestnut and brown	1·10	50
1431	1l.10 lilac and violet	2·20	1·00	

DESIGNS—VERT: 25q. La Marseillaise; 50q. Women Communards. HORIZ: 1l.10, Firing squad.

299 Conflict of Race

1971. Racial Equality Year.

1432	**299**	25q. black and brown	35	20
1433	–	1l.10 black and red	1·10	50
1434	–	1l.15 black and red	1·30	65

DESIGNS—VERT: 1l.10, Heads of three races; 1l.15, Freedom fighters.

300 Tulip

1971. Hybrid Tulips.

1435	**300**	5q. multicoloured	15	10
1436	-	10q. multicoloured	20	10
1437	-	15q. multicoloured	35	10
1438	-	20q. multicoloured	45	15
1439	-	25q. multicoloured	55	20
1440	-	80q. multicoloured	1·60	50
1441	-	1l. multicoloured	2·75	1·00
1442	-	1l.45 multicoloured	4·25	2·10

DESIGNS: 10q. to 1l.45, Different varieties of tulips.

301 Postrider

1971. 500th Birth Anniv of Albrecht Durer (painter and engraver).

1443	**301**	10q. black and green	20	10
1444	-	15q. black and blue	45	15
1445	-	25q. black and blue	55	20
1446	-	45q. black and purple	1·10	50
1447	-	65q. multicoloured	2·20	1·00
1448	-	2l.40 multicoloured	6·50	2·10
MS1449	93×90 mm. 2l.50 multicoloured. Imperf		5·50	3·75

DESIGNS—VERT: 15q. *Three Peasants*; 25q. *Peasant Dancers*; 45q. *The Bagpiper.* HORIZ: 65q. *View of Kalchreut*; 2l.40, *View of Trient.* LARGER: 2l.50, Self-portrait.

302 Globe and Satellite (1970)

1971. Chinese Space Achievements. Multicoloured.

1450	60q. Type **302**	1·10	50
1451	1l.20 Public Building, Tirana	2·20	1·60
1452	2l.20 Globe and satellite (1971)	4·25	3·25
MS1453	65×112 mm. 2l.50 Globe and arrow. Imperf	6·50	3·75

The date on No. 1451 refers to the passage of Chinese satellite over Tirana.

303 Mao Tse-tung

1971. 50th Anniv of Chinese Communist Party. Multicoloured.

1454	25q. Type **303**	85	50
1455	1l.05 Party Birthplace (horiz)	2·20	1·60
1456	1l.20 Chinese celebrations (horiz)	3·25	2·50

304 Crested Tit

1971. Birds. Multicoloured.

1457	5q. Type **304**	35	10
1458	10q. European serin	45	15

1459	15q. Linnet	65	15
1460	25q. Firecrest	1·10	20
1461	45q. Rock thrush	1·60	40
1462	60q. Blue tit	2·40	1·00
1463	2l.40 Chaffinch	9·75	8·25

305 Running

1971. Olympic Games (1972). (1st issue). Multicoloured.

1464	5q. Type **305**	10	10
1465	10q. Hurdling	15	10
1466	15q. Canoeing	20	15
1467	25q. Gymnastics	55	20
1468	80q. Fencing	1·10	40
1469	1l.05 Football	1·30	50
1470	3l.60 Diving	4·50	1·60
MS1471	70×83 mm. 2l. Runner breasting tape (47×54 mm). Imperf	4·00	3·00

See also Nos. 1522/**MS**1530.

306 Workers with Banner

1971. Sixth Workers' Party Congress. Multicoloured.

1472	25q. Type **306**	55	20
1473	1l.05 Congress hall	1·60	1·40
1474	1l.20 "VI", flag, star and rifle (vert)	2·20	1·60

307 'XXX' and Red Flag

1971. 30th Anniv of Albanian Workers' Party. Multicoloured.

1475	15q. Workers and industry (horiz)	20	10
1476	80q. Type **307**	1·40	1·00
1477	1l.55 Enver Hoxha and flags (horiz)	2·75	1·90

308 *Young Man* (R. Kuci)

1971. Albanian Paintings. Multicoloured.

1478	5q. Type **308**	10	10
1479	15q. *Building Construction* (M. Fushekati)	15	10
1480	25q. *Partisan* (D. Jukniu)	20	15
1481	80q. *Fighter Pilots* (S. Kristo) (horiz)	1·10	20
1482	1l.20 *Girl Messenger* (A. Sadikaj) (horiz)	1·40	85
1483	1l.55 *Medieval Warriors* (S. Kamberi) (horiz)	1·60	1·40
MS1484	89×70 mm. 2l. *Partisans in the Mountains* (I. Lulani). Imperf	4·00	3·00

309 Emblems and Flags

1971. 30th Anniv of Albanian Young Communists' Union.

1485	**309** 15q. multicoloured	20	10
1486	**309** 1l.35 multicoloured	2·00	1·00

310 Village Girls

1971. Albanian Ballet *Halili and Hajria.* Multicoloured

1487	5q. Type **310**	15	10
1488	10q. Parting of Halili and Hajria	20	10
1489	15q. Hajria before Sultan Suleiman	20	15
1490	50q. Hajria's marriage	75	50
1491	80q. Execution of Halili	1·30	75
1492	1l.40 Hajria killing her husband	2·20	1·30

311 Rifle-shooting (Biathlon)

1972. Winter Olympic Games, Sapporo, Japan. Multicoloured.

1493	5q. Type **311**	10	10
1494	10q. Tobogganing	15	10
1495	15q. Ice-hockey	15	10
1496	20q. Bobsleighing	20	10
1497	50q. Speed skating	85	50
1498	1l. Slalom skiing	1·30	85
1499	2l. Ski jumping	2·40	1·90
MS1500	71×91 mm. 2l.50 Figure skating. Imperf	4·00	3·00

312 Wild Strawberries

1972. Wild Fruits. Multicoloured.

1501	5q. Type **312**	15	10
1502	10q. Blackberries	15	10
1503	15q. Hazelnuts	20	10
1504	20q. Walnuts	45	15
1505	25q. Strawberry-tree fruit	55	20
1506	30q. Dogwood berries	75	50
1507	2l.40 Rowanberries	4·25	1·60

313 Human Heart

1972. World Health Day. Multicoloured.

1508	1l.10 Type **313**	1·80	1·30
1509	1l.20 Treatment of cardiac patient	2·00	1·40

314 Congress Delegates

1972. Seventh Albanian Trade Unions Congress. Multicoloured

1510	25q. Type **314**	75	50
1511	2l.05 Congress Hall	3·00	1·80

315 Memorial Flame

1972. 30th Anniv of Martyrs' Day, and Death of Qemal Stafa.

1512	**315** 15q. multicoloured	20	10
1513	- 25q. black, orge & grey	55	20
1514	- 1l.90 black and ochre	2·75	1·30

DESIGNS—VERT: 25q. *Spirit of Defiance* (statue). HORIZ: 1l.90, Qemal Stafa.

316 *Camellia japonica Kamelie*

1972. Camellias.

1515	**316** 5q. multicoloured	15	10
1516	- 10q. multicoloured	20	10
1517	- 15q. multicoloured	25	15
1518	- 25q. multicoloured	55	20
1519	- 45q. multicoloured	75	30
1520	- 50q. multicoloured	1·30	50
1521	- 2l.50 multicoloured	5·00	2·50

DESIGNS: Nos. 1516/21, Various camellias as Type **316**.

317 High Jumping

1972. Olympic Games, Munich (2nd issue). Multicoloured.

1522	5q. Type **317**	10	10
1523	10q. Running	15	10
1524	15q. Putting the shot	20	10
1525	20q. Cycling	35	15
1526	25q. Pole-vaulting	45	20
1527	50q. Hurdling	55	30
1528	75q. Hockey	1·10	50
1529	2l. Swimming	3·25	1·00
MS1530	59×76 mm. 2l.50 High-diving (vert). Imperf	4·00	3·00

318 Articulated Bus

1972. Modern Transport. Multicoloured.

1531	15q. Type **318**	20	10
1532	25q. Czechoslovakian Class T699 diesel locomotive	55	15
1533	80q. Freighter *Tirana*	75	20
1534	1l.05 Motor-car	1·30	50
1535	1l.20 Container truck	2·20	1·00

319 Trial of Strength

1972. First Nat Festival of Traditional Games. Multicoloured

1536	5q. Type **319**	10	10
1537	10q. Pick-a-back ball game	15	10
1538	15q. Leaping game	20	10
1539	25q. Rope game	55	20
1540	90q. Leap-frog	1·60	75
1541	2l. Women's throwing game	2·75	2·10

320 Newspaper Mastheads

1972. 30th Anniv of Press Day.

1542	**320** 15q. black and blue	20	10
1543	- 25q. green, red & black	35	15
1544	- 1l.90 black and mauve	2·20	1·60

DESIGNS: 25q. Printing-press and partisan; 1l.90, Workers with newspaper.

321 Location Map and Commemorative Plaque

1972. 30th Anniv of Peza Conference. Multicoloured

1545	15q. Type **321**	35	20
1546	25q. Partisans with flag	55	30
1547	1l.90 Conference Memorial	3·00	1·90

322 *Partisans Conference* (S. Capo)

1972. Albanian Paintings. Multicoloured.

1548	5q. Type **322**	10	10
1549	10q. *Head of Woman* (I. Lulani) (vert)	15	10
1550	15q. *Communists* (L. Shkreli) (vert)	20	10
1551	20q. *Nendorit*, 1941 (S. Shijaku) (vert)	35	15
1552	50q. *Farm Woman* (Z. Shoshi) (vert)	65	20
1553	1l. *Landscape* (D. Trebicka)	1·30	75
1554	2l. *Girls with Bicycles* (V. Kilica)	2·75	2·10
MS1555	55×83 mm. 2l.30 *Folk Dance* (A. Buza) (vert, 40×67 mm). Imperf	4·00	3·00

323 Congress Emblem

1972. Sixth Congress of Young Communists' Union.

1556	**323** 25q. gold, red and silver	75	50
1557	- 2l.05 multicoloured	3·00	1·80

DESIGN: 2l.05, Young worker and banner.

324 Lenin

1972. 55th Anniv of Russian October Revolution. Multicoloured.

1558	1l.10 multicoloured	1·60	1·00
1559	**324** 1l.20 red, blk & pink	3·25	1·30

DESIGN: 1l.10, Hammer and Sickle.

325 Albanian Soldiers

1972. 60th Anniv of Independence.

1560	**325** 15q. blue, red and black	15	15
1561	- 25q. black, red & yellow	35	20
1562	- 65q. multicoloured	85	50
1563	- 1l.25 black and red	2·75	1·30

DESIGNS—VERT: 25q. Ismail Qemali; 1l.25, Albanian double-eagle emblem. HORIZ: 65q. Proclamation of Independence, 1912.

326 Cockerel (mosaic)

1972. Ancient Mosaics from Apolloni and Butrint (3rd series). Multicoloured.

1564	5q. Type **326**	10	10
1565	10q. Bird (vert)	15	10
1566	15q. Partridges (vert)	20	10
1567	25q. Warrior's leg	45	30
1568	45q. Nude on dolphin (vert)	55	40
1569	50q. Fish (vert)	75	50
1570	2l.50 Warrior's head	3·75	2·50

327 Nicolas Copernicus

1973. 500th Birth Anniv of Copernicus. Multicoloured.

1571	5q. Type **327**	10	10
1572	10q. Copernicus and signatures	15	10
1573	25q. Engraved portrait	20	15
1574	80q. Copernicus at desk	75	40
1575	1l.20 Copernicus and planets	2·20	1·00
1576	1l.60 Planetary diagram	3·25	1·60

328 Policeman and Industrial Scene

1973. 30th Anniv of State Security Police.

1577	**328** 25q. black, blue & lt blue	55	40
1578	- 1l.80 multicoloured	3·00	1·80

DESIGN: 1l.80, Prisoner under escort.

329/30 Cactus Flowers

1973. Cacti. As T 329/30.

1579	**329** 10q. multicoloured	10	10
1580	**330** 15q. multicoloured	15	10
1581	- 20q. multicoloured	20	10
1582	- 25q. multicoloured	55	15
1583	- 30q. multicoloured	4·25	2·50
1584	- 65q. multicoloured	85	40
1585	- 80q. multicoloured	1·10	50
1586	- 2l. multicoloured	2·20	1·30

Nos. 1579/86 were issued together *se-tenant* within the sheet and in alternate formats as Types **329/30**.

331 Common Tern

1973. Sea Birds. Multicoloured.

1587	5q. Type **331**	25	15
1588	15q. White-winged black tern	45	20
1589	25q. Black-headed gull	55	30
1590	45q. Great black-headed gull	1·10	75
1591	80q. Slender-billed gull	2·20	1·60
1592	2l.40 Sandwich tern	4·25	3·25

332 Postmark of 1913, and Letters

1973. 60th Anniv of First Albanian Stamps. Multicoloured.

1593	25q. Type **332**	1·10	50
1594	1l.80 Postman and postmarks	4·25	2·10

333 Albanian Woman

1973. Seventh Albanian Women's Congress.

1595	**333** 25q. red and pink	55	30
1596	- 1l.80 black, orge & yell	3·25	2·30

DESIGN: 1l.80, Albanian female workers.

334 *Creation of the General Staff* (G. Madhi)

1973. 30th Anniv of Albanian People's Army. Multicoloured

1597	25q. Type **334**	16·00	10·50
1598	40q. *August 1949* (sculpture by Sh. Haderi) (vert)	16·00	10·50
1599	60q. *Generation after Generation* (Statue by H. Dule) (vert)	16·00	10·50
1600	80q. *Defend Revolutionary Victories* (M. Fushekati)	16·00	10·50

335 *Electrification* (S. Hysa)

1973. Albanian Paintings. Multicoloured.

1601	5q. Type **335**	10	10
1602	10q. *Textile Worker* (E. Nallbani) (vert)	15	10
1603	15q. *Gymnastics Class* (M. Fushekati)	15	10
1604	50q. *Aviator* (F. Stamo) (vert)	65	40
1605	1l.20 *Downfall of Fascism* (A. Lakuriqi)	75	50
1606	1l.20 *Koci Bako* (demonstrators (P. Mele)) (vert)	1·10	85
1607	1l.30 *Peasant Girl* (Z. Shoshi) (vert)	2·20	1·60
MS1608	100×69 mm. 2l.05 *Battle of Tendes se Qypit* (F. Haxhiu) (88×47 mm). Imperf	4·00	3·00

336 *Mary Magdalene*

1973. 400th Birth Anniv of Caravaggio. Paintings. Multicoloured.

1609	5q. Type **336**	10	10
1610	10q. *The Guitar Player* (horiz)	15	10
1611	15q. Self-portrait	20	10
1612	50q. *Boy carrying Fruit*	65	40
1613	80q. *Basket of Fruit* (horiz)	85	65
1614	1l.20 *Narcissus*	1·30	1·00
1615	1l.30 *Boy peeling Apple*	2·20	1·60
MS1616	80×102 mm. 2l.05 *Man in Feathered Hat*. Imperf	6·00	5·25

337 Goalkeeper with Ball

1973. World Cup Football Championship, Munich (1974) (1st issue). Multicoloured.

1617	**337** 5q. multicoloured	10	10
1618	- 10q. multicoloured	15	10
1619	- 15q. multicoloured	15	10
1620	- 20q. multicoloured	20	15
1621	- 25q. multicoloured	25	15
1622	- 90q. multicoloured	1·30	40
1623	- 1l.20 multicoloured	1·50	75
1624	- 1l.25 multicoloured	2·20	1·00
MS1625	80×50 mm. 2l.05 multicoloured (Ball in net, and list of Championships). Imperf	4·50	3·25

DESIGNS: Nos. 1618/24 are similar to Type **337**, showing goalkeepers saving goals.
See also Nos. 1663/70.

338 Weightlifting

1973. World Weightlifting Championships, Havana, Cuba.

1626	**338** 5q. multicoloured	10	10
1627	- 10q. multicoloured	15	10
1628	- 25q. multicoloured	20	10
1629	- 90q. multicoloured	75	40
1630	- 1l.20 mult (horiz)	1·10	75
1631	- 1l.60 mult (horiz)	2·20	1·20

DESIGNS: Nos. 1627/31 are similar to Type **338**, showing various lifts.

339 Ballet Scene

1973. Albanian Life and Work. Multicoloured.

1632	5q. Cement Works, Kavaje	10	10
1633	10q. Ali Kelmendi truck factory and trucks (horiz)	20	10
1634	15q. Type **339**	55	10
1635	20q. Combine-harvester (horiz)	25	10
1636	25q. "Telecommunications"	85	20
1637	35q. Skier and hotel, Dajt (horiz)	65	20
1638	60q. Llogora holiday village (horiz)	1·10	45
1639	80q. Lake scene	1·80	50
1640	1l. Textile mill (horiz)	45	20
1641	1l.20 Furnacemen (horiz)	1·30	50
1642	2l.40 Welder and pipeline (horiz)	2·75	1·60
1643	3l. Skanderbeg Statue, Tirana	4·25	2·50
1644	5l. Roman arches, Durres	5·00	3·25

340 Mao Tse-tung

1973. 80th Birth Anniv of Mao Tse-tung. Multicoloured.

1645	85q. Type **340**	2·75	1·60
1646	1l.20 Mao Tse-tung at parade	3·75	2·50

341 *Horse's Head* (Gericault)

1974. 150th Death Anniv of Jean-Louis Gericault (French painter).

1647	**341** 10q. multicoloured	15	10
1648	- 15q. multicoloured	15	10
1649	- 20q. black and gold	20	10
1650	- 25q. black, lilac and gold	55	30
1651	- 1l.20 multicoloured	2·20	75
1652	- 2l.20 multicoloured	3·75	2·10
MS1653	90×68 mm. 2l.05 multicoloured. Imperf	4·00	3·00

DESIGNS—VERT: 15q. *Male Model* (Gericault); 20q. *Man and Dog*; 25q. *Head of a Negro*; 1l.20, Self-portrait. HORIZ: 2l.20, *Battle of the Giants*.

342 *Lenin with Crew of the Aurora* (D. Trebicka)

1974. 50th Death Anniv of Lenin. Multicoloured.

1654	25q. Type **342**	55	30
1655	60q. *Lenin* (P. Mele) (vert)	1·10	50
1656	1l.20 *Lenin* (seated) (V. Kilica) (vert)	3·25	2·10

343 Duck

1974. Ancient Mosaics from Butrint, Pogradec and Apolloni (4th series). Multicoloured.

1657	5q. Duck (different)	10	10
1658	10q. Bird and flower	15	10
1659	15q. Ornamental basket and grapes	20	15
1660	25q. Type **343**	35	20
1661	40q. Donkey and cockerel	45	30
1662	2l.50 Dragon	2·75	2·10

344 Shooting at Goal

1974. World Cup Football Championship, Munich (2nd issue).

1663	**344**	10q. multicoloured	15	10
1664	-	15q. multicoloured	15	10
1665	-	20q. multicoloured	20	10
1666	-	25q. multicoloured	35	15
1667	-	40q. multicoloured	55	20
1668	-	80q. multicoloured	1·10	50
1669	-	1l. multicoloured	1·30	75
1670	-	1l.20 multicoloured	1·80	1·40

MS1671 72×75 mm. 2l.05 multicoloured (Trophy and names of competing countries). Imperf 4·00 3·00

DESIGNS: Nos. 1664/70, Players in action similar to Type **344**.

345 Memorial and Arms

1974. 30th Anniv of Permet Congress. Multicoloured.

| 1672 | 25q. Type **345** | 55 | 30 |
| 1673 | 1l.80 Enver Hoxha and text | 2·20 | 1·60 |

346 *Solanum dulcamara*

1974. Useful Plants. Multicoloured.

1674	10q. Type **346**	15	10
1675	15q. *Arbutus uva-ursi* (vert)	15	10
1676	20q. *Convallaria majalis* (vert)	20	10
1677	25q. *Colchicum autumnale* (vert)	55	10
1678	40q. *Borago officinalis*	75	20
1679	80q. *Saponaria officinalis*	1·30	50
1680	2l.20 *Gentiana lutea*	3·75	2·10

347 Revolutionaries

1974. 50th Anniv of 1924 Revolution.

| 1681 | **347** | 25q. mauve, black & red | 55 | 30 |
| 1682 | - | 1l.80 multicoloured | 2·20 | 1·60 |

DESIGN—VERT: 1l.80, Prominent revolutionaries.

348 Redwing

1974. Song Birds. Multicoloured.

1683	10q. Type **348**	20	10
1684	15q. European robin	25	15
1685	20q. Western greenfinch	35	15
1686	25q. Northern bullfinch (vert)	55	20
1687	40q. Hawfinch (vert)	85	25
1688	80q. Blackcap (vert)	2·40	75
1689	2l.20 Nightingale (vert)	4·25	2·10

349 Globe and Post Office Emblem

1974. Centenary of Universal Postal Union. Multicoloured.

| 1690 | **349** | 85q. multicoloured | 1·80 | 85 |
| 1691 | - | 1l.20 green, lilac & violet | 2·75 | 1·30 |

MS1692 78×78 mm. 2l.05 multicoloured. Imperf 25·00 33·00

DESIGNS—Vert: 1l.20, U.P.U. emblem. Square: (70×70 mm.) 2l.50, Text on globe.

350 *Widows* (Sali Shijaku)

1974. Albanian Paintings. Multicoloured.

1693	10q. Type **350**	10	10
1694	15q. *Road Construction* (Danish Jukniu) (vert)	20	10
1695	20q. *Fulfilling the Plans* (Clirim Ceka)	25	10
1696	25q. *The Call to Action* (Spiro Kristo) (vert)	45	20
1697	40q. *The Winter Battle* (Sabaudin Xhaferi)	55	20
1698	80q. *Three Comrades* (Clirim Ceka) (vert)	1·10	50
1699	1l. *Step by Step, Aid the Partisans* (Guri Madhi)	1·60	1·00
1700	1l.20 *At the War Memorial* (Kleo Nini)	2·20	1·30

MS1701 87×78 mm. 2l.05 *Comrades* (Guri Madhi). Imperf 4·00 3·00

351 Chinese Festivities

1974. 25th Anniv of Chinese People's Republic. Multicoloured.

| 1702 | **351** | 85q. multicoloured | 3·50 | 2·10 |
| 1703 | - | 1l.20 black, red and gold | 5·50 | 3·25 |

DESIGN—VERT: 1l.20, Mao Tse-tung.

352 Volleyball

1974. National Spartakiad. Multicoloured.

1704	10q. Type **352**	10	10
1705	15q. Hurdling	10	10
1706	20q. Hoop exercises	15	10
1707	25q. Stadium parade	20	15
1708	40q. Weightlifting	55	20
1709	80q. Wrestling	75	40
1710	1l. Rifle shooting	1·10	45
1711	1l.20 Football	1·60	50

353 Berat

1974. 30th Anniv of Second Berat Liberal Council Meeting.

1712	**353**	25q. red and black	55	30
1713	-	80q. yellow, brown and black	1·60	75
1714	-	1l. purple and black	3·25	1·60

DESIGNS—HORIZ: 80q. "Liberation" frieze. VERT: 1l. Council members walking to meeting.

354 Security Guards patrolling Industrial Plant

1974. 30th Anniv of Liberation. Multicoloured.

1715	25q. Type **354**	15	10
1716	35q. Chemical industry	20	10
1717	50q. Agricultural produce	35	15
1718	80q. Cultural activities	45	25
1719	1l. Scientific technology	85	50
1720	1l.20 Railway construction	1·20	75

MS1721 81×70 mm. 2l.05 Albanians with book (60×40 mm.). Imperf 4·00 3·25

355 Head of Artemis

1974. Archaeological Discoveries. Multicoloured.

1722	**355**	10q. black, mauve & sil	10	10
1723	-	15q. black, green and silver	20	10
1724	-	20q. black, buff & silver	35	20
1725	-	25q. black, mauve & sil	55	40
1726	-	40q. multicoloured	1·10	85
1727	-	80q. black, blue & silver	1·60	1·30
1728	-	1l. black, green & silver	2·20	1·60
1729	-	1l.20 black, sepia & sil	3·75	2·10

MS1730 96×96 mm. 2l.05 multicoloured. Imperf 4·00 3·25

DESIGNS: 15q. Statue of Zeus; 20q. Statue of Poseidon; 25q. Illyrian helmet; 40q. Greek amphora; 80q. Bust of Agrippa; 1l. Bust of Demosthenes; 1l.20, Bust of Bilia. Square: (84×84 mm.) 2l.50, Head of Artemis and Greek vase.

356 Clasped Hands

1975. 30th Anniv of Albanian Trade Unions. Multicoloured

| 1731 | 25q. Type **356** | 55 | 20 |
| 1732 | 1l.80 Workers with arms raised (horiz) | 2·20 | 1·40 |

357 *Cichorium intybus*

1975. Albanian Flowers. Multicoloured.

1733	5q. Type **357**	10	10
1734	10q. *Sempervivum montanum*	10	10
1735	15q. *Aquilegia alpina*	10	10
1736	20q. *Anemone hortensis*	15	10
1737	25q. *Hibiscus trionum*	15	10
1738	30q. *Gentiana kochiana*	20	10
1739	35q. *Lavatera arborea*	55	10
1740	2l.70 *Iris graminea*	3·00	1·90

358 Head of Jesus (detail, Doni Tondo)

1975. 500th Birth Anniv of Michelangelo. Multicoloured

| 1741 | **358** | 5q. multicoloured | 10 | 10 |

1742	-	10q. brown, grey & gold	10	10
1743	-	15q. brown, grey & gold	15	10
1744	-	20q. sepia, grey and gold	20	10
1745	-	25q. multicoloured	20	10
1746	-	30q. brown, grey & gold	20	10
1747	-	1l.20 brn, grey & gold	1·10	65
1748	-	3l.90 multicoloured	2·75	1·90

MS1749 77×86 mm. 2l.05 multicoloured. Imperf 4·50 3·25

DESIGNS: 10q. *The Heroic Captive*; 15q. *Head of Dawn*; 20q. *Awakening Giant* (detail); 25q. *Cumaenian Sybil* (detail, Sistine chapel); 30q. *Lorenzo di Medici*; 1l.20, Head and shoulders of *David*; 3l.90, "Delphic Sybil" (detail, Sistine chapel). 70×77 mm. 2l.05, Head of Michelangelo.

359 Horseman

1975. Albanian Transport of the Past. Multicoloured.

1750	5q. Type **359**	10	10
1751	10q. Horse and cart	15	10
1752	15q. Ferry	25	10
1753	20q. Barque	25	15
1754	25q. Horse-drawn cab	35	15
1755	3l.35 Early car	3·75	1·60

360 Frontier Guard

1975. 30th Anniv of Frontier Force. Multicoloured

| 1756 | 25q. Type **360** | 55 | 30 |
| 1757 | 1l.80 Guards patrolling industrial plant | 2·20 | 1·60 |

361 Patriot affixing Anti-fascist Placard

1975. 30th Anniv of Victory over Fascism. Multicoloured.

1758	25q. Type **361**	35	20
1759	60q. Partisans in battle	75	50
1760	1l.20 Patriot defeating Nazi soldier	1·60	1·00

362 European Wigeon

1975. Albanian Wildfowl. Multicoloured.

1761	5q. Type **362**	10	10
1762	10q. Red-crested pochard	15	10
1763	15q. White-fronted goose	20	10
1764	20q. Pintail	20	10
1765	25q. Red-breasted merganser	35	15
1766	30q. Eider	65	15
1767	35q. Whooper swans	85	20
1768	2l.70 Common shoveler	5·00	2·50

363 *Shyqyri Kanapari* (Musa Qarri)

1975. Albanian Paintings. People's Art Exhibition, Tirana. Multicoloured.

1769	5q. Type 363	10	10
1770	10q. Sea Rescue (Agim Faja)	10	10
1771	15q. 28 November 1912 (Petri Ceno) (horiz)	10	10
1772	20q. Workers' Meeting (Sali Shijaka)	15	10
1773	25q. Shota Galica (Ismail Lulani)	15	10
1774	30q. Victorious Fighters (Nestor Jonuzi)	20	15
1775	80q. Partisan Comrades (Vilson Halimi)	65	40
1776	2l.25 Republic Day Celebration (Fatmir Haxhiu) (horiz)	3·00	2·10
MS1777 68×98 mm. 2l.05 Folk Dance (Abdurahim Buza). Imperf		3·75	3·25

364 Farmer with Declaration of Reform

1975. 30th Anniv of Agrarian Reform. Multicoloured

1778	15q. Type 364	55	30
1779	2l. Agricultural scene	2·75	1·80

365 Dead Man's Fingers

1975. Marine Corals. Multicoloured.

1780	5q. Type 365	10	10
1781	10q. Paramuricea chamaeleon	15	10
1782	20q. Red Coral	20	10
1783	25q. Tube Coral or Sea Fan	35	15
1784	3l.70 Cladocora cespitosa	5·50	2·50

366 Cycling

1975. Olympic Games, Montreal (1976). Multicoloured

1785	5q. Type 366	10	10
1786	10q. Canoeing	10	10
1787	15q. Handball	20	10
1788	20q. Basketball	35	15
1789	25q. Water-polo	45	15
1790	30q. Hockey	55	20
1791	1l.20 Pole vaulting	1·60	85
1792	2l.05 Fencing	2·75	1·60
MS1793 73×77 mm. 2l.15 Games emblem and sportsmen. Imperf		6·50	6·50

367 Power Lines leading to Village

1975. Fifth Anniv of Electrification of Albanian Countryside. Multicoloured.

1794	367	15q. multicoloured	20	10
1795	-	25q. violet, red and lilac	35	20
1796	-	80q. black, turq & green	1·10	50
1797	-	85q. buff, brn & ochre	2·20	1·80

DESIGNS: 25q. High power insulators; 80q. Dam and power station; 85q. T.V. pylons and emblems of agriculture and industry.

368 Berat

1975. Air. Tourist Resorts. Multicoloured.

1798	20q. Type 368	35	20
1799	40q. Gjirokaster	55	20
1800	65q. Sarande	85	30
1801	90q. Durres	1·60	50
1802	1l.20 Krujae	2·20	1·00
1803	2l.40 Boga	4·25	2·10
1804	4l.05 Tirana	6·50	3·75

369 Child, Rabbit and Bear planting Saplings

1975. Children's Tales. Multicoloured.

1805	5q. Type 369	10	10
1806	10q. Mrs. Fox and cub	20	10
1807	15q. Ducks in school	25	10
1808	20q. Bears building	35	10
1809	25q. Animals watching television	45	10
1810	30q. Animals with log and electric light bulbs	50	10
1811	35q. Ants with spade and guitar	55	20
1812	2l.70 Boy and girl with sheep and dog	2·75	1·90

370 Arms and Rejoicing Crowd

1976. 30th Anniv of Albanian People's Republic. Multicoloured.

1813	25q. Type 370	55	30
1814	1l.90 Folk-dancers	3·75	1·60

371 Ice Hockey

1976. Winter Olympic Games, Innsbruck. Multicoloured

1815	5q. Type 371	10	10
1816	10q. Speed skating	15	10
1817	15q. Rifle shooting (biathlon)	20	10
1818	50q. Ski jumping	35	15
1819	1l.20 Skiing (slalom)	1·10	40
1820	2l.30 Bobsleighing	2·00	1·00
MS1821 66×80 mm. 2l.15 Figure skating (pairs)		3·25	2·10

372 Colchicum autumnale

1976. Medicinal Plants. Multicoloured.

1822	5q. Type 372	10	10
1823	10q. Atropa belladonna	15	10
1824	15q. Gentiana lutea	20	10
1825	20q. Aesculus hippocastanum	20	10
1826	70q. Polystichum filix	75	20
1827	80q. Althaea officinalis	1·10	40
1828	2l.30 Datura stamonium	2·75	2·10

373 Wooden Bowl and Spoon

1976. Ethnographical Studies Conference, Tirana. Albanian Artifacts. Multicoloured.

1829	10q. Type 373	10	10
1830	15q. Flask (vert)	15	10
1831	20q. Ornamental handles (vert)	20	10
1832	25q. Pistol and dagger	25	15
1833	80q. Hand-woven rug (vert)	75	30
1834	1l.20 Filigree buckle and earrings	1·10	50
1835	1l.40 Jugs with handles (vert)	2·20	1·40

374 Founding the Co-operatives (Zef Shoshi)

1976. Albanian Paintings. Multicoloured.

1836	5q. Type 374	10	10
1837	10q. Going to Work (Agim Zajmi) (vert)	15	10
1838	20q. Listening to Broadcast (Vilson Kilica) (vert)	20	10
1839	40q. Female Welder (Sabaudin Xhaferi) (vert)	45	20
1840	50q. Steel Workers (Isuf Sulovari) (vert)	85	30
1841	1l.20 1942 Revolt (Lec Shkreli) (vert)	1·10	85
1842	1l.60 Returning from Work (Agron Dine)	1·60	1·00
MS1843 93×79 mm. 2l.05 The Young Pioneer (Andon Lakuriqi)		3·25	2·10

375 Demonstrators attacking Police

1976. 35th Anniv of Hoxha's Anti-fascist Demonstration. Multicoloured.

1844	25q. Type 375	55	20
1845	1l.90 Crowd with flag	3·25	2·10

376 Party Flag, Industry and Agriculture

1976. Seventh Workers' Party Congress. Multicoloured.

1846	25q. Type 376	55	20
1847	1l.20 Hand holding Party symbols, and flag	2·20	1·60

377 Communist Advance

1976. 35th Anniv of Workers' Party. Multicoloured.

1848	15q. Type 377	20	10
1849	25q. Hands holding emblems and revolutionary army	55	30
1850	80q. "Reconstruction"	1·10	50
1851	1l.20 "Heavy Industry and Agriculture"	1·60	1·00
1852	1l.70 "The Arts" (ballet)	2·20	1·60

378 Young Communist

1976. 35th Anniv of Young Communists' Union. Multicoloured.

1853	80q. Type 378	2·10	1·00
1854	1l.25 Young Communists in action	2·75	2·10

379 Ballet Dancers

1976. Albanian Ballet Cuca e Malexe.

1855	379	10q. multicoloured	10	30
1856	-	15q. multicoloured	20	50
1857	-	20q. multicoloured	35	1·00
1858	-	25q. multicoloured	45	2·10
1859	-	80q. multicoloured	1·30	3·25
1860	-	1l.20 multicoloured	1·80	3·75
1861	-	1l.40 multicoloured	2·20	4·25
MS1862 77×67 mm. 2l.05 multicoloured. Imperf			5·00	5·25

DESIGNS: 15q. to 2l.50, Various ballet scenes.

380 Bashtoves Castle

1976. Albanian Castles.

1863	380	10q. black and blue	10	10
1864	-	15q. black and green	15	10
1865	-	20q. black and grey	20	15
1866	-	25q. black and ochre	35	20
1867	-	80q. black, pink and red	1·10	50
1868	-	1l.20 black and blue	1·60	95
1869	-	1l.40 black, red & pink	1·70	1·00

DESIGNS: 15q. Gjirokaster; 20q. All Pash Tepelenes; 25q. Petreles; 80q. Berat; 1l.20, Durres; 1l.40, Krujes.

381 Skanderbeg's Shield and Spear

1977. Crest and Arms of Skanderbeg's Army. Multicoloured

1870	15q. Type 381	2·20	50
1871	80q. Helmet, sword and scabbard	7·50	3·75
1872	1l. Halberd, spear, bow and arrows	12·00	9·50

382 Ilya Oiqi

1977. Albanian Heroes. Multicoloured.

1873	5q. Type 382	10	10
1874	10q. Ilia Dashi	20	20
1875	25q. Fran Ndue Ivanaj	55	30
1876	80q. Zeliha Allmetaj	1·60	50
1877	1l. Ylli Zaimi	1·80	75
1878	1l.90 Isuf Plloci	3·75	1·30

383 Polyvinyl-chloride Plant, Vlore

1977. Sixth Five-year Plan. Multicoloured.

1879	15q. Type 383	35	30
1880	25q. Naphtha plant, Ballsh	55	40
1881	65q. Hydroelectric station, Fjerzes	1·60	85
1882	1l. Metallurgical combinate, Elbasan	2·40	1·00

384 Shote Galica

1977. 50th Death Anniv of Shote Galica (Communist partisan).

1883	**384**	80q. red and pink	1·60	85
1884	-	1l.25 grey and blue	2·40	1·50

DESIGN: 1l.25, Shote Galica and father.

385 Crowd and Martyrs' Monument, Tirana

1977. 35th Anniv of Martyrs' Day. Multicoloured.

1885		25q. Type **385**	55	30
1886		80q. Clenched fist and Albanian flag	1·80	75
1887		1l.20 Bust of Qemal Stafa	3·25	1·60

386 Doctor calling at Village House

1977. Socialist Transformation of Villages. Multicoloured.

1888		5q. Type **386**	10	10
1889		10q. Cowherd with cattle	15	10
1890		20q. Harvesting	20	20
1891		80q. Modern village	1·60	75
1892		2l.95 Tractor and greenhouse	6·00	1·60

387 Workers outside Factory

1977. Eighth Trade Unions Congress. Multicoloured.

1893		25q. Type **387**	55	30
1894		1l.80 Three workers with flags	3·75	2·10

388 Advancing Soldiers

1977. All the People are Soldiers. Multicoloured.

1895		15q. Type **388**	40	20
1896		25q. Enver Hoxha and marching soldiers	55	30
1897		80q. Soldiers and workers	1·60	1·00
1898		1l. The Armed Forces	2·75	2·10
1899		1l.90 Marching soldiers and workers	4·25	3·75

389 Two Girls with Handkerchiefs

1977. National Costume Dances (1st series). Multicoloured

1900		5q. Type **389**	10	10
1901		10q. Two male dancers	15	10
1902		15q. Man and woman in kerchief dance	15	15
1903		25q. Two male dancers (different)	20	15
1904		80q. Two women dancers with kerchiefs	75	40
1905		1l.20 "Elbow dance"	1·10	50
1906		1l.55 Two women with kerchiefs (different)	1·60	1·00
MS1907		56×74 mm. 2l.05 Sabre dance	4·00	3·25

See also Nos. 1932/6 and 1991/5.

390 Armed Worker with Book

1977. New Constitution.

1908	**390**	25q. gold, red and black	55	30
1909	-	1l.20 gold, red and black	2·20	1·00

DESIGN: 1l.20, Industrial and agricultural symbols and hand with book.

391 Beni Ecen Vet

1977. Albanian Films.

1910	**391**	10q. green and grey	20	10
1911	-	15q. multicoloured	35	10
1912	-	25q. green, black & grey	55	30
1913	-	80q. multicoloured	2·20	1·60
1914	-	1l.20 brown and grey	3·25	2·50
1915	-	1l.60 multicoloured	3·75	3·25

DESIGNS: 15q. *Rruge te Bardha*; 25q. *Rrugicat qe Kerkonin Diell*; 80q. *Ne Fillim te Veres*; 1l.20, *Lulekuqet Mbi Mure*; 1l.60, *Zonja nga Qyteti*.

392 Rejoicing Crowd and Independence Memorial, Tirana

1977. 65th Anniv of Independence. Multicoloured.

1916		15q. Type **392**	15	15
1917		25q. Independence leaders marching in Tirana	55	30
1918		1l.65 Albanians dancing under national flag	3·75	2·10

393 Farm Workers

1977. Paintings by V. Mio. Multicoloured.

1919		5q. Type **393**	10	10
1920		10q. *Landscape in the Snow*	10	10
1921		15q. *Sheep under a Walnut Tree, Springtime*	15	10
1922		25q. *Street in Korce*	25	10
1923		65q. *Riders in the Mountains*	65	30
1924		1l. *Boats by the Seashore*	1·10	65
1925		1l.75 *Tractors Ploughing*	1·80	1·30
MS1926		67×102 mm. 2l.05 *Self-portrait*	4·00	3·25

394 Pan Flute

1978. Folk Music Instruments.

1927	**394**	15q. red, black and green	55	30
1928	-	25q. yellow, black & vio	1·10	50
1929	-	80q. red, black and blue	2·75	1·60
1930	-	1l.20 yellow, blk & blue	5·50	3·25
1931	-	1l.70 lilac, black & grn	7·00	7·25

DESIGNS: 25q. Single-string goat's head fiddle; 80q. Trumpet; 1l.20, Drum; 1l.70, Bagpipes.

1978. National Costume Dances (2nd series). As T **389**. Multicoloured.

1932		5q. Girl dancers with scarves	20	10
1933		25q. Male dancers	35	20
1934		80q. Kneeling dancers	85	50
1935		1l. Female dancers	1·10	85
1936		2l.30 Male dancers with linked arms	2·75	2·10

395 Tractor Drivers (D. Trebicka)

1978. Paintings of the Working Class. Multicoloured

1937		20q. Type **395**	20	10
1938		80q. *Steeplejack* (S. Kristo)	55	30
1939		85q. *A Point in the Discussion* (S. Milori)	65	40
1940		90q. *Oil Rig Crew* (A. Cini) (vert)	75	50
1941		1l.60 *Metal Workers* (R. Karanxha)	1·60	1·00
MS1942		73×99 mm. 2l.20 *The Political Discussion* (S. Sholla)	7·50	4·75

396 Boy and Girl

1978. International Children's Day. Multicoloured.

1943		5q. Type **396**	20	10
1944		10q. Boy and girl with pickaxe and rifle	35	20
1945		25q. Children dancing	75	50
1946		1l.80 Classroom scene	4·00	3·25

397 Woman with Pickaxe and Rifle

1978. Eighth Women's Union Congress.

1947	**397**	25q. red and gold	55	30
1948	-	1l.95 red and gold	8·25	5·25

DESIGN: 1l.95, Peasant, Militia Guard and industrial installation.

398 Battle of Mostar Bridge

1978. Centenary of the League of Prizren.

1949	**398**	10q. multicoloured	20	10
1950	-	25q. multicoloured	35	20
1951	-	80q. multicoloured	1·60	1·00
1952	-	1l.20 blue, black & vio	2·20	1·60
1953	-	1l.65 multicoloured	3·25	2·50
1954	-	2l.60 lt grn, blk & grn	5·50	4·75
MS1955		75×69 mm. 2l.20 multicoloured	4·25	4·25

DESIGNS: 25q. Spirit of Skanderbeg; 80q. Albanians marching under national flag; 1l.20, Riflemen; 1l.65, Abdyl Frasheri (founder); 2l.20, League building, crossed rifles, pens and paper; 2l.60, League Headquarters, Prizren.

399 Guerillas and Flag

1978. 35th Anniv of People's Army.

1956		5q. Type **399**	55	30
1957		25q. Men of armed forces (horiz)	1·10	50
1958		1l.90 Men of armed forces, civil guards and Young Pioneers	7·00	6·25

1978. International Fair, Riccione. No. 1832 surch **3.30L. RICCIONE 78 26.8.78.**

1959		3l.30 on 25q. multicoloured	17·00	15·00

401 Man with Target Rifle

1978. 32nd National Shooting Championships.

1960	**401**	25q. black and yellow	35	20
1961	-	80q. black and orange	75	65
1962	-	95q. black and red	1·10	85
1963	-	2l.40 black and red	2·75	2·50

DESIGNS—VERT: 80q. Woman with machine carbine; 2l.40, Pistol shooting. HORIZ: 95q. Shooting from prone position.

402 Kerchief Dance

1978. National Folklore Festival, Gjirokaster. Multicoloured.

1964		10q. Type **402**	10	10
1965		15q. Musicians	15	10
1966		25q. Fiddle player	20	15
1967		80q. Singers	55	30
1968		1l.20 Sabre dance	1·20	75
1969		1l.90 Girl dancers	2·40	1·80

403 Enver Hoxha (after V. Kilica)

1978. Enver Hoxha's 70th Birthday.

1970	**403**	80q. multicoloured	55	30
1971	**403**	1l.20 multicoloured	1·10	50
1972	**403**	2l.40 multicoloured	2·20	1·60
MS1973		68×88 mm. **403** 2l.20 multicoloured	4·25	3·25

404 Woman with Wheatsheaf

1978. Agriculture and Stock Raising. Multicoloured.

1974		15q. Type **404**	55	30
1975		25q. Woman with boxes of fruit	75	50
1976		80q. Shepherd and flock	2·75	2·10
1977		2l.60 Dairymaid and cattle	9·75	7·25

405 Pupils entering School

1978

1978	**405**	5q. brown, lt brn & gold	15	10
1979	-	10q. blue, lt bl & gold	20	10
1980	-	15q. violet, lilac and gold	35	15
1981	-	20q. brown, drab & gold	45	20
1982	-	25q. red, pink and gold	55	30
1983	-	60q. green, lt grn & gold	1·60	50
1984	-	80q. blue, lt blue & gold	2·20	50
1985	-	1l.20 magenta, mauve and gold	3·25	1·00
1986	-	1l.60 blue, lt blue & gold	4·25	1·00
1987	-	2l.40 grn, lt grn & gold	6·50	3·25
1988	-	3l. blue, lt blue & gold	7·50	5·25

DESIGNS: 10q. Telephone, letters, telegraph wires and switchboard operators; 15q. Pouring molten iron; 20q. Dancers, musical instruments, book and artist's materials; 25q. Newspapers, radio, television and broadcasting tower; 60q. Assistant in clothes shop; 80q. Militiamen and women, tanks, ships, aircraft and radar equipment; 1l.20, Industrial complex and symbols of industry; 1l.60, Train and truck; 2l.40, Workers hoeing fields, cattle and girl holding wheat sheaf; 3l. Microscope and nurse holding up baby.

406 Dora D'Istria

1979. 150th Birth Anniv of Dora D'Istria (pioneer of women's rights).

1989	**406**	80q. green and black	1·60	1·00
1990	-	1l.10 grey and black	2·75	2·10

DESIGN: 1l.10, Full-face portrait.

1979. National Costume Dances (3rd series). As T **389**. Multicoloured.

1991	15q. Girl dancers with scarves	35	20
1992	25q. Male dancers	55	30
1993	80q. Girl dancers with scarves (different)	2·20	1·00
1994	1l.20 Male dancers with pistols	2·75	1·60
1995	1l.40 Female dancers with linked arms	3·25	2·10

407 Stone-built Galleried House

1979. Traditional Albanian Houses (1st series). Multicoloured.

1996	15q. Type **407**	20	10
1997	25q. Tower house (vert)	35	15
1998	80q. House with wooden galleries	1·10	50
1999	1l.20 Galleried tower house (vert)	1·60	75
2000	1l.40 Three-storied fortified house (vert)	2·20	1·30
MS2001	62×75 mm. 1l.90 Fortified tower house	8·75	5·25

See also Nos. 2116/19.

408 Aleksander Moissi

1979. Birth Cententary of Aleksander Moissi (actor).

2002	**408**	80q. green, black & gold	1·60	65
2003	-	1l.10 brown, blk & gold	2·20	1·60

DESIGN: 1l.10, Aleksander Moissi (different).

409 Vasil Shanto

1979. Anti-fascist Heroes (1st series). Multicoloured.

2004	15q. Type **409**	25	10
2005	25q. Qemal Stafa	55	30
2006	60q. Type **409**	2·20	1·00
2007	90q. As 25q.	3·25	2·10

See also Nos. 2052/5, 2090/3, 2126/9, 2167/70, 2221/4, 2274/7 and 2313/5.

410 Soldier, Crowd and Coat of Arms

1979. 35th Anniv of Permet Congress. Multicoloured.

2008	25q. Soldier, factories and wheat	1·10	50
2009	1l.65 Type **410**	5·00	2·50

411 Albanian Flag

1979. Fifth Albanian Democratic Front Congress.

2010	**411**	25q. multicoloured	1·10	50
2011	**411**	1l.65 multicoloured	5·00	3·25

412 Ne Stervitje (Arben Basha)

1979. Paintings. Multicoloured.

2012	15q. Type **412**	10	10
2013	25q. Shtigje Lufte (Ismail Lulani)	20	10
2014	80q. Agim me Fitore (Myrteza Fushekati)	1·10	50
2015	1l.20 Gjithe Populli ushtare (Muhamet Deliu)	1·80	75

2016	1l.40 Zjarret Ndezur Mbajme (Jorgji Gjikopulli)	2·20	1·00
MS2017	78×103 mm. 1l.90 Cajime Rrethime (Fatmir Haxhiu)	4·00	3·00

413 Athletes round Party Flag

1979. 35th Anniv of Liberation Spartakiad. Multicoloured.

2018	15q. Type **413**	10	10
2019	25q. Shooting	20	10
2020	80q. Girl gymnast	1·10	50
2021	1l.10 Football	1·60	1·00
2022	1l.40 High jump	1·80	1·30

414 Founder-president

1979. Centenary of Albanian Literary Society.

2023	-	25q. black, brown and gold	35	20
2024	**414**	80q. black, brown and gold	1·10	65
2025	-	1l.20 black, blue & gold	1·60	1·00
2026	-	1l.55 black, vio & gold	2·00	1·30
MS2027	78×66 mm. 1l.90 black, buff and gold		3·75	3·25

DESIGNS: 25q. Foundation document and seal of 1880; 1l.20, Headquarters building, 1979; 1l.55, Headquarters building, 1879; 1l.90, Four founder members, book and quill.

415 Congress Building

1979. 35th Anniv of Berat Congress. Multicoloured.

2028	25q. Arms and congress document	1·40	1·00
2029	1l.65 Type **415**	4·75	3·75

416 Workers and Industrial Complex

1979. 35th Anniv of Liberation. Multicoloured.

2030	25q. Type **416**	35	20
2031	80q. Wheat and hand grasping hammer and pickaxe	1·10	65
2032	1l.20 Open book, star and musical instrument	1·60	1·00
2033	1l.55 Open book, compasses and gear wheel	2·20	1·30

417 Joseph Stalin

1979. Birth Centenary of Joseph Stalin.

2034	**417**	80q. blue and red	1·60	1·00
2035	-	1l.10 blue and red	2·20	1·60

DESIGN: 1l.10, Stalin and Enver Hoxha.

418 Fireplace and Pottery, Korce

1980. Interiors (1st series). Multicoloured.

2036	25q. Type **418**	35	20
2037	80q. Carved bed alcove and weapons, Shkoder	75	50
2038	1l.20 Cooking hearth and carved chair, Mirdite	1·60	1·00
2039	1l.35 Turkish-style chimney, dagger and embroidered jacket, Gjirokaster	2·20	1·60

See also Nos. 2075/8.

419 Lacework

1980. Handicrafts. Multicoloured.

2040	25q. Pipe and flask	35	20
2041	80q. Leather handbags	75	50
2042	1l.20 Carved eagle and embroidered rug	1·60	1·00
2043	1l.35 Type **419**	2·20	1·60

420 Aleksander Xhuvani

1980. Birth Centenary of Dr. Aleksander Xhuvani.

2044	**420**	80q. blue, grey and black	2·20	1·60
2045	**420**	1l. brown, grey and black	2·75	2·10

421 Insurrectionists

1980. 70th Anniv of Kosovo Insurrection.

2046	**421**	80q. black and red	2·20	1·60
2047	-	1l. black and red	3·25	2·50

DESIGN: 1l. Battle scene.

422 Soldiers and Workers helping Stricken Population (D. Jukniu and L. Lulani)

1980. 1979 Earthquake Relief.

2048	**422**	80q. multicoloured	2·20	1·60
2049	**422**	1l. multicoloured	3·25	2·50

423 Lenin

1980. 110th Birth Anniv of Lenin.

2050	**423**	80q. grey, red and pink	2·20	1·60
2051	**423**	1l. multicoloured	3·25	2·50

424 Misto Mame and Ali Demi

1980. Anti-fascist Heroes (2nd series). Multicoloured.

2052	25q. Type **424**	35	20
2053	80q. Sadik Staveleci, Vojo Kushi and Xhoxhi Martini	1·10	75

2054	1l.20 Bule Naipi and Persefoni Kokedhima	1·80	1·00
2055	1l.35 Ndoc Deda, Hydajet Lezha, Naim Gjylbegu, Ndoc Mazi and Ahmet Haxhia	2·20	1·60

425 Mirela

1980. Children's Tales. Multicoloured.

2056	15q. Type **425**	10	10
2057	25q. Shkarravina	20	15
2058	80q. Ariu Artist	1·10	75
2059	2l.40 Pika e Ujit	4·00	3·25

426 The Enver Hoxha Tractor Combine (S. Shijaku and M. Fushekati)

1980. Paintings from Gallery of Figurative Arts, Tirana. Multicoloured.

2060	25q. Type **426**	35	20
2061	80q. The Welder (Harilla Dhima)	1·10	75
2062	1l.20 Steel Erector (Petro Kokushta)	1·80	1·60
2063	1l.35 Harvest Festival (Pandeli Lena)	2·20	1·80
MS2064	65×82 mm. 1l.80 Communists (Vilson Kilica) (48×71 mm)	5·00	5·00

427 Decorated Door (Pergamen miniature)

1980. Art of the Middle Ages. Each black and gold.

2065	25q. Type **427**	35	20
2066	80q. Bird (relief)	75	50
2067	1l.20 Crowned lion (relief)	1·40	1·00
2068	1l.35 Pheasant (relief)	1·60	1·30

428 Divjaka

1980. National Parks. Multicoloured.

2069	80q. Type **428**	1·10	85
2070	1l.20 Lura	1·60	1·30
2071	1l.60 Thethi	2·75	2·30
MS2072	89×90 mm. 1l.80 Llogara (77×80 mm)	5·50	5·50

429 Flag, Arms and rejoicing Albanians

1981. 35th Anniv of Albanian People's Republic. Multicoloured.

2073	80q. Type **429**	1·60	85
2074	1l. Crowd and flags outside People's Party headquarters	2·20	1·00

1981. Interiors (2nd series). Multicoloured.

2075	25q. As T **418**	20	15
2076	80q. Sleeping mats and spirit keg, Labara	65	50
2077	1l.20 Fireplace and covered dish mat	1·30	75
2078	1l.35 Interior and embroidered jacket, Dibres	1·80	1·40

430 Wooden Cot

1981. Folk Art. Multicoloured.

2079	25q. Type **430**	35	20
2080	80q. Bucket and flask	85	75
2081	1l.20 Embroidered slippers	1·20	1·00
2082	1l.35 Jugs	1·50	1·40

431 Footballers

1981. World Cup Football Championship Eliminating Rounds. Multicoloured.

2083	25q. Type **431**	1·30	60
2084	80q. Tackle	3·75	2·20
2085	1l.20 Player kicking ball	5·50	3·75
2086	1l.35 Goalkeeper saving goal	6·75	4·25

432 Rifleman

1981. Cent of Battle of Shtimje. Each purple & red.

2087	80q. Type **432**	1·20	85
2088	1l. Albanian with sabre	1·50	1·00
MS2089	84×68 mm. 1l.80 Albanian with pistol	5·00	5·00

1981. Anti-fascist Heroes (3rd series). As T 424. Multicoloured.

2090	25q. Perlat Rexhepi and Branko Kadia	35	20
2091	80q. Xheladin Beqiri and Hajdah Dushi	1·10	50
2092	1l.20 Koci Bako, Vasil Laci and Mujo Ulqinaku	1·30	1·00
2093	1l.35 Mine Peza and Zoja Cure	2·20	1·30

433 Acrobats

1981. Children's Circus.

2094	-	15q. black, green & stone	15	10
2095	-	25q. black, blue and grey	20	15
2096	**433**	80q. black, mve & pink	65	50
2097	-	2l.40 black, orge & yell	2·20	2·00

DESIGNS: 15q. Monocyclists. 25q. Human pyramid; 2l.40, Acrobats spinning from marquee pole.

434 *Rallying to the Flag, December 1911* (A. Zajmi)

1981. Paintings. Multicoloured.

2098	25q. *Allies* (Sh. Hysa) (horiz)	55	20
2099	80q. *Azem Galica breaking the Ring of Turks* (A. Buza) (horiz)	85	50
2100	1l.20 Type **434**	1·30	1·00
2101	1l.35 *My Flag is my Heart* (L. Cefa)	1·60	1·40
MS2102	81×109 mm. 1l.80 *Unite under the Flag* (N. Vasia) (55×79 mm)	5·00	5·00

435 Weightlifting

1981. Albanian Participation in Inter. Sports. Multicoloured

2103	25q. Rifle shooting	35	20
2104	80q. Type **435**	75	50
2105	1l.20 Volleyball	1·10	85
2106	1l.35 Football	1·30	1·00

436 Flag and Hands holding Pickaxe and Rifle

1981. Eighth Workers' Party Congress.

2107	**436**	80q. red, brown & black	85	65
2108	-	1l. red and black	1·30	1·20

DESIGN: 1l. Party flag, hammer and sickle.

437 Industrial and Agricultural Symbols

1981. 40th Anniv of Workers' Party. Multicoloured.

2109	80q. Type **437**	55	30
2110	2l.80 Albanian flag and hand holding pickaxe and rifle	2·75	2·10
MS2111	79×98 mm. 1l.80 Enver Hoxha and book (50×68 mm)	5·50	5·50

438 Pickaxe, Rifle and Young Communists Flag

1981. 40th Anniv of Young Communists' Union. Multicoloured.

2112	80q. Type **438**	1·30	1·00
2113	1l. Workers' Party flag and Young Communists emblem	2·20	1·90

439 F. S. Noli

1981. Birth Centenary of F. S. Noli (author).

2114	**439**	80q. green and gold	1·40	75
2115	**439**	1l.10 brown and gold	1·80	1·00

1982. Traditional Albanian Houses (2nd series). As T 407, but vert. Multicoloured.

2116	25q. House in Bulqize	35	20
2117	80q. House in Kosovo	1·60	1·00
2118	1l.20 House in Bicaj	2·20	1·60
2119	1l.55 House in Mat	3·00	1·90

440 Map, Globe and Bacillus

1982. Centenary of Discovery of Tubercle Bacillus.

2120	**440**	80q. multicoloured	5·50	2·10
2121	-	1l.10 brown & dp brown	7·50	3·75

DESIGN: 1l.10, Robert Koch (discoverer), microscope and bacillus.

441 *Prizren Castle* (G. Madhi)

1982. Paintings of Kosovo. Multicoloured.

2122	25q. Type **441**	55	30
2123	80q. *House of the Albanian League, Prizren* (K. Buza) (horiz)	1·60	1·30
2124	1l.20 *Mountain Gorge, Rogove* (K. Buza)	2·75	1·60
2125	1l.55 *Street of the Hadhji, Zekes* (G. Madhi)	3·75	2·10

1982. Anti-fascist Heroes (4th series). As T 424. Multicoloured.

2126	25q. Hibe Palikuqi and Liri Gero	55	30
2127	80q. Mihal Duri and Kojo Karafili	1·30	85
2128	1l.20 Fato Dudumi, Margarita Tutulani and Shejnaze Juka	2·00	1·40
2129	1l.55 Memo Meto and Gjok Doci	2·75	1·50

442 Factories and Workers

1982. Ninth Trade Unions Congress. Multicoloured.

2130	80q. Type **442**	3·75	2·20
2131	1l.10 Congress emblem	5·00	3·00

443 Ship in Harbour

1982. Children's Paintings. Multicoloured.

2132	15q. Type **443**	55	20
2133	80q. Forest camp	1·10	75
2134	1l.20 House	1·60	1·30
2135	1l.65 House and garden	3·25	2·00

444 *Village Festival* (Danish Jukniu)

1982. Paintings from Gallery of Figurative Arts, Tirana. Multicoloured.

2136	25q. Type **444**	35	20
2137	80q. *The Hydroelectric Station Builders* (Ali Miruku)	1·30	1·00
2138	1l.20 *Steel Workers* (Clirim Ceka)	1·60	1·30
2139	1l.55 *Oil Drillers* (Pandeli Lena)	2·75	1·60
MS2140	75×90 mm. 1l.90 *First Tapping of the Furnace* (Jorgji Gjikopulli)	5·50	3·75

445 *Voice of the People* (party newspaper)

1982. 40th Anniv of Popular Press. Multicoloured.

2141	80q. Type **445**	£120	£100
2142	1l.10 Hand duplicator producing first edition of *Voice of the People*	£120	£100

446 Heroes of Peza Monument

1982. 40th Anniv of Democratic Front. Multicoloured.

2143	80q. Type **446**	8·25	4·00
2144	1l.10 Peza Conference building and marchers with flag	12·00	5·50

447 Congress Emblem

1982. Eighth Young Communists' Union Congress.

2145	**447**	80q. multicoloured	7·25	4·25
2146	**447**	1l.10 multicoloured	11·50	6·25

448 Tapestry

1982. Handicrafts. Multicoloured.

2147	25q. Type **448**	55	30
2148	80q. Bags (vert)	1·30	75
2149	1l.20 Butter churns	1·80	1·00
2150	1l.55 Jug (vert)	2·75	1·60

449 Freedom Fighters

1982. 70th Anniv of Independence.

2151	**449**	20q. deep red, red & blk	45	30
2152	-	1l.20 black, grn & red	2·20	1·30
2153	-	2l.40 brown, buff and red	4·00	2·50
MS2154		90×89 mm. 1l.90 multicoloured	6·50	4·25

DESIGNS: 20q. Ismail Qemali (patriot) and crowd around building; 2l.40, Six freedom fighters. (58×55 mm) 1l.90, Independence Monument, Tirana.

450 Dhermi

1982. Coastal Views. Multicoloured.

2155	25q. Type **450**	35	20
2156	80q. Sarande	1·10	75
2157	1l.20 Ksamil	1·60	1·00
2158	1l.55 Lukove	2·40	1·60

451 Male Dancers

1983. Folk Dance Assemblies Abroad. Multicoloured

2159	25q. Type **451**	20	10
2160	80q. Male dancers and drummer	75	50
2161	1l.20 Musicians	1·30	1·00
2162	1l.55 Group of female dancers	1·60	1·50

452 Karl Marx

1983. Death Centenary of Karl Marx.

2163	**452**	80q. multicoloured	2·20	1·00
2164	**452**	1l.10 multicoloured	2·75	1·60

453 Electricity Generation

1983. Energy Development.

2165	**453**	80q. blue and orange	1·40	85
2166	-	1l.10 mauve and green	1·80	1·30

DESIGN: 1l.10, Gas and oil production.

1983. Anti-fascist Heroes (5th series). As T 424. Multicoloured.

2167	25q. Asim Zeneli and Nazmi Rushiti	35	20
2168	80q. Shyqyri Ishmi, Shyqyri Alimerko and Myzafer Asqeriu	1·10	50
2169	1l.20 Qybra Sokoli, Qeriba Derri and Ylbere Bilibashi	1·80	1·00
2170	1l.55 Themo Vasi and Abaz Shehu	2·75	1·60

454 Congress Emblem

1983. Ninth Women's Union Congress.
2171	**454**	80q. multicoloured	1·50	1·00
2172	**454**	1l.10 multicoloured	2·00	1·60

455 Cycling

1983. Sport and Leisure. Multicoloured.
2173	25q. Type **455**		35	20
2174	80q. Chess		1·10	50
2175	1l.20 Gymnastics		1·80	1·00
2176	1l.55 Wrestling		2·20	1·40

456 Soldier and Militia

1983. 40th Anniv of People's Army.
2177	**456**	20q. gold and red	35	20
2178	-	1l.20 gold and red	1·80	1·00
2179	-	2l.40 gold and brown	3·25	1·90

DESIGNS: 1l.20, Soldier; 2l.40 Factory guard.

457 Sunny Day (Myrteza Fushekati)

1983. Paintings from Gallery of Figurative Arts, Tirana. Multicoloured.
2180	25q. Type **457**		35	20
2181	80q. *Morning Gossip* (Niko Progri)		1·30	75
2182	1l.20 *29th November, 1944* (Harilla Dhimo)		1·60	1·00
2183	1l.55 *Demolition* (Pandi Mele)		2·20	1·40

MS2184 111×74 mm. 1l.90 *Partisan Assault* (Sali Shijaku and Myrteza Fushekati) (99×59 mm) | 11·00 | 7·50

1983. National Folklore Festival, Gjirokaster. As T **402**. Multicoloured.
2185	25q. Sword dance		25	15
2186	80q. Kerchief dance		1·80	1·00
2187	1l.20 Musicians		2·40	1·60
2188	1l.55 Women dancers with garlands		3·75	2·50

458 Enver Hoxha

1983. 75th Birthday of Enver Hoxha.
2189	**458**	80q. multicoloured	80	65
2190	**458**	1l.20 multicoloured	1·30	1·00
2191	**458**	1l.80 multicoloured	1·80	1·40

MS2192 77×98 mm. 1l.90 multicoloured (as T **458** but with inscriptions differently arranged) | 4·25 | 4·25

459 W.C.Y. Emblem and Globe

1983. World Communications Year.
2193	**459**	60q. multicoloured	75	50
2194	**459**	1l.20 blue, orange & blk	2·00	1·60

460 Combine to Triumph (J. Keraj)

1983. Skanderbeg Epoch in Art. Multicoloured.
2195	25q. Type **460**		55	20
2196	80q. *The Heroic Resistance at Krujes* (N. Bakalli)		1·60	1·00
2197	1l.20 *United we are Unconquerable by our Enemies* (N. Progri)		2·20	1·30
2198	1l.55 *Assembly at Lezhe* (B. Ahmeti)		3·25	1·80

MS2199 77×90 mm. 1l.90 *Victory over the Turks* (G. Madhi) | 8·25 | 7·75

461 Amphitheatre, Butrint (Buthrotum)

1983. Graeco-Roman Remains in Illyria. Multicoloured
2200	80q. Type **461**		2·20	1·60
2201	1l.20 Colonnade, Apoloni Cesma (Apollonium)		2·75	2·10
2202	1l.80 Vaulted gallery of amphitheatre, Dyrrah (Epidamnus)		3·25	2·50

462 Man's Head from Apoloni

1984. Archaeological Discoveries (1st series). Multicoloured
2203	15q. Type **462**		20	15
2204	25q. Tombstone from Korce		35	20
2205	80q. Woman's head from Apoloni		1·30	85
2206	1l.10 Child's head from Tren		1·60	1·00
2207	1l.20 Man's head from Dyrrah		2·00	1·30
2208	2l.20 Bronze statuette of Eros from Dyrrah		3·25	1·60

See also Nos. 2258/61.

463 Clock Tower, Gjirokaster

1984. Clock Towers.
2209	**463**	15q. purple	20	15
2210	-	25q. brown	35	20
2211	-	80q. violet	1·10	75
2212	-	1l.10 red	1·30	1·00
2213	-	1l.20 green	2·00	1·40
2214	-	2l.20 brown	3·25	2·30

DESIGNS: 25q. Kavaje; 80q. Elbasan; 1l.10, Tirana; 1l.20, Peqin; 2l.20, Kruje.

464 Student with Microscope

1984. 40th Anniv of Liberation (1st issue). Multicoloured.
2215	15q. Type **464**		20	15
2216	25q. Soldier with flag		35	20
2217	80q. Schoolchildren		1·30	85
2218	1l.10 Soldier, ships, airplanes and weapons		1·60	1·00
2219	1l.20 Workers with flag		2·00	1·30
2220	2l.20 Armed guards on patrol		3·25	1·60

See also Nos. 2255/6.

1984. Anti-fascist Heroes (6th series). As T **424**. Multicoloured.
2221	15q. Manush Alimani, Mustafa Matohiti and Kastriot Muco		65	20
2222	25q. Zaho Koka, Reshit Collaku and Maliq Muco		1·30	55
2223	1l.20 Lefter Talo, Tom Kola and Fuat Babani		2·40	1·40
2224	2l.20 Myslysm Shyri, Dervish Hekali and Skender Caci		4·25	2·75

465 Enver Hoxha

1984. 40th Anniv of Permet Congress.
2225	**465**	80q. brown, orge & red	3·25	2·10
2226	-	1l.10 black, yell & lilac	4·00	2·50

DESIGN: 1l.10, Resistance fighter (detail of monument).

466 Children reading Comic

1984. Children. Multicoloured.
2227	15q. Type **466**		55	20
2228	25q. Children with toys		1·10	50
2229	60q. Children gardening and rainbow		2·20	1·00
2230	2l.80 Children flying kite bearing Albanian arms		5·00	2·50

467 Football in Goal

1984. European Football Championship Finals. Multicoloured.
2231	15q. Type **467**		1·10	30
2232	25q. Referee and football		1·60	50
2233	1l.20 Football and map of Europe		3·25	1·00
2234	2l.20 Football and pitch		3·75	2·10

468 Freedom is Here (Myrteza Fushekati)

1984. Paintings from Gallery of Figurative Arts, Tirana. Multicoloured.
2235	15q. Type **468**		55	20
2236	25q. *Morning* (Zamir Mati) (vert)		1·10	65
2237	80q. *My Darling* (Agim Zajmi) (vert)		2·75	1·60
2238	2l.60 *For the Partisans* (Arben Basha)		4·25	2·30

MS2239 80×93 mm. 1l.90 *Albania* (Zamir Mati) | 11·00 | 9·00

469 Mulberry

1984. Flowers. Multicoloured.
2240	15q. Type **469**		3·25	85
2241	25q. Plantain		4·25	1·30
2242	1l.20 Hypericum		12·00	4·75
2243	2l.20 Edelweiss		24·00	9·00

470 Sabre Dance

1984. Ausipex 84 International Stamp Exhibition, Melbourne. Sheet 72×88 mm.
MS2244 **470** 1l.90 multicoloured | 4·50 | 4·50

471 Truck driving through Forest

1984. Forestry. Multicoloured.
2245	15q. Type **471**		1·10	65
2246	25q. Transporting logs on overhead cable		1·60	1·00
2247	1l.20 Sawmill in forest		5·50	3·25
2248	2l.20 Lumberjack sawing down trees		8·25	4·50

472 Gjirokaster

1984. Eurphila '84 Int Stamp Exhibition, Rome.
2249	**472**	1l.20 multicoloured	2·75	2·50

473 Football

1984. Fifth National Spartakiad. Multicoloured.
2250	15q. Type **473**		20	15
2251	25q. Running		55	20
2252	80q. Weightlifting		1·10	65
2253	2l.20 Pistol shooting		3·00	2·10

MS2254 70×90 mm. 1l.90 Opening ceremony | 4·25 | 3·50

474 Agriculture and Industry

1984. 40th Anniv of Liberation (2nd issue). Multicoloured.
2255	80q. Type **474**		2·20	1·00
2256	1l.10 Soldiers and flag		2·75	1·60

MS2257 68×89 mm. 1l.90 Enver Hoxha making liberation speech | 5·00 | 4·00

1985. Archaeological Discoveries (2nd series). As T **462**, showing Illyrian finds. Multicoloured.
2258	15q. Pot		55	20
2259	80q. Terracotta head of woman		2·20	1·00
2260	1l.20 Terracotta bust of Aphrodite		2·75	1·40
2261	1l.70 Bronze statuette of Nike		4·25	2·10

476 Kapo (bust)

1985. 70th Birthday of Hysni Kapo (politician).

2262	476	90q. black and red	2·20	1·60
2263	476	1l.10 black and blue	2·75	2·10

477 Running

1985. Olymphile '85 Olympic Stamps Exhibition, Lausanne. Multicoloured.

2264		25q. Type **477**	35	20
2265		60q. Weightlifting	85	65
2266		1l.20 Football	1·60	1·30
2267		1l.50 Pistol shooting	2·75	1·60

478 Bach

1985. 300th Birth Anniv of Johann Sebastian Bach (composer).

2268	**478**	80q. orange, brn & blk	22·00	13·00
2269	-	1l.20 blue, dp blue & blk	27·00	16·00

DESIGN—1l.20, Bach's birthplace, Eisenach.

479 Hoxha

1985. Enver Hoxha Commemoration.

2270	**479**	80q. multicoloured	2·75	2·10
MS2271 67×90 mm. **479** 1l.90 multicoloured			4·25	4·25

480 Frontier Guards

1985. 40th Anniv of Frontier Force. Multicoloured.

2272		25q. Type **480**	1·60	1·00
2273		80q. Frontier guard	3·75	3·25

1985. Anti-fascist Heroes (7th series). As T **424**. Multicoloured.

2274		25q. Mitro Xhani, Nimete Progonati and Kozma Nushi	85	50
2275		40q. Ajet Xhindoli, Mustafa Kacaci and Estref Caka	1·30	1·00
2276		60q. Celo Sinani, Llambro Andoni and Meleo Gosnishti	2·20	1·30
2277		1l.20 Thodhori Mastora, Fejzi Micoli and Hysen Cino	3·75	3·00

481 Scarf on Rifle Barrel

1985. 40th Anniv of V.E. (Victory in Europe) Day. Multicoloured.

2278		25q. Type **481**	33·00	50·00
2279		80q. Crumpled swastika and hand holding rifle butt	85·00	£130

482 Primary School (Thoma Malo)

1985. Paintings from Gallery of Figurative Arts, Tirana. Multicoloured.

2280		25q. Type **482**	35	20
2281		80q. *Heroes and Mother* (Hysen Devolli) (vert)	1·30	1·00

2282		90q. *Mother writing* (Angjelin Dodmasej) (vert)	1·60	1·30
2283		1l.20 *Women off to Work* (Ksenofen Dilo)	2·20	1·80
MS2284 74×88 mm. 1l.90 *Foundry Workers* (Mikel Gurashi)			5·00	3·75

483 Scoring a Goal

1985. Tenth World Basketball Championship, Spain.

2285	**483**	25q. blue and black	25	15
2286	-	80q. green and black	1·30	75
2287	-	1l.20 violet and black	1·80	1·30
2288	-	1l.60 red and black	2·75	2·10

DESIGNS: 80q. Player running with ball; 1l.20, Defending goal; 1l.60, Defender capturing ball.

484 Oranges

1985. Fruit Trees. Multicoloured.

2289		25q. Type **484**	55	30
2290		80q. Plums	2·75	1·60
2291		1l.20 Apples	4·25	2·10
2292		1l.60 Cherries	5·50	3·25

485 Kruja

1985. Architecture.

2293	**485**	25q. black and red	55	30
2294	-	80q. black, grey and brown	2·75	1·60
2295	-	1l.20 black, brown & bl	3·25	2·10
2296	-	1l.60 black, brown & red	4·25	2·50

DESIGNS: 80q. Gjirokastra; 1l.20, Berat; 1l.60, Shkoder.

486 War Horse Dance

1985. National Folklore Festival. Dances.

2297	**486**	25q. brown, red & black	55	30
2298	-	80q. brown, red & black	1·60	1·00
2299	-	1l.20 brown, red & blk	2·20	1·30
2300	-	1l.60 brown, red & blk	2·75	1·80
MS2301 56×82 mm. 1l.90 multicoloured. Imperf			4·25	3·75

DESIGNS: 80q. Pillow dance; 1l.20, Ladies' kerchief dance; 1l.60, Men's one-legged pair dance; 1l.90, Fortress dance.

487 State Arms

1986. 40th Anniv of Albanian People's Republic.

2302	**487**	25q. gold, red and black	1·60	1·00
2303	-	80q. multicoloured	3·25	2·10

DESIGN: 80q. *Comrade Hoxha announcing the News to the People* (Vilson Kilica) and arms.

488 Dam across River Drin

1986. Enver Hoxha Hydroelectric Power Station. Multicoloured.

2304		25q. Type **488**	5·50	2·10
2305		80q. Control building	12·00	7·25

489 *Gymnospermium shqipetarum*

1986. Flowers. Multicoloured.

2306		25q. Type **489**	2·20	1·00
2307		1l.20 *Leucojum valentinum*	8·75	4·25

490 Maksim Gorki (writer)

1986. Anniversaries.

2308	**490**	25q. brown	55	30
2309	-	80q. violet	2·20	1·30
2310	-	1l.20 green	3·75	2·10
2311	-	2l.40 green	7·50	4·75
MS2312 88×72 mm. 1l.90 violet, blue and yellow			5·50	4·25

DESIGNS: 25q. Type **490** (50th death anniv); 80q. Andre Ampere (physicist and mathematician, 150th death anniv); 1l.20, James Watt (inventor, 250th birth); 2l.40, Franz Liszt (composer, death cent). 88×72 mm. 1l.90, Heads of Gorki, Ampere, Watt and Liszt.

1986. Anti-fascist Heroes (8th series). As T **424**. Multicoloured.

2313		25q. Ramiz Aranitasi, Inajete Dumi and Laze Nuro Ferraj	2·20	1·60
2314		80q. Dine Kalenja, Kozma Naska, Met Hasa and Fahri Raalbani	5·50	2·50
2315		1l.20 Hiqmet Buzi, Bajram Tusha, Mumin Selami and Hajredin Bylyshi	8·75	5·25

491 Trophy on Globe

1986. World Cup Football Championship, Mexico. Multicoloured.

2316		25q. Type **491**	55	30
2317		1l.20 Goalkeeper's hands and ball	2·75	2·10
MS2318 97×63 mm. 1l.90 Globefootball (40×32 mm)			4·25	3·25

492 Car Tyre within Ship's Wheel, Diesel Train and Traffic Lights

1986. 40th Anniv of Transport Workers' Day.

2319	**492**	1l.20 multicoloured	14·00	7·75

493 Naim Frasheri (poet)

1986. Anniversaries. Multicoloured.

2320	**493**	30q. Type **493** (140th birth anniv)	75	50
2321		60q. Ndre Mjeda (poet, 120th birth anniv)	1·30	1·00
2322		90q. Petro Nini Luarasi (journalist, 75th death anniv)	2·20	1·60
2323		1l. Andon Zaka Cajupi (poet, 120th birth anniv)	2·75	1·90
2324		1l.20 Millosh Gjergj Nikolla (Migjeni) (revolutionary writer, 75th birth anniv)	3·25	2·30
2325		2l.60 Urani Rumbo (women's education pioneer, 50th death anniv)	8·75	4·25

494 Congress Emblem

1986. Ninth Workers' Party Congress, Tirana.

2326	**494**	30q. multicoloured	11·00	7·75

495 Party Stamp and Enver Hoxha's Signature

1986. 45th Anniv of Workers' Party.

2327	**495**	30q. red, grey and gold	3·25	1·60
2328	-	1l.20 red, orange & gold	8·75	3·75

DESIGNS: 1l.20, Profiles of Marx, Engels, Lenin and Stalin and Tirana house where Party was founded.

496 'Mother Albania'

1986.

2329	496	10q. blue	10	10
2330	496	20q. red	10	10
2331	496	30q. red	10	10
2332	496	50q. brown	20	15
2333	496	60q. green	35	20
2334	496	80q. red	55	30
2335	496	90q. blue	75	50
2336	496	1l.20 green	1·10	75
2337	496	1l.60 purple	1·60	10
2338	496	2l.20 green	2·20	1·60
2339	496	3l. brown	2·75	2·10
2340	496	6l. yellow	5·50	3·75

497 Marble Head of Aesculapius

1987. Archaeological Discoveries (3rd series). Multicoloured.

2341		30q. Type **497**	1·10	65
2342		80q. Terracotta figure of Aphrodite	2·20	1·00
2343		1l. Bronze figure of Pan	3·25	1·50
2344		1l.20 Limestone head of Jupiter	4·25	2·75

498 Monument and Centenary Emblem

1987. Centenary of First Albanian School.

2345	**498**	30q. brown, lt brn & yell	55	30
2346	-	80q. multicoloured	1·60	75
2347	-	1l.20 multicoloured	2·20	1·60

DESIGNS: 80q. First school building; 1l.20, Woman soldier running, girl reading book and boy doing woodwork.

499 Victor Hugo (writer, 185th birth anniv)

1987. Anniversaries.

2348	**499**	30q. vio, lavender & blk	55	30
2349	-	80q. brown, lt brn & blk	1·30	75
2350	-	90q. dp blue, blue & blk	2·00	1·30
2351	-	1l.30 dp grn, grn & brn	2·75	2·10

DESIGNS: 80q. Galileo Galilei (astronomer, 345th death); 90q. Charles Darwin (naturalist, 105th death); 1l.30. Miguel de Cervantes Saavedra (writer, 440th birth).

500 Forsythia europaea

1987. Flowers. Multicoloured.

2352		30q. Type **500**	75	40
2353		90q. Moltkia doerfleri	1·40	1·00
2354		2l.10 Wulfenia baldacii	3·25	2·75

501 Congress Emblem

1987. Tenth Trade Unions Congress, Tirana.

2355	**501**	1l.20 dp red, red & gold	5·50	4·25

502 The Bread of Industry (Myrteza Fushekati)

1987. Paintings from Gallery of Figurative Arts, Tirana. Multicoloured.

2356		30q. Type **502**	55	30
2357		80q. Partisan Gift (Skender Kokobobo)	1·10	85
2358		1l. Sowers (Bujar Asllani) (horiz)	1·60	1·30
2359		1l.20 At the Foundry (Clirim Ceka) (horiz)	2·20	1·90

503 Throwing the Hammer

1987. World Light Athletics Championships, Rome. Multicoloured.

2360		30q. Type **503**	55	30
2361		90q. Running	1·50	1·00
2362		1l.10 Putting the shot	1·60	1·30

MS2363 85×59 mm. 1l.90 Runner, winners' podium and banner (64×24 mm) | 4·25 | 4·25

504 Themistokli Germenji (revolutionary, 70th death)

1987. Anniversaries.

2364	**504**	30q. brown, red & black	35	25
2365	-	80q. red, scarlet & black	1·30	65
2366	-	90q. violet, red and black	1·60	1·00
2367	-	1l.30 green, red & black	2·75	1·90

DESIGNS: 80q. Bajram Curri (organizer of Albanian League, 125th birth); 90q. Aleks Stavre Drenova (poet, 40th death); 1l.30, Gjerasim Qiriazi (educational pioneer, 126th birth).

505 Emblem

1987. Ninth Young Communists' Union Congress, Tirana.

2368	**505**	1l.20 multicoloured	7·00	5·25

506 National Flag

1987. 75th Anniv of Independence.

2369	**506**	1l.20 multicoloured	7·00	5·25

507 Post Office Emblem

1987. 75th Anniv of Albanian Postal Administration. Multicoloured.

2370		90q. Type **507**	7·50	5·25
2371		1l.20 National emblem on bronze medallion	11·00	10·50

508 Lord Byron (writer, bicentenary)

1988. Birth Anniversaries.

2372	**508**	30q. black and orange	5·50	4·25
2373	-	1l.20 black and mauve	22·00	17·00

DESIGN: 1l.20, Eugene Delacroix (painter, 190th anniv.).

509 Oil Derrick, Tap, Houses and Wheat Ears

1988. 40th Anniv of W.H.O.

2374	**509**	90q. multicoloured	30·00	25·00
2375	**509**	1l.20 multicoloured	41·00	33·00

510 Sideritis raeseri

1988. Flowers. Multicoloured.

2376		30q. Type **510**	11·00	6·25
2377		90q. Lunaria telekiana	22·00	14·50
2378		2l.10 Sanguisorba albanica	33·00	21·00

511 Flag and Woman with Book

1988. Tenth Women's Union Congress, Tirana.

2379	**511**	90q. black, red & orange	13·00	10·50

512 Footballers

1988. Eighth European Football Championship, West Germany. Multicoloured.

2380		30q. Type **512**	2·20	1·90
2381		80q. Players jumping for ball	3·25	3·00
2382		1l.20 Tackling	5·50	5·00

MS2383 78×67 mm. 1l.90 Goalkeeper saving ball. Imperf | 13·00 | 13·00

513 Clasped Hands

1988. 110th Anniv of League of Prizren. Multicoloured.

2384		30q. Type **513**	45·00	45·00
2385		1l.20 League Headquarters, Prizren	75·00	75·00

514 Flag, Woman with Rifle and Soldier

1988. 45th Anniv of People's Army. Multicoloured.

2386		60q. Type **514**	45·00	45·00
2387		90q. Army monument, partisans and Labinot house	75·00	75·00

515 Mihal Grameno (writer)

1988. Multicoloured.

2388		30q. Type **515**	16·00	16·00
2389		90q. Bajo Topulli (revolutionary)	27·00	27·00
2390		1l. Murat Toptani (sculptor and poet)	33·00	33·00
2391		1l.20 Jul Variboba (poet)	43·00	43·00

516 Migjeni

1988. 50th Death Anniv of Millosh Gjergj Nikolla (Migjeni) (writer).

2392	**516**	90q. silver and brown	13·00	12·50

517 Dede Skurra

1988. Ballads. Each black and grey.

2393		30q. Type **517**	11·00	8·25
2394		90q. Young Omer	27·00	23·00
2395		1l.20 Gjergj Elez Alia	33·00	26·00

518 Bride wearing Fezzes, Mirdita

1988. National Folklore Festival, Gjirokaster. Wedding Customs. Multicoloured.

2396		30q. Type **518**	33·00	31·00
2397		1l.20 Pan Dance, Gjirokaster	£120	95·00

519 Hoxha

1988. 80th Birth Anniv of Enver Hoxha. Multicoloured.

2398		90q. Type **519**	5·50	5·25
2399		1l.20 Enver Hoxha Museum (horiz)	8·25	7·75

520 Detail of Congress Document

1988. 80th Anniv of Monastir Language Congress. Multicoloured.

2400		60q. Type **520**	27·00	23·00
2401		90q. Alphabet book and Congress building	43·00	37·00

521 Steam Locomotive and Map showing 1947 Railway Line

1989. Railway Locomotives. Multicoloured.

2402		30q. Type **521**	45	10
2403		90q. Polish steam locomotive and map of 1949 network	1·30	50
2404		1l.20 Diesel locomotive and 1978 network	1·70	85
2405		1l.80 Diesel locomotive and 1985 network	2·50	1·00
2406		2l.40 Czechoslovakian diesel-electric locomotive and 1988 network	5·00	2·10

522 Entrance to Two-storey Tomb

1989. Archaeological Discoveries in Illyria.

2407	**522**	30q. black, brown & grey	35	10
2408	-	90q. black and green	1·30	1·00
2409	-	2l.10 multicoloured	2·20	1·90

DESIGNS: 90q. Buckle showing battle scene; 2l.10, Earring depicting head.

523 Mother mourning Son

1989. Kostandini and Doruntina (folk tale). Multicoloured.

2410		30q. Type **523**	55	30
2411		80q. Mother weeping over tomb and son rising from dead	1·10	75
2412		1l. Son and his sister on horseback	1·30	1·00
2413		1l.20 Mother and daughter reunited	1·60	1·30

524 *Aster albanicus*

1989. Flowers. Multicoloured.
2414	30q. Type **524**	35	10
2415	90q. *Orchis paparisti*	1·30	1·00
2416	2l.10 *Orchis albanica*	2·20	1·90

525 Johann Strauss
(composer, 90th
death anniv)

1989. Anniversaries. Each brown and gold.
2417	30q. Type **525**	55	20
2418	80q. Marie Curie (physicist, 55th death anniv)	1·10	75
2419	1l. Federico Garcia Lorca (writer, 53rd death anniv)	1·60	1·30
2420	1l.20 Albert Einstein (physicist, 110th birth anniv)	2·20	1·80

526 State Arms, Workers'
Party Flag and Crowd

1989. Sixth Albanian Democratic Front Congress, Tirana.
2421	**526** 1l.20 multicoloured	9·75	5·25

527 Storming of the Bastille

1989. Bicentenary of French Revolution. Multicoloured
2422	90q. Type **527**	75	50
2423	1l.20 Monument	1·40	85

528 Galley

1989. Ships.
2424	**528** 30q. green and black	55	20
2425	- 80q. blue and black	1·00	75
2426	- 90q. blue and black	1·10	95
2427	- 1l.30 lilac and black	1·60	1·40

DESIGNS: 80q. Kogge; 90q. Schooner; 1l.30, *Tirana* (freighter).

529 Pjeter Bogdani
(writer, 300th
anniv)

1989. Death Anniversaries. Multicoloured.
2428	30q. Type **529**	20	15
2429	80q. Gavril Dara (writer, centenary)	75	50
2430	90q. Thimi Mitko (writer, centenary (1990))	1·40	85
2431	1l.30 Kole Idromeno (painter, 50th anniv)	2·00	1·00

530 Engels, Marx
and Marchers

1989. 125th Anniv of First International. Multicoloured.
2432	90q. Type **530**	1·10	50
2433	1l.20 Factories, marchers and worker with pickaxe and rifle	1·60	75

531 Gymnastics

1989. Sixth National Spartakiad.
2434	**531** 30q. black, orange & red	35	10
2435	- 80q. black, lt grn & grn	75	50
2436	- 1l. black, blue & dp blue	85	65
2437	- 1l.20 black, pur & red	1·30	1·00

DESIGNS: 80q. Football; 1l. Cycling; 1l.20, Running.

532 Soldier

1989. 45th Anniv of Liberation. Multicoloured.
2438	30q. Type **532**	55	20
2439	80q. Date	1·00	50
2440	1l. State arms	1·10	75
2441	1l.20 Young couple	1·60	1·30

533 Chamois

1990. Endangered Animals. The Chamois. Multicoloured.
2442	10q. Type **533**	35	10
2443	30q. Mother and young	75	30
2444	80q. Chamois keeping lookout	2·10	1·00
2445	90q. Head of chamois	2·20	1·30

534 Eagle Mask

1990. Masks. Multicoloured.
2446	30q. Type **534**	35	10
2447	90q. Sheep	75	50
2448	1l.20 Goat	1·10	75
2449	1l.80 Stork	1·60	1·00

535 Caesar's Mushroom

1990. Fungi. Multicoloured.
2450	30q. Type **535**	35	20
2451	90q. Parasol mushroom	85	50
2452	1l.20 Cep	1·40	1·20
2453	1l.80 *Clathrus cancelatus*	2·00	1·60

536 Engraving Die

1990. 150th Anniv of the Penny Black. Multicoloured.
2454	90q. Type **536**	75	50
2455	1l.10 Mounted postal messenger	1·10	85
2456	1l.80 Mail coach passengers reading letters	2·20	1·80

537 Mascot and Flags

1990. World Cup Football Championship, Italy. Multicoloured.
2457	30q. Type **537**	35	15
2458	90q. Mascot running	75	50
2459	1l.20 Mascot preparing to kick ball	1·30	1·00
MS2460	80×62 mm. 3l.30 Mascot as goalkeeper. Imperf	3·75	3·75

538 Young Van Gogh and
Paintings

1990. Death Centenary of Vincent van Gogh (painter). Multicoloured.
2461	30q. Type **538**	45	20
2462	90q. Van Gogh and woman in field	85	50
2463	2l.10 Van Gogh in asylum	2·00	1·60
MS2464	88×73 mm. 2l.40 Van Gogh and *Wheatfield with Crows*. Imperf	3·25	3·25

539 Gjergj Elez Alia lying Wounded

1990. Gjergj Elez Alia (folk hero). Multicoloured.
2465	30q. Type **539**	35	20
2466	90q. Alia being helped onto horse	75	50
2467	1l.20 Alia fighting Bajloz	1·10	85
2468	1l.80 Alia on horseback and severed head of Bajloz	1·60	1·00

540 Mosque

1990. 2400th Anniv of Berat. Multicoloured.
2469	30q. Type **540**	10	10
2470	90q. Triadha's Church	60	40
2471	1l.20 River	70	50
2472	1l.80 Onufri (artist)	1·20	95
2473	2l.40 Nikolla	1·40	1·20

541 Pirrroja

1990. Illyrian Heroes. Each black.
2474	30q. Type **541**	20	10
2475	90q. Teuta	65	40
2476	1l.20 Bato	75	50
2477	1l.80 Bardhyli	1·10	85

542 School and Globe
of Books

1990. International Literacy Year.
2478	542 90q. multicoloured	75	50
2479	542 1l.20 multicoloured	1·10	85

543 *Albanian Horsemen*
(Eugene Delacroix)

1990. Albanians in Art. Multicoloured.
2480	30q. Type **543**	35	10
2481	1l.20 *Albanian Woman* (Camille Corot)	1·00	75
2482	1l.80 *Skanderbeg* (anon)	1·40	1·20

544 Boletini

1991. 75th Death Anniv of Isa Boletini (revolutionary). Multicoloured.
2483	90q. Type **544**	65	40
2484	1l.20 Boletini and flag	1·00	75

545 Armorial Eagle

1991. 800th Anniv (1990) of Founding of Arberi State.
2485	**545** 90q. multicoloured	65	50
2486	**545** 1l.20 multicoloured	1·00	75

546 *Woman reading*

1991. 150th Birth Anniv of Pierre Auguste Renoir (artist). Multicoloured.
2487	30q. Type **546**	55	10
2488	90q. *The Swing*	85	75
2489	1l.20 *The Boat Club* (horiz)	1·30	1·00
2490	1l.80 Still life (detail) (horiz)	2·20	1·80
MS2491	94×75 mm. 3l. *Portrait of Artist with Beard*. Imperf	4·25	4·25

547 *Cistus
albanicus*

1991. Flowers. Multicoloured.
2492	30q. Type **547**	35	10
2493	90q. *Trifolium pilczii*	85	75
2494	1l.80 *Lilium albanicum*	1·60	1·30

548 Rozafa
breastfeeding Child

1991. Imprisonment of Rozafa (folk tale). Multicoloured.

2495	30q. Type **548**	20	10
2496	90q. The three brothers talking to old man	65	50
2497	1l.20 Building of walls around Rozafa	1·10	75
2498	1l.80 Figures symbolizing water flowing between stones	1·50	1·20

549 Mozart
conducting

1991. Death Bicentenary of Wolfgang Amadeus Mozart (composer). Multicoloured.

2499	90q. Type **549**	75	50
2500	1l.20 Mozart and score	1·20	85
2501	1l.80 Mozart composing	2·10	1·50
MS2502	88×69 mm. 3l. Mozart medallion and score. Imperf	6·50	6·50

550 Vitus Bering

1992. Explorers. Multicoloured.

2503	30q. Type **550**	35	20
2504	90q. Christopher Columbus and his flagship *Santa Maria*	75	40
2505	1l.80 Ferdinand Magellan and his flagship *Vitoria*	1·60	95

551 Otto Lilienthal's Biplane
Glider, 1896

1992. Aircraft.

2506	**551**	30q. black, red and blue	35	20
2507	-	80q. multicoloured	55	40
2508	-	90q. multicoloured	75	65
2509	-	1l.20 multicoloured	1·00	85
2510	-	1l.80 multicoloured	1·30	1·20
2511	-	2l.40 black, grey & mve	1·60	1·50

DESIGNS: 80q. Clement Ader's *Avion III*, 1897; 90q. Wright Brothers' Type A, 1903; 1l.20, Concorde supersonic jetliner; 1l.80, Tupolev Tu-144 jetliner (wrongly inscr '114'); 2l.40, Dornier Do-31E (wrongly inscr 'Dernier').

552 Ski Jumping

1992. Winter Olympic Games, Albertville. Multicoloured.

2512	30q. Type **552**	35	20
2513	90q. Skiing	75	65
2514	1l.20 Ice skating (pairs)	1·10	85
2515	1l.80 Luge	1·60	1·40

553 'Europe' and Doves

1992. Admission of Albania to European Security and Co-operation Conference at Foreign Ministers' Meeting, Berlin. Multicoloured.

2516	90q. Type **553**	1·20	1·00
2517	1l.20 Members' flags and map of Europe	1·50	1·30

554 Envelopes and Emblem

1992. Admission of Albania to E.P.T. Conference. Multicoloured.

2518	90q. Type **554**	1·30	1·20
2519	1l.20 Emblem and tape reels	1·60	1·50

555 Everlasting Flame

1992. National Martyrs' Day. Multicoloured.

2520	90q. Type **555**	70	65
2521	4l.10 Poppies (horiz)	3·25	2·75

556 Pictograms

1992. European Football Championship, Sweden.

2522	**556**	30q. light green & green	60	30
2523	-	90q. red and blue	1·20	75
2524	-	1l.80 ochre and brown	7·00	5·25
MS2525	90×69 mm. 5l. pink, ochre and green. Imperf		4·00	4·00

DESIGNS: 90q. to 5l., Different pictograms.

557 Lawn Tennis

1992. Olympic Games, Barcelona. Multicoloured.

2526	30q. Type **557**	45	20
2527	90q. Baseball	1·40	85
2528	1l.80 Table tennis	2·75	1·90
MS2529	89×69 mm. 5l. Torch bearer and running tracks. Imperf	4·75	4·75

558 Map and Doves

1992. European Unity.

2530	**558**	1l.20 multicoloured	1·40	1·00

559 Native Pony

1992. Horses. Multicoloured.

2531	30q. Type **559**	35	20
2532	90q. Hungarian nonius	60	40
2533	1l.20 Arab (vert)	80	65
2534	10l.60 Haflinger (vert)	7·50	6·00

560 Map of Americas,
Columbus and Ships

1992. Europa. 500th Anniv of Discovery of America by Columbus. Multicoloured.

2535	60q. Type **560**	60	40
2536	3l.20 Map of Americas and Columbus meeting Amerindians	4·00	3·75
MS2537	90×70 mm. 5l. Map of America and Columbus. Imperf	85·00	85·00

561 Mother
Teresa and Child

1992. Mother Teresa (Agnes Gonxhe Bojaxhi) (founder of Missionaries of Charity).

2538	**561**	40q. red	10	10
2539	**561**	60q. brown	10	10
2540	**561**	1l. violet	10	10
2541	**561**	1l.80 grey	15	10
2542	**561**	2l. red	35	20
2543	**561**	2l.40 green	45	30
2544	**561**	3l.20 blue	60	50
2545	**561**	5l. violet	70	65
2546	**561**	5l.60 purple	95	85
2547	**561**	7l.20 green	1·20	1·00
2548	**561**	10l. orange	1·40	1·30
2549	**561**	18l. orange	1·50	1·40
2550	**561**	20l. purple	60	50
2551	**561**	25l. green	2·30	2·10
2552	**561**	60l. green	2·50	2·40

562 Pope John
Paul II

1993. Papal Visit.

2555	**562**	16l. multicoloured	3·00	2·50

1993. Nos. 2329/32 and 2335 surch **POSTA SHQIPTARE** and new value.

2556	**496**	3l. on 10q. blue	25	20
2557	**496**	6l.50 on 20q. red	80	75
2558	**496**	13l. on 30q. red	2·30	2·10
2559	**496**	20l. on 90q. blue	3·50	3·25
2560	**496**	30l. on 50q. brown	5·25	4·75

564 Lef Nosi (first Postal
Minister)

1993. 80th Anniv of First Albanian Stamps.

2561	**564**	6l.50 brown and green	1·20	1·00

565 *Life Weighs
Heavily on Man* (A.
Zajmi)

1993. Europa. Contemporary Art. Multicoloured.

2562	**565**	3l. Type **565**	1·20	1·00
2563		7l. *The Green Star* (E. Hila) (horiz)	4·75	4·25
MS2564	116×121 mm. 20l. *Gjirokaster* (B. Ahmeti). Imperf		8·25	8·25

566 Running

1993. Mediterranean Games, Agde and Roussillon (Languedoc), France. Multicoloured.

2565	3l. Type **566**	25	20
2566	16l. Canoeing	2·30	2·10
2567	21l. Cycling	3·25	3·00
MS2568	117×84 mm. 20l. Map of Mediterranean. Imperf	4·00	4·00

567 Bardhi

1993. 350th Death Anniv of Frang Bardhi (scholar).

2569	**567**	6l.50 brown and stone	1·40	1·30
MS2570	94×107 mm. 20l. brown and gold. Imperf		4·75	4·75

DESIGN: 20l. Bardhi writing at desk.

568 Mascot and
Flags around
Stadium

1994. World Cup Football Championship, U.S.A. Multicoloured.

2571	42l. Type **568**	1·40	1·30
2572	68l. Mascot kicking ball	2·10	1·90

569 Gjovalin Gjadri
(construction
engineer)

1994. Europa. Discoveries and Inventions.

2573	**569**	50l. dp brn, ches & brn	2·30	2·10
2574	-	100l. dp brn, ches & brn	3·50	3·25
MS2575	60×80 mm. 150l. drab and brown. Imperf		5·75	5·75

DESIGN: 100l. Karl Ritter von Ghega (railway engineer); 150l. Sketch of traffic project.

570 Emblem and Benz

1995. 150th Birth Anniv (1994) of Karl Benz (motor manufacturer). Multicoloured.

2576	5l. Type **570**	10	10
2577	10l. Mercedes-Benz C-class saloon, 1995 Daimler motor carriage, 1886	25	20
2578	60l. First four-wheel Benz motor-car, 1886	1·40	1·30
2579	125l. Mercedes-Benz 540 K cabriolet, 1936	4·00	3·75

571 Richard
Wagner

1995. Composers. Each brown and gold.

2580	3l. Type **571**	10	10
2581	6l.50 Edvard Grieg	25	20
2582	11l. Charles Gounod	35	30
2583	20l. Pyotr Tchaikovsky	80	75

572 Intersections

1995. 50th Anniv (1994) of Liberation.
2584	**572**	50l. black and red	1·70	1·60

573 Ali Pasha

1995. 250th Birth Anniv (1994) of Ali Pasha of Tepelene (Pasha of Janina, 1788–1820).
2585	**573**	60l. black, yellow & brn	2·00	1·80
MS2586 80×60 mm. 100l. brown and orange (Administration building, Tepelene). Imperf			3·50	3·50

574 Veskopoja, 1744
(left half)

1995. 250th Anniv (1994) of Veskopoja Academy. Multicoloured.
2587	**574**	42l. Type **574**	1·20	1·00
2588		68l. Veskopoja, 1744 (right half)	1·70	1·60

Nos. 2587/8 were issued together, *se-tenant*, forming a composite design.

575 Olympic Rings and Map

1995. Centenary of International Olympic Committee. Sheet 60×80 mm. Imperf.
MS2589 **575** 80l. multicoloured		2·50	2·50

576 Palace of Europe, Strasbourg

1995. Admission of Albania to Council of Europe. Multicoloured.
2590	**576**	25l. Type **576**	95	85
2591		85l. State arms and map of Europe	3·75	3·25

577 Hands holding Olive Branch

1995. Europa. Peace and Freedom. Multicoloured.
2592	**577**	50l. Type **577**	2·30	2·10
2593		100l. Dove flying over hands	4·75	4·25
MS2594 80×60 mm. 150l. Figure stretching out hands. Imperf			7·00	7·00

578 Mice sitting around Table and Stork with Fox

1995. 300th Death Anniv of Jean de La Fontaine (writer). Multicoloured.
2595		2l. Type **578**	15	10
2596		3l. Stork with foxes around table	25	10
2597		25l. Frogs under tree	95	85
MS2598 80×60 mm. 60l. La Fontaine and animals. Imperf			2·30	2·30

579 Bee on Flower

1995. The Honey Bee. Multicoloured.
2599		5l. Type **579**	25	10
2600		10l. Bee and honeycomb	35	20
2601		25l. Bee on comb	1·60	1·30

580 Fridtjof Nansen

1995. Polar Explorers. Multicoloured.
2602		25l. Type **580**	80	70
2603		25l. James Cook	80	70
2604		25l. Roald Amundsen	80	70
2605		25l. Robert Scott	80	70

Nos. 2602/5 were issued together, *se-tenant*, forming a composite design.

581 Flags outside U.N. Building, New York

1995. 50th Anniv of U.N.O. Multicoloured.
2606		2l. Type **581**	25	10
2607		100l. Flags flying to right outside U.N. building, New York	3·25	3·00

582 Male Chorus

1995. National Folklore Festival, Berat. Multicoloured.
2608		5l. Type **582**	35	20
2609		50l. Female participant	1·70	1·60

583 Poet

1995. Jan Kukuzeli (11th-century poet, musician and teacher). Abstract representations of Kukuzeli. Multicoloured.
2610		18l. Type **583**	70	65
2611		20l. *Musician*	75	70
MS2612 80×80 mm. 100l. *Teacher.* Imperf			3·50	3·50

584 Church and Preacher, Berat Kruje

1995. 20th Anniv of World Tourism Organization. Multicoloured.
2613		18l. Type **584**	70	65
2614		20l. Street, Shkoder	80	75
2615		42l. Buildings, Gjirokaster	2·00	1·80

585 Paul Eluard

1995. Poets' Birth Centenaries. Multicoloured.
2616		25l. Type **585**	80	75
2617		50l. Sergei Yessenin	1·60	1·50

586 Louis, Film Reel and Projector

1995. Centenary of Motion Pictures. Lumiere Brothers (developers of cine camera). Multicoloured
2618		10l. Type **586**	25	20
2619		85l. Auguste, film reel and cinema audience	2·30	2·10

587 Presley

1995. 60th Birth Anniv of Elvis Presley (entertainer). Multicoloured.
2620		3l. Type **587**	25	20
2621		60l. Presley (different)	2·10	1·90

588 Banknotes of 1925

1995. 70th Anniv of Albanian National Bank. Multicoloured
2622		10l. Type **588**	35	20
2623		25l. Modern banknotes	95	85

589 '5', Crumbling Star, Open Book and Peace Dove

1995. Fifth Anniv of Democratic Movement. Multicoloured
2624		5l. Type **589**	25	10
2625		50l. Woman planting tree	1·90	1·70

590 Mother Teresa

1996. Europa. Famous Women. Mother Teresa (founder of Missionaries of Charity).
2626	**590**	25l. multicoloured	1·20	1·00
2627	**590**	100l. multicoloured	4·00	3·75
MS2628 60×80 mm. 150l. Mother Teresa (different). Imperf			8·25	8·25

591 Football, Union Flag, Map of Europe and Stadium

1996. European Football Championship, England. Multicoloured.
2629	**591**	25l. Type **591**	95	85
2630		100l. Map of Europe, ball and player	3·75	3·25

592 Satellite and Radio Mast

1996. Inauguration of Cellular Telephone Network. Multicoloured.
2631		10l. Type **592**	35	20
2632		60l. User, truck, container ship and mobile telephone (vert)	2·00	1·80

593 Running

1996. Olympic Games, Atlanta, U.S.A. Multicoloured.
2633		5l. Type **593**	25	10
2634		25l. Throwing the hammer	95	85
2635		60l. Long jumping	2·30	2·10
MS2636 60×80 mm. 100l. Games emblem. Imperf			3·00	3·00

594 Linked Hands

1996. 75th Anniv of Albanian Red Cross.
2637	**594**	50l.+10l. mult	2·10	1·90

595 Gottfried Wilhelm Leibniz (350th)

1996. Philosopher and Mathematicians' Birth Anniversaries. Multicoloured.
2638		10l. Type **595**	60	40
2639		85l. Rene Descartes (400th)	3·00	2·50

596 The Naked Maja

1996. 250th Birth Anniv of Francisco de Goya (artist). Multicoloured.
2640		10l. Type **596**	60	40
2641		60l. *Dona Isabel Cobos de Porcel*	2·10	1·90
MS2642 80×60 mm. 100l. *Self-portrait* (24×29 mm)			3·00	3·00

597 Book Binding

1996. Christian Art Exhibition. Multicoloured.

2643	5l. Type **597**	25	10
2644	25l. Book clasp showing crucifixion	95	85
2645	85l. Book binding (different)	3·00	2·50

598 Princess

1996. 50th Anniv of UNICEF Children's Paintings. Multicoloured.

2646	5l. Type **598**	25	10
2647	10l. Woman	35	20
2648	25l. Sea life	1·20	1·00
2649	50l. Harbour	1·70	1·60

599 State Arms, Book and Fishta

1996. 125th Birth Anniv of Gjergj Fishta (writer and politician). Multicoloured.

2650	10l. Type **599**	35	20
2651	60l. Battle scene and Fishta	2·00	1·80

600 Omar Khayyam and Writing Materials

1997. 950th Birth Anniv of Omar Khayyam (astronomer and poet). Multicoloured.

2652	20l. Type **600**	60	40
2653	50l. Omar Khayyam and symbols of astronomy	1·40	1·30

Nos. 2652/3 are inscribed '850' in error.

601 Gutenberg

1997. 600th Birth Anniv of Johannes Gutenberg (printer). Multicoloured.

2654	20l. Type **601**	60	40
2655	60l. Printing press	1·70	1·60

Nos. 2654/5 were issued together, *se-tenant*, forming a composite design.

602 Pelicans

1997. The Dalmatian Pelican. Multicoloured.

2656	10l. Type **602**	25	20
2657	80l. Pelicans on shore and in flight	2·30	2·10

Nos. 2656/7 were issued together, *se-tenant*, forming a composite design.

603 Dragon

1997. Europa. Tales and Legends. The Blue Pool. Multicoloured.

2658	30l. Type **603**	1·20	1·00
2659	100l. Dragon drinking from pool	4·00	3·75

604 Konica

1997. 55th Death Anniv of Faik Konica (writer and politician).

2660	**604**	10l. brown and black	35	20
2661	**604**	25l. blue and black	1·00	95
MS2662		60×80 mm. **604** 80l. brown	3·00	3·00

605 Male Athlete

1997. Mediterranean Games, Bari. Multicoloured.

2663	20l. Type **605**	60	40
2664	30l. Female athlete and rowers	1·20	1·00
MS2665	60×80 mm. 100l. Discus-thrower, javelin-thrower and runner. Imperf	3·00	3·00

606 Skanderbeg

1997

2666	**606**	5l. red and brown	25	10
2667	**606**	10l. green and olive	35	25
2668	**606**	20l. green and deep green	65	50
2669	**606**	25l. mauve and purple	75	65
2670	**606**	30l. violet and lilac	95	80
2671	**606**	50l. grey and black	1·50	1·30
2672	**606**	60l. lt brown & brown	1·80	1·60
2673	**606**	80l. lt brown & brown	2·40	2·20
2674	**606**	100l. red and lake	3·00	2·75
2675	**606**	110l. blue and deep blue	3·25	3·00

1997. Mother Teresa (founder of Missionaries of Charity) Commemoration. No. 2627 optd **HOMAZH 1910–1997**.

2676	**590**	100l. multicoloured	4·00	3·50

608 Codex Aureus (11th century)

1997. Codices (1st series). Multicoloured.

2677	10l. Type **608**	25	10
2678	25l. Codex Purpureus Beratinus (7th century) showing mountain and scribe	70	65
2679	60l. Codex Purpureus Beratinus showing church and scribe	1·60	1·50

See also Nos. 2712/14.

609 Twin-headed Eagle (postal emblem)

1997. 85th Anniv of Albanian Postal Service.

2680	**609**	10l. multicoloured	25	10
2681	**609**	30l. multicoloured	95	85

The 30l. differs from Type **609** in minor parts of the design.

610 Nikete of Ramesiana

1998. Nikete Dardani, Bishop of Ramesiana (philosopher and composer).

2682	**610**	30l. multicoloured	70	50
2683	**610**	100l. multicoloured	2·20	2·00

There are minor differences of design between the two values.

611 Man sitting at Table

1998. Legend of Pogradeci Lake. Multicoloured.

2684	30l. Type **611**	70	50
2685	50l. The Three Graces	1·00	85
2686	60l. Women drawing water	1·30	1·20
2687	80l. Man of ice	1·70	1·60

612 Stylized Dancers

1998. Europa. National Festivals. Multicoloured.

2688	60l. Type **612**	2·30	2·10
2689	100l. Female dancer	3·00	2·50
MS2690	60×80 mm. 150l. Two dancers. Imperf	5·25	5·25

613 Abdyl Frasheri (founder)

1998. 120th Anniv of League of Prizren. Multicoloured

2691	30l. Type **613**	70	50
2692	50l. Sulejman Vokshi and partisan	1·00	85
2693	60l. Iljaz Pashe Dibra and crossed rifles	1·30	1·20
2694	80l. Ymer Prizreni and partisans	1·70	1·60

614 Player with Ball

1998. World Cup Football Championship, France. Multicoloured.

2695	60l. Type **614**	1·30	1·20
2696	100l. Player with ball (different)	2·20	2·00
MS2697	60×80 mm. 120l. Championship mascot. Imperf	3·00	3·00

615 Wrestlers in National Costume

1998. European Junior Wrestling Championship. Multicoloured.

2698	30l. Type **615**	60	40
2699	60l. Ancient Greek wrestlers	1·30	1·20

616 Cacej

1998. 90th Birth Anniv of Eqerem Cabej (linguist).

2700	**616**	60l. black and yellow	80	65
2701	**616**	80l. yellow, black & red	1·20	1·00

617 Diana, Princess of Wales

1998. Diana, Princess of Wales Commemoration. Multicoloured.

2702	60l. Type **617**	1·70	1·60
2703	100l. With Mother Teresa	2·30	2·10

618 Mother Teresa holding Child

1998. Mother Teresa (founder of Missionaries of Charity) Commemoration. Multicoloured.

2704	60l. Type **618**	1·40	1·30
2705	100l. Mother Teresa (vert)	2·30	2·10

619 Detail of Painting

1998. 150th Birth Anniv of Paul Gauguin (artist). Multicoloured.

2706	60l. Type **619**	1·20	1·00
2707	80l. *Women of Tahiti*	1·60	1·50
MS2708	60×80 mm. 120l. Face. Imperf	3·00	3·00

620 Epitaph

1998. 625th Anniv of Epitaph of Gllavenica (embroidery of dead Christ). Multicoloured.

2709	30l. Type **620**	60	40
2710	80l. Close-up of upper body	1·60	1·50
MS2711	80×60 mm. 100l. Detail of epitaph (24×29 mm)	2·00	2·00

621 Page of Codex

1998. Codices (2nd series). 11th-century Manuscripts. Multicoloured.

2712	30l. Type **621**	60	40
2713	50l. Front cover of manuscript	95	75
2714	80l. Page showing mosque	1·60	1·50

1998. Italia '98 International Stamp Exhibition. No. **MS**2628 optd **Italia 98**.

MS2715	60×80 mm. 150l. mult	7·50	7·50

623 Koliqi

1998. First Death Anniv of Cardinal Mikel Koliqi (first Albanian Cardinal). Multicoloured.

| 2716 | 30l. Type **623** | 60 | 40 |
| 2717 | 100l. Koliqi (different) | 2·00 | 1·80 |

624 George Washington (first President, 1789–97)

1999. American Anniversaries. Multicoloured.

2718	150l. Type **624** (death bicentenary)	3·50	3·25
2719	150l. Abraham Lincoln (President 1861–65, 190th birth anniv)	3·50	3·25
2720	150l. Martin Luther King Jr. (civil rights campaigner, 70th birth anniv)	3·50	3·25

625 Monk Seals

1999. The Monk Seal. Multicoloured.

2721	110l. Type **625**	2·50	2·30
2722	110l. Two seals (both facing left)	2·50	2·30
2723	150l. As No. 2722 but both facing right	3·50	3·25
2724	150l. As Type **625** but seal at back facing left and seal at front facing right	3·50	3·25

Nos. 2721/4 were issued together, *se-tenant*, forming a composite design.

1999. 50th Anniv of Council of Europe. No. 2590 surch **150 LEKE** and emblem.

| 2725 | **576** | 150l. on 25l. mult | 4·00 | 3·50 |

1999. iBRA '99 International Stamp Exhibition, Nuremberg, Germany. No. 2496 surch **150 LEKE** in black (new value) and multicoloured (emblem).

| 2726 | 150l. on 90q. multicoloured | 3·75 | 3·25 |

628 Dove, Airplane and NATO Emblem

1999. 50th Anniv of North Atlantic Treaty Organization.

2727	**628**	10l. multicoloured	35	20
2728	**628**	100l. multicoloured	2·50	2·30
MS2729	69×85 mm. 250l. multicoloured		5·75	5·75

629 Mickey Mouse

1999. Mickey Mouse (cartoon film character). Multicoloured.

2730	60l. Type **629**	1·40	1·30
2731	80l. Mickey writing letter	2·10	1·90
2732	110l. Mickey thinking	2·30	2·10
2733	150l. Wearing black and red jumper	3·50	3·25

630 Thethi National Park, Shkoder

1999. Europa. Parks and Gardens. Multicoloured.

2734	90l. Type **630**	3·00	2·50
2735	310l. Lura National Park, Dibra	7·50	6·75
MS2736	80×60 mm. 350l. Divjaka National Park, Lushnje. Imperf	10·50	10·50

631 Coin

1999. Illyrian Coins. Multicoloured.

2737	10l. Type **631**	25	10
2738	20l. Coins from Labeateve, Bylisi and Scutari	45	30
2739	200l. Coins of King Monuni	5·00	4·50
MS2740	80×60 mm. 310l. Coin of King Gent (29×49 mm)	7·50	7·50

1999. Philexfrance 99 International Stamp Exhibition, Paris. No. 2512 surch with new value and Exhibition logo.

| 2741 | **552** | 150l. on 30q. mult | 3·75 | 3·25 |

633 Chaplin

1999. 110th Birth Anniv of Charlie Chaplin (film actor and director). Multicoloured.

2742	30l. Type **633**	70	50
2743	50l. Raising hat	1·20	1·00
2744	250l. Dancing	6·50	6·50

634 Neil Armstrong on Moon

1999. 30th Anniv of First Manned Moon Landing. Multicoloured.

2745	30l. Type **634**	70	50
2746	150l. Lunar module	3·75	3·25
2747	300l. Astronaut and American flag	7·50	6·75
MS2748	60×80 mm. 280l. Launch of "Apollo 1" (25×29 mm)	7·00	7·00

Nos. 2745/7 were issued together, *se-tenant*, forming a composite design.

635 Prisoner behind Bars

1999. The Nazi Holocaust.

| 2749 | **635** | 30l. multicoloured | 80 | 70 |
| 2750 | **635** | 150l. black and yellow | 4·00 | 3·75 |

636 UPU Emblem

1999. 125th Anniv of Universal Postal Union.

| 2751 | **636** | 20l. multicoloured | 45 | 30 |
| 2752 | **636** | 60l. multicoloured | 1·50 | 1·40 |

1999. China 1999 International Stamp Exhibition, Peking. No. 2497 surch **150 LEKE**.

| 2753 | 150l. on 1l.20 multicoloured | 3·75 | 3·25 |

638 Javelin

1999. 70th Anniv of National Athletic Championships. Multicoloured.

2754	10l. Type **638**	25	10
2755	20l. Discus	45	30
2756	200l. Running	5·00	4·50

639 Madonna and Child

1999. Icons by Onufri Shek (artist). Multicoloured.

| 2757 | 30l. Type **639** | 90 | 80 |
| 2758 | 300l. The Resurrection | 7·00 | 6·25 |

640 Bilal Golemi (veterinary surgeon)

1999. Birth Anniversaries. Multicoloured.

2759	10l. Type **640** (centenary)	25	10
2760	20l. Azem Galica (revolutionary) (centenary)	45	30
2761	50l. Viktor Eftimiu (writer) (centenary)	1·30	1·20
2762	300l. Lasgush Poradeci (poet) (centenary (2000))	7·50	6·75

641 Carnival Mask

1999. Carnivals. Multicoloured.

| 2763 | 30l. Type **641** | 1·10 | 95 |
| 2764 | 300l. Turkey mask | 7·50 | 6·75 |

642 Bell and Flowers

2000. New Millennium. The Peace Bell. Multicoloured

| 2765 | 40l. Type **642** | 1·00 | 90 |
| 2766 | 90l. Bell and flowers (different) | 2·30 | 2·00 |

643 Woman's Costume, Librazhdi

2000. Regional Costumes (1st series). Multicoloured.

2767	5l. Type **643**	10	10
2768	10l. Woman's costume, Malesia E Madhe	25	15
2769	15l. Man's costume, Malesia E Madhe	35	20
2770	20l. Man's costume, Tropoje	45	30
2771	30l. Man's costume, Dumrea	70	50
2772	35l. Man's costume, Tirana	80	65
2773	40l. Woman's costume, Tirana	95	75
2774	45l. Woman's costume, Arbereshe	1·00	85

2775	50l. Man's costume, Gjirokastra	1·20	1·00
2776	55l. Woman's costume, Lunxheri	1·30	1·20
2777	70l. Woman's costume, Cameria	1·60	1·50
2778	90l. Man's costume, Laberia	2·10	1·90

See also Nos. 2832/43, 2892/2903, 2943/54, 3053/64, 3080/91 and 3171/82.

644 Majer

2000. 150th Birth Anniv of Gustav Majer (etymologist).

| 2779 | **644** | 50l. green | 1·20 | 1·00 |
| 2780 | **644** | 130l. red | 3·00 | 2·75 |

645 Donald Duck

2000. Donald and Daisy Duck (cartoon film characters). Multicoloured.

2781	10l. Type **645**	25	10
2782	30l. Donald Duck	70	50
2783	90l. Daisy Duck	2·10	1·90
2784	250l. Donald Duck	5·75	5·25

646 Early Racing Car

2000. Motor Racing. Multicoloured.

2785	30l. Type **646**	1·00	90
2786	30l. Two-man racing car	1·00	90
2787	30l. Racing car with wire nose	1·00	90
2788	30l. Racing car with solid wheels	1·00	90
2789	30l. Car No. 1	1·00	90
2790	30l. Car No. 2	1·00	90
2791	30l. White Formula 1 racing car (facing left)	1·00	90
2792	30l. Blue Formula 1 racing car	1·00	90
2793	30l. Red Formula 1 racing car	1·00	90
2794	30l. White Formula 1 racing car (front view)	1·00	90

647 Ristoz of Mborja Church, Korca

2000. Birth Bimillenary of Jesus Christ. Multicoloured.

2795	15l. Type **647**	45	30
2796	40l. St. Kolli Church, Voskopoja	1·30	1·20
2797	90l. Church of Flori and Lauri, Kosovo	3·00	2·50
MS2798	80×60 mm. 250l. Fountain of Shengjin (mosaic), Tirana (37×37 mm)	5·25	5·25

648 'Building Europe'

2000. Europa. Multicoloured.

| 2799 | 130l. Type **648** | 4·00 | 3·75 |
| MS2800 | 60×80 mm. 300l. Detail of design showing boy holding star (24×29 mm) | 10·50 | 10·50 |

649 Wolf

2000. Animals. Multicoloured.

2801	10l. Type **649**	25	10
2802	40l. Brown bear	95	75
2803	90l. Wild boar	2·10	1·90
2804	220l. Red fox	5·00	4·50

650 Gustav Mahler (composer) (40th death anniv)

2000. WIPA 2000 International Stamp Exhibition, Vienna.

2805	**650**	130l. multicoloured	3·00	2·75

651 Footballer saving Ball

2000. European Football Championship, Belgium and The Netherlands. Multicoloured.

2806	10l. Type **651**	25	10
2807	120l. Footballer heading ball	3·00	2·50
MS2808 80×60 mm. 260l. Footballer kicking ball. Imperf		6·25	6·25

652 Musicans

2000. Paintings by Picasso. Multicoloured.

2809	30l. Type **652**	70	50
2810	40l. Abstract face	1·00	85
2811	250l. Two women running along beach	5·75	5·25
MS2812 60×80 mm. 400l. Painting of man (24×29 mm)		9·25	9·25

653 Basketball

2000. Olympic Games, Sydney. Multicoloured.

2813	10l. Type **653**	25	10
2814	40l. Football	95	75
2815	90l. Athletics	2·10	1·90
2816	250l. Cycling	5·75	5·25

654 LZ-1 (first Zeppelin airship) over Lake Constance, Friedrichshafen (first flight)

2000. Centenary of First Zeppelin Flight. Airship Development. Multicoloured.

2817	15l. Type **654**	35	20
2818	30l. Santos-Dumont airship *Ballon No. 5* and Eiffel Tower C attempted round trip from St. Cloud via Eiffel Tower, 1901	70	50
2819	300l. Beardmore airship *R-34* over New York (first double crossing of Atlantic)	6·50	5·75
MS2820 80×60 mm. 300l. Ferdinand von Zeppelin and airship (24×28 mm)		6·50	6·50

655 *Self-portrait* (Picasso)

2000. Espana 2000 World Stamp Exhibition, Madrid.

2821	**655**	130l. multicoloured	3·25	3·00

656 Yellow Gentian (*Gentiana lutea*)

2000. Medicinal Plants. Multicoloured.

2822	50l. Type **656**	1·30	1·20
2823	70l. Cross-leaved gentian (*Gentiana cruciata*)	1·60	1·50

657 Naim Frasheri (poet) and Landscape

2000. Personalities. Multicoloured.

2824	30l. Type **657**	70	50
2825	50l. Bajram Curri (revolutionary) and landscape	1·30	1·20

Nos. 2824/5 were issued together, *se-tenant*, forming a composite design.

658 Mother holding Child

2000. 50th Anniv of United Nations High Commission for Refugees. Multicoloured.

2826	50l. Type **658**	1·40	1·30
2827	90l. Mother breastfeeding child	2·10	1·90

659 Dede Ahmed Myftar Ahmataj

2001. Religious Leaders. Multicoloured.

2828	90l. Type **659**	2·30	2·10
2829	90l. Dede Sali Njazi	2·30	2·10

2001. For Kosovo. Nos. 2592/3 surch **PER KOSOVEN** and new value.

2830	80l.+10l. on 50l. multicoloured	5·25	4·75
2831	130l.+20l. on 100l. multicoloured	8·75	7·75

2001. Regional Costumes (2nd series). As T **643**. Multicoloured.

2832	20l. Man's costume, Tropoje	60	50
2833	20l. Woman's costume, Lume	60	50
2834	20l. Woman's costume, Mirdite	60	50
2835	20l. Man's costume, Lume	60	50
2836	20l. Woman's costume, Zadrime	60	50
2837	20l. Woman's costume, Shpati	60	50
2838	20l. Man's costume, Kruje	60	50
2839	20l. Woman's costume, Macukulli	60	50
2840	20l. Woman's costume, Dardhe	60	50
2841	20l. Man's costume, Lushnje	60	50
2842	20l. Woman's costume, Dropulli	60	50
2843	20l. Woman's costume, Shmili	60	50

661 Southern Magnolia (*Magnolia gandiflora*)

2001. Scented Flowers. Multicoloured.

2844	10l. Type **661**	35	20
2845	20l. Virginia rose (*Rosa virginiana*)	60	40
2846	90l. *Dianthus barbatus*	2·30	2·10
2847	140l. Lilac (*Syringa vulgaris*)	3·75	3·25

662 Goofy in Shorts

2001. Goofy (cartoon film character). Multicoloured.

2848	20l. Type **662**	45	30
2849	50l. Goofy in blue hat	1·20	1·00
2850	90l. Goofy in red trousers	2·10	1·90
2851	140l. Goofy in purple waistcoat	3·25	3·00

663 Vincenzo Bellini

2001. Composers' Anniversaries. Multicoloured.

2852	90l. Type **663** (birth centenary)	2·20	2·00
2853	90l. Guiseppe Verdi (death centenary)	2·20	2·00
MS2854 90×90 mm. 300l. Bellini and Verdi (75×38 mm)		7·00	7·00

664 Cliffs and Stream

2001. Europa. Water Resources. Multicoloured.

2855	40l. Type **664**	1·20	1·00
2856	110l. Waterfall	2·30	2·10
2857	200l. Lake	4·75	4·25
MS2858 60×80 mm. 350l. Ripples (24×78 mm)		10·50	10·50

665 Horse

2001. Domestic Animals. Multicoloured.

2859	10l. Type **665**	25	10
2860	15l. Donkey	35	20
2861	80l. Siamese cat	1·90	1·70
2862	90l. Dog	2·20	2·00
MS2863 80×60 mm. 300l. Head of Siamese cat (49×29 mm)		7·00	7·00

666 Swimming

2001. Mediterranean Games, Tunis. Multicoloured.

2864	10l. Type **666**	35	20
2865	90l. Athletics	2·30	2·10
2866	140l. Cycling	3·75	3·25
MS2867 60×80 mm. 260l. Discus (29×24 mm)		6·50	6·50

667 *Eole* (first powered take-off by Clement Ader, 1890)

2001. Aviation History. Multicoloured.

2868	40l. Type **667**	1·20	1·00
2869	40l. *Bleriot XI* (first powered crossing of English channel by Louis Bleriot, 1909)	1·20	1·00
2870	40l. *Spirit of St. Louis* (first solo non-stop crossing of North Atlantic from Paris to New York by Charles Lindbergh, 1927)	1·20	1·00
2871	40l. First flight to Tirana, 1925	1·20	1·00
2872	40l. Antonov AH-10 (first flight, 1956)	1·20	1·00
2873	40l. Concorde (first flight, 1969)	1·20	1·00
2874	40l. Concorde (first commercial flight, 1970)	1·20	1·00
2875	40l. Space shuttle *Colombia* (first flight, 1981)	1·20	1·00

668 Tabakeve

2001. Old Bridges.

2876	**668**	10l. multicoloured	25	10
2877	-	20l. multicoloured	35	20
2878	-	40l. multicoloured	1·00	85
2879	-	90l. black	2·10	1·90
MS2880 80×60 mm. 2l.50 multicoloured			6·50	6·50

DESIGNS: 20l. Kamares; 40l. Golikut; 90l. Mesit. 49×22 mm—2l.50, Tabakeve.

669 Dimitri of Arber

2001. Arms (1st series).

2881	20l. Type **669**	60	40
2882	45l. Balsha pricipality	1·20	1·00
2883	50l. Muzaka family	1·20	1·00
2884	90l. George Castriot (Skanderbeg)	2·30	2·10

See also Nos. 2921/4 and 2965/8.

670 Children encircling Globe

2001. United Nations Year of Dialogue among Civilizations. Multicoloured, background colours given.

2885	**670**	45l. red, yellow and black	1·20	1·00
2886	**670**	50l. orange and green	1·20	1·00
2887	**670**	120l. black and red	3·00	2·50

There are minor differences in Nos. 2886/7, with each colour forming a solid block above and below the central motif.

671 Award Ceremony (Medicins sans Frontieres, 1999 Peace Prize) and Medal

2001. Centenary of Nobel Prizes. Showing winners and Nobel medal. Multicoloured.

2888	10l. Type **671**	25	10
2889	20l. Wilhelm Konrad Rontgen (1901 Physics prize)	45	30
2890	90l. Ferid Murad (1998 Medicine Prize)	2·30	2·10
2891	200l. Mother Teresa (1979 Peace Prize)	4·75	4·25

2002. Regional Costumes (3rd series). As T **643**. Multicoloured.

2892	30l. Woman's costume, Gjakova	70	65
2893	30l. Woman's costume, Prizreni	70	65
2894	30l. Man's costume, Shkodra	70	65
2895	30l. Woman's costume, Shkodra	70	65
2896	30l. Man's costume, Berati	70	65
2897	30l. Woman's costume, Berati	70	65
2898	30l. Woman's costume, Elbasani	70	65
2899	30l. Man's costume, Elbasani	70	65
2900	30l. Woman's costume, Vlora	70	65
2901	30l. Man's costume, Vlora	70	65

2902	30l. Woman's costume, Gjirokastra	70	65
2903	30l. Woman's costume, Delvina	70	65

672 Bambi and Thumper

2002. Bambi (cartoon film character). Multicoloured.

2904	20l. Type 672	45	30
2905	50l. Bambi alone amongst flowers	1·20	1·00
2906	90l. Bambi and Thumper looking right	2·00	1·80
2907	140l. Bambi with open mouth	3·00	2·50

673 Fireplace

2002. Traditional Fireplaces. T 673 and similar vert designs showing fireplaces. Multicoloured.

MS2908	30l. Type 673: 40l. With columns at each side; 50l. With foliage arch; 90l. With three medallions in arch	4·75	4·75

674 Acrobatic Jugglers

2002. Europa. Circus. Multicoloured.

2909	40l. Type 674	95	75
2910	90l. Female acrobat	2·00	1·80
2911	220l. Tightrope performers	5·75	5·25
MS2912	60×80 mm. 350l. Equestrienne performer (38×38 mm)	11·50	11·50

675 Heading the Ball

2002. Football World Championship, Japan and South Korea. Multicoloured.

2913	20l. Type 675	45	30
2914	30l. Catching the ball	70	50
2915	90l. Kicking the ball from horizontal position	2·10	1·90
2916	120l. Player and ball	2·50	2·30
MS2917	80×60 mm. 360l. Emblem (50×30)	8·25	8·25

2002. Arms (2nd series). As T 669. Multicoloured.

2918	20l. Gropa family	45	30
2919	45l. Skurra family	1·00	85
2920	50l. Bua family	1·20	1·00
2921	90l. Topia family	2·30	2·10

676 Opuntia catingiola

2002. Cacti. T 676 and similar triangular designs. Multicoloured.

MS2922	50l. Type 676; 50l. Neoporteria pseudoreicheana; 50l. Lobivia shaferi 50l. Hylocereus undatus; 50l. Borzicactus madisoniorum	5·25	5·25

677 Blood Group Symbols with Wings

2002. 50th Anniv of Blood Bank Service. Multicoloured.

2923	90l. Type 677	2·30	2·10
2924	90l. Blood group symbols containing figures	2·30	2·10

678 Naim Kryeziu (footballer)

2002. Sports Personalities. Multicoloured.

2925	50l. Type 678	1·20	1·00
2926	50l. Riza Lushta (footballer)	1·20	1·00
2927	50l. Ymer Pampuri (weight lifter)	1·20	1·00
MS2928	61× 81 mm. 300l. Loro Boriçi (footballer) (vert). Imperf	7·00	7·00

679 Stamp, Torso and Emblem

2002. 50th Anniv International Federation of Stamp Dealers' Associations (IFSDA). Multicoloured.

2929	50l. Type 679	1·20	1·00
2930	100l. Part of stamp enlarged and emblem	2·40	2·20

680 Statue of Liberty

2002. First Anniv of Attacks on World Trade Centre, New York. Multicoloured.

2931	100l. Type 680	2·40	2·20
2932	150l. Burning towers and skyline	3·50	3·25
MS2933	61×81 mm. 350l. Statue of Liberty and World Trade Centre tower (vert)	8·50	8·50

681 Loggerhead Turtle (Caretta caretta)

2002. Fauna of Mediterranean Sea. Sheet 100×107 mm containing T 681 and similar horiz designs. Multicoloured.

MS2934	50l. Type 681; 50l. Common dolphin (Delphinus delphis); 50l. Blue shark (Prionace glauca); 50l. Fin whale (Balenoptera physalus); 50l. Ray (Torpedo torpedo); 50l. Octopus (Octopus vulgaris)	7·25	7·25

682 Tefta Tashko Koço

2002. Personalities. The Stage. Multicoloured.

2935	50l. Type 682 (singer)	1·20	1·10
2936	50l. Naim Frasheri (actor)	1·20	1·10
2937	50l. Kristaq Antoniu (singer)	1·20	1·10
2938	50l. Panajot Kanaçi (choreographer)	1·20	1·10

683 Flags

2002. 90th Anniv of Independence. Multicoloured.

2939	20l. Type 683	55	50
2940	90l. People and Albanian flag	2·20	2·00

684 Satellite Dish and Outline of Stamp

2002. 90th Anniv of Albanian Post and Telecommunications. Multicoloured.

2941	20l. Type 684	55	50
2942	90l. Airmail envelope and telegraph machine	2·20	2·00

2003. Regional Costumes (4th series). As T 643. Multicoloured.

2943	30l. Woman's costume, Kelmendi	90	85
2944	30l. Man's costume, Zadrime	90	85
2945	30l. Woman's costume, Zerqani	90	85
2946	30l. Man's costume, Peshkopi	90	85
2947	30l. Woman's costume, Malesia Tiranes	90	85
2948	30l. Woman's costume, Malesia Tiranes	90	85
2949	30l. Woman's costume, Fushe Kruje	90	85
2950	30l. Man's costume, Shpati	90	85
2951	30l. Woman's costume, Myzeqe	90	85
2952	30l. Woman's costume, Labinoti	90	85
2953	30l. Man's costume, Korce	90	85
2954	30l. Woman's costume, Laberi	90	85

685 Popeye and Bluto

2003. Popeye (cartoon film character). Multicoloured.

2955	40l. Type 685	1·20	1·10
2956	50l. Popeye running	1·50	1·30
2957	80l. Popeye and Olive Oyl	2·40	2·20
2958	150l. Popeye	4·25	3·75

686 Port Palermo Castle

2003. Castles. Sheet 118×98 mm. T 686 and similar horiz designs.

MS2959	10l. grey and black; 20l. green and black; 50l. grey and black; 20l. mauve and black	6·00	6·00

DESIGNS: 10l. Type 686; 20l. Petrela; 50l. Kruja; 120l. Preza.

687 Bearded Man

2003. Europa. Poster Art. Multicoloured.

2960	150l. Type 687	4·50	4·25
2961	200l. Eye, apple and piano	6·00	5·50
MS2962	80×61 mm. 350l. Detail of No. 2960	10·50	10·50

688 Envelopes

2003. 90th Anniv of Albanian Post and Telecommunications (2nd series). Multicoloured.

2963	50l. Type 688	1·30	1·20
2964	1000l. Outline of stamps	29·00	26·00

2003. Arms (3rd series). As T 669. Multicoloured.

2965	10l. Ariantet family	25	10
2966	20l. Jonimajt family	65	60
2967	70l. Dukagjini family	2·00	1·80
2968	120l. Kopili family	3·50	3·00

689 Pomegranate (Punica granatum)

2003. Fruit. Multicoloured. Self-adhesive.

MS2969	50l. Citron (Citrus medica); 70l. Cantaloupe (Cucumis melo); 80l. Fig (Ficus) (inscr "Fieus")	7·25	7·25

690 Diocletian

2003. Roman Emperors. Multicoloured.

2970	70l. Type 690	2·00	1·80
2971	70l. Justinian	2·00	1·80
2972	70l. Claudius II	2·00	1·80
2973	70l. Constantine	2·00	1·80

691 White Stork (Cicona cicona)

2003. Birds. Sheet 100×119 mm containing T 691 and similar vert designs. Multicoloured.

MS2974	70l. Type 691; 70l. Golden eagle (Aquila chrysaetos); 70l. Eagle owl (Bubo bubo); 70l. Capercaillie (Tetrao urogallus)	8·25	8·25

692 Players

2003. 90th Anniv of Albanian Football. Each grey, black and red.

2975	80l. Type 692	2·20	2·00
2976	80l. Group of players	2·20	2·00

Nos. 2975/6 were issued together, *se-tenant*, forming a composite design.

693 *The Luncheon* (detail)

2003. 120th Death Anniv of Edouard Manet (artist). Multicoloured.

2977	40l. Type 693	1·10	95
2978	100l. *The Fifer*	3·00	2·75
MS2979	80×60 mm. 250l. Edouard Manet (horiz)	7·00	7·00

694 Odhise Paskall

2003. Albanian Sculptors. Multicoloured.

2980	40l. Type 694	1·30	1·20
2981	50l. Llazar Nikolla	1·30	1·20
2982	50l. Janaq Paco	1·30	1·20
2983	50l. Murat Toptani	1·30	1·20

695 Profile of Mother Teresa

2003. Mother Teresa (humanitarian) Commemoration. Multicoloured.
2984	401.	Type **695**	1·30	1·20
2985	2501.	Mother Teresa facing front	6·50	6·00
MS2986	60×60 mm. 3501. Mother Teresa (statue) (40×40 mm)		9·25	9·25

696 Lake, Pelicans and Pine Trees (Divjaka)

2003. Natural Heritage. Multicoloured.
2987	20l.	Type **696**	55	50
2988	30l.	House and fir trees (Hotova forest)	85	75
2989	200l.	Snow-covered fir trees (Drenova forest)	6·25	5·75

697 Stylized Cyclist and Map of France

2003. Centenary of Tour de France Cycle Race.
2990	**697**	50l. blue, red and black	1·40	1·30
2991	–	100l. multicoloured	2·75	2·50

DESIGN: 100l. Two cyclists.

698 Trees, Lake and Mountain, Pushimet

2004. Europa. Holidays. Multicoloured.
2992	200l.	Type **698**	6·00	5·50
2993	200l.	Grassland, hills and mountains, Pushimet	6·00	5·50
MS2994	61×81 mm. 350l. Island, Pushimet		11·00	11·00

699 Goalkeeper

2004. European Football Championship 2004, Portugal. Multicoloured.
2995	20l.	Type **699**	75	70
2996	40l.	Two players and goalkeeper catching ball	1·40	1·30
2997	50l.	Two players	1·70	1·50
2998	200l.	Players jumping for ball	7·00	6·50
MS2999	81×61 mm. 350l. Player with raised arms (38×38 mm) (circular)		11·00	11·00

700 Discus Thrower (statue)

2004. Olympic Games, Athens. Multicoloured.
3000	10l.	Type **700**	30	25
3001	200l.	Face (statue)	6·25	5·75
MS3002	61×81 mm. 350l. Athlete carrying Olympic torch (39×55 mm)		11·00	11·00

701 Wilhelm von Wied

2004. Wilhelm von Wied (ruler, February 6th—September 5th, 1914) Commemoration. Multicoloured.
3003	40l.	Type **701**	1·30	1·20
3004	150l.	Facing left	4·75	4·25

702 Bugs Bunny

2004. Bugs Bunny (cartoon character). Multicoloured.
3005	40l.	Type **702**	1·30	1·20
3006	50l.	With crossed arms	1·60	1·50
3007	80l.	Wearing dinner jacket	2·75	2·40
3008	150l.	Facing left	4·75	4·25

703 Damaged Painting

2004. Mural Paintings by Nikolla Onufri, Church of Saint Mary Vllherna. Multicoloured.
3009	10l.	Type **703**	45	40
3010	20l.	Mary	75	70
3011	1000l.	Saint	34·00	31·00
MS3012	80×65 mm. 400l. Crowned Christ		12·50	12·50

704 Ladybird

2004. Ladybird (*Coccinella*). Sheet 120×95 mm containing T **704** and similar horiz designs showing ladybirds. Multicoloured.
MS3013	80l.×4, Type **704**; Six-spot; With open wings; 12-spot		10·00	10·00

705 Norek Luca

2004. Personalities. Multicoloured.
3014	50l.	Type **705** (actor) (80th birth anniv)	1·50	1·40
3015	50l.	Jorgjia Truja (singer) (10th death anniv)	1·50	1·40
3016	50l.	Maria Kraja (singer) (5th death anniv)	1·50	1·40
3017	50l.	Zina Andri (actor) (80th birth anniv)	1·50	1·40

706 Dushmani Principality

2004. Arms. Multicoloured.
3018	20l.	Type **706**	80	75
3019	40l.	Gjuraj family	1·40	1·30
3020	80l.	Zahariaj family	2·75	2·50
3021	150l.	Spani principality	5·00	4·75

707 Cactus-type Dahlia

2004. Dahlias. Sheet 164×77 mm containing T **707** and similar triangular designs showing dahlias. Multicoloured.
MS3022	80l.×4, Type **707**; Water lily type; Anemone type; Dahlia		10·00	10·00

708 *Madonna and Child* (Anonim Shen Meria)

2004. 50th Anniv of National Art Gallery. Multicoloured.
3023	20l.	Type **708**	60	55
3024	20l.	*Saint* (Mihal Anagnosti)	60	55
3025	20l.	*Angel* (Onufer Qiprioti)	60	55
3026	20l.	*Enthroned saint holding open book* (Cetiret)	60	55
3027	20l.	*God and saints* (Onuferi)	60	55
3028	20l.	*Woman wearing scarf* (Kel Kodheli)	60	55
3029	20l.	*Crying woman* (Vangjush Mio)	60	55
3030	20l.	*Woman wearing hat* (Abdurahim Buza)	60	55
3031	20l.	*Semi-naked woman* (Mustapha Arapi)	60	55
3032	20l.	*Man with moustache* (Guri Madhi)	60	55
3033	20l.	*Soldier* (sculpture) (Janaq Paco)	60	55
3034	20l.	*Still life with grapes* (Zef Kolombi)	60	55
3035	20l.	*Flowers* (Hasan Reci)	60	55
3036	20l.	*Still life with onions* (Vladimir Jani)	60	55
3037	20l.	*Woman's head* (sculpture) (Halim Beqiri)	60	55
3038	20l.	*Men seated* (Edison Gjergo)	60	55
3039	20l.	*Men wearing traditional dress* (Naxhi Bakalli)	60	55
3040	20l.	*Family* (Agron Bregu)	60	55
3041	20l.	*Tree planting* (Edi Hila)	60	55
3042	20l.	*Holding paintbrushes* (Artur Muharremi)	60	55
3043	20l.	*Old man* (Rembrandt)	60	55
3044	20l.	*Winged horseman* (Gazmend Leka)	60	55
3045	20l.	*Multicoloured circle* (Damien Hirst)	60	55
3046	20l.	*Corpse in cave* (Edvin Rama)	60	55
3047	20l.	*Viking* (Ibrahim Kodra)	60	55

709 Bunting and NATO Emblem

2004. Fifth Anniv of NATO Peacekeeping in Kosovo. Multicoloured.
3048	100l.	Type **709**	3·00	2·75
3049	200l.	Doves and United Nations flag	6·00	5·50
MS3050	80×60 mm. 350l. Houses flying Kosovo flag		11·00	11·00

710 Two Doves

2004. 60th Anniv of Liberation. Multicoloured.
3051	50l.	Type **710**	1·70	1·60
3052	200l.	One dove	6·25	5·75

2004. Regional Costumes (5th series). As T **643**. Multicoloured.
3053	30l.	Back view of woman's costume, Gramshi	90	85
3054	30l.	Front view of woman's costume, Gramshi	90	85
3055	30l.	Woman's costume, Korca	90	85
3056	30l.	Man's costume, Kolonja	90	85
3057	30l.	Woman's costume, Korca (different)	90	85
3058	30l.	Woman's costume, Librazhdi	90	85
3059	30l.	Woman's costume, Permeti	90	85
3060	30l.	Woman's costume, Pogradeci	90	85
3061	30l.	Man's costume, Skrapari	90	85
3062	30l.	Woman's costume, Skrapari	90	85
3063	30l.	Woman's costume, Tepelena	90	85
3064	30l.	Woman's costume, Vlora	90	85

711 Emblem

2005. 50th Anniv of Europa Stamps. Multicoloured.
3065	200l.	Type **711**	9·00	8·50
3066	250l.	Stylized figure grasping '50'	10·50	10·00

712 Triangular Pies

2005. Europa. Gastronomy. Multicoloured.
3068	200l.	Type **712**	7·00	6·50
3069	200l.	Stew	7·00	6·50

713 Emblem

2005. 50th Anniv of United Nations Membership.
3071	**713**	40l. multicoloured	1·90	1·70

714 Tom and Jerry

2005. Tom and Jerry (cartoon characters). Multicoloured.
3072	40l.	Type **714**	1·00	90
3073	50l.	Heads of Tom and Jerry	1·30	1·20
3074	80l.	Jerry	2·00	1·80
3075	150l.	Tom	3·50	3·25

715 Mountain, City and Lake

2005. Art. Albanian Landscapes. Multicoloured.
3076	10l.	Type **715**	30	30
3077	20l.	Aqueduct and castle	65	60
3078	95l.	Crowd and minaret	95	90
3079	1000l.	Lake and mountain fortress	27·00	25·00

2005. Regional Costumes (6th series). As T **643**. Multicoloured.
3080	30l.	Man's costume, Tirane	1·10	1·00
3081	30l.	Woman's costume, Bende Tirane	1·10	1·00
3082	30l.	Back of woman's costume, Zall Dajt	1·10	1·00
3083	30l.	Man's costume, Kavaje-Durres	1·10	1·00
3084	30l.	Woman's costume, Has	1·10	1·00
3085	30l.	Man's costume, Mat	1·10	1·00
3086	30l.	Woman's costume, Liqenas	1·10	1·00
3087	30l.	Woman's costume, Klenje	1·10	1·00
3088	30l.	Woman's costume, Maleshove	1·10	1·00
3089	30l.	Woman's costume, German	1·10	1·00
3090	30l.	Woman's costume, Kruje	1·10	1·00
3091	30l.	Man's costume, Rec	1·10	1·00

716 Starting Blocks

2005. Mediterranean Games, Almera. Multicoloured.
3092	20l. Type **716**	85	70
3093	60l. Rings	2·10	1·80
3094	120l. Relay baton	4·25	3·50
MS3095 60×80 mm. 300l. Diver (30×50 mm)		14·50	14·50

717 Globe and Emblem

2005. Centenary of Rotary International. Multicoloured.
3096	30l. Type **717**	1·00	90
3097	150l. Emblem (vert)	5·25	4·50

2005. Arms (5th series). As T **706**. Multicoloured.
3098	10l. Bua	40	35
3099	20l. Karl Topia	1·00	90
3100	70l. Dukagjini II	3·50	3·00
3101	120l. Engjej	5·25	4·50

718 Yellow-flowered Portulaca

2005. Portulaca. Sheet 203×60 mm containing T **718** and similar triangular designs showing portulacas. Multicoloured.
MS3102 70l.×5, Type **718**; White flowers; Red and yellow flowers; Pale pink flowers; Double dark pink flower		12·50	12·50

719 Cyclists

2005. 80th Anniv of Cycle Race.
3103	**719**	50l. multicoloured	1·70	1·60
3104	**719**	60l. multicoloured	2·20	2·00
3105	**719**	120l. multicoloured	4·25	4·00

720 Battle Scene

2005. 600th Birth Anniv of Gjergj Kastrioti (Skanderbeg). Sheet 240×82 mm containing T **720** and similar multicoloured designs.
MS3106 40l. Type **720**; 50l. Chariot and fallen horse and rider; 60l. Archers, emblem and foot soldiers with spears; 70l. Shield bearer and archers; 80l. Soldier with raised sword and archers on rocks (30×30 mm) (circular); 90l. Archers firing from cliff ledge (30×30 mm) (circular)		14·00	14·00

The stamps and margins of **MS**3106 form a composite design of battle.

721 Roses growing through Helmet

2005. 60th Anniv of End of World War II. Multicoloured.
3107	50l. Type **721**	1·70	1·50
3108	200l. Allied flags and statues	7·25	6·50

722 Matia Kodheli-Marubi

2005. National Marubi Photograph Collection. Multicoloured.
3109	10l. Type **722**	30	25
3110	20l. Gege Marubi	70	65
3111	70l. Pjeter Marubi (Pietro Marubbi) (photographer, artist and architect)	2·50	2·30
3112	200l. Kel Marubi (Mikel Kodheli)	7·25	6·50

2006. Various stamps, numbers given in brackets, surch **40 lek**.
3113	40l. on 30q. multicoloured (2531)	1·40	1·30
3114	40l. on 18l. multicoloured (2549)	1·40	1·30
3115	40l. on 2l. multicoloured (2567)	1·40	1·30
3116	40l. on 2l. multicoloured (2595)	1·40	1·30
3117	40l. on 3l. multicoloured (2596)	1·40	1·30
3118	40l. on 25l. multicoloured (2597)	1·40	1·30
3119	40l. on 2l. multicoloured (2606)	1·40	1·30
3120	40l. on 18l. multicoloured (2610)	1·40	1·30
3121	40l. on 18l. multicoloured (2613)	1·40	1·30
3122	40l. on 25l. multicoloured (2620)	1·40	1·30
3123	40l. on 25l. multicoloured (2629)	1·40	1·30

724 Pres. George Bush

2007. President George Bush's visit to Albania. Multicoloured.
3124	20l. Type **724**	75	70
3125	40l. As Type **724** (suffused green)	1·50	1·40
3126	80l. As Type **724** (multicoloured)	3·00	2·75
MS3127 97×73 mm. 200l. Statue of Liberty		6·75	6·75

725 Arms of Italy and Albania

2007. Tenth Anniv of Italians in Albania.
3128	**725**	40l. multicoloured	1·80	1·60

Nos. 3129/41 and Type **726** have been left for 'Flags', issued 5 October 2007, not yet received.

727 Flags and Scouts

2007. Centenary of Scouting. Multicoloured.
3153	100l. Type **727**	4·00	3·75
3154	150l. Flags and scouts (different)	6·00	5·75
MS3155 Sheet 80×60 mm. 250l. Knot (30×25 mm)		10·00	10·00

728 Pink Panther

2007. Pink Panther (cartoon character). Multicoloured.
3156	40l. Type **728**	1·60	1·40
3157	50l. With Inspector Clouseau	2·10	2·00
3158	80l. Leaning	3·00	2·75
3159	150l. Wearing tunic	6·50	6·00

729 Roads (Arkida)

2007. Children's Drawings. Multicoloured.
3160	10l. Type **729**	40	35
3161	40l. Boy and flowers (Amarilda Prifti)	1·70	1·60
3162	50l. Outline of houses and viaduct (Iliaz Kasa)	2·10	2·00
3163	80l. Buildings (K. Mezini) (horiz)	3·50	3·25

730 Galerio Maksimiliani

2007. Rulers. Multicoloured.
3164	30l. Type **730**	1·40	1·20
3165	120l. Flavio Anastasi	5·00	4·75

731 Sower (fresco by David Selenica)

2007. Art. Multicoloured.
3166	70l. Type **731**	3·00	2·75
3167	110l. Flowers and garlands (wall painting) (Et'hem Bey Mosque, Tirana)	4·75	4·25

732 Young People, Map and Stars

2007. Europa. Integration. Multicoloured.
3168	200l. Type **732**	6·75	6·25
3169	200l. Young people and double-headed eagle	6·75	6·25
MS3170 Sheet 80×60 mm. 350l. Young people and flag (30×25 mm)		12·00	12·00

2007. Regional Costumes (7th series). As T **643**. Multicoloured.
3171	40l. Woman's costume (inscr 'German')	1·30	1·20
3172	40l. Man's costume, Kubrin	1·30	1·20
3173	40l. Woman's costume, Golloborde	1·30	1·20
3174	40l. Man's costume, Kerrabe Malesi	1·30	1·20
3175	40l. Man's costume, Gur I Bardhe	1·30	1·20
3176	40l. Woman's costume, Martanesh	1·30	1·20
3177	40l. Woman's costume, Puke	1·30	1·20
3178	40l. Woman's costume Serice Labinot	1·30	1·20
3179	40l. Woman's costume Shen Gjergj	1·30	1·20
3180	40l. Woman's costume, Tirane Qytet	1·30	1·20
3181	40l. Man's costume, Zalle Dajt	1·30	1·20
3182	40l. Woman's costume, Zaranike Godolesh	1·30	1·20

Nos. 3183/94 have been left for 'Regional Costumes (8th series)' (Vert designs as T **643**), issued on 2 November 2007, not yet received.

733 Thethi National Park (Inscr 'Parku Kombetar I Thethit')

2007. Tourism. Multicoloured.
3195	40l. Type **733**	1·60	1·40
3196	50l. Luras Lake (Inscr 'Liqenet e Lures')	2·00	1·80
3197	60l. Canine's Castle (Inscr 'Kalaja Kanines')	2·30	2·10
3198	70l. Laguna Karavastase	2·75	2·50

734 Plane Tree

2007. Natural Heritage. Elbasan Plane Trees. Multicoloured.
3199	70l. Type **734**	3·00	2·75
3200	90l. Hollow tree	3·50	3·25

735 Pope Clement II

2007. Pope Clement II
3201	**735**	30l. multicoloured	1·20	1·10
3202	**735**	90l. multicoloured	4·75	4·25

736 Leopold Senghor

2007. Birth Centenary (2006) of Leopold Sedar Senghor (poet and first President of Senegal 1960–80).
3203	**736**	40l. multicoloured	1·60	1·40
3204	**736**	80l. multicoloured	3·00	2·75

737 Team

2007. 60th Anniv of Albania as Balkan Football Champions.
3205	**737**	10l. multicoloured	80	70
3206	**737**	80l. multicoloured	7·00	6·25

738 Cannon

2007. World Heritage Site. Gjirokastra. Sheet 120×100 mm containing T **738** and similar vert designs. Multicoloured.
MS3207 10l. Type **738**; 20l. Flowers in a roundel; 30l. 'Kule' (building with tall basement, a first floor for use in the cold season, and a second floor for the warm season); 60l. Bridge; 80l. Aerial view; 90l. Clock tower		12·00	12·00

739 Soldier wearing Gas Mask

2007. Tenth Anniv of Albania's Participation in International Military Missions. Multicoloured.

| 3208 | 10l. Type **739** | 45 | 40 |
| 3209 | 100l. Soldiers in inflatable boat | 4·25 | 3·75 |

740 Mother Teresa

2007. Tenth Death Anniv of Agnes Ganzhou Bojaxhiu (Mother Teresa). Multicoloured.

| 3210 | **740** | 60l. multicoloured | 3·00 | 2·75 |
| 3211 | **740** | 130l. multicoloured No. | 5·50 | 5·00 |

MS3212 has been left for miniature sheet, not yet received.

741 Gaia (statue)

2007. Archaeology. Durres City. Multicoloured.

| 3213 | 30l. Type **741** | 1·20 | 1·10 |
| 3214 | 120l. Gaia (close up) | 4·75 | 4·25 |

No. MS3215 has been left for miniature sheet, not yet received.

742 Drawings

2007. Cultural History. Tren Cave System (first occupied during Eneolithic period c. 2500–2000 BC). Multicoloured.

3216	20l. Type **742**	1·10	1·00
3217	100l. Drawings (different)	4·25	3·75
MS3218	81×61 mm. 300l. Cave (horiz)	12·50	12·50

743 Osman Kazazi

2007. Personalities (1st issue). Multicoloured.

3219	10l. Type **743** (politician)	40	35
3220	20l. Pjeter Arbnori (politician)	80	75
3221	60l. Llazar Sotir Gusho (Lagush Poradeci) (poet)	2·50	2·40
3222	100l. Cesk Zadeja (composer)	4·25	4·00

744 Abdurrahim Buza

2007. Personalities (2nd issue). Multicoloured.

3223	50l. Type **744** (artist)	2·00	1·90
3224	50l. Aleks Buda (historian)	2·00	1·90
3225	50l. Thimi Mitko (folklorist and nationalist)	2·00	1·90
3226	50l. Martin Camaj (writer)	2·00	1·90

745 Spheres as Player

2007. World Cup Football Championship, Germany. Multicoloured.

3227	30l. Type **745**	1·80	1·70
3228	60l. Triangles as player	3·00	2·75
3229	120l. Rectangles as player	5·25	4·75
MS3230	61×82 mm. 350l. Emblems	13·50	13·50

The stamp and margin of **MS**3230 form a composite design.

746 Ismail Kemal Bej Vlora (Ismail Qemali) (first head of state and government) and Arms

2007. 95th Anniv of Independence. Multicoloured.

| 3231 | 50l. Type **746** | 2·00 | 1·90 |
| 3232 | 110l. Ismail Qemali | 4·50 | 4·00 |

747 Garlic

2007. Domestic Plants. Multicoloured.

3233	80l. Type **747**	3·00	2·75
3234	80l. Onions	3·00	2·75
3235	80l. Peppers	3·00	2·75
3236	80l. Tomatoes	3·00	2·75

748 Blooms and Leaves

2007. *Wulfenia baldacci.* Multicoloured.

| 3237 | 70l. Type **748** | 3·00 | 2·75 |
| 3238 | 100l. Flowers on single stem | 4·25 | 4·00 |

749 Emblem

2007. 95th Anniv of National Post Office.

| 3239 | **749** | 80l. agate and vermilion | 3·25 | 3·00 |
| 3240 | **749** | 90l. vermilion and black | 3·75 | 3·25 |

750 New Road Surfacing

2007. Infrastructure Improvements. Sheet 133×107 mm containing T **750** and similar horiz designs. Multicoloured.

| MS3241 | 10l. Type **750**; 20l. Durres port; 30l. New building, Tirana; 40l. Mother Teresa airport; 50l. Shkodra street, Hani i Hotit; 60l. Tepelene road, Gijirokastra; 70l. Fier road, Lushnje; 80l. Kalimash road, Morine | 13·50 | 13·50 |

751 Emblem and Member Flags

2008. Albania in NATO. Multicoloured.

| 3242 | 40l. Type **751** | 2·00 | 1·90 |
| 3243 | 60l. Arms and emblem | 2·50 | 2·40 |

752 Map of Switzerland

2008. EURO 2008–European Football Championships, Austria and Switzerland. Multicoloured.

3244	50l. Type **752**	2·20	2·10
3245	250l. Map of Austria	10·50	10·00
MS3246	60×80 mm. 200l. Mascots (vert)	9·50	9·50

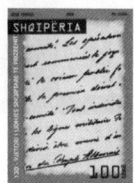

753 Script

2008. 130th Anniv of Albanian League of Prizren. Multicoloured.

| 3247 | 100l. Type **753** | 4·25 | 4·00 |
| 3248 | 150l. Building | 7·00 | 6·75 |

754 Postmark

2008. 95th Anniv of Postal Service.

| 3249 | **754** | 40l. multicoloured | 2·00 | 1·90 |

755 John Belushi (actor)

2008. Personalities of Albanian Descent. Multicoloured.

3250	5l. Type **755**	20	15
3251	10l. Gjon Mili (photographer)	40	35
3252	20l. Koca Mi'mar Sinan Aga (Sinan) (Ottoman architect)	80	75
3253	200l. Ibrahim Kodra (artist)	8·75	8·50

756 Hand holding Quill

2008. Europa. The Letter. Multicoloured.

3254	100l. Type **756**	4·50	4·25
3255	150l. Hand holding quill writing Europa	7·00	6·75
MS3256	81×61 mm. 250l. 'Europa' (horiz)	11·50	11·50

757 Two Poppies

2008. Poppy (*Papaver rhoeas*). Multicoloured.

| 3257 | 50l. Type **757** | 2·20 | 2·10 |
| 3258 | 150l. Poppy | 7·00 | 6·75 |

758 Swallows

2008. Universal Language of Art. Multicoloured.

| 3259 | 40l. Type **758** | 2·00 | 1·90 |
| 3260 | 70l. Parachutists | 3·00 | 2·75 |

759 Football

2008. Olympic Games, Beijing. Multicoloured.

3261	20l. Type **759**	80	75
3262	30l. Water polo	1·50	1·40
3263	40l. Athletics	2·00	1·90
3264	50l. Cycling	2·20	2·10

760 Osumi Canyons

2008. Tourism. Multicoloured.

| 3265 | 60l. Type **760** | 2·50 | 2·40 |
| 3266 | 250l. Komani Lake | 10·50 | 10·00 |

761 Ahmet Zogu

2008. 80th Anniv of Coronation of King Ahmet Zogu.

| 3267 | **761** | 40l. multicoloured | 2·00 | 1·90 |
| 3268 | **761** | 100l. multicoloured | 4·50 | 4·25 |

762 Azem Hajdari (politician)

2008. Personalities. Multicoloured.

| 3269 | 40l. Type **762** | 2·00 | 1·90 |
| 3270 | 200l. Adem Jashari (Kosovo nationalist) | 8·75 | 8·50 |

763 Ymer Prizreni

2008. Kosovo Nationalists. Multicoloured.

3271	20l. Type **763**	80	75
3272	30l. Isa Boletini	1·50	1·40
3273	40l. Ibrahim Rugova	2·00	1·90
3274	50l. Azem Galica	2·20	2·10
3275	70l. Adem Jashari	3·00	2·75

764 Decius

2008. Roman Emperors of Illyrian Ancestry. Multicoloured.

| 3276 | 30l. Type **764** | 1·50 | 1·40 |

No. 3277 has been left for stamp not yet recieved.

765 Harry Potter (Daniel Radcliffe) and Professor Dumbledore (Michael Gambon)

2008. Youth Stamps. Harry Potter (character created by J. K. Rowling). Designs showing Harry Potter and other characters. Multicoloured.

3278	20l. Type **765**	80	75
3279	30l. With Dobby	1·50	1·40
3280	50l. With Hermione (Emma Watson) and friends	2·20	2·10
3281	100l. With Voldemort (Ralph Fiennes)	4·50	4·25

766 Congress Buildings, Monastir, Macedonia

2008. Centenary of Congress of Monastir (to decide on the use of Latin script for written Albanian). Multicoloured.

3282	40l. Type **766**	2·00	1·90
3283	100l. Albanian script using Latin alphabet	4·50	4·25

767 Sinagogue, Saranda

2008. Archaeological Excavations. Multicoloured.

3284	10l. Type **767**	80	75
3285	50l. Orikum	2·20	2·10
3286	80l. Antigonea	3·25	3·00

767a Emblem

2009. 135th Anniv of Universal Postal Union

3286a	**767a** 100l. multicoloured	9·50	9·50
3286aa	200l. As Type **767a** (vert)	4·50	4·50

767b Laurel and Hardy

2009. Laurel and Hardy (Arthur Stanley Jefferson and Norvell Hardy) (comedians). Multicoloured.

3286b	150l. Type **767b**	6·50	6·50
3286ba	200l. Wearing bowler hats	7·50	7·50
MS3286c	80×60 mm. 300l. Type **767b**	14·00	14·00

768 Completed Lift

2009. Weightlifting. Multicoloured.

3287	10l. Type **768**	80	75
3288	60l. Jerk and lunge	3·00	3·75
3289	120l. Squattin with barbell at shoulder hieght	4·75	4·25
3290	150l. Squatting and grasping barbell	7·00	6·75

769 Stylized Buildings

2009. 50th Anniv of Court of Human Rights.

3291	**769** 200l. multicoloured	9·00	8·50

770 Flags as Map of Europe

2009. 60th Anniv of Council of Europe.

3292	**770** 150l. multicoloured	7·00	6·75

771 Abidin Dino

2009. Painters of the Diaspora. Multicoloured.

3293	40l. Type **771**	2·00	1·90
3294	50l. Lin Delija	2·20	2·10
3295	60l. Lika Janko	3·00	2·75
3296	150l. Artur Tashko	7·00	6·75

772 Car and Traffic Controller

2009. Road Traffic Control. Multicoloured.

3297	5l. Type **772**	55	55
3298	1000l. Zebra crossing	30·00	30·00

773 Dove and Dragon

2009. Albania–China Diplomatic Relations.

3299	**773** 20l. multicoloured	1·50	1·40

774 Choir

2009. Albanian Folk Iso-Polyphony-UNESCO Oral and Intangible Cultural Heritage of Humanity (2005). Multicoloured.

3300	40l. Type **774**	2·00	2·00
3301	250l. Musicians	9·00	9·00

775 Soldier and Arms

2009. 65th Anniv of Liberation. Multicoloured.

3302	70l. Type **775**	3·00	2·75
3303	200l. Arms and aircraft	9·00	9·25

776 Mujit Dhe e Halilit

2009. Albanian Folklore. Mujo and Halili (epic poem). Multicoloured.

3304	30l. Type **776**	2·00	2·00
3305	200l. Couple on horseback	9·00	9·00

777 Mosque, Berat (1827)

2009. Religious Art. Multicoloured.

3306	90l. Type **777**	4·25	4·25
3307	100l. Fresco, Church of Mary and St. Ristozit, Mborje, Korce (1389)	4·75	4·75
3308	120l. Frescoes, Church of St. Venerandes, Pllane-Lezhe Shek, 18th-19th century	5·00	5·00

778 Satellite Receiver and Planets

2009. Europa. Multicoloured.

3309	200l. Type **778**	8·50	9·00
3310	200l. Landing craft and vehicles on the moon	9·00	8·50
MS3311	80×60 mm. Size 30×24 mm. 350l. Satellite.	10·50	10·00

779 Fortress of Tirana

2009. Archaeology. Multicoloured.

3312	30l. Type **779**	2·50	2·50
3313	250l. Artefacts, Tumulus of Kamenica	10·50	10·50

780 Rainy Beach

2009. National Theatre. Multicoloured.

3314	20l. Type **780**	2·25	2·25
3315	80l. *Pallati 176*	3·25	3·25
3316	200l. *True Apology of Socrates* (Apologjia e vertete e Sokratit)	8·50	8·50

781 Frontispiece

2009. 60th Anniv of State Archives. Multicoloured.

3317	40l. Type **781**	2·00	2·00
3318	60l. Roll of parchment	3·00	3·00

782 Emblems

2010. Albania–Italy Friendship

3319	**782** 40l. multicoloured	2·00	2·00

783 Mother Teresa

2010. Birth Centenary of Agnes Gonxha Bojaxhiu (Mother Teresa) (founder of Missionaries of Charity)

3320	**783** 100l. multicoloured	4·50	4·50

784 Double-headed Eagle and European Stars

2010. Introduction of Visa-free Travel for Albanians in the EU

3321	**784** 40l. multicoloured	2·20	2·20

785 Reading in Library

2011. 90th Anniv of State Library. Multicoloured.

3322	10l. Type **785**	5·00	5·00
3323	1000l. Using computer in library	45·00	45·00

Nos. 3322/3 were printed, *se-tenant*, forming a composite design

786 Students

2011. 20th Anniv of Student Unrest. Multicoloured.

3324	40l. Type **786**	2·50	2·50
3325	60l. Students protesting, rear view	3·00	3·00
MS3326	70×90 mm. 200l. Students making 'V' sign (vert)	9·75	9·75

787 Cockerel, Donkey and Sun

2011. Europa (2010). Children's Books. Multicoloured.

3327	100l. Type **787**	4·50	4·50
3328	150l. Girl, pigeon and cat	7·50	7·50
MS3329	80×60 mm. 250l. Girl with pile of books (horiz)	12·00	12·00

788 Bull's Head

2011. Underwater Archaeology. Multicoloured.

3330	50l. Type **788**	3·00	3·00
3331	250l. Amphorae	12·00	12·00

789 Player

2011. World Cup Football Championships, South Africa. Multicoloured.

3332	80l. Type **789**	4·50	4·50
3333	120l. Two players	5·25	5·25
MS3333a	60×80 mm. 200l. Two players (different)	9·75	9·75

790 Soldiers and Helicopter

2011. Albanian Peacekeepers. Multicoloured.

3334	50l. Type **790**	2·50	2·50
3335	200l. Soldier, wearing beret, and tank	10·00	10·00

791 Handstamp

2011. 90th (2010) Anniv of Congress of Lushnjë. Multicoloured.

| 3336 | 70l. Type **791** | 3·50 | 3·50 |
| 3337 | 150l. Building | 7·50 | 7·50 |

792 House of Zacat, Gjirokäster

2011. National Day of Cultural Heritage. Multicoloured.

3338	10l. Type **792**	85	85
3339	70l. Woven skirt from Dumre	3·25	3·25
3340	80l. Castle, Petrela	5·75	5·75
3341	120l. Lute, Shkodër	5·75	5·75
MS3341a	80×60 mm. 200l. Woman from Buzdrin, Zadrimë	9·75	9·75

793 Basket with Handle

2011. Silverwork. Multicoloured.

3342	20l. Type **793**	1·30	1·30
3343	30l. Evening bag	1·70	1·70
3344	50l. Butterfly	3·75	3·75
3345	100l. Closed cigarette case and holder	4·50	4·50
MS3346	80×60 mm. 200l. Open cigarette case and holder	9·75	9·75

794 Roadway and Plan of Junction

2011. Upgrade of Durres to Kukes Road. Multicoloured.

3347	40l. Type **794**	2·50	2·50
3348	60l. Roadworks and plan of roundabout	3·75	3·75
3349	90l. Tunnnel and plan of junction	5·50	5·50
3350	150l. Viaduct and plan	6·25	6·25

795 House with Balcony

2011. World Heritage Sites. Berat. Each black and scarlet-vermilion.

| MS3351 | 10l. Type **795**; 20l. Hillside houses facing left; 30l. Bridge; 50l. Archway and gated courtyard; 60l. Hillside houses facing right; 80l. Church in castle grounds | 12·00 | 12·00 |

796 Tree containing Map of Europe

2011. Europa. Forests. Multicoloured.

| 3352 | 200l. Type **796** | 11·50 | 11·50 |
| MS3353 | 80×60 mm. 250l. As Type **796** but with colour change | 9·50 | 9·50 |

797 Two Boxers

2011. Boxing. Multicoloured.

3354	50l. Type **797**	2·50	2·50
3355	100l. Two boxers (different)	4·50	4·50
MS3356	80×60 mm. 250l. Boxer wearing blue with raised fist	11·50	11·50

798 Ballot Box

2011. 20th Anniv of First Free Elections

| 3357 | **798** | 150l. multicoloured | 7·00 | 7·00 |

799 Ismail Kadare

2011. 75th Birth Anniv of Ismail Kadare

| 3358 | **799** | 40l. multicoloured | 2·10 | 2·10 |

800 Wooded Valley and River

2011. Tourism. Valbona River. Multicoloured.

| 3354 | 80l. Type **800** | 3·00 | 3·00 |
| 3355 | 120l. Boulders in river | 6·50 | 6·50 |

801 Worker holding Red Cross Parcel, Expectant Mother and Worker binding Injured Arm

2011. 90th Anniv of Albanian Red Cross. Each black and carmine-vermilion.

| 3361 | 70l. + 10l. Type **801** | 3·00 | 3·00 |
| 3362 | 120l. Giving and receiving aid | 6·50 | 6·50 |

802 Pigeon wearing Helmet with Goggles and carrying Mail Bag and Globe

2011. Stamp Day. Carrier Pigeons. Multicoloured.

| 3363 | 10l. Type **802** | 5·00 | 5·00 |
| 3364 | 1000l. Globe and pigeon (blue background) | 42·00 | 42·00 |

EXPRESS LETTER STAMPS
ITALIAN OCCUPATION

E67 King Victor Emmanuel

1940

| E373 | **E67** | 25q. violet | 9·75 | 10·50 |
| E374 | **E67** | 50q. red | 18·00 | 19·00 |

No. E374 is inscr "POSTAT EXPRES".

1943. Optd **14 Shtator 1943**.

| E402 | 25q. violet | 27·00 | 33·00 |

POSTAGE DUE STAMPS

1914. Optd **TAKSE** through large letter **T**.

D33	**4**	2q. brown and yellow	13·00	5·25
D34	**4**	5q. green and yellow	13·00	5·25
D35	**4**	10q. red and pink	18·00	5·25
D36	**4**	25q. blue	22·00	5·25
D37	**4**	50q. mauve and red	33·00	17·00

1914. Nos. 40/4 optd **TAKSE**.

D46	10pa. on 5q. green & yell	6·50	5·25
D47	20pa. on 10q. red and pink	6·50	5·25
D48	1g. on 25q. blue	6·50	5·25
D49	2g. on 50q. mauve and red	6·50	5·25

1919. Fiscal stamps optd **TAXE**.

D89	**12**	4q. on 4h. pink	16·00	12·50
D90	**12**	10q. on 10k. red on grn	16·00	12·50
D91	**12**	20q. on 2k. orge on lilac	16·00	12·50
D92	**12**	50q. on 5k. brown on yell	16·00	12·50

D20 Fortress of Shkoder

1920. Optd with posthorn.

D129	**D20**	4q. olive	1·30	5·25
D130	**D20**	10q. red	2·50	7·75
D131	**D20**	20q. brown	2·50	7·75
D132	**D20**	50q. black	6·50	21·00

D22

1922

D141	**D22**	4q. black on red	1·80	5·25
D142	**D22**	10q. black on red	1·80	5·25
D143	**D22**	20q. black on red	1·80	5·25
D144	**D22**	50q. black on red	1·80	5·25

1922. Optd **Republika Shiqiptare**.

D186	4q. black on red	5·50	5·25
D187	10q. black on red	5·50	5·25
D188	20q. black on red	5·50	5·25
D189	50q. black on red	5·50	5·25

D35

1925

D204	**D35**	10q. blue	2·20	4·25
D205	**D35**	20q. green	2·20	4·25
D206	**D35**	30q. brown	4·25	8·25
D207	**D35**	50q. dark brown	7·50	16·00

D53 Arms of Albania

1930

D288	**D53**	10q. blue	18·00	26·00
D289	**D53**	20q. red	6·50	16·00
D290	**D53**	30q. violet	6·50	16·00
D291	**D53**	50q. green	6·50	16·00

1936. Optd **Takse**.

| D312 | **50** | 10q. red | 16·00 | 47·00 |

D67

1940

D373	**D67**	4q. red	43·00	65·00
D374	**D67**	10q. violet	43·00	65·00
D375	**D67**	20q. brown	43·00	65·00
D376	**D67**	30q. blue	43·00	65·00
D377	**D67**	50q. red	43·00	65·00

ALEXANDRETTA

The territory of Alexandretta. Autonomous under French control from 1923 to September 1938.

1938. 100 centiemes = 1 piastre.

1938. Stamps of Syria of 1930/1 optd **Sandjak d'Alexandrette** (Nos. 1, 4, 7 and 11) or **SANDJAK D'ALEXANDRETTE** (others), Nos. 7 and 11 surch also.

1	0p.10 purple	1·40	5·50
2	0p.20 red	1·50	5·75
3	0p.50 violet	1·70	4·50
4	0p.75 red	2·40	5·50
5	1p. brown	2·00	4·25
6	2p. violet	2·00	4·75
7	2p.50 on 4p. orange	3·50	3·50
8	3p. green	3·00	8·25
9	4p. orange	4·00	2·75
10	6p. black	4·25	4·25
11	12p.50 on 15p. red (No. 267)	7·50	8·25
12	25p. purple	10·00	29·00

1938. Air. Stamps of Syria of 1937 (Nos. 322 etc.) optd **SANDJAK D'ALEXANDRETTE**.

13	½p. violet	1·70	3·00
14	1p. black	1·50	4·25
15	2p. green	3·25	5·50
16	3p. blue	3·75	9·75
17	5p. mauve	9·00	25·00
18	10p. brown	8·75	25·00
19	15p. brown	9·25	28·00
20	25p. blue	16·00	34·00

1938. 10Death of Kemal Ataturk. Nos. 4, 5, 7, 9 and 11 optd **10-11-1938** in frame.

27	0p.75 red	43·00	70·00
28	1p. brown	29·00	65·00
29	2p.50 on 4p. orange	16·00	13·00
30	4p. orange	10·00	17·00
31	12p.50 on 15p. red	65·00	80·00

POSTAGE DUE STAMPS

1938. Postage Due stamps of Syria of 1925 optd **SANDJAK D'ALEXANDRETTE**.

D21	**D20**	0p.50 brown on yellow	3·00	6·75
D22	**D20**	1p. purple on pink	2·30	7·25
D23	**D20**	2p. black on blue	3·00	8·00
D24	**D20**	3p. black on red	3·75	14·00
D25	**D20**	5p. black on green	5·75	11·00
D26	**D20**	8p. black on blue	8·25	11·50

Pt. 6

ALEXANDRIA

Issues of the French P.O. in this Egyptian port. The French Post Offices in Egypt closed on 31 March 1931.

1899. 100 centimes = 1 franc.
1921. 10 milliemes = 1 piastre.

1899. Stamps of France optd **ALEXANDRIE.**

1	10	1c. black on blue	1·50	1·80
2	10	2c. brown on yellow	2·50	2·50
3	10	3c. grey	1·80	2·30
4	10	4c. brown on grey	1·40	2·30
5	10	5c. green	3·75	2·10
7	10	10c. black on lilac	8·75	10·00
9	10	15c. green	7·25	5·50
10	10	20c. red on green	9·25	8·50
11	10	25c. black on red	10·50	90
12	10	30c. brown	13·50	9·25
13	10	40c. red on yellow	13·00	11·00
15	10	50c. red	38·00	11·00
16	10	1f. olive	28·00	12·00
17	10	2f. brown on blue	90·00	£100
18	10	5f. mauve on lilac	£130	£100

1902. 'Blanc', 'Mouchon' and 'Merson' key-types, inscr 'ALEXANDRIE'.

19	A	1c. grey	1·80	1·20
20	A	2c. purple	60	1·90
21	A	3c. red	75	1·60
22	A	4c. brown	65	1·50
24	A	5c. green	75	60
25	B	10c. red	3·25	1·20
26	B	15c. red	7·00	2·50
27	B	15c. orange	2·50	2·50
28	B	20c. brown	3·50	1·80
29	B	25c. blue	2·00	20
30	B	30c. mauve	5·00	3·75
31	C	40c. red and blue	6·00	2·30
32	C	50c. brown and lilac	12·00	90
33	C	1f. red and green	22·00	2·30
34	C	2f. lilac and buff	18·00	7·25
35	C	5f. blue and buff	22·00	12·50

1915. Red Cross. Surch **5c** and Red Cross.

36	B	10c. + 5c. red	30	7·00

1921. Surch thus, **15 Mill.**, in one line (without bars).

37	A	2m. on 5c. green	4·00	9·25
38	A	3m. on 3c. red	10·50	16·00
39	B	4m. on 10c. red	3·75	6·50
40	A	5m. on 1c. grey	13·00	19·00
41	A	5m. on 4c. brown	10·50	19·00
42	B	6m. on 15c. orange	2·75	7·75
43	B	8m. on 20c. brown	5·00	14·00
44	B	10m. on 25c. blue	3·75	6·50
45	B	12m. on 30c. mauve	17·00	32·00
46	A	15m. on 2c. purple	7·75	14·00
47	C	15m. on 40c. red and blue	17·00	32·00
48	C	15m. on 50c. brown & lilac	9·50	25·00
49	C	30m. on 1f. red and green	£140	£140
50	C	60m. on 2f. lilac and buff	£160	£160
51	C	150m. on 5f. blue and buff	£250	£250

1921. Surch thus, **15 MILLIEMES**, in two lines (without bars).

53	A	1m. on 1c. grey	4·50	6·75
54	A	2m. on 5c. green	3·50	5·50
55	B	4m. on 10c. red	5·00	10·50
65	B	4m. on 10c. green	3·50	4·50
56	A	5m. on 3c. orange	6·50	10·00
57	B	6m. on 15c. orange	3·25	6·00
58	B	8m. on 20c. brown	3·75	3·75
59	B	10m. on 25c. blue	1·80	2·75
60	B	10m. on 30c. mauve	7·25	6·50
61	C	15m. on 50c. brown & lilac	7·75	6·50
66	B	15m. on 50c. blue	3·00	3·00
62	C	30m. on 1f. red and green	6·00	3·75
63	C	60m. on 2f. lilac and buff	£2000	£2000
67	C	60m. on 2f. red and green	20·00	23·00
64	C	150m. on 5f. blue and buff	21·00	25·00

1925. Surch in milliemes with bars over old value.

68	A	1m. on 1c. grey	20	4·00
69	A	2m. on 5c. orange	45	3·00
70	A	2m. on 5c. green	3·25	4·75
71	B	4m. on 10c. green	1·00	5·00
72	A	5m. on 3c. red	1·70	3·00
73	B	6m. on 15c. orange	1·50	4·50
74	B	8m. on 20c. brown	1·10	4·50
75	B	10m. on 25c. blue	65	1·60
76	B	15m. on 50c. blue	2·50	1·70
77	C	30m. on 1f. red and green	1·70	1·00
78	C	60m. on 2f. red and green	4·25	12·00

79	C	150m. on 5f. blue and buff	6·25	12·50

1927. Altered key-types, inscr 'Mm' below value.

80	A	3m. orange	2·75	6·25
81	B	15m. blue	2·50	1·40
82	B	20m. mauve	6·00	13·00
83	C	50m. red and green	13·00	24·00
84	C	100m. blue and yellow	16·00	27·00
85	C	250m. green and red	20·00	44·00

1927. Sinking Fund. As No. 81, colour changed, surch **+ 5 Mm Caisse d'Amortissement.**

86	B	15m.+5m. orange	3·75	12·00
87	B	15m.+5m. red	6·00	12·00
88	B	15m.+5m. brown	11·50	25·00
89	B	15m.+5m. lilac	15·00	40·00

POSTAGE DUE STAMPS

1922. Postage Due Stamps of France surch in milliemes.

D65	D11	2m. on 5c. blue	1·80	10·00
D66	D11	4m. on 10c. brown	3·75	10·00
D67	D11	10m. on 30c. red	3·00	11·00
D68	D11	15m. on 50c. purple	1·80	11·00
D69	D11	30m. on 1f. pur on yell	2·00	16·00

D10

1928.

D90	D10	1m. grey	1·00	9·00
D91	D10	2m. blue	3·75	8·75
D92	D10	4m. pink	4·00	9·50
D93	D10	5m. olive	3·75	8·75
D94	D10	10m. red	4·25	9·50
D95	D10	20m. purple	5·50	8·75
D96	D10	30m. green	10·50	16·00
D97	D10	40m. lilac	7·25	16·00

This set was issued for use in both Alexandria and Port Said.

Pt. 6, Pt. 12

ALGERIA

French territory in N. Africa. Stamps of France were used in Algeria from July 1958 until 3 July 1962, when the country achieved independence following a referendum.

1924. 100 centimes = 1 franc.
1964. 100 centimes = 1 dinar.

1924. Stamps of France optd **ALGERIE.**

1	11	½c. on 1c. grey	55	80
2	11	1c. grey	60	2·50
3	11	2c. red	55	2·75
4	11	3c. red	70	2·50
5	11	4c. brown	70	1·90
6	18	5c. orange	1·40	70
7	11	5c. green	70	15
8	30	10c. green	1·60	1·40
9	18	10c. green	40	50
10	15	15c. green	1·60	1·40
11	30	15c. green	70	2·75
12	18	15c. brown	1·40	1·10
13	18	20c. brown	1·40	50
14	18	25c. blue	85	25
15	30	30c. red	85	90
16	18	30c. blue	70	15
17	18	30c. red*	85	1·50
18	18	35c. violet	1·50	1·70
19	13	40c. red and blue	2·50	2·10
20	18	40c. olive	1·80	1·90
21	13	45c. green and blue	1·40	2·30
22	30	45c. red	90	75
23	30	50c. blue	1·40	90
24	15	60c. violet	1·40	65
25	15	65c. red	55	65
26	30	75c. blue	70	40
27	15	80c. red	1·20	75
28	15	85c. red	1·00	40
29	13	1f. red and green	2·10	45
30	18	1f.05 red	1·10	1·50
31	13	2f. red and green	2·30	3·75
32	13	3f. violet and blue	2·50	3·00
33	13	5f. blue and yellow	11·00	16·00

*No. 17 was only issued pre-cancelled and the price in the unused column is for stamps with full gum.

3 Street in the Casbah

4 Mosque of Sidi Abderahman

5 Grand Mosque

6 Bay of Algiers

1926.

34	3	1c. green	30	1·50
35	3	2c. purple	30	1·50
36	3	3c. orange	20	1·50
37	3	5c. green	45	15
38	3	10c. mauve	45	15
39	4	15c. brown	45	30
40	4	20c. green	40	15
41	4	20c. red	1·50	20
45	4	25c. blue	70	35
46	4	30c. blue	1·40	1·50
47	4	30c. green	1·70	60
48	4	35c. violet	1·70	5·25
49	4	40c. green	15	15
50	5	45c. purple	50	15
51	5	50c. blue	50	15
53	5	50c. red	1·60	15
54	5	60c. green	30	75
55	5	65c. brown	2·00	1·80
56	3	65c. blue	20	30
57	5	75c. red	75	15
58	5	75c. blue	3·25	30
59	5	80c. orange	1·20	2·50
60	5	90c. red	2·50	2·20
61	6	1f. purple and green	1·20	15
62	5	1f.05 brown	1·10	2·30
63	5	1f.10 mauve	4·50	7·25
64	6	1f.25 ultramarine and blue	1·90	6·75
65	6	1f.50 ultramarine and blue	3·75	1·50
66	6	2f. brown and green	2·75	45
67	6	3f. red and mauve	4·25	2·20
68	6	5f. mauve and red	5·25	3·00
69	6	10f. red and brown	75·00	50·00
70	6	20f. green and violet	11·50	13·00

1926. Surch ½ centime.

71	3	½c. on 1c. olive	40	2·40

1927. Wounded Soldiers of Moroccan War Charity Issue. Surch with star and crescent and premium.

72		5c.+5c. green	1·00	6·00
73		10c.+10c. mauve	1·20	6·00
74	4	15c.+15c. brown	1·50	6·00
75	4	20c.+20c. red	1·50	6·00
76	4	25c.+25c. green	1·00	6·00
77	4	30c.+30c. blue	2·10	6·00
78	4	35c.+35c. violet	65	6·00
79	4	40c.+40c. olive	1·00	6·00
80	5	50c.+50c. blue	1·50	6·50
81	5	80c.+80c. orange	1·30	6·50
82	6	1f.+1f. purple and green	1·50	6·50
83	6	2f.+2f. brown and green	32·00	70·00
84	6	5f.+5f. mauve and red	70·00	90·00

1927. Surch in figures.

85	4	10 on 35c. violet	40	90
86	4	25 on 30c. blue	55	10
87	4	30 on 25c. green	40	10
88	5	65 on 60c. green	95	90
89	5	90 on 80c. orange	20	10
90	5	1f.10 on 1f.05 brown	15	10
91	6	1f.50 on 1f.25 ultramarine and blue	1·00	1·00

1927. Surch **5c.**

92	11	5c. on 4c. brown (No. 5)	90	1·60

11 Railway Terminus, Oran

1930. Centenary of French Occupation.

93		5c.+5c. orange	9·75	29·00
94	-	10c.+10c. olive	9·75	22·00
95	-	15c.+15c. brown	8·25	22·00
96	-	25c.+25c. grey	8·25	20·00
97	-	30c.+30c. red	7·00	28·00
98	-	40c.+40c. green	5·50	26·00
99	-	50c.+50c. blue	5·50	24·00
100	-	75c.+75c. purple	4·75	24·00
101	-	1f.+1f. orange	5·50	26·00
102	-	1f.50+1f.50 blue	6·25	24·00
103	-	2f.+2f. red	5·50	26·00
104	-	3f.+3f. green	7·00	26·00
105	-	5f.+5f. red and green	14·00	55·00

DESIGNS—HORIZ: 10c. Constantine; 15c. Admiralty, Algiers; 25c. Algiers; 30c. Ruins of Timgad; 40c. Ruins of Djemila; 50c. Ruins of Djemila; 75c. Tlemcen; 1f. Ghardaia; 1f.50, Tolga; 2f. Tuaregs; 3f. Native quarter, Algiers; 5f. Mosque, Algiers.

12 Bay of Algiers, after painting by Verecque

1930. N. African International Philatelic Exn.

106	12	10f.+10f. brown	34·00	65·00

15 Admiralty and Penon Lighthouse, Algiers

1936.

107	A	1c. blue	35	1·50
108	F	2c. purple	30	75
109	B	3c. green	75	2·10
110	C	5c. mauve	45	15
111	15	10c. green	90	75
112	D	15c. red	45	15
113	G	20c. green	50	15
114	E	25c. green	2·20	60
115	C	30c. green	60	20
116	D	40c. purple	90	20
117	G	45c. blue	1·30	3·75
118	15	50c. red	3·00	60
119	A	65c. brown	8·75	11·50
120	A	65c. red	1·90	60
121	A	70c. brown	75	90
122	F	75c. slate	75	20
124	B	90c. red	75	90
125	E	1f. brown	75	20
126	15	1f.25 violet	2·10	75
127	15	1f.25 red	75	1·50
128	F	1f.50 blue	2·75	90
129	F	1f.50 red	3·00	4·50
130	C	1f.75 orange	1·50	75
131	B	2f. purple	1·00	15
132	A	2f.25 green	19·00	26·00
133	E	2f.25 blue	1·90	2·00
134	C	2f.50 blue	2·20	3·25
135	G	3f. mauve	75	30
136	E	3f.50 blue	2·50	3·50
137	15	5f. slate	1·50	1·60
138	F	10f. orange	1·00	2·75
139	D	20f. blue	1·90	3·75

DESIGNS—HORIZ: A, In the Sahara; B, Arc de Triomphe, Lambese; C, Ghardaia, Mzab; D, Marabouts, Touggourt; E, El Kebir Mosque, Algiers. VERT: F, Colomb Bechar-Oued; G, Cemetery, Tlemcen.

17 Exhibition Pavilion

1937. Paris International Exhibition.

140	17	40c. green	1·00	65
141	17	50c. red	65	35
142	17	1f.50 blue	90	1·00
143	17	1f.75 black	1·90	1·70

18 Constantine in 1837

1937. Centenary of Capture of Constantine.

144	18	65c. red	1·00	50
145	18	1f. brown	3·00	65
146	18	1f.75 blue	30	75
147	18	2f.15 purple	45	50

19 Ruins of Roman Villa

1938. Centenary of Philippeville.

148	19	30c. green	1·50	2·50
149	19	65c. blue	45	50
150	19	75c. purple	1·80	2·75
151	19	3f. red	3·75	4·25
152	19	5f. brown	4·50	5·75

1938. 20th Anniv of Armistice Day. No. 132 surch **1918 - 11 Nov. - 1938 0.65 + 0.35.**

153		65c.+35c. on 2f.25 green	1·50	4·00

1938. Surch **0,25**.

154	15	25c. on 50c. red	45	15

22 Caillie, Lavigerie and Duveyrier

1939. Sahara Pioneers' Monument Fund.

155	22	30c.+20c. green	2·30	7·50
156	22	90c.+60c. red	2·20	5·75
157	22	2f.25+75c. blue	11·50	50·00
158	22	5f.+5f. black	29·00	75·00

23 *Extavia* (freighter) in Algiers Harbour

1939. New York World's Fair.

159	23	20c. green	1·50	3·75
160	23	40c. purple	1·90	4·25
161	23	90c. brown	2·10	65
162	23	1f.25 red	6·50	8·25
163	23	2f.25 blue	2·75	3·25

1939. Surch with new values and bars or cross.

173	3	50c. on 65c. blue	1·50	50
164	3	1f. on 90c. red	75	35
173c	B	90c.+60c. red (No. 124)	90	35

25 Algerian Soldiers

1940. Soldiers' Dependants' Relief Fund. Surch + and premium.

166	25	1f.+1f. blue	1·90	5·00
167	25	1f.+2f. red	1·90	5·75
168	25	1f.+4f. green	2·20	6·50
169	25	1f.+9f. brown	2·50	8·25

26 Algiers

1941

170	26	30c. blue	1·40	1·70
171	26	70c. brown	1·10	35
172	26	1f. red	1·10	35

28 Marshal Petain

1941

174	28	1f. blue	60	1·50

1941. National Relief Fund. As No. 174, but surch **+4 f** and colour changed.

175		1f.+4f. black	1·00	35

1942. National Relief Fund. Surch **SECOURS NATIONAL +4f**

176		1f.+4f. blue (No. 174)	1·20	6·50

1942. Various altered types. (a) As T **26**, but without 'RF'.

177	26	30c. blue	60	3·25

(b) As T **5**, but without 'REPUBLIQUE FRANCAISE'.

178	5	40c. grey	1·20	5·00
179	5	50c. red	75	1·30

(c) As No. 129 but without 'RF'.

180	F	1f.50 red	1·80	1·10

32 Arms of Oran

1942. Coats-of-Arms.

190	A	10c. lilac	1·30	3·50
191	32	30c. green	1·00	3·75
181	B	40c. violet	75	4·25
192	B	40c. lilac	2·10	3·75
182	32	60c. red	1·30	2·50
194	B	70c. blue	90	2·30
195	A	80c. green	1·00	3·75
183	B	1f.20 green	1·30	3·00
184	A	1f.50 red	45	50
198	32	2f. blue	45	90
186	B	2f.40 red	1·80	3·00
187	A	3f. blue	45	65
188	B	4f. blue	1·20	1·50
201	32	4f.50 purple	90	15
189	32	5f. green	1·30	1·70

ARMS: A, Algiers; B, Constantine.

34 Marshal Petain

1943

202	34	1f.50 red	45	3·25

35 "La Marseillaise" 36 Allegory of Victory

1943

203	35	1f.50 red	1·00	3·00
204	36	1f.50 blue	30	65

1943. Surch **2f.**

205	32	2f. on 5f. orange	45	1·20

38 Summer Palace, Algiers

1943

206	38	15f. grey	1·50	2·10
207	38	20f. green	1·50	2·10
208	38	50f. red	1·20	1·30
209	38	100f. blue	3·00	3·25
210	38	200f. brown	4·50	5·00

39 Mother and Children

1943. Prisoners-of-war Relief Fund.

211	39	50c.+4f.50 pink	90	6·50
212	39	1f.50+8f.50 green	90	6·50
213	39	3f.+12f. blue	90	6·50
214	39	5f.+15f. brown	90	6·50

40 "Marianne"

1944

215	40	10c. grey	20	75
216	40	30c. lilac	20	50
217	40	50c. red	20	15
218	40	80c. green	45	90
219	40	1f.20 lilac	75	1·70
220	40	1f.50 blue	20	15
221	40	2f.40 red	30	50
222	40	3f. violet	45	25
223	40	4f.50 black	60	35

41 Gallic Cock

1944

224	41	40c. red	45	3·25
225	41	1f. green	50	15
226	41	2f. red	45	35
227	41	2f. brown	60	75
228	41	4f. blue	1·30	35
229	41	10f. black	1·50	2·50

1944. Surch **0f.30**.

230	4	0f.30 on 15c. brown	60	1·30

No. 230 was only issued pre-cancelled and the price in the unused column is for stamps with full gum.

1945. Types of France optd **ALGERIE**.

247	239	10c. black and blue	30	3·75
231	217	40c. mauve	15	50
232	217	50c. blue	30	35
248	-	50c. brown, yellow and red (No. 973)	90	50
233	218	60c. blue	60	85
236	136	80c. green	1·20	1·70
234	218	1f. red	60	50
237	136	1f. blue	90	50
238	136	1f.20 violet	90	4·25
235	218	1f.50 lilac	90	1·30
239	136	2f. brown	30	15
240	136	2f.40 red	1·00	2·10
242	219	2f. green	75	25
241	136	3f. orange	65	85
243	219	3f. red	45	15
244	219	4f.50 blue	2·10	50
245	219	5f. green	35	25
246	219	6f. blue	1·80	2·00

1945. Airmen and Dependants Fund. As No. 742 of France (bombers) optd **RF ALGERIE**.

249	169	1f.50+3f.50 blue	1·20	5·75

1945. Postal Employees War Victims' Fund. As No. 949 of France overprinted **ALGERIE**.

250	223	4f.+6f. brown	90	5·75

1945. Stamp Day. As No. 955 of France (Louis XI) optd **ALGERIE**.

251	228	2f.+3f. purple	1·20	5·00

1946. No. 184 surch **0f50 RF**.

252		50c. on 1f.50 red	30	50

1946. Type of France optd **ALGERIE** and surch **2F**.

253	136	2f. on 1f.50 brown	30	35

46 Potez 56 over Algiers

1946. Air.

254	46	5f. red	1·60	85
255	46	10f. blue	35	15
256	46	15f. green	1·50	75
257a	46	20f. brown	1·50	35
258	46	25f. violet	1·30	50
259	46	40f. black	1·90	1·70

1946. Stamp Day. As No. 975 of France (De la Varane), optd **ALGERIE**.

260	241	3f.+2f. red	90	6·50

47 Children at Spring

1946. Charity. Inscr as in T **47**.

261	47	3f.+17f. green	3·00	8·25
262	47	4f.+21f. red	3·25	7·50
263	47	8f.+27f. purple	4·00	18·00
264	47	10f.+35f. blue	3·75	8·25

DESIGNS—VERT: 4f. Boy gazing skywards; 8f. Laurel-crowned head. HORIZ: 10f. Soldier looking at Algerian coast.

1947. Air. Surch **-10%**.

265	46	"-10%" on 5f. red	45	60

1947. Stamp Day. As No. 1008 of France (Louvois), optd **ALGERIE**.

266	253	4f.50+5f.50 blue	1·20	7·00

49 Arms of Constantine

1947. Various Arms.

267	49	10c. green and red	15	2·50
268	A	50c. black and orange	15	35
269	B	1f. blue and yellow	15	15
270	49	1f.30 black and blue	1·50	4·25
271	A	1f.50 violet and yellow	30	15
272	B	2f. black and green	30	15
273	49	2f.50 black and red	1·20	1·30
274	A	3f. red and green	45	65
275	B	3f.50 green and purple	45	35
276	49	4f. brown and green	15	15
277	A	4f.50 blue and red	60	15
278	A	5f. black and blue	20	15
279	B	6f. brown and red	45	15
280	B	8f. brown and blue	30	15
281	49	10f. pink and brown	60	25
282	A	15f. black and red	1·80	15

ARMS: A, Algiers; B, Oran. See also Nos. 364/8 and 381/3.

1947. Air. Seventh Anniv of Gen. de Gaulle's Call to Arms. Surch with Lorraine Cross and **18 Juin 1940 + 10 Fr**.

283	46	10f.+10f. blue	3·25	8·25

1947. Resistance Movement. Type of France surch **ALGERIE+10f**.

284	261	5f.+10f. grey	1·80	8·25

1948. Stamp Day. Type of France (Arago) optd **ALGERIE**.

285	267	6f.+4f. green	1·50	8·25

1948. Air. Eighth Anniv of Gen. de Gaulle's Call to Arms. Surch with Lorraine Cross and **18 JUIN 1940 + 10 Fr.**

286	46	5f.+10f. red	3·00	6·50

1948. General Leclerc Memorial. Type of France surch **ALGERIE + 4f**.

287	270	6f.+4f. red	1·50	6·25

57 Battleship *Richelieu*

1949. Naval Welfare Fund.

288	57	10f.+15f. blue	5·75	25·00
289	-	18f.+22f. red	8·75	25·00

DESIGN: 18f. Aircraft-carrier *Arromanches*.

58 White Storks over Minaret

1949. Air.

290	58	50f. green	4·50	1·30
291	-	100f. brown	3·00	85
292	58	200f. red	8·75	4·25
293	-	500f. blue	31·00	46·00

DESIGN—HORIZ: 100, 500f. Dewoitine D-338 trimotor airplane over valley dwellings.

1949. Stamp Day. As No. 1054 of France (Choiseul) optd **ALGERIE**.

294	278	15f.+5f. mauve	95	6·50

60 French Colonials

1949. 75th Anniv of U.P.U.

295	60	5f. green	2·40	5·75
296	60	15f. red	3·00	5·75
297	60	25f. blue	4·75	15·00

61 Statue of Duke of Orleans

1949. Air. 25th Anniv of First Algerian Postage Stamp.

298	61	15f.+20f. brown	6·00	20·00

62 Grapes

1950

299	62	20f. purple, green & dp pur	1·20	65
300	-	25f. brown, green & black	2·40	1·00
301	-	40f. orange, green & brown	3·00	2·00

DESIGNS: 25f. Dates; 40f. Oranges and lemons.

1950. Stamp Day. As No. 1091 of France (Postman), optd **ALGERIE**.

302	292	12f.+3f. brown	2·40	9·00

63 Foreign Legionary

1950. Foreign Legion Welfare Fund.
303 63 15f.+5f. green 2·30 8·25

64 R. P. de Foucauld and Gen. Laperrine

1950. 50th Anniv of French in the Sahara (25f.) and Unveiling of Monument to Abd-el-Kader (40f.).
304 64 25f.+5f. black and green 6·00 20·00
305 – 40f.+10f. dp brown & brn 6·00 20·00
DESIGN: 40f. Emir Abd-el-Kader and Marshal Bugeaud.

65 Col. C. d'Ornano

1951. Col. d'Ornano Monument Fund.
306 65 15f.+5f. purple, brn blk 1·20 5·75

1951. Stamp Day. As No. 1107 of France (Travelling Post Office sorting van), optd **ALGERIE**.
307 300 12f.+3f. brown 4·25 8·25

66 Apollo of Cherchel

1952.
308 66 10f. sepia 50 15
309 – 12f. brown 60 25
310 – 15f. blue 50 25
311 – 18f. red 70 50
312 – 20f. green 50 25
313 66 30f. blue 85 50
STATUES: 12, 18f. Isis of Cherchel; 15, 20f. Boy and eagle.

1952. Stamp Day. As No. 1140 of France (Mail Coach), optd **ALGERIE**.
314 319 12f.+3f. blue 2·40 11·50

67 Algerian War Memorial

1952. African Army Commemoration.
315 67 12f. green 95 2·50

68 Medaille Militaire

1952. Military Medal Centenary.
316 68 15f.+5f. brown, yell & grn 2·40 6·50

69 Fossil ("Berbericeras sekikensis")

1952. 19th Int Geological Convention, Algiers.
317 69 15f. red 3·50 5·75
318 – 30f. blue 2·40 4·25

DESIGN: 30f. Phonolite Dyke, Hoggar.

1952. Tenth Anniv of Battle of Bir-Hakeim. As No. 1146 of France surch **ALGERIE+5 F.**
319 325 30f.+5f. blue 2·30 6·50

72 Bou-Nara

1952. Red Cross Fund.
320 – 8f.+2f. red and blue 1·20 5·00
321 72 12f.+3f. red 1·80 8·25
DESIGN: 8f. El-Oued and map of Algeria.

73 Members of Corps and Camel

1952. 50th Anniv of Sahara Corps.
322 73 12f. brown 1·80 3·50

1953. Stamp Day. As No. 1161 of France (Count D'Argenson), optd **ALGERIE**.
323 334 12f.+3f. violet 1·20 8·25

74 "Victory" of Cirta

1954. Army Welfare Fund.
324 74 15f.+5f. brown and sepia 85 3·75

75 E. Millon

1954. Military Health Service.
325 75 25f. sepia and green 95 65
326 – 40f. red and brown 85 50
327 – 50f. indigo and blue 1·20 60
DOCTORS—VERT: 40f. F. Maillot. HORIZ: 50f. A. Laveran.

1954. Stamp Day. As No. 1202 of France (Lavalette), optd **ALGERIE**.
328 346 12f.+3f. red 95 5·25

76 French and Algerian Soldiers

1954. Old Soldiers' Welfare Fund.
329 76 15f.+5f. sepia 1·80 5·75

77 Foreign Legionary

1954. Foreign Legion Welfare Fund.
330 77 15f.+5f. green 2·50 8·25

78

1954. Third International Congress of Mediterranean Citrus Fruit Culture.
331 78 15f. blue and indigo 1·30 3·00

1954. Tenth Anniv of Liberation. As No. 1204 of France ("D-Day") optd **ALGERIE**.
332 348 15f. red 70 2·00

79 Darguinah Hydroelectric Station

1954. Inauguration of River Agrioun Hydroelectric Installations.
333 79 15f. purple 1·20 4·00

80 Courtyard of Bardo Museum

1954
334 80 10f. brown & light brown 70 15
335 80 12f. orange and brown (I) 95 20
336 80 12f. orange and brown (II) 60 50
337 80 15f. blue and light blue 70 20
338 80 18f. carmine and red 70 50
339 80 20f. green and light green 90 1·30
340 80 25f. lilac and mauve 95 30
12f. "POSTES" and "ALGERIE" in orange (I) or in white (II).

1954. 150th Anniv of Presentation of First Legion of Honour. As No. 1223 of France, optd **ALGERIE**.
341 356 12f. green 95 4·00

81 Red Cross Nurses

1954. Red Cross Fund. Cross in red.
342 81 12f.+3f. blue 3·50 9·00
343 – 15f.+5f. violet 4·75 12·00
DESIGN: 15f. J.H. Dunant and Djemila ruins.

82 St. Augustine

1954. 1600th Birth Anniv of St. Augustine.
344 82 15f. brown 1·20 2·20

83 Earthquake Victims and Ruins

1954. Orleansville Earthquake Relief Fund. Inscr as in T **83**.
345 83 12f.+4f. brown 1·40 6·25
346 83 15f.+5f. blue 1·50 6·50
347 – 18f.+6f. mauve 1·70 6·50
348 – 20f.+7f. violet 1·80 7·00
349 – 25f.+8f. lake 2·30 7·25
350 – 30f.+10f. turquoise 1·80 8·25
DESIGNS—HORIZ: 18, 20f. Red Cross workers. 25, 30f. Stretcher-bearers.

1955. Stamp Day. As No. 1245 of France (Balloon Post), optd **ALGERIE**.
351 364 12f.+3f. blue 65 5·00

84 Statue of Aesculapius and El Kettar Hospital

1955. 30th French Medical Congress.
352 84 15f. red 35 80

85 Ruins of Tipasa

1955. Bimillenary of Tipasa.
353 85 50f. brown 40 20

1955. 50th Anniv of Rotary International. As No. 1235 of France optd **ALGERIE**.
354 361 30f. blue 45 2·30

1955. As Nos. 1238 and 1238b of France ("France") inscr 'ALGERIE'.
355 362 15f. red 70 20
356 362 20f. blue 2·10 1·50

86 Widows and Children

1955. War Victims' Welfare Fund.
357 86 15f.+5f. indigo and blue 1·40 3·25

87 Grand Kabylia

1955
358 87 100f. indigo and blue 2·40 50

88

1956. Anti-cancer Fund.
359 88 15f.+5f. brown 1·60 5·50

1956. Stamp Day. As No. 1279 of France ("Francis of Taxis"), optd **ALGERIE**.
360 383 12f.+3f. red 95 4·50

89 Foreign Legion Retirement Home, Sidi Bel Abbes

1956. Foreign Legion Welfare Fund.
361 89 15f.+5f. green 1·70 6·00

90 Marshal Franchet d'Esperey (after J. Ebstein)

1956. Birth Cent of Marshal Franchet d'Esperey.
362 90 15f. indigo and blue 2·00 4·25

91 Marshal Leclerc and Memorial

1956. Marshal Leclerc Commemoration.
363 91 15f. brown and sepia 50 4·00

1956. Various arms as T **49**.
364 – 1f. green and red 85 70
365 – 3f. blue and green 80 2·75

366		5f. blue and yellow	1·10	50
367		6f. green and red	1·40	3·00
368		12f. blue and red	1·60	4·50

DESIGNS: 1f. Bone; 3f. Mostaganem; 5f. Tlemcen; 6f. Algiers; 12f. Orleansville.

92 Oran

1956

369	92	30f. purple	1·40	30
370	92	35f. red	1·90	5·25

1957. Stamp Day. As No. 1322 of France ("Felucca") optd **ALGERIE.**

371	403	12f.+3f. purple	1·80	5·00

93 Electric Train Crossing Viaduct

1957. Electrification of Bone-Tebessa Railway Line.

372	93	40f. turquoise and green	1·80	50

94 Fennec Fox

1957. Red Cross Fund. Cross in red.

373	94	12f.+3f. brown	3·50	15·00
374	-	15f.+5f. sepia (White storks)	3·50	15·00

1957. 17th Anniv of Gen. de Gaulle's Call to Arms. Surch **18 JUIN 1940 + 5F.**

375	91	15f.+5f. red and carmine	95	5·25

96 Beni Bahdel Barrage, Tlemcen

1957. Air.

376	96	200f. red	9·50	11·00

97 "Horseman Crossing Ford" (after Delacroix)

1957. Army Welfare Fund. Inscr 'OEUVRES SOCIALES DE L'ARMEE'.

377	97	15f.+5f. red	4·75	11·00
378	-	20f.+5f. green	4·25	11·50
379	-	35f.+10f. blue	4·25	12·00

DESIGNS—HORIZ: 20f. "Lakeside View" (after Fromentin). VERT: 35f. "Arab Dancer" (after Chasseriau).

1958. Stamp Day. As No. 1375 of France (Rural Postal Service), optd **ALGERIE.**

380	421	15f.+5f. brown	1·60	5·00

1958. Arms. As T **49** but inscr 'REPUBLIQUE FRANCAISE' instead of 'RF' at foot.

381		2f. red and blue	60	4·00
382		6f. green and red	36·00	60·00
383		10f. purple and green	1·20	4·50

ARMS: 2f. Tizi-Ouzou; 6f. Algiers; 10f. Setif.

99 "Strelitzia Reginae"

1958. Algerian Child Welfare Fund.

384	99	20f.+5f. orge, vio & grn	3·50	7·00

100

1958. Marshal de Lattre Foundation.

385	100	20f.+5f. red, grn & bl	3·50	7·00

INDEPENDENT STATE

1962. Stamps of France optd **EA** and with bars obliterating "REPUBLIQUE FRANCAISE".

386	344	10c. green	95	40
387	463	25c. grey and red	70	30
393	-	45c. violet, purple and sepia (No. 1463)	6·75	4·50
394	-	50c. pur & grn (No. 1464)	6·75	4·50
395	-	1f. brown, blue and myrtle (No. 1549)	4·50	1·80

103a Maps of Africa and Algeria

1962. War Orphans' Fund.

395a	103a	1f.+9f. green, black and red		£350

1962. As pictorial types of France but inscr 'REPUBLIQUE ALGERIENNE'.

396	-	5c. turquoise, grn & brn	25	10
397	438	10c. blue and sepia	25	10
398	-	25c. red, slate & brown	55	15
399	-	95c. blue, buff and sepia	3·50	1·10
400	-	1f. sepia and green	2·50	1·60

DESIGNS—VERT: 5c. Kerrata Gorges; 25c. Tlemcen Mosque; 95c. Oil derrick and pipeline at Hassi-Massaoud, Sahara. HORIZ: 1f. Medea.

104 Flag, Rifle and Olive Branch

1963. Return of Peace. Flag in green and red. Inscription and background colours given.

401	104	5c. bistre	25	10
402	104	10c. blue	25	10
403	104	25c. red	1·90	30
404	104	95c. violet	1·80	15
405	-	1f. green	2·20	15
406	-	2f. brown	3·75	80
407	-	5f. purple	7·00	3·00
408	-	10f. black	25·00	14·50

DESIGN: 1f. to 10f. As Type **104** but with dove and broken chain added.

105 Campaign Emblem and Globe

1963. Freedom from Hunger.

409	105	25c. yellow, green and red	70	25

106 Clasped Hands

1963. National Solidarity Fund.

410	106	50c.+20c. red, grn & blk	1·40	65

107 Map and Emblems

1963. First Anniv of Independence.

411	107	25c. multicoloured	70	25

108 "Arab Physicians" (13th-century MS.)

1963. Second Arab Physicians Union Congress.

412	108	25c. brown, green & bistre	2·10	55

109 Branch of Orange Tree

1963

413	109	8c. orange and bronze*	10	10
414	109	20c. orange and green*	25	15
415	109	40c. orange & turq*	75	35
416	109	55c. orange and green*	95	55

*These stamps were only issued pre-cancelled, the unused prices being for stamps with full gum.

110 "Constitution"

1963. Promulgation of Constitution.

417	110	25c. red, green and sepia	70	40

111 "Freedom Fighters"

1963. Ninth Anniv of Revolution.

418	111	25c. red, green and brown	70	25

112 Centenary Emblem

1963. Red Cross Centenary.

419	112	25c. blue, red and yellow	95	55

113 Globe and Scales of Justice

1963. 15th Anniv of Declaration of Human Rights.

420	113	25c. black and blue	70	25

114 Labourers

1964. Labour Day.

421	114	50c. multicoloured	1·40	45

115 Map of Africa and Flags

1964. First Anniv of Africa Day, and African Unity Charter.

422	115	45c. red, orange and blue	90	40

116 Tractors

1964

423	116	5c. purple	10	10
424	-	10c. brown	10	10
425	-	12c. green	50	25
426	-	15c. blue	45	25
427	-	20c. yellow	45	10
428	116	25c. red	55	10
429	-	30c. violet	55	15
430	-	45c. lake	70	25
431	-	50c. blue	70	10
432	-	65c. orange	90	25
433	116	85c. green	1·40	25
434	-	95c. red	1·80	25

DESIGNS: 10, 30, 65c. Apprentices; 12, 15, 45c. Research scientist; 20, 50, 95c. Draughtsman and bricklayer.

117 Rameses II in War Chariot, Abu Simbel

1964. Nubian Monuments Preservation.

435	117	20c. purple, red and blue	95	40
436	-	30c. ochre, turq & red	1·20	55

DESIGN: 30c. Heads of Rameses II.

118 Hertzian-wave Radio Transmitting Pylon

1964. Inauguration of Algiers–Annaba Radio-Telephone Service.

437	118	85c. black, blue & brown	2·10	65

119 Fair Emblems

1964. Algiers Fair.

438	119	30c. blue, yellow and red	55	25

120 Gas Plant

1964. Inauguration of Natural Gas Plant at Arzew.

439	120	25c. blue, yellow & violet	90	50

121 Planting Trees

1964. Reafforestation Campaign.

440	121	25c. green, red and yellow	55	25

122 Children

1964. Children's Charter.
441 **122** 15c. blue, green and red 50 25

123 Mehariste Saddle

1965. Saharan Handicrafts.
442 **123** 20c. multicoloured 55 25

124 Books Aflame

1965. Reconstitution of Algiers University Library.
443 **124** 20c.+5c. red, blk & grn 55 40

125 I.C.Y. Emblem

1965. International Co-operation Year.
444 **125** 30c. black, green and red 95 45
445 **125** 60c. black, green and blue 1·40 60

126 I.T.U. Emblem and Symbols

1965. Centenary of I.T.U.
446 **126** 60c. violet, ochre & green 95 50
447 **126** 95c. brown, ochre & lake 1·40 55

127 Musicians playing Rebbah and Lute

1965. Mohamed Racim's Miniatures (1st series). Multicoloured.
448 **127** 30c. Type **127** 1·80 65
449 60c. Musicians playing derbouka and tarr 2·75 1·50
450 5d. Algerian princess and sand gazelle 14·50 7·75
 See also Nos. 471/3.

128 Cattle

1966. Rock-paintings of Tassili-N-Ajjer (1st series).
451 **128** 1d. brown, ochre & purple 5·25 2·75
452 - 1d. multicoloured 5·25 2·75
453 - 2d. dp brown, buff & brn 11·00 4·75

454 - 3d. multicoloured 12·00 6·25
DESIGNS—VERT: No. 452, Peuhl shepherd; 454, Peuhl girls. HORIZ: No. 453, Ostriches.
 See also Nos. 474/7.

129 Pottery

1966. Grand Kahylie Handicrafts.
455 **129** 40c. brown, sepia and blue 55 40
456 - 50c. orange, green & bl 90 40
457 - 70c. black, red and blue 1·40 50
DESIGNS—HORIZ: 50c. Weaving. VERT: 70c. Jewellery.

130 Meteorological Instruments

1966. World Meteorological Day.
458 **130** 1d. purple, green and blue 1·40 50

131 Open Book, Cogwheel and Ear of Corn

1966. Literacy Campaign.
459 **131** 30c. black and ochre 50 25
460 - 60c. red, black and grey 75 40
DESIGN: 60c. Open primer, cogwheel and ear of corn.

132 W.H.O. Building

1966. Inauguration of W.H.O. Headquarters, Geneva.
461 **132** 30c. turq, grn & brn 45 40
462 **132** 60c. slate, blue and brown 90 40

133 Mohammedan Scout Emblem and Banner

1966. 30th Anniv of Algerian Mohammedan Scouts, and Seventh Arab Scout Jamboree, Jedaid (Tripoli). Multicoloured.
463 30c. Type **133** 70 40
464 1d. Jamboree emblem 1·80 65

134 Soldiers and Battle Casualty

1966. Freedom Fighters' Day.
465 **134** 30c.+10c. mult 95 65
466 **134** 95c.+10c. mult 1·80 1·30

135 Massacre Victims

1966. Deir Yassin Massacre (1948).
467 **135** 30c. black and red 55 25

136 Emir Abd-el-Kader

1966. Return of Emir Abd-el-Kader's Remains.
468 **136** 30c. multicoloured 25 10
469 **136** 95c. multicoloured 1·10 40
 See also Nos. 498/502.

137 UNESCO Emblems

1966. 20th Anniv of UNESCO.
470 **137** 1d. multicoloured 1·10 40

1966. Mohamed Racim's Miniatures (2nd series). As T **127**. Multicoloured.
471 1d. Horseman 4·50 1·50
472 1d.50 Algerian bride 6·75 2·00
473 2d. Barbarossa 10·00 3·50

1967. Rock-paintings of Tassili-N-Ajjer (2nd series). As T **128**.
474 1d. violet, buff and purple 4·50 1·90
475 2d. brown, buff and purple 6·75 3·75
476 2d. brown, purple and buff 7·50 4·00
477 3d. brown, buff and black 10·50 5·50
DESIGNS: No. 474, Cow; No. 475, Antelope; No. 476, Archers; No. 477, Warrior.

138 Bardo Museum

1967. Musulman Art. Multicoloured.
478 35c. Type **138** 45 25
479 95c. La Kalaa minaret (vert) 95 45
480 1d.30 Sedrata ruins 1·70 65

139 Ghardaia

1967. Air.
481 **139** 1d. brown, green & purple 1·40 55
482 - 2d. brown, green and blue 3·25 1·40
483 - 5d. brown, green and blue 8·50 2·50
DESIGNS: 2d. Sud Aviation SE210 Caravelle over El Oued (Souf); 5d. Tipasa.

140 View of Moretti

1967. International Tourist Year. Multicoloured.
484 40c. Type **140** 70 40
485 70c. Tuareg, Tassili (vert) 1·40 55

141 Boy and Girl, and Red Crescent

1967. Algerian Red Crescent Organization.
486 **141** 30c.+10c. brn, red & grn 90 50

142 Ostrich

1967. Saharan Fauna. Multicoloured.
487 5c. Shiny-tailed Lizard (horiz) 50 40
488 20c. Type **142** 90 50
489 40c. Sand gazelle 1·40 65
490 70c. Fennec foxes (horiz) 1·90 1·00

143 Dancers with Tambourines

1967. National Youth Festival.
491 **143** 50c. black, yellow & blue 95 40

144 "Athletics"

1967. Fifth Mediterranean Games, Tunis.
492 **144** 30c. black, blue and red 70 40

145 Skiing

1967. Winter Olympic Games, Grenoble (1968).
493 **145** 30c. blue, green & ultram 95 40
494 - 95c. green, violet & brown 1·80 85
DESIGN—HORIZ (36×26 mm): 95c. Olympic rings and competitors.

1967
498 **136** 5c. purple 25 10
499 **136** 10c. green 10 10
500 **136** 25c. orange 35 10
501 **136** 30c. black 45 10
502 **136** 30c. violet 45 10
496 **136** 50c. red 70 25
497 **136** 70c. blue 90 25
The 10c. value exists in two versions, differing in the figures of value and inscription at bottom right.

146 Scouts supporting Jamboree Emblem

1967. World Scout Jamboree, Idaho.
503 **146** 1d. multicoloured 2·10 75

1967. No. 428 surch.
504 **116** 30c. on 25c. red 70 25

148 Kouitra

1968. Musical Instruments. Multicoloured.
505	30c. Type **148**	55	25
506	40c. Lute	90	40
507	1d.30 Rebbah	3·00	1·10

149 Nememcha Carpet

1968. Algerian Carpets. Multicoloured.
509	30c. Type **149**	95	55
510	70c. Guergour	1·80	85
511	95c. Djebel-Amour	3·00	1·20
512	1d.30 Kalaa	3·75	1·40

150 Human Rights Emblem and Globe

1968. Human Rights Year.
| 513 | **150** | 40c. red, yellow and blue | 75 | 40 |

151 W.H.O. Emblem

1968. 20th Anniv of W.H.O.
| 514 | **151** | 70c. yellow, black & blue | 90 | 40 |

152 Emigrant

1968. Emigration of Algerians to Europe.
| 515 | **152** | 30c. brown, slate & blue | 55 | 25 |

153 Scouts holding Jamboree Emblem

1968. Eighth Arab Scouts Jamboree, Algiers.
| 516 | **153** | 30c. multicoloured | 70 | 25 |

154 Torch and Athletes

1968. Olympic Games, Mexico. Multicoloured.
517	30c. Type **154**	60	45
518	50c. Football	1·10	65
519	1d. Allegory of Games (horiz)	1·80	95

155 Barbary Sheep

1968. Protected Animals. Multicoloured.
| 520 | 40c. Type **155** | 90 | 40 |
| 521 | 1d. Red deer | 2·10 | 65 |

156 "Neptune's Chariot", Timgad

1968. Roman Mosaics. Multicoloured.
| 522 | 40c. "Hunting Scene" (Djemila) (vert) | 70 | 25 |
| 523 | 95c. Type **156** | 1·50 | 55 |

157 Miner

1968. Industry, Energy and Mines.
524	**157**	30c. multicoloured	50	25
525	-	30c. silver and red	50	25
526	-	95c. red, black and silver	1·40	40

DESIGNS: No. 525, Coiled spring ("Industry"); No. 526, Symbol of radiation ("Energy").

158 Opuntia

1969. Algerian Flowers. Multicoloured.
527	25c. Type **158**	70	50
528	40c. Dianthus	1·10	65
529	70c. Rose	1·80	75
530	95c. Strelitzia	3·25	1·30

See also Nos. 621/4.

159 Djorf Torba Dam, Oued Guir

1969. Saharan Public Works. Multicoloured.
| 531 | 30c. Type **159** | 70 | 25 |
| 532 | 1d.50 Route Nationale No. 51 | 2·10 | 80 |

160 Desert Mail-coach of 1870

1969. Stamp Day.
| 533 | **160** | 1d. sepia, brown and blue | 2·75 | 85 |

161 The Capitol, Timgad

1969. Roman Ruins in Algeria. Multicoloured.
| 534 | 30c. Type **161** | 55 | 25 |
| 535 | 1d. Septimius Temple, Djemila (horiz) | 1·50 | 60 |

162 I.L.O. Emblem

1969. 50th Anniv of I.L.O.
| 536 | **162** | 95c. red, yellow and black | 1·30 | 45 |

1969. No. 425 surch.
| 537 | 20c. on 12c. green | 45 | 10 |

164 Carved Bookcase

1969. Handicrafts. Multicoloured.
538	30c. Type **164**	50	25
539	60c. Copper tray	90	40
540	1d. Arab saddle	1·60	60

165 "Africa" Head

1969. First Pan-African Cultural Festival, Algiers.
| 541 | **165** | 30c. multicoloured | 55 | 25 |

166 Astronauts on Moon

1969. First Man on the Moon.
| 542 | **166** | 50c. multicoloured | 1·10 | 45 |

167 Bank Emblem

1969. Fifth Anniv of African Development Bank.
| 543 | **167** | 30c. black, yellow blue | 55 | 25 |

168 Flood Victims

1969. Aid for 1969 Flood Victims.
| 544 | **168** | 30c.+10c. black, flesh and blue | 75 | 45 |
| 545 | - | 95c.+25c. brown, blue and purple | 1·60 | 95 |

DESIGN: 95c. Helping hand for flood victims.

169 *Algerian Women* (Dinet)

1969. Dinet's Paintings. Multicoloured.
| 546 | 1d. Type **169** | 2·10 | 85 |
| 547 | 1d.50 *The Look-outs* (Dinet) | 2·75 | 1·20 |

170 "Mother and Child"

1969. Protection of Mother and Child
| 548 | **170** | 30c. multicoloured | 70 | 40 |

171 "Agriculture"

1970. Four Year Plan.
549	**171**	25c. multicoloured	30	25
550	-	30c. multicoloured	55	25
551	-	50c. black and purple	55	25

DESIGNS: (LARGER, 49×23 mm): 30c. "Industry and Transport"; 50c. "Industry" (abstract).

172 Postal Deliveries by Donkey and Renault R4 Mail Van

1970. Stamp Day.
| 552 | **172** | 30c. multicoloured | 70 | 25 |

173 Royal Prawn

1970. Marine Life. Multicoloured.
553	30c. Type **173**	70	25
554	40c. Noble pen (mollusc)	90	40
555	75c. Neptune's basket	1·40	50
556	1d. Red coral	2·10	75

174 Oranges

1970. Expo 70 World Fair, Osaka, Japan. Multicoloured.
557	30c. Type **174**	70	25
558	60c. Algerian Pavilion	70	40
559	70c. Bunches of grapes	1·40	60

175 Olives and Bottle of Olive-oil

1970. World Olive-oil Year.
| 560 | **175** | 1d. multicoloured | 1·90 | 80 |

176 New U.P.U. H.Q. Building

1970. Inauguration of New U.P.U. Headquarters Building.
| 561 | **176** | 75c. multicoloured | 1·10 | 40 |

177 Crossed Muskets

1970. Algerian 18th-century Weapons. Multicoloured.
562	40c. Type **177**		90	65
563	75c. Sabre (vert)		1·60	85
564	1d. Pistol		2·30	1·10

178 Arab League Flag, Arms and Map

1970. 25th Anniv of Arab League.
565	**178**	30c. multicoloured	55	25

179 Lenin

1970. Birth Centenary of Lenin.
566	**179**	30c. bistre and ochre	2·75	40

180 Exhibition Palace

1970. Seventh International Algiers Fair.
567	**180**	60c. green	70	40

181 I.E.Y. and Education Emblems

1970. International Education Year. Multicoloured.
568	**181**	30c. Type **181**	55	25
569		3d. Illuminated Koran (30×41 mm)	3·50	1·80

182 Great Mosque, Tlemcen

1970. Mosques.
570	**182**	30c. multicoloured	45	25
571		40c. brown and bistre	55	25
572		1d. multicoloured	1·00	40
DESIGNS—VERT: 40c. Ketchaoua Mosque, Algiers; 1d. Sidi-Okba Mosque.

183 Fine Arts

1970. Algerian Fine Arts.
573	**183**	1d. orange, grn & lt grn	1·10	45

184 G.P.O., Algiers

1971. Stamp Day.
574	**184**	30c. multicoloured	1·10	40

185 Hurdling

1971. Sixth Mediterranean Games, Izmir (Turkey).
575	**185**	20c. grey and blue	50	25
576	-	40c. grey and green	55	40
577	-	75c. grey and brown	1·10	65
DESIGNS—VERT: 40c. Gymnastics; 75c. Basket-ball.

186 "Racial Equality"

1971. Racial Equality Year.
578	**186**	60c. multicoloured	70	40

187 Symbols of Learning, and Students

1971. Inauguration of Technological Institutes.
579	**187**	70c. multicoloured	90	30

188 Red Crescent Banner

1971. Red Crescent Day.
580	**188**	30c.+10c. red and green	70	40

189 Casbah, Algiers

1971. Air.
581	**189**	2d. multicoloured	2·50	1·10
582	-	3d. violet and black	3·75	1·60
583	-	4d. multicoloured	4·25	2·00
DESIGNS: 3d. Port of Oran; 4d. Rhumel Gorges.

190 Aures Costume

1971. Regional Costumes (1st series). Multicoloured.
584	**190**	50c. Type **190**	1·30	60
585		70c. Oran	1·60	75
586		80c. Algiers	1·90	95
587		90c. Djebel-Amour	2·30	1·10
See also Nos. 610/13 and 659/62.

191 UNICEF Emblem, Tree and Animals

1971. 25th Anniv of UNICEF.
588	**191**	60c. multicoloured	90	45

192 Lion of St. Mark's

1971. UNESCO 'Save Venice' Campaign. Multicoloured.
589	**192**	80c. Type **192**	1·40	55
590		1d.15 Bridge of Sighs	2·30	95

193 Cycling

1972. Olympic Games, Munich. Multicoloured.
591	**193**	25c. Type **193**	45	25
592		40c. Throwing the javelin (vert)	60	25
593		60c. Wrestling (vert)	1·10	50
594		1d. Gymnastics (vert)	1·60	55

194 Book and Bookmark

1972. International Book Year.
595	**194**	1d.15 red, black and brown	90	45

195 Algerian Postmen

1972. Stamp Day.
596	**195**	40c. multicoloured	70	25

196 Jasmine

1972. Flowers. Multicoloured.
597	**196**	50c. Type **196**	70	40
598		60c. Violets	70	40
599		1d.15 Tuberose	2·10	65

197 Olympic Stadium

1972. Inauguration of Cheraga Olympic Stadium.
600	**197**	50c. green, brown & violet	70	40

198 Festival Emblem

1972. First Festival of Arab Youth.
601	**198**	40c. brown, yellow & grn	55	25

199 Rejoicing Algerians

1972. Tenth Anniv of Independence.
602	**199**	1d. multicoloured	1·30	60

1972. Regional Costumes (2nd series). As T **190**. Multicoloured.
610		50c. Hoggar	1·40	65
611		60c. Kabylie	1·80	65
612		70c. Mzab	1·90	85
613		90c. Tlemcen	2·40	1·10

201 Child posting Letter

1973. Stamp Day.
614	**201**	40c. multicoloured	55	25

202 Ho-Chi-Minh and Map

1973. Homage to the Vietnamese People
615	**202**	40c. multicoloured	90	40

203 Annaba Embroidery

1973. Algerian Embroidery. Multicoloured.
616		40c. Type **203**	55	25
617		60c. Algiers embroidery	90	50
618		80c. Constantine embroidery	1·30	70

204 "Food Cultivation"

1973. Tenth Anniv of World Food Programme.
619	**204**	1d.15 multicoloured	90	40

205 Serviceman and Flag

1973. National Service.
620	**205**	40c. multicoloured	55	25

1973. Algerian Flowers. As T **158**. Multicoloured.
621		30c. Type **158**	70	25
622		40c. As No. 529	90	40
623		1d. As No. 528	1·80	65
624		1d.15 As No. 530	2·75	1·10

206 O.A.U. Emblem

1973. Tenth Anniv of Organization of African Unity.
625	**206**	40c. multicoloured	55	25

207 Peasant Family

1973. Agrarian Revolution.
626 **207** 40c. multicoloured ... 70 25

208 Scout Badge
on Map

1973. 24th World Scouting Congress, Nairobi, Kenya.
627 **208** 80c. mauve ... 75 40

209 P.T.T. Symbol

1973. Inauguration of New P.T.T. Symbol.
628 **209** 40c. orange and blue ... 55 25

210 Conference
Emblem

1973. Fourth Summit Conference of Non-Aligned
Countries, Algiers.
629 **210** 40c. multicoloured ... 45 25
630 **210** 80c. multicoloured ... 90 40

211 "Skikda Harbour"

1973. Opening of Skikda Port.
631 **211** 80c. multicoloured ... 70 25

212 Young Workers

1973. Volontariat Students' Volunteer Service.
632 **212** 40c. multicoloured ... 55 25

213 Arms of Algiers

1973. Millenary of Algiers.
633 **213** 2d. multicoloured ... 3·00 1·40

214 "Protected Infant"

1974. Anti-TB Campaign.
634 **214** 80c. multicoloured ... 90 45

215 Industrial Scene

1974. Four Year Plan.
635 **215** 80c. multicoloured ... 90 40

216 Arabesque Motif

1974. Birth Millenary of Abu-al Rayhan al-Biruni
(mathematician and philosopher).
636 **216** 1d.50 multicoloured ... 2·50 1·40

217 Map and Arrows

1974. Meeting of Maghreb Committee for Co-ordination
of Posts and Telecommunications, Tunis.
637 **217** 40c. multicoloured ... 55 25

218 Upraised
Weapon and Fist

1974. Solidarity with South African People's Campaign.
638 **218** 80c. black and red ... 70 25

219 Algerian
Family

1974. Homage to Algerian Mothers.
639 **219** 85c. multicoloured ... 70 25

220 Urban Scene

1974. Children's Drawings. Multicoloured.
640 70c. Type **220** ... 75 35
641 80c. Agricultural scene ... 90 40
642 90c. Tractor and sunrise ... 1·10 65
Nos. 641/2 are size 49×33 mm.

1974. Floralies 1974 Flower Show, Algiers. Nos. 623/4
optd **FLORALIES 1974.**
643 1d. multicoloured ... 1·80 85
644 1d.15 multicoloured ... 2·30 1·30

222 Automatic
Stamp-vending
Machine

1974. Stamp Day.
645 **222** 80c. multicoloured ... 80 35

223 U.P.U. Emblem on
Globe

1974. Centenary of U.P.U.
646 **223** 80c. multicoloured ... 80 35

224 Revolutionaries

1974. 20th Anniv of Revolution. Multicoloured.
647 40c. Type **224** ... 55 25
648 70c. Armed soldiers (vert) ... 75 25
649 95c. Raising the flag (vert) ... 90 40
650 1d. Algerians looking to Inde-
pendence ... 1·20 40

225 "Towards the
Horizon"

1974. Horizon 1980.
651 **225** 95c. red, brown & black ... 75 40

226 Ewer

1974. Algerian 17th-century Brassware. Multicoloured.
652 50c. Type **226** ... 60 30
653 60c. Coffee pot ... 75 40
654 95c. Sugar basin ... 1·00 55
655 1d. Bath vessel ... 1·40 75

1975. No. 622 surch.
656 50c. on 40c. multicoloured ... 2·75 55

228 Games Emblem

1975. Seventh Mediterranean Games (1st issue).
657 **228** 50c. violet, green &
yellow ... 50 25
658 **228** 1d. orange, violet & blue ... 90 40
See also Nos. 671/5.

1975. Regional Costumes (3rd series). As T **190.**
Multicoloured.
659 1d. Algiers ... 1·60 85
660 1d. The Hogger ... 1·60 85
661 1d. Oran ... 1·60 85
662 1d. Tlemcen ... 1·60 85

229 Labour Emblems

1975. Tenth Anniv of Arab Labour Organization.
663 **229** 50c. brown ... 55 10

230 Transfusion

1975. Blood Collection and Transfusion Service.
664 **230** 50c. multicoloured ... 90 40

231 El Kantara
Post Office

1975. Stamp Day.
665 **231** 50c. multicoloured ... 70 25

232 Policeman and
Oil Rig on Map of
Algeria

1975. Police Day.
666 **232** 50c. multicoloured ... 1·10 40

233 Ground Receiving Aerial

1975. Satellite Telecommunications. Multicoloured.
667 50c. Type **233** ... 55 15
668 1d. Map of receiving sites ... 90 25
669 1d.20 Main and subsidiary
ground stations ... 1·20 50

234
Revolutionary
with Flag

1975. 20th Anniv of 'Skikda' Revolution.
670 **234** 1d. multicoloured ... 75 40

235 Swimming

1975. Seventh Mediterranean Games, Algiers (2nd issue).
Multicoloured.
671 25c. Type **235** ... 20 10
672 50c. Wrestling ... 45 25
673 70c. Football (vert) ... 70 30
674 1d. Athletics (vert) ... 90 40
675 1d.20 Handball (vert) ... 1·20 65
MS676 136×136 mm. Nos. 671/5 ... 7·75 6·75

236
"Setif-Guelma-
Kherrata"

1975. 30th Anniv of Setif, Guelma and Kherrata
Massacres (1st issue).
677 **236** 5c. black and orange ... 10 10
678 **236** 10c. black and green ... 10 10
679 **236** 25c. black and blue ... 25 10
680 **236** 30c. black and brown ... 45 10
681 **236** 50c. black and green ... 45 10
682 **236** 70c. black and red ... 55 25
683 **236** 1d. black and red ... 90 40
See also No. 698.

237 Map of the Maghreb
and A.P.U. Emblem

1975. Tenth Arab Postal Union Congress, Algiers.
684 **237** 1d. multicoloured 75 40

238 Mosaic, Palace of
the Bey, Constantine

1975. Historic Buildings.
685 **238** 1d. multicoloured 1·10 40
686 - 2d. multicoloured 2·20 95
687 - 2d.50 black and brown 3·00 1·40
DESIGNS—VERT: 2d. Medersa Sidi-Boumedienne Oratory,
Tlemcen. HORIZ: 2d.50, Palace of the Dey, Algiers.

239 University Building

1975. Millenary of Al-Azhar University, Cairo.
688 **239** 2d. multicoloured 2·10 80

240 Red-billed
Fire Finch

1976. Algerian Birds (1st series). Multicoloured.
689 50c. Type **240** 1·30 65
690 1d.40 Black-headed bush shrike
 (horiz) 2·50 1·30
691 2d. Blue-tit 3·25 1·40
692 2d.50 Black-bellied sand-grouse
 (horiz) 3·75 2·00
 See also Nos. 722/5.

241 Early and
Modern Telephones

1976. Telephone Centenary.
693 **241** 1d.40 multicoloured 1·10 55

242 Map and
Angolan Flag

1976. Solidarity with Republic of Angola
694 **242** 50c. multicoloured 65 25

243 Child on Map

1976. Solidarity with People of Western Sahara.
695 **243** 50c. multicoloured 55 25

244 Postman

1976. Stamp Day.
696 **244** 1d.40 multicoloured 1·10 40

245 People, Microscope
and Slide

1976. Campaign Against Tuberculosis.
697 **245** 50c. multicoloured 1·10 35

246
"Setif-
Guelma-
Kherrata"

1976. 30th Anniv of Setif, Guelma and Kherrata
 Massacres (2nd issue)
698 **246** 50c. yellow and blue 55 10

247 Ram's Head
and Landscape

1976. Sheep Raising.
699 **247** 50c. multicoloured 65 25

248 Algerians
holding Torch

1976. National Charter.
700 **248** 50c. multicoloured 55 25

249 Flag and
Map

1976. Solidarity with the Palestinian People.
701 **249** 50c. multicoloured 70 25

250 Map of Africa

1976. Second Pan-African Commercial Fair, Algiers.
702 **250** 2d. multicoloured 1·70 65

251 Blind Man making
Brushes

1976. Rehabilitation of the Blind. Multicoloured.
703 1d.20 Type **251** 1·40 45
704 1d.40 *The Blind Man* (E. Dinet)
 (horiz) 2·10 65

252 Open Book

1976. The Constitution.
705 **252** 2d. multicoloured 1·70 65

253 Soldiers
planting Seedlings

1976. Protection against Saharan Encroachment.
706 **253** 1d.40 multicoloured 1·40 55

254 Arabic Inscription

1976. Election of President Boumedienne.
707 **254** 2d. multicoloured 1·70 65

255 Map of
Telephone Centres

1977. Inauguration of Automatic Telephone Dialling
 System.
708 **255** 40c. multicoloured 50 25

256 "Pyramid" of
Heads

1977. Second General Population and Housing Census.
709 **256** 60c. on 50c. mult 60 25

257 Museum Building

1977. Sahara Museum, Ouargla.
710 **257** 60c. multicoloured 75 40

258 El Kantara
Gorges

1977
711 **258** 20c. green and cream 10 10
712 **258** 60c. mauve and cream 25 10
713 **258** 1d. brown and cream 60 25

259 Assembly in Session

1977. National Assembly.
714 **259** 2d. multicoloured 1·40 55

260 Soldiers with
Flag

1977. Solidarity with People of Zimbabwe.
715 **260** 2d. multicoloured 1·40 50

261 Soldier with
Flag

1977. Solidarity with People of Namibia.
716 **261** 3d. multicoloured 2·30 75

262 *Winter*

1977. Roman Mosaics. The Seasons. Multicoloured.
717 1d.20 Type **262** 1·60 85
718 1d.40 *Autumn* 1·60 85
719 2d. *Summer* 2·50 1·30
720 3d. *Spring* 3·50 1·70
MS721 101×145 mm. Nos. 717/20 13·50 12·00

1977. Algerian Birds (2nd series). As T **240**. Multicoloured.
722 60c. Tristram's warbler 1·20 70
723 1d.40 Moussier's redstart (horiz) 2·10 1·10
724 2d. Temminck's horned lark
 (horiz) 3·25 1·50
725 3d. Hoopoe 4·00 2·00

263 Horseman

1977. The Cavaliers (performing horsemen).
 Multicoloured.
726 2d. Type **263** 2·10 85
727 5d. Three horsemen (horiz) 4·75 1·90

264 Ribbon and Games Emblem

1977. Third African Games, Algiers (1978) (1st issue). Multicoloured.
728		60c. Type **264**	55	25
729		1d.40 Symbolic design and emblem	1·50	50

See also Nos. 740/4.

265 Tessala el Merdja

1977. Socialist Agricultural Villages.
730	**265**	1d.40 multicoloured	1·00	40

266 12th-century Almohad Dirham

1977. Ancient Coins. Multicoloured.
731		60c. Type **266**	70	40
732		1d.40 12th-century Alomhad dinar	1·30	65
733		2d. 11th-century Almorarid dinar	1·90	95

267 Cherry (*Cerasus avium*)

1978. Fruit Tree Blossom. Multicoloured.
734		60c. Type **267**	70	25
735		1d.20 *Persica vulgaris* (peach)	1·10	75
736		1d.30 *Amygdalus communis* (almond)	1·10	75
737		1d.40 *Malus communis* (crab apple)	1·60	80

1978. Surch.
738	**236**	60c. on 50c. black & grn	70	25

269 Children with Traffic Signs opposing Car

1978. Road Safety for Children.
739	**269**	60c. multicoloured	60	25

270 Boxing and Map of Africa

1978. Third African Games, Algiers (2nd issue). Multicoloured.
740		40c. Sports emblems and volleyball (horiz)	25	10
741		60c. Olympic rings and table tennis symbol	40	25
742		1d.20 Basketball symbol (horiz)	1·00	40
743		1d.30 Hammerthrowing symbol	1·00	5·00
744		1d.40 Type **270**	1·30	60

271 Patient returning to Family

1978. Anti-tuberculosis Campaign.
745	**271**	60c. multicoloured	60	25

272 Ka'aba, Mecca

1978. Pilgrimage to Mecca.
746	**272**	60c. multicoloured	70	25

273 Road-building

1978. African Unity Road.
747	**273**	60c. multicoloured	70	25

274 Triangular Brooch

1978. Jewellery (1st series). Multicoloured.
748		1d.20 Type **274**	1·20	55
749		1d.35 Circular brooch	1·50	70
750		1d.40 Anklet	1·80	80

See also Nos. 780/2 and 833/5.

275 President Houari Boumedienne

1979. President Boumedienne Commem (1st issue).
751	**275**	60c. brown, red & turq	55	25

See also No. 753.

276 Books and Hands holding Torch

1979. National Liberation Front Party Congress.
752	**276**	60c. multicoloured	55	25

277 President Houari Boumedienne

1979. President Boumedienne Commem (2nd issue).
753	**277**	1d.40 multicoloured	1·40	50

278 Arabic Inscription

1979. Election of President Chadli Bendjedid.
754	**278**	2d. multicoloured	1·60	40

279 White Storks

1979. Air.
755	**279**	10d. blue, black and red	6·75	2·50

280 Ben Badis

1979. 90th Birth Anniv of Sheikh Abdelhamid Ben Badis (journalist and education pioneer).
756	**280**	60c. multicoloured	55	25

281 Globe within Telephone Dial

1979. Telecom 79 Exhibition. Multicoloured.
757		1d.20 Type **281**	90	35
758		1d.40 Sound waves	1·20	45

282 Children dancing on Globe

1979. International Year of the Child. Multicoloured.
759		60c. Picking Dates	55	10
760		1d.40 Type **282** (vert)	1·10	45

283 Kabylie Nuthatch

1979.
761	**283**	1d.40 multicoloured	2·00	95

284 Fighting for the Revolution and Construction work

1979. 25th Anniv of Revolution. Multicoloured.
762		1d.40 Type **284**	1·00	30
763		3d. Algerians with flag	1·70	85

285 Arabic Inscription

1979. 1400th Anniv of Hegira.
764	**285**	3d. gold, turquoise & blue	2·10	80

286 Return of Dionysus (right detail)

1980. Dionysus Mosaic, Setif. Multicoloured.
765		1d.20 Type **286**	1·30	40
766		1d.35 Centre detail	1·30	55
767		1d.40 Left detail	1·60	80

Nos. 765/7 were issued together, *se-tenant*, forming a composite design.

287 Books

1980. Day of Knowledge.
768	**287**	60c. brown, yellow & grn	55	10

288 Five Year Plan

1980. Extraordinary Congress of National Liberation Front Party.
769	**288**	60c. multicoloured	55	25

289 Olympic Flame

1980. Olympic Games, Moscow. Multicoloured.
770		50c. Type **289**	50	10
771		1d.40 Olympic sports (horiz)	95	45

290 Figures supporting O.P.E.C. Emblem

1980. 20th Anniv of Organization of Petroleum Exporting Countries.
772	**290**	60c. green, blue and red	65	10
773	–	1d.40 green and blue	1·20	45

DESIGN: 1d.40, O.P.E.C. emblem on world map.

291 Aures

1980. World Tourism Conference, Manila. Multicoloured.
774	50c. Type **291**		50	25
775	1d. El Oued		90	25
776	1d.40 Tassili		1·10	40
777	2d. Algiers		1·90	65

292 Ibn Sina

1980. Birth Millenary of Ibn Sina (Avicenna) (philosopher).
778	**292**	3d. multicoloured	2·10	80

293 Earthquake Devastation

1980. El Asnam Earthquake Relief.
779	**293**	3d. multicoloured	2·10	55

1980. Jewellery (2nd series). As T **274**. Multicoloured.
780	60c. Necklace		60	25
781	1d.40 Earrings and bracelet		1·10	55
782	2d. Diadem (horiz)		1·60	70

294 Emblem

1981. Five Year Plan.
783	**294**	60c. multicoloured	40	10

295 Basket-worker

1981. Traditional Arts. Multicoloured.
784	40c. Type **295**		35	10
785	60c. Spinning		45	20
786	1d. Copper-smith		75	25
787	1d.40 Jeweller		1·20	40

296 Cedar *Cedrus atlantica*

1981. World Tree Day. Multicoloured.
788	60c. Type **296**		45	10
789	1d.40 Cypress *Cupressus dupreziana*		1·10	40

297 Mohamed Bachir el Ibrahimi

298 Children and Blackboard (Basic Schooling)

1981. Day of Knowledge.
790	**297**	60c. multicoloured	45	10
791	**298**	60c. multicoloured	45	10

299 Archer, Dog and Internal Organs

1981. 12th Int Hydatidological Congress, Algiers.
792	**299**	2d. multicoloured	1·80	55

300 Dish Aerial and Caduceus

1981. World Telecommunications Day.
793	**300**	1d.40 multicoloured	1·10	25

301 "Disabled"

1981. International Year of Disabled People.
794	**301**	1d.20 blue, red & orange	90	25
795	-	1d.40 multicoloured	1·00	30

DESIGN: 1d.40, Disabled people and hand holding flower.

302 *Papilio machaon*

1981. Butterflies. Multicoloured.
796	60c. Type **302**		70	35
797	1d.20 *Rhodocera rhamni gonepteryx rhamni*		1·20	50
798	1d.40 *Charaxes jasius*		1·60	85
799	2d. *Papilio podalirius*		2·10	90

303 Mediterranean Monk Seal

1981. Nature Protection. Multicoloured.
800	60c. Type **303**		80	40
801	1d.40 Barbary ape		1·60	85

304 Man holding Ear of Wheat

1981. World Food Day.
802	**304**	2d. multicoloured	1·30	50

305 Cattle, Jabbaren

1981. Cave Paintings. Multicoloured.
803	60c. Mouflon, Tan Zoumaitek		55	25
804	1d. Type **305**		95	40
805	1d.60 Cattle, Iherir (horiz)		1·30	55

806	2d. One-horned bull, Jabbaren (horiz)		1·80	85

306 Galley

1981. Algerian Ships of 17th and 18th Centuries. Multicoloured.
807	60c. Type **306**		80	50
808	1d.60 Xebec		1·80	1·00

307 Footballers with Cup

1982. World Cup Football Championship, Spain. Multicoloured.
809	80c. Type **307**		60	25
810	2d.80 Footballers and ball (horiz)		1·90	75

308 Microscope

1982. Centenary of Discovery of Tubercle Bacillus.
811	**308**	80c. blue, lt blue & orge	55	25

309 Mirror

1982. Popular Traditional Arts. Multicoloured.
812	80c. Type **309**		60	25
813	2d. Whatnot		1·30	40
814	2d.40 Chest (48×32 mm)		1·70	75

310 New Mosque, Algiers

1982. Views of Algeria before 1830 (1st series). Size 32×22 mm.
815	**310**	80c. brown	45	15
816	-	2d.40 violet	1·20	50
817	-	3d. green	1·60	65

DESIGNS: 2d.40, Sidi Boumedienne Mosque, Tlemcen; 3d. Garden of Dey, Algiers.
 See also Nos. 859/62, 873/5, 880/2, 999/1001, 1054/6 and 1075/86.

311 *Callitris articulata*

1982. Medicinal Plants. Multicoloured.
818	50c. Type **311**		45	10
819	80c. *Artemisia herba-alba*		55	25
820	1d. *Ricinus communis*		90	35
821	2d.40 *Thymus fontanesii*		1·90	75

312 Independence Fighter

1982. 20th Anniv of Independence. Multicoloured.
822	50c. Type **312**		40	15
823	80c. Modern soldiers		55	25
824	2d. Algerians and symbols of prosperity		1·40	55
MS825	74×82 mm. 5d. Sun rising over flames (31×39 mm)		4·25	4·00

313 Congress House

1982. Soumman Congress.
826	**313**	80c. multicoloured	55	15

314 Scout and Guide releasing Dove

1982. 75th Anniv of Boy Scout Movement.
827	**314**	2d.80 multicoloured	1·90	55

315 Child

1982. Palestinian Children.
828	**315**	1d.60 multicoloured	95	30

316 Waldrapp

1982. Nature Protection. Multicoloured.
829	50c. Type **316**		70	40
830	80c. Houbara bustard (vert)		95	65
831	2d. Tawny eagle		2·20	1·10
832	2d.40 Lammergeier (vert)		2·75	1·40

317 Mirror

1983. Silver Work.
833	**317**	50c. silver, black and red	35	10
834	-	1d. multicoloured	55	40
835	-	2d. silver, black, & purple	1·20	60

DESIGNS—VERT. 1d. Perfume flasks. HORIZ: 2d. Belt buckle.

318 *Abies numidica*

1983. World Tree Day. Multicoloured.
836	80c. Type **318**		70	25
837	2d.80 *Acacia raddiana*		2·10	75

319 Mineral

1983. Mineral Resources.
838	**319**	70c. multicoloured	90	35
839	**319**	80c. multicoloured	1·00	50
840	**319**	1d.20 mult (horiz)	1·20	65
841	**319**	2d.40 mult (horiz)	2·50	1·20

320 Customs Officer

1983. 30th Anniv of Customs Co-operation Council.
842 **320** 80c. multicoloured 70 25

321 Emir Abdelkader

1983. Death Centenary of Emir Abdelkader.
843 **321** 4d. multicoloured 2·30 95

322 Fly Agaric

1983. Mushrooms. Multicoloured.
844 50c. Type **322** 80 25
845 80c. Death cap 1·10 65
846 1d.40 *Pleurotus eryngii* 2·40 1·00
847 2d.80 *Terfezia leonis* 3·75 1·70

323 Ibn Khaldoun

1983. Ibn Khaldoun Commemoration.
848 **323** 80c. multicoloured 70 25

324 W.C.Y. Emblem and Post Office

1983. World Communications Year. Multicoloured.
849 80c. Type **324** 55 25
850 2d.40 W.C.Y. emblem and
telephone switch box 1·50 65

325 Goat and Tassili Mountains

1983. Tassili World Patrimony. Multicoloured.
851 50c. Type **325** 40 10
852 80c. Touaregs 55 25
853 2d.40 Rock paintings 1·40 55
854 2d.80 Rock formation 1·80 75

326 Sloughi

1983. Sloughi. Multicoloured.
855 80c. Type **326** 80 35
856 2d.40 Sloughi 2·10 1·00

327 Symbols of Economic Progress

1983. Fifth National Liberation Front Party Congress.
Multicoloured.
857 80c. Type **327** 80 35
MS858 75×82 mm. 5d. Party emblem
(31×38 mm) 4·25 4·00

1984. Views of Algeria before 1830 (2nd series). As T **310**.
859 10c. blue 10 10
860 1d. purple 45 10
861 2d. blue 95 45
862 4d. red 2·10 65
DESIGNS: 10c. Oran; 1d. Sidi Abderahmane Mosque, Et
Taalibi; 2d. Bejaia; 4d. Constantine.

328 Jug

1984. Pottery. Multicoloured.
863 80c. Type **328** 55 25
864 1d. Dish (horiz) 75 40
865 2d. Lamp 1·40 60
866 2d.40 Jug (horiz) 1·60 75

329 Fountain

1984. Fountains of Old Algiers.
867 **329** 50c. multicoloured 20 10
868 – 80c. multicoloured 55 40
869 – 2d.40 multicoloured 1·30 65
DESIGNS: 80c., 2d.40, Different fountains.

330 Dove, Flames and Olympic Rings

1984. Olympic Games, Los Angeles.
870 **330** 1d. multicoloured 90 40

331 Stallion

1984. Horses. Multicoloured.
871 80c. Type **331** 70 40
872 2d.40 Mare 1·90 1·00

1984. Views of Algeria before 1830 (3rd series). As T **310**.
873 5c. purple 10 10
874 20c. blue 10 10
875 70c. violet 40 10
DESIGNS: 5c. Mustapha Pacha; 20c. Bab Azzoun; 70c.
Mostaganem.

332 Lute

1984. Musical Instruments. Multicoloured.
876 80c. Type **332** 55 25
877 1d. Drum 90 40
878 2d.40 One-stringed instrument 1·80 75
879 2d.80 Bagpipes 2·00 1·00

1984. Views of Algeria before 1830 (4th series). As T **310**.
880 30c. red and black 25 10
881 40c. black 25 10
882 50c. brown 25 10
DESIGNS: 30c. Algiers from Admiralty; 40c. Kolea; 50c. Algiers from aqueduct.

333 Partisans in Mountains and Flag

1984. 30th Anniv of Revolution. Multicoloured.
883 80c. Type **333** 70 25
MS884 75×82 mm. 5d. Algerian flags
(31×39 mm) 4·25 4·00

334 Map of M'Zab Valley

1984. M'Zab Valley. Multicoloured.
885 80c. Type **334** 65 10
886 2d.40 M'Zab town 1·70 60

335 Coffee Pot

1985. Ornamental Tableware.
887 **335** 80c. black, silver &
yellow 55 25
888 – 2d. black, silver and
green 1·20 60
889 – 2d.40 black, silver & pink 1·60 70
DESIGNS—HORIZ: 2d. Bowl. VERT: 2d.40, Lidded jar.

336 Blue-finned Tuna

1985. Fishes. Multicoloured.
890 50c. Type **336** 55 25
891 80c. Gilthead seabream 95 40
892 2d.40 Dusky grouper 2·20 1·10
893 2d.80 Smooth hound 2·75 1·20

337 Birds in Flight and Emblem

1985. National Games.
894 **337** 80c. multicoloured 65 25

338 Stylized Trees

1985. Environmental Protection. Multicoloured.
895 80c. Type **338** 80 25
896 1d.40 Stylized waves 90 40

339 Algiers Casbah

1985
897 **339** 20c. blue and cream 10 10
898 **339** 80c. green and cream 55 10
899 **339** 2d.40 brown and cream 1·70 10

340 Dove within "40"

1985. 40th Anniv of U.N.O.
900 **340** 1d. multicoloured 90 25

341 Figures linking arms and Emblem

1985. First National Youth Festival.
901 **341** 80c. multicoloured 70 25

342 Figures linking arms on Globe and Dove

1985. International Youth Year. Multicoloured.
902 80c. Type **342** 60 25
903 1d.40 Doves making globe
with laurels 90 35

343 O.P.E.C. Emblem

1985. 25th Anniv of Organization of Petroleum Exporting
Countries.
904 **343** 80c. multicoloured 70 25

344 Mother and Children

1985. Family Planning. Multicoloured.
905 80c. Type **344** 55 25
906 1d.40 Doctor weighing baby 90 40
907 1d.70 Mother breast-feeding
baby 1·10 50

345 Chetaibi Bay

1985. Tourist Sites.
908 **345** 80c. blue, green & brown 45 25
909 – 2d. brown, green & blue 1·30 40
910 – 2d.40 brown, green & bl 1·60 65
DESIGNS—VERT: 2d. El Meniaa. HORIZ: 2d.40, Bou Noura.

346 Palm Grove

1985. Paintings by N. Dinet. Multicoloured.
911 2d. Type **346** 1·50 75
912 3d. Palm Grove (different) 2·10 1·20

347 Line Pattern

1985. Weavings. Multicoloured.

913	80c. Type **347**	70	45
914	1d.40 Diamond pattern	1·40	65
915	2d.40 Patterned horizontal stripes	2·00	1·10
916	2d.80 Vertical and horizontal stripes	2·50	1·60

348 Felis margarita

1986. Wild Cats. Multicoloured.

917	80c. Type **348**	80	45
918	1d. Caracal	1·00	60
919	2d. Wild cat	1·90	1·10
920	2d.40 Serval (vert)	2·50	1·40

349 Oral Vaccination

1986. UNESCO Child Survival Campaign. Multicoloured.

921	80c. Type **349**	55	25
922	1d.40 Sun behind mother and baby	1·20	55
923	1d.70 Children playing	1·50	75

350 Industrial Skyline, Clasped Hands and Emblem

1986. 30th Anniv of Algerian General Workers' Union.

924	**350**	2d. multicoloured	1·50	55

351 Books and Crowd

1986. National Charter.

925	**351**	4d. multicoloured	2·75	1·20

352 Emblem on Book and Drawing Instruments

1986. Disabled Persons' Day.

926	**352**	80c. multicoloured	70	30

353 Children playing

1986. Anti-tuberculosis Campaign.

927	**353**	80c. multicoloured	70	35

354 Sombrero on Football

1986. World Cup Football Championship, Mexico. Multicoloured.

928	2d. Type **354**	1·40	55
929	2d.40 Players and ball	1·60	70

355 Courtyard with Fountain

1986. Traditional Dwellings. Multicoloured.

930	80c. Type **355**	70	30
931	2d.40 Courtyard with two beds of shrubs	1·80	1·00
932	3d. Courtyard with plants in tall pot	2·30	1·30

356 Heart forming Drop over Patient

1986. Blood Donors.

933	**356**	80c. multicoloured	1·40	40

357 Transmission Mast as Palm Tree

1986. Opening of Hertzian Wave Communications (Southern District).

934	**357**	60c. multicoloured	45	25

358 Studded Gate

1986. Mosque Gateways. Multicoloured.

935	2d. Type **358**	1·30	55
936	2d.40 Ornate gateway	1·60	75

359 Dove

1986. International Peace Year.

937	**359**	2d.40 multicoloured	1·60	55

360 Girl dancing

1986. Folk Dances. Multicoloured.

938	80c. Type **360**	70	25
939	2d.40 Woman with purple dress dancing	1·70	65
940	2d.80 Veiled sword dancer	1·90	85

361 Narcissus tazetta

1986. Flowers. Multicoloured.

941	80c. Type **361**	70	30
942	1d.40 Iris unguicularis	1·20	55
943	2d.40 Capparis spinosa	1·70	90
944	2d.80 Gladiolus segetum	2·10	1·10

362 Algerian Family

1987. Paintings by Mohammed Issiakhem in National Museum. Multicoloured.

945	2d. Type **362**	1·50	75
946	5d. Man and Books	3·50	2·00

363 Earrings

1987. Jewellery from Aures. Multicoloured.

947	1d. Type **363**	75	40
948	1d.80 Bangles	1·20	60
949	2d.90 Brooches	1·70	1·10
950	3d.30 Necklace (horiz)	2·00	1·20

364 Boy and Girl

1987. Rock Carvings. Multicoloured.

951	1d. Type **364**	90	55
952	2d.90 Goat	2·00	1·30
953	3d.30 Animals	2·30	1·40

365 Baby holding Syringe "Umbrella"

1987. African Vaccination Year.

954	**365**	1d. multicoloured	55	25

366 Workers and Circles

1987. Voluntary Service.

955	**366**	1d. multicoloured	55	30

367 People and Buildings

1987. Third General Population Census.

956	**367**	1d. multicoloured	55	25

368 1962 War Orphans Fund Stamps and Magnifying Glass

1987. 25th Anniv of Independent Algeria Stamps.

957	**368**	1d.80 multicoloured	1·80	60

369 Hand holding Torch

1987. 25th Anniv of Independence. Multicoloured.

958	1d. Type **369**	55	25
MS959	75×82 mm. 5d. Sun, dove and "25" (32×39 mm)	3·50	3·25

370 Actors in Spotlight

1987. Amateur Theatre Festival, Mostaganem. Multicoloured.

960	1d. Type **370**	55	85
961	1d.80 Theatre	90	55

371 Discus Thrower

1987. Mediterranean Games, Lattaquie. Multicoloured.

962	1d. Type **371**	55	30
963	2d.90 Tennis player (vert)	1·50	70
964	3d.30 Footballer	1·80	95

372 Greater Flamingo

1987. Birds. Multicoloured.

965	1d. Type **372**	75	40
966	1d.80 Purple swamphen	1·30	80
967	2d.50 Black-shouldered kite	2·00	95
968	2d.90 Red kite	1·90	85

373 Reservoir

1987. Agriculture. Multicoloured.

969	1d. Type **373**	60	25
970	1d. Forestry (36×28 mm)	60	25
971	1d. Foodstuffs (25×37 mm)	60	25
972	1d. Erecting hedge against desert (25×37 mm)	55	25

374 Map,
Transmitter and
Radio Waves

1987. African Telecommunications Day.
973 **374** 1d. multicoloured 70 25

375 Motorway

1987. Transport. Multicoloured.
974 2d.90 Type **375** 1·50 60
975 3d.30 Diesel locomotive and
passenger train 2·75 1·20

376 Houari Boumedienne
University, Algiers

1987. Universities. Multicoloured.
976 1d. Type **376** 55 25
977 2d.50 Oran University 1·30 45
978 2d.90 Constantine University 1·50 60
979 3d.30 Emir Abdelkader Univer-
sity, Constantine (vert) 1·90 75

377 Wheat, Sun and
Farmer ploughing with
Oxen

1988. Tenth Anniv of International Agricultural
Development Fund.
980 **377** 1d. multicoloured 70 25

378 Emblem as
Sun above
Factories

1988. Autonomy of State-owned Utilities.
981 **378** 1d. multicoloured 55 25

379 Woman's Face
and Emblem

1988. International Women's Day.
982 **379** 1d. multicoloured 55 25

380 Globe, Flag,
Wood Pigeon and
Scout Salute

1988. 75th Anniv of Arab Scouting.
983 **380** 2d. multicoloured 1·10 45

381 Bau-Hanifia

1988. Spas. Multicoloured.
984 1d. Type **381** 55 25
985 2d.90 Chellala 1·50 55
986 3d.30 Righa-Ain Tolba 1·70 70

382 Running

1988. Olympic Games, Seoul.
987 **382** 2d.90 multicoloured 1·90 90

383 Pencil and
Globe

1988. International Literacy Day.
988 **383** 2d.90 multicoloured 1·40 70

384 Barbary Ape

1988. Endangered Animals. Barbary Ape. Multicoloured.
989 50c. Type **384** 80 40
990 90c. Ape family 1·20 65
991 1d. Ape's head and shoulders
(vert) 1·60 85
992 1d.80 Ape in tree (vert) 2·75 1·50

385 Family Group

1988. 40th Anniv of W.H.O.
993 **385** 2d.90 multicoloured 1·30 60

386 Different Races
raising Fists

1988. Anti-apartheid Campaign.
994 **386** 2d.50 multicoloured 1·20 50

387 Emblem

1988. Sixth National Liberation Front Party Congress.
995 **387** 1d. multicoloured 55 25

388 Man irrigating Fields

1988. Agriculture. Multicoloured.
996 1d. Type **388** 55 25
997 1d. Fields, cattle and man
picking fruit 55 25

389
Constantine

1989
998 **389** 1d. deep green and
green 40 85

1989. Views of Algeria before 1830 (5th series). As T **310**.
999 2d.50 green 90 25
1000 2d.90 green 1·00 25
1001 5d. brown and black 2·10 40
DESIGNS: 2d.50, Bay; 2d.90, Harbour; 5d. View of harbour
through archway.

390 Courtyard

1989. National Achievements. Multicoloured.
1002 1d. Type **390** 55 25
1003 1d. Flats (housing) 55 25
1004 1d. Gateway, Timimoun
(tourism) 55 25
1005 1d. Dish aerial and telephones
(communications) 55 25

391 Oran Es Senia Airport

1989. Airports. Multicoloured.
1006 2d.90 Type **391** 1·20 45
1007 3d.30 Tebessa airport 1·40 60
1008 5d. Tamanrasset airport (vert) 2·10 1·20

392 Irrigation

1989. Development of South. Multicoloured.
1009 1d. Type **392** 50 25
1010 1d.80 Ouargla secondary school 70 40
1011 2d.50 Gas complex, Hassi R'mel
(vert) 1·10 50

393 Soldiers at
Various Tasks

1989. 20th Anniv of National Service.
1012 **393** 2d. multicoloured 1·30 65

394 Locusts and Crop
Spraying

1989. Anti-locusts Campaign.
1013 **394** 1d. multicoloured 55 25

395 Mother and
Baby

1989. International Children's Day.
1014 **395** 1d.+30c. mult 65 40

396 Moon

1989. 20th Anniv of First Manned Landing on Moon.
Multicoloured.
1015 2d.90 Type **396** 1·20 50
1016 4d. Astronaut on moon 1·50 80

397 Globe and Emblem

1989. Centenary of Interparliamentary Union.
1017 **397** 2d.90 mauve, brn & gold 1·20 40

398 Fruits and Vegetables

1989. National Production.
1018 **398** 2d. multicoloured 75 40
1019 — 3d. multicoloured 1·10 60
1020 — 5d. multicoloured 1·90 1·10
DESIGNS: 3, 5d. Various fruits and vegetables.

399 Atlantic Bonito

1989. Fish. Multicoloured.
1021 1d. Type **399** 60 30
1022 1d.80 John dory 1·10 45
1023 2d.90 Red seabream 1·60 60
1024 3d.30 Swordfish 1·80 75

400 "35" and
Soldier with Rifle

1989. 35th Anniv of Revolution.
1025 **400** 1d. multicoloured 50 15

401 Bank Emblem,
Cogwheel, Factory
and Wheat

1989. 25th Anniv of African Development Bank.
1026 **401** 1d. multicoloured 45 25

402 Satan's Mushroom

1989. Fungi. Multicoloured.
1027	1d. Type **402**		70	30
1028	1d.80 Yellow stainer		1·20	45
1029	2d.90 Parasol mushroom		1·90	75
1030	3d.30 Saffron milk cap		2·20	95

403 Emblem

1990. Tenth Anniv of Pan-African Postal Union.
1031	**403**	1d. multicoloured	50	25

404 Sun, Arm and Face

1990. Rational Use of Energy.
1032	**404**	1d. multicoloured	60	25

405 Emblem

1990. African Nations Cup Football Championship.
1033	**405**	3d. multicoloured	1·30	50

406 Ceramics

1990. Industries. Multicoloured.
1034	2d. Type **406**	70	35
1035	2d.90 Car maintenance	1·10	45
1036	3d.30 Fishing	1·70	65

407 Pictogram and Olympic Rings

1990. World Cup Football Championship, Italy. Multicoloured.
1037	2d.90 Type **407**	1·10	50
1038	5d. Trophy, ball and flag	1·90	95

408 Pylons on Map

1990. Rural Electrification.
1039	**408**	2d. multicoloured	80	30

409 Young Workers

1990. Youth. Multicoloured.
1040	2d. Type **409**	80	30
1041	3d. Youth in crowd (vert)	1·20	45

410 Members' Flags

1990. Arab Maghreb Union Summit Conference.
1042	**410**	1d. multicoloured	50	25

411 Anniversary Emblem

1990. 30th Anniv of O.P.E.C.
1043	**411**	2d. multicoloured	80	30

412 House and Hand holding Coin

1990. Savings Day.
1044	**412**	1d. multicoloured	40	15

413 Flag, Rifle and Hands with Broken Manacles

1990. Namibian Independence.
1045	**413**	3d. multicoloured	1·00	30

414 Duck

1990. Domestic Animals. Multicoloured.
1046	1d. Type **414**	50	15
1047	2d. Hare (horiz)	95	35
1048	2d.90 Common turkey	1·30	55
1049	3d.30 Red junglefowl (horiz)	1·60	75

415 Dome of the Rock and Palestinians

1990. Palestinian "Intifada" Movement.
1050	**415**	1d.+30c. mult	60	40

416 Crowd with Banners

1990. 30th Anniv of 11 December 1960 Demonstration.
1051	**416**	1d. multicoloured	30	10

417 Families in Countryside

1990. Campaign against Respiratory Diseases.
1052	**417**	1d. multicoloured	30	10

418 Sunburst, Torch and Open Book

1991. Second Anniv of Constitution.
1053	**418**	1d. multicoloured	30	10

1991. Views of Algeria before 1830 (6th series). As T 310.
1054	1d.50 red	50	10
1055	4d.20 green	1·40	55
DESIGNS: 1d.50, Kolea; 4d.20, Constantine.

419 Bejaia

1991. Air. Multicoloured.
1056	10d. Type **419**	2·75	1·20
1057	20d. Annaba	5·50	2·75

420 *Jasminum fruticans*

1991. Flowers. Multicoloured.
1058	2d. Type **420**	70	30
1059	4d. *Dianthus crinitus*	1·40	55
1060	5d. *Cyclamen africanum*	1·80	80

421 *Trip to the Country* (Mehdi Medrar)

1991. Children's Drawings. Multicoloured.
1061	3d. Type **421**	90	25
1062	4d. *Children playing* (Ouidad Bounab)	1·20	40

422 Emblem

1991. Third Anniv of Arab Maghreb Union Summit Conference, Zeralda.
1063	**422**	1d. multicoloured	30	10

423 Figures and Emblem

1991. 40th Anniv of Geneva Convention on Status of Refugees.
1064	**423**	3d. multicoloured	1·00	35

424 Coded Letter and Target

1991. World Post Day (1065) and "Telecom 91" International Telecommunications Exhibition, Geneva (1066). Multicoloured.
1065	1d.50 Type **424**	55	25
1066	4d.20 Exhibition and I.T.U. emblems (vert)	1·20	45

425 Spanish Festoon

1991. Butterflies. Multicoloured.
1067	2d. Type **425**	60	30
1068	4d. *Melitaea didyma*	1·00	45
1069	6d. Red admiral	1·40	65
1070	7d. Large tortoiseshell	1·70	95

426 Chest Ornament

1991. Silver Jewellery from South Algeria. Multicoloured.
1071	3d. Necklaces	60	30
1072	4d. Type **426**	80	45
1073	5d. Enamelled ornament	90	65
1074	7d. Bangles (horiz)	1·50	1·00

1992. Views of Algeria before 1830. As previous issues and new values. Size 30½×21 mm.
1075	5c. purple	60	30
1076	10c. blue	70	1·80
1077	20c. blue	90	50
1078	30c. red and black	1·30	35
1079	50c. brown	1·30	35
1080	70c. lilac	1·80	85
1081	80c. brown	2·00	75
1082	1d. brown	1·50	65
1083	2d. blue	2·75	1·30
1084	3d. green	3·75	95
1085	4d. red	5·25	1·30
1086	6d.20 blue	90	25
1087	7d.50 red	1·20	25
DESIGNS: 5c., 6d.20, As No. 873; 10c., 7d.50, As No. 859; 20c. As No. 1000; 30c. As No. 1001; 50c. As No. 882; 70c. As No. 875; 80c. Type **310**; 1d. As No. 860; 2d. As No. 861; 3d. As No. 817; 4d. As No. 1055.

427 Woman

1992. International Women's Day.
1095	**427**	1d.50 multicoloured	40	10

428 Dorcas Gazelle

1992. Gazelles. Multicoloured.
1096	1d.50 Type **428**	40	10
1097	6d.20 Edmi gazelle	1·10	60
1098	8d.60 Addra gazelle	1·50	75

429 Algiers

1992
1099	**429**	1d.50 brown & lt brown	25	10

1132	429	2d. blue	30	10
1147	429	3d. blue	50	10

430 Runners

1992. Olympic Games, Barcelona.

1100	430	6d.20 multicoloured	1·20	45

431 Doves and Flags

1992. 30th Anniv of Independence.

1101	431	5d. green, red and black	90	30

432 *Ajuga iva*

1992. Medicinal Plants. Multicoloured.

1102		1d.50 Type **432**	25	10
1103		5d.10 Buckthorn	90	40
1104		6d.20 Milk thistle	1·20	50
1105		8d.60 French lavender	1·60	70

433 Computerized Post Office Equipment

1992. World Post Day. Modernization of Postal Service.

1106	433	1d.50 multicoloured	40	10

434 Boudiaf

1992. Mohammed Boudiaf (chairman of Committee of State) Commemoration.

1107	434	2d. multicoloured	45	25
1108	434	8d.60 multicoloured	1·50	75

435 2nd-century B.C. Numidian Coin

1992. Coinage. Multicoloured.

1109		1d.50 Type **435**	20	10
1110		2d. 14th-century Zianide dinar	30	15
1111		5d.10 11th-century Almoravid dinar	85	40
1112		6d.20 19th-century Emir Abd-el-Kader coin	1·20	55

436 Short-snouted Seahorse

1992. Marine Animals. Multicoloured.

1113		1d.50 Type **436**	35	10

1114		2d.70 Loggerhead turtle	55	25
1115		6d.20 Mediterranean moray	1·20	55
1116		7d.50 Lobster	1·40	70

437 Algiers Door Knocker

1993. Door Knockers. Multicoloured.

1117		2d. Type **437**	30	10
1118		5d.60 Constantine	90	35
1119		8d.60 Tlemcen	1·40	70

438 Medlar Blossom

1993. Fruit-tree Blossom. Multicoloured.

1120		4d.50 Type **438**	80	40
1121		8d.60 Quince (vert)	1·40	70
1122		11d. Apricot (vert)	1·80	95

439 Patrol Boat, Emblem and Flag

1993. 20th Anniv of Coastguard Service.

1123	439	2d. multicoloured	95	35

440 Grain Storage Jar

1993. Traditional Utensils. Multicoloured.

1124		2d. Type **440**	50	10
1125		5d.60 Grindstone	90	50
1126		8d.60 Oil-press	1·40	65

441 Mauretanian Royal Mausoleum, Tipaza

1993. Mausoleums. Multicoloured.

1127		8d.60 Type **441**	1·10	50
1128		12d. Royal Mausoleum, El Khroub	1·80	80

442 Jijelienne Coast

1993. Air.

1129	442	50d. green, brown & blue	5·75	2·00

443 Annaba

1993. Ports. Multicoloured.

1130		2d. Type **443**	40	10
1131		8d.60 Arzew	1·40	50

444 Chameleon

1993. Reptiles. Multicoloured.

1133		2d. Type **444**	50	10
1134		8d.60 Desert monitor (horiz)	1·60	85

445 Tipaza

1993. Tourism. Multicoloured.

1135		2d. Type **445**	40	10
1136		8d.60 Kerzaz	1·10	50

446 Map, Processing Plant and Uses of Hydrocarbons

1993. 30th Anniv of Sonatrach (National Society for Transformation and Commercialization of Hydrocarbons).

1137	446	2d. multicoloured	50	10

447 Dove, Flag and "18"

1994. National Chahid Day.

1138	447	2d. multicoloured	55	10

448 Crown of Statue of Liberty, Football, U.S. Flag and Trophy

1994. World Cup Football Championship, U.S.A.

1139	448	8d.60 multicoloured	2·75	85

449 Monkey Orchid

1994. Orchids. Multicoloured.

1140		5d.60 Type **449**	1·20	65
1141		8d.60 *Orphrys lutea*	1·50	85
1142		11d. Bee orchid	2·20	1·30

450 Hoggar Script on Stone

1994. Ancient Communication. Multicoloured.

1143		3d. Type **450**	80	25
1144		10d. Abizar stele	1·80	75

451 Flags and Olympic Rings

1994. Cent of International Olympic Committee.

1145	451	12d. multicoloured	1·90	65

452 Figures and City on Globe

1994. World Population Day.

1146	452	3d. multicoloured	50	10

453 Sandstone

1994. Minerals. Multicoloured.

1148		3d. Type **453**	55	25
1149		5d. Cipolin	90	45
1150		10d. Turitella shells in chalk	2·00	1·00

454 Brooches

1994. Saharan Silver Jewellery. Multicoloured.

1151		3d. Type **454**	65	15
1152		5d. Belt (horiz)	1·10	40
1153		12d. Bracelets (horiz)	2·75	1·00

455 Soldiers

1994. 40th Anniv of Revolution.

1154	455	3d. multicoloured	45	10

456 Ladybirds on Leaves

1994. Insects. Multicoloured.

1155		3d. Type **456**	50	15
1156		12d. Beetle (*Buprestidae*) on plant	1·90	75

457 Virus and Family

1994. World Anti-AIDS Campaign Day.

1157	457	3d. black, blue & mauve	50	10

458 Algiers

1994. Regional Dances. Multicoloured.
1158	3d. Type **458**	50	10
1159	10d. Constantine	1·30	65
1160	12d. Alaoui	1·40	75

459 Southern Algeria

1995. 20th Anniv of World Tourism Organization.
| 1161 | **459** | 3d. multicoloured | 40 | 10 |

460 Honey Bee on Comb

1995. Bee-keeping. Multicoloured.
| 1162 | 3d. Type **460** | 40 | 10 |
| 1163 | 13d. Bee on flower (horiz) | 1·50 | 85 |

461 Dahlia

1995. Flowers. Multicoloured.
1164	3d. Type **461**	55	10
1165	10d. Zinnias	1·60	70
1166	13d. Lilac	1·80	85

462 Circular Design

1995. Stucco Work from Sedrata (4th century after Hegira).
1167	**462**	3d. brown	30	10
1168	-	4d. green	50	10
1169	-	5d. brown	55	25
DESIGNS—4d. Circular design within square; 5d. Stylized flowers.

463 Doves, Graves, Victims and Soldiers

1995. 50th Anniv of End of Second World War. Multicoloured.
| 1170 | 3d. Type **463** | 40 | 10 |
| MS1171 | 70×80 mm. 13d. National flag on dove (25×27 mm) | 4·50 | 3·50 |

464 Water Pollution

1995. Environmental Protection. Multicoloured.
| 1172 | 3d. Type **464** | 35 | 10 |
| 1173 | 13d. Air pollution | 1·50 | 65 |

465 Players and Anniversary Emblem

1995. Centenary of Volleyball.
| 1174 | **465** | 3d. multicoloured | 30 | 10 |

466 Map and Pylon

1995. Electrification.
| 1175 | **466** | 3d. multicoloured | 35 | 10 |

467 Children and Schoolbag Contents

1995. National Solidarity.
| 1176 | **467** | 3d.+50c. mult | 50 | 35 |

468 Doves and Anniversary Emblem

1995. 50th Anniv of U.N.O.
| 1177 | **468** | 13d. multicoloured | 1·40 | 75 |

469 Pitcher from Lakhdaria

1995. Traditional Pottery.
1178	**469**	10d. brown	1·10	40
1179	-	20d. brown	2·10	65
1180	-	21d. brown	2·10	65
1181	-	30d. brown	3·00	90
DESIGNS: 20d. Water jug (Aokas); 21d. Jar (Larbaa nath Iraten); 30d. Jar (Ouadhia).

470 Common Shelduck

1995. Water Birds. Multicoloured.
| 1182 | 3d. Type **470** | 55 | 25 |
| 1183 | 5d. Common snipe | 90 | 35 |

471 Doves flying over Javelin Thrower and Olympic Rings

1996. Centenary of Modern Olympic Games and Olympic Games, Atlanta.
| 1184 | **471** | 20d. multicoloured | 2·20 | 1·10 |

472 Fringed Bag

1996. Handicrafts. Leather Bags. Multicoloured.
| 1185 | 5d. Type **472** | | 1·20 | 50 |
| 1186 | 16d. Shoulder bag with handle (vert) | | 2·20 | 95 |

473 Pasteur Institute

1996. Centenary (1994) of Algerian Pasteur Institute.
| 1187 | **473** | 5d. multicoloured | 55 | 20 |

474 Arabic Script and Computer

1996. Scientific and Technical Education Day. Multicoloured.
1188	5d. Type **474**	55	25
1189	16d. Dove, fountain pen and symbols (vert)	1·40	60
1190	23d. Pencil, pen, dividers and satellite over Earth on pages of open book (vert)	2·40	1·10

475 Iron Ore, Djebel Quenza

1996. Minerals. Multicoloured.
| 1191 | 10d. Type **475** | 1·20 | 50 |
| 1192 | 20d. Gold, Tirek-Amesmessa | 2·20 | 95 |

476 *Pandoriana pandora*

1996. Butterflies. Multicoloured.
1193	5d. Type **476**	65	25
1194	10d. *Coenonympha pamphilus*	1·10	50
1195	20d. Painted lady	2·30	1·10
1196	23d. Marbled white	2·50	1·30

477 Globe, Drug Addict and Drugs

1996. World Anti-drugs Day.
| 1197 | **477** | 5d. multicoloured | 50 | 15 |

478 *Woman with Pigeons*

1996. Paintings by Ismail Samsom. Multicoloured.
| 1198 | 20d. Type **478** | 1·50 | 80 |
| 1199 | 30d. *Interrogation* | 2·30 | 1·30 |

479 Ambulance and Paramedic holding Child (Medical Aid)

1996. Civil Defence. Multicoloured.
| 1200 | 5d. Type **479** | 50 | 25 |
| 1201 | 23d. Globe resting in cupped hands (natural disaster prevention) (vert) | 1·80 | 85 |

480 Children, Syringe and Pens

1996. 50th Anniv of UNICEF Multicoloured.
| 1202 | 5d. Type **480** | 40 | 10 |
| 1203 | 10d. Family holding pencil, key, syringe and flower | 90 | 35 |

481 Dar Hassan Pacha

1996. Algiers Courtyards. Multicoloured.
1204	5d. Type **481**	40	15
1205	10d. Dar Kedaoudj el Amia	75	40
1206	20d. Palais des Rais	1·50	90
1207	30d. Villa Abdellatif	2·40	1·40

482 Minbar Inscription, Nedroma Mosque

1997. Mosque Carvings. Multicoloured.
| 1208 | 5d. Type **482** | 40 | 15 |
| 1209 | 23d. Doors, Ketchaoua Mosque, Algiers | 1·80 | 95 |

483 Outline Map, Graph and Roofs over People

1997. Fourth General Population and Housing Census.
| 1210 | **483** | 5d. multicoloured | 40 | 10 |

484 Soldiers controlling Crowd with Flags

1997. 35th Anniv of Oargla Protest.
| 1211 | **484** | 5d. multicoloured | 40 | 10 |

485 Doves above Crowd with Flags

1997. 35th Anniv of Victory Day.
| 1212 | **485** | 5d. multicoloured | 40 | 10 |

486 *Ficaria verna*

1997. Flowers. Multicoloured.
1213	**486**	5d. Type 486	50	20
1214		16d. Honeysuckle	1·20	70
1215		23d. Common poppy	1·80	1·00

487 "No Smoking" Sign on Map

1997. World No Smoking Day.
1216	**487**	5d. multicoloured	40	10

488 Crowd and Map

1997. Legislative Elections.
1217	**488**	5d. multicoloured	40	10

489 "Buthus occitanus"

1997. Scorpions. Multicoloured.
1218	**489**	5d. Type 489	45	15
1219		10d. "Androctonus australis"	80	45

490 Crowd with Flags

1997. 35th Anniv of Independence. Multicoloured.
1220	**490**	5d. Type 490	40	10
MS1221		70×80 mm. 10d. National flag behind doves and "35" between broken chain-link (25×36 mm)	1·10	85

491 Zakaria

1997. 20th Death Anniv of Moufdi Zakaria (poet).
1222	**491**	5d. multicoloured	40	10

492 Dokkali Design, Tidikelt

1997. Textiles. Multicoloured.
1223		3d. Type 492	30	10
1224		5d. Tellis design, Aures	45	25
1225		10d. Bou Taleb design, M'Sila	80	40
1226		20d. Ddil design, Ait-Hichem	1·50	85

493 Map, Emblem and Rainbow

1997. 25th Anniv of Pan-Arab Security Forces Organization.
1227	**493**	5d. multicoloured	40	15

494 Packages and Express Mail Service Emblem

1997. World Post Day.
1228	**494**	5d. multicoloured	40	15

495 Rising Sun on Map

1997. Local Elections.
1229	**495**	5d. multicoloured	40	15

496 Tenes Lighthouse

1997. Lighthouses. Multicoloured.
1230		5d. Type 496	50	25
1231		10d. Cap Caxine, Algiers (vert)	1·00	50

497 Mail Plane and Mail Van

1997. First Anniv of Aeropostale.
1232	**497**	5d. multicoloured	50	15

498 Variable Scallop

1997. Sea Shells. Multicoloured.
1233		5d. Type 498	55	15
1234		10d. Bolinus brandaris	1·00	40
1235		20d. Hinia reticulata (vert)	1·90	80

499 National Flag and Columned Facade

1997. Inauguration of Council of the Nation (upper parliamentary chamber).
1236	**499**	5d. multicoloured	40	15

500 Flag, Ballot Box, Constitution and People

1997. Completion of Government Reform. Multicoloured.
1237		5d. Type 500 (presidential election)	40	15
1238		5d. Constitution and torch (constitution referendum)	40	15
1239		5d. Ballot box and voting papers (elections to National Assembly (lower chamber of Parliament))	40	15
1240		5d. Flag, sun and rose (local elections)	40	15
1241		5d. Flag and Parliament (elections to National Council (upper chamber))	40	15

Nos. 1237/41 were issued together, *se-tenant*, forming a composite design.

501 Exhibition Emblem

1998. "Expo 98" World's Fair, Lisbon. Multicoloured.
1242		5d. Type 501	40	15
MS1243		80×70 mm. 24d. Mosaic of fishes (40×31 mm) Imperf	2·00	1·80

502 Aerial Bombardment

1998. 40th Anniv of Bombing of Sakiet Sidi Youcef.
1244	**502**	5d. multicoloured	40	15

503 Archives Building

1998. National Archives.
1245	**503**	5d. multicoloured	40	15

504 Lalla Fadhma N'Soumeur

1998. International Women's Day.
1246	**504**	5d. multicoloured	35	15

505 Players and Eiffel Tower

1998. World Cup Football Championship, France.
1247	**505**	24d. multicoloured	1·90	55

506 View from Land

1998. Algiers Kasbah. Multicoloured.
1248		5d. Type 506	40	30
1249		10d. Street	80	40
1250		24d. View from sea (horiz)	1·50	95

507 Crescent and Flag

1998. Red Crescent.
1251	**507**	5d.+1d. red, green and black	45	25

508 Battle Scene

1998. 150th Anniv of Insurrection of the Zaatcha.
1252	**508**	5d. multicoloured	40	15

509 Parent and Child and Hand holding Rose

1998. International Children's Day. National Solidarity. Multicoloured.
1253		5d.+1d. Type 509	45	25
1254		5d.+1d. Children encircling emblem (horiz)	45	25

510 "Tourism and the Environment"

1998. Tourism. Multicoloured.
1255		5d. Type 510	40	15
1256		10d. Young tourists and methods of transportation (horiz)	90	35
1257		24d. Taghit (horiz)	1·80	95

511 Map of North Africa and Arabia

1998. Arab Post Day.
1258	**511**	5d. multicoloured	90	10

512 Interpol and Algerian Police Force Emblems

1998. 75th Anniv of Interpol.
1259	**512**	5d. multicoloured	40	10

513 Provisional Government and State Flag

1998. 40th Anniv of Creation of Provisional Government of Algerian Republic.
1260	**513**	5d. multicoloured	40	15

514 Arrows leading from Algeria around the World

1998. National Diplomacy Day.
1261	**514**	5d. multicoloured	40	10

515 Dove and Olympic
Rings

1998. 35th Anniv of Algerian Olympic Committee.
1262 **515** 5d. multicoloured 40 10

516 Osprey

1998. Birds. Multicoloured.
1263 5d. Type **516** 55 25
1264 10d. Audouin's gull 1·10 45
1265 24d. Shag (vert) 2·20 1·10
1266 30d. Common cormorant (vert) 2·75 1·40

517 Anniversary Emblem
and Profiles

1998. 50th Anniv of Universal Declaration of Human
Rights. Multicoloured.
1267 5d. Type **517** 55 10
1268 24d. Anniversary emblem, dove
and people 2·00 90

518 Comb

1999. Spinning and Weaving Implements. Multicoloured.
1269 5d. Type **518** 50 25
1270 10d. Carding (horiz) 90 40
1271 20d. Spindle 1·90 90
1272 24d. Loom 2·20 1·00

519 Dove, Torch,
Flag and Soldiers

1999. National Chahid Day.
1273 **519** 5d. multicoloured 40 15

520 Pear

1999. Fruit Trees. Multicoloured.
1274 5d. Type **520** 45 25
1275 10d. Plum 80 45
1276 24d. Orange (vert) 2·00 1·10

521 Calligraphy

1999. Presidential Election.
1277 **521** 5d. multicoloured 40 15

522 14th-century
Ceramic Mosaic,
Tlemcen

1999. Crafts. Multicoloured.
1278 5d. Type **522** 45 25
1279 10d. 11th-century ceramic mo-
saic, Kalaa des Beni Hammad 80 40
1280 20d. Cradle (horiz) 1·80 90
1281 24d. Table with raised rim
(horiz) 2·00 1·00

523 Pictograms
on Map of Africa
and South African
Flag

1999. Seventh African Games, Johannesburg.
Multicoloured.
1282 5d. Type **523** 45 25
1283 10d. Pictograms of athletes and
South African flag (horiz) 90 40

524 Gneiss

1999. Minerals. Multicoloured.
1284 5d. Type **524** 40 25
1285 20d. Granite 1·60 90
1286 24d. Sericite schist 2·00 1·10

525 Emblem

1999. Organization of African Unity Summit, Algiers.
1287 **525** 5d. multicoloured 40 15

526 Family and
Map of Africa

1999. 40th Anniv of Organization of African Unity
Convention on Refugees.
1288 **526** 5d. multicoloured 40 15

527 Emblem and
Police Officers

1999. Police Day.
1289 **527** 5d. multicoloured 90 15

528 Linked Hands and
"2000"

1999. International Year of Culture and Peace.
1290 **528** 5d. multicoloured 40 15

529 Dentex Seabream

1999. Fish. Multicoloured.
1291 5d. Type **529** 55 25
1292 10d. Striped red mullet 95 45
1293 20d. Pink dentex 2·00 1·00
1294 24d. White seabream 2·75 1·20

530 Rainbow

1999. Referendum.
1295 **530** 5d. multicoloured 40 15

531 Emblem and
Rainbow

1999. 125th Anniv of Universal Postal Union.
Multicoloured.
1296 5d. Type **531** 55 15
1297 5d. Globe, satellite and stamps 55 15

532 Woman's Face

1999. Rural Women's Day.
1298 **532** 5d. multicoloured 55 15

533 Partisans and
Helicopters

1999. 45th Anniv of Revolution. Multicoloured.
1299 5d. Type **533** 55 20
1300 5d. Partisans and fires 55 20
Nos. 1299/300 were issued together, *se-tenant*, forming
a composite design.

534 Chaoui

1999. Folk Dances. Multicoloured.
1301 5d. Type **534** 55 25
1302 10d. Targuie 1·00 45
1303 24d. M'zab 2·00 1·10

535 Doves

2000. New Millennium. Multicoloured. Self-adhesive.
1304 5d. Type **535** (peace) 55 40
1305 5d. Plants and tree (environ-
ment) 55 40
1306 5d. Umbrella over ears of grain
(food security) 55 40
1307 5d. Wind farm (new energy
sources) 55 40
1308 5d. Globe and ballot box
(democracy) 55 40
1309 5d. Microscope (health) 55 40
1310 5d. Cargo ship at quayside
(commerce) 55 40
1311 5d. Space satellite, dish aerial,
jet plane and train (com-
munications) 55 40
1312 5d. Astronaut and lunar buggy
on Moon (space) 55 40
1313 5d. Film cave paintings,
mandolin and music notes
(culture) 55 40
1314 5d. Outline of dove (peace) 55 40
1315 5d. Hand above flora and fauna
(environment) 55 40
1316 5d. Space satellites, computer
and printed circuits forming
maps of Europe and Africa
(communications) 55 40
1317 5d. Sun, clouds, flame and
water (new energy sources) 55 40
1318 5d. Hand holding seedling
(food security) 55 40
1319 5d. Staff of Aesculapius and
heart (health) 55 40
1320 5d. Arrows around globe (com-
munication) 55 40
1321 5d. Cave paintings, book, paint-
ing and violin (culture) 55 40
1322 5d. Parthenon and envelopes
(democracy) 55 40
1323 5d. Space satellite, solar system,
space shuttle and astronaut
(space) 55 40

536 Chaffinches

2000. Birds. Multicoloured.
1324 5d. Type **536** 50 35
1325 5d. Northern serin (horiz) 50 35
1326 10d. Northern bullfinch (horiz) 95 60
1327 24d. Eurasian goldfinch 2·50 1·40

537 Emblem

2000. "EXPO 2000" World's Fair, Hanover.
1328 **537** 5d. multicoloured 50 30

538 Sydney Opera
House and Sports
Pictograms

2000. Olympic Games, Sydney.
1329 **538** 24d. multicoloured 2·20 85

539 Emblem

2000. Telethon 2000 (fundraising event).
1330 **539** 5d. multicoloured 50 25

540 Crowd,
Linked Hands and
White Doves

2000. "Concorde Civile". Multicoloured.
1331	5d. Type **540**	50	15
1332	10d. Hands releasing doves (horiz)	95	40
1333	20d. Flag, doves and hands forming heart (horiz)	1·90	80
1334	24d. Doves and clasped hands above flowers	2·20	1·00

541 Building

2000. National Library.
| 1335 | **541** | 5d. multicoloured | 50 | 20 |

542 Hand
holding Blood
Droplet

2000. Blood Donation Campaign.
| 1336 | **542** | 5d. multicoloured | 50 | 25 |

543 Lock

2000. Touareg Cultural Heritage. Multicoloured.
| 1337 | 5d. Type **543** | 50 | 40 |
| 1338 | 10d. Lock (vert) | 95 | 40 |

544 Mohamed Racim (artist)

2000. Personalities. Multicoloured.
1339	10d. Type **544**	95	40
1340	10d. Mohammed Dib (writer)	95	40
1341	10d. Mustapha Kateb (theatre director)	95	40
1342	10d. Ali Maachi (musician)	95	40

545 Cock-chafer

2000. Insects. Multicoloured.
1343	5d. Type **545**	50	30
1344	5d. Carpet beetle	50	30
1345	10d. Drugstore beetle	95	55
1346	24d. Carabus	2·50	1·20

546 Jug

2000. Roman Artefacts, Tipasa. Multicoloured.
1347	5d. Type **546**	50	25
1348	10d. Vase	95	50
1349	24d. Jug	2·40	1·10

547 Limodorum
abortivum

2000. Orchids. Multicoloured.
1350	5d. Type **547**	50	25
1351	10d. Orchis papilionacea	95	50
1352	24d. Orchis provincialis	2·40	1·10

548 Greylag Goose
(Anser anser)

2001. Waterfowl. Multicoloured.
1353	5d. Type **548**	50	25
1354	5d. Avocet (Recurvirostra avosetta) (vert)	50	25
1355	10d. Eurasian bittern (Botaurus stellaris) (vert)	95	55
1356	24d. Western curlew (Numenius arquata)	2·50	1·10

549 Painted
Table

2001. Traditional Crafts. Multicoloured.
1357	5d. Type **549**	50	25
1358	10d. Decorated shelf (horiz)	95	60
1359	24d. Ornate mirror	2·40	95

550 Forest,
Belezma National
Park, Batna

2001. National Parks. Multicoloured.
1360	5d. Type **550**	50	25
1361	10d. Headland, Gouraya National Park, Bejaia (horiz)	95	45
1362	20d. Forest and mountains, Theneit el Had National Park, Tissemsilt (horiz)	1·90	80
1363	24d. El Tarf National Park	2·40	1·00

551 St. Augustine
as Child (statue)

2001. St. Augustine of Hippo Conference, Algiers and Annaba. Multicoloured.
| 1364 | 5d. Type **551** | 50 | 25 |
| 1365 | 24d. 4th-century Christian mosaic (43×31 mm) | 2·40 | 1·10 |

552 Obverse and Reverse of
Ryal Boudjou, 1830

2001. Coins. Multicoloured.
1366	5d. Type **552**	50	25
1367	10d. Obverse and reverse of Double Boudjou, 1826	95	45
1368	24d. Obverse and reverse of Ryal Drahem, 1771	2·40	1·00

553 Emblem and Scouts

2001. National Scouts' Day.
| 1369 | **553** | 5d. multicoloured | 50 | 30 |

554 Child
throwing Stones

2001. Intifida.
| 1370 | **554** | 5d. multicoloured | 50 | 15 |

555 Asthma
Sufferer

2001. National Asthma Day.
| 1371 | **556** | 5d. multicoloured | 45 | 15 |

556 Hopscotch

2001. Children's Games. Multicoloured.
1372	5d. Type **556**	50	15
1373	5d. Jacks	50	15
1374	5d. Spinning top	50	15
1375	5d. Marbles	50	15

557 Runners

2001. 50th Anniv of Mediterranean Games. Multicoloured.
| 1376 | 5d. Type **557** | 45 | 15 |
| 1377 | 5d. Race winners and tile decoration | 45 | 15 |

558 Emblem

2001. 15th World Festival of Youth and Students, Algiers.
| 1378 | **558** | 5d. multicoloured | 45 | 15 |

559 Burning Lorry

2001. Freedom Fighters' Day.
| 1379 | **559** | 5d. multicoloured | 45 | 15 |

560 Tree of
Pencils

2001. Teacher's Day.
| 1380 | **560** | 5d. multicoloured | 45 | 15 |

561 Children
encircling Globe

2001. United Nations Year of Dialogue among Civilisations.
| 1381 | **561** | 5d. multicoloured | 45 | 15 |

562 Dove and Explosion

2001. National Immigration Day. 40th Anniv of Demonstrations in Paris.
| 1382 | **562** | 5d. multicoloured | 45 | 20 |

563 El Mokrani

2001. Resistance Fighters. Multicoloured.
| 1383 | 5d. Type **563** | 45 | 20 |
| 1384 | 5d. Cheikh Bouamama | 45 | 20 |

564 Bab el Oued
(flood damaged
town)

2001. Flood Victims Relief Fund.
| 1385 | **564** | 5d.+5d. multicoloured | 90 | 40 |

565 Earring

2002. Silver Jewellery from Aures Region. Multicoloured.
1386	5d. Type **565**	45	25
1387	5d. Fibula	45	25
1388	24d. Pendant	1·60	1·10

566 Ball, Net and
Goalkeeper

2002. World Cup Football Championship, Japan and South Korea. Multicoloured.
| 1389 | 5d. Type **566** | 45 | 25 |
| 1390 | 24d. Monk holding football (vert) | 1·80 | 1·60 |

567 Flag, Doves and Soldiers

2002. 40th Anniv of Victory Day.
1391	**567**	5d. multicoloured	45	30

568 Ksar Sidi Ouali Tamentit, Touat

2002. Fortified Castles. Multicoloured.
1392		5d. Type **568**	45	30
1393		5d. Ksar Ighzar, Gourara	45	30

569 Basket, Ball and Players

2002. World Basketball Championship, Indianapolis, U.S.A.
1394	**569**	5d. multicoloured	45	10

570 Child and Table

2002. Children's Day. Multicoloured.
1395		5d. Type **570**	45	10
1396		5d. Two girls	45	10

571 Book Illustration

2002. 14th Death Anniv of Mohamed Temmam (artist and musician). Multicoloured.
1397		10d. Type **571**	90	40
1398		10d. Self-portrait	90	40

572 Anniversary Emblem

2002. 40th Anniv of Independence. Multicoloured.
1399		5d. Type **572**	45	10
1400		24d. Flags and crowd	1·30	1·00

573 Calcite

2002. Minerals. Multicoloured.
1401		5d. Type **573**	30	10
1402		5d. Feldspar	30	10
1403		5d. Galena (horiz)	30	10
1404		5d. Conglomerate (pudding stone) (horiz)	30	10

574 Cherchell

2002. Lighthouses. Multicoloured.
1405		5d. Type **574**	30	10
1406		10d. Cap de Fer	60	40
1407		24d. Rachgoun island	1·50	1·00

575 Postal Emblem

2002. Re-organization of Algerian Posts.
1408	**575**	5d. multicoloured	30	10

576 Small Jug

2002. Pots. Multicoloured.
1409		5d. Type **576**	30	10
1410		5d. Pot for cooking cous-cous	30	10
1411		5d. Two-handled jar	30	10
1412		5d. Oil lamp	30	10

577 Dove and Rainbow

2002. International Day of Tolerance.
1413	**577**	24d. multicoloured	1·50	1·00

578 *Venus verrucosa*

2002. Shells. Multicoloured.
1414		5d. Type **578**	30	10
1415		5d. *Acanthocardia aculeate*	30	10
1416		5d. *Xenophora crispa*	30	10
1417		5d. *Epitonium commune*	30	10

579 *Eucalyptus globules*

2002. Medicinal Plants. Multicoloured.
1418		5d. Type **579**	30	10
1419		10d. Mallow (*Malva sylvestris*)	60	40
1420		24d. Laurel (*Laurus nobilis*)	1·50	1·00

580 Eiffel Tower, Paris and Martyr's Monument, Algiers

2003. Djazair 2003, Year of Algeria in France. Multicoloured.
1421		5d. Type **580**	30	15
1422		24d. French and Algerian flags (horiz)	1·50	1·00

581 Emblem

2003. Tenth Arab Games.
1423	**581**	5d. multicoloured	30	10

582 El Maadjen, Relizane (oasis)

2003. International Year of Freshwater. Multicoloured.
1424		5d. Type **582**	30	10
1425		10d. Traditional well, M'zab valley	60	40
1426		24d. Kesria (irrigation), Timimoun	1·50	1·00

583 Slave Sale Contract (5 June 494)

2003. Vandal Carved Tablets. Multicoloured.
1427		10d. Type **583**	60	40
1428		24d. Mathematical chart (5 April 493) (vert)	1·50	1·00

584 Building Facade, Face and Books

2003. Student's Day.
1429	**584**	5d. multicoloured	30	10

585 *Rumina decollate*

2003. Snails. Multicoloured.
1430		5d. Type **585**	30	10
1431		24d. *Helix aspera*	1·50	1·00

586 Candle, Map of Africa and Members' Flags

2003. First Anniv of African Union.
1432	**586**	5d. multicoloured	30	10

587 *Ulva lactuca*

2003. Seaweeds. Multicoloured.
1433		5d. Type **587**	30	10
1434		24d. *Gymnogongrus crenulatus*	1·50	1·00

588 Ploughing with Oxen

2003. Roman Mosaics. Multicoloured.
1435		5d. Type **588**	30	10
1436		10d. Ulysses and the Sirens	60	40
1437		24d. Hunting scene	1·50	1·00

589 Maouche Mohand Amokrane (founder) and Emblem

2003. 40th Anniv of Algerian Olympic Committee.
1438	**589**	5d. multicoloured	30	10

590 Heart, Hand, Foot and Eye

2003. World Diabetes Awareness Day.
1439	**590**	5d. multicoloured	30	10

591 Ruins

2003. Support for Earthquake Victims (21 May 2003).
1440	**591**	5d.+5d. multicoloured	60	40

592 Doors

2003. Decorative Art. Multicoloured.
1441		5d. Type **592**	30	15
1442		10d. Window	60	40
1443		24d. Ceiling	1·50	1·00

593 Flags

2003. 45th Anniv of Algeria—China Diplomatic Relations.
1444	**593**	5d. multicoloured	30	10

594 Hurdler

2004. Olympic Games, Athens. Multicoloured.
1445		5d. Type **594**	30	10
1446		10d. Parthenon and hand holding Olympic torch	60	40

595 Woman with Raised Arms

2004. Women's Day.
1447 **595** 5d. multicoloured 30 10

596 Juba I

2004. Numidian Kings. Each brown, bronze and black.
1448 5d. Type **596** 30 10
1449 5d. Juba II 30 10
1450 5d. Micipsa 30 10
1451 5d. Massinassa 30 10
1452 5d. Jugurtha 30 10

597 Olive Tree

2004. Tree Day. Multicoloured.
1453 5d. Type **597** 30 10
1454 10d. Date palm (vert) 60 40

598 Entrance to Presidential Palace

2004. Presidential Elections.
1455 **598** 24d. multicoloured 1·50 1·00

599 Player catching Ball

2004. Centenary of FIFA (Federation Internationale de Football Association). Multicoloured.
1456 5d. Type **599** 30 10
1457 24d. Anniversary emblem 1·50 1·00

600 Dromedary

2004
1458 **600** 24d. multicoloured 1·50 1·00

601 Giving and Receiving Blood

2004. International Blood Donation Day.
1459 **601** 5d. vermilion and black 30 10

602 Tradesmen

2004. Acquiring a Trade.
1460 **602** 5d. multicoloured 30 10

603 Chess Pieces and Board

2004. 80th Anniv of World Chess Federation (FIDE).
1461 **603** 5d. multicoloured 30 10

604 Emblems and Currency

2004. 40th Anniv of CNEP Bank. Multicoloured.
1462 5d. Type **604** 30 10
1463 24d. Harbour 1·50 1·00

605 Yellow Rose

2004. Roses. Multicoloured.
1464 15d. Type **605** 1·30 65
1465 20d. Yellow rose (different) 1·40 85
1466 30d. Orange rose 1·80 1·30
1467 50d. Pink rose 2·75 2·10

606 Map and Flags

2004. Sixth Pan African Conference, Algiers.
1470 **606** 24d. multicoloured 1·50 1·00

607 In Tehaq Rock Formation

2004. Tourism. Sahara. Multicoloured.
1471 5d. Type **607** 30 15
1472 24d. Ekanassay (vert) 1·50 1·00

608 TeleFood Emblem, Houses and Flowers

2004. World Food Day. TeleFood (UN food agency). Multicoloured.
1473 5d.+1d. Type **608** 35 25
1474 5d.+1d. House and fruit trees 35 25

609 Group of Six

2004. 50th Anniv of Revolution. Multicoloured.
1475 15d. Type **609** 1·30 65
MS1476 70×80 mm. 30d. Emblem (30×40 mm) 1·80 1·80

610 Satellite and Earth

2004. Second Anniv of Launch of D'ALSAT 1 Satellite.
1477 **610** 30d. multicoloured 1·80 1·30

611 Rainbow and Plants

2004. Protection of the Environment.
1478 **611** 15d. multicoloured 1·10 60

612 Rabah Bitat

2004. Fourth Death Anniv of Rabah Bitat (politician).
1479 **612** 15d. multicoloured 1·10 60

613 Wood Pigeon (*Columba palumbus*)

2005. Pigeons. Multicoloured.
1480 10d. Type **613** 60 35
1481 15d. Rock dove (*Columba livia*) 1·10 60

614 *Echium australis*

2005. Flowers. Multicoloured.
1482 15d. Type **614** 1·30 65
1483 30d. *Borago officinalis* 1·80 1·30

615 Eye and Hands

2005. National Day for the Disabled.
1484 **615** 15d. multicoloured 1·10 60

616 Emblem

2005. Arab League Summit, Algeria (1485). 60th Anniv of Arab League (1486). Multicoloured.
1485 15d. Type **616** 1·10 60
1486 30d. Emblem and "2005–1945" (vert) 1·80 1·30

617 Medersa D'Alger

2005. Medersa (seats of learning). Multicoloured.
1487 10d. Type **617** 60 35
1488 15d. Medersa de Constantine 1·10 60
1489 30d. Medersa de Tlemcen 1·80 1·30

618 Emblem

2005. World Intellectual Property Day.
1490 **618** 15d. multicoloured 1·10 60

619 Workers and Hand holding Apple

2005. World Day for Safety and Health at Work.
1491 **619** 15d. multicoloured 1·10 60

620 "60" and Dove

2005. 60th Anniv of Massacre.
1492 **620** 15d. multicoloured 1·10 60

621 Medal and Stylized Sports

2005. 15th Mediterranean Games, Almeria. Multicoloured.
1493 15d. Type **621** 1·10 60
1494 30d. Emblem (horiz) 1·80 1·30

622 Lakhdar Ben Khlouf

2005. Poets. Multicoloured.
1495 10d. Type **622** 60 35
1496 15d. Ben M'sayeb 1·10 60
1497 20d. Si Mohand Ou M'Hand 1·40 85
1498 30d. Aissa El Djermouni 1·80 1·30

623 Children

2005. International Day against Drug Abuse.
1499 **623** 15d. multicoloured 1·10 60

624 Student and Soldiers

2005. 50th Anniv of UGEMA (General Union of the Algerian Moslem Students).
1500 **624** 15d. multicoloured 1·10 60

625 Cheetah

2005. Cheetah (inscr "Guepard"). Multicoloured.
1501	15d. Type **625**		1·10	60
1502	30d. Standing		1·80	1·30

626 Emblem

2005. World Information Society Summit, Tunis.
1503	**626**	15d. multicoloured	1·10	60

627 "50" and Soldiers

2005. 50th Anniv of Uprising.
1504	**627**	15d. multicoloured	1·10	60

628 Phare Fort

2005. Forts. Multicoloured.
1505	10d. Type **628**		60	35
1506	15d. Cap Matifou		1·10	60
1507	30d. Santa Cruz		1·80	1·30

629 Emblem and Runners

2005. International Year of Sports Education.
1508	**629**	30d. multicoloured	1·80	1·30

630 Clasped Hands

2005. National Reconciliation.
1509	**630**	15d. multicoloured	1·10	60

631 Flag

2005. Referendum.
1510	**631**	15d. multicoloured	1·10	60

632 Flag, Emblem and Buildings

2005. Recovery of National Sovereignty.
1511	**632**	30d. multicoloured	1·80	1·30

633 Saddle

2005. Emir Abdelkader's Possessions. Multicoloured.
1512	15d. Type **633**		1·10	60
1513	30d. Boots		1·80	1·30
1514	40d. Jacket (vert)		2·40	1·70
1515	50d. Seal (vert)		2·75	2·10

634 Miguel de Cervantes

2005. Miguel de Cervantes Saavedra (writer) Commemoration.
1516	**634**	30d. multicoloured	1·80	1·30

635 Amputee

2005. Anti-Personnel Mine Destruction Campaign.
1517	**635**	30d. multicoloured	1·80	1·30

636 Emblem

2005. International AIDS Awareness Day.
1518	**636**	30d. multicoloured	1·80	1·30

637 Ptolemy

2005. Kings. Multicoloured.
1519	15d. Type **637**		1·10	60
1520	30d. Syphax		1·80	1·30

638 Building Facade

2006. Posts.
1521	**638**	30d. multicoloured	1·80	1·30

639 *Ciconia ciconia*

2006. Waterside Birds. Multicoloured.
1522	10d. Type **639**		60	35
1523	15d. *Ciconia nigra*		1·10	60
1524	20d. *Platalea leucorodia*		1·40	85
1525	30d. *Grus grus*		1·80	1·30

640 Skier

2006. Winter Olympic Games, Turin.
1526	**640**	15d. multicoloured	1·10	60

641 Aissat Idir (founder)

2006. 50th Anniv of UGTA Trade Union.
1527	**641**	15d. multicoloured	1·10	60

642 Ball and Globe

2006. World Cup Football Championship, Germany.
1528	**642**	30d. multicoloured	1·80	1·30

643 Airport

2006. New Air Terminal, Algiers.
1529	**643**	30d. multicoloured	1·80	1·30

645 Students

2006. 50th Anniv of Student's Day.
1532	**645**	20d. multicoloured	1·40	85

646 Trees

2006. International Environment Day.
1533	**646**	30d. multicoloured	1·80	1·30

647 Powder Holder

2006. Poire a Poudre (powder holders). Multicoloured.
1534	15d. Type **647**		1·10	60
1535	20d. Powder holder (different)		1·40	85

648 Map

2006. 50th Anniv of La Soummam Congress.
1536	**648**	20d. multicoloured	1·40	85

649 Emblem

2006. 16th Arab School Games.
1537	**649**	30d. multicoloured	1·80	1·30

649a Hand holding Pencils

2006. Teacher's Day
1537a	**649a**	20d. multicoloured	1·40	85

649b Inscr "Pistachier de l'Atlas"

2006. Fruiting Trees. Multicoloured.
1537b	20d. Type **649b**		1·40	85
1537c	30d. Inscr "Grenadier"		1·80	1·30

649c Globe

2006. Sino-African Forum Summit, Beijing
1537d	**649c**	30d. multicoloured	1·80	1·30

650 Dunes and Oasis

2006. International Year of Deserts and Desertification. Multicoloured.
1538	**650**	15d. multicoloured	1·10	60
1538a		15d. Ain Hammou-Tinerkouk-Adar	1·10	60

650a Map and building

2006. First Anniv of Arab Transient Parliament.
1538b	**650a**	15d. multicoloured	1·10	60

650b Early Edition

2006. 50th Anniv of El-Moudjohid (journal).
1538c	**650b**	30d. multicoloured	1·80	1·30

650c Desalination Plant

2006. Desalination Plant
1538d	**650c**	20d. multicoloured	1·40	85

651 Traditional Designs

2007. Algiers-Arab Cultural Capital-2007. Multicoloured.
1539	15d. Type **651**	1·10	60
1540	30d. "2007"	1·80	1·30

652 L'îlot d'Arzew

2007. Lighthouses. Multicoloured.
1541	15d. Type **652**	1·10	60
1542	20d. Cap Sigli	1·40	85
1543	38d. Ras-Afia	2·20	1·50

653 Women

2007. Development of Women's Employment.
1544	**653**	15d. multicoloured	1·10	60

653a Mohamed
Ameziane Belhaddad

2007. Mohamed Ameziane Belhaddad Commemoration.
1545	**653a**	15d. multicoloured	1·10	60

654 Ksar de Kenadsa

2007. Cultural Heritage. Multicoloured.
1546	15d. Type **654**	1·10	60
1547	15d. Ksar de Temacine (vert)	1·10	60

655 Emblem, Map and
'JEUX AFRO-ASIATIQUES
D'ALGER'

2007. Sport Events in Algiers. Multicoloured.
1548	15d. Type **655**	1·10	60
1549	15d. Emblem, map and 'ALL AFRICAN GAMES' (vert)	1·10	60

656 Count Landon's Garden,
Biskra

2007. Gardens. Multicoloured.
1550	15d. Type **656**	1·10	60
1551	20d. Ibn Badis garden, Oran	1·40	85
1552	38d. Jardin d' Essai du Hamma, Algiers	2·20	1·50

657 Theatre de Setif

2007. Theatres. Multicoloured.
1553	15d. Type **657**	1·10	60
1554	15d. Theatre d'Oranen, Oran	1·10	60
1555	20d. Theatre de Annaba (horiz)	1·40	85
1555a	38d. Theatre d'Algers	2·20	1·50

658 Demonstrators

2007. 45th Anniv of Festival of Independence and Youth. Multicoloured.
1556	15d. Type **658**	1·10	60

MS1557 60×77 mm. 20d. Satellite,
computer and inkwell. Imperf 1·40 1·40

659 Bottle

2007. Ceramics. Multicoloured.
1558	15d. Type **659**	1·10	60
1559	15d. Two handled jug	1·10	60
1560	20d. Censer	1·40	85
1561	38d. Oil lamp (horiz)	2·20	1·50

660 Emblem

2007. 45th Anniv of National Police. Multicoloured.
1562	15d. Type **660**	1·10	60
1563	38d. Policeman and patrol vehicle	2·20	1·50

661 Hyena

2007. Endangered Species. Multicoloured.
1564	15d. Type **661**	1·10	60
1565	38d. White-tailed red fox	2·20	1·50

662 Encyclopaedia of
Algerian Postage
Stamps

2007
1566	**662**	15d. multicoloured	1·10	60

663 Ahmed Bey

2007. Ahmed Bey (resistance fighter) Commemoration.
1567	**663**	15d. multicoloured	1·10	60

664 Emblem

2007. National Artisans' Day.
1568	**664**	15d. multicoloured	1·10	60

665 Nile Tilapia

2007. Nile Tilapia (*Oreochromis niloticus*).
1569	**665**	15d. multicoloured	1·10	60

666 Abd el-kader

2007. Birth Bicentenary of Abd al-Qadir al-Jaza'iri (Abd el-kader) (Islamic scholar, Sufi, political and military leader). Sheet 158×108 mm containing T **666** and similar vert designs.
MS1570 15d. Type **666**; 15d. Facing
left; 38d. Wearing medals and belt 3·25 3·25

667 Emblem

2008. Census.
1571	**667**	15d. multicoloured	1·10	60

668 Doves and
Emblem

2008. 50th Anniv of Bombing of Sakiet Sid Youcef, Tunisia.
1572	**668**	15d. multicoloured	1·10	60

A stamp of a similar design was issued by Tunisia.

669 Ain de la
Grande Rue

2008. Fountains. Sheet 110×90 mm containing T **669** and similar vert designs. Multicoloured.
MS1573 10d. Type **669**; 15d. Ain Bir
Djebbah; 20d. Ain Sidi Abdellah;
38d. Ain bir Chebana 5·00 5·00

670 Issakarassen
Wetland, Tamanrasset

2008. Zaragoza 2008 International Water and Sustainable Development Exhibition. Sheet 110×90 mm containing T **670** and similar vert designs. Multicoloured.
MS1574 10d. Type **670**; 15d. Reghaia
wetland; 20d. Guerbes wetland,
Skikda; 38d. Emblem 2·75 2·75

671 '50'

2008. 50th Anniv of National Liberation Front Football Team. Sheet 158×108 mm.
MS1575 **671** 38d. multicoloured 2·30 2·30

672 Redha Houhou

2008. Writers. Multicoloured (background colour given).
1576	15d. Type **672** (green)	95	50
1577	15d. Abdelhamid Benhadouga (magenta)	95	50
1578	15d. Malek Bennabi (brown)	95	50
1579	15d. Kateb Yacine (blue)	95	50

It has been reported that No. 1577 (Abdelhamid Ben-hadouga) has been withdrawn by Algeria Posts due to a design error.

672a Fencing

2008. Olympic Games, Beijing. Multicoloured.
1580	15d. Type **672a**	95	50
1581	15d. Wrestling	95	50

673 Boy with
Balloons

2008. Children and New Technologies.
1582	**673**	15d. multicoloured	95	50

674 Self Portrait

2008. Art from National Museums. 10th Death Anniv of Baya Mahieddine (artist). Sheet 88×80 mm containing T **674** and similar horiz design. Multicoloured.
MS1583 15d. Type **674**; 38d. Femme et
oiseau en cage 3·25 3·25

675 Gare d'Alger

2008. Stations. Multicoloured.
1584	10d. Type **675**	60	35
1585	15d. Gare de Constantine	95	50
1586	20d. Gare d'Oran	1·25	65
1587	38d. Gare de Skikda	2·30	2·10

676 Ferhat Abbas

2008. Ferhat Abbas (political leader) Commemoration.
1588 **676** 15d. multicoloured 95 50

677 Script

2008. National Anthem.
1589 **677** 15d. multicoloured 95 50

678 Emblem

2008. Government Postage Stamp Printers' Association Conference.
1590 **678** 15d. multicoloured 95 50

679 Arms

2008. National Army.
1591 **679** 15d. multicoloured 95 50

680 Pont de Sidi M'Cid, Constantine

2008. Bridges. Sheet 110×88 mm containing T **680** and similar horiz designs. Multicoloured.
MS1592 10d. Type **680**; 15d. Pont de Sidi Rached; 20d. Pont d'El Knatara; 38d. Pont de la Medersa 5·00 5·00

681 Tebessa

2008. Towns. Multicoloured.
1593 10d. Type **681** 60 35
1594 15d. Saida 95 50
1595 20d. Miliana 1·25 65
1596 38d. Biskra 2·30 2·10

682 Globe and Flags

2008. 50th Anniv of Algeria–China Diplomatic Relations.
1597 **682** 15d. multicoloured 95 50

683 Emblem

2008. 60th Anniv of Anniv of Declaration of Human Rights.
1598 **683** 15d. multicoloured 95 50

684 Louis Braille and Alphabets

2009. Birth Bicentenary of Louis Braille (inventor of Braille writing for the blind).
1599 **684** 15d. multicoloured 95 50

685 Abderrahmene's Mausoleum, Algers

2009. Islamic Heritage. Mausoleums. Multicoloured.
1600 15d. Type **685** 95 50
1601 20d. Ibrahim El Atteuf, Mausoleum (horiz) 1·25 65

686 Figures

2009. National Day of Disabled Persons. Multicoloured.
1602 15d. Type **686** 95 50
1603 20d. Emblems 1·25 65

687 Polar Map and Hands enclosing Snowflake

2009. Preserve Polar Regions and Glaciers.
1604 **687** 38d. multicoloured 2·30 1·10

688 Emblem

2009. Presidential Elections.
1605 **688** 15d. multicoloured 95 50

689 Wooden Shoes

2009. Museum Exhibits. Multicoloured.
1606 15d. Type **689** 95 50
1607 20d. Silver brooch fragment 1·20 65
1608 30d. 19th-century waistcoat 1·90 1·00

690 Students and University Building

2009. Centenary of Universite d'Alger (university).
1609 **690** 15d. multicoloured 95 50

691 Silver Fibulae

2009. Jewellery.
1610 1d. dull green 10 10
1611 5d. pale brown-purple 30 20
1612 9d. bright reddish violet 50·00 30·00
1613 10d. olive-sepia 60 35
DESIGNS: 1d. Type **691**; 5d. Collar with amulets; 9d. Pectoral ornament; 10d. Circular brooch.

692 Digital Code, World Map and Children on Crossing

2009. Protection for Children using the Internet.
1614 **692** 15d. multicoloured 95 50

693 Windsurfing

2009. Mediterranean Games. Multicoloured.
1615 15d. Type **693** 95 50
1616 20d. Show jumping (horiz) 1·20 65

694 Madaure

2009. Roman Sites and Monuments. Multicoloured.
1617 15d. Type **694** 95 50
1618 20d. Khemissa 1·20 65
1619 30d. Theatre, Guelma 1·90 1·00

695 Symbols of Culture

2009. Pan African Cultural Festival, Algiers. Multicoloured.
1620 15d. Type **695** 95 50
1621 20d. Map of Africa as design 1·20 65

696 Symbols of Youth Development

2009. Algerian Youth. Multicoloured.
1622 15d. Type **696** 95 50
1623 20d. Heart, national flag and dove 1·20 65

697 '40'

2009. 40th Anniv of SONELGAZ.
1624 **697** 15d. multicoloured 95 50

698 Hand and Upturned Car

2009. Road Safety Campaign.
1625 **698** 15d. multicoloured 95 50

699 Bouharoun Fishing Port

2009. Fishing Ports. Multicoloured.
1626 15d. Type **699** 95 50
1627 20d. Beni Saf 1·20 65
1628 30d. Stora 1·90 1·00

700 Assistance

2009. Protection for the Elderly.
1629 **700** 15d. multicoloured 95 50

701 Symbols of Armed Forces

2009. National Army.
1630 **701** 15d. multicoloured 90 50

702 Women picking Olives

2009. Olive Cultivation. Multicoloured.
1631 15d. Type **702** 95 50
1632 20d. Pressing olives (vert) 1·20 65

703 La fée colombe

2009. Popular Tales. Multicoloured.
1633 15d. Type **703** 95 50
1634 15d. La rose rouge 95 50
1635 15d. Loundja la fille de l'ogre 95 50
1636 15d. Badra 95 50

704 Aquila chrysaetos (golden eagle)

2010. Raptors. Multicoloured.
1637 15d. Type **704** 95 50

| 1638 | 20d. *Falco biarmicus* (Lanner falcon) (vert) | 1·20 | 65 |
| 1639 | 30d. *Falco peregrinus* (peregrine falcon) (vert) | 1·90 | 1·00 |

705 Victim, Blast Fallout and Radiation

2010. Victims of Nuclear Testing.
| 1640 | **705** | 15d. multicoloured | 95 | 50 |

706 Fort de l'Empereur (Bordj Moulay Hassan), Alger

2010. Forts. Multicoloured.
| 1641 | | 15d. Type **706** | 95 | 50 |
| 1642 | | 20d. Fort Gouraya, Bejaia | 1·20 | 65 |

707 Family and Emblem

2010. Expo 2010, Shanghai. Multicoloured.
| 1643 | | 15d. Type **707** | 95 | 50 |
| 1644 | | 38d. China pavillion | 2·30 | 1·10 |

708 Refinery and Conference Emblem

2010. International Conference on Natural Liquid Gas. Multicoloured.
| 1645 | | 15d. Type **708** | 95 | 50 |
| 1646 | | 20d. Hill fort, coast line and conference emblem (horiz) | 1·20 | 65 |

709 Jules Rimet Trophy and Flags

2010. World Cup Football Championship, South Africa. Multicoloured.
1647		15d. Type **709**	95	50
1648		15d. Algerian player and home crowd	95	50
MS1649	108×88 mm. 15d. ×2 Desert fox as footballer; Player and colours	1·90	1·90

710 Martyrs

2010. 65th Anniv of May 8th Massacre.
| 1650 | **710** | 15d. multicoloured | 95 | 50 |

711 Singers

2010. L'Ahellil du Gourara
| 1651 | **711** | 15d. multicoloured | 95 | 50 |

712 Shrine

2010. Martyrs Shrine
| 1652 | **712** | (-) multicoloured | 95 | 50 |

713 Hands, Dove and Map

2010. Year of Peace and Security in Africa
| 1653 | **713** | 15d. multicoloured | 95 | 50 |

714 Caves of Gor Beni-Add

2010. Caves and Grottoes. Multicoloured.
| 1654 | | 15d. Type **714** | 95 | 50 |
| 1655 | | 15d. Ziama Mansouriah-Jijel Grotto | 95 | 50 |

715 Anniversary Emblem

2010. 50th Anniv of Organization of Petroleum Exporting Countries. Multicoloured.
| 1656 | | 15d. Type **715** | 95 | 50 |
| 1657 | | 38d. Emblem and oil tanker | 2·30 | 1·10 |

716 El Hanafi-Blida Mosque

2010. Mosques. Multicoloured.
1658		15d. Type **716**	95	50
1659		20d. Ali Dib-Skida	1·20	65
1660		30d. Nedroma Gran Mosque	1·90	1·00

717 Dates (inscr 'Degla Beida')

2010. Dates. Multicoloured.
1661		15d. Type **717**	95	50
1662		15d. Inscr 'Akerbuch'	95	50
1663		15d. Inscr 'Deglet Noir' (vert)	95	50
1664		15d. Inscr 'Ghars' (vert)	95	50

718 Ceramic Candlestick

2010. Traditional Crafts. Multicoloured.
1665		15d. Type **718**	95	50
1666		20d. Quanoun (musical instrument)	1·20	65
1667		30d. Tuareg leather chest (horiz)	2·30	1·10

719 Ears of Corn

2010. Cereal
| 1668 | **719** | 1d. light green | 20 | 15 |
| 1669 | **719** | 2d. blue | 35 | 25 |

720 Cork Oak Tree

2011. International Year of Forests. Multicoloured.
1670		15d. Type **720**	95	50
1671		20d. Carob	1·20	65
1672		30d. Soapnut	2·30	1·10
1673		38d. Argan	2·30	1·10

721 Minaret of Mansourah Ruins, Tlemcen

2011. Tlemcen, Capital of Islamic Culture, 2011. Multicoloured.
| 1674 | | 15d. Type **721** | 1·10 | 60 |
| 1675 | | 20d. Open work pendant | 1·40 | 75 |

722 Horned Viper (inscr 'VIPERE A CORNES')

2011. Reptiles. Multicoloured.
| 1676 | | 15d. Type **722** | 1·10 | 60 |
| 1677 | | 15d. Awl-headed snake (inscr 'COULEUVRE A DIADEME') | 1·10 | 60 |

723 Symbols of Census

2011. First Algerian Economic Census
| 1678 | **723** | 15d. multicoloured | 1·10 | 60 |

724 18th-century Couscous Dish

2011. Cultural Heritage. Culinary Utensils. Multicoloured.
| 1679 | | 15d. Type **724** | 1·10 | 60 |
| 1680 | | 30d. 18th-century copper-plated butter dish | 2·40 | 2·30 |

725 Computer Users and Satellite Dish

2011. Telecentres
| 1681 | **725** | 15d. multicoloured | 1·10 | 60 |

726 AIDS Ribbon and Building

2011. 30th Anniv of Discovery of AIDS
| 1682 | **726** | 15d. multicoloured | 1·10 | 60 |

727 Benyoucef Benkhadda

2011. Benyoucef Benkhadda (pharmacist, politician and Minister of Social Affairs and Chairman of the Provisional Government of the Algerian Republic (GPRA), August 1961-July 1962) Commemoration
| 1683 | **727** | 15d. multicoloured | 1·10 | 60 |

728 Fez and Monument of Martyrs (Maquam E' chahid) in Algiers

2011. International Comics Festival of Algiers (Festival International de la Bande Dessinée d'Alger, FIBDA). Multicoloured.
| 1684 | | 15d. Type **728** | 1·10 | 60 |
| 1685 | | 15d. M'Quidèch | 1·10 | 60 |

729 Oran Post Office

2011. Stamp Day. Post Offices. Multicoloured.
| 1686 | | 15d. Type **729** | 1·10 | 60 |
| 1687 | | 15d. Constantine | 1·10 | 60 |

730 Eiffel Tower and Protestors

2011. 50th Anniv of Day of Emmigration

1688	730	15d. multicoloured	1·10	60

731 Anniversary Emblem

2011. 50th Anniv of Algeria Press Service Agency

1689	731	15d. multicoloured	1·10	60

732 Museum Façade

2011. Central Army Museum

1690	732	15d. multicoloured	1·10	60

733 Locomotive in Station

2011. Algiers Metro. Multicoloured.

MS1691	15d.×2, Type 733; Locomotive facing right	2·25	1·25

734 Ouled-Djellal Sheep

2011. Algerian Sheep. Multicoloured.

1692	15d. Type 734	1·10	60
1693	15d. Hamra sheep (brown with horns)	1·10	60

735 Bougainvillea

2011. Flora

1694	15d. Type 735	1·10	60
1695	20d. Wisteria (inscr 'Glycine')	1·20	65
1696	30d. Mimosa (horiz)	2·30	1·10
1697	38d. Night flowering jasmine (inscr 'Galant de Nuit (Mesk Ellil)') (horiz)	2·30	1·10

736 Door

2012. Traditional Crafts. Woodwork. Multicoloured. Multicoloured.

1698	15d. Type 736	1·10	60
1699	20d. Ceiling	1·20	65
1700	30d. Window shutters	2·30	1·10

737 Theba pisana

2012. Snails. Multicoloured.

1701	15d. Type 737	1·10	60
1702	20d. Eobania vermiculata	1·20	65

738 Jubilant Demonstrators

2012. 50th Anniv of Ceasefire

1703	738	15d. multicoloured	1·10	60

739 Emblem

2012. Expo 2012, Yeosu

1704	739	15d. multicoloured	1·10	60

740 Larbi Djedri Tebessi

2012. Personalities. Multicoloured.

1705	15d. Type 740	1·10	60
1706	20d. Embarek El-Mili	1·20	65
1707	30d. Ahmed Hamani	2·30	1·10

741 Street Scene, Dellys

2012. Casbahs. Multicoloured.

1708	15d. Type 741	1·10	60
1709	20d. Bab El Bahr (Sarrazine Gate), Bejaia	1·20	65
1710	30d. Street Scene, Constantine	2·30	1·10

742 Judo

2012. Olympic Games, London

1711	15d. Type 742	1·10	60
1712	38d. Single sculls	2·30	1·10

743 Anniversary Emblem

2012. 50th Anniv of Independence and Day Youth Festival

MS1713	743	15d. multicoloured	1·20	1·00

744 Airforce

2012. Armed Forces. Multicoloured.

1714	15d. Type 744	1·10	60
1715	15d. Navy	1·10	60
1716	15d. Tank patrol (army)	1·10	60
1717	15d. Rocket array (aerial defence)	1·10	60
1718	15d. Motorcycle policeman (National police)	1·10	60
1719	15d. Horseman (Republican guard)	1·10	60
MS1720	132×112 mm. 15d.×3 As Nos. 1714, 1715 and 1719	3·25	3·00

POSTAGE DUE STAMPS

1926. As Postage Due stamps of France, but inscr "ALGERIE".

D34	D11	5c. blue	70	6·00
D35	D11	10c. brown	60	1·20
D36	D11	20c. olive	1·70	4·75
D37	D11	25c. red	1·40	7·25
D38	D11	30c. red	50	10
D39	D11	45c. green	2·50	7·75
D40	D11	50c. purple	25	35
D41	D11	60c. green	2·50	6·50
D42	D11	1f. red on yellow	55	95
D249	D11	1f.50 lilac	2·30	6·00
D250	D11	2f. blue	2·75	5·75
D43	D11	2f. mauve	1·10	3·00
D44	D11	3f. blue	85	1·80
D251	D11	5f. red	2·50	6·00
D252	D11	5f. green	4·00	8·25

1926. As Postage Due stamps of France, but inscr "ALGERIE".

D45	D19	1c. olive	25	4·75
D46	D19	10c. violet	1·20	2·75
D47	D19	30c. bistre	80	15
D48	D19	60c. red	1·30	15
D49	D19	1f. violet	9·00	1·90
D50	D19	2f. blue	13·00	2·75

1927. Nos. D36, D39 and D37 surch.

D92	D11	60 on 20c. olive	1·70	1·10
D93	D11	2f. on 45c. green	2·75	5·50
D94	D11	3f. on 25c. red	1·50	6·50

1927. Nos. D45/8 surch.

D95	D19	10c. on 30c. bistre	4·25	13·00
D96	D19	1f. on 1c. olive	2·75	4·50
D97	D19	1f. on 60c. red	14·00	75
D98	D19	2f. on 10c. violet	9·75	42·00

1942. As 1926 issue, but without "RF".

D181	D11	30c. red	2·20	8·25
D182	D11	2f. mauve	3·00	7·50

1944. No. 208 surch TAXE P. C. V. DOUANE 20Fr.

D230	38	20f. on 50f. red	3·00	5·25

1944. Surch T 0.50.

D231	4	50c. on 20c. green	1·50	5·25

1947. Postage Due Stamps of France optd ALGERIE.

D283	10c. brown (No. D985)	45	5·75
D284	30c. purple (No. D986)	45	5·75

D53

1947

D285	D53	20c. red	45	6·50
D286	D53	60c. blue	75	7·00
D287	D53	1f. brown	45	4·50
D288	D53	1f.50 olive	1·50	8·25
D289	D53	2f. red	35	3·75
D290	D53	3f. violet	60	4·25
D291	D53	5f. blue	60	1·70
D292	D53	6f. black	60	3·75
D293	D53	10f. purple	1·50	1·30
D294	D53	15f. myrtle	3·00	6·50
D295	D53	20f. green	1·50	1·30
D296	D53	30f. red	5·75	6·25
D297	D53	50f. black	6·50	10·00
D298	D53	100f. blue	28·00	28·00

1962. Postage Due stamps of France optd EA and with bar obliterating "REPUBLIQUE FRANCAISE".

D391	D457	5c. mauve	20·00	17·00
D392	D457	10c. red	20·00	17·00
D393	D457	20c. brown	20·00	17·00
D394	D457	50c. green	40·00	34·00
D395	D457	1f. green	60·00	55·00

The above also exist with larger overprint applied with handstamps.

D107 Scales of Justice

1963

D411	D107	5c. red and olive	10	10
D412	D107	10c. olive and red	10	10
D413	D107	20c. blue and black	50	30
D414	D107	50c. brown and green	1·10	75
D415	D107	1f. violet and orange	2·20	1·80

1968. No. D415 surch.

D508	60c. on 1f. violet and orange	80	60

D200 Ears of Corn

1972

D603	D200	10c. brown	10	10
D604	D200	20c. brown	10	10
D605	D200	40c. orange	25	10
D606	D200	50c. blue	30	10
D607	D200	80c. brown	65	30
D608	D200	1d. green	85	50
D609	D200	2d. blue	1·60	95
D610	D200	3d. violet	50	25
D611	D200	4d. purple	55	40

D644 Post Office

2006. Postage Due.

D1530	D644	5d. blue	15	10
D1531	D644	10d. green	20	10

Pt. 7

ALLENSTEIN

A district of E. Prussia retained by Germany as the result of a plebiscite in 1920. Stamps issued during the plebiscite period.

100 pfennig = 1 mark.

1920. Stamps of Germany inscr "DEUTSCHES REICH" optd PLEBISCITE OLSZTYN ALLENSTEIN.

1	17	5pf. green	60	1·40
2	17	10pf. red	60	1·40
3	24	15pf. violet	60	1·40
4	24	15pf. purple	8·25	14·00
5	17	20pf. blue	60	1·90
6	17	30pf. black & orge on buff	60	1·90
7	17	40pf. black and red	60	1·40
8	17	50pf. black & pur on buff	60	1·40
9	17	75pf. black and green	60	1·40
10	18	1m. red	2·40	6·00
11	18	1m.25 green	2·40	6·00
12	18	1m.50 brown	1·40	4·75
13b	20	2m.50 red	3·50	14·00
14	21	3m. black	3·50	6·00

1920. Stamps of Germany inscr "DEUTSCHES REICH" optd TRAITE DE VERSAILLES etc. in oval.

15	17	5pf. green	60	1·40
16	17	10pf. red	60	1·40
17	24	15pf. violet	60	1·40
18	24	15pf. purple	29·00	60·00
19	17	20pf. blue	95	2·40
20	17	30pf. black & orge on buff	60	1·40
21	17	40pf. black and red	60	1·40
22	17	50pf. black & pur on buff	60	1·40
23	17	75pf. black and green	95	2·40
24	18	1m. red	2·40	4·25
25	18	1m.25 green	2·40	4·25
26	18	1m.50 brown	1·70	4·25
27	20	2m.50 red	4·25	10·50
28	21	3m. black	2·50	4·25

Pt. 6

ALSACE AND LORRAINE

Stamps used in parts of France occupied by the German army in the war of 1870 -71, and afterwards temporarily in the annexed provinces of Alsace and Lorraine

100 pfennig = 1 mark

1

1870

1	1	1c. green	80·00	£140
3	1	2c. brown	£100	£200
5	1	4c. grey	£100	£100
8	1	5c. green	65·00	14·00
10	1	10c. brown	90·00	20·00
14	1	20c. blue	90·00	16·00
16	1	25c. brown	£140	£110

For 1940 issues see separate lists for Alsace and Lorraine under German Occupations.

Pt. 1

ALWAR

A state of Rajputana, N. India. Now uses Indian stamps.

12 pies = 1 anna; 16 annas = 1 rupee

1 Native Dagger

1877. Roul or perf.

1b	¼a. blue	6·00	1·10
2c	1a. brown	3·25	1·50
5	¼a. green	8·00	2·50

Pt. 6, Pt. 9

ANDORRA (FRENCH)

An independent state in the Pyrenees under the joint suzerainty of France and Spain.

French Post Office
1931. 100 centimes = 1 franc.
2002. 100 cents = 1 euro.

Spanish Post Office
1928. 100 centimos = 1 peseta.
2002. 100 cents = 1 euro.

FRENCH POST OFFICES

1931. Stamps of France optd **ANDORRE.**

F1	11	½c. on 1c. grey	1·10	6·50
F2	11	1c. grey	1·20	1·70
F3	11	2c. red	1·60	8·00
F4	11	3c. orange	2·10	4·25
F5	11	5c. green	3·25	8·25
F6	11	10c. lilac	5·25	10·00
F7	18	15c. brown	9·00	9·75
F8	18	20c. mauve	14·50	15·00
F9	18	25c. brown	12·50	17·00
F10	18	30c. green	12·50	15·00
F11	18	40c. blue	13·50	23·00
F12	18	45c. green	26·00	31·00
F13	15	50c. red	18·00	20·00
F14	15	65c. green	37·00	41·00
F15	15	75c. mauve	42·00	46·00
F16	15	90c. green	55·00	70·00
F17	15	1f. blue	60·00	70·00
F18	18	1f.50 blue	65·00	80·00
F19	13	2f. red and green	60·00	90·00
F20	13	3f. mauve and red	£110	£150
F21	13	5f. blue and buff	£150	£250
F22	13	10f. green and red	£325	£450
F23	13	20f. mauve and green	£425	£500

F3 Our Lady's Chapel, Meritxell

F5 St. Michael's Church, Engolasters

1932

F24	F3	1c. slate	75	2·75
F25	F3	2c. violet	1·10	2·30
F26	F3	3c. brown	1·20	2·50

F27	F3	5c. green	95	2·75
F28	A	10c. lilac	1·80	3·25
F29	A	15c. red	2·75	3·50
F30	A	20c. mauve	13·50	17·00
F31	F5	25c. brown	5·75	7·50
F32	A	25c. brown	13·50	34·00
F33	A	30c. green	3·75	4·50
F34	A	40c. blue	10·50	9·25
F35	A	40c. brown	1·60	4·00
F36	A	45c. red	15·00	29·00
F37	A	45c. green	7·50	22·00
F38	F5	50c. mauve	16·00	17·00
F39	A	50c. violet	7·50	20·00
F40	A	50c. green	2·10	10·50
F41	A	55c. violet	32·00	70·00
F42	A	60c. brown	2·10	7·50
F43	F5	65c. green	70·00	75·00
F44	A	65c. blue	19·00	33·00
F45	A	70c. red	2·40	5·75
F46	F5	75c. green	11·50	12·50
F47	A	75c. blue	5·25	17·00
F48	A	80c. green	28·00	70·00
F49	B	80c. green	1·70	6·25
F50	B	90c. red	9·50	9·25
F51	B	90c. green	7·50	15·00
F52	B	1f. green	34·00	23·00
F53	B	1f. red	32·00	34·00
F54	B	1f. blue	1·40	3·50
F55	B	1f. 20 violet	1·30	6·50
F56	F3	1f. 25 mauve	65·00	80·00
F57	F3	1f.25 red	8·00	20·00
F58	B	1f.30 brown	1·70	6·50
F59	C	1f.50 blue	26·00	37·00
F60	B	1f.50 red	1·10	6·50
F61	B	1f.75 violet	£110	£140
F62	B	1f.75 blue	60·00	75·00
F63	B	2f. mauve	10·50	23·00
F64	F3	2f. red	2·10	8·50
F65	F3	2f. green	1·20	8·50
F66	F3	2f.15 violet	60·00	90·00
F67	F3	2f.25 blue	10·50	30·00
F68	F3	2f.40 red	1·40	6·50
F69	F3	2f.50 black	12·50	36·00
F70	F3	2f.50 blue	2·75	10·50
F71	B	3f. brown	25·00	41·00
F72	F3	3f. brown	2·20	7·00
F73	F3	4f. blue	1·60	6·25
F74	F3	4f.50 violet	2·10	8·25
F75	C	5f. brown	1·80	7·00
F76	C	10f. violet	2·40	7·00
F78	C	15f. blue	1·60	4·00
F79	C	20f. red	2·10	3·75
F81	A	50f. green	3·00	9·25

DESIGNS—HORIZ: A, St. Anthony's Bridge; C, Andorra la Vella. VERT: B, Valley of Sant Julia.

1935. No. F38 surch **20c.**

F82	F5	20c. on 50c. purple	16·00	29·00

F9

1936

F83	F9	1c. black	55	3·25
F84	F9	2c. blue	55	3·25
F85	F9	3c. brown	55	3·25
F86	F9	5c. red	40	3·25
F87	F9	10c. blue	40	3·25
F88	F9	15c. mauve	3·25	5·25
F89	F9	20c. green	40	3·25
F90	F9	30c. red	75	7·00
F91	F9	30c. black	1·50	6·50
F92	F9	35c. green	60·00	90·00
F93	F9	40c. brown	1·10	6·25
F94	F9	50c. green	1·20	6·50
F95	F9	60c. blue	1·60	6·50
F96	F9	70c. violet	1·60	6·50

F13 Andorra la Vella

F10

F14 Councillor Jaume Bonell

1944

F97	F10	10c. violet	20	4·00
F98	F10	30c. red	20	4·00

F99	F10	40c. blue	40	4·00
F100	F10	50c. red	20	4·50
F101	F10	60c. black	40	4·00
F102	F10	70c. mauve	30	5·75
F103	F10	80c. green	20	5·75
F104	F10	1f. blue	1·10	2·40
F105	D	1f. purple	20	6·25
F106	D	1f.20 blue	20	6·25
F107	D	1f.50 red	20	6·25
F108	D	2f. green	20	4·00
F109	E	2f.40 violet	20	4·00
F110	E	2f.50 red	4·25	7·00
F111	E	3f. brown	60	2·75
F112	D	3f. red	4·25	5·75
F113	E	4f. blue	55	6·25
F114	E	4f. green	1·10	7·50
F115	E	4f. brown	2·30	10·50
F116	E	4f.50 brown	60	5·75
F117	F 13	4f.50 blue	5·25	20·00
F118	F 13	5f. blue	55	6·25
F119	F 13	5f. green	1·40	6·50
F120	E	5f. green	3·25	11·50
F121	E	5f. violet	4·25	8·00
F122	F 13	6f. red	55	3·75
F123	F 13	6f. purple	55	5·75
F124	E	6f. green	3·25	7·50
F125	F 13	8f. blue	1·60	8·00
F126	E	8f. brown	1·10	3·50
F127	F 13	10f. green	40	5·75
F128	F 13	10f. blue	1·60	1·80
F129	F 13	12f. red	1·40	7·50
F130	F 13	12f. green	1·60	5·75
F131	F 14	15f. purple	65	6·50
F132	F 13	15f. red	85	3·50
F133	F 13	15f. brown	7·50	4·50
F134	F 14	18f. blue	3·25	12·00
F135	F 13	18f. red	12·50	26·00
F136	F 14	20f. blue	1·10	6·50
F137	F 14	20f. violet	3·25	10·00
F138	F 14	25f. red	3·75	10·50
F139	F 14	25f. blue	2·10	8·50
F140	F 14	30f. blue	21·00	29·00
F141	F 14	40f. green	3·25	9·25
F142	F 14	50f. brown	1·80	4·25

DESIGNS—HORIZ: D, Church of St. John of Caselles; E, House of the Valleys.

F15 Chamois and Pyrenees

1950. Air.

F143	F15	100f. blue	£110	£110

F16 Les Escaldes

1955

F144	F16	1f. blue (postage)	20	2·75
F145	F16	2f. green	55	2·10
F146	F16	3f. red	65	2·10
F147	F16	5f. brown	65	2·10
F148	-	6f. green	2·20	2·75
F149	-	8f. red	2·40	3·25
F150	-	10f. violet	4·25	2·75
F151	-	12f. blue	2·30	2·10
F152	-	15f. red	3·00	2·30
F153	-	18f. blue	2·75	3·75
F154	-	20f. violet	3·25	2·30
F155	-	25f. brown	3·50	4·00
F156	-	30f. blue	26·00	34·00
F157	-	35f. blue	13·50	14·50
F158	-	40f. green	35·00	55·00
F159	-	50f. red	4·25	4·50
F160	-	65f. violet	9·50	29·00
F161	-	70f. brown	9·25	22·00
F162	-	75f. blue	45·00	90·00
F163	-	100f. green (air)	10·50	15·00
F164	-	200f. red	21·00	23·00
F165	-	500f. blue	85·00	90·00

DESIGNS—VERT: 15f. to 25f. Gothic cross, Andorra la Vella; 100f. to 500f. East Valira River. HORIZ: 6f. to 12f. Santa Coloma Church; 30f. to 75f. Les Bons village.

F21

F22 Gothic Cross, Meritxell

1961

F166	F21	1c. grey, blue and slate (postage)	65	1·60
F167	F21	2c. lt orge, blk & orge	65	1·60
F168	F21	5c. lt grn, blk & grn	40	1·60
F169	F21	10c. pink, blk & red	45	45
F170a	F21	12c. yell, pur & grn	2·20	4·50
F171	F21	15c. lt bl, blk & bl	75	1·60
F172	F21	18c. pink, blk & mve	1·40	3·25
F173	F21	20c. lt yell, brn & yell	80	55
F174	F22	25c. blue, vio & grn	1·10	1·10
F175	F22	30c. pur, red & grn	1·10	80
F175a	F22	40c. green and brown	1·30	2·00
F176	F22	45c. blue, ind & grn	21·00	34·00
F176a	F22	45c. brown, bl & vio	1·30	2·75
F177	F22	50c. multicoloured	2·75	2·75
F177a	F22	60c. brown & chestnut	1·60	2·10
F178	F22	65c. olive, bl & brn	23·00	55·00
F179	F22	85c. multicoloured	23·00	40·00
F179a	F22	90c. green, bl & brn	1·60	3·50
F180	F22	1f. blue, brn & turq	2·75	2·75
F181	-	2f. green, red and purple (air)	2·20	2·30
F182	-	3f. purple, bl & grn	2·40	2·20
F183	-	5f. orange, pur & red	4·00	4·00
F184	-	10f. green and blue	6·00	5·50

DESIGNS—As Type F **22**: 60c. to 1f. Engolasters Lake; 2f. to 10f. Incles Valley.

F23 "Telstar" Satellite and part of Globe

1962. First Trans-Atlantic TV Satellite Link.

F185	F23	50c. violet and blue	1·60	2·75

F24 "La Sardane" (dance)

1963. Andorran History (1st issue).

F186	F24	20c. purple, mve & grn	3·75	6·50
F187	-	50c. red and green	6·75	12·50
F188	-	1f. green, blue & brn	9·50	21·00

DESIGNS—LARGER (48½×27 mm): 50c. Charlemagne crossing Andorra. (48×27 mm): 1f. Foundation of Andorra by Louis le Debonnaire.
See also Nos. F190/1.

F25 Santa Coloma Church and Grand Palais, Paris

1964. "PHILATEC 1964" International Stamp Exhibition, Paris.

F189	F25	25c. green, pur & brn	1·60	3·25

1964. Andorran History (2nd issue). As Nos. F187/8, inscribed "1964".

F190	-	60c. green, chestnut and brown	11·50	32·00
F191	-	1f. blue, sepia and brown	16·00	32·00

DESIGNS (48½×27 mm): 60c. "Napoleon re-establishes the Andorran Statute, 1806"; 1f. "Confirmation of the Co-government, 1288".

F26 Virgin of Santa Coloma

1964. Red Cross Fund.

F192	F26	25c.+10c. red, green and blue	21·00	38·00

F27 "Syncom",
Morse Key and
Pleumeur-
Bodou centre

1965. Centenary of I.T.U.
F193 **F27** 60c. violet, blue and red 4·75 8·00

F28 Andorra
House, Paris

1965. Opening of Andorra House, Paris.
F194 **F28** 25c. brown, olive & bl 1·10 2·30

F29 Chair-lift

1966. Winter Sports.
F195 **F29** 25c. green, purple & bl 1·30 3·25
F196 - 40c. brown, blue & red 2·10 4·00
DESIGN—HORIZ: 40c. Ski-lift.

F30 Satellite "FR 1"

1966. Launching of Satellite "FR 1".
F197 **F30** 60c. blue, emer & grn 2·10 4·25

F31 Europa
"Ship"

1966. Europa.
F198 **F31** 60c. brown 3·50 6·25

F32 Cogwheels

1967. Europa.
F199 **F32** 30c. indigo and blue 4·25 5·75
F200 **F32** 60c. red and purple 5·50 10·50

F33 "Folk
Dancers"
(statue)

1967. Centenary (1966) of New Reform.
F201 **F33** 30c. green, olive & slate 1·50 3·50

F34 Telephone
and Dial

1967. Inaug of Automatic Telephone Service.
F202 **F34** 60c. black, violet & red 1·60 3·75

F35 Andorran Family

1967. Institution of Social Security.
F203 **F35** 2f.30 brown & purple 8·50 18·00

F36 "The Temptation"

1967. 16th-century Frescoes in House of the Valleys (1st
series).
F204 **F36** 25c. red and black 1·10 2·75
F205 - 30c. purple and violet 1·20 3·50
F206 - 60c. blue and indigo 1·60 4·50
FRESCOES: 30c. *The Kiss of Judas*; 60c. *The Descent from
the Cross*.
 See also Nos. F210/12.

F37 Downhill
Skiing

1968. Winter Olympic Games, Grenoble.
F207 **F37** 40c. purple, orge & red 1·40 3·75

F38 Europa "Key"

1968. Europa.
F208 **F38** 30c. blue and slate 5·25 8·50
F209 **F38** 60c. violet & brown 8·50 14·00

1968. 16th-century Frescoes in House of the Valleys (2nd
series). Designs as Type **F36**.
F210 25c. deep green and green 95 3·25
F211 30c. purple and brown 1·20 4·75
F212 60c. brown and red 2·10 6·50
FRESCOES: 25c. "The Beating of Christ"; 30c. "Christ
Helped by the Cyrenians"; 60c. "The Death of Christ".

F39 High Jumping

1968. Olympic Games, Mexico.
F213 **F39** 40c. brown and blue 2·10 3·75

F40 Colonnade

1969. Europa.
F214 **F40** 40c. grey, blue and red 9·50 11·50
F215 **F40** 70c. red, green and blue 13·00 22·00

F41 Canoeing

1969. World Kayak-Canoeing Championships, Bourg-St.
Maurice.
F216 **F41** 70c. dp blue, bl & grn 2·10 5·25

F41a "Diamond
Crystal" in Rain
Drop

1969. European Water Charter.
F217 **F41a** 70c. black, blue and
 ultramarine 5·25 9·75

F42 The Apocalypse

1969. Altar-screen, Church of St. John of Caselles (1st
series). "The Revelation of St. John".
F218 **F42** 30c. red, violet & brn 1·10 2·10
F219 - 40c. bistre, brn & grey 1·60 2·75
F220 - 70c. purple, lake & red 2·10 3·50
DESIGNS: 40c. Angel "clothed with cloud with face as the
sun, and feet as pillars of fire" (Rev. 10); 70c. Christ with
sword and stars, and seven candlesticks.
 See also Nos. F225/7, F233/5 and F240/2.

F43 Handball
Player

1970. Seventh World Handball Championships, France.
F221 **F43** 80c. blue, brn & dp bl 2·75 5·25

F44 "Flaming Sun"

1970. Europa.
F222 **F44** 40c. orange 9·50 8·00
F223 **F44** 80c. violet 12·00 13·00

F45 Putting the
Shot

1970. First European Junior Athletic Championships,
Paris.
F224 **F45** 80c. purple and blue 2·75 5·50

1970. Altar-screen, Church of St. John of Caselles (2nd
series). Designs as Type **F42**.
F225 30c. violet, brown and red 1·50 2·50
F226 40c. green and violet 1·60 2·75
F227 80c. red, blue and green 3·25 4·00
DESIGNS: 30c. Angel with keys and padlock; 40c. Angel
with pillar; 80c. St. John being boiled in cauldron of oil.

F46 Ice Skaters

1971. World Ice Skating Championships, Lyon.
F228 **F46** 80c. violet, pur & red 3·00 4·75

F47 Western
Capercaillie

1971. Nature Protection.
F229 **F47** 80c. multicoloured 4·75 6·25
F230 - 80c. brown, green & bl 4·75 6·25
DESIGN: No. F230, Brown bear.

F48 Europa Chain

1971. Europa.
F231 **F48** 50c. red 10·50 12·50
F232 **F48** 80c. green 16·00 20·00

1971. Altar-screen, Church of St. John of Caselles (3rd
series). As Type **F42**.
F233 30c. green, brown and myrtle 1·80 4·50
F234 50c. brown, orange and lake 2·40 5·25
F235 90c. blue, purple and brown 3·75 7·00
DESIGNS: 30c. St. John in temple at Ephesus; 50c. St.
John with cup of poison; 90c. St. John disputing with pa-
gan philosophers.

F49 "Communications"

1972. Europa.
F236 **F49** 50c. multicoloured 10·00 10·50
F237 **F49** 90c. multicoloured 15·00 18·00

F50 Golden Eagle

1972. Nature Protection.
F238 **F50** 60c. olive, green & pur 4·75 6·25

F51 Rifle-shooting

1972. Olympic Games, Munich.
F239 **F51** 1f. purple 3·25 4·50

1972. Altar-screen, Church of St. John of Caselles (4th
series). As Type **F42**.
F240 30c. purple, grey and green 1·40 2·30
F241 50c. grey and blue 1·70 2·75
F242 90c. green and blue 2·75 4·00
DESIGNS: 30c. St. John in discussion with bishop; 50c. St.
John healing a cripple; 90c. Angel with spear.

F52 General De
Gaulle

1972. Fifth Anniv of Gen. De Gaulle's Visit to Andorra.
F243 **F52** 50c. blue 3·50 5·75
F244 - 90c. red 4·75 7·75
DESIGN: 90c. Gen. De Gaulle in Andorra la Vella, 1967.
 See also Nos. F434/5.

F53 Europa "Posthorn"

1973. Europa.
F245	**F53**	50c. multicoloured	10·00	10·50
F246	**F53**	90c. multicoloured	10·50	21·00

F54 *Virgin of Canolich*
(wood carving)

1973. Andorran Art.
F247	**F54**	1f. lilac, blue and drab	3·00	4·25

F55 Lily

1973. Pyrenean Flowers (1st series). Multicoloured.
F248	30c. Type **F55**	1·10	3·25
F249	50c. Columbine	2·10	4·50
F250	90c. Wild pinks	1·60	3·50
See also Nos. F253/5 and F264/6.

F56 Blue Tit
("Mesange
Bleue")

1973. Nature Protection. Birds. Multicoloured.
F251	**F56**	90c. Type **F56**	2·75	5·25
F252		1f. Lesser spotted woodpecker ("Pic Epeichette")	3·00	5·75
See also Nos. F259/60.

1974. Pyrenean Wild Flowers (2nd series). As Type **F 55**. Multicoloured.
F253	45c. Iris	55	4·00
F254	65c. Tobacco Plant	65	4·50
F255	90c. Narcissus	1·40	4·75

F57 The Virgin of
Pal

1974. Europa. Church Sculptures. Multicoloured.
F256	50c. Type **F 57**	17·00	11·50
F257	90c. "The Virgin of Santa Coloma"	23·00	18·00

F58 Arms of
Andorra

1974. Meeting of Co-Princes, Cahors.
F258	**F58**	1f. blue, violet & orge	1·40	5·75

1974. Nature Protection. Birds. As Type **F56**. Multicoloured.
F259	60c. Citril finch ("Venturon Montagnard")	4·25	7·00
F260	80c. Northern bullfinch ("Boureuil")	4·25	7·00

F59 Letters crossing
Globe

1974. Centenary of U.P.U.
F261	**F59**	1f.20 red, grey & brn	2·30	4·25

F60 Calvary

1975. Europa. Paintings from La Cortinada Church. Multicoloured.
F262	80c. Type **F60**	8·50	15·00
F263	1f.20 Coronation of St. Martin (horiz)	10·50	23·00

1975. Pyrenean Flowers (3rd series). As Type **F55**.
F264	60c. multicoloured	65	3·25
F265	80c. multicoloured	1·80	4·00
F266	1f.20 yellow, red and green	1·30	3·50
DESIGNS: 60c. Gentian; 80c. Anemone; 1f.20, Colchicum.

F61 "Arphila" Motif

1975. "Arphila 75" International Stamp Exhibition, Paris.
F267	**F61**	2f. red, green and blue	2·00	4·50

F62 Pres.
Pompidou
(Co-prince of
Andorra)

1976. President Pompidou of France Commem.
F268	**F62**	80c. black and violet	1·10	3·25

F63 "La Pubilla"
and Emblem

1976. International Women's Year.
F269	**F63**	1f.20 black, pur & bl	2·10	3·75

F64 Skier

1976. Winter Olympic Games, Innsbruck.
F270	**F64**	1f.20 black, green & bl	1·60	3·50

F65 Telephone
and Satellite

1976. Telephone Centenary.
F271	**F65**	1f. green, black and red	1·60	3·75

F66 Catalan Forge

1976. Europa.
F272	**F66**	80c. brown, blue & grn	4·25	4·50
F273	-	1f.20 red, green & blk	5·25	5·75
DESIGN: 1f.20, Andorran folk-weaving.

F67 Thomas
Jefferson

1976. Bicentenary of American Revolution.
F274	**F67**	1f.20 dp grn, brn & grn	1·40	3·50

F68 Ball-trap
(clay pigeon)
Shooting

1976. Olympic Games, Montreal.
F275	**F68**	2f. brown, violet & grn	2·10	4·00

F69 New Chapel

1976. New Chapel of Our Lady, Meritxell.
F276	**F69**	1f. green, purple & brn	1·20	3·25

F70 Apollo

1976. Nature Protection. Butterflies. Multicoloured.
F277	80c. Type **F70**	3·25	6·50
F278	1f.40 Camberwell beauty	4·00	7·00

F71 Stoat

1977. Nature Protection.
F279	**F71**	1f. grey, black & blue	2·40	3·75

F72 Church of
St. John of
Caselles

1977. Europa.
F280	**F72**	1f. purple, green & bl	6·75	5·75
F281	-	1f.40 indigo, grn & bl	11·00	7·00
DESIGN: 1f.40, St. Vicens Chateau.

F73 Book and
Flowers

1977. Frist Anniv of Institute of Andorran Studies.
F282	**F73**	80c. brown, green & bl	1·20	2·75

F74 St. Roma

1977. Reredos, St. Roma's Chapel, Les Bons.
F283	**F74**	2f. multicoloured	2·75	3·50

F75 General Council
Assembly Hall

1977. Andorran Institutions.
F284	**F75**	1f.10 red, blue & brn	2·75	4·00
F285	-	2f. brown and red	2·75	4·00
DESIGN—VERT. 2f. Don Guillem d'Areny Plandolit.

F76 Eurasian
Red Squirrel

1978. Nature Protection.
F286	**F76**	1f. brown, grn & olive	1·30	2·75

F77 Escalls Bridge

1978. 700th Anniv of Parity Treaties (1st issue).
F287	**F77**	80c. green, brown & bl	85	2·75
See also No. F292.

F78 Church at Pal

1978. Europa.
F288	**F78**	1f. brown, green & red	7·00	5·75
F289	-	1f.40 brown, bl & red	11·50	7·50
DESIGN: 1f.40, Charlemagne's House.

F79 *Virgin of Sispony*

1978. Andorran Art.
F290	**F79**	2f. multicoloured	2·10	3·50

F80 Tribunal Meeting

1978. Tribunal of Visura.
F291 **F80** 1f.20 multicoloured 1·80 2·75

F81 Treaty Text

1978. 700th Anniv of Parity Treaties (2nd issue).
F292 **F81** 1f.50 brown, grn & red 1·30 2·75

F82 Chamois

1978. Nature Protection.
F293 **F82** 1f. brown, lt brn & bl 85 2·40

F83 Rock
Ptarmigans
("Perdiu
Blanca")

1979. Nature Protection.
F294 **F83** 1f.20 multicoloured 1·70 3·25

F84 Early 20th
Century Postman
and Church of
St. John of
Caselles

1979. Europa.
F295 **F84** 1f.20 black, brn & grn 3·25 4·75
F296 - 1f.70 brown, grn & mve 5·25 5·75
DESIGN: 1f.70, Old French Post Office, Andorra.

F85 Wall painting, Church
of St. Cerni, Nagol

1979. Pre-Romanesque Art.
F297 **F85** 2f. green, pink and
 brown 1·60 2·75
See also No. F309.

F86 Boy with
Sheep

1979. International Year of the Child.
F298 **F86** 1f.70 multicoloured 1·30 2·75

F87 Co-princes
Monument
(Luigiteruggi)

1979. Co-princes Monument.
F299 **F87** 2f. dp green, grn & red 1·60 3·25

F88 Judo

1979. World Judo Championships, Paris.
F300 **F88** 1f.30 black, dp bl & bl 1·10 2·75

F89 Cal Pal, La
Cortinada

1980
F301 **F89** 1f.10 brown, bl & grn 85 2·40

F90 Cross-country Skiing

1980. Winter Olympics, Lake Placid.
F302 **F90** 1f.80 ultram, bl & red 1·50 3·25

F91
Charlemagne

1980. Europa.
F303 **F91** 1f.30 brn, chest & red 2·10 3·50
F304 - 1f.80 green and brown 2·75 4·00
DESIGN: 1f.80, Napoleon I.

F93 Dog's-tooth
Violet

1980. Nature Protection. Multicoloured.
F305 1f.30 Pyrenean lily 85 2·40
F306 1f.10 Type F 93 95 2·50

F94 Cyclists

1980. World Cycling Championships.
F307 **F94** 1f.20 violet, mve & brn 1·20 2·50

F95 House of the Valleys

1980. 400th Anniv of Restoration of House of the Valleys
(meeting place of Andorran General Council).
F308 **F95** 1f.40 brown, vio & grn 1·20 2·50

1980. Pre-Romanesque Art. As Type **F85**. Multicoloured.
F309 2f. Angel (wall painting, Church
 of St. Cerni, Nagol) (horiz) 1·70 3·25

F97 Shepherds' Huts,
Mereig

1981. Architecture.
F310 **F97** 1f.40 brown and blue 1·10 1·70

F98 Bear Dance (Emcamp
Carnival)

1981. Europa.
F311 **F98** 1f.40 black, green & bl 1·60 2·30
F312 - 2f. black, blue and red 2·10 3·50
DESIGN: 2f. El Contrapas (dance).

F99 Bonelli's
Warbler

1981. Nature Protection. Birds. Multicoloured.
F313 1f.20 Type **F99** 1·10 2·75
F314 1f.40 Wallcreeper 1·30 2·75

F100 Fencing

1981. World Fencing Championships, Clermont-Ferrand.
F315 **F100** 2f. blue and black 1·30 2·75

F101 Chasuble of St.
Martin (miniature)

1981. Art.
F316 **F101** 3f. multicoloured 1·80 2·75

F102 Fountain,
Sant Julia de
Loria

1981. International Decade of Drinking Water.
F317 **F102** 1f.60 blue and brown 1·10 2·50

F103 Symbolic
Disabled

1981. International Year of Disabled Persons.
F318 **F103** 2f.30 blue, red & grn 1·50 2·75

F104 Scroll and Badge
(creation of Andorran
Executive Council, 1981)

1982. Europa.
F319 **F104** 1f.60 blue, brn & orge 2·10 2·75
F320 - 2f.30 blue, blk & orge 2·75 3·25
DESIGN: 2f.30, Hat and cloak (creation of Land Council,
1419).

F105 Footballer
running to right

1982. World Cup Football Championship, Spain.
F321 **F105** 1f.60 brown and red 1·30 2·40
F322 - 2f.60 brown and red 1·90 2·75
DESIGN: 2f.60, Footballer running to left.

F106 1933 1f.25 Stamp

1982. First Official Exhibition of Andorran Postage
Stamps.
MSF323 **F106** 5f. black and red 2·75 4·00

F107 Wall Painting, La Cortinada
Church

1982. Romanesque Art.
F324 **F107** 3f. multicoloured 1·60 4·75

F108 Wild Cat

1982. Nature Protection.
F325 **F108** 1f.80 blk, grn & grey 1·60 3·75
F326 - 2f.60 brown & green 1·40 4·00
DESIGN: 2f.60, Scots Pine.

F109 Dr. Robert
Koch

1982. Centenary of Discovery of Tubercle Bacillus.
F327 **F109** 2f.10 lilac 1·40 2·75

F110 St.
Thomas
Aquinas

1982. St. Thomas Aquinas Commemoration.
F328 **F110** 2f. deep brown, brown
 and grey 1·30 2·75

F111 Montgolfier and
Charles Balloon over
Tuileries, Paris

1983. Bicentenary of Manned Flight.
F329 **F111** 2f. green, red and brown 1·30 2·75

F112 Silver Birch

1983. Nature Protection.
F330 **F112** 1f. red, brown and green 1·50 3·75
F331 – 1f.50 green, bl & brn 1·60 4·00
DESIGN: 1f.50, Brown trout.

F113 Mountain Cheesery

1983. Europa.
F332 **F113** 1f. purple and violet 2·40 3·75
F333 – 2f.60 red, mve & pur 2·75 4·00
DESIGN: 2f.60, Catalan forge.

F114 Royal Edict of Louis XIII

1983. 30th Anniv of Customs Co-operation Council.
F334 **F114** 3f. black and slate 2·00 5·50

F115 Early Coat of Arms

1983. Inscr "POSTES".
F335 **F115** 5c. green and red 1·10 2·30
F336 **F115** 10c. dp green & green 1·10 2·30
F337 **F115** 20c. violet and mauve 1·10 2·30
F338 **F115** 30c. purple and violet 1·10 2·30
F339 **F115** 40c. blue & ultram 1·10 2·30
F340 **F115** 50c. black and red 1·10 2·30
F341 **F115** 1f. lake and red 1·10 2·30
F342 **F115** 1f.90 green 3·75 4·75
F343 **F115** 2f. red and brown 1·50 1·60
F344 **F115** 2f.10 green 1·50 2·75
F345 **F115** 2f.20 red 1·10 3·75
F346 **F115** 2f.30 red 1·40 3·75
F347 **F115** 3f. green and mauve 1·60 4·00
F348 **F115** 4f. orange and brown 3·25 6·25
F349 **F115** 5f. brown and red 2·10 5·75
F350 **F115** 10f. red and brown 4·25 6·25
F351 **F115** 15f. green & dp green 6·25 9·00
F352 **F115** 20f. blue and brown 8·00 9·25
For design as Type **F115** but inscribed "LA POSTE" see Nos. F446/9.

F116 Wall Painting, La Cortinada Church

1983. Romanesque Art.
F354 **F116** 4f. multicoloured 2·10 4·00

F117 Plandolit House

1983
F355 **F117** 1f.60 brown & green 1·10 1·70

F118 Snowflakes and Olympic Torch

1984. Winter Olympic Games, Sarajevo.
F356 **F118** 2f.80 red, blue & grn 1·70 2·75

F119 Pyrenees and Council of Europe Emblem

1984. Work Community of Pyrenees Region.
F357 **F119** 3f. blue and brown 1·80 3·25

F120 Bridge

1984. Europa.
F358 **F120** 2f. green 3·75 4·00
F359 **F120** 2f.80 red 4·75 5·25

F121 Sweet Chestnut

1984. Nature Protection.
F360 **F121** 1f.70 grn, brn & pur 1·30 3·75
F361 – 2f.10 green & brown 1·60 4·00
DESIGN: 2f.10, Walnut.

F122 Centre Members

1984. Pyrenean Cultures Centre, Andorra.
F362 **F122** 3f. blue, orange & red 1·80 3·50

F123 St. George (detail of fresco, Church of St. Cerni, Nagol)

1984. Pre-Romanesque Art.
F363 **F123** 5f. multicoloured 2·75 4·00

F124 Sant Julia Valley

1985
F364 **F124** 2f. green, olive & brn 1·50 2·75

F125 Title Page of "Le Val d'Andorre" (comic opera)

1985. Europa.
F365 **F125** 2f.10 green 3·75 4·00
F366 – 3f. brown & dp brown 4·75 5·25
DESIGN: 3f. Musical instruments within frame.

F126 Teenagers holding up ball

1985. International Youth Year.
F367 **F126** 3f. red and brown 1·60 3·25

F127 Mallard

1985. Nature Protection. Multicoloured.
F368 1f.80 Type **F127** 1·40 3·50
F369 2f.20 Eurasian goldfinch 1·70 4·00

F128 St. Cerni and Angel (fresco, Church of St. Cerni, Nagol)

1985. Pre-Romanesque Art.
F370 **F128** 5f. multicoloured 2·30 4·00

F130 1979 Europa Stamp

1986. Inauguration of Postal Museum.
F381 **F130** 2f.20 brown & green 1·40 3·25

F131 Ansalonga

1986. Europa.
F382 **F131** 2f.20 black and blue 4·25 4·50
F383 – 3f.20 black and green 5·25 5·50
DESIGN: 3f.20, Pyrenean chamois.

F132 Players

1986. World Cup Football Championship, Mexico.
F384 **F132** 3f. grn, blk & dp grn 2·10 3·50

F133 Angonella Lakes

1986
F385 **F133** 2f.20 multicoloured 1·40 2·75

F134 Title Page of *Manual Digest*, 1748

1986. *Manual Digest.*
F386 **F134** 5f. black, grn & brn 2·75 4·00

F135 Dove with Twig

1986. International Peace Year.
F387 **F135** 1f.90 blue and indigo 1·30 2·75

F136 St. Vincent's Chapel, Enclar

1986
F388 **F136** 1f.90 brn, blk & grn 1·30 2·75

F137 Arms

1987. Visit of French Co-prince (French president).
F389 **F137** 2f.20 multicoloured 2·00 4·00

F138 Meritxell Chapel

1987. Europa.
F390 **F138** 2f.20 purple and red 5·25 4·50
F391 – 3f.40 violet and blue 7·50 6·25
DESIGN: 3f.40, Ordino.

F139 Ransol

1987
F392 **F139** 1f.90 multicoloured 1·50 3·50

F140 Horse

1987. Nature Protection. Multicoloured.
F393 1f.90 Type **F140** 1·70 4·25
F394 2f.20 Isabel (moth) 2·00 4·50

F141 Arualsu (fresco, La Cortinada Church)

1987. Romanesque Art.
F395 **F141** 5f. multicoloured — 3·00 4·25

F142 Walker with Map by Signpost

1987. Walking.
F396 **F142** 2f. pur, grn & dp grn — 1·40 2·75

F143 Key

1987. La Cortinada Church Key.
F397 **F143** 3f. multicoloured — 1·70 3·50

F144 Arms

1988
F398 **F144** 2f.20 red — 1·40 2·75
F399 **F144** 2f.30 red — 1·60 4·50
F400 **F144** 2f.50 red — 1·70 4·50
F401 **F144** 2f.80 red — 1·80 4·25
Nos. F400/1 are inscribed "LA POSTE".

F145 Bronze Boot and Mountains

1988. Archaeology.
F407 **F145** 3f. multicoloured — 1·70 3·75

F146 Players

1988. Rugby.
F408 **F146** 2f.20 blk, yell & grn — 1·40 4·50

F147 Enclar Aerial

1988. Europa. Transport and Communications. Each green, brown and blue.
F409 2f.20 Type **F147** — 3·75 4·00
F410 3f.60 Hand pointing to map on screen (tourist information) — 4·75 5·75

F148 Les Escaldes Hot Spring

1988
F411 **F148** 2f.20 blue, brn & grn — 1·40 2·75

F149 Ansalonga Pass

1988
F412 **F149** 2f. blue, green & olive — 1·20 2·75

F150 Pyrenean Shepherd Dog

1988. Nature Protection. Multicoloured.
F413 2f. Type **F150** — 1·90 4·50
F414 2f.20 Hare — 2·00 4·50

F151 Fresco, Andorra La Vella Church

1988. Romanesque Art.
F415 **F151** 5f. multicoloured — 3·00 4·00

F152 Birds

1989. Bicentenary of French Revolution.
F416 **F152** 2f.20 violet, blk & red — 1·50 2·75

F153 Pal

1989
F417 **F153** 2f.20 violet and blue — 1·50 2·75

F154 The Strong Horse

1989. Europa. Children's Games. Each brown and cream.
F418 2f.20 Type **F154** — 3·25 3·50
F419 3f.60 The Handkerchief — 4·25 4·75

F155 Wounded Soldiers

1989. 125th Anniv of International Red Cross.
F420 **F155** 3f.60 brn, blk & red — 2·10 3·50

F156 Archaeological Find and St. Vincent's Chapel, Enclar

1989. Archaeology.
F421 **F156** 3f. multicoloured — 1·60 3·50

F157 Wild Boar

1989. Nature Protection.
F422 **F157** 2f.20 blk, grn & brn — 1·60 3·50
F423 — 3f.60 black, green and deep green — 2·10 4·50
DESIGN: 3f.60, Palmate newt.

F158 Retable of St. Michael de la Mosquera, Encamp

1989
F424 **F158** 5f. multicoloured — 3·25 5·50

F159 La Margineda Bridge

1990
F425 **F159** 2f.30 blue, brn & turq — 1·60 2·75

F160 Llorts Iron Ore Mines

1990
F426 **F160** 3f.20 multicoloured — 2·10 3·25

F161 Exterior of Old Post Office, Andorra La Vella

1990. Europa. Post Office Buildings.
F427 **F161** 2f.30 red and black — 4·25 5·25
F428 — 3f.20 violet and red — 6·25 7·00
DESIGN: 3f.20, Interior of modern post office.

F162 Censer, St. Roma's Chapel, Les Bons

1990
F429 **F162** 3f. multicoloured — 2·10 3·25

F163 Wild Roses

1990. Nature Protection. Multicoloured.
F430 2f.30 Type **F163** — 1·60 3·25
F431 3f.20 Otter (horiz) — 2·10 3·50

F164 Tobacco-drying Sheds, Les Bons

1990
F432 **F164** 2f.30 yell, blk & red — 1·60 2·75

F165 Part of Mural from Santa Coloma Church

1990
F433 **F165** 5f. multicoloured — 2·75 3·75

1990. Birth Centenary of Charles de Gaulle (French statesman). As Nos. F243/4 but values and inscriptions changed.
F434 **F52** 2f.30 blue — 2·10 3·25
F435 **F52** 3f.20 red — 2·50 3·50

F166 Coin from St. Eulalia's Church, Encamp

1990
F436 **F166** 3f.20 multicoloured — 2·10 3·25

F167 Chapel of Sant Roma Dels Vilars

1991
F437 **F167** 2f.50 blue, blk & grn — 1·60 2·75

F168 Emblem and Track

1991. Fourth European Small States Games.
F438 **F168** 2f.50 multicoloured — 1·50 2·75

F169 Television Satellite

1991. Europa. Europe in Space. Multicoloured.
F439 2f.50 Type **F169** — 4·25 4·50
F440 3f.50 Globe, telescope and eye (horiz) — 7·50 8·00

F170 Bottles

1991. Artefacts from Tomb of St. Vincent of Enclar.
F441 **F170** 3f.20 multicoloured — 1·80 2·75

F171 Sheep

1991. Nature Protection.
F442 **F171** 2f.50 brown, bl & blk — 2·10 4·50
F443 — 3f.50 brn, mve & blk — 2·20 4·75
DESIGN: 3f.50, Pyrenean cow.

F172 Players

1991. World Petanque Championship, Engordany.
F444 **F172** 2f.50 blk, bistre & red — 1·80 2·75

F173 Mozart, Quartet and Organ Pipes

1991. Death Bicentenary of Wolfgang Amadeus Mozart (composer).
F445 **F173** 3f.40 blue, blk & turq — 2·20 3·25

1991. As Type **F115** but inscr "LA POSTE".
F446 **F115** 2f.20 green — 1·40 4·00
F447 **F115** 2f.40 green — 3·00 4·50
F448 **F115** 2f.50 red — 1·60 4·00
F449 **F115** 2f.70 green — 2·75 4·00
F450 **F115** 2f.80 red — 2·75 4·00
F451 **F115** 3f. red — 2·75 4·00

F174 *Virgin of the Remedy of Sant Julia and Sant Germa*

1991
| F455 | **F174** | 5f. multicoloured | 3·25 | 3·75 |

F175 Slalom

1992. Winter Olympic Games, Albertville. Multicoloured.
| F456 | 2f.50 Type **F175** | | 2·40 | 2·75 |
| F457 | 3f.40 Figure skating | | 2·75 | 3·25 |

F176 St. Andrew's Church, Arinsal

1992
| F458 | **F176** | 2f.50 black and buff | 1·80 | 2·20 |

F177 Navigation Instrument and Columbus's Fleet

1992. Europa. 500th Anniv of Discovery of America by Columbus. Multicoloured.
| F459 | 2f.50 Type **F177** | | 4·75 | 4·50 |
| F460 | 3f.40 Fleet, Columbus and Amerindians | | 7·50 | 5·75 |

F178 Canoeing

1992. Olympic Games, Barcelona. Multicoloured.
| F461 | 2f.50 Type **F178** | | 1·90 | 2·30 |
| F462 | 3f.40 Shooting | | 2·20 | 2·50 |

F179 Globe Flowers

1992. Nature Protection. Multicoloured.
| F463 | 2f.50 Type **F179** | | 1·70 | 2·40 |
| F464 | 3f.40 Griffon vulture ("El Voltor") (horiz) | | 2·30 | 2·75 |

F180 *Martyrdom of St. Eulalia* (altarpiece, St. Eulalia's Church, Encamp)

1992
| F465 | **F180** | 4f. multicoloured | 2·40 | 2·75 |

F181 *Ordino Arcalis 91* (Mauro Staccioli)

1992. Modern Sculpture. Multicoloured.
| F466 | 5f. Type **F181** | | 3·25 | 3·50 |
| F467 | 5f. *Storm in a Teacup* (Dennis Oppenheim) (horiz) | | 3·25 | 3·50 |

F182 Grau Roig

1993. Ski Resorts. Multicoloured.
F468	2f.50 Type **F182**		1·60	2·30
F469	2f.50 Ordino		1·60	2·30
F470	2f.50 Soldeu el Tarter		1·60	2·30
F471	3f.40 Pal		2·30	2·75
F472	3f.40 Arinsal		2·30	2·75

F183 *Estructures Autogeneradores* (Jorge du Bon)

1993. Europa. Contemporary Art.
| F473 | **F183** | 2f.50 dp bl, bl & vio | 2·20 | 3·25 |
| F474 | - | 3f.40 multicoloured | 2·40 | 3·50 |
DESIGN—HORIZ: 3f.40, *Fisicromia per Andorra* (Carlos Cruz-Diez).

F184 Common Blue

1993. Nature Protection. Butterflies. Multicoloured.
| F475 | 2f.50 Type **F184** | | 2·10 | 3·25 |
| F476 | 4f.20 *Nymphalidae* | | 3·00 | 4·00 |

F185 Cyclist

1993. Tour de France Cycling Road Race.
| F477 | **F185** | 2f.50 multicoloured | 2·20 | 3·50 |

F186 Smiling Hands

1993. Tenth Anniv of Andorran School.
| F478 | **F186** | 2f.80 multicoloured | 2·50 | 3·50 |

F187 *A Pagan Place* (Michael Warren)

1993. Modern Sculpture.
| F479 | **F187** | 5f. black and blue | 3·50 | 3·00 |
| F480 | - | 5f. multicoloured | 3·50 | 3·00 |
DESIGN: No. F480, *Pep, Lu, Canolic, Ton, Meritxell, Roma, Anna, Pau, Carles, Eugenia... and Others* (Erik Dietman).

F188 Cross-country Skiing

1994. Winter Olympic Games, Lillehammer, Norway.
| F481 | **F188** | 3f.70 multicoloured | 2·20 | 2·50 |

F189 Constitution Monument

1994. First Anniv of New Constitution.
| F482 | **F189** | 2f.80 multicoloured | 1·90 | 2·00 |
| F483 | - | 3f.70 blk, yell & mve | 2·40 | 3·50 |
DESIGN: 3f.70, Stone tablet.

F190 AIDS Virus

1994. Europa. Discoveries and Inventions. Multicoloured.
| F484 | 2f.80 Type **F190** | | 2·50 | 2·50 |
| F485 | 3f.70 Radio mast | | 3·00 | 3·00 |

F191 Competitors' Flags and Football

1994. World Cup Football Championship, U.S.A.
| F486 | **F191** | 3f.70 multicoloured | 2·50 | 2·75 |

F192 Horse Riding

1994. Tourist Activities. Multicoloured.
F487	2f.80 Type **F192**		1·90	1·90
F488	2f.80 Mountain biking		1·90	1·90
F489	2f.80 Climbing		1·90	1·90
F490	2f.80 Fishing		1·90	1·90

F193 Scarce Swallowtail

1994. Nature Protection. Butterflies. Multicoloured.
| F491 | 2f.80 Type **F193** | | 2·50 | 2·75 |
| F492 | 4f.40 Small tortoiseshell | | 3·75 | 4·00 |

F194 "26 10 93"

1994. Meeting of Co-princes.
| F493 | **F194** | 2f.80 multicoloured | 1·70 | 2·00 |

F195 Emblem

1995. European Nature Conservation Year.
| F494 | **F195** | 2f.80 multicoloured | 1·90 | 2·10 |

F196 Globe, Goal and Player

1995. Third World Cup Rugby Championship, South Africa.
| F495 | **F196** | 2f.80 multicoloured | 1·90 | 2·10 |

F197 Dove and Olive Twig ("Peace")

1995. Europa. Peace and Freedom. Multicoloured.
| F496 | 2f.80 Type **F197** | | 2·50 | 2·75 |
| F497 | 3f.70 Flock of doves ("Freedom") | | 2·75 | 3·00 |

F198 Emblem

1995. 15th Anniv of Caritas Andorrana (welfare organization).
| F498 | **F198** | 2f.80 multicoloured | 1·90 | 2·30 |

F199 Caldea Thermal Baths, Les Escaldes-Engordany

1995
| F499 | **F199** | 2f.80 multicoloured | 1·90 | 2·30 |

F200 National Auditorium, Ordino

1995
| F500 | **F200** | 3f.70 black and buff | 2·50 | 2·75 |

F201 "Virgin of Meritxell"

1995
| F501 | **F201** | 4f.40 multicoloured | 2·75 | 3·00 |

F202 Brimstone

1995. Nature Protection. Butterflies. Multicoloured.
| F502 | 2f.80 Type **F202** | | 2·50 | 2·75 |
| F503 | 3f.70 Marbled white (horiz) | | 3·00 | 3·25 |

F203 National Flag over U.N. Emblem

1995. 50th Anniv of U.N.O. Multicoloured.
| F504 | 2f.80 Type **F203** | | 2·50 | 2·75 |
| F505 | 3f.70 Anniversary emblem over flag | | 2·75 | 3·00 |

F204 National Flag and
Palace of Europe,
Strasbourg

1995. Admission of Andorra to Council of Europe.
F506 **F204** 2f.80 multicoloured 1·90 2·00

F205 Emblem

1996. Fourth Borrufa Trophy Skiing Competition.
F507 **F205** 2f.80 multicoloured 1·90 2·00

F206 Basketball

1996
F508 **F206** 3f.70 red, blk & yell 3·00 3·75

F207 Children

1996. 25th Anniv of Our Lady of Meritxell Special School.
F509 **F207** 2f.80 multicoloured 1·90 2·10

F208 European Robin

1996. Nature Protection. Multicoloured.
F510 3f. Type **F208** 2·50 3·00
F511 3f.80 Great tit 3·00 3·25

F209 Cross, St.
James's Church,
Engordany

1996. Religious Objects. Multicoloured.
F512 3f. Type **F209** 2·50 2·75
F513 3f.80 Censer, St. Eulalia's
 Church, Encamp (horiz) 2·75 3·00

F210
Ermessenda de
Castellbo

1996. Europa. Famous Women.
F514 **F210** 3f. multicoloured 2·50 2·75

F211 Chessmen

1996. Chess.
F515 **F211** 4f.50 red, black & bl 2·50 2·75

F212 Canillo

1996. No value expressed. Self-adhesive.
F516 **F212** (3f.) multicoloured 3·00 3·25

F213 Cycling, Running
and Throwing the Javelin

1996. Olympic Games, Atlanta.
F517 **F213** 3f. multicoloured 1·90 2·00

F214 Singers

1996. Fifth Anniv of National Youth Choir.
F518 **F214** 3f. multicoloured 1·90 2·00

F215 Man and Boy with
Animals

1996. Livestock Fair.
F519 **F215** 3f. yellow, red and black 1·90 2·00

F216 St. Roma's Chapel,
Les Bons

1996. Churches. Multicoloured.
F520 6f.70 Type **F216** 4·00 4·25
F521 6f.70 Santa Coloma 4·00 4·25

F217 Mitterrand

1997. Francois Mitterrand (President of France and Co-
prince of Andorra, 1981–95) Commemoration.
F522 **F217** 3f. multicoloured 1·90 2·00

F218 Parish
Emblem

1997. Parish of Encamp. No value expressed. Self-
adhesive.
F523 **F218** (3f.) blue 1·90 2·00

F219 Volleyball

1997
F524 **F219** 3f. multicoloured 1·90 2·00

F220 The White
Lady

1997. Europa. Tales and Legends.
F525 **F220** 3f. multicoloured 2·50 2·75

F221 House Martin
approaching Nest

1997. Nature Protection.
F526 **F221** 3f.80 multicoloured 1·90 2·00

F222 Mill and
Saw-mill, Cal Pal

1997. Tourism. Paintings by Francesc Galobardes.
Multicoloured.
F527 3f. Type **F222** 2·50 2·75
F528 4f.50 Mill and farmhouse, Sole
 (horiz) 3·00 3·25

F223 Monstrance, St. Iscle
and St. Victoria's Church

1997. Religious Silver Work. Multicoloured.
F529 3f. Type **F223** 2·50 2·75
F530 15f.50 Pax, St. Peter's Church,
 Aixirivall 7·50 8·00

F224 The
Legend of
Meritxell

1997. Legends. Multicoloured.
F531 3f. Type **F224** 1·90 2·10
F532 3f. The Seven-armed Cross 1·90 2·10
F533 3f.80 Wrestlers (The Fountain of
 Esmelicat) 3·00 3·25

F225 St. Michael's Chapel,
Engolasters

1997. International Stamp Exn, Monaco.
F534 **F225** 3f. multicoloured 1·90 2·10

F226 Harlequin
juggling
Candles

1998. Birthday Greetings Stamp.
F535 **F226** 3f. multicoloured 1·90 2·10

F227 Super
Giant Slalom

1997. Winter Olympic Games, Nagano, Japan.
F536 **F227** 4f.40 multicoloured 3·25 3·50

F228 Arms of
Ordino

1998. No value expressed. Self-adhesive.
F537 **F228** (3f.) multicoloured 1·90 2·10

F229 Altarpiece and Vila Church

1998
F538 **F229** 4f.50 multicoloured 3·25 3·50

F230 Emblem and
Cogwheels

1998. 20th Anniv of Rotary Int in Andorra.
F539 **F230** 3f. multicoloured 1·90 2·10

F231 Chaffinch and
Berries

1998. Nature Protection.
F540 **F231** 3f.80 multicoloured 3·00 3·25

F232 Players

1998. World Cup Football Championship, France.
F541 **F232** 3f. multicoloured 1·90 2·10

F233 Treble Score and
Stylized Orchestra

1998. Europa. National Festivals. Music Festival.
F542 **F233** 3f. multicoloured 1·90 2·10

F234 River

1998. "Expo '98" World's Fair, Lisbon, Portugal.
F543 **F234** 5f. multicoloured 3·75 4·25

F235 Chalice

1998. Chalice from the House of the Valleys.
F544 **F235** 4f.50 multicoloured 3·25 3·75

1998. French Victory in World Cup Football Championship. No. F541 optd **FINAL FRANCA/BRASIL 3-0.**
F545 **F232** 3f. multicoloured 3·75 4·25

F237 Andorra, 1717

1998. Relief Maps. Multicoloured.
F546 3f. Type **F237** 1·90 2·10
F547 15f.50 Andorra, 1777 (horiz) 9·75 10·50

F238 Museum

1998. Inauguration of Postal Museum.
F548 **F238** 3f. multicoloured 1·90 2·10

F239 Front Page of First Edition

1998. 250th Anniv of *Manual Digest.*
F549 **F239** 3f.80 multicoloured 3·00 3·25

F240 Arms of La Massana

1999. No value expressed. Self-adhesive.
F550 **F240** (3f.) multicoloured 1·90 2·10

F241 House and Recycling Bins

1999. "Green World". Recycling of Waste.
F551 **F241** 5f. multicoloured 3·75 4·25

F242 Vall de Sorteny

1999. Europa. Parks and Gardens.
F552 **F242** 3f. multicoloured 1·90 2·10

F243 Council Emblem and Seat, Strasbourg

1999. 50th Anniv of Council of Europe.
F553 **F243** 3f.80 multicoloured 3·00 3·25

F244 "The First Mail Coach"

1999.
F554 **F244** 2f.70 multicoloured 1·70 1·90

F245 Footballer and Flags

1999. Andorra–France Qualifying Match for European Nations Football Championship.
F555 **F245** 4f.50 multicoloured 3·50 4·00

F246 St. Michael's Church, Engolasters, and Emblem

1999. "Philexfrance 99" International Stamp Exhibition, Paris, France.
F556 **F246** 3f. multicoloured 1·80 2·00

F247 Winter Scene

1999. Paintings of Pal by Francesc Galobardes. Multicoloured.
F557 3f. Type F **247** 1·80 2·00
F558 3f. Summer scene (horiz) 1·80 2·00

F248 Emblem and "50"

1999. 50th Anniv of International Photographic Art Federation.
F559 **F248** 4f.40 multicoloured 2·75 3·00

F249 Rull House, Sispony

1999.
F560 **F249** 15f.50 multicoloured 7·25 8·00

F250 Chest with Six Locks

1999.
F561 **F250** 6f.70 multicoloured 3·25 3·50

F251 Angels

1999. Christmas.
F562 **F251** 3f. multicoloured 1·80 2·00

F252 Revellers

2000. New Millennium.
F563 **F252** 3f. multicoloured 1·80 2·00

F253 Arms of La Vella

2000. No value expressed. Self-adhesive.
F564 **F253** (3f.) multicoloured 1·80 2·00

F254 Snow Boarder

2000
F565 **F254** 4f.50 blue, brown and black 2·75 3·00

F255 Emblem

2000. Montserrat Caballe International Opera Competition, Saint Julia de Loria.
F566 **F255** 3f.80 yellow and blue 2·30 2·50

F256 *Campanula cochleariifolia*

2000
F567 **F256** 2f.70 multicoloured 1·80 2·00

F257 "Building Europe"

2000. Europa.
F568 **F257** 3f. multicoloured 2·50 2·75

F258 Church (Canolich Festival)

2000. Festivals. Multicoloured.
F569 3f. Type **F258** 1·80 2·00
F570 3f. People at Our Lady's Chapel, Meritxell (Meritxell Festival) 1·80 2·00

F259 Sparrow

2000
F571 **F259** 4f.40 multicoloured 2·75 3·00

F260 Hurdling

2000. Olympic Games, Sydney.
F572 **F260** 5f. multicoloured 3·00 3·50

F261 Goat, Skier and Walker

2000. Tourism Day.
F573 **F261** 3f. multicoloured 1·80 2·00

F262 Flower, Text, Circuit Board and Emblems

2000. "EXPO 2000" World's Fair, Hanover.
F574 **F262** 3f. multicoloured 1·80 2·00

F263 Stone Arch and Flag

2000. European Community.
F575 **F263** 3f.80 multicoloured 2·30 2·50

F264 Pottery

2000. Prehistoric Pottery.
F576 **F264** 6f.70 multicoloured 3·25 3·50

F265 Drawing

2000. 25th Anniv of National Archives.
F577 **F265** 15f.50 multicoloured 7·25 8·00

F266 Arms of Saint Julia de Loria

2001. No value expressed. Self-adhesive.
F578 **F266** (3f.) multicoloured 1·80 2·00

F267 Ski Lift

2001. Canillo Aliga Club.
F579 **F267** 4f.50 multicoloured 2·75 3·00

F268 Decorative Metalwork

2001. Casa Cristo Museum.
F580 **F268** 6f.70 multicoloured 3·25 3·50

F269 Legend of
Lake
Engolasters

2001. Legends. Multicoloured.
F581 3f. Type F **269** 1·80 2·00
F582 3f. Lords before King (founda-
 tion of Andorra) 1·80 2·00

F270 Globe
and Books

2001. World Book Day.
F583 **F270** 3f.80 multicoloured 2·30 2·50

F271 Water
Splash

2001. Europa. Water Resources.
F584 **F271** 3f. multicoloured 2·50 2·75

F272 Raspberry

2001. Multicoloured.
F585 3f. Type F**272** 2·30 2·50
F586 4f.40 Jay (horiz) 3·00 3·50

F273 Profiles talking

2001. European Year of Languages.
F587 **F273** 3f.80 multicoloured 2·75 3·25

F274 Trumpeter

2001. Jazz Festival, Escaldes-Engordany.
F588 **F274** 3f. multicoloured 2·30 2·50

F275 Kitchen

2001
F589 **F275** 5f. multicoloured 3·00 3·50

F276 Chapel

2001. 25th Anniv of Chapel of Our Lady, Meritxell.
F590 **F276** 3f. multicoloured 2·30 2·50

F277 Hotel Pla

2001
F591 **F277** 15f.50 black, violet and
 green 7·75 8·75

F278 Cross

2001. Grossa Cross (boundary cross at the crossroads
between Avinguda Meritxell and Carrer Bisbe
Iglesias).
F592 **F278** 2f.70 multicoloured 1·60 1·70

F279 State
Arms

2002. (a) With Face Value. Ordinary gum.
F593 **F279** 1c. multicoloured 30 35
F594 **F279** 2c. multicoloured 30 35
F595 **F279** 5c. multicoloured 30 35
F596 **F279** 60c. multicoloured 1·90 2·10

 (b) No value expressed.
F598 (46c.) multicoloured 2·30 2·50
F599 (46c.) multicoloured 2·30 2·50

 (ii) Size 17×23 mm. Self-adhesive gum.
F599a (52c.) multicoloured 1·70 1·90
 Nos. F598/9 were sold at the rate for inland letters up
to 20 grammes.

F280 The
Legend of
Meritxell

2002. Legends. Designs as Nos. F525, F531/3 and F581/2
but with values in new currency as Type **F280**.
Multicoloured.
F600 10c. Type **F280** 55 60
F601 20c. Wrestlers (The Fountain of
 Esmelicat) 55 60
F602 41c. The Piper (La joueurde
 cornemuse) 1·40 1·60
F603 45c. Legend of Saint Vincent
 Castle 1·40 1·60
F604 48c. Port Rat (horiz) 2·10 2·30
F604a 48c. The Cave of Ourses 1·40 1·60
F604b 49c. The Testament of Ilop 1·40 1·60
F604c 50c. El tresor de la font del
 Manego 1·40 1·60
F605 50c. The Seven-armed Cross 1·40 1·60
F606 51c. The Devils of Aiscirivall
 Ches Diables d'Aixirivall 2·10 2·30
F606a 75c. 'Le joueur de cornemuse' 2·75 3·00
F606b 90c. Legende du pin de la
 "Margin eda" 1·20 1·80
F610 €1 Lords before King (founda-
 tion of Andorra) 2·75 3·00
F611 €2 Legend of Lake Engolasters 5·50 6·25
F612 €5 The White Lady 12·50 14·00

F281 Pedestrians
on Crossing

2002. Schools' Road Safety Campaign.
F615 **F281** 69c. multicoloured 2·50 2·75

F282 Skier

2002. Winter Olympic Games, Salt Lake City, U.S.A.
F616 **F282** 58c. multicoloured 1·90 2·10

F283 Hotel Rosaleda

2002
F617 **F283** 46c. multicoloured 1·70 1·80

F284 Water
Droplet and
Clouds

2002. World Water Day.
F618 **F284** 67c. multicoloured 2·10 2·30

F285 Clown

2002. Europa. Circus.
F619 **F285** 46c. multicoloured 2·50 2·75

F286 Myrtle

2002
F620 **F286** 46c. multicoloured 1·70 1·80

F287 Seated Nude
(Josep Viladomat)

2002
F621 **F287** €2.26 multicoloured 6·50 7·00

F288 Mountains from Tunnel
Entrance

2002. Completion of the Envalira Road Tunnel between
Andorra and France.
F622 **F288** 46c. multicoloured 1·70 1·80

F289 Mural (detail) (Santa Coloma
Church, Andorra la Vella)

2002
F623 **F289** €1.02 multicoloured 3·25 3·50

F290 Arms of
Escaldes
– Engordany

2003. Arms. No value expressed. Self-adhesive.
F624 **F 290** (46c.) multicoloured 1·90 2·10
 No. F624 was sold at the rate for inland letters up to
20 grammes.

2003. Legends. 'Legende du pinde la Margineda'. As T
F280.
F625 69c. multicoloured 1·90 2·10

F291 State Arms

2003. Tenth Anniv of Constitution.
F626 **F 291** €2.36 multicoloured 6·50 7·00

F292 Les Bons

2003. Architecture.
F627 **F 292** 67c. multicoloured 2·50 2·10

F293 Hotel Mirador

2003
F628 **F 293** €1.02 multicoloured 3·25 3·50

F294 Man, Dog
and Sheep

2003. Europa. Poster Art.
F629 **F 294** 46c. multicoloured 2·50 2·75

F295 Dancers and Fire

2003. Fires of St. John the Baptist Festival.
F630 **F 295** 50c. multicoloured 1·90 2·10

F296 Cyclist
and Map

2003. Centenary of Tour de France (cycle race).
F631 **F 296** 50c. multicoloured 1·90 2·10

F297 Pole Vault

2003. World Athletics Championship, Paris.
F632 **F 297** 90c. multicoloured 2·75 3·25

F298 *Greixa sparassis crispa*

2003
F633 **F298** 45c. multicoloured 1·30 1·40

F299 Red Currant

2003
F634 **F299** 75c. multicoloured 2·50 2·75

F300 Telephone, Satellite and Globe

2003. Centenary of First Telephone in Andorra.
F635 **F300** 50c. multicoloured 1·90 2·10

F301 *Maternity* (Paul Gauguin)

2003
F636 **F301** 75c. multicoloured 2·75 3·00

F302 St. Anthony's Market

2004
F637 **F302** 50c. multicoloured 1·90 2·10

F303 Children

2004
F638 **F303** 50c. multicoloured 1·90 2·10

F304 Hotel Valira

2004
F639 **F304** €1.11 multicoloured 3·50 3·75

F305 Woman and Andorra Sign

2004. Europa. Holidays.
F640 **F305** 50c. orange, red and black 2·10 2·30

F306 Madriu-Perafita-Claror Valley

2004. UNESCO World Heritage Site.
F641 **F306** 75c. multicoloured 2·50 2·75

F307 Poblet de Fontaneda

2004
F642 **F307** 50c. multicoloured 1·90 2·10

F308 Runner and Swimmer

2004. Olympic Games, Athens 2004.
F643 **F308** 90c. multicoloured 3·00 3·25

F309 *Pont de la Margineda* (sketch)

2004. Arts. Margineda Bridge by Joaquim Mir (Spanish artist). Multicoloured.
F644 €1 Type **F309** 3·00 3·25
F645 €2 *Pont de la Margineda* (painting) 5·75 6·25

F310 Town Names and Post Codes

2004. Introduction of Postal Codes.
F646 **F310** 50c. vermilion, black and lemon 1·90 2·10

F311 Emblem

2004. Tenth Anniv of Entry into Council of Europe.
F647 **F311** €2.50 multicoloured 7·75 8·50

F312 Children's Nativity

2004. Christmas.
F648 **F312** 50c. black, brown and bistre 1·90 2·10

F313 Three Kings visiting Child

2005
F649 **F313** 50c. multicoloured 1·90 2·10

F314 Mountains and Lake

2005. World Heritage Site. Madriu-Claror-Perafita Valley.
F650 **F314** 50c. multicoloured 1·90 2·10

F315 Tengmalm's Owl (*Aegolius funereus*)

2005
F651 **F315** 90c. multicoloured 2·75 3·25

F316 Bottle, Glass, Jug and Fruit

2005. Europa. Gastronomy.
F652 **F316** 55c. multicoloured 2·00 2·20

F317 Marksman

2005. Small States of Europe Games. Sheet 151×70 mm containing Type **F317** and similar vert designs. Each black and magenta.
MSF653 53c. Type **F317**; 55c. Runner; 82c. Swimmer; €1 Diver 9·00 9·50

F318 Mountain Hut, Bordes d'Ensegur

2005
F654 **F318** €2.50 multicoloured 8·00 8·75

F319 Motorcycle

2005
F655 **F319** 53c. sepia, brown and black 1·60 1·70

F320 *Prats de Santa Coloma* (Joaquim Mir)

2005. Art.
F656 **F320** 82c. multicoloured 2·75 2·75

F321 Hostel Calones

2005
F657 **F321** €1.98 multicoloured 6·25 6·50

F322 Lorry in Snow (Josep Alsina)

2005. Photography.
F658 **F322** 53c. multicoloured 1·70 1·80

F323 Emblem

2005. Centenary of Rotary International.
F659 **F323** 55c. multicoloured 1·90 2·00

F324 *Adoration of the Shepherds* (A. Viladomat)

2005. Christmas.
F660 **F324** €1.22 multicoloured 4·00 4·25

F325 *Ursus arctos*

2006. Fauna. Multicoloured.
F661 53c. Type **F325** 1·70 1·80
F662 53c. *Rupicapra pyrenaica* (vert) 1·70 1·80

F326 Alpine Skier

2006. Winter Olympic Games, Turin. Multicoloured.
F663 55c. Type **F326** 1·70 1·80
F664 75c. Cross country skier 2·30 2·50

F326a Tobacco Leaves

2006. Tobacco Museum, Sant Julia de Loria.
F665 **F326a** 82c. multicoloured 2·75 2·75

F327 Napoleon

2006. Bicentenary of Napoleon's Decree restoring Statute of Co-Principality.
F666 **F327** 53c. blue, azure and black 1·70 1·80

F328 Coloured blocks

2006. Europa. Integration.
F667 **F328** 53c. multicoloured 2·00 2·10

F329 Sorteny Valley Nature Reserve

2006
F668 **F329** 55c. multicoloured 1·90 2·00

F330 Pablo Casals

2006. 130th Birth Anniv of Pablo Casals (cellist).
F669 **F330** 90c. multicoloured 3·00 3·25

F331 Model T Ford

2006
F670 **F331** 85c. multicoloured 2·75 3·00

F332 *Montserrat Procession* (Josep Borrell)

2006
F671 **F332** €1.30 multicoloured 4·25 4·50

F333 Reredos (retable), Sant Marti de la Cortinada, Ordino

2006
F672 **F333** 54c. multicoloured 1·90 2·00

F334 Marmot (*Marmota marmota*)

2007. Fauna. Multicoloured.
F673 54c. Type **F334** 1·90 2·00
F674 60c. Eurasian red squirrel (*Sciurus vulgaris*) (horiz) 2·00 2·10

F335 *Predel-la de Prats* (Master of Canillo)

2007. *Pradel la des Prats.*
F675 **F335** €1.30 multicoloured 4·25 4·50

F336 Heart enclosing Rose

2007. Saint George.
F676 **F336** 86c. multicoloured 3·00 3·25

F337 Salute

2007. Europa. Centenary of Scouting.
F677 **F337** 54c. multicoloured 1·90 2·00

F338 Virgin, Meritxell

2007. Twinning of Meritxell and Sabart. Multicoloured.
F678 54c. Type **F338** 1·90 2·00
F679 54c. Virgin, Sabart 1·90 2·00

F339 'Pinette'

2007
F680 **F339** 60c. multicoloured 2·00 2·10

F340 Players

2007. Rugby World Cup, France.
F681 **F340** 85c. multicoloured 2·75 3·00

F341 Vall del Comapedrosa

2007
F682 **F341** €3.04 multicoloured 10·00 10·50

F341a Prehistoric Family

2007. Pre-Historic Sites. El Cedre.
F683 **F341a** 85c. multicoloured 3·00 3·25

F342 Cave Dwellers

2007. Pre-Historic Sites. La Barma de la Marginada.
F684 **F342** 60c. multicoloured 2·00 2·10

F343 Altarpiece, Sant Marti de la Cortinada

2007. Christmas.
F685 **F343** 54c. multicoloured 1·90 2·00

F344 *Vulpes vulpes* (red fox)

2008. Fauna. Multicoloured.
F686 54c. Type **F344** 2·00 2·10
F687 60c. *Sus scrofa* (wild boar) (vert) 2·20 2·30

F345 Predella's Altar of St. Michaels d'Pratts church

2008. Easter.
F688 **F345** €1.33 multicoloured 5·00 5·25

F346 Cartercar, 1906

2008
F689 **F346** 65c. multicoloured 2·75 2·75

F347 Symbols of Writing

2008. Europa. The Letter.
F690 **F347** 55c. multicoloured 2·30 2·40

F348 Rowing

2008. Olympic Games, Beijing. Sheet 210×60 mm containing Type **F348** and similar horiz designs. Multicoloured.
MSF691 55c.×4, Type **F348**; Running; Swimming; Judo 8·25 8·50
The stamps of **MS**F691 were not for sale separately.

F349 *Narcissus poeticus*

2008
F692 **F349** 55c. multicoloured 2·30 2·40

F350 Vall d'Incles (Incles valley)

2008
F693 **F350** €2.80 multicoloured 10·50 11·00

F351 Men

2008. 75th Anniv of Male Suffrage.
F694 **F351** 55c. multicoloured 2·30 2·40

F352 Valley

2008. Sustainable Development.
F695 **F352** 88c. multicoloured 3·75 4·00

F353 El roc d'Enclar

2008
F696 **F353** 85c. multicoloured 3·50 3·75

F354 St. Mark and St. Mary (alterpiece (reredos))

2008
F697 **F354** 55c. multicoloured 2·75 2·75

F355 Louis Braille

2009. Birth Bicentenary of Louis Braille (inventor of Braille writing for the blind).
F698 **F355** 88c. blue and brown 4·00 4·00

F356 *Equus mulus* (mule)

2009. Domestic Animals. Multicoloured.
F699 55c. Type **F356** 2·30 2·40
F700 65c. *Bos taurus* (cow) (horiz) 2·50 2·50

F357 Penguins

2009. Preserve Polar Regions and Glaciers. Sheet 143×120 mm containing Type **F357** and similar multicoloured design.
MSF701 56c. Type **F357**; 85c. Polar ice 6·25 6·50

F358 *Pradel la des Prats* (detail)

2009
F702 **F358** €1.35 multicoloured 6·00 6·25

F359 Nebula

2009. Europa. Astronomy.
F703 **F359** 56c. multicoloured 2·50 2·50

F360 Renault Voiturette, 1898

2009. First Car manufactured by Renault.
F704 **F360** 70c. multicoloured 3·00 3·25

F361 *Sant Joan de Caselles* (Maurice Utrillo)

2009. Art.
F705 **F361** 90c. multicoloured 4·00 4·00

F362 Cercle dels Pessons

2009
F706 **F362** €2.80 multicoloured 11·50 12·00

F363 Cyclist

2009. Tour de France (cycle race).
F707 **F363** 56c. multicoloured 2·50 2·50

F364 Allegory

2009. 40th Anniv of Circle of Arts and Letters.
F708 **F364** 51c. multicoloured 2·40 2·40

F365 Santa Coloma Church

2009. Romanesque Art in Andorra.
F709 **F365** 85c. multicoloured 3·75 3·75

F366 The Nativity

2009. Christmas.
F710 **F366** 56c. multicoloured 2·50 2·50

F366a Arms

2010. State Arms. Background colour given. (a) With face value.
F710a **F366a** 1c. multicoloured (pale lemon) 20 25
F711 5c. multicoloured (cobalt) 25 30
F712 10c. multicoloured (bright yellow-orange) 55 60
F713 20c. multicoloured (lavender) 55 60
F714 50c. multicoloured (olive-bistre) 1·40 1·60

(b) No value expressed.
F715 (60c.) multicoloured (aquamarine) 2·40 2·50
Nos. F710a/F715 are as No. **F279** but with different inscriptions.

F367 Athlete

2010. Winter Olympic Games, Vancouver.
F716 **F367** 85c. multicoloured 3·75 3·75

F368 Casamanya Peak

2010. Mountains.
F717 **F368** €2.80 multicoloured 11·50 12·00

F369 Anniversary Emblem

2010. 20th Anniv of Convention on Rights of the Child. UNICEF
F718 **F369** 56c. multicoloured 2·50 2·50

F370 *Gyps fulvus* (griffon vulture)

2010. Vulture
F719 **F370** 56c. multicoloured 2·50 2·50

F371 Ovis aries (sheep)

2010. Sheep
F720 **F371** 90c. multicoloured 3·50 3·50

F372 Embassy of Andorra in Brussels

2010. Antverpia 2010–International Stamp Exhibition, Antwerp
F721 **F372** 70c. multicoloured 3·00 3·00

No. F722 and Type **F373** are left for Legends issued on 26 April 2010, not yet received.

F374 Mirror and 'Mirror, Magic Mirror, tell me which is' (from Snow White)

2010. Europa. Children's Books
F723 **F374** 56c. silver and bright rose-red 2·50 2·50

F375 Radio Andorra

2010. Radio Andorra
F724 **F375** 56c. multicoloured 2·50 2·50

F377 Ferrari 328 GTS

2010. Classic Cars
F725 **F377** 70c. multicoloured 3·00 3·00

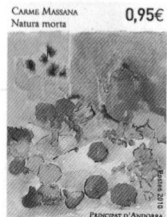

F378 Still Life (Carme Massana)

2010. Art
F726 **F378** 95c. multicoloured 3·75 3·75

F379 The Crucifixion of Christ, Predella of the Altar of Saint-Michel De Prats Church (detail)

2010. Religious Art
F727 **F379** €1.40 multicoloured 2·50 2·50
See also No. F702.

F380 Sant Joan de Caselles

2010. Romanesque Art in Andorra. Multicoloured.
MSF728 58c.×2, Type **F380**; Sant Romà de les Bons (horiz) 5·75 5·75

2010. State Arms. No value expressed.
F729 **F366a** (58c.) multicoloured (bright vermilion) 2·75 2·75
As Type **F366a**

F381 Signing of Paréage of Andorra on Escalls Bridge

2010. Feudal Andorra. Signing of Paréages of Andorra (Parity Treaties)
F730 **F381** 87c. multicoloured 3·75 3·75

F382 The Epiphany

2010. Christmas
F731 **F382** 58c. multicoloured 2·50 2·50

F383 *Saint Joan de Caselle*

2011. Legends. 'Saint Joan de Caselle'
F732 **F383** €2.80 multicoloured 11·50 11·50

F384 Lighthouse Beam showing French Flag Colours

2011. Francophone
F733 **F384** 87c. multicoloured 4·00 4·00

F385 Taking of Christ, Predella of the Altar of Saint-Michel De Prats Church (detail)

2010. Religious Art
F734	**F385**	€1.40 multicoloured	5·75	5·75

See also No. F702 and F727

F386 Tree Bark

2011. Europa. Forests.
F735	**F386**	58c. multicoloured	2·75	2·75

F387 Francesc Borras

2011. Francesc Borras
F736	**F387**	95c. multicoloured	4·25	4·25

F388 Placeta de Sant Esteve

2012. Placeta de la Consòrcia
F737	**F388**	58c. multicoloured	2·75	2·75

F389 Soriano Pedroso Type P, 1922

2011. Soriano Pedroso Automobile Manufacturer
F738	**F389**	75c. m ulticoloured	3·50	3·50

F390 Games Emblem as Maori Shield

2011. Rugby World Cup Championship, New Zealand
F739	**F390**	89c. mutlicoloured	4·00	4·00

F391 Dansa de les 7 Parròquies, Placa Benlloch, Andorra la Vella

2011. Folk Dances. Sheet 105×71 mm.
MSF740	**F391**	€1.45 multicoloured	6·50	6·50

F392 Rhododendron ferrugineum

2011. Flowers and Fruit. Multicoloured.
F741		60c. Type **F392**	2·75	2·75
F742		€1 Rose hips (Rosa semper-virens)	4·50	4·50

F393 Consell de la Terra

2011. Conseil de la Terra, 1866 (forerunner of Parliament)
F743	**F393**	89c. multicoloured	4·00	4·00

F394 Angel del Retaule de Santa Eulalia d'Encamp

2011. Angel from the Reredos of Santa Eulalia d'Encamp Church
F744	**F394**	60c. multicoloured	2·75	2·75

POSTAGE DUE STAMPS

1931. Postage Due stamps of France optd **ANDORRE**.
FD24	D11	5c. blue	2·10	5·75
FD25	D11	10c. brown	2·10	4·50
FD26	D11	30c. red	1·10	5·25
FD27	D11	50c. purple	2·10	5·75
FD28	D11	60c. green	26·00	55·00
FD29	D11	1f. brown on yellow	2·10	7·00
FD30	D11	2f. mauve	17·00	41·00
FD31	D11	3f. mauve	4·25	9·75

1931. Postage Due stamps of France optd **ANDORRE**.
FD32	D43	1c. green	3·25	5·75
FD33	D43	10c. red	6·25	14·00
FD34	D43	60c. red	31·00	48·00
FD35	D43	1f. green	95·00	£140
FD36	D43	1f.20 on 2f. blue	90·00	£160
FD37	D43	2f. brown	£180	£275
FD38	D43	5f. on 1f. purple	95·00	£130

FD7

1935
FD82	**FD7**	1c. green	4·25	9·25

FD10

1937
FD97	**FD10**	5c. blue	7·50	16·00
FD98	**FD10**	10c. brown	5·25	30·00
FD99	**FD10**	2f. mauve	11·50	16·00
FD100	**FD10**	5f. orange	25·00	40·00

FD11 Wheat Sheaves

1943
FD101a	**FD11**	10c. brown	65	2·10
FD102	**FD11**	30c. mauve	1·90	2·75
FD103	**FD11**	50c. green	1·40	3·25
FD104	**FD11**	1f. blue	2·10	4·75
FD105	**FD11**	1f.50 red	5·75	14·50
FD106	**FD11**	2f. blue	2·10	5·25
FD107	**FD11**	3f. red	2·50	9·75
FD108	**FD11**	4f. violet	5·25	15·00
FD109	**FD 11**	5f. mauve	4·25	14·50
FD110	**FD 11**	10f. orange	5·75	15·00
FD111	**FD 11**	20f. brown	8·00	22·00

1946. As Type **FD11**, but inscr "TIMBRE-TAXE".
FD143	10c. brown	1·10	7·25
FD144	1f. blue	1·30	4·00
FD145	2f. blue	1·40	4·00
FD146	3f. brown	2·75	6·00
FD147	4f. violet	3·75	7·25
FD148	5f. red	2·10	5·75
FD149	10f. orange	3·75	7·50
FD150	20f. brown	7·50	13·00
FD151	50f. green	60·00	55·00
FD152	100f. green	£110	£160

1961. As Nos. FD143/52 but new values and colours.
FD185	5c. red	4·25	8·25
FD186	10c. orange	9·50	17·00
FD187	20c. brown	13·50	29·00
FD188	50c. green	26·00	47·00

1964. Designs as Nos. D1650/6 of France, but inscr "ANDORRE".
FD192	5c. red, green and purple	55	4·25
FD193	10c. blue, grn & pur	85	4·25
FD194	15c. red, green and brown	95	4·25
FD195	20c. purple, green & turq	1·10	4·25
FD196	30c. blue, grn & brn	85	2·50
FD197	40c. yellow, red and green	2·10	2·75
FD198	50c. red, green and blue	1·70	1·70

FD129 Holly Berries

1985. Fruits.
FD371	**FD129**	10c. red and green	1·70	2·75
FD372	-	20c. brown & blue	1·70	2·75
FD373	-	30c. green and red	1·70	2·75
FD374	-	40c. brown & blk	1·70	2·75
FD375	-	50c. olive & violet	1·70	2·75
FD376	-	1f. green and blue	1·70	2·75
FD377	-	2f. red and brown	1·80	3·00
FD378	-	3f. purple & green	2·10	3·50
FD379	-	4f. olive and blue	2·75	3·75
FD380	-	5f. olive and red	3·25	4·25

DESIGNS: 20c. Wild plum; 30c. Raspberry; 40c. Dogberry; 50c. Blackberry; 1f. Juniper; 2f. Rose hip; 3f. Elder; 4f. Bilberry; 5f. Strawberry.

SPANISH POST OFFICES

1928. Stamps of Spain optd **CORREOS ANDORRA**.
1B	68	2c. green	1·70	2·30
2B	68	5c. red	2·30	2·75
3B	68	10c. green	3·50	4·00
5B	68	15c. blue	3·50	4·00
6B	68	20c. violet	3·75	4·25
7A	68	25c. red	8·50	8·50
8A	68	30c. brown	29·00	29·00
9A	68	40c. blue	34·00	34·00
10A	68	50c. orange	37·00	37·00
11B	69	1p. grey	34·00	36·00
12A	69	4p. red	£180	£180
13A	69	10p. brown	£250	£250

2 House of the Valleys **3** General Council of Andorra

1929
14A	2	2c. green	2·00	2·30
26	2	2c. brown	1·40	2·30
15A	-	5c. purple	3·75	4·00
27	-	5c. brown	2·10	2·75
16A	-	10c. green	3·75	4·00
17A	-	15c. blue	5·50	5·75
30	-	15c. green	5·75	7·00
18A	-	20c. violet	5·50	6·25
33	-	25c. red	2·75	3·50
20A	2	30c. brown	£150	£160
34	2	30c. red	2·75	4·00
21A	-	40c. blue	11·50	8·00
36	2	45c. red	2·30	2·75
22A	-	50c. orange	11·50	7·00
38	2	60c. blue	4·50	5·75
23A	3	1p. slate	23·00	29·00
39	3	4p. purple	46·00	50·00
40	3	10p. brown	70·00	75·00

DESIGNS: 5, 40c. Church of St. John of Caselles; 10, 20, 50c. Sant Julia de Loria; 15, 25c. Santa Coloma Church.

7 Councillor Manuel Areny Bons **11** Map

1948
41	F	2c. olive	1·10	1·70
42	F	5c. orange	1·10	1·70
43	F	10c. blue	1·10	1·70
44	7	20c. purple	10·50	7·00
45	7	25c. orange	7·00	3·50
46	G	30c. green	23·00	11·50
47	H	50c. green	34·00	15·00
48	I	75c. blue	33·00	16·00
49	H	90c. purple	17·00	11·50
50	I	1p. red	29·00	15·00
51	G	1p.35 violet	11·50	11·50
52	11	4p. blue	34·00	29·00
53	11	10p. brown	65·00	34·00

DESIGNS—VERT: F. Edelweiss; G. Arms; H. Market Place, Ordino; I. Shrine near Meritxell Chapel.

12 Andorra La Vella

1951. Air.
54	12	1p. brown	40·00	26·00

13 St. Anthony's Bridge

1963
55	13	25c. brown and black	25	30
56	-	70c. black and green	35	55
57	-	1p. lilac and grey	90	1·50
58	-	2p. violet and lilac	1·10	1·70
59	-	2p.50 deep red and purple	90	1·40
60	-	3p. slate and black	1·10	1·60
61	-	5p. purple and brown	3·50	3·75
62	-	6p. red and brown	4·50	4·00

DESIGNS—VERT: 70c. Anyos meadows (wrongly inscr "AYNOS"); 1p. Canillo; 2p. Santa Coloma Church; 2p.50 Arms; 6p. Virgin of Meritxell. HORIZ: 3p. Andorra la Vella; 5p. Ordino.

14 Daffodils

1966. Pyrenean Flowers.
63	14	50c. blue and slate	55	1·10
64	-	1p. purple and brown	1·10	1·30
65	-	5p. blue and green	3·25	3·50
66	-	10p. slate and violet	1·70	2·75

DESIGNS: 1p. Carnation; 5p. Narcissus; 10p. Anemone (wrongly inscr "HELEBORUS CONI").

15 "Communications"

1972. Europa.
67	15	8p. multicoloured	£150	£140

16 Encamp Valley

1972. Tourist Views. Multicoloured.
68	1p. Type **16**		1·00	1·20
69	1p.50 La Massana		1·10	1·20
70	2p. Skis and snowscape, Pas de la Casa		2·10	2·40
71	5p. Lake Pessons (horiz)		2·30	2·40

17 Volleyball

1972. Olympic Games, Munich. Multicoloured.
72	2p. Type **17**		50	55
73	5p. Swimming (horiz)		70	75

18 St. Anthony's Auction

1972. Andorran Customs. Multicoloured.
74	1p. Type **18**		35	35
75	1p.50 "Les Caramelles" (choir)		35	35
76	2p. Nativity play (Christmas)		55	60
77	5p. Giant cigar (vert)		90	1·00
78	8p. Carved shrine, Meritxell (vert)		1·10	1·20
79	15p. "La Marratxa" (dance)		3·00	3·25

19 "Peoples of Europe"

1973. Europa.
80	**19**	2p. black, red and blue	55	60
81	-	8p. red, brown and black	1·70	1·90

DESIGN: 8p. Europa "Posthorn".

20 The Nativity

1973. Christmas. Frescoes from Meritxell Chapel. Multicoloured.
82	2p. Type **20**		55	60
83	5p. "Adoration of the Kings"		1·70	1·90

21 Virgin of Ordino

1974. Europa. Sculptures. Multicoloured.
84	2p. Type **21**		2·75	3·00
85	8p. Cross		4·00	4·25

22 Oak Cupboard and Shelves

1974. Arts and Crafts. Multicoloured.
86	10p. Type **22**		2·75	3·00
87	25p. Crown of the Virgin of the Roses		6·25	6·75

23 U.P.U. Monument, Berne

1974. Centenary of Universal Postal Union.
88	**23**	15p. multicoloured	3·50	3·75

24 The Nativity

1974. Christmas. Carvings from Meritxell Chapel. Multicoloured.
89	2p. Type **24**		1·10	1·20
90	5p. Adoration of the Kings		3·50	3·75

25 19th-century Postman and Church of St. John of Caselles

1975. "Espana 75" Int Stamp Exhibition, Madrid.
91	**25**	3p. multicoloured	55	60

26 Peasant with Knife

1975. Europa. 12th-century Romanesque Paintings from La Cortinada Church. Multicoloured.
92	3p. Type **26**		2·75	3·00
93	12p. Christ		5·75	6·25

27 Cathedral and Consecration Text

1975. 1100th Anniv of Consecration of Urgel Cathedral.
94	**27**	7p. multicoloured	3·50	3·75

28 The Nativity

1975. Christmas. Paintings from La Cortinada Church. Multicoloured.
95	3p. Type **28**		55	60
96	7p. Adoration of The Kings		1·10	1·20

29 Copper Cauldron

1976. Europa. Multicoloured.
97	3p. Type **29**		70	75
98	12p. Wooden marriage chest (horiz)		2·10	2·30

30 Slalom Skiing

1976. Olympic Games, Montreal. Multicoloured.
99	7p. Type **30**		70	75
100	15p. Canoeing (horiz)		2·10	2·30

31 The Nativity

1976. Christmas. Carvings from La Massana Church. Multicoloured.
101	3p. Type **31**		40	45
102	25p. Adoration of the Kings		2·50	2·75

32 Ansalonga

1977. Europa. Multicoloured.
103	3p. Type **32**		70	75
104	12p. Xuclar		2·10	2·30

33 Boundary Cross

1977. Christmas. Multicoloured.
105	5p. Type **33**		55	60
106	12p. St. Michael's Church, Engolasters		2·50	2·75

34 Map of Andorran Post Offices

1978. 50th Anniv of Spanish Post Offices. Sheet 105×149 mm containing T **34** and similar vert designs. Multicoloured.
MS107	5p. Type **34**; 10p. Postman delivering letter, 1923; 20p. Spanish Post Office, Andorra la Vella, 1928; 25p. Andorran arms	2·75	3·00

35 House of the Valleys

1978. Europa. Multicoloured.
108	5p. Type **35**		55	75
109	12p. Church of St. John of Caselles		1·40	2·30

36 Crown, Mitre and Crook

1978. 700th Anniv of Parity Treaties.
110	**36**	5p. multicoloured	85	1·50

37 Holy Family

1978. Christmas. Frescoes in St. Mary's Church, Encamp. Multicoloured.
111	5p. Type **37**		40	45
112	25p. Adoration of the Kings		95	1·10

38 Young Woman's Costume

1979. Local Costumes. Multicoloured.
113	3p. Type **38**		30	30
114	5p. Young man's costume		40	45
115	12p. Newly-weds		70	75

39 Old Mail Bus

1979. Europa.
116	**39**	5p. green & blue on yellow	70	75
117	-	12p. lilac and red on yellow	1·40	1·50

DESIGN: 12p. Pre-stamp letters.

40 Drawing of Boy and Girl

1979. International Year of the Child.
118	**40**	19p. blue, red and black	1·40	1·50

41 Agnus Dei, Santa Coloma Church

1979. Christmas. Multicoloured.
119	8p. Santa Coloma Church		40	45
120	25p. Type **41**		95	1·10

42 Pere d'Urg

1979. Bishops of Urgel, Co-princes of Andorra (1st series).
121	**42**	1p. blue and brown	30	30
122	-	5p. red and violet	40	45
123	-	13p. brown and green	85	90

DESIGNS: 5p. Joseph Caixal; 13p. Joan Benlloch. See also Nos. 137/8, 171, 182 and 189.

43 Antoni Fiter i Rossell

1980. Europa.

124	**43**	8p. brown, ochre and green	40	45
125	-	19p. black, green & dp grn	1·70	1·80

DESIGN: 19p. Francesc Cairat i Freixes.

44 Skiing

1980. Olympic Games, Moscow.

126	**44**	5p. turquoise, red and blk	30	30
127	-	8p. multicoloured	40	45
128	-	50p. multicoloured	1·50	1·70

DESIGNS: 8p. Boxing; 50p. Shooting.

45 Nativity

1980. Christmas. Multicoloured.

129	10p. Type **45**	40	45
130	22p. Epiphany	95	1·10

46 Santa Anna Dance

1981. Europa. Multicoloured.

131	12p. Type **46**	70	75
132	30p. Festival of the Virgin of Canolich	1·40	1·50

47 Militia Members

1981. 50th Anniv of People's Militia.

133	**47**	30p. green, grey and black	1·40	1·50

48 Handicapped Child learning to Write

1981. International Year of Disabled Persons.

134	**48**	50p. multicoloured	2·10	2·30

49 The Nativity

1981. Christmas. Carvings from Encamp Church. Multicoloured.

135	12p. Type **49**	70	75
136	30p. *The Adoration*	1·40	1·50

1981. Bishops of Urgel, Co-princes of Andorra (2nd series). As T **42**.

137	7p. purple and blue	40	45
138	20p. brown and green	95	1·10

DESIGNS: 7p. Salvador Casanas; 20p. Josep de Boltas.

50 Arms of Andorra

1982. With "PTA" under figure of value.

139	**50**	1p. mauve	30	30
140	**50**	3p. brown	30	30
141	**50**	7p. red	30	30
142	**50**	12p. red	30	30
143	**50**	15p. blue	40	45

144	**50**	20p. green	70	75
145	**50**	30p. red	70	75
146	**50**	50p. green (25×31 mm)	1·70	1·90
147	**50**	100p. blue (25×31 mm)	3·00	3·50

See also Nos. 203/6.

51 The New Reforms, 1866

1982. Europa. Multicoloured.

154	14p. Type **51**	95	1·10
155	33p. Reform of the Institutions, 1981	1·80	2·00

52 Footballers

1982. World Cup Football Championship, Spain. Multicoloured.

156	14p. Type **52**	1·40	1·50
157	33p. Tackle	2·75	3·00

53 Arms and 1929 1p. stamp

1982. National Stamp Exhibition.

158	**53**	14p. black and green	1·40	1·50

54 Spanish and French Permanent Delegations Buildings

1982. Anniversaries.

159	**54**	9p. brown and blue	40	45
160	-	23p. blue and brown	70	75
161	-	33p. black and green	1·10	1·20

DESIGNS—VERT: 9p. Type **54** (centenary of Permanent Delegations); 23p. *St. Francis feeding the Birds* (after Ciambue) (800th birth anniv of St. Francis of Assisi); 33p. Title page of *Relacio sobre la Vall de Andorra* (birth centenary of Tomas Junoy (writer)).

55 *Virgin and Child* (statue from Andorra la Vella Parish Church)

1982. Christmas. Multicoloured.

162	14p. Type **55**	70	75
163	33p. Children beating log with sticks	2·10	2·30

56 Building Romanesque Church

1983. Europa.

164	**56**	16p. green, purple & black	70	75
165	-	38p. brown, blue and black	2·10	2·30

DESIGN: 38p. 16th-century water mill.

57 *Lactarius sanguifluus*

1983. Nature Protection.

166	**57**	16p. multicoloured	70	75

58 Ballot Box on Map and Government Building

1983. 50th Anniv of Universal Suffrage in Andorra.

167	**58**	10p. multicoloured	70	75

59 Mgr. Cinto Verdaguer

1983. Centenary of Mgr. Cinto Verdaguer's Visit.

168	**59**	50p. multicoloured	2·10	2·30

60 Jaume Sansa Nequi

1983. Air. Jaume Sansa Nequi (Verger-Episcopal) Commemoration.

169	**60**	20p. deep brown & brown	70	75

61 Wall Painting, Church of San Cerni, Nagol

1983. Christmas.

170	**61**	16p. multicoloured	70	75

1983. Bishops of Urgel, Co-princes of Andorra (3rd series). As T **42**.

171	26p. brown and red	1·40	1·50

DESIGN: 26p. Joan Laguarda.

62 Ski Jumping

1984. Winter Olympic Games, Sarajevo.

172	**62**	16p. multicoloured	95	1·10

63 Exhibition and F.I.P. Emblems

1984. "Espana 84" Int Stamp Exhibition, Madrid.

173	**63**	26p. multicoloured	1·40	1·50

64 Bridge

1984. Europa.

174	**64**	16p. brown	70	75
175	**64**	38p. blue	2·10	2·30

65 Hurdling

1984. Olympic Games, Los Angeles.

176	**65**	40p. multicoloured	2·10	2·30

66 Common Morel

1984. Nature Protection.

177	**66**	11p. multicoloured	4·25	7·50

67 Pencil, Brush and Pen

1984. Pyrenean Cultures Centre, Andorra.

178	**67**	20p. multicoloured	85	90

68 The Holy Family (wood carvings)

1984. Christmas.

179	**68**	17p. multicoloured	70	75

69 Mossen Enric Marfany and Score

1985. Europa.

180	**69**	18p. green, purple & brown	95	1·10
181	-	45p. brown and green	1·80	2·00

DESIGN: 45p. Musician with viola (fresco detail, La Cortinada Church).

1985. Air. Bishops of Urgel, Co-princes of Andorra (4th series). As T **42**.

182	20p. brown and ochre	70	75

DESIGN: 20p. Ramon Iglesias.

70 Beefsteak Morel

1985. Nature Protection.

183	**70**	30p. multicoloured	1·40	1·50

71 Pal

1985

184	**71**	17p. deep blue and blue	70	75

72 Angels (St. Bartholomew's Chapel)

1985. Christmas.

185	**72**	17p. multicoloured	70	75

73 Scotch Bonnet

1986. Nature Protection.
186 **73** 30p. multicoloured 1·40 1·50

74 Sun, Rainbow, Lighthouse and Fish

1986. Europa. Each blue, red and green.
187 17p. Type **74** 1·40 1·50
188 45p. Sun and trees on rocks 2·10 2·30

1986. Bishops of Urgel, Co-princes of Andorra (5th series). As T **42**.
189 35p. blue and brown 1·40 1·50
DESIGN: 35p. Justi Guitart.

75 Bell of St. Roma's Chapel, Les Bons

1986. Christmas.
190 **75** 19p. multicoloured 70 75

76 Arms

1987. Meeting of Co-princes.
191 **76** 48p. multicoloured 1·40 1·50

77 Interior of Chapel

1987. Europa. Meritxell Chapel.
192 **77** 19p. brown and blue 70 75
193 - 48p. blue and brown 1·40 1·50
DESIGN: 48p. Exterior of Chapel.

78 Emblem and House of Valleys

1987. Olympic Games, Barcelona (1992). Sheet 122×86 mm containing T **78** and similar horiz designs. Multicoloured.
MS194 20p. Type **78**; 50p. Torch carrier and St. Michael's Chapel, Fontaneda, bell tower 5·50 6·00

79 Cep

1987. Nature Protection.
195 **79** 100p. multicoloured 3·50 3·75

80 Extract from *Doctrina Pueril* by Ramon Llull

1987. Christmas.
196 **80** 20p. multicoloured 70 75

81 Copper Lance Heads

1988. Archaeology.
197 **81** 50p. multicoloured 1·70 1·80

82 Early 20th-century Trader and Pack Mules

1988. Europa. Communications. Each blue and red.
198 20p. Ancient road, Les Bons 70 75
199 45p. Type **82** 2·10 2·30

83 Pyrenean Mountain Dog

1988. Nature Protection.
200 **83** 20p. multicoloured 1·40 1·50

84 Commemorative Coin

1988. 700th Anniv of Second Parity Treaty.
201 **84** 20p. black, grey and brown 70 75

85 Church of St. John of Caselles

1988. Christmas.
202 **85** 20p. multicoloured 70 75

1988. As T **50** but without "PTA" under figure of value.
203 20p. green 70 75
204 50p. green (25×31 mm) 2·10 2·30
205 100p. blue (25×31 mm) 3·75 4·25
206 500p. brown (25×31 mm) 12·50 13·50

86 Leap-frog

1989. Europa. Children's Games. Multicoloured.
210 20p. Type **86** 1·40 1·50
211 45p. Girl trying to pull child from grip of other children (horiz) 2·10 2·30

87 St. Roma's Chapel, Les Bons

1989
212 **87** 50p. black, green and blue 2·10 2·30

88 Anniversary Emblem

1989. 125th Anniv of International Red Cross.
213 **88** 20p. multicoloured 70 75

89 "Virgin Mary" (detail of altarpiece, Les Escaldes Church)

1989. Christmas.
214 **89** 20p. multicoloured 70 75

90 Old French and Spanish Post Offices, Andorra La Vella

1990. Europa. Post Office Buildings. Multicoloured.
215 20p. Type **90** 70 75
216 50p. Modern Spanish post office, Andorra La Vella (vert) 2·10 2·30

91 *Gomphidius rutilus*

1990. Nature Protection.
217 **91** 45p. multicoloured 2·10 2·30

92 Plandolit House

1990
218 **92** 20p. brown and yellow 70 75

93 Angel, La Massana Church

1990. Christmas.
219 **93** 25p. brown, stone and red 85 90

94 Throwing the Discus

95 "Olympus 1" Satellite

1991. European Small States' Games. Multicoloured.
220 25p. Type **94** 95 1·10
221 45p. High jumping and running 1·80 2·00

1991. Europa. Europe in Space. Multicoloured.
222 25p. Type **95** 2·10 2·30
223 55p. Close-up of "Olympus I" telecommunications satellite (horiz) 3·50 3·75

96 Parasol Mushroom

1991. Nature Protection.
224 **96** 45p. multicoloured 2·10 2·30

97 *Virgin of the Three Hands* (detail of triptych in Meritxell Chapel by Maria Assumpta Ortado i Maimo)

1991. Christmas.
225 **97** 25p. multicoloured 1·40 1·50

98 Woman fetching Water from Public Tap

1992
226 **98** 25p. multicoloured 1·40 1·50

99 *Santa Maria*

1992. Europa. 500th Anniv of Discovery of America by Columbus.
227 **99** 27p. multicoloured 2·10 2·30
228 - 45p. brown, red and orange 2·75 3·00
DESIGN—HORIZ: 45p. Engraving of King Ferdinand from map sent by Columbus to Ferdinand and Queen Isabella the Catholic.

100 White-water Canoeing

1992. Olympic Games, Barcelona.
229 **100** 27p. multicoloured 1·40 1·50

101 Benz Velo, 1894 and Sedanca de ville, 1920s

1992. National Motor Car Museum, Encamp.
230 **101** 27p. multicoloured 1·40 1·50

102 *Nativity* (Fra Angelico)

1992. Christmas.
231 **102** 27p. multicoloured 1·40 1·50

103 Chanterelle

1993. Nature Protection.
232 **103** 28p. multicoloured 1·40 1·50

104 *Upstream* (J. A. Morrison)

1993. Europa. Contemporary Art. Multicoloured.
233 28p. Type **104** 1·40 1·50
234 45p. *Ritme* (Angel Calvente) (vert) 2·10 2·30

105 Society Emblem on National Colours

1993. 25th Anniv of Andorran Arts and Letters Circle.
235 **105** 28p. multicoloured 1·40 1·50

106 Illuminated "P" (Galceran de Vilanova Missal)

1993. Christmas.
236 **106** 28p. multicoloured 1·40 1·50

107 National Colours

1994. First Anniv of New Constitution. Sheet 105×78 mm.
MS237 **107** 29p. multicoloured 2·10 2·30

108 Sir Alexander Fleming and Penicillin

1994. Europa. Discoveries.
238 **108** 29p. multicoloured 1·40 1·50
239 – 55p. blue and black 2·75 3·00
DESIGN: 55p. Test tube and AIDS virus.

109 *Hygrophorus gliocyclus*

1994. Nature Protection.
240 **109** 29p. multicoloured 1·40 1·50

110 *Madonna and Child* (anon)

1994. Christmas.
241 **110** 29p. multicoloured 1·40 1·50

111 Madriu Valley (south)

1995. European Nature Conservation Year. Multicoloured.
242 30p. Type **111** 85 90
243 60p. Madriu Valley (north) 1·90 2·10

112 Sun, Dove and Barbed Wire

1995. Europa. Peace and Freedom.
244 **112** 60p. green, orange & blk 2·10 2·30

113 *Flight into Egypt* (altarpiece, St. Mark and St. Mary Church, Encamp)

1995. Christmas.
245 **113** 30p. multicoloured 1·40 1·50

114 Palace of Europe, Strasbourg

1995. Admission of Andorra to Council of Europe.
246 **114** 30p. multicoloured 1·40 1·50

115 *Ramaria aurea*

1996. Nature Protection. Multicoloured.
247 30p. Type **115** 1·40 1·50
248 60p. Black truffles 2·30 2·50

116 Isabelle Sandy (writer)

1996. Europa. Famous Women.
249 **116** 60p. multicoloured 2·75 3·00

117 Old Iron

1996. International Museums Day.
250 **117** 60p. multicoloured 2·10 2·30

118 *The Annunciation* (altarpiece, St. Eulalia's Church, Encamp)

1996. Christmas.
251 **118** 30p. multicoloured 1·40 1·50

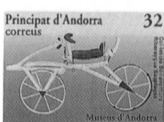

119 Drais Velocipede, 1818

1997. Bicycle Museum (1st series). Multicoloured.
252 32p. Type **119** 95 1·10
253 65p. Michaux velocipede, 1861 1·90 2·10
See also Nos. 258/9 and 264/5.

120 The Bear and The Smugglers

1997. Europa. Tales and Legends.
254 **120** 65p. multicoloured 2·75 3·00

121 Dove and Cultural Symbols

1997. National UNESCO Commission.
255 **121** 32p. multicoloured 70 75

122 Catalan Crib Figure

1997. Christmas.
256 **122** 32p. multicoloured 70 75

123 Giant Slalom

1998. Winter Olympic Games, Nagano, Japan.
257 **123** 35p. multicoloured 70 75

1998. Bicycle Museum (2nd series). As T **119**. Multicoloured.
258 35p. Kangaroo bicycle, Great Britain, 1878 95 1·10
259 70p. The Swallow, France, 1889 1·90 2·10

124 Harlequins of Canillo

1998. Europa. National Festivals.
260 **124** 70p. multicoloured 2·10 2·30

125 Front Page of First Edition and Landscape

1998. 250th Anniv of *Manual Digest*.
261 **125** 35p. multicoloured 70 75

126 Emblem

1998. Inauguration of Postal Museum.
262 **126** 70p. violet and yellow 2·10 2·30

127 St. Lucia Fair

1998. Christmas.
263 **127** 35p. multicoloured 1·40 1·50

1999. Bicycle Museum (3rd series). As T **119**. Multicoloured.
264 35p. Salvo tricycle, 1878 (vert) 95 1·10
265 70p. Rudge tricycle, Coventry, England 1·90 2·10

128 Mules

1999. Postal History.
266 **128** 35p. black and brown 1·40 1·50

129 Palace of Human Rights, Strasbourg

1999. 50th Anniv of Council of Europe.
267 **129** 35p. multicoloured 1·40 1·50

130 Vall d'Incles National Park, Canillo

1999. Europa. Parks and Gardens.
268 **130** 70p. multicoloured 2·10 2·30

131 Rull House, Sispony

1999
269 **131** 35p. multicoloured 1·40 1·50

132 Angel (detail of altarpiece, St. Serni's Church, Canillo)

1999. Christmas.
270 **132** 35p. brown and light brown 1·40 1·50

133 Santa
Coloma Church

1999. European Heritage.
271 **133** 35p. multicoloured · 1·40 1·50

134 "Building
Europe"

2000. Europa.
272 **134** 70p. multicoloured · 2·75 3·00

135 Angonella Lakes,
Ordino

2000
273 **135** 35p. multicoloured · 1·40 1·50

136 Casa Lacruz

2000. 131st Birth Anniv of Josep Cadafalch (architect).
274 **136** 35p. multicoloured · 1·40 1·50

137 Dinner
Service

2000. D'Areny-Plandolit Museum.
275 **137** 70p. multicoloured · 2·10 2·30

138 Hurdling

2000. Olympic Games, Sydney.
276 **138** 70p. multicoloured · 2·10 2·30

139 United Nations
Headquarters, Strasbourg

2000. 50th Anniv of United Nations Declaration of
Human Rights.
277 **139** 70p. multicoloured · 2·10 2·30

140 Gradual, St.
Roma, Les Bons

2000. 25th Anniv of the National Archives.
278 **140** 35p. multicoloured · 70 75

141 *Quadre de les
Animes* (Joan
Casanovas)

2000. Christmas.
279 **141** 35p. multicoloured · 70 75

142 Rec del Sola

2001. Natural Heritage.
280 **142** 40p. multicoloured · 1·20 1·40

143 Roc del Metge
(thermal spring),
Escaldes-Engordany

2001. Europa. Water Resources.
281 **143** 75p. multicoloured · 2·10 2·30

144 Casa Palau,
Sant

2001
282 **144** 75p. multicoloured · 2·10 2·30

145 Part of
Sanctuary, Julia
de Loria Meritxell

2001. 25th Anniv of Chapel of Our Lady, Meritxell.
283 **145** 40p. multicoloured · 1·40 1·50

146 Building

2001. Tenth Anniv of National Auditorium, Ordino.
284 **146** 75p. multicoloured · 2·10 2·30

147 Angel (detail of
altarpiece, Church of St.
John of Caselles)

2001. Christmas.
285 **147** 40p. multicoloured · 1·40 1·50

148 State
Arms

2002
286 **148** 25c. orange · 70 75
286a **148** 27c. blue · 70 75
286b **148** 28c. blue · 85 90
286c **148** 29c. sepia · 85 90
286d **148** 30c. carmine · 85 90
287 **148** 50c. red · 1·40 1·50
288 **148** 52c. yellow · 1·50 1·70
289 **148** 53c. green · 1·50 1·70
289a **148** 57c. blue · 1·70 1·80
289b **148** 58c. black · 1·70 1·80
290 **148** 77c. orange · 2·20 2·40
291 **148** 78c. magenta · 2·20 2·40

149 Alpine Accentor
(*Prunella collaris*)

2002. Native Birds. Multicoloured.
300 25c. Type **149** · 95 1·10
301 50c. Snow finch (*Montifringilla
nivalis*) · 1·90 2·10

150 Emblem

2002. International Year of the Mountain.
302 **150** 50c. multicoloured · 2·10 2·30

151 Tightrope Walker

2002. Europa. Circus.
303 **151** 50c. multicoloured · 14·00 15·00

152 Casa Fusile,
Escaldes-
Engordany

2002. Architectural Heritage. Multicoloured.
304 €1.80 Type **152** · 5·50 6·00
305 €2.10 Farga Rossell Iron Mu-
seum, La Massana · 6·25 6·75

153 Pinette
Minim

2002. History of the Motor Car (1st series). Multicoloured.
306 25c. Type **153** · 95 1·10
307 50c. Rolls Royce Silver Wraith · 1·90 2·10
See also Nos. 317/18 and 324/5.

154 Placa Benlloch,
Areny-Plandolit

2002. Christmas.
308 **154** 25c. multicoloured · 1·40 1·50

155 Painted
Medallion

2002. Cultural Heritage. Romanesque Murals from Santa
Coloma Church, Andorra la Vella.. Multicoloured.
309 25c. Type **155** · 70 75

310 50c. Part of damaged fresco
showing seated figure · 1·40 1·50
311 75c. Frieze · 2·10 2·30

156 Sassanat Bridge

2003
312 **156** 26c. multicoloured · 1·40 1·50

157 State Arms

2003. Tenth Anniv of Constitution.
313 **157** 76c. multicoloured · 2·75 3·00

158 Man
drinking, Donkey
and Market Stalls

2003. Europa. Poster Art.
314 **158** 76c. multicoloured · 2·75 3·00

159 Northern
Wheatear
(*Oenanthe
oenanthe*)

2003. Native Birds.
315 **159** 50c. multicoloured · 1·40 1·50

160 Multicoloured Stripes

2003. Tenth Anniv of Andorras' Membership of United
Nations.
316 **160** 76c. multicoloured · 2·75 3·00

161 Carter (1908)

2003. History of the Motor Car (2nd series).
Multicoloured.
317 51c. Type **161** · 1·70 1·80
318 76c. Peugeot (1928) (horiz) · 2·50 2·75

162 Roadside Cross,
Andorra la Vella

2003. Christmas.
319 **162** 26c. multicoloured · 1·40 1·50

163 *Fira del Bestiar*
(Joaquim Mir)

2004
320 **163** 27c. multicoloured 1·10 1·20

164 *L'Escorxador*
(Joaquim Mir)

2004
321 **164** 52c. multicoloured 1·90 2·10

165 Coaches and
Skiers in Snow

2004. Europa. Holidays.
322 **165** 77c. black 2·75 3·00

166 Chaffinch (*Fringilla
coelebs*)

2004. Native Birds.
323 **166** 27c. multicoloured 1·10 1·20

167 Simca 508 C (1939)

2004. History of the Motor Car (3rd series).
324 €1.90 Type **167** 6·50 7·25
325 €2.19 Messerschmitt KR 1
 (1955) 7·25 8·00

168 Map showing
Postal Districts

2004. Introduction of Postal Codes.
326 **168** 52c. orange, magenta
 and black 2·10 2·30

169 Stars and Flag as
Jigsaw Pieces

2004. Tenth Anniv of Entry into Council of Europe.
327 **169** 52c. multicoloured 2·10 2·30

170 Nativity

2004. Christmas.
328 **170** 27c. multicoloured 1·10 1·20

171 Madriu-
Perafita-Claror
Valley

2005. UNESCO World Heritage Site.
329 **171** 28c. multicoloured 1·10 1·20

172 *Endless* (Mark Brusse)

2005
330 **172** 53c. multicoloured 2·20 2·40

174 Cyclist

2005. Europa. Gastronomy.
331 **173** 78c. multicoloured 3·00 3·50

174 Cyclist

2005. Small States of Europe Games.
332 **174** €1.95 brown and black 5·50 6·00

175 Shrine

2005. 25th Anniv of Caritas Andorra (humanitarian
organization).
333 **175** 28c. multicoloured 1·10 1·20

176 Dipper (*Cinclus cinclus*)

2005. Native Birds.
334 **176** €2.21 multicoloured 6·25 6·75

177 *The Nativity* (Sergei
Mas)

2005. Christmas.
335 **177** 28c. multicoloured 1·10 1·20

178 Skiers

2006. Winter Olympic Games, Turin.
336 **178** 29c. multicoloured 1·40 1·50

179 *Ruta del Hierro*
(sculpture) (Satora
Sato)

2006. Cultural Heritage.
337 **179** 78c. multicoloured 2·50 2·75

180 Stylized People of
Many Colours and Abilities

2006. Europa. Integration.
338 **180** 57c. multicoloured 2·20 2·40

181 Grey Partridge (*Perdix
perdix*)

2006. Natural Heritage.
339 **181** €2.39 multicoloured 8·25 9·00

182 Scrabble Letters

2006. Fulbright Scholarships.
340 **182** 57c. multicoloured 2·20 2·40

183 Head
Containing World
Map

2006. 60th Anniv of UNESCO and 10th Anniv of CNAU.
341 **183** €2.33 multicoloured 8·00 8·75

184 Nativity

2006. Christmas.
342 **184** 29c. multicoloured 1·20 1·20

185 *Encamp 1994*
(F. Galobardes)

2007. Cultural Heritage.
343 **185** 30c. multicoloured 1·20 1·20

186 Doves and
Emblem

2007. Europa. Centenary of Scouting.
344 **186** 58c. multicoloured 2·30 2·50

187 *La Familia
Jordino* (sculpture
by Rachid
Khimoune)

2007. Cultural Heritage. The Iron Route (historical trail).
345 **187** €2.43 multicoloured 8·50 9·00

188 Capercaillie (*Tetrao
urogallus*)

2007. Natural Heritage.
346 **188** €2.49 multicoloured 8·75 9·25

189 *Casa de la Vall* (Francesc
Galobardes)

2007. Cultural Heritage.
347 **189** 78c. multicoloured 3·00 3·25

190 Stylized Figures

2007. 25th Anniv of Andorra Red Cross.
348 **190** 30c. carmine and black 1·20 1·20

191 *Lamb kneeling before
Infant Jesus* (painting by
Sergi Mas)

2007. Christmas.
349 **191** 30c. multicoloured 1·20 1·20

192 *Gypaetus barbatus*
(Lammergeier or bearded
vulture)

2008. Natural Heritage.
350 **192** 31c. multicoloured 1·40 1·50

193 *Carro Vortiu*
(sculpture by Jordi
Casamajor)

2008. Cultural Heritage.
351 **193** 60c. multicoloured 2·50 2·75

194 Flag and Ballot
Box

2008. 15th Anniv of Constitution.
352 **194** 31c. multicoloured 1·80 2·10

195 Envelope

2008. Europa. The Letter.
353 **195** 60c. blue and black 2·75 3·00

196 Adam, Eve and Graph

2008. 25th Anniv of National Science Society.
354 **196** 78c. blue and black 3·75 4·00

197 Fluvi (exhibition mascot)

2008. Zaragoza 2008 International Water and Sustainable Development Exhibition. Sheet 105×79 mm.
MS355 **197** €2.60 multicoloured 10·50 11·50

198 Games Emblem

2008. Olympic Games, Beijing.
356 **198** 60c. multicoloured 2·75 3·00

199 Vall del Comapedrosa

2008. Natural Heritage.
357 **199** €2.44 multicoloured 9·25 10·00

200 Sispony (Carme Massana)

2008. Cultural Heritage.
358 **200** 31c. multicoloured 1·60 1·80

201 Midnight Mass

2008. Christmas.
359 **201** 31c. multicoloured 1·60 1·80

202 Narcissus

2009. Natural Heritage. Flora. Self adhesive.
360 **202** 32c. multicoloured 1·60 1·80

203 '25'

2009. 25th Anniv of Escola Andorrana.
361 **203** 62c. multicoloured 2·75 3·00

204 Merce Rodoreda

2009. Merce Rodoreda (Catalan writer) Commemoration.
362 **204** 78c. black 3·50 3·75

205 Emblem

2009. 60th Anniv of Council of Europe.
363 **205** 32c. multicoloured 1·60 1·80

206 Figures and Stars

2009. Europa. Astronomy.
364 **206** 62c. multicoloured 2·75 3·00

207 Bridge Strut

2009. Pont de Madrid (bridge designed by Carlos Fernandez Casado). Sheet 106×80 mm.
MS365 **207** €2.70 multicoloured 12·00 13·00

208 Eurasian Sparrowhawk

2009. Natural Heritage. Accipiter nisus.
366 **208** €2.47 multicoloured 9·25 10·00

209 *El Tarter* (Francesc Galobardes)

2009. Cultural Heritage. Multicoloured.
367 62c. Type **209** 2·75 3·00
368 78c. *Contrallum a Canillo* (Carme Massana) 3·50 3·75

210 Three Wise Men as Musicians (homage to National Classical Orchestra of Andorra by Sergei Mas)

2009. Christmas
369 **210** 32c. multicoloured 1·30 1·50

211 Iris

2010. Flora. Self-adhesive.
370 **211** 34c. multicoloured 1·70 1·90

212 Jacint Verdaguer

2010. 165th Birth Anniv of Jacint Verdaguer i Santaló (Catalan poet).
371 **212** 64c. black 2·75 3·00

213 Central Section

2010. Pont de Paris (bridge designed by Carlos Fernandez Casado).
372 **213** €2.75 multicoloured 12·00 13·00

214 Boy, Book and Fairy

2010. Europa
373 **214** 64c. multicoloured 2·75 3·00

215 Circle of Flame

2010. Cultural Heritage
374 **215** 64c. multicoloured 3·25 3·50

216 Emblem and Globe

2010. World Cup Football Championship, South Africa
375 **216** 78c. multicoloured 4·00 4·25

217 Multicoloured Ribbon

2010. Civic Values. Recycling
376 **217** €2.49 multicoloured 11·50 12·00

218 Mural (by Josep Oromi), Sant Joan de Sispony Church

2010. Christmas
377 **218** 34c. multicoloured 1·90 2·10

219 Capital of Culture Year Emblem

2011. Escaldes-Engordany, Capital of Catalan Culture
378 **219** 35c. multicoloured 2·00 2·20

220 Miquel Marti i Pol

2011. Personalities. Miquel Marti i Pol (poet) Commemoration
379 **220** 65c. black 3·25 3·50

221 Sorobilles Forest

2011. Europa. Forests
380 **221** 65c. multicoloured 4·00 4·25

222 Casa Farras

2011. Architecture. Casa Farras
381 **222** 80c. multicoloured 4·00 4·25

223 Decorated Stonework (Pedro Clau Sant Esteve)

2011. Cultural Heritage
382 **223** €2.55 multicoloured 12·00 13·00

224 Untitled (Helena Guàrdia)

2011. Venice Bienniale. Multicoloured.
383 80c. Type **224** 4·00 4·25
384 €2.55 Untitled (Francisco Sanchez) 11·00 12·00

225 Female and Masculine Figure

2011. Civic Values. Equality

385	**225**	80c. multicoloured	4·00	4·25

226 Mailbox

2011. America. Mailboxes

386	**226**	80c. multicoloured	4·00	4·25

227 Christmas Tree Baubles

2011. Christmas

387	**227**	35c. multicoloured	2·00	2·10

EXPRESS LETTER STAMPS

1928. Express Letter stamp of Spain optd **CORREOS ANDORRA**.

E15	**E53**	20c. red	70·00	90·00

E4 Lammergeier over Pyrenees

1929

E41	**E4**	20c. red	8·00	10·50

E12 Eurasian Red Squirrel (after Durer) and Arms

1949

E54	**E12**	25c. red	7·00	8·00

Pt. 9, Pt. 12

ANGOLA

Republic of Southern Africa. Independent of Portugal since 11 November 1975.

1870. 1000 reis = 1 milreis.
1913. 100 centavos = 1 escudo.
1932. 100 centavos = 1 angolar.
1954. 100 centavos = 1 escudo.
1977. 100 lweis = 1 kwanza.

1870. "Crown" key-type inscr "ANGOLA".

7	P	5r. black	3·50	2·10
17	P	10r. yellow	25·00	15·00
31	P	10r. green	9·75	5·50
9	P	20r. bistre	2·75	2·30
26	P	20r. red	23·00	16·00
10	P	25r. red	14·00	9·50
27	P	25r. purple	16·00	5·75
19b	P	40r. blue	£275	£190
33	P	40r. yellow	46·00	7·00
12	P	50r. green	65·00	17·00
30	P	50r. blue	50·00	10·50
21a	P	100r. lilac	6·25	3·75
22	P	200r. orange	5·25	2·30
23a	P	300r. brown	6·25	3·75

1886. "Embossed" key-type inscr "PROVINCIA DE ANGOLA".

35	Q	5r. black	20·00	8·00
36	Q	10r. green	20·00	8·00
37	Q	20r. red	29·00	16·00
39	Q	25r. mauve	20·00	5·25
40	Q	40r. brown	24·00	9·25
41	Q	50r. blue	30·00	5·75
42	Q	100r. brown	46·00	12·50
43	Q	200r. violet	55·00	17·00
44	Q	300r. orange	55·00	21·00

1894. "Figures" key-type inscr "ANGOLA".

49	R	5r. orange	4·00	1·60
62	R	10r. mauve	5·25	3·25
63	R	15r. brown	7·00	2·75
54	R	20r. lavender	8·00	3·50
74	R	25r. green	5·75	2·50
66	R	50r. blue	7·50	3·50
67	R	75r. red	14·00	11·50
68	R	80r. green	20·00	10·50
69	R	100r. brown on buff	20·00	10·50
70	R	150r. red on rose	25·00	18·00
77	R	200r. blue on blue	32·00	17·00
78	R	300r. blue on brown	32·00	17·00

1894. No. N51 with circular surch **CORREIOS DE ANGOLA 25 REIS**.

79b	V	25r. on 2½r. brown	80·00	70·00

1898. "King Carlos" key-type inscr "ANGOLA".

80	S	2½r. grey	70	55
81	S	5r. orange	70	55
82	S	10r. green	70	55
83	S	15r. brown	4·00	2·10
142	S	15r. green	2·00	1·80
84	S	20r. lilac	80	70
85	S	25r. green	2·10	80
143	S	25r. red	90	55
86	S	50r. blue	3·75	1·10
144	S	50r. brown	9·75	5·75
145	S	65r. blue	10·50	7·00
87	S	75r. red	12·50	8·00
146	S	75r. purple	4·00	2·50
88	S	80r. mauve	11·50	4·00
89	S	100r. blue on blue	2·50	1·60
147	S	115r. brown on pink	16·00	9·75
148	S	130r. brown on yellow	16·00	9·75
90	S	150r. brown on buff	12·50	7·50
91	S	200r. purple on pink	7·00	2·30
92	S	300r. blue on pink	8·00	7·00
149	S	400r. blue on yellow	7·00	4·50
93	S	500r. black on blue	8·00	7·00
94	S	700r. mauve on yellow	39·00	25·00

1902. "Embossed", "Figures" and "Newspaper" key-types of Angola surch.

98	R	65r. on 5r. orange	11·50	8·50
100	R	65r. on 10r. mauve	15·00	8·50
102	R	65r. on 20r. violet	13·50	8·50
104	R	65r. on 25r. green	14·00	10·50
95	Q	65r. on 40r. brown	14·00	8·50
96	Q	65r. on 300r. orange	14·00	8·50
106	R	115r. on 10r. green	11·50	8·00
109	R	115r. on 80r. green	20·00	11·50
111	R	115r. on 100r. brn on buff	16·00	10·50
113	R	115r. on 150r. red on rose	21·00	12·50
108	R	115r. on 200r. violet	11·50	8·00
120	R	130r. on 15r. brown	9·25	6·25
116	Q	130r. on 50r. blue	16·00	6·25
124	R	130r. on 75r. red	11·50	10·50
118	Q	130r. on 100r. brown	10·50	6·25
126	R	130r. on 300r. blue on brn	29·00	18·00
136	V	400r. on 2½r. brown	2·30	2·00
127	Q	400r. on 5r. black	23·00	17·00
128	Q	400r. on 20r. red	£110	70·00
130	Q	400r. on 25r. mauve	28·00	14·00
131	R	400r. on 50r. pale blue	10·50	7·00
133	R	400r. on 200r. blue on blue	11·50	9·75

1902. "King Carlos" key-type of Angola optd **PROVISORIO**.

138	S	15r. brown	2·75	1·80
139	S	25r. green	2·30	1·00
140	S	50r. blue	4·75	2·30
141	S	75r. red	8·00	6·25

1905. No. 145 surch **50 REIS** and bar.

150		50r. on 65r. blue	7·00	3·75

1911. "King Carlos" key-type optd **REPUBLICA**.

151		2½r. grey	55	45
152		5r. orange	55	45
153		10r. green	55	45
154		15r. green	80	70
155		20r. lilac	85	75
156		25r. red	85	75
157		50r. brown	3·25	4·00
232		50r. blue (No. 140)	2·50	2·10
224		75r. purple	2·50	1·30
234		75r. red (No. 141)	5·75	4·25
225		100r. blue on blue	4·00	3·75
160		115r. brown on pink	4·00	2·30
161		130r. brown on yellow	4·00	2·30
226		200r. purple on pink	2·75	1·80
163		400r. blue on yellow	4·50	2·00
164		500r. black on blue	4·50	2·30
165		700r. mauve on yellow	4·50	2·50

1912. "King Manoel" key-type inscr "ANGOLA" optd **REPUBLICA**.

166	T	2½r. lilac	70	45
167	T	5r. black	70	45
168	T	10r. green	70	45
169	T	20r. red	70	45
170	T	25r. brown	70	45
171	T	50r. blue	1·80	1·40
172	T	75r. brown	2·10	1·80
173	T	100r. brown on green	4·00	2·30
174	T	200r. green on pink	4·00	2·30
175	T	300r. black on blue	4·00	2·30

1912. "King Carlos" key-type of Angola optd **REPUBLICA** and surch.

176	S	2½ on 15r. green	5·75	3·25
177	S	5 on 15r. green	6·25	3·25
178	S	10 on 15r. green	6·25	3·25
179	S	25 on 75r. red (No. 141)	90·00	65·00
180	S	25 on 75r. purple	6·25	5·75

1913. Surch **REPUBLICA ANGOLA** and value in figures on "Vasco da Gama" issues of (a) Portuguese Colonies.

181		¼c. on 2½r. green	1·30	90
182		½c. on 5r. red	1·30	90
183		1c. on 10r. purple	1·30	90
184		2½c. on 25r. green	1·30	90
185		5c. on 50r. blue	1·30	90
186		7½c. on 75r. brown	7·50	6·25
187		10c. on 100r. brown	2·75	1·80
188		15c. on 150r. bistre	2·75	2·30

(b) Macao.

189		¼c. on ½a. green	2·75	2·20
190		½c. on 1a. red	2·75	2·20
191		1c. on 2a. purple	2·75	2·20
192		2½c. on 4a. green	2·30	1·60
193		5c. on 8a. blue	2·30	1·60
194		7½c. on 12a. brown	9·25	5·75
195		10c. on 16a. brown	3·50	2·50
196		15c. on 24a. bistre	4·25	2·50

(c) Timor.

197		¼c. on ½a. green	2·75	2·20
198		½c. on 1a. red	2·75	2·20
199		1c. on 2a. purple	2·75	2·20
200		2½c. on 4a. green	2·30	1·60
201		5c. on 8a. blue	2·30	1·60
202		7½c. on 12a. brown	9·25	5·75
203		10c. on 16a. brown	3·50	2·50
204		15c. on 24a. bistre	4·25	2·50

1914. "Ceres" key-type inscr "ANGOLA".

296	U	¼c. olive	40	35
297	U	½c. black	40	35
298	U	1c. green	40	35
299	U	1½c. brown	40	35
300	U	2c. red	40	35
301	U	2c. grey	70	55
281	U	2½c. violet	40	35
303	U	3c. orange	35	30
304	U	4c. red	35	30
305	U	4½c. grey	35	30
284a	U	5c. blue	40	35
307	U	6c. mauve	35	30
308	U	7c. blue	35	30
309	U	7½c. brown	45	40
288	U	8c. grey	45	40
311	U	10c. brown	40	35
312	U	12c. brown	70	55
313	U	12c. green	70	55
291	U	15c. purple	40	35
314	U	15c. pink	40	35
315	U	20c. green	2·00	1·70
316	U	24c. blue	1·70	1·40
317	U	25c. brown	1·70	1·40
217	U	30c. brown on green	2·75	2·50
318	U	30c. green	70	55
218	U	40c. brown on pink	2·75	2·50
319	U	40c. blue	1·40	70
219	U	50c. orange on pink	11·50	8·00
320	U	50c. purple	1·40	70
321	U	60c. blue	1·70	1·00
322	U	60c. red	£100	60·00
322a	U	80c. pink	2·10	1·00
220	U	1e. green on blue	8·50	5·25
323	U	1e. red	2·10	1·00
325	U	1e. blue	3·50	2·10
326	U	2e. purple	2·75	1·40
327	U	5e. brown	18·00	15·00
328	U	10e. pink	38·00	31·00
329	U	20e. green	£110	80·00

1914. Provisional stamps of 1902 optd **REPUBLICA**.

233	S	50r. on 65r. blue	5·50	3·75
256	R	115r. on 10r. green	2·40	2·30
258	R	115r. on 80r. green	2·00	1·90
261	R	115r. on 100r. brn on buff	2·50	2·10
263	R	115r. on 150r. red on rose	1·90	1·90

266	Q	115r. on 200r. violet	2·75	2·30
267	R	130r. on 15r. brown	2·00	1·90
246	Q	130r. on 50r. blue	32·00	32·00
269	R	130r. on 75r. red	3·75	2·30
273	Q	130r. on 100r. brown	2·30	1·90
274	R	130r. on 300r. blue on brn	2·30	2·30
254	V	400r. on 2½r. brown	1·10	85

1919. Stamps of 1911, 1912 or 1914 surch.

331	T	½c. on 75r. brown	1·60	1·30
332	S	½c. on 75r. purple	1·80	1·60
336	S	1c. on 50r. brown	1·80	1·60
334	S	2½c. on 100r. brown on grn	3·00	2·30
335	S	2½c. on 100r. blue on blue	2·30	1·70
337	S	4c. on 130r. brown on yell	2·50	1·80
339	U	$04 on 15c. purple	2·50	1·80
340	U	$04 on 15c. pink	25·00	
341	U	$00.5 on 75r. brown	1·80	1·60
342	U	$00.5 on 7½c. brown	2·50	2·10

1925. Nos. 136 and 133 surch **Republica 40 C**.

343	R	40c. on 400r. on 200r. blue on blue	1·00	1·00
345	V	40c. on 400r. on 2½r. brn	1·50	1·10

1931. "Ceres" key-type of Angola surch.

347	U	50c. on 60c. red	2·30	2·00
348	U	70c. on 80c. pink	4·50	3·50
349	U	70c. on 1e. blue	4·25	3·50
350	U	1e.40 on 2e. purple	2·75	2·10

17 Ceres

1932

351	17	1c. brown	35	25
352	17	5c. sepia	35	35
353	17	10c. mauve	35	35
354	17	15c. black	35	35
355	17	20c. grey	35	35
356	17	30c. green	35	35
357	17	35c. green	9·25	4·25
358	17	40c. red	45	35
359	17	45c. blue	1·70	1·40
360	17	50c. brown	35	25
361	17	60c. olive	1·10	35
362	17	70c. brown	1·10	35
363	17	80c. green	70	25
364	17	85c. red	5·75	2·50
365	17	1a. red	1·10	35
366	17	1a.40 blue	11·50	3·50
367	17	1a.75 blue	20·00	5·25
368	17	2a. mauve	5·75	55
369	17	5a. green	11·50	1·80
370	17	10a. brown	23·00	5·75
371	17	20a. orange	55·00	5·75

1934. Surch.

380		5c. on 80c. green (A)	1·00	55
419		5c. on 80c. green (B)	1·00	55
413		10c. on 45c. blue	2·00	1·30
381		10c. on 80c. green	1·80	90
414		15c. on 45c. blue	2·00	1·30
382		15c. on 80c. green	2·50	90
415		20c. on 85c. red	2·00	1·30
374		30c. on 1a.40 blue	3·75	2·75
416		35c. on 85c. red	2·00	1·30
417		50c. on 1a.40 blue	2·00	1·30
418		60c. on 1a. red	11·00	8·50
375		70c. on 2a. mauve	6·25	2·75
376		80c. on 5a. green	2·00	1·30

(A) surch **0,05 Cent.** in one line; (B) surch **5 CENTAVOS** in two lines.

1935. "Due" key-type surch CORREIOS and new value.

377	W	5c. on 6c. brown	2·50	1·60
378	W	30c. on 50c. grey	2·50	1·60
379	W	40c. on 50c. grey	2·50	1·60

22 Vasco da Gama

27 Airplane over Globe

1938. Name and value in black.

383	22	1c. olive (postage)	25	25
384	22	5c. brown	35	35
385	22	10c. red	45	35
386	22	15c. purple	45	35

387	22	20c. grey	45	35
388	-	30c. purple	55	45
389	-	35c. green	1·10	80
390	-	40c. brown	35	25
391	-	50c. mauve	55	25
392	-	60c. black	1·10	35
393	-	70c. violet	1·10	35
394	-	80c. orange	1·10	35
395	-	1a. red	1·10	35
396	-	1a.75 blue	2·30	1·00
397	-	2a. red	3·50	1·10
398	-	5a. olive	16·00	1·10
399	-	10a. blue	32·00	1·30
400	-	20a. brown	44·00	4·00
401	27	10c. red (air)	45	40
402	27	20c. violet	45	40
403	27	50c. orange	45	40
404	27	1a. blue	45	40
405	27	2a. red	1·00	45
406	27	3a. green	1·80	70
407	27	5a. brown	7·00	1·00
408	27	9a. red	8·00	2·00
409	27	10a. mauve	11·00	2·75

DESIGNS: 30c. to 50c. Mousinho de Albuquerque; 60c. to 1a. "Fomento" (symbolizing Progress); 1a.75, 2, 5a. Prince Henry the Navigator; 10, 20a. Afonso de Albuquerque.

28 Portuguese Colonial Column

1938. President's Colonial Tour.

410	28	80c. green	3·50	2·20
411	28	1a.75 blue	23·00	6·25
412	28	20a. brown	70·00	40·00

1945. Nos. 394/6 surch.

420		5c. on 80c. orange	1·00	55
421		50c. on 1a. red	1·00	55
422		50c. on 1a.75 blue	1·00	55

31 Arms of Angola

1947. Air.

423a	31	1a. brown	11·50	7·00
423b	31	2a. green	12·50	8·00
423c	31	3a. orange	12·50	8·00
423d	31	3a.50 orange	23·00	8·00
423e	31	5a. green	£110	29·00
423f	31	6a. pink	£110	23·00
423g	31	9a. red	£350	£225
423h	31	10a. green	£225	£100
423i	31	20a. blue	£375	£110
423j	31	50a. black	£500	£275
423k	31	100a. yellow	£800	£700

32 Sao Miguel Fortress, Luanda

1948. Tercentenary of Restoration of Angola. Inscr "Tricentenario da Restauracao de Angola 1648–1948".

424	32	5c. violet	35	25
425	-	10c. brown	90	35
426	-	30c. green	35	25
427	-	50c. purple	35	25
428	-	1a. red	90	25
429	-	1a.75 blue	1·60	25
430	-	2a. green	1·60	25
431	-	5a. black	3·75	70
432	-	10a. mauve	12·50	90
433	-	20a. blue	28·00	5·75
MS433a 162×225 mm. Nos. 424/33 (sold at 42a.50)			£140	£140

DESIGNS—HORIZ: 10c. Our Lady of Nazareth Hermitage, Luanda; 1a. Surrender of Luanda; 5a. Inscribed Rocks of Yelala; 20a. Massangano Fortress. VERT (portraits): 30c. Don John IV; 50c. Salvador Correia de Sa Benevides; 1a.75, Dioga Cao; 7a. Manuel Cerveira Pereira; 10a. Paulo Dias de Novais.

33 Our Lady of Fatima

1948. Honouring Our Lady of Fatima.

434	33	50c. red	2·75	1·70
435	33	3a. blue	11·00	3·50
436	33	6a. orange	34·00	8·50
437	33	9a. red	90·00	11·00

35 River Chiumbe **36** Pedras Negras

1949

438	35	20c. blue	80	25
439	36	40c. brown	80	25
440	-	50c. red	80	25
441	-	2a.50 blue	4·00	50
442	-	3a.50 grey	4·00	2·30
443	-	15a. green	29·00	2·30
444	-	50a. green	£160	9·25

DESIGNS—As T **35**: 50c. Luanda; 2a.50, Bandeira; 3a.50, Mocamedes; 50a. Braganza Falls. 31×26 mm: 15a. River Cubal.

37 Aircraft and Globe

1949. Air.

445	37	1a. orange	80	25
446	37	2a. brown	1·70	25
447	37	3a. mauve	2·30	25
448	37	6a. green	4·25	90
449	37	9a. purple	6·25	2·20

38 Tentativa Feliz

1949. Centenary of Founding of Mocamedes.

450	38	1a. purple	9·25	1·00
451	38	4a. green	28·00	2·75

39 Letter and Globe

1949. 75th Anniv of U.P.U.

452	39	4a. green	14·00	3·50

40 Reproduction of "Crown" key-type

1950. Philatelic Exhibition and 80th Anniv of First Angolan Stamp.

454	40	1a. red	1·70	90
455	40	4a. black	6·25	2·10
453	40	50a. green	1·70	55
MS455a 120×79 mm. Nos. 453/5 (sold at 6a.50)			34·00	29·00

41 Bells and Dove **42** Angels holding Candelabra

1950. Holy Year.

456	41	1a. violet	1·60	35
457	42	4a. black	6·25	1·10

43 Dark Chanting Goshawk

1951. Birds. Multicoloured.

458	43	5c. Type **43**	55	20
459		10c. Racquet-tailed roller	55	20
460		15c. Bateleur	90	20
461		20c. European bee eater	1·00	45
462		50c. Giant kingfisher	1·00	20
463		1a. Anchieta's barbet	1·00	20
464		1a.50 African open-bill stork	1·50	20
465		2a. Southern ground hornbill	4·00	20
466		2a.50 African skimmer	2·20	20
467		3a. Shikra	1·50	20
468		3a.50 Senham's bustard	2·20	20
469		4a. African golden oriole	2·50	20
470		4a.50 Magpie shrike	2·50	20
471		5a. Red-shouldered glossy starling	8·00	70
472		6a. Sharp-tailed glossy starling	10·50	1·70
473		7a. Fan-tailed whydah	11·50	2·30
474		10a. Half-collared kingfisher	46·00	2·75
475		12a.50 White-crowned shrike	14·50	4·00
476		15a. White-winged starling	13·00	4·00
477		20a. Southern yellow-billed hornbill	£100	9·75
478		25a. Violet starling	48·00	8·00
479		30a. Sulphur-breasted bush shrike	48·00	8·50
480		40a. Secretary bird	65·00	12·50
481		50a. Peach-faced lovebird	£140	30·00

The 10, 15 and 20c., 2a.50, 3a., 4a.50, 12a.50 and 30a. are horiz, the remainder vert.

44 Our Lady of Fatima

1951. Termination of Holy Year.

482	44	4a. orange	4·50	1·70

45 Laboratory

1952. First Tropical Medicine Congress, Lisbon.

483	45	1a. grey and blue	1·30	45

46 The Sacred Face

1952. Missionary Art Exhibition.

484	46	10c. blue and flesh	20	20
485	46	50c. green and stone	1·00	25
486	46	2a. purple and flesh	3·75	70

47 Leopard

1953. Angolan Fauna. Multicoloured.

487	47	5c. Type **47**	25	25
488		10c. Sable antelope (vert)	25	25
489		20c. African elephant (vert)	25	25
490		30c. Eland (vert)	25	25
491		40c. Crocodile	25	25
492		50c. Impala (vert)	25	25
493		1a. Mountain zebra (vert)	35	25
494		1a.50 Sitatunga (vert)	35	25
495		2a. Black rhinoceros	35	25
496		2a.30 Gemsbok (vert)	35	25
497		2a.50 Lion (vert)	45	25
498		3a. African buffalo	55	25
499		3a.50 Springbok (vert)	55	25
500		4a. Blue wildebeest (vert)	20·00	25
501		5a. Hartebeest (vert)	90	25
502		7a. Warthog (vert)	1·40	25
503		10a. Waterbuck (vert)	2·75	25
504		12a.50 Hippopotamus (vert)	7·50	1·50
505		15a. Greater kudu (vert)	9·25	1·50
506		20a. Giraffe (vert)	11·50	90

48 Stamp of 1853 and Colonial Arms

1953. Portuguese Stamp Centenary.

507	48	50c. multicoloured	1·30	55

49 Father M. da Nobrega and Sao Paulo

1954. Fourth Centenary of Sao Paulo.

508	49	1e. black and buff	80	35

50 Route of President's Tour

1954. Presidential Visit.

509	50	35c. multicoloured	15	15
510	50	4e.50 multicoloured	1·70	80

51 Map of Angola

1955. Map mult. Angola territory in colour given.

511	51	5c. white	20	20
512	51	20c. salmon	20	20
513	51	50c. blue	20	20
514	51	1e. orange	20	20
515	51	2e.30 yellow	1·30	45
516	51	4e. blue	2·50	25
517	51	10e. green	3·00	25
518	51	20e. white	4·25	1·80

52 Col. A. de Paiva

1956. Birth Centenary of De Paiva.

519	52	1e. black, blue and orange	45	35

53 Quela Chief

1957. Natives. Multicoloured.

520	53	5c. Type **53**	20	20
521		10c. Andulo flute player	20	20
522		15c. Dembos man and woman	20	20
523		20c. Quissama dancer (male)	20	20
524		30c. Quibala family	20	20

525	40c. Bocolo dancer (female)		20	20
526	50c. Quissama woman		20	20
527	80c. Cuanhama woman		45	45
528	1e.50 Luanda widow		2·75	45
529	2e.50 Bocolo dancer (male)		3·50	25
530	4e. Muquixe man		1·40	25
531	10e. Cabinda chief		3·00	55

54 Father J. M.
Antunes

1957. Birth Centenary of Father Antunes.
532	**54**	1e. multicoloured	90	45

55 Exhibition Emblem,
Globe and Arms

1958. Brussels International Exhibition.
533	**55**	1e.50 multicoloured	80	70

56 *Securidaca
longipedunculata*

1958. Sixth Int Tropical Medicine Congress.
534	**56**	2e.50 multicoloured	3·50	1·00

57 Native Doctor
and Patient

1958. 75th Anniv of Maria Pia Hospital, Luanda.
535	**57**	1e. brown, black and blue	55	35
536	-	1e.50 multicoloured	1·40	70
537	-	2e.50 multicoloured	2·50	1·30

DESIGNS: 1e.50, 17th-century doctor and patient; 2e.50, Present-day doctor, orderly and patients.

58 Welwitschia (plant)

1959. Centenary of Discovery of Welwitschia.
538	**58**	1e.50 multicoloured	1·10	55
539	-	2e.50 multicoloured	1·70	70
540	-	5e. multicoloured	2·75	70
541	-	10e. multicoloured	6·25	2·30

DESIGNS: 2e.50, 5, 10e. Various types of Welwitschia (*Welwitschia mirabilis*).

59 Old Map of West
Africa

1960. 500th Death Anniv of Prince Henry the Navigator.
542	**59**	2e.50 multicoloured	70	35

60 "Agriculture"
(distribution of seeds)

1960. Tenth Anniv of African Technical Co-operation Commission.
543	**60**	2e.50 multicoloured	80	35

61

1961. Angolan Women. As T **61**. Portraits multicoloured; background colours given.
544	10c. green	10	10
545	15c. blue	10	10
546	30c. yellow	10	10
547	40c. grey	10	10
548	60c. brown	10	10
549	1e.50 turquoise	15	10
550	2e. lilac	1·30	10
551	2e.50 lemon	1·30	10
552	3e. pink	4·50	35
553	4e. olive	2·30	35
554	5e. blue	1·50	35
555	7e.50 yellow	2·10	1·00
556	10e. buff	1·50	80
557	15e. brown	2·30	1·00
558	25e. red	3·25	1·50
559	50e. grey	5·75	3·25

62 Weightlifting

1962. Sports. Multicoloured.
560	50e. Flying	20	20
561	1e. Rowing	1·40	25
562	1e.50 Water polo	90	35
563	2e.50 Throwing the hammer	1·10	35
564	4e.50 High jumping	90	70
565	15e. Type **62**	2·30	1·70

63 *Anopheles
funestus*
(mosquito)

1962. Malaria Eradication.
566	**63**	2e.50 multicoloured	2·10	90

64 Gen. Norton
de Matos
(statue)

1962. 50th Anniv of Nova Lisboa.
567	**64**	2e.50 multicoloured	70	35

65 Red Locusts

1963. 15th Anniv of Int Locust Eradication Service.
568	**65**	2e.50 multicoloured	2·10	55

66 Arms of St. Paul of the
Assumption, Luanda

1963. Angolan Civic Arms (1st series). Multicoloured.
569	5c. Type **66**	20	20
570	10c. Massangano	20	20
571	30c. Muxima	20	20
572	50c. Carmona	20	20
573	1e. Salazar	80	20
574	1e.50 Malanje	1·50	20

575	2e. Henry of Carvalho	80	20
576	2e.50 Mocamedes	4·50	70
577	3e. Novo Redondo	1·10	20
578	3e.50 St. Salvador (Congo)	1·30	20
579	5e. Luso	1·10	35
580	7e.50 St. Philip (Benguela)	1·50	1·30
581	10e. Lobito	1·80	1·10
582	12e.50 Gabela	2·10	1·80
583	15e. Sa da Bandeira	2·10	1·80
584	17e.50 Silva Porto	3·50	3·00
585	20e. Nova Lisboa	3·50	2·50
586	22e.50 Cabinda	3·50	3·00
587	30e. Serpa Pinto	4·25	4·00

See also Nos. 589/610.

67 Rear-Admiral
A. Tomas

1963. Presidential Visit.
588	**67**	2e.50 multicoloured	70	25

68 Arms of
Sanza-Pombo

1963. Angolan Civic Arms (2nd series). Multicoloured.
589	15c. Type **68**	25	20
590	20c. St. Antonio do Zaire	25	20
591	25c. Ambriz	25	20
592	40c. Ambrizete	25	20
593	50c. Catete	25	20
594	70c. Quibaxe	25	20
595	1e. Maquela do Zombo	25	20
596	1e.20 Bembe	25	20
597	1e.50 Caxito	80	20
598	1e.80 Dondo	80	70
599	2e.50 Damba	3·00	25
600	4e. Cuimba	70	25
601	6e.50 Negage	70	45
602	7e. Quitexe	1·00	70
603	8e. Mucaba	1·00	80
604	9e. 31 de Janeiro	1·50	1·30
605	11e. Novo Caipemba	1·70	1·50
606	14e. Songo	2·00	1·70
607	17e. Quimbele	2·10	2·00
608	25e. Noqui	2·50	2·00
609	35e. Santa Cruz	3·75	3·00
610	50e. General Freire	4·75	2·50

69 Map of
Africa, Boeing
707 and
Lockheed Super
Constellation
Airliners

1963. Tenth Anniv of T.A.P. Airline.
611	**69**	1e. multicoloured	1·40	45

70 Bandeira
Cathedral

1963. Angolan Churches. Multicoloured.
612	10c. Type **70**	10	10
613	20c. Landana	10	10
614	30c. Luanda (Cathedral)	10	10
615	40c. Gabela	10	10
616	50c. St. Martin, Bay of Tigers (Chapel)	10	10
617	1e. Melange (Cathedral) (horiz)	25	20
618	1e.50 St. Peter, Chibia	25	20
619	2e. Benguela (horiz)	35	20
620	2e.50 Jesus, Luanda	35	20
621	3e. Camabatela (horiz)	45	20
622	3e.50 Cabinda Mission	55	20
623	4e. Vila Folgares (horiz)	70	30
624	4e.50 Arrabida, Lobito (horiz)	90	35

625	5e. Cabinda	90	45
626	7e.50 Cacuso, Malange (horiz)	1·50	80
627	10e. Lubanga Mission	2·00	80
628	12e.50 Huila Mission (horiz)	2·30	1·30
629	15e. Island Cape, Luanda (horiz)	2·50	1·40

71 Dr. A. T. de Sousa

1964. Centenary of National Overseas Bank.
630	**71**	2e.50 multicoloured	90	45

72 Arms and Palace of
Commerce, Luanda

1964. Cent of Luanda Commercial Association.
631	**72**	1e. multicoloured	45	25

73 I.T.U. Emblem
and St. Gabriel

1965. Centenary of I.T.U.
632	**73**	2e.50 multicoloured	1·40	70

74 Boeing 707
over Petroleum
Refinery

1965. Air. Multicoloured.
633	1e.50 Type **74**	1·40	20
634	2e.50 Cambabe Dam	1·40	20
635	3e. Salazar Dam	2·00	20
636	4e. Captain Trofilo Duarte Dam	2·00	25
637	4e.50 Creveiro Lopes Dam	1·40	25
638	5e. Cuango Dam	1·40	35
639	6e. Quanza Bridge	2·20	45
640	7e. Captain Trofilo Duarte Railway Bridge	3·25	45
641	8e.50 Dr. Oliveira Salazar Bridge	4·00	1·30
642	12e.50 Captain Silva Carvalho Railway Bridge	4·25	1·70

Nos. 634/42 are horiz and each design includes a Boeing 707 airliner overhead.

75 Fokker F.27
Friendship over
Luanda Airport

1965. 25th Anniv of Direccao dos Transportes Aereos (Angolan airline).
643	**75**	2e.50 multicoloured	1·40	35

76 Arquebusier,
1539

1966. Portuguese Military Uniforms. Multicoloured.
644	50c. Type **76**	10	10
645	1e. Arquebusier, 1640	15	15
646	1e.50 Infantry officer, 1777	20	15
647	2e. Infantry standard-bearer, 1777	35	15
648	2e.50 Infantryman, 1777	40	15
649	3e. Cavalry officer, 1783	45	15
650	4e. Trooper, 1783	70	25
651	4e.50 Infantry officer, 1807	80	35
652	5e. Infantryman, 1807	90	35
653	6e. Cavalry officer, 1807	1·30	70
654	8e. Trooper, 1807	1·70	1·50
655	9e. Infantryman, 1873	2·10	1·70

77 St. Paul's Hospital, Luanda, and Sarmento Rodrigues Commercial and Industrial School

1966. 40th Anniv of National Revolution.
656 **77** 1e. multicoloured 45 25

78 Emblem of Brotherhood

1966. Centenary of Brotherhood of the Holy Spirit.
657 **78** 1e. multicoloured 45 25

79 Mendes Barata and Cruiser *Don Carlos I*

1967. Centenary of Military Naval Assn. Multicoloured.
658 1e. Type **79** 1·00 45
659 2e.50 Augusto de Castilho and sail/steam corvette *Mindelo* 1·40 80

80 Basilica of Fatima

1967. 50th Anniv of Fatima Apparitions.
660 **80** 50c. multicoloured 45 25

81 17th-century Map and M. C. Pereira (founder)

1967. 350th Anniv of Benguela.
661 **81** 50c. multicoloured 45 25

82 Town Hall, Uige-Carmona

1967. 50th Anniv of Uige-Carmona.
662 **82** 1e. multicoloured 25 20

83 "The Three Orders"

1967. Portuguese Civil and Military Orders. Multicoloured.
663 50c. Type **83** 20 20
664 1e. "Tower and Sword" 20 20
665 1e.50 "Avis" 20 20
666 2e. "Christ" 20 20
667 2e.50 "St. James of the Sword" 20 20
668 3e. "Empire" 35 20
669 4e. "Prince Henry" 45 40
670 5e. "Benemerencia" 70 45
671 10e. "Public Instruction" 1·30 55
672 20e. "Agricultural and Industrial Merit" 2·75 1·50

84 Belmonte Castle

1968. 500th Birth Anniv of Pedro Cabral (explorer). Multicoloured.
673 50c. Our Lady of Hope (vert) 20 20
674 1e. Type **84** 55 20
675 1e.50 St. Jeronimo's hermitage (vert) 70 20
676 2e.50 Cabral's fleet (vert) 1·30 45

85 Francisco Inocencio de Souza Countinho

1969. Bicent of Novo Redondo (Angolan city).
677 **85** 2e. multicoloured 45 15

86 Gunboat *Loge* and Admiral Coutinho

1969. Birth Centenary of Admiral Gago Coutinho.
678 **86** 2e.50 multicoloured 1·00 35

87 Compass

1969. 500th Birth Anniv of Vasco da Gama (explorer).
679 **87** 1e. multicoloured 45 20

88 L. A. Rebello de Silva

1969. Cent of Overseas Administrative Reforms.
680 **88** 1e.50 multicoloured 25 20

89 Gate of Jeronimos

1969. 500th Birth Anniv of King Manoel I.
681 **89** 3e. multicoloured 45 20

90 *Angolasaurus bocagei*

1970. Fossils and Minerals. Multicoloured.
682 50c. Type **90** 55 25
683 1e. Ferro-meteorite 55 25
684 1e.50 Dioptase 90 55
685 2e. *Gondwanidium validium* 90 55
686 2e.50 Diamonds 90 55
687 3e. Estromatolitos 90 55
688 3e.50 Giant-toothed shark (*Procarcharodon megalodon*) 1·50 90
689 4e. Dwarf lungfish (*Microceratodus angolensis*) 1·50 90
690 4e.50 Muscovite (mica) 1·50 90
691 5e. Barytes 1·50 90
692 6e. *Nostoceras helicinum* 2·75 1·30
693 10e. *Rotula orbiculus angolensis* 3·00 1·80

91 Marshal Carmona

1970. Birth Centenary of Marshal Carmona.
694 **91** 2e.50 multicoloured 45 20

92 Cotton-picking

1970. Centenary of Malanje Municipality.
695 **92** 2e.50 multicoloured 55 35

93 Mail Steamers *Infante Dom Henrique* and *Principe Perfeito* and 1870 5r. Stamp

1970. Stamp Centenary. Multicoloured.
696 1e.50 Type **93** (postage) 55 35
697 4e.50 Beyer-Garratt steam locomotive and 25r. stamp of 1870 3·00 3·00
698 2e.50 Fokker F.27 Friendship and Boeing 707 mail planes and 10r. stamp of 1870 (air) 2·10 90
MS699 150×105 mm. Nos. 696/8 (sold at 15e.) 14·00 14·00

94 Map and Emblems

1971. Fifth Regional Soil and Foundation Engineering Conference, Luanda.
700 **94** 2e.50 multicoloured 45 20

96 16th-century Galleon at Mouth of Congo

1972. 400th Anniv of Camoens' *The Lusiads* (epic poem).
704 **96** 1e. multicoloured 70 25

97 Sailing Yachts

1972. Olympic Games, Munich.
705 **97** 50c. multicoloured 70 25

98 Fairey IIID Seaplane *Santa Cruz* near Fernando de Noronha

1972. 50th Anniv of First Flight Lisbon–Rio de Janeiro.
706 **98** 1e. multicoloured 35 20

99 W.M.O. Emblem

1974. Centenary of W.M.O.
707 **99** 1e. multicoloured 45 20

100 Dish Aerials

1974. Inauguration of Satellite Communications Station Network.
708 **100** 2e. multicoloured 45 20

101 Doris Harp

1974. Sea Shells. Multicoloured.
709 25c. Type **101** 10 10
710 30c. West African murex 10 10
711 50c. Scaly-ridged venus 10 10
712 70c. Filose latirus 20 10
713 1e. *Cymbium cisium* 20 10
714 1e.50 West African helmet 20 10
715 2e. Rat cowrie 20 10
716 2e.50 Butterfly cone 30 10
717 3e. Bubonian conch 40 20
718 3e.50 *Tympanotonus fuscatus* 45 20
719 4e. Great ribbed cockle 45 20
720 5e. Lightning moon 55 20
721 6e. Lion's-paw scallop 70 30
722 7e. Giant tun 85 30
723 10e. Rugose donax 1·10 45
724 25e. Smith's distorsio 3·50 1·30
725 30e. *Olivancilaria acuminata* 3·50 1·50
726 35e. Giant hairy melongena 3·75 2·00
727 40e. Wavy-leaved turrid 5·25 2·10
728 50e. American sundial 6·50 2·50

1974. Youth Philately. No. 511 optd **1974 FILATELIA JUVENIL.**
729 **51** 5c. multicoloured 25 80

103 Arm with Rifle and Star

1975. Independence.
730 **103** 1e.50 multicoloured 10 10

104 Diquiche-ua-Puheue Mask

1975. Angolan Masks. Multicoloured.
731 50c. Type **104** 10 10
732 3e. Bui ou Congolo mask 15 10

105 Workers

1976. Workers' Day.
733 **105** 1e. multicoloured 10 10

1976. Stamp Day. Optd **DIA DO SELO 15 Junho 1976 REP. POPULAR DE.**
734 **51** 10e. multicoloured 1·50 1·25

107 Pres. Agostinho Neto

1976. First Anniv of Independence.
735 **107** 50c. black and grey 10 10
736 **107** 2e. purple and grey 10 10
737 **107** 3e. blue and grey 10 10
738 **107** 5e. brown and buff 15 10
739 **107** 10e. brown and drab 25 10
MS740 59×75 mm. No. 739, but without President's name. Imperf 2·00

1976. St. Silvestre Games. Optd **S Silvestre Rep. Popular de**.

741	**62**	15e. multicoloured	55	35

1977. Nos. 518, 724/5 and 728 optd **REPUBLICA POPULAR DE**.

742	20e. Type **51**		3·50	3·50
743	25e. "Cymatium trigonum"		60	15
744	30e. "Olivancilaria acuminata"		75	25
745	50e. "Solarium granulatum"		1·25	40

111 Child receiving Vaccine

1977. Polio Vaccination Campaign.

746	**111**	2k.50 blue and black	10	10

112 Map of Africa and Flag

1977. MPLA Congress.

747	**112**	6k. multicoloured	20	15

113 Human Rights Flame

1979. 30th Anniv of Declaration of Human Rights.

748	**113**	2k.50 yellow, red & black	15	10

114 Emblem

1979. International Anti-apartheid Year.

749	**114**	1k. multicoloured	10	10

115 Child raising Arms to Light

1980. International Year of the Child (1979).

750	**115**	3k.50 multicoloured	15	10

1980. Nos. 697/8 optd **REPUBLICA POPULAR DE**.

751	4e.50 multicoloured (postage)		2·75	1·75
752	2e.50 multicoloured (air)		15	10

117 Pres. Agostinho Neto

1980. National Heroes Day. Multicoloured.

753	**117**	4k.50 Type **117**	15	10
754		50k. Pres. Neto with machine-gun	1·25	70

118 Arms and Workers

1980. "Popular Power".

755	**118**	40k. blue and black	1·00	55

119 *The* Liberated Angolan (A. Vaz de Carvalho)

1980. Fifth Anniv of Independence.

756	**119**	5k.50 multicoloured	15	10

120 Running

1980. Olympic Games, Moscow.

757	**120**	9k. pink and red	20	10
758	–	12k. light blue and blue	30	10

DESIGN: 12k. Swimming.

121 Millet

1980. Angolan Produce. Multicoloured.

759	**121**	50l. Type **121**	10	10
760		5k. Coffee	15	10
761		7k.50 Sunflower	20	10
762		13k.50 Cotton	30	15
763		14k. Petroleum	30	15
764		16k. Diamonds	35	20

1981. Nos. 708, 713/16 and 718/27 with "REPUBLICA PORTUGUESA" inscr obliterated. (a) Dish aerials.

765	**100**	2e. multicoloured	10	10

(b) Sea Shells. Multicoloured.

766	1e. *Cymbium cisium*	10	10
767	1e.50 West African helmet	15	10
768	2e. Rat cowrie	20	10
769	2e.50 Butterfly cone	25	10
770	3e.50 *Tympanotonus fuscatus*	30	10
771	4e. Great ribbed cockle	35	15
772	5e. Lightning moon	40	15
773	6e. Lion's-paw scallop	45	20
774	7e. Giant tun	50	20
775	10e. Rugose donax	70	25
776	25e. Smith's distorsio	1·75	30
777	30e. *Olivancilaria acuminata*	1·90	65
778	35e. Giant hairy melongena	2·40	90
779	40e. Wavy-leaved turrid	3·00	1·00

122 Prisoner and Protesting Crowd

1981. Fifth Anniv of Soweto Riots in South Africa.

780	**122**	4k.50 black, red & silver	20	15

123 Basketball and Volleyball

1981. Second Central African Games. Multicoloured.

781		50l. Cycling and Tennis	10	10
782		5k. Judo and Boxing	20	15
783		6k. Type **123**	25	15
784		10k. Handball and football	40	20

MS784a 116×129 mm. 15k. Swimming and javelin. Imperf ... 80 ... 85

124 Statuette

1981. "Turipex 81".

785	**124**	9k. multicoloured	40	20

125 *Charaxes kahldeni* f. *homeyri*

1982. Butterflies. Multicoloured.

787		50l. Type **125**	10	10
788		1k. *Abantis gambesiaca*	10	10
789		5k. *Catacroptera cloanthe*	25	30
790		9k. *Myrina ficedula* (vert)	60	25
791		10k. *Colotis danae*	60	25
792		15k. *Acraea acrita bella*	80	30
793		100k. *Precis hierta cebrese*	5·25	2·40

MS793a 154×104 mm. Nos. 787/93. Imperf (sold at 30k.) ... 1·40 ... 1·40

126 Silence of Night

1982. Fifth Anniv of Admission to United Nations. Multicoloured.

794		5k.50 Type **126**	25	15
795		7k.50 Cotton Fields	35	15

127 Worker and Building

1982. 20th Anniv of Angola Laboratory of Engineering. Multicoloured.

797		9k. Laboratory building (horiz)	40	20
798		13k. Type **127** (Research in construction materials)	45	25
799		100k. Geotechnical equipment	4·00	2·25

128 Albizzia versicolor

1983. Flowers (1st series). Multicoloured.

800		5k. *Dichrostachys glomerata*	25	10
801		12k. *Amblygonocarpus obtu-sangulus*	45	20
802		50k. Type **128**	2·00	1·10

129 Angolan Woman and Emblem

1983. First Angolan Women's Organization Congress.

803	**129**	20k. multicoloured	80	25

130 M'pungi (horn)

1983. World Communications Year. Multicoloured.

804		6k.50 Type **130**	25	20
805		12k. Mondu (drum)	50	45

131 Spear breaking Chain around South Africa

1983. 30th Anniv of Organization of African Unity.

806	**131**	6k.50 multicoloured	30	25

132 Antestiopsis lineaticollis intricata

1983. "Brasiliana 83" International Stamp Exn, Rio de Janeiro. Harmful Insects. Multicoloured.

807		4k.50 Type **132**	25	15
808		6k.50 *Stephanoderes hampei*	35	25
809		10k. *Zonocerus variegatus*	60	45

133 Map of Africa and E.C.A. Emblem

1983. 25th Anniv of Economic Commission for Africa.

810	**133**	10k. multicoloured	45	40

134 Collecting Mail

1983. 185th Anniv of Postal Service. Multicoloured.

811		50l. Type **134**	10	10
812		3k.50 Unloading mail from aircraft (horiz)	20	15
813		5k. Sorting mail (horiz)	35	25
814		15k. Posting letter	85	80
815		30k. Collecting mail from private box (horiz)	1·75	1·50

MS816 142×78 mm. Nos. 812, 813 and 815 ... 2·20 ... 1·90

135 Parasa karschi

1984. Moths. Multicoloured.

817		50l. Type **135**	10	10
818		1k. *Diaphone angolensis*	10	10
819		3k.50 *Choeropais jucunda*	30	15
820		6k.50 *Hespagarista rendalli*	50	35
821		15k. *Euchromia guineensis*	95	80
822		17k.50 *Mazuca roseistriga*	1·10	95
823		20k. *Utetheisa callima*	1·40	1·25

136 Dove

1984. First National Union of Angolan Workers Congress.

824	**136**	30k. multicoloured	1·75	1·50

137 Flag and Agostinho Neto

1984. Fifth National Heroes Day. Multicoloured.

825	10k.50 Type **137**	50	45
826	36k.50 Flag and Agostinho Neto (different)	1·60	1·50

138 Southern Ground Hornbill

1984. Birds. Multicoloured.

827	10k.50 Type **138**	90	90
828	14k. Palm-nut vulture	1·25	1·25
829	16k. Goliath heron	1·50	1·50
830	19k.50 Eastern white pelican	1·75	1·75
831	22k. African spoonbill	2·00	2·00
832	26k. South African crowned crane	2·40	2·40

139 Greater Kudu

1984. Mammals. Multicoloured.

833	1k. Type **139**	10	10
834	4k. Springbok	25	15
835	5k. Chimpanzee	30	25
836	10k. African buffalo	55	50
837	15k. Sable antelope	80	65
838	20k. Aardvark	1·25	1·10
839	25k. Spotted hyena	1·50	1·25

140 Sao Pedro da Barra Fortress

1985. Monuments. Multicoloured.

840	5k. Type **140**	25	20
841	12k.50 Nova Oerias ruins	60	55
842	18k. Antiga cathedral ruins, M'Banza Kongo	80	75
843	26k. Massangano fortress	1·25	1·10
844	39k. Escravatura museum	1·75	1·60

141 Flags on World Map

1985. Fifth Anniv of Southern Africa Development Co-ordination Conference. Multicoloured.

845	1k. Type **141**	10	10
846	11k. Offshore drilling	1·25	50
847	57k. Conference session	2·50	2·40

142 Flags and "XXV"

1985. 25th Anniv of National Union of Angolan Workers.

848	**142** 77k. multicoloured	3·50	3·25

143 Lonchocarpus sericeus

1985. Medicinal Plants. Multicoloured.

849	1k. Type **143**	10	10
850	4k. Gossypium sp.	20	15
851	11k. Senna	50	45
852	25k.50 Gloriosa superba	1·10	1·00
853	55k. Cochlospermum angolensis	2·50	2·40

144 Map of Angola as Dove and Conference Emblem

1984. Ministerial Conference of Non-aligned Countries, Luanda.

854	**144** 35k. multicoloured	1·60	1·50

145 Dove and U.N. Emblem

1985. 40th Anniv of U.N.O.

855	**145** 12k.50 multicoloured	60	55

146 Cement Works

1985. Tenth Anniv of Independence. Multicoloured.

856	50l. Type **146**	10	10
857	5k. Timber yard	20	15
858	7k. Quartz	30	25
859	10k. Iron works	50	45
MS860	210×123 mm. Nos. 856/9	1·10	95

147 Emblem, Open Book, Soldier, Farmer and Factory

1985. Second MPLA Congress.

861	**147** 20k. multicoloured	90	85

148 Runner on Track

1985. 30th Anniv of Demostenes de Almeida Clington Races. Multicoloured.

862	50l. Type **148**	10	10
863	5k. Two runners on road	20	15
864	6k.50 Three runners on road	30	25
865	10k. Two runners on track	50	45

149 Map, Stadium and Players

1986. World Cup Football Championship, Mexico.

866	**149** 50l. multicoloured	10	10
867	- 3k.50 multicoloured	15	15
868	- 5k. multicoloured	30	25
869	- 7k. multicoloured	35	30
870	- 10k. multicoloured	50	45
871	- 18k. multicoloured	85	70

DESIGNS: 3k.50 to 18k. Different footballers.

150 Crowd

1986. 25th Anniv of Armed Independence Movement.

872	**150** 15k. multicoloured	75	70

151 Soviet Space Project

1985. 25th Anniv of First Man in Space. Multicoloured.

873	50l. Type **151**	10	10
874	1k. "Voskhod 1"	10	10
875	5k. Cosmonaut on space walk	20	15
876	10k. Moon vehicle	50	45
877	13k. "Soyuz"–"Apollo" link-up	60	55

152 National Flag and U.N. Emblem

1986. Tenth Anniv of Angolan Membership of U.N.O.

878	**152** 22k. multicoloured	1·00	90

153 People at Work

1986. 30th Anniv of Popular Movement for the Liberation of Angola. Multicoloured.

879	5k. Type **153**	20	15
880	5k. Emblem and people (29×36 mm)	20	15
881	5k. Soldiers fighting	20	15

Nos. 879/81 were printed together, *se-tenant*, forming a composite design.

154 Lecturer and Students (Faculty of Engineering)

1986. Tenth Anniv of Agostinho Neto University. Multicoloured.

882	50l. Type **154**	10	10
883	7k. Students and Judges (Faculty of Law)	30	25
884	10k. Students using microscopes and surgeons operating (Faculty of Medicine)	50	45

155 Ouioca

1987. Traditional Hairstyles. Multicoloured.

885	1k. Type **155**	10	10
886	1k.50 Luanda	10	10
887	5k. Humbe	20	15
888	7k. Muila	35	25
889	20k. Muila (different)	80	70
890	30k. Lunda, Dilolo	1·25	1·00

156 Lenin in the Smolny Institute (detail, Serov)

1987. 70th Anniv of Russian Revolution.

891	**156** 15k. multicoloured	60	25

157 Pambala Beach

1987. Scenic Spots. Multicoloured.

892	50l. Type **157**	10	10
893	1k.50 Quedas do Dala (waterfalls)	10	10
894	3k.50 Black Feet Rocks, Pungo Adongo (vert)	15	10
895	5k. Cuango River valley	20	15
896	10k. Luanda shore (vert)	40	35
897	20k. Serra da Leba road	80	75

158 Emblem

1988. Second Angolan Women's Organization Congress. Multicoloured.

898	2k. Type **158**	10	10
899	10k. Women engaged in various pursuits	40	35

159 Dancers

1988. Tenth Anniv of Vitoria Carnival. Multicoloured.

900	5k. Type **159**	15	10
901	10k. Revellers	40	35

160 Augusto N'Gangula (child revolutionary)

1989. Pioneers. Multicoloured.

902	12k. Type **160** (20th death anniv)	50	45
903	15k. Pioneers (25th anniv (1988) of Agostinho Neto Pioneers Organization)	60	55

161 Luanda 1st August Sports Club (1979–81)

1989. Tenth National Football League Championship. Championship Winners. Multicoloured.

904	5k. Type **161**	15	15
905	5k. Luanda Petro Atletico (1982, 1984, 1986–88)	15	15
906	5k. Benguela 1st May Sports Club (1983, 1985)	15	15

162 Watering Cabbages

1990. Tenth Anniv (1987) of International Fund for Agricultural Development.

907	**162** 10k. multicoloured	1·60	1·30

163 19th-century Middle-class Houses, Luanda

1990. Historical Buildings. Multicoloured.

908	1k. Type **163**	25	25
909	2k. Cidade Alta railway station, Luanda	50	30
910	5k. National Anthropology Museum	60	40
911	15k. Palace of Ana Joaquina dos Santos	1·20	1·20
912	23k. Iron Palace	1·60	2·00
913	36k. Meteorological observatory (vert)	2·75	2·50
914	50k. Governor's palace	3·75	3·50

164 *General Machado* and Route Map

1990. Benguela (915) and Luanda Railways. Multicoloured.
915	5k. Type **164**	1·00	1·00
916	12k. Beyer-Garratt steam locomotive (facing left)	2·00	2·00
917	12k. Beyer-Garratt steam locomotive (facing right)	2·00	2·00
918	14k. Mikado steam locomotive	2·50	2·50
MS919	88×69 mm. 25k. Diesel-electric locomotive (39×29 mm)	4·25	4·25

165 Hydroelectric Production

1990. Tenth Anniv of Southern Africa Development Co-ordinating Conference. Multicoloured.
920	5k. Type **165**	1·00	80
921	9k. Oil industry	2·00	1·75

166 Map in Envelope

1990. Tenth Anniv of Pan-African Postal Union. Multicoloured.
922	4k. Type **166**	90	70
923	10k. Map consisting of stamps and envelopes	2·60	1·80

167 *Muxima*

1990. "Stamp World London 90" International Stamp Exn. Paintings by Raul Indipwo. Multicoloured.
924	6k. *Three Graces* (horiz)	1·00	90
925	9k. Type **167**	1·80	1·25

168 Antelope

1990. Protected Animals. Sable Antelope. Multicoloured.
926	5k. Type **168**	2·60	1·90
927	5k. Male and female	2·60	1·90
928	5k. Female	2·60	1·90
929	5k. Female and young	2·60	1·90

169 Porcelain Rose

1990. "Belgica 90" International Stamp Exhibition, Brussels. Flowers. Multicoloured.
930	5k. Type **169**	55	60
931	8k. Indian carnation	90	80
932	10k. Allamanda	1·10	90
MS933	113×139 mm. 40k. Hibiscus and "Mannequin Pis", Brussels (49×39 mm)	4·50	4·00

170 Zebra Drinking

1990. International Literacy Year. Multicoloured.
934	5k. Type **170**	1·10	80
935	5k. Butterfly	1·10	80
936	5k. Horse's head	1·10	80
MS937	210×260 mm. 30×1k. Composite jungle-scene showing various animals and plants	7·50	7·00

171 Flag and People

1990. Tenth Anniv of People's Assembly.
938	**171**	10k. multicoloured	50	30

172 Dove, Flag and Workers

1990. Third Popular Movement for the Liberation of Angola–Labour Party Congress.
939	**172**	14k. multicoloured	80	50

173 Uniform, 1961

1991. 30th Anniv of Armed Independence Movement. Freedom Fighters' Uniforms. Multicoloured.
940	6k. Type **173**	1·40	1·00
941	6k. Pau N'Dulo, 1962–63	1·40	1·00
942	6k. Military uniform, 1968	1·40	1·00
943	6k. Military uniform from 1972	1·40	1·00

174 Marimba

1991. Musical Instruments. Multicoloured.
944	6k. Type **174**	1·20	85
945	6k. Ngoma ya Mucupela (double-ended drum)	1·20	85
946	6k. Ngoma la Txina (floor-standing drum)	1·20	85
947	6k. Kissange	1·20	85

175 Iona National Park

1991. African Tourism Year. Multicoloured.
948	3k. Type **175**	50	40
949	7k. Kalandula Falls	1·00	80
950	35k. Lobito Bay	3·00	2·40
951	60k. *Welwitschia mirabilis*	5·00	4·50

176 Kabir of the Dembos

1991. "Espamer '91" Spain–Latin America Stamp Exhibition, Buenos Aires. Dogs. Multicoloured.
953	5k. Type **176**	60	50
954	7k. Ombua	90	70
955	11k. Kabir massongo	1·50	1·10
956	12k. Kawa tchowe	1·60	1·20

177 Judo

1991. Olympic Games, Barcelona (1992) (1st issue). Multicoloured.
957	4k. Type **177**	30	20
958	6k. Yachting	40	30
959	10k. Marathon	70	50
960	100k. Swimming	6·50	5·25

178 Mother and Child

1991. 13th Anniv of Angolan Red Cross. Multicoloured.
961	20k.+5k. Type **178**	1·40	1·40
962	40k.+5k. Zebra and foal	2·40	2·40

179 Quadrant and Galleon

1991. "Iberex '91" Stamp Exhibition. Navigational Instruments. Multicoloured.
963	5k. Type **179**	50	35
964	15k. Astrolabe and caravel	1·40	1·00
965	20k. Cross-staff and caravel	1·80	1·30
966	50k. Navigation chart by Francisco Rodrigues and galleon	4·50	3·25

180 Common Eagle Ray

1992. Rays. Multicoloured.
967	40k. Type **180**	1·20	50
968	50k. Spotted eagle ray	1·50	80
969	66k. Manta ray	2·20	1·20
970	80k. Brown ray	2·75	1·60
MS971	112×140 mm. 25k. "Atlantic manta"	3·00	3·00

181 Mukixi wa Mbwesu Mask

1992. Quioca Painted Masks (1st series).
972	–	60k. orange and brown	50	35
973	–	100k. black, verm & red	70	60
974	**181**	150k. pink and orange	1·00	95
975	–	250k. red and brown	1·70	1·50

DESIGNS: 60k. Kalelwa mask; 100k. Mikixe wa Kino mask; 250k. Cikunza mask.
See also Nos. 1006/7 and 1021/4.

182 *Ptaeroxylon obliquum*

1992. "Lubrapex 92" Brazilian–Portuguese Stamp Exhibition, Lisbon. Medicinal Plants. Each brown, stone and deep brown.
976	200k. Type **182**	1·00	65
977	300k. *Spondias mombin*	1·50	1·00
978	500k. *Parinari curatellifolia*	2·50	1·60
979	600k. *Cochlospermum angolense*	3·00	1·90

183 King and Missionaries

1992. 500th Anniv (1991) of Baptism of First Angolans. Multicoloured.
980	150k. Type **183**	80	50
981	420k. Ruins of M'Banza Congo Church	2·20	1·40
982	470k. Muxima Church	2·40	1·50
983	500k. Cross superimposed on children's faces	2·60	1·60

184 Dimba House

1992. "Expo '92" World's Fair, Seville. Traditional Houses. Multicoloured.
984	150k. Type **184**	4·00	4·00
985	330k. Cokwe house	2·20	1·40
986	360k. Mbali house	2·40	1·60
987	420k. Ambwela house	2·60	1·80
988	500k. House of the Upper Zambezi	3·00	2·50

185 Lovebirds

1992. Nature Protection. Peach-faced Lovebirds. Multicoloured.
989	150k. Type **185**	1·20	80
990	200k. Birds feeding	1·50	1·00
991	250k. Bird in hand	1·90	1·30
992	300k. Bird on perch	2·30	1·50

186 *Crucifixion*

1992. Visit of Pope John Paul II. Sheet 151×90 mm containing T **186** and similar vert design plus two labels.
MS993	340k. Type **186** 370k. *The Lost Soul*	5·50	4·50

187 Hurdling

1992. Olympic Games, Barcelona (2nd issue). Multicoloured.
994	120k. Type **187**	70	60
995	180k. Cycling	1·30	1·10
996	240k. Roller hockey	1·50	1·30
997	360k. Basketball	2·20	1·80

188 Women with Nets

1992. Fishing. Multicoloured.
998	65k. Type **188**	60	50
999	90k. Fishermen pulling in nets	80	70
1000	100k. Fishermen checking traps	90	80
1001	120k. Fishing canoes	1·10	95

189 *Santa Maria*

1992. 500th Anniv of Discovery of America by Columbus and Genova 92 International Thematic Stamp Exhibition. Sheet 95×70 mm.
MS1002	**189** 500k. multicoloured	7·50	7·00

190 Crowd with Ballot Papers around Ballot Box

1992. First Free Elections. Multicoloured.
1003	120k. Type **190**	90	75
1004	150k. Doves, map, people and ballot box	1·10	1·10
1005	200k. Dove, crowd and ballot box	1·50	1·20

1992. Quioca Painted Masks (2nd series). As T **181**.
1006	72k. brown, black and yellow	60	50
1007	80k. red, black and brown	70	60
1008	120k. pink, black and red	1·00	90
1009	210k. black and yellow	1·70	1·50

DESIGNS: 72k. Cihongo mask; 80k. Mbwasu mask; 120k. Cinhanga mask; 210k. Kalewa mask.

191 Mail Van

1992. Introduction of Express Mail Service in Angola. Multicoloured.
1010	450k. Type **191**	4·75	4·50
1011	550k. Boeing 707 airplane	6·75	5·50

192 Weather Balloon

1993. World Meteorology Day. Meteorological Instruments. Multicoloured.
1012	250k. Type **192**	2·75	1·80
1013	470k. Actinometer	3·75	3·00
1014	500k. Rain-gauge	4·00	3·25

193 Rayed Hat

1993. Molluscs. Multicoloured.
1015	210k. Type **193**	75	60
1016	330k. Bubonian conch	1·20	90
1017	400k. African pelican's foot	1·50	1·20
1018	500k. White spindle	1·80	1·40
MS1019	70×90 mm. 1000k. "Pusionella nifat"	3·50	3·50

194 Leopard

1993. Africa Day. Sheet 95×70 mm.
MS1020	**194** 1500k. multicoloured	6·00	4·50

1993. Quioca Art (1st series). As T **181**.
1021	72k. grey, red and brown	25	20
1022	210k. pink and brown	60	55
1023	420k. black, brown & orge	1·80	1·50
1024	600k. black, red and brown	10	10

DESIGNS: 72k. Men with vehicles; 210k. Rider on antelope; 420k. Bird-plane; 600k. Carrying "soba".
See also Nos. 1038/41 and 1050/3.

195 Sansevieria cylindrica

1993. Cacti and Succulents. Multicoloured.
1025	360k. Type **195**	1·40	1·60
1026	400k. Milk-bush	1·80	1·60
1027	500k. Indian fig	2·00	2·30
1028	600k. *Dracaena aubryana*	2·75	2·40

196 Atlantic Hawksbill Turtle laying Eggs and Green Turtle

1993. Sea Turtles. Multicoloured.
1029	180k. Type **196**	80	70
1030	450k. Head of Atlantic hawksbill turtle and newly hatched turtles	2·00	1·70
1031	550k. Leather-back turtle	2·30	2·00
1032	630k. Loggerhead turtles	3·00	2·50

Nos. 1029/32 were issued together, *se-tenant*, forming a composite design.

197 People Dancing

1993. Union of Portuguese speaking Capital Cities. Sheet 95×71 mm.
MS1033	**197** 1500k. multicoloured	6·00	5·00

198 Vimbundi Pipe

1993. Tobacco Pipes. Multicoloured.
1034	72k. Type **198**	30	25
1035	200k. Vimbundi pipe (different)	9·00	70
1036	420k. Mutopa calabash water pipe	1·80	1·50
1037	600k. Pexi carved-head pipe	2·50	2·20

1993. Quioca Art (2nd series). As T **181**.
1038	300k. brown and orange	95	80
1039	600k. red and brown	2·00	1·60
1040	800k. black, orange and deep orange	2·50	2·20
1041	1000k. orange and brown	3·25	2·75

DESIGNS: 300k. Leopard and dog; 600k. Rabbits; 800k. Birds; 1000k. Birds and cockerel.

199 St. George's Mushroom

1993. Fungi. Multicoloured.
1042	300k. Type **199**	1·20	95
1043	500k. Death cap	2·00	1·50
1044	600k. *Amanita vaginata*	2·20	1·80
1045	1000k. Parasol mushroom	3·75	3·00

200 *Cinganji* (figurine of dancer, Bie province)

1994. National Culture Day. "Hong Kong '94" International Stamp Exhibition. Multicoloured.
1046	500k. Type **200**	80	75
1047	1000k. Chief's staff with carved woman's head (Bie province)	1·60	1·50
1048	1200k. Statuette of traveller riding ox (Huambo province)	2·00	1·80
1049	2200k. Corn pestle (Ovimbundu)	3·50	3·25

1994. Quioca Art (3rd series). As T **181**.
1050	500k. multicoloured	80	75
1051	2000k. red and brown	1·60	1·50
1052	2500k. red and brown	3·00	2·50
1053	3000k. carmine and red	3·50	3·25

DESIGNS: 500k. Bird on plant; 2000k. Plant with roots; 2500k. Plant; 3000k. Fern.

201 Orgy

1994. AIDS Awareness Campaign. Multicoloured.
1054	500k. Type **201**	1·00	80
1055	1000k. Masked figure using infected syringe passing box of condoms to young couple	2·00	1·70
1056	3000k. Victims	5·00	4·50

202 Flag, Arrows and Small Ball

1994. World Cup Football Championship, U.S.A. Multicoloured.
1057	500k. Type **202**	8·00	70
1058	700k. Flag, four arrows and large ball	1·10	1·00
1059	2200k. Flag, goal net and ball	3·50	3·00
1060	2500k. Flag, ball and boot	4·00	3·50

203 Brachiosaurus

1994. "Philakorea 1994" International and "Singpex '94" Stamp Exhibitions. Dinosaurs. Multicoloured.
1061	1000k. Type **203**	1·00	50
1062	3000k. Spinosaurus	1·50	1·00
1063	5000k. Ouranosaurus	2·00	1·50
1064	10000k. Lesothosaurus	3·50	3·00
MS1065	102×145 mm. 19000k. Lesothosaurus and map (43×34 mm)	4·50	4·50

204 Brown Snake Eagle, Ostrich, Yellow-billed Stork and Pink-backed Pelican

1994. Tourism. Multicoloured.
1066	2000k. Type **204**	1·00	80
1067	4000k. Animals	1·50	1·30
1068	8000k. Women	2·40	2·00
1069	10000k. Men	3·00	2·50

205 Dual-service Wall-mounted Post Box

1994. Post Boxes. Multicoloured.
1070	500k. Type **205**	70	65
1071	7500k. Wall-mounted philatelic post box	1·30	1·20
1072	10000k. Free-standing post box	2·60	2·40
1073	21000k. Multiple service wall-mounted post box	3·50	3·00

206 *Heliothis armigera* (moth)

1994. Cotton Pests (Insects). Multicoloured.
1074	5000k. Type **206**	60	50
1075	6000k. *Bemisia tabasi*	75	60
1076	10000k. *Dysdercus* sp. (bug)	1·20	1·00
1077	27000k. *Spodoptera exigua* (moth)	3·25	2·50

207 "100"

1994. Cent of International Olympic Committee.
1078	**207** 27000k. red, yell & blk	2·40	2·00

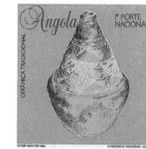

208 Pot

1995. Traditional Ceramics. With service indicator. Multicoloured. (a) INLAND POSTAGE. Inscr "PORTE NACIONAL".
1079	(1°) Type **208**	8·00	70
1080	(2°) Pot with figure of woman on lid	80	70

(b) INTERNATIONAL POSTAGE. Inscr "PORTE INTERNACIONAL".
1081	(1°) Pot with man's head on lid	1·60	1·50
1082	(2°) Duck-shaped pot	1·80	1·70

209 Making Fire

1995. The !Kung (Khoisan tribe). Multicoloured.
1083	10000k. Type **209**	60	55
1084	15000k. Tipping darts with poison	95	80
1085	20000k. Smoking	1·30	1·00
1086	25000k. Hunting	1·50	1·40
1087	28000k. Women and children	1·75	1·50
1088	30000k. Painting animals on walls	1·90	1·60

210 Vaccinating Child against Polio

1995. 90th Anniv of Rotary International. Multicoloured. (a) Inscr in Portuguese.
1089	27000k. Type **210**	2·00	2·00
1090	27000k. Examining baby	2·00	2·00
1091	27000k. Giving child vaccination	2·00	2·00

(b) Inscr in English.
1092	27000k. Type **210**	2·00	2·00
1093	27000k. As No. 1090	2·00	2·00
1094	27000k. As No. 1091	2·00	2·00
MS1095	Two sheets, each 110×80 mm. 81000k. Dove flying over map. (a) Inscr in Portuguese; (b) Inscr in English Set of 2 sheets	15·00	15·00

Nos. 1089/91 and 1092/4 respectively were issued together, *se-tenant*, forming composite designs.

211 "Sputnik 1" (satellite)

1995. World Telecommunications Day. Multicoloured.
1096	27000k. Type **211**	1·70	1·70
1097	27000k. "Intelsat" satellite and space shuttle	1·70	1·70
MS1098	100×80 mm. Nos. 1096/7	3·50	3·50

212 Doves above Baby on Daisy-covered Map

1995. 20th Anniv of Independence.
1099	**212** 2900k. multicoloured	1·75	1·75

213 Child, Containers and Fork-lift Truck

1996. Goods Transportation. Multicoloured.

1100	200k. Type **213**	25	20
1101	1265k. Sailing boats and *Mount Cameroon* (ferry)	1·00	80
1102	2583k. Fork-lift trucks loading and unloading *Mount Cameroon* (ferry)	2·00	1·70
1103	2583k. Truck	3·00	1·70
MS1104	106×76 mm. 1265k. Ferry	1·50	1·20

214 Women in Agriculture

1996. Fourth World Conference on Women, Peking (1995). Multicoloured.

1105	375k. Type **214**	30	30
1106	1106k. Women in education	90	75
1107	1265k. Women in business	1·00	80
1108	2900k. Dimba servant girl (vert)	2·30	1·80
MS1109	106×76 mm. 1500k. Traditional education (vert)	1·30	1·30

215 Verdant Hawk Moth

1996. Flora and Fauna. Multicoloured.

1110	1500k. Type **215**	60	50
1111	1500k. Western honey buzzard	40	30
1112	1500k. Bateleur	40	30
1113	1500k. Common kestrel	40	30
1114	4400k. Water lily	90	60
1115	4400k. Red-crested turaco	45	35
1116	4400k. Giraffe	40	35
1117	4400k. African elephant	45	35
1118	5100k. Panther toad	1·10	70
1119	5100k. Hippopotamus	50	40
1120	5100k. Cattle egret	50	40
1121	5100k. Lion	50	40
1122	6000k. African hunting ("wild") dog	1·30	1·10
1123	6000k. Helmeted turtle	60	50
1124	6000k. African pygmy goose	60	50
1125	6000k. Egyptian plover	60	50
MS1126	100×70 mm. 12000k. Spotted hyena	2·00	1·60

Nos. 1111/13, 1115/17, 1119/21 and 1123/5 respectively were issued together, *se-tenant*, forming composite designs.

216 California Quail

1997. Birds. Multicoloured.

1127	5500k. Type **216**	50	35
1128	5500k. Prairie chicken ("Greater Prairie Chicken")	50	35
1129	5500k. Indian blue quail ("Painted Quail")	50	35
1130	5500k. Golden pheasant	50	35
1131	5500k. Crested wood partridge ("Roulroul Partridge")	50	35
1132	5500k. Ceylon spurfowl ("Ceylon Sourfowl")	50	35
1133	5500k. Himalayan snowcock	50	35
1134	5500k. Temminck's tragopan ("Temminicks Tragopan")	50	35
1135	5500k. Lady Amherst's pheasant	50	35
1136	5500k. Great curassow	50	35
1137	5500k. Red-legged partridge	50	35
1138	5500k. Himalayan monal pheasant ("Impeyan Pheasant")	50	35
1139	5500k. Anna's hummingbird	1·30	75
1140	5500k. Blue-throated hummingbird	1·30	75
1141	5500k. Broad-tailed hummingbird	1·30	75
1142	5500k. Costa's hummingbird	1·30	75
1143	5500k. White-eared hummingbird	1·30	75
1144	5500k. Calliope hummingbird	1·30	75
1145	5500k. Violet-crowned hummingbird	1·30	75
1146	5500k. Rufous hummingbird	1·30	75
1147	5500k. Crimson topaz ("Crimson Topaz Hummingbird")	1·30	75
1148	5500k. Broad-billed hummingbird	1·30	75
1149	5500k. Frilled coquette ("Frilled Coquette Hummingbird")	1·70	75
1150	5500k. Ruby-throated hummingbird	1·70	75
MS1151	Two sheets, each 100×70 mm. (a) 12000k. Ring-necked pheasant; (b) 12000k. Racquet-tailed hummingbird Set of 2 sheets	8·50	6·00

217 Lions attacking Zebra

1996. African Wildlife. Multicoloured.

1152	180k. Type **217**	80	55
1153	180k. Lions watching zebras	80	55
1154	180k. African hunting dogs attacking gnu	80	55
1155	180k. Pack of hunting dogs chasing herd of gnu	80	55
1156	450k. Lions stalking isolated zebra	80	55
1157	450k. Male lion	80	55
1158	450k. Hunting dogs surrounding gnu	80	55
1159	450k. Close-up of African hunting dog	80	55
1160	550k. Cheetah	80	55
1161	550k. Cheetah chasing springbok	80	55
1162	550k. Leopard	80	55
1163	550k. Leopard stalking oryx	80	55
1164	630k. Cheetah running beside herd of springbok	80	55
1165	630k. Cheetah overpowering springbok	80	55
1166	630k. Leopard approaching oryx	80	55
1167	630k. Leopard leaping at oryx	80	55

Nos. 1152/67 were issued together, *se-tenant*, in sheetlets with each horizontal strip forming a composite design of lions, cheetah, hunting dogs or leopard attacking prey.

218 Couple with Elderly Woman

1996. 50th Anniv of U.N.O. Multicoloured.

1168	3500k. Type **218**	2·30	1·70
1169	3500k. Children at water pump	2·30	1·70
MS1170	104×74 mm. 8000k. Unloading sacks from ship	5·50	4·50

219 *Styrbjorn* (Swedish sail warship), 1789

1996. Ships. Multicoloured.

1171	6000k. Type **219**	75	55
1172	6000k. U.S.S. *Constellation* (United States frigate), 1797	75	55
1173	6000k. *Taureau* (French torpedo-boat), 1865	75	55
1174	6000k. French bomb ketch	75	55
1175	6000k. *Sardegna* (Italian battleship), 1881	75	55
1176	6000k. H.M.S. *Glasgow* (frigate), 1867	75	55
1177	6000k. U.S.S. *Essex* (frigate), 1812	75	55
1178	6000k. H.M.S. *Inflexible* (battleship), 1881	75	55
1179	6000k. H.M.S. *Minotaur* (ironclad), 1863	75	55
1180	6000k. *Napoleon* (French steam ship of the line), 1854	75	55
1181	6000k. *Sophia Amalia* (Danish galleon), 1650	75	55
1182	6000k. *Massena* (French battleship), 1887	75	55
MS1183	Two sheets, each 105×74 mm. (a) 12000k. *Royal Prince* (English galleon), 1666 (vert); (b) 12000k. H.M.S. *Tremendous* (British ship of the line), 1806 (vert) Set of 2 sheets	5·00	4·00

220 Mask and Drilling Platform

1996. 20th Anniv of Sonangol. Multicoloured.

1184	1000k. Type **220**	60	40
1185	1000k. Storage tanks and mask of woman's face	50	40
1186	2500k. Mask with beard and gas bottles	1·10	90
1187	5000k. Refuelling airplane and mask of monkey's face	2·00	1·70

221 Slaves in Ship's Hold

1996. "Brapex 96" National Stamp Exhibition, Recife, Brazil. Multicoloured.

1188	20000k. Type **221**	3·00	2·50
1189	20000k. Ship capsizing	3·00	2·50
1190	30000k. Boats punting out to ship	4·75	3·50
1191	30000k. Inspection of slaves	4·75	3·50
MS1192	100×70 mm. 50000k. Boats (close-up of detail of No. 1190)	7·50	6·00

222 Mission Church, Huila

1996. Churches. Multicoloured.

1193	5000k. Type **222**	75	65
1194	10000k. Church of Our Lady, PoPulo	1·50	1·30
1195	10000k. Church of Our Lady, Nazare	1·50	1·30
1196	25000k. St. Adriao's Church	3·75	3·25

223 Handball

1996. Olympic Games, Atlanta, U.S.A. Multicoloured.

1197	5000k. Type **223**	10	10
1198	10000k. Swimming (horiz)	15	10
1199	25000k. Athletics	2·75	2·00
1200	35000k. Shooting (horiz)	3·75	3·00
MS1201	76×106 mm. 65000k. Basketball (horiz)	7·00	6·50

224 Dolphins, and Angola on Map of Africa

1996. 40th Anniv of Popular Movement for the Liberation of Angola (MPLA).

1202	**224**	30000k. multicoloured	4·50	4·00

The face value of No. 1202 is wrongly inscr as "300.00.00".

225 AVE, Spain

1997. Trains. Multicoloured.

1203	100000k. Type **225**	1·80	1·30
1204	100000k. "Hikari", Japan	1·80	1·30
1205	100000k. "Warbonnet" diesel locomotives, U.S.A.	1·80	1·30
1206	100000k. "Deltic" diesel locomotive, Great Britain	1·80	1·30
1207	100000k. "Eurostar", France and Great Britain	1·80	1·30
1208	100000k. ETR 450, Italy	1·80	1·30
1209	140000k. Class E1300 diesel locomotive, Morocco	2·30	1·70
1210	140000k. ICE, Germany	2·30	1·70
1211	140000k. Class X2000, Sweden	2·30	1·70
1212	140000k. TGV, France	2·30	1·70
1213	250000k. Steam locomotive	3·25	3·00
1214	250000k. Garratt steam locomotive	3·25	3·00
1215	250000k. General Electric electric locomotive	3·25	3·00
MS1216	Two sheets, each (a) 106×76 mm. 11000k. Via Rail diesel locomotive, Canada (49×37 mm); (b) 76×106 mm. 11000k. Canadian Pacific steam locomotive, Canada (37×49 mm) Set of 2 sheets	12·50	11·00

Nos. 1203/8 were issued together, *se-tenant*, forming a composite design.

226 Thoroughbred

1997. Horses. Multicoloured.

1217	100000k. Type **226**	1·30	1·10
1218	100000k. Palomino and Appaloosa	1·30	1·10
1219	100000k. Grey and white Arabs	1·30	1·10
1220	100000k. Arab colt	1·30	1·10
1221	100000k. Thoroughbred colt	1·30	1·10
1222	100000k. Mustang (with hind quarters of another mustang)	1·30	1·10
1223	100000k. Head of mustang and hind quarters of Furioso	1·30	1·10
1224	100000k. Head and shoulders of Furioso	1·30	1·10
1225	120000k. Thoroughbred	1·70	1·30
1226	120000k. Arab and palomino	1·70	1·30
1227	120000k. Arab and Chincoteague	1·70	1·30
1228	120000k. Pintos	1·70	1·30
1229	120000k. Przewalski's Horse	1·70	1·30
1230	120000k. Thoroughbred colt	1·70	1·30
1231	120000k. Arabs	1·70	1·30
1232	120000k. New Forest pony	1·70	1·30
1233	140000k. Selle Francais	1·90	1·60
1234	140000k. Fjord	1·90	1·60
1235	140000k. Percheron	1·90	1·60
1236	140000k. Italian heavy draught horse	1·90	1·60
1237	140000k. Shagya Arab	1·90	1·60
1238	140000k. Avelignese	1·90	1·60
1239	140000k. Czechoslovakian warmblood	1·90	1·60
1240	140000k. New Forest pony	1·90	1·60
MS1241	Two sheets, each 100×70 mm. (a) 215000k. Thoroughbred mother and foal; (b) 220000k. Head and shoulders of thoroughbred Set of 2 sheets	8·00	6·00

Stamps of the same value were issued together, *se-tenant*, Nos. 1217/24 and 1225/32 respectively forming composite designs.

227 Jules Rimet Trophy (Uruguay, 1930)

1997. World Cup Football Championship, France.

1242	**227**	100000k. black	1·90	1·40
1243	–	100000k. black	1·90	1·40
1244	–	100000k. multicoloured	1·90	1·40
1245	–	100000k. multicoloured	1·90	1·40
1246	–	100000k. multicoloured	1·90	1·40
1247	–	100000k. black	1·90	1·40
1248	–	100000k. multicoloured	1·90	1·40
1249	–	100000k. black	1·90	1·40
1250	–	100000k. multicoloured	1·90	1·40
1251	–	100000k. multicoloured	1·90	1·40
1252	–	100000k. black	1·90	1·40
MS1253	Two sheets. (a) 127×102 mm. 220000k. multicoloured (Angola team); (b) 76×102 mm. 250000k. multicoloured (Angola team, 1997) Set of 2 sheets	10·00	8·50	

DESIGNS—Victory celebrations: No. 1243, Germany (1954); 1244, Brazil (1970); 1245, Maradona holding trophy (Argentina, 1986); 1246, Brazil (1994). Official team photographs: 1247, Germany (1954); 1248, Uruguay (1958); 1249, Italy (1938); 1250, Brazil (1962); 1251, Brazil (1970); 1252, Uruguay (1930).

228 House
Insurance

1998. 20th Anniv of ENSA Insurance. Multicoloured.
1254	240000k. Type **228**	2·10	1·80
1255	240000k. Forklift truck carrying egg (industrial risks)	2·10	1·80
1256	240000k. Egg on cross (personal accidents)	2·10	1·80
1257	240000k. Egg on waves (pleasure boating)	2·10	1·80
MS1258 99×155 mm. 350000k. Emblem (59×39 mm)		3·00	2·50

229 Coral

1998. "Expo '98" World's Fair, Lisbon, Portugal. Multicoloured.
1259	100000k. Type **229**	1·70	1·30
1260	100000k. Sea urchin	1·70	1·30
1261	100000k. Seahorses	1·70	1·30
1262	100000k. Sea anemone	1·70	1·30
1263	240000k. Sea slug	4·00	3·00
1264	240000k. Finger coral	4·00	3·00

230 Royal Assyrian
(*Terinos terpander*)

1998. Butterflies. Multicoloured.
1265	120000k. Type **230**	1·60	1·30
1266	120000k. Wanderer (*Bematistes aganice*)	1·60	1·30
1267	120000k. Great orange-tip (*Hebomoia glaucippe*)	1·60	1·30
1268	120000k. Alfalfa butterfly (*Colias eurytheme*)	1·60	1·30
1269	120000k. Red-banded perelite (*Pereute leucodrosime*)	1·60	1·30
1270	120000k. Large copper (*Lycaena dispar*)	1·60	1·30
1271	120000k. Malachite (*Metamorpha stelenes*)	1·60	1·30
1272	120000k. Tiger swallowtail (*Papilio glaucus*)	1·60	1·30
1273	120000k. Monarch (*Danaus plexippus*)	1·60	1·30
1274	120000k. Grecian shoemaker (*Catonephele numili*)	1·60	1·30
1275	120000k. Silver-studded blue (*Plebejus argus*)	1·60	1·30
1276	120000k. Common eggfly (*Hypolimnas bolina*)	1·60	1·30
1277	120000k. Brazilian dynastor (*Dynastor napolean*) (horiz)	1·60	1·30
1278	120000k. Saturn butterfly (*Zeuxidia amethystus*) (horiz)	1·60	1·30
1279	120000k. Pipevine swallowtail (*Battus philenor*) (horiz)	1·60	1·30
1280	120000k. Orange-barred sulphur (*Phoebis philea*) (horiz)	1·60	1·30
1281	120000k. African monarch (*Danaus chrysippus*) (horiz)	1·60	1·30
1282	120000k. Green-underside blue (*Glaucopsyche alexis*) (horiz)	1·60	1·30
MS1283 Three sheets. (a) 68×98 mm. 250000k. Gold-banded forester (*Euphaedra neophron*); (b) 98×68 mm. 250000k. Hewitson's uraneis (*Uraneis ucubis*) on *Armillaria straminea* (fungus); (c) 98×68 mm. 250000k. Brown hairstreak (*Thecla betulae*) (horiz) Set of 3 sheets		23·00	19·00

Nos. 1265/70, 1271/6 and 1277/82 respectively were issued together, *se-tenant*, forming composite designs.

231 British Tortoiseshell

1998. Cats and Dogs. Multicoloured.
1284	140000k. Type **231**	1·10	95
1285	140000k. Chinchilla	1·10	95

1286	140000k. Russian blue	1·10	95
1287	140000k. Black persian (longhair) (wrongly inscribed "Longhiar")	1·10	95
1288	140000k. British red tabby	1·10	95
1289	140000k. Birman	1·10	95
1290	140000k. West Highland white terrier	1·10	95
1291	140000k. Red setter	1·10	95
1292	140000k. Dachshund	1·10	95
1293	140000k. St. John water-dog	1·10	95
1294	140000k. Shetland sheep-dog	1·10	95
1295	140000k. Dalmatian	1·10	95
MS1296 Two sheets, each 91×73 mm. (a) 500000k. Turkish van (swimming cat); (b) 500000k. Labrador retriever Set of 2 sheets		12·00	11·00

232 Dolphin, Yacht and Container Ship

1998. First Anniv of Government of Unity and National Reconciliation. Multicoloured.
1297	100000k. Type **232**	1·50	1·20
1298	100000k. Yacht, dolphin and container ship (different)	1·50	1·20
1299	100000k. Yacht, container ship and railway line	1·50	1·20
1300	100000k. Coastline and electricity pylons	1·50	1·20
1301	200000k. Grapes, goat and railway	3·00	2·40
1302	200000k. Village	3·00	2·40
1303	200000k. Tractor, grapes and railway	3·00	2·40
1304	200000k. Coal train	3·00	2·40
1305	200000k. Railway line with branch and pylons	3·00	2·40
1306	200000k. Elephant and tip of tree	3·00	2·40
1307	200000k. Edge of coastline with pylon	3·00	2·40
1308	200000k. Tree trunk and coastline	3·00	2·40

Nos. 1297/1308 were issued together, *se-tenant*, forming a composite design.

233 Ostrich,
Children and
Blackboard

1998. Decade of Education in Africa. Sheet 100×70 mm.
MS1309 **233** 400000k. mult — 5·00 4·00

234 Lion

1998. Animals of the Grande Porte. Multicoloured.
1310	100000k. Type **234**	1·50	1·20
1311	100000k. Hippopotamus (*Hippopotamus amphibius*)	1·50	1·20
1312	100000k. African elephant (*Loxodonta africana*)	1·50	1·20
1313	100000k. Giraffe (*Giraffa campelopardalis*)	1·50	1·20
1314	220000k. African buffalo (*Synceros caffer*)	3·00	2·40
1315	220000k. Gorilla (*Gorilla gorilla*)	3·00	2·40
1316	220000k. White rhinoceros (*Ceratotherium simum*)	3·00	2·40
1317	220000k. Gemsbok (*Oryx gazella*)	3·00	2·40

There are errors in the Latin inscriptions.

236 Diana,
Princess of Wales

1998. Diana, Princess of Wales Commemoration. Multicoloured.
1319	100000k. Type **236**	1·40	1·20
1320	100000k. Wearing white balldress	1·40	1·20
1321	100000k. Holding handbag	1·40	1·20
1322	100000k. Wearing black evening dress	1·40	1·20
1323	100000k. Holding bouquet (white jacket)	1·40	1·20
1324	100000k. Wearing pearl necklace (looking down)	1·40	1·20
1325	100000k. Wearing pearl necklace (head raised)	1·40	1·20
1326	100000k. Speaking, wearing green velvet jacket	1·40	1·20
1327	100000k. Wearing sunglasses	1·40	1·20
1328	100000k. Wearing black jacket and white blouse	1·40	1·20
1329	100000k. Wearing green blouse	1·40	1·20
1330	100000k. Holding flowers (black jacket)	1·40	1·20
1331	150000k. With young girl amputee	2·20	1·80
1332	150000k. With two amputees	2·20	1·80
1333	150000k. Walking through minefield	2·20	1·80
MS1334 76×106 mm. 400000k. In mine protective clothing		6·50	5·50

237 *Pagurites* sp.

1998. International Year of the Ocean. Multicoloured.
1335	100000k. Type **237**	45	35
1336	100000k. *Callinectes marginatus* (crab)	90	80
1337	100000k. *Thais forbesi*	90	90
1338	100000k. *Ostrea tulipa*	90	80
1339	100000k. *Balanus amphitrite*	90	80
1340	100000k. *Uca tangeri*	90	80
1341	170000k. *Littorina angulifera*	1·60	1·40
1342	170000k. Great hairy melongena (*Semifusus morio*)	1·60	1·40
1343	170000k. *Thais coronata*	1·60	1·40
1344	170000k. *Cerithium atratum* on red branch	1·60	1·40
1345	170000k. *Ostrea tulipa* (different)	1·60	1·40
1346	170000k. *Cerithium atratum* on green branch	1·60	1·40
MS1347 Two sheets, each 85×110 mm. (a) 300000k. *Goniopsis* (crab) (horiz); (b) 300000k. Shell Set of 2 sheets		6·00	5·50

238 Mangos

1998. "Portugal 98" International Stamp Exhibition, Lisbon. Fruit and Vegetables. Multicoloured.
1348	100000k. Type **238**	1·40	1·10
1349	100000k. Guava	1·40	1·10
1350	120000k. Chillies	1·60	1·30
1351	120000k. Sweet corn	1·60	1·30
1352	140000k. Sliced bananas	1·90	1·50
1353	140000k. Avocadoes	1·90	1·50

239 Bimba Canoe

1998. Canoes. Multicoloured.
1354	250000k. Type **239**	2·75	2·50
1355	250000k. Sailing canoe, Ndongo	2·75	2·50
1356	250000k. Building canoes in Ndongo	2·75	2·50

240 *Titanic*

1998. The *Titanic* (liner that sank on maiden voyage, 1912). Sheet 200×160 mm containing T **240** and similar designs. Multicoloured.
MS1357 350000k. Type **240**; 350000k. Stern of *Titanic*; 350000k. *Titanic* under full steam (75×30 mm); 350000k. Bow of *Titanic* (37×60 mm) — 11·00 10·00

241 Ultralight Plane

1998. Aircraft. Multicoloured.
1358	150000k. Type **241**	1·00	80
1359	150000k. Gyroplane	1·00	80
1360	150000k. Business jet	1·00	80
1361	150000k. Convertible plane	1·00	80
1362	150000k. Chuterplane	1·00	80
1363	150000k. Twin-rotor craft	1·00	80
1364	150000k. Skycrane	1·00	80
1365	150000k. British Aerospace/ Aerospatiale Concorde Supersonic airliner	1·00	80
1366	150000k. Flying boat	1·00	80
1367	200000k. Boeing 737-100	1·80	1·40
1368	200000k. Ilyushin Il-62M	1·80	1·40
1369	250000k. Pedal-powered plane	1·20	90
1370	250000k. Sail plane	1·20	90
1371	250000k. Aerobatic plane	1·20	90
1372	250000k. Hang-gliding	1·20	90
1373	250000k. Balloon	1·20	90
1374	250000k. Glidercraft	1·20	90
1375	250000k. Model airplane	1·20	90
1376	250000k. Air racing	1·20	90
1377	250000k. Solar-celled plane	1·20	90
MS1378 Four sheets. (a) 110×85 mm. 1000000k. Boeing 777 (84×28 mm); (b) 85×110 mm. 1000000k. Space shuttle Columbia (28×84 mm); (c) 100×70 mm. 1000000k. Boeing 737-200 (84×28 mm); (d) 100×70 mm. 1000000k. Boeing 747-300 (84×28 mm) Set of 4 sheets		18·00	15·00

Nos. 1358/66 and 1369/77 respectively were issued together, *se-tenant*, forming composite designs.

242 *Parasaurolophus*

1998. Prehistoric Animals. Multicoloured.
1379	120000k. Type **242**	90	80
1380	120000k. Elaphosaurus	90	80
1381	120000k. Iguanodon	90	80
1382	120000k. Maiasaura	90	80
1383	120000k. Brontosaurus	90	80
1384	120000k. Plateosaurus	90	80
1385	120000k. Brachiosaurus	90	80
1386	120000k. Anatosaurus	90	80
1387	120000k. Tyrannosaurus rex	90	80
1388	120000k. Carnotaurus	90	80
1389	120000k. Corythosaurus	90	80
1390	120000k. Stegosaurus	90	80
1391	120000k. Iguanodon (different)	90	80
1392	120000k. Hadrosaurus (horiz)	90	80
1393	120000k. Ouranosaurus (horiz)	90	80
1394	120000k. Hypsilophodon (horiz)	90	80
1395	120000k. Brachiosaurus (horiz)	90	80
1396	120000k. Shunosaurus (horiz)	90	80
1397	120000k. Amargasaurus (horiz)	90	80
1398	120000k. Tuojiangosaurus (horiz)	90	80
1399	120000k. Monoclonius (horiz)	90	80
1400	120000k. Struthiosaurus (horiz)	90	80
MS1401 Two sheets, each 85×110 mm. (a) 550000k. Tyrannosaurus (different); (b) 550000k. Triceratops Set of 2 sheets		48·00	48·00

243 Head

1999. Endangered Species. The Lesser Flamingo (*Phoenicopterus minor*). Multicoloured.

1402	300000k. Type **243**	1·60	1·30
1403	300000k. Flamingo with wings outstretched	1·60	1·30
1404	300000k. Flamingo facing left	1·60	1·30
1405	300000k. Front view of flamingo	1·40	1·30

244 Hyacinth Macaw (*Anodorhynchus hyacinthinus*)

1999. Animals and Birds. Multicoloured.

1406	300000k. Type **244**	1·60	1·30
1407	300000k. Penguin (*Sphenisciformes*) (vert)	1·60	1·30
1408	300000k. Przewalski's horse (*Equus caballus przewalski*) (wrongly inscr "Equis")	1·60	1·30
1409	300000k. American bald eagle (*Haliaetus leucocephalus*) (vert)	1·60	1·30
1410	300000k. Spectacled bear (*Tremarctos ornatus*)	1·50	1·20
1411	300000k. Jay (*Aphelocoma*)	1·50	1·20
1412	300000k. Bare-legged scops owl (*Otus insularis*)	1·50	1·20
1413	300000k. Whale-headed stork (*Balaeniceps rex*)	1·50	1·20
1414	300000k. Atlantic ridley turtle (*Lepidochelys kempii*)	1·50	1·20
1415	300000k. Canadian river otter (*Lutra canadensis*)	1·50	1·20
1416	300000k. Swift fox (*Vulpes velox hebes*)	1·50	1·20
1417	300000k. Deer (*Odocoileus*)	1·50	1·20
1418	300000k. Orang-utan (*Pongo pygmaeus*)	1·50	1·20
1419	300000k. Golden lion tamarin (*Leontopithecus rosalia rosalia*) (inscr "Leontopitecus")	1·50	1·20
1420	300000k. Tiger (*Panthera tigris altaica*)	1·50	1·20
1421	300000k. Polecat (wrongly inscr "Tragelaphus eurycerus")	1·50	1·20
MS1422	Two sheets, each 110×85 mm. (a) 1000000k. Brown bear (*Ursus arctos horribilis*): (b) 1000000k. Giant panda (*Ailuropoda melanoleuca*)	10·00	9·00

245 Satellite circling Earth

1999. International Telecommunications Day.

1423	**245** 500000k. multicoloured	2·30	2·00

246 Waterfall, Andulo, Bie

1999. Waterfalls. Multicoloured.

1424	500000k. Type **246**	2·30	2·00
1425	500000k. Chiumbo, Lunda	2·30	2·00
1426	500000k. Ruacana, Cunene	2·30	2·00
1427	500000k. Coemba, Moxico	2·30	2·00

247 Emblem

1999. "Afrobasket '99" (Men's African Basketball Championship). Multicoloured.

1428	15000000k. Type **247**	1·30	1·30
1429	15000000k. Ball teetering on the edge of net, and players' hands	1·60	1·30
1430	15000000k. Hand scooping ball from edge of net	1·60	1·30
1431	15000000k. Flower holding ball	1·60	1·30

MS1432	95×83 mm. 25000000k. Enlarged detail from No. 1441 (39×29 mm)	7·25	2·20

248 African Continent

1999. South African Development Community (S.A.D.C.).

1433	**248** 1000000k. multicoloured	2·00	1·80

249 Duke and Duchess of York, 1923

1999. 100th Birthday of Queen Elizabeth, the Queen Mother. Multicoloured.

1434	**249** 200000k. black and gold	1·50	90
1435	- 200000k. mult	1·50	90
1436	- 200000k. mult	1·50	90
1437	- 200000k. mult	1·50	90
MS1438	154×157 mm. 500000k. Queen Mother in academic robes (37×50 mm)	3·00	2·50

DESIGNS: No. 1435, Portrait of Queen Mother wearing Star of the Garter; 1436, Queen Mother wearing fur stole; 1437, Queen Mother wearing blue hat.

250 Ekuikui II

1999. Rulers. Multicoloured.

1439	500000k. Type **250**	2·20	1·90
1440	500000k. Mvemba Nzinga	2·20	1·90
1441	500000k. Mwata Yamvu Nawej II	2·20	1·90
1442	500000k. Njinga Mbande	2·20	1·90
MS1443	104×76 mm. 1000000k. Mandume Ndemufayo	5·00	4·50

251 13th-century B.C. Pharaonic Barque

1999. Ships. Multicoloured.

1444	950000k. Type **251**	1·10	80
1445	950000k. Flemish carrack, 1480	1·10	80
1446	950000k. H.M.S. *Beagle* (Darwin), 1830	1·10	80
1447	950000k. *North Star* (paddle-steamer), 1852	1·10	80
1448	950000k. *Fram* (schooner, Amundsen and Nansen), 1892	1·10	80
1449	950000k. *Unyo Maru* (sail/steam freighter), 1909 (inscr "Unyon")	1·10	80
1450	950000k. *Juan Sebastian de Elcano* (cadet schooner), 1927	1·10	80
1451	950000k. *Tovarishch*, (three-masted cadet barque), 1933	1·10	80
1452	950000k. *Bucentaur* (Venetian state galley), 1728	1·10	80
1453	950000k. *Clermont* (first commercial paddle-steamer), 1807	1·10	80
1454	950000k. *Savannah* (paddle-steamer), 1819	1·10	80
1455	950000k. *Dromedary* (steam tug), 1844	1·10	80
1456	950000k. *Iberia* (steam freighter), 1881	1·10	80
1457	950000k. *Gluckauf* (tanker), 1886	1·10	80
1458	950000k. *Cidade de Paris* (ocean steamer), 1888	1·10	80
1459	950000k. *Mauretania* (liner), 1906	1·10	80
1460	950000k. *La Gloire* (first armoured-hull ship), 1859	1·10	80
1461	950000k. *L'Ocean*, (French battery ship), 1868	1·10	80

1462	950000k. *Dandolo* (Italian cruiser), 1876 (inscr "Dandalo") and stern of H.M.S. *Dreadnought*	1·10	80
1463	950000k. H.M.S. *Dreadnought* (battleship), 1906	1·10	80
1464	950000k. *Bismarck* (battleship), 1939 and stern of U.S.S. *Cleveland*	1·10	80
1465	950000k. U.S.S. *Cleveland* (cruiser), 1946	1·10	80
1466	950000k. U.S.S. *Boston* (first guided-missile cruiser), 1942 and stern of U.S.S. *Long Beach*	1·10	80
1467	950000k. U.S.S. *Long Beach* (first nuclear-powered cruiser), 1959	1·10	80
MS1468	Four sheets, each 75×70 mm. (a) 5000000k. 18th-century junk; (b) 5000000k. *Madre de Dios* (carrack) (wrongly inscr "Deus"), 1609; (c) 5000000k. Catamaran, 1861; (d) 5000000k. *Natchez* (Mississippi paddle-steamer), 1870	22·00	16·00

Nos. 1474/5, 1476/7 and 1478/9 respectively were issued together, *se-tenant*, forming a composite design.

252 Fly Agaric (*Amanita muscaria*)

1999. Fungi. Multicoloured.

1469	1000000k. Type **252** (wrongly inscr "Aminita")	1·00	75
1470	1000000k. Bronze boletus (*Boletus*)	1·00	75
1471	1000000k. Lawyer's wig (*Coprinus comatus*)	1·00	75
1472	1000000k. The blusher (*Amanita rubescens*) (inscr "Aminita")	1·00	75
1473	1000000k. Slimy-branded cort (*Cortinarius collinitus*)	1·00	75
1474	1000000k. Devil's boletus (*Boletus satanas*)	1·00	75
1475	1000000k. Parasol mushroom (*Lepiota procera*)	1·00	75
1476	1000000k. Trumpet agaric (*Clitocybe geotropa*)	1·00	75
1477	1000000k. Morchella crassipes	1·00	75
1478	1000000k. Boletus rufescens	1·00	75
1479	1000000k. Death cap (*Amanita phalloides*)	1·00	75
1480	1000000k. Collybia iocephala	1·00	75
1481	1000000k. Tricholoma aurantium	1·00	75
1482	1000000k. Cortinarius violaceus	1·00	75
1483	1000000k. Mycena polygramma	1·00	75
1484	1000000k. Psalliota augusta	1·00	75
1485	1000000k. Russula nigricans	1·00	75
1486	1000000k. Granulated boletus (*Boletus granulatus*)	1·00	75
1487	1000000k. Mycena strobilinoides	1·00	75
1488	1000000k. Caesar's mushroom (*Amanita caesarea*)	1·00	75
1489	1000000k. Fly agaric (*Amanita muscaria*) (different)	1·00	75
1490	1000000k. Boletus crocipodius	1·00	75
1491	1000000k. Cracked green russula (*Russula virescens*)	1·00	75
1492	1000000k. Saffron milk cap (*Lactarius deliciosus*)	1·00	75
1493	1250000k. Caesar's mushroom (*Amanita caesarea*) (different)	1·50	1·40
1495	1250000k. Red cracked boletus (*Boletus chrysenteron*) (wrongly inscr "chyrsenteron")	1·50	1·40
1496	1250000k. Butter mushroom (*Boletus luteus*)	1·50	1·40
1497	1250000k. Lawyer's wig (*Coprinus comatus*) (different)	1·50	1·40
1498	1250000k. Witch's hat (*Hygrocybe conica*)	1·50	1·40
1499	1250000k. Psalliota xanthoderma	1·50	1·40
MS1500	Two sheets, each 75×105 mm. (a) 5000000k. Mycena lilacifolia; (b) 5000000k. Psalliota haemorrhoidaria	11·00	8·00

253 Mercury and Venus

1999. 30th Anniv of First Manned Moon Landing. Multicoloured.

1501	3500000k. Type **253**	1·10	75
1502	3500000k. Jupiter	1·10	75
1503	3500000k. Neptune and Pluto	1·10	75

1504	3500000k. Earth and Mars	1·10	75
1505	3500000k. Saturn	1·10	75
1506	3500000k. Uranus	1·10	75
1507	3500000k. Explorer 17 satellite, 1963	1·10	75
1508	3500000k. Intelsat 4A satellite, 1975	1·10	75
1509	3500000k. GOES-D (Geostationary Operational Environmental Satellite), 1980	1·10	75
1510	3500000k. Intelsat 2 satellite, 1966	1·10	75
1511	3500000k. Navstar 2 (Navigation System with Timing And Ranging), 1978	1·10	75
1512	3500000k. S.M.S. (Solar Maximum Mission) satellite, 1980	1·10	75
1513	3500000k. Earth and astronaut walking in space	1·10	75
1514	3500000k. Mariner 8 spacecraft	1·10	75
1515	3500000k. Viking 10 spacecraft	1·10	75
1516	3500000k. Ginga satellite	1·10	75
1517	3500000k. Soyuz 19 spacecraft (inscr "satelite")	1·10	75
1518	3500000k. Voyager spacecraft	1·10	75
1519	3500000k. Hubble space telescope (vert)	1·10	75
1520	3500000k. Launch of space shuttle *Atlantis* (vert)	1·10	75
1521	3500000k. Uhuru satellite (vert)	1·10	75
1522	3500000k. Mir space station (vert)	1·10	75
1523	3500000k. Gemini 7 spacecraft (vert)	1·10	75
1524	3500000k. Venera 7 spacecraft (vert)	1·10	75
MS1525	Five sheets (a) 95×85 mm. 6000000k. Astronaut from Apollo 17 walking on moon (vert); (b) 95×85 mm. 6000000k. Astronaut driving moon buggy (vert); (c) 85×110 mm. 12000000k. Launch of commercial satellite SBS 4 (vert); (d) 85×110 mm. Neil Armstrong (astronaut) (vert); (e) 110×85 mm. 12000000k. Earth and *Columbia* spacecraft	18·00	15·00

No. 1523 is inscribed "GEMNI" in error.

254 Night Attack by 47 Ronin

1999. 150th Death Anniv of Katushika Hokusai (artist). Multicoloured.

1526	3500000k. Type **254**	1·10	75
1527	3500000k. *Usigafuchi no Kudan*	1·10	75
1528	3500000k. Sketch of seated man	1·10	75
1529	3500000k. Sketch of animals and birds	1·10	75
1530	3500000k. *Autumn Pheasant*	1·10	75
1531	3500000k. Rural landscape	1·10	75
1532	3500000k. *Survey of the region*	1·10	75
1533	3500000k. Kabuki theatre	1·10	75
1534	3500000k. Sketch of hen	1·10	75
1535	3500000k. Sketch of wheelwright	1·10	75
1536	3500000k. *Excursion to Enoshima*	1·10	75
1537	3500000k. Sumida River landscape	1·10	75
MS1538	Two sheets, each 100×70 mm. (a) 12000000k. Japanese calligraphy between woman and child (vert); (b) 12000000k. Woman dressing hair (vert)	8·00	6·50

255 SNCF Class 242 Steam Locomotive

2000. "PHILEX FRANCE 99" International Stamp Exhibition, Paris. Locomotives. Two sheets, each 111×80 mm containing T **255** and similar horiz design. Multicoloured.

MS1539	(a) 12k. Type **255** (b) 12k. Prototype Linear Propulsion Hover Train	13·50	12·00

257 Zebra

2000. Fauna. Multicoloured.

1540	1k.50 Type **256**	1·00	90
1541	2k. Short-tailed fruit bat	1·30	1·20
1542	3k. California condor	1·90	1·80
1543	5k.50 Lion	3·50	3·25

MS1544 Eight sheets:—140×179 mm.
(a) 3k.50×6, Florida white-tailed deer; Turkey; Bullfrog; Manatee; Greenback cutthroat trout; (b) 3k.50×6, White-faced sapajou; Toucan; Eyelash viper; Tree frog; Golden lion tamarin; Harpy eagle:—140×179 mm. (vert) (c) 3k.50×6, Mountain gorilla; Black rhino; Cape buffalo; Jackson chameleon; Cape cobra; Meerkats; (d) 3k.50×6, Kangaroo; Koala; Rainbow bee-eater; Red-eyed tree frog; Townsville blue-eye; Snake-necked tortoise:—107×77 mm. (vert) (e) 12k. Three-toed sloth; (f) 12k. Cheetah; (g) 12k. Orangutan:—70×100 mm. (vert) 12k. Ring-tailed lemur ... 40·00 ... 34·00

256 Harpy Eagle

2000. Birds. Multicoloured.

1545	1k.50 Type **257**	1·40	1·10
1546	2k. Andean condor	1·50	1·40
1547	3k. Lappet-faced vulture (vert)	2·30	2·00
1547a	5k.50 Vulture	4·25	4·00

MS1548 Eight sheets 128×127 mm.
(a) 3k.50×6, American kestrel (*Falco sparverius*) (inscr "sperterius"); Spectacled owl (*Pulsatrix perspicillata*); White-tailed kite (*Eleanus leucurus*) (inscr "Elemus"); Boobook owl (*Ninox novaeseelandiae*) (inscr "novaseeeelandiar"); *Polemaetus bellicosus* (inscr "Polmactus"); Caracara (*Polyborus plancus*); (b) 3k.50×6, Northern goshawk (*Accipiter gentiles*) (inscr "Acolpiler genttlis"); Hawk owl (*Surnia ulula*) (wrongly inscr "Surnis"); Peregrine falcon (*Falco prregrinus*); Eastern screech owl (*Otus asio*); African fish eagle (*Haliaeetus vocifer*) (inscr "Haliaectus"); Laughing falcon (*Herpetotheres cachinnans*) (inscr "Herpetothers"):—85×127 mm. (c) 6k.50×3, Verreaux's eagle; Bonelli's eagle; African fish eagle:—127×85 mm. (d) 6k.50×3, Bald eagle (vert); Tawny eagle (vert); Eagle (vert); (e) 85×110 mm. 12k. Lanner falcon (vert); (f) 110×85 mm. 12k. King vultures; (g) 85×111 mm. 15k. Secretary bird (*Sagittarius serpentarius*); (h) 15k. Golden eagle (*Aquila chrysaetos*) (inscr "chrysctos") ... 40·00 ... 40·00

258 Zebra (*Equs zebra*)

2000. Animals and Birds. Multicoloured.

1549	1k.50 Type **258**	1·00	80
1550	1k.50 Golden palm weaver (*Ploceus xanthops*)	1·00	80
1551	1k.50 Hunting dog (*Lycaon pictus*)	1·00	80
1552	1k.50 Cheetah (*Acinonyx jubatus*)	1·30	1·00
1553	1k.50 Gemsbok (*Oryx gazelle*)	1·00	80
1554	1k.50 Cape fox (*Vulpes chama*) (inscr "Otocyon megalotis")	1·00	80
1555	1k.50 Giraffe (*Giraffa camelopardalis*)	1·00	80
1556	1k.50 Golden jackal (*Canis aureus*) (inscr "adustus")	1·00	80
1557	1k.50 Potto (*Perodicticus potto*)	1·00	80
1558	1k.50 Lion (*Panthera leo*)	1·00	80
1559	1k.50 Lilac-breasted roller (*Coracias caudate*) (inscr "Coracus")	1·30	1·00
1560	1k.50 Bat-eared fox (*Otocyon megalotis*)	1·00	80
1561	2k. Ostrich (*Struthio camelus*)	1·50	1·20
1562	2k. African wild cat (*Felis lybica*)	1·50	1·20
1563	2k. Impala (*Aepyceros melampus*)	1·50	1·20
1564	2k. Savanna monkey (*Cercopithecus aethiops*)	1·50	1·20
1565	2k. Black rhino (*Diceros bicornis*)	1·50	1·20
1566	2k. Baboon (*Papio*)	1·50	1·20
1567	2k. Caracal (*Felis caracal*)	1·50	1·20
1568	2k. Secretary bird (*Sagittarius serpentarius*)	1·75	1·50
1569	2k. Warthog (*Phacochoerus aethiopicus*)	1·50	1·20
1570	2k. Afro-Australian fur seal (*Arctocephalus pusillus*)	1·50	1·20
1571	2k. Malachite kingfisher (*Alcedo cristata*)	2·00	1·75
1572	2k. Hippopotamus (*Hippopotamus amphibius*)	1·50	1·20

MS1573 Two sheets. a) 85×110 mm.12k. Savanna monkey (vert); (b) 110×85 mm. 12k. Elephant (*Loxodonta Africana*) (vert) ... 13·00 ... 13·00

259 Flowers and Birds (Lai-Ji)

2000. Millennium (1st issue). Cultural Events of the 16th-century. Multicoloured.

1574	2k.50 Type **259**	2·75	1·50
1575	2k.50 *Last Judgement*, Orvieto Cathedral (Luca Signorelli)	2·75	1·50
1576	2k.50 *Enchanted Garden* (Hieronymus Bosch)	2·75	1·50
1577	2k.50 Machiavelli (author of *O Principe* (beginning of modern politics))	2·75	1·50
1578	2k.50 Illustration from Utopia (Sir Thomas More)	2·75	1·50
1579	2k.50 Martin Luther (church reform)	2·75	1·50
1580	2k.50 Charles I of Spain (holy Roman Emperor (unification of Europe))	2·75	1·50
1581	2k.50 "School of Athens" (Rafael)	2·75	1·50
1582	2k.50 Juan Sebastion Elcano (first circumnavigation of the world)	3·25	1·50
1583	2k.50 Henry VIII (separation from Catholic church)	3·25	1·50
1584	2k.50 Spanish conquering Aztecs and Incas (exploration of Americas)	2·75	1·50
1585	2k.50 Plasencia Cathedral (beginning of Romanesque architecture)	2·75	1·50
1586	2k.50 Potatoes (first introduction into Europe)	3·25	1·50
1587	2k.50 Astrolabe (Copernicus' theory of the universe)	3·25	1·50
1588	2k.50 Priest and courtiers (Portuguese-Japanese trade)	2·75	1·50
1589	2k.50 Self Portrait (Albrecht Durer (death, 1528)) (60×40 mm)	2·75	1·50
1590	2k.50 Woman, hourglass, inkwell and cross (declaration of rights of indigenous Americans by Queen Isabel of Castille)	2·75	1·50

260 Henry II of Germany

2000. Millennium (2nd issue). Monarchs and Popes. Multicoloured.

MS1591 Twelve sheets:—165×198 mm. (a) 3k.×4, Type **260**; Marina Mniszech, Queen Consort of Tsar Lzhedmitry (false Dmitri); Tsar Ivan IV; Tsar Ivan III; (b) 3k.×4, Charles II of England; Lady Jane Grey; Leopold III of Belgium; Louis XV of France; (c) 3k.×6, James I of England; James II of England; James VI of Scotland; Brian Boru, King of Ireland; William I of Prussia (inscr "William I of Germany"); Edward VI of England; (d) 3k.×6, Pope Nicholas II; Pope Pascal II; Pope Sergius IV; Pope Victor II; Pope Victor III; Pope Urban III; Pope Innocent II; (e) 3k.×6, Pope John XIII; Pope Agapetus II; Pope John XVIII; Pope Lucius II; (f) 3k.×6, Pope Celestine II; Pope Clement II; Pope Clement III; Pope Gelasius II; Pope Benedict VII; Pope Gregory V:—109×129 mm. (g) 12k. William IV of England; (h) 12k. Tsar Fyodor I; (i) 12k. Tsar Lzhedmitry; (j) 12k. Pope Gregory VII; (k) 12k. Pope Leo XIII; (l) 12k. Pope Leo IX ... 60·00 ... 60·00

261 Damaged Building, Kuito

2000. Buildings and People. Multicoloured.

1592	3k. Type **261**	1·90	1·90
1593	3k. People and Kunje–Kuito road	1·90	1·90
1594	4k. Post Office building	2·50	2·50
1595	4k. Police headquarters	2·50	2·50
1596	5k. Damaged apartments	3·25	3·25

1597	5k. Independence Plaza	3·25	3·25
1598	6k. Children	3·75	3·75
1599	6k. Man carrying sack	3·75	3·75

262 Trees

2000. Children's Paintings. Multicoloured.

1600	3k. Type **262**	1·50	1·50
1601	4k. Wall	1·90	1·90
1602	5k. Rural scene	2·40	2·40

263 Directorate of Communications, Telephones and Telegraphs, Luanda

2000. Postal Buildings. Multicoloured.

1603	5k. Type **263**	2·30	2·00
1604	5k. ETP building, Mbanza Congo	2·30	2·00
1605	5k. CTT building, Namibe	2·30	2·00
1606	8k. ECP building, Luanda	3·75	3·50
1607	8k. ETP building, Lobito	3·75	3·50
1608	8k. ECP building, Luanda (different)	3·75	3·50

264 Tank, Rifle and Dove

2001. 25th Anniv of Independence. Sheet 140×47 mm containing T 264 and similar horiz design. Multicoloured.

MS1609 12k. Type **264**; 12k. Dove, mattock and tractor ... 6·00 ... 6·00

265 Radio Studio

2001. 25th Anniv of Public Radio (MS1613a, MS1613c) and Television (others). Four sheets containing T 265 and similar multicoloured designs.

MS1610 (a) 154×80 mm. 9k.50, Type **265**; 9k.50, Reporter in war zone; 9k.50 Carrying stretcher from burning aeroplane. (b) 154×80 mm. 9k.50, Television studio; 9k.50, Cameraman filming tank; 9k.50, Women and children crossing water. (c) 99×60 mm. 12k. Reporter in war zone (detail) (42×28 mm). (d) 99×60 mm. 12k. Cameraman filming tank (detail) (28×42 mm) (vert) ... 30·00 ... 30·00

266 Hands holding Book

2001. Africa Day. Multicoloured.

1611	10k. Type **266**	2·75	2·30
1612	10k. Hands and xylophone	2·75	2·30

MS1613 130×90 mm. 30k. Map of Africa ... 8·00 ... 8·00

267 *Nicolaia speciosa*

2001. Flowers. Belgica 2001 International Stamp Exhibition. Multicoloured.

1614	8k. Type **267**	2·75	2·50
1615	9k. *Allamanda cathartica* (inscr "cathartca")	3·00	2·75
1616	10k. *Welwitschia mirabilis*	3·50	3·00
1617	10k. *Tagetes patula*	3·50	3·00

MS1618 130×90 mm. 30k. No. 1616 ... 10·50 ... 10·00

268 Man wearing Dark Glasses

2001. Total Eclipse of the Sun, 21 June 2001. Sheet 130×90 mm.

MS1619 30k. multicoloured ... 7·50 ... 7·50

269 West African Lungfish (*Protopterus annectens*)

2001. Freshwater Fish. Multicoloured.

1620	11k. Type **269**	2·00	1·50
1621	17k. *Protopterus amphibious*	3·00	2·40
1622	18k. *Tilapia ruweti*	3·25	2·50

MS1623 130×90 mm. 36k. Redbreasted tilapia (*Tilapia rendalli*) ... 6·50 ... 6·50

270 Ovambo Efundula, Cunene

2001. Traditional Dances. Multicoloured.

1624	11k. Type **270**	1·50	1·30
1625	11k. Massembo, Luanda	1·60	1·30
1626	17k. Macolo Batuque, Uige	2·50	2·00
1627	18k. Mukixi, Lunda Tchokwe	2·60	2·20
1628	18k. Humbi Puberdade, Namibe	2·60	2·20

MS1629 130×90 mm. 36k. Carnival Juvenil, Luanda ... 5·50 ... 5·50

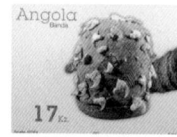
271 Hand-woven Hat, Banda

2001. Woven Crafts. Sheet 130×90 mm containing T 271 and similar horiz design. Multicoloured.

MS1630 17k. Type **271**; 18k. Hat with extensions, Kijinga ... 5·25 ... 5·25

272 Malachite

2001. Minerals. Multicoloured.

1631	11k. Type **272**	2·00	1·80
1632	11k. Hematite	2·00	1·80
1633	18k. Diamond	3·25	2·75
1634	18k. Psilomelane	3·25	2·75

273 Mwana Mpwevo

2002. Masks. Multicoloured.

1635	10k. Type **273** (Ngangela animistic ritual)	1·40	1·30
1636	11k. Mukixi (Cokwe circumcision ritual)		
1637	11k. Mbunda (comic)		
1638	17k. Mwana Pwo (Cok circumcision ritual)		
1639	18k. Likisi-Cinganji (supernatural incarnation)		

MS1640 90×80 mm. 36k. Ndem (Bakongo circumcision ritual)

274 Players and Football

2002. Football World Cup Championship, Japan and South Korea. Multicoloured.
1641	35k.	Type **274**	4·50	3·00
1642	37k.	Players and ball (different)	4·75	3·25
MS1643	55×120 mm. Nos. 1641/2		8·50	6·50

275 Figure with Target on Chest

2002. Socialist International Congress. Multicoloured.
1644	10k.	Type **275** (abolition of the death penalty)	1·20	80
1645	10k.	Woman (end to violence against women)	1·20	80
1646	10k.	Faces (combating poverty)	1·20	80
1647	10k.	Map and dollar sign (eliminate foreign debt)	1·20	80
1648	10k.	Map ("Africa in Peril" combating poverty)	1·20	80
MS1649	40×30 mm. Nos. 1644/7		6·50	6·00

276 National Map, Rainbow and Dove

2002. Peace and Reconciliation Commission.
1650	**276**	35k. multicoloured	2·00	1·60

277 Python (*Python anchietae*) (inscr "pithon")

2002. Reptiles. Multicoloured.
1651	21k.	Type **277**	1·50	1·10
1652	35k.	*Lacerta* (lizard)	2·50	1·90
1653	37k.	*Naja Nigricollis* (spitting cobra)	2·60	2·00
1654	40k.	*Crocodylus niloticus*	2·75	2·20

278 Lighthouse, Barra do Dande

2002. Lighthouses and Buoys. Multicoloured.
1655	45k.	Type **278**	3·50	2·50
1656	45k.	Snake Head lighthouse, Soyo	3·50	2·50
1657	45k.	Tafe lighthouse, Cabinda Bay	3·50	2·50
1658	45k.	Moita Seca lighthouse, South Margin Bay	3·50	2·50
1659	45k.	Red buoy no. 9, Luanda Bay	3·50	2·50
1660	45k.	Green buoy no. 1, Luanda Bay	3·50	2·50

279 Partial Eclipse (one third)

2002. Total Eclipse of the Sun (21 June 2001). Sheet 155×80 mm containing T **279** and similar horiz designs showing stages of eclipse. Multicoloured.
21k. Type **279**; 35k. Two thirds; total eclipse			6·00	6·00

280 Antonio Manuel (17th-century Congolese ambassador to Pope Paul V) and Lion

2002. Angola–Italy Friendship. Multicoloured.
1662	35k.	Type **280**	2·20	1·80
1663	45k.	Antonio Manuel and papal plaque	3·00	2·20
MS1664	120×72 mm. Nos. 1662/3		4·00	4·00

281 Omolingui (Ovimbundo water pot)

2002. Pottery. Multicoloured.
1665	27k.	Type **281**	2·00	1·20
1666	45k.	Mulondo (Luvale drinking jar)	3·00	2·00
1667	47k.	Ombya Yo Tuma (Ovimbundo food pot)	3·25	2·20
MS1668	120×72 mm. 51k. Sanga (Bakongo drinking vessel)		4·00	3·00

282 Trees, Satellite Dish and UN Emblem

2003. Third United Nations Science, Technology and Development Meeting.
1669	**282**	50k. multicoloured	2·75	2·20

283 Stylized Bi-plane

2003. Centenary of Powered Flight.
1670	**283**	25k. multicoloured	2·75	2·75

284 Antonio Jacinto

2003. Writers. Multicoloured.
1671	27k.	Type **284**	1·50	1·20
1672	45k.	Antonio Agostinho Neto	2·20	1·70
MS1673	121×90 mm. 27k. Antonio Jacinto wearing cap; 45k. Agostinho Neto as younger man		3·75	3·75

285 Two Antelope

2003. Sable Antelope (Hippotragus niger). Multicoloured.
1674	27k.	Type **285**	1·50	1·20
1675	45k.	Two antelope with straight horns	2·20	1·70
1676	47k.	One antelope with curved horns	2·50	2·00

286 Mbunda Woman

2003. Traditional Women's Hairstyles. Sheet 130×120 mm containing T **286** and similar vert designs.
MS1677	25k.×6, Type **286**; Soyo; Huila; Humbi; Cabinda; Quipungu		8·00	8·00

287 Musicians (detail, *Ascensao*) (Jorge Afonso)

2003. Christmas. Multicoloured.
1678	27k.	Type **287**	1·50	1·20
1679	27k.	*Adoraçao dos Pastores* (Andre Reinoso)	1·50	1·20
1680	45k.	Holy Family (detail, *Adoraçao dos Pastores*) (Josefa de Obidos)	2·20	1·70
1681	45k.	Cherubs (detail, *Adoraçao dos Pastores*) (Josefa de Obidos)	2·20	1·70
MS1682	110×92 mm. Nos. 1678/81		7·50	7·50

288 Bryde's Whale (*Balaenoptera edeni*)

2003. Marine Mammals. Multicoloured.
1683	27k.	Type **288**	2·50	2·20
1684	45k.	Heaviside's dolphin (*Cephalorhynchus heavisidii*)	4·50	3·50
MS1685	120×84 mm. 27k. Type **288**; 47k. Pilot whale (*Globicephala melaena*) (inscr "Giobiocephaia")		7·00	6·00

289 Tawny Eagle (*Aquila rapax*)

2003. Eagles. Multicoloured.
1686	20k.	Type **289**	2·00	1·70
1687	20k.	Martial eagle (*Hieraaetus bellicosus*) (inscr "Polemaetus")	2·00	1·70
1688	25k.	African fish eagle (*Haliaeetus vocifer*)	2·50	2·20
1689	25k.	Bateleur (*Terathopius ecaudatus*)	2·50	2·20
MS1690	120×80 mm. 45k. Verreaux's eagle (*Aquila verreauxi*)		5·50	5·00

290 Chess Pieces

2003. Chess. Multicoloured.
1691	45k.	Type **290**	3·50	3·00
1692	45k.	Board and pieces	3·50	3·00

291 Pope John Paul II

2003. 25th Anniv of the Pontificate of Pope John Paul II. Multicoloured.
1693	27k.	Type **291**	2·20	1·70
1694	27k.	Pope John Paul II with raised hand	2·20	1·70

292 *Adansonia digitata*

2004. Southern African Development Community. Plants. Multicoloured.
1695	27k.	Type **292**	1·80	1·30
1695a	27k.	*Psidium guayava*	1·80	1·30
1696	45k.	*Carica papaya*	3·00	2·20
1697	45k.	*Cymbopogon citrates*	3·00	2·20
MS1698	129×105 mm. Nos. 1695/7		8·00	6·00

293 Basketball

2004. Olympic Games, Athens. Multicoloured.
1699	27k.	Type **293**	1·50	1·10
1700	27k.	Handball	1·50	1·10
1701	45k.	Running	2·50	1·80
1702	45k.	Volleyball	2·50	1·80

294 Humpback Whales (*Megaptera novaeangliae*)

2004. Sea Mammals. Multicoloured.
1703	27k.	Type **294**	1·50	1·10
1704	27k.	Heaviside's dolphin (*Cephalorhynchus heavisidii*)	1·50	1·10
1705	45k.	Bottlenose dolphin (*Tursiops truncates*)	2·50	1·80
MS1706	135×80 mm. 99k. *Megaptera novaeangliae* (different)		5·50	5·00

Nos. 1703/5 were issued together, *se-tenant*, forming a composite design.

295 Saddle Tanker (Benguela)

2004. Trains. Multicoloured.
1707	27k.	Type **295**	1·50	1·10
1708	27k.	Diesel locomotive (Mocamedes)	1·50	1·10
1709	27k.	Locomotive CFB 225 (Benguela)	1·50	1·10

296 Fireman and Campaign Emblem

2004. Fire Emergency Phone Number Publicity Campaign. Multicoloured.
1710	27k.	Type **296**	1·50	1·10
1711	27k.	Fire appliance	1·50	1·10
1712	45k.	Fire appliance facing right	2·50	1·80
MS1713	130×80 mm. Nos. 1710/12		5·00	5·50

297 Globe and Footballers

2004. Centenary of FIFA (Federation Internationale de Football Association).
1714	**297**	45k. multicoloured	2·00	1·60

298 Three Kings

2004. Christmas. Multicoloured.
1715	27k.	Type **298**	1·20	95
1716	45k.	Nativity	2·00	1·60

Nos. 1715/16 were issued together, *se-tenant*, forming a composite design.

299 Family of Monkeys

2004. Colobus Monkey (*Colobus angolensis*). Multicoloured.

1717	27k. Type **299**	1·20	1·20
1718	27k. Mother and baby	1·20	1·20
1719	27k. Male	1·20	1·20
1720	27k. Facing left	1·20	1·20

300 Woman and City Skyline

2005. 50th Anniv of Rotary of Luanda (45k.) and Centenary of Rotary (51k.). Multicoloured.

1721	45k. Type **300**	2·00	1·60
1722	51k. Woman and countryside	2·75	2·00
MS1723	120×80 mm. Nos. 1721/2	5·50	5·00

Nos. 1724/7 and Type **301** are left for Basketry, issued on 6 September 2005, not yet received.

Nos. 1728/9 and Type **302** are left for 30th Anniv of Independence, issued on 8 November 2005, not yet received.

Nos. 1730/1and Type **303** are left for World Summit on the Information Society (WSIS), issued on 8 November 2005, not yet received.

Nos. 1732/5 and Type **304** are left for Ministerial Conference of African Oil Producers , issued on 24 April 2006, not yet received.

Nos. 1736/7 and Type **305** are left for World Cup, issued on 30 August 2006, not yet received.

306 Dogs

2006. Tenth Anniv of Countries of Portuguese Language Community. Lubrapex International Stamp Exhibition, Rio de Janeiro, Brazil. Multicoloured.

1738	27k. Type **306**	35	15
1739	45k. Grey parrots	65	25
1740	45k. Helmeted guinea fowl	65	25

307 Currency

2006. 30th Anniv of National Bank. Multicoloured.
MS1745 200×136 mm. 90k. Type **307** 1·90 1·90

No. 1746 and Type **308** are left for Paralympic Committee, issued on 29 December 2006, not yet received.

No. 1747 and Type **309** are left for Five Years of Peace, issued on 20 April 2007, not yet received.

Nos. 1748/9 and Type **310** are left for Venice Biennial, issued on 20 April 2007, not yet received.

No. 1750 and Type **311** are left for Africa Day, issued on 25 May 2007, not yet received.

Nos. 1751/5 and Type **312** are left for Centenary of Scouting, issued on 1 June 2007, not yet received.

No. 1756 and Type **313** are left for 27th Anniv of SADC , issued on 17 August 2007, not yet received.

No. 1757 and Type **314** are left for Olympic Games, Beijing, issued on 20 September 2007, not yet received.

315 Malange

2007. World Post Day. Multicoloured.
MS1758 45k.×2, Type **315**; Huambo 1·10 1·10

316 *Caretta caretta*

2007. Marine Turtles. Multicoloured.
MS1759 126×104 mm. 27k. Type **316**; 27k. *Chelonia mydas*; 45k. *Eretmochelys imbricata*; 45k. *Lepidochelys olivacea* 45 45

MS1760 142×108 mm. 130k. *Dermochelys coriacea* (37×39 mm) 1·30 1·30

317 Meat and Dumplings

2008. Angolan Gastronomy. Multicoloured.

1761	37k. Type **317**	40	14
1762	40k. Greens and dumplings	40	15
1763	59k. Stew with greens (Calulu)	1·10	35
MS1764	160×90 mm. 153k. Chicken stew (Muamba)	1·90	1·90

318 Rio Kuebe

2008. Rivers. Multicoloured.

1765	37k. Type **318**	40	15
1766	37k. Rapidos do Kuanza (Rapids of Kwanza)	40	15
1767	40k. Rio Kuanza	55	20
1768	40k. Foz do Rio Mbridge (Mbridge rivermouth)	55	20
MS1769	160×90 mm. 153k. Recursos Hidricos (waterfall (water resources))	1·90	1·10

319 Landmine Clearance

2008. Tenth Anniv of Lwini Social Solidarity Fund (to help landmine victims). Multicoloured.
MS1770 37k. Type **319**; 40k. Information literature (horiz); 40k. Princess Diana and Ana Paula dos Santos (foundation president) (horiz); 59k. Children in wheelchairs (horiz); 59k. Landmine victims making baskets (horiz) 2·75 2·75

320 Water Jug

2008. Water Jugs. Multicoloured.

1771	37k. Type **320**	40	15
1772	37k. Incised jug with several handles	40	15
1773	40k. Green jug with spout, handle and lid	55	20
1774	40k. White jug with figure as lid	55	20

321 Mangroves

2008. Mangroves on Rio Chiloango. Multicoloured.

1775	37k. Mangroves	60	25
1776	37k. River bordered by mangroves	60	25
1777	59k. Type **321**	85	35

322 Coffee Berries

2009. Angolan Coffee, Amboim. Multicoloured.

1778	37k. Type **322**	40	15
1779	45k. Branches of coffee plant	55	30
1780	45k. Woman picking coffee (horiz)	55	30

323 Antonio Agostinho Neto

2009. Antonio Agostinho Neto (first president of Angola) Commemoration.

1781	40k. black and scarlet-vermilion	45	30
1782	50k. multicoloured	45	35
MS1783	160×90 mm. 150k. multicoloured	1·20	1·20

DESIGNS: 40k. Type **323**; 50k. Wearing uniform; 150k. With school children.

324 Pope Benedict XVI

2009. Visit of Pope Benedict XVI to Angola
MS1784 **324** 150×60mm. 100k. multicoloured 2·75 2·75

325 Cabinda Stadium

2010. COCAN 2010, African Cup of Nations Football Competition. Multicoloured.

1785	40k. Type **325**	40	15
1786	40k. Benguela	40	15
1787	50k. Huila	45	20
1788	50k. Luanda	45	20

APPENDIX

1995

90th Anniv of Rotary International (on gold foil). 81000k.

CHARITY TAX STAMPS

Used on certain days of the year as an additional tax on internal letters. If one was not used in addition to normal postage, postage due stamps were used to collect the deficiency and the fine.

1925. Marquis de Pombal Commemorative stamps of Portugal but inscr "ANGOLA".

C343	**C73**	15c. violet	1·10	90
C344	-	15c. violet	1·10	90
C345	**C75**	15c. violet	1·10	90

C15

1929

C347	**C15**	50c. blue	7·00	2·00

C29

1939. No gum.

C413	**C29**	50c. green	4·00	35
C414	**C29**	1a. red	9·25	2·50

C52 Old Man

1955. Heads in brown.

C646	**C52**	50c. orange	35	25
C647	-	1e. red (Boy)	35	25
C648	-	1e.50 green (Girl)	55	35
C522	-	2e.50 blue (Old woman)	1·00	55

1957. Surch.

C535	**C52**	10c. on 50c. orange	35	35
C534	**C52**	30c. on 50c. orange	35	35

C58 Mother and Child

1959

C538	**C58**	10c. black and orange	35	35
C539	-	30c. black and slate	35	35

DESIGN: 30c. Boy and girl.

C65 Yellow, White and Black Men

1962. Provincial Settlement Committee.

C568	**C65**	50c. multicoloured	35	35
C569	**C65**	1e. multicoloured	55	25

C75 "Full Employment"

1965. Provincial Settlement Committee.

C644	**C75**	1e. multicoloured	55	35
C645	**C75**	2e. multicoloured	55	35
C643	**C75**	50e. multicoloured	55	35

C95 Planting Tree

1972. Provincial Settlement Committee.

C701	**C95**	50c. red and brown	35	35
C702	-	1e. black and green	35	35
C703	-	2e. black and brown	35	35

DESIGNS: 1e. Agricultural workers; 2e. Corncobs and flowers.

NEWSPAPER STAMP

1893. "Newspaper" key-type inscr "ANGOLA".

N51	**V**	2½r. brown	3·50	2·10

POSTAGE DUE STAMPS

1904. "Due" key-type inscr "ANGOLA".

D150	**W**	5r. green	45	45
D151	**W**	10r. grey	45	45
D152	**W**	20r. brown	1·00	70
D153	**W**	30r. orange	1·00	70
D154	**W**	50r. brown	1·30	1·00
D155	**W**	60r. brown	11·00	7·50
D156	**W**	100r. mauve	4·50	3·50
D157	**W**	130r. blue	4·50	3·50
D158	**W**	200r. red	14·00	9·25
D159	**W**	500r. lilac	11·50	7·50

See also Nos. D343/52.

1911. Nos. D150/9 optd **REPUBLICA**.

D166	5r. green	35	30
D167	10r. grey	35	30
D168	20r. brown	35	30
D169	30r. orange	55	45
D170	50r. brown	55	45
D171	60r. brown	1·50	1·10
D172	100r. mauve	1·50	1·10
D173	130r. blue	1·70	1·30
D174	200r. red	2·20	1·30
D175	500r. lilac	2·30	2·20

1921. Values in new currency.

D343	½c. green	40	35
D344	1c. grey	40	35
D345	2c. brown	40	35
D346	3c. orange	40	35
D347	5c. brown	40	35
D348	6c. brown	40	35
D349	10c. mauve	55	45
D350	13c. blue	1·00	90
D351	20c. red	1·00	90
D352	50c. grey	1·00	90

1925. Marquis de Pombal stamps of Angola, as Nos. C343/5, optd **MULTA**.

D353	**C73**	30c. violet	1·10	90
D354	-	30c. violet	1·10	90
D355	**C75**	30c. violet	1·10	90

1949. Surch **PORTEADO** and value.

D438	17	10c. on 20c. grey	45	40
D439	17	20c. on 30c. green	55	50
D440	17	30c. on 50c. brown	1·00	90
D441	17	40c. on 1a. red	1·30	1·10
D442	17	50c. on 2a. mauve	2·00	1·80
D443	17	1a. on 5a. green	3·00	2·75

D45

1952. Numerals in red, name in black.

D483	D45	10c. brown and olive	35	30
D484	D45	30c. green and blue	35	30
D485	D45	50c. brown & lt brn	35	30
D486	D45	1a. blue, green & orge	65	55
D487	D45	2a. brown and red	80	75
D488	D45	5a. brown and blue	80	75

<div style="text-align:right">**Pt. 9**</div>

ANGRA

A district of the Azores, which used the stamps of the Azores except from 1892 to 1905.

1000 reis = 1 milreis.

1892. As T **4** of Funchal, inscr "ANGRA".

16		5r. yellow	4·25	2·50
5		10r. mauve	4·75	2·50
6		15r. brown	5·50	3·75
7		20r. violet	5·50	3·75
8		25r. green	7·50	1·70
9		50r. blue	11·00	5·75
10		75r. red	13·00	7·50
11		80r. green	15·00	14·00
24		100r. brown on yellow	55·00	20·00
13		150r. red on rose	75·00	60·00
14		200r. blue on blue	75·00	60·00
15		300r. blue on brown	75·00	60·00

1897. "King Carlos" key-type inscr "ANGRA".

28	S	2½r. grey	1·00	65
29	S	5r. red	1·00	65
30	S	10r. green	1·00	65
31	S	15r. brown	13·00	8·50
43	S	15r. green	1·30	80
32	S	20r. lilac	2·50	1·90
33	S	25r. green	4·25	1·70
44	S	25r. red	90	80
34	S	50r. blue	7·75	2·40
46	S	65r. blue	1·80	80
35	S	75r. red	4·75	2·30
47	S	75r. brown on yellow	19·00	15·00
36	S	80r. mauve	2·10	1·70
37	S	100r. blue on blue	3·75	2·40
48	S	115r. red on pink	3·75	2·75
49	S	130r. brown on cream	3·75	2·75
38	S	150r. brown on yellow	3·75	2·40
50	S	180r. grey on pink	4·75	4·25
39	S	200r. purple on pink	7·75	6·75
40	S	300r. blue on pink	11·50	8·75
41	S	500r. black on blue	24·00	19·00

<div style="text-align:right">**Pt. 1**</div>

ANGUILLA

St. Christopher, Nevis and Anguilla were granted Associated Statehood on 27 February 1967, but following a referendum Anguilla declared her independence and the St. Christopher authorities withdrew. On 7 July 1969, the Anguilla post office was officially recognised by the Government of St. Christopher, Nevis and Anguilla and normal postal communications via St. Christopher were resumed.

By the Anguilla Act of 27 July 1971, the island was restored to direct British control.

100 cents = 1 West Indian dollar.

1967. Nos. 129/44 of St. Kitts-Nevis optd **Independent Anguilla** and bar.

1	–	½c. sepia and blue	70·00	26·00
2	33	1c. multicoloured	80·00	11·00
3	–	2c. multicoloured	75·00	2·25
4	–	3c. multicoloured	75·00	6·50
5	–	4c. multicoloured	80·00	6·50
6	–	5c. multicoloured	£300	35·00
7	–	6c. multicoloured	£130	18·00
8	–	10c. multicoloured	75·00	10·00
9	–	15c. multicoloured	£150	16·00
10	–	20c. multicoloured	£350	23·00
11	–	25c. multicoloured	£250	40·00
12	–	50c. multicoloured	£4750	£800
13	–	60c. multicoloured	£5500	£1600
14	–	$1 yellow and blue	£4250	£750
15	–	$2.50 multicoloured	£3250	£475
16	–	$5 multicoloured	£3500	£500

Owing to the limited stocks available for overprinting, the sale of the stamps was personally controlled by the Postmaster and no orders from the trade were accepted.

2 Mahogany Tree, The Quarter

1967

17	2	1c. green, brown and orange	10	1·00
18	–	2c. turquoise and black	10	3·00
19	–	3c. black and green	10	10
20	–	4c. blue and black	10	10
21	–	5c. multicoloured	10	10
22	–	6c. red and black	10	10
23	–	10c. multicoloured	15	10
24	–	15c. multicoloured	2·50	20
25	–	20c. multicoloured	1·25	2·75
26	–	25c. multicoloured	60	20
27	–	40c. green, blue and black	1·00	25
28	–	60c. multicoloured	4·50	4·75
29	–	$1 multicoloured	1·75	3·25
30	–	$2.50 multicoloured	2·00	7·50
31	–	$5 multicoloured	3·00	4·25

DESIGNS: 2c. Sombrero Lighthouse; 3c. St. Mary's Church; 4c. Valley Police Station; 5c. Old Plantation House, Mt. Fortune; 6c. Valley Post Office; 10c. Methodist Church, West End; 15c. Wall Blake Airport; 20c. Beech A90 King Air aircraft over Sandy Ground; 25c. Island harbour; 40c. Map of Anguilla; 60c. Hermit crab and starfish; $1, Hibiscus; $2.50, Local scene; $5, Spiny lobster.

17 Yachts in Lagoon

1968. Anguillan Ships. Multicoloured.

32		10c. Type **17**	35	10
33		15c. Boat on beach	40	10
34		25c. Schooner *Warspite*	55	15
35		40c. Schooner *Atlantic Star*	65	20

18 Purple-throated Carib

1968. Anguillan Birds. Multicoloured.

36		10c. Type **18**	65	15
37		15c. Bananaquit	80	20
38		25c. Black-necked stilt (horiz)	85	20
39		40c. Royal tern (horiz)	90	30

19 Guides' Badge and Anniversary Years

1968. 35th Anniv of Anguillan Girl Guides. Multicoloured.

40		10c. Type **19**	10	15
41		15c. Badge and silhouettes of guides (vert)	15	15
42		25c. Guides' badge and Headquarters	20	20
43		40c. Association and proficiency badges (vert)	25	25

20 The Three Kings

1968. Christmas.

44	20	1c. black and red	10	10
45	–	10c. black and blue	10	10
46	–	15c. black and brown	15	10
47	–	40c. black and blue	15	10
48	–	50c. black and green	20	15

DESIGNS—VERT: 10c. The Wise Men; 15c. Holy Family and manger. HORIZ: 40c. The Shepherds; 50c. Holy Family and donkey.

21 Bagging Salt

1969. Anguillan Salt Industry. Multicoloured.

49		10c. Type **21**	25	15
50		15c. Packing salt	30	15
51		40c. Salt pond	35	15
52		50c. Loading salt	35	35

1969. Expiration of Interim Agreement on Status of Anguilla. Nos. 17/22, 23, 24 and 26/7 optd **INDEPENDENCE JANUARY 1969**.

52a		1c. green, brown and orange	10	40
52b		2c. green and black	10	40
52c		3c. black and green	10	40
52d		4c. blue and black	10	40
52e		5c. multicoloured	10	20
52f		6c. red and black	10	20
52g		10c. multicoloured	10	30
52h		15c. multicoloured	90	30
52i		15c. multicoloured	80	30
52j		40c. green, blue and black	10	40

The remaining values of the 1967 series, nos. 17/31, also come with this overprint but these are outside the scope of this catalogue.

22 *The Crucifixion* (Studio of Massys)

1969. Easter Commemoration. Multicoloured.

53		25c. Type **22**	25	15
54		40c. *The Last Supper* (ascribed to Roberti)	35	15

23 Amaryllis

1969. Flowers of the Caribbean. Multicoloured.

55		10c. Type **23**	15	20
56		15c. Bougainvillea	15	25
57		40c. Hibiscus	20	50
58		50c. *Cattleya* orchid	1·00	1·60

24 Superb Gaza, Channelled Turban, Chestnut Turban and Carved Star Shell

1969. Sea Shells. Multicoloured.

59		10c. Type **24**	20	20
60		15c. American thorny oysters	20	20
61		40c. Scotch, royal and smooth scotch bonnets	30	30
62		50c. Atlantic trumpet triton	40	30

1969. Christmas. Nos. 17 and 25/8 optd with different seasonal emblems.

63		1c. green, brown and orange	10	10
64		20c. multicoloured	20	10
65		25c. multicoloured	20	10
66		40c. green, blue and black	25	15
67		60c. multicoloured	40	20

30 Spotted Goatfish

1969. Fish. Multicoloured.

68		10c. Type **30**	45	15
69		15c. Blue-striped grunt	60	15
70		40c. Nassau grouper	75	20
71		50c. Banded butterflyfish	80	20

31 "Morning Glory"

1970. Flowers. Multicoloured.

72		10c. Type **31**	25	10
73		15c. Blue petrea	35	10
74		40c. Hibiscus	50	20
75		50c. "Flame Tree"	60	25

32 The Crucifixion (Masaccio)

1970. Easter. Multicoloured.

76		10c. *The Ascent to Calvary* (Tiepolo) (horiz)	15	10
77		20c. Type **32**	20	10
78		40c. *Deposition* (Rosso Fiorentino)	25	15
79		60c. *The Ascent to Calvary* (Murillo) (horiz)	25	15

33 Scout Badge and Map

1970. 40th Anniv of Scouting in Anguilla. Multicoloured.

80		10c. Type **33**	15	20
81		15c. Scout camp, and cubs practising first aid	20	20
82		40c. Monkey bridge	25	30
83		50c. Scout H.Q. building and Lord Baden-Powell	35	40

34 Boatbuilding

1970. Multicoloured.

84		1c. Type **34**	30	40
85		2c. Road construction	30	40
86		3c. Quay, Blowing Point	30	20
87		4c. Broadcaster, Radio Anguilla	30	50
88		5c. Cottage Hospital extension	40	50
89		6c. Valley Secondary School	30	50
90		10c. Hotel extension	30	30
91		15c. Sandy Ground	30	30
92		20c. Supermarket and cinema	70	30
93		25c. Bananas and mangoes	35	1·00
94		40c. Wall Blake Airport	4·00	3·25
95		60c. Sandy Ground jetty	65	3·50
96		$1 Administration buildings	1·25	1·40
97		$2.50 Livestock	1·50	4·00
98		$5 Sandy Hill Bay	3·25	3·75

35 *The Adoration of the Shepherds* (Reni)

1970. Christmas. Multicoloured.

99		1c. Type **35**	10	15
100		20c. *The Virgin and Child* (Gozzoli)	30	20
101		25c. *Mystic Nativity* (detail, Botticelli)	30	25
102		40c. *The Santa Margherita Madonna* (detail, Mazzola)	40	25
103		50c. *The Adoration of the Magi* (detail, Tiepolo)	40	25

36 *Ecce Homo* (detail, Correggio)

1971. Easter. Paintings. Multicoloured.
104	10c. Type **36**		25	10
105	15c. *Christ appearing to St. Peter* (detail, Carracci)		25	10
106	40c. *Angels weeping over the Dead Christ* (detail, Guercino) (horiz)		30	10
107	50c. *The Supper at Emmaus* (detail, Caravaggio) (horiz)		30	15

37 *Hypolimnas misippus*

1971. Butterflies. Multicoloured.
108	10c. Type **37**		1·60	70
109	15c. *Junonia evarete*		1·60	80
110	40c. *Agraulis vanillae*		2·00	1·25
111	50c. *Danaus plexippus*		2·00	1·50

38 *Magnanime* and *Aimable* in Battle

1971. Sea-battles of the West Indies. Multicoloured.
112	10c. Type **38**		1·10	1·40
113	15c. H.M.S. *Duke*, *Glorieux* and H.M.S. *Agamemnon*		1·25	1·60
114	25c. H.M.S. *Formidabl* and H.M.S. *Namur* against *Ville de Paris*		1·50	1·75
115	40c. H.M.S. *Canada*		1·60	1·90
116	50c. H.M.S. *St. Albans* and wreck of *Hector*		1·75	2·00

Nos. 112/116 were issued together, *se-tenant*, forming a composite design.

39 *The Ansidei Madonna* (detail, Raphael)

1971. Christmas. Multicoloured.
117	20c. Type **39**		30	30
118	25c. *Mystic Nativity* (detail, Botticelli)		30	30
119	40c. *Adoration of the Shepherds* (detail, ascr to Murillo)		35	40
120	50c. *The Madonna of the Iris* (detail, ascr to Durer)		40	70

40 *Map of Anguilla and St. Martin by Thomas Jefferys, 1775*

1972. Caribbean Maps depicting Anguilla. Multicoloured.
121	10c. Type **40**		25	10
122	15c. *Samuel Fahlberg's Map, 1814*		35	15
123	40c. *Thomas Jefferys' Map, 1775* (horiz)		50	25
124	50c. *Captain E. Barnett's Map, 1847* (horiz)		60	25

41 "Jesus Buffeted"

1972. Easter. Multicoloured.
125	10c. Type **41**		25	25
126	15c. *The Way of Sorrows*		30	30
127	25c. *The Crucifixion*		30	30
128	40c. *Descent from the Cross*		35	35
129	50c. *The Burial*		40	40

42 *Loblolly Tree*

1972. Multicoloured.
130	1c. Spear fishing		10	40
131	2c. Type **42**		10	40
132	3c. Sandy Ground		10	40
133	4c. Ferry at Blowing Point		1·75	20
134	5c. Agriculture		15	1·00
135	6c. St. Mary's Church		25	20
136	10c. St. Gerard's Church		25	40
137	15c. Cottage hospital extension		25	30
138	20c. Public library		30	35
139	25c. Sunset at Blowing Point		40	2·00
140	40c. Boat building		5·00	1·50
141	60c. Hibiscus		4·00	4·00
142	$1 Magnificent frigate bird ("Man-o'-War")		10·00	8·00
143	$2.50 Frangipani		5·00	10·00
144	$5 Brown pelican		17·00	17·00
144a	$10 Green-back turtle		16·00	18·00

1972. Royal Silver Wedding. As T **52** of Ascension, but with Schooner and Common dolphin in background.
145	25c. green		50	75
146	40c. brown		50	75

44 *Flight into Egypt*

1972. Christmas. Multicoloured.
147	1c. Type **44**		10	10
148	20c. Star of Bethlehem		20	20
149	25c. Holy Family		20	20
150	40c. Arrival of the Magi		20	25
151	50c. Adoration of the Magi		25	25

45 *The Betrayal of Christ*

1973. Easter. Multicoloured.
152	1c. Type **45**		10	10
153	10c. *The Man of Sorrows*		10	10
154	20c. *Christ bearing the Cross*		10	15
155	25c. *The Crucifixion*		15	15
156	40c. *The Descent from the Cross*		15	15

157	50c. *The Resurrection*		15	20
MS158	140×141 mm. Nos. 152/7. Bottom panel in gold and mauve		70	80

46 *Santa Maria*

1973. Columbus Discovers the West Indies. Multicoloured.
159	1c. Type **46**		10	10
160	20c. Early map		1·50	1·25
161	40c. Map of voyages		1·60	1·40
162	70c. Sighting land		1·90	1·75
163	$1.20 Landing of Columbus		2·50	2·25
MS164	193×93 mm. Nos. 159/63		6·75	7·00

47 *Princess Anne and Captain Mark Phillips*

1973. Royal Wedding. Multicoloured. Background colours given.
165	**47**	60c. green	20	15
166	**47**	$1.20 mauve	30	15

48 *The Adoration of the Shepherds* (Reni)

1973. Christmas. Multicoloured.
167	1c. Type **48**		10	10
168	10c. *The Madonna and Child with Saints Dominic and Dominic* (Filippino Lippi)		10	10
169	20c. *The Nativity* (Master of Brunswick)		15	15
170	25c. *Madonna of the Meadow* (Bellini)		15	15
171	40c. *Virgin and Child* (Cima)		20	20
172	50c. *Adoration of the Kings* (Geertgen)		20	20
MS173	148×149 mm. Nos. 167/72		80	1·60

49 *The Crucifixion* (Raphael)

1974. Easter.
174	**49**	1c. multicoloured	10	10
175	-	15c. multicoloured	10	10
176	-	20c. multicoloured	15	15
177	-	25c. multicoloured	15	15
178	-	40c. multicoloured	15	15
179	-	$1 multicoloured	20	25
MS180	123×141 mm. Nos. 174/9		1·00	1·25

DESIGNS: 15c. to $1, Details of Raphael's *Crucifixion*.

50 *Churchill Making "Victory" Sign*

1974. Birth Centenary of Sir Winston Churchill. Multicoloured.
181	1c. Type **50**		10	10
182	20c. Churchill with Roosevelt		20	20
183	25c. Wartime broadcast		20	20
184	40c. Birthplace, Blenheim Palace		30	30
185	60c. Churchill's statue		30	35
186	$1.20 Country residence, Chartwell		45	55
MS187	195×96 mm. Nos. 181/6		1·40	2·50

51 *U.P.U. Emblem*

1974. Centenary of U.P.U.
188	**51**	1c. black and blue	10	10
189	**51**	20c. black and orange	15	15
190	**51**	25c. black and yellow	15	15
191	**51**	40c. black and mauve	20	25
192	**51**	60c. black and green	30	40
193	**51**	$1.20 black and blue	50	60
MS194	195×96 mm. Nos. 188/93		1·25	2·25

52 *Anguillan pointing to Star*

1974. Christmas. Multicoloured.
195	1c. Type **52**		10	10
196	20c. Child in Manger		10	20
197	25c. King's offering		10	20
198	40c. Star over map of Anguilla		15	20
199	60c. Family looking at star		15	20
200	$1.20 Angels of Peace		20	30
MS201	177×85 mm. Nos. 195/200		1·10	1·75

53 *Mary, John and Mary Magdalene* (Matthias Grunewald)

1975. Easter. Details from Isenheim Altarpiece, Colmar Museum. Multicoloured.
202	1c. Type **53**		10	10
203	10c. *The Crucifixion*		15	15
204	15c. *St. John the Baptist*		15	15
205	20c. *St. Sebastian and Angels*		15	20
206	$1 *The Entombment* (horiz)		20	35
207	$1.50 *St. Anthony the Hermit*		25	45
MS208	134×127 mm. Nos. 202/7 (imperf)		1·00	2·00

54 *Statue of Liberty*

1975. Bicentenary of American Revolution. Multicoloured.
209	1c. Type **54**		10	10
210	10c. The Capitol		20	10
211	15c. "Congress voting for Independence" (Pine and Savage)		30	15
212	20c. Washington and map		30	15
213	$1 Boston Tea Party		45	40
214	$1.50 Bicentenary logo		50	60
MS215	198×97 mm. Nos. 209/14		1·25	2·50

55 *Madonna, Child and the Infant John the Baptist* (Raphael)

1975. Christmas. "Madonna and Child" paintings by artists named. Multicoloured.
216	1c. Type **55**		10	10
217	10c. Cima		15	15
218	15c. Dolci		20	15
219	20c. Durer		20	20
220	$1 Bellini		35	25
221	$1.50 Botticelli		45	35
MS222	130×145 mm. Nos. 216/21		2·00	2·25

1976. New Constitution. Nos. 130 etc optd **NEW CONSTITUTION 1976** or surch also.

223	1c. Spear fishing	30	50
224	2c. on 1c. Spear fishing	30	50
225	2c. Type **42**	7·50	1·75
226	3c. on 40c. Boat building	75	70
227	4c. Ferry at Blowing Point	1·00	1·00
228	5c. on 40c. Boat building	30	60
229	6c. St. Mary's Church	30	60
230	10c. on 20c. Public library	30	50
231	10c. St. Gerard's Church	9·50	4·75
232	15c. Cottage Hospital extension	30	1·25
233	20c. Public library	30	50
234	25c. Sunset at Blowing Point	30	50
235	40c. Boat building	1·00	70
236	60c. Hibiscus	70	70
237	$1 Magnificent frigate bird	6·50	2·25
238	$2.50 Frangipani	2·25	2·25
239	$5 Brown pelican	8·00	10·00
240	$10 Green-back turtle	3·00	6·00

57 Almond

1976. Flowering Trees. Multicoloured.

241	1c. Type **57**	10	10
242	10c. Autograph	20	20
243	15c. Calabash	20	20
244	20c. Cordia	20	20
245	$1 Papaya	30	45
246	$1.50 Flamboyant	35	55
MS247	194×99 mm. Nos. 241/6	1·50	2·00

58 The Three Marys

1976. Easter. Showing portions of the Altar Frontal Tapestry, Rheinau. Multicoloured.

248	1c. Type **58**	10	10
249	10c. The Crucifixion	10	10
250	15c. Two Soldiers	15	15
251	20c. The Annunciation	15	15
252	$1 The complete tapestry (horiz)	65	65
253	$1.50 The Risen Christ	80	80
MS254	138×130 mm. Nos. 248/53 (imperf)	1·75	2·10

59 French Ships approaching Anguilla

1976. Bicentenary of Battle of Anguilla. Multicoloured.

255	1c. Type **59**	10	10
256	3c. *Margaret* (sloop) leaving Anguilla	1·25	35
257	15c. Capture of *Le Desius*	1·50	55
258	25c. *La Vaillante* forced aground	1·50	80
259	$1 H.M.S. *Lapwing*	2·00	1·25
260	$1.50 *Le Desius* burning	2·25	1·75
MS261	205×103 mm. Nos. 255/60	7·50	6·00

60 *Christmas Carnival* (A. Richardson)

1976. Christmas. Children's Paintings. Multicoloured.

262	1c. Type **60**	10	10
263	3c. *Dreams of Christmas Gifts* (J. Connor)	10	10
264	15c. *Carolling* (P. Richardson)	15	15
265	25c. *Candle-light Procession* (A. Mussington)	20	20
266	$1 *Going to Church* (B. Franklin)	30	30
267	$1.50 *Coming Home for Christmas* (E. Gumbs)	40	40
MS268	232×147 mm. Nos. 262/7	1·50	1·75

61 Prince Charles and H.M.S. *Minerva* (frigate)

1977. Silver Jubilee. Multicoloured.

269	25c. Type **61**	15	10
270	40c. Prince Philip landing by launch at Road Bay, 1964	15	10
271	$1.20 Coronation scene	20	20
272	$2.50 Coronation regalia and map of Anguilla	25	30
MS273	145×96 mm. Nos. 269/72	65	90

62 Yellow-crowned Night Heron

1977. Multicoloured.

274	1c. Type **62**	30	1·25
275	2c. Great barracuda	30	2·75
276	3c. Queen or pink conch	2·00	3·75
277	4c. Spanish bayonet (flower)	40	70
278	5c. Honeycomb trunkfish	1·50	30
279	6c. Cable and Wireless building	30	30
280	10c. American kestrel ("American Sparrow Hawk")	5·50	4·00
281	15c. Ground orchid	3·50	1·75
282	20c. Stop-light parrotfish	3·50	75
283	22c. Lobster fishing boat	50	60
284	35c. Boat race	1·40	70
285	50c. Sea bean	90	50
286	$1 Sandy Island	60	50
287	$2.50 Manchineel	1·00	1·00
288	$5 Ground lizard	2·00	2·00
289	$10 Red-billed tropic bird	9·00	4·50

No. 290 is vacant.

63 The Crucifixion (Massys)

1977. Easter. Paintings by Castagno ($1.50) or Ugolino (others). Multicoloured.

291	1c. Type **63**	10	10
292	3c. *The Betrayal*	10	10
293	22c. *The Way to Calvary*	20	20
294	30c. *The Deposition*	25	25
295	$1 *The Resurrection*	40	40
296	$1.50 *The Crucifixion*	45	45
MS297	192×126 mm. Nos. 291/6	1·60	1·75

1977. Royal Visit. Nos. 269/72 optd **ROYAL VISIT TO WEST INDIES.**

298	25c. Type **61**	10	10
299	40c. Prince Philip landing at Road Bay, 1964	10	15
300	$1.20 Coronation scene	20	25
301	$1.50 Coronation regalia and map of Anguilla	25	35
MS302	145×96 mm. Nos. 298/301	80	60

65 *Le Chapeau de Paille*

1977. 400th Birth Anniv of Rubens. Multicoloured.

303	25c. Type **65**	15	15
304	40c. *Helene Fourment and her Two Children*	20	25
305	$1.20 *Rubens and his Wife*	60	65
306	$2.50 *Marchesa Brigida Spinola-Doria*	75	95
MS307	90×145 mm. Nos. 303/6	2·00	2·10

1977. Christmas. Nos. 262/7 with old date blocked out and additionally inscr "1977", some also surch.

308	1c. Type **60**	10	10
309	5c. on 3c. *Dreams of Christmas Gifts*	10	10
310	12c. on 15c. *Carolling*	15	15

311	18c. on 25c. *Candle-light Procession*	20	20
312	$1 *Going to Church*	45	45
313	$2.50 on $1.50 *Coming Home for Christmas*	90	90
MS314	232×147 mm. Nos. 308/13	2·50	2·50

1978. Easter. Nos. 303/6 optd **EASTER 1978.**

315	25c. Type **65**	15	20
316	40c. *Helene Fourment with her Two Children*	15	20
317	$1.20 *Rubens and his Wife*	35	40
318	$2.50 *Marchesa Brigida Spinola-Doria*	45	60
MS319	93×145 mm. Nos. 315/18	1·25	1·50

68 Coronation Coach at Admiralty Arch

1978. 25th Anniv of Coronation. Multicoloured.

320	22c. Buckingham Palace	10	10
321	50c. Type **68**	10	10
322	$1.50 Balcony scene	15	15
323	$2.50 Royal coat of arms	25	25
MS324	138×92 mm. Nos. 320/3	60	60

1978. Anniversaries. Nos. 283/4 and 287 optd **VALLEY SECONDARY SCHOOL 1953–1978** and Nos. 285/6 and 288 optd **ROAD METHODIST CHURCH 1878–1978,** or surch also.

325	22c. Lobster fishing boat	25	15
326	35c. Boat race	35	20
327	50c. Sea bean	35	30
328	$1 Sandy Island	40	40
329	$1.20 on $5 Ground lizard	45	45
330	$1.50 on $2.50 Manchineel	50	55

71 Mother and Child

1978. Christmas. Children's Paintings. Multicoloured.

331	5c. Type **71**	10	10
332	12c. Christmas masquerade	15	10
333	18c. Christmas dinner	15	10
334	22c. Serenading	15	10
335	$1 Child in manger	35	20
336	$2.50 Family going to church	55	40
MS337	191×101 mm. Nos. 331/6	1·25	1·75

1979. International Year of the Child. As Nos. 331/6, but additionally inscr "1979 INTERNATIONAL YEAR OF THE CHILD" and emblem. Borders in different colours.

338	5c. Type **71**	10	10
339	12c. Christmas masquerade	10	10
340	18c. Christmas dinner	10	10
341	22c. Serenading	10	10
342	$1 Child in manger	30	30
343	$2.50 Family going to church	50	50
MS344	205×112 mm. Nos. 338/43	1·75	2·50

1979. Nos. 274/7 and 279/80 surch.

345	12c. on 2c. Great barracuda	50	50
346	14c. on 4c. Spanish bayonet	40	50
347	18c. on 3c. Queen conch	1·00	55
348	25c. on 6c. Cable and Wireless building	55	50
349	38c. on 10c. American kestrel	2·50	70
350	40c. on 1c. Type **62**	2·75	70

73 Valley Methodist Church

1979. Easter. Church Interiors. Multicoloured.

351	5c. Type **73**	10	10
352	12c. St. Mary's Anglican Church, The Valley	10	10
353	18c. St. Gerard's Roman Catholic Church, The Valley	15	15
354	22c. Road Methodist Church	15	15
355	$1.50 St. Augustine's Anglican Church, East End	40	40
356	$2.50 West End Methodist Church	50	50
MS357	190×105 mm. Nos. 351/6	1·50	2·25

74 Cape of Good Hope 1d. "Woodblock" of 1881

1979. Death Centenary of Sir Rowland Hill. Multicoloured.

358	1c. Type **74**	10	10
359	1c. U.S.A. "inverted Jenny" of 1918	10	10
360	22c. Penny Black ("V.R." Official)	15	15
361	35c. Germany 2m, *Graf Zeppelin* of 1928	20	20
362	$1.50 U.S.A. $5 *Columbus* of 1893	40	60
363	$2.50 Great Britain £5 orange of 1882	60	95
MS364	187×123 mm. Nos. 358/63	1·25	2·40

75 Wright *Flyer I* (1st powered Flight, 1903)

1979. History of Powered Flight. Multicoloured.

365	5c. Type **75**	20	10
366	12c. Louis Bleriot at Dover after Channel crossing, 1909	25	10
367	18c. Vickers FB-27 Vimy (1st non-stop crossing of Atlantic, 1919)	30	15
368	22c. Ryan NYP Special *Spirit of St Louis* (1st solo Atlantic flight by Charles Lindbergh, 1927)	30	20
369	$1.50 Airship LZ 127 *Graf Zeppelin*, 1928	65	60
370	$2.50 Concorde, 1979	3·50	90
MS371	200×113 mm. Nos. 365/70	4·25	3·25

76 Sombrero Island

1979. Outer Islands. Multicoloured.

372	5c. Type **76**	15	10
373	12c. Anguillita Island	15	10
374	18c. Sandy Island	15	15
375	25c. Prickly Pear Cays	15	15
376	$1 Dog Island	40	40
377	$2.50 Scrub Island	60	70
MS378	180×91 mm. Nos. 372/7	2·75	2·25

77 Red Poinsettia

1979. Christmas. Multicoloured.

379	22c. Type **77**	15	20
380	35c. Kalanchoe	20	30
381	$1.50 Cream poinsettia	40	50
382	$2.50 White poinsettia	60	70
MS383	146×164 mm. Nos. 379/82	1·75	2·25

78 Exhibition Scene

1979. "London 1980" International Stamp Exhibition (1st issue). Multicoloured.

384	35c. Type **78**	15	20
385	50c. Earls Court Exhibition Centre	15	25
386	$1.50 Penny Black and Two-penny Blue stamps	25	60
387	$2.50 Exhibition Logo	45	95
MS388	150×94 mm. Nos. 384/7	1·40	2·00

See also Nos. 407/9.

79 Games Site

1980. Winter Olympic Games, Lake Placid, U.S.A. Multicoloured.

389	5c. Type **79**	10	10
390	18c. Ice hockey	20	10
391	35c. Ice skating	20	20
392	50c. Bobsleighing	20	20
393	$1 Skiing	20	35
394	$2.50 Luge-tobogganing	40	80
MS395	136×128 mm. Nos. 389/94	1·00	2·00

80 Salt ready for "Reaping"

1980. Salt Industry. Multicoloured.

396	5c. Type **80**	10	10
397	12c. Tallying salt	10	10
398	18c. Unloading salt flats	15	15
399	22c. Salt storage heap	15	15
400	$1 Salt for bagging and grinding	30	40
401	$2.50 Loading salt for export	50	70
MS402	180×92 mm. Nos. 396/401	1·10	1·75

1980. Anniversaries. Nos. 280, 282 and 287/8 optd **50th Anniversary Scouting 1980** (10c., $2.50) or **75th Anniversary Rotary 1980** (others).

403	10c. American kestrel	1·75	20
404	20c. Stop-light parrotfish	1·00	20
405	$2.50 Manchineel	1·75	1·50
406	$5 Ground lizard	2·50	2·50

83 Palace of Westminster and Great Britain 1970 9d. "Philympia" Commemoration

1980. "London 1980" International Stamp Exhibition (2nd issue). Multicoloured.

407	50c. Type **83**	55	75
408	$1.50 City Hall, Toronto and "Capex 1978" stamp of Canada	85	1·25
409	$2.50 Statue of Liberty and 1976 "Interphil" stamp of U.S.A.	1·10	1·60
MS410	157×130 mm. Nos. 407/9	2·25	3·00

84 Queen Elizabeth the Queen Mother

1980. 80th Birthday of The Queen Mother.

411	**84**	35c. multicoloured	70	40
412	**84**	50c. multicoloured	85	50
413	**84**	$1.50 multicoloured	1·25	1·50
414	**84**	$3 multicoloured	2·00	2·50
MS415		160×110 mm. Nos. 411/14	4·75	4·75

85 Brown Pelicans ("Pelican")

1980. Christmas. Birds. Multicoloured.

416	5c. Type **85**	45	10
417	22c. Great blue heron ("Great Grey Heron")	1·00	20
418	$1.50 Barn swallow ("Swallow")	2·00	60
419	$3 Ruby-throated hummingbird ("Hummingbird")	2·25	1·40
MS420	126×160 mm. Nos. 416/19	10·00	7·50

1980. Separation from St. Kitts. Nos. 274, 277, 280/9, 334 and 418/19 optd **SEPARATION 1980** or surch also.

421	1c. Type **62**	20	80
422	2c. on 4c. Spanish bayonet	20	80
423	5c. on 15c. Ground orchid	1·75	80
424	5c. on $1.50 Barn swallow	1·75	80
425	5c. on $3 Ruby-throated hummingbird	1·75	80
426	10c. American kestrel	2·25	80
427	12c. on $1 Sandy Island	30	80
428	14c. on $2.50 Manchineel	30	80
429	15c. Ground orchid	2·00	80
430	18c. on $5 Ground lizard	35	80
431	20c. Stop-light parrotfish	35	80
432	22c. Lobster fishing boat	35	80
433	25c. on 15c. Ground orchid	2·00	85
434	35c. Boat race	35	85
435	38c. on 22c. Serenading	35	85
436	40c. on 1c. Type **62**	1·00	85
437	50c. Sea bean	40	95
438	$1 Sandy Island	50	1·25
439	$2.50 Manchineel	1·25	3·00
440	$5 Ground lizard	2·25	4·00
441	$10 Red-billed tropic bird	5·00	6·00
442	$10 on 6c. Cable and Wireless Building	5·00	6·00

87 First Petition for Separation, 1825

1980. Separation from St. Kitts. Multicoloured.

443	18c. Type **87**	10	10
444	22c. Referendum ballot paper, 1967	15	10
445	35c. Airport blockade, 1967	40	15
446	50c. Anguillan flag	70	30
447	$1 Separation celebration, 1980	40	45
MS448	178×92 mm. Nos. 443/7	1·40	1·25

88 Nelson's Dockyard (R. Granger Barrett)

1981. 175th Death Anniv of Lord Nelson. Multicoloured.

449	22c. Type **88**	2·50	50
450	35c. Ships in which Nelson Served (Nicholas Pocock)	2·50	70
451	50c. H.M.S. Victory (Monamy Swaine)	3·00	1·50
452	$3 Battle of Trafalgar (Clarkson Stanfield)	3·75	6·50
MS453	82×63 mm. $5 Horatio Nelson (L. F. Abbott) and coat of arms	3·00	3·25

89 Minnie Mouse being chased by Bees

1981. Easter. Walt Disney Cartoon Characters. Multicoloured.

454	1c. Type **89**	10	10
455	2c. Pluto laughing at Mickey Mouse	10	10
456	3c. Minnie Mouse tying ribbon round Pluto's neck	10	10
457	5c. Minnie Mouse confronted by love-struck bird who fancies her bonnet	10	10
458	7c. Dewey and Huey admiring themselves in mirror	10	10
459	9c. Horace Horsecollar and Clarabelle Cow out for a stroll	10	10
460	10c. Daisy Duck with hat full of Easter eggs	10	10
461	$2 Goofy unwrapping Easter hat	1·40	1·40
462	$3 Donald Duck in his Easter finery	1·60	1·60
MS463	134×108 mm. $5 Chip and Dale making off with hat	3·50	3·50

90 Prince Charles, Lady Diana Spencer and St. Paul's Cathedral

1981. Royal Wedding. Multicoloured.

464	50c. Type **90**	15	20
465	$2.50 Althorp	30	50
466	$3 Windsor Castle	35	60
MS467	90×72 mm. Buckingham Palace	1·25	1·50

91 Children playing in Tree

1981. 35th Anniv of UNICEF Multicoloured.

470	5c. Type **91**	20	30
471	10c. Children playing by pool	20	30
472	15c. Children playing musical instruments	20	30
473	$3 Children playing with pets	2·50	3·00
MS474	78×106 mm. Children playing football (vert)	3·50	5·00

1981. Christmas. Designs as T **89** showing scenes from Walt Disney's cartoon film *The Night before Christmas*.

475	1c. multicoloured	10	10
476	2c. multicoloured	10	10
477	3c. multicoloured	10	10
478	5c. multicoloured	15	10
479	7c. multicoloured	15	10
480	10c. multicoloured	15	10
481	12c. multicoloured	15	10
482	$2 multicoloured	3·75	1·25
483	$3 multicoloured	3·75	1·60
MS484	130×105 mm. $5 multicoloured	5·50	3·50

92 Red Grouper

1982. Multicoloured.

485	1c. Type **92**	15	1·25
486	5c. Ferry service, Blowing Point	30	1·25
487	10c. Island dinghies	20	60
488	15c. Majorettes	20	60
489	20c. Launching boat, Sandy Hill	40	60
490	25c. Corals	1·50	60
491	30c. Little Bay cliffs	30	75
492	35c. Fountain Cave interior	1·50	80
493	40c. Sunset over Sandy Island	30	75
494	45c. Landing at Sombrero	50	80
495	60c. Seine fishing	3·25	3·25
496	75c. Boat race at sunset, Sandy Ground	1·00	2·00
497	$1 Bagging lobster at Island Harbour	2·25	2·00
498	$5 Brown pelicans	17·00	14·00
499	$7.50 Hibiscus	11·00	16·00
500	$10 Queen triggerfish	17·00	16·00

1982. No. 494 surch **50c.**

501	50c. on 45c. Landing at Sombrero	50	35

94 Anthurium and *Heliconius charithonia*

1982. Easter. Flowers and Butterflies. Multicoloured.

502	10c. Type **94**	1·10	15
503	35c. Bird of paradise and *Junonia evarete*	2·00	40
504	75c. Allamanda and *Danaus plexippus*	2·25	70
505	$3 Orchid tree and *Biblis hyperia*	3·50	2·25
MS506	65×79 mm. $5 Amaryllis and *Dryas julia*	2·75	3·50

95 Lady Diana Spencer in 1961

1982. 21st Birthday of Princess of Wales. Multicoloured.

507	10c. Type **95**	50	20
508	30c. Lady Diana Spencer in 1968	1·75	25
509	40c. Lady Diana in 1970	50	30
510	60c. Lady Diana in 1974	55	35
511	$2 Lady Diana in 1981	80	1·10
512	$3 Lady Diana in 1981 (different)	5·50	1·40
MS513	72×90 mm. $5 Princess of Wales	7·50	3·00
MS514	125×125 mm. As Nos. 507/12, but with buff borders	9·50	7·00

96 Pitching Tent

1982. 75th Anniv of Boy Scout Movement. Multicoloured.

515	10c. Type **96**	45	20
516	35c. Scout band	85	50
517	75c. Yachting	1·25	90
518	$3 On parade	3·00	2·75
MS519	90×72 mm. $5 Cooking	4·50	4·00

1982. World Cup Football Championship, Spain. Horiz designs as T **89** showing scenes from Walt Disney's cartoon film *Bedknobs and Broomsticks*.

520	1c. multicoloured	10	10
521	3c. multicoloured	10	10
522	4c. multicoloured	10	10
523	5c. multicoloured	10	10
524	7c. multicoloured	10	10
525	9c. multicoloured	10	10
526	10c. multicoloured	10	10
527	$2.50 multicoloured	2·50	1·75
528	$3 multicoloured	2·50	2·00
MS529	126×101 mm. $5 multicoloured	9·00	8·50

1982. Commonwealth Games, Brisbane. Nos. 487, 495/6 and 498 optd **COMMONWEALTH GAMES 1982.**

530	10c. Island dinghies	15	25
531	60c. Seine fishing	45	60
532	75c. Boat race at sunset, Sandy Ground	60	80
533	$5 Brown pelicans	3·25	3·75

1982. Birth Cent of A. A. Milne (author). As T **89**.

534	1c. multicoloured	25	20
535	2c. multicoloured	25	20
536	3c. multicoloured	25	20
537	5c. multicoloured	35	20
538	7c. multicoloured	35	25
539	10c. multicoloured	50	15
540	12c. multicoloured	60	20
541	20c. multicoloured	90	25
542	$5 multicoloured	9·00	9·50
MS543	120×93 mm. $5 multicoloured	7·50	9·00

DESIGNS—HORIZ: 1c. to $5 Scenes from various *Winnie the Pooh* stories.

98 Culture

1983. Commonwealth Day. Multicoloured.

544	10c. Type **98**	10	15
545	35c. Anguilla and British flags	30	30
546	75c. Economic co-operation	60	1·00
547	$2.50 Salt industry (salt pond)	3·75	5·25
MS548	76×61 mm. World map showing positions of Commonwealth countries	2·50	2·50

99 "I am the Lord Thy God"

1983. Easter. The Ten Commandments. Multicoloured.

549	1c. Type **99**	10	10
550	2c. "Thou shalt not make any graven image"	10	10
551	3c. "Thou shalt not take My Name in vain"	10	10
552	10c. "Remember the Sabbath Day"	25	10
553	35c. "Honour thy father and mother"	65	20
554	60c. "Thou shalt not kill"	1·00	40
555	75c. "Thou shalt not commit adultery"	1·25	50
556	$2 "Thou shalt not steal"	2·75	1·50
557	$2.50 "Thou shalt not bear false witness"	3·00	1·50
558	$5 "Thou shalt not covet"	4·25	2·75
MS559	126×102 mm. $5 "Moses receiving the Tablets" (16th-century woodcut)	2·75	3·00

100 Leatherback Turtle

1983. Endangered Species. Turtles. Multicoloured.

560	10c. Type **100**	4·00	80
561	35c. Hawksbill turtle	7·00	1·25
562	75c. Green turtle	8·00	3·50
563	$1 Loggerhead turtle	9·00	7·50
MS564	93×72 mm. $5 Leatherback turtle (different)	22·00	4·00

101 Montgolfier Hot Air Balloon, 1783

1983. Bicentenary of Manned Flight. Multicoloured.

565	10c. Type **101**	50	50
566	60c. Blanchard and Jefferies crossing English Channel by balloon, 1785	1·25	85
567	$1 Henri Giffard's steam-powered dirigible airship, 1852	1·75	1·50
568	$2.50 Otto Lillienthal and biplane glider, 1890–96	3·00	3·00
MS569	72×90 mm. $5 Wilbur Wright flying round Statue of Liberty, 1909	2·75	3·50

102 Boys' Brigade Band and Flag

1983. Centenary of Boys' Brigade. Multicoloured.

570	10c. Type **102**	50	15
571	$5 Brigade members marching	3·50	2·75
MS572	96×115 mm. Nos. 570/1	3·25	4·50

1983. 150th Anniv of Abolition of Slavery (1st issue). Nos. 487, 493 and 497/8 optd **150TH ANNIVERSARY ABOLITION OF SLAVERY ACT.**

573	10c. Island dinghies	20	10
574	40c. Sunset over Sandy Island	30	25
575	$1 Bagging lobster at Island Harbour	80	50
576	$5 Brown pelicans	10·00	2·75

See also Nos. 616/23.

104 Jiminy on Clock ("Cricket on the Hearth")

1983. Christmas. Walt Disney Cartoon Characters. Multicoloured.

577	1c. Type **104**	10	10
578	2c. Jiminy with fiddle (*Cricket on the Hearth*)	10	10
579	3c. Jiminy among toys (*Cricket on the Hearth*)	10	10
580	4c. Mickey as Bob Cratchit (*A Christmas Carol*)	10	10
581	5c. Donald Duck as Scrooge (*A Christmas Carol*)	10	10
582	6c. Mini and Goofy in *The Chimes*	10	10
583	10c. Goofy sees an imp appearing from bells (*The Chimes*)	10	10
584	$2 Donald Duck as Mr. Pickwick (*The Pickwick Papers*)	3·50	2·75
585	$3 Disney characters as Pickwickians (*The Pickwick Papers*)	4·00	2·25
MS586	130×104 mm. Donald Duck as Mr. Pickwick with gifts (*The Pickwick Papers*)	10·00	11·00

105 100 Metres Race

1984. Olympic Games, Los Angeles. Multicoloured

(a) Inscr "1984 Los Angeles".

587A	1c. Type **105**	10	10
588A	2c. Long jumping	10	10
589A	3c. Shot-putting	10	10
590A	4c. High jumping	10	10
591A	5c. 400 metres race	10	10
592A	6c. Hurdling	10	10
593A	10c. Discus-throwing	10	10
594A	$1 Pole-vaulting	3·25	1·25
595A	$4 Javelin-throwing	6·00	3·50
MS596A	117×93 mm. $5 1500 metres race	7·50	4·50

(b) Inscr "1984 Olympics Los Angeles" and Olympic emblem.

587B	1c. Type **105**	10	10
588B	2c. Long jumping	10	10
589B	3c. Shot-putting	10	10
590B	4c. High jumping	10	10
591B	5c. 400 metres race	10	10
592B	6c. Hurdling	10	10
593B	10c. Discus-throwing	10	10
594B	$1 Pole-vaulting	3·75	3·00
595B	$4 Javelin-throwing	7·50	8·50
MS596B	117×93 mm. $5 1500 metres race	8·00	4·50

106 Justice

1984. Easter. Multicoloured.

597	10c. Type **106**	15	10
598	25c. "Poetry"	20	20
599	35c. "Philosophy"	30	30
600	40c. "Theology"	30	30
601	$1 "Abraham and Paul"	85	95
602	$2 "Moses and Matthew"	1·60	1·75
603	$3 "John and David"	2·25	3·00
604	$4 "Peter and Adam"	2·50	3·00
MS605	83×110 mm. $5 "Astronomy"	3·00	3·00

Nos. 597/605 show details from "*La Stanza della Segnatura*" by Raphael.

1984. Nos. 485, 491, 498/500 surch.

606	25c. on $7.50 Hibiscus	65	35
607	35c. on 30c. Little Bay cliffs	50	40
608	60c. on 1c. Type **92**	55	45
609	$2.50 on $5 Brown pelicans	3·00	1·50
610	$2.50 on $10 Queen triggerfish	1·75	1·50

108 1913 1d. Kangaroo Stamp

1984. "Ausipex 84" International Stamp Exhibition. Multicoloured.

611	10c. Type **108**	40	30
612	75c. 1914 6d. Laughing Kookaburra	1·50	1·25
613	$1 1932 2d. Sydney Harbour Bridge	2·00	1·75
614	$2.50 1938 10s. King George VI	2·25	4·00
MS615	95×86 mm. $5 £1 Bass and £2 Admiral King	5·00	7·00

109 Thomas Fowell Buxton

1984. 150th Anniv of Abolition of Slavery (2nd issue). Multicoloured.

616	10c. Type **109**	15	10
617	25c. Abraham Lincoln	30	25
618	35c. Henri Christophe	40	35
619	60c. Thomas Clarkson	60	50
620	75c. William Wilberforce	70	60
621	$1 Olaudah Equiano	80	70
622	$2.50 General Charles Gordon	1·75	1·60
623	$5 Granville Sharp	3·00	3·00
MS624	150×121 mm. Nos. 616/23	7·50	10·00

1984. Universal Postal Union Congress, Hamburg. Nos. 486/7 and 498 optd **U.P.U. CONGRESS HAMBURG 1984** or surch also (No 626).

625	5c. Ferry service, Blowing Point	30	10
626	20c. on 10c. Island dinghies	30	15
627	$5 Brown pelicans	5·50	3·50

1984. Birth of Prince Henry. Nos. 507/12 optd **PRINCE HENRY BIRTH 15.9.84.**

628	10c. Type **95**	20	10
629	30c. Lady Diana Spencer in 1968	40	25
630	40c. Lady Diana in 1970	20	30
631	60c. Lady Diana in 1974	30	45
632	$2 Lady Diana in 1981	75	1·25
633	$3 Lady Diana in 1981 (different)	1·25	1·75
MS634	72×90 mm. $5 Princess of Wales	2·00	3·00
MS635	125×125 mm. As Nos. 628/33, but with buff borders	2·00	4·00

112 Christmas in Sweden

1984. Christmas. Walt Disney Cartoon Characters. National Scenes. Multicoloured.

636	1c. Type **112**	10	10
637	2c. Italy	10	10
638	3c. Holland	10	10
639	4c. Mexico	10	10
640	5c. Spain	10	10
641	10c. Disneyland, U.S.A.	10	10
642	$1 Japan	3·00	2·00
643	$2 Anguilla	4·00	4·50
644	$4 Germany	6·50	7·50
MS645	126×102 mm. $5 England	7·00	5·00

113 Icarus in Flight

1984. 40th Anniv of International Civil Aviation Authority. Multicoloured.

646	60c. Type **113**	60	75
647	75c. *Solar Princess* (abstract)	80	90
648	$2.50 I.C.A.O. emblem (vert)	2·25	3·00
MS649	65×49 mm. $5 Map of air routes serving Anguilla	3·00	4·50

114 Barn Swallow

1985. Birth Bicentenary of John J. Audubon (ornithologist). Multicoloured.

650	10c. Type **114**	1·25	75
651	60c. American wood stork ("Woodstork")	1·75	1·50
652	75c. Roseate tern	1·75	1·50
653	$5 Osprey	4·75	6·50
MS654	Two sheets, each 73×103 mm. $4 Western tanager (horiz); (b) $4 Solitary vireo (horiz) Set of 2 sheets	10·00	6·00

115 The Queen Mother visiting King's College Hospital, London

1985. Life and Times of Queen Elizabeth the Queen Mother. Multicoloured.

655	10c. Type **115**	10	10
656	$2 The Queen Mother inspecting Royal Marine Volunteer Cadets, Deal	80	1·25
657	$3 The Queen Mother outside Clarence House	1·10	1·50
MS658	56×85 mm. $5 At Ascot, 1979	1·75	2·50

116 White-tailed Tropic Bird

1985. Birds. Multicoloured.

659	5c. Brown pelican	1·75	1·75
660	10c. Mourning dove ("Turtle Dove")	1·75	1·75
661	15c. Magnificent frigate bird (inscr "Man-o-War")	1·75	1·75
662	20c. Antillean crested hummingbird	1·75	1·75
663	25c. Type **116**	1·75	1·75
664	30c. Caribbean elaenia	1·75	1·75
665	35c. Black-whiskered vireo	7·50	5·50
665a	35c. Lesser Antillean bullfinch	6·00	3·00
666	40c. Yellow-crowned night heron	2·00	1·75
667	45c. Pearly-eyed thrasher	1·75	1·75
668	50c. Laughing gull	1·75	1·75
669	65c. Brown booby	1·75	1·75
670	80c. Grey kingbird	2·25	3·00
671	$1 Audubon's shearwater	2·25	3·00
672	$1.35 Roseate tern	2·00	3·00
673	$2.50 Bananaquit	6·00	8·50
674	$5 Belted kingfisher	5·00	8·50
675	$10 Green-backed heron ("Green Heron")	7·00	11·00

1985. 75th Anniv of Girl Guide Movement. Nos. 486, 491, 496 and 498 optd **GIRL GUIDES 75TH ANNIVERSARY 1910–1985** and anniversary emblem.

676	5c. Ferry service, Blowing Point	30	30
677	30c. Little Bay cliffs	40	35
678	75c. Boat race at sunset, Sandy Ground	60	85
679	$5 Brown pelicans	10·00	10·00

118 Goofy as Huckleberry Finn Fishing

1985. 150th Birth Anniv of Mark Twain (author). Walt Disney cartoon characters in scenes from *Huckleberry Finn*. Multicoloured.

680	10c. Type **118**	70	20
681	60c. Pete as Pap surprising Huck	2·25	85
682	$1 "Multiplication tables"	2·75	1·25
683	$3 The Duke reciting Shakespeare	4·00	4·00
MS684	127×102 mm. $5 "In school but out"	8·50	8·00

119 Hansel and Gretel (Mickey and Minnie Mouse) awakening in Forest

1985. Birth Bicentenaries of Grimm Brothers (folklorists). Designs showing Walt Disney cartoon characters in scenes from *Hansel and Gretel*. Multicoloured.

685	5c. Type **119**	55	55
686	50c. Hansel and Gretel find the gingerbread house	1·50	60

687	90c. Hansel and Gretel meeting the Witch	2·00	1·00
688	$4 Hansel and Gretel captured by the Witch	3·50	5·00
MS689	128×101 mm. $5 Hansel and Gretel riding on swan	8·00	9·00

120 Statue of Liberty and *Danmark* (Denmark)

1985. Centenary of the Statue of Liberty (1986). The Statue of Liberty and Cadet ships.

690	10c. Type **120**	1·00	85
691	20c. *Eagle* (U.S.A.)	1·25	90
692	60c. *Amerigo Vespucci* (Italy)	1·60	1·50
693	75c. *Sir Winston Churchill* (Great Britain)	1·60	1·50
694	$2 *Nippon Maru* (Japan)	1·75	4·00
695	$2.50 *Gorch Fock* (West Germany)	1·75	4·00
MS696	96×69 mm. $5 Statue of Liberty (vert)	7·50	4·50

1985. 80th Anniv of Rotary (10, 35c.) and International Youth Year (others). Nos. 487, 491 and 497 optd or surch **80TH ANNIVERSARY ROTARY 1985** and emblem (10, 35c.) or **INTERNATIONAL YOUTH YEAR** and emblem ($1, $5).

697	10c. Island dinghies	30	25
698	35c. on 30c. Little Bay cliffs	60	45
699	$1 Bagging lobster at Island Harbour	1·50	1·25
700	$5 on 30c. Little Bay cliffs	4·25	5·25

123 Johannes Hevelius (astronomer) and Mayan Temple Observatory

1986. Appearance of Halley's Comet. Multicoloured.

701	5c. Type **123**	55	55
702	10c. "Viking Lander" space vehicle on Mars, 1976	55	55
703	60c. Comet in 1664 (from *Theatri Cosmicum*, 1668)	1·50	85
704	$4 Comet over Mississippi riverboat, 1835 (150th birth anniv of Mark Twain)	4·50	5·00
MS705	101×70 mm. $5 Halley's Comet over Anguilla	4·50	6·00

124 "The Crucifixion"

1986. Easter.

706	**124**	10c. multicoloured	20	20
707	-	25c. multicoloured	35	35
708	-	45c. multicoloured	65	65
709	-	$4 multicoloured	3·75	5·00
MS710	– 93×75 mm. $5 multicoloured (horiz)		6·00	8·50

DESIGNS: 25c. to $5 Different stained glass windows from Chartres Cathedral.

125 Princess Elizabeth inspecting Guards, 1946

1986. 60th Birthday of Queen Elizabeth II.

711	**125**	20c. black and yellow	40	20
712	-	$2 multicoloured	1·75	1·50
713	-	$3 multicoloured	1·75	1·75
MS714	– 120×85 mm. $5 black and brown		2·75	3·75

DESIGNS: $2 Queen at Garter Ceremony; $3 At Trooping the Colour; $5 Duke and Duchess of York with baby Princess Elizabeth, 1926.

1986. "Ameripex" International Stamp Exhibition, Chicago. Nos. 659, 667, 671, 673 and 675 optd **AMERIPEX 1986.**

715	5c. Brown pelican	60	1·00
716	45c. Pearly-eyed thrasher	1·25	50
717	$1 Audubon's shearwater	2·00	1·25
718	$2.50 Bananaquit	2·75	3·25
719	$10 Green-backed heron	6·50	9·50

127 Prince Andrew and Miss Sarah Ferguson

1986. Royal Wedding. Multicoloured.

720	10c. Type **127**	50	15
721	35c. Prince Andrew	85	35
722	$2 Miss Sarah Ferguson	2·25	1·50
723	$3 Prince Andrew and Miss Sarah Ferguson (differrent)	2·50	2·00
MS724	119×90 mm. $6 Westminster Abbey	5·50	6·50

1986. International Peace Year. Nos. 616/23 optd **INTERNATIONAL YEAR OF PEACE.**

725	10c. Type **109**	90	60
726	25c. Abraham Lincoln	1·25	50
727	35c. Henri Christophe	1·40	55
728	60c. Thomas Clarkson	2·00	80
729	75c. William Wilberforce	2·00	1·00
730	$1 Olaudah Equiano	2·00	1·25
731	$2.50 General Gordon	3·75	4·75
732	$5 Granville Sharp	4·25	7·00
MS733	150×121 mm. Nos. 725/32	15·00	17·00

129 Trading Sloop

1986. Christmas. Ships. Multicoloured.

734	10c. Type **129**	1·75	60
735	45c. *Lady Rodney* (cargo liner)	3·25	1·10
736	80c. *West Derby* (19th-century sailing ship)	4·25	2·50
737	$3 *Warspite* (local sloop)	8·50	10·00
MS738	130×100 mm. $4 Boat-race day (vert)	18·00	20·00

130 Christopher Columbus with Astrolabe

1986. 500th Anniv (1992) of Discovery of America by Columbus (1st issue). Multicoloured.

739	5c. Type **130**	60	60
740	10c. Columbus on board ship	1·00	60
741	35c. *Santa Maria*	2·10	1·10
742	80c. King Ferdinand and Queen Isabella of Spain (horiz)	1·50	1·75
743	$4 Caribbean Indians smoking tobacco (horiz)	3·25	5·00
MS744	Two sheets, each 96×66 mm. (a) $5 Caribbean manatee (horiz). (b) $5 Dragon tree Set of 2 sheets	15·00	17·00

See also Nos. 902/6.

131 *Danaus plexippus*

1987. Easter. Butterflies. Multicoloured.

745	10c. Type **131**	1·50	70
746	80c. *Anartia jatrophae*	4·00	2·75
747	$1 *Heliconius charithonia*	4·25	2·75
748	$2 *Junonia evarete*	7·00	8·50
MS749	90×69 mm. $6 *Dryas julia*	11·00	13·00

132 Old Goose Iron and Modern Electric Iron

1987. 20th Anniv of Separation from St. Kitts-Nevis. Multicoloured.

750	10c. Type **132**	70	40
751	35c. Old East End School and Albena Lake-Hodge Comprehensive College	75	45
752	45c. Past and present markets	85	50
753	80c. Previous sailing ferry and new motor ferry, Blowing Point	2·50	1·25
754	$1 Original mobile post office and new telephone exchange	2·50	1·40
755	$2 Open-air meeting, Burrowes Park and House of Assembly in session	2·75	3·25
MS756	159×127 mm. Nos. 750/5	13·00	16·00

1987. "Capex '87" International Stamp Exhibition, Toronto. Nos. 665a, 667, 670 and 675 optd **CAPEX'87.**

757	35c. Lesser Antillean bullfinch	2·50	1·00
758	45c. Pearly-eyed thrasher	2·50	1·00
759	80c. Grey kingbird	3·75	1·50
760	$10 Green-backed heron	12·00	14·00

1987. 20th Anniv of Independence. Nos. 659, 661/4 and 665a/75 optd **20 YEARS OF PROGRESS 1967–1987,** No. 762 surch also.

761	5c. Brown pelican	3·25	3·25
762	10c. on 15c. Magnificent frigate bird	3·25	3·25
763	15c. Magnificent frigate bird	3·25	3·25
764	20c. Antillean crested hummingbird	3·25	3·25
765	25c. Type **116**	3·25	3·25
766	30c. Caribbean elaenia	3·25	3·25
767	35c. Lesser Antillean bullfinch	3·25	3·25
768	40c. Yellow-crowned night heron	3·25	3·25
769	45c. Pearly-eyed thrasher	3·25	3·25
770	50c. Laughing gull	3·25	3·25
771	65c. Brown booby	3·50	3·50
772	80c. Grey kingbird	3·50	3·50
773	$1 Audubon's shearwater	3·50	3·50
774	$1.35 Roseate tern	4·00	4·25
775	$2.50 Bananaquit	5·00	7·00
776	$5 Belted kingfisher	7·00	9·50
777	$10 Green-backed heron	9·00	12·00

135 Wicket Keeper and Game in Progress

1987. Cricket World Cup. Multicoloured.

778	10c. Type **135**	2·50	80
779	35c. Batsman and local Anguilla team	2·50	70
780	45c. Batsman and game in progress	3·00	75
781	$2.50 Bowler and game in progress	6·00	9·00
MS782	100×75 mm. $6 Batsman and game in progress (different)	16·00	17·00

136 West Indian Top Shell

1987. Christmas. Sea Shells and Crabs. Multicoloured.

783	10c. Type **136**	1·75	55
784	35c. Ghost crab	2·50	60
785	50c. Spiny Caribbean vase	3·25	1·40
786	$2 Great land crab	6·50	8·50
MS787	101×75 mm. $6 Queen or pink conch	14·00	15·00

1987. Royal Ruby Wedding. Nos. 665a, 671/2 and 675 optd **40TH WEDDING ANNIVERSARY H.M. QUEEN ELIZABETH II H.R.H. THE DUKE OF EDINBURGH.**

788	35c. Lesser Antillean bullfinch	1·50	55
789	$1 Audubon's shearwater	2·25	80
790	$1.35 Roseate tern	2·50	90
791	$10 Green-backed heron	6·50	10·00

138 *Crinum erubescens*

1988. Easter. Lilies. Multicoloured.

792	30c. Type **138**	70	25
793	45c. Spider lily	70	25
794	$1 *Crinum macowanii*	2·00	85
795	$2.50 Day lily	2·00	3·00
MS796	100×75 mm. $6 Easter lily	2·75	4·50

139 Relay Racing

1988. Olympic Games, Seoul. Multicoloured.

797	35c. Type **139**	45	30
798	45c. Windsurfing	55	45
799	50c. Tennis	1·50	1·10
800	80c. Basketball	6·50	2·75
MS801	104×78 mm. $6 Athletics	3·00	4·50

140 Common Sea Fan

1988. Christmas. Marine Life. Multicoloured.

802	35c. Type **140**	1·00	30
803	80c. Coral crab	1·75	70
804	$1 Grooved brain coral	2·00	1·00
805	$1.60 Queen triggerfish	2·75	3·25
MS806	103×78 mm. $6 West Indian spiny lobster	3·00	4·50

1988. Visit of Princess Alexandra. Nos. 665a, 670/1 and 673 optd **H.R.H. PRINCESS ALEXANDRA'S VISIT NOVEMBER 1988.**

807	35c. Lesser Antillean bullfinch	3·00	70
808	80c. Grey kingbird	4·00	1·40
809	$1 Audubon's shearwater	4·00	1·60
810	$2.50 Bananaquit	6·00	6·00

142 Wood Slave

1989. Lizards. Multicoloured.

811	45c. Type **142**	1·75	50
812	80c. Slippery back	2·50	85
813	$2.50 *Iguana delicatissima*	4·50	4·75
MS814	101×75 mm. $6 Tree lizard	14·00	4·75

143 *Christ Crowned with Thorns* (detail) (Bosch)

1989. Easter. Religious Paintings. Multicoloured.

815	35c. Type **143**	80	25
816	80c. *Christ bearing the Cross* (detail) (Gerard David)	1·25	75
817	$1 *The Deposition* (detail) (Gerard David)	1·40	80
818	$1.60 *Pieta* (detail) (Rogier van der Weyden)	2·00	2·75
MS819	103×77 mm. $6 *Crucified Christ with the Virgin Mary and Saints* (detail) (Raphael)	2·75	4·25

144 University Arms

1989. 40th Anniv of University of the West Indies.

820	**144**	$5 multicoloured	4·50	5·00

1989. 20th Anniv of First Manned Landing on Moon. Nos. 670/2 and 674 optd **20TH ANNIVERSARY MOON LANDING.**

821	80c. Grey kingbird	3·25	90
822	$1 Audubon's shearwater	3·25	1·00
823	$1.35 Roseate tern	3·75	1·75
824	$5 Belted kingfisher	9·00	12·00

146 Lone Star (house), 1930

1989. Christmas. Historic Houses. Multicoloured.

825	5c. Type **146**	50	1·50
826	35c. Whitehouse, 1906	1·00	45
827	45c. Hodges House	1·10	50
828	80c. Warden's Place	1·75	1·75
MS829	102×77 mm. $6 Wallblake House, 1787	4·25	6·50

147 Bigeye ("Blear Eye")

1990. Fish. Multicoloured.

830B	5c. Type **147**	75	1·00
831B	10c. Long-spined squirrelfish ("Redman")	75	1·00
832A	15c. Stop-light parrotfish ("Speckletail")	80	60
833A	25c. Blue-striped grunt	1·00	80
834A	30c. Yellow jack	1·00	80
835B	35c. Red hind	1·00	75
836A	40c. Spotted goatfish	1·25	80
837A	45c. Queen triggerfish ("Old wife")	1·25	60
838A	50c. Coney ("Butter fish")	1·25	80
839A	65c. Smooth trunkfish ("Shell fish")	1·75	1·00
840A	80c. Yellow-tailed snapper	1·50	90
841A	$1 Banded butterflyfish ("Katy")	1·50	1·00
842A	$1.35 Nassau grouper	2·25	1·50
843A	$2.50 Blue tang ("Doctor fish")	2·50	3·75
844A	$5 Queen angelfish	3·00	6·00
845A	$10 Great barracuda	4·75	9·00

148 The Last Supper

1990. Easter. Multicoloured.

846	35c. Type **148**	1·25	40
847	45c. The Trial	1·25	40
848	$1.35 The Crucifixion	3·00	2·25
849	$2.50 The Empty Tomb	3·50	5·00
MS850	114×84 mm. $6 The Resurrection	12·00	14·00

149 G.B. 1840 Penny Black

1990. "Stamp World London 90" International Stamp Exhibition. Multicoloured.

851	25c. Type **149**	1·25	35
852	50c. G.B. 1840 Twopenny Blue	1·75	50
853	$1.50 Cape of Good Hope 1861 1d. "woodblock" (horiz)	3·00	3·25
854	$2.50 G.B. 1882 £5 (horiz)	3·50	4·25
MS855	86×71 mm. $6 Penny Black and Twopence Blue (horiz)	13·00	16·00

1990. Anniversaries and Events. Nos. 841/4 optd.

856	$1 Banded butterflyfish (optd **EXPO '90**)	1·75	1·25
857	$1.35 Nassau grouper (optd **1990 INTERNATIONAL LITERACY YEAR**)	1·75	1·25
858	$2.50 Blue tang (optd **WORLD CUP FOOTBALL CHAMPIONSHIPS 1990**)	7·00	7·00
859	$5 Queen angelfish (optd **90TH BIRTHDAY H.M. THE QUEEN MOTHER**)	12·00	12·00

151 Mermaid Flag

1990. Island Flags. Multicoloured.

860	50c. Type **151**	2·25	70
861	80c. New Anguilla official flag	2·75	1·00
862	$1 Three Dolphins flag	3·00	1·25
863	$5 Governor's official flag	7·50	10·00

152 Laughing Gulls

1990. Christmas. Sea Birds. Multicoloured.

864	10c. Type **152**	60	50
865	35c. Brown booby	1·00	50
866	$1.50 Bridled tern	2·00	2·00
867	$3.50 Brown pelican	3·25	5·50
MS868	101×76 mm. $6 Least tern	9·50	12·00

1991. Easter. Nos. 846/9 optd **1991.**

869	35c. Type **148**	1·50	60
870	45c. The Trial	1·60	60
871	$1.35 The Crucifixion	3·00	2·00
872	$2.50 The Empty Tomb	4·25	7·50
MS873	114×84 mm. $6 The Resurrection	13·00	16·00

154 Angel

1991. Christmas.

874	**154** 5c. violet, brown & black	1·00	1·00
875	- 35c. multicoloured	2·50	55
876	- 80c. multicoloured	2·50	2·25
877	- $1 multicoloured	3·50	2·25
MS878	131×97 mm. $5 multicoloured	13·00	15·00

DESIGNS—VERT: 35c. Father Christmas. HORIZ: 80c. Church and house; $1 Palm trees at night; $5 Anguilla village.

155 Angels with Palm Branches outside St. Gerard's Church

1992. Easter. Multicoloured.

879	30c. Type **155**	1·40	45
880	45c. Angels singing outside Methodist Church	1·60	45
881	80c. Village (horiz)	2·75	90
882	$1 Congregation going to St. Mary's Church	2·75	1·25
883	$5 Dinghy regatta (horiz)	7·00	11·00

1992. No. 834 surch **$1.60.**

884	$1.60 on 30c. Yellow jack	3·25	2·50

157 Anguillan Flags

1992. 25th Anniv of Separation from St. Kitts-Nevis. Multicoloured.

885	80c. Type **157**	3·25	1·50
886	$1 Present official seal	3·25	1·75
887	$1.60 Anguillan flags at airport	5·00	4·00
888	$2 Royal Commissioner's official seal	5·00	6·00
MS889	116×117 mm. $10 "Independent Anguilla" overprinted stamps of 1967 (85×85 mm)	16·00	18·00

158 Dinghy Race

1992. Sailing Dinghy Racing.

890	**158** 20c. multicoloured	2·00	1·00
891	- 35c. multicoloured	2·50	75
892	- 45c. multicoloured	2·75	75
893	- 80c. multicoloured	3·50	5·00
894	- 80c. black and blue	3·50	5·00
895	- $1 multicoloured	3·50	3·00
MS896	129×30 mm. $6 multicoloured	11·00	13·00

DESIGNS—VERT: 35c. Stylized poster; 80c. (No. 893) "Blue Bird" in race; 80c. (No. 894) Construction drawings of "Blue Bird" by Douglas Pyle; $1 Stylized poster (different). HORIZ: 45c. Dinghies on beach. (97×32 mm)—$6 Composite designs as 20 and 45c. values.

159 Mucka Jumbie on Stilts

1992. Christmas. Local Traditions. Multicoloured.

897	20c. Type **159**	1·25	40
898	70c. Masqueraders	2·50	60
899	$1.05 Baking in old style oven	2·75	1·25
900	$2.40 Collecting presents from Christmas tree	5·50	7·00
MS901	128×101 mm. $5 As No. 900	4·00	6·50

160 Columbus landing in New World

1992. 500th Anniv of Discovery of America by Columbus (2nd issue).

902	**160** 80c. multicoloured	3·25	1·25
903	- $1 black and brown	3·25	1·25
904	- $2 multicoloured	5·00	5·00
905	- $3 multicoloured	5·50	7·00
MS906	78×54 mm. $6 multicoloured	15·00	14·00

DESIGNS—VERT: $1 Christopher Columbus; $6 Columbus and map of West Indies. HORIZ: $2 Fleet of Columbus; $3 "Pinta".

161 Kite Flying (Kyle Brooks)

1993. Easter. Children's Paintings. Multicoloured.

907	20c. Type **161**	2·00	75
908	45c. Clifftop Village Service (Kara Connor)	2·50	70
909	80c. Morning Devotion on Sombrero (Junior Carty)	3·25	1·40
910	$1.50 Hill Top Church Service (Leana Harris)	4·50	7·00
MS911	90×110 mm. $5 Good Friday Kites (Marvin Hazel and Kyle Brooks) (39×53 mm)	5·50	7·50

162 Salt Picking

1993. Traditional Industries. Multicoloured.

912	20c. Type **162**	4·00	1·25
913	80c. Tobacco growing	2·75	1·25
914	$1 Cotton picking	2·75	1·25
915	$2 Harvesting sugar cane	5·00	7·00
MS916	111×85 mm. $6 Fishing	12·00	14·00

163 Lord Great Chamberlain presenting Spurs of Charity to Queen

1993. 40th Anniv of Coronation. Multicoloured.

917	80c. Type **163**	2·50	80
918	$1 The Benediction	2·75	90
919	$2 Queen Elizabeth II in Coronation robes	3·50	3·50
920	$3 St. Edward's Crown	4·00	4·50
MS921	114×95 mm. $6 The Queen and Prince Philip in Coronation coach	14·00	15·00

164 Carnival Pan Player

1993. Anguilla Carnival. Multicoloured.

922	20c. Type **164**	1·00	50
923	45c. Revellers dressed as pirates	1·50	40
924	80c. Revellers dressed as stars	2·50	80
925	$1 Mas dancing	2·75	3·25
926	$2 Masked couple	3·75	4·75
927	$3 Revellers dressed as commandos	4·25	6·00
MS928	123×94 mm. $5 Revellers in fantasy costumes	13·00	15·00

165 Mucka Jumbies Carnival Characters

1993. Christmas. Multicoloured.

929	20c. Type **165**	1·25	80
930	35c. Local carol singers	1·60	70
931	45c. Christmas home baking	1·75	70
932	$3 Decorating Christmas tree	5·50	7·50
MS933	123×118 mm. $4 Mucka Jumbies and carol singers (58½×47 mm)	3·50	5·00

166 Travelling Branch Post Van at Sandy Ground

1994. Delivering the Mail. Multicoloured.

934	20c. Type **166**	2·25	80
935	45c. Betsy R (mail schooner) at The Forest (vert)	2·75	80
936	80c. Mail van at old Post Office	3·25	1·60
937	$1 Jeep on beach, Island Harbour (vert)	3·25	1·60
938	$4 New Post Office	5·00	8·00

167 Princess
Alexandra, 1988

1994. Royal Visitors. Multicoloured.
939	45c. Type **167**	2·00	1·00
940	50c. Princess Alice, 1960	2·00	1·00
941	80c. Prince Philip, 1993	3·00	1·50
942	$1 Prince Charles, 1973	3·00	1·75
943	$2 Queen Elizabeth II, 1994	4·50	5·50
MS944	162×90 mm. Nos. 939/43	14·00	15·00

168 The
Crucifixion

1994. Easter. Stained-glass Windows. Multicoloured.
945	20c. Type **168**	1·25	60
946	45c. The Empty Tomb	1·60	45
947	80c. The Resurrection	2·25	90
948	$3 Risen Christ with Disciples	5·00	8·50

169 Cameroun Player and
Pontiac Silverdome, Detroit

1994. World Cup Football Championship, U.S.A.
Multicoloured.
949	20c. Type **169**	1·00	50
950	70c. Argentine player and Foxboro Stadium, Boston	1·75	70
951	$1.80 Italian player and RFK Memorial Stadium, Washington	2·75	3·25
952	$2.40 German player and Soldier Field, Chicago	3·75	4·75
MS953	112×85 mm. $6 American and Colombian players	13·00	14·00

170 The Nativity
(Gustave Doré)

1994. Christmas. Religious Paintings. Multicoloured.
954	20c. Type **170**	1·00	80
955	30c. The Wise Men guided by the Star (Doré)	1·25	80
956	35c. The Annunciation (Doré)	1·25	80
957	45c. Adoration of the Shepherds (detail) (Poussin)	1·40	80
958	$2.40 "The Flight into Egypt" (Doré)	5·00	7·25

171 Pair of Zenaida Doves

1995. Easter. Zenaida Doves. Multicoloured.
959	20c. Type **171**	65	40
960	45c. Dove on branch	85	50
961	50c. Guarding nest	90	55
962	$5 With chicks	5·50	7·00

172 Trygve Lie (first
Secretary-General) and General
Assembly

1995. 50th Anniv of United Nations. Multicoloured.
963	20c. Type **172**	30	30
964	80c. Flag and building showing "50"	60	65
965	$1 Dag Hammarskjold and U Thant (former Secretaries-Generals) and U.N. Charter	70	75
966	$5 U.N. Building (vert)	4·00	7·00

173 Anniversary Emblem and
Map of Anguilla

1995. 25th Anniv of Caribbean Development Bank.
Multicoloured.
967	45c. Type **173**	1·75	2·00
968	$5 Bank building and launches	3·75	4·50

174 Blue Whale

1995. Endangered Species. Whales. Multicoloured.
969	20c. Type **174**	2·50	85
970	45c. Right whale (vert)	2·75	75
971	$1 Sperm whale	3·25	1·75
972	$5 Humpback whale	8·50	9·00

175 Palm Tree

1995. Christmas. Multicoloured.
973	10c. Type **175**	1·00	1·00
974	25c. Balloons and fishes	1·40	60
975	45c. Shells	1·75	60
976	$5 Fishes in shape of Christmas tree	10·00	11·00

176 Deep Water
Gorgonia

1996. Corals. Multicoloured.
977	20c. Type **176**	1·75	80
978	80c. Common sea fan	2·75	1·00
979	$5 Venus sea fern	8·00	10·00

177 Running

1996. Olympic Games, Atlanta. Multicoloured.
980	20c. Type **177**	1·00	60
981	80c. Javelin throwing and wheelchair basketball	3·50	1·50
982	$1 High jumping and hurdles	1·50	1·50
983	$3.50 Olympic rings and torch with Greek and American flags	6·00	6·00

178 Siege of
Sandy Hill Fort

1996. Bicentenary of the Battle for Anguilla.
Multicoloured.
984	60c. Type **178**	1·50	1·25
985	75c. French troops destroying church (horiz)	1·50	1·25
986	$1.50 Naval battle (horiz)	3·25	3·00
987	$4 French troops landing at Rendezvous Bay	4·50	6·00

179 Gooseberry

1997. Fruit. Multicoloured.
988	10c. Type **179**	60	85
989	20c. West Indian cherry	70	40
990	40c. Tamarind	85	30
991	50c. Pomme-surette	90	40
992	60c. Sea almond	1·00	55
993	75c. Sea grape	1·25	85
994	80c. Banana	1·25	85
995	$1 Genip	1·50	1·00
996	$1.10 Coco plum	1·50	1·60
997	$1.25 Pope	2·00	2·25
998	$1.50 Pawpaw	2·00	2·25
999	$2 Sugar apple	2·75	3·25
1000	$3 Soursop	3·50	4·00
1001	$4 Pomegranate	4·50	4·75
1002	$5 Cashew	5·50	6·50
1003	$10 Mango	8·50	9·50

180 West Indian Iguanas
hatching

1997. Endangered Species. West Indian Iguanas.
Multicoloured.
1004	20c. Type **180**	1·75	1·50
1005	50c. On rock	2·00	1·60
1006	75c. On branch	2·25	2·00
1007	$3 Head of West Indian iguana	3·25	4·00

181 "Juluca, Rainbow
Deity"

1997. Ancient Stone Carvings from Fountain Cavern.
Multicoloured.
1008	30c. Type **181**	75	35
1009	$1.25 "Lizard with front legs extended"	1·50	1·00
1010	$2.25 "Chief"	2·50	2·75
1011	$2.75 "Jocahu, the Creator"	3·00	3·50

182 Diana, Princess
of Wales

1998. Diana, Princess of Wales Commemoration.
Multicoloured.
1012	15c. Type **182**	2·00	1·25
1013	$1 Wearing yellow blouse	2·75	1·60
1014	$1.90 Wearing tiara	3·00	3·00
1015	$2.25 Wearing blue short-sleeved Red Cross blouse	3·25	3·25

183 Treasure Island (Valarie
Alix)

1998. International Arts Festival. Multicoloured.
1016	15c. Type **183**	60	60
1017	30c. Posing in the Light (Melsadis Fleming) (vert)	60	40
1018	$1 Pescadores de Anguilla (Juan Garcia) (vert)	90	80
1019	$1.50 Fresh Catch (Verna Hart)	1·25	1·75
1020	$1.90 The Bell Tower of St. Mary's (Ricky Racardo Edwards) (vert)	1·50	2·25

184 Roasting Corn-cobs on
Fire

1998. Christmas. Hidden Beauty of Anguilla. Children's
Paintings. Multicoloured.
1021	15c. Type **184**	35	30
1022	$1 Fresh fruit and market stallholder	80	50
1023	$1.50 Underwater scene	1·00	1·25
1024	$3 Cacti and view of sea	1·60	2·50

185 University of West Indies
Centre, Anguilla

1998. 50th Anniv of University of West Indies.
Multicoloured.
1025	$1.50 Type **185**	1·00	1·00
1026	$1.90 Man with torch and University arms	1·40	2·00

186 Sopwith Camel and Bristol
F2B Fighters

1998. 80th Anniv of Royal Air Force. Multicoloured.
1027	30c. Type **186**	1·25	60
1028	$1 Supermarine Spitfire Mk II and Hawker Hurricane Mk I	2·25	90
1029	$1.50 Avro Lancaster	2·50	2·25
1030	$1.90 Panavia Tornado F3 and Harrier GR7	3·00	3·50

187 Saturn 5 Rocket and
"Apollo 11" Command Module

1999. 30th Anniv of First Manned Landing on Moon.
Multicoloured.
1031	30c. Type **187**	55	35
1032	$1 Astronaut Edwin Aldrin, Lunar Module Eagle and first footprint on Moon	1·00	70
1033	$1.50 Lunar Module leaving Moon's surface	1·00	1·00
1034	$1.90 Recovery of Command Module	1·40	2·00

188 Albena Lake
Hodge

1999. Anguillan Heroes and Heroines (1st series). Each
black, green and cream.
1035	30c. Type **188**	40	30
1036	$1 Collins O. Hodge	80	65
1037	$1.50 Edwin Wallace Rey	1·00	1·25
1038	$1.90 Walter G. Hodge	1·25	2·00

189 Library and Resource Centre

1999. Modern Architecture. Multicoloured.

1039	30c. Type **189**	45	35
1040	65c. Parliamentary building and Court House	75	70
1041	$1 Caribbean Commercial Bank	1·00	90
1042	$1.50 Police Headquarters	3·00	2·25
1043	$1.90 Post Office	2·00	3·00

190 Beach Barbeque and Fireworks

1999. Christmas and New Millennium. Multicoloured.

1044	30c. Type **190**	70	30
1045	$1 Musicians around globe	1·50	55
1046	$1.50 Family at Christmas dinner	2·25	1·75
1047	$1.90 Celebrations around decorated shrub	2·75	3·50

191 Shoal Bay (East)

2000. Beaches. Multicoloured.

1048	15c. Type **191**	40	60
1049	30c. Maundys Bay	45	30
1050	$1 Rendezvous Bay	90	60
1051	$1.50 Meads Bay	1·25	1·25
1052	$1.90 Little Bay	1·50	2·25
1053	$2 Sandy Ground	1·50	2·25
MS1054	144×144 mm. Nos. 1048/53	5·00	6·00

192 Toy Banjo (Casey Reid)

2000. Easter. Indigenous Toys. Multicoloured.

1055	25c. Type **192**	40	30
1056	30c. Spinning top (Johniela Harrigan)	40	30
1057	$1.50 Catapult (Akeem Rogers)	1·10	1·10
1058	$1.90 Roller (Melisa Mussington)	1·40	1·75
1059	$2.50 Killy Ban (trap) (Casey Reid)	1·75	2·25
MS1060	145×185 mm. 75c. Rag Doll (Jahia Esposito) (vert); $1 Kite (Javed Maynard) (vert); $1.25, Cricket ball (Jevon Lake) (vert); $4 Pond boat (Corvel Flemming) (vert)	4·75	5·50

193 Lanville Harrigan

2000. West Indies Cricket Tour and 100th Test Match at Lord's. Multicoloured.

1061	$2 Type **193**	2·25	2·25
1062	$4 Cardigan Connor	3·25	4·50
MS1063	119×102 mm. $6 Lord's Cricket Ground (horiz)	9·50	9·00

2000. "The Stamp Show 2000" International Stamp Exhibition, London. Beaches. As No. **MS1054**, but with exhibition logo on bottom margin. Multicoloured.

MS1064	144×144 mm. Nos. 1048/53	4·75	6·00

194 Prince William and Royal Family after Trooping the Colour

2000. 18th Birthday of Prince William. Multicoloured.

1065	30c. Type **194**	1·75	50
1066	$1 Prince and Princess of Wales with sons	2·50	85
1067	$1.90 With Prince Charles and Prince Harry	3·00	3·00
1068	$2.25 Skiing with father and brother	3·50	3·50
MS1069	125×95 mm. $8 Prince William as pupil at Eton	8·00	9·00

195 Queen Elizabeth the Queen Mother and Prince William

2000. 100th Birthday of Queen Elizabeth the Queen Mother. Showing different portraits. Multicoloured.

1070	30c. Type **195**	65	40
1071	$1.50 Island scene	1·50	1·00
1072	$1.90 Clarence House	1·75	1·60
1073	$5 Castle of Mey	3·25	4·00

196 Anguilla Montage (Weme Caster)

2000. International Arts Festival. Multicoloured.

1074	15c. Type **196**	30	40
1075	30c. Serenity (Damien Carty)	35	35
1076	65c. Inter Island Cargo (Paula Walden)	55	45
1077	$1.50 Rainbow City where Spirits find Form (Fiona Percy)	1·25	1·50
1078	$1.90 Sailing Silver Seas (Valerie Carpenter)	1·40	2·00
MS1079	75×100 mm. $7 Historic Anguilla (Melsadis Fleming) (42×28 mm)	4·75	6·00

197 Dried Flower Arrangement

2000. Christmas. Flower and Garden Show.

1080	**197**	15c. multicoloured	25	25
1081	-	25c. multicoloured	30	25
1082	-	30c. multicoloured	30	25
1083	-	$1 multicoloured	80	60
1084	-	$1.50 multicoloured	1·25	1·50
1085	-	$1.90 multicoloured	1·50	2·50

DESIGNS: 25c. to $1.90, Different floral arrangements.

198 Winning Primary School Football Team (Bank Sponsorship)

2000. 15th Anniv of National Bank of Anguilla. Multicoloured.

1086	30c. Type **198**	30	25
1087	$1 De-Chan (yacht) (Bank sponsorship) (vert)	70	60
1088	$1.50 Bank crest (vert)	1·25	1·50
1089	$1.90 New Bank Headquarters	1·50	2·25

199 Ebenezer Methodist Church in 19th Century

2000. 170th Anniv of Ebenezer Methodist Church.

1090	**199**	30c. brown and black	30	20
1091	-	$1.90 multicoloured	1·50	2·00

DESIGN: $1.90, Church in 2000.

200 Soroptomist Day Care Centre

2001. United Nations Women's Human Rights Campaign. Multicoloured.

1092	25c. Type **200**	30	30
1093	30c. Britannia Idalia Gumbs (Anguillan politician) (vert)	30	30
1094	$2.25 Caribbean Woman II (Leisel Renee Jobity) (vert)	1·60	2·25

201 John Paul Jones and U.S.S. Ranger (frigate)

2001. 225th Anniv of American War of Independence. Multicoloured.

1095	30c. Type **201**	1·75	80
1096	$1 George Washington and Battle of Yorktown	2·50	1·25
1097	$1.50 Thomas Jefferson and submission of Declaration of Independence to Congress	2·75	3·00
1098	$1.90 John Adams and the signing of the Treaty of Paris	3·00	4·00

202 Bahama Pintail

2001. Anguillian Birds. Multicoloured.

1099	30c. Type **202**	1·00	65
1100	$1 Black-faced grassquit (vert)	1·50	1·00
1101	$1.50 Common noddy	2·00	1·60
1102	$2 Black-necked stilt (vert)	2·50	2·50
1103	$3 Kentish plover ("Snowy Plover")	3·50	4·00
MS1104	124×88 mm. 25c. Snowy egret; 65c. Red-billed tropic bird; $1.35, Greater yellowlegs; $2.25, Sooty tern	6·50	6·50

203 "Children encircling Globe" (Urska Golob)

2001. U.N. Year of Dialogue among Civilisations.

1105	**203** $1.90 multicoloured	1·60	2·25

204 Triangle

2001. Christmas. Indigenous Musical Instruments. Multicoloured.

1106	15c. Type **204**	25	30
1107	25c. Maracas	35	35
1108	30c. Guiro (vert)	35	35
1109	$1.50 Marimba	1·25	1·25
1110	$1.90 Tambu (hand drum) (vert)	1·50	1·75
1111	$2.50 Bass pan	2·00	2·50
MS1112	110×176 mm. 75c. Banjo (vert); $1 Quatro (vert); $1.25, Ukelele (vert); $3 Cello (vert)	5·00	6·00

205 Sombrero Lighthouse, 1962

2002. Commissioning of New Sombrero Lighthouse. Multicoloured.

1113	30c. Type **205**	1·00	65
1114	$1.50 Old and new lighthouses (horiz)	2·00	1·75
1115	$1.90 New, fully-automated lighthouse, 2001	2·50	3·00

206 Artist, Entertainer and Sportsmen

2002. 20th Anniv of Social Security Board. Multicoloured (except 30c.).

1116	30c. Type **206** (ultramarine and blue)	40	30
1117	75c. Anguillans of all ages	70	65
1118	$2.50 Anguillan workers (horiz)	2·25	3·50

207 H.M.S. *Antrim* (destroyer), 1967

2002. Ships of the Royal Navy. Multicoloured.

1119	30c. Type **207**	1·25	65
1120	50c. H.M.S. *Formidable* (aircraft carrier), 1939	1·75	85
1121	$1.50 H.M.S. *Dreadnought* (battleship), 1906	2·50	2·00
1122	$2 H.M.S. *Warrior* (ironclad), 1860	3·00	4·00
MS1123	102×77 mm. H.M.S. *Ark Royal* (aircraft carrier), 1981 (vert)	8·00	9·00

208 Princess Elizabeth with Prince Charles

2002. Golden Jubilee. Multicoloured.

1124	30c. Type **208**	75	45
1125	$1.50 Queen Elizabeth wearing white coat	1·40	1·10
1126	$1.90 Queen Elizabeth in evening dress	2·00	1·75
1127	$5 Wearing yellow hat and coat	4·75	6·00
MS1128	106×75 mm. $8 Queen Elizabeth sitting at desk	10·00	11·00

209 Valley Health Centre

2002. Centenary of Pan American Health Organization. Multicoloured.

1129	30c. Type **209**	45	40
1130	$1.50 Centenary of PAHO logo	1·25	1·60

210 Finance (sloop)

2003. Past Sailing Vessels of Anguilla. Multicoloured.

1131	15c. Type **210**	50	40
1132	30c. Tiny Gull	60	30
1133	65c. Lady Laurel (schooner)	80	40
1134	75c. Spitfire (gaff rigged sloop)	80	40
1135	$1 Liberator (schooner)	1·00	50
1136	$1.35 Excelsior (schooner)	1·25	70
1137	$1.50 Rose Millicent	1·50	1·00
1138	$1.90 Betsy R. (sloop)	1·75	1·10
1139	$2 Sunbeam R. (sloop)	2·00	1·60
1140	$2.25 New London	2·25	2·25
1141	$3 Ismay (schooner)	2·75	3·00
1142	$10 Warspite (schooner)	7·50	8·50

211 Stone Pestle

2003. Artifacts of Anguilla. Multicoloured.
1143	30c. Type **211**	50	25
1144	$1 Frog worked shell ornament	1·00	75
1145	$1.50 Pottery	1·25	1·25
1146	$1.90 Mask worked shell ornament	1·50	2·00

212 Frangipani Beach Club

2003. Hotels of Anguilla. Multicoloured.
1147	75c. Type **212**	70	45
1148	$1 Pimms, Cap Juluca	85	55
1149	$1.35 Cocoloba Beach Resort	1·00	1·00
1150	$1.50 Malliouhana Hotel	1·25	1·10
1151	$1.90 Carmiar Beach Club	1·40	1·40
1152	$3 Covecastles	2·00	3·00

213 Eudice's Garden (Eunice Summer)

2004. International Arts Festival. Multicoloured.
1153	15c. Type **213**	50	40
1154	30c. *Hammocks* (Lisa Davenport)	60	30
1155	$1 *Conched Out* (Richard Shaffett)	1·00	70
1156	$1.50 *Islands Rhythms* (Carol Garvin)	1·40	1·25
1157	$1.90 *Party at the Beach* (Jean–Pierre Ballagny)	1·75	1·75
1158	$3 *Shoal Bay before Luis* (Jacqueline Mariethoz)	2·50	3·25

214 Athlete (400 Metres)

2004. Olympic Games, Athens. Multicoloured.
1159	30c. Type **214**	60	30
1160	$1 Laser dinghies (sailing)	1·00	60
1161	$1.50 Gymnastics (rings)	1·40	1·25
1162	$1.90 The Acropolis, Athens, Pierre de Coubertin (founder of modern Olympics) and Dimetrios Vikelas (first IOC President) (horiz)	1·75	2·25

215 Goat

2004. Goats of Anguilla. Multicoloured.
1163	30c. Type **215**	60	30
1164	50c. Black and white goat	70	35
1165	$1 Black and tan goat (vert)	1·00	60
1166	$1.50 Chestnut goat	1·40	1·25
1167	$1.90 Chestnut and white goat (vert)	1·75	2·00
1168	$2.25 Two kids	2·00	2·50

216 Cordless Telephone

2004. Development of the Telephone. Multicoloured.
1169	30c. Type **216**	40	30

1170	$1 Touch tone telephone	1·00	70
1171	$1.50 Cellular phone	1·40	1·40
1172	$1.90 Circular dial telephone (horiz)	1·75	1·75
1173	$3.80 Magneto telephone	3·50	5·00

217 Santa baking in Traditional Rock Oven

2004. Christmas. Multicoloured.
1174	30c. Type **217**	45	25
1175	$1.50 Santa climbing coconut tree	1·40	1·40
1176	$1.90 Santa's string band	1·60	1·60
1177	$3.80 Santa delivering gifts by donkey	3·00	4·50
MS1178 107×76 mm. $8 Santa delivering gifts by boat		6·50	8·00

218 AIDS, Remember it's Real. Don't let it take over the World (Owean Hodge)

2005. World AIDS Day 2004—"AIDS through the Eyes of a Child". Children's paintings. Multicoloured.
1179	30c. Type **218**	45	30
1180	$1.50 *Arm Yourself against AIDS* (Lydia Fleming)	1·50	1·50
1181	$1.90 *AIDS is Your Concern* (Nina Rodriguez)	1·75	2·00
MS1182 144×144 mm. 15c. Classroom (Kenswick Richardson); 75c. Dancer, Schoolgirl, Teacher, Smoker (Toniquewah Ruan); $1 Girls and Tree (Elizabeth Anne Orchard); $2"*Even I can get AIDS* (Tricia Watty-Beard)		3·00	3·50

219 Arms of Anguilla and Rotary Emblem

2005. Centenary of Rotary International and 25th Anniv of Anguilla Rotary Club. Multicoloured.
1183	30c. Type **219**	40	30
1184	$1 Brown pelican and palm tree (District 7020)	1·25	85
1185	$1.50 Paul Harris (founder)	1·40	1·40
1186	$1.90 Children on slide (School Playground Project)	1·60	2·00

220 Grey Dog

2005. Dogs of Anguilla. Multicoloured.
1187	30c. Type **220**	65	40
1188	$1.50 Black and tan dog with puppy (vert)	1·75	1·40
1189	$2 Black and tan dog (vert)	2·00	2·00
1190	$2.25 Tan dog	2·50	2·75

221 Air Anguilla Cessna 402

2006. Early Airlines. Multicoloured.
1191	30c. Type **221**	65	40
1192	40c. LIAT DHC Dash 8	70	55
1193	60c. Winair Foxtrot DHC Twin Otter	1·00	80
1194	$1 Anguilla Airways Piper Aztec	1·50	1·00
1195	$1.50 St. Thomas Air Transport Piper Aztec	2·00	1·75
1196	$1.90 Carib Air Service Piper Aztec	2·25	2·50

222 Appias drusillia

2006. Butterflies. Multicoloured.
1197	30c. Type **222**	65	40
1198	$1.50 *Danaus plexippus megalippe*	1·75	1·40
1199	$1.90 *Phoebis sennae*	2·25	2·25
1200	$2.75 *Papilio demoleus*	3·50	4·00
MS1201 126×88 mm. 40c. *Aphrissa statira*; 60c. *Eurema elathea*; $1 *Danaus plexippus megalippe*; $3 *Agraulis vanillae*		4·75	5·00

223 Soroptimist International Logo

2007. 25th Anniv (2006) of Anguilla Soroptimist Club. Multicoloured.
1202	$1.90 Type **223**	1·75	1·90
1203	$2.75 Alecia Ballin	2·75	3·25

224 St. Bruno (Carthusian founder)

2007. Bronze Devotional Medallions. Designs showing medallions from Spanish ship El Buen Consejo, sunk in 1772 off Anguilla coast. Multicoloured.
1204	30c. Type **224**	40	30
1205	$1.50 Our Lady of Sorrows	1·40	1·40
1206	$1.90 Five Wounds of Jesus	1·60	1·75
1207	$2.75 Virgin and Child	2·50	3·25

225 Hyacinth Carty

2008. 40th Anniv of the Revolution (independence from St. Kitts-Nevis). Multicoloured.
1208	30c. Type **225**	40	30
1209	$1 Edward Duncan	1·00	80
1210	$1.50 Connell Harrigan	1·40	1·40
1211	$1.90 Reverend Leonard Carty	1·75	1·75
1212	$2.25 Jeremiah Gumbs	2·00	2·50
1213	$3.75 Atlin Harrigan	3·50	3·25

226 White-painted House with Gabled Roof and Lean-to

2008. Historical Architecture. Local Houses of the 1930s–1960s. Multicoloured.
1214	30c. Type **226**	15	30
1215	$1 House with gabled roof and lean-to at back	1·00	65
1216	$1.25 House with double hipped roof and flight of steps	1·25	1·00
1217	$1.50 House on seashore with hipped roof	1·50	1·10
1218	$1.90 House with double gabled roof	1·90	1·75
1219	$2.40 House with double hipped roof and verandah	2·50	2·75
1220	$2.75 House with hipped roof and verandah	3·00	3·50
1221	$3.75 House with gabled roof and flight of steps	4·50	5·00

227 Three Legged Pot

2009. Traditional Household Items. Multicoloured.
1222	30c. Type **227**	40	30
1223	$1 Mortar and pestle	1·10	70
1224	$1.50 Gas and coal irons	1·60	1·25
1225	$1.90 Oil and gas lamps	2·00	1·75
1226	$2 Coal pots	2·25	2·50
1227	$2.25 Enamel and aluminium utensils (wrongly inscr 'USTENSILS')	3·25	3·50

228 Tabebuia heterophylla

2009. Wild Flowers. Multicoloured.
1228	30c. Type **228**	55	50
1229	$1 *Argemone mexicana*	1·25	1·00
1230	$1.50 *Catharanthus roseus*	1·60	1·40
1231	$1.90 *Datura stramonium*	2·00	2·00
1232	$2 *Centrosema virginianum*	2·50	2·50
1233	$2.25 *Tetramicra canaliculata*	3·00	3·50

229 Sombrero Island Ground Lizard (*Ameiva corvina*)

2010. Endemics of Anguilla. Multicoloured.
1234	$1.50 Type **229**	1·75	2·00
1235	$2 Little Scrub Island ground lizard (*Ameiva corax*)	2·75	3·00
1236	$2.25 Anguilla bush (*Rondeletia anguillensis*)	3·25	3·50

230 Prince William and Miss Catherine Middleton

2011. Royal Wedding. Multicoloured.
1237	$4 Type **230**	5·00	5·25
1238	$5 Engagement photograph (horiz)	6·25	6·50
1239	$6 Prince William and Miss Catherine Middleton (wearing black hat)	7·50	7·75
1240	$10 Photos of Prince William and Miss Catherine Middleton and arms (horiz)	12·50	13·00

231 Anguilla 1967 Liberty Dollar (on Panama Balboa)

2012. Revolutionary Coins. Multicoloured.
1241	15c. Type **231**	25	30
1242	40c. Liberty Dollar on Mexican peso	75	80
1243	$2.50 1968 commemorative coin for first year of independence	3·50	3·75
1244	$5 1967 $4 coin showing Anguilla coat of arms	6·25	6·50

Pt. 6

ANJOUAN

One of the Comoro Is. between Madagascar and the East coast of Africa. Used stamps of Madagascar from 1914 and became part of the Comoro Islands in 1950.

100 centimes = 1 franc.

1892. "Tablet" key-type inscr "SULTANAT D'ANJOUAN".

1	D	1c. black on blue	1·40	2·00
2	D	2c. brown on buff	2·10	2·30
3	D	4c. brown on grey	3·25	3·75
4	D	5c. green on green	5·50	7·75
5	D	10c. black on lilac	7·75	7·25
14	D	10c. red	25·00	33·00
6	D	15c. blue	11·00	11·50
15	D	15c. grey	13·00	21·00
7	D	20c. red on green	12·00	15·00
8	D	25c. black on pink	12·00	15·00
16	D	25c. blue	16·00	28·00
9	D	30c. brown on grey	27·00	30·00
17	D	35c. black on yellow	8·25	9·25
10	D	40c. red on yellow	32·00	27·00
18	D	45c. black on green	£100	£120
11	D	50c. red on pink	36·00	48·00
19	D	50c. brown on blue	22·00	40·00
12	D	75c. brown on orange	33·00	55·00
13	D	1f. green	70·00	90·00

1912. Surch in figures.

20A		05 on 2c. brown on buff	2·75	5·50
21A		05 on 4c. brown on grey	1·40	3·00
22A		05 on 5c. blue	1·40	3·00
23A		05 on 20c. red on green	2·30	7·00
24A		05 on 25c. black on pink	1·60	3·50
25A		05 on 30c. brown on grey	2·50	3·00
26A		10 on 40c. red on yellow	1·50	1·80
27A		10 on 45c. black on green	1·40	1·70
28A		10 on 50c. red on pink	2·40	10·50
29A		10 on 75c. brown on orange	3·00	9·00
30A		10 on 1f. green	4·25	8·25

Pt. 6

ANNAM AND TONGKING

Later part of Indo-China and now included in Vietnam

100 centimes = 1 franc.

1888. Stamps of French Colonies, "Commerce" type, surch **A & T** and value in figures.

1	J	1 on 2c. brown on yellow	65·00	55·00
2	J	1 on 4c. lilac on grey	55·00	37·00
3	J	5 on 10c. black on lilac	50·00	50·00

Pt. 1

ANTIGUA

One of the Leeward Is., Br. W. Indies. Used general issues for Leeward Islands, concurrently with Antiguan stamps until 1 July 1956. Ministerial Government introduced on 1 January 1960. Achieved Associated Statehood on 3 March 1967 and Independence within the Commonwealth on 1 November 1981. Nos. 718/21 and 733 onwards are inscribed "Antigua and Barbuda".

1862. 12 pence = 1 shilling; 20 shillings = 1 pound.
1951. 100 cents = 1 West Indian dollar.

1

5	1	1d. mauve	£130	75·00
25	1	1d. red	2·25	3·75
29	1	6d. green	60·00	£120

3

1879

21	3	½d. green	4·00	18·00
22	3	2½d. brown	£190	55·00
27	3	2½d. blue	7·00	14·00
23	3	4d. blue	£275	15·00
28	3	4d. brown	2·25	3·00
30	3	1s. mauve	£160	£140

4

1903

31	4	½d. black and green	3·75	6·50
41	4	½d. green	4·75	4·75
32	4	1d. black and red	11·00	1·25
44	4	1d. red	7·50	3·25
45	4	2d. purple and brown	4·75	32·00
34	4	2½d. black and blue	14·00	21·00
46	4	2½d. blue	22·00	17·00
47	4	3d. green and brown	6·50	19·00
48	4	6d. purple and black	7·50	40·00
49	4	1s. blue and purple	24·00	70·00
50	4	2s. green and violet	£110	£130
39	4	2s.6d. black and purple	27·00	70·00
40	5	5s. green and violet	£110	£160

5

1913. Head of King George V.

51	5	5s. green and violet	95·00	£150

1916. Optd **WAR STAMP**.

53	4	½d. green	1·50	2·75
54	4	1½d. orange	1·25	1·25

8

1921

62	8	½d. green	3·00	50
63	8	1d. red	4·25	50
64	8	1d. violet	7·00	1·50
67	8	1½d. orange	5·50	6·00
68	8	1½d. red	9·00	1·75
69	8	1½d. brown	3·00	60
70	8	2d. grey	4·25	75
72	8	2½d. yellow	2·50	17·00
73	8	2½d. blue	13·00	4·50
74	8	3d. purple on yellow	12·00	8·50
56	8	4d. black and red on yellow	2·25	5·50
75	8	6d. purple	7·00	4·25
57	8	1s. black on green	4·25	9·00
58	8	2s. purple and blue on blue	13·00	29·00
78	8	2s.6d. black and red on blue	50·00	38·00
79	8	3s. green and violet	50·00	£100
80	8	4s. black and red	50·00	75·00
60	8	5s. green and red on yellow	8·50	50·00
61	8	£1 purple and black on red	£250	£375

9 Old Dockyard, English Harbour

10 Government House, St. John's

1932. Tercentenary. Designs with medallion portrait of King George V.

81	9	½d. green	4·50	7·50
82	-	1d. red	4·00	7·50
83	-	1½d. brown	4·00	4·75
84	10	2d. grey	8·00	26·00
85	10	2½d. blue	8·00	8·50
86	10	3d. orange	8·00	12·00
87	-	6d. violet	15·00	12·00
88	-	1s. olive	20·00	32·00
89	-	2s.6d. purple	55·00	80·00
90	-	5s. black and brown	£120	£160

DESIGNS—HORIZ: 6d. to 2s.6d. Nelson's *Victory*; 5s. Sir Thomas Warner's *Concepcion*.

13 Windsor Castle

1935. Silver Jubilee.

91	13	1d. blue and red	3·00	4·00
92	13	1½d. blue and grey	2·75	1·50
93	13	2½d. brown and blue	7·00	1·60
94	13	1s. grey and purple	8·50	17·00

1937. Coronation. As T **2** of Aden.

95		1d. red	70	3·00
96		1½d. brown	60	2·75
97		2½d. blue	2·25	3·00

15 English Harbour

16 Nelson's Dockyard

1938

98	15	½d. green	40	1·25
99	16	1d. red	3·50	2·50
100a	16	1½d. brown	2·75	4·00
101	15	2d. grey	1·00	1·25
102	16	2½d. blue	1·50	80
103	-	3d. orange	1·25	1·00
104	-	6d. violet	4·75	1·25
105	-	1s. black and brown	7·00	2·00
106a	-	2s.6d. purple	35·00	19·00
107	-	5s. olive	17·00	13·00
108	16	10s. mauve	22·00	35·00
109	-	£1 green	45·00	65·00

DESIGNS—HORIZ: 3d., 2s.6d., £1, Fort James. VERT: 6d., 1s., 5s. St. John's Harbour.

1946. Victory. As T **9** of Aden.

110		1½d. brown	30	10
111		3d. orange	30	50

1949. Silver Wedding. As T **10/11** of Aden.

112		2½d. blue	50	2·75
113		5s. green	15·00	13·00

20 Hermes, Globe and Forms of Transport

21 Hemispheres, Jet-powered Vickers Viking Airliner and Steamer

22 Hermes and Globe

23 U.P.U. Monument

1949. 75th Anniv of U.P.U.

114	20	2½d. blue	40	75
115	21	3d. orange	2·00	3·50
116	22	6d. purple	45	3·50
117	23	1s. brown	45	1·25

24 Arms of University

25 Princess Alice

1951. Inauguration of B.W.I. University College.

118	24	3c. black and brown	75	2·00
119	25	12c. black and violet	1·00	2·00

1953. Coronation. As T **13** of Aden.

120		2c. black and green	30	75

27 Martello Tower

1953. Designs as 1938 issues but with portrait of Queen Elizabeth II as in T **27**.

120a	-	½c. brown	40	40
121	15	1c. grey	30	2·00
122	16	2c. green	30	10
123	16	3c. black and yellow	40	20
153	15	4c. red	30	2·75
154	16	5c. black and lilac	20	10
155	-	6c. yellow	60	30
156	27	8c. blue	30	20
157	-	12c. violet	1·75	20
129	-	24c. black and brown	1·50	20
130	27	48c. purple and blue	11·00	3·00
131	-	60c. purple	9·00	80
132a	-	$1.20 olive	3·75	1·00
133	16	$2.40 purple	18·00	12·00
134	-	$4.80 slate	24·00	28·00

DESIGNS—HORIZ: ½, 6, 60c., $4.80, Fort James. VERT: 12, 24c., $1.20, St John's Harbour.

28 Federation Map

1958. Inaug of British Caribbean Federation.

135	28	3c. green	1·25	30
136	28	6c. blue	1·40	2·75
137	28	12c. red	1·60	75

1960. New Constitution. Nos. 123 and 157 optd **COMMEMORATION ANTIGUA CONSTITUTION**.

138	16	3c. black and yellow	20	15
139	-	12c. violet	20	15

30 Nelson's Dockyard and Admiral Nelson

1961. Restoration of Nelson's Dockyard.

140	30	20c. purple and brown	1·75	1·60
141	30	30c. green and blue	2·00	2·50

31 Stamp of 1862 and R.M.S.P. *Solent I* at English Harbour

1962. Stamp Centenary.

142	31	3c. purple and green	90	10
143	31	10c. blue and green	1·00	10
144	31	12c. sepia and green	1·10	10
145	31	50c. brown and green	1·50	2·25

1963. Freedom from Hunger. As T **28** of Aden.

146		12c. green	15	15

33 Red Cross Emblem

1963. Centenary of Red Cross.

147	33	3c. red and black	30	1·00
148	33	12c. red and blue	45	1·25

34 Shakespeare and Memorial Theatre, Stratford-upon-Avon

1964. 400th Birth Anniv of Shakespeare.

164	34	12c. brown	30	10

1965. No. 157 surch **15c**.

165		15c. on 12c. violet	10	10

36 I.T.U. Emblem

1965. Centenary of I.T.U.

166	36	2c. blue and red	25	15
167	36	50c. yellow and blue	75	1·25

37 I.C.Y. Emblem

1965. International Co-operation Year.

| 168 | 37 | 4c. purple and turquoise | 25 | 10 |
| 169 | 37 | 15c. green and lavender | 40 | 20 |

38 Sir Winston Churchill, and St. Paul's Cathedral in Wartime

1966. Churchill Commemoration. Designs in black, red and gold with background in colours given.

170	38	½c. blue	10	1·75
171	38	4c. green	65	10
172	38	25c. brown	1·50	45
173	38	35c. violet	1·50	55

39 Queen Elizabeth II and Duke of Edinburgh

1966. Royal Visit.

| 174 | 39 | 6c. black and blue | 1·50 | 1·10 |
| 175 | 39 | 15c. black and mauve | 1·50 | 1·40 |

40 Footballer's Legs, Ball and Jules Rimet Cup

1966. World Cup Football Championship.

| 176 | 40 | 6c. multicoloured | 20 | 75 |
| 177 | 40 | 35c. multicoloured | 60 | 25 |

41 W.H.O. Building

1966. Inaug of W.H.O. Headquarters, Geneva.

| 178 | 41 | 2c. black, green and blue | 20 | 25 |
| 179 | 41 | 15c. black, purple & brn | 1·25 | 25 |

42 Nelson's Dockyard

1966

180	42	½c. green and blue	10	1·25
181	-	1c. purple and mauve	10	30
182	-	2c. blue and orange	10	20
183a	-	3c. red and black	15	15
184a	-	4c. violet and brown	15	30
185	-	5c. blue and green	10	10
186a	-	6c. orange and purple	15	1·00
187	-	10c. green and red	15	10
188a	-	15c. brown and blue	55	10
189	-	25c. blue and brown	35	20
190a	-	35c. mauve and brown	60	1·00
191a	-	50c. green and black	70	2·25
192	-	75c. blue and ultramarine	4·50	2·50
193b	-	$1 mauve and green	1·25	5·00
194a	-	$2.50 black and mauve	1·50	8·00
195	-	$5 green and violet	13·00	6·50

DESIGNS: 1c. Old Post Office, St John's; 2c. Health Centre; 3c. Teachers' Training College; 4c. Martello Tower, Barbuda; 5c. Ruins of Officers' Quarters, Shirley Heights; 6c. Government House, Barbuda; 10c. Princess Margaret School; 15c. Air terminal building; 25c. General Post Office; 35c. Clarence House; 50c. Government House, St. John's; 75c. Administration building; $1 Court-house, St. John's; $2.50 Magistrates' Court; $5 St. John's Cathedral.

54 "Education"

55 "Science"

56 "Culture"

1966. 20th Anniv of UNESCO.

196	54	4c. violet, yellow & orange	20	10
197	55	25c. yellow, violet and olive	45	10
198	56	$1 black, purple and orange	90	2·25

57 State Flag and Maps

1967. Statehood. Multicoloured.

199	57	4c. Type 57	10	10
200		15c. State Flag	10	20
201		25c. Premier's Office and State Flag	10	25
202		35c. As 15c.	15	25

60 Gilbert Memorial Church

1967. Attainment of Autonomy by the Methodist Church.

203	60	4c. black and red	10	10
204	-	25c. black and green	15	15
205	-	35c. black and blue	15	15

DESIGNS: 25c. Nathaniel Gilbert's House; 35c. Caribbean and Central American map.

63 Coat of Arms

1967. 300th Anniv of Treaty of Breda and Grant of New Arms.

| 206 | 63 | 15c. multicoloured | 20 | 10 |
| 207 | 63 | 35c. multicoloured | 20 | 10 |

64 Susan Constant (settlers' ship)

1967. 300th Anniv of Barbuda Settlement.

208	64	4c. blue	45	10
209	-	6c. purple	45	1·25
210	64	25c. green	50	20
211	-	35c. black	55	25

DESIGN: 6, 35c. Blaeu's Map of 1665.

66 Tracking Station

1968. N.A.S.A. Apollo Project. Inauguration of Dow Hill Tracking Station.

212	66	4c. blue, yellow and black	10	10
213	-	15c. blue, yellow and black	20	10
214	-	25c. blue, yellow and black	20	10
215	-	50c. blue, yellow and black	30	40

DESIGNS: 15c. Antenna and spacecraft taking off; 25c. Spacecraft approaching Moon; 50c. Re-entry of space capsule.

70 Limbo-dancing

1968. Tourism. Multicoloured.

216	½c. Type 70		10	50
217	15c. Water-skier and bathers		30	10
218	25c. Yachts and beach		30	10
219	35c. Underwater swimming		30	10
220	50c. Type 70		35	1·25

74 Old Harbour in 1768

1968. Opening of St. John's Deep Water Harbour.

221	74	2c. blue and red	10	40
222	-	15c. green and sepia	35	10
223	-	25c. yellow and blue	40	10
224	-	35c. salmon and emerald	50	10
225	74	$1 black	90	2·00

DESIGNS: 15c. Old harbour in 1829; 25c. Freighter and chart of new harbour; 35c. New harbour.

78 Parliament Buildings

1969. Tercentenary of Parliament. Multicoloured.

226	78	4c. Type 78	10	10
227		15c. Antigua Mace and bearer	20	10
228		25c. House of Representative's Room	20	10
229		50c. Coat of arms and Seal of Antigua	30	1·60

82 Freight Transport

1969. First Anniv of Caribbean Free Trade Area.

230	82	4c. black and purple	10	10
231	82	15c. black and blue	20	30
232	-	25c. brown, black & ochre	25	30
233	-	35c. chocolate, blk & brn	25	30

DESIGN—VERT: 25, 35c. Crate of cargo.

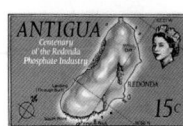

84 Island of Redonda (Chart)

1969. Centenary of Redonda Phosphate Industry. Multicoloured.

249	15c. Type 84		20	10
250	25c. View of Redonda from the sea		20	10
251	50c. Type 84		45	75

86 The Adoration of the Magi (Marcillat)

1969. Christmas. Stained Glass Windows. Multicoloured.

252	6c. Type 86		10	10
253	10c. The Nativity (unknown German artist, 15th century)		10	10
254	35c. Type 86		25	10
255	50c. As 10c.		50	40

1970. Surch 20c. and bars.

| 256 | 20c. on 25c. (No. 189) | | 10 | 10 |

89 Coat of Arms

1970. Coil Stamps.

257A	89	5c. blue	10	40
258A	89	10c. green	10	35
259A	89	25c. red	20	35

90 Sikorsky S-38 Flying Boat

1970. 40th Anniv of Antiguan Air Services. Multicoloured.

260	5c. Type 90		50	10
261	20c. Dornier Do-X flying boat		80	10
262	35c. Hawker Siddeley H.S.748		1·00	10
263	50c. Douglas C-124C Globemaster II		1·00	1·50
264	75c. Vickers Super VC-10		1·25	2·00

91 Dickens and Scene from Nicholas Nickleby

1970. Death Centenary of Charles Dickens.

265	91	5c. bistre, sepia and black	10	10
266	-	20c. turq, sepia & blk	20	10
267	-	35c. blue, sepia and black	30	10
268	-	$1 red, sepia and black	75	80

DESIGNS: All stamps show Dickens and scene from: 20c. "Pickwick Papers"; 35c. "Oliver Twist"; $1 "David Copperfield".

92 Carib Indian and War Canoe

1970. Nelson. Multicoloured..

323	½c. Type 92		20	50
270	1c. Columbus and Nina		30	1·50
271	2c. Sir Thomas Warner's emblem and Concepcion		40	3·25
325	3c. Viscount Hood and H.M.S. Barfleur		1·00	1·25
273	4c. Sir George Rodney and H.M.S. Formidable		40	3·00
274	5c. Nelson and H.M.S. Boreas		50	40
275	6c. William IV and H.M.S. Pegasus		1·75	4·25
276	10c. Blackbeard and pirate ketch		80	20
277	15c. Collingwood and H.M.S. Pelican		12·00	1·00
278	20c. Nelson and H.M.S. Victory		1·25	40
279	25c. Solent I (paddle-steamer)		1·25	40
280	35c. George V (when Prince George) and H.M.S. Canada (screw corvette)		2·75	80
281	50c. H.M.S. Renown (battle cruiser)		4·00	6·00
331	75c. Federal Maple (freighter)		7·50	3·00

332		$1 *Sol Quest* (yacht) and class emblem	3·00	1·75
333		$2.50 H.M.S. *London* (destroyer)	2·75	6·50
285		$5 *Pathfinder* (tug)	2·50	6·00

93 The Small Passion (detail) (Durer).

1970. Christmas.

286	**93**	3c. black and blue	10	10
287	-	10c. purple and pink	10	10
288	**93**	35c. black and red	30	10
289	-	50c. black and lilac	45	50

DESIGN: 10, 50c. *Adoration of the Magi* (detail) (Durer).

94 4th King's Own Regiment, 1759

1970. Military Uniforms (1st series). Multicoloured.

290		½c. Type **94**	10	10
291		10c. 4th West India Regiment, 1804	65	10
292		20c. 60th Regiment, The Royal American, 1809	1·00	10
293		35c. 93rd Regiment, Sutherland Highlanders, 1826–34	1·25	10
294		75c. 3rd West India Regiment, 1851	1·75	2·00
MS295		128×164 mm. Nos. 290/4	5·50	11·00

See also Nos. 303/8, 313/18, 353/8 and 380/5.

95 Market Woman casting Vote

1971. 20th Anniv of Adult Suffrage.

296	**95**	5c. brown	10	10
297	-	20c. olive	10	10
298	-	35c. purple	10	10
299	-	50c. blue	15	30

DESIGNS: People voting: 20c. Executive; 35c. Housewife; 50c. Artisan.

96 The Last Supper

1971. Easter. Works by Durer.

300	**96**	5c. black grey and red	10	10
301	-	35c. black, grey and violet	10	10
302	-	75c. black, grey and gold	20	30

DESIGNS: 35c. *The Crucifixion*; 75c. *The Resurrection*.

1971. Military Uniforms (2nd series). As T 94. Multicoloured.

303		½c. Private, 12th Regiment, The Suffolk (1704)	10	10
304		10c. Grenadier, 38th Regiment, South Staffordshire (1751)	35	10
305		20c. Light Company, 5th Regiment, Royal Northumberland Fusiliers (1778)	50	10
306		35c. Private, 48th Regiment, The Northamptonshire (1793)	60	10
307		75c. Private, 15th Regiment, East Yorks (1805)	1·00	3·00
MS308		127×144 mm. Nos. 303/7	4·50	6·50

97 *Madonna and Child* (detail, Veronese)

1971. Christmas. Multicoloured.

309		3c. Type **97**	10	10
310		5c. *Adoration of the Shepherds* (detail, Veronese)	10	10
311		35c. Type **97**	25	10
312		50c. As 5c.	40	30

1972. Military Uniforms (3rd series). As T 94. Multicoloured.

313		½c. Battalion Company Officer, 25th Foot, 1815	10	10
314		10c. Sergeant, 14th Foot, 1837	70	10
315		20c. Private, 67th Foot, 1853	1·25	15
316		35c. Officer, Royal Artillery, 1854	1·40	20
317		75c. Private, 29th Foot, 1870	1·75	4·00
MS318		125×141 mm. Nos. 313/17	7·00	8·50

98 Reticulated Cowrie Helmet

1972. Shells. Multicoloured.

319		3c. Type **98**	50	10
320		5c. Measled cowrie	50	10
321		35c. West Indian fighting conch	1·40	15
322		50c. Hawk-wing conch	1·60	3·00

99 St. John's Cathedral, Side View

1972. Christmas and 125th Anniv of St. John's Cathedral. Multicoloured.

335		35c. Type **99**	20	10
336		50c. Cathedral interior	25	25
337		75c. St. John's Cathedral	30	60
MS338		165×102 mm. Nos. 335/7	65	1·00

1972. Royal Silver Wedding. As T 52 of Ascension, but with floral background.

339		20c. blue	15	15
340		35c. blue	15	15

101 Batsman and Map

1972. 50th Anniv of Rising Sun Cricket Club. Multicoloured.

341		5c. Type **101**	55	15
342		35c. Batsman and wicket-keeper	65	10
343		$1 Club badge	1·00	2·25
MS344		88×130 mm. Nos. 341/3	3·25	7·50

102 Yacht and Map

1972. Inauguration of Antigua and Barbuda Tourist Office in New York. Multicoloured.

345		35c. Type **102**	15	10
346		50c. Yachts	20	15
347		75c. St. John's G.P.O.	25	25
348		$1 Statue of Liberty	25	25
MS349		100×94 mm. Nos. 346, 348	75	1·25

103 "Episcopal Coat of Arms"

1973. Easter. Multicoloured.

350	**103**	5c. Type **103**	10	10
351	-	35c. "The Crucifixion"	15	10
352	-	75c. "Arms of 1st Bishop of Antigua"	25	30

Nos. 350/2 show different stained-glass windows from St. John's Cathedral.

1973. Military Uniforms (4th series). As T 94. Multicoloured.

353		½c. Private, Zachariah Tiffin's Regiment of Foot, 1701	10	10
354		10c. Private, 63rd Regiment of Foot, 1759	40	10
355		20c. Light Company Officer, 35th Regiment of Foot, 1828	50	15
356		35c. Private, 2nd West India Regiment, 1853	65	15
357		75c. Sergeant, 49th Regiment, 1858	1·00	1·25
MS358		127×145 mm. Nos. 353/7	3·75	3·25

104 Butterfly Costumes

1973. Carnival. Multicoloured.

359		5c. Type **104**	10	10
360		20c. Carnival street scene	15	10
361		35c. Carnival troupe	20	10
362		75c. Carnival Queen	30	30
MS363		134×95 mm. Nos. 359/62	65	1·00

105 *Virgin of the Milk Porridge* (Gerard David)

1973. Christmas. Multicoloured.

364		3c. Type **105**	10	10
365		5c. *Adoration of the Magi* (Stomer)	10	10
366		20c. *The Granducal Madonna* (Raphael)	15	10
367		35c. *Nativity with God the Father and Holy Ghost* (Battista)	20	10
368		$1 *Madonna and Child* (Murillo)	40	60
MS369		130×128 mm. Nos. 364/8	1·10	1·75

106 Princess Anne and Captain Mark Phillips

1973. Royal Wedding.

370	**106**	35c. multicoloured	10	10
371	-	$2 multicoloured	25	25
MS372		78×100 mm. Nos. 370/1	50	40

The $2 is as Type **106** but has a different border.

1973. Nos. 370/1 optd HONEYMOON VISIT DECEMBER 16TH 1973.

373	**106**	35c. multicoloured	15	10
374	-	$2 multicoloured	30	30
MS375		78×100 mm. Nos. 373/4	55	55

108 Coat of Arms of Antigua and University

1974. 25th Anniv of University of West Indies. Multicoloured.

376		5c. Type **108**	15	10
377		20c. Extra-mural art	20	10
378		35c. Antigua campus	20	10
379		75c. Antigua chancellor	25	35

1974. Military Uniforms (5th series). As T 94. Multicoloured.

380		½c. Officer, 59th Foot, 1797	10	10
381		10c. Gunner, Royal Artillery, 1800	35	10
382		20c. Private, 1st West India Regiment, 1830	50	10
383		35c. Officer, 92nd Foot, 1843	60	10
384		75c. Private, 23rd Foot, 1846	75	2·25
MS385		125×145 mm. Nos. 380/4	2·25	2·50

109 English Postman, Mailcoach and Westland Dragonfly Helicopter

1974. Centenary of U.P.U. Multicoloured.

386		½c. Type **109**	10	20
387		1c. Bellman, mail steamer *Orinoco* and satellite	10	20
388		2c. Train guard, post-bus and hydrofoil	10	20
389		5c. Swiss messenger, Wells Fargo coach and Concorde	60	50
390		20c. Postilion, Japanese post-men and carrier pigeon	35	10
391		35c. Antiguan postman, Sikorsky S-88 flying boat and tracking station	45	15
392		$1 Medieval courier, American express train and Boeing 747-100	1·75	2·00
MS393		141×161 mm. Nos. 386/92	3·00	2·50

On the ½c. English is spelt "Enlish" and on the 2c. Postal is spelt "Fostal".

110 Traditional Player

1974. Antiguan Steel Bands.

394	**110**	5c. dp red, red and black	10	10
395	-	20c. brown, lt brn & blk	10	10
396	-	35c. lt green, green & blk	10	10
397	-	75c. blue, dp blue & blk	20	1·10
MS398		115×108 mm. Nos. 394/7	35	1·25

DESIGNS—HORIZ: 20c. Traditional band; 35c. Modern band. VERT: 75c. Modern player.

111 Footballers

1974. World Cup Football Championship.

399	**111**	5c. multicoloured	10	10
400	-	35c. multicoloured	15	10
401	-	75c. multicoloured	30	30
402	-	$1 multicoloured	35	40
MS403		135×130 mm. Nos. 399/402	85	90

Nos. 400/2 show various footballing designs similar to Type **111**.

1974. Earthquake Relief Fund. Nos. 400/2 and 397 optd or surch EARTHQUAKE RELIEF.

404		35c. multicoloured	20	10
405		75c. multicoloured	30	30
406		$1 multicoloured	40	40
407		$5 on 75c. deep blue, blue and black	1·25	2·25

113 Churchill as Schoolboy and School College Building, Harrow

1974. Birth Centenary of Sir Winston Churchill. Multicoloured.

408	5c. Type **113**	15	10
409	35c. Churchill and St. Paul's Cathedral	20	10
410	75c. Coat of arms and catafalque	30	65
411	$1 Churchill, "reward" notice and South African escape route	45	1·00
MS412	107×82 mm. Nos. 408/11	1·00	1·50

114 Madonna of the Trees (Bellini)

1974. Christmas. Madonna and Child paintings by named artists. Multicoloured.

413	½c. Type **114**	10	10
414	1c. Raphael	10	10
415	2c. Van der Weyden	10	10
416	3c. Giorgione	10	10
417	5c. Mantegna	10	10
418	20c. Vivarini	20	10
419	35c. Montagna	30	10
420	75c. Lorenzo Costa	55	1·10
MS421	139×126 mm. Nos. 413/20	1·00	1·40

1975. Nos. 390/2 and 331 surch.

422	50c. on 20c. multicoloured	1·25	2·00
423	$2.50 on 35c. multicoloured	2·00	5·50
424	$5 on $1 multicoloured	6·50	7·00
425	$10 on 75c. multicoloured	2·00	7·50

116 Carib War Canoe, English Harbour, 1300

1975. Nelson's Dockyard. Multicoloured.

427	5c. Type **116**	20	10
428	15c. Ship of the line, English Harbour, 1770	80	15
429	35c. H.M.S. Boreas at anchor, and Lord Nelson, 1787	1·00	15
430	50c. Yachts during "Sailing Week", 1974	1·00	1·50
431	$1 Yacht Anchorage, Old Dockyard, 1970	1·00	2·25
MS432	130×134 mm. As Nos. 427/31, but in larger format, 43×28 mm	3·00	2·00

117 Lady of the Valley Church

1975. Antiguan Churches. Multicoloured.

433	5c. Type **117**	10	10
434	20c. Gilbert Memorial	10	10
435	35c. Grace Hill Moravian	15	10
436	50c. St. Phillips	20	20
437	$1 Ebenezer Methodist	35	50
MS438	91×101 mm. Nos. 435/7	65	1·25

118 Map of 1721 and Sextant of 1640

1975. Maps of Antigua. Multicoloured.

439	5c. Type **118**	30	15
440	20c. Map of 1775 and galleon	55	15
441	35c. Maps of 1775 and 1955	70	15
442	$1 1973 maps of Antigua and English Harbour	1·40	2·25
MS443	130×89 mm. Nos. 439/42	3·00	3·25

119 Scout Bugler

1975. World Scout Jamboree, Norway. Multicoloured.

444	15c. Type **119**	25	15
445	20c. Scouts in camp	30	15
446	35c. "Lord Baden-Powell" (D. Jagger)	50	20
447	$2 Scout dancers from Dahomey	1·50	2·25
MS448	145×107 mm. Nos. 444/7	2·75	3·50

120 Eurema elathea

1975. Butterflies. Multicoloured.

449	½c. Type **120**	10	30
450	1c. Danaus plexippus	10	30
451	2c. Phoebis philea	15	30
452	5c. Hypolimnas misippus	30	10
453	20c. Eurema proterpia	1·00	40
454	35c. Battus polydamas	1·50	50
455	$2 Cynthia cardui	4·25	9·00
MS456	147×94 mm. Nos. 452/5	6·00	11·00

No. 452 is incorrectly captioned "Marpesia petreus thetys".

121 Madonna and Child (Correggio)

1975. Christmas. Madonna and Child paintings by named artists. Multicoloured.

457	½c. Type **121**	10	10
458	1c. El Greco	10	10
459	2c. Durer	10	10
460	3c. Antonello	10	10
461	5c. Bellini	10	10
462	10c. Durer (different)	10	10
463	35c. Bellini (different)	40	10
464	$2 Durer (different again)	1·00	1·00
MS465	138×119 mm. Nos. 461/4	1·50	1·60

122 Vivian Richards

1975. World Cricket Cup Winners. Multicoloured.

466	5c. Type **122**	1·25	20
467	35c. Andy Roberts	2·25	60
468	$2 West Indies team (horiz)	4·25	8·00

123 Antillean Crested Hummingbird

1976. Multicoloured.

469A	½c. Type **123**	40	50
470A	1c. Imperial amazon ("Imperial Parrot")	1·40	50
471A	2c. Zenaida dove	1·40	50
472A	3c. Loggerhead kingbird	1·40	60
473A	4c. Red-necked pigeon	1·40	2·25
474A	5c. Rufous-throated solitaire	2·00	10
475A	6c. Orchid tree	30	2·00
476A	10c. Bougainvillea	30	10
477A	15c. Geiger tree	35	10
478A	20c. Flamboyant	35	35
479A	25c. Hibiscus	40	15
480A	35c. Flame of the wood	40	40
481A	50c. Cannon at Fort James	55	60
482A	75c. Premier's Office	60	2·00
483A	$1 Potworks Dam	75	1·00
484A	$2.50 Diamond irrigation scheme (44×28 mm)	1·00	5·00
485B	$5 Government House (44×28 mm)	1·50	7·50
486A	$10 Coolidge International Airport (44×28 mm)	3·75	8·00

124 Privates, Clark's Illinois Regiment

1976. Bicentenary of American Revolution. Multicoloured.

487	½c. Type **124**	10	10
488	1c. Rifleman, Pennsylvania Militia	10	10
489	2c. Powder horn	10	10
490	5c. Water bottle	10	10
491	35c. American flags	40	10
492	$1 Montgomery (American brig)	75	30
493	$5 "Ranger" (privateer sloop)	1·50	1·75
MS494	71×84 mm. $2.50, Congress flag	1·00	1·40

125 High Jump

1976. Olympic Games, Montreal.

495	**125**	½c. brown, yellow & black	10	10
496	-	1c. violet, blue and black	10	10
497	-	2c. green and black	10	10
498	-	15c. blue and black	15	10
499	-	30c. brown, yell & blk	20	15
500	-	$1 orange, red and black	40	40
501	-	$2 red and black	60	80
MS502		88×138 mm. Nos. 498/501	1·75	1·25

DESIGNS: 1c. Boxing; 2c. Pole vault; 15c. Swimming; 30c. Running; $1 Cycling; $2 Shot put.

126 Water Skiing

1976. Water Sports. Multicoloured.

503	½c. Type **126**	10	10
504	1c. Sailing	10	10
505	2c. Snorkeling	10	10
506	20c. Deep sea fishing	50	10
507	50c. Scuba diving	75	35
508	$2 Swimming	1·25	1·25
MS509	89×114 mm. Nos. 506/8	1·75	1·75

127 French Angelfish

1976. Fish. Multicoloured.

510	15c. Type **127**	40	15
511	30c. Yellow-finned grouper	55	30
512	50c. Yellow-tailed snapper	70	50
513	90c. Shy hamlet	90	1·50

128 The Annunciation

1976. Christmas. Multicoloured.

514	8c. Type **128**	10	10
515	10c. The Holy Family	10	10
516	15c. The Magi	10	10
517	50c. The Shepherds	20	25
518	$1 Epiphany scene	30	50

129 Mercury and U.P.U. Emblem

1976. Special Events, 1976. Multicoloured.

519	½c. Type **129**	10	10
520	1c. Alfred Nobel	10	10
521	10c. Space satellite	30	10
522	50c. Viv Richards and Andy Roberts	3·50	1·75
523	$1 Bell and telephones	1·00	2·00
524	$2 Yacht Freelance	2·25	4·50
MS525	127×101 mm. Nos. 521/4	7·50	13·00

130 Royal Family

1977. Silver Jubilee. Multicoloured

(a) Perf

526	10c. Type **130**	10	10
527	30c. Royal Visit, 1966	10	10
528	50c. The Queen enthroned	15	15
529	90c. The Queen after Coronation	15	25
530	$2.50 Queen and Prince Charles	30	55
MS531	116×78 mm. $5 Queen and Prince Philip	65	85

(a) Perf

581	10c. Type **138**	10	10
582	30c. Crowning	10	10
583	50c. Coronation procession	15	10
584	90c. Queen seated in St. Edward's Chair	20	15
585	$2.50 Queen wearing Imperial State Crown	40	40
MS586	114×104 mm. $5 Queen and Prince Philip	80	80

(b) Roul×imperf. Self-adhesive.

532	50c. As 90c.	35	75
533	$5 The Queen and Prince Philip	2·00	3·75

Nos. 532/3 come from booklets.

131 Making Camp

1977. Caribbean Scout Jamboree, Jamaica. Multicoloured.

534	½c. Type **131**	10	10
535	1c. Hiking	10	10
536	2c. Rock-climbing	10	10
537	10c. Cutting logs	15	10
538	30c. Map and sign reading	40	10
539	50c. First aid	65	25
540	$2 Rafting	1·25	2·50
MS541	127×114 mm. Nos. 538/40	3·00	4·00

132 Carnival Costume

1977. 21st Anniv of Carnival. Multicoloured.

542	10c. Type **132**	10	10
543	30c. Carnival Queen	25	10
544	50c. Butterfly costume	30	15
545	90c. Queen of the band	40	25
546	$1 Calypso King and Queen	40	30
MS547	140×120 mm. Nos. 542/6	1·10	1·60

1977. Royal Visit. Nos. 526/30 optd **ROYAL VISIT 28TH OCTOBER 1977.**

548	10c. Type **130**	10	10
549	30c. Royal Visit, 1966	15	10
550	50c. The Queen enthroned	20	10
551	90c. The Queen after Coronation	30	20
552	$2.50 Queen and Prince Charles	50	35
MS553	116×178 mm. $5 Queen and Prince Philip	1·00	1·00

134 *Virgin and Child Enthroned (Tura)*

1977. Christmas. Paintings by named artists. Multicoloured.

554	½c. Type **134**	10	20
555	1c. Crivelli	10	20
556	2c. Lotto	10	20
557	8c. Pontormo	15	10
558	10c. Tura (different)	15	10
559	25c. Lotto (different)	30	10
560	$2 Crivelli (different)	85	1·00
MS561	144×118 mm. Nos. 557/60	1·75	2·75

135 Pineapple

1977. Tenth Anniv of Statehood. Multicoloured.

562	10c. Type **135**	10	10
563	15c. State flag	60	20
564	50c. Police band	2·50	80
565	90c. Premier V. C. Bird	55	80
566	$2 State Coat of Arms	90	2·00
MS567	129×99 mm. Nos. 563/6	3·50	3·00

136 Wright Glider III, 1902

1978. 75th Anniv of Powered Flight. Multicoloured.

568	½c. Type **136**	10	10
569	1c. Wright *Flyer I*, 1903	10	10
570	2c. Launch system and engine	10	10
571	10c. Orville Wright (vert)	30	10
572	50c. Wright *Flyer III*, 1905	60	15
573	90c. Wilbur Wright (vert)	80	30
574	$2 Wright Type B, 1910	1·00	80
MS575	90×75 mm. $2.50, Wright *Flyer I* on launch system	1·25	2·75

137 Sunfish Regatta

1978. Sailing Week. Multicoloured.

576	10c. Type **137**	20	10
577	50c. Fishing and work boat race	35	20
578	90c. Curtain Bluff race	60	35
579	$2 Power boat rally	1·10	1·25
MS580	110×77 mm. $2.50, Guadeloupe–Antigua race	1·50	1·75

138 Queen Elizabeth and Prince Philip

1978. 25th Anniv of Coronation. Multicoloured.

(a) Perf

581	10c. Type **138**	10	10
582	30c. Crowning	10	10
583	50c. Coronation procession	15	10
584	90c. Queen seated in St. Edward's Chair	20	15
585	$2.50 Queen wearing Imperial State Crown	40	40
MS586	114×104 mm. $5 Queen and Prince Philip	80	80

(b) Roul×imperf. Self-adhesive. Horiz designs as Type **138**.

587	25c. Glass Coach	15	30
588	50c. Irish State Coach	25	50
589	$5 Coronation Coach	1·75	3·00

Nos. 587/9 come from booklets.

140 Player running with Ball

1978. World Cup Football Championship, Argentina. Multicoloured.

590	10c. Type **140**	15	10
591	15c. Players in front of goal	15	10
592	$3 Referee and player	1·50	1·75
MS593	126×88 mm. 25c. Player crouching with ball; 30c. Players heading ball; 50c. Players running with ball; $2 Goalkeeper diving. All horiz	3·25	2·50

141 Petrea

1978. Flowers. Multicoloured.

594	25c. Type **141**	20	10
595	50c. Sunflower	30	20
596	90c. Frangipani	50	30
597	$2 Passion flower	90	2·00
MS598	118×85 mm. $2.50, Hibiscus	1·40	1·60

142 St. Ildefonso receiving the Chasuble from the Virgin (Rubens)

1978. Christmas. Multicoloured.

599	8c. Type **142**	10	10
600	25c. *The Flight of St. Barbara* (Rubens)	20	10
601	$2 *Madonna and Child, with St. Joseph, John the Baptist and Donor*	65	55
MS602	170×113 mm. $4 *The Annunciation* (Rubens)	1·25	1·50

The painting shown on No. 601 is incorrectly attributed to Rubens on the stamp. The artist was Sebastiano del Piombo.

143 1d. Stamp of 1863

1979. Death Centenary of Sir Rowland Hill. Multicoloured.

603	25c. Type **143**	10	10
604	50c. 1840 Penny Black	20	15
605	$1 Mail coach and woman posting letter, c. 1840	30	20
606	$2 Modern transport	1·10	60
MS607	108×82 mm. $2.50, Sir Rowland Hill	80	90

144 *The Deposition from the Cross (painting)*

1979. Easter. Works by Durer.

608	**144** 10c. multicoloured	10	10
609	— 50c. multicoloured	35	20
610	— $4 black, mauve and yellow	1·00	90
MS611	114×99 mm. $2.50, multicoloured	80	80

DESIGNS: 50c., $2.50, *Christ on the Cross–The Passion* (wood engravings) (both different); $4 *Man of Sorrows with Hands Raised* (wood engraving).

145 Toy Yacht and Child's Hand

1979. International Year of the Child. Multicoloured.

612	25c. Type **145**	10	10
613	50c. Rocket	25	15
614	90c. Car	40	25
615	$2 Toy train	1·00	90
MS616	80×112 mm. $5 Aeroplane	1·10	1·10

Nos. 612/16 also show the hands of children of different races.

146 Yellow Jack

1979. Fish. Multicoloured.

617	30c. Type **146**	35	15
618	50c. Blue-finned tuna	40	25
619	90c. Sailfish	60	40
620	$3 Wahoo	1·50	1·75
MS621	122×75 mm. $2.50, Great barracuda	1·50	1·40

147 Cook's Birthplace, Marton

1979. Death Bicentenary of Captain Cook. Multicoloured.

622	25c. Type **147**	65	25
623	50c. H.M.S. *Endeavour*	1·25	60
624	90c. Marine chronometer	75	80
625	$3 Landing at Botany Bay	1·75	3·00
MS626	110×85 mm. $2.50, H.M.S. *Resolution*	2·25	1·50

148 The Holy Family

1979. Christmas. Multicoloured.

627	8c. Type **148**	10	10
628	25c. Virgin and Child on ass	15	10
629	50c. Shepherd and star	25	35
630	$4 Wise Men with gifts	85	2·50
MS631	113×94 mm. $3 Angel with trumpet	1·00	1·50

149 Javelin Throwing

1980. Olympic Games, Moscow. Multicoloured.

632	10c. Type **149**	20	10
633	25c. Running	20	10
634	$1 Pole vault	50	50
635	$2 Hurdles	70	1·75
MS636	127×96 mm. $3 Boxing (horiz)	80	90

150 Mickey Mouse and Airplane

1980. International Year of the Child. Walt Disney Cartoon Characters. Multicoloured.

637	½c. Type **150**	10	10
638	1c. Donald Duck driving car (vert)	10	10
639	2c. Goofy driving taxi	10	10
640	3c. Mickey and Minnie Mouse on motorcycle	10	10
641	4c. Huey, Dewey and Louie on a bicycle for three	10	10
642	5c. Grandma Duck and truck of roosters	10	10
643	10c. Mickey Mouse in jeep (vert)	10	10
644	$1 Chip and Dale in yacht	2·00	2·00
645	$4 Donald Duck riding toy train (vert)	4·00	6·50
MS646	101×127 mm. $2.50, Goofy flying biplane	4·50	3·25

1980. "London 1980" International Stamp Exhibition. Nos. 603/6 optd **LONDON 1980**.

647	25c. Type **143**	25	15
648	50c. Penny Black	35	35
649	$1 Stage-coach and woman posting letter, c. 1840	60	70
650	$2 Modern mail transport	3·25	3·00

152 *David* (statue, Donatello)

1980. Famous Works of Art. Multicoloured.

651	10c. Type **152**	10	10
652	30c. *The Birth of Venus* (painting, Botticelli) (horiz)	30	15
653	50c. *Reclining Couple* (sarcophagus), Cerveteri (horiz)	40	40
654	90c. *The Garden of Earthly Delights* (painting by Bosch) (horiz)	55	65
655	$1 *Portinari Altarpiece* (painting, van der Goes) (horiz)	65	75
656	$4 *Eleanora of Toledo and her Son, Giovanni de'Medici* (painting, Bronzino)	1·75	3·00
MS657	99×124 mm. $5 *The Holy Family* (painting, Rembrandt)	2·50	1·75

153 Anniversary Emblem and Headquarters, U.S.A.

1980. 75th Anniv of Rotary International. Multicoloured.

658	30c. Type **153**	30	30
659	50c. Rotary anniversary emblem and Antigua Rotary Club banner	40	50
660	90c. Map of Antigua and Rotary emblem	60	70
661	$3 Paul P. Harris (founder) and Rotary emblem	2·00	3·50
MS662	102×78 mm. $5 Antiguan flags and Rotary emblems	1·25	2·00

154 Queen Elizabeth the Queen Mother

1980. 80th Birthday of The Queen Mother.

663	**154** 10c. multicoloured	40	10
664	**154** $2.50 multicoloured	1·00	1·75
MS665	68×90 mm. As T **154**. $3 multicoloured	1·40	2·25

155 Ringed Kingfisher

1980. Birds. Multicoloured.

666	10c. Type 155	70	30
667	30c. Plain pigeon	1·00	50
668	$1 Green-throated carib	1·50	50
669	$2 Black-necked stilt	2·00	4·00
MS670	73×73 mm. $2.50, Roseate tern	7·00	6·00

1980. Christmas. Walt Disney's "Sleeping Beauty". As T 150. Multicoloured.

671	½c. The Bad Fairy with her raven	10	10
672	1c. The good fairies	10	10
673	2c. Aurora	10	10
674	4c. Aurora pricks her finger	10	10
675	8c. The prince	10	10
676	10c. The prince fights the dragon	15	10
677	25c. The prince awakens Aurora with a kiss	20	20
678	$2 The prince and Aurora's betrothal	2·25	2·25
679	$2.50 The prince and princess	2·50	2·50
MS680	126×101 mm. $4 multicoloured (vert)	5·00	3·25

156 Diesel Locomotive No. 15

1981. Sugar Cane Railway Locomotives. Multicoloured.

681	25c. Type 156	15	15
682	50c. Narrow-gauge steam locomotive	30	30
683	90c. Diesel locomotives Nos. 1 and 10	55	60
684	$3 Steam locomotive hauling sugar cane	2·00	2·25
MS685	82×111 mm. $2.50, Antiguan sugar factory, railway yard and sheds	1·75	1·75

1981. Independence. Nos. 475/6 and 478/86 optd "INDEPENDENCE 1981".

686B	6c. Orchid tree	10	50
687B	10c. Bougainvillea	10	10
688B	20c. Flamboyant	10	10
689B	25c. Hibiscus	15	15
690B	35c. Flame of the wood	20	20
691B	50c. Cannon at Fort James	35	45
692B	75c. Premier's Office	40	60
693B	$1 Potworks Dam	55	75
694B	$2.50 Irrigation scheme, Diamond Estate	75	2·00
695B	$5 Government House	1·40	3·50
696B	$10 Coolidge International Airport	3·25	6·00

158 Pipes of Pan

1981. Birth Centenary of Picasso. Multicoloured.

697	10c. Type 158	10	10
698	50c. Seated Harlequin	30	30
699	90c. Paulo as Harlequin	55	55
700	$4 Mother and Child	2·00	2·00
MS701	115×140 mm. $5 Three Musicians (detail)	1·75	2·75

159 Prince Charles and Lady Diana Spencer

1981. Royal Wedding (1st issue). Multicoloured.

702	25c. Type 159	10	10
703	50c. Glamis Castle	10	10
704	$4 Prince Charles skiing	80	80
MS705	96×82 mm. $5 Glass coach	80	80

160 Prince of Wales at Investiture, 1969

1981. Royal Wedding (2nd issue). Multicoloured. Roul×imperf. Self-adhesive.

706	25c. Type 160	15	25
707	25c. Prince Charles as baby, 1948	15	25
708	$1 Prince Charles at R.A.F. College, Cranwell, 1971	25	50
709	$1 Prince Charles attending Hill House School, 1956	25	50
710	$2 Prince Charles and Lady Diana Spencer	50	75
711	$2 Prince Charles at Trinity College, 1967	50	75
712	$5 Prince Charles and Lady Diana (different)	1·00	1·50

161 Irene Joshua (founder)

1981. 50th Anniv of Antigua Girl Guide Movement. Multicoloured.

713	10c. Type 161	15	10
714	50c. Campfire sing-song	45	35
715	90c. Sailing	75	65
716	$2.50 Animal tending	1·50	2·00
MS717	110×85 mm. $5 Raising the flag	4·50	3·00

162 Antigua and Barbuda Coat of Arms

1981. Independence. Multicoloured.

718	10c. Type 162	25	10
719	50c. Pineapple, with Antigua and Barbuda flag and map	2·00	60
720	90c. Prime Minister Vere Bird	55	55
721	$2.50 St. John's Cathedral (38×25 mm)	1·50	3·50
MS722	105×79 mm. $5 Map of Antigua and Barbuda (42×42 mm)	4·50	2·75

163 Holy Night (Jacques Stella)

1981. Christmas. Paintings. Multicoloured.

723	8c. Type 163	15	10
724	30c. Mary with Child (Julius Schnorr von Carolfeld)	40	15
725	$1 Virgin and Child (Alonso Cano)	75	90
726	$3 Virgin and Child (Lorenzo di Credi)	1·10	3·75
MS727	77×111 mm. $5 Holy Family (Pieter von Avon)	2·50	4·50

164 Swimming

1981. International Year of Disabled People. Sports for the Disabled. Multicoloured.

728	10c. Type 164	10	10
729	50c. Discus-throwing	20	30
730	90c. Archery	40	55
731	$2 Baseball	1·00	1·40
MS732	108×84 mm. $4 Basketball	5·00	2·75

165 Scene from Football Match

1982. World Cup Football Championship, Spain.

733	165	10c. multicoloured	30	10
734	-	50c. multicoloured	60	35
735	-	90c. multicoloured	1·10	70
736	-	$4 multicoloured	3·00	3·50
MS737		– 75×92 mm. $5 multicoloured	6·00	10·00

DESIGNS: 50c. to $5, Scenes from various matches.

166 Airbus Industrie A300

1982. Coolidge International Airport. Multicoloured.

738	10c. Type 166	10	10
739	50c. Hawker-Siddeley H.S.748	30	30
740	90c. de Havilland DHC-6 Twin Otter	60	60
741	$2.50 Britten Norman Islander	1·75	1·75
MS742	99×73 mm. $5 Boeing 747-100 (horiz)	2·75	4·00

167 Cordia

1982. Death Centenary of Charles Darwin. Fauna and Flora. Multicoloured.

743	10c. Type 167	30	10
744	50c. Small Indian mongoose (horiz)	70	40
745	90c. Corallita	1·10	75
746	$2 Mexican bulldog bat (horiz)	2·50	3·25
MS747	107×85 mm. $5 Carribbean monk seal	7·50	8·00

168 Queen's House, Greenwich

1982. 21st Birthday of Princess of Wales. Multicoloured.

748	90c. Type 168	45	45
749	$1 Prince and Princess of Wales	65	50
750	$4 Princess Diana	3·00	2·00
MS751	102×75 mm. $5 Type 169	3·75	2·50

170 Boy Scouts decorating Streets for Independence Parade

1982. 75th Anniv of Boy Scout Movement. Multicoloured.

752	10c. Type 170	25	10
753	50c. Boy Scout giving helping hand during street parade	50	40
754	90c. Boy Scouts attending H.R.H. Princess Margaret at Independence Ceremony	80	75
755	$2.20 Cub Scout giving directions to tourists	1·50	2·75
MS756	102×72 mm. $5 Lord Baden-Powell	4·50	5·50

1982. Birth of Prince William of Wales. Nos. 748/50 optd ROYAL BABY 21.6.82.

757	90c. Type 168	45	45
758	$1 Prince and Princess of Wales	50	50
759	$4 Princess Diana	1·50	1·50
MS760	102×75 mm. $5 Type 169	2·40	2·50

172 Roosevelt in 1940

1982. Birth Centenary of Franklin D. Roosevelt. (Nos. 761, 763 and 765/6) and 250th Birth Anniv of George Washington (others). Multicoloured.

761	10c. Type 172	20	10
762	25c. Washington as blacksmith	45	15
763	45c. Churchill, Roosevelt and Stalin at Yalta Conference	1·75	40
764	60c. Washington crossing the Delaware (vert)	1·00	40
765	$1 "Roosevelt Special" train (vert)	1·75	90
766	$3 Portrait of Roosevelt (vert)	1·40	2·40
MS767	92×87 mm. $4 Roosevelt and Wife	2·00	1·75
MS768	92×87 mm. $4 Portrait of Washington (vert)	2·00	1·75

No. MS768 also exists imperf.

173 Annunciation

1982. Christmas. Religious Paintings by Raphael. Multicoloured.

769	10c. Type 173	10	10
770	30c. Adoration of the Magi	15	15
771	$1 Presentation at the Temple	50	40
772	$4 Coronation of the Virgin	1·75	1·90
MS773	95×124 mm. $5 Marriage of the Virgin	2·75	2·50

174 Tritons and Dolphins

1983. 500th Birth Anniv of Raphael. Details from Galatea Fresco. Multicoloured.

774	45c. Type 174	20	25
775	50c. Sea nymph carried off by Triton	25	30
776	60c. Winged angel steering dolphins (horiz)	30	35
777	$4 Cupids shooting arrows (horiz)	1·60	2·00
MS778	101×125 mm. $5 Galatea pulled along by dolphins	1·50	2·25

175 Pineapple Produce

1983. Commonwealth Day. Multicoloured.

779	25c. Type 175	15	15
780	45c. Carnival	20	25
781	60c. Tourism	30	35
782	$3 Airport	1·00	1·50

176 T.V. Satellite Coverage of Royal Wedding

1983. World Communications Year. Multicoloured.

783	15c. Type 176	40	20
784	50c. Police communications	2·25	1·50
785	60c. House-to-train telephone call	2·25	1·50
786	$3 Satellite earth station with planets Jupiter and Saturn	4·75	5·00
MS787	100×90 mm. $5 "Comsat" satellite over West Indies	2·00	3·75

177 Bottle-nosed Dolphin

1983. Whales. Multicoloured.

788	15c. Type **177**	85	20
789	50c. Fin whale	1·75	1·25
790	60c. Bowhead whale	2·00	1·25
791	$3 Spectacled porpoise	3·75	4·25
MS792	122×101 mm. $5 Narwhal	8·50	6·00

178 Cashew Nut

1983. Fruits and Flowers. Multicoloured.

793	1c. Type **178**	15	1·25
794	2c. Passion fruit	15	1·25
795	3c. Mango	15	1·25
796	5c. Grapefruit	20	1·25
797a	10c. Pawpaw	30	20
798	15c. Breadfruit	75	20
799	20c. Coconut	50	20
800a	25c. Oleander	75	20
801	30c. Banana	60	40
802a	45c. Pineapple	75	30
803a	45c. Cordia	85	40
804	50c. Cassia	90	60
805	60c. Poui	1·50	1·00
806a	$1 Frangipani	2·00	1·50
807a	$2 Flamboyant	3·50	4·50
808	$2.50 Lemon	3·75	6·50
809	$5 Linum vitae	5·00	13·00
810	$10 National flag and coat of arms	8·00	17·00

179 Dornier Do-X Flying Boat

1983. Bicentenary of Manned Flight. Multicoloured.

811	30c. Type **179**	1·00	30
812	50c. Supermarine S.6B seaplane	1·25	60
813	60c. Curtiss F-9C Sparrowhawk biplane and airship U.S.S. Akron	1·40	85
814	$4 Hot-air balloon *Pro Juventute*	3·25	6·00
MS815	80×105 mm. $5 Airship LZ-127 *Graf Zeppelin*	1·75	2·25

180 Sibyls and Angels (detail) (Raphael)

1983. Christmas. 500th Birth Anniv of Raphael.

816	**180** 10c. multicoloured	30	20
817	- 30c. multicoloured	65	35
818	- $1 multicoloured	1·50	1·50
819	- $4 multicoloured	2·50	5·00
MS820	101×103 mm. $5 multicoloured	1·50	2·25

DESIGNS—HORIZ: 10c. to $4, Different details from *Sibyls and Angels*. VERT: $5 *The Vision of Ezekiel*.

181 John Wesley (founder)

1983. Bicentenary of Methodist Church (1984). Multicoloured.

821	15c. Type **181**	25	15
822	50c. Nathaniel Gilbert (founder in Antigua)	70	50
823	60c. St. John Methodist Church steeple	75	65
824	$3 Ebenezer Methodist Church, St. John's	2·00	4·00

182 Discus

1984. Olympic Games, Los Angeles. Multicoloured.

825	25c. Type **182**	20	15
826	50c. Gymnastics	35	30
827	90c. Hurdling	65	70
828	$3 Cycling	2·50	4·25
MS829	82×67 mm. $5 Volleyball	2·75	3·00

183 *Booker Vanguard* (freighter)

1984. Ships. Multicoloured.

830	45c. Type **183**	1·00	55
831	50c. S.S. *Canberra* (liner)	1·25	80
832	60c. Yachts	1·50	1·00
833	$4 *Fairwind* (cargo liner)	3·00	7·00
MS834	107×80 mm. $5 18th-century British man-of-war (vert)	1·75	3·50

184 Chenille

1984. Universal Postal Union Congress, Hamburg. Multicoloured.

835	15c. Type **184**	40	15
836	50c. Shell flower	75	70
837	60c. Anthurium	75	1·10
838	$3 Angels trumpet	2·25	6·50
MS839	100×75 mm. $5 Crown of Thorns	1·50	3·25

1984. Various stamps surch

(a) Nos. 702/4.

840	$2 on 25c. Type **159**	2·50	2·50
841	$2 on 50c. Glamis Castle	2·50	2·50
842	$2 on $4 Prince Charles skiing	2·50	2·50
MS843	96×82 mm. $2 on $5 Glass coach	4·00	4·00

(b) Nos. 748/50.

844	$2 on 90c. Type **168**	2·50	2·50
845	$2 on $1 Prince and Princess of Wales	2·50	2·50
846	$2 on $4 Princess Diana	2·50	2·50
MS847	102×75 mm. Type **169**	4·00	4·00

(c) Nos. 757/9.

848	$2 on 90c. Type **168**	2·00	2·00
849	$2 on $1 Prince and Princess of Wales	2·00	2·00
850	$2 on $4 Princess Diana	2·00	2·00
MS851	102×75 mm. $2 on $5 Type **169**	4·00	4·00

(d) Nos. 779/82.

852	$2 on 25c. Type **175**	2·75	1·25
853	$2 on 45c. Carnival	2·75	1·25
854	$2 on 60c. Tourism	2·75	1·25
855	$2 on $3 Airport	2·75	1·25

187 Abraham Lincoln

1984. Presidents of the United States of America. Multicoloured.

856	10c. Type **187**	15	10
857	20c. Harry S. Truman	20	15
858	30c. Dwight D. Eisenhower	30	25
859	40c. Ronald W. Reagan	50	30
860	90c. Gettysburg Address, 1863	90	90
861	$1.10 Formation of N.A.T.O.,1949	1·00	1·25

188 View of Moravian Mission

862	$1.50 Eisenhower during the war	1·60	1·75
863	$2 Reagan and Caribbean Basin Initiative	1·75	2·00

1984. 150th Anniv of Abolition of Slavery. Multicoloured.

864	40c. Type **188**	90	50
865	50c. Antigua Courthouse, 1823	1·00	65
866	60c. Planting sugar-cane, Monks Hill	1·10	75
867	$3 Boiling house, Delaps' estate	4·25	6·00
MS868	95×70 mm. $5 Loading sugar, Willoughby Bay	6·50	4·75

189 Rufous-sided Towhee

1984. Songbirds. Multicoloured.

869	40c. Type **189**	1·25	85
870	50c. Parula warbler	1·40	1·10
871	60c. House wren	1·50	1·50
872	$2 Ruby-crowned kinglet	2·00	3·75
873	$3 Common flicker ("Yellow-shafted Flicker")	2·75	5·00
MS874	76×76 mm. $5 Yellow-breasted chat	2·50	6·00

190 Grass-skiing

1984. "Ausipex" International Stamp Exhibition, Melbourne, Australian Sports. Multicoloured.

875	$1 Type **190**	1·25	1·50
876	$5 Australian football	3·25	4·75
MS877	108×78 mm. $5 Boomerang-throwing	2·00	3·50

191 *The Virgin and Infant with Angels and Cherubs*

1984. 450th Death Anniv of Correggio (painter). Multicoloured.

878	25c. Type **191**	40	20
879	60c. *The Four Saints*	80	50
880	90c. *St. Catherine*	1·10	90
881	$3 *The Campori Madonna*	2·25	4·25
MS882	90×60 mm. $5 *St. John the Baptist*	1·75	2·75

192 *The Blue Dancers*

1984. 150th Birth Anniv of Edgar Degas (painter). Multicoloured.

883	15c. Type **192**	35	15
884	50c. *The Pink Dancers*	80	60
885	70c. *Two Dancers*	1·10	85
886	$4 *Dancers at the Bar*	2·50	4·75
MS887	90×60 mm. *The Folk dancers* (40×27 mm)	2·00	2·75

193 Sir Winston Churchill

1984. Famous People. Multicoloured.

888	60c. Type **193**	1·10	1·50
889	60c. Mahatma Gandhi	1·10	1·50
890	60c. John F. Kennedy	1·10	1·50
891	60c. Mao Tse-tung	1·10	1·50
892	$1 Churchill with General De Gaulle, Paris, 1944 (horiz)	1·25	1·75
893	$1 Gandhi leaving London by train, 1931 (horiz)	1·25	1·75
894	$1 Kennedy with Chancellor Adenauer and Mayor Brandt, Berlin, 1963 (horiz)	1·25	1·75
895	$1 Mao Tse-tung with Lin Piao, Peking, 1969 (horiz)	1·25	1·75
MS896	114×80 mm. $5 Flags of Great Britain, India, the United States and China	9·50	8·00

194 Donald Duck fishing

1984. Christmas. 50th Birthday of Donald Duck. Walt Disney Cartoon Characters. Multicoloured.

897	1c. Type **194**	10	10
898	2c. Donald Duck lying on beach	10	10
899	3c. Donald Duck and nephews with fishing rods and fishes	10	10
900	4c. Donald Duck and nephews in boat	10	10
901	5c. Wearing diving masks	10	10
902	10c. In deckchairs reading books	10	10
903	$1 With toy shark's fin	2·25	1·25
904	$2 In sailing boat	2·50	3·00
905	$5 Attempting to propel boat	4·00	6·00
MS906	Two sheets, each 125×100 mm. (a) $5 Nephews with crayon and paintbrushes (horiz). (b) $5 Donald Duck in deckchair Set of 2 sheets	7·50	13·00

195 Torch from Statue in Madison Square Park, 1885

1985. Centenary (1986) of Statue of Liberty (1st issue). Multicoloured.

907	25c. Type **195**	30	20
908	30c. Statue of Liberty and scaffolding ("Restoration and Renewal") (vert)	30	20
909	50c. Frederic Bartholdi (sculptor) supervising construction, 1876	40	40
910	90c. Close-up of statue	60	75
911	$1 Statue and cadet ship ("Operation Sail", 1976) (vert)	1·60	1·40
912	$3 Dedication ceremony, 1886	1·75	3·00
MS913	110×80 mm. $5 Port of New York	3·75	3·75

See also Nos. 1110/19.

196 Arawak Pot Sherd and Indians making Clay Utensils

1985. Native American Artefacts. Multicoloured.

914	15c. Type **196**	15	10
915	50c. Arawak body design and Arawak Indians tattooing	30	40
916	60c. Head of the god "Yocahu" and Indians harvesting manioc	40	50
917	$3 Carib war club and Carib Indians going into battle	1·25	2·50
MS918	97×68 mm. $5 Taino Indians worshipping stone idol	1·50	2·50

197 Triumph 2hp "Jap", 1903

1985. Centenary of the Motorcycle. Multicoloured.
919	10c. Type **197**		65	15
920	30c. "Indian Arrow", 1949		1·10	40
921	60c. BMW "R100RS", 1976		1·60	1·25
922	$4 Harley-Davidson "Model II", 1916		5·50	9·00
MS923 90×93 mm. $5 Laverda "Jota", 1975			5·50	7·00

198 Slavonian Grebe ("Horned Grebe")

1985. Birth Bicentenary of John J. Audubon (ornithologist) (1st issue). Multicoloured. Designs showing original paintings.
924	90c. Type **198**		1·75	1·25
925	$1 British storm petrel ("Least Petrel")		2·00	1·25
926	$1.50 Great blue heron		2·50	3·25
927	$3 Double-crested cormorant		3·75	6·00
MS928 103×72 mm. $5 White-tailed tropic bird (vert)			7·00	6·00

See also Nos. 990/4.

199 Anaea cyanea

1985. Butterflies. Multicoloured.
929	25c. Type **199**		1·00	30
930	60c. Leodonta dysoni		2·25	1·25
931	90c. Junea doraete		2·75	1·50
932	$4 Prepona pylene		7·50	10·50
MS933 132×105 mm. $5 Caerois gerdtrudlus			4·50	6·50

200 Cessna 172D Skyhawk

1985. 40th Anniv of International Civil Aviation Organization. Multicoloured.
934	30c. Type **200**		1·25	30
935	90c. Fokker D.VII		2·75	1·25
936	$1.50 SPAD VII		3·75	3·25
937	$3 Boeing 747-100		5·50	7·50
MS938 97×83 mm. $5 de Havilland DHC-6 twin otter			4·50	6·50

201 Maimonides

1985. 850th Birth Anniv of Maimonides (physician, philosopher and scholar).
939	**201** $2 green		4·25	3·25
MS940 70×84 mm. Type **201** $5 brown			7·00	4·50

202 Young Farmers with Produce

1985. International Youth Year. Multicoloured.
941	25c. Type **202**		25	20
942	50c. Hotel management trainees		40	50
943	60c. Girls with goat and boys with football ("Environment")		1·00	70
944	$3 Windsurfing ("Leisure")		2·75	5·50
MS945 102×72 mm. $5 Young people with Antiguan flags			2·75	3·25

203 The Queen Mother attending Church

1985. Life and Times of Queen Elizabeth the Queen Mother. Multicoloured.
946	$1 Type **203**		45	60
947	$1.50 Watching children playing in London garden		60	85
948	$2.50 The Queen Mother in 1979		90	1·40
MS949 56×85 mm. $5 With Prince Edward at Royal Wedding, 1981			5·50	3·00

Stamps as Nos. 946/8, but with face values of 90c., $1 and $3 exist from additional sheetlets with changed background colours.

204 Magnificent Frigate Bird

1985. Marine Life. Multicoloured.
950	15c. Type **204**		1·00	30
951	45c. Brain coral		2·00	95
952	60c. Cushion star		2·25	1·75
953	$3 Spotted moray		7·00	9·00
MS954 110×80 mm. $5 Elkhorn coral			9·00	7·00

205 Girl Guides Nursing

1985. 75th Anniv of Girl Guide Movement. Multicoloured.
955	15c. Type **205**		75	20
956	45c. Open-air Girl Guide meeting		1·40	60
957	60c. Lord and Lady Baden-Powell		1·75	90
958	$3 Girl Guides gathering flowers		4·25	4·50
MS959 67×96 mm. $5 Barn swallow (Nature study)			6·50	8·50

206 Bass Trombone

1985. 300th Birth Anniv of Johann Sebastian Bach (composer).
960	**206** 25c. multicoloured		1·40	55
961	– 50c. multicoloured		1·75	1·10
962	– $1 multicoloured		3·25	1·75
963	– $3 multicoloured		6·00	7·00
MS964 – 104×73 mm. $5 black and grey			4·50	4·75

DESIGNS: 50c. English horn; $1 Violino piccolo; $3 Bass rackett; $5 Johann Sebastian Bach.

207 Flags of Great Britain and Antigua

1985. Royal Visit. Multicoloured.
965	60c. Type **207**		1·00	65
966	$1 Queen Elizabeth II (vert)		1·50	1·25
967	$4 Royal Yacht "Britannia"		3·25	7·00
MS968 110×83 mm. $5 Map of Antigua			3·00	3·25

1985. 150th Birth Anniv of Mark Twain (author). As T **118** of Anguilla showing Walt Disney cartoon characters in scenes from Roughing It. Multicoloured.
969	25c. Donald Duck and Mickey Mouse meeting Indians		1·00	20
970	50c. Mickey Mouse, Donald Duck and Goofy canoeing		1·50	55
971	$1.10 Goofy as Pony Express rider		2·50	2·25
972	$1.50 Donald Duck and Goofy hunting buffalo		3·00	3·75
973	$2 Mickey Mouse and silver mine		3·50	4·50
MS974 127×101 mm. $5 Mickey Mouse driving stagecoach			8·00	7·50

1985. Birth Bicentenaries of Grimm Brothers (folklorists). As T **119** of Anguilla showing Walt Disney cartoon characters in scenes from "Spindle, Shuttle and Needle". Multicoloured.
975	30c. The Prince (Mickey Mouse) searches for a bride		1·25	40
976	60c. The Prince finds the Orphan Girl (Minnie Mouse)		1·75	80
977	70c. The Spindle finds the Prince		2·00	1·40
978	$1 The Needle tidies the Girl's home		2·50	1·75
979	$3 The Prince proposes		4·75	7·50
MS980 125×101 mm. $5 The Orphan Girl and spinning wheel on Prince's horse			8·00	7·50

208 Benjamin Franklin and U.N. (New York) 1953 U.P.U. 5c. Stamp

1985. 40th Anniv of United Nations Organization. Multicoloured.
981	40c. Type **208**		1·00	70
982	$1 George Washington Carver (agricultural chemist) and 1982 Nature Conservation 28c. stamp		2·00	2·00
983	$3 Charles Lindbergh (aviator) and 1978 I.C.A.O. 25c. stamp		4·75	7·50
MS984 101×77 mm. $5 Marc Chagall (artist) (vert)			6·50	4·75

Nos. 981/4 each include a United Nations (New York) stamp design.

209 Madonna and Child (De Landi)

1985. Christmas. Religious Paintings. Multicoloured.
985	10c. Type **209**		30	15
986	25c. Madonna and Child (Berlinghiero)		55	25
987	60c. The Nativity (Fra Angelico)		70	60
988	$4 Presentation in the Temple (Giovanni di Paolo)		1·75	4·25
MS989 113×81 mm. $5 The Nativity (Antoniazzo Romano)			3·00	3·75

1986. Birth Bicentenary of John J. Audubon (ornithologist) (2nd issue). As T **198** showing original paintings. Multicoloured.
990	60c. Mallard		2·25	1·50
991	90c. North American black duck ("Dusky Duck")		2·75	2·00
992	$1.50 Pintail ("Common Pintail")		3·50	4·50
993	$3 American wigeon ("Wigeon")		4·75	6·50
MS994 102×73 mm. Eider ("Common Eider")			7·00	5·50

210 Football, Boots and Trophy

1986. World Cup Football Championship, Mexico. Multicoloured.
995	30c. Type **210**		1·50	40
996	60c. Goalkeeper (vert)		2·00	85
997	$1 Referee blowing whistle (vert)		2·50	1·75
998	$4 Ball in net		6·50	9·00
MS999 87×76 mm. $5 Two players competing for ball			8·50	7·50

1986. Appearance of Halley's Comet (1st issue). As T **123** of Anguilla. Multicoloured.
1000	5c. Edmond Halley and Old Greenwich Observatory		30	20
1001	10c. Messerschmitt Me 163B Komet (fighter aircraft), 1944		30	15
1002	60c. Montezuma (Aztec emperor) and Comet in 1517 (from Historias de las Indias de Neuva Espana)		1·50	70
1003	$4 Pocahontas saving Capt. John Smith and Comet in 1607		4·50	5·50
MS1004 101×70 mm. $5 Halley's Comet over English Harbour, Antigua			3·50	3·75

See also Nos. 1047/51.

1986. 60th Birthday of Queen Elizabeth II. As T **125** of Anguilla.
1005	60c. black and yellow		30	35
1006	$1 multicoloured		50	55
1007	$4 multicoloured		1·40	1·90
MS1008 120×85 mm. $5 black and brown			2·00	3·00

DESIGNS: 60c. Wedding photograph, 1947; $1 Queen at Trooping the Colour; $4 In Scotland; $5 Queen Mary and Princess Elizabeth, 1927.

211 Tug

1986. Local Boats. Multicoloured.
1009	30c. Type **211**		25	20
1010	60c. Game fishing boat		45	35
1011	$1 Yacht		75	60
1012	$4 Lugger with auxiliary sail		2·50	3·25
MS1013 108×78 mm. $5 Boats under construction			3·00	4·00

212 Hiawatha express

1986. "Ameripex '86" International Stamp Exhibition, Chicago. Famous American Trains. Multicoloured.
1014	25c. Type **212**		1·25	50
1015	50c. Grand Canyon express		1·50	80
1016	$1 Powhattan Arrow express		1·75	1·75
1017	$3 Empire State express		3·00	6·00
MS1018 116×87 mm. $5 Southern Pacific Daylight express			6·00	11·00

213 Prince Andrew and Miss Sarah Ferguson

1986. Royal Wedding. Multicoloured.
1019	45c. Type **213**		70	35
1020	60c. Prince Andrew		80	45
1021	$4 Prince Andrew with Prince Philip		2·75	3·50
MS1022 88×88 mm. $5 Prince Andrew and Miss Sarah Ferguson (different)			5·00	4·50

214 Fly-specked Cerith

1986. Sea Shells. Multicoloured.
1023	15c. Type **214**		75	50
1024	45c. Smooth Scotch bonnet		1·75	1·25
1025	60c. West Indian crown conch		2·00	2·00
1026	$3 Ciboney murex		5·50	10·00
MS1027 109×75 mm. $5 Colourful Atlantic moon (horiz)			7·50	8·50

215 Water Lily

1986. Flowers. Multicoloured.

1028	10c. Type **215**	20	15
1029	15c. Queen of the night	20	15
1030	50c. Cup of gold	55	55
1031	60c. Beach morning glory	70	70
1032	70c. Golden trumpet	80	80
1033	$1 Air plant	90	1·10
1034	$4 Purple wreath	1·75	3·00
1035	$4 Zephyr lily	2·00	3·75
MS1036	Two sheets, each 102×72 mm. (a) $4 Dozakie. (b) $5 Four o'clock flower Set of 2 sheets	5·00	7·50

1986. World Cup Football Championship Winners, Mexico. Nos. 995/8 optd WINNERS Argentina 3 W.Germany 2.

1037	30c. Type **210**	1·25	40
1038	60c. Goalkeeper (vert)	1·75	75
1039	$1 Referee blowing whistle (vert)	2·25	1·10
1040	$4 Ball in net	5·50	4·50
MS1041	87×76 mm. $5 Two players competing for ball	5·50	4·00

217 *Hygrocybe occidentalis var. scarletina*

1986. Mushrooms. Multicoloured.

1042	10c. Type **217**	30	25
1043	50c. *Trogia buccinalis*	70	55
1044	$1 *Collybia subpruinosa*	1·00	1·25
1045	$4 *Leucocoprinus brebissonii*	2·50	4·50
MS1046	102×82 mm. $5 *Pyrrhoglossum pyrrhum*	13·00	11·00

(218)

1986. Appearance of Halley's Comet (2nd issue). Nos. 1000/3 optd with T 218.

1047	5c. Edmond Halley and Old Greenwich Observatory	20	10
1048	10c. Messerschmitt Me 163B Komet (fighter aircraft), 1944	50	10
1049	60c. Montezuma (Aztec emperor) and Comet in 1517 (from *Historias de las Indias de Neuva Espana*)	1·25	65
1050	$4 Pocahontas saving Capt. John Smith and Comet in 1607	4·50	4·00
MS1051	101×70 mm. $5 Halley's Comet over English Harbour, Antigua	6·00	6·50

219 Auburn "Speedster" (1933)

1986. Centenary of First Benz Motor Car. Multicoloured.

1052	10c. Type **219**	20	10
1053	15c. Mercury "Sable" (1986)	25	10
1054	50c. Cadillac (1950)	60	30
1055	60c. Studebaker (1950)	75	45
1056	70c. Lagonda "V-12" (1939)	85	55
1057	$1 Adler "Standard" (1930)	1·25	75
1058	$3 DKW (1956)	2·50	3·00
1059	$4 Mercedes "500K" (1936)	3·00	3·00
MS1060	Two sheets, each 99×70 mm. (a) $5 Daimler (1896). (b) $5 Mercedes "Knight" (1921) Set of 2 sheets	9·00	6·50

220 Young Mickey Mouse playing Santa Claus

1986. Christmas. Designs showing Walt Disney cartoon characters as babies. Multicoloured.

1061	25c. Type **220**	60	35
1062	30c. Mickey and Minnie Mouse building snowman	70	40
1063	40c. Aunt Matilda and Goofy baking	75	45
1064	60c. Goofy and Pluto	1·00	85
1065	70c. Pluto, Donald and Daisy Duck carol singing	1·10	1·00

1066	$1.50 Donald Duck, Mickey Mouse and Pluto stringing popcorn	1·75	2·50
1067	$3 Grandma Duck and Minnie Mouse	3·00	4·50
1068	$4 Donald Duck and Pete	3·25	4·50
MS1069	Two sheets, each 127×102 mm. (a) $5 Goofy, Donald Duck and Minnie Mouse playing with reindeer. (b) $5 Mickey Mouse, Donald and Daisy Duck playing with toys Set of 2 sheets	13·00	14·00

221 Arms of Antigua

1986

1070	**221**	10c. blue	1·00	1·00
1071	-	25c. red	1·00	1·00

DESIGN: 25c. Flag of Antigua.

222 *Canada I* (1981)

1987. America's Cup Yachting Championship. Multicoloured.

1072	30c. Type **222**	45	20
1073	60c. *Gretel II* (1970)	60	50
1074	$1 *Sceptre* (1958)	85	1·00
1075	$3 *Vigilant* (1893)	1·75	3·00
MS1076	113×84 mm. $5 *Australia II* defeating *Liberty* (1983) (horiz)	4·00	5·00

223 Bridled Burrfish

1987. Marine Life. Multicoloured.

1077	15c. Type **223**	2·50	50
1078	30c. Common noddy ("Brown Noddy")	5·00	60
1079	40c. Nassau grouper	3·00	70
1080	50c. Laughing gull	6·00	1·50
1081	60c. French angelfish	3·50	1·50
1082	$1 Porkfish	3·50	1·75
1083	$2 Royal tern	8·00	6·00
1084	$3 Sooty tern	8·00	8·00
MS1085	Two sheets, each 120×94 mm. (a) $5 Banded butterflyfish. (b) $5 Brown booby Set of 2 sheets	17·00	14·00

Nos. 1078, 1080 and 1083/5 are without the World Wildlife Fund logo shown on Type **223**.

224 Handball

1987. Olympic Games, Seoul (1988) (1st issue). Multicoloured.

1086	10c. Type **224**	60	10
1087	60c. Fencing	85	35
1088	$1 Gymnastics	1·00	80
1089	$3 Football	2·25	4·00
MS1090	100×72 mm. $5 Boxing gloves	3·00	4·25

See also Nos. 1222/6.

225 *The Profile*

1987. Birth Centenary of Marc Chagall (artist). Multicoloured.

1091	10c. Type **225**	30	15
1092	30c. *Portrait of the Artist's Sister*	45	30
1093	40c. *Bride with Fan*	50	40
1094	60c. *David in Profile*	55	45
1095	90c. *Fiancee with Bouquet*	75	60

1096	$1 *Self Portrait with Brushes*	75	65
1097	$3 *The Walk*	1·75	2·25
1098	$4 *Three Candles*	2·00	2·50
MS1099	Two sheets, each 110×95 mm. (a) $5 *Fall of Icarus* (104×89 mm). (b) $5 *Myth of Orpheus* (104×89 mm). Imperf Set of 2 sheets	6·50	6·00

226 *Spirit of Australia* (fastest powerboat), 1978

1987. Milestones of Transportation. Multicoloured.

1100	10c. Type **226**	80	40
1101	15c. Werner von Siemens's electric locomotive, 1879	1·50	50
1102	30c. U.S.S. *Triton* (first submerged circum-navigation), 1960	1·25	50
1103	50c. Trevithick's steam carriage (first passenger-carrying vehicle), 1801	1·75	60
1104	60c. U.S.S. *New Jersey* (battleship), 1942	1·75	85
1105	70c. Draisaine bicycle, 1818	2·00	1·00
1106	90c. *United States* (liner) (holder of Blue Riband), 1952	1·75	1·00
1107	$1.50 Cierva C.4 (first autogyro), 1923	1·75	2·75
1108	$2 Curtiss NC-4 flying boat (first transatlantic flight), 1919	2·00	3·00
1109	$3 *Queen Elizabeth 2* (liner), 1969	3·50	4·50

227 Lee Iacocca at Unveiling of Restored Statue

1987. Centenary of Statue of Liberty (1986) (2nd issue). Multicoloured.

1110	15c. Type **227**	15	15
1111	30c. Statue at sunset (side view)	20	20
1112	45c. Aerial view of head	30	30
1113	50c. Lee Iacocca and torch	35	35
1114	60c. Workmen inside head of Statue (horiz)	35	35
1115	90c. Restoration work (horiz)	50	50
1116	$1 Head of Statue	55	55
1117	$2 Statue at sunset (front view)	1·00	1·50
1118	$3 Inspecting restoration work (horiz)	1·00	2·00
1119	$5 Statue at night	1·75	3·50

228 Grace Kelly

1987. Entertainers. Multicoloured.

1120	15c. Type **228**	90	40
1121	30c. Marilyn Monroe	2·75	80
1122	45c. Orson Welles	90	60
1123	50c. Judy Garland	90	65
1124	60c. John Lennon	4·25	1·25
1125	$1 Rock Hudson	1·40	1·10
1126	$2 John Wayne	2·50	2·00
1127	$3 Elvis Presley	10·00	4·50

229 Scouts around Camp Fire and Red Kangaroo

1987. 16th World Scout Jamboree, Australia. Multicoloured.

1128	10c. Type **229**	65	20
1129	60c. Scouts canoeing and blue-winged kookaburra	1·25	80
1130	$1 Scouts on assault course and ring-tailed rock wallaby	1·00	85
1131	$3 Field kitchen and koala	1·50	4·25
MS1132	103×78 mm. $5 Flags of Antigua, Australia and Scout Movement	3·25	3·50

230 Whistling Frog

1987. "Capex '87" International Stamp Exhibition, Toronto. Reptiles and Amphibians. Mult.

1133	30c. Type **230**	55	20
1134	60c. Croaking lizard	75	40
1135	$1 Antiguan anole	1·00	70
1136	$3 Red-footed tortoise	2·00	3·00
MS1137	106×76 mm. $5 Ground lizard	2·25	2·75

1987. Tenth Death Anniv of Elvis Presley (entertainer). No. 1127 optd 10th ANNIVERSARY 16th AUGUST 1987.

1138	$3 Elvis Presley	8·00	4·75

232 House of Burgesses, Virginia ("Freedom of Speech")

1987. Bicentenary of U.S. Constitution. Multicoloured.

1139	15c. Type **232**	10	10
1140	45c. State Seal, Connecticut	20	25
1141	60c. State Seal, Delaware	25	35
1142	$4 Governor Morris (Pennsylvania delegate) (vert)	1·75	2·25
MS1143	105×75 mm. $5 Roger Sherman (Connecticut delegate) (vert)	2·00	2·75

233 *Madonna and Child* (Bernardo Daddi)

1987. Christmas. Religious Paintings. Multicoloured.

1144	45c. Type **233**	50	15
1145	60c. St. Joseph (detail, *The Nativity* (Sano di Pietro))	65	30
1146	$1 Virgin Mary (detail, *The Nativity* (Sano di Pietro))	85	55
1147	$4 *Music-making Angel* (Melozzo da Forli)	2·25	3·50
MS1148	99×70 mm. $5 *The Flight into Egypt* (Sano di Pietro)	2·25	2·75

234 Wedding Photograph, 1947

1988. Royal Ruby Wedding.

1149	**234**	25c. brown, black and blue	30	15
1150	-	60c. multicoloured	60	40
1151	-	$2 brown, black and green	1·10	1·10
1152	-	$3 multicoloured	1·50	1·60
MS1153	107×77 mm. $5 multicoloured		2·50	2·75

DESIGNS: 60c. Queen Elizabeth II; $2 Princess Elizabeth and Prince Philip with Prince Charles at his christening, 1948; $3 Queen Elizabeth (from photo by Tim Graham), 1980; $5 Royal family, 1952.

235 Great Blue Heron

1988. Birds of Antigua. Multicoloured.

1154	10c. Type **235**	50	40
1155	15c. Ringed kingfisher (horiz)	55	40
1156	50c. Bananaquit (horiz)	1·00	50
1157	60c. American purple gallinule ("Purple Gallinule") (horiz)	1·00	50
1158	70c. Blue-hooded euphonia (horiz)	1·10	55

1159	$1 Brown-throated conure ("Caribbean Parakeet")	1·40	75
1160	$3 Troupial (horiz)	2·50	3·50
1161	$4 Purple-throated carib ("Hummingbird") (horiz)	2·50	3·50
MS1162	Two sheets, each 115×86 mm. (a) $5 Greater flamingo. (b) $5 Brown pelican Set of 2 sheets	4·50	5·50

236 First Aid at Daycare Centre, Antigua

1988. Salvation Army's Community Service. Multicoloured.

1163	25c. Type **236**	80	65
1164	30c. Giving penicillin injection, Indonesia	80	65
1165	40c. Children at daycare centre, Bolivia	90	75
1166	45c. Rehabilitation of the handicapped, India	90	75
1167	50c. Training blind man, Kenya	1·00	1·25
1168	60c. Weighing baby, Ghana	1·00	1·25
1169	$1 Training typist, Zambia	1·40	1·75
1170	$2 Emergency food kitchen, Sri Lanka	2·00	3·50
MS1171	152×83 mm. $5 General Eva Burrows	3·75	4·50

237 Columbus's Second Fleet, 1493

1988. 500th Anniv (1992) of Discovery of America by Columbus (1st issue). Multicoloured.

1172	10c. Type **237**	80	40
1173	30c. Painos. Indian village and fleet	80	45
1174	45c. *Santa Mariagalante* (flagship) and Painos. village	1·25	45
1175	60c. Painos Indians offering Columbus fruit and vegetables	80	50
1176	90c. Painos Indian and Columbus with scarlet macaw	2·50	1·00
1177	$1 Columbus landing on island	1·75	1·00
1178	$3 Spanish soldier and fleet	2·50	3·25
1179	$4 Fleet under sail	2·75	3·25
MS1180	Two sheets, each 110×80 mm. (a) $5 Queen Isabella's cross. (b) $5 Gold coin of Ferdinand and Isabella Set of 2 sheets	6·50	7·00

See also Nos. 1267/71, 1360/8, 1503/11, 1654/60 and 1670/1.

238 Bust of Christ

1988. Easter. 500th Birth Anniv of Titian (artist). Multicoloured.

1181	30c. Type **238**	40	20
1182	40c. *Scourging of Christ*	45	25
1183	45c. *Madonna in Glory with Saints*	45	25
1184	50c. *The Averoldi Polyptych* (detail)	45	35
1185	$1 *Christ Crowned with Thorns*	70	55
1186	$2 *Christ Mocked*	1·10	1·25
1187	$3 *Christ and Simon of Cyrene*	1·50	1·75
1188	$4 *Crucifixion with Virgin and Saints*	1·75	2·25
MS1189	Two sheets, each 110×95 mm. (a) $5 *Ecce Homo* (detail). (b) $5 *Noli me Tangere* (detail) Set of 2 sheets	5·50	7·50

239 Two Yachts rounding Buoy

1988. Sailing Week. Multicoloured.

1190	30c. Type **239**	35	20
1191	60c. Three yachts	50	40
1192	$1 British yacht under way	60	55
1193	$3 Three yachts (different)	1·10	2·50
MS1194	103×92 mm. $5 Two yachts	1·75	3·25

240 Mickey Mouse and Diver with Porpoise

1988. Disney EPCOT Centre, Orlando, Florida. Designs showing cartoon characters and exhibits. Multicoloured.

1195	1c. Type **240**	10	10
1196	2c. Goofy and Mickey Mouse with futuristic car (vert)	10	10
1197	3c. Mickey Mouse and Goofy as Atlas (vert)	10	10
1198	4c. Mickey Mouse and "Edaphosaurus" (prehistoric reptile)	10	10
1199	5c. Mickey Mouse at Journey into Imagination exhibit	15	10
1200	10c. Mickey Mouse collecting vegetables (vert)	20	10
1201	25c. Type **240**	55	25
1202	30c. As 2c.	55	25
1203	40c. As 3c.	60	30
1204	60c. As 4c.	85	50
1205	70c. As 5c.	95	60
1206	$1.50 As 10c.	2·00	2·00
1207	$3 Goofy and Mickey Mouse with robot (vert)	2·50	2·75
1208	$4 Mickey Mouse and Clarabelle at Horizons exhibit	2·50	2·75
MS1209	Two sheets, each 125×99 mm. (a) $5 Mickey Mouse and monorail (vert). (b) $5 Mickey Mouse flying over EPCOT Centre Set of 2 sheets	7·00	6·50

1988. Stamp Exhibitions. Nos. 1083/4 optd.

1210	$2 Royal tern (optd **Praga '88**, Prague)	7·00	3·50
1211	$3 Sooty tern (optd **INDEPENDENCE 40**, Israel)	7·00	4·00
MS1212	Two sheets, each 120×94 mm. (a) $5 Banded butterflyfish (optd **"OLYM-PHILEX '88"**, Seoul). (b) $5 brown booby (optd **"FINLANDIA 88"**, Helsinki). Set of 2 sheets	23·00	14·00

242 Jacaranda

1988. Flowering Trees. Multicoloured.

1213	10c. Type **242**	30	20
1214	30c. Cordia	40	20
1215	50c. Orchid tree	60	40
1216	90c. Flamboyant	70	50
1217	$1 African tulip tree	75	55
1218	$2 Potato tree	1·40	1·60
1219	$3 Crepe myrtle	1·60	2·00
1220	$4 Pitch apple	1·75	2·75
MS1221	Two sheets, each 106×76 mm. (a) $5 Cassia. (b) $5 Chinaberry Set of 2 sheets	5·00	6·00

243 Gymnastics

1988. Olympic Games, Seoul (2nd issue). Multicoloured.

1222	40c. Type **243**	30	25
1223	60c. Weightlifting	40	30
1224	$1 Water polo (horiz)	80	50
1225	$3 Boxing (horiz)	1·50	2·25
MS1226	114×80 mm. $5 Runner with Olympic torch	2·00	3·00

244 *Danaus plexippus*

1988. Caribbean Butterflies. Multicoloured.

1227	1c. Type **244**	60	1·25
1228	2c. *Greta diaphanus*	70	1·25
1229	3c. *Calisto archebates*	70	1·25
1230	5c. *Hamadryas feronia*	85	1·25
1231	10c. *Mestra dorcas*	1·00	30
1232	15c. *Hypolimnas misippus*	1·50	30
1233	20c. *Dione juno*	1·60	30
1234	25c. *Heliconius charithonia*	1·60	30
1235	30c. *Eurema pyro*	1·60	30
1236	40c. *Papilio androgeus*	1·60	30
1237	45c. *Anteos maerula*	1·60	30
1238	50c. *Aphrissa orbis*	1·75	45
1239	60c. *Astraptes xagua*	2·00	60
1240	$1 *Heliopetes arsalte*	2·25	1·00
1241	$2 *Polites baracoa*	3·25	3·75
1242	$2.50 *Phocides pigmalion*	4·00	5·00
1243	$5 *Prepona amphitoe*	5·50	8·00
1244	$10 *Oarisma nanus*	7·50	12·00
1244a	$20 *Parides lycimenes*	17·00	22·00

245 President Kennedy and Family

1988. 25th Death Anniv of John F. Kennedy (American statesman). Multicoloured.

1245	1c. Type **245**	10	10
1246	2c. Kennedy commanding "PT109"	10	10
1247	3c. Funeral cortege	10	10
1248	4c. In motorcade, Mexico City	10	10
1249	30c. As 1c.	35	15
1250	60c. As 4c.	1·00	40
1251	$1 As 3c.	1·10	75
1252	$4 As 2c.	3·00	3·50
MS1253	105×75 mm. $5 Kennedy taking presidential oath of office	2·50	3·25

246 Minnie Mouse carol singing

1988. Christmas. "Mickey's Christmas Chorale". Design showing Walt Disney cartoon characters. Multicoloured.

1254	10c. Type **246**	40	30
1255	25c. Pluto	55	45
1256	30c. Mickey Mouse playing ukelele	55	45
1257	70c. Donald Duck and nephew	90	80
1258	$1 Mordie and Ferdie carol singing	90	1·00
1259	$1 Goofy carol singing	90	1·00
1260	$1 Chip n'Dale sliding off roof	90	1·00
1261	$1 Two of Donald Duck's nephews at window	90	1·00
1262	$1 As 10c.	90	1·00
1263	$1 As 25c.	90	1·00
1264	$1 As 30c.	90	1·00
1265	$1 As 70c.	90	1·00
MS1266	Two sheets, each 127×102 mm. (a) $7 Donald Duck playing trumpet and Mickey and Minnie Mouse in carriage. (b) $7 Mickey Mouse and friends singing carols on roller skates (horiz) Set of 2 sheets	8·50	8·50

Nos. 1258/65 were printed together, *se-tenant*, forming a composite design.

247 Arawak Warriors

1989. 500th Anniv of Discovery of America by Columbus (1992) (2nd issue). Pre-Columbian Arawak Society. Multicoloured.

1267	$1.50 Type **247**	1·10	1·40
1268	$1.50 Whip dancers	1·10	1·40
1269	$1.50 Whip dancers and chief with pineapple	1·10	1·40
1270	$1.50 Family and camp fire	1·10	1·40
MS1271	71×84 mm. $6 Arawak chief	2·75	3·00

Nos. 1267/70 were printed together, *se-tenant*, forming a composite design.

248 de Havilland Comet 4 Airliner

1989. 50th Anniv of First Jet Flight. Multicoloured.

1272	10c. Type **248**	90	45
1273	30c. Messerschmitt Me 262 fighter	1·50	45
1274	40c. Boeing 707 airliner	1·50	45
1275	60c. Canadair CL-13 Sabre (inscr "F-86") fighter	1·90	55
1276	$1 Lockheed F-104 Starfighters	2·25	1·10
1277	$2 McDonnell Douglas DC-10 airliner	3·00	3·00
1278	$3 Boeing 747-300/400 airliner	3·25	4·50
1279	$4 McDonnell Douglas F-4 Phantom II fighter	3·25	4·50
MS1280	Two sheets, each 114×83 mm. (a) $7 Grumman F-14A Tomcat fighter. (b) $7 Concorde airliner Set of 2 sheets	11·00	13·00

249 *Festivale*

1989. Caribbean Cruise Ships. Multicoloured.

1281	25c. Type **249**	2·00	50
1282	45c. *Southward*	2·25	50
1283	50c. *Sagafjord*	2·25	50
1284	60c. *Daphne*	2·25	60
1285	75c. *Cunard Countess*	2·50	1·00
1286	90c. *Song of America*	2·75	1·10
1287	$3 *Island Princess*	4·25	5·50
1288	$4 *Galileo*	4·25	6·00
MS1289	(a) 113×87 mm. $6 *Norway*. (b) 111×82 mm. $6 *Oceanic* Set of 2 sheets	7·50	11·00

250 Fish swimming by Duck half-submerged in Stream

1989. Japanese Art. Paintings by Hiroshige. Multicoloured.

1290	25c. Type **250**	1·00	50
1291	45c. *Crane and Wave*	1·25	50
1292	50c. *Sparrows and Morning Glories*	1·40	50
1293	60c. *Crested Blackbird and Flowering Cherry*	1·50	60
1294	$1 *Great Knot sitting among Water Grass*	1·75	80
1295	$2 *Goose on a Bank of Water*	2·50	2·50
1296	$3 *Black Paradise Flycatcher and Blossoms*	3·00	3·00
1297	$4 *Sleepy Owl perched on a Pine Branch*	3·00	3·00
MS1298	Two sheets, each 102×75 mm. (a) $5 *Bullfinch flying near a Clematis Branch*. (b) $5 *Titmouse on a Cherry Branch* Set of 2 sheets	9·00	9·50

251 Mickey and Minnie Mouse in Helicopter over River Seine

1989. "Philexfrance 89" International Stamp Exhibition, Paris. Walt Disney cartoon characters in Paris. Multicoloured.

1299	1c. Type **251**	10	10
1300	2c. Goofy and Mickey Mouse passing Arc de Triomphe	10	10
1301	3c. Mickey Mouse painting picture of Notre Dame	10	10
1302	4c. Mickey and Minnie Mouse with Pluto leaving Metro station	10	10
1303	5c. Minnie Mouse as model in fashion show	10	10
1304	10c. Daisy Duck, Minnie Mouse and Clarabelle as Folies Bergere dancers	10	10

1305 $5 Mickey and Minnie Mouse
 shopping in street market 7·00 7·00

1306 $6 Mickey and Minnie Mouse,
 Jose Carioca and Donald
 Duck at pavement cafe 7·00 7·00

MS1307 Two sheets, each 127×101
 mm. (a) $5 Mickey and Minnie
 Mouse in hot air balloon. (b) $5
 Mickey Mouse at Pompidou Centre
 cafe (vert) Set of 2 sheets 11·00 13·00

252 Goalkeeper

1989. World Cup Football Championship, Italy (1990).
Multicoloured.

1308 15c. Type **252** 85 30
1309 25c. Goalkeeper moving
 towards ball 90 30
1310 $1 Goalkeeper reaching for ball 1·50 1·25
1311 $4 Goalkeeper saving goal 3·00 5·00

MS1312 Two sheets, each 75×105 mm.
 (a) $5 Three players competing for
 ball (horiz). (b) $5 Ball and player'
 legs (horiz) Set of 2 sheets 7·00 10·00

253 *Mycena pura*

1989. Fungi. Multicoloured.

1313 10c. Type **253** 75 50
1314 25c. *Psathyrella tuberculata*
 (vert) 1·10 40
1315 50c. *Psilocybe cubensis* 1·50 60
1316 60c. *Leptonia caeruleocapitata*
 (vert) 1·50 70
1317 75c. *Xeromphalina tenuipes*
 (vert) 1·75 1·10
1318 $1 *Chlorophyllum molybdites*
 (vert) 1·75 1·25
1319 $3 *Marasmius haematocephalus* 2·75 3·75
1320 $4 *Cantharellus cinnabarinus* 2·75 3·75

MS1321 Two sheets, each 88×62 mm.
 (a) $6 *Leucopaxillus gracillimus*
 (vert). (b) $6 *Volvariella volvacea* Set
 of 2 sheets 13·00 15·00

254 Desmarest's Hutia

1989. Local Fauna. Multicoloured.

1322 25c. Type **254** 80 50
1323 45c. Caribbean monk seal 2·50 1·00
1324 80c. Mustache bat (vert) 1·50 1·00
1325 $4 American manatee (vert) 3·50 5·50

MS1326 113×87 mm. $5 West Indian
 giant rice rat 7·00 9·00

255 Goofy and Old
Printing Press

1989. "American Philately". Walt Disney cartoon
characters with stamps and the logo of the
American Philatelic Society. Multicoloured.

1327 1c. Type **255** 10 10
1328 2c. Donald Duck cancelling first
 day cover for Mickey Mouse 10 10
1329 3c. Donald Duck's nephews
 reading recruiting poster for
 Pony Express riders 10 10
1330 4c. Morty and Ferdie as early
 radio broadcasters 10 10
1331 5c. Donald Duck and water buf-
 falo watching television 10 10
1332 10c. Donald Duck with stamp
 album 10 10
1333 $4 Daisy Duck with computer
 system 4·75 6·00

1334 $6 Donald's nephews with
 stereo radio, trumpet and
 guitar 6·00 7·00

MS1335 Two sheets, each 127×102
 mm. (a) $5 Donald's nephews donat-
 ing stamps to charity. (b) $5 Minnie
 Mouse flying mailplane upside down
 (horiz) Set of 2 sheets 11·00 13·00

256 Mickey Mouse and Donald
Duck with Camden and Amboy
Locomotive *John Bull*, 1831

1989. "World Stamp Expo '89" International Stamp
Exhibition, Washington. Walt Disney cartoon
characters and locomotives. Mult.

1336 25c. Type **256** 90 50
1337 45c. Mickey Mouse and friends
 with *Atlantic*, 1832 1·10 50
1338 50c. Mickey Mouse and Goofy
 with *William Crooks*, 1861 1·10 50
1339 60c. Mickey Mouse and Goofy
 with *Minnetonka*, 1869 1·10 65
1340 $1 Chip n'Dale with *Thatcher
 Perkins*, 1863 1·40 75
1341 $2 Mickey and Minnie Mouse
 with *Pioneer*, 1848 2·25 2·25
1342 $3 Mickey Mouse and Donald
 Duck with cog railway loco-
 motive *Peppersass*, 1869 3·00 4·00
1343 $4 Mickey Mouse with Huey,
 Dewey and Louie aboard
 N.Y. World's Fair *Gimbels
 Flyer*, 1939 3·25 4·00

MS1344 Two sheets, each 127×101
 mm. (a) $6 Mickey Mouse and loco-
 motive *Thomas Jefferson*, 1835 (vert).
 (b) $6 Mickey Mouse and friends
 at Central Pacific *Golden Spike*
 ceremony, 1869 Set of 2 sheets 8·50 10·00

258 Launch of
"Apollo II"

1989. 20th Anniv of First Manned Landing on Moon.
Multicoloured.

1346 10c. Type **258** 50 30
1347 45c. Aldrin on Moon 1·25 30
1348 $1 Module "Eagle" over Moon
 (horiz) 1·75 1·10
1349 $4 Recovery of "Apollo II" crew
 after splashdown (horiz) 2·75 5·00

MS1350 107×77 mm. $5 Astronaut Neil
 Armstrong 4·50 5·50

259 *The Small
Cowper Madonna*
(Raphael)

1989. Christmas. Paintings by Raphael and Giotto.
Multicoloured.

1351 10c. Type **259** 30 15
1352 25c. *Madonna of the Goldfinch*
 (Raphael) 45 20
1353 30c. *The Alba Madonna*
 (Raphael) 45 20
1354 50c. Saint (detail, "Bologna
 Altarpiece") (Giotto) 65 30
1355 60c. Angel (detail, "Bologna
 Altarpiece") (Giotto) 70 35
1356 70c. Angel slaying serpent
 (detail, "Bologna Altarpiece")
 (Giotto) 80 40
1357 $4 Evangelist (detail, "Bologna
 Altarpiece") (Giotto) 3·00 4·50
1358 $5 *Madonna of Foligno* (detail)
 (Raphael) 3·00 4·50

MS1359 Two sheets, each 71×96 mm.
 (a) $5 "The Marriage of the Virgin (de-
 tail) (Raphael). (b) $5 Madonna and
 Child (detail, "Bologna Altarpiece")
 (Giotto) Set of 2 sheets 9·00 12·00

260 Star-eyed
Hermit Crab

1990. 500th Anniv (1992) of Discovery of America by
Columbus (3rd issue). New World Natural History–
Marine Life. Multicoloured.

1360 10c. Type **260** 45 20
1361 20c. Spiny lobster 65 25
1362 25c. Magnificent banded
 fanworm 65 25
1363 45c. Cannonball jellyfish 80 40
1364 60c. Red-spiny sea star 1·00 60
1365 $2 Peppermint shrimp 2·00 1·50
1366 $3 Coral crab 2·25 3·75
1367 $4 Branching fire coral 2·25 3·75

MS1368 Two sheets, each 100×69 mm.
 (a) $5 Common sea fan. (b) $5 Por-
 tuguese man-of-war Set of 2 sheets 8·00 9·00

261 *Vanilla
mexicana*

1990. "Expo '90" International Garden and Greenery
Exhibition, Osaka. Orchids. Multicoloured.

1369 15c. Type **261** 75 50
1370 45c. *Epidendrum ibaguense* 1·10 50
1371 50c. *Epidendrum secundum* 1·25 55
1372 60c. *Maxillaria conferta* 1·40 55
1373 $1 *Oncidium altissimum* 1·50 1·00
1374 $2 *Spiranthes lanceolata* 2·00 2·50
1375 $3 *Tonopsis utricularioides* 2·25 3·50
1376 $5 *Epidendrum nocturnum* 3·25 4·50

MS1377 Two sheets, each 102×70
 mm. (a) $6 *Octomeria graminifolia*.
 (b) $6 *Rodriguezia lanceolata* Set
 of 2 sheets 6·50 8·00

262 Queen Victoria and
Queen Elizabeth II

1990. 150th Anniv of the Penny Black.

1378 **262** 45c. green 1·25 40
1379 - 60c. mauve 1·50 65
1380 - $5 blue 3·75 5·50

MS1381 102×80 mm. Type **262** $6
 purple 5·00 6·50

DESIGNS: 60c., $5 As Type **262**, but with different back-
grounds.

263 *"Britannia"* (mail
paddle-steamer), 1840

1990. "Stamp World London '90" International Stamp
Exhibition.

1382 **263** 50c. green and red 1·25 35
1383 - 75c. brown and red 1·50 90
1384 - $4 blue and red 4·00 5·50

MS1385 – 104×81 mm. $6 brown
 and red 4·50 6·00

DESIGNS: 75c. Travelling Post Office sorting van, 1892; $4
Short S.23 Empire "C" Class flying boat *Centaurus*, 1938;
$6 Post Office underground railway, London, 1927.

264 Flamefish

1990. Reef Fish. Multicoloured.

1386 10c. Type **264** 65 55
1387 15c. Coney 80 55
1388 50c. Long-spined squirrelfish 1·25 60
1389 60c. Sergeant major 1·25 60
1390 $1 Yellow-tailed snapper 1·50 85

1391 $2 Rock beauty 2·25 2·75
1392 $3 Spanish hogfish 2·75 3·75
1393 $4 Striped parrotfish 2·75 3·75

MS1394 Two sheets, each 90×70 mm.
 (a) $5 Black-barred soldierfish. (b)
 $4 Four-eyed butterflyfish Set of
 2 sheets 10·00 11·00

265 "Voyager 2"
passing Saturn

1990. Achievement in Space. Multicoloured.

1395 45c. Type **265** 1·10 85
1396 45c. "Pioneer 11" photograph-
 ing Saturn 1·10 85
1397 45c. Astronaut in transporter 1·10 85
1398 45c. Space shuttle "Columbia" 1·10 85
1399 45c. "Apollo 10" command
 module on parachutes 1·10 85
1400 45c. "Skylab" space station 1·10 85
1401 45c. Astronaut Edward White
 in space 1·10 85
1402 45c. "Apollo" spacecraft on joint
 mission 1·10 85
1403 45c. "Soyuz" spacecraft on joint
 mission 1·10 85
1404 45c. "Mariner 1" passing Venus 1·10 85
1405 45c. "Gemini 4" capsule 1·10 85
1406 45c. "Sputnik 1" 1·10 85
1407 45c. Hubble space telescope 1·10 85
1408 45c. North American X-15
 rocket plane 1·10 85
1409 45c. Bell XS-1 airplane 1·10 85
1410 45c. "Apollo 17" astronaut and
 lunar rock formation 1·10 85
1411 45c. Lunar Rover 1·10 85
1412 45c. "Apollo 14" lunar module 1·10 85
1413 45c. Astronaut Buzz Aldrin
 on Moon 1·10 85
1414 45c. Soviet "Lunokhod" lunar
 vehicle 1·10 85

266 Queen Mother
in Evening Dress

1990. 90th Birthday of Queen Elizabeth the Queen
Mother.

1415 **266** 15c. multicoloured 55 20
1416 - 35c. multicoloured 75 25
1417 - 75c. multicoloured 1·00 85
1418 - $3 multicoloured 2·50 3·50

MS1419 – 67×98 mm. mult 4·00 4·50

DESIGNS: Nos. 1416/19, Recent photographs of the
Queen Mother.

267 Mickey Mouse as Animator

1990. Mickey Mouse in Hollywood. Walt Disney cartoon
characters. Multicoloured.

1420 25c. Type **267** 60 25
1421 45c. Minnie Mouse learning
 lines while being dressed 80 25
1422 50c. Mickey Mouse with clap-
 per board 90 30
1423 60c. Daisy Duck making-up
 Mickey Mouse 1·00 35
1424 $1 Clarabelle Cow as Cleopatra 1·25 70
1425 $2 Mickey Mouse directing
 Goofy and Donald Duck 1·75 2·25
1426 $3 Mickey Mouse directing
 Goofy as birdman 2·25 3·50
1427 $4 Donald Duck and Mickey
 Mouse editing film 2·25 3·50

MS1428 Two sheets, each 132×95 mm.
 (a) $5 Minnie Mouse, Daisy Duck
 and Clarabelle as musical stars. (b)
 $5 Mickey Mouse on set as director
 Set of 2 sheets 7·00 9·00

268 Men's 20
Kilometres Walk

1990. Olympic Games, Barcelona (1992) (1st issue). Multicoloured.

1429	50c. Type **268**	75	40
1430	75c. Triple jump	1·00	75
1431	$1 Men's 10,000 metres	1·25	85
1432	$5 Javelin	3·50	6·00

MS1433 100×70 mm. $6 Athlete lighting Olympic flame at Los Angeles Olympics — 5·50 7·00

See also Nos. 1553/61 and 1609/17.

269 Huey and Dewey
asleep (*Christmas Stories*)

1990. International Literacy Year. Walt Disney cartoon characters illustrating works by Charles Dickens. Multicoloured.

1434	15c. Type **269**	65	35
1435	45c. Donald Duck as Poor Jo looking at grave (*Bleak House*)	1·00	45
1436	50c. Dewey as Oliver asking for more (*Oliver Twist*)	1·10	50
1437	60c. Daisy Duck as The Marchioness (*Old Curiosity Shop*)	1·25	55
1438	$1 Little Nell giving nosegay to her grandfather (*Little Nell*)	1·40	85
1439	$2 Scrooge McDuck as Mr. Pickwick (*Pickwick Papers*)	2·00	2·50
1440	$3 Minnie Mouse as Florence and Mickey Mouse as Paul (*Dombey and Son*)	2·25	3·50
1441	$5 Minnie Mouse as Jenny Wren (*Our Mutual Friend*)	2·75	4·50

MS1442 Two sheets, each 126×102 mm. (a) $6 Artful Dodger picking pocket (*Oliver Twist*). (b) $6 Unexpected arrivals at Mr. Peggoty's (*David Copperfield*) Set of 2 sheets — 10·00 12·00

1990. World Cup Football Championship Winners, Italy. Nos. 1308/11 optd **Winners West Germany 1 Argentina 0.**

1443	15c. Type **252**	75	40
1444	25c. Goalkeeper moving towards ball	75	40
1445	$1 Goalkeeper reaching for ball	1·50	1·60
1446	$4 Goalkeeper saving goal	3·25	5·50

MS1447 Two sheets, each 75×105 mm. (a) $5 Three players competing for ball (horiz). (b) $5 Ball and players' legs (horiz) Set of 2 sheets — 9·50 11·00

271 Pearly-eyed Thrasher

1990. Birds. Multicoloured.

1448	10c. Type **271**	55	30
1449	25c. Purple-throated carib	60	35
1450	50c. Common yellowthroat	75	40
1451	60c. American kestrel	1·00	70
1452	$1 Yellow-bellied sapsucker	1·25	80
1453	$2 American purple gallinule ("Purple Gallinule")	2·25	2·50
1454	$3 Yellow-crowned night heron	2·50	3·25
1455	$4 Blue-hooded euphonia	2·50	3·50

MS1456 Two sheets, each 76×60 mm. (a) $6 Brown pelican. (b) $6 Magnificent frigate bird Set of 2 sheets — 14·00 16·00

272 Madonna and Child with Saints
(detail, Sebastiano del Piombo)

1990. Christmas. Paintings by Renaissance Masters. Multicoloured.

1457	25c. Type **272**	80	30
1458	30c. *Virgin and Child with Angels* (detail, Grunewald) (vert)	90	30
1459	40c. *The Holy Family and a Shepherd* (detail, Titian)	1·00	30
1460	60c. *Virgin and Child* (detail, Lippi) (vert)	1·40	40
1461	$1 *Jesus, St. John and Two Angels* (Rubens)	2·00	70
1462	$2 *Adoration of the Shepherds* (detail, Vincenzo Catena)	2·50	2·75
1463	$4 *Adoration of the Magi* (detail, Giorgione)	4·00	5·50
1464	$5 *Virgin and Child adored by Warrior* (detail, Vincenzo Catena)	4·00	5·50

MS1465 Two sheets, each 71×101 mm. (a) $6 *Allegory of the Blessings of Jacob* (detail, Rubens) (vert). (b) $6 *Adoration of the Magi* (detail, Fra Angelico) (vert) Set of 2 sheets — 7·00 8·50

273 *Rape of the Daughters of Leucippus* (detail)

1991. 350th Death Anniv of Rubens. Multicoloured.

1466	25c. Type **273**	1·00	40
1467	45c. *Bacchanal* (detail)	1·50	45
1468	50c. *Rape of the Sabine Women* (detail)	1·50	50
1469	60c. *Battle of the Amazons* (detail)	1·60	65
1470	$1 *Rape of the Sabine Women* (different detail)	2·00	1·00
1471	$2 *Bacchanal* (different detail)	2·50	2·50
1472	$3 *Rape of the Sabine Women* (different detail)	3·50	4·25
1473	$4 *Bacchanal* (different detail)	3·50	5·25

MS1474 Two sheets, each 101×71 mm. (a) $6 *Rape of Hippoda-meia* (detail). (b) $6 *Battle of the Amazons* (different detail) Set of 2 sheets — 8·50 10·00

274 U.S. Troops cross into
Germany, 1944

1991. 50th Anniv of Second World War. Multicoloured.

1475	10c. Type **274**	1·10	65
1476	15c. Axis surrender in North Africa, 1943	1·25	50
1477	25c. U.S. tanks invade Kwalajalein, 1944	1·25	50
1478	45c. Roosevelt and Churchill meet at Casablanca, 1943	2·75	70
1479	50c. Marshal Badoglio, Prime Minister of Italian anti-fascist government, 1943	1·50	70
1480	$1 Lord Mountbatten, Supreme Allied Commander Southeast Asia, 1943	3·25	1·50
1481	$2 Greek victory at Koritza, 1940	2·25	2·75
1482	$4 Anglo-Soviet mutual assistance pact, 1941	3·25	4·25
1483	$5 Operation Torch landings, 1942	3·50	4·25

MS1484 Two sheets, each 108×80 mm. (a) $6 Japanese attack on Pearl Harbor, 1941. (b) $6 U.S.A.A.F. daylight raid on Schweinfurt, 1943 Set of 2 sheets — 11·00 12·00

275 Locomotive *Prince Regent*, Middleton Colliery, 1812

1991. Cog Railways. Multicoloured.

1485	25c. Type **275**	1·25	55
1486	30c. Snowdon Mountain Railway	1·25	55
1487	40c. First railcar at Hell Gate, Manitou Pike's Peak Railway, U.S.A	1·40	65
1488	60c. P.N.K.A. rack railway, Java	1·60	70
1489	$1 Green Mountain Railway, Maine, 1883	2·00	1·00
1490	$2 Rack locomotive *Pike's Peak*, 1891	3·00	3·00

1491	$4 Vitznau–Rigi Railway, Switzerland, and Mt. Rigi hotel local post stamp	3·75	4·75
1492	$5 Leopoldina Railway, Brazil	3·75	4·75

MS1493 Two sheets, each 100×70 mm. (a) $6 Electric towing locomotives, Panama Canal. (b) $6 Gornergracht Railway, Switzerland (vert) Set of 2 sheets — 12·00 13·00

276 *Heliconius charithonia*

1991. Butterflies. Multicoloured.

1494	10c. Type **276**	65	50
1495	35c. *Marpesia petreus*	1·10	50
1496	50c. *Anartia amathea*	1·25	60
1497	75c. *Siproeta stelenes*	1·50	1·00
1498	$1 *Battus polydamas*	1·75	1·10
1499	$2 *Historis odius*	2·25	2·75
1500	$4 *Hypolimnas misippus*	3·25	4·25
1501	$5 *Hamadryas feronia*	3·25	4·25

MS1502 Two sheets. (a) 73×100 mm. $6 *Vanessa cardui* caterpillar (vert) (b) 100×73 mm. $6 "*Danaus plexippus* caterpillar (vert) Set of 2 sheets — 14·00 16·00

277 Hanno the Phoenician,
450 B.C.

1991. 500th Anniv of Discovery of America by Columbus (1992) (4th issue). History of Exploration.

1503	**277**	10c. multicoloured	70	40
1504	-	15c. multicoloured	80	40
1505	-	45c. multicoloured	1·25	50
1506	-	60c. multicoloured	1·40	60
1507	-	$1 multicoloured	1·75	85
1508	-	$2 multicoloured	2·25	2·75
1509	-	$4 multicoloured	3·00	4·00
1510	-	$5 multicoloured	3·00	4·00

MS1511 – Two sheets, each 106×76 mm. (a) $6 black and red. (b) $6 black and red Set of 2 sheets — 7·00 9·00

DESIGNS—HORIZ: 15c. Pytheas the Greek, 325 B.C.; 45c. Erik the Red discovering Greenland, 985 A.D.; 60c. Leif Eriksson reaching Vinland, 1000 A.D.; $1 Scylax the Greek in the Indian Ocean, 518 B.C.; $2 Marco Polo sailing to the Orient, 1259 A.D.; $4 Ship of Queen Hatshepsut of Egypt, 1493 B.C.; $5 St. Brendan's coracle, 500 A.D. VERT: $6 (No. MS1511a) Engraving of Columbus as Admiral; $6 (No. MS1511b) Engraving of Columbus bare-headed.

278 Camille Roulin (Van Gogh)

1991. Death Centenary (1990) of Vincent van Gogh (artist). Multicoloured.

1512	5c. Type **278**	70	85
1513	10c. Armand Roulin	70	60
1514	15c. *Young Peasant Woman with Straw Hat sitting in the Wheat*	85	50
1515	25c. *Adeline Ravoux*	1·00	50
1516	30c. *The Schoolboy*	1·00	50
1517	40c. *Doctor Gachet*	1·10	50
1518	50c. *Portrait of a Man*	1·25	50
1519	75c. *Two Children*	1·75	80
1520	$2 *The Postman Joseph Roulin*	2·75	2·75
1521	$3 *The Seated Zouave*	3·75	4·00
1522	$4 *L'Arlesienne*	4·00	4·50
1523	$5 *Self-Portrait, November/December 1888*	4·00	4·50

MS1524 Three sheets, each 102×76 mm. (a) $5 *Farmhouse in Provence* (horiz). (b) $5 *Flowering Garden* (horiz). (c) $6 *The Bridge at Trinquetaille* (horiz) Imperf Set of 3 sheets — 16·00 18·00

279 Mickey Mouse as
Champion Sumo Wrestler

1991. "Philanippon '91" International Stamp Exhibition, Tokyo. Walt Disney cartoon characters participating in martial arts. Multicoloured.

1525	10c. Type **279**	80	20
1526	15c. Goofy using the tonfa (horiz)	90	25
1527	45c. Donald Duck as a Ninja	1·60	50
1528	60c. Mickey armed for Kung fu	2·00	65
1529	$1 Goofy with Kendo sword	2·50	1·25
1530	$2 Mickey and Donald demonstrating Aikido (horiz)	3·00	3·00
1531	$4 Mickey and Donald in Judo bout (horiz)	4·00	5·00
1532	$5 Mickey performing Yabusame (mounted archery)	4·00	5·00

MS1533 Two sheets, each 127×102 mm. (a) $6 Mickey delivering Karate kick (horiz). (b) $6 Mickey demonstrating Tamashiwara Set of 2 sheets — 10·00 12·00

280 Queen Elizabeth and
Prince Philip in 1976

1991. 65th Birthday of Queen Elizabeth II. Multicoloured.

1534	15c. Type **280**	40	10
1535	20c. The Queen and Prince Philip in Portugal, 1985	40	10
1536	$2 Queen Elizabeth II	1·75	1·50
1537	$4 The Queen and Prince Philip at Ascot, 1986	2·75	3·25

MS1538 68×90 mm. $4 The Queen at National Theatre, 1986, and Prince Philip — 3·50 4·00

1991. Tenth Wedding Anniv of Prince and Princess of Wales. As T **280**. Multicoloured.

1539	10c. Prince and Princess of Wales at party, 1986	50	10
1540	40c. Separate portraits of Prince, Princess and sons	1·00	25
1541	$1 Prince Henry and Prince William	1·25	70
1542	$5 Princess Diana in Australia and Prince Charles in Hungary	4·50	4·50

MS1543 68×90 mm. $4 Prince Charles in Hackney and Princess and sons in Majorca, 1987 — 5·50 5·50

281 Daisy Duck teeing-off

1991. Golf. Walt Disney cartoon characters. Multicoloured.

1544	10c. Type **281**	70	50
1545	15c. Goofy playing ball from under trees	75	50
1546	45c. Mickey Mouse playing deflected shot	1·25	50
1547	60c. Mickey hacking divot out of fairway	1·50	65
1548	$1 Donald Duck playing ball out of pond	1·75	1·10
1549	$2 Minnie Mouse hitting ball over pond	2·50	2·75
1550	$4 Donald in a bunker	3·25	4·00
1551	$5 Goofy trying snooker shot into hole	3·25	4·00

MS1552 Two sheets, each 127×102 mm. (a) $6 Grandma Duck in senior tournament. (b) $6 Mickey and Minnie Mouse on course (horiz) Set of 2 sheets — 10·00 12·00

282 Moose receiving
Gold Medal

1991. 50th Anniv of Archie Comics, and Olympic Games, Barcelona (1992) (2nd issue). Multicoloured.

1553	10c. Type **282**	55	40
1554	25c. Archie playing polo on a motorcycle (horiz)	85	40
1555	40c. Archie and Betty at fencing class	1·10	45
1556	60c. Archie joining girls' volleyball team	1·40	65
1557	$1 Archie with tennis ball in his mouth	1·75	1·10
1558	$2 Archie running marathon	2·50	3·00
1559	$4 Archie judging women's gymnastics (horiz)	3·75	4·50
1560	$5 Archie watching the cheerleaders	3·75	4·50

MS1561 Two sheets, each 128×102 mm. (a) $6 Archie heading football. (b) $6 Archie catching baseball (horiz) Set of 2 sheets 11·00 13·00

283 Presidents De Gaulle and Kennedy, 1961

1991. Birth Centenary of Charles de Gaulle (French statesman). Multicoloured.

1562	10c. Type **283**	80	50
1563	15c. General De Gaulle with President Roosevelt, 1945 (vert)	80	50
1564	45c. President De Gaulle with Chancellor Adenauer, 1962 (vert)	1·25	50
1565	60c. De Gaulle at Arc de Triomphe, Liberation of Paris, 1944 (vert)	1·50	65
1566	$1 General De Gaulle crossing the Rhine, 1945	1·75	1·25
1567	$2 General De Gaulle in Algiers, 1944	2·50	3·00
1568	$4 Presidents De Gaulle and Eisenhower, 1960	3·25	4·50
1569	$5 De Gaulle returning from Germany, 1968 (vert)	3·25	4·50

MS1570 Two sheets. (a) 76×106 mm. $6 De Gaulle with crowd. (b) 106×76 mm. $6 De Gaulle and Churchill at Casablanca, 1943 Set of 2 sheets 15·00 13·00

284 Parliament Building and Map

1991. Tenth Anniv of Independence.
1571 **284** 10c. multicoloured 75 50

MS1572 87×97 mm. $6 Old Post Office, St. Johns, and stamps of 1862 and 1981 (50×37 mm) 6·00 7·50

285 Germans celebrating Reunification

1991. Anniversaries and Events. Multicoloured.

1573	25c. Type **285**	30	30
1574	75c. Cubs erecting tent	70	50
1575	$1.50 *Don Giovanni* and Mozart	5·50	3·00
1576	$2 Chariot driver and Gate at night	1·10	2·00
1577	$2 Lord Baden-Powell and members of 3rd Antigua Methodist cub pack (vert)	3·25	2·75
1578	$2 Lilienthal's signature and glider *Flugzeug Nr. 5*	3·50	2·75
1579	$2.50 Driver in Class P36 steam locomotive (vert)	6·50	4·00
1580	$3 Statues from podium	1·75	3·25
1581	$3.50 Cubs and camp fire	2·50	3·25
1582	$4 St. Peter's Cathedral, Salzburg	10·00	7·50

MS1583 Two sheets. (a) 100×72 mm. $4 Detail of chariot and helmet; (b) 89×117 mm. $5 Antiguan flag and Jamboree emblem (vert) Set of 2 sheets 9·00 11·00

ANNIVERSARIES AND EVENTS: Nos. 1573, 1576, 1580, **MS**1583a, Bicentenary of Brandenburg Gate, Germany; 1574, 1577, 1581, **MS**1583b, 17th World Scout Jamboree, Korea; 1575, 1582, Death bicentenary of Mozart (composer); 1578, Centenary of Otto Lilienthal's gliding experiments; 1579, Centenary of Trans-Siberian Railway.

286 "Nimitz" Class Carrier and "Ticonderoga" Class Cruiser

1991. 50th Anniv of Japanese Attack on Pearl Harbor. Multicoloured.

1585	$1 Type **286**	2·50	1·75
1586	$1 Tourist launch	2·50	1·75
1587	$1 U.S.S. *Arizona* memorial	2·50	1·75
1588	$1 Wreaths on water and aircraft	2·50	1·75
1589	$1 White tern	2·50	1·75
1590	$1 Mitsubishi A6M Zero-Sen fighters over Pearl City	2·50	1·75
1591	$1 Mitsubishi A6M Zero-Sen fighters attacking	2·50	1·75
1592	$1 Battleship Row in flames	2·50	1·75
1593	$1 U.S.S. *Nevada* (battleship) underway	2·50	1·75
1594	$1 Mitsubishi A6M Zero-Sen fighters returning to carriers	2·50	1·75

287 The Annunciation

1991. Christmas. Religious Paintings by Fra Angelico. Multicoloured.

1595	10c. Type **287**	40	30
1596	30c. *Nativity*	65	30
1597	40c. *Adoration of the Magi*	75	30
1598	60c. *Presentation in the Temple*	1·00	45
1599	$1 *Circumcision*	1·25	65
1600	$3 *Flight into Egypt*	2·50	3·50
1601	$4 *Massacre of the Innocents*	2·50	4·00
1602	$5 *Christ teaching in the Temple*	2·50	4·00

MS1603 Two sheets, each 102×127 mm. (a) $6 *Adoration of the Magi* (Cook Tondo). (b) $6 *Adoration of the Magi* (different) Set of 2 sheets 13·00 14·00

288 Queen Elizabeth II and Bird Sanctuary

1992. 40th Anniv of Queen Elizabeth II's Accession. Multicoloured.

1604	10c. Type **288**	1·25	40
1605	30c. Nelson's Dockyard	1·50	40
1606	$1 Ruins on Shirley Heights	1·50	70
1607	$3 Beach and palm trees	3·00	4·25

MS1608 Two sheets, each 75×98 mm. (a) $6 Beach. (b) $6 Hillside foliage Set of 2 sheets 8·50 9·00

289 Mickey Mouse awarding Swimming Gold Medal to Mermaid

1992. Olympic Games, Barcelona (3rd issue). Walt Disney cartoon characters. Multicoloured.

1609	10c. Type **289**	70	30
1610	15c. Huey, Dewey and Louie with kayak	80	30
1611	30c. Donald Duck and Uncle Scrooge in yacht	1·00	35
1612	50c. Donald and horse playing water polo	1·40	50
1613	$1 Big Pete weightlifting	2·00	85
1614	$2 Donald and Goofy fencing	3·00	3·00
1615	$4 Mickey and Donald playing volleyball	4·00	4·50
1616	$5 Goofy vaulting	4·00	4·50

MS1617 Four sheets, each 123×98 mm. (a) $6 Mickey playing football. (b) $6 Mickey playing basketball (horiz). (c) $6 Minnie Mouse on uneven parallel bars (horiz). (d) $6 Mickey, Goofy and Donald judging gymnastics (horiz) Set of 4 sheets 14·00 15·00

290 Pteranodon

1992. Prehistoric Animals. Multicoloured.

1618	10c. Type **290**	65	40
1619	15c. Brachiosaurus	65	40
1620	30c. Tyrannosaurus Rex	85	40
1621	50c. Parasaurolophus	1·00	50
1622	$1 Deinonychus (horiz)	1·50	1·00
1623	$2 Triceratops (horiz)	2·00	2·00
1624	$4 Protoceratops hatching (horiz)	2·25	3·25
1625	$5 Stegosaurus (horiz)	2·25	3·25

MS1626 Two sheets, each 100×70 mm. (a) $6 Apatosaurus (horiz). (b) $6 Allosaurus (horiz) Set of 2 sheets 8·50 9·50

291 Supper at Emmaus (Caravaggio)

1992. Easter. Religious Paintings. Multicoloured.

1627	10c. Type **291**	65	25
1628	15c. *The Vision of St. Peter* (Zurbaran)	80	25
1629	30c. *Christ driving the Money-changers from the Temple* (Tiepolo)	1·25	40
1630	40c. *Martyrdom of St. Bartholomew* (detail) (Ribera)	1·40	50
1631	$1 *Christ driving the Money-changers from the Temple* (detail) (Tiepolo)	2·25	1·00
1632	$2 *Crucifixion* (detail) (Altdorfer)	3·25	3·00
1633	$4 *The Deposition* (detail) (Fra Angelico)	4·25	5·00
1634	$5 *The Deposition* (different detail) (Fra Angelico)	4·25	5·00

MS1635 Two sheets. (a) 102×71 mm. $6 *The Last Supper* (detail, Masip). (b) 71×102 mm. $6 *Crucifixion* (detail, Altdorfer) (vert) Set of 2 sheets 9·50 12·00

292 The Miracle at the Well (Alonso Cano)

1992. "Granada '92" International Stamp Exhibition, Spain. Spanish Paintings. Multicoloured.

1636	10c. Type **292**	50	30
1637	15c. *The Poet Luis de Goingora y Argote* (Velazquez)	65	30
1638	30c. *The Painter Francisco Goya* (Vincente Lopez Portana)	85	40
1639	40c. *Maria de las Nieves Michaela Fourdinier* (Luis Paret y Alcazar)	95	50
1640	$1 *Carlos III eating before his Court* (Alcazar) (horiz)	1·75	1·25
1641	$2 *Rain Shower in Granada* (Antonio Munoz Degrain) (horiz)	2·50	2·75
1642	$4 *Sarah Bernhardt* (Santiago Rusinol i Prats)	3·50	4·00
1643	$5 *The Hermitage Garden* (Joaquim Mir Trinxet)	3·50	4·00

MS1644 Two sheets, each 120×95 mm. (a) $6 *The Ascent of Monsieur Boucle's Montgolfier Balloon in the Gardens of Aranjuez* (Antonio Carnicero) (112×87 mm). (b) $6 *Olympus: Battle with the Giants* (Francisco Bayeu y Subías) (112×87 mm). Imperf Set of 2 sheets 15·00 16·00

293 Amanita caesarea

1992. Fungi. Multicoloured.

1645	10c. Type **293**	70	40
1646	15c. *Collybia fusipes*	85	40
1647	30c. *Boletus aereus*	1·25	40
1648	40c. *Laccaria amethystina*	1·25	50
1649	$1 *Russula virescens*	2·00	1·25
1650	$2 *Tricholoma equestre* ("Tricholoma auratum")	2·75	2·75
1651	$4 *Calocybe gambosa*	3·50	4·00
1652	$5 *Lentinus tigrinus* ("Panus tigrinus")	3·50	4·00

MS1653 Two sheets, each 100×70 mm. (a) $6 *Clavariadelphus truncatus*. (b) $6 *Auricularia auricula-judae* Set of 2 sheets 12·00 13·00

294 Memorial Cross and Huts, San Salvador

1992. 500th Anniv of Discovery of America by Columbus (5th issue). World Columbian Stamp "Expo '92", Chicago. Multicoloured.

1654	15c. Type **294**	30	25
1655	30c. Martin Pinzon with telescope	55	25
1656	40c. Christopher Columbus	80	35
1657	$1 *Pinta*	2·75	1·50
1658	$2 *Nina*	3·00	3·00
1659	$4 *Santa Maria*	3·75	6·00

MS1660 Two sheets, each 108×76 mm. (a) $6 Ship and map of West Indies. (b) $6 Sea monster Set of 2 sheets 10·00 12·00

295 Antillean Crested Hummingbird and Wild Plantain

1992. "Genova '92" International Thematic Stamp Exhibition. Hummingbirds and Plants. Multicoloured.

1661	10c. Type **295**	45	50
1662	25c. Green mango and parrot's plantain	60	40
1663	45c. Purple-throated carib and lobster claws	80	45
1664	60c. Antillean mango and coral plant	90	55
1665	$1 Vervain hummingbird and cardinal's guard	1·40	85
1666	$2 Rufous-breasted hermit and heliconia	2·00	2·00
1667	$4 Blue-headed hummingbird and red ginger	3·00	3·75
1668	$5 Green-throated carib and ornamental banana	3·00	3·75

MS1669 Two sheets, each 100×70 mm. (a) $6 Bee hummingbird and jungle flame. (b) $6 Western streamertail and bignonia Set of 2 sheets 10·00 12·00

296 Columbus meeting Amerindians

1992. 500th Anniv of Discovery of America by Columbus (6th issue). Organization of East Caribbean States. Multicoloured.

1670	$1 Type **296**	85	65
1671	$2 Ships approaching island	1·40	1·60

297 Ts'ai Lun and Paper

1992. Inventors and Inventions. Multicoloured.

1672	10c. Type **297**	25	25
1673	25c. Igor Sikorsky and "Bolshoi Baltiskii" (first four-engined airplane)	1·75	40
1674	30c. Alexander Graham Bell and early telephone	55	45
1675	40c. Johannes Gutenberg and early printing press	55	45
1676	60c. James Watt and stationary steam engine	4·00	1·25
1677	$1 Anton van Leeuwenhoek and early microscope	2·00	1·60
1678	$4 Louis Braille and hands reading braille	5·00	5·50
1679	$5 Galileo and telescope	5·00	5·50

MS1680 Two sheets, each 100×73 mm. (a) $6 Edison and Latimer's phonograph. (b) $6 *Clermont* (first commercial paddle-steamer) Set of 2 sheets — 9·50 12·00

298 Elvis looking Pensive

1992. 15th Death Anniv of Elvis Presley. Multicoloured.

1681	$1 Type **298**	1·90	1·25
1682	$1 Wearing black and yellow striped shirt	1·90	1·25
1683	$1 Singing into microphone	1·90	1·25
1684	$1 Wearing wide-brimmed hat	1·90	1·25
1685	$1 With microphone in right hand	1·90	1·25
1686	$1 In Army uniform	1·90	1·25
1687	$1 Wearing pink shirt	1·90	1·25
1688	$1 In yellow shirt	1·90	1·25
1689	$1 In jacket and bow tie	1·90	1·25

299 Madison Square Gardens

1992. Postage Stamp Mega Event, New York. Sheet 100×70 mm.

MS1690 **299** $6 multicoloured — 4·50 6·00

300 Virgin and Child with Angels (detail) (School of Piero della Francesca)

1992. Christmas. Details of the Holy Child from various paintings. Multicoloured.

1691	10c. Type **300**	60	30
1692	25c. *Madonna degli Alberelli* (Giovanni Bellini)	90	30
1693	30c. *Madonna and Child with St. Anthony Abbot and St. Sigismund* (Neroccio)	95	30
1694	40c. *Madonna and the Grand Duke* (Raphael)	1·00	30
1695	60c. *The Nativity* (Georges de la Tour)	1·50	60
1696	$1 *Holy Family* (Jacob Jordaens)	1·75	1·00
1697	$4 *Madonna and Child Enthroned* (Magaritone)	3·75	4·75
1698	$5 *Madonna and Child on a Curved Throne* (Byzantine school)	3·75	4·75

MS1699 Two sheets, each 76×102 mm. (a) $6 *Madonna and Child* (Domenco Ghirlando). (b) $6 *The Holy Family* (Pontormo) Set of 2 sheets — 9·50 12·00

301 Russian Cosmonauts

1992. Anniversaries and Events. Multcoloured.

1700	10c. Type **301**	80	60
1701	40c. *Graf Zeppelin* (airship), 1929	1·75	65
1702	45c. Bishop Daniel Davis	50	40
1703	75c. Konrad Adenauer making speech	65	65
1704	$1 Bus Mosbacher and *Weatherly* (yacht)	1·25	1·25
1705	$1.50 Rain forest	1·75	1·75
1706	$2 Tiger	7·00	4·00
1707	$2 National flag, plant and emblem (horiz)	5·50	3·00
1708	$2 Members of Community Players company (horiz)	2·00	3·00
1709	$2.25 25 Women carrying pots	2·00	3·00
1710	$3 Lions Club emblem	2·25	3·25
1711	$4 Chinese rocket on launch tower	4·25	5·00
1712	$4 West German and N.A.T.O. flags	5·50	5·50
1713	$6 Hugo Eckener (airship pioneer)	5·00	6·00

MS1714 Four sheets, each 100×71 mm. (a) $6 Projected European space station. (b) $6 Airship LZ-129 *Hindenburg*, 1936. (c) $6 Brandenburg Gate on German flag. (d) $6 *Danaus plexippu*" (butterfly) Set of 4 sheets — 23·00 25·00

ANNIVERSARIES AND EVENTS: Nos. 1700, 1711, **MS**1714a, International Space Year; 1701, 1713, **MS**1714b, 75th death anniv of Count Ferdinand von Zeppelin; 1702, 150th anniv of Anglican Diocese of North-eastern Caribbean and Aruba; 1703, 1712, **MS**1714c, 25th death anniv of Konrad Adenauer (German statesman); 1704, Americas Cup yachting championship; 1705/6, **MS**1714d, Earth Summit '92, Rio; 1707, 50th anniv of Inter-American Institute for Agricultural Co-operation; 1708, 40th anniv of Cultural Development; 1709, United Nations World Health Organization Projects; 1710, 75th anniv of International Association of Lions Clubs.

302 Boy Hiker resting

1993. Hummel Figurines. Multicoloured.

1715	15c. Type **302**	35	15
1716	30c. Girl sitting on fence	55	25
1717	40c. Boy hunter	65	35
1718	50c. Boy with umbrella	75	45
1719	$1 Hikers at signpost	1·25	75
1720	$2 Boy hiker with pack and stick	1·75	2·25
1721	$4 Girl with young child and goat	2·75	3·50
1722	$5 Boy whistling	2·75	3·50

MS1723 Two sheets, each 97×122 mm. (a) $1.50×4, As Nos. 1715/18. (b) $1.50×4, As Nos. 1719/22 Set of 2 sheets — 13·00 14·00

303 Goofy playing Golf

1993. Opening of Euro-Disney Resort, Paris. Multicoloured.

1724	10c. Type **303**	80	30
1725	25c. Chip and Dale at Davy Crockett's campground	1·00	30
1726	30c. Donald Duck at the Cheyenne Hotel	1·00	35
1727	40c. Goofy at the Santa Fe Hotel	1·10	35
1728	$1 Mickey and Minnie Mouse at the New York Hotel	2·25	1·25
1729	$2 Mickey, Minnie and Goofy in car	2·75	2·25
1730	$4 Goofy at Pirates of the Caribbean	4·00	5·00
1731	$5 Donald at Adventureland	4·00	5·00

MS1732 Four sheets, each 127×102 mm. (a) $6 Mickey in bellboy outfit. (b) $6 Mickey on star (vert). (c) $6 Mickey on opening poster (vert). (d) $6 Mickey and balloons on opening poster (vert) Set of 2 sheets — 16·00 18·00

304 Cardinal's Guard

1993. Flowers. Multicoloured.

1733	15c. Type **304**	1·00	40
1734	25c. Giant granadilla	1·10	40
1735	30c. Spider flower	1·10	40
1736	40c. Gold vine	1·25	40
1737	$1 Frangipani	2·00	1·25
1738	$2 Bougainvillea	2·75	2·75
1739	$4 Yellow oleander	3·75	4·50
1740	$5 Spicy jatropha	3·75	4·50

MS1741 Two sheets, each 100×70 mm. (a) $6 Birdlime tree. (b) Fairy lily Set of 2 sheets — 9·00 12·00

305 The Destiny of Marie de' Medici (upper detail)

1993. Bicentenary of the Louvre, Paris. Paintings by Peter Paul Rubens. Multicoloured.

1742	$1 Type **305**	95	85
1743	$1 *The Birth of Marie de' Medici*	95	85
1744	$1 *The Education of Marie de' Medici*	95	85
1745	$1 *The Destiny of Marie de' Medici* (lower detail)	95	85
1746	$1 *Henry VI receiving the Portrait of Marie*	95	85
1747	$1 *The Meeting of the King and Marie at Lyons*	95	85
1748	$1 *The Marriage by Proxy*	95	85
1749	$1 *The Birth of Louis XIII*	95	85
1750	$1 *The Capture of Juliers*	95	85
1751	$1 *The Exchange of the Princesses*	95	85
1752	$1 *The Regency*	95	85
1753	$1 *The Majority of Louis XIII*	95	85
1754	$1 *The Flight from Blois*	95	85
1755	$1 *The Treaty of Angouleme*	95	85
1756	$1 *The Peace of Angers*	95	85
1757	$1 *The Reconciliation of Louis and Marie de' Medici*	95	85

MS1758 70×100 mm. $6 *Helene Faurment with a Coach* (52×85 mm) — 5·50 7·00

Nos. 1742/57 depict details from *The Story of Marie de' Medici*.

306 St. Lucia Amazon ("St. Lucia Parrot")

1993. Endangered Species. Multicoloured.

1759	$1 Type **306**	90	90
1760	$1 Cahow	90	90
1761	$1 Swallow-tailed kite	90	90
1762	$1 Everglade kite ("Everglades Kite")	90	90
1763	$1 Imperial amazon ("Imperial Parrot")	90	90
1764	$1 Humpback whale	90	90
1765	$1 Plain pigeon ("Puerto Rican Plain Pigeon")	90	90
1766	$1 St. Vincent amazon ("St. Vincent Parrot")	90	90
1767	$1 Puerto Rican amazon ("Puerto Rican Parrot")	90	90
1768	$1 Leatherback turtle	90	90
1769	$1 American crocodile	90	90
1770	$1 Hawksbill turtle	90	90

MS1771 Two sheets, each 100×70 mm. (a) As No. 1764. (b) West Indian manatee Set of 2 sheets — 8·00 10·00

Nos. 1759/70 were printed together, *se-tenant*, with the background forming a composite design.

307 Queen Elizabeth II at Coronation (photograph by Cecil Beaton)

1993. 40th Anniv of Coronation (1st issue).

1772	**307**	30c. multicoloured	60	60
1773	-	40c. multicoloured	70	70
1774	-	$2 blue and black	1·75	2·00
1775	-	$4 multicoloured	2·25	2·50

MS1776 70×100 mm. $6 multicoloured — 5·00 6·00

DESIGNS: 40c. Queen Elizabeth the Queen Mother's Crown, 1937; $2 Procession of heralds; $4 Queen Elizabeth II and Prince Edward. (28½×42½ mm)—$6 "Queen Elizabeth II" (detail) (Dennis Fildes).

308 Princess Margaret and Antony Armstrong-Jones

1993. 40th Anniv of Coronation (2nd issue).

1777-	$1×32 either grey and black or		
1808	multicoloured	26·00	28·00

DESIGNS: Various views as Type **308** from each decade of the reign.

309 Edward Stanley Gibbons and Catalogue of 1865

1993. Famous Professional Philatelists (1st series).

1809	**309**	$1.50 brown, black & grn	1·75	1·50
1810	-	$1.50 multicoloured	1·75	1·50
1811	-	$1.50 multicoloured	1·75	1·50
1812	-	$1.50 multicoloured	1·75	1·50
1813	-	$1.50 multicoloured	1·75	1·50
1814	-	$1.50 multicoloured	1·75	1·50

MS1815 98×69 mm. $3 black; $3 black — 5·50 6·50

DESIGNS: No. 1810, Theodore Champion and France 1849 1f. stamp; 1811, J. Walter Scott and U.S.A. 1918 24c. "Inverted Jenny" error; 1812, Hugo Michel and Bavaria 1849 1k. stamp; 1813, Alberto and Giulio Bolaffi with Sardinia 1851 5c. stamp; 1814, Richard Borek and Brunswick 1865 1gr. stamp; **MS**1815, Front pages of "*Mekeel's Weekly Stamp News*" in 1891 (misdated 1890) and 1993.

See also No. 1957.

310 Paul Gascoigne

1993. World Cup Football Championship, U.S.A. (1st issue). English Players. Multicoloured.

1816	$2 Type **310**	1·50	1·40
1817	$2 David Platt	1·50	1·40
1818	$2 Martin Peters	1·50	1·40
1819	$2 John Barnes	1·50	1·40
1820	$2 Gary Lineker	1·50	1·40
1821	$2 Geoff Hurst	1·50	1·40
1822	$2 Bobby Charlton	1·50	1·40
1823	$2 Bryan Robson	1·50	1·40
1824	$2 Bobby Moore	1·50	1·40
1825	$2 Nobby Stiles	1·50	1·40
1826	$2 Gordon Banks	1·50	1·40
1827	$2 Peter Shilton	1·50	1·40

MS1828 Two sheets, each 135×109 mm. (a) $6 Bobby Moore holding World Cup. (b) $6 Gary Lineker and Bobby Robson Set of 2 sheets — 9·00 11·00

See also Nos. 2039/45.

311 Grand
Inspector W. Heath

1993. Anniversaries and Events. Multicoloured.

1829	10c. Type 311	2·50	1·00
1830	15c. Rodnina and Oulanov (U.S.S.R.) (pairs figure skating) (horiz)	1·25	50
1831	30c. Present Masonic Hall, St. John's (horiz)	2·75	1·00
1832	30c. Willy Brandt with Helmut Schmidt and George Leber (horiz)	70	40
1833	30c. *Cat and Bird* (Picasso) (horiz)	70	40
1834	40c. Previous Masonic Hall, St. John's (horiz)	2·75	1·00
1835	40c. *Fish on a Newspaper* (Picasso) (horiz)	70	50
1836	40c. Early astronomical equipment	70	50
1837	40c. Prince Naruhito and engagement photographs (horiz)	70	50
1838	60c. Grand Inspector J. Jeffery	4·00	1·25
1839	$1 *Woman combing her Hair* (W. Slewinski) (horiz)	1·25	1·25
1840	$3 Masako Owada and engagement photographs (horiz)	2·50	3·00
1841	$3 *Artist's Wife with Cat* (Konrad Kryzanowski) (horiz)	2·50	3·00
1842	$4 Willy Brandt and protest march (horiz)	3·00	3·50
1843	$4 Galaxy	3·00	3·50
1844	$5 Alberto Tomba (Italy) (giant slalom) (horiz)	3·00	3·50
1845	$5 *Dying Bull* (Picasso) (horiz)	3·00	3·50
1846	$5 Pres. Clinton and family (horiz)	3·00	3·50

MS1847 Seven sheets. (a) 106×75 mm. $5 Copernicus. (b) 106×75 mm. $6 Womens' 1500 metre speed skating medallists (horiz). (c) 106×75 mm. $6 Willy Brandt at Warsaw Ghetto Memorial (horiz). (d) 106×75 mm. $6 *Woman with a Dog* (detail) (Picasso) (horiz). (e) 106×75 mm. $6 Masako Owada. (f) 70×100 mm. $6 *General Confusion* (S. I. Witkiewicz). (g) 106×75 mm. $6 Pres. Clinton taking the Oath (42½×57 mm) Set of 7 sheets ... 28·00 30·00

ANNIVERSARIES AND EVENTS: Nos. 1829, 1831, 1834, 1838, 150th anniv of St. John's Masonic Lodge No. 492; 1830, 1844, MS1847c, Winter Olympic Games '94, Lillehammer; 1832, 1842, MS1847c, 80th birth anniv of Willy Brandt (German politician); 1833, 1835, 1845, MS1847d, 20th death anniv of Picasso (artist); 1836, 1843, MS1847a, 450th death anniv of Copernicus (astronomer); 1837, 1840, MS1847e, Marriage of Crown Prince Naruhito of Japan; 1839, 1841, MS1847f, "Polska '93" International Stamp Exhibition, Poznan; 1846, MS1847g, Inauguration of U.S. President William Clinton.

312 Hugo Eckener and Dr. W. Beckers with Airship "Graf Zeppelin" over Lake George, New York

1993. Aviation. Multicoloured.

1848	30c. Type 312	1·00	70
1849	40c. Chicago World's Fair from *Graf Zeppelin*	1·00	1·00
1850	40c. Gloster Whittle E.28/39, 1941	1·00	1·00
1851	40c. George Washington writing balloon mail letter (vert)	1·00	1·00
1852	$4 Pres. Wilson and Curtiss JN-4 Jenny	3·75	4·50
1853	$5 Airship *Hindenburg* over Ebbets Field baseball stadium, 1937	3·75	4·50
1854	$5 Gloster Meteor in dogfight	3·75	4·50

MS1855 Three sheets. (a) 86×105 mm. $6 Hugo Eckener (vert). (b) 105×86 mm. $6 Consolidated PBY-5 Catalina flying boat (57×42½ mm). (c) 105×86 mm. $6 Alexander Hamilton, Washington and John Jay watching Blanchard's balloon, 1793 (horiz) Set of 3 sheets ... 16·00 18·00

ANNIVERSARIES: Nos. 1848/9, 1853, MS1855a, 125th birth anniv of Hugo Eckener (airship commander); 1850, 1854, MS1855b, 75th anniv of Royal Air Force; 1851/2, MS1855c, Bicentenary of first airmail flight.

313 Lincoln Continental

1993. Centenaries of Henry Ford's First Petrol Engine (Nos. 1856, 1858), and Karl Benz's First Four-wheeled Car (others). Multicoloured.

1856	30c. Type 313	1·00	75
1857	40c. Mercedes racing car, 1914	1·00	75
1858	$4 Ford "GT40", 1966	4·00	4·50
1859	$5 Mercedes Benz "gull-wing" coupe, 1954	4·00	4·50

MS1860 Two sheets. (a) 114×87 mm. $6 Ford's Mustang emblem. (b) 87×114 mm. $6 Germany 1936 12pf. Benz and U.S.A. 1968 12c. Ford stamps Set of 2 sheets ... 9·00 12·00

314 *The Musical Farmer*, 1932

1993. Mickey Mouse Film Posters. Multicoloured.

1861	10c. Type 314	75	30
1862	15c. *Little Whirlwind*, 1941	85	35
1863	30c. *Pluto's Dream House*, 1940	1·00	40
1864	40c. *Gulliver Mickey*, 1934	1·00	40
1865	50c. *Alpine Climbers*, 1936	1·00	50
1866	$1 *Mr. Mouse Takes a Trip*, 1940	1·50	1·00
1867	$2 *The Nifty Nineties*, 1941	2·25	2·50
1868	$4 *Mickey Down Under*, 1948	3·25	4·50
1869	$5 *The Pointer*, 1939	3·25	4·50

MS1870 Two sheets, each 125×105 mm. (a) $6 *The Simple Things*, 1953. (b) $6 *The Prince and the Pauper*, 1990 Set of 2 sheets ... 11·00 14·00

315 Marie and Fritz with Christmas Tree

1993. Christmas. Mickey's Nutcracker. Walt Disney cartoon characters in scenes from *The Nutcracker*. Multicoloured.

1871	10c. Type 315	75	40
1872	15c. Marie receives Nutcracker from Godfather Drosselmeir	80	40
1873	20c. Fritz breaks Nutcracker	80	40
1874	30c. Nutcracker with sword	90	40
1875	40c. Nutcracker and Marie in the snow	95	40
1876	50c. Marie and the Prince meet Sugar Plum Fairy	1·00	60
1877	60c. Marie and Prince in Crystal Hall	1·00	60
1878	$3 Huey, Dewey and Louie as Cossack dancers	3·25	4·00
1879	$6 Mother Ginger and her puppets	4·50	6·50

MS1880 Two sheets, each 127×102 mm. (a) $6 Marie and Prince in sleigh. (b) $6 The Prince in sword fight (vert) Set of 2 sheets ... 9·00 12·00

316 *Hannah and Samuel* (Rembrandt)

1993. Famous Paintings by Rembrandt and Matisse. Multicoloured.

1881	15c. Type 316	40	30
1882	15c. *Guitarist* (Matisse)	40	30
1883	30c. *The Jewish Bride* (Rembrandt)	55	30
1884	40c. *Jacob wrestling with the Angel* (Rembrandt)	60	30
1885	60c. *Interior with a Goldfish Bowl* (Matisse)	80	50
1886	$1 *Mlle Yvonne Landsberg* (Matisse)	1·25	80
1887	$4 *The Toboggan* (Matisse)	3·00	4·25
1888	$5 *Moses with the Tablets of the Law* (Rembrandt)	3·00	4·25

MS1889 Two sheets. (a) 124×99 mm. $6 *The Blinding of Samson by the Philistines* (detail) (Rembrandt). (b) 99×124 mm. $6 *The Three Sisters* (detail) (Matisse) Set of 2 sheets ... 10·00 11·00

317 Hong Kong 1981 $1 Golden Threadfin Bream Stamp and Sampans, Shau Kei Wan

1994. "Hong Kong '94" International Stamp Exhibition (1st issue). Multicoloured.

1890	40c. Type 317	80	80
1891	40c. Antigua 1990 $2 Rock beauty stamp and sampans, Shau Kei Wan	80	80

Nos. 1890/1 were printed together, *se-tenant*, forming a composite design.
See also Nos. 1892/7 and 1898/1905.

318 Terracotta Warriors

1994. "Hong Kong '94" International Stamp Exhibition (2nd issue). Qin Dynasty Terracotta Figures. Multicoloured.

1892	40c. Type 318	60	60
1893	40c. Cavalryman and horse	60	60
1894	40c. Warriors in armour	60	60
1895	40c. Painted bronze chariot and team	60	60
1896	40c. Pekingese dog	60	60
1897	40c. Warriors with horses	60	60

319 Mickey Mouse in Junk

1994. "Hong Kong '94" International Stamp Exhibition (3rd issue). Walt Disney cartoon characters. Multicoloured.

1898	10c. Type 319	70	30
1899	15c. Minnie Mouse as mandarin	75	35
1900	30c. Donald and Daisy Duck on houseboat	90	45
1901	50c. Mickey holding bird in cage	1·10	60
1902	$1 Pluto and ornamental dog	1·75	1·00
1903	$2 Minnie and Daisy celebrating Bun Festival	2·50	2·50
1904	$4 Goofy making noodles	3·50	4·50
1905	$5 Goofy pulling Mickey in rickshaw	3·50	4·50

MS1906 Two sheets, each 133×109 mm. (a) $5 Mickey and Donald on harbour ferry (horiz). (b) $5 Mickey in traditional dragon dance (horiz) Set of 2 sheets ... 7·00 9·00

320 Sumatran Rhinoceros lying down

1994. Centenary (1992) of Sierra Club (environmental protection society). Endangered Species. Multicoloured.

1907	$1.50 Type 320	1·25	1·25
1908	$1.50 Sumatran rhinoceros feeding	1·25	1·25
1909	$1.50 Ring-tailed lemur on ground	1·25	1·25
1910	$1.50 Ring-tailed lemur on branch	1·25	1·25
1911	$1.50 Red-fronted brown lemur on branch	1·25	1·25
1912	$1.50 Head of red-fronted brown lemur	1·25	1·25
1913	$1.50 Head of red-fronted brown lemur in front of trunk	1·25	1·25
1914	$1.50 Sierra Club Centennial emblem	80	80
1915	$1.50 Head of Bactrian camel	1·25	1·25
1916	$1.50 Bactrian camel	1·25	1·25
1917	$1.50 African elephant drinking	1·25	1·25
1918	$1.50 Head of African elephant	1·25	1·25
1919	$1.50 Leopard sitting upright	1·25	1·25
1920	$1.50 Leopard in grass (emblem at right)	1·25	1·25
1921	$1.50 Leopard in grass (emblem at left)	1·25	1·25

MS1922 Four sheets. (a) 100×70 mm. $1.50, Sumatran rhinoceros (horiz). (b) 70×100 mm. $1.50, Ring-tailed lemur (horiz). (c) 70×100 mm. $1.50, Bactrian camel (horiz). (d) 100×70 mm. $1.50, African elephant (horiz) Set of 4 sheets ... 6·00 8·00

321 West Highland White Terrier

1994. Dogs of the World. Chinese New Year ("Year of the Dog"). Multicoloured.

1923	50c. Type 321	75	65
1924	50c. Beagle	75	65
1925	50c. Scottish terrier	75	65
1926	50c. Pekingese	75	65
1927	50c. Dachshund	75	65
1928	50c. Yorkshire terrier	75	65
1929	50c. Pomeranian	75	65
1930	50c. Poodle	75	65
1931	50c. Shetland sheepdog	75	65
1932	50c. Pug	75	65
1933	50c. Shih Tzu	75	65
1934	50c. Chihuahua	75	65
1935	75c. Mastiff	75	65
1936	75c. Border collie	75	65
1937	75c. Samoyed	75	65
1938	75c. Airedale terrier	75	65
1939	75c. English setter	75	65
1940	75c. Rough collie	75	65
1941	75c. Newfoundland	75	65
1942	75c. Weimarana	75	65
1943	75c. English springer spaniel	75	65
1944	75c. Dalmatian	75	65
1945	75c. Boxer	75	65
1946	75c. Old English sheepdog	75	65

MS1947 Two sheets, each 93×58 mm. (a) $6 Welsh corgi. (b) $6 Labrador retriever Set of 2 sheets ... 9·00 12·00

322 *Spiranthes lanceolata*

1994. Orchids. Multicoloured.

1948	10c. Type 322	70	60
1949	20c. *Ionopsis utricularioides*	1·00	50
1950	30c. *Tetramicra canaliculata*	1·25	50
1951	50c. *Oncidium picturatum*	2·00	1·25
1952	$1 *Epidendrum difforme*	3·00	2·75
1953	$2 *Epidendrum ciliare*	4·00	4·25
1954	$4 *Epidendrum ibaguense*	4·00	4·25
1955	$5 *Epidendrum nocturnum*	4·00	4·25

MS1956 Two sheets, each 100×73 mm. (a) $6 *Rodriguezia lanceolata*. (b) $6 *Encyclia cochleata* Set of 2 sheets ... 9·00 12·00

323 Hermann E. Sieger, Germany 1931 1m. Zeppelin Stamp and Airship LZ-127 *Graf Zeppelin*

1994. Famous Professional Philatelists (2nd series).

1957	323	$1.50 multicoloured	3·00	2·50

324 *Danaus plexippus*

1994. Butterflies. Multicoloured.

1958	10c. Type **324**	85	75
1959	15c. *Appias drusilla*	1·00	45
1960	30c. *Eurema lisa*	1·25	55
1961	40c. *Anaea troglodyta*	1·25	60
1962	$1 *Urbanus proteus*	2·00	1·25
1963	$2 *Junonia evarete*	2·75	2·75
1964	$4 *Battus polydamas*	3·50	4·50
1965	$5 *Heliconius charitonia*	3·50	4·50
MS1966	Two sheets, each 102×72 mm. (a) $6 *Phoebis sennae*. (b) $6 *Hemiargus hanno* Set of 2 sheets	9·00	12·00

No. 1959 is inscribed "Appisa drusilla" and No. 1965 "Heliconius charitonius", both in error.

325 Bottlenose Dolphin

1994. Marine Life. Multicoloured.

1967	50c. Type **325**	75	75
1968	50c. Killer whale	75	75
1969	50c. Spinner dolphin	75	75
1970	50c. Oceanic sunfish	75	75
1971	50c. Caribbean reef shark and short fin pilot whale	75	75
1972	50c. Copper-banded butterflyfish	75	75
1973	50c. Mosaic moray	75	75
1974	50c. Clown triggerfish	75	75
1975	50c. Red lobster	75	75
MS1976	Two sheets, each 106×76 mm. (a) $6 Seahorse. (b) $6 Swordfish ("Blue Marlin") (horiz) Set of 2 sheets	11·00	12·00

326 Edwin Aldrin (astronaut)

1994. 25th Anniv of First Manned Moon Landing. Multicoloured.

1977	$1.50 Type **326**	2·00	1·50
1978	$1.50 First lunar footprint	2·00	1·50
1979	$1.50 Neil Armstrong (astronaut)	2·00	1·50
1980	$1.50 Aldrin stepping onto Moon	2·00	1·50
1981	$1.50 Aldrin and equipment	2·00	1·50
1982	$1.50 Aldrin and U.S.A. flag	2·00	1·50
1983	$1.50 Aldrin at Tranquility Base	2·00	1·50
1984	$1.50 Moon plaque	2·00	1·50
1985	$1.50 "Eagle" leaving Moon	2·00	1·50
1986	$1.50 Command module in lunar orbit	2·00	1·50
1987	$1.50 First day cover of U.S.A. 1969 10c. First Man on Moon stamp	2·00	1·50
1988	$1.50 Pres. Nixon and astronauts	2·00	1·50
MS1989	72×102 mm. $6 Armstrong and Aldrin with postal official	5·00	4·00

327 Edwin Moses (U.S.A.) (400 m hurdles, 1984)

1994. Centenary of International Olympic Committee. Gold Medal Winners. Multicoloured.

1990	50c. Type **327**	40	30
1991	$1.50 Steffi Graf (Germany) (tennis, 1988)	2·00	1·75
MS1992	79×110 mm. $6 Johann Olav Koss (Norway) (500, 1500 and 10,000 metre speed skating), 1994	5·00	5·50

328 Antiguan Family

1994. International Year of the Family.

1993	**328** 90c. multicoloured	1·00	1·00

329 Mike Atherton (England) and Wisden Trophy

1994. Centenary (1995) of First English Cricket Tour to the West Indies. Multicoloured.

1994	35c. Type **329**	1·25	65
1995	75c. Viv Richards (West Indies) (vert)	2·00	1·25
1996	$1.20 Richie Richardson (West Indies) and Wisden Trophy	2·75	2·50
MS1997	80×100 mm. $3 English team, 1895 (black and brown)	2·50	3·00

330 Entrance Bridge, Songgwangsa Temple

1994. "Philakorea '94" International Stamp Exhibition, Seoul. Multicoloured.

1998	40c. Type **330**	50	40
1999	75c. Long-necked bottle	70	75
2000	75c. Punch'ong ware jar with floral decoration	70	75
2001	75c. Punch'ong ware jar with blue dragon pattern	70	75
2002	75c. Ewer in shape of bamboo shoot	70	75
2003	75c. Punch'ong ware green jar	70	75
2004	75c. Pear-shaped bottle	70	75
2005	75c. Porcelain jar with brown dragon pattern	70	75
2006	75c. Porcelain jar with floral pattern	70	75
2007	90c. Song-op Folk Village, Cheju	70	75
2008	$3 Port Sogwipo	1·75	2·25
MS2009	104×71 mm. $4 Ox herder playing flute (vert)	3·25	4·00

331 Short S.25 Sunderland (flying boat)

1994. 50th Anniv of D-Day. Multicoloured.

2010	40c. Type **331**	1·25	40
2011	$2 Lockheed P-38 Lightning fighters attacking train	3·00	2·75
2012	$3 Martin B-26 Marauder bombers	3·25	3·75
MS2013	108×78 mm. $6 Hawker Typhoon fighter bomber	6·75	6·25

332 Travis Tritt

1994. Stars of Country and Western Music. Multicoloured.

2014	75c. Type **332**	70	70
2015	75c. Dwight Yoakam	70	70
2016	75c. Billy Ray Cyrus	70	70
2017	75c. Alan Jackson	70	70
2018	75c. Garth Brooks	70	70
2019	75c. Vince Gill	70	70
2020	75c. Clint Black	70	70
2021	75c. Eddie Rabbit	70	70
2022	75c. Patsy Cline	70	70
2023	75c. Tanya Tucker	70	70
2024	75c. Dolly Parton	70	70
2025	75c. Anne Murray	70	70
2026	75c. Tammy Wynette	70	70
2027	75c. Loretta Lynn	70	70
2028	75c. Reba McEntire	70	70
2029	75c. Skeeter Davis	70	70

2030	75c. Hank Snow	70	70
2031	75c. Gene Autry	70	70
2032	75c. Jimmie Rodgers	70	70
2033	75c. Ernest Tubb	70	70
2034	75c. Eddy Arnold	70	70
2035	75c. Willie Nelson	70	70
2036	75c. Johnny Cash	70	70
2037	75c. George Jones	70	70
MS2038	Three sheets. (a) 100×70 mm. $6 Hank Williams Jr. (b) 100×70 mm. $6 Hank Williams Sr. (c) 70×100 mm. $6 Kitty Wells (horiz) Set of 3 sheets	15·00	15·00

333 Hugo Sanchez (Mexico)

1994. World Cup Football Championship, U.S.A. (2nd issue). Multicoloured.

2039	15c. Type **333**	75	30
2040	35c. Jurgen Klinsmann (Germany)	1·25	45
2041	65c. Antiguan player	1·50	55
2042	$1.20 Cobi Jones (U.S.A.)	2·00	1·75
2043	$4 Roberto Baggio (Italy)	3·25	4·00
2044	$5 Bwalya Kalusha (Zambia)	3·25	4·00
MS2045	Two sheets. (a) 72×105 mm. $6 Maldive Islands player (vert). (b) 107×78 mm. $6 World Cup trophy (vert) Set of 2 sheets	8·50	9·00

No. 2040 is inscribed "Klinsman" in error.

334 Sir Shridath Ramphal

1994. First Recipients of Order of the Caribbean Community. Multicoloured.

2046	65c. Type **334**	50	40
2047	90c. William Demas	65	60
2048	$1.20 Derek Walcott	2·50	1·75

335 Pair of Magnificent Frigate Birds

1994. Birds. Multicoloured.

2049	10c. Type **335**	60	45
2050	15c. Bridled quail dove	70	40
2051	30c. Magnificent frigate bird chick hatching	1·00	70
2052	40c. Purple-throated carib (vert)	1·00	70
2053	$1 Male magnificent frigate bird in courtship display (vert)	1·40	1·40
2054	$1 Broad-winged hawk (vert)	1·40	1·40
2055	$3 Young magnificent frigate bird	2·50	3·25
2056	$4 Yellow warbler	2·75	3·25
MS2057	Two sheets. (a) 70×100 mm. $6 Female magnificent frigate bird (vert). (b) 100×70 mm. $6 Black-billed whistling duck ducklings Set of 2 sheets	8·00	9·00

Nos. 2049, 2051, 2053 and 2055 also show the W.W.F. Panda emblem.

336 *The Virgin and Child by the Fireside* (Robert Campin)

1994. Christmas. Religious Paintings. Multicoloured.

2058	15c. Type **336**	80	30
2059	35c. *The Reading Madonna* (Giorgione)	1·10	30
2060	40c. *Madonna and Child* (Giovanni Bellini)	1·25	30
2061	45c. *The Litta Madonna* (Da Vinci)	1·25	30
2062	65c. *The Virgin and Child under the Apple Tree* (Lucas Cranach the Elder)	1·60	55
2063	75c. *Madonna and Child* (Master of the Female Half-lengths)	1·75	70

2064	$1.20 *An Allegory of the Church* (Alessandro Allori)	2·25	2·00
2065	$5 *Madonna and Child wreathed with Flowers* (Jacob Jordaens)	3·75	5·50
MS2066	Two sheets. (a) 123×88 mm. $6 *Madonna and Child with Commissioners* (detail) (Palma Vecchio) (b) 88×123 mm. $6 *The Virgin Enthroned with Child* (detail) (Bohemian master) Set of 2 sheets	13·00	9·00

337 Magnificent Frigate Bird

1995. Birds. Multicoloured.

2067	15c. Type **337**	45	20
2068	25c. Blue-hooded euphonia	60	20
2069	35c. Eastern meadowlark ("Meadowlark")	70	20
2070	40c. Red-billed tropic bird	75	20
2071	65c. Greater flamingo	75	25
2072	60c. Yellow-faced grassquit	1·00	30
2073	65c. Yellow-billed cuckoo	1·00	30
2074	70c. Purple-throated carib	1·00	35
2075	75c. Bananaquit	1·00	35
2076	90c. Painted bunting	1·10	40
2077	$1.20 Red-legged honeycreeper	1·50	65
2078	$2 Northern jacana ("Jacana")	2·50	1·75
2079	$5 Greater Antillean bullfinch	4·00	4·25
2080	$10 Caribbean elaenia	7·00	8·00
2081	$20 Brown trembler ("Trembler")	11·00	15·00

338 Head of Pachycephalosaurus

1995. Prehistoric Animals. Multicoloured.

2082	15c. Type **338**	60	60
2083	20c. Head of afrovenator	60	60
2084	65c. Centrosaurus	85	80
2085	75c. Kronosaurus (horiz)	85	85
2086	75c. Ichthyosaurus (horiz)	85	85
2087	75c. Plesiosaurus (horiz)	85	85
2088	75c. Archelon (horiz)	85	85
2089	75c. Pair of tyrannosaurus (horiz)	85	85
2090	75c. Tyrannosaurus (horiz)	85	85
2091	75c. Parasaurolophus (horiz)	85	85
2092	75c. Pair of parasaurolophus (horiz)	85	85
2093	75c. Oviraptor (horiz)	85	85
2094	75c. Protoceratops with eggs (horiz)	85	85
2095	75c. Pteranodon and protoceratops (horiz)	85	85
2096	75c. Pair of protoceratops (horiz)	85	85
2097	90c. Pentaceratops drinking	1·00	1·00
2098	$1.20 Head of tarbosaurus	1·25	1·25
2099	$5 Head of styracosaurus	3·50	4·50
MS2100	Two sheets, each 101×70 mm. (a) $6 Head of Corythosaurus (horiz). (b) $6 Head of Carnotaurus (horiz) Set of 2 sheets	11·00	13·00

339 Al Oerter (U.S.A.) (discus – 1956, 1960, 1964, 1968)

1995. Olympic Games, Atlanta (1996). Previous Gold Medal Winners (1st issue). Multicoloured.

2101	15c. Type **339**	60	30
2102	20c. Greg Louganis (U.S.A.) (diving – 1984, 1988)	60	30
2103	65c. Naim Suleymanoglu (Turkey) (weightlifting – 1988)	75	50
2104	90c. Louise Ritter (U.S.A.) (high jump – 1988)	1·00	70
2105	$1.20 Nadia Comaneci (Rumania) (gymnastics –1976)	2·00	1·40
2106	$5 Olga Bondarenko (Russia) (10,000 metres – 1988)	3·25	5·00
MS2107	Two sheets, each 106×76 mm. (a) $6 United States crew (eight-oared shell – 1964). (b) $6 Lutz Hesslich (Germany) (cycling — 1988) (vert) Set of 2 sheets	11·00	12·00

No. 2106 is inscribed "BOLDARENKO" in error.
See also Nos. 2302/23.

340 Map of Berlin showing Russian Advance

1995. 50th Anniv of End of Second World War in Europe. Multicoloured.

2108	$1.20 Type **340**	1·50	1·25
2109	$1.20 Russian tank and infantry	1·50	1·25
2110	$1.20 Street fighting in Berlin	1·50	1·25
2111	$1.20 German tank exploding	1·50	1·25
2112	$1.20 Russian air raid	1·50	1·25
2113	$1.20 German troops surrendering	1·50	1·25
2114	$1.20 Hoisting the Soviet flag on the Reichstag	1·50	1·25
2115	$1.20 Captured German standards	1·50	1·25
MS2116	104×74 mm. $6 Gen. Konev (vert)	4·50	5·50

See also Nos. 2132/8.

341 Signatures and Earl of Halifax

1995. 50th Anniv of United Nations. Multicoloured.

2117	75c. Type **341**	70	1·00
2118	90c. Virginia Gildersleeve	70	1·00
2119	$1.20 Harold Stassen	70	1·00
MS2120	100×70 mm. $6 Pres. Franklin D. Roosevelt	3·50	4·25

Nos. 2117/19 were printed together, *se-tenant*, forming a composite design.

342 Woman buying Produce from Market

1995. 50th Anniv of F.A.O. Multicoloured.

2121	75c. Type **342**	70	1·00
2122	90c. Women shopping	70	1·00
2123	$1.20 Women talking	70	1·00
MS2124	100×70 mm. $6 Tractor	3·00	3·75

Nos. 2121/3 were printed together, *se-tenant*, forming a composite design.

343 Beach and Rotary Emblem

1995. 90th Anniv of Rotary International.

2125	**343** $5 multicoloured	3·50	4·00
MS2126	74×104 mm. $6 National flag and emblem	3·50	4·00

344 Queen Elizabeth the Queen Mother

1995. 95th Birthday of Queen Elizabeth the Queen Mother.

2127	-	$1.50 brown, light brown and black	1·50	1·50
2128	**344**	$1.50 multicoloured	1·50	1·50
2129	-	$1.50 multicoloured	1·50	1·50
2130	-	$1.50 multicoloured	1·50	1·50

MS2131	100×127 mm. $6 multicoloured	5·50	5·50

DESIGNS: No. 2127, Queen Elizabeth the Queen Mother (pastel drawing); 2129, At desk (oil painting); 2130, Wearing green dress; **MS**2131, Wearing blue dress.

1995. 50th Anniv of End of Second World War in the Pacific. As T **340**. Multicoloured.

2132	$1.20 Gen. Chang Kai-Shek and Chinese guerrillas	1·10	1·25
2133	$1.20 Gen. Douglas MacArthur and beach landing	1·10	1·25
2134	$1.20 Gen. Claire Chennault and U.S. fighter aircraft	1·10	1·25
2135	$1.20 Brig. Orde Wingate and supply drop	1·10	1·25
2136	$1.20 Gen. Joseph Stilwell and U.S. supply plane	1·10	1·25
2137	$1.20 Field-Marshal Bill Slim and loading cow into plane	1·10	1·25
MS2138	108×76 mm. $3 Admiral Nimitz and aircraft carrier	2·75	3·50

345 Family ("Caring")

1995. Tourism. Sheet 95×72 mm, containing T **345** and similar horiz designs. Multicoloured.

MS2139	$2 Type **345**; $2 Market trader ("Marketing"); $2 Workers and housewife ("Working"); $2 Leisure pursuits ("Enjoying Life")	5·50	7·00

346 Purple-throated Carib

1995. Birds. Multicoloured.

2140	75c. Type **346**	1·10	1·00
2141	75c. Antillean crested hummingbird	1·10	1·00
2142	75c. Bananaquit	1·10	1·00
2143	75c. Mangrove cuckoo	1·10	1·00
2144	75c. Troupial	1·10	1·00
2145	75c. Green-throated carib	1·10	1·00
2146	75c. Yellow warbler	1·10	1·00
2147	75c. Antillean euphonia ("Blue-hooded Euphonia")	1·10	1·00
2148	75c. Scaly-breasted thrasher	1·10	1·00
2149	75c. Burrowing owl	1·10	1·00
2150	75c. Carib grackle	1·10	1·00
2151	75c. Adelaide's warbler	1·10	1·00
2152	75c. Ring-necked duck	1·10	1·00
2153	75c. Ruddy duck	1·10	1·00
2154	75c. Green-winged teal	1·10	1·00
2155	75c. Wood duck	1·10	1·00
2156	75c. Hooded merganser	1·10	1·00
2157	75c. Lesser scaup	1·10	1·00
2158	75c. Black-billed whistling duck ("West Indian Tree Duck")	1·10	1·00
2159	75c. Fulvous whistling duck	1·10	1·00
2160	75c. Bahama pintail	1·10	1·00
2161	75c. Northern shoveler	1·10	1·00
2162	75c. Masked duck	1·10	1·00
2163	75c. American wigeon	1·10	1·00
MS2164	Two sheets, each 104×74 mm. (a) $6 American purple gallinule. (b) $6 Heads of Blue-winged teal Set of 2 sheets	13·00	13·00

Nos. 2140/51 and 2152/63 respectively were printed together, *se-tenant*, forming composite designs.

347 Original Church, 1845

1995. 150th Anniv of Greenbay Moravian Church. Multicoloured.

2165	20c. Type **347**	70	30
2166	60c. Church in 1967	1·00	40
2167	75c. Present church	1·25	50
2168	90c. Revd. John Buckley (first minister of African descent)	1·40	60
2169	$1.20 Bishop John Ephraim Knight (longest-serving minister)	1·75	1·75
2170	$2 As 75c.	2·75	3·50

MS2171	110×81 mm. $6 Front of present church	4·50	6·00

348 Mining Bees

1995. Bees. Multicoloured.

2172	90c. Type **348**	1·00	70
2173	$1.20 Solitary bee	1·40	90
2174	$1.65 Leaf-cutter bee	2·00	2·00
2175	$1.75 Honey bees	2·00	2·00
MS2176	110×80 mm. $6 Solitary mining bee	4·00	5·00

349 Narcissus

1995. Flowers. Multicoloured.

2177	75c. Type **349**	80	80
2178	75c. Camellia	80	80
2179	75c. Iris	80	80
2180	75c. Tulip	80	80
2181	75c. Poppy	80	80
2182	75c. Peony	80	80
2183	75c. Magnolia	80	80
2184	75c. Oriental lily	80	80
2185	75c. Rose	80	80
2186	75c. Pansy	80	80
2187	75c. Hydrangea	80	80
2188	75c. Azaleas	80	80
MS2189	80×100 mm. $6 Calla lily	4·00	5·00

No. 2186 is inscribed "Pansie" in error.

350 Somali

1995. Cats. Multicoloured.

2190	45c. Type **350**	80	60
2191	45c. Persian and butterflies	80	60
2192	45c. Devon rex	80	60
2193	45c. Turkish angora	80	60
2194	45c. Himalayan	80	60
2195	45c. Maine coon	80	60
2196	45c. Ginger non-pedigree	80	60
2197	45c. American wirehair	80	60
2198	45c. British shorthair	80	60
2199	45c. American curl	80	60
2200	45c. Black non-pedigree and butterfly	80	60
2201	45c. Birman	80	60
MS2202	104×74 mm. $6 Siberian kitten (vert)	7·50	7·50

Nos. 2190/2201 were printed together, *se-tenant*, forming a composite design.

351 The Explorer Tent

1995. 18th World Scout Jamboree, Netherlands. Tents. Multicoloured.

2203	$1.20 Type **351**	1·60	1·60
2204	$1.20 Camper tent	1·60	1·60
2205	$1.20 Wall tent	1·60	1·60
2206	$1.20 Trail tarp	1·60	1·60
2207	$1.20 Miner's tent	1·60	1·60
2208	$1.20 Voyager tent	1·60	1·60
MS2209	Two sheets, each 76×106 mm. (a) $6 Scout and camp fire. (b) $6 Scout with back pack (vert) Set of 2 sheets	8·50	10·00

352 Trans-Gabon Diesel-electric Train

1995. Trains of the World. Multicoloured.

2210	35c. Type **352**	1·00	65
2211	65c. Canadian Pacific diesel-electric locomotive	1·50	90
2212	75c. Santa Fe Railway diesel-electric locomotive, U.S.A.	1·60	1·00
2213	90c. High Speed Train, Great Britain	1·60	1·00
2214	$1.20 TGV express train, France	1·60	1·00
2215	$1.20 Diesel-electric locomotive, Australia	1·60	1·60
2216	$1.20 Pendolino "ETR 450" electric train, Italy	1·60	1·60
2217	$1.20 Diesel-electric locomotive, Thailand	1·60	1·60
2218	$1.20 Pennsylvania Railroad Type K4 steam locomotive, U.S.A.	1·60	1·60
2219	$1.20 Beyer-Garratt steam locomotive, East African Railways	1·60	1·60
2220	$1.20 Natal Government steam locomotive	1·60	1·60
2221	$1.20 Rail gun, American Civil War	1·60	1·60
2222	$1.20 Locomotive *Lion* (red livery), Great Britain	1·60	1·60
2223	$1.20 William Hedley's *Puffing Billy* (green livery), Great Britain	1·60	1·60
2224	$6 Amtrak high speed diesel locomotive, U.S.A.	3·75	4·50
MS2225	Two sheets, each 110×80 mm. (a) $6 Locomotive *Iron Rooster*, China (vert). (b) $6 *Indian-Pacific* diesel-electric locomotive, Australia (vert) Set of 2 sheets	14·00	14·00

353 Dag Hammarskjold (1961 Peace)

1995. Centenary of Nobel Prize Trust Fund. Multicoloured.

2226	$1 Type **353**	1·10	1·10
2227	$1 Georg Wittig (1979 Chemistry)	1·10	1·10
2228	$1 Wilhelm Ostwald (1909 Chemistry)	1·10	1·10
2229	$1 Robert Koch (1905 Medicine)	1·10	1·10
2230	$1 Karl Ziegler (1963 Chemistry)	1·10	1·10
2231	$1 Alexander Fleming (1945 Medicine)	1·10	1·10
2232	$1 Hermann Staudinger (1953 Chemistry)	1·10	1·10
2233	$1 Manfred Eigen (1967 Chemistry)	1·10	1·10
2234	$1 Arno Penzias (1978 Physics)	1·10	1·10
2235	$1 Shmuel Agnon (1966 Literature)	1·10	1·10
2236	$1 Rudyard Kipling (1907 Literature)	1·10	1·10
2237	$1 Aleksandr Solzhenitsyn (1970 Literature)	1·10	1·10
2238	$1 Jack Steinberger (1988 Physics)	1·10	1·10
2239	$1 Andrei Sakharov (1975 Peace)	1·10	1·10
2240	$1 Otto Stern (1943 Physics)	1·10	1·10
2241	$1 John Steinbeck (1962 Literature)	1·10	1·10
2242	$1 Nadine Gordimer (1991 Literature)	1·10	1·10
2243	$1 William Faulkner (1949 Literature)	1·10	1·10
MS2244	Two sheets, each 100×70 mm. (a) $6 Elie Wiesel (1986 Peace) (vert). (b) $6 The Dalai Lama (1989 Peace) (vert) Set of 2 sheets	9·00	10·00

354 Elvis Presley

1995. 60th Birth Anniv of Elvis Presley. Multicoloured.

2245	$1 Type **354**	1·25	95
2246	$1 Holding microphone in right hand	1·25	95
2247	$1 In blue shirt and with neck of guitar	1·25	95
2248	$1 Wearing blue shirt and smiling	1·25	95
2249	$1 On wedding day	1·25	95
2250	$1 In army uniform	1·25	95
2251	$1 Wearing red shirt	1·25	95
2252	$1 Wearing white shirt	1·25	95

2253	$1 In white shirt with microphone	1·25	95

MS2254 101×71 mm. $6 "Ghost" image of Elvis amongst the stars — 7·50 5·50

355 John Lennon and Signature

1995. 15th Death Anniv of John Lennon (entertainer). Multicoloured.

2255	45c. Type **355**	50	40
2256	50c. In beard and spectacles	50	50
2257	65c. Wearing sunglasses	55	55
2258	75c. In cap with heart badge	65	65

MS2259 103×73 mm. $6 As 75c. — 5·50 6·50

1995. Hurricane Relief. Nos. 2203/8 optd **"Hurricane Relief"**.

2260	$1.20 Type **351**	1·25	1·25
2261	$1.20 Camper tent	1·25	1·25
2262	$1.20 Wall tent	1·25	1·25
2263	$1.20 Trail tarp	1·25	1·25
2264	$1.20 Miner's tent	1·25	1·25
2265	$1.20 Voyager tent	1·25	1·25

MS2266 Two sheets, each 76×106 mm. (a) $6 Scout and camp fire. (b) $6 Scout with back pack (vert) Set of 2 sheets — 12·00 15·00

357 Rest on the Flight into Egypt (Paolo Veronese)

1995. Christmas. Religious Paintings. Multicoloured.

2267	15c. Type **357**	35	30
2268	35c. Madonna and Child (Van Dyck)	50	40
2269	65c. Sacred Conversation Piece (Veronese)	70	50
2270	75c. Vision of St. Anthony (Van Dyck)	80	60
2271	90c. Virgin and Child (Van Eyck)	90	65
2272	$6 The Immaculate Conception (Giovanni Tiepolo)	3·25	4·75

MS2273 Two sheets, each 101×127 mm. $5 Christ appearing to his Mother (detail) (Van der Weyden). (b) 127×101 mm. $6 The Infant Jesus and Young St. John (Murillo) Set of 2 sheets — 8·00 9·00

358 Hygrophoropsis aurantiaca

1996. Fungi. Multicoloured.

2274	75c. Type **358**	60	70
2275	75c. Hygrophorus bakerensis	60	70
2276	75c. Hygrophorus conicus	60	70
2277	75c. Hygrophorus miniatus ("Hygrocybe miniata")	60	70
2278	75c. Suillus brevipes	60	70
2279	75c. Suillus luteus	60	70
2280	75c. Suillus granulatus	60	70
2281	75c. Suillus caerulescens	60	70

MS2282 Two sheets, each 105×75 mm. (a) $6 Conocybe filaris. (b) $6 Hygrocybe flavescens Set of 2 sheets — 7·00 8·00

359 H.M.S. Resolution (Cook)

1996. Sailing Ships. Multicoloured.

2283	15c. Type **359**	1·25	75
2284	25c. Mayflower (Pilgrim Fathers)	1·25	65
2285	45c. Santa Maria (Columbus)	1·50	65
2286	75c. Aemilia (Dutch galleon)	1·50	1·50
2287	75c. Sovereign of the Seas (English galleon)	1·50	1·50
2288	90c. H.M.S. Victory (Nelson)	1·75	1·25
2289	$1.20 As No. 2286	1·75	1·60
2290	$1.20 As No. 2287	1·75	1·60
2291	$1.20 Royal Louis (French galleon)	1·75	1·60
2292	$1.20 H.M.S. Royal George (ship of the line)	1·75	1·60
2293	$1.20 Le Protecteur (French frigate)	1·75	1·60
2294	$1.20 As No. 2288	1·75	1·60
2295	$1.50 As No. 2285	1·75	1·60
2296	$1.50 Vitoria (Magellan)	1·75	1·75
2297	$1.50 Golden Hind (Drake)	1·75	1·75
2298	$1.50 As No. 2284	1·75	1·75
2299	$1.50 Griffin (La Salle)	1·75	1·75
2300	$1.50 Type **359**	1·75	1·75

MS2301 Two sheets. (a) 102×72 mm. $6 U.S.S. Constitution (frigate). (b) 98×67 mm. $6 Grande Hermine (Cartier) Set of 2 sheets — 10·00 11·00

360 Florence Griffith Joyner (U.S.A.) (Gold – track, 1988)

1996. Olympic Games, Atlanta. Previous Medal Winners (2nd issue). Multicoloured.

2302	65c. Type **360**	60	60
2303	75c. Olympic Stadium, Seoul (1988) (horiz)	65	65
2304	90c. Allison Jolly and Lynne Jewell (U.S.A.) (Gold – yachting, 1988) (horiz)	75	70
2305	90c. Wolfgang Nordwig (Germany) (Gold – pole vaulting, 1972)	75	75
2306	90c. Shirley Strong (Great Britain) (Silver – 100 metres hurdles, 1984)	75	75
2307	90c. Sergei Bubka (Russia) (Gold – pole vault, 1988)	75	75
2308	90c. Filbert Bayi (Tanzania) (Silver – 3000 metres steeplechase, 1980)	75	75
2309	90c. Victor Saneyev (Russia) (Gold – triple jump, 1968, 1972, 1976)	75	75
2310	90c. Silke Renk (Germany) (Gold – javelin, 1992)	75	75
2311	90c. Daley Thompson (Great Britain) (Gold – decathlon, 1980, 1984)	75	75
2312	90c. Robert Richards (U.S.A.) (Gold – pole vault, 1952, 1956)	75	75
2313	90c. Parry O'Brien (U.S.A.) (Gold – shot put, 1952, 1956)	75	75
2314	90c. Ingrid Kramer (Germany) (Gold – women's platform diving, 1960)	75	75
2315	90c. Kelly McCormick (U.S.A.) (Silver – women's springboard diving, 1984)	75	75
2316	90c. Gary Tobian (U.S.A.) (Gold – men's springboard diving, 1960)	75	75
2317	90c. Greg Louganis (U.S.A.) (Gold – men's diving, 1984 and 1988)	75	75
2318	90c. Michelle Mitchell (U.S.A.) (Silver – women's platform diving, 1984 and 1988)	75	75
2319	90c. Zhou Jihong (China) (Gold – women's platform diving, 1984)	75	75
2320	90c. Wendy Wyland (U.S.A.) (Bronze – women's platform diving, 1984)	75	75
2321	90c. Xu Yanmei (China) (Gold – women's platform diving, 1988)	75	75
2322	90c. Fu Mingxia (China) (Gold – women's platform diving, 1992)	75	75
2323	$1.20 2000 metre tandem cycle race (horiz)	1·00	1·00

MS2324 Two sheets, each 106×76 mm. (a) $5 Bill Toomey (U.S.A.) (Gold—Decathlon, 1968) (horiz). (b) $6 Mark Lenzi (U.S.A.) (Gold—Men's springboard diving, 1992) Set of 2 sheets — 7·50 8·00

Nos. 2305/13 and 2314/22 respectively were printed together, se-tenant, with the background forming a composite design.

361 Black Skimmer

1996. Sea Birds. Multicoloured.

2325	75c. Type **361**	90	90
2326	75c. Black-capped petrel	90	90
2327	75c. Sooty tern	90	90
2328	75c. Royal tern	90	90
2329	75c. Pomarine skua ("Pomarine Jaegger")	90	90
2330	75c. White-tailed tropic bird	90	90
2331	75c. Northern gannet	90	90
2332	75c. Laughing gull	90	90

MS2333 Two sheets, each 105×75 mm. (a) $5 Magnificent frigate bird ("Great Frigate Bird"). (b) $6 Brown pelican Set of 2 sheets — 8·00 9·00

362 Mickey and Goofy on Elephant (Around the World in Eighty Days)

1996. Novels of Jules Verne. Walt Disney cartoon characters in scenes from the books. Multicoloured.

2334	1c. Type **362**	15	25
2335	2c. Mickey, Donald and Goofy entering cave ("A Journey to the Centre of the Earth")	20	25
2336	5c. Mickey and Minnie driving postcart ("Michel Strogoff")	35	25
2337	10c. Mickey, Donald and Goofy in space rocket ("From the Earth to the Moon")	50	20
2338	15c. Mickey and Goofy in balloon ("Five Weeks in a Balloon")	50	20
2339	20c. Mickey and Goofy in China ("Around the World in Eighty Days")	50	20
2340	$1 Mickey, Goofy and Pluto on island ("The Mysterious Island")	2·25	85
2341	$2 Mickey, Pluto, Goofy and Donald on Moon ("From the Earth to the Moon")	2·75	2·75
2342	$3 Mickey being lifted by bird ("Captain Grant's Children")	3·25	3·50
2343	$5 Mickey with seal and squid ("Twenty Thousand Leagues Under the Sea")	4·25	5·00

MS2344 Two sheets, each 124×99 mm. (a) $6 Mickey on "Nautilus" ("Twenty Thousand Leagues Under the Sea"). (b) $6 Mickey and Donald on raft ("A Journey to the Centre of the Earth") Set of 2 sheets — 12·50 12·50

363 Bruce Lee

1996. "CHINA '96" 9th Asian International Stamp Exhibition, Peking. Bruce Lee (actor). Multicoloured.

2345	75c. Type **363**	60	70
2346	75c. Bruce Lee in white shirt and red tie	60	70
2347	75c. In plaid jacket and tie	60	70
2348	75c. In mask and uniform	60	70
2349	75c. Bare-chested	60	70
2350	75c. In mandarin jacket	60	70
2351	75c. In brown jumper	60	70
2352	75c. In fawn shirt	60	70
2353	75c. Shouting	60	70

MS2354 76×106 mm. $5 Bruce Lee — 3·75 4·00

364 Queen Elizabeth II

1996. 70th Birthday of Queen Elizabeth II. Multicoloured.

2355	$2 Type **364**	1·25	1·50
2356	$2 With bouquet	1·25	1·50
2357	$2 In Garter robes	1·25	1·50

MS2358 96×111 mm. $6 Wearing white dress — 5·50 6·00

365 Ancient Egyptian Cavalryman

1996. Cavalry through the Ages. Multicoloured.

2359	60c. Type **365**	50	55
2360	60c. 13th-century English knight	50	55
2361	60c. 16th-century Spanish lancer	50	55
2362	60c. 18th-century Chinese cavalryman	50	55

MS2363 100×70 mm. $6 19th-century French cuirassier — 3·25 3·75

366 Girl in Red Sari

1996. 50th Anniv of UNICEF Multicoloured.

2364	75c. Type **366**	60	60
2365	90c. South American mother and child	70	70
2366	$1.20 Nurse with child	90	1·00

MS2367 114×74 mm. $6 Chinese child — 3·25 3·75

367 Tomb of Zachariah and "Verbascum sinuatum"

1996. 3000th Anniv of Jerusalem. Multicoloured.

2368	75c. Type **367**	75	65
2369	90c. Pool of Siloam and Hyacinthus orientalis	85	75
2370	$1.20 Hurva Synagogue and Ranunculus asiaticus	1·25	1·10

MS2371 66×80 mm. $6 Model of Herrod's Temple and Cerics siliquastrum — 6·50 6·00

368 Kate Smith

1996. Cent of Radio. Entertainers. Multicoloured.

2372	65c. Type **368**	50	50
2373	75c. Dinah Shore	60	60
2374	90c. Rudy Vallee	75	70
2375	$1.20 Bing Crosby	1·10	1·00

MS2376 72×104 mm. $6 Jo Stafford (28×42 mm) — 3·25 3·75

369 Madonna Enthroned

1996. Christmas. Religious Paintings by Filippo Lippi. Multicoloured.

2377	60c. Type **369**	80	40
2378	90c. Adoration of the Child and Saints	1·00	55
2379	$1 The Annunciation	1·10	90

2380	$1.20 *Birth of the Virgin*	1·25	1·25
2381	$1.60 *Adoration of the Child*	1·60	1·90
2382	$1.75 *Madonna and Child*	1·90	2·50

MS2383 Two sheets, each 76×106 mm. (a) $6 *Madonna and Child* (different). (b) $6 *The Circumcision* Set of 2 sheets 11·00 12·00

370 Robert Preston (*The Music Man*)

1997. Broadway Musical Stars. Multicoloured.

2384	$1 Type **370**	90	90
2385	$1 Michael Crawford (*Phantom of the Opera*)	90	90
2386	$1 Zero Mostel (*Fiddler on the Roof*)	90	90
2387	$1 Patti Lupone (*Evita*)	90	90
2388	$1 Raul Julia (*Threepenny Opera*)	90	90
2389	$1 Mary Martin (*South Pacific*)	90	90
2390	$1 Carol Channing (*Hello Dolly*)	90	90
2391	$1 Yul Brynner (*The King and I*)	90	90
2392	$1 Julie Andrews (*My Fair Lady*)	90	90

MS2393 106×76 mm. $6 Mickey Rooney (*Sugar Babies*) 4·00 5·00

371 Goofy and Wilbur

1997. Walt Disney Cartoon Characters. Multicoloured.

2394	1c. Type **371**	10	10
2395	2c. Donald and Goofy in boxing ring	10	10
2396	5c. Donald, Panchito and Jose Carioca	10	10
2397	10c. Mickey and Goofy playing chess	20	15
2398	15c. Chip and Dale with acorns	20	15
2399	20c. Pluto and Mickey	20	15
2400	$1 Daisy and Minnie eating ice-cream	90	75
2401	$2 Daisy and Minnie at dressing table	1·50	1·75
2402	$3 Gus Goose and Donald	2·00	2·50

MS2403 Two sheets. (a) 102×127 mm. $6 Goofy. (b) 127×102 mm. $6 Donald Duck playing guitar (vert) Set of 2 sheets 8·50 9·00

372 Charlie Chaplin as Young Man

1997. 20th Death Anniv of Charlie Chaplin (film star). Multicoloured.

2404	$1 Type **372**	80	70
2405	$1 Pulling face	80	70
2406	$1 Looking over shoulder	80	70
2407	$1 In cap	80	70
2408	$1 In front of star	80	70
2409	$1 In *The Great Dictator*	80	70
2410	$1 With movie camera and megaphone	80	70
2411	$1 Standing in front of camera lens	80	70
2412	$1 Putting on make-up	80	70

MS2413 76×106 mm. $6 Charlie Chaplin 4·00 4·25

Nos. 2404/12 were printed together, *se-tenant*, with the backgrounds forming a composite design.

373 *Charaxes porthos*

1997. Butterflies. Multicoloured.

2414	90c. Type **373**	80	50
2415	$1.10 *Charaxes protoclea protoclea*	80	80
2416	$1.10 *Byblia ilithyia*	80	80
2417	$1.10 Black-headed tchagra (bird)	80	80
2418	$1.10 *Charaxes nobilis*	80	80
2419	$1.10 *Pseudacraea boisduvali trimeni*	80	80
2420	$1.10 *Charaxes smaragdalis*	80	80
2421	$1.10 *Charaxes lasti*	80	80
2422	$1.10 *Pseudacrea poggei*	80	80
2423	$1.10 *Graphium colonna*	80	80
2424	$1.10 Carmine bee eater (bird)	80	80
2425	$1.10 *Pseudacraea eurytus*	80	80
2426	$1.10 *Hypolimnas monteironis*	80	80
2427	$1.10 *Charaxes anticlea*	80	80
2428	$1.10 *Graphium leonidas*	80	80
2429	$1.10 *Graphium illyris*	80	80
2430	$1.10 *Nephronia argia*	80	80
2431	$1.10 *Graphium policenes*	80	80
2432	$1.10 *Papilio dardanus*	80	80
2433	$1.20 *Aethiopana honorius*	80	80
2434	$1.60 *Charaxes hadrianus*	1·25	1·10
2435	$1.75 *Precis westermanni*	1·25	1·40

MS2436 Three sheets, each 106×76 mm. (a) $6 *Charaxes lactitinctus* (horiz). (b) $6 *Eupheadra neophron*. (c) $6 *Euxanthe tiberius* (horiz) Set of 3 sheets 11·00 13·00

Nos. 2415/23 and 2424/32 respectively were printed together, *se-tenant*, with the backgrounds forming a composite design.

No. 2430 is inscribed "Nepheronia argia" in error.

374 Convent of The Companions of Jesus, Morelia, Mexico

1997. 50th Anniv of UNESCO Multicoloured.

2437	60c. Type **374**	70	35
2438	90c. Fortress at San Lorenzo, Panama (vert)	80	50
2439	$1 Canaima National Park, Venezuela (vert)	80	55
2440	$1.10 Aerial view of church with tower, Guanajuato, Mexico (vert)	80	90
2441	$1.10 Church facade, Guanajuato, Mexico (vert)	80	90
2442	$1.10 Aerial view of churches with domes, Guanajuato, Mexico (vert)	80	90
2443	$1.10 Jesuit Missions of the Chiquitos, Bolivia (vert)	80	90
2444	$1.10 Huascaran National Park, Peru (vert)	80	90
2445	$1.10 Jesuit Missions of La Santisima, Paraguay (vert)	80	90
2446	$1.10 Cartagena, Colombia (vert)	80	90
2447	$1.10 Fortification, Havana, Cuba (vert)	80	90
2448	$1.20 As No. 2444 (vert)	85	90
2449	$1.60 Church of San Fransisco, Guatemala (vert)	1·25	1·40
2450	$1.65 Tikal National Park, Guatemala	1·50	1·60
2451	$1.65 Rio Platano Reserve, Honduras	1·50	1·60
2452	$1.65 Ruins of Copan, Honduras	1·50	1·60
2453	$1.65 Antigua ruins, Guatemala	1·50	1·60
2454	$1.65 Teotihuacan, Mexico	1·50	1·60
2455	$1.75 Santo Domingo, Dominican Republic (vert)	1·75	1·90

MS2456 Two sheets, each 127×102 mm. (a) $6 Tikal National Park, Guatemala. (b) $6 Teotihuacan pyramid, Mexico Set of 2 sheets 9·00 9·50

No. 2446 is inscribed "Columbia" in error.

375 Red Bishop

1997. Endangered Species. Multicoloured.

2457	$1.20 Type **375**	1·40	1·40
2458	$1.20 Yellow baboon	1·40	1·40
2459	$1.20 Superb starling	1·40	1·40
2460	$1.20 Ratel	1·40	1·40
2461	$1.20 Hunting dog	1·40	1·40
2462	$1.20 Serval	1·40	1·40
2463	$1.65 Okapi	1·40	1·40
2464	$1.65 Giant forest squirrel	1·40	1·40
2465	$1.65 Lesser masked weaver	1·40	1·40
2466	$1.65 Small-spotted genet	1·40	1·40
2467	$1.65 Yellow-billed stork	1·40	1·40
2468	$1.65 Red-headed agama	1·40	1·40

MS2469 Three sheets, each 106×76 mm. (a) $6 South African crowned crane. (b) $6 Bat-eared fox. (c) $6 Malachite kingfisher Set of 3 sheets 15·00 16·00

Nos. 2457/62 and 2463/8 respectively were printed together, *se-tenant*, with the backgrounds forming composite designs.

376 Child's Face and UNESCO Emblem

1997. Tenth Anniv of Chernobyl Nuclear Disaster. Multicoloured.

2470	$1.65 Type **376**	1·40	1·50
2471	$2 As Type **376**, but inscr "CHABAD'S CHILDREN OF CHERNOBYL" at foot	1·75	2·00

377 Paul Harris and James Grant

1997. 50th Death Anniv of Paul Harris (founder of Rotary International). Multicoloured.

2472	$1.75 Type **377**	1·25	1·50

MS2473 78×107 mm. $6 Group study exchange, New Zealand 3·75 4·25

378 Queen Elizabeth II

1997. Golden Wedding of Queen Elizabeth and Prince Philip. Multicoloured.

2474	$1 Type **378**	1·10	1·10
2475	$1 Royal coat of arms	1·10	1·10
2476	$1 Queen Elizabeth and Prince Philip at reception	1·10	1·10
2477	$1 Queen Elizabeth and Prince Philip in landau	1·10	1·10
2478	$1 Balmoral	1·10	1·10
2479	$1 Prince Philip	1·10	1·10

MS2480 100×71 mm. $6 Queen Elizabeth with Prince Philip in naval uniform 4·25 4·50

379 Kaiser Wilhelm I and Heinrich von Stephan

1997. "Pacific '97" International Stamp Exhibition, San Francisco. Death Centenary of Heinrich von Stephan (founder of the U.P.U.).

2481	**379**	$1.75 blue	1·25	1·40
2482	–	$1.75 brown	1·25	1·40
2483	–	$1.75 mauve	1·25	1·40

MS2484 82×119 mm. $6 violet 3·75 4·50

DESIGNS: No. 2482, Von Stephan and Mercury; 2483, Carrier pigeon and loft; **MS**2484, Von Stephan and 15th-century Basle messenger.

No. 2483 is inscribed "PIDGEON" in error.

380 The Two Ugly Sisters and their Mother

1997. 175th Anniv of Brothers Grimm's Third Collection of Fairy Tales. *Cinderella*. Multicoloured.

2485	$1.75 Type **380**	1·60	1·60
2486	$1.75 Cinderella and her Fairy Godmother	1·60	1·60
2487	$1.75 Cinderella and the Prince	1·60	1·60

MS2488 124×96 mm. $6 Cinderella trying on slipper 4·25 4·50

381 *Marasmius rotula*

1997. Fungi. Multicoloured.

2489	45c. Type **381**	50	30
2490	65c. *Cantharellus cibarius*	60	40
2491	70c. *Lepiota cristata*	60	40
2492	90c. *Auricularia mesenteric*	70	50
2493	$1 *Pholiota alnicola*	75	55
2494	$1.65 *Leccinum aurantiacum*	1·10	1·25
2495	$1.75 *Entoloma serrulatum*	1·25	1·40
2496	$1.75 *Panaeolus sphinctrinus*	1·25	1·40
2497	$1.75 *Volvariella bombycina*	1·25	1·40
2498	$1.75 *Conocybe percincta*	1·25	1·40
2499	$1.75 *Pluteus cervinus*	1·25	1·40
2500	$1.75 *Russula foetens*	1·25	1·40

MS2501 Two sheets, each 106×76 mm. (a) $6 *Amanita cothurnata*. (b) $6 *Panellus serotinus* Set of 2 sheets 7·50 8·50

382 *Odontoglossum cervantesii*

1997. Orchids of the World. Multicoloured.

2502	45c. Type **382**	60	30
2503	65c. *Phalaenopsis* Medford Star	70	40
2504	75c. "Vanda Motes" Resplendent	75	45
2505	90c. *Odontonia* Debutante	80	50
2506	$1 *Iwanagaara* Apple Blossom	90	70
2507	$1.65 *Cattleya* Sophia Martin	1·25	1·25
2508	$1.65 Dogface Butterfly	1·25	1·25
2509	$1.65 *Laeliocattleya* Mini Purple	1·25	1·25
2510	$1.65 *Cymbidium* Showgirl	1·25	1·25
2511	$1.65 *Brassolaeliocattleya* Dorothy Bertsch	1·25	1·25
2512	$1.65 *Disa Blackii*	1·25	1·25
2513	$1.65 *Paphiopedilum leeanum*	1·25	1·25
2514	$1.65 *Paphiopedilum macranthum*	1·25	1·25
2515	$1.65 *Brassocattleya* Angel Lace	1·25	1·25
2516	$1.65 *Saphrolae liocattleya* Precious Stones	1·25	1·25
2517	$1.65 Orange Theope Butterfly	1·25	1·25
2518	$1.65 *Promenaea xanthina*	1·25	1·25
2519	$1.65 *Lycaste macrobulbon*	1·25	1·25
2520	$1.65 *Amestella philippinensis*	1·25	1·25
2521	$1.65 *Masdevallia* Machu Picchu	1·25	1·25
2522	$1.65 *Phalaenopsis* Zuma Urchin	1·25	1·25
2523	$2 *Dendrobium victoria-reginae*	1·60	1·60

MS2524 Two sheets, each 76×106 mm. (a)"*Mitonia* Seine. (b) *Pouphiopedilum gratrixanum* Set of 2 sheets 8·00 9·00

Nos. 2507/14 and 2515/22 respectively were printed together, *se-tenant*, with the backgrounds forming composite designs.

383 Maradona holding World Cup Trophy, 1986

1997. World Cup Football Championship, France (1998).

2525	**383**	60c. multicoloured	50	35
2526	-	75c. brown	60	45
2527	-	90c. multicoloured	70	50
2528	-	$1 brown	75	75
2529	-	$1 brown	75	75
2530	-	$1 brown	75	75
2531	-	$1 black	75	75
2532	-	$1 brown	75	75
2533	-	$1 brown	75	75
2534	-	$1 brown	75	75
2535	-	$1 brown	75	75
2536	-	$1.20 multicoloured	75	75
2537	-	$1.65 multicoloured	1·10	1·25
2538	-	$1.75 multicoloured	1·10	1·40

MS2539 Two sheets, each 102×127 mm. (a) $6 multicoloured. (b) $6 mult Set of 2 sheets — 7·50 8·50

DESIGNS—HORIZ: No. 2526, Fritzwalter, West Germany, 1954; 2527, Zoff, Italy, 1982; 2536, Moore, England, 1966; 2537, Alberto, Brazil, 1970; 2538, Matthaus, West Germany, 1990; MS2539 (b) West German players celebrating, 1990. VERT: No. 2528, Ademir, Brazil, 1950; 2529, Eusebio, Portugal, 1966; 2530, Fontaine, France, 1958; 2531, Schillaci, Italy, 1990; 2532, Leonidas, Brazil, 1938; 2533, Stabile, Argentina, 1930; 2534, Nejedly, Czechoslovakia, 1934; 2535, Muller, West Germany, 1970; MS2539 (a) Bebeto, Brazil.

384 Scottish Fold Kitten

1997. Cats and Dogs. Multicoloured.

2540		$1.65 Type **384**	1·50	1·25
2541		$1.65 Japanese bobtail	1·50	1·25
2542		$1.65 Tabby manx	1·50	1·25
2543		$1.65 Bicolor American shorthair	1·50	1·25
2544		$1.65 Sorrel Abyssinian	1·50	1·25
2545		$1.65 Himalayan blue point	1·50	1·25
2546		$1.65 Dachshund	1·50	1·25
2547		$1.65 Staffordshire terrier	1·50	1·25
2548		$1.65 Shar-pei	1·50	1·25
2549		$1.65 Beagle	1·50	1·25
2550		$1.65 Norfolk terrier	1·50	1·25
2551		$1.65 Golden retriever	1·50	1·25

MS2552 Two sheets, each 107×77 mm. (a) $6 Red tabby (vert). (b) $6 Siberian husky (vert) Set of 2 sheets — 8·50 9·00

385 Original Drawing by Trevithick, 1803

1997. Railway Locomotives of the World. Multicoloured.

2553	$1.65 Type **385**	1·50	1·25
2554	$1.65 William Hedley's *Puffing Billy*, (1813–14)	1·50	1·25
2555	$1.65 Crampton locomotive of French Nord Railway, 1858	1·50	1·25
2556	$1.65 Lawrence Machine Shop locomotive, U.S.A., 1860	1·50	1·25
2557	$1.65 Natchez and Hamburg Railway steam locomotive *Mississippi*, U.S.A., 1834	1·50	1·25
2558	$1.65 Bury *Coppernob* locomotive, Furness Railway, 1846	1·50	1·25
2559	$1.65 David Joy's *Jenny Lind*, 1847	1·50	1·25
2560	$1.65 Schenectady Atlantic locomotive, U.S.A., 1899	1·50	1·25
2561	$1.65 Kitsons Class 1800 tank locomotive, Japan, 1881	1·50	1·25
2562	$1.65 Pennsylvania Railroad express frieght	1·50	1·25
2563	$1.65 Karl Golsdorf's 4 cylinder locomotive, Austria	1·50	1·25
2564	$1.65 Series "E" locomotive, Russia, 1930	1·50	1·25

MS2565 Two sheets, each 72×100 mm. (a) $6 George Stephenson "Patentee" type locomotive, 1843. (b) $6 Brunel's trestle bridge over River Lynher, Cornwall Set of 2 sheets — 8·00 9·00

No. 2554 is dated "1860" in error.

386 The Angel leaving Tobias and his Family (Rembrandt)

1997. Christmas. Religious Paintings. Multicoloured.

2566	15c. Type **386**	30	15
2567	25c. *The Resurrection* (Martin Knoller)	40	20
2568	60c. *Astronomy* (Raphael)	60	40
2569	75c. *Music-making Angel* (Melozzo da Forli)	70	55
2570	90c. *Amor* (Parmigianino)	80	60
2571	$1.20 *Madonna and Child with Saints* (Rosso Fiorentino)	1·00	1·25

MS2572 Two sheets, each 105×96 mm. (a) $6 *The Wedding of Tobias* (Gianantonio and Francesco Guardi) (horiz). (b) $6 *The Portinari Altarpiece* (Hugo van der Goes) (horiz) Set of 2 sheets — 7·50 8·50

387 Diana, Princess of Wales

1998. Diana, Princess of Wales Commemoration. Multicoloured (except Nos. 2574 and 2581/2).

2573	$1.65 Type **387**	1·10	1·10
2574	$1.65 Wearing hoop earrings (red and black)	1·10	1·10
2575	$1.65 Carrying bouquet	1·10	1·10
2576	$1.65 Wearing floral hat	1·10	1·10
2577	$1.65 With Prince Harry	1·10	1·10
2578	$1.65 Wearing white jacket	1·10	1·10
2579	$1.65 In kitchen	1·10	1·10
2580	$1.65 Wearing black and white dress	1·10	1·10
2581	$1.65 Wearing hat (brown and black)	1·10	1·10
2582	$1.65 Wearing floral print dress (brown and black)	1·10	1·10
2583	$1.65 Dancing with John Travolta	1·10	1·10
2584	$1.65 Wearing white hat and jacket	1·10	1·10

MS2585 Two sheets, each 70×100 mm. (a) $6 Wearing red jumper. (b) $6 Wearing black dress for papal audience (brown and black) Set of 2 sheets — 7·50 8·00

388 Yellow Damselfish

1998. Fish. Multicoloured.

2586	75c. Type **388**	55	40
2587	90c. Barred hamlet	65	50
2588	$1 Yellow-tailed damselfish ("Jewelfish")	70	55
2589	$1.20 Blue-headed wrasse	75	60
2590	$1.50 Queen angelfish	85	85
2591	$1.65 Jackknife-fish	95	95
2592	$1.65 Spot-finned hogfish	95	95
2593	$1.65 Sergeant major	95	95
2594	$1.65 Neon goby	95	95
2595	$1.65 Jawfish	95	95
2596	$1.65 Flamefish	95	95
2597	$1.65 Rock beauty	95	95
2598	$1.65 Yellow-tailed snapper	95	95
2599	$1.65 Creole wrasse	95	95
2600	$1.65 Slender filefish	95	95
2601	$1.65 Long-spined squirrelfish	95	95
2602	$1.65 Royal gramma ("Fairy Basslet")	95	95
2603	$1.75 Queen triggerfish	1·00	1·10

MS2604 Two sheets, each 80×110 mm. (a) $6 Porkfish. (b) $6 Black-capped basslet Set of 2 sheets — 8·00 9·00

Nos. 2591/6 and 2597/2602 respectively were printed together, *se-tenant*, with the backgrounds forming composite designs.

389 First Church and Manse, 1822–40

1998. 175th Anniv of Cedar Hall Moravian Church. Multicoloured.

2605	20c. Type **389**	20	20
2606	45c. Cedar Hall School, 1840	35	30
2607	75c. Hugh A. King, minister 1945–53	55	45
2608	90c. Present Church building	65	50
2609	$1.20 Water tank, 1822	75	75
2610	$2 Former Manse, demolished 1978	1·25	2·00

MS2611 100×70 mm. $6 Present church building (different) (50×37 mm.) — 3·25 4·25

390 Europa Point Lighthouse, Gibraltar

1998. Lighthouses of the World. Multicoloured.

2612	45c. Type **390**	65	40
2613	65c. Tierra del Fuego, Argentina (horiz)	75	55
2614	75c. Point Loma, California, U.S.A. (horiz)	80	55
2615	90c. Groenpoint, Cape Town, South Africa	90	60
2616	$1 Youghal, Cork, Ireland	1·00	90
2617	$1.20 Launceston, Tasmania, Australia	1·10	1·10
2618	$1.65 Point Abino, Ontario, Canada (horiz)	1·40	1·75
2619	$1.75 Great Inagua, Bahamas	1·50	2·00

MS2620 99×70 mm. $6 Cap Hatteras, North Carolina, U.S.A. — 5·50 6·00

No. 2613 is inscribed "Terra Del Fuego" in error.

391 Pooh and Tigger (January)

1998. Through the Year with Winnie the Pooh. Multicoloured.

2621	$1 Type **391**	1·00	1·00
2622	$1 Pooh and Piglet indoors (February)	1·00	1·00
2623	$1 Piglet hang-gliding with scarf (March)	1·00	1·00
2624	$1 Tigger, Pooh and Piglet on pond (April)	1·00	1·00
2625	$1 Kanga and Roo with posy of flowers (May)	1·00	1·00
2626	$1 Pooh on balloon and Owl (June)	1·00	1·00
2627	$1 Pooh, Eeyore, Tigger and Piglet gazing at stars (July)	1·00	1·00
2628	$1 Pooh and Piglet by stream (August)	1·00	1·00
2629	$1 Christopher Robin going to school (September)	1·00	1·00
2630	$1 Eeyore in fallen leaves (October)	1·00	1·00
2631	$1 Pooh and Rabbit gathering pumpkins (November)	1·00	1·00
2632	$1 Pooh and Piglet skiing (December)	1·00	1·00

MS2633 Four sheets, each 126×101 mm. (a) $6 Pooh and Piglet with blanket (Spring). (b) $6 Pooh by pond (Summer). (c) $6 Pooh sweeping fallen leaves (Autumn). (d) $6 Pooh and Eeyore on ice (Winter) Set of 4 sheets — 16·00 16·00

392 Miss Nellie Robinson (founder)

1998. Centenary of Thomas Oliver Robinson Memorial School.

2634	**392**	20c. green and black	20	20
2635	-	45c. multicoloured	40	25
2636	-	65c. green and black	55	50
2637	-	75c. multicoloured	60	60
2638	-	90c. multicoloured	70	65
2639	-	$1.20 brown, green and black	90	1·40

MS2640 106×76 mm. $6 brown — 3·25 4·00

DESIGNS—HORIZ: 45c. School photo, 1985; 65c. Former school building, 1930–49; 75c. Children with Mrs. Natalie Hurst (present headmistress); $1.20, Present school building, 1950. VERT: 90c. Miss Ina Loving (former teacher); $6 Miss Nellie Robinson (different).

393 Spotted Eagle Ray

1998. International Year of the Ocean. Multicoloured.

2641-2665	40c.×25 Type **393**; Manta ray; Hawksbill turtle; Jellyfish; Queen angelfish; Octopus; Emperor angelfish; Regal angelfish; Porkfish; Racoon butterflyfish; Atlantic barracuda; Sea horse; Nautilus; Trumpetfish; White tip shark; Sunken Spanish galleon; Black-tip shark; Long-nosed butterflyfish; Green moray eel; Captain Nemo; Treasure chest; Hammerhead shark; Divers; Lionfish; Clownfish	7·00	8·00
2666-2677	75c.×12 Maroon-tailed conure; Cocoi heron; Common tern; Rainbow lory ("Rainbow Lorikeet"); Saddleback butterflyfish; Goatfish and cat shark; Blue shark and stingray; Majestic snapper; Nassau grouper; Black-cap gramma and blue tang; Stingrays; Stingrays and giant starfish	7·00	8·00

MS2678 Two sheets. (a) 68×98 mm. $6 Humpback whale. (b) 98×68 mm. $6 Fiddler ray Set of 2 sheets — 9·00 9·50

Nos. 2641/65 and 2666/77 respectively were printed together, *se-tenant*, with the backgrounds forming composite designs.

394 *Savannah* (paddle-steamer)

1998. Ships of the World. Multicoloured.

2679	$1.75 Type **394**	1·50	1·50
2680	$1.75 Viking longship	1·50	1·50
2681	$1.75 Greek galley	1·50	1·50
2682	$1.75 Sailing clipper	1·50	1·50
2683	$1.75 Dhow	1·50	1·50
2684	$1.75 Fishing catboat	1·50	1·50

MS2685 Three sheets, each 100×70 mm. (a) $6 13th-century English warship (41×22 mm). (b) $6 Sailing dory (22×41 mm). (c) $6 Baltimore clipper (41×22 mm) Set of 3 sheets — 13·00 14·00

395 Flags of Antigua and CARICOM

1998. 25th Anniv of Caribbean Community.

2686	**395**	$1 multicoloured	1·25	1·25

396 Ford, 1896

1998. Classic Cars. Multicoloured.

2687	$1.65 Type **396**		1·10	1·10
2688	$1.65 Ford A, 1903		1·10	1·10
2689	$1.65 Ford T, 1928		1·10	1·10
2690	$1.65 Ford T, 1922		1·10	1·10
2691	$1.65 Ford Blackhawk, 1929		1·10	1·10
2692	$1.65 Ford Sedan, 1934		1·10	1·10
2693	$1.65 Torpedo, 1911		1·10	1·10
2694	$1.65 Mercedes 22, 1913		1·10	1·10
2695	$1.65 Rover, 1920		1·10	1·10
2696	$1.65 Mercedes-Benz, 1956		1·10	1·10
2697	$1.65 Packard V-12, 1934		1·10	1·10
2698	$1.65 Opel, 1924		1·10	1·10

MS2699 Two sheets, each 70×100 mm.
(a) $6 Ford, 1908 (60×40 mm). (b)
$6 Ford, 1929 (60×40 mm) Set of
2 sheets 7·50 8·00

397 Lockheed-Boeing
General Dynamics Yf-22

1998. Modern Aircraft. Multicoloured.

2700	$1.65 Type **397**		1·25	1·25
2701	$1.65 Dassault-Breguet Rafale BO 1		1·25	1·25
2702	$1.65 MiG 29		1·25	1·25
2703	$1.65 Dassault-Breguet Mirage 2000D		1·25	1·25
2704	$1.65 Rockwell B-1B "Lancer"		1·25	1·25
2705	$1.65 McDonnell-Douglas C-17A		1·25	1·25
2706	$1.65 Space Shuttle		1·25	1·25
2707	$1.65 SAAB "Grippen"		1·25	1·25
2708	$1.65 Eurofighter EF-2000		1·25	1·25
2709	$1.65 Sukhoi SU 27		1·25	1·25
2710	$1.65 Northrop B-2		1·25	1·25
2711	$1.65 Lockheed F-117 "Nighthawk"		1·25	1·25

MS2712 Two sheets, each 110×85 mm.
(a) $6 F18 Hornet. (b) $6 Sukhoi SU
35 Set of 2 sheets 8·50 9·00

No. **MS**2712b is inscribed "Sukhi" in error.

398 Karl Benz
(internal-
combustion
engine)

1998. Millennium Series. Famous People of the Twentieth Century. Inventors. Multicoloured.

2713	$1 Type **398**		1·00	1·00
2714	$1 Early Benz car and Mercedes-Benz racing car (53×38 mm)		1·00	1·00
2715	$1 Atom bomb mushroom cloud (53×38 mm)		1·00	1·00
2716	$1 Albert Einstein (theory of relativity)		1·00	1·00
2717	$1 Leopold Godowsky Jr. and Leopold Damrosch Mannes (Kodachrome film)		1·00	1·00
2718	$1 Camera and transparencies (53×38 mm)		1·00	1·00
2719	$1 Heinkel He 178 (first turbo jet plane) (53×38 mm)		1·00	1·00
2720	$1 Dr. Hans Pabst von Ohain (jet turbine engine)		1·00	1·00
2721	$1 Rudolf Diesel (diesel engine)		1·00	1·00
2722	$1 Early Diesel engine and forms of transport (53×38 mm)		1·00	1·00
2723	$1 Zeppelin airship (53×38 mm)		1·00	1·00
2724	$1 Count Ferdinand von Zeppelin (airship pioneer)		1·00	1·00
2725	$1 Wilhelm Conrad Rontgen (X-rays)		1·00	1·00
2726	$1 X-ray of hand (53×38 mm)		1·00	1·00
2727	$1 Launch of Saturn rocket (53×38 mm)		1·00	1·00
2728	$1 Wernher von Braun (rocket research)		1·00	1·00

MS2729 Two sheets, each 106×76 mm. (a) $6 Hans Geiger (Geiger counter). (b) $6 William Shockley (research into semi-conductors) Set of 2 sheets 9·50 10·00

No. 2713 is inscribed "CARL BENZ" in error.

399 Stylized Americas

1998. 50th Anniv of Organization of American States.

2730	**399**	$1 multicoloured	80	90

400 Figures on the Seashore

1998. 25th Death Anniv of Pablo Picasso (painter). Multicoloured.

2731	$1.20 Type **400**		75	70
2732	$1.65 Three Figures under a Tree (vert)		85	1·00
2733	$1.75 Two Women running on the Beach		95	1·25

MS2734 126×102 mm. $6 Bullfight 3·25 3·75

401 Dino 246 GT-GTS

1998. Birth Centenary of Enzo Ferrari (car manufacturer). Multicoloured.

2735	$1.75 Type **401**		2·25	2·25
2736	$1.75 Front view of Dino 246 GT-GTS		2·25	2·25
2737	$1.75 365 GT4 BB		2·25	2·25

MS2738 104×72 mm. $6 Dino 246 GT-GTS (91×34 mm) 6·00 6·00

402 Scout Handshake

1998. 19th World Scout Jamboree, Chile. Multicoloured.

2739	90c. Type **402**		60	55
2740	$1 Scouts hiking		75	90
2741	$1.20 Scout salute		90	1·25

MS2742 68×98 mm. $6 Lord Baden-Powell 3·25 3·75

403 Mahatma Gandhi

1998. 50th Death Anniv of Mahatma Gandhi. Multicoloured.

2743	90c. Type **403**		1·00	60
2744	$1 Gandhi seated		1·25	85
2745	$1.20 As young man		1·60	1·25
2746	$1.65 At primary school in Rajkot, aged 7		2·25	2·25

MS2747 100×70 mm. $6 Gandhi with staff 4·00 4·25

404 McDonnell Douglas
Phantom F-GR1

1998. 80th Anniv of Royal Air Force. Multicoloured.

2748	$1.75 Type **404**		1·60	1·60
2749	$1.75 Two Sepecat Jaguar GR1As		1·60	1·60
2750	$1.75 Panavia Tornado F3		1·60	1·60
2751	$1.75 McDonnell Douglas Phantom F-GR2		1·60	1·60

MS2752 Two sheets, each 90×68 mm.
(a) $6 Golden eagle (bird) and Bristol
F2B Fighter. (b) $6 Hawker Hurricane
and EF-2000 Eurofighter Set of 2
sheets 10·00 10·00

405 Diana, Princess
of Wales

1998. First Death Anniv of Diana, Princess of Wales.

2753	**405**	$1.20 multicoloured	1·00	1·00

406 Brown Pelican

1998. Sea Birds of the World. Multicoloured.

2754	15c. Type **406**		30	20
2755	25c. Dunlin		40	20
2756	45c. Atlantic puffin		50	25
2757	75c. King eider		65	70
2758	75c. Inca tern		65	70
2759	75c. Little auk ("Dovekie")		65	70
2760	75c. Ross's gull		65	70
2761	75c. Common noddy ("Brown Noddy")		65	70
2762	75c. Marbled murrelet		65	70
2763	75c. Northern gannet		65	70
2764	75c. Razorbill		65	70
2765	75c. Long-tailed skua ("Long-tailed Jaegar")		65	70
2766	75c. Black guillemot		65	70
2767	75c. Whimbrel		65	70
2768	75c. American oystercatcher ("Oystercatcher")		30	35
2769	90c. Pied cormorant		65	70

MS2770 Two sheets, each 100×70 mm.
(a) $6 Black skimmer. (b) $6 Wandering albatross Set of 2 sheets 8·00 9·00

Nos. 2757/68 were printed together, se-tenant, with the backgrounds forming a composite design.
No. 2760 is inscribed "ROSS' BULL" in error.

407 Border Collie

1998. Christmas. Dogs. Multicoloured.

2771	15c. Type **407**		45	25
2772	25c. Dalmatian		55	25
2773	65c. Weimaraner		90	50
2774	75c. Scottish terrier		95	50
2775	90c. Long-haired dachshund		1·10	55
2776	$1.20 Golden retriever		1·40	1·25
2777	$2 Pekingese		2·00	2·50

MS2778 Two sheets, each 75×66 mm.
(a) $6 Dalmatian. (b) $6 Jack Russell
terrier Set of 2 sheets 8·50 9·00

408 Mickey Mouse
Sailing

1999. 70th Birthday of Mickey Mouse. Walt Disney characters participating in water sports. Multicoloured.

2779	$1 Type **408**		95	95
2780	$1 Mickey and Goofy sailing		95	95
2781	$1 Goofy windsurfing		95	95
2782	$1 Mickey sailing and seagull		95	95
2783	$1 Goofy sailing		95	95
2784	$1 Mickey windsurfing		95	95
2785	$1 Goofy running with surfboard		95	95
2786	$1 Mickey surfing		95	95
2787	$1 Donald Duck holding surfboard		95	95
2788	$1 Donald on surfboard (face value at right)		95	95
2789	$1 Minnie Mouse surfing in green shorts		95	95

2790	$1 Goofy surfing		95	95
2791	$1 Goofy in purple shorts waterskiing		95	95
2792	$1 Mickey waterskiing		95	95
2793	$1 Goofy waterskiing with Mickey		95	95
2794	$1 Donald on surfboard (face value at left)		95	95
2795	$1 Goofy in yellow shorts waterskiing		95	95
2796	$1 Minnie in pink shorts surfing		95	95

MS2797 Four sheets, each 127×102
mm. (a) $6 Goofy (horiz). (b) $6 Donald Duck. (c) $6 Minnie Mouse. (d)
$6 Mickey Mouse Set of 4 sheets 15·00 16·00

409 Hell's Gate Steel
Orchestra, 1996

1999. 50th Anniv of Hell's Gate Steel Orchestra. Multicoloured.

2798	20c. Type **409**		25	20
2799	60c. Orchestra members, New York, 1992		50	40
2800	75c. Orchestra members with steel drums, 1950		60	50
2801	90c. Eustace Henry, 1964		70	55
2802	$1.20 Alston Henry playing double tenor		1·00	1·40

MS2803 Two sheets. (a) 100×70 mm.
$4 Orchestra members, 1950 (vert).
(b) 70×100 mm. $4 Eustace Henry,
1964 (vert) Set of 2 sheets 5·50 6·50

410 Tulips

1999. Flowers. Multicoloured.

2804	60c. Type **410**		40	30
2805	75c. Fuschia		50	35
2806	90c. Morning glory (horiz)		60	60
2807	90c. Geranium (horiz)		60	60
2808	90c. Blue hibiscus (horiz)		60	60
2809	90c. Marigolds (horiz)		60	60
2810	90c. Sunflower (horiz)		60	60
2811	90c. Impatiens (horiz)		60	60
2812	90c. Petunia (horiz)		60	60
2813	90c. Pansy (horiz)		60	60
2814	90c. Saucer magnolia (horiz)		60	60
2815	$1 Primrose (horiz)		70	70
2816	$1 Bleeding heart (horiz)		70	70
2817	$1 Pink dogwood (horiz)		70	70
2818	$1 Peony (horiz)		70	70
2819	$1 Rose (horiz)		70	70
2820	$1 Hellebores (horiz)		70	70
2821	$1 Lily (horiz)		70	70
2822	$1 Violet (horiz)		70	70
2823	$1 Cherry blossom (horiz)		70	70
2824	$1.20 Calla lily		75	75
2825	$1.65 Sweet pea		90	1·10

MS2826 Two sheets. (a) 76×100 mm.
$6 Sangria lily. (b) 106×76 mm. $6
Zinnias Set of 2 sheets 7·50 8·00

Nos. 2806/14 and 2815/23 respectively were each printed together, se-tenant, forming composite designs.

411 Elle
Macpherson

1999. "Australia '99" International Stamp Exhibition, Melbourne (1st issue). Elle Macpherson (model). Multicoloured.

2827	$1.20 Type **411**		1·00	1·00
2828	$1.20 Lying on couch		1·00	1·00
2829	$1.20 In swimsuit		1·00	1·00
2830	$1.20 Looking over shoulder		1·00	1·00
2831	$1.20 Wearing cream shirt		1·00	1·00
2832	$1.20 Wearing stetson		1·00	1·00
2833	$1.20 Wearing black T-shirt		1·00	1·00
2834	$1.20 Holding tree branch		1·00	1·00

See also Nos. 2875/92.

412 "Luna 2" Moon Probe

1999. Satellites and Spacecraft. Multicoloured.

2835	$1.65 Type **412**	1·10	1·10
2836	$1.65 "Mariner 2" space probe	1·10	1·10
2837	$1.65 "Giotto" space probe	1·10	1·10
2838	$1.65 Rosat satellite	1·10	1·10
2839	$1.65 International Ultraviolet Explorer	1·10	1·10
2840	$1.65 "Ulysses" space probe	1·10	1·10
2841	$1.65 "Mariner 10" space probe	1·10	1·10
2842	$1.65 "Luna 9" Moon probe	1·10	1·10
2843	$1.65 Advanced X-ray Astrophysics Facility	1·10	1·10
2844	$1.65 "Magellan" space probe	1·10	1·10
2845	$1.65 "Pioneer – Venus 2" space probe	1·10	1·10
2846	$1.65 Infra-red Astronomy Satellite	1·10	1·10

MS2847 Two sheets, each 106×76 mm.
(a) $6 "Salyut 1" space station (horiz).
(b) $6 "MIR" space station (horiz) Set of 2 sheets — 7·50 / 8·00

Nos. 2835/40 and 2841/46 respectively were each printed together, *se-tenant*, with the backgrounds forming composite designs.

413 John Glenn entering "Mercury" Capsule, 1962

1999. John Glenn's Return to Space. Multicoloured.

2848	$1.75 Type **413**	1·25	1·25
2849	$1.75 Glenn in "Mercury" mission spacesuit	1·25	1·25
2850	$1.75 Fitting helmet for "Mercury" mission	1·25	1·25
2851	$1.75 Outside pressure chamber	1·25	1·25

414 Brachiosaurus

1999. Prehistoric Animals. Multicoloured.

2852	65c. Type **414**	65	40
2853	75c. Oviraptor (vert)	70	40
2854	$1 Homotherium	80	45
2855	$1.20 Macrauchenia (vert)	90	60
2856	$1.65 Struthiomimus	1·00	1·00
2857	$1.65 Corythosaurus	1·00	1·00
2858	$1.65 Dsungaripterus	1·00	1·00
2859	$1.65 Compsognathus	1·00	1·00
2860	$1.65 Prosaurolophus	1·00	1·00
2861	$1.65 Montanoceratops	1·00	1·00
2862	$1.65 Stegosaurus	1·00	1·00
2863	$1.65 Deinonychus	1·00	1·00
2864	$1.65 Ouranosaurus	1·00	1·00
2865	$1.65 Leptictidium	1·00	1·00
2866	$1.65 Ictitherium	1·00	1·00
2867	$1.65 Plesictis	1·00	1·00
2868	$1.65 Hemicyon	1·00	1·00
2869	$1.65 Diacodexis	1·00	1·00
2870	$1.65 Stylinodon	1·00	1·00
2871	$1.65 Kanuites	1·00	1·00
2872	$1.65 Chriacus	1·00	1·00
2873	$1.65 Argyrolagus	1·00	1·00

MS2874 Two sheets, each 110×85 mm. (a) $6 Eurhinodelphis. (b) $6 Pteranodon Set of 2 sheets — 7·50 / 8·00

Nos. 2856/64 and 2865/73 respectively were each printed together, *se-tenant*, with the backgrounds forming composite designs.

415 Two White Kittens

1999. "Australia '99" International Stamp Exhibition, Melbourne (2nd issue). Cats. Multicoloured.

2875	35c. Type **415**	40	30
2876	45c. Kitten with string	50	35
2877	60c. Two kittens under blanket	60	50
2878	75c. Two kittens in basket	70	55
2879	90c. Kitten with ball	80	55
2880	$1 White kitten	90	80
2881	$1.65 Two kittens playing	1·10	1·10
2882	$1.65 Black and white kitten	1·10	1·10
2883	$1.65 Black kitten and sleeping cream kitten	1·10	1·10
2884	$1.65 White kitten with green string	1·10	1·10
2885	$1.65 Two sleeping kittens	1·10	1·10
2886	$1.65 White kitten with black tip to tail	1·10	1·10
2887	$1.65 Kitten with red string	1·10	1·10
2888	$1.65 Two long-haired kittens	1·10	1·10
2889	$1.65 Ginger kitten	1·10	1·10
2890	$1.65 Kitten playing with mouse	1·10	1·10
2891	$1.65 Kitten asleep on blue cushion	1·10	1·10
2892	$1.65 Tabby kitten	1·10	1·10

MS2893 Two sheets, each 70×100 mm.
(a) $6 Cat carrying kitten in mouth.
(b) $6 Kitten in tree Set of 2 sheets — 8·50 / 9·00

416 Early Leipzig–Dresden Railway Carriage and Caroline Islands 1901 Yacht Type 5m. Stamp

1999. "iBRA '99" International Stamp Exhibition, Nuremberg. Multicoloured.

2894	$1 Type **416**	70	60
2895	$1.20 Golsdorf steam locomotive and Caroline Islands 1901 Yacht type 1m.	80	70
2896	$1.65 Early Leipzig–Dresden Railway carriage and Caroline Islands 1899 20pf. optd on Germany	1·00	1·10
2897	$1.90 Golsdorf steam locomotive and Caroline Islands 1901 Yacht type 5pf. and 20pf.	1·40	2·00

MS2898 165×110 mm. $6 Registration label for Ponape, Caroline Islands — 3·25 / 3·75

417 People on Balcony of Sazaido (Hokusai)

1999. 150th Death Anniv of Katsushika Hokusai (Japanese artist). Multicoloured.

2899	$1.65 Type **417**	1·00	1·00
2900	$1.65 Nakahara in Sagami Province	1·00	1·00
2901	$1.65 Defensive Positions (two wrestlers)	1·00	1·00
2902	$1.65 Defensive Positions (three wrestlers)	1·00	1·00
2903	$1.65 Mount Fuji in Clear Weather	1·00	1·00
2904	$1.65 Nihonbashi in Edo	1·00	1·00
2905	$1.65 Asakusa Honganji	1·00	1·00
2906	$1.65 Dawn at Isawa in Kai Province	1·00	1·00
2907	$1.65 Samurai with Bow and Arrow (with arrows on ground)	1·00	1·00
2908	$1.65 Samurai with Bow and Arrow (trees in background)	1·00	1·00
2909	$1.65 Kajikazawa in Kai Province	1·00	1·00
2910	$1.65 A Great Wave	1·00	1·00

MS2911 Two sheets, each 100×71 mm.
(a) $6 A Netsuke Workshop (vert).
(b) $6 Gotenyama at Shinagawa on Tokaido Highway (vert) Set of 2 sheets — 7·50 / 8·00

No. 2903 is inscribed "MOUNT FUGI" in error.

418 Sophie Rhys-Jones

1999. Royal Wedding. Multicoloured.

2912	$3 Type **418**	1·75	2·00
2913	$3 Sophie and Prince Edward	1·75	2·00
2914	$3 Prince Edward	1·75	2·00

MS2915 108×78 mm. $6 Prince Edward with Sophie Rhys-Jones and Windsor Castle (horiz) — 3·50 / 4·00

419 Three Children

1999. Tenth Anniv of United Nations Rights of the Child Convention. Multicoloured.

2916	$3 Type **419**	1·75	2·00
2917	$3 Adult hand holding child's hand	1·75	2·00
2918	$3 Dove and U.N. Headquarters	1·75	2·00

MS2919 112×70 mm. $6 Dove — 3·25 / 3·75

Nos. 2916/18 were printed together, *se-tenant*, forming a composite design.

420 Crampton Type Railway Locomotive, 1855–69

1999. "PhilexFrance '99" International Stamp Exhibition, Paris. Railway Locomotives. Two sheets, each 106×81 mm, containing T 420 and similar design. Multicoloured.

MS2920 (a) $6 Type **420**. (b) $6 Compound type No. 232-U1 steam locomotive, 1949 Set of 2 sheets — 7·50 / 8·00

421 Three Archangels from *Faust*

1999. 250th Birth Anniv of Johann von Goethe (German writer).

2921	**421**	$1.75 purple, mauve and black	1·10	1·25
2922	-	$1.75 blue, violet and black	1·10	1·25
2923	-	$1.75 green and black	1·10	1·25

MS2924 – 79×101 mm. $6 black and brown — 3·25 / 3·75

DESIGNS: No. 2922, Von Goethe and Von Schiller; 2923, Faust reclining with spirits; MS2924 Wolfgang von Goethe.

422 Missa Ferdie (fishing launch)

1999. Local Ships and Boats. Multicoloured.

2925	25c. Type **422**	25	25
2926	45c. Yachts in 32nd Annual Antigua International Sailing Week	40	30
2927	60c. Jolly Roger (tourist ship)	50	40
2928	90c. Freewinds (cruise liner) (10th anniv of first visit)	70	60
2929	$1.20 Monarch of the Seas (cruise liner)	95	1·25

MS2930 98×62 mm. $4 Freewinds (11th anniv of maiden voyage) (50×37 mm) — 2·75 / 3·25

423 Fiery Jewel

1999. Butterflies. Multicoloured.

2931	65c. Type **423**	70	45
2932	75c. Hewitson's blue hairstreak	80	55
2933	$1 California dog face (horiz)	90	90
2934	$1 Small copper (horiz)	90	90
2935	$1 Zebra swallowtail (horiz)	90	90
2936	$1 White "M" hairstreak (horiz)	90	90
2937	$1 Old world swallowtail (horiz)	90	90
2938	$1 Buckeye (horiz)	90	90
2939	$1 Apollo (horiz)	90	90
2940	$1 Sonoran blue (horiz)	90	90
2941	$1 Purple emperor (horiz)	90	90
2942	$1.20 Scarce bamboo page (horiz)	1·00	1·00
2943	$1.65 Paris peacock (horiz)	1·25	1·50

MS2944 Two sheets. (a) 85×110 mm. $6 Monarch. (b) 110×85 mm. $6 Cairns birdwing (horiz) Set of 2 sheets — 9·00 / 9·50

Nos. 2933/41 were printed together, *se-tenant*, forming a composite design.

424 "Madonna and Child in Wreath of Flowers" (Rubens)

1999. Christmas. Religious Paintings.

2945	**424**	15c. multicoloured	25	15
2946	-	25c. black, stone & yellow	30	15
2947	-	45c. multicoloured	50	25
2948	-	60c. multicoloured	60	30
2949	-	$2 multicoloured	1·75	1·75
2950	-	$4 black, stone & yell	3·00	4·00

MS2951 – 76×106 mm. $6 multicoloured — 4·00 / 4·25

DESIGNS: 25c. *Shroud of Christ held by Two Angels* (Durer); 45c. *Madonna and Child enthroned between Two Saints*"(Raphael); 60c. *Holy Family with Lamb* (Raphael); $2 *The Transfiguration* (Raphael); $4 *Three Putti holding Coat of Arms* (Durer); $6 *Coronation of St. Catharine* (Rubens).

425 Katharine Hepburn (actress)

2000. Senior Celebrities of the 20th Century. Multicoloured.

2952	90c. Type **425**	85	85
2953	90c. Martha Graham (dancer)	85	85
2954	90c. Eubie Blake (jazz pianist)	85	85
2955	90c. Agatha Christie (novelist)	85	85
2956	90c. Eudora Welty (American novelist)	85	85
2957	90c. Helen Hayes (actress)	85	85
2958	90c. Vladimir Horowitz (concert pianist)	85	85
2959	90c. Katharine Graham (newspaper publisher)	85	85
2960	90c. Pablo Casals (cellist)	85	85
2961	90c. Pete Seeger (folk singer)	85	85
2962	90c. Andres Segovia (guitarist)	85	85
2963	90c. Frank Lloyd Wright (architect)	85	85

426 Sir Cliff Richard

2000. 60th Birthday of Sir Cliff Richard (entertainer).

2964	**426**	$1.65 multicoloured	1·25	1·25

427 Charlie Chaplin

2000. Charlie Chaplin (actor and director) Commemoration. Showing film scenes. Multicoloured.

2965	$1.65 Standing in street (*Modern Times*)	95	95
2966	$1.65 Hugging man (*The Gold Rush*)	95	95
2967	$1.65 Type **427**	95	95
2968	$1.65 Wielding tools (*Modern Times*)	95	95
2969	$1.65 With hands on hips (*The Gold Rush*)	95	95
2970	$1.65 Wearing cape (*The Gold Rush*)	95	95

428 Streamertail

2000. "The Stamp Show 2000" International Stamp Exhibition, London. Birds of the Caribbean. Multicoloured.

2971	75c. Type **428**	50	35
2972	90c. Yellow-bellied sapsucker	60	40
2973	$1.20 Rufous-tailed jacamar	75	75
2974	$1.20 Scarlet macaw	75	75
2975	$1.20 Yellow-crowned amazon ("Yellow-fronted Amazon")	75	75
2976	$1.20 Golden conure ("Queen-of-Bavaria")	75	75
2977	$1.20 Nanday conure	75	75
2978	$1.20 Jamaican tody	75	75
2979	$1.20 Smooth-billed ani	75	75
2980	$1.20 Puerto Rican woodpecker	75	75
2981	$1.20 Ruby-throated hummingbird	75	75
2982	$1.20 Common ground dove	75	75
2983	$1.20 American wood ibis ("Wood Stork")	75	75
2984	$1.20 Saffron finch	75	75
2985	$1.20 Green-backed heron	75	75
2986	$1.20 Lovely cotinga	75	75
2987	$1.20 St. Vincent amazon ("St. Vincent Parrot")	75	75
2988	$1.20 Cuban grassquit	75	75
2989	$1.20 Red-winged blackbird	75	75
2990	$2 Spectacled owl	1·40	1·50

MS2991 Two sheets, each 80×106 mm. (a) $6 Vermillion flycatcher (50×37 mm). (b) $6 Red-capped manakin (37×50 mm) Set of 2 sheets ... 9·50 10·00

Nos. 2974/81 and 2982/9 were each printed together, *se-tenant*, with the backgrounds forming composite designs.

No. 2981 is inscribed "Arhilochus colubria" in error.

429 Arthur Goodwin

2000. 400th Birth Anniv of Sir Anthony Van Dyck (Flemish painter). Multicoloured.

2992	$1.20 Type **429**	75	75
2993	$1.20 *Sir Thomas Wharton*	75	75
2994	$1.20 *Mary Villiers, Daughter of Duke of Buckingham*	75	75
2995	$1.20 *Christina Bruce, Countess of Devonshire*	75	75
2996	$1.20 *James Hamilton, Duke of Hamilton*	75	75
2997	$1.20 *Henry Danvers, Earl of Danby*	75	75
2998	$1.20 *Marie de Raet, Wife of Philippe le Roy*	75	75
2999	$1.20 *Jacomo de Cachopin*	75	75
3000	$1.20 *Princess Henrietta of Lorraine attended by a Page*	75	75
3001	$1.20 *Portrait of a Man*	75	75
3002	$1.20 *Portrait of a Woman*	75	75
3003	$1.20 *Philippe le Roy, Seigneur de Ravels*	75	75
3004	$1.20 *Charles I in State Robes*	75	75
3005	$1.20 *Queen Henrietta Maria (in white dress)*	75	75
3006	$1.20 *Queen Henrietta Maria with Sir Jeffrey Hudson*	75	75
3007	$1.20 *Charles I in Armour*	75	75
3008	$1.20 *Queen Henrietta Maria in Profile facing right*	75	75
3009	$1.20 *Queen Henrietta Maria (in black dress)*	75	75

MS3010 Six sheets. (a) 102×128 mm. $5 *Charles I on Horseback.* (b) 102×128 mm. $5 *Charles I Hunting.* (c) 128×102 mm. $5 *Charles I with Queen Henrietta Maria.* (d) 128×102 mm. $5 *Charles I (from Three Aspects portrait).* (e) 102×128 mm. $6 *William, Lord Russell.* (f) 102×128 mm. $6 *Two Sons of Duke of Lennox* Set of 6 sheets ... 20·00 22·00

No. 2994 is inscribed "Mary Villers", 3002 "Portrait of a Women", 3005 "Henrieta Maria" and **MS**3010f "Duke of Lenox", all in error.

430 *Eupolea miniszeki*

2000. Butterflies. Multicoloured.

3011	$1.65 Type **430**	90	90
3012	$1.65 *Heliconius doris*	90	90
3013	$1.65 *Evenus coronata*	90	90
3014	$1.65 *Papilio anchisiades*	90	90
3015	$1.65 *Syrmatia dorilas*	90	90
3016	$1.65 *Morpho patroclus*	90	90
3017	$1.65 *Mesosemia loruhama*	90	90
3018	$1.65 *Bia actorion*	90	90
3019	$1.65 *Anteos clorinde*	90	90
3020	$1.65 *Menander menande*	90	90
3021	$1.65 *Catasticta manco*	90	90
3022	$1.65 *Urania leilus*	90	90
3023	$1.65 *Theope eudocia* (vert)	90	90
3024	$1.65 *Uranus sloanus* (vert)	90	90
3025	$1.65 *Helicopis cupido* (vert)	90	90
3026	$1.65 *Papilio velovis* (vert)	90	90
3027	$1.65 *Graphium androcles* (vert)	90	90
3028	$1.65 *Mesene phareus* (vert)	90	90

MS3029 Three sheets. (a) 110×85 mm. $6 *Graphium enceladus.* (b) 110×85 mm. $6 *Graphium milon.* (c) 85×110 mm. $6 *Hemlargus isola* (vert) Set of 3 sheets ... 13·00 14·00

Nos. 3011/16, 3017/22 and 3023/8 were each printed together, *se-tenant*, with the backgrounds forming composite designs.

431 Boxer

2000. Cats and Dogs. Multicoloured.

3030	90c. Type **431**	75	45
3031	$1 Alaskan malamute	85	70
3032	$1.65 Bearded collie	1·10	1·10
3033	$1.65 Cardigan Welsh corgi	1·10	1·10
3034	$1.65 Saluki (red)	1·10	1·10
3035	$1.65 Basset hound	1·10	1·10
3036	$1.65 White standard poodle	1·10	1·10
3037	$1.65 Boston terrier	1·10	1·10
3038	$1.65 Long-haired blue and white cat (horiz)	1·10	1·10
3039	$1.65 Snow shoe (horiz)	1·10	1·10
3040	$1.65 Persian (horiz)	1·10	1·10
3041	$1.65 Chocolate lynx point (horiz)	1·10	1·10
3042	$1.65 Brown and white sphynx (horiz)	1·10	1·10
3043	$1.65 White tortoiseshell (horiz)	1·10	1·10
3044	$2 Wirehaired pointer	1·40	1·40
3045	$4 Saluki (black)	2·50	3·00

MS3046 Two sheets. (a) 106×71 mm. $6 Cavalier King Charles spaniel. (b) 111×81 mm. $6 Lavender tortie Set of 2 sheets ... 12·00 12·00

432 *Epidendrum pseudepidendrum*

2000. Flowers of the Caribbean. Multicoloured.

3047	45c. Type **432**	85	35
3048	65c. *Odontoglossum cervantesii*	1·00	50
3049	75c. *Cattleya dowiana*	1·00	50
3050	90c. *Beloperone guttata*	1·00	50
3051	$1 *Colliandra haematocephala*	1·00	70
3052	$1.20 *Brassavola nodosa*	1·00	80
3053	$1.65 *Pseudocalymna alliaceum*	1·10	1·10
3054	$1.65 *Datura candida*	1·10	1·10

3055	$1.65 *Ipomoea tuberosa*	1·10	1·10
3056	$1.65 *Allamanda cathartica*	1·10	1·10
3057	$1.65 *Aspasia epidendroides*	1·10	1·10
3058	$1.65 *Maxillaria cucullata*	1·10	1·10
3059	$1.65 *Anthurium andreanum*	1·10	1·10
3060	$1.65 *Doxantha unguiscati*	1·10	1·10
3061	$1.65 *Hibiscus rosa-sinensis*	1·10	1·10
3062	$1.65 *Canna indica*	1·10	1·10
3063	$1.65 *Heliconius umilis*	1·10	1·10
3064	$1.65 *Strelitzia reginae*	1·10	1·10
3065	$1.65 *Masdevallia coccinea*	1·10	1·10
3066	$1.65 *Paphinia cristata*	1·10	1·10
3067	$1.65 *Vanilla planifolia*	1·10	1·10
3068	$1.65 *Cattleya forbesii*	1·10	1·10
3069	$1.65 *Lycaste skinneri*	1·10	1·10
3070	$1.65 *Cattleya percivaliana*	1·10	1·10

MS3071 Three sheets, each 74×103 mm. (a) $6 *Cattleya leopoldiie.* (b) $6 *Strelitzia reginae.* (c) $6 *Rossioglossum grande* Set of 3 sheets ... 13·00 14·00

No. 3061 is inscribed "rosa-senensis" and **MS**3071b "regenae", both in error.

433 Prince William

2000. 18th Birthday of Prince William. Multicoloured.

3072	$1.65 Prince William waving	1·40	1·40
3073	$1.65 Wearing Eton school uniform	1·40	1·40
3074	$1.65 Wearing grey suit	1·40	1·40
3075	$1.65 Type **433**	1·40	1·40

MS3076 100×80 mm. $6 Princess Diana with Princes William and Harry (37×50 mm) ... 4·25 4·50

434 "Sputnik I"

2000. "EXPO 2000" World Stamp Exhibition, Anaheim, U.S.A. Space Satellites. Multicoloured.

3077	$1.65 Type **434**	1·10	1·10
3078	$1.65 "Explorer I"	1·10	1·10
3079	$1.65 "Mars Express"	1·10	1·10
3080	$1.65 "Lunik I Solnik"	1·10	1·10
3081	$1.65 "Ranger 7"	1·10	1·10
3082	$1.65 "Mariner 4"	1·10	1·10
3083	$1.65 "Mariner 10"	1·10	1·10
3084	$1.65 "Soho"	1·10	1·10
3085	$1.65 "Mariner 2"	1·10	1·10
3086	$1.65 "Giotto"	1·10	1·10
3087	$1.65 "Exosat"	1·10	1·10
3088	$1.65 "Pioneer Venus"	1·10	1·10

MS3089 Two sheets, each 106×76 mm. (a) $6 "Vostok I". (b) $6 Hubble Space Telescope Set of 2 sheets ... 8·50 9·50

Nos. 3077/82 and 3083/8 were each printed together, *se-tenant*, with the backgrounds forming composite designs.

435 Alexei Leonov (Commander of "Soyuz 19")

2000. 25th Anniv of "Apollo–Soyuz" Joint Project. Multicoloured.

3090	$3 Type **435**	1·75	2·00
3091	$3 "Soyuz 19"	1·75	2·00
3092	$3 Valeri Kubasov ("Soyuz 19" engineer)	1·75	2·00

MS3093 71×88 mm. $6 Alexei Leonov and Thomas Stafford (Commander of "Apollo 18") ... 3·25 3·75

436 Anna Karina in *Une Femme est Une Femme*, 1961

2000. 50th Anniv of Berlin Film Festival. Designs showing actors, directors and film scenes. Multicoloured.

3094	$1.65 Type **436**	1·00	1·00
3095	$1.65 *Carmen Jones*, 1955	1·00	1·00
3096	$1.65 *Die Ratten*, 1955	1·00	1·00
3097	$1.65 *Die Vier im Jeep*, 1951	1·00	1·00
3098	$1.65 Sidney Poitier in *Lilies of the Field*, 1963	1·00	1·00
3099	$1.65 *Invitation to the Dance*, 1956	1·00	1·00

MS3100 97×103 mm. $6 Kate Winslet in *Sense and Sensibility*, 1996 ... 3·25 3·75

No. 3096 is inscribed "GOLDER BERLIN BEAR" and **MS**3100 shows the award date "1966" in error.

437 George Stephenson and *Locomotion No. 1*, 1825

2000. 175th Anniv of Stockton and Darlington Line (first public railway). Multicoloured.

3101	$3 Type **437**	2·50	2·50
3102	$3 Camden and Amboy Railroad locomotive *John Bull*, 1831	2·50	2·50

438 Statue of Johann Sebastian Bach

2000. 250th Death Anniv of Johann Sebastian Bach (German composer). Sheet 77×88 mm.

MS3103 $6 multicoloured ... 4·00 4·50

439 Albert Einstein

2000. Election of Albert Einstein (mathematical physicist) as Time Magazine "Man of the Century". Sheet 117×91 mm.

MS3104 $6 multicoloured ... 3·75 4·25

440 LZ-1 Airship, 1900

2000. Centenary of First Zeppelin Flight.

3105	**440**	$3 brown, black and blue	2·50	2·50
3106	-	$3 brown, black and blue	2·50	2·50
3107	-	$3 multicoloured	2·50	2·50

MS3108 – 93×66 mm. $6 multicoloured ... 3·75 4·00

DESIGNS: No. 3106, LZ-2, 1906; 3107, LZ-3, 1906. (50×37 mm)—No. **MS**3108, LZ-7 *Deutschland*, 1910.

Nos. 3105/7 were printed together, *se-tenant*, with the backgrounds forming a composite design.

441 Marcus Latimer Hurley (cycling), St. Louis (1904)

2000. Olympic Games, Sydney. Multicoloured.

3109	$2 Type **441**	2·25	2·25
3110	$2 Diving	2·25	2·25
3111	$2 Flaminio Stadium, Rome (1960) and Italian flag	2·25	2·25
3112	$2 Ancient Greek javelin thrower	2·25	2·25

442 Richie Richardson

2000. West Indies Cricket Tour and 100th Test Match at Lord's. Multicoloured.

3113	90c. Type **442**	1·50	70
3114	$5 Viv Richards	5·50	6·00
MS3115	121×104 mm. $6 Lord's Cricket Ground (horiz)	5·50	6·00

No. 3114 is inscribed "Viv Richard" in error.

443 Outreach Programme at Sunshine Home for Girls

2000. Girls Brigade. Multicoloured.

3116	20c. Type **443**	25	20
3117	60c. Ullida Rawlins Gill (International Vice President) (vert)	50	35
3118	75c. Officers and girls	60	45
3119	90c. Girl with flag (vert)	80	55
3120	$1.20 Members of 8th Antigua Company with flag (vert)	1·10	1·40
MS3121	102×124 mm. $5 Girl Brigade badge (vert)	3·25	3·75

444 Lady Elizabeth Bowes-Lyon as Young Girl

2000. "Queen Elizabeth the Queen Mother's Century".

3122	**444**	$2 multicoloured	1·75	1·75
3123	-	$2 black and gold	1·75	1·75
3124	-	$2 black and gold	1·75	1·75
3125	-	$2 multicoloured	1·75	1·75
MS3126		– 153×157 mm. $6 multicoloured	4·00	4·25

DESIGNS: No. 3123, Queen Elizabeth in 1940; 3124, Queen Mother with Princess Anne, 1951; 3125, Queen Mother in Canada, 1989; **MS**3126, Queen Mother inspecting guard of honour.

No. **MS**3126 also shows the Royal Arms embossed in gold.

445 Thumbscrew (Expansion of Inquisition, 1250)

2000. New Millennium. People and Events of Thirteenth Century (1250–1300). Multicoloured (except No. 3127).

3127	60c. Type **445** (black and red)	90	90
3128	60c. Chartres Cathedral (completed, 1260)	90	90
3129	60c. Donor's sculpture, Naumberg (completed, 1260)	90	90
3130	60c. Delegates (Simon de Montfort's Parliament, 1261)	90	90
3131	60c. *Maestà* (Cimabue) (painted 1270)	90	90
3132	60c. Marco Polo (departure from Venice, 1271)	90	90
3133	60c. *Divine Wind* (Kamikaze wind saves Japan from invasion, 1274)	90	90
3134	60c. St. Thomas Aquinas (died 1274)	90	90
3135	60c. Arezzo Cathedral (completed 1277)	90	90

3136	60c. Margrethe ("The Maid of Norway") (crowned Queen of Scotland, 1286)	90	90
3137	60c. Jewish refugees (Expulsion of Jews from England, 1290)	90	90
3138	60c. Muslim horseman (capture of Acre, 1291)	90	90
3139	60c. Moshe de Leon (compiles *The Zohar*, 1291)	90	90
3140	60c. Knights in combat (German Civil War, 1292–98)	90	90
3141	60c. Kublai Khan (died 1294)	90	90
3142	60c. Dante (writes *La Vita Nuova*, 1295) (59×39 mm)	90	90
3143	60c. *Autumn Colours on Quiao and Hua Mountains* (Zhan Mengfu) (painted 1296)	90	90

446 *Admonishing the Court Ladies* (after Ku K'ai-Chih)

2000. New Millennium. Two Thousand Years of Chinese Paintings. Multicoloured.

3144	25c. Type **446**	40	40
3145	25c. *Ink on silk drawing from Zhan Jadashan*	40	40
3146	25c. *Ink and colour on silk drawing from Mawangdui Tomb*	40	40
3147	25c. *Scholars collating Texts* (attr Yang Zihua)	40	40
3148	25c. *Spring Outing* (attr Zhan Ziqian)	40	40
3149	25c. *Portrait of the Emperors* (attr Yen Liben)	40	40
3150	25c. *Sailing Boats and Riverside Mansion* (attr Li Sixun)	40	40
3151	25c. *Two Horses and Groom* (Han Kan)	40	40
3152	25c. *King's Portrait* (attr Wu Daozi)	40	40
3153	25c. *Court Ladies wearing Flowered Headdresses* (attr Zhou Fang)	40	40
3154	25c. *Distant Mountain Forest* (mountain) (Juran)	40	40
3155	25c. *Mount Kuanglu* (Jiang Hao)	40	40
3156	25c. *Pheasant and Small Birds* (Huang Jucai)	40	40
3157	25c. *Deer among Red Maples* (anon)	40	40
3158	25c. *Distant Mountain Forest* (river and fields) (Juran)	40	40
3159	25c. *Literary Gathering* (Han Huang) (57×39 mm)	40	40
3160	25c. *Birds and Insects* (Huang Quan)	40	40

No. 3148 is inscribed "SPRINTING", No. 3150 "MASION" and No. 3153 "HEADRESSES", all in error.

447 King Donald III of Scotland

2000. Monarchs of the Millennium.

3161	**447**	$1.65 black, stone and brown	1·50	1·50
3162	-	$1.65 black, stone and brown	1·50	1·50
3163	-	$1.65 black, stone and brown	1·50	1·50
3164	-	$1.65 black, stone and brown	1·50	1·50
3165	-	$1.65 black, stone and brown	1·50	1·50
3166	-	$1.65 black, stone and brown	1·50	1·50
3167	-	$1.65 multicoloured	1·50	1·50
3168	-	$1.65 multicoloured	1·50	1·50
3169	-	$1.65 multicoloured	1·50	1·50
3170	-	$1.65 multicoloured	1·50	1·50
3171	-	$1.65 multicoloured	1·50	1·50
3172	-	$1.65 multicoloured	1·50	1·50
MS3173		– Two sheets, each 115×135 mm. (a) $6 mult. (b) $6 mult Set of 2 sheets	8·50	9·50

DESIGNS: No. 3162, King Duncan I of Scotland; 3163, King Duncan II of Scotland; 3164, King Macbeth of Scotland; 3165, King Malcolm III of Scotland; 3166, King Edgar of Scotland; 3167, King Charles I of England and Scotland; 3168, King Charles II of England and Scotland; 3169, Prince Charles Edward Stuart ("The Young Pretender"); 3170, King James II of England and VII of Scotland; 3171, King James II of Scotland; 3172, King James III of Scotland; **MS**3173a, King Robert I of Scotland; **MS**3173b, Queen Anne of Great Britain.

No. 3169 is inscribed "George III 1760–1820 Great Britain" in error.

2000. Popes of the Millennium. As T 447. Each black, yellow and green.

3174	$1.65 Alexander VI (bare-headed)	1·50	1·50
3175	$1.65 Benedict XIII	1·50	1·50
3176	$1.65 Boniface IX	1·50	1·50
3177	$1.65 Alexander VI (wearing cap)	1·50	1·50
3178	$1.65 Clement VIII	1·50	1·50
3179	$1.65 Clement VI	1·50	1·50
3180	$1.65 John Paul II	1·50	1·50
3181	$1.65 Benedict XV	1·50	1·50
3182	$1.65 John XXIII	1·50	1·50
3183	$1.65 Pius XI	1·50	1·50
3184	$1.65 Pius XII	1·50	1·50
3185	$1.65 Paul VI	1·50	1·50
MS3186	Two sheets, each 115×135 mm. (a) $6 Pius II (black, yellow and black). (b) $6 Pius VII (black, yellow and black) Set of 2 sheets	9·00	9·50

No. 3181 is inscribed "BENIDICT XV" in error.

448 Agouti

2000. Fauna of the Rain Forest. Multicoloured.

3187	75c. Type **448**	60	45
3188	90c. Capybara	70	50
3189	$1.20 Basilisk lizard	80	70
3190	$1.65 Green violetear ("Green Violet-Ear Hummingbird")	1·10	1·10
3191	$1.65 Harpy eagle	1·10	1·10
3192	$1.65 Three-toed sloth	1·10	1·10
3193	$1.65 White uakari monkey	1·10	1·10
3194	$1.65 Anteater	1·10	1·10
3195	$1.65 Coati	1·10	1·10
3196	$1.75 Red-eyed tree frog	1·10	1·10
3197	$1.75 Black spider monkey	1·10	1·10
3198	$1.75 Emerald toucanet	1·10	1·10
3199	$1.75 Kinkajou	1·10	1·10
3200	$1.75 Spectacled bear	1·10	1·10
3201	$1.75 Tapir	1·10	1·10
3202	$2 Heliconid butterfly	1·25	1·40
MS3203	Two sheets. (a) 90×65 mm. $6 Keel-billed toucan (horiz). (b) 65×90 mm. $6 Scarlet macaw Set of 2 sheets	10·00	11·00

Nos. 3190/5 and 3196/201 were printed together, se-tenant, forming composite designs.

449 "Sea Cliff" Submarine

2000. Submarines. Multicoloured.

3204	65c. Type **449**	85	45
3205	75c. "Beaver Mark IV"	1·00	50
3206	90c. "Reef Ranger"	1·10	50
3207	$1 "Cubmarine"	1·25	70
3208	$1.20 "Alvin"	1·40	80
3209	$2 H.M.S. *Revenge*	2·00	2·00
3210	$2 *Walrus*, Netherlands	2·00	2·00
3211	$2 U.S.S. *Los Angeles*	2·00	2·00
3212	$2 *Daphne*, France	2·00	2·00
3213	$2 U.S.S. *Ohio*	2·00	2·00
3214	$2 U.S.S. *Skipjack*	2·00	2·00
3215	$3 "*Argus*", Russia	2·50	2·75
MS3216	Two sheets, each 107×84 mm. (a) $6 "Trieste". (b) $6 Type 209 U-boat, Germany Set of 2 sheets	10·00	11·00

Nos. 3209/14 were printed together, se-tenant, with the backgrounds forming a composite design.

450 German Lookout

DESIGNS: No. 3162, King Duncan I of Scotland; 3163, King Duncan II of Scotland; 3164, King Macbeth of Scotland; 3165, King Malcolm III of Scotland; 3166, King Edgar of Scotland; 3167, King Charles I of England and Scotland; 3168, King Charles II of England and Scotland; 3169, Prince Charles Edward Stuart ("The Young Pretender"); 3170, King James II of England and VII of Scotland; 3171, King James II of Scotland; 3172, King James III of Scotland; MS3173a, King Robert I of Scotland; MS3173b, Queen Anne of Great Britain.

2000. 60th Anniv of Battle of Britain. Multicoloured (except No. 3222).

3217	$1.20 Type **450**	1·50	1·50
3218	$1.20 Children's evacuation train	1·50	1·50
3219	$1.20 Evacuating hospital patients	1·50	1·50
3220	$1.20 Hawker Hurricane (fighter)	1·50	1·50
3221	$1.20 Rescue team	1·50	1·50
3222	$1.20 Churchill cartoon (black)	1·50	1·50
3223	$1.20 King George VI and Queen Elizabeth inspecting bomb damage	1·50	1·50
3224	$1.20 Barrage balloon above Tower Bridge	1·50	1·50
3225	$1.20 Bristol Blenheim (bomber)	1·50	1·50
3226	$1.20 Prime Minister Winston Churchill	1·50	1·50
3227	$1.20 Bristol Blenheim and barrage balloons	1·50	1·50
3228	$1.20 Heinkel (fighter)	1·50	1·50
3229	$1.20 Supermarine Spitfire (fighter)	1·50	1·50
3230	$1.20 German rescue launch	1·50	1·50
3231	$1.20 Messerschmitt 109 (fighter)	1·50	1·50
3232	$1.20 R.A.F. rescue launch	1·50	1·50
MS3233	Two sheets, each 90×60 mm. (a) $6 Junkers 87B (dive bomber). (b) $6 Supermarine Spitfires at dusk Set of 2 sheets	12·00	13·00

No. **MS**3233a is inscribed "JUNKERS 878" in error.

451 *The Defence of Cadiz* (Zurbaran)

2000. "Espana 2000" International Stamp Exhibition, Madrid. Paintings from the Prado Museum. Multicoloured.

3234	$1.65 Type **451**	1·25	1·25
3235	$1.65 *The Defence of Cadiz* (General and galleys)	1·25	1·25
3236	$1.65 *The Defence of Cadiz* (officers)	1·25	1·25
3237	$1.65 *Vulcan's Forge* (Vulcan) (Velazquez)	1·25	1·25
3238	$1.65 *Vulcan's Forge* (working metal)	1·25	1·25
3239	$1.65 *Vulcan's Forge* (workers with hammers)	1·25	1·25
3240	$1.65 *Family Portrait* (three men) (Adriaen Key)	1·25	1·25
3241	$1.65 *Family Portrait* (one man)	1·25	1·25
3242	$1.65 *Family Portrait* (three women)	1·25	1·25
3243	$1.65 *The Devotion of Rudolf I* (horseman with lantern) (Rubens and Jan Wildens)	1·25	1·25
3244	$1.65 *The Devotion of Rudolf I* (priest on horseback)	1·25	1·25
3245	$1.65 *The Devotion of Rudolf I* (huntsman)	1·25	1·25
3246	$1.65 *The Concert* (lute player) (Vincente Gonzalez)	1·25	1·25
3247	$1.65 *The Concert* (lady with fan)	1·25	1·25
3248	$1.65 *The Concert* (two gentlemen)	1·25	1·25
3249	$1.65 *The Adoration of the Magi* (Wise Man) (Juan Maino)	1·25	1·25
3250	$1.65 *The Adoration of the Magi* (two Wise Men)	1·25	1·25
3251	$1.65 *The Adoration of the Magi* (Holy Family)	1·25	1·25
MS3252	Three sheets. (a) 115×90 mm. $6 *The Deliverance of St. Peter* (Jose de Ribera) (horiz). (b) 110×90 mm. $6 *The Fan Seller* (Jose del Castillo). (c) 110×90 mm. $6 *Family in a Garden* (Jan van Kessel the Younger) Set of 3 sheets	11·00	13·00

Nos. 3246/8 are inscribed "Gonzalez" with No. 3248 additionally inscribed "Francisco Rizi", all in error.

452 Two Angels

2000. Christmas and Holy Year. Multicoloured.

3253	25c. Type **452**	20	15

3254	45c. Heads of two angels looking down	35	25
3255	90c. Heads of two angels, one looking up	60	40
3256	$1.75 Type **452**	1·25	1·50
3257	$1.75 As 45c.	1·25	1·50
3258	$1.75 As 90c.	1·25	1·50
3259	$1.75 As $5	1·25	1·50
3260	$5 Two angels with drapery	3·00	3·75
MS3261	110×120 mm. $6 Holy Child	3·50	4·00

453 Dr. Ephraim Bueno (Rembrandt)

2000. Bicentenary of Rijksmuseum, Amsterdam. Dutch Paintings. Multicoloured.

3262	$1 Type **453**	85	85
3263	$1 Woman writing a Letter (Frans van Meris de Oude)	85	85
3264	$1 Mary Magdalen (Jan van Scorel)	85	85
3265	$1 Anna Coddle (Maerten van Heemskerck)	85	85
3266	$1 Cleopatra's Banquet (Gerard Lairesse)	85	85
3267	$1 Titus in Friar's Habit (Rembrandt)	85	85
3268	$1.20 Saskia (Rembrandt)	90	90
3269	$1.20 In the Month of July (Paul Joseph Constantin Gabriel)	90	90
3270	$1.20 Maria Trip (Rembrandt)	90	90
3271	$1.20 Still Life with Flowers (Jan van Huysum)	90	90
3272	$1.20 Haesje van Cleyburgh (Rembrandt)	90	90
3273	$1.20 Girl in a White Kimono (George Hendrick Breitner)	90	90
3274	$1.65 Man and Woman at a Spinning Wheel (Pieter Pietersz)	1·10	1·10
3275	$1.65 Self-portrait (Rembrandt)	1·10	1·10
3276	$1.65 Jeremiah lamenting the Destruction of Jerusalem (Rembrandt)	1·10	1·10
3277	$1.65 The Jewish Bride (Rembrandt)	1·10	1·10
3278	$1.65 Anna accused by Tobit of stealing a Kid (Rembrandt)	1·10	1·10
3279	$1.65 The Prophetess Anna (Rembrandt)	1·10	1·10
MS3280	Three sheets, each 118×88 mm. (a) $6 Doubting Thomas (Hendrick ter Brugghen). (b) $6 Still Life with Cheeses (Floris van Dijck); (c) $6 Isaac Blessing Jacob (Govert Flinck) Set of 3 sheets	11·00	13·00

454 "Starmie No. 121"

2001. Characters from "Pokemon" (children's cartoon series). Multicoloured.

3281	$1.75 Type **454**	1·10	1·10
3282	$1.75 "Misty"	1·10	1·10
3283	$1.75 "Brock"	1·10	1·10
3284	$1.75 "Geodude No. 74"	1·10	1·10
3285	$1.75 "Krabby No. 98"	1·10	1·10
3286	$1.75 "Ash"	1·10	1·10
MS3287	74×114 mm. $6 "Charizard No. 6"	3·25	3·50

455 Blue-toothed Entoloma

2001. "Hong Kong 2001" Stamp Exhibition. Tropical Fungi. Multicoloured.

3288	25c. Type **455**	45	30
3289	90c. Common morel	90	50
3290	$1 Red cage fungus	1·00	70
3291	$1.65 Copper trumpet	1·10	1·10

3292	$1.65 Field mushroom ("Meadow Mushroom")	1·10	1·10
3293	$1.65 Green gill ("Green-gilled Parasol")	1·10	1·10
3294	$1.65 The panther	1·10	1·10
3295	$1.65 Death cap	1·10	1·10
3296	$1.65 Royal boletus ("King Bolete")	1·10	1·10
3297	$1.65 Lilac fairy helmet ("Lilac Bonnet")	1·10	1·10
3298	$1.65 Silky volvar	1·10	1·10
3299	$1.65 Agrocybe mushroom ("Poplar Field Cap")	1·10	1·10
3300	$1.65 Saint George's mushroom	1·10	1·10
3301	$1.65 Red-stemmed tough shank	1·10	1·10
3302	$1.65 Fly agaric	1·10	1·10
3303	$1.75 Common fawn agaric ("Fawn Shield-Cap")	1·25	1·50
MS3304	Two sheets, each 70×90 mm. (a) $6 Yellow parasol. (b) $6 Mutagen milk cap Set of 2 sheets	8·50	9·50

Nos. 3291/6 and 3297/302 were each printed together, se-tenant, with the backgrounds forming composite designs.

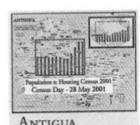

456 Map and Graphs

2001. Population and Housing Census.

3305	**456** 15c. multicoloured	15	15
3306	– 25c. multicoloured	20	20
3307	– 65c. multicoloured	55	55
3308	– 90c. multicoloured	70	70
MS3309	– 55×50 mm. $6 multicoloured (Map and census logo)	5·50	6·00

DESIGNS: 25c. to 90c. Map and different form of graph.

457 Yuna (Bath-house Women) (detail)

2001. "PHILANIPPON 2001" International Stamp Exhibition, Tokyo. Traditional Japanese Paintings. Multicoloured.

3310	45c. Type **457**	50	30
3311	60c. Yuna (Bath-house Women) (different detail)	60	50
3312	65c. Yuna (Bath-house Women) (different detail)	60	50
3313	75c. The Hikone Screen (detail)	70	50
3314	$1 The Hikone Screen (different detail)	75	60
3315	$1.20 The Hikone Screen (different detail)	80	70
3316	$1.65 Galleon and Dutch merchants with horse	95	95
3317	$1.65 Galleon and merchants with tiger	95	95
3318	$1.65 Merchants unpacking goods	95	95
3319	$1.65 Merchants with parasol and horse	95	95
3320	$1.65 Women packing food	95	95
3321	$1.65 Picnic under the cherry tree	95	95
3322	$1.65 Palanquins and resting bearers	95	95
3323	$1.65 Women dancing	95	95
3324	$1.65 Three samurai	95	95
3325	$1.65 One samurai	95	95
MS3326	Three sheets, each 80×110 mm. (a) $6 Harunobu Suzuki (Shiba Kokani) (38×50 mm). (b) $6 Daruma (Tsujo Kako) (38×50 mm). (c) $6 Visiting a Shrine on a Rainy Night (Harunobu Suziki) (38×50 mm) Set of 3 sheets	9·50	11·00

Nos. 3316/19 (The Namban Screen by Kano Nizen) and Nos. 3320/5 (Merry-making under the Cherry Blossoms by Kano Naganobu) were each printed together, se-tenant, with both sheetlets forming the entire painting.

458 Lucille Ball leaning on Mantelpiece

2001. Scenes from I Love Lucy (American T.V. comedy series). Eight sheets each containing multicoloured design as T **458**.

MS3327	(a) 118×92 mm. $6 Type **458**. (b) 98×120 mm. $6 Desi Arnaz laughing. (c) 93×130 mm. $6 William Frawley at table. (d) 114×145 mm. $6 Lucille Ball with William Frawley. (e) 114×145 mm. $6 Lucille Ball in blue dress. (f) 119×111 mm. $6 Lucille Ball sitting at table. (g) 128×100 mm. $6 Lucille Ball as scarecrow. (h) 93×125 mm. $6 William Frawley shouting at Desi Arnaz (horiz) Set of 8 sheets	22·00	24·00

459 Hintleya burtii

2001. Caribbean Orchids. Multicoloured.

3328	45c. Type **459**	50	25
3329	75c. Neomoovea irrovata	65	45
3330	90c. Comparettia speciosa	70	50
3331	$1 Cyprepedium crapeanum	80	70
3332	$1.20 Trichoceuos muralis (vert)	90	90
3333	$1.20 Dracula rampira (vert)	90	90
3334	$1.20 Psychopsis papilio (vert)	90	90
3335	$1.20 Lycaste clenningiana (vert)	90	90
3336	$1.20 Telipogon nevuosus (vert)	90	90
3337	$1.20 Masclecallia ayahbacana (vert)	90	90
3338	$1.65 Cattleya dowiana (vert)	1·10	1·10
3339	$1.65 Dendiobium cruentum (vert)	1·10	1·10
3340	$1.65 Bulbophyllum lobb (vert)	1·10	1·10
3341	$1.65 Chysis laevis (vert)	1·10	1·10
3342	$1.65 Ancistrochilus rothschildicanus (vert)	1·10	1·10
3343	$1.65 Angraecum sororium (vert)	1·10	1·10
3344	$1.65 Rhyncholaelia glanca (vert)	1·10	1·10
3345	$1.65 Oncidium barbatum (vert)	1·10	1·10
3346	$1.65 Phaius tankervillege (vert)	1·10	1·10
3347	$1.65 Ghies brechtiana (vert)	1·10	1·10
3348	$1.65 Angraecum leonis (vert)	1·10	1·10
3349	$1.65 Cycnoches loddigesti (vert)	1·10	1·10
MS3350	Two sheets. (a) 68×104 mm. $6 Symphalossum sanquinem (vert). (b) 104×68 mm. $6 Trichopilia fragrans (vert) Set of 2 sheets	8·50	9·50

460 Yellowtail Damselfish

2001. Tropical Marine Life. Multicoloured.

3351	25c. Type **460**	35	25
3352	45c. Indigo hamlet	55	30
3353	65c. Great white shark	70	40
3354	90c. Bottle-nose dolphin	80	65
3355	90c. Palette surgeonfish	80	65
3356	$1 Octopus	80	65
3357	$1.20 Common dolphin	90	90
3358	$1.20 Franklin's gull	90	90
3359	$1.20 Rock beauty	90	90
3360	$1.20 Bicoloured angelfish	90	90
3361	$1.20 Beaugregory	90	90
3362	$1.20 Banded butterflyfish	90	90
3363	$1.20 Common tern	90	90
3364	$1.20 Flying fish	90	90
3365	$1.20 Queen angelfish	90	90
3366	$1.20 Blue-striped grunt	90	90
3367	$1.20 Porkfish	90	90
3368	$1.20 Blue tang	90	90
3369	$1.65 Red-footed booby	1·10	1·10
3370	$1.65 Bottle-nose dolphin	1·10	1·10
3371	$1.65 Hawksbill turtle	1·10	1·10
3372	$1.65 Monk seal	1·10	1·10
3373	$1.65 Great white shark (inscr "Bull Shark")	1·10	1·10
3374	$1.65 Lemon shark	1·10	1·10
3375	$1.65 Dugong	1·10	1·10
3376	$1.65 White-tailed tropicbird	1·10	1·10

3377	$1.65 Bull shark	1·10	1·10
3378	$1.65 Manta ray	1·10	1·10
3379	$1.65 Green turtle	1·10	1·10
3380	$1.65 Spanish grunt	1·10	1·10
MS3381	Four sheets. each 68×98 mm. $5 Sailfish. (b) 68×98 mm. $5 Brown pelican and beaugregory (vert). (c) 98×68 mm. $6 Queen triggerfish. (d) 96×68 mm. $6 Hawksbill turtle Set of 4 sheets	18·00	19·00

Nos. 3357/62, 3363/8, 3369/74 and 3375/80 were each printed together, se-tenant, the backgrounds forming composite designs.

461 Freewinds (liner) and Police Band, Antigua

2001. Work of Freewinds (Church of Scientology flagship) in Caribbean. Multicoloured.

3382	30c. Type **461**	40	30
3383	45c. At anchor off St. Barthelemy	45	30
3384	75c. At sunset	70	60
3385	90c. Off Bonaire	90	90
3386	$1.50 Freewinds anchored off Bequia	1·25	1·40
MS3387	Two sheets, each 85×60 mm. (a) $4 Freewinds alongside quay, Curacao. (b) $4 Decorated with lights Set of 2 sheets	5·50	6·00

462 Young Queen Victoria in Blue Dress

2001. Death Centenary of Queen Victoria. Multicoloured.

3388	$2 Type **462**	1·40	1·60
3389	$2 Queen Victoria wearing red head-dress	1·40	1·60
3390	$2 Queen Victoria with jewelled hair ornament	1·40	1·60
3391	$2 Queen Victoria, after Chalon, in brooch	1·40	1·60
MS3392	70×82 mm. $5 Queen Victoria in old age	3·00	3·75

463 Water Lilies

2001. 75th Death Anniv of Claude-Oscar Monet (French painter). Multicoloured.

3393	$2 Type **463**	1·50	1·50
3394	$2 Rose Portals, Giverny	1·50	1·50
3395	$2 Water Lily Pond, Harmony in Green	1·50	1·50
3396	$2 Artist's Garden, Irises	1·50	1·50
MS3397	136×111 mm. $5 Jerusalem Artichoke Flowers (vert)	3·25	3·75

No. 3396 is inscribed "Artists's" in error.

464 Duchess of York with Baby Princess Elizabeth (1926)

2001. 75th Birthday of Queen Elizabeth II. Multicoloured.

3398	$1 Type **464**	1·25	1·25
3399	$1 Queen in Coronation robes (1953)	1·25	1·25
3400	$1 Young Princess Elizabeth (1938)	1·25	1·25
3401	$1 Queen Elizabeth in Garter robes (1956)	1·25	1·25
3402	$1 Princess Elizabeth with pony (1939)	1·25	1·25
3403	$1 Queen Elizabeth in red dress and pearls (1985)	1·25	1·25

MS3404 90×72 mm. $6 Princess Eliza-
beth and Queen Elizabeth (1940) 4·50 5·00

465 Verdi in Top
Hat

2001. Death Centenary of Giuseppe Verdi (Italian
composer). Multicoloured.
3405	$2 Type **465**	2·75	2·75
3406	$2 Don Carlos and part of opera score	2·75	2·75
3407	$2 Conductor and score for *Aida*	2·75	2·75
3408	$2 Musicians and score for *Rigoletto*	2·75	2·75
MS3409	77×117 mm. $5 Verdi in evening dress	6·50	6·50

Nos. 3405/8 were printed together, *se-tenant*, the back-
grounds forming a composite design.

466 *Georges-Henri Manuel*

2001. Death Centenary of Henri de Toulouse-Lautrec
(French painter). Multicoloured.
3410	$2 Type **466**	1·75	1·75
3411	$2 *Louis Pascal*	1·75	1·75
3412	$2 *Romain Coolus*	1·75	1·75
3413	$2 *Monsieur Fourcade*	1·75	1·75
MS3414	67×84 mm. $5 *Dancing at the Moulin de la Galette*	5·00	5·00

No 3412 is inscribed "ROMAN" in error.

467 Marlene Dietrich
smoking

2001. Birth Centenary of Marlene Dietrich (actress and
singer).
3415	**467**	$2 black, purple and red	1·50	1·50
3416	-	$2 black, purple and red	1·50	1·50
3417	-	$2 multicoloured	1·50	1·50
3418	-	$2 black, purple and red	1·50	1·50

DESIGNS: No. 3416, Marlene Dietrich, in evening gown,
sitting on settee; 3417, In black dress; 3418, Sitting on
piano.

468 Collared Peccary

2001. Vanishing Fauna of the Caribbean. Multicoloured.
3419	25c. Type **468**	45	30
3420	30c. Baird's tapir	45	30
3421	45c. Agouti	60	30
3422	75c. Bananaquit	1·25	55
3423	90c. Six-banded armadillo	1·00	55
3424	$1 Roseate spoonbill	1·50	80
3425	$1.80 Mouse opossum	2·00	2·00
3426	$1.80 Magnificent black frig-ate bird	2·00	2·00
3427	$1.80 Northern jacana	2·00	2·00
3428	$1.80 Painted bunting	2·00	2·00
3429	$1.80 Haitian solenodon	2·00	2·00
3430	$1.80 St. Lucia iguana	2·00	2·00
3431	$2.50 West Indian iguana	2·75	2·75
3432	$2.50 Scarlet macaw	2·75	2·75
3433	$2.50 Cotton-topped tamarin	2·75	2·75
3434	$2.50 Kinkajou	2·75	2·75
MS3435	Two sheets. (a) 117×85 mm. $6 Ocelot (vert). (b) 162×116 mm. $6 King vulture (vert) Set of 2 sheets	14·00	15·00

469 Sara Crewe (*The
Little Princess*) reading a
Letter

2001. Shirley Temple Films. Multicoloured. Showing film
scenes

(a) The Little Princess. Multicoloured.
3436	$1.50 Type **469**	95	95
3437	$1.50 Sara in pink dressing gown	95	95
3438	$1.50 Sara cuddling doll	95	95
3439	$1.50 Sara as Princess on throne	95	95
3440	$1.50 Sara talking to man in frock coat	95	95
3441	$1.50 Sara blowing out candles	95	95
3442	$1.80 Sara with Father (horiz)	1·10	1·10
3443	$1.80 Sara scrubbing floor (horiz)	1·10	1·10
3444	$1.80 Sara and friend with Headmistress (horiz)	1·10	1·10
3445	$1.80 Sara with Queen Victoria (horiz)	1·10	1·10
MS3446	106×76 mm. $6 Sara with wounded Father	3·25	3·75

(b) Baby, Take a Bow.
3447	$1.65 Shirley in dancing class (horiz)	95	95
3448	$1.65 Shirley cuddling Father (horiz)	95	95
3449	$1.65 Shirley at bedtime with parents (horiz)	95	95
3450	$1.65 Shirley in yellow dress with Father (horiz)	95	95
3451	$1.65 Shirley and Father at Christmas party (horiz)	95	95
3452	$1.65 Shirley and gangster looking in cradle (horiz)	95	95
3453	$1.65 Shirley in spotted dress	95	95
3454	$1.65 Shirley on steps with gangster	95	95
3455	$1.65 Shirley with gangster holding gun	95	95
3456	$1.65 Shirley with Mother	95	95
MS3457	106×76 mm. $6 Shirley in spotted dress	3·25	3·75

470 Rudolph Valentino in
Blood and Sand, 1922

2001. 75th Death Anniv of Rudolph Valentino (Italian film
actor).
3458	**470**	$1 brown and black	75	75
3459	-	$1 lilac and black	75	75
3460	-	$1 brown and black	75	75
3461	-	$1 brown and black	75	75
3462	-	$1 red and black	75	75
3463	-	$1 lilac and black	75	75
3464	-	$1 multicoloured	75	75
3465	-	$1 multicoloured	75	75
3466	-	$1 multicoloured	75	75
3467	-	$1 multicoloured	75	75
3468	-	$1 multicoloured	75	75
3469	-	$1 multicoloured	75	75
MS3470	Two sheets. (a) 90×125 mm. $6 multicoloured. (b) 68×95 mm. $6 multicoloured Set of 2 sheets	7·50	8·50

DESIGNS: No. 3459, In *Eyes of Youth* with Clara Kimbal
Young, 1919; 3460, In *All Night Long* with Carmel Mey-
ers, 1918; 3461, Valentino in 1926; 3462, In *Camille* with
Alla Nazimova, 1921; 3463, In *Cobra* with Nita Naldi, 1925;
3464, In *The Son of the Sheik* with Vilma Banky, 1926;
3465, In *The Young Rajah*, 1922; 3466, In *The Eagle* with
Vilma Banky, 1925; 3467, In *The Sheik* with Agnes Ayres,
1921; 3468, In *A Sainted Devil*, 1924; 3469, In *Monsieur
Beaucaire*, 1924; MS3470, (a) Valentino with Natacha Ram-
bova. (b) In *The Four Horseman of the Apocalypse*, 1921.

Nos. 3464 and 3466 are inscribed "BLANKY" and No.
3467 "AYERS", all in error.

471 Queen
Elizabeth

2001. Golden Jubilee (1st issue).
| 3471 | **471** | $1 multicoloured | 1·50 | 1·50 |

No. 3471 was printed in sheetlets of 8, containing
two vertical rows of four, separated by a large illustrated
central gutter. Both the stamp and the illustration on
the central gutter are made up of a collage of miniature
flower photographs.
See also Nos. 3535/8.

472 Melvin Calvin,
1961

2001. Centenary of Nobel Prizes. Chemistry Winners.
Multicoloured.
3472	$1.50 Type **472**	1·25	1·25
3473	$1.50 Linus Pauling, 1954	1·25	1·25
3474	$1.50 Vincent du Vigneaud, 1955	1·25	1·25
3475	$1.50 Richard Synge, 1952	1·25	1·25
3476	$1.50 Archer Martin, 1952	1·25	1·25
3477	$1.50 Alfred Werner, 1913	1·25	1·25
3478	$1.50 Robert Curl Jr., 1996	1·25	1·25
3479	$1.50 Alan Heeger, 2000	1·25	1·25
3480	$1.50 Michael Smith, 1993	1·25	1·25
3481	$1.50 Sidney Altman, 1989	1·25	1·25
3482	$1.50 Elias Corey, 1990	1·25	1·25
3483	$1.50 William Giauque, 1949	1·25	1·25
MS3484	Three sheets, each 107×75 mm. (a) $6 Ernest Rutherford, 1908. (b) $6 Ernst Fischer, 1973. (c) $6 American volunteers, International Red Cross (Peace Prize, 1944) Set of 3 sheets	12·50	13·00

473 *Madonna and
Child with Angels
(Filippo Lippi)*

2001. Christmas. Italian Religious Paintings.
Multicoloured.
3485	25c. Type **473**	35	20
3486	45c. *Madonna of Corneto Tarquinia* (Lippi)	55	25
3487	50c. *Madonna and Child* (Do-menico Ghirlandaio)	60	30
3488	75c. *Madonna and Child* (Lippi)	1·00	55
3489	$4 *Madonna Delceppo* (Lippi)	5·00	6·00
MS3490	106×136 mm. $6 *Madonna enthroned with Angels and Saints* (Lippi)	4·50	5·00

474 Final between
Uruguay and
Brazil, Brazil 1950

2001. World Cup Football Championship, Japan and
Korea (2002). Multicoloured.
3491	$1.50 Type **474**	95	95
3492	$1.50 Ferenc Puskas (Hungary), Switzerland 1954	95	95
3493	$1.50 Raymond Kopa (France), Sweden 1958	95	95
3494	$1.50 Mauro (Brazil), Chile 1962	95	95
3495	$1.50 Gordon Banks (England), England 1966	95	95
3496	$1.50 Pele (Brazil), Mexico 1970	95	95
3497	$1.50 Daniel Passarella (Argen-tina), Argentina 1978	95	95
3498	$1.50 Karl-Heinz Rummenigge (Germany), Spain 1982	95	95

3499	$1.50 World Cup Trophy, Mexico 1986	95	95
3500	$1.50 Diego Maradona (Argen-tina), Italy 1990	95	95
3501	$1.50 Roger Milla (Cameroun), U.S.A. 1994	95	95
3502	$1.50 Zinedine Zidane (France), France 1998	95	95
MS3503	Two sheets, each 88×75 mm. (a) $6 Detail of Jules Rimet Trophy, Uruguay, 1930. (b) $6 Detail of World Cup Trophy, Japan/Korea, 2002 Set of 2 sheets	7·50	8·50

No. 3500 is inscribed "Deigo" in error.

475 Battle of Nashville,
1864

2002. American Civil War. Multicoloured.
3504	45c. Type **475**	85	85
3505	45c. Capture of Atlanta, 1864	85	85
3506	45c. Battle of Spotsylvania, 1864	85	85
3507	45c. Battle of The Wilderness, 1864	85	85
3508	45c. Battle of Chickamauga Creek, 1863	85	85
3509	45c. Battle of Gettysburg, 1863	85	85
3510	45c. Lee and Jackson at Chan-cellorsville, 1863	85	85
3511	45c. Battle of Fredericksburg, 1862	85	85
3512	45c. Battle of Antietam, 1862	85	85
3513	45c. Second Battle of Bull Run, 1862	85	85
3514	45c. Battle of Five Forks, 1865	85	85
3515	45c. Seven Days' Battles, 1862	85	85
3516	45c. First Battle of Bull Run, 1861	85	85
3517	45c. Battle of Shiloh, 1862	85	85
3518	45c. Battle of Seven Pines, 1862	85	85
3519	45c. Bombardment of Fort Sumter, 1861	85	85
3520	45c. Battle of Chattanooga, 1863	85	85
3521	45c. Grant and Lee at Ap-pomattox, 1865	85	85
3522	50c. General Ulysses S. Grant (vert)	1·00	1·00
3523	50c. President Abraham Lincoln (vert)	1·00	1·00
3524	50c. President Jefferson Davis (vert)	1·00	1·00
3525	50c. General Robert E. Lee (vert)	1·00	1·00
3526	50c. General George Custer (vert)	1·00	1·00
3527	50c. Admiral Andrew Hull Foote (vert)	1·00	1·00
3528	50c. General "Stonewall" Jackson (vert)	1·00	1·00
3529	50c. General Jeb Stuart (vert)	1·00	1·00
3530	50c. General George Meade (vert)	1·00	1·00
3531	50c. General Philip Sheridan (vert)	1·00	1·00
3532	50c. General James Longstreet (vert)	1·00	1·00
3533	50c. General John Mosby (vert)	1·00	1·00
MS3534	Two sheets, each 105×76 mm. (a) $6 Confederate ironclad *Merrimack* attacking *Cumberland* (Federal sloop) (51×38 mm). (b) $6 *Monitor* (Federal ironclad) Set of 2 sheets	13·00	14·00

476 Queen Elizabeth
presenting Rosettes

2002. Golden Jubilee (2nd issue). Multicoloured.
3535	$2 Type **476**	2·50	2·50
3536	$2 Queen Elizabeth at garden party	2·50	2·50
3537	$2 Queen Elizabeth in evening dress	2·50	2·50
3538	$2 Queen Elizabeth in cream coat	2·50	2·50
MS3539	76×108 mm. $6 Princesses Elizabeth and Margaret as brides-maids	4·50	5·00

477 U.S. Flag as Statue of Liberty and Antigua & Barbuda Flag

2002. "United We Stand". Support for Victims of 11 September 2001 Terrorist Attacks.
| 3540 | **477** | $2 multicoloured | 1·25 | 1·40 |

478 Sir Vivian Richards waving Bat

2002. 50th Birthday of Sir Vivian Richards (West Indian cricketer). Multicoloured.
3541	25c. Type **478**	1·40	55
3542	30c. Sir Vivian Richards receiving presentation from Antigua Cricket Association	1·40	55
3543	50c. Sir Vivian Richards wearing sash	1·75	65
3544	75c. Sir Vivian Richards batting	2·00	90
3545	$1.50 Sir Vivian Richards and Lady Richards	3·25	3·50
3546	$1.80 Sir Vivian Richards with enlarged action photograph of himself	3·50	4·00

MS3547 Two sheets, each 68×95 mm. (a) $6 Sir Vivian Richards with guard of honour. (b) $6 Sir Vivian Richards in Indian traditional dress Set of 2 sheets — 16·00 16·00

479 Thick-billed Parrot

2002. Flora and Fauna. Multicoloured.
3548	50c. Type **479**	1·00	55
3549	75c. Lesser long-nosed bat	1·00	60
3550	90c. Quetzal	1·25	1·25
3551	90c. Two-toed sloth	1·25	1·25
3552	90c. Lovely cotinga	1·25	1·25
3553	90c. *Pseudolycaena marsyas* (butterfly)	1·25	1·25
3554	90c. Magenta-throated woodstar	1·25	1·25
3555	90c. *Automeris rubrescens* (moth)	1·25	1·25
3556	90c. *Bufo periglenes* (toad)	1·25	1·25
3557	90c. Collared peccary	1·25	1·25
3558	90c. Tamandua anteater	1·25	1·25
3559	$1 St. Lucia parrot	1·25	1·25
3560	$1 Cuban kite	1·25	1·25
3561	$1 West Indian whistling-duck	1·25	1·25
3562	$1 *Eurema amelia* (butterfly)	1·25	1·25
3563	$1 Scarlet ibis	1·25	1·25
3564	$1 Black-capped petrel	1·25	1·25
3565	$1 *Cnemidophorus vanzoi* (lizard)	1·25	1·25
3566	$1 Cuban solenodon	1·25	1·25
3567	$1 *Papilio thersites* (butterfly)	1·25	1·25
3568	$1.50 Montserrat oriole	2·00	2·00
3569	$1.80 *Leptotes perkinsae* (butterfly)	2·50	2·50

MS3570 Two sheets, each 110×85 mm. (a) $6 Olive Ridley turtle. (b) $6 Margay Set of 2 sheets — 11·00 12·00

Nos. 3550/8 and 3559/67 were each printed together, *se-tenant*, with the backgrounds forming composite designs.

480 Community Players

2002. 50th Anniv of Community Players. Multicoloured. Showing scenes from various productions.
3571	20c. Type **480**	35	30
3572	25c. Men in suits with women in long dresses	35	30
3573	30c. In *Pirates of Penzance*	40	30

3574	75c. Female choir	75	50
3575	90c. In Mexican dress	90	55
3576	$1.50 Members at a reception	1·25	1·50
3577	$1.80 Production in the open air	1·50	2·00

MS3578 Two sheets, each 76×84 mm. (a) $4 Mrs. Edie Hill-Thibou (former President) (vert). (b) $4 Miss Yvonne Maginley (Acting President and Director of Music) (vert) Set of 2 sheets — 7·00 8·00

481 Mount Fuji, Japan

2002. International Year of Mountains. Multicoloured.
3579	$2 Type **481**	1·50	1·50
3580	$2 Machu Picchu, Peru	1·50	1·50
3581	$2 The Matterhorn, Switzerland	1·50	1·50

482 Cross-country Skiing

2002. Winter Olympic Games, Salt Lake City. Multicoloured.
| 3582 | $2 Type **482** | 1·75 | 2·00 |
| 3583 | $2 Pairs figure skating | 1·75 | 2·00 |

MS3584 84×114 mm. Nos. 3582/3 — 3·50 4·00

483 Amerigo Vespucci wearing Skullcap

2002. 500th Anniv of Amerigo Vespucci's Third Voyage. Multicoloured.
3585	$2.50 Type **483**	2·50	2·50
3586	$2.50 Vespucci as an old man	2·50	2·50
3587	$2.50 16th-century map	2·50	2·50

MS3588 49×68 mm. $5 Vespucci holding dividers (vert) — 4·50 5·00

484 *Spirit of St. Louis* and Charles Lindbergh (pilot)

2002. 75th Anniv of First Solo Transatlantic Flight. Multicoloured.
3589	$2.50 Type **484**	2·50	2·50
3590	$2.50 *Spirit of St. Louis* at Le Bourget, Paris, 1927	2·50	2·50
3591	$2.50 Charles Lindbergh in New York ticker-tape parade, 1927	2·50	2·50

MS3592 80×110 mm. $6 Charles Lindbergh wearing flying helmet — 4·50 5·00

485 Princess Diana

2002. Fifth Death Anniv of Diana, Princess of Wales. Multicoloured.
3593	$1.80 Type **485**	1·40	1·40
3594	$1.80 Princess Diana in tiara (looking left)	1·40	1·40
3595	$1.80 Wearing hat	1·40	1·40
3596	$1.80 Princess Diana wearing pearl drop earrings and black dress	1·40	1·40
3597	$1.80 Wearing tiara (facing front)	1·40	1·40
3598	$1.80 Princess Diana wearing pearl drop earrings	1·40	1·40

MS3599 91×106 mm. $6 Princess Diana — 4·50 5·00

486 Kennedy Brothers

2002. Presidents John F. Kennedy and Ronald Reagan Commemoration. Multicoloured.
3600	$1.50 Type **486**	1·60	1·60
3601	$1.50 John Kennedy with Danny Kaye (American entertainer)	1·60	1·60
3602	$1.50 Delivering Cuban Blockade speech, 1962	1·60	1·60
3603	$1.50 With Jacqueline Kennedy	1·60	1·60
3604	$1.50 Meeting Bill Clinton (future president)	1·60	1·60
3605	$1.50 Family at John Kennedy's funeral	1·60	1·60
3606	$1.50 President and Mrs. Reagan with Pope John Paul II, 1982	1·60	1·60
3607	$1.50 As George Gipp in *Knute Rockne - All American*, 1940	1·60	1·60
3608	$1.50 With General Matthew Ridgeway, Bitburg Military Cemetery, Germany, 1985	1·60	1·60
3609	$1.50 With George H. Bush and Secretary Mikhail Gorbachev of U.S.S.R., 1988	1·60	1·60
3610	$1.50 Presidents Reagan, Ford, Carter and Nixon at the White House, 1981	1·60	1·60
3611	$1.50 Horse riding with Queen Elizabeth, Windsor, 1982	1·60	1·60

MS3612 Two sheets, each 88×22 mm. (a) $6 President Kennedy at press conference (vert). (b) $6 President Reagan (vert) Set of 2 sheets — 11·00 12·00

487 Red-billed Tropicbird

2002. Endangered Species of Antigua. Multicoloured.
3613	$1.50 Type **487**	2·00	2·00
3614	$1.50 Brown pelican	2·00	2·00
3615	$1.50 Magnificent frigate bird	2·00	2·00
3616	$1.50 Ground lizard	2·00	2·00
3617	$1.50 West Indian whistling duck	2·00	2·00
3618	$1.50 Antiguan racer snake	2·00	2·00
3619	$1.50 Spiny lobster	2·00	2·00
3620	$1.50 Hawksbill turtle	2·00	2·00
3621	$1.50 Queen conch	2·00	2·00

488 Elvis Presley

2002. 25th Death Anniv of Elvis Presley (American entertainer).
| 3622 | **488** | $1 multicoloured | 1·75 | 1·40 |

489 Cheerleader Teddy

2002. Centenary of the Teddy Bear. Girl Teddies. Multicoloured.
3623	$2 Type **489**	1·25	1·40
3624	$2 Figure skater	1·25	1·40
3625	$2 Ballet dancer	1·25	1·40
3626	$2 Aerobics instructor	1·25	1·40

490 "Croconaw No. 159"

2002. Pokemon (children's cartoon series). Multicoloured.
3627	$1.50 Type **490**	90	90
3628	$1.50 "Mantine No. 226"	90	90
3629	$1.50 "Feraligatr No. 160"	90	90
3630	$1.50 "Qwilfish No. 211"	90	90
3631	$1.50 "Remoraid No. 223"	90	90
3632	$1.50 "Quagsire No. 195"	90	90

MS3633 80×106 mm. $6 "Chinchou No. 170" — 3·25 3·50

491 Charlie Chaplin

2002. 25th Death Anniv of Charlie Chaplin (British actor). Each black, grey and light grey.
3634	$1.80 Type **491**	1·75	1·75
3635	$1.80 Wearing waistcoat and spotted bow-tie	1·75	1·75
3636	$1.80 In top hat	1·75	1·75
3637	$1.80 Wearing coat and bowler hat	1·75	1·75
3638	$1.80 Charlie Chaplin in old age	1·75	1·75
3639	$1.80 With finger on chin	1·75	1·75

MS3640 90×105 mm. $6 Charlie Chaplin as The Tramp — 4·50 4·75

492 Bob Hope

2002. Bob Hope (American entertainer) Commemoration. Designs showing him entertaining American troops. Multicoloured.
3641	$1.50 Type **492**	1·50	1·50
3642	$1.50 Wearing bush hat,Vietnam, 1972	1·50	1·50
3643	$1.50 On board U.S.S. *John F. Kennedy* (aircraft carrier)	1·50	1·50
3644	$1.50 With hawk badge on sleeve, Berlin, 1948	1·50	1·50
3645	$1.50 Wearing desert fatigues	1·50	1·50
3646	$1.50 In white cap and stars on collar	1·50	1·50

493 Lee Strasberg

2002. 20th Death Anniv of Lee Strasberg (pioneer of "Method Acting").
| 3647 | **493** | $1 black and stone | 1·00 | 1·00 |

494 Marlene Dietrich

2002. 10th Death Anniv of Marlene Dietrich (actress and singer). Each black and grey.
3648	$1.50 Type **494**	90	90
3649	$1.50 Wearing top hat	90	90
3650	$1.50 In chiffon dress	90	90

3651	$1.50 Resting chin on left hand	90	90
3652	$1.50 In cloche hat	90	90
3653	$1.50 Wearing black evening gloves	90	90
MS3654	83×108 mm. $6 Marlene Dietrich wearing chiffon scarf	3·25	3·75

495 Ferrari 801, 1957

2002. Ferrari Racing Cars. Multicoloured.

3655	20c. Type **495**	30	30
3656	25c. Ferrari 256, 1959	30	30
3657	30c. Ferrari 246 P, 1960	35	30
3658	90c. Ferrari 246, 1966	85	55
3659	$1 Ferrari 312 B2, 1971	95	70
3660	$1.50 Ferrari 312, 1969	1·40	1·40
3661	$2 Ferrari F310 B, 1997	1·75	2·00
3662	$4 Ferrari F2002, 2002	3·00	3·50

496 Antigua & Barbuda Flag

2002. 21st Anniv of Independence. Multicoloured.

3663	25c. Type **496**	50	35
3664	30c. Antigua & Barbuda coat of arms (vert)	50	35
3665	$1.50 Mount St. John's Hospital under construction	1·75	1·75
3666	$1.80 Parliament Building, St. John's	2·00	2·25
MS3667	Two sheets, each 77×81 mm. (a) $6 Sir Vere Bird (Prime Minister, 1967–94) (38×51 mm). (b) $6 Lester Bird (Prime Minister since 1994) (38×51 mm) Set of 2 sheets	10·00	11·00

497 Juan Valeron (Spain)

2002. World Cup Football Championship, Japan and Korea. Multicoloured.

3668	$1.65 Type **497**	1·00	1·00
3669	$1.65 Iker Casillas (Spain)	1·00	1·00
3670	$1.65 Fernando Hierro (Spain)	1·00	1·00
3671	$1.65 Gary Kelly (Ireland)	1·00	1·00
3672	$1.65 Damien Duff (Ireland)	1·00	1·00
3673	$1.65 Matt Holland (Ireland)	1·00	1·00
3674	$1.65 Pyo Lee (South Korea)	1·00	1·00
3675	$1.65 Ji Sung Park (South Korea)	1·00	1·00
3676	$1.65 Jung Hwan Ahn (South Korea)	1·00	1·00
3677	$1.65 Filippo Inzaghi (Italy)	1·00	1·00
3678	$1.65 Paolo Maldini (Italy)	1·00	1·00
3679	$1.65 Dammiano Tommasi (Italy)	1·00	1·00
MS3680	Four sheets, each 82×82 mm. (a) $3 Jose Camacho (Spanish coach); $3 Raul Gonzales Blanco (Spain). (b) $3 Robbie Keane (Ireland); $3 Mick McCarthy (Irish coach). (c) $3 Guus Hiddink (South Korean coach); $3 Chul Sang Yoo (South Korea). (d) $3 Francesco Totti (Italy); $3 Giovanni Trapattoni (Italian coach) Set of 4 sheets	13·00	14·00

No. **MS**3680a is inscribed "Carlos Gamarra" in error.

498 Coronation of the Virgin (Domenico Ghirlandaio)

2002. Christmas. Religious Paintings. Multicoloured.

3681	25c. Type **498**	40	20
3682	45c. Adoration of the Magi (detail) (D. Ghirlandaio)	60	25
3683	75c. Annunciation (Simone Martini) (vert)	1·00	45
3684	90c. Adoration of the Magi (different detail) (D. Ghirlandaio)	1·25	55
3685	$5 Madonna and Child (Giovanni Bellini)	5·00	6·00
MS3686	76×110 mm. $6 "Madonnna and Child (S. Martini)	5·00	6·00

499 Antiguan Racer Snake Head

2002. Endangered Species. Antiguan Racer Snake. Multicoloured.

3687	$1 Type **499**	1·25	1·25
3688	$1 Coiled Antiguan racer snake with tail at right	1·25	1·25
3689	$1 Antiguan racer snake with pebbles and leaves	1·25	1·25
3690	$1 Coiled Antiguan racer snake with tail at left	1·25	1·25

500 Magnificent Frigate Bird

2002. Fauna and Flora. Multicoloured.

3691	$1.50 Type **500**	1·75	1·75
3692	$1.50 Sooty tern	1·75	1·75
3693	$1.50 Bananaquit	1·75	1·75
3694	$1.50 Yellow-crowned night heron	1·75	1·75
3695	$1.50 Greater flamingo	1·75	1·75
3696	$1.50 Belted kingfisher	1·75	1·75
3697	$1.50 Killer whale	1·75	1·75
3698	$1.50 Sperm whale	1·75	1·75
3699	$1.50 Minke whale	1·75	1·75
3700	$1.50 Blainville's beaked whale	1·75	1·75
3701	$1.50 Blue whale	1·75	1·75
3702	$1.50 Cuvier's beaked whale	1·75	1·75
3703	$1.80 Epidendrum fragans	1·75	1·75
3704	$1.80 Dombeya wallichii	1·75	1·75
3705	$1.80 Abebuia serratifolia	1·75	1·75
3706	$1.80 Cryptostegia grandiflora	1·75	1·75
3707	$1.80 Hylocereus undatus	1·75	1·75
3708	$1.80 Rodriguezia lanceolata	1·75	1·75
3709	$1.80 Diphthera festiva	1·75	1·75
3710	$1.80 Hypocrita dejanira	1·75	1·75
3711	$1.80 Eupseudosoma involutum	1·75	1·75
3712	$1.80 Composia credula	1·75	1·75
3713	$1.80 Citheronia magnifica	1·75	1·75
3714	$1.80 Divana diva	1·75	1·75
MS3715	Four sheets, each 75×45 mm. (a) $5 Snowy egret. (b) $5 Rothschildia orizaba (moth). (c) $6 Humpback whale. (d) $6 Ionopsis utricularioides (flower) Set of 4 sheets	22·00	23·00

Nos. 3691/6 (birds), 3697/702 (whales), 3703/8 (moths) and 3709/14 (flowers) were each printed together, se-tenant, with the backgrounds forming composite designs.

501 Dr. Margaret O'garro

2002. Centenary of Pan American Health Organization. Health Professionals. Multicoloured.

3716	$1.50 Type **501**	1·40	1·40
3717	$1.50 Ineta Wallace (nurse)	1·40	1·40
3718	$1.50 Vincent Edwards (public health official)	1·40	1·40

502 Antiguan Brownie

2002. 20th World Scout Jamboree, Thailand. Each lilac and brown (Nos. 3719/21) or multicoloured (others).

3719	$3 Type **502**	3·00	3·00
3720	$3 Brownie with badge on cap	3·00	3·00
3721	$3 Brownie without badge on cap	3·00	3·00
3722	$3 Robert Baden-Powell on horseback, 1896 (horiz)	3·00	3·00
3723	$3 Ernest Thompson Seton (founder, Boy Scouts of America), 1910, and American scout badge (horiz)	3·00	3·00
3724	$3 First black scout troop, Virginia, 1928 (horiz)	3·00	3·00
MS3725	Two sheets. (a) 80×113 mm. $6 Ernest Thompson Seton. (b) 110×83 mm. $6 Scout salute Set of 2 sheets	11·00	12·00

Nos. 3719/21 were printed together, se-tenant, forming a composite design.

503 Scene from *2001: A Space Odyssey* (Arthur C. Clarke)

2002. Famous Science Fiction Authors. Three sheets, each 150×108 mm, containg vert designs as T **503**. Multicoloured.

MS3726	Three sheets. (a) $6 Type **503**. (b) $6 Scene from *The Monuments of Mars* (Richard C. Hoagland). (c) $6 Nostradamus with globe Set of 3 sheets	13·00	14·00

504 "Goat and Kids" (Liu Jiyou)

2003. Chinese New Year ("Year of the Goat").

3727	**504**	$1.80 multicoloured	1·60	1·60

505 Lucretia

2003. 450th Death Anniv of Lucas Cranach the Elder (artist). Multicoloured.

3728	75c. Type **505**	75	55
3729	90c. Venus and Cupid (detail)	90	65
3730	$1 Judith with Head of Holofernes (c. 1530)	1·00	1·00
3731	$1.50 Portrait of a Young Lady (detail)	1·25	1·75
MS3732	152×188 mm. $2 Portrait of the Wife of a Jurist; $2 Portrait of a Jurist; $2 Johannes Cuspinian; $2 Portrait of Anna Cuspinian	4·75	5·50
MS3733	120×100 mm. $6 Judith with Head of Holofernes (c. 1532)	4·75	5·50

506 A High Class Maid training in a Samurai Household

2003. Japanese Art of Taiso Yoshitoshi. Multicoloured.

3734	25c. Type **506**	35	20
3735	50c. A Castle-Toppler known as a Keisei	55	30
3736	$1 Stylish Young Geisha battling a Snowstorm on her Way to Work	90	65
3737	$5 A Lady in Distress being treated with Moxa	3·50	4·25
MS3738	178×140 mm. $2 A Lady of the Imperial Court wearing Four Layers of Robes; $2 Young Mother adoring her Infant Son; $2 Lady-in-Waiting looking amused over a Veranda in the Household of a Great Lord; $2 A High Ranking Courtesan known as an "Oiran", waiting for a Private Assignation	5·50	6·50
MS3739	135×67 mm. $6 A Girl teasing her Cat	4·50	5·00

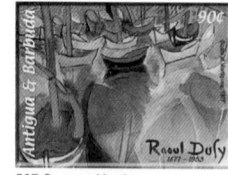

507 Boats at Martigues

2003. 50th Death Anniv of Raoul Dufy (artist). Multicoloured.

3740	90c. Type **507**	75	45
3741	$1 Harvesting	90	60
3742	$1.80 Sailboats in the Port of Le Havre	1·40	1·40
3743	$5 The Big Bather (vert)	4·00	4·50
MS3744	173×124 mm. $2 The Beach and the Pier at Trouville; $2 Port with Sailing Ships; $2 Black Cargo; $2 Nice, The Bay of Anges	5·50	6·00
MS3745	Two sheets, each 95×76 mm. (a) $6 Vence. (b) $6 The Interior with an Open Window. Both Imperf	8·50	9·50

508 Queen Elizabeth II at Trooping the Colour

2003. 50th Anniv of Coronation. Multicoloured.

MS3746	155×93 mm. $3 Type **508**; $3 Queen wearing fawn beret with single feather; $3 Queen wearing feathered hat	8·50	9·00
MS3747	105×75 mm. $6 Princess Elizabeth	5·00	5·50

509 Prince William

2003. 21st Birthday of Prince William of Wales. Multicoloured.

MS3748	147×77 mm. $3 Type **509**; $3 Prince william wearing polo helmet; $3 Wearing blue T-shirt	8·00	8·50
MS3749	67×97 mm. $6 As teenager holding bouquet	4·75	5·00

510 Tamarind Tree, Parham

2003. Centenary of Salvation Army in Antigua. Multicoloured.

3750	30c. Type **510**	60	30
3751	90c. Salvation Army pre-school	1·25	55
3752	$1 Meals on wheels (horiz)	1·40	80
3753	$1.50 St. John Citadel band (horiz)	1·75	1·75
3754	$1.80 Salvation Army Citadel (horiz)	2·00	2·50
MS3755	146×78 mm. $6 As Type **510** but without badge and centenary inscription	5·50	6·00

511 First Anglican
Scout Troop, 1931

2003. 90th Anniv of Antigua and Barbuda Scouts Association. Multicoloured (except No. 3756).

3756	30c. Type **511** (black and brown)	50	30
3757	$1 National Scout Camp, 2002	1·25	80
3758	$1.50 Woodbadge Training course, 2000 (horiz)	1·60	1·60
3759	$1.80 Visitors to National Camp, 1986 (horiz)	1·90	2·25

MS3760 136×96 mm. 90c. Edris George; 90c. Theodore George; 90c. Edris James (all Deputy Commissioners) ... 3·00 3·25

MS3761 74×101 mm. $6 Scout leader demonstrating semaphore ... 5·00 5·50

512 Cesar Garin (1903)

2003. Centenary of Tour de France Cycle Race. Past winners. Multicoloured.

MS3762 160×100 mm. $2 Type **512**; $2 Caricature of Henri Cornet (1904); $2 Louis Trousselier (1905); $2 Rene Pottier (1906) ... 8·00 8·00

MS3763 160×100 mm. $2 Lucien Petit-Breton (1907); $2 Lucien Petit-Breton (1908); $2 Francois Faber (1909); $2 Octave Lapize (1910) ... 8·00 8·00

MS3764 160×100 mm. $2 Gustave Garrigou (1911); $2 Odile Defraye (1912); $2 Phillipe Thys (1913); $2 Phillipe Thys (1914) ... 8·00 8·00

MS3765 Three sheets, each 100×70 mm. (a) $6 Henri Desgranges (editor of *L'Auto*). (b) $6 Pierre Giffard (editor of *Le Velo*). (c) $6 Le Compte de Dion (sponsor) Set of 3 sheets ... 13·00 14·00

513 Frigate Bird and Emblem

2003. 30th Anniv of CARICOM.

3766	**513**	$1 multicoloured	1·25	1·00

514 Cadillac Eldorado Convertible (1955)

2003. Centenary of General Motors Cadillac. Multicoloured.

MS3767 110×150 mm. $2 Type **514**; $2 Cadillac Series 60 (1937); $2 Cadillac Eldorado (1959); $2 Cadillac Eldorado (2002) ... 6·00 6·50

MS3768 102×76 mm. $6 Cadillac Eldorado (1953) ... 3·75 4·00

515 Chutes de Carbet Waterfall, Guadeloupe

2003. International Year of Freshwater. Multicoloured.

MS3769 94×180 mm. $2 Type **515**; $2 Foot of Chutes de Carbet waterfall; $2 Rapids at foot of Chutes de Carbet waterfall ... 4·50 4·75

MS3770 96×67 mm. $6 Waterfall, Ocho Rios, Jamaica (vert) ... 4·50 4·75

516 Corvette Convertible (1954)

2003. 50th Anniv of General Motors Chevrolet Corvette. Multicoloured.

MS3771 110×151 mm. $2 Type **516**; $2 Corvette Sting Ray (1964); $2 Corvette Sting Ray Convertible (1964); $2 Corvette Convertible (1998) ... 6·00 6·50

MS3772 102×74 mm. $6 Corvette Convertible (1956) ... 3·75 4·00

517 *Flyer I* (first manned powered flight), 1903

2003. Centenary of Powered Flight. Multicoloured.

MS3773 176×106 mm. $2 Type **517**; $2 Paul Cornu's helicopter on first helicopter flight, 1907; $2 E.B. Ely's biplane making first landing on ship, 1911; $2 Curtiss A-1 (first seaplane), 1911 ... 8·00 8·00

MS3774 176×106 mm. $2 Bell X-5 research aircraft with variable wings, 1951; $2 Convair XFY-1 vertical take-off and landing; $2 North American X-15 rocket aircraft, 1959; $2 Alexei Leonov on first spacewalk, 1965 ... 8·00 8·00

MS3775 176×106 mm. $2 Concorde, 1969; $2 Martin X-24 Lifting Body Vehicle Pre-Space Shuttle, 1969; $2 Apollo-Soyuz, 1975; $2 Viking Robot Mars Expedition, 1976 ... 8·00 8·00

MS3776 Three sheets, each 106×76 mm. (a) $6 Boeing Model 200 Monomail with retractable landing gear, 1930. (b) $6 Bell XS-1 rocket plane breaking sound barrier, 1947. (c) $6 Grumman X-29 with forward swept wings, 1984 ... 13·00 14·00

2003. As Nos. 2067/81, with country name overprint smaller and bird inscriptions in English only.

3777	$5 Greater Antillean bullfinch	4·50	5·00
3778	$10 Caribbean elaenia	8·50	9·50

518 *Psychopsis papilio*

2003. Orchids. Multicoloured.

MS3779 96×138 mm. $2.50 Type **518**; $2.50 *Amesiella philippinensis*; $2.50 *Maclellanara* "Pagan Dove Song"; $2.50 *Phalaenopsis* "Little Hal" ... 8·00 8·00

MS3780 205×124 mm. $2.50 *Daeliocattleya* "Amber Glow"; $2.50 *Hygrochilus parishii*; $2.50 *Dendrobium crystallinum*; $2.50 *Disa* hybrid (all horiz) ... 8·00 8·00

MS3781 98×68 mm. $5 *Cattleya deckeri* (horiz) ... 5·00 5·00

519 Bull Shark

2003. Sharks. Multicoloured.

MS3782 128×128 mm. $2 Type **519**; $2 Grey reef shark; $2 Black tip shark; $2 Leopard shark ... 8·00 8·00

MS3783 88×88 mm. $5 Great white shark ... 5·00 5·00

520 Esmeralda

2003. Butterflies. Multicoloured.

MS3784 105×86 mm. $2 Type **520**; $2 Tiger pierid; $2 Blue night butterfly; $2 *Charaxes nobilis* ... 8·00 8·00

MS3785 205×132 mm. $2.50 Orange-barred sulphur; $2.50 Scarce bamboo page; $2.50 *Charaxes latona*; $2.50 Hewitson's blue hairstreak ... 8·00 8·00

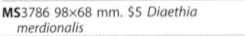

MS3786 98×68 mm. $5 *Diaethia merdionalis* ... 5·00 5·00

521 Apes

2003. Centenary of Circus Clowns. Multicoloured.

MS3787 119×195 mm. $1.80 Type **521**; $1.80 Mo Lite; $1.80 Gigi; $1.80 "Buttons" M. C. Bride ... 4·75 5·50

MS3788 145×218 mm. $1.80 Chun Group; $1.80 Casselly Sisters (acrobats); $1.80 Oliver Groszer; $1.80 Keith Nelson (sword swallower) ... 4·75 5·50

No. MS3787 is cut in the shape of a clown on a bicycle and No. MS3788 in the shape of a circus elephant.

522 Madonna and Child (detail) (Bartolommeo Vivarini)

2003. Christmas. Multicoloured.

3789	25c. Type **522**	35	20
3790	30c. *Holy Family* (detail) (Pompeo Girolano Batoni)	35	20
3791	45c. *Madonna and Child* (detail) (Benozzo Gozzoli)	50	25
3792	50c. *Madonna and Child* (detail) (Benozzo Gozzoli), Calci Parish Church	50	30
3793	75c. *Madonna and Child giving Blessings* (Benozzo Gozzoli)	75	50
3794	90c. *Madonna and Child* (detail) (Master of the Female Half-Figures)	90	55
3795	$2.50 *The Benois Madonna* (detail) (da Vinci)	2·50	3·25

MS3796 70×110 mm. $6 *The Virgin and Child with Angels* (Rosso Fiorentino) ... 5·50 6·00

523 Blue and Yellow Macaw ("Blue and Gold Macaw")

2003. Birds. Multicoloured.

MS3797 96×137 mm. $2.50 Type **523**; $2.50 Green-winged macaw; $2.50 Rainbow lory ("Green-naped Lorikeet"); $2.50 Lesser sulphur-crested cockatoo ... 8·50 8·50

MS3798 205×133 mm. $2.50 Chestnut-fronted macaw ("Severe Macaw"); $2.50 Blue-headed parrot; $2.50 Budgerigar; $2.50 Sun conure (all horiz) ... 8·50 8·50

MS3799 98×68 mm. $5 Waldrapp ("Bald Ibis") (horiz) ... 5·50 5·50

524 Diana Monkey

2004. Chinese New Year ("Year of the Monkey"). Multicoloured.

MS3800 152×95 mm. $1.50 Type **524**; $1.50 Mandrill; $1.50 Lar gibbon; $1.50 Red howler monkey ... 4·50 4·75

525 Mountain Landscape

2004. Hong Kong 2004 International Stamp Exhibition. Paintings by Ren Xiong. Multicoloured.

MS3801 131×138 mm. $1.50 Type **525**; $1.50 *Myriad Bamboo in Misty Rain*; $1.50 Winter landscape; $1.50 House and tree ... 4·50 4·75

MS3802 170×137 mm. $1.50 *Myriad Sceptres worshipping Heaven*; $1.50 Misty mountain landscape; $1.50 Myriad cherry trees; $1.50 Mountain landscape with two streams; $1.50 *Myriad Valleys with competing Streams*; $1.50 Myriad lights ... 5·50 6·00

MS3803 74×153 mm. $2.50 Bird singing from flowering cherry branch; $2.50 Bird in maple tree ... 3·75 4·00

Nos. MS3801/2 show paintings from *The Ten Myriads* album and No. MS3803 paintings from *Album after the Poems of Yao Xie*.

526 Binky skating

2004. Arthur the Aardvark by Marc Brown (children's books and TV programme). T **526** and similar vert designs. Multicoloured.

MS3804 150×183 mm. $1.50 Type **526**; $1.50 Buster skating; $1.50 Francine skating; $1.50 D.W.; $1.50 Sue Ellen; $1.50 Muffy skating ... 6·00 6·50

MS3805 150×183 mm. $1.80 Binky in baseball game; $1.80 Muffy with bat; $1.80 Francine running; $1.80 Buster catching ball ... 5·00 5·50

MS3806 150×183 mm. $2.50 Arthur hitting ball; $2.50 Sue Ellen with bat; $2.50 Binky holding bat; $2.50 Arthur with bat batting ... 5·00 5·50

No. MS3804 shows Arthur characters skating and MS3805/6 show them playing baseball.

527 Freedom of Speech

2004. 25th Death Anniv of Norman Rockwell (artist) (2003). T **527** and similar vert designs. Multicoloured.

MS3807 135×145 mm. $2 Type **527**; $2 *Freedom to Worship*; $2 "Freedom from Want"; $2 "Freedom from Fear ... 6·00 6·50

MS3808 62×82 mm. $6 *Do Unto Others as you would have them Do Unto You*. Imperf ... 6·00 6·50

No. MS3807 shows a series of posters and MS3808 a painting for Saturday Evening Post cover, 1961.

528 *Woman with a Flower*

2004. 30th Death Anniv of Pablo Picasso (artist). T **528** and similar vert designs. Multicoloured.

MS3809 177×127 mm. $2 Type **528**; $2"*Marie-Therese Seated*; $2 *The Red Armchair (Marie-Therese) Seated*; $2 *The Dream (Marie-Therese) Seated* ... 6·00 6·50

MS3810 58×69 mm. $5 *Bust of a Girl (Marie-Therese)*. Imperf ... 4·50 4·75

529 *The Smile of Flaming Wings, 1953*

2004. 20th Death Anniv of Joan Miro (artist). Multicoloured.

3811	75c. Type **529**	70	45
3812	90c. *The Bird's Song in the Dew of the Moon, 1955*	85	50
3813	$1 *Dancer II, 1957* (vert)	90	70
3814	$4 *Painting, 1954* (vert)	3·50	4·50

MS3815 Sheet 181×152 mm containing four different $2 designs, each entitled *Painting Based on a Collage, 1933* | 6·50 | 7·00 |

MS3816 Two sheets. (a) 102×83 mm. $5 *Bather, 1932.* (b) 83×102 mm. $6 *Flame in Space and Nude Woman, 1932*" Both imperf. Set of 2 sheets | 8·50 | 9·50 |

530 *Vaite Goupil*

2004. Death Centenary of Paul Gauguin (2003) (artist). Multicoloured.

3817	25c. Type **530**	40	25
3818	30c. *Autoportrait. Pres du Golgotha*	40	25
3819	75c. *Le Moulin David A Pont-Aven* (horiz)	85	60
3820	$2.50 *Moisson en Bretagne*	2·75	3·25

MS3821 77×62 mm. $4 *Cavaliers sur la Plage*. Imperf | 4·25 | 4·50 |

531 *Felipe de Borbon and Letizia Ortiz*

2004. Marriage of Crown Prince Felipe de Borbon and Letizia Ortiz. Multicoloured.

3822	30c. Type **531**	40	25
3823	50c. Felipe de Borbon and Letizia Ortiz in gardens	55	30
3824	75c. Letizia Ortiz	80	55
3825	90c. Felipe de Borbon	1·00	60
3826	$1 Felipe de Borbon and Letizia Ortiz wearing dark coats	1·10	85
3827	$5 Felipe de Borbon and Letizia Ortiz at social function	4·00	5·00

MS3828 190×174 mm. $1.80 Family photo; $1.80 Felipe de Borbon swearing allegiance to the Flag; $1.80 Felipe de Borbon with father and grandfather; $1.80 With King Juan Carlos I and Queen Sofia (horiz); $1.80 As No. 3824; $1.80 As No. 3825 | 9·00 | 10·00 |

MS3829 Six sheets, each 138×123 mm. (a) $5 Family photo. (b) $5 Felipe de Borbon with father and grandfather. (c) $5 Felipe de Borbon and Letizia Ortiz laughing. (d) $6 With King Juan Carlos I and Queen Sofia (horiz). (e) $6 Felipe de Borbon swearing allegiance to the Flag. (f) $6 Letizia Ortiz reading news Set of 6 sheets | 26·00 | 29·00 |

532 *Dove carrying Olive Branch*

2004. United Nations International Year of Peace. Sheet 146×86 mm containing T **532** and similar horiz designs. Multicoloured.

MS3830 $3 Type **532**; $3 Dove with olive branch and globe; $3 Dove with olive branch and United Nations emblem | 6·00 | 7·00 |

533 *King Class 4-6-0*

2004. Bicentenary of Steam Locomotives. Six sheets containing T **533** and similar multicoloured designs.

MS3831 Three sheets. (a) 147×175 mm. $1 Type **533**; $1 Argentinian 11B Class 2-8-0; $1 Baldwin Mikado; $1 Track signal; $1 Signal block instrument; $1 Forders Sidings signal box; $1 Signal on line; $1 Signal in snow; $1 Interior of signal box; $1 Two light signals. (b) 147×176 mm. $1 Class 2-4-0T, Douglas–Port Erin line; $1 Class 4-8-2S, South African; $1 Class 2-8-2, China; $1 St. Pancras Station; $1 Ulverston Station; $1 Bolton Station; $1 Liverpool Street Station; $1 Cannon Street Station; $1 Malvern Station. (c) 146×177 mm. $1 Evening Star (horiz); $1 Indian Railways XC Pacific (horiz); $1 German Kreigslokomotive (horiz); $1 Bullied Light Pacific and Corfe Castle (horiz); $1 Copper cap chimney (horiz); $1 Tallylyn Railway (horiz); $1 Preservation volunteers (horiz); $1 Class Y7 0-4-0T (horiz); $1 Asmara Locoshed and Breda 0-4-0, Eritrea (horiz) Set of 3 sheets | 26·00 | 28·00 |

MS3832 Three sheets, each 97×67 mm. (a) $5 Settle–Carlisle line (horiz). (b) $6 Lake Egridir (horiz). (c) $6 Douro Valley railway (horiz) Set of 3 sheets | 16·00 | 17·00 |

534 *Pope John Paul II and Mother Teresa*

2004. 25th Anniv of the Pontificate of Pope John Paul II. Sheet 162×152 mm containing T **534** and similar horiz designs. Multicoloured.

MS3833 $1.80 Type **534**; $1.80 At the Wailing Wall; $1.80 With Pres. George W. Bush; $1.80 Waving with left hand; $1.80 Waving with right hand | 13·00 | 13·00 |

535 *Poster of 1964 Olympic Games, Tokyo*

2004. Olympic Games, Athens. Multicoloured.

3834	$1 Type **535**	1·00	60
3835	$1.65 Commemorative medal of 1964 Olympic Games, Tokyo	1·50	1·25
3836	$1.80 Fencing (horiz)	1·60	1·60
3837	$2 Pankration (wrestling, Greek art) (horiz)	1·75	2·25

536 *Milan Galic (Yugoslav player)*

2004. European Football Championship 2004, Portugal. Commemoration of First European Football Championship (1960). T **536** and similar multicoloured designs.

MS3838 147×86 mm. $2 Type **536**; $2 Slava Metreveli (USSR player); $2 Igor Netto (USSR player); $2 Parc des Princes stadium | 6·50 | 7·00 |

MS3839 98×85 mm. $6 USSR football team, 1960 (50×37 mm) | 4·50 | 4·75 |

537 *Derrick Tysoe (Durham Light Infantry)*

2004. 60th Anniv of D-Day Landings.

3840	**537** 30c. multicoloured	50	30
3841	- 45c. multicoloured	65	30
3842	- $1.50 multicoloured	1·75	1·75
3843	- $3 multicoloured	3·00	3·75

MS3844 Two sheets, each 177×107 mm. (a) $2 purple, mauve and black; $2 multicoloured; $2 purple; $2 lilac and black. (b) $2 deep blue and black; $2 blue and black; $2 slate and black; $2 slate violet and black Set of 2 sheets | 17·00 | 17·00 |

MS3845 Two sheets, each 100×69 mm. (a) $6 purple and black. (b) $6 brown and black Set of 2 sheets | 13·00 | 13·00 |

DESIGNS: No. 3840 Type **537**; No. 3841 Lt. Gen. Walter Bedell Smith; 3842 Les Perry, 1st Battalion, Suffolk Regiment; 3843 Major Gen. Percy Hobart; **MS**3844 (a) $2 Tiger II tank; $2 Kurt Meyer and tactics; $2 Canadian infantry; $2 British infantry; (b) $2 Hamilcar and Tetrarch tank; $2 Horsa Glider and soldiers; $2 Beachheads; $2 Soldiers and civilians; **MS**3845 (a) $6 Mulberry Harbour; (b) $6 Sherman tank.

538 *Queen Juliana*

2004. Queen Juliana of the Netherlands. Sheet, 170×180 mm, containing T **538** and similar horiz designs. Multicoloured.

MS3846 $2 Type **538**; $2 With Prince Bernhard; $2 With Princess Beatrix; $2 With Princess Irene; $2 With Princess Margriet; $2 With Princess Christina | 12·00 | 12·00 |

539 *Mike Bibby*

2004. National Basketball Association, China. Sheet, 204×140 mm, containing T **539** and similar vert designs. Multicoloured.

MS3847 Type **539**; $1.50 Jim Jackson; $1.50 Tracy McGrady; $1.50 Chris Webber; $1.50 Peja Stojakovic; $1.50 Yao Ming | 12·00 | 12·00 |

540 *Zinedine Zidane (France)*

2004. Centenary of FIFA (Federation Internationale de Football Association). T **540** and similar horiz designs. Multicoloured.

MS3848 193×97 mm. $2 Type **540**; $2 Roberto Baggio (Italy); $2 Franz Beckenbauer (Germany); $2 Ossie Ardiles (Argentina) | 6·00 | 6·50 |

MS3849 108×87 mm. $6 Jimmy Greaves (England) | 5·00 | 5·50 |

541 *George Herman "Babe" Ruth*

2004. Centenary of Baseball World Series. Sheet 127×118 mm containing T **541** and similar vert designs showing portraits of George Herman Ruth Jr ("Babe Ruth"). Multicoloured.

MS3850 $1.80 Type **541**; $1.80 Wearing crown; $1.80 Wearing striped cap; $1.80 Holding baseball bat over shoulder | 4·50 | 5·00 |

542 *John Denver*

2004. John Denver Commemoration. Sheet 117×107 mm containing T **542** and similar vert designs. Multicoloured.

MS3851 $1.50 Type **542**; $1.50 John Denver (wearing pale waistcoat); $1.50 Wearing dark waistcoat; $1.50 Facing left | 4·50 | 4·75 |

543 *"If you had wider shoulders…"*

2004. *The Family Circus* (cartoon). T **543** and similar vert designs. Multicoloured.

MS3852 115×176 mm. $2 Type **543**; $2 "Billy attacked me too hard!" (red border); $2 "Who tee-peed the mummies?"; $2 "Looking out there makes me realize its indeed the little things that count" | 6·00 | 6·50 |

MS3853 115×176 mm. $2 "Billy attacked me too hard!" (purple border); $2 "His ears came from where his eyes are"; $2 "Tennessee!"; $2 "One candy, or one bowl?" | 6·00 | 6·50 |

MS3854 176×115 mm. $2 "Someday I might travel to another planet, but I'm not sure why"; $2 "Adam and Eve were lucky. They didn't have any history to learn"; $2 "My backpack is too full. Will somebody help me to stand up?"; $2 "I tripped because one foot tried to hug the other foot" | 6·00 | 6·50 |

MS3855 176×115 mm. $2 "If you don't put enough stamps on it the mailman will only take it part way"; $2 "Gee, Grandma, you have a lot of thoughts on your wall"; $2 "Shall I play for you, pa-rum-pa-rum-pummm…"; $2 "You have to do that when you're married" | 6·00 | 6·50 |

MS3856 192×105 mm. $2 Billy; $2 Jeffy; $2 PJ; $2 Dolly | 6·00 | 6·50 |

544 *People holding Balloons forming AIDS Ribbon*

2004. World AIDS Day.

3857	**544** $2 multicoloured	2·00	2·00

545 *Madonna in Floral Wreath* (Bruegel the Elder with Rubens)

546 *Santa on Skis*

2004. Christmas. Multicoloured

(a) As T **545**.

3858	20c. Type **545**	30	25
3859	25c. *Madonna and Child* (detail) (Mabuse (Jan Gossaert))	30	25
3860	$1 *Floral Wreath with Virgin and Child* (detail) (Daniel Seghers)	1·00	75
3861	$1.80 *Madonna and Child* (detail) (Andrea Mantegna)	1·75	2·00

MS3862 70×100 mm. $6 *Madonna in a Floral Wreath* (Daniel Seghers) | 5·50 | 6·00 |

(b) As T **546**.

3863	30c. Type **546**	30	25
3864	45c. Santa ornament with arms raised	50	25
3865	50c. Santa on chimney	55	35

547 American Pit (inscr "Pitt") Bull Terrier

2005. Cats and Dogs. Multicoloured.

3866	30c. Type **547**	50	30
3867	75c. Golden Persian	90	50
3868	90c. Maltese (dog)	1·10	55
3869	$1 Calico shorthair (cat)	1·25	80
3870	$1.50 Siamese	1·40	1·60
3871	$1.50 Rottweiler	1·40	1·60
3872	$3 Tabby Persian	2·75	3·50
3873	$3 Australian terrier	2·75	3·50

MS3874 Two sheets, each 100×70 mm.
(a) $5 Turkish cat. (b) $5 German shepherd dog (horiz) 10·00 11·00

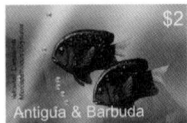

548 Yellowtail Damselfish

2005. Tropical Sea Life. Multicoloured.
MS3875 143×84 mm. $2 Type **548**; $2 French angelfish; $2 Horseshoe crab; $2 Emerald mithrax crab 8·00 8·00
MS3876 100×70 mm. $6 Spanish hogfish 5·50 6·00
The stamps within **MS**3875 form a composite design of a coral reef.

549 Figure-of-eight Butterfly

2005. Insects. Multicoloured.
MS3877 143×83 mm. $2 Type **549**; $2 Honey bee; $2 Migratory grasshopper; $2 Hercules beetle 8·00 8·00
MS3878 100×70 mm. $5 Cramer's mesene butterfly (vert) 5·00 5·50

550 Mammuthus imperator

2005. Prehistoric Animals. Multicoloured.
MS3879 Three sheets, each 140×110 mm. (a) $2 Type **550**; $2 Brontops; $2 Hyracotherium; $2 Propaleotherium. (b) $2.50 Ceratosaurs; $2.50 Coelurosaurs; $2.50 Ornitholestes; $2.50 Baryonyx. (c) $3 Plateosaurus; $3 Yangchuanosaurus; $3 Ceolophysis; $3 Lystrosaurus 25·00 27·00
MS3880 Three sheets, each 98×70 mm. (a) $4 Triceratops. (b) $5 Stegosaurus. (c) $6 Coelodonta 12·00 13·00
The stamps within Nos. **MS**3879a/c each form composite background designs.

551 Uruguay Team, 1930

2005. 75th Anniv of First World Cup Football Championship, Uruguay. Multicoloured.

3881	$2.50 Type **551**	2·00	2·00
3882	$2.50 Hector Castro scoring goal against Argentina, World Cup final, 1930	2·00	2·00
3883	$2.50 Estadio Centenario	2·00	2·00
3884	$2.50 Hector Castro	2·00	2·00

MS3885 111×86 mm. $6 Players after victory of Uruguay, 1930 5·00 6·00

552 Bust of Von Schiller (C. L. Richter), Central Park, New York

2005. Death Bicentenary of Friedrich von Schiller (poet and dramatist). Multicoloured.

3886	$3 Type **552**	2·50	2·50
3887	$3 Modern performance of *Kabale und Liebe*	2·50	2·50
3888	$3 Von Schiller's birthplace, Marbach, Germany	2·50	2·50

MS3889 66×95 mm. $6 Von Schiller and statue, Lincoln Park, Chicago 4·75 5·50

553 *Misterio en la Isla de los Monstruos*, 1961

2005. Death Centenary of Jules Verne (writer). Posters from films of Jules Verne's novels. Multicoloured.

3890	$2 Type **553**	2·25	2·25
3891	$2 *Journey to the Centre of the Earth*, 1961	2·25	2·25
3892	$2 *From the Earth to the Moon*, 1956	2·25	2·25
3893	$2 *Los Diablos del Mar*, 1961	2·25	2·25

MS3894 103×97 mm. $5 Michael Strogoff (56×41 mm) 5·00 5·00

554 British attempting to Board Spanish Ship *Santisma Trinidad*

2005. Bicentenary of the Battle of Trafalgar. Multicoloured.

3895	90c. Type **554**	1·75	1·00
3896	$1 Sailors clinging to wreckage and HMS *Royal Sovereign*, *Santa Ana*, HMS *Mars*, *Fouguex* and HMS *Temeraire*	2·00	1·25
3897	$1.50 HMS *Britannia* firing on crippled French *Bucentaure*	2·50	2·50
3898	$1.80 French *Redoubtable* and HMS *Victory*	3·00	3·50

MS3899 90×122 mm. $6 Crew of HMS *Victory* firing during battle 8·00 8·00

555 Ronald Reagan

2005. Ronald Reagan (US President 1981–9) Commemoration.
3900 **555** $1.50 multicoloured 1·25 1·50

556 Defeated German Soldiers, Red Square, 9 May 1945

2005. 60th Anniv of Victory in Europe Day. Multicoloured.

3901	$1.50 Type **556**	2·00	2·00
3902	$1.50 General Montgomery	2·00	2·00
3903	$1.50 Marshal Zhukov	2·00	2·00
3904	$1.50 General Bradley	2·00	2·00

557 Churchill, Roosevelt and Stalin at Yalta Summit, 1945

2005. 60th Anniv of Victory in Japan Day. Multicoloured.

3905	$2 Type **557**	2·50	2·50
3906	$2 US troops raising flag on Mt. Suribachi	2·50	2·50
3907	$2 Gen. McArthur signing Japanese surrender documents	2·50	2·50
3908	$2 Surrendering Japanese officials, 2 September 1945	2·50	2·50

558 *Mother Hen and her Brood* (Wang Ning)

2005. Chinese New Year ("Year of the Rooster"). Multicoloured.
3909 $1 Type **558** 1·25 1·25
MS3910 75×105 mm. $4 *Mother Hen and her Brood* (Wang Ning) 3·50 4·00

559 Dwight Howard, Orlando Magic

2005. US National Basketball Association Players. Multicoloured.

3911	75c. Type **559**	1·25	90
3912	75c. Lucious Harris, Cleveland Cavaliers	1·25	90
3913	75c. Emeka Okafor, Charlotte Bobcats	1·25	90
3914	75c. Antonio McDyess, Detroit Pistons	1·25	90
3915	75c. Ray Allen, Seattle Supersonics	1·25	90

560 Pope John Paul II with Rabbi Meir Lau (Chief Rabbi of Israel, 1993–2003)

2005. Pope John Paul II Commemoration.
3916 **560** $3 multicoloured 3·75 3·50

561 Italy 1979 World Rotary Congress Stamp

2005. Centenary of Rotary International. Multicoloured.

3917	$3 Type **561**	2·25	2·25
3918	$3 Paul Harris medallion and "Sow the Seeds of Love"	2·25	2·25
3919	$3 Paul Harris (founder), Tokyo, 1935	2·25	2·25

MS3920 100×70 mm. $6 Young African children (horiz) 4·75 5·00

562 Albert Einstein

2005. 50th Death Anniv of Albert Einstein (physicist). Multicoloured.

3921	$3 Type **562**	2·50	2·50
3922	$3 On bicycle	2·50	2·50
3923	$3 Albert Einstein (grey background)	2·50	2·50

563 Hans Christian Andersen

2005. Birth Bicentenary of Hans Christian Andersen (writer). Multicoloured.

3924	$3 Type **563**	2·25	2·25
3925	$3 Statue in Central Park, New York	2·25	2·25
3926	$3 Tombstone	2·25	2·25

MS3927 100×70 mm. $6 Hans Christian Andersen seated in chair 4·50 5·00

564 Pope Benedict XVI

2005. Election of Pope Benedict XVI.
3928 **564** $2 multicoloured 2·50 2·50

565 Gilbert's Memorial Methodist Church

2005. Christmas. Churches. Multicoloured.

3929	25c. Type **565**	35	20
3930	30c. The People's Church, Barbuda	40	30
3931	30c. Tyrell's Roman Catholic Church	40	30
3932	45c. St. Barnabas Anglican Church	55	25
3933	50c. St. Peter's Anglican Church	60	35
3934	75c. Spring Gardens Moravian Church	75	75
3935	75c. St. Steven's Anglican Church	75	75
3936	90c. Pilgrim Holiness Church (vert)	90	90
3937	90c. Holy Family Catholic Cathedral	90	90
3938	$1 Ebenezer Methodist Church	1·00	1·00

MS3939 Two sheets, each 100×70 mm. (a) $5 St. John's Cathedral. (b) $5 Service at Spring Gardens Moravian Church (vert) 8·50 9·50

566 The Joiners Loft, Nelson's Dockyard

2005. National Parks of Antigua. Multicoloured.

3940	20c. Type **566**	30	30
3941	20c. Pay Office, Nelson's Dockyard (vert)	30	30
3942	30c. Bakery, Nelson's Dockyard	45	45
3943	30c. Admirals House Museum, Nelson's Dockyard	45	45
3944	75c. Devil's Bridge National Park	80	80
3945	75c. View from Shirley Heights Lookout, Nelson's Dockyard National Park	80	80
3946	90c. Green Castle Hill National Park	95	95
3947	90c. Fort Berkeley, Nelson's Dockyard National Park	95	95

3948	$1.50 Pigeon Point Beach, Nelson's Dockyard National Park	1·50	1·75
3949	$1.50 Half Moon Bay National Park	1·50	1·75
3950	$1.80 Cannon at Fort Berkeley	1·75	2·00

MS3951 Two sheets. (a) 96×67 mm. $5 Frigate birds nesting at Codrington Lagoon National Park, Barbuda. (b) 65×96 mm. $5 Cannon and Admirals House Museum, Nelson's Dockyard (vert) 10·00 11·00

567 Yellowstone National Park

2006. National Parks of the USA. Multicoloured.

3952	$1.50 Type **567**	1·40	1·40
3953	$1.50 Olympic National Park	1·40	1·40
3954	$1.50 Glacier National Park	1·40	1·40
3955	$1.50 Grand Canyon National Park	1·40	1·40
3956	$1.50 Yosemite National Park	1·40	1·40
3957	$1.50 Great Smoky Mountains National Park	1·40	1·40

MS3958 95×70 mm. $6 Mount Rainier National Park (42×28 mm) 4·75 5·50

568 Bishop John Ephraim Knight

2006. 250th Anniv of Moravian Church in Antigua. Moravian Church Antigua Conference. Multicoloured.

3959	30c. Type **568**	35	20
3960	$1 John Andrew Buckley (minister 1856–79)	1·00	85
3961	$1.50 Old Spring Gardens Moravian Church, 1854–1963 (horiz)	1·40	1·75

MS3962 Three sheets, each 95×60 mm. (a) $5 Westerby Memorial, St. John's. (b) $5 Sandbox Tree (site of beginnings of Antigua Moravian Church). (c) $5 Spring Gardens Teachers College, 1854–1958 (horiz) 12·00 13·00

569 Princess Elizabeth

2006. 80th Birthday of Queen Elizabeth II. Multicoloured.

3963	$2 Type **569**	2·25	2·25
3964	$2 Princess Elizabeth wearing cream dress and pearl necklace	2·25	2·25
3965	$2 Princess Elizabeth wearing white blouse	2·25	2·25
3966	$2 Queen Elizabeth II wearing diadem and red dress	2·25	2·25

MS3967 120×120 mm. $6 Queen Elizabeth II wearing diadem and drop earrings 6·00 6·00

570 Marilyn Monroe

2006. 80th Birth Anniv of Marilyn Monroe (actress).

3968	**570** $3 multicoloured	2·50	2·50

571 Austria 2s.20 Ice Hockey Stamp

2006. Winter Olympic Games, Turin. Showing Austrian stamps issued for 1964 Olympic Games, Innsbruck (Nos. 3964/6) or poster (No. 3967). Multicoloured.

3969	75c. Type **571**	75	65
3970	75c. Poster for Winter Olympic Games, Sapporo, 1972 (vert)	75	65
3971	90c. Japan 1972 Winter Olympics 20y. skiing stamp (vert)	75	65
3972	90c. (1s.80) Figure skating stamp	75	65
3973	$2 4s. Bobsleighing stamp	1·75	2·00
3974	$3 Poster for Winter Olympic Games, Innsbruck, 1964 (vert)	2·75	3·25

572 Benjamin Franklin

2006. Washington 2006 International Stamp Exhibition. Showing Benjamin Franklin. Multicoloured.

MS3975 Two sheets, each 140×152 mm. (a) $3×4 Type **572**,Wearing red in oval portrait in gold frame (84×93 mm) (imperf); USA 1847 5c. stamp; Close-up portrait. (b) $3×3 Round portraits in gold frames: Wearing red; Sitting at desk; In close-up 17·00 19·00

573 Mozart's Viola

2006. 250th Birth Anniv of Wolfgang Amadeus Mozart (composer). Multicoloured.

3976	$3 Type **573**	3·50	3·00
3977	$3 Mozart aged eleven	3·50	3·00
3978	$3 Young Mozart	3·50	3·00
3979	$3 Mozart in Verona, 1770	3·50	3·00

574 Elvis Presley in Charro!

2006. 50th Anniv of Elvis Presley's Film Debut. Sheet 190×127 mm containing T **574** and similar vert designs showing film posters. Multicoloured.

3980	$3 Type **574**	2·50	2·50
3981	$3 Follow That Dream	2·50	2·50
3982	$3 G I Blues	2·50	2·50
3983	$3 Blue Hawaii	2·50	2·50

575 Leaders after Garbage Collection Race, 2002

2006. 75th Anniv of Antigua and Barbuda Girl Guides. Multicoloured.

3984	25c. Type **575**	35	20
3985	30c. Girl guides colour party (horiz)	35	20
3986	45c. Uniformed and non-uniformed members	55	25
3987	50c. Girl guides marching band (horiz)	60	30
3988	$1 Leeward Islands leaders training camp, 1946 (horiz)	1·00	1·25

MS3989 Three sheets, each 100×70 mm. (a) $5 Enrolment ceremony, 2006 (horiz). (b) $5 Girl guides gathering at Fort James, 1935 (horiz). (c) $5 Lisa Simon, Assistant Commissioner 12·00 13·00

576 HS-748 Hawker Siddely Avro

2006. 50th Anniv of LIAT (Leeward Islands Air Transport) Airline. Multicoloured.

3990	30c. Type **576**	50	25
3991	50c. BN2 Islanders on ground	70	70
3992	50c. BN2 Norman Islander	70	70
3993	50c. Beechcraft Twin Bonanza (vert)	70	70
3994	$1.50 BAC111-orange and HS748-pink/lilac on ground	2·00	2·00
3995	$2.50 Present brand DH8-300 50 seater De Havilland on ground	3·25	3·50

MS3996 70×100 mm. $5 Sir Frank Delisle (founder) and first Beechcraft Twin Bonanza N9614R (vert) 5·50 6·00

577 Magnificent Frigate Bird

2006. 25th Anniv of Independence. Multicoloured.

3997	25c. Type **577**	50	50
3998	25c. Fallow deer hinds	50	50
3999	25c. Fallow deer stag on beach	50	50
4000	25c. Magnificent frigate birds in flight and on nest	50	50
4001	30c. Pineapple	50	20
4002	$1 National flag	1·50	1·00
4003	$1.50 Coat of Arms	1·75	2·00

MS4004 100×70 mm. $5 New Parliament building (38×49 mm) 4·50 5·00

578 JSC Shuttle Mission Simulator (SMS)

2006. Space Anniversaries. Multicoloured

(a) 25th Anniv of First Flight of Space Shuttle "Columbia".

4005	$2 Type **578**	2·25	2·25
4006	$2 STS-1 prime crew during classroom session	2·25	2·25
4007	$2 STS-1 "Columbia" on launch pad	2·25	2·25
4008	$2 STS-1 "Columbia" blast-off	2·25	2·25
4009	$2 Pre-touchdown landing of "Columbia" at Edwards AFB, California	2·25	2·25
4010	$2 Space shuttle "Columbia" landing at Edwards Air Force Base	2·25	2·25

(b) 40th Anniv of "Luna 9" Moon Landing.

4011	$3 Molniya 8K78M rocket on launch vehicle	3·00	3·00
4012	$3 "Luna 9" flight apparatus	3·00	3·00
4013	$3 Image of Moon's surface transmitted by "Luna 9"	3·00	3·00
4014	$3 "Luna 9" capsule	3·00	3·00

(c) 30th Anniv (2005) of "Apollo-Soyuz" Test Project.

4015	$3 "Apollo" crew boarding transfer van	3·00	3·00
4016	$3 Handshake after "Apollo-Soyuz" linkup	3·00	3·00
4017	$3 Display of ASTP commemorative plaque	3·00	3·00
4018	$3 Recovery of ASTP Apollo command module	3·00	3·00

MS4019 Three sheets, each 100×70 mm. (a) $6 Calipso satellite. (b) $6 SS *Atlantis* docking on Space Station "MIR". (c) $6 Artist's concept of a NASA spaceship to orbit the Moon 16·00 16·00

579 Dalai Lama (Tibetan leader)

2006. Civil Rights. Multicoloured.

4020	$2 Type **579**	2·75	2·75
4021	$2 Abraham Lincoln (slavery abolitionist)	2·75	2·75
4022	$2 Susan Anthony (women's suffragist)	2·75	2·75
4023	$2 Harriet Tubman (slave liberator)	2·75	2·75
4024	$2 Mahatma Gandhi (Indian leader)	2·75	2·75
4025	$2 Nelson Mandela (anti-apartheid leader)	2·75	2·75
4026	$2 Rosa Parks (civil rights activist)	2·75	2·75

MS4027 70×100 mm. $5 Martin Luther King (civil rights leader) 4·50 5·00

580 Landscape with the Baptism of the Eunuch (detail)

2006. 400th Birth Anniv of Rembrandt Harmenszoon van Rijn (artist). Multicoloured.

4028	50c. Type **580**	60	30
4029	75c. Landscape with a Coach (detail)	1·00	55
4030	$1 River Landscape with Ruins (detail)	1·10	80
4031	$2 Landscape with a Castle (detail)	1·75	1·75
4032	$2 Samson Posing the Riddle to the Wedding Guests (detail, Samson's bride)	1·75	1·75
4033	$2 Samson Posing the Riddle to the Wedding Guests (detail, two men)	1·75	1·75
4034	$2 Samson Posing the Riddle to the Wedding Guests (detail, two guests listening)	1·75	1·75
4035	$2 Samson Posing the Riddle to the Wedding Guests (detail, woman)	1·75	1·75
4036	$2 The Holy Family (detail, man sitting at table)	1·75	1·75
4037	$2 The Good Samaritan arriving at the Inn (detail)	1·75	1·75
4038	$2 Rebecca Taking Leave of her Family (detail)	1·75	1·75
4039	$2 The Holy Family (detail, man sitting)	1·75	1·75

MS4040 Two sheets, each 70×100 mm. (a) $5 Self-Portrait. (b) $5 Rembrandt's Mother. Both imperf 8·00 9·00

581 Bauble

2006. Christmas. Multicoloured.

4041	30c. Type **581**	40	20
4042	90c. Gold star	1·10	55
4043	$1 Red bell	1·25	75
4044	$1.50 Miniature tree	1·75	2·00

MS4045 100×150 mm. $2×4 As Nos. 4041/4 8·00 9·00

MS4046 100×70 mm. $6 Santa on beach with wrapped presents 4·75 5·00

Nos. 4041/5 show Christmas tree decorations.
Stamps from MS4045 are in similar designs to Nos. 4041/4 but have the country inscription at top and no coloured panel at the foot of the stamp.
The background of MS4045 forms a composite design showing a decorated Christmas tree.

582 Betty Boop

2006. Betty Boop. Multicoloured.

4047	$1.50 Type **582**	1·00	1·00
4048	$1.50 Leaning forward	1·00	1·00
4049	$1.50 Holding mirror	1·00	1·00
4050	$1.50 Holding microphone	1·00	1·00
4051	$1.50 Seated, looking over shoulder	1·00	1·00
4052	$1.50 Wearing red heart garter	1·00	1·00

MS4053 70×100 mm. $3 "BETTY BOOP"; $3 With yellow fur stole 3·50 4·00

583 Columbus landing in New World

2007. 500th Death Anniv of Christopher Columbus. Multicoloured.

4054	75c. Type **583**	1·00	60
4055	90c. Christopher Columbus	1·10	65
4056	$2 Columbus (portrait in oval frame)	2·00	2·00
4057	$3 Columbus (in profile)	2·75	3·25
MS4058	100×70 mm. $6 Nina, Pinta and Santa Maria	5·50	6·00

584 National Flags forming Knot

2007. Centenary of World Scout Movement. Multicoloured.

| 4059 | $4 Type **584** | 4·00 | 4·25 |
| **MS**4060 | 110×80 mm. $6 National flags forming knot | 5·50 | 6·00 |

585 Ensign Kennedy

2007. 90th Birth Anniv of John F. Kennedy (American President 1960–3). Multicoloured.

4061	$3 Type **585**	2·50	2·50
4062	$3 Kennedy and crew members	2·50	2·50
4063	$3 Kennedy at the USS PT-109	2·50	2·50
4064	$3 Kennedy in the South Pacific	2·50	2·50
4065	$3 Campaigning on crutches	2·50	2·50
4066	$3 "The New Congressman"	2·50	2·50
4067	$3 John F. Fitzgerald, Joseph Kennedy and John F. Kennedy	2·50	2·50
4068	$3 "Celebrating Victory"	2·50	2·50

Nos. 4061/4 (showing John Kennedy in the Navy, 1941–5) and 4065/8 (showing his election to the House of Representatives, 1947–53).

586 Alamanda

587 Callicore maimuna (figure-of-eight butterfly)

2007. Flowers. Multicoloured.

4069	75c. Type **586**	90	50
4070	90c. Bidens sulphurea	1·00	50
4071	$1 Alstroemeria caryophyllacea	1·10	80
4072	$2 Canna limbata (horiz)	2·00	2·00
4073	$2 Gazania rigens (horiz)	2·00	2·00
4074	$2 Gloriosa rothschildiana (horiz)	2·00	2·00
4075	$2 Hibiscus sinensis (horiz)	2·00	2·00
4076	$4 Bougainvillea	3·50	4·00
MS4077	100×70 mm. $6 Caesalpinia pulcherrima	5·50	6·00

2007. Butterflies of the Caribbean. Multicoloured.

4078	75c. Type **587**	1·00	60
4079	90c. Dismorphia amphione (tiger pierid)	1·25	65
4080	$1 Eryphanis polyxena (purple mort bleu)	1·40	90
4081	$4 Colobura dirce (mosaic butterfly)	4·75	5·50
MS4082	130×108 mm. $2×4 Actinote pellenea (small lacewing); Anteos clorinde (clorinde); Morpho peleides (common morpho); Anartia jatrophae (white peacock)	8·00	8·00

| **MS**4083 | 70×99 mm. $5 Catonephele numilia (Grecian shoemaker) | 5·00 | 5·00 |

The stamps and margins of No. **MS**4082 form a composite design of palm tree foliage.

588 Cantharellus cibarius

590 Kenneth Benjamin

589 Oncidium flexuosum

2007. Mushrooms of the Caribbean. Multicoloured.

| **MS**4084 | 131×108 mm. $2×4 Type **588**; Auricularia auricula-judae; Mycena acicula; Peziza vesiculosa | 8·00 | 8·00 |
| **MS**4085 | 100×70 mm. $6 Pleurotus djamor | 6·00 | 6·00 |

The stamps and margins of No. **MS**4084 form a composite design.

2007. Orchids. Multicoloured.

4086	$3 Type **589**	1·75	1·75
4087	$3 Paphiopedilum Pinocchio	1·75	1·75
4088	$3 Cattleyopsis lindenii	1·75	1·75
4089	$3 Cattleyopsis cubensis	1·75	1·75
MS4090	100×70 mm. $6 Osmoglossum pulchellum (vert)	3·00	3·25

2007. World Cup Cricket, West Indies. Famous West Indian Cricketers. Multicoloured.

4091	25c. Type **590**	15	10
4092	30c. Anderson Roberts	20	15
4093	90c. Ridley Jacobs	60	45
4094	$1 Curtly Ambrose	70	55
4095	$1.50 Richard (Richie) Richardson	90	75
MS4096	117×90 mm. $5 Sir Vivian Richards	2·75	3·00

591 Princess Elizabeth and Duke of Edinburgh

2007. Diamond Wedding of Queen Elizabeth II and Duke of Edinburgh. Multicoloured.

4097	$1.50 Type **591**	90	75
4098	$1.50 Wedding shoes	90	75
MS4099	101×70 mm. $6 On wedding day with family (vert)	3·00	3·25

592 Camellias and Butterfly

2007. 50th Death Anniv of Qi Baishi (artist). Paintings on Fans. Multicoloured.

4100	$1.50 Type **592**	90	75
4101	$1.50 Two shrimps and arrowhead leaves	90	75
4102	$1.50 Gourd and ladybug	90	75
4103	$1.50 Bird	90	75
4104	$1.50 Landscape	90	75
4105	$1.50 Five shrimps	90	75
MS4106	(a) 102×72 mm. $3 Chrysanthemums; $3 Maple leaves (both vert). (b) 72×102 mm. $6 Wisteria (vert)	7·00	7·50

593 Ferrari 365 GTS4, 1969

2007. Ferrari Classic Cars. Multicoloured.

4107	$1.40 Type **592**	85	70
4108	$1.40 Superamerica, 2005	85	70
4109	$1.40 F1 90, 1990	85	70
4110	$1.40 400 Automatic, 1976	85	70
4111	$1.40 250 GT Coupe, 1954	85	70
4112	$1.40 156 F2, 1960	85	70
4113	$1.40 312 P, 1972	85	70
4114	$1.40 D 50, 1956	85	70

594 Concorde 01 rolled out, Filton, 20 Sept 1971

2007. Concorde. Multicoloured.

4115	$1.50 Type **594**	90	75
4116	$1.50 Concorde 01 (G-AXDN) in flight (green border)	90	75
4117	$1.50 As Type **594** (violet border)	90	75
4118	$1.50 As No. 4116 (magenta)	90	75
4119	$1.50 As Type **594** (green border)	90	75
4120	$1.50 As No. 4116 (violet border)	90	75
4121	$1.50 Concorde and London Eye (green inscr)	90	75
4122	$1.50 Concorde and Sydney Opera House (black inscr)	90	75
4123	$1.50 As No. 4121 (magenta inscr)	90	75
4124	$1.50 As No. 4122 (orange inscr)	90	75
4125	$1.50 As No. 4121 (black inscr)	90	75
4126	$1.50 As No. 4122 (blue inscr)	90	75

Nos. 4115/20 show Concorde 01, the first pre-production aircraft.

Nos. 4121/6 commemorate the London to Sydney flight record set on 13 February 1985. The colours given for Nos. 4121/6 are those of the country inscription 'ANTIGUA & BARBUDA'.

595 NH-90 Helicopter

2007. Centenary of the Helicopter. Multicoloured.

4127	$1.50 Type **595**	90	75
4128	$1.50 BO 105 helicopter carrying pipes	90	75
4129	$1.50 NH-90 helicopter on ground	90	75
4130	$1.50 AS-61 helicopter 6-15 over sea	90	75
4131	$1.50 BO 105 helicopter and lighthouse	2·25	2·00
4132	$1.50 AS-61 helicopter 6-26	90	75
MS MS4133	100×71 mm. $6 Bell UH-1 Iroquois 'Huey' troop carrier (vert)	7·50	7·00

596 Pope Benedict XVI

2007. 80th Birthday of Pope Benedict XVI.

| 4134 | **596** $1.40 multicoloured | 85 | 75 |

597 Elvis Presley

2007. 30th Death Anniv of Elvis Presley. Multicoloured.

4135	$1.50 Type **597**	90	90
4136	$1.50 Wearing striped shirt, seen in profile	90	97
4137	$1.50 Holding guitar, wearing jacket and bow tie	90	97
4138	$1.50 Wearing striped shirt, smiling	90	97
4139	$1.50 Wearing red shirt	90	97
4140	$1.50 Holding guitar, seen in half-profile	90	97

598 Diana, Princess of Wales

2007. Tenth Death Anniv of Diana, Princess of Wales. Multicoloured.

4141	$2 Type **598**	1·25	1·25
4142	$2 Wearing pale mauve and drop earrings	1·25	1·25
4143	$2 Wearing purple jacket with black edging on collar	1·25	1·25
4144	$2 Wearing brownish grey and white dress and hat	1·25	1·25
MS4145	70×100 mm. $6 Wearing headscarf	3·00	2·75

599 Strelitzia parvifolia (bird of paradise)

2007. Plants and Trees. Multicoloured.

4146	15c. Type **599**	15	10
4147	20c. Thespesia populnea (seaside mahoe)	20	15
4148	30c. Hibiscus rosa sinensis	25	15
4149	50c. Agave karatto	30	20
4150	70c. Barringtonia asiatica	45	35
4151	75c. Cocos nucifera (coconut)	50	40
4152	90c. Prosopis chilensis (mesquite) (horiz)	60	45
4153	$1 Tamarindus indica	70	55
4154	$1.50 Capparis cynophallophora (black willow) (horiz)	90	75
4155	$1.80 Baobab (horiz)	1·10	1·10
4156	$2 Petrea volubilis	1·25	1·25
4157	$2.50 Opuntia cochenillifera (cactus) (horiz)	1·50	1·50
4158	$5 Hymenaea courbaril (locust fruit) (horiz)	2·75	3·00
4159	$10 Caesalpinia ciliata (Barbuda black warri)	5·25	5·50
4160	$20 Ricinus communis (castor oil plant)	10·00	10·50

600 John W. Ashe, Antigua &; Barbuda

2007. Holocaust Remembrance. Multicoloured.

4161	$1.40 Type **600**	85	70
4162	$1.40 Alfred Capelle, Marshall Islands	85	70
4163	$1.40 Masao Nakayama, Micronesia	85	70
4164	$1.40 Gilles Noghes, Monaco	85	70
4165	$1.40 Baatar Choisuren, Mongolia	85	70
4166	$1.40 Filipe Chiduma, Mozambique	85	70
4167	$1.40 Marlene Moses, Nauru	85	70
4168	$1.40 Franciscus Majoor, Netherlands	85	70

601 Antigua and Barbuda on Bauble

2007. Christmas. Multicoloured.

4169	30c. Type **601**	25	15
4170	90c. Decorated palm tree and parade dancers on beach	65	50
4171	$1 Cake decorations	75	55
4172	$1.50 Parade costume	90	75

602 Hands

2007. World Hospice and Palliative Care Day. Multicoloured.

| 4173 | 30c. Type **602** | 25 | 15 |
| 4174 | 30c. Clock | 25 | 15 |

603 King Court (Prince Klaas), 1691–1736

2008. National Heroes. Multicoloured.

4175	90c. Type **603**	65	50
4176	90c. Dame Georgiana E. (Nellie) Robinson, 1880–1972	65	50
4177	$1 Sir Vivian Richards	75	60
4178	$1.50 Sir V. C. Bird Snr, 1909–99	1·25	1·00

603a Field Marshal William 'Bill' Slim

2008. Field Marshal William 'Bill' Slim Commemoration.

| 4178a | **603a** | $1·20 multicoloured | 1·25 | 1·10 |

604 Americas Cup Yachts

2008. 32nd Americas Cup Yachting Championship, Valencia, Spain. Multicoloured.

4179	$1.20 Type **604**	90	75
4180	$1.80 Two yachts, yellow-hulled *Lladro* at right	1·40	1·40
4181	$3 Two yachts	2·25	1·50
4182	$5 Five yachts	3·75	4·00

605 Pierre de Coubertin (founder of modern Olympics), 1896

2008. Olympic Games, Beijing. Multicoloured.

4183	$1.40 Type **605**	1·10	1·10
4184	$1.40 Poster for first modern Olympic Games, Athens, 1896	1·10	1·10
4185	$1.40 Spiridon Louis of Greece, marathon gold medallist, 1896	1·10	1·10
4186	$1.40 Paul Masson of France, cycling gold medallist, 1896	1·10	1·10

606 King's Garden, Walls of Old City and Al-Aqsa Mosque, Jerusalem (image scaled to 44% of original size)

2008. Israel 2008 World Stamp Championship. Sheet 110×100 mm.

| MS4187 | **606** | $6 multicoloured | 4·50 | 4·75 |

607 Applying Eye Drops

2008. World Glaucoma Day. Multicoloured.

4188	30c. Type **607**	25	30
4189	50c. Normal and glaucomatous optic nerves	40	25
4190	$1 Using braille typewriter	75	60

608 Pope Benedict XVI

2008. Frist Visit of Pope Benedict XVI to the United States

| 4191 | **608** | $2 multicoloured | 1·50 | 1·25 |

609 Elvis Presley

2008. 50th Anniv of Elvis Presley's Induction into the US Army. Sheet 160×130 mm containing T **609** and similar vert designs. Multicoloured.

MS4192 Type **609**; In light grey uniform; In dark grey uniform; In light grey uniform with cap — 6·00 5·75

The stamps within No. **MS**4192 share a composite background design.

610 *Vanguard I*, 1958

2008. 50 Years of Space Exploration and Satellites. Multicoloured.

4193	$1.50 Type **610**	1·25	1·00
4194	$1.50 *Vanguard I* (green and white background)	1·25	1·00
4195	$1.50 *Vanguard I* (sphere and base)	1·25	1·00
4196	$1.50 *Explorer III*, 1958	1·25	1·00
4197	$1.50 *Explorer III* orbiting Earth	1·25	1·00
4198	$1.50 Van Allen radiation belt (discovered by Explorer programme)	1·25	1·00
4199	$2 *Vanguard I* and Moon	1·50	1·25
4200	$2 *Vanguard I* orbiting Earth at sunrise	1·50	1·25
4201	$2 *Explorer III* (deep brown-red and light green background)	1·50	1·25
4202	$2 *Explorer III*	1·50	1·25

MS4203 Two sheets, each 100×70 mm.
(a) $6 *Vanguard I* above Earth (horiz).
(b) $6 *Explorer III* and Earth (horiz) — 9·00 8·75

611 Capt Kirk and Mr. Spock

2008. Star Trek. Multicoloured.

4204	$1.50 Type **611**	1·25	1·10
4205	$1.50 Mr. Spock, Capt. Kirk, Dr. Leonard McCoy and Lt. Cmdr Scott	1·25	1·10
4206	$1.50 Mr. Spock and Lt. Uhura	1·25	1·10
4207	$1.50 Enterprise crew in alien city	1·25	1·10
4208	$1.50 Lt. Uhura (Nichelle Nichols) on bridge of Enterprise	1·25	1·10
4209	$1.50 Lt. Cmdr Scott (James Doohan)	1·25	1·10
4210	$2 Dr. Leonard McCoy (DeForest Kelley) (50×37 mm)	1·50	1·25
4211	$2 Mr. Spock (Leonard Nimoy) (50×37 mm)	1·50	1·25
4212	$2 Captain Kirk (William Shatner) (50×37 mm)	1·50	1·25
4213	$2 Hikaru Sulu (George Takei) (50×37 mm)	1·50	1·25

612 Muhammad Ali

2008. Muhammad Ali (world heavyweight boxing champion, 1964, 1974–8). Multicoloured.

| 4214– 4219 | $1.50×6 Type **612** and similar designs showing Muhammad Ali speaking | 7·00 | 6·75 |
| 4220– 4223 | $2×4 Hitting punchbag; Wearing white robe, speaking; With white robe over back of shoulders; Wearing helmet (all 37×50 mm) | 6·00 | 6·75 |

613 John F. Kennedy (in profile)

2008. John F. Kennedy (US President 1960–3) Commemoration. Sheet 100×130 mm containing T **613** and similar vert designs showing President Kennedy. Multicoloured.

MS4224 Type **613**; Facing straight ahead; Head turned to left; With hand raised to chin — 6·00 5·75

614 Marilyn Monroe

2008. Marilyn Monroe Commemoration. Sheet 100×140 mm containing T **614** and similar horiz designs. Multicoloured.

MS4225 Type **614**; Head turned to left; Wearing deep orange; Wearing mauve sweater — 6·00 7·75

615 Holy Family

2009. Christmas. Designs showing stained glass windows. Multicoloured.

4226	30c. Type **615**	25	15
4227	90c. Baby Jesus in manger	60	50
4228	$1 Mary and infant Jesus with hands held together in prayer (vert)	75	60
4229	$1.50 Mary and infant Jesus standing on her lap (vert)	1·25	1·10

616 Baseball

2009. Olympic Games, Beijing (2008). Sports of the Summer Games. Sheet 130×94 mm containing T **616** and similar vert designs. Multicoloured.

MS4230 Type **616**; Beach volleyball; Gymnastics; Judo — 4·25 4·00

617 First Inaugural Address of Pres. Lincoln, 4 March 1861

2009. Birth Bicentenary of Abraham Lincoln (US President 1861–5). Sheet 130×100 mm containing T **617** and similar horiz designs. Multicoloured.

MS4231 Type **617**; Abraham Lincoln; Crowd at his second inaugural address, 4 March 1865; Crowd and Abraham Lincoln — 6·00 5·75

The stamps and margins of No. **MS**4231 form composite designs.

618 Pres. Barack Obama (in profile)

2009. Inauguration of President Barack Obama. Multicoloured.

MS4232 130×100 mm. $2.75 Type **618**×4 — 6·50 7·50

MS4232aa 100×70 mm. $10 Pres. Obama (in front of US flag) (37×50 mm) — 8·00 8·50

619 Ox

2009. Chinese New Year. Year of the Ox. Sheet 190×78 mm.

MS4233 $1 Type **619**×4 multicoloured — 4·00 3·75

620 Xian

2009. China 2009 World Stamp Exhibition, Luoyang (1st issue). Sites and Scenes of China. Multicoloured.

MS4234 100×145 mm. $1.40×4 Type **620**; Harbinn; Chongqing; Tianjin — 1·40 1·40

621 Emperor Quin Shi Huang

2009. China 2009 World Stamp Exhibition, Luoyang (2nd issue). First Emperor Quin Shi Huang (221–210BC) and his Terracotta Army. Multicoloured.

MS4235 120×150 mm. $1.40×4 Type **621**; Horses; Warriors; Excavation with army in columns — 1·40 1·40

622 Peony

2009. China 2009 World Stamp Exhibition, Luoyang (3rd issue). Peonies. Multicoloured.

| 4236 | $1 Type **622** | 95 | 90 |

MS4237 100×70 mm. $5 Black and dull pink peony design (triangular 35×30 mm) — 4·75 4·75

623 Elvis Presley

2009. Elvis Presley Commemoration. Multicoloured.
MS4238 185×125 mm. $1.50×6 Type
623; Wearing jacket and tie (orange
background); Standing with hands
on hips; Wearing pale orange jacket
with white stripe; Playing guitar,
wearing lei; Wearing jacket and tie
(sky background) 3·25 3·25

624

2009. National Stamp Day.
4239 **624** $4 multicoloured 3·75 3·50

625 Labrador Retriever

2009. 125th Anniv of the American Kennel Club. Two
sheets, each 100×120 mm, containing T **625** and
similar horiz designs showing Labrador Retriever
puppies (**MS**4240) or Dachshunds (**MS**4241).
Multicoloured.
MS4240 $2.50×4 Type **625**; Two golden
labrador puppies; Black and golden
labrador puppies carrying stick;
Golden labrador puppy in tub 9·75 9·75
MS4241 $2.50×4 Black and tan
dachshund pawing case; Tan dachs-
hund in green wooden crate; Two
dachshund puppies in wooden trug;
Wire-haired dachshund 9·75 9·75

626 Michael Jackson

2009. Michael Jackson Commemoration. Multicoloured.
MS4242 158×112 mm. $2.50×4 Type
626; Wearing black with gold
crossbelts and waistband; Wearing
orange-red with black diagonal
band; Wearing silver jacket with
eagle design 9·75 9·75
MS4243 130×100 mm. $2.50×4 Wear-
ing plain white shirt; Wearing white
jacket with black armbands 9·75 9·75
MS4244 150×110 mm. $6 Wearing
white T-shirt and white shirt (38×51
mm) 4·75 4·75

627 Flypast of Fighter Jets

2009. Centenary of Chinese Aviation and Aeropex 2009
Exhibition, Beijing. T **627** and similar horiz designs.
Multicoloured.
MS4245 145×95 mm. $2×4 (All show-
ing Chengdu J-7 fighters) Type **627**;
Flying to right; Flying to left; Flying
in fan formation 3·75 3·75
MS4246 120×80 mm. $6 Chengdu
J–7GB fighter jet (50×38 mm) 3·75 3·75

628 Pres. Barack
Obama

2009. Meeting of US President Barack Obama and Pope
Benedict XVI, Vatican, 10 July 2009. Multicoloured.
MS4247 150×100 mm. $2.75×3 Type
628; Pope Benedict XVI; Michelle
Obama 2·75 2·75
MS4248 110×90 mm. $6 Pope Benedict
XVI and Pres. Barack Obama (horiz) 3·75 3·75

629 Apollo 11 Emblem

2009. 40th Anniv of First Manned Moon Landing and
International Year of Astronomy. Multicoloured.
MS4249 151×100 mm. $2.50×4 Type
629; Lunar Module *Eagle*; Passive
Seismic Experiment Package;
Apollo 11 9·75 9·75
MS4250 101×71 mm. $6 Apollo 11
orbiting Moon 5·75 5·75

630 Poster for *King Creole*,
1958

2009. Elvis Presley in Film *King Creole*. Multicoloured.
MS4251 125×90 mm. $6 Type **630** 3·75 3·75
MS4252 90×125 mm. $6 Elvis Presley
playing guitar 3·75 3·75
MS4253 90×125 mm. $6 Elvis Presley
with arms raised (horiz) 3·75 3·75
MS4254 125×90 mm. $6 Elvis Presley
playing guitar (horiz) 3·75 3·75

631 Candles and
Wreath

2009. Christmas. Showing Christmas lights. Multicoloured.
4255 90c. Type **631** 90 85
4256 $1 Gold, red and green lights 95 90
4257 $1.80 Three bells and tree
 branches 1·75 1·60
4258 $3 Nativity 2·75 2·50

632 Pair of Caribbean Coot

2009. Endangered Species. Caribbean Coot (*Fulica
caribaea*). Multicoloured.
4259 $2.65 Type **632** 2·50 2·50
4260 $2.65 Pair landing 2·50 2·50
4261 $2.65 Pair with chick 2·50 2·50
4262 $2.65 Adult feeding chick 2·50 2·50
MS4263 112×165 mm. Nos. 4259/62,
 each ×2 20·00 20·00

633 Sir Vere
Cornwall Bird

2009. Birth Centenary of Rt. Honourable Dr. Sir Vere
Cornwall Bird Sr. (first Chief Minister, Premier
and Prime Minister of Antigua and Barbuda).
Multicoloured.
4264 30c. Type **633** 30 25
4265 75c. Sir V. C. Bird (Antigua flag
 in background) 75 70
4266 90c. Wearing red jacket and hat 90 85
4267 $1.50 Sir V. C. Bird (black and
 white photo) 1·40 1·25
MS4268 160×110 mm. $2.50×4 As
 Nos. 4265/7 9·75 9·75

2009.
MS4269 100×70 mm. $6 Sir V. C. Bird
(Antigua flag and outline map in
background) 5·75 5·75

634 Glossy Ibis (*Plegadis
falcinellus*)

2009. Birds of Antigua and Barbuda. Multicoloured.
4270 $1.20 Type **634** 1·25 1·10
4271 $1.80 Green-winged teal (*Anas
 carolinensis*) 1·75 1·60
4272 $3 California clapper rail (*Rallus
 longirostris obsoletus*) 2·75 2·50
4273 $5 Cattle egret (*Bubulcus ibis*)
 (vert) 4·75 4·50
MS4274 90×90 mm. $2.50×4 Green
heron (*Butorides virescens*); Com-
mon ground dove (*Columbina
passerina*); White-tailed hawk (*Buteo
albicaudatus*); Black-faced grassquit
(*Tiaris bicolor*) 6·50 6·50
MS4275 70×100 mm. $3×2 Bananaquit
(*Coereba flaveola*); Osprey (*Pandion
haliaetus*) 5·75 5·75

634a Nurse Shark
(*Ginglymostoma cirratum*)

2010. Sharks of the Caribbean. Multicoloured.
4275a $1.20 Type **634a** 1·25 1·10
4275b $1.80 Caribbean reef shark
 (*Carcharhinus perezi*) 1·75 1·60
4275c $3 Tiger Shark (*Galeocerdo
 cuvier*) 2·25 2·00
4275d $5 Whale shark (*Rhincodon
 typus*) 3·50 3·25
MS4275e $2.75x4 170×100 mm.
$2.75×4 Caribbean sharpnose shark
(*Rhizoprionodon porosus*); Blacktip
shark (*Carcharhinus limbatus*);
Oceanic whitetip shark (*Carcharhinus
longimanus*); Bull shark (*Carcharhinus
leucas*) 5·50 5·25
The stamps and margins of **MS**4275e form a compos-
ite design.

634b Rat

2010. Chinese Lunar Calendar.. Multicoloured.
MS4275f 60c.x12 Type **634b**; Ox; Tiger;
Rabbit; Dragon; Snake; Horse; Ram;
Monkey; Rooster; Dog; Pig 3·50 3·25

634c Bronze Tiger, Western
Han Dynasty, China

2010. Chinese New Year (Year of the Tiger)..
Multicoloured.
MS4275g $5 Type **634c**; $5 Bronze
tiger, Shang Dynasty, China 4·75 4·50

635 Risso's Dolphin
(*Grampus griseus*)

2010. Whales and Dolphins of the Caribbean.
Multicoloured.
4276 $1.20 Type **635** 1·25 1·10
4277 $1.80 Common dolphin (*Delphi-
 nus delphis*) 1·75 1·60
4278 $3 Humpback whale (*Meg-
 aptera novaeangliae*) 2·25 2·00
4279 $5 Sperm whale (*Physeter
 macrocephalus*) 3·75 3·50
MS4280 100×140 mm. $2×6 Short-
snout dolphin (*Lagenodelphis hosei*);
Spotted dolphin (*Stenella frontalis*);
Cuvier's beaked whale (*Ziphius
cavirostris*); Shortfin pilot whale
(*Globicephala macrorhynchus*); Gulf
Stream beaked whale (*Mesoplodon
europaeus*); Rough-toothed dolphin
(*Stenobredanensis*) 9·00 8·75

636 Diana, Princess
of Wales

2010. Diana, Princess of Wales Commemoration. Sheet
130×90 mm containing T **636** and similar vert
designs. Multicoloured.
MS4281 $2×4 Type **636**; Wearing
pink; Wearing pale mauve; Wearing
pale green 6·00 5·75

637 Airfoil of Ferrari 312
F1-68, 1968

2010. Ferrari Cars. Multicoloured.
4282 $1.25 Type **637** 3·75 3·50
4283 $1.25 Ferrari 312 F1-68, 1968 75 70
4284 $1.25 Engine of Ferrari 246 P
 F1, 1960 75 70
4285 $1.25 Ferrari 246 P F1, 1960
 (car no. 34) 75 70
4286 $1.25 Interior of Ferrari 365 P
 Speciale, 1966 75 70
4287 $1.25 Ferrari 365 P Speciale,
 1966 75 70
4288 $1.25 Engine of Ferrari 158
 F1, 1964 75 70
4289 $1.25 Ferrari 158 F1, 1964 (car
 no. 20) 75 70

638 Common Buckeye
(*Junonia coenia*)

2010. Butterflies of the Caribbean. Multicoloured.
4290 $1.20 Type **638** 1·20 1·10
4291 $1.80 Red postman (*Heliconius
 erato*) 1·75 1·60
4292 $3 Red admiral (*Vanessa
 atalanta*) 2·20 2·10
4293 $5 Zebra longwing (*Heliconius
 charithonia*) 3·50 3·25
MS4294 140×100 mm. $2×6 Orange
sulphur (inscr 'sulfur') (*Colias
eurytheme*); Blue morpho (*Morpho
peleides*); Queen butterfly (*Danaus
gilippus*); Zebra swallowtail (*Eurytides
marcellus*); Malachite (*Siproata
stelenes*); Gatekeeper butterfly
(*Pyronia tithonus*) 6·00 3·75
The stamps and margins of **MS**4294 form a composite
background design of a flowering plant.

639 Dancers,
Shanghai
International Culture
and Art Festival

2010. Expo 2010, Shanghai, China. Multicoloured.
MS4295 $1.50×4 Type **639**; China Na-
tional Grand Theatre, Beijing; Green
rice terrace, Guangxi Province, China;
Dance performance, Beijing (yellow
background) 3·25 3·00

640 Mother Teresa with
Princess Diana

2010. Birth Centenary of Mother Teresa. Multicoloured.
MS4296 $2.50×4 Type **640**; Receiving
Order of Merit from Queen Elizabeth
II, India; Receiving Medal of Freedom
from Pres. Reagan; With Pope John
Paul II, Calcutta, India 5·25 5·00

641 Scout giving Lecture ('Citizenship and Leadership')

2010. Centenary of Boy Scouts of America. Multicoloured.
MS4297 $2.50 Type **641**×2; $2.50 Two scouts in kayak ('Aquatic sport adventures')×2 5·25 5·00
MS4298 $2.50 Statue of Liberty giving Scout salute×2; $2.50 Two scouts ('Navigation with map and compass')×2 5·25 5·00

642 Elvis Presley

2010. 75th Birth Anniv of Elvis Presley. Multicoloured.
MS4299 $2.75×4 Type **642**; Facing forward, singing; Facing left, guitar strap over face; Three images of Elvis Presley 5·25 5·00
MS4300 $2.75×4 Wearing white with pattern; Wearing open neck shirt; Two images of Elvis Presley; Wearing white jacket with dark piping 7·50 8·00
The stamps and margins of **MS**4299 form a composite design spelling out 'ELV75'.

643 Pres. Obama holding Nobel Peace Prize

2010. Pres. Barack Obama's Nobel Peace Prize (2009). Multicoloured.
MS4301 $2.75×4 Type **643**; Speaking (side view); Speaking from podium; Holding Nobel Peace Prize, smiling 5·50 5·00

644 Princess Diana on Visit to Hindu Mission, UK

2010. Princess Diana Commemoration. Multicoloured.
MS4302 $2.75×4 Type **644**; Visit to Pakistan; Visit to Dubai; Visit to Japan 5·50 5·00
MS4303 $2.75×4 Wearing tiara with pearls and pearl drop earrings; Wearing tiara and sapphire and diamond earrings; Wearing tiara and pearl drop earrings; Wearing tiara and white jacket with stand-up collar 5·50 5·00

645 Rainbows

2010. Centenary of Girlguiding. Multicoloured.
MS4304 150×100 mm. $2.75×4 Type **645**; Brownies in kayaks; Three guides; Three Senior Section guides hiking 5·50 5·00
MS4305 70×100 mm. $6 Guides 4·25 4·00

646 Abraham Lincoln

2010. Birth Bicentenary (2009) of Abraham Lincoln (US President 1861–5). Multicoloured.
MS4306 $2.75×4 Type **646**; With beard, facing forward; With beard, looking to left; Profile, facing left 5·50 5·25
MS4307 $2.75×4 Type **646**; With beard, facing forward; With beard, looking to left; Profile, facing left 5·50 5·25

647 Pope John Paul II

2010. Pope John Paul II Commemoration. Multicoloured.
4308 $2.75 Type **647** 2·50 2·50

648 Pres. John F. Kennedy

2010. 50th Anniv of Election of Pres. John F. Kennedy. Multicoloured.
MS4309 $2.75×4 Type **648**; Pres. John F. Kennedy; Seated in chair (bookcase in background); Speaking 5·50 5·25

649 Three Stooges

2010. The Three Stooges. Multicoloured.
MS4310 $2.50×4 Type **649**; The Three Stooges as decorators, Curly holding cloth to Moe's neck; The Three Stooges as doctors and patient, Larry holding scissors to Curly's nose; Larry and Moe with Curly's head in guillotine 6·50 7·00

650 Maximiliano Pereira (Uruguay)

2010. World Cup Football Championship, South Africa. Multicoloured.
MS4311 130×150 mm. $1.50×6 Type **650**; John Heitinga (Netherlands); Edinson Cavani (Uruguay); Mark Van Bommel (Netherlands); Martin Caceres (Uruguay); Giovanni van Bronckhorst (Netherlands) 8·00 7·25
MS4312 85×90 mm. $3.50 Oscar Tabarez (Uruguay coach); $3.50 Uruguay flag on football 5·50 5·25
MS4313 85×90 mm. $3.50 Bert van Marwijk (Dutch coach); $3.50 Dutch flag on football 5·50 5·25

651 California Spangled Cat

2010. Cats of the World. Multicoloured.
MS4314 150×100 mm. $2.50×6 Type **651**; Siamese; British shorthair; Norwegian forest; Egyptian mau; American curl longhair 3·75 3·75
MS4315 100×70 mm. $6 Manx cat 3·75 3·75

652 Henri Dunant and Nurses with Wounded Soldiers

2010. Death Centenary of Henri Dunant (instigator of Red Cross). Multicoloured.
MS4316 150×100 mm. $2.50×4 Type **652**; Wounded laying on battlefield; Cavalry; Cavalry and soldiers 2·40 2·40
MS4317 70×100 mm. $6 Battle of Solferino 3·75 3·75

653 Pope Benedict XVI

2010. Fifth Anniv of Papacy of Pope Benedict XVI. Multicoloured.
MS4318 142×153 mm. $2.75 Type **653**×4 9·75 9·75
MS4319 171×113 mm. $2.75 Pope Benedict XVI (facing left)×4 9·75 9·75

654 Rabbit

2011. Chinese New Year (Year of the Rabbit)
MS4320 $4 Type **654**; $4 Chinese rabbit symbol 6·00 6·00

655 Giant Panda

2011. Beijing 2010 International Stamp and Coin Exposition. Giant Panda. Multicoloured.
MS4321 170×95 mm. $2×4 Type **655**; Close-up of face; Panda with bamboo plant; Panda eating leaves (side view) 2·40 2·40
MS4322 62×90 mm. $5 Giant panda (facing right) 3·25 3·25

656 Casini Madonna (Masaccio)

2011. Christmas. Multicoloured.
4323 30c. Type **656** 30 25
4324 75c. Madonna of the Stars (Tintoretto) 70 65
4325 90c. Wall mosaic showing magi from Basilica of Sant Apollinare Nuovo, Ravenna, Italy 90 85
4326 $1.50 The Annunciation (Fra Angelico) 1·40 1·25

657 Prince William and Miss Catherine Middleton

2011. Royal Engagement. Multicoloured.
4327 $2.50 Type **657** 2·50 2·25
4328 $2.50 Prnce William 2·50 2·25
4329 $2.50 Miss Catherine Middleton 2·50 2·25

MS4330 120×70 mm. $6 Prince William (smiling) 3·25 3·25
MS4331 120×70 mm. $6 Prince William (speaking) 3·25 3·25

658 Mahatma Gandhi

2011. Indipex 2011 World Philatelic Exhibition, Delhi. Mahatma Gandhi. Multicoloured.
MS4332 $2.75×4 Type **658**; Gandhi and Asokan capital; Gandhi and towers and gateway; Gandhi and Taj Mahal, India 3·00 2·75
MS4333 $2.75×4 Gandhi (in profile, wearing white) and crowd; Gandhi (facing forward) and crowd; Gandhi (in profile, looking down) and crowd; Gandhi (looking to right) and crowd 3·00 2·75

659 Pope John Paul II praying

2011. Beatification of Pope John Paul II. Multicoloured.
MS4334 176×91 mm. $2 Type **659**×3; $2 Pope John Paul II wearing red cape×3 10·00 10·00
MS4335 100×70 mm. $6 Pope John Paul II 10·00 10·00

660 Stephen Mallory, Lt-Commander Murray and Warships of Atlantic Blockading Squadron

2011. 150th Anniv of the American Civil War. Multicoloured.
MS4336 $2.50×4 Type **660**; Stephen Mallory (Confederate Secretary of Navy), Union Lt. Commander Alexander Murray and flotilla of Union warships; Mallory, Murray and Confederate privateers near Delaware Bay; Mallory, Murray and flagship USS *Minnesota* 10·00 10·00
MS4337 $2.50×4 Confederate General Henry Jackson, Union General Joseph Reynolds and map of battle of Greenbriar River by A. T. McRae of the Quitman Guards; Jackson, Reynolds and skirmish along the Greenbriar River; Jackson, Reynolds and Union forces assembling near Greenbriar River; Jackson, Reynolds and battle of Greenbriar River 10·00 10·00
MS4338 $2.50×4 Confederate Brigadier General Richard Anderson, Union Colonel Harvey Brown and Fort Pickens; Anderson, Brown and battle at Santa Rosa Island; Anderson, Brown and Union ships cutting off Confederate dispatch galley; Anderson, Brown and Colonel Brown in command of 3rd US Infantry 10·00 10·00

661 *Tylopilus potamogeton*

2011. Mushrooms of the Caribbean. Multicoloured.
MS4339 170×100 mm. $2×6 Type **661**; *Amanita campinaranae*; *Cantharellus atratus*; *Tylopilus orsonianus*; *Boletellus ananas*; *Amanita craseoderma* 10·00 10·00
MS4340 170×100 mm. $2.50×4 *Amanita cyanopus*; *Phyllobolites miniatus*; *Chroogomphus jamaicensis*; *Coltricia cf. montagnei* 9·00 9·00
MS4341 101×70 mm. $6 *Austroboletus festivus* 9·00 9·00
MS4342 101×70 mm. $6 *Austroboletus rostrupii* 6·00 6·00

662 Princess Diana in Barbuda, April 1997

2011. 50th Birth Anniv of Princess Diana. Multicoloured.
MS4343 150×100 mm. $10 Type **662**×5 10·00 10·00
MS4344 150×100 mm. $10 Princess Diana, Prince William and Prince Harry in Barbuda, April 1997×5 10·00 10·00
MS4345 101×70 mm. $50 Princess Diana wearing red dress and beach (horiz) 22·00 22·00

663 Pope Benedict XVI and Church

2011. Pope Benedict XVI visits Germany. Multicoloured.
MS4346 $3×3 Type **663**; Pope Benedict XVI and church with blue roof; Pope Benedict XVI and Brandenburg Gate, Berlin 10·50 10·50
MS4347 $3×3 Pope Benedict XVI and St. Mary's Cathedral and Church of St. Severus, Erfurt; Pope Benedict XVI and church with turquoise roof; Pope Benedict XVI and Bavarian houses and bell tower 10·50 10·50

664 Duke and Duchess of Cambridge

2011. Royal Wedding. Multicoloured.
MS4348 100×134 mm. $2.50 Type **664**×2; $2.50 Prince William (in profile); $2.50 Duchess of Cambridge (in profile) 9·00 9·00
MS4349 100×134 mm. $2.50 Prince William waving; $2.50 Duke and Duchess of Cambridge kissing×2; $2.50 Duchess of Cambridge 9·00 9·00
MS4350 100×106 mm. $6 Duke and Duchess of Cambridge 7·00 7·00

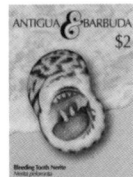

665 Bleeding Tooth Nerite (*Nerita peloronta*)

2011. Shells of the Caribbean. Multicoloured.
MS4351 100×150 mm. $2×6 Type **665**; Pen shell (*Atrina rigida*); Banded tulip shell (*Fasciolaria lillium*); Chank shell (*Turbinella pyrum*); Flame helmet (*Cassis flammea*); Atlantic partridge tun (*Tonna maculosa*) 10·00 10·00
MS4352 101×131 mm. $2.75×4 Pink conch (*Strombus gigas*); Sunrise tellin (*Tellina radiata*); Flamingo tongue (*Cyphoma gibbosum*); Queen's helmet (*Cassis madagascariensis*) 10·00 10·00
MS4353 101×101 mm. $6 King's helmet (*Cassis tuberosa*) 6·00 6·00
MS4354 101×101 mm. $6 Triton's trumpet (*Charonia tritonis*) (horiz) 6·00 6·00

666 Pres. Kennedy inspects Mercury Capsule, 23 February 1962

2011. 50th Anniv of Inauguration of Pres. John F. Kennedy. Multicoloured.
MS4355 150×110 mm. $2.75×4 Type **666**; Cape Canaveral tour, 16 November 1963; Saturn rocket briefing, 16 November 1963; Pres. Kennedy at Cape Canaveral, 16 November 1963 10·00 10·00
MS4356 100×100 mm. $6 Pres. John F. Kennedy (51×38 mm) 6·00 6·00

667 Elvis Presley

2011. Elvis Presley Commemoration. Multicoloured.
MS4357 90×140 mm. $2×3 Type **667**; Wearing white suit, boarding train; On motorbike 10·00 10·00
MS4358 138×80 mm. $2.75×4 Elvis Presley in army uniform: Head and shoulders portrait; Leaning on railing; Wearing overalls; Reading letter (all vert) 10·00 10·00
MS4359 176×124 mm. $2.75×4 In concert: Wearing red shirt; Wearing blue jacket and white shirt; Wearing white jacket with silver studs; Wearing white jacket with patterned collar (all vert) 10·00 10·00
MS4360 140×90 mm. $3 On stage, wearing black; $3 Wearing sweater with two shoulder stripes (both vert) 10·00 10·00

668 Pres. Barack Obama

2011. Pres. Barack Obama. Multicoloured.
MS4361 150×110 mm. $2.75×4 Type **668**; Pres. Obama facing forward, speaking; Facing forward; Facing left 10·00 10·00
MS4362 100×70 mm. $6 Pres. Barack Obama 10·00 10·00

669 Liftoff of Vostok 1, 1961

2011. 50th Anniv of the First Man in Space. Multicoloured.
MS4363 150×100 mm. $2.75×4 Type **669**; Kosmonaut Yuri Gagarin (tracking ship), 1970-91; Vostok 1 mission logo; Alan Shepard (first American astronaut) and Freedom 7, 1961 10·00 10·00
MS4364 150×100 mm. $2.75×4 Globe showing flightpath of Yuri Gagarin; Vostok 8K72K rocket; Yuri Gagarin in space; US astronaut Virgil Gus Grissom and rocket 10·00 10·00
MS4365 100×71 mm. $6 Vostok 1 orbiting Earth 6·00 6·00
MS4366 100×71 mm. $6 Yuri Gagarin 6·00 6·00

670 Princess Diana

2011. 50th Birth Anniv of Princess Diana. Multicoloured.
MS4367 150×100 mm. $2.75×4 Type **670**; Princess Diana wearing beige top with white lapels and beige pleated skirt; Wearing white; On honeymoon with Prince Charles at Balmoral, 1981 10·00 10·00
MS4368 101×101 mm. $6 Princess Diana wearing pale mauve and white patterned dress (51×38 mm) 10·00 10·00

671 Queen Angelfish (*Holacanthus ciliaris*)

2011. Tropical Fish. Multicoloured.
MS4369 161×100 mm. $3.50×4 Type **671**; Ocean surgeonfish (*Acanthurus bahianus*); Rock beauty (*Holacanthus tricolor*); Gray angelfish (*Pomacanthus arcuatus*) 11·00 11·00
MS4370 161×100 mm. $3.50×4 Foureye butterflyfish (*Chaetodon capistratus*); French grunt (*Haemulon flavolineatum*); French angelfish (*Pomacanthus paru*); Spotfin butterflyfish (*Chaetodon ocellatus*) 11·00 11·00
MS4371 121×81 mm. $9 Great barracuda (*Sphyraena barracuda*) (80×30 mm) 14·00 14·00
MS4372 121×81 mm. $9 Banded butterflyfish (*Chaetodon striatus*) (40×40 mm) 14·00 14·00

Pt. 20

ANTIOQUIA

One of the states of the Granadine Confederation. A department of Colombia from 1886, now uses Colombian stamps.

100 centavos = 1 peso.

1

1868. Various arms designs. Imperf.

1	1	2½c. blue	£1200	£700
2	-	5c. green	£900	£500
3	-	10c. lilac	£2750	£900
4	-	1p. red	£700	£450

5 **6**

1869. Various frames. Imperf.

5	5	2½c. blue	5·00	4·25
6	5	5c. green	7·75	7·00
8	5	10c. mauve	10·00	5·00
9	5	20c. brown	10·00	5·00
10	6	1p. red	20·00	17·00

7

1873. Arms designs inscr "E.S." (or "Eo. So." or "Estado Soberano") "de Antioquia". Imperf.

11	7	1c. green	7·25	5·25
12	-	5c. green	12·00	8·50
13	-	10c. mauve	35·00	28·00
14	-	20c. brown	12·00	10·00
15	-	50c. blue	2·75	2·10
16	-	1p. red	5·00	3·75
17	-	2p. black on yellow	12·00	10·50
18	-	5p. black on red	90·00	75·00

The 5p. is larger (25½×31½ mm).

15

1875. Imperf.

20	15	1c. black on green	2·40	3·25
21	15	1c. black	1·80	3·25
43	15	1c. mauve	3·50	5·25
52	15	1c. green	3·50	5·25
22	-	2½c. blue (Arms)	3·50	2·75
23	-	5c. green ("Liberty")	22·00	19·00
25	-	10c. mauve (J. Berrio)	35·00	28·00

20 **21** Liberty **23** Liberty

1879. Imperf.

30	20	2½c. blue	3·75	3·50
38	20	2½c. green	3·50	2·75
45	20	2½c. black on buff	10·00	8·50
39	21	5c. green	6·00	5·00
40	21	5c. violet	13·00	10·00
32	-	10c. violet (Arms)	£1400	£900

36	23	10c. violet	£275	85·00
41	23	10c. red	3·50	2·75
42	21	20c. brown	6·00	5·00

25 Liberty

1883. Various frames. Head of Liberty to left. Imperf.

47	25	5c. yellow	7·75	5·75
48	25	5c. green	£225	£100
53	25	5c. brown	7·25	4·50
49	25	10c. green	7·75	7·00
50	25	10c. mauve	17·00	10·00
55	25	10c. blue	7·75	5·75
51	25	20c. blue	7·25	5·75

28

1886. Imperf.

57	28	1c. green on pink	90	75
65	28	1c. red on lilac	65	55
58	28	2½c. black on orange	90	75
66	28	2½c. mauve on pink	65	75
59	28	5c. blue on buff	5·00	4·25
67	28	5c. red on green	5·00	2·30
68	28	5c. lake on buff	90	85
60	28	10c. red on buff	1·00	1·20
69	28	10c. brown on green	1·00	1·20
61	28	20c. purple on buff	2·40	2·10
62	28	50c. yellow on buff	4·50	3·75
63	28	1p. yellow on green	7·25	5·75
64	28	2p. green on lilac	7·25	5·75

31

1888. Various sizes and frames. Inscr "MEDELLIN". Imperf.

70	31	2½c. black on yellow	22·00	19·00
71	31	2½c. red on white	11·00	9·00
72	31	5c. black on yellow	12·00	10·00
73	31	5c. red on orange	7·25	5·75

34

1889. Arms in various frames.

74	34	1c. black on red	35	30
75	34	2½c. black on blue	35	30
76	34	5c. black on yellow	45	45
77	34	10c. black on green	45	45
95	34	10c. brown	35	30
78	34	20c. blue	2·00	1·90
79	34	50c. brown	3·75	3·75
80	34	50c. green	2·75	2·75
81	34	1p. red	2·75	2·75
82	34	2p. black on mauve	20·00	19·00
83	34	5p. black on red	29·00	28·00

35

1890. Perf.

84	35	2½c. black on buff	2·75	2·75
85	35	5c. black on yellow	2·75	2·75
86	35	10c. black on buff	9·25	9·00
87	35	10c. black on red	12·00	11·50
88	35	20c. black on yellow	12·00	11·50

36

1892.

89	36	1c. brown on buff	55	55

90	36	1c. blue	35	30
91	36	2½c. violet on lilac	55	55
92	36	2½c. green	55	55
93	36	5c. black	1·50	75
94	36	5c. red	35	30

37

1896

96	37	2c. grey	35	30
107	37	2c. red	35	55
97	37	2½c. brown	35	30
108	37	2½c. blue	35	30
98	37	3c. red	35	30
109	37	3c. olive	35	30
99	37	5c. green	35	30
110	37	5c. yellow	45	45
100	37	10c. lilac	75	75
111	37	10c. brown	75	75
101	37	20c. brown	2·00	1·90
112	37	20c. blue	2·00	1·90
102	37	50c. sepia	2·00	1·90
113	37	50c. red	1·80	1·70
103	37	1p. black and blue	24·00	23·00
114	37	1p. black and red	24·00	23·00
104	37	2p. black and orange	75·00	75·00
115	37	2p. black and green	75·00	75·00
105	37	5p. black and mauve	£130	£130

39 Gen. Cordoba

1899

118	39	½c. blue	20	20
119	39	1c. blue	20	20
120	39	2c. black	20	20
121	39	3c. red	20	20
122	39	4c. brown	20	20
123	39	5c. green	20	20
124	39	10c. red	20	20
125	39	20c. violet	20	20
126	39	50c. yellow	20	20
127	39	1p. green	20	20
128	39	2p. green	20	20

43

1901. Various frames.

132	43	1c. red	35	30
133	43	1c. brown	90	85
134	43	1c. blue	90	85

Nos. 132 and 134 also exist with "CENTAVO" inside the rectangle below figure "1".

46 47 48 Girardot

1902

138	46	1c. red	35	30
139	46	1c. blue	35	30
140	46	2c. blue	35	30
141	46	2c. violet	35	30
142	46	3c. green	35	30
143	46	4c. purple	35	30
144	47	5c. red	35	30
145	47	10c. mauve	35	30
147	47	20c. green	35	30
148	47	30c. red	35	30
149	48	40c. blue	35	30
150	48	50c. brown on yellow	35	30
152	-	1p. black and violet	1·10	1·10
153	-	2p. black and red	1·10	1·10
154	-	5p. black and blue	2·00	1·90

DESIGN: 1p. to 5p. Dr. J. Felix de Restrepo.
No. 145 also exists with smaller head.

54 55 56 Zea

1903

159	54	4c. brown	35	30
160	54	5c. blue	35	30
161	55	10c. yellow	35	30
162	55	20c. lilac	35	30
163	55	30c. brown	90	85
164	55	40c. green	90	85
165	55	50c. red	35	30
166	56	1p. green	90	85
167	56	2p. mauve (Rovira)	90	85
168	56	3p. blue (La Pola)	90	85
169	56	4p. red (Restrepo)	1·50	1·50
170	56	5p. brown (Madrid)	4·50	2·10
171	56	10p. red (Corral)	9·25	5·25

ACKNOWLEDGEMENT OF RECEIPT STAMPS

AR53

1902

AR157	AR53	5c. black on red	1·40	1·40
AR158	AR53	5c. green	45	45

REGISTRATION STAMPS

R38

1896

R106	R38	2½c. pink	1·80	1·80
R117	R38	2½c. blue	1·80	1·70

R41 Gen. Cordoba R42

1899

R130	R41	2½c. blue	35	30
R131	R42	10c. red	35	30

R52

1902

R156	R52	10c. violet on green	45	45

TOO LATE STAMPS

L40 Gen. Cordoba

1899

L129	L40	2½c. green	35	30

1901. As T **43**, but inscr "RETARDO" at sides.

L137a		2½c. purple	1·10	1·10

L51

1902

L155	L51	2½c. lilac	35	30

ARBE
Pt. 8

During the period of D'Annunzio's Italian Regency of Carnaro (Fiume), separate issues were made for Arbe (now Rab).

100 centesimi = 1lira

1920. No. 148, etc of Fiume optd **ARBE**.

1B		5c. green	10·50	10·50
2B		10c. red	21·00	21·00
3B		20c. brown	55·00	32·00
4B		25c. blue	32·00	32·00
5		50c. on 20c. brown	55·00	32·00
6		55c. on 5c. green	55·00	32·00

EXPRESS LETTER STAMPS

1920. Nos. E163/4 of Fiume optd **ARBE**.

E7		30c. on 20c. brown	£190	£110
E8		30c. on 5c. green	£130	£110

ARGENTINE REPUBLIC
Pt. 20

A republic in the S.E. of S. America formerly part of the Spanish Empire.

1858. 100 centavos = 1 peso.
1985. 100 centavos = 1 austral.
1992. 100 centavos = 1 peso (= 10000 old australs)

1 Argentine Confederation

1858. Imperf.

1	1	5c. red	1·00	25·00
2	1	10c. green	1·50	55·00
3	1	15c. blue	14·00	£160

3 Argentine Confederation

1862. Imperf.

10	3	5c. red	16·00	18·00
8	3	10c. green	£150	60·00
9	3	15c. blue	£300	£190

5 Rivadavia 6 Rivadavia

1864. Imperf.

24	5	5c. red	£190	80·00
14	6	10c. green	£2250	£1300
15	5	15c. blue	£7500	£4500

1864. Perf.

16	5	5c. red	26·00	10·50
17	6	10c. green	70·00	24·00
18	5	15c. blue	£200	80·00

9 Rivadavia 10 Gen. Belgrano 11 Gen. San Martin

1867. Perf.

28	9	5c. red	12·50	1·00
29	10	10c. green	41·00	8·75
30a	11	15c. blue	85·00	16·00

12 Balcarce

1873. Portraits. Perf.

31	12	1c. violet	6·25	2·00
32	-	4c. brown (Moreno)	5·00	45
33	-	30c. orange (Alvear)	£100	19·00
34	-	60c. black (Posadas)	£100	4·50
35	-	90c. blue (Saavedra)	26·00	2·75

1877. Surch with large figure of value.

37	9	1 on 5c. red	55·00	20·00

38	9	2 on 5c. red	95·00	60·00
39	10	8 on 10c. green	£110	29·00

22 Sarsfield

1876. Roul.

36	9	5c. red	£180	75·00
40	9	8c. lake	21·00	35
41	10	16c. green	10·00	1·20
42	22	20c. blue	12·50	2·75
43	11	24c. blue	21·00	2·75

24 Lopez

1877. Perf.

46	24	2c. green	4·50	85
44	9	8c. lake	4·25	50
45	11	24c. blue	24·00	1·80
47	-	25c. lake (Alvear)	22·00	6·00

1882. Surch 1/2 (PROVISORIO).

51	9	½ on 5c. red	1·40	1·40

29

1882

52	29	½c. brown	1·60	1·00
55	29	1c. red	3·50	1·00
54	29	12c. blue	50·00	8·75

1884. Surch 1884 and value in figures or words.

90	9	½c. on 5c. red	2·75	2·20
92	11	½c. on 15c. blue	11·00	8·00
94	11	1c. on 15c. blue	11·00	8·75
100	9	4c. on 5c. red	7·00	4·50

33

1884

101	33	½c. brown	1·30	50
102	33	1c. red	6·25	50
103	33	12c. blue	30·00	1·20

34 Urquiza 45 Mitre

1888. Portrait types, inscr "CORREOS ARGENTINOS".

108	34	½c. blue	1·00	50
110	-	2c. green (Lopez)	12·00	7·25
111	-	3c. green (Celman)	2·10	75
113	-	5c. red (Rivadavia)	15·00	1·30
114	-	6c. red (Sarmiento)	31·00	18·00
115	-	10c. brown (Avellaneda)	18·00	1·00
116	-	15c. orange (San Martin)	21·00	1·60
117a	-	20c. green (Roca)	14·50	1·20
118	-	25c. violet (Belgrano)	21·00	2·50
119	-	30c. brown (Dorrego)	26·00	3·00
120a	-	40c. grey (Moreno)	31·00	3·50
121	45	50c. blue	£120	7·75

51 Rivadavia 60 Paz

1888. Portrait types, inscr "CORREOS Y TELEGRAFOS" except No. 126.

137	60	¼c. green	50	30
122	-	½c. blue (Urquiza)	50	30
123	-	1c. brown (Sarsfield)	1·00	50
125	-	2c. violet (Derqui)	1·00	50
126	-	3c. green (Celman)	3·00	80
127	51	5c. red	3·00	50
129	-	6c. blue (Sarmiento)	2·10	55
130	-	10c. brown (Avellaneda)	3·00	50

131	-	12c. blue (Alberti)	6·25	2·00
132	-	40c. grey (Moreno)	6·25	1·00
133	-	50c. orange (Mitre)	6·25	1·00
134	-	60c. black (Posadas)	15·00	3·00

1890. No. 131 surch 1/4 and bars.

135		¼ on 12c. blue	35	35

52 Rivadavia

1890

128a	52	5c. red	1·80	20

63 La Madrid

1891. Portraits.

139	-	1p. blue (San Martin)	55·00	9·75
140	63	5p. blue	£275	50·00
141	-	20p. green (G. Brown)	£425	£130

61 Rivadavia

1891

138	61	8c. red	1·30	50

65 Rivadavia **66** Belgrano **67** San Martin

1892

142	65	½c. blue	30	15
143	65	1c. brown	50	15
144	65	2c. green	60	20
145	65	3c. orange	1·20	20
146	65	5c. red	1·20	20
147	66	10c. red	9·50	35
148	66	12c. blue	7·25	35
149	66	16c. slate	12·00	45
150	66	24c. sepia	12·00	45
257	66	30c. orange	32·00	2·00
151	66	50c. green	18·00	45
188	66	80c. lilac	8·50	45
152a	67	1p. red	8·75	65
190	67	1p.20 black	8·50	1·70
153	67	2p. green	18·00	1·80
154	67	5p. blue	24·00	1·80

70 Fleet of Columbus

1892. Fourth Centenary of Discovery of America by Columbus.

219	70	2c. blue	7·75	3·25
220	70	5c. blue	8·25	4·00

71 "Liberty" and Shield

1899

221	71	½c. brown	30	20
222	71	1c. brown	1·30	40
223	71	2c. grey	40	20
224	71	3c. orange	40	35
225	71	4c. yellow	65	40
226	71	5c. red	40	20
227	71	6c. black	40	40
228	71	10c. green	1·00	25
229a	71	12c. blue	65	40
230	71	12c. green	65	40
231	71	15c. blue	1·40	40
232	71	16c. orange	5·50	4·00
233	71	20c. red	1·10	20
234	71	24c. purple	2·75	70

235	71	30c. red	5·00	40
237	71	50c. blue	2·75	35
238	71	1p. black and blue	8·50	70
239	71	5p. black and orange	32·00	6·00
240	71	10p. black and green	42·00	10·00
241	71	20p. black and red	£110	20·00

The peso values are larger (19×32 mm).

73 Port Rosario

1902. Completion of Port Rosario Docks.

290	73	5c. blue	4·00	1·70

74 Gen. San Martin

1908

291B	74	½c. violet	35	20
292B	74	1c. brown	35	20
293B	74	2c. brown	40	20
294B	74	3c. green	40	25
295B	74	4c. mauve	85	25
296B	74	5c. red	40	20
297B	74	6c. green	60	40
298B	74	10c. green	1·30	20
299A	74	12c. brown	40	40
300B	74	12c. blue	1·30	20
301A	74	15c. green	4·25	1·20
302B	74	20c. blue	85	20
303B	74	24c. red	2·50	40
304B	74	30c. red	4·25	40
305B	74	50c. black	4·25	35
306A	74	1p. red and blue	12·50	1·70

The 1p. is larger (21½×27 mm) with portrait at upper left.

76 Pyramid of May **78** Azcuenaga and Alberti

80 Saavedra

1910. Cent of Deposition of the Spanish Viceroy.

366	76	½c. blue and grey	50	30
367	-	1c. black and green	50	30
368	-	2c. black and green	50	30
369	78	3c. green	1·00	40
370	-	4c. green and blue	1·00	40
371	80	5c. red	75	30
372	-	10c. black and brown	1·10	50
373	-	12c. blue	1·10	50
374	-	20c. black and brown	3·00	70
375	-	24c. blue and brown	2·75	1·20
376	-	30c. black and lilac	2·75	1·00
377	-	50c. black and red	6·25	1·20
378	-	1p. blue	9·50	3·00
379	-	5p. purple and orange	75·00	36·00
380	-	10p. black and orange	£100	60·00
381	-	20p. black and blue	£160	£100

DESIGNS—VERT: 50c. Crowds on 25 May 1810; 10p. Centenary Monument; 20p. San Martin. HORIZ: 1c. Pena and Vieytes; 2c. Meeting at Pena's house; 4c. Fort of the Viceroys, Buenos Aires; 10c. Distribution of cockades; 12c. Congress Building; 20c. Castelli and Matheu; 24c. First National Council; 30c. Belgrano and Larrea; 1p. Moreno and Paso; 5p. "Oath of the Junta".

90 Sarmiento

1911. Birth Centenary of Pres. Sarmiento.

382	90	5c. black and brown	85	40

91 Ploughman

1911

383	91	5c. red	40	15
384	91	12c. blue	5·25	45

92 **94**
Ploughman

1911

395	92	½c. violet	45	45
396	92	1c. brown	45	45
397	92	2c. brown	65	45
398	92	3c. green	65	65
399a	92	4c. purple	75	75
400	92	5c. red	55	45
401	92	10c. green	2·20	45
402	92	12c. blue	75	45
403	92	20c. blue	4·00	65
404	92	24c. brown	8·25	2·75
405	92	30c. red	9·25	1·40
406	92	50c. black	13·00	1·30
408	94	1p. red and blue	13·00	1·40
409	94	5p. green and grey	24·00	8·00
410	94	10p. blue and violet	£100	20·00
411	94	20p. red and blue	£225	£100

95 Dr. F. N. Laprida **96** Declaration of Independence **97** San Martin

1916. Centenary of Independence.

417	95	½c. violet	75	45
418	95	1c. brown	75	55
419	95	2c. brown	75	45
420	95	3c. green	75	75
421	95	4c. purple	75	75
422	96	5c. red	75	9·50
423	96	10c. green	2·10	45
424	97	12c. blue	75	45
425	97	20c. blue	75	75
426	97	24c. red	3·25	1·60
427	97	30c. red	3·25	95
428	97	50c. black	5·00	95
429	97	1p. red and blue	13·00	7·00
430	97	5p. green and grey	£130	80·00
431	97	10p. blue and violet	£200	£160
432	97	20p. red and grey	£170	£130

98 San Martin

1917

450A	98	½c. violet	45	20
451A	98	1c. buff	45	20
452A	98	2c. brown	45	20
453A	98	3c. green	65	20
454A	98	4c. purple	65	20
455B	98	5c. red	45	20
439A	98	10c. green	45	45
457B	-	12c. blue	1·70	20
458B	-	20c. blue	1·70	20
459B	-	24c. red	3·25	20
460B	-	30c. red	4·00	45
461B	-	50c. black	8·25	65
445B	-	1p. red and blue	8·25	75
446B	-	5p. green and grey	21·00	3·75
447B	-	10p. blue and violet	65·00	16·00
448B	-	20p. red and grey	£130	75·00

The 12c. to 20p. values are larger (21×27 mm).

100 Dr. Juan Pujol

1918. Birth Centenary of Juan Pujol, First P.M.G. of Argentina.

449	100	5c. grey and bistre	1·00	45

102 Mausoleum of Belgrano **103** Creation of Argentine Flag

1920. Death Centenary of Gen. Manuel Belgrano.

478	102	2c. red	70	15
479	103	5c. blue and red	70	15
480	-	12c. blue and green	1·40	60

DESIGN—VERT: 12c. Gen. Belgrano.

106 General Urquiza

1920. Gen. Urquiza's Victory at Cepada.

488	106	5c. blue	55	30

107 General Mitre

1921. Birth Centenary of Gen. Mitre.

490	107	2c. brown	55	30
491	107	5c. blue	55	30

108

1921. First Pan-American Postal Congress.

492	108	3c. lilac	75	45
493	108	5c. blue	1·90	10
494	108	10c. brown	2·20	45
495	108	12c. red	2·75	95

1921. As T 108, but smaller. Inscr "BUENOS AIRES AGOSTO DE 1921".

496A		5c. red	40	25

1921. As No. 496, but inscr "REPUBLICA ARGENTINA" at foot.

511A		5c. red	3·00	25

112

1923. With or without stop below "c".

529	112	½c. purple	35	15
530	112	1c. brown	35	15
531	112	2c. brown	35	15
516A	112	3c. green	35	25
517A	112	4c. red	35	25
534	112	5c. red	35	15
535	112	10c. green	35	20
536	112	12c. blue	40	20
537	112	20c. blue	65	20
538	112	24c. brown	1·80	80
539	112	25c. violet	85	20
540	112	30c. red	1·80	20
541	112	50c. black	4·25	20
542	-	1p. red and blue	7·00	35
543	-	5p. green and lilac	21·00	4·00
544	-	10p. blue and red	65·00	10·00
545	-	20p. lake and slate	85·00	30·00

The peso values are larger (21×27 mm).

114 B. Rivadavia

1926. Rivadavia Centenary.

546	114	5c. red	55	30

115 Rivadavia **116** San Martin **117** G.P.O., 1926

118 G.P.O., 1826

1926. Postal Centenary.

547	115	3c. green	35	20
548	116	5c. red	35	20
549	117	12c. blue	1·10	30
550	118	25c. brown	2·75	85

120 Biplane and Globe **122**

1928. Air.

558	120	5c. red	1·80	75
559	120	10c. blue	2·75	1·10
560	–	15c. brown	2·75	1·10
561	120	18c. violet	5·00	3·75
562	–	20c. blue	3·25	1·10
563	–	24c. blue	5·50	3·75
564	122	25c. violet	5·50	1·70
565	122	30c. red	6·50	1·30
566	–	35c. red	5·50	1·20
567a	120	36c. brown	3·00	1·50
568	–	50c. black	5·50	75
569	122	54c. brown	5·50	2·30
570	–	72c. green	6·50	2·30
571	122	90c. purple	12·00	2·30
572	122	1p. red and blue	14·50	1·10
573	122	1p.08 blue and red	22·00	5·75
574	–	1p.26 green and violet	29·00	10·50
575	–	1p.80 red and blue	29·00	10·50
576	–	3p.60 blue and grey	55·00	23·00

DESIGNS—VERT: 15, 20, 24, 54, 72c. Yellow-headed Ca-racara over sea. HORIZ: 35, 50c., 1p.26, 1p.80, 3p.60, Andean Condor on mountain top.

124 Arms of Argentina and Brazil

1928. Centenary of Peace with Brazil.

577	124	5c. red	1·90	65
578	124	12c. blue	3·25	85

125 Torch illuminating New World

1929. "Day of the Race" issue.

579	125	2c. brown	2·75	55
580	–	5c. red	2·75	45
581	–	12c. blue	8·25	1·30

DESIGNS: 5c. Symbolical figures, Spain and Argentina; 12c. American offering laurels to Columbus.

(128)

1930. Air. Zeppelin Europe–Pan-America Flight. Optd with T 128.

587	–	20c. blue (No. 562)	14·50	8·50
588	–	50c. black (No. 568)	19·00	13·00
589	122	90c. purple	13·00	8·50
584	122	1p. red and blue	29·00	14·00
585	–	1p.80 (No. 575)	85·00	37·00
586	–	3p.60 (No. 576)	£225	£110

129 Soldier and Civilian Insurgents **130** The Victorious March, 6 September 30

1930. Revolution of 6 September 1930.

592	129	½c. violet	55	30
611	130	½c. mauve	45	30
593	129	1c. green	55	35
612	130	1c. black	1·30	1·10
594	130	2c. lilac	65	30
595	130	3c. green	55	45
613	130	3c. green	90	65
596	129	4c. violet	55	45
614	130	4c. lake	55	45
597	130	5c. red	45	30
615	130	5c. red	45	30
598	129	10c. black	1·10	55
616	130	10c. green	1·90	65
599	130	12c. blue	90	45
600	130	20c. buff	90	35
601	130	24c. brown	3·50	2·30
602	130	25c. green	4·25	2·30
603	130	30c. violet	6·50	3·50
604	130	50c. black	9·25	4·50
605	130	1p. red and blue	19·00	14·00
606	130	2p. orange and black	33·00	16·00
607	130	5p. black and green	£100	49·00
608	130	10p. blue and lake	£130	60·00
609	130	20p. blue and green	£350	£130
610	130	50p. violet and green	£1000	£750

1931. First Anniv of 1930 Revolution. Optd 6 Septembre 1930 - 1931.

617	112	3c. green (postage)	45	45
618	112	10c. green	90	85
624	129	18c. violet (air)	2·75	1·60
619	112	30c. red	5·00	4·50
620	112	50c. black	5·00	4·50
625	–	72c. green (No. 570)	22·00	14·00
626	122	90c. purple	22·00	14·00
621	112	1p. red and blue	6·00	4·50
627	–	1p.80 red & bl (No. 575)	44·00	34·00
623	130	2p. orange and black	19·00	13·00
628	–	3p.60 bl & grey (No. 576)	85·00	60·00
622	112	5p. green and lilac	£100	28·00

1932. Zeppelin Air stamps. Optd GRAF ZEPPELIN 1932.

629	120	5c. red	3·25	2·10
630	120	18c. violet	14·00	9·50
631	122	90c. purple	50·00	28·00

134 Refrigerating Plant

1932. Sixth International Refrigerating Congress.

632	134	3c. green	1·30	65
633	134	10c. red	2·75	55
634	134	12c. blue	7·75	1·90

135 Port La Plata

1933. 50th Anniv of La Plata City.

635	135	3c. brown and green	55	35
636	–	10c. purple and orange	65	30
637	–	15c. blue	5·00	2·30
638	–	20c. brown and lilac	2·20	1·40
639	–	30c. red and green	21·00	8·00

DESIGNS: 10c. President J. A. Roca; 15c. Municipal buildings; 20c. La Plata Cathedral; 30c. Dr. D. Rocha.

139 Christ of the Andes

1934. 32nd Int Eucharistic Congress, Buenos Aires.

640	139	10c. red	1·10	30
641	–	15c. blue	2·20	65

DESIGN—HORIZ: 15c. Buenos Aires Cathedral.

141 "Liberty" with Arms of Brazil and Argentina

1935. Visit of President Vargas of Brazil. Inscr "MAYO DE 1935".

642	141	10c. red	1·10	30
643	–	15c. blue	2·20	65

DESIGN: 15c. Clasped hands and flags.

143 D. F. Sarmiento

1935. Portraits.

644		½c. purple (Belgrano)	30	20
645		1c. brown (Type 143)	30	20
646		2c. brown (Urquiza)	35	20
647		3c. green (San Martin)	35	20
648		4c. grey (G. Brown)	35	20
653b		5c. brown (Moreno)	70	20
650		6c. green (Alberdi)	40	20
653d		10c. red (Rivadavia)	2·10	20
651		12c. purple (Mitre)	45	30
708		15c. grey (Martin Guemes)	55	35
652		20c. blue (Juan Martin Guemes)	90	20
653		20c. blue (Martin Guemes)	55	20

See also Nos. 671 etc.

1935. Philatelic Exhibition, Buenos Aires (Ex. Fl. B.A.). Sheet 83×100 mm.

MS654	112	10c. green ×4 (sold at 1p.)	95·00	45·00

146 Prize Bull **151** With Boundary Lines

1936. Production and Industry.

676	146	15c. blue	55	30
677a	146	20c. blue (19½×26 mm)	35	20
755	146	20c. blue (22×33 mm)	2·75	10
656	–	25c. red and pink	45	20
757	–	30c. brown and yellow	1·20	10
658	–	40c. purple and mauve	55	20
659	–	50c. red and salmon	45	20
660	151	1p. blue and brown	24·00	1·20
760	–	1p. blue and brown	5·00	10
661	–	2p. blue and purple	1·30	20
662	–	5p. green and blue	6·50	45
763	–	10p. black and purple	22·00	2·00
764	–	20p. brown and blue	19·00	2·00

DESIGNS—VERT: 25c. Ploughman; 50c. Oil well; 1p. (No. 760) as Type **151** but without country boundaries; 5p. Iguazu Falls; 10p. Grapes; 20p. Cotton plant. HORIZ: 30c. Patagonian ram; 40c. Sugar cane and factory; 2p. Fruit products.

157

1936. Pan-American Peace Conference.

665	157	10c. red	90	25

158 Pres. Sarmiento

1938. President's 50th Death Anniv.

666	158	3c. green	65	55
667	158	5c. red	65	55
668	158	15c. blue	1·30	65
669	158	50c. orange	4·25	1·40

159 Presidente Sarmiento

1939. Last Voyage of Cadet Ship Presidente Sarmiento.

670	159	5c. green	55	30

1939. Portraits as T 143.

671		2½c. black	30	20
672		3c. grey (San Martin)	40	20
672a		3c. grey (Moreno)	40	20
673		4c. green	35	20
894		5c. brown (16½×22½ mm)	25	10
674		8c. orange	35	20
678		10c. purple	30	20
675		12c. red	30	20
895		20c. lilac (21×27 mm)	90	20
895b		20c. lilac (19½×25½ mm)	90	20

PORTRAITS: 2½c. L. Braille; 4c. G. Brown; 5c. Jose Hernandez; 8c. N. Avellaneda; 10c. B. Rivadavia; 12c. B. Mitre; 20c. G. Brown.

160 Allegory of the Post

1939. 11th U.P.U. Congress, Buenos Aires.

679	160	5c. red	90	20
680	–	15c. grey	90	45
681	–	20c. blue	90	20
682	–	25c. green	1·30	45
683	–	50c. brown	2·20	85
684	–	1p. purple	5·50	2·10
685	–	2p. mauve	24·00	13·00
686	–	5p. violet	55·00	27·00

DESIGNS—VERT: 20c. Seal of Argentina; 1p. Symbols of postal communications; 2p. Argentina, Land of Promise from a pioneer painting. HORIZ: 15c. G.P.O.; 25c. Iguazu Falls; 50c. Mt. Bonete; 5p. Lake Frias.

1939. International Philatelic Exhibition, Buenos Aires. Two sheets se-tenant horiz or vert, each comprising Nos. 679, 681/3 arranged differently.

MS686a	Two sheets, 190×95 mm or 95×190 mm		17·00	16·00

165 Working-class Family and New Home

1939. First Pan-American Housing Congress.

687	165	5c. green	45	20

167 North and South America

1940. 50th Anniv of Pan-American Union.

688	167	15c. blue	55	20

168 Corrientes Type 5

1940. Centenary of First Adhesive Postage Stamps and Philatelic Exhibition, Cordoba. Sheet 111×111 mm containing early Argentine issues as T 168.

MS688a	5c. blue (Type **168**); 5c. blue (Cordoba T 3); 5c. red (Type **1**); 5c. red (Type **3**); 10c. blue (Buenos Aires T 1)		13·00	10·50

169 Airplane and Envelope

1940. Air.

689	**169**	30c. orange	8·75	45
690	–	50c. brown	13·00	45
691	**169**	1p. red	3·25	10
692	–	1p.25 green	90	10
693	**169**	2p.50 blue	2·75	50

DESIGNS—VERT: 50c. "Mercury"; 1p.25, Douglas DC-2 in clouds.

172 Gen. French, Col. Beruti and Rosette of the "Legion de Patricios"

1941. 131st Anniv of Rising against Spain.

694	**172**	5c. blue	45	20

173 Marco M. de Avellaneda

1941. Death Centenary of Avellaneda (patriot).

695	**173**	5c. blue	45	20

174 Statue of Gen. J. A. Roca

1941. Dedication of Statue of Gen. Roca.

696	**174**	5c. green	45	20

175 Pellegrini (founder) and National Bank

1941. 50th Anniv of National Bank.

697	**175**	5c. lake	45	20

176 Gen. Juan Lavalle

1941. Death Centenary of Gen. Lavalle.

698	**176**	5c. blue	45	20

177 New P.O. Savings Bank

1942. Inauguration of P.O. Savings Bank.

699	**177**	1c. green	35	20

178 Jose Manuel Estrada

1942. Birth Centenary of Estrada (patriot).

700	**178**	5c. purple	45	20

180 G.P.O., Buenos Aires

1942. Postage and Express Stamps.

717	**180**	35c. blue	4·75	20
746	**180**	35c. blue	1·90	30

No. 717 is inscr "PALACIO CENTRAL DE CORREOS Y TEL-EGRAFOS" and No. 746 "PALACIO CENTRAL DE CORREOS Y TELECOMUNICACIONES".

181 Proposed Columbus Lighthouse

1942. 450th Anniv of Discovery of America by Columbus.

721b	**181**	15c. blue	6·50	65

182 Dr. Paz (founder of "La Prensa")

1942. Birth Centenary of Dr. Jose C. Paz.

722	**182**	5c. blue	45	15

183 Flag of Argentina and Books

1943. First National Book Fair.

723	**183**	5c. blue	45	15

184 Arms of Argentina

1943. Revolution of 4 June 1943.

724	**184**	5c. red	35	15
725	**184**	15c. green	1·00	20
726	**184**	20c. blue (larger)	1·50	20

185 National Independence House

1943. Restoration of Tucuman Museum.

727b	**185**	5c. green	45	15

186 Head of Liberty, Money-box and Laurels

1943. First Savings Bank Conference.

728	**186**	5c. brown	35	10

187 Buenos Aires in 1800

1944. Export Day.

729	**187**	5c. black	35	10

188 Postal Union of the Americas and Spain

189 Alexander Graham Bell

1944. Postmen's Benefit Fund. Inscr "PRO-CARTERO".

730	–	3c.+2c. black and violet	80	65
731	**188**	5c.+5c. black and red	1·10	30
732	**189**	10c.+5c. black and orge	2·20	75
733	–	25c.+15c. black and brn	2·75	1·30
734	–	1p.+50c. black and green	13·00	10·50

DESIGNS: 3c. Samuel Morse; 25c. Rowland Hill; 1p. Columbus landing in America.

191 Liner, Warship and Yacht

1944. Naval Week.

735	**191**	5c. blue	35	10

192 Argentina

1944. San Juan Earthquake Relief Fund.

736	**192**	5c.+10c. black & olive	1·40	65
737	**192**	5c.+50c. black and red	5·50	2·30
738	**192**	5c.+1p. black & orange	17·00	10·50
739	**192**	5c.+20p. black & blue	40·00	21·00

193 Arms of Argentina

1944. First Anniv of Revolution of 4 June 1943.

740	**193**	5c. blue	45	15

193a National Flag

1944. National Anthem and Aid for La Rioja and Catamarca Provinces. Two sheets 75×110 mm each containing T **193a**.

MS740a	5c.+1p. blue and plum	22·00	7·00
MS740b	5c.+50p. blue and indigo	£650	£650

194 Archangel Gabriel

195 Cross of Palermo

1944. Fourth National Eucharistic Congress.

741	**194**	3c. green	50	20
742	**195**	5c. red	50	20

196 Allegory of Savings

1944. 20th Anniv of Universal Savings Day.

743	**196**	5c. black	35	15

197 Reservists

1944. Reservists' Day.

744	**197**	5c. blue	35	15

198 Bernardino Rivadavia

199 Rivadavia's Mausoleum

1945. Rivadavia's Death Centenary.

770	**198**	3c. green	45	15
771	–	5c. red	45	15
772	**199**	20c. blue	55	20

DESIGN—As Type **198**: 5c. Rivadavia and Scales of Justice.

200 San Martin

1945

773	**200**	5c. red	35	15

201 Monument to Andes Army, Mendoza

1946. "Homage to the Unknown Soldier of Independence".

776	**201**	5c. purple	45	15

202 Pres. Roosevelt

1946. First Death Anniv of Pres. Franklin Roosevelt.

777	**202**	5c. grey	35	15

203 "Affirmation"

1946. Installation of Pres. Juan Peron.

778	**203**	5c. blue	35	15

204 Airplane over Iguazu Falls

1946. Air.

779	**204**	15c. red	45	15
780	–	25c. green	45	15

DESIGN: 25c. Airplane over Andes.

205 "Flight"

1946. Aviation Week.

781	**205**	15c. green on green	90	30
782	–	60c. purple on buff	90	30

DESIGN: 60c. Hand upholding globe.

207 "Argentina and Populace"

1946. First Anniv of Peron's Defeat of Counter-revolution.

783	**207**	5c. mauve	65	45
784	**207**	10c. green	90	55
785	**207**	15c. blue	1·10	85
786	**207**	50c. brown	90	65
787	**207**	1p. red	2·10	1·70

208 Money-box and Map

1946. Annual Savings Day.

788	**208**	30c. red	90	30

209 Industry

1946. Industrial Exhibition.

789	**209**	5c. purple	55	15

210 Argentine–Brazil International Bridge

1947. Opening of Bridge between Argentina and Brazil.

790	**210**	5c. green	45	15

211 South Pole

1947. 43rd Anniv of 1st Argentine Antarctic Mail.

791	**211**	5c. violet	65	20
792	**211**	20c. red	1·40	20

212 "Justice"

1947. First Anniv of Col. Juan Peron's Presidency.

793	**212**	5c. purple and buff	45	15

213 Icarus Falling

1947. "Week of the Wing".

794	**213**	15c. purple	45	15

214 *Presidente Sarmiento*

1947. 50th Anniv of Launching of Cadet Ship *Presidente Sarmiento*.

795	**214**	5c. blue	45	15

215 Cervantes and "Don Quixote"

1947. 400th Birth Anniv of Cervantes.

796	**215**	5c. green	45	15

216 Gen. San Martin and Urn

1947. Arrival from Spain of Ashes of Gen. San Martin's Parents.

797	**216**	5c. green	45	15

217 Young Crusaders

1947. Educational Crusade for Universal Peace.

798	**217**	5c. green	45	15
799	**217**	20c. brown	55	15

218 Statue of Araucarian Indian

1948. American Indian Day.

801	**218**	25c. brown	45	15

219 Phrygian Cap and Sprig of Wheat

1948. Fifth Anniv of Anti-isolationist Revolution of 4 June 1943.

802	**219**	5c. blue	35	15

220 "Stop"

1948. Safety First Campaign.

803	**220**	5c. yellow and brown	40	15

221 Posthorn and Oak Leaves

1948. Bicent of Postal Service in Rio de la Plata.

804	**221**	5c. mauve	40	15

222 Argentine Farmers

1948. Agriculture Day.

805	**222**	10c. brown	35	15

223 "Liberty and Plenty"

1948. Re-election of President Peron.

806	**223**	25c. red	55	20

225 Statue of Atlas **226** Map, Globe and Compasses

1948. Air. Fourth Meeting of Pan-American Cartographers.

807	**225**	45c. brown	65	20
808	**226**	70c. green	1·30	55

226a Buenos Aires

1948. Bicentenary of Postal Service in Rio de la Plata (2nd issue). Two sheets containing designs as T **226a**.

MS808a 144×101 mm. (horiz designs). 15c. green (Mail coach, 1865); 45c. brown (Type **226a**); 55c. brown (First train, 1857); 85c. ultramarine (Sailing ship, 1767) — 8·75 / 3·75

MS808b 102×144 mm (vert designs). 85c. brown (Domingo de Basavilbaso); 1p.50 green (Postrider, 1748); 1p.20 indigo (Sailing ship, 1798); 1p.90 purple (Courier in the Andes, 1772) Price for 2 sheets — 60·00 / 13·00

227 Winged Railway Wheel

1949. First Anniv of Nationalization of Argentine Railways.

809	**227**	10c. blue	55	20

228 Head of Liberty

1949. Constitution Day.

810	**228**	1p. purple and red	70	30

229 Trophy and Target

1949. Air. International Shooting Championship.

811	**229**	75c. brown	1·20	30

230 "Intercommunication"

1949. 75th Anniv of U.P.U.

812	**230**	25c. green and olive	35	15

231 San Martin **232** San Martin at Boulogne

1950. San Martin's Death Cent. Dated "1850 1950".

813	-	10c. purple and blue	20	10
814	**231**	20c. brown and red	20	10
815	**232**	25c. brown	35	10
816	-	50c. blue and green	75	30
817	-	75c. green and brown	75	30
818	-	1p. green	2·00	30
819	-	2p. purple	1·10	55

MS819a 120×150 mm. Nos. 813/14 and 816/17. Imperf — 3·75 / 2·75

DESIGNS—As Type **231**: 10, 50, 75c. Portraits of San Martin; 2p. San Martin Mausoleum. As Type **232**: 1p. House where San Martin died.

233 Stamp Designer

1950. Int Philatelic Exhibition, Buenos Aires.

820	**233**	10c.+10c. violet (postage)	20	15
821	-	45c.+45c. blue (air)	35	30
822	-	70c.+70c. brown	55	50
823	-	1p.+1p. red	2·20	1·60
824	-	2p.50+2p.50 olive	12·00	8·00
825	-	5p.+5p. green	19·00	13·00

MS825a 120×150 mm. Nos. 820/2. Imperf — 8·75 / 8·00

DESIGNS: 45c. Engraver; 70c. Proofing; 1p. Printer; 2p.50, Woman reading letter; 5p. San Martin.

234 S. America and Antarctic

1951

826	**234**	1p. blue and brown	1·00	20

235 Douglas DC-3 and Andean Condor

1951. Air. Tenth Anniv of State Airlines.

827	**235**	20c. olive	70	20

236 Pegasus and Steam Locomotive

1951. Five-year Plan.

828	**236**	5c. brown (postage)	1·20	20
829	-	25c. green	2·40	35
830	-	40c. purple	3·25	35
831	-	20c. blue (air)	95	20

DESIGNS—HORIZ: 25c. *President Peron* (liner) and common dolphin. VERT: 20c. Douglas DC-4 and Andean condor; 40c. Head of Mercury and telephone.

237 Woman Voter and "Argentina"

1951. Women's Suffrage in Argentina.

832	**237**	10c. purple	55	15

238 "Piety"

1951. Air. Eva Peron Foundation Fund.
833 **238** 2p.45+7p.55 olive 34·00 20·00

239 Eva Peron **240** Eva Peron

1952. (a) Size 20×26 mm.
834	**239**	1c. brown	35	15
835	**239**	5c. grey	35	15
836	**239**	10c. red	35	15
837	**239**	20c. red	35	15
838	**239**	25c. green	35	15
839	**239**	40c. purple	35	15
841	**239**	45c. blue	70	20
840	**239**	50c. bistre	70	20

(b) Size 22×33 mm. Without inscr "EVA PERON".
842	**240**	1p. brown	70	20
843	**240**	1p.50 green	3·50	20
844	**240**	2p. red	70	20
845	**240**	3p. blue	2·10	20

(c) Size 22×33 mm. Inscr "EVA PERON".
846		1p. brown	55	20
847		1p.50 green	2·10	20
848		2p. red	2·10	20
849		3p. blue	5·25	75

(d) Size 30½×40 mm. Inscr "EVA PERON".
850		5p. brown	5·25	1·00
851	**239**	10p. red	12·50	2·20
852	**240**	20p. green	21·00	5·25
853	**239**	50p. blue	37·00	13·00

241 Indian Funeral Urn

1953. Fourth Centenary of Santiago del Estero.
854 **241** 50c. green 35 10

242 Rescue Ship *Uruguay*

1953. 50th Anniv of Rescue of the *Antarctic*.
855 **242** 50c. blue 1·90 65

243 Planting Flag in S. Orkneys

1954. 50th Anniv of Argentine P.O. in South Orkneys.
856 **243** 1p.45 blue 1·70 45

244 "Telegraphs"

1954. International Telecommunications Conference. Symbolical designs inscr as in T **244**.
857 **244** 1p.50 purple 70 20

858	-	3p. blue	2·10	35
859	-	5p. red	2·75	65

DESIGNS—VERT: 3p. "Radio". HORIZ: 5p. "Television".

245 Pediment, Buenos Aires Stock Exchange

1954. Centenary of Argentine Stock Exchange.
860 **245** 1p. green 70 10

246 Eva Peron

1954. Second Death Anniv of Eva Peron.
861 **246** 3p. red 3·00 55

247 San Martin **249** Wheat

250 Mt. Fitz Roy

1954
862	**247**	20c. red	25	10
863	**247**	40c. red	35	10
868	-	50c. blue (33×22 mm)	35	10
869	-	50c. blue (32×21 mm)	75	20
870	**249**	80c. brown	35	10
871	-	1p. brown	45	10
872	-	1p.50 blue	35	10
873	-	2p. red	55	20
874	-	3p. purple	55	20
875a	-	5p. green	10·50	25
876	-	10p. green and grey	11·00	25
877	**250**	22p. violet	16·00	70
1018	-	22p. blue	2·40	25
878	-	50p. indigo and blue (30½×40½ mm)	13·50	1·40
1023	-	50p. blue (29½×40 mm)	12·00	70
1287	-	50p. blue (22½×32½ mm)	1·80	25

DESIGNS—As Type **249**: HORIZ: 50c. Port of Buenos Aires; 1p. Cattle; 2p. Eva Peron Foundation; 3p. El Nihuil Dam. As Type **250**: VERT: 1p.50, 22p. Industrial Plant; 5p. Iguazu Falls; 10p. San Martin. HORIZ: 10p. Humahuaca Ravine.
For 43p. in the design of the 1p.50 and 22p. see No. 1021.
For 65c. in same design see No. 1313.

248 "Prosperity"

1954. Centenary of Argentine Corn Exchange.
867 **248** 1p.50 grey 1·00 25

251 Clasped Hands and Congress Emblem

1955. Productivity and Social Welfare Congress.
879 **251** 3p. brown 1·70 35

252 Father and Son with Model Airplane

1955. 25th Anniv of Commercial Air Services.
880 **252** 1p.50 grey 1·40 25

253 "Liberation"

1955. Anti-Peronist Revolution of 16 Sept. 1955.
881 **253** 1p.50 olive 1·00 25

254 Forces Emblem

1955. Armed Forces Commemoration.
882 **254** 3p. blue 70 20

255 Gen. Urquiza (after J. M. Blanes)

1956. 104th Anniv of Battle of Caseros.
883 **255** 1p.50 green 1·10 35

256 Detail from *Antiope* (Correggio)

1956. Infantile Paralysis Relief Fund.
884 **256** 20c.+30c. grey 45 30

257 Coin and Die

1956. 75th Anniv of National Mint.
885 **257** 2p. brown and sepia 45 25

258 Corrientes Stamp of 1856 **259** Dr. J. G. Pujol

1956. Centenary of First Argentine Stamps.
886	**258**	40c. blue and green	35	10
887	**258**	2p.40 mauve and brown	45	20
888	**259**	4p.40 blue	1·00	35

The 40c. shows a 1r. stamp of 1856.

260 Cotton, Chaco

1956. New Provinces.
889	-	50c. blue	80	20
890	**260**	1p. lake	90	20
891	-	1p.50 green	1·00	20

DESIGNS—HORIZ: 50c. Lumbering, La Pampa. VERT: 1p.50, Mate tea plant, Misiones.

261 "Liberty"

1956. First Anniv of Revolution.
892 **261** 2p.40 mauve 1·10 35

262 Detail from *Virgin of the Rocks* (Leonardo)

1956. Air. Infantile Paralysis Victims, Gratitude for Help.
893 **262** 1p. purple 1·10 35

1956. Argentine Stamp Centenary (2nd issue) and Corrientes Stamp Centenary Exhibition. Nos. 886/7 but in litho and colours changed and No. 888 in sheet.
MS893a 147×169 mm. 40c. indigo
and green; 2p.40 claret and purple;
4p.40 blue 7·50 7·25

264 Esteban Echeverria (writer) **265** F. Ameghino (anthropologist) **266** Roque Saenz Pena (statesman)

1956
896	**264**	2p. purple	35	20
897	**265**	2p.40 brown	45	20
898	**266**	4p.40 green	70	30

267 Franklin

1956. 250th Birth Anniv of Benjamin Franklin.
899 **267** 40c. blue 45 20

268 *Hercules* (sail frigate) **269** Admiral G. Brown

1957. Death Cent of Admiral Guillermo Brown.
900	**268**	40c. blue (postage)	25	10
902	-	60c. grey (air)	35	10
903	-	1p. mauve	25	10
904	**269**	2p. brown	35	10
901	-	2p.40 green	55	10

DESIGNS—HORIZ: 60c. *Zefiro* and *Nancy* (sail warships) at Battle of Montevideo; 1p. L. Rosales and T. Espora. VERT: 2p.40, Admiral Brown in later years.

270 Church of Santo Domingo

1957. 150th Anniv of Defence of Buenos Aires.
905 **270** 40c. green 35 10

271 Map of the Americas and Badge of Buenos Aires

1957. Air. Inter-American Economic Conference.
906 **271** 2p. purple 55 15

272 *La Portena*, 1857

1957. Centenary of Argentine Railways.
907 **272** 40c. sepia (postage) 1·40 35
908 – 60c. grey (air) 1·40 35
DESIGN: 60c. Diesel locomotive.

273 Globe, Flag and Compass Rose

1957. Air. Int Tourist Congress, Buenos Aires.
909 **273** 1p. brown 35 25
910 – 2p. turquoise 35 25
DESIGN: 2p. Symbolic key of tourism.

274 Head of Liberty

1957. Reform Convention.
911 **274** 40c. red 45 15

275

1957. Air. International Correspondence Week.
912 **275** 1p. blue 70 30

276 "Wealth in Oil"

1957. 50th Anniv of Argentine Oil Industry.
913 **276** 40c. blue 1·00 35

277 La Plata Museum

1958. 75th Anniv of Founding of La Plata.
914 **277** 40c. black 35 15

278 Health Emblem and Flower

1958. Air. Child Welfare.
915 **278** 1p.+50c. red 45 45

279 Stamp of 1858 and River Ferry **280** Stamp of 1858

1958. Centenary of Argentine Confederation Stamps and Philatelic Exhibition, Buenos Aires.
916 **279** 40c.+20c. purple and green (postage) 85 60
917 – 2p.40+1p.20 blue and black 90 65
918 – 4p.40+2p.20 pur & bl 95 70
919 **280** 1p.+50c. blue and olive (air) 90 85
920 **280** 2p.+1p. violet and red 1·10 95
921 **280** 3p.+1p.50 brown & grn 1·10 1·00
922 **280** 5p.+2p.50 red and olive 1·40 1·30
923 **280** 10p.+5p. sepia & olive 2·30 1·80
DESIGNS—HORIZ: 2p.40, Magnifier, stamp album and stamp of 1858; 4p.40, P.O. building of 1858.

281 Steam Locomotive and Arms of Argentina and Bolivia

1958. Argentine–Bolivian Friendship. (a) Inauguration of Yacuiba–Santa Cruz Railway.
924 **281** 40c. red and slate 90 30

282 Douglas DC-6 over Map of Argentine-Bolivian Frontier

(b) Exchange of Presidential Visits.
925 **282** 1p. brown 90 30

283 "Liberty and Flag"

1958. Transfer of Presidential Mandate. Head of "Liberty" in grey; inscr black; flag yellow and blue; background colours given.
926 **283** 40c. buff 15 10
927 **283** 1p. salmon 35 10
928 **283** 2p. green 70 35

284 Farman H.F.20 Biplane

1958. 50th Anniv of Argentine Aero Club.
929 **284** 2p. brown 35 20

285 National Flag Monument, Rosario

1958. First Anniv of Inauguration of National Flag Monument.
930 **285** 40c. grey and blue 35 20

286 Map of Antarctica

1958. International Geophysical Year.
931 **286** 40c. black and red 1·10 35

287 Confederation Stamp and *The Santa Fe Mail* (after J. L. Palliere)

1958. Cent of Argentine Confederation Stamps.
932 – 40c. grn & blue (postage) 35 25
933 – 80c. blue & yellow (air) 45 25
934 **287** 1p. blue and orange 40 25
DESIGNS: 40c. First local Cordoba 5c. stamp of 1858 and mail coach; 80c. Buenos Aires Type **1** of 1858 and *View of Buenos Aires* (after Deroy).

288 Aerial view of Flooded Town

1958. Flood Disaster Relief Fund. Inscr as in T **288**.
935 **288** 40c.+20c. brn (postage) 35 25
936 – 1p.+50c. plum (air) 35 25
937 – 5p.+2p.50 blue 1·20 1·10
DESIGNS—HORIZ: 1p. Different aerial view of flooded town; 5p. Truck in flood water and garage.

289 Child receiving Blood

1958. Leukaemia Relief Campaign.
938 **289** 1p.+50c. red and black 1·30 35

290 U.N. Emblem and *Dying Captive* (after Michelangelo)

1959. Tenth Anniv of Declaration of Human Rights.
939 **290** 40c. grey and brown 35 20

291 Hawker Siddeley Comet 4

1959. Air. Inauguration of Comet Jet Airliners by Argentine National Airlines.
940 **291** 5p. black and green 50 10

292 Orchids and Globe

1959. First Int Horticultural Exn, Buenos Aires.
941 **292** 1p. purple 35 20

293 Pope Pius XII

1959. Pope Pius XII Commemoration.
942 **293** 1p. black and yellow 50 20

294 William Harvey

1959. 21st International Physiological Science Congress. Medical Scientists.
943 **294** 50c. green 25 10
944 – 1p. red 30 10
945 – 1p.50 brown 35 10
PORTRAITS: 1p. Claude Bernard; 1p.50, Ivan P. Pavlov.

295 Creole Horse **296** Tierra del Fuego

1959
946 10c. green 60 20
947 20c. purple 60 20
948 50c. ochre 60 20
950 **295** 1p. red 60 20
1016 – 1p. brown 25 10
1027 – 1p. brown 25 10
1035 – 2p. red 50 10
951 – 3p. blue 50 20
1036 – 4p. red 1·50 25
952 **296** 5p. green 75 30
1037 – 8p. red 75 15
1038 – 10p. red 1·00 20
1286 – 10p. brown 75 20
1017 – 12p. purple 1·50 25
954 – 20p. green 4·25 25
1039 – 20p. red 50 10
1019 – 23p. green 7·25 25
1020 – 25p. lilac 2·20 25
1021 – 43p. lake 10·50 25
1022 – 45p. brown 6·00 25
1025 – 100p. blue 11·00 25
1026 – 300p. violet 5·50 25
1032 – 500p. green 2·20 25
1290 – 1000p. blue 5·25 85
DESIGNS—As Type **295**—HORIZ: 10c. Spectacled caiman; 20c. Llama; 50c. Puma. VERT: 2, 4, 8, 10p. (No 1038), 20p. (No. 1039) San Martin. As Type **296**—HORIZ: 3p. Zapata Hill, Catamarca; 300p. Mar del Plata (40×29½ mm). VERT: 1p. (No. 1016) Sunflowers; 1p. (No. 1027) Sunflower (22×32 mm); 10p. (No. 1286) Inca Bridge, Mendoza; 12, 23, 25p. Red quebracho tree; 20p. (No. 954) Lake Nahuel Huapi; 43, 45p. Industrial plant (30×39½ mm); 100p. Ski-jumper; 500p. Red deer (stag); 1,000p. Leaping salmon.
 For these designs with face values in revalued currency, see Nos. 1300 etc.

298 Runner

1959. Third Pan-American Games, Chicago. Designs embody torch emblem. Centres and torch in black.
955 **298** 20c.+10c. green (postage) 25 10
956 – 50c.+20c. yellow 35 20
957 – 1p.+50c. purple 50 25
958 – 2p.+1p. blue (air) 60 25
959 – 3p.+1p.50 olive 85 70
DESIGNS—VERT: 50c. Basketball; 1p. Boxing. HORIZ: 2p. Rowing; 3p. High-diving.

299

1959. Red Cross Hygiene Campaign.
960 **299** 1p. red, blue and black 35 15

300 Child with Toys

1959. Mothers' Day.
961 **300** 1p. red and black 35 15

301 Buenos Aires 1p. stamp of 1859

1959. Stamp Day.
962 **301** 1p. blue and grey 35 15

302 B. Mitre and J. J. de Urquiza

1959. Centenary of Pact of San Jose de Flores.
963 **302** 1p. plum 35 15

303 Andean Condor

1960. Child Welfare. Birds.
964 **303** 20c.+10c. blue (postage) 1·50 25
965 — 50c.+20c. violet 1·80 25
966 — 1p.+50c. brown 1·50 25
967 — 2p.+1p. mauve (air) 1·50 35
968 — 3p.+1p.50 green 1·50 70
BIRDS: 50c. Fork-tailed flycatcher; 1p. Magellanic woodpecker; 2p. Red-winged tinamou; 3p. Greater rhea.

304 "Uprooted Tree"

1960. World Refugee Year.
969 **304** 1p. red and brown 50 25
970 **304** 4p.20 purple and green 50 25
MS971 113×85 mm. No. 969/70 with premium added for aid to refugees 1p.50c. and 4p.20+2p.10. Imperf 2·10 1·90

305 Abraham Lincoln

1960. 150th Birth Anniv of Abraham Lincoln.
972 **305** 5p. blue 60 25

306 Saavedra and Chapter Hall, Buenos Aires

1960. 150th Anniv of May Revolution.
973 **306** 1p. purple (postage) 25 10
974 — 2p. green 25 10
975 — 4p.20 green and grey 35 20
976 — 10p.70 blue and slate 60 25
977 — 1p.80 brown (air) 25 10
978 — 5p. purple and brown 50 20
MS979 Two sheets each 104×156 mm. Nos. 973/4, 977 in red-brown. Nos. 975/6, 978 in green 5·25 5·00
DESIGNS—Chapter Hall and: 1p.80, Moreno; 2p. Paso; 4p.20, Alberti and Azcuenaga; 5p. Belgrano and Castelli; 10p.70, Larrea and Matheu.

307 Dr. L. Drago

1960. Birth Centenary of Drago.
980 **307** 4p.20 brown 35 20

308 "Five Provinces"

1960. Air. New Argentine Provinces.
981 **308** 1p.80 blue and red 35 20

309 "Market Place 1810" (Buenos Aires)

1960. Air. Inter-American Philatelic Exhibition, Buenos Aires ("EFIMAYO") and 150th Anniv of Revolution. Inscr "EFIMAYO 1960".
982 **309** 2p.+1p. lake 25 10
983 — 6p.+3p. grey 50 20
984 — 10p.70+5p.30 blue 85 45
985 — 20p.+10p. turquoise 1·50 1·20
DESIGNS: 6p. "The Water Carrier"; 10p.70, "The Landing Place"; 20p. "The Fort".

310 J. B. Alberdi

1960. 150th Birth Anniv of J. B. Alberdi (statesman).
986 **310** 1p. green 35 20

311 Seibo (Argentine National Flower)

1960. Air. Chilean Earthquake Relief Fund. Inscr "AYUDA CHILE".
987 **311** 6p.+3p. red 50 25
988 — 10p.70+5p.30 red 75 45
DESIGN: 10p.70, Copihue (Chilean national flower).

312 Map of Argentina

1960. Census.
989 **312** 5p. lilac 1·20 35

313 Galleon

1960. Eighth Spanish-American P.U. Congress.
990 **313** 1p. green (postage) 35 10
991 **313** 5p. brown 85 25
992 **313** 1p.80 purple (air) 35 10
993 **313** 10p.70 turquoise 1·10 35

1960. Air. U.N. Day. Nos. 982/5 optd **DIA DE LAS NACIONES UNIDAS 24 DE OCTUBRE.**
994 **309** 2p.+1p. red 25 10
995 — 6p.+3p. black 50 35
996 — 10p.70+5p.30 blue 75 60
997 — 20p.+10p. turquoise 1·30 1·10

315 Blessed Virgin of Lujan

1960. First Inter-American Marian Congress.
998 **315** 1p. blue 1·00 25

316 Jacaranda

1960. International Thematic Stamp Exhibition ("TEMEX"). Inscr "TEMEX-61".
999 **316** 50c.+50c. blue 10 10
1000 — 1p.+1p. turquoise 20 10
1001 — 3p.+3p. brown 60 25
1002 — 5p.+5p. brown 85 60
FLOWERS: 1p. Passion flowers; 3p. Hibiscus; 5p. Black lapacho.

317 Argentine Scout Badge

1961. International Scout (Patrol) Camp.
1003 **317** 1p. red and black 50 20

318 *Shipment of Cereals* (after B. Q. Martin)

1961. Export Campaign.
1004 **318** 1p. brown 50 20

319 Emperor Penguin and Chick

1961. Child Welfare. Inscr "PRO-INFANCIA".
1005 — 4p.20+2p.10 brown (postage) 1·70 95
1006 **319** 1p.80+90c. black (air) 85 60
DESIGN: 4p.20, Blue-eyed cormorant.

320 *America*

1961. 150th Anniv of Battle of San Nicolas.
1007 **320** 2p. black 50 20

321 Dr. M. Moreno

1961. 150th Death Anniv of Dr. M. Moreno.
1008 **321** 2p. blue 35 15

322 Emperor Trajan

1961. Visit of President of Italy.
1009 **322** 2p. green 35 15

1961. Americas Day. Nos. 999/1002 optd **14 DE ABRIL DE LAS AMERICAS.**
1010 **316** 50c.+50c. blue 25 10
1011 — 1p.+1p. turquoise 25 10
1012 — 3p.+3p. brown 35 25
1013 — 5p.+5p. brown 75 45

324 Tagore

1961. Birth Centenary of Rabindranath Tagore (Indian poet).
1014 **324** 2p. violet on green 1·10 25

325 San Martin Monument, Madrid

1961. Inaug of Spanish San Martin Monument.
1015 **325** 1p. black 35 20

331a Gen. Belgrano (after monument by Rocha, Buenos Aires)

1961. Gen. Manuel Belgrano Commemoration.
1034 **331a** 2p. blue 1·00 25

333 Antarctic Scene

1961. Tenth Anniv of San Martin Antarctic Base.
1044 **333** 2p. black 1·00 25

334 Conquistador and Sword

1961. Fourth Centenary of Jujuy City.
1045 **334** 2p. red and black 35 20

335 Sarmiento Statue (Rodin)

1961. 150th Birth Anniv of Sarmiento.
1046 **335** 2p. violet 35 20

336 Cordoba Cathedral

1961. "Argentina 62" International Philatelic Exn.
1047 **336** 2p.+2p. purple (postage) 35 25
1048 — 3p.+3p. green 50 35
1049 — 10p.+10p. blue 1·10 95

MS1050 86×86 mm. Nos. 1047/9 each
indigo. Imperf ... 3·75 2·50
DESIGNS-HORIZ: 10p. Buenos Aires Cathedral. VERT: 3p,
As Type **336** but showing 10c. value and different inscr.

337

1961. World Town-planning Day.
1052 **337** 2p. blue and yellow ... 35 20

338 "The Flight
into Egypt" (after
Ana Maria
Moncalvo)

1961. Child Welfare.
1053 **338** 2p.+1p. brown & lilac ... 25 10
1054 **338** 10p.+5p. purple & mve ... 75 20

339 Belgrano
Statue (C.
Belleuse)

1962. 150th Anniv of National Flag.
1055 **339** 2p. blue ... 35 20

340 Mounted
Grenadier

1962. 150th Anniv of Gen. San Martin's Mounted
Grenadiers.
1056 **340** 2p. red ... 1·00 25

341 Mosquito and
Emblem

1962. Malaria Eradication.
1057 **341** 2p. black and red ... 60 20

342 Lujan
Basilica

1962. 75th Anniv of Coronation of the Holy Virgin of
Lujan.
1058 **342** 2p. black and brown ... 35 10

343 15c. Stamp
of 1862

1962. Argentina 62 Philatelic Exhibition
1059 **343** 6p.50+6p.50 blue and
turquoise (air) ... 1·00 85

344 Juan Jufre
(founder)

1962. 400th Anniv of San Juan.
1060 **344** 2p. blue ... 35 20

345 UNESCO Emblem

1962. Air. 15th Anniv of UNESCO.
1061 **345** 13p. brown and ochre ... 60 35

346 "Flight"

1962. 50th Anniv of Argentine Air Force.
1062 **346** 2p. blue, black & purple ... 35 20

347 Juan
Vucetich
(fingerprints
pioneer)

1962. Vucetich Commem.
1063 **347** 2p. green ... 35 15

348 19th-century Mail
Coach

1962. Air. Postman's Day.
1064 **348** 5p.60 black and drab ... 1·00 25

1962. Air. Surch *AEREO* and value.
1065 **296** 5p.60 on 5p. brown ... 35 25
1066 **296** 18p. on 5p. brn on grn ... 1·50 35

350 U.P.A.E.
Emblem

1962. Air. 50th Anniv of Postal Union of Latin America.
1067 **350** 5p.60 blue ... 50 15

351 Pres.
Sarmiento

1962
1073 **351** 2p. green ... 1·00 25
1069 - 4p. red ... 75 25
1071 - 6p. brown ... 50 10
1075 - 6p. red ... 2·40 25
1072 - 90p. bistre ... 4·00 45
PORTRAITS: 4, 6p. Jose Hernandez; 90p. G. Brown.

352 Chalk-browed
Mockingbird

1962. Child Welfare.
1076 **352** 4p.+2p. sepia, turquoise
and brown ... 2·00 1·10
1077 - 12p.+6p. brown, yellow
and slate ... 3·00 1·50
DESIGN—VERT: 12p. Rufous-collared sparrow.
See also Nos. 1101/2, 1124/5, 1165/6, 1191/2, 1214/15,
1264/5, 1293/4, 1394/5, 1415/16 and 1441/2.

353 Skylark 3
Glider

1963. Air. Ninth World Gliding Championships, Junin.
1078 **353** 5p.60 black and blue ... 25 10
1079 - 11p. black, red and blue ... 60 35
DESIGN: 11p. Super Albatross glider.

354 "20 de
Febrero"
Monument, Salta

1963. 150th Anniv of Battle of Salta.
1080 **354** 2p. green ... 1·00 25

355 Cogwheels

1963. 75th Anniv of Argentine Industrial Union.
1081 **355** 4p. red and grey ... 1·00 25

356 National
College

1963. Centenary of National College, Buenos Aires.
1082 **356** 4p. black and buff ... 1·10 35

357 Child
drinking Milk

1963. Freedom from Hunger.
1083 **357** 4p. ochre, black and red ... 35 20

358 "Flight"

1963. Air. (a) As T **358**.
1084 **358** 5p.60 green, mve & pur ... 35 20
1085 **358** 7p. black & yellow (I) ... 85 25
1086 **358** 7p. black & yellow (II) ... 7·25 1·40
1087 **358** 11p. purple, green & blk ... 35 20
1088 **358** 18p. blue, red and
mauve ... 1·50 35
1089 **358** 21p. grey, red and
brown ... 2·40 45
Two types of 7p. I, "ARGENTINA" reads down, and II,
"ARGENTINA" reads up as in Type **358**.

(b) As T **358** but inscr "REPUBLICA ARGENTINA" reading
down.
1147 12p. lake and brown ... 2·30 35
1148 15p. blue and red ... 1·60 35
1291 26p. ochre ... 25 10
1150 27p.50 green and black ... 2·50 60
1151 30p.50 brown and blue ... 3·25 95
1292 40p. lilac ... 4·00 25
1153 68p. green ... 5·75 70
1154 78p. blue ... 2·40 95
See also Nos. 1374/80 in revalued currency.

359 Football

1963. Fourth Pan-American Games, Sao Paulo.
1090 **359** 4p.+2p. green, black and
pink (postage) ... 35 20
1091 - 12p.+6p. purple, black
and salmon ... 75 60
1092 - 11p.+5p. red, black and
green (air) ... 85 70
DESIGNS: 11p. Cycling; 12p. Show-jumping.

360 Frigate *La
Argentina* (after
Bouchard)

1963. Navy Day.
1093 **360** 4p. blue ... 1·10 35

361 Assembly House
and Seal

1963. 150th Anniv of 1813 Assembly.
1094 **361** 4p. black and blue ... 1·00 25

362 Battle Scene

1963. 150th Anniv of Battle of San Lorenzo.
1095 **362** 4p. black & green on grn ... 1·00 25

363 Queen Nefertari
(bas-relief)

1963. UNESCO Campaign for Preservation of Nubian
Monuments.
1096 **363** 4p. black, green & buff ... 1·00 25

364 Government House

1963. Presidential Installation.
1097 **364** 5p. brown and pink ... 1·00 25

365 "Science"

1963. Tenth Latin-American Neurosurgery Congress.
1098 **365** 4p. blue, black & brown ... 1·10 35

366 Blackboards

1963. "Alliance for Progress".
1099 **366** 5p. red, black and blue 35 20

367 F. de las
Carreras
(President of
Supreme Court)

1963. Centenary of Judicial Power.
1100 **367** 5p. green 35 20

1963. Child Welfare. As T **352**. Multicoloured.
1101 4p.+2p. Vermilion flycatcher
(postage) 1·80 60
1102 11p.+5p. Great kiskadee (air) 2·40 95

368 Kemal
Ataturk

1963. 25th Death Anniv of Kemal Ataturk.
1103 **368** 12p. grey 75 25

369 "Payador"
(after
Castagnino)

1964. Fourth National Folklore Festival.
1104 **369** 4p. black, blue & ultram 1·00 25

370 Map of Antarctic
Islands

1964. Antarctic Claims Issue.
1105 **370** 2p. bl & ochre (postage) 2·50 35
1106 - 4p. bistre and blue 3·75 45
1107 - 18p. bl & bistre (air) 3·75 85
DESIGNS—VERT: (30×39½ mm): 4p. Map of Argentina and
Antarctica. HORIZ: (as Type **291**): 18p. Map of "Islas Malvi-
nas" (Falkland Islands).

371 Jorge Newbery in
Airplane

1964. 50th Death Anniv of Jorge Newbery (aviator).
1108 **371** 4p. green 1·10 35

372 Pres. Kennedy

1964. President Kennedy Memorial Issue.
1109 **372** 4p. blue and mauve 75 25

373 Father
Brochero

1964. 50th Death Anniv of Father J. G. Brochero.
1110 **373** 4p. brown 1·10 35

374 U.P.U. Monument,
Berne

1964. Air. 15th U.P.U. Congress, Vienna.
1111 **374** 18p. purple and red 90 35

375 Soldier of the
Patricios Regiment

1964. Army Day.
1112 **375** 4p. multicoloured 1·30 25
See also Nos. 1135, 1170, 1201, 1223, 1246, 1343,
1363, 1399, 1450, 1515, 1564, 1641 and 1678.

376 Pope John XXIII

1964. Pope John Commemoration.
1113 **376** 4p. black and orange 40 20

377 Olympic Stadium

1964. Olympic Games, Tokyo.
1114 **377** 4p.+2p. brown, yellow
and red (postage) 40 20
1115 - 12p.+6p. black & green 75 35
1116 - 11p.+5p. blk & bl (air) 1·50 70
DESIGNS—VERT: 11p. Sailing; 12p. Fencing.

378 University
Arms

1964. 350th Anniv of Cordoba University.
1117 **378** 4p. yellow, blue & black 40 10

379 Olympic
Flame and
Crutch

1964. Air. Invalids Olympic Games, Tokyo.
1118 **379** 18p.+9p. multicoloured 1·00 85

380 The Discovery of
America (Florentine
woodcut)

1964. Air. "Columbus Day" (or "Day of the Race").
1119 **380** 13p. black and drab 1·40 45

381 Pigeons and
U.N.
Headquarters

1964. United Nations Day.
1120 **381** 4p. ultramarine and blue 65 20

382 J. V.
Gonzalez
(medallion)

1964. Birth Centenary of J. V. Gonzalez.
1121 **382** 4p. red 1·00 25

383 Gen. J. Roca

1964. 50th Death Anniv of General Julio Roca.
1122 **383** 4p. blue 40 10

384 Market-place,
Montserrat Square
(after C. Morel)

1964. "Argentine Painters".
1123 **384** 4p. sepia 50 35

1964. Child Welfare. As T **352**. Multicoloured.
1124 4p.+2p. Red-crested cardinal
(postage) 1·60 45
1125 18p.+9p. Chilean swallow (air) 3·25 1·20

385 Icebreaker General
San Martin and Bearded
Penguin

1965. "National Territory of Tierra del Fuego, Antarctic
and South Atlantic Isles".
1126 - 2p. purple (postage) 75 20
1127 **385** 4p. blue 1·90 35
1128 - 11p. red (air) 90 25
DESIGNS: 2p. General Belgrano Base (inscr "BASE DE EJER-
CITO" etc); 11p. Teniente Matienzo Joint Antarctic Base
(inscr "BASE CONJUNTA" etc).

1965. Air. First Rio Plata Philatelists' Day. Optd **PRIMERAS
JORNADAS FILATELICAS RIOPLATENSES**.
1129 **358** 7p. black & yellow (II) 40 20

387 Young Saver

1965. 50th Anniv of National Postal Savings Bank.
1130 **387** 4p. black and red 35 10

388 I.T.U.
Emblem

1965. Air. Centenary of I.T.U.
1131 **388** 18p. multicoloured 65 25

389 I.Q.S.Y. Emblem

1965. Int Quiet Sun Year and Space Research.
1132 **389** 4p. black, orange and
blue (postage) 1·00 35
1133 - 18p. red (air) 1·10 45
1134 - 50p. blue 1·60 95
DESIGNS—VERT: 18p. Rocket launching. HORIZ: 50p.
Earth, trajectories and space phenomena (both inscr "IN-
VESTIGACIONES ESPACIALES").

391 Ricardo
Guiraldes

1965. Army Day (29 May).
1135 **390** 8p. multicoloured 90 35
See also Nos. 1170, 1201, 1223, 1246, 1343, 1363,
1399, 1450, 1515, 1564 and 1641.

391 Ricardo
Guiraldes

1965. Argentine Writers (1st series). Each brown.
1136 8p. Type **391** 65 25
1137 8p. E. Larreta 65 25
1138 8p. L. Lugones 65 25
1139 8p. R. J. Payro 65 25
1140 8p. R. Rojas 65 25
See also Nos 1174/8.

392 H. Yrigoyen
(statesman)

1965. Hipolito Yrigoyen Commemoration.
1141 **392** 8p. black and red 40 20

393 "Children looking
through a Window"

1965. International Mental Health Seminar.
1142 **393** 8p. black and brown 1·00 45

394 Ancient Map and Funeral Urn

1965. 400th Anniv of San Miguel de Tucuman.
1143 **394** 8p. multicoloured 50 25

395 Mgr. Dr. J. Cagliero

1965. Cagliero Commemoration.
1144 **395** 8p. violet 40 10

396 Dante (statue in Church of the Holy Cross, Florence)

1965. 700th Birth Anniv of Dante.
1145 **396** 8p. blue 1·00 25

397 Sail Merchantman *Mimosa*

1965. Centenary of Welsh Colonisation of Chubut and Foundation of Rawson.
1146 **397** 8p. black and red 50 20

398 Police Emblem on Map of Buenos Aires

1965. Federal Police Day.
1155 **398** 8p. red 50 35

399 Schoolchildren

1965. 81st Anniv of Law 1420 (Public Education).
1156 **399** 8p. black and green 50 20

400 St. Francis's Church, Catamarca

1965. Brother Mamerto Esquiu Commemoration.
1157 **400** 8p. brown and yellow 40 10

401 R. Dario (Nicaraguan poet)

1965. 50th Death Anniv of Ruben Dario.
1158 **401** 15p. violet on grey 40 20

402 *The Orange-seller* (detail)

1966. Prilidiano Pueyrredon's Paintings. Designs show details from the original works, each green.
1159 8p. Type **402** 1·10 60
1160 8p. *A Halt at the Village Grocer's Shop* 1·10 60
1161 8p. *San Fernando Landscape* 1·10 60
1162 8p. *Bathing Horses on the Banks of the River Plate* 1·10 60

403 Rocket "Centaur" and Antarctic Map

1966. Air. Rocket Launches in Antarctica.
1163 **403** 27p.50 red, black & blue 1·50 1·20

404 Dr. Sun Yat-sen

1966. Birth Centenary of Dr. Sun Yat-sen.
1164 **404** 8p. brown 1·10 25

1966. Child Welfare. As T **352**, inscr "R. ARGENTINA". Multicoloured.
1165 8p.+4p. Southern lapwing (postage) 2·00 85
1166 27p.50+12p.50 Rufous hornero (air) 1·60 1·20

405 "Rivadavia" 5c. stamp of 1864

1966. Second Rio Plata Philatelists Days and Exhibition. Miniature sheet containing designs as T **405**.
MS1167 141×100 mm. 4p. red and grey (T **405**); 5p. green and grey (10c. stamp); 8p. blue and grey (15c. stamp) 1·60 1·50

406 "Human Races"

1966. Inaug of W.H.O. Headquarters, Geneva.
1168 **406** 8p. black and brown 50 20

407 Magellan Gull

1966. Air. 50th Anniv of Naval Aviation School, Puerto Militar.
1169 **407** 12p. multicoloured 75 35

1966. Army Day (29 May). As T **390**.
1170 8p. multicoloured 1·00 25
DESIGN: 8p. Militiaman of Guemes's "Infernals".

408 Arms of Argentina

1966. Air. "Argentina '66" Philatelic Exhibition, Buenos Aires.
1171 **408** 10p.+10p. multicoloured 2·75 1·90

409

1966. 150th Anniv of Independence. Sheet of 25 (5×5) comprising different 10p. designs–national, federal and provincial arms and maps, as T **409**. Inscr "1816–1966". Multicoloured.
MS1172 Sheet of 25 stamps 65·00 60·00

410 "Charity" Emblem

1966. Argentine Charities.
1173 **410** 10p. blue, black & green 40 10

1966. Argentine Writers (2nd series). Portraits as T **391**. Each green.
1174 10p. H. Ascasubi 65 25
1175 10p. Estanislao del Campo 65 25
1176 10p. M. Cane 65 25
1177 10p. Lucio V. Lopez 65 25
1178 10p. R. Obligado 65 25

411 Anchor

1966. 25th Anniv of Argentine Mercantile Marine.
1179 **411** 4p. multicoloured 40 20

412 L. Agote

1966. Argentine Scientists. Each violet.
1180 10p. Type **412** 65 25
1181 10p. J. B. Ambrosetti 65 25
1182 10p. M. I. Lillo 65 25
1183 10p. F. P. Moreno 65 25
1184 10p. F. J. Muniz 65 25

413 Map and Flags of the American States

1966. Seventh American Armies Conf, Buenos Aires.
1185 **413** 10p. multicoloured 40 10

414 Bank Facade

1966. 75th Anniv of Argentine National Bank.
1186 **414** 10p. green 40 10

415 La Salle Statue and College

1966. 75th Anniv of La Salle College, Buenos Aires.
1187 **415** 10p. black and brown 40 10

416 Antarctic Map with Expedition Route

1966. Argentine South Pole Expedition, 1965–66.
1188 **416** 10p. multicoloured 1·30 25

417 Gen. J. M. de Pueyrredon

1966. Gen. J. M. de Pueyrredon Commemoration.
1189 **417** 10p. red 50 20

418 Gen. J. G. de Las Heras

1966. Gen. Juan G. de Las Heras Commemoration.
1190 **418** 10p. black 40 10

1967. Child Welfare. As T **352**, inscr "R. ARGENTINA". Multicoloured.
1191 10p.+5p. Scarlet-headed black-bird (horiz) (postage) 2·30 1·10
1192 15p.+7p. Blue and yellow tanager (air) 2·75 1·70

419 Ancient Pot

1967. 20th Anniv of UNESCO.
1193 **419** 10p. multicoloured 50 20

420 *The Meal* (after F. Fader)

1967. Fernando Fader (painter).
1194 **420** 10p. brown 50 20

421 Juana Azurduy de Padilla

1967. Famous Argentine Women. Each sepia.
1195 6p. Type **421** 65 25
1196 6p. J. M. Gorriti 65 25
1197 6p. C. Grierson 65 25
1198 6p. J. P. Manson 65 25
1199 6p. A. Storni 65 25

422 Schooner *Invencible*

1967. Navy Day.
1200 **422** 20p. multicoloured 1·80 45

1967. Army Day (29 May). As T **390**.
1201 20p. multicoloured 1·10 25
DESIGN: 20p. Soldier of the Arribenos Regiment.

423 M. Belgrano (6p.) and J. G. de Artigas (22p.)

1967. Third Rio Plata Philatelists Days and Exhibition. Sheet 63×55 mm comprising designs as T **423**.
MS1202 6p. and 22p. each brown and grey 75 70

424 Suitcase and Dove

1967. International Tourist Year.
1203 **424** 20p. multicoloured 50 20

425 PADELAI Emblem and Sun

1967. 75th Anniv of PADELAI (Argentine Children's Welfare Association).
1204 **425** 20p. multicoloured 40 10

426 Teodoro Fels's Bleriot XI

1967. Air. 50th Anniv of First Argentine–Uruguay Airmail Flight.
1205 **426** 26p. brown, olive & blue 40 10

427 Ferreyra's Oxwagon and Skyscrapers

1967. Centenary of Villa Maria.
1206 **427** 20p. multicoloured 40 10

428 *General San Martin* (from statue by M. P. Nunez de Ibarra)

1967. 150th Anniv of Battle of Chacabuco.
1207 **428** 20p. brown and yellow 90 25
1208 - 40p. blue 1·40 45
DESIGN—(48×31 mm)—HORIZ: 40p. *Battle of Chacabuco* (from painting by P. Subercaseaux).

429 Interior of Museum

1967. Tenth Anniv of Government House Museum.
1209 **429** 20p. blue 40 20

430 Pedro Zanni and "Provincia de Buenos Aires"

1967. Aeronautics Week.
1210 **430** 20p. multicoloured 50 20

431 Cadet Ship *General Brown* (from painting by E. Biggeri)

1967. "Temex 67" Stamp Exhibition and 95th Anniv of Naval Military School.
1211 **431** 20p. multicoloured 1·90 60

432 Ovidio Lagos and Front Page of *La Capital* (newspaper)

1967. Centenary of *La Capital*.
1212 **432** 20p. brown 40 10

433 St. Barbara (from altar-painting, Segovia, Spain)

1967. Artillery Day (4 Dec).
1213 **433** 20p. red 50 15

1967. Child Welfare. Bird designs as T **352**. Multicoloured.
1214 20p.+10p. Amazon kingfisher (postage) 2·00 60
1215 26p.+13p. Toco toucan (air) 2·50 85

434 *Sivori's Wife*

1968. 50th Death Anniv of Eduardo Sivori (painter).
1216 **434** 20p. green 50 20

435 *Almirante Brown* Scientific Station

1968. "Antarctic Territories".
1217 - 6p. multicoloured 90 20
1218 **435** 20p. multicoloured 1·30 25
1219 - 40p. multicoloured 2·10 85
DESIGNS—VERT (22½×32 mm): 6p. Map of Antarctic radio-postal stations. HORIZ (as Type **435**): 40p. Aircraft over South Pole ("Trans-Polar Round Flight").

436 Man in Wheelchair

1968. Rehabilitation Day for the Handicapped.
1220 **436** 20p. black and green 40 25

437 "St. Gabriel" (detail from *The Annunciation* by Leonardo da Vinci)

1968. St. Gabriel (patron saint of army communications).
1221 **437** 20p. mauve 40 25

438 Children and W.H.O. Emblem

1968. 20th Anniv of W.H.O.
1222 **438** 20p. blue and red 40 25

1968. Army Day (29 May). As T **390**.
1223 20p. multicoloured 1·30 25
DESIGN: 20p. Iriarte's artilleryman.

439 Full-rigged Cadet Ship *Libertad* (E. Biggeri)

1968. Navy Day.
1224 **439** 20p. multicoloured 2·10 35

440 G. Rawson and Hospital

1968. Centenary of Guillermo Rawson Hospital.
1225 **440** 6p. bistre 50 25

441 Vito Dumas and *Legh II*

1968. Air. Vito Dumas' World Voyage in Yacht *Legh II*.
1226 **441** 68p. multicoloured 1·00 60

442 Children using Zebra crossing

1968. Road Safety.
1227 **442** 20p. multicoloured 1·00 35

443 O'Higgins greeting San Martin (P. Subercaseaux)

1968. 150th Anniv of Battle of the Maipu.
1228 **443** 40p. blue 1·10 45

444 Dr. O. Magnasco (lawyer)

1968. Magnasco Commemoration.
1229 **444** 20p. brown 65 30

445 *The Sea* (E. Gomez) **446** *Grandmother's Birthday* (P. Lynch)

1968. Children's Stamp Design Competition.
1230 **445** 20p. multicoloured 50 20
1231 **446** 20p. multicoloured 50 20

447 Mar del Plata at Night

1968. Fourth Plenary Assembly of Int Telegraph and Telephone Consultative Committee, Mar del Plata.
1232 **447** 20p. black, yellow and blue (postage) 40 20
1233 - 40p. black, mauve and blue (air) 75 20
1234 - 68p. multicoloured 1·10 45
DESIGNS (as Type **447**): 40p. South America in Assembly hemisphere. (Larger, 40×30 mm): 68p. Assembly emblem.

448 Mounted Gendarme

1968. National Gendarmerie.
1235 **448** 20p. multicoloured 50 20

449 Coastguard Cutter Lynch

1968. National Maritime Prefecture (Coastguard).
1236 **449** 20p. black, grey and blue 50 20

450 A. de Anchorena and *Pampero*

1968. Aeronautics Week.
1237 **450** 20p. multicoloured 50 20

451 St. Martin
of Tours (A.
Guido)

1968. St. Martin of Tours (patron saint of Buenos Aires).
1238 **451** 20p. brown and lilac 40 20

452 Bank Emblem

1968. Municipal Bank of Buenos Aires.
1239 **452** 20p. black, green & yell 40 20

453 Anniversary and
A.L.P.I. Emblems

1968. 25th Anniv of "Fight Against Polio Association"
(A.L.P.I.).
1240 **453** 20p. green and red 40 20

454 My Grandmother's Birthday
(Patricia Lynch)

1968. First "Solidarity" Philatelic Exn, Buenos Aires.
1241 **454** 40p.+20p. multicoloured 90 60

455 The Potter
Woman (Ramon
Gomez Cornet)

1968. Cent of Whitcomb Gallery, Buenos Aires.
1242 **455** 20p. red 90 60

456 Emblem of
State Coalfields

1968. Coal and Steel Industries. Multicoloured.
1243 20p. Type **456** 50 20
1244 20p. Ladle and emblem of
 Military Steel-manufacturing
 Agency ("FM") 50 20

457 Illustration from
Schmidl's book Journey to
the River Plate and Paraguay

1969. Ulrich Schmidl Commemoration.
1245 **457** 20p. yellow, red & black 90 60

1969. Army Day (29 May). As T **390**.
1246 20p. Sapper, Buenos Aires
 Army, 1856 1·50 25

459 Sail Frigate
Hercules

1969. Navy Day.
1247 **459** 20p. multicoloured 2·75 45

460 Freedom
and Equality
(from poster by
S. Zagorski)

1969. Human Rights Year.
1254 **460** 20p. black and yellow 40 20

461 I.L.O.
Emblem within
Honeycomb

1969. 50th Anniv of I.L.O.
1255 **461** 20p. multicoloured 40 20

462 P. N. Arata
(biologist)

1969. Argentine Scientists.
1256 **462** 6p. brown on yellow 75 30
1257 - 6p. brown on yellow 75 30
1258 - 6p. brown on yellow 75 30
1259 - 6p. brown on yellow 75 30
1260 - 6p. brown on yellow 75 30
PORTRAITS: No. 1257, M. Fernandez (zoologist); 1258, A. P.
Gallardo (biologist); 1259, C. M. Hicken (botanist); 1260, E.
L. Holmberg (botanist).

463 Dish Aerial
and Satellite

1969. Satellite Communications.
1261 **463** 20p. blk & yell (postage) 50 20
1262 - 40p. blue (air) 1·10 35
DESIGN—HORIZ: 40p. Earth station and dish aerial.

464 Nieuport 28 and
Route Map

1969. 50th Anniv of First Argentine Airmail Service.
1263 **464** 20p. multicoloured 50 20

1969. Child Welfare. As T **352**, inscr "R. ARGENTINA".
Multicoloured.
1264 20p.+10p. White-faced whistling
 duck (postage) 2·50 70
1265 26p.+13p. Lineated woodpecker
 (air) 2·75 85

465 College Entrance

1969. Centenary of Argentine Military College.
1266 **465** 20p. multicoloured 50 20

466 General
Pacheco (from
painting by R.
Guidice)

1969. Death Centenary of General Angel Pacheco.
1267 **466** 20p. green 40 20

467 Bartolome Mitre
and Logotypes of La
Nacion

1969. Centenary of Newspapers La Nacion and La Prensa.
1268 **467** 20p. black, emer & grn 1·10 45
1269 - 20p. black orange & yell 1·10 45
DESIGN: No. 1269 "The Lantern" (masthead) and logo-
types of "La Prensa".

468 J. Aguirre

1969. Argentine Musicians.
1270 **468** 6p. green and blue 1·10 45
1271 - 6p. green and blue 1·10 45
1272 - 6p. green and blue 1·10 45
1273 - 6p. green and blue 1·10 45
1274 - 6p. green and blue 1·10 45
MUSICIANS: No. 1271, F. Boero; 1272, C. Gaito; 1273, C. L.
Buchardo; 1274, A. Williams.

469 Hydro-electric Project
on Rivers Limay and
Neuquen

1969. National Development Projects. Multicoloured.
1275 6p. Type **469** (postage) 90 25
1276 20p. Parana–Santa Fe river
 tunnel 1·80 35
1277 26p. Atomic power plant,
 Atucha (air) 2·50 1·30

470 Lieut. B. Matienzo and
Nieuport 28 Biplane

1969. Aeronautics Week.
1278 **470** 20p. multicoloured 90 20

471 Capital "L" and Lions
Emblem

1969. 50th Anniv of Lions International.
1279 **471** 20p. olive, orge & green 1·10 25

472 Madonna and
Child (after R. Soldi)

1969. Christmas.
1280 **472** 20p. multicoloured 1·10 35

1970. Child Welfare. As T **352**, but differently arranged
and inscr "REPUBLICA ARGENTINA". Multicoloured.
1293 20c.+10c. Slender-tailed wood-
 star (postage) 2·00 70
1294 40c.+20c. Chilean flamingo (air) 2·50 85
 See also Nos. 1394/5, 1415/16 and 1441/2.

474 General
Belgrano (lithograph
by Gericault)

1970. Birth Bicent of General Manuel Belgrano.
1295 **474** 20c. brown 65 20
1296 - 50c. black, flesh & blue 1·30 35
DESIGN—HORIZ (56×15 mm): 50c. Monument to the Flag
(bas-relief by Jose Fioravanti).

475 Early Fire Engine

1970. Air. Centenary of Buenos Aires Fire Brigade.
1297 **475** 40c. multicoloured 2·30 45

476 Naval Schooner Juliet,
1814

1970. Navy Day.
1298 **476** 20c. multicoloured 2·00 60

477 San Jose Palace

1970. President Justo de Urquiza Commemoration.
1299 **477** 20c. multicoloured 40 20

478
General
Belgrano

1970. Revalued currency. Previous designs with values
in centavos and pesos as T **478**. Inscr "REPUBLICA
ARGENTINA" or "ARGENTINA".
1300 1c. green (No. 1016) 25 10
1301 3c. red (No. 951) 25 10
1302 **296** 5c. blue 25 10
1303 **478** 6c. blue 40 15
1304 **478** 8c. green 25 10
1305 - 10c. brown (No. 1286)* 50 15
1306 - 10c. red (No. 1286) 2·40 45
1307 - 10c. brown (No. 1286)* 65 25
1308 **478** 10c. brown ˙25 10
1309 - 25c. brown 65 15
1310 **478** 30c. purple 50 20
1311 - 50c. red 1·50 30
1312 **478** 60c. yellow 50 25
1313 - 65c. brown (No. 878) 1·50 25
1314 - 70c. blue 25 15
1315 - 90c. green (No. 878) 4·50 30

1316a	-	1p. brown (as No. 1027, but 23×29 mm)	4·50	25
1317	-	1p.15 blue (No. 1072)	1·50	25
1318	-	1p.20 orange (No. 878)	1·60	30
1319	-	1p.20 red	50	20
1320	-	1p.80 brn (as No. 1072)	50	25
1321	478	1p.80 blue	50	25
1322	-	2p. brown	50	15
1323	-	2p.70 bl (as No. 878)	50	25
1323a	478	3p. grey	50	20
1392	-	4p.50 green (as No. 1288) (G. Brown)	1·10	20
1325	-	5p. green (as No. 1032)	1·90	35
1326	-	6p. red	50	20
1327	-	6p. green	50	20
1328	-	7p.50 grn (as No. 878)	1·60	30
1329	-	10p. blue (as No. 1033)	2·50	25
1329a	-	12p. green	65	20
1329b	-	12p. red	65	20
1330	-	13p.50 red (as No. 1072)	1·60	60
1331	-	13p.50 red (as No. 1072 but larger, 16×24 mm)	75	25
1332	-	15p. red	50	15
1333	-	15p. blue	50	15
1334	-	20p. red	50	20
1335	-	22p.50 blue (as No. 878) (22×32½ mm)	1·30	25
1393	-	22p.50 blue (as No. 878) (26×39 mm)	2·20	70
1336	-	30p. red	65	20
1337	478	40p. green	1·80	25
1338	-	40p. red	50	15
1339	478	60p. blue	2·50	30
1340	-	70p. blue	2·50	45
1340a	478	90p. green	1·30	30
1340b	-	100p. red	1·30	30
1340c	-	110p. red	65	25
1340d	-	120p. red	50	30
1340e	-	130p. red	90	35

DESIGNS—VERT (as Type **478**): 25, 50, 70c., 1p.20, 2, 6, 12, 15p. (No. 1332), 20, 30, 40p. (No. 1338), 100, 110, 120, 130p. General Jose de San Martin; 15p. (No. 1333), 70p. Guillermo Brown.

*No. 1307 differs from Nos. 1305/6 in being without imprint. It also has "CORREOS" at top right.

482 Wireless Set of 1920 and Radio "Waves"

1970. 50th Anniv of Argentine Radio Broadcasting.
1341	**482**	20c. multicoloured	75	45

483 Emblem of Education Year

1970. Air. International Education Year.
1342	**483**	68c. black and blue	65	30

1970. Military Uniforms. As T **390**. Multicoloured.
1343		20c. Military courier, 1879	1·50	25

484 Liberation Fleet leaving Valparaiso (A. Abel)

1970. 150th Anniv of Peruvian Liberation.
1344	**484**	26c. multicoloured	1·90	60

485 "United Nations"

1970. 25th Anniv of U.N.
1345	**485**	20c. multicoloured	40	20

486 Cordoba Cathedral

1970. 400th Anniv of Tucuman Diocese.
1346	**486**	50c. blk & grey (postage)	1·40	35
1347	-	40c. multicoloured (air)	1·50	60

DESIGN—HORIZ: 40c. Chapel, Sumampa.

487 Planetarium

1970. Air. Buenos Aires Planetarium.
1348	**487**	40c. multicoloured	1·10	35

488 "Liberty" and Mint Building

1970. 25th Anniv of State Mint Building, Buenos Aires.
1349	**488**	20c. black, green & gold	40	10

489 The Manger (H. G. Gutierrez)

1970. Christmas.
1350	**489**	20c. multicoloured	90	60

490 Jorge Newbery and Morane Saulnier Type L Airplane

1970. Air. Aeronautics Week.
1351	**490**	26c. multicoloured	65	25

491 St. John Bosco and College Building

1970. Salesian Mission in Patagonia.
1352	**491**	20c. black and green	40	20

492 "Planting the Flag"

1971. Fifth Anniv of Argentine Expedition to the South Pole.
1353	**492**	20c. multicoloured	2·30	35

493 Dorado

1971. Child Welfare. Fishes. Multicoloured.
1354		20c.+10c. Type **493** (postage)	2·00	70
1355		40c.+20c. River Plate pejerrey (air)	1·80	60

494 Einstein and Scanners

1971. Electronics in Postal Development.
1356	**494**	25c. multicoloured	75	45

495 E. I. Alippi

1971. Argentine Actors and Actresses. Each black and brown.
1357		15c. Type **495**	50	15
1358		15c. J. A. Casaberta	50	15
1359		15c. R. Casaux	50	15
1360		15c. Angelina Pagano	50	15
1361		15c. F. Parravicini	50	15

496 Federation Emblem

1971. Inter-American Regional Meeting of International Roads Federation.
1362	**496**	25c. black and blue	50	20

1971. Army Day. As T **390**.
1363		25c. multicoloured	2·10	25

DESIGN: 25c. Artilleryman of 1826.

1971. Navy Day. As T **476**.
1364		25c. multicoloured	2·30	25

DESIGN: Sloop Carmen.

498 General Guemes (L. Gigli)

1971. 150th Death Anniv of General M. de Guemes. Multicoloured.
1365		25c. Type **498**	90	25
1366		25c. Death of Guemes (A. Alice) (84×29 mm)	90	25

499 Order of the Peruvian Sun

1971. 150th Anniv of Peruvian Independence.
1367	**499**	31c. yellow, black & red	1·10	25

500 Stylized Tulip

1971. Third Int and 8th Nat Horticultural Exhibition.
1368	**500**	25c. multicoloured	65	20

501 Dr. A. Saenz (founder) (after Jose Gut)

1971. 150th Anniv of Buenos Aires University.
1369	**501**	25c. multicoloured	50	20

502 Arsenal Emblem

1971. 30th Anniv of Fabricaciones Militares (Arsenals).
1370	**502**	25c. multicoloured	50	20

503 Road Transport

1971. Nationalized Industries.
1371	**503**	25c. mult (postage)	90	15
1372	-	65c. multicoloured	2·30	45
1373	-	31c. yell, blk & red (air)	1·00	35

DESIGNS: 31c. Refinery and formula ("Petrochemicals"); 65c. Tree and paper roll ("Paper and Cellulose").

1971. Air. Revalued currency. Face values in centavos.
1374	**358**	45c. brown	4·50	60
1375	**358**	68c. red	65	25
1376a	**358**	70c. blue	3·25	25
1377	**358**	90c. green	3·25	25
1378	**358**	1p.70 blue	1·00	25
1379	**358**	1p.95 green	1·00	25
1380	**358**	2p.65 purple	1·00	25

504 Constellation and Telescope

1971. Centenary of Cordoba Observatory.
1381	**504**	25c. multicoloured	1·10	25

505 Capt. D. L. Candelaria and Morane Saulnier Type P Airplane

1971. 25th Aeronautics and Space Week.
1382	**505**	25c. multicoloured	65	20

506 Stamps (Mariette Lydis)

1971. Second Charity Stamp Exhibition
1383	**506**	1p.+50c. multicoloured	75	45

507 Christ in Majesty (tapestry by Butler)

1971. Christmas.
1384	**507**	25c. multicoloured	40	20

1972. Child Welfare. As T **352**, but differently arranged and inscr "REPUBLICA ARGENTINA".
1394		25c.+10c. Saffron finch (vert)	1·90	45
1395		65c.+30c. Rufous-bellied thrush (horiz)	2·50	60

508 *Maternity* (J. Castagnino)

1972. 25th Anniv of UNICEF.
1396 **508** 25c. black and brown ... 40 ... 15

509 Treaty Emblem, *Libertad* (liner) and Almirante Brown Base

1972. Tenth Anniv of Antarctic Treaty.
1397 **509** 25c. multicoloured ... 1·10 ... 45

510 Postman's Mail Pouch

1972. Bicentenary of First Buenos Aires Postman.
1398 **510** 25c. multicoloured ... 35 ... 10

1972. Army Day. As T **390**. Multicoloured.
1399 25c. Sergeant of Negro and Mulatto Battalion (1806–7) ... 1·10 ... 45

1972. Navy Day. As T **476**. Multicoloured.
1400 25c. Brigantine "Santisima Trinidad" ... 1·60 ... 50

512 Sonic Balloon

1972. National Meteorological Service.
1401 **512** 25c. multicoloured ... 50 ... 15

513 Oil Pump

1972. 50th Anniv of State Oilfields (Y.P.F.).
1402 **513** 45c. black, blue & gold ... 1·40 ... 25

514 Forest Centre

1972. Seventh World Forestry Congress, Buenos Aires.
1403 **514** 25c. black, blue & lt bl ... 1·10 ... 35

515 Arms and Cadet Ship *Presidente Sarmiento*

1972. Centenary of Naval School.
1404 **515** 25c. multicoloured ... 1·30 ... 25

516 Baron A. de Marchi, Balloon and Voisin *Boxkite*

1972. Aeronautics Week.
1405 **516** 25c. multicoloured ... 75 ... 40

517 Bartolome Mitre

1972. 150th Birth Anniv of General Bartolome Mitre.
1406 **517** 25c. blue ... 70 ... 40

518 Heart and Flower

1972. World Health Day.
1407 **518** 90c. blk, violet & blue ... 90 ... 45

519 *Martin Fierro* (J. C. Castignino)

1972. Int Book Year and Cent of *Martin Fierro* (poem by Jose Hernandez). Multicoloured.
1408 50c. Type **519** ... 50 ... 15
1409 90c. *Spirit of the Gaucho* (V. Forte) ... 1·00 ... 45

520 Iguazu Falls

1972. American Tourist Year.
1410 **520** 45c. multicoloured ... 50 ... 20

521 *Wise Man on Horseback* (18th-century wood-carving)

1972. Christmas.
1411 **521** 50c. multicoloured ... 75 ... 25

522 Cockerel Emblem

1973. 150th Anniv of Federal Police Force.
1412 **522** 50c. multicoloured ... 50 ... 20

523 Bank Emblem and First Coin

1973. 150th Anniv of Provincial Bank of Buenos Aires.
1413 **523** 50c. multicoloured ... 40 ... 15

524 Douglas DC-3 Aircraft and Polar Map

1973. Tenth Anniv of Frist Argentine Flight to South Pole.
1414 **524** 50c. multicoloured ... 2·50 ... 95

1973. Child Welfare. As T **473**, but differently arranged and inscr "R. ARGENTINA". Multicoloured.
1415 50c.+25c. Crested screamer (vert) ... 2·00 ... 95
1416 90c.+45c. Saffron-cowled blackbird (horiz) ... 2·50 ... 1·50

525 Presidential Chair

1973. Presidential Inauguration.
1417 **525** 50c. multicoloured ... 40 ... 10

526 San Martin and Bolivar

1973. San Martin's Farewell to People of Peru. Multicoloured.
1418 50c. Type **526** ... 50 ... 20
1419 50c. "San Martin" (after Gil de Castro) (vert) ... 50 ... 20

527 "Eva Peron – Eternally with her People"

1973. Eva Peron Commemoration.
1420 **527** 70c. multicoloured ... 40 ... 15

528 House of Viceroy Sobremonte (H. de Virgilio)

1973. Fourth Centenary of Cordoba.
1421 **528** 50c. multicoloured ... 45 ... 15

529 *Woman* (L. Spilimbergo)

1973. Philatelists' Day. Argentine Paintings. Multicoloured.
1422 15c.+15c. *Nature Study* (A. Guttero) (horiz) ... 50 ... 10
1423 70c. Type **529** ... 1·30 ... 25
1424 90c.+90c. *Nude* (M. C. Victorica) (horiz) ... 1·60 ... 1·10
See also Nos. 1434/6 and 1440.

530 *La Argentina* (sail frigate)

1973. Navy Day.
1425 **530** 70c. multicoloured ... 1·30 ... 25

531 Early and Modern Telephones

1973. 25th Anniv of National Telecommunications Enterprise (E.N.T.E.L.).
1426 **531** 70c. multicoloured ... 65 ... 15

532 Quill Pen of Flags

1973. 12th International Latin Notaries Congress.
1427 **532** 70c. multicoloured ... 40 ... 15

533 Lujan Basilica

1973
1428 **533** 18c. brown and yellow ... 25 ... 10
1429 **533** 50c. purple and black ... 25 ... 10
1429a **533** 50c. blue and brown ... 25 ... 10
1430 **533** 50c. purple ... 25 ... 10

1973. Transfer of Presidency of General Juan Peron. No. 1318 optd **TRANSMISION DEL MANDO PRESIDENCIAL 12 OCTUBRE 1973**.
1431 1p.20 orange ... 1·40 ... 25

535 *Virgin and Child* (stained-glass window)

1973. Christmas. Multicoloured.
1432 70c. Type **535** ... 65 ... 25
1433 1p.20 "The Manger" (B. Venier) ... 1·10 ... 45

1974. Argentine Paintings. As T **529**. Multicoloured.
1434 50c. *Houses* (E. Daneri) (horiz) ... 65 ... 20
1435 70c. *The Lama* (J. B. Planas) (horiz) ... 70 ... 25
1436 90c. *Homage to the Blue Grotto* (E. Pettoruti) (horiz) ... 75 ... 35

536 View of Mar del Plata

1974. Centenary of Mar del Plata.
1437 **536** 70c. multicoloured ... 50 ... 20

537 Fray Justo Santa Maria de Oro (anon.)

1974. Birth Bicentenary of Fray Justo Santa Maria de Oro.
| 1438 | **537** | 70c. multicoloured | 40 | 10 |

538 Weather Contrasts

1974. Cent of World Meteorological Organization.
| 1439 | **538** | 1p.20 multicoloured | 1·00 | 35 |

1974. "Prenfil 74" Philatelic Press Exhibition, Buenos Aires. As No. 1435.
| 1440 | 70c.+30c. multicoloured | 75 | 30 |

1974. Child Welfare. As T **352** but differently arranged and inscr "REPUBLICA ARGENTINA". Multicoloured.
| 1441 | 70c.+30c. Double-collared seedeater | 2·00 | 60 |
| 1442 | 1p.20+60c. Hooded siskin | 2·50 | 85 |

539 B. Roldan

1974. Birth Centenary of Belisario Roldan (writer).
| 1443 | **539** | 70c. brown and blue | 35 | 15 |

540 O.E.A. Member Countries

1974. 25th Anniv of Organization of American States' Charter.
| 1444 | **540** | 1p.38 multicoloured | 40 | 15 |

541 Posthorn Emblem

1974. Creation of State Posts and Telecommunications Enterprise (E.N.C.O.T.E.L.).
| 1445 | **541** | 1p.20 blue, black & gold | 75 | 15 |

542 Flags of Member Countries

1974. Sixth Meeting of River Plate Countries' Foreign Ministers.
| 1446 | **542** | 1p.38 multicoloured | 40 | 20 |

543 El Chocon Hydro-electric Complex

1974. Nationalized Industries. Multicoloured.
| 1447 | 70c. Type **543** | 65 | 15 |

| 1448 | 1p.20 Blast furnace, Somisa steel mills | 1·00 | 45 |
| 1449 | 4p.50 General Belgrano Bridge (61×25 mm) | 3·25 | 70 |

1974. Army Day. As T **390**. Multicoloured.
| 1450 | 1p.20 Mounted Grenadier | 1·00 | 20 |
See also Nos. 1515 and 1564.

544 A. Mascias and Bleriot XI

1974. Air Force Day.
| 1451 | **544** | 1p.20 multicoloured | 1·00 | 20 |

545 Brigantine Belgrano

1974. 150th Anniv of San Martin's Departure into Exile.
| 1452 | **545** | 1p.20 multicoloured | 1·80 | 45 |

546 San Francisco Convent, Santa Fe

1974. 400th Anniv of Santa Fe.
| 1453 | **546** | 1p.20 multicoloured | 65 | 15 |

547 Symbolic Posthorn

1974. Centenary of U.P.U.
| 1454 | **547** | 2p.65 multicoloured | 1·40 | 35 |

548 Mariano Necochea

1974. 150th Anniv of Battles of Junin and Ayacucho. Sheet 143×134 mm comprising T **548** and similar vert designs. Multicoloured.
MS1455 (a) 1p. Type **548**; (b) 1p.20 San Martin; (c) 1p.70 Manuel Isidoro Suarez; (d) 1p.90 Juan Pascual Pringles; (e) 2p.70 Latin American flags; (f) 4p.50 Jose Felix Bogado
| | | | 5·25 | 5·00 |

549 Congress Building, Buenos Aires

1974
| 1456 | **549** | 30p. purple and yellow | 3·25 | 25 |

550 Boy examining Stamp

1974. International Year of Youth Philately.
| 1457 | **550** | 1p.70 black and yellow | 65 | 15 |

551 Christmas in Peace (V. Campanella)

1974. Christmas. Multicoloured.
| 1458 | 1p.20 Type **551** | 1·10 | 25 |
| 1459 | 2p.65 St. Anne and the Virgin Mary | 1·30 | 45 |

552 Space Monsters (R. Forner)

1975. Contemporary Argentine Paintings. Multicoloured.
| 1460 | 2p.70 Type **552** | 1·50 | 35 |
| 1461 | 4p.50 Sleep (E. Centurion) | 2·75 | 60 |

553 Cathedral and Weaver, Catamarca (image scaled to 58% of original size)

1975. Tourist Views (1st series). Multicoloured.
1462	1p.20 Type **553**	40	20
1463	1p.20 Street scene and carved pulpit, Jujuy	40	20
1464	1p.20 Monastery and tree- felling, Salta	40	20
1465	1p.20 Dam and vase, Santiago del Estero	40	20
1466	1p.20 Colombres Museum and farm cart, Tucuman	40	20
See also Nos. 1491/3.

554 We're Vaccinated Now (M. L. Alonso)

1975. Children's Vaccination Campaign.
| 1467 | **554** | 2p. multicoloured | 75 | 20 |

555 Don Quixote (Zuloaga)

1975. Air. "Espana 75" International Stamp Exhibition, Madrid.
| 1468 | **555** | 2p.75 black, yell & red | 1·00 | 40 |

556 Hugo S. Acuna and South Orkneys Base

1975. Antarctic Pioneers. Multicoloured.
1469	2p. Type **556**	50	15
1470	2p. Francisco P. Moreno and Quetrihue Peninsula	50	15
1471	2p. Capt. Carlos M. Moyano and Cerra Torre, Santa Cruz	50	15
1472	2p. Lt. Col. Luis Piedra Buena and naval cutter Luisito in the Antarctic	50	15
1473	2p. Ensign Jose M. Sobral and Snow Hill House	50	15

557 Valley of the Moon, San Juan Province

1975
1474	**557**	50p. multicoloured	4·00	45
1474a	**557**	300p. multicoloured	4·50	45
1474b	-	500p. multicoloured	8·75	1·20
1474c	-	1000p. multicoloured	7·00	1·40
DESIGNS—HORIZ: 500p. Admiral Brown Antarctic Station; 1000p. San Francisco Church, Salta.

1975. Air. Surch.
1475	358	9p.20 on 5p.60 green, mauve and purple	1·50	35
1476	358	19p.70 on 5p.60 green, mauve and purple	2·10	70
1477	358	100p. on 5p.60 green, mauve and purple	9·50	3·75

559 Eduardo Bradley and Balloon

1975. Air Force Day.
| 1478 | **559** | 6p. multicoloured | 75 | 25 |

560 Sail Frigate 25 de Mayo

1975. Navy Day.
| 1479 | **560** | 6p. multicoloured | 1·50 | 35 |

561 Oath of the 33 Orientales on the Beach of La Agraciada (J. Blanes)

1975. 150th Anniv of Uruguayan Independence.
| 1480 | **561** | 6p. multicoloured | 1·30 | 35 |

1975. Air. Surch. **REVALORIZADO** and value.
| 1481 | 358 | 9p.20 on 5p.60 green, mauve and purple | 1·10 | 45 |
| 1482 | 358 | 19p.70 on 5p.60 green, mauve and purple | 2·00 | 95 |

563 Flame Emblem

1975. 30th Anniv of Pres. Peron's Seizure of Power.
| 1483 | **563** | 6p. multicoloured | 65 | 25 |

1975. Surch **REVALORIZADO** and value.
| 1484 | **533** | 5p. on 18c. brown & yell | 75 | 15 |

565 Bridge and Flags of Argentina and Uruguay

1975. "International Bridge" between Colon (Argentina) and Paysandu (Uruguay).
| 1485 | **565** | 6p. multicoloured | 75 | 20 |

566 Posthorn Emblem

1975. Introduction of Postal Codes.
1486	**566**	10p. on 20c. yellow, black and green	90	20

1975. Nos. 951 and 1288 surch **REVALORIZADO** and value.
1487		6c. on 3p. blue	40	10
1488		30c. on 90p. bistre	40	10

568 *The Nativity* (stained-glass window)

1975. Christmas.
1489	**568**	6p. multicoloured	75	20

569 Stylized Nurse and Child

1975. Centenary of Children's Hospital.
1490	**569**	6p. multicoloured	1·30	35

1975. Tourist Views (2nd series). As T **553**. Multicoloured.
1491		6p. Mounted patrol and oil rig, Chubut	90	25
1492		6p. Glacier and sheep-shearing, Santa Cruz	90	25
1493		6p. Lake Lapataia, Tierra del Fuego, and Antarctic scene	90	25

570 "Numeral"

1976
1494	**570**	12c. grey and black	40	15
1495	**570**	50c. slate and green	40	15
1496	**570**	1p. red and black	40	15
1497	**570**	4p. blue and black	40	15
1498	**570**	5p. yellow and black	50	15
1499	**570**	6p. brown and black	50	15
1500	**570**	10p. grey and violet	90	20
1501	**570**	27p. green and black	65	20
1502	**570**	30p. blue and black	3·25	25
1503	**570**	45p. yellow and black	1·80	25
1504	**570**	50p. green and black	1·80	25
1505	**570**	100p. green and red	1·80	25

571 Airliner in Flight

1976. 25th Anniv of "Aerolineas Argentinas".
1513	**571**	30p. multicoloured	2·00	25

572 Sail Frigate *Heroina* and Map of Malvinas

1976. Argentine Claims to Falkland Islands (Malvinas).
1514	**572**	6p. multicoloured	5·75	60

1976. Army Day. As T **390**. Multicoloured.
1515		12p. Infantryman of Conde's 7th Regiment	75	20

573 Louis Braille

1976. Louis Braille (inventor of characters for the Blind) Commemoration.
1516	**573**	19p.70 blue	50	15

574 Plush-crested Jay

1976. Argentine Philately. Multicoloured.
1517	**574**	7p.+3p.50 Type **574**	1·40	80
1518		13p.+6p.50 Yellow-collared macaw	1·50	80
1519		20p.+10p. *Begonia micranthera*	1·70	85
1520		40p.+20p. *Echinopsis shaferi* (teasel)	2·10	1·00

575 Schooner *Rio de la Plata*

1976. Navy Day.
1521	**575**	12p. multicoloured	95	25

576 Dr. Bernardo Houssay (Medicine)

1976. Argentine Nobel Prize Winners.
1522	**576**	10p. black, orge & grey	50	15
1523	-	15p. black, yell & grey	50	15
1524	-	20p. black, brn & grey	65	25

DESIGNS:—15p. Dr. Luis Leloir (chemistry); 20p. Dr. Carlos Lamas (peace).

577 Bridge and Ship

1976. "International Bridge" between Unzue (Argentina) and Fray Bentos (Uruguay).
1525	**577**	12p. multicoloured	1·30	25

578 Cooling Tower and Pipelines

1976. General Mosconi Petrochemical Project.
1526	**578**	28p. multicoloured	75	20

579 Teodoro Fels and Bleriot XI

1976. Air Force Day.
1527	**579**	15p. multicoloured	65	15

580 *Nativity* (E. Chiapetto)

1976. Christmas.
1528	**580**	20p. multicoloured	1·10	45

581 Dr. D. Velez Sarsfield (statesman)

1977. Death Cent (1975) of Dr. D. V. Sarsfield.
1529	**581**	50p. brown and red	1·30	45

582 Conference Emblem

1977. United Nations Water Conference.
1530	**582**	70p. multicoloured	1·10	35

583 *The Visit* (Horacio Butler)

1977. Plastic Arts. Multicoloured.
1531		50p. Type **583**	1·00	25
1532		70p. *Consecration* (M. P. Caride) (vert)	1·40	45

584 World Cup Emblem

1977. World Cup Football Championship, Argentina. Multicoloured.
1533		30p. Type **584**	75	25
1534		70p. Stadium and flags (vert)	1·40	35

585 City of La Plata Museum

1977
1535	**585**	5p. black and brown	40	10
1536	-	10p. black and blue	25	10
1538	-	20p. black and yellow	40	10
1539	-	40p. black and blue	50	10
1540	-	50p. black and yellow	65	20
1541	-	50p. black and brown	65	15
1542	-	100p. black and pink	50	10
1543	-	100p. black and orange	65	15
1544	-	100p. black and green	50	10
1545	-	200p. black and blue	75	25
1546	-	280p. black and lilac	11·50	1·30
1547b	-	300p. black and yellow	1·20	25
1548	-	480p. black and yellow	1·80	35
1549b	-	500p. black and green	2·20	25
1550	-	520p. black and orange	2·40	35
1551	-	800p. black and purple	2·75	35
1552a	-	1000p. black and gold	3·75	35
1553	-	1000p. black and yellow	3·25	45
1554	-	2000p. multicoloured	2·75	45

DESIGNS—HORIZ: 10p. House of Independence, Tucuman; 20p. Type **585**; 50p. (No. 1541), Cabildo, Buenos Aires; 100p. (Nos. 1542/3), Columbus Theatre, Buenos Aires; 280p., 300p. Rio Grande Museum Chapel, Tierra del Fuego; 480p., 520p., 800p. San Ignacio Mission Church ruins; 500p. Candonga Chapel; 1000p. General Post Office, Buenos Aires (No. 1552 39×29 mm, No. 1553 32×21 mm); 2000p. Civic Centre, Bariloche. VERT: 40p. Cabildo, Salta; 50p. (No. 1540), Cabildo, Buenos Aires; 200p. Monument to the Flag, Rosario.

586 Morse Key and Satellite

1977. "Argentine Philately". Multicoloured.
1560		10p.+5p. Type **586**	55	30
1561		20p.+10p. Old and modern mail vans	65	65
1562		60p.+30p. Old and modern ships	1·30	1·00
1563		70p.+35p. SPAD XIII and Boeing 707 aircraft	1·60	1·00

1977. Army Day. As T **390**. Multicoloured.
1564		30p. Trooper of 16th Lancers	1·50	35

587 Schooner *Sarandi*

1977. Navy Day.
1565	**587**	30p. multicoloured	1·50	35

1977. 150th Anniv of Uruguay Post Office. As No. 1325 but colour changed. Surch **100 PESOS 150 ANIV. DEL CORREO NACIONAL DEL URUGUAY.**
1566		100p. on 5p. brown	2·50	1·10

1977. "Argentina '77" Exhibition. As No. 1474c, but inscr "EXPOSICION ARGENTINA '77".
1567		160p.+80p. multicoloured	4·50	3·00

589 Admiral Guillermo Brown

1977. Birth Bicent of Admiral Guillermo Brown.
1568	**589**	30p. multicoloured	65	20

590 Civic Centre, Santa Rosa (La Pampa)

1977. Provinces of the Argentine. Multicoloured.
1569		30p. Type **590**	65	25
1570		30p. Sierra de la Ventana (Buenos Aires)	65	25
1571		30p. Skiers at Chapelco, San Martin de los Andes (Neuquen)	65	25
1572		30p. Lake Fonck (Rio Negro)	65	25

591 Savoia S.16 ter Flying Boat over Rio de la Plata

1977. Air Force and 1926 Buenos Aires–New York Flight Commemoration.
1573	**591**	40p. multicoloured	50	20

592 Jet Fighter Outline

1977. 50th Anniv of Military Aviation Factory.
1574	**592**	30p. blue, pale blue and black	40	10

593 *The Adoration of the Kings* (stained-glass window, Holy Sacrament Basilica, Buenos Aires)

1977. Christmas.
| 1575 | 593 | 100p. multicoloured | 1·60 | 25 |

1978. World Cup Football Championship, Argentina. Sheet 102×133 mm containing No. 1567×4 optd **Argentina 78** and logo.
| MS1576 | | 160p.+80p. multicoloured | 33·00 | 31·00 |

595 World Cup Emblem

1978. World Cup Football Championship, Argentina.
| 1577 | 595 | 200p. green and blue | 1·50 | 45 |

596 Rosario

1978. World Cup Football Championship (3rd issue). Match Sites. Multicoloured.
1578	596	50p. Type 596	50	20
1579		100p. Cordoba	50	20
1580		150p. Mendoza	90	25
1581		200p. Mar del Plata	90	25
1582		300p. Buenos Aires	1·60	45

597 Children and Institute Emblem

1978. 50th Anniv of Inter-American Children's Institute.
| 1583 | 597 | 100p. multicoloured | 65 | 30 |

598 *The Working Day* (B. Quinquela Martin)

1978. Argentine Art. Multicoloured.
| 1584 | 598 | 100p. Type 598 | 90 | 25 |
| 1585 | | 100p. *Bust of an Unknown Woman* (Orlando Pierri) | 90 | 25 |

599 Players from Argentina, Hungary, France and Italy (Group One)

1978. World Cup Football Championship, Argentina. Multicoloured.
1586	599	100p. Type 599	50	20
1587		200p. Group Two players	1·30	25
1588		300p. Group Three players	1·80	35
1589		400p. Group Four players	2·40	45
MS1590		89×60 mm. 700p. black and flesh	5·00	4·75

DESIGN: (39×26 mm) 700p. River Plate Stadium.

600 Hooded Siskin

1978. Inter-American Philatelic Exhibition. Multicoloured.
1591		50p.+50p. Type 600	2·10	1·50
1592		100p.+100p. Double-collared seedeater	2·30	1·50
1593		150p.+150p. Saffron-cowled blackbird	3·25	2·20
1594		200p.+200p. Vermilion flycatcher	3·50	2·50
1595		500p.+500p. Great kiskadee	7·50	6·00

601 Young Tree with Support

1978. Technical Co-operation among Developing Countries Conference, Buenos Aires.
| 1596 | 601 | 100p. multicoloured | 65 | 20 |

602 River Plate Stadium

1978. Argentina's Victory in World Cup Football Championship. Sheet 88×60 mm.
| MS1597 | 602 | 1000p. black, stone and red | 6·25 | 6·00 |

603 Bank Emblems of 1878 and 1978

1978. Centenary of Bank of Buenos Aires.
| 1598 | 603 | 100p. multicoloured | 65 | 20 |

604 General Manuel Savio and Steel Production

1978. 30th Death Anniv of General Manuel Savio (director of military manufacturing).
| 1599 | 604 | 100p. multicoloured | 65 | 20 |

605 San Martin

1978. Birth Bicentenary of Gen. San Martin.
| 1600 | 605 | 2000p. green | 7·50 | 45 |
| 1600a | 605 | 10000p. blue | 11·50 | 60 |

606 Numeral

1978
1601	606	150p. blue and light blue	65	25
1602	606	180p. blue and light blue	65	25
1603	606	200p. blue and light blue	60	25

607 Chessboard, Pawn and Queen

1978. 23rd Chess Olympiad, Buenos Aires.
| 1604 | 607 | 200p. multicoloured | 6·25 | 95 |

608 Argentine Flag supporting Globe

1978. 12th Int Cancer Congress, Buenos Aires.
| 1605 | 608 | 200p. multicoloured | 1·40 | 25 |

609 "Correct Franking"

1978. Postal Publicity.
1606	609	20p. blue	25	10
1607	-	30p. green	40	15
1608	-	50p. red	65	15

DESIGN—VERT: 30p. "Collect postage stamps". HORIZ: 50p. "Indicate the correct post code".

610 Push-pull Tug

1978. 20th Anniv of Argentine River Fleet. Multicoloured.
1609		100p. Type 610	50	20
1610		200p. Tug *Legador*	90	25
1611		300p. Tug *Rio Parana Mini*	1·30	35
1612		400p. River passenger ship *Ciudad de Parana*	1·80	35

611 Bahia Blanca and Arms

1978. 150th Anniv of Bahia Blanca.
| 1613 | 611 | 200p. multicoloured | 90 | 35 |

612 *To Spain* (Arturo Dresco)

1978. Visit of King and Queen of Spain.
| 1614 | 612 | 300p. multicoloured | 5·00 | 60 |

613 Stained-glass Window, San Isidro Cathedral, Buenos Aires

1978. Christmas.
| 1615 | 613 | 200p. multicoloured | 1·10 | 25 |

614 *Chacabuco Slope* (Pedro Subercaseaux)

1978. Birth Bicent of General Jose de San Martin.
| 1616 | 614 | 500p. Type 614 | 3·25 | 45 |
| 1617 | | 1000p. *The Embrace of Maipo* (Pedro Subercaseaux) (vert) | 6·25 | 60 |

615 San Martin Stamp of 1877 and U.P.U. Emblem

1979. Cent of Argentine Membership of U.P.U.
| 1618 | 615 | 200p. blue, black & brn | 90 | 20 |

616 Mariano Moreno (revolutionary)

1979. Celebrities.
| 1619 | 616 | 200p. yellow, blk & red | 90 | 20 |
| 1620 | - | 200p. blue, blk & dp bl | 90 | 20 |

DESIGNS: No. 1620, Adolfo Alsina (statesman).

617 *Still Life* (Ernesto de la Carcova)

1979. Argentine Paintings. Multicoloured.
| 1621 | | 200p. Type 617 | 75 | 25 |
| 1622 | | 300p. *The Washer-woman* (F. Brughetti) | 1·50 | 45 |

618 Balcarce Antenna and Radio Waves

1979. Third Inter-American Telecommunications Conference.
| 1623 | 618 | 200p. multicoloured | 1·00 | 35 |

619 Rosette

1979
1624	619	240p. blue and brown	65	25
1625	619	260p. blue and black	65	25
1626	619	290p. blue and brown	75	25
1627	619	310p. blue and purple	75	25
1628	619	350p. blue and red	1·00	25
1629	619	450p. blue and ultram	90	25
1630	619	600p. blue and green	90	25
1631	619	700p. blue and black	1·10	25
1632	619	800p. blue and orange	75	25
1632a	619	1100p. blue and grey	1·60	25
1632b	619	1500p. blue and black	90	2·40
1632c	619	1700p. blue and green	90	25

620 Olives

1979. Agricultural Products. Multicoloured.
1633		100p. Type 620	75	45
1634		200p. Tea	1·00	60
1635		300p. Sorghum	1·90	70
1636		400p. Flax	2·10	95

621 "75" and Symbol

1979. 75th Anniv of Argentine Automobile Club.
1637 **621** 200p. multicoloured 65 30

622 Laurel Leaves
and Army Emblem

1979. Naming of Village Subteniente Berdina, Tucuman.
1638 **622** 200p. multicoloured 70 30

623 Wheat Exchange and
Emblem

1979. 125th Anniv of Wheat Exchange, Buenos Aires.
1639 **623** 200p. blue, gold & black 65 30

624 *Uruguay* (sail/steam gunboat)

1979. Navy Day.
1640 **624** 250p. multicoloured 1·50 60

1979. Army Day. As T **390.** Multicoloured.
1641 200p. Trooper of Mounted
Chasseurs, 1817 1·80 45

625 *Comodoro Rivadavia* (hydrographic
survey ship)

1979. Naval Hydrographic Service.
1642 **625** 250p. multicoloured 1·50 60

626 Tree and Man
Symbol

1979. Ecology Day.
1643 **626** 250p. multicoloured 1·00 35

627 SPAD XIII and Vicente
Almandos

1979. Air Force Day.
1644 **627** 250p. multicoloured 1·30 35

628 *Military Occupation of
Rio Negro by Gen. Julio A.
Roca's Expedition* (detail, J. M.
Blanes)

1979. Centenary of Conquest of the Desert.
1645 **628** 250p. multicoloured 1·30 35

629 Caravel *Magdalena*

1979. "Buenos Aires '80" International Stamp Exhibition.
Multicoloured.
1646 400p.+400p. Type **629** 6·25 3·75
1647 500p.+500p. Three-masted
sailing ship 7·50 4·25
1648 600p.+600p. Corvette *Descu-
bierta* 10·50 8·75
1649 1500p.+1500p. Yacht *Fortuna* 25·00 13·00

630 Rowland Hill

1979. Death Centenary of Sir Rowland Hill.
1650 **630** 300p. black, grey & red 1·00 35

631 Francisco de
Viedma y Narvaez
Monument (A. Funes
and J. Agosta)

1979. Bicentenary of Founding of Viedma and Carmen
de Patagones Towns.
1651 **631** 300p. multicoloured 1·50 35

632 Pope Paul VI

1979. Election of Pope John Paul I.
1652 **632** 500p. black 1·80 45
1653 – 500p. black 1·80 45
DESIGN: No. 1653, Pope John Paul I.

633 Molinas Church

1979. Churches. Multicoloured.
1654 100p.+50p. Purmamarca Church 50 20
1655 200p.+100p. Type **633** 75 25
1656 300p.+150p. Animana Church 1·10 45
1657 400p.+200p. San Jose de Lules
Church 1·60 70

1979. 75th Anniv of Rosario Philatelic Society. No.
1545 optd **75 ANIV. SOCIEDAD FILATELICA DE
ROSARIO.**
1658 200p. blue and black 1·10 35

635 Children's Faces,
and Sun on Map of
Argentina

1979. Resettlement Policy.
1659 **635** 300p. yellow, black & bl 1·30 45

636 Stained-glass Window,
Salta Cathedral

1979. Christmas.
1660 **636** 300p. multicoloured 1·10 35

637 Institute Emblem

1979. Centenary of Military Geographical Institute.
1661 **637** 300p. multicoloured 1·30 45

638 General Mosconi and Oil Rig

1979. Birth Centenary of General Enrique Mosconi.
1662 **638** 1000p. blue and black 2·75 85

639 Buenos Aires 3p. Stamp
of 1858

1979. Prenfil 80 International Exhibition of Philatelic
Literature and Journalism, Buenos Aires. Four sheets
89×60 mm containing designs as T **639**.
MS1663 (a) 250p.+250p. black, stone
and vermilion; (b) 750p.+750p. flesh
and black; (c) 1000p.+1000p. multi-
coloured; (d) 2000p.+2000p. black,
green and vermilion 32·00 30·00
DESIGNS—VERT: 750p. Rowland Hill; 2000p. International
Year of the Child emblem. HORIZ: 1000p. Argentine 5c.
Columbus stamp of 1892.

640 Rotary Emblem and
Globe

1979. 75th Anniv of Rotary International.
1664 **640** 300p. multicoloured 3·25 60

641 Girl with Ruddy
Ground Doves

1979. International Year of the Child.
1665 **641** 500p. brown, blue & blk 1·40 60
1666 – 1000p. multicoloured 2·75 70
DESIGN: 1000p. "Family".

642 Guillermo Brown

1980
1667 **642** 5000p. black 9·50 35
1668 **642** 30000p. black and blue 5·75 1·10

643 I.T.U. Emblem and Microphone

1980. Regional Administrative Conference on
Broadcasting, Buenos Aires.
1669 **643** 500p. blue, gold &
ultram 2·50 35

644 Organization of
American States
Emblem

1980. Day of the Americas.
1670 **644** 500p. multicoloured 1·00 30

645 Angel

1980. Centenary of Argentinian Red Cross.
1671 **645** 500p. multicoloured 1·00 30

646 Salto Grande
Hydro-electric Complex

1980. National Development Projects. Multicoloured.
1672 **646** 300p. Type **646** 90 35
1673 300p. Zarate-Brazo Largo
bridge 90 35
1674 300p. Dish aerials, Balcarce 90 35

647 Hipolito Bouchard and Sail Frigate *La
Argentina*

1980. Navy Day.
1675 **647** 500p. multicoloured 1·30 45

648 *Villarino* and Woodcut of San Martin
Theodore by Gericault

1980. Centenary of Return of General Jose de San
Martin's Remains.
1676 **648** 500p. multicoloured 1·30 45

649 *Gazeta de Buenos-Ayres*
and Signature of Dr. Mariano
Moreno (first editor)

1980. Journalists' Day.
1677 **649** 500p. multicoloured 1·00 25

650 Part of Mural

1980. 400th Anniv of Buenos Aires. Sheet 249×103 mm
containing T **650** and similar vert designs forming
a composite design depicting the ceramic mural by
Rodolfo Franco in Cathedral Underground Station.
MS1678 500p.×14 multicoloured 23·00 21·00

651 Soldier feeding Dove

1980. Army Day.
1679 **651** 500p. green, blk & gold 1·50 45

652 Lt. Gen. Aramburu

1980. Tenth Death Anniv of Lt. Gen. Pedro Eugenio Aramburu.
1680 **652** 500p. yellow and black 1·00 35

653 Gen. Juan Gregorio de Las Heras

1980. National Heroes.
1681 **653** 500p. stone and black 1·00 35
1682 - 500p. yellow, blk & pur 1·00 35
1683 - 500p. mauve and black 1·00 35
DESIGNS: No. 1682, Bernardino Rivadavia; 1683, Brigadier-General Jose Matias Zapiola.

654 University of La Plata

1980. 75th Anniv of La Plata University.
1684 **654** 500p. multicoloured 1·00 30

655 Major Francisco de Arteaga and Avro 504K

1980. Air Force Day.
1685 **655** 500p. multicoloured 1·10 30

656 Flag and "Pencil" Figure

1980. National Census.
1686 **656** 500p. black and blue 2·00 30

657 King Penguin

1980. 75th Anniv of Argentine Presence in South Orkneys and 150th Anniv of Political and Military Command for the Malvinas. Two sheets each 151×174 mm containing T 657 and similar vert designs. Multicoloured.
MS1687 Two sheets (a) 150p.×12
 Centre two stamps depict South
 Orkneys Naval Station; (b) 500p.×12
 Centre two stamps depict "Puerto
 Soledad 1829" by Luisa Vernet 44·00 41·00

658 Congress Emblem

1980. National Marian Congress, Mendoza.
1688 **658** 700p. multicoloured 1·50 35

659 Heart pierced by Cigarette

1980. Anti-smoking Campaign.
1689 **659** 700p. multicoloured 1·60 35

660 Part of Mural

1980. Buenos Aires 80 International Stamp Exhibition. Sheet 251×105 mm containing T **660** and similar vert designs forming a composite design depicting the ceramic mural by Alfredo Guido in the 9th July Underground Station.
MS1690 500p.×14 multicoloured 20·00 19·00

661 Radio Antenna and Call Sign

1980. Radio Amateurs.
1691 **661** 700p. blue, black & green 1·40 35

662 Academy Emblem

1980. 50th Anniv of Technical Military Academy.
1692 **662** 700p. multicoloured 1·40 35

663 Commemorative Medallion

1980. Christmas. 150th Anniv of Appearance of Holy Virgin to St. Catherine Laboure.
1693 **663** 700p. multicoloured 1·40 35

664 Plan of Lujan Cathedral and Outline of Virgin

1980. Christmas. 350th Anniv of Appearance of Holy Virgin at Lujan.
1694 **664** 700p. green and brown 1·40 35

665 Simon Bolivar

1980. 150th Death Anniv of Simon Bolivar.
1695 **665** 700p. multicoloured 1·40 35

666 Football and Flags of Competing Nations

1981. Gold Cup Football Competition, Montevideo.
1696 **666** 1000p. multicoloured 2·00 35

667 *Lujan Landscape* (Marcos Tiglio)

1981. Paintings. Multicoloured.
1697 1000p. Type **667** 1·60 60
1698 1000p. *Effect of Light on Lines* (Miguel Angel Vidal) 1·60 60

668 Congress Emblem

1981. International Congress on Medicine and Sciences applied to Sport.
1699 **668** 1000p. blue, brown & blk 1·40 35

669 Esperanza Army Base, Antarctica

1981. 20th Anniv of Antarctic Treaty. Multicoloured.
1700 1000p. Type **669** 2·50 70
1701 2000p. Map of Vicecomodoro Marambio Island and De Havilland Twin Otter airplane (59½×25 mm) 4·50 95
1702 2000p. Icebreaker *Almirante Irizar* 4·50 95

670 Military Club

1981. Centenary of Military Club. Multicoloured.
1703 1000p. Type **670** 1·30 35
1704 2000p. Blunderbusses 1·50 45

671 *Minuet* (Carlos E. Pellegrini)

1981. "Espamer '81" International Stamp Exhibition, Buenos Aires (1st issue).
1705 **671** 500p.+250p. purple, gold and brown 1·40 70
1706 - 700p.+350p. green, gold and brown 2·00 1·20
1707 - 800p.+400p. brown, gold and deep brown 2·10 1·50
1708 - 1000p.+500p. mult 2·75 2·10

DESIGNS: 700p. *La Media Cana* (Carlos Morel); 800p. *Cielito* (Carlos E. Pellegrini); 1000p. *El Gato* (Juan Leon Palliere).
 See also Nos. 1719 and 1720/1.

672 Juan A. Alvarez de Arenales

1981. Celebrities' Anniversaries.
1709 **672** 1000p. black, yell & brn 1·30 35
1710 - 1000p. blk, pink & lilac 1·30 35
1711 - 1000p. black, pale green and green 1·30 35
DESIGNS: No. 1709, Type **672** (patriot, 150th death anniv); 1710, Felix G. Frias (writer and politician, death centenary); 1711, Jose E. Uriburu (statesman, 150th birth centenary).

1981. 50th Anniv of Bahia Blanca Philatelic and Numismatic Society. No. 1553 optd **50 ANIV DE LA ASOCIACION FILATELICA Y NUMISMATICA DE BAHIA BLANCA.**
1712 1000p. black and yellow 3·25 60

674 World Map divided into Time Zones and Sun

1981. Centenary of Naval Observatory.
1713 **674** 1000p. multicoloured 1·90 45

675 *St. Cayetano* (detail, stained-glass window, San Cayetano Basilica)

1981. 500th Death Anniv of St. Cayetano (founder of Teatino Order).
1714 **675** 1000p. multicoloured 1·30 35

676 Pablo Castaibert and Bleriot XI

1981. Air Force Day.
1715 **676** 1000p. multicoloured 2·10 45

677 First Argentine Blast Furnace, Sierra de Palpala

1981. 22nd Latin American Steel-makers Congress, Buenos Aires.
1716 **677** 1000p. multicoloured 1·10 30

678 Emblem of National Directorate for Special Education

1981. International Year of Disabled People.
1717 **678** 1000p. multicoloured 1·30 30

679 Sperm Whale and Map of Argentina and Antarctica

1981. Campaign against Indiscriminate Whaling.
| 1718 | **679** | 1000p. multicoloured | 9·25 | 60 |

680 "Espamer 81"
Emblem and
15th-century Caravel

1981. "Espamer 81" International Stamp Exhibition,
Buenos Aires (2nd issue).
| 1719 | **680** | 1300p. pink, brn & blk | 1·60 | 60 |

681 San Martin at the
Battle of Bailen
(equestrian statuette)

1981. "Espamer 81" International Stamp Exhibition,
Buenos Aires (3rd issue).
| 1720 | **681** | 1000p. multicoloured | 65 | 30 |
| 1721 | **681** | 1500p. multicoloured | 90 | 35 |

682 Argentine Army
Emblem

1981. Argentine Army. 175th Anniv of Infantry Regiment
No. 1 "Patricios". Multicoloured.
| 1722 | | 1500p. Type **682** | 75 | 35 |
| 1723 | | 1500p. "Patricios" badge | 75 | 35 |

1981. Philatelic Services Course, Postal Union of the
Americas and Spain Technical Training School,
Buenos Aires. Optd **CURSO SUPERIOR DE
ORGANIZACION DE SERVICIOS FILATELICOS-
UPAE-BUENOS AIRES-1981.**
| 1724 | **680** | 1300p. pink, brn & blk | 2·50 | 45 |

684 Football

1981. Espamer 81 International Stamp Exhibition, Buenos
Aires (4th issue). Sheet 137×130 mm containing T
684 and similar vert designs. Multicoloured.
MS1725 2000p. Type **684**; 3000p.
Tackle; 5000p. Dribbling; 15000p.
Goalkeeper 12·50 12·00

685 "Patacon" (one peso
piece)

1981. Centenary of First Argentine Coins.
| 1726 | **685** | 2000p. silver, blk & pur | 90 | 25 |
| 1727 | – | 3000p. gold, black & bl | 1·10 | 35 |
DESIGN: 3000p. Argentine oro (five pesos piece).

686 Stained-glass
Window, Church of
Our Lady of Mercy,
Tucuman

1981. Christmas.
| 1728 | **686** | 1500p. multicoloured | 3·75 | 85 |

687 "Drive Carefully"

1981. Road Safety. Multicoloured.
1729		1000p. "Observe traffic lights"	2·50	60
1730		2000p. Type **687**	1·30	70
1731		3000p. Zebra Crossing ("Cross at the white lines") (horiz)	1·90	75
1732		4000p. Headlights ("Don't dazzle") (horiz)	2·10	85

688 Francisco Luis
Bernardez

1982. Authors. Multicoloured.
1733		1000p. Type **688**	2·50	60
1734		2000p. Lucio V. Mansilla	1·30	65
1735		3000p. Conrado Nale Roxlo	1·90	85
1736		4000p. Victoria Ocampo	2·50	95

689 Emblem

1982. 22nd American Air Force Commanders Conference,
Buenos Aires.
| 1737 | **689** | 2000p. multicoloured | 2·00 | 45 |

690 Dr. Robert Koch

1982. 25th World Tuberculosis Conf, Buenos Aires.
| 1738 | **690** | 2000p. brown, red & blk | 1·90 | 45 |

691 Pre-Columbian Artwork
and Signature of Hernando
de Lerma (founder)

1982. 400th Anniv of Salta City.
| 1739 | **691** | 2000p. green, blk & gold | 2·50 | 45 |
MS1740 89×60 mm. **691** 5000p. green,
black and gold (39×26 mm) 5·00 4·75

1982. Argentine Invasion of the Falkland Islands. Optd
LAS MALVINAS SON ARGENTINAS.
| 1741 | **619** | 1700p. blue and green | 1·00 | 35 |

693 Poseidon with Trophies of War
(sculpture) and Naval Centre Arms

1982. Centenary of Naval Centre.
| 1742 | **693** | 2000p. multicoloured | 1·30 | 45 |

694 Chorisia
speciosa

1982. Flowers. Multicoloured.
1743		200p. Zinnia peruviana	50	15
1744		300p. Ipomoea purpurea	50	15
1745		400p. Tillandsia aeranthos	50	15
1746		500p. Type **694**	50	15
1747		800p. Oncidium bifolium	50	15
1748		1000p. Erythrina crista-galli	50	15
1749		2000p. Jacaranda mimosifolia	55	15
1750		3000p. Bauhinia candicans	1·00	35
1751		5000p. Tecoma stans	1·00	35
1752		10000p. Tabebuia ipe	1·80	35
1753		20000p. Passiflora coerulea	1·90	35
1754		30000p. Aristolochia littoralis	2·75	60
1755		50000p. Oxalis enneaphylla	5·25	85

695 Juan C. Sanchez

1982. Tenth Death Anniv of Lt. Gen. Juan C. Sanchez.
| 1761 | **695** | 5000p. multicoloured | 1·50 | 35 |

696 Don Luis Verne (first
Commander)

1982. 153rd Anniv of Political and Military Command for
the Malvinas.
| 1762 | **696** | 5000p. black and brown | 2·50 | 85 |
| 1763 | – | 5000p. light bl, blk & bl | 1·90 | 60 |
DESIGN (82×28 mm): No. 1763, Map of the South Atlantic
Islands.

697 Pope John Paul II

1982. Papal Visit.
| 1764 | **697** | 5000p. multicoloured | 3·25 | 85 |

698 San Martin

1982
| 1765 | **698** | 50000p. brown and red | 12·00 | 1·40 |

699 The Organ Player
(detail, Aldo Severi)

1982. Paintings. Multicoloured.
| 1766 | | 2000p. Type **699** | 1·30 | 40 |
| 1767 | | 3000p. Flowers (Santiago Cogorno) | 1·40 | 45 |

700 Gen. de Sombras
(Sylvia Sieburger)

1982. "Argentine Philately". Tapestries. Multicoloured.
1768		1000p.+500p. Type **700**	75	60
1769		2000p.+1000p. Inter-pretation of a Rectangle (Silke Haupt)	90	70
1770		3000p.+1500p. Canal (detail, Beatriz Bongliani) (horiz)	1·00	85
1771		4000p.+2000p. Pueblito de Tilcara (Tana Sachs) (horiz)	1·10	95

701 Petrol Pump and
Sugar Cane

1982. Alconafta (petrol-alcohol mixture) Campaign.
| 1772 | **701** | 2000p. multicoloured | 1·40 | 35 |

1982. 50th Anniv of Tucuman Philatelic Society. No. 1751
optd **50 ANIVERSARIO SOCIEDAD FILATELICA DE
TUCUMAN.**
| 1773 | | 5000p. multicoloured | 3·75 | 1·40 |

703 Belt Buckle with
Argentine Scout Emblem

1982. 75th Anniv of Boy Scout Movement.
| 1774 | **703** | 5000p. multicoloured | 3·50 | 60 |

704 Map of Africa
showing Namibia

1982. Namibia Day.
| 1775 | **704** | 5000p. multicoloured | 1·50 | 35 |

705 Rio Tercero Nuclear
Power Station

1982. Atomic Energy. Multicoloured.
| 1776 | | 2000p. Type **705** | 65 | 15 |
| 1777 | | 2000p. Control room of Rio Tercero power station | 65 | 15 |

706 Our Lady of Itati,
Corrientes

1982. Churches and Cathedrals of the North-east
Provinces.
1778	**706**	2000p. green and black	90	55
1779	–	3000p. grey and purple	1·00	60
1780	–	5000p. blue and purple	1·60	65
1781	–	10000p. brown and black	2·50	85
DESIGNS—VERT: 3000p. Resistencia Cathedral, Chaco.
HORIZ: 5000p. Formosa Cathedral; 10000p. Ruins of San
Ignacio, Misiones.

707 *Sidereal Tension* (M. A. Agatiello)

1982. Art. Multicoloured.
1782		2000p. Type **707**	1·40	60
1783		3000p. *Sugerencia II* (E. MacEntyre)	1·50	65
1784		5000p. *Storm* (Carlos Silva)	2·10	70

708 Games Emblem and Santa Fe Bridge

1982. 2nd "Southern Cross" Games, Rosario and Santa Fe.
1785	**708**	2000p. blue and black	90	35

709 Volleyball

1982. Tenth Men's Volleyball World Championship.
1786	**709**	2000p. multicoloured	50	25
1787	**709**	5000p. multicoloured	1·00	35

710 Road Signs

1982. 50th Anniv of National Roads Administration.
1788	**710**	5000p. multicoloured	1·00	30

711 Monument to the Army of the Andes

1982. Centenary of *Los Andes* Newspaper.
1789	**711**	5000p. multicoloured	90	25

712 La Plata Cathedral

1982. Centenary of La Plata. Multicoloured.
1790		5000p. Type **712**	1·40	35
1791		5000p. Municipal Palace	1·40	35

MS1792 120×115 mm. 2500p.×6 (a) Cathedral; (b) Allegorical head (top); (c) Observatory; (d) Municipal Palace; (e) Allegorical head (bottom); (f) Natural Sciences Museum ... 4·00 3·75

713 First Oil Rig

1982. 75th Anniv of Discovery of Oil in Comodoro Rivadavia.
1793	**713**	5000p. multicoloured	1·90	35

714 Dr. Carlos Pellegrini (founder) (after J. Sorolla y Bastida)

1982. Cent of Buenos Aires Jockey Club. Multicoloured.
1794		5000p. Jockey Club emblem	1·50	35
1795		5000p. Type **714**	1·50	35

715 Cross of St. Damian, Assisi

1982. 800th Birth Anniv of St. Francis of Assisi.
1796	**715**	5000p. multicoloured	2·10	35

716 "St. Vincent de Paul" (stained-glass window, Our Lady of the Miraculous Medal, Buenos Aires)

1982. Christmas.
1797	**716**	3000p. multicoloured	3·25	60

717 Pedro B. Palacios

1982. Authors. Each red and green.
1798		1000p. Type **717**	40	10
1799		2000p. Leopoldo Marechal	50	15
1800		3000p. Delfina Bunge de Galvez	65	20
1801		4000p. Manuel Galvez	75	25
1802		5000p. Evaristo Carriego	90	30

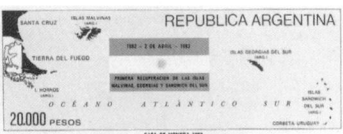

718 Argentine Flag and Map of South Atlantic Islands (image scaled to 58% of original size)

1983. First Anniv of Argentine Invasion of Falkland Islands.
1803	**718**	20000p. multicoloured	2·50	85

719 Sitram (automatic message transmission service) Emblem

1983. Information Technology. Multicoloured.
1804	**719**	5000p. Type **719**	2·00	95
1805		5000p. Red Arpac (data communications system) emblem	2·00	95

720 Naval League Emblem

1983. Navy Day. 50th Anniv of Naval League.
1806	**720**	5000p. multicoloured	1·00	35

721 Allegorical Figure (Victor Rebuffo)

1983. 25th Anniv of National Arts Fund.
1807	**721**	5000p. multicoloured	75	25

722 Golden Saloon

1983. 75th Anniv of Columbus Theatre, Buenos Aires. Multicoloured.
1808		5000p. Type **722**	1·10	60
1809		10000p. Stage curtain	1·60	70

723 Marbles

1983. Argentine Philately. Children's Games (1st series). Multicoloured.
1810		20c.+10c. Type **723**	50	30
1811		30c.+15c. Skipping	65	35
1812		50c.+25c. Hopscotch	1·40	45
1813		1p.+50c. Boy with kite	1·80	70
1814		2p.+1p. Boy with spinning top	2·50	95

See also Nos. 1870/4.

724 Maned Wolf

1983. Protected Animals (1st series). Multicoloured.
1815		1p. Type **724**	1·60	35
1816		1p.50 Pampas deer	2·40	45
1817		2p. Giant anteater	2·50	60
1818		2p.50 Jaguar	3·00	70

See also Nos 1883/87.

1983. Flowers. As T **694** but inscr in new currency. Multicoloured.
1819		5c. Type **694**	75	20
1820		10c. Erythrina crista-galli	25	10
1821		20c. Jacaranda mimosifolia	25	10
1822		30c. Bauhinia candicans	65	20
1823		40c. Eichhornia crassipes	40	10
1824		50c. Tecoma stans	25	10
1825		1p. Tabebuia ipe	50	10
1826		1p.80 Mutisia retusa	40	10
1827		2p. Passiflora coerulea	50	10
1828		3p. Aristolochia littoralis	65	10
1829		5p. Oxalis enneaphylla	90	15
1830		10p. Alstroemeria aurantiaca	1·50	25
1831		20p. Ipomoea purpurea	65	10
1832		30p. Embothrium coccineum	3·25	25
1833		50p. Tillandsia aeranthos	90	25
1834		100p. Oncidium bifolium	2·50	25
1835		300p. Cassia carnaval	2·75	70

725 Founding of City of Catamarca (detail, Luis Varela Lezana)

1983. 300th Anniv of San Fernando del Valle de Catamarca.
1836	**725**	1p. multicoloured	65	30

726 Brother Mamerto Esquiu

1983. Death Centenary of Brother Mamerto Esquiu, Bishop of Cordoba.
1837	**726**	1p. black, red and grey	65	30

727 Bolivar (painting by Herrera Toro after engraving by C. Turner)

1983. Birth Bicentenary of Simon Bolivar.
1838	**727**	1p. multicoloured	65	30
1839	–	2p. red and black	1·00	45

DESIGN: 2p. Bolivar (engraving by Kepper).

728 San Martin

1983
1840	**728**	10p. green and black	4·50	60
1841		20p. blue and black	4·00	2·40
1842	**728**	50p. brown and blue	3·50	2·50
1843	–	200p. black and blue	3·25	1·80
1844	–	500p. blue and brown	3·50	85

DESIGNS: 20, 500p. Guillermo Brown; 200p. Manuel Belgrano.

729 Gen. Toribio de Luzuriaga

1983. Birth Bicentenary (1982) of Gen. Toribio de Luzuriaga.
1845	**729**	1p. multicoloured	90	35

730 Grand Bourg House, Buenos Aires

1983. 50th Anniv of Sanmartinian National Institute.
1846	**730**	2p. brown and black	1·00	35

731 Dove and Rotary Emblem

1983. Rotary International South American Regional Conference, Buenos Aires.
| 1847 | **731** | 1p. multicoloured | 1·00 | 35 |

732 Running Track and Games Emblem

1983. Ninth Pan-American Games, Venezuela.
| 1848 | **732** | 1p. red, green & black | 75 | 25 |
| 1849 | - | 2p. multicoloured | 1·00 | 35 |

DESIGN: 2p. Games emblem.

733 W.C.Y. Emblem

1983. World Communications Year (1st issue).
| 1850 | **733** | 2p. multicoloured | 1·00 | 35 |

See also Nos. 1853/6 and 1857.

734 The Squash Peddler (Antonio Berni)

1983. Argentine Paintings. Multicoloured.
| 1851 | 1p. Type **734** | 75 | 25 |
| 1852 | 2p. Figure in Yellow (Luis Seoane) | 1·00 | 35 |

735 Ox-drawn Wagon

1983. World Communications Year (2nd issue). Mail Transport. Multicoloured.
1853	1p. Type **735**	90	45
1854	2p. Horse-drawn mail cart	1·00	60
1855	4p. Locomotive La Portena	1·50	65
1856	5p. Tram	1·60	70

736 Central Post Office, Buenos Aires (Lola Frexas)

1983. World Communications Year (3rd issue).
| 1857 | **736** | 2p. multicoloured | 65 | 30 |

737 Rockhopper Penguin

1983. Fauna and Pioneers of Southern Argentina. Multicoloured.
1858a	2p. Type **737**	65	35
1858b	2p. Wandering albatross	65	35
1858c	2p. Black-browed albatross	65	35
1858d	2p. Macaroni penguin	65	35
1858e	2p. Luis Piedra Buena (after Juan R. Mezzadra)	65	35
1858f	2p. Carlos Maria Moyano (after Mezzadra)	65	35
1858g	2p. Luis Py (after Mezzadra)	65	35
1858h	2p. Augusto Lasserre (after Horacio Alvarez Boero)	65	35
1858i	2p. Light-mantled sooty albatross	65	35
1858j	2p. Leopard seal	65	35
1858k	2p. Crabeater seal	65	35
1858l	2p. Weddell seal	65	35

738 Coin of 1813

1983. Transfer of Presidency.
| 1859 | **738** | 2p. silver, black and blue | 1·00 | 20 |

739 "Christmas Manger" (tapestry by Silke)

1983. Christmas. Multicoloured.
| 1860 | 2p. Type **739** | 95 | 20 |
| 1861 | 3p. Stained-glass window, San Carlos de Bariloche Church | 1·50 | 45 |

740 Printing Cylinder and Newspaper

1984. Centenary of El Dia Newspaper.
| 1862 | **740** | 4p. multicoloured | 75 | 20 |

741 Compass Rose

1984. "Espana 84" (Madrid) and "Argentina 85" (Buenos Aires) International Stamp Exhibitions (1st issue). Multicoloured.
1863	5p.+2p.50 Type **741**	1·30	45
1864	5p.+2p.50 Arms of Spain and Argentine Republic	1·30	45
1865	5p.+2p.50 Arms of Christopher Columbus	1·30	45
1866	5p.+2p.50 Nina	1·30	45
1867	5p.+2p.50 Pinta	1·30	45
1868	5p.+2p.50 Santa Maria	1·30	45

See also Nos. 1906/10, 1917/18 and 1920/4.

742 College

1984. Centenary of Alejandro Carbo Teacher Training College, Cordoba.
| 1869 | **742** | 10p. multicoloured | 75 | 30 |

1984. Argentine Philately. Children's Games (2nd series). As T **723**. Multicoloured.
1870	2p.+1p. Blind man's buff	65	35
1871	3p.+1p.50 Girls throwing hoop	70	40
1872	4p.+2p. Leap frog	75	55
1873	5p.+2p.50 Boy rolling hoop	90	60
1874	6p.+3p. Ball and stick	1·10	85

743 Rowing and Basketball

1984. Olympic Games, Los Angeles. Multicoloured.
1875	5p. Type **743**	50	35
1876	5p. Weightlifting and discus	50	35
1877	10p. Cycling and swimming	90	45
1878	10p. Pole vault and fencing	90	45

744 Wheat

1984. Food Supplies. Multicoloured.
1879	10p. Type **744** (18th F.A.O. Latin American Regional Conference, Buenos Aires)	1·00	45
1880	10p. Sunflowers (World Food Day)	1·00	45
1881	10p. Maize (3rd National Maize Congress, Pergamino)	1·00	45

745 Stock Exchange

1984. Centenary of Rosario Stock Exchange.
| 1882 | **745** | 10p. multicoloured | 90 | 45 |

1984. Protected Animals (2nd series). As T **724**. Multicoloured.
1883	20p. Brazilian merganser	1·60	45
1884	20p. Black-fronted piping guan	1·60	45
1885	20p. Hooded grebes	1·60	45
1886	20p. Vicunas	1·60	45
1887	20p. Chilean guemal	1·60	45

746 Festival Emblem

1984. First Latin American Theatre Festival, Cordoba.
| 1888 | **746** | 20p. multicoloured | 65 | 35 |

747 Apostles' Communion (detail, Fra Angelico)

1984. 50th Anniv of Buenos Aires International Eucharist Congress.
| 1889 | **747** | 20p. multicoloured | 75 | 45 |

748 Antonio Oneto and Railway Station (Puerto Deseado)

1984. City Centenaries. Multicoloured.
| 1890 | 20p. Type **748** | 1·30 | 45 |
| 1891 | 20p. 19th-century view and sail/steam corvette Parana (Ushuaia) | 1·30 | 45 |

749 Glacier

1984. World Heritage Site. Los Glaciares National Park. Multicoloured.
| 1892 | 20p. Glacier (different) | 1·10 | 35 |
| 1893 | 30p. Type **749** | 1·90 | 45 |

1984. 50th Anniv of Buenos Aires Philatelic Centre. No. 1830 optd **1934–50°ANIVERSARIO-1984 CENTRO FILATELICO BUENOS-AIRES**.
| 1894 | 10p. multicoloured | 75 | 55 |

751 Jesus and the Star (Diego Aguero)

1984. Christmas. Multicoloured.
1895	20p. Type **751**	1·00	40
1896	30p. The Three Kings (Leandro Ruiz)	1·30	45
1897	50p. The Holy Family (Maria Castillo) (vert)	1·40	55

752 Sheds (La Boca) (Marcos Borio)

1984. Argentine Paintings. Multicoloured.
1898	20p. Type **752**	90	40
1899	20p. View of the Zoo (Fermin Eguia) (horiz)	90	40
1900	20p. Floodlit Congress Building (Francisco Travieso)	90	40

753 Angel J. Carranza (historian, 150th)

1985. Birth Anniversaries.
1901	**753**	10p. deep blue & blue	75	35
1902	-	20p. deep brown & brn	90	45
1903	-	30p. deep blue & blue	1·00	60
1904	-	40p. black and green	1·60	65

DESIGNS: 20p. Estanislao del Campo (poet, 150th); 30p. Jose Hernandez (journalist, 150th); 40p. Vicente Lopez y Planes (President of Argentine Confederation 1827–28, birth bicent).

754 Guemes and "Infernal" (soldier)

1985. Birth Bicentenary of General Martin Miguel de Guemes (Independence hero).
| 1905 | **754** | 30p. multicoloured | 50 | 30 |

755 Teodoro Fels's Bleriot XI Gnome

1985. "Argentina '85" International Stamp Exhibition, Buenos Aires (2nd issue). First Airmail Flights. Multicoloured.
1906	20p. Type **755** (Buenos Aires–Montevideo, 1917)	40	20
1907	40p. Junkers F-13L (Cordoba–Villa Dolores, 1925)	65	35
1908	60p. Saint-Exupery's Latecoere 25 (first Bahia Blanca–Comodoro Rivadavia, 1929)	1·00	40
1909	80p. Graf Zeppelin airship (Argentina-Germany, 1934)	1·30	60
1910	100p. Consolidated PBY-5A Catalina amphibian (to Argentine Antarctic, 1952)	1·80	70

756 Central Bank

1985. 50th Anniv of Central Bank, Buenos Aires.
1911	756	80p. multicoloured	1·10	35

757 Jose A. Ferreyra and "Munequitas Portenas"

1985. Argentine Film Directors. Multicoloured.
1912	100p. Type **757**	1·30	60
1913	100p. Leopoldo Torre Nilsson and "Martin Fierro"	1·30	60

758 Carlos Gardel
(Hermenegildo Sabat)

1985. 50th Death Anniv of Carlos Gardel (entertainer). Multicoloured.
1914	200p. Type **758**	2·50	70
1915	200p. Carlos Gardel (Carlos Alonso)	2·50	70
1916	200p. Carlos Gardel (Aldo Severi and Martiniano Arce)	2·50	70

759 The Arrival (Pedro Figari)

1985. "Argentina '85" International Stamp Exhibition (3rd issue). Multicoloured.
1917	20c. Type **759**	1·50	60
1918	30c. Mail Coach Square (detail, Cesareo B. de Quiros)	1·80	65
MS1919	146×74 mm. 20c. (29×39 mm), 30c. (39×29 mm) Details of Halt in the Country (Prilidiano Pueyrredon)	6·25	6·00

760 Cover of 1917 Teodoro Fels Flight

1985. "Argentina '85" International Stamp Exhibition (4th issue). Multicoloured.
1920	10c. Type **760**	75	35
1921	10c. Cover of 1925 Cordoba– Villa Dolores flight	75	35
1922	10c. Cover of 1929 Saint- Exupery flight	75	35
1923	10c. Cover of 1934 Graf Zep- pelin flight	75	35
1924	10c. Cover of 1952 Antarctic flight	75	35

1985. Flowers. As T **694** but with currency expressed as "A". Multicoloured.
1930	½c. Oxalis enneaphylla	90	15
1931	1c. Alstroemeria aurantiaca	50	10
1932	2c. Ipomoea purpurea	50	10
1933	3c. Embothrium coccineum	50	10
1934a	5c. Tillandsia aeranthos	50	10
1927	8½c. Erythrina crista-galli	50	10
1935a	10c. Oncidium bifolium	90	15
1936a	20c. Chorisia speciosa	65	35
1937	30c. Cassia carnaval	1·50	60
1938	50c. Zinnnia peruviana	1·90	45
1941	1a. Begonia micranthera var. Hieronymi	2·50	45
1941a	2a. Bauhinia candicans	1·00	30
1942	5a. Gymnocalycium bruchii	6·25	4·25
1942a	10a. Eichhornia crassipes	50	30
1942b	20a. Mutisia retusa	15	10
1942c	50a. Passion flower	50	30
1943	100a. Alstroemeria aurantiaca	65	20
1943a	300a. Ipomoea purpurea	2·00	95
1943b	500a. Embothrium coccineum	3·25	1·50

1943c	1000a. Aristolochia littoralis	1·00	60
1943d	5000a. Erythrina crista-galli	4·75	65
1943e	10000a. Jacaranda mimosifolia	7·50	4·75

No. 1927 is 15×23 mm, the remainder 22×32 mm.

761 Woman with Bird (Juan del Prete)

1985. Argentine Paintings. Multicoloured.
1944	20c. Type **761**	1·50	60
1945	30c. Illuminated Fruits (Fortu- nato Lacamera)	1·80	70

762 Musical Bow

1985. Traditional Musical Instruments. Multicoloured.
1946	20c. Type **762**	1·00	40
1947	20c. Long flute with drum ac- companiment	1·00	40
1948	20c. Frame drum	1·00	40
1949	20c. Pan's flute	1·00	40
1950	20c. Jew's harp	1·00	40

763 Juan Bautista Alberdi (writer)

1985. Anniversaries. Multicoloured.
1951	10c. Type **763** (death centenary (1984))	40	20
1952	20c. Nicolas Avellaneda (President 1874–80, death centenary)	75	35
1953	30c. Brother Luis Beltran (Independence hero, birth bicentenary (1984))	1·10	60
1954	40c. Ricardo Levene (historian) (birth centenary)	2·00	70

764 Roller Skaters

1985. International Youth Year.
1955	**764**	20c. black and blue	1·00	40	
1956	–	30c. multicoloured	1·10	45
MS1957	146×74 mm. 1a. multicol- oured. Imperf			6·25	6·00

DESIGNS: 30c. "Disappointment". 137×66 mm "Halt in the Country" (Prilidiano Pueyrredon).

765 Rothschildia jacobaeae

1985. Argentine Philately. Butterflies.
1958	5c.+2c. Type **765**	1·40	45
1959	10c.+5c. Heliconius erato phyllis	1·50	60
1960	20c.+10c. Precis evarete hilaris	2·10	1·10
1961	25c.+13c. Cyanopepla pretiosa	3·25	1·80
1962	40c.+20c. Papilio androgeus	4·25	2·50

766 Forclaz Windmill (Entre Rios)

1985. Tourism. Argentine Provinces. Multicoloured.
1963	10c. Type **766**	75	20
1964	10c. Sierra de la Ventana (Buenos Aires)	75	20
1965	10c. Potrero de los Funes artificial lake (San Luis)	75	20
1966	10c. Church belfry (North-west Argentina)	75	20
1967	10c. Magellanic penguins, Punta Tombo (Chubut)	75	20
1968	10c. Sea of Mirrors (Cordoba)	75	20

767 Hand holding White Stick

1985. National Campaign for the Prevention of Blindness.
1969	767	10c. multicoloured	65	20

768 Birth of Our Lord (Carlos Cortes)

1985. Christmas. Multicoloured.
1970	10c. Type **768**	65	25
1971	20c. Christmas (Hector Viola)	1·40	70

769 Rio Gallegos Cathedral

1985. Centenary of Rio Gallegos.
1972	769	10c. multicoloured	2·50	60

770 Grape Harvesting

1986. 50th Anniv of Grape Harvest Nat Festival.
1973	770	10c. multicoloured	75	15

771 House of Valentin Alsina (Italian Period)

1986. Buenos Aires Architecture, 1880–1930. Multicoloured.
1974	20c. Type **771**	1·00	45
1975	20c. 1441 Calle Cerrito (French period)	1·00	45
1976	20c. Customs House (Academic period) (horiz)	1·00	45
1977	20c. House, Avenido de Mayo (Art Nouveau)	1·00	45
1978	20c. Isaac Fernandez Blanco Museum (National Restora- tion period) (horiz)	1·00	45

772 Jubany Base

1986. Argentine Antarctic Research. Multicoloured.
1979	10c. Type **772**	1·50	1·00
1980	10c. Kerguelen fur seal	1·50	1·00
1981	10c. Southern sealion	1·50	1·00
1982	10c. General Belgrano Base	1·50	1·00
1983	10c. Pintado petrel	1·50	1·00
1984	10c. Black-browed albatross	1·50	1·00
1985	10c. King penguin	1·50	1·00
1986	10c. Giant petrel	1·50	1·00
1987	10c. Hugo Alberto Acuna (explorer)	1·50	1·00
1988	10c. Magellanic penguin	1·50	1·00
1989	10c. Magellan snipe	1·50	1·00
1990	10c. Capt. Augustin Servando del Castillo (explorer)	1·50	1·00

773 Foundation of Nereid (detail, Lola Mora)

1986. Sculpture. Multicoloured.
1991	20c. Type **773**	1·40	45
1992	30c. Work Song (detail, Rogelio Yrurtia)	1·50	55

774 Dr. Alicia Moreau de Justo (suffragist, d. 1986)

1986. Anniversaries.
1993	**774**	10c. black, yellow & brn	75	35
1994	–	10c. black, turq & blue	75	35
1995	–	30c. black, red & mauve	2·30	1·10

DESIGNS: No. 1994, Dr. Emilio Ravignani (historian, birth centenary); 1995, Indira Gandhi (Prime Minister of India, 1st death anniv).

775 Dr. Francisco Narciso Laprida

1986. Birth Bicentenaries of Independence Heroes. Each brown, yellow and black.
1996	20c. Type **775**	90	45
1997	20c. Brig. Gen. Estanislao Lopez	90	45
1998	20c. Gen. Francisco Ramirez	90	45

776 Namuncura

1986. Birth Centenary of Ceferino Namuncura (first Indian seminary student).
1999	776	20c. multicoloured	1·00	60

777 Drawing by Nazarena Pastor

1986. Argentine Philately. Children's Drawings. Multicoloured.

2000	5c.+2c. Type **777**	40	20
2001	10c.+5c. Girl and boy holding flowers and balloon (Tatiana Valleistein) (horiz)	65	30
2002	20c.+10c. Boy and girl (Juan Manel Flores)	1·00	95
2003	25c.+13c. Town and waterfront (Marcelo E. Pezzuto) (horiz)	1·40	1·20
2004	40c.+20c. Village (Esteban Diehl) (horiz)	2·00	1·80

1986. No. 1825 surch **A0,10.**

2005	10c. on 1p. *Tabebuia ipe*	1·90	85

779 Argentine Team (value top left)

1986. Argentina, World Cup Football Championship (Mexico) Winners. Multicoloured.

2006	75c. Type **779**	2·10	1·80
2007	75c. Argentine team (value top right)	2·10	1·80
2008	75c. Argentine team (value bottom left)	2·10	1·80
2009	75c. Argentine team (value bottom right)	2·10	1·80
2010	75c. Player shooting for goal	2·10	1·80
2011	75c. Player tackling and goalkeeper on ground	2·10	1·80
2012	75c. Player number 11	2·10	1·80
2013	75c. Player number 7	2·10	1·80
2014	75c. Crowd and Argentina player	2·10	1·80
2015	75c. West German player	2·10	1·80
2016	75c. Goalkeeper on ground	2·10	1·80
2017	75c. Footballers' legs	2·10	1·80
2018	75c. Hand holding World Cup trophy	2·10	1·80
2019	75c. Raised arm and crowded stadium	2·10	1·80
2020	75c. People with flags and cameras	2·10	1·80
2021	75c. Player's body and crowd	2·10	1·80

Nos. 2006/13 were printed together *se-tenant* in a sheetlet of eight stamps arranged in two blocks, each block forming a composite design. Nos. 2014/21 were similarly arranged in a second sheetlet.

780 Municipal Building

1986. Centenary of San Francisco City.

2022	**780** 20c. multicoloured	90	55

781 Old Railway Station

1986. Centenary of Trelew City.

2023	**781** 20c. multicoloured	90	55

782 Emblem and Colours

1986. Mutualism Day.

2024	**782** 20c. multicoloured	90	55

783 *Primitive Retable* (Aniko Szabo)

1986. Christmas. Multicoloured.

2025	20c. Type **783**	1·60	60
2026	30c. *Everybody's Tree* (Franca Delacqua)	1·90	70

784 St. Rosa of Lima

1986. 400th Birth Anniv of St. Rosa de Lima.

2027	**784** 50c. multicoloured	2·50	1·20

785 Municipal Building

1986. Anniversaries. Multicoloured.

2028	20c. Type **785** (bicentenary of Rio Cuarto city)	1·50	45
2029	20c. Palace of Justice, Cordoba (50th anniv)	1·50	45

786 Marine Biology

1987. 25th Anniv of Antarctic Treaty. Multicoloured.

2030	20c. Type **786**	1·50	60
2031	30c. Study of native birds	2·10	70
MS2032	159×89 mm. As Nos. 2030/1 but each 39×49 mm	9·50	8·75

787 Emblem

1987. Centenary of National Mortgage Bank.

2033	**787** 20c. yellow, brown & blk	1·30	70

788 Stylized Pine Trees

1987. Argentine Co-operative Movement.

2034	**788** 20c. multicoloured	1·30	70

789 Pope

1987. Second Visit of Pope John Paul II.

2035	**789** 20c. blue and red	65	35
2036	- 80c. brown and green	2·50	1·20
MS2037	160×90 mm. 1a. multicoloured (34×45 mm)	4·50	4·25

DESIGNS: 80c. Pope in robes with Crucifix; 1a. Pope and children.

790 Flag forming "PAZ" (peace)

1987. International Peace Year.

2038	**790** 20c. blue, dp blue & blk	1·10	35
2039	- 30c. multicoloured	1·20	45

DESIGN: 30c. Pigeon (sculpture, Victor Kaniuka).

791 Polo Players (Alejandro Moy)

1987. World Polo Championships, Palermo.

2040	**791** 20c. multicoloured	1·50	35

792 *Supplicant* (Museum of Natural Sciences, La Plata)

1987. 14th International Museums Council General Conference, Buenos Aires. Multicoloured.

2041	25c. Conference emblem	75	35
2042	25c. Shield of Potosi (National History Museum, Buenos Aires)	75	35
2043	25c. Statue of St. Bartholomew (Enrique Larreta Spanish Art Museum, Buenos Aires)	75	35
2044	25c. Cudgel with animal design (Patagonia Museum, San Carlos de Bariloche)	75	35
2045	25c. Type **792**	75	35
2046	25c. Grate from Argentine Confederation House (Entre Rios Historical Museum, Parana)	75	35
2047	25c. Statue of St. Joseph (Northern Historical Museum, Salta)	75	35
2048	25c. Funeral urn (Provincial Archaeological Museum, Santiago del Estero)	75	35

793 Pillar Box

1987. No value expressed. (a) Inscr "C" and "TARIFA INTERNA/HASTA 10 GRAMOS".

2049	**793** (18c.) red, black & yell	1·60	45

(b) Inscr "C" and "TARIFA INTERNA/DE 11 A 20 GRAMOS".

2050	(33c.) black, yell & grn	1·90	60

794 Spotted Metynis (*Metynnis maculatus*)

1987. Argentine Philately. River Fish. Mulicoloured.

2051	10c.+5c. Type **794**	45	15
2052	10c.+5c. Black-finned pearlfish (*Cynolebias nigripinnis*)	45	15
2053	10c.+5c. Solar's leporinus (*Leporinus solarii*)	45	15
2054	10c.+5c. Red-flanked bloodfin (*Aphyocharax rathbuni*)	45	15
2055	10c.+5c. Bronze catfish (*Corydoras aeneus*)	45	15
2056	10c.+5c. Giant hatchetfish (*Thoracocharax securis*)	45	15
2057	10c.+5c. Black-striped pearlfish (*Cynolebias melanotaenia*)	45	15
2058	10c.+5c. Chanchito cichlid (*Cichlasoma facetum*)	45	15
2059	20c.+10c. Silver tetra (*Tetragonopterus argente*)	80	30
2060	20c.+10c. Buenos Aires tetra (*Hemigrammus caudovittatus*)	80	30
2061	20c.+10c. Two-spotted astyanax (*Astyanax bimaculatus*)	80	30
2062	20c.+10c. Black widow tetra (*Gymnocorymbus ternetzi*)	80	30
2063	20c.+10c. Trahira (*Hoplias malabaricus*)	80	30
2064	20c.+10c. Blue-finned tetra (*Aphyocharax rubripinnis*)	80	30
2065	20c.+10c. Agassiz's dwarf cichlid (*Apistogramma agassizi*)	80	30
2066	20c.+10c. Fanning pyrrhulina (*Pyrrhulina rachoviana*)	80	30

795 College Facade and Arms

1987. 300th Anniv of Montserrat College, Cordoba and Montserrat/87 National Stamp Exhibition. Sheet 75×110 mm. Imperf.

MS2067	**795** 1a. multicoloured	2·50	2·40

796 Jorge Luis Borges (writer)

1987. Anniversaries. Multicoloured.

2068	20c. Type **796** (1st death anniv)	65	15
2069	30c. Armando Discepolo, (dramatist and theatre director, birth cent)	75	25
2070	50c. Dr Carlos Alberto Pueyrredon (historian, birth centenary)	90	40

797 Drawing by Leonardo da Vinci

1987. "The Post, a Medium for Communication and Prevention of Addictions".

2071	**797** 30c. multicoloured	1·90	45

798 *The Sower* (Julio Vanzo)

1987. 75th Anniv of Argentine Farmers' Union.

2072	**798** 30c. multicoloured	1·30	45

799 Basketball

1987. Tenth Pan-American Games, Indianapolis. Multicoloured.

2073	20c. Type **799**	75	35
2074	30c. Rowing	90	40
2075	50c. Dinghies	1·00	45

800 Col. Maj. Ignacio Alvarez Thomas

1987. Anniversaries. Multicoloured.
2076	25c. Type **800** (birth bicent)	90	35
2077	25c. Col. Manuel Dorrego (birth bicentenary)	90	35
2078	50c. 18th-century Spanish map of Falkland Islands (death bicentenary of Jacinto de Altolaguirre, governor of Islands) (horiz)	1·80	60
2079	50c. *Signing the Accord* (Rafael del Villar) (50th anniv of House of Accord Museum, San Nicolas) (horiz)	1·80	60

801 Children as Nurse and Mother

1987. UNICEF Child Vaccination Campaign.
2080	**801**	30c. multicoloured	90	30

802 Balloon

1987. Anniversaries. Multicoloured.
2081	50c. Type **802** (50th anniv of LRA National Radio)	1·30	70
2082	50c. Celendonio Galvan Moreno (first editor) (50th anniv of *Postas Argentinas* magazine)	1·30	70
2083	1a. Dr. Jose Marco del Pont (founder) (centenary of Argentine Philatelic Society)	2·50	95

803 *Nativity* (tapestry, Alisia Frega)

1987. Christmas. Multicoloured.
2084	50c. Type **803**	1·00	35
2085	1a. Doves and flowers (tapestry, Silvina Trigos)	2·10	95

804 Crested Oropendola, Baritu National Park

1987. National Parks (1st series). Multicoloured.
2086	50c. Type **804**	2·30	60
2087	50c. Otter, Nahuel Huapi National Park	2·30	60
2088	50c. Night monkey, Rio Pilcomayo National Park	2·30	60
2089	50c. Kelp goose, Tierra del Fuego National Park	2·30	60
2090	50c. Alligator, Iguazu National Park	2·30	60

See also Nos. 2150/4, 2222/6 and 2295/9.

805 *Caminito* (Jose Canella)

1988. Historical and Tourist Sites. Multicoloured.
2090a	3a. *Purmamarca* (Nestor Martin) (33×22 mm)	1·10	45
2091	5a. Type **805**	4·00	2·00
2092	10a. *Old Almacen* (Jose Canella) (A)	8·25	4·25
2092a	10a. *Old Almacen* (Jose Canella) (B)	2·10	95
2095	20a. *Ushuaia* (Nestor Martin) (vert)	7·50	3·00
2099	50a. Type **805**	2·10	95

10a. A. Inscr "Viejo Almacen". B. Inscr "El Viejo Almacen".

806 Minstrel singing in a Grocer's Shop (Carlos Morel)

1988. Argentine Paintings. Multicoloured.
2105	1a. Type **806**	1·50	60
2106	1a. *Curuzu* (detail, Candido Lopez)	1·50	60

807 Hand arranging Coloured Cubes

1988. Argentine–Brazil Economic Co-operation.
2107	**807**	1a. multicoloured	1·00	45

808 St. Anne's Chapel, Corrientes

1988. 400th Annivs of Corrientes and Alta Gracia. Multicoloured.
2108	1a. Type **808**	1·50	60
2109	1a. Alta Gracia church	1·50	60

809 Men Stacking Sacks

1988. Labour Day. Details of mural *Cereals* (Nueve de Julio station, Buenos Aires underground railway). Multicoloured.
2110	50c. Type **809**	90	75
2111	50c. Sacks	90	75
2112	50c. Men unloading truck	90	75
2113	50c. Horse and cart	90	75

Nos. 2110/13 were printed together, *se-tenant*, forming a composite design.

810 Steam Locomotive *Yatay* and Tender, 1888 (image scaled to 54% of original size)

1988. "Prenfil '88" Philatelic Literature Exhibition, Buenos Aires (1st issue). Railways. Multicoloured.
2114	1a.+50c. Type **810**	1·30	85
2115	1a.+50c. Electric passenger coach, 1914	1·30	85
2116	1a.+50c. Type B-15 loco-motive and tender, 1942	1·30	85
2117	1a.+50c. Type GT-22 diesel loco-motive, 1988	1·30	85

See also Nos. 2134/7.

811 Running

1988. Olympic Games, Seoul. Multicoloured.
2118	1a. Type **811**	65	35

2119	2a. Football	1·60	45
2120	3a. Hockey	2·30	95
2121	4a. Tennis	2·75	1·20

812 Bank Facade

1988. Centenary of Bank of Mendoza.
2122	**812**	2a. multicoloured	1·30	55

813 Arms of Guemes and National Guard Emblem

1988. 50th Anniv of National Guard.
2123	**813**	2a. multicoloured	1·30	55

814 *St. Cayetano* (patron saint of workers)" (C. Quaglia)

1988. Philatelic Anniversaries and Events. Multicoloured.
2124	2a. Type **814** (50th anniv of Liniers (Buenos Aires) Philatelic Circle)	1·40	70
2125	3a. *Our Lady of Carmen* (patron saint of Cuyo) (window, Carlos Quaglia) (50th anniv of West Argentina Philatelic Society)	1·50	85
MS2126	145×73 mm. 5a. *Love* (mural, Antonio Berni) (Li-men 88 national stamp exhibition, Buenos Aires) (39×29 mm)	4·50	4·25

815 Sarmiento (after Mario Chierico) and Cathedral of the North School

1988. Death Centenary of Domingo Faustino Sarmiento (President, 1868–74).
2127	**815**	3a. multicoloured	2·10	85

816 San Isidro (Enrique Castro)

1988. Horse Paintings. Multicoloured.
2128	2a.+1a. Type **816**	1·90	95
2129	2a.+1a. *Waiting* (Gustavo Solari)	1·90	95
2130	2a.+1a. *Beside the Pond* (F. Romero Carranza)	1·90	95
2131	2a.+1a. *Mare and Colt* (Enrique Castro)	1·90	95
2132	2a.+1a. *Under the Tail* (Enrique Castro)	1·90	95

1988. 21st International Urological Society Congress. No. 2091 optd **XXI CONGRESO DE LA SOCIEDAD INTERNACIONAL DE UROLOGIA SIU 88.**
2133	**805**	5a. multicoloured	7·50	2·40

818 Cover of *References de la Poste*

1988. "Prenfil '88" Philatelic Literature Exhibition, Buenos Aires (2nd issue). Designs showing magazine covers. Multicoloured.
2134	1a.+1a. Type **818**	75	35
2135	1a.+1a. *Cronaca Filatelica*	75	35
2136	1a.+1a. *Co Fi*	75	35
2137	2a.+2a. *Postas Argentinas*	95	60

819 *Immaculate Conception*

1988. Arbrafax 88 Argentinian–Brazilian Stamp Exhibition, Buenos Aires. Sheet 156×80 mm containing T **819** and similar horiz design. Multicoloured.
MS2138 2a.+2a. *Candle Delivery at San Ignacio* (Leonie Matthis); 3a.+3a. Type **819** ... 5·00 4·75

820 Underground Train

1988. 75th Anniv of Buenos Aires Underground Railway.
2139	**820**	5a. multicoloured	2·10	95

821 *Virgin of Tenderness*

1988. Christmas. Virgins in Ucrania Cathedral, Buenos Aires. Multicoloured.
2140	5a. Type **821**	1·90	70
2141	5a. Virgin of Protection	1·90	70

822 Ushuaia and St. John

1989. Death Centenary (1988) of St. John Bosco (founder of Salesian Brothers).
2142	**822**	5a. multicoloured	1·30	35

823 *Rincon de los Areneros* (Justo Lynch)

1989. Paintings. Multicoloured.
2143	5a. Type **823**	2·75	45
2144	5a. *Blancos* (Fernando Fader)	2·75	45

824 *Crowning with Thorns* and Church of Our Lady of Carmen, Tandil

1989. Holy Week. Multicoloured.
2145	2a. Type **824**	50	25

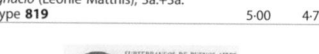

2146	2a. *Jesus of Nazareth* and Buenos Aires Cathedral	50	25
2147	3a. *Our Lady of Sorrows* and Humahuaca Church, Jujuy	65	30
2148	3a. *Jesus Meets His Mother* (statue) and La Quebrada Church, San Luis	65	30

825 Shattering Drinking Glass

1989. Anti-alcoholism Campaign.

2149	**825** 5a. multicoloured	1·30	45

1989. National Parks (2nd series). As T 804. Multicoloured.

2150	5a. Crested gallito (*Gallito Capeton*), Lihue Calel National Park	1·30	45
2151	5a. Lizard, El Palmar National Park	1·30	45
2152	5a. Tapirs, Calilegua National Park	1·30	45
2153	5a. Howler monkey, Chaco National Park	1·30	45
2154	5a. Magellanic wood-pecker (*Carpintero Negro Patagonico*), Los Glaciares National Park	1·30	45

826 Emblem

1989. Cent of Argentine Membership of I.T.U.

2155	**826** 10a. multicoloured	2·75	60

827 Class 1A Glider Entries

1989. World Model Airplane Championships, La Cruz-Embals-Cordoba. Multicoloured.

2156	5a. Type **827**	1·00	35
2157	5a. Class 1B rubber-powered entries	1·00	35
2158	10a. Class 1C petrol-engined entries	1·80	50

828 Otuno (*Diplomystes viedmensis*)

1989. Argentine Philately. Fish. Multicoloured.

2159	10a.+5a. Type **828**	1·00	60
2160	10a.+5a. Striped galaxiid (*Hap-lochiton taeniatus*)	1·00	60
2161	10a.+5a. Creole perch (*Jenyns percichthys tucha*)	1·00	60
2162	10a.+5a. River Plate galaxiid (*Galaxias platei*)	1·00	60
2163	10a.+5a. Brown trout (*Salmo fario*)	1·00	60

829 "All Men are Born Free and Equal"

1989. Bicentenary of French Revolution.

2164	**829** 10a. red, blue and black	1·00	45
2165	- 15a. black, red and blue	1·10	50
MS2166	146×74 mm. 25a. multicoloured	2·10	2·00

DESIGNS: 15a. *Marianne* (Gandon) and French flag; 25a. *Liberty guiding the People* (detail, E. Delacroix).

830 *Weser* (steamer)

1989. Immigration. Multicoloured.

2167	150a. Type **830**	2·75	85
2168	200a. Immigrants' hostel	3·25	1·10
MS2169	155×80 mm. As Nos. 2167/8 but each 35×25 mm	5·00	4·75

831 "Republic" (bronze bust)

1989. Transference of Presidency. Unissued stamp surch as in T 831.

2170	**831** 300a. on 50a. mult	2·75	85

832 Arms of Columbus and Title Page of *Book of Privileges*

1989. "Espamer '90" Spain–Latin America Stamp Exhibition. Chronicles of Discovery. Each yellow, black and red.

2171	100a.+50a. Type **832**	75	70
2172	150a.+50a. Illustration from *New Chronicle and Good Government* (Guaman Poma de Ayala)	1·00	95
2173	200a.+100a. Illustration from *Discovery and Conquest of Peru* (Pedro de Cieza de Leon)	1·50	1·40
2174	250a.+100a. Illustration from *A Journey to the River Plate* (Ulrico Schmidl)	1·80	1·70

833 Fr. Guillermo Furlong and Title Page of *Los Jesuitas*

1989. Birth Anniversaries.

2175	**833** 150a. black, light green and green (centenary)	90	55
2176	- 150a. black, buff and brown (centenary)	90	55
2177	- 200a. black, light blue and blue (bicentenary)	1·00	60

DESIGNS: No. 2176, Dr. Gregorio Alvarez (physician) and title page of *Canto A Chos Mala*; 2177, Brigadier Gen. Enrique Martinez and *Battle of Maipu* (detail of lithograph, Theodore Gericault).

834 Wooden Mask from Atajo

1989. America. Pre-Columbian Artefacts. Multicoloured.

2178	200a. Type **834**	1·60	60
2179	300a. Urn from Punta de Balastro	2·10	65

835 *Policewoman with Children* (Diego Molinari)

1989. Federal Police Week. Winning entries in a schools' painting competition.

2180	100a. Type **835**	95	35
2181	100a. *Traffic policeman* (Carlos Alberto Sarago)	95	35
2182	150a. *Adults and child by traffic lights* (Roxana Andrea Osuna)	1·30	60
2183	150a. *Policeman and child stop-ping traffic at crossing* (Pablo Javier Quaglia)	1·30	60

836 *Dream of Christmas* (Maria Carballido)

1989. Christmas. Multicoloured.

2184	200a. Type **836**	1·10	35
2185	200a. *Cradle Song for Baby Jesus* (Gato Frias)	1·10	35
2186	300a. *Christ of the Hills* (statue, Chipo Cespedes) (vert)	1·30	45

837 *Battle of Vuelta de Obligado* (Ulde Todo)

1989

2187	**837** 300a. multicoloured	2·10	45

838 Port Building

1990. Cent of Buenos Aires Port. Multicoloured.

2188	200a. Type **838**	2·50	1·00
2189	200a. Crane and bows of con-tainer and sailing ships	2·50	1·00
2190	200a. Truck on quay and ships in dock	2·50	1·00
2191	200a. Van and building	2·50	1·00

Nos. 2188/91 were printed together, *se-tenant*, forming a composite design.

839 Aconcagua Peak and Los Horcones Lagoon

1990. Aconcagua International Fair. Multicoloured.

2192	500a. Type **839**	1·80	75
2193	500a. Aconcagua Peak and Los Horcones Lagoon (right-hand detail)	1·80	75

Nos. 2192/3 were printed together, *se-tenant*, forming a composite design.

840 "75" and Girl with Savings Box

1990. 75th Anniv of National Savings and Insurance Fund.

2194	**840** 1000a. multicoloured	1·00	45

841 Footballer in Striped Shirt

1990. World Cup Football Championship, Italy. Multicoloured.

2195	2500a. Type **841**	2·20	1·00
2196	2500a. Upper body of foot-baller in blue shirt	2·20	1·00
2197	2500a. Ball and footballers' legs	2·20	1·00
2198	2500a. Lower body of foot-baller	2·20	1·00

Nos. 2195/8 were printed together, *se-tenant*, forming a composite design.

842 Flowers

1990. Anti-drugs Campaign.

2199	**842** 2000a. multicoloured	1·90	85

843 School Emblem and Pellegrini

1990. Centenary of Carlos Pellegrini Commercial High School.

2200	**843** 2000a. multicoloured	1·90	85

844 *Calleida suturalis*

1990. Argentine Philately. Insects. Multicoloured.

2201	1000a.+500a. Type **844**	1·80	1·20
2202	1000a.+500a. *Adalia bipunctata*	1·80	1·20
2203	1000a.+500a. *Hippodamia convergens*	1·80	1·20
2204	1000a.+500a. *Nabis punctipennis*	1·80	1·20
2205	1000a.+500a. *Podisus nigrispinus*	1·80	1·20

845 Letters and Globe

1990. International Literacy Year.

2206	**845** 2000a. multicoloured	1·50	85

846 Marcos Zar and Savoia S-16 Flying Boat

1990. Air. Aerofildae 90 National Air Mail Exhibition, Buenos Aires. Sheet 158×78 mm containing T 846 and similar horiz design. Multicoloured.

MS2207	2000a.+ 2000a. Type **846**; 3000a.+3000a. Capt. Antonio Parodi and biplane	12·50	12·00

847 Players

1990. World Basketball Championship. Multicoloured.
2208 2000a. Type **847** 3·25 2·10
MS2209 5000a. Detail of No. 2208
(29×39 mm) 8·25 7·00

848 Junkers Ju 52/3m

1990. Air. 50th Anniv of LADE (airline). Multicoloured.
2210 2500a. Type **848** 2·10 1·10
2211 2500a. Grumman SA-16 Alba-
tross flying boat 2·10 1·10
2212 2500a. Fokker Friendship 2·10 1·10
2213 2500a. Fokker Fellowship 2·10 1·10

849 Arms of West Indies
Maritime Post

1990. 14th Postal Union of the Americas and Spain
Congress, Buenos Aires.
2214 **849** 3000a. brown & black 2·50 1·00
2215 - 3000a. multicoloured 2·50 1·00
2216 - 3000a. multicoloured 2·50 1·00
2217 - 3000a. multicoloured 2·50 1·00
DESIGNS: No. 2215, Sailing packet and despatch boat;
2216, *Rio Carcarana* (cargo liner); 2217, Boeing 707 air-
plane and mail van.

850 Descubierta

1990. Espamer 91 Spain–Latin America Stamp Exhibition,
Buenos Aires. Sheet 109×114 mm containing T **850**
and similar vert designs. Multicoloured.
MS2218 2000a.+1000a.x4: Type **850**;
Alejandro Malaspina (explorer) and
Atrevide; Amerindians; Artist drawing
Amerindians 12·50 12·00

851 *Hamelia erecta* and
Iguazu Falls

1990. America. Natural World. Multicoloured.
2219 3000a. Type **851** 2·50 1·00
2220 3000a. Sea cow, Puerto
Deseado 2·50 1·00

852 U.P.U. Emblem on
"Stamp"

1990. World Post Day.
2221 **852** 3000a. multicoloured 2·30 85

1990. National Parks (3rd series). As T **804**. Multicoloured.
2222 3000a. Anteater, El Rey National
Park 2·40 95
2223 3000a. Black-necked swans
(*Cisne de Cuello Negro*), La-
guna Blanca National Park 2·40 95
2224 3000a. Black-chested buzzard
eagle (*Aguila Mora*), Lanin
National Park 2·40 95
2225 3000a. Armadillo, Perito
Moreno National Park 2·40 95
2226 3000a. Pudu, Puelo National
Park 2·40 95

853 Hands (after
Michelangelo) and Army
Emblem

1990. Cent of Salvation Army in Argentina (2227) and
Nat University of the Littoral (2228). Multicoloured.
2227 3000a. Type **853** 2·30 1·10
2228 3000a. University building and
emblem 2·30 1·10

854 Archangel
Gabriel

1990. Christmas. Stained-glass windows by Carlos
Quaglia from Church of Immaculate Conception,
Villaguay. Multicoloured.
2229 3000a. Dove's wing and hand 2·10 1·10
2230 3000a. Dove and Mary 2·10 1·10
2231 3000a. Type **854** 2·10 1·10
2232 3000a. Lower half of Mary and
open book 2·10 1·10
2233 3000a. Joseph 2·10 1·10
2234 3000a. Star, shepherds and
head of Mary 2·10 1·10
2235 3000a. Manger 2·10 1·10
2236 3000a. Baby Jesus in Mary's
arms 2·10 1·10
2237 3000a. Joseph with two doves
and Mary 2·10 1·10
2238 3000a. Simeon 2·10 1·10
2239 3000a. Lower halves of Joseph
and Mary 2·10 1·10
2240 3000a. Lower half of Simeon
and altar 2·10 1·10
Nos. 2229/32, 2233/6 and 2237/40 were printed to-
gether in *se-tenant* sheetlets of four stamps, each sheet-
let forming a composite design of stained glass windows
entitled *Incarnation of Son of God*, *The Birth of Christ* and
Presentation of Jesus in the Temple.

855 Putting the Shot

1990. Espamer 91 Spain–Latin America Stamp Exhibition,
Buenos Aires (2nd issue) and Olympic Games,
Barcelona (1992). Sheet 103×125 mm containing T
855 and similar vert designs. Multicoloured.
MS2241 2000a.+2000a.x4: Type **855**;
High jumping; Hurdling; Pole
vaulting 19·00 18·00

856 *Landscape* (Pio
Collivadino)

1991. Paintings. Multicoloured.
2242 4000a. Type **856** 1·80 1·00
2243 4000a. *Weeping Willows* (Atilio
Malinverno) (horiz) 1·80 1·00

857 Juan Manuel
Fangio

1991. Espamer 91 Spain–Latin America Stamp Exhibition,
Buenos Aires (3rd issue). Racing Drivers. Sheet
104×125 mm containing T **857** and similar vert
designs. Multicoloured.
MS2244 2500a.+2500a.x4: Type **857**;
Juan Manuel Bordeau; Carlos Alberto
Reutemann; Oscar and Juan Galvez 9·50 9·25

858 Rosas

1991. Return of Remains of Brig. Gen. Juan Manuel de
Rosas.
2245 **858** 4000a. multicoloured 1·80 1·00

859 Freestyle
Gymnastics

1991. Espamer 91 Spain–Latin America Stamp Exhibition,
Buenos Aires (4th issue) and Olympic Games,
Barcelona (1992) (2nd issue). Gymnastics. Sheet
103×125 mm containing T **859** and similar vert
designs. Multicoloured.
MS2246 2500a.+2500a.x4: Type **859**;
Asymmetric bars; Beam; Hoop
exercise 9·50 9·25

860 Hernan, the Pirate
(Jose Salinas)

1991. Comic Strips. Each black and blue.
2247 4000a. Type **860** 1·80 1·00
2248 4000a. *Don Fulgencio* (Lino
Palacio) 1·80 1·00
2249 4000a. *Tablas Medicas de
Salerno* (Oscar Conti) 1·80 1·00
2250 4000a. *Buenos Aires en Camiseta*
(Alejandro del Prado) 1·80 1·00
2251 4000a. *Girls!* (Jose Divito) 1·80 1·00
2252 4000a. *Langostino* (Eduardo
Ferro) 1·80 1·00
2253 4000a. *Mafalda* (Joaquin
Lavado) 1·80 1·00
2254 4000a. *Mort Cinder* (Alberto
Breccia) 1·80 1·00

861 "Flags" (Maria Augustina
Ferreyra)

1991. 700th Anniv of Swiss Confederation.
2255 **861** 4000a. multicoloured 1·80 85

862 Divine Child
Mayor

1991. 400th Anniv of La Rioja City.
2256 **862** 4000a. multicoloured 1·80 85

863 Eduardo Bradley, Angel Zuloaga and
Balloon *Eduardo Newbery*

1991. 75th Anniv of Crossing of Andes by Balloon.
2257 **863** 4000a. multicoloured 1·80 85

864 *Vitoria* (Magellan's
galleon)

1991. America. Voyages of Discovery. Multicoloured.
2258 4000a. Type **864** 2·50 1·00
2259 4000a. Juan Diaz de Solis's fleet 2·50 1·00

865 "Virgin of the
Valley, Catamarca"
(top half)

1991. Christmas. Stained-glass Windows from Church of
Our Lady of Lourdes, Santos Lugares, Buenos Aires.
Multicoloured.
2260 4000a. Type **865** 2·10 1·00
2261 4000a. "Virgin of the Valley"
(bottom half) 2·10 1·00
2262 4000a. Church and "Virgin of
the Rosary of the Miracle,
Cordoba" (top half) 2·10 1·00
2263 4000a. "Virgin of the Rosary of
the Miracle" (bottom half) 2·10 1·00
Nos. 2260/3 were issued together, *se-tenant*, Nos.
2260/1 and 2262/3 forming composite designs.

866 Enrique Pestalozzi (editor)
and Masthead

1991. Centenaries. Multicoloured.
2264 4000a. Type **866** ("Argen-
tinisches Tageblatt" (1989)) 1·80 85
2265 4000a. Leandro Alem (founder)
and flags (Radical Civic
Union) 1·80 85
2266 4000a. Marksman (Argentine
Shooting Federation) 1·80 85
2267 4000a. Dr. Nicasio Etchepare-
borda (first professor) and
emblem (Buenos Aires
Faculty of Odontology) 1·80 85
2268 4000a. Dalmiro Huergo and
emblem (Graduate School of
Economics) 1·80 85

867 Gen. Juan Lavalle and
Medal

1991. Anniversaries. Multicoloured.
2269 4000a. Type **867** (150th death
anniv) 1·80 85
2270 4000a. Gen. Jose Maria Paz and
Battle of Ituzaingo medal
(birth bicentenary) 1·80 85

2271	4000a. Dr. Marco Avellaneda and opening words of *Ode to the 25th May* (politician and writer, 150th death anniv)	1·80	85	
2272	4000a. William Henry Hudson and title page of *Far Away and Long Ago* (writer, 150th birth anniv)	1·80	85	

868 *Castor* (rocket)

1991. "Iberoprenfil '92" Iberia–Latin America Philatelic Literature Exhibition, Buenos Aires (1st issue). Multicoloured.

2273	4000a.+4000a. Type **868**	4·00	1·60
2274	4000a.+4000a. "Lusat-1" satellite	4·00	1·60

See also Nos. 2313/14 and 2325/8.

869 Guiana Crested Eagle (*Morphnu guianensis*)

1991. Birds. Multicoloured.

2275	4000a. Type **869**	2·50	1·10
2276	4000a. Green-winged macaw (*Ara chloroptera*)	2·50	1·10
2277	4000a. Lesser rhea (*Pterocnemia pennata*)	2·50	1·10

870 Gaucho with Woman

1992. Abrafex 92 Argentinian–Brazilian Stamp Exhibition, Porto Algere, Brazil. Sheet 103×126 mm containing T **870** and similar vert designs. Multicoloured.

MS2278 38c. Type **870**; 38c. Gaucho with horse; 38c. Gaucho in grocer's shop; 38c. Ranch owner ... 8·25 8·00

871 Golden Tops

1992. Fungi.

2279	10c. Type **871**	75	25
2280	25c. Common ink cap	1·30	35
2281	38c. Type **871**	1·30	45
2282	48c. As 25c.	1·50	55
2283	50c. Granulated boletus	2·50	70
2284	51c. Common morel	1·60	60
2285	61c. Fly agaric	2·00	65
2286	68c. Lawyer's wig	3·25	80
2289	1p. As 61c.	5·00	1·10
2290	1p.25 As 50c.	5·00	1·10
2293	2p. As 51c.	9·50	2·75

For redrawn, smaller, designs see Nos. 2365/77.

1992. National Parks (4th series). As T **804**. Multicoloured.

2295	38c. Chucao tapaculo (*Chucao*), Los Alerces National Park	1·50	85
2296	38c. Opossum, Los Arrayanes National Park	1·50	85
2297	38c. Giant armadillo, Formosa Nature Reserve	1·50	85
2298	38c. Cavy, Petrified Forests Natural Monument	1·50	85
2299	38c. James's flamingo (*Parina chica*), Laguna de los Pozuelos Natural Monument	1·50	85

872 Soldier and Truck

1992. National Heroes Commem. Multicoloured.

2300	38c. Type **872**	1·30	70
2301	38c. "General Belgrano" (cruiser)	1·30	70
2302	38c. FMA Pucara fighter	1·30	70

873 "Carnotaurus sastrei"

1992. Dinosaurs. Multicoloured.

2303	38c.+38c. Type **873**	2·75	1·80
2304	38c.+38c. "Amargasaurus cazaui"	2·75	1·80

874 *Tileforo Areco*

1992. Birth Centenary (1991) of Florencio Molina Campios (painter). Multicoloured.

2305	38c. Type **874**	1·50	85
2306	38c. *In the Shade* (horiz)	1·50	85

875 Deer

1992. Conference on Environment and Development, Rio de Janeiro. Sheet 85×82 mm containing T **875** and similar square designs. Multicoloured.

MS2307 38c. Type **875**; 38c. Birds; 38c. Butterflies; 38c. Whale ... 12·00 12·00

876 General Lucio N. Mansilla and *San Martin* (frigate)

1992. Birth Anniversaries. Multicoloured.

2308	38c. Type **876** (bicentenary)	1·50	85
2309	38c. Jose Manuel Estrada (historian, 150th)	1·50	85
2310	38c. General Jose I. Garmendia (150th)	1·50	85

877 Hearts as Flowers

1992. Anti-drugs Campaign.

2311	**877**	38c. multicoloured	1·90	95

878 Steam Pump Fire Engine and Calaza

1992. 140th Birth Anniv of Col. Jose Calaza (founder of fire service).

2312	**878**	38c. multicoloured	1·60	90

879 *The Party*

1992. "Iberoprenfil '92" Iberia–Latin America Philatelic Literature Exhibition, Buenos Aires (2nd issue). Paintings by Raul Soldi. Multicoloured.

2313	76c.+76c. Type **879**	6·25	4·75
2314	76c.+76c. Church of St. Anne of Glew	6·25	4·75

880 Columbus, European Symbols and *Santa Maria*

1992. America. 500th Anniv of Discovery of America by Columbus. Multicoloured.

2315	38c. Type **880**	2·50	1·20
2316	38c. American symbols and Columbus	2·50	1·20

1992. 50th Anniv of Neuquen and Rio Negro Philatelic Centre. Unissued stamp as T **871** optd **50°ANIVERSARIO CENTRO FILATELICO DE NEUQUEN Y RIO NEGRO**. Multicoloured.

2317	1p.77 Verdigris agaric	7·50	4·75

882 *God Pays You*

1992. Argentine Films. Advertising posters. Multicoloured.

2318	38c. Type **882**	1·80	85
2319	38c. *The Turbid Waters*	1·80	85
2320	38c. *Un Guapo del 900*	1·80	85
2321	38c. *The Truce*	1·80	85
2322	38c. *The Official Version*	1·80	85

883 Flags of Paraguay and Argentina as Stamps

1992. "Parafil '92" Paraguay–Argentina Stamp Exhibition, Buenos Aires.

2323	**883**	76c.+76c. mult	6·00	4·50

884 Angel and Baby Jesus

1992. Christmas.

2324	**884**	38c. multicoloured	1·80	85

885 Punta Mogotes Lighthouse

1992. "Iberoprenfil '92" Iberia–Latin America Philatelic Literature Exhibition, Buenos Aires (3rd issue). Lighthouses. Multicoloured.

2325	38c. Type **885**	1·80	85
2326	38c. Rio Negro	1·80	85
2327	38c. San Antonio	1·80	85
2328	38c. Cabo Blanco	1·80	85

886 Campaign Emblem

1992. Anti-AIDS Campaign.

2329	**886**	10c. black, red and blue	3·25	60
2330	-	26c. multicoloured	5·75	1·00

DESIGN: 26c. AIDS cloud over house of life.

887 "SAC-B" Research Satellite

1992. International Space Year.

2331	**887**	38c. multicoloured	2·00	95

888 *The Lord of the Miracle* (Matriz Church, Salta)

1992. 400th Anniv of Arrival of the *Lord of the Miracle* in America. Sheet 72×112 mm.

MS2332 **888** 76c. multicoloured ... 7·00 4·75

889 Footballers and Emblem

1993. Centenary of Argentine Football Assn.

2333	**889**	38c. multicoloured	1·80	85

890 Arquebusier and Arms of Francisco de Arganaras (founder)

1993. 400th Anniv of Jujuy.

2334	**890**	38c. multicoloured	1·80	85

891 Government Tower, Poznan

1993. International Stamp Exhibitions. Sheet 84×119 mm containing T **891** and similar square designs. Multicoloured.

MS2335 38c. Type **891** (Polska 93); 48c. "Christ the Redeemer" (Statue), Rio de Janeiro (Brasiliana 93); 76c. Palace dome, Bangkok (Bangkok 1993) ... 6·50 6·50

892 Order of San Martin

1993. Anniversaries. Multicoloured.

2336	38c. Type **892** (50th anniv)	1·80	85
2337	38c. Entrance to and emblem of National History Academy (centenary)	1·80	85

893 Flag-bearer and Arms of Gendarmerie

1993. National Heroes Commemoration. Multicoloured.
2338	38c. Type **893**	1·80	85
2339	38c. "Rio Iguazu" (coastguard corvette)	1·80	85

894 Luis Candelaria and Morane Saulnier Type P Monoplane

1993. 75th Anniv of First Flight over the Andes.
2340	**894** 38c. multicoloured	1·90	95

895 Snowy Egret (Egretta thula)

1993. Paintings of Birds by Axel Amuchastegui. Multicoloured.
2341	38c.+38c. Type **895**	2·75	2·10
2342	38c.+38c. Scarlet-headed blackbird (Amblyramphus holosericeus)	2·75	2·10
2343	38c.+38c. Red-crested cardinal (Paroaria coronata)	2·75	2·10
2344	38c.+38c. Amazon kingfisher (Chloroceryle amazona)	2·75	2·10

896 Coming Home (Adriana Zaefferer)

1993. Paintings. Multicoloured.
2345	38c. Type **896**	1·80	85
2346	38c. The Old House (Norberto Russo)	1·80	85

897 Pato

1993. 40th Anniv of Declaration of Pato as National Sport.
2347	**897** 1p. multicoloured	3·75	2·20

898 Segurola's Pacara (Enterolobium contortisiliquum)

1993. Old Trees in Buenos Aires. Multicoloured.
2348	75c. Type **898** (Puan and Baldomero Fernandez Moreno Streets)	2·50	1·40
2349	75c. Pueyrredon's carob tree (Prosopis alba) (Pueyrredon Square)	2·50	1·40
2350	1p.50 Alvear's coral tree (Erythrina falcata) (Lavalle Square)	5·25	2·50
2351	1p.50 Avellaneda's magnolia (Magnolia grandiflora) (Adolfo Berro Avenue)	5·25	2·50

899 Southern Right Whale

1993. America. Endangered Animals. Multicoloured.
2352	50c. Type **899**	2·00	1·10
2353	75c. Commerson's dolphin	3·00	1·80

900 Star, Leaf and Bell (Christmas)

1993. Christmas and New Year. Festive Symbols. Multicoloured.
2354	75c. Type **900**	3·00	1·80
2355	75c. Leaf, sun and moon (New Year)	3·00	1·80
2356	75c. Leaf and fir tree (Christmas)	3·00	1·80
2357	75c. Fish and moon (New Year)	3·00	1·80

Nos. 2354/7 were issued together, *se-tenant*, forming a composite design.

901 Cave Painting

1993. Cave of Hands, Santa Cruz.
2358	**901** 1p. multicoloured	3·75	2·20

902 Emblem

1994. New Argentine Post Emblem.
2359	**902** 75c. multicoloured	5·00	1·70

903 Brazil Player

1994. World Cup Football Championship, U.S.A. (1st issue). Multicoloured.
2360	25c. German player	1·00	60
2361	50c. Type **903**	1·90	1·20
2362	75c. Argentine player	2·50	1·80
2363	1p. Italian player	3·75	2·40
MS2364	151×99 mm. 1p.50 As No. 2362 but 39×49 mm	5·75	5·25

See also Nos. 2380/3.

904 Golden Tops

1994. Fungi. Multicoloured.
2365	10c. Type **904**	50	25
2366	25c. Common ink cap	75	45
2369	50c. Granulated boletus	1·50	95
2374	1p. Fly agaric	3·25	1·90
2377	2p. Common morel	6·25	3·75

Correo Argentino

905 Argentine Player with Ball (Matias Taylor)

1994. World Cup Football Championship, U.S.A. (2nd issue). Winning entries in children's competition. Multicoloured.
2380	75c. Type **905**	2·75	1·20
2381	75c. Tackle (Torcuato Santiago Gonzalez Agote)	2·75	1·20
2382	75c. Players (Julian Lisenberg) (horiz)	2·75	1·20
2383	75c. Match scene (Maria Paula Palma) (horiz)	2·75	1·20

906 Black-throated Finch

1994. Animals of the Falkland Islands (Islas Malvinas). Multicoloured.
2384	25c. Type **906**	1·00	60
2385	50c. Gentoo penguins	1·50	85
2386	75c. Falkland Islands flightless steamer ducks	2·50	1·20
2387	1p. Southern elephant-seal	3·25	2·10

907 Town Arms

1994. Anniversaries. Multicoloured.
2388	75c. Type **907** (400th anniv of San Luis)	2·75	1·20
2389	75c. Arms (3rd anniv of provincial status of Tierra del Fuego, Antarctica and South Atlantic Islands)	3·75	1·80

908 Ladislao Jose Biro

1994. Inventors. Multicoloured.
2390	75c. Type **908** (ball-point pen)	2·75	1·20
2391	75c. Raul Pateras de Pescara (helicopter)	2·75	1·20
2392	75c. Quirino Cristiani (animated films)	2·75	1·20
2393	75c. Enrique Finochietto (surgical instruments)	2·75	1·20

909 Star, Purple Bauble and Bell

1994. UNICEF Children's Fund in Argentina. Multicoloured.
2394	50c. Type **909**	1·90	85
2395	75c. Bell, red bauble and star	2·75	1·20

910 Children holding Globe (Ivana Mirna de Caro)

1994. Care of the Planet. Children's Painting Competition. Multicoloured.
2396	25c. Type **910**	90	40
2397	25c. Girl polishing sunbeam and boy tending tree (Elena Tsouprik)	90	40
2398	50c. Children of all races around globe (Estefania Navarro) (horiz)	1·90	85
2399	50c. Globe as house (Maria Belen Gidoni) (horiz)	1·90	85

911 Star and Angel (The Annunciation)

1994. Christmas. Multicoloured.
2400	50c. Type **911**	1·90	85
2401	75c. Madonna and Child (Nativity)	2·75	1·20

912 Running

1995. 12th Pan-American Games, Mar del Plata. Multicoloured.
2402	75c. Type **912**	2·75	1·20
2403	75c. Cycling	2·75	1·20
2404	75c. Diving	2·75	1·20
2405	1p.25 Football (vert)	3·75	1·80
2406	1p.25 Gymnastics (vert)	3·75	1·80

913 Postal Emblem

1995. Self-adhesive.
2407	**913** 25c. yellow, blue & black	10·00	95
2408	**913** 75c. yellow, blue & black	3·50	1·70

914 National Congress Building and "The Republic Triumphant" (statue, detail)

1995. New Constitution, August 1994.
2409	**914** 75c. multicoloured	2·75	1·80

915 Letters and Disk

1995. 21st International Book Fair.
2410	**915** 75c. multicoloured	2·75	1·80

916 Bay-winged Cowbird

1995. Birds. Multicoloured.
2412	5p. Hooded siskin	16·00	12·00
2413	9p.40 Type **916**	27·00	21·00
2414	10p. Rufous-collared sparrow	29·00	23·00

917 Clouds seen through Atrium

1995. Centenary of Argentine Engineers' Centre, Buenos Aires.

| 2420 | **917** | 75c. multicoloured | 2·75 | 1·70 |

918 Antoine de Saint-Exupery (pilot and writer)

1995. Aerofila 96 Latin American Airmail Exhibition. Sheet 130×90 mm containing T **918** and similar multicoloured design.

MS2421 25c.+25c. Type **918**; 75c.+75c. Illustration from *The Little Prince* 12·50 12·00

919 *Bahia Aguirre* (supply ship)

1995. Argentine Antarctic. Sheet 171×91 mm containing T **919** and similar horiz design. Multicoloured.

MS2422 75c.+25c. Type **919**; 1p.25+75c. Lockheed C-130 Hercules transport plane 14·00 14·00

920 Jose Marti

1995. Revolutionaries' Anniversaries. Multicoloured.

| 2423 | 1p. Type **920** (death cent) | 3·75 | 2·40 |
| 2424 | 1p. Antonio de Sucre (birth bicentenary) | 3·75 | 2·40 |

921 Greater Rhea

1995. Birds. Multicoloured.

2425	5c. Type **921**	15	10
2425a	10c. Giant wood rail ("ipecae")	65	25
2426	25c. King penguin	90	40
2427	50c. Toco toucan	1·90	80
2428	75c. Andean condor	2·75	1·60
2429	1p. Barn owl	5·00	2·40
2430	2p. Olivaceous cormorant	8·75	4·75
2431	2p.75 Southern lapwing	10·50	6·25
2432	3p.25 Southern lapwing	15·00	7·75

1995. Animals. As T **921**. Multicoloured.

2436	25c. Alligator	90	55
2437	50c. Red fox	1·90	1·20
2438	75c. Anteater	2·75	1·70
2439	75c. Vicuna	2·75	1·70
2440	75c. Sperm whale	2·75	1·70

922 Cave Painting (Patagonia)

1995. Archaeology. Multicoloured.

2441	75c. Type **922**	2·75	1·70
2442	75c. Stone mask (Tafi culture, Tucuman)	2·75	1·70
2443	75c. Anthropomorphic vase (Catamarca)	2·75	1·70
2444	75c. Woven cloth (North Patagonia)	2·75	1·70

923 Peron

1995. Birth Centenary of Juan Peron (President, 1946–55 and 1973–74).

| 2445 | **923** | 75c. blue and bistre | 2·75 | 1·70 |

924 Postal Emblem on Sunflower

1995

| 2446 | **924** | 75c. multicoloured | 8·75 | 2·40 |

925 "50" Emblem

1995. Anniversaries. Sheet 110×80 mm containing T **925** and similar horiz designs. Multicoloured.

MS2447 75c. Type **925** (50th anniv of United Nations Organization); 75c. "50" and emblem (50th anniv of International Civil Aviation Organization); 75c. "50" and emblem (50th anniv of Food and Agriculture Organization); 75c. "75" and emblem (75th anniv of International Labour Organization) 12·00 12·00

926 Christmas Tree

1995. Christmas. Multicoloured.

2448	75c. Type **926**	2·75	1·70
2449	75c. "1996"	2·75	1·70
2450	75c. Glasses of champagne	2·75	1·70
2451	75c. Present	2·75	1·70
2452	75c. Type **926**	2·75	1·70

927 *Les 400 Coups* (dir. Francois Truffaut)

1995. Centenary of Motion Pictures. Each black, grey and orange.

2453	75c. *Battleship Potemkin* (dir. Sergei Eisenstein)	2·75	1·70
2454	75c. *Casablanca* (dir. Michael Curtiz)	2·75	1·70
2455	75c. *Bicycle Thieves* (dir. Vittorio de Sica)	2·75	1·70
2456	75c. Charlie Chaplin in *Limelight*	2·75	1·70
2457	75c. Type **927**	2·75	1·70
2458	75c. *Chronicle of an Only Child* (dir. Leonardo Favio)	2·75	1·70

928 Horse-drawn Mail Coach

1995. America (1994). Postal Transport. Multicoloured.

| 2459 | 75c. Type **928** | 2·75 | 1·70 |
| 2460 | 75c. Early postal van | 2·75 | 1·70 |

929 Dirigible Airship

1995. The Sky. Multicoloured.

| 2461 | 25c. Type **929** | 1·00 | 65 |
| 2462 | 25c. Kite | 1·00 | 65 |

2463	25c. Hot-air balloon	1·00	65
2464	50c. Balloons	2·00	1·30
2465	50c. Paper airplane	2·00	1·30
2466	75c. Airplane	2·75	1·70
2467	75c. Helicopter	2·75	1·70
2468	75c. Parachute	2·75	1·70

930 Ancient Greek and Modern Runners

1996. Multicoloured. (a) Centenary of Modern Olympic Games. Horiz designs.

| 2471 | 75c. Type **930** | 2·75 | 1·70 |
| 2472 | 1p. *The Discus Thrower* (ancient Greek statue, Miron) and modern thrower | 4·00 | 2·50 |

(b) Olympic Games. Vert designs.

| 2473 | 75c. Torch bearer (Buenos Aires, 2004) | 2·75 | 1·70 |
| 2474 | 1p. Rowing (Atlanta, 1996) | 4·00 | 2·50 |

931 Francisco Muniz (founder of Academy of Medicine and Public Hygiene Council)

1996. Physicians' Anniversaries. Multicoloured.

2475	50c. Type **931** (birth bicentenary (1995)	2·00	1·30
2476	50c. Ricardo Gutierrez (founder of Children's Hospital and co-founder of periodical *La Patria Argentina*, death centenary)	2·00	1·30
2477	50c. Ignacio Pirovano (death centenary (1995))	2·00	1·30
2478	50c. Esteban Maradona (birth centenary (1995) and first death anniv)	2·00	1·30

932 Mosaic Map of Jerusalem (left-hand detail)

1996. 3000th Anniv of Jerusalem. Multicoloured.

| 2479 | 75c. Type **932** | 2·75 | 1·70 |
| 2480 | 75c. Map (right-hand detail) | 2·75 | 1·70 |

Nos. 2479/80 were issued together, *se-tenant*, forming a composite design.

933 Capybaras

1996. America. Endangered Species. Multicoloured.

| 2481 | 75c. Type **933** | 2·75 | 1·70 |
| 2482 | 75c. Guanacos | 2·75 | 1·70 |

934 Ramon Franco's Seaplane *Plus Ultra*

1996. "Aerofila '96" Latin American Airmail Exhibition. Aircraft. Multicoloured.

2483	25c.+25c. Type **934**	2·00	1·30
2484	25c.+25c. Alberto Santos-Dumont's biplane *14 bis*	2·00	1·30
2485	50c.+50c. Charles Lindbergh's *Spirit of St. Louis*	4·00	2·50
2486	50c.+50c. Eduardo Olivero's biplane *Buenos Aires*	4·00	2·50

1996. As Nos. 2407/8. Self-adhesive. Imperf.

| 2486a | 913 | 25c. yellow and blue | 2·40 | 1·50 |
| 2486b | 913 | 75c. yellow and blue | 4·50 | 2·75 |

935 Dusky-legged Guan, Diamante National Park

1996. National Parks. Multicoloured.

2487	75c. Type **935**	2·75	1·70
2488	75c. Mountain viscacha, El Leoncito Nature Reserve	2·75	1·70
2489	75c. Marsh deer, Otamendi Nature Reserve	2·75	1·70
2490	75c. Red-spectacled amazon, San Antonio Nature Reserve	2·75	1·70

936 Dragon

1996. Murals from Buenos Aires Underground Railway. Multicoloured.

| 2491 | 1p.+50c. Type **936** | 5·25 | 2·75 |
| 2492 | 1p.50+1p. Bird | 8·75 | 4·75 |

937 *San Antonio* (tank landing ship)

1996. Cent of Port Belgrano Naval Base. Multicoloured.

2493	25c. Type **937**	1·30	80
2494	50c. *Rosales* (corvette)	2·00	1·30
2495	75c. *Hercules* (destroyer)	2·75	1·70
2496	1p. *25 de Mayo* (aircraft carrier)	3·75	2·40

938 Decorative Panel

1996. Carousel. Multicoloured.

2497	25c. Type **938**	1·00	65
2498	25c. Child on horse	1·00	65
2499	25c. Carousel	1·00	65
2500	50c. Fairground horses	2·00	1·30
2501	50c. Child in airplane	2·00	1·30
2502	50c. Pig	2·00	1·30
2503	75c. Child in car	2·75	1·70

939 Head Post Office, Buenos Aires

1996. Size 24½×34½ mm. Self-adhesive. Imperf.

| 2504 | **939** | 75c. multicoloured | 3·75 | 2·00 |

See also Nos. 2537/8.

940 *Adoration of the Wise Men* (Gladys Rinaldi)

1996. Christmas. Tapestries. Multicoloured.

| 2505 | 75c. Type **940** | 2·75 | 1·70 |
| 2506 | 1p. *Abstract* (Norma Bonet de Maekawa) (horiz) | 4·00 | 2·50 |

941 Melchior Base

1996. Argentinian Presence in Antarctic. Multicoloured.
2507	75c. Type **941**	2·75	1·70
2508	1p.25 "Irizar" (ice-breaker)	5·00	3·25

942 *Vahine no te Miti* (Gauguin)

1996. Cent of National Gallery of Fine Arts. Multicoloured.
2509	75c. Type **942**	2·50	1·60
2510	1p. *The Nymph surprised* (Edouard Manet)	3·25	2·00
2511	1p. *Figure of Woman* (Amedeo Modigliani)	3·25	2·00
2512	1p.25 *Woman lying down* (Pablo Picasso) (horiz)	3·75	2·40

943 Granite Mining, Cordoba

1997. Mining Industry. Multicoloured.
2513	75c. Type **943**	2·75	1·70
2514	1p.25 Borax mining, Salta	5·00	3·25

944 *They amuse Themselves in Dancing* (Raul Soldi)

1997. America (1996). National Costume.
2515	**944**	75c. multicoloured	2·75	1·70

945 Arms, Sabre and Shako

1997. Centenary of Repatriation of General San Martin's Sabre.
2516	**945**	75c. multicoloured	2·75	1·70

946 Match Scene

1997. 29th World Rugby Youth Championship, Argentina.
2517	**946**	75c. multicoloured	2·75	1·70

947 *Fortuna* (yacht)

1997. 50th Anniv of Buenos Aires to Rio de Janeiro Regatta.
2518	**947**	75c. multicoloured	2·75	1·70

948 Ceres Design, France (1849–52)

1997. "Mevifil '97" First Int Exn of Philatelic Audio-visual and Computer Systems. Multicoloured.
2519	50c.+50c. Type **948**	4·50	2·75
2520	50c.+50c. Queen Isabella II design, Spain (1851)	4·50	2·75
2521	50c.+50c. Rivadavia design, Argentine Republic (1864)	4·50	2·75
2522	50c.+50c. Paddle-steamer design, Buenos Aires (1858)	4·50	2·75

Nos. 2519/22 were issued together, *se-tenant*, with the centre of the block forming the composite design of an eye.

949 Museum

1997. Centenary of National History Museum, Buenos Aires.
2523	**949**	75c. multicoloured	2·75	1·70

950 Seal and Oak Leaf

1997. Centenary of La Plata National University.
2524	**950**	75c. multicoloured	2·75	1·70

951 Carcano (after Dolores Capdevila)

1997. 50th Death Anniv (1996) of Ramon Carcano (postal reformer).
2525	**951**	75c. multicoloured	2·75	1·70

952 Cabo Virgenes Lighthouse

1997. Lighthouses. Multicoloured.
2526	75c. Type **952**	2·75	1·70
2527	75c. Isla Pinguino	2·75	1·70
2528	75c. San Juan de Salvamento	2·75	1·70
2529	75c. Punta Delgada	2·75	1·70

953 Condor and Olympic Rings

1997. Inclusion of Buenos Aires in Final Selection Round for 2004 Olympic Games.
2530	**953**	75c. multicoloured	2·75	1·70

954 Lacroze Company Suburban Service, 1912

1997. Centenary of First Electric Tramway in Buenos Aires. Illustrations from *History of the Tram* by Marcelo Mayorga. Multicoloured.
2531	75c. Type **954**	2·75	1·70
2532	75c. Lacroze Company urban service, 1907	2·75	1·70
2533	75c. Anglo Argentina Company tramcar, 1930	2·75	1·70
2534	75c. City of Buenos Aires Transport Corporation tramcar, 1942	2·75	1·70
2535	75c. Fabricaciones Militares tramcar, 1956	2·75	1·70
2536	75c. Electricos de Sur Company tramcar, 1908	2·75	1·70

Nos. 2531/6 were issued together, *se-tenant*, showing a composite design of a tram in a city street.

1997. As No. 2504 but size 23×35 mm. Self-adhesive. Imperf.
2537	**939**	25c. multicoloured	1·00	65
2538	**939**	75c. multicoloured	2·75	1·70

955 Monument (by Mauricio Molina)

1997. Inauguration of Monument to Joaquin Gonzalez (politician) at La Rioja.
2539	**955**	75c. multicoloured	2·75	1·70

956 Alberto Ginastera (after Carlos Nine)

1997. Composers. Multicoloured.
2540	75c. Type **956**	2·75	1·70
2541	75c. Astor Piazzolla (after Carlos Alonso)	2·75	1·70
2542	75c. Anibal Troilo (after Hermenegildo Sabat)	2·75	1·70
2543	75c. Atahualpa Yupanqui (after Luis Scafati)	2·75	1·70

957 "Tren a las Nubes", Salta

1997. Trains. Multicoloured.
2544	50c.+50c. Type **957**	4·50	2·75
2545	50c.+50c. Preserved steam locomotive, Buenos Aires	4·50	2·75
2546	50c.+50c. Patagonian express *La Trochita* Rio Negro–Chubut	4·50	2·75
2547	50c.+50c. Austral Fueguino Railway locomotive No. 2, Tierra del Fuego	4·50	2·75

958 Eva Peron (after Raul Manteola)

1997. 50th Anniv of Women's Suffrage.
2548	**958**	75c. pink and grey	2·75	1·70

959 Jorge Luis Borges and Maze

1997. Writers. Multicoloured.
2549	1p. Type **959**	3·75	2·40
2550	1p. Julio Cortazar and hop-scotch grid	3·75	2·40

1997. 70th Anniv of Air Mail in Argentina. No. **MS**2421 optd **1927 1997 ANIVERSARIO AEROPOSTA ARGENTINA** in margin.
MS2551	25c.+25c. multicoloured; 75c.+75c. multicoloured	12·00	7·50

961 Members' Flags and Southern Cross

1997. Mercosur (South American Common Market).
2552	**961**	75c. multicoloured	3·25	2·00

962 *Presidente Sarmiento* (Hugo Leban)

1997. Centenary of Launch of *Presidente Sarmiento* (cadet ship). Multicoloured.
2553	75c. Type **962**	3·25	2·00
MS2554	150×100 mm. 75c. *Presidente Sarmiento* at sea; 75c. Figurehead (vert)	8·75	5·50

963 Guevara

1997. 30th Death Anniv of Ernesto "Che" Guevara (revolutionary).
2555	**963**	75c. brown, red & black	3·75	2·00

964 Vicuna (Julian Chiapparo)

1997. "Draw an Ecostamp" Children's Competition Winners. Multicoloured.
2556	50c. Type **964**	2·10	1·30
2557	50c. Vicuna (Leandro Lopez Portal)	2·10	1·30
2558	75c. Seal (Andres Lloren) (horiz)	3·00	1·90
2559	75c. Ashy-headed goose (Jose Saccone) (horiz)	3·00	1·90

965 *Nativity* (Mary Jose)

1997. Christmas. Tapestries of the Nativity. Designs by artists named. Multicoloured. (a) Size 45×34 mm.
2560	75c. Type **965**	3·00	2·00

(b) Size 44×27 mm. Self-adhesive. Imperf.
2561	25c. Elena Aguilar	95	65
2562	25c. Silvia Pettachi	95	65

2563	50c. Ana Escobar	2·00	1·30
2564	50c. Alejandra Martinez	2·00	1·30
2565	75c. As No. 2560 but with inscriptions differently arranged	3·00	2·00
2566	75c. Nidia Martinez	3·00	2·00

966 Mother Teresa

1997. Mother Teresa (founder of the Missionaries of Charity) Commemoration.

2567	**966**	75c. multicoloured	3·00	2·00

967 Houssay

1998. 50th Anniv (1997) of Award to Bernardo Houssay of Nobel Prize for Medicine and Physiology.

2568	**967**	75c. multicoloured	3·00	2·00

968 Mountaineers

1998. Cent of First Ascent of Mt. Aconcagua.

2569	**968**	1p.25 multicoloured	5·25	3·50

969 San Martin de los Andes and Lake Lacar

1998. Centenary of San Martin de los Andes.

2570	**969**	75c. multicoloured	3·00	2·00

970 Grenadier Monument (Juan Carlos Ferraro)

1998. Declaration as National Historical Monument of Palermo Barracks of General San Martin Horse Grenadiers. Multicoloured.

2571	**970**	75c. Type **970**	3·00	2·00
2572		75c. Sevres urn with portrait of San Martin	3·00	2·00
2573		75c. Regiment coat of arms	3·00	2·00
2574		75c. Main facade of barracks	3·00	2·00

971 Globe and Baby

1998. Protection of Ozone Layer.

2575	**971**	75c. multicoloured	3·00	2·00

972 Postman, 1920

1998. America. The Postman. Multicoloured.

2576	75c. Type **972**	3·00	2·00
2577	75c. Postman, 1998	3·00	2·00

973 El Reino del Reves

1998. Stories by Maria Elena Walsh. Illustrations by Eduardo and Ricardo Fuhrmann. Multicoloured. Self-adhesive.

2578	75c. Type **973**	3·00	2·00
2579	75c. Zoo Loco	3·00	2·00
2580	75c. Dailan Kifki	3·00	2·00
2581	75c. Manuelita	3·00	2·00

974 St Peter's, Fiambala, Catamarca

1998. Historic Chapels. Multicoloured.

2582	75c. Type **974**	3·00	2·00
2583	75c. Huacalera, Jujuy	3·00	2·00
2584	75c. St. Dominic's, La Rioja	3·00	2·00
2585	75c. Tumbaya, Jujuy	3·00	2·00

975 Raised Hands

1998. White Helmets (volunteer humanitarian workers).

2586	**975**	1p. multicoloured	4·25	2·75

976 Argentine Player

1998. World Cup Football Championship, France. Multicoloured.

2587	75c. Type **976**	3·00	2·00
2588	75c. Croatian player	3·00	2·00
2589	75c. Jamaican player	3·00	2·00
2590	75c. Japanese player	3·00	2·00

977 Typewriter, Camera, Pen, Computer and Satellite

1998. Journalism Day.

2591	**977**	75c. multicoloured	3·00	2·00

978 Corrientes 1860 3c. Stamps and Postal Emblem

1998. 250th Anniv of Establishment of Regular Postal Service in Rio de la Plata (Spanish dominion in South America). Multicoloured.

2592	75c. Type **978**	3·00	2·00
2593	75c. Buenos Aires Post Office and pillar box	3·00	2·00

979 Jesuit Ruins, San Ignacio Mini

1998. Mercosur Missions.

2594	**979**	75c. multicoloured	3·00	2·00

980 Aberdeen Angus

1998. Cattle. Multicoloured.

2595	25c. Type **980**	1·20	80
2596	25c. Brahman	1·20	80
2597	50c. Hereford	2·10	1·40
2598	50c. Criolla	2·10	1·40
2599	75c. Holando-Argentina	3·00	2·00
2600	75c. Shorthorn	3·00	2·00

981 Map and Base

1998. 50th Anniv of Decepcion Antarctic Base.

2601	**981**	75c. multicoloured	3·25	2·00

982 Anniversary Emblem

1998. 50th Anniv of State of Israel.

2602	**982**	75c. multicoloured	3·25	2·00

983 Bridge in Japanese Garden, Buenos Aires

1998. Cent of Argentina–Japan Friendship Treaty.

2603	**983**	75c. multicoloured	3·25	2·00

984 Facade and clock

1998. 70th Anniv of Head Post Office, Buenos Aires. Multicoloured.

2604	75c. Type **984**	3·25	2·00
2605	75c. Capital and bench	3·25	2·00

985 Patoruzu (Quinterno)

1998. Comic Strip Characters. Multicoloured.

2606	75c. Type **985**	3·25	2·00
2607	75c. Matias (Sendra)	3·25	2·00
2608	75c. Clemente (Caloi)	3·25	2·00

2609	75c. El Eternauta (Oesterheld Solano Lopez)	3·25	2·00
2610	75c. Loco Chavez (Trillo Altuna)	3·25	2·00
2611	75c. Inodoro Pereyra (Fontanarrosa)	3·25	2·00
2612	75c. Tia Vicenta (Landru)	3·25	2·00
2613	75c. Gaturro (Nik)	3·25	2·00

986 Heart with Arms holding Baby

1998. 220th Anniv of Dr. Pedro de Elizalde Children's Hospital.

2614	**986**	75c. multicoloured	3·25	2·00

987 Post Banner and Pennant, 1785, and Arms of Maritime Post

1998. "Espamer '98" Iberian–Latin American Stamp Exhibition, Buenos Aires. Multicoloured. Self-adhesive.

2615	25c. Type **987**	1·10	70
2616	75c. Mail brigantine	3·25	2·00
2617	75c.+75c. Mail brigantine (different)	6·50	4·25
2618	1p.25+1p.25 Mail brig	10·50	7·00

988 Passport and Wallenberg

1998. Raoul Wallenberg (Swedish diplomat in Hungary who helped Jews escape, 1944–45) Commemoration.

2619	**988**	75c. multicoloured	3·00	2·00

989 Aguada Culture Bird

1998. 50th Anniv of Organization of American States.

2620	**989**	75c. multicoloured	3·00	2·00

990 Eoraptor

1998. Prehistoric Animals. Multicoloured.

2621	75c. Type **990**	3·50	2·40
2622	75c. Gasparinisaura	3·50	2·40
2623	75c. Giganotosaurus	3·50	2·40
2624	75c. Patagosaurus	3·50	2·40

Nos. 2621/4 were issued together, *se-tenant*, forming a composite design.

991 Child as Angel, Stars and Score

1998. Christmas.

2625	**991**	75c. multicoloured	3·00	2·00

992 Juan Figueroa
(founder) and First Issue

1998. Centenary of *El Liberal* (newspaper).
2626 **992** 75c. multicoloured 3·00 2·00

993 Postman

1998. Postman. Size 25×35 mm. Multicoloured. Self-adhesive.
2627 25c. Type **993** 95 65
2628 75c. Modern postman 3·00 2·00
For 75c. in reduced size see No. 2640.

1998. Birds. As T **921**. Multicoloured. Self-adhesive.
2629 60c. Red-tailed comet 2·10 1·40

994 Child (painting, Francisco
Ramirez)

1998. 50th Anniv of Universal Declaration of Human Rights.
2635 **994** 75c. multicoloured 3·00 2·00

995 Enrique Julio
(founder) and Newspaper
Offices

1998. Cent of *La Nueva Provincia* (newspaper).
2636 **995** 75c. multicoloured 3·00 2·00

996 *Haggadah* of Pessah
(exhibit) and Carving on
Cathedral

1998. Permanent Exhibition commemorating Holocaust Victims, Buenos Aires Cathedral.
2637 **996** 75c. multicoloured 3·00 2·00

1999. Postmen. Size 21×27 mm. Multicoloured. Self-adhesive.
2638 25c. Type **993** 85 55
2639 50c. Postman, 1950 1·50 1·00
2640 75c. As No. 2628 2·40 1·60

997 Oil-smeared
Magellanic Penguin

1999. International Year of the Ocean. Multicoloured.
2641 50c. Type **997** 1·70 1·10
2642 75c. Dolphins (horiz) 2·50 1·70

998 Buildings and
Draughtsman's Instruments

1999. National Arts Fund.
2643 **998** 75c. multicoloured 2·40 1·60

999 Computer and Book

1999. 25th Book Fair, Buenos Aires. Multicoloured.
2644 75c. Type **999** 2·75 1·80
2645 75c. Obelisk, compact disk case and readers 2·75 1·80
Nos. 2644/5 were issued together, *se-tenant*, forming a composite design.

1000 Rugby Balls and Player

1999. Centenary of Argentine Rugby Union. Multicoloured.
2646 75c. Type **1000** 2·75 1·80
MS2647 120×90 mm. 1p.50 19th-century and modern players 5·00 4·00

1001 Glass, La
Giralda

1999. Cafes. Multicoloured. Self-adhesive.
2648 25c. Type **1001** 85 55
2649 75c. Two glasses, Cafe Homero Manzi 2·50 1·70
2650 75c. Hatstand, Confiteria Ideal 2·50 1·70
2651 1p.25 Cup and saucer, Cafe Tortoni 4·25 2·75

1002 Pierre de
Coubertin, 1924
Olympic Gold Medal
and Olympic Rings

1999. 75th Anniv of Argentine Olympic Committee.
2652 **1002** 75c. multicoloured 2·50 1·70

1003 Enrico Caruso (Italian
tenor)

1999. Opera. Multicoloured.
2653 75c. Type **1003** (125th birth anniv and centenary of American debut) 2·50 1·60
2654 75c. Singer and musical instruments 2·50 1·60
2655 75c. Buenos Aires Opera House 2·50 1·60
2656 75c. Scene from *El Matrero* (Felipe Boero) 2·50 1·60

1004 Rosario Vera
Penaloza (educationist)

1999. America (1998). Famous Women. Multicoloured.
2659 75c. Type **1004** 2·50 1·70
2660 75c. Julieta Lanteri (women's rights campaigner) 2·50 1·70

1005 *Portrait of L. E. S.*
(Carlos Alonso)

1999. Paintings. Two sheets each 150×100 mm containing multicoloured designs as T **1005**.
MS2661 Two sheets. (a) 75c. *Anarchy of Year 20* (Luis Felipe Noe) (78×39 mm); 75c. Type **1005**. (b) 75c. *Typical Orchestra* (Antonio Berni) (69×49 mm); 75c. Unititled (Aida Carballo) (39×49 mm) 10·00 10·00

1006 Local Road
Network

1999. Bulk Mailing Stamps. Multicoloured. Self-adhesive.
2662 35c. Type **1006** 1·20 80
2663 40c. Town plan 1·30 85
2664 50c. Regional map 1·70 1·10

1007 Carrier Pigeon

1999
2665 **1007** 75c. multicoloured 2·75 1·90

1008 Boxer

1999. Dogs. Multicoloured.
2666 25c. Type **1008** 70 45
2667 25c. Old English sheepdog 70 45
2668 50c. Welsh collie 1·30 85
2669 50c. St. Bernard 1·30 85
2670 75c. German shepherd 2·10 1·40
2671 75c. Siberian husky 2·10 1·40

1009 Telephone
Keypad

1999. National Telecommunications Day.
2672 **1009** 75c. multicoloured 2·50 1·70

1010 College Gates

1999. 150th Anniv of Justo Jose de Urquiza College, Concepcion del Uruguay.
2673 **1010** 75c. multicoloured 2·50 1·70

1011 Krause (engineer) and
Industrial Instruments

1999. Centenary of Technical School No. 1 Otto Krause.
2674 **1011** 75c. multicoloured 2·50 1·70

1012 Nativity

1999. Bethlehem 2000.
2675 **1012** 75c. blue, gold and red 3·50 2·00

1013 Brotherhood among
Men

1999. America. A New Millennium without Arms. Multicoloured.
2676 75c. Type **1013** 2·50 1·70
2677 75c. Liberty Tree (vert) 2·50 1·70

1014 Coypu (*Myocastor coypus*), Mburucuya
National Park

1999. National Parks. Multicoloured.
2678 50c. Type **1014** 1·70 1·00
2679 50c. Andean condor, Quebrada de los Condoritos National Park 1·70 1·00
2680 50c. Vicuna, San Guillermo National Park 1·70 1·00
2681 75c. Puma, Sierra de las Quijadas National Park 2·50 1·70
2682 75c. Argentine grey fox (*Dusicyon griseus*), Talampaya National Park 2·50 1·70

1015 Map of the
Americas, Road
Network and
Wickerwork

1999. 40th Anniv of Inter-American Development Bank.
2683 **1015** 75c. multicoloured 2·50 1·70

1016 *Evidencias VI* (Carlos
Gallardo)

1999. 125th Anniv of Universal Postal Union.
2684 **1016** 1p.50 multicoloured 5·00 3·25

1017 *Fournier* and Map

1999. 50th Anniv of Sinking of the *Fournier* (minesweeper) in Antarctica.
2685 **1017** 75c. multicoloured 2·50 1·70

1018 *Nothofagus pumillio*

1999. Trees (1st series). Multicoloured.

2686		75c. Type **1018**	2·50	1·70
2687		75c. *Prosopis caldenia*	2·50	1·70
2688		75c. *Schinopsis balansae*	2·50	1·70
2689		75c. *Cordia trichotoma*	2·50	1·70

Nos. 2686/9 were issued together, *se-tenant*, forming a composite design.

1019 Latecoere 25 Mailplane

1999. 50th Anniv of World Record for Consecutive Parachute Jumps. Multicoloured.

2690		75c. Type **1019**	2·50	1·70
2691		75c. Parachutists	2·50	1·70

1020 Accordionist *The Tango*

1999. The New Millennium. Three sheets each 150×100 mm containing multicoloured designs as T **1020**.

MS2692 Three sheets. (a) 50, 75c. *The Tango*; (b) 50, 75c. Jorge Luis Borges (writer); (c) 50, (horiz), 75c. Football	12·00 12·00

1021 Boca Juniors Club Supporters

1999. Football. Multicoloured. (a) Size 42×33 mm.

2693		75c. Type **1021**	2·50	1·70
2694		75c. River Plate Club supporters	2·50	1·70

(b) Size 37×34 mm (1p.50) or 37×27 mm (others) (i) Boca Juniors.

2695		25c. Two players and ball	85	55
2696		50c. Club badge	1·50	1·00
2697		50c. Players hugging	1·50	1·00
2698		75c. Supporters and balloons	2·40	1·60
2699		75c. Club banner	2·40	1·60
2700		75c. Players	2·40	1·60
2701		1p.50 Player making high kick	4·75	3·25

(ii) River Plate.

2702		25c. Stadium	85	55
2703		50c. Players arriving on pitch	1·50	1·00
2704		50c. Supporters waving flags	1·50	1·00
2705		75c. Club badge	2·40	1·60
2706		75c. Trophy	2·40	1·60
2707		75c. Supporters with banner	2·40	1·60
2708		1p.50 Player preparing to kick ball	4·75	3·25

Nos. 2695/708 are self-adhesive.

1022 Planisphere of Central South America (Pierre Descelliers, 1546)

1999. Maps. Multicoloured.

2709		25c.+25c. Type **1022**	1·50	1·00
2710		50c.+50c. 17th-century map of estuary of the River Plate (Claes Voogt)	3·00	2·00

2711		50c.+50c. Buenos Aires (Military Geographical Institute, 1910)	3·00	2·00
2712		75c.+75c. Mouth of Riachuelo river and Buenos Aires harbour (satellite picture, 1999)	4·75	3·25

1023 Valdivielso and St. Peter's Cathedral, Rome

1999. Canonization of Hector Valdivielso Saez (Brother of the Christian Schools).

2713	**1023**	75c. multicoloured	2·50	1·70

1024 *San Francisco Xavier* (brig)

1999. Bicentenary of Manuel Belgrano Naval Academy.

2714	**1024**	75c. multicoloured	2·50	1·70

1025 *Uruguay*

1999. 125th Anniv of Launch of *Uruguay* (sail/steam corvette). Sheet 150×100 mm.

MS2715 **1025** 1p.50 multicoloured	4·75 4·75

1026 Holy Family

1999. Christmas. Multicoloured.

2716		25c. Wise Man (29×29 mm)	85	55
2717		25c. Bell (29×29 mm)	85	55
2718		50c. Two kings and camels (39×29 mm)	1·70	1·10
2719		50c. Holly leaf (39×29 mm)	1·70	1·10
2720		75c. Angel with star (39×30 mm)	2·50	1·70
2721		75c. Star (29×30 mm)	2·50	1·70
2722		75c. Nativity (39×29 mm)	2·50	1·70
2723		75c. Tree decorations (29×29 mm)	2·50	1·70
2724		75c. Type **1026**	2·50	1·70

1027 Grape on Vine

2000. Wine Making. Multicoloured.

2725		25c. Type **1027**	85	55
2726		25c. Glass and bottle of wine	85	55
2727		50c. Wine bottles	1·70	1·10
2728		50c. Cork screw and cork	1·70	1·10

1028 Mathematical Symbol and "2000"

2000. International Mathematics Year.

2729	**1028**	75c. multicoloured	2·50	1·70

1029 White-fronted Dove

2000. Doves and Pigeon. Mult. Self-adhesive.

2730		75c. Type **1029**	2·75	2·00
2731		75c. Picazuro pigeon (*Columba picazuro*)	2·75	2·00
2732		75c. Picui dove (*Columbina picni*)	2·75	2·00
2733		75c. Eared dove (*Fenaida auriculata*)	2·75	2·00

1030 *Venda coerulea*

2000. Bangkok 2000 International Stamp Exhibition. Plants. Sheet 100×76 mm containing T **1030** and similar horiz design. Multicoloured.

MS2734 25c. Type **1030**; 75c. Coral tree	3·50 3·50

1031 Open Book (CONABIP Library)

2000. Libraries. Multicoloured.

2735		25c. Type **1031**	90	65
2736		50c. Building facade (Jujuy library)	1·80	1·30
2737		75c. Hands and braille book (Argentine Library for the Blind)	2·75	2·00
2738		$1 Open book and building (National Library)	3·50	2·75

No. 2737 has an inscription in braille across the stamp.

1032 Caravel, Compass Rose and Letter

2000. 500th Anniv of the Discovery of Brazil. Multicoloured.

2739		25c. Type **1032**	90	65
2740		75c. Pedro Alvares Cabral (discoverer) and map of South America	2·75	2·00

1033 Lieutenant General Luis Maria Campos (founder)

2000. Centenary of the Higher Military Academy.

2741	**1033**	75c. multicoloured	2·75	2·00

1034 Penny Black and *La Portena* (steam locomotive), 1857

2000. The Stamp Show 2000 International Stamp Exhibition, London. Sheet 99×76 mm containing T **1034** and similar horiz design. Multicoloured.

MS2742 25c. Type **1034**; 75c. Two 1862 15c. stamps and modern pillar box	3·50 3·50

1035 Convention Emblem

2000. 91st Rotary International Convention, Buenos Aires.

2743	**1035**	75c. multicoloured	2·75	2·10

1036 Futuristic Houses and Emblems (Rocio Casado)

2000. "Stampin' the Future". Winning Entries in Children's International Painting Competition. Multicoloured.

2744		25c. Type **1036**	1·00	75
2745		50c. Sea and clouds (Carolina Cacerez) (vert)	1·90	1·40
2746		75c. Flower (Valeria A. Pizarro)	3·00	2·30
2747		$1 Flying cars (Cristina Ayala Castro) (vert)	3·75	2·75

1037 Ribbon

2000. America. AIDS Awareness. Multicoloured.

2748		75c. Type **1037**	3·00	2·30
2749		75c. Arms circling faces	3·00	2·30

1038 Potez 25 Biplane

2000. Birth Centenary of Antoine de Saint-Exupery (novelist and pilot). Multicoloured.

2750		25c. Type **1038**	1·00	75
2751		50c. Late 28	2·00	1·50

1039 Potez 25 Biplane

2000. "Aerofila 2000" Mercosur Air Philately Exhibition, Buenos Aires. Multicoloured.

2752		25c. As Type **1039**	1·00	75
2753		25c. Antoine de Saint-Exupery (novelist and pilot) (29×29 mm)	1·00	75
2754		50c. Late 28	2·00	1·50
2755		50c. Henri Guillaumet, Almonacid and Jean Mermoz (aviation pioneers) (29×29 mm)	2·00	1·50
2756		50c. Map of South America and tail of Late 25 (39×39 mm)	2·00	1·50
2757		$1 Late 25 and cover (39×29 mm)	4·00	3·00

1040 Illia

2000. Birth Centenary of Arturo U. Illia (President, 1963–66).

2758	**1040**	75c. multicoloured	3·00	2·30

1041 San Martin

2000. 150th Death Anniv of General Jose de San Martin.

2759	**1041**	75c. multicoloured	3·00	2·30

1042 Siku Pipes

2000. Argentine Culture. Multicoloured.

2760	10c. Ceremonial axe	30	25
2761	25c. Type **1042**	90	60
2762	50c. Andean loom	1·80	1·20
2763	60c. Pampeana poncho	2·30	1·50
2764	75c. Funeral mask	2·75	1·80
2765	$1 Basket	3·50	2·40
2766	$2 Kultun ritual drum	7·25	4·75
2767	$3.25 Ceremonial tiger mask	11·50	7·50
2768	$5 Funeral urn	18·00	12·00
2770	$9.40 Suri ceremonial costume	34·00	23·00

1043 Sarsfield, Signature and Cordoba Province Arms

2000. Birth Bicentenary of Dalmacio Velez Sarsfield (lawyer).

2775	**1043**	75c. multicoloured	3·25	2·40

1044 Windsurfing

2000. Olympic Games, Sydney. Multicoloured.

2776	75c. Type **1044**	3·25	2·40
2777	75c. Hockey	3·25	2·40
2778	75c. Volleyball	3·25	2·40
2779	75c. High jump and pole vault	3·25	2·40

1045 Argentine Petiso

2000. "Espana 2000" International Stamp Exhibition, Madrid. Horses. Multicoloured.

2780	25c. Type **1045**	1·00	75
2781	25c. Carriage horse	1·00	75
2782	50c. Peruvian horse	2·00	1·50
2783	50c. Criolla	2·00	1·50
2784	75c. Saddle horse	3·25	2·40
2785	75c. Polo horse	3·25	2·40
MS2786	100×75 mm. 25c. Stagecoach (39×29 mm); 75c. Horse's head (39×29 mm)	4·25	4·25

1046 Man on Bicycle and Las Nereidas Fountain

2000. Transportation. Multicoloured.

2787	25c.+25c. Type **1046**	2·00	1·50
2788	50c.+50c. Graf Zeppelin over Buenos Aires	4·25	3·25
2789	50c.+50c. Ganz (diesel locomotive)	4·25	3·25
2790	75c.+75c. Tram	6·25	4·75

1047 Nuclear Reactor

2000. 50th Anniv of National Commission for Atomic Energy.

2791	**1047**	75c. multicoloured	3·25	2·40

1048 Filete (left-hand detail)

2000. Fileteado (painting genre) (Nos. 2792/3) and Tango (dance) (Nos. 2794/5). Multicoloured.

2792	75c. Type **1048**	3·25	2·40
2793	75c. Filete (right-hand detail) (Brunetti brothers)	3·25	2·40
2794	75c. Tango orchestra	3·25	2·40
2795	75c. Couple dancing	3·25	2·40

1049 Human Bodies on Jigsaw

2000. 40th Anniv of Organ Donation Publicity Campaign.

2796	**1049**	75c. multicoloured	3·25	2·40

1050 Birth of Jesus (stained glass window, Sanctuary of Our Lady of the Rosary, New Pompeii)

2000. Christmas.

2797	**1050**	75c. multicoloured	3·25	2·40

1051 Commelina erecta

2000. Medicinal Plants. Multicoloured.

2798	75c. Type **1051**	3·25	2·40
2799	75c. Senna corymbosa	3·25	2·40
2800	75c. Mirabilis jalapa	3·25	2·40
2801	75c. Eugenia uniflora	3·25	2·40

1052 Human-shaped Vessel, Cienaga

2000. Traditional Crafts. Multicoloured.

2802	75c. Type **1052**	3·25	2·40
2803	75c. Painted human-shaped vase, Vaquerias	3·25	2·40
2804	75c. Animal-shaped vessel, Condorhuasi	3·25	2·40
2805	75c. Human-shaped vase, Candelaria	3·25	2·40

1053 "U. P." Unidad Postal

2001. Postal Agents' Stamps. Multicoloured, background colours given. Self-adhesive gum.

2806	**1053**	10c. turquoise	25	20
2807	**1053**	25c. green	70	55
2808	**1053**	60c. yellow	1·60	1·20
2809	**1053**	75c. red	2·20	1·70
2810	**1053**	$1 blue	3·00	2·20
2811	**1053**	$3 red	9·00	6·75
2812	**1053**	$3.25 yellow	9·75	7·25
2813	**1053**	$5.50 mauve	16·00	12·00

Nos. 2806/13 were issued for use by Postal Agents as opposed to branches of the Argentine Post Office.

1054 Megatherium americanum ("Megaterio")

2001. Cainozoic Mammals. Multicoloured.

2820	75c. Type **1054**	3·25	2·40
2821	75c. Doedicurus clavcaudatus ("Gliptodonte")	3·25	2·40
2822	75c. Macrauchenia patachonica ("Macrauqueria")	3·25	2·40
2823	75c. Toxodon platensis ("Toxodonte")	3·25	2·40

1055 Map, South Polar Skua and San Martin Base

2001. 50th Anniv of San Martín and Brown Antarctic Bases. Multicoloured.

2824	75c. Type **1055**	3·25	2·40
2825	75c. Blue-eyed cormorant, map and Brown Base	3·25	2·40

1056 Bees on Clover Flower

2001. Apiculture. Multicoloured.

2826	75c. Type **1056**	3·25	2·40
2827	75c. Bees on honeycomb	3·25	2·40
2828	75c. Bees and bee-keeper attending hives	3·25	2·40
2829	75c. Jar of honey and swizzle	3·25	2·40

Nos. 2826/9 were issued together, se-tenant, forming a composite design.

1057 Scientist with Fossilized Bones

2001. 50th Anniv of Argentine Antarctic Institute. Sheet 150×99 mm containing T **1057** and similar horiz design. Multicoloured.

MS2830	75c. Type **1057**; 75c. Scientist and surveying equipment	6·25	6·25

1058 Dornier Do-j Wal Flying Boat Plus Ultra and Route Map

2001. 75th Anniv of Major Ramon Franco's Flight from Spain to Argentina.

2831	**1058**	75c. multicoloured	3·25	2·40

1059 Horse's Bridle Fittings

2001. Silver Work. Each blue, silver and black.

2832	75c. Type **1059**	3·25	2·40
2833	75c. Stirrups	3·25	2·40
2834	75c. Spurs	3·25	2·40
2835	75c. Rastra (gaucho belt decoration)	3·25	2·40

1060 Washerwoman by the Banks of Belgrano (detail, Prilidiano Pueyrredon)

2001. Belgica 2001 International Stamp Exhibition, Brussels. 500th Anniv of European Postal Service. Sheet 99×75 mm containing T **1060** and similar horiz design. Multicoloured.

MS2836	25c. Type **1060**; 75c. Hay Harvest (detail, Pieter Bruegel, the Elder)	4·50	4·50

1061 Goalkeeper catching Ball

2001. Under 20's World Youth Football Championship, Argentine Republic. Multicoloured.

2837	75c. Type **1061**	3·25	2·40
2838	75c. Player kicking ball	3·25	2·40

1062 People and Buildings

2001. National Census.

2839	**1062**	75c. multicoloured	3·25	2·40

1063 SAC-C Satellite, Seagulls and Sunflowers

2001. Environmental Protection. Satellite Tracking Project.

2840	**1063**	75c. multicoloured	3·25	2·40

1064 Puma

2001. Wild Cats. Multicoloured.

2841	25c. Type **1064**	1·00	75
2842	25c. Jaguar	1·00	75
2843	50c. Jaguarundi	2·00	1·50
2844	50c. Ocelot	2·00	1·50
2845	75c. Geoffroy's Cat	3·25	2·40
2846	75c. Kodkod	3·25	2·40

1065 Bandoneon Recital (painting, Aldo Severi)

2001

2847	**1065**	75c. multicoloured	3·25	2·40

1066 Couple dancing the Tango

2001. PHILA NIPPON 01 International Stamp Exhibition, Tokyo. Sheet 100×75 mm containing T **1066** and similar horiz design. Multicoloured.

MS2848	75c. Type **1066**; 75c. Kabuki performer	6·25	6·25

1067 Discepolo

2001. Birth Centenary of Enriques Santos Discepolo (actor and lyric writer).
2849	**1067**	75c. multicoloured	3·50	2·50

1068 Courtyard, Caroya Estancia, Angel and Chapel, Estancia Santa Catalina

2001. UNESCO World Heritage Sites. Multicoloured.
2850		75c. Type **1068**	3·50	2·50
2851		75c. Emblem and chapel, Estancia La Candelaria, dome of Estancia Alta Gracia and belfry, Estancia Jesus Maria	3·50	2·50

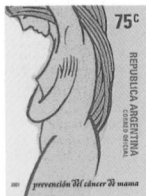

1069 Woman

2001. Breast Cancer Awareness.
2852	**1069**	75c. multicoloured	3·50	2·50

1070 Burmeister's Porpoise

2001. Marine Mammals. Multicoloured.
2853	25c.+25c. Type **1070**	2·30	2·10
2854	50c.+50c. La Plata River dolphin	4·75	4·25
2855	50c.+50c. Minke whale	4·75	4·25
2856	75c.+75c. Humpback whale	7·25	6·50

1071 Alfa Romeo 159 Alfetta, Spain, 1951

2001. Formula 1 Racing Cars driven by Juan Manuel Fangio. Multicoloured.
2857	75c. Type **1071**	3·25	2·40
2858	75c. Mercedes Benz W 196, France, 1954	3·25	2·40
2859	75c. Lancia-Ferrari D50, Monaco, 1956	3·25	2·40
2860	75c. Maserati 250 F, Germany, 1957	3·25	2·40

1072 Palo Santo Tree (*Bulnesia sarmientoi*)

2001. Mercosur (South American Common Market).
2861	**1072**	75c. multicoloured	3·25	2·40

1073 Justo Jose de Urquiza

2001. Birth Anniversaries. Multicoloured.
2862	75c. Type **1073** (politician) (bicentenary)	3·25	2·40
2863	75c. Roque Saenz Pena (President 1910—14) (150th anniv)	3·25	2·40

1074 18th-century Mail Courier

2001. HAFNIA 01 International Stamp Exhibition, Copenhagen. Sheet 100×75 mm containing T **1074** and similar horiz design. Multicoloured.
MS2864	25c. Type **1074**; 75c. 17th-century mail courier	5·00	5·00

1075 "La Pobladora" Carriage (Enrique Udaondo Graphic Museum Complex)

2001. Museums. Multicoloured.
2865	75c. Type **1075**	3·25	2·40
2866	75c. Ebony and silver crucifix (Brigadier General Juan Martin de Pueyrredon Museum) (vert)	3·25	2·40
2867	75c. Funerary urn (Emilio and Duncan Wagner Museum of Anthropological and Natural Sciences) (vert)	3·25	2·40
2868	75c. Skeleton of Carnotaurus sastrei (Argentine Natural Science Museum)	3·25	2·40

1076 *The Power of the Most High will Overshadow You* (Martin La Spina)

2001. Christmas.
2869	**1076** 75c. multicoloured	3·25	2·40

1077 Carola Lorenzini and Focke Wulf 44-J

2001. Aviation. Multicoloured.
2870	75c. Type **1077**	3·25	2·40
2871	75c. Jean Mermoz and Arc-en-Ciel	3·25	2·40

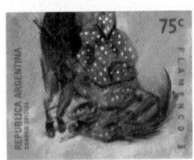

1078 Dancers (Flamenco)

2001. Dances. Multicoloured.
2872	75c. Type **1078**	3·25	2·40
2873	75c. Dancers (purple skirt) (Vals)	3·25	2·40
2874	75c. Dancers (orange skirt) (Zamba)	3·25	2·40
2875	75c. Dancers (Tango)	3·25	2·40

1079 Scene from *Apollon Musagete* (Igor Stravinsky)

2001. National Day of the Dancer.
2876	**1079** 75c. multicoloured	3·25	2·40

1080 Television Set, Camera and Microphone

2001. 50th Anniv of Television in Argentina. Multicoloured.
2877	75c. Type **1080**	3·25	2·40
2878	75c. Television set and video tapes	3·25	2·40
2879	75c. Satellite dish and astronaut	3·25	2·40
2880	75c. Colour television cables and remote control	3·25	2·40

1081 Consolidated PBY-5A Catalina (amphibian) and Cancellation

2002. 50th Anniv of Argentine Antarctic Programme. Multicoloured.
2881	75c. Type **1081** (first air and sea courier service)	3·25	2·40
2882	75c. Chiriguano (minesweeper) and buildings (foundation of Esparanza Base)	3·25	2·40

1082 House and Flag

2002. America. Education and Literacy Campaign. Multicoloured.
2883	75c. Type **1082**	3·25	2·40
2884	75c. Children playing hopscotch	3·25	2·40

1083 Two-banded Plover (*Charadrius falklandicus*)

2002. Birds. Multicoloured.
2885	50c. Type **1083**	1·80	1·30
2886	50c. Dolphin gull (*Larus scoresbii*)	1·80	1·30
2887	75c. Ruddy-headed goose (*Chloephaga rubidiceps*) (vert)	2·75	2·00
2888	75c. King penguin (*Aptenodytes patagonicus*) (vert)	2·75	2·00

1084 Flags of Championship Winners and Football

2002. 20th-century World Cup Football Champions. Multicoloured.
2889	75c. Type **1084**	2·75	2·00
2890	75c. Argentine footballer	2·75	2·00

1085 Parana River and Emblem

2002. Anniversaries. Multicoloured.
2891	25c. Type **1085** (150th anniv of Rosario City)	90	65
2892	25c. National flag and monument	90	65

2002. 50c. Mount Fitzroy (150th birth anniv of Francisco Pascasio Moreno (Perito) (explorer and founder of Argentine Scouts movement))
2893	50c. Mount Fitzroy (150th birth anniv of Francisco Pascasio Moreno (Perito) (explorer and founder of Argentine Scouts movement))	1·80	1·30
2894	50c. Dr. Moreno	1·80	1·30
2895	75c. Flower and view of city (centenary of foundation San Carlos de Bariloche)	2·75	2·00
2896	75c. Capilla San Eduardo (St. Edward's chapel) and city plan	2·75	2·00

1086 Fruit, Mother, Boy, Bread and Health Centre

2002. Centenary of Pan-American Health Organization.
2897	**1086**	75c. multicoloured	2·75	2·00

1087 Cosme Mariano Argerich, 1758–1820

2002. Doctors. Multicoloured.
2898	50c. Type **1087**	1·80	1·30
2899	50c. Jose Maria Ramos Mejia, 1849–1914	1·80	1·30
2900	50c. Salvador Mazza, 1886–1946	1·80	1·30
2901	50c. Carlos Arturo Giananonio, 1926–1995	1·80	1·30

1088 Hill of Seven Colours, Jujuy

2002. Landscapes. Multicoloured.
2902	75c. Type **1088**	2·75	2·00
2903	75c. Iguazu waterfall, Misiones	2·75	2·00
2904	75c. Talampaya National Park	2·75	2·00
2905	75c. Agoncagua mountain, Mendoza	2·75	2·00
2906	75c. Rosedal Park, Buenos Aires	2·75	2·00
2907	75c. San Jorge lighthouse, Chubut	2·75	2·00
2908	75c. Perito Moreno glacier, Santa Cruz	2·75	2·00
2909	75c. Lapataia Bay, Tierra del Fuego	2·75	2·00

See also Nos. 2980/7 and 3022/9.

1089 Pampas Deer (*Ozotoceros bezoarticus*)

2002. Endangered Species. Multicoloured.
2910	$1 Type **1089**	3·25	2·20
2911	$1 Vicuna (*Vicugna vicugna*)	3·25	2·20
2912	$1 Southern pudu (*Pudu pudu*)	3·25	2·20
2913	$1 Chaco peccary (*Catgonus wagneri*)	3·25	2·20

1090 Eva Peron

2002. 50th Death Anniv of Eva Peron. Multicoloured.
2914	75c. Type **1090**	2·75	2·00
2915	75c. In cameo	2·75	2·00
2916	75c. At microphone	2·75	2·00
2917	75c. In profile wearing earrings	2·75	2·00

1091 Argentine Footballer

2002. Philakorea 2002 International Stamp Exhibition. Sheet 100×75 mm containing T **1091** and similar horiz design. Multicoloured.
MS2918 $1.50 Type **1091**; $1.50 Korean footballer 6·75 6·75

1092 Boa Constrictor (*Boa lampalagua*)

2002. Reptiles. Multicoloured.
2919	25c.+25c. Type **1092**		1·10	80
2920	50c.+50c. Caiman (*Caiman yacare*)		2·30	1·60
2921	50c.+50c. Argentine black and white tegu (*Tupinambis merianae*)		2·30	1·60
2922	75c.+75c. Red-footed tortoise (*Chelonoidis carbonaria*)		3·50	2·40

1093 Whale's Head

2002. Mercosur (South American Common Market). Multicoloured.
2923	75c. Type **1093**		1·30	85
2924	75c. Whale's tail		1·30	85

1094 *Edessa meditabunda*

2002. Insects. Multicoloured.
2925	25c. Type **1094**		65	45
2926	50c. *Elaeochlora viridis*		1·30	85
2927	75c. *Chrysodina aurata*		1·90	1·30
2928	75c. *Steirastoma breve*		2·50	1·70

1095 Players, Ball and Net

2002. World Men's Volleyball Championships. Multicoloured.
2929	75c. Type **1095**		1·90	1·30
2930	75c. Two players ball and net		1·90	1·30
2931	75c. Hands, net, ball and head		1·90	1·30
2932	75c. Players congratulating one another		1·90	1·30

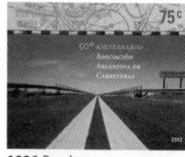

1096 Roadway

2002. 50th Anniv of Argentine Highways Department.
2933	**1096** 75c. multicoloured		1·90	1·30

1097 Roberto Arlt

2002. Death Anniversaries. Multicoloured.
2934	75c. Type **1097** (writer, 60th)		1·90	1·30
2935	75c. Luis Sandrini (actor and director, 22nd)		1·90	1·30
2936	75c. Nini Marshall (actor, 6th)		1·90	1·30
2937	75c. Beatriz Guido (writer, 14th)		1·90	1·30

1101 Andres Chazarreta (composer)

2002. Folklorists. Multicoloured.
2945	75c. Type **1101**		1·90	1·30
2946	75c. Gustavo "Cuchi" Leguiza-mon (songwriter)		1·90	1·30
2947	75c. Carlos Vega (guitarist)		1·90	1·30
2948	75c. Armando Tejada Gomez (poet and songwriter)		1·90	1·30

1098 Immigrant Hotel, Mother and Child

2002. Immigration. Multicoloured.
2938	75c. Type **1098**		1·90	1·30
2939	75c. Two men and ship		1·90	1·30
2940	75c. Two men and immigrant hotel		1·90	1·30
2941	75c. Horse-drawn farm imple-ment and family		1·90	1·30

Nos. 2938/41 were issued in horizontal *se-tenant* strips of four stamps within the sheet, each pair (2938/9 and 2940/1) forming a composite design.

1099 Envelope, Horse-drawn Coach and Head

2002. 50th Anniv of Argentine Federation of Philatelic Entities (FAEF). Multicoloured.
2942	75c. Type **1099**		1·90	1·30
2943	75c. Flag, figure, ship and arms		1·90	1·30

1100 Joseph leading Donkey carrying Mary and Jesus

2002. Christmas.
2944	**1100** 75c. multicoloured		1·90	1·30

1102 Girl (rod puppet)

2002. Puppets. Multicoloured.
2949	75c. Type **1102**		1·90	1·30
2950	75c. Fish and king (marionettes)		1·90	1·30
2951	75c. Man (marote puppet)		1·90	1·30
2952	75c. Figures (shadow puppets)		1·90	1·30

1103 Cabbage containing Hands

2003. "Pro Huerta" (communal gardens initiative). Multicoloured.
2953	75c. Type **1103**		1·90	1·30
2954	75c. Street map as corn cob (vert)		1·90	1·30

1104 Woven Bag and Band

2003. Mercosur (South American Common Market). Multicoloured.
2955	75c. Type **1104** (Pilaga and Toba people, Formosa province)		1·90	1·30
2956	75c. Basketwork sieve (Mbya people, Misiones province) and wooden servers (Wichi people, Salta province)		1·90	1·30

1105 Squirrel Cuckoo (*Piaya cayana*) (Colonia Benitez reserve)

2003. National Parks. Multicoloured.
2957	50c. Type **1105**		1·30	85
2958	50c. Grey brocket (*Mazama gouzoupira*) (Copo park)		1·30	85
2959	50c. Guanaco (*Lama guanicoe*) (Los Cardones)		1·30	85
2960	75c. Magellanic penguin (*Speniscus magellanicus*) (Monte Leon)		1·90	1·30
2961	75c. *Tinamotis pentlandii* (Campo de los Alisos)		1·90	1·30

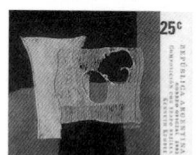

1106 *Composition with Rag Grid* (Kenneth Kemble)

2003. Art. Multicoloured.
2962	25c. Type **1106**		65	45
2963	25c. *Painting* (Roberto Aizen-berg) (vert)		65	45
2964	50c. *Screen* (Romulo Maccio) (vert)		1·30	85
2965	75c. *La Gioconda* (Guillemo Roux)		1·90	1·30
2966	75c. *To Flee* (Antonio Segui)		1·90	1·30
2967	$1 *San P.* (Xul Solar) (vert)		2·50	1·70

1107 Hockey Player

2003. Sport. Multicoloured.
2968	75c. Type **1107** (Women's Hockey World Champions, 2002)		1·90	1·30
2969	75c. Footballer (World Blind Football Champions, 2002)		1·90	1·30

No. 2969 was embossed with the face value in Braille.

1108 Mago Fafa (Broccoli)

2003. Cartoons. Sheet 156×120 mm containing T **1108** and similar vert designs. Multicoloured.
MS2970 25c. Type **1108**; 25c. Astro-nauta (Crist); 50c. Hijitus (Garcia Ferre); 50c. Savarese (Mandrafina and Robin Wood); 75c. Sonoman (Oswal); 75c. El Tipito (Daniel Paz and Rudy); 75c. La Vaca Aurora (Mirco); 75c. Diogenes y el Linyera (Tabare) 7·50 7·50

1109 19th-century Soup Tureen

2003. Silver Work. Multicoloured.
2971	75c. Type **1109**		1·90	1·30
2972	75c. Kettle, *mate de campana* and drinking tube		1·90	1·30
2973	75c. Chocolate pot and jug		1·90	1·30
2974	75c. 19th-century sugar bowl		1·90	1·30

Nos. 2971/4 were issued together, *se-tenant*, forming a composite design.

1110 Empanadas

2003. Traditional Foods. Multicoloured.
2975	75c. Type **1110** (turnovers)		1·90	1·30
2976	75c. Locro (corn and bean stew)		1·90	1·30
2977	75c. Parillada (mixed grill)		1·90	1·30
2978	75c. Pastilitos (miniature pastries)		1·90	1·30

1111 El Elastico (elastic)

2003. Children's Games. Sheet 108×88 mm containing T **1111** and similar horiz designs. Multicoloured.
MS2979 50c.×4 Type **1111**; La escon-dida (hide and seek); La mancha (tag); Martin pescador (Martin the fisherman) 4·50 4·50

2003. Landscapes. As T **1088**. Multicoloured.
2980	75c. Mbigua marsh, Formosa		1·90	1·30
2981	75c. Dead Man's salt flat, Catamarca		1·90	1·30
2982	75c. Quilmes ruins, Tucuman		1·90	1·30
2983	75c. Ibera marshland, Corrientes		1·90	1·30
2984	75c. Moon Valley, Ischigualasto park, San Juan		1·90	1·30
2985	75c. Mar del Plata city, Buenos Aires		1·90	1·30
2986	75c. Caleu Caleu, La Pampa		1·90	1·30
2987	75c. Lanin National Park, Neuqueen		1·90	1·30

1112 Velocipede (1855)

2003. Evolution of the Bicycle. Multicoloured.
2988	25c.+25c. Type **1112**		1·10	80
2989	50c.+50c. Penny farthing (1867)		2·30	1·60
2990	50c.+50c. Touring bicycle		2·30	1·60
2991	75c.+75c. Racing bicycle		3·50	2·40

1113 Bridge

2003. Inauguration of Nuestra Senora de Rosario Bridge over Parana River. Multicoloured.
2992	25c. Type **1113**		65	45
2993	75c. Ship and bridge		1·90	1·30

Nos. 2992/3 were issued together, *se-tenant*, forming a composite design of the bridge.

1114 Provincial
Emblem

2003. Rio Negro Province.

| 2994 | **1114** 75c. multicoloured | 1·90 | 1·30 |

1115 Dr. Vicente Fidel Lopez

2003. Anniversaries. Multicoloured.

2995	75c. Type **1115** (politician) (death centenary)	1·90	1·30
2996	75c. General San Martin Regiment (centenary of modern regiment)	1·90	1·30
2997	75c. Script and Bautista Alberdi (constitutional pioneer) (150th anniv of constitution)	1·90	1·30
2998	75c. Presidential palace and symbols of office	1·90	1·30

1116 Demon Mask

2003. Bangkok 2003 International Stamp Exhibition. Sheet 150×100 mm containing T **1116** and similar vert design. Multicoloured.

MS2999 75c.×2 Type **1116** (Quebrada de Humahuaca carnival, Argentine); Spirit mask (Phi Ta Khon festival, Thailand) ... 3·50 ... 3·50

1117 Andean Condor (*Vultur gryphus*)

2003. America. Flora and Fauna. Multicoloured.

| 3000 | 75c. Type **1117** | 1·90 | 1·30 |
| 3001 | 75c. *Nothofagus pumilio* (tree), forest and mountains | 1·90 | 1·30 |

1118 Map, Laboratory and Tres Hermanos Mountain

2003. 50th Anniv of Jubany Antarctic Base.

| 3002 | **1118** 75c. multicoloured | 1·90 | 1·30 |

1119 Cattle

2003. National Products. Multicoloured.

3003	75c. Type **1119** (livestock)	1·90	1·30
3004	75c. Soya beans (agriculture)	1·90	1·30
3005	75c. Telecobalt therapy machines (nuclear medicine)	1·90	1·30
3006	75c. Drums and bars (aluminium production)	1·90	1·30

1120 Corvette *Uruguay*

2003. Centenary of Rescue of Swedish Scientists by Argentine Corvette Uruguay. Multicoloured.

| 3007 | 75c. Type **1120** | 1·90 | 1·30 |

MS3008 150×99 mm. 75c.×2 Swedish ship (40×30 mm); Captain Julian Irizar and *Uruguay* (40×30 mm) ... 3·50 ... 3·50

1121 The Nativity (clay figures)

2003. Christmas. Multicoloured.

| 3009 | 75c. Type **1121** | 1·90 | 1·30 |
| 3010 | 75c. "Guacho Birth" (wooden carving) (Eloy Lopez) | 1·90 | 1·30 |

1122 Savings Bank Building, Cordoba

2003. 20th-Century Architecture. Multicoloured.

3011	75c. Type **1122**	1·90	1·30
3012	75c. Bank, San Miguel de Tucuman	1·90	1·30
3013	75c. Minetti Palace, Rosario	1·90	1·30
3014	75c. Barolo Palace, Buenos Aires	1·90	1·30

1123 Helicopter over Orcados Base

2004. Centenary of Orcados Base and Orcados del Sud Post Office, Antarctica. Multicoloured.

| 3015 | 75c. Type **1123** | 1·90 | 1·30 |

MS3016 150×100 mm. 75c.×2, 5 cent 1904 stamp and "Orcados del Sud" 1904 postmark; Orcados meteorological observatory, 1904 ... 3·50 ... 3·50

1124 Llama, Cave Painting, Painted Door and Rio Grande Valley

2004. UNESCO World Heritage Site. Quebrada de Humahuaca. Multicoloured.

| 3017 | 75c. Type **1124** | 1·90 | 1·30 |
| 3018 | 75c. Church, festival procession and valley | 1·90 | 1·30 |

Nos. 3017/18 were issued together, *se-tenant*, forming a composite design.

1125 Green Forest

2004. America. Endangered Species. Destruction of the Rainforest. Multicoloured.

| 3019 | 75c. Type **1125** | 1·90 | 1·30 |

| 3020 | 75c. Dying forest | 1·90 | 1·30 |

Nos. 3019/20 were issued together, *se-tenant*, forming a composite design.
The centre of No. 3020 has been removed to simulate burning.

1126 Masthead of First Edition and Modern Copy

2004. Centenary of *La Voz del Interior* Newspaper.

| 3021 | **1126** 75c. multicoloured | 1·90 | 1·30 |

2004. Landscapes. As T **1088**. Multicoloured.

3022	75c. Drying peppers, Molinas, Salta	1·90	1·30
3023	75c. Man leading donkey, Pampa del Indio Park, Chaco	1·90	1·30
3024	75c. Dam on Rio Dulce river, Rio Hondo, Santiago del Estero	1·90	1·30
3025	75c. Bridge over Setubal lagoon, Santa Fe de la Vera Cruz	1·90	1·30
3026	75c. San Roque lake, Cordoba	1·90	1·30
3027	75c. Palm Grove National Park, Entre Rios	1·90	1·30
3028	75c. Potero de los Funes, San Luis	1·90	1·30
3029	75c. Tronador mountain, Rio Negro	1·90	1·30

1127 Street Football

2004. Centenary of FIFA (Federation Internationale de Football Association). Paintings by Ruben Ramonda. Multicoloured.

| 3030 | 75c. Type **1127** | 1·90 | 1·30 |
| 3031 | 75c. The Tunnel | 1·90 | 1·30 |

1128 *Back from Fishing* (Joaquin Sorolla y Bastida)

2004. Espana 2004 International Stamp Exhibition, Valencia. Sheet 150×100 mm containing T **1128** and similar multicoloured design.

MS3032 75c. Type **1128**; 75c. "At Rest in the Pampa" (Angel Della Valle) (vert) ... 3·50 ... 3·50

1129 Compass in Case

2004. 125th Anniv of Naval Hydro-Graphic Service. Multicoloured.

3033	75c. Type **1129**	1·90	1·30
3034	75c. Sextant	1·90	1·30
3035	75c. Cabo Virgenes lighthouse	1·90	1·30
3036	75c. *Puerto Deseado* (hydrographic ship)	1·90	1·30

1130 Performing Dogs

2004. Circus. Sheet 109×88 mm containing T **1130** and similar horiz designs. Multicoloured.

MS3037 75c. Type **1130**; 50c. Trapeze artiste; 50c. Clown riding unicycle; 50c. Equestrienne ... 4·00 ... 4·00

The stamps of No. **MS**3037 form a composite design of a circus ring.

1131 Isidorito

2004. Patorutzito (character from graphic magazine by Dante Quinterno). Designs showing characters. Multicoloured.

3038	75c. Patoruzito (20×60 mm)	1·90	1·30
3039	75c. Pamperito (20×60 mm)	1·90	1·30
3040	75c. Isidorito (30×29 mm)	1·90	1·30
3041	75c. Malen	1·90	1·30
3042	75c. Upita	1·90	1·30
3043	75c. Chacha	1·90	1·30

MS3044 167×118 mm. 25c. Type **1131**; 25c. Upita (different); 50c. Patoruzito; 50c. Malen (different); 75c. Pamperito; 75c. Chacha plus 2 stamp size labels ... 7·00 ... 7·00

The stamps and labels contained in **MS**3044 form a composite design.

1132 Woman and Guide Dog

2004. Working Dogs. Multicoloured.

| 3045 | 75c. Type **1132** | 1·90 | 1·30 |
| 3046 | 75c. Rescue dog (horiz) | 1·90 | 1·30 |

1133 *Patagonotothen ramsay*

2004. Endangered Species. Fish. Multicoloured.

3047	75c. Type **1133**	1·90	1·30
3048	75c. *Bathyraja griseocauda*	1·90	1·30
3049	75c. *Salilota australis*	1·90	1·30
3050	75c. *Dissostichus eleginoides*	1·90	1·30

1134 Cycling

2004. Olympic Games, Athens 2004. Multicoloured.

3051	75c. Type **1134**	1·90	1·30
3052	75c. Judo	1·90	1·30
3053	75c. Swimming	1·90	1·30
3054	75c. Tennis	1·90	1·30

1135 Villarino

2004. Naval Carriers. Multicoloured.

3055	25c.+25c. Type **1135**	90	70
3056	50c.+50c. *Pampa*	1·80	1·30
3057	50c.+50c. *Bahia Thetis*	1·80	1·30
3058	75c.+75c. *Cabo de Hornis*	2·50	2·20

Nos. 3055/8 were issued together, *se-tenant*, forming a composite design.

1136 Queen Palm Fruit (*Syagrus romanzoffiana*)

2004. Singapore 2004 International Stamp Exhibition. Fruit. Sheet 150×100 mm containing T **1136** and similar vert designs.
MS3059 75c.×2, Type **1136**; Mango 2·50 1·70

1137 El Pehuen

2004. Legends and Traditions. Multicoloured.
3060	75c. Type **1137** (legend of araucaria tree)	1·60	1·10
3061	75c. La Yacumama (Diaguita water goddess)	1·60	1·10
3062	75c. La Pachamama (earth goddess)	1·60	1·10
3063	75c. La Difunta Correa (legend of mother who died of thirst)	1·60	1·10

1138 Early Students and Microscope

2004. Centenaries. Multicoloured.
3064	75c. Type **1138** (Agronomy and Veterinary Science Institute)	1·60	1·10
3065	75c. Jose san Martin (statue) and road and rail bridges over Nequen river (Neuqin city)	1·60	1·10
3066	75c. Monument and cover of *La Coleccionista* (Rosario Philatelic Association)	1·60	1·10

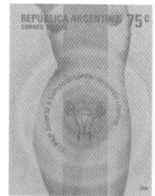
1139 Woman's Torso and Campaign Emblem

2004. Cervical Cancer Awareness Campaign.
3067 **1139** 75c. multicoloured 1·60 1·10

1140 Hourglass containing Clear Water

2004. Mercosur. Water Conservation Campaign. Multicoloured.
3068	75c. Type **1140**	1·60	1·10
3069	75c. Hourglass containing contaminated water	1·60	1·10

1141 Mary

2004. Christmas. Multicoloured.
3070	75c. Type **1141**	1·60	1·10
3071	75c. The Nativity	1·60	1·10

1142 Reverse

2004. 1813 One Ounce Gold Coin. Multicoloured.
3072	75c. Type **1142**	1·60	1·10
3073	75c. Obverse	1·60	1·10

Nos. 3072/3 were issued together, *se-tenant*, forming a composite design.

1143 "Spanish Grammar for Americans" and Andres Bello (author)

2004. Third International Spanish Language Congress.
3074 **1143** 75c. multicoloured 1·60 1·10

1144 Exchange Building

2004. 150th Anniv of Buenos Aires Commodities Exchange.
3075 **1144** 75c. multicoloured 1·60 1·10

1145 *Aloysia citriodora*

2004. Aromatic Plants. Multicoloured.
3076	75c. Type **1145**	1·60	1·10
3077	75c. *Minthostachys mollis*	1·60	1·10
3078	75c. *Tagetes minuta*	1·60	1·10
3079	75c. *Lippia turbinate*	1·60	1·10

1146 Emblem and Scout

2005. 12th Pan American Scout Jamboree, Mendoza.
3080 **1146** 75c. multicoloured 1·60 1·10

1147 Ram Klong Yao Dance (Thailand)

2005. 50th Anniv of Thailand—Argentina Diplomatic Relations. Multicoloured.
3081	75c. Type **1147**	1·60	1·10
3082	75c. Tango (Argentina)	1·60	1·10

1148 *Woman in Red Sweater*

2005. Birth Centenary of Alberto Berni (artist). Details from painting. Multicoloured.
3083 75c. Type **1148** 1·60 1·10
MS3084 150×99 mm. 75c.×2 Face (detail); Baby and men wearing hats (detail) (horiz) 3·25 3·25

The stamps and margin of No. MS3084 form a composite design of *Manifestation*.

1149 Rotary International Emblem, Children and Vaccine

2005. Centenary of Rotary International (charitable organization). Eradication of Polio Campaign.
3085 **1149** 75c. multicoloured 1·60 1·10

1150 Silvina Ocampo

2005. Mercosaur. Writers. Multicoloured.
3086	75c. Type **1150** (1903–1993)	1·60	1·10
3087	75c. Ezequiel Martinez Estrada (1895–1964)	1·60	1·10

1151 Sedan Graciela

2005. National Motor Industry. Multicoloured.
3088	75c. Type **1151**	1·60	1·10
3089	75c. Justicalista sport	1·60	1·10
3090	75c. Rastrojero diesel	1·60	1·10
3091	75c. Siam di Tella 1500	1·60	1·10
3092	75c. Torino 380W	1·60	1·10

1152 Jose Antonio Balseiro (founder) and Nuclear Reactor

2005. 50th Anniv of Balseiro Institute. International Year of Physics. Multicoloured.
3093	75c. Type **1152**	1·60	1·10
3094	75c. Albert Einstein and frontispiece of *Theory of Special Relativity*	1·60	1·10

1153 Pope John Paul II

2005. Pope John Paul II Commemoration. Multicoloured.
3095 75c. Type **1153** 1·60 1·10
MS3096 150×99 mm. 75c.×2, (each 40×50 mm) Wearing mitre and carrying pastoral staff; Saying farewell 3·25 3·25

1154 Workers at Machines and Demonstrators

2005. Anniversaries. Multicoloured.
3097	75c. Type **1154** (75th anniv of Workers Confederation)	1·60	1·10
3098	75c. Mar del Plata and *La Capital* (centenary of *La Capital* newspaper)	1·60	1·10
3099	75c. Alfredo Palacios (centenary of Sunday blue law)	1·60	1·10

1155 Cesar Milstein

2005. Cesar Milstein (Nobel Prize for Medicine, 1984) Commemoration.
3100 **1155** 75c. multicoloured 1·60 1·10

1156 Orestes Liberti (1st Commander) and Horse-drawn Fire Engine

2005. Volunteer Fire Fighters. Multicoloured.
3101	75c. Type **1156**	1·60	1·10
3102	75c. Fighting fire and modern engine	1·60	1·10

1157 Early and Modern Red Cross Workers

2005. 125th Anniv of Argentine Red Cross Society.
3103 **1157** 75c. multicoloured 1·60 1·10

1158 Abyssinian

2005. Cats. Sheet 117×166 mm containing T **1158** and similar horiz designs. Multicoloured.
MS3104 25c. Birman; 25c. Siamese; 50c. Oriental shorthair; 50c. Persian; 75c. Type **1158**; 75c. European shorthair 5·00 5·00

1159 Juan Filloy

2005. Fifth Death Anniv of Juan Filloy (writer).
3105 **1159** 75c. multicoloured 1·60 1·10

1160 Malbec

2005. Tourism. Wine. Multicoloured.
3106	75c. Type **1160** (Mendoza, Tupungato Valley)	1·60	1·10
3107	75c. Merlot (Rio Negro, Alto Valle de Rio Negro)	1·60	1·10
3108	75c. Syrah (San Juan - Zonda Valley)	1·60	1·10
3109	75c. Torrontes (Salta - Cafayate, Calchaquies Valleys)	1·60	1·10

See also Nos. 3202/4.

1161 Our Lady of the Rosary Candonga Chapel, Sierras Chicas, Cordoba

2005. Places of Worship. Multicoloured.
3110	75c. Type **1161**	1·60	1·10
3111	75c. Al Ahmad Mosque, Buenos Aires	1·60	1·10

3112	75c. Israelite Congregation of Argentine Temple, Buenos Aires	1·60	1·10
3113	75c. Vision of the Middle Buddhist Temple, Buenos Aires	1·60	1·10

1162 Pulperia Perucho, Gral, Lavalle, Mendoza

2005. Stores (Pulperias). Multicoloured.

3114	75c. Type **1162**	1·60	1·10
3115	75c. El Torito, Baradero, Buenos Aires	1·60	1·10
3116	75c. Impini, Larroque, Entre Rios	1·60	1·10
3117	75c. Pulperia de Cacho di Catarina	1·60	1·10

1163 Rio De la Plata (merchant vessel)

2005. Ships. Multicoloured.

3118	25c.+25c. Type **1163**	95	60
3119	50c.+50c. Libertad (passenger ship)	1·80	1·00
3120	50c.+50c. Camopo Duran (tanker)	1·80	1·00
3121	75c.+75c. Isla Soledad (container ship)	2·50	2·20

Nos. 3118/21 were issued together, *se-tenant*, forming a composite design.

1164 Julio Bocca (dancer)

2005. Colon Theatre. Multicoloured.

3122	75c. Type **1164**	1·60	1·10
3123	75c. Theatre orchestra, opera singers and choir	1·60	1·10

1165 Ice Flow

2005. First Anniv of Antarctic Treaty Secretariat, Buenos Aires (3124). General Hernan Pujato's Expeditions to Antarctica (MS3125). Mult.

3124	75c. Type **1165**	1·60	1·10
MS3125	150×100 mm. 75c.×2, Divers and boat; General Pujato and team members	3·25	3·25

1166 Virgin and Child (detail)

2005. Christmas. Showing parts of the painting *Retablo* by Elena Strorni. Multicoloured.

3126	75c. Type **1166**	1·60	1·10
MS3127	150×100 mm. 75c.×4, The Annunciation (40×40 mm); The Nativity (40×40 mm); Three Wise Men (40×40 mm); Presenting Jesus in the temple (40×40 mm)	6·25	6·25

1167 Solar Panel and Light Bulb

2005. Alternative Energy. Multicoloured.

3128	75c. Type **1167**	1·60	1·10
3129	$4 Wind generators	6·25	4·75

1168 Mar de Plata Port and Summit Emblem

2005. Fourth Americas' Summit.

3130	**1168** 75c. multicoloured	1·60	1·10

1169 German Immigrants, Canada de Gomez, Santa Fe

2005. Immigration. Multicoloured.

3131	75c. Type **1169**	1·60	1·10
3132	75c. Slovakian women and children, Immigrant Hotel, Buenos Aires	1·60	1·10
3133	75c. Welsh immigrants, Chubut Central Railway, Trelew	1·60	1·10
3134	75c. Jewish colony, Moises Ville, Santa Fe	1·60	1·10

1170 Luis Angel Firpo

2005. Sport. Boxers. Multicoloured.

3135	75c. Type **1170**	1·60	1·10
3136	75c. Nicolino Locche	1·60	1·10

1171 Man (film, *Ivan & Eva*)

2005. Design. Multicoloured.

3137	75c. Type **1171**	1·60	1·10
3138	75c. Dress (Nadine Zlotogora) (clothes and textile) (vert)	1·60	1·10
3139	75c. Aluminium chair (Ricardo Blanco) (industrial design) (vert)	1·60	1·10
3140	75c. CD case (Claudia Smith) (graphic design)	1·60	1·10

1172 Bartolme Mitre

2006. Death Centenary of Bartolme Mitre (journalist and president 1862–8).

3141	**1172** 75c. multicoloured	1·60	1·10

1173 Snow-covered City

2006. Centenary of Esquel.

3142	**1173** 75c. multicoloured	1·60	1·10

2006. Tourism. Wine. As T **1160**. Multicoloured.

3143	50c. Vineyard, Alto Valle del Rio Negro (Merlot wine) (Rio Negro) (70×30 mm)	1·10	75
3144	75c. Wine barrels (Salta)	1·60	1·10
3145	1p. Grape harvest (San Juan)	2·20	1·50
3146	1p.25 Vineyard, Valle del Tupungato (Malbec wine) (Mendoza) (70×30 mm)	2·40	1·60
3147	2p.75 Wine tasting (Mendoza)	2·50	1·70
3148	3p. Vineyard, Valle del Zonda (Syrah wine) (San Juan) (70×30 mm)	2·75	1·90
3149	3p.25 Vineyard, Cafayate, Valles Calchaquies (Torrentes wine) (Salta) (70×30 mm)	3·00	2·00
3150	3p.50 Wine vats (Rio Negro)	3·25	2·20

1175 Ramon Carrillo

2006. Birth Centenary of Ramon Carrillo (health care specialist).

3151	**1175** 75c. multicoloured	1·60	95

1176 Guitar

2006. Mercosur. Musical Instruments. Multicoloured.

3152	75c. Type **1176**	1·60	95
3153	$3.50 Drum	5·00	3·50

1177 1 de Mayo Lighthouse

2006. Lighthouses. Multicoloured.

3154	75c. Type **1177**	1·60	90
3155	75c. Ano Nuevo	1·60	90
3156	75c. El Rincon	1·60	90
3157	75c. Recalada a Bahia Blanca	1·60	90

1178 Escuela de Mecanica de la Armada (concentration camp) (1976)

2006. *From Horror to Hope*. 30th Anniv of Military Dictatorship. Sheet 151×99 mm containing T **1178** and similar vert design. Multicoloured.

MS3158	75c.×2, Type **1178**; Escuela de Mecanica de la Armada (memorial museum) (2006)	3·25	3·25

1179 Crown

2006. 18th-century Religious Silverware. Multicoloured.

3159	75c. Type **1179**	1·60	95
3160	75c. Candelabra	1·60	95
3161	75c. Chalice	1·60	95
3162	75c. Viaticum	1·60	95

1180 Toyota Corolla WRC (Luis Perez Companc—Rally Nacional A8 category)

2006. National Motor Racing Champions. Multicoloured.

3163	75c. Type **1180**	1·60	95
3164	75c. Ford Falcon (Juan Manuel Silva—Turismo Carretera category)	1·60	95
3165	75c. Ford Focus (Gabriel Ponce de Leon—Turismo Competición 2000 category)	1·60	95
3166	75c. Ford Escort (Patricio di Palma—Class 3 Nacional category)	1·60	95

1181 Springer Spaniel

2006. Dogs. Sheet 117×166 mm containing T **1181** and similar horiz designs. Multicoloured.

MS3167	25c. Type **1181**; 25c. Yorkshire terrier; 50c. Argentine dogo (Argentinian mastiff); 50c. Miniature schnauzer; 75c. Poodle; 75c. Chow	6·50	2·75

No. **MS**3167 also contains two illustrated stamp size labels forming a composite design.

1182 Argentine Player

2006. World Cup Football Championship, Germany. Multicoloured.

3168	1p. Type **1182**	1·90	1·90
3169	1p. Serbia and Montenegro	1·90	1·90
3170	1p. Ivory Coast	1·90	1·90
3171	1p. Netherlands	1·90	1·90
3172	4p. Football in net	5·75	4·25
MS3173	149×100 mm. 1p.50 As No. 3168 (detail)	2·75	2·75

1183 Knotted Cigarette (image scaled to 49% of original size)

2006. World Health Organization No Tobacco Day.

3174	**1183** 75c. multicoloured	1·60	95

1184 Lizard Outline and Dead Tree

2006. International Year of Deserts and Desertification. Multicoloured.

3175	75c. Type **1184**	1·60	95
3176	75c. Lilotaemus (lizard) and Calycera crassifolia	1·60	95

1185 Mauricio Borensztein (Tato Bores) (actor)

2006. Personalities. Multicoloured.

3177	75c. Type **1185**	1·60	95
3178	75c. Rodolfo Walsh (journalist)	1·60	95

1186 Alpine Skiing

2006. Winter Sports. Multicoloured.

3179	75c. Type **1186**	1·60	95
3180	75c. Snowboarding	1·60	95
3181	75c. Cross-country skiing	1·60	95
3182	75c. Biathlon	1·60	95

1187 Musician

2006. Tango. Multicoloured.
3183	75c. Type **1187**	1·60	95
3184	$4 Dancers	1·60	95

Stamps of a similar design were issued by France.

1188 Patoruzito riding Pamperito

2006. Patoruzito (character from graphic magazine by Dante Quinterno). Opening of *Patoruzito—La Gran Adventura* (film).
3185	**1188** 75c. multicoloured	1·60	95

1189 Taruca (*Hippocamelus antisensis*)

2006. Natural Monuments. Multicoloured.
3186	75c. Type **1189**	1·60	95
3187	75c. Southern right whale (*Eubaluena australis*)	1·60	95
3188	75c. Huemul (*Hippocamelus bisculus*)	1·60	95
3189	75c. Jaguar (*Panthera onca*)	1·60	95

1190 House as Money Box and Plug connected to Sun (Florencia Tovi)

2006. America. Energy Conservation. Winning Designs in Children's Drawing Competition. Multicoloured.
3190	75c. Type **1190**	1·60	95
3191	75c. Window, table and standard lamp (Camila Suarez)	1·60	95

1191 *The Re-conquest of Buenos Aires* (Charles Fouqueray)

2006. Bicentenary of British Invasion and Defeat. Sheet 99×75 mm.
MS3192	**1191** 1p.50 multicoloured	2·75	2·75

1192 Flags as Ribbons

2006. 30th Council of the Common Market. Mercosur and Associate States' Presidents' Summit.
3193	**1192** 3p.50 multicoloured	1·60	95

1193 *Ciudad de Buenos Aires* (image scaled to 49% of original size)

2006. River Transport. Multicoloured.
3194	25c.+25c. Type **1193**	1·60	95
3195	50c.+50c. *Lambare*	1·60	95
3196	50c.+50c. *Madrid*	1·60	95
3197	75c.+75c. *Rawson*	1·60	95

1194 "150 Anos"

2006. 150th Anniv of First Argentine Stamp. Multicoloured.
3198	75c. Type **1194**	1·60	95

MS3199 151×99 mm. $1.50 As Type **3**
(1856 1 real stamp) (40×40 mm)	2·75	2·75

1195 Colorado River Basin

2006. 30th Anniv of Comite Interjurisdiccional de Rio Colorado (COIRCO) (inter-jurisdictional committee on the Colorado river).
3200	**1195** 75c. multicoloured	1·60	95

1196 Legion de Patricios Rifleman (1806–9)

2006. Bicentenary of Infantry Corps "Patricios".
3201	**1196** 75c. multicoloured	1·60	95

2006. Tourism. Wine. As T **1160**. Multicoloured.
3202	75c. Syrah (Catamarcaungato Valley)	1·60	95
3203	75c. Torrontes Riojano (La Rioja)	1·60	95
3204	75c. Pinot noir (Neuquen)	1·60	95

1197 Cadets

2006. Centenary of Ramon L. Falcon Cadet School.
3205	**1197** 75c. multicoloured	1·60	95

1198 Puente San Roque Gonzalez de Santa Cruz, between Argentina and Paraguay

2006. International Bridges in Argentina. Multicoloured.
3206	75c. Type **1198**	1·60	95
3207	75c. Puente Presidente Tancredo Neves, between Argentina and Brazil	1·60	95

1199 *Madona y Paloma*

2006. Christmas. Paintings by Alfredo Guttero. Multicoloured.
3208	75c. Type **1199**	1·60	95
3209	75c. *Anunciacion* (horiz)	1·60	95

1200 Research Activities

2006. National Institute of Farming Technology.
3210	**1200** 75c. multicoloured	1·60	95

1201 Norberto Napolitano (Pappo)

2006. 40th Anniv of Argentinean Rock Music. Multicoloured.
3211	75c. Type **1201**	1·60	95
3212	75c. Luca George (Luca) Prodan	1·60	95
3213	75c. Miguel Angel Peralta (Miguel Abuelo)	1·60	95
3214	75c. Jose Alberto Iglesias (Tanguito)	1·60	95

1202 Valentin Sayhueque

2006. Caciques (tribal chiefs). Multicoloured.
3215	75c. Type **1202** (Huilliche people)	1·60	95
3216	75c. Casimiro Bigua (Tehuelche people)	1·60	95

1203 *Hercules* (detail from painting *Combate de Marin Garcia* by Emilio Biggeri)

2007. 150th Death Anniv of Admiral William Brown.
3217	**1203** 75c. multicoloured	1·60	95

1204 Grapes (Neuquen)

2007. Tourism. Wine. Multicoloured.
3218	75c. Type **1204**	1·60	95
3219	75c. Grapes (Catamarca)	1·60	95
3220	75c. Grapes (La Rioja)	1·60	95
3221	3p.25 Bottle (Neuquen)	3·75	2·40
3222	3p.25 Bottle (Catamarca)	3·75	2·40
3223	3p.25 Bottle (La Rioja)	3·75	2·40

1205 1982 18 pesos Stamp and Ofincina Radiopostal Islas Malvinas Postmark

2007. 25th Anniv of South Atlantic Conflict. Multicoloured.
3224	75c. Type **1205**	1·60	95
3225	75c. IAI Dagger Fighter aircraft	1·60	95
3226	75c. Battle Cruiser *General Belgrano*	1·60	95
3227	75c. Decorated veteran	1·60	95
3228	75c. Decoration awarded to all veterans (*vert*)	1·60	95

1206 Postal Workers (detail from painting by Jose Murcia)

2007. 50th Anniv of Postal and Telecommunications Workers Federation (FOECYT).
3229	**1206** 75c. multicoloured	1·60	95

1207 *Phalacrocorax atriceps* (Imperial or blue-eyed cormorant)

2007. Argentina in Antarctica. Multicoloured..
3230	75c. Type **1207**	1·60	95
3231	75c. *Leptonychotes weddellii* (Weddell seal)	1·60	95
3232	75c. *Sterna vittata* (Antarctic tern)	1·60	95
3233	75c. *Sterna vittata* (Antarctic tern)	1·60	95
3234	75c. *Pysoscelis adeliae* (Adelie penguin)	1·60	95
3235	75c. *Chionis alba* (snowy or yellow-billed sheathbill)	1·60	95
3236	75c. *Pygoscelis papua* (gentoo penguins)	1·60	95
3237	75c. *Pygoscelis papua* (gentoo penguins)	1·60	95
3238	4p. *Almirante Irizar* (ice breaker)	5·00	3·50

Nos. 3232/3 and 3236/7 were issued together, *se-tenant*, forming a composite design.

1208 Latin American Art Museum, Buenos Aires

2007. Architecture. Multicoloured.
3239	75c. Type **1208**	1·60	95
3240	3p.25. High Mountain Archaeological Museum, Salta	4·50	3·00

1209 Rocking Horse

2007. Toys. Multicoloured.
3241	75c. Type **1209**	1·60	95
3242	75c. Tea set	1·60	95
3243	75c. Train set	1·60	95
3244	75c. Soldiers	1·60	95

1210 Emblem

2007. National Road Safety Campaign.
3245	**1210** 75c. red and silver	1·60	95

1211 Argentine Bases

2007. International Polar Year. Sheet 150×98 mm.
MS3246	**1211** 4p. multicoloured	5·00	3·50

1212 *Combate de Santo Domingo* (Eleodora Marenco)

2007. Bicentenary of Defence of Buenos Aires.
3247 **1212** 75c. multicoloured 1·60 95

1213 Radiation and
Fluorescence Detectors

2007. Pierre Auger Observatory.
3248 **1213** 75c. multicoloured 1·60 95

1214 St. Jose de
Calasanz and Pupils
(stained glass window,
San Jose de Calasanz
Church, Buenos Aires)

2007. 450th Birth Anniv of Jose de Calasanz (founder of
first free school in modern Europe).
3249 **1214** 1p. multicoloured 1·90 1·20

1215 Campfire

2007. Centenary of Scouting. Multicoloured.
3250 25c.+25c. Type **1215** 90 60
3251 50c.+50c. Tent and scout
saluting 1·80 1·20
3252 75c.+75c. Scout wearing pack 2·20 1·50
3253 1p.+1p. Scouts pulling guy rope 2·50 1·70
Nos. 3250/3 were issued together, *se-tenant*, forming a
composite design.

1216 *El Chaco* (meteorite)

2007. Meteorites of Campo Del Cielo. Sheet 148×99 mm.
MS3254 6p. multicoloured 6·25 6·00

1217 *Homero Manzi*
(Hermenegildo Sabat)

2007. Birth Centenary of Homero Nicolas Manzione
Prestera (Homero Manzi) (lyricist).
3255 **1217** 1p. multicoloured 1·60 95

1218 Road leading
to S. C. de Bariloche
(Rio Negro)

2007. Tourism. National Route 40. Sheet 496×99 mm
containing T **1218** and similar horiz designs.
Multicoloured.
MS3256 50c. Type **1218**; 50c. Abra
El Acay (40×30 mm); 1p. Road to
Perito Moreno (Santa Cruz) (70×30
mm); 1p. *La Trochita* locomotive
(Chubut) (40×30 mm); 1p. Lanin
volcano (Neuquen) (40×30 mm),
1p. Rio Grande (Mendoza) (50×30
mm); 1p. Goats, San Jose Jachal (San
Juan) (40×30 mm); 1p. Cuesta de
Miranda (La Rioja) (50×30 mm); 1p.
Capel Nuestra Senora del Transito
(Catamarca); 1p. Ruins of Quilmes
(Tucuman); 1p. Road leading to
Oratorio (Jujuy) (40×30 mm) 10·00 9·50

1219 Houses with Blocked
and Free-flowing Chimneys
(Julieta Saavedra Barrgan)

2007. Carbon Monoxide Inhalation Prevention Campaign.
Winning Designs in Children's Drawing Competition.
Multicoloured.
3257 1p. Type **1219** 1·80 1·20
3258 1p. Dirty and clean flames
(Efrain Osvaldo Rost) (vert) 1·80 1·20
3259 1p. Engineer and gas cooker
(Camila Micaela Alvarez
Petrone) (vert) 1·80 1·20
3260 1p. Smoking fire (Leandro
Ventancour) 1·80 1·20

1220 Accordion

2007. 150th Anniv of Argentine–Germany Bilateral
Relations. Sheet 150×100 mm.
MS3261 4p. multicoloured 5·25 5·25

1221 Emblem

2007. Centenary of Club Atletico San Lorenzo de
Almagro.
3262 **1221** 1p. multicoloured 1·80 1·20

1222 Ceferino Namuncura

2007. Beatification of Ceferino Namuncura.
3263 **1222** 1p. multicoloured 1·80 1·20

1223 *Corrientes esquina
Uruguay* (Horacio Cuppola)

2007. Contemporary Art. Multicoloured.
3264 1p. Type **1223** 1·80 1·20
3265 1p. *Dialogo* (Liliana Porter)
(vert) 1·80 1·20
3266 1p. *0611* (detail) (Pablo Siqier) 1·80 1·20
3267 1p. *Imaginando el estupor* (de-
tail) (Marta Minujin) (vert) 1·80 1·20

1224 Three Wise
Men

2007. Christmas. Showing detail from The Birth (stained
glass window)). Multicoloured.
3268 25c. Type **1224** 1·80 1·20
3269 1p. Holy Family 1·80 1·20

1225 Early Drilling Site

2007. Centenary of Oil and Gas Discovery in Argentina.
3270 **1225** 1p. multicoloured 1·80 1·20

1226 *Pampero* (balloon) and
River Plate

2007. Centenary of Aaron de Anchorena and Jorge
Newbery's Balloon Flight across the River Plate.
3271 **1226** 1p. multicoloured 1·80 1·20

1227 Ceremonial Staff

2007. Presidential Inauguration. 24th Anniv of
Democracy.
3272 **1227** 1p. multicoloured 1·80 1·20

1228 Accordionist and
Dancers

2007. Festivals. Multicoloured.
3273 1p. Type **1228** (National
Chamame (dance) festival) 1·80 1·20
3274 1p. Ponchos and dancers
(National and International
Poncho festival) 1·80 1·20
3275 1p. Horseman, fireworks, guitar
and dancers (National and
International Dressage and
Folklore festival) 1·80 1·20
3276 1p. Snow Queen and skier
(National Snow festival) 1·80 1·20

1234 Piper Aircraft

2008. Centenary of Aero Club
3290 **1234** 1p. multicoloured 1·90 1·30

1235 Leonardo Realde performing 'pas de
l'ange' from, Diane and Actaen (ballet)

2008. Centenary of Teatro Colon
3291 **1235** 1p. multicoloured 1·90 1·30

1236 Aimé Bonpland, Script,
Yerba Mate Leaf and Flower

2008. 150th Death Anniv of Aimé Jacques Alexandre
Bonpland (explorer and botanist)
3292 **1236** 1p. multicoloured 1·90 1·30

1239 'MAMRRACHOS POR
CARTA' (Ricardo Mariño)

2008. Youth Philately
3296 1p. Type **1239** 1·90 1·30
3297 1p. 'CARTA A PAPÁ NOEL' (Luis
Maria Pescetti) 1·90 1·30
3298 1p. 'CANCION DEL CORREO'
(Maria Elena Walsh) (vert) 1·90 1·30
3299 1p. 'GRAN HERMANO' (Silvia
Schujer) (vert) 1·90 1·30

1240 *Callistoma
militaris*

2008. Shells. Multicoloured.
3314 25c. +25c. Type **1240** 35 25
3315 50c. +50c. *Epitonium fabrizioi* 75 55
3316 75c. +75c. *Odontocymbiola
magellanica* 1·40 95
3317 1p. +1p. *Trophon geverrrsianus* 1·90 1·30

1241 Tiles and Guitar
(Portugal)

2008. Immigration. Multicoloured.
3318 1p. Type **1241** (Portugal) 1·90 1·30
3319 1p. *Two Swimmers* (koi carp)
(Kobayashi Katsushiro)and
cherry blossom (Japan) 1·90 1·30
3320 1p. Virgin and child (plate) and
Arabic script (Lebanon) 1·90 1·30
3321 1p. Wooden box, embroidered
silk and Ugarithic alphabet
tablet (Syria) 1·90 1·30

1242 Carnation, Lily and Delphinium

2008. National Flower Festival. Multicoloured.
MS3322 5p. Type **1242** 9·50 9·50
MS3323 5p. Gerbera, gardenia and rose 9·50 9·50

1243 Basket and Ball (Emanuel Ginóbili)

2008. Argentine Sporting Idols. Multicoloured.
MS3324 100×150 mm. 5p. Type **1243** 9·50 9·50
MS3325 100×150 mm. 5p. Golf ball and hole (Roberto de Vicenzo) 9·50 9·50
MS3326 100×150 mm. 5p. Rugby goal posts, ball and player silhouette (horiz) 9·50 9·50
MS3327 150×100 mm. 5p. Driver and race car (Juan Manuel Fangio) 9·50 9·50

1244 Symbols of Science and Scientists

2008. 2008-Teaching of Sciences Year
3328 **1244** 1p. greenish blue, bright light green and silver 1·90 1·30

1245 Nelumbo nucifera

2008. 35th Anniv of Argentine-Vietnam Diplomatic Relations. Multicoloured.
3329 1p. Type **1245** 1·90 1·30
3330 1p. Ceiba chodatii 1·90 1·30

1246 First Stamp of Cordoba

2008. 150th Anniv of First Postage Stamps
MS3331 1p.×3, Type **1246**; Buenos Aires (40×30 mm); Argentine Federation (30×40 mm) 5·50 5·50

1247 Angel Gabriel (Renée T. Pietrantonio)

2008. Christmas
3332 **1247** 1p. multicoloured 1·90 1·30

1253 Sugar Cane, Soya Beans and Microscope

2009. Bishop Colombres Memorial Agribusiness Experimental Centre, Tucumán
3342 **1253** 1p. multicoloured 1·90 1·30

1254 Bull (Chinese New Year. Year of the Ox)

2009. China 2009 International Stamp Exhibition, Luoyang. Sheet 75×100 mm
MS3343 **1254** 5p. multicoloured 9·50 9·50

1255 Parish Church

2009. Centenary of Holy Cross Exaltation Parish Church, Puerto Santa Cruz
3344 **1255** 1p. multicoloured 1·90 1·30

1256 Aguila coronada (crowned eagle)

2009. Endangered Species. Multicoloured.
3345 1p. Type **1256** 1·90 1·30
3346 1p. Chelonoidis chilensis (Argentine tortoise) (horiz) 1·90 1·30

1257 Vintage Wine

2009. Mercosur. Exports. Multicoloured.
3347 1p. Type **1257** 1·90 1·30
3348 1p. Containers and tractor 1·90 1·30

No. 3349 and Type **1258** are left for R. R. Alfonsin, issued on 9 May 2009, not yet received.
No. 3350 and Type **1259** are left for R. S. Ortiz, issued on 23 May 2009, not yet received.
No. 3351 and Type **1260** are left for 150th Anniv of the Children of Holy Virgin at Orchard Congregation in Argentina , issued on 23 May 2009, not yet received.
Nos. 3352/3 and Type **1261** are left for 180th Anniv of Political and Military Command, issued on 13 June 2009, not yet received.

1262 Beads of Water

2009. Environmental Protection. Water
MS3354 5p.×2, Type **1262**; Hand and large water droplet (vert) 18·00 18·00

1263 Polybetes pythagoricus

2009. Native Flora and Fauna. Multicoloured .
3355 1p. Type **1263** 1·90 1·30
3356 1p. Passiflora caerulea 1·90 1·30

1264 Bumper Cars

2009. Youth Philately. Amusement Parks. Multicoloured.
3357 1p. Type **1264** 1·90 1·30
3358 1p. Roller coaster 1·90 1·30
3359 1p. Ferris wheel 1·90 1·30
3360 1p. Ghost train 1·90 1·30

Nos. 3357/60, plus stamp size label, were printed, se-tenant, in horizontal strips of four stamps plus label, the whole forming a composite design

1265 Merino Ram

2009. Sheep. Multicoloured.
MS3361 1p.×6, Type **1265**; Romney Marsh yearling; Corriedale ewe and lamb; Hampshire Down ewe and lamb; Lincoln ewe; Frisian ewe 11·00 11·00

Nos. 3362/5 and Type **1266** are left for Astronomy, issued on 22 August 2009, not yet received
Nos. 3366/7 and Type **1267** are left for Education, issued on 12 September 2009, not yet received

1268 Rainfall Damage, Erosion and Area under Conservation Management

2009. Natural Resources. The Soil. Multicoloured.
3368 1p. Type **1268** 1·90 1·30
3369 1p. Wind erosion of arid land and arid area under conservation management 1·90 1·30

Nos. 3368/9 were printed, se-tenant, in horizontal pairs within the sheet, each pair forming a composite design.

Nos. 3370/3 and Type **1269** are left for Sport, issued on 26 September 2009, not yet received.
Nos. 3374 and Type **1270** are left for 50th Anniv of UTN, issued on 17 October 2009, not yet received.
Nos. 3375/8 and Type **1271** are left for Italia 2009, issued on 24 October 2009, not yet received.
Nos. 3379/80 and Type **1272** are left for Astronomy, issued on 24 October 2009, not yet received.
Nos. 3381/4 and Type **1273** are left for TB Awareness, issued on 14 November 2009, not yet received.
Nos. 3385 and Type **1274** are left for Christmas, issued on 21 November 2009, not yet received.
Nos. 3386/93 and Type **1275** are left for Architecture, issued on 12 December 2009, not yet receivedNos. 3394/7 and Type **1276** are left for Festivals, issued on 20 February 2010, not yet received.
Nos. 3398/9 and Type **1277** are left for Ships, issued on 20 February 2010, not yet received.
No. 3400 and Type **1278** are left for Bicentenary, issued on 27 March 2010, not yet received.
Nos. 3401/2 and Type **1279** are left for America, issued on 27 March 2010, not yet received.
No. 3403 and Type **1280** are left for Centenary of Orchestra, issued on 24 April 2010, not yet received.
Nos. 3404/5 and Type **1281** are left for Mercosur, issued on 8 May 2010, not yet received.
No. 3406 and Type **1282** are left for Bicentenary, issued on 8 May 2010, not yet received.
Nos. 3407 and Type **1283** are left for Bicentenary, issued on 29 May 2010, not yet received.

1284 Buenos Aires Town Hall

2010. Bicentenary Mural (by Miguel Rep). Black, carmine and silver.
MS3408 1p.50×12, Type **1284**; General Manuel Belgrano creating National Flag; General San Martin crossing Andes (40×80 mm); National Constitution; Ships with immigrants; Confrontation (70×30 mm); National Congress; Symbols of literary expression (40×30 mm); People celebrating Loyalty Day (30×60 mm); 1976 Coup (30×40 mm); Mothers of May Square (40×60 mm); Symbols of Nineties economics (40×60 mm) 11·00 11·00

1285 First Issue of Gazeta de Buenos Aires

2010. Bicentenary of Gazeta de Buenos Ayres (newspaper)
3409 **1285** 1p.50 multicoloured 2·00 1·40

1286 Player, Greece

2010. World Cup Football Championship, South Africa. Multicoloured.
3410 1p.50 Type **1286** 1·90 1·30
3411 1p.50 Player, Nigeria (horiz) 1·90 1·30
3412 5p. Player, South Korea (horiz) 2·75 2·30
3413 7p. Player, Argentina 3·00 2·40
MS3414 100×75 mm. 5p. Goalkeeper making a save (40×60 mm) 9·50 9·50
MS3415 100×75 mm. 5p. Player diving for ball (70×40 mm) 9·50 9·50
MS3416 100×75 mm. 5p. Player heading ball towards goal (70×40 mm) 9·50 9·50
MS3417 100×75 mm. 5p. Player kicking ball into air with left leg raised (60×40 mm) 9·50 9·50

1287 Players

2010. Junior World Rugby Championship, Argentina
3418 **1287** 1p.50 multicoloured 1·90 1·30

1288 Dog and Hobby Horse

2010. Children's Games. Multicoloured.
3419 2p. Type **1288** 1·90 1·30
3420 2p. Boy with whip and ball (El balero) 1·90 1·30
3421 2p. Spinning top (El trompo) 1·90 1·30
3422 2p. Girls with hoops (El aro) 1·90 1·30
3423 2p. Girl with doll (La muñeca) 1·90 1·30

1289 Members of Provisional Government Junta take the Oath on 25 May 1810 (Guillermo Da Ré)

2010. Bicentenary of the First Argentine Government Junta. Sheet 100×75 mm
MS3424 **1289** 5p. multicoloured 9·50 9·50

1290 Balea Lake, Romania

2010. 80th Anniv of Argentina–Romania Diplomatic Relations. Multicoloured.
3425 1p.50 Type **1290** 1·90 1·30
3426 7p. Nahuel Huapi Lake, Argentina 3·00 2·40

Stamps of a similar design were issued by Romania.

1291 Jorge Luis Borges

2010. Frankfurt Bookfair
3427 **1291** 7p. black, silver and scarlet-vermilion 3·00 2·40

1292 'Be Prepared' ('siempre LISTA')

2010. Centenary of Girl Guiding and Girl Scouting. Multicoloured.

3428	75c. +75c. Type **1292**		1·40	95
3429	75c. +75c. Clasped hands ('Always better' ('siempre MEJOR'))		1·40	95
3430	1p. +1p. Clasped hands and campfire ('Always forward' ('siempre ADELANTE'))		1·90	1·30
3431	1p. +1p. Hand on shoulder ('To serve' ('SERVIR'))		1·90	1·30

1293 Player's Silhouette and Pitch

2010. Women's World Hockey Championships, Argentina 2010

3432	**1293**	1p.50 multicoloured	2·00	1·40

1294 Bowls

2010. America. Traditional Games. Multicoloured.

3433	1p.50 Type **1294**		1·90	1·30
3434	1p.50 Cards ('truco')		1·90	1·30

1295 Symbols of Census

2010. Census-2010

3435	**1295**	1p.50 multicoloured	1·90	1·30

1296 Juan Bautista Alberdi (Liliana Ferrari)

2010. Birth Bicentenary of Juan Bautista Alberdi (writer and politician)

3436	**1296**	1p.50 multicoloured	1·90	1·30

1297 Library Building and Antique Books

2010. Bicentenary of National Library

3437	**1297**	1p.50 multicoloured	1·90	1·30

1298 Cherub (tiles, Carmo Church (Igreja do Carmo) (image scaled to 40% of original size)

2010. Portugal 2010, International Stamp Exhibition. Multicoloured.

MS3438 151×98 mm. 5p.×2,Querandi Lighthouse, Buenos Aires; Santa Marta lighthouse, Cascais, Lisbon		18·00	18·00
MS3439 120×120 mm. 10p.Type **1298**, Porto, Portugal) (50×50 mm)		18·00	18·00

1299 Postman (statue), World Map, FOECOP (postal workers' union) Emblem and Envelopes

2010. World Post Day. The Postman

3440	**1299**	1p.50 multicoloured	1·90	1·30

1300 Austria-Hungarian Community Meteorological Station, Botanical Garden, Buenos Aires

2010. Meteorological Architecture. Multicoloured.

MS3441 5p.×2, Type **1300**; Weather Station, City Park, Vienna		18·00	18·00

1301 Canto al Trabajo (statue) (Rogelio Yrurtia)

2010. Argentinian Workers

3442	**1301**	1p.50 multicoloured	1·90	1·30

1302 The Child of Bethlehem (Aldo Severi)

2010. Christmas

3443	**1302**	1p.50 multicoloured	1·90	1·30

1303 Map and Symbols of Electricity Generation and Distribution

2010. 50th Anniv of Electrical Power Federal Council

3444	**1303**	1p.50 multicoloured	1·90	1·30

1304 Race Start, Buenos Aires

2010. Dakar Rally, Argentina, 2009 and 2010. Multicoloured.

MS3445 480×100 mm (open), 140×100 mm. (closed). 1p.50 Type **1304**;1p.50 Philippe Peillon, Motor cycle No. 107 (Dakar 2009) (50×50 mm.);1p.50 Stephane Peterhansel, Car No. 303 (Dakar 2009) (60×40 mm.);1p.50 Ales Loprais, Lorry No. 502 (Dakar 2009) (50×50 mm.);1p.50 Caravan of vehicles (Dakar 2009) (50×50 mm.); 5p. Marcos Patronelli, Quad No. 251 (Dakar 2010) (40×80 mm.); 7p. Alejandro Patronelli Quad No. 277 (Dakar 2010) (40×80 mm.)		19·00	19·00
MS3446 492×100 mm (open) 170×100 mm. (closed). 1p.50 Jun Mitsuhashi, Car No. 375 (Dakar 2009) (60×50 mm.);1p.50 Patronelli Brothers, Quads Nos. 252 and 277 (Dakar 2010) (60×40 mm.);1p.50 Roman Cabot, Car No. 377 (Dakar 2009) (40×50 mm.);1p.50 Marc Coma Motor cycle No. 1 (Dakar 2010) (60×40 mm.);1p.50 Laguna del Pescado, Entre Rios (40×50 mm.); 1p.50 Tafi del Valle, Tucuman (40×50 mm.);1p.50 Purmamarca, Jujuy (40×50 mm.); 10p. Firdaus Kabirov Lorry No. 500 (Dakar 2010) (70×50 mm.)		19·00	19·00

No. 3447 and Type **1305** are left for Year of Forests, issued on 19 March 2011, not yet received.
No. 3448 and Type **1306** are left for America, issued on 19 March 2011, not yet received.
Nos. 3449/50 and Type **1307** are left for Capital of Books, issued on 16 April 2011, not yet received.

1308 Ice Floe streaked with Colours

2011. 50th Anniv of Antarctic Treaty. 34th Antarctic Treaty Consultative Meeting. Multicoloured.

3451	2p. Type **1308**		1·90	1·30
MS3452 150×98 mm. Triangular Size 51×51mm. 8p.×2, Pygocelis papua; Researcher and equipment			7·50	7·50

1309 Mariano Moreno and Masthead of Gazeta de Buenos Ayres

2011. Death Bicentenary of Mariano Moreno (lawyer, journalist and politician.)

3453	**1309**	2p. multicoloured	1·90	1·30

1310 Blood Droplet

2011. Blood Donor Day

3453a	**1310**	5p. multicoloured	9·50	6·00

1311 Silhouettes of Workers' Heads

2011. 2011, Year of Decent Labour, Health and Safety for Workers

3454	**1311**	2p. multicoloured	1·90	1·30

1312 Pirámide de Mayo

2011. Pirámide de Mayo, Buenos Aires (constructed to celebrate first anniversary of 1810 May Revolution)

3455	**1312**	2p.50 multicoloured	2·00	1·40

1313 Domingo Faustino Sarmiento

2011. Birth Bicentenary of Domingo Faustino Sarmiento (activist, intellectual, writer, statesman and seventh President of Argentina, 1868–74)

3456	**1313**	2p.50 multicoloured	2·00	1·40

1314 Argentina and Bolivia Players

2011. Copa America 2011, Argentina. Multicoloured.

MS3457 5p.×2, Group A, Type **1314**; Costa rica goalkeeper making save		18·00	18·00
MS3458 5p.×2, Group B, Venezuela and Brazil players tackling for ball (facing right); Paraguay and Ecuador players heading ball (facing left)		18·00	18·00
MS3459 5p.×2, Group C, Uruguay player wearing blue (facing right); Chile player preparing for goal kick (facing left)		18·00	18·00

1315 Satellite Sac-D/Aquarius

2011. Satellite Sac-D/Aquarius

3460	**1315**	2p.50 multicoloured	2·00	1·40

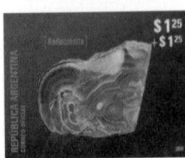

1316 Rhodochrosite

2011. Minerals. Multicoloured.

3461	1p.25 +1p.25 Type **1316**		2·00	1·40
3462	1p.25 +1p.25 Sulphur		2·00	1·40
3463	1p.25 +1p.25 Pyrite		2·00	1·40
3464	1p.25 +1p.25 Quartz		2·00	1·40

1317 Decorated Postbox

2011. America. Post Boxes

3465	2p.50 Type **1317**		2·00	1·40
3466	2p.50 Pillarbox (vert)		2·00	1·40

1318 National Beer Festival, Villa General Belgrano, Córdoba

2011. Festivals. Multicoloured.

3467	2p.50 Type **1318**	2·00	1·40
3468	2p.50 National Day of the Horse, San Cristobal, Santa Fe	2·00	1·40
3469	2p.50 Foreign Communities Fair, Comodoro Rivadavia, Chubut	2·00	1·40
3470	2p.50 National Tea Party, Campo Viera, Missiones.	2·00	1·40

1319 *Sacoila lanceolata*

2011. Orchids

3471	2p.50 Type **1319**	2·00	1·40
3472	2p.50 *Zygopetalum maxillare* (horiz)	2·00	1·40

1320 Carriages

2011. Tourism. Train to the Clouds. Multicoloured.

MS3473	5p.×4, Type **1320**; Locomotive; Rear of train crossing bridge; Crossing bridge viewed from below	18·00	18·00

1321 Physician and Hand holding Baby

2011. Centenary of Argentine Pediatric Society

3474	**1321**	2p.50 multicoloured	2·00	1·40

1322 Star of Bethlehem and Three Kings

2011. Christmas

3475	**1322**	2p.50 multicoloured	2·00	1·40

1323 Landrace

2011. Pigs. Multicoloured.

MS3476	2p.50×6, Type **1323**; Hampshire; Pietrain; Duroc Jersey; Spotted Poland; Yorkshire	12·00	12·00

1324 Nestor Carlos Kirchner and Casa Rosada (detail)

2011. Nestor Carlos Kirchner (president 2003-7) Commemoration. Sheet 100×150 mm

MS3477	**1324** 5p. multicoloured	9·50	9·50

1325 Polo Horse (Adolfo Cambiaso)

2011. Sports Personalities. Multicoloured.

MS3478	100×150 mm. 10p. Type **1325**	9·50	9·50
MS3479	100×150 mm. 10p. Skaters legs (Nora Vega) (60×40 mm)	9·50	9·50
MS3480	150×100 mm. 10p. Stylised windsurfer (Carlos Espinola) (50×60 mm)	9·50	9·50
MS3481	150×100 mm. 10p. Chessboard and Miguel Najdorf (50×60 mm)	9·50	9·50

1326 Family (Nicolas Agustin Bernachea)

2011. Rights of Children and Women. Centenary of Argentine Pediatrics Society . Multicoloured.

3482	2p.50 Type **1326**	2·00	1·40
3483	2p.50 Crying child and hand (Catalano Segesso)	2·00	1·40
3484	2p.50 Mother and child (Florencia Martinesi)	2·00	1·40
3485	2p.50 Girl jumping (Sofia Panagópulo)	2·00	1·40

1327 Douglas DC-3 making First Landing and Map showing Flight Route

2012. 50th Anniv of First Argentine Landing at South Pole

3486	**1327**	2p.50 multicoloured	2·00	1·40

1328 Creation of the Flag (detail, bas-relief) (Jose Fioravanti), Flag and Sun

2012. Bicentenary of National Flag. Sheet 100×75 mm

MS3487	**1328** 5p. multicoloured	9·50	9·25

1329 Gen. Manuel Belgrano Monument, Buenos Aires

2012. General Manuel Belgrano Commemoration

3488	**1329**	2p.50 multicoloured	2·00	1·40

1330 'Islas Malvinas'

2012. Falkland Islands (Malvinas). Multicoloured.

3489	2p.50 Type **1330**	2·00	1·40
3490	2p.50 Inscr 'Islas Georgias del Sur'	2·00	1·40
3491	2p.50 Inscr 'Islas Sandwich del Sur' (28×67 mm)	2·00	1·40

1331 Presidential Staff and Flag

2012. Second Presidential Mandate of Cristina Elisabet Fernández de Kirchner

3492	**1331** 2p.50 multicoloured	2·00	1·40

1332 First Deed (detail) and Jose de San Martin Monument

2012. Centenary of Rio Gallegos Town Council

3493	**1332** 2p.50 multicoloured	2·00	1·40

1333 Mounting Dahlia (elephant), 1943

2012. Bicentenary of Natural Science Museum

3494	2p.50 Type **1333**	2·00	1·40
3495	2p.50 Skull of Bonatitan reigi (sauropod)	2·00	1·40
3496	2p.50 Feather function display, Birds' Hall (44×34 mm)	2·00	1·40
3497	2p.50 *Agrias narcissus* butterflies (44×34 mm)	2·00	1·40

1334 Biogas, BioMass and Biofuel piped into House

2012. Mercosur. Alternative Energy. Multicoloured.

3498	2p.50 Type **1334**	2·00	1·40
3499	9p.50 Solar, Wind and Hydroelectric Energy piped into house	7·50	7·25

BULK MAIL STAMPS

BP999 Post Office Building, Buenos Aires

1999. Bulk Mail. Self-adhesive. Imperf.

BP2644	**BP999** $7 black and blue	21·00	14·00
BP2645	**BP999** $11 black and red	33·00	22·00
BP2646	**BP999** $16 black and yellow	50·00	35·00
BP2647	**BP999** $23 black and green	70·00	47·00

BP1069

2001. Bulk Mail. Additionally overprinted UP. Imperf.

BP2853	**BP1069** $7 black and blue	19·00	17·00
BP2854	**BP1069** $11 black and red	29·00	26·00

EXPRESS SERVICE MAIL

E999 Express Service Emblem

1999. Self-adhesive.

E2644	**E999** 8p.75 blue and silver	30·00	20·00
E2645	- 17p.50 blue and gold	65·00	43·00

DESIGN: 24-hour service emblem.
No. E2644 was for express service mail and No. E2645 for use on 24-hour express service mail.

OFFICIAL STAMPS

1884. Optd OFICIAL.

O66	33	½c. brown	15·00	12·00
O69	33	1c. red	60	40
O70	24	2c. green	60	40
O71	-	4c. brown (No. 32)	60	40
O72	9	8c. red	60	55
O73	10	10c. green	50·00	30·00
O76	33	12c. blue	1·00	80
O77	10	16c. green	2·00	1·20
O78	22	20c. blue	10·00	8·25
O79	11	24c. blue (roul)	12·50	8·50
O80	11	24c. blue (perf)	1·20	90
O81	-	25c. red (No. 47)	20·00	15·00
O82	-	30c. orange (No. 48)	42·00	24·00
O83	-	60c. black (No. 34)	25·00	15·00
O84	-	90c. blue (No. 35)	25·00	19·00

O73

1901

O275	**O73**	1c. grey	20	15
O276	**O73**	2c. brown	20	15
O277	**O73**	5c. red	20	15
O278	**O73**	10c. green	40	15
O279	**O73**	30c. blue	2·75	80
O280	**O73**	50c. orange	1·80	70

1938. (a) Optd SERVICIO OFICIAL in two lines.

O668	143	1c. brown (No. 645)	45	20
O669	-	2c. brown (No. 646)	45	20
O670	-	3c. green (No. 647)	1·20	20
O679	-	3c. grey (No. 672)	45	20
O771	-	3c. grey (No. 672a)	3·50	1·40
O671	-	5c. brown (No. 653b)	45	20
O782	200	5c. red (No. 773)	10	10
O667	-	10c. red (No. 653d)	55	20
O773	-	10c. purple (No. 678)	55	20
O681	146	15c. blue (No. 676)	55	20
O683	146	20c. blue (19½×26 mm)	1·40	45
O774	-	15c. grey (No. 708)	65	20
O872	247	20c. red	45	10
O813	-	25c. (No. 673)	65	20
O674	-	40c. (No. 658)	1·80	45
O675	-	50c. (No. 659)	45	20
O676	152	1p. (No. 760)	55	45
O827	234	1p. (No. 826)	90	20
O778	-	2p. (No. 661)	55	20
O779	-	5p. (No. 662)	55	20
O780	-	10p. (No. 763)	65	45
O781	-	20p. (No. 764)	1·80	1·40

(b) Optd SERVICIO OFICIAL in one line.

O897	20c. lilac (No. 895)	45	20

1953. Eva Peron stamps optd SERVICIO OFICIAL.

O854	239	5c. grey	45	15
O855	239	10c. red	45	15
O856	239	20c. red	45	15
O857	239	25c. green	45	15
O858	239	40c. purple	45	15
O859	239	45c. blue	55	45
O860	239	50c. bistre	45	15
O862	240	1p. brown (No. 846)	55	20

O863	240	1p.50 green (No. 847)	55	20
O864	240	2p. red (No. 848)	55	20
O865	240	3p. blue (No. 849)	70	45
O866	240	5p. brown	1·40	65
O867	239	10p. red	7·50	6·00
O868	240	20p. green	65·00	35·00

1955. Stamps of 1954 optd **SERVICIO OFICIAL** in one line.

O869	247	20c. red	45	10
O870	247	40c. red	45	10
O880	-	1p. brown (No. 871)	45	20
O882	-	3p. purple (No. 874)	55	20
O883	-	5p. green (No. 875)	55	20
O884	-	10p. green and grey (No. 876)	65	20
O886	250	20p. violet	1·50	70

1955. Various stamps optd. (a) Optd **S. OFICIAL.**

O896	-	5c. brown (No. 894)	45	20
O955	-	10c. green (No. 946)	50	20
O956	-	20c. purple (No. 947)	60	20
O879	-	50c. blue (No. 868)	45	20
O957	-	50c. ochre (No. 948)	50	20
O1034	-	1p. brn (No. 1016)	60	35
O899	264	2p. purple	45	20
O1050	-	2p. red (No. 1035)	50	10
O959	-	3p. blue (No. 951)	50	20
O1051	-	4p. red (No. 1036)	75	10
O961	296	5p. brown	60	20
O1052	-	8p. red (No. 1037)	50	20
O962	-	10p. brown (No. 1286)	60	20
O1036	-	12p. dull purple (No. 1028)	1·10	25
O1053	-	10p. red (No. 1038)	60	10
O964	-	20p. green (No. 954)	60	20
O1055	-	20p. blue (No. 1039)	55	25
O1037	-	22p. blue (No. 1018)	1·30	45
O1038	-	23p. green (No. 1019)	1·60	60
O1039	-	25p. lilac (No. 1020)	1·30	60
O1040	-	43p. lake (No. 1021)	3·00	1·30
O1041	-	45p. brn (No. 1022)	3·00	1·30
O1042	-	50p. blue (No. 1023)	5·00	1·50
O1043	-	50p. blue (No. 1287)	6·75	1·50
O1045	-	100p. blue (No. 1289)	3·25	1·30
O1046	-	300p. violet (No. 1026)	9·75	4·75

(b) Optd **SERVICIO OFICIAL.**

O900	265	2p.40 brown	45	20
O958	-	3p. blue (No. 951)	50	20
O901	266	4p.40 green	45	20
O960	296	5p. brown	60	20
O887	-	50p. ind & bl (No. 878)	3·00	1·30
O1049	-	500p. grn (No. 1032)	16·00	7·75

For lists of stamps optd **M.A., M.G., M.H., M.I., M.J.I., M.M., M.O.P.** or **M.R.C.** for use in ministerial offices see the Stanley Gibbons Catalogue Part 20 (South America).

1963. Nos. 1068, etc., optd **S. OFICIAL.**

O1076	351	2p. green	60	10
O1080	-	4p. red (No. 1069)	75	15
O1081	-	6p. red (No. 1070)	85	45
O1078	-	90p. bistre (No. 1288)	8·00	3·75

RECORDED MESSAGE STAMPS

RM166 Winged Messenger

1939. Various symbolic designs inscr "CORREOS FONOPOSTAL".

RM688	RM166	1p.18 blue	19·00	10·50
RM689	-	1p.32 blue	19·00	10·50
RM690	-	1p.50 brown	65·00	45·00

DESIGNS—VERT: 1p.32, Head of Liberty and National Arms. HORIZ: 1p.50, Record and winged letter.

TELEGRAPH STAMPS USED FOR POSTAGE

PT34 PT35 (Sun closer to "NACIONAL")

1887

PT104	PT34	10c. red	1·10	15
PT105	PT35	10c. red	1·10	15
PT106	PT34	40c. blue	1·20	15
PT107	PT35	40c. blue	1·20	15

Pt. 10

ARMENIA

Formerly part of Transcaucasian Russia. Temporarily independent after the Russian revolution of 1917. From 12 March 1922, Armenia, Azerbaijan and Georgia formed the Transcaucasian Federation. Issues for the federation were superseded by those of the Soviet Union in 1924.

With the dissolution of the Soviet Union in 1991 Armenia once again became independent.

NOTE. Only one price is given for Nos. 3/245, which applies to unused or cancelled to order. Postally used copies are worth more.

All the overprints and surcharges were hands-tamped and consequently were applied upright or inverted indiscriminately, some occurring only inverted.

1919. 100 kopeks = 1 rouble.
1994. 100 luna = 1 dram.

NATIONAL REPUBLIC

28 May 1918 to 2 December 1920 and 18 February to 2 April 1921.

1919. Arms type of Russia and unissued Postal Savings Bank stamp (No. 6) surch. Imperf or perf. (a) Surch thus **k. 60 k** with or without stops.

3	22	60k. on 1k. orange		65
6	-	60k. on 1k. red on buff		12·00

(b) Surch in figures only.

7	22	60k. on 1k. orange		30·00
8	22	120k. on 1k. orange		30·00

(6)

1919. Stamps of Russia optd as T **6** in various sizes, with or without frame. Imperf or perf. (a) Arms types.

53B	22	1k. orange	12·50
54B	22	2k. green	3·00
55B	22	3k. red	2·40
11B	23	4k. red	80
12B	22	5k. red	1·30
13B	23	10k. blue	90
14B	22	10k. on 7k. blue	1·20
15B	10	15k. blue and purple	1·50
16B	14	20k. red and blue	1·60
17B	10	25k. mauve and green	2·00
45B	10	35k. green and purple	2·20
19B	14	50k. green and purple	1·00
30aB	22	60k. on 1k. orange (No. 3)	2·50
31B	10	70k. orange and brown	1·00
32B	15	1r. orange and brown	2·20
33B	11	3r.50 green and brown	3·50
23B	20	5r. green and blue	5·00
24B	11	7r. pink and green	9·00
62B	11	7r. yellow and black	40·00
52B	20	10r. grey, red and yellow	11·00

(b) Romanov type.

63B	20	4k. red (No. 129)	2·00

(c) Unissued Postal Savings Bank stamp.

64A		1k. red on buff	6·50

5r
(8)

1920. Stamps of Russia surch as T **8** in various types and sizes. Imperf or perf. (a) Arms types.

65B	22	1r. on 1k. orange	3·25
94B	22	1r. on 60k. on 1k. orange (No. 3)	4·50
66B	22	3r. on 3k. red	2·10
67B	22	3r. on 4k. red	7·25
97B	22	5r. on 2k. green	2·50
69B	23	5r. on 4k. red	1·30
70B	22	5r. on 5k. red	1·80
71B	22	5r. on 7k. blue	1·20
72B	23	5r. on 10k. blue	1·60
73B	22	5r. on 10 on 7k. blue	2·10
74B	10	5r. on 14k. red and blue	2·30
75B	10	5r. on 15k. blue and purple	2·10
76aB	10	5r. on 20 on 14k. red and blue	8·50
76B	14	5r. on 20k. red and blue	2·10
77B	10	5r. on 25k. mauve and green	8·50
111B	22	5r. on 3r. on 5k. red	11·00
78B	10	10r. on 25k. mauve and green	2·00
79B	10	10r. on 35k. green and purple	1·50
80B	14	10r. on 50k. green and purple	4·00

80aB	9	25r. on 1k. orange	40·00
80bB	9	25r. on 3k. red	40·00
80cB	9	25r. on 5k. purple	40·00
80dB	22	25r. on 10 on 7k. blue	40·00
80eB	10	25r. on 15k. blue and purple	40·00
81B	14	25r. on 20k. red and blue	4·50
82B	10	25r. on 25k. mauve and green	3·75
83B	10	25r. on 35k. green and purple	2·75
84B	14	25r. on 50k. green and purple	3·50
85B	10	25r. on 70k. orange and brown	5·00
104aB	9	50r. on 1k. orange	45·00
104bB	9	50r. on 3k. red	48·00
85bB	14	50r. on 4k. red	45·00
104cB	14	50r. on 5k. purple	48·00
85cB	10	50r. on 15k. blue and purple	45·00
85dB	14	50r. on 20k. red and blue	45·00
85eB	10	50r. on 35k. green & purple	45·00
85fB	14	50r. on 50k. green & purple	25·00
105B	10	50r. on 70k. orange and brown	6·25
106B	15	50r. on 1r. orange and brown	6·50
107B	15	100r. on 1r. orange and brown	6·00
108B	11	100r. on 3r.50 green and brown	18·00
88B	20	100r. on 5r. green and blue	15·00
89B	11	100r. on 7r. yellow and black	19·00
90B	11	100r. on 7r. pink and green	10·00
93B	20	100r. on 10r. grey, red and yellow	15·00

(b) Romanov issue of 1913.

112	20	1r. on 1k. orange	10·50
113	20	3r. on 3k. red	13·00
114	20	5r. on 4k. red	5·50
115	20	5r. on 10 on 7k. brown	3·25
116	20	5r. on 14k. green	39·00
117	20	5r. on 20 on 14k. green	5·25
118	20	25r. on 4k. red	6·50
118a	20	100r. on 1k. orange	65·00
119	20	100r. on 2k. green	65·00
120	20	100r. on 3r. violet	65·00

(c) War Charity issues of 1914 and 1915.

121	15	25r. on 1k. green and red on yellow	39·00
122	15	25r. on 3k. green and red on rose	39·00
123	15	50r. on 7k. green and brown on buff	48·00
124	15	50r. on 10k. brown and blue	48·00
125	15	100r. on 1k. green and red on yellow	48·00
126	15	100r. on 1k. grey and brown	48·00
127	15	100r. on 3k. green and red on rose	48·00
128	15	100r. on 7k. green and brown on buff	48·00
129	15	100r. on 10k. brown and blue	48·00

1920. Arms types of Russia optd as T **6** in various sizes with or without frame, and surch T **8** or with value only in various types and sizes. Imperf or perf.

155B	22	1r. on 60k. on 1k. orange (No. 3)	1·30
156A	22	3r. on 3k. red	2·50
157A	22	5r. on 2k. green	1·10
141A	23	5r. on 4k. red	4·50
158A	22	5r. on 5k. red	4·25
142A	23	5r. on 10k. blue	4·50
143A	22	5r. on 10 on 7k. blue	4·50
144A	10	5r. on 15k. blue & pur	2·40
145A	14	5r. on 20k. red and blue	2·40
132B	10	10r. on 15k. blue & pur	12·00
145aB	14	10r. on 20k. red & blue	1·20
146A	10	10r. on 25k. mauve and green	2·40
147B	10	10r. on 35k. green and purple	1·20
148A	14	10r. on 50k. green and purple	3·00
159A	10	10r. on 70k. orange and brown	14·00
163A	22	10r. on 5r. on 5k. green	30·00
164A	10	10r. on 5r. on 25k. mauve and green	32·00
165A	10	10r. on 5r. on 35k. green and purple	11·00
138A	20	25r. on 70k. orange and brown	8·00
161B	10	50r. on 1r. orange and brown	2·75

135B	11	100r. on 3r.50 green and brown	3·00
151A	20	100r. on 5r. green & bl	8·00
136A	11	100r. on 7r. pink and green	9·00
154aA	20	100r. on 10r. grey, red and yellow	12·00
166A	20	100r. on 25r. on 5r. green and blue	30·00

1920. Stamps of Russia optd as T **6** in various sizes, with or without frame. Perf. (a) Arms types.

168	14	10 on 20k. red and blue	30·00
169	10	10 on 25k. mauve and green	30·00
170	10	10 on 35k. green and purple	20·00
171	14	10 on 50k. green and purple	24·00

(b) Romanov type.

172		10 on 4k. red (No. 129)	48·00

1920. Stamps of Russia optd with monogram as in T **8** in various types and sizes and surch **10**. Imperf or perf. (a) Arms types.

173	23	10 on 4k. red	48·00
174	22	10 on 5k. red	48·00
175	10	10 on 15k. blue & purple	48·00
176	14	10 on 20k. red and blue	45·00
176a	10	10 on 20 on 14k. red and blue	24·00
177	10	10 on 25k. mauve & green	24·00
178	10	10 on 35k. green & purple	24·00
179	14	10 on 50k. green & purple	24·00

(b) Romanov type.

181		10 on 4k. red (No. 129)	60·00

SOVIET REPUBLIC

Stamps in Types **11, 12** and a similar horizontal type showing a woman spinning were printed in Paris to the order of the Armenian National Government, but were not issued in Armenia as the Bolshevists had assumed control. (Price 10p. each).

11 12 Mt. Ararat

(13)

1921. Arms types of Russia surch with T **13**. Perf.

182	15	5000r. on 1r. orange and brown	6·50
183	11	5000r. on 3r.50 grn & brn	6·50
184	20	5000r. on 5r. green & blue	6·50
185	11	5000r. on 7r. pink and green	6·50
186	20	5000r. on 10r. grey, red & yellow	6·50

TRANSCAUCASIAN FEDERATION ISSUES FOR ARMENIA

14 Common Crane 16 Village Scene

1922. Unissued stamps surch in gold kopeks. Imperf.

187	14	1 on 250r. red	9·75
188	14	1 on 250r. slate	13·00
189	16	2 on 500r. red	5·25
190	16	3 on 500r. slate	5·25
191	-	4 on 1000r. red	5·25
192	-	4 on 1000r. slate	9·75
193	-	5 on 2000r. slate	30·00
194	-	10 on 2000r. slate	30·00
195	-	15 on 5000r. red	23·00
196	-	20 on 5000r. slate	5·25

DESIGNS (sizes in mm): 1000r. Woman at well (17×26); 2000r. Erivan railway station (35×24½); 5000r. Horseman and Mt. Ararat (39½×24½).

17 Soviet Emblems

18 Wall Sculpture at Ani

19 Mt. Aragatz

1922. Unissued stamps as T **17/19** surch in gold kopeks in figures. Imperf or perf.

210	**17**	1 on 1r. green	9·75	
198	**18**	2 on 2r. slate	15·00	
212	-	3 on 3r. red	18·00	
213	-	4 on 25r. green	3·75	
201	-	5 on 50r. red	5·00	
215	-	10 on 100r. orange	13·00	
203	-	15 on 250r. blue	2·20	
204a	**19**	20 on 500r. purple	3·00	
205	-	35 on 20,000r. red	24·00	
206a	-	50 on 25,000r. green	48·00	
209	-	50 on 25,000r. blue	6·50	

DESIGNS (sizes in mm): 3r. (29×22) and 250r. (21×35) Soviet emblems; 25r. (30×22½); 100r. (34½×23) and 20,000r. (43×27) Mythological sculptures, Ani. 50r. (25½×37). Armenian soldier; 25,000r. (45½×27½) Mt. Ararat.

The above and other values were not officially issued without the surcharges.

1923. As T **19**, etc., surch in gold kopeks in figures. Imperf or perf.

219	-	1 on 250r. blue	6·50	
217	**19**	2 on 500r. purple	6·50	
218	-	3 on 20000r. lake	13·00	

26 Mt. Ararat and Soviet Emblems

28 Ploughing

1923. Unissued stamps in various designs as T **26/28** surch in Transcaucasian roubles in figures. Perf.

227	**26**	10,000r. on 50r. green and red	1·80	
228	-	15,000r. on 300r. blue and buff	1·80	
229	-	25,000r. on 400r. blue and pink	1·80	
240B	-	30,000r. on 500r. violet and lilac	2·00	
231	-	50,000r. on 1000r. blue	1·80	
232	-	75,000r. on 3000r. black and green	2·00	
233	-	100,000r. on 2000r. black and grey	2·40	
243	-	200,000r. on 4000r. black and brn	1·20	
235	-	300,000r. on 5000r. black and red	3·25	
245	**28**	500,000r. on 10,000r. black and red	1·50	

DESIGNS (sizes in mm): 300r. (26×35) Star over Mt. Ararat; 400r. (26×34½) Soviet emblems; 500r. (26×34½) Crane (bird); 1000r. (19×25) Peasant in punt; 2000r. (26×31) Human-headed bird from old bas-relief; 3000r. (26½×36) Sower; 4000r. (26×31½) Star and dragon; 5000r. (26×32) Blacksmith.

INDEPENDENT REPUBLIC

31 Mount Ararat and National Colours

1992. Independence Day.

246	**31**	20k. multicoloured	15	15
247	**31**	2r. multicoloured	70	70
248	**31**	5r. multicoloured	1·70	1·70
MS249		80×80 mm. 7r. multicoloured (Mt. Ararat and eagle)	43·00	43·00

32 Dish Aerial and World Map

1992. Inauguration of International Direct-dial Telephone System.

250	**32**	50k. multicoloured	3·00	3·00

33 Ancient Greek Wrestling

1992. Olympic Games, Barcelona. Multicoloured.

251		40k. Type **33**	10	35
252		3r.60 Boxing	40	40
253		5r. Weightlifting	60	60
254		12r. Gymnastics (ring exercises)	1·40	1·40

34 National Flag

1992

255	**34**	20k. multicoloured (postage)	10	10
256	-	1r. black	15	15
257	-	3r. brown	45	45
258	-	3r. brown	30	30
259	-	5r. black	60	60
260	-	20r. grey	65	65
261	-	2r. blue (air)	30	30

DESIGNS: 1r. Goddess Waroubini statuette from Orgov radio-optical telescope; 2r. Zvartnots Airport, Yerevan; 3r. (No. 257) Goddess Anahit; 3r. (No. 258) Runic inscription Karmir-Blour; 5r. U.P.U. Monument, Berne, Switzerland; 20r. Silver cup from Karashamb.
See also Nos. 275/82.

35 Noah's Descent from Mt. Ararat

1993. 175th Birth Anniv of Hovhannes Aivazovsky (painter). Sheet 95×63 mm.

MS262	**35**	7r. multicoloured	2·10	2·10

36 Engraved 10th-century Tombstone, Makenis

1993. Armenian Cultural History. Multicoloured.

263		40k. Type **36**	10	10
264		80k. Illuminated page from Gospel of 1295	20	20
265		3r.60 13th-century bas-relief, Gandzasar	75	75
266		5r. *Glorious Mother of God* (18th-century painting, H. Hovnatanian)	1·30	1·30
MS267		93×73mm. 12r. *David of Sassoun,* 1922 (painting, H. Kojoian)	6·25	5·75

37 Garni Canyon

1993. Landscapes. Multicoloured.

268		40k. Type **37**	10	10
269		80k. Shaki Falls, Zangezur	10	10
270		3r.60 River Arpa gorge, Vike	35	35
271		5r. Lake Sevan (horiz)	50	50
272		12r. Mount Ararat (horiz)	1·20	1·20

38 Temple of Garni

1993. "YEREVAN '93" International Stamp Exn.

273	**38**	10r. red, black and brown	10	10
MS274		133×111 mm. No. 273×6 plus two labels	4·50	4·25

1994. As T **34** but new currency.

275		10l. agate and brown	10	10
277		50l. deep brown and brown	60	60
280		10d. brown and grey	60	60
282		25d. gold and red	1·50	1·50

DESIGNS: 10l. Shivini, Sun God (Karmir-Blour); 50l. Tayshaba, God of the Elements (Karmir-Blour); 10d. Khaldi, Supreme God (Karmir-Blour); 25d. National arms.

39 Reliquary for Arm of St. Thaddeus (17th cent)

1994. Treasures of Etchmiadzin (seat of Armenian church). Multicoloured.

286		3d. Descent from the Cross (9th-century wooden panel)	10	10
287		5d. Gilded silver reliquary of Holy Cross of Khotakerats (1300)	10	10
288		12d. Cross with St. Karapet's right hand (14th century)	1·00	1·00
289		30d. Type **39**	50	50
290		50d. Gilded silver chrism vessel (1815)	1·40	1·40

40
(40)

40
(41)

1994. Stamp Exhibitions, Yerevan. (a) "Armenia '94" National Exn. No. 273 surch with T **40**.

291		40d. on 10r. red, blk & brn	3·75	3·75

(b) "Armenia–Argentina" Exhibition. No. 273 surch with T **41**.

292		40d. on 10r. red, blk & brn	3·75	3·75

42 Cancelled Stamps of 1919

1994. 75th Anniv of First Stamp Issue.

293	**42**	16d. multicoloured	30	30

43 Stadium and Arms of National Committee

1994. Olympic Committees. Multicoloured.

294		30d. Type **43**	45	45
295		40d. Olympic rings (centenary of Int Olympic Committee)	65	65

44 Haroutune Shmavonian

1994. Bicentenary of *Azdarar* (first Armenian periodical).

296	**44**	30d. brown and green	40	40

45 Ervand Otian

1994. 125th Birth Anniversaries.

297	**45**	50d. drab and brown	30	30
298	-	50d. brown	30	30

DESIGN—HORIZ: 50d. Levon Shant.

46 *Cross* (from Gospel)

1995. 1700th Anniv (2001) of Christianity in Armenia (1st issue). Works of art. Multicoloured.

299		60d. Type **46**	55	55
300		70d. St. Bartholomew and St. Thaddeus the Apostles (Hovnatan Hovnatanian) (45×39 mm)	55	55
301		70d. Kings Abhar and Trdat (Mkrtoum Hovnatanian) (45×39 mm)	55	55
302		80d. *St. Gregory the Illuminator*	70	70
303		90d. *The Baptism of Armenian People* (H. Aivazovsky)	85	85
MS304		97×71 mm. 400d. black and ochre (*Echmiadzin Monastery* (detail of engraving by Jacob Peeters))	2·75	2·75

See also Nos. **MS**331, 362/**MS**367, 382/**MS**387 and **MS**401.

47 Vazgen I

1995. First Death Anniv of Vazgen I (Patriarch of Armenian Orthodox Church).

305	**47**	150d. black and grey	70	70

48 Black-polished Pottery

1995. Museum Artefacts (1st series). Multicoloured.

306		30d. Type **48**	25	25
307		60d. Silver horn	50	50
308		130d. Gohar carpet	1·20	1·20

See also Nos. 332/4.

49 Red Kite and Oak

1995. Birds and Trees. Multicoloured.

309		40d. Type **49**	40	55
310		60d. Golden eagle and juniper	50	60

50 Workers building "Honeycomb" Map

1995. Hyastan All-Armenian Fund.

311	**50**	90d. multicoloured	65	65

51 Rainbows around U.N. Emblem

1995. 50th Anniv of U.N.O.

312	**51**	90d. multicoloured	65	65

52 Commander P. Kitsook (408th Rifle Division)

1995. 50th Anniv of End of Second World War. (a) Size 40×23 mm. Each black, orange and blue.

313	60d. Type **52**		40	40
314	60d. Commanders S. Chernikov, N. Tavartkeladze and V. Penkovsky (76th Mountain Rifle Red-banner (51st Guard) Division)		40	40
315	60d. Commanders S. Zakian, H. Babayan and I. Lyudnikov (390th Rifle Division)		40	40
316	60d. Commanders A. Vasilian, M. Dobrovolsky, Y. Grechany and G. Sorokin (409th Rifle Division)		40	40
317	60d. Commanders A. Sargissian and N. Safarian (89th Taman Triple Order Bearer Rifle Division)		40	40

(b) Size 23×35 mm. Each blue, orange and brown.

318	60d. Marshal Hovhannes Baghramian	60	60	
319	60d. Admiral Hovhannes Issakov	60	60	
320	60d. General Marshal Hamazasp Babajanian	60	60	
321	60d. Marshal Sergey Khoud-yakov	60	60	
MS322	120×90 mm. 300d. *Return of the Hero* (Mariam Aslamazian)	2·50	2·50	

53 Ghevond Alishan (historian and geographer)

1995. Writers' Anniversaries.

323	**53**	90d. green and black	55	55
324	-	90d. sepia, brown & yellow	55	55
325	-	90d. blue and red	60	60

DESIGNS: No. 323, Type **53** (175th birth); 324, Grigor Artsruni (journalist, 150th birth); 325, Franz Werfel (50th death).

54 Sports and Concert Complex

1995. Yerevan.

326		60d. black and orange	30	30
327		80d. black and pink	40	40
328	**54**	90d. black and buff	45	45
329	-	100d. black and buff	60	60
330	-	120d. black and pink	80	80
MS331	90×65 mm. 400d. multicoloured		2·40	2·40

DESIGNS—As T **54**: 60d. Brandy distillery and wine cellars; 80d. Abovian Street; 400d. Panoramic view of Yerevan. 60×23 mm: 100d. Baghramian Avenue; 120d. Republic Square.

No. **MS**331 also commemorates the 1700th anniv (2001) of Christianity in Armenia.

1995. Museum Artefacts (2nd series). As T 48. Multicoloured.

332	40d. Four-wheeled carriages (horiz)		25	25
333	60d. Bronze model of solar system		45	45
334	90d. Tombstone from Loriberd		65	65

55 Katsian and Spectators watching Flight

1995. Air. 86th Anniv of Artiom Katsian's 1909 World Record for Range and Altitude.

335	**55**	90d. ochre, brown and blue	60	60

Երyրthnus 40

(56)

1996. No. 275 surch as T 56.

336	40d. on 10l. agate and brown		95	95
337	100d. on 10l. agate and brown		2·30	2·30
338	150d. on 10l. agate and brown		3·50	3·50
339	200d. on 10l. agate and brown		5·00	5·00

57 Griboedov

1996. Birth Bicentenary of Aleksandr Griboedov (historian).

340	**57**	90d. stone, brown and red	65	65

58 Hayrik Khrimian (patriarch of Armenian Orthodox Church, 175th birth anniv (1995))

1996. Anniversaries.

341	**58**	90d. blue & brn (postage)	55	55
342	-	90d. multicoloured	55	55
343	-	90d. grey, blue & red (air)	55	55

DESIGNS—HORIZ: No. 342, Lazar Serebryakov (Admiral of the Fleet, and 19th-century Russian warships, birth bicentenary (1995)). VERT: No. 343, Nelson Stepanian (Second World War pilot, 50th death anniv (1994)).

59 Opening Frame from First Armenian Film

1996. Centenary of Motion Pictures.

344	**59**	60d. black, grey and blue	40	40

60 Angel and Red Cross

1996. 75th Anniv of Armenian Red Cross Society.

345	**60**	60d. multicoloured	40	40

61 Wild Goats

1996. Mammals. Multicoloured.

346	40d. Type **61**		60	20
347	60d. Leopards		55	65

62 Nansen and *Fram*

1996. Centenary of Return of Fridtjof Nansen's Arctic Expedition.

348	**62**	90d. multicoloured	70	70

63 Cycling

1996. Olympic Games, Atlanta. Multicoloured.

349	40d. Type **63**		25	25
350	60d. Triple jumping		40	40
351	70d. Wrestling		70	70

Nos. 349/51 were issued together, *se-tenant*, the backgrounds forming a composite design showing ancient Greek athletes.

64 Torch Bearer

1996. Centenary of Modern Olympic Games.

352	**64**	60d. multicoloured	35	35

65 Genrikh Kasparian (first prize winner, "Chess in USSR" competition, 1939)

1996. 32nd Chess Olympiad, Yerevan. Designs showing positions from previous games. Multicoloured.

353	40d. Type **65**		35	35
354	40d. Tigran Petrosian v. Mikhail Botvinnik (World Championship, Moscow, 1963)		35	35
355	40d. Gary Kasparov v. Anatoly Karpov (World Championship, Leningrad, 1986)		35	35
356	40d. Olympiad emblem		35	35

66 Tigran Petrosian (World chess champion, 1963–69) and Tigran Petrosian Chess House, Yerevan

1996

357	**66**	90d. multicoloured	65	65

67 Goats

1996. The Wild Goat. Multicoloured.

358	70d. Type **67**		35	35
359	100d. Lone female		45	45
360	130d. Lone male		60	60
361	350d. Heads of male and female		1·70	1·70

68 Church of the Holy Mother, Samarkand, Uzbekistan

1997. 1700th Anniv (2001) of Christianity in Armenia (2nd issue). Armenian Apostolic Overseas Churches. Multicoloured.

362	100d. Type **68**		50	50
363	100d. Church of the Holy Mother, Kishinev, Moldova		50	50
364	100d. St. Hripsime's Church, Yalta, Ukraine		50	50
365	100d. St. Catherine's Church, St. Petersburg, Russia		50	50
366	100d. Church, Lvov, Ukraine		50	50
MS367	92×66 mm. 500d. St. George of Echmiadzin's Church, Tbilisi, Georgia		2·50	2·50

69 Man operating Printing Press

1997. 225th Anniv of First Printing Press in Armenia.

368	**69**	70d. multicoloured	85	85

70 Jivani and Mount Ararat

1997. 150th Birth Anniv of Jivani (folk singer).

369	**70**	90d. multicoloured	45	45

71 Babajanian and Score of *Heroic Ballad*

1997. 75th Birth Anniv (1996) of Arno Babajanian (composer and pianist).

370	**71**	90d. black, lilac & purple	45	45

72 *Countryside* (Gevorg Bashinjaghian)

1997. Exhibits in National Gallery of Armenia (1st series). Multicoloured.

371	150d. Type **72**		75	75
372	150d. *One of My Dreams* (Eghishe Tadevossian)		75	75
373	150d. *Portrait of Natalia Tehumian* (Hakob Hovnatanian) (vert)		75	75
374	150d. *Salome* (Vardges Sureniants) (vert)		75	75

See also Nos. 390/2 and 512/13.

73 Mamulian

1997. Birth Centenary of Rouben Mamulian (film director).

375	**73**	150d. multicoloured	80	80

74 St. Basil's Cathedral, Moscow

1997. "Moscow 97" Int Stamp Exhibition.
376 **74** 170d. multicoloured 85 85

75 Hayk and Bel

1997. Europa. Tales and Legends. Multicoloured.
377 170d. Type **75** 2·00 2·00
378 250d. The Song of Vahagn 2·50 2·50

76 Charents

1997. Birth Centenary of Eghishe Charents (poet).
379 **76** 150d. brown and red 75 75

77 Iris lycotis

1997. Irises. Multicoloured.
380 40d. Type **77** 15 15
381 170d. "Iris elegantissima" 75 75

78 St. Gregory the Illuminator Cathedral, Anthelias, Libya

1997. 1700th Anniv (2001) of Christianity in Armenia (3rd issue). Armenian Overseas Educational Centres. Multicoloured.
382 100d. Type **78** 50 50
383 100d. St. Khach Armenian Church, Nakhijevan, Rostov-on-Don 50 50
384 100d. St. James's Monastery, Jerusalem (horiz) 50 50
385 100d. Nercissian School, Tblisi, Georgia (60×21 mm) 50 50
386 100d. San Lazzaro Mekhitarian Congregation, Venice (horiz) 50 50
MS387 90×45 mm. 500d. Lazarian Seminary, Moscow (horiz) 2·40 2·40

79 Baby Jesus, Angel and Mary

1997. Christmas.
388 **79** 40d. multicoloured 30 30

80 Eagle and Demonstrator with Flag

1998. Tenth Anniv of Karabakh Movement.
389 **80** 250d. multicoloured 1·60 1·60

1998. Exhibits in National Gallery of Armenia (2nd series). As T **72**. Multicoloured.
390 150d. Family. Generations (Yervand Kochar) (vert) 75 75
391 150d. Tartar Women's Dance (Alexander Bazhbeouk-Melikian) 75 75
392 150d. Spring in Our Yard (Haroutiun Kalents) (vert) 75 75

81 Diana, Princess of Wales

1998. Diana, Princess of Wales Commemoration.
393 **81** 250d. multicoloured 90 90

82 Eiffel Tower, Ball and Pitch

1998. World Cup Football Championship, France.
394 **82** 250d. multicoloured 1·20 1·20

83 Couple leaping through Flames (Trndez)

1998. Europa. National Festivals. Multicoloured.
395 170d. Type **83** 1·30 1·30
396 250d. Girls in traditional costume (Ascension) 2·20 2·20

84 Southern Swallowtail

1998. Insects. Multicoloured.
397 170d. Type **84** 85 85
398 250d. Rethera komarovi (moth) 1·20 1·20

85 Ayrarat Couple

1998. Traditional Costumes (1st series). Multicoloured.
399 170d. Type **85** 85 85
400 250d. Vaspurakan family 1·20 1·20
See also Nos. 408/9, 492/3, 591/2 and 620/1.

86 St. Forty Children's Church, Milan

1998. 1700th Anniv (2001) of Christianity in Armenia (4th issue). Sheet 143×71 mm. Multicoloured.
MS401 100d. Type **86**; 100d. St. Sargis's Church, London; 100d. St. Vardan's Cathedral, New York; 100d. St. Hovhannes's Cathedral, Paris; 100d. St. Gregory the Illuminator's Cathedral, Buenos Aires 2·50 2·50

87 Fissure in Earth's Surface

1998. Tenth Anniv of Armenian Earthquake.
402 **87** 250d. black, red and lilac 1·20 1·20

88 Pyrite

1998. Minerals. Multicoloured.
403 170d. Type **88** 90 90
404 250d. Agate 1·30 1·30

89 Briusov

1998. 125th Birth Anniv of Valery Briusov (Russian translator of Armenian works).
405 **89** 90d. multicoloured 45 45

90 Parajanov

1999. 75th Birth Anniv of Sergei Parajanov (film director and artist). Sheet 74 ×65 mm.
MS406 **90** 500d. multicoloured 2·75 2·75
MS407 As No. MS406 but with emblem in margin of "iBRA" International Stamp Exhibition, Nuremberg, Germany 3·00 3·00

1999. Traditional Costumes (2nd series). As T **85**.
408 170d. Mother and child from Karin 90 90
409 250d. Zangezour couple 1·30 1·30

91 Khosrov Reserve

1999. Europa. Parks and Gardens. Multicoloured.
410 170d. Type **91** 85 85
411 250d. Dilijan Reserve 1·00 1·00

92 Anniversary Emblem on Flag

1999. 50th Anniv of Council of Europe.
412 **92** 170d. multicoloured 1·80 1·80

93 Medieval Kogge and Map

1999. Ships of the Armenian Kingdom of Cilicia (11–14th centuries). Multicoloured.
413 170d. Type **93** 85 85
414 250d. Medieval single-masted sailing ships 1·30 1·30
415 250d. As No. 414 but with emblem of "Philexfrance 99" International Stamp Exhibition, Paris, France, in lower right corner 1·30 1·30

94 Armenian Gampr

1999. Domestic Pets. Multicoloured.
416 170d. Type **94** 85 85
417 250d. Turkish van cat 1·30 1·30
418 250d. As No. 417 but with emblem of "China 1999" International Stamp Exhibition, Peking, China, in lower right corner 1·40 1·40

95 Obverse and Reverse of Medal

1999. First Pan-Armenian Games, Yerevan. Sheet 58×40 mm.
MS419 **95** 250d. multicoloured 2·20 2·20

96 St. Gregory the Illuminator's Church, Cairo

1999. 1700th Anniv (2001) of Christianity in Armenia (5th issue). Sheet 121×65 mm containing T **96** and similar horiz designs. Multicoloured.
MS420 70d. Type **96**; 70d. St. Gregory the Illuminator's Church, Singapore; 70d. St. Khach's Church, Suchava; 70d. St. Saviour's Church, Worcester; 70d. Church of the Holy Mother, Madras 1·90 1·90

97 House made of Envelopes

1999. 125th Anniv of Universal Postal Union.
421 **97** 270d. multicoloured 1·60 1·60

98 Karen Demirchyan (Speaker of the National Assembly)

2000. Commemoration of Victims of Attack on National Assembly. Multicoloured.
422 250d. Type **98** 1·40 1·40
423 250d. Vazgen Sargsyan (Prime Minister) 1·40 1·40
MS424 60×40 mm. 540d. Demirchyan Sargsyan, Yuri Bakhshyan, Ruben Mirochyan, Henrik Abrahamyan, Armenak Armenakyan, Leonard Petrossyan and Mikael Kotanyan 3·00 3·00

99 Sevan Trout

2000. Fish. Multicoloured.
425 50d. Type **99** 35 35
426 270d. Sevan barbel 1·50 1·50

100 The Liar Hunter

2000. National Fairy Tales. Multicoloured.
427 70d. Type **100** 40 40
428 130d. The King and the Peddler 70 70

101 "Building Europe"

2000. Europa.
429 **101** 40d. multicoloured 35 35
430 **101** 500d. multicoloured 4·25 4·25

102 St. Gayane Church, Vagharshapat

2000. 1700th Anniv (2001) of Christianity in Armenia (6th issue). Sheet 121×65 mm containing T **102** and similar horiz designs. Multicoloured.
MS431 70d. Type **102**; 70d. Etchmiadzin Cathedral, Vagharshapat; 70d. Church of the Holy Mother, Khor Virap; 70d. St. Shoghakat Church, Vagharshapat; 70d. St. Hrip'sime Church, Vagharshapat 2·75 2·75

103 Basketball

2000. Olympic Games, Sydney. Multicoloured.

432		10d. Type **103**	10	10
433		30d. Tennis	25	25
434		500d. Weightlifting	4·25	4·25

104 Quartz

2000. Minerals. Multicoloured.

435		170d. Type **104**	1·30	1·30
436		250d. Molybdenite	1·90	1·90

105 Shnorhali

2000. 900th Birth Anniv of Nerses Shnorhali (writer and musician).

437	**105**	270d. multicoloured	1·60	1·60

106 Adoration of the Magi

2000. Christmas.

438	**106**	170d. multicoloured	1·00	1·00

107 Issahakian

2000. 125th Birth Anniv of Avetik Issahakian (poet).

439	**107**	130d. multicoloured	60	60

108 Dhol

2000. Musical Instruments. Multicoloured.

440		170d. Type **108**	95	95
441		250d. Duduk (wind instrument)	1·30	1·30

109 Viktor Hambartsoumian (astrophysicist)

2000. New Millennium. Famous Armenians. Multicoloured.

442		110d. Type **109**	65	65
443		110d. Abraham Alikhanov (physicist)	65	65
444		110d. Andranik Iossifan (electrical engineer)	65	65
445		110d. Sargis Saltikov (metallurgist)	65	65
446		110d. Samval Kochariants (electrical engineer)	65	65
447		110d. Artem Mikoyan (aircraft designer)	65	65
448		110d. Norayr Sisisakian (biochemist)	65	65
449		110d. Ivan Knunyants (chemist)	65	65
450		110d. Nikoghayos Yenikolopian (physical chemist)	65	65
451		110d. Nikoghayos Adonts (historian)	65	65
452		110d. Manouk Abeghian (folklore scholar)	65	65
453		110d. Hovhannes Toumanian (poet)	65	65
454		110d. Hrachya Ajarian (linguist)	65	65
455		110d. Gevorg Emin (poet)	65	65
456		110d. Yervand Lalayan (anthropologist)	65	65
457		110d. Daniel Varoujan (poet)	65	65
458		110d. Paruyr Sevak (poet)	65	65
459		110d. William Saroyan (dramatist and novelist)	65	65
460		110d. Hamo Beknazarian (film director)	65	65
461		110d. Alexandre Tamanian (architect)	65	65
462		110d. Vahram Papazian (actor)	65	65
463		110d. Vasil Tahirov (viticulturist)	65	65
464		110d. Leonid Yengibarian (mime artist)	65	65
465		110d. Haykanoush Danielian (singer)	65	65
466		110d. Sergo Hambartsoumian (weight lifter)	65	65
467		110d. Hrant Shahinian (gymnast)	65	65
468		110d. Toros Toramanian (architect)	65	65
469		110d. Komitas (composer)	65	65
470		110d. Aram Khachatourian (composer)	65	65
471		110d. Martiros Sarian (artist)	65	65
472		110d. Avet Terterian (composer)	65	65
473		110d. Alexandre Spendiarian (composer)	65	65
474		110d. Arshile Gorky (artist)	65	65
475		110d. Minas Avetissian (artist)	65	65
476		110d. (Levon Orbeli physiologist)	65	65
477		110d. Hripsimeh Simonian (ceramics artist)	65	65

110 Soldiers

2001. 1550th Anniv of Battle of Avarayr. Sheet 90×65 mm containing T **110** and similar vert design. Multicoloured.

MS478		170d. Type **110**; 270d. Vardan Mamikonian	3·00	3·00

111 Narekatsi and Text

2001. Millenary of A Record of Lamentations by Grigor Narekatsi.

479	**111**	25d. multicoloured	55	55

112 Lake Sevan

2001. Europa. Water Resources. Multicoloured.

480		50d. Type **112**	25	25
481		500d. Spandarian Reservoir	2·75	2·75

113 Emblem

2001. Armenian Membership of Council of Europe.

482	**113**	240d. multicoloured	1·10	1·10

114 Trophy

2001. Second Pan-Armenian Games. Sheet 58×40 mm.

MS483	**114**	300d. multicoloured	2·20	2·20

115 Persian Squirrel

2001. Endangered Species. Persian Squirrel (*Sciurus persicus*). Multicoloured.

484	**113**	40d. Type **115**	40	40
485	**113**	50d. Adult sitting on branch with young in tree hole	50	50
486	**113**	80d. Head of squirrel	85	85
487	**113**	120d. On ground	1·30	1·30

116 Cathedral Facade

2001. 1700th Anniv of Christianity in Armenia (7th issue). St. Gregory the Illuminator Cathedral, Yerevan. Multicoloured.

488		50d. Type **116**	35	35
489		205d. Interior elevation of Cathedral (44×30 mm)	1·40	1·40
490		240d. Exterior elevation of Cathedral (44×30 mm)	1·70	1·70

117 Lazarian and Institute

2001. Death Bicentenary of Hovhannes Lazarian (founder of Institute of Oriental Languages, Moscow).

491	**117**	300d. multicoloured	1·70	1·70

A stamp in a similar design was issued by Russia.

2001. Traditional Costumes (3rd series). As T **85**. Multicoloured.

492		50d. Javakhch couple	40	40
493		250d. Artzakh couple	1·70	1·70

118 Emblem

2001. Sixth World Wushu Championships, Yerevan.

494	**118**	180d. black	1·00	1·00

119 Children encircling Globe

2001. United Nations Year of Dialogue among Civilizations.

495	**119**	275d. multicoloured	1·60	1·60

120 Emblem

2001. Tenth Anniv of Commonwealth of Independent States.

496	**120**	205d. multicoloured	1·20	1·20

121 Profiles

2001. European Year of Languages.

497	**121**	350d. multicoloured	2·30	2·30

122 Flag

2001. Tenth Anniv of Independence.

498	**122**	300d. multicoloured	1·70	1·70

123 Cart

2001. Transport. Multicoloured.

499		180d. Type **123**	1·30	1·30
500		205d. Phaeton	1·40	1·40

124 *Hypericum perforatum*

2001. Medicinal Plants. Multicoloured.

501		85d. Type **124**	60	60
502		205d. *Thymus serpyllum*	1·50	1·50

125 Eagle

2002.

503	**125**	10d. brown	10	10
504	**125**	25d. green	20	20
506	**125**	50d. blue	35	35
507	**125**	70d. rose	20	20
508	**125**	300d. blue	1·50	1·50
509	**125**	500d. brown	1·90	1·90

126 Calendar Belt (2000 B.C.) and Copper Works

2002. Traditional Production. Multicoloured.

510		120d. Type **126**	75	75
511		350d. Beer vessels (7th century B.C.) and modern brewing equipment	2·10	2·10

2002. Exhibits in National Gallery of Armenia (3rd series). Vert designs as T **72**.

512		200d. black, grey and green	1·00	1·00
513		200d. black, grey and red	1·00	1·00

DESIGNS: No. 512, *Lily* (Edgar Chahine); 513, *Salome* (sculpture, Hakob Gurjian).

127 Football and Maps of Japan and South Korea

2002. World Cup Football Championship, Japan and South Korea.

514	**127**	350d. multicoloured	1·90	1·90

128 Pushman and *The Silent Order* (detail, painting)

2002. 125th Birth Anniv of Hovsep Pushman (artist). Sheet 75×65 mm.

MS515	**128**	650d. multicoloured	3·50	3·50

129 Technical Drawings, Tevossian and Factory

2002. Birth Centenary of Hovhannes Tevossian (metallurgical engineer).

516	**129**	350d. multicoloured	1·90	1·90

130 Birds, Playing Cards, Ribbons and Magician's Hat

2002. Europa. Circus. Multicoloured.
517		70d. Type **130**	40	40
518		500d. Clown juggling	2·10	2·10

131 Aivazian

2002. Birth Centenary of Artemy Aivazian (composer).
519	**131**	600d. multicoloured	3·25	3·25

132 Ani Cathedral

2002. Sheet 90×60 mm.
MS520	**132**	550d. multicoloured	2·75	2·75

133 Kaputjugh Mountain

2002. International Year of Mountains.
521	**133**	350d. multicoloured	2·10	2·10

134 Armenian Lizard (*Lacerta armeniaca*)

2002. Reptiles. Multicoloured.
522		170d. Type **134**	1·10	1·10
523		220d. Radde's viper (*Vipera raddei*)	1·40	1·40

135 Woman and Dove

2002. United Nations Development Fund for Women.
524	**135**	220d. multicoloured	1·60	1·60

136 Steam Locomotive

2002. Centenary of Alexandrapol–Yerevan Railway.
525	**136**	350d. multicoloured	2·50	2·50

137 *Galanthus artjuschenkoae*

2002. Flowers. Multicoloured.
526		150d. Type **137**	1·00	1·00
527		200d. *Merendera mirzoevae*	1·50	1·50

138 Research Station, Yerevan Physics Institute

2002. Space Research. Multicoloured.
528		120d. Type **138**	85	85
529		220d. Orion 1 and Orion 2 space observatories	1·50	1·50

139 *Handle with Care* (Artak Baghdassaryan)

2003. Europa. Poster Art. Multicoloured.
530		170d. Type **139**	1·30	1·30
531		250d. *Armenia our Home* (Kearen Kojoyan)	1·70	1·70

140 Aram Khachatourian

2003. Birth Centenary of Aram Khachatourian (composer).
532	**140**	350d. multicoloured	1·90	1·90

141 Armenian Gull (*Larus Armenicus*)

2003. World Environment Day. Rehabilitation of Lake Gilli.
533	**141**	220d. multicoloured	1·30	1·30

142 Viaduct and Emblem

2003. Tenth Anniv of TRACEA (transport corridor Europe–Caucasus–Asia) Programme. Sheet 74×55 mm.
MS534	**142**	480d. multicoloured	2·75	2·75

143 Horse-drawn Cart, Map of Route and First Postal Seal

2003. 175th Anniv of First Armenian Postal Dispatch.
535	**143**	70d. multicoloured	40	40

144 Siamanto and Script

2003. 125th Birth Anniv of Siamanto (Atom Yarchanyan) (writer).
536	**144**	350d. multicoloured	1·90	1·90

145 Coins and Currency Notes

2003. Tenth Anniv of Armenian Currency.
537	**145**	170d. multicoloured	95	95

146 Vahan Tekeyan

2003. 125th Birth Anniv of Vahan Tekeyan (writer).
538	**146**	200d. multicoloured	1·10	1·10

147 Profile showing Brain

2003. Neurophysiology.
539	**147**	120d. multicoloured	65	65

148 Sports and Culture Complex, Yerevan

2003. Third Armenian Games. Sheet 58×40 mm.
MS540	**148**	350d. multicoloured	2·00	2·00

149 *The Baptism* (6–7th century), Gospel of Ejmiatsin

2003. Armenian Miniatures (1st series). Sheet 65×74 mm.
MS541	**149**	550d. multicoloured	3·25	3·25

150 *Still Life* (Alexander Shevchenko)

2004. Art. Multicoloured.
542		200d. Type **150**	1·20	1·20
543		220d. *In a Restaurant* (Konstantin Roudakon)	1·30	1·30

151 "100" and Football

2004. Centenary of FIFA (Federation Internationale de Football Association).
544	**151**	350d. multicoloured	1·70	1·70

152 White Voskehat Grapes

2004. Grapes. Multicoloured.
545		170d. Type **152**	1·00	1·00
546		220d. Black Areni grapes	1·20	1·20

153 17th-century Frescos, Vifliem Church

2004. 400th Anniv of New Julfa (Armenian settlement in Iran). Sheet 55×56 mm.
MS547	**153**	590d. multicoloured	3·00	3·00

154 *The Cat and the Dog*, 1937

2004. Animated Films. Multicoloured.
548		70d. Type **154**	40	40
549		120d. *Foxbook*, 1975	70	70

155 Aramayis Yerznkian

2004. 125th Birth Anniv of Aramayis Yerznkian (politician).
550	**155**	220d. multicoloured	1·10	1·10

156 Karabakh Horse

2005.
551	**156**	350d. multicoloured	1·80	1·80

157 Hand and Olympic Rings

2005. Olympic Games, Athens (2004). Multicoloured.
552		70d. Type **157**	40	40
553		170d. Hand as runner	1·00	1·00
554		350d. Hand as pistol	2·10	2·10

158 Hands enclosing Seedling

2005. International Day against Desertification.
555	**158**	360d. multicoloured	1·90	1·90

159 Laboratory Vessel and Chemical Formula

2005. Chemistry.
556	**159**	220d. multicoloured	1·10	1·10

160 Michael Nalbandian and Script

2005. 175th Birth Anniv of Michael Nalbandian (writer).
557 **160** 220d. multicoloured 1·10 1·10

161 Mouratsan and Forest

2005. 150th Birth Anniv of Grigor Ter–Hovhanissian (Mouratsan) (writer).
558 **161** 350d. multicoloured 1·80 1·80

162 Tigran petrossian

2005. 75th Birth Anniv of Tigran Petrossian (chess player).
559 **162** 220d. multicoloured 1·10 1·10

163 Man sitting on Flower

2005. Europa. Holidays (2004). Multicoloured.
560 70d. Type **163** 25 25
561 350d. Footprint in sand 1·70 1·70

164 Goshavank Church

2005. Goshavank Monastery (12th–13th century). Sheet 84×84 mm.
MS562 **164** 480d. multicoloured 2·40 2·40

165 Armen Tigranian, Musical Scores and Landscape

2005. 125th Birth Anniv of Armen Tigranian (composer and musician).
563 **165** 220d. multicoloured 1·10 1·10

166 Xachkar (cross)

2005. 90th Anniv of Armenian Genocide.
564 **166** 350d. multicoloured 1·90 1·90

167 Mother Armenia (statue)

2005. 60th Anniv of End of World War II.
565 **167** 350d. multicoloured 1·90 1·90

168 Anushavan Arzumanian

2005. Birth Centenary of Anushavan Arzumanian (economist).
566 **168** 220d. multicoloured 1·10 1·10

169 *Self Portrait*

2005. 125th Birth Anniv of Martiros Sarian (artist). Multicoloured.
567 170d. Type **169** 80 80
568 200d. *Mount Aragats* 90 90

170 Lavash Bread

2005. Europa. Gastronomy. Multicoloured.
569 70d. Type **170** 25 25
570 350d. Harisa porridge 1·90 1·90

171 Fragment of 16th-century Khachkar

2005. Mother's Day.
571 **171** 350d. multicoloured 1·90 1·90

172 Alphabet and Mesrob Mashots (inventor) (statue)

2005. 1600th Anniv of Armenian Alphabet.
572 **172** 70d. multicoloured 25 25

173 Vardan Ajemian (actor and theatre director)

2005. Anniversaries. Multicoloured.
573 70d. Type **173** (birth centenary) 25 25
574 170d. Anania Shirakatsi (scientist) (1400th birth anniv) 80 80

174 Carpet (Artzakh) (19th-century)

2005. Carpets. Multicoloured.
575 60d. Type **174** 15 15
576 350d. Carpet (Zangezour) (1904) 1·90 1·90
MS577 92×65 mm. 480d. Carpet (Artzakh) (18th-century) (28×42 mm) 2·50 2·50

175 Mher Mkrtchian (actor)

2005. Anniversaries. Multicoloured.
578 120d. Type **175** (75th birth anniv) 45 45
579 350d. Artem Mikoyan (aircraft designer) (birth centenary) 1·90 1·90

176 Armenian and Russian Flags and Arms

2006. Year of Armenia in Russia.
580 **176** 350d. multicoloured 1·90 1·90
A stamp of the same design was issued by Russia.

177 Alexandre Melik-Pashaev (conductor)

2006. Birth Centenaries. Multicoloured.
581 70d. Type **177** 25 25
582 170d. Vakhtang Ananian (writer) 80 80

178 Emblem

2006. Winter Olympic Games, Turin. Multicoloured.
583 120d. Type **178** 45 45
584 170d. Map of Italy on skis 80 80

179 Cathedral Facade

2006. St. Mary's Cathedral of Russian Orthodox.
585 **179** 170d. multicoloured 80 80

180 Raphael Patakanian

2006. 175th Birth Anniv of Raphael Patkanian (writer).
586 **180** 220d. multicoloured 1·10 1·10

181 "P" and Emblem

2006. 50th Anniv of Europa Stamps. Multicoloured.
587 70d. Type **181** 20 20
588 70d. "T" and emblem 20 20
589 70d. "C" and emblem 20 20
590 70d. "E" and emblem 20 20

2006. Traditional Costumes (4th series). As T **85**.
591 170d. Sassoun family 60 60
592 200d. Shatakhk couple 65 65

182 *Porphyrophora hamelii*

2006. Insects. Multicoloured.
593 170d. Type **182** 60 60
594 220d. *Procerus fallettianus* 70 70

183 Spiridon Melikian

2006. 125th (2005) Birth Anniv of Spiridon Melikian (composer).
595 **183** 350d. multicoloured 90 90

184 *Adoration of the Magi* (1391), Gospel of Vostan

2006. Armenian Miniatures (2nd series). Sheet 75×65 mm.
MS596 **184** 480d. multicoloured 1·40 1·40

185 "15"

2006. 15th Anniv of Republic of Armenia. Sheet 70×70 mm.
MS597 **185** 480d. multicoloured 1·80 1·80

186 Dove

2006. Peace.
598 **186** 50d. multicoloured 1·00 1·00

187 *To Jerusalem* (1211), Gospel of Haghpat

2006. Armenian Miniatures (3rd series). Sheet 65×76 mm.
MS599 **187** 220d. multicoloured 2·75 2·75

188 Watch Mechanism

2006. Europa. Integration. Multicoloured.
600 200d. Type **188** 2·75 2·75
601 350d. Golden key and rusty keys 4·50 4·50

189 Ball, Trophy, Flags and Emblem

2006. World Cup Football Championship, Germany.
602 **189** 350d. multicoloured 4·50 4·50

190 Boghos Nubar

2006. Centenary of General Benevolent Union. Sheet 110×77 mm containing T **190** and similar vert designs. Multicoloured.

MS603 120d.×3, Type **190** (benefactor); Minutes of first meeting; Alex Manoogian (benefactor) 4·50 4·50

191 Sergey Merkurov and "Naked" (sculpture)

2006. 125th Birth Anniv of Sergey Merkurov (artist and sculptor).
604 **191** 230d. multicoloured 2·75 2·75

192 *Testudo horsfieldii*

2007. Endangered Species. *Testudo horsfieldii.* Multicoloured.
605 **192** 70d. Type **192** 95 95
606 70d. Facing left 95 95
607 70d. Facing right 95 95
608 70d. Amongst leaves 95 95

193 Trophy

2007. Armenia—37th World Chess Olympiad Champions. Multicoloured.
609 **193** 170d. Type **193** 2·20 2·20
610 220d. Medal 2·75 2·75
611 280d. Chess pieces 2·75 2·75
612 350d. Queen 4·50 4·50

194 Decorated Tree

2007. Christmas and New Year.
613 **194** 70d. multicoloured 95 95

195 Clown and Circus Building

2007. 50th Anniv of National Circus Collective.
614 **195** 70d. multicoloured 95 95

196 Stepan Shahumian Monument

2007. Armenian Settlements. Stepanavan. Multicoloured.
615 **196** 110d. Type **196** 1·40 1·40
616 120d. Memorial fountain 1·50 1·50
617 170d. Rock of Lori Bridge 2·25 2·25
618 200d. Bear Rock 2·50 2·50

197 Sculpture

2007. 50th Anniv of Yerevan Mathematical Machines Scientific Research Institute.
619 **197** 120d. multicoloured 1·50 1·50

2007. Traditional Costumes (5th series). As T **85**.
620 170d. Taron couple 2·25 2·25
621 230d. Shirak couple 2·75 2·75

198 Voski

2007. Apricot (*Armeniaca vulgaris*). Multicoloured.
622 230d. Type **198** 2·25 2·25
623 230d. Yerevani 2·25 2·25
624 230d. Ghevondi 2·25 2·25
625 230d. Karmir Nakhijevanik 2·25 2·25
626 230d. Deghin Nakhijevanik 2·25 2·25
627 230d. Khosroveni karmir 2·25 2·25
628 230d. Deghnanush vaghahas 2·25 2·25
629 230d. Vaghahas vardaguyn 2·25 2·25
630 230d. Karmreni 2·25 2·25
631 230d. Sateni deghin 2·25 2·25

199 Earrings (8th–7th century BC)

2007. Jewellery. Multicoloured.
632 280d. Type **199** 2·75 2·75
633 280d. Pendant (3rd century BC) 2·75 2·75
634 280d. Earrings with pendants (10th–11th century) 2·75 2·75
635 280d. Gospel with encrusted cover (1484) 2·75 2·75
636 280d. Chalice (1623) 2·75 2·75
637 280d. Mitre (1765) 2·75 2·75
638 280d. Dove-shaped vessel (1797) 2·75 2·75
639 280d. Knar-diadem (19th century) 2·75 2·75
640 280d. Bracelet (early 20th century) 2·75 2·75
641 280d. Incensory (19th century) 2·75 2·75

200 *Pallas Athena or Armoured Figure*

2007. 400th Birth Anniv (2006) of Rembrandt Harmenszoon van Rijn (artist). Multicoloured.
642 70d. Type **200** 95 95
643 350d. Portrait of an Old Man 4·50 4·50

MS644 128×89 mm. 70d. *Self Portrait with Saskia*; 170d. *Juno*; 280d. *Woman with Fan*; 350d. *Portrait of Jan Six* 10·00 10·00

201 Mozart as a Young Man (detail)

2007. 250th Birth Anniv (2006) of Wolfgang Amadeus Mozart (composer and musician). Multicoloured.
645 70d. Type **201** 95 95
646 350d. Mozart facing left (vert) 4·50 4·50

MS647 128×89 mm. 70d. Mozart and score (42×28 mm); 170d. Mozart and script (42×28 mm); 280d. Mozart and stringed instrument (42×28 mm); 350d. Mozart as young man (28×42 mm) 10·00 10·00

202 Artashes Shahinian

2007. Birth Centenary of Artashes Shahinian (scientist).
648 **202** 230d. multicoloured 1·90 1·90

203 Blue Mosque

2007
649 **203** 350d. multicoloured 4·50 4·50

204 'L'Ange au Sourire' (the angel with a smile), Rheims Cathedral

2007. Year of Armenia in France. Multicoloured.
650 70d. Type **204** 1·00 1·00
651 350d. The Nativity (15th-century miniature) 4·50 4·50

205 Apricot

2007
652 **205** 350d. multicoloured 4·25 4·25

206 Tirgran the Great

2007
653 **206** 50d. multicoloured 80 80
654 **206** 60d. multicoloured 90 90
655 **206** 70d. multicoloured 1·00 1·00
656 **206** 120d. multicoloured 1·80 1·80

207 Hands

2007. Centenary of Scouting.
657 **207** 350d. multicoloured 4·50 4·50

208 Gusan Sheram

2007. 150th Birth Anniv of Talyan Grigor Karapet (Gusan Sheram) (composer and singer).
658 **208** 280d. multicoloured 3·75 3·75

209 Margar Sedrakyan

2007. Birth Centenary of Margar Sedrakyan (Cognac maker).
659 **209** 170d. multicoloured 2·30 2·30

210 Memorial

2007. 40th Anniv of Genocide Museum. Sheet 74×65 mm.
MS660 480d. multicoloured 6·00 6·00

211 *Sparrows* (Yeva Karapetyan)

2007. Children's Drawings.
661 **211** 35d. multicoloured 1·00 1·00

212 Gevorg Bashinjaghyan and *Gyughakan Tesaran*

2007. 150th Birth Anniv of Gevorg Bashinjaghyan (artist). Multicoloured.
662 160d. Type **212** 2·30 2·30
663 220d. *Aragats* 3·00 3·00

213 Jean Garzou in his Studio

2007. Birth Centenary of Garnik Zulumyan (Jean Garzou) (artist). Multicoloured.
664 180d. Type **213** 2·50 2·50
665 220d. *Portrait of Seda* (vert) 2·75 2·75

214 Hands holding Trophy

2007. Pan Armenian Games, Yerevan. Sheet 40×58 mm.
MS666 360d. multicoloured 4·75 4·75

215 Norayr Sisakyan

2007. Birth Centenary of Norayr Sisakyan (biochemist).
667 **215** 120d. multicoloured 1·60 1·60

216 Kamancha

2007. Traditional Instruments.
668 **216** 110d. multicoloured 1·60 1·60

217 *Pelecanus crispus* (Dalmatian pelican)

2007. Endangered Species. Multicoloured.
669 **217** 120d. Type **217** 1·50 1·50
670 200d. *Aegypius monachus* (Eurasian black vulture) 2·75 2·75

218 Matenadaran

2007. Matenadaran Manuscript and Book Depository.
671	**218**	200d. multicoloured	2·50	2·50

219 Bagrat Nalbandyan

2007. Bagrat Nalbandyan (communications commissar) Commemoration.
672	**219**	230d. multicoloured	3·00	3·00

220 Nemrut Baghdasaryan

2007. Birth Centenary of Nemrut Baghdasaryan (photojournalist).
673	**220**	200d. multicoloured	2·50	2·50

221 Sun and Earth

2007. International Year of Solar Physics. 50th Anniv of Geophysics.
674	**221**	170d. multicoloured	2·30	2·30

222 *Aphrodite* (Greek)

2007. Statues. Multicoloured.
675	70d. Type **222**		1·00	1·00
676	350d. *Anahit* (Armenian)		4·50	4·50

Stamps of the same design were issued by Greece.

223 Family (Eduard Ghazaryan)

2008. International Children's Day.
677	**223**	70d. multicoloured	1·50	1·50

No. 677 includes the *se-tenant* premium-carrying tab shown in Type **223**, the premium for the benefit of children's charities.

224 Chinese Dragon

2008. Olympic Games, Beijing.
678	**224**	350d. multicoloured	5·00	5·00

225 Carving

2008. Woodcraft.
679	**225**	120d. multicoloured	7·75	7·75

226 Envelopes and Map

2008. Europa. The Letter.
680	**226**	350d. multicoloured	5·00	5·00

227 Alexander Shirvanzade

2008. 150th Birth Anniv of Alexander Shirvanzade (writer).
681	**227**	280d. multicoloured	4·00	4·00

2008. Tigran the Great.
682	**206**	10d. multicoloured	30	30
683	**206**	20d. multicoloured	55	55
684	**206**	50d. multicoloured	1·30	1·30
685	**206**	1100d. multicoloured	13·75	13·75

See also Nos. 653/6.

228 *Anemone fasciculata*

2008. Flowers. Multicoloured.
686	120d. Type **228**		2·75	2·75
687	280d. *Scabiosa caucasica*		4·00	4·00

229 Building Facade

2008. 75th Anniv of Polytechnic Institute.
688	**229**	220d. multicoloured	3·75	3·75

230 William Saroyan

2008. Birth Centenary of William Saroyan (dramatist and writer).
689	**230**	350d. multicoloured	5·75	5·75

231 Viktor Ambartsumyan

2008. Birth Centenary of Viktor Amazaspovich Ambartsumyan (scientist).
690	**231**	120d. multicoloured	2·00	2·00

232 Peyo Yavorov (Bulgarian poet and revolutionary)

2008. Nationalist Liberation Movements of Bulgaria and Armenia. Multicoloured.
691	70d. Type **232**		1·00	1·00
692	350d. Andranik Ozanyan (Armenian general in Balkan Wars of Independence)		4·75	4·75

2009. Tigran the Great. Size 19×23 mm.
693	**206**	10d. multicoloured (dull yellow-green)	15	15
694	**206**	25d. multicoloured (orange-yellow)	25	25
695	**206**	50d. multicoloured (bright magenta)	55	55
696	**206**	70d. multicoloured (olive-sepia)	75	75
697	**206**	120d. multicoloured (reddish violet)	1·30	1·30
698	**206**	220d. multicoloured (deep blue)	2·75	2·75
699	**206**	280d. multicoloured (deep dull violet blue)	3·75	3·75
700	**206**	350d. multicoloured (bright crimson)	4·25	2·25

See also Nos. 653/6 and 682/5.

233 Dancer holding Sword

2009. Dances. Multicoloured.
701	70d. Type **233**		1·20	1·20
702	350d. Couple		3·75	3·75

234 Ruins

2009. Tushpa-Van–Ancient Capital of Armenia.
703	**234**	220d. multicoloured	2·50	2·50

235 Observatory

2009. Europa. Astronomy.
704	**235**	350d. multicoloured	4·75	4·75

236 Armenian Chess Team

2009. Armenia Gold Medalists at Chess Olympiad 2008, Dresden, Germany. Multicoloured.
705	70d. Type **236**		2·50	2·50
706	280d. Chess pieces		11·00	11·00

237 Stylized Buildings

2009. 50th Anniv of European Court of Human Rights.
707	**237**	70d. multicoloured	95	95

238 '60' and Emblem

2009. 60th Anniv of Council of Europe
708	**238**	280d. multicoloured	3·50	3·50

239 Braille Dots as Eyes

2009. Birth Bicentenary of Louis Braille (inventor of Braille writing for the blind).
709	**239**	110d. multicoloured	1·40	1·40

240 Daniel Varuzhan

2009. 125th Birth Anniv of Daniel Varuzhan (writer).
710	**240**	230d. multicoloured	2·75	2·75

241 Monument

2009. 50th Anniv of Monument to Davit of Sasun (epic hero). Sheet 69×90 mm.
MS711	**241**	multicoloured	4·50	4·50

242 Hrant Shahinyan, Helsinki–1952

2009. Olympic Champions. Sheet 119×59 mm containing T **242** and square designs. Multicoloured.
MS712 70d. Type **242**; 120d. Igor Novikov, Melbourne–1956; 160d. Albert Azaryan, Melbourne–1956; 160d. Rome–1960 4·50 4·50

Tokyo–1964;160d. Albert Azaryan, Melbourne–1956; 160d. Rome–1960

243 Khachatur Abovyan

2009. Birth Bicentenary of Khachatur Abovyan (educator, poet and advocate of modernization).
713	**243**	170d. multicoloured	2·00	2·00

244 *Panna Paskevich* (Georgi Yakulov)

2009. Art from National Gallery. Multicoloured.
714	200d. Type **244**		2·50	2·50
715	200d. *Autumn. A Corner in Yerevan* (Sedrak Arakelyan)		2·50	2·50

245 *Lutra lutra meridionalis* (European otter)

2009. Fauna. Multicoloured.
716	120d. Type **245**		2·10	2·10
717	160d. *Ursus arctos syriacus* (Syrian brown bear)		2·75	2·75

246 Zvartnots Church, 642 AD,

2009. Churches in Vagharshapat. Sheet 145×69 mm containing T **246** and similar vert designs. Multicoloured.
MS718 70d.×4, Type **246**; St. Hripsime church, 618 AD; Mother See of Holy Etchmiadzin, 301–303 AD; St. Gayane church, 630 AD 3·50 3·50

247 Decorated Tree

2009. New Year.
719	**247**	120d. multicoloured	1·60	1·60

The tree shown on No. 719 was printed with a flocked surface and simulated baubles.

248 Virgin and Child

2009. Christmas. Multicoloured.
720		280d. Type **248**	3·50	3·50

MS721 80×105 mm. Size 60×30 mm. 650d. As Type **248** but design enlarged 8·00 8·00

2010. Tirgran the Great

(a) Ordinary gum
722	**206**	10d. magenta	40	40
723		25d. ultramarine	60	60
724		50d. yellow-ochre	75	75
725		70d. bright vermilion	1·00	1·00
726		100d. purple-brown	1·50	1·50
727		120d. claret	1·80	1·80
728		200d. pale greenish grey	2·50	2·50
729		220d. bright reddish violet	2·75	2·75
730		280d. scarlet	3·75	3·75
731		650d. apple green	4·50	4·50

(b) Self-adhesive
732	**206**	10d. magenta	40	40
733		25d. ultramarine	60	60
734		50d. yellow-ochre	75	75
735		70d. bright vermilion	1·00	1·00
736		100d. purple-brown	1·50	1·50
737		120d. claret	1·80	1·80
738		200d. pale greenish grey	2·50	2·50
739		220d. bright reddish violet	2·75	2·75
740		280d. scarlet	3·75	3·75
741		650d. apple green	4·50	4·50

249 Henrik Kasparyan and Chessboard

2010. Birth Centenary of Henrik Kasparyan
742	**249**	870d. multicoloured	9·50	9·50

250 Victory Monument

2010. 65th Anniv of End of World War II
743	**250**	350d. multicoloured	4·75	4·75

251 Memorial Complex

2010. Russian Officer Cemetery. Multicoloured.
744		350d. Type **251**	5·00	5·00

MS745 102×77 mm. 650d. As Type **251** 5·00 8·00

252 Mount Ararat

2010. Independence Day
746		350d. Type **252**	4·50	4·50
747		650d. National flag (30×30 mm)	8·50	8·50

253 Armenian Pavillion

2010. Expo 2010, Shanghai. Multicoloured.
748		280d. Type **253**	3·75	3·75
749		280d. View of Yerevan and Mount Ararat (50×30 mm)	3·75	3·75

254 Medieval Women

2010. Europa
750	**254**	350d. multicoloured	4·50	4·50

255 Vladimir Yengibaryan (Melbourne, 1956)

2010. Olympic Champions. Multicoloured.
MS751 160d.×3, Type **255**; Faina Melnik (Munich, 1972); Yuri Vardanyan (Moscow, 1980) 6·50 6·50

256 Cross Country Skier

2010. Winter Olympic Games, Vancouver. Multicoloured.
MS752 350d. Type **256**; 500d. Alpine houses and cross country skier; 600d. Alpine skier 19·00 19·00

257 Games Emblem and Pictograms

2010. Olympic Youth Games, Singapore
753	**257**	870d. multicoloured	11·50	11·50

258 Ball and Globe

2010. World Cup Football Championship, South Africa
754	**258**	1100d. multicoloured	14·50	14·50

259 Arakel Babakhanyan

2010. 150th Birth Anniv of Araqel Babakhanyan (Leo) (historian and publicist)
755	**259**	220d. multicoloured	2·75	2·75

260 Raffi

2010. 175th Birth Anniv of Hakob Melik- Hakobyan (Raffi) (writer and publicist)
756	**260**	220d. multicoloured	2·75	2·75

261 Tigran the Great

2011. Tigran the Great. Background colour given in brackets.
757	**261**	10d. multicoloured (blue)	40	40
758	**261**	35d. multicoloured (deep brown)	60	60
759	**261**	50d. multicoloured (apple green)	75	75
760	**261**	70d. multicoloured pale (turquoise)	1·00	1·00
761	**261**	120d. multicoloured (orange-red)	1·80	1·80
762	**261**	160d. multicoloured (deep claret)	2·20	2·20
763	**261**	220d. multicoloured (deep rose-red)	3·75	3·75
764	**261**	280d. multicoloured (ultramarine)	3·75	3·75
765	**261**	350d. multicoloured (ochre)	4·00	4·00
766	**261**	1100d. multicoloured (brown)	14·00	14·00

262 Avet Avetisyan as Zimzimow and Davit Malyan as Kakuli

2011. First Armenian Sound Film - *Pepo* (1935). Each black and scarlet-vermilion.
MS767 170d. Type **262**; 200d. Hrachya Nercissyan as Pepo; 500d. Tatiana Makhmuryan as Kekel 11·00 11·00

263 Leonid Yengibarov

2011. Leonid Yengibarov (actor) Commemoration
768	**263**	220d. chrome yellow and black	3·00	3·00

264 Ruben Sevak

2011. 125th Birth Anniv of Ruben Chilinkiryan (Ruben Sevak) (writer, publicist and doctor)
769	**264**	280d. multicoloured	3·75	3·75

265 Vahan Teryan

2011. 125th Birth Anniv of Vahan Ter-Grigoryan (Vahan Teryan) (writer and politician)
770	**265**	280d. multicoloured	3·75	3·75

266 Fritillaria armena

2011. Flora and Fruit. Multicoloured.
771	**266**	280d. Type **266**	3·75	3·75
772		280d. *Sambucus tigranii*	3·75	3·75

267 Portrait of Actress Khmara (Haroutyun Kalents)

2011. Paintings from National Gallery. Multicoloured.
773	**267**	450d. Type **267**	5·75	5·75
774		450d. *Mkrtich Khriyan* (writer, newspaper editor, political and religious leader, Armenian Patriarch of Constantinople (1869–1873), Prelate of Van (1880–1885) and Catholicos of All Armenians (1892–1907)) (Vardghes Sourenyants)	5·75	5·75

268 Angel (detail from Resurrection (manuscript, c. 1319))

2011. Easter. Sheet 80×115 mm
MS775 **268** 1100d. multicoloured 14·00 14·00

269 Andranik Iosifyan

2011. Andranik Iosifyan (constructor of meteorological satellites) Commemoration
776	**269**	200d. multicoloured	2·50	2·50

270 Yuri Gagarin

2011. 50th Anniv of First Manned Space Flight
777	**270**	350d. multicoloured	4·00	4·00

271 Hovhannes Toumanyan

2011. Personalities. Writers. Multicoloured.
778		120d. Type **271**	1·80	1·80
779		230d. Valeri Bryusov	2·75	2·75

272 Minsk

2011. Capital Cities. Multicoloured.
780		200d. Type **272**	2·40	2·40

| 781 | 200d. Museum of Art and History, Yerevan | 2·40 | 2·40 |

273 Globe and Commonwealth Emblem

2011. 20th Anniv of Regional Communication Community (RCC). Sheet 108×78 mm

| MS782 **273** 200d. multicoloured | 2·40 | 2·40 |

274 Athletes

2011. Pan Armenian Games. Sheet 120×104 mm

| MS783 **274** 380d. multicoloured | 4·25 | 4·25 |

275 *Luscinia scecica* (Bluethroat)

2011. Birds. Multicoloured.

| 784 | 230d. Type **275** | 2·75 | 2·75 |
| 785 | 330d. *Parus major* (Great Tit) | 2·75 | 2·75 |

276 Emblem and '20'

2011. 20th Anniv of Independence. Multicoloured.

| 786 | 330d. Type **276** | 4·25 | 4·25 |
| 787 | 380d. National Arms and '2011' | 4·25 | 4·25 |

277 Fridtjof Nansen

2011. 150th Birth Anniv of Fridtjof Nansen (explorer)

| 788 | **277** 350d. multicoloured | 4·25 | 4·25 |

278 Anniversary Emblem

2011. 20th Anniv of Community of Independent States (CIS)

| 789 | **278** 280d. multicoloured | 3·75 | 3·75 |

279 AIDS Ribbon

2011. United Nations AIDS Awareness Programme. Multicoloured.

| MS790 200d. Right side of AIDS ribbon; 280d. Type **279** | 6·50 | 6·50 |

280 Karen Demirchyan Sports and Concerts Complex, Yerevan

2011. Junior Eurovision Song Contest, Yerevan

| 791 | **280** 230d. multicoloured | 3·25 | 3·25 |

281 Dilijan Forest

2011. Europa. Forests. Multicoloured.

| 792 | 350d. Type **281** | 4·25 | 4·25 |
| 793 | 350d. Dilijan Forest, younger trees | 4·25 | 4·25 |

282 Grigor Zohrap

2011. 150th Birth Anniv of Grigor Zohrap (Krikor Zohrab) (writer)

| 794 | **282** 170d. multicoloured | 2·50 | 2·50 |

283 Girl

2011. Youth Stamps. Multicoloured.

| 779 | 100d. Type **283** | 1·50 | 1·50 |
| 796 | 120d. Boy | 1·80 | 1·80 |

284 Santa Claus

2011. Christmas and New Year

| 797 | **284** 220d. multicoloured | 3·00 | 3·00 |

285 Sanahin Monastery

2011. World Heritage Sites. Multicoloured.

| MS798 230d. Type **285**; 330d. Haghpat Monastery | 8·00 | 8·00 |

286 Armed Forces

2012. 20th Anniv of Armenian Army. Multicoloured.

| 799 | 200d. Type **286** | 2·40 | 2·40 |
| 800 | 280d. Flag and arms | 3·75 | 3·75 |

287 Anniversary Emblem

2012. 20th Anniv of Armenia's Membership of United Nations Organization

| 801 | **287** 350d. multicoloured | 4·25 | 4·25 |

288 Hakob Meghapart (first Armenian printer), Logotype of his Printing House and Urbatagirk, Book of Friday (first printed book in Armenian)

2012. Yerevan - World Book Capital 2012. Sheet 90×70 mm

| MS802 **288** 560d. multicoloured | 7·50 | 7·50 |

289 Garegin Nzhdeh

2012. 125th Birth Anniv of Garegin Ter-Harutyunyan (Garegin Njdeh) (nationalist)

| 803 | **289** 200d. multicoloured | 2·40 | 2·40 |

290 Misak Metsarents

2012. 125th Birth Anniv of Misak Metsadourian (Misak Metsarents)

| 804 | **290** 280d. black | 3·75 | 3·75 |

291 'a'

2012. The Armenian Alphabet. Multicoloured.

805	10d. Type **291**	40	40
806	25d. 'b'	50	50
807	50d. 'g'	75	75
808	70d. 'd'	1·00	1·00
809	100d. 'e'	1·50	1·50
810	120d. 'z'	1·80	1·80
811	280d. 'ē'	3·75	3·75

292 Khachkar (Cross-stone)

2012. Traditional Handicrafts. Stone Carving. Cross-stones (Khachkars). Multicoloured.

| 812 | 200d. Type **292** | 2·40 | 2·40 |
| 813 | 280d. Khachkar (different) | 3·75 | 3·75 |

293 Eduard Azaryan (Moscow, 1980)

2012. Olympic Champions. Multicoloured.

| MS814 160d.×3, Type **293**; Levon Julfalakyan (Seoul, 1988); Oksen Mirzoyan (Seoul, 1988) | 6·50 | 6·50 |

294 Mesrop Mashtots

2012. 1650th Birth Anniv of Mesrop Mashtots (monk, theologian, linguist and inventor of Armenian alphabet). Sheet 84×108 mm

| MS815 **294** 560d. multicoloured | 7·50 | 7·50 |

295 Hagigadar Monastery Church

2012. 500th Anniv of Hagigadar Monastery Church

| 816 | **295** 380d. multicoloured | 5·00 | 5·00 |
| MS817 128×82 mm. No. 816×2 | 10·00 | 10·00 |

296 Hofburg Conference Centre, Vienna

2012. 20th Anniv of Membership of Organization for Security and Co-operation in Europe

| 818 | **296** 330d. multicoloured | 4·00 | 4·00 |

297 Ancient Artashat (capital of Armenia from 185 BC - 120 AD)

2012. Historical Capitals of Armenia

| 819 | **297** 220d. multicoloured | 3·00 | 3·00 |

298 Aleksandr Myasnikyan and Mount Ararat

2012. 125th Birth Anniv of Aleksandr Teodorosi Myasnikyan (Aleksandr Fyodorovich Myasnikov) (politician and writer)

| 820 | **298** 230d. multicoloured | 3·25 | 3·25 |

299 Hrachya Petikyan

2012. Olympic Champions (Barcelona, 1992 or Atlanta, 1996). Multicoloured.

| MS821 120d.×4, Type **299**; Israyel Militosyan; Mnatsakan Iskandaryan; Armen Nazaryan (Atlanta, 1996) | 7·00 | 7·00 |

300 Boxing

2012. Olympic Games, London. Multicoloured.

822	170d. Type **300**	2·50	2·50
823	200d. Weightlifting	2·40	2·40
824	230d. Wrestling	3·25	3·25

301 Samvel Kocharyants

2012. Birth Centenary (2009) of Samvel Kocharyants (nuclear scientist)
825 **301** 350d. multicoloured 4·25 4·25

302 Perch Proshyan

2012. 175th Birth Anniv of Perch Proshyan (Ovanes Stepanovich Ter-Arakelyan) (writer)
826 **302** 170d. multicoloured 2·50 2·50

303 Reliquary of Geghard, 1687

2012. Treasures of Etchmiadzin. Multicoloured.
827 200d. Type **303** 2·50 2·50
828 220d. Cross with relic, 1746 3·00 3·00
829 450d. Reliquary, 13th-century (inscr 'Aragadz. St. Nshan') 6·00 6·00

304 Lusine Zakaryan

2012. 75th Birth Anniv of Lusine (Svetlana) Zakaryan (soprano)
830 **304** 220d. multicoloured 3·00 3·00

305 Ashot Hovhannissyan

2012. 125th Birth Anniv of Ashot Hovhannisyan (politician)
831 **305** 170d. multicoloured 2·50 2·50

306 Gai (Hayk Bzhishkyan)

2012. 125th Birth Anniv of Gai (Hayk Bzhishkyan) (soldier and lecturer)
832 **306** 280d. multicoloured 3·75

307 Hofsep Orbeli

2012. 125th Birth Anniv of Hofsep Abgari Orbeli (historian, orientalist and founder of Armenian Academy of Sciences)
833 **307** 280d. multicoloured 3·75 3·75

308 Tigran Tchoukhadjian

2012. 175th Birth Anniv of Tigran Tchoukhadjian (composer, conductor, creator of first Armenian opera)
834 **308** 330d. multicoloured 4·00 4·00

309 Anniversary Emblem

2012. 20th Anniv of Hayastan All-Armenian Fund (uniting Armenians in Armenia and overseas to overcome the country's difficulties and to help establish sustainable development in Armenia)
835 **309** 380d. multicoloured 4·25 4·25

310 Emblem

2012. Collective Security Treaty Organization
836 **310** 230d. multicoloured 3·25 3·25

311 Tadevos Minasyants

2012. Birth Centenary of Tadevos Minasyants (Minister of Communication)
837 **311** 170d. multicoloured 2·50 2·50

312 *Dacha* (Mark Chagall)

2012. Art. Multicoloured.
838 220d. Type **312** 3·00 3·00
839 280d. *Self-portrait* (Rudolf Khachatryan) 3·75 3·75

313 Tatev Monastery (8th-century) and Cable Car

2012. Europa. Visit Armenia
840 **313** 350d. multicoloured 4·25 4·25

314 Monument to Sayat-Nova

2012. 300th Birth Anniv of Sayat-Nova (Harutyun Sayadyan) (poet and musician). Sheet 90×70 mm
MS841 **314** 560d. multicoloured 7·50 7·50

315 Trees and Mountains

2012. Children's Drawings. Multicoloured.
842 100d. Type **315** 1·50 1·50
843 120d. Boy kicking football against house 1·80 1·80

316 Decorated Tree and Night Scene

2012. Christmas and New Year
844 **316** 220d. multicoloured 3·00 3·00

317 *Allactaga elater* (Small Five-toed Jerboa)

2012. Fauna. Multicoloured.
845 230d. Type **317** 3·25 3·25
846 330d. *Ovis orientalis gmelinii* (Armenian Mouflon) 4·00 4·00

Pt. 4

ARUBA

An island in the Caribbean, formerly part of Netherlands Antilles. In 1986 became an autonomous country within the Kingdom of the Netherlands.

100 cents = 1 gulden.

1 Map

1986. New Constitution.
1 **1** 25c. yellow, blue and black 1·70 55
2 - 45c. multicoloured 2·00 1·10
3 - 55c. black, grey and red 2·50 1·50
4 - 100c. multicoloured 3·25 2·50
DESIGNS—VERT: 45c. Aruban arms; 55c. National anthem. HORIZ: 100c. Aruban flag.

2 House

1986
5 **2** 5c. black and yellow 55 10
6 - 15c. black and blue 1·20 55
7 - 20c. black and grey 90 35
8 - 25c. black and violet 1·70 55
9 - 30c. black and red 1·70 90
10 - 35c. black and bistre 1·70 90
12 - 45c. black and blue 2·00 1·20
14 - 55c. black and grey 1·70 90
15 - 60c. black and blue 1·90 1·10
16 - 65c. black and blue 1·80 1·50
18 - 75c. black and brown 2·00 1·50
20 - 85c. black and orange 2·00 1·10
21 - 90c. black and green 2·20 1·50
22 - 100c. black and brown 2·20 1·50
23 - 150c. black and green 3·75 2·20
24 - 250c. black and green 5·25 4·50
DESIGNS: 15c. Clock tower; 20c. Container crane; 25c. Lighthouse; 30c. Snake; 35c. Burrowing owl; 45c. Caribbean vase (shell); 55c. Frog; 60c. Water-skier; 65c. Fisherman casting net; 75c. Hurdy-gurdy; 85c. Pot; 90, 250c. Different cacti; 100c. Maize; 150c. Watapana Tree.

3 People and Two Ropes

1986. "Solidarity". Multicoloured.
25 30c.+10c. Type **3** 2·00 1·10
26 35c.+15c. People and three ropes 2·00 1·10
27 60c.+25c. People and one rope 2·75 1·70

4 Dove between Scenes of Peace and War

1986. International Peace Year. Multicoloured.
28 60c. Type **4** 5·00 1·70
29 100c. Doves flying over broken barbed wire 10·00 3·25

5 Boy and Caterpillar

1986. Child Welfare. Multicoloured.
30 45c.+20c. Type **5** 2·75 1·10

31 70c.+25c. Boy and shell 3·25 1·70
32 100c.+40c. Girl and butterfly 4·00 2·50

6 Engagement Picture

1987. Golden Wedding of Princess Juliana and Prince Bernhard.
33 **6** 135c. orange, black and gold 4·50 2·50

7 Queen Beatrix and Prince Claus

1987. Royal Visit. Multicoloured.
34 55c. Type **7** 2·20 1·10
35 60c. Prince Willem-Alexander 2·20 1·10

8 Woman looking at Beach

1987. Tourism. Multicoloured.
36 60c. Type **8** 2·20 1·50
37 100c. Woman looking at desert landscape 3·25 2·00

9 Child with Book on Beach

1987. Child Welfare. Multicoloured.
38 25c.+10c. Type **9** 1·70 90
39 45c.+20c. Children drawing Christmas tree 2·20 1·10
40 70c.+30c. Child gazing at Nativity crib 3·25 1·70

10 Plantation

1988. *Aloe vera*. Multicoloured.
41 45c. Type **10** 2·00 1·10
42 60c. Stem and leaves of plant 2·20 1·50
43 100c. Harvesting aloes 2·75 1·70

11 25c. Coin

1988. Coins. Multicoloured.
44 25c. Type **11** 1·50 55
45 55c. Square 50c. coin 2·00 1·10
46 65c. 5c. and 10c. coins 2·20 1·50
47 150c. 1 gulden coin 4·00 2·50

12 Bananaquits, Country Scene and "Love"

1988. Greetings Stamps. Multicoloured.
48 70c. Type **12** 2·00 1·10
49 135c. West Indian crown conch, West Indian chank (shells), seaside scene and "Love" 2·75 2·00

13 White Triangle on Shaded Background

1988. "Solidarity". 11th Y.M.C.A. World Council. Multicoloured.
50	45c.+20c. Type **13**	2·20	1·10
51	60c.+25c. Interlocking triangles	2·20	1·70
52	100c.+50c. Shaded triangle on white background	2·75	2·20

14 Torch

1988. Olympic Games, Seoul. Multicoloured.
| 53 | 35c. Type **14** | 1·70 | 90 |
| 54 | 100c. Games and Olympic emblems | 2·75 | 1·70 |

15 Jacks

1988. Child Welfare. Toys. Multicoloured.
55	45c.+20c. Type **15**	2·20	1·10
56	70c.+30c. Spinning top	2·20	1·70
57	100c.+50c. Kite	2·75	2·20

16 Children

1989. Carnival. Multicoloured.
58	45c. Type **16**	2·20	1·10
59	60c. Girl in costume	2·20	1·10
60	100c. Lights	2·75	1·70

17 Maripampun

1989. Maripampun. Multicoloured.
61	35c. Type **17**	1·70	85
62	55c. Seed pods	1·70	1·10
63	200c. Pod distributing seeds	4·50	3·25

18 Emblem

1989. Universal Postal Union.
| 64 | **18** | 250c. multicoloured | 6·75 | 4·25 |

19 Snake

1989. South American Rattlesnake.
65	**19**	45c. multicoloured	1·70	90
66	-	55c. multicoloured	2·00	1·10
67	-	60c. multicoloured	2·00	1·10
DESIGNS: 55, 60c. Snake (different).

20 Spoon in Child's Hand

1989. Child Welfare. Multicoloured.
| 68 | 45c +20c. Type **20** | 2·00 | 1·10 |
| 69 | 60c.+30c. Child playing football | 2·20 | 1·20 |

| 70 | 100c.+50c. Child's hand in adult's hand (vert) | 3·25 | 2·20 |

21 Violin, Tambour and Cuatro Players

1989. New Year. Dande Musicians. Multicoloured.
71	25c. Type **21**		1·10	55
72	70c. Guitar and cuatro players and singer with hat	1·60	1·10
73	150c. Cuatro, accordion and wiri players	3·00	2·20

22 Tractor and Natural Vegetation

1990. Environmental Protection. Multicoloured.
74	45c. Type **22**	1·50	1·10
75	55c. Face and wildlife (vert)	1·70	1·10
76	100c. Marine life	2·75	2·00

23 Giant Caribbean Anemone and Pederson's Cleaning Shrimp

1990. Marine Life. Multicoloured.
77	60c. Type **23**	1·70	1·10
78	70c. Queen angelfish and red coral	2·20	1·70
79	100c. Banded coral shrimp, fire sponge and yellow boring sponge	3·25	2·50

24 Ball

1990. World Cup Football Championship, Italy. Multicoloured.
| 80 | 35c. Type **24** | 1·50 | 90 |
| 81 | 200c. Mascot | 4·50 | 3·25 |

25 Emblem of Committee of Tanki Leendert Association Youth Centre

1990. "Solidarity". Multicoloured.
| 82 | 55c.+25c. Type **25** | 2·20 | 1·80 |
| 83 | 100c.+50c. Emblem of Foundation for Promotion of Responsible Parenthood | 4·00 | 3·00 |

26 Clay Painting Stamps

1990. Archaeology. Multicoloured.
84	45c. Type **26**	1·50	1·10
85	60c. Stone figure	1·70	1·10
86	100c. Dabajuroid-style jar	2·75	1·70

27 Sailboards and Fishes

1990. Child Welfare. Multicoloured.
87	45c.+20c. Type **27**	1·70	1·10
88	60c.+30c. Parakeets and coconut trees	2·20	1·70
89	100c.+50c. Kites and lizard	3·25	2·75

28 Mountain and Shoreline

1991. Landscapes. Multicoloured.
90	55c. Type **28**	1·40	1·10
91	65c. Cacti and Haystack mountain	1·70	1·50
92	100c. House, mountain and ocean, Jaburibari	2·50	2·20

29 Woman holding Herbs ("Carer")

1991. Women and Work. Multicoloured.
93	35c. Type **29**	1·10	55
94	70c. Women and kitchen ("Housewife")	1·70	1·50
95	100c. Women and telephone ("Woman in the World")	2·20	2·00

30 Ocimum sanctum

1991. Medicinal Plants. Multicoloured.
96	65c. Type **30**	1·70	1·10
97	75c. *Jatropha gossypifolia*	2·00	1·50
98	95c. *Croton flavens*	2·20	1·70

31 Fishing Net, Float and Needle

1991. Traditional Crafts.
| 99 | **31** | 35c. black, ultram & blue | 1·10 | 90 |
| 100 | - | 250c. black, lilac & purple | 5·00 | 4·25 |
DESIGNS: 250c. Hat, straw and hat-block.

32 Child's Hand taking Book from Shelf

1991. Child Welfare. Multicoloured.
101	45c.+25c. Type **32**	1·70	1·50
102	60c.+35c. Child's finger pointing to letter "B"	2·20	1·70
103	100c.+50c. Child reading	3·25	2·50

33 Toucan saying "Welcome"

1991. Tourism. Multicoloured.
104	35c. Type **33**	1·10	1·10
105	70c. Aruban youth welcoming tourist	1·70	1·10
106	100c. Windmill and Bubali swamp	2·75	2·20

34 Government Decree of 1892 establishing first Aruban Post Office

1992. Centenary of Postal Service (1st issue). Multicoloured.
107	60c. Type **34**	1·40	1·10
108	75c. Lt.-Governor's building (mail service office, 1892–1908) (horiz)	1·70	1·10
109	80c. Present Oranjestad P.O. (horiz)	2·20	1·70
See also Nos. 117/19.

35 Equality of Sexes

1992. Equality. Multicoloured.
| 110 | 100c. Type **35** | 2·20 | 1·70 |
| 111 | 100c. People of different races (equality of nations) | 2·20 | 1·70 |

36 Aruban Flag, Guide Emblem and Girl Guides

1992. "Solidarity". Multicoloured.
| 112 | 55c.+30c. Type **36** | 2·20 | 1·70 |
| 113 | 100c.+50c. Open hand with Cancer Fund emblem | 3·25 | 2·50 |

37 Columbus, Map and Clouds

1992. 500th Anniv of Discovery of America by Columbus. Multicoloured.
114	30c. Type **37**	1·70	55
115	40c. Caravel (from navigation chart, 1525)	1·70	90
116	50c. Indians, queen conch shell and 1540 map	1·70	1·10

38 I Love Post (Jelissa Boekhoudt)

1992. Child Welfare. Centenary of Postal Service (2nd issue). Children's Drawings. Multicoloured.
117	50c.+30c. Type **38**	2·00	1·50
118	70c.+35c. Airplane dropping letters (Marianne Fingal)	2·20	1·70
119	100c.+50c. Pigeon carrying letter in beak (Minorenti Jacobs) (vert)	3·25	2·50

39 Seroe Colorado Bridge

1992. Natural Bridges. Multicoloured.
| 120 | 70c. Type **39** | 1·60 | 1·10 |
| 121 | 80c. Natural Bridge | 2·00 | 1·70 |

41 Rocks at Ayo

1993. Rock Formations. Multicoloured.

123	50c. Type **41**	1·10	1·10
124	60c. Casibari	1·50	1·10
125	100c. Ayo (different)	2·20	2·00

42 Traditional Instruments

1993. Cock's Burial (part of St. John's Feast celebrations). Multicoloured.

126	40c. Type **42**	1·10	1·10
127	70c. *Cock's Burial* (painting, Leo Kuiperi)	1·50	1·10
128	80c. Verses of song, yellow flag, and calabashes	1·70	1·70

43 Sailfish dinghy

1993. Sports. Multicoloured.

129	50c. Type **43**	1·10	1·10
130	65c. Land sailing	1·50	1·10
131	75c. Sailboard	1·70	1·50

44 Young Iguana

1993. The Iguana. Multicoloured.

132	35c. Type **44**	1·50	90
133	60c. Young adult	1·70	1·50
134	100c. Adult (vert)	2·20	2·20

45 Aruban House, Landscape and Cacti

1993. Child Welfare. Multicoloured.

135	50c.+30c. Type **45**	1·60	1·50
136	75c.+40c. Face, bridge and sea (vert)	2·20	2·20
137	100c.+50c. Bridge, buildings and landscape	3·00	2·75

46 Owls

1994. The Burrowing Owl. Multicoloured.

138	5c. Type **46**	1·80	40
139	10c. Pair with young	1·80	90
140	35c. Owl with locust in claw (vert)	2·10	1·10
141	40c. Owl (vert)	2·10	1·70

47 Athlete

1994. Centenary of Int Olympic Committee. Multicoloured.

142	50c. Type **47**	1·30	1·10
143	90c. Baron Pierre de Coubertin (founder)	2·00	1·70

48 Family in House

1994. "Solidarity". Int Year of The Family. Multicoloured.

144	50c.+35c. Type **48**	1·70	1·60
145	100c.+50c. Family outside house	3·00	3·00

49 Flags of U.S.A. and Aruba, Ball and Players

1994. World Cup Football Championship, U.S.A. Multicoloured.

146	65c. Type **49**	1·70	1·50
147	150c. Mascot	3·25	2·75

50 West Indian Cherry

1994. Wild Fruits. Multicoloured.

148	40c. Type **50**	1·10	1·10
149	70c. Geiger tree	1·70	1·10
150	85c. *Pithecellobium unguis-cati*	2·00	1·70
151	150c. Sea grape	3·75	2·75

51 Children with Umbrella sitting on Anchor (shelter and security)

1994. Child Welfare. Influence of the Family. Multicoloured.

152	50c.+30c. Type **51**	2·00	1·70
153	80c.+35c. Children in smiling sun (warmth of nurturing home)	2·50	2·20
154	100c.+50c. Child flying on owl (wisdom guiding the child)	2·75	2·75

52 Government Building, 1888

1995. Historic Buildings. Multicoloured.

155	35c. Type **52**	90	75
156	60c. Ecury Residence, 1929 (vert)	1·50	1·10
157	100c. Protestant Church, 1846 (vert)	2·20	2·00

53 Dove, Emblem and Flags

1995. 50th Anniv of U.N.O. Multicoloured.

158	30c. Type **53**	1·50	90
159	200c. Emblem, flags, globe and doves	4·00	3·75

54 Casanova II and Rosettes

1995. Interpaso Horses. Multicoloured.

160	25c. Type **54**	90	50
161	75c. Horse performing Paso Fino	1·70	1·50
162	80c. Horse performing Figure 8 (vert)	1·70	1·70
163	90c. Girl on horseback (vert)	2·00	1·70

55 Cowpea

1995. Vegetables. Multicoloured.

164	25c. Type **55**	85	50
165	50c. Apple cucumber	1·40	1·10
166	70c. Okra	1·60	1·40
167	85c. Pumpkin	1·80	1·70

56 Hawksbill Turtle

1995. Turtles. Multicoloured.

168	15c. Type **56**	1·70	40
169	50c. Green turtle	2·10	90
170	95c. Loggerhead turtle	2·30	1·70
171	100c. Leatherback turtle	2·75	1·70

57 Children holding Balloons outside House (Christina Trejo)

1995. Child Welfare. Children's Drawings. Multicoloured.

172	50c.+25c. Type **57**	1·70	1·40
173	70c.+35c. Children at seaside (Julysses Tromp)	2·20	2·00
174	100c.+50c. Children and adults gardening (Ronald Tromp)	3·25	2·75

58 Henry Eman

1996. Tenth Anniv of Internal Autonomy. Politicians. Multicoloured.

175	100c. Type **58**	2·00	1·70
176	100c. Juancho Irausquin	2·00	1·70
177	100c. Shon Eman	2·00	1·70
178	100c. Betico Croes	2·00	1·70

59 Woman

1996. America. Traditional Costumes. Multicoloured.

179	65c. Type **59**	2·20	1·10
180	70c. Man	2·20	1·10
181	100c. Couple dancing (horiz)	2·75	1·70

60 Running

1996. Olympic Games, Atlanta. Multicoloured.

182	85c. Type **60**	2·20	1·50
183	130c. Cycling	2·75	2·50

61 Mathematical Instruments, "G" and Rising Sun

1996. "Solidarity". 75th Anniv of Freemasons' Lodge El Sol Naciente. Multicoloured.

184	60c.+30c. Type **61**	2·50	1·50

185	100c.+50c. Globes on top of columns and doorway	3·25	2·50

62 Livia Ecury (teacher and nurse)

1996. Anniversaries. Multicoloured.

186	60c. Type **62** (5th death)	1·50	1·50
187	60c. Laura Wernet-Paskel (teacher and politician, 85th birth)	1·50	1·50
188	60c. Lolita Euson (poet, 2nd death)	1·50	1·50

63 Rabbits at Bus-stop

1996. Child Welfare. Comic Strips. Multicoloured.

189	50c.+25c. Type **63**	1·90	1·50
190	70c.+35c. Mother accompanying young owl to school	2·30	2·00
191	100c.+50c. Boy flying kite with friend	2·75	2·50

64 Children at the Seaside and Words on Signpost

1997. "Year of Papiamento" (Creole language). Multicoloured.

192	50c. Type **64**	1·10	1·10
193	140c. Sunrise over ocean	2·75	2·75

65 Postman on Bicycle, 1936–57

1997. America. The Postman. Multicoloured.

194	60c. Type **65**	2·75	1·70
195	70c. Postman delivering package by jeep, 1957–88	2·75	1·70
196	80c. Postman delivering letter from motor scooter, 1995	2·75	1·70

66 Decorated Cunucu House

1997. Aruban Architecture. Multicoloured.

197	30c. Type **66**	90	60
198	65c. Bannistered steps	1·70	1·50
199	100c. Arends Building (vert)	2·20	2·00

67 Merlin and Lighthouse

1997. "Pacific 97" International Stamp Exhibition, San Francisco. Multicoloured.

200	90c. Type **67**	2·75	2·20
201	90c. Windswept trees and dolphin	2·75	2·20
202	90c. Iguana on rock and cacti	2·75	2·20
203	90c. Three types of fishes and one dolphin	2·75	2·20
204	90c. Two dolphins and fishes	2·75	2·20
205	90c. Burrowing owl on shore, turtle and lionfish	2·75	2·20
206	90c. Stingray, rock beauty, angelfishes, squirrelfish and coral reef	2·75	2·20

207	90c. Diver and stern of shipwreck	2·75	2·20
208	90c. Shipwreck, reef and fishes	2·75	2·20

Nos. 200/8 were issued together, *se-tenant*, forming a composite design.

68 Passengers approaching Cruise Liner

1997. Cruise Tourism. Multicoloured.

209	35c. Type **68**	1·10	90
210	50c. Passengers disembarking	1·50	1·10
211	150c. Cruise liner at sea and launch at shore	3·00	2·75

69 Coral Tree

1997. Trees. Multicoloured.

212	50c. Type **69**	1·50	1·10
213	60c. *Cordia dentata*	1·70	1·50
214	70c. *Tabebuia billbergii*	2·00	1·50
215	130c. *Lignum vitae*	2·75	2·20

70 Girl among Aloes

1997. Child Welfare. Child and Nature. Multicoloured.

216	50c.+25c. Type **70**	1·70	1·40
217	70c.+35c. Boy and butterfly (vert)	2·50	2·20
218	100c.+50c. Girl swimming underwater by coral reef	2·50	2·75

71 Fort Zoutman

1998. Bicentenary of Fort Zoutman.

219	**71**	30c. multicoloured	1·10	90
220	**71**	250c. multicoloured	4·75	4·25

Each design consists of alternating strips in brown tones or black and white. When the 250c. is laid on top of the 30c., the brown strips form a composite design of the fort in its early years and the black and white strips a composite design of the fort after 1929, when various alterations were made.

72 Stages of Eclipse

1998. Total Solar Eclipse. Multicoloured.

221	85c. Type **72**	2·20	1·50
222	100c. Globe showing path of eclipse and map of Aruba plotting duration of total darkness	2·50	1·70

73 Globe, Emblem and Wheelchair balanced on Map of Aruba

1998. "Solidarity" Anniversaries. Multicoloured.

223	60c.+30c. Type **73** (50th anniv of Lions Club of Aruba)	2·20	1·60
224	100c.+50c. Boy reading, emblem and grandmother in rocking chair (60th anniv of Rotary Club of Aruba)	3·25	2·50

74 Tropical Mockingbird

1998. Birds. Multicoloured.

225	50c. Type **74**	1·90	1·10

226	60c. American kestrel (vert)	2·20	1·50
227	70c. Troupial (vert)	2·20	1·50
228	150c. Bananaquit	3·75	3·25

75 Villagers processing Corn

1998. World Stamp Day.

229	**75**	225c. multicoloured	6·25	5·00

76 Ribbon Dance

1998. Child Welfare. Multicoloured.

230	50c.+25c. Type **76**	1·60	1·50
231	80c.+40c. Boy playing cuarta (four-string guitar)	2·50	2·50
232	100c. + 50c. Basketball	3·25	2·75

77 Two Donkeys

1999. The Donkey. Multicoloured.

233	40c. Type **77**	1·60	90
234	65c. Two adults and foal	1·80	1·50
235	100c. Adult and foal	2·75	2·20

78 Opuntia wentiana

1999. Cacti. Multicoloured.

236	50c. Type **78**	1·50	1·00
237	60c. *Lemaireocereus griseus*	1·70	1·20
238	70c. *Cephalocereus lanuginosus* ("Cadushi di carona")	1·70	1·50
239	75c. *Cephalocereus lanuginosus* ("Cadushi")	2·00	1·70

79 Creole Dog

1999. Creole Dogs (*Canis familiaris*). Multicoloured.

240	40c. Type **79**	1·70	1·10
241	60c. White dog standing on rock	2·00	1·50
242	80c. Dog sitting by sea	2·20	1·50
243	165c. Black and tan dog sitting on rock	3·75	3·25

80 Indian Cave Drawings and Antique Map

1999. 500 Years of Cultural Diversity. Multicoloured.

244	150c. Type **80**	2·75	2·50
245	175c. Indian cave drawings and carnival headdress	3·25	3·00
MS246	90×60 mm. Nos. 244/5	6·75	5·50

81 Public Library and Children

1999. 50th Anniv of Public Library Service. Multicoloured.

247	70c. Type **81**	1·60	1·70
248	100c. Library, Santa Cruz	2·30	2·00

82 Boy with Fisherman

1999. Child Welfare. Multicoloured.

249	60c.+30c. Type **82**	1·70	1·50
250	80c.+40c. Man reading to children	2·50	2·20
251	100c.+50c. Woman with child (vert)	3·25	2·75

83 Three Wise Men

1999. Christmas. Multicoloured. Self-adhesive.

252	40c. Type **83**	1·80	1·10
253	70c. Shepherds	2·20	1·50
254	100c. Holy Family	2·75	2·00

84 Norops lineatus

2000. Reptiles. Multicoloured.

255	40c. Type **84**	7·75	80
256	60c. Greeen iguana (vert)	1·60	1·50
257	75c. Annulated snake (vert)	1·80	1·50
258	150c. Racerunner	3·75	2·50

85 Flags

2000. America. A.I.D.S. Awareness. Multicoloured.

259	75c. Type **85**	2·00	2·00
260	175c. Ribbon on globe (vert)	3·75	3·75

86 Bank Facade

2000. Anniversaries. Multicoloured.

261	150c. Type **86** (75th anniv of Aruba Bank)	3·25	2·50
262	165c. Chapel (250th anniv of Alto Vista Chapel)	3·25	2·75

87 West Indian Top Shell

2000. Aspects of Aruba. Multicoloured.

263	15c. Type **87**	50	40
264	25c. Guadirikiri cave	85	50
265	35c. Mud-house (vert)	1·00	90
267	55c. Cacti	1·50	1·10
269	85c. Hooiberg	2·00	1·70
271	100c. Gold smelter, Balashi (vert)	2·50	2·00
272	250c. Rock crystal	5·00	4·50
275	500c. Conchi	9·50	8·25

88 Children at Beach Playground

2000. "Solidarity". Multicoloured.

280	75c.+35c. Type **88**	2·10	1·80
281	100c.+50c. Children building sandcastles	3·50	2·75

89 Solar Energy (Nikki Johanna Teresia Willems)

2000. Child Welfare. "Stampin' the Future". Winning Entries in Children's International Painting Competition. Multicoloured.

282	60c.+30c. Type **89**	2·10	1·70
283	80c.+40c. *Environmental Protection* (Samantha Jeanne Tromp)	2·30	2·00
284	100c.+50c. *Future Vehicles* (Jennifer Huntington)	3·25	2·75

90 Cat

2001. Domestic Animals. Multicoloured.

285	5c. Type **90**	65	35
286	30c. Tortoise	1·70	1·10
287	50c. Rabbit	1·70	1·10
288	200c. Brown-throated conure	4·50	4·00

91 Shaman preparing for Sun Ceremony

2001. 40 Years of Mascaruba (amateur theatre group). Depicting scenes from *Macuarima, History or Legend?* (musical play). Multicoloured.

289	60c. Type **91**	1·60	1·10
290	150c. Love scene between Guadarikiri and Blanco	3·00	2·75

92 Ford Model A Roadster, 1930

2001. Motor Cars. Multicoloured.

291	25c. Type **92**	1·80	1·10
292	40c. Citroen Comerciale saloon, 1933	1·80	1·10
293	70c. Plymouth Pick-up, 1948	2·00	1·70
294	75c. Edsel corsair convertable, 1959	2·10	1·70

93 Rock Drawings

2001. Universal Postal Union. United Nations Year of Dialogue among Civilizations.

295	**93**	175c. multicoloured	4·00	3·25

94 Pedestrians using Crossing

2001. Child Welfare. International Year of Volunteers. Multicoloured.

296	40c. + 20c. Type **94**	1·60	1·10
297	60c. + 30c. Boys walking dogs	2·10	1·70
298	100c. + 50c. Children putting litter in bin	3·25	2·75

95 Dakota Airport, 1950

2002. Queen Beatrix Airport. Multicoloured.

299	30c. Type **95**	1·00	55
300	75c. Queen Beatrix Airport, 1972	1·90	1·50
301	175c. Queen Beatrix Airport, 2000	3·75	3·25

Dakota Airport was re-named Princess Beatrix Airport in 1955 and Queen Beatrix Airport in 1972.

96 Prince Willem-Alexander and Princess Maxima

2002. Wedding of Crown Prince Willem-Alexander to Maxima Zorreguieta. Multicoloured.

| 302 | 60c. Type **96** | 1·50 | 1·10 |
| 303 | 300c. Prince Willem-Alexander and Princess Máxima facing right | 5·50 | 5·50 |

97 Tap and Water Droplet

2002. 70th Anniv of Water Company (W. E. B.). Multicoloured.

304	60c. Type **97**	1·20	1·10
305	85c. Water pipes (horiz)	1·70	1·60
306	165c. Water meter and meter reader	3·25	3·25

98 Hand holding Quill Pen

2002. America. Literacy Campaign. Multicoloured.

| 307 | 25c. Type **98** | 1·10 | 90 |
| 308 | 100c. Alphabet on wall and boy on step-ladder | 2·20 | 1·90 |

99 *U-156* Submarine firing on Lago Oil Refinery

2002. Second World War. Multicoloured.

309	60c. Type **99**	2·20	1·10
310	75c. *Pedernales* (oil-tanker) in flames	2·20	1·40
311	150c. "Boy" Ecury (resistance fighter) (statue) (vert)	3·25	2·75

100 Boy, Iguana and Goat

2002. Child Welfare. Animals. Multicoloured.

312	40c.+20c. Type **100**	1·20	1·10
313	60c.+30c. Girl, turtle and crab (horiz)	2·50	1·70
314	100c.+50c. Pelicans, boy and parakeet	3·00	2·75

101 House at Fontein

2003. Mud Houses. Multicoloured.

315	40c. Type **101**	90	80
316	60c. House at Ari Kok	1·20	1·10
317	75c. House at Fontein	1·60	1·50

102 The Trupialen Boys Choir

2003. 50th Anniv of "De Trupialen" (boys' organization). Multicoloured.

318	30c. Type **102**	65	55
319	50c. Puppet theatre posters	1·10	1·00
320	100c. Organization emblems	2·20	1·90

103 *Schomburgkia humboldtii*

2003. Orchids. Multicoloured.

| 321 | 75c. Type **103** | 1·80 | 1·70 |
| 322 | 500c. *Brassavola nodosa* | 11·00 | 9·00 |

104 Orange-barred Sulphur Butterfly

2003. Butterflies. Multicoloured.

323	40c. Type **104**	1·30	1·10
324	75c. Monarch	1·90	1·60
325	85c. Hairstreak	2·20	1·80
326	175c. Gulf fritillary	3·75	3·25

105 Hawksbill Turtle (*Eretmochelys imbricate*)

2003. Endangered Species. Turtles. Multicoloured.

327	25c. Type **105**	1·20	1·00
328	60c. Leatherback turtle (*Dermochelys coricea*) (horiz)	1·40	1·20
329	75c. Green turtle (*Chelonia mydas*)	1·80	1·50
330	150c. Loggerhead turtle (*Caretta caretta*) (horiz)	3·50	3·00

106 Baseball

2003. Child Welfare. Children and Sport.. Multicoloured.

331	40c.+20c. Type **106**	1·20	1·00
332	60c.+30c. Volleyball	1·80	1·50
333	100c.+50c. Football	3·50	3·00

107 Masks and Headdresses

2004. 50th Anniv of Carnival. Multicoloured.

334	60c. Type **107**	95	80
335	75c. Woman's face (vert)	1·40	1·20
336	150c. Heads wearing carnival headdresses	3·00	2·50

108 Sandwich Tern (*Sterna sandvicensis*)

2004. Birds. Multicoloured.

337	70c. Type **108**	1·40	1·20
338	75c. Brown pelican (*Pelecanus occidentalis*)	1·60	1·30
339	80c. Frigate bird (*Fregata magnificens*)	1·70	1·40
340	90c. Laughing gull (*Larus atricilla*)	1·80	1·50

109 Parrotfish

2004. Fish. Multicoloured.

341	40c. Type **109**	1·10	90
342	60c. Queen angelfish	1·30	1·10
343	75c. Squirrelfish	1·60	1·30
344	100c. Small-mouthed grunt	1·90	1·60

110 Children holding Maracas

2004. Child Welfare. Musical Instruments. Multicoloured.

345	60c.+30c. Type **110**	1·80	1·50
346	85c.+40c. Three children and steel drum	2·40	2·10
347	100c.+50c. Boy playing wiri and girl holding tambourine	3·00	2·50

111 Presents and Decorated Tree

2004. Christmas and New Year. Multicoloured.

348	50c. Type **111**	95	80
349	85c. Parcels, carol singers and candle	1·70	1·40
350	125c. Fireworks	2·40	2·10

112 Interconnecting Islands (Aruba, Curacao, Bonaire, Saba, St. Maarten and St. Eustatius)

2004. 50th Anniv of Charter of the Kingdom (statute establishing partial autonomy). Multicoloured.

| 351 | 160c. Type **112** | 2·30 | 2·00 |
| 352 | 165c. Kingdom Statute monument | 2·40 | 2·10 |

113 Sun and Flower

2004. Greetings Stamps. Multicoloured.

353	60c. Type **113** ("Thank you")	1·10	90
354	75c. Two rabbits ("Love")	1·20	1·00
355	135c. Fish ("Get well soon")	1·90	1·60
356	215c. Balloons ("Congratulations")	3·50	3·00

114 Race Car and Spectators

2005. Drag Racing. Multicoloured.

357	60c. Type **114**	1·20	1·00
358	85c. Parachute opening at race end	1·80	1·50
359	185c. Race start	3·00	2·50

115 Queen Beatrix and Prince Claus

2005. 25th Anniv of Coronation of Queen Beatrix. Sheet 144×75 mm containing T **115** and similar vert designs. Multicoloured.

| MS360 | 30c. Type **115**; 60c. Seated; 75c. With Nelson Mandela; 105c.Wearing glasses; 215c. Wearing hat | 7·75 | 7·75 |

116 Sunset

2005. Tourism. Sunsets. Multicoloured.

361	60c. Type **116**	95	80
362	100c. Palm tree	1·60	1·30
363	205c. Pelicans	3·25	2·75

117 American Kestrel (*Falco sparverius*)

2005. Birds. Multicoloured.

364	60c. Type **117**	1·20	1·00
365	75c. Burrowing owl (*Athene cunicularia*)	1·60	1·30
366	135c. Osprey (*Pandion haliaetus*)	2·30	2·00
367	200c. Common caracara (*Polyborus plancus*)	3·50	3·00
MS368	110×70 mm. Nos. 364/7	7·75	7·75

118 *Acropora cervicornis*

2005. Corals. Multicoloured.

369	60c. Type **118**	1·10	95
370	75c. *Millepora complanata*	1·40	1·20
371	100c. *Iciligorgia schrammi*	1·80	1·50
372	215c. *Diploria strigosa*	3·75	3·25

119 Girl and Stamps

2005. Child Welfare. Philately. Multicoloured.

373	75c. Type **119**	1·50	1·30
374	85c. Boy holding magnifier and album	1·60	1·40
375	125c. Boy putting stamps in album	2·30	2·00

120 "House of Savaneta" (Jean George Pandellis)

2006. Art. Multicoloured.

376	60c. Type **120**	1·20	1·00
377	75c. *Haf di Rei* (Mateo Hayde)	1·50	1·30
378	185c. *Landscape* (Julie Oduber)	3·50	3·00

121 Emblem

2006. 50th Anniv of YMCA. Multicoloured.

| 379 | 75c. Type **121** | 1·50 | 1·30 |
| 380 | 205c. Children at play (horiz) | 3·75 | 3·25 |

122 Tree and Log Bridge

2006. Washington 2006 International Stamp Exhibition. Sheet 98×88 mm containing T **122** and similar multicoloured design.

| MS381 | 500c.×2, Type **122**; Cacti and boats (vert) | 13·50 | 13·50 |

The stamps and margins of **MS**381 form a composite design.

123 Goalkeeper

2006. World Cup Football Championship, Germany. Multicoloured.

| 382 | 75c. Type **123** | 1·40 | 1·20 |
| 383 | 215c. Hands holding globe as football | 3·75 | 3·25 |

124 Surf Boards, Boats,
Windsurfers and
Kitesurfer

2006. 20th Anniv of Hi-Winds Windsurfing Competition.
Multicoloured.

384	60c. Type **124**	1·00	85
385	100c. Leaping kitesurfer	1·60	1·30
386	125c. Windsurfers	2·00	1·70

125 Fire Hazards

2006. Fire Prevention. Multicoloured.

387	60c. Type **125**	1·00	85
388	100c. Firefighters	1·60	1·30
389	205c. Fire appliances	3·25	2·75

126 House and Goat

2006. Arikok National Park. Multicoloured.

390	75c. Type **126**	1·30	1·10
391	100c. Cacti, valley and eagle (vert)	1·60	1·30
392	200c. Cacti and owl	3·25	2·75

127 Dancers and Boar

2007. New Year. Year of the Pig. Sheet 78×62 mm
containing T **127** and similar multicoloured design.
MS393 205c. Type **127**; 215c. Dragon
(vert) 6·50 6·50

The stamp and margin of **MS**393 form a composite
design.

128 Luciana Maria
Koolman and Original
Building

2007. 50th Anniv of Casa Cuna Children's Home
Foundation. Multicoloured.

394	50c. Type **128**	85	70
395	125c. Children enclosed in hands	2·00	1·70
396	150c. New building	2·40	2·10

129 Museum of
Antiquities

2007. Museums. Multicoloured.

397	70c. Type **129**	1·10	95
398	85c. Numismatic museum	1·30	1·10
399	100c. Archaeological museum	1·50	1·30
400	135c. Historical museum	2·10	1·80

130 Pipeline of
Pedernalis (wrecked oil
tanker)

2007. Wrecks and Reefs. Sheet 87×70 mm containing T
130 and similar horiz designs. Multicoloured.
MS401 200c. Type **130**; 300c. Convair
400 aircraft wreck; 500c. Sea turtle
and *Jane* (wrecked freighter); 500c.
Antilla (wrecked freighter) and fish 17·00 17·00

The stamps and margins of **MS**401 form a composite
design.

131 Mother and Child

2007. Christmas. Multicoloured.

402	70c. Type **131**	1·20	1·10
403	100c. Girl with presents	1·70	1·50
404	150c. Child with balloon	2·50	2·30

132 Beached
Catamarans

2007. Catamaran Regatta. Multicoloured.

405	40c. Type **132**	70	60
406	80c. Two catamarans and buoy	1·40	1·20
407	125c. Tacking	2·10	1·90
408	130c. Racing	2·20	2·00

133 As Small
Child

2008. 70th Birth Anniv of Queen Beatrix. Multicoloured.

409	75c. Type **133**	1·30	1·10
410	125c. With Prince Claus and new born Prince Willem Alexander	2·10	1·90
411	250c. Wearing regalia on day of accession	4·25	3·75
412	300c. With Crown Prince Willem Alexander and his family	5·00	4·50

134 Carnival

2008. Cultural Heritage. Multicoloured.

413	80c. Type **134**	1·40	1·20
414	130c. Street entertainers	2·20	2·00
415	250c. Musicians, dancers, cockerel and campfire	3·50	3·00
416	300c. Musicians and house-holders	4·75	4·25

135 Athletics

2008. Olympic Games, Beijing. Multicoloured.

417	50c. Type **135**	85	75
418	75c. Synchronised swimming	1·30	1·10
419	100c. Gymnastics (vert)	1·70	1·50
420	175c. Judo	2·10	1·90

136 Burrowing
Owl

2008. Aruban Cultural Year. Burrowing Owl Athene
cunicularia arubensis . Multicoloured.

421	100c. Type **136**	1·80	1·60
422	150c. Two owls (horiz)	2·75	2·40
423	350c. Head	6·25	5·75

137 FRX Super Glide
Big Boy

2008. Harley Davidson Motorcycles. Multicoloured.

424	175c. Type **137**	3·25	3·00
425	225c. Knucklehead	4·00	3·50
426	305c. Roadking	5·25	4·75

138 Script (poem by
Frederico Oduber)

2008. Netherlands and Beyond. Sheet 145×75 mm
containing T **138** and similar multicoloured designs.
MS427 240c. Type **138**; 240c. *Wata-
pana* (first magazine in Papiamento
(local language)) (vert); 240c. Henry
Habibe and poem (vert) 14·50 14·50

No. **MS**427 also includes a Netherlands Antilles 5c.
stamp (Houses (architecture)) and a Netherlands 92c.
stamp (chillies and cheese (food)).

The 'foreign' stamps could only be used in their coun-
try of origin.

139 *Calatropis procea*

2008. Flowers. Multicoloured.

428	100c. Type **139**	1·80	1·60
429	185c. *Thespesia populnea*	3·50	3·00
430	200c. *Cryptostegia grandiflora*	3·50	3·25
431	215c. *Passiflora foetida*	3·75	3·50

140 Self Portrait

2008. International Culture. Drawings by Rembrandt.
Multicoloured.

432	350c. Type **140**	7·00	6·25
433	425c. *Self Portrait*	8·25	7·50
434	500c. Beggars at the Door	9·75	9·00

141 Donkeys
transporting Water

2008. Aruba in the Old Days. Each brown and ochre.

435	100c. Type **141**	2·00	1·80
436	200c. Two roomed clay house	4·00	3·50
437	215c. Harvesting *Aloe vera*	4·25	3·75

142 Louis
Braille

2009. Birth Bicentenary of Louis Braille (inventor of
Braille writing for the blind). Multicoloured.

438	200c. Type **142**	4·00	3·50
439	215c. Hand holding white stick	4·25	3·75

143 Carnival Queen

2009. 55th Anniv of Aruba Carnival. Sheet 115×95
mm containing T **143** and similar horiz designs.
Multicoloured.
MS440 75c. Type **143**; 100c. Float with
clown; 175c. Float with champagne
bottle, large '55' bottom left; 225c.
Dancers 11·00 11·50

143a Kapel Alto Vista

2009. Architecture

440a	**143a** 5c. multicoloured	10	10
440b	10c. multicoloured	15	10
440c	25c. multicoloured	40	25
440d	50c. multicoloured	85	65
440e	85c. multicoloured	1·20	1·00
440f	90c. multicoloured	1·50	1·30
440g	100c. multicoloured	1·70	1·50
440h	125c. multicoloured	2·40	1·90
440i	130c. multicoloured	2·50	1·90
440j	135c. multicoloured	2·60	2·20
440k	140c. multicoloured	2·60	2·20

440l	200c. multicoloured	3·50	2·75
440m	215c. multicoloured	3·75	3·25
440n	220c. multicoloured	4·00	3·50

144 Tunnel of Love
(Baranca Suna) Cave

2009. Caves. Multicoloured.

441	175c. Type **144**	3·50	3·25
442	200c. Fountain (Fontein)	4·00	3·50
443	225c. Guardirikiri (Quadirikiri Grot)	4·25	4·00

145 Ozone Layer

2009. Global Warming Awareness Campaign. Sheet
82×64 mm containing T **145** and similar horiz
designs. Multicoloured.
MS444 200c. Type **145**; 250c. Melting
ice caps; 250c. Pollution; 300c.
Alternative energy sources 17·00 17·00

146 California
Lighthouse

2009. Architecture. Sheet 86×86 mm containing T **146**
and similar multicoloured designs.
MS445 175c. Type **146**; 250c. Plaza
Daniel Leo, Oranjestad (horiz); 275c.
Henriquez Building (horiz); 325c.
Main Building, Ecury Complex 18·00 18·00

147 Girl Reading

2009. 60th Anniv of National Library. Each black and new
blue.

446	185c. Type **147**	3·50	3·25
447	300c. Woman reading	6·00	5·25

148 *Stenella frontalis*
(Atlantic spotted
dolphin)

2009. Dophins. Multicoloured.

448	125c. Type **148**	1·90	1·50
449	200c. *Steno bredanensis* (rough-toothed dolphin)	4·00	3·50
450	300c. Two Atlantic spotted dolphins facing right	6·00	5·25
451	325c. Several rough-toothed dolphins	6·50	5·75

149 Virgin and Child

2009. Christmas. Multicoloured.

452	75c. Type **149**	1·30	1·10
453	120c. Angel	1·90	1·70
454	125c. Hands holding globe, '2009' and 'Peace'	2·10	1·90
455	210c. Shepherds and star	4·50	3·50

150 Palm Tree, Wall
and Fish (paper)

2010. Recycle. Multicoloured.

456	90c. Type **150**	1·80	1·60
457	180c. House and cow (cardboard and pasta)	3·50	3·25
458	325c. Fish and boat (paper, bottle tops and lolly sticks)	6·50	5·75

151 Seaplane

2010. Historic Aircraft. Multicoloured.

459	250c. Type **151**	4·50	4·25
460	500c. Curtiss NC-4	8·75	8·50

152 Two Junior Scouts

2010. Scouting. Multicoloured.

461	85c. Type **152**	60	55
462	95c. Two scouts and campfire	75	70
463	135c. Scout emerging from tent	1·50	1·40
464	180c. Four scouts map reading	2·00	1·90

153 Soldiers in Gun Placement

2010. 65th Anniv of End of World War II. Multicoloured.

465	140c. Type **153**	1·60	1·50
466	200c. Soldiers and missile	2·50	2·40
467	275c. Guns on foundering ship	3·00	2·75

154 Blue and Gold Macaw

2010. Parrots. Multicoloured.

468	85c. Type **154**	70	55
469	90c. Green Amazonian	90	65
470	180c. Scarlet macaw	2·00	1·70

155 Self-Portrait

2010. Art. 120th Death Anniv of Vincent Willem van Gogh (artist). Multicoloured.

471	200c. Type **155**	1·30	1·00
472	250c. *Vase with Fifteen Sunflowers*	1·90	1·50
473	305c. *The Starry Night*	3·00	2·50
474	500c. *Wheat Field Under Threatening Skies* (detail)	5·25	4·75

156 Essoville Rum Shop

2010. Rum Shops. Multicoloured.

475	100c. Type **156**	2·50	2·20
476	200c. Aruba Rum Shop	4·50	4·25
477	255c. Caribbean Store	5·50	5·25

157 *Caesalpinia pulcherrima*

2010. Flowers. Multicoloured.

478	200c. Type **157**	3·25	2·75
479	200c. *Dipladenia sanderi*	3·25	2·75
480	200c. *Dipladenia sanderi*	3·25	2·75
481	200c. *Adenium obesum*	3·25	2·75
482	200c. *Bougainvillea*	3·25	2·75
483	200c. *Ixora*	3·25	2·75

484	200c. *Eichhornia crassipes*	3·25	2·75
485	200c. *Passiflora caerulea*	3·25	2·75
486	200c. *Allamanda cathartica*	3·25	2·75
487	200c. *Nerium oleander*		

158 Beth Israel Synagogue

2010. Places of Worship. Multicoloured.

488	85c. Type **158**	1·50	1·20
489	90c. Protestant Church	1·90	1·50
490	135c. St. Fransiscus Catholic Church	3·00	2·50
491	240c. Interior, St. Fransiscus Church	5·50	2·00

159 *Falco sparverius* (American kestrel)

2010. Birds. Multicoloured.

492	200c. Type **159**	4·25	3·75
493	200c. *Icterus icterus* (troupial)	4·25	3·75
494	200c. *Mimus gilvus* (tropical mockingbird)	4·25	3·75
495	200c. *Egretta alba* (great white egret)	4·25	3·75
496	200c. *Aratinga pertinax* (brown-throated parakeet)	4·75	3·75
497	200c. *Pelicanus occidentalis* (eastern brown pelican)	4·25	3·75
498	200c. *Athena cunicularia* (burrowing owl)	4·25	3·75
499	200c. *Coereba flaveola* (bananaquit)	4·25	3·75
500	200c. *Polyborus plancus* (caracara)	4·25	3·75
501	200c. *Colibri thalassinus* (green violet-ear)	4·25	3·75

160 Caribbean Reef Octopus

2010. Caribbean Reef Octopus (*Octopus briareus*). Multicoloured.

502	100c. Type **160**	2·10	1·90
503	175c. With tenacles extended downwards	4·25	3·75
504	255c. With tenacles extended upwards	5·00	4·50
505	300c. Coiled on sea bed	6·00	5·50

161 *Heliconius hecale*

2010. Butterflies. Multicoloured.

506	200c. Type **161**	4·00	3·50
507	200c. *Morpho peleides* (inscr 'Morpho paleides')	4·00	3·50
508	200c. *Danaus plexippus*	4·00	3·50
509	200c. *Anartia jatrophae*	5·00	3·50
511	200c. *Phoebis sennae*	4·00	3·50
511	200c. *Heliconius charithorius* (inscr 'Heliconius charithorius')	4·00	3·50
512	200c. *Siproeta stelenes*	4·00	3·50
513	200c. *Caligo memmon*	4·00	3·50
514	200c. *Heliconius melpomene*	4·00	3·50
515	200c. *Agraulis vanilla*	4·00	3·50

162 Flag

2011. 25th Anniv of Status Aparte (status of an autonomous state within Kingdom of the Netherlands). Multicoloured.

516	200c. Type **162**	4·50	4·50
517	300c. 'STATUS APARTE'	6·75	6·75
518	300c. Filipe Tromp and Henny Eman	6·75	6·75
519	400c. Fredis Refunjol and Betico Croes	6·75	6·75

163 *Delonix regia*

2011. Flowers. Multicoloured.

520	160c. Type **163**	3·50	3·50
521	160c. *Cassia fistula*	3·50	3·50
522	160c. *Ipomoea pes-caprae*	3·50	3·50
523	160c. *Allamanda cathartica*	3·50	3·50
524	160c. *Catharanthus roseus* (inscr 'Catharantus roseus')	3·50	3·50
525	160c. *Nerium oleander*	3·50	3·50
526	160c. *Bougainvillea glabra*	3·50	3·50
527	160c. *Hibiscus rosa-sinensis*	3·50	3·50
528	160c. *Cordia sebestena*	3·50	3·50
529	160c. *Echinopsis lageniformis*	3·50	3·50

164 Hands as Flags of Portugal, Cuba, USA and Brazil

2011. Centenary of UPAEP (Unión Postal de las Américas, España y Portugal). Multicoloured.

530	200c. Type **164**	4·50	5·50
531	250c. Canada, Argentina and Colombia	6·75	6·75
532	350c. Brazil, USA and Panama	6·75	6·75
533	400c. Suriname, Portugal and Chile	8·75	8·75
MS534	108×78 mm. 300c.×4, As Nos. 530/3	28·00	28·00

165 Indonesia 1965 25sen Note

2011. 25th Anniv of Papermoney Fair, Maastricht. Multicoloured.

535	167c. Type **165**	3·50	3·50
536	167c. Bhutan 1986 - 2 Ngultrum	3·50	3·50
537	167c. Phippines 1949 - 50 centavos	3·50	3·50
538	167c. Sudan 1987 - 25 piastres	3·50	3·50
539	167c. Mozambique 1976 - 100 Escudos	3·50	3·50
540	167c. Haiti 1993 - 25 Gourdes	3·50	3·50
541	167c. Gottingen 1917 - 25 pt.	3·50	3·50
542	167c. Turkey 1997 - 250000 l.	3·50	3·50
543	167c. Solomon Islands 1977 - 10 dollars	3·50	3·50
544	167c. Lille 1915 - 25 centimes	3·50	3·50
545	167c. Egypt 1985 - 25 piastres	3·50	3·50
546	167c. Albania 1976 - 100 leke	3·50	3·50

166 Peony Flower

2011. Peonies. Multicoloured.

547	110c. Type **166**	1·90	1·90
548	110c. Yellow flowered peony	1·90	1·90
549	110c. White flowered peony	1·90	1·90
550	110c. Large pale pink flowered peony with black centre	1·90	1·90
MS551	50×75 mm. 350c. Medium flowered pink peony	7·75	7·75

167 *Holocanthus ciliaris*

2011. Fish. Multicoloured.

552	120c. Type **167**	1·90	1·70
553	120c. *Chaetodon caristratus*	1·90	1·70

554	120c. *Sparisoma viride*	1·90	1·70
555	120c. *Pomacanthus para*	1·90	1·70
556	120c. *Balistes vetula*	1·90	1·70
557	120c. *Lactophrys triqueter*	1·90	1·70
558	120c. *Holocentrus rufus*	1·90	1·70
559	120c. *Holocentrus striatus*	1·90	1·70
560	120c. *Didon holocanthus*	1·90	1·70
561	120c. *Equetus puncatus*	1·90	1·70

168 White Queen

2011. Chess. Multicoloured.

562	180c. Type **168**	3·50	3·25
563	180c. Black pawn	3·50	3·25
564	180c. Black king	3·50	3·25
565	180c. White knight	3·50	3·25
566	180c. Black bishop	3·50	3·25
567	180c. White pawn	3·50	3·25
568	180c. Black knight	3·50	3·25
569	180c. Black rook	3·50	3·25
570	180c. White king	3·50	3·25

169 Square Pillarbox

2011. America. Mailboxes. Multicoloured.

571	150c. Type **169**	2·75	2·50
572	150c. Estonian red wall-mounted box	2·75	2·50
573	150c. Yellow wall-mounted box	2·75	2·50
574	150c. American blue post box on legs	2·75	2·50
575	150c. Early German yellow wall-mounted box with decorative top	2·75	2·50
576	150c. Blue Russian wall-mounted box	2·75	2·50
577	150c. Green Chinese pillarbox	2·75	2·50
578	150c. Red Dutch wall-mounted box	2·75	2·50
579	150c. Ornate green box on two legs	2·75	2·50
580	150c. Royal mail pillarbox	2·75	2·50

170 Girl with a Red Hat

2011. Art. Paintings by Johannes Vermeer. Multicoloured.

581	200c. Type **170**	4·00	3·50
582	250c. *The Kitchen Maid*	5·00	4·50
583	250c. *The Lacemaker*	5·00	4·50
584	300c. *Girl with the Pearl Earring*	5·75	5·50

171 Barquentine

2011. Ships. Classic Sail Ships.

585	200c. Type **171**	4·00	3·50
586	225c. Two-masted barque (horiz)	4·50	4·00
587	250c. Schooner (horiz)	5·00	4·50
588	250c. Galleon (horiz)	5·00	4·50
589	275c. Three-masted barque (horiz)	5·50	5·00
590	300c. Three-masted barque under partial sail	5·75	5·50

172 *Diaethria neglecta*

2010. Butterflies. Multicoloured.

591	160c. Type **172**	3·00	2·75
592	160c. *Lycaena cupreus lapidicola*	3·00	2·75
593	160c. *Pyrrhogyra edocla*	3·00	2·75

594	160c. *Anartia amathea amathea*	3·00	2·75
595	160c. *Anglais urticae*	3·00	2·75
596	160c. *Morpho aega*	3·00	2·75
597	160c. *Junio coenia coenia*	3·00	2·75
598	160c. *Junio coenia coenia* (different)	3·00	2·75
599	160c. *Dione juno juno*	3·00	2·75
600	160c. *Lycaena heteronea austin*	3·00	2·75

173 *Pithecophaga jefferyi*

2012. Raptors and Vulture. Multicoloured.

601	150c. Type **159** (Philippine Eagle)	2·75	2·50
602	150c. *Harpia harpyja* (Harpy Eagle)	2·75	2·50
603	150c. *Morphnus guianensis* (Crested Eagle)	2·75	2·50
604	150c. *Caracara plancus* (Southern Crested Caracara)	2·75	2·50
605	150c. *Lophaetus occipitalis* (Long-crested Eagle)	2·75	2·50
606	150c. *Stephanoaetus coronatus* (Crowned Eagle)	2·75	2·50
607	150c. *Haliaeetus leucocephalus* (Bald Eagle)	2·75	2·50
608	150c. *Vultur gryphus* (Andean Condor)	2·75	2·50
609	150c. *Aquila chrysaetos* (Golden Eagle)	2·75	2·50
610	150c. *Falco sparverius* (American Kestrel)	2·75	2·50

174 White Goat

2012. Aruban Goats

611	175c. Type **174**	3·25	3·00
612	225c. Dark coloured goat against sunset (horiz)	3·25	3·00
613	275c. Light brown goat with large horns (horiz)	3·25	3·00
614	300c. Head of small brown goat with immature horns	3·25	3·00

175 Hurdler

2012. Olympic Games, London. Multicoloured.

615	500c. Type **175**	8·00	7·75
616	500c. Hand holding Olympic torch	8·00	7·75
617	500c. 'OLYMPIA' (laid horizontally)	8·00	7·75
618	500c. Swimmer	8·00	7·75
MS619	80×65 mm. Nos. 615/18	20·00	20·00

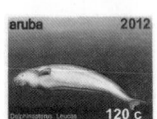

176 *Delphinapterus leucas*

2012. Whales. Multicoloured.

620	120c. Type **176** (Beluga Whale)	1·90	1·80
621	120c. *Kogia breviceps* (Pygmy Sperm Whale)	1·90	1·80
622	120c. *Balaena mysticetus* (Bowhead Whale)	1·90	1·80
623	120c. *Orcinus orca* (Killer Whale)	1·90	1·80
624	120c. *Physeter macrocephalus* (Sperm Whale)	1·90	1·80
625	120c. *Balaenoptera musculus* (Blue Whale)	1·90	1·80
626	120c. *Globicephala macrorhynchus* (Short-finned Pilot Whale)	1·90	1·80
627	120c. *Megaptera novaeangliae* (Humpback Whale)	1·90	1·80
628	120c. *Balaenoptera edeni*	1·90	1·80
629	120c. *Megaptera novaeangliae*	1·90	1·80

177 White Dress with Blue Underskirt

2012. Caribbean Dresses. Multicoloured.

630	175c. Type **177**	3·00	2·75
631	200c. White dress with red underskirt	4·00	3·50
632	200c. Two dancers wearing halter tops and white skirts	4·00	3·50
633	250c. Two women wearing yellow dresses with red and black bodices	5·00	4·50

178 Sailfish

2012. Rembrandt Regatta

634	150c. Type **178**	2·75	2·50
635	150c. Three-masted yacht (horiz)	2·75	2·50
636	175c. Twin-sailed yacht	3·00	2·75
637	175c. Three man keel boat (horiz)	3·00	2·75
638	200c. J 35 yacht	4·00	3·50
639	200c. Sailfish (horiz)	4·00	3·50

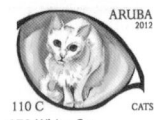

179 White Cat

2012. Cats. Multicoloured.

640	110c. Type **179**	1·80	1·70
641	110c. Tabby leaping	1·80	1·70
642	110c. Tabby laying on back	1·80	1·70
643	110c. Tabby kitten (head)	1·80	1·70
644	110c. Tabby and white with open mouth	1·80	1·70
645	110c. Tabby kitten looking up and right	1·80	1·70
646	110c. Silver tabby sleeping in curled position	1·80	1·70
647	110c. Tortoiseshell and white cat on tree trunk	1·80	1·70

180 Baubles

2012. Christmas. Multicoloured.

648	75c. Type **180**	90	75
649	120c. Presents and The Nativity	1·90	1·80
650	125c. Candles	2·00	2·25
651	210c. Wine glasses and fireworks	4·25	4·00

181 Yellow Tube Sponges

2012. Underwater Exploration. Multicoloured.

652	100c. Type **181**	1·50	1·25
653	100c. Flat yellow coral	1·50	1·25
654	100c. Manta Ray	1·50	1·25
655	100c. Blue Angelfish	1·50	1·25
656	100c. Turtle	1·50	1·25
657	100c. Encrusted spars of shipwreck	1·50	1·25
658	100c. Modern shipwreck	1·50	1·25
659	100c. Coral encrusted deck and rails of shipwreck	1·50	1·25
660	100c. Dark-coloured encrusted shipwrecks	1·50	1·25
661	100c. Aircraft	1·50	1·25

182 *Orchidaceae laelia xanthina*

2012. Orchids. Multicoloured.

662	200c. Type **182**	4·00	3·50
663	200c. *Orchidaceae dendrobium*	4·00	3·50
664	200c. *Orchidaceae dendrobium convolutum*	4·00	3·50
665	200c. *Orchidaceae brassavola nodosa*	4·00	3·50
666	200c. *Orchidaceae rossioglossum grande*	4·00	3·50
667	200c. *Orchidaceae cattleya aclandiae*	4·00	3·50
668	200c. *Orchidaceae cattleya*	4·00	3·50
669	200c. *Orchidaceae epidendrum cinnabarinum*	4·00	3·50
670	200c. *Orchidaceae phragmipedium cardinale*	4·00	3·50
671	200c. *Orchidaceae phragmipedium*	4·00	3·50
672	200c. *Orchidaceae phalaenopsis*	4·00	3·50
673	200c. *Orchidaceae cattleya gaskelliana*	4·00	3·50

EXPRESS MAIL SERVICE

E40 Globe, Planets and Aruban Arms

1993

E122	**E40**	200c. multicoloured	4·50	3·25

<table><tr><td align="right">Pt. 1</td></tr></table>

ASCENSION

An island in South Atlantic. A dependency of St. Helena.

1922. 12 pence = 1 shilling; 20 shillings = 1 pound.

1971. 100 pence = 1 pound.

1922. Stamps of St. Helena of 1912 optd **ASCENSION**.

1	½d. black and green	6·50	26·00
2	1d. green	6·50	25·00
3	1½d. red	17·00	48·00
4	2d. black and slate	17·00	13·00
4b	2d. black and slate	£425	£450
5	3d. blue	13·00	26·00
6	8d. black and purple	27·00	50·00
9	1s. black on green	28·00	48·00
7	2s. black and blue on blue	£119	£130
8	3s. black and violet	£140	£160

2 Badge of St. Helena

1924

10	**2**	½d. black	6·00	18·00
11	**2**	1d. black and green	6·00	13·00
12	**2**	1½d. red	10·00	42·00
13	**2**	2d. black and grey	20·00	12·00
14	**2**	3d. blue	8·00	18·00
15	**2**	4d. black on yellow	50·00	95·00
15d	**2**	5d. purple and green	19·00	26·00
16	**2**	6d. black and purple	60·00	£120
17	**2**	8d. black and violet	17·00	45·00
18	**2**	1s. black and brown	21·00	55·00
19	**2**	2s. black and blue on blue	75·00	£100
20	**2**	3s. black on blue	£100	£100

3 Georgetown **4** Ascension Island

1934. Medallion portrait of King George V (except 1s.).

21	**3**	½d. black and violet	90	80
22	**4**	1d. black and green	1·75	1·50
23	-	1½d. black and red	1·75	2·25
24	**4**	2d. black and orange	1·75	2·50
25	-	3d. black and blue	2·50	1·50
26	-	5d. black and blue	2·25	3·25
27	**4**	8d. black and brown	4·25	5·50
28	-	1s. black and red	18·00	11·00
29	**4**	2s.6d. black and purple	45·00	48·00

30	-	5s. black and brown	55·00	60·00

DESIGNS—HORIZ: 1½d. The Pier; 3d. Long Beach; 5d. Three Sisters; 1s. Sooty tern ("Wideawake Fair"); 5s. Green mountain.

1935. Silver Jubilee. As T **13** of Antigua.

31		1½d. black and red	3·50	14·00
32		2d. blue and grey	11·00	38·00
33		5d. green and blue	23·00	32·00
34		1s. grey and purple	23·00	40·00

1937. Coronation. As T **2** of Aden.

35		1d. green	50	1·40
36		2d. orange	1·00	60
37		3d. blue	1·00	50

11 Green Mountain

1938

38b	**A**	½d. black and violet	1·40	3·25
39	**11**	1d. black and green	45·00	13·00
39b	**11**	1d. black and orange	45	60
39d	**C**	1d. black and green	60	1·50
40b	**B**	1½d. black and red	1·00	80
40d	**B**	1½d. black and pink	1·50	1·00
41a	**11**	2d. black and orange	80	40
41c	**11**	2d. black and red	1·25	1·75
42	**D**	3d. black and blue	£100	29·00
42b	**D**	3d. black and grey	70	80
42d	**11**	4d. black and blue	5·00	3·00
43	**C**	6d. black and blue	10·00	2·25
44a	**A**	1s. black and brown	4·75	2·00
45	**B**	2s.6d. black and red	42·00	9·50
46a	**D**	5s. black and brown	38·00	40·00
47a	**C**	10s. black and purple	48·00	60·00

DESIGNS: A, Georgetown; B, The Pier; C, Three Sisters; D, Long Beach.

1946. Victory. As T **9** of Aden.

48	2d. orange	40	1·00
49	4d. blue	40	60

1948. Silver Wedding. As T **10/11** of Aden.

50	3d. black	50	30
51	10s. mauve	55·00	50·00

1949. U.P.U. As T **20/23** of Antigua.

52	3d. red	1·00	2·00
53	4d. blue	4·00	1·50
54	6d. olive	2·00	3·50
55	1s. black	2·00	1·50

1953. Coronation. As T **13** of Aden.

56	3d. black and grey	1·00	2·25

15 Water Catchment

1956

57	**15**	½d. black and brown	10	50
58	-	1d. black and mauve	4·25	2·50
59	-	1½d. black and orange	1·00	1·00
60	-	2d. black and red	5·50	3·25
61	-	2½d. black and brown	2·00	3·00
62	-	3d. black and blue	5·50	1·25
63	-	4d. black and turquoise	1·25	2·00
64	-	6d. black and blue	1·50	2·50
65	-	7d. black and olive	3·75	1·50
66	-	1s. black and red	1·00	1·25
67	-	2s.6d. black and purple	29·00	8·50
68	-	5s. black and green	40·00	18·00
69	-	10s. black and purple	50·00	40·00

DESIGNS: 1d. Map of Ascension; 1½d. Georgetown; 2d. Map showing Atlantic cables; 2½d. Mountain road; 3d. White-tailed tropic bird ("Boatswain Bird"); 4d. Yellow-finned tuna; 6d. Rollers on seashore; 7d. Turtles; 1s. Land crab; 2s.6d. Sooty tern ("Wideawake"); 5s. Perfect Crater; 10s. View of Ascension from north-west.

28 Brown Booby

1963. Birds. Multicoloured.

70	1d. Type **28**	1·50	30
71	1½d. White-capped noddy ("Black Noddy")	2·00	1·00
72	2d. White tern ("Fairy Tern")	1·25	30
73	3d. Red-billed tropic bird	1·75	30
74	4½d. Common noddy ("Brown Noddy")	1·75	30
75	6d. Sooty tern ("Wideawake Tern")	1·25	30

76	7d. Ascension frigate bird ("Frigate bird")	1·25	30
77	10d. Blue-faced booby ("White Booby")	1·25	50
78	1s. White-tailed tropic bird ("Yellow-billed Tropicbird")	1·25	30
79	1s.6d. Red-billed tropic bird	4·50	1·75
80	2s.6d. Madeiran storm petrel	8·50	11·00
81	5s. Red-footed booby (brown phase)	10·00	11·00
82	10s. Ascension frigate birds ("Frigate birds")	13·00	14·00
83	£1 Red-footed booby (white phase)	20·00	16·00

1963. Freedom from Hunger. As T 28 of Aden.

84	1s.6d. red	75	40

1963. Centenary of Red Cross. As T 33 of Antigua.

85	3d. red and black	1·00	1·25
86	1s.6d. red and blue	1·50	2·25

1965. Centenary of I.T.U. As T 36 of Antigua.

87	3d. mauve and violet	50	65
88	6d. turquoise and brown	75	65

1965. I.C.Y. As T 37 of Antigua.

89	1d. purple and turquoise	40	60
90	6d. green and lavender	60	90

1966. Churchill Commemoration. As T 38 of Antigua.

91	1d. blue	50	75
92	3d. green	1·75	1·00
93	6d. brown	2·00	1·25
94	1s.6d. violet	2·50	1·50

1966. World Cup Football Championship. As T 40 of Antigua.

95	3d. multicoloured	1·50	60
96	6d. multicoloured	1·50	80

1966. Inauguration of W.H.O. Headquarters, Geneva. As T 41 of Antigua.

97	3d. black, green and blue	1·75	1·00
98	1s.6d. black, purple and ochre	4·75	2·00

36 Satellite Station

1966. Opening of Apollo Communication Satellite Earth Station.

99	36	4d. black and violet	10	10
100	36	8d. black and green	15	15
101	36	1s.3d. black and brown	15	20
102	36	2s.6d. black and blue	15	15

37 B.B.C. Emblem

1966. Opening of B.B.C. Relay Station.

103	37	1d. gold and blue	10	10
104	37	3d. gold and green	15	15
105	37	6d. gold and violet	15	15
106	37	1s.6d. gold and red	15	15

1967. 20th Anniv of UNESCO As T 54/56 of Antigua.

107	3d. multicoloured	2·25	1·50
108	6d. yellow, violet and olive	3·00	2·00
109	1s.6d. black, purple and orange	4·75	2·50

44 Human Rights Emblem and Chain Links

1968. Human Rights Year.

110	44	6d. orange, red and black	30	15
111	44	1s.6d. blue, red and black	40	25
112	44	2s.6d. green, red and black	40	30

45 Black Durgon ("Ascension Black-Fish")

1968. Fish (1st series).

113	45	4d. black, grey and blue	30	35
114	-	8d. multicoloured	35	60
115	-	1s.9d. multicoloured	40	65
116	-	2s.3d. multicoloured	40	65

DESIGNS: 8d. Scribbled filefish ("Leather-jacket"); 1s.9d. Yellow-finned tuna; 2s.3d. Short-finned mako. See also Nos. 117/20 and 126/9.

1969. Fish (2nd series). As T 45. Multicoloured.

117	4d. Sailfish	65	80
118	6d. White seabream ("Old wife")	80	1·00
119	1s.6d. Yellowtail	1·00	2·25
120	2s.11d. Rock hind ("Jack")	1·25	2·50

46 H.M.S. Rattlesnake

1969. Royal Navy Crests (1st series).

121	46	4d. multicoloured	60	30
122	-	9d. multicoloured	75	35
123	-	1s.9d. blue and gold	1·10	45
124	-	2s.3d. multicoloured	1·25	55
MS125		165×105 mm. Nos. 121/4	6·50	13·00

DESIGNS: 9d. H.M.S. *Weston*; 1s.9d. H.M.S. *Undaunted*; 2s.3d. H.M.S. *Eagle*. See also Nos. 130/3, 149/52, 154/7 and 166/9.

1970. Fish (3rd series). As T 45. Multicoloured.

126	4d. Wahoo	4·50	2·75
127w	9d. Ascension jack ("Coalfish")	3·00	1·25
128	1s.9d. Pompouno dolphin	5·50	3·50
129w	2s.3d. Squirrelfish ("Soldier")	3·00	1·50

1970. Royal Navy Crests (2nd series). As T 46. Multicoloured.

130	4d. H.M.S. *Penelope*	1·00	1·00
131	9d. H.M.S. *Carlisle*	1·25	1·50
132	1s.6d. H.M.S. *Amphion*	1·75	2·00
133	2s.6d. H.M.S. *Magpie*	1·75	2·00
MS134	159×96 mm. Nos. 130/3	9·00	15·00

50 Early Chinese Rocket

1971. Decimal Currency. Evolution of Space Travel. Multicoloured.

135	½p. Type **50**	15	20
136	1p. Medieval Arab astronomers	20	20
137	1½p. Tycho Brahe's observatory, quadrant and supernova (horiz)	30	30
138	2p. Galileo, Moon and telescope (horiz)	40	30
139	2½p. Isaac Newton, instruments and apple (horiz)	1·75	1·00
140	3½p. Harrison's chronometer and H.M.S. *Deptford* (frigate), 1735 (horiz)	2·50	1·50
141	4½p. Space rocket taking off	1·25	1·00
142	5p. World's largest telescope, Palomar (horiz)	1·00	1·00
143	7½p. World's largest radio telescope, Jodrell Bank (horiz)	4·00	1·75
144	10p. "Mariner VII" and Mars (horiz)	3·50	1·75
145	12½p. "Sputnik II" and Space dog, Laika (horiz)	5·00	2·00
146	25p. Walking in Space	6·00	2·25
147	50p. "Apollo XI" crew on Moon (horiz)	5·00	2·75
148	£1 Future Space Research station (horiz)	5·00	4·50

1971. Royal Navy Crests (3rd series). As T 46. Multicoloured.

149	2p. H.M.S. "Phoenix"	1·00	30
150	4p. H.M.S. "Milford"	1·00	55
151	9p. H.M.S. "Pelican"	1·25	80
152	15p. H.M.S. "Oberon"	1·25	1·00
MS153	151×104 mm. Nos. 149/52	4·00	15·00

1972. Royal Navy Crests (4th series). As T 46. Multicoloured.

154	1½p. H.M.S. *Lowestoft*	50	50
155	3p. H.M.S. *Auckland*	55	75
156	6p. H.M.S. *Nigeria*	60	1·25
157	17½p. H.M.S. *Bermuda*	90	2·50
MS158	157×93 mm. Nos. 154/7	2·25	7·50

51 Course of the Quest

1972. 50th Anniv of Shackleton's Death. Multicoloured.

159	2½p. Type **51**	30	60
160	4p. Shackleton and *Quest* (horiz)	35	60
161	7½p. Shackleton's cabin and *Quest* (horiz)	35	65
162	11p. Shackleton statue and memorial	40	80
MS163	139×114 mm. Nos. 159/62	1·25	6·00

52 Land Crab and Short-finned Mako

1972. Royal Silver Wedding. Multicoloured.

164	52	2p. violet	15	10
165	52	16p. red	35	30

1973. Royal Naval Crests (5th series). As T 46. Multicoloured.

166	2p. H.M.S. *Birmingham*	2·00	1·50
167	4p. H.M.S. *Cardiff*	2·25	1·50
168	9p. H.M.S. *Penzance*	3·00	1·75
169	13p. H.M.S. *Rochester*	3·25	1·75
MS170	109×152 mm. Nos. 166/9	28·00	10·00

53 Green Turtle

1973. Turtles. Multicoloured.

171	4p. Type **53**	2·75	1·75
172	9p. Loggerhead turtle	3·00	2·00
173	12p. Hawksbill turtle	3·25	2·25

54 Sergeant, R.M. Light Infantry, 1900

1973. 50th Anniv of Departure of Royal Marines from Ascension. Multicoloured.

174	2p. Type **54**	1·50	1·50
175	6p. R.M. Private, 1816	2·25	1·50
176	12p. R.M. Light Infantry Officer, 1880	2·50	2·25
177	20p. R.M. Artillery Colour Sergeant, 1910	3·00	2·50

1973. Royal Wedding. As T 47 of Anguilla. Multicoloured. Background colours given.

178	2p. brown	15	10
179	18p. green	20	20

55 Letter and H.Q., Berne

1974. Centenary of Universal Postal Union. Multicoloured.

180	2p. Type **55**	20	30
181	9p. Hermes and U.P.U. monument	30	45

56 Churchill as a Boy, and Birthplace, Blenheim Palace

1974. Birth Centenary of Sir Winston Churchill. Multicoloured.

182	5p. Type **56**	20	35
183	25p. Churchill as statesman, and U.N. Building	30	75
MS184	93×87 mm. Nos. 182/3	1·00	2·50

57 "Skylab 3" and Photograph of Ascension

1975. Space Satellites. Multicoloured.

185	2p. Type **57**	20	30
186	18p. "Skylab 4" Command module and photograph	30	40

58 U.S.A.F. Lockheed C-141A Starlifter

1975. Wideawake Airfield. Multicoloured.

187	2p. Type **58**	80	65
188	5p. R.A.F. Lockheed C-130 Hercules	80	85
189	9p. Vickers Super VC-10	80	1·40
190	24p. U.S.A.F. Lockheed C-5A Galaxy	1·25	2·50
MS191	144×99 mm. Nos. 187/90	14·00	22·00

1975. "Apollo-Soyuz" Space Link. Nos. 141 and 145/6 optd APOLLO-SOYUZ LINK 1975.

192	4½p. multicoloured	15	20
193	12½p. multicoloured	15	25
194	25p. multicoloured	25	40

60 Arrival of Royal Navy, 1815

1975. 160th Anniv of Occupation. Multicoloured.

195	2p. Type **60**	25	25
196	5p. Water supply, Dampiers Drip	25	40
197	9p. First landing, 1815	25	60
198	15p. The garden on Green Mountain	35	85

61 Yellow Canaries ("Canary")

1976. Multicoloured.. Multicoloured..

199	1p. Type **61**	40	1·50
200	2p. White tern ("Fairy Tern") (vert)	50	1·50
201	3p. Common waxbill ("Waxbill")	50	1·50
202	4p. White-capped noddy ("Black Noddy") (vert)	50	1·50
203	5p. Common noddy ("Brown Noddy")	70	1·50
204	6p. Common mynah	70	1·50
205	7p. Madeiran storm petrel (vert)	70	1·50
206	8p. Sooty tern	70	1·50
207	9p. Blue-faced booby ("White Booby") (vert)	70	1·50
208	10p. Red-footed booby	70	1·50
209	15p. Red-necked spurfowl ("Red-throated Francolin") (vert)	85	1·50
210	18p. Brown booby (vert)	85	1·50
211	25p. Red-billed tropic bird ("Red-billed Bo'sun Bird")	90	1·50
212	50p. White-tailed tropic bird ("Yellow-billed Tropic Bird")	1·00	1·75
213	£1 Ascension frigate-bird (vert)	1·00	2·25
214	£2 Boatswain Bird Island Sanctuary (50×38 mm)	2·00	5·00

63 G.B. Penny Red with Ascension Postmark

1976. Festival of Stamps, London.

215	**63**	5p. red, black and brown	15	15
216	-	9p. green, black and brown	15	20
217	-	25p. multicoloured	25	45

MS218 133×121 mm. No. 217 with St. Helena No. 318 and Tristan da Cunha No. 206 1·75 2·00

DESIGNS—VERT: 9p. ½d. stamp of 1922. HORIZ: 25p. *Southampton Castle* (liner).

64 U.S. Base, Ascension

1976. Bicentenary of American Revolution. Multicoloured.

219	8p. Type **64**	30	40
220	9p. NASA Station at Devils Ashpit	30	45
221	25p. "Viking" landing on Mars	50	80

65 Visit of Prince Philip, 1957

1977. Silver Jubilee. Multicoloured.

222	8p. Type **65**	15	15
223	12p. Coronation Coach leaving Buckingham Palace (horiz)	20	20
224	25p. Coronation Coach (horiz)	35	40

66 Tunnel carrying Water Pipe

1977. Water Supplies. Multicoloured.

225	3p. Type **66**	15	15
226	5p. Breakneck Valley wells	20	20
227	12p. Break tank (horiz)	30	35
228	25p. Water catchment (horiz)	45	65

67 Mars Bay Location, 1877

1977. Centenary of Visit of Professor Gill (astronomer). Multicoloured.

229	3p. Type **67**	15	20
230	8p. Instrument sites, Mars Bay	15	25
231	12p. Sir David and Lady Gill	20	40
232	25p. Maps of Ascension	60	70

68 Lion of England

1978. 25th Anniv of Coronation.

233	**68**	25p. yellow, brown and silver	35	50
234	-	25p. multicoloured	35	50
235	-	25p. yellow, brown and silver	35	50

DESIGNS: No 234, Queen Elizabeth II; No 235, Green turtle.

70 Flank of Sisters, Sisters' Red Hill and East Crater

1978. Ascension Island Volcanic Rock Formations. Multicoloured.

236	3p. Type **70**	15	20
237	5p. Holland's Crater (Hollow Tooth)	20	30
238	12p. Street Crater, Lower Valley Crater and Bear's Back	25	40
239	15p. Butt Crater, Weather Post and Green Mountain	30	45
240	25p. Flank of Sisters, Thistle Hill and Two Boats Village	35	50

MS241 185×100 mm. Nos. 236/40, each × 2 2·00 5·00

Nos. 236/40 were issued as a *se-tenant* strip within the sheet, forming a composite design.

71 *The Resolution* (H. Roberts)

1979. Bicentenary of Captain Cook's Voyages, 1768–79. Multicoloured.

242	3p. Type **71**	30	25
243	8p. Cook's chronometer	25	40
244	12p. Green turtle	30	50
245	25p. Flaxman/Wedgwood medallion of Cook	30	70

72 St. Mary's Church, Georgetown

1979. Ascension Day. Multicoloured.

246	8p. Type **72**	10	20
247	12p. Map of Ascension	15	30
248	50p. *The Ascension* (painting by Rembrandt)	30	90

73 Landing Cable, Comfortless Cove

1979. 80th Anniv of Eastern Telegraph Company's Arrival on Ascension.

249	**73**	3p. black and red	10	10
250	-	8p. black and green	15	15
251	-	12p. black and yellow	20	20
252	-	15p. black and violet	20	25
253	-	25p. black and brown	25	35

DESIGNS—HORIZ: 8p. C.S. *Anglia*; 15p. C.S. *Seine*; 25p. Cable and Wireless earth station. VERT: 12p. Map of Atlantic cable network.

74 1938 6d. Stamp

1979. Death Centenary of Sir Rowland Hill.

254	**74**	3p. black and blue	10	10
255	-	8p. black, green and pale green	15	20
256	-	12p. black, blue and pale blue	15	25
257	-	50p. black and red	40	90

DESIGNS—HORIZ: 8p. 1956 5s. definitive. VERT: 12p. 1924 3s. stamp; 50p. Sir Rowland Hill.

75 *Anogramma ascensionis*

1980. Ferns and Grasses. Multicoloured.

258	3p. Type **75**	10	15
259	6p. *Xiphopteris ascensionense*	10	20
260	8p. *Sporobolus caespitosus*	10	20
261	12p. *Sporobolus durus* (vert)	15	30
262	18p. *Dryopteris ascensionis* (vert)	15	40
263	24p. *Marattia purpurascens* (vert)	20	55

76 17th-Century Bottle Post

1980. "London 1980" International Stamp Exhibition. Multicoloured.

264	8p. Type **76**	15	20
265	12p. 19th-century chance calling ship	20	25
266	15p. *Garth Castle* (regular mail service from 1863)	20	30
267	50p. *St. Helena* (mail services, 1980)	60	90

MS268 102×154 mm. Nos. 264/7 1·00 2·40

77 H.M. Queen Elizabeth the Queen Mother

1980. 80th Birthday of The Queen Mother.

269	**77**	15p. multicoloured	40	40

78 Lubbock's Yellowtail

1980. Fish. Multicoloured.

270	3p. Type **78**	20	25
271	10p. Resplendent angelfish	20	25
272	25p. Bicoloured butterflyfish	30	55
273	40p. Marmalade razorfish	40	75

79 H.M.S. *Tortoise*

1980. 150th Anniv of Royal Geographical Society. Multicoloured.

274	10p. Type **79**	20	40
275	15p. *Wideawake Fair*	25	45
276	60p. Mid-Atlantic Ridge (38×48 mm)	65	1·25

80 Green Mountain Farm, 1881

1981. Green Mountain Farm. Multicoloured.

277	12p. Type **80**	15	35
278	15p. Two Boats, 1881	15	40
279	20p. Green Mountain and Two Boats, 1981	20	50
280	30p. Green Mountain Farm, 1981	30	70

81 Cable and Wireless Earth Station

1981. "Space Shuttle" Mission and Opening of 2nd Earth Station.

281	**81**	15p. black, blue and pale blue	30	35

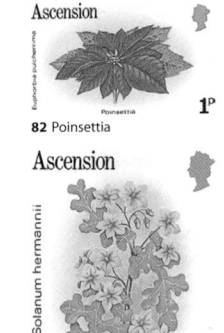

82 Poinsettia

83 Solanum

1981. Flowers. Multicoloured.

282A	1p. Type **82**	70	1·25
283B	2p. Clustered wax flower	50	1·25
284B	3p. Kolanchoe (vert)	50	1·25
285A	4p. Yellow pops	80	1·25
286A	5p. Camels foot creeper	80	1·25
287A	8p. White oleander	80	1·25
288B	10p. Ascension lily (vert)	45	75
289A	12p. Coral plant (vert)	1·50	1·10
290B	15p. Yellow allamanda	50	75
291B	20p. Ascension euphorbia	1·00	75
292A	30p. Flame of the forest (vert)	1·25	1·25
293A	40p. Bougainvillea "King Leopold"	1·25	3·00
294A	50p. Type **83**	1·75	3·25
295B	£1 Ladies petticoat	2·00	3·00
296A	£2 Red hibiscus	3·50	6·00

Nos. 294/6 are as Type **83**.

84 Map by Maxwell, 1793

1981. Early Maps of Ascension.

297	**84**	10p. black, gold and blue	20	35
298	-	12p. black, gold and green	20	35
299	-	15p. black, gold and stone	20	35
300	-	40p. black, gold and yellow	50	70

MS301 – 79×64 mm. 5p. × 4 multicoloured 60 75

DESIGNS: 12p. Maxwell, 1793 (different); 15p. Ekeberg and Chapman, 1811; 40p. Campbell, 1819; miniature sheet, Linschoten, 1599.

Stamps from **MS**301 form a composite design.

85 Wedding Bouquet from Ascension

1981. Royal Wedding. Multicoloured.

302	10p. Type **85**	15	15
303	15p. Prince Charles in Fleet Air Arm flying kit	30	30
304	50p. Prince Charles and Lady Diana Spencer	65	90

87 "Interest"

1981. 25th Anniv of Duke of Edinburgh Award Scheme. Multicoloured.

305	5p. Type **87**	15	15
306	10p. "Physical activities"	15	15
307	15p. "Service"	20	20
308	40p. Duke of Edinburgh	45	45

88 Scout crossing Rope Bridge

1982. 75th Anniv of Boy Scout Movement.

309	**88**	10p. black, blue and light blue	15	35
310	-	15p. black, brown and yellow	15	50
311	-	25p. black, mve & lt mve	20	60
312	-	40p. black, red and orange	30	85

MS313 – 121×121 mm. 10, 15, 25, 40p. As Nos. 309/12 (each diamond 40×40 mm) 1·00 2·50

DESIGNS: 15p. 1st Ascension Scout Group flag; 25p. Scouts learning to use radio; 40p. Lord Baden-Powell.

89 Charles Darwin

1982. 150th Anniv of Charles Darwin's Voyage. Multicoloured.

314	10p. Type **89**	20	40
315	12p. Darwin's pistols	20	50
316	15p. Rock crab	25	55
317	40p. H.M.S. *Beagle*	60	95

90 Fairey Swordfish Torpedo Bomber

1982. 40th Anniv of Wideawake Airfield. Multicoloured.

318	5p. Type **90**	75	35
319	10p. North American B-25C Mitchell	1·00	40
320	15p. Boeing EC-135N Aria	1·25	55
321	50p. Lockheed C-130 Hercules	1·75	1·10

91 Ascension Coat of Arms

1982. 21st Birthday of Princess of Wales. Multicoloured.

322	12p. Type **91**	20	20
323	15p. Lady Diana Spencer in Music Room, Buckingham Palace	20	20
324	25p. Bride and Earl Spencer leaving Clarence House	30	30
325	50p. Formal portrait	65	65

1982. Commonwealth Games, Brisbane. Nos. 290/1 optd **1st PARTICIPATION COMMON-WEALTH GAMES 1982**.

326	15p. Yellow allamanda	30	40
327	20p. Ascension euphorbia	40	45

94 Bush House, London

1982. Christmas. 50th Anniv of B.B.C. External Broadcasting. Multicoloured.

328	5p. Type **94**	15	20
329	10p. Atlantic relay station	20	30
330	25p. Lord Reith, first Director-General	30	60
331	40p. King George V making his first Christmas broadcast, 1932	45	75

95 *Marasmius thwaitesii* (*Marasmius echinosphaerus*)

1983. Fungi. Multicoloured.

332	7p. Type **95**	25	30
333	12p. *Chlorophyllum molybdites*	35	45
334	15p. *Leucocoprinus cepaestripes*	40	50
335	20p. *Lycoperdon marginatum*	45	65
336	50p. *Marasmiellus distantifolius*	55	1·25

96 Aerial View of Georgetown

1983. Island Views (1st series). Multicoloured.

337	12p. Type **96**	15	25
338	15p. Green Mountain farm	15	25
339	20p. Boatswain Bird Island	20	40
340	60p. Telemetry Hill by night	40	80

See also Nos. 367/70.

97 Westland Wessex 5 Helicopter of No. 845 Naval Air Squadron

1983. Bicentenary of Manned Flight. British Military Aircraft. Multicoloured.

341	12p. Type **97**	40	65
342	15p. Avro Vulcan B.2 of No. 44 Squadron	40	75
343	20p. Hawker Siddeley Nimrod M.R.2P of No. 20 Squadron	40	85
344	60p. Handey Page Victor K2 of No. 55 Squadron	60	2·00

98 Iguanid

1983. Introduced Species. Multicoloured.

345	12p. Type **98**	25	30
346	15p. Common rabbit	30	35
347	20p. Cat	40	45
348	60p. Donkey	75	1·40

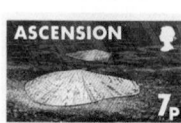

99 Speckled Tellin (*Tellina listeri*)

1983. Sea Shells. Multicoloured.

349	7p. Type **99**	15	20
350	12p. Lion's paw scallop	15	30
351	15p. Lurid cowrie	20	35
352	20p. Ascension nerite	20	45
353	50p. Miniature melo	40	1·10

100 1922 1½d. Stamp

1984. 150th Anniv of St. Helena as a British Colony. Multicoloured.

354	12p. Type **100**	20	45
355	15p. 1922 2d. stamp	20	50
356	20p. 1922 8d. stamp	20	55
357	60p. 1922 1s. stamp	50	1·40

101 Prince Andrew

1984. Visit of Prince Andrew. Sheet 124×90 mm.
MS358 12p. Type **101**; 70p. Prince Andrew in naval uniform 1·00 1·60

102 Naval Semaphore

1984. 250th Anniv of *Lloyd's List* (newspaper). Multicoloured.

359	12p. Type **102**	50	30
360	15p. *Southampton Castle* (liner)	50	35
361	20p. Pier head	55	45
362	70p. *Dane* (screw steamer)	1·25	1·50

103 Penny Coin and Yellow-finned Tuna

1984. New Coinage. Multicoloured.

363	12p. Type **103**	35	35
364	15p. Twopenny coin and donkey	40	40
365	20p. Fifty pence coin and green turtle	45	50
366	70p. Pound coin and sooty tern	80	1·75

1984. Island Views (2nd series). As T **96**. Multicoloured.

367	12p. The Devil's Riding-school	20	30
368	15p. St. Mary's Church	25	35
369	20p. Two Boats Village	25	45
370	70p. Ascension from the sea	80	1·50

104 Bermuda Cypress

1985. Trees. Multicoloured.

371	7p. Type **104**	20	20
372	12p. Norfolk Island pine	25	30
373	15p. Screwpine	25	35
374	20p. Eucalyptus	25	45
375	65p. Spore tree	70	1·40

105 The Queen Mother with Prince Andrew at Silver Jubilee Service

1985. Life and Times of Queen Elizabeth the Queen Mother. Multicoloured.

376	12p. With the Duke of York at Balmoral, 1924	25	35
377	15p. Type **105**	25	40
378	20p. The Queen Mother at Ascot	30	55
379	70p. With Prince Henry at his christening (from photo by Lord Snowdon)	80	1·75

MS380 91×73 mm. 75p. Visiting the *Queen Elizabeth 2* at Southampton, 1968 1·10 1·60

106 32 Pdr. Smooth Bore Muzzle-loader, *c* 1820, and Royal Marine Artillery Hat Plate, *c* 1816

1985. Guns on Ascension Island. Multicoloured.

381	12p. Type **106**	40	90
382	15p. 7 inch rifled muzzle-loader, c. 1866, and Royal Cypher on barrel	40	1·00
383	20p. 7 pdr rifled muzzle-loader, c. 1877, and Royal Artillery Badge	40	1·25
384	70p. 5.5 inch gun, 1941, and crest from H.M.S. *Hood*	80	3·00

107 Guide Flag

1985. 75th Anniv of Girl Guide Movement and International Youth Year. Multicoloured.

385	12p. Type **107**	30	70
386	15p. Practising first aid	30	80
387	20p. Camping	30	90
388	70p. Lady Baden-Powell	80	2·50

108 *Clerodendrum fragrans*

1985. Wild Flowers. Multicoloured.

389	12p. Type **108**	30	75
390	15p. Shell ginger	30	90
391	20p. Cape daisy	35	90
392	70p. Ginger lily	70	2·50

109 Newton's Reflector Telescope

1986. Appearance of Halley's Comet. Multicoloured.

393	12p. Type **109**	40	1·10
394	15p. Edmond Halley and Old Greenwich Observatory	40	1·25
395	20p. Short's Gregorian telescope and comet, 1759	40	1·25
396	70p. Ascension satellite tracking station and ICE spacecraft	1·10	3·50

110 Princess Elizabeth in 1926

1986. 60th Birthday of Queen Elizabeth II. Multicoloured.

397	7p. Type **110**	15	25
398	15p. Queen making Christmas broadcast, 1952	15	40
399	20p. At Garter ceremony, Windsor Castle, 1983	20	50
400	35p. In Auckland, New Zealand, 1981	30	80
401	£1 At Crown Agents' Head Office, London, 1983	75	2·25

111 1975 Space Satellites 2p. Stamp

1986. "Ameripex '86" International Stamp Exhibition, Chicago. Designs showing previous Ascension stamps. Multicoloured.

402	12p. Type **111**	25	60
403	15p. 1980 "London 1980" International Stamp Exhibition 50p.	20	70
404	20p. 1976 Bicentenary of American Revolution 8p.	25	90
405	70p. 1982 40th anniv of Wide-awake Airfield 10p.	70	2·00
MS406	60×75 mm. 75p. Statue of Liberty	1·50	2·75

112 Prince Andrew and Miss Sarah Ferguson

1986. Royal Wedding. Multicoloured.

407	15p. Type **112**	25	50
408	35p. Prince Andrew aboard H.M.S. *Brazen*	50	1·00

113 H.M.S. *Ganymede* (c 1811)

1986. Ships of the Royal Navy. Multicoloured.

409	1p. Type **113**	55	1·50
410	2p. H.M.S. *Kangaroo* (c.1811)	60	1·50
411	4p. H.M.S. *Trinculo* (c.1811)	60	1·50
412	5p. H.M.S. *Daring* (c.1811)	60	1·50
413	9p. H.M.S. *Thais* (c.1811)	70	1·50
414	10p. H.M.S. *Pheasant* (1819)	70	1·50
415	15p. H.M.S. *Myrmidon* (1819)	80	1·75
416	18p. H.M.S. *Atholl* (1825)	90	1·75
417	20p. H.M.S. *Medina* (1830)	90	1·75
418	25p. H.M.S. *Saracen* (1840)	1·00	2·00
419	30p. H.M.S. *Hydra* (c.1845)	1·00	2·00
420	50p. H.M.S. *Sealark* (1849)	1·00	2·50
421	70p. H.M.S. *Rattlesnake* (1868)	1·00	3·00
422	£1 H.M.S. *Penelope* (1889)	1·25	3·75
423	£2 H.M.S. *Monarch* (1897)	2·50	6·50

114 Cape Gooseberry

1987. Edible Bush Fruits. Multicoloured.

424	12p. Type **114**	65	90
425	15p. Prickly pear	65	1·00
426	20p. Guava	70	1·10
427	70p. Loquat	1·10	2·75

115 Ignition of Rocket Motors

1987. 25th Anniv of First American Manned Earth Orbit. Multicoloured.

428	15p. Type **115**	55	75
429	18p. Lift-off	60	80
430	25p. Re-entry	75	95
431	£1 Splashdown	2·50	3·25
MS432	92×78 mm. 70p. "Friendship 7" capsule	1·75	2·00

116 Captains in Full Dress raising Red Ensign

1987. 19th-century Uniforms (1st series). Royal Navy, 1815–20. Multicoloured.

433	25p. Type **116**	50	60
434	25p. Surgeon and seamen	50	60
435	25p. Seaman with water-carrying donkey	50	60
436	25p. Midshipman and gun	50	60
437	25p. Commander in undress uniform surveying	50	60

See also Nos. 478/82.

117 *Cynthia cardui*

1987. Insects (1st series). Multicoloured.

438	15p. Type **117**	55	65
439	18p. *Danaus chrysippus*	60	75
440	25p. *Hypolimnas misippus*	75	85
441	£1 *Lampides boeticus*	1·50	2·50

See also Nos. 452/5 and 483/6.

118 Male Ascension Frigate Birds

1987. Sea Birds (1st series). Multicoloured.

442	25p. Type **118**	1·60	2·00
443	25p. Juvenile Ascension frigate bird, brown booby and blue-faced boobies	1·60	2·00
444	25p. Male Ascension frigate bird and blue-faced boobies	1·60	2·00
445	25p. Female Ascension frigate bird	1·60	2·00
446	25p. Adult male feeding juvenile Ascension frigate bird	1·60	2·00

Nos. 442/6 were printed together, *se-tenant*, forming a composite design.
See also Nos. 469/73.

1987. Royal Ruby Wedding. Nos. 397/401 optd **40TH WEDDING ANNIVERSARY.**

447	7p. Type **110**	15	15
448	15p. Queen making Christmas broadcast, 1952	20	20
449	20p. At Garter ceremony, Windsor Castle, 1983	25	25
450	35p. In Auckland, New Zealand, 1981	40	45
451	£1 At Crown Agents' Head Office, London, 1983	1·00	1·10

1988. Insects (2nd series). As T **117**. Multicoloured.

452	15p. *Gryllus bimaculatus* (field cricket)	30	30
453	18p. *Ruspolia differeus* (bush cricket)	35	35
454	25p. *Chilomenus lunata* (ladybird)	40	40
455	£1 *Diachrysia orichalcea* (moth)	1·50	1·50

120 Bate's Memorial, St. Mary's Church

1988. 150th Death Anniv of Captain William Bate (garrison commander, 1828–38). Multicoloured.

456	9p. Type **120**	25	25
457	15p. Commodore's Cottage	30	30
458	18p. North East Cottage	35	35
459	25p. Map of Ascension	45	45
460	70p. Captain Bate and marines	1·00	1·00

121 H.M.S. *Resolution* (ship of the line), 1667

1988. Bicentenary of Australian Settlement. Ships of the Royal Navy. Multicoloured.

461	9p. Type **121**	1·25	45
462	18p. H.M.S. *Resolution* (Captain Cook), 1772	1·75	70
463	25p. H.M.S. *Resolution* (battleship), 1892	1·75	85
464	65p. H.M.S. *Resolution* (battleship), 1916	2·50	1·50

1988. "Sydpex '88" National Stamp Exhibition, Sydney. Nos. 461/4 optd **SYDPEX 88 30.7.88 - 7.8.88**.

465	9p. Type **121**	50	40
466	18p. H.M.S. *Resolution* (Captain Cook), 1772	75	60
467	25p. H.M.S. *Resolution* (battleship), 1892	85	70
468	65p. H.M.S. *Resolution* (battleship), 1916	1·60	1·40

1988. Sea Birds (2nd series). Sooty Tern. As T **118**. Multicoloured.

469	25p. Pair displaying	1·60	1·25
470	25p. Turning egg	1·60	1·25
471	25p. Incubating egg	1·60	1·25
472	25p. Feeding chick	1·60	1·25
473	25p. Immature sooty tern	1·60	1·25

Nos. 469/73 were printed together, *se-tenant*, forming a composite design of a nesting colony.

123 Lloyd's Coffee House, London, 1688

1988. 300th Anniv of Lloyd's of London. Multicoloured.

474	8p. Type **123**	25	25
475	18p. *Alert IV* (cable ship) (horiz)	65	65
476	25p. Satellite recovery in space (horiz)	80	80
477	65p. *Good Hope Castle* (cargo liner) on fire off Ascension, 1973	1·75	1·75

1988. 19th-century Uniforms (2nd series). Royal Marines 1821–34. As T **116**. Multicoloured.

478	25p. Marines landing on Ascension, 1821	1·10	1·60
479	25p. Officer and Marine at semaphore station, 1829	1·10	1·60
480	25p. Sergeant and Marine at Octagonal Tank, 1831	1·10	1·60
481	25p. Officers at water pipe tunnel, 1833	1·10	1·60
482	25p. Officer supervising construction of barracks, 1834	1·10	1·60

1989. Insects (3rd series). As T **117**. Multicoloured.

483	15p. *Trichoptilus wahlbergi* (moth)	75	50
484	18p. *Lucilia sericata* (fly)	80	55
485	25p. *Alceis ornatus* (weevil)	1·10	70
486	£1 *Polistes fuscatus* (wasp)	3·00	2·40

124 Two Land Crabs

1989. Ascension Land Crabs. Multicoloured.

487	15p. Type **124**	40	45
488	18p. Crab with claws raised	45	50
489	25p. Crab on rock	60	70
490	£1 Crab in surf	2·00	2·50
MS491	98×101 mm. Nos. 487/90	3·00	3·75

125 1949 75th Anniversary of U.P.U. 1s. Stamp

1989. "Philexfrance '89" International Stamp Exhibition, Paris, and "World Stamp Expo '89", Washington (1st issue). Sheet 104×86 mm.

MS492	**125** 75p. multicoloured	3·00	3·75

See also Nos. 498/503.

126 "Apollo 7" Tracking Station, Ascension

1989. 20th Anniv of First Manned Landing on Moon. Multicoloured.

493	15p. Type **126**	65	45
494	18p. Launch of "Apollo 7" (30×30 mm)	70	50
495	25p. "Apollo 7" emblem (30×30 mm)	90	70
496	70p. "Apollo 7" jettisoning expended Saturn rocket	1·75	1·75
MS497	101×83 mm. £1 Diagram of "Apollo 11" mission	2·00	2·10

127 *Queen Elizabeth 2* (liner) and U.S.S. *John F. Kennedy* (aircraft carrier) in New York Harbour

1989. "Philexfrance 89" International Stamp Exhibition, Paris, and "World Stamp Expo '89", Washington (1st issue). Designs showing Statue of Liberty and Centenary celebrations. Multicoloured.

498	15p. Type **127**	50	50
499	15p. Cleaning statue	50	50
500	15p. Statue of Liberty	50	50
501	15p. Crown of statue	50	50
502	15p. Warships and New York skyline	50	50
503	15p. *Jean de Vienne* (French destroyer) and skyscrapers	50	50

128 Devil's Ashpit Tracking Station

1989. Closure of Devil's Ashpit Tracking Station, Ascension. Multicoloured.

504	18p. Type **128**	80	50
505	25p. Launch of shuttle "Atlantis"	80	55

129 Bubonian Conch (*Strombus latus*)

1989. Sea Shells. Multicoloured.

506	8p. Type **129**	40	30
507	18p. Giant tun	70	50
508	25p. Doris loup	90	65
509	£1 Atlantic trumpet triton	2·75	2·50

130 Donkeys

1989. Ascension Wildlife. Multicoloured.
510	18p. Type **130**	1·00	1·25
511	25p. Green turtle	1·00	1·25

131 Seaman's Pistol, Hat and Cutlass

1990. Royal Navy Equipment, 1815–20. Multicoloured.
512	25p. Type **131**	70	70
513	25p. Midshipman's belt plate, button, sword and hat	70	70
514	25p. Surgeon's hat, sword and instrument chest	70	70
515	25p. Captain's hat, telescope and sword	70	70
516	25p. Admiral's epaulette, megaphone, hat and pocket	70	70

See also Nos. 541/5.

132 Pair of Ascension Frigate Birds with Young

1990. Endangered Species. Ascension Frigate Bird. Multicoloured.
517	9p. Type **132**	1·50	1·00
518	10p. Fledgling	1·50	1·00
519	11p. Adult male in flight	1·50	1·00
520	15p. Female and immature birds in flight	1·75	1·25

133 Penny Black and Twopence Blue

1990. "Stamp World London 90" International Stamp Exhibition. Multicoloured.
521	9p. Type **133**	50	40
522	18p. Ascension postmarks used on G.B. stamps	70	60
523	25p. Unloading mail at Wideawake Airfield	95	85
524	£1 Mail van and Main Post Office	2·25	2·75

134 Queen Elizabeth, 1940 (Sir Gerald Kelly)

1990. 90th Birthday of Queen Elizabeth the Queen Mother.
525	**134** 25p. multicoloured	75	75
526	- £1 black and lilac	2·25	2·25

DESIGN—29×37 mm: £1 King George VI and Queen Elizabeth with Bren-gun carrier.

136 Madonna and Child (sculpture, Dino Felici)

1990. Christmas. Works of Art. Multicoloured.
527	8p. Type **136**	70	70
528	18p. *Madonna and Child* (anon)	1·25	1·25
529	25p. *Madonna and Child with St. John* (Johann Gebhard)	1·75	1·75
530	65p. *Madonna and Child* (Giacomo Gritti)	3·00	4·00

137 *Garth Castle* (mail steamer), 1910

1990. Maiden Voyage of *St. Helena II*. Multicoloured.
531	9p. Type **137**	90	90
532	18p. *St. Helena I* during Falkland Islands campaign, 1982	1·25	1·25
533	25p. Launch of *St. Helena II*	1·75	1·75
534	70p. Duke of York launching *St. Helena II*	3·00	4·25
MS535	100×100 mm. £1 *St. Helena II* and outline map of Ascension	3·50	5·00

1991. 175th Anniv of Occupation. Nos. 418, 420 and 422 optd **BRITISH FOR 175 YEARS.**
536	25p. H.M.S. *Saracen* (1840)	2·00	2·50
537	50p. H.M.S. *Sealark* (1849)	2·50	3·50
538	£1 H.M.S. *Penelope* (1889)	3·75	5·00

139 Queen Elizabeth II at Trooping the Colour

1991. 65th Birthday of Queen Elizabeth II and 70th Birthday of Prince Philip. Multicoloured.
539	25p. Type **139**	1·25	1·60
540	25p. Prince Philip in naval uniform	1·25	1·60

1991. Royal Marines Equipment, 1821–1844. As T **131**. Multicoloured.
541	25p. Officer's shako, epaulettes, belt plate and button	1·10	1·60
542	25p. Officer's cap, sword, epaulettes and belt plate	1·10	1·60
543	25p. Drum major's shako and staff	1·10	1·60
544	25p. Sergeant's shako, chevrons, belt plate and canteen	1·10	1·60
545	25p. Drummer's shako and side-drum	1·10	1·60

140 B.B.C. World Service Relay Station

1991. 25th Anniv of B.B.C. Atlantic Relay Station. Multicoloured.
546	15p. Type **140**	90	1·10
547	18p. Transmitters at English Bay	1·00	1·25
548	25p. Satellite receiving station (vert)	1·25	1·40
549	70p. Antenna support tower (vert)	2·50	4·00

141 St. Mary's Church

1991. Christmas. Ascension Churches. Multicoloured.
550	8p. Type **141**	55	55
551	18p. Interior of St. Mary's Church	1·00	1·00
552	25p. Our Lady of Ascension Grotto	1·25	1·25
553	65p. Interior of Our Lady of Ascension Grotto	2·75	5·00

142 Black Durgon ("Blackfish")

1991. Fish. Multicoloured.
554	1p. Type **142**	1·25	60
555	2p. Sergeant major ("Five finger")	1·25	60
556	4p. Resplendent angelfish	1·50	60
557	5p. Derbio ("Silver fish")	1·50	70
558	9p. Spotted scorpionfish ("Gurnard")	1·75	80
559	10p. St. Helena parrotfish ("Blue dad")	1·75	80
560	15p. St. Helena butterflyfish ("Cunning fish")	2·25	1·00
561	18p. Rock hind ("Grouper")	2·25	1·00
562	20p. Spotted moray	2·25	1·25
563	25p. Squirrelfish ("Hardback soldierfish")	2·25	1·25
564	30p. Blue marlin	2·25	1·40
565	50p. Wahoo	3·00	2·00
566	70p. Yellow-finned tuna	3·00	2·75
567	£1 Blue shark	3·25	3·50
568	£2.50 Bottlenose dolphin	7·00	7·00

143 Holland's Crater

1992. 40th Anniv of Queen Elizabeth II's Accession. Multicoloured.
569	9p. Type **143**	30	30
570	15p. Green Mountain	50	50
571	18p. Boatswain Bird Island	60	60
572	25p. Three portraits of Queen Elizabeth	80	80
573	70p. Queen Elizabeth II	2·00	2·00

The portraits shown on the 25p. are repeated from the three lower values of the set.

144 Compass Rose and *Eye of the Wind* (cadet brig)

1992. 500th Anniv of Discovery of America by Columbus and Re-enactment Voyages. Mult.
574	9p. Type **144**	1·25	80
575	18p. Map of re-enactment voyages and *Soren Larsen* (cadet brigantine)	1·75	1·25
576	25p. *Santa Maria, Pinta* and *Nina*	2·25	1·50
577	70p. Columbus and *Santa Maria*	3·75	3·50

145 Control Tower, Wideawake Airfield

1992. 50th Anniv of Wideawake Airfield. Multicoloured.
578	15p. Type **145**	65	65
579	18p. Nose hangar	70	70
580	25p. Site preparation by U.S. Army engineers	90	90
581	70p. Laying fuel pipeline	2·25	2·25

146 Hawker Siddeley Nimrod

1992. Tenth Anniv of Liberation of Falkland Islands. Aircraft. Multicoloured.
582	15p. Type **146**	1·50	1·75
583	18p. Vickers VC-10 landing at Ascension	1·50	1·75
584	25p. Westland Wessex HU Mk 5 helicopter lifting supplies	2·00	1·75
585	65p. Avro Vulcan B.2 over Ascension	3·25	4·75
MS586	116×116 mm. 15p.+3p. Type **146**; 18p.+4p. As No. 583; 25p.+5p. As No. 584; 65p.+13p. As No. 585	4·00	6·00

The premiums on No. **MS586** were for the S.S.A.F.A.

147 Christmas in Great Britain and Ascension

1992. Christmas. Children's Paintings. Multicoloured.
587	8p. Type **147**	80	1·00
588	18p. Santa Claus riding turtle	1·25	1·50
589	25p. Nativity	1·50	1·75
590	65p. Nativity with rabbit	2·75	5·00

148 Male Canary Singing

1993. Yellow Canary. Multicoloured.
591	15p. Type **148**	75	80
592	18p. Adult male and female	85	90
593	25p. Young birds calling for food	95	1·10
594	70p. Adults and young birds on the wing	2·50	4·00

149 Sopwith Snipe

1993. 75th Anniv of Royal Air Force. Multicoloured.
595	20p. Type **149**	2·00	1·75
596	25p. Supermarine Southampton	2·00	1·75
597	30p. Avro Type 652 Anson	2·00	1·90
598	70p. Vickers-Armstrong Wellington	3·25	4·50
MS599	110×77 mm. 25p. Westland Lysander; 25p. Armstrong-Whitworth Meteor (*Gloster Meteor*); 25p. de Havilland D.H.106 Comet; 25p. Hawker Siddeley H.S.801 Nimrod	3·00	4·00

150 Map of South Atlantic Cable

1993. 25th Anniv of South Atlantic Cable Company. Multicoloured.
600	20p. Type **150**	80	90
601	25p. *Sir Eric Sharpe* laying cable	90	1·00
602	30p. Map of Ascension	1·00	1·25
603	70p. *Sir Eric Sharpe* (cable ship) off Ascension	2·25	2·75

151 Lanatana Camara

1993. Local Flowers. Multicoloured.
604	20p. Type **151**	1·50	1·00
605	25p. Moonflower	1·60	1·10
606	30p. Hibiscus	1·60	1·25
607	70p. Frangipani	3·00	3·25

152 Posting Christmas Card to Ascension

1993. Christmas. Multicoloured.
608	12p. Type **152**	45	45
609	20p. Loading mail onto R.A.F. Lockheed TriStar at Brize Norton	95	70
610	25p. TriStar over South Atlantic	1·25	90
611	30p. Unloading mail at Wideawake Airfield	1·40	1·10
612	65p. Receiving card and Georgetown Post Office	1·60	3·25
MS613	161×76 mm. Nos. 608/12	10·00	10·00

153 Ichthyosaurus

1994. Prehistoric Aquatic Reptiles. Multicoloured.

614	12p. Type **153**	70	1·10
615	20p. Metriorhynchus	85	1·25
616	25p. Mosasaurus	90	1·40
617	30p. Elasmosaurus	90	1·50
618	65p. Plesiosaurus	1·75	2·75

1994. "Hong Kong '94" International Stamp Exhibition. Nos. 614/18 optd **HONG KONG '94** and emblem.

619	12p. Type **153**	1·00	1·50
620	20p. Metriorhynchus	1·25	1·60
621	25p. Mosasaurus	1·25	1·90
622	30p. Elasmosaurus	1·40	2·00
623	65p. Plesiosaurus	2·50	4·00

155 Young Green Turtles heading towards Sea

1994. Green Turtles. Multicoloured.

624	20p. Type **155**	2·25	2·25
625	25p. Turtle digging nest	2·25	2·25
626	30p. Turtle leaving sea	2·25	2·25
627	65p. Turtle swimming	3·75	6·00
MS628	116×90 mm. 30p. Turtle leaving sea (different); 30p. Turtle digging nest (different); 30p. Young turtles heading towards sea (different); 30p. Young turtle leaving nest	12·00	12·00

156 Yorkshireman (tug)

1994. Civilian Ships used in Liberation of Falkland Islands, 1982. Multicoloured.

629	20p. Type **156**	2·75	2·25
630	25p. St. Helena I (minesweeper support ship)	2·75	2·25
631	30p. British Esk (tanker)	2·75	2·50
632	65p. Uganda (hospital ship)	5·00	6·00

157 Sooty Tern Chick

1994. Sooty Tern. Multicoloured.

633	20p. Type **157**	90	1·50
634	25p. Juvenile bird	95	1·50
635	30p. Brooding adult	1·10	1·60
636	65p. Adult male performing courting display	1·75	2·75
MS637	77×58 mm. £1 Flock of sooty terns	3·50	5·50

158 Donkey Mare with Foal

1994. Christmas. Donkeys. Multicoloured.

638	12p. Type **158**	1·60	1·40
639	20p. Juvenile	1·90	1·75
640	25p. Foal	1·90	1·75
641	30p. Adult and cattle egrets	1·90	1·90
642	65p. Adult	3·75	5·00

159 Leonurus japonicus

1995. Flowers. Multicoloured.

643	20p. Type **159**	2·75	2·25
644	25p. Catharanthus roseus (horiz)	2·75	2·25
645	30p. Mirabilis jalapa	3·00	2·50
646	65p. Asclepias curassavica (horiz)	3·75	5·50

160 Two Boats and Green Mountain

1995. Late 19th-century Scenes. Each in cinnamon and brown.

647	12p. Type **160**	50	80
648	20p. Island Stewards' Store	70	90
649	25p. Navy headquarters and barracks	90	1·10
650	30p. Police office	1·75	1·75
651	65p. Pierhead	2·00	3·50

161 5.5-inch Coastal Battery

1995. 50th Anniv of End of Second World War. Multicoloured.

652	20p. Type **161**	1·75	2·00
653	25p. Fairey Swordfish aircraft	2·00	2·00
654	30p. H.M.S. Dorsetshire (cruiser)	2·25	3·25
655	65p. H.M.S. Devonshire (cruiser)	3·75	4·50
MS656	75×85 mm. £1 Reverse of 1939–45 War Medal (vert)	2·50	3·25

162 Male and Female Lampides boeticus

1995. Butterflies. Multicoloured.

657	20p. Type **162**	1·50	1·50
658	25p. Vanessa cardui	1·75	1·75
659	30p. Male Hypolimnas misippus	1·75	1·75
660	65p. Danaus chrysippus	2·75	3·50
MS661	114×85 mm. £1 Vanessa atalanta	5·50	6·00

No. **MS**661 includes the "Singapore '95" International Stamp Exhibition logo on the sheet margin.

163 Santa Claus on Boat (Phillip Stephens)

1995. Christmas. Children's Drawings. Multicoloured.

662	12p. Type **163**	1·75	1·25
663	20p. Santa sitting on Wall (Kelly Lemon)	2·00	1·75
664	25p. Santa in Chimney (Mario Anthony)	2·00	1·75
665	30p. Santa riding Dolphin (Verena Benjamin)	2·00	1·75
666	65p. Santa in Sleigh over Ascension (Tom Butler)	3·50	5·00

164 Cypraea lurida oceanica

1996. Molluscs. Multicoloured.

667	12p. Type **164**	2·75	3·00
668	25p. Cypraea spurca sanctae-helenae	3·00	3·25
669	30p. Harpa doris	3·00	3·25
670	65p. Umbraculum umbraculum	3·75	4·00

Nos. 667/70 were printed together, se-tenant, forming a composite design.

165 Queen Elizabeth II and St. Mary's Church

1996. 70th Birthday of Queen Elizabeth II. Multicoloured.

671	20p. Type **165**	55	55
672	25p. The Residency	60	60
673	30p. The Roman Catholic Grotto	70	75
674	65p. The Exiles' Club	1·75	2·00

166 American Army Jeep

1996. "CAPEX '96" International Stamp Exhibition, Toronto. Island Transport. Multicoloured.

675	20p. Type **166**	1·50	1·50
676	25p. Citroen 7.5hp two-seater car, 1924	1·60	1·60
677	30p. Austin ten tourer car, 1930	1·60	1·60
678	65p. Series 1 Land Rover	2·75	3·25

167 Madeiran Storm Petrel

1996. Birds and their Young. Multicoloured.

679	1p. Type **167**	75	1·00
680	2p. Red-billed tropic bird	75	1·00
681	4p. Common mynah	75	1·00
682	5p. House sparrow	75	1·00
683	7p. Common waxbill	1·00	1·25
684	10p. White tern	1·25	1·25
685	12p. Red-necked spurfowl	1·50	1·25
686	15p. Common noddy ("Brown Noddy")	1·50	1·50
687	20p. Yellow canary	1·75	1·50
688	25p. White-capped noddy ("Black Noddy")	1·75	1·50
689	30p. Red-footed booby	1·75	1·50
690	40p. White-tailed tropic bird ("Yellow-billed Tropicbird")	2·00	2·00
691	65p. Brown booby	2·75	3·00
692	£1 Blue-faced booby ("Masked Booby")	3·25	3·50
693	£2 Sooty tern	5·00	6·00
694	£3 Ascension frigate bird	7·00	8·00

See also Nos. 726/7.

168 Pylons

1996. 30th Anniv of B.B.C. Atlantic Relay Station. Multicoloured.

695	20p. Type **168**	75	75
696	25p. Pylons (different)	80	80
697	30p. Pylons and station buildings	90	90
698	65p. Dish aerial, pylon and beach	1·90	1·90

169 Santa Claus on Dish Aerial

1996. Christmas. Santa Claus. Multicoloured.

699	12p. Type **169**	50	50
700	20p. Playing golf	75	75
701	25p. In deck chair	75	75
702	30p. On top of aircraft	85	85
703	65p. On funnel of St. Helena II (mail ship)	1·90	2·25

170 Date Palm

1997. "Hong Kong '97" International Stamp Exhibition. Trees. Multicoloured.

704	20p. Type **170**	75	75
705	25p. Mauritius hemp	85	85
706	30p. Norfolk Island pine	95	95
707	65p. Dwarf palm	2·00	2·50

1997. "HONG KONG '97" International Stamp Exhibition. Sheet 130×90 mm containing design as No. 691. Multicoloured.

MS708	65p. Brown booby	1·50	1·75

171 Red Ensign and Maersk Ascension (tanker)

1997. Flags. Multicoloured.

709	12p. Type **171**	1·00	80
710	25p. R.A.F. flag and Tristar airliner	1·40	1·10
711	30p. N.A.S.A. emblem and Space Shuttle "Atlantis" landing	1·40	1·25
712	65p. White Ensign and H.M.S. Northumberland (frigate)	2·75	2·75

172 Solanum sodomaeum

1997. Wild Herbs. Multicoloured.

713	30p. Type **172**	1·40	1·60
714	30p. Ageratum conyzoides	1·40	1·60
715	30p. Leonurus sibiricus	1·40	1·60
716	30p. Cerastium vulgatum	1·40	1·60
717	30p. Commelina diffusa	1·40	1·60

Nos. 713/17 were printed together, se-tenant, with the backgrounds forming a composite design.

1997. Return of Hong Kong to China. Sheet 130×90 mm containing design as No. 692, but with "1997" imprint date.

MS718	£1 Blue-faced booby	1·50	2·10

173 Queen Elizabeth II

1997. Golden Wedding of Queen Elizabeth and Prince Philip. Multicoloured.

719	20p. Type **173**	1·50	2·00
720	20p. Prince Philip on horseback	1·50	2·00
721	25p. Queen Elizabeth with polo pony	1·50	2·00
722	25p. Prince Philip in Montserrat	1·50	2·00
723	30p. Queen Elizabeth and Prince Philip	1·50	2·00
724	30p. Prince William and Prince Harry on horseback	1·50	2·00
MS725	110×70 mm. $1.50, Queen Elizabeth and Prince Philip in landau (horiz)	3·50	3·50

Nos. 719/20, 721/2 and 723/4 respectively were printed together, se-tenant, with the backgrounds forming composite designs.

1997. Birds and their Young. As Nos. 683 and 687, but smaller, size 20×24 mm. Multicoloured.

726	15p. Common waxbill	2·00	2·25
727	35p. Yellow canary	2·00	2·25

174 Black Marlin

1997. Gamefish. Multicoloured.

728	12p. Type **174**	75	75
729	20p. Atlantic sailfish	1·00	1·00
730	25p. Swordfish	1·10	1·10
731	30p. Wahoo	1·25	1·25
732	£1 Yellowfin tuna	3·00	4·00

175 Interior of St.
Mary's Church

1997. Christmas. Multicoloured.

733	15p. Type **175**	1·00	1·00
734	35p. Falklands memorial window showing Virgin and child	1·60	1·60
735	40p. Falklands memorial window showing Archangel	1·75	1·90
736	50p. Pair of stained glass windows	2·00	2·25

176 *Cactoblastis cactorum* (caterpillar and moth)

1998. Biological Control using Insects. Multicoloured.

737	15p. Type **176**	2·00	1·75
738	35p. *Teleonemia scrupulosa* (lace-bug)	2·50	2·25
739	40p. *Neltumius arizonensis* (beetle)	2·50	2·75
740	50p. *Algarobius prosopis* (beetle)	2·75	3·25

177 Diana, Princess of Wales, 1985

1998. Diana, Princess of Wales Commemoration. Sheet 145×70 mm, containing T 177 and similar vert designs. Multicoloured.

MS741	35p. Type **177**; 35p. Wearing yellow blouse, 1992; 35p. Wearing grey jacket, 1984; 35p. Carrying bouquets (sold at £1.40+20p. charity premium)	2·25	3·75

178 Fairey Fawn

1998. 80th Anniv of Royal Air Force. Multicoloured.

742	15p. Type **178**	1·50	1·25
743	35p. Vickers Vernon	2·25	2·25
744	40p. Supermarine Spitfire F.22	2·25	2·50
745	50p. Bristol Britannia C.2	2·50	3·00
MS746	110×77 mm. 50p. Blackburn Kangaroo; 50p. S.E.5a; 50p. Curtiss Kittyhawk III; 50p. Boeing Fortress II	4·75	4·75

179 Barn Swallow

1998. Migratory Birds. Multicoloured.

747	15p. Type **179**	1·25	1·25
748	25p. House martin	1·50	1·50
749	35p. Cattle egret	1·75	1·75
750	40p. Eurasian swift ("Swift")	1·90	1·90
751	50p. Allen's gallinule	2·00	2·00

180 Cricket

1998. Sporting Activities. Multicoloured.

752	15p. Type **180**	2·75	1·75
753	35p. Golf	3·50	2·25
754	40p. Football	2·00	2·50
755	50p. Shooting	2·00	2·50

181 Children in Nativity Play

1998. Christmas. Multicoloured.

756	15p. Type **181**	1·25	1·25
757	35p. Santa Claus arriving on Ascension	1·75	1·75
758	40p. Santa Claus on carnival float	1·75	1·75
759	50p. Carol singers	1·75	1·75

182 Curtiss C-46 Commando

1999. Aircraft. Multicoloured.

760	15p. Type **182**	1·75	1·75
761	35p. Douglas C-47 Dakota	2·25	2·25
762	40p. Douglas C-54 Skymaster	2·25	2·25
763	50p. Consolidated Liberator Mk. V	2·25	2·50
MS764	120×85 mm. $1.50, Consolidated Liberator LB-30	11·00	11·00

No. **MS**764 also commemorates the 125th birth anniv of Sir Winston Churchill.

183 *Glengorm Castle* (mail ship), 1929

1999. "Australia '99" World Stamp Exhibition, Melbourne. Ships. Multicoloured.

765	15p. Type **183**	1·75	1·75
766	35p. *Gloucester Castle* (mail ship), 1930	2·25	2·25
767	40p. *Durham Castle* (mail ship), 1930	2·25	2·25
768	50p. *Garth Castle* (mail ship), 1930	2·25	2·50
MS769	121×82 mm. £1 H.M.S. *Endeavour* (Cook)	3·00	4·00

184 Pair of White Terns ("Fairy Terns")

1999. Endangered Species. White Tern ("Fairy Tern"). Multicoloured.

770	10p. Type **184**	45	55
771	10p. On branch	45	55
772	10p. Adult and fledgeling	45	55
773	10p. In flight	45	55

185 Prince Edward and Miss Sophie Rhys-Jones

1999. Royal Wedding. Multicoloured.

774	50p. Type **185**	1·25	1·25
775	£1 Engagement photograph	2·25	2·75

186 Command and Service Modules

1999. 30th Anniv of First Manned Landing on Moon. Multicoloured.

776	15p. Type **186**	75	1·10
777	35p. Moon from "Apollo 11"	1·25	1·60
778	40p. Devil's Ashpit Tracking Station and command module	1·25	1·60
779	50p. Lunar module leaving Moon	1·25	1·60
MS780	90×80 mm. $1.50, Earth as seen from Moon (circular, 40 mm diam)	3·75	5·00

187 King George VI, Queen Elizabeth and Prime Minister Winston Churchill, 1940

1999. "Queen Elizabeth the Queen Mother's Century". Multicoloured.

781	15p. Type **187**	1·25	1·25
782	35p. With Prince Charles at Coronation, 1953	1·75	1·75
783	40p. On her 88th Birthday, 1988	1·75	1·75
784	50p. With Guards' drummers, 1988	1·75	1·75
MS785	145×70 mm. £1.50, Lady Elizabeth Bowes-Lyon, and *Titanic* (liner) (black)	3·75	5·00

188 Babies with Toys

1999. Christmas. Multicoloured.

786	15p. Type **188**	1·50	1·50
787	35p. Children dressed as clowns	2·00	2·00
788	40p. Getting ready for bed	2·00	2·00
789	50p. Children dressed as pirates	2·00	2·00

189 *Anglia* (cable ship), 1900

1999. Centenary of Cable & Wireless Communications plc on Ascension.

790	**189**	15p. black, brown and bistre	1·75	1·75
791	-	35p. black, brown and bistre	2·25	2·25
792	-	40p. multicoloured	2·25	2·25
793	-	50p. black, brown and bistre	2·50	2·50
MS794		105×90 mm. £1.50, multicoloured	3·75	4·00

DESIGNS: 35p. *Cambria* (cable ship), 1910; 40p. Cable network map; 50p. *Colonia* (cable ship), 1910; £1.50, *Seine* (cable ship), 1899.

190 Baby Turtles

2000. Turtle Project on Ascension. Multicoloured.

795	15p. Type **190**	1·25	1·25
796	35p. Turtle on beach	1·75	1·75
797	40p. Turtle with tracking device	1·75	1·75
798	50p. Turtle heading for sea	1·75	1·75
MS799	197×132 mm. 25p. Head of turtle; 25p. Type **190**; 25p. Turtle on beach; 25p. Turtle entering sea (each 40×26 mm)	5·00	5·50

2000. "The Stamp Show 2000" International Stamp Exhibition, London. As No. MS799, but with "The Stamp Show 2000" added to the bottom right corner of the margin.

MS800	197×132 mm. 25p. Head of turtle; 25p. Type **190**; 25p. Turtle on beach; 25p. Turtle entering sea (each 40×26 mm)	2·75	3·25

191 Prince William as Toddler, 1983

2000. 18th Birthday of Prince William. Multicoloured.

801	15p. Type **191**	1·00	1·00
802	35p. Prince William in 1994	1·50	1·50
803	40p. Skiing at Klosters, Switzerland (horiz)	1·50	1·50
804	50p. Prince William in 1997 (horiz)	1·50	1·50
MS805	175×95 mm. 10p. As baby with toy mouse (horiz) and Nos. 801/4	7·00	7·00

192 Royal Marine and Early Fort, 1815

2000. Forts. Multicoloured.

806	15p. Type **192**	1·75	1·75
807	35p. Army officer and Fort Thornton, 1817	2·50	2·50
808	40p. Soldier and Fort Hayes, 1860	2·50	2·50
809	50p. Naval lieutenant and Fort Bedford, 1940	2·75	2·75

193 Ships and Dockside Crane (*I saw Three Ships*)

2000. Christmas. Carols. Multicoloured.

810	15p. Type **193**	1·50	1·20
811	25p. Choir and musicians on beach (*Silent Night*)	1·75	1·25
812	40p. Donkeys and church (*Away in a Manger*)	2·50	2·00
813	90p. Carol singers outside church (*Hark the Herald Angels Sing*)	4·50	7·00

194 Green Turtle

2001. "Hong Kong 2001" Stamp Exhibition. Sheet 150×90 mm, containing T 194. Multicoloured.

MS814	25p. Type **194**; 40p. Loggerhead turtle	3·75	4·50

195 Captain William Dampier

2001. Centenary of Wreck of the Roebuck. Multicoloured.

815	15p. Type **195**	2·25	2·25
816	35p. Construction drawing (horiz)	2·75	2·75
817	40p. Cave dwelling at Dampier's Drip (horiz)	2·75	2·75
818	50p. Map of Ascension	3·50	3·50

196 Alfonso de Albuquerque

2001. 500th Anniv of the Discovery of Ascension Island. Multicoloured.

819	15p. Type **196**	2·25	2·25
820	35p. Portuguese caravel	3·25	3·25
821	40p. Cantino map	3·50	3·50
822	50p. Rear Admiral Sir George Cockburn	3·50	3·50

197 Great Britain 1d. Stamp used on Ascension, 1855

2001. Death Centenary of Queen Victoria. Multicoloured.

823	15p. Type **197**	1·25	1·25
824	25p. Navy church parade, 1901 (horiz)	1·50	1·50
825	35p. H.M.S. *Phoebe* (cruiser) (horiz)	2·00	2·00
826	40p. The Red Lion, 1863 (horiz)	2·00	2·00
827	50p. "Queen Victoria"	2·00	2·00
828	65p. Sir Joseph Hooker (botanist)	2·00	2·75

MS829 105×80 mm. £1.50, Queen Victoria's coffin on the steps of St. George's Chapel, Windsor (horiz) — 5·50 — 6·50

198 Islander Hostel

2001. "BELGICA 2001" International Stamp Exhibition, Brussels. Tourism. Multicoloured.

830	35p. Type **198**	2·50	3·00
831	35p. The Residency	2·50	3·00
832	40p. The Red Lion	2·50	3·00
833	40p. Turtle Ponds	2·50	3·00

199 Female Ascension Frigate Bird

2001. Birdlife World Bird Festival (1st series). Ascension Frigate Birds. Multicoloured.

834	15p. Type **199**	1·25	1·25
835	35p. Fledgeling	1·75	1·75
836	40p. Male bird in flight (horiz)	1·75	1·75
837	50p. Male bird with pouch inflated (horiz)	1·75	1·75

MS838 175×80 mm. 10p. Male and female birds on rock (horiz) and Nos. 834/7 — 6·50 — 7·50

See also Nos. 889/94 and 921/**MS**926.

200 Princess Elizabeth and Dog

2002. Golden Jubilee.

839	**200**	15p. agate, mauve and gold	1·50	1·50
840	-	35p. multicoloured	2·00	2·00
841	-	40p. multicoloured	2·00	2·00
842	-	50p. multicoloured	2·00	2·00

MS843 – 162×95 mm. Nos. 839/42 and 60p. multicoloured — 7·50 — 8·50

DESIGNS—HORIZ: 35p. Queen Elizabeth wearing tiara, 1978; 40p. Princess Elizabeth, 1946; 50p. Queen Elizabeth visiting Henley-on-Thames, 1998. VERT: (38×51 mm)—50p. Queen Elizabeth after Annigoni.

201 Royal Marines landing at English Bay

2002. 20th Anniv of Liberation of the Falkland Islands. Multicoloured.

844	15p. Type **201**	1·25	1·25
845	35p. Weapons testing	1·60	1·60
846	40p. H.M.S. *Hermes* (aircraft carrier)	1·60	1·60
847	50p. R.A.F. Vulcan at Wideawake Airfield	1·60	1·60

202 Duchess of York at Harrow Hospital, 1931

2002. Queen Elizabeth the Queen Mother Commemoration.

848	**202**	35p. black, gold and purple	1·40	1·40
849	-	40p. multicoloured	1·40	1·40

MS850 – 145×70 mm. 50p. brown and gold; £1 multicoloured — 6·50 — 7·50

DESIGNS: 40p. Queen Mother on her birthday, 1997; 50p. Duchess of York, 1925; £1 Queen Mother, Scrabster, 1992.

203 Travellers Palm and Vinca

2002. Island Views. Multicoloured.

851	10p. Type **203**	75	1·00
852	15p. Broken Tooth (volcanic crater) and Mexican poppy	1·00	75
853	20p. St. Mary's Church and Ascension lily	1·00	75
854	25p. Boatswain Bird Island and goatweed	1·40	1·25
855	30p. Cannon and Mauritius hemp	1·40	1·40
856	35p. The Guest House and frangipani	1·50	1·25
857	40p. Wideawake tern and Ascension spurge	2·00	2·00
858	50p. The Pier Head and lovechaste	2·00	2·25
859	65p. Sisters' Peak and yellowboy	2·25	2·75
860	90p. Two Boats School and Persian lilac	3·00	3·25
861	£2 Green turtle and wild currant	6·00	7·00
862	£5 Wideawake Airfield and coral tree	13·00	14·00

204 *Ecce Ancilla Dominii* (Dante Rossetti)

2002. Christmas. Religious Paintings. Multicoloured.

863	15p. Type **204**	70	70
864	25p. *The Holy Family and Shepherd* (Titian) (horiz)	95	95
865	35p. *Christ carrying the Cross* (A. Bergognone)	1·25	1·25
866	75p. Sketch for *The Ascension* (Benjamin West)	2·50	2·50

205 Ariane 4 Rocket on Gantry

2003. Ariane Downrange Station. Multicoloured.

867	35p. Type **205**	1·40	1·40
868	40p. Map of Ariane Downrange stations (horiz)	1·50	1·50
869	65p. Automated Transfer Vehicle (ATV) in Space (horiz)	2·50	2·50
870	90p. Launch of Ariane 5	3·75	4·25

MS871 170×88 mm. Nos. 867/70 — 8·25 — 8·25

206 Coronation Coach in Procession

2003. 50th Anniv of Coronation. Multicoloured.

872	40p. Type **206**	1·50	1·00
873	£1 Newly crowned Queen with bishops and peers	3·25	3·75

MS874 95×115 mm. As Nos. 872/3 — 4·75 — 4·75

Nos. 872/3 have red frame; stamps from **MS**874 have no frame and country name in mauve panel.

207 Queen Elizabeth II

2003

875	**207**	£3 black, green and myrtle	6·50	7·00

208 Prince William at Tidworth Polo Club and on Skiing Holiday, 2002

2003. 21st Birthday of Prince William of Wales. Multicoloured.

876	75p. Type **208**	2·75	2·75
877	75p. On Raleigh International Expedition, 2000 and at Queen Mother's 101st Birthday, 2001	2·75	2·75

209 Bleriot XI

2003. Centenary of Powered Flight. Multicoloured.

878	15p. Type **209**	85	85
879	20p. Vickers VC-10	90	90
880	35p. BAe Harrier FRS Mk1	1·60	1·60
881	40p. Westland Sea King HAS Mk. 4 helicopter	1·75	1·75
882	50p. Rockwell Space Shuttle	1·75	1·75
883	90p. General Dynamics F-16 Fighting Falcon	3·25	3·50

MS884 115×65 mm. £1.50 Fairey Swordfish Mk II. — 6·50 — 7·00

210 Casting Vote into Ballot Box

2003. Christmas. First Anniv of Democracy on Ascension. Multicoloured.

885	15p. Type **210**	75	55
886	25p. Island Council session	90	65
887	40p. Students ("HIGHER EDUCATION")	1·40	1·10
888	£1 Government Headquarters	2·75	3·50

211 Adult with Fledgling

2004. Birdlife International (2nd series). Masked Booby. Multicoloured.

889	15p. Type **211**	85	75
890	35p. Pair (vert)	1·40	1·00
891	40p. In flight (vert)	1·40	1·25
892	50p. Adult calling	1·50	1·50
893	90p. Masked booby	3·00	3·50

MS894 175×80 mm. Nos. 889/93 — 7·00 — 7·50

212 *Bougainvillea glabra* (orange)

2004. Bicentenary of the Royal Horticultural Society. Multicoloured.

895	15p. Type **212**	75	75
896	35p. *Bougainvillea glabra* (pink)	1·40	1·00
897	40p. *Bougainvillea glabra* (white)	1·50	1·10
898	90p. *Bougainvillea spectabilis* (red)	2·75	3·50

MS899 105×80 mm. £1.50 *Pteris adscensionis* — 6·00 — 6·50

213 Blue Marlin

2004. Sport Fishing (1st series). Multicoloured.

900	15p. Type **213**	75	75
901	35p. Swordfish	1·40	1·00
902	40p. Sailfish	1·50	1·10
903	90p. White marlin	2·75	3·50

MS904 61×51 mm. £1.50 Blue marlin — 5·00 — 6·00

See also Nos. 927/**MS**931.

214 Moon over Hummock Point

2004. Lunar Eclipse. Multicoloured.

905	15p. Type **214**	75	75
906	25p. Yellow moon over Sisters Peak (North side)	1·25	1·00
907	35p. Orange moon over Daly's Craggs	1·50	1·00
908	£1.25 Red moon and birds over Mars Bay	3·75	4·50

MS909 130×55 mm. £1.25 As No. 908 — 4·00 — 5·00

215 MV *Ascension*

2004. Merchant Ships. Multicoloured.

910	15p. Type **215**	1·25	1·00
911	35p. *St. Helena* (mail ship)	2·00	1·25
912	40p. *Caronia* (mail ship)	2·00	1·50
913	£1.25 MV *Maersk Gannet*	6·00	7·50

216 British Carronade on Sliding Carriage

2005. Bicentenary of Battle of Trafalgar (1st issue). Multicoloured.

914	15p. Type **216**	75	65
915	25p. Royal Marine drummer boy, 1805 (vert)	1·25	90
916	35p. HMS *Britannia* (vert)	1·40	1·25
917	40p. Admiral Nelson	1·50	1·50
918	50p. HMS *Neptune* and *Santissima Trinidad* (vert)	1·60	1·60
919	90p. HMS *Victory*	2·75	4·00

MS920 120×80 mm. £1 Lord Nelson (vert); £1 *Neptune* (vert) — 6·50 — 7·50

No. 919 contains traces of powdered wood from HMS *Victory*.

See also Nos. 937/9.

217 White Tern ("Fairy Tern")

2005. Birdlife International (3rd series). "The Sea Birds Return". Multicoloured.

921	15p. Type **217**	55	55
922	35p. White-tailed tropic bird	1·10	1·10
923	40p. Brown booby	1·25	1·40
924	50p. Common noddy ("Brown Noddy")	1·40	1·40
925	£1.25 Red-billed tropic bird	3·25	4·25
MS926	170×80 mm. Nos. 921/5	8·00	8·50

218 Yellowfin Tuna

2005. Sport Fishing (2nd series). Tuna. Multicoloured.

927	35p. Type **218**	1·25	1·25
928	40p. Skipjack tuna	1·40	1·40
929	50p. Albacore tuna	1·50	1·50
930	£1.25 Bigeye tuna	3·50	4·00
MS931	61×51 mm. £1.50 Yellowfin tuna hunting herrings	4·50	5·50

219 Pope John Paul II

2005. Pope John Paul II Commemoration.

932	**219**	40p. multicoloured	1·75	1·75

220 The Little Fir Tree

2005. Christmas. Birth Bicentenary of Hans Christian Andersen (writer). Multicoloured.

933	15p. Type **220**	1·00	1·00
934	25p. The Mail-Coach Passengers	1·25	1·25
935	35p. The Little Match Girl	1·50	1·50
936	£1.25 The Snow Man	4·00	5·00

221 HMS Victory

2005. Bicentenary of the Battle of Trafalgar (2nd issue). Multicoloured.

937	40p. Type **221**	1·50	1·40
938	65p. Ships engaged in battle (horiz)	2·50	3·00
939	90p. Admiral Lord Nelson	3·50	4·00

222 Black Jack

2006. Sport Fishing (3rd series). Jacks. Multicoloured.

940	20p. Type **222**	1·00	1·00
941	35p. Almaco jack	1·60	1·40
942	50p. Horse-eye jack	2·00	2·00
943	£1 Rainbow runner	3·50	4·25
MS944	61×50 mm. £1.50 Longfin crevalle jack	4·50	5·50

223 Princess Elizabeth

2006. 80th Birthday of Queen Elizabeth II. Multicoloured.

945	20p. Type **223**	80	80
946	40p. Queen Elizabeth II, c. 1952	1·00	1·25
947	50p. Queen Elizabeth II	1·75	1·90
948	£1.30 Wearing Garter robes	4·25	8·00
MS949	144×75 mm. £1 Queen, c. 1952; £1 Queen in 1960s	6·00	7·00

224 HMS Beagle (175th anniv of Darwin's voyage)

2006. Exploration and Innovation. Anniversaries. Multicoloured.

950	20p. Type **224**	1·25	1·25
951	20p. Charles Darwin (originator of theory of evolution)	1·25	1·25
952	35p. Great Britain (steam/sail)	2·00	2·00
953	35p. Isambard Kingdom Brunel (engineer, birth bicentenary)	2·00	2·00
954	40p. Nina (Columbus)	2·25	2·25
955	40p. Christopher Columbus (discoverer of New World, 500th death anniv)	2·25	2·25
956	50p. World map with lines of magnetic variation	2·25	2·25
957	50p. Edmund Halley (astronomer, 350th birth anniv) and Halley's comet	2·25	2·25

Nos. 950/1, 952/3, 954/5 and 956/7 were each printed together, se-tenant, forming a composite background design.

225 Long Beach ("Greetings from Ascension")

2006. Christmas. Views of Ascension Island. Multicoloured.

958	15p. Type **225**	85	85
959	25p. Coastal rocks at sunset ("Merry Christmas")	1·25	1·25
960	35p. Dewpond ("Seasons Greetings")	1·60	1·25
961	£1.25 Coast and Boatswain Bird Island ("Happy New Year")	4·25	5·00

226 Resplendent Angelfish

2007. Endangered Species. Resplendent Angelfish (Centropyge resplendens). Multicoloured.

962	35p. Type **226**	1·40	1·10
963	40p. Shoal of resplendent angelfish	1·60	1·60
964	50p. Three angelfish near red coral and rocks	1·60	1·60
965	£1.25 Large male angelfish and three smaller females	4·00	4·50

227 Handley Page Victor K Mk2 Tanker

2007. 25th Anniv of the Liberation of the Falkland Islands. Multicoloured.

966	35p. Type **227**	1·50	1·10
967	40p. HMS Dumbarton Castle (offshore patrol vessel) and Chinook helicopter	1·90	1·90
968	50p. HMS Fearless with helicopter and landing craft	1·90	1·90
969	£1.25 Vulcan XM607 taking off	4·50	5·00

MS970 Two sheets, each 183×89 mm. (a) As Type **227**; 40p. Vickers VC10 Transport; 50p. Nimrod MR2 Maritime Reconnaissance; As No. 969. (b) 35p. RFA Tidespring refuelling HMS Antrim; As No. 967; As No. 968; £1.25 Atlantic Conveyor and Harrier fighter 9·00 10·00

Stamps from the two miniature sheets **MS**970a/b do not have white borders.
The 50p. stamp from **MS**970(a) has an incorrect spelling "Reconaissance".

228 Ascension Scouts forming Fleur-de-Lis Emblem

2007. Centenary of Scouting. Multicoloured.

971	35p. Type **228**	1·40	1·10
972	40p. Scouts rescuing stranded turtle	1·60	1·60
973	50p. Ascension Scout Troop sitting on gun from HMS Hood	1·60	1·60
974	£1.25 Scouts on top of their Land Rover near Butt Crater	4·00	5·00

229 Mother Teresa and Princess Diana, Rome, 1992

2007. Tenth Death Anniv of Diana, Princess of Wales.

975	**229**	50p. multicoloured	1·60	1·60

230 Engagement Photograph, July 1947

2007. Diamond Wedding of Queen Elizabeth II and Duke of Edinburgh. Multicoloured.

976	35p. Type **230**	2·00	2·50
977	90p. Wedding programme	4·00	4·50
978	£1.25 Queen and Duke of Edinburgh at St. Paul's Cathedral for 80th birthday Thanksgiving Service	4·25	4·75

231 BOU Base Camp near Mars Bay

2007. 50th Anniv of the British Ornithologists' Union Centenary Expedition (1957–9). Multicoloured.

979	15p. Type **231**	1·00	1·25
980	15p. Peter Mundy's drawing of extinct flightless rail, 1656	1·00	1·25
981	25p. Team member recording sooty tern ('Wideawake')	1·25	1·50
982	25p. Sooty terns ('Wideawake')	1·25	1·50
983	40p. BOU outpost, Boatswainbird Island	4·50	5·00
984	40p. Masked booby	2·25	2·50
985	50p. Team members with expedition dinghy Overdraft	2·25	2·50
986	50p. Red-footed booby	2·25	2·50

232 Lampides boeticus (long-tailed blue butterfly)

2008. Fauna and their Eggs. Multicoloured.

987	15p. Type **232**	45	50
988	20p. Cheilomenes lunata (ladybird)	60	65
989	25p. Panulirus echinatus (spiny lobster)	75	80
990	30p. Schistocerca gregaria (desert locust)	90	85
991	35p. Chelonia mydas (green turtle)	1·10	1·20
992	40p. Gecarcinus lagostoma (landcrab)	1·20	1·30
993	50p. Sula sula (red-footed booby)	1·50	1·60
994	65p. Hemdactylus mercatorius (coconut-palm gecko)	1·90	2·00
995	90p. Estrilda astrild (common waxbill)	2·75	3·00
996	£1 Stegastes lubbocki (yellowtail damselfish)	3·00	3·25
997	£2.50 Oceanodroma castro (Madeiran storm-petrel)	7·50	7·75
998	£5 Francolinus afer (red-necked francolin)	15·00	15·00

233 Bluntnose Sixgill Shark

2008. Sharks. Multicoloured.

999	35p. Type **233**	1·75	2·25
1000	40p. Scalloped hammerhead	1·75	2·25
1001	50p. Shortfin mako	1·75	2·25
1002	£1.25 Whale shark	3·75	2·25
MS1003	70×45 mm. £1.50 Bigeye thresher	5·00	5·50

234 Bell X-1E NACA X-Plane, 1958

2008. 50th Anniv of NASA. Multicoloured.

1004	35p. Type **234**	1·10	1·20
1005	35p. Apollo 11 Moon Walk, 1969	1·10	1·20
1006	40p. Apollo 17 Lunar Roving Vehicle, 1972	1·10	1·20
1007	50p. STS1 Space Shuttle Columbia, 1981	1·50	1·60
1008	65p. The Hubble Space Telescope, 1990	1·90	1·80
1009	90p. International Space Station, 2006	2·75	3·00

235 Sopwith 7F.1 Snipe

2008. 90th Anniv of the Royal Air Force. Multicoloured.

1010	15p. Type **235**	1·10	90
1011	35p. Vickers Wellington Mk 1C	1·90	1·75
1012	40p. Supermarine Spitfire Mk IX	2·00	2·00
1013	50p. Gloster Meteor F.IV	2·00	2·00
1014	65p. BAe Hawk	2·50	2·75
1015	90p. Typhoon F2 (Eurofighter)	3·25	3·50

236 Valerius Cordus (1515–44) and Cordia sebestena

2008. Botanists and Plants named after them. Multicoloured.

1016	35p. Type **236**	1·50	1·25
1017	40p. Nehemiah Grew (1641–1712) and Grewia occidentalis	1·75	1·75
1018	50p. Charles Plumier (1646–1704) and Plumeria rubra	1·75	1·75
1019	£2 Carl Peter Thunberg (1743–1828) and Thunbergia grandiflora	6·50	7·00

237 Father Christmas

2008. Christmas. Designs showing illustrations of Father Christmas from Father Christmas and Father Christmas Goes on Holiday by Raymond Briggs superimposed over Ascension Island scenes. Multicoloured.

1020	15p. Type **237**	70	70
1021	25p. Father Christmas in reindeer-drawn sleigh above surf of western coast	1·00	1·00
1022	50p. Father Christmas lying on inflatable	1·75	1·75
1023	£2 Father Christmas and his laden sleigh above Green Mountain and Two Boats Village	6·50	7·00

238 King Henry III (1216–72) and the Tower of London

2008. Britain's Longest Reigning Monarchs. Multicoloured.

1024	35p. Type **238**	1·90	1·60
1025	40p. King James VI (1567–1625) and Stirling Castle	2·00	2·00
1026	50p. King George III (1760–1820) and Windsor Castle	2·25	2·25
1027	65p. Queen Victoria (1837–1901) and Osborne House	2·50	2·75
1028	£1.25 Queen Elizabeth II (from 1952) and Buckingham Palace	4·75	5·50

239 Bottlenose Dolphin (*Tursiops truncatus*)

2009. Whales and Dolphins. Multicoloured.

1029	35p. Type **239**	1·10	1·20
1030	40p. Pantropical spotted dolphin (*Stenella attenuata*)	1·20	1·30
1031	50p. Sperm whale (*Physeter macrocephalus*) and squid (prey)	1·50	1·60
1032	£1.25 Gervais' beaked whale (*Mesoplodon europeus*)	3·75	4·00
MS1033	111×65 mm. £2 Humpback whale (*Megaptera novaeangliae*)	6·00	6·25

240 Flt. SLt. Rex Warneford

2009. Centenary of Naval Aviation. Victoria Cross of the Fleet Air Arm. Multicoloured.

1034	35p. Type **240**	1·75	1·75
1035	35p. Moraine-Saulnier L destroys Zeppelin LZ37, Belgium, 6/7 June 1915	1·75	1·75
1036	35p. Sqn. Cdr. Richard Bell Davies	1·75	1·75
1037	35p. Nieuport 10 takes off pursued by enemy soldiers, Bulgaria, 19 November 1915	1·75	1·75
1038	40p. Lt. Cdr. (A) Eugene Esmonde	1·75	1·75
1039	40p. Fairey Swordfish aircraft attacking German heavy cruisers, 12 February 1942	1·75	1·75
1040	50p. Lt. Robert Hampton Gray	1·75	1·75
1041	50p. Corsair bombing Japanese warship	1·75	1·75

241 Blue Water Lily (*Nymphaea capensis*)

2009. Introduced Plant Species. Multicoloured.

1042	35p. Type **241**	1·10	1·20
1043	35p. Raspberry (*Rubus rosifolius*)	1·10	1·20
1044	40p. Prickly pear (*Optunia vulgaris*)	1·20	1·30
1045	50p. Ascension lily (*Hippeastrum reginae*)	1·50	1·60
1046	65p. Yellowboy (*Tecoma stans*)	1·90	2·00
1047	90p. Portraits of young and old Joseph Dalton Hooker (botanist)	2·75	3·00

242 Dr. Archie Carr with Early Turtle Tracking Equipment

2009. Turtle Research and Conservation and Birth Centenary of Dr. Archie Carr (sea turtle biologist). T **242** and similar horiz designs, each showing either head of turtle at left (Nos. 1048, 1050, 1052, 1054) or outline map of Ascension Island at right (others). Multicoloured.

1048	15p. Type **242**	80	1·00
1049	15p. Dr. Archie Carr attaching tracking floats to turtle	80	2·00
1050	35p. Female laying eggs	1·40	1·60
1051	35p. Turtle hatchlings	1·40	1·60
1052	40p. Beach raking to remove turtle tracks after counting	1·40	1·75
1053	40p. Population monitoring	1·40	1·75
1054	65p. Rescuer with turtle	2·00	2·50
1055	65p. Two rescuers with turtle	2·00	2·50

Nos. 1048/9, 1050/1, 1052/3 and 1054/5 were each printed together, *se-tenant*, each pair forming a composite design.

243 Charles Darwin and Woodpecker Finch

2009. Birth Bicentenary of Charles Darwin (naturalist and evolutionary theorist). Each showing a different portrait. Multicoloured.

1056	35p. Type **243**	1·75	1·50
1057	40p. Charles Darwin (in profile) and marine iguanas	1·75	1·75
1058	50p. Charles Darwin and Galapagos tortoise	1·75	1·75
1059	£2 Charles Darwin as old man, Galapagos penguins and *Beagle*	6·50	7·00

244 Juvenile White-tailed Tropic Bird

2009. White-tailed Tropic Bird (*Phaethon lepturus*). Multicoloured.

1060	35p. Type **244**	1·75	2·00
1061	40p. Adult feeding juvenile	1·75	2·00
1062	50p. Juvenile in flight	1·75	2·00
1063	£1.25 Adult in flight	3·50	4·00

245 Hardback Soldier Fish (*Holocentrus adscensionis*)

2010. Reef Fish. Multicoloured.

1064	35p. Type **245**	1·60	1·60
1065	40p. Grouper (*Epinephelus adscensionis*)	1·75	1·75
1066	50p. Five fingers (*Abudefduf saxatilis*)	1·75	1·75
1067	£1.25 Rock bullseye (*Heteropriacanthus cruentatus*)	3·50	4·00
MS1068	84×59 mm. £2 Softback soldier fish (*Myripristis jacobus*)	6·50	7·00

246 Guides

2010. Centenary of Girl Guiding. Multicoloured.

1069	40p. Type **246**	1·60	1·60
1070	50p. Guides and large fish catch	1·75	1·75
1071	90p. Guide leaders and 'Celebrating 100 Years of Guiding' celebration cake	3·00	3·25
1072	£1.25 Guide abseiling	3·75	4·00
MS1073	160×80 mm. £1×3 Olave, Lady Baden-Powell (Chief Guide 1918–77); Agnes Baden-Powell (founder); Lord Baden-Powell (founder of Scout Movement) (all vert)	9·00	9·00

247 Supermarine Spitfire R6803, 65 Squadron

2010. London 2010 Festival of Stamps. 70th Anniv of the Battle of Britain. Multicoloured.

1074	50p. Type **247**	1·75	2·00
1075	50p. Hawker Hurricane V7383, 615 Squadron	1·75	2·00
1076	50p. Supermarine Spitfire X4036, 234 Squadron	1·75	2·00
1077	50p. Hawker Hurricane R4175, 303 Squadron	1·75	2·00
1078	50p. Supermarine Spitfire R6885, 41 Squadron	1·75	2·00
1079	50p. Hawker Hurricane V6684, 303 Squadron	1·75	2·00
1080	50p. Supermarine Spitfire K9998, 603 Squadron	1·75	2·00
1081	50p. Hawker Hurricane R4118, 605 Squadron	1·75	2·00

Nos. 1080/1 were printed together, *se-tenant*, forming composite background design.

248 Juvenile Yellow Canary

2010. Yellow Canary (*Serinus flaviventris*). Multicoloured.

1082	15p. Type **248**	70	70
1083	35p. Adult male (perched)	1·25	1·25
1084	60p. Adult female	2·00	2·00
1085	90p. Adult male (on ground)	2·75	2·75

249 Christmas Lunch

2010. Christmas on Ascension Island. Multicoloured.

1086	15p. Type **249**	45	50
1087	40p. Santa riding in decorated pick-up truck in Christmas parade	1·10	1·20
1088	50p. Three children at Christingle service	1·50	1·60
1089	£1.25 Children's nativity play	3·50	3·75

250 HMS Erebus and Terror approaching Ascension

2011. Parsley Fern (*Anogramma ascensionis*). Multicoloured.

1090	15p. Type **250**	15	15
1091	25p. Parsley fern	80	80
1092	35p. Parsley fern in situ	1·10	1·10
1093	40p. Parsley fern seedlings	1·25	1·25
1094	£1 Parsley fern cultivation, Kew Gardens	3·00	3·00

251 Queen Elizabeth II, Westminster Abbey, 12 April 2001

2011. Queen Elizabeth II and Prince Philip 'A Lifetime of Service'. Multicoloured.

1095	15p. Type **251**	45	45
1096	25p. Queen Elizabeth and Prince Philip, 1953	80	80
1097	35p. Queen Elizabeth and Prince Philip, Buckingham Palace, 1999	1·10	1·10
1098	40p. Queen Elizabeth and Prince Philip, The Mall, London, 24 February 2009	1·25	1·25
1099	60p. Queen Elizabeth and Prince Philip in Balmoral Castle grounds, September 1960	1·75	1·75
1100	£1.25 Duke of Edinburgh, Westminster Abbey, 12 April 2001	3·75	3·75
MS1101	174×163 mm. Nos. 1095/100 and three stamp-size labels	9·00	9·00
MS1102	110×70 mm. £2 Queen Elizabeth II and Prince Philip, Westminster Abbey, 1977	6·00	6·00

252 Unloading Sea King Helicopter from Hold of Short Belfast Aircraft, 8 May 1982

2011. 70th Anniv of RAF Search and Rescue. Multicoloured.

1103	35p. Type **252**	1·10	1·25
1104	40p. Westland Sea King HAR3 helicopter XZ593 over Ascension Island	1·25	1·40
1105	90p. Sea King helicopter XZ593 delivering stores to HMS *Dumbarton Castle* (Castle Class patrol ship), 1982	2·75	3·00
1106	£1 Sea King helicopter XZ593 airlifting casualty from nuclear submarine HMS *Spartan*, 1982	3·00	3·25
MS1107	64×94 mm. £2.50 Sea King helicopter XZ593	7·50	7·50

253 Red and Yellow Peonies

2011. The Peony. Multicoloured.

MS1108	50p.×4 Type **253**; White peony; Apricot peony; Pale yellow peony	5·25	5·25

254 Prince William and Miss Catherine Middleton at Friend's Wedding, 23 October 2010

2011. Royal Wedding. Multicoloured.

1109	35p. Type **254**	1·10	1·10
1110	90p. Prince William and Miss Catherine Middleton at St. James's Palace, November 2010	2·75	2·75
1111	£1.25 Duke and Duchess of Cambridge in carriage on their wedding day	3·75	3·75
MS1112	94×64 mm. £2 Duke and Duchess of Cambridge leaving Westminster Abbey after wedding (vert)	5·25	5·25

255 Red-billed Tropic Bird on Nest

2011. Endangered Species. Red-billed Tropicbird (*Phaethon aethereus*). Multicoloured.

1113	35p. Type **255**	90	90
1114	40p. Pair in flight	1·10	1·10
1115	50p. Adult and juvenile on nest	1·40	1·40
1116	£1.25 Red-billed tropic bird in flight over sea	3·50	3·50

256 Mother Goose

2011. Christmas. Pantomimes. Multicoloured.

1117	15p. Type **256**		45	45
1118	40p. Jack and the Beanstalk		1·25	1·25
1119	50p. Aladdin		1·50	1·50
1120	£1.25 Cinderella		3·75	3·75

257 Queen Elizabeth II, Windsor, 2011

2012. Diamond Jubilee. Multicoloured.

1121	15p. Type **257**		45	45
1122	25p. At reception on eve of Prince Charles' 50th birthday, Buckingham Palace, 13 November 1998		75	75
1123	35p. Attending Maundy Service, Lichfield, 1988		1·10	1·10
1124	40p. Official portrait by Peter Grugeon, Windsor Castle, October 1975		1·25	1·25
1125	60p. Formal photograph, Buckingham Palace, 1961		1·75	1·75
1126	£1.25 Wearing Coronation gown, 4 June 1953		3·75	3·75
MS1127	174×164 mm. Nos. 1121/6 and three stamp-size labels		9·00	9·00
MS1129	111×70 mm. £2 In Westminster Abbey, 1977		6·00	6·00

2012. Reef Fish (2nd series). Multicoloured.

1129	35p. Trumpetfish (*Aulostomus strigosus*)		1·10	1·10
1130	40p. Peacock flounder (*Bothus lunatus*)		1·25	1·25
1131	90p. Queen triggerfish (*Balistes vetula*)		2·50	2·50
1132	£1 Scrawled filefish (*Aluterus scriptus*)		2·75	2·75
MS1133	85×61 mm. £2 Yellow goatfish (*Mulloidichthys martinicus*)		6·00	6·00

258 The Departure of *Titanic*

2012. Centenary of Sinking of the *Titanic*. Multicoloured.

1134	20p. Type **258**		60	60
1135	45p. The Boat Deck		1·40	1·40
1136	50p. The Iceberg		1·50	1·50
1137	£1 The Sinking		3·00	3·00
MS1138	94×64 mm. £2 Abandoning Ship		6·00	6·00

259 Sir Ernest Shackleton

2012. Shackleton-Rowett Expedition, 1921-2

1139	45p. Type **259**		1·40	1·40
1140	45p. John Quiller Rowett (expedition sponsor) (18×36 mm)		1·40	1·40
1141	45p. Frank Wild		1·40	1·40
1142	50p. *Quest* leaving London		1·50	1·50
1143	50p. *Quest* at Ascension Island (18×36 mm)		1·50	1·50
1144	50p. *Quest* in ice		1·50	1·50

260 Scrooge

2012. Christmas. *A Christmas Carol* by Charles Dickens.

1145	25p. Type **260**		75	75
1146	40p. Ghost of Jacob Marley appearing to Scrooge		1·25	1·25
1147	50p. Scrooge carrying Tiny Tim (vert)		1·50	1·50
1148	£1.25 Scrooge giving Christmas turkey to Bob Cratchit (vert)		3·75	3·75

261 Sooty Tern ('Wideawake Tern')

2012. 70th Anniv of Wideawake Airfield. Multicoloured.

MS1149	45p. Type **261**; 50p. Douglas DC-3 Dakota; £1 Eurofighter Typhoon; £1.45 Masked booby	10·00	10·00

262 Fairey Swordfish

2013. Aircraft. Multicoloured.

1150	15p. Type **262**		45	45
1151	20p. North American B-25 Mitchell		60	60
1152	25p. Lockheed C-130K Hercules		75	75
1153	30p. Hawker Siddeley Nimrod MR2		90	90
1154	40p. BAE Sea Harrier FRS1		1·25	1·25
1155	45p. Lockheed C-5 Galaxy		1·40	1·40
1156	50p. Douglas DC-3 Dakota		1·50	1·50
1157	65p. Avro Vulcan		1·90	1·90
1158	90p. McDonnell Douglas Phantom F-4		2·75	2·75
1159	£1 Eurofighter Typhoon		3·00	3·00
1160	£2.50 Lockheed C-121		7·00	7·00
1161	£5 Short's Belfast		10·00	10·00

263 Queen Victoria, Soldiers and Cavalry ("Battles of Her Majestys Reign")

2013. 60th Anniv of Coronation

1162	45p. Type **263**		1·40	1·40
1163	50p. King Edward VII and Queen Alexandra		1·50	1·50
1164	70p. King George V and Queen Mary		2·10	2·10
1165	£1.10 King George VI, Queen Elizabeth, Princess Elizabeth and Princess Margaret		3·00	3·00
1166	£1.25 Queen Elizabeth II in Coronation Coach		3·75	3·75
MS1167	110×70 mm. £2 Coronation photograph of Queen Elizabeth II with Orb and Sceptre (32×48 mm)		11·00	11·00

264 Empress Josephine of France, c. 1801 (Francis Pascal Simon Gerard)

2013. Bicentenary of British Settlement (2015) (1st issue). The Napoleonic Years. Multicoloured.

1168	45p. Type **264**		1·40	1·40
1169	50p. Bonaparte at the Bridge of Arcole (Antoine-Jean Gros) (Italian Campaign, 1796)		1·50	1·50
1170	60p. Napolean and his General Staff (oil on panel) (Egyptian Campaign, 1798)		1·75	1·75
1171	£1.45 Napolean as First Consul (after Jean-Baptiste Isabey, 1799)		4·25	4·25

265 Conservative Party Leader Margaret Thatcher outside her Chelsea Home, November 1976

2013. Margaret Thatcher (1925-2013, Prime Minister 1979-90) Commemoration. Multicoloured.

1172	45p. Type **265**		1·40	1·40

1173	50p. Prime Minister Margaret Thatcher inspecting Sea Harrier at British Aerospace factory, Dunsfold, Surrey, 18 December 1982		1·50	1·50
1174	60p. The Residency, Ascension Island, June 1992		1·75	1·75
1175	£1.45 Baroness Thatcher, appointed Lady of the Garter, 1995		4·25	4·25

POSTAGE DUE STAMPS

D1 Outline Map of Ascension

1986

D1	**D1**	1p. deep brown and brown	15	30
D2	**D1**	2p. brown and orange	15	30
D3	**D1**	5p. brown and orange	15	30
D4	**D1**	7p. black and violet	20	40
D5	**D1**	10p. black and blue	25	45
D6	**D1**	25p. black and green	65	1·10

Pt. 1

AUSTRALIA

An island continent to the S.E. of Asia. A Commonwealth consisting of the states of New S. Wales, Queensland, S. Australia, Tasmania, Victoria and W. Australia.

1913. 12 pence = 1 shilling; 20 shillings = 1 pound.
1966. 100 cents = 1 dollar.

1 Eastern Grey Kangaroo

1913

1	1	½d. green	8·50	5·00
2	1	1d. red	15·00	1·75
35	1	2d. grey	48·00	8·00
36	1	2½d. blue	24·00	10·00
37	1	3d. olive	40·00	4·75
6	1	4d. orange	85·00	25·00
8	1	5d. brown	75·00	40·00
38	1	6d. blue	80·00	7·50
73	1	6d. brown	26·00	1·75
133	1	9d. violet	38·00	2·25
40	1	1s. green	50·00	6·00
41	1	2s. brown	£225	13·00
134	1	2s. purple	9·00	1·00
135	1	5s. grey and yellow	£150	19·00
136	1	10s. grey and pink	£400	£140
15	1	£1 brown and blue	£2500	£2500
137	1	£1 grey	£650	£275
138	1	£2 black and pink	£4000	£550

3

1913

20	3	½d. green	3·75	1·00
94	3	½d. orange	2·25	1·00
17	3	1d. red	3·50	5·00
57	3	1d. violet	6·00	1·50
125	3	1d. green	2·00	20
59a	3	1½d. brown	7·00	60
61	3	1½d. green	4·25	80
77	3	1½d. red	2·25	40
62	3	2d. orange	12·00	1·00
98	3	2d. brown	13·00	9·50
127	3	2d. red	1·75	10
128	3	3d. blue	18·00	1·25
22	3	4d. orange	35·00	2·50
64	3	4d. violet	15·00	15·00
65	3	4d. blue	48·00	8·50
129	3	4d. olive	19·00	1·25
92	3	4½d. violet	19·00	3·75
130	3	5d. brown	15·00	20
131	3	1s.4d. blue	50·00	2·75

4 Laughing Kookaburra

1913

19	4	6d. purple	75·00	55·00

8 Parliament House, Canberra

1927. Opening of Parliament House.

105	8	1½d. lake	50	50

1928. National Stamp Exhibition, Melbourne.

106	4	3d. blue	4·25	6·50
MS106a	65×70 mm. No. 106×4		£110	£200

9 de Havilland Hercules and Pastoral Scene

1929. Air.

115	9	3d. green	8·50	4·25

10 Black Swan

1929. Centenary of Western Australia.

116	10	1½d. red	1·25	1·60

11 "Capt. Chas Sturt" (J. H. Crossland)

1930. Centenary of Sturt's Exploration of River Murray.

117	11	1½d. red	1·25	1·00
118	11	3d. blue	7·50	9·00

1930. Surch in words.

119	3	2d. on 1½d. red	1·50	1·00
120	3	5d. on 4½d. violet	12·00	14·00

13 The *Southern Cross* above Hemispheres

1931. Kingsford Smith's Flights.

(a) POSTAGE

121	13	2d. red (postage)	1·00	1·00
122	13	3d. blue	7·00	5·50

(b) AIR

123	13	6d. violet (air)	5·50	16·00

1931. Air. As T 13 but inscr "AIR MAIL SERVICE".

139		6d. brown	19·00	17·00

1931. Air. No. 139 optd O S.

139a		6d. brown	30·00	55·00

17 Superb Lyrebird

1932

140	17	1s. green	42·00	2·75

18 Sydney Harbour Bridge

1932. Opening of Sydney Harbour Bridge.

144	18	2d. red	5·50	1·40
142	18	3d. blue	8·50	9·50
143	18	5s. green	£425	£200

19 Laughing
Kookaburra

1932

146	**19**	6d. brown		17·00	55

20 Melbourne and
River Yarra

1934. Centenary of Victoria.

147	**20**	2d. red		3·00	1·75
148	**20**	3d. blue		4·00	5·50
149	**20**	1s. black		55·00	20·00

21 Merino Ram

1934. Death Centenary of Capt. John Macarthur (founder
of Australian sheep-farming).

150	**21**	2d. red		8·00	1·50
151	**21**	3d. blue		15·00	18·00
152	**21**	9d. purple		35·00	50·00

22 Hermes

1934

153b	**22**	1s.6d. purple		2·00	1·40

23 Cenotaph,
Whitehall

1935. 20th. Anniv of Gallipoli Landing.

154	**23**	2d. red		2·50	30
155	**23**	1s. black		50·00	45·00

24 King George
V on "Anzac"

1935. Silver Jubilee.

156	**24**	2d. red		2·75	30
157	**24**	3d. blue		8·50	11·00
158	**24**	2s. violet		35·00	48·00

25 Amphitrite and
Telephone Cable

1936. Opening of Submarine Telephone Cable to
Tasmania.

159	**25**	2d. red		2·75	50
160	**25**	3d. blue		4·50	2·75

26 Site of Adelaide,
1836; Old Gum Tree,
Glenelg; King William
Street, Adelaide

1936. Centenary of South Australia.

161	**26**	2d. red		3·00	40
162	**26**	3d. blue		9·50	3·50
163	**26**	1s. green		17·00	10·00

27 Wallaroo

28 Queen
Elizabeth

29 King
George VI

 (not detected labels)

30 King
George VI

31 King
George VI

33 Merino Ram

38 Queen
Elizabeth

40 King George VI and
Queen Elizabeth

1937

228	**27**	½d. orange		20	10
165	**28**	1d. green		1·00	50
180	-	1d. green		7·50	60
181	-	1d. purple		1·50	50
182	**29**	1½d. purple		5·50	15·00
183	**29**	1½d. green		1·25	1·75
167	**30**	2d. red		1·00	50
184	-	2d. red		6·50	20
185	**30**	2d. purple		50	2·00
186	**31**	3d. blue		45·00	3·75
187	**31**	3d. brown		40	10
188	-	4d. green		1·00	10
189	**33**	5d. purple		50	2·25
190a	-	6d. brown		1·75	10
191	-	9d. brown		1·00	30
192	-	1s. green		2·25	10
175	**31**	1s.4d. mauve		3·00	2·50
176a	**38**	5s. purple		4·50	2·75
177	-	10s. purple		50·00	17·00
178	**40**	£1 slate		70·00	35·00

DESIGNS—As Type **28**: 4d. Koala; 6d. Kookaburra; 1s.
Lyrebird. As Type **33**: 9d. Platypus. As Type **38**: 10s. King
George VI.

Nos. 180 and 184 are as Types **28** and **30** but with
completely shaded background.

41 Governor Phillip at
Sydney Cove (J. Alcott)

1937. 150th Anniv of New South Wales.

193	**41**	2d. red		3·25	30
194	**41**	3d. blue		7·50	2·25
195	**41**	9d. purple		25·00	14·00

42 A.I.F. and
Nurse

1940. Australian Imperial Forces.

196	**42**	1d. green		2·50	2·75
197	**42**	2d. red		2·00	1·50
198	**42**	3d. blue		17·00	10·00
199	**42**	6d. purple		32·00	28·00

1941. Surch with figures and bars.

200	**30**	2½d. on 2d. red		1·00	70
201	**31**	3½d. on 3d. blue		2·50	2·25
202	**33**	5½d. on 5d. purple		4·25	6·00

46a Queen
Elizabeth

47 King
George VI

48 King
George VI

49 King
George VI

50 Emu

1942

203	**46a**	1d. purple		2·25	10
204	**46a**	1½d. green		2·75	10

205	**47**	2d. purple		1·75	2·00
206	**48**	2½d. red		50	10
207	**49**	3½d. blue		3·25	60
208	**50**	5½d. grey		1·00	20

52 Duke and
Duchess of
Gloucester

1945. Royal Visit.

209	**52**	2½d. red		20	10
210	**52**	3½d. blue		40	1·25
211	**52**	5½d. grey		50	1·25

53 Star and Wreath

1946. Victory. Inscr "PEACE 1945".

213	**53**	2½d. red		20	10
214	-	3½d. blue		55	1·75
215	-	5½d. green		60	1·00

DESIGNS—HORIZ: 3½d. Flag and dove. VERT: 5½d. Angel.

56 Sir Thomas
Mitchell and
Queensland

1946. Centenary of Mitchell's Central Queensland
Exploration.

216	**56**	2½d. red		25	10
217	**56**	3½d. blue		75	1·75
218	**56**	1s. green		75	65

57 Lt. John
Shortland,
R.N.

58 Steel
Foundry

1947. 150th Anniv of City of Newcastle.

219	**57**	2½d. lake		20	10
220	**58**	3½d. blue		60	1·50
221	-	5½d. green		60	75

DESIGNS—As Type **58**: HORIZ: 5½d. Coal carrier cranes.

60 Queen
Elizabeth II
when Princess

1947. Wedding of Princess Elizabeth.

222a	**60**	1d. purple		10	10

61 Hereford
Bull

61a Hermes
and Globe

62 Aboriginal
Art

62a
Commonwealth
Coat of Arms

1948

223	**61**	1s.3d. brown		2·50	1·10
223a	**61a**	1s.6d. brown		1·00	10
224	**62**	2s. brown		1·50	10
224a	**62a**	5s. red		3·75	20
224b	**62a**	10s. purple		19·00	85
224c	**62a**	£1 blue		40·00	4·25
224d	**62a**	£2 green		85·00	16·00

63 William J.
Farrer

1948. W. J. Farrer (wheat research) Commem.

225	**63**	2½d. red		40	10

64 Ferdinand
von Mueller

1948. Sir Ferdinand von Mueller (botanist)
Commemoration.

226	**64**	2½d. red		30	10

65 Boy Scout

1948. Pan-Pacific Scout Jamboree, Wonga Park.

227	**65**	2½d. lake		30	10

For 3½d. value dates "1952–53", see No. 254.

66 "Henry
Lawson" (Sir
Lionel
Lindsay)

1949. Henry Lawson (poet) Commemoration.

231	**66**	2½d. purple		40	10

67 Mounted Postman
and Convair CV 240
Aircraft

1949. 75th Anniv of U.P.U.

232	**67**	3½d. blue		60	60

68 John,
Lord Forrest
of Bunbury

1949. John, Lord Forrest (explorer and politician)
Commemoration.

233	**68**	2½d. red		55	10

69 Queen
Elizabeth

70 King
George VI

71 Aborigine

80 King
George VI

81 King
George VI

82 King George
VI

1950

236	**69**	1½d. green		70	40
237	**69**	2d. green		15	10
234	**70**	2½d. red		10	10
237c	**70**	2½d. brown		10	35
235	**70**	3d. red		15	25
237d	**70**	3d. green		15	10
247	**80**	3½d. purple		10	10
248	**81**	4½d. red		15	1·25
249	**81**	6½d. brown		20	1·50
250	**81**	6½d. green		30	45
251	**80**	7½d. blue		15	80
238	**71**	8½d. brown		30	1·00
252	**82**	1s.0½d. blue		1·25	60
253	**71**	2s.6d. brown (21×25½ mm)		2·25	1·00

72 Reproduction of First Stamp of N.S.W.

73 Reproduction of First Stamp of Victoria

1950. Centenary of Australian States Stamps.

239	**72**	2½d. purple	50	10
240	**73**	2½d. purple	50	10

75 Sir Henry Parkes

77 Federal Parliament House, Canberra

1951. 50th Anniv of Commonwealth. Inscr as in T **75** and **77**.

241	**75**	3d. lake	1·50	10
242	-	3d. lake	1·50	10
243	-	5½d. blue	65	2·25
244	**77**	1s.6d. brown	1·25	50

DESIGNS—As Type **70**: No. 242, Sir Edmund Barton. As Type **77**: No. 243, Opening first Federal Parliament.

78 E. H. Hargraves

79 C. J. Latrobe

1951. Centenaries. Discovery of Gold in Australia and of Responsible Government in Victoria.

245	**78**	3d. purple	1·00	10
246	**79**	3d. purple	1·00	10

1952. Pan-Pacific Scout Jamboree, Greystanes. As T **65** but dated "1952–53".

254	**65**	3½d. lake	20	10

83 Butter

1953. Food Production. Inscr "PRODUCE FOOD!".

255	**83**	3d. green	30	10
256	-	3d. green (Wheat)	30	10
257	-	3d. green (Beef)	30	10
258	**83**	3½d. red	30	10
259	-	3½d. red (Wheat)	30	10
260	-	3½d. red (Beef)	30	10

86 Queen Elizabeth II

1953

261	**86**	1d. purple	15	15
261a	**86**	2½d. blue	20	15
262	**86**	3d. green	20	10
263	**86**	3½d. red	20	10
263a	**86**	6½d. orange	2·50	50

87 Queen Elizabeth II

1953. Coronation.

264	**87**	3½d. red	40	10
265	**87**	7½d. violet	75	1·40
266	**87**	2s. green	2·50	1·40

88 Young Farmers and Calf

1953. 25th Anniv of Australian Young Farmers' Clubs.

267	**88**	3½d. brown and green	10	10

89 Lt.-Gov. D. Collins

90 Lt.-Gov. W. Paterson

91 Sullivan Cove, Hobart, 1804

1953. 150th Anniv of Settlement in Tasmania.

268	**89**	3½d. purple	35	10
269	**90**	3½d. purple	35	10
270	**91**	2s. green	1·25	3·00

92 Stamp of 1853

1953. First Centenary of Tasmania Postage Stamps.

271	**92**	3d. red	10	40

93 Queen Elizabeth II and Duke of Edinburgh

94 Queen Elizabeth II

1954. Royal Visit.

272	**93**	3½d. red	20	10
273	**94**	7½d. purple	30	1·25
274	**93**	2s. green	60	65

95 "Telegraphic Communications"

1954. Centenary of Telegraph.

275	**95**	3½d. brown	10	10

96 Red Cross and Globe

1954. 40th Anniv of Australian Red Cross Society.

276	**96**	3½d. blue and red	10	10

97 Mute Swan

1954. Centenary of Western Australian Stamps.

277	**97**	3½d. black	20	10

98 Locomotives of 1854 and 1954

1954. Centenary of Australian Railways.

278	**98**	3½d. purple	30	10

99 Territory Badge

1954. Australian Antarctic Research.

279	**99**	3½d. black	15	10

100 Olympic Games Symbol

1954. Olympic Games Propaganda.

280	**100**	2s. blue	1·75	1·00
280a	**100**	2s. green	2·00	2·50

101 Rotary Symbol, Globe and Flags

1955. 50th Anniv of Rotary International.

281	**101**	3½d. red	10	10

101a Queen Elizabeth II **102** Queen Elizabeth II

1955

282a	**101a**	4d. lake	20	10
282b	**101a**	7½d. violet	1·25	1·50
282c	**101a**	10d. blue	60	1·00
282	**102**	1s.0½d. blue	1·25	1·25
282d	**102**	1s.7d. brown	1·25	45

103 American Memorial, Canberra

1955. Australian–American Friendship.

283	**103**	3½d. blue	10	10

104 Cobb & Co. Coach (from etching by Sir Lionel Lindsay)

1955. Mail-coach Pioneers Commemoration.

284	**104**	3½d. sepia	25	10
285	**104**	2s. brown	1·00	1·40

105 Y.M.C.A. Emblem and Map of the World

1955. World Centenary of Y.M.C.A.

286	**105**	3½d. green and red	10	10

106 Florence Nightingale and Young Nurse

1955. Nursing Profession Commemoration.

287	**106**	3½d. lilac	10	10

107 Queen Victoria

1955. Centenary of South Australian Postage Stamps.

288	**107**	3½d. green	10	10

108 Badges of N.S.W., Victoria and Tasmania

1956. Centenary of Responsible Government in N.S.W., Victoria and Tasmania.

289	**108**	3½d. lake	10	10

109 Arms of Melbourne

110 Olympic Torch and Symbol

111 Collins Street, Melbourne

1956. Olympic Games, Melbourne.

290	**109**	4d. red	30	10
291	**110**	7½d. blue	70	1·40
292	**111**	1s. multicoloured	80	30
293	-	2s. multicoloured	1·60	2·00

DESIGN—As Type **111**: 2s. Melbourne across River Yarra.

115 South Australia Coat of Arms

1957. Centenary of Responsible Government in South Australia.

296	**115**	4d. brown	10	10

116 Map of Australia and Caduceus

1957. Royal Flying Doctor Service of Australia.

297	**116**	7d. blue	15	10

117 "The Spirit of Christmas" (after Sir Joshua Reynolds)

1957. Christmas.

298	**117**	3½d. red	10	20
299	**117**	4d. purple	10	10

118 Lockheed Super Constellation Airliner

1958. Inaug of Australian "Round-the-World" Air Service.

301	**118**	2s. blue	1·00	1·00

119 Hall of Memory, Sailor and Airman

1958

302	119	5½d. lake	60	30
303	-	5½d. lake	60	30

No. 303 shows a soldier and servicewoman instead of the sailor and airman.

120 Sir Charles Kingsford Smith and the *Southern Cross*

1958. 30th Anniv of First Air Crossing of the Tasman Sea.

304	120	8d. blue	60	1·00

121 Silver Mine, Broken Hill

1958. 75th Anniv of Founding of Broken Hill.

305	121	4d. brown	30	10

122 The Nativity

1958. Christmas Issue.

306	122	3½d. red	20	30
307	122	4d. violet	20	10

124 Queen Elizabeth II **126** Queen Elizabeth II **127** Queen Elizabeth II

128 Queen Elizabeth II **129** Queen Elizabeth II

1959

308	-	1d. purple	10	10
309	124	2d. brown	50	20
311	126	3d. turquoise	15	10
312	127	3½d. green	15	15
313	128	4d. red	2·00	10
314	129	5d. blue	1·25	10

No. 308 shows a head and shoulders portrait as in Type **128** and is vert.

131 Numbat **137** Christmas Bells

142 Aboriginal Stockman

1959

316	131	6d. brown	1·50	10
317	-	8d. brown	75	10
318	-	9d. sepia	2·00	55
319	-	11d. blue	1·00	15
320	-	1s. green	1·75	40
321	-	1s.2d. purple	1·00	15
322	137	1s.6d. red on yellow	1·75	1·00
323	-	2s. blue	70	10
324	-	2s.3d. green on yellow	1·00	10
324a	-	2s.3d. green	2·50	75
325	-	2s.5d. brown on yellow	3·50	75
326	-	3s. red	1·75	20
327	142	5s. brown	12·00	2·75

DESIGNS—As Type **131**: VERT: 8d. Tiger Cat; 9d. Eastern grey kangaroo; 11d. Common rabbit bandicoot; 1s. Platypus. HORIZ: 1s.2d. Thylacine. As Type **137**: 2s. Flannel flower; 2s.3d. Wattle; 2s.5d. Banksia (plant); 3s. Waratah.

143 Postmaster Isaac Nichols boarding the Brig *Experiment*

1959. 150th Anniv of Australian P.O.

331	143	4d. slate	15	10

144 Parliament House, Brisbane, and Arms of Queensland

1959. Centenary of Queensland Self-Government.

332	144	4d. lilac and green	10	10

145 "The Approach of the Magi"

1959. Christmas.

333	145	5d. violet	10	10

146 Girl Guide and Lord Baden-Powell

1960. 50th Anniv of Girl Guide Movement.

334	146	5d. blue	30	15

147 *The Overlanders* (after Sir Daryl Lindsay)

1960. Centenary of Northern Territory Exploration.

335	147	5d. mauve	50	15

148 *Archer* and Melbourne Cup

1960. 100th Melbourne Cup Race Commemoration.

336	148	5d. sepia	20	10

149 Queen Victoria

1960. Centenary of Queensland Stamps.

337	149	5d. green	25	10

150 Open Bible and Candle

1960. Christmas Issue.

338	150	5d. lake	10	10

151 Colombo Plan Bureau Emblem

1961. Colombo Plan.

339	151	1s. brown	30	10

152 Melba (after bust by Sir Bertram Mackennal)

1961. Birth Centenary of Dame Nellie Melba (singer).

340	152	5d. blue	30	15

153 Open Prayer Book and Text

1961. Christmas Issue.

341	153	5d. brown	10	10

154 J. M. Stuart

1962. Centenary of Stuart's South to North Crossing of Australia.

342	154	5d. red	40	10

155 Flynn's Grave and Nursing Sister

1962. 50th Anniv of Australian Inland Mission.

343	155	5d. multicoloured	30	10

156 "Woman"

1962. "Associated Country Women of the World" Conference, Melbourne.

344	156	5d. green	10	10

157 "Madonna and Child"

1962. Christmas.

345	157	5d. violet	15	10

158 Perth and Kangaroo Paw (plant)

1962. British Empire and Commonwealth Games, Perth. Multicoloured.

346		5d. Type **158**	50	10
347		2s.3d. Arms of Perth and running track	2·00	2·75

160 Queen Elizabeth II

1963. Royal Visit.

348	160	5d. green	35	10
349	-	2s.3d. lake	1·50	3·00

DESIGN: 2s.3d. Queen Elizabeth II and Duke of Edinburgh.

162 Arms of Canberra and W. B. Griffin (architect)

1963. 50th Anniv of Canberra.

350	162	5d. green	15	10

163 Centenary Emblem

1963. Centenary of Red Cross.

351	163	5d. red, grey and blue	60	10

164 Blaxland, Lawson and Wentworth on Mount York

1963. 150th Anniv of First Crossing of Blue Mountains.

352	164	5d. blue	15	10

165 "Export"

1963. Export Campaign.

353	165	5d. red	10	10

1963. As T **160** but smaller 17½×21½ mm "5D" at top right replacing "ROYAL VISIT 1963" and oak leaves omitted.

354		5d. green	1·00	10
354c		5d. red	55	10

167 Tasman and *Heemskerk*

1963. Navigators.

355	167	4s. blue	3·00	55
356	-	5s. brown	3·75	1·75
357	-	7s.6d. olive	21·00	19·00
358	-	10s. purple	25·00	5·00
359	-	£1 violet	35·00	16·00
360	-	£2 sepia	55·00	75·00

DESIGNS—As Type **167**: 7s.6d. Captain Cook; 10s. Flinders and *Investigator*. 20½×5½ mm: 5s. Dampier and *Roebuck* £1 Bass and *Tom Thumb* (whale boat); £2 Admiral King and *Mermaid* (survey cutter).

173 "Peace on Earth..."

1963. Christmas.

361	173	5d. blue	10	10

174 "Commonwealth Cable"

1963. Opening of COMPAC (Trans-Pacific Telephone Cable).

362	174	2s.3d. multicoloured	1·50	2·75

176 Black-backed Magpie

1964. Birds.

363	-	6d. multicoloured	1·00	25

364	176	9d. black, grey and green	1·00	2·75
365	-	1s.6d. multicoloured	75	1·40
366	-	2s. yellow, black and pink	1·40	50
367	-	2s.5d. multicoloured	1·75	3·50
368	-	2s.6d. multicoloured	2·50	4·00
369	-	3s. multicoloured	1·40	2·00

BIRDS—HORIZ: 6d. Yellow-tailed thornbill; 2s.6d. Scarlet robin. VERT: 1s.6d. Galah (cockatoo); 2s. Golden whistler (Thickhead); 2s.5d. Blue wren; 3s. Straw-necked ibis.

182 Bleriot XI Aircraft (type flown by M. Guillaux, 1914)

1964. 50th Anniv of 1st Australian Airmail Flight.

370	182	5d. green	30	10
371	182	2s.3d. red	1·50	2·75

183 Child looking at Nativity Scene

1964. Christmas.

372	183	5d. red, blue, buff and black	10	10

184 "Simpson and his Donkey"

1965. 50th Anniv of Gallipoli Landing.

373	184	5d. brown	50	10
374	184	8d. blue	75	2·50
375	184	2s.3d. purple	1·50	2·50

185 "Telecommunications"

1965. Centenary of I.T.U.

376	185	5d. black, brown and blue	60	10

186 Sir Winston Churchill

1965. Churchill Commemoration.

377	186	5d. multicoloured	30	10

HELECON PAPER. All stamps from No. 378 were on Helecon paper, unless otherwise stated.

187 General Monash

1965. Birth Centenary of General Sir John Monash (engineer and soldier).

378	187	5d. multicoloured	15	10

188 Hargrave and *Multiplane* Seaplane (1902)

1965. 50th Death Anniv of Lawrence Hargrave (aviation pioneer).

379	188	5d. multicoloured	25	10

189 I.C.Y. Emblem

1965. International Co-operation Year.

380	189	2s.3d. green and blue	65	1·50

190 "Nativity Scene"

1965. Christmas.

381	190	5d. multicoloured	15	10

191 Queen Elizabeth II **192** Blue-faced Honeyeater

1966. Decimal currency. As earlier issues but with values in cents and dollars as in T 191/2. Also some new designs.

382	191	1c. brown	25	10
383	191	2c. green	70	10
384	191	2c. green	70	10
404	191	3c. black, pink and green	45	1·25
385	191	4c. red	20	10
405	191	4c. black, brown and red	35	60
386	-	5c. multicoloured (as 363)	25	10
386c	191	5c. blue	70	10
405a	191	5c. black, brown and blue	40	10
387	192	6c. multicoloured	1·25	1·00
387a	191	6c. orange	1·00	10
388	-	7c. multicoloured	60	10
388a	191	7c. purple	1·25	10
389	-	8c. multicoloured	60	1·00
390	-	9c. multicoloured	60	20
391	-	10c. multicoloured	60	10
392	-	13c. multicoloured	1·50	25
393	-	15c. multicoloured (as 365)	1·25	2·00
394	-	20c. yellow, black and pink (as 366)	1·50	15
395	-	24c. multicoloured	65	1·25
396	-	25c. multicoloured (as 368)	1·50	30
397	-	30c. multicoloured (as 369)	3·50	1·25
398	167	40c. blue	3·00	10
399	-	50c. brown (as 356)	3·00	10
400	-	75c. olive (as 357)	1·00	1·00
401	-	$1 purple (as 358)	1·50	20
402	-	$2 violet (as 359)	6·00	1·00
403	-	$4 brown (as 360)	6·00	6·50

DESIGNS—VERT: 7c. White-tailed Dascyllus ("Humbug fish"); 8c. Copper-banded butterflyfish ("Coral fish"); 9c. Hermit crab; 10c. Orange clownfish ("Anemone fish"); 13c. Red-necked avocet. HORIZ: 24c. Azure kingfisher.

200 "Saving Life"

1966. 75th Anniv of Royal Life Saving Society.

406	200	4c. black, lt bl & bl	15	10

201 "Adoration of the Shepherds"

1966. Christmas.

407	201	4c. black and olive	10	10

202 Eendracht

1966. 350th Anniv of Dirk Hartog's Landing in Australia.

408	202	4c. multicoloured	10	10

203 Open Bible

1967. 150th Anniv of British and Foreign Bible Society in Australia.

409	203	4c. multicoloured	10	10

204 Ancient Keys and Modern Lock

1967. 150th Anniv of Australian Banking.

410	204	4c. black, blue and green	10	10

205 Lions Badge and 50 Stars

1967. 50th Anniv of Lions International.

411	205	4c. black, gold and blue	10	10

206 Y.W.C.A. Emblem

1967. World Y.W.C.A. Council Meeting, Monash University, Melbourne.

412	206	4c. multicoloured	10	10

207 Anatomical Figures

1967. Fifth World Gynaecology and Obstetrics Congress, Sydney.

413	207	4c. black, blue and violet	10	10

1967. No. 385 surch.

414	191	5c. on 4c. red	25	10

209 Christmas Bells and Gothic Arches

1967. Christmas. Multicoloured.

415	209	5c. Type 209	20	10
416	-	25c. Religious symbols (vert)	1·00	1·90

211 Satellite in Orbit

1968. World Weather Watch. Multicoloured.

417	211	5c. Type 211	30	10
418	-	20c. World weather map	1·10	3·00

213 Radar Antenna

1968. World Telecommunications via Intelsat II.

419	213	25c. blue, black and green	1·00	2·00

214 Kangaroo Paw (Western Australia)

1968. State Floral Emblems. Multicoloured.

420	214	6c. Type 214	45	1·25
421	-	13c. Pink Heath (Victoria)	50	70
422	-	15c. Tasmanian Blue Gum (Tasmania)	50	40
423	-	20c. Sturt's Desert Pea (South Australia)	1·00	75
424	-	25c. Cooktown Orchid (Queensland)	1·10	75
425	-	30c. Waratah (New South Wales)	50	10

220 Soil Sample Analysis

1968. International Soil Science Congress and World Medical Association Assembly. Multicoloured.

426	220	5c. Type 220	10	10
427	-	5c. Rubber-gloved hands, syringe and head of Hippocrates	10	10

222 Athlete carrying Torch and Sunstone Symbol

1968. Olympic Games, Mexico City. Multicoloured.

428	222	5c. Type 222	30	10
429	-	25c. Sunstone symbol and Mexican flag	40	1·50

224 Houses and Dollar Signs

1968. Building and Savings Societies Congress.

430	224	5c. multicoloured	10	40

225 Church Window and View of Bethlehem

1968. Christmas.

431	225	5c. multicoloured	10	10

226 Edgeworth David (geologist)

1968. Famous Australians (1st series).

432	226	5c. green on myrtle	25	20
433	-	5c. black on blue	25	20
434	-	5c. brown on buff	25	20
435	-	5c. violet on lilac	25	20

DESIGNS: No. 433, A. B. Paterson (poet); No. 434, Albert Namatjira (artist); No. 435, Caroline Chrisholm (social worker).

Nos. 432/5 were only issued in booklets and exist with one or two sides imperf.

See also Nos. 446/9, 479/82, 505/8, 537/40, 590/5, 602/7 and 637/40.

230 Macquarie Lighthouse

1968. 150th Anniv of Macquarie Lighthouse.

436	**230**	5c. black and yellow	50	70

231 Pioneers and Modern Building, Darwin

1969. Centenary of Northern Territory Settlement.

437	**231**	5c. brown, olive and ochre	10	10

232 Melbourne Harbour

1969. Sixth Biennial Conference of International Association of Ports and Harbours, Melbourne.

438	**232**	5c. multicoloured	20	10

233 Concentric Circles (symbolizing Management, Labour and Government)

1969. 50th Anniv of I.L.O.

439	**233**	5c. multicoloured	15	10

234 Sugar Cane

1969. Primary Industries. Multicoloured.

440	7c. Type **234**	50	1·50
441	15c. Timber	75	2·50
442	20c. Wheat	30	60
443	25c. Wool	50	1·50

238 *The Nativity* (stained glass window)

1969. Christmas. Multicoloured.

444	5c. Type **238**	20	10
445	25c. *Tree of Life*, Christ in crib and Christmas Star (abstract)	1·00	2·00

240 Edmund Barton

1969. Famous Australians (2nd series). Prime Ministers.

446	**240**	5c. black on green	30	20
447	-	5c. black on green	30	20
448	-	5c. black on green	30	20
449	-	5c. black on green	30	20

DESIGNS: No. 447, Alfred Deakin; 448, J. C. Watson; 449, G. H. Reid.

Nos. 446/9 were only issued in booklets and only exist with one or two adjacent sides imperf.

244 Capt. Ross Smith's Vickers Vimy, 1919

1969. 50th Anniv of First England–Australia Flight.

450	**244**	5c. multicoloured	15	10
451	-	5c. red, black and green	15	10
452	-	5c. multicoloured	15	10

DESIGNS: No. 451, Lt. H. Fysh and Lt. P. McGinness on 1919 survey with Ford Model T runabout; 452, Capt. Wrigley and Sgt. Murphy in Royal Aircraft Factory B.E.2E taking off to meet the Smiths.

247 Symbolic Track and Diesel Locomotive

1970. Sydney–Perth Standard Gauge Railway Link.

453	**247**	5c. multicoloured	15	10

248 Australian Pavilion, Osaka

1970. World Fair, Osaka.

454	**248**	5c. multicoloured	15	10
455	-	20c. red and black	35	65

DESIGN: 20c., *Southern Cross* and "from the Country of the south with warm feelings" (message).

251 Australian Flag

1970. Royal Visit.

456		5c. black and ochre	35	15
457	**251**	30c. multicoloured	1·10	2·50

DESIGN: 5c. Queen Elizabeth II and Duke of Edinburgh.

252 Lucerne Plant, Bull and Sun

1970. 11th International Grasslands Congress, Queensland.

458	**252**	5c. multicoloured	10	80

253 Captain Cook and H.M.S. *Endeavour*

1970. Bicentenary of Captain Cook's Discovery of Australia's East Coast. Multicoloured.

459	5c. Type **253**	30	10
460	5c. Sextant and H.M.S. *Endeavour*	30	10
461	5c. Landing at Botany Bay	30	10
462	5c. Charting and exploring	30	10
463	5c. Claiming possession	30	10
464	30c. Captain Cook, H.M.S. *Endeavour*, sextant, aborigines and kangaroo (63×30 mm)	1·00	2·50

MS465 157×129 mm. Nos. 459/64. Imperf | 5·50 | 6·50 |

Nos. 459/63 were issued together, *se-tenant*, forming a composite design.

259 Sturt's Desert Rose

1970. Coil Stamps. Multicoloured.

465a	2c. Type **259**	40	20
466	4c. Type **259**	85	2·25
467	5c. Golden wattle	20	10
468	6c. Type **259**	1·25	1·00
468b	7c. Sturt's desert pea	40	70
468d	10c. As 7c.	60	1·50

264 Snowy Mountains Scheme

1970. National Development (1st series). Multicoloured.

469	7c. Type **264**	20	1·00
470	8c. Ord River scheme	10	15
471	9c. Bauxite to aluminium	15	15
472	10c. Oil and natural gas	30	10

See also Nos. 541/4.

265 Rising Flames

1970. 16th Commonwealth Parliamentary Association Conference, Canberra.

473	**265**	6c. multicoloured	10	10

266 Milk Analysis and Dairy Herd

1970. 18th International Dairy Congress, Sydney.

474	**266**	6c. multicoloured	10	10

267 "The Nativity"

1970. Christmas.

475	**267**	6c. multicoloured	10	10

268 U.N. "Plant" and Dove of Peace

1970. 25th Anniv of United Nations.

476	**268**	6c. multicoloured	15	10

269 Boeing 707 and Avro 504

1970. 50th Anniv of QANTAS Airline.

477	**269**	6c. multicoloured	30	10
478	-	30c. multicoloured	70	1·50

DESIGN: 30c. Avro 504 and Boeing 707.

1970. Famous Australians (3rd series). As T **226**.

479	6c. blue	35	20
480	6c. black on brown	35	20
481	6c. purple on pink	35	20
482	6c. red on pink	35	20

DESIGNS: No. 479, The Duigan brothers (pioneer aviators); 480, Lachlan Macquarie (Governor of New South Wales); 481, Adam Lindsay Gordon (poet); 482, E. J. Eyre (explorer).

271 "Theatre"

1971. "Australia–Asia". 28th International Congress of Orientalists, Canberra. Multicoloured.

483	**271**	7c. Type **271**	40	50
484		15c. "Music"	60	75
485		20c. "Sea Craft"	60	70

272 The Southern Cross

1971. Centenary of Australian Natives' Association.

486	**272**	6c. black, red and blue	10	10

273 Market "Graph"

1971. Centenary of Sydney Stock Exchange.

487	**273**	6c. multicoloured	10	10

274 Rotary Emblem

1971. 50th Anniv of Rotary International in Australia.

488	**274**	6c. multicoloured	15	10

275 Dassault Mirage Jets and de Havilland D.H.9A Biplane

1971. 50th Anniv of R.A.A.F.

489	**275**	6c. multicoloured	70	10

276 Draught-horse, Cat and Dog

1971. Animals. Multicoloured.

490	6c. Type **276**	20	10
491	12c. Vet and lamb ("Animal Science")	45	20
492	18c. Red Kangaroo ("Fauna Conservation")	1·25	35
493	24c. Guide-dog ("Animals Aid to Man")	1·00	1·50

The 6c. commemorates the Centenary of the Australian R.S.P.C.A.

277 Bark Painting

1971. Aboriginal Art. Multicoloured.

494	20c. Type **277**	20	20
495	25c. Body decoration	20	55
496	30c. Cave painting (vert)	65	20
497	35c. Grave posts (vert)	30	15

278 The Three Kings and the Star

1971. Christmas. Colours of star and colour of "AUSTRALIA" given.

498	**278**	7c. blue, mauve and brown	40	15
499	**278**	7c. mauve, brown and white	40	15
500	**278**	7c. mauve, white and black	2·50	80
501	**278**	7c. black, green and black	40	15
502	**278**	7c. lilac, green and mauve	40	15
503	**278**	7c. black, brown and white	40	15

504 **278** 7c. blue, mauve and green 11·00 2·25

1972. Famous Australians. (4th series). As T **240**. Prime Ministers.
505 7c. blue 30 20
506 7c. blue 30 20
507 7c. red 30 20
508 7c. red 30 20
DESIGNS: No. 505, Andrew Fisher; 506, W. M. Hughes; 507, Joseph Cook; 508, S. M. Bruce.

280 Cameo Brooch

1972. 50th Anniv of Country Women's Association.
509 **280** 7c. multicoloured 20 10

281 Fruit

1972. Primary Industries. Multicoloured.
510 20c. Type **281** 1·00 2·50
511 25c. Rice 1·00 4·00
512 30c. Fish 1·00 1·00
513 35c. Beef 2·25 75

282 Worker in Wheelchair

1972. Rehabilitation of the Disabled.
514 **282** 12c. brown and green 10 10
515 - 18c. green and orange 1·00 35
516 - 24c. blue and brown 15 10
DESIGNS—HORIZ: 18c. Patient and teacher. VERT: 24c. Boy playing with ball.

283 Telegraph Line

1972. Centenary of Overland Telegraph Line.
517 **283** 7c. multicoloured 15 15

284 Athletics

1972. Olympic Games, Munich. Multicoloured.
518 7c. Type **284** 25 25
519 7c. Rowing 25 25
520 7c. Swimming 25 25
521 35c. Equestrian 1·25 3·50

285 Numerals and Computer Circuit

1972. Tenth Int Congress of Accountants, Sydney.
522 **285** 7c. multicoloured 15 15

286 Australian-built Harvester

1972. Pioneer Life. Multicoloured.
523 5c. Pioneer family (vert) 10 10
524 10c. Water-pump (vert) 20 10
525 15c. Type **286** 15 10

526 40c. House 15 30
527 50c. Stage-coach 35 20
528 60c. Morse key (vert) 30 80
529 80c. *Gem* (paddle-steamer) 30 80

287 Jesus with Children

1972. Christmas. Multicoloured.
530 7c. Type **287** 30 10
531 35c. Dove and spectrum motif (vert) 2·75 5·00

288 "Length"

1973. Metric Conversion. Multicoloured.
532 7c. Type **288** 35 60
533 7c. "Volume" 35 60
534 7c. "Mass" 35 60
535 7c. "Temperature" (horiz) 35 60

289 Caduceus and Laurel Wreath

1973. 25th Anniv of World Health Organization.
536 **289** 7c. multicoloured 30 15

1973. Famous Australians (5th series). As T **226**.
537 7c. brown and black 35 45
538 7c. lilac and black 35 45
539 7c. brown and black 35 45
540 7c. lilac and black 35 45
PORTRAITS: No. 537, William Wentworth (statesman and explorer); 538, Isaac Issacs (1st Australian-born Governor-General); 539, Mary Gilmore (writer); 540, Marcus Clarke (author).

291 Shipping

1973. National Development (2nd series). Multicoloured.
541 20c. Type **291** 1·50 2·75
542 25c. Iron ore and steel 1·50 2·75
543 30c. Beef roads 1·50 2·75
544 35c. Mapping 2·25 2·75

292 Banded Coral Shrimp

1973. Marine Life and Gemstones. Multicoloured.
545 1c. Type **292** 10 10
546 2c. Fiddler crab 10 10
547 3c. Coral crab 10 10
548 4c. Mauve stinger 15 65
549 6c. Chrysoprase (vert) 65 1·00
550 7c. Agate (vert) 20 10
551 8c. Opal (vert) 35 10
552 9c. Rhodonite (vert) 50 15
552a 10c. Star sapphire (vert) 75 10

293 Children at Play

1973. 50th Anniv of Legacy (welfare organization).
553 **293** 7c. brown, red and green 30 10

294 John baptizing Jesus

1973. Christmas. Multicoloured.
554 7c. Type **294** 35 10
555 30c. The Good Shepherd 1·75 2·50

295 Sydney Opera House

1973. Architecture.
556 **295** 7c. blue and pale blue 30 15
557 - 10c. ochre and brown 80 70
558 - 40c. grey, brown and black 1·25 2·50
559 - 50c. multicoloured 1·25 3·00
DESIGNS—HORIZ: 10c. Buchanan's Hotel, Townsville; 40c. Como House, Melbourne. VERT: 50c. St. James's Church, Sydney.

296 Wireless Receiver and Speaker

1973. 50th Anniv of Regular Radio Broadcasting.
560 **296** 7c. blue, red and black 15 10

297 Common Wombat

1974. Animals. Multicoloured.
561 20c. Type **297** 25 10
562 25c. Short-nosed echidna (inscr "Spiny Anteater") 60 60
563 30c. Brush-tailed possum 75 15
564 75c. Pygmy (inscr "Feather-tailed") glider 80 1·00

298 *Sergeant of Light Horse* (G. Lambert)

1974. Australian Paintings. Multicoloured.
565 $1 Type **298** 1·00 10
566 $2 *Red Gums of the Far North* (H. Heysen) (horiz) 1·25 25
566b $4 *Shearing the Rams* (Tom Roberts) (horiz) 2·00 2·25
567 $5 *McMahon's Point* (Sir Arthur Streeton) 3·00 2·25
567a $10 *Coming South* (Tom Roberts) 4·00 3·50

299 Supreme Court Judge

1974. 150th Anniv of Australia's Third Charter of Justice.
568 **299** 7c. multicoloured 20 10

300 Rugby Football

1974. Non-Olympic Sports. Multicoloured.
569 7c. Type **300** 40 50
570 7c. Bowls 40 50
571 7c. Australian football (vert) 40 50
572 7c. Cricket (vert) 40 50
573 7c. Golf (vert) 40 50
574 7c. Surfing (vert) 40 50
575 7c. Tennis (vert) 40 50

301 "Transport of Mails"

1974. Centenary of U.P.U. Multicoloured.
576 7c. Type **301** 40 20
577 30c. Three-part version of T **301** (vert) 85 2·25

302 Letter "A" and W. C. Wentworth (co-founder)

1974. 150th Anniv of First Independent Newspaper, *The Australian*.
578 **302** 7c. black and brown 50 40

1974. No. 551 surch.
579 9c. on 8c. multicoloured 15 15

304 The Adoration of the Magi

1974. Christmas. Woodcuts by Durer.
580 **304** 10c. black on cream 25 10
581 - 35c. black on cream 80 1·00
DESIGN: 35c. *The Flight into Egypt*.

305 "Pre-school Education"

1974. Education in Australia. Multicoloured.
582 5c. Type **305** 25 40
583 11c. "Correspondence Schools" 25 60
584 15c. "Science Education" 40 40
585 60c. "Advanced Education" (vert) 50 2·00

306 "Road Safety"

1975. Environment Dangers. Multicoloured.
586 10c. Type **306** 50 50
587 10c. "Pollution" (horiz) 50 50
588 10c. "Bush Fires" (horiz) 50 50

307 Australian Women's Year Emblem

1975. International Women's Year.

589	**307**	10c. blue, green and violet	20	15

308 J. H. Scullin

1975. Famous Australians (6th series). Prime Ministers. Multicoloured.

590	10c. Type **308**	25	35
591	10c. J. A. Lyons	25	35
592	10c. Earle Page	25	35
593	10c. Arthur Fadden	25	35
594	10c. John Curtin	25	35
595	10c. J. B. Chifley	25	35

309 Atomic Absorption Spectrophotometry

1975. Scientfic Development. Multicoloured.

596	11c. Type **309**	70	75
597	24c. Radio astronomy	1·25	2·00
598	33c. Immunology	1·25	2·25
599	48c. Oceanography	1·50	2·75

310 Logo of Australian Postal Commission

1975. Inauguration of Australian Postal and Tele-communications Commissions.

600	**310**	10c. black, red and grey	25	10
601	-	10c. black, orange and grey	25	10

DESIGN: No. 601, Logo of Australian Tele-communications Commission.

311 Edith Cowan

1975. Famous Australians (7th series). Australian Women. Multicoloured.

602	10c. Type **311**	55	75
603	10c. Louisa Lawson	55	75
604	10c. "Henry Richardson" (pen name of Ethel Richardson)	55	75
605	10c. Catherine Spence	55	75
606a	10c. Constance Stone	55	75
607	10c. Truganini	55	75

312 *Helichrysum thomsonii*

1975. Wild Flowers. Multicoloured.

608	18c. Type **312**	25	10
609	45c. *Callistemon teretifolius* (horiz)	50	10

313 "Tambaran" House and Sydney Opera House

1975. Independence of Papua New Guinea. Multicoloured.

610	18c. Type **313**	20	10
611	25c. "Freedom" (bird in flight) (horiz)	50	1·50

314 Epiphany Scene

1975. Christmas.

612	**314**	15c. multicoloured	40	10
613	-	45c. violet, blue and silver	1·00	3·00

DESIGN—HORIZ: 45c. "Shining Star".

315 Australian Coat of Arms

1976. 75th Anniv of Nationhood.

614	**315**	18c. multicoloured	40	20

316 Telephone-user, c. 1878

1976. Centenary of Telephone.

615	**316**	18c. multicoloured	20	15

317 John Oxley

1976. 19th Century Explorers. Multicoloured.

616	18c. Type **317**	35	50
617	18c. Hume and Hovell	35	50
618	18c. John Forrest	35	50
619	18c. Ernest Giles	35	50
620	18c. William Gosse	35	50
621	18c. Peter Warburton	35	50

318 Measuring Stick, Graph and Computer Tape

1976. 50th Anniv of Commonwealth Scientific and Industrial Research Organization.

622	**318**	18c. multicoloured	20	15

319 Football

1976. Olympic Games, Montreal. Multicoloured.

623	18c. Type **319**	20	20
624	18c. Gymnastics (vert)	20	20
625	25c. Diving (vert)	35	80
626	40c. Cycling	1·25	1·25

320 Richmond Bridge, Tasmania

1976. Australian Scenes. Multicoloured.

627	5c. Type **320**	20	10
628	25c. Broken Bay, N.S.W	65	10
629	35c. Wittenoom Gorge, W.A	45	20
630	50c. Mt. Buffalo, Victoria (vert)	70	20
631	70c. Barrier Reef	1·00	1·25
632	85c. Ayers Rock, N.T	1·25	2·25

321 Blamire Young (designer of first Australian stamp)

1976. National Stamp Week.

633	**321**	18c. multicoloured	15	15
MS634	101×112 mm. Nos. 633×4		75	1·50

322 *Virgin and Child* (detail, Simone Contarini)

1976. Christmas.

635	**322**	15c. mauve and blue	20	10
636	-	45c. multicoloured	50	90

DESIGN: 45c. Toy koala bear and decorations.

323 John Gould

1976. Famous Australians. (8th series). Scientists. Multicoloured.

637	18c. Type **323**	35	50
638	18c. Thomas Laby	35	50
639	18c. Sir Baldwin Spencer	35	50
640	18c. Griffith Taylor	35	50

324 "Music"

1977. Performing Arts. Multicoloured.

641	20c. Type **324**	15	25
642	30c. Drama	20	35
643	40c. Dance	25	40
644	60c. Opera	1·50	1·75

325 Queen Elizabeth II

1977. Silver Jubilee. Multicoloured.

645	18c. Type **325**	30	10
646	45c. The Queen and Duke of Edinburgh	70	90

326 Fielder and Wicket Keeper

1977. Centenary of Australia–England Test Cricket. Multicoloured.

647	18c. Type **326**	40	50
648	18c. Umpire and batsman	40	50
649	18c. Fielders	40	50
650	18c. Batsman and umpire	40	50
651	18c. Bowler and fielder	40	50
652	45c. Batsman facing bowler	50	1·00

327 Parliament House

1977. 50th Anniv of Opening of Parliament House, Canberra.

653	**327**	18c. multicoloured	15	10

328 Trade Union Workers

1977. 50th Anniv of Australian Council of Trade Unions.

654	**328**	18c. multicoloured	15	10

329 Surfing Santa

1977. Christmas. Multicoloured.

655	15c. Type **329**	25	10
656	45c. Madonna and Child	75	1·25

330 National Flag

1978. Australia Day.

657	**330**	18c. multicoloured	20	15

331 Harry Hawker and Sopwith Atlantic

1978. Early Australian Aviators. Multicoloured.

658	18c. Type **331**	40	50
659	18c. Bert Hinkler and Avro Type 581 Avian	40	50
660	18c. Sir Charles Kingsford Smith and *Southern Cross*	40	50
661	18c. Charles Ulm and *Southern Cross*	40	50
MS662	100×112 mm. Nos. 658/61×2. Imperf	75	1·75

332 Piper PA-31 Navajo landing at Station Airstrip

1978. 50th Anniv of Royal Flying Doctor Service.

663	**332**	18c. multicoloured	20	15

333 Illawarra Flame Tree

1978. Trees. Multicoloured.

664	18c. Type **333**	20	15
665	25c. Ghost gum	35	1·40
666	40c. Grass tree	45	2·00
667	45c. Cootamundra wattle	45	70

334 Sturt's Desert Rose and Map

1978. Establishment of State Government for the Northern Territory.

668	**334**	18c. multicoloured	20	15

335 Hooded Plover

1978. Birds (1st series). Multicoloured.

669	1c. Spotted-sided ("Zebra") finch	10	20
670	2c. Crimson finch	10	20
671	5c. Type **335**	50	10
672	15c. Forest kingfisher (vert)	20	20
673	20c. Australian dabchick ("Little Grebe")	70	10
674	20c. Yellow robin ("Eastern Yellow Robin")	75	10
675	22c. White-tailed kingfisher (22×29 mm)	30	10
676	25c. Masked ("Spur-wing") plover	1·00	1·25
677	30c. Pied oystercatcher	1·00	25
678	40c. Variegated ("Lovely") wren (vert)	30	45
679	50c. Flame robin (vert)	1·00	1·00
680	55c. Comb-crested jacana ("Lotus-Bird")	1·40	60

See also Nos. 734/40.

336 1928 3d. National Stamp Exhibition Commemorative

1978. 50th Anniv of National Stamp Week, and National Stamp Exhibition.

694	**336**	20c. multicoloured	15	15
MS695	78×113 mm. No. 694×4		75	1·50

337 *The Madonna and the Child* (after van Eyck)

1978. Christmas. Multicoloured.

696	15c. Type **337**	25	10
697	25c. *The Virgin and Child* (Marmion)	35	65
698	55c. *The Holy Family* (del Vaga)	50	1·00

338 *Tulloch*

1978. Horse Racing. Multicoloured.

699	20c. Type **338**	30	10
700	35c. *Bernborough* (vert)	45	85
701	50c. *Phar Lap* (vert)	60	1·25
702	55c. *Peter Pan*	60	1·10

339 *Raising the Flag, Sydney Cove, 26 January 1788*

1979. Australia Day.

703	**339**	20c. multicoloured	15	15

340 *Canberra* (paddle-steamer)

1979. Ferries and Murray River Steamers. Multicoloured.

704	20c. Type **340**	20	10
705	35c. *Lady Denman*	40	70
706	50c. *Murray River Queen* (paddle-steamer)	50	1·40
707	55c. *Curl Curl* (hydrofoil)	55	1·25

341 Port Campbell, Victoria

1979. National Parks. Multicoloured.

708	20c. Type **341**	20	30
709	20c. Uluru, Northern Territory	20	30
710	20c. Royal, New South Wales	20	30
711	20c. Flinders Ranges, South Australia	20	30
712	20c. Nambung, Western Australia	20	30
713	20c. Girraween, Queensland (vert)	20	30
714	20c. Mount Field, Tasmania (vert)	20	30

342 *Double Fairlie* Type Locomotive, Western Australia

1979. Steam Railways. Multicoloured.

715	20c. Type **342**	30	10
716	35c. Locomotive, Puffing Billy Line, Victoria	60	70
717	50c. Locomotive, Pichi Richi Line, South Australia	70	1·50
718	55c. Locomotive, Zig Zag Railway, New South Wales	80	1·40

343 Symbolic Swan

1979. 150th Anniv of Western Australia.

719	**343**	20c. multicoloured	15	15

344 Children playing on Slide

1979. International Year of the Child.

720	**344**	20c. multicoloured	15	10

345 Letters and Parcels

1979. Christmas. Multicoloured.

721	15c. *Christ's Nativity* (Eastern European icon)	15	10
722	25c. Type **345**	15	65
723	55c. *Madonna and Child* (Buglioni)	25	80

346 Fly-fishing

1979. Fishing.

724	**346**	20c. multicoloured	15	10
725	-	35c. blue and violet	25	70
726	-	50c. multicoloured	35	90
727	-	55c. multicoloured	35	85

DESIGNS: 35c. Spinning; 50c. Deep sea game-fishing; 55c. Surf-fishing.

347 Matthew Flinders

1980. Australia Day.

728	**347**	20c. multicoloured	20	10

348 Dingo

1980. Dogs. Multicoloured.

729	20c. Type **348**	40	10
730	25c. Border collie	40	50
731	35c. Australian terrier	45	70
732	50c. Australian cattle dog	80	2·25
733	55c. Australian kelpie	80	1·40

1980. Birds (2nd series). As T **335**. Multicoloured.

734	10c. Golden-shouldered parrot (vert)	50	10
734b	18c. Spotted catbird (vert)	50	2·25
735	28c. Australian bee eater ("Rainbow Bird") (vert)	50	10
736	35c. Regent bower bird (vert)	50	10
737	45c. Masked wood swallow	50	10
738	60c. Australian king parrot ("King Parrot") (vert)	50	15
739	80c. Rainbow pitta	1·00	60
740	$1 Black-backed magpie ("Western Magpie") (vert)	1·00	10

349 Queen Elizabeth II

1980. Birthday of Queen Elizabeth II.

741	**349**	22c. multicoloured	30	20

350 Once a jolly Swagman camp'd by a Billabong

1980. Folklore. *Waltzing Matilda*. Multicoloured.

742	22c. Type **350**	25	40
743	22c. "And he sang as he shoved that jumbuck in his tuckerbag"	25	40
744	22c. "Up rode the squatter mounted on his thorough-bred"	25	40
745	22c. "Down came the troopers one, two, three"	25	40
746	22c. "And his ghost may be heard as you pass by that billabong"	25	40

351 High Court Building, Canberra

1980. Opening of High Court Building.

747	**351**	22c. multicoloured	20	20

352 Salvation Army

1980. Community Welfare. Multicoloured.

748	22c. Type **352**	30	30
749	22c. St. Vincent de Paul Society (vert)	30	30
750	22c. Meals on Wheels (vert)	30	30
751	22c. "Life. Be in it"	30	30

353 Postbox, c. 1900

1980. National Stamp Week. Multicoloured.

752	22c. Type **353**	25	40
753	22c. Postman, facing left	25	40
754	22c. Ford Model T mail van	25	40
755	22c. Postman, facing right	25	40
756	22c. Postman and postbox	25	40
MS757	95×100 mm. Nos. 752, 754 and 756	1·10	1·60

354 *Holy Family* (painting, Prospero Fontana)

1980. Christmas. Multicoloured.

758	15c. *The Virgin Enthroned* (Justin O'Brien) (detail)	15	10
759	28c. Type **354**	25	40
760	60c. *Madonna and Child* (sculpture by School of M. Zuern)	50	1·10

355 Commonwealth Aircraft Factory Wackett, 1941

1980. Australian Aircraft. Multicoloured.

761	22c. Type **355**	30	10
762	40c. Commonwealth Aircraft Factory Winjeel, 1955	50	75
763	45c. Commonwealth Aircraft Factory Boomerang, 1944	50	85
764	60c. Government Aircraft Factory Nomad, 1975	65	1·40

356 Flag in shape of Australia

1981. Australia Day.

765	**356**	22c. multicoloured	20	20

357 Caricature of Darby Munro (jockey)

1981. Sporting Personalities. Caricatures. Multicoloured.

766	22c. Type **357**	20	10
767	35c. Victor Trumper (cricket)	40	60
768	55c. Sir Norman Brookes (tennis)	40	1·00
769	60c. Walter Lindrum (billiards)	40	1·25

358 1931 Kingsford Smith's Flights 6d. Commemorative

1981. 50th Anniversary of Official Australia–U.K. Airmail Service.

770	**358**	22c. lilac, red and blue	15	10
771	-	60c. lilac, red and blue	40	90

DESIGN—HORIZ: 60c. As T **358**, but format changed.

359 Apex Emblem and Map of Australia

1981. 50th Anniv of Apex (young men's service club).
| 772 | **359** | 22c. multicoloured | 20 | 20 |

360 Queen's Personal Standard for Australia

1981. Birthday of Queen Elizabeth II.
| 773 | **360** | 22c. multicoloured | 20 | 20 |

361 Licence Inspected

1981. Gold Rush Era. Sketches by S. T. Gill. Multicoloured.
774	22c. Type **361**	20	25
775	22c. Puddling	20	25
776	22c. Quality of washing stuff	20	25
777	22c. On route to deposit gold	20	25

362 On the Wallaby Track (Fred McCubbin)

1981. Paintings. Multicoloured.
| 778 | $2 Type **362** | 1·00 | 20 |
| 779 | $5 A Holiday at Mentone, 1888 (Charles Conder) | 3·00 | 50 |

363 Thylacine **363a** Blue Mountain Tree Frog

363b Papilio ulysses (butterfly)

1981. Wildlife. Multicoloured.
781	1c. Lace monitor	10	20
782	3c. Corroboree frog	10	10
783	4c. Regent skipper (butterfly) (vert)	55	80
784	5c. Queensland hairy-nosed wombat (vert)	10	10
785	10c. Cairns birdwing (butterfly) (vert)	60	10
786	15c. Eastern snake-necked tortoise	1·00	1·00
787	20c. MacLeay's swallowtail (butterfly) (vert)	80	35
788	24c. Type **363**	45	10
789	25c. Greater Bilby (vert)	40	1·00
790a	27c. Type **363a**	1·00	1·00
791	27c. Type **363b**	1·00	30
792	30c. Bridle nail-tailed wallaby (vert)	90	20
792a	30c. Chlorinda hairstreak (butterfly) (vert)	1·00	20
793	35c. Blue tiger (butterfly) (vert)	1·00	30
794	40c. Smooth knob-tailed gecko	45	30
795	45c. Big greasy (butterfly) (vert)	1·00	30
796	50c. Leadbeater's possum	50	10
797	55c. Stick-nest rat (vert)	50	30
798	60c. Wood white (butterfly) (vert)	1·10	30
799	65c. Yellow-faced whip snake	1·75	1·50
800	70c. Crucifix toad	65	1·75
801	75c. Eastern water dragon	1·25	90
802	80c. Amaryllis azure (butterfly) (vert)	1·40	2·00
803	85c. Centralian blue-tongued lizard	1·10	1·25

804	90c. Freshwater crocodile	1·60	1·25
805	95c. Thorny devil	1·60	2·00
806	$1 Sword-grass brown (butterfly) (vert)	1·40	30

364 Prince Charles and Lady Diana Spencer

1981. Royal Wedding.
| 821 | **364** | 24c. multicoloured | 20 | 10 |
| 822 | **364** | 60c. multicoloured | 55 | 1·00 |

365 Cortinarius cinnabarinus

1981. Australian Fungi. Multicoloured.
823	24c. Type **365**	20	10
824	35c. Coprinus comatus	40	80
825	55c. Armillaria luteobubalina	55	1·00
826	60c. Cortinarius austro-venetus	60	1·10

366 Disabled People playing Basketball

1981. International Year for Disabled Persons.
| 827 | **366** | 24c. multicoloured | 20 | 20 |

367 Christmas Bush for His Adorning

1981. Christmas. Scenes and Verses from Carols by W. James and J. Wheeler. Multicoloured.
828	18c. Type **367**	20	10
829	30c. The Silver Stars are in the Sky	25	25
830	60c. Noeltime	40	1·10

368 Globe depicting Australia

1981. Commonwealth Heads of Government Meeting, Melbourne.
| 831 | **368** | 24c. black, blue and gold | 15 | 10 |
| 832 | **368** | 60c. black, blue and silver | 45 | 75 |

369 Ragamuffin ocean racing yacht

1981. Yachts. Multicoloured.
833	24c. Type **369**	20	10
834	35c. Sharpie	30	55
835	55c. 12 Metre	40	1·50
836	60c. Sabot	50	1·50

370 Aborigine, Governor Phillip (founder of N.S.W., 1788) and Post World War II Migrant

1982. Australia Day. "Three Great Waves of Migration".
| 837 | **370** | 24c. multicoloured | 35 | 25 |

371 Humpback Whale

1982. Whales. Multicoloured.
838	24c. Sperm whale	25	10
839	35c. Black (inscr "Southern") right whale (vert)	35	50
840	55c. Blue whale (vert)	50	1·25
841	60c. Type **371**	60	1·25

372 Queen Elizabeth II

1982. Birthday of Queen Elizabeth II.
| 842 | **372** | 27c. multicoloured | 35 | 15 |

373 "Marjorie Atherton"

1982. Roses. Multicoloured.
843	27c. Type **373**	25	15
844	40c. "Imp"	30	60
845	65c. "Minnie Watson"	50	2·00
846	75c. "Satellite"	50	1·25

374 Radio Announcer and 1930-style Microphone

1982. 50th Anniv of ABC (Australian Broadcasting Commission). Multicoloured.
| 847 | 27c. Type **374** | 30 | 65 |
| 848 | 27c. ABC logo | 30 | 65 |

375 Forbes Post Office

1982. Historic Australian Post Offices. Multicoloured.
849	27c. Type **375**	25	40
850	27c. Flemington Post Office	25	40
851	27c. Rockhampton Post Office	25	40
852	27c. Kingston S. E. Post Office (horiz)	25	40
853	27c. York Post Office (horiz)	25	40
854	27c. Launceston Post Office	25	40
855	27c. Old Post and Telegraph Station, Alice Springs (horiz)	25	40

376 Early Australian Christmas Card

1982. Christmas. Multicoloured.
856	21c. Bushman's Hotel with Cobb's coach arriving (horiz)	25	10
857	35c. Type **376**	40	60
858	75c. Little girl offering Christmas pudding to swagman	60	1·60

377 Boxing

1982. Commonwealth Games, Brisbane.
859	**377**	27c. stone, yellow and red	20	25
860	-	27c. yellow, stone and green	20	25
861	-	27c. stone, yellow and brown	20	25
862	-	75c. multicoloured	50	1·25
MS863	130×95 mm. Nos. 859/61		1·00	1·75
DESIGNS: No. 860, Archery; No. 861, Weight-lifting; No. 862, Pole-vaulting.

378 Sydney Harbour Bridge 5s. Stamp of 1932

1982. National Stamp Week.
| 864 | **378** | 27c. multicoloured | 35 | 30 |

379 Yirawala Bark Painting

1982. Opening of Australian National Gallery.
| 865 | **379** | 27c. multicoloured | 30 | 25 |

380 Mimi Spirits Dancing

1982. Aboriginal Culture. Music and Dance.
866	**380**	27c. multicoloured	20	10
867	-	40c. multicoloured	30	60
868	-	65c. multicoloured	45	1·00
869	-	75c. multicoloured	50	1·00
DESIGN: 40c. to 75c. Aboriginal bark paintings of Mimi Spirits.

381 Eucalyptus calophylla "Rosea"

1982. Eucalyptus Flowers. Multicoloured.
870	1c. Type **381**	10	30
871	2c. Eucalyptus casia	10	30
872	3c. Eucalyptus ficifolia	1·25	2·25
873	10c. Eucalyptus globulus	1·25	2·25
874	27c. Eucalyptus forrestiana	30	40

382 Shand Mason Steam Fire Engine, 1891

1983. Historic Fire Engines. Multicoloured.
875	27c. Type **382**	35	10
876	40c. Hotchkiss fire engine, 1914	45	75
877	65c. Ahrens-Fox fire engine, 1929	70	1·60
878	75c. Merryweather manual fire appliance, 1851	70	1·40

383 H.M.S. Sirius

1983. Australia Day. Multicoloured.
| 879 | 27c. Type **383** | 40 | 75 |
| 880 | 27c. H.M.S.*Supply* | 40 | 75 |

384 Stylized Kangaroo and Kiwi

1983. Closer Economic Relationship Agreement with New Zealand.
| 881 | **384** | 27c. multicoloured | 30 | 30 |

385 Equality and Dignity

1983. Commonwealth Day. Multicoloured.
882	27c. Type **385**	20	25
883	27c. Liberty and Freedom	20	25
884	27c. Social Justice and Co-operation	20	25
885	75c. Peace and Harmony	50	1·50

386 R.Y. *Britannia* passing Sydney Opera House

1983. Birthday of Queen Elizabeth II.
| 886 | **386** | 27c. multicoloured | 50 | 30 |

387 "Postal and Telecommunications Services"

1983. World Communications Year.
| 887 | **387** | 27c. multicoloured | 30 | 30 |

388 Badge of the Order of St. John

1983. Centenary of St. John Ambulance in Australia.
| 888 | **388** | 27c. black and blue | 35 | 30 |

389 Jaycee Members and Badge

1983. 50th Anniv of Australian Jaycees.
| 889 | **389** | 27c. multicoloured | 30 | 30 |

390 "The Bloke"

1983. Folklore. *The Sentimental Bloke* (humorous poem by C. J. Dennis). Multicoloured.
890	27c. Type **390**	30	50
891	27c. "Doreen—The Intro"	30	50
892	27c. "The Stror' at Coot"	30	50
893	27c. "Hitched"	30	50
894	27c. "The Mooch o' Life"	30	50

391 Nativity Scene

1983. Christmas. Children's Paintings. Multicoloured.
895	24c. Type **391**	20	10
896	35c. Kookaburra	30	45
897	85c. Father Christmas in sleigh over beach	60	1·40

392 Sir Paul Edmund de Strzelecki

1983. Explorers of Australia. Multicoloured.
898	30c. Type **392**	25	40
899	30c. Ludwig Leichhardt	25	40
900	30c. William John Wills and Robert O'Hara Burke	25	40
901	30c. Alexander Forrest	25	40

393 Cook Family Cottage, Melbourne

1984. Australia Day.
| 902 | **393** | 30c. black and stone | 30 | 35 |

394 Charles Ulm, *Faith in Australia* and Trans-Tasman Cover

1984. 50th Anniv of First Official Airmail Flights. New Zealand–Australia and Australia–Papua New Guinea. Multicoloured.
| 903 | 45c. Type **394** | 75 | 1·25 |
| 904 | 45c. As Type **394** but showing flown cover to Papua New Guinea | 75 | 1·25 |

395 Thomson "Steamer", 1898

1984. Veteran and Vintage Cars. Multicoloured.
905	30c. Type **395**	35	60
906	30c. Tarrant two seater, 1906	35	60
907	30c. Gordon & Co "Australian Six" two seater, 1919	35	60
908	30c. Summit tourer, 1923	35	60
909	30c. Chic two seater, 1924	35	60

396 Queen Elizabeth II

1984. Birthday of Queen Elizabeth II.
| 910 | **396** | 30c. multicoloured | 30 | 35 |

397 Cutty Sark

1984. Clipper Ships. Multicoloured.
911	30c. Type **397**	35	25
912	45c. Orient (horiz)	50	80
913	75c. Sobraon (horiz)	70	1·75
914	85c. Thermopylae	70	1·50

398 Freestyle

1984. Skiing. Multicoloured.
915	30c. Type **398**	30	45
916	30c. Downhill racer	30	45
917	30c. Slalom (horiz)	30	45
918	30c. Nordic (horiz)	30	45

399 Coral Hopper

1984. Marine Life. Multicoloured.
919	2c. Type **399**	10	30
920	3c. Jimble	40	30
921	5c. Tasselled frogfish ("Anglerfish")	15	10
922	10c. Rough stonefish	1·25	50
923	20c. Red handfish	65	40
924	25c. Orange-lipped cowrie	45	40
925	30c. Choat's wrasse	45	40
926	33c. Leafy seadragon	65	10
927	40c. Red velvetfish	85	1·75
928	45c. Textile or cloth of gold cone	1·75	50
929	50c. Clown surgeonfish	80	50
930	55c. Bennet's nudibranch	80	50
931	60c. Zebra lionfish	1·75	70
932	65c. Banded stingray	1·75	2·25
933	70c. Southern blue-ringed octopus	1·75	1·75
934	80c. Pineconefish ("Pineapple fish")	1·25	1·75
935	85c. Royal angelfish	90	70
936	90c. Crab-eyed goby	1·60	75
937	$1 Crown of thorns starfish	1·50	80

400 Before the Event

1984. Olympic Games, Los Angeles. Multicoloured.
941	30c. Type **400**	25	40
942	30c. During the event	25	40
943	30c. After the event (vert)	25	40

401 Australian 1913 1d. Kangaroo Stamp

1984. "Ausipex '84" International Stamp Exhibition, Melbourne.
| 944 | **401** | 30c. multicoloured | 35 | 30 |

MS945 126×175 mm. 30c. × 7, Victoria 1850 3d. "Half Length"; New South Wales 1850 1d. "Sydney View"; Tasmania 1853 1d.; South Australia 1855 1d.; Western Australia 1854 1d. "Black Swan"; Queensland 1860 6d.; Type **401**
| | | 3·50 | 4·50 |

402 *Angel* (stained-glass window, St. Francis's Church, Melbourne)

1984. Christmas. Stained-glass Windows. Multicoloured.
946	24c. *Angel and Child* (Holy Trinity Church, Sydney)	15	10
947	30c. *Veiled Virgin and Child* (St. Mary's Catholic Church, Geelong)	20	10
948	40c. Type **402**	30	75
949	50c. *Three Kings* (St. Mary's Cathedral, Sydney)	40	90

| 950 | 85c. *Madonna and Child* (St. Bartholomew's Church, Norwood) | 50 | 1·60 |

403 "Stick Figures" (Cobar Region)

1984. Bicentenary (1988) of Australian Settlement (1st issue). The First Australians. Multicoloured.
951	30c. Type **403**	20	45
952	30c. "Bunjil" (large figure), Grampians	20	45
953	30c. "Quikans" (tall figures), Cape York	20	45
954	30c. "Wandjina Spirit and Baby Snakes" (Gibb River)	20	45
955	30c. "Rock Python" (Gibb River)	20	45
956	30c. "Silver Barramundi" (fish) (Kakadu National Park)	20	45
957	30c. Bicentenary emblem	20	45
958	85c. "Rock Possum" (Kakadu National Park)	50	1·40

See also Nos. 972/5, 993/6, 1002/7, 1019/22, 1059/63, 1064/6, 1077/81, 1090/2, 1110, 1137/41, 1145/8 and 1149.

404 Yellow-tufted Honeyeater

1984. 150th Anniv of Victoria. Multicoloured.
| 959 | 30c. Type **404** | 40 | 65 |
| 960 | 30c. Leadbeater's possum | 40 | 65 |

405 Musgrave Ranges (Sidney Nolan)

1985. Australia Day. Birth Bicentenary of Dorothea Mackellar (author of poem *My Country*). Multicoloured.
| 961 | 30c. Type **405** | 50 | 80 |
| 962 | 30c. *The Walls of China* (Russell Drysdale) | 50 | 80 |

406 Young People of Different Races and Sun

1985. International Youth Year.
| 963 | **406** | 30c. multicoloured | 40 | 30 |

407 Royal Victorian Volunteer Artillery

1985. 19th-Century Australian Military Uniforms. Multicoloured.
964	33c. Type **407**	40	65
965	33c. Western Australian Pinjarrah Cavalry	40	65
966	33c. New South Wales Lancers	40	65
967	33c. New South Wales Contingent to the Sudan	40	65
968	33c. Victorian Mounted Rifles	40	65

408 District
Nurse of early
1900s

1985. Centenary of District Nursing Services.

969	**408**	33c. multicoloured	45	35

409 Sulphur-crested Cockatoos

1985. Multicoloured, background colour given.

970	**409**	1c. flesh	2·50	4·00
971	**409**	33c. turquoise	50	55

410 Abel Tasman and
Journal Entry

1985. Bicentenary (1988) of Australian Settlement (2nd issue). Navigators. Multicoloured.

972		33c. Type **410**	40	35
973		33c. Dirk Hartog's *Eendracht* (detail, Aert Anthonisz)	40	35
974		33c. *William Dampier* (detail, T. Murray)	40	35
975		90c. Globe and hand with extract from Dampier's journal	75	2·50
MS976		150×115 mm. As Nos. 972/5, but with cream-coloured margins	1·75	4·50

411 Sovereign's
Badge of Order
of Australia

1985. Queen Elizabeth II's Birthday.

977	**411**	33c. multicoloured	40	30

412 Tree, and
Soil running
through
Hourglass ("Soil")

1985. Conservation. Multicoloured.

978		33c. Type **412**	25	20
979		50c. Washing on line and smog ("air")	40	75
980		80c. Tap and flower ("water")	50	1·25
981		90c. Chain encircling flames ("energy")	60	1·75

413 *Elves and
Fairies* (Annie
Rentoul and Ida
Rentoul
Outhwaite)

1985. Classic Australian Children's Books. Multicoloured.

982		33c. Type **413**	40	75
983		33c. *The Magic Pudding* (Norman Lindsay)	40	75
984		33c. *Ginger Meggs* (James Charles Bancks)	40	75
985		33c. *Blinky Bill* (Dorothy Wall)	40	75
986		33c. *Snugglepot and Cuddlepie* (May Gibbs)	40	75

414 Dish Aerials

1985. Electronic Mail Service.

987	**414**	33c. multicoloured	35	30

415 Angel in Sailing Ship

1985. Christmas. Multicoloured.

988		27c. Angel with holly wings	20	10
989		33c. Angel with bells	25	10
990		45c. Type **415**	30	25
991		55c. Angel with star	40	75
992		90c. Angel with Christmas tree bauble	65	2·25

416 Astrolabe
("Batavia", 1629)

1985. Bicentenary (1988) of Australian Settlement (3rd issue). Relics from Early Shipwrecks. Multicoloured.

993		33c. Type **416**	35	15
994		50c. German beardman jug (*Vergulde Draeck*, 1656)	60	1·00
995		90c. Wooden bobbins (*Batavia*, 1629) and encrusted scissors (*Zeewijk*, 1727)	1·00	3·75
996		$1 Silver and brass buckle (*Zeewijk*, 1727)	1·00	2·25

417 Aboriginal
Wandjina Spirit,
Map of Australia
and Egg

1986. Australia Day.

997	**417**	33c. multicoloured	40	30

418 AUSSAT
Satellite, Moon
and Earth's
Surface

1986. AUSSAT National Communications Satellite System. Multicoloured.

998		33c. Type **418**	30	10
999		80c. AUSSAT satellite in orbit	70	2·00

419 H.M.S. *Buffalo*

1986. 150th Anniv of South Australia. Multicoloured.

1000		33c. Type **419**	70	1·25
1001		33c. *City Sign* sculpture (Otto Hajek), Adelaide	70	1·25

Nos. 1000/1 were printed together *se-tenant*, the background of each horiz pair showing an extract from the colony's Letters Patent of 1836.

420 *Banksia serrata*

1986. Bicentenary (1988) of Australian Settlement (4th issue). Cook's Voyage to New Holland. Multicoloured.

1002		33c. Type **420**	50	35
1003		33c. *Hibiscus meraukensis*	50	35
1004		50c. *Dillenia alata*	70	1·10
1005		80c. *Correa reflexa*	1·50	2·75
1006		90c. *Joseph Banks* (botanist) (Reynolds) and Banks with Dr. Solander	2·00	2·75
1007		90c. *Sydney Parkinson* (self-portrait) and Parkinson drawing	2·00	2·75

421 Radio
Telescope, Parkes,
and Diagram of
Comet's Orbit

1986. Appearance of Halley's Comet.

1008	**421**	33c. multicoloured	50	35

422 Queen
Elizabeth II

1986. 60th Birthday of Queen Elizabeth.

1009	**422**	33c. multicoloured	55	35

423 Brumbies (wild
horses)

1986. Australian Horses. Multicoloured.

1010		33c. Type **423**	60	15
1011		80c. Mustering	1·50	2·25
1012		90c. Show-jumping	1·50	2·50
1013		$1 Child on pony	1·75	2·25

424 *The Old
Shearer stands*

1986. Folklore. Scenes and Verses from the Folksong *Click go the Shears*. Multicoloured.

1014		33c. Type **424**	45	80
1015		33c. "The ringer looks around"	45	80
1016		33c. "The boss of the board"	45	80
1017		33c. "The tar-boy is there"	45	80
1018		33c. "Shearing is all over"	45	80

Nos. 1014/18 were printed together, *se-tenant*, forming a composite design.

425 *King George III* (A. Ramsay) and Convicts

1986. Bicentenary (1988) of Australian Settlement (5th issue). Convict Settlement in New South Wales. Multicoloured.

1019		33c. Type **425**	40	45
1020		33c. *Lord Sydney* (Gilbert Stuart) and convicts	40	45
1021		33c. *Captain Arthur Phillip* (F. Wheatley) and ship	40	45
1022		$1 *Captain John Hunter* (W. B. Bennett) and aborigines	1·25	4·50

426 Red
Kangaroo

1986. Australian Wildlife (1st series). Multicoloured.

1023		36c. Type **426**	70	95
1024		36c. Emu	70	95
1025		36c. Koala	70	95
1026		36c. Laughing kookaburra ("Kookaburra")	70	95
1027		36c. Platypus	70	95

See also Nos. 1072/6.

427 Royal
Bluebell

1986. Alpine Wildflowers. Multicoloured.

1028		3c. Type **427**	50	75
1029		5c. Alpine marsh marigold	2·00	3·25
1030		25c. Mount Buffalo sunray	2·00	3·25
1031		36c. Silver snow daisy	45	30

428 Pink Enamel
Orchid

1986. Native Orchids. Multicoloured.

1032		36c. Type **428**	75	20
1033		55c. *Dendrobium nindii*	1·50	1·25
1034		90c. Duck orchid	2·25	4·00
1035		$1 Queen of Sheba orchid	2·25	2·75

429 *Australia II*
crossing Finishing
Line

1986. Australian Victory in America's Cup, 1983. Multicoloured.

1036		36c. Type **429**	75	75
1037		36c. Boxing kangaroo flag of winning syndicate	75	75
1038		36c. America's Cup trophy	75	75

430 Dove with
Olive Branch and
Sun

1986. International Peace Year.

1039	**430**	36c. multicoloured	65	40

431 Mary and
Joseph

1986. Christmas. Scenes from children's nativity play. Multicoloured.

1040		30c. Type **431**	40	30
1041		36c. Three Wise Men leaving gifts	50	20
1042		60c. Angels (horiz)	90	2·00
MS1043		147×70 mm. 30c. Three angels and shepherd (horiz); 30c. Kneeling shepherds (horiz); 30c. Mary, Joseph and three angels; 30c. Innkeeper and two angels; 30c. Three Wise Men (horiz)	3·00	4·00

432 Australian Flag on Printed Circuit Board

1987. Australia Day. Multicoloured.

| 1044 | 36c. Type **432** | 55 | 75 |
| 1045 | 36c. "Australian Made" Campaign logos | 55 | 75 |

433 Aerial View of Yacht

1987. America's Cup Yachting Championship. Multicoloured.

1046	36c. Type **433**	30	20
1047	55c. Two yachts tacking	50	75
1048	90c. Two yachts beating	60	2·50
1049	$1 Two yachts under full sail	65	1·25

434 Grapes and Melons

1987. Australian Fruit. Multicoloured.

1050	36c. Type **434**	30	20
1051	65c. Tropical and sub-tropical fruits	60	1·25
1052	90c. Citrus fruit, apples and pears	1·00	2·50
1053	$1 Stone and berry fruits	1·00	1·25

435 Livestock

1987. Agricultural Shows. Multicoloured.

1054	36c. Type **435**	60	20
1055	65c. Produce	1·00	1·75
1056	90c. Sideshows	1·25	3·25
1057	$1 Competitions	1·50	2·50

436 Queen Elizabeth in Australia, 1986

1987. Queen Elizabeth II's Birthday.

| 1058 | **436** | 36c. multicoloured | 55 | 60 |

437 Convicts on Quay

1987. Bicentenary (1988) of Australian Settlement (6th issue). Departure of the First Fleet. Multicoloured.

1059	36c. Type **437**	55	1·00
1060	36c. Royal Marines officer and wife	55	1·00
1061	36c. Sailors loading supplies	55	1·00
1062	36c. Officers being ferried to ships	55	1·00
1063	36c. Fleet in English Channel	55	1·00

See also Nos. 1064/6, 1077/81 and 1090/2.

1987. Bicentenary (1988) of Australian Settlement (7th issue). First Fleet at Tenerife. As T **437**. Multicoloured.

1064	36c. Ferrying supplies, Santa Cruz	55	1·00
1065	36c. Canary Islands fishermen and departing fleet	55	1·00
1066	$1 Fleet arriving at Tenerife	1·40	2·25

Nos. 1064/5 were printed together, *se-tenant*, forming a composite design.

438 *At the Station*

1987. Folklore. Scenes and Verses from Poem *The Man from Snowy River*. Multicoloured.

1067	36c. Type **438**	65	1·00
1068	36c. "Mountain bred"	65	1·00
1069	36c. "That terrible descent"	65	1·00
1070	36c. "At their heels"	65	1·00
1071	36c. "Brought them back"	65	1·00

Nos. 1067/71 were printed together, *se-tenant*, forming a composite background design of mountain scenery.

1987. Australian Wildlife (2nd series). As T **426**. Multicoloured.

1072	37c. Common brushtail possum	55	85
1073	37c. Sulphur-crested cockatoo ("Cockatoo")	55	85
1074	37c. Common wombat	55	85
1075	37c. Crimson rosella ("Rosella")	55	85
1076	37c. Echidna	55	85

1987. Bicentenary (1988) of Australian Settlement (8th issue). First Fleet at Rio de Janeiro. As T **437**. Multicoloured.

1077	37c. Sperm whale and fleet	60	1·10
1078	37c. Brazilian coast	60	1·10
1079	37c. British officers in market	60	1·10
1080	37c. Religious procession	60	1·10
1081	37c. Fleet leaving Rio	60	1·10

Nos. 1077/81 were printed together, *se-tenant*, forming a composite design.

439 Bionic Ear

1987. Australian Achievements in Technology. Multicoloured.

1082	37c. Type **439**	25	15
1083	53c. Microchips	40	35
1084	63c. Robotics	50	60
1085	68c. Ceramics	55	65

440 Catching Crayfish

1987. "Aussie Kids". Multicoloured.

1086	37c. Type **440**	30	10
1087	55c. Playing cat's cradle	50	55
1088	90c. Young football supporters	75	2·25
1089	$1 Children with kangaroo	75	1·25

1987. Bicentenary (1988) of Australian Settlement (9th issue). First Fleet at Cape of Good Hope. As T **437**. Multicoloured.

1090	37c. Marine checking list of livestock	65	1·00
1091	37c. Loading livestock	65	1·00
1092	$1 First Fleet at Cape Town	1·50	2·50

Nos. 1090/1 were printed together, *se-tenant*, forming a composite design.

441 Detail of Spearthrower, Western Australia

1987. Aboriginal Crafts. Multicoloured.

1093	3c. Type **441**	1·10	1·60
1094	15c. Shield pattern, New South Wales	5·50	9·50
1095	37c. Basket weave, Queensland	1·10	1·60
1096	37c. Bowl design, Central Australia	90	1·25
1097	37c. Belt pattern, Northern Territory	1·10	1·60

442 Grandmother and Granddaughters with Candles

1987. Christmas. Designs showing carol singing by candlelight. Multicoloured.

1098	30c. Type **442**	50	65
1099	30c. Father and daughters	50	65
1100	30c. Four children	50	65
1101	30c. Family	50	65
1102	30c. Six teenagers	50	65
1103	37c. Choir (horiz)	50	35
1104	63c. Father and two children (horiz)	85	1·60

1988. Bicentenary of Australian Settlement (10th issue). Arrival of First Fleet. As T **437**. Multicoloured.

1105	37c. Aborigines watching arrival of Fleet, Botany Bay	65	95
1106	37c. Aborigine family and anchored ships	65	95
1107	37c. Fleet arriving at Sydney Cove	65	95
1108	37c. Ship's boat	65	95
1109	37c. Raising the flag, Sydney Cove, 26 January 1788	65	95

Nos. 1105/9 were printed together, *se-tenant*, forming a composite design.

443 Koala with Stockman's Hat and Eagle dressed as Uncle Sam

1988. Bicentenary of Australian Settlement (11th issue). Joint issue with U.S.A.

| 1110 | **443** | 37c. multicoloured | 60 | 35 |

444 *Religion* (A. Horner)

1988. "Living Together". Designs showing cartoons. Multicoloured (except 30c.).

1111	1c. Type **444**	50	70
1112	2c. *Industry* (P. Nicholson)	50	60
1113	3c. *Local Government* (A. Collette)	50	60
1114	4c. *Trade Unions* (Liz Honey)	10	20
1115	5c. *Parliament* (Bronwyn Halls)	50	50
1116	10c. *Transport* (Meg Williams)	30	50
1117	15c. *Sport* (G. Cook)	1·75	60
1118	20c. *Commerce* (M. Atcherson)	70	1·00
1119	25c. *Housing* (C. Smith)	45	40
1120	30c. *Welfare* (R. Tandberg) (black and lilac)	55	1·25
1121	39c. *Postal Services* (P. Viska)	45	50
1121b	39c. *Tourism* (J. Spooner)	65	50
1122	40c. *Recreation* (R. Harvey)	70	70
1123	45c. *Health* (Jenny Coopes)	70	1·25
1124	50c. *Mining* (G. Haddon)	70	50
1125	53c. *Primary Industry* (S. Leahy)	1·75	2·25
1126	55c. *Education* (Victoria Roberts)	1·50	2·25
1127	60c. *Armed Forces* (B. Green)	1·50	70
1128	63c. *Police* (J. Russell)	2·50	1·40
1129	65c. *Telecommunications* (B. Petty)	1·50	2·75
1130	68c. *The Media* (A. Langoulant)	2·25	3·50
1131	70c. *Science and Technology* (J. Hook)	1·75	1·75
1132	75c. *Visual Arts* (G. Dazeley)	1·00	1·00
1133	80c. *Performing Arts* (A. Stitt)	1·25	1·00
1134	90c. *Banking* (S. Billington)	1·50	1·50
1135	95c. *Law* (C. Aslanis)	1·00	2·25
1136	$1 *Rescue and Emergency* (M. Leunig)	1·10	1·00

445 *Government House, Sydney, 1790* (George Raper)

1988. Bicentenary of Australian Settlement (12th issue). *The Early Years, 1788–1809.* Multicoloured.

1137	37c. Type **445**	65	1·00
1138	37c. *Government Farm, Parramatta, 1791* ("The Port Jackson Painter")	65	1·00
1139	37c. *Parramatta Road, 1796* (attr Thomas Watling)	65	1·00
1140	37c. *View of Sydney Cove, c. 1800* (detail) (Edward Dayes)	65	1·00
1141	37c. *Sydney Hospital, 1803,* (detail) (George William Evans)	65	1·00

Nos. 1137/41 were printed together, *se-tenant*, forming a composite background design from the painting *View of Sydney from the East Side of the Cove, c. 1808* by John Eyre.

446 Queen Elizabeth II (from photo by Tim Graham)

1988. Queen Elizabeth II's Birthday.

| 1142 | **446** | 37c. multicoloured | 50 | 40 |

447 Expo '88 Logo

1988. "Expo '88" World Fair, Brisbane.

| 1143 | **447** | 37c. multicoloured | 50 | 40 |

448 New Parliament House

1988. Opening of New Parliament House, Canberra.

| 1144 | **448** | 37c. multicoloured | 50 | 40 |

449 Early Settler and Sailing Clipper

1988. Bicentenary of Australian Settlement (13th issue). Multicoloured.

1145	37c. Type **449**	75	1·00
1146	37c. Queen Elizabeth II with British and Australian Parliament Buildings	75	1·00
1147	$1 W. G. Grace (cricketer) and tennis racquet	1·50	2·25
1148	$1 Shakespeare, John Lennon (entertainer) and Sydney Opera House	1·50	2·25

Stamps in similar designs were also issued by Great Britain.

450 Kiwi and Koala at Campfire

1988. Bicentenary of Australian Settlement (14th issue).

| 1149 | **450** | 37c. multicoloured | 65 | 40 |

A stamp in a similar design was also issued by New Zealand.

451 *Bush Potato Country* (Turkey Tolsen Tjupurrula and David Corby Tjapaltjarri)

1988. Art of the Desert. Aboriginal Paintings from Central Australia. Multicoloured.

1150	37c. Type **451**		25	20
1151	55c. *Courtship Rejected* (Limpi Puntungka Tjapangati)		45	70
1152	90c. *Medicine Story* (artist unknown)		65	2·50
1153	$1 *Ancestor Dreaming* (Tim Leura Tjapaltjarri)		65	1·50

452 Basketball

1988. Olympic Games, Seoul. Multicoloured.

1154	37c. Type **452**	40	25
1155	65c. Athlete crossing finish line	45	1·75
1156	$1 Gymnast with hoop	60	1·75

453 Rod and Mace

1988. 34th Commonwealth Parliamentary Conference, Canberra.

1157	**453** 37c. multicoloured	50	60

454 Necklace by Peter Tully

1988. Australian Crafts. Multicoloured.

1158	2c. Type **454**	4·00	6·50
1159	5c. Vase by Colin Levy	4·00	6·50
1160	39c. Teapot by Frank Bauer	50	35

455 Pinnacles Desert

1988. Panorama of Australia. Multicoloured.

1161	39c. Type **455**	55	20
1162	55c. Flooded landscape, Arnhem Land	75	75
1163	65c. Twelve Apostles, Victoria	1·00	2·00
1164	70c. Mountain Ash wood	1·00	2·00

456 The Nativity (Danielle Hush)

1988. Christmas. Multicoloured.

1165	32c. Type **456**	35	10
1166	39c. *Koala as Father Christmas* (Kylie Courtney)	35	10
1167	63c. *Christmas Cockatoo* (Benjamin Stevenson)	70	1·40

457 Sir Henry Parkes

1989. Australia Day. Centenary of Federation Speech by Sir Henry Parkes (N.S.W. Prime Minister).

1168	**457** 39c. multicoloured	45	40

458 Bowls

1989. Sports. Multicoloured.

1169	1c. Type **458**	10	50
1170	2c. Tenpin-bowling	10	20
1171	3c. Australian football	1·00	1·50
1172	5c. Kayaking and canoeing	15	10
1174	10c. Sailboarding	15	15
1176	20c. Tennis	20	25
1179	39c. Fishing	45	40
1180	41c. Cycling	40	35
1181	43c. Skateboarding	50	40
1184	55c. Kite-flying	50	45
1186	65c. Rock-climbing	80	70
1187	70c. Cricket	1·90	80
1188	75c. Netball	70	1·50
1189	80c. Squash	1·00	65
1190	85c. Diving	1·75	80
1191	90c. Soccer	1·75	2·00
1192	$1 Fun-run	1·00	50
1193	$1.10 Golf	4·50	1·00
1194	$1.20 Hang-gliding	5·50	1·10

459 Merino

1989. Sheep in Australia. Multicoloured.

1195	39c. Type **459**	70	50
1196	39c. Poll Dorset	70	50
1197	85c. Polwarth	1·75	3·50
1198	$1 Corriedale	1·75	2·00

460 Adelaide Botanic Garden

1989. Botanic Gardens. Multicoloured.

1199	$2 Noroo, New South Wales	1·50	30
1200	$5 Mawarra, Victoria	4·25	60
1201	$10 Type **460**	6·50	1·00
1201a	$20 *A View of the Artist's House and Garden in Mills Plains, Van Diemen's Land* (John Glover)	19·00	8·00

461 *Queen Elizabeth II* (sculpture, John Dowie)

1989. Queen Elizabeth II's Birthday.

1202	**461** 39c. multicoloured	55	50

462 Arrival of Immigrant Ship, 1830s

1989. Colonial Development (1st issue). Pastoral Era 1810–1850. Multicoloured.

1203	39c. Type **462**	40	55
1204	39c. Pioneer cottage and wool dray	40	55
1205	39c. Squatter's homestead	40	55
1206	39c. Shepherd with flock (from Joseph Lycett's *Views of Australia*)	40	55
1207	39c. Explorer in desert (after watercolour by Edward Frome)	40	55

See also Nos. 1254/8 and 1264/8.

463 Gladys Moncrieff and Roy Rene

1989. Australian Stage and Screen Personalities. Multicoloured.

1208	39c. Type **463**	30	25
1209	85c. Charles Chauvel and Chips Rafferty	70	2·00
1210	$1 Nellie Stewart and J. C. Williamson	70	1·00
1211	$1.10 Lottie Lyell and Raymond Longford	70	1·25

464 *Impression* (Tom Roberts)

1989. Australian Impressionist Paintings. Multicoloured.

1212	41c. Type **464**	45	50
1213	41c. *Impression for Golden Summer* (Sir Arthur Streeton)	45	50
1214	41c. *All on a Summer's Day* (Charles Conder) (vert)	45	50
1215	41c. *Petit Dejeuner* (Frederick McCubbin)	45	50

465 Freeways

1989. The Urban Environment.

1216	**465** 41c. black, purple and green	80	1·40
1217	- 41c. black, purple and mauve	80	1·25
1218	- 41c. black, purple and blue	80	1·40

DESIGNS: No. 1217, City buildings, Melbourne; No. 1218, Commuter train at platform.

466 Hikers outside Youth Hostel

1989. 50th Anniv of Australian Youth Hostels.

1219	**466** 41c. multicoloured	55	50

467 Horse Tram, Adelaide, 1878

1989. Historic Trams. Multicoloured.

1220	41c. Type **467**	60	75
1221	41c. Steam tram, Sydney, 1884	60	75
1222	41c. Cable tram, Melbourne, 1886	60	75
1223	41c. Double-deck electric tram, Hobart, 1893	60	75
1224	41c. Combination electric tram, Brisbane, 1901	60	75

468 *Annunciation* (15th-century Book of Hours)

1989. Christmas. Illuminated Manuscripts. Multicoloured.

1225	36c. Type **468**	30	10
1226	41c. *Annunciation to the Shepherds* (Wharncliffe Book of Hours, c. 1475)	35	10
1227	80c. *Adoration of the Magi* (15th-century Parisian Book of Hours)	1·00	1·75

469 Radio Waves and Globe

1989. 50th Anniv of Radio Australia.

1228	**469** 41c. multicoloured	55	50

470 Golden Wattle

1990. Australia Day.

1229	**470** 41c. multicoloured	55	50

471 Australian Wildflowers

1990. Greetings Stamps.

1230	**471** 41c. multicoloured	60	65
1231	**471** 43c. multicoloured	50	50

472 Dr. Constance Stone (first Australian woman doctor), Modern Doctor and Nurses

1990. Centenary of Women in Medical Practice.

1232	**472** 41c. multicoloured	50	45

473 Greater Glider

1990. Animals of the High Country. Multicoloured.

1233	41c. Type **473**	60	45
1234	65c. Tiger cat ("Spotted-tailed Quoll")	90	1·90
1235	70c. Mountain pygmy-possum	95	1·90
1236	80c. Brush-tailed rock-wallaby	1·10	1·90

474 "Stop Smoking"

1990. Community Health. Multicoloured.

1237	41c. Type **474**	55	55
1238	41c. "Drinking and driving don't mix"	55	55
1239	41c. "No junk food, please"	55	55
1240	41c. "Guess who's just had a check up?"	55	55

475 Soldiers from Two World Wars

1990. "The Anzac Tradition". Multicoloured.

1241	41c. Type **475**	80	40

1242	41c. Fighter pilots and munitions worker	80	40
1243	65c. Veterans and Anzac Day parade	1·25	1·25
1244	$1 Casualty evacuation, Vietnam, and disabled veteran	1·75	1·40
1245	$1.10 Letters from home and returning troopships	1·75	1·50

476 Queen at Australian Ballet Gala Performance, London, 1988

1990. Queen Elizabeth II's Birthday.

1246	**476**	41c. multicoloured	1·00	50

477 New South Wales 1861 5s. Stamp

1990. 150th Anniv of the Penny Black. Designs showing stamps. Multicoloured.

1247	41c. Type **477**	75	1·00
1248	41c. South Australia 1855 unissued 1s.	75	1·00
1249	41c. Tasmania 1853 4d.	75	1·00
1250	41c. Victoria 1867 5s.	75	1·00
1251	41c. Queensland 1897 unissued 6d.	75	1·00
1252	41c. Western Australia 1855 4d. with inverted frame	75	1·00
MS1253	122×85 mm. Nos. 1247/52	4·00	5·50

478 Gold Miners on Way to Diggings

1990. Colonial Development (2nd issue). Gold Fever. Multicoloured.

1254	41c. Type **478**	85	1·00
1255	41c. Mining camp	85	1·00
1256	41c. Panning and washing for gold	85	1·00
1257	41c. Gold Commissioner's tent	85	1·00
1258	41c. Moving gold under escort	85	1·00

479 Glaciology Research

1990. Australian–Soviet Scientific Co-operation in Antarctica. Multicoloured.

1261	41c. Type **479**	65	40
1262	$1.10 Krill (marine biology research)	1·60	2·00
MS1263	85×65 mm. Nos. 1261/2	2·25	2·25

Stamps in similar designs were also issued by Russia.

480 Auctioning Building Plots

1990. Colonial Development (3rd issue). Boomtime. Multicoloured.

1264	41c. Type **480**	55	55
1265	41c. Colonial mansion	55	55
1266	41c. Stock exchange	55	55
1267	41c. Fashionable society	55	55
1268	41c. Factories	55	55

481 Salmon Gums (Robert Juniper)

1990. Heidelberg and Heritage Art Exhibition. Multicoloured.

1269	28c. Type **481**	2·50	4·25
1270	43c. The Blue Dress (Brian Dunlop)	40	45

482 Adelaide Town Hall (Edmund Gouldsmith)

1990. 150th Anniv of Local Government.

1271	**482**	43c. multicoloured	75	50

483 Laughing Kookaburras and Gifts

1990. Christmas. Multicoloured.

1272	38c. Type **483**	50	15
1273	43c. Baby Jesus with koalas and wallaby (vert)	50	15
1274	80c. Possum on Christmas tree	1·50	3·50

484 National Flag

1991. Australia Day. 90th Anniv of Australian Flag.

1275	**484**	43c. blue, red and grey	55	25
1276	-	90c. multicoloured	1·25	1·25
1277	-	$1 multicoloured	1·25	1·40
1278	-	$1.20 red, blue and grey	1·60	1·75

DESIGNS: 90c. Royal Australian Navy ensign; $1 Royal Australian Air Force standard; $1.20, Australian merchant marine ensign.

485 Black-necked Stork

1991. Waterbirds. Multicoloured.

1279	43c. Type **485**	80	60
1280	43c. Black swan (horiz)	80	60
1281	85c. Cereopsis goose ("Cape Barren")	2·25	3·50
1282	$1 Chestnut-breasted teal ("Chestnut Teal") (horiz)	2·25	2·50

486 Recruitment Poster (Women's Services)

1991. Anzac Day. 50th Anniversaries.

1283	**486**	43c. multicoloured	60	40
1284	-	43c. black, green & brn	60	40
1285	-	$1.20 multicoloured	2·25	2·00

DESIGNS: 43c. (No. 1284) Patrol (Defence of Tobruk); $1.20, "V-P Day Canberra" (Harold Abbot) (Australian War Memorial).

487 Queen Elizabeth at Royal Albert Hall, London

1991. Queen Elizabeth II's Birthday.

1286	**487**	multicoloured	1·00	50

488 Tectocoris diophthalmus (bug)

1991. Insects. Multicoloured.

1287	43c. Type **488**	75	45
1288	43c. Cizara ardeniae (hawk moth)	75	45
1289	80c. Petasida ephippigera (grasshopper)	2·25	2·00
1290	$1 Castiarina producta (beetle)	2·25	1·50

489 Bondi (Max Dupain)

1991. 150 Years of Photography in Australia.

1291	**489**	43c. black, brown and blue	80	65
1292	-	43c. black, green & brn	80	65
1293	-	70c. black, green & brn	1·50	1·50
1294	-	$1.20 black, brn & grn	2·00	1·50

DESIGNS: No. 1292, Gears for the Mining Industry, Vickers Ruwolt, Melbourne (Wolfgang Sievers): 1293, The Wheel of Youth (Harold Cazneaux): 1294, Teacup Ballet (Olive Cotton).

490 Singing Group

1991. Australian Radio Broadcasting. Designs showing listeners and scenes from radio programmes. Multicoloured.

1295	43c. Type **490**	70	45
1296	43c. "Blue Hills" serial	70	45
1297	85c. "The Quiz Kids"	1·40	2·25
1298	$1 "Argonauts' Club" children's programme	1·60	1·40

491 Puppy

1991. Domestic Pets. Multicoloured.

1299	43c. Type **491**	70	45
1300	43c. Kitten	70	45
1301	70c. Pony	1·40	2·50
1302	$1 Sulphur-crested cockatoo	1·90	1·50

492 George Vancouver (1791) and Edward Eyre (1841)

1991. Exploration of Western Australia.

1303	**492**	$1.05 multicoloured	1·25	1·10
MS1304	100×65 mm. No. 1303		1·25	1·40

493 Seven Little Australians (Ethel Turner)

1991. Australian Writers of the 1890s. Multicoloured.

1305	43c. Type **493**	50	45
1306	75c. On Our Selection (Steele Rudd)	80	1·00
1307	$1 Clancy of the Overflow (poem, A. B. Paterson) (vert)	1·10	1·00
1308	$1.20 The Drover's Wife (short story, Henry Lawson) (vert)	1·25	1·60

494 Shepherd

1991. Christmas. Multicoloured.

1309	38c. Type **494**	40	15
1310	43c. Infant Jesus	45	15
1311	90c. Wise Man	1·50	1·75

495 Parma Wallaby

1992. Threatened Species. Multicoloured. Ordinary or self-adhesive gum.

1312	45c. Type **495**	80	90
1313	45c. Ghost bat	80	90
1314	45c. Long-tailed dunnart	80	90
1315	45c. Little pygmy-possum	80	90
1316	45c. Dusky hopping-mouse	80	90
1317	45c. Squirrel glider	80	90

496 Basket of Wild Flowers

1992. Greetings Stamp.

1318	**496**	45c. multicoloured	50	50

497 Noosa River, Queensland

1992. Wetlands and Waterways. Multicoloured.

1319	20c. Type **497**	1·75	2·50
1320	45c. Lake Eildon, Victoria	40	45

498 "Young Endeavour" (brigantine)

1992. Australia Day and 500th Anniv of Discovery of America by Columbus (**MS**1337). Multicoloured. Sailing Ships.

1333	45c. Type **498**	80	50
1334	45c. Britannia (yacht) (vert)	80	50
1335	$1.05 Akarana (cutter) (vert)	1·75	2·75
1336	$1.20 John Louis (pearling lugger)	2·00	2·00
MS1337	147×64 mm. Nos. 1333/6	4·75	5·50

499 Bombing of Darwin

1992. 50th Anniv of Second World War Battles. Multicoloured.

1338	45c. Type **499**	90	45
1339	75c. Anti-aircraft gun and fighters, Milne Bay	1·75	1·90
1340	75c. Infantry on Kokoda Trail	1·75	1·90
1341	$1.05 H.M.A.S. Australia (cruiser) and U.S.S. Yorktown (aircraft carrier), Coral Sea	2·00	2·25
1342	$1.20 Australians advancing, El Alamein	2·25	2·00

500 Helix Nebula

1992. International Space Year. Multicoloured.

1343	45c. Type **500**	85	45
1344	$1.05 *The Pleiades*	2·00	1·25
1345	$1.20 *Spiral Galaxy, NGC 2997*	2·25	1·50
MS1346	133×70 mm. Nos. 1343/5	4·50	4·50

501 Hunter Valley, New South Wales

1992. Vineyard Regions. Multicoloured.

1347	45c. Type **501**	80	1·10
1348	45c. North-east Victoria	80	1·10
1349	45c. Barossa Valley, South Australia	80	1·10
1350	45c. Coonawarra, South Australia	80	1·10
1351	45c. Margaret River, Western Australia	80	1·10

502 3½d. Stamp of 1953

1992. Queen Elizabeth II's Birthday.

1352	**502**	45c. multicoloured	1·00	60

503 Salt Action

1992. Land Conservation. Multicoloured.

1353	45c. Type **503**	85	1·10
1354	45c. Farm planning	85	1·10
1355	45c. Erosion control	85	1·10
1356	45c. Tree planting	85	1·10
1357	45c. Dune care	85	1·10

504 Cycling

1992. Olympic Games and Paralympic Games (No. 1359), Barcelona. Multicoloured.

1358	45c. Type **504**	60	25
1359	$1.20 High jumping	1·50	1·75
1360	$1.20 Weightlifting	1·50	1·75

505 Echidna

1992. Australian Wildlife (1st series). Multicoloured.

1361	30c. Saltwater crocodile	35	20
1362	35c. Type **505**	65	30
1363	40c. Platypus	2·25	1·50
1364	50c. Koala	60	35
1365	60c. Common bushtail possum	1·50	1·75
1366	70c. Laughing kookaburra ("Kookaburra")	2·25	1·00
1367	85c. Australian pelican ("Pelican")	1·00	70
1368a	90c. Eastern grey kangaroo	2·75	3·25
1369	95c. Common wombat	1·00	2·50
1370a	$1 Major Mitchell's cockatoo ("Pink Cockatoo")	2·00	1·40
1371	$1.35 Emu	2·50	3·00

See also Nos. 1459/64.

506 Sydney Harbour Tunnel (value at left)

1992. Opening of Sydney Harbour Tunnel. Multicoloured.

1375b	45c. Type **506**	1·90	1·90
1376b	45c. Sydney Harbour Tunnel (value at right)	1·90	1·90

Nos. 1375/6 were printed together, *se-tenant*, forming a composite design.

507 Warden's Courthouse, Coolgardie

1992. Centenary of Discovery of Gold at Coolgardie and Kalgoorlie. Multicoloured.

1377	45c. Type **507**	90	50
1378	45c. Post Office, Kalgoorlie	90	50
1379	$1.05 York Hotel, Kalgoorlie	2·00	3·00
1380	$1.20 Town Hall, Kalgoorlie	2·25	2·50

508 Bowler of 1892

1992. Centenary of Sheffield Shield Cricket Tournament. Multicoloured.

1381	45c. Type **508**	1·00	50
1382	$1.20 Batsman and wicket-keeper	2·00	3·00

509 Children's Nativity Play

1992. Christmas. Multicoloured.

1383	40c. Type **509**	40	15
1384	45c. Child waking on Christmas Day	60	15
1385	$1 Children carol singing	2·00	1·75

510 Ghost Gum, Central Australia (Namatjira)

1993. Australia Day. Paintings by Albert Namatjira. Multicoloured.

1386	45c. Type **510**	90	1·40
1387	45c. *Across the Plain to Mount Giles*	90	1·40

511 *Wild Onion Dreaming* (Pauline Nakamarra Woods)

1993. "Dreamings". Paintings by Aboriginal Artists. Multicoloured.

1388	45c. Type **511**	50	15
1389	75c. *Yam Plants* (Jack Wunu-wun) (vert)	80	90
1390	85c. *Goose Egg Hunt* (George Milpurrurru) (vert)	85	1·40
1391	$1 *Kalumpiwarra-Ngulalintji* (Rover Thomas)	1·10	1·25

512 Uluru (Ayers Rock) National Park

1993. World Heritage Sites (1st series). Multicoloured.

1392	45c. Type **512**	60	30
1393	85c. Rain forest, Fraser Island	1·50	1·75
1394	95c. Beach, Shark Bay	1·50	1·75
1395	$2 Waterfall, Kakadu	2·75	3·50

See also Nos. 1582/5.

513 Queen Elizabeth II on Royal Visit, 1992

1993. Queen Elizabeth II's Birthday.

1396	**513**	45c. multicoloured	1·00	65

514 H.M.A.S. *Sydney* (cruiser, launched 1934) in Action

1993. Second World War Naval Vessels. Multicoloured.

1397	45c. Type **514**	1·00	45
1398	85c. H.M.A.S. *Bathurst* (mine-sweeper)	2·25	1·75
1399	$1.05 H.M.A.S. *Arunta* (de-stroyer)	2·50	2·75
1400	$1.20 *Centaur* (hospital ship) and tug	2·50	2·75

515 "Work in the Home"

1993. Working Life in the 1890s. Multicoloured.

1401	45c. Type **515**	35	35
1402	45c. "Work in the Cities"	35	35
1403	$1 "Work in the Country"	70	90
1404	$1.20 Trade Union banner	80	1·40

516 *Centenary Special,* Tasmania, 1971

1993. Australian Trains. Multicoloured.

(a) Ordinary gum

1405	45c. Type **516**	65	95
1406	45c. *Spirit of Progress*, Victoria	65	95
1407	45c. *Western Endeavour*, Western Australia, 1970	65	95
1408	45c. *Silver City Comet*, New South Wales	65	95
1409	45c. Cairns–Kuranda tourist train, Queensland	65	95
1410	45c. *The Ghan*, Northern Territory	65	95

(b) Self-adhesive

1411	45c. Type **516**	95	1·25
1412	45c. "Spirit of Progress", Victoria	95	1·25
1413	45c. "Western Endeavour", Western Australia, 1970	95	1·25
1414	45c. "Silver City Comet", New South Wales	95	1·25
1415	45c. Cairns-Kuranda tourist train, Queensland	95	1·25
1416	45c. "The Ghan", Northern Territory	95	1·25

517 *Black Cockatoo Feather* (Fiona Foley)

1993. International Year of Indigenous Peoples. Aboriginal Art. Multicoloured.

1417	45c. Type **517**	30	20
1418	75c. *Ngarrgooroon Country* (Hector Jandany) (horiz)	50	1·25
1419	$1 *Ngak Ngak* (Ginger Riley Munduwalawala) (horiz)	65	1·25
1420	$1.05 *Untitled* (Robert Cole)	65	1·75

518 Conference Emblem

1993. Inter-Parliamentary Union Conference and 50th Anniv of Women in Federal Parliament. Multicoloured.

1421	45c. Type **518**	50	1·00
1422	45c. Dame Enid Lyons and Senator Dorothy Tangney	50	1·00

519 Ornithocheirus

1993. Prehistoric Animals. Multicoloured.

(a) Ordinary gum

1423	45c. Type **519**	40	40
1424	45c. Leaellynasaura (25×30 mm)	40	40
1425	45c. Timimus (26×33 mm)	40	40
1426	45c. Allosaurus (26×33 mm)	40	40
1427	75c. Muttaburrasaurus (30×50 mm)	70	90
1428	$1.05 Minmi (50×30 mm)	80	1·50
MS1429	166×73 mm. Nos. 1423/8	3·00	5·50

(b) Self-adhesive

1430	45c. Type **519**	55	80
1431	45c. Leaellynasaura (25×30 mm)	55	80

520 "Goodwill"

1993. Christmas. Multicoloured.

1432	40c. Type **520**	40	10
1433	45c. "Joy"	55	10
1434	$1 "Peace"	1·50	1·60

521 *Shoalhaven River Bank—Dawn* (Arthur Boyd)

1994. Australia Day. Landscape Paintings. Multicoloured.

1435	45c. Type **521**	40	20
1436	85c. *Wimmera* (Sir Sidney Nolan)	80	90
1437	$1.05 *Lagoon, Wimmera* (Nolan)	90	1·25
1438	$2 *White Cockatoos with Flame Trees* (Boyd) (vert)	1·60	2·10

522 Teaching Lifesaving Techniques

1994. Centenary of Organized Life Saving in Australia. Multicoloured.

(a) Ordinary gum

1439	45c. Type **522**	35	25
1440	45c. Lifeguard on watch	35	25
1441	95c. Lifeguard team	70	1·00
1442	$1.20 Lifeguards on surf boards	1·00	1·25

(b) Self-adhesive

1443	45c. Type **522**	55	1·00
1444	45c. Lifeguard on watch	55	1·00

523 Rose

1994. Greetings Stamps. Flower photographs by Lariane Fonseca. Multicoloured.
1445	45c. Type **523**		40	45
1446	45c. Tulips		40	45
1447	45c. Poppies		40	45

524 Bridge and National Flags

1994. Opening of Friendship Bridge between Thailand and Laos.
1448	**524**	95c. multicoloured	1·25	1·40

525 Queen Elizabeth II (Sir William Dargie)

1994. Queen Elizabeth II's Birthday.
1449	**525**	45c. multicoloured	1·00	70

526 Family in Field (Bobbie-Lea Blackmore)

1994. International Year of the Family. Children's Paintings. Multicoloured.
1450	45c. Type **526**		45	10
1451	75c. Family on Beach (Kathryn Teoh)		60	80
1452	$1 Family around Fire (Maree McCarthy)		85	1·00

1994. Australian Wildlife (2nd series). As T **505**. Multicoloured. Ordinary or self-adhesive gum.
1459	45c. Kangaroo	60	85
1460	45c. Female kangaroo with young	60	85
1461	45c. Two kangaroos	60	85
1462	45c. Family of koalas on branch	60	85
1463	45c. Koala on ground	60	85
1464	45c. Koala asleep in tree	60	85

527 Suffragettes

1994. Centenary of Women's Emancipation in South Australia.
1465	**527**	45c. multicoloured	60	60

528 Bunyip from Aboriginal Legend

1994. The Bunyip (mythological monster). Multicoloured.
1466	45c. Type **528**	45	70
1467	45c. Nature spirit bunyip	45	70
1468	90c. "The Bunyip of Berkeley's Creek" (book illustration)	70	1·50
1469	$1.35 Bunyip as natural history	1·00	1·75

529 Robert Menzies (Sir Ivor Hele)

1994. Wartime Prime Ministers. Multicoloured.
1470	45c. Type **529**	1·25	1·50
1471	45c. Arthur Fadden (William Dargie)	1·25	1·50
1472	45c. John Curtin (Anthony Dattilo-Rubbo)	1·25	1·50
1473	45c. Francis Forde (Joshua Smith)	1·25	1·50
1474	45c. Joseph Chifley (A. D. Colquhoun)	1·25	1·50

530 Lawrence Hargrave and Box Kites

1994. Aviation Pioneers.
1475	**530**	45c. brown, green and cinnamon	1·25	55
1476	-	45c. brown, red and lilac	1·25	55
1477	-	$1.35 brown, violet and blue	3·00	4·00
1478	-	$1.80 brown, deep green and green	3·25	4·00

DESIGNS: No. 1476, Ross and Keith Smith with Vickers Vimy (first England–Australia flight); 1477, Ivor McIntyre, Stanley Goble and Fairey IIID seaplane (first aerial circumnavigation of Australia); 1478, Freda Thompson and de Havilland Moth Major *Christopher Robin* (first Australian woman to fly solo from England to Australia).

531 Scarlet Macaw

1994. Australian Zoos. Endangered Species. Multicoloured.

(a) Ordinary gum
1479	45c. Type **531**	90	55
1480	45c. Cheetah (25×30 mm)	90	55
1481	45c. Orang-utan (26×37 mm)	90	55
1482	45c. Fijian crested iguana (26×37 mm)	90	55
1483	$1 Asian elephants (49×28 mm)	2·75	1·60
MS1484	166×73 mm. Nos. 1479/83	4·00	4·50

(b) Self-adhesive
1485	45c. Type **531**	1·50	1·75
1486	45c. Cheetah	1·50	1·75

532 Madonna and Child (detail)

1994. Christmas. *The Adoration of the Magi* by Giovanni Toscani. Multicoloured.
1487	40c. Type **532**	40	15
1488	45c. Wise Man and Horse (detail) (horiz)	40	15
1489	$1 Wise Man and St. Joseph (detail) (horiz)	80	85
1490	$1.80 Complete painting (49×29 mm)	1·50	2·25

533 Yachts outside Sydney Harbour

1994. 50th Sydney to Hobart Yacht Race. Multicoloured

(a) Ordinary gum
1491	45c. Type **533**	1·00	80
1492	45c. Yachts passing Tasmania coastline	1·00	80

(b) Self-adhesive
1493	45c. Type **533**	80	1·25
1494	45c. Yachts passing Tasmania coastline	80	1·25

534 Symbolic Kangaroo

1994. Self-adhesive. Automatic Cash Machine Stamps.
1495	**534**	45c. gold, emerald and green	55	90
1496	**534**	45c. gold, green and blue	55	90
1497	**534**	45c. gold, green and lilac	55	90
1498	**534**	45c. gold, emerald and green	55	90
1499	**534**	45c. gold, emerald and green	55	90
1500	**534**	45c. gold, green and pink	55	90
1501	**534**	45c. gold, green and red	55	90
1502	**534**	45c. gold, green and brown	55	90

535 Back Verandah (Russell Drysdale)

1995. Australia Day. Paintings. Multicoloured.
1503	45c. Type **535**	35	35
1504	45c. Skull Springs Country (Guy Grey-Smith)	35	35
1505	$1.05 Outcamp (Robert Juniper)	1·00	1·25
1506	$1.20 Kite Flying (Ian Fairweather)	1·10	1·25

536 Red Heart and Rose

1995. St. Valentine's Day. Multicoloured.
1507	45c. Type **536**	55	55
1508	45c. Gold and red heart with rose	55	55
1509	45c. Gold heart and roses	85	1·25

537 Endeavour Replica at Sea

1995. Completion of *Endeavour* Replica. Multicoloured.

(a) Sheet stamps
1510	45c. Type **537**	1·50	1·75
1511	45c. Captain Cook's Endeavour (detail) (Oswald Brett)	1·50	1·75

(b) Booklet stamps
1512	20c. Type **537** (44×26 mm)	1·25	3·25

538 Coalport Plate and Bracket Clock, Old Government House, Parramatta

1995. 50th Anniv of Australian National Trusts.
1514	**538**	45c. blue and brown	30	45
1515	-	45c. green and brown	30	45
1516	-	$1 red and blue	70	70
1517	-	$2 green and blue	1·40	1·90

DESIGNS: No. 1515, Steiner doll and Italian-style chair, Ayers House, Adelaide; 1516, "Advance Australia" teapot and parian-ware statuette, Victoria; 1517, Silver bowl and china urn, Old Observatory, Perth.

539 Light Opal (hologram)

1995. Opals. Multicoloured.
1518	$1.20 Type **539**		3·50	1·25
1519	$2.50 Black opal (hologram)		4·50	3·75

540 Queen Elizabeth II at Gala Concert, 1992

1995. Queen Elizabeth II's Birthday.
1520	**540**	45c. multicoloured	75	75

541 Sir Edward Dunlop and P.O.W. Association Badge

1995. Australian Second World War Heroes (1st series). Multicoloured

(a) Ordinary gum
1521	45c. Type **541**	50	60
1522	45c. Mrs. Jessie Vasey and War Widows' Guild badge	50	60
1523	45c. Sgt. Tom Derrick and Victoria Cross	50	60
1524	45c. Flt. Sgt. Rawdon Middleton and Victoria Cross	50	60

(b) Self-adhesive
1525	45c. Type **541**	65	1·00
1526	45c. Mrs. Jessie Vasey and War Widows' Guild badge	65	1·00
1527	45c. Sgt. Tom Derrick and Victoria Cross (I)	65	1·00
1528	45c. Flt. Sgt. Rawdon Middleton and Victoria Cross (I)	65	1·00

See also Nos. 1545/8.

542 Children and Globe of Flags

1995. 50th Anniv of United Nations.
1529	**542**	45c. multicoloured	75	75

543 The Story of the Kelly Gang

1995. Centenary of Cinema. Scenes from Films. Multicoloured

(a) Size 23×35 mm
1530	45c. Type **543**	1·00	1·50
1531	45c. On Our Selection	1·00	1·50
1532	45c. Jedda	1·00	1·50
1533	45c. Picnic at Hanging Rock	1·00	1·50
1534	45c. Strictly Ballroom	1·00	1·50

(b) Self-adhesive. Size 19×30½ mm.
1535	45c. Type **543**	1·00	1·50
1536	45c. On Our Selection	1·00	1·50
1537	45c. Jedda	1·00	1·50
1538	45c. Picnic at Hanging Rock	1·00	1·50
1539	45c. Strictly Ballroom	1·00	1·50

544 Man in Wheelchair flying Kite

1995. People with Disabilities. Multicoloured.
1540	45c. Type **544**	1·00	1·40
1541	45c. Blind woman playing violin	1·00	1·40

1995. 50th Anniv of Peace in the Pacific. Designs as 1946 Victory Commemoration (Nos. 213/15) redrawn with new face values.

1542	**53**	45c. red	70	70
1543	-	45c. green	70	70
1544	-	$1.50 blue	1·75	3·00

DESIGNS—VERT: No. 1543, Angel. HORIZ: No. 1544, Flag and dove.

1995. Australian Second World War Heroes (2nd series). As T **541**. Multicoloured.

1545	45c. Sister Ellen Savage and George Medal	1·25	1·75
1546	45c. Chief Petty Officer Percy Collins and Distinguished Service Medal and Bar	1·25	1·75
1547	45c. Lt-Comm. Leon Goldsworthy and George Cross	1·25	1·75
1548	45c. Warrant Officer Len Waters and R.A.A.F. wings	1·25	1·75

545 Koala with Cub

1995. Australia–China Joint Issue. Endangered Species. Multicoloured.

1549	45c. Type **545**	70	1·00
1550	45c. Giant panda with cubs	70	1·00
MS1551	Two sheets, each 106×70 mm. (a) No. 1549. (b) No. 1550 Set of 2 sheets	2·00	2·25

546 Father Joseph Slattery, Thomas Lyle and Walter Filmer (Radiology)

1995. Medical Scientists. Multicoloured.

1552	45c. Type **546**	1·50	1·50
1553	45c. Dame Jean Macnamara and Sir Macfarlane Burnet (viruses)	1·50	1·50
1554	45c. Fred Hollows (ophthalmology) (vert)	1·50	60
1555	$2.50 Sir Howard Florey (antibiotics) (vert)	6·00	7·00

547 Flatback Turtle

1995. Marine Life. Multicoloured

(a) Ordinary gum

1556	45c. Type **547**	55	55
1557	45c. Flame angelfish and nudibranch	55	55
1558	45c. Potato grouper ("Potato cod") and hump-headed wrasse ("Maori wrasse")	55	55
1559	45c. Giant trevally	55	55
1560	45c. Black marlin	55	55
1561	45c. Mako and tiger sharks	55	55
MS1562	166×73 mm. Nos. 1556/61	3·00	3·00

(b) Self-adhesive

1563	45c. Type **547**	55	90
1564	45c. Flame Angelfish and Nudibranch	55	90
1565	45c. Potato Cod and Maori Wrasse	55	90
1566	45c. Giant Trevally	55	90
1567	45c. Black Marlin	55	90
1568	45c. Mako and Tiger Sharks	55	90

548 Madonna and Child

1995. Christmas. Stained-glass Windows from Our Lady Help of Christians Church, Melbourne. Multicoloured.

(a) Ordinary gum

1569	40c. Type **548**	80	15
1570	45c. Angel carrying the Gloria banner	80	15
1571	$1 Rejoicing Angels	3·00	3·25

(b) Self-adhesive

1572	40c. Type **548**	40	45

549 West Australian Banksia (Margaret Preston)

1996. Australia Day. Paintings. Multicoloured.

1573	45c. Type **549**	1·00	30
1574	85c. The Babe is Wise (Lina Bryans)	2·00	2·50
1575	$1 The Bridge in Curve (Grace Cossington Smith) (horiz)	2·25	2·00
1576	$1.20 Beach Umbrellas (Vida Lahey) (horiz)	2·50	3·50

550 Gold Heart and Rose

1996. St. Valentine's Day.

1577	**550**	45c. multicoloured	1·00	1·00

551 Bristol Type 156 Beaufighter and Curtiss P-40E Kittyhawk I

1996. Military Aviation. Multicoloured.

1578	45c. Type **551**	2·00	2·00
1579	45c. Hawker Sea Fury and Fairey Firefly	2·00	2·00
1580	45c. Bell Kiowa helicopters	2·00	2·00
1581	45c. Government Aircraft Factory Hornets	2·00	2·00

552 Tasmanian Wilderness

1996. World Heritage Sites (2nd series). Multicoloured.

1582	45c. Type **552**	90	45
1583	75c. Willandra Lakes	2·25	3·00
1584	95c. Naracoorte Fossil Cave	2·50	4·25
1585	$1 Lord Howe Island	2·50	2·25

553 Australian Spotted Cuscus

1996. Australia–Indonesia Joint Issue. Multicoloured.

1586	45c. Type **553**	90	1·50
1587	45c. Indonesian bear cuscus	90	1·50
MS1588	106×70 mm. Nos. 1586/7	2·25	3·50

554 Head of Queen Elizabeth II

1996. Queen Elizabeth II's Birthday.

1589	**554**	45c. multicoloured	1·25	1·00

555 North Melbourne Players

1996. Centenary of Australian Football League. Players from different teams. Multicoloured. Ordinary or self-adhesive gum.

1606	45c. Type **555**	50	90
1607	45c. Brisbane (red and yellow shirt)	50	90
1608	45c. Sydney (red and white shirt)	50	90
1609	45c. Carlton (black shirt with white emblem)	50	90
1610	45c. Adelaide (black, red and yellow shirt)	50	90
1611	45c. Fitzroy (yellow, red and blue shirt)	50	90
1612	45c. Richmond (black shirt with yellow diagonal stripe)	50	90
1613	45c. St. Kilda (red, white and black shirt)	50	90
1614	45c. Melbourne (black shirt with red top)	50	90
1615	45c. Collingwood (black and white vertical striped shirt)	50	90
1616	45c. Fremantle (green, red, white and blue shirt)	50	90
1617	45c. Footscray (blue, white and red shirt)	50	90
1618	45c. West Coast (deep blue shirt with yellow stripes)	50	90
1619	45c. Essendon (black shirt with red stripe)	50	90
1620	45c. Geelong (black and white horizontal striped shirt)	50	90
1621	45c. Hawthorn (black and yellow vertical striped shirt)	50	90

556 Leadbeater's Possum

1996. Fauna and Flora (1st series). Central Highlands Forest, Victoria. Multicoloured.

1622	5c. Type **556**	30	25
1623	10c. Powerful owl	1·75	45
1624	$2 Blackwood wattle	1·40	1·25
1625	$5 Soft tree fern and mountain ash (30×50 mm)	11·00	3·75

See also Nos. 1679/90, 1854/66, 2130/33, 2200/3, 2272/6 and 2377/80.

1996. "China '96" 9th Asian International Stamp Exhibition, Peking. Sheet 120×65 mm, containing Nos. 1453b, 1454b and 1455b. Multicoloured.

MS1626	45c. Kangaroo; 45c. Female kangaroo with young; 45c. Two kangaroos	2·00	2·25

557 Edwin Flack (800 and 1500 metres gold medal winner, 1896)

1996. Centennial Olympic Games and Tenth Paralympic Games, Atlanta. Multicoloured.

1627	45c. Type **557**	90	90
1628	45c. Fanny Durack (100 metres freestyle swimming gold medal winner, 1912)	90	90
1629	$1.05 Wheelchair athletes	2·25	2·25

558 Animalia (Graeme Base)

1996. 50th Anniv of Children's Book Council Awards. Designs taken from book covers. Multicoloured

(a) Ordinary gum

1630	45c. Type **558**	60	60
1631	45c. Greetings from Sandy Beach (Bob Graham)	60	60
1632	45c. Who Sank the Boat? (Pamela Allen)	60	60
1633	45c. John Brown, Rose and the Midnight Cat (Jenny Wagner, illustrated by Ron Brooks)	60	60

(b) Self-adhesive

1634	45c. Type **558**	60	75
1635	45c. Greetings from Sandy Beach (Bob Graham)	60	75
1636	45c. Who Sank the Boat? (Pamela Allen)	60	75
1637	45c. John Brown, Rose and the Midnight Cat (Jenny Wagner, illustrated by Ron Brooks)	60	75

559 American Bald Eagle, Kangaroo and Olympic Flame

1996. Passing of Olympic Flag to Sydney.

1638	**559**	45c. multicoloured	55	50

560 Margaret Windeyer

1996. Centenary of the National Council of Women.

1639	**560**	45c. purple and yellow	50	50
1640	-	$1 blue and yellow	1·25	2·00

DESIGN: $1 Rose Scott.

561 Pearl

1996. Pearls and Diamonds. Multicoloured.

1641	45c. Type **561**	60	50
1642	$1.20 Diamond	1·40	1·50

The pearl on the 45c. is shown as an exelgram (holographic printing on ultra thin plastic film) and the diamond on the $1.20 as a hologram, each embossed on to the stamp.

562 Silhouettes of Female Dancer and Musician on Rural Landscape

1996. 50th Anniv of Arts Councils. Multicoloured.

1643	20c. Type **562**	1·40	2·50
1644	45c. Silhouettes of musician and male dancer on landscape	35	45

563 Ginger Cats

1996. Australian Pets. Multicoloured.

(a) Ordinary gum

1645	45c. Type **563**	65	75
1646	45c. Blue heeler dogs	65	75
1647	45c. Sulphur-crested cockatoo (30×25 mm)	65	75
1648	45c. Duck with ducklings (25×30 mm)	65	75
1649	45c. Dog and cat (25×30 mm)	65	75
1650	45c. Ponies (30×50 mm)	65	75
MS1651	166×73 mm. Nos. 1645/50	3·50	4·00

(b) Self-adhesive

1652	45c. Type **563**	75	1·25
1653	45c. Blue Heeler dogs	75	1·25

564 Ferdinand von Mueller

1996. Australia–Germany Joint Issue. Death Centenary of Ferdinand von Mueller (botanist).

1654	**564**	$1.20 multicoloured	1·25	2·00

565 Willem de Vlamingh

1996. 300th Anniv of the Visit of Willem de Vlamingh to Western Australia.

| 1655 | **565** | 45c. multicoloured | 1·00 | 1·50 |

566 Madonna and Child

1996. Christmas. Multicoloured.

(a) Ordinary gum

1656		40c. Type **566**	55	15
1657		45c. Wise man with gift	55	15
1658		$1 Shepherd boy with lamb	1·25	1·50

(b) Self-adhesive

| 1659 | | 40c. Type **566** | 75 | 60 |

567 Landscape '74 (Fred Williams)

1997. Australia Day. Contemporary Paintings. Multicoloured.

1660		85c. Type **567**	1·10	1·10
1661		90c. The Balcony 2 (Brett Whiteley)	1·10	1·10
1662		$1.20 Fire Haze at Gerringong (Lloyd Rees)	1·40	1·40

568 Sir Donald Bradman

1997. Australian Legends (1st series). Sir Donald Bradman (cricketer). Multicoloured.

| 1663 | | 45c. Type **568** | 55 | 55 |
| 1664 | | 45c. Bradman playing stroke | 55 | 55 |

See also Nos. 1731/42, 1838/9, 1947/50, 2069/70, 2165/9, 2264/7, 2348/9, 2473/8, 2577/81 and 2741/58.

569 Red Roses

1997. St. Valentine's Day

(a) Ordinary gum

| 1665 | **569** | 45c. multicoloured | 50 | 50 |

(b) Self-adhesive

| 1666 | | 45c. multicoloured | 75 | 1·25 |

570 Ford Coupe Utility, 1934

1997. Classic Cars. Multicoloured.

(a) Ordinary gum

1667		45c. Type **570**	50	75
1668		45c. Holden 48-215 (FX) sedan, 1948	50	75
1669		45c. Austin Lancer sedan, 1958	50	75
1670		45c. Chrysler Valiant "R" Series sedan, 1962	50	75

(b) Self-adhesive

1671		45c. Type **570**	45	65
1672		45c. GMH Holden 48-215 (FX), 1948	45	65
1673		45c. Austin Lancer, 1958	45	65
1674		45c. Chrysler Valiant "R" Series, 1962	45	65

571 May Wirth and Horse

1997. 150th Anniv of the Circus in Australia. Multicoloured.

1675		45c. Type **571**	55	75
1676		45c. Con Colleano on tightrope	55	75
1677		45c. Clowns	55	75
1678		45c. Acrobats	55	75

1997. Fauna and Flora (2nd series). Kakadu Wetlands, Northern Territory. As T **556**. Multicoloured.

1679		20c. Saltwater crocodile	60	20
1680		25c. Northern dwarf tree frog	60	25
1681		45c. Comb-crested jacana ("Jacana")	75	75
1682		45c. Mangrove kingfisher ("Little Kingfisher")	75	75
1683		45c. Brolga	75	75
1684		45c. Black-necked stork ("Jabiru")	75	75
1685		$1 "Cressida cressida" (butterfly)	70	75
1686		$10 Kakadu Wetlands (50×30 mm)	7·00	5·00
MS1686a		106×70 mm. No. 1686	9·00	11·00

Nos. 1681/84 also come self-adhesive.

572 Royal Wedding 1d. Stamp of 1947

1997. Queen Elizabeth II's Birthday.

| 1691 | **572** | 45c. purple | 60 | 60 |

573 Hand holding Globe and Lion's Emblem

1997. 50th Anniv of First Australian Lions Club.

| 1692 | **573** | 45c. blue, brown and purple | 50 | 50 |

574 Doll holding Teddy Bear (Kaye Wiggs)

1997. Dolls and Teddy Bears. Multicoloured.

1693		45c. Type **574**	40	50
1694		45c. Teddy bear standing (Jennifer Laing)	40	50
1695		45c. Doll wearing white dress with teddy bear (Susie McMahon)	40	50
1696		45c. Doll in brown dress and bonnet (Lynda Jacobson)	40	50
1697		45c. Teddy bear sitting (Helen Williams)	40	50

575 Police Rescue Helicopter

1997. Emergency Services. Multicoloured.

1698		45c. Type **575**	1·50	1·00
1699		45c. Emergency Service volunteers carrying victim	1·50	1·00
1700		$1.05 Fire service at fire	2·75	2·25
1701		$1.20 Loading casualty into ambulance	3·00	2·00

576 George Peppin Jnr (breeder) and Merino Sheep

1997. Bicentenary of Arrival of Merino Sheep in Australia. Multicoloured.

| 1702 | | 45c. Type **576** | 70 | 1·00 |
| 1703 | | 45c. Pepe chair, cloth and wool logo | 70 | 1·00 |

577 Dumbi the Owl

1997. The Dreaming. Cartoons from Aboriginal Stories. Multicoloured.

1704		45c. Type **577**	40	20
1705		$1 The Two Willy-Willies	70	50
1706		$1.20 How Brolga became a Bird	75	1·25
1707		$1.80 Tuggan-Tuggan	1·25	2·75

578 "Rhoetosaurus brownei"

1997. Prehistoric Animals. Multicoloured.

1708		45c. Type **578**	45	60
1709		45c. "Mcnamaraspis kaprios"	45	60
1710		45c. "Ninjemys oweni"	45	60
1711		45c. "Paracylotosaurus davidi"	45	60
1712		45c. "Woolungasaurus glendowerensis"	45	60

579 Spotted-tailed Quoll

1997. Nocturnal Animals. Multicoloured.

(a) Ordinary gum

1713		45c. Type **579**	70	90
1714		45c. Barking owl	70	90
1715		45c. Platypus (30×25 mm)	70	90
1716		45c. Brown antechinus (30×25 mm)	70	90
1717		45c. Dingo (30×25 mm)	70	90
1718		45c. Yellow-bellied glider (50×30 mm)	70	90
MS1719		166×78 mm. Nos. 1713/18	4·75	4·75

(b) Self-adhesive

| 1720 | | 45c. Type **579** | 1·10 | 1·00 |
| 1721 | | 45c. Barking Owl | 1·10 | 1·00 |

580 Woman

1997. Breast Cancer Awareness Campaign.

| 1722 | **580** | 45c. multicoloured | 1·25 | 60 |

581 Two Angels

1997. Christmas. Children's Nativity Play. Multicoloured.

(a) Ordinary gum

1723		40c. Type **581**	50	15
1724		45c. Mary	55	15
1725		$1 Three Kings	1·25	1·50

(b) Self-adhesive

| 1726 | | 40c. Type **581** | 35 | 40 |

582 Flying Cloud (clipper) (J. Scott)

1998. Ship Paintings. Multicoloured.

1727		45c. Type **582**	60	30
1728		85c. Marco Polo (full-rigged ship) (T. Robertson)	1·00	1·00
1729		$1 Chusan I (steamship) (C. Gregory)	1·25	1·10
1730		$1.20 Heather Belle (clipper)	1·50	1·75

583 Betty Cuthbert (1956)

1998. Australian Legends (2nd series). Olympic Gold Medal Winners. Multicoloured. Ordinary or self-adhesive gum

1731		45c. Type **583**	35	55
1732		45c. Betty Cuthbert running	35	55
1733		45c. Herb Elliott (1960)	35	55
1734		45c. Herb Elliott running	35	55
1735		45c. Dawn Fraser (1956, 1960 and 1964)	35	55
1736		45c. Dawn Fraser swimming	35	55
1737		45c. Marjorie Jackson (1952)	35	55
1738		45c. Marjorie Jackson running	35	55
1739		45c. Murray Rose (1956)	35	55
1740		45c. Murray Rose swimming	35	55
1741		45c. Shirley Strickland (1952 and 1956)	35	55
1742		45c. Shirley Strickland hurdling	35	55

584 "Champagne" Rose

1998. Greeting Stamp. Ordinary or self-adhesive gum.

| 1755 | **584** | 45c. multicoloured | 55 | 50 |

585 Queen Elizabeth II

1998. Queen Elizabeth II's Birthday.

| 1757 | **585** | 45c. multicoloured | 70 | 50 |

586 Sea Hawk (helicopter) landing on Frigate

1998. 50th Anniv of Royal Australian Navy Fleet Air Arm.

| 1758 | **586** | 45c. multicoloured | 1·00 | 50 |

587 Sheep Shearer and Sheep

1998. Farming. Multicoloured. Ordinary or self-adhesive gum.

1759		45c. Type **587**	45	50
1760		45c. Barley and silo	45	50
1761		45c. Farmers herding beef cattle	45	50
1762		45c. Sugar cane harvesting	45	50
1763		45c. Two dairy cows	45	50

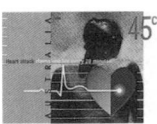

588 Cardiograph Trace and Heart

1998. Heart Disease Awareness.
1769 **588** 45c. multicoloured 75 50

589 Johnny OKeefe (*The Wild One*, 1958)

1998. Australian Rock and Roll. Multicoloured. Ordinary or self-adhesive gum.

1770	45c. Type **589**		30	40
1771	45c. Col Joye (*Oh Yeah Uh Huh*, 1959)		30	40
1772	45c. Little Pattie (*He's My Blonde Headed Stompie Wompie Real Gone Surfer Boy*, 1963)		30	40
1773	45c. Normie Rowe (*Shakin all Over*, 1965)		30	40
1774	45c. Easybeats (*She's so Fine*, 1965)		30	40
1775	45c. Russell Morris (*The Real Thing*, 1969)		30	40
1776	45c. Masters Apprentices (*Turn Up Your Radio*, 1970)		30	40
1777	45c. Daddy Cool (*Eagle Rock*, 1971)		30	40
1778	45c. Billy Thorpe and the Aztecs (*Most People I know think I'm Crazy*, 1972)		30	40
1779	45c. Skyhooks (*Horror Movie*, 1974)		30	40
1780	45c. AC/DC (*It's a Long Way to the Top*, 1975)		30	40
1781	45c. Sherbet (*Howzat*, 1976)		30	40

590 Yellow-tufted Honeyeater ("Helmeted Honeyeater")

1998. Endangered Species. Multicoloured.

1794	5c. Type **590**		45	45
1795	5c. Orange-bellied parrot		45	45
1796	45c. Red-tailed cockatoo ("Red-tailed Black-Cockatoo")		80	80
1797	45c. Gouldian finch		80	80

591 French Horn and Cello Players

1998. Youth Arts, Australia. Multicoloured.
1798 45c. Type **591** 50 50
1799 45c. Dancers 50 50

592 *Phalaenopsis rosenstromii*

1998. Australia–Singapore Joint Issue. Orchids. Multicoloured.

1800	45c. Type **592**		55	40
1801	85c. *Arundina graminifolia*		1·00	1·00
1802	$1 *Grammatophyllum speciosum*		1·40	1·25
1803	$1.20 *Dendrobium phalaenopsis*		1·50	1·60
MS1804	138×72 mm. Nos. 1800/3		4·00	3·75

593 Flying Angel with Teapot (cartoon by Michael Leunig)

1998. *The Teapot of Truth* (cartoons by Michael Leunig). Multicoloured.
1805 45c. Type **593** 75 80

1806	45c. Two birds in heart-shaped tree		75	80
1807	45c. Pouring tea		75	80
1808	$1 Mother and child (29×24 mm)		1·40	1·75
1809	$1.20 Cat with smiling face (29×24 mm)		1·40	1·75

594 Red Lacewing

1998. Butterflies. Multicoloured. Ordinary or self-adhesive gum

1815	45c. Type **594**		75	1·00
1816	45c. Dull oakblue		75	1·00
1817	45c. Meadow argus		75	1·00
1818	45c. Ulysses butterfly		75	1·00
1819	45c. Common red-eye		75	1·00

595 Flinders' Telescope and Map of Tasmania

1998. Bicentenary of the Circumnavigation of Tasmania by George Bass and Matthew Flinders. Multicoloured.

1820	45c. Type **595**		75	65
1821	45c. Sextant and letter from Bass		75	65

596 Weedy Seadragon

1998. International Year of the Ocean. Multicoloured.

1822	45c. Type **596**		55	55
1823	45c. Bottlenose dolphin		55	55
1824	45c. Fiery squid (24×29 mm)		55	55
1825	45c. Manta ray (29×24 mm)		55	55
1826	45c. White pointer shark (29×49 mm)		55	55
1827	45c. Southern right whale (49×29 mm)		55	55
MS1828	166×73 mm. Nos. 1822/7		2·75	2·75

Nos. 1822/3 also come self-adhesive.

597 Rose of Freedom

1998. 50th Anniv of Universal Declaration of Human Rights.
1831 **597** 45c. multicoloured 50 50

598 Three Kings

1998. Christmas. Multicoloured.

1832	40c. Type **598**		40	15
1833	45c. Nativity scene		40	15
1834	$1 Mary and Joseph		1·10	1·10

No. 1832 also comes self-adhesive.

599 Australian Coat of Arms

1999. 50th Anniv of Australian Citizenship. Ordinary or self-adhesive gum
1837 **599** 45c. multicoloured 40 40

600 Arthur Boyd

1999. Australian Legends (3rd series). Arthur Boyd (painter). Multicoloured. Ordinary or self-adhesive gum.

1838	45c. Type **600**		50	50
1839	45c. *Nebuchadnezzer on fire falling over Waterfall* (Arthur Boyd)		50	50

601 Red Roses

1999. Greetings Stamp. Romance. Ordinary or self-adhesive gum
1843 **601** 45c. multicoloured 40 40

602 Elderly Man and Grandmother with Boy

1999. International Year of Older Persons. Multicoloured.

1844	45c. Type **602**		50	50
1845	45c. Elderly woman and grandfather with boy		50	50

603 Polly Woodside (barque)

1999. Sailing Ships. Multicoloured.

1846	45c. Type **603**		60	35
1847	85c. *Alma Doepel* (topsail schooner)		1·00	1·10
1848	$1 *Enterprize* replica (topsail schooner)		1·25	1·10
1849	$1.05 *Lady Nelson* replica (topsail schooner)		1·40	1·90

1999. Australia—Ireland Joint Issue. *Polly Woodside* (barque). Sheet 137×72 mm. Multicoloured.
MS1850 45c. Type **603**; 30p. Type **374** of Ireland (No. **MS**1850 was sold at $1.25 in Australia) 1·25 1·40

1999. Australia—Canada. Joint Issue. *Marco Polo* (emigrant ship). Sheet 160×95 mm. Multicoloured.
MS1851 85c. As No. 1728; 46c. Type **701** of Canada (No. **MS**1851 was sold at $1.30 in Australia) 1·25 1·40

1999. "Australia '99" International Stamp Exhibition, Melbourne. Two sheets, each 142×76 mm, containing designs as Nos. 398/403 and all with face value of 45c.
MS1852 (a) 45c. ultramarine (Type **167**); 45c. grey (Captain Cook); 45c. brown (Flinders). (b) 45c. red (Type **168**); 45c. brown (Bass); 45c. purple (King) Set of 2 sheets 2·50 2·75

604 Olympic Torch and 1956 7½d. Stamp

1999. Olympic Torch Commemoration.
1853 **604** $1.20 multicoloured 1·10 1·10

605 *Correa reflexa* (native fuchsia)

1999. Fauna and Flora (3rd series). Coastal Environment. Multicoloured.

1854	45c. Type **605**		50	60
1855	45c. *Hibbertia scandens* (guinea flower)		50	60
1856	45c. *Ipomoea pre-caprae* (beach morning glory)		50	60
1857	45c. *Wahlenbergia stricta* (Australian bluebells)		50	60
1858	70c. Humpback whales and zebra volute shell (29×24 mm)		1·00	70
1859	90c. Brahminy kite and checkerboard helmet shell (29×24 mm)		90	1·00
1860	90c. Fraser Island and chambered nautilus (29×24 mm)		90	1·00
1861	$1.05 Loggerhead turtle and melon shell (29×24 mm)		1·00	80
1862	$1.20 White-bellied sea eagle and Campbell's stromb shell (29×24 mm)		1·25	90

Nos. 1859/60 were printed together, *se-tenant*, forming a composite design.
Nos. 1854/7 also come self-adhesive.

606 Queen Elizabeth II with The Queen Mother

1999. Queen Elizabeth II's Birthday.
1870 **606** 45c. multicoloured 70 50

607 *Here's Humphrey*

1999. Children's Television Programmes. Multicoloured. Ordinary or self-adhesive gum.

1871	45c. Type **607**		40	45
1872	45c. *Bananas in Pyjamas*		40	45
1873	45c. *Mr. Squiggle*		40	45
1874	45c. *Play School* (teddy bears)		40	45
1875	45c. *Play School* (clock, toy dog and doll)		40	45

608 Obverse and Reverse of 1899 Sovereign

1999. Centenary of the Perth Mint.
1881 **608** $2 gold, blue and green 2·00 1·75

609 Lineout against New Zealand

1999. Centenary of Australian Test Rugby. Multicoloured.

1882	45c. Type **609**		50	40
1883	45c. Kicking the ball against England		50	40
1884	$1 Try against South Africa (horiz)		1·00	85
1885	$1.20 Passing the ball against Wales (horiz)		1·10	1·25

Nos. 1882/3 also come self-adhesive.

610 Drilling at Burn's Creek and Rock Bolting in Tumut 2 Power Station Hall

1999. 50th Anniv of Snowy Mountain Scheme (hydro-electric project). Multicoloured. Ordinary or self-adhesive gum.
1888 45c. Type **610** 65 65

1889	45c. English class for migrant workers, Cooma	65	65
1890	45c. Tumut 2 Tailwater Tunnel and Eucumbene Dam	65	65
1891	45c. German carpenters and Island Bend Dam	65	65

611 Calligraphy Pen and Letter

1999. Greetings Stamps. Multicoloured.

1896	45c. Type **611**	50	55
1897	45c. Wedding rings	50	55
1898	45c. Birthday cake	50	55
1899	45c. Christmas decoration	50	55
1900	45c. Teddy bear	50	55
1901	$1 Koala	1·00	1·25

See also No. 1921.

612 Sydney Olympic Emblem

1999. Olympic Games, Sydney (2000) (1st issue).

1902	**612** 45c. multicoloured	1·50	60

See also Nos. 2015/24.

613 Australia Post Symbol, 1975

1999. "Sydney Design '99" International Congress and Exhibition. Multicoloured.

1903	45c. Type **613**	35	20
1904	90c. Embryo chair, 1988	65	70
1905	$1.35 Possum skin textile, c.1985	1·00	1·25
1906	$1.50 Storey Hall, R.M.I.T. University, 1995	1·00	1·25

614 Magnificent Tree Frog

1999. National Stamp Collecting Month, Small Pond Life. Multicoloured. Ordinary or self-adhesive gum.

1907	45c. Type **614**	55	55
1908	45c. Sacred kingfisher	55	55
1909	45c. Roth's tree frog (29×24 mm)	55	55
1910	45c. Dragonfly (29×24 mm)	55	55
1911	50c. Javelin frog (24×29 mm)	65	65
1912	50c. Northern dwarf tree frog (24×29 mm)	65	65
MS1913	166×73 mm. Nos. 1907/12	3·00	3·25

615 Madonna and Child

1999. Christmas. Multicoloured.

1918	40c. Type **615**	50	15
1919	$1 Tree of Life (horiz)	1·00	1·10

No. 1918 also comes self-adhesive.

616 Fireworks and Hologram

1999. Millennium Greetings stamp.

1921	**616** 45c. multicoloured	50	50

617 Rachel Thomson (college administrator)

2000. New Millennium. "Face of Australia". Multicoloured.

1922	45c. Nicholle and Meghan Triandis (twin babies)	35	60
1923	45c. David Willis (cattleman)	35	60
1924	45c. Natasha Bramley (scuba diver)	35	60
1925	45c. Cyril Watson (Aborigine boy)	35	60
1926	45c. Mollie Dowdall (wearing red hat) (vineyard worker)	35	60
1927	45c. Robin Dicks (flying instructor)	35	60
1928	45c. Mary Simons (retired nurse)	35	60
1929	45c. Peta and Samantha Nieuwerth (mother and baby)	35	60
1930	45c. John Matthews (doctor)	35	60
1931	45c. Edith Dizon-Fitzimmons (wearing drop earrings) (music teacher)	35	60
1932	45c. Philippa Weir (wearing brown hat) (teacher)	35	60
1933	45c. John Thurgar (in bush hat and jacket) (farmer)	35	60
1934	45c. Miguel Alzona (with face painted) (schoolboy)	35	60
1935	45c. Type **617**	35	60
1936	45c. Necip Akarsu (wearing blue shirt) (postmaster)	35	60
1937	45c. Justin Allan (R.A.N. sailor)	35	60
1938	45c. Wadad Dennaoui (wearing checked shirt) (student)	35	60
1939	45c. Jack Laity (market gardener)	35	60
1940	45c. Kelsey Stubbin (wearing cricket cap) (schoolboy)	35	60
1941	45c. Gianna Rossi (resting chin on hand) (church worker)	35	60
1942	45c. Paris Hansch (toddler)	35	60
1943	45c. Donald George Whatham (in blue shirt and tie) (retired teacher)	35	60
1944	45c. Stacey Coull (wearing pendant)	35	60
1945	45c. Alex Payne (wearing cycle helmet) (schoolgirl)	35	60
1946	45c. John Lodge (Salvation Army member)	35	60

618 Walter Parker

2000. Australian Legends (4th series). *The Last Anzacs*. Multicoloured. Ordinary or self-adhesive gum.

1951	45c. Type **618**	35	40
1952	45c. Roy Longmore	35	40
1953	45c. Alec Campbell	35	40
1954	45c. 1914–15 Star (medal)	35	40

619 Scenes from *Cloudstreet* (play) (Perth Festival)

2000. Arts Festivals. Multicoloured.

1955	45c. Type **619**	45	50
1956	45c. Belgian dancers from Rosas Company (Adelaide Festival)	45	50
1957	45c. *Guardian Angel* (sculpture) and dancer (Sydney Festival)	45	50
1958	45c. Musician and Balinese dancer (Melbourne Festival)	45	50
1959	45c. Members of Vusa Dance Company of South Africa (Brisbane Festival)	45	50

620 Coast Banksia, False Sarsaparilla and Swamp Bloodwood (plants)

2000. Gardens. Multicoloured. Ordinary or self-adhesive gum.

1965	45c. Type **620**	40	55
1966	45c. Eastern spinebill on swamp bottlebrush in foreground	40	55
1967	45c. Border of cannas	40	55
1968	45c. Roses, lake and ornamental bridge	40	55
1969	45c. Hibiscus with bandstand in background	40	55

621 Queen Elizabeth II in 1996

2000. Queen Elizabeth II's Birthday.

1970	**621** 45c. multicoloured	80	50

622 Medals and Korean Landscape

2000. 50th Anniv of Korean War.

1971	**622** 45c. multicoloured	60	50

623 Daisy

2000. Nature and Nation. Greeting stamps. Multicoloured.

1972	45c. Type **623**	45	50
1973	45c. Australia on globe	45	50
1974	45c. Red kangaroo and flag	45	50
1975	45c. Sand, sea and sky	45	50
1976	45c. Rainforest	45	50

624 Taking the Vote, New South Wales

2000. Centenary of Commonwealth of Australia Constitution Act. Multicoloured.

1977	45c. Type **624**	45	40
1978	45c. Voters waiting for results, Geraldton, Western Australia	45	40
1979	$1.50 Queen Victoria (29×49 mm)	1·25	1·40
1980	$1.50 Women dancing ("The Fair New Nation") (29×49 mm)	1·25	1·40
MS1981	155×189 mm. Nos. 1977/80	3·00	3·25

625 Sydney Opera House, New South Wales

2000. International Stamps. Views of Australia (1st series). Multicoloured.

1982	50c. Type **625**	90	20
1983	$1 Nandroya Falls, Queensland	1·60	30
1984	$1.50 Sydney Harbour Bridge, New South Wales	2·00	75
1985	$2 Cradle Mountain, Tasmania	2·25	75
1986	$3 The Pinnacles, Western Australia	2·50	1·25
1987	$4.50 Flinders Ranges, South Australia (51×24 mm)	3·75	2·25
1988	$5 Twelve Apostles, Victoria (51×24 mm)	4·00	2·25

1989	$10 Devils Marbles, Northern Territory (51×24 mm)	8·25	4·50

Nos. 1982/9 were intended for international postage which, under changes in Australian tax laws from 1 July 2000, remained exempt from General Sales Tax.

From 1 February 2001 only international stamps were valid on overseas mail and from that date could not be used on items posted to Australian addresses.

See also Nos. 2121/4 and 2195/9.

626 Tennis Player in Wheelchair

2000. Paralympic Games, Sydney (1st issue). Multicoloured. Ordinary or self-adhesive gum.

1990	45c. Type **626**	40	40
1991	45c. Amputee sprinting	40	40
1992	49c. Basketball player in wheelchair	40	40
1993	49c. Blind cyclist	40	40
1994	49c. Amputee putting the shot	40	40

See also Nos. 2053/4.

627 Sir Neville Howse (first Australian recipient of Victoria Cross, 1900)

2000. Cent of Australia's First Victoria Cross Award.

2000	**627** 45c. multicoloured	70	50
2001	– 45c. brown, gold and black	70	50
2002	– 45c. multicoloured	70	50
2003	– 45c. multicoloured	70	50
2004	– 45c. brown, gold and black	70	50

DESIGNS: No. 2001, Sir Roden Cutler, 1941; 2002, Victoria Cross; 2003, Private Edward Kenna, 1945; 2004, Warrant Officer Keith Payne, 1969.

628 Water Polo

2000. Olympic Games, Sydney (2nd issue). Multicoloured. Ordinary or self-adhesive gum. Competitors highlighted in varnish.

2005	45c. Type **628**	35	45
2006	45c. Hockey	35	45
2007	45c. Swimming	35	45
2008	45c. Basketball	35	45
2009	45c. Cycling (triathlon)	35	45
2010	45c. Horse riding	35	45
2011	45c. Tennis	35	45
2012	45c. Gymnastics	35	45
2013	45c. Running	35	45
2014	45c. Rowing	35	45

Nos. 2005/14 were printed together, *se-tenant*, with the backgrounds forming a composite design.

629 Olympic Flag, Flame and Parthenon

2000. Transfer of Olympic Flag from Sydney to Athens. Joint issue with Greece. Multicoloured.

2025	45c. Type **629**	40	20
2026	$1.50 Olympic Flag, Flame and Sydney Opera House	1·25	1·25

Stamps in similar designs were issued by Greece.

630 Ian Thorpe (Men's
400m Freestyle
Swimming)

2000. Australian Gold Medal Winners at Sydney Olympic
Games. Multicoloured.

2027A	45c. Type **630**		40	45
2028A	45c. Australian team (Men's 4×100 m Freestyle Swimming Relay)		40	45
2029A	45c. Michael Diamond (Men's Trap Shooting)		40	45
2030A	45c. Australian team (Three Day Equestrian Event)		40	45
2031A	45c. Susie O'Neill (Women's 200 m Freestyle Swimming)		40	45
2032A	45c. Australian team (Men's 4×200 m Freestyle Swimming Relay)		40	45
2033A	45c. Simon Fairweather (Men's Individual Archery)		40	45
2034A	45c. Australian team (Men's Madison Cycling)		40	45
2035A	45c. Grant Hackett (Men's 1500 m Freestyle Swimming)		40	45
2036A	45c. Australian team (Women's Water Polo)		40	45
2037A	45c. Australian team (Women's Beach Volleyball)		40	45
2038A	45c. Cathy Freeman (Women's 400 m Athletics)		40	45
2039A	45c. Lauren Burns (Women's under 49 kg Taekwondo)		40	45
2040A	45c. Australian team (Women's Hockey)		40	45
2041A	45c. Australian crew (Women's 470 Dinghy Sailing)		40	45
2042A	45c. Australian crew (Men's 470 Dinghy Sailing)		40	45

631 Martian
Terrain

2000. Stamp Collecting Month. Exploration of Mars.
Multicoloured

(a) Ordinary gum

2043	45c. Type **631**		35	35
2044	45c. Astronaut using thruster		35	35
2045	45c. Spacecraft (50×30 mm)		35	35
2046	45c. Flight crew (30×25 mm)		35	35
2047	45c. Launch site (30×50 mm)		35	35
2048	45c. Robots on kelp rod (25×30 mm)		35	35
MS2049	166×73 mm. Nos. 2043/8		1·90	2·25

(b) Self-adhesive. Designs 21×32 mm.

2050	45c. Type **631**		45	45
2051	45c. Astronaut using thruster		45	45

632 Cathy Freeman
with Olympic Torch
and Ring of Flames

2000. Opening Ceremony, Olympic Games, Sydney.

2052	**632**	45c. multicoloured	1·00	50

633 Blind Athlete
carrying Olympic
Torch

2000. Paralympic Games, Sydney (2nd issue).
Multicoloured.

2053	45c. Type **633**		55	50
2054	45c. Paralympic Games logo		55	50

634 Siobhan Paton
(swimmer)

2000. Siobhan Paton, Paralympian of the Year.

2055	**634**	45c. multicoloured	1·25	75

635 "Sleep in
Heavenly Peace"

2000. Christmas. Silent Night (carol). Multicoloured

(a) Ordinary gum

2056	40c. Type **635**		50	25
2057	45c. "All is Calm, All is Bright"		50	25
MS2058	165×75 mm. Nos. 2056/7		1·00	1·00

(b) Self-adhesive.

2059	40c. Type **635**		45	35

(c) International Mail. As T **625** inscr "Season's Greetings".

2060	80c. Byron Bay, New South Wales		70	85

2001. International Mail. No. 1901 optd **International POST**.

2061	$1 Koala		2·75	1·75

637 Parade
passing
Federation Arch,
Sydney

2001. Centenary of Federation. Multicoloured

(a) Ordinary gum.

2062	49c. Type **637**		50	50
2063	49c. Edmund Barton (first Federal Prime Minister)		50	50
2064	$2 Australia For Ever (song sheet) and celebration picnic (50×30 mm)		1·75	1·75
2065	$2 State Banquet, Sydney (30×50 mm)		1·75	1·75
MS2066	166×73 mm. Nos. 2062/5		4·50	5·00

(b) Self-adhesive.

2067	49c. Type **637**		50	60
2068	49c. Edmund Barton (first Federal Prime Minister)		50	60

638 Slim Dusty with
Guitar in 1940s

2001. Australian Legends (5th series). Slim Dusty (country
music singer). Multicoloured. Ordinary or self-adhesive gum.

2069	45c. Type **638**		50	50
2070	45c. Slim Dusty wearing "Sundowner" hat		50	50

639 Light Horse Parade,
1940, and Command
Post, New Guinea, 1943

2001. Centenary of Australian Army. Multicoloured.

2073	45c. Type **639**		1·00	65
2074	45c. Soldier carrying Rwandan child and officers on the Commando Selection Course		1·00	65

640 Entry Canopy,
Skylights and Site Plan

2001. Opening of the National Museum, Canberra.
Multicoloured.

2075	49c. Type **640**		50	50
2076	49c. Skylights and "Pangk" (wallaby sculpture)		50	50

2001. Sir Donald Bradman (cricketer) Commemoration.
Nos. 1663/4 additionally inscribed "1908–2001" in
red. Multicoloured.

2077	45c. Type **568**		50	50
2078	45c. Bradman playing stroke		50	50

641 Khe Sanh (Cold
Chisel), 1978

2001. Australian Rock and Pop Music. Multicoloured.
Ordinary or self-adhesive gum

2089	45c. Type **641**		35	50
2090	45c. Down Under (Men at Work), 1981		35	50
2091	45c. Power and the Passion (Midnight Oil), 1983		35	50
2092	45c. Original Sin (INXS), 1984		35	50
2093	45c. You're the Voice (John Farnham), 1986		35	50
2094	45c. Don't Dream it's Over (Crowded House), 1986		35	50
2095	45c. Treaty (Yothu Yindi), 1991		35	50
2096	45c. Tomorrow (Silverchair), 1994		35	50
2097	45c. Confide in Me (Kylie Minogue), 1994		35	50
2098	45c. Truly, Madly, Deeply (Savage Garden), 1997		35	50

642 Queen
Elizabeth II
holding Bouquet

2001. Queen Elizabeth II's Birthday.

2099	**642**	45c. multicoloured	1·75	65

643 Party Balloons

2001. "Colour My Day". Greetings Stamps

(a) Domestic Mail.

2100	45c. Type **643**		30	35
2101	45c. Smiling Flower		30	35
2102	45c. Hologram and party streamers		30	35

(b) International Mail.

2103	$1 Kangaroo and joey		1·00	80
2104	$1.50 The Bayulu Banner		1·40	1·75

644 Opening of the First
Federal Parliament
(Charles Nuttall)

2001. Centenary of Federal Parliament. Paintings.
Multicoloured.

2105	45c. Type **644**		50	25
2106	$2.45 45 Prince George opening the First Parliament of the Commonwealth of Australia (Tom Roberts)		1·75	2·25
MS2107	Two sheets, each 166×75 mm. (a) No. 2105. (b) No. 2106 Set of 2 sheets		2·75	3·00

645 Telecommunications
Tower

2001. Outback Services. Multicoloured. Ordinary or self-
adhesive gum.

2108	45c. Type **645**		1·00	75
2109	45c. Road train		1·00	75
2110	45c. School of the Air pupil		1·00	75
2111	45c. Outback family and mail box		1·00	75
2112	45c. Royal Flying Doctor Service aircraft and ambulance		1·00	75

646 Dragon Boat and
Hong Kong Convention
and Exhibition Centre

2001. Joint Issue with Hong Kong. Dragon Boat Racing.
Multicoloured

(a) Domestic Mail

2118	45c. Type **646**		50	45

(b) International Mail.

2119	$1 Dragon boat and Sydney Opera House		1·00	1·00
MS2120	115×70 mm. Nos. 2118/19		1·40	1·40

2001. International Stamps. Views of Australia (2nd
series). As T **625**. Multicoloured.

2121	50c. The Three Sisters, Blue Mountains, New South Wales		1·50	40
2122	$1 The Murrumbidgee River, Australian Capital Territory		2·50	40
2123	$1.50 Four Mile Beach, Port Douglas, Queensland		3·50	1·00
2124	$20 Uluru Rock at dusk, Northern Territory (52×24 mm)		28·00	16·00

647 Variegated
Wren ("Variegated
Fairy-Wren")

2001. Fauna and Flora (4th series). Desert Birds.
Multicoloured. Ordinary or self-adhesive gum

2130	45c. Type **647**		50	50
2131	45c. Painted finch ("Painted Firetail")		50	50
2132	45c. Crimson chat		50	50
2133	45c. Budgerigar		50	50

648 Daniel Solander
(Swedish botanist) and
Mango Tree

2001. Australia–Sweden Joint Issue. Daniel Solander's
Voyage with Captain Cook. Multicoloured

(a) Domestic Mail

2134	45c. Type **648**		1·00	50

(b) International Mail

2135	$1.50 H.M.S. Endeavour on reef and Kapok tree		3·50	3·50

649 Christmas
Tree

2001. Christmas (1st issue). Multicoloured.

(a) Domestic Mail

2136	40c. Type **649**		50	20

(b) International Mail.

2137	80c. Star		1·50	1·10

See also Nos. 2157/8.

650 Australia on Globe

2001. Commonwealth Heads of Government Meeting (No. 2138) and Commonwealth Parliamentary Conference (No. 2139). Multicoloured.

2138	45c. Type **650**	50	50
2139	45c. Southern Cross	50	50

651 Wedge-tailed Eagle

2001. Centenary of Birds of Australia. Birds of Prey. Multicoloured.

2140	49c. Type **651**	1·00	75
2141	49c. Australian kestrel ("Nankeen Kestrel")	1·00	75
2142	98c. Red goshawk (vert)	2·00	2·00
2143	98c. Spotted harrier (vert)	2·00	2·00

652 Cockatoos dancing to Animal Band

2001. National Stamp Collecting Month. "Wild Babies" (cartoons). Multicoloured.

Ordinary or self-adhesive gum

2144	45c. Type **652**	55	45
2145	45c. Kevin Koala with birthday cake	55	45
2146	45c. Ring-tailed possums eating	55	45
2147	45c. Bilbies at foot of tree	55	45
2148	45c. James Wombat on rope ladder	55	45
2149	45c. Wallaby, echidna and platypus on rope ladder	55	45
MS2150	Two sheets, each 175×75 mm. (a) Nos. 2144/6. (b) 2147/9. Ordinary gum	2·50	2·50

653 *Adoration of the Magi*

2001. Christmas (2nd issue). Miniatures from *Wharncliffe Hours Manuscript*. Multicoloured.

2157	40c. Type **653**	1·10	30
2158	45c. *Flight into Egypt*	1·10	35

No. 2157 also comes self-adhesive.

654 Sir Gustav Nossal (immunologist)

2002. Australian Legends. (6th series). Medical Scientists. Multicoloured. Ordinary or self-adhesive gum

2165	45c. Type **654**	40	55
2166	45c. Nancy Millis (microbiologist)	40	55
2167	45c. Peter Doherty (immunologist)	40	55
2168	45c. Fiona Stanley (epidemiologist)	40	55
2169	45c. Donald Metcalf (haematologist)	40	55

655 Queen Elizabeth in 1953

2002. Golden Jubilee. Multicoloured.

2170	45c. Type **655**	75	35
2171	$2.45 45 Queen Elizabeth in Italy, 2000	2·25	3·75
MS2172	160×77 mm. Nos. 2170/1	3·00	3·75

656 Steven Bradbury (Men's 1000m Short Track Speed Skating)

2002. Australian Gold Medal Winners at Salt Lake City Winter Olympic Games. Multicoloured.

2173	45c. Type **656**	95	60
2174	45c. Alisa Camplin (Women's Aerials Freestyle Skiing)	95	60

657 Austin 7 and Bugatti Type 40, Australian Grand Prix, Phillip Island, 1928

2002. Centenary of Motor Racing in Australia and New Zealand. Multicoloured. Ordinary or self-adhesive gum

2175	45c. Type **657**	60	80
2176	45c. Jaguar Mark II, Australian Touring Car Championship, Mallala, 1963	60	80
2177	45c. Repco-Brabham, Tasman Series, Sandown, 1966	60	80
2178	45c. Holden Torana and Ford Falcon, Hardie-Ferodo 500, Bathurst, 1972	60	80
2179	45c. William's Ford, Australian Grand Prix, Calder, 1980	60	80
2180	45c. Benetton-Renault, Australian Grand Prix, Albert Park, 2001	60	80

658 Macquarie Lighthouse

2002. Lighthouses. Multicoloured. Ordinary or self-adhesive gum

2187	45c. Type **658**	75	35
2188	49c. Cape Naturaliste	90	80
2189	49c. Troubridge Island	90	80
2190	$1.50 Cape Bruny	2·25	2·25

659 Nicolas Baudin, Kangaroo, *Geographe* (ship) and Map

2002. Australia—France Joint Issue. Bicentenary of Flinders—Baudin Meeting at Encounter Bay. Multicoloured

(a) Domestic Mail

2193	45c. Type **659**	60	40

(b) International Mail.

2194	$1.50 Matthew Flinders, Port Lincoln Parrot, *Investigator* (ship) and Map	2·00	1·75

2002. International Stamps. Views of Australia (3rd series). As T **625**. Multicoloured. Ordinary or self-adhesive gum

2195	50c. Walker Flat, River Murray, South Australia	65	40
2196	$1 Mt. Roland, Tasmania	1·25	60
2197	$1.50 Cape Leveque, Western Australia	1·60	1·25

660 Desert Star Flower

2002. Fauna and Flora (5th series). Great Sandy Desert. Multicoloured.

2200	50c. Type **660**	40	35
2201	$1 Bilby	80	65
2202	$1.50 Thorny Devil	1·20	1·60
2203	$2 Great Sandy Desert landscape (50×30 mm)	1·60	1·90

No. 2200 also comes self-adhesive.

661 *Ghost Gum, Mt Sonder* (Albert Namatjira)

2002. Birth Centenary of Albert Namatjira (artist). Multicoloured.

(a) Ordinary gum

2204	45c. Type **661**	50	50
2205	45c. "Mt Hermannsburg"	50	50
2206	45c. "Glen Helen Country"	50	50
2207	45c. "Simpsons Gap"	50	50
MS2208	133×70 mm. Nos. 2204/7	1·75	1·75

(b) Self-adhesive

2209	45c. Type **661**	40	55
2210	45c. *Mt Hermannsburg*	40	55
2211	45c. *Glen Helen Country*	40	55
2212	45c. *Simpsons Gap*	40	55

662 *Nelumbo nucifera*

2002. Australia–Thailand Joint Issue. 50th Anniv of Diplomatic Relations. Water Lilies. Multicoloured.

(a) Domestic Mail

2213	45c. Type **662**	60	35

(b) International Mail.

2214	$1 *Nymphaea immutabilis*	1·40	75
MS2215	107×70 mm. Nos. 2214/15	2·00	1·75

663 Star, Presents and Baubles

2002. International Greetings. Multicoloured.

2216	90c. Type **663**	85	80
2217	$1.10 10 Koala	1·00	95
2218	$1.65 65 *Puja* (painting by Ngarralja Tommy May)	1·50	1·40

2002. International Stamps. Views of Australia (4th series). As T **625**. Multicoloured.

2219	$1.10 Coonawarra, South Australia	2·25	70
2220	$1.65 Gariwerd (Grampians), Victoria	3·00	1·40
2221	$2.20 National Library, Canberra	3·75	3·50
2222	$3.30 Cape York, Queensland	5·50	5·50

664 Lilly-pilly

2002. "Bush Tucker". Edible Plants from the Outback. Multicoloured. Ordinary or self-adhesive gum

2228	49c. Type **664**	55	55
2229	49c. Honey Grevillea	55	55
2230	49c. Quandong	55	55
2231	49c. Acacia seeds	55	55
2232	49c. Murnong	55	55

665 Bunyip

2002. Stamp Collecting Month. *The Magic Rainforest*, (book by John Marsden). Multicoloured.

2233	45c. Type **665**	50	50
2234	45c. Fairy on branch	50	50
2235	45c. Gnome with sword	50	50
2236	45c. Goblin with stock whip	50	50
2237	45c. Wizard	50	50
2238	45c. Sprite	50	50
MS2239	170×90 mm. Nos. 2234/9	3·00	3·00

Nos. 2233/8, ordinary or self-adhesive gum.

666 Wakeful

2002. Champion Racehorses. Multicoloured.

2246	45c. Type **666**	1·40	1·40
2247	45c. *Rising Fast*	1·40	1·40
2248	45c. *Manikato*	1·40	1·40
2249	45c. *Might and Power*	1·40	1·40
2250	45c. *Sunline*	1·40	1·40

667 Nativity

2002. Christmas. Multicoloured.

2251	40c. Type **667**	75	35
2252	45c. The Three Wise Men	75	35

No. 2251 also comes self-adhesive.

668 Two Daisies

2003. Greetings Stamps. Some adapted from previous issues. Multicoloured.

2254	50c. Type **668**	40	45
2255	50c. Wedding rings and yellow roses	40	45
2256	50c. Hearts and pink roses	40	45
2257	50c. Birthday cake and present	40	45
2258	50c. Seated teddy bear	40	45
2259	50c. Balloons	40	45
2260	50c. Red kangaroo and flag	40	45
2261	50c. Australia on globe	40	45
2262	50c. Sports car	40	45
2263	$1 Wedding rings and pink rose	80	85

669 Margaret Court with Wimbledon Trophy

2003. Australian Legends (7th series). Tennis Players. Ordinary or self-adhesive gum. Multicoloured.

2264	50c. Type **669**	65	50
2265	50c. Margaret Court in action	65	50
2266	50c. Rod Laver with Wimbledon Trophy	65	50
2267	50c. Rod Laver in action	65	50

670 Blue Orchid

2003. Fauna and Flora (6th series). Rainforest, Daintree National Park. Multicoloured. Ordinary or self-adhesive gum.

2272	50c. Orange-thighed tree frog	85	75
2273	50c. Green-spotted triangle (butterfly)	85	75
2274	50c. Striped possum	85	75

2275	50c. Yellow-bellied sunbird	85	75
2276	$1.45 Type **670**	2·25	1·25

671 Snapper and Fishing from Beach

2003. Angling in Australia. Multicoloured.

2282	50c. Type **671**	60	60
2283	50c. Murray cod and flooded wood	60	60
2284	50c. Brown trout and fly-fishing	60	60
2285	50c. Yellow-finned tuna and sea-fishing from launch	60	60
2286	50c. Barramundi and anglers in mangrove swamp	60	60

672 "Hari Withers" Camellia

2003. Australian Horticulture. Multicoloured

(a) Size 25×36 mm. Ordinary gum.

2287	50c. Type **672**	55	50
2288	50c. "Victoria Gold" rose	55	50
2289	50c. "Superb" grevillea	55	50
2290	50c. "Bush Tango" kangaroo paw	55	50
2291	50c. "Midnight" rhododendron	55	50

(b) Size 21×33 mm. Self-adhesive.

2292	50c. Type **672**	50	60
2293	50c. "Victoria Gold" rose	50	60
2294	50c. "Superb" grevillea	50	60
2295	50c. "Bush Tango" kangaroo paw	50	60
2296	50c. "Midnight" rhododendron	50	60

673 Ned Kelly (Sir Sidney Nolan)

2003. Australian Paintings (1st series). Multicoloured.

2297	$1 Type **673**	1·50	1·75
2298	$1 *Family Home, Suburban Exterior* (Howard Arkley)	1·50	1·75
2299	$1.45 *Cord Long Drawn, Expectant* (Robert Jacks)	2·00	2·00
2300	$2.45 *Girl* (Joy Hester)	3·00	3·50

674 Queen Elizabeth II, 1953 (photograph by Cecil Beaton)

2003. 50th Anniv of Coronation. Multicoloured.

2301	50c. Type **674**	75	45
2302	$2.45 St. Edward's Crown	2·50	3·50
MS2303	105×70 mm. Nos. 2301/2	3·25	4·25

No. 2301 also comes self-adhesive.

675 Untitled Painting by Ningura Napurrula

2003. International Stamps. Art of Papunya Tula Movement. Showing untitled paintings by Aboriginal artists. Multicoloured.

2305	$1.10 Type **675**	1·75	70
2306	$1.65 Naata Nungurrayi	2·75	1·40
2307	$2.20 Graham Tjupurrula (55×24 mm)	3·25	2·00
2308	$3.30 Dini Campbell Tjampitjinpa (55×24 mm)	4·50	3·50

676 Kangaroo Chromosomes

2003. 50th Anniv of Discovery of DNA. Multicoloured.

2309	50c. Type **676**	1·00	1·00
2310	50c. DNA double helix	1·00	1·00

677 *Oscar W* (paddle-steamer)

2003. 150th Anniv of Murray River Shipping. Multicoloured. Ordinary or self-adhesive gum.

2311	50c. Type **677**	65	55
2312	50c. *Marion* (paddle-steamer)	65	55
2313	50c. *Ruby* (paddle-steamer)	65	55
2314	50c. *Pyap* (cruise vessel)	65	55
2315	50c. *Adelaide* (paddle-steamer)	65	55

678 Christmas Tree

2003. Greetings Stamps. Peace and Goodwill. Design, adapted from Christmas 2001 (1st issue) (Nos. 2136/7). Multicoloured

(a) Domestic Mail

2321	50c. Type **678**	40	30

(b) International Mail.

2322	90c. Star	75	95

679 Sir Samuel Griffith (first Chief Justice)

2003. Centenary of High Court of Australia.

2323	**679**	50c. purple, black and red	55	45
2324	–	$1.45 vermilion, red and black	1·50	1·50
MS2325		105×70 mm. Nos. 2323/4	2·50	2·25

DESIGN: $1.45, "JUSTICE".

680 Ulysses Butterfly

2003. Stamp Collecting Month. Bugs and Butterflies. Multicoloured. Ordinary or self-adhesive.

2326	50c. Type **680**	50	45
2327	50c. Leichhardt's grasshopper	50	45
2328	50c. Vedalia ladybird	50	45
2329	50c. Green mantid and captured damselfly	50	45
2330	50c. Emperor gum moth caterpillar	50	45
2331	50c. Fiddler beetle	50	45
MS2332	170×85 mm. Nos. 2326/31	3·25	3·00

681 Hands passing Ball and Players

2003. Rugby World Cup Championship, Australia. Multicoloured

(a) Domestic Mail

2339	50c. Type **681**	55	45

(b) International Mail.

2340	$1.10 Trophy (Webb Ellis Cup) and Telstra Stadium	1·10	1·00
2341	$1.65 Hand grasping ball and player taking shot at goal	1·50	2·00
MS2342	115×70 mm. Nos. 2339/41	2·75	3·00

682 "Active with ASTHMA" and Silhouettes of Sportspeople

2003. National Asthma Week Campaign.

2343	**682**	50c. multicoloured	1·00	45

683 Mary, Baby Jesus and Angels

2003. Christmas. Multicoloured.

2344	45c. Type **683**	45	15
2345	50c. Three Wise Men	45	15
2346	90c. Angel appearing to shepherds	80	90

No. 2344 also comes self-adhesive.

684 Joan Sutherland as *Lucia di Lammermoor*, 1980

2004. Australian Legends (8th series). Dame Joan Sutherland (opera singer). Multicoloured. Ordinary or self-adhesive gum.

2350	50c. Type **684**	80	80
2351	50c. Joan Sutherland	80	80

685 Aboriginal shell necklace and bracelet

2004. Bicentenary of Settlement of Hobart, Tasmania. Multicoloured.

2352	50c. Type **685**	85	70
2353	50c. Cheshunt House, Deloraine	85	70
2354	$1 Mount Wellington and Hobart Town from Kangaroo Point (John Glover)	1·75	1·75
2355	$1 Mountains, south west Tasmania	1·75	1·75
MS2356	135×72 mm. Nos. 2352/5	4·25	4·25

686 Ross Bridge, Tasmania, 1836

2004. Landmark Bridges. Multicoloured. Ordinary or self-adhesive gum.

2357	50c. Type **686**	1·00	70
2358	50c. Lockyer Creek Bridge, Queensland, 1911	1·00	70
2359	50c. Sydney Harbour Bridge, 1932	1·00	70
2360	50c. Birkenhead Bridge, Adelaide, 1940	1·00	70
2361	50c. Bolte Bridge, Melbourne, 1999	1·00	70

687 Stylized "Southern Cross"

2004. Greetings Stamp.

2367	**687**	50c. multicoloured	70	55

688 Solar Systems CS500 Dish ("solar")

2004. Renewable Energy. Multicoloured. Ordinary or self-adhesive gum.

2368	50c. Type **688**	85	85
2369	50c. Wind turbines ("wind")	85	85
2370	50c. Snowy Mountains Hydro-electric Scheme ("hydro")	85	85
2371	50c. Sugar cane field, bagasse (waste plant fibre) and sugar mill ("biomass")	85	85

689 Queen Elizabeth II (from photo by Dorothy Wilding)

2004. 50th Anniv of Royal Tour to Australia.

2376	**689**	50c. purple, black and grey	1·25	55

690 Red Lacewing

2004. Fauna and Flora (7th series). Rainforest Butterflies. Multicoloured.

2377	5c. Type **690**	20	15
2378	10c. Blue-banded eggfly	20	15
2379	75c. Cruiser	1·25	50
2380	$2 Ulysses and red lacewing butterflies and Daintree Rainforest (50×30 mm)	3·25	2·50

691 Cockatoos and Aircraft

2004. Australian Innovations. Multicoloured. Ordinary or self-adhesive gum.

2381	50c. Type **691** (black box flight recorder, 1961)	1·10	1·10
2382	50c. Pregnant woman (ultra-sound imaging equipment, 1976)	1·10	1·10
2383	50c. Driver's hands on wheel (Racecam TV sport coverage, 1979)	1·10	1·10
2384	50c. Kangaroo with joey and car (baby safety capsule, 1984)	1·10	1·10
2385	50c. Portion of banknote and tree (polymer banknotes, 1988)	1·10	1·10

692 Shaw Savill Lines *Dominion Monarch*

2004. "Bon Voyage". Ocean Liners. Advertising posters. Multicoloured.

2391	50c. Type **692**	90	45
2392	$1 Union Steam Ship Co. *Awatea*	1·50	85
2393	$1.45 Orient Line *Ormonde & Orsova*	2·00	2·00
2394	$2 Aberdeen & Commonwealth Line liner passing under bridge	2·75	2·75

No. 2395 also comes self-adhesive.

693 Eureka Flag (Southern Cross)

2004. 150th Anniv of Eureka Stockade. Multicoloured.

2396	50c. Type **693**	60	45
2397	$2.45 Peter Lalor (gold diggers leader) and detail from *Swearing allegiance to the Southern Cross 1854* (Alphonse Doudiet)	2·75	3·00
MS2398	106×69 mm. Nos. 2396/7	3·25	3·25

694 Koala

2004. "Impressions". Australian Wildlife and Heritage. Multicoloured.

2399	$1 Type **694**	1·50	1·75
2400	$1 Little penguin	1·50	1·75
2401	$1.45 Clown anemonefish (horiz)	1·75	1·75
2402	$2.45 Gold Coast (horiz)	2·75	3·50

695 Swimming

2004. Olympic Games, Athens, Greece. Multicoloured.

2403	50c. Type **695**	60	45
2404	$1.65 Sprinting	1·90	1·90
2405	$1.65 Cycling	2·75	1·90

696 Ian Thorpe (Men's 400m Freestyle Swimming)

2004. Australian Gold Medal Winners at Olympic Games, Athens. Multicoloured.

2406	50c. Type **696**	65	65
2407	50c. Women's 4×100m relay team	65	65
2408	50c. Sara Carrigan (Road Race Cycling)	65	65
2409	50c. Petria Thomas (Women's 100m Butterfly Swimming)	65	65
2410	50c. Suzanne Balogh (Women's Trap Shooting)	65	65
2411	50c. Ian Thorpe (Men's 200m Freestyle Swimming)	65	65
2412	50c. Jodie Henry (Women's 100m Freestyle Swimming)	65	65
2413	50c. Anna Meares (Women's 500m Time Trial Cycling)	65	65
2414	50c. James Tomkins and Drew Ginn (Men's Pair Rowing)	65	65
2415	50c. Grant Hacket (Men's 1500m Freestyle Swimming)	65	65
2416	50c. Women's 4×100m Medley Relay Swimming Team	65	65
2417	50c. Chantelle Newberry (Women's 10m Platform Diving)	65	65
2418	50c. Men's 4000m pursuit cycling team	65	65
2419	50c. Ryan Bayley (Men's Individual Sprint Cycling)	65	65
2420	50c. Graeme Brown and Stuart O'Grady (Men's Madison Cycling)	65	65
2421	50c. Ryan Bayley (Men's Keirin Cycling)	65	65
2422	50c. Men's hockey team	65	65

697 Entrance Beach, Broome, Western Australia

2004. International Stamps. Coastlines. Multicoloured.

2423	$1.20 Type **697**	2·00	50
2424	$1.80 Mt. William National Park, Tasmania	2·50	90
2425	$2.40 Potato Point, Bodalla, New South Wales	3·25	1·50
2426	$3.60 Point Gibbon, Eyre Peninsula, South Australia	4·50	2·75

698 Sheet of Early Australian Stamp (No. 16) (image scaled to 47% of original size)

2004. Treasures from the Archives (1st series). Ordinary or self-adhesive gum.

2427	**698**	$5 multicoloured	8·00	9·50

See also No. 2555.

699 Stephenson 2-4-0 (Melbourne–Sandridge, 1854)

2004. 150th Anniv of Australian Railways. Multicoloured. Ordinary or self-adhesive gum.

2429	50c. Type **699**	1·00	1·10
2430	50c. Locomotive No. 1 (Sydney–Parramatta, 1855)	1·00	1·10
2431	50c. B12 Class locomotive (Helidon–Toowoomba, 1867)	1·00	1·10
2432	50c. G Class train (Kalgoorlie–Port Augusta, 1917)	1·00	1·10
2433	50c. *The Ghan* (Alice Springs–Darwin, 2004)	1·00	1·10

700 "Ezzie" (black and white cat)

2004. Stamp Collecting Months. Cats and Dogs. Multicoloured

(a) Ordinary gum

2439	50c. Type **700**	1·25	1·25
2440	50c. "Tinkerbell" (ginger and white kitten)	1·25	1·25
2441	50c. "Max" (Labrador puppy)	1·25	1·25
2442	50c. "Bridie" and "Lily" (West Highland terriers)	1·25	1·25
2443	$1 "Edward" (Jack Russell terrier)	2·25	1·50
MS2444	170×85 mm. Nos. 2439/43	6·50	6·00

(b) Self-adhesive.

2445	50c. "Max" (Labrador puppy)	70	80
2446	50c. Type **700**	70	80
2447	50c. "Bridie" and "Lily" (West Highland Terriers)	70	80
2448	50c. "Tinkerbell" (ginger and white kitten)	70	80
2449	$1 "Edward" (Jack Russell terrier)	1·50	1·60

701 Mick Doohan (Repsol)

2004. Formula 1 Motorcycle Racing. Multicoloured. Ordinary or self-adhesive gum.

2455	50c. Type **701**	80	90
2456	50c. Wayne Gardner (Racing Honda)	80	90
2457	50c. Troy Bayliss (Ducati)	80	90
2458	50c. Daryl Beattie (Team Suzuki)	80	90
2459	50c. Garry McCoy (Red Bull)	80	90

702 Mary and Jesus

2004. Christmas. Multicoloured

(a) Domestic mail

2460	45c. Type **702**	40	15
2461	50c. The Angel and the shepherds	45	15

(b) International mail.

2462	$1 The Three Wise Men (horiz)	80	80

(c) Self-adhesive.

2464	$1 The Three Wise Men (horiz)	90	1·25

703 Tennis Player and Match, Warehousemen's Cricket Ground, Melbourne, c. 1905

2005. Centenary of Australian Open Tennis Championships. Multicoloured.

(a) Domestic Mail

2465	50c. Type **703**	1·50	50

(b) International Post

2466	$1.80 Woman player and match, Melbourne Park, c. 2005	3·00	2·75

704 Prue Acton

2005. Australian Legends (9th series). Fashion Designers. Multicoloured. Ordinary or self-adhesive gum.

2473	50c. Type **704**	90	1·10
2474	50c. Jenny Bannister	90	1·10
2475	50c. Collette Dinnigan	90	1·10
2476	50c. Akira Isogawa	90	1·10
2477	50c. Joe Saba	90	1·10
2478	50c. Carla Zampatti	90	1·10

705 Princess Parrot

2005. Australian Parrots. Multicoloured. Ordinary or self-adhesive gum.

2484	50c. Type **705**	1·10	1·10
2485	50c. Rainbow lorikeet	1·10	1·10
2486	50c. Green rosella	1·10	1·10
2487	50c. Red-capped parrot	1·10	1·10
2488	50c. Purple-crowned lorikeet	1·10	1·10

706 Sir Donald Bradman's Cap

2005. Sporting Treasures. Multicoloured.

2489	50c. Type **706**	1·25	85
2490	50c. Lionel Rose's boxing gloves	1·25	85
2491	$1 Marjorie Jackson's running spikes	1·50	1·50
2492	$1 Phar Lap's racing silks	1·50	1·50

707 Bumble Bee Toy

2005. Greetings Stamps (1st series). "Marking the Occasion". Multicoloured.

(i) Domestic Mail

2493	50c. Type **707**	1·00	1·10
2494	50c. Red roses	1·00	1·10
2495	50c. Wrapped presents	1·00	1·10
2496	50c. Kangaroos at sunset	1·00	1·10
2497	50c. Bouquet of white flowers	1·00	1·10
2498	$1 Hand holding bouquet of cream roses	1·75	1·25

(ii) International Post

2499	$1.10 Koala	1·75	1·50
2500	$1.20 Shell on sandy beach	2·00	2·25
2501	$1.80 Sydney Opera House	3·50	3·50

Nos. 2493/8 are for domestic use and 2499/51 are for international use.

See also Nos. 2556/7.

708 Greater Blue Mountains Area, New South Wales

2005. World Heritage Sites. Multicoloured.

2502	50c. Type **708**	1·00	85
2503	50c. Blenheim Palace, England	1·00	85
2504	50c. Wet Tropics, Queensland	1·00	85
2505	50c. Stonehenge, England	1·00	85
2506	$1 Purnululu National Park, West Australia	1·75	1·50
2507	$1 Heart of Neolithic Orkney, Scotland	1·75	1·50
2508	$1.80 Uluru-Kata Tjuta National Park, Northern Territories	2·50	2·75
2509	$1.80 Hadrian's Wall, England	2·50	2·75

Nos. 2502/7 are for domestic use and 2508/9 are for international use.

Stamps in similar designs were also issued by Great Britain.

709 Tribrachidium

2005. Creatures of the Slime (Ediacaran fossils). Multicoloured.

2510	50c. Type **709**	1·40	1·00
2511	50c. Dickinsonia	1·40	1·00
2512	50c. Spriggina	1·40	1·00
2513	50c. Kimberella	1·40	1·00
2514	50c. Inaria	1·40	1·00
2515	$1 Charniodiscus 1.501	2·00	1·50
MS2516	170×210 mm. Nos. 2510/15	6·00	5·50

710 Rotary Emblem and Man supporting Globe

2005. Centenary of Rotary International. Ordinary or self-adhesive gum.

2517	**710**	50c. multicoloured	1·25	85

711 Obverse of Coin showing Head of Queen Victoria

2005. 150th Anniv of First Australian Coin. Design showing one sovereign coin and Sydney Mint building. Multicoloured.

2519	50c. Type **711**	1·50	85
2520	$2.45 Reverse of coin showing olive wreath	4·25	3·25
MS2521	105×69 mm. As Nos. 2519/20 but coins in gold foil	6·00	4·75

712 Queen at Opening Ceremony for Commonwealth Heads of Government Meeting, Queensland, 2002

2005. Queen's Birthday.

2522	**712**	50c. multicoloured	1·50	60

713 Superb Lyrebird

2005. International Stamps. Bush Wildlife. Multicoloured.

2523	$1 Type **713**	1·50	60
2524	$1.10 Laughing kookaburra	1·50	65
2525	$1.20 Koala	1·60	80
2526	$1.80 Red kangaroo	2·50	1·50

Nos. 2524/6 also come self-adhesive.

714 Sturt's Desert Pea

2005. Australian Wildflowers (1st series). Multicoloured. Ordinary or self-adhesive gum.

2530	50c. Type **714**	1·00	1·00
2531	50c. Coarse-leaved mallee	1·00	1·00
2532	50c. Common fringe lily	1·00	1·00
2533	50c. Swamp daisy	1·00	1·00

See also Nos. 2590/**MS**2594 and 2759/62.

715 Vineyard

2005. Australian Wine. Multicoloured.

2538	50c. Type **715**	1·00	1·00
2539	50c. Ripening grapes	1·00	1·00
2540	$1 Harvesting grapes	1·90	1·75
2541	$1 Casks of wine	1·90	1·75
2542	$1.45 Glasses of red and white wine and cheese	2·75	2·50

Nos. 2538/9 also come self-adhesive.

716 Snowgum

2005. Native Trees. Multicoloured. Ordinary or self-adhesive gum.

2550	50c. Type **716**	80	1·00
2551	50c. Wollemi pine	80	1·00
2552	50c. Boab	80	1·00
2553	50c. Karri	80	1·00
2554	50c. Moreton Bay fig	80	1·00

717 1888 20s. New South Wales Stamps (image scaled to 47% of original size)

2005. Treasures from the Archives (2nd issue).

2555	**717** $5 multicoloured	12·00	14·00

718 Christmas Tree with Lights

2005. Greeting Stamps. "Marking the Occasion" (2nd series). Multicoloured.

2556	45c. Type **718**	85	85
2557	50c. Map of Australia with stars	85	85

719 Chloe the Chicken

2005. Stamp Collecting Month. "Down on the Farm". Multicoloured

(a) Ordinary gum

2558	50c. Type **719**	85	85
2559	50c. Lucy the Lamb	85	85
2560	50c. Gilbert the Goat	85	85
2561	50c. Ralph the Piglet	85	85
2562	50c. Abigail the Cow	85	85
2563	$1 Harry the Horse	1·40	1·40
MS2564	170×85 mm. Nos. 2558/63	5·00	5·50

(b) Self-adhesive

2565	50c. Type **719**	1·00	1·25
2566	50c. Lucy the Lamb	1·00	1·25
2567	50c. Gilbert the Goat	1·00	1·25
2568	50c. Ralph the Piglet	1·00	1·25
2569	50c. Abigail the Cow	1·00	1·25
2570	$1 Harry the Horse	2·00	3·00

720 Madonna and Child

2005. Christmas. Multicoloured. Ordinary or self-adhesive gum

(i) Domestic mail

2571	45c. Type **720**	75	15

(ii) International Mail.

2572	$1 Adoring angel (horiz)	1·50	85

721 Emblem

2006. Commonwealth Games, Melbourne (1st issue). Ordinary or self-adhesive gum.

2575	**721** 50c. multicoloured	60	45

See also Nos. 2596/2600 and **MS**2607/**MS**2623.

722 Mrs. Norm Everage, 1969

2006. Australian Legends (10th series). Barry Humphries (satirist and actor). Multicoloured. Ordinary or self-adhesive gum.

2582	50c. Type **722**	1·00	1·50
2583	50c. As Mrs. Edna Everage, 1973	1·00	1·50
2584	50c. As Dame Edna Everage, 1982	1·00	1·50
2585	50c. As Dame Edna Everage, 2004	1·00	1·50
2586	50c. Barry Humphries	1·00	1·50

723 Red Rose

2006. Greetings Stamp. Roses. Ordinary or self-adhesive gum.

2587	**723** 50c. multicoloured	1·00	45

724 Pincushion Hakea

2006. Australian Wildflowers (2nd series). Multicoloured.

2590	$1 Type **724**	1·75	50
2591	$2 Donkey orchid	3·75	1·25
2592	$5 Mangles kangaroo paw (49×29 mm)	7·00	4·50
2593	$10 Waratah (49×29 mm)	13·00	9·00
MS2594	105×70 mm. $10 As No. 2593 (49×29 mm)	11·00	12·00

725 Dale Begg-Smith

2006. Dale-Begg Smith's Gold Medal for Men's Moguls Skiing at Winter Olympic Games, Turin.

2595	**725** 50c. multicoloured	1·00	1·00

726 Athlete at Start

2006. Commonwealth Games, Melbourne (2nd issue). Multicoloured

(a) Ordinary gum. (i) Domestic Mail

2596	50c. Type **726**	50	45

(ii) International Post.

2597	$1.25 Cyclist	2·25	2·00
2598	$1.85 Netball	2·75	3·25
MS2599	142×75 mm. Nos. 2596/8	5·50	5·50

(b) Self-adhesive.

2600	50c. Type **726**	75	80

727 Platypus

2006. International Post. Native Wildlife. Multicoloured.

2601	5c. Type **727**	40	30
2602	25c. Short-beaked echidna	60	25
2603	$1.25 Common wombat	2·50	70
2604	$1.85 Tasmanian devil	3·50	1·40
2605	$2.50 Greater bilby	4·50	1·75
2606	$3.70 Dingo	6·50	3·25

728 Tram with Feathered "Wings" (Opening Ceremony)

2006. Commonwealth Games (3rd issue). Seventeen sheets each 180×200 mm containing horiz designs as T **728** showing opening/closing ceremonies (Nos. **MS**2607, **MS**2622) or Australian gold medal winners (others). Multicoloured.

MS2607	50c.×5 No. 1 Opening Ceremony	2·50	3·25
MS2608	50c.×5 No. 2	2·50	3·25
MS2609	50c.×10 No. 3	4·00	6·00
MS2610	50c.×5 No. 4	2·50	3·25
MS2611	50c.×10 No. 5	4·00	6·00
MS2612	50c.×5 No. 6	2·50	3·25
MS2613	50c.×5 No. 7	2·50	3·25
MS2614	50c.×10 No. 8	4·00	6·00
MS2615	50c.×5 No. 9	2·50	3·25
MS2616	50c.×10 No. 10	4·00	6·00
MS2617	50c.×5 No. 11	2·50	3·25
MS2618	50c.×10 No. 12	4·00	6·00
MS2619	50c.×10 No. 13	4·00	6·00
MS2620	50c.×10 No. 14	4·00	6·00
MS2621	50c.×5 No. 15	2·50	3·25
MS2622	50c.×5 No. 16 Closing Ceremony	2·50	3·25
MS2623	50c.×10 No. 17 Most memorable moment Kerryn McCann's Marathon victory	4·00	6·00

Nos. **MS**2607/23 are numbered from 1 to 17 at the foot of the sheet.

729 Queen Elizabeth II in Garter Robes (Pietro Annigoni)

2006. 80th Birthday of Queen Elizabeth II. Multicoloured

(a) Ordinary gum

2624	50c. Type **729**	1·50	45
2625	$2.45 Queen Elizabeth II (photo by Cecil Beaton)	4·75	4·00
MS2626	105×70 mm. Nos. 2624/5	6·25	4·25

No. **MS**2626 also commemorates the 50th anniversary of the portrait by Annigoni.

(b) Self-adhesive

2627	50c. Type **729**	75	1·00

730 Point Lonsdale, Victoria, 1902

2006. Lighthouses of the 20th Century. Ordinary or self-adhesive gum. Multicoloured.

2628	50c. Type **730**	1·10	1·00
2629	50c. Cape Don, Northern Territory, 1916	1·10	1·00
2630	50c. Wollongong Head, New South Wales, 1937	1·10	1·00
2631	50c. Casuarina Point, West Australia, 1971	1·10	1·00
2632	50c. Point Cartwright, Queensland, 1979	1·10	1·00

731 Koala with Cub

2006. International Stamps. "Greetings from Australia". Ordinary or self-adhesive gum. Multicoloured.

2638	$1.25 Type **731**	2·75	1·25
2639	$1.85 Royal Exhibition Building, Melbourne	3·75	2·75

732 Boy heading Ball ("PLAY")

2006. World Cup Football Championship, Germany. Soccer in Australia. Multicoloured

(a) Ordinary gum. (i) Domestic Mail.

2642	50c. Type **732**	70	80
2643	50c. Player kicking ball ("GOAL")	70	80

(ii) International Post.

2644	$1.25 $1.25 Goalkeeper ("SAVE")	1·75	1·50
2645	$1.85 $1.85 Player with ball ("SHOT")	2·40	2·75
MS2646	Circular 170×170 mm. Nos. 2642/5	4·75	4·75

(b) Self-adhesive.

2647	50c. Type **732**	75	90
2648	50c. As No. 2643	75	90

733 Kate sorting Mail

2006. "Postie Kate". Ordinary or self-adhesive gum. Multicoloured.

2649	50c. Type **733**	90	80
2650	50c. On motorcycle, giving letter to woman	90	80
2651	50c. With van, delivering parcel	90	80
2652	50c. Riding motorcycle. passing mailbox	90	80
2653	50c. With mail satchel on shoulder	90	80

734 Blue Whale

2006. Endangered Species. Whales. Multicoloured

(a) Ordinary gum. (i) Domestic Mail.

2659	50c. Type **734**	75	65
2660	50c. Humpback whale	75	65

	(ii) International Post.		
2661	$1.25 Fin whale	1·75	1·25
2662	$1.85 Southern bottlenose whale	2·75	2·75
MS2663	69×66 mm. Nos. 2659/62	5·50	5·00

	(b) Self-adhesive. (i) Domestic Mail.		
2664	50c. Type 734	75	90
2665	50c. As No. 2660	75	90

	(ii) International Post.		
2666	$1.25 As No. 2661	1·60	2·25
2667	$1.85 As No. 2662	2·40	3·75

2006. Le Salon du Timbre Stamp Exhibition, Paris. No. MS2646 inscr "LE SALON DU TIMBRE & DE L'ECRIT 17 AU 25 JUIN 2006 PARC FLORAL DE PARIS www. salondutimbre.fr" on sheet margin.

MS2668	Circular 170×170 mm. Nos. 2642/5	4·75	4·75

735 Surfing

2006. Extreme Sports. Multicoloured.

2669	50c. Type 735	90	50
2670	$1 Snowboarding	1·75	1·25
2671	$1.45 Skateboarding	2·00	2·50
2672	$2 Freestyle motoX	3·50	4·00

736 Ford TT Truck, 1917

2006. Driving through the Years. Multicoloured. Ordinary or self-adhesive gum.

2678	50c. Type 736	70	1·00
2679	50c. Holden FE, 1956	70	1·00
2680	50c. Morris 850 (Mini Minor), 1961	70	1·00
2681	50c. Holden Sandman HX panel van, 1976	70	1·00
2682	50c. Toyota LandCruiser FJ60, 1985	70	1·00

737 "Sunbury Rock Festival" (1972)

2006. Rock Posters (1st series). Multicoloured. Ordinary or self-adhesive gum.

2683	50c. Type 737	95	1·00
2684	50c. "Magic Dirt" (2002)	95	1·00
2685	50c. "Masters Apprentices" (1969)	95	1·00
2686	50c. "Goanna's Spirit of Place" (1983)	95	1·00
2687	50c. "Angels/Sports/Paul Kelly" (c. 1979)	95	1·00
2688	50c. "Midnight Oil" (c. 1979)	95	1·00
2689	50c. "Big Day Out" (2003)	95	1·00
2690	50c. "Apollo Bay Music Festival" (1999)	95	1·00
2691	50c. "Rolling Stones Australian Tour" (1973)	95	1·00
2692	50c. "Mental as Anything" (1990)	95	1·00

See also Nos. 2808/11.

738 White Shark

2006. Stamp Collecting Month. Dangerous Australians. Multicoloured

	(a) Ordinary gum.		
2703	50c. Type 738	1·25	1·25
2704	50c. Eastern brown snake	1·25	1·25
2705	50c. Box jellyfish	1·25	1·25
2706	50c. Saltwater crocodile	1·25	1·25
2707	50c. Blue-ringed octopus	1·25	1·25
2708	$1 Yellow-bellied sea snake	1·75	1·50
MS2709	130×90 mm. Nos. 2703/8	6·00	6·00

	(b) Self-adhesive.		
2710	50c. Type 738	90	1·10
2711	50c. As No. 2704	90	1·10
2712	50c. As No. 2705	90	1·10
2713	50c. As No. 2706	90	1·10
2714	50c. As No. 2707	90	1·10
2715	$1 As No. 2708	1·40	1·75

739 In Melbourne Tonight

2006. 50th Anniv of Television in Australia. Multicoloured. Ordinary or self-adhesive gum.

2716	50c. Type 739	70	70
2717	50c. Homicide	70	70
2718	50c. Dateline	70	70
2719	50c. Neighbours	70	70
2720	50c. Kath and Kim	70	70

2006. China 2006 Stamp and Coin Expo. Two sheets, each 110×80 mm containing No. 2638, design on sheet margin given.

MS2726	731 (a) $1.25 multicoloured (Great Wall of China). (b) $1.25 multi-coloured (Sydney Opera House)	4·25	4·00

740 2s. Melbourne across River Yarra Stamp

2006. 50th Anniv of Olympic Games, Melbourne. Showing Australia 1956 Olympic Games stamps and contemporary photographs of Melbourne. Multicoloured.

2727	50c. Type 740	1·25	1·25
2728	50c. River Yarra, Melbourne	1·25	1·25
2729	$1 1s. Collins Street stamp	1·75	2·00
2730	$1 Collins Street, Melbourne	1·75	2·00

741 Virgin Mary and Baby Jesus

2006. Christmas. Multicoloured

	(a) Ordinary gum. (i) Domestic mail.		
2731	45c. Type 741	80	30
2732	50c. Magi with gift	80	35

	(ii) International Mail.		
2733	$1.05 Young shepherd with lamb	1·40	1·10

	(b) Self-adhesive. Smaller design 22×33 mm. (i) Domestic mail.		
2734	45c. Type 741	70	60

	(ii) International Mail.		
2735	$1.05 As No. 2733	1·25	1·50

742 Victorious Australian Cricketers

2007. "Australia wins the Ashes". Multicoloured

	(a) Ordinary gum. (i) Domestic Mail.		
2736	50c. Type 742	1·50	1·00

	(ii) International Post.		
2737	$1.85 Australian team with Ashes Urn	4·50	4·50
MS2738	160×80 mm. Nos. 2736/7	6·00	6·00

	(b) Self-adhesive. (i) Domestic Mail.		
2739	50c. As No. 2736	1·00	1·00

	(ii) International Post.		
2740	$1.85 As No. 2737	3·00	4·00

743 Scobie Breasley (jockey), 1936

2007. Australian Legends (11th series). Legends of Australian Horse Racing. Multicoloured

	(a) Ordinary gum		
2741	50c. Type 743	1·25	1·25
2742	50c. Scobie Breasley on Santa Claus after winning English Derby	1·25	1·25
2743	50c. Bart Cummings (trainer) holding binoculars, 1966	1·25	1·25
2744	50c. Bart Cummings holding Melbourne Cup	1·25	1·25
2745	50c. Roy Higgins (jockey), 1965	1·25	1·25
2746	50c. Roy Higgins riding Light Fingers to win Melbourne Cup, 1965	1·25	1·25
2747	50c. Bob Ingham (breeder), c. 1972	1·25	1·25
2748	50c. Bob Ingham leading Lonhro, 2004	1·25	1·25
2749	50c. George Moore (jockey), 1957	1·25	1·25
2750	50c. George Moore riding Tul-loch, 1960	1·25	1·25
2751	50c. John Tapp (race commen-tator), 1972	1·25	1·25
2752	50c. John Tapp at microphone, 1998	1·25	1·25

	(b) Self-adhesive.		
2753	50c. Type 743	1·00	1·25
2754	50c. As No. 2743	1·00	1·25
2755	50c. As No. 2746	1·00	1·25
2756	50c. As No. 2748	1·00	1·25
2757	50c. As No. 2749	1·00	1·25
2758	50c. As No. 2751	1·00	1·25

744 Tasmanian Christmas Bell

2007. Australian Wildflowers (3rd series). Multicoloured. Ordinary or self-adhesive gum.

2759	50c. Type 744	1·40	1·50
2760	50c. Green spider flower	1·40	1·50
2761	50c. Sturt's desert rose	1·40	1·50
2762	50c. Phebalium whitei	1·40	1·50

745 Swimmer

2007. 12th FINA (Federation Internationale de Natation) World Championships, Melbourne. Ordinary or self-adhesive gum.

2767	745	50c. multicoloured	70	70

746 Maria Island, Tasmania

2007. International Post. Island Jewels. Multicoloured

	(a) Ordinary gum.		
2769	10c. Type 746	15	10
2770	30c. Rottnest Island, West Australia	45	40
2771	$1.30 Green Island, Queensland	2·00	2·10
2772	$1.95 Fraser Island, Queensland	2·50	2·50
2773	$2.60 Kangaroo Island, South Australia	3·25	3·25
2774	$3.85 Lord Howe Island, New South Wales	3·75	4·00

	(b) Self-adhesive gum.		
2775	$1.30 As No. 2771	2·50	3·00
2776	$1.95 As No. 2772	3·00	4·25

747 Female Lifeguard with Reel

2007. Year of the Surf Lifesaver. Multicoloured

	(a) Ordinary gum		
2777	50c. Type 747	70	90
2778	50c. Male lifeguards	70	90
2779	$1 Surf boat	2·50	2·25
2780	$2 "Nippers" (life saving club's children's programme)	3·50	4·50

	(b) Self-adhesive gum.		
2781	50c. As No. 2778	70	1·00
2782	50c. Type 747	70	1·00
MS2783	160×90 mm. $2.45 Inflatable rescue boat ×2	6·50	7·00

748 Aries

2007. Signs of the Zodiac. Multicoloured. Ordinary or self-adhesive gum.

2784	50c. Type 748	60	80
2785	50c. Taurus	60	80
2786	50c. Gemini	60	80
2787	50c. Cancer	60	80
2788	50c. Leo	2·25	80
2789	50c. Virgo	60	80
2790	50c. Libra	60	80
2791	50c. Scorpio	60	80
2792	50c. Sagittarius	60	80
2793	50c. Capricorn	60	80
2794	50c. Aquarius	60	80
2795	50c. Pisces	60	80

749 At the Beach (Percy Trompf)

2007. Poster Art (2nd series). Nostalgic Tourism. Showing 1930s tourism posters. Multicoloured.

2808	50c. Type 749	70	70
2809	$1 Fishing (John Vickery)	1·40	1·25
2810	$2 Riding in the Country (James Northfield)	3·00	3·75
2811	$2.45 Winter Sport (James Northfield)	3·75	5·50

750 Queen Elizabeth II in Australia, March 2006

2007. Queen's Birthday.

2812	750	50c. multicoloured	1·50	1·25

751 Admella (steamship), 1859

2007. Historic Shipwrecks. Multicoloured.

2813	50c. Type 751	1·00	70
2814	$1 Loch Ard (clipper), 1878	1·75	1·25
2815	$2 Dunbar (clipper), 1857	3·00	4·50

752 Yellow-footed Rock-wallaby

2007. International Post. "Country to Coast". Multicoloured.

2816	$1.30 Type **752**	3·00	1·75
2817	$1.95 Sydney Harbour Bridge	5·00	2·75

753 "The Burning Bicycle"

2007. Circus: Under the Big Top. Multicoloured. Ordinary or self-adhesive gum.

2818	50c. Type **753**	80	1·00
2819	50c. "The Inside-out Man"	80	1·00
2820	50c. "The Dental Trapeze"	80	1·00
2821	50c. "The Banana Lady"	80	1·00
2822	50c. "The Human Cannonball"	80	1·00

754 Big Golden Guitar, Tamworth, New South Wales

2007. Big Things. Multicoloured.

2828	50c. Type **754**	80	85
2829	50c. Big lobster, Kingston SE, South Australia	80	85
2830	50c. Big banana, Coffs Harbour, New South Wales	80	85
2831	50c. Big Merino ram, Goulburn, New South Wales	80	85
2832	50c. Big pineapple, Nambour, Queensland	80	85

755 Sydney Harbour Bridge

2007. International Post. 75th Anniv of Sydney Harbour Bridge. Sheet 130×90 mm.

MS2838 (a) $1.95×2 multicoloured. (b) $1.95×2 multicoloured (emblem and '15 JUNE 2007 SYDNEY NSW 2000' inscr in gold on sheet margin) Set of 2 sheets 11·00 11·00

756 Grey-headed flying-fox

2007. Threatened Wildlife. Multicoloured.

(i) Domestic Mail

2839	50c. Type **756**	1·50	1·25
2840	50c. Mountain Pygmy-possum	1·50	1·25

(ii) International Post.

2841	$1.25 Flatback turtle	2·75	2·50
2842	$1.30 Wandering albatross	3·00	2·50

757 Former ICI House, Melbourne, 1973

2007. Landmarks: Modernist Australian Architecture. Multicoloured.

2843	50c. Type **757**	90	90
2844	50c. Academy of Science, Canberra, 1958	90	90
2845	$1 Council House, Perth, 1962	1·60	1·25
2846	$2.45 Sydney Opera House, 1973	4·00	4·50

MS2847 90×90 mm. Nos. 2843/6 6·75 6·75

758 Delicatessen, Dairy Produce Hall, Queen Victoria Market, Melbourne

2007. Market Feast. Multicoloured. Ordinary or self-adhesive gum.

2848	50c. Type **758**	1·00	1·25
2849	50c. Banana seller, Rusty's Market, Cairns	1·00	1·25
2850	50c. Sydney Fish Market	1·00	1·25
2851	50c. Vegetable stall, Adelaide Central Market	1·00	1·25
2852	50c. Potato seller, Hume Murray Farmers Market, Albury Wodonga	1·00	1·25

2007. BANGKOK 2007

MS2857b 130×90 mm. **755** $1.95×2 multicoloured 8·50 8·00

759 APEC Logo and Half Globe

2007. Asia-Pacific Economic Cooperation Forum, Australia. Ordinary or self-adhesive gum.

2858	**759** 50c. multicoloured	70	70

760 SAS Soldiers, Helicopter and Parachutist

2007. 50th Anniv of the Special Air Service.

2860	**760** 50c. multicoloured	1·50	1·00

761 Brisbane Botanic Gardens, Mt. Coot-tha

2007. Australian Botanic Gardens (1st issue). Multicoloured. Ordinary or self-adhesive gum.

2861	50c. Type **761**	1·25	1·25
2862	50c. Kings Park and Botanic Garden, Perth	1·25	1·25
2863	50c. Royal Botanic Gardens and Domain, Sydney	1·25	1·25
2864	50c. Royal Botanic Gardens, Melbourne	1·25	1·25
2865	50c. Botanic Gardens of Adelaide	1·25	1·25

2007. Collectors International Fair, Prague. No. MS2838 inscr 'SBERATEL SAMMLER COLLECTOR' and emblem on sheet margin.

MS2871 130×90 mm. **755** $1.95×2 multicoloured 5·75 5·75

762 Sputnik (first satellite), 1957

2007. Stamp Collecting Month. Blast Off! 50 Years in Space. Multicoloured.

2872	50c. Type **762**	70	80
2873	50c. Cosmonaut Alexei Leonov on first space walk, 1965	70	80
2874	50c. Neil Armstrong walking on Moon, 1969	70	80
2875	50c. *Voyager* space probe, 1977	70	80
2876	50c. International Space Station, 1998	70	80
2877	$1 Hubble Space Telescope and galaxy, 1990	1·25	1·50

MS2878 160×90 mm. Nos. 2872/7 and as No. 2877 but 51×37 mm 8·50 8·50

Nos. 2872/6 also come self-adhesive.

763 Family Picnic outside Caravan, 1950s

2007. Caravanning through the Years. Multicoloured. Ordinary or self-adhesive gum.

2884	50c. Type **763**	1·40	1·40
2885	50c. Family with kangaroos outside caravan, 1960s	1·40	1·40
2886	50c. Family outside caravan, 1970s	1·40	1·40
2887	50c. Woman and girl outside caravan, 1980s	1·40	1·40
2888	50c. Elderly couple sitting outside caravan, c. 2007	1·40	1·40

764 Surfing Santa Stamp Design by Roger Roberts, 1977

2007. Christmas. 50 Years of Christmas Stamps. Multicoloured designs showing Christmas stamp designs from previous years redrawn without the face values

(a) Ordinary gum. (i) Domestic Mail

2894	45c. Type **764**	80	20
2895	45c. Bush Nativity (Baby Jesus with koalas and wallaby) by Marg Towt, 1990	80	1·00
2896	45c. Madonna and Child	80	1·00
2897	50c. The Spirit of Christmas	80	70

(ii) International Post.

2898	$1.10 Madonna and Child from stained-glass window, 1984	1·50	1·50

(b) Self-adhesive. (i) Domestic Mail.

2899	45c. As Type **764**	65	60
2900	45c. As No. 2895	90	90
2901	45c. As No. 2896	90	90
2902	50c. As No. 2897	90	1·25

(ii) International Post.

2903	$1.10 As No. 2898	1·75	2·00

MS2904 156×100 mm. As No. 2899 and Nos. 2900/3 4·75 4·75

765 Red Rose

2008. Greetings stamp. 'Love Blooms'. Ordinary or self-adhesive gum.

2905	**765** 50c. multicoloured	80	70

766 Dame Elisabeth Murdoch

2008. Australian Legends (12th series). Philanthropists. Multicoloured. Ordinary or self-dhesive gum.

2907	50c. Type **766**	1·40	1·40
2908	50c. Victor Smorgon and Loti Smorgon	1·40	1·40
2909	50c. Lady (Mary) Fairfax	1·40	1·40
2910	50c. Frank Lowy	1·40	1·40

767 Human Body showing Organs

2008. Organ and Tissue Donation. Ordinary or self-adhesive gum.

2915	**767** 50c. multicoloured	75	75

768 Scout Camp

2008. Centenary of Scouting in Australia. T **768** and similar horiz designs. Multicoloured

(a) Ordinary gum. (i) Domestic Mail

2917	50c. Type **768**	75	75

(ii) International Post.

2918	$1.35 Scouts in circle	1·90	2·00
2919	$2 Lord Baden-Powell (founder)	2·75	3·75

(b) Self-adhesive. (i) Domestic Mail.

2920	50c. As Type **768**	75	1·00

(ii) International Post.

2921	$1.35 As No. 2918	4·50	5·50
2922	$2 As No. 2919	6·50	8·50

769 Hanging Rock, Grose River Gorge, New South Wales

2008. International Post. 'Gorgeous Australia'. Multicoloured

(a) Ordinary gum.

2923	$1.35 Type **769**	1·90	1·90
2924	$2 Walpa Gorge, Northern Territory	3·00	2·75
2925	$2.70 Katherine Gorge, Northern Territory (horiz)	4·00	4·00
2926	$4 Geikie Gorge, West Australia (horiz)	6·50	6·50

(b) Self-adhesive

2927	$1.35 As Type **769**	3·50	4·50
2928	$2 As No. 2924	4·75	7·00

770 Pope Benedict XVI

2008. World Youth Day, Sydney. Multicoloured

(a) Ordinary gum (i) Domestic Mail

2929	50c. Type **770**	1·00	75

(ii) International Post

2930	$1.35 Pope holding crosier	2·50	2·50
2931	$2 Pope giving blessing	3·00	3·25

(b) Self-adhesive. (ii) International Post

2932	$1.35 As No. 2930	3·00	4·00
2933	$2 As No. 2931	4·50	6·00

2008. Canberra Stamp Show. Sheet 130×90 mm containing No. 2919×2. Multicoloured.

MS2934 $2×2 Lord Baden-Powell 8·50 7·50

771 Bulldogs

2008. Centenary of Rugby League. Multicoloured

(a) Ordinary gum.

2935	50c. Type **771**	80	90
2936	50c. Titans	80	90
2937	50c. Sharks	80	90
2938	50c. Knights	80	90
2939	50c. Cowboys	80	90
2940	50c. Broncos	80	90
2941	50c. Sea Eagles	80	90
2942	50c. Storm	80	90
2943	50c. Roosters	80	90
2944	50c. Raiders	80	90

2945	50c. Rabbitohs	80	90
2946	50c. Panthers	80	90
2947	50c. Dragons	80	90
2948	50c. Eels	80	90
2949	50c. Wests Tigers	80	90
2950	50c. Warriors	80	90

(b) Self-adhesive.

2951	50c. As No. 2942	75	1·00
2952	50c. As No. 2937	75	1·00
2953	50c. As No. 2943	75	1·00
2954	50c. As Type **771**	75	1·00
2955	50c. As No. 2938	75	1·00
2956	50c. As No. 2939	75	1·00
2957	50c. As No. 2945	75	1·00
2958	50c. As No. 2944	75	1·00
2959	50c. As No. 2948	75	1·00
2960	50c. As No. 2949	75	1·00
2961	50c. As No. 2947	75	1·00
2962	50c. As No. 2941	75	1·00
2963	50c. As No. 2940	75	1·00
2964	50c. As No. 2936	75	1·00
2965	50c. As No. 2946	75	1·00
2966	50c. As No. 2950	75	1·00

772 Face Shovel in Mine

2008. Heavy Haulers. Multicoloured. Ordinary or self-adhesive gum.

2967	50c. Type **772**	1·75	1·50
2968	50c. 200 tonne mine haul truck	1·75	1·50
2969	50c. Road train	1·75	1·50
2970	50c. Ore train, West Australia	1·75	1·50
2971	50c. MS *Berge Stahl* (world?s largest bulk carrier)	1·75	1·50

773 Veterans marching

2008. 'Lest We Forget': ANZAC Day. Multicoloured

(a) Ordinary gum.

2977	50c. Type **773**	1·75	1·75
2978	50c. Laying wreaths at war memorial	1·75	1·75
2979	50c. Playing the *Last Post*	1·75	1·75
2980	50c. War veteran and young boy	1·75	1·75
2981	50c. Young Australians at Gallipoli	1·75	1·75
MS2982	160×90 mm. Nos. 2977/81	7·00	7·00

(b) Self-adhesive.

2983	50c. As Type **773**	1·40	1·50
2984	50c. As No. 2978	1·40	1·50
2985	50c. As No. 2979	1·40	1·50
2986	50c. As No. 2980	1·40	1·50
2987	50c. As No. 2981	1·40	1·50

774 Queen Elizabeth II at Official Dinner, Parliament House, Canberra, 2006

2008. Queen's Birthday. Multicoloured

(i) Domestic Mail

2988	50c. Type**774**	1·75	75

(ii) International Post.

2989	$2 Sovereign's badge, Order of Australia	5·00	4·00
MS2990	106×70 mm. Nos. 2988/9	7·50	7·00

775 Balloons over Sydney, New South Wales

2008. 'Up Up and Away'. 150th Anniv of First Hot Air Balloon Flight in Australia. Multicoloured. Ordinary or self adhesive gum.

2991	50c. Type **775**	2·00	2·00
2992	50c. Orange and white balloons over Mt. Feathertop, Victoria	2·00	2·00
2993	50c. Multicoloured balloons over the Western MacDonnell Ranges, Northern Territories	2·00	2·00
2994	50c. Balloons over Canberra, Australian Central Territory	2·00	2·00

2008. WSC Israel 2008 World Stamp Championship, Tel-Aviv. Sheet 130×90 mm containing No. 2979×4. Multicoloured.

MS2999	50c.× 4 Playing *The Last Post*	9·00	7·50

776 German Shepherd Dog

2008. Working Dogs. Multicoloured. Ordinary or self-adhesive gum.

3005	50c. Type **776**	1·25	1·40
3006	50c. Australian cattle dog	1·25	1·40
3007	50c. Beagle	1·25	1·40
3008	50c. Border collie	1·25	1·40
3009	50c. Labrador	1·25	1·40

777 Chinese Dragon

2008. Olympic Games, Beijing. Ordinary or self-adhesive gum.

3010	**777** 50c. multicoloured	1·50	1·00

778 Watering Can and Rubber Duck ('SAVE WATER')

2008. Living Green. Ordinary or self-adhesive gum. Mulitcoloured.

3012	50c. Type **778**	1·10	80
3013	50c. Hand holding bin ('RE-DUCE WASTE')	1·10	80
3014	50c. Bus with legs ('TRAVEL SMART')	1·10	80
3015	50c. Crescent moon with light switch ('SAVE ENERGY')	1·10	80

779 Quarantine Detector Dog and Handler

2008. Centenary of the Quarantine Act. Ordinary or self-adhesive gum.

3020	**779** 50c. multicoloured	1·25	1·00

780 Pilgrims with Flags at Barangaroo for Opening Mass

2008. World Youth Day (2nd issue). Multicoloured.

3022	50c. Type **780**	2·25	2·00
3023	50c. Pope Benedict XVI at Barangaroo	2·25	2·00
3024	50c. Re-enactment of Stations of the Cross	2·25	2·00
3025	50c. Start of Pilgrimage Walk at Sydney Harbour Bridge	2·25	2·00
3026	50c. Pope Benedict XVI at Final Mass, Southern Cross Precinct	2·25	2·00

781 Football Game, Melbourne, 1866

2008. 150th Anniv of Australian Football.

3027	**781** 50c. multicoloured	1·00	1·00

782 Basketball

2008. Olympic Games, Beijing. Multicoloured.

(a) Ordinary gum. (i) Domestic Mail

3028	50c. Type **782**	2·00	65

(ii) International Post

3029	$1.30 Cycling	4·00	3·00
3030	$1.35 Gymnastics	4·00	3·00

Nos. 3029/3030 also come self-adhesive.

783 Bristol Tourer

2008. Aviation. Multicoloured

(a) Ordinary gum. (i) Domestic mail

3033	50c. Type **783**	1·40	1·40
3034	50c. Short S.30 Empire flying boat	1·40	1·40
3035	50c. Lockheed Super Constellation	1·40	1·40

(ii) International Post.

3036	$2 Airbus A320	4·50	4·50

(b) Self-adhesive.

3037	$2 As No. 3036	4·50	5·50

784 Stephanie Rice (swimming: women's 400m individual medley)

2008. Ausralian Gold Medal Winners at Olympic Games, Beijing. Multicoloured.

3038A	50c. Type **784**	1·50	1·50
3039A	50c. Lisbeth Trickett (swimming: women's 100m butterfly)	1·50	1·50
3040A	50c. Leisel Jones (swimming: women's 100m breaststroke)	1·50	1·50
3041A	50c. Stephanie Rice (swimming: women's 200m individual medley)	1·50	1·50
3042A	50c. Women's 4×200m freestyle relay swimming team	1·50	1·50
3043A	50c. Drew Ginn and Duncan Free (rowing: men's pair)	1·50	1·50
3044A	50c. David Crawshay and Scott Brennan (rowing: men's double sculls)	1·50	1·50
3045A	50c. Women's 4×100m medley relay swimming team	1·50	1·50
3046A	50c. Emma Snowsill (women's triathlon)	1·50	1·50
3047A	50c. Malcolm Page and Nathan Wilmott (sailing: men's 470)	1·50	1·50
3048A	50c. Tessa Parkinson and Elise Rechichi (sailing: women's 470)	1·50	1·50
3049A	50c. Ken Wallace (canoe/kayak: men's K-1 500m)	1·50	1·50
3050A	50c. Steven Hooker (athletics: men's pole vault)	1·50	1·50
3051A	50c. Matthew Mitcham (diving: men's 10m platform)	1·50	1·50

2008. SunStamp 2008 National Stamp Exhibition, Brisbane. Sheet 130×90 mm containing Nos. 2998 and 3036, each ×2. Multicoloured.

MS3052	50c.×2 Multicoloured balloons over the Western MacDonnell Ranges, Northern Territories; $2×2 Airbus A320	16·00	16·00

785 Luna Park, Melbourne

2008. Tourist Precincts. Multicoloured.

3053	55c. Type **785**	90	90
3054	55c. South Bank, Brisbane	90	90
3055	55c. The Rocks, Sydney	90	90
3056	55c. Fisherman's Wharf, Fremantle	90	90
3057	$1.10 Foreshore, Cairns	1·75	1·40
3058	$1.65 Salamanca Place, Hobart	2·75	2·25
3059	$2.75 Glenelg, Adelaide (50×30 mm)	4·25	4·75

Nos. 3053/3056 also come self-adhesive.

786 Russell Falls, Tasmania

2008. International Post. Waterfalls of Australia. Multicoloured.

3064	$1.40 Type **786**	2·00	1·25
3065	$2.05 Jim Jim Falls, Northern Territory	3·00	3·00
3066	$2.80 Spa Pool, Hamersley Gorge, Western Australia	4·00	4·00
3067	$4.10 Mackenzie Falls, Victoria	6·00	6·00

Nos. 3064/3065 also come self-adhesive.

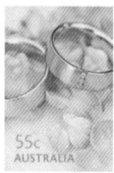

787 Silver Rings

2008. Greetings Stamps. 'For Every Occasion'. Multicoloured.

3070	55c. Type **787**	1·40	1·40
3071	55c. Gold rings	1·40	1·40
3072	55c. Baby's feet	1·40	1·40
3073	55c. Gold heart and pink roses	1·40	1·40
3074	55c. Balloons	1·40	1·40
3075	55c. Bird flying over beach	1·40	1·40
3076	55c. Outline map of Australia as sun and stylised landscape	1·40	1·40
3077	55c. Sparklers	1·40	1·40
3078	55c. Australia and Antarctica on globe (30×30 mm)	1·40	1·10
3079	$1.10 Embroidery from wedding dress and pale pink roses	2·00	2·00

788 Genyornis

2008. Stamp Collecting Month. Megafauna of Australia. Multicoloured.

3080	55c. Type **788**	1·50	1·25
3081	55c. Diprotodon	1·50	1·25
3082	55c. Thylacoleo	1·50	1·25
3083	55c. Thylacine	1·50	1·25
3084	$1.10 Megalania (52×37 mm)	2·00	2·00
3085	$1.10 Procoptodon (52×37 mm)	2·00	2·00
MS3086	170×90 mm. Nos. 3080/5	8·00	8·00

Nos. 3080/3083 also come self-adhesive.

2008. Beijing Expo. No. MS3086 optd with emblem and **BEIJING 24-27 OCTOBER 2008.**

MS3091	170×90 mm. Nos. 3080/5	7·00	7·00

789 Matthew Cowdrey

2008. Paralympian of the Year.

3092	**789**	55c. multicoloured	1·50	1·00

790 Baubles

2008. Christmas. Multicoloured

(a) Ordinary gum. (i) Domestic Mail

3093	50c. Type **790**	75	75
3094	50c. Virgin Mary and baby Jesus	75	75
3095	55c. Angel	75	30

(ii) International Post.

3096	$1.20 Wise man carrying gift	1·75	2·50

(b) Self-adhesive. (i) Domestic Mail.

3097	50c. As Type **790**	85	85
3098	50c. As Type **790** but gold foil star on bottom left bauble	85	85
3099	50c. As No. 3094	85	85

(ii) International Post.

3100	$1.20 As No. 3096	1·75	2·00

791 The Adventures of Priscilla, Queen of the Desert

2008. Favourite Australian Films. Multicoloured. Self-adhesive.

3106	55c. Type **791**	85	95
3107	55c. The Castle	85	95
3108	55c. Muriel's Wedding	85	95
3109	55c. Lantana	85	95
3110	55c. Gallipoli	85	95

Nos. 3106/3110 also came with ordinary gum.

2008. Discovery of the HMAS Sydney. Sheet 130×90 mm containing Nos. 2977/8, each ×2. Multicoloured.

MS3111	50c.×2 Type **773**; 50c.×2 Laying wreaths at war memorial	4·00	4·00

2008. 90th Anniv of the End of World War I. Sheet 160×90 mm containing Nos. 2978/9, each ×2. Multicoloured.

MS3112	50c.×2 Laying wreaths at war memorial; 50c.×2 Playing the *Last Post*	4·00	4·00

792 Nicole Kidman

2009. Australian Legends (13th series). 'Legends of the Screen'. Multicoloured.

3113	55c. Type **792**	1·75	1·25
3114	55c. Russell Crowe	1·75	1·25
3115	55c. Geoffrey Rush	1·75	1·25
3116	55c. Cate Blanchett	1·75	1·25
3117	55c. Russell Crowe in *Gladiator*, 2000	1·75	1·25
3118	55c. Nicole Kidman in *Moulin Rouge!*, 2001	1·75	1·25
3119	55c. Cate Blanchett in *Elizabeth: The Golden Age*, 2007	1·75	1·25
3120	55c. Geoffrey Rush in *Shine*, 1996	1·75	1·25

Nos. 3113/3120 also come self-adhesive.

793 Red Roses

2009. Greetings Stamps. 'With Love'. Azure (3131, 3134, 3136) or multicoloured (others)

(a) Ordinary gum.

3129	55c. Type **793**	1·25	70
3130	55c. Heart flowers	1·25	1·50
3131	55c. Fiigree heart	1·25	1·50

(b) Self-adhesive

3132	55c. Type **793**	95	95
3133	55c. As No. 3130 but with white border	95	95
3134	55c. As No. 3131 but with white border	95	95
3135	55c. As No. 3130 but with red foil applied to hearts and white border	95	95
3136	55c. As No. 3131 but with flocking applied to filigree heart and white border	95	95

794 Esky (coolbox) and Wine Cask

2009. Inventive Australia. Designs showing Australian inventions. Multicoloured

(a) Ordinary gum

3137	55c. Type **794**	1·60	1·60
3138	55c. Girl swinging on Hills hoist (rotary clothes line)	1·60	1·60
3139	55c. Girl wearing Speedo swimsuit and boy and girl wearing zinc cream	1·60	1·60
3140	55c. Ute and B&D Roll-a-Door (garage door)	1·60	1·60
3141	55c. Victa rotary lawnmower	1·60	1·60
MS3142	170×84 mm. Nos. 3137/41	7·25	7·25

(b) Self-adhesive

3143	55c. As Type **794**	1·10	1·60
3144	55c. As No. 3138	1·10	1·60
3145	55c. As No. 3139	1·10	1·60
3146	55c. As No. 3140	1·10	1·60
3147	55c. As No. 3141	1·10	1·60

2009. Greetings Stamps. 'For Every Occasion' (2nd series). As Nos. 3071/2, 3074, 3077 and 3079. Multicoloured. Self-adhesive.

3148	55c. Gold rings (3071)	95	95
3149	55c. Baby's feet (3072)	95	95
3150	55c. Balloons (3074)	95	95
3151	55c. Sparklers (3077)	95	95
3152	$1.10 Embroidery from wedding dress and pale pink roses (3079)	2·50	2·50

Nos. 3149/51 differ from Nos. 3072, 3074 and 3077 by having white borders.

795 Possum ('LIGHTS OUT')

2009. Earth Hour. Multicoloured

(a) Ordinary gum. (i) Domestic Mail

3153	55c. Type **795**	1·00	1·00
3154	55c. Owl ('SWITCH OFF')	1·00	1·00

(ii) International Post

3155	$2.05 Orang-utan ('SAVE ENERGY')	3·50	3·50

(b) Self-adhesive.

3156	55c. As Type **795**	90	90
3157	55c. As No. 3154	90	90

796 Isaac Nicholls, First Postmaster of New South Wales, boarding Ship to Collect Incoming Mail, 1809

2009. Bicentenary of Postal Services in Australia (1st issue). Multicoloured. Ordinary or self-adhesive gum.

3158	55c. Type **796**	1·75	1·40
3159	55c. Menzies Creek Post Office, Victoria, 1900s ('Early post office')	1·75	1·40
3160	55c. Early posting box	1·75	1·40
3161	55c. Australian soldiers reading letters, France, 1918 ('News from home')	1·75	1·40
3162	55c. First Qantas air mail service, Brisbane–Charleville, 1929 ('Early air mail')	1·75	1·40
3163	55c. Home delivery	1·75	1·40
3164	55c. Family reading letter ('Post-war immigration')	1·75	1·40
3165	55c. Retail PostShop	1·75	1·40
3166	55c. Express Post	1·75	1·40
3167	55c. Australia Post lorry ('Part of every day')	1·75	1·40

797 *Mamu* (Nura Rupert), 2002

2009. Indigenous Culture. Designs showing aboriginal paintings. Multicoloured

(a) Ordinary gum. (i) Domestic Mail

3178	55c. Type **797**	1·00	1·00
3179	55c. *All the Jila* (Jan Billycan), 2006	1·00	1·00
3180	55c. *Mina Mina* (Judy Napangardi Watson), 2004	1·00	1·00

(ii) International Post

3181	$1.40 Untitled (from the Mission series) (Elaine Russell), 2006	2·75	2·75
3182	$2.05 *Natjula* (Tjuruparu Watson), 2003	3·25	3·25

(b) Self-adhesive.

3183	$1.40 As No. 3181	2·25	2·50
3184	$2.05 As No. 3182	3·25	3·25

798 Queen Elizabeth II riding Side Saddle at Trooping the Colour

2009. Queen's Birthday. Multicoloured.

3185	55c. Type **798**	1·75	80
3186	$2.05 Queen Elizabeth and Prince Philip riding in carriage at Trooping the Colour	6·00	4·50
MS3187	106×70 mm. Nos. 3185/6	7·50	7·00

2009. 23rd Asian International Stamp Exhibition, Hong Kong. Sheet 130×90 mm containing Nos. 3053/6. Multicoloured.

MS3188	55c. Type **785**; 55c. South Bank, Brisbane; 55c. The Rocks, Sydney; 55c. Fisherman's Wharf, Fremantle	3·50	3·50

799 Anna Pavlova (ballerina) and Pavlova (meringue, whipped cream and fruit)

2009. 'Not Just Desserts'. Multicoloured.

3189	55c. Type **799**	2·00	2·00
3190	55c. Dame Nellie Melba (opera singer) and peach melba	2·00	2·00

3191	55c. Second Baron Lamington (Governor of Queensland, 1896–1901), Lady Lamington and lamingtons (sponge cake squares with chocolate and coconut)	2·00	2·00
3192	55c. ANZAC soldiers of 1915 and Anzac biscuits	2·00	2·00

Nos. 3189/3192 also come self-adhesive.

800 Indian Ocean ('Spotted') Bottlenose Dolphin

2009. Endangered Species. Dolphins of the Australian Coastline. Multicoloured.

(a) Ordinary gum. (i) Domestic Mail

3197	55c. Type **800**	1·75	90

(ii) International Post.

3198	$1.35 Hourglass dolphin	3·50	2·25
3199	$1.40 Southern right whale dolphin	3·50	2·25
3200	$5.50 Dusky dolphin	5·50	4·50
MS3201	136×70 mm. Nos. 3197/200	12·50	10·00

(b) Self-adhesive.

3202	$1.35 As No. 3198	2·50	2·75
3203	$1.40 As No. 3199	2·50	2·75
3204	$2.05 As No. 3200	3·75	4·50

801 Queensland Parliament House, Brisbane, Windmill and Outback Red Sands

2009. 150th Anniv of Queensland. Multicoloured.

3205	55c. Type **801**	1·00	90
3206	$2.75 Great Barrier Reef, red-eyed tree frog, rainforest and beach	4·50	5·00
MS3207	106×70 mm. Nos. 3205/6	5·25	5·25

802 1913 £2 Kangaroo and Map Stamp

2009. Bicentenary of Postal Services in Australia (2nd issue). Australia's Favourite Stamps. Multicoloured.

3208	55c. Type **802**	1·75	1·75
3209	55c. 1932 5s. Sydney Harbour Bridge stamp	1·75	1·75
3210	55c. 1946 Victory Commemoration 2½d. 'Peace' stamp	1·75	1·75
3211	55c. 1950 8½d. Aborigine stamp	1·75	1·75
3212	55c. 1914 6d. Kookaburra stamp	1·75	1·75

Nos. 3208/3212 also come self-adhesive.

803 Koala (*Phascolarctos cinereus*)

2009. International Post. Australian Bush Babies. Multicoloured.

3218	$1.45 Type **803**	3·00	1·75
3219	$2.10 Eastern grey kangaroo (*Macropus giganteus*)	5·00	3·00
3220	$2.90 Brushtail possum (*Trichosurus vulpecula*)	7·00	5·50
3221	$4.20 Common wombat (*Vombatus ursinus*)	9·50	7·50

Nos. 3218/3219 also come self-adhesive.

804 Fitzroy Gardens,
Melbourne

2009. Australian Parks and Gardens. Multicoloured.

3224	55c. Type **804**	1·75	1·40
3225	55c. Roma Street Parkland, Brisbane	1·75	1·40
3226	55c. St. David's Park, Hobart	1·75	1·40
3227	55c. Commonwealth Park, Canberra	1·75	1·40
3228	55c. Hyde Park, Sydney	1·75	1·40

Nos. 3224/3228 also come self-adhesive.

2009. Melbourne Stampshow 2009 National Stamp Exhibition. Sheet 140×95 mm. Sheet containing Nos. 3192, 3208, 3212 and 3224.

MS3234	55c.×4 ANZAC soldiers of 1915 and Anzac biscuits; Type **802**; 1914 6d. Kookaburra stamp; Type **804**	3·50	3·50

805 Hatchet Wasp

2009. Micro Monsters. Multicoloured.

3235	55c. Type **805**	1·10	1·10
3236	55c. Praying mantis	1·10	1·10
3237	55c. Ground beetle	1·10	1·10
3238	55c. Jumping spider	1·10	1·10
3239	55c. Ant	1·10	1·10
3240	$1.10 Weevil	2·10	2·10
MS3241	160×85 mm. As Nos. 3235/40	6·75	6·75

Nos. 3235/3239 also come self-adhesive.

806 Bridled
Nailtail Wallaby
(Australia)

2009. Species at Risk. Multicoloured.

3247	55c. Type **806**	2·00	2·00
3248	55c. Norfolk Island green parrot (Norfolk Island)	2·00	2·00
3249	55c. Subantarctic fur seal (Australian Antarctic Territory)	2·00	2·00
3250	55c. Christmas Island blue-tailed skink) (Christmas Island)	2·00	2·00
3251	55c. Green turtle (Cocos (Keeling) Islands)	2·00	2·00
MS3252	150×85 mm. As Nos. 3247/51	9·00	9·00

Nos. 3247/3251 also come self-adhesive.

807 Water Tank,
Fleurieu Peninsula,
South Australia

2009. Corrugated Landscapes. Multicoloured.

3258	55c. Type **807**	1·10	1·10
3259	55c. Traditional home, Broken Hill, New South Wales	1·10	1·10
3260	55c. Nissen hut converted into shearing shed, Bushy Park Cattle Station, Queensland	1·10	1·10
3261	55c. Magney House, Bingie Bingie Point, New South Wales	1·10	1·10

Nos. 3258/3261 also come self-adhesive.

808 Sombrero Galaxy
M104

2009. International Year of Astronomy. Stargazing: The Southern Skies. Multicoloured

(i) Domestic Mail

3266	55c. Type **808**	1·25	1·00

(ii) International Post.

3267	$1.45 Reflection nebula M78	2·75	2·75
3268	$2.10 Spiral galaxy M83	3·75	4·00
MS3269	141×75 mm. Nos. 3266/8	7·00	7·00

809 Green
Catbird
(*Ailuroedus
crassirostris*)

2009. Australian Songbirds. Multicoloured.

3270	55c. Type **809**	1·75	60
3271	$1.10 Noisy scrub-bird (*Atrichornis clamosus*)	3·00	1·90
3272	$1.65 Mangrove golden whistler (*Pachycephala melanura*) (male)	4·00	3·50
3273	$2.75 Pair of scarlet honeyeaters (*Myzomela sanguinolenta*)	6·00	7·00

No. 3270 also comes self-adhesive.

810 Cyclops
Pedal Car

2009. Classic Toys. Multicoloured.

3275	55c. Type **810**	1·75	1·75
3276	55c. Test Match board game	1·75	1·75
3277	55c. Barbie doll	1·75	1·75
3278	55c. Malvern Star Dragstar bicycle	1·75	1·75
3279	55c. Cabbage Patch Kids doll	1·75	1·75

Nos. 3275/3279 also come self-adhesive.

811 Australian
Rules Football

2009. Stamp Collecting Month. 'Let's Get active!'. Multicoloured.

3285	55c. Type **811**	1·10	1·25
3286	55c. Basketball	1·10	1·25
3287	55c. Soccer	1·10	1·25
3288	55c. Netball	1·10	1·25
3289	55c. Cricket	1·10	1·25
3290	55c. Tennis	1·10	1·25
MS3291	160×89 mm. Nos. 3285/90	6·00	6·75

Nos. 3285/3290 come self-adhesive.

812 Patrica Crabb

2009. Bicentenary of Postal Services in Australia (3rd issue). 'Our People Your Post'. Multicoloured.

3298	55c. Type **812**	1·25	1·25
3299	55c. Shirley Freeman (behind counter, wearing red blouse)	1·25	1·25
3300	55c. Vinko Romank (carrying box of Express Post)	1·25	1·25
3301	55c. Valda Knott (in front of shelving)	1·25	1·25
3302	55c. Gordon Morgan (in front of Australia Post motorcycles)	1·25	1·25
3303	55c. Vongpradith Phongsavan (wearing striped shirt and fluorescent tabard)	1·25	1·25
3304	55c. Norma Thomas and Australia Post contractor's van	1·25	1·25
3305	55c. John Marsh (wearing pale blue shirt)	1·25	1·25
3306	55c. Anne Brun (behind counter)	1·25	1·25
3307	55c. Russell Price (wearing blue jacket with Australia Post emblem)	1·25	1·25

813 Virgin
Mary and
Infant Jesus

2009. Christmas (1st issue). Multicoloured

(a) Ordinary gum. (i) Domestic mail

3308	50c. Type **813**	95	50

(ii) International Post.

3309	$1.25 The Magi	2·40	2·75
MS3310	106×70 mm. Nos. 3308/9	3·25	3·25

(b) Self-adhesive. (i) Domestic mail.

3311	50c. As Type **813**	1·00	1·00

(ii) International Post.

3312	$1.25 As No. 3309	2·25	2·25

814 Candles
enclosed in Star

2009. Christmas (2nd issue). Multicoloured.

(a) Ordinary gum

3313	50c. Type **814**	95	95
3314	50c. Decorated Christmas tree	95	95
3315	50c. Wrapped gifts enclosed in Santa hat	95	95
3316	50c. Baubles enclosed in bell	95	95
3317	50c. Candy canes enclosed in stocking	95	95

(b) Self-adhesive.

3318	50c. As Type **814**	95	95
3319	50c. As No. 3314	95	95
3320	50c. As No. 3315	95	95
3321	50c. As No. 3316	95	95
3322	50c. As No. 3317	95	95

(c) Self-adhesive.

3323	50c. As Type **814** but gold foil star outline	1·00	1·00
3324	50c. As No. 3314 but gold foil Christmas tree outline	1·00	1·00
3325	50c. As No. 3315 but gold foil Santa hat outline	1·00	1·00
3326	50c. As No. 3316 but gold foil bell outline	1·00	1·00
3327	50c. As No. 3317 but gold foil stocking outline	1·00	1·00

815 Peter Carey

2010. Australian Legends (14th series). 'Legends of the Written Word'. Multicoloured

(a) Ordinary gum

3328	55c. Type **815**	1·10	1·10
3329	55c. Peter Carey (black/white photo)	1·10	1·10
3330	55c. David Malouf (black/white photo)	1·10	1·10
3331	55c. David Malouf	1·10	1·10
3332	55c. Colleen McCullough	1·10	1·10
3333	55c. Colleen McCullough (black/ white photo)	1·10	1·10
3334	55c. Bryce Courtenay (black/ white photo)	1·10	1·10
3335	55c. Bryce Courtenay	1·10	1·10
3336	55c. Thomas Keneally	1·10	1·10
3337	55c. Thomas Keneally (black/ white photo)	1·10	1·10
3338	55c. Tim Winton (black/white photo)	1·10	1·10
3339	55c. Tim Winton	1·10	1·10

(b) Self-adhesive.

3340	55c. As Type **815**	1·00	1·00
3341	55c. As No. 3331	1·00	1·00
3342	55c. As No. 3332	1·00	1·00
3343	55c. As No. 3335	1·00	1·00
3344	55c. As No. 3336	1·00	1·00
3345	55c. As No. 3339	1·00	1·10

816 Governor Macquarie
and North View of
Sydney

2010. Bicentenary of Arrival of Governor Lachlan Macquarie in New South Wales. Multicoloured.

3346	55c. Type **816**	1·40	1·40
3347	55c. Port Jackson and Sydney Town	1·40	1·40
3348	55c. Parramatta Female Penitentiary, 1818	1·40	1·40
3349	55c. Government Stables, Sydney, 1817	1·40	1·40

817 Coat of Arms on
Reverse of Florin

2010. Centenary of First Australian Commonwealth Coins. Multicoloured.

3350	55c. Type **817**	1·25	60
3351	$2.75 King Edward VII on Obverse of Florin	6·50	7·00
MS3352	106×70 mm. As Nos. 3350/1	7·50	7·50

818 Torah Bright
(snowboard – halfpipe)

2010. Australian Gold Medallists at Olympic Winter Games, Vancouver. Multicoloured.

3353	55c. Type **818**	1·10	90
3354	55c. Lydia Lassila (freestyle skiing - aerials)	1·10	90

819 Colin Defries flying
modified Wright Model A
The Stella, Victoria Park
Racecourse, Sydney, 9
December 1909

2010. Centenary of Powered Flight. Multicoloured

(a) Ordinary gum. (i) Domestic Mail

3355	55c. Type **819** (first powered flight in Australia)	1·25	60

(ii) International Post.

3356	$1.45 John Duigan's flight, Mia Mia, Victoria, 7 October 1910 (first flight by Australian in Australian plane)	3·00	2·75
3357	$2.10 Harry Houdini flying Voisin aircraft, Diggers Rest, Victoria, 18 March 1910	4·00	5·00

(b) Self-adhesive.

3358	$1.45 As No. 3356	2·75	3·00
3359	$2.10 As No. 3357	3·75	5·00

2010. Canberra Stampshow 2010. Sheet 140×95 mm containing Nos. 3346, 3351, and 3355/6.

MS3360	55c. Type **816**; 55c. Type **819**; $1.45 John Duigan's flight, Mia Mia, Victoria, 7 October 1910 (first flight by Australian in Australian plane); $2.75 King Edward VII on obverse of florin coin	9·00	9·00

820 Prize Bull

2010. 'Come to the Show'. Multicoloured.

3361	55c. Type **820**	1·75	1·75
3362	55c. Cake decorating	1·75	1·75
3363	55c. Winning show horse	1·75	1·75
3364	55c. Wood chopping	1·75	1·75
3365	55c. Prizewinning dog	1·75	1·75
MS3366	170×85 mm. Nos. 3361/5	8·00	8·00

Nos. 3361/3365 also come self-adhesive.

821 Queen Elizabeth II leaving St. Andrew's Cathedral, Sydney, 2006

2010. Queen's Birthday. Ordinary or self-adhesive gum.

3372	**821**	55c. multicoloured	1·50	60

822 Australian Soldiers on Kokoda Trail, 1942

2010. Kokoda. Multicoloured

(a) Ordinary gum. (i) Domestic mail

3374	55c. Type **822**	1·25	1·25
3375	55c. Papua New Guineans help- ing wounded soldiers along trail, 1942	1·25	1·25
3376	55c. Kokoda veterans	1·25	1·25
3377	55c. Trekker, guide and memorial	1·25	1·25

(ii) International Post.

3378	$1.45 Veterans at Kokoda Isurava Memorial	3·00	3·00
MS3379	160×90 mm. Nos. 3374/8	7·25	7·25

(b) Self-adhesive.

3380	55c. As Type **822**	1·25	1·40
3381	55c. As No. 3375	1·25	1·40
3382	55c. As No. 3376	1·25	1·40
3383	55c. As No. 3377	1·25	1·40

Stamps in similar designs were issued by Papua New Guinea.

823 The Ghan'

2010. Great Australian Railway Journeys. Multicoloured.

(a) Ordinary gum. (i) Domestic Mail.

3384	55c. Type **823**	1·60	1·25
3385	55c. West Coast Wilderness Railway, Tasmania	1·60	1·25
3386	55c. 'The Indian Pacific'	1·60	1·25

(ii) International Post. Size 50×30 mm.

3387	$2.10 Kuranda Scenic Railway, Queensland	5·50	4·25
MS3388	140×90 mm. No. 3387	7·00	7·50

(b) Self-adhesive. Phosphor over parts of design. (i) Domestic Mail.

3389	55c. As Type **823**	1·25	1·10
3390	55c. As No. 3385	1·10	1·25
3391	55c. As No. 3386	1·10	1·25

(ii) International Post. Size 50×30 mm.

3392	$2.10 As No. 3387	5·50	6·50

824 Queen Victoria

2010. Colonial Heritage: Empire (1st issue)

3393	**824**	$5 multicoloured	9·50	11·00
MS3394	140×90 mm. No. 3393		9·50	11·00

2010. London 2010 Festival of Stamps. Multicoloured.

MS3395	140×90 mm. Type 819×2; No. 3356×2	4·00	4·00
MS3396	140×90 mm. Type **821**; Type 774; Type 798; Type 729	9·50	9·50
MS3397	140×90 mm. No. 3387	7·50	7·50
MS3398	140×90 mm. No. 3393	4·00	4·00

825 Peng Peng (Australian kookaburra mascot)

2010. Expo 2010, Shanghai, China. Multicoloured.

3399	55c. Type **825**	1·10	1·10
3400	55c. Australian pavilion	1·10	1·10

826 Purnululu National Park, Western Australia

2010. Australian UNESCO World Heritage Sites. Multicoloured.

(a) Ordinary gum.

3401	55c. Type **826**	1·25	1·25
3402	55c. Kakadu National Park, Northern Territory	1·25	1·25
3403	$1.10 Mount Warning, Gond- wana Rainforests (horiz)	2·50	2·50
3404	$1.10 Tasmanian Wilderness (horiz)	2·50	2·50

(b) Self-adhesive. Partial phosphor frame (at left and foot).

3405	55c. As No. 3402	1·10	1·10
3406	55c. As Type **826**	1·10	1·10

827 Coral Rabbitfish

2010. Fish of the Reef. Multicoloured.

(a) Ordinary gum

3407	5c. Type **827**	20	20
3408	60c. Clown triggerfish	1·25	1·25
3409	60c. Spotted sweetlips	1·25	1·25
3410	60c. Golden damselfish	1·25	1·25
3411	50c. Regal angelfish	1·25	1·25
3413	$1.80 Chevron butterflyfish	3·00	2·75
3414	$3 Orangefin anemonefish (50×30 mm)	5·50	6·00

(b) Self-adhesive

3415	5c. As Type **827**	20	30
3416	60c. As No. 3408	1·10	1·10
3417	60c. As No. 3409	1·10	1·10
3418	60c. As No. 3410	1·10	1·10
3419	60c. As No. 3411	1·10	1·10

Nos. 3420/5 are left vacant for possible additions to this series of definitive stamps.

828 Bay of Fires, Tasmania

2010. International Stamps. Australian Beaches. Multicoloured.

(a) Ordinary gum

3426	$1.50 Type **828**	3·50	3·25
3427	$2.20 Cape Tribulation, Queensland	4·50	4·25
3428	$4.30 Hellfire Bay, Western Australia (50×30 mm)	8·50	9·00

(b) Self-adhesive

3429	$1.50 As Type **828**	3·25	3·50
3430	$2.20 As No. 3427	4·25	4·75

829 'Piper'

2010. Adopted and Adored. Dogs. Multicoloured.

(a) Ordinary gum

3431	60c. Type **829**	1·90	1·40
3432	60c. Jessie	1·90	1·40
3433	60c. Buckley	1·90	1·40
3434	60c. Daisy	1·90	1·40
3435	60c. Tigger	1·90	1·40

(b) Self-adhesive

3436	60c. As Type **829**	1·60	1·75
3437	60c. As No. 3432	1·60	1·75
3438	60c. As No. 3433	1·60	1·75
3439	60c. As No. 3434	1·60	1·75
3440	60c. As No. 3435	1·60	1·75

830 'STAY FOCUSED STAY RELEVANT STAY ON LINE'

2010. Emergency Services. Multicoloured.

(a) Ordinary gum

3441	60c. Type **830**	1·75	1·75
3442	60c. Police helicopter	1·75	1·75
3443	60c. Fire emblem	1·75	1·75
3444	60c. Ambulance service emblem	1·75	1·75

(b) Self-adhesive

3445	60c. As Type **830**	1·60	1·75
3446	60c. As No. 3442	1·60	1·75
3447	60c. As No. 3443	1·60	1·75
3448	60c. As No. 3444	1·60	1·75

831 Gold and White Design

2010. Greetings Stamps. 'For Special Occasions'. Multicoloured.

(a) Ordinary gum

3449	60c. Type **831**	1·25	1·25
3450	60c. Pink tulips	1·25	1·25
3451	60c. Cream roses	1·25	1·25
3452	60c. Glasses of champagne	1·25	1·25
3453	60c. Three balloons	1·25	1·25
3454	60c. Teddy bear holding daisy	1·25	1·25
3455	60c. Wattle flowers	1·25	1·25
3456	60c. Southern Cross (deep blue background) (30×30 mm)	1·25	1·25
3457	60c. Southern Cross (orange and pink background) (30×30 mm)	1·25	1·25
3458	$1.20 Wedding and engage- ment rings	2·50	2·50

(b) Self-adhesive

3459	60c. As No. 3450	1·10	1·25
3460	60c. As No. 3451	1·10	1·25
3461	60c. As No. 3453	1·10	1·25
3462	60c. As No. 3454	1·10	1·25
3463	60c. As No. 3455	1·10	1·25
3464	$1.20 As No. 3458	2·50	2·75

832 Construction Worker, Doctor and Teacher

2010. Centenary of Australian Taxation Office

3465	**832**	60c. multicoloured	1·10	1·10

833

2010. 150th Anniv of Departure of Burke and Wills Expedition. Multicoloured.

(a) Ordinary gum

3466	60c. Type **833**	1·60	1·60
3467	60c. Expedition leaving Mel- bourne, August 1860	1·60	1·60
3468	$1.20 Return of Burke, Wills and John King from Gulf of Carpentaria to Cooper's Creek, April 1861	3·25	3·25
3469	$1.20 Burke, Wills and King on journey to Mount Hopeless	3·25	3·25

(b) Self-adhesive

3470	60c. As No. 3467	1·60	1·60
3471	60c. As Type **833**	1·60	1·60

2010. Bangkok 2010 25th Asian International Stamp Exhibition. Multicoloured.

MS3472	5c. Coral Rabbitfish×2; 60c. Oriental sweetlips; 60c. Clown triggerfish	3·00	3·00

2010. Stampex '10 National Stamp Exhibition, Adelaide. Multicoloured.

MS3473	60c. Type **833**; $2.05 Jade iceberg	7·50	7·50

834 Guide

2010. Centenary of Girl Guides Australia. Multicoloured.

(a) Ordinary gum. (i) Domestic Mail

3474	60c. Type **834**	1·50	1·50

(ii) International Mail

3475	$1.50 Two guides making guide sign	3·00	2·75
3476	$2.20 Olave Baden-Powell (founder)	5·25	5·50

(b) Self-adhesive. (i) Domestic Mail

3477	60c. As Type **834**	1·50	1·50

(ii) International Post

3478	$1.50 As No. 3475	3·00	4·75
3479	$2.20 As No. 3476	5·25	6·50

835

2010. National Service Memorial, Canberra

(a) Ordinary gum

3480	**835**	60c. multicoloured	1·50	1·25

(b) Self-adhesive. Irregular partial phosphor frame.

3481	**835**	60c. multicoloured	1·25	1·40

836 Children on Beach, 1950s

2010. 'Long Weekend'. Multicoloured.

(a) Ordinary gum

3482	60c. Type **836**	1·50	1·50
3483	60c. Family camping, 1960s	1·50	1·50
3484	60c. Surfers on beach, 1970s	1·50	1·50
3485	60c. Family on shore and houseboat on Lake Eildon, Victoria, 1980s	1·50	1·50
3486	60c. Children playing in snow, 1990s	1·50	1·50

(b) Self-adhesive. Phosphor over parts of design

3487	60c. As Type **836**	1·75	1·75
3488	60c. As No. 3483	1·75	1·75
3489	60c. As No. 3484	1·75	1·75
3490	60c. As No. 3485	1·75	1·75
3491	60c. As No. 3486	1·75	1·75

837 Common
Wombat

2010. Wildlife Caring: Rescue to Release. Multicoloured.

(a) Ordinary gum

3492	60c. Type **837**	1·75	1·75
3493	60c. Eastern grey kangaroo	1·75	1·75
3494	60c. Koala	1·75	1·75
3495	60c. Grey-headed flying fox	1·75	1·75
3496	60c. Southern boobook owl	1·75	1·75
3497	$1.20 Ringtail possum	3·25	3·25
MS3498	170×85 mm. Nos. 3492/7	11·00	11·00

(b) Self-adhesive

3499	60c. As Type **837**	1·40	1·75
3500	60c. As No. 3493	1·40	1·75
3501	60c. As No. 3494	1·40	1·75
3502	60c. As No. 3495	1·40	1·75
3503	60c. As No. 3496	1·40	1·75

838 Mary
MacKillop

2010. Canonisation of Mary MacKillop (Mother Mary of the Cross, founder of Sisters of St. Joseph of the Sacred Heart)

3504	**838** 60c. multicoloured	1·50	1·25

839
Red-backed
Kingfisher
(Todiramphus
pyrrhopygius)

2010. Australian Kingfishers. Multicoloured.

(a) Ordinary gum

3505	60c. Type **839**	1·75	1·50
3506	$1.20 Sacred kingfisher (To-diramphus sanctus)	2·50	1·75
3507	$1.80 Blue-winged kookaburra (Dacelo leachii)	3·50	3·25
3508	$3 Yellow-billed kingfisher (Syma torotoro)	6·25	7·00

(b) Self-adhesive

3509	60c. As Type **839**	1·50	1·75

840 Melbourne
Cup, 2010

2010. 150th Anniv of Melbourne Cup Horse Race. Multicoloured.

(a) Ordinary gum

3510	60c. Type **840**	1·60	1·25
3511	60c. Carbine, 1890 (horiz)	1·60	1·60
3512	60c. Phar Lap, 1930 (horiz)	1·60	1·60
3513	60c. Saintly, 1996 (horiz)	1·60	1·60
MS3514	160×85 mm. Nos. 3510/13	6·00	6·00

(b) Self-adhesive

3515	60c. As No. 3511	1·25	1·50
3516	60c. As No. 3512	1·25	1·50
3517	60c. As No. 3513	1·25	1·50

841 Young Girl
writing Letter

2010. Christmas (1st issue). Dear Santa. Multicoloured.

(a) Ordinary gum

3518	55c. Type **841**	1·25	1·25
3519	55c. Santa reading letter	1·25	1·25

(b) Self-adhesive

3520	55c. As No. 3519	1·25	1·25
3521	55c. As Type **841**	1·25	1·25
3522	55c. As Type **841** but foil 'AUSTRALIA' and varnish on letter and stocking	1·25	1·25
3523	55c. As No. 3519 but foil 'AUSTRALIA' and varnish on Santa's beard, cuffs and boots	1·25	1·25

842 Madonna
and Child

2010. Christmas (2nd issue). Multicoloured.

(a) Ordinary gum

(i) Domestic mail

3524	55c. Type **842**	1·25	50

(ii) International Post

3525	$1.30 Angel and shepherds	3·00	3·00

(b) Self-adhesive

(i) Domestic mail

3526	55c. As Type **842**	1·25	1·00

(ii) International Post

3527	$1.30 As No. 3525	3·00	3·50

843 'LOVE' and
Red Roses

2011. Greetings Stamps. Special Occasions. 'LOVE'. Multicoloured.

(a) Ordinary gum

3528	60c. Type **843**	1·25	1·25
3529	60c. Pattern of hearts, flowers and vine leaves	1·25	1·25

(b) Self-adhesive

3530	60c. As Type **843**	1·25	1·50
3531	60c. As No. 3529	1·25	1·50
3532	60c. As No. 3452	1·25	1·50

844 Eva Cox
(feminist)

2011. Australian Legends (15th series). Multicoloured.

(a) Ordinary gum

3533	60c. Type **844**	1·25	1·25
3534	60c. Germaine Greer (feminist author)	1·25	1·25
3535	60c. Elizabeth Evatt (former chief judge)	1·25	1·25
3536	60c. Anne Summers (writer and co-founder of first women's refuge)	1·25	1·25

(b) Self-adhesive

3537	60c. As Type **844**	1·25	1·50
3538	60c. As No. 3534	1·25	1·50
3539	60c. As No. 3535	1·25	1·50
3540	60c. As No. 3536	1·25	1·50

Nos. 3541/50, T **845** are left for Premier's Flood Relief Appeal sheetlet, issued 27 January 2011, not yet received.

845 Rescuer
carrying Baby

2011. Premier's Flood Relief Appeal. Multicoloured.

3541	60c. Type **845**	1·50	1·50
3542	60c. House surrounded by floodwater	1·50	1·50
3543	60c. Rescuing cat from flooded house	1·50	1·50
3544	60c. Wallaby on debris in floodwater	1·50	1·50
3545	60c. Aerial view of flooded houses and street	1·50	1·50

Each sheetlet was sold at $8, a $2 premium over face value. This premium went to the Premier's Flood Relief Appeal.

Nos. 3546/50 are vacant.

846 Women's Eyes

2011. Centenary of International Women's Day

3551	**846**	60c. multicoloured	1·40	1·40

847 F-111 ('Pig')

2011. Royal Australian Air Force (RAAF) Aviation. Multicoloured.

(a) Ordinary gum

3552	60c. Type **847**	1·75	1·75
3553	60c. F/A -18F	1·75	1·75
3554	$1.20 Wedgetail	3·50	3·50
3555	$3 C-17 Globemaster III	7·00	7·00
MS3556	135×72 mm. Nos. 3552/5	12·50	12·50

(b) Self-adhesive

3557	60c. As Type **847**	1·60	1·75
3558	60c. As No. 3553	1·60	1·75

Nos. 3552/3 were printed together, se-tenant, as horizontal pairs, each pair forming a composite background design. The stamps and margins of **MS**3556 form a composite design.

848 Gerbera

2011. Floral Festivals Australia. Multicoloured.

(a) Ordinary gum

3559	60c. Type **848** (Melbourne International Flower and Garden Show)	1·50	1·50
3560	60c. Jacaranda (Jacaranda Festival, Grafton)	1·50	1·50
3561	60c. Australian everlasting (Kings Park Festival, Perth)	1·50	1·50
3562	60c. Violet (Toowoomba Carnival of Flowers)	1·50	1·50
3563	60c. Tulip (Floriade, Canberra)	1·50	1·50

(b) Self-adhesive

3564	60c. As Type **848**	1·50	1·60
3565	60c. As No. 3560	1·50	1·60
3566	60c. As No. 3561	1·50	1·60
3567	60c. As No. 3562	1·50	1·60
3568	60c. As No. 3563	1·50	1·60

849 A Bunch of Flowers
(Nora Heysen), 1930

2011. The Gallery Series. National Gallery of Victoria: Flowers (1st series). Multicoloured.

(a) Ordinary gum

3569	60c. Type **849**	1·50	1·50
3570	60c. Camellias (Arnold Shore), 1937	1·50	1·50

3571	60c. Fruit and Flowers (Vida Lahey), c. 1924	1·50	1·50
3572	60c. Still Life, Zinnias (Roy de Maistre), 1925–30	1·50	1·50
3573	60c. A Cottage Bunch (Hans Heysen), 1930	1·50	1·50

(b) Self-adhesive

3574	60c. As Type **849**	1·50	1·60
3575	60c. As No. 3570	1·50	1·60
3576	60c. As No. 3571	1·50	1·60
3577	60c. As No. 3572	1·50	1·60
3578	60c. As No. 3573	1·50	1·60

2011. Sydney Stamp Expo 2011. Multicoloured.

MS3578a 60c. Type **847**; 60c. Type **833**; $1.20 Return of Burke, Wills and John King from Gulf of Carpentaria to Cooper's Creek, April 1861; $1.20 Wedgetail 7·75 7·75

850 Salt Pan ('The Dry')

2011. Lake Eyre. Multicoloured.

(a) Ordinary gum. (i) Domestic mail

3579	60c. Type **850**	1·75	1·25

(ii) Internatonal Post

3580	$1.55 Green land with pools of water ('New Growth')	4·50	3·50
3581	$2.25 Australian pelican flying over breeding colony on island ('Bird Life')	5·50	4·50
3582	$3.10 Lake Eyre ('In Flood')	8·50	8·00

(b) Self-adhesive

3583	$1.55 As No. 3580	4·00	4·00
3584	$2.25 As No. 3581	5·00	6·00

851 Queen
Elizabeth II, 1984
(Brian Dunlop)

2011. 85th Birthday of Queen Elizabeth II. Multicoloured.

(i) Domestic Mail

3585	60c. Type **851**	1·75	1·25

(ii) International Post

3586	$2.25 Queen Elizabeth II, 2005 (Rolf Harris)	6·50	7·00
MS3587	106×70 mm. Nos. 3585/6	8·25	8·25

852 Prince
William and Miss
Catherine
Middleton

2011. Royal Wedding (1st issue). Multicoloured.

(a) Ordinary gum. (i) Domestic mail

3588	60c. Type **852**	1·75	1·25

(ii) International Post

3589	$2.25 As Type **852** but white background	6·50	7·00
MS3590	106×70 mm. Nos. 3588/9	9·00	9·00

(b) Self-adhesive

3591	60c. As Type **852**	1·50	1·50

853 Wedding of
Prince William and
Miss Catherine
Middleton

2011. Royal Wedding (2nd issue)

(a) Ordinary gum

3592	**853**	60c. multicoloured	1·75	1·50

	(b) Self-adhesive		
3593	**853** 60c. multicoloured	1·50	1·50

854 *Madame Melba* (Rupert Bunny)

2011. 150th Birth Anniv of Dame Nellie Melba (soprano)

	(a) Ordinary paper		
3594	**854** 60c. multicoloured	1·75	1·50
	(b) Self-adhesive		
3595	**854** 60c. multicoloured	1·75	1·50

855 Eucalyptus Oil and Blue Mallee

2011. Farming Australia (1st series). Native Plants. Multicoloured.

	(a) Ordinary gum		
3596	60c. Type **855**	1·75	1·75
3597	60c. Eucalyptus flowers and honeycomb ('Australian Honey')	1·75	1·75
3598	60c. Macadamia nuts	1·75	1·75
3599	60c. Tea tree and tea tree oil	1·75	1·75
	(b) Self-adhesive		
3600	60c. As Type **855**	1·50	1·75
3601	60c. As No. 3597	1·50	1·75
3602	60c. As No. 3598	1·50	1·75
3603	60c. As No. 3599	1·50	1·75

856 HMAS *Australia* (I) (1913-22)

2011. Centenary of Royal Australian Navy. Multicoloured.

	(a) Ordinary paper		
3604	60c. Type **856**	2·00	1·75
3605	60c. HMAS *Sydney* (IV)	2·00	1·75
	(b) Self-adhesive		
3606	60c. As Type **856**	1·75	1·75
3607	60c. As No. 3605	1·75	1·75

857 Bilby

2011. Australian Bush Babies. Multicoloured.

	(a) Ordinary paper. (i) Domestic mail		
3608	60c. Type **857**	1·75	1·50
	(ii) International Post		
3609	$1.60 Dingo pup	4·00	4·00
3610	$1.65 Red kangaroo joey	4·00	4·00
3611	$2.35 Koala	6·00	6·00
3612	$4.70 Sugar glider	11·00	12·00
	(b) Self-adhesive		
3613	$1.65 As No. 3610	3·75	4·25
3614	$2.35 As No. 3611	6·00	7·50

858 Man and Dog ('Best Friends')

2011. 'Living Australian' (1st issue). Winning Entries from Photography Competition. Multicoloured.

	(a) Ordinary paper		
3615	60c. Type **858**	1·75	1·75
3616	60c. Two girls ('Embrace Friendship')	1·75	1·75
3617	60c. Spectators reflected in sunglasses ('Cricket at the GABBA')	1·75	1·75
3618	60c. Aborigine boy performing Wedge Tail Eagle Dance ('Little Man's Business')	1·75	1·75
3619	60c. Red kangaroo lying on beach ('This is So Relaxing')	1·75	1·75
	(b) Self-adhesive		
3620	60c. As Type **858**	1·75	1·75
3621	60c. As No. 3616	1·75	1·75
3622	60c. As No. 3617	1·75	1·75
3623	60c. As No. 3618	1·75	1·75
3624	60c. As No. 3619	1·75	1·75

859 Hand enclosing Candle wrapped in Barbed Wire

2011. 50th Anniv of Amnesty International

3625	**859** 60c. black and greenish yellow	1·50	1·50

860 Child learning to Ski

2011. Skiing Australia. Multicoloured.

	(a) Ordinary paper. (i) Domestic mail		
3626	60c. Type **860**	1·75	1·50
	(ii) International Post		
3627	$1.60 Snowboarder (horiz)	3·75	3·75
3628	$1.65 Skiier (horiz)	4·00	4·25
	(b) Self-adhesive. (i) Domestic mail		
3629	60c. As Type **860**	1·50	1·50
	(ii) International Post		
3630	$1.60 As No. 3627	3·50	4·00
3631	$1.65 As No. 3628	3·75	4·50

2011. Colonial Heritage: Emerging Identity (2nd issue). As T 824. Multicoloured.

3632	$2 Kangaroo	4·50	5·00
3633	$2 Black swan	4·50	5·00
MS3634	141×90 mm. Nos. 3632/3	9·00	10·00

2011. Phila Nippon '11 World Stamp Exhibition, Yokohama, Japan. Sheet 130×90 mm containing Nos. 3609/10. Multicoloured.

MS3635	$1.60 Dingo pup; $1.65 Red kangaroo joey	7·50	7·50

861 Quokka (*Setonix brachyurus*)

2011. 50th Anniv of Worldwide Fund for Nature (formerly World Wildlife Fund). Multicoloured.

3636	60c. Type **861**	1·90	1·90
3637	60c. Southern elephant seal (*Mirounga leonina*) (Australian Antarctic Territory)	1·90	1·90
3638	60c. Dugong (*Dugong dugon*) (Cocos (Keeling) Islands)	1·90	1·90
3639	60c. Christmas Island shrew (*Crocidura trichura*) (Christmas Island)	1·90	1·90
MS3640	135×72 mm. Nos. 3636/9	7·00	7·00

Nos. 3637/9 were all inscr 'AUSTRALIA' and also 'AUSTRALIAN ANTARCTIC TERRITORY' (3637), 'COCOS (KEELING) ISLANDS' (3638) or 'CHRISTMAS ISLAND' (3639).

862 Hand holding Golf Club

2011. Golf. Multicoloured.

	(a) Ordinary paper. (i) Domestic mail		
3641	60c. Type **862**	1·90	1·90
3642	60c. The President's Cup	1·90	1·90
3643	60c. Golf shoes	1·90	1·90
	(ii) International Post		
3644	$1.65 Golf club and ball	4·25	3·25
3645	$2.35 Golf clubs	6·00	6·50
MS3646	170×85 mm. Nos. 3641/5	14·50	14·50
	(b) Self-adhesive. (i) Domestic mail		
3647	60c. As Type **862**	1·75	1·90
3648	60c. As No. 3642	1·75	1·90
3649	60c. As No. 3643	1·75	1·90
	(ii) International Post		
3650	$1.65 As No. 3644	4·00	4·50
3651	$2.35 As No. 3645	6·00	7·50

863 Fairy

2011. Stamp Collecting Month. Mythical Creatures. Multicoloured.

	(a) Ordinary paper		
3652	60c. Type **863**	1·50	1·60
3653	60c. Troll	1·50	1·60
3654	60c. Mermaid	1·50	1·60
3655	60c. Griffin	1·50	1·60
3656	60c. Unicorn	1·50	1·60
3657	$1.20 Dragon	3·00	3·25
MS3658	170×85 mm. Nos. 3652/7	9·50	10·00
	(b) Self-adhesive		
3659	60c. As Type **863**	1·25	1·40
3660	60c. As No. 3653	1·25	1·40
3661	60c. As No. 3654	1·25	1·40
3665	60c. As No. 3655	1·50	1·25
3666	60c. As No. 3656	3·50	3·75

864 Perth Skyline and Southern Cross

2011. Commonwealth Heads of Government Meeting, Perth

3664	**864** 60c. multicoloured		

865 Haegeum Musician

2011. Australia - Korea Friendship. Multicoloured.

	(a) Ordinary gum		
	(i) Domestic Mail		
3665	60c. Type **865**	1·50	1·25
	(ii) International Post		
3666	$1.65 Didgeridoo musician	3·50	3·75
	(b) Self-adhesive		
3667	$1.65 As No. 3666	3·25	4·00

866 Virgin Mary and Baby Jesus **867** Christmas Tree

2011. Christmas. Multicoloured.

	(a) Ordinary gum. (i) Domestic mail		
3668	55c. Type **866**	1·25	50
	(ii) International Post		
3669	$1.50 Wise men following Star (horiz)	3·25	3·75
	(b) Self-adhesive.		
	(i) Domestic mail		
3670	55c. As Type **866**	1·25	1·00
	(ii) International Post		
3671	$1.50 As No. 3669	3·25	3·25

2011. Christmas (2nd issue). Multicoloured.

	(a) Ordinary gum		
3672	55c. Type **867**	1·40	1·40
3673	55c. Wrapped present	1·40	1·40
3674	60c. Star and berry decorations	1·40	1·40
	(b) Self-adhesive		
3675	55c. As Type **867**	1·25	1·25
3676	55c. As No. 3673	1·25	1·25
3677	55c. As Type **867** but gold and red foil tree decorations	1·25	1·25
3678	55c. As No. 3673 but gold foil on parcel, silver foil on bow and red foil on star and berry decorations	1·25	1·25

868 Poppy and Bugler

2011. Remembrance Day. Multicoloured.

	(a) Ordinary gum		
3679	60c. Type **868**	1·50	1·25
3680	$1.20 Two poppies and two soldiers	2·75	3·00
MS3681	Nos. 3679/80	4·25	4·25
	(b) Self-adhesive		
3682	60c. As Type **868**	1·25	1·40

2011. China 2011 27th Asian International Stamp Exhibition, Wuxi, China. Two sheets, each 130×90 mm. Multicoloured.

MS3683	No. 3609	4·00	4·00
MS3684	No. 3610	4·00	4·00

869 Lieut-Gen Rowell (Australia), Admiral Radford (US) and Maj-Gen Gentry (New Zealand), 1952

2011. 50th Anniv of ANZUS Treaty

3685	**869** 60c. multicoloured	1·75	1·50

870 Cupcake

2012. Greetings Stamps. 'Precious Moments'. Multicoloured.

	(a) Ordinary gum		
3686	60c. Type **870**	1·40	1·40
3687	60c. Teddy bear and stars within stars	1·40	1·40
3688	60c. Multicoloured balloons	1·40	1·40
3689	60c. 'LOVE' and hearts on strings	1·40	1·40
3690	60c. Love birds, 'with love' and branch of flowering tree	1·40	1·40
3691	$1.20 Pale gold rose	2·75	2·75
	(b) Self-adhesive		
3692	60c. As Type **870**	1·40	1·40
3693	60c. As No. 3687	1·40	1·40
3694	60c. As No. 3688	1·40	1·40
3695	60c. As No. 3689	1·40	1·40
3696	60c. As No. 3690	1·40	1·40

871 Ron Barassi (Australian rules football)

2012. Australian Legends (16th series). Legends of Football. Multicoloured.

(a) Ordinary gum

3697	60c. Type **871**	1·40	1·40
3698	60c. Gary Ablett (Australian rules football)	1·40	1·40
3699	60c. John Raper (Rugby League)	1·40	1·40
3700	60c. Billy Slater (Rugby League)	1·40	1·40
3701	60c. David Campese (Rugby Union)	1·40	1·40
3702	60c. David Pocock (Rugby Union)	1·40	1·40
3703	60c. Joe Marston (soccer)	1·40	1·40
3704	60c. Mark Schwarzer (soccer)	1·40	1·40

(b) Self-adhesive

3705	60c. As Type **871**	1·40	1·40
3706	60c. As No. 3698	1·40	1·40
3707	60c. As No. 3699	1·40	1·40
3708	60c. As No. 3700	1·40	1·40
3709	60c. As No. 3701	1·40	1·40
3710	60c. As No. 3702	1·40	1·40
3711	60c. As No. 3703	1·40	1·40
3712	60c. As No. 3704	1·40	1·40

872 Early Telephone and Modern 4G Phone

2012. Technology - Then and Now. Multicoloured.

(a) Ordinary gum

3713	60c. Type **872**	1·40	1·40
3714	60c. Ice chest and modern refrigerator	1·40	1·40
3715	60c. Early and modern television	1·40	1·40
3716	60c. Record player and digital media player	1·40	1·40
3717	60c. Road map and GPS (global positioning system)	1·40	1·40
MS3718	170×85 mm. Nos. 3713/17	7·00	7·00

(b) Self-adhesive

3719	60c. As Type **872**	1·40	1·40
3720	60c. As No. 3714	1·40	1·40
3721	60c. As No. 3715	1·40	1·40
3722	60c. As No. 3716	1·40	1·40
3723	60c. As No. 3717	1·40	1·40

873 O-Bahn Bus, Adelaide

2012. City Transport. Multicoloured.

(a) Ordinary gum

3724	60c. Type **873**	1·40	1·40
3725	60c. *Charlotte* (ferry) passing Luna Park, Sydney	1·40	1·40
3726	60c. Train running alongside roads, Perth	1·40	1·40
3727	60c. W-class tram, Melbourne	1·40	1·40
3728	60c. Double-decker train, Sydney	1·40	1·40

(b) Self-adhesive

3729	60c. As Type **873**	1·40	1·40
3730	60c. As No. 3725	1·40	1·40
3731	60c. As No. 3726	1·40	1·40
3732	60c. As No. 3727	1·40	1·40
3733	60c. As No. 3728	1·40	1·40

874 Radjah Shelduck (*Tadorna radjah*)

2012. Australian Waterbirds. Multicoloured.

(a) Ordinary gum. (i) Domestic mail

3734	60c. Type **874**	1·40	1·40
3735	60c. Pink-eared duck (*Malacorhynchus membranaceus*)	1·40	1·40

(ii) International Post

3736	$1.65 Australian shelduck (*Tadorna tadornoides*)	3·75	3·75
3737	$2.35 Plumed whistling duck (*Dendrocygna eytoni*)	5·50	5·50

(b) Self-adhesive. (i) Domestic mail

3738	60c. As Type **874**	1·40	1·40
3739	60c. As No. 3735	1·40	1·40

(ii) International Post

3740	$1.65 As No. 3736	3·75	3·75
3741	$2.35 As No. 3737	5·50	5·50

875 Jersey Cattle (Dairy)

2012. Farming Australia (2nd series). Multicoloured.

(a) Ordinary gum

3742	10c. Type **875**	25	25
3743	20c. Pineapples	50	50
3744	60c. Beef cattle (26 June)	1·40	1·40
3745	60c. Oranges (26 June)	1·40	1·40
3746	60c. Sugar cane (26 June)	1·40	1·40
3747	60c. Sheep (Wool) (26 June)	1·40	1·40
3748	$1 Bunch of grapes and vine-yard (Wine) (50×30 mm)	2·40	21·40
3749	$3 Sunflowers (50×30 mm)	7·00	7·00
3750	$5 Apples (50×30 mm)	11·50	11·50

(b) Self-adhesive

3751	60c. As No. 3744 (26 June)	2·40	2·40
3752	60c. As No. 3745 (26 June)	1·40	1·40
3753	60c. As No. 3746 (26 June)	1·40	1·40
3754	60c. As No. 3747 (26 June)	1·40	1·40

876 'enrol to vote'

2012. Centenary of Compulsory Enrolment to Vote

3755	**876** 60c. multicoloured	1·40	1·40

877 Queen Elizabeth II, c. 1952

2012. Diamond Jubilee. Multicoloured.

(a) Ordinary gum. (i) Domestic mail

3756	60c. Type **877**	1·40	1·40

(ii) International Post

3757	$2.35 Queen Elizabeth II, c. 2012	5·50	5·50
MS3758	106×71 mm. Nos. 3756/7	7·00	7·00

(b) Self-adhesive. International Post

3759	$2.35 As No. 3757	5·50	5·50

878 Professor Chris O'Brien (1952-2009, head and neck surgeon)

2012. Medical Doctors. Multicoloured.

(a) Ordinary gum

3760	60c. Type **878**	1·40	1·40
3761	60c. Professor Fred Hollows (1929-93, ophthalmologist)	1·40	1·40
3762	60c. Victor Chang (1936-91, cardiac surgeon)	1·40	1·40
3763	60c. Dame Kate Campbell (1899-1986, paediatrician)	1·40	1·40
3764	60c. Jane Stocks Greig (1872-1939, public health specialist)	1·40	1·40

(b) Self-adhesive

3765	60c. As Type **878**	1·40	1·40
3766	60c. As No. 3761	1·40	1·40
3767	60c. As No. 3762	1·40	1·40
3768	60c. As No. 3763	1·40	1·40
3769	60c. As No. 3764	1·40	1·40

879 Rising Sun Badge, 1902-4

2012. Rising Sun Badge (Australian Army General Service badge). Multicoloured.

(a) Ordinary gum

3770	60c. Type **879**	1·40	1·40
3771	60c. Rising Sun badge, 1904-49	1·40	1·40
3772	60c. Rising Sun badge, 1954-69	1·40	1·40
3773	60c. Rising Sun badge, 1969-91	1·40	1·40
3774	60c. Rising Sun badge, from 1991	1·40	1·40
MS3775	130×80 mm. Nos. 3770/4	7·00	7·00

(b) Self-adhesive

3776	60c. As Type **879**	1·40	1·40
3777	60c. As No. 3771	1·40	1·40
3778	60c. As No. 3772	1·40	1·40
3779	60c. As No. 3773	1·40	1·40
3780	60c. As No. 3774	1·40	1·40

880 *Chromodoris westraliensis*

2012. Underwater World. Nudibranchs. Multicoloured.

(a) Ordinary gum

3781	60c. Type **880**	1·40	1·40
3782	60c. *Godiva* sp.	1·40	1·40
3783	60c. *Flabellina rubrolineata*	1·40	1·40
3784	$1.20 *Phyllidia ocellata*	2·75	2·75
3785	$1.20 *Thorunna florens*	2·75	2·75
3786	$1.80 *Nembrotha purpureo-lineata*	4·25	4·25
MS3787	170×80 mm. Nos. 3781/6	14·00	14·00

(b) Self-adhesive

3788	60c. As Type **880**	1·40	1·40
3789	60c. As No. 3782	1·40	1·40
3790	60c. As No. 3783	1·40	1·40

881 Double-decker Bus, St. Paul's Cathedral, the London Eye and Big Ben

2012. Olympic Games (1st issue). The Road to London

(a) Ordinary gum

3791	**881** 60c. multicoloured	1·40	1·40

(b) Self-adhesive

3792	**881** 60c. multicoloured	1·40	1·40

2012. Indonesia 2012 World Stamp Championship, Jakarta. Sheet 130×90 mm containing No. 3611×2. Multicoloured.

MS3793	$2.35 Koala baby×2	11·00	11·00

2012. Australia 2013 World Stamp Expo, Melbourne. Sheet 130×90 mm containing stamp as No. 2639 but 52×37 mm with Australia 2013 World Stamp Expo emblem at left. Multicoloured.

MS3794	$1.85 Australia 2013 kangaroo on map emblem and Royal Exhibition Building, Melbourne	4·25	4·25

No. MS3794 was issued for Indonesia 2012 World Stamp Championship and has the Indonesia 2012 emblem on the lower right sheet margin.

2012. Colonial Heritage: Visualising Australia (3rd issue). As T **824**

3795	$2 'Sydney View' (figure of Industry receiving three convicts)	4·75	4·75
3796	$2 Hobart	4·75	4·75
MS3797	140×90 mm. Nos. 3795/6	9·50	9·50

882 Emblem

2012. Olivia Newton-John Cancer and Wellness Centre, Austin Hospital, Melbourne

3798	**882** 60c. multicoloured	1·90	1·90

No. 3798 was issued in sheetlets of ten stamps, each sheetlet sold for $8, the $2 premium over face value going to the Olivia Newton-John Cancer and Wellness Centre Appeal.

883 Blue Mountain Pioneers (engraving by Emile Ulm from *Sydney Mail*, 1880)

2012. Inland Explorers. Bicentenary of Gregory Blaxland, William Lawson and William Wentworth's crossing of the Blue Mountains and 150th Anniv of John McDouall Stuart's Overland Crossing of Australia. Multicoloured.

3799	60c. Type **883**	1·40	1·40
3800	60c. Gregory Blaxland, William Lawson and William Charles Wentworth	1·40	1·40
3801	$1.20 John McDouall Stuart and desert landscape	2·75	2·75
3802	$1.20 *Planting the Flag on the Shores of the Indian Ocean Coast* (engraving by George French Angas from *Journals of John McDouall Stuart*, 1865)	2·75	2·75
MS3803	135×72 mm. Nos. 3799/802	8·25	8·25

884 Swimming

2012. Olympic Games, London (2nd issue). Multicoloured.

(a) Ordinary gum. (i) Domestic mail

3804	60c. Type **884**	1·40	1·40

(ii) International Post

3805	$1.60 Pole vault	3·75	3·75
3806	$2.35 Rowing	5·50	5·50

(b) Self-adhesive. Domestic mail

3807	60c. As Type **884**	1·40	1·40

International Post

3808	$1.60 As No. 3805	3·75	3·75
3809	$2.35 As No. 3806	5·50	5·50

885 'Little Wonders' (Ann Clarke)

2012. Living Australian (2nd issue). Winning Entries from Photography Competition. Multicoloured.

(a) Ordinary gum

3810	60c. Type **885**	1·40	1·40
3811	60c. Merino sheep ('The Godfa-thers', Chevelle Williams)	1·40	1·40
3812	60c. Rural letter boxes ('Is there a Letter for Me?', Wanda Lach)	1·40	1·40
3813	60c. Seagull with chip in beak ('Lunch on the Harbour', Damian Madden)	1·40	1·40
3814	60c. Rural service station ('Fuel Ask at the Store across the Road', Ronald Rockman)	1·40	1·40

(b) Self-adhesive

3815	60c. As No. 3814	1·40	1·40
3816	60c. As Type **885**	1·40	1·40
3817	60c. As No. 3812	1·40	1·40
3818	60c. As No. 3811	1·40	1·40
3819	60c. As No. 3813	1·40	1·40

886 Alicia Coutts, Cate Campbell, Brittany Elmslie and Melanie Schlanger (swimming: women's 4×100m freestyle relay)

2012. Australian Gold Medal Winners at Olympic Games, London. Multicoloured.

3820	60c. Type **886**	1·40	1·40
3821	60c. Tom Slingsby (sailing: men's laser) (9 Aug)	1·40	1·40

3822	60c. Anna Meares (cycling: women's sprint) (10 Aug)	1·40	1·40
3823	60c. Sally Pearson (athletics: women's 100m hurdles) (13 Aug)	1·40	1·40
3824	60c. Iain Jensen and Nathan Outteridge (sailing: men's 49er class) (13 Aug)	1·40	1·40
3825	60c. Tate Smith, David Smith, Murray Stewart and Jacob Clear (canoe/kayak: men's K4 1000m) (13 Aug)	1·40	1·40
3826	60c. Mathew Belcher and Malcolm Page (sailing: men's 470 class) (13 Aug)	1·40	1·40

887 Sir Frank Macfarlane Burnet (physiology or medicine, 1960) (Clifton Pugh)

2012. Australian Nobel Prize Winners. Multicoloured.

(a) Ordinary gum

3827	60c. Type **887**	1·40	1·40
3828	60c. *Sir John Carew Eccles* (physiology or medicine, 1963) (Judy Cassab)	1·40	1·40
3829	60c. *Patrick White* (Literature, 1973) (Brett Whiteley)	1·40	1·40
3830	60c. *Sir Howard Walter Florey* (physiology or medicine, 1945) (Allan Gwynne-Jones)	1·40	1·40
3831	60c. *William Lawrence Bragg* (physics, 1915) (Sir William Dargie)	1·40	1·40

(b) Self-adhesive

3832	60c. As Type **887**	1·40	1·40
3833	60c. As No. 3828	1·40	1·40
3834	60c. As No. 3829	1·40	1·40
3835	60c. As No. 3830	1·40	1·40
3836	60c. As No. 3831	1·40	1·40

888 Car arriving at Port Arthur

2012. Road Trip Australia. Multicoloured.

(a) Ordinary gum. (i) Domestic mail

3837	60c. Type **888**	1·40	1·40
3838	60c. Motor caravan on coast road, diver's goggles and Great Barrier Reef fish and corals	1·40	1·40
3839	60c. Motorcyclists picnicking and vineyard, Margaret River	1·40	1·40

(ii) International Post

3840	$1.65 Little penguins and laden family car on Phillip Island	3·75	3·75
3841	$2.35 Car and finish of Camel Cup, Alice Springs	5·50	5·50
MS3842	170×80 mm. Nos. 3837/41	13·50	13·50

(b) Self-adhesive. (i) Domestic mail

3843	60c. As No. 3838	1·40	1·40
3844	60c. As No. 3839	1·40	1·40
3845	60c. As Type **888**	1·40	1·40

(ii) International Post

3846	$1.65 As No. 3840	3·75	3·75
3847	$2.35 As No. 3841	5·50	5·50

889 Nullarbor Plain

2012. International Stamps. Wilderness Australia. Multicoloured.

(a) Ordinary gum

3848	$1.65 Type **889**	3·75	3·75
3849	$2.35 Daintree National Park, Queensland	5·50	5·50
3850	$4.50 Cradle Mountain, Tasmania	10·50	10·50

(b) Self-adhesive

3851	$1.65 As Type **889**	3·75	3·75
3852	$2.35 As No. 3849	5·50	5·50

890 Black Rhino, Taronga Western Plains Zoo, NSW

2012. Stamp Collecting Month. Australian Zoos. Multicoloured.

(a) Ordinary gum

3853	60c. Type **890**	1·40	1·40
3854	60c. Giraffe, Taronga Zoo, New South Wales	1·40	1·40
3855	60c. Giant panda, Adelaide Zoo	1·40	1·40
3856	60c. Sumatran orangutan, Perth Zoo	1·40	1·40
3857	60c. Saltwater crocodile, Australia Zoo, Queensland	1·40	1·40
3858	60c. Wedge-tailed eagle, Healesville Sanctuary, Victoria	1·40	1·40
3859	60c. Sumatran tiger, Melbourne Zoo (50×30 mm)	1·40	1·40
MS3860	160×80 mm. Nos. 3853/9	9·75	9·75

(b) Self-adhesive

3861	60c. As Type **890**	1·40	1·40
3862	60c. As No. 3854	1·40	1·40
3863	60c. As No. 3855	1·40	1·40
3864	60c. As No. 3856	1·40	1·40
3865	60c. As No. 3857	1·40	1·40
3866	60c. As No. 3858	1·40	1·40

891 Peter Brock's Torana Touring Car

2012. 50th Anniv (2013) of Bathurst Endurance Race (touring car race). Multicoloured.

(a) Ordinary gum

3867	60c. Type **891**	1·40	1·40
3868	60c. Mt. Panorama track	1·40	1·40
3869	60c. Will Davison's Ford	1·40	1·40
3870	60c. Russell Ingall's Holden	1·40	1·40
MS3871	160×80 mm. Nos. 3867/70	5·50	5·50

(b) Self-adhesive

3872	60c. As Type **891**	1·40	1·40
3873	60c. As No. 3870	1·40	1·40
3874	60c. As No. 3869	1·40	1·40
3875	60c. As No. 3868	1·40	1·40

892 Susie O'Neill

2012. Sporting Legends: Susie O'Neill. Multicoloured.

3876	60c. Type **892**	1·40	1·40
3877	60c. Susie O'Neill swimming	1·40	1·40

893 Ballet Dancer

2012. 50th Anniv of the Australian Ballet. Multicoloured.

(a) Ordinary gum

3878	60c. Type **893**	1·40	1·40
3879	60c. Two dancers	1·40	1·40

(b) Self-adhesive

3880	60c. As No. 3879	1·40	1·40
3881	60c. As Type **893**	1·40	1·40

894 Madonna and Christ Child (from tapestry)

2012. Christmas (1st issue)

(a) Ordinary gum. (i) Domestic mail

3882	55c. Type **894**	1·25	1·25

(ii) International Post. Size 50×30 mm

3883	$1.60 *Adoration of the Magi* (tapestry)	3·75	3·75

(b) Self-adhesive. (i) Domestic mail

3884	55c. As Type **894**	1·25	1·25

(ii) International Post. Size 50×30 mm.

3885	$1.60 As No. 3883	3·75	3·75

895 Reindeer

2012. Christmas (2nd issue). Multicoloured.

(a) Ordinary gum

3886	55c. Type **895**	1·25	1·25
3887	55c. Wrapped presents	1·25	1·25
3888	60c. Bells and holly	1·40	1·40

(b) Self-adhesive

3889	55c. As Type **895**	1·25	1·25
3890	55c. As No. 3887	1·25	1·25
3891	55c. As Type **895** but silver foil snowflake and red foil on reindeer's nose and neck ribbon	1·25	1·25
3892	55c. As No. 3890 but red foil ribbon on green parcel	1·25	1·25

896 Lawn Bowls

2012. Lawn Bowls. Multicoloured.

3893	60c. Type **896**	1·40	1·40
3894	$1.20 Lawn bowls (men)	2·75	2·75
MS3895	135×80 mm. Nos. 3893/4	4·25	4·25

897 Jacqueline Freney

2012. Paralympian of the Year (winner of eight swimming gold medals at Olympic Games, London)

3896	**897**	60c. multicoloured	1·40	1·40

898 Paul Kelly

2013. Australian Legends (17th series). Legends of Music. Multicoloured.

(a) Ordinary gum

3897	60c. Type **898**	1·40	1·40
3898	60c. INXS (*Listen Like Thieves* album cover)	1·40	1·40
3899	60c. Kylie Minogue	1·40	1·40
3900	60c. Ian "Molly" Meldrum	1·40	1·40
3901	60c. Olivia Newton-John	1·40	1·40
3902	60c. John Farnham	1·40	1·40
3903	60c. AC/DC (*Back in Black* album cover)	1·40	1·40
3904	60c. Cold Chisel (album cover)	1·40	1·40
3905	60c. Men at Work (*Business as Usual* album cover)	1·40	1·40
3906	60c. The Seekers (album cover)	1·40	1·40

(b) Self-adhesive

3907	60c. As Type **898**	1·40	1·40
3908	60c. As No. 3898	1·40	1·40
3909	60c. As No. 3899	1·40	1·40
3910	60c. As No. 3900	1·40	1·40
3911	60c. As No. 3901	1·40	1·40
3912	60c. As No. 3902	1·40	1·40
3913	60c. As No. 3903	1·40	1·40
3914	60c. As No. 3904	1·40	1·40
3915	60c. As No. 3905	1·40	1·40
3916	60c. As No. 3906	1·40	1·40

899 Sprig of Eucalyptus Leaves

2013. Greetings Stamps. Special Occasions. Multicoloured.

(a) Ordinary gum

3917	60c. Type **899**	1·40	1·40
3918	60c. Outline map of Australia on globe (green and blue)	1·40	1·40
3919	60c. Outline map of Australia on globe (red and yellow)	1·40	1·40
3920	60c. Rose petal ('Love')	1·40	1·40
3921	60c. Green orchid	1·40	1·40
3922	$1.20 Wedding gift in silver box and two glasses of champagne	1·40	1·40

(b) Self-adhesive

3923	60c. As Type **899**	2·80	2·80
3924	60c. As No. 3918	1·40	1·40
3925	60c. As No. 3919	1·40	1·40
3926	60c. As No. 3920	1·40	1·40
3927	60c. As No. 3921	1·40	1·40
3928	$1.20 As No. 3922	1·40	1·40

900 Women and Surfboards

2013. 50th Anniv of Surfing Australia. Multicoloured.

(a) Ordinary paper

3929	60c. Type **900**	2·80	2·80
3930	60c. Poster of surfer and shore	1·40	1·40
3931	60c. Van carrying surfboards parked on beach	1·40	1·40
3932	60c. Surfer on crest of wave	1·40	1·40
MS3933	130×80 mm. Nos. 3929/32	5·50	5·50

(b) Self-adhesive

3934	60c. As Type **900**	1·40	1·40
3935	60c. As No. 3930	1·40	1·40
3936	60c. As No. 3931	1·40	1·40
3937	60c. As No. 3932	1·40	1·40

901 Miniature Schnauzer

2013. Top Dogs. Multicoloured.

(a) Ordinary paper

3938	60c. Type **901**	1·40	1·40
3939	60c. Miniature Dachshund	1·40	1·40
3940	60c. Cavalier King Charles Spaniel	1·40	1·40
3941	60c. Pug	1·40	1·40
3942	60c. Australian Terrier	1·40	1·40

(b) Self-adhesive

3943	60c. As Type **901**	1·40	1·40
3944	60c. As No. 3939	1·40	1·40
3945	60c. As No. 3940	1·40	1·40
3946	60c. As No. 3941	1·40	1·40
3947	60c. As No. 3942	1·40	1·40

902 National Portrait Gallery, Canberra

2013. Centenary of Canberra. Multicoloured.

(a) Ordinary gum. (i) Domestic mail

3948	60c. Type **902**	1·40	1·40

(ii) International Post

3949	$2.35 Parliament House, Canberra	5·50	5·50

(b) Self-adhesive

3950	60c. As Type **902**	1·40	1·40

903 *Dandenong Ranges from 'Beleura'* (detail) (Eugene von Guérard), 1870

2013. The Gallery Series. National Gallery of Australia. Landscape Paintings. Multicoloured.

(a) Ordinary gum

3951	60c. Type **903**	1·40	1·40
3952	60c. *In the Flinders - Far North* (detail) (Hans Heysen), 1951	1·40	1·40
3953	60c. *Land of the Golden Fleece* (detail) (Arthur Streeton), 1926	1·40	1·40
3954	60c. *Mr. Robinson's house on the Derwent, Van Diemen's Land* (detail) (John Glover) c. 1838	1·40	1·40
3955	60c. *Studley Park at sunrise* (detail) (Nicholas Chevalier), 1861	1·40	1·40

(b) Self-adhesive

3956	60c. As Type **903**	1·40	1·40
3957	60c. As No. 3952	1·40	1·40
3958	60c. As No. 3953	1·40	1·40
3959	60c. As No. 3954	1·40	1·40
3960	60c. As No. 3955	1·40	1·40

2013. International Post. Bush Babies (2nd issue). Vert designs as T **857**. Multicoloured.

(a) Ordinary paper

3961	$1.70 Kookaburra	4·00	4·00
3962	$1.75 Wombat joey	4·00	4·00
3963	$2.60 Echidna	6·00	6·00
3964	$4.65 Platypus	11·00	11·00
3965	$6.45 Brush-tailed Possum	15·00	15·00

(b) Self-adhesive

3966	$1.70 As No. 3961	4·00	4·00
3967	$1.75 As No. 3962	4·00	4·00
3968	$2.60 As No. 3963	6·00	6·00

905 Gold State Coach

2013. 60th Anniv of the Coronation.

(a) Ordinary gum. (i) Domestic mail

3969	60c. Type **905**	1·40	1·40

(ii) International Post

3970	$2.60 Portrait photograph by Cecil Beaton (26×37 mm)	6·00	6·00
MS3971	125×80 mm. Nos. 3969/70	7·00	7·00

(b) Self-adhesive. International Post

3972	$2.60 As No. 3970	6·00	6·00

906 Wall and Borders at Royal Tasmanian Botanical Gardens, Hobart

2013. Australian Botanic Gardens (2nd issue). Multicoloured.

(a) Ordinary gum

3973	60c. Type **906**	1·40	1·40
3974	60c. Australian National Botanic Gardens, Canberra	1·40	1·40
3975	60c. Blue Mountains Botanic Garden, Mount Tomah, New South Wales	1·40	1·40
3976	60c. George Brown Darwin Botanic Gardens	1·40	1·40
3977	60c. Royal Botanic Gardens, Cranbourne, Victoria	1·40	1·40

(b) Self-adhesive

3978	60c. As Type **906**	1·40	1·40
3979	60c. As No. 3974	1·40	1·40
3980	60c. As No. 3975	1·40	1·40
3981	60c. As No. 3976	1·40	1·40
3982	60c. As No. 3977	1·40	1·40

OFFICIAL STAMPS

1931. Optd **O.S.** (a) Kangaroo issue.

O133	**1**	6d. brown	32·00	20·00

1931. Optd **O.S.** (b) King George V issue.

O128	**3**	½d. orange	7·50	1·50
O129	**3**	1d. green	3·50	45
O130	**3**	2d. red	20·00	55
O131	**3**	3d. blue	7·50	4·50
O126	**3**	4d. olive	22·00	3·00
O132	**3**	5d. brown	45·00	27·00

1931. Optd **O.S.** (c) Various issues.

O123	**13**	2d. red	75·00	25·00
O134	**18**	2d. red	8·00	2·00
O124	**13**	3d. blue	£250	27·00
O135	**18**	3d. blue	16·00	5·00
O136	**17**	1s. green	50·00	28·00

POSTAGE DUE STAMPS

D1

1902. White space below value at foot.

D1	**D1**	½d. green	3·50	5·00
D2	**D1**	1d. green	23·00	11·00
D3	**D1**	2d. green	55·00	13·00
D4	**D1**	3d. green	48·00	28·00
D5	**D1**	4d. green	48·00	14·00
D6	**D1**	6d. green	60·00	10·00
D7	**D1**	8d. green	95·00	80·00
D8	**D1**	5s. green	£200	70·00

D3

1902. White space filled in.

D22	**D3**	½d. green	18·00	14·00
D23	**D3**	1d. green	17·00	4·50
D24	**D3**	2d. green	45·00	3·00
D25	**D3**	3d. green	70·00	16·00
D26	**D3**	4d. green	60·00	18·00
D17	**D3**	5d. green	60·00	15·00
D28	**D3**	6d. green	65·00	10·00
D29	**D3**	8d. green	£130	55·00
D18	**D3**	10d. green	85·00	19·00
D19	**D3**	1s. green	65·00	16·00
D20	**D3**	2s. green	£120	18·00
D33	**D3**	5s. green	£350	22·00
D43	**D3**	10s. green	£1900	£1800
D44	**D3**	20s. green	£4250	£2250

1908. As Type D **3**, but stroke after figure of value, thus "5/-".

D58	1s. green	£110	13·00
D60	2s. green	£1000	£15000
D59	5s. green	£250	48·00
D61	10s. green	£2500	£24000
D62	20s. green	£6500	£48000

D7

1909.

D132	**D7**	½d. red and green	4·50	4·25
D133	**D7**	1d. red and green	2·50	3·00
D93	**D7**	1½d. red and green	1·50	9·00
D121	**D7**	2d. red and green	6·00	1·25
D134	**D7**	3d. red and green	1·75	3·00
D109	**D7**	4d. red and green	10·00	4·25
D124	**D7**	5d. red and green	18·00	9·00
D137	**D7**	6d. red and green	2·50	2·00
D126	**D7**	7d. red and green	2·25	1·50
D127	**D7**	8d. red and green	3·25	15·00
D139	**D7**	10d. red and green	3·25	1·75
D128	**D7**	1s. red and green	17·00	1·75
D70	**D7**	2s. red and green	70·00	8·50
D71	**D7**	5s. red and green	90·00	11·00
D72	**D7**	10s. red and green	£250	£150
D73	**D7**	£1 red and green	£500	£300

D10

1953.

D140	**D10**	1s. red and green	5·50	1·25
D130	**D10**	2s. red and green	14·00	5·00
D131a	**D10**	5s. red and green	12·00	1·00

Pt. 1

AUSTRALIAN ANTARCTIC TERRITORY

By an Order in Council of 7 February 1933, the territory S. of latitude 60°S. between 160th and 145th meridians of East longitude (excepting Adelie Land) was placed under Australian administration. Until 1957 stamps of Australia were used from the base.

1957. 12 pence = 1 shilling; 20 shillings = 1 pound.
1966. 100 cents = 1 dollar.

1 1954 Expedition at Vestfold Hills and Map

1957

1	**1**	2s. blue	1·00	65

2 Members of Shackleton Expedition at S. Magnetic Pole, 1909

3 Weazel and Team

1959

2	**2**	5d. on 4d. black and sepia	60	15
3	**3**	8d. on 7d. black and blue	1·75	2·25
4	-	1s. myrtle	2·25	2·00
5	-	2s.3d. green	7·00	3·00

DESIGNS—VERT (as Type **3**): 1s. Dog-team and iceberg; 2s.3d. Map of Antarctica and emperor penguins.

6

1961

6	**6**	5d. blue	1·00	20

7 Sir Douglas Mawson (Expedition leader)

1961. 50th Anniv of 1911–14 Australian Antarctic Expedition.

7	**7**	5d. myrtle	35	20

8 Aurora and Camera Dome

1966. Antarctic Scenery. Multicoloured.

8	**8**	1c. Type **8**	70	30
9		2c. Emperor penguins	3·00	80
10		4c. Ship and iceberg	1·00	90
11		5c. Banding southern elephant-seals	2·25	1·75
12		7c. Measuring snow strata	80	80
13		10c. Wind gauges	1·25	1·10
14		15c. Weather balloon	5·00	2·00
15		20c. Bell Trooper helicopter (horiz)	9·50	2·50

16		25c. Radio operator (horiz)	1·75	2·25
17		50c. Ice-compression tests (horiz)	2·50	4·00
18		$1 Parahelion ("mock sun") (horiz)	19·00	12·00

11 Sastrugi (Snow Ridges)

1971. Tenth Anniv of Antarctic Treaty.

19	**11**	6c. blue and black	75	1·00
20	-	30c. multicoloured	2·75	7·00

DESIGN: 30c. Pancake ice.

12 Capt. Cook, Sextant and Compass

1972. Bicentenary of Cook's Circumnavigation of Antarctica. Multicoloured.

21	**12**	7c. Type **12**	1·00	75
22		35c. Chart and H.M.S. *Resolution*	2·50	1·25

13 Plankton

1973. Multicoloured.

23		1c. Type **13**	30	20
24		5c. Mawson's de Havilland Gipsy Moth, 1931	55	1·00
25		7c. Adelie penguin	1·50	1·00
26		8c. de Havilland Fox Moth, 1934–37	60	1·25
27		9c. Leopard seal (horiz)	40	1·25
28		10c. Killer whale (horiz)	2·25	2·00
29		20c. Wandering albatross ("Albatross") (horiz)	1·50	1·00
30		25c. Wilkins's Lockheed Vega *San Francisco*, 1928 (horiz)	55	1·00
31		30c. Ellsworth's Northrop Gamma *Polar Star*, 1935	55	1·00
32		35c. Christensen's Avro Type 581 Avian, 1934 (horiz)	55	1·00
33		50c. Byrd's Ford Trimotor *Floyd Bennett*, 1929	55	1·25
34		$1 Sperm whale	75	1·40

14 Admiral Byrd (expedition leader), Ford Trimotor *Floyd Bennett* and Map of South Pole

1979. 50th Anniv of First Flight over South Pole. Multicoloured.

35		20c. Type **14**	25	60
36		55c. Admiral Byrd, aircraft and Antarctic terrain	50	1·25

15 Thala Dan (supply ship)

1979. Ships. Multicoloured.

37		1c. *Aurora* (horiz)	15	10
38		2c. *Penola* (Rymill's ship)	40	10
39		5c. Type **15**	30	40
40		10c. H.M.S. *Challenger* (survey ship) (horiz)	50	1·50
41		15c. *Morning* (bow view) (whaling ship) (horiz)	2·00	3·00
42		15c. *Nimrod* (stern view) (Shackleton's ship) (horiz)	1·40	2·50
43		20c. *Discovery II* (supply ship) (horiz)	1·50	1·50
44		22c. *Terra Nova* (Scott's ship)	1·00	1·25
45		25c. *Endurance* (Shackleton's ship)	1·00	1·00
46		30c. *Fram* (Amundsen's ship) (horiz)	60	1·75

47	35c. *Nella Dan* (supply ship) (horiz)	80	1·75
48	40c. *Kista Dan* (supply ship)	1·25	2·50
49	45c. *L'Astrolabe* (D'Urville's ship) (horiz)	70	1·50
50	50c. *Norvegia* (supply ship) (horiz)	70	70
51	55c. *Discovery* (Scott's ship)	1·00	2·00
52	$1 H.M.S. *Resolution* (Cook's ship)	1·90	2·50

No. 41 is incorrectly inscr "S.Y. Nimrod".

16 Sir Douglas Mawson in Antarctic Terrain

1982. Birth Centenary of Sir Douglas Mawson (Antarctic explorer). Multicoloured.

53	27c. Type **16**	25	25
54	75c. Sir Douglas Mawson and map of Australian Antarctic Territory	75	1·50

17 Light-mantled Sooty Albatross

1983. Regional Wildlife. Multicoloured.

55	27c. Type **17**	60	90
56	27c. King cormorant ("Macquarie Island shag")	60	90
57	27c. Southern elephant seal	60	90
58	27c. Royal penguin	60	90
59	27c. Dove prion ("Antarctic prion")	60	90

18 Antarctic Scientist

1983. 12th Antarctic Treaty Consultative Meeting, Canberra.

60	**18** 27c. multicoloured	55	1·00

19 Prismatic Compass and Lloyd-Creak Dip Circle

1984. 75th Anniv of Magnetic Pole Expedition. Multicoloured.

61	30c. Type **19**	30	30
62	85c. Aneroid barometer and theodolite	70	1·25

20 Dog Team pulling Sledge

1984. Antarctic Scenes. Multicoloured.

63	2c. Summer afternoon, Mawson Station	20	1·00
64	5c. Type **20**	20	30
65	10c. Late summer evening, MacRobertson Land	20	40
66	15c. Prince Charles Mountains	20	1·00
67	20c. Summer morning, Wilkesland	20	1·50
68	25c. Sea-ice and iceberg	60	1·50
69	30c. Mount Coates	25	50
70	33c. "Iceberg Alley", Mawson	25	1·00
71	36c. Early winter evening, Casey Station	1·25	50
72	45c. Brash ice (vert)	70	2·00
73	60c. Midwinter shadows, Casey Station	50	65
74	75c. Coastline	2·25	3·00
75	85c. Landing strip	2·50	3·00

76	90c. Pancake ice (vert)	75	80
77	$1 Emperor penguins	3·00	1·50

21 Prince Charles Mountains near Mawson Station

1986. 25th Anniv of Antarctic Treaty.

78	**21** 36c. multicoloured	1·25	1·10

22 Hourglass Dolphins and *Nella Dan*

1988. Environment, Conservation and Technology. Multicoloured.

79	37c. Type **22**	1·25	1·40
80	37c. Emperor penguins and Davis Station	1·25	1·40
81	37c. Crabeater seal and Hughes 500D helicopters	1·25	1·40
82	37c. Adelie penguins and tracked vehicle	1·25	1·40
83	37c. Grey-headed albatross and photographer	1·25	1·40

23 *Antarctica*

1989. Antarctic Landscape Paintings by Sir Sidney Nolan. Multicoloured.

84	39c. Type **23**	1·50	1·75
85	39c. *Iceberg Alley*	1·50	1·75
86	60c. *Glacial Flow*	2·50	2·75
87	80c. *Frozen Sea*	3·00	3·25

24 "Aurora Australis"

1991. 30th Anniv of Antarctic Treaty (43c.) and Maiden Voyage of *Aurora Australis* (research ship) ($1.20). Multicoloured.

88	43c. Type **24**	75	60
89	$1.20 *Aurora Australis* off Heard Island	2·75	4·25

25 Adelie Penguin and Chick

1992. Antarctic Wildlife. Multicoloured.

90	45c. Type **25**	1·00	50
91	75c. Elephant seal with pup	1·40	90
92	85c. Hall's giant petrel ("Northern giant petrel") on nest with fledgeling	2·00	1·00
93	95c. Weddell seal and pup	1·75	1·00
94	$1 Royal penguin	2·00	1·00
95	$1.20 Emperor penguins with chicks (vert)	2·50	1·40
96	$1.40 Fur seal	2·00	1·75
97	$1.50 King penguin (vert)	2·50	2·25

26 Head of Husky

1994. Departure of Huskies from Antarctica. Multicoloured.

104	45c. Type **26**	1·75	75

105	75c. Dogs pulling sledge (horiz)	2·00	2·25
106	85c. Husky in harness	2·25	2·50
107	$1.05 Dogs on leads (horiz)	2·50	3·00

27 Humpback Whale with Calf

1995. Whales and Dolphins. Multicoloured.

108	45c. Type **27**	1·75	80
109	45c. Pair of hourglass dolphins (vert)	1·75	2·00
110	45c. Pair of minke whales (vert)	1·75	2·00
111	$1 Killer whale	3·00	3·00
MS112	146x64 mm. Nos. 108/11	8·00	8·00

Nos. 109/10 were printed together, *se-tenant*, forming a composite design.

28 *Rafting Sea Ice* (Christian Clare Robertson)

1996. Paintings by Christian Clare Robertson. Multicoloured.

113	45c. Type **28**	90	1·40
114	45c. *Shadow on the Plateau*	90	1·40
115	$1 *Ice Cave*	1·90	2·00
116	$1.20 *Twelve Lake*	2·25	2·75

29 Apple Huts

1997. 50th Anniv of Australian National Antarctic Research Expeditions (A.N.A.R.E.). Multicoloured.

117	45c. Type **29**	1·00	1·25
118	45c. Tuning a radio receiver	1·00	1·25
119	95c. Summer surveying	1·60	2·25
120	$1.05 Scientists in cage above sea ice	1·75	2·25
121	$1.20 Scientists and tents	1·90	2·50

30 *Aurora Australis* (research ship)

1998. Antarctic Transport. Multicoloured.

122	45c. Type **30**	2·25	2·50
123	45c. Skidoo	2·25	2·50
124	$1 Helicopter lifting quad motorcycle (vert)	4·50	3·25
125	$2 Hagglunds tractor and trailer (vert)	5·00	6·50

31 Sir Douglas Mawson (expedition leader, 1911–14) and *Aurora* (research ship)

1999. Restoration of Mawson's Huts, Cape Denison. Each including a background drawing of a hut. Multicoloured.

126	45c. Type **31**	2·00	2·25
127	45c. Huts in blizzard	2·00	2·25
128	90c. Husky team	3·25	3·75
129	$1.35 Conservation in progress	3·25	3·75

32 Emperor Penguins

2000. Penguins. Multicoloured.

130	45c. Type **32**	3·50	3·50
131	45c. Adelie penguins	3·50	3·50

33 Adelie Penguins with Egg

2001. Centenary of Australian Antarctic Exploration. Multicoloured.

132	5c. Type **33**	90	1·00
133	5c. Louis Bernacchi (physicist)	90	1·00
134	5c. *Nimrod* (Shackleton)	90	1·00
135	5c. Mackay, Edgeworth David and Mawson at South Magnetic Pole, 1909	90	1·00
136	5c. Taylor and Debenham (geologists)	90	1·00
137	10c. Early radio set	90	1·00
138	10c. Lockheed-Vega aircraft and husky team	90	1·00
139	10c. Sir Douglas Mawson	90	1·00
140	10c. Members of BANZARE Expedition, 1929–31	90	1·00
141	10c. Hoisting Union Jack	90	1·00
142	25c. Hoisting Australian flag, 1948	1·10	1·25
143	25c. Hagglund vehicle and helicopter	1·10	1·25
144	25c. *Aurora australis* over Casey	1·10	1·25
145	25c. Scientist with weather balloon	1·10	1·25
146	25c. Modern Antarctic clothing and "apple" hut	1·10	1·25
147	45c. *Nella Dan* (supply ship) and emperor penguins	1·10	1·25
148	45c. Male and female scientists taking ice sample	1·10	1·25
149	45c. Scientist using satellite phone	1·10	1·25
150	45c. Weddell seal and tourists	1·10	1·25
151	45c. Satellite photograph of Antarctica	1·10	1·25

Nos. 132/51 were printed together, *se-tenant*, with the backgrounds forming a composite design.

Each stamp carries an inscription on the reverse, printed over the gum.

34 Female Leopard Seal and Pup

2001. Endangered Species. Leopard Seal. Multicoloured.

152	45c. Type **34**	2·00	2·25
153	45c. Male seal on ice floe chasing adelie penguins	2·00	2·25
154	45c. Female seal and pup swimming underwater	2·00	2·25
155	45c. Adult seal chasing adelie penguins underwater	2·00	2·25

35 Light Detection and Ranging Equipment, Davis Base

2002. Antarctic Research. Multicoloured.

156	45c. Type **35**	2·50	2·75
157	45c. Magnified diatom and coastline, Casey Base	2·50	2·75
158	45c. Wandering albatross, Macquarie Base	2·50	2·75
159	45c. Adelie penguin, Mawson Base	2·50	2·75

36 *Kista Dan* in Heavy Seas

2003. Antarctic Supply Ships. Multicoloured.

160	50c. Type **36**	3·00	3·25
161	50c. *Magga Dan* entering pack ice	3·00	3·25
162	$1 *Thala Dan* and iceberg (vert)	4·50	2·75
163	$1.45 *Nella Dan* unloading in Antarctic (vert)	5·50	6·50

37 Naming Ceremony, 1954

2004. 50th Anniv of Mawson Station. Multicoloured.
164	50c. Type **37**		2·75	3·25
165	50c. Mawson Station, 2004		2·75	3·25
166	$1 Accomodation "caravan", 1950s		3·50	2·75
167	$1.45 Emperor penguin rookery		4·50	5·50

38 Hughes 500 Helicopter

2005. Aviation in the Australian Antarctic Territory. Multicoloured.
168	50c. Type **38**		2·00	2·00
169	50c. de Haviland DHC-2 Beaver		2·00	2·00
170	$1 Pilatus PC06 Porter		3·00	2·25
171	$1.45 Douglas DC-3/Dakota C-47		3·75	3·75

39 Mackerel Icefish

2006. Fish of the Australian Antarctic Territory. Multicoloured.
172	50c. Type **39**		2·00	2·25
173	50c. Lanternfish		2·00	2·25
174	$1 Eaton's skate		2·50	2·75
175	$1 Patagonian toothfish		2·50	2·75

40 Royal Penguins

2007. Endangered Species. Royal Penguins (*Eudyptes schlegeli*). Multicoloured.
176	50c. Type **40**		2·75	2·75
177	50c. Penguin with egg		2·75	2·75
178	$1 Two penguins sparring		3·00	3·00
179	$1 Pair snuggling together		3·00	3·00

41 Telescope, AASTINO Observatory, Stars and Gas Cloud (Astronomy from the Polar Plateaus)

2008. International Polar Year 2007–08. Multicoloured.
180	55c. Type **41**		2·75	2·75
181	55c. Scientists drilling through sea ice (Sea Ice Physics and Ecosystem Experiment)		2·75	2·75
182	$1.10 Pteropod, pelagic snail *Limacina helicina* and emperor penguin (marine biology)		3·50	3·50
183	$1.10 CTD (conductivity-temperature-depth) probe and ocean (Climate of Antarctica and the Southern Ocean project)		3·50	3·50
MS184	160×90 mm. Nos. 180/3		11·00	11·00

42 Unloading *Nimrod*

2009. Centenary of the First Expedition to the South Magnetic Pole. Each black, grey and blue.
185	55c. Type **42**		2·25	2·25
186	55c. Arroll-Johnston car towing provisions on sledge		2·25	2·25
187	$1.10 Northern Party camp		3·00	3·00

188	$1.10 Alistair Mackay, Douglas Mawson and Edgeworth David raising Union Jack at South Magnetic Pole		3·00	3·00
MS189	170×85 mm. Nos. 185/8		9·50	9·50

43 Snow Petrel

2009. Preserve the Polar Regions and Glaciers. Multicoloured

(i) Domestic Mail
190	55c. Type **43**		2·25	1·25

(ii) International Post
191	$2.05 Jade iceberg		7·00	8·00
MS192	120×80mm. Nos. 190/1		9·00	9·00

44 Pleurophyllum hookeri

2010. Macquarie Island. Multicoloured.
193	60c. Type **44**		2·25	2·25
194	60c. Southern elephant seal		2·25	2·25
195	$1.20 Mawson Point Stacks		3·75	3·75
196	$1.20 Caroline Cove		3·75	3·75
MS197	159×85 mm. Nos. 193/6		11·00	11·00

45 Greenish Iceberg with Pinnacle

2011. Icebergs. Multicoloured.

(a) Ordinary paper
198	60c. Type **45**		1·75	1·75
199	60c. Flat-topped iceberg with overhang at left		1·75	1·75
200	60c. Dark iceberg with fluted sides		1·75	1·75
201	60c. Iceberg with low ridge in foreground and higher ridge with pinnacle at right		1·75	1·75
MS202	135×72 mm. Nos. 198/201		7·00	7·00

(b) Self-adhesive
203	60c. As Type **45**		1·40	1·60
204	60c. As No. 199		1·40	1·60
205	60c. As No. 200		1·40	1·60
206	60c. As No. 201		1·40	1·60

46 SY *Aurora* leaving Hobart, December 1911

2011. Centenary of the Australasian Antarctic Expedition, 1911-14 (1st issue). Departure and Journey. Multicoloured.
207	60c. Type **46**		1·75	1·75
208	60c. Captain John King Davis of the SY *Aurora*		1·75	1·75
209	60c. SY *Aurora* on Antarctic voyage		1·75	1·75
210	60c. Landing at Macquarie Island		1·75	1·75
211	60c. Birdlife on Macquarie Island		1·75	1·75
MS212	169×85 mm. Nos. 207/11		8·00	8·00

Nos. 207/11 were printed together in horizontal strips of five stamps throughout the sheets, each strip forming a composite background design of sea and coast.

47 (image scaled to 36% of original size)

2011. 50th Anniv of Worldwide Fund for Nature (formerly World Wildlife Fund). Sheet 135×72 mm containing Nos. 3637/9 and 3636 of Australia. Multicoloured.
MS213	47 60c.×4 Southern elephant seal (*Mirounga leonina*) (Australian Antarctic Territory); Dugong (*Dugong dugon*) (Cocos (Keeling) Islands); Christmas Island shrew (*Crocidura trichura*) (Christmas Island); Type **861** of Australia		6·50	6·50

48 Phillip Law

2012. Birth Centenary of Dr. Phillip Law (Antarctic explorer). Multicoloured.
214	60c. Type **48**		1·75	1·75
215	$1.20 Phillip Law in Antarctic snow, landed helicopter and map of Antarctic		3·75	3·75
216	$1.80 Researchers, Australian flag and map of Antarctica		4·50	4·50
MS217	160×90 mm. Nos. 214/16		9·00	9·00

2012. Centenary of the Australasian Antarctic Expedition, 1911-14 (2nd issue). Arrival and Exploration. Multicoloured.
218	60c. Main Hut, Cape Denison		1·50	1·50
219	60c. Xavier Mertz and dog team		1·50	1·50
220	60c. Dog handler Belgrave Ninnis and sled		1·50	1·50
221	$1.20 SY *Aurora* anchored off Cape Denison, January 1912		3·00	3·00
222	$1.20 Unloading supplies from SY *Aurora*		3·00	3·00
MS223	171×86 mm. Nos. 218/22		9·50	9·50

Nos. 218/20 were printed together in horizontal strips of three stamps throughout the sheets, each strip forming a composite background design.

Nos. 221/2 were printed together in horizontal pairs throughout the sheets, each pair forming a composite background design.

49 Mt. Parsons

2013. Mountains. Multicoloured.
224	60c. Type **49**		1·50	1·50
225	60c. Mawson Escarpment		1·50	1·50
226	$1.20 South Masson Range		3·00	3·00
227	$1.80 David Range		4·50	4·50
MS228	135×72 mm. Nos. 224/7		10·00	10·00

Pt. 2

AUSTRIA

A state of central Europe, part of the Austro-Hungarian Monarchy and Empire until 1918. At the end of the First World War the Empire was dismembered and German-spealing Austria became a Republic.

Austria was absorbed into the German Reich in 1938 and remained part of Germany until 1945. Following occupation of the four Allied Powers the Austrian Republic was re-established on 14 May 1945.

1850. 60 kreuzer = 1 gulden.
1858. 100 kreuzer = 1 gulden.
1899. 100 heller = 1 krone.
1925. 100 groschen = 1 schilling.
1938. 100 pfennig = 1 German reichsmark.
1945. 100 groschen = 1 schilling.
2002. 100 cents = 1 euro.

1 Arms of Austria

1850. Imperf.
6a	1	1k. yellow	£1800	£110
7	1	2k. black	£2250	£100
8a	1	3k. red	£600	4·75
9	1	6k. brown	£1300	8·50
10	1	9k. blue	£1300	3·75

For stamps in Type **1** with values in "CENTES", see Lombardy and Venetia.

4 **5**

1858
22a	5	2k. yellow	£1500	70·00
23	4	3k. black	£2250	£375
24	4	3k. green	£1900	£225
25a	5	5k. red	£500	2·75
26a	5	10k. brown	£1200	4·25
27a	5	15k. blue	£1100	2·75

For stamps in Types **4** and **5** with values in "SOLDI", see Lombardy and Venetia.

The portraits on Austrian stamps to 1906 are of the Emperor Francis Joseph I.

10

1860
33	10	2k. yellow	£550	43·00
34	10	3k. green	£475	38·00
35	10	5k. red	£350	1·10
36	10	10k. brown	£450	2·75
37	10	15k. blue	£600	1·90

12 Arms of Austria

1863
45	12	2k. yellow	£250	17·00
46	12	3k. green	£250	17·00
47	12	5k. red	70·00	55
48	12	10k. blue	£300	4·25
49	12	15k. brown	£300	2·40

A H14 **A H16**

1867
59	AH14	2k. yellow	19·00	1·10
60	AH14	3k. green	95·00	1·10
62	AH14	5k. red	3·00	20
63	AH14	10k. blue	£225	1·10
64	AH14	15k. brown	21·00	17·00
AH56a	AH14	25k. grey	65·00	24·00
66	AH16	50k. brown	19·00	£250

20

1883
70c	20	2k. brown	8·25	45
71c	20	3k. green	8·25	30
72c	20	5k. red	£150	20
73c	20	10k. blue	21·00	45
74c	20	20k. grey	£200	4·25
75a	20	50k. mauve	£475	£160

23 **24**

1890
79	23	1k. grey	2·10	55
80	23	2k. brown	50	20
81	23	3k. green	60	20
82	23	5k. red	60	20
83	23	10k. blue	1·50	20
84	23	12k. purple	3·50	55
85	23	15k. purple	3·50	55
86	23	20k. green	55·00	3·25
87	23	24k. blue	3·00	1·90
88	23	30k. brown	3·00	1·30
89	23	50k. mauve	8·25	15·00
90	24	1g. blue	6·25	4·25
105	24	1g. lilac	£100	6·50
91	24	2g. red	10·50	38·00
106	24	2g. green	41·00	65·00

25

1891. Figures in black.

92	25	20k. green	5·25	20
93	25	24k. blue	7·25	1·30
94	25	30k. brown	5·25	20
95	25	50k. mauve	6·25	55

27 28 29

30

1899. Corner numerals in black on heller values.

107	27	1h. mauve	1·00	20
108	27	2h. grey	4·25	85
140	27	3h. brown	1·00	20
141b	27	5h. green	1·00	20
142b	27	6h. orange	1·00	20
143b	28	10h. red	1·00	20
144b	28	20h. brown	1·00	20
145b	28	25h. blue	1·00	20
146b	28	30h. mauve	2·10	1·10
147b	29	35h. green	1·50	30
148b	29	40h. green	2·10	5·25
149b	29	50h. blue	5·25	13·00
150b	29	60h. brown	2·10	1·10
119a	30	1k. red	11·50	65
120	30	2k. lilac	£150	65
121	30	4k. green	26·00	32·00

33 35

1904. Types as before, but with corners containing figures altered as T 33 and 35. Figures in black on white on 10h. to 30h. only.

169	33	1h. purple	20	65
170	33	2h. black	20	45
171	33	3h. brown	40	10
173	33	6h. orange	60	10
160a	28	10h. red	2·30	10
a161	28	20h. brown	37·00	1·30
162a	28	25h. blue	37·00	1·10
a163	28	30h. mauve	55·00	2·10
178	35	35h. green	5·25	55
179	35	40h. purple	5·25	1·40
180	35	50h. blue	5·25	4·75
181	35	60h. brown	5·25	1·30
168	35	72h. red	6·25	2·10

1906. Figures on plain white ground and stamps printed in one colour.

183	28	5h. yellow-green	40	10
184	28	10h. red	50	20
185	28	12h. violet	1·50	1·10
186	28	20h. brown	5·00	30
187	28	25h. blue	5·00	75
188	28	30h. red	12·50	55

37 Francis Joseph I 38 Francis Joseph I

41 Schonbrunn 42 Francis Joseph I

1908. 60th Anniv of Emperor's Accession.

189A	-	1h. black	40	20
190A	-	2h. violet	40	20
191B	-	3h. purple	30	10
192B	37	5h. green	20	10
193A	-	6h. brown	95	1·10
194B	37	10h. red	20	10
195A	-	12h. red	2·10	1·60
196B	-	20h. brown	2·75	50
197B	37	25h. blue	2·50	40
198B	-	30h. green	6·25	65
199A	-	35h. grey	6·00	40
200	38	50h. green	2·00	55

201	-	60h. red	40	20
202	38	72h. brown	5·00	55
203	-	1k. violet	21·00	55
204	41	2k. green and red	36·00	1·10
205	-	5k. purple and brown	65·00	8·50
206	42	10k. brown, blue & ochre	£300	£110

DESIGNS—As Type 37: 1h. Charles VI; 2h. Maria Theresa; 3h. Joseph II; 6h. Leopold II; 12h. Francis I; 20h. Ferdinand; 30h. Francis Joseph I in 1848; 35h. Same in 1878. As Type 38: 60h. Francis Joseph I on horseback; 1k. Same in ceremonial robes. As Type 41: 5k. Hofburg.

45

1910. 80th Birthday of Francis Joseph I. As issue of 1908 but with dates added as T 45.

223	1h. black	6·25	10·50
224	2h. violet	8·25	21·00
225	3h. purple	7·25	18·00
226	5h. green	20	45
227	6h. brown	4·25	16·00
228	10h. red	20	45
229	12h. red	5·25	18·00
230	20h. brown	13·50	20·00
231	25h. blue	4·25	4·25
232	30h. green	5·25	16·00
233	35h. grey	5·25	17·00
234	50h. green	7·25	20·00
235	60h. red	7·25	20·00
236	1k. violet	5·75	9·50
237	2k. green and red	£200	£325
238	5k. purple and brown	£150	£300
239	10k. brown, blue and ochre	£275	£475

47

1914. War Charity Funds.

240	47	5h.+(2h.) green	30	45
241	47	10h.+(2h.) red	40	75

48 Cavalry

1915. War Charity Funds.

242	-	3h.+1h. brown	10	55
243	48	5h.+2h. green	10	10
244	-	10h.+2h. red	10	10
245	-	20h.+3h. green	60	3·25
246	-	35h.+3h. blue	3·00	7·50

DESIGNS: 3h. Infantry; 10h. Artillery; 20h. Battleship *Viribus Unitas* (Navy); 35h. Lohner Pfeilflieger B-1 biplane (Air Force).

49 Imperial Austrian Crown 50 Francis Joseph I 51 Arms of Austria

52

1916

247	49	3h. violet	10	10
248	49	5h. green	10	10
249	49	6h. orange	40	1·60
250	49	10h. red	10	10
251	49	12h. blue	40	2·75
252	50	15h. red	60	10
253	50	20h. brown	3·75	40
254	50	25h. blue	8·25	75
255	50	30h. slate	7·50	1·30
256	51	40h. olive	20	10
257	51	50h. green	20	10
258	51	60h. blue	20	10

259	51	80h. brown	20	10
260	51	90h. purple	20	10
261	51	1k. red on yellow	40	15
262aa	52	2k. blue	10	20
263aa	52	3k. red	30	1·10
264a	52	4k. green	4·25	40
265aa	52	10k. violet	10·50	43·00

On Nos. 254/5 the portrait is full face. The 1k. has floral sprays each side of the coat-of-arms.

60 Charles I

1917

290	60	15h. red	20	30
291a	60	20h. green	20	30
292	60	25h. blue	1·00	30
293	60	30h. violet	1·00	30

1918. Air. Optd FLUGPOST or surch also.

296A	52	1k.50 on 2k. mauve	2·10	9·75
297B	52	2k.50 on 3k. brown	10·50	32·00
298A	52	4k. grey	7·25	23·00

1918. Optd Deutschosterreich.

299	49	3h. violet	10	10
300	49	5h. green	10	10
301	49	6h. orange	30	2·75
302	49	10h. red	10	10
303	49	12h. blue	30	2·75
304	60	15h. red	30	1·60
305	60	20h. green	10	10
306	60	25h. blue	10	30
307	60	30h. violet	10	10
308	51	40h. olive	10	10
309	51	50h. green	60	2·10
310	51	60h. blue	55	2·00
311	51	80h. brown	20	20
312	51	90h. red	20	65
313	51	1k. red on yellow	20	30
314	52	2k. blue	10	10
315	52	3k. red	40	1·10
316	52	4k. green	2·10	4·25
317	52	10k. violet	10·50	27·00

64 Posthorn 65 Republican Arms 66 "New Republic"

1919. Imperf or perf.

336	64	3h. grey	10	10
337	65	5h. green	10	10
338	65	5h. grey	10	10
339	64	6h. orange	10	65
340	65	10h. red	10	10
342	64	12h. blue	10	1·30
343a	64	15h. brown	10	10
344	66	20h. green	10	10
346	65	25h. blue	10	10
347	66	25h. violet	10	10
348	66	30h. brown	10	10
349	66	40h. violet	10	10
350	66	40h. red	10	10
351	66	45h. green	20	1·10
352	66	50h. blue	10	10
353	64	60h. green	10	10
354	65	1k. red on yellow	10	10
355	65	1k. blue	40	1·10

67 Parliament Building

1919

356	67	2k. black and red	30	1·10
357	67	2½k. bistre	20	55
358	67	3k. brown and blue	10	10
359	67	4k. black and red	10	10
360	67	5k. black	10	30
361	67	7½k. purple	30	55
362	67	10k. brown and green	25	55
363	67	20k. brown and violet	10	55
364	67	50k. violet on yellow	70	1·60

71 Republican Arms

1920

402	71	80h. red	10	20
403	71	1k. brown	10	20
404	71	1½k. green	30	20
405	71	2k. blue	10	20
406	71	3k. black and green	10	30
407	71	4k. claret and red	10	20
408	71	5k. red and lilac	10	20
409	71	7½k. brown and orange	10	30
410	71	10k. blue and violet	10	20

The frames of the 3 to 10k. differ.

1920. Issues for Carinthian Plebiscite. Optd Karnten Abstimmung (T 65/7 in new colours). (a) Perf.

411	65	5h. (+10h.) grey on yell	70	2·10
412	65	10h. (+20h.) red on pink	70	1·60
413	64	15h. (+30h.) brn on yell	30	1·10
414	66	20h. (+40h.) green on bl	30	85
415	64	25h. (+50h.) pur on pink	30	90
416	66	30h. (+60h.) brn on buff	1·80	3·75
417	64	40h. (+80h.) red on yell	30	1·10
418	66	50h. (+100h.) indigo on blue	30	85
419	64	60h. (+120h.) green on bl	1·80	3·75
420	71	80h. (+160h.) red	45	95
421	71	1k. (+2k.) brown	45	1·10
422	71	2k. (+4k.) blue	45	1·10

(b) Imperf.

423	67	2½k. (+5k.) brown	50	1·40
424	67	3k. (+6k.) green & blue	60	1·70
425	67	4k. (+8k.) violet & red	85	2·00
426	67	5k. (+10k.) blue	75	1·70
427	67	7½k. (+15k.) green	75	1·70
428	67	10k. (+20k.) red & green	85	1·90
429	67	20k. (+40k.) brn & lilac	95	2·40

The plebiscite was to decide whether Carinthia should be part of Austria or Yugoslavia, and the premium was for a fund to promote a vote in favour of remaining in Austria. The result was a vote for Austria.

1921. Flood Relief Fund. Optd Hochwasser 1920 (colours changed).

430	65	5h. (+10h.) grey on yell	30	1·10
431	65	10h. (+20h.) brown	30	1·10
432	64	15h. (+30h.) grey	30	1·10
433	66	20h. (+40h.) green on yell	30	1·10
434	64	25h. (+50h.) blue on yell	30	1·10
435	66	30h. (+60h.) purple on bl	65	2·10
436	66	40h. (+80h.) brn on red	75	2·75
437	66	50h. (+100h.) green on bl	1·70	4·75
438	64	60h. (+120h.) pur on yell	50	2·10
439	71	80h. (+160h.) blue	50	2·10
440	71	1k. (+2k.) orange on blue	45	2·10
441	71	1½k. (+3k.) green on yell	25	1·10
442	71	2k. (+4k.) brown	25	1·10
443	67	2½k. (+5k.) blue	30	1·10
444	67	3k. (+6k.) red & green	30	1·10
445	67	4k. (+8k.) brown & lilac	1·00	3·75
446	67	5k. (+10k.) green	30	2·10
447	67	7½k. (+15k.) red	30	2·10
448	67	10k. (+20k.) green & blue	30	2·10
449	67	20k. (+40k.) pur & red	60	3·25

80 Pincers and Hammer 81 Ear of Corn

1922

461	81	½k. brown	10	85
462	80	1k. brown	10	10
463	81	2k. blue	10	10
464	81	2½k. brown	10	10
465	81	4k. purple	10	1·40
466	80	5k. green	10	10
467	81	7½k. violet	10	10
468	80	10k. red	10	10
469	81	12½k. green	10	10
470	81	15k. turquoise	10	10
471	80	20k. blue	10	10
472	81	25k. red	10	10
473	80	30k. grey	10	10
474	80	45k. red	10	10
475	80	50k. brown	10	10
476	80	60k. green	10	10
477	80	75k. blue	10	10

478	80	80k. yellow	10	10
479	81	100k. grey	10	10
480	81	120k. brown	10	10
481	81	150k. orange	10	10
482	81	160k. green	10	10
483	81	180k. red	10	10
484	81	200k. pink	10	10
485	81	240k. violet	10	10
486	81	300k. blue	10	10
487	81	400k. green	1·50	55
488	81	500k. yellow	10	10
489	81	600k. slate	10	10
490	81	700k. brown	2·50	20
491	81	800k. violet	1·00	2·75
492	80	1000k. mauve	1·30	20
493	80	1200k. red	85	65
494	80	1500k. orange	85	20
495	80	1600k. slate	4·25	4·25
496	80	2000k. blue	5·25	3·75
497	80	3000k. brown	15·00	20
498	80	4000k. blue on blue	7·75	3·75

82

1922

499	82	20k. sepia	10	20
500	82	25k. blue	10	20
501	82	50k. red	10	20
502	82	100k. green	10	20
503	82	200k. purple	10	20
504	82	500k. orange	40	2·10
505	82	1000k. violet on yellow	10	20
506	82	2000k. green on yellow	10	20
507	82	3000k. red	13·00	1·10
508	82	5000k. black	2·40	2·10
509	82	10,000k. brown	5·75	7·50

85 Mozart

1922. Musicians' Fund.

519b	85	2½k. brown	9·25	13·00
520	85	5k. blue	1·50	2·75
521	-	7½k. black	2·50	4·25
522	-	10k. purple	3·00	5·25
523	-	25k. purple	5·75	10·50
524	-	50k. red	3·00	5·25
525	-	100k. green	9·25	21·00

COMPOSERS: 2½k. Haydn; 7½k. Beethoven; 10k. Schubert; 25k. Bruckner; 50k. J. Strauss; 100k. Wolf.

87 Hawk 88 W. Kress

1922. Air.

546	87	300k. red	40	2·40
547	87	400k. green	6·25	21·00
548	87	600k. olive	40	2·10
549	87	900k. red	40	2·10
550	88	1200k. purple	40	2·10
551	88	2400k. slate	40	2·10
552	88	3000k. brown	4·25	13·00
553	88	4800k. blue	4·25	13·00

89 Bregenz

1923. Artists' Charity Fund.

554	89	100k. green	5·25	10·50
555	-	120k. blue	5·25	10·50
556	-	160k. purple	5·25	10·50
557	-	180k. purple	5·25	10·50
558	-	200k. red	5·25	10·50
559	-	240k. brown	5·25	10·50
560	-	400k. brown	5·25	10·50
561	-	600k. green	6·25	10·50
562	-	1000k. black	9·25	17·00

DESIGNS: 120k. Salzburg; 160k. Eisenstadt; 180k. Klagenfurt; 200k. Innsbruck; 240k. Linz; 400k. Graz; 600k. Melk; 1000k. Vienna.

90 "Art the Comforter"

1924. Artists' Charity Fund.

563	90	100k.+300k. green	5·25	13·00
564	-	300k.+900k. brown	5·25	13·00
565	-	500k.+1500k. purple	5·25	14·00
566	-	600k.+1800k. turquoise	10·50	25·00
567	-	1000k.+3000k. brown	15·00	31·00

DESIGNS: 300k. "Agriculture and Handicraft"; 500k. "Mother Love"; 600k. "Charity"; 1000k. "Fruitfulness".

 91 92 Plains 93 Minorite Church, Vienna

1925

568	91	1g. grey	25	20
569	91	2g. red	50	20
570	91	3g. red	50	20
571	91	4g. blue	1·50	20
572	91	5g. brown	2·10	20
573	91	6g. blue	1·50	20
574	91	7g. brown	2·10	20
575	91	8g. green	5·25	20
576	92	10g. brown	1·00	20
577	92	15g. red	1·00	20
578	92	16g. blue	1·00	20
579	92	18g. green	1·50	1·10
580	-	20g. violet	1·00	20
581	-	24g. red	1·20	55
582	-	30g. violet	1·50	20
583	-	40g. blue	1·90	20
584	-	45g. brown	2·10	20
585	-	50g. grey	2·10	30
586	-	80g. blue	4·75	6·00
587	93	1s. green	23·00	2·10
588	-	2s. red	8·75	14·00

DESIGN—As T 92—20g. to 80g. Golden eagle on mountains.

 96 Pilot and Hansa Brandenburg C-1 97 de Havilland D.H.34 and Common Crane

1925. Air.

616	96	2g. brown	50	1·30
617	96	5g. red	30	45
618	96	6g. blue	1·00	2·10
619	96	8g. green	1·00	2·40
620	97	10g. red	1·30	3·75
621	96	10g. orange	1·30	2·75
622	97	15g. red	1·00	2·10
623	96	15g. mauve	50	1·10
624	96	20g. brown	14·00	16·00
625	96	25g. violet	6·25	12·00
626	97	30g. purple	1·20	3·75
627	96	30g. bistre	10·50	13·00
628	97	50g. grey	1·20	3·75
629	96	50g. blue	18·00	19·00
630	97	80g. green	3·00	5·25
631	97	1s. blue	10·50	14·00
632	97	2s. green	2·10	5·25
633	97	3s. brown	65·00	85·00
634	97	5s. blue	18·00	38·00
635	97	10s. brown on grey (25×32 mm)	10·50	32·00

98 Siegfried and Dragon

1926. Child Welfare. Scenes from the Nibelung Legend.

636	98	3g.+2g. brown	1·20	1·20
637	-	8g.+2g. blue	20	55
638	-	15g.+5g. red	40	55
639	-	20g.+5g. green	60	1·10
640	-	24g.+6g. violet	60	1·10
641	-	40g.+10g. brown	4·25	7·00

DESIGNS: 8g. Gunther's voyage; 15g. Kriemhild and Brunhild; 20g. Hagen and the Rhine maidens; 24g. Rudiger and the Nibelungs; 40g. Dietrich's fight with Hagen.

99 Dr. Michael Hainisch

1928. Tenth Anniv of Republic and War Orphans and Invalid Children's Fund.

642	99	10g. (+10g.) brown	6·25	16·00
643	99	15g. (+15g.) red	6·25	16·00
644	99	30g. (+30g.) black	6·25	16·00
645	99	40g. (+40g.) blue	6·25	16·00

 100 Gussing 101 National Library, Vienna

1929. Views. Size 25½×21½ mm.

646	100	10g. orange	1·00	10
647	100	10g. brown	1·00	10
648	-	15g. purple	1·00	1·80
649	-	16g. black	20	10
650	-	18g. green	50	65
651	-	20g. black	50	10
653	-	24g. purple	7·25	75
654	-	30g. violet	8·25	10
655	-	40g. blue	10·50	30
656	-	50g. violet	39·00	30
657	-	60g. green	31·00	55
658	101	1s. brown	8·25	55
659	-	2s. green	19·00	17·00

VIEWS—As T 100: 15g. Hochosterwitz; 16, 20g. Durnstein; 18g. Traunsee; 24g. Salzburg; 30g. Seewiesen; 40g. Innsbruck; 50g. Worthersee; 60g. Hohenems. As T 101: 2s. St. Stephen's Cathedral, Vienna.
See also Nos. 678/91.

102 Pres. Wilhelm Miklas

1930. Anti-tuberculosis Fund.

660	102	10g. (+10g.) brown	10·50	30·00
661	102	20g. (+20g.) red	10·50	30·00
662	102	30g. (+30g.) purple	10·50	30·00
663	102	40g. (+40g.) blue	10·50	30·00
664	102	50g. (+50g.) green	10·50	30·00
665	102	1s. (+1s.) brown	10·50	30·00

1930. Rotarian Congress. Optd with Rotary Int emblem and CONVENTION WIEN 1931.

666	100	10g. (+10g.) brown	50·00	85·00
667	-	20g. (+20g.) grey (No. 651)	50·00	85·00
668	-	30g. (+30g.) vio (No. 654)	50·00	85·00
669	-	40g. (+40g.) bl (No. 655)	50·00	85·00
670	-	50g. (+50g.) vio (No. 656)	50·00	85·00
671	101	1s. (+1s.) brown	50·00	85·00

104 Johann Nestroy

1931. Austrian Writers and Youth Unemployment Fund.

672	-	10g. (+10g.) purple	21·00	45·00
673	-	20g. (+20g.) grey	21·00	45·00
674	104	30g. (+30g.) red	21·00	45·00
675	-	40g. (+40g.) blue	21·00	45·00
676	-	50g. (+50g.) green	21·00	45·00
677	-	1s. (+1s.) brown	21·00	45·00

DESIGNS: 10g. F. Raimund; 20g. E. Grillparzer; 40g. A Stifter; 50g. L. Anzengruber; 1s. P. Rosegger.

105

1932. Designs as No. 646 etc, but size reduced to 20½×16 mm as T 105.

678	105	10g. brown	1·00	20
679	-	12g. green	2·10	20
680	-	18g. green	2·10	3·50
681	-	20g. black	1·00	20
682	-	24g. red	6·75	20
683	-	24g. violet	4·25	20
684	-	30g. violet	23·00	20
685	-	30g. blue	8·25	30
686	-	40g. blue	27·00	2·10
687	-	40g. violet	10·50	55
688	-	50g. violet	31·00	55
689	-	50g. blue	10·50	55
690	-	60g. green	70·00	5·25
691	-	64g. green	23·00	55

DESIGNS (new values): 12g. Traunsee; 64g. Hohenems.

106 Dr. Ignaz Seipel

1932. Death of Dr. Seipel (Chancellor), and Ex-servicemen's Fund.

692	106	50g. (+50g.) blue	19·00	38·00

107 Hans Makart

1932. Austrian Painters.

693	-	12g. (+12g.) green	31·00	65·00
694	-	24g. (+24g.) purple	31·00	65·00
695	-	30g. (+30g.) red	31·00	65·00
696	107	40g. (+40g.) grey	31·00	65·00
697	-	64g. (+64g.) brown	31·00	65·00
698	-	1s. (+1s.) red	31·00	65·00

DESIGNS: 12g. F. G. Waldmuller; 24g. Von Schwind; 30g. Alt; 64g. Klimt; 1s. A. Egger-Lienz.

108 The Climb

1933. International Ski Championship Fund.

699	108	12g. (+12g.) green	10·50	27·00
700	-	24g. (+24g.) violet	£140	£190
701	-	30g. (+30g.) red	21·00	38·00
702	-	50g. (+50g.) blue	£140	£190

DESIGNS: 24g. Start; 30g. Race; 50g. Ski jump.

109 The Honeymoon (M. von Schwind)

1933. International Philatelic Exn, Vienna (WIPA).

703	109	50g. (+50g.) blue	£200	£350
MS705		127×105 mm. As No. 703 (+1s.60 admission) in block of four	£3500	£5000

111 John Sobieski

1933. 250th Anniv of Relief of Vienna and Pan-German Catholic Congress.

706	-	12g. (+12g.) green	33·00	55·00
707	-	24g. (+24g.) violet	31·00	48·00
708	-	30g. (+30g.) red	31·00	48·00
709	111	40g. (+40g.) grey	44·00	85·00
710	-	50g. (+50g.) blue	31·00	48·00
711	-	64g. (+64g.) brown	36·00	75·00

DESIGNS—VERT: 12g. Vienna in 1683; 24g. Marco d'Aviano; 30g. Count von Starhemberg; 50g. Charles of Lorraine; 64g. Burgomaster Liebenberg.

1933. Winter Relief Fund. Surch with premium and Winterhilfe (5g.) or WINTERHILFE (others).

712	91	5g.+2g. green	20	75
713	-	12g.+3g. blue (as 679)	30	1·10
714	-	24g.+6g. brn (as 682)	20	75
715	101	1s.+50g. red	41·00	95·00

114 **115**

1934

716	**114**	1g. violet	10	10
717	**114**	3g. red	10	10
718	-	4g. green	10	10
719	-	5g. purple	10	10
721	-	6g. blue	20	10
722	-	8g. green	10	10
723	-	12g. brown	10	10
724	-	20g. brown	20	10
725	-	24g. turquoise	10	10
726	-	25g. violet	20	25
727	-	30g. red	20	10
728	-	35g. red	40	50
729	**115**	40g. grey	50	30
730	**115**	45g. brown	45	20
731	-	60g. blue	70	55
732	-	64g. brown	1·00	20
733	-	1s. purple	1·50	85
735	-	2s. green	4·75	8·50
736	-	3s. orange	18·00	32·00
737	-	5s. black	41·00	70·00

DESIGNS (Austrian costumes of the districts named)—As Type **114**: 1, 3g. Burgenland; 4, 5g. Carinthia; 6, 8g. Lower Austria; 12, 20g. Upper Austria; 24, 25g. Salzburg; 30, 35g. Styria (Steiermark). As Type **115**: 40, 45g. Tyrol; 60, 64g. Vorarlberg; 1s. Vienna; 2s. Army officer and soldiers. 30×31 mm: 3s. Harvesters; 5s. Builders.

117 Chancellor Dollfuss

1934. Dollfuss Mourning Stamp.

738	**117**	24g. black	60	1·10

See also No. 762.

118 Anton Pilgram

1934. Welfare Funds. Austrian Architects.

739	**118**	12g. (+12g.) black	14·50	32·00
740	-	24g. (+24g.) violet	14·50	32·00
741	-	30g. (+30g.) red	14·50	32·00
742	-	40g. (+40g.) brown	14·50	32·00
743	-	60g. (+60g.) blue	14·50	32·00
744	-	64g. (+64g.) green	14·50	32·00

DESIGNS: 24g. Fischer von Erlach; 30g. J. Prandtauer; 40g. A. von Siccardsburg and E. van der Null; 60g. H. von Ferstel; 64g. Otto Wagner.

119 *Mother and Child (J. Danhauser)*

1935. Mothers Day.

745	**119**	24g. blue	70	55

1935. First Anniv of Assassination of Dr. Dollfuss.

762	**117**	24g. blue	1·50	1·40

121 Maria Worth Castle, Carinthia

122 Zugspitze Aerial Railway

1935. Air. Designs showing Junkers airplane (except 10s.) and landscape.

763	-	5g. purple	30	85
764	**121**	10g. orange	10	55
765	-	15g. green	1·00	2·75
766	-	20g. blue	10	55
767	-	25g. purple	10	55
768	-	30g. red	10	55
769	-	40g. green	10	55
770	-	50g. blue	20	95

771	-	60g. sepia	40	1·40
772	-	80g. brown	50	1·80
773	-	1s. red	40	1·60
774	-	2s. green	3·00	8·50
775	-	3s. brown	9·25	32·00
776	**122**	5s. green	5·25	23·00
777	-	10s. blue	85·00	£170

DESIGNS—As T **121**: 5g. Gussing Castle; 15g. Durnstein; 20g. Hallstatt; 25g. Salzburg; 30g. Dachstein Mts.; 40g. Wettersee; 50g. Stuben am Arlberg; 60g. St. Stephen's Cathedral, Vienna; 80g. Minorite Church, Vienna. As T **122**: 1s. River Danube; 2s. Tauern railway viaduct; 3s. Grossglockner mountain roadway; 10s. Glider and yachts on the Attersee.

1935. Winter Relief Fund. As Nos. 719, 723, 725 and 733, but colours changed, surch Winterhilfe (778/80) or WINTERHILFE (781) and premium.

778	-	5g.+2g. green	70	1·60
779	-	12g.+3g. blue	1·20	2·10
780	-	24g.+6g. brown	70	1·60
781	-	1s.+50g. red	41·00	90·00

123 Prince Eugene of Savoy (born 1663, not 1667 as given)

1935. Welfare Funds. Austrian Heroes.

782	**123**	12g. (+12g.) brown	15·00	32·00
783	-	24g. (+24g.) green	15·00	32·00
784	-	30g. (+30g.) purple	15·00	32·00
785	-	40g. (+40g.) blue	15·00	32·00
786	-	60g. (+60g.) blue	15·00	32·00
787	-	64g. (+64g.) violet	15·00	32·00

PORTRAITS: 24g. Baron von Laudon; 30g. Archduke Charles; 40g. Field-Marshal Radetzky; 60g. Vice-Admiral von Tegetthoff; 64g. Field-Marshal Conrad von Hotzendorff.

124 Slalom Course Skier

1936. International Ski Championship Fund. Inscr "WETTKAMPFE 1936".

788	**124**	12g. (+12g.) green	3·00	6·50
789	-	24g. (+24g.) violet	5·25	8·50
790	-	35g. (+35g.) red	31·00	75·00
791	-	60g. (+60g.) blue	31·00	75·00

DESIGNS: 24g. Skier on mountain slope; 35g. Woman slalom course skier; 60g. View of Maria Theresienstrasse, Innsbruck.

125 Madonna and Child

1936. Mothers' Day.

792	**125**	24g. blue	40	1·30

126 Chancellor Dollfuss

1936. Second Anniv of Assassination of Dr. Dollfuss.

793	**126**	10s. blue	£950	£1500

127 'St. Martin sharing Cloak

1936. Winter Relief Fund. Inscr "WINTERHILFE 1936/37".

794	**127**	5g.+2g. green	35	1·10
795	-	12g.+3g. violet	35	1·10

796	-	24g.+6g. blue	35	1·10
797	-	1s.+1s. red	9·25	25·00

DESIGNS: 12g. "Healing the sick"; 24g. "St. Elizabeth feeding the hungry"; 1s. "Warming the poor".

128 J. Ressel

1936. Welfare Funds. Austrian Inventors.

798	**128**	12g. (+12g.) brown	3·50	10·00
799	-	24g. (+24g.) violet	3·50	10·00
800	-	30g. (+30g.) red	3·50	10·00
801	-	40g. (+40g.) black	3·50	10·00
802	-	60g. (+60g.) blue	3·50	10·00
803	-	64g. (+64g.) green	3·50	10·00

PORTRAITS: 24g. Karl Ritter von Ghega; 30g. J. Werndl; 40g. Carl Freih. Auer von Welsbach; 60g. R. von Lieben; 64g. V. Kaplan.

129 Mother and Child

1937. Mothers' Day.

804	**129**	24g. red	30	55

130 *Maria Anna*

1937. Centenary of Regular Danube Services of Danube Steam Navigation Co. Paddle-steamers.

805	**130**	12g. red	85	1·10
806	-	24g. blue	85	1·10
807	-	64g. green	85	2·10

DESIGNS: 24g. "Helios"; 64g. "Oesterreich".

131 "Child Welfare"

1937. Winter Relief Fund. Inscr "WINTERHILFE 1937 1938".

808	**131**	5g.+2g. green	20	65
809	-	12g.+3g. brown	20	65
810	-	24g.+6g. blue	20	65
811	-	1s.+1s. red	4·75	18·00

DESIGNS: 12g. "Feeding the Children"; 24g. "Protecting the Aged"; 1s. "Nursing the Sick".

132 Steam Locomotive *Austria*, 1837

1937. Railway Centenary.

812	**132**	12g. brown	20	40
813	-	25g. violet	85	1·60
814	-	35g. red	2·50	3·75

DESIGNS: 25g. Steam locomotive, 1936; 35g. Electric locomotive.

133 Dr. G. Van Swieten

1937. Welfare Funds. Austrian Doctors.

815	**133**	5g. (+5g.) brown	2·75	7·50
816	-	8g. (+8g.) red	2·75	7·50
817	-	12g. (+12g.) brown	2·75	7·50
818	-	20g. (+20g.) green	2·75	7·50
819	-	24g. (+24g.) violet	2·75	7·50
820	-	30g. (+30g.) red	2·75	7·50
821	-	40g. (+40g.) olive	2·75	7·50
822	-	60g. (+60g.) blue	2·75	7·50
823	-	64g. (+64g.) purple	2·75	7·50

DESIGNS: 8g. L. A. von Auenbrugg; 12g. K. von Rokitansky; 20g. J. Skoda; 25g. F. von Hebra; 30g. F. von Arlt; 40g. J. Hyrtl; 60g. T. Billroth; 64g. T. Meynert.

134 Nosegay and Signs of the Zodiac

1937. Christmas Greetings.

824	-	12g. green	10	30
825	**134**	24g. red	10	30

ALLIED OCCUPATION. Nos. 826/905 were issued in the Russian Zone of occupation and Nos. 906/22 were a joint issue for use in the British, French and American zones.

1945. Hitler portrait stamps of Germany optd. (a) Optd Osterreich only.

826	**173**	5pf. green	30	1·40
827	**173**	8pf. red	40	1·10

(b) Optd Osterreich and bar.

828		6pf. violet	60	1·60
829		12pf. red	60	1·60

(137)

1945. 1941 and 1944 Hitler stamps of Germany optd as T 137.

830	**137**	1pf. grey	6·25	13·00
831	**137**	3pf. brown	3·25	11·00
832	**137**	4pf. grey	17·00	38·00
833	**137**	5pf. green	4·25	11·00
834	**137**	6pf. violet	1·60	2·20
835	**137**	8pf. red	1·30	3·25
836	**137**	10pf. brown	4·25	11·00
837	**137**	12pf. red	60	1·10
838	**137**	15pf. red	1·60	5·50
839	**137**	16pf. green	40·00	85·00
840	**137**	20pf. blue	4·25	8·50
841	**137**	24pf. brown	37·00	85·00
842	**173**	25pf. blue	5·25	11·00
843	**173**	30pf. green	5·25	11·00
844	**173**	40pf. mauve	5·75	11·50
845	**225**	42pf. green	8·25	19·00
846	**173**	50pf. green	6·75	13·00
847	**173**	60pf. brown	7·25	16·00
848	**173**	80pf. blue	6·25	15·00
853	**182**	1rm. green	34·00	70·00
850	**182**	2rm. violet	29·00	60·00
855	**182**	3rm. red	60·00	£130
856	**182**	5rm. blue	£425	£900

1945. Stamps of Germany surch OSTERREICH and new value.

857	**186**	5pf. on 12+88pf. green	85	2·75
858	-	6pf. on 6+14pf. brown and blue (No. 811)	10·50	24·00
859	**220**	8pf. on 42+108pf. brn	1·40	4·75
860	-	12pf. on 3+7pf. blue (No. 810)	85	2·75

(140)

1945. 1941 and 1944 Hitler stamps of Germany optd as T 140.

862	**173**	5pf. green	1·60	5·50
863	**173**	6pf. violet	1·00	4·25
864	**173**	8pf. red	85	4·50
865	**173**	12pf. red	1·00	5·50
866	**173**	30pf. green	10·50	27·00
867a	**225**	42pf. green	23·00	44·00

141 New National Arms

142 New National Arms

1945

868	**141**	3pf. brown	20	20
869	**141**	4pf. blue	20	45
870	**141**	5pf. green	20	25

871	141	6pf. purple	20	25
872	141	8pf. orange	20	25
873	141	10pf. brown	20	25
874	141	12pf. red	20	25
875	141	15pf. orange	20	30
876	141	16pf. green	25	65
877	141	20pf. blue	20	30
878	141	24pf. orange	20	45
879	141	25pf. blue	20	35
880	141	30pf. green	20	35
881	141	38pf. blue	20	35
882	141	40pf. purple	20	40
883	141	42pf. grey	30	45
884	141	50pf. green	20	55
885	141	60pf. red	20	55
886	141	80pf. violet	20	45
887	142	1rm. green	40	1·10
888	142	2rm. violet	45	1·20
889	142	3rm. purple	50	1·70
890	142	5rm. brown	70	2·30

Nos. 877/86 are 24×28 mm.

144 Allegorical of the Home Land

1945. Austrian Welfare Charities.

905	144	1s.+10s. green	1·80	3·50

145 Posthorn

1945

906	145	1g. blue	20	85
907	145	3g. orange	20	30
908	145	4g. brown	20	30
909	145	5g. green	20	25
910	145	6g. purple	20	25
911	145	8g. red	20	25
912	145	10g. grey	20	25
913	145	12g. brown	20	25
914	145	15g. red	20	30
915	145	20g. brown	20	30
916	145	25g. blue	20	30
917	145	30g. mauve	20	30
918	145	40g. brown	20	30
919	145	60g. olive	20	45
920	145	1s. violet	40	85
921	145	2s. yellow	50	1·70
922	145	5s. blue	55	1·80

146 Salzburg **148** Durnstein

1945. Views as T **146/8.**

923	-	3g. blue	20	20
924	-	4g. red	20	20
925	-	5g. red	20	20
926	146	6g. green	20	20
927	-	8g. brown	20	20
928	-	8g. purple	20	20
929	-	8g. green	20	20
930	-	10g. green	20	20
931	-	10g. purple	20	20
932	-	12g. brown	20	20
933	-	15g. blue	20	20
934	-	16g. brown	20	20
935	-	20g. blue	20	20
936	-	24g. green	20	20
937	-	25g. grey	20	20
938	-	30g. red	20	20
939	-	30g. blue	50	55
940	-	35g. red	20	20
941	-	38g. green	20	20
942	-	40g. grey	20	20
943	-	42g. red	20	20
944	-	45g. blue	30	55
945	-	50g. blue	20	20
946	-	50g. purple	85	85
947	-	60g. blue	30	30
948	-	60g. violet	3·00	3·75
949	-	70g. blue	35	55
950	-	80g. brown	40	75
951	-	90g. green	1·70	3·25
952A	148	1s. brown	1·00	1·60
953A	-	2s. grey	3·50	5·50

954A	-	3s. green	1·20	2·75
955A	-	5s. red	2·10	3·75

DESIGNS—As Type **146:** 3g. Lermoos; 4g. Iron-ore mine, Erzberg; 5g. Leopoldsberg, Vienna; 8g. (927), Prater Woods, Vienna; 8g. (928/9), Town Hall Park, Vienna; 10g. (930/1), Hochosterwitz; 12g. Schafberg; 15g. Forchtenstein; 16g. Gesauseeingang; 23½×29 mm: 20g. Gebhartsberg; 24g. Holdrichsmuhle, near Modling; 25g. Vent im Otztal; 30g. (938/9), Neusiedler Lake; 35g. Belvedere Palace, Vienna; 38g. Langbath Lake; 40g. Mariazell; 42g. Traunstein; 45g. Burg Hartenstein; 50g. (945/6), Silvretta Peaks, Vorarlberg; 60g. (947/8), Semmering; 70g. Badgastein; 80g. Kaisergebirge; 90g. Wayside shrine near Tragoss. As T **148:** 2s. St. Christof; 3s. Heiligenblut; 5s. Schonbrunn Palace, Vienna.

See also Nos. 1072/86a.

1946. 1st Anniv of U.N.O. No. 938 surch **26. JUNI 1945+20 g 26. JUNI 1946** and globe.

971		30g.+20g. red	3·00	6·50

151 Dr. Karl Renner

1946. First Anniv of Establishment of Renner Government.

972	151	1s.+1s. green	6·25	11·00
973	151	2s.+2s. violet	6·25	11·00
974	151	3s.+3s. purple	6·25	11·00
975	151	5s.+5s. brown	6·25	11·00

MS976 Four sheets, each 180×155 mm, each with block of 8 of one value (972/5) and Arms in centre. Imperf
Set 4 sheets £2500 £17000

152 Dagger and Map

1946. "Anti-Fascist" Exhibition.

977	152	5g.+3g. sepia	60	1·30
978	-	6g.+4g. green	40	95
979	-	8g.+6g. orange	40	95
980	-	12g.+12g. blue	40	95
981	-	30g.+30g. violet	40	1·10
982	-	42g.+42g. brown	60	1·10
983	-	1s.+1s. red	50	1·60
984	-	2s.+2s. red	1·20	2·75

DESIGNS: 6g. Broom sweeping Nazi and Fascist emblems; 8g. St. Stephen's Cathedral in flames; 12g. Hand and barbed wire; 30g. Hand strangling snake; 42g. Hammer and broken column; 1s. Hand and Austrian flag; 2s. Eagle and smoking Nazi emblem.

(153)

1946. Congress of Society for Promotion of Cultural and Economic Relations with the Soviet Union. No. 932 optd with T **153.**

985		12g. brown	20	55

154 Mare and Foal

1946. Austria Prize Race Fund.

986	154	16g.+16g. red	2·50	5·50
987	-	24g.+24g. violet	2·10	4·25
988	-	60g.+60g. green	2·10	4·25
989	-	1s.+1s. blue	2·10	4·25
990	-	2s.+2s. brown	7·25	11·00

DESIGNS: 24g. Two horses' heads; 60g. Racehorse clearing hurdle; 1s. Three racehorses; 2s. Three horses' heads.

155 Ruprecht's Church, Vienna

1946. 950th Anniv of First recorded use of name "Osterreich".

991	155	30g.+70g. red	50	1·10

156 Statue of Duke Rudolf

1946. St. Stephen's Cathedral Reconstruction Fund. Architectural and Sculptural designs.

992	156	3g.+12g. brown	20	1·10
993	-	5g.+20g. purple	20	1·10
994	-	6g.+24g. blue	20	1·10
995	-	8g.+32g. green	20	1·10
996	-	10g.+40g. blue	20	1·10
997	-	12g.+48g. violet	50	2·20
998	-	30g.+1s.20 red	1·80	2·20
999	-	50g.+1s.80 blue	2·30	6·50
1000	-	1s.+5s. purple	3·00	8·50
1001	-	2s.+10s. brown	6·25	11·00

DESIGNS: 5g. Tomb of Frederick III; 6g. Pulpit; 8g. Statue of St. Stephen; 10g. Statue of Madonna and Child; 12g. Altar; 30g. Organ; 50g. Anton Pilgram; 1s. N.E. Tower; 2s. S.W. Spire.

157 Franz Grillparzer (dramatic poet)

1947. Famous Austrians.

1002		12g. green	30	55
1003	157	18g. purple	30	30
1004	-	20g. green	50	30
1005	-	40g. brown	10·50	6·00
1006	-	40g. green	10·50	11·00
1007	-	60g. lake	45	45

PORTRAITS: 12g. Franz Schubert (composer); 20g. Carl Michael Ziehrer (composer); 40g. (No. 1005), Adalbert Stifter (poet); 40g. (No. 1006), Anton Bruckner (composer); 60g. Friedrich Amerling (painter).

158 Harvesting

1947. Vienna Fair Fund.

1009	158	3g.+2g. brown	50	1·10
1010	-	8g.+2g. green	50	1·10
1011	-	10g.+5g. slate	50	1·10
1012	-	12g.+8g. violet	50	1·10
1013	-	18g.+12g. olive	50	1·10
1014	-	30g.+10g. purple	50	1·10
1015	-	35g.+15g. red	50	1·60
1016	-	60g.+20g. blue	50	1·70

DESIGNS: 8g. Logging; 10g. Factory; 12g. Pithead; 18g. Oil wells; 30g. Textile machinery; 35g. Foundry; 60g. Electric cables.

159 Airplane over Hinterstoder

1947. Air.

1017		50g. brown	50	1·10
1018	-	1s. purple	50	1·10
1019	-	2s. green	50	2·20
1020	159	3s. brown	3·50	7·50
1021	-	4s. green	2·50	7·50
1022	-	5s. blue	2·50	7·50
1023	-	10s. blue	1·30	13·00

DESIGNS—Airplane over: 50g. Windmill at St. Andra; 1s. Heidentor; 2s. Gmund; 4s. Pragraten; 5s. Torsaule; 10s. St. Charles's Church, Vienna.

160 Beaker (15th century)

1947. National Art Exhibition Fund.

1024	160	3g.+2g. brown	50	85
1025	-	8g.+2g. brown	50	85
1026	-	10g.+5g. red	50	85
1027	-	12g.+8g. violet	50	85
1028	-	18g.+8g. brown	50	85
1029	-	20g.+10g. violet	50	1·10
1030	-	30g.+10g. green	50	1·10
1031	-	35g.+15g. red	50	1·10
1032	-	48g.+12g. purple	1·60	1·40
1033	-	60g.+20g. blue	1·60	1·40

DESIGNS: 8g. Statue of "Providence" (Donner); 10g. Benedictine Monastery, Melk; 12g. "Wife of Dr. Brante of Vienna"; 18g. "Children in a Window" (Waldmuller); 20g. Belvedere Palace Gateway; 30g. Figure of "Egeria" on fountain at Schonbrunn; 35g. National Library, Vienna; 48g. "Copper Printer's (Ernst Rohm) Workshop" (Ferdinand Schmutzer); 60g. "Girl in Straw Hat" (Amerling).

161 Racehorse

1947. Vienna Prize Race Fund.

1034	161	60+20g. blue on pink	30	1·40

163 Prisoner-of-war

1947. Prisoners-of-war Relief Fund.

1063	163	8g.+2g. green	30	85
1064	-	12g.+8g. brown	30	85
1065	-	18g.+12g. black	30	85
1066	-	35g.+15g. purple	30	85
1067	-	60g.+20g. blue	30	85
1068	-	1s.+40g. brown	30	1·60

DESIGNS: 12g. Letter from home; 18g. Gruesome camp visitor; 35g. Soldier and family reunited; 60g. Industry beckons returned soldier; 1s. Soldier sowing.

1947. Nos. 934 and 941 surch.

1069		75g. on 38g. green	50	1·60
1070		1s.40 on 16g. brown	30	55

165 Globe and Tape Machine

1947. Telegraph Centenary.

1071	165	40g. violet	40	65

1947. Currency Revaluation. (a) As T **146.**

1072		3g. red (Lermoos)	40	20
1073		5g. red (Leopoldsberg)	40	20
1074		10g. red (Hochosterwitz)	40	20
1075		15g. red (Forchtenstein)	2·50	2·40

(b) As T **146** but larger (23½×29 mm).

1076		20g. red (Gebhartsberg)	50	20
1077		30g. red (Neusiedler Lake)	60	30
1078		40g. red (Mariazell)	1·00	20
1079		50g. red (Silvretta Peaks)	1·00	20
1080		60g. red (Semmering)	12·50	2·75
1081		70g. red (Badgastein)	5·25	20
1082		80g. red (Kaisergebirge)	5·25	55
1083		90g. red (Wayside shrine, Tragoss)	6·25	1·40

(c) As T **148.**

1084		1s. violet (Durnstein)	1·30	30
1085		2s. violet (St. Christof)	1·60	55
1086		3s. violet (Heiligenblut)	31·00	2·20
1086a		5s. violet (Schonbrunn)	31·00	2·75

Nos. 1072/86a in new currency replaced previous issue at rate of 3s. (old) = 1s. (new).

166 Sacred
Olympic Flame

1948. Fund for Entries to 5th Winter Olympic Games, St. Moritz.

| 1087 | **166** | 1s.+50g. blue | 50 | 85 |

167 Laabenbach
Viaduct,
Neulenbach

1948. Reconstruction Fund.

1088	**167**	10g.+5g. grey	20	30
1089	-	20g.+10g. violet	20	30
1090	-	30g.+10g. green	50	65
1091	-	40g.+20g. green	20	30
1092	-	45g.+20g. blue	20	30
1093	-	60g.+30g. red	20	30
1094	-	75g.+35g. purple	30	45
1095	-	80g.+40g. purple	30	45
1096	-	1s.+50g. blue	30	45
1097	-	1s.40+70g. lake	60	75

DESIGNS (showing reconstruction): 20g. Vermunt Lake Dam; 30g. Danube Port, Vienna; 40g. Erzberg open-cast mine; 45g. Southern Railway Station, Vienna; 60g. Flats; 75g. Vienna Gas Works; 80g. Oil refinery; 1s. Mountain roadway; 1s.40, Parliament Building.

169 Violets

1948. Anti-tuberculosis Fund.

1098	**169**	10g.+5g. violet, mauve and green	35	35
1099	-	20g.+10g. green, light green and yellow	35	35
1100	-	30g.+10g. brown, yellow and green	4·50	4·50
1101	-	40g.+20g. green, yellow and orange	85	85
1102	-	45g.+20g. purple, mauve and yellow	30	30
1103	-	60g.+30g. red, mauve and green	30	30
1104	-	75g.+35g. green, pink and yellow	30	30
1105	-	80g.+40g. blue, pink and green	40	40
1106	-	1s.+50g. blue, ultramarine and green	40	40
1107	-	1s.40+70g. green, blue and yellow	2·75	2·75

FLOWERS: 20g. Anemone; 30g. Crocus; 40g. Primrose; 45g. Pasque flower; 60g. Rhododendron; 75g. Wild rose; 80g. Cyclamen; 1s. Gentian; 1s.40, Edelweiss.

170 Vorarlberg
Montafon

1948. Provincial Costumes.

1108		3g. grey	85	1·10
1109	-	5g. green	30	20
1110	-	10g. brown	30	20
1111	-	15g. brown	50	20
1112	**170**	20g. green	30	20
1113	-	25g. brown	30	20
1114	-	30g. red	3·50	20
1115	-	30g. violet	1·00	20
1116	-	40g. violet	4·25	20
1117	-	40g. green	85	20
1118	-	45g. blue	4·25	75
1119	-	50g. brown	1·20	20
1120	-	60g. red	85	20
1121	-	70g. green	85	20
1122	-	75g. blue	7·25	75
1123	-	80g. rose	1·00	20
1124	-	90g. purple	55·00	55
1125	-	1s. blue	16·00	20

1126	-	1s. red	£130	20
1127	-	1s. green	70	20
1128	-	1s.20 violet	1·00	20
1129	-	1s.40 brown	3·00	30
1130	-	1s.45 red	2·50	20
1131	-	1s.50 blue	2·10	20
1132	-	1s.60 red	85	20
1133	-	1s.70 blue	4·25	1·30
1134	-	2s. green	1·60	20
1135	-	2s.20 slate	8·25	30
1136	-	2s.40 blue	2·10	25
1137	-	2s.50 brown	5·75	2·20
1138	-	2s.70 brown	1·00	1·40
1139	-	3s. lake	4·25	20
1140	-	3s.50 green	34·00	30
1141	-	4s.50 purple	1·00	1·30
1142	-	5s. purple	1·60	20
1143	-	7s. olive	6·25	2·20
1144	-	10s. grey	50·00	7·50

DESIGNS—As T **170**: 3g. "Tirol Inntal"; 5g. "Salzburg Pinzgau"; 10, 75g. "Steiermark Salzkammergut" (different designs); 15g. "Burgenland Lutzmannsburg"; 25g., 1s.60, "Wien 1850" (two different designs); 30g. (2) "Salzburg Pongau"; 40g. (2) "Wien 1840"; 45g. "Karnten Lesachtal"; 50g. "Vorarlberg Bregenzerwald"; 60g. "Karnten Lavanttal"; 70g. "Niederosterreich Wachau"; 80g. "Steiermark Ennstal"; 90g. "Steiermark Mittelsteier"; 1s. (3) "Tirol Pustertal"; 1s.20, "Niederosterreich Wienerwald"; 1s.40, "Oberosterreich Innviertel"; 1s.45, "Wilter bei Innsbruck"; 1s.50, "Wien 1853"; 1s.70, "Ost Tirol Kals"; 2s. "Oberosterreich"; 2s.20, "Ischl 1820"; 2s.40, "Kitzbuhel"; 2s.50, "Obersteiermark 1850"; 2s.70, "Kleines Walsertal"; 3s. "Burgenland"; 3s.50, "Niederosterreich 1850"; 4s.50, "Gailtal"; 5s. "Zillertal"; 7s. "Steiermark Sumltal". 25×35 mm: 10s. "Wien 1850".

172 Kunstlerhaus **173** Hans Makart

1948. 80th Anniv of Creative Artists' Association.

1145	**172**	20g.+10g. green	10·50	8·50
1146	**173**	30g.+15g. brown	3·50	4·25
1147	-	40g.+20g. blue	3·50	4·25
1148	-	50g.+25g. violet	6·25	7·50
1149	-	60g.+30g. red	7·25	6·50
1150	-	1s.+50g. blue	7·25	8·50
1151	-	1s.40+70g. brown	21·00	26·00

PORTRAITS: 40g. K. Kundmann; 50g. A. von Siccardsburg; 60g. H. Canon; 1s. W. Unger; 1s.40, Friedr. Schmidt.

174 St. Rupert

1948. Salzburg Cathedral Reconstruction Fund.

1152	**174**	20g.+10g. green	10·50	11·00
1153	-	30g.+15g. brown	3·00	4·25
1154	-	40g.+20g. green	3·50	4·25
1155	-	50g.+25g. brown	1·00	1·10
1156	-	60g.+30g. red	1·00	1·10
1157	-	80g.+40g. purple	1·00	1·10
1158	-	1s.+50g. blue	1·00	1·60
1159	-	1s.40+70g. green	3·00	4·25

DESIGNS: 30, 40, 50, 80g. Views of Salzburg Cathedral; 60g. St. Peter's; 1s. Cathedral and Fortress; 1s.40, Madonna.

175 Pres. Renner

1948. 30th Anniv of Republic.

| 1160 | **175** | 1s. blue | 3·00 | 2·75 |

See also Nos. 1224 and 1333.

176 F. Gruber and J.
Mohr

1948. 130th Anniv of Composition of Carol *Silent Night, Holy Night*.

| 1161 | **176** | 60g. brown | 8·50 | 8·50 |

177 Boy and Hare

1949. Child Welfare Fund.

1162	**177**	40g.+10g. purple	22·00	24·00
1163	-	60g.+20g. red	22·00	24·00
1164	-	1s.+25g. blue	22·00	24·00
1165	-	1s.40+35g. green	25·00	27·00

DESIGNS: 60g. Two girls and apples in boot; 1s. Boy and birthday cake; 1s.40, Girl praying before candle.

178 Boy and Dove

1949. U.N. Int. Children's Emergency Fund.

| 1166 | **178** | 1s. blue | 16·00 | 4·25 |

179 Johann Strauss

1949. 50th Death Anniv of Johann Strauss the Younger (composer).

| 1167 | **179** | 1s. blue | 4·25 | 3·00 |

See also Nos. 1174, 1207 and 1229.

180 Esperanto Star

1949. Esperanto Congress, Vienna.

| 1168 | **180** | 20g. green | 1·40 | 1·40 |

181 St. Gebhard

1949. Birth Millenary of St. Gebhard (Bishop of Vorarlberg).

| 1169 | **181** | 30g. violet | 2·50 | 2·50 |

182 Seal of Duke
Friedrich II, 1230

1949. Prisoners-of-war Relief Fund. Arms.

1170	**182**	40g.+10g. yell & brn	14·00	13·00
1171	-	60g.+15g. pink & pur	12·00	11·00
1172	-	1s.+25g. red & blue	12·00	11·00
1173	-	1s.60+40g. pink and green	16·00	16·00

ARMS: 60g. Princes of Austria, 1450; 1s. Austria, 1600; 1s.60, Austria, 1945.

1949. Death Centenary of Johann Strauss the Elder (composer). Portrait as T **179**.

| 1174 | - | 30g. purple | 2·20 | 2·75 |

183 Allegory of U.P.U.

1949. 75th Anniv of U.P.U.

| 1175 | **183** | 40g. green | 5·50 | 5·50 |

| 1176 | - | 60g. red | 6·50 | 5·50 |
| 1177 | - | 1s. blue | 11·00 | 9·75 |

DESIGNS: 60g. Children holding "75"; 1s. Woman's head.

185 Magnifying
Glass and Covers

1949. Stamp Day.

| 1206 | **185** | 60g.+15g. brown | 4·25 | 3·75 |

1949. 50th Death Anniv of Karl Millocker (composer). Portrait as T **179**.

| 1207 | | 1s. blue | 22·00 | 17·00 |

186 M. M.
Daffinger

1950. 160th Birth Anniv of Moritz Michael Daffinger (painter).

| 1208 | **186** | 60g. brown | 11·00 | 8·50 |

187 A. Hofer

1950. 140th Death Anniv of Andreas Hofer (patriot).

| 1209 | **187** | 60g. violet | 17·00 | 13·00 |

See also Nos. 1211, 1223, 1232, 1234, 1243, 1253, 1288 and 1386.

188 Stamp of 1850

1950. Austrian Stamp Centenary.

| 1210 | **188** | 1s. black on yellow | 2·75 | 2·20 |

1950. Death Centenary of Josef Madersperger (sewing machine inventor). Portrait as T **187**.

| 1211 | | 60g. violet | 9·75 | 5·50 |

189 Arms of
Austria and
Carinthia

1950. 30th Anniv of Carinthian Plebiscite.

1212	**189**	60g.+15g. grn & brn	43·00	38·00
1213	-	1s.+25g. red & orange	55·00	43·00
1214	-	1s.70+40g. blue and turquoise	55·00	49·00

DESIGNS: 1s. Carinthian waving Austrian flag; 1s.70, Hand and ballot box.

190 Rooks

1950. Air.

1215	**190**	60g. violet	6·50	5·50
1216	-	1s. violet (Barn swallows)	32·00	30·00
1217	-	2s. blue (Black-headed gulls)	22·00	11·00
1218	-	3s. turquoise (Great cormorants)	£190	£160
1219	-	5s. brown (Common buzzard)	£190	£160
1220	-	10s. purple (Grey heron)	85·00	75·00
1221	-	20s. sepia (Golden eagle)	16·00	4·25

191 Philatelist

1950. Stamp Day.
1222 **191** 60g.+15g. green 13·00 11·00

1950. Birth Centenary of Alexander Girardi (actor). Portrait as T 187.
1223 30g. blue 2·40 1·90

192 Dr. Renner

1951. Death of Pres. Karl Renner.
1224 **192** 1s. black on lemon 1·90 85

193 Miner

1951. Reconstruction Fund.
1225 **193** 40g.+10g. purple 22·00 24·00
1226 – 60g.+15g. purple 22·00 24·00
1227 – 1s.+25g. brown 22·00 24·00
1228 – 1s.70+40g. blue 22·00 24·00
DESIGNS: 60g. Bricklayer; 1s. Bridge-builder; 1s.70, Telegraph engineer.

1951. 150th Birth Anniv of Joseph Lanner (composer). Portrait as T 179.
1229 60g. green 7·00 3·75

194 Martin Johann Schmidt

1951. 150th Death Anniv of Schmidt (painter).
1230 **194** 1s. red 10·00 4·75

195 Scout Badge

1951. Boy Scout Jamboree.
1231 **195** 1s. red, yellow & green 7·00 6·50

1951. Tenth Death Anniv of Wilhelm Kienzl (composer). Portrait as T 187.
1232 1s.50 blue 4·75 3·25

196 Laurel Branch and Olympic Emblem

1952. Sixth Winter Olympic Games, Oslo.
1233 **196** 2s.40+60g. green 32·00 30·00

1952. 150th Birth Anniv of Karl Ritter von Ghega (railway engineer). Portrait as T 187.
1234 1s. green 11·00 3·25

197 Schrammel

1952. Birth Cent of Josef Schrammel (composer).
1235 **197** 1s.50 blue 11·00 3·25
See also No. 1239.

198 Cupid and Letter

1952. Stamp Day.
1236 **198** 1s.50+35g. purple 32·00 31·00

199 Breakfast Pavilion

1952. Bicentenary of Schonbrunn Menagerie.
1237 **199** 1s.50 green 9·75 3·25

200

1952. Int Union of Socialist Youth Camp, Vienna.
1238 **200** 1s.50 blue 11·00 2·20

1952. 150th Birth Anniv of Nikolaus Lenau (writer). Portrait as T 197.
1239 1s. green 11·00 3·25

202

1952. International Children's Correspondence.
1240 **202** 2s.40 blue 18·00 4·25

203 *Christus Pantocrator* (sculpture)

1952. Austrian Catholics' Day.
1241 **203** 1s.+25g. olive 16·00 15·00

204 Hugo Wolf

1953. 50th Death Anniv of Wolf (composer).
1242 **204** 1s.50 blue 12·00 3·25

1953. President Korner's 80th Birthday. As T 187 but portrait of Korner.
1243 1s.50 blue 12·00 3·25
For 1s.50 black, see No. 1288.

1953. 60th Anniv of Austrian Trade Union Movement. As No. 955 (colour changed) surch GEWERKSCHAFTS BEWEGUNG 60 JAHRE 1s+25g.
1244 1s.+25g. on 5s. blue 4·75 4·25

207 Meeting-house, Steyr

1953. Vienna Evangelical School Rebuilding Fund.
1246 **207** 70g.+15g. purple 45 45
1247 – 1s.+25g. blue 45 45
1248 – 1s.50+40g. brown 1·10 1·10
1249 – 2s.40+60g. green 4·75 4·75
1250 – 3s.+75g. lilac 12·00 12·00
DESIGNS: 1s. J. Kepler (astronomer); 1s.50, Lutheran Bible, 1534; 2s.40, T. von Hansen (architect); 3s. School after reconstruction.

208 Child and Christmas Tree

1953. Christmas.
1251 **208** 1s. green 1·80 1·10
See also No. 1266.

209

1953. Stamp Day.
1252 **209** 1s.+25g. brown 12·00 11·00

1954. 150th Birth Anniv of M. Von Schwind (painter). As T 187 but portrait of Von Schwind.
1253 1s.50 lilac 23·00 4·25

210 Baron K. von Rokitansky

1954. 150th Birth Anniv of Von Rokitansky (anatomist).
1254 **210** 1s.50 violet 26·00 4·25
See also No. 1264.

1954. Avalanche Fund. As No. 953 (colour changed) surch LAWINENOPFER 1954 1s+20g.
1255 1s.+20g. blue 55 55

212 Surgeon with Microscope

1954. Health Service Fund.
1256 – 30g.+10g. violet 1·60 1·60
1257 **212** 70g.+15g. brown 55 55
1258 – 1s.+25g. blue 55 55
1259 – 1s.45+35g. green 85 1·10
1260 – 1s.50+35g. red 7·75 11·00
1261 – 2s.40+60g. purple 9·25 12·00
DESIGNS: 30g. Boy patient and sun-ray lamp; 1s. Mother and children; 1s.45, Operating theatre; 1s.50, Baby on scales; 2s.40, Red Cross nurse and ambulance.

213 Esperanto Star

1954. 50th Anniv of Esperanto in Austria.
1262 **213** 1s. green and brown 7·50 75

214 J. M. Rottmayr von Rosenbrunn

1954. Birth Tercentenary of Rottmayr von Rosenbrunn (painter).
1263 **214** 1s. green 19·00 4·75

1954. 25th Death Anniv of Dr. Auer von Welsbach (inventor). Portrait as T 210.
1264 1s.50 blue 55·00 4·25

216 Great Organ, Church of St. Florian

1954. Second International Congress of Catholic Church Music, Vienna.
1265 **216** 1s. brown 3·50 65

1954. Christmas. As No. 1251, but colour changed.
1266 **208** 1s. blue 6·00 1·10

217 18th-century River Boat

1954. Stamp Day.
1267 **217** 1s.+25g. green 11·00 9·75

218 Arms of Austria and Newspapers

1954. 150th Anniv of State Printing Works and 250th Anniv of *Wiener-Zeitung* (newspaper).
1268 **218** 1s. black and red 4·25 85

219 "Freedom"

1955. Tenth Anniv of Re-establishment of Austrian Republic.
1269 – 70g. purple 3·25 55
1270 – 1s. blue 8·50 55
1271 **219** 1s.45 red 14·00 7·00
1272 – 1s.50 brown 36·00 60
1273 – 2s.40 green 14·00 9·75
DESIGNS: 70g. Parliament Buildings; 1s. Western Railway terminus, Vienna; 1s.50, Modern houses; 2s.40, Limberg Dam.

1955. Austrian State Treaty. As No. 888, but colour changed, optd STAATSVERTRAG 1955.
1274 **142** 2s. grey 4·25 1·10

221 "Strength through Unity"

1955. Fourth World Trade Unions Congress, Vienna.
1275 **221** 1s. blue 4·25 3·75

222 "Return to Work"

1955. Returned Prisoners-of-war Relief Fund.
1276 **222** 1s.+25g. brown 3·75 3·25

223 Burgtheater, Vienna

1955. Re-opening of Burgtheater and State Opera House, Vienna.

1277	223	1s.50 brown	6·00	85
1278	-	2s.40 blue (Opera House)	8·00	4·50

224 Globe and Flags

1955. Tenth Anniv of U.N.O.

1279	224	2s.40 green	24·00	5·50

225 Stamp Collector

1955. Stamp Day.

1280	225	1s.+25g. brown	6·50	6·00

226 Mozart

1956. Birth Bicentenary of Mozart (composer).

1281	226	2s.40 blue	9·75	2·75

227

1956. Admission of Austria into U.N.

1282	227	2s.40 brown	19·00	3·75

228

1956. Fifth World Power Conference, Vienna.

1283	228	2s.40 blue	17·00	4·25

229 Vienna and Five New Towns

1956. 23rd International Town Planning Congress.

1284	229	1s.45 red, black & green	5·50	1·70

230 J. B. Fischer von Erlach

1956. Birth Tercentenary of Fischer von Erlach (architect).

1285	230	1s.50 brown	1·80	1·80

231 "Stamp Day"

1956. Stamp Day.

1286	231	1s.+25g. red	5·50	5·50

1956. Hungarian Relief Fund. As No. 1173, but colours changed, surch **1956 1.50 +50 UNGARNHILFE.**

1287		1s.50+50g. on 1s.60+40g. red and grey	1·10	1·10

1957. Death of Pres. Korner. As No. 1243, but colour changed.

1288		1s.50 black	3·25	2·75

233 J. Wagner von Jauregg

1957. Birth Centenary of Wagner von Jauregg (psychiatrist).

1289	233	2s.40 brown	6·50	4·25

234 Anton Wildgans

1957. 25th Death Anniv of Anton Wildgans (poet).

1290	234	1s. blue	85	75

235 Daimber (1907), Graf and Stift (1957) Post Buses

1957. 50th Anniv of Postal Coach Service.

1291	235	1s. black on yellow	85	75

237 Mt. Gasherbrum II

1957. Austrian Himalaya–Karakorum Expedition, 1956.

1293	237	1s.50 blue	75	75

236 Mariazell Basilica

1957. Buildings. (a) Size 20½×24½ mm.

1295	-	20g. purple	55	20
1296	-	30g. green	65	20
1297	-	40g. red	45	20
1298	-	50g. grey	45	20
1299	-	60g. brown	45	20
1300	-	70g. blue	90	20
1301	-	80g. brown	70	20
1302	**236**	1s. brown	1·90	30
1303	-	1s. brown	1·20	20
1304	-	1s.20 purple	1·30	45
1305	-	1s.30 green	30	20
1306	-	1s.40 blue	1·10	30
1307	-	1s.50 red	1·30	20
1308	-	1s.80 blue	1·40	20
1309	-	2s. blue	6·50	30
1310	-	2s. blue	2·20	60
1311	-	2s.20 green	1·40	20
1312	-	2s.50 violet	3·00	1·10
1313	-	3s. blue	1·60	20
1314	-	3s.40 green	2·30	1·10
1315	-	3s.50 mauve	2·40	65
1316	-	4s. violet	2·50	55
1317	-	4s.50 green	3·25	85
1318	-	5s.50 green	2·40	1·20
1319	-	6s. violet	2·50	50
1320	-	6s.40 blue	4·00	1·10
1321	-	8s. purple	5·50	1·10

(b) Larger.

1322		10s. green	5·50	55
1323		20s. purple	6·50	1·70

(c) Smaller, size 17½×21 mm.

1324		50g. grey	45	30
1325	**236**	1s. brown	45	30
1326	-	1s.50 purple	55	30

DESIGNS: 20g. Old Courtyard, Morbisch; 30g. Vienna Town Hall; 40g. Porcia Castle, Spittal; 50g. Heiligenstadt flats; 60g. Lederer Tower, Wells; 70g. Archbishop's Palace, Salzburg; 80g. Old farmhouse, Pinzgau; 1s. (1303) Millstatt; 1s.20, Corn Measurer's House, Bruck-on-the-Mur; 1s.30, Schattenburg Castle; 1s.40, Klagenfurt Town Hall; 1s.50, "Rabenhof" Flats, Erdberg, Vienna; 1s.80, Mint Tower, Hall-in-Tyrol; 2s. (1309) Christkindl Church; 2s. (1310) Dragon Fountain, Klagenfurt; 2s.20, Beethoven's House, Heiligenstadt, Vienna; 2s.50, Danube Bridge, Linz; 3s. "Swiss Portal", Imperial Palace, Vienna; 3s.40, Stein Gate, Krems-on-the-Danube; 3s.50, Esterhazy Palace, Eisenstadt; 4s. Vienna Gate, Hainburg; 4s.50, Schwechat Airport; 5s.50, Chur Gate, Feldkirch; 6s. Graz Town Hall; 6s.40, "Golden Roof", Innsbruck; 8s. Steyr Town Hall. 22×28½ mm: 10s. Heidenreichstein Castle. 28½×37½ mm: 20s. Melk Abbey.

238 Post Office, Linz

1957. Stamp Day.

1327	238	1s.+25g. green	4·75	4·25

239 Badgastein

1958. International Alpine Ski Championships, Badgastein.

1328	239	1s.50 blue	65	55

240 Vickers Viscount 800 OE-LAB

1958. Austrian Airlines Inaugural Flight, Vienna–London.

1329	240	4s. red	1·60	85

241 Mother and Child

1958. Mothers' Day.

1330	241	1s.50 blue	65	55

242 Walther von der Vogelweide (after 12th-century manuscript)

1958. Third Austrian Choir Festival, Vienna.

1331	242	1s.50 multicoloured	65	55

243 Dr. O. Redlich

1958. Birth Cent of Dr. Oswald Redlich (historian).

1332	243	2s.40 blue	95	65

1958. 40th Anniv of Republic. As T **175** but inscr "40 JAHRE".

1333	**175**	1s.50 green	1·10	95

244 Post Office, Kitzbuhel

1958. Stamp Day.

1334	244	2s.40+60g. blue	1·60	1·40

245 "E" building on Map of Europe

1959. Europa.

1335	245	2s.40 green	3·75	75

246 Monopoly Emblem and Cigars

1959. 175th Anniv of Austrian Tobacco Monopoly.

1336	246	2s.40 brown	95	55

247 Archduke Johann

1959. Death Cent of Archduke Johann of Austria.

1337	247	1s.50 green	65	45

248 Western Capercailie

1959. International Hunting Congress, Vienna.

1338	248	1s. purple	55	30
1339	-	1s.50 blue (Roebuck)	85	20
1340	-	2s.40 grn (Wild boar)	1·40	1·50
1341	-	3s.50 brown (Red deer family)	95	65

249 Haydn

1959. 150th Death Anniv of Haydn.

1342	249	1s.50 purple	85	55

250 Tyrolean Eagle

1959. 150th Anniv of Tyrolese Rising.

1343	250	1s.50 red	65	40

251 Microwave
Transmitting
Aerial, Zugspitze

1959. Inaug of Austrian Microwave Network.
1344 **251** 2s.40 blue 85 55

252 Handball
Player

1959. Sports.
1345	-	1s. violet	65	30
1346	**252**	1s.50 green	95	65
1347	-	1s.80 red	65	55
1348	-	2s. purple	55	45
1349	-	2s.20 blue	65	55

DESIGNS: 1s. Runner; 1s.80, Gymnast; 2s. Hurdling; 2s.20, Hammer thrower.

253 Orchestral
Instruments

1959. Vienna Philharmonic Orchestra's World Tour.
1350 **253** 2s.40 black and blue 85 60

254 Roman Coach

1959. Stamp Day.
1351 **254** 2s.40+60g. blk & mve 1·30 1·20

255 Refugees

1960. World Refugee Year.
1352 **255** 3s. turquoise 95 70

256 Pres. Adolf
Scharf

1960. President's 70th Birthday.
1353 **256** 1s.50 green 95 50

257 Youth Hostellers

1960. Youth Hostels Movement.
1354 **257** 1s. red 55 50

258 Dr. Eiselsberg

1960. Birth Cent of Dr. Anton Eiselsberg (surgeon).
1355 **258** 1s.50 sepia and cream 1·10 50

259 Gustav Mahler

1960. Birth Centenary of Gustav Mahler (composer).
1356 **259** 1s.50 brown 1·10 50

260 Jakob
Prandtauer

1960. 300th Birth Anniv of Jakob Prandtauer (architect).
1357 **260** 1s.50 brown 1·10 50

261 Grossglockner
Highway

1960. 25th Anniv of Grossglockner Alpine Highway.
1358 **261** 1s.80 blue 2·20 90

262 Ionic Capital

1960. Europa.
1359 **262** 3s. black 2·75 2·30

263 Griffen, Carinthia

1960. 40th Anniv of Carinthian Plebiscite.
1360 **263** 1s.50 green 85 50

264 Examining Proof of
Engraved Stamp

1960. Stamp Day.
1361 **264** 3s.+70g. brown 2·20 2·00

265 "Freedom"

1961. Austrian Freedom Martyrs' Commem.
1362 **265** 1s.50 red 95 60

266 Hansa Brandenburg
C-1

1961. "LUPOSTA" Exhibition, Vienna, and First Austrian Airmail Service Commemoration.
1363 **266** 5s. blue 1·60 1·50

267 Transport and
Multi-unit Electric
Train

1961. European Transport Ministers' Meeting.
1364 **267** 3s. olive and red 1·10 1·00

268 *Mower in the
Alps* (Detail, A.
Egger-Lienz)

1961. Centenary of Kunstlerhaus, Vienna. Inscr as in T **268**.
1365	**268**	1s. purple and brown	55	30
1366	-	1s.50 lilac and brown	55	30
1367	-	3s. green and brown	1·60	1·20
1368	-	5s. violet and brown	1·60	1·20

PAINTINGS: 1s.50, *The Kiss* (after A. von Pettenkofen). 3s. *Portrait of a Girl* (after A. Romako). 5s. *The Triumph of Ariadne* (detail of Ariadne, after Hans Makart).

269 Observatory
on Sonnblick
Mountain

1961. 75th Anniv of Sonnblick Meteorological Observatory.
1369 **269** 1s.80 blue 85 60

270 Lavanttaler
Colliery

1961. 15th Anniv of Nationalized Industries. Inscr "JAHRE VERSTAATLICHTE UNTERNEHMUNGEN".
1370	**270**	1s. black	30	25
1371	-	1s.50 green	30	25
1372	-	1s.80 red	95	90
1373	-	3s. mauve	1·30	1·20
1374	-	5s. blue	1·60	1·40

DESIGNS: 1s.50, Turbine; 1s.80, Industrial plant; 3s. Steelworks, Linz; 5s. Oil refinery, Schwechat.

271 Mercury

1961. World Bank Congress, Vienna.
1375 **271** 3s. black 95 90

272 Arms of
Burgenland

1961. 40th Anniv of Burgenland.
1376 **272** 1s.50 red, yellow & sepia 65 60

273 Liszt

1961. 150th Birth Anniv of Franz Liszt (composer).
1377 **273** 3s. brown 85 60

274 Rust Post Office

1961. Stamp Day.
1378 **274** 3s.+70g. green 2·00 2·00

275 Court of Accounts

1961. Bicentenary of Court of Accounts.
1379 **275** 1s. sepia 55 50

276 Glockner-Kaprun Power
Station

1962. 15th Anniv of Electric Power Nationalization. Inscr as in T **276**.
1380	**276**	1s. blue	20	25
1381	-	1s.50 purple	45	40
1382	-	1s.80 green	1·20	1·10
1383	-	3s. brown	85	80
1384	-	4s. red	95	90
1385	-	6s.40 black	2·75	2·50

DESIGNS: 1s.50, Ybbs-Persenbeug (Danube); 1s.80, Luner See; 3s. Grossraming (Enns River); 4s. Bisamberg Transformer Station; 6s.40, St. Andra Power Stations.

1962. Death Cent of Johann Nestroy (playwright). Portrait as T **187**.
1386 1s. violet 65 60

277 F. Gauermann

1962. Death Cent of Friedrich Gauermann (painter).
1387 **277** 1s.50 blue 65 60

278 Scout Badge
and Handclasp

1962. 50th Anniv of Austrian Scout Movement.
1388 **278** 1s.50 green 85 80

279 Forest and Lake

1962. "The Austrian Forest".
1389	**279**	1s. grey	75	70
1390	-	1s.50 brown	85	80
1391	-	3s. myrtle	2·75	2·50

DESIGNS: 1s.50, Deciduous forest; 3s. Fir and larch forest.

280 Electric Locomotive
and Steam Locomotive
Austria (1837)

1962. 125th Anniv of Austrian Railways.
1392 **280** 3s. black and buff 2·20 1·50

281 Engraving Die

1962. Stamp Day.
1393 **281** 3s.+70g. violet 2·75 2·50

282 Postal Officials
of 1863

1963. Centenary of Paris Postal Conference.
1394 **282** 3s. sepia and yellow 1·30 90

283 Hermann Bahr

1963. Birth Centenary of Hermann Bahr (writer).
1395 **283** 1s.50 sepia and blue 85 40

284 St. Florian
(statue)

1963. Cent of Austrian Voluntary Fire Brigade.
1396 **284** 1s.50 black and pink 85 50

285 Flag and Emblem

1963. Fifth Austrian Trade Unions Federation Congress.
1397 **285** 1s.50 red, sepia & grey 65 40

286 Crests of Tyrol and
Austria

1963. 600th Anniv of Tyrol as an Austrian Province.
1398 **286** 1s.50 multicoloured 65 40

287 Prince Eugene
of Savoy

1963. Birth Tercent of Prince Eugene of Savoy.
1399 **287** 1s.50 violet 65 40

288 Centenary
Emblem

1963. Centenary of Red Cross.
1400 **288** 3s. silver, red and black 95 80

289 Skiing (slalom)

1963. Winter Olympic Games, Innsbruck, 1964. Centres
black; inscr gold; background colours given.

1401	**289**	1s. grey	30	20
1402	-	1s.20 blue	45	30
1403	-	1s.50 grey	55	40
1404	-	1s.80 purple	65	60
1405	-	2s.20 green	1·10	1·00
1406	-	3s. slate	75	60
1407	-	4s. blue	1·30	1·20

DESIGNS: 1s.20, Skiing (biathlon); 1s.50, Ski jumping;
1s.80, Figure skating; 2s.20, Ice hockey; 3s. Tobogganing;
4s. Bobsleighing.

290 Vienna "101" P.O. and
Railway Shed

1963. Stamp Day.
1408 **290** 3s.+70g. black & drab 1·10 1·00

291 *The Holy
Family* (Josef
Stammel)

1963. Christmas.
1409 **291** 2s. green 65 40

292 Nasturtium

1964. Int Horticultural Exn, Vienna. Multicoloured.

1410	1s. Type **292**	30	20
1411	1s.50 Peony	40	25
1412	1s.80 Clematis	45	40
1413	2s.20 Dahlia	95	90
1414	3s. Convolvulus	1·10	1·00
1415	4s. Mallow	1·60	1·50

293 Gothic Statue and
Stained-glass Window

1964. Romanesque Art Exhibition, Vienna.
1416 **293** 1s.50 blue and black 65 60

294 Pallas Athene
and Interior of
Assembly Hall,
Parliament Building

1964. Second Parliamentary and Scientific Conference,
Vienna.
1417 **294** 1s.80 black and green 55 50

295 *The Kiss* (Gustav Klimt)

1964. Re-opening of "Viennese Secession" Exn Hall.
1418 **295** 3s. multicoloured 95 90

296 "Comforting
the Sick"

1964. 350th Anniv of Order of Brothers of Mercy in
Austria.
1419 **296** 1s.50 blue 75 70

297 *Bringing News of the
Victory at Kunersdorf*
(Bellotto)

1964. 15th U.P.U. Congress, Vienna. Paintings.

1420	**297**	1s. purple	20	15
1421	-	1s.20 brown	45	30
1422	-	1s.50 blue	30	25
1423	-	1s.80 violet	65	60
1424	-	2s.20 black	85	80
1425	-	3s. purple	55	50
1426	-	4s. green	1·10	1·00
1427	-	6s.40 purple	3·50	3·25

PAINTINGS: 1s.20, *Changing Horses"* (Hormann); 1s.50, *The
Wedding Trip* (Schwind); 1s.80, *Postboys returning Home*
(Raffalt); 2s.20, *The Vienna Mail Coach* (Klein); 3s. *Changing
Horses* (Gauermann); 4s. *Postal Tracked-vehicle in Mountain
Village* (Pilch); 6s.40, *Saalbach Post Office and Post-bus*
(Pilch).

298 Vienna, from the
Hochhaus (N.)

1964. "WIPA" Stamp Exhibition, Vienna (1965) (1st issue).
Multicoloured.

1428	1s.50+30g. Type **298**	65	65
1429	1s.50+30g. N.E.	65	65
1430	1s.50+30g. E.	65	65
1431	1s.50+30g. S.E.	65	65
1432	1s.50+30g. S.	65	65
1433	1s.50+30g. S.W.	65	65
1434	1s.50+30g. W.	65	65
1435	1s.50+30g. N.W.	65	65

The designs show a panoramic view of Vienna, looking
to different points of compass (indicated on stamps). The
inscription reads "Vienna welcomes you to WIPA 1965".
See also Nos. 1447/52.

299 "Workers"

1964. Centenary of Austrian Workers' Movement.
1436 **299** 1s. black 55 45

300 Europa
"Flower"

301 Radio Receiver Dial

1964. Europa.
1437 **300** 3s. blue 2·40 85

1964. 40th Anniv of Austrian Broadcasting Service.
1438 **301** 1s. sepia and red 55 45

302 Old Printing
Press

1964. Sixth International Graphical Federation Congress,
Vienna.
1439 **302** 1s.50 black and drab 55 45

303 Post-bus Station, St.
Gilgen

1964. Stamp Day.
1440 **303** 3s.+70g. multicoloured 1·60 1·30

304 Dr. Adolf Scharf

1965. Pres. Scharf Commemoration.
1441 **304** 1s.50 blue and black 85 45

305
"Reconstruction"

1965. "20 Years of Reconstruction".
1442 **305** 1s.80 lake 65 50

306 University
Seal, 1365

1965. 600th Anniv of Vienna University.
1443 **306** 3s. red and gold 95 80

307 St. George (after
engraving by
Altdorfer)

1965. Danubian Art.
1444 **307** 1s.80 blue 65 50

308 I.T.U. Emblem,
Morse Key and T.V.
Aerial

1965. Centenary of I.T.U.
1445 **308** 3s. violet 95 50

309 F. Raimund

1965. 175th Birth Anniv of Ferdinand Raimund (actor and playwright).
1446 **309** 3s. purple 85 45

310 Egyptian Hieroglyphs on Papyrus

1965. "WIPA" Stamp Exhibition, Vienna (2nd issue). "Development of the Letter".
1447 **310** 1s.50+40g. black and pink 55 45
1448 - 1s.80+50g. black and yellow 65 50
1449 - 2s.20+60g. black and lilac 1·20 95
1450 - 3s.+80g. black & yell 95 80
1451 - 4s.+1s. black & blue 1·50 1·20
1452 - 5s.+1s.20 black & grn 2·20 1·70
DESIGNS: 1s.80, Cuneiform writing; 2s.20, Latin; 3c. Ancient letter and seal; 4s.19th-century letter; 5s. Typewriter.

311 Gymnasts with Wands

1965. Fourth Gymnaestrada, Vienna.
1453 **311** 1s.50 black and blue 55 25
1454 - 3s. black and brown 85 45
DESIGNS: 3s. Girls exercising with tambourines.

312 Dr. I. Semmelweis

1965. Death Cent of Ignaz Semmelweis (physician).
1455 **312** 1s.50 lilac 55 25

313 F. G. Waldmuller (self-portrait)

1965. Death Cent of F. G. Waldmuller (painter).
1456 **313** 3s. black 95 50

314 Red Cross and Gauze

1965. Red Cross Conference, Vienna.
1457 **314** 3s. red and black 95 45

315 Flag and Crowned Eagle

1965. 50th Anniv of Austrian Towns Union.
1458 **315** 1s.50 multicoloured 85 50

316 Austrian Flag, U. N. Emblem and Headquarters

1965. Tenth Anniv of Austria's Membership of U.N.O.
1459 **316** 3s. sepia, red and blue 95 50

317 University Building

1965. 150th Anniv of University of Technology, Vienna.
1460 **317** 1s.50 violet 65 35

318 Bertha von Suttner

1965. 60th Anniv of Nobel Peace Prize Award to Bertha von Suttner (writer).
1461 **318** 1s.50 black 65 35

319 Postman delivering Mail

1965. Stamp Day.
1462 **319** 3s.+70g. green 1·60 1·30

320 Postal Code Map

1966. Introduction of Postal Code System.
1463 **320** 1s.50 black, red & yell 65 35

321 P.T.T. Headquarters

1966. Centenary of Austrian Posts and Telegraphs Administration.
1464 **321** 1s.50 black on cream 65 35

322 M. Ebner-Eschenbach

1966. 50th Death Anniv of Maria Ebner-Eschenbach (writer).
1465 **322** 3s. purple 95 45

323 Big Wheel

1966. Bicentenary of Vienna Prater.
1466 **323** 1s.50 green 65 25

324 Josef Hoffmann

1966. Tenth Death Anniv of Josef Hoffmann (architect).
1467 **324** 3s. brown 95 50

325 Bank Emblem

1966. 150th Anniv of Austrian National Bank.
1468 **325** 3s. brown, grn & drab 95 50

326 Arms of Wiener Neustadt

1966. "Wiener Neustadt 1440–93" Art Exhibition.
1469 **326** 1s.50 multicoloured 65 35

327 Puppy

1966. 120th Anniv of Vienna Animal Protection Society.
1470 **327** 1s.80 black and yellow 65 50

328 Columbine

1966. Alpine Flora. Multicoloured.
1471 **328** 1s.50 Type **328** 50 25
1472 - 1s.80 Turk's cap 55 25
1473 - 2s.20 Wulfenia 65 40
1474 - 3s. Globe flower 75 45
1475 - 4s. Orange lily 85 60
1476 - 5s. Alpine anemone 1·90 85

329 Fair Building

1966. Wels International Fair.
1477 **329** 3s. blue 95 45

330 Peter Anich

1966. Death Bicent of Peter Anich (cartographer).
1478 **330** 1s.80 black 65 35

331 "Suffering"

1966. 15th International Occupational Health Congress, Vienna.
1479 **331** 3s. black and red 95 50

332 *Eunuchus* by Terence (engraving, Johann Gruninger)

1966. Austrian National Library, Vienna. Multicoloured.
1480 1s.50 Type **332** (Theatre collection) 45 20
1481 1s.80 Detail of title page of Willem Blaeu's atlas (Cartography collection) 50 25
1482 2s.20 *Herrengasse, Vienna* (Anton Stutzinger (Pictures and portraits collection)) 55 35
1483 3s. Illustration from Rene of Anjou's *Livre du Cuer d'Amours Espris* (Manuscripts collection) 1·10 50

333 Young Girl

1966. Austrian "Save the Children" Fund.
1484 **333** 3s. black and blue 85 45

334 Strawberries

1966. Fruits. Multicoloured.
1485 50g. Type **334** 55 25
1486 1s. Grapes 55 20
1487 1s.50 Apple 55 25
1488 1s.80 Blackberries 85 70
1489 2s.20 Apricots 85 70
1490 3s. Cherries 95 80

335 16th-century Postman

1966. Stamp Day.
1491 **335** 3s.+70g. multicoloured 1·10 85

336 Arms of Linz University

1966. Inauguration of Linz University.
1492 **336** 3s. multicoloured 95 50

337 Skater of
1867

1967. Centenary of Vienna Skating Assn.
1493 **337** 3s. indigo and blue 95 50

338 Dancer with
Violin

1967. Centenary of "Blue Danube" Waltz.
1494 **338** 3s. purple 95 45

339 Dr. Schonherr

1967. Birth Cent of Dr. Karl Schonherr (poet).
1495 **339** 3s. brown 95 50

340 Ice Hockey
Goalkeeper

1967. World Ice Hockey Championships, Vienna.
1496 **340** 3s. blue and green 95 80

341 Violin and
Organ

1967. 125th Anniv of Vienna Philharmonic Orchestra.
1497 **341** 3s.50 blue 95 45

342 *Mother and Children*
(aquarelle, Peter Fendi)

1967. Mother's Day.
1498 **342** 2s. multicoloured 65 50

343 *Madonna*
(Gothic
wood-carving)

1967. "Gothic Art in Austria" Exhibition, Krems.
1499 **343** 3s. green 95 35

344 Jewelled
Cross

1967. "Salzburg Treasures" Exhibition, Salzburg Cathedral.
1500 **344** 3s.50 multicoloured 95 50

345 "The White
Swan" (from
Kokoschkas
tapestry *Cupid
and Psyche*)

1967. "Art of the Nibelungen District" Exhibition,
Pochlarn.
1501 **345** 2s. multicoloured 65 35

346 Vienna

1967. Tenth European Talks, Vienna.
1502 **346** 3s. black and red 85 45

347 Champion Bull

1967. Centenary of Ried Fair.
1503 **347** 2s. purple 65 35

348 Colorado Potato
Beetle

1967. Sixth Int Plant Protection Congress, Vienna.
1504 **348** 3s. multicoloured 95 50

349 Locomotive No. 671

1967. Centenary of Brenner Railway.
1505 **349** 3s.50 green and brown 95 50

350 *Christ* (fresco
detail)

1967. Lambach Frescoes.
1506 **350** 2s. multicoloured 65 45

351 Prater Hall, Vienna

1967. International Trade Fairs Congress, Vienna.
1507 **351** 2s. purple and cream 85 45

352 Rector's
Medallion and
Chain

1967. 275th Anniv of Fine Arts Academy, Vienna.
1508 **352** 2s. brown, yellow & blue 85 45

353 Bible on Rock
(from
commemorative
coin of 1717)

1967. 450th Anniv of the Reformation.
1509 **353** 3s.50 blue 85 45

354 Forest Trees

1967. 100 Years of Austrian University Forestry Studies.
1510 **354** 3s.50 green 1·30 70

355 Memorial,
Vienna

1967. 150th Anniv of Land Registry.
1511 **355** 2s. green 55 25

356 *St. Leopold*
(stained-glass
window,
Heiligenkreuz
Monastery)

1967. Margrave Leopold the Holy.
1512 **356** 1s.80 multicoloured 55 25

357 "Music and Art"

1967. 150th Anniv of Academy of Music and Dramatic
Art, Vienna.
1513 **357** 3s.50 black and violet 95 50

358 St. Mary's
Altar, Nonnberg
Convent, Salzburg

1967. Christmas.
1514 **358** 2s. green 65 35

359 "The
Letter- carrier"
(from
playing-card)

1967. Stamp Day.
1515 **359** 3s.50+80g. mult 1·60 85

360 Ski Jump,
Stadium and
Mountains

1968. Winter University Games, Innsbruck.
1516 **360** 2s. blue 65 35

361 C. Sitte

1968. 125th Birth Anniv of Camillo Sitte (architect).
1517 **361** 2s. brown 55 45

362 Mother and Child

1968. Mothers' Day.
1518 **362** 2s. olive 55 45

363 "Veterinary
Medicine"

1968. Bicentenary of Vienna Veterinary College.
1519 **363** 3s.50 gold, pur & drab 85 70

364 Bride with Lace
Veil

1968. Centenary of Vorarlberg Lace.
1520 **364** 3s.50 blue 85 70

365 Etrich Limousine

1968. "IFA Wien 1968" Airmail Stamp Exhibition, Vienna.
1521 **365** 2s. brown 55 45
1522 - 3s.50 green 95 80
1523 - 5s. blue 1·70 1·40
DESIGNS: 3s.50, Sud Aviation SE 210 Caravelle; 5s. Douglas DC-8 A-8021.

366 Horse-racing

1968. Centenary of Freudenau Gallop Races.
1524 **366** 3s.50 brown ... 95 ... 50

367 Landsteiner

1968. Birth Centenary of Dr. Karl Landsteiner (physician and pathologist).
1525 **367** 3s.50 blue ... 95 ... 50

368 P. Rosegger

1968. 50th Death Anniv of Peter Rosegger (writer).
1526 **368** 2s. green ... 65 ... 35

369 A. Kauffmann (self-portrait)

1968. Exhibition of Angelica Kauffmann's Paintings, Bregenz.
1527 **369** 2s. violet ... 65 ... 45

370 Statue of Young Man (Helenenberg site)

1968. Magdalensberg Excavations, Carinthia.
1528 **370** 2s. black and green ... 55 ... 35

371 The Bishop (Romanesque carving)

1968. 750th Anniv of Graz-Seckau Diocese.
1529 **371** 2s. grey ... 55 ... 35

372 K. Moser

1968. 50th Death Anniv of Koloman Moser (graphic artist).
1530 **372** 2s. brown and red ... 55 ... 35

373 Human Rights Emblem

1968. Human Rights Year.
1531 **373** 1s.50 red, green & grey ... 95 ... 50

374 Arms and Provincial Shields

1968. 50th Anniv of Republic. Multicoloured.
1532 2s. Type **374** ... 55 ... 35
1533 2s. Karl Renner (first President of Second Republic) ... 55 ... 35
1534 2s. First Article of Constitution ... 55 ... 35

375 Crib, Oberndorf, Salzburg

1968. 150th Anniv of *Silent Night, Holy Night* (carol).
1535 **375** 2s. green ... 65 ... 35

376 Mercury

1968. Stamp Day.
1536 **376** 3s.50+80g. green ... 1·10 ... 1·10

377 Fresco (Troger), Melk Monastery

1968. Baroque Frescoes. Designs showing frescoes in locations given. Multicoloured.
1537 2s. Type **377** ... 65 ... 60
1538 2s. Altenburg Monastery ... 65 ... 60
1539 2s. Rohrenbach-Greillenstein ... 65 ... 60
1540 2s. Ebenfurth Castle ... 65 ... 60
1541 2s. Halbthurn Castle ... 65 ... 60
1542 2s. Maria Treu Church, Vienna ... 65 ... 60
 Nos. 1537/9 are the work of Anton Troger and Nos. 1540/2 that of Franz Maulbertsch.

378 "Madonna and Child"

1969. 500th Anniv of Vienna Diocese. Statues in St. Stephen's Cathedral, Vienna.
1543 **378** 2s. blue ... 65 ... 60
1544 – 2s. grey ... 65 ... 60
1545 – 2s. green ... 65 ... 60
1546 – 2s. purple ... 65 ... 60
1547 – 2s. black ... 65 ... 60
1548 – 2s. brown ... 65 ... 60
DESIGNS: No. 1544, "St. Christopher"; No. 1545, "St. George"; No. 1546, "St. Paul"; No. 1547, "St. Sebastian"; No. 1548, "St. Stephen".

379 Parliament Building, Vienna

1969. Interparliamentary Union Meeting, Vienna.
1549 **379** 2s. green ... 55 ... 35

380 Colonnade

1969. Europa.
1550 **380** 2s. multicoloured ... 1·60 ... 45

381 "Council Members"

1969. 20th Anniv of Council of Europe.
1551 **381** 3s.50 multicoloured ... 95 ... 60

382 Soldiers

1969. Austrian Armed Forces.
1552 **382** 2s. brown and red ... 65 ... 35

383 *Don Giovanni*

1969. Centenary of State Opera, Vienna. Sheet 182×212 mm. T **383** and similar scenes.
MS1553 2s.×8 each brown, red and gold ... 6·50 ... 6·50
DESIGNS—Scenes from Opera and Ballet: *Don Giovanni* (Mozart), *The Magic Flute* (Mozart), *Fidelio* (Beethoven), *Lohengrin* (Wagner), *Don Carlos* (Verdi), *Carmen* (Bizet), *Der Rosenkavlier* (R. Strauss) and *Swan Lake* (Tchaikovsky).

384 Maximilian's Armour

1969. "Maximilian I" Exhibition, Innsbruck.
1554 **384** 2s. black ... 65 ... 35

385 Viennese "Privilege" Seal

1969. 19th International Union of Local Authorities Congress, Vienna.
1555 **385** 2s. red, brown & ochre ... 65 ... 35

386 Young Girl

387 Hands clasping Spanner

1969. 20th Anniv of "SOS" Children's Villages Movement.
1556 **386** 2s. brown and green ... 65 ... 35

1969. 50th Anniv of Int Labour Organization.
1557 **387** 2s. green ... 65 ... 35

388 Austrian "Flag" encircling Globe

1969. "Austrians Living Abroad" Year.
1558 **388** 3s.50 red and green ... 95 ... 50

389 *El Cid killing a Bull* (Goya)

1969. Bicentenary of Albertina Art Collection, Vienna. Multicoloured.
1559 2s. Type **389** ... 55 ... 55
1560 2s. *Young Hare* (Durer) ... 55 ... 55
1561 2s. *Madonna with Pomegranate* (Raphael) ... 55 ... 55
1562 2s. *The Painter and the Amateur* (Bruegel) ... 55 ... 55
1563 2s. *Rubens's Son, Nicholas* (Rubens) ... 55 ... 55
1564 2s. *Self-portrait* (Rembrandt) ... 55 ... 55
1565 2s. *Madame de Pompadour* (detail, Guerin) ... 55 ... 55
1566 2s. *The Artist's Wife* (Schiele) ... 55 ... 55

390 Pres. Jonas

1969. Pres. Franz Jonas's 70th Birthday.
1567 **390** 2s. blue and grey ... 55 ... 45

391 Posthorn and Lightning over Globe

1969. 50th Anniv of Post and Telegraph Employees Union.
1568 **391** 2s. multicoloured ... 55 ... 45

392 Savings Bank (c. 1450)

1969. 150th Anniv of Austrian Savings Bank.
1569 **392** 2s. green and silver ... 55 ... 45

393 *The Madonna*
(Egger-Lienz)

1969. Christmas.
1570	**393**	2s. purple and yellow	55	45

394 Unken,
Salzburg,
Post-house Sign
(after F. Zeller)

1969. Stamp Day.
1571	**394**	3s.50+80g. black, red and stone	95	85

395 J. Schoffel

1970. 60th Death Anniv of Josef Schoffel ("Saviour of the Vienna Woods").
1572	**395**	2s. purple	45	35

396 St. Clement
Hofbauer

1970. 150th Death Anniv of St. Clement Hofbauer (theologian).
1573	**396**	2s. brown and green	45	35

397 Chancellor Leopold Figl

1970. 25th Anniv of Austrian Republic.
1574	**397**	2s. olive	65	35
1575	-	2s. brown	65	35

DESIGN: No. 1575, Belvedere Castle.

398 Krimml
Waterfalls

1970. Nature Conservation Year.
1576	**398**	2s. green	1·10	70

399 Oldest
University Seal

1970. 300th Anniv of Leopold Franz University, Innsbruck.
1577	**399**	2s. black and red	55	45

400 "Musikverein" Organ

1970. Centenary of "Musikverein" Building.
1578	**400**	2s. purple and gold	55	45

401 Tower Clock,
1450–1550

1970. Antique Clocks.
1579	**401**	1s.50 brown and cream	55	45
1580	-	1s.50 green & lt green	55	45
1581	-	2s. blue and pale blue	65	50
1582	-	2s. red and purple	65	50
1583	-	3s.50 brown and buff	1·10	85
1584	-	3s.50 purple and lilac	1·10	85

DESIGNS: No. 1580, Empire "lyre" clock, 1790–1815; No. 1581, Pendant ball clock, 1600–50; No. 1582, Pocket-watch and signet, 1800–30; No. 1583, Bracket clock, 1720–60; No. 1584, "Biedermeier" pendulum clock and musical-box, 1820–50.

402 *The Beggar
Student*
(Millocker)

1970. Famous Operettas.
1585	**402**	1s.50 turquoise & green	55	45
1586	-	1s.50 blue and yellow	55	45
1587	-	2s. purple and pink	65	50
1588	-	2s. brown and green	65	50
1589	-	3s.50 blue and light blue	1·10	85
1590	-	3s.50 blue and buff	1·10	85

OPERETTAS: No. 1586, *Die Fledermaus* (Johann Strauss the younger); 1587, *A Waltz Dream* (O. Straus); 1588, *The Birdseller* (C. Zeller); 1589, *The Merry Widow* (F. Lehar); 1590,"*Two Hearts in Waltz-time* (R. Stoiz).

403 Scene from *The
Gipsy Baron* (J. Strauss)

1970. 25th Anniv of Bregenz Festival.
1591	**403**	3s.50 blue, buff & ult	95	50

404 Festival Emblem

1970. 50th Anniv of Salzburg Festival.
1592	**404**	3s.50 multicoloured	95	50

405 T. Koschat

1970. 125th Birth Anniv of Thomas Koschat (composer and poet).
1593	**405**	2s. brown	55	45

406 "Head of St. John",
from sculpture *Mount
of Olive*, Ried Church
(attribs, Ried Church
(attributed to T.
Schwanthaler)

1970. 13th World Veterans Federation General Assembly.
1594	**406**	3s.50 sepia	95	50

407 Climbers and
Mountains

1970. "Walking and Mountaineering".
1595	**407**	2s. blue and mauve	55	35

408 A. Cossmann

1970. Birth Cent of Alfred Cossmann (engraver).
1596	**408**	2s. brown	55	35

409 Arms of
Carinthia

1970. 50th Anniv of Carinthian Plebiscite.
1597	**409**	2s. multicoloured	55	35

410 U.N. Emblem

1970. 25th Anniv of United Nations.
1598	**410**	3s.50 blue and black	95	50

411 *Adoration of the
Shepherds* (carving,
Garsten Monastery)

1970. Christmas.
1599	**411**	2s. blue	45	35

412 Saddle, Harness
and Posthorn

1970. Stamp Day.
1600	**412**	3s.50+80g. black, yellow and grey	1·10	1·10

413 Pres. K. Renner

1970. Birth Centenary of Pres. Renner.
1601	**413**	2s. purple	55	35

414 Beethoven
(after painting by
Waldmuller)

1970. Birth Bicentenary of Beethoven.
1602	**414**	3s.50 black and stone	95	60

415 E.
Handel-Mazzetti

1971. Birth Centenary of Enrica Handel-Mazzetti (novelist).
1603	**415**	2s. brown	45	25

416 "Safety for Children"

1971. Road Safety.
1604	**416**	2s. multicoloured	65	35

417 Florentine Bowl, c.
1580

1971. Austrian Art Treasures (1st series). Sculpture and Applied Art.
1605	**417**	1s.50 green and grey	55	45
1606	-	2s. purple and grey	85	70
1607	-	3s.50 yellow, brn & grey	1·30	1·00

DESIGNS: 2s. Ivory equestrian statuette of Joseph I, 1693 (Matthias Steinle); 3s.50, Salt-cellar, c. 1570 (Cellini). See also Nos. 1609/11, 1632/4 and 1651/3.

418 Shield of Trade
Association

1971. 23rd International Chamber of Commerce Congress, Vienna.
1608	**418**	3s.50 multicoloured	85	50

419 *Jacopo de
Strada* (Titian)

1971. Austrian Art Treasures (2nd series).
1609	**419**	1s.50 purple	55	45
1610	-	2s. black	85	70
1611	-	3s.50 brown	1·30	1·00

PAINTINGS: 2s. *The Village Feast* (Brueghel); 3s.50, *Young Venetian Woman* (Durer).

420 Notary's Seal

1971. Austrian Notarial Statute Cent Congress.
1612 **420** 3s.50 purple and brown 85 45

421 "St. Matthew" (altar sculpture)

1971. "Krems Millennium of Art" Exhibition.
1613 **421** 2s. brown and purple 45 25

422 Dr. A. Neilreich

1971. Death Cent of Dr. August Neilreich (botanist).
1614 **422** 2s. brown 45 25

423 Singer with Lyre

1971. International Choir Festival, Vienna.
1615 **423** 4s. blue, gold & lt blue 95 80

424 Arms of Kitzbuhel

1971. 700th Anniv of Kitzbuhel.
1616 **424** 2s.50 multicoloured 55 45

425 Stock Exchange Building

1971. Bicentenary of Vienna Stock Exchange.
1617 **425** 4s. brown 85 50

426 Old and New Fair Halls

1971. "50 Years of Vienna International Fairs".
1618 **426** 2s.50 purple 55 45

427 O.G.B. Emblem

1971. 25th Anniv of Austrian Trade Unions Federation.
1619 **427** 2s. multicoloured 45 35

428 Arms and Insignia

1971. 50th Anniv of Burgenland Province.
1620 **428** 4s. multicoloured 45 35

429 "Marcus" Veteran Car

1971. 75th Anniv of Austrian Automobile, Motor Cycle and Touring Club.
1621 **429** 4s. black and green 85 60

430 Europa Bridge, Brenner Highway

1971. Inauguration of Brenner Highway.
1622 **430** 4s. blue 85 60

431 Iron-ore Workings, Erzberg

1971. 25 Years of Nationalized Industries.
1623 **431** 1s.50 brown 55 45
1624 – 2s. blue 55 45
1625 – 4s. green 1·10 85
DESIGNS: 2s. Nitrogen Works, Linz; 4s. Iron and Steel works, Linz.

432 Electric Train on the Semmering Line

1971. Railway Anniversaries.
1626 **432** 2s. purple 55 45

433 E. Tschermak-Seysenegg

1971. Birth Centenary of Dr. E. Tshermak-Seysenegg (biologist).
1627 **433** 2s. purple and grey 45 35

434 Angling

1971. Sports.
1628 **434** 2s. brown 45 35

435 The Infant Jesus as Saviour (from miniature by Durer)

1971. Christmas.
1629 **435** 2s. multicoloured 55 45

436 "50 Years"

1971. 50th Anniv of Austrian Philatelic Clubs Association.
1630 **436** 4s.+1s.50 pur & gold 1·30 1·00

437 Franz Grillparzer (from miniature by Daffinger)

1972. Death Centenary of Grillparzer (dramatist).
1631 **437** 2s. black, brown & stone 65 35

438 Roman Fountain, Friesach

1972. Austrian Art Treasures (3rd series). Fountains.
1632 **438** 1s.50 purple 55 45
1633 – 2s. brown 85 70
1634 – 2s.50 green 1·30 1·00
DESIGNS: 2s. Lead Fountain, Heiligenkreuz Abbey; 2s.50. Leopold Fountain, Innsbruck.

439 Hofburg Palace

1972. Fourth European Postal Ministers' Conf, Vienna.
1635 **439** 4s. violet 95 80

440 Heart Patient

1972. World Heart Month.
1636 **440** 4s. brown 95 80

441 Woman's Head (sculpture, Gurk Cathedral)

1972. 900th Anniv of Gurk Diocese.
1637 **441** 2s. purple and gold 65 50

442 Vienna Town Hall and Congress Emblem

1972. Ninth International Public and Co-operative Economy Congress, Vienna.
1638 **442** 4s. black, red and yellow 1·10 70

443 Lienz–Pelos Pylon Line

1972. 25th Anniv of Electric Power Nationalization.
1639 **443** 70g. violet and grey 45 35
1640 – 2s.50 brown and grey 65 50
1641 – 4s. blue and grey 1·10 85
DESIGNS: 2s.50, Vienna-Semmering Power Station; 4s. Zemm Dam and lake.

444 Runner with Torch

1972. Passage of the Olympic Torch through Austria.
1642 **444** 2s. brown and red 55 45

445 Hermes (C. Laib)

1972. "Late Gothic Art" Exhibition, Salzburg.
1643 **445** 2s. purple 55 45

446 Pears

1972. Amateur Gardeners' Congress, Vienna.
1644 **446** 2s.50 multicoloured 75 60

447 "Spanish Walk"

1972. 400th Anniv of the Spanish Riding School, Vienna. Sheet 136×181 mm containing T **447** and similar square designs each in purple, red and gold.
MS1645 2s. Type **447**; 2s. "Piaffe"; 2s.50 "Levade"; 2s.50 "On the long rein"; 4s. "Capriole"; 4s. "Courbette" 5·50 5·50

448 University Arms

1972. Cent of University of Agriculture, Vienna.
1646 **448** 2s. multicoloured 55 45

449 Old University Buildings (after F. Danreiter)

1972. 350th Anniv of Paris Lodron University, Salzburg.
1647	**449**	4s. brown	95	80

450 C. M. Ziehrer

1972. 50th Death Anniv of Carl M. Ziehrer (composer and conductor).
1648	**450**	2s. red	55	45

451 "Virgin and Child", Inzersdorf Church

1972. Christmas.
1649	**451**	2s. purple and green	65	50

452 18th-century Viennese Postman

1972. Stamp Day.
1650	**452**	4s.+1s. green	1·30	1·00

453 State Sledge of Maria Theresa

1972. Austrian Art Treasures (4th series). Carriages from the Imperial Coach House.
1651	**453**	1s.50 brown and bistre	55	45
1652	-	2s. green and bistre	85	70
1653	-	2s.50 purple and bistre	1·30	1·00

DESIGNS: 2s. Coronation landau; 2s.50, Hapsburg State Coach.

454 Telephone Network

1972. Completion of Austrian Telephone System Automation.
1654	**454**	2s. black and yellow	55	45

455 "Drug Addict"

1973. Campaign against Drug Abuse.
1655	**455**	2s. multicoloured	75	45

456 A. Petzold

1973. 50th Death Anniv of Alfons Petzold (writer).
1656	**456**	2s. purple	55	45

457 Korner

1973. Birth Centenary of Pres. Theodor Korner (President, 1951–57).
1657	**457**	2s. purple and grey	55	45

458 McDonell DC-9 OE-LDA

1973. Austrian Aviation Anniversaries.
1658	**458**	2s. blue and red	55	45

459 Otto Loewi

1973. Birth Cent of Otto Loewi (pharmacologist).
1659	**459**	4s. violet	95	70

460 "Succour"

1973. 25th Anniv of National Federation of Austrian Social Insurance Institutes.
1660	**460**	2s. blue	55	45

461 Telephone Dial within Posthorn

1973. Europa.
1661	**461**	2s.50 black, yell & orge	2·20	70

462 Fair Emblem

1973. 25th Dornbirn Fair.
1662	**462**	2s. multicoloured	65	35

463 Military Pentathlon

1973. 25th Anniv of International Military Sports Council and 23rd Military Pentathlon Championships, Wiener Neustadt.
1663	**463**	4s. green	1·00	55

464 Leo Slezak

1973. Birth Centenary of Leo Slezak (operatic tenor).
1664	**464**	4s. brown	1·00	55

465 Main Entrance, Hofburg Palace

1973. 39th International Statistical Institute's Congress, Vienna.
1665	**465**	2s. brown, red and grey	55	30

466 *Admiral Tegetthof Icebound* (J. Payer)

1973. Centenary of Discovery of Franz Josef Land.
1666	**466**	2s.50 green	80	45

467 I.U.L.C.S. Arms

1973. 13th International Union of Leather Chemists' Societies Congress, Vienna.
1667	**467**	4s. multicoloured	1·00	65

468 *Academy of Sciences, Vienna* (B. Bellotto)

1973. Cent of Int Meteorological Organization.
1668	**468**	2s.50 violet	80	45

469 Max Reinhardt

1973. Birth Centenary of Max Reinhardt (theatrical director).
1669	**469**	2s. purple	55	45

470 F. Hanusch

1973. 50th Death Anniv of Ferdinand Hanusch (politician).
1670	**470**	2s. purple	55	30

471 Light Harness Racing

1973. Centenary of Vienna Trotting Assn.
1671	**471**	2s. green	65	55

472 Radio Operator

1973. 50th Anniv of International Criminal Police Organization (Interpol).
1672	**472**	4s. violet	90	65

473 Petzval Camera Lens

1973. "Europhot" (professional photographers) Congress, Vienna.
1673	**473**	2s.50 multicoloured	90	55

474 Aqueduct, Hollen Valley

1973. Centenary of Vienna's 1st Mountain-spring Aqueduct.
1674	**474**	2s. brown, red & blue	55	30

475 Almsee

1973. Views. (a) Size 23×29 mm.
1674a	-	20g. blue and light blue	90	45
1675	-	50g. green & lt green	45	25
1676	-	1s. sepia and brown	45	25
1677	-	1s.50 purple and pink	65	30
1678	-	2s. indigo and blue	80	30
1679	-	2s.50 deep lilac & lilac	90	30
1680	-	3s. ultramarine & blue	1·10	30
1680a	-	3s.50 brown & orange	1·10	45
1681	**475**	4s. violet and lilac	1·10	30
1681a	-	4s.20 black and grey	1·70	95
1682	-	4s.50 dp green & green	1·50	45
1683	-	5s. violet and lilac	1·50	45
1683a	-	5s.50 blue and violet	2·50	1·90
1683b	-	5s.60 olive and green	3·25	2·75
1684	-	6s. lilac and pink	2·10	30
1684a	-	6s.50 blue & turquoise	2·00	45
1685	-	7s. deep green & green	2·75	45
1685a	-	7s.50 purple & mauve	3·25	45
1686	-	8s. brown and pink	2·75	65
1686a	-	9s. red and pink	3·25	65
1687	-	10s. myrtle and green	3·25	45
1688	-	11s. red and orange	4·00	45
1688a	-	12s. sepia and brown	4·00	95
1688b	-	14s. myrtle and green	5·00	95
1688c	-	16s. brown and orange	5·50	95
1688d	-	20s. green and bistre	6·75	95

(b) Size 28×37 mm.
1689	-	50s. violet and grey	20·00	2·40

(c) Size 17×20 mm.
1690	-	3s. ultramarine and blue	80	65

DESIGNS: 20g. Friedstadt Keep, Muhlviertel; 50g. Zillertal; 1s. Kahlenbergerdorf, Vienna; 1s.50, Bludenz; 2s. Old bridge, Finstermunz; 2s.50, Murau, Styria; 3s. Bischofsmutze and Alpine farm; 3s.50, Osterkirche, Oberwart; 4s.20, Hirschegg, Kleinwalsertal; 4s.50, Windmill, Retz; 5s. Ruins of Aggstein Castle; 5s.50, Peace Chapel, Stoderzinken; 5s.60, Riezlern, Kleinwalsertal; 6s. Lindauer Hut, Ratikon Massif; 6s.50, Villach, Carinthia; 7s. Falkenstein Castle; 7s.50, Hohensalzburg Fortress; 8s. Votive column, Reiteregg, Styria; 9s. Asten valley; 10s. Neusiedlersee; 11s. Enns; 12s. Kufstein Fortress; 14s. Weisszee, Salzburg; 16s. Bad Tatzmannsdorf open-air museum; 20s. Myra Falls, Muggendorf; 50s. Hofburg, Vienna.

476 The Nativity (stained-glass window, St. Erhard Church, Bretenau)

1973. Christmas.
1691	**476**	2s. multicoloured	55	30

477 *Archangel Gabriel* (carving by Lorenz Luchsperger)

1973. Stamp Day.
1692 **477** 4s.+1s. purple 1·20 1·20

478 Dr. Fritz Pregl

1973. 50th Anniv of Award of Nobel Prize for Chemistry to Fritz Pregl.
1693 **478** 4s. blue 1·00 65

479 Telex Machine and Globe

1974. 50th Anniv of Radio Austria.
1694 **479** 2s.50 blue & ultramarine 80 45

480 Hugo Hofmannsthal

1974. Birth Cent of Hugo Hofmannsthal (writer).
1695 **480** 4s. blue 1·00 65

481 Anton Bruckner (composer)

1974. Inaug of Bruckner Memorial Centre, Linz.
1696 **481** 4s. brown 1·10 65

482 Vegetables

1974. Second Int Horticultural Show, Vienna. Multicoloured.
1697 **482** 2s. Type 482 55 45
1698 2s.50 Fruit 90 75
1699 4s. Flowers 1·10 95

483 Head from Ancient Seal

1974. 750th Anniv of Judenburg.
1700 **483** 2s. multicoloured 65 40

484 Karl Kraus

1974. Birth Centenary of Karl Kraus (poet).
1701 **484** 4s. red 1·00 65

485 *St. Michael* (wood-carving, Thomas Schwanthaler)

1974. "Sculptures by the Schwanthaler Family" Exhibition, Reichersberg.
1702 **485** 2s.50 green 90 45

486 *King Arthur* (statue, Innsbruck)

1974. Europa.
1703 **486** 2s.50 blue and brown 2·20 95

487 *Early De Dion-Bouton Motor-tricycle*

1974. 75th Anniv of Austrian Association of Motoring, Motor Cycling and Cycling.
1704 **487** 2s. brown and grey 55 45

488 *Mask of Satyr's Head*

1974. "Renaissance in Austria" Exhibition, Schallaburg Castle.
1705 **488** 2s. black, brown & gold 55 45

489 I.R.U. Emblem

1974. 14th International Road Haulage Union Congress, Innsbruck.
1706 **489** 4s. black and orange 1·10 65

490 F. A. Maulbertsch

1974. 205th Birth Anniv of Franz Maulbertsch (painter).
1707 **490** 2s. brown 65 30

491 Gendarmes of 1849 and 1974

1974. 125th Anniv of Austrian Gendarmerie.
1708 **491** 2s. multicoloured 65 30

492 Fencing

1974. Sports.
1709 **492** 2s.50 black and orange 80 45

493 Transport Emblems

1974. European Transport Ministers' Conference, Vienna.
1710 **493** 4s. multicoloured 1·00 65

494 *St. Virgilius* (wood-carving)

1974. 1200 Years of Christianity in Salzburg.
1711 **494** 2s. blue 65 30

495 Pres. F. Jonas

1974. Pres. Franz Jonas Commemoration.
1712 **495** 2s. black 65 30

496 F. Stelzhamer

1974. Death Cent of Franz Stelzhamer (poet).
1713 **496** 2s. blue 65 30

497 Diving

1974. 13th European Swimming, Diving and Water-polo Championships.
1714 **497** 4s. brown and blue 1·10 65

498 *F. R. von Hebra* (founder of German scientific dermatology)

1974. 30th Meeting of German-speaking Dermatologists Association, Graz.
1715 **498** 4s. brown 1·00 65

499 A. Schonberg

1974. Birth Cent of Arnold Schonberg (composer).
1716 **499** 2s.50 purple 90 45

500 Broadcasting Studios, Salzburg

1974. 50th Anniv of Austrian Broadcasting.
1717 **500** 2s. multicoloured 65 30

501 E. Eysler

1974. 25th Death Anniv of Edmund Eysler (composer).
1718 **501** 2s. green 55 45

502 19th-century Postman and Mail Transport

1974. Centenary of U.P.U.
1719 **502** 2s. brown and mauve 65 55
1720 – 4s. blue and grey 1·00 85
DESIGN: 4s. Modern postman and mail transport.

503 Sports Emblem

1974. 25th Anniv of Football Pools in Austria.
1721 **503** 70g. red, black and green 55 30

504 Steel Gauntlet grasping Rose

1974. Nature Protection.
1722 **504** 2s. multicoloured 90 55

505 C. D. von Dittersdorf

1974. 175th Death Anniv of Carl Ditters von Dittersdorf (composer).
1723 **505** 2s. green 65 30

506 Mail Coach and P.O., 1905

1974. Stamp Day.
1724 **506** 4s.+2s. blue 1·50 95

507 *Virgin Mary and Child* (wood-carving)

1974. Christmas.
1725 **507** 2s. brown and gold 55 40

508 F. Schmidt

1974. Birth Centenary of Franz Schmidt (composer).
1726 **508** 4s. black and stone 1·00 65

509 *St. Christopher and Child* (altarpiece)

1975. European Architectural Heritage Year and 125th Anniv of Austrian Commission for Preservation of Monuments.
1727 **509** 2s.50 brown and grey 80 40

510 Slalom

1975. Winter Olympics, Innsbruck (1976) (1st issue). Multicoloured.
1728 **510** 1s.+50g. Type **510** 35 30
1729 1s.50+70g. Ice hockey 45 40
1730 2s.+90g. Ski-jumping 65 55
1731 4s.+1s.90 Bobsleighing 1·30 1·10
 See also Nos. 1747/50.

511 Seat-belt around Skeletal Limbs

1975. Car Safety-belts Campaign.
1732 **511** 70g. multicoloured 45 40

512 Stained-glass Window, Vienna Town Hall

1975. 11th European Communities' Day.
1733 **512** 2s.50 multicoloured 65 45

513 "The Buffer State"

1975. 30th Anniv of Foundation of Austrian Second Republic.
1734 **513** 2s. black and brown 55 30

514 Forest Scene

1975. 50th Anniv of Foundation of Austrian Forests Administration.
1735 **514** 2s. green 80 40

515 The High Priest (M. Pacher)

1975. Europa.
1736 **515** 2s.50 multicoloured 2·20 45

516 Gosaukamm Cable-way

1975. Fourth International Ropeways Congress, Vienna.
1737 **516** 2s. blue and red 65 30

517 J. Misson

1975. Death Centenary of Josef Misson (poet).
1738 **517** 2s. brown and red 55 30

518 "Setting Sun"

1975. Nat Pensioners' Assn Meeting, Vienna.
1739 **518** 1s.50 multicoloured 55 30

519 F. Porsche

1975. Birth Centenary of Prof. Ferdinand Porsche (motor engineer).
1740 **519** 1s.50 purple & green 55 30

520 L. Fall

1975. 50th Death Anniv of Leo Fall (composer).
1741 **520** 2s. violet 55 30

521 Judo "Shoulder Throw"

1975. World Judo Championships, Vienna.
1742 **521** 2s.50 multicoloured 80 45

522 Heinrich Angeli

1975. 50th Death Anniv of Heinrich Angeli (court painter).
1743 **522** 2s. purple 65 30

523 J. Strauss

1975. 150th Birth Anniv of Johann Strauss the Younger (composer).
1744 **523** 4s. brown and ochre 1·10 65

524 "The Cellist"

1975. 75th Anniv of Vienna Symphony Orchestra.
1745 **524** 2s.50 blue and silver 65 40

525 "One's Own House"

1975. 50th Anniv of Austrian Building Societies.
1746 **525** 2s. multicoloured 55 30

1975. Winter Olympic Games, Innsbruck (1976) (2nd issue). As T **510**. Multicoloured.
1747 70g.+30g. Figure-skating (pairs) 45 40
1748 2s.+1s. Cross-country skiing 55 45
1749 2s.50+1s. Tobogganing 90 75
1750 4s.+2s. Rifle-shooting (biathlon) 1·30 1·10

526 Scene on Folding Fan

1975. Bicentenary of Salzburg State Theatre.
1751 **526** 1s.50 multicoloured 55 30

527 Austrian Stamps of 1850, 1922 and 1945

1975. Stamp Day. 125th Anniv of Austrian Postage Stamps.
1752 **527** 4s.+2s. multicoloured 1·30 1·10

528 *Virgin and Child* (Schottenaltar, Vienna)

1975. Christmas.
1753 **528** 2s. lilac and gold 65 40

529 "Spiralbaum" (F. Hundertwasser)

1975. Modern Austrian Art.
1754 **529** 4s. multicoloured 1·70 1·20

530 Old Theatre Building

1976. Bicentenary of the Burgtheatre, Vienna. Sheet 130×60 mm containing T **530** and similar horiz design.
MS1755 3s. blue (Type **530**); 3s. brown (Interior of the modern theatre) 2·00 2·00

531 Dr. R. Barany

1976. Birth Centenary of Dr. Robert Barany (Nobel prizewinner for Medicine, 1915).
1756 **531** 3s. brown and blue 1·00 45

532 Ammonite Fossil

1976. Cent Exn, Vienna Natural History Museum.
1757 **532** 3s. multicoloured 1·00 45

533 9th-century Coronation Throne

1976. Millenary of Carinthia.
1758 **533** 3s. black and yellow 1·00 45

534 Stained-glass Window, Klosterneuburg

1976. Babenberg Exhibition, Lilienfeld.
1759 **534** 3s. multicoloured 1·00 45

535 *The Siege of Linz* (contemporary engraving)

1976. 350th Anniv of the Peasants' War in Upper Austria.
1760 **535** 4s. black and green 1·00 55

536 Bowler delivering Ball

1976. 11th World Skittles Championships, Vienna.
1761 **536** 4s. black and orange 1·00 55

537 *St. Wolfgang* (altar painting by Michael Pacher)

1976. International Art Exhibition, St. Wolfgang.
1762 **537** 6s. purple 1·70 95

538 Tassilo Cup, Kremsmunster

1976. Europa.
1763 **538** 4s. multicoloured 2·75 95

539 Fair Emblem

1976. 25th Austrian Timber Fair, Klagenfurt.
1764 **539** 3s. multicoloured 1·00 45

540 Constantin Economo

1976. Birth Centenary of Constantin Economo (brain specialist).
1765 **540** 3s. brown 1·00 45

541 Bohemian Court Chancellery, Vienna

1976. Centenary of Administrative Court.
1766 **541** 6s. brown 1·70 95

542 Arms of Lower Austria

1976. Millenary of Austria. Sheet 135×180 mm containing T **542** and similar vert designs showing provincial arms.
MS1767 2s.×9 multicoloured 5·00 5·00
DESIGNS: Arms of Lower Austria, Upper Austria, Styria, Carinthia, Vorarlberg, Salzburg, Burgenland and Vienna.

543 Cancer the Crab

1976. Fight against Cancer.
1768 **543** 2s.50 multicoloured 80 45

544 U.N. Emblem and Bridge

1976. Tenth Anniv of U.N. Industrial Development Organization.
1769 **544** 3s. blue and gold 1·00 55

545 Punched Tapes and Map of Europe

1976. 30th Anniv of Austrian Press Agency.
1770 **545** 1s.50 multicoloured 45 30

546 V. Kaplan

1976. Birth Centenary of Viktor Kaplan (inventor of turbine).
1771 **546** 2s.50 multicoloured 65 55

547 *The Birth of Christ* (Konrad von Friesach)

1976. Christmas.
1772 **547** 3s. multicoloured 90 45

548 Postilion's Hat and Posthorn

1976. Stamp Day.
1773 **548** 6s.+2s. black & lilac 1·80 1·50

549 R. M. Rilke

1976. 50th Death Anniv of Rainer Maria Rilke (poet).
1774 **549** 3s. violet 90 45

550 *Augustin the Piper* (Arik Brauer)

1976. Austrian Modern Art.
1775 **550** 6s. multicoloured 1·70 95

551 City Synagogue

1976. 150th Anniv of Vienna City Synagogue.
1776 **551** 1s.50 multicoloured 45 30

552 N. J. von Jacquin

1977. 250th Birth Anniv of Nikolaus Joseph Freiherrn von Jacquin (botanist).
1777 **552** 4s. brown 1·00 65

553 Oswald von Wolkenstein

1977. 600th Birth Anniv of Oswald von Wolkenstein (poet).
1778 **553** 3s. multicoloured 90 45

554 Handball

1977. World Indoor Handball Championships, Group B, Austria.
1779 **554** 1s.50 multicoloured 45 30

555 A. Kubin

1977. Birth Centenary of Alfred Kubin (writer and illustrator).
1780 **555** 6s. blue 1·70 95

556 Cathedral Spire

1977. 25th Anniv of Re-opening of St. Stephen's Cathedral, Vienna.
1781 **556** 2s.50 brown 90 75
1782 - 3s. blue 1·00 85
1783 - 4s. purple 1·50 1·20
DESIGNS: 3s. West front; 4s. Interior.

557 F. Herzmanovsky-Orlando

1977. Birth Centenary of Fritz Herzmanovsky-Orlando (writer).
1784 **557** 6s. green and gold 1·70 95

558 I.A.E.A. Emblem

1977. 20th Anniv of Int Atomic Energy Agency.
1785 **558** 3s. lt blue, gold & blue 90 45

559 Arms of Schwanenstadt

1977. 350th Anniv of Schwanenstadt.
1786 **559** 3s. multicoloured 90 45

560 Attersee

1977. Europa.
1787 **560** 6s. green 4·00 1·40

561 Globe (Vincenzo Coronelli)

1977. Fifth International Symposium and 25th Anniv of Coronelli World Federation of Globe Friends.
1788 **561** 3s. black and stone 90 45

562 Canoeist

1977. World "White Water" Canoe Championships.
1789 **562** 4s. multicoloured 1·00 55

563 *The Samaritan* (Francesco Bassano)

1977. 50th Anniv of Austrian Workers' Samaritan Federation.
1790 **563** 1s.50 multicoloured 55 30

564 Papermakers' Arms

1977. 17th Conference of European Committee of Pulp and Paper Technology.
1791 **564** 3s. multicoloured 90 45

565 "Freedom"

1977. Martyrs for Austrian Freedom.
1792 **565** 2s.50 blue and red 80 45

566 Steam Locomotive, Austria, 1837

1977. 140th Anniv of Austrian Railways. Multicoloured.
1793 1s.50 Type **566** 65 55
1794 2s.50 Type 214 steam locomotive, 1928 1·00 85
1795 3s. Type 1044 electric locomotive, 1974 1·70 1·40

567 *Madonna and Child* (wood carving, Mariastein Pilgrimage Church)

1977. Christmas.
1796 **567** 3s. multicoloured 90 45

568 *Danube Maiden*
(Wolfgang Hutter)

1977. Austrian Modern Art.
1797 **568** 6s. multicoloured 1·70 95

569 Emanuel
Herrmann
(inventor of
postcard)

1977. Stamp Day.
1798 **569** 6s.+2s. brown and cin-
namon 2·00 1·40

570 Egon Friedell

1978. Birth Centenary of Egon Friedell (writer).
1799 **570** 3s. black and blue 90 45

571 Underground Train

1978. Opening of Vienna Underground Railway.
1800 **571** 3s. multicoloured 1·10 55

572 Rifleman and Skier

1978. Biathlon World Championships, Hochfilzen.
1801 **572** 4s. multicoloured 1·10 65

573 Aztec Feather Shield

1978. 30th Anniv of Museum of Ethnology, Vienna.
1802 **573** 3s. multicoloured 1·00 45

574 Leopold
Kunschak

1978. 25th Death Anniv of Leopold Kunschak (politician).
1803 **574** 3s. blue 1·00 45

575 "Mountain
Peasants"

1978. Birth Centenary of Suitbert Lobisser (wood
engraver).
1804 **575** 3s. brown and stone 1·00 45

576 Black Grouse,
Hunting Satchel and
Fowling Piece

1978. International Hunting Exn, Marchegg.
1805 **576** 6s. blue, brown & turq 1·70 95

577 Map of Europe
and Austrian
Parliament Building

1978. Third Interparliamentary European Security
Conference, Vienna.
1806 **577** 4s. multicoloured 1·00 65

578 Riegersburg Castle,
Styria

1978. Europa.
1807 **578** 6s. purple 4·00 95

579 *Admont Pieta*
(Salzburg Circle
Master)

1978. "Gothic Art in Styria" Exhibition.
1808 **579** 2s.50 black and ochre 65 55

580 Ort Castle

1978. 700th Anniv of Gmunden Town Charter.
1809 **580** 3s. multicoloured 1·10 45

581 Face
surrounded by
Fruit and Flowers

1978. 25th Anniv of Austrian Association for Social
Tourism.
1810 **581** 6s. multicoloured 1·70 95

582 Franz Lehar
and Villa at Bad
Ischl

1978. International Lehar Congress.
1811 **582** 6s. blue 1·70 95

583 Tools and Globe

1978. 15th Congress of International Federation of
Building and Wood Workers.
1812 **583** 1s.50 black, yellow & red 55 45

584 Knights Jousting

1978. 700th Anniv of Battle of Durnkrut and
Jedenspeigen.
1813 **584** 3s. multicoloured 1·10 65

585 Bridge over River
Drau

1978. 1100th Anniv of Villach.
1814 **585** 3s. multicoloured 1·10 65

586 City Seal, 1440

1978. 850th Anniv of Graz.
1815 **586** 4s. brown, green & grey 1·30 75

587 Angler

1978. 25th Sport Fishing Championships, Vienna.
1816 **587** 4s. multicoloured 1·30 75

588 Distorted Pattern

1978. Handicapped People.
1817 **588** 6s. black and brown 1·70 95

589 Concrete Chain

1978. Ninth International Concrete and Prefabrication
Industry Congress, Vienna.
1818 **589** 2s.50 multicoloured 65 55

590 *Grace* (Albin
Egger-Lienz)

1978. European Family Congress.
1819 **590** 6s. multicoloured 1·70 95

591 Lise Meitner

1978. Birth Centenary of Lise Meitner (physicist).
1820 **591** 6s. violet 1·70 95

592 Victor Adler (bust,
Anton Hamek)

1978. 60th Death Anniv of Victor Adler (statesman).
1821 **592** 3s. black and red 1·10 45

593 Franz Schubert
(after Josef
Kriehuber)

1978. 150th Death Anniv of Franz Schubert (composer).
1822 **593** 6s. brown 2·00 95

594 *Madonna
and Child*
(Martino
Altomonte,
Wilhering
Collegiate
Church)

1978. Christmas.
1823 **594** 3s. multicoloured 1·00 45

595 Postbus, 1913

1978. Stamp Day.
1824 **595** 10s.+5s. multicoloured 3·00 2·50

596 *Archduke Johann Hut,
Grossglockner* (E. T.
Compton)

1978. Centenary of Austrian Alpine Club.
1825 **596** 1s.50 violet and gold 55 45

597 *Adam* (Rudolf
Hausner)

1978. Austrian Modern Art.
1826 **597** 6s. multicoloured 1·70 95

598 Bound Hands

1978. 30th Anniv of Declaration of Human Rights.
1827 598 6s. purple 1·70 95

599 "CCIR"

1979. 50th Anniv of International Radio Consultative Committee.
1828 599 6s. multicoloured 1·50 75

600 Adult protecting Child

1979. International Year of the Child.
1829 600 2s.50 multicoloured 65 55

601 Air Rifle, Pistol and Target

1979. Centenary of Austrian Shooting Club, and European Air Rifle and Air Pistol Shooting Championships.
1830 601 6s. multicoloured 1·70 75

602 *Franz I* (paddle-steamer)

1979. 150th Anniv of Danube Steam Navigation Company.
1831 602 1s.50 blue 55 45
1832 - 2s.50 brown 80 65
1833 - 3s. red 1·50 1·20
DESIGNS: 2s.50, Pusher tug "Linz"; 3s. "Theodor Korner" (passenger vessel).

603 Skater

1979. World Ice Skating and Dancing Championships. Vienna.
1834 603 4s. multicoloured 1·10 75

604 Fashion Drawing by Theo Zache, 1900

1979. 50th Viennese Int Ladies' Fashion Week.
1835 604 2s.50 multicoloured 65 55

605 Wiener Neustadt Cathedral

1979. 700th Anniv of Wiener Neustadt Cathedral.
1836 605 4s. blue and grey 1·10 65

606 Relief from Emperor Joseph II Monument, Vienna

1979. Bicentenary of Education for the Deaf.
1837 606 2s.50 green, black & gold 80 45

607 Population Graph

1979. 150th Anniv of Austrian Central Statistical Office.
1838 607 2s.50 multicoloured 90 45

608 Laurenz Koschier (postal reformer)

1979. Europa.
1839 608 6s. brown and ochre 3·75 95

609 Section through Diesel Engine

1979. 13th Congress of International Combustion Engine Council.
1840 609 4s. multicoloured 1·10 65

610 Town Arms of Ried, Braunau and Scharding

1979. Bicentenary of Innviertel District.
1841 610 3s. multicoloured 1·10 45

611 Water Pollution

1979. Prevention of Water Pollution.
1842 611 2s.50 green and grey 90 45

612 Arms of Rottenmann

1979. 700th Anniv of Rottenmann.
1843 612 3s. multicoloured 1·70 45

613 Jodok Fink

1979. 50th Death Anniv of Jodok Fink (politician).
1844 613 3s. brown 1·10 45

614 Arms of Wels and Returned Soldiers League Badge

1979. Fifth European Meeting of Returned Soldiers.
1845 614 4s. green and black 1·10 65

615 Flower

1979. U.N. Conference on Science and Technology for Development, Vienna.
1846 615 4s. blue 1·10 65

616 Vienna International Centre

1979. Opening of U.N.O. Vienna Int Centre.
1847 616 6s. slate 1·70 95

617 Eye and Blood Vessels of Diabetic

1979. Tenth World Congress of International Diabetes Federation, Vienna.
1848 617 2s.50 multicoloured 80 45

618 Stanzer Valley seen from Arlberg Road Tunnel

1979. 16th World Road Congress, Vienna.
1849 618 4s. multicoloured 1·10 65

619 Steam-driven Printing Press

1979. 175th Anniv of State Printing Works.
1850 619 3s. black and stone 90 55

620 Richard Zsigmondy

1979. 50th Death Anniv of Dr. Richard Zsigmondy (Nobel Prize winner for Chemistry).
1851 620 3s. brown 1·70 95

621 Bregenz Festival and Congress Hall

1979. Bregenz Festival and Congress Hall.
1852 621 2s.50 lilac 90 45

622 Burning Match

1979. "Save Energy".
1853 622 2s.50 multicoloured 90 45

623 Lions Emblem

1979. 25th European Lions Forum, Vienna.
1854 623 4s. yellow, gold and lilac 1·10 65

624 Wilhelm Exner (founder)

1979. Centenary of Industrial Museum and Technical School, Vienna.
1855 624 2s.50 dp purple & purple 80 45

625 *The Suffering Christ* (Hans Fronius)

1979. Austrian Modern Art.
1856 625 4s. black and stone 1·10 75

626 Series 52 Goods Locomotive

1979. Centenary of Raab (Gyor)–Odenburg (Sopron)-Ebenfurt Railway.
1857 626 2s.50 multicoloured 1·10 75

627 August Musger

1979. 50th Death Anniv of August Musger (pioneer of slow-motion photography).
1858 627 2s.50 black and grey 80 45

628 *Nativity* (detail of icon by Moses Subotic, St. Barbara Church, Vienna)

1979. Christmas.
1859 628 4s. multicoloured 1·10 65

629 Neue Hofburg, Vienna

1979. "WIPA 1981" International Stamp Exhibition, Vienna (1st issue). Inscr "1. Phase".
1860 629 16s.+8s. multicoloured 4·75 4·50
See also No. 1890.

630 Arms of Baden

1980. 500th Anniv. of Baden.
1861	**630**	4s. multicoloured	1·10	65

631 Loading Exports

1980. Austrian Exports.
1862	**631**	4s. blue, red and black	1·10	65

632 Rheumatic Hand holding Stick

1980. Fight against Rheumatism.
1863	**632**	2s.50 red and blue	80	45

633 Emblems of 1880 and 1980

1980. Centenary of Austrian Red Cross.
1864	**633**	2s.50 multicoloured	80	45

634 Kirchschlager

1980. Pres. Rudolf Kirchschlager's 65th Birthday.
1865	**634**	4s. brown and red	1·10	65

635 Robert Hamerling

1980. 150th Birth Anniv of Robert Hamerling (writer).
1866	**635**	2s.50 green	80	45

636 Town Seal

1980. 750th Anniv of Hallein.
1867	**636**	4s. black and red	1·10	65

637 *Maria Theresa as a Young Woman* (Andreas Moller)

1980. Death Bicentenary of Empress Maria Theresa.
1868	**637**	2s.50 purple	1·10	95
1869	-	4s. blue	1·50	1·20

1870	-	6s. brown	2·50	2·10

DESIGNS: 4s. *Maria Theresa with St. Stephen's Crown* (Martin van Meytens); 6s. *Maria Theresa as Widow* (Joseph Ducreux).

638 Flags of Treaty Signatories

1980. 25th Anniv of Austrian State Treaty.
1871	**638**	4s. multicoloured	1·10	65

639 St. Benedict (statue, Meinrad Guggenbichler)

1980. Congress of Austrian Benedictine Orders, Mariazell.
1872	**639**	2s.50 green	80	45

640 *Hygieia* (Gustav Klimt)

1980. 175th Anniv of Hygiene Education.
1873	**640**	4s. multicoloured	1·10	65

641 Dish Aerial, Aflenz

1980. Inauguration of Aflenz Satellite Communications Earth Station.
1874	**641**	6s. multicoloured	1·70	95

642 Steyr (copperplate engraving, 1693)

1980. Millenary of Steyr.
1875	**642**	4s. brown, black & gold	1·10	65

643 Oil Driller

1980. 50th Anniv of Oil Production in Austria.
1876	**643**	2s.50 multicoloured	80	45

644 Town Seal of 1267

1980. 800th Anniv of Innsbruck.
1877	**644**	2s.50 yellow, blk & red	80	45

645 Ducal Crown

1980. 800th Anniv of Elevation of Styria to Dukedom.
1878	**645**	4s. multicoloured	1·10	65

646 Leo Ascher

1980. Birth Cent of Leo Ascher (composer).
1879	**646**	3s. violet	80	45

647 "Abraham" (illustration from *Viennese Genesis*)

1980. Tenth Congress of International Organization for Study of the Old Testament.
1880	**647**	4s. multicoloured	1·10	65

648 Robert Stolz

1980. Europa and Birth Centenary of Robert Stolz (composer).
1881	**648**	6s. red	3·25	95

649 Falkenstein Railway Bridge

1980. 11th International Association of Bridge and Structural Engineering Congress, Vienna.
1882	**649**	4s. multicoloured	1·10	65

650 *Moon Figure* (Karl Brandstatter)

1980. Austrian Modern Art.
1883	**650**	4s. multicoloured	1·10	65

651 Customs Officer

1980. 150th Anniv of Customs Service.
1884	**651**	2s.50 brown and red	80	45

652 Masthead of 1810

1980. 350th Anniv of *Linzer Zeitung* (Linz newspaper).
1885	**652**	2s.50 black, red & gold	80	45

653 Frontispiece of Waidhofen Municipal Book

1980. 750th Anniv of Waidhofen.
1886	**653**	2s.50 multicoloured	80	45

654 Heads

1980. 25th Anniv of Federal Army.
1887	**654**	2s.50 green and red	80	45

655 Alfred Wegener

1980. Birth Centenary of Alfred Wegener (explorer and geophysicist).
1888	**655**	4s. blue	1·10	65

656 Robert Musil

1980. Birth Centenary of Robert Musil (writer).
1889	**656**	4s. brown	1·10	65

1980. "WIPA 1981" International Stamp Exhibition, Vienna (2nd issue). Inscr "2. Phase".
1890	**629**	16s.+8s. mult	4·75	4·50

657 *Adoration of the Kings* (stained-glass window, Viktring Collegiate Church)

1980. Christmas.
1891	**657**	4s. multicoloured	1·10	65

658 Ribbon in National Colours

1981. 25th Anniv of General Social Insurance Act.
1892	**658**	2s.50 red, green & black	55	45

1981. WIPA. 1981 International Stamp Exhibtion, Vienna (3rd issue). Sheet 90×71 mm. containing horiz designs as T **629** but in finished state.
MS1893	16s. + 8s. multicoloured		5·50	5·50

659 Unissued Design for 1926 Child Welfare Stamps

1981. Birth Centenary of Wilhelm Dachauer (artist).
1894	**659**	3s. brown	80	45

660 Disabled Person operating Machine Tool

1981. Third European Regional Conference of Rehabilitation International.
1895 **660** 6s. brown, blue and red ... 1·30 ... 85

661 Sigmund Freud

1981. 125th Birth Anniv of Sigmund Freud (psychoanalyst).
1896 **661** 3s. purple ... 80 ... 45

662 Long-distance Heating System

1981. 20th International Union of Long-distance Heat Distributors Congress, Vienna.
1897 **662** 4s. multicoloured ... 1·10 ... 65

663 *Azzo and his Vassals* (cover of Monastery's "bearskin" Manuscript)

1981. Kuenring Exhibition, Zwettl Monastery.
1898 **663** 3s. multicoloured ... 80 ... 45

664 Maypole

1981. Europa.
1899 **664** 6s. multicoloured ... 4·50 ... 1·40

665 Early Telephone

1981. Centenary of Austrian Telephone System.
1900 **665** 4s. multicoloured ... 1·10 ... 65

666 "The Frog King"

1981. Art Education in Schools.
1901 **666** 3s. multicoloured ... 80 ... 45

667 Research Centre

1981. 25th Anniv of Seibersdorf Research Centre.
1902 **667** 4s. blue, dp blue & orge ... 1·10 ... 65

668 Town Hall and Seal

1981. 850th Anniv of St. Veit-on-Glan.
1903 **668** 4s. yellow, brown & red ... 1·10 ... 65

669 Johann Florian Heller (chemist)

1981. 11th Int Clinical Chemistry Congress, Vienna.
1904 **669** 6s. brown ... 1·30 ... 95

670 Boltzmann

1981. 75th Death Anniv of Ludwig Boltzmann (physicist).
1905 **670** 3s. green ... 80 ... 45

671 Otto Bauer

1981. Birth Centenary of Otto Bauer (writer and politician).
1906 **671** 4s. multicoloured ... 1·10 ... 65

672 Chemical Balance

1981. International Pharmaceutical Federation Congress, Vienna.
1907 **672** 6s. black, brown and red ... 1·20 ... 75

673 Impossible Construction (M. C. Escher)

1981. Tenth International Austrian Mathematicians' Congress, Innsbruck.
1908 **673** 4s. lt blue, blue & dp blue ... 1·10 ... 65

674 *Coronation of Virgin Mary* (detail)

1981. 500th Anniv of Michael Pacher's Altarpiece at St. Wolfgang, Abersee.
1909 **674** 3s. blue ... 80 ... 45

675 Compass Rose

1981. 75th Anniv of Graz S.E. Exhibition.
1910 **675** 4s. multicoloured ... 1·10 ... 65

676 *Holy Trinity* (illuminated MS, 12th century)

1981. 16th International Congress of Byzantine Scholars, Vienna.
1911 **676** 6s. multicoloured ... 1·20 ... 75

677 Josef II

1981. Bicentenary of Toleration Act (giving freedom of worship to Protestants).
1912 **677** 4s. black, blue & bistre ... 1·10 ... 65

678 Hans Kelsen

1981. Bicentenary of Hans Kelsen (law lecturer and contributor to shaping of Austrian Constitution).
1913 **678** 3s. red ... 80 ... 45

679 Full and Empty Bowls and F.A.O. Emblem

1981. World Food Day.
1914 **679** 6s. multicoloured ... 1·20 ... 75

680 *Between the Times* (Oscar Asboth)

1981. Austrian Modern Art.
1915 **680** 4s. multicoloured ... 1·10 ... 65

681 Workers and Emblem

1981. Seventh International Catholic Employees' Meeting, Vienna-Lainz.
1916 **681** 3s. multicoloured ... 80 ... 45

682 Hammer-Purgstall

1981. 125th Death Anniv of Josef Hammer-Purgstall (orientalist).
1917 **682** 3s. multicoloured ... 80 ... 45

683 Julius Raab

1981. 90th Birth Anniv of Julius Raab (politician).
1918 **683** 6s. purple ... 1·10 ... 95

684 Stefan Zweig

1981. Birth Centenary of Stefan Zweig (writer).
1919 **684** 4s. lilac ... 90 ... 75

685 Christmas Crib, Burgenland

1981. Christmas.
1920 **685** 4s. multicoloured ... 90 ... 75

686 Arms of St. Nikola

1981. 800th Anniv of St. Nikola-on-Danube.
1921 **686** 4s. multicoloured ... 90 ... 75

687 Volkswagen Transporter Ambulance

1981. Cent of Vienna's Emergency Medical Service.
1922 **687** 3s. multicoloured ... 80 ... 45

688 Skier

1982. Alpine Skiing World Championship, Schladming-Haus.
1923 **688** 4s. multicoloured ... 80 ... 45

689 Dorotheum Building

1982. 275th Anniv of Dorotheum Auction, Pawn and Banking Society.
1924 **689** 4s. multicoloured ... 80 ... 45

690 Lifesaving

1982. 25th Anniv of Austrian Water Lifesaving Service.
1925 **690** 5s. blue, red & light blue ... 1·00 ... 85

691 St. Severin

1982. "St. Severin and the End of the Roman Period" Exhibition, Enns.
1926 **691** 3s. multicoloured ... 80 ... 45

692 Sebastian Kneipp (pioneer of holistic medicine)

1982. International Kneipp Congress, Vienna.
1927 **692** 4s. multicoloured 80 65

693 Printers' Coat-of-arms

1982. 500th Anniv of Printing in Austria.
1928 **693** 4s. multicoloured 80 65

694 Urine Analysis from *Canon Medicinae* by Avicenna

1982. Fifth European Union for Urology Congress, Vienna.
1929 **694** 6s. multicoloured 1·10 95

695 St. Francis preaching to Animals (miniature)

1982. "Franciscan Art and Culture in the Middle Ages" Exhibition, Krems-Stein.
1930 **695** 3s. multicoloured 80 45

696 Haydn and Birthplace, Rohrau

1982. "Joseph Haydn and His Time" Exhibition, Eisenstadt.
1931 **696** 3s. green 1·10 95

697 Globe within Milk Churn

1982. World Dairying Day.
1932 **697** 7s. multicoloured 1·70 95

698 Town Arms (1804 flag)

1982. 800th Anniv of Gfohl.
1933 **698** 4s. multicoloured 80 65

699 Tennis Player

1982. 80th Anniv of Austrian Lawn Tennis Assn.
1934 **699** 3s. multicoloured 80 45

700 Main Square, Langenlois

1982. 900th Anniv of Langenlois.
1935 **700** 4s. multicoloured 90 45

701 Town Arms

1982. 800th Anniv of Weiz.
1936 **701** 4s. multicoloured 1·70 75

702 Linz–Freistadt–Budweis Horse-drawn Railway

1982. Europa.
1937 **702** 6s. brown 5·00 1·00

703 Ignaz Seipel

1982. 50th Death Anniv of Ignaz Seipel (Federal Chancellor).
1938 **703** 3s. purple 80 50

704 Postbus

1982. 75th Anniv of Post-bus Service.
1939 **704** 4s. multicoloured 90 80

705 Rocket Launch

1982. Second U.N. Conference on the Exploration and Peaceful Uses of Outer Space, Vienna.
1940 **705** 4s. multicoloured 1·10 1·00

706 Globe (Federal Office for Standardization and Surveying, Vienna)

1982. Geodesists' Day.
1941 **706** 3s. multicoloured 80 50

707 Great Bustard ("Grosstrappe")

1982. Endangered Animals. Multicoloured.
1942 3s. Type **707** 80 70
1943 4s. Eurasian beaver 1·00 90
1944 6s. Western capercaillie ("Au-erhahn") 1·60 1·40

708 Institute Building, Laxenburg

1982. Tenth Anniv of International Institute for Applied Systems Analysis.
1945 **708** 3s. black and brown 65 60

709 St. Apollonia (patron saint of dentists)

1982. 70th International Dentists Federation Congress, Vienna.
1946 **709** 4s. multicoloured 90 80

710 Emmerich Kalman

1982. Birth Cent of Emmerich Kalman (composer).
1947 **710** 3s. blue 80 50

711 Max Mell

1982. Birth Centenary of Max Mell (writer).
1948 **711** 3s. multicoloured 80 50

712 Christmas Crib, Damuls Church

1982. Christmas.
1949 **712** 4s. multicoloured 90 80

713 Aerial View of Bosphorus

1982. Centenary of St. George's Austrian College, Istanbul.
1950 **713** 4s. multicoloured 90 80

714 "Mainz-Weber" Mailbox, 1870

1982. Stamp Day.
1951 **714** 6s.+3s. multicoloured 2·20 2·00

715 *Muse of the Republic* (Ernst Fuchs)

1982. Austrian Modern Art.
1952 **715** 4s. red and violet 1·10 1·00

716 Bank, Vienna

1983. Centenary of Postal Savings Bank.
1953 **716** 4s. yellow, black and blue 90 80

717 Hildegard Burjan

1983. Birth Centenary of Hildegard Burjan (founder of Caritas Socialis (religious sisterhood)).
1954 **717** 4s. red 90 80

718 Linked Arms

1983. World Communications Year.
1955 **718** 7s. multicoloured 1·50 1·00

719 Young Girl

1983. 75th Anniv of Children's Friends Organization.
1956 **719** 4s. black, blue and red 90 80

720 Josef Matthias Hauer

1983. Birth Centenary of Josef Matthias Hauer (composer).
1957 **720** 3s. purple 65 60

721 Douglas DC-9-80 Super Eighty

1983. 25th Anniv of Austrian Airlines.
1958 **721** 6s. multicoloured 1·30 1·20

722 Hands protecting Workers

1983. Cent of Government Work Inspection Law.
1959　**722**　4s. grn, dp grn & brn　90　80

723 Wels (engraving, Matthaeus Merian)

1983. "Millenary of Upper Austria" Exn, Wels.
1960　**723**　3s. multicoloured　65　60

724 Human Figure, Heart and Electrocardiogram

1983. Seventh World Symposium on Pacemakers.
1961　**724**　4s. red, mauve and blue　90　80

725 Monastery Arms

1983. 900th Anniv of Gottweig Monastery.
1962　**725**　3s. multicoloured　65　60

726 Weitra

1983. 800th Anniv of Weitra.
1963　**726**　4s. black, red and gold　90　80

727 Cap, Stick, Ribbon and Emblems

1983. 50th Anniv of MKV and CCV Catholic Students' Organizations.
1964　**727**　4s. multicoloured　90　80

728 Glopper Castle and Town Arms

1983. 650th Anniv of Hohenems Town Charter.
1965　**728**　4s. multicoloured　90　80

729 Hess

1983. Europa. Birth Centenary of Viktor Franz Hess (physicist and Nobel Prize winner).
1966　**729**　6s. green　5·00　1·00

730 Vienna City Hall

1983. 25th Anniv of Vienna City Hall.
1967　**730**　4s. multicoloured　90　80

731 Kiwanis Emblem and View of Vienna

1983. Kiwanis International, World and European Conference, Vienna.
1968　**731**　5s. multicoloured　1·10　1·00

732 Congress Emblem

1983. Seventh World Psychiatry Congress, Vienna.
1969　**732**　4s. multicoloured　90　60

733 Hasenauer and Natural History Museum, Vienna

1983. 150th Birth Anniv of Carl Freiherr von Hasenauer (architect).
1970　**733**　3s. brown　90　50

734 Institute for Promotion of Trade and Industry, Linz

1983. 27th International Professional Competition for Young Skilled Workers, Linz.
1971　**734**　4s. multicoloured　1·10　70

735 Symbols of Penicillin V Efficacy and Cancer

1983. 13th Int Chemotherapy Congress, Vienna.
1972　**735**　5s. red and green　1·10　80

736 Pope John Paul II

1983. Papal Visit.
1973　**736**　6s. black, red and gold　1·70　1·00

737 Relief of Vienna, 1683 (Franz Geffels)

1983. 300th Anniv of Relief of Vienna. Sheet 90×70 mm.
MS1974　**737**　6s. multicoloured　2·20　2·00

738 Spectrum around Cross

1983. Austrian Catholics' Day.
1975　**738**　3s. multicoloured　80　50

739 Vienna Town Hall

1983. Centenary of Vienna Town Hall.
1976　**739**　4s. multicoloured　1·10　60

740 Karl von Terzaghi

1983. Birth Centenary of Karl von Terzaghi (soil mechanics and foundations engineer).
1977　**740**　3s. blue　90　50

741 Initials of Federation

1983. Tenth Austrian Trade Unions Federation Congress.
1978　**741**　3s. red and black　80　50

742 Evening Sun in Burgenland (Gottfried Kumpf)

1983. Austrian Modern Art.
1979　**742**　4s. multicoloured　1·10　80

743 Tram No. 5, 1883

1983. Centenary of Modling–Hinterbruhl Electric Railway.
1980　**743**　3s. multicoloured　1·10　50

744 Boy looking at Stamped Envelope

1983. Stamp Day.
1981　**744**　6s.+3s. multicoloured　2·00　1·60

745 Francisco Carolinum Museum, Linz

1983. 150th Anniv of Upper Austrian Provincial Museum.
1982　**745**　4s. multicoloured　1·10　70

746 Crib by Johann Giner the Elder, Kitzbuhel Church

1983. Christmas.
1983　**746**　4s. multicoloured　90　80

747 Parliament Building

1983. Centenary of Parliament Building, Vienna.
1984　**747**　4s. blue　1·10　70

748 "St. Nicholas" (Maria Freund)

1983. Youth Stamp.
1985　**748**　3s. multicoloured　80　50

749 Wolfgang Pauli

1983. 25th Death Anniv of Wolfgang Pauli (Nobel Prize winner for Physics).
1986　**749**　6s. brown　1·30　1·00

750 Gregor Mendel

1984. Death Cent of Gregor Mendel (geneticist).
1987　**750**　4s. ochre and brown　90　80

751 Hanak at Work

1984. 50th Death Anniv of Anton Hanak (sculptor).
1988　**751**　3s. brown and black　80　50

752 Disabled Skier

1984. Third World Winter Games for the Disabled, Innsbruck.
1989　**752**　4s.+2s. multicoloured　1·30　1·20

753 Memorial, Wollersdorf

1984. 50th Anniv of 1934 Insurrections.
1990　**753**　4s.50 red and black　90　60

754 Founders'
Stone

1984. 900th Anniv of Reichersberg Monastery.
1991 **754** 3s.50 stone, brown & bl 80 50

755 Geras
Monastery

1984. Monasteries and Abbeys.
1992 - 50g. yellow, black & grey 20 20
1993 - 1s. yellow, black & mve 45 20
1994 - 1s.50 yellow, red & blue 45 25
1995 - 2s. yellow, green & black 80 30
1996 **755** 3s.50 yellow, sep & brn 1·30 40
1997 - 4s. yellow, purple & red 1·30 30
1998 - 4s.50 yellow, lilac & blue 1·50 50
1999 - 5s. yellow, purple & orge 1·50 50
2000 - 5s.50 yell, dp vio & vio 1·80 50
2001 - 6s. yellow, green & emer 1·80 30
2002 - 7s. yellow, green & blue 2·75 40
2003 - 7s.50 yell, dp brn & brn 2·50 50
2004 - 8s. yellow, blue and red 2·50 50
2005 - 10s. yellow, red & grey 3·00 50
2006 - 11s. yellow, black & brn 3·25 80
2007 - 12s. yellow, brn & orge 5·00 1·20
2008 - 17s. yellow, ultram & bl 5·50 1·30
2009 - 20s. yellow, brown & red 6·75 1·50
DESIGNS: 50g. Vorau Monastery; 1s. Wettingen Abbey,
Mehrerau; 1s.50, Monastery of Teutonic Order, Vienna;
2s. Michaelbeuern Benedictine Monastery, Salzburg; 4s.
Stams Monastery; 4s.50, Schlagl Monastery; 5s. St. Paul's
Monastery, Lavanttal; 5s.50, St. Gerold's Priory, Vorarlberg;
6s. Rein Monastery; 7s. Loretto Monastery; 7s.50, Domini-
can Monastery, Vienna; 8s. Cistercian Monastery, Zwettl;
10s. Premonstratensian Monastery, Wilten; 11s. Trappist
Monastery, Engelszell; 12s. Monastery of the Hospitallers,
Eisenstadt; 17s. St. Peter's Abbey, Salzburg; 20s. Wernberg
Convent, Carinthia.

756 Cigar Band showing
Tobacco Plant

1984. Bicentenary of Tobacco Monopoly.
2012 **756** 4s.50 multicoloured 90 60

757 Kostendorf

1984. 1200th Anniv of Kostendorf.
2013 **757** 4s.50 multicoloured 90 60

758 Wheel Bearing

1984. 20th International Federation of Automobile
Engineers' Associations World Congress, Vienna.
2014 **758** 5s. multicoloured 1·10 80

759 Bridge

1984. Europa. 25th Anniv of E.P.T. Conference.
2015 **759** 6s. blue and ultramarine 4·50 1·00

760 Archduke
Johann (after
Schnorr von
Carolsfeld)

1984. 125th Death Anniv of Archduke Johann.
2016 **760** 4s.50 multicoloured 90 60

761 Aragonite

1984. "Ore and Iron in the Green Mark" Exhibition,
Eisenerz.
2017 **761** 3s.50 multicoloured 65 50

762 Binding of *Das
Buch vom Kaiser*, by
Max Herzig

1984. Lower Austrian *Era of Emperor Franz Joseph: From
Revolution to Grunderzeit* Exhibition, Grafenegg
Castle.
2018 **762** 3s.50 red and gold 90 50

763 Upper City
Tower and Arms

1984. 850th Anniv of Vocklabruch.
2019 **763** 4s.50 multicoloured 1·10 80

764 Dionysus
(Virunum mosaic)

1984. Centenary of Carinthia Provincial Museum,
Klagenfurt.
2020 **764** 3s.50 stone, brn & grey 80 50

765 *Meeting of
Austrian Army with
South Tyrolean
Reserves* (detail,
Schnorr von
Carolsfeld)

1984. "Jubilee of Tyrol Province" Exhibition.
2021 **765** 3s.50 multicoloured 80 50

766 Ralph
Benatzky

1984. Birth Cent of Ralph Benatzky (composer).
2022 **766** 4s. brown 90 60

767 Flood Control
Barriers

1984. Centenary of Flood Control Systems.
2023 **767** 4s.50 green 1·10 70

768 Christian von
Ehrenfels

1984. 125th Death Anniv of Christian von Ehrenfels
(philosopher).
2024 **768** 3s.50 multicoloured 80 50

769 Models of European
Monuments

1984. 25th Anniv of Minimundus (model world),
Worthersee.
2025 **769** 4s. yellow and black 90 80

770 Blockheide Eibenstein
National Park

1984. Natural Beauty Spots.
2026 **770** 4s. pink and olive 90 80

771 Electric Train on
Schanatobel Bridge
(Arlberg Railway
Centenary)

1984. Railway Anniversaries.
2027 **771** 3s.50 brown, gold & red 1·10 1·00
2028 - 4s.50 blue, silver and red 1·30 1·20
DESIGN: 4s.50, Electric train on Falkenstein Bridge (75th
anniv of Tauern Railway).

772 Johann Georg
Stuwer's Flight in
Montgolfier Balloon

1984. Bicentenary of First Manned Balloon Flight in
Austria.
2029 **772** 6s. multicoloured 1·50 90

773 Lake Neusiedl

1984. Natural Beauty Spots.
2030 **773** 4s. purple and blue 90 80

774 Palace of
Justice, Vienna

1984. 20th Int Bar Assn Congress, Vienna.
2031 **774** 7s. multicoloured 1·50 1·30

775 *Joseph Hyrtl*
(window,
Innsbruck
Anatomy
Institute)

1984. Seventh European Anatomists' Congress, Innsbruck.
2032 **775** 6s. multicoloured 1·30 80

776 *Window* (Karl
Korab)

1984. Austrian Modern Art.
2033 **776** 4s. multicoloured 1·10 80

777 Clock of Imms
(astrolabe)

1984. 600th Birth Anniv of Johannes von Gmunden
(astronomer and mathematician).
2034 **777** 3s.50 multicoloured 80 50

778 Quill

1984. 125th Anniv of Concordia Press Club.
2035 **778** 4s.50 black, gold & red 90 60

779 Fanny
Elssler

1984. Death Centenary of Fanny Elssler (dancer).
2036 **779** 4s. multicoloured 1·00 60

780 *Holy Family* (detail,
Aggsbach Old High Altar)

1984. Christmas.
2037 **780** 4s.50 multicoloured 1·00 90

781 Detail from Burial Chamber Wall of Seschemnofer III

1984. Stamp Day.
2038 **781** 6s.+3s. multicoloured 2·00 1·60

782 Coat of Arms

1985. 400th Anniv of Graz University.
2039 **782** 3s.50 multicoloured 80 70

783 Dr. Lorenz Bohler

1985. Birth Centenary of Prof. Dr. Lorenz Bohler (surgeon).
2040 **783** 4s.50 purple 90 60

784 Ski Jumping, Skiing and Emblem

1985. World Nordic Skiing Championship, Seefeld.
2041 **784** 4s. multicoloured 1·00 90

785 Linz Cathedral

1985. Bicentenary of Linz Diocese.
2042 **785** 4s.50 multicoloured 90 60

786 Alban Berg

1985. Birth Centenary of Alban Berg (composer).
2043 **786** 6s. blue 1·30 1·00

787 Institute Emblem

1985. 25th Anniv of Institute for Vocational Advancement.
2044 **787** 4s.50 multicoloured 90 60

788 Stylized "B" and Clouds

1985. 2000th Anniv of Bregenz.
2045 **788** 4s. black, ultram & blue 80 50

789 1885 Registration Label

1985. Centenary of Registration Labels in Austria.
2046 **789** 4s.50 black, yell & grey 90 60

790 Josef Stefan

1985. 150th Birth Anniv of Josef Stefan (physicist).
2047 **790** 6s. brown, stone and red 1·30 90

791 St. Leopold (Margrave and patron saint)

1985. Lower Austrian Provincial Exhibition, Klosterneuburg Monastery.
2048 **791** 3s.50 multicoloured 80 50

792 The Story-teller

1985. 150th Birth Anniv of Franz Defregger (artist).
2049 **792** 3s.50 multicoloured 80 70

793 Barbed Wire, Broken Tree and New Shoot

1985. 40th Anniv of Liberation.
2050 **793** 4s.50 multicoloured 90 60

794 Johann Joseph Fux (composer)

1985. Europa. Music Year.
2051 **794** 6s. brown and grey 4·25 1·00

795 Flags and Caduceus

1985. 25th Anniv of European Free Trade Association.
2052 **795** 4s. multicoloured 1·00 70

796 Town and Arms

1985. Millenary of Boheimkirchen.
2053 **796** 4s.50 multicoloured 1·00 70

797 Bishop's Gate, St. Polten

1985. Bicentenary of St. Polten Diocese.
2054 **797** 4s.50 multicoloured 1·00 70

798 Johannes von Nepomuk Church, Innsbruck

1985. Gumpp Family (architects) Exn, Innsbruck.
2055 **798** 3s.50 multicoloured 80 60

799 Garsten (copperplate, George Matthaus Fischer)

1985. Millenary of Garsten.
2056 **799** 4s.50 multicoloured 1·10 80

800 U.N. Emblem and Austrian Arms

1985. 40th Anniv of U.N.O. and 30th Anniv of Austrian Membership.
2057 **800** 4s. multicoloured 1·00 70

801 Association Headquarters, Vienna

1985. 13th International Suicide Prevention Association Congress, Vienna.
2058 **801** 5s. brown, lt yell & yell 1·10 80

802 Woodland

1985. Forestry Year. Sheet 90×70 mm.
MS2059 **802** 6s. multicoloured 2·20 2·20

803 Operetta Emblem and Spa Building

1985. 25th Bad Ischl Operetta Week.
2060 **803** 3s.50 multicoloured 1·00 70

804 Fireman and Emblem

1985. Eighth International Fire Brigades Competition, Vocklabruck.
2061 **804** 4s.50 black, green & red 1·30 80

805 Grossglockner Mountain Road

1985. 50th Anniv of Grossglockner Mountain Road.
2062 **805** 4s. multicoloured 1·00 70

806 Chessboard as Globe

1985. World Chess Association Congress, Graz.
2063 **806** 4s. multicoloured 90 80

807 "Founding of Konigstetten" (August Stephan)

1985. Millenary of Konigstetten.
2064 **807** 4s.50 multicoloured 1·00 70

808 Webern Church and Arms of Hofkirchen and Taufkirchen

1985. 1200th Anniversaries of Hofkirchen, Weibern and Taufkirchen.
2065 **808** 4s.50 multicoloured 1·00 70

809 Dr. Adam Politzer

1985. 150th Birth Anniv of Dr. Adam Politzer (otologist).
2066 **809** 3s.50 violet 90 60

810 Emblem and View of Vienna

1985. International Association of Forwarding Agents World Congress, Vienna.
2067 **810** 6s. multicoloured 1·30 90

811 "Clowns Riding High Bicycles" (Paul Flora)

1985. Austrian Modern Art.
2068 **811** 4s. multicoloured 1·10 1·00

812 St. Martin, Patron Saint of Burgenland

1985. 25th Anniv of Eisenstadt Diocese.
2069 **812** 4s.50 black, bistre & red 1·10 80

813 Roman Mounted Courier

1985. 50th Anniv of Stamp Day.
2070 **813** 6s.+3s. multicoloured 2·00 1·80

814 Hanns Horbiger

1985. 125th Birth Anniv of Hanns Horbiger (design engineer).
2071 **814** 3s.50 purple and gold 90 80

815 *Adoration of the Christ Child* (marble relief)

1985. Christmas.
2072 **815** 4s.50 multicoloured 80 50

816 Aqueduct

1985. 75th Anniv of Second Vienna Waterline.
2073 **816** 3s.50 black, red & blue 80 50

818 Chateau de la Muette (headquarters)

1985. 25th Anniv of Organization of Economic Co-operation and Development.
2080 **818** 4s. black, gold & mauve 95 85

819 Johann Bohm

1986. Birth Centenary of Johann Bohm (founder of Austrian Trade Unions Federation).
2081 **819** 4s.50 black and red 1·00 70

820 Dove and Globe

1986. International Peace Year.
2082 **820** 6s. multicoloured 1·30 85

821 Push-button Dialling

1986. Introduction of Digital Preselection Telephone System.
2083 **821** 5s. multicoloured 1·00 60

822 Albrechtsberger and Organ

1986. 250th Birth Anniv of Johann Georg Albrechtsberger (composer).
2084 **822** 3s.50 multicoloured 80 70

823 Main Square and Arms

1986. 850th Anniv of Korneuburg.
2085 **823** 5s. multicoloured 1·20 70

824 Kokoschka (self-portrait)

1986. Birth Centenary of Oskar Kokoschka (artist).
2086 **824** 4s. black and pink 1·00 60

825 Council Flag

1986. 30th Anniv of Membership of Council of Europe.
2087 **825** 6s. black, red and blue 1·30 85

826 Holzmeister and Salzburg Festival Hall

1986. Birth Centenary of Professor Clemens Holzmeister (architect).
2088 **826** 4s. grey, brown & lt brn 80 70

827 Road, Roll of Material, and Congress Emblem

1986. Third International Geotextile Congress, Vienna.
2089 **827** 5s. multicoloured 1·00 60

828 Schlosshof Palace (after Bernardo Bellotto) and Prince Eugene

1986. "Prince Eugene and the Baroque Era" Exhibition, Schlosshof and Niederweiden.
2090 **828** 4s. multicoloured 95 70

829 St. Florian Monastery

1986. Upper Austrian "World of Baroque" Exhibition, St. Florian Monastery.
2091 **829** 4s. multicoloured 1·00 70

830 Herberstein Castle and Styrian Arms

1986. "Styria – Bridge and Bulwark" Exhibition, Herberstein Castle, near Stubenberg.
2092 **830** 4s. multicoloured 1·00 70

831 Large Pasque Flower

1986. Europa.
2093 **831** 6s. multicoloured 3·50 1·00

832 Wagner and Scene from Opera *Lohengrin*

1986. International Richard Wagner (composer) Congress, Vienna.
2094 **832** 4s. multicoloured 95 85

833 Antimonite Crystal

1986. Burgenland "Mineral and Fossils" Exhibition, Oberpullendorf.
2095 **833** 4s. multicoloured 95 85

834 Martinswall, Zirl

1986. Natural Beauty Spots.
2096 **834** 5s. brown and blue 1·20 85

835 Waidhofen

1986. 800th Anniv of Waidhofen on Ybbs.
2097 **835** 4s. multicoloured 1·20 85

836 Tschauko Falls, Ferlach

1986. Natural Beauty Spots.
2098 **836** 5s. green and brown 1·20 85

837 19th-century Steam and Modern Articulated Trams

1986. Cent of Salzburg Local Transport System.
2099 **837** 4s. multicoloured 1·20 1·00

838 Enns and Seals of Signatories

1986. 800th Anniv of Georgenberg Treaty (between Duke Leopold V of Austria and Duke Otakar IV of Styria).
2100 **838** 5s. multicoloured 1·20 85

839 Tandler

1986. 50th Death Anniv of Julius Tandler (social reformer).
2101 **839** 4s. multicoloured 95 85

840 *Observatory, 1886* (A. Heilmann)

1986. Centenary of Sonnblick Observatory.
2102 **840** 4s. black, blue and gold 95 85

841 Man collecting Mandragora (from "Codex Tacuinum Sanitatis")

1986. Seventh European Anaesthesia Congress, Vienna.
2103 **841** 5s. multicoloured 1·20 85

842 Fire Assistant

1986. 300th Anniv of Vienna Fire Brigade.
2104 **842** 4s. multicoloured 1·70 1·00

843 Stoessl

1986. 50th Death Anniv of Otto Stoessl (writer).
2105 **843** 4s. multicoloured 95 85

844 Viennese Hunting Tapestry (detail)

1986. Fifth International Oriental Carpets and Tapestry Conference, Vienna and Budapest.
2106 **844** 5s. multicoloured 1·20 85

845 Minister in Pulpit

1986. 125th Anniv of Protestants Act and 25th Anniv of Protestants Law.
2107 **845** 5s. black and violet 1·20 85

846 Decomposition (Walter Schmogner)

1986. Austrian Modern Art.
2108 **846** 4s. multicoloured 1·20 85

847 Liszt, Birthplace and Score

1986. 175th Birth Anniv of Franz Liszt (composer).
2109 **847** 5s. green and brown 1·20 85

848 Aerial View of Vienna

1986. European Security and Co-operation Conference Review Meeting, Vienna. Sheet 90×70 mm.
MS2110 **848** 6s. multicoloured 1·70 1·60

849 Strettweg Religious Carriage

1986. 175th Anniv of Styrian Joanneum Museum.
2111 **849** 4s. multicoloured 95 85

850 Nuremberg Letter Messenger (16th century woodcut)

1986. Stamp Day.
2112 **850** 6s.+3s. multicoloured 2·20 1·70

851 Adoration of the Shepherds (woodcut, Johann Georg Schwanthaler)

1986. Christmas.
2113 **851** 5s. brown and gold 1·20 85

852 Headquarters

1986. 40th Anniv of Federal Chamber of Trade and Industry.
2114 **852** 5s. multicoloured 1·20 85

853 Foundry Worker

1986. Austrian World of Work (1st series).
2115 **853** 4s. multicoloured 95 85
See also Nos. 2144, 2178, 2211, 2277, 2386, 2414, 2428, 2486, 2520, 2572 and 2605.

854 "The Educated Eye"

1987. Centenary of Adult Education in Vienna.
2116 **854** 5s. multicoloured 1·20 85

855 Large Blue Madonna (Anton Faistauer)

1987. Painters' Birth Centenaries. Multicoloured.
2117 4s. Type **855** 95 85
2118 6s. "Self-portrait" (Albert Paris Gutersloh) 1·40 1·20

856 Hundertwasser House, Vienna

1987. Europa and "Europalia 1987 Austria" Festival, Belgium.
2119 **856** 6s. multicoloured 6·50 2·10

857 Ice Hockey Players

1987. World Ice Hockey Championships, Vienna, and 75th Anniv of Austrian Ice Hockey Association.
2120 **857** 5s. multicoloured 1·50 1·00

858 Austria Centre

1987. Inaug of Austria Conference Centre, Vienna.
2121 **858** 5s. multicoloured 1·50 1·00

859 Salzburg

1987. 700th Anniv of Salzburg Town Charter.
2122 **859** 5s. multicoloured 1·50 1·00

860 Machine Shop, 1920

1987. Upper Austrian "Work–Men–Machines, the Route to Industrialized Society" Exhibition, Steyr.
2123 **860** 4s. black and red 1·20 70

861 Man and Woman

1987. Equal Rights for Men and Women.
2124 **861** 5s. multicoloured 1·20 85

862 Adele Bloch-Bauer I (detail, Gustav Klimt)

1987. Lower Austrian "Era of Emperor Franz Joseph: Splendour and Misery" Exhibition, Grafenegg Castle.
2125 **862** 4s. multicoloured 1·20 70

863 Archbishop and Salzburg

1987. 400th Anniv of Election of Prince Wolf Dietrich von Raitenau as Archbishop of Salzburg.
2126 **863** 4s. multicoloured 95 85

864 Schnitzler

1987. 125th Birth Anniv of Arthur Schnitzler (dramatist).
2127 **864** 6s. multicoloured 1·30 95

865 Lace and Arms

1987. 1100th Anniv of Lustenau.
2128 **865** 5s. multicoloured 1·20 85

866 Anniversary Emblem (William Slattery)

1987. 150th Anniv of Austrian Railways. Sheet 90×70 mm.
MS2129 **866** 6s. silver, red and black 2·30 2·10

867 Dachstein Giant Ice Cave

1987. Natural Beauty Spots.
2130 **867** 5s. green and black 1·20 85

868 Engraver at Work

1987. Eighth European Association of Engravers and Flexographers International Congress, Vienna.
2131 **868** 5s. brown, pink and grey 1·20 60

869 Dr. Karl Josef Bayer (chemist)

1987. Eighth International Light Metal Meeting, Leoben and Vienna.
2132 **869** 5s. multicoloured 1·20 60

870 Passenger Ferry

1987. Centenary of 1st Achensee Steam Service.
2133 **870** 4s. multicoloured 1·20 1·00

871 Office Building, Vienna

1987. Tenth Anniv of Office of Ombudsmen.
2134 **871** 5s. black, yellow and red 1·20 85

872 Schrodinger

1987. Birth Cent of Erwin Schrodinger (physicist).
2135 **872** 5s. brown, cream and bistre 1·20 85

873 Freistadt Town Square

1987. 125th Anniv of Freistadt Exhibitions.
2136 **873** 5s. multicoloured 1·20 60

874 Arbing Church

1987. 850th Anniv of Arbing.
2137 **874** 5s. multicoloured 1·20 60

875 Gauertal and Montafon
Valleys, Voralberg

1987. Natural Beauty Spots.
2138 **875** 5s. brown and yellow 1·20 85

876 Cyclist

1987. World Cycling Championship, Vienna and Villach.
2139 **876** 5s. multicoloured 1·20 1·00

877 Emblem

1987. World Congress of International Institute of
Savings Banks, Vienna.
2140 **877** 5s. multicoloured 1·20 85

878 Hofhaymer at
Organ

1987. 450th Death Anniv of Paul Hofhaymer (composer
and organist).
2141 **878** 4s. blue, black and gold 95 85

879 Haydn and Salzburg

1987. 250th Birth Anniv of Michael Haydn (composer).
2142 **879** 4s. lilac 95 85

880 Lammergeier
("Bartgeier")

1987. 25th Anniv of Alpine Zoo, Innsbruck.
2143 **880** 4s. multicoloured 95 85

881 Woman using Word
Processor

1987. Austrian World of Work (2nd series).
2144 **881** 4s. multicoloured 1·00 70

882 *Tree Goddesses* (Arnulf
Neuwirth)

1987. Austrian Modern Art.
2145 **882** 5s. multicoloured 1·20 85

883 Lottery Wheel

1987. Bicentenary of Gambling Monopoly.
2146 **883** 5s. multicoloured 1·20 85

884 Helmer

1987. Birth Centenary of Oskar Helmer (politician).
2147 **884** 4s. multicoloured 95 85

885 Gluck

1987. Death Bicentenary of Christoph Willibald Gluck
(composer).
2148 **885** 5s. brown and ochre 1·20 85

886 Stagecoach and
Passengers (lithograph,
Carl Schuster)

1987. Stamp Day.
2149 **886** 6s.+3s. multicoloured 2·20 1·80

887 Josef Mohr and Franz
Xaver Gruber (composers
of *Silent Night*)

1987. Christmas.
2150 **887** 5s. multicoloured 1·70 1·00

888 Bosco and Boys

1988. International Educational Congress of St. John
Bosco's Salesian Brothers, Vienna.
2151 **888** 5s. purple and orange 1·20 85

889 Cross-country
Sledging

1988. Fourth World Winter Games for the Disabled,
Innsbruck.
2152 **889** 5s.+2s.50 multicoloured 2·00 1·30

890 Mach

1988. 150th Birth Anniv of Ernst Mach (physicist and
philosopher).
2153 **890** 6s. multicoloured 1·40 95

891 *Village with
Bridge*

1988. 25th Death Anniv of Franz von Zulow (artist).
2154 **891** 4s. multicoloured 1·20 85

892 *The Confiscation*
(Ferdinand Georg
Waldmuller)

1988. "Patriotism and Protest: Viennese Biedermeier and
Revolution" Exhibition, Vienna.
2155 **892** 4s. multicoloured 1·20 85

893 Barbed Wire, Flag and
Crosses

1988. 50th Anniv of Annexation of Austria by Germany.
2156 **893** 5s. green, brown and red 1·40 90

894 Steam Locomotive
Aigen, Muhlkreis Railway,
1887

1988. Railway Centenaries. Multicoloured.
2157 4s. Type **894** 1·20 1·00
2158 5s. Modern electric tram and
Josefsplatz stop (Viennese
Local Railways Stock Cor-
poration) 1·50 1·30

895 European
Bee Eater

1988. 25th Anniv of World Wildlife Fund, Austria.
2159 **895** 5s. multicoloured 1·40 1·00

896 Decanter and
Beaker

1988. Styrian "Glass and Coal" Exn, Barnbach.
2160 **896** 4s. multicoloured 95 85

897 Late Gothic
Silver Censer

1988. Lower Austrian "Art and Monastic Life at the Birth
of Austria" Exhibition, Seitenstetten Benedictine
Monastery.
2161 **897** 4s. multicoloured 95 85

898 Taking Casualty to
Volkswagen Transporter
Ambulance and Red
Cross

1988. 125th Anniv of Red Cross.
2162 **898** 12s. black, red and green 2·50 1·90

899 Dish Aerials, Aflenz

1988. Europa. Telecommunications.
2163 **899** 6s. multicoloured 4·75 1·60

900 Mattsee
Monastery

1988. Salzburg "Bajuvars from Severin to Tassilo"
Exhibition, Mattsee Monastery.
2164 **900** 4s. multicoloured 95 85

901 Weinberg Castle

1988. Upper Austrian "Muhlviertel: Nature, Culture, Life"
Exhibition, Weinberg Castle, near Kefermarkt.
2165 **901** 4s. multicoloured 95 85

902 Horvath

1988. 50th Death Anniv of Odon von Horvath (writer).
2166 **902** 6s. black and bistre 1·40 95

903 Stockerau Town Hall

1988. 25th Anniv of Stockerau Festival.
2167 **903** 5s. multicoloured 1·20 85

904 Motorway

1988. Completion of Tauern Motorway.
2168 **904** 4s. multicoloured 95 85

905 Brixlegg

1988. 1200th Anniv of Brixlegg.
2169 **905** 5s. multicoloured 1·20 85

906 Klagenfurt (after Matthaus Merian)

1988. 400th Anniv of Regular Postal Services in Carinthia.
2170 **906** 5s. multicoloured 1·20 85

907 Parish Church and Dean's House

1988. 1200th Anniv of Brixen im Thale, Tyrol.
2171 **907** 5s. multicoloured 1·20 85

908 Krimml Waterfalls, Upper Tauern National Park

1988. Natural Beauty Spots.
2172 **908** 5s. black and blue 1·20 85

909 Town Arms

1988. 1100th Anniv of Feldkirchen, Carinthia.
2173 **909** 5s. multicoloured 1·20 85

910 Feldbach

1988. 800th Anniv of Feldbach.
2174 **910** 5s. multicoloured 1·20 85

911 Ansfelden

1988. 1200th Anniv of Ansfelden.
2175 **911** 5s. multicoloured 1·20 85

912 Hologram of Export Emblem

1988. Federal Economic Chamber Export Congress.
2176 **912** 8s. multicoloured 3·00 2·30

913 Concert Hall

1988. 75th Anniv of Vienna Concert Hall.
2177 **913** 5s. multicoloured 1·20 85

914 Laboratory Assistant

1988. Austrian World of Work (3rd series).
2178 **914** 4s. multicoloured 1·00 70

915 *Guards* (Giselbert Hoke)

1988. Austrian Modern Art.
2179 **915** 5s. multicoloured 1·20 85

916 Schonbauer

1988. Birth Centenary of Dr. Leopold Schonbauer (neurosurgeon and politician).
2180 **916** 4s. multicoloured 1·00 70

917 Carnation

1988. Cent of Austrian Social Democratic Party.
2181 **917** 4s. multicoloured 95 85

918 Loading Railway Mail Van at Pardubitz Station, 1914

1988. Stamp Day.
2182 **918** 6s.+3s. multicoloured 2·30 1·70

919 *Nativity* (St. Barbara's Church, Vienna)

1988. Christmas.
2183 **919** 5s. multicoloured 1·20 85

920 *Madonna* (Lucas Cranach)

921 Margrave Leopold II leading Abbot Sigibold and Monks to Melk (detail of fresco, Paul Troger)

1989. 25th Anniv of Diocese of Innsbruck.
2184 **920** 4s. multicoloured 95 60

1989. 900th Anniv of Melk Benedictine Monastery.
2185 **921** 5s. multicoloured 1·20 85

922 Marianne Hainisch

1989. 150th Birth Anniv of Marianne Hainisch (women's rights activist).
2186 **922** 6s. multicoloured 1·40 1·00

923 Glider and Paraskier

1989. World Gliding Championships, Wiener Neustadt, and World Paraskiing Championships, Damuls.
2187 **923** 6s. multicoloured 1·40 1·00

924 *The Painting*

1989. 50th Death Anniv of Rudolf Jettmar (painter).
2188 **924** 5s. multicoloured 1·20 85

925 *Bruck an der Leitha* (17th-century engraving, Georg Vischer)

1989. 750th Anniv of Bruck an der Leitha.
2189 **925** 5s. multicoloured 1·20 85

926 Wittgenstein

1989. Birth Centenary of Ludwig Wittgenstein (philosopher).
2190 **926** 5s. multicoloured 1·20 70

927 Holy Trinity Church, Stadl-Paura

1989. 250th Death Anniv of Johann Michael Prunner (architect).
2191 **927** 5s. multicoloured 1·20 70

928 Suess (after Josef Kriehuber) and Map

1989. 75th Death Anniv of Eduard Suess (geologist and politician).
2192 **928** 6s. multicoloured 1·30 85

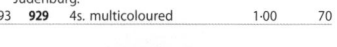

929 *Judenburg* (17th-century engraving, Georg Vischer)

1989. Upper Styrian "People, Coins, Markets" Exhibition, Judenburg.
2193 **929** 4s. multicoloured 1·00 70

930 Steam Engine (Vinzenz Prick)

1989. Lower Austrian "Magic of Industry" Exhibition, Pottenstein.
2194 **930** 4s. blue and gold 1·00 70

931 Radstadt

1989. 700th Anniv of Radstadt.
2195 **931** 5s. multicoloured 1·20 85

932 Wooden Salt Barge from Viechtau

1989. Europa. Children's Toys.
2196 **932** 6s. multicoloured 4·00 1·00

933 *St. Adalbero and Family before Madonna and Child* (Monastery Itinerary Book)

1989. Upper Austrian "Graphic Art" Exhibition and 900th Anniv of Lambach Monastery Church.
2197 **933** 4s. multicoloured 1·00 70

934 *Gisela* (paddle-steamer)

1989. 150th Anniv of Passenger Shipping on Traunsee.
2198 **934** 5s. multicoloured 1·70 1·00

935 Hansa
Brandenburg C-1 Mail
Biplane at Vienna, 1918

1989. Stamp Day.
2199 **935** 6s.+3s. multicoloured 2·00 1·70

936 St. Andra (after
Matthaus Merian)

1989. 650th Anniv of St. Andra.
2200 **936** 5s. multicoloured 1·20 85

937 Strauss

1989. 125th Birth Anniv of Richard Strauss (composer).
2201 **937** 6s. red, brown and gold 1·40 1·00

938 Locomotive

1989. Centenary of Achensee Steam Rack Railway.
2202 **938** 5s. multicoloured 1·50 85

939 Parliament Building,
Vienna

1989. Centenary of Interparliamentary Union.
2203 **939** 6s. multicoloured 1·40 95

940 Anniversary
Emblem

1989. Centenary of National Insurance in Austria.
2204 **940** 5s. multicoloured 1·20 70

941 U.N. Building, Vienna

1989. Tenth Anniv of U.N. Vienna Centre.
2205 **941** 8s. multicoloured 2·00 1·00

942 Lusthaus Water, Prater
Woods, Vienna

1989. Natural Beauty Spots.
2206 **942** 5s. black and buff 1·20 1·00

943 Wildalpen and
Hammerworks

1989. 850th Anniv of Wildalpen.
2207 **943** 5s. multicoloured 1·20 85

944 Emblem

1989. 33rd Congress of European Organization for
Quality Control, Vienna.
2208 **944** 6s. multicoloured 1·40 95

945 Palace of Justice,
Vienna

1989. 14th Congress of Int Assn of Criminal Law.
2209 **945** 6s. multicoloured 1·30 90

946 Tree of Life
(Ernst Steiner)

1989. Austrian Modern Art.
2210 **946** 5s. multicoloured 1·40 95

947 Bricklayer

1989. Austrian World of Work (4th series).
2211 **947** 5s. multicoloured 1·40 95

948 Ludwig
Anzengruber
(150th birth anniv)

1989. Writers' Anniversaries. Multicoloured.
2212 4s. Type **948** 1·20 85
2213 4s. Georg Trakl (75th death
 anniv) 1·20 85

949 Fried

1989. 125th Birth Anniv of Alfred Fried (Peace Movement
worker).
2214 **949** 6s. multicoloured 1·50 1·00

950 Adoration of the
Shepherds (detail, Johann
Carl von Reslfeld)

1989. Christmas.
2215 **950** 5s. multicoloured 1·20 85

951 "Courier"
(Albrecht Durer)

1990. 500th Anniv of Regular European Postal Services.
2216 **951** 5s. chocolate, cinnamon
 and brown 1·30 85

952 Streif Downhill
and Ganslern Slalom
Runs

1990. 50th Hahnenkamm Ski Championships, Kitzbuhel.
2217 **952** 5s. multicoloured 1·20 85

953 Sulzer

1990. Death Centenary of Salomon Sulzer (creator of
modern Synagogue songs).
2218 **953** 4s.50 multicoloured 1·00 60

954 Emich

1990. 50th Death Anniv of Friedrich Emich
(microchemist).
2219 **954** 6s. purple and green 1·20 85

955 Emperor Friedrich III
(miniature by Ulrich
Schreier)

1990. 500th Anniv of Linz as Capital of Upper Austria.
2220 **955** 5s. multicoloured 1·20 85

956 University Seals

1990. 625th Anniv of Vienna University and 175th Anniv
of Vienna University of Technology.
2221 **956** 5s. red, gold and lilac 1·20 85

957 South Styrian
Vineyards

1990. Natural Beauty Spots.
2222 **957** 5s. black and yellow 1·20 85

958 Parish Church

959 1897 May Day
Emblem

1990. Centenary of Labour Day.
2224 **959** 4s.50 multicoloured 1·00 95

960 "Our Dear
Housewife of
Seckau" (relief)

1990. 850th Anniv of Seckau Abbey.
2225 **960** 4s.50 blue 1·00 70

961 Ebene Reichenau
Post Office

1990. Europa. Post Office Buildings.
2226 **961** 7s. multicoloured 5·25 1·20

962 Thematic Stamp
Motifs

1990. Stamp Day.
2227 **962** 7s.+3s. multicoloured 2·30 1·90

963 Makart
(self-portrait)

1990. 150th Birth Anniv of Hans Makart (painter).
2228 **963** 4s.50 multicoloured 1·20 1·00

964 Schiele
(self-portrait)

1990. Birth Centenary of Egon Schiele (painter).
2229 **964** 5s. multicoloured 1·20 1·00

965 Raimund

1990. Birth Bicentenary of Ferdinand Raimund (actor and
playwright).
2230 **965** 4s.50 multicoloured 1·20 1·00

1990. 1200th Anniv of Anthering.
2223 **958** 7s. multicoloured 1·90 95

966 *The Hundred Guilden Note* (Rembrandt)

1990. Second Int Christus Medicus Congress, Bad Ischl.
2231 **966** 7s. multicoloured 1·90 95

967 Hardegg

1990. 700th Anniv of Hardegg's Elevation to Status of Town.
2232 **967** 4s.50 multicoloured 1·20 85

968 Oberdrauburg (copperplate engraving, Freiherr von Valvasor)

1990. 750th Anniv of Oberdrauburg.
2233 **968** 5s. multicoloured 1·30 60

969 Church and Town Hall

1990. 850th Anniv of Gumpoldskirchen.
2234 **969** 5s. multicoloured 1·30 60

970 Zdarsky skiing

1990. 50th Death Anniv of Mathias Zdarsky (developer of alpine skiing).
2235 **970** 5s. multicoloured 1·30 60

971 *Telegraph*, 1880, and *Anton Chekhov*, 1978

1990. 150th Anniv of Modern (metal) Shipbuilding in Austria.
2236 **971** 9s. multicoloured 2·10 1·20

972 Perkonig

1990. Birth Centenary of Josef Friedrich Perkonig (writer).
2237 **972** 5s. sepia, brown & gold 1·20 85

973 "Man of Rainbows" (Robert Zeppel-Sperl)

1990. Austrian Modern Art.
2238 **973** 5s. multicoloured 1·20 85

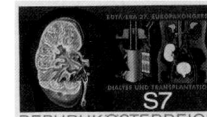

974 Kidney, Dialysis Machine and Anatomical Diagram

1990. 27th European Dialysis and Transplantation Federation Congress, Vienna.
2239 **974** 7s. multicoloured 1·90 95

975 Werfel

1990. Birth Centenary of Franz Werfel (writer).
2240 **975** 5s. multicoloured 1·20 85

976 U.N. and Austrian Flags

1990. 30th Anniv of Austrian Participation in U.N. Peace-keeping Forces.
2241 **976** 7s. multicoloured 1·90 95

977 Arms of Provinces

1990. 45th Anniv of First Provinces Conference (established Second Republic as Federal State).
2242 **977** 5s. multicoloured 1·20 60

978 University Seal

1990. 150th Anniv of Mining University, Leoben.
2243 **978** 4s.50 black, red & green 1·00 60

979 Vogelsang

1990. Death Centenary of Karl von Vogelsang (Christian social reformer).
2244 **979** 4s.50 multicoloured 1·00 60

980 Metal Workers

1990. Centenary of Metal, Mining and Energy Trade Union.
2245 **980** 5s. multicoloured 1·20 60

981 Player

1990. Third World Ice Curling Championships, Vienna.
2246 **981** 7s. multicoloured 1·90 95

982 Greenhouse

1990. Re-opening of Schonbrunn Greenhouse.
2247 **982** 5s. multicoloured 1·20 60

983 "Birth of Christ"

1990. Christmas. Detail of Altarpiece by Master Nikolaus of Verdun, Klosterneuburg Monastery.
2248 **983** 5s. multicoloured 1·20 60

984 Grillparzer

1991. Birth Bicent of Franz Grillparzer (dramatist).
2249 **984** 4s.50 multicoloured 1·20 60

985 Skier

1991. World Alpine Skiing Championships, Saalbach-Hinterglemm.
2250 **985** 5s. multicoloured 1·20 85

986 Kreisky

1991. 80th Birth Anniv of Bruno Kreisky (Chancellor, 1970–82).
2251 **986** 5s. multicoloured 1·20 85

987 Schmidt and Vienna Town Hall

1991. Death Centenary of Friedrich von Schmidt (architect).
2252 **987** 7s. multicoloured 1·90 1·20

988 Fountain, Vienna

1991. Anniversaries. Multicoloured.
2253 4s.50 Type **988** (250th death anniv of Georg Raphael Donner (sculptor)) 1·00 95
2254 5s. *Kitzbuhel in Winter* (birth centenary of Alfons Walde (artist and architect)) 1·20 1·00
2255 7s. Vienna Stock Exchange (death centenary of Theophil von Hansen (architect)) 1·70 1·60

See also No. 2269.

989 M. von Ebner-Eschenbach

1991. 75th Death Anniv of Marie von Ebner-Eschenbach (writer).
2256 **989** 4s.50 purple 1·20 85

990 Mozart

1991. Death Bicentenary of Wolfgang Amadeus Mozart (composer). Sheet 115×69 mm containing T **990** and similar vert design, each purple, mauve and gold.
MS2257 5s. Type **990**; 5s. *The Magic Flute* (statue, Vienna) 3·50 3·00

991 Obir Stalactite Caverns, Eisenkappel

1991. Natural Beauty Spots.
2258 **991** 5s. multicoloured 1·30 90

992 Spittal an der Drau (after Matthaus Merian)

1991. 800th Anniv of Spittal an der Drau.
2259 **992** 4s.50 multicoloured 1·30 90

993 "ERS-1" European Remote Sensing Satellite

1991. Europa. Europe in Space.
2260 **993** 7s. multicoloured 6·00 1·30

994 "Garden Party" (Anthoni Bays)

1991. Vorarlberg "Clothing and People" Exhibition, Hohenems.
2261 **994** 5s. multicoloured 1·30 90

995 Grein

1991. 500th Anniv of Grein Town Charter.
2262 **995** 4s.50 multicoloured 1·30 90

996 Bedding Plants forming Arms

1991. 1200th Anniv of Tulln.
2263 **996** 5s. multicoloured 1·30 90

997 Military History Museum

1991. Vienna Museum Centenaries. Multicoloured.
2264	5s. Type **997**	1·30	1·10
2265	7s. Museum of Art History	1·60	1·50

998 "B" and "P"

1991. Stamp Day.
2266	**998**	7s.+3s. brown, sepia and black	2·30	2·00

This is the first of a series of ten annual stamps, each of which will illustrate two letters. The complete series will spell out the words "Briefmarke" and "Philatelie".

999 Tunnel Entrance

1991. Opening of Karawanken Road Tunnel between Carinthia and Slovenia.
2267	**999**	7s. multicoloured	1·60	1·20

1000 Town Hall

1991. Fifth Anniv of St. Polten as Capital of Lower Austria.
2268	**1000**	5s. multicoloured	1·40	90

1991. 150th Birth Anniv of Otto Wagner (architect). As T **988**. Multicoloured.
2269		4s.50 Karlsplatz Station, Vienna City Railway	1·30	1·10

1001 Rowing

1991. Junior World Canoeing Championships and World Rowing Championships, Vienna.
2270	**1001**	5s. multicoloured	1·30	90

1002 X-ray Tube

1991. European Radiology Congress, Vienna.
2271	**1002**	7s. multicoloured	1·60	1·10

1003 Paracelsus

1991. 450th Death Anniv of Theophrastus Bombastus von Hohenheim (Paracelsus) (physician and scientist).
2272	**1003**	4s. black, red & brown	1·30	90

1004 "Mir" Space Station

1991. "Austro Mir 91" Soviet–Austrian Space Flight.
2273	**1004**	9s. multicoloured	2·10	1·50

1005 Almabtrieb (driving cattle from mountain pastures) (Zell, Tyrol)

1991. Folk Customs and Art (1st series). Multicoloured. . Multicoloured.
2274	4s.50 Type **1005**	1·00	90
2275	5s. Vintage Crown (Neustift, Vienna)	1·10	1·00
2276	7s. Harvest monstrance (Nestelbach, Styria)	1·60	1·50

See also Nos. 2305/7, 2349/51, 2363/5, 2393/5, 2418, 2432/3, 2450, 2482, 2491, 2500/1, 2508, 2524, 2546, 2547, 2550, 2552, 2569, 2581, 2587, 2595, 2718, 2776 and 2815.

1006 Weaver

1991. Austrian World of Work (5th series).
2277	**1006**	4s.50 multicoloured	1·10	80

1007 The General (Rudolf Pointner)

1991. Austrian Modern Art.
2278	**1007**	5s. multicoloured	1·30	90

1008 Raab

1991. Birth Centenary of Julius Raab (Chancellor, 1953–61).
2279	**1008**	4s.50 brown & chestnut	1·30	90

1009 "Birth of Christ" (detail of fresco, Baumgartenberg Church)

1991. Christmas.
2280	**1009**	5s. multicoloured	1·30	1·10

1010 Clerks

1992. Centenary of Trade Union of Clerks in Private Enterprise.
2281	**1010**	5s.50 multicoloured	1·40	1·00

1011 Emblems of Games and Olympic Rings

1992. Winter Olympic Games, Albertville, and Summer Games, Barcelona.
2282	**1011**	7s. multicoloured	2·00	1·10

1012 Competitor

1992. Eighth World Toboggan Championships on Natural Runs, Bad Goisern.
2283	**1012**	5s. multicoloured	1·30	90

1013 Hollow Stone, Klostertal

1992. Natural Beauty Spots.
2284	**1013**	5s. multicoloured	1·30	90

1014 Saiko

1992. Birth Centenary of George Saiko (writer).
2285	**1014**	5s.50 brown	1·40	1·00

1015 *Athlete with Ball* (Christian Attersee)

1992. Centenary of Workers' Sport Movement.
2286	**1015**	5s.50 multicoloured	1·40	1·00

1016 Franz Joseph Muller (chemist and mineralogist)

1992. Scientific Anniversaries. Multicoloured.
2287	5s. Type **1016** (250th birth anniv)	1·30	1·10
2288	5s.50 Paul Kitaibel (botanist, 175th death anniv)	1·40	1·20
2289	6s. Christian Doppler (physicist) (150th anniv of observation of Doppler Effect)	1·50	1·30
2290	7s. Richard Kuhn (chemist, 25th death anniv)	1·60	1·50

1017 Angels playing Instruments

1992. 150th Anniv of Vienna Philharmonic Orchestra. Sheet 90×70 mm.
MS2291	**1017**	5s.50 black, brown and gold	2·30	2·00

1018 First and Present Emblems

1992. Centenary of Railway Workers' Trade Union.
2292	**1018**	5s.50 red and black	1·30	80

1019 Hanrieder

1992. 150th Birth Anniv of Norbert Hanrieder (writer).
2293	**1019**	5s.50 lilac & brown	1·40	90

1020 Scenes from *"The Birdseller"* (Zeller) and *The Beggar Student* (Millocker)

1992. 150th Birth Anniversaries of Carl Zeller and Karl Millocker (composers).
2294	**1020**	6s. multicoloured	1·50	1·10

1021 Foundry and Process

1992. Ironworks Day. 40th Anniv of First LD-Process Steel Works, Linz.
2295	**1021**	5s. multicoloured	1·30	90

1022 Woodcut of the Americas by Sebastian Munster (from *Geographia Universalis* by Claudius Ptolomaus)

1992. Europa. 500th Anniv of Discovery of America by Columbus.
2296	**1022**	7s. multicoloured	6·00	1·70

1023 Dredger

1992. Centenary of Treaty for International Regulation of the Rhine.
2297	**1023**	7s. multicoloured	2·00	1·30

1024 Rieger

1992. Centenary of Adoption of Pseudonym Reimmichl by Sebastian Rieger (writer).
2298	**1024**	5s. brown	1·30	90

1025 Flags and Alps

1992. Alpine Protection Convention.
2299 **1025** 5s.50 multicoloured 1·40 1·00

1026 Dr. Anna Dengel

1992. Birth Centenary of Dr. Anna Dengel (founder of Medical Missionary Sisters).
2300 **1026** 5s.50 multicoloured 1·50 90

1027 "R" and "H"

1992. Stamp Day.
2301 **1027** 7s.+3s. multicoloured 2·30 2·00
See note below No. 2266.

1028 Town Hall

1992. 750th Anniv of First Documentation of Lienz as a Town.
2302 **1028** 5s. multicoloured 1·30 90

1029 "Billroth in Lecture Room" (A. F. Seligmann)

1992. Austrian Surgery Society International Congress, Eisenstadt.
2303 **1029** 6s. multicoloured 1·40 1·00

1030 Waldheim

1992. Presidency of Dr. Kurt Waldheim.
2304 **1030** 5s.50 black, red & grey 1·30 90

1992. Folk Customs and Art (2nd series). As T **1005**. Multicoloured.
2305 5s. Target with figure of Zieler, Lower Austria, 1732 1·30 1·10
2306 5s.50 Chest, Carinthia 1·50 1·30
2307 7s. Votive tablet from Venser Chapel, Vorarlberg 1·60 1·50

1031 Bridge over Canal

1992. Completion of Marchfeld Canal System.
2308 **1031** 5s. multicoloured 1·30 90

1032 "The Purification of Sea Water" (Peter Pongratz)

1992. Austrian Modern Art.
2309 **1032** 5s.50 multicoloured 1·50 1·10

1033 Gateway, Hofburg Palace (venue)

1992. Fifth Int Ombudsmen's Conference, Vienna.
2310 **1033** 5s.50 multicoloured 1·30 90

1034 Academy Seal

1992. 300th Anniv of Academy of Fine Arts, Vienna.
2311 **1034** 5s. blue and red 1·30 90

1035 The Annunciation

1992. Death Bicentenary of Veit Koniger (sculptor).
2312 **1035** 5s. multicoloured 1·30 1·10

1036 Birth of Christ (Johann Georg Schmidt)

1992. Christmas.
2313 **1036** 5s.50 multicoloured 1·40 90

1037 Earth and Satellite

1992. Birth Centenary of Hermann Potocnik (alias Noordung) (space travel pioneer).
2314 **1037** 10s. multicoloured 2·30 1·70

1038 Dome of Michael Wing, Hofburg Palace, Vienna

1993. Architects' Anniversaries. Multicoloured.
2315 5s. Type **1038** (Joseph Emanuel Fischer von Erlach, 300th birth) 1·10 1·00
2316 5s.50 Kinsky Palace, Vienna (Johann Lukas von Hildebrandt, 325th birth) 1·20 1·10
2317 7s. State Opera House, Vienna (Eduard van der Null and August Siccard von Siccardsburg, 125th death annivs) 1·80 1·70

1039 Emergency Vehicle's Flashing Lantern

1993. 25th Anniv of Radio-controlled Emergency Medical Service.
2318 **1039** 5s. multicoloured 1·20 90

1040 Wilder Kaiser Massif, Tyrol

1993. Natural Beauty Spots.
2319 **1040** 6s. multicoloured 1·40 1·00

1041 Mitterhofer Typewriter

1993. Death Centenary of Peter Mitterhofer (typewriter pioneer).
2320 **1041** 17s. multicoloured 4·25 2·75

1042 "Strada del Sole" (record sleeve)

1993. "Austro Pop" (1st series). Rainhard Fendrich (singer).
2321 **1042** 5s.50 multicoloured 1·40 1·10
See also Nos. 2356 and 2368.

1043 Games Emblem

1993. Winter Special Olympics, Salzburg and Schladming.
2322 **1043** 6s.+3s. multicoloured 3·50 2·00

1044 Sealsfield

1993. Birth Bicent of Charles Sealsfield (novelist).
2323 **1044** 10s. red, blue and gold 3·50 1·50

1045 Girl realizing her Rights

1993. Ratification of U.N. Convention on Children's Rights.
2324 **1045** 7s. multicoloured 1·80 1·10

1046 "Death" (detail of sculpture, Josef Stammel), Admont Monastery, Styria

1993. Monasteries and Abbeys.

2325	-	1s. brown, black & grn	35	35
2326	**1046**	5s.50 black, yell & grn	2·40	55
2327	-	6s. black, mauve & yell	1·40	35
2328	-	7s. brown, black & grey	2·40	1·50
2329	-	7s.50 brown, bl & blk	2·40	55
2330	-	8s. orange, black & bl	3·00	90
2331	-	10s. black, blue & orge	3·25	1·30
2332	-	20s. black, blue & yell	7·25	1·10
2333	-	26s. orange, black & bis	7·75	1·10
2334	-	30s. red, yellow & black	10·50	1·80

DESIGNS: 1s. The Annunciation (detail of crosier of Abbess), St. Gabriel Benedictine Abbey, Bertholdstein; 6s. St. Benedict of Nursia (glass painting), Mariastern Abbey, Gwiggen; 7s. Marble lion, Franciscan Monastery, Salzburg; 7s.50, Virgin Mary (detail of cupola painting by Paul Troger), Altenburg Monastery; 8s. Early Gothic doorway, Wilhering Monastery; 10s. The Healing of St. Peregrinus (altarpiece), Maria Luggau Monastery; 20s. Hartmann Crosier, St. Georgenberg Abbey, Fiecht; 26s. Master Dolorosa (sculpture), Franciscan Monastery, Schwaz; 30s. Madonna and Child, Monastery of the Scottish Order, Vienna.

1047 "Flying Harlequin" (Paul Flora)

1993. Europa. Contemporary Art.
2345 **1047** 7s. multicoloured 4·50 1·10

1048 Silhouette, Script and Signature

1993. 150th Birth Anniv of Peter Rosegger (writer and newspaper publisher).
2346 **1048** 5s.50 black and green 1·20 1·10

1049 Hohentwiel (lake steamer) and Flags

1993. Lake Constance European Region.
2347 **1049** 6s. multicoloured 1·80 1·10

1050 Knights in Battle and "I"s

1993. Stamp Day.
2348 **1050** 7s.+3s. gold, black and blue 2·20 2·00
See note below No. 2266.

1005 Almabtrieb (driving cattle from mountain pastures) (Zell, Tyrol)

1993. Folk Customs and Art (3rd series). As T **1005**. Multicoloured.
2349 5s. Corpus Christi Day procession, Hallstatt, Upper Austria 1·10 1·00
2350 5s.50 Drawing the block (log), Burgenland 1·20 1·10
2351 7s. Aperschnalzen (whipping the snow away), Salzburg 1·60 1·50

1051 Human Rights Emblem melting Bars

1993. U.N. World Conf on Human Rights, Vienna.
2352 **1051** 10s. multicoloured 2·20 1·50

1052 Jagerstatter

1993. 50th Death Anniv of Franz Jagerstatter (conscientious objector).
2353 **1052** 5s.50 multicoloured 1·20 1·10

1053 Train approaching Wolfgangsee

1993. Centenary of Schafberg Cog Railway.
2354 **1053** 6s. multicoloured 1·60 1·10

1054 Self-portrait with Doll

1993. Birth Centenary of Rudolf Wacker (artist).
2355 **1054** 6s. multicoloured 1·20 1·10

1993. "Austro Pop" (2nd series). Ludwig Hirsch (singer and actor). As T **1042**. Multicoloured.
2356 5s.50 "Die Omama" (record sleeve) 1·40 1·10

1055 Concert in Dornbacher Park (Balthasar Wigand)

1993. 150th Anniv of Vienna Male Choral Society.
2357 **1055** 5s. multicoloured 1·20 90

1056 Easter (Max Weiler)

1993. Austrian Modern Art.
2358 **1056** 5s.50 multicoloured 1·20 90

1057 "99 Heads" (detail, Friedensreich Hundertwasser)

1993. Council of Europe Heads of State Conference, Vienna.
2359 **1057** 7s. multicoloured 3·00 2·00

1058 Statue of Athene, Parliament Building

1993. 75th Anniv of Austrian Republic.
2360 **1058** 5s. multicoloured 1·20 90

1059 Workers

1993. Cent of First Austrian Trade Unions Congress.
2361 **1059** 5s.50 multicoloured 1·20 90

1060 "Birth of Christ" (Krainburg Altar, Styria)

1993. Christmas.
2362 **1060** 5s.50 multicoloured 1·20 90

1994. Folk Customs and Art (4th series). As T **1005**. Multicoloured.
2363 5s.50 Rocking cradle, Vorarlberg 1·20 1·10
2364 6s. Carved sleigh, Styria 1·40 1·30
2365 7s. Godparent's bowl and lid, Upper Austria 1·60 1·50

1061 Winter Sports

1994. Winter Olympic Games, Lillehammer, Norway.
2366 **1061** 7s. multicoloured 1·40 1·30

1062 Early Production of Coins

1994. 800th Anniv of Vienna Mint.
2367 **1062** 6s. multicoloured 1·20 1·10

1994. "Austro Pop" (3rd series). Falco (Johann Holzel) (singer). As T **1042**. Multicoloured.
2368 6s. "Rock Me Amadeus" (record sleeve) 1·40 1·10

1063 Reclining Lady (detail, Herbert Boeckl)

1994. Birth Centenary of Herbert Boeckl (painter).
2369 **1063** 5s.50 multicoloured 1·20 1·10

1064 N.W. Tower of City Wall

1994. 800th Anniv of Wiener Neustadt.
2370 **1064** 6s. multicoloured 1·20 1·10

1065 Lurgrotte (caves), Styria

1994. Natural Beauty Spots.
2371 **1065** 6s. multicoloured 1·20 1·10

1066 Lake Rudolf (Teleki–Hohnel expedition to Africa, 1887)

1994. Europa. Discoveries.
2372 **1066** 7s. multicoloured 3·75 1·80

1067 "E" and "L" as Ruins in Landscape

1994. Stamp Day.
2373 **1067** 7s.+3s. multicoloured 2·20 2·00
See note below No. 2266.

1068 "Allegory of Theology, Justice, Philosophy and Medicine" (detail of fresco, National Library)

1994. 300th Birth Anniv of Daniel Gran (artist).
2374 **1068** 20s. multicoloured 4·75 3·25

1069 Scene from The Prodigal Son (opera, Benjamin Britten)

1994. 25th Anniv of Carinthian Summer Festival, Ossiach and Villach.
2375 **1069** 5s.50 gold and red 1·20 1·10

1070 Steam Locomotive and Diesel Railcar (Gailtal)

1994. Railway Centenaries. Multicoloured.
2376 5s.50 Type **1070** 1·40 1·30
2377 6s. Steam locomotive and diesel railcar (Murtal) 1·60 1·50

1071 Gmeiner and Children

1994. 75th Birth Anniv of Hermann Gmeiner (founder of S.O.S. children's villages).
2378 **1071** 7s. multicoloured 1·40 1·30

1072 Seitz (bust, G. Ambrosi)

1994. 125th Birth Anniv of Karl Seitz (acting President, 1920).
2379 **1072** 5s.50 multicoloured 1·20 90

1073 Bohm

1994. Birth Centenary of Karl Bohm (conductor).
2380 **1073** 7s. blue and gold 1·40 1·30

1074 Ethnic Minorities on Map

1994. Legal and Cultural Protection of Ethnic Minorities.
2381 **1074** 5s.50 multicoloured 1·20 1·00

1075 Franz Theodor Csokor (dramatist and poet)

1994. Writers' Anniversaries. Multicoloured.
2382 6s. Type **1075** (25th death anniv) 1·20 1·10
2383 7s. Joseph Roth (novelist, birth cent) 1·40 1·30

1076 Head (Franz Ringel)

1994. Austrian Modern Art.
2384 **1076** 6s. multicoloured 1·40 1·10

1077 Money Box

1994. 175th Anniv of Savings Banks in Austria.
2385 **1077** 7s. multicoloured 1·40 1·00

1078 Air Hostess and Child

1994. Austrian World of Work (6th series).
2386 **1078** 6s. multicoloured 1·20 90

1079 Coudenhove-Kalergi and Map of Europe

1994. Birth Cent of Richard Coudenhove-Kalergi (founder of Paneuropa Union).
2387 **1079** 10s. multicoloured 2·10 1·20

1080 Birth of Christ (Anton Wollenek)

1994. Christmas.
2388 **1080** 6s. multicoloured 1·20 90

1081 Map and Austrian and E.U. Flags

1995. Austria's Entry into E.U.
2389 **1081** 7s. multicoloured 1·40 90

1082 Loos House, Michaelerplatz, Vienna

1995. 125th Birth Anniv of Adolf Loos (architect).
2390 **1082** 10s. multicoloured 1·90 1·50

1083 Sporting Activities

1995. 50th Anniv of Austrian Gymnastics and Sports Association.
2391 **1083** 6s. multicoloured 1·20 90

1084 Workers

1995. 75th Anniv of Workers' and Employees' Chambers (advisory body).
2392 **1084** 6s. multicoloured 1·20 80

1995. Folk Costumes and Art (5th series). As T **1005**. Multicoloured.
2393 5s.50 Belt, Carinthia 1·20 1·10
2394 6s. Costume of Hiata (vineyard guard), Vienna 1·40 1·30
2395 7s. Gold bonnet, Wachau 1·60 1·50

1085 State Seal

1995. 50th Anniv of Second Republic.
2396 **1085** 6s. multicoloured 1·20 90

1086 Heft Ironworks

1995. Carinthian "History of Mining and Industry" Exhibition, Heft, Huttenberg.
2397 **1086** 5s.50 multicoloured 1·20 90

1087 Hiker in Mountains

1995. Centenary of Friends of Nature.
2398 **1087** 5s.50 multicoloured 1·20 90

1088 Heidenreichstein National Park

1995. Natural Beauty Spots.
2399 **1088** 6s. multicoloured 1·30 1·00

1089 Woman and Barbed Wire around Skull

1995. Europa. Peace and Freedom.
2400 **1089** 7s. multicoloured 4·50 1·90

1090 Map, Woman and Child and Transport

1995. Meeting of European Ministers of Transport Conference, Vienna.
2401 **1090** 7s. multicoloured 1·40 90

1091 "F" and "A" on Vase of Flowers

1995. Stamp Day.
2402 **1091** 10s.+5s. multicoloured 3·00 2·75
See note below No. 2266.

1092 Set for *The Flying Dutchman*

1995. 50th Bregenz Festival.
2403 **1092** 6s. multicoloured 1·20 80

1093 St. Gebhard (stained-glass window, Martin Hausle)

1995. Death Millenary of St. Gebhard, Bishop of Konstanz (patron saint of Vorarlberg chuches).
2404 **1093** 7s.50 multicoloured 1·40 90

1094 Members' Flags

1995. 50th Anniv of U.N.O.
2405 **1094** 10s. multicoloured 2·10 1·20

1095 Loschmidt

1995. Death Centenary of Josef Loschmidt (physical chemist).
2406 **1095** 20s. black, stone & brn 5·75 3·00

1096 K. Leichter

1995. Birth Cent of Kathe Leichter (sociologist).
2407 **1096** 6s. cream, black & red 1·20 90

1097 Scene from *Jedermann* (Hugo von Hofmannsthal)

1995. 75th Anniv of Salzburg Festival.
2408 **1097** 6s. multicoloured 1·20 90

1098 *European Scene* (Adolf Frohner)

1995. Austrian Modern Art.
2409 **1098** 6s. multicoloured 1·20 90

1099 Franz von Suppe and *The Beautiful Galatea*

1995. Composers' Anniversaries. Scenes from operettas. Multicoloured.
2410 6s. Type **1099** (death cent) 1·20 1·10
2411 7s. Nico Dostal and *The Hungarian Wedding* (birth centenary) 1·40 1·30

1100 University Building

1995. 25th Anniv of Klagenfurt University.
2412 **1100** 5s.50 multicoloured 1·20 80

1101 Hollenburg Castle

1995. 75th Anniv of Carinthian Referendum.
2413 **1101** 6s. multicoloured 1·20 80

1102 Postman

1995. Austrian World of Work (7th series).
2414 **1102** 6s. multicoloured 1·20 80

1103 Anton von Webern (50th death)

1995. Composers' Anniversaries.
2415 **1103** 6s. blue and orange 1·20 1·10
2416 - 7s. red and orange 1·40 1·30
DESIGN: 7s. Ludwig van Beethoven (225th birth).

1104 Christ Child

1995. Christmas. 300th Anniv of Christkindl Church.
2417 **1104** 6s. multicoloured 1·20 80

1996. Folk Customs and Art (6th series). As T **1005**.
2418 6s. multicoloured 1·30 1·20
DESIGN: 6s. Masked figures Roller and Scheller (Imst masquerades, Tyrol).

1105 Empress Maria Theresia and Academy Building

1996. 250th Anniv of Theresian Academy, Vienna.
2419 **1105** 6s. multicoloured 1·30 1·20

1106 Ski Jumping

1996. World Ski Jumping Championships, Tauplitz and Bad Mitterndorf.
2420 **1106** 7s. multicoloured 1·60 90

1107 Terminal

1996. Completion of West Terminal, Vienna International Airport.
2421 **1107** 7s. multicoloured 1·60 90

1108 Hohe Tauern National Park

1996. Natural Beauty Spots.
2422 **1108** 6s. multicoloured 1·40 80

1109 "Mother and Child" (Peter Fendi)

1996. Artists' Birth Bicentenaries. Multicoloured.
2423 6s. Type **1109** 1·30 1·20
2424 7s. *Self-portrait* (Leopold Kupelwieser) 1·70 1·60

1110 Organ and Music

1996. Death Cent of Anton Bruckner (composer).
2425	**1110**	5s.50 multicoloured	1·30	80

1111 Kollmitz Castle (from copper engraving)

1996. 300th Death Anniv of Georg Vischer (cartographer and engraver).
2426	**1111**	10s. black and stone	2·20	1·30

1112 Old Market Square

1996. 800th Anniv of Klagenfurt.
2427	**1112**	6s. multicoloured	1·60	90

1113 Hotel Chef and Waitress

1996. Austrian World of Work (8th series).
2428	**1113**	6s. multicoloured	1·20	90

1114 Paula von Preradovic (writer)

1996. Europa. Famous Women.
2429	**1114**	7s. stone, brown & grey	1·60	1·10

1115 "M" and "T" and Bluebirds (mosaic)

1996. Stamp Day.
2430	**1115**	10s.+5s. mult	3·50	2·50

See note below No. 2266.

1116 Mascot with Olympic Flag

1996. Olympic Games, Atlanta.
2431	**1116**	10s. multicoloured	2·20	1·50

1996. Folk Customs and Art (7th series). As T **1005**.
2432		5s.50 Flower-bedecked poles, Salzburg	1·40	1·30
2433		7s. Tyrol militia	1·60	1·50

1117 Landscape

1996. 75th Anniv of Burgenland.
2434	**1117**	6s. multicoloured	1·20	80

1118 Mountaineers

1996. Cent of Austrian Mountain Rescue Service.
2435	**1118**	6s. multicoloured	1·20	80

1119 Deed of Otto III, 996

1996. Millenary of Austria. Multicoloured.
2436		6s. Type **1119**	1·20	90
2437		6s. Archduke Joseph II (after Georg Weikert) and Archduchess Maria Theresia (after Martin van Meytens)	1·20	90
2438		7s. *Duke Heinrich II* (stained-glass window, Monastery of the Holy Cross)	1·30	1·10
2439		7s. Arms in flames (1848 Revolution)	1·30	1·10
2440		7s. Rudolf IV, the Founder	1·30	1·10
2441		7s. Karl Renner (first Federal Republic president)	1·30	1·10
2442		10s. Archduke Maximilian I (Holy Roman Emperor) (miniature from Statute Book of Order of the Golden Fleece)	2·20	1·60
2443		10s. Seal and signature of Leopold Figl (State Treaty of 1955)	2·20	1·60
2444		20s. Imperial crown of Rudolf II	4·25	3·25
2445		20s. State arms, stars of Europe and *The Horsebreaker* (bronze by Josef Lax) (Austria and Europe)	4·25	3·25

1120 *Power Station* (Reinhard Artberg)

1996. Austrian Modern Art.
2446	**1120**	7s. multicoloured	1·60	1·10

1121 Children of Different Nations

1996. 50th Anniv of UNICEF.
2447	**1121**	10s. multicoloured	2·20	1·30

1122 Nativity and Vienna Town Hall

1996. Christmas.
2448	**1122**	6s. multicoloured	1·20	90

1123 Kramer

1997. Birth Centenary of Theodor Kramer (poet).
2449	**1123**	5s.50 blue	1·20	80

1997. Folk Customs and Art (8th series). As T **1005**. Multicoloured.
2450	7s. Epiphany carol singers, Eisenstadt Burgenland	1·60	1·50

1124 Vineyards on the Nussberg, Vienna

1997. Natural Beauty Spots.
2451	**1124**	6s. multicoloured	1·30	90

1125 Academy and Light

1997. 150th Anniv of Austrian Academy of Sciences, Vienna.
2452	**1125**	10s. multicoloured	2·30	1·30

1126 Emblem

1997. 50th Anniv of Verbund Electricity Company.
2453	**1126**	6s. multicoloured	1·20	90

1127 The Cruel Rosalia of Forchtenstein

1997. Myths and Legends.
2454	-	6s.50 grn, pink & blk	2·20	90
2455	**1127**	7s. black, stone & brn	2·40	65
2456	-	8s. orange, blk & lilac	2·20	1·10
2457	-	9s. black, stone & pur	3·00	1·70
2458	-	10s. black, grey & red	3·50	2·00
2459	-	13s. black, brn & pur	4·25	2·20
2460	-	14s. black, lt blue & bl	4·25	1·90
2461	-	20s. green, blk & stone	6·00	2·75
2462	-	22s. black, bl & stone	5·50	4·50
2463	-	23s. black, ochre and green	7·75	5·00
2464	-	25s. stone, black and yellow	7·25	3·25
2465	-	32s. black, brn & pink	11·00	5·50

DESIGNS: 6s.50, Lindworm of Klagenfurt; 8s. The Black Lady of Hardegg; 9s. Charming Augustin; 10s. Basilisk of Vienna; 13s. The Pied Piper of Korneuburg; 14s. The Strudengau Water-nymph; 20s. St. Notburga; 22s. Witches Whirl; 23s. Loaf Agony; 25s. St. Konrad and Altems Castle; 32s. The Discovery of Erzberg (Mountain of Ore).

1128 Stage Set for 'Die tote Stadt'

1997. Birth Cent of Erich Korngold (composer).
2470	**1128**	20s. black, blue & gold	5·75	2·75

1129 Stadium, Badge and Players

1997. Rapid Vienna, National Football Champions, 1995–96.
2471	**1129**	7s. multicoloured	1·80	90

1130 Red Deer

1997. Hunting and the Environment. Deer Feeding in Winter.
2472	**1130**	7s. multicoloured	1·60	90

1131 Canisius and Children (altar by Josef Bachlechner in Innsbruck Seminary)

1997. 400th Death Anniv of St. Petrus Canisius (patron saint of Innsbruck).
2473	**1131**	7s.50 multicoloured	1·60	90

1132 Johannes Brahms (after L. Michalek)

1997. Composers' Anniversaries.
2474	**1132**	6s. violet and gold	1·30	1·20
2475	-	10s. purple and gold	2·30	2·10

DESIGNS: 6s. Type **1132** (death centenary); 10s. Franz Schubert (birth bicentenary).

1133 "A" and "E"

1997. Stamp Day.
2476	**1133**	7s. multicoloured	1·80	1·10

See note below No. 2266.

1134 The Four Friends

1997. Europa. Tales and Legends. *The Town Band of Bremen* by the Brothers Grimm.
2477	**1134**	7s. multicoloured	4·25	1·10

1135 1850 9k. Stamp and Postman

1997. "WIPA 2000" International Stamp Exhibition, Vienna (1st issue).
2478	**1135**	27s.+13s. mult	9·00	6·75

See also Nos. 2521, 2543, **MS**2551 and **MS**2564.

1136 Train on Hochschneeberg Line

1997. Railway Anniversaries. Multicoloured.
2479		6s. Type **1136** (centenary of Hochschneeberg rack-railway)	1·40	1·30

2480 7s.50 Steam locomotive
Licaon and viaduct near
Mattersburg (150th anniv of
Odenburg–Wiener Neustadt
line) 1·90 1·80

1137 Cogwheels

1997. 125th Anniv of Austrian Technical Supervisory
Association.
2481 **1137** 7s. multicoloured 1·70 90

1997. Folk Customs and Art (9th series). As T **1005**.
Multicoloured.
2482 6s.50 Tyrolean brass band 1·60 1·10

1138 Waggerl
(self-portrait)

1997. Birth Centenary of Karl Waggerl (writer).
2483 **1138** 7s. green, yellow & blue 1·70 90

1139 Adolf Lorenz (founder
of German Society of
Orthopaedia)

1997. Orthopaedics Congress, Vienna.
2484 **1139** 8s. multicoloured 1·80 1·10

1140 Emblem

1997. 125th Anniv of College of Agricultural Sciences,
Vienna.
2485 **1140** 9s. multicoloured 2·10 1·30

1141 Patient, Nurse and Doctor

1997. Austrian World of Work (9th series).
2486 **1141** 6s.50 multicoloured 1·40 90

1142 Blind Man with
Guide Dog

1997. Cent of Austrian Association for the Blind.
2487 **1142** 7s. multicoloured 1·60 90

1143 *House in Wind*
(Helmut Schickhofer)

1997. Austrian Modern Art.
2488 **1143** 7s. multicoloured 1·80 90

1144 Klestil

1997. 65th Birthday of Pres. Thomas Klestil.
2489 **1144** 7s. multicoloured 1·80 90

1145 Werner

1997. 75th Birth Anniv of Oskar Werner (actor).
2490 **1145** 7s. black, orge & grey 1·80 90

1997. Folk Customs and Art (10th series). As T **1005**.
Multicoloured.
2491 6s.50 Tower wind-band, Upper
 Austria 1·40 1·10

1146 Glowing Light

1997. 25th Anniv of Light in Darkness (umbrella
organization of children's charities).
2492 **1146** 7s. blue 1·60 90

1147 "Mariazell
Madonna"

1997. Christmas.
2493 **1147** 7s. multicoloured 1·60 90

1148 Kalkalpen National
Park

1998. Natural Beauty Spots.
2494 **1148** 7s. multicoloured 1·40 90

1149 Courting Pair

1998. Hunting and the Environment. Preservation of
Breeding Habitat of the Black Grouse.
2495 **1149** 9s. multicoloured 1·80 1·30

1150 Ice Skaters

1998. Winter Olympic Games, Nagano, Japan.
2496 **1150** 14s. multicoloured 2·75 2·00

1151 Austrian Poster
Exposition
Advertising Poster,
1928

1998. Birth Cent of Joseph Binder (designer).
2497 **1151** 7s. multicoloured 1·60 1·10

1152 Alois Senefelder
(inventor) on
Lithographic Stone

1998. Bicentenary of Invention of Lithography (printing
process).
2498 **1152** 7s. blue, yellow & black 1·40 90

1153 Facade

1998. Centenary of Vienna Secession (exn hall).
2499 **1153** 8s. brown, gold & blue 1·80 1·10

1998. Folk Customs and Art (11th series). As T **1005**.
Multicoloured.
2500 6s.50 Fiacre, Vienna 1·40 1·30
2501 7s. Palm Sunday procession,
 Thaur, Tyrol 1·60 1·50

1154 Player and Team
Emblem

1998. Austria Memphis Football Club.
2502 **1154** 7s. multicoloured 1·80 1·00

1155 "St. Florian"
(glass painting)

1998. St. Florian, Patron Saint of Firemen.
2503 **1155** 7s. multicoloured 1·80 1·00

1156 Rupertus Cross

1998. 1200th Anniv of Salzburg Archdiocese.
2504 **1156** 7s. multicoloured 1·80 1·00

1157 Series Yv
Locomotive No. 2, 1895

1998. Centenary of Completion of Ybbs Valley Railway.
2505 **1157** 6s.50 multicoloured 1·80 1·10

1158 "Tyrolia"
(Ferdinand Cosandier)

1998. 175th Anniv of Tyrol Ferdinandeum (state
museum), Innsbruck.
2506 **1158** 7s. multicoloured 1·60 1·00

1159 Vienna Town
Hall (Viennese
festive weeks)

1998. Europa. National Festivals.
2507 **1159** 7s. multicoloured 4·00 1·10

1998. Folk Customs and Art (12th series). As T **1005**.
Multicoloured.
2508 6s.50 Samson and the dwarves,
 Salzburg 1·80 1·10

1160 Christine Lavant

1998. 25th Death Anniv of Christine Lavant (poet).
2509 **1160** 7s. multicoloured 1·80 1·10

1161 Electric Railcar No.
1

1998. Centenary of Postlingberg Railway.
2510 **1161** 6s.50 multicoloured 1·80 1·10

1162 "R" and "L"

1998. Stamp Day.
2511 **1162** 7s. multicoloured 1·80 1·10
See note below No. 2266.

1163 Presidency
Emblem

1998. Austrian Presidency of E.U.
2512 **1163** 7s. multicoloured 1·80 1·10

1164 Railcar No. 5090

1998. Centenary of Pinzgau Railway.
2513 **1164** 6s.50 multicoloured 1·80 1·10

1165 Volksoper, Vienna

1998. Centenary of Volksoper (theatre) and 50th Death Anniv of Franz Lehar (composer).
2514 **1165** 6s.50 multicoloured 1·60 1·10

1166 Empress Elisabeth (after Franz Winterhalter)

1998. Death Centenary of Empress Elisabeth.
2515 **1166** 7s. multicoloured 1·80 1·50

1167 School Building

1998. Centenary of Vienna Business School.
2516 **1167** 7s. multicoloured 1·80 1·50

1168 Kudlich and Farmers

1998. 175th Birth Anniv of Hans Kudlich (promoter of 1848 "Peasants' Liberation" Law).
2517 **1168** 6s.50 multicoloured 1·60 1·00

1169 *My Garden* (Hans Staudacher)

1998. Austrian Modern Art.
2518 **1169** 7s. multicoloured 1·80 1·10

1170 Town Hall and Arms

1998. 350th Anniv of Declaration of Eisenstadt as a Free Town.
2519 **1170** 7s. multicoloured 1·60 1·10

1171 Photographer and Reporter

1998. Austrian World of Work (10th series). Art, Media and Freelances.
2520 **1171** 6s.50 multicoloured 1·40 1·00

1172 1929 2s. Stamp and Post Van

1998. "WIPA 2000" International Stamp Exhibition, Vienna (2nd issue).
2521 **1172** 32s.+13s. mult 9·75 7·75

1173 "Nativity" (fresco, Tainach Church)

1998. Christmas.
2522 **1173** 7s. multicoloured 1·40 1·00

1174 Cross-country Skiing

1999. World Nordic Skiing Championships, Ramsau.
2523 **1174** 7s. multicoloured 1·80 1·20

1999. Folk Customs and Art (13th series). As T **1005**. Multicoloured.
2524 6s.50 Walking pilgrimage to Mariazell 1·40 1·10

1175 Stingl Rock, Bohemian Forest

1999. Natural Beauty Spots.
2525 **1175** 7s. multicoloured 1·40 1·10

1176 Books and Compact Disc

1999. Centenary of Austrian Patent Office.
2526 **1176** 7s. multicoloured 1·40 1·10

1177 Player and Club Emblem

1999. SK Puntigamer Sturm Graz Football Club.
2527 **1177** 7s. multicoloured 1·80 1·10

1178 Palace Facade

1999. World Heritage Site. Schonbrunn Palace, Vienna.
2528 **1178** 13s. multicoloured 2·75 2·20

1179 Partridges

1999. Hunting and the Environment. Living Space for Grey Partridges.
2529 **1179** 6s.50 multicoloured 1·40 1·10

1180 Snowboarder

1999. 50th Anniv of Austrian General Sport Federation.
2530 **1180** 7s. multicoloured 1·60 1·10

1181 Council Building, Strasbourg

1999. 50th Anniv of Council of Europe.
2531 **1181** 14s. multicoloured 3·00 2·20
No. 2531 is denominated both in Austrian schillings and in euros.

1182 Steyr Type 50 Baby Saloon

1999. Birth Centenary of Karl Jenschke (engineer and car manufacturer).
2532 **1182** 7s. multicoloured 1·60 1·20

1183 "St. Martin" (marble relief, Peuerbach Church)

1999. Ancient Arts and Crafts (1st series).
2533 **1183** 8s. brown, blue & orange 1·80 1·30
See also Nos. 2542, 2575, 2600 and 2602.

1184 Symbols of Aid and Emblem

1999. 125th Anniv of Diakonie (professional charitable services).
2534 **1184** 7s. multicoloured 1·40 1·10

1185 Johann Strauss, the Younger

1999. Composers' Death Anniversaries. Multicoloured.
2535 7s. Type **1185** (centenary) 1·70 1·60
2536 8s. Johann Strauss, the Elder (150th anniv) 1·80 1·70

1186 Rural Gendarmes

1999. 150th Anniv of National Gendarmerie.
2537 **1186** 7s. multicoloured 1·60 1·10

1187 Donau-auen National Park

1999. Europa. Parks and Gardens.
2538 **1187** 7s. multicoloured 1·80 1·10

1188 "K" and "I"

1999. Stamp Day.
2539 **1188** 7s. multicoloured 1·80 1·10
See note below No. 2266.

1189 Iron Stage Curtain

1999. Centenary of Graz Opera.
2540 **1189** 6s.50 multicoloured 1·80 1·10

1190 Couple on Bench

1999. International Year of the Elderly.
2541 **1190** 7s. multicoloured 1·40 1·10

1191 "St. Anne with Mary and Child Jesus" (wood-carving, St. George's Church, Purgg)

1999. Ancient Arts and Crafts (2nd series).
2542 **1191** 9s. multicoloured 2·20 2·00

1192 1949 25g. Stamp and Vienna Airport

1999. "WIPA 2000" International Stamp Exhibition, Vienna (3rd issue).
2543 **1192** 32s.+16s. mult 11·50 8·50

1193 "Security throughout Life"

1999. 14th Congress of Federation of Austrian Trade Unions.
2544 **1193** 6s.50 multicoloured 1·40 1·10

1194 "Cafe Girardi" (Wolfgang Herzig)

1999. Austrian Modern Art.
2545 **1194** 7s. multicoloured 1·80 1·10

1999. Folk Customs and Art (14th series). As T **1005**. Multicoloured.
2546 8s. Pumpkin Festival, Lower
Austria 1·80 1·10

1999. Folk Customs and Art (15th series). As T **1005**. Multicoloured.
2547 7s. The Pummerin (great bell of St. Stephen's Cathedral) ringing in the New Year 1·80 1·10

1195 Institute and Fossils

1999. 150th Anniv of National Institute of Geology.
2548 **1195** 7s. multicoloured 1·80 1·10

1196 "Nativity" (altar painting, Pinkafeld Church)

1999. Christmas.
2549 **1196** 7s. multicoloured 1·40 1·10

2000. Folk Customs and Art (16th series). As T 1005. Multicoloured.
2550 7s. Chapel procession, Carinthia 1·40 1·30

2000. "WIPA 2000" International Stamp Exhibition, Vienna (4th issue). Sheet 150×95 mm.
MS2551 27s.+13s. No. 2478; 32s.+13s.
No. 2521; 32s.+16s. No. 2543 36·00 39·00

2000. Folk Customs and Art (17th series). As T 1005. Multicoloured.
2552 6s.50 Three men wearing masks
(Cavalcade of Beautiful
Masks, Telfs) 1·40 1·10

1197 Zantadeschica aethiopica

2000. International Garden Show, Graz.
2553 **1197** 7s. multicoloured 1·80 1·10

1198 Ibex

2000. Hunting and the Environment. Return of Ibex to Austrian Mountains.
2554 **1198** 7s. multicoloured 1·60 1·10

1199 Players

2000. F.C. Tirol Innsbruck, National Football Champion 2000.
2555 **1199** 7s. multicoloured 1·60 1·10

1200 Mt. Grossglockner and Viewing Point

2000. Bicentenary of First Ascent of Mt. Grossglockner.
2556 **1200** 7s. multicoloured 1·60 1·10

1201 Weisssee Lake

2000. Natural Beauty Spots.
2557 **1201** 7s. multicoloured 1·40 1·20

1202 "Building Europe"

2000. Europa.
2558 **1202** 7s. multicoloured 1·80 1·70

1203 Junkers F13 Airplane and Air Traffic Control Tower

2000. 75th Anniv of Civil Aviation at Klagenfurt Airport.
2559 **1203** 7s. multicoloured 1·40 1·30

1204 Madonna of Altenmarkt (statue) and Glass Roof, Palm House, Burggarten, Vienna

2000. 150th Anniv of Protection of Historic Monuments.
2560 **1204** 8s. multicoloured 1·80 1·50

1205 Illuminated Letter and Text

2000. Life of St. Malachy (treatise) by St. Bernard of Clairvaux.
2561 **1205** 9s. multicoloured 2·40 2·20

1206 "E" and "E"

2000. Stamp Day.
2562 **1206** 7s. multicoloured 1·80 1·30
See note below No. 2266.

1207 1850 9 Kreuzer and 2000 Stamp Day Stamps

2000. 150th Anniv of Austrian Stamps.
2563 **1207** 7s. multicoloured 1·80 1·30

2000. "WIPA 2000" International Stamp Exhibition, Vienna (5th series). Sheet 65×90 mm.
MS2564 10s. As No. 2458 36·00 34·00

1208 "Confetti"

2000. Confetti (children's television programme).
2565 **1208** 7s. multicoloured 1·60 1·30

1209 Blue Blues

2000. Death Commemoration of Friedensreich Hundertwasser (artist). Sheet 129×126 mm, containing four versions of T **1209** identified by the colours of the vertical strips at the top of the design.
MS2566 7s. silver; 7s. red; 7s. mauve;
7s. black 9·75 9·00

1210 Blood Droplets

2000. Centenary of Discovery of Blood Groups by Karl Landsteiner (pathologist).
2567 **1210** 8s. pink, silver & black 1·60 1·50

1211 Daimler Cannstatter Bus

2000. Centenary of First Regular Bus Route between Purkersdorf and Gablitz.
2568 **1211** 9s. black, blue and light
blue 2·40 2·00

2000. Folk Customs and Art (18th series). As T 1005. Multicoloured.
2569 7s. Men on raft (International
Rafting Meeting, Carinthia) 1·40 1·30

1212 Dachstein River and Hallstatt

2000. Natural Beauty Spots.
2570 **1212** 7s. multicoloured 1·40 1·30

1213 String Instrument and Emblem

2000. Centenary of Vienna Symphony Orchestra.
2571 **1213** 7s. multicoloured 1·40 1·30

1214 Dinghies

2000. Olympic Games, Sydney.
2572 **1214** 9s. multicoloured 2·20 1·80

1215 Old and Modern Paper Production Methods

2000. Austrian World of Work (11th series). Printing and Paper.
2573 **1215** 6s.50 multicoloured 1·40 1·30

1216 Turf Turkey (Ida Szigethy)

2000. Austrian Modern Art.
2574 **1216** 7s. multicoloured 1·40 1·30

1217 Codex 965 (National Library)

2000. Ancient Arts and Crafts (3rd series).
2575 **1217** 8s. multicoloured 1·80 1·70
See also Nos. 2600 and 2602.

1218 Child receiving Vaccination

2000. Bicentenary of Vaccination in Austria.
2576 **1218** 7s. black and cinnamon 1·40 1·30

1219 Urania Building, Vienna

2000. 50th Anniv of Adult Education Association.
2577 **1219** 7s. brown, grey & gold 1·40 1·30

1220 The Nativity (altar piece, Ludesch Church)

2000. Christmas.
2578 **1220** 7s. multicoloured 1·40 1·30

1221 Downhill Skier

2000. World Skiing Championship (2001), St. Anton am Arlberg.
2579 **1221** 7s. multicoloured 1·60 1·50

1222 Pair of Mallards

2001. Hunting and the Environment. Protection of Wetlands.
2580 **1222** 7s. multicoloured 1·60 1·50

2001. Folk Customs and Art (19th series). As T **1005**. Multicoloured.
2581 8s. Boat mill, Mureck, Styria 1·80 1·50

1223 Steam Locomotive No. 3

2001. Centenary of Zillertal Railway.
2582 **1223** 7s. multicoloured 1·60 1·50

1224 Players and Club Emblem

2001. SV Casino Salzburg, National Football Champion.
2583 **1224** 7s. multicoloured 1·80 1·30

1225 Rolf Rudiger

2001. Confetti (children's television programme).
2584 **1225** 7s. multicoloured 1·80 1·30

1226 Fieseler Fi-156 Storch and Airport

2001. 75th Anniv of Salzburg Airport.
2585 **1226** 14s. multicoloured 3·25 2·75

1227 Baerenschuetz Gorge

2001. Natural Beauty Spots.
2586 **1227** 7s. multicoloured 1·60 1·50

2001. Folk Customs and Art (20th series). As T **1005**. Multicoloured.
2587 7s. Lent season cloth from Eastern Tyrol 1·60 1·50

1228 Water Droplet

2001. Europa. Water Resources.
2588 **1228** 15s. multicoloured 4·75 3·25

1229 Post Office Railway Car

2001. Stamp Day.
2589 **1229** 20s.+10s. mult 11·00 10·00

1230 Air Balloon

2001. Centenary of Austrian Flying Club.
2590 **1230** 7s. multicoloured 1·80 1·50

1231 Refugee

2001. 50th Anniv of United Nations High Commissioner for Refugees.
2591 **1231** 21s. multicoloured 4·75 4·50

1232 Kalte Rinne Viaduct

2001. UNESCO World Heritage Site. The Semmering Railway.
2592 **1232** 35s. multicoloured 11·00 10·00

1233 "Seppl" (mascot) (Michelle Schneeweiss)

2001. Seventh International Hiking Olympics, Seefeld.
2593 **1233** 7s. multicoloured 1·60 1·50

1234 Field Post Office at Famagusta

2001. Army Postal Services Abroad.
2594 **1234** 7s. multicoloured 1·60 1·50

2001. Folk Customs and Art (21st series). As T **1005**. Multicoloured.
2595 7s. Rifle and Clubhouse, Preberschiessen, Salzburg (Rifleman's gathering) 1·60 1·50

1235 Taurus (Railway Engine)

2001. Conversion of East–West Railway to Four-tracked Railway.
2596 **1235** 7s. multicoloured 1·80 1·70

1236 19th-century Theatrical Scene

2001. Birth Bicentenary of Johann Nestroy (playwright and actor).
2597 **1236** 7s. multicoloured 1·60 1·50

1237 The Continents (detail Helmut Leherb)

2001. Austrian Modern Art.
2598 **1237** 7s. multicoloured 1·60 1·50

1238 False Friends (Von Fuehrich)

2001. 125th Death Anniv of Joseph Ritter von Fuehrich (artist and engraver).
2599 **1238** 8s. deep green & green 1·70 1·60

1239 Pluviale (embroidered religious robe)

2001. Ancient Arts and Crafts (4th series).
2600 **1239** 10s. multicoloured 2·40 2·20

1240 Dobler

2001. Birth Bicentenary of Leopold Ludwig Dobler (magician and inventor).
2601 **1240** 7s. multicoloured 1·60 1·50

1241 Dalmatika (religious vestment) (Carmelite Monastery, Silbergrasse, Vienna)

2001. Ancient Arts and Crafts (5th series).
2602 **1241** 7s. multicoloured 1·60 1·50

1242 Building and Scientific Equipment

2001. 150th Anniv of the Central Institute for Meteorology and Geodynamics, Vienna.
2603 **1242** 12s. multicoloured 3·00 2·20

1243 Cat

2001
2604 **1243** 19s. multicoloured 6·00 5·50

1244 Civil Servants

2001. Austrian World of Work (12th series). Civil Service.
2605 **1244** 7s. multicoloured 1·60 1·50

1245 Figure of Infant Jesus

2001. Christmas. Glass Shrine, Fitzmoos Church.
2606 **1245** 7s. multicoloured 1·40 1·30

New Currency

1246 House of the Basilisk, Vienna

2002. Tourism.

2607	-	4c. multicoloured	25	10
2608	-	7c. blue and black	35	20
2609	-	13c. multicoloured	50	35
2610	-	17c. violet and black	60	45
2611	-	20c. multicoloured	70	65
2612	-	25c. multicoloured	85	80
2613	-	27c. blue and black	95	90
2614	-	45c. multicoloured	1·20	1·10
2615	**1246**	51c. multicoloured	1·40	1·30
2616	-	55c. multicoloured	1·40	1·20
2617	-	58c. multicoloured	1·60	1·50
2618	-	73c. multicoloured	1·80	1·70
2619	-	75c. multicoloured	2·10	1·80
2620	-	87c. multicoloured	2·40	2·20
2621	-	€1 multicoloured	2·75	2·20
2622	-	€1.25 multicoloured	3·25	2·50
2623	-	€2.03 multicoloured	6·00	5·50
2624	-	€3.75 multicoloured	9·25	8·50

DESIGNS: 4c. As No. 2615; 7c. As No. 2623; 13c. As No. 2620; 17c. As No. 2617; 20c. Yachts, Worthersee, Carinta; 25c. Crucifixes on rock, Mondsee, Upper Austria; 27c. As No. 2618; 45c. Snow covered chalet, Jungholz, Kleinwasler; 55c. Gothic houses, Steyr, Upper Austria; 58c. Wine cellars, Hadres, Lower Austria; 73c. Alpine chalet, Salzburg; 75c. Boat on Bodensee, Voralberg; 87c. Alpach Valley, Tyrol; €1 Farmhouse, Rossegg, Styria; €1.25 Wine press building, Eisenburg, Burgenland; €2.03 Heligenkreuz, Lower Austria; €3.75 Gothic shrine, Hochhosterwitz, Carinthia.

1247 Stars, Map of Europe and €1 Coin

2002. Euro Currency.
2630 **1247** €3.27 multicoloured 9·75 9·00
No. 2630 is printed on the back under the gum with examples of Austrian schilling coins.

1248 Skiers and Olympic Rings

2002. Winter Olympic Games, Salt Lake City, U.S.A.
2631 **1248** 73c. multicoloured 2·20 2·00

1249 Bouquet of Flowers

2002
2632 **1249** 87c. multicoloured 2·30 2·10

1250 Woman and Skyline

2002. Women's Day.
2633 **1250** 51c. multicoloured 3·50 3·25

1251 Mel and Lucy

2002. "Philis" (children's stamp awareness programme) (1st issue).
2634 **1251** 58c. multicoloured 2·20 2·00
See also Nos. 2639 and 2662.

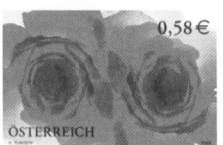

1252 Red Roses

2002. Greetings Stamp.
2635 **1252** 58c. multicoloured 1·80 1·70

1253 Kubin

2002. 125th Birth Anniv of Alfred Kubin (artist).
2636 **1253** 87c. black and buff 2·30 2·10

1254 St. Elizabeth of Thuringia and Sick Man

2002. Caritas (Catholic charity organization).
2637 **1254** 51c. multicoloured 1·90 1·80

1255 Tiger, Clown and Circus Tent

2002. Europa. The Circus.
2638 **1255** 87c. multicoloured 3·50 3·25

1256 Sisko and Mauritius

2002. "Philis" (children's stamp awareness programme) (2nd issue)
2639 **1256** 58c. multicoloured 1·90 1·80

1257 The Nativity

2002. 800th Anniv of Lilienfeld Abbey.
2640 **1257** €2.03 multicoloured 5·75 5·50

1258 Mimi

2002. Confetti (children's television programme).
2641 **1258** 51c. multicoloured 1·80 1·70

1259 Railway Carriage, 1919

2002. Stamp Day.
2642 **1259** €1.60+80c. multicoloured 8·50 7·75

1260 Cheetah, Zebra and Orang-utan

2002. 250th Anniv of Schonbrunn Zoo. Multicoloured.
2643 51c. Type **1260** 1·70 1·60
2644 58c. Gulls, flamingos and pelicans 1·80 1·70
2645 87c. Lion, turtle and crocodile 2·40 2·20
2646 €1.38 Elephant, birds and fish 3·50 3·25
Nos. 2643/6 were issued together, *se-tenant*, forming a composite design.

1261 Teddy Bears

2002. Centenary of the Teddy Bear.
2647 **1261** 51c. multicoloured 1·90 1·80

1262 Chair No. 14 (Michael Thonet)

2002. 75th Anniv of "Design Austria" (design group) (1st issue).
2648 **1262** €1.38 multicoloured 3·50 3·25
See also Nos. 2661 and 2670.

1263 Crystal Cup

2002. Ancient Arts and Crafts.
2649 **1263** €1.60 multicoloured 4·25 4·00

1264 Museum Buildings

2002. Museumsquartier (MQ), Messepalast, Vienna.
2650 **1264** 58c. multicoloured 2·20 2·00

1265 Figures supporting Emblem

2002. 50th Anniv of Union of Austrians Abroad.
2651 **1265** €2.47 multicoloured 6·75 6·25

1266 Clown Doctor

2002. "Rote Nasen" (Red Noses (charity)).
2652 **1266** 51c. multicoloured 1·80 1·70

1267 Head

2002. Linzer Klangwolke (sound and light performance), Linz.
2653 **1267** 58c. multicoloured 1·90 1·80

1268 Graf & Stift Type 40/45

2002
2654 **1268** 51c. multicoloured 1·60 1·50

1269 Dog

2002
2655 **1269** 51c. multicoloured 1·60 1·50

1270 Steam Locomotive 109

2002
2656 **1270** 51c. multicoloured 1·80 1·70

1271 *Schutzenhaus* (Karl Goldammer)

2002. Austrian Modern Art.
2657 **1271** 51c. multicoloured 1·80 1·70

1272 Lottery Ball

2002. 250th Anniv of Austrian Lottery. Sheet 72×90 mm.
MS2658 **1272** 87c. multicoloured 3·00 2·75

1273 Thayatal National Park

2002
2659 **1273** 58c. multicoloured 1·80 1·70

1274 Puch 175 SV

2002
2660 **1274** 58c. multicoloured 1·90 1·80

1275 "Eye"

2002. 75th Anniv of "Design Austria" (design group) (2nd issue). Winning Entry in Design Competition.
2661 **1275** €1.38 multicoloured 4·25 4·00

1276 Edison and Gogo

2002. "Philis" (children's stamp awareness programme) (3rd issue).
2662 **1276** 58c. multicoloured 2·20 2·00

1277 Crib Aureola, Thaur, Tyrol

2002. Christmas.
2663 **1277** 51c. multicoloured 1·60 1·50

1278 Emblem

2003. Make-up Rate Stamp.
2664 **1278** 45c. yellow, silver and black 6·75 4·50

1279 Amphitheatre on River Mur

2003. Graz, Cultural Capital of Europe, 2003.
2665 **1279** 58c. multicoloured 1·80 1·70

1280 Billy Wilder

2003. First Death Anniv of Billy Wilder (film director).
2666 **1280** 58c. multicoloured 1·90 1·80

1281 Heart, Linked Rings and Doves

2003. Greetings Stamp. Wedding.
2667 **1281** 58c. multicoloured 1·90 1·80

1282 Kasperl

2003. Confetti (children's television programme). 45th Anniv of Kasperl (puppet).
2668 **1282** 51c. multicoloured 1·60 1·50

1283 Emblem

2003. Tenth Anniv of Recycling Enterprise.
2669 **1283** 55c. multicoloured 1·40 1·30

1284 Carafe and Glasses (Adolf Loos)

2003. 75th Anniv of "Design Austria" (design group) (3rd issue).
2670 **1284** €1.38 blue, black and orange 3·50 3·25

1285 Seated Pandas

2003. Schönbrunn Zoo's Acquisition of Pandas from People's Republic of China. Sheet 110×76 mm containing T **1285** and similar multicoloured design.
MS2671 75c. Pandas nuzzling (40×34 mm) (horiz); €1 Type **1285** 8·50 6·75

1286 St. George's Monastery

2003. Millenary of St. George's Monastery, Carintha.
2672 **1286** 87c. multicoloured 2·20 2·00

1287 Marcel Prawy

2003. Marcel Prawy Commemoration (musician). Sheet 100×100 mm.
MS2673 **1287** €1.75 multicoloured 6·75 6·75

1288 Face

2003. Europa. Poster Art.
2674 **1288** €1.02 multicoloured 3·00 2·75

1289 Siemmens M 320 Postal Wagon

2003. Stamp Day.
2675 **1289** €2.54+€1.26 multicoloured 11·00 10·00

1290 Series 5045 Locomotive *Blue Flash*

2003.
2676 **1290** 75c. multicoloured 2·30 2·10

1291 Bridge over Salzach River

2003. Centenary of Oberndorf–Laufen Bridge.
2677 **1291** 55c. multicoloured 2·40 2·20
A stamp of the same design was issued by Germany.

1292 Ford Model T

2003. Centenary of Ford Motor Company. Sheet 150×81 mm containing T **1292** and similar horiz designs. Multicoloured.
MS2678 Type **1292**; 55c. Henry Ford; 55c. Ford Streetka 6·75 6·25

1293 Keith Richards

2003. Rolling Stones. Sheet 101×101 mm containing T **1293** and similar vert designs. Multicoloured.
MS2679 Type **1293**; 55c. Mick Jagger; 55c. Charlie Watts; 55c. Ronnie Woods 9·00 8·50

1294 Panther Airport Fire Appliance

2003
2688 **1294** 55c. multicoloured 1·80 1·70

1295 Apostle and Scribe

2003. Year of the Bible.
2689 **1295** 55c. multicoloured 1·40 1·30

1296 "Prenez le temps d'aimer" (Take time to enjoy) (Kiki Kogelnik)

2003
2690 **1296** 55c. multicoloured 1·80 1·70

1297 Lake

2003. UNESCO World Heritage Site. Lake Neusiedlersee.
2691 **1297** €1 multicoloured 3·00 2·75

1298 Geisha and Samurai

2003. Japan Exhibition, Leoben.
2692 **1298** 55c. multicoloured 1·80 1·70

1299 Princess Turandot

2003. Performance of Puccini's Opera *Turandot*, St. Margarethen Roman Quarry.
2693 **1299** 55c. multicoloured 1·80 1·70

1300 Family (Eva Wallner)

2003. Children's Stamp.
2694 **1300** 55c. multicoloured 1·80 1·70

1301 Water Tower

2003. 50th Anniv Local Government Conference, Wiener Neustadt.
2695 **1301** 55c. multicoloured 1·60 1·50

1302 TomTom (cartoon character) and Bouquet

2003. Greetings stamp.
2696 **1302** 55c. multicoloured 2·20 2·00

1303 TomTom throwing Parcel from Hot Air Balloon

2003
2697 **1303** 55c. multicoloured 2·20 2·00

1304 Werner Schlager

2003. Werner Schlager, World Table Tennis Champion, 2003.
2698 **1304** 55c. multicoloured 2·40 2·20

1305 Stylized Head (Cornelia Zell)

2003. Jugend-Phila '03 International Youth Stamp Exhibition, Graz.
2699 **1305** 55c. multicoloured 1·40 1·30

1306 Fan and *Elisabeth*

2003. Elisabeth, the Musical (musical based on life of Empress Elisabeth).
2700 **1306** 55c. multicoloured 1·90 1·80

1307 *Judith*

2003. 185th Death Anniv of Gustav Klimt (artist). Sheet 80×100 mm.
MS2701 **1307** €2.10 multicoloured 7·75 7·25

1308 Hands enclosing Light

2003. 30th Anniv of "Licht ins Dunkel" (Bringing light into darkness) (fund raising campaign).
2702 **1308** 55c. multicoloured 1·40 1·30

1309 Grand Piano

2003. 175th Anniv of Bosendorfer (piano manufacturer).
2703 **1309** 75c. multicoloured 2·20 2·00

1310 Oscar Peterson

2003. 78th Birth Anniv of Oscar Peterson (pianist).
2704 **1310** €1.25 multicoloured 3·50 3·25

1311 Stained Glass Window

2003. Christmas.
2705 **1311** 55c. multicoloured 1·90 1·80

1312 Postal Emblem

2003. Greeting Stamps. T **1312** and similar design. Each yellow, black and gold.
2706 **1312** 55c. Type **1312** 1·40 1·30
2707 55c. Postal emblem (horiz) 1·40 1·30
 Nos. 2706/7 could be personalised by the addition of photograph or logo, replacing the design shown on the stamp.

1313 Ricardo Muti

2004. Vienna Philharmonic Orchestra's New Year Concert conducted by Ricardo Muti (principal conductor, La Scala Milan).
2708 **1313** €1 multicoloured 3·50 3·25

1314 Seiji Ozawa

2004. Second Anniv of Seija Ozawa's Appointment as Musical Director of Vienna State Opera House.
2709 **1314** €1 multicoloured 3·50 3·25

1315 Jose Carreras

2004. 30th Anniv of Jose Carreras Association with Vienna State Opera House.
2710 **1315** €1 multicoloured 3·50 3·25

1316 Gerard Hanappi

2004. Centenary of Austrian Football. Sheet 196×113 mm containing T **1316** and similar vert designs. Multicoloured.
MS2711 55c.×10, Type **1316**; Mathias Sindelar; Football and anniversary emblem; Bruno Pezzey; Ernst Ocwirk; Walter Zeman; Herbert Prohaska; Hans Krankl; Andreas Herzog; Anton Polster 16·00 16·00

1317 Crucifixion (Werner Berg)

2004. Easter.
2712 **1317** 55c. multicoloured 1·40 1·30

1318 Dancers

2004. Life Ball (AIDS charity).
2713 **1318** 55c. multicoloured 1·60 1·30

1319 Cardinal Franz Konig

2004. Cardinal Franz Konig Commemoration.
2714 **1319** €1 multicoloured 3·00 2·75

1320 Emperor Franz Joseph and Empress Elisabeth

2004. 150th Anniv of the Marriage of Emperor Franz Joseph and Empress Elisabeth. Sheet 157×109 mm containing T **1320** and similar vert designs. Multicoloured.
MS2715 €1.25 Type **1320**; €1.50 Wedding procession; €1.75 Emperor Franz Joseph and Empress Elisabeth (35×42 mm) 13·50 13·50

1321 Catholics' Day Emblem

2004. Catholics' Day. Sheet 110×160 mm containing T **1321** and similar vert designs. Multicoloured.
MS2716 55c. Type **1321**; €1.25 Pope John Paul II; €1.25 Magna Mater Austriae (Romanesque statue) (Chapel of Grace, Basilica, Mariazell); €1.25 Mother of God on Column of the Blessed Virgin (Treasury Altar, Mariazell); €1.25 Virgin Mary (Treasury Altar, Mariazell); €1.25 Crucifix (High Altar, Basilica, Mariazell) 19·00 19·00

1322 Oeffag C.11 Mail Plane

2004. Stamp Day.
2717 **1322** €2.65+€1.30 multicoloured 11·50 10·50

2004. Folk Customs and Art (22nd series). As T **1005**. Multicoloured.
2718 55c. Barrel sliding, Kosterneuburgs 1·80 1·70

1323 Joe Zawinul (musician)

2004.
2719 **1323** 55c. multicoloured 1·80 1·70

1324 Sun and Flowers

2004. Europa. Holidays.
2720 **1324** 75c. multicoloured 2·10 1·90

1325 Holy Sepulchre, Jerusalem

2004. Papal Order of the Holy Sepulchre.
2721 **1325** 125c. multicoloured 3·25 3·00

1326 Imperial and Royal Southern State Railway Locomotive *Engerth*

2004.
2722 **1326** 55c. multicoloured 1·70 1·60

1327 Fireworks and Bubbles

2004. Danube Island Festival, Vienna.
2723 **1327** 55c. multicoloured 1·40 1·30

1328 Theodor Herzl

2004. Death Centenary of Theodor Herzl (writer and Zionist pioneer).
2724 **1328** 55c. multicoloured 2·30 2·10
 A stamp of the same design was issued by Israel and Hungary.

1329 Arnold Schwarzenegger (governor of California)

2004.
2725 **1329** 100c. multicoloured 5·50 5·00

1330 Ernst Happel

2004. 12th Death Anniv of Ernst Happel (football trainer).
2726 **1330** 100c. black and scarlet 5·50 5·00

1331 Tom Turbo (bicycle) (Andreas Wolkerstorfer)

2004. Tom Turbo (character from children's television series). Winning Entry in Children's Drawing Competition.
2727 **1331** 55c. multicoloured 1·70 1·60

1332 TomTom (cartoon character) greeting Snail

2004. Greetings Stamp.
2728 **1332** 55c. multicoloured 1·90 1·80

1333 Town Hall and Steam Tram

2004. Incorporation of Floridsdorf into Vienna.
2729 **1333** 55c. multicoloured 1·90 1·80

1334 Crystal

2004. Crystal Worlds (tourist attraction), Wattens. Sheet 147×85 mm containing T **1334** and similar horiz design. Multicoloured.
MS2730 375c.×2, Type **1334**; Swan 21·00 21·00
 The stamps of **MS**2730 have crystals applied to the surface.

1335 Hermann Maier

2004. Hermann Maier—World Champion Giant Slalom Skier.
2731 **1335** 55c. multicoloured 2·40 2·20

1336 Kaspar *Winterbild* (Josef Bramer)

2004
2732	**1336**	55c. multicoloured	1·60	1·50

2004. No. 2607 surch **BASILISK**.
2733	55c. on 51c. multicoloured	1·80	1·70

1338 *Die Wartende*
(Sylvia Gredenberg)

2004
2734	**1338**	55c. multicoloured	1·40	1·30

1339 *Junge
Sonnenblume* (Max
Weiler)

2004. Sheet 80×100 mm.
MS2735	**1339**	€2.10 multicoloured	6·75	6·75

1340 Campaign
Poster (Friednsreich
Hundertwasser)

2004. 20th Anniv of Campaign to save Danube Meadows
(now National Park).
2736	**1340**	55c. multicoloured	3·50	3·25

1341 Soldier and National Arms

2004. 50th Anniv of Federal Army.
2737	**1341**	55c. multicoloured	1·60	1·50

1342 Nikolaus Harnoncourt

2004. 75th Birthday of Nikolaus Harnoncourt (musician).
2738	**1342**	€1 multicoloured	2·75	2·50

1343 Salzburg
Christmas Market

2004. Christmas.
2739	**1343**	55c. multicoloured	1·40	1·30

1344 Lorin Maazel

2005. Vienna Philharmonic Orchestra's New Year Concert
conducted by Lorin Maazel.
2740	**1344**	€1 multicoloured	2·75	2·50

1345 Herbert von Karajan

2005. Tenth Anniv of Herbert von Karajan Centre.
2741	**1345**	55c. blue, black and		
deep blue | 1·40 | 1·30 |

1346 Stephan Eberharter

2005. Stephan Eberharter—World Champion Skier.
2742	**1346**	55c. multicoloured	1·90	1·80

2005. Nos. 2607, 2609/10, 2613, 2617/18, 2620 and 2623
variously surch.
2743	55c. on 4c. multicoloured	1·40	1·30
2744	55c. on 13c. multicoloured	1·40	1·30
2745	55c. on 17c. multicoloured	1·40	1·30
2746	55c. on 27c. multicoloured	1·40	1·30
2747	55c. on 58c. multicoloured	1·40	1·30
2748	55c. on 73c. multicoloured	1·40	1·30
2749	55c. on 87c. multicoloured	1·40	1·30
2750	55c. on €2.03 multicoloured	1·40	1·30

1355 Globe and Rotary
Emblem

2005. Centenary of Rotary International (charitable
organization).
2751	**1355**	55c. multicoloured	1·60	1·50

1356 Max Schmeling

2005. Death Centenary of Max Schmeling (boxer).
2752	**1356**	100c. multicoloured	2·75	2·50

1357 *Venus in Front of
the Mirror* (Peter Paul
Rubens)

2005. Liechtenstein Museum, Garden Palace, Vienna.
2753	**1357**	125c. multicoloured	3·50	3·25

1358 Carl Djerassi

2005. 82nd Birth Anniv of Carl Djerassi (chemist and
writer). Sheet 60×80 mm.
MS2754	**1358**	100c. multicoloured	3·50	3·50

1359 Pope John Paul II

2005. Pope John Paul II Commemoration.
2755	**1359**	€1 multicoloured	2·75	2·50

1360 Taurus

2005. Astrology (1st issue). Multicoloured. Self-adhesive
gum.
2756	55c. Type **1360**		1·60	1·50
2757	55c. Gemini		1·60	1·50
2758	55c. Cancer		1·60	1·50
2759	55c. Rooster (Year of the			
Rooster) (Chinese astrology)
(red) | | 1·60 | 1·50 |

See also Nos. 2772/5, 2784/7 and 2799/2802.

1361 Post Office Building
and Carriages

2005. Imperial Post Office in Jerusalem (1859–1914).
2760	**1361**	100c. multicoloured	2·75	2·50

1362 Saint Florian

2005. Saints (1st issue). Saint Florian (National Patron
Saint).
2761	**1362**	55c. multicoloured	1·60	1·50

See also Nos. 2767, 2829, 2857, 2890, 2932 and 2959.

1363 Tracks

2005. 60th Anniv of Liberation of Mauthausen
Concentration Camp.
2762	**1363**	55c. multicoloured	1·60	1·50

1364 State Arms

2005. 60th Anniv of Second Republic and 50th Anniv of
State Treaty. Sheet 120×80 mm containing T **1364**
and similar multicoloured design.
MS2763	55c.×2, Type **1364**; Seals and			
signatures on treaty (42×35 mm) | | 3·50 | 3·50 |

1365 Heidi Klum

2005. Life Ball (AIDS charity).
2764	**1365**	75c. multicoloured	2·20	2·00

1366 Junkers F13 Flying
Boat

2005. Stamp Day.
2765	**1366**	265c.+130c. mult	11·00	11·00

1367 Waiter in Cup of
Coffee

2005. Europa. Gastronomy.
2766	**1367**	75c. multicoloured	2·30	2·10

1368 Saint Joseph

2005. Saints (2nd issue).
2767	**1368**	55c. multicoloured	1·60	1·50

1369 Jochen Rindt

2005. 25th Death Anniv of Karl Jochen Rindt (1970—
Formula 1 World Champion).
2768	**1369**	55c. multicoloured	1·80	1·70

1370 Melman,
Marty, Alex and
Gloria (characters)

2005. Madagascar (animated film).
2769	**1370**	55c. multicoloured	1·60	1·50

1371 Peacock Butterfly
(*Inachis io*)

2005
2770	**1371**	55c. multicoloured	1·60	1·50

1372 Edelweiss

2005. Vorarlberg Embroidery.
2771	**1372**	375c. green	9·75	9·50

2005. Astrology (2nd issue). As T **1360**. Multicoloured.
Self-adhesive.
2772	55c. Leo	1·60	1·50
2773	55c. Virgo	1·60	1·50
2774	55c. Libra	1·60	1·50
2775	55c. As No. 2759 (yellow)	1·60	1·50

2005. Customs and Art (23rd series). As T **1005**.
Multicoloured.
2776	55c. Game of dice, Frankenburg	1·60	1·50

1373 Nikki Lauda

2005. Nikki Lauda (Formula 1 World Champion—1975,
1977 and 1984).
2777	**1373**	55c. multicoloured	1·70	1·60

1374 Pumpkin

2005. Halloween.
2778 **1374** 55c. multicoloured 1·60 1·50

1375 "Houses" (Egon Schiele)

2005. Art. Sheet 100×80 mm.
MS2779 **1375** 210c. multicoloured 6·75 6·75

1376 ET 10.103 Railcar

2005. Centenary of Montafon Railway.
2780 **1376** 55c. multicoloured 1·60 1·50

1377 Presentation of Deed

2005. Landhaus (provincial government building), Klagenfurt.
2781 **1377** 75c. multicoloured 2·10 1·90

1378 *Master of the Woods* (Karl Hodina)

2005
2782 **1378** 55c. multicoloured 1·60 1·50

1379 Adalbert Stifter

2005. Birth Bicentenary of Adalbert Stifter (writer).
2783 **1379** 55c. multicoloured 2·40 2·20

2005. Astrology (3rd issue). As T **1360**. Multicoloured. Self-adhesive.
2784 55c. Scorpio 1·60 1·50
2785 55c. Sagittarius 1·60 1·50
2786 55c. Capricorn 1·60 1·50
2787 55c. As No. 2759 (orange) 1·60 1·50

1380 National Theatre

2005. 50th Anniv of Re-opening of National Theatre and Opera House. Sheet 130×60 mm containing T **1380** and similar horiz design.
MS2788 55c. sepia and agate; 55c. indigo and black 4·75 4·75
DESIGNS: 55c.×2, Type **1380**; State Opera House.

1381 Hills

2005. Restoration of Sattler's Cyclorama of Salzburg. Sheet 155×56 mm containing T **381** and similar horiz design. Multicoloured.
MS2789 125c.×2, Type **1381**;
Townscape 7·75 7·75

1382 "Nude" (Veronika Zillner)

2005
2790 **1382** 55c. multicoloured 1·60 1·50

1383 Aslan (character)

2005. *The Chronicles of Narnia* (film of book by C. S. Lewis).
2791 **1383** 55c. multicoloured 1·60 1·50

1384 *Maria Heimsuchung* (Reinhold Stecher)

2005. Advent.
2792 **1384** 55c. multicoloured 1·40 1·30

1385 Shields

2005. 800th Anniv of Order of Teutonic Knights.
2793 **1385** 55c. multicoloured 1·40 1·30

1386 Snow-covered Houses

2005. Christmas.
2794 **1386** 55c. multicoloured 1·40 1·30

1387 Mariss Jansons

2006. Vienna Philharmonic Orchestra's New Year Concert conducted by Mariss Jansons.
2795 **1387** 75c. multicoloured 1·90 1·80

1388 Building Facade

2006. Austria's Presidency of European Union.
2796 **1388** 75c. multicoloured 1·90 1·80

1389 "Post" Philatelic Shop

2006. Greeting Stamp.
2797 **1389** 55c. multicoloured 1·40 1·30

1390 Muhammad Ali

2006. Muhammad Ali (boxer).
2798 **1390** €1.25 multicoloured 3·50 3·25

1391 Dog ("Year of the Dog")

2006. Astrology (4th issue). Multicoloured. Self-adhesive.
2799 55c. Type **1391** 1·60 1·50
2800 55c. Aquarius 1·60 1·50
2801 55c. Pisces 1·60 1·50
2802 55c. Aries 1·60 1·50

1392 Wolfgang Mozart

2006. 250th Birth Anniv of Wolfgang Amadeus Mozart (composer and musician).
2803 **1392** 55c. red and silver 1·60 1·50

1393 Europa (sculpture) (R. Chavanon)

2006. 50th Anniv of Europa Stamps.
2804 **1393** 125c. multicoloured 3·50 3·25

1394 *Lost in her Dreams* (Friedrich von Amerling)

2006. Liechtenstein Museum, Garden Palace, Vienna.
2805 **1394** 125c. multicoloured 3·50 3·25
A stamp of the same design was issued by Liechtenstein.

1395 Meteorite

2006. Post from another World. Meteorite H-chondrite on Stamps. Sheet 81×60 mm.
MS2806 **1395** 375c. multicoloured 11·00 11·00
No. **MS**2806 contains ground meteorite dust and is sold in a folder.

1396 Almaz and Karl Heinz Bohm (founders)

2006. 25th Anniv of Menschen fur Menschen (charity).
2807 **1396** 100c. multicoloured 2·50 2·40

1397 Initiation

2006. Freemasonry in Austria. Sheet 81×61 mm.
MS2808 **1397** 100c. multicoloured 3·50 3·50

1398 Couch

2006. 150th Birth Anniv of Sigmund Freud (psychoanalysis).
2809 **1398** 55c. multicoloured 1·30 1·20

1399 Franz Beckenbauer (Andy Warhol)

2006. Franz Beckenbauer (footballer).
2810 **1399** 75c. multicoloured 1·90 1·80

2006. Flood Relief. No. 2612 surch **75+425 HOCH WASSER HILFE 2006.**
2811 75c.+425c. on 25c. multicoloured 9·75 9·50
The surcharge was for the victims of the Marchfeld floods.

2006. No. 2608 surch **HEILIGENKREUZ NIEDEROSTERRICH** and tree.
2812 55c. on 7c. multicoloured 1·40 1·30

1402 Falco

2006. Hans Holzl (Falco) (rock musician) Commemoration.
2813 **1402** 55c. multicoloured 1·60 1·50

1403 Naomi Campbell

2006. Life Ball (AIDS charity).
2814 **1403** 75c. multicoloured 2·30 2·10

2006. Customs and Art (24th series). As T **1005**. Multicoloured.
2815 55c. Weitensfeld Kranzlreiten (race) 1·40 1·30

1404 Emblem

2006. Privatization of Post Office.
2816 **1404** 55c. multicoloured 1·40 1·30

1405 Jim Clark

2006. Formula I Motor Racing Legends. Sheet 140×185 mm containing T **1405** and similar horiz designs. Multicoloured.
MS2817 55c.×4, Type **1405**; Jacky Ickx; Jackie Stewart; Alain Prost; 75c.×2, Stirling Moss; Mario Andretti; 100c. Bruce McLaren; 125c. Jack Brabham 16·00 16·00
See also No. **MS2868**.

1406 Saint Hemma

2006
2818 **1406** 55c. multicoloured 1·40 1·30

1407 Emblem

2006. 60th Anniv of Federal Chamber of Industry and Commerce.
2819 **1407** 55c. silver, vermilion and black 1·80 1·70

1408 Mozart

2006. 250th Birth Anniv of Wolfgang Amadeus Mozart (composer and musician). Viva Mozart Exhibition, Salzburg.
2820 **1408** 55c. multicoloured 1·40 1·30

1409 Ottfried Fischer

2006. Ottfried Fischer (actor).
2821 **1409** 55c. multicoloured 1·40 1·30

1410 Figures

2006. Europa. Integration.
2822 **1410** 75c. multicoloured 1·90 1·80

1411 Airbus A310-300

2006. Stamp Day.
2823 **1411** 265c.+130c. multicoloured 10·50 10·50

1412 St. Anne's Column, Innsbruck

2006
2824 **1412** 55c. multicoloured 1·40 1·30

1413 K. K. STB Reihe 106 Locomotive

2006. Centenary of Pyhrn Railway.
2825 **1413** 55c. multicoloured 1·40 1·30

1414 Fireworks over Victoria Harbour, Hong Kong

2006. Fireworks. Sheet 146×85 mm containing T **1414** and similar horiz design. Multicoloured.
MS2826 €3.75×2, Type **1414**; Fireworks over Giant Ferris Wheel, Vienna, Austria 21·00 21·00
 MS2826 has crystals applied to the surface of the stamps and was sold in a folder.
 Stamps of a similar design were issued by Hong Kong.

1415 European Lynx (Lynx lynx)

2006. Fauna.
2827 **1415** 55c. multicoloured 1·40 1·30

1416 Emblem

2006. WIPA 2008 International Stamp Exhibition.
2828 **1416** 55c.+20c. multicoloured 2·20 2·00

1417 Saint Gebhard

2006. Saints (3rd issue).
2829 **1417** 55c. multicoloured 1·40 1·30

1418 Steyr 220 Motor Car

2006
2830 **1418** 55c. multicoloured 1·40 1·30

1419 KTM R 125 Tarzan Motorbike

2006
2831 **1419** 55c. multicoloured 1·40 1·30

1420 Benjamin Raich

2006. Benjamin Raich—World Champion Skier.
2832 **1420** 55c. multicoloured 1·40 1·30

1421 Piano

2006. Musical Instruments. Multicoloured.
2833 55c. Type **1421** 1·40 1·30
2834 55c. Guqin 1·40 1·30
 Stamps of a similar design were issued by China.

1422 "Young Boy" (Cornelia Schlesinger)

2006
2835 **1422** 55c. multicoloured 1·40 1·30

1423 Alte Saline (salt refinery) and Saint Rupert

2006. German and Austrian Philatelic Exhibition, Bad Reichenhall.
2836 **1423** 55c.+20c. multicoloured 1·90 1·80

1424 Homo sapiens (detail) (Valentin Oman)

2006. Modern Art.
2837 **1424** 55c. multicoloured 1·40 1·30

1425 Pond Turtle

2006. Self-adhesive.
2838 **1425** 55c. multicoloured 1·40 1·30

1426 Bald Ibis

2006. Fauna. Multicoloured. Self-adhesive.
2839 55c. Type **1426** 1·40 1·30
2840 55c. Brown bear 1·40 1·30

1427 The Holy Family at Rest (Franz Weiss)

2006. Christmas (1st issue).
2841 **1427** 55c. multicoloured 1·40 1·30

1428 Christkindl Pilgrimage Church (Reinhold Stecher)

2006. Christmas (2nd issue).
2842 **1428** 55c. multicoloured 1·40 1·30

1429 Ferdinand Square (T. Chyshkovskii)

2006. 750th Anniv of Lvov.
2843 **1429** 55c. multicoloured 1·40 1·30
 A stamp of a similar design was issued by Ukraine.

1430 Michael Schumacher **1430a** Michael Schumacher

2006. Michael Schumacher (Formula 1 World Champion–1994/5 and 2000/4).
2844 **1430** 75c. multicoloured 2·20 2·00
2844a **1430a** 75c. multicoloured 3·25 3·00
 No. 2844a has different (incorrect) championship year dates and includes designer and year of issue at lower margin.

1431 "Zinnoberroten Merkur" (No. N13 "Mercury")

2006. Centenary of National Stamp and Coin Dealers' Association.
2845 **1431** 55c. cerise and gold 1·40 1·30

1432 Zubin Mehta

2007. Vienna Philharmonic Orchestra's New Year Concert conducted by Zubin Mehta.
2846 **1432** 75c. multicoloured 1·90 1·80

1433 Alpine Flowers

2007. Flowers. Multicoloured.

2847	55c. Type **1433**	1·30	1·20
2848	75c. Hellebores	1·80	1·70
2849	€1.25 Spring flowers	3·00	2·75

1434 Symbols of Technology and Figure

2007. Mankind and Technology. Self-adhesive.

2850	**1434**	55c. multicoloured	1·40	1·30

1435 Fire and Earth

2007. Lower Austrian Provincial Exhibition.

2851	**1435**	55c. multicoloured	1·40	1·30

1436 Outline of Robert Baden-Powell

2007. Centenary of Scouting. Sheet 170×130 mm containing T **1436** and similar horiz designs. Multicoloured.

MS2852 55c.×4, Type **1436**; Campfire; Tent; Guitar 6·00 6·00

1437 Roe Deer

2007

2853	**1437**	75c. multicoloured	1·90	1·80

1438 *Portrait of a Lady* (Bernardino Zaganelli da Cottignola)

2007

2854	**1438**	€1.25 multicoloured	3·25	3·00

1439 Injured Woman

2007. Stop Violence against Women Campaign.

2855	**1439**	55c. multicoloured	1·40	1·30

1440 Easter Rattles

2007. Traditional Customs.

2856	**1440**	55c. multicoloured	1·40	1·30

1441 Saint Klemens Maria Holbauer

2007. Saints (4th issue).

2857	**1441**	55c. multicoloured	1·40	1·30

1442 Emblem

2007. WIPA 2008 International Stamp Exhibition.

2858	**1442**	55c.+20c. multicoloured	2·20	2·00

1443 Roses

2007. Mourning Stamp. No value expressed.

2859	**1443**	(55c.) multicoloured	1·40	1·30

1444 Flowers

2007. Greetings Stamp. No value expressed.

2860	**1444**	(55c.) multicoloured	1·40	1·30

1445 Salamander (*Salamandra salamandra*)

2007. Fauna. Multicoloured. Self-adhesive.

2861	55c. Type **1445**	1·40	1·30
2862	55c. Crayfish (*Astacus astacus*)	1·40	1·30

1446 Pope Benedict XVI

2007. 80th Birth Anniv of Pope Benedict XVI.

2863	**1446**	100c. multicoloured	2·75	2·50

1447 Inscr "Myotis brandtii"

2007. Whiskered Bat. Self-adhesive.

2864	**1447**	55c. multicoloured	1·40	1·30

No. 2864 is described as "Whiskered Bat", that is Myotis mystacinus but is inscribed "Myotis brandtii", that is Brandt's Bat.

1448 Violet

2007

2865	**1448**	100c. multicoloured	2·40	2·20

1449 'The Good Samaritan' (fresco, Franciscan Monastery, Schwaz)

2007. 80th Anniv of Austrian Workers Samaritan Federation (medical assistance organization).

2866	**1449**	55c. multicoloured	1·40	1·30

1450 'Untitled' (painting by Hermann Nitsch)

2007. Modern Art. Sheet 61×80 mm. Imperf.

MS2867 **1450** scarlet and black 3·00 3·00

2007. Formula I Motor Racing Legends. Sheet 140×185 mm containing horiz designs (size 50×32 mm) as T **1405**. Multicoloured.

MS2868 55c.×8, Phil Hill; Clay Regazzoni; Gerhard Berger; Juan Manuel Fangio; John Surtees; Mika Hakkinen; Graham Hill; Emerson Fittipaldi 11·50 11·50

1451 Krause & Comp Electric Locomotive

2007. Centenary of Mariazell Narrow Gauge Railway.

2869	**1451**	55c. multicoloured	1·40	1·30

1452 Church Facade and Tower

2007. 850th Anniv of Mariazell Basilica.

2870	**1452**	55c. multicoloured	1·40	1·30

1453 Trix and Flix

2007. European Football Championships (Euro 2008), Austria and Switzerland. Sheet 100×80 mm containing T **1453** and similar horiz designs. Multicoloured.

MS2871 20c. Type **1453**; 25c. Holding trophy; 30c.Tackling for the ball; 35c. With arms around each other 3·00 3·00

1454 *Self-portrait* (painting by Angelika Kauffmann)

2007. Modern Art. Sheet 81×101 mm.

MS2872 **1454** 210c. scarlet and black 6·00 6·00

1455 *Wien* (steamer) (painting by Harry Heusser)

2007. Stamp Day.

2873	**1455**	265c.+130c. multicoloured	9·75	9·00

1456 Globe as Scout

2007. Europa. Centenary of Scouting.

2874	**1456**	55c. multicoloured	1·40	1·30

1457 Ignaz Pleyel

2007. 250th Birth Anniv of Ignaz Joseph Pleyel (composer).

2875	**1457**	£1 multicoloured	2·40	2·20

1458 Shrek and Fiona

2007. *Shrek the Third* (animated film).

2876	**1458**	55c. multicoloured	1·40	1·30

1459 Museum Building

2007. Essel Museum. Self-adhesive.

2877	**1459**	55c. multicoloured	1·40	1·30

1460 Wilhelm Kienzl

2007. 150th Birth Anniv of Wilhelm Kienzl (composer).

2878	**1460**	75c. multicoloured	1·80	1·70

1461 U Series Steam Locomotive

2007. Bregenz Forest Railway.

2879	**1461**	75c. multicoloured	1·90	1·80

1462 *Man* (Astrid Bernhart)

2007

2880	**1462**	55c. multicoloured	1·40	1·30

1463
Dandelion

2007. Flora. Multicoloured.

2881	**1463**	4c. Type **1463**	25	20
2882		10c. Scottish laburnum	35	35
2883		65c. Gelder rose	1·60	1·50
2884		115c. *Gentiana ciliate*	2·75	2·50
2885		140c. Clematis	3·50	3·25

1464 *Haliaeetus albicilla* (white-tailed eagle)

2007

| 2886 | **1464** | 55c. multicoloured | 1·40 | 1·30 |

1465 Ivory and Gold Medallions (Necklace, 1916) (image scaled to 60% of original size)

2007. Josef Hoffman (designer and architect) Commemoration. Sheet 81×51 mm. Imperf.

| **MS**2887 | **1465** | 265c. multicoloured | 7·75 | 7·75 |

1466 Oil Derrick

2007. 75th Anniv of Austrian Oil Production.

| 2888 | **1466** | 75c. multicoloured | 1·90 | 1·80 |

No. 2888 was impregnated with scent of oil which was released by rubbing part of the design.

1467 Stag and Hind

2007. Birth Bicentenary of Friedrich Gauermann (artist).

| 2889 | **1467** | 55c. multicoloured | 1·40 | 1·30 |

1468 Saint Rupert

2007. Saints (5th issue).

| 2890 | **1468** | 55c. multicoloured | 1·40 | 1·30 |

1469 Niki Hosp

2007. Niki Hosp–Women's World Cup Alpine Ski Champion, 2006–2007.

| 2891 | **1469** | 55c. multicoloured | 1·40 | 1·30 |

1470 *Lucanus cervus* (stag beetle)

2007. Self-adhesive.

| 2892 | **1470** | 75c. multicoloured | 2·10 | 1·90 |

1471 Key

2007. Michel Blumelhuber (iron and steel carver) Commemoration.

| 2893 | **1471** | 75c. multicoloured | 2·10 | 1·90 |

1472 Christiane Horbiger

2007. Christiane Horbiger (actress and recipient of Cross of Honour for Science and Art).

| 2894 | **1472** | 55c. multicoloured | 1·40 | 1·30 |

1473 Scene from *Queen of Spades* (Peter Illyich Tchaikovsky)

2007. Vienna State Opera Opening Nights (1st issue).

| 2895 | **1473** | 55c. multicoloured | 1·40 | 1·30 |

See also No. 2914.

1474 Nativity (altar painting, Oberwollan)

2007. Christmas. Multicoloured.

| 2896 | | 55c. Type **1474** | 1·40 | 1·30 |
| 2897 | | 65c. Nativity (icon, Church of St. Barbara) | 1·60 | 1·50 |

1475 Clownfish

2007. 50th Anniv of Haus des Meeres (Aqua Terra Zoo).

| 2898 | **1475** | 55c. multicoloured | 1·40 | 1·30 |

1476 Thomas Gottschalk

2007. Thomas Gottschalk and 'Wetten dass?' (TV presenter and game show).

| 2899 | **1476** | 65c. multicoloured | 1·70 | 1·60 |

1477 *Cypripedium calceolus* (lady's slipper orchid)

2008

| 2900 | **1477** | 15c. multicoloured | 35 | 35 |

1478 Vienna

2008. EURO 2008 Football Championships (1st issue). Venues. Sheet 150×90 mm containing T **1478** and similar square designs. Multicoloured.

| **MS**2901 | | 55c.×4, Type **1478**; Salzburg; Klagenfurt; Innsbruck, 65c.×4, Zurich; Basel; Bern; Geneva | 12·00 | 12·00 |

The stamps of No. **MS**2901 share a common background design.

See also Nos. 2903/4, 2906/7, 2909, 2910, 2917, 2918, 2919, 2912, 2922, 2926, 2925, **MS**2929, 2930, **MS**2931 and 2951.

1479 Emblem and St Stephen's Cathedral

2008. WIPA 2008 International Stamp Exhibition.

| 2902 | **1479** | 55c.+20c. multicoloured | 2·20 | 2·00 |

See also Nos. 2828 and 2858.

1480 Trix and Flix (mascots)

2008. EURO 2008 Football Championships (2nd issue). Multicoloured. Self-adhesive.

| 2903 | | 55c. Type **1480** | 1·40 | 1·30 |
| 2904 | | 65c. Emblem | 1·60 | 1·50 |

1481 *Portrait of Martina* (Hans Robert Pippal)

2008. Modern Art.

| 2905 | **1481** | 65c. multicoloured | 1·60 | 1·50 |

1482 Trix and Flix (Alexandra Payer)

2008. EURO 2008 Football Championships (3rd issue). Children's Drawings. Multicoloured.

| 2906 | | 55c. Type **1482** | 1·40 | 1·30 |
| 2907 | | 55c. Footballs as map of Europe (Corina Payr) | 1·40 | 1·30 |

2008. WIPA 2008 International Stamp Exhibition. Gold. Sheet 126×73 mm containing triangular designs as T **1479**. Multicoloured.

| **MS**2908 | | 55c. As No. 2828; 55c. As No. 2858; 65c. As No. 2902 | 5·75 | 5·75 |

1483 Map of Europe, Football and Euro Stars (Saskia Puchegger)

2008. EURO 2008 Football Championships (4th issue). Children's Drawings.

| 2909 | **1483** | 65c. multicoloured | 1·60 | 1·50 |

1484 *Defence* (Maria Lassnig)

2008. EURO 2008 Football Championships (5th issue).

| 2910 | **1484** | 55c. multicoloured | 1·40 | 1·30 |

1485 *Hyla arborea* (tree frog)

2008. Fauna. Multicoloured. Self-adhesive.

| 2911 | | 65c. Type **1485** | 1·70 | 1·60 |
| 2912 | | 65c. *Alcedo atthis* (kingfisher) | 1·70 | 1·60 |

1486 Airbus A320

2008. 50th Anniv of Austrian Airlines.

| 2913 | **1486** | 140c. multicoloured | 3·50 | 3·25 |

No. 2913 includes an area, which when scratched, could win a prize.

1487 Scene from *La Forza del Destino* (Giuseppe Verdi)

2008. Vienna State Opera Opening Nights (2nd issue).

| 2914 | **1487** | 55c. multicoloured | 1·40 | 1·30 |

1488 *Princess Marie Franziska von Liechtenstein* (Friedrich von Amerling)

2008

| 2915 | **1488** | 125c. multicoloured | 3·50 | 3·25 |

A stamp of a similar design was issued by Liechtenstein.

1489 *Imaginary Landscape*

2008. Modern Art. Sysanne Sculler (Soshana).

| 2916 | **1489** | 55c. multicoloured | 1·40 | 1·30 |

1490 Football

2008. EURO 2008 Football Championships (6th issue). Self-adhesive.

| 2917 | **1490** | 375c. multicoloured | 9·75 | 9·25 |

No. 2917 is made from a synthetic mixture containing polyurethane, as the original ball used for the EURO 2008 (known as the 'Europass').

1491 Football Field, Ball and Player's Legs

2008. EURO 2008 Football Championships (7th issue).
2918 **1491** 55c. multicoloured 1·40 1·30

1492 Lindwurm (symbol of Klagenfurt) on Football and Karawanken Mountains (Bolona Jencic)

2008. EURO 2008 Football Championships (8th issue). Children's Drawings.
2919 **1492** 125c. multicoloured 3·00 2·75

1493 View from River

2008. World Heritage Site. Wachau.
2920 **1493** 100c. multicoloured 2·40 2·20

1494 Austrian and Swiss Flags, Alps and Turf (Stefan Gritsch)

2008. EURO 2008 Football Championships (9th issue). Children's Drawings.
2921 **1494** 55c. multicoloured 1·40 1·30

1495 Football wearing Lederhosen (Vanessa Schennach)

2008. EURO 2008 Football Championships (10th issue). Children's Drawings.
2922 **1495** 100c. multicoloured 2·40 2·20

1496 Traditional Clothes

2008. Centenary of Tyrolean Federation of Traditional Provincial Costumes.
2923 **1496** 75c. multicoloured 2·00 1·90

1497 *Erinaceus concolor* (southern white-breasted hedgehog)

2008. Fauna. Multicoloured. Self-adhesive.
2924 55c. Type **1497** 1·40 1·30
2925 55c. *Lepus europaeus* (hare) 1·40 1·30

1498 Preparation and Goal

2008. EURO 2008 Football Championships (11th issue). Andreas Herzog's Winning Goal—World Cup Qualifier, 1997. Self-adhesive.
2926 **1498** 545c. multicoloured 14·00 14·00

1499 Mare and Foal

2008. Federal Lipizzaner Stud, Piber.
2927 **1499** 55c. multicoloured 1·50 1·40

1500 Turf (Silvia Holemar, Denise Prossegger and Guso Aldijana)

2008. EURO 2008 Football Championships (12th issue). Children's Drawings.
2928 **1500** 75c. multicoloured 2·00 1·90

1501 Italy

2008. EURO 2008 Football Championships (13th issue). Participating Teams. Two sheets 150×90 mm containing T **1501** and similar square designs showing faces painted with team flag.
MS2929 (a) 10c. Type **1501**; 10c. Croatia; 15c. Sweden; 15c. Greece; 20c. Austria; 20c. Portugal; 65c. Spain; 65c. Czech Republic. (b) 25c. Switzerland; 25c. Germany; 30c. Romania; 30c. Turkey; 35c. Netherlands; 35c. Poland; 55c. Russia; 55c. France 12·50 12·50

1502 Ball and Chairs (Andrea Kastrun)

2008. EURO 2008 Football Championships (14th issue). Children's Drawings.
2930 **1502** 55c. multicoloured 1·50 1·40

1503 Henri Delaunay Cup (EURO 2008 trophy)

2008. EURO 2008 Football Championships (15th issue). Sheet 65×75 mm.
MS2931 **1503** 375c. multicoloured 10·00 10·00
No. **MS**2931 contains four crystals and was issued contained in a folder.

1504 Saint Notburga

2008. Saints (6th issue).
2932 **1504** 55c. multicoloured 1·50 1·40

1505 Script, Hand, Pen and Ink

2008. Europa. The Letter.
2933 **1505** 65c. multicoloured 1·80 1·60

1506 *Upupa epops* (hoopoe)

2008. Fauna. Multicoloured. Self-adhesive.
2934 75c. Type **1506** 1·90 1·70
2935 75c. *Hemaris fuciformis* (broad-bordered bee hawk-moth) 1·90 1·70

1507 Steam Locomotive

2008. 110th Anniv of Vienna Urban Railway.
2936 **1507** 75c. multicoloured 2·00 1·90

1508 Letterbox

2008. Death Centenary of Josef Maria Olbrich (artist and architect).
2937 **1508** 65c. multicoloured 1·80 1·60

1509 Statuette

2008. Centenary of Discovery of Willendorf Venus. Self-adhesive.
2938 **1509** 375c. multicoloured 10·00 9·75

1510 Columbine

2008. Flowers.
2939 **1510** 50c. multicoloured 1·40 1·30

1512 Skyline

2008. WIPA 2008 International Stamp Exhibition. Self-adhesive.
2941 **1512** 55c. multicoloured 1·50 1·40
See also No. 2828, 2858 and 2902.

1513 Series 4130 Rail Car Set

2008. 150th Anniv of Empress Elizabeth Western Railway.
2942 **1513** 100c. multicoloured 2·75 2·50

1514 Express Mail (detail) (painting by K. Schorpfeil)

2008. Praga 2008 and WIPA 2008, International Stamp Exhibitions. Sheet 120×80 mm.
MS2943 **1514** 265c. multicoloured 7·25 7·00
Stamp of the same design was issued by Czech Republic.

1515 Maze

2008. 80th Birth Anniv of Friedensreich Hundertwasser (artist). Sheet 97×127 mm containing T **1515** and similar vert designs. Multicoloured.
MS2944 55c. Type **1515**; 75c. House; 100c. Stylized lamps; 125c. Maze (different) 10·00 10·00

2008. WIPA 2008 International Stamp Exhibition. Silver. Sheet 126×73 mm containing triangular designs as T **1479**. Multicoloured.
MS2945 55c.+20c.×3, As No. 2828; As No. 2902; As No. 2858 6·25 6·25

1516 Schonbrunn (paddle steamer)

2008. Stamp Day.
2946 **1516** 265c.+130c. multicoloured 10·50 10·00

1517 Nude (Dina Larot)

2008
2947 **1517** 55c. multicoloured 1·50 1·40

1518 Gentian

2008. Vorarlberg Embroidery. Self-adhesive.
2948　**1518**　375c. blue　　　　10·00　9·75

1519 *Maximilian Schell*
((Arnulf Rainer)

2008. Maximilian Schell (actor).
2949　**1519**　100c. multicoloured　　2·75　2·50

1520 Romy Schneider

2008. 70th Birth Anniv of Romy Schneider (actress).
2950　**1520**　100c. multicoloured　　2·75　2·50

1521 Iker Casillas (winning
Spanish team captain)
holding Trophy

2008. Euro 2008 Football Championships (16th issue).
2951　**1521**　65c. multicoloured　　1·80　1·60

1522 Thomas Morgenstern

2008. Thomas Morgenstern—World Champion Ski-
jumper, 2007 and Olympic Gold Medallist.
2952　**1522**　100c. multicoloured　　2·75　2·50

1523 Markus Rogan

2008. Markus Rogan—World Champion Backstroke
Swimmer, 2008.
2953　**1523**　100c. multicoloured　　2·75　2·50

1524 Heinz Fischer

2008. 70th Birth Anniv of Heinz Fischer (federal president
2004—present).
2954　**1524**　55c. multicoloured　　1·50　1·40

1525 Manner
Neapolitan Biscuits

2008. Classic Trademarks.
2955　**1525**　55c. multicoloured　　1·50　1·40

1526 Koloman
Moser

2008. Koloman Moser (artist and stamp designer)
Commemoration.
2956　**1526**　130c. multicoloured　　3·75　3·50

1527 Trieste Imperial and
Royal Post Office Building

2008. Old Austria.
2957　**1527**　65c. multicoloured　　2·00　1·90

1528 *First Christmas Tree
in Ried* (Felix Ignaz
Pollingger)

2008. Art History.
2958　**1528**　65c. multicoloured　　2·00　1·90

1529 Saint Martin

2008. Saints (7th issue).
2959　**1529**　55c. multicoloured　　1·50　1·40

1530 Karl Schranz

2008. 70th Birth Anniv of Karl Schranz (World Champion
skier).
2960　**1530**　65c. multicoloured　　2·00　1·90

1531 Adoration of the Magi
(ceiling fresco, Collegiate
Monastery and Parish
Church of St Michael,
Flachgau)

2008. Christmas.
2961　**1531**　55c. multicoloured　　1·80　1·60

1532 Female Figure

2009. Saliera (salt cellar) by Benvento Cellini. Sheet
110×75 mm containing T **1532** and similar vert
design. Multicoloured.
MS2962 210c.×2, Type **1532**; Male
figure　　　　　　　14·00　14·00
　　The stamps of **MS**2962 form a composite design of the
salt cellar.

1533 Landskron
Castle

2009. Self-adhesive.
2963　**1533**　55c. multicoloured　　1·90　1·70

1534 Pez Peppermint
Sweets

2009. Classic Trademarks.
2964　**1534**　55c. multicoloured　　1·90　1·70

1535 Post Building, Cracow

2009. Old Austria.
2965　**1535**　100c. multicoloured　　3·00　2·75

1536 Raimondo
Montecuccoli

2009. 400th Birth Anniv of Raimondo Montecuccoli
(soldier and writer).
2966　**1536**　130c. multicoloured　　4·00　3·75

1537 Girl

2009. 60th Anniv of SOS Children's Villages.
2967　**1537**　55c. multicoloured　　1·90　1·70

1538 Lewis Hamilton and McLaren
Race Car

2009. Lewis Hamilton (Formula I World Champion–2008).
2968　**1538**　100c. multicoloured　　3·00　2·75

1539 Mercedes W 196 Silver Arrow

2009. Centenary of Technical Museum, Vienna. Self-
adhesive.
2969　**1539**　265c. multicoloured　　8·00　8·00

1540 Schonbrunn Imperial
Palace

2009
2970　**1540**　65c. multicoloured　　2·00　1·90

1541 Venediger
Glacier

2009. Preserve Polar Regions and Glaciers.
2971　**1541**　65c. multicoloured　　2·00　1·90

1542 Haflinger

2009. 50th Anniv of Steyr Daimler Puch Haflinger All
Terrain Vehicle.
2972　**1542**　55c. murlticoloured　　1·90　1·70

1543 Joseph Haydn

2009. Death Bicentenary of Franz Joseph Haydn
(composer).
2973　**1543**　65c. multicoloured　　2·00　1·90

1544 *Tyto alba*
(barn owl)

2009. Self-adhesive.
2974　**1544**　55c. multicoloured　　1·90　1·70

1545 Wrapped Flak
Tower

2009. Art. Works by Christo Vladimirov Javashev (Christo,
the packaging artist). Sheet 78×80 mm containing T
1545 and similar vert design. Multicoloured.
MS2975 55c.×2, Type **1545**; The 21st
Century Collection　　3·75　3·75

1546 Fred Zinnemann

2009. Austrians in Hollywood. Fred Zinnemann (director)
Commemoration
2976　**1546**　55c. multicoloured　　1·60　1·40

1547 Old Town

2009. 850th Anniv of St Pölten
2977　**1547**　55c. multicoloured　　1·60　1·40

1548 Burning Ring

2009. *The Ring of the Nibelungen* (opera) performed at Vienna State Opera House
2978	**1548**	100c. multicoloured	1·60	1·40

1549 *Thalia*

2009. Centenary of *Thalia* (pleasure steamer)
2979	**1549**	55c. multicoloured	1·60	1·60

1550 Baptismal Font, Old Cathedral, Linz

2009. Religious Art
2980	**1550**	55c. multicoloured	6·25	6·00

1551 State Opera House

2009. 140th Anniv of Vienna State Opera House
2981	**1551**	100c. multicoloured	3·00	2·75

1552 Wolfgang Graf Berghe von Trips

2009. Formula I Motor Racing Legends. Multicoloured.
MS2982 55c.×4, Type **1552**; Gilles Villeneuve; James Hunt; Bernie Ecclestone 6·25 6·25

1553 Napoleon

2009. Bicentenary of Battle of Aspern and Essling. Sheet 73×87 mm
MS2983 **1553** 110c. multicoloured 3·00 3·00

1554 TUGSAT-1 (nano-satellite)

2009.
2984	**1554**	65c. multicoloured	2·10	1·90

1555 Graz

2009. Old Town, Graz–World Heritage Site
2985	**1555**	100c. multicoloured	3·00	2·75

1556 Early Aircraft

2009. Centenary of Wiener Neustadt Airfield
2986	**1556**	140c. multicoloured	4·00	3·75

1557 *Rosalia alpina* (longhorn beetle)

2009. Longhorn Beetle
2987	**1557**	75c. multicoloured	2·10	1·90

1558 Steam Locomotive

2009. Centenary of Wachau Railway
2988	**1558**	75c. multicoloured	2·10	1·90

1559 *Apis mellifera* (honeybee)

2009. Fauna. Multicoloured.
2989	55c. Type **1559**		1·60	1·40
2990	55c. *Merops apiaster* (bee-eater)		1·60	1·40

Nos. 2989/90 were issued in *se-tenant* 'hang sell' sheetlets of ten stamps

1560 Anemones

2009

1561 Film Poster

2009. 60th Anniv of *The Third Man* (film by Carol Reed, based on book by Graham Greene)
2992	**1562**	65c. multicoloured	1·90	1·70

1562 '20'

2009. 20th Anniv of Opening of Border between Austria and Hungary
2993	**1562**	65c. multicoloured	1·90	1·70

1563 Gateway and Soldier, Carnuntum

2009. Archaeology. Multicoloured.
MS2994 55c. Type **1563**; 65c. Bas-relief and mounted soldier, Gerulata 5·00 5·00

Stamps of a similar design were issued by Slovakia.

1564 *MS Österreich* (oldest motor powered passenger ship on Lake Constance)

2009. Stamp Day
2995	**1564**	265c.+130c. multicoloured	11·50	10·00

1565 Berta von Suttner

2009. 120th Anniv of *Lay Down Your Arms!* (antiwar novel by Berta von Suttner)
2996	**1565**	55c. multicoloured	1·60	1·40

1566 The Glorious Rosary

2009. Tenth Anniv of the Return of Rosary Triptych (painted by Ernst Fuchs), Parish Church of Hetzendorf, Vienna. Multicoloured.
MS2997 55c. Type **1566**; 75c. *The Joyful Rosary*; 100c. *The Sorrowful Rosary* 6·75 6·75

1567 Wolfgang Loitzl (Four Hills Champion)

2009. Champion Ski Jumpers. Multicoloured.
2998	100c. Type **1567**		3·00	2·75
2999	100c. Gregor Schlierenzauer (World Cup winner 2008–9)		3·00	2·75

1568 5042 Series Rail Car in Zistersdorf Station

2009. 120th Anniv of Drösing–Zistersdorf Local Railway
3000	**1568**	100c. multicoloured	3·00	2·75

1569 *Woman rocking on a Chair* (Leander Kaiser)

2009. Modern Art
3001	**1569**	55c. multicoloured	1·90	1·70

1571 *Las Meninas* (The Royal Family of Felipe IV)

2009. Diego Rodríguez de Silva y Velázquez (artist) Commemoration. Multicoloured.
MS3003 55c. Type **1571**; 65c.*The Infanta Margarita Teresa in a Blue Dress* 4·25 4·25

Stamps of the same design were issued by Spain

1572 Ranui Church, Vilnös Valley, South Tyrol

2009. Christmas
3004	**1572**	65c. multicoloured	2·00	1·90

1573 Palmers Underwear

2009. Classic Trademarks
3005	**1573**	55c. multicoloured	1·90	1·70

1574 St. Leopold

2009. Patron Saints
3006	**1574**	55c. multicoloured	1·90	1·70

1575 Zum gnadenreichen Christkindl (Blessed Holy Child)

2009. Christmas
3007	**1575**	55c. multicoloured	1·90	1·70

1576 *Tribute to Vedova* (George Baselitz)

2009. Tenth Anniv of Essl Art Museum
3008	**1576**	55c. multicoloured	1·90	1·70

1577 Ape holding Book

(*Following image 21 column*)

1570 *Emilie Flöge* (Gustav Klimt)

2009. Austria–Japan Year. Multicoloured.
MS3002 140c.×2, Type **1570**; *Autumn Clothes* (Shoen Uemura) 8·50 8·50

2009. Birth Bicentenary of Charles Darwin (naturalist and evolutionary theorist). Multicoloured.
MS3009 55c.×3, Type **1577**; Cherub with head in hands and mirror; Ape holding mirror to cherub 5·75 5·75
The stamps and margins of **MS**3009 form a composite design

1578 *Lutra lutra* (otter)

2010. Fauna (1st issue). Multicoloured.
3010 75c. Type **1578** 2·10 2·00
3011 75c. *Salmo trutta fario* (brown trout) 2·10 2·00

1579 *Felis silvestris* (wild cat)

2010. Fauna (2nd issue)
3012 **1579** 65c. multicoloured 2·00 1·90

1580 View from Salzach River

2010. World Heritage Site
3013 **1580** 100c. multicoloured 3·00 2·75

1581 *Annual Rings of Scent and Bliss* (Helmut Kand)

2010. Modern Art
3014 **1581** 55c. multicoloured 1·90 1·70

1582 *Prince Eugene as Victor over the Turks* (Jacob van Schuppen)

2010. Prince Eugene of Savoy Exhibition, Belvedere, Vienna
3015 **1582** 65c. multicoloured 2·00 1·90

1583 Kleinbahn Model Railways

2010. Classic Trade Marks
3016 **1583** 55c. multicoloured 1·90 1·70

1584 *The Tyrolean Land Army Year Nine* (Joseph Anton Koch)

2010. Death Bicentenary of Andreas Hofer (revolutionary leader)
MS3017 **1584** 175c. multicoloured 5·75 5·75

1585 Stage Setting for *Medea* (by Marco Auturo Marelli)

2010. Vienna State Opera House
3018 **1585** 100c. multicoloured 3·00 2·75

1586 Otto Preminger

2010. Austrians in Hollywood. Otto Ludwig Preminger (film director) Commemoration
3019 **1586** 55c. multicoloured 1·90 1·70

1587 Roger Federer

2010. Roger Federer (world champion tennis player)
3020 **1587** 65c. multicoloured 2·00 1·90

1588 *Soon the Sun will rise*

2010. Birth Centenary of Max Weiler (artist)
3021 **1588** 75c. multicoloured 2·10 2·00

1589 *Lady in Yellow* (Max Kurzwell)

2010. Wien Museum
3022 **1589** 65c. multicoloured 2·00 1·90

1590 Upper Belvedere

2010. Belvedere Palace, Vienna
3023 **1590** 65c. multicoloured 2·00 1·90

1591 671 Steam Locomotive (1860 (oldest operational steam locomotive in the world)

2010. 150th Anniv of Graz Köflach Railway
3024 **1591** 100c. multicoloured 3·00 2·75

1592 Prague Castle and St Vitus Cathedral.

2010. Old Austria
3025 **1592** 65c. multicoloured 2·00 1·90

1593 Empress Elisabeth (Sisi)

2010. Expo 2010, Shanghai
MS3026 **1593** 55c. multicoloured 1·50 1·50

1594 Railway

2010. Centenary (2003) of Mendel (Mendola) Railway (first electric funicular railway)
3027 **1594** 65c. multicoloured 1·90 1·80

1595 Post Box on Legs

2010. Post–Publicity Campaign 2010
3028 **1595** 55c. multicoloured 1·90 1·80

1596 Palace during Early 19th Century

2010. Imperial Festival Palace Hof
3029 **1596** 55c. multicoloured 1·50 1·40

1597 Baroque Church (painting by Franz Knapp)

2010. 350th Anniv of Maria Taferl
3030 **1597** 55c. multicoloured 1·50 1·40

1598 Gustav Mahler

2010. 150th Birth Anniv of Gustav Mahler (composer and conductor)
3031 **1598** 100c. multicoloured 3·00 2·75

1599 Festival Poster, 1928 (by Leopoldine (Poldi) Wojtek)

2010. 90th Anniv of Salzburg Festival
3032 **1599** 55c. multicoloured 1·50 1·50

1600 *Coracias garrulus* (European roller)

2010. Fauna. Multicoloured.
3033 55c. Type **1600** 1·50 1·40
3034 75c. *Aquila chrysaetos* (golden eagle) 2·10 2·00

1601 Crozier

2010. Religious Art
3035 **1601** 75c. multicoloured 2·10 2·00

1602 Fridolin Fuchs (post fox) on Skateboard (illustration by Carola Holland)

2010. Europa
3036 **1602** 65c. multicoloured 1·90 1·80

1603 *Self Portrait with Black Vase*

2010. 120th Birth Anniv of Egon Schiele (artist)
3037 **1603** 140c. multicoloured 4·00 3·75

1604 Mountain Spring and Fountain in Front of Vienna City Hall

2010. Centenary of Second Pipeline carrying Mountain Spring Water to Vienna
3038 **1604** 55c. multicoloured 2·10 2·00

1605 Simon Wiesenthal in Star of David

2010. Simon Wiesenthal (holocaust survivor and pursuer of war criminals) Commemoration
3039 **1605** 75c. multicoloured 2·10 2·00

1606 Opera House Interior and Ioan Holender

2010. 75th Birth Anniv of Ioan Holender (director of Vienna State Opera)
3040 **1606** 100c. multicoloured 2·75 2·50

1607 Karnburg Church

2010. Churches
3041 **1607** 100c multicoloured 2·75 2·50

1608 Johann Flux

2010. 350th Birth Anniv of Johann Joseph Fux (composer and musical theorist)
3042 **0608** 100c. multicoloured 3·00 2·75

1609 Grete Rehor and Parliament Building, Vienna

2010. Birth Centenary of Grete Rehor (politician and first female Federal Minister)
3043 **1609** 55c. multicoloured 1·50 1·40

1610 'PARADE'

2010. 15th Anniv of Rainbow Parade
3044 **1610** 55c. multicoloured 3·00 2·75

1611 Steam Locomotive

2010. 125th Anniv of Spielfeld Strass-Bad Radkersburg Railway
3045 **1611** 65c. multicoloured 1·90 1·80

1612 Castle and Grounds

2010. Grafenegg Castle
3046 **1612** 55c. multicoloured 1·50 1·40

1613 Zodiac

2010. 150th Birth Anniv of Alfons Maria Mucha (artist)
3047 **1613** 115c. multicoloured 3·25 3·00

1614 Church

2010. 50th Anniv of Eisenstadt Diocese
3048 **1614** 55c. multicoloured 1·50 1·40

1615 Mother Teresa

2010. Birth Centenary of Agnes Gonxha Bojaxhiu (Mother Teresa) (founder of Missionaries of Charity)
3049 **1615** 130c. multicoloured 3·50 3·25

1616 Railjet Train and Gmunden

2010. Stamp Day
3050 **1616** 265c.+130c. multicoloured 11·00 10·50

1618 Steam Locomotive, Salzburg, Austria

2010. *Orient Express*. Multicoloured.
MS3052 65c.×2, Type **1618**; Steam locomotive, Sinaia, Romania 3·50 3·50

1619 Crucifix (Jakob Adhart), ArchAbbey of St. Peter, Salzburg

2010. Sacred Art
3052a **1619** 100c. multicoloured 2·75 2·50

1620 Anniversary Emblem and Members Flags

2010. 50th Anniv of OPEC (Organization of Petroleum Exporting Countries)
3053 **1620** 140c. multicoloured 4·00 4·00

1621 Rose

2010. Petit Point
MS3054 multicoloured 7·25 7·25

1622 Imperial and Royal State Railways Series 199 Locomotive

2010. Centenary of Wechsel Railway
3055 **1622** 100c. multicoloured 2·75 2·50

1623 Andreas and Wolfgang Linger

2010. Andreas and Wolfgang Linger–Winners of Luge Olympic Gold Medal at Winter Olympic Games, Vancouver
3056 **1623** 100c. multicoloured 2·75 2·50

1624 Desk

2010. Austrian Design. Peter Zuchi (cabinet maker)
3057 **1624** 65c. multicoloured 1·90 1·80

1625 Maria Theresa (Martin van Meytens)

2010. 230th Death Anniv of Archduchess Maria Theresia Walburga Amalia Christina von Österreich (Maria Theresa of Austria) (Archduchess of Austria and Queen of Hungary and Bohemia)
3058 65c. multicoloured 1·90 1·80

1626 Weather Station, City Park, Vienna

2010. Meteorological Architecture. Multicoloured.
MS3059 65c. Type **1626**; 140c. Austria-Hungarian community meteorological station, Botanical Garden, Buenos Aires 5·50 5·50

1627 Ornithopter (first controlled flight, November 1808)

2010. 250th Birth Anniv of Jakob Degen (inventor)
3060 **1627** 125c multicoloured 1·90 1·80

1628 Flag and Soldier

2010. 50th Anniv of Austrian Armed Forces International Assignments
3061 **1628** 65c. multicoloured 1·90 1·80

1629 St Stephen's Cathedral and St Peter's Church, Vienna

2010. Cultural Heritage
3062 **1629** 199c. multicoloured 3·00 2·75

1630 Goldenes Dachl, Innsbruck

2010. Advent
3063 **1630** 65c. multicoloured 2·00 1·90

1631 Three Wise Men (detail from 12th-century missal), St Florian's Monastery

2010. Christmas (1st issue)
3064 **1631** (55c.) multicoloured 1·50 1·40

1632 The Nativity (detail of antiphonal from Cistercian monastery, Rein, Styria)

2010. Christmas (2nd issue)
3065 **1632** 55c. multicoloured 1·50 1·40

1632a Emperor Franz Joseph and Dr. Anton Freiherr von Eiselsberg

2011. Centenary of Austrian Cancer Aid
3065a **1632a** 55c. multicoloured 1·50 1·40

1633 Post Office

2011. Old Austria
3066 **1633** 65c. multicoloured 1·90 1·80

1634 Violin

2011. Musical Instruments
3067 **1634** 75c. multicoloured 2·20 2·10

1635 Bruno Kreisky

2011. Birth Centenary of Bruno Kreisky (politician)
3068 **1635** 55c. multicoloured 1·60 1·50

1636 Stylized Joanneum Graz and Kunsthaus Graz

2011. Bicentenary of Joanneum Graz Museum
3069 **1636** 100c. multicoloured 3·00 2·75

1637 Franz Liszt

2011. Birth Bicentenary of Franz Liszt
3070 **1637** 65c. multicoloured 1·90 1·90

1638 Hedy Lamarr

2011. Austrians in Hollywood. Hedwig Eva Maria Kiesler (Hedy Lamarr) (film actor) Commemoration
3071 **1638** 55c. multicolured 1·60 1·50

1639 Niemetz Confectioners

2010. Classic Trade Marks
3072 **1639** 55c. multicoloured 1·90 1·80

1640 Luigi Hussak, Walter Nausch, Ernst Fiala and Herbert Prohaska (former captains) and Club Emblem

2011. Centenary of FC Austria Vienna
3073 **1640** 65c. multicoloured 2·00 1·90

1641 KTM 125 D.O.H.C. Apfelbeck

2011. Motorcycles
3074 **1641** 75c. multicoloured 2·25 2·10

1642 Puch 500

2011. Cars
3075 **1642** 65c. multicoloured 2·00 1·90

1643 Series 310 Locomotive and Karl Golsdorf

2011. 150th Birth Anniv of Karl Golsdorf (engineer and designer)
3076 **1643** 65c. multicoloured 2·00 1·90

1644 Museum Building

2011. 20th Anniv of Kunst Haus, Vienna
3077 **1644** 175c. multicoloured 5·25 5·00

1645 Cup of Coffee and Café Entrance

2011. Dining with Tradition. Cafe Hawelka
3078 **1645** 62c. multicoloured 2·00 1·90

1646 Space Walk

2011. 50th Anniv of Manned Space Flight
3079 **1646** 65c. multicoloured 2·00 1·90

1647 Roman Structures

2011. Lower Austrian Regional Exhibition 2011
3080 **1647** 62c. multicoloured 1·90 1·80

1648 Ars Electronica Centre, Linz

2011. Modern Architecture. All designs black, background colour given.
3081 7c. grey-brown 30 25
3082 62c. azure 1·90 1·80
3083 62c. azure 1·90 1·80
3084 62c. azure (vert) 1·90 1·80
3085 62c. azure (vert) 1·90 1·80
3086 70c. chrome yellow 2·20 2·10
3087 70c. pale yellow 2·20 2·10
3088 90c. pale lilac 2·50 2·40
3089 90c. pale lilac 2·50 2·40
3090 145c. pale turquoise-green 4·75 4·50
3091 170c. pale buff 5·75 5·50
3092 340c. pale greenish yellow (vert) 10·50 10·00

Designs: 7c. Type **1648**; 62c. Kunsthaus Graz Universalmuseum, Joanneum; 62c. Museum of Modern Art Ludwig Foundation, Vienna (Museum Moderner Kunst Stiftung Ludwig, Wien); 62c. Kunsthaus Bregenz; 62c. Kunsthalle Krems; 70c. Museum der Moderne Monchsberg, Salzburg; 70c. Lentos Art Museum, Linz (Lentos Kunstmuseum, Linz); 90c. Forum Stadtpark, Graz; 90c. Essl Museum, Klosterneuburg; 145c. Kunsthalle Wien Project Space Karlsplatz, Vienna; 170c. MAK Centre Schindler Chase House, Los Angeles; 340c. Austrian Cultural Forum, New York.

1649 Horse pulling Railway Wagons

2011. 175 Years of Budweis (Budejowice)-Linz-Gmunden Horse-drawn Railway
3093 **1649** 62c. multicoloured 1·70 1·60

1650 Smiling Child

2011. 25th Anniv of CARE (humanitarian organization) Austria
3094 **1650** 70c. multicoloured 5·25 5·00

1651 Antique Bookcase from Mekhitarist's Library

2011. Bicentenary of Mekhitarists (congregation of Benedictine monks of Armenian Catholic Church founded in 1712 by Mechitar of Sebaste) in Vienna
3095 **1651** 90c. multicoloured 2·75 2·50

1652 Graz

2011. Stamp Day
3096 **1652** 272c. +136c. multicoloured 12·50 12·00

1653 Church

2011. Churches
3097 **1653** 62c. multicoloured 1·70 1·70

1654 Tower of Babel (Pieter Bruegel the Elder)

2011. Art. Old Masters
3098 **1654** 145c. multicoloured 4·50 4·25

1655 Portrait of Dora Fournier-Gabillon

2011. Art. Works by Hans Makart. Multicoloured.
MS3099 70c. Type **1655**; 170c. The Triumph of Ariadne 6·75 6·75

1656 Pheasant, Badger, Deer and Fungi

2011. Country of Forests. International Year of Forests
3100 **1656** 90c. multicoloured 2·50 2·25

2011. Modern Architecture. Horiz design as Type **1648**.
3101 5c. Liaunig Museum 1·00 90

1657 Etrich Taube Aircraft and Black Hawk Helicopter

2011. Centenary of Military Aviation
3102 **1657** 62c. multicoloured 2·00 1·90

1658 Chalice

2011. Religious Art
3103 **1658** 145c. multicoloured 4·50 4·25

1659 St Christoph Hospice

2011. 625th Anniv of St Christopher Brotherhood
3104 **1659** 62c. multicoloured 2·00 1·90

1660 Anniversary Emblem

2011. 50th Anniv of Organisation for Economic Co-operation and Development (OECD) (Organisation de coopération et de développement économiques, OCDE)
3105 **1660** 70c. multicoloured 2·25 2·10

1661 BBÖ 378 series Locomotive and Old Railway Station Building

2011. Centenary of Stammersdorf Railway
3106 **1661** 90c. multicoloured 2·50 2·25

1662 Curing a
Woman (Ulrich Henn)

2011. Religious Art (2nd issue). Bronze Relief, Rankwil
Basilica
3107 **1662** 90c. multicoloured 2·50 2·25

1663 Girl and Peddler

2011. 175th Death Anniv of Ferdinand Jakob Raimann
(Ferdinand Raimund) (dramatist)
3108 **1663** 62c. multicoloured 2·00 1·90

1664 Football Boot

2011. Centenary of Austrian Football Championship
3109 **1664** 62c. multicoloured 2·00 1·90

1665 Vienna Künstlerhaus

2011. Centenary of Vienna Visual Artists Cooperative
(Austrian Society of Artists, Künstlerhaus)
3110 **1665** 62c. multicoloured 2·00 1·90

1666 Lotto Ball

2011. 25th Anniv of Lottery. Sheet 70×90 mm
MS3111 **1666** 145c. multicoloured 4·50 4·25

1667 Coniferous Forest

2011. Europa. Forests. Sheet 112×73 mm
MS3112 **1667** 170c. multicoloured 4·25 2·25

1668 'C02 NEUTRAL
ZUGESTELLT'

2011. C0₂ Neutral Post Delivery
3113 **1668** 62p. green 2·00 1·90

1669 Hand holding
Globe of Stamps

2011. 90th Anniv of Federation of Austrian Philatelist
Societies
3114 **1669** 62c. +20c. multicoloured 2·50 2·25

1670 Early Steam
Locomotive

2011. 120th Anniv of Erzberg Railway
3115 **1670** 90c. multicoloured 2·50 2·25

1671 *Portrait of Walburga
Neuzil* (Wally) (Egon Schiele)

2011. Tenth Anniv of Leopold Museum
3116 **1671** 62c. multicoloured 2·00 1·90

1672 Elisabeth Görgl

2011. Elisabeth Görgl (skiier) (gold medalist in Super-G
and Downhill Race at World Skiing Championships,
Garmisch-Partenkirchen)
3117 **1672** 62c. multicoloured 2·00 1·90

1673 Diana, the
Huntress (As Type
2342 of USA)

2011. Breast Cancer Awareness Campaign
3118 **1673** 90c. +10c. multicoloured 3·00 2·75

1674 *Angst* (Arnulf
Rainer)

2011. Modern Art
3119 **1674** 62c multicoloured 2·00 1·90

1675 *o.T. 014, 2003*

2011. Photo Art Austria. Eva Schlegel
3120 **1675** 70c. multicoloured 2·25 1·10

1676 Looking down on
Pasterze Glacier

2011. Trademark Austria. Winning Design in Austrian
Identity Competition
3121 **1676** 62c. multicoloured 2·00 1·90

1677 Loisium Visitors' Centre,
Langenlois (Steven Holl)

2011. Modern Architecture in Austria
3122 **1677** 62c. multicoloured 2·00 1·90

1678 *The Song of
Songs* (Arik Brauer)

2011. Art
3123 **1678** 170c. multicoloured 5·00 4·75

1679 Nesting Storks

2011. 90th Anniv of Burgenland in Austria
3124 **1679** 90c. multicoloured 2·50 2·25

1680 St Quirinus
Chapel

2011. Advent
3125 **1680** 70c. multicoloured 2·10 2·00

1681 Madonna
of Plain

2011. Christmas (1st issue). Coil Stamp
3126 **1681** 62c. multicoloured 1·90 1·80

1682 Vienna BahnhofCity
West Station

2011. Re-opening of Vienna BahnhofCity West
3127 **1682** 70c. multicoloured 2·10 2·00

1683 Birth of Christ
(anon)

2011. Christmas (2nd issue)
3128 **1683** 62c. multicoloured 1·90 1·80

1684 Wolfgang
Amadeus Mozart
(detail)

2011. 220th Death Anniv of Wolfgang Amadeus Mozart
3129 **1684** 70c. multicoloured 2·10 2·00

1685 Interior of Great Hall
and Caryatid

2012. Bicentenary of Gesellschaft der Musikfreunde
(Friends of Music Society) in Vienna
3130 **1685** 90c. multicoloured 2·50 2·40

1686 Lohner L 125

2012. Motorcycles
3131 **1686** €1.45 multicoloured 4·00 3·75

1687 Carl Ritter von Ghega
and Railway

2012. 210th Birth Anniv of Carl Ritter von Ghega
(designer of Semmering Railway from Gloggnitz to
Mürzzuschlag)
3132 **1687** 70c. multicoloured 2·00 1·90

1688 Early Mountaineer and
Edelweiss

2012. 150th Anniv of Alpine Association
3133 **1688** 62c. multicoloured 1·75 1·60

1689 Locomotives

2012. 50th Anniv of Vienna Rapid Transit Railway
3134 **1689** 62c. multicoloured 1·75 1·60

2012. Modern Architecture
3135 145c. pale apple green and
black 4·75 4·50
3136 170c. pale buff and black 5·75 5·50
Design: 145c. Frauenmuseum, Hittisau; 170c. As No.3091
(MAK Centre Schindler Chase House, Los Angeles)

2012. Modern Architecture
3137 62c. azure and black 1·90 1·80
3138 62c. azure and black (vert) 1·90 1·80
3139 70c. pale yellow and black 2·10 2·00
Design: 62c. As No. 3082 (Kunsthaus Graz Universalmuse-
um, Joanneum); 62c. As No. 3084 (Kunsthaus Bregenz);
70c. As No. 3087 (Museum der Moderne Monchsberg,
Salzburg)

1691 Wind-up Dancer
(Zoé Byland)

2012. Young Art in Austria. Vienna Opera Ball
3140 **1691** 70c. multicoloured 2·10 1·90

1692 Stöckl

2012. Photo Art Austria. Elfie Semotan
3141 **1692** 70c. multicoloured 2·10 2·00

1693 Steyr XII Taxi –
Landaulet

2012. Vintage Cars
3142 **1693** 70c. multicoloured 2·10 2·00

1694 Viennese Oboe

2012. Musical Instruments
3143 **1694** 90c. multicoloured 2·50 2·40

1695 The Small 'I am I'

2012. 40th Anniv of *Das Kleine Ich-bin-ich* (children's
book)
3144 **1695** 62c. multicoloured 1·75 1·60

1696 Turhan Bey

2012. Austrians in Hollywood. Turhan Gilbert Selahattin
Sahultavy (Turhan Bey) (film actor) Commemoration
3145 **1696** 70c. multicoloured 2·10 2·00

1697 Stadtturm
(town tower) (1564),
and Square

2012. 800th Anniv of Enns
3146 **1697** 145c. multicoloured 4·75 4·00

1698 Golden Bull of Holy
Roman Emperor Charles IV

2012. 'Verbundet-Verfeindet-Verschwagert', Upper Austria
and Bavaria State Exhibition, Braunau, Mattighofen
and Burghausen
3147 **1698** 70c. multicoloured 2·10 2·00

2012. Modern Architecture
3148 70c. chrome yellow and black 2·10 2·00
3149 90c. pale lilac and black 2·50 2·40
3150 145c. pale apple green and
 black 4·75 4·50
Designs: 70c. As No. 3086 (Museum der Moderne
Monchsberg, Salzburg); 90c. As No. 3089 (Forum Stadt-
park, Graz); 145c. As No. 3135 (Frauenmuseum, Hittisau).

1699 St George (statue) and
Anniversary Emblem

2012. 900th Anniv of Herzogenburg Priory
3151 **1699** 90c. multicoloured 2·50 2·40

1700 Victor Hess and Symbols of
Cosmic Rays

2012. Centenary of Confirmation of Existence of Cosmic
Rays by Victor Hess (Nobel Prize Winner for Physics,
1936)
3152 **1700** 145c. multicoloured 4·75 4·50

1701 Team Members
and Trophy

2012. Centenary of SV Reid Football Club, Ried im
Innkreis
3153 **1701** 62c. multicoloured 1·75 1·60

1702 Ferris Wheel, Vienna
Prater Amusement Park

2012. Europa. Visit Austria. Sheet 100×80 mm
MS3154 **1702** 70c. multicoloured 2·10 2·00

1703 St. Charles's Church,
Vienna and Subway Train set
on the Vienna – Baden
Route

2012. Stamp Day
3155 **1703** 272c. +136c. multicol-
 oured 10·00 9·00

1704 *Schönbrunn* on
the Donau (Walter
Ofner)

2012. Centenary of *Schönbrunn* Steamship
3156 **1704** 90c. multicoloured 2·50 2·40

2012. Modern Architecture
3156a 90c. azure 2·50 2·40
Designs: 62c. As No. 3083 (Museum of Modern Art Lud-
wig Foundation, Vienna (Museum Moderner Kunst Stif-
tung Ludwig, Wien))

1705 Johann Nestroy
as Willibald in *Worst
Boy in the School*
(lithograph by
Melchior Fritsch)

2012. 150th Death Anniv of Johann Nestroy (singer, actor
and playwright)
3157 **1705** 145c. multicoloured 4·75 4·50

1706 Self-portrait

2012. 125th Birth Anniv of Anton Faistauer (artist)
3158 **1706** 70c. multicoloured 2·10 2·00

1707 City Parish Church

2012. Millenary of Stockerau
3159 **1707** 62c. multicoloured 1·90 1·90

1708 Mary Crowned

2012. Religious Art. Stained Glass Window, Cistercian
Monastery, Lilienfeld
3160 **1708** 145c. multicoloured 4·75 4·50

1709 Johann Puch
and Puch Model IV

2012. 150th Birth Anniv of Johann Puch (engineer)
3161 **1709** 145c. multicoloured 4·75 4·50

1710 Boy holding
Handful of Corn

2012. Caritas and You, For a World without Hunger
Campaign
3162 **1710** 62c. multicoloured 1·90 1·80

1711 Map of Austria as
Flag

2012. Austria. No Value Expressed. Multicoloured.
3163 INLAND Type **1711** 1·90 1·80
3164 EUROPA Map of Austria as flag
 in Europe 2·50 2·40
3165 WELT Map of Austria as flag
 on globe 4·00 3·75

1712 Wolkenturm Event
Centre, Grafenegg (the
next ENTERprise)

2012. Modern Architecture in Austria
3166 **1712** 70c. multicoloured 2·10 2·00

1713 Post Office
Building

2012. Old Austria. Zagreb
3167 **1713** 70c. multicoloured 2·10 2·00

1714 Portrait of Fritza
Riedler

2012. 150th Birth Anniv of Gustav Klimt (artist)
3168 **1714** 170c. multicoloured 5·25 4·75

1715 Votivkirche,
Vienna

2012. Birth Bicentenary of Rudolf von Alt (artist)
3169 **1715** 170c. multicoloured 5·75 5·50

1716 Gmunden
Ceramics

2012. Classic Trade Marks
3170 **1716** 62c. multicoloured 1·90 1·80

1717 Dray Horse and Dray

2012. Dining with Tradition. Stieglbrauerei Brewery
3171 **1717** 62c. multicoloured 1·90 1·80

1718 Children
encircling Globe (Bianca
Haselmayer)

2012. Youth for Integration. Children's Drawing
Competition Winning Design
3172 **1718** 62c. +20c. multicoloured 2·50 2·40

1719 *Vulpes vulpes* (Fox)

2012. Wildlife and Hunting
3173	**1719**	90c. multicoloured	2·50	2·40

2012. Modern Architecture
3174	90c. pale lilac	2·50	2·40
3175	340c. pale greenish yellow (vert)	10·50	5·50

Designs: 90c. As No. 3089 (Essl Museum, Klosterneuburg); 340c. As No. 3092 (Austrian Cultural Forum, New York)

1720 St. Stephan Church, Baden

2012. Churches. 700th Anniv of St. Stephan, Baden
3176	**1720**	90c. multicoloured	2·50	2·40

1721 Alpine Ibex

2012. 50th Anniv of Alpine Zoo, Innsbruck
3177	**1721**	70c. multicoloured	2·20	2·10

1722 Gerlinde Kaltenbrunner

2012. Gerlinde Kaltenbrunner (mountaineer)
3178	**1722**	62c. multicoloured	1·90	1·80

1723 Train exiting Tunnel

2012. Centenary of Mittenwald Railway
3179	**1723**	145c. multicoloured	4·75	4·50

1724 Archangel Michael (sculpture by Hans Waldburger), High Altar, Basilica of St. Michael, Mondsee

2012. Religious Art (2nd issue)
3180	**1724**	145c. multicoloured	4·75	4·50

1725 Penguins and Alex the Lion (lower face)

2012. *Madagascar 3 - Europe's Most Wanted* (animated film)
MS3181	62c. Type **1725**; 62c. Marty the Zebra and Gloria the hippotomas; 70c. Penguins and Alex (upper face); 90c. Melman the giraffe	8·00	8·00

1726 Ants (Peter Kogler)

2012. Art. Contemporary Art
MS3182	62c. silver, black and bright vermilion; 70c. bright vermilion, black and silver	5·50	5·50

Design: 62c. *Ants* ; 70c. *Ants* (different)

1727 *Sleeping Child* (Bernardo Strozzi)

2012. Art. Old Masters
3183	**1727**	170c. multicoloured	5·75	5·50

1728 *Self-portrait with Red Hat* (Marie-Louise von Motesiczky)

2011. Art
3184	**1728**	62c. multicoloured	1·90	1·80

1729 Gas Lamp and Carl Auer von Welsbach (inventor)

2012. Austrian Inventions. Gas Lamp Mantle
3185	**1729**	62c. multicoloured	1·90	1·80

1730 Modern Electric Locomotive, Early Steam Locomotive and Arms of Györ, Sopron and Ebenfurt

2012. 140th Anniv of Raab - Ödenburg - Ebenfurter Railway
3186	**1730**	62c. multicoloured	1·90	1·80

1731 Grüner Veltliner Grapes and Wine Glass

2012. Wine Regions of Austria. Weinviertel
3187	**1731**	62c. multicoloured	1·90	1·80

1732 Scene form *Une Catastrophe* (directed by Jean-Luc Godard)

2012. 50th Anniv of Vienna International Film Festival (Viennale)
3188	**1732**	70c. multicoloured	2·20	2·10

1733 Emperor Franz Josef I

2012. 115th Anniv of Meeting between Emperor Franz Josef I and King Rama V. Multicoloured.
MS3189	70c. Type **1733**; 170c. King Rama V of Thailand	7·50	7·50

1734 Kals St George Church, Tyrol

2012. Christmas (1st issue)
3190	**1734**	70c. multicoloured	2·20	2·10

1735 *Adoration of the Magi* (Jacopo Bassano)

2012. Christmas (2nd issue). Coil Stamp
3191	**1735**	70c. multicoloured	2·20	2·10

1736 Lenz Moser Winery

2012. Classic Trade Marks
3192	**1736**	62c. multicoloured	1·90	1·80

1737 Locomotive inscribed with Anniversary Emblem

2012. 175th Anniv of Austrian Railways
3193	**1737**	90c. multicoloured	2·50	2·40

1738 Arndorfer Altar, Maria Saal Church, Carinthia

2012. Christmas (3rd issue)
3194	**1738**	62c. multicoloured	1·90	1·80

1739 Hunters in the Snow (Pieter Breughel the Elder)

2012. Christmas (4th issue). Coil Stamp
3195	**1739**	90c. multicoloured	1·90	1·80

1740 Bergisel Ski Jump (Zaha Hadid)

2013. Modern Architecture in Austria
3196	**1740**	62c. multicoloured	1·25	1·75

1741 Sun, Fiddle playing Skier and Female Skier

2013. FIS Alpine World Ski Championships 2013, Schladming, Styria, Austria. Multicoloured.
3197		62c. Type **1741**	1·75	90
3198		70c. Ski run, skiers, Alpine flowers, cow, sheep, fruit and heart	3·50	2·25
3199		90c. Ski run, skier and Austrian flag	3·50	2·25

1742 'FALTIN' etc

2013. Europe - Unity in Diversity
3199a	**1742**	70c. multicoloured	1·00	90

1743 HMW Z50 Motorcycle (1953)

2013. Motorcycles
3199b	**1743**	220c. multicoloured	2·25	2·10

IMPERIAL JOURNAL STAMPS

J18

1853. Imperf.
J67		1k. blue	15·00	2·10
J15	**J18**	2k. green	£4250	£120
J68		2k. brown	13·50	3·00
J32		4k. brown	£550	£1600

The 2k. green has different corner ornaments. For similar values in black or red, see Lombardy and Venetia Imperial Journal stamps, Nos. J22/4.

J21 Arms of Austria

1890. Imperf.
J76	**J21**	1k. brown	15·00	2·10
J77	**J21**	2k. green	13·50	3·00

J22 Arms of
Austria

1890. Perf.
J78	**J22**	25k. red	£140	£300

NEWSPAPER STAMPS

N2 Mercury

1851. Imperf.
N11b	**N2**	(0.6k.) blue	£225	£160
N12	**N2**	(6k.) yellow	£37000	£12000
N13	**N2**	(6k.) red	£62000	£108000
N14	**N2**	(30k.) red	£42000	£17000

N8 Francis
Joseph I

1858. Imperf.
N28	**N8**	(1k.05) blue	£800	£900
N29	**N8**	(1k.05) lilac	£1100	£425

N11 Francis
Joseph I

1861. Imperf.
N38	**N11**	(1k.05) grey	£250	£225

N13 Arms of
Austria

1863. Imperf.
N44	**N13**	(1k.05) lilac	55·00	21·00

AHN17
Mercury

1867. Imperf.
AHN58b	**AHN17**	(1k.) lilac	50	30

N19 Mercury

1880. Imperf.
N69	**N19**	½k. green	11·50	1·60

N31 Mercury

1899. Imperf.
N122	**N31**	2h. blue	30	20
N123	**N31**	6h. orange	3·00	3·00
N124	**N31**	10h. brown	2·10	1·60
N125	**N31**	20h. pink	2·10	3·00

N43 Mercury

1908. Imperf.
N207C	**N43**	2h. blue	1·50	45
N208C	**N43**	6h. orange	6·75	1·10
N209C	**N43**	10h. red	6·75	85
N210C	**N43**	20h. brown	6·75	85

N53 Mercury

1916. Imperf.
N266	**N53**	2h. brown	10	20
N267	**N53**	4h. green	50	1·60
N268	**N53**	6h. blue	40	1·70
N269	**N53**	10h. orange	1·00	2·10
N270	**N53**	30h. orange	50	1·90

N54 Mercury

1916. For Express. Perf.
N271	**N54**	2h. red on yellow	1·50	4·25
N272	**N54**	5h. green on yellow	1·50	4·25

N61 Mercury

1917. For Express. Perf.
N294	**N61**	2h. red on yellow	20	55
N295	**N61**	5h. green on yellow	20	55

1919. Optd **Deutschosterreich**. Imperf.
N318	**N53**	2h. brown	20	1·10
N319	**N53**	4h. green	50	8·50
N320	**N53**	6h. blue	30	10·50
N321	**N53**	10h. orange	1·20	16·00
N322	**N53**	30h. red	60	21·00

1919. For Express. Optd Deutschosterreich. Perf.
N334	**N61**	2h. red on yellow	10	30
N335	**N61**	5h. green on yellow	10	30

N68 Mercury

1920. Imperf.
N365A	**N68**	2h. violet	10	20
N366A	**N68**	4h. brown	10	30
N367A	**N68**	5h. slate	10	20
N368A	**N68**	6h. blue	15	20
N369A	**N68**	8h. green	10	55
N370A	**N68**	9h. bistre	10	20
N371A	**N68**	10h. red	10	20
N372A	**N68**	12h. blue	10	55
N373A	**N68**	15h. mauve	10	25
N374A	**N68**	18h. turquoise	10	30
N375A	**N68**	20h. orange	10	30
N376A	**N68**	30h. brown	10	20
N377A	**N68**	45h. green	10	55
N378A	**N68**	60h. red	10	30
N379A	**N68**	72h. brown	20	55
N380A	**N68**	90h. violet	30	85
N381A	**N68**	1k.20 red	30	1·10
N382A	**N68**	2k.40 green	30	1·10
N383A	**N68**	3k. grey	30	1·10

1921. For Express. No. N334 surch **50 50**.
N450	**N 61**	50 on 2h. red on yell	10	45

N78 Mercury

1921. Imperf.
N452	**N78**	45h. grey	20	20
N453	**N78**	75h. red	10	55
N454	**N78**	1k.50 green	10	75
N455	**N78**	1k.80 blue	10	95
N456	**N78**	2k.25 brown	10	1·30
N457	**N78**	3k. green	10	1·10
N458	**N78**	6k. purple	10	1·20
N459	**N78**	7k.50 brown	20	1·60

N79 Posthorn and
Arrow

1921. For Express. Perf.
N460	**N79**	50h. lilac on yellow	20	2·10

POSTAGE DUE STAMPS

D26

1894. Perf.
D96	**D26**	1k. brown	6·25	2·10
D97	**D26**	2k. brown	8·25	4·25
D98	**D26**	3k. brown	10·50	2·10
D99	**D26**	5k. brown	10·50	75
D100	**D26**	6k. brown	8·25	9·25
D101	**D26**	7k. brown	4·25	9·25
D102	**D26**	10k. brown	8·25	85
D103	**D26**	20k. brown	4·25	9·25
D104	**D26**	50k. brown	90·00	£120

1899. As Type **D26**, but value in heller. Perf or imperf.
D126		1h. brown	75	30
D127		2h. brown	75	20
D128d		3h. brown	75	20
D129		4h. brown	95	20
D130		5h. brown	1·00	20
D131d		6h. brown	75	75
D132		10h. brown	1·20	10
D133		12h. brown	1·50	75
D134		15h. brown	1·20	1·40
D135		20h. brown	1·70	45
D136		40h. brown	3·00	75
D137d		100h. brown	8·25	4·25

D44

1908. Perf.
D210B	**D44**	1h. red	1·00	2·10
D211C	**D44**	2h. red	60	45
D212C	**D44**	4h. red	40	20
D213C	**D44**	6h. red	40	20
D214C	**D44**	10h. red	60	20
D215C	**D44**	14h. red	7·25	3·00
D216C	**D44**	20h. red	15·00	20
D217C	**D44**	25h. red	19·00	6·75
D218C	**D44**	30h. red	10·50	45
D219C	**D44**	50h. red	35·00	55
D220C	**D44**	100h. red	29·00	75
D221C	**D44**	5k. violet	85·00	20·00
D222C	**D44**	10k. violet	£300	5·25

D55　　　　　　D56

1916
D273	**D55**	5h. red	10	20
D274	**D55**	10h. red	10	20
D275	**D55**	15h. red	10	20
D276	**D55**	20h. red	10	20
D277	**D55**	25h. red	25	1·30
D278	**D55**	30h. red	30	55
D279	**D55**	40h. red	20	85
D280	**D55**	50h. red	1·20	3·75
D281	**D 56**	1k. blue	1·00	55
D282	**D 56**	5k. blue	3·00	4·25
D283	**D 56**	10k. blue	4·25	2·30

1916. Nos. 189/90 optd **PORTO** or surch **15 15** also.
D284		1h. black	10	20
D285		15 on 2h. violet	35	75

1917. Unissued stamps as T **50** surch **PORTO** and value.
D286	**50**	10 on 24h. blue	2·10	75
D287	**50**	15 on 36h. violet	60	30
D288	**50**	20 on 54h. orange	35	55
D289	**50**	50 on 42h. brown	40	30

The above differ from Type **50** by showing a full-face portrait.

1919. Optd **Deutschosterreich**.
D323	**D55**	5h. red	10	20
D324	**D55**	10h. red	10	20
D325	**D55**	15h. red	30	55
D326	**D55**	20h. red	30	55
D327	**D55**	25h. red	10·50	32·00
D328	**D55**	30h. red	30	55
D329	**D55**	40h. red	30	1·10
D330	**D55**	50h. red	35	1·60
D331	**D 56**	1k. blue	5·75	19·00
D332	**D 56**	5k. blue	11·50	19·00
D333	**D 56**	10k. blue	13·50	5·25

D69　　　　　D70

1920. Imperf or perf (D 69), perf (D 70).
D384A	**D69**	5h. pink	20	45
D385A	**D69**	10h. pink	10	20
D386A	**D69**	15h. pink	10	1·60
D387A	**D69**	20h. pink	10	20
D388A	**D69**	25h. pink	20	1·60
D389A	**D69**	30h. pink	10	45
D390A	**D69**	40h. pink	10	45
D391A	**D69**	50h. pink	10	30
D392A	**D69**	80h. pink	10	55
D393A	**D 70**	1k. blue	10	40
D394A	**D 70**	1½k. blue	10	40
D395A	**D 70**	2k. blue	10	40
D396Aa	**D 70**	3k. blue	10	65
D397Aa	**D 70**	4k. blue	10	85
D398A	**D 70**	5k. blue	10	40
D399A	**D 70**	8k. blue	10	1·10
D400A	**D 70**	10k. blue	10	55
D401A	**D 70**	20k. blue	50	2·75

1921. No. 343a surch **Nachmarke 7½ K**. Perf.
D451	**64**	7½k. on 15h. brown	10	55

D83

1921
D510	**D83**	1k. brown	20	45
D511	**D83**	2k. brown	20	55
D512	**D83**	4k. brown	20	95
D513	**D83**	5k. brown	20	45
D514	**D83**	7½k. brown	20	1·30
D515	-	10k. blue	20	55
D516	-	15k. blue	20	75
D517	-	20k. blue	20	85
D518	-	50k. blue	20	75

The 10k. to 50k. are larger (22×30 mm).

D86

1922
D526	**D83**	10k. turquoise	10	65
D527	**D83**	15k. turquoise	10	95
D528	**D83**	20k. turquoise	10	75
D529	**D83**	25k. turquoise	10	1·60
D530	**D83**	40k. turquoise	10	55
D531	**D83**	50k. turquoise	10	1·90
D532	**D 86**	100k. purple	10	20
D533	**D 86**	150k. purple	10	20
D534	**D 86**	200k. purple	10	20
D535	**D 86**	400k. purple	10	20
D536	**D 86**	600k. purple	25	65
D537	**D 86**	800k. purple	10	20
D538	**D 86**	1000k. purple	10	20
D539	**D 86**	1200k. purple	1·50	9·25
D540	**D 86**	1500k. purple	10	55
D541	**D 86**	1800k. purple	4·25	18·00
D542	**D 86**	2000k. purple	50	1·30
D543	**D 86**	3000k. purple	9·25	37·00
D544	**D 86**	4000k. purple	6·25	30·00
D545	**D 86**	6000k. purple	10·50	47·00

D94

1925
D589	**D94**	1g. red	10	10
D590	**D94**	2g. red	10	10
D591	**D94**	3g. red	10	10
D592	**D94**	4g. red	10	10
D593	**D94**	5g. red	10	10
D594	**D94**	6g. red	30	45
D595	**D94**	8g. red	20	20
D596	**D94**	10g. blue	30	10
D597	**D94**	12g. blue	10	10
D598	**D94**	14g. blue	10	10
D599	**D94**	15g. blue	10	10
D600	**D94**	16g. blue	30	25
D601	**D94**	18g. blue	2·10	3·75
D602	**D94**	20g. blue	20	10

D603	D94	23g. blue	60	20
D604	D94	24g. blue	3·00	10
D605	D94	28g. blue	2·75	25
D606	D94	30g. blue	1·30	10
D607	D94	31g. blue	3·00	25
D608	D94	35g. blue	3·00	10
D609	D94	39g. blue	3·50	10
D610	D94	40g. blue	1·50	2·10
D611	D94	60g. blue	1·50	1·90
D612	-	1s. green	6·75	95
D613	-	2s. green	36·00	3·75
D614	-	5s. green	£140	60·00
D615	-	10s. green	55·00	5·25

DESIGN: 1 to 10s. Horiz bands of colour.

D120

1935

D746	D120	1g. red	10	20
D747	D120	2g. red	10	20
D748	D120	3g. red	10	20
D749	D120	5g. red	10	20
D750	-	10g. blue	10	10
D751	-	12g. blue	10	10
D752	-	15g. blue	30	65
D753	-	20g. blue	30	20
D754	-	24g. blue	35	20
D755	-	30g. blue	35	20
D756	-	39g. blue	40	20
D757	-	60g. blue	85	1·60
D758	-	1s. green	1·00	45
D759	-	2s. green	2·10	1·30
D760	-	5s. green	4·25	4·00
D761	-	10s. green	6·25	85

DESIGNS: 10 to 60g. As Type D **120** but with background of horizontal lines; 1 to 10s. As last, but with positions of figures, arms and inscriptions reversed.

D143

1945

D891	D143	1pf. red	20	20
D892	D143	2pf. red	20	20
D893	D143	3pf. red	20	20
D894	D143	5pf. red	20	20
D895	D143	10pf. red	20	20
D896	D143	12pf. red	20	25
D897	D143	20pf. red	20	25
D898	D143	24pf. red	20	45
D899	D143	30pf. red	20	50
D900	D143	60pf. red	20	55
D901	D143	1rm. violet	20	60
D902	D143	2rm. violet	20	95
D903	D143	5rm. violet	30	1·10
D904	D143	10rm. violet	30	1·30

1946. Optd **PORTO.**

D956	145	3g. orange	10	10
D957	145	5g. green	10	10
D958	145	6g. purple	10	10
D959	145	8g. red	10	10
D960	145	10g. grey	10	20
D961	145	12g. brown	10	10
D962	145	15g. red	10	10
D963	145	20g. brown	10	10
D964	145	25g. blue	20	20
D965	145	30g. mauve	10	10
D966	145	40g. blue	10	10
D967	145	60g. green	10	10
D968	145	1s. violet	20	10
D969	145	2s. yellow	70	1·20
D970	145	5s. blue	30	95

D162

1947

D1035	D162	1g. brown	10	10
D1036	D162	2g. brown	10	10
D1037	D162	3g. brown	10	20
D1038	D162	5g. brown	10	10
D1039	D162	8g. brown	10	10
D1040	D162	10g. brown	10	10
D1041	D162	12g. brown	10	10
D1042	D162	15g. brown	10	10
D1043	D162	16g. brown	50	95
D1044	D162	17g. brown	40	95
D1045	D162	18g. brown	40	95
D1046	D162	20g. brown	95	10
D1047	D162	24g. brown	40	1·10
D1048	D162	30g. brown	20	30
D1049	D162	36g. brown	95	1·60
D1050	D162	40g. brown	10	10
D1051	D162	42g. brown	1·10	1·60
D1052	D162	48g. brown	1·10	1·60
D1053	D162	50g. brown	95	30
D1054	D162	60g. brown	20	30
D1055	D162	70g. brown	20	25
D1056	D162	80g. brown	6·00	2·75
D1057	D162	1s. blue	20	10
D1058	D162	1s.15 blue	4·25	55
D1059	D162	1s.20 blue	4·50	2·20
D1060	D162	2s. blue	40	30
D1061	D162	5s. blue	50	40
D1062	D162	10s. blue	60	45

D184

1949

D1178	D184	1g. red	20	20
D1179	D184	2g. red	20	20
D1180	D184	4g. red	65	65
D1181	D184	5g. red	2·75	75
D1182	D184	8g. red	2·75	2·20
D1183	D184	10g. red	45	10
D1184	D184	20g. red	45	10
D1185	D184	30g. red	45	10
D1186	D184	40g. red	45	10
D1187	D184	50g. red	45	10
D1188	D184	60g. red	14·00	75
D1189	D184	63g. red	6·75	4·25
D1190	D184	70g. red	45	10
D1191	D184	80g. red	45	20
D1192	D184	90g. red	75	55
D1193	D184	1s. violet	75	10
D1194	D184	1s.20 violet	75	30
D1195	D184	1s.35 violet	45	20
D1196	D184	1s.40 violet	75	45
D1197	D184	1s.50 violet	75	25
D1198	D184	1s.65 violet	65	45
D1199	D184	1s.70 violet	65	45
D1200	D184	2s. violet	1·10	20
D1201	D184	2s.50 violet	75	20
D1202	D184	3s. violet	75	30
D1203	D184	4s. violet	1·20	1·10
D1204	D184	5s. violet	1·60	45
D1205	D184	10s. violet	1·80	60

D817

1985

D2074	D817	10g. yellow & black	10	10
D2075	D817	20g. red and black	10	10
D2076	D817	50g. orange & black	10	10
D2077	D817	1s. blue and black	20	20
D2078	D817	2s. brown & black	40	30
D2079	D817	3s. violet and black	50	40
D2080	D817	5s. yellow & black	90	60
D2081	D817	10s. green & black	1·80	90

`Pt. 2`

AUSTRIAN TERRITORIES ACQUIRED BY ITALY

Italian territory acquired from Austria at the close of the war of 1914-18, including Trentino and Trieste.

1918. 100 heller = 1 krone.
1918. 100 centesimi = 1 lira.
1919. 100 centesimi = 1 corona.

TRENTINO

1918. Stamps of Austria optd **Regno d'Italia Trentino 3 nov 1918.**

1	49	3h. purple	6·25	12·50
2	49	5h. green	4·25	6·25
3	49	6h. orange	70·00	£110
4	49	10h. red	4·25	9·25
5	49	12h. green	£200	£300
6	60	15h. brown	6·25	11·50
7	60	20h. green	3·00	10·50
8	60	25h. blue	55·00	70·00
9	60	30h. violet	17·00	26·00
10	51	40h. green	60·00	£100
11	51	50h. green	36·00	50·00
12	51	60h. blue	50·00	90·00
13	51	80h. brown	85·00	£130
14	51	90h. red	£1700	£3000
15	51	1k. red on yellow	85·00	£120
16	52	2k. blue	£500	£850
17	52	4k. green	£2000	£4000
18	52	10k. violet	£94000	

1918. Stamps of Italy optd **Venezia Tridentina.**

19	30	1c. brown	3·00	10·50
20	31	2c. brown	3·00	10·50
21	37	5c. green	3·00	10·50
22	37	10c. red	3·00	10·50
23	41	20c. orange	3·00	10·50
24	39	40c. brown	65·00	90·00
25	39	45c. olive	37·00	90·00
26	39	50c. mauve	37·00	90·00
27	34	1l. brown and green	37·00	90·00

1919. Stamps of Italy surch **Venezia Tridentina** and value.

28	37	5h. on 5c. green	3·00	5·25
29	37	10h. on 10c. red	3·00	5·25
30	41	20h. on 20c. orange	3·00	5·25

VENEZIA GIULIA

For use in Trieste and territory, Gorizia and province, and in Istria.

1918. Stamps of Austria optd **Regno d'Italia Venezia Giulia 3. XI. 18.**

31	49	3h. purple	1·60	3·00
32	49	5h. green	1·60	3·00
33	49	6h. orange	1·80	4·25
34	49	10h. red	5·25	5·25
35	49	12h. green	2·50	5·25
36	60	15h. brown	1·60	3·00
37	60	20h. green	1·60	3·00
38	60	25h. blue	8·25	13·50
39	60	30h. purple	3·00	6·25
40	51	40h. green	£100	£300
41	51	50h. green	8·25	12·50
42	51	60h. blue	29·00	36·00
43	51	80h. brown	18·00	23·00
44	51	1k. red on yellow	18·00	23·00
45	52	2k. blue	£275	£500
46	52	3k. red	£350	£600
47	52	4k. green	£1200	
48	52	10k. violet	£65000	£69000

1918. Stamps of Italy optd **Venezia Giulia.**

49	30	1c. brown	3·00	7·25
50	31	2c. brown	3·00	7·25
51	37	5c. green	2·10	3·00
52	37	10c. red	2·10	3·00
53	41	20c. orange	2·10	4·25
54	39	25c. blue	2·10	5·25
55	39	40c. brown	16·00	31·00
56	39	45c. green	5·25	11·50
57	39	50c. mauve	10·50	14·50
58	39	60c. red	90·00	£180
59	34	1l. brown and green	41·00	70·00

1919. Stamps of Italy surch **Venezia Giulia** and value.

60	37	5h. on 5c. green	2·10	4·25
61	41	20h. on 20c. orange	2·10	4·25

EXPRESS LETTER STAMPS

1919. Express Letter stamp of Italy optd **Venezia Giulia.**

E60	E35	25c. red	70·00	£120

POSTAGE DUE STAMPS

1918. Postage Due Stamps of Italy optd **Venezia Giulia.**

D60	D 12	5c. mauve and orange	1·00	2·10
D61	D 12	10c. mauve & orange	1·60	2·10
D62	D 12	20c. mauve & orange	1·60	4·25
D63	D 12	30c. mauve & orange	4·25	8·25
D64	D 12	40c. mauve & orange	36·00	55·00
D65	D 12	50c. mauve & orange	60·00	£160
D66	D 12	1l. mauve and blue	£200	£500

GENERAL ISSUE

For use throughout the liberated area of Trentino, Venezia Giulia and Dalmatia.

1919. Stamps of Italy surch in new currency.

62	30	1ce. di cor on 1c. brown	2·10	3·00
64	31	2ce. di cor on 2c. brown	2·10	3·00
65	37	5ce. di cor on 5c. green	2·10	2·10
67	37	10ce. di cor on 10c. red	2·10	2·10
68	41	20ce. di cor on 20c. orange	2·10	2·10
70	39	25ce. di cor on 25c. blue	2·10	5·25
71	39	40ce. di cor on 40c. brown	2·10	5·25
72	33	45ce. di cor on 45c. green	2·10	5·25
73	39	50ce. di cor on 50c. mauve	2·10	5·25
74	39	60ce. di cor on 60c. red	2·10	9·25
75	34	1cor. on 1l. brown & green	4·25	8·25
76	34	una corona on 1l. brn & grn	5·25	21·00
82	34	5cor. on 5l. blue and red	50·00	£120
83	34	10cor. on 10l. green & red	50·00	£120

EXPRESS LETTER STAMPS

1919. Express Letter stamps of Italy surch in new currency.

E76	E35	25ce. di cor on 25c. red	2·10	4·25
E77	E41	30ce. di cor on 30c. red and blue	3·00	8·25

POSTAGE DUE STAMPS

1919. Postage Due stamps of Italy surch in new currency.

D76	D12	5ce. di cor on 5c. mauve and orange	1·00	3·00
D77	D12	10ce. di cor. on 10c. mauve and orange	1·00	3·00
D78	D12	20ce. di cor on 20c. mauve and orange	2·10	3·00
D79	D12	30ce. di cor on 30c. mauve and orange	2·30	5·25
D80	D12	40ce. di cor on 40c. mauve and orange	2·30	5·25
D81	D12	50ce. di cor on 50c. mauve and orange	5·25	10·50
D82	D12	una corona on 1l. mauve and blue	5·25	12·50
D83	D12	due corona on 2l. mauve and blue	80·00	£180
D84	D12	cinque corona on 5l. mauve and blue	80·00	£180
D86	D12	1cor. on 1l. mve & blue	5·25	14·50
D87	D12	2cor. on 2l. mve & blue	50·00	£110
D88	D12	5cor. on 5l. mve & blue	50·00	£110

`Pt. 2`

AUSTRO-HUNGARIAN MILITARY POST

A. General Issues.
100 heller = 1 krone.

B. Issues for Italy.
100 centesimi = 1 lira.

C. Issues for Montenegro.
100 heller = 1 krone.

D. Issues for Romania.
100 bani = 1 leu.

E. Issues for Serbia.
100 heller = 1 krone.

A. GENERAL ISSUES

1915. Stamps of Bosnia and Herzegovina optd **K.U.K. FELDPOST.**

1	25	1h. olive	50	55
2	25	2h. blue	50	55
3	25	3h. lake	50	55
4	25	5h. green	40	30
5	25	6h. black	50	55
6	25	10h. red	30	30
7	25	12h. olive	50	75
8	25	20h. brown	60	1·10
9	25	25h. blue	50	75
10	25	30h. red	4·25	8·50
11	26	35h. green	3·00	7·50
12	26	40h. violet	3·00	7·50
13	26	45h. brown	3·00	7·50
14	26	50h. blue	3·00	7·50
15	26	60h. purple	60	1·40
16	26	72h. blue	3·00	6·25
17	25	1k. brown on cream	3·00	7·00
18	25	2k. indigo on blue	3·00	7·00
19	26	3k. red on green	31·00	70·00
20	26	5k. lilac on grey	28·00	47·00
21	26	10k. black on grey	£200	£375

2

1915

22	2	1h. green	10	30
23	2	2h. blue	10	45
24	2	3h. brown	10	30
25	2	5h. green	10	30
26	2	6h. black	10	45
27	2	10h. red	10	30
28	2	10h. blue	10	45
29	2	12h. green	10	55
30	2	15h. red	10	30
31	2	20h. brown	40	55
32	2	20h. green	40	65
33	2	25h. blue	20	45
34	2	30h. red	20	65
35	2	35h. green	40	95
36	2	40h. violet	40	95
37	2	45h. brown	40	95
38	2	50h. deep green	40	95
39	2	60h. purple	40	95
40	2	72h. blue	40	95

41	2	80h. brown	40	45
42	2	90h. red	1·10	1·80
43	-	1k. purple on cream	2·10	3·25
44	-	2k. green on blue	1·20	2·40
45	-	3k. red on green	1·10	7·50
46	-	4k. violet on green	1·10	12·00
47	-	5k. violet on grey	27·00	49·00
48	-	10k. blue on grey	4·75	22·00

The kronen values are larger, with profile portrait.

1917. As 1917 issue of Bosnia, but inscr "K.u.K. FELDPOST".

49		1h. blue	10	20
50		2h. orange	10	20
51		3h. grey	10	20
52		5h. green	10	20
53		6h. violet	10	20
54		10h. brown	10	20
55		12h. blue	10	20
56		15h. red	10	20
57		20h. brown	10	20
58		25h. blue	40	65
59		30h. grey	10	20
60		40h. bistre	10	20
61		50h. green	10	20
62		60h. red	10	55
63		80h. blue	10	30
64		90h. purple	40	95
65		2k. red on buff	20	55
66		3k. green on blue	1·40	5·50
67		4k. red on green	22·00	38·00
68		10k. violet on grey	2·30	16·00

The kronen values are larger and the border is different.

1918. Imperial and Royal Welfare Fund. As 1918 issue of Bosnia, but inscr "K. UND K. FELDPOST".

69	40	10h. (+10h.) green	50	1·10
70		20h. (+10h.) red	50	1·10
71	40	45h. (+10h.) blue	50	1·10

NEWSPAPER STAMPS

N4
Mercury

1916

N49	N4	2h. blue	20	45
N50	N4	6h. orange	60	1·60
N51	N4	10h. red	60	1·60
N52	N4	20h. brown	60	1·60

B. ISSUES FOR ITALY

1918. General Issue stamps of 1917 surch in figs and words.

1		2c. on 1h. blue	10	55
2		3c. on 2h. orange	10	55
3		4c. on 3h. grey	10	55
4		6c. on 5h. green	10	55
5		7c. on 6h. violet	20	55
6		11c. on 10h. brown	10	55
7		13c. on 12h. blue	10	55
8		16c. on 15h. red	10	55
9		22c. on 20h. brown	10	55
10		27c. on 25h. blue	40	1·60
11		32c. on 30h. grey	20	1·50
12		43c. on 40h. bistre	30	1·20
13		53c. on 50h. green	20	1·10
14		64c. on 60h. red	30	1·60
15		85c. on 80h. blue	20	1·10
16		95c. on 90h. purple	20	1·10
17		2l.11 on 2k. red on buff	30	2·20
18		3l.16 on 3k. green on blue	70	3·25
19		4l.22 on 4k. red on green	85	4·25

NEWSPAPER STAMPS

1918. Newspaper stamps of General Issue surch in figs and words.

N20		3c. on 2h. blue	20	45
N21		7c. on 6h. orange	40	1·40
N22		11c. on 10h. red	40	1·40
N23		22c. on 20h. brown	50	1·40

1918. For Express. Newspaper stamps of Bosnia surch in figs and words.

N24	N35	3c. on 2h. red on yell	7·25	26·00
N25	N35	6c. on 5h. green on yell	7·25	26·00

POSTAGE DUE STAMPS

1918. Postage Due stamps of Bosnia surch in figs and words.

D20	D 35	6c. on 5h. red	4·25	11·00
D21	D 35	11c. on 10h. red	2·50	13·00
D22	D 35	16c. on 15h. red	1·00	5·50
D23	D 35	27c. on 25h. red	1·00	5·50
D24	D 35	32c. on 30h. red	1·00	5·50
D25	D 35	43c. on 40h. red	1·00	5·50
D26	D 35	53c. on 50h. red	1·00	5·50

C. ISSUES FOR MONTENEGRO

1917. Nos. 28 and 30 of General Issues optd **K.U.K. MILIT. VERWALTUNG MONTENEGRO.**

1	2	10h. blue	20·00	16·00
2	2	15h. red	20·00	16·00

D. ISSUES FOR ROMANIA

1917. General Issue stamps of 1917 optd **BANI** or **LEI.**

1		3b. grey	3·50	5·75
2		5b. green	3·50	4·00
3		6b. violet	3·50	4·00
4		10b. brown	60	1·20
5		12b. blue	2·30	4·00
6		15b. red	2·30	4·00
7		20b. brown	60	1·20
8		25b. blue	60	1·20
9		30b. grey	1·20	1·70
10		40b. bistre	1·20	1·70
11		50b. green	1·20	1·70
12		60b. red	1·20	1·70
13		80b. blue	60	1·20
14		90b. purple	1·20	2·30
15		2l. red on buff	1·70	3·00
16		3l. green on blue	1·70	3·50
17		4l. red on green	2·30	4·00

3 Charles I

1918

18	3	3b. grey	60	1·20
19	3	5b. green	60	1·20
20	3	6b. violet	60	1·70
21	3	10b. brown	60	1·70
22	3	12b. blue	60	1·70
23	3	15b. red	60	1·20
24	3	20b. brown	60	1·20
25	3	25b. blue	60	1·20
26	3	30b. grey	60	1·20
27	3	40b. bistre	60	1·20
28	3	50b. green	60	1·70
29	3	60b. red	60	1·70
30	3	80b. blue	60	1·70
31	3	90b. purple	60	1·20
32	3	2l. red on buff	60	1·70
33	3	3l. green on blue	1·20	4·00
34	3	4l. red on green	1·70	4·00

E. ISSUES FOR SERBIA

1916. Stamps of Bosnia optd **SERBIEN.**

22	25	1h. olive	2·75	6·50
23	25	2h. blue	2·75	6·50
24	25	3h. lake	2·75	6·50
25	25	5h. green	45	95
26	25	6h. black	1·90	4·75
27	25	10h. red	45	95
28	25	12h. olive	95	2·75
29	25	20h. brown	95	95
30	25	25h. blue	95	2·75
31	25	30h. red	95	1·90
32	26	35h. green	95	1·90
33	26	40h. violet	95	1·90
34	26	45h. brown	95	1·90
35	26	50h. blue	95	1·90
36	26	60h. brown	95	1·90
37	26	72h. blue	95	1·90
38	25	1k. brown on cream	1·90	2·75
39	25	2k. indigo on blue	1·90	2·75
40	26	3k. red on green	1·90	2·75
41	26	5k. lilac on grey	1·90	2·75
42	26	10k. blue on grey	19·00	37·00

Pt. 2

AUSTRO-HUNGARIAN POST OFFICES IN THE TURKISH EMPIRE

A. Lombardy and Venetia Currency.
100 soldi = 1 florin.

B. Turkish Currency.
40 paras = 1 piastre.

C. French Currency.
100 centimes = 1 franc.

A. LOMBARDY AND VENETIA CURRENCY

1 2

1867

1	1	2s. yellow	3·25	38·00
9	1	3s. green	1·60	38·00

10	1	5s. red	55	27·00
11	1	10s. blue	£140	1·70
5	1	15s. brown	36·00	11·00
6	1	25s. lilac	37·00	55·00
7a	2	50s. brown	1·60	85·00

3

1883

14	3	2s. black and brown	20	£225
15	3	3s. black and green	1·60	49·00
16	3	5s. black and red	30	28·00
17	3	10s. black and blue	1·10	85
18	3	20s. black and grey	8·00	13·00
19	3	50s. black and mauve	1·60	28·00

B. TURKISH CURRENCY

1886. Surch **10 PARA 10.**

21a		10p. on 3s. green	45	11·00

1888. Nos. 71/75a of Austria surch.

22	20	10pa. on 3k. green	5·50	17·00
23	20	20pa. on 5k. red	65	13·00
24	20	1pi. on 10k. blue	95·00	2·20
25	20	2pi. on 20k. grey	2·40	6·50
26	20	5pi. on 50k. purple	2·75	27·00

1890. Stamps of Austria of 1890, the kreuzer values with lower figures of value removed, surch at foot.

27	23	8pa. on 2k. brown	20	85
28	23	10pa. on 3k. green	75	85
29	23	20pa. on 5k. red	85	85
30	23	1pi. on 10k. blue	55	30
31	23	2pi. on 20k. olive	11·00	43·00
32	23	5pi. on 50k. mauve	16·00	95·00
33	24	10pi. on 1g. blue	14·00	60·00
37	24	10pi. on 1g. lilac	27·00	32·00
34	24	20pi. on 2g. red	22·00	90·00
38	24	20pi. on 2g. green	55·00	£110

1890. Stamps of Austria of 1891, with lower figures of value removed, surch at foot.

35	25	2pi. on 20k. green	8·50	2·20
36	25	5pi. on 50k. mauve	3·25	4·25

1900. Stamps of Austria of 1899, the heller values with lower figures of value removed, surch at foot.

46	27	10pa. on 5h. green	3·25	4·00
40	28	20pa. on 10h. red	7·50	1·20
48	28	1pi. on 25h. blue	2·20	1·10
49	29	2pi. on 50h. blue	5·50	8·50
43d	30	5pi. on 1k. red	75	55
44d	30	10pi. on 2k. lavender	3·25	4·75
45d	30	20pi. on 4k. green	3·25	13·00

1903. Stamps of Austria of 1899, with all figures of value removed, surch at top and at foot.

55	27	10pa. green	75	2·75
56	28	20pa. red	1·60	1·60
57	28	30pa. mauve	75	5·50
58	28	1pi. blue	1·10	55
59	29	2pi. blue	1·10	1·20

11 Francis Joseph I 12 Francis Joseph I

1908. 60th Anniv of Emperor's Accession.

60	11	10pa. green on yellow	20	55
61	11	20pa. red on pink	30	55
62	11	30pa. brown on buff	55	75
63	11	60pa. purple on blue	1·10	6·50
70	11	1pi. ultramarine on blue	45	75
65	12	2pi. red on yellow	1·10	85
66	12	5pi. brown on grey	1·10	1·30
67	12	10pi. green on yellow	1·60	2·75
68	12	20pi. blue on grey	3·75	5·50

POSTAGE DUE STAMPS

1902. Postage Due stamps as Type D32 of Austria, but with value in heller, surch with new value.

D50	D32	10pa. on 5h. green	1·60	4·25
D51	D32	20pa. on 10h. green	1·60	6·25
D52	D32	1pi. on 20h. green	2·20	6·25
D53	D32	2pi. on 40h. green	2·20	6·25
D54	D32	5pi. on 100h. green	2·20	6·00

D13

1908

D71A	D13	¼pi. green	4·25	16·00
D72A	D13	½pi. green	2·75	13·00
D73A	D13	1pi. green	3·25	13·00
D74A	D13	1½pi. green	1·60	30·00
D75A	D13	2pi. green	2·20	27·00
D76A	D13	5pi. green	3·25	19·00
D77A	D13	10pi. green	23·00	£190
D78A	D13	20pi. green	15·00	£225
D79A	D13	30pi. green	23·00	19·00

C. FRENCH CURRENCY

1903. Stamps of Austria surch **CENTIMES** or **FRANC.**

F1A	27	5c. on 5h. green and black	1·60	6·50
F2A	28	10c. on 10h. red and black (No. 143)	1·20	6·50
F3A	28	25c. on 25h. blue and black (No. 145)	55·00	43·00
F4A	29	50c. on 50h. blue and black	14·00	£225
F5	30	1f. on 1k. red	1·60	£190
F6	30	2f. on 2k. lilac	14·00	£550
F7	30	4f. on 4k. green	16·00	£850

1904. Stamps of Austria surch **CENTIMES.**

F14	33	5c. on 5h. green	1·10	6·00
F13	28	10c. on 10h. red and black (No. 160)	75	22·00
F10B	28	25c. on 25h. blue and black (No. 176)	75	£170
F11A	35	50c. on 50h. blue	75	£750

1906. Type of Austria surch **CENTIMES.**

F15	28	10c. on 10h. red (No. 184)	1·60	55·00
F16	28	15c. on 15h. violet and black (as No. 185)	1·10	55·00

No. F16 was not issued without the surch.

1908. 60th Anniv of Emperor's Accession. As T **11/12** but in centimes or franc.

F17	11	5c. green on yellow	20	1·30
F18	11	10c. red on pink	45	1·60
F19	11	15c. brown on buff	65	9·75
F20	11	25c. blue on blue	19·00	8·50
F21	12	50c. red on yellow	5·50	49·00
F22	12	1f. brown on grey	7·50	75·00

Pt. 10

AZERBAIJAN

Formerly part of the Russian Empire. Became independent on 27 May 1918, following the Russian Revolution. Soviet troops invaded the country on 27 April 1920, and a Soviet Republic followed. From 1 October 1923 stamps of the Transcaucasian Federation were used but these were superseded by those of the Soviet Union in 1924.

With the dissolution of the Soviet Union in 1991, Azerbaijan once again became an independent state.

1919. 100 kopeks = 1 rouble.
1992. 100 qopik = 1 manat.
2006. 1 manat = 100 qepik.

1
Standard-bearer

1919. Imperf. Various designs.

1B	1	10k. multicoloured	20	20
2B	-	20k. multicoloured	20	20
3B	-	40k. olive, black and yellow	20	20
4B	-	60k. orange, black & yellow	20	25
5B	-	1r. blue, black and yellow	30	30
6B	-	2r. red, black and yellow	30	30
7B	-	5r. blue, black and yellow	40	55
8B	-	10r. olive, black & yellow	60	60
9B	-	25r. blue, black and red	1·00	1·00
10B	-	50r. olive, black and red	1·30	1·10

DESIGNS—HORIZ: 40k. to 1r. Reaper; 2r. to 10r. Citadel, Baku; 25r., 50r. Temple of Eternal Fires.

3 "Labour" 4 Petroleum Well

1921. Imperf.

11	3	1r. green	35	75
12	4	2r. brown	50	80

13	-	5r. brown	35	75
14	-	10r. grey	50	85
15	-	25r. orange	35	75
16	-	50r. violet	35	75
17	-	100r. orange	40	80
18	-	150r. blue	40	80
19	-	250r. violet and buff	40	80
20	-	400r. blue	40	80
21	-	500r. black and lilac	40	80
22	-	1000r. red and blue	40	80
23	-	2000r. black and blue	40	80
24	-	3000r. brown and blue	40	80
25	-	5000r. green on olive	55	90

DESIGNS—HORIZ: 5r., 3000r. Bibi Eibatt Oilfield; 100r., 5000r. Goukasoff House (State Museum of Arts); 400r., 1000r. Hall of Judgment, Khan's Palace. VERT: 10r., 2000r. Minaret of Friday Mosque, Khan's Palace, Baku; 25r., 250r. Globe and Workers; 50r. Malden's Tower, Baku; 150r., 500r. Blacksmiths.

6 Famine Supplies

1921. Famine Relief. Imperf.

26	**6**	500r. blue	50	1·50
27	-	1000r. brown	85	2·50

DESIGN—VERT: 1000r. Starving family.
For stamps of the above issues surch with new values, see Stanley Gibbons Part 10 (Russia) Catalogue.

13 Azerbaijan Map and Flag

1992. Independence.

83	**13**	35q. multicoloured	90	90

1992. Unissued stamp showing Caspian Sea surch **AZARBAYCAN** and new value.

84B		25q. on 15k. multicoloured	45	45
85B		35q. on 15k. multicoloured	65	65
86B		50q. on 15k. multicoloured	85	85
87B		1m.50 on 15k. multicoloured	2·75	2·75
88B		2m.50 on 15k. multicoloured	4·25	4·25

16 Maiden's Tower, Baku

1992. Dated "1992".

89	**16**	10q. green and black	15	15
90	**16**	20q. red and black	15	15
91	**16**	50q. yellow and black	20	20
92	**16**	1m.50 blue and black	85	85

See also Nos. 101/4.

17 Akhalteka Horse

1993. Horses. Multicoloured.

93	**17**	20q. Type **17**	10	10
94		30q. Kabarda horse	10	10
95		50q. Qarabair horse	10	10
96		1m. Don horse	10	10
97		2m.50 Yakut horse	45	45
98		5m. Orlov horse	85	85
99		10m. Diliboz horse	1·70	1·70
MS100		80×60 mm. 8m. Qarabag horse	1·70	1·70

1993. Dated "1993".

101		50q. blue and black	25	25
102		1m. mauve and black	15	15
103		2m.50 yellow and black	30	30
104		5m. green and black	55	55

18 *Tulipa eichleri*

1993. Flowers. Multicoloured.

105		25q. Type **18**	10	10
106		50q. *Puschkinia scilloides*	10	10
107		1m. *Iris elegantissima*	15	15
108		1m.50 *Iris acutiloba*	20	20
109		5m. *Tulipa florenskyii*	70	70
110		10m. *Iris reticulata*	1·30	1·30
MS111		78×58 mm. 10m. *Muscari elecostomum* (31×39 mm)	1·20	1·20

19 Russian Sturgeon

1993. Fish. Multicoloured.

112		25q. Type **19**	10	10
113		50q. Stellate sturgeon	10	10
114		1m. Iranian roach	15	10
115		1m.50 Caspian roach	25	25
116		5m. Caspian trout	90	90
117		10m. Black-backed shad	1·80	1·80
MS118		76×58 mm. 10m. Beluga (*Huso huso*) (39×31 mm)	1·60	1·20

20 Map of Nakhichevan

1993. 70th Birthday of President Heydar Aliev.

119	-	25m. black and red	1·50	1·50
120	**20**	25m. multicoloured	1·50	1·50
MS121a		110×90 mm. Nos. 119/20 (map inscr "Naxcivan")	9·50	9·50

DESIGN: No. 119, President Aliev.

21 Government Building, Baku

1993

122	**21**	25q. black and yellow	15	15
123	**21**	30q. black and green	15	15
124	**21**	50q. black and blue	30	30
125	**21**	1m. black and red	60	60

22 Flags, and Dish Aerials on Maps

1993. Azerbaijan–Iran Telecommunications Co-operation.

126	**22**	15q. multicoloured	80	80

23 National Colours and Islamic Crescent

1994. National Day.

127	**23**	5m. multicoloured	35	35

24 State Arms

1994

128	**24**	8m. multicoloured	65	65

25 Sirvan Palace

1994. Baku Architecture.

129	**25**	2m. red, silver and black	15	15
130	-	4m. green, silver and black	25	25
131	-	8m. blue, silver and black	55	55

DESIGNS: 4m. 15th-century tomb; 8m. Divan-Khana.

26 Fuzuli

1994. 500th Birth Anniv (1992) of Mohammed ibn Suleiman Fuzuli (poet).

132	**26**	10m. multicoloured	45	45

1994. No. 126 surch **IRAN–AZERBAYGAN** and value.

133	**22**	2m. on 15q. multicoloured	30	30
134	**22**	20m. on 15q. multicoloured	85	85
135	**22**	25m. on 15q. multicoloured	1·00	1·00
136	**22**	50m. on 15q. multicoloured	2·40	2·40

1994. Nos. 122/5 surch.

137	**21**	5m. on 1m. black and red	30	30
138	**21**	10m. on 30q. black & grn	30	30
139	**21**	20m. on 30q. black & grn	30	30
140	**21**	20m. on 50q. black & blue	30	30
141	**21**	25m. on 1m. black & red	35	35
142	**21**	40m. on 50q. black & blue	65	65
143	**21**	50m. on 25q. black & yell	85	85
144	**21**	100m. on 25q. black & yell	1·70	1·70

29 Rasulzade

1994. 110th Birth Anniv of Mammed Amin Rasulzade (politician).

145	**29**	15m. brown, ochre & black	85	85

30 Mamedquluzade

1994. 125th Birth Anniv of Jalil Mamedquluzade (writer).

146	**30**	20m. black, gold and blue	85	85

31 Temple of the Fire Worshippers of Atashgah

1994. 115th Anniv of Nobel Partnership to Exploit Black Sea Oil. Multicoloured.

147	**31**	15m. Type **31**	25	25
148		20m. Oil wells	35	35
149		25m. *Zoroastr* (first oil tanker in Caspian Sea)	40	40
150		50m. Nobel brothers and Petr Bilderling (partners)	1·00	1·00
MS151		110×73 mm. No. 150	1·10	1·10

32 Laumontite

1994. Minerals. Multicoloured.

152		5m. Type **32**	25	25
153		10m. Epidot calcite	40	40
154		15m. Andradite	65	65
155		20m. Amethyst	85	85
MS156		120×110 mm. Nos. 152/5	2·10	2·10

33 Players

1994. World Cup Football Championship, U.S.A.

157	**33**	5m. multicoloured	10	10
158	-	10m. multicoloured	10	10
159	-	20m. multicoloured	25	25
160	-	25m. multicoloured	35	35
161	-	30m. multicoloured	40	40
162	-	50m. multicoloured	70	70
163	-	80m. multicoloured	1·10	1·10
MS164		90×65 mm. 100m. multicoloured (31×39 mm)	1·30	1·30

DESIGNS: 10m. to 100m. Match scenes.

34 Posthorn

1994

165	**34**	5m. red and black	10	10
166	**34**	10m. green and black	10	10
167	**34**	20m. blue and black	30	20
168	**34**	25m. yellow and black	30	30
169	**34**	40m. brown and black	55	55

35 Coelophysis and Segisaurus

1994. Prehistoric Animals. Multicoloured.

170		5m. Type **35**	10	15
171		10m. Pentaceratops and tyrannosaurids	10	15
172		20m. Segnosaurus and oviraptor	40	40
173		25m. Albertosaurus and corythosaurus	50	50
174		30m. Iguanodons	60	60
175		50m. Stegosaurus and allosaurus	1·10	1·10
176		80m. Tyrannosaurus and saurolophus	1·70	1·70
MS177		81×61 mm. 100m. Phobetor (39×31 mm)	1·80	1·80

36 Nesting Grouse

1994. The Caucasian Black Grouse. Multicoloured.

178		50m. Type **36**	60	60
179		80m. Grouse on mountain	95	95
180		100m. Pair of grouse	1·40	1·40
181		120m. Grouse in spring meadow	2·00	2·00

1994. No. 84 further surch **400 M.**

182		400m. on 25q. on 15k. multi-coloured	1·60	1·60

38 Kapitan Razhabov (tug)

1994. Ships. Multicoloured.

183		50m. Type **38**	30	30
184		50m. *Azerbaijan* (ferry)	30	30
185		50m. *Merkuri 1* (ferry)	30	30
186		50m. *Tovuz* (container ship)	30	30
187		50m. *Ganzha* (tanker)	30	30

Nos. 183/7 were issued together, se-tenant, the backgrounds of which form a composite design of a map.

39 Pres. Aliev

1994. President Haidar Aliev. Sheet 102×72 mm.

MS188	**39**	150m. multicoloured	2·40	2·40

40 White-tailed Sea Eagle

1994. Birds of Prey. Multicoloured.

189		10m. Type **40**	60	60
190		15m. Imperial eagle	70	70
191		20m. Tawny eagle	85	85
192		25m. Lammergeier (vert)	1·00	1·00
193		50m. Saker falcon (vert)	2·40	2·40
MS194		83×64 mm. 100m. Golden eagle (*Aquila chrysaetos*) (39×31 mm)	1·60	1·60

Nos. 190/1 and **MS**194 are wrongly inscr "Aguila".

41 *Felis libica caudata*

1994. Wild Cats. Multicoloured.

195		10m. Type **41**	60	60
196		15m. Manul cat	70	70
197		20m. Lynx	85	85
198		25m. Leopard (horiz)	1·00	1·00
199		50m. Tiger (horiz)	2·40	2·40
MS200		64×56 mm. 100m. Tiger with cub (31×39 mm)	1·60	1·60

No. 197 is wrongly inscribed "Felis lyns lyns".

42 Ancient Greek and Modern Javelin Throwers

1994. Centenary of Int Olympic Committee. Multicoloured.

201		100m. Type **42**	60	60
202		100m. Ancient Greek and modern discus throwers	60	60
203		100m. Baron Pierre de Coubertin (founder of modern games) and flame	60	60

1995. Nos. 89/92 and 101/4 surch.

204	**15**	250m. on 10q. green & blk	50	50
205	**15**	250m. on 20q. red & black	50	50
206	**15**	250m. on 50q. yell & blk	50	50
207	**15**	250m. on 1m.50 bl & blk	50	50
208	**15**	500m. on 50q. blue & blk	1·10	1·10
209	**15**	500m. on 1m. mve & blk	1·10	1·10

210	**15**	500m. on 2m.50 yellow and black	1·10	1·10
211	**15**	500m. on 5m. green & blk	1·10	1·10

44 Apollo

1995. Butterflies. Multicoloured.

212		10m. Type **44**	30	30
213		25m. *Zegris menestho*	70	70
214		50m. *Manduca atropos*	1·40	1·40
215		60m. *Pararge adrastoides*	1·80	1·80
MS216		103×157 mm. Nos. 212/15	4·25	4·25

45 Aleksei Urmanov (Russia) (gold, men's figure skating)

1995. Winter Olympic Games, Lillehammer, Norway, Medal Winners. Multicoloured.

217		10m. Type **45**	10	10
218		25m. Nancy Kerrigan (U.S.A.) (silver, women's figure skating)	25	25
219		40m. Bonnie Blair (U.S.A.) (gold, women's 500m. speed skating) (horiz)	40	45
220		50m. Takanori Kano (Japan) (gold, men's ski jumping) (horiz)	40	40
221		80m. Philip Laros (Canada) (silver, men's freestyle skiing)	75	75
222		100m. German team (gold, three-man bobsleigh)	1·00	1·00
MS223		102×71 mm. 200m. Katya Seizinger (Germany) (gold, women's skiing)	2·20	2·20

46 Mary Cleave

1995. 25th Anniv (1994) of First Manned Moon Landing. Female Astronauts. Two sheets, each 137×78 mm, containing T **46** and similar vert designs. Multicoloured.

MS224		(a) 100m. Type **46**; 100m. Valentina Tereshkova; 100m. Tamara Jernigen; 100m. Wendy Lawrence. (b) 100m. Mae Jemison; 100m. Cathy Coleman; 100m. Ellen Shulman; 100m. Mary Weber	3·75	3·75

1995. Nos. 165/7 surch.

225	**34**	100m. on 5m. red & black	15	15
226	**34**	250m. on 10m. grn & blk	45	45
227	**34**	500m. on 20m. blue & blk	90	90

48 *Polyorchis karafutoensis*

1995. Marine Animals. Multicoloured.

228		50m. *Loligo vulgaris* (horiz)	15	15
229		100m. *Orchistoma pileus* (horiz)	40	40
230		150m. *Pegea confoederata* (horiz)	60	60
231		250m. Type **48**	1·00	1·00
232		300m. *Agalma okeni*	1·20	1·20
MS233		89×60 mm. 500m. *Corolla spectabilis* (39×31 mm)	3·00	2·00

49 Matamata Turtle

1995. Tortoises and Turtles. Multicoloured.

234		50m. Type **49**	15	15
235		100m. Loggerhead turtle	40	40
236		150m. Leopard tortoise	60	60
237		250m. Indian star tortoise	1·00	1·00
238		300m. Hermann's tortoise	1·20	1·20
MS239		79×65 mm. 500m. Alligator-snapping turtle (*Macroclemys temmincki*) (31×39 mm)	1·70	1·70

50 Uzeyir Hacibeyov (composer, 110th)

1995. Birth Anniversaries.

240	**50**	250m. silver and black	40	40
241	–	400m. gold and black	60	60

DESIGN: 400m. Vakhid (poet, centenary).

1995. Nos. 84/88 surch.

242		200m. on 2m.50 on 15k. mult	60	60
243		400m. on 25q. on 15k. mult	1·00	1·00
244		600m. on 35q. on 15k. mult	1·80	1·80
245		800m. on 50q. on 15k. mult	2·30	2·30
246		1000m. on 1m.50 on 15k. multicoloured	3·00	3·00

1995. Nos. 168/9 surch.

247	**34**	400m. on 25m. yell & blk	1·10	1·10
248	**34**	900m. on 40m. brn & blk	2·50	2·50

53 Charles's Hydrogen Balloon, 1783

1995. History of Airships. Multicoloured.

249		100m. Type **53**	15	15
250		150m. Tissandier Brothers' electrically-powered airship, 1883	30	30
251		250m. J.-B. Meusnier's elliptical balloon design, 1784 (horiz)	50	50
252		300m. Baldwin's dirigible airship, 1904 (horiz)	60	60
253		400m. U.S. Navy dirigible airship, 1917 (horiz)	85	85
254		500m. Pedal-powered airship, 1909 (horiz)	1·00	1·00
MS255		79×62 mm. 800m. First rigid dirigible airship by Hugo Eckener, 1924 (horiz)	1·70	1·70

No. 249 is wrongly dated.

54 *Gymnopilus spectabilis*

1995. Fungi. Multicoloured.

256		100m. Type **54**	35	35
257		250m. Fly agaric	95	95
258		300m. Parasol mushroom	1·10	1·10
259		400m. *Hygrophorus spectosus*	1·40	1·40
MS260		110×80 mm. 500m. Fly agaric (different)	2·40	2·40

The 250m. and 500m. are wrongly inscr "agaris".

55 *Paphiopedilum argus* and *Paphiopedilum barbatum*

1995. "Singapore '95" International Stamp Exhibition. Orchids. Multicoloured.

261		100m. Type **55**	35	35
262		250m. *Maxillaria picta*	95	95
263		300m. *Laeliocattleya*	1·10	1·10
264		400m. *Dendrobium nobile*	1·40	1·40
MS265		110×80 mm. 500m. *Cattleya gloriette*	1·30	1·30

56 Pres. Aliev and U.N. Secretary-General Boutros Boutros Ghali

1995. 50th Anniv of U.N.O.

266	**56**	250m. multicoloured	2·10	2·10

57 Players

1995. World Cup Football Championship, France (1998). Multicoloured.

267		100m. Type **57**	35	35
268		150m. Dribbling	50	50
269		250m. Tackling	85	85
270		300m. Preparing to kick ball	1·00	1·00
271		400m. Contesting for ball	1·30	1·30
MS272		79×60 mm. 600m. Goalkeeper diving for ball	2·20	2·20

58 American Bald Eagle

1995. Air.

273	**58**	2200m. multicoloured	2·50	2·50

59 Persian

1995. Cats. Multicoloured.

274		100m. Type **59**	15	15
275		150m. Chartreux	30	30
276		250m. Somali	50	50
277		300m. Longhair Scottish fold	60	60
278		400m. Cymric	85	85
279		500m. Turkish angora	1·00	1·00
MS280		85×75 mm. 800m. Birman (31×39 mm)	1·70	1·70

60 Horse

1995. Flora and Fauna. Multicoloured.

281		100m. Type **60**	15	15
282		200m. Grape hyacinths (vert)	40	40
283		250m. Beluga	50	50
284		300m. Golden eagle	60	60
285		400m. Tiger	75	75
286		500m. Georgian black grouse nesting	1·00	1·00
287		1000m. Georgian black grouse in meadow	2·00	2·00

61 Lennon and Signature

1995. 15th Death Anniv of John Lennon (entertainer).

288	**61**	500m. multicoloured	1·10	1·10

62 Early Steam Locomotive, U.S.A.

1996. Railway Locomotives. Multicoloured.

289	100m. Type **62**	45	45
290	100m. New York Central Class J3 locomotive	45	45
291	100m. Steam locomotive on bridge	45	45
292	100m. Steam locomotive No. 1959, Germany	45	45
293	100m. Steam locomotive No. 4113, Germany	45	45
294	100m. Steam locomotive, Italy	45	45
295	100m. Class 59 steam locomotive, Japan	45	45
296	100m. Class QJ steam locomotive, China	45	45
297	100m. Class Sn 23 steam locomotive, China	45	45
MS298	110×80 mm. 500m. Electric train (vert)	2·75	2·75

63 Operating Theatre and Topcubasov

1996. Birth Centenary of M. Topcubasov (surgeon).

299	**63** 300m. multicoloured	1·00	1·00

64 Feast and Woman wearing Traditional Costume

1996. New Year.

300	**64** 250m. multicoloured	90	90

65 Carl Lewis (athletics, Los Angeles, 1984)

1996. Olympic Games, Atlanta. Previous Gold Medallists. Multicoloured.

301	50m. Type **65** (wrongly inscr "1994")	15	15
302	100m. Mohammed Ali (Cassius Clay) (boxing, Rome, 1960)	35	35
303	150m. Li Ning (gymnastics, Los Angeles, 1984)	55	55
304	200m. Said Aouita (5000m, Los Angeles, 1984)	70	70
305	250m. Olga Korbut (gymnastics, Munich, 1972)	90	90
306	300m. Nadia Comaneci (gymnastics, Montreal, 1976)	1·10	1·10
307	400m. Greg Louganis (diving, Los Angeles, 1984)	1·30	1·30
MS308	74×104 mm. 500m. Nazim Goussinev (bantamweight boxing, Barcelona, 1992) (vert)	1·80	1·80

66 *Maral-Gol*

1996. Fifth Death Anniv of G. Aliev (painter). Multicoloured.

309	100m. *Reka Cura*	55	55
310	200m. Type **66**	1·10	1·10

67 Behbudov and Globe

1996. Seventh Death Anniv of Resid Behbudov (singer).

311	**67** 100m. multicoloured	95	95

68 Mammadaliev and Flasks

1996. First Death Anniv of Yusif Mammadaliev (scientist).

312	**68** 100m. multicoloured	95	95

69 National Flag and Government Building

1996. Fifth Anniv of Republic.

313	**69** 250m. multicoloured	90	90

70 Dome of the Rock

1996. 3000th Anniv of Jerusalem. Multicoloured.

314	100m. Praying at the Wailing Wall	70	70
315	250m. Interior of church	1·70	1·70
316	300m. Type **70**	2·00	2·00
MS317	73×104 mm. 500m. Montefiore Windmill	3·50	3·50

71 German Shepherd

1996. Dogs. Multicoloured.

318	50m. Type **71**	10	10
319	100m. Basset hounds	40	40
320	150m. Collies	60	60
321	200m. Bull terriers	85	85
322	300m. Boxers	1·30	1·30
323	400m. Cocker spaniels	1·70	1·70
MS324	70×80 mm. 500m. Shar-pei (38×30 mm)	2·10	2·10

72 Shaft-tailed Whydah

1996. Birds. Multicoloured.

325	50m. Type **72**	10	10
326	100m. Blue-naped mousebird	40	40
327	150m. Asian black-headed oriole	60	60
328	200m. Golden oriole	85	85
329	300m. Common starling	1·30	1·30
330	400m. Yellow-fronted canary	1·70	1·70
MS331	60×80 mm. 500m. European bee eater (*Merops apaister*) (31×39 mm)	2·10	2·10

73 "Burgundy"

1996. Roses. Multicoloured.

332	50m. Type **73**	10	10
333	100m. "Virgo"	40	40
334	150m. "Rose Gaujard"	60	60
335	200m. "Luna"	85	85
336	300m. "Lady Rose"	1·30	1·30
337	400m. "Landora"	1·70	1·70
MS338	90×70 mm. 500m. "Luxor" (39×31 mm)	2·10	2·10

74 Child

1996. 50th Anniv of UNICEF.

339	**74** 500m. multicoloured	90	90

75 Spain v. Bulgaria

1996. European Football Championship, England. Multicoloured.

340	100m. Type **75**	25	25
341	150m. Rumania v. France	40	40
342	200m. Czech Republic v. Germany	50	50
343	250m. England v. Switzerland	70	70
344	300m. Croatia v. Turkey	75	75
345	400m. Italy v. Russia	1·10	1·10
MS346	110×80 mm. 500m. Detail of cup	1·40	1·40

76 Chinese Junk

1996. Ships. Multicoloured.

347	100m. Type **76**	25	25
348	150m. *Danmark* (Danish full-rigged cadet ship)	40	40
349	200m. *Nippon-Maru II* (Japanese cadet ship)	60	60
350	250m. *Mircea* (Rumanian barque)	75	75
351	300m. *Kruzenshtern* (Russian cadet barque)	95	95
352	400m. *Ariadne* (German cadet schooner)	1·30	1·30
MS353	107×77 mm. 500m. *Tovarishch* (Russian four-masted cadet barque) (vert)	2·75	2·75

77 Baxram Gur killing Dragon (fountain by A. Shulgin at Baku)

1997

354	**77**	100m. purple and black	35	35
356	**77**	250m. black and yellow	40	40
357	**77**	400m. black and red	55	55
358	**77**	500m. black and green	65	65
359	**77**	1000m. black and blue	1·30	1·30

78 Nariman Narimanov (politician and writer)

1997. Anniversaries. Multicoloured.

365	250m. Type **78** (125th birth anniv (1995))	80	80
366	250m. Fatali Xoyskin (politician, 120th birth anniv (1995))	80	80
367	250m. Aziz Mammed-Kerim ogli Aliyev (politician, birth centenary)	80	80

368	250m. Ilyas Afendiyev (writer, 1st death anniv)	80	80

79 Bulls

1997. Qobustasn Rock Carvings. Sheet 127×84 mm containing T **79** and similar vert designs. Multicoloured.

MS369	500m. Type **79**; 500m. Goats; 500m. Dancers	4·50	4·50

1997. Red Cross. Various stamps optd **Red Cross** and cross. (a) Nos. 93/99.

370	20q. multicoloured	10	10
371	30q. multicoloured	10	10
372	50q. multicoloured	10	10
373	1m. multicoloured	35	35
374	2m.50 multicoloured	1·00	1·00
375	5m. multicoloured	2·00	2·00
376	10m. multicoloured	4·25	4·25
MS377	80×60 mm. 8m. multicoloured	4·25	4·25

(b) Nos. 195/9.

378	10m. multicoloured	40	40
379	15m. multicoloured	70	70
380	20m. multicoloured	95	95
381	25m. multicoloured	1·20	1·20
382	50m. multicoloured	2·40	2·40
MS383	64×56 mm. 100m. multicoloured	4·25	4·25

1997. 50th Anniv of Rotary Club International in Azerbaijan. Various stamps optd 50th Anniversary of the Rotary Club and emblem. (a) Nos. 314/16.

384	100m. multicoloured	95	95
385	250m. multicoloured	2·20	2·20
386	300m. multicoloured	2·75	2·75
MS387	74×103 mm. 500m. multicoloured	2·50	2·50

(b) Nos. 347/52.

388	100m. multicoloured	40	40
389	150m. multicoloured	70	70
390	200m. multicoloured	85	85
391	250m. multicoloured	1·10	1·10
392	300m. multicoloured	1·30	1·30
393	400m. multicoloured	1·70	1·70
MS394	106×76 mm. 500m. multicoloured	4·50	4·50

82 Dog

1997. *The Town Band of Bremen* by the Brothers Grimm. Multicoloured.

395	250m. Type **82**	1·50	1·50
396	250m. Donkey and cat	1·50	1·50
397	250m. Rooster	1·50	1·50
MS398	125×96 mm. 500m. Animals frightening robbers from hideaway	3·50	3·50

Nos. 395/7 were issued together, *se-tenant*, forming a composite design.

83 Seal Pup

1997. The Caspian Seal. Multicoloured.

399	250m. Type **83**	65	65
400	250m. Bull and mountain peak	65	65
401	250m. Bull and gull	65	65
402	250m. Cow (profile)	65	65
403	250m. Cow (full face)	65	65
404	250m. Young seal (three-quarter face)	65	65
MS405	106×77 mm. 500m. Cow (vert)	3·50	3·50

Nos. 399/404 were issued together, *se-tenant*, forming a composite design.

84 Tanbur

1997. Traditional Musical Instruments. Multicoloured.
406	250m. Type **84**	60	60
407	250m. Gaval (tambourine)	60	60
408	500m. Jang (harp)	1·20	1·20

85 19th-century
Oil Derricks,
Aspheron
Peninsula

1997. 125th Anniv of First Industrial Oil Well in Azerbaijan. Sheet 115×91 mm containing T **85** and similar vert design. Multicoloured.
MS409 500m. Type **85**; 500m. Modern drilling platform, Caspian Sea ... 2·50 ... 2·50

86 Sirvani

1997. 870th Birth Anniv (1996) of Xanqani Sirvani (poet).
| 410 | **86** | 250m. multicoloured | 85 | 85 |

87 Taza-pir Mosque, Baku

1997. Mosques. Multicoloured.
411	250m. Type **87**	75	75
412	250m. Momuna-Xatun Mosque, Nakhichevan	75	75
413	250m. Govharaga Mosque, Shusha	75	75

88 Rasulbekov and Baku T.V. Tower

1997. 80th Birth Anniv of G. D. Rasulbekov (former Minister of Telecommunications).
| 414 | **88** | 250m. multicoloured | 75 | 75 |

89 Italy, 1938

1997. World Cup Football Championship, France (1998).
415	**89**	250m. black	70	70
416	-	250m. black	70	70
417	-	250m. black	70	70
418	-	250m. multicoloured	70	70
419	-	250m. multicoloured	70	70
420	-	250m. multicoloured	70	70
MS421	85×90 mm. 1500m. black and blue (Tofiq Bahramov (referee)		3·25	3·25

DESIGNS—World Champion Teams: No. 416, Argentina, 1986; 417, Uruguay, 1930 (wrongly inscr "1980"); 418, Brazil, 1994; 419, England, 1966; 420, West Germany, 1990.

90 Katarina Wit, East Germany

1997. Winter Olympic Games, Nagano, Japan. Multicoloured.
422	250m. Type **90** (figure skating gold medal, 1984 and 1988)	3·75	50
423	250m. Elvis Stoyko, Canada (figure skating silver medal, 1994)	50	50
424	250m. Midori Ito, Japan (figure skating silver medal, 1992)	50	50
425	250m. Azerbaijan flag and silhouettes of sports	50	50
426	250m. Olympic torch and mountain	50	50
427	250m. Kristin Yamaguchi, U.S.A. (figure skating gold medal, 1992)	50	50
428	250m. John Curry, Great Britain (figure skating gold medal, 1976)	50	50
429	250m. Cen Lu, China (figure skating bronze medal, 1994)	50	50
MS430	76×106 mm. 500m. Yekaterina Gordeyeva and Sergi Grinkov, Russia (figure skating gold medal, 1984 and 1988)	3·00	3·00

91 Diana, Princess of Wales

1998. Diana, Princess of Wales Commem. Multicoloured.
| 431 | 400m. Type **91** | 50 | 50 |
| 432 | 400m. Wearing black polo-neck jumper | 50 | 50 |

92 Aliyev and Mountain Landscape

1998. 90th Birth Anniv of Hasan Aliyev (ecologist).
| 433 | **92** | 500m. multicoloured | 85 | 85 |

93 Tourist Map, Flag and Pres. Aliev

1998. 75th Birthday of President Haidar Aliev. Sheet 114×89 mm.
MS434 **93** 500m. multicoloured ... 2·10 ... 2·10

1998. "Israel 98" International Stamp Exhibition, Tel Aviv. No. **MS**369 optd **98** and emblem on each stamp and **Israel 98–WORLD STAMP EXHIBITION TEL–AVIV 13–21 MAY 1998** in margin.
MS435 500m. ×3 multicoloured ... 5·50 ... 5·50

95 Ashug Alesker (singer)

1998. Birth Anniversaries. Multicoloured.
436	250m. Type **95** (175th anniv)	60	60
437	250m. Magomedhuseyn Shakhriyar (poet, 90th anniv)	60	60
438	250m. Qara Qarayev (composer, 80th anniv)	60	60

96 Bul-Bul

1998. Birth Centenary of Bul-Bul (Murtuz Meshadirza ogli Mamedov) (singer).
| 439 | **96** | 500m. multicoloured | 85 | 85 |

97 Mickey and Minnie Mouse playing Chess

1998. World Rapid Chess Championship, Georgia. Multicoloured.
440	250m. Type **97**	2·10	2·10
441	500m. Mickey, Minnie, pawn and rook	2·40	2·40
442	500m. Goofy, bishop and knight	2·40	2·40
443	500m. Donald Duck, king and bishop	2·40	2·40
444	500m. Pluto, rook, pawn and clockwork pawn	2·40	2·40
445	500m. Minnie and queen	2·40	2·40
446	500m. Daisy Duck, bishop and king	2·40	2·40
447	500m. Goofy, Donald and pawn	2·40	2·40
448	500m. Mickey, queen and rook	2·40	2·40
MS449	Two sheets, each 127×101 mm. (a) 4000m. Mickey, Minnie, Pluto and queen; (b) 4000m. Donald, Mickey and pawn	19·00	19·00

98 Preparing Pastries

1998. Europa. National Festivals: New Year. Multicoloured.
| 450 | 1000m. Type **98** | 1·20 | 1·20 |
| 451 | 3000m. Acrobat and wrestlers | 3·00 | 3·00 |

1999. "iBRA" International Stamp Exhibition, Nuremberg, Germany. Nos. 450/1 optd with exhibition emblem.
| 452 | 1000m. multicoloured | 75 | 75 |
| 453 | 3000m. multicoloured | 2·30 | 2·30 |

100 Greater Flamingo, Gizilagach National Park

1999. Europa. Parks and Gardens. Multicoloured.
| 454 | 1000m. Type **100** | 1·20 | 1·20 |
| 455 | 3000m. Stag, Girkan National Park | 3·00 | 3·00 |

101 14th-century Square Tower

1999. Towers at Mardakyan.
| 456 | **101** | 1000m. black and blue | 60 | 60 |
| 457 | - | 3000m. black and red | 2·30 | 1·90 |
DESIGN: 3000m. 13th-century round tower. See also Nos. 547 and 557.

102 President Aliev and Flag

1999. 75th Anniv of Nakhichevan Autonomous Region. Multicoloured.
460	1000m. Type **102**	1·00	1·00
461	1000m. Map of Nakhichevan	1·00	1·00
MS462	110×90 mm. Nos. 460/1	1·90	1·90

103 Cabbarli

1999. Birth Centenary of Cafar Cabbarli (dramatist).
| 463 | **103** | 250m. multicoloured | 75 | 75 |

104 40k. Stamp

1999. 80th Anniv of First Azerbaijani Stamps. Sheet 131×106 mm containing T **104** and similar multicoloured designs showing stamps of 1919.
MS464 500m. 10k. stamp (Type **1**) (25×35 mm); 500m. Type **104**; 500m. 5r. stamp; 500m. 50r. stamp (Type **2**) ... 3·25 ... 3·25

105 Flag, Pigeon and Emblem on Scroll

1999. 125th Anniv of Universal Postal Union. Multicoloured.
| 465 | 250m. Type **105** | 10 | 10 |
| 466 | 300m. Satellite, computer and emblem | 3·00 | 3·00 |

106 Caravanserai Inner Court and Maiden's Tower, Baku

1999. 19th-century Caravanserais. Multicoloured.
| 467 | 500m. Type **106** | 1·30 | 1·30 |
| 468 | 500m. Camels outside caravanserai, Sheki | 1·30 | 1·30 |

107 Anniversary Emblem

1999. 50th Anniv of Council of Europe.
| 469 | **107** | 1000m. multicoloured | 95 | 95 |

108 Beybur Khan's Son fighting Camel

1999. 1300th Anniv of Kitabi Dada Qorqud (folk epic). Sheet 90×125 mm containing T **108** and similar horiz designs. Multicoloured.
MS470 1000m. Type **108**; 1000m. Wounded Tural slumped on horse; 1000m. Gaza Khan asleep beside horse ... 2·75 ... 2·75

109 "Building
Europe"

2000. Europa.
| 471 | **109** | 1000m. multicoloured | 90 | 90 |
| 472 | **109** | 3000m. multicoloured | 3·25 | 3·25 |

110 Phaeton

2000. Baku City Transport. Sheet 111×88 mm containing T **110** and similar horiz designs. Multicoloured.
MS473 500m. Type **110**; 500m. Konka; 500m. Electric tram; 500m. Trolleybus 3·50 3·50

111 14th-century
Square Tower,
Ramana

2000. Towers of Mardakyan.
| 474 | **111** | 100m. black and orange | 40 | 40 |
| 475 | - | 250m. black and green | 1·00 | 1·00 |

DESIGN: 250m. 14th-century round tower, Nardaran.
See also Nos. 499/500.

112 Wrestling

2000. Olympic Games, Sydney. Multicoloured.
476	500m. Type **112**	95	95
477	500m. Weightlifting	95	95
478	500m. Boxing	95	95
479	500m. Relay	95	95

113 Duck flying

2000. The Ferruginous Duck. Multicoloured.
480	500m. Type **113**	70	70
481	500m. Ducks in water and standing on rocks	70	70
482	500m. Duck standing on rock and others swimming by grasses	70	70
483	500m. Ducks at sunset	70	70

114 Satellite
Picture of
Azerbaijan and
Emblem

2000. 50th Anniv of World Meteorological Organization.
| 484 | **114** | 1000m. multicoloured | 85 | 85 |

115 Quinces

2000. Fruits. Multicoloured.
485	500m. Type **115**	75	75
486	500m. Pomegranates (*Punica granatum*)	75	75
487	500m. Peaches (*Persica*)	75	75
488	500m. Figs (*Ficus carica*)	75	75

116 Ringed-necked
Pheasant

2000. The Ringed-necked Pheasant (*Phasanus colchicus*). Sheet 102×72 mm.
MS489 **116** 2000m. multicoloured 2·50 2·50

117 Rasul-Rza

2000. 90th Birth Anniv of Rasul-Rza (poet).
| 490 | **117** | 250m. multicoloured | 80 | 80 |

118 Levantine Viper

2000. Reptiles. Multicoloured.
491	500m. Type **118**	1·10	1·10
492	500m. Rock lizard (*Lacerta saxicola*) (wrongly inscr "Laserta saxcola")	1·10	1·10
493	500m. Ottoman viper (*Vipera xanthina*)	1·10	1·10
494	500m. Toad-headed agama (*Phrynocephalus mystaceus*)	1·10	1·10

MS495 90×63 mm. 500m. Watersnake (*Natrix tessellate*) and sunwatcher (*Phrynocephalus heliscopus*) (vert) 1·30 1·30

119 Rahman

2000. 90th Birth Anniv of Sabit Rahman (writer).
| 496 | **119** | 1000m. multicoloured | 1·40 | 1·40 |

120 Emblem

2000. UNESCO International Year of Culture and Peace.
| 497 | **120** | 3000m. multicoloured | 2·75 | 2·75 |

121 Namig Abullayev (gold,
freestyle flyweight
wrestling)

2001. Olympic Games, Sydney. Medal Winners. Sheet 99×127 mm containing T **121** and similar horiz designs. Multicoloured.
MS498 1000m. Type **121**; 1000m. Zemfira Meftahaddinova (gold, skeet shooting); 1000m. Vugar Alakbarov (bronze, middle-weight boxing) 3·00 3·00

122 Seal, Lesser
White-fronted
Goose and Oil
Rig

2001. Europa. Water Resources. The Caspian Sea. Multicoloured.
| 499 | 1000m. Type **122** | 1·00 | 1·00 |
| 500 | 3000m. Sturgeon, crab and oil rig | 3·25 | 3·25 |

123 Building and Flags

2001. Admission of Azerbaijan to Council of Europe.
| 501 | **123** | 1000m. multicoloured | 1·00 | 1·00 |

2001. Towers of Sheki. As T **111**.
| 502 | 100m. black and lilac | 30 | 30 |
| 503 | 250m. black and yellow | 80 | 80 |

DESIGNS: 100m. 18th-century round tower; 250m. Ruin of 12th-century tower.

124 Refugee Camp

2001. 50th Anniv of United Nations High Commissioner for Refugees. Sheet 100×73 mm.
MS504 **124** 3000m. black and blue 2·50 2·50

125 Tusi, Globe and Books

2001. 800th Birth Anniv of Nasraddin Tusi (mathematician and astronomer). Sheet 110×78 mm.
MS505 **125** 3000m. multicoloured 2·50 2·50

126 Handshake
and Emblem

2001. Tenth Anniv of Union of Independent States.
| 506 | **126** | 1000m. multicoloured | 1·00 | 1·00 |

127 Yuri Gagarin, "Vostok 1"
and Globe

2001. 40th Anniv of First Manned Space Flight. Sheet 83×56 mm.
MS507 **127** 3000m. multicoloured 2·20 2·20

128 Short-eared
Owl (*Asio
flammeus*)

2001. Owls. Multicoloured.
508	1000m. Type **128**	75	75
509	1000m. Tawny owl (*Strix aluco*)	75	75
510	1000m. Scops owl (*Otus scops*)	75	75
511	1000m. Long-eared owl (*Asio otus*)	75	75
512	1000m. Eagle owl on branch (*Bubo bubo*)	75	75
513	1000m. Little owl (*Athene noctua*)	75	75

MS514 91×68 mm. 1000m. Eagle owl (*Bubo bubo*) in flight 1·90 1·90

129 Pres. Heydar Aliyev

2001. Tenth Anniv of Independence.
| 515 | **129** | 5000m. multicoloured | 7·75 | 7·75 |

130 Pres. Vladimir Putin
and Pres. Heydar Aliyev

2001. Visit of President Putin to Azerbaijan.
| 516 | **130** | 1000m. multicoloured | 85 | 80 |

131 Emblem and Athletes

2002. Tenth Anniv of National Olympic Committee.
| 517 | **131** | 3000m. multicoloured | 2·20 | 2·20 |

132 Circus
Performers

2002. Europa. Circus. Multicoloured.
| 518 | 1000m. Type **132** | 1·00 | 1·00 |
| 519 | 3000m. Equestrian juggler and trapeze artist | 3·25 | 3·25 |

133 Presidents Heydar
Aliyev and Jiang Zemin

2002. Tenth Anniv of Azerbaijan--China Diplomatic Relations.
| 520 | **133** | 1000m. multicoloured | 90 | 90 |

134 Molla
Panah Vagif's
Mausoleum,
Susa

2002. Towers of Karabakh.
| 521 | **134** | 100m. black and green | 20 | 20 |
| 522 | - | 250m. black and cinnamon | 50 | 50 |

DESIGNS: 250m. 19th-century mosque, Aghdam.

2002. Tenth Anniv of Azermarka Stamp Company. No. 83 surch **Azermarka 1992--2002 1000m.**
| 523 | **13** | 1000m. on 35q. multicoloured | 85 | 85 |

136 Emblem

2002. Tenth Anniv of New Azerbaijan Party.
| 524 | **136** | 3000m. multicoloured | 2·20 | 2·20 |

137 African Monarch
(*Danaus chrysippus*)

2002. Butterflies and Moths. Multicoloured.

525	1000m. Type **137** (inscr "Danais")	95	95
526	1000m. Southern swallowtail (*Papilio alexanor*)	95	95
527	1000m. *Thaleropis jonia*	95	95
528	1000m. Red admiral (*Vanessa atalanta*)	95	95
529	1000m. *Argynnis alexandra*	95	95
530	1000m. *Brahmaea christoph* (moth)	95	95

138 Pres. Heydar Aliyev
and Pope John Paul II

2002. Pope John Paul II's Visit to Azerbaijan. Sheet 80×65 mm.

MS531 **138** 1500m. multicoloured 2·00 2·00

139 Telegraph
Machine, Building
Facade and
Emblem

2002. 70th Anniv of Baku Telegraph Office.

532 **139** 3000m. multicoloured 2·00 2·00

140 Gadjiyev and Piano

2002. 80th Birth Anniv of Ruaf Gadjiyev (composer).

533 **140** 5000m. multicoloured 2·50 2·50

141 Bearded Men with
Swords, Black Pawns, White
Pawn and White Rook

2002. European Junior Chess Championships, Baku. Showing chess board and views of Baku. Multicoloured.

534	1500m. Type **141**	1·20	1·20
535	1500m. Two knights on horseback	1·20	1·20
536	1500m. Two elephants	1·20	1·20
537	1500m. Black rook, black pawn, bearded men with swords and fallen knight	1·20	1·20

Nos. 534/7 were issued together, *se-tenant*, forming a composite design showing a chess game and views of ancient Baku.

142 World Trade
Centre, New
York, U.S.A. and
Azerbaijan Flags
and Globe

2002. First Anniv of Attack on World Trade Centre, New York. Sheet 130×65 mm containing vert design as T **142**. Multicoloured.

MS538 1500m. ×3 Type **142** 2·30 2·30

143 Turkish Football Team

2002. Football World Cup Championship, Japan and South Korea. Sheet 102×110 mm.

MS539 **143** 5000m. multicoloured 3·50 3·50

144 Dove, Woman,
Flag and Emblems

2002. United Nations Development Fund for Women.

540 **144** 3000m. multicoloured 2·10 2·10

145 Siamese
Fighting Fish (*Betta
splendens*)

2002. Aquarium Fish. Multicoloured.

541	100m. Type **145**	75	75
542	100m. Blue discus (*Symphysodon aequifasciatus*)	75	75
543	100m. Freshwater angelfish (*Pterophyllum scalare*)	75	75
544	100m. Black moor (*Carassius auratus auratus*)	75	75
545	100m. Boeseman's rainbowfish (*Melanotaenia boesemani*)	75	75
546	1000m. Firemouth cichlid (*Cichlasoma meeki*)	75	75

2003. Towers of Karabakh. As T **101**.

547 250m. black and blue 45 45

DESIGN: No. 547, Askeran tower and fortress.

146 Bomb and Scissors
("Stop Terrorism")

2003. Europa. Poster Art. Multicoloured.

548	1000m. Type **146**	85	85
549	3000m. Wrestlers ("Sport is the Health of the Nation")	2·50	2·50

147 Flag and UPU
Emblem

2003. Tenth Anniv of Azerbaijan Membership of Universal Postal Union.

550 **147** 3000m. multicoloured 2·10 2·10

148 H. Djavid Mausoleum
and Hacha Mountain

2003. Nakhichevan.

551 **148** 3000m. multicoloured 2·10 2·10

149 Map and Pipeline

2003. Baku–Tbilisi–Jeychan Oil Pipeline.

552 **149** 3000m. multicoloured 2·10 2·10

150 Zarifa Aliyeva and Eye

2003. 80th Birth Anniv of Zarifa Aliyeva (ophthalmologist).

553 **150** 3000m. multicoloured 2·10 2·10

151 Heydar Aliyev

2003. 80th Birth Anniv of Pres. Heydar Aliyev. Sheet 130×160 mm.

MS554 **151** 10000m. multicoloured 6·00 6·00

2003. Nos. 131 and 168 surch.

555	500m. on 25m. yellow and black	50	50
556	1000m. on 8m. blue, silver and black	1·00	1·00

2003. Towers of Karabakh. As T **101**.

557 1000m. black 75 75

DESIGN: No. 557, Archway, walls and tower, Shusha Town.

153 QAZ-11-73 Saloon Car

2003. Cars. Sheet 100×77 mm containing T **153** and similar horiz designs. Multicoloured.

MS558 500m.×4 Type **153**; QAZ-M-20 Pobeda; QAZ 12 Zim; QAZ-21 Volga (inscr "Volqa") 2·40 2·00

154 Textile Seller

2003. 90th Anniv of U. Hajibekov's Musical Comedy *Arshin Mal Alan*.

559 **154** 10000m. multicoloured 5·00 5·00

2003. Nos. 91, 129, 130, 152/5, 165 and 169 surch.

560	500m. on 50q. yellow and black	40	40
561	500m. on 2m. red, silver and black	40	40
562	500m. on 4m. green, silver and black	40	40
563	500m. on 5m. multicoloured	40	40
567	500m. on 5m. red and black	40	40
564	500m. on 10m. multicoloured	40	40
565	500m. on 15m. multicoloured	40	40
566	500m. on 20m. multicoloured	40	40
568	500m. on 40m. brown and black	40	40

155 Bear (*Ursus arctos*)
(inscr "arctors")

2003. Sheki National Park. Sheet 106×84 mm containing T **155** and similar horiz designs. Multicoloured.

MS569 3000m. Type **155**; Racoon (*Procyon lotor*); Wild boar (*Sus scrofa*); Fox (*Vulpes vulpes*) 6·75 6·75

156 Map and
Monument

157 Dove
of Peace
(sculpture)

2004. 80th Anniversary of Nakhichevan Autonomous Republic.

570 **156** 3000m. multicoloured 1·70 1·70

2004. Samgayit Town.

571 **157** 500m. blue and black 60 60

158 Geygel Lake

2004. Europa. Holidays. Multicoloured.

572	1000m. Type **158**	85	85
573	3000m. Baku at night	2·50	2·50

159 Molla Cuma

2004. 150th Birth Anniversary of Molla Cuma (singer).

574 **159** 500m. multicoloured 75 75

160 High Jump

2004. Olympic Games, 2004, Greece. Multicoloured.

575	500m. Type **160**	70	70
576	500m. Wrestlers	70	70
577	500m. Runner	70	70
578	500m. Greek vase	70	70

Nos. 575/8 were issued together, *se-tenant*, forming a composite design.

161 World Cup Trophy

2004. Centenary of FIFA (Federation Internationale de Football Association). Multicoloured.

579	500m. Type **161**	70	70
580	500m. Player facing left	70	70
581	500m. Player facing right	70	70
582	500m. Goalkeeper	70	70

Nos. 579/82 were issued together, *se-tenant*, forming a composite design.

162 Heydar
Aliyev

2004. Heydar Aliyev Commemoration (president, 1993–2003) (1st issue).

583 **162** 500m. multicoloured 60 60

See also Nos. MS590, 607 and 632.

163 Mosques and
Camels

2004. The Great Silk Route.

584 **163** 3000m. multicoloured 2·10 2·10

164 Carpet and Couple wearing 19th-century Costume, Baku

2004. Traditional Costumes. Carpets and 19th-century costumes.

585	500m. Type **164**		65	65
586	500m. Couple holding instruments, Karabakh		65	65
587	500m. Woman wearing long headdress, man with cane, Nakhichevan		65	65
588	500m. Man with dagger		65	65

165 Globe, Honeywell DDP 516 and Modern Computer

2004. 35th Anniv of the Internet.

589	**165**	3000m. multicoloured	1·80	1·80

166 Heydar Aliyev

2004. Heydar Aliyev Commemoration (president, 1993–2003) (2nd issue). Sheet 60×80 mm.

MS590	**166**	1000m. multicoloured	5·50	5·50

167 Leopard in Tree

2005. Endangered Species. Leopards. Multicoloured.

591	1000m. Type **167**		80	80
592	1000m. Two cubs		80	80
593	1000m. Adult		80	80
594	1000m. Mother and cubs		80	80

2005. Nos. 212/15 surch **1000 mm.**

595	1000m. on 10m. multicoloured		60	60
596	1000m. on 25m. multicoloured		60	60
597	1000m. on 50m. multicoloured		60	60
598	1000m. on 60m. multicoloured		60	60

169 Ministry Building and Emblem

2005. Fifth Anniv of Ministry of Taxes.

599	**169**	3000m. multicoloured	2·50	1·80

170 Observatory

2005. Shemakha Town.

600	**170**	500m. mauve and black	1·40	45

171 *Cephalanthera rubra*

2005. Orchids. Multicoloured.

601	500m. Type **171**		40	40
602	1000m. *Orchis papilionacea*		85	85
603	1500m. *Epipactis atrorubens*		1·30	1·30
604	3000m. *Orchis purpurea*		3·00	3·00
MS605	135×190 mm. Nos. 601/4		3·75	3·75

172 Aircraft, Tanks and Oil Tankers

2005. 60th Anniv of the End of World War II.

606	**172**	1000m. multicoloured	60	60

173 Heydar Aliyev

2005. Heydar Aliyev (president, 1993–2003) Commemoration (3rd issue).

607	**173**	1000m. multicoloured	60	60

174 Pilaf

2005. Europa. Gastronomy. Multicoloured.

608	1000m. Type **174**		70	70
609	3000m. Dolmasi		3·00	3·00

175 Rock Paintings and Academy Building

2005. 60th Anniv of Academy of Science.

610	**175**	1000m. multicoloured	45	45

176 Astronaut

2005. 40th Anniv of First Space Walk. Sheet 86×58 mm.

MS611	**176**	3000m. multicoloured	2·00	2·00

177 Computers and Emblem

2005. Tunis 2005 (World Summit on Information Society).

612	**177**	1000m. multicoloured	45	45

178 Pope John Paul II

2005. Pope John Paul II Commemoration.

613	**178**	3000m. multicoloured	2·00	2·00

179 *Paravespula germanica*

2005. Insects. Sheet 101×80 mm containing T **179** and similar horiz designs. Multicoloured.

MS614 500m. Type **179**; 1000m. *Bombus terrestris*; 1500m. *Vespa crabro*; 3000m. *Apis mellifera caucasica*	3·25	3·25

180 Emblem and Nos. 450/1

2005. 50th Anniv of Europa Stamps. Showing previous Europa stamps. Multicoloured.

615	3000m. Type **180**		1·40	1·40
616	3000m. Emblem and Nos. 471/2		1·40	1·40
617	3000m. Emblem and Nos. 548/9		1·40	1·40
618	3000m. Emblem and Nos. 1167/8 of West Germany		1·40	1·40
MS619	Four sheets, each 88×88 mm. (a) As No. 615; (b) As No. 616; (c) As No. 617; (d) As No. 618		5·00	5·00

Note: On 1 January 2006 the manat was re-valued at the rate 1 new manat = 5000 old manat.

2006. Nos. 131, 110, 114, 168, 521, 113, 457, 146 and 127/8 surch.

620	5q. on 8m. blue, silver and black (No. 131)		1·00	1·00
621	10q. on 1m. multicoloured (No. 110)		1·30	1·30
622	10q. on 1m. multicoloured (No. 114)		1·30	1·30
623	10q. on 25m. yellow and black (No. 168)		1·30	1·30
624	10q. on 100m. black and green (No. 521)		1·30	1·30
625	20q. on 50q. multicoloured (No. 113)		1·75	1·75
627	20q. on 20m. black, gold and blue (No. 146)		1·75	1·75
626	20q. on 3000m. black and scarlet (No. 457)		1·75	1·75
628	60q. on 5m. multicoloured (No. 127)		2·50	2·50
629	60q. on 8m. multicoloured (No. 128)		2·50	2·50

182 19th-century Mosque, Lankaran

2006. Towns.

630	**182**	10q. blue and black	1·00	1·00
631	–	20q. buff and brown	1·50	1·50

DESIGNS: Type **182**; 20q. 9th-century fortress, Lachin. See also Nos. 652/3.

2006. Heydar Aliyev (president, 1993–2003) Commemoration (4th issue).

632	**162**	60q. multicoloured	4·25	4·25

183 Emblem

2006. 30th Anniv of OPEC Fund for International Development.

633	**183**	5q. multicoloured	1·00	1·00

184 Hands from Many Nations

2006. Europa. Integration. Multicoloured.

634	20q. Type **184**		2·50	2·50
635	60q. Globe enclosed in star		7·50	7·50

185 Emblem

2006. World Cup Football Championship, Germany. Multicoloured.

636	20q. Type **185**		1·50	1·50

637	60q. Player and map of Germany		1·40	1·40

186 Samad Vurgun

2006. Writers Birth Centenaries. Multicoloured.

638	10q. Type **186**		80	80
639	60q. Suleyman Rustam		2·40	2·40

187 Russian Flag and Arms and St. Basil's Cathedral, Moscow

2006. Year of Russia in Azerbaijan. Multicoloured.

640	10q. Type **187**		1·00	1·00
641	20q. Azerbaijan flag and arms and Taza Pir mosque, Baku		1·30	1·30
642	30q. Azerbaijan flag and arms and Maiden Tower, Baku		1·50	1·50
643	60q. Russian flag and arms and Kremlin, Moscow		2·50	2·50

188 Gulustan Mausoleum, Nakhichivan (13th-century)

2006

644	**188**	20q. multicoloured	1·40	1·40

189 Globe and Binary Code

2006. World Information Organization Day.

645	**189**	1m. multicoloured	6·00	6·00

190 Khan (1867)

2006. Karabakh Horses. Multicoloured.

646	20q. Type **190**		1·50	1·50
647	20q. Zaman (1952)		1·50	1·50
648	20q. Sarvan (1987)		1·50	1·50
649	20q. Gar-gar (2001)		1·50	1·50
MS650	122×94 mm. Size 52×37 mm. Nos. 646/9		9·00	9·00
MS651	82×65 mm. 60q. Rearing horse (vert)		6·50	6·50

2006. Towns. As T **182**. Multicoloured.

652	10q. lilac and black		1·00	1·00
653	20q. pink and black		1·50	1·50

DESIGNS: 10q. Sumuggala tower, Gakh; 20q. Nizami's mausoleum, Ganja.

2006. 50th Anniv of Europa Stamps. Nos. 608/609 surch. Multicoloured.

654	20q. on 1000m. multicoloured (Type **174**)		2·50	2·50
655	60q. on 3000m. multicoloured (Dolmasi)		8·00	8·00

192 Emblem

2006. 15th Anniv of Regional Concord of Communication.

656	**192**	20q. multicoloured	1·60	1·60

193 Arms and Flag

2006. 15th Anniv of Independence.
| 657 | 193 | 20q. multicoloured | 1·60 | 1·60 |

194 Fire Appliance AMO-F15 (1926)

2006. Fire Engines. Sheet 101×76 mm containing T **194** and similar horiz designs showing fire engines. Multicoloured.
MS658 10q. Type **194**; 20q. PMQ-1 (1932); 60q. PMQ-9 (1950); 1m. ATS 2,5 (1998) 10·50 10·50

195 Pigeons and Tower

2007. Pigeons. Multicoloured.
659	20q. Type **195**	1·60	1·60
660	20q. Iridescent pigeons and domes	1·60	1·60
661	20q. Brown and white pigeons and oil derricks	1·60	1·60
662	20q. White pigeon, brown and white pigeon and buildings	1·60	1·60
663	20q. Dark pigeons and gateways	1·60	1·60
664	20q. Spotted pigeons and windmills	1·60	1·60
MS665 54×78 mm. 1m. White pigeon with feathered feet (vert) 5·00 5·00

The stamp and margins of MS665 form a composite design.

196 Baku Customs' Building

2007. Bicentenary of Baku Customs Services (20q.) or 15th Anniv of Azerbaijan Customs Services (60q.). Multicoloured.
| 666 | 20q. Type **196** | 1·60 | 1·60 |
| 667 | 60q. Azerbaijan Customs' building | 4·50 | 4·50 |

197 Monument to Victims

2007. 15th Anniv of Khojali Tragedy. Sheet 99×72 mm.
MS668 **197** multicoloured 6·25 6·25

198 Emblem

2007. Europa. Centenary of Scouting. Multicoloured.
| 669 | 20q. Type **198** | 2·50 | 2·50 |
| 670 | 60q. Emblem on kite | 7·00 | 7·00 |

199 Symbols of Azerbaijan and Japan

2007. Azerbaijan—Japan Friendly Relations.
| 671 | **199** | 1m. multicoloured | 5·50 | 5·50 |

200 Mosque, Goycay

2007. Towns.
| 672 | **200** | 10q. yellow and black | 1·00 | 1·00 |

(201) (202)

(203)

2007. Nos. 551 and 613 surch as T **201**, 615/18 surch as T **202** and 570 surch as T **203**.
673	60q. on 3000m. multicoloured (No. 551)	4·50	4·50
674	60q. on 3000m. multicoloured (No. 570)	4·50	4·50
675	60q. on 3000m. multicoloured (No. 613)	4·50	4·50
676	60q. on 3000m. multicoloured (No. 615)	3·75	3·75
677	60q. on 3000m. multicoloured (No. 616)	3·75	3·75
678	60q. on 3000m. multicoloured (No. 617)	3·75	3·75
679	60q. on 3000m. multicoloured (No. 618)	3·75	3·75

204 Dog Fight

2007. Azim Azimzade (artist) Commemoration. Paintings. Multicoloured.
| 680 | 20q. Type **204** | 1·50 | 1·50 |
| 681 | 20q. Wedding | 1·50 | 1·50 |

205 Emblem

2007. 15th Anniv of Azermarka (postal company).
| 682 | **205** | 50q. multicoloured | 3·75 | 3·75 |

206 Polar Bear Cub

2007. Polar Bear (*Ursus maritimus*). Multicoloured.
| 683 | 60q. Type **206** | 4·50 | 4·50 |
MS684 76×122 mm 1m. Cub with stick (*vert*) 8·50 8·50

No. MS684 was cut around in the shape of a bear cub.

207 *Gagea alexeenkoana*

2007. Local Flora. Two sheets containing T **207** and similar horiz designs. Multicoloured.
MS685 182×50 mm 10q. Type **207**; 20q. *Centaurea ficher*; 40q. *Galanthus caucasica*; 60q. *Ophrys caucasica* 7·00 7·00
MS686 50×54 mm 1m. *Ophrys caucasica* (different) 6·50 6·50

The stamp and margin of No. MS686 form a composite design.

208 Huseyn Cavid

2007. 160th Birth Anniv of Huseyn Cavid.
| 687 | **208** | 20q. multicoloured | 1·60 | 1·60 |

209 Khudafarin Bridge, Jabrail

2007. Azim Azimzade (artist) Commemoration. Bridges. Multicoloured.
688	10q. Type **209**	80	80
689	20q. Gazanchi, Nakhchivan	1·60	1·60
690	30q. Gudyalchay, Guba	2·40	2·40
691	50q. Ganjachay, Ganja	3·00	3·00
MS692 74×58 mm 60q. 11th century bridge, Jabrail 4·00 4·00

The stamps and margin of No. MS692 form a composite design.

(210)

2007. No. 145 surch as T **210**.
| 693 | 10q. on 15m. brown, ochre and black | 1·20 | 1·20 |

211 11th-century Bridge, Jabrail

2007. Towns.
| 694 | **211** | 10q. pink and black | 90 | 90 |
| 695 | – | 20q. emerald and black | 1·00 | 1·00 |
DESIGNS: 10q. Type **211**; 20q. Fortress, Kalbajar.

212 Sputnik

2007. 50th Anniv of Space Exploration. Sheet 100×72 mm.
MS696 **212** multicoloured 6·75 6·75

213 Karim Karimov

2007. 90th Birth Anniv of Karim Karimov (Chairman of the Aeronautics Commission). Sheet 61×76 mm.
MS697 **213** multicoloured 6·25 6·25

214 Judo

2008. Olympic Games, Beijing. Showing stylized athletes. Multicoloured.
698	20q. Type **214**	1·60	1·60
699	30q. Weight lifting	2·20	2·20
700	40q. Wrestling	3·25	3·25
701	60q. Boxing	4·00	4·00

215 Stylized Envelope

2008. Europa. The Letter. Multicoloured.
| 702 | 20q. Type **215** | 2·50 | 2·50 |
| 703 | 60q. Stylized computer screen | 6·75 | 6·75 |
MS704 110×65 mm. 1m. Dove (20×27 mm) 10·00 10·00

216 17th-century Tower, Gazakh

2008. Towns.
| 705 | **216** | 10q. pink and black | 1·50 | 1·50 |

217 Theatre Facade

2008. 125th Anniv of Musical Drama Theatre, Nakhchivan.
| 706 | **217** | 20q. multicoloured | 2·50 | 2·50 |

218 Zafira Aliyeva

2008. 85th Birth Anniv of Zafira Aliyeva (ophthalmologist). Multicoloured.
| 707 | 1m. Type **218** | 6·50 | 6·50 |
| 708 | 1m. Zafira Aliyeva (painting) | 6·50 | 6·50 |

219 Heydar Aliyev

2008. 85th Birth Anniv of Heydar Aliyev (president, 1993–2003). Multicoloured.
| 709 | 1m. Type **219** | 7·50 | 7·50 |
| 710 | 1m. Heydar Aliyev with national flag | 7·50 | 7·50 |

220 Map as Flag and Meeting

2008. 90th Anniv of Independence.
| 711 | **220** | 20q. multicoloured | 1·50 | 1·50 |

221 Mikayil Mushvig and Shirvan-Shakh Palace

2008. Birth Centenary of Mikayil Mushvig (writer).
| 712 | **221** | 20q. multicoloured | 1·50 | 1·50 |

222 Lev Davidovich Landau

2008. Academicians. Multicoloured.
| 713 | 20q. Type **222** (physicist, winner of 1962 Nobel Prize for Physics) (birth centenary) | 1·50 | 1·50 |
| 714 | 20q. Hasan Abdullayev (President of Academy of Science, 1970–1983) (90th birth anniv) | 1·50 | 1·50 |

223 Heydar Aliyev (tanker)

2008. 150th Anniv of Caspian Shipping Company. Sheet 175×110 mm containing T **223** and similar horiz designs. Multicoloured.
MS715 20q. Type **223**; 30q. *Azerbaijan* (ferry); 50q. *Composer G. Garayev* (cargo boat); 60q. *Maestro Niyazi* (cargo); 1m. *Vandal* (tanker) 16·00 16·00

224 Earring (12th—13th century)

2008. Jewellery. Multicoloured.
716 60q. Type **224** 5·00 5·00
717 60q. Pendant (19th century) 5·00 5·00
Stamps of a similar design were issued by Ukraine.

225 Khanagah Mausoleum, Djulfa

2008. Towns.
718 10q. brown and black 1·25 1·25
719 20q. bgrey and black (vert) 2·00 2·00
DESIGNS: Type **225**; 20q. Garabaglar Mausoleum, Sharur.

226 *Galeodes araneoides*

2008. Arachnids. Two sheets containing T **226** and similar multicoloured designs.
MS720 100×106 mm. 5q. Type **226**; 10q. *Buthus occitanus*; 20q. *Pisaura mirabilis*; 30q. *Latrodectus tredecim-guttatus*; 40q. *Araneus diadematus*; 60q. *Tegenaria domestica*
MS721 40×28 mm. 1m. *Argyroneta aquatica* (horiz) 6·50 6·50

227 Mir Jalal Pashayev

2008. Birth Centenary of Mir Jalal Pashayev (writer).
722 **227** 60q. multicoloured 15·00 15·00

228 Huseyn Javid Mausoleum

2009. 85th Anniv of Nakhchivan Autonomous Republic. Multicoloured.
723 20q. Type **228** 1·60 1·60
724 20q. Heydar Aliev School 1·60 1·60
725 20q. Ministry of Finance 1·60 1·60
726 20q. Nakhchivan State University Library 1·60 1·60
727 20q. Nakhchivan State University Conservatoire 1·60 1·60
728 20q. Physiotherapy Centre 1·60 1·60
729 20q. Tebriz Hotel 1·60 1·60
730 20q. Diagnostic Medical Centre 1·60 1·60

229 Emblem

2009. Baku–Islamic Cultural Centre–2009. Multicoloured.
731 10q. Type **229** 1·50 1·50

230 Ice Cliffs, Emblem Antarctica Outline

2009. Preserve Polar Regions and Glaciers. Sheet 120×72 mm containing T **230** and similar vert design. Multicoloured.
MS733 1m.×2, Type **230**; Arctic outline 13·00 13·00
The stamps and margins of **MS733** form a composite polar design.

231 Emblem and Map

2009. Tenth Economic Cooperation Organization Summit, Tehran.
734 **231** 1m. multicoloured 6·50 6·50

232 Nasiruddin Tusi (astronomer)

2009. Europa. Astronomy. Multicoloured.
735 20q. Type **232** 2·50 2·50
736 60q. Observatory, Shamakhi region 7·50 7·50
MS737 80×80 mm. 1m. First telescope invented by Galileo Galilei, 1609 10·00 10·00

233 Flags

2009. 15th Anniv of Azerbaijan–NATO Co-operation.
738 **233** 20q. multicoloured 1·90 1·90

234 '60', European Stars and Council Building

2009. 60th Anniv of Council of Europe.
739 **234** 60q. multicoloured 5·00 5·00

235 Court Building

2009. 50th Anniv of European Court of Human Rights.
740 **235** 60q. multicoloured 5·00 5·00

236 '60'

2009. 60th Anniv of Sumgait.
741 **236** 10q. multicoloured 1·00 1·00

237 *Vanessa atalanta*

2009. Butterflies. Multicoloured.
742 10q. Type **237** 1·00 1·00
743 20q. *Papilio alexanor* 1·10 1·10

238 Anniversary Emblem

2009. 90th Anniv of Diplomatic Service.
744 **238** 60q. multicoloured 5·00 5·00

239 Jalil Mammadguluzadeh

2009. 140th Birth Anniv of Jalil Huseyngulu oglu Mammadguluzadeh (writer).
745 **239** 20q. multicoloured 1·60 1·60

240 Leyla Mammadbekova

2009. Birth Centenary of Leyla Mammadbekova (first Azerbaijani woman pilot).
746 **240** 20q. multicoloured 5·75 5·75

241 Anniversary Emblem

2009. Tenth Anniv of State Oil Fund
747 **241** 60q. multicoloured 5·00 5·00

242 Anniversary Emblem

2009. 135th Anniv of Universal Postal Union.
748 **242** 20q. multicoloured 2·50 2·50
749 **242** 60q. multicoloured 7·50 7·50

243 *Platalea leucorodia* (spoonbill)

2009. Marsh Waterfowl. Sheet 100×72 mm containing T **243** and similar horiz designs. Multicoloured.
MS750 10q. Type **243**; 20q. *Phalacrocorax pygmaeus* (pygmy cormorant); 60q. *Numenius tenuirostris* (slender-billed curlew); 1m. *Porphyrio porphyrio* (gallinule) 11·50 11·50

244 Chess Pieces on Map of Europe and Azerbaijan

2009. Azerbaijan–European Chess Champion 2009. Sheet 92×70 mm containing T **244** and similar square design. Multicoloured.
MS751 50q. Type **244**; 1m. Chess pieces on map of Azerbaijan 12·00 12·00

245 Ancient Shamakha

2009. Azerbaijan Art. Paintings by Sattar Bahlulzade. Sheet 135×100 mm containing T **245** and similar horiz designs. Multicoloured.
MS752 20q.×6, Type **245**; *Still-life with Pomegranates; Buzovna. Shore; Landscape; Poppies; Red View* 11·00 11·00

246 *Thaleropis jonia fisch*

2010. Butterflies. Multicoloured.
753 10q. Type **246** 70 70
754 20q. *Danais chrysippus* 1·40 1·40

247 Bodies

2010. 20th Anniv of 20 January 1990–National Day of Mourning Sheet 99×74 mm
MS755 **247** black and bright rose-red 1·90 1·90

248 Sunrise over Sea

2010. Tenth Anniv of Ministry of Taxes.
756 **248** 60q. multicoloured 5·00 5·00

249 Tiger

2010. Chinese New Year. Year of the Tiger.
757 **249** 60q. multicoloured 5·00 5·00

250 Hands

2010. 90th Anniv of Azerbaijan Red Crescent Society.
758 **250** 60q. multicoloured 5·00 5·00

251 Bear's Dream

2010. Europa. Children's Books. Multicoloured.
759 20q. Type **251** 1·40 1·40
760 60q. *Lion and Fox* 5·00 5·00
MS761 175×110 mm. Size 32×42 mm. 1m. *Jirtdan* 2·20 2·20

252 Yellow Peony

2010. Peonies. Two sheets containing T **252** and similar square designs. Multicoloured.
MS762 152×104 mm. 10q.×4, Type **252**; Pink peony; White peony; Magenta peony 4·75 4·75
MS763 104×72 mm. 20q. Vase of Peonies 5·00 5·00

253 Soldiers
celebrating
Victory in Berlin

2010. 65th Anniv of End of World War II. Multicoloured.
MS764 10q. Type **253**×2; 20q. Hoisting
Soviet Flag over Reichstag×2; 60q.
Oil container inscribed 'Baku - for
front'×2 7·00 7·00

254 Player and
Championship Emblem

2010. World Cup Football Championships, South Africa.
Multicoloured.
765 Type **254** 1·50 1·50
766 60q. Horiz pair. Nos. 765/6 5·50 5·50

255 Shanghai Skyline

2010. Expo 2010, Shanghai
MS767 **255** 60q. multicoloured 4·75 4·75

256 Cinefilm and A.
Alekperov

2010. Birth Centenary of Alesker Gadzhi Aga ogly
Alekperov (actor)
768 **256** 20q. multicoloured 2·20 2·20

257
*Argynnis
alexandra*

2010. Butterflies. Multicoloured.
769 10q. Type **257** 1·00 1·00
770 20q. *Brahmaea christophi* 1·00 1·10

258 Noah's
Mausoleum,
Nakhchivan

2010. Architectural Heritage
771 **258** 60q. multicoloured 4·75 4·75

259 Maiden Tower (6th
century)

2010. Icheri Sheher Fortress, Baku Old City. Multicoloured.
MS772 10q. Type **259**; 20q. Maham-
mad mosque (11th century); 30q.
Fortress walls (12th century); 40q.
Palace Mosque (15th century); 50q.
Shirvanshahlar tomb (15th century);
60q. Court-house (15th century) 9·25 9·25

MS773 Horiz. 10q. Palace building
(12th-15th centuries); 20q. Bazar
square (15th century); 30q. Two
fortress archways (6th century); 40q.
Jame mosque (14th century); 50q.
Gasim Bay bathhouse (15th century);
60q. Multam and Bukhara Caravan-
saries (15th century) 9·25 9·25
MS774 Horiz. 1m. Shirvanshahlar Pal-
ace complex (12th–16th centuries) 6·50 6·50

260 Ateshgah (Zoroastrian
fire temple), Baku

2010. Ancient Architecture. Multicoloured.
MS775 60q.×2, Type **260**; Pyramid of
the Moon, Teotihuacan (Mexico) 7·50 7·50
Stamps of a similar design were issued by Mexico.

261 Shafaat Mehdiyev

2010. Birth Centenary of Shafaat Farhad Mehdiyev
(academician)
776 **261** 60q. multicoloured 5·00 5·00

262 Scottish
Fold Kitten

2010. Cats. Multicoloured.
MS777 104×104 mm. 10q. Type **262**;
20q. Persian kitten; 30q. Somali
kitten; 40q. British Shorthair kitten;
50q. Birman kitten; 60q. Maine
coon kitten 9·25 9·25
MS778 28x40 mm. 1m. Turkish Angora
cat with kitten (28×40 mm) 6·50 6·50

263 *Phoenicopterus
roseus* (greater
flamingo)

2010. Ecology of Caspian Sea. Multicoloured.
779 60q. Type **263** 5·00 5·00
780 60q. *Ardeola ralloides* (Squacco
heron) 5·00 5·00
Stamps of a similar design were issued by Kazakhstan.

264
*Parnassius
apollo*

2010. Butterflies
781 **264** 10q. multicoloured 1·00 1·00

265
Centaurea
(inscr
'Centaurea
Ficher')

2011. Garabagh Flora. Multicoloured.
782 20q. Type **265** 1·60 1·60
783 50q. *Gagea* (inscr 'Gagea
alexxeenkoana') 3·50 3·50

266 Samani and
Fire (symbols of
Novruz)

2011. Novruz Holiday
784 **266** 30q. multicoloured 2·20 2·20

267 Rabbit

2011. Chinese New Year. Year of the Rabbit
785 **267** 1m. multicoloured 6·25 6·25

268 '10'

2011. Tenth Anniversary of Azerbaijan Republic Joining
to the Council of Europe
786 **268** 1m. multicoloured 6·25 6·25

269 *Ulmus densa*

2011. Europa. Multicoloured.
787 20q. Type **259** 2·25 2·25
788 60q. *Platanus orientalis* 7·50 7·50
MS789 109×170 mm. 1m. *Parrotia
persica* 11·00 11·00

270 International Space
Station

2011. 50th Anniv of First Manned Space Flight.
Multicoloured.
MS790 20q. Type **270**; 50q. Spaceship
Vostok-1 i(n which Yuri Gagarin
made first space flight); 1m. *To you
mankind* (painting by Tahir Salakhov)
(80×28 mm) 6·25 6·25

271 Huseyn Aliyev

2011. Birth Centenary of Huseyn Aliyev (painter)
791 **271** 60q. multicoloured 4·50 4·50

272 Wheel Lyra

2011. Musical Instruments. Multicoloured.
792 50q. Type **272** 3·50 3·50
793 50q. Tar 3·50 3·50

273 *Ophrys
Caucasica*

2011. Flowers of Garabagh. Multicoloured.
794 10q. Type **273** 85 85
795 30q. *Galanthus Caucasicus* 2·50 2·50

274 Ell and Nikki

2011. Azerbaijan, Winners of Eurovision 2011, Dusseldorf.
Sheet 83×92 mm
MS796 **274** 1m. multicoloured 2·25 2·25

275 Heydar Aliyev Palace

2011. Heydar Aliyev Palace, Nakhchivan
797 **275** 60q. multicoloured 4·75 4·75

276 Behbud aga
Shakhtakhtinsky

2011. Anniversaries. 130th Birth Anniv of Behbud aga
Shakhtakhtinsky (politician) (No. 798) or 90th
Anniv of International Treaty of Kars (No. 799).
Multicoloured.
798 60q. Type **276** 4·75 4·75
799 60q. Map of Azerbaijan at time
of treaty 4·75 4·75

277
Chrysanthemums

2011. Chrysanthemums. Multicoloured.
800 10q. Type **277** 85 85
801 20q. Chrysanthemums (dif-
ferent) 1·75 1·75

278 Two Bayonets

2011. Customs Museum Exhibits. Multicoloured.
802 20q. Type **278** 90 90
803 20q. Curved poniard and
decorated sheath 90 90
804 20q. Poniard, metal sheath with
chain and detail of poniard
handle 90 90
805 20q. Wide decorated bladed
knife with decorative sheath 90 90
806 20q. Dagger and sheath 90 90
807 20q. Decorated rifle and pistol
with tassel 90 90
808 20q. Short barreled rifle 90 90
809 20q. Rifle with inlaid stock and
powder flask 90 90
810 60q. Gold-coloured metal belt
with solid rectangular links
and large three piece buckle 2·50 2·50
811 60q. Bronze-coloured metal
belt with solid vertical links
and three piece buckle, all
inlaid with black decorations 2·50 2·50
812 60q. Wide leather belt with
coins and large buckle with
raised decoration 2·50 2·50
813 60q. Cylindrical metal snuff
box, with five suspended
medallions and chain 2·50 2·50
814 60q. Bronze-coloured metal
belt with solid interlocking
links and raised circular
buckle 2·50 2·50
815 60q. Two bronze animal statues,
the left carrying two figures,
the right, one figure 2·50 2·50
816 60q. Lute with tassels 2·50 2·50
817 60q. Five-headed metal dog
and mounted horse-like
statues 2·50 2·50

279 Order of Heydar Aliyev

2011. Orders of the Republic of Azerbaijan. Multicoloured.

818	60q. Type **279**	2·50	2·50
819	60q. Gold Star medal	2·50	2·50
820	60q. Order of Independence	2·50	2·50
821	60q. Order of Şah Ismayil	2·50	2·50
822	60q. Order of Azerbaijan Flag	2·50	2·50
823	60q. Order of Honour	2·50	2·50
824	60q. Order of Glory	2·50	2·50
825	60q. Order of Friendship	2·50	2·50
825	60q. Order of Service to Motherland	2·50	2·50

280 Nizami Ganjavi

2011. 870th Birth Anniv of Nizami Ganjavi (poet). Multicoloured.

827	30q. Type **280**	1·25	1·25
828	30q. Nizami Ganjavi, facing left	1·25	1·25

281 Clasped Hands and Emblem

2011. 20th Anniv of Regional Communication Community (RCC)

829	**281**	50q. multicoloured	2·25	2·25

282 Anniversary Emblem

2011. 20th Anniv of Community of Independent States (CIS)

830	**282**	60q. multicoloured	2·50	2·50

283 National Coat of Arms

2011. 20th Anniv of Independence. Multicoloured.

831	1m. Type **283**	1·90	1·90
832	1m. National flag	1·90	1·90
833	1m. National anthem	1·90	1·90
834	1m. Map of Azerbaijan	1·90	1·90
MS835	74×108 mm. 2m. National flag and map	3·75	3·75
MS836	74×108 mm. 2m. Heydar Aliyev (president 1993-2003)	3·75	

284 Emblem and UN Building, New York

2011. Azerbaijan Candidate for the United Nations Security Council

837	**284**	60q. multicoloured	2·50	2·50

285 *Circaetus gallicus* (short-toed snake eagle)

2011. Endangered Species. Short-toed Snake Eagle (*Circaetus gallicus*). Multicoloured.

838	20q. Type **285**	90	90
839	30q. Pair and chick on nest	1·25	1·25
840	50q. Pair and fledgling on nest	2·25	2·25
841	60q. Diving for snake	2·50	2·50
MS842	180×130mm. Nos. 838/41, each×2	13·00	13·00
MS843	105×140 mm. Nos. 838/41	6·50	6·50

286 National Flag Square

2011. Ninth November, National Flag Day

844	**286**	30q. multicoloured	1·25	1·25

287 Chestnut Garabagh Horse

2011. Garabagh Horses. Multicoloured.

845	10q. Type **287**	85	85
846	20q. Palomino	1·25	1·25
847	30q. Yellow dun	1·25	1·25
848	50q. Bay	2·25	2·25

288 Abbas Zamanov

2011. Birth Centenary of Abbas Zamanov (literary critic)

849	**288**	60q. multicoloured	2·50	2·50

289 Telephone, Satellite and Globe

2011. 130th Anniv of Telephone Communication in Azerbaijan

850	**289**	1m. multicoloured	1·90	1·90

290 Shir Pai Puppy

2011. Dogs. Multicoloured.

MS851 105×105 mm. Puppies. 10q. Type **290**; 20q. Dalmatian; 30q. Labrador; 40q. Doberman; 50q. Chow Chow; 60q. German shepherd 3·75 3·75

MS852 70×75 mm. 1m. Caucasian Shepherd dogs (mother and two puppies) 1·90 1·90

291 Team Members

2011. Rabita Baku Volleyball Club - Fédération Internationale de Volleyball (FIVB) World Champions, 2011. Sheet 102×110 mm

MS853	**291**	1m. multicoloured	90	90

292 Dragon

2012. Chinese New Year. Year of the Dragon

854	**292**	20q. multicoloured	2·25	2·25

293 Anniversary Emblem

2012. 20th Anniv of Central Bank of Azerbaijan

855	**293**	50q. multicoloured	90	90

294 Bahruz Kengerli

2012. 120th Birth Anniv of Bahruz Kengerli (artist)

856	**294**	20q. multicoloured	90	90

295 Beach on Caspian Sea

2012. Europa. Visit Azerbaijan. Multicoloured.

857	20q. Type **295**	90	90
858	60q. Skiing	1·90	1·90
MS859	86×61 mm. 1m. Baku International Airport (vert)	2·50	2·50

295a State Symbols

2012. My Stamp. Multicoloured.

859a	60q. Type **295a**	1·90	1·90
859b	60q. Baku and coastline (horiz)	1·90	1·90

296 Heydar Aliyev Palace

2012. Eurovision Song Contest, 2012, Baku. Multicoloured.

MS860 137×137 mm. 10q. Type **296**; 20q. Opera and Ballet Theatre; 30q. Philharmonic Hall; 40q. Green Theatre; 50q. Mugham Center; 60q. Song Theatre 3·75 3·50

MS861 137×137 mm. 10q. Shitvanshahs Palace; 20q. Government House; 30q. City Hall; 40q. Museum of Literature; 50q. Heydar Aliyev Foundation; 60q. National Academy of Science 3·75 3·50

MS862 137×137 mm. 10q. Flame Towers; 20q. Heydar Aliyev Center; 30q.SOCAR Tower; 40q. Hotel 'Hilton Baku'; 50q. Complex 'Port Baku Residence'; 60q. Hotel 'Absheron Marriot' 3·75 3·50

MS863 84×93 mm. 60q. Eurovision emblem 2·00 1·75

MS864 84×93 mm. 60q. Eurovision emblem and Shitvanshahs Palace 2·00 1·75

297 Maiden Tower, Azerbaijan and Great Wall of China

2012. 20th Anniv of Azerbaijan - China Diplomatic Relations

865	**297**	50q. multicoloured	1·00	75

298 Mirza Fatali Axundzaden

2012. Birth Bicentenary of Mirza Fatali Axundzaden (writer)

866	**298**	20q. multicoloured	90	90

299 Mirza Alakbar Sabir

2012. 150th Birth Anniv of Mirza Alakbar Sabir (poet)

867	**299**	20q. multicoloured	90	90

300 Anniversary Emblem

2012. 20th Anniv of 'Azermarka'. Sheet 116×116 mm

MS868	**300**	1m. multicoloured	2·75	2·75

301 Mammad Said Ordubadi

2012. 140th Birth Anniv of Mammad Said Ordubadi (writer)

869	**301**	50q. multicoloured	1·75	1·75

302 Muslim Magomayev

2012. 70th Birth Anniv of Muslim Magomayev (singer)

870	**302**	50q. multicoloured	1·75	1·75

303 *Aythya nyroca* (Ferruginous Duck)

2012. Endangered Species. Ferruginous Duck (*Aythya nyroca*). Multicoloured.

871	10q. Type **303**	70	70
872	20q. In flight	90	90
873	50q. At water's edge, facing left	1·75	1·75

304 Maiden Tower and
Shirvanshah's Palace,
Baku, Azerbaijan

2012. 20th Anniv of Azerbaijan - Egypt Diplomatic
Relations. Multicoloured.
MS874 60q.×2, Type **304**; Sphinx and
pyramids, Egypt 3·00 3·00

305 Hüseyn
Cavid

2012. 130th Birth Anniv of Hüseyn Cavid (writer)
875 **305** 20q. multicoloured 90 90

306 Woman and
Girl

2012. Traditional Costumes from Shusha, Karabakh.
Multicoloured.
876 50q.×2, Type **306**; Man and boy 2·75 2·75

307 Hasan
Bayandour (Uzun
Hassan) of
Azerbaijan

2012. Azerbaijan - Poland Diplomatic Relations.
Multicoloured.
MS877 60q.×2, Type **307**; Casimir IV
Jagiellon, King of Poland 3·00 3·00

308 Goose

2012. Poultry. Multicoloured.
MS878 104×104 mm.10q. Type **308**;
20q. Turkey; 30q. Hen; 40q. Guinea
fowl; 50q. Duck; 60q. Quail 3·25 3·25
MS879 70×76 mm. 1m. Hen and chicks 2·75 2·75

309 Committee Emblem,
Flag and Runners

2012. 20th Anniv of National Olympic Committee
880 **309** 20q. multicoloured 90 90

310 Route from Kars to
Tbilisi

2012. Baku - Tbilisi - Kars Railway. Multicoloured.
MS881 60q.×2, Type **310**; Route from
Tiblisi to Baku 3·00 3·00

AZORES
Pt. 9

A group of islands in the Atlantic Ocean.

1868. 1000 reis = 1 milreis.
1912. 100 centavos = 1 escudo.
2002. 100 cents = 1 euro.

NOTE. Except where otherwise stated, Nos. 1/393 are
all stamps of Portugal optd **ACORES**.

1868. Curved value labels. Imperf.

1	14	5r. black	£4250	£2500
2	14	10r. yellow	£1800	£12000
3	14	20r. bistre	£250	£200
4	14	50r. green	£250	£200
5	14	80r. orange	£275	£225
6	14	100r. purple	£275	£225

1868. Curved value labels. Perf.

7		5r. black	85·00	85·00
9		10r. yellow	£110	85·00
10		20r. bistre	85·00	75·00
11		25r. pink	85·00	13·00
12		50r. green	£250	£225
13		80r. orange	£250	£225
14		100r. lilac	£250	£225
16		120r. blue	£225	£140
17		240r. lilac	£750	£475

1871. Straight value labels.

38	15	5r. black	16·00	10·50
39	15	10r. yellow	65·00	40·00
73	15	10r. green	£100	80·00
29	15	15r. brown	21·00	19·00
31	15	20r. bistre	36·00	21·00
109	15	20r. red	£170	£140
32	15	25r. pink	21·00	5·00
33	15	50r. green	£110	40·00
54	15	50r. blue	£190	£100
101b	15	80r. orange	90·00	70·00
103	15	100r. mauve	70·00	60·00
25	15	120r. blue	£200	£170
49	15	150r. blue	£225	£190
104	15	150r. yellow	70·00	60·00
26	15	240r. lilac	£1100	£800
50	15	300r. lilac	£110	70·00
94	15	1000r. black	£170	£140

1880

58	16	5r. black	29·00	12·50
60	17	25r. grey	£170	50·00
61	16	25r. grey	65·00	10·00
61b	16	25r. brown	65·00	10·00
67	16	50r. blue	£200	55·00

1882

136	19	5r. grey	17·00	6·25
125	19	10r. green	34·00	15·00
139	19	20r. red	38·00	20·00
126	19	25r. brown	34·00	5·00
141	19	25r. mauve	38·00	3·25
142	19	50r. blue	30·00	5·00
128	19	500r. black	£200	£180
129	19	500r. mauve	£170	£110

1894. Prince Henry the Navigator.

143	32	5r. orange	3·75	3·25
144	32	10r. red	3·75	3·25
145	32	15r. brown	4·75	4·25
146	32	20r. lilac	5·00	4·50
147	32	25r. green	5·50	4·75
148	32	50r. blue	13·50	7·25
149	32	75r. red	25·00	10·00
150	32	80r. green	29·00	11·00
151	32	100r. brown on buff	29·00	8·75
152	32	150r. red	39·00	29·00
153	32	300r. blue on buff	45·00	32·00
154	32	500r. purple	85·00	48·00
155	32	1000r. black on buff	£180	90·00

1895. St. Anthony of Padua.

156	35	2½r. black	3·25	1·30
157	-	5r. orange	10·50	3·25
158	-	10r. mauve	10·50	4·75
159	-	15r. brown	16·00	7·25
160	-	20r. grey	18·00	10·50
161	-	25r. purple and green	11·00	3·25
162	37	50r. brown and blue	37·00	16·00
163	37	75r. brown and red	55·00	45·00
164	37	80r. brown and green	60·00	50·00
165	37	100r. black and brown	60·00	46·00
166	-	150r. red and brown	£130	£110
167	-	200r. blue and brown	£130	£110
168	-	300r. black and brown	£160	£120
169	-	500r. brown & green	£225	£160
170	-	1000r. lilac and green	£375	£275

1898. Vasco da Gama stamps as Nos. 378/385 of
Portugal but inscr "ACORES".

171		2½r. green	3·75	1·40
172		5r. red	3·75	1·70
173		10r. purple	7·50	3·25
174		25r. green	7·50	3·25
175		50r. blue	11·00	10·00
176		75r. brown	23·00	15·00
177		100r. brown	29·00	16·00
178		150r. bistre	46·00	32·00

1906. "King Carlos" key-type inscr "ACORES" and optd
with letters **A**, **H** and **PD** in three of the corners.

179	S	2½r. grey	45	40
180	S	5r. orange	45	40
181	S	10r. green	45	40
182	S	20r. lilac	75	55
183	S	25r. red	75	40
184	S	50r. blue	6·75	5·00
185	S	75r. brown on yellow	2·30	1·40
186	S	100r. blue on blue	2·30	1·40
187	S	200r. purple on pink	2·40	1·40
188	S	300r. blue on pink	7·25	6·00
189	S	500r. black on blue	17·00	15·00

7 King Manoel

1910

190	7	2½r. lilac	50	40
191	7	5r. black	50	40
192	7	10r. green	50	40
193	7	15r. brown	1·00	70
194	7	20r. red	1·40	1·10
195	7	25r. brown	50	50
196	7	50r. blue	3·25	1·70
197	7	75r. brown	3·25	1·70
198	7	80r. grey	3·25	1·70
199	7	100r. brown on green	5·25	4·00
200	7	200r. green on pink	5·25	4·00
201	7	300r. black on blue	3·25	3·00
202	7	500r. brown and olive	10·50	11·00
203	7	1000r. black and blue	24·00	20·00

1910. Optd **REPUBLICA**.

204		2½r. lilac	40	35
205		5r. black	40	35
206		10r. green	45	35
207		15r. brown	2·00	1·40
208b		20r. red	2·00	1·40
209		25r. brown	40	30
210a		50r. blue	1·40	1·30
211		75r. brown	1·50	1·00
212		80r. grey	1·50	1·00
213		100r. brown on green	1·40	1·10
214		200r. green on orange	1·40	1·10
215		300r. black on blue	4·00	2·50
216		500r. brown and green	4·75	3·50
217		1000r. black and blue	12·00	7·00

1911. Vasco da Gama stamps of Azores optd
REPUBLICA, some surch also.

218		2½r. green	70	50
219		15r. on 5r. red	70	50
220		25r. green	70	50
221		50r. blue	2·40	1·60
222		75r. brown	2·00	1·90
223		80r. on 150r. brown	2·10	2·00
224		100r. brown	2·40	2·10
225		1000r. on 10r. purple	22·00	16·00

1911. Postage Due stamps optd or surch **REPUBLICA
ACORES**.

226	D48	5r. black	1·40	1·20
227	D48	10r. mauve	3·00	1·20
228	D48	20r. orange	5·75	4·00
229	D48	200r. brown on buff	25·00	22·00
230	D48	300r. on 50r. grey	24·00	21·00
231	D48	500r. on 100r. red on pink	24·00	20·00

1912. "Ceres" type.

250	56	¼c. brown	60	45
273	56	½c. black	60	60
252	56	1c. green	1·20	85
274	56	1c. brown	60	60
254	56	1½c. brown	1·20	85
255	56	1½c. green	60	60
256	56	2c. red	85	70
257	56	2c. orange	60	60
258	56	2½c. lilac	85	70
259	56	3c. red	60	60
278	56	3c. blue	45	35
260	56	3½c. green	60	60
261	56	4c. green	60	60
401	56	4c. orange	75	60
262	56	5c. blue	85	70
280	56	5c. brown	60	60
264	56	6c. purple	60	60
282	56	6c. brown	65	55
403	56	6c. red	50	35
265	56	7½c. brown	7·25	4·00
266	56	7½c. blue	2·00	1·80
267	56	8c. grey	85	70
283	56	8c. green	85	60
284	56	8c. orange	1·10	1·00
268	56	10c. brown	7·25	3·00
285	56	10c. red	60	60
286	56	12c. blue	3·00	1·90
287	56	12c. green	1·00	80
288	56	13½c. blue	3·00	1·90
249	56	14c. blue on yellow	2·50	2·50
269	56	15c. purple	90	70
289	56	15c. black	60	60
290	56	16c. blue	1·00	95
243	56	20c. brown on green	13·50	7·75
291	56	20c. brown	1·00	80
292	56	20c. green	1·30	1·00
293	56	20c. drab	85	70
294	56	24c. blue	1·00	65
295	56	25c. pink	75	60
244	56	30c. brown on pink	85·00	65·00
245	56	30c. brown on yellow	2·50	2·50
296	56	30c. brown	2·10	1·80
406	56	32c. green	3·50	2·40
298	56	36c. red	90	70
299	56	40c. blue	1·10	70
300	56	40c. brown	2·00	1·10
407	56	40c. green	1·90	95
408	56	48c. pink	4·50	3·75
246	56	50c. orange on orange	7·00	3·00
247	56	50c. orange on yellow	7·00	4·00
302	56	50c. yellow	2·00	1·60
410	56	50c. red	6·00	4·50
303	56	60c. blue	2·00	1·60
304	56	64c. blue	5·25	2·40
411	56	64c. red	6·00	4·50
305	56	75c. pink	5·50	4·25
412	56	75c. red	6·00	4·50
306	56	80c. purple	2·75	2·20
307	56	80c. lilac	3·00	2·10
413	56	80c. green	6·00	3·75
308	56	90c. blue	2·75	2·40
309	56	96c. red	8·25	3·75
248	56	1e. green on blue	7·75	6·50
310	56	1e. lilac	2·75	2·20
314	56	1e. purple	4·00	3·50
414	56	1e. red	55·00	36·00
311	56	1e.10 brown	3·00	2·20
312	56	1e.20 green	3·50	2·20
315	56	1e.20 buff	9·00	6·50
415	56	1e.25 blue	3·50	3·00
316	56	1e.50 purple	10·50	7·00
317	56	1e.50 lilac	9·25	7·25
400	56	1e.60 blue	5·25	2·20
313	56	2e. green	11·50	7·00
319	56	2e.40 green	80·00	50·00
320	56	3e. pink	90·00	55·00
321	56	3e.20 green	10·50	10·50
322	56	5e. green	20·00	11·00
323	56	10e. pink	55·00	30·00
324	56	20e. blue	£130	90·00

1925. C. C. Branco Centenary.

325	65	2c. orange	25	25
326	65	3c. green	25	25
327	65	4c. blue	25	25
328	65	5c. red	25	25
329	-	10c. blue	25	25
330	-	16c. orange	40	30
331	67	25c. red	40	30
332	-	32c. green	60	55
333	67	40c. black and green	60	55
334	67	48c. purple	1·30	1·30
335	-	50c. green	1·30	1·10
336	-	64c. brown	1·30	1·10
337	-	75c. grey	1·30	1·10
338	67	80c. brown	1·30	1·10
339	-	96c. red	1·50	1·30
340	-	1e.50 blue on blue	1·50	1·30
341	67	1e.60 red	1·70	1·50
342	-	2e. green on green	2·75	2·40
343	-	2e.40 red on orange	3·75	2·50
344	-	3e.20 black on green	6·50	5·75

1926. First Independence Issue.

345	76	2c. black and orange	45	35
346	-	3c. black and blue	45	35
347	76	4c. black and green	45	35
348	-	5c. black and brown	45	35
349	76	6c. black and orange	45	35
350	-	15c. black and green	80	75
351	77	20c. black and violet	80	75
352	-	25c. black and red	80	75
353	77	32c. black and green	80	75
354	-	40c. black and brown	80	75
355	-	50c. black and olive	1·80	1·70
356	-	75c. black and red	1·90	1·80
357	-	1e. black and violet	2·40	2·30
358	-	4e.50 black and green	9·50	9·50

1927. Second Independence Issue.

359	**80**	2c. black and brown	35	35
360	-	3c. black and blue	35	35
361	**80**	4c. black and orange	35	35
362	-	5c. black and brown	35	35
363	-	6c. black and brown	35	35
364	-	15c. black and brown	45	35
365	**80**	25c. black and grey	1·70	1·70
366	-	32c. black and green	1·70	1·70
367	-	40c. black and green	95	95
368	-	96c. black and red	4·25	4·00
369	-	1e.60 black and blue	4·50	4·25
370	-	4e.50 black and yellow	11·50	11·50

1928. Third Independence Issue.

371		2c. black and blue	45	35
372	**84**	3c. black and green	45	35
373	-	4c. black and red	45	35
374	-	5c. black and olive	45	35
375	-	6c. black and brown	45	35
376	**84**	15c. black and grey	85	80
377	-	16c. black and purple	95	95
378	-	25c. black and blue	95	95
379	-	32c. black and green	1·00	1·00
380	-	40c. black and brown	1·00	1·00
381	-	50c. black and red	2·20	2·10
382	**84**	80c. black and grey	2·20	2·10
383	-	96c. black and red	4·25	4·00
384	-	1e. black and mauve	4·25	4·00
385	-	1e.60 black and blue	4·25	4·00
386	-	4e.50 black and yellow	11·00	10·50

1929. "Ceres" type surch **ACORES** and new value.

387	**56**	4c. on 25c. pink	95	95
388	**56**	4c. on 60c. blue	1·90	1·80
389	**56**	10c. on 25c. pink	1·90	1·80
390	**56**	12c. on 25c. pink	1·90	1·80
391	**56**	15c. on 25c. pink	1·90	1·80
392	**56**	20c. on 25c. pink	3·25	3·00
393	**56**	40c. on 1e.10 brown	6·25	6·00

14 10r. Stamp of 1868

1980. 112th Anniv of First Azores Stamps.

416	**14**	6e.50 black, yellow & red	45	25
417	-	19e.50 blk, purple & blue	1·50	1·00

MS418 140×115 mm. Nos. 416/17 (sold at 30e.) 6·75 6·75
DESIGN: 19e.50, 100r. stamp of 1868.

15 Map of the Azores

1980. World Tourism Conference, Manila, Philippines. Multicoloured.

419		50c. Type **15**	20	15
420		1e. Church	30	20
421		5e. Windmill	75	40
422		6e.50 Traditional costume	95	45
423		8e. Coastal scene	1·40	65
424		30e. Coastal village	2·75	1·10

16 St. Peter's Cavalcade, Sao Miguel Island

1981. Europa. Folklore.

425	**16**	22e. multicoloured	1·90	95

MS426 140×116 mm. No. 425×2 8·50 8·50

17 Bulls attacking Spanish Soldiers

1981. 400th Anniv of Battle of Salga. Multicoloured.

427		8e.50 Type **17**	80	10
428		33e.50 Friar Don Pedro leading attack	3·00	1·40

18 Myosotis azorica

1981. Regional Flowers. Multicoloured.

429		4e. Type **18**	20	10
430		7e. Tolpis azorica	45	30
431		8e.50 Ranunculus azoricus	60	30
432		10e. Lactuca watsoniana	85	30
433		12e.50 Hypericum foliosum	40	10
434		20e. Platanthera micranta	1·00	70
435		27e. Vicia dennesiana	1·90	1·20
436		30e. Rubus hochstetterorum	1·20	50
437		33e.50 Azorina vidalii	2·10	1·40
438		37e.50 Vaccinium cylindraceum	1·70	1·00
439		50e. Laurus azorica	2·75	1·50
440		100e. Juniperus brevifolia	3·50	1·60

19 Embarkation of the Heroes of Mindelo

1982. Europa. Multicoloured.

445	**19**	33e.50 multicoloured	2·75	1·40

MS446 140×113 mm. No. 445×3 21·00 21·00

20 Chapel of the Holy Ghost

1982. Regional Architecture. Multicoloured.

447		27e. Type **20**	2·00	1·20
448		33e.50 Chapel of the Holy Ghost (different)	2·75	1·60

21 Geothermal Power Station, Pico Vermeilho, São Miguel

1983. Europa.

449	**21**	37e.50 multicoloured	2·75	1·10

MS450 114×140 mm. No. 449×3 23·00 23·00

22 Flag of Azores

1983. Flag.

451	**22**	12e.50 multicoloured	1·10	20

23 Two "Holy Ghost" Jesters, São Miguel

1984. Traditional Costumes. Multicoloured.

452		16e. Type **23**	85	20
453		51e. Two women wearing Terceira cloak	3·00	2·10

23a Bridge

1984. Europa.

454	**23a**	51e. multicoloured	4·00	1·90

MS455 114×139 mm. No. 454×3 20·00 20·00

24 Megabombus ruderatus

1984. Insects (1st series). Multicoloured.

456		16e. Type **24**	50	10
457		35e. Large white (butterfly)	1·50	1·00
458		40e. Chrysomela banksi (leaf beetle)	2·20	1·00
459		51e. Phlogophora interrupta (moth)	2·50	1·60

1985. Insects (2nd series). As T **24**. Multicoloured.

460		20e. Polyspilla polyspilla (leaf beetle)	55	10
461		40e. Sphaerophoria nigra (hover fly)	1·60	85
462		46e. Clouded yellow (butterfly)	2·30	1·20
463		60e. Southern grayling (butterfly)	2·50	1·40

25 Drummer

1985. Europa. Music Year.

464	**25**	60e. multicoloured	4·00	1·70

MS465 140×114 mm. No. 464×3 25·00 25·00

26 Jeque

1985. Traditional Boats. Multicoloured.

466		40e. Type **26**	2·10	1·20
467		60e. Bote	2·75	1·50

27 Northern Bullfinch

1986. Europa.

468	**27**	68e.50 multicoloured	4·75	1·90

MS469 140×114 mm. No. 468×3 21·00 21·00

28 Alto das Covas Fountain, Terceira

1986. Regional Architecture. Drinking Fountains. Multicoloured.

470		22e.50 Type **28**	90	20
471		52e.50 Faja de Baixo, Sao Miguel	2·75	1·40
472		68e.50 Portoes de S. Pedro, Terceira	4·00	1·80
473		100e. Agua d'Alto, Sao Miguel	5·50	1·60

29 Ox Cart, Santa Maria

1986. Traditional Carts. Multicoloured.

474		25e. Type **29**	90	10
475		75e. Ram cart, Sao Miguel	4·00	2·30

30 Regional Assembly Building (Correia Fernandes and Luis Miranda)

1987. Europa. Architecture.

476	**30**	74e.50 multicoloured	4·25	1·90

MS477 140×114 mm. No. 476×4 25·00 25·00

31 Santa Cruz, Graciosa

1987. Windows and Balconies. Multicoloured.

478		51e. Type **31**	2·50	1·40
479		74e.50 Ribeira Grande, São Miguel	3·00	1·40

32 A. C. Read's Curtiss NC-4 Flying Boat, 1919

1987. Historic Airplane Landings in the Azores. Multicoloured.

480		25e. Type **32**	75	10
481		57e. E. F. Christiansen's Dornier Do-X flying boat, 1932	2·75	1·90
482		74e.50 Italo Balbo's Savoia Marchetti S-55X flying boat, 1933	4·00	1·70
483		125e. Charles Lindbergh's Lockheed 8 Sirius seaplane *Tingmissartoq*, 1933	4·50	2·40

33 19th-century Mule-drawn Omnibus

1988. Europa. Transport and Communications.

484	**33**	80e. multicoloured	5·00	1·50

MS485 140×112 mm. As No. 484 ×4 but with cream background 25·00 25·00

34 Wood Pigeon

1988. Nature Protection. Birds (1st series). Multicoloured.

486		27e. Type **34**	90	30
487		60e. Eurasian woodcock	2·75	1·40
488		80e. Roseate tern	3·00	1·60
489		100e. Common buzzard	3·75	1·60

See also Nos. 492/5 and 500/3.

35 Azores Arms

1988. Coats-of-arms. Multicoloured.

490		55e. Type **35**	2·30	1·20
491		80e. Bettencourt family arms	3·00	1·60

1989. Nature Protection (2nd series). Goldcrest. As T **34**. Multicoloured.

492		30e. Goldcrest perched on branch	1·30	40
493		30e. Pair	1·30	40
494		30e. Goldcrest on nest	1·30	40
495		30e. Goldcrest with outspread wings	1·30	40

36 Boy in Boat

1989. Europa. Children's Games and Toys.

496	**36**	80e. multicoloured	3·75	1·60

MS497 139×112 mm. 80e. ×2, Type **36**; 80e. ×2, Boy with toy boat 25·00 25·00

37 Pioneers

1989. 550th Anniv of Portuguese Settlement in Azores. Multicoloured.
498	29e. Type **37**		85	30
499	87e. Settler breaking land		3·50	1·90

1990. Nature Protection (3rd series). Northern Bullfinch. As T **34**. Multicoloured.
500	32e. Two bullfinches		1·70	55
501	32e. Bullfinch on branch		1·70	55
502	32e. Bullfinch landing on twig		1·70	55
503	32e. Bullfinch on nest		1·70	55

38 Vasco da Gama P.O.

1990. Europa. P.O. Buildings.
504	**38**	80e. multicoloured	3·00	1·50
MS505	139×111 mm. 80e. ×2, Type **38**; 80e. ×2, Maia Post Office		23·00	23·00

39 Cart Maker

1990. Traditional Occupations. Multicoloured.
506	5e. Type **39**		20	15
507	10e. Viol maker		20	15
508	32e. Potter		80	40
509	35e. Making roof tiles		75	30
510	38e. Carpenter		75	35
511	60e. Tinsmith		2·30	1·20
512	65e. Laying pavement mosaics		1·80	1·10
513	70e. Quarrying		2·00	1·20
514	85e. Basket maker		1·90	1·00
515	100e. Cooper		3·25	1·80
516	110e. Shaping stones		3·00	1·40
517	120e. Boat builders		2·50	1·20

40 *Hermes* Spaceplane

1991. Europa. Europe in Space.
520	**40**	80e. multicoloured	5·25	4·00
MS521	140×112 mm. 80e. ×2, Type **40**; 80e. ×2, *Sanger* spaceplane		20·00	20·00

41 *Helena* (schooner)

1991. Inter-island Transport. Multicoloured.
522	35e. Type **41**		75	25
523	60e. Beech Model 18 airplane, 1947		1·50	85
524	80e. *Cruzeiro do Canal* (ferry), 1987		2·30	1·40
525	110e. British Aerospace ATP airliner, 1991		2·75	1·60

42 *Santa Maria* off Azores

1992. Europa. 500th Anniv of Discovery of America by Columbus.
526	**42**	85e. multicoloured	2·40	1·10

43 *Insulano* (steamer, 1868)

1992. The Empresa Insulana de Navegacao Shipping Fleet. Multicoloured.
527	38e. Type **43**		75	30
528	65e. *Carvalho Araujo* (ferry, 1930)		1·50	1·00
529	85e. *Funchal* (ferry, 1961)		1·90	1·20
530	120e. *Terceirense* (freighter, 1948)		2·50	1·40

44 Ox-mill

1993. Traditional Grinders. Multicoloured.
531	42e. Type **44**		75	35
532	130e. Hand-mill		3·00	1·80

45 *Two Sirens at the Entrance of a Grotto* (Antonio Dacosta)

1993. Europa. Contemporary Art.
533	**45**	90e. multicoloured	2·75	1·20
MS534	140×112 mm. 90e. ×2, Type **45**; 90e. ×2, *Acorinan III*		15·00	15·00

46 Main Entrance, Praia da Vitoria Church, Terceira

1993. Doorways. Multicoloured.
535	42e. Type **46**		75	35
536	70e. South door, Praia da Vitoria Church		1·40	85
537	90e. Main door, Ponta Delgada Church, Sao Miguel		1·80	1·10
538	130e. South door, Ponta Delgada Church		2·75	1·40

47 Floral Decoration, Our Lady of Sorrows, Caloura, Sao Miguel

1994. Tiles. Multicoloured.
539	40e. Type **47**		60	35
540	70e. Decoration of crosses, Our Lady of Sorrows, Caloura, Sao Miguel		1·40	80
541	100e. *Adoration of the Wise Men*, Our Lady of Hope Monastery, Ponta Delgada, Sao Miguel		1·80	1·10
542	150e. *St. Bras* (altar frontal), Our Lady of Anjos, Santa Maria		2·75	1·70

48 Monkey and Explorer with Model Caravel

1994. Europa. Discoveries. Multicoloured.
543	**48**	100e. multicoloured	2·20	1·10
MS544	140×112 mm. 100e. ×2, Type **48**; 100e. ×2, Armadilo and explorer with model caravel		12·50	12·50

49 Doorway, St. Barbaras Church, Cedros, Faial

1994. Manoeline Architecture. Multicoloured.
545	45e. Type **49**		65	35
546	140e. Window, Ribeira Grande, Sao Miguel		2·40	1·60

50 Aristides Moreira da Motta

1995. Centenary of Decree decentralizing Government of the Azores and Madeira Islands. Pro-autonomy activists. Multicoloured.
547	42e. Type **50**		65	35
548	130e. Gil Mont' Alverne de Sequeira		2·20	1·40

51 Santana Palace, Ponta Delgada

1995. Architecture of Sao Miguel. Multicoloured.
549	45e. Type **51**		65	35
550	80e. Chapel of Our Lady of the Victories, Furnas		1·30	75
551	95e. Hospital, Ponta Delgada		1·50	80
552	135e. Ernesto do Canto's villa, Furnas		1·80	1·10

52 Contendas Lighthouse, Terceira

1996. Lighthouses. Multicoloured.
553	47e. Type **52**		60	35
554	78e. Molhe Lighthouse, Sao Miguel		1·30	85
555	98e. Arnel Lighthouse, Sao Miguel		1·50	1·00
556	140e. Santa Clara Lighthouse, Sao Miguel		2·10	1·30
MS557	110×140 mm. 200e. Ponta da Barca Lighthouse, Graciosa		3·00	3·00

53 Natalia Correia (poet)

1996. Europa. Famous Women.
558	**53**	98e. multicoloured	1·70	85
MS559	140×112 mm. No. 558×3		5·75	5·75

54 Bird eating Grapes (St. Peter's Church, Ponta Delgada)

1997. Gilded Wooden Altarpieces. Multicoloured.
560	49e. Type **54**		65	35
561	80e. Cherub (St. Peter of Alcantara Convent, Sao Roque)		1·20	55
562	100e. Cherub with wings (All Saints Church, Jesuit College, Ponta Delgada)		1·40	1·00
563	140e. Caryatid (St. Joseph's Church, Ponta Delgada)		2·00	1·20

55 Island of the Seven Cities

1997. Europa. Tales and Legends.
564	**55**	100e. multicoloured	1·70	85
MS565	140×106 mm. No. 564×3		5·50	5·50

56 Emperor and Empress and young Bulls (Festival of the Holy Spirit)

1998. Europa. National Festivals.
566	**56**	100e. multicoloured	1·60	85
MS567	140×109 No. 566×3		4·75	4·75

57 Spotted Dolphin

1998. "Expo '98" World's Fair, Lisbon. Marine Life. Multicoloured.
568	50e. Type **57**		65	35
569	140e. Sperm whale (79×30 mm)		1·90	1·20

58 Mt. Pico Nature Reserve

1999. Parks and Gardens.
570	**58**	100e. multicoloured	1·40	85
MS571	154×109 mm. No. 570×3		4·75	4·75

59 Emigrants (Domingos Rebelo)

1999. Paintings. Multicoloured.
572	51e. Type **59**		65	35
573	95e. *Portrait of Vitorino Nemesio* (Antonio Dacosta) (vert)		1·30	85
574	100e. *Cattle loose on the Alto das Covas* (Ze van der Hagen Bretao)		1·30	85
575	140e. *Vila Franca Island* (Duarte Maia)		1·70	1·20

60 "Building Europe"

2000. Europa.
576	**60**	100e. multicoloured	1·70	95
MS577	154×108 mm. No. 576×3		5·25	5·25

61 Fishermen retrieving Mail Raft

2000. History of Mail Delivery in the Azores. Multicoloured.
578	85e. Type **61**		1·30	80
579	140e. Zeppelin airship dropping mail sacks		2·10	1·40

62 Coast Line

2001. Europa. Water Resources.
580	**62**	105e. multicoloured	1·70	95
MS581		140×110 mm. No. 580×3	5·25	5·25

63 Arch and Town

2001. UNESCO World Heritage Site, Angra do Heroismo. Multicoloured.
582	**63**	53e. Type **63**	70	35
583		85e. Monument and town	1·30	85
584		140e. Balcony and view over town	2·00	1·30
MS585		140×112 mm. 350e. Map of town	5·00	5·00

64 Clown

2002. Europa. Circus.
586	**64**	54c. multicoloured	1·70	1·90
MS587		140×110 mm. No. 586×3	5·00	5·00

65 Faial Island, Azores

2002. Windmills. Multicoloured.
588	**65**	43c. Type **65**	1·10	70
589		54c. Onze-Lieve-Vrouw-Lombeek, Roosdaal	1·50	85

Stamps of a similar design were issued by Belgium.

66 Birds (Sebastiao Rodrigues)

2003. Europa. Poster Art.
590	**66**	55c. multicoloured	1·80	95
MS591		140×113 mm. No. 591×2	3·25	3·25

67 Pineapple Groves

2003. Sao Miguel Island. Multicoloured.
592	**67**	30c. Type **67**	80	30
593		43c. Vineyards and grapes	1·10	70
594		55c. Date growing	1·40	90
595		70c. Coffee growing	1·80	1·20
MS596		140×112 mm. €1 Dancers and ceramic figure; €2 Fruit and ceramic bird (Espirito Santos festival)	8·00	8·00

68 Figures, Flowers and Island

2004. Europa. Holidays.
597	**68**	56c. multicoloured	1·60	90
MS598		141×112 mm. No. 597×2	3·25	3·25

69 Blue Marlin (*Makaira nigricans*)

2004. Endangered Species. Atlantic Marlin. Multicoloured.
599		30c. Type **69**	80	55
600		30c. Fin, body and tail	80	55
601		30c. White marlin (*Tetrapturus albidus*)	80	55
602		30c. Back and tail	80	55

Nos. 599/602 were issued together, *se-tenant*, forming a composite design.

70 Torresmos (marinated pork)

2005. Europa. Gastronomy. Multicoloured.
603		57c. Type **70**	1·60	90
MS604		125×95 mm. 57c.×2, *Polvo guisado* (octopus)×2	4·25	4·25

71 Cow

2005. Tourism. Multicoloured.
605		30c. Type **71**	70	50
606		30c. Arched window and lake	70	50
607		45c. Decorated house	1·10	75
608		45c. Windmill	1·10	75
609		57c. Whale's tail	1·40	90
610		74c. Pineapple and hot spring	1·80	1·30
MS611		125×95 mm. 30c. Santo Cristo dos Milagres (statue); €1.55 Bird	4·50	4·50

Nos. 605/10 were issued together, *se-tenant*, forming a composite design.

72 Figures standing on Head (Joao Dinis)

2006. Europa. Integration. Winning Entries in ANACED (association for art and creativity by and for people with disabilities) Painting Competition. Multicoloured.
612		60c. Type **72**	1·50	85
MS613		125×95 mm. 60c.×2, One legged figure; Figures with irregular outlines	3·00	3·00

73 Crabs, Lucky Strike

2006. Hydrothermal Springs. Multicoloured.
614		20c. Type **73**	45	30
615		30c. Fish, Lucky Strike	70	45
616		75c. Plumes, Rainbow	1·70	1·10
617		€2 Fish tower, Rainbow	4·50	3·00
MS618		125×95 mm. €2 No. 617	4·75	4·75

74 Mountain

2006. Wine from Pico Island. Multicoloured.
619		30c. Type **74**	70	45
620		60c. Terraces	1·30	85
621		75c. Wine barrel	1·70	1·10
622		€1 Harvesting	2·20	1·50
MS623		125×95 mm. 45c. Young vines; 60c. Harvesting; 75c. Winery; €1 Barrels	6·50	6·50

75 Scarf

2007. Europa. Centenary of Scouting. Multicoloured.
624		61c. Type **75**	1·40	85
MS625		125×95 mm. 61c.×2, Reef knot; Scouts in camp	3·00	3·00

The stamps of **MS625** form a composite design.

76 Sao Miguel

2007. Windmills. Multicoloured.
626		30c. Type **76**	65	45
627		45c. Sao Jorge	95	65
628		61c. Corvo	1·30	85
629		75c. Blue windmill, Sao Jorge	1·70	1·10
MS630		125×95 mm. 45c. Sao Miguel (different); €2 Red windmill, Sao Jorge	5·50	5·50

77 Capelinhos Volcano

2007. 50th Anniv of Eruption of Capelinhos Volcano, Faial Island. Multicoloured.
631		30c. Type **77**	65	45
632		75c. Erupting volcano and lighthouse	1·70	1·10
MS633		125×95 mm. €2.45 Island showing lighthouse (80×30 mm)	5·75	5·75

The stamp and margin of **MS633** form a composite design.

78 Envelope as Boat

2008. Europa. The Letter. Multicoloured.
634		61c. Type **78**	1·50	85
MS635		125×95 mm. 61c.×2, Windmill and envelopes; As Type **78**	3·00	3·00

The stamps of **MS635** each form a composite design.

79 Cock Bird

2008. Azores Bullfinch (*Pyrrhula murina*). Multicoloured.
636		30c. Type **79**	75	45
637		61c. Female	1·50	85
638		75c. Male facing right	1·80	1·00
639		€1 Male facing left	2·50	1·40
MS640		Two sheets, each 125×95 mm. (a) €2.45 Head of male eating seed. (b) €2.95 Head of male with open beak	14·00	14·00

The stamps and margins of **MS640**a/b form a composite design.

80 Ponta do Arnel

2008. Lighthouse.
641	**80**	61c. multicoloured	1·50	85

81 Woodcock (Lagoa Comprida)

2009. Biodiversity. Lakes. Multicoloured.
642		32c. Type **81**	95	45
643		68c. Brown butterfly (Lagoa do Caldeirao)	2·10	1·00
644		80c. Dragonfly (Lagoa do Capitao)	2·40	1·20
645		€2 Azores juniper (Lagoinha)	6·00	3·00
MS646		125×95 mm. €2.50 Tessellate moray (80×30 mm)	7·50	7·50
MS647		125×95 mm. €2.50 Tufted duck, teal and capped heron (80×30 mm)	7·50	7·50

82 European Space Agency Satellite Tracking Station, Santa Maria Island, Azores

2009. Europa. Astronomy. Multicoloured.
648		68c. Type **82**	2·10	1·00
MS649		125×95 mm. 68c.×2, Ribeira Grande Astronomical Observatory, Sao Miguel Island, Azores; As Type **82**	4·25	4·25

The stamps and margins of **MS649** form a composite design.

83 Milho (maize bread)

2009. Bread. Sheet 125×95 mm.
MS650	**83**	€2 multicoloured	6·00	6·00

84 Girl

2010. Europa. Children's Books. Multicoloured.
651		68c. Type **84**	2·10	1·00
MS652		125×96 mm. 68c.× 2 King on horseback; As Type **84**	4·25	4·25

85 Dardanus callidus

2010. Invertebrates. Multicoloured.
653		32c. Type **85**	95	45
654		68c. *Alicia mirabilis*	2·10	1·00
655		80c. *Orphidiaster orphidianus*	2·40	1·20
MS656		125×95 mm. €2 *Grapsus adscencionis*	6·00	6·00
MS657		125×95 mm. €2 *Sphaerechinus granularis*	6·00	6·00

CHARITY TAX STAMPS

Used on certain days of the year as an additional postal tax on internal letters. The proceeds were devoted to public charities. If one was not affixed in addition to the ordinary postage, postage due stamps were used to collect the deficiency and the fine.

1911. No. 206 optd **ASSISTENCIA**.
C218a	**7**	10r. green	1·50	1·20

1913. No. 252 optd **ASSISTENCIA**.
C250	**56**	1c. green	5·25	4·00

1915. For the Poor. Charity stamp of Portugal optd **ACORES**.
C251	**C58**	1c. red	70	35

1925. No. C251 surch **15 ctvs**.
C325		15c. on 1c. red	1·20	95

1925. Portuguese Army in Flanders issue of Portugal optd **ACORES**.
C345	**C71**	10c. red	1·20	1·20
C346	**C71**	10c. green	1·20	1·20
C347	**C71**	10c. blue	1·20	1·20
C348	**C71**	10c. brown	1·20	1·20

1925. As Marquis de Pombal issue of Portugal, inscr "ACORES".
C349	**C73**	20c. green	1·20	1·20
C350	-	20c. green	1·20	1·20
C351	**C75**	20c. green	1·20	1·20

NEWSPAPER STAMPS

1876. Stamps of Portugal optd **ACORES**.
N146	**N16**	2r. black	7·00	3·25
N150a	**N17**	2½r. brown	6·50	1·90
N150b	**N17**	2½r. green	6·50	1·90

PARCEL POST STAMPS

1921. Stamps of Portugal optd **ACORES**.
P325	**P59**	1c. brown	60	50
P326	**P59**	2c. orange	60	50
P327	**P59**	5c. brown	60	50
P328	**P59**	10c. brown	80	50
P329	**P59**	20c. blue	80	50
P330	**P59**	40c. red	80	50
P331	**P59**	50c. black	1·60	1·10
P332	**P59**	60c. blue	1·60	1·10

P333	**P59**	70c. brown	3·00	2·50
P334	**P59**	80c. blue	3·00	2·50
P335	**P59**	90c. violet	3·00	2·50
P336	**P59**	1e. green	3·00	2·50
P337	**P59**	2e. lilac	4·75	3·75
P338	**P59**	3e. olive	8·50	4·00
P339	**P59**	4e. blue	10·00	4·00
P340	**P59**	5e. lilac	10·50	8·00
P341	**P59**	10e. brown	43·00	24·00

POSTAGE DUE STAMPS

Nos. D179/351 are stamps of Portugal overprinted **ACORES**.

1904

D179	**D49**	5r. brown	1·40	1·20
D180	**D49**	10r. orange	1·50	1·20
D181	**D49**	20r. mauve	2·50	1·40
D182	**D49**	30r. green	2·50	1·90
D183	**D49**	40r. lilac	4·25	2·50
D184	**D49**	50r. red	7·25	4·75
D185	**D49**	100r. blue	9·00	8·75

1911. As last, optd **REPUBLICA**.

D218		5r. brown	80	70
D219		10r. orange	80	70
D220		20r. mauve	1·00	90
D221		30r. green	1·00	90
D222		40r. lilac	1·60	1·20
D223		50r. red	8·50	8·00
D224		100r. blue	3·00	3·00

1918. Value in centavos.

D325		½c. brown	85	80
D326		1c. orange	85	80
D327		2c. purple	85	85
D328		3c. green	85	80
D329		4c. lilac	85	80
D330		5c. red	85	80
D331		10c. blue	85	80

1922

D332		½c. green	40	40
D333		1c. green	65	50
D334		2c. green	65	50
D335		3c. green	1·10	50
D336		8c. green	1·10	50
D337		10c. green	1·10	50
D338		12c. green	1·10	50
D339		16c. green	1·10	50
D340		20c. green	1·10	50
D341		24c. green	1·10	50
D342		32c. green	1·10	50
D343		36c. green	1·10	70
D344		40c. green	1·10	70
D345		48c. green	1·10	70
D346		50c. green	1·10	70
D347		60c. green	1·20	75
D348		72c. green	1·20	75
D349		80c. green	5·50	4·50
D350		1e.20 green	6·25	5·00

1925. Portuguese Army in Flanders.

D351	**D72**	20c. brown	1·20	1·20

1925. As Nos. C349/51, optd **MULTA**.

D352	**D73**	40c. green	1·20	1·20
D353	-	40c. green	1·20	1·20
D354	**D75**	40c. green	1·20	1·20

Pt. 7

BADEN

In S.W. Germany. Formerly a Grand Duchy, now part of the German Federal Republic.

60 kreuzer = 1 gulden.

1

1851. Imperf.

1a	**1**	1k. black on buff	£650	£375
8	**1**	1k. black on white	£275	41·00
3	**1**	3k. black on yellow	£325	23·00
9	**1**	3k. black on green	£250	11·50
10	**1**	3k. black on blue	£1100	47·00
5	**1**	6k. black on green	£1100	70·00
11	**1**	6k. black on orange	£450	41·00
6a	**1**	9k. black on red	£275	35·00

2

1860. Shaded background behind Arms. Perf.

13	**2**	1k. black	£130	41·00
16	**2**	3k. blue	£120	35·00
17	**2**	6k. orange	£150	£110
22	**2**	6k. blue	£225	£150
19	**2**	9k. red	£350	£250
25	**2**	9k. brown	£150	£190

1862. Uncoloured background behind Arms.

27		1k. black	65·00	21·00
28		3k. red	80·00	5·75
30		6k. blue	16·00	42·00
33		9k. brown	22·00	42·00
36		18k. green	£550	£800
38		30k. orange	45·00	£3250

1868. "K R." instead of "KREUZER".

39		1k. green	5·50	14·00
41		3k. red	3·25	7·00
44		7k. blue	28·00	55·00

RURAL POSTAGE DUE STAMPS

D4

1862

D39	**D4**	1k. black on yellow	6·75	£475
D40	**D4**	3k. black on yellow	4·00	£180
D41	**D4**	12k. black on yellow	50·00	£20000

For later issues of 1947 to 1964 see Germany: Allied Occupation (French Zone).

Pt. 1

BAGHDAD

A city in Iraq. Special stamps issued during British occupation in the War of 1914–18.

1917. 16 annas = 1 rupee.

1917. Various issues of Turkey surch **BAGHDAD IN BRITISH OCCUPATION** and new value in annas. A. Pictorial issues of 1913.

1	**32**	¼a. on 2pa. red	£325	£375
2	**34**	¼a. on 5pa. purple	£225	£250
3	-	½a. on 10pa. green (No. 516)	£1200	£1400
4	**31**	½a. on 10pa. green	£2500	£2750
5	-	1a. on 20pa. red (No. 504)	£800	£900
6	-	2a. on 1pi. blue (No. 518)	£375	£400

B. As last, but optd with small star.

7		1a. on 20pa. red	£550	£600
8		2a. on 1pi. blue	£6500	£7000

C. Postal Jubilee issue.

9	**60**	½a. on 10pa. red	£850	£950
10b	**60**	1a. on 20pa. blue	£2000	£2500
11b	**60**	2a. on 1pi. black & violet	£250	£275

D. Optd with Turkish letter "B".

12	**30**	2a. on 1pi. blue	£950	£1100

E. Optd with star and Arabic date within crescent.

13		½a. on 10pa. green	£225	£250
14		1a. on 20pa. red	£800	£850
15	**23**	1a. on 20pa. red	£850	£950
16	**21**	1a. on 20pa. red (No. N185)	£7500	£9500
17	**30**	2a. on 1pi. blue	£250	£275
18	**21**	2a. on 1pi. blue	£375	£425

F. Optd as last, but with date between star and crescent.

19	**23**	½a. on 10pa. green	£250	£300
20	**60**	½a. on 10pa. red	£375	£400
21	**30**	1a. on 20pa. green	£250	£300
22	**28**	1a. on 20pa. red	£850	£900
23	**15**	1a. on 10pa. on 20pa. red	£425	£450
24	**30**	2a. on 1pi. blue	£375	£425
25	**28**	2a. on 1pi. blue	£3000	£3250

Pt. 1

BAHAMAS

A group of islands in the Br. W. Indies, S.E. of Florida. Self-Government introduced on 7 January 1964. The islands became an independent member of the British Commonwealth on 10 July 1973.

1859. 12 pence = 1 shilling; 20 shillings = 1 pound.
1966. 100 cents = 1 dollar.

1

1859. Imperf.

2	**1**	1d. red	65·00	£1500

2 **3**

1860. Perf.

33	**1**	1d. red	70·00	15·00
26	**2**	4d. red	£300	60·00
31	**2**	6d. violet	£160	60·00
39ba	**3**	1s. green	8·00	9·50

1883. Surch **FOURPENCE**.

45	**2**	4d. on 6d. violet	£550	£400

5

1884

48	**5**	1d. red	7·50	2·00
52	**5**	2½d. blue	11·00	1·75
53	**5**	4d. yellow	9·50	4·00
54	**5**	6d. mauve	6·00	35·00
56	**5**	5s. green	85·00	95·00
57	**5**	£1 red	£275	£225

6 Queen's Staircase, Nassau

1901

111	**6**	1d. black and red	3·50	3·50
76a	**6**	3d. purple on buff	7·00	9·00
77	**6**	3d. black and brown	2·75	2·25
59	**6**	5d. black and orange	8·50	50·00
78	**6**	5d. black and mauve	3·50	5·50
113	**6**	2s. black and blue	22·00	22·00
61	**6**	3s. black and green	50·00	65·00

7

1902

71	**7**	½d. green	5·00	3·25
62	**7**	1d. red	1·50	1·50
63	**7**	2½d. blue	8·00	1·25
64	**7**	4d. yellow	15·00	60·00
66	**7**	6d. brown	6·00	28·00
67	**7**	1s. black and red	22·00	55·00
69	**7**	5s. purple and blue	75·00	95·00
70	**7**	£1 green and black	£300	£350

8

1912

115	**8**	½d. green	50	40
116	**8**	1d. red	1·00	15
117	**8**	1½d. brown	13·00	1·00
118	**8**	2d. grey	1·50	2·25
119	**8**	2½d. blue	1·00	2·25
120	**8**	3d. purple on yellow	6·50	16·00
121	**8**	4d. yellow	1·50	2·75
122	**8**	6d. brown	70	1·25
123	**8**	1s. black and red	6·00	5·50
124	**8**	5s. purple and blue	42·00	65·00
125	**8**	£1 green and black	£170	£350

1917. Optd **1.1.17.** and Red Cross.

90	**6**	1d. black and red	40	2·00

1918. Optd **WAR TAX** in one line.

96	**8**	½d. green	1·75	1·75
93		1d. black and red	3·75	8·50
97	**8**	1d. red	3·50	35
98	**6**	3d. purple on yellow	1·00	1·50
100	**6**	3d. black and brown	1·00	5·00
99	**8**	1s. black and red	11·00	5·00

1919. Optd **WAR CHARITY 3.6.18.**

101		1d. black and red	30	2·50

1919. Optd **WAR TAX** in two lines.

102	**8**	½d. green	30	1·25
103	**8**	1d. red	1·50	1·50
105	**6**	3d. black and brown	1·00	8·00
104	**8**	1s. black and red	27·00	55·00

16

1920. Peace Celebration.

106	**16**	½d. green	1·00	5·50
107	**16**	1d. red	2·75	1·00
108	**16**	2d. grey	2·75	7·50
109	**16**	3d. brown	2·75	9·00
110	**16**	1s. green	15·00	38·00

17 Seal of the Colony

1930. Tercentenary of the Colony.

126	**17**	1d. black and red	3·50	2·75
127	**17**	3d. black and brown	5·50	15·00
128	**17**	5d. black and violet	5·50	15·00
129	**17**	2s. black and blue	18·00	50·00
130	**17**	3s. black and green	48·00	85·00

1931. As T **17**, but without dates at top.

131b		2s. black and blue	15·00	9·00
132a		3s. black and green	13·00	4·50

1935. Silver Jubilee. As T **13** of Antigua.

141		1½d. blue and red	1·00	3·50
142		2½d. brown and blue	5·00	9·50
143		6d. blue and olive	7·00	15·00
144		1s. grey and purple	7·00	14·00

19 Greater Flamingo (in flight)

1935

145	**19**	8d. blue and red	8·50	3·25

1937. Coronation. As T **2** of Aden.

146		½d. green	15	15
147		1½d. brown	40	1·10
148		2½d. blue	55	1·10

20 King George VI **21** Sea Garden, Nassau

1938

149	**20**	½d. green	2·75	1·25
149e	**20**	½d. purple	1·00	3·75
150	**20**	1d. red	8·50	2·00
150ab	**20**	1d. grey	60	70
151	**20**	1½d. brown	1·50	1·25
152	**20**	2d. grey	19·00	3·50
152b	**20**	2d. red	1·00	65
152c	**20**	2d. green	2·00	80
153	**20**	2½d. blue	3·25	1·50
153a	**20**	2½d. violet	1·25	1·25
154	**20**	3d. violet	16·00	3·00
154a	**20**	3d. blue	2·50	1·50
154b	**20**	3d. red	2·25	3·25
158	**21**	4d. blue and orange	1·50	1·00
159	-	6d. green and blue	1·25	1·00
160	-	8d. blue and red	16·00	3·50
154c	**20**	10d. orange	2·50	20
155d	**20**	1s. black and red	17·00	1·50
156e	**20**	5s. purple and blue	24·00	24·00
157a	**20**	£1 green and black	60·00	55·00

DESIGNS—As Type **21**: 6d. Fort Charlotte; 8d. Greater flamingos.

1940. Surch **3d.**

161	**20**	3d. on 2½d. blue	1·50	3·00

1942. 450th Anniv of Landing of Columbus. Optd **1492 LANDFALL OF COLUMBUS 1942**.

162		½d. green	30	60
163		1d. grey	30	60
164		1½d. brown	40	60
165		2d. red	50	65
166		2½d. blue	50	65
167		3d. blue	30	65
168	**21**	4d. blue and orange	40	90
169	-	6d. green & blue (No. 159)	40	1·75
170	-	8d. blue and red (No. 160)	3·50	70

171	20	1s. black and red	12·00	5·00
172a	17	2s. black and blue	8·50	10·00
173	17	3s. black and green	9·00	6·50
174a	20	5s. purple and blue	23·00	14·00
175a	20	£1 green and black	30·00	25·00

1946. Victory. As T **9** of Aden.

176	1½d. brown	10	60
177	3d. blue	10	60

26 Infant Welfare Clinic

1948. Tercentenary of Settlement of Island of Eleuthera. Inscr as in T **26**.

178	26	½d. orange	40	1·75
179	-	1d. olive	40	35
180	-	1½d. yellow	40	80
181	-	2d. red	40	40
182	-	2½d. brown	70	75
183	-	3d. blue	2·50	85
184	-	4d. black	60	70
185	-	6d. green	2·50	80
186	-	8d. violet	1·25	70
187	-	10d. red	1·25	35
188	-	1s. brown	3·00	50
189	-	2s. purple	5·00	8·50
190	-	3s. blue	13·00	8·50
191	-	5s. mauve	20·00	5·50
192	-	10s. grey	17·00	13·00
193	-	£1 red	17·00	17·00

DESIGNS: 1d. Agriculture; 1½d. Sisal; 2d. Straw work; 2½d. Dairy; 3d. Fishing fleet; 4d. Island settlement; 6d. Tuna fishing; 8d. Paradise Beach; 10d. Modern hotels; 1s. Yacht racing; 2s. Water sports—skiing; 3s. Shipbuilding; 5s. Transportation; 10s. Salt production; £1 Parliament Buildings.

1948. Silver Wedding. As T **10/11** of Aden.

194	1½d. brown	20	25
195	£1 grey	45·00	32·00

1949. 75th Anniv of U.P.U. As T **20/23** of Antigua.

196	2½d. violet	35	75
197	3d. blue	2·25	3·50
198	6d. blue	55	3·25
199	1s. red	55	75

1953. Coronation. As T **13** of Aden.

200	6d. black and blue	1·50	60

42 Infant Welfare Clinic

1954. Designs as Nos. 178/93 but with portrait of Queen Elizabeth II and without commemorative inscr as in T **42**.

201	42	½d. black and red	10	1·50
202	-	1d. olive and brown	10	30
203	-	1½d. black and blue	15	80
204	-	2d. brown and green	15	30
205	-	3d. black and red	65	1·25
206	-	4d. turquoise and purple	30	30
207	-	5d. brown and blue	1·40	2·25
208	-	6d. blue and black	2·25	20
209	-	8d. black and lilac	70	40
210	-	10d. black and blue	30	10
211	-	1s. blue and brown	1·75	10
212	-	2s. orange and black	3·00	70
213	-	2s.6d. black and blue	3·50	2·00
214	-	5s. green and orange	22·00	75
215	-	10s. black and slate	35·00	2·50
216	-	£1 black and violet	29·00	7·00

DESIGNS: 1½d. Hatchet Bay, Eleuthera; 4d. Water sports—skiing; 5d. Dairy; 6d. Transportation; 2s. Sisal; 2s.6d. Shipbuilding; 5s. Tuna fishing. Other values the same as for the corresponding values in Nos. 178/93.

43 Queen Elizabeth II

1959. Centenary of 1st Bahamas Postage Stamp.

217	43	1d. black and red	50	20
218	43	2d. black and green	50	1·00
219	43	6d. black and blue	60	40
220	43	10d. black and brown	60	1·00

44 Christ Church Cathedral

1962. Centenary of Nassau.

221	44	8d. green	65	55
222		10d. violet	65	25

DESIGN: 10d. Nassau Public Library.

1963. Freedom from Hunger. As T **28** of Aden.

223	8d. sepia	40	40

1963. Bahamas Talks. Nos. 209/10 optd **BAHAMAS TALKS 1962.**

224	8d. black and lilac	65	75
225	10d. black and blue	65	75

1963. Centenary of Red Cross. As T **33** of Antigua.

226	1d. red and black	50	75
227	10d. red and blue	1·75	2·50

1964. New Constitution. Nos. 201/16 optd **NEW CONSTITUTION 1964.**

228	42	½d. black and red	15	1·50
229	-	1d. olive and brown	15	15
230	-	1½d. blue and black	70	1·50
231	-	2d. brown and green	15	20
232	-	3d. black and red	2·00	1·75
233	-	4d. turquoise and purple	70	55
234	-	5d. brown and blue	70	1·50
235	-	6d. blue and black	3·25	30
236	-	8d. black and lilac	70	30
237	-	10d. black and blue	30	15
238	-	1s. blue and brown	1·50	15
239	-	2s. brown and black	2·00	1·75
240	-	2s.6d. black and blue	3·00	2·75
241	-	5s. green and orange	7·00	3·25
242	-	10s. black and slate	7·00	5·50
243	-	£1 black and violet	7·50	25·00

1964. 400th Birth Anniv of Shakespeare. As T **34** of Antigua.

244	6d. turquoise	30	10

1964. Olympic Games, Tokyo. No. 211 surch **8d.** and Olympic rings.

245	8d. on 1s. blue and brown	45	15

49 Colony's Badge

1965

247	49	½d. multicoloured	15	2·25
248	-	1d. slate, blue and orange	50	1·00
249	-	1½d. red, green and brown	15	3·75
250	-	2d. slate, green and blue	15	10
251	-	3d. red, blue and purple	4·50	20
252	-	4d. green, blue and brown	5·00	3·50
253	-	6d. green, blue and red	1·25	10
254	-	8d. purple, blue & bronze	50	30
255	-	10d. brown, green and violet	25	10
256a	-	1s. multicoloured	75	10
257	-	2s. brown, blue and green	1·00	1·25
258	-	2s.6d. olive, blue and red	2·50	3·00
259	-	5s. brown, blue and green	2·75	1·00
260	-	10s. red, blue and brown	16·00	3·50
261	-	£1 brown, blue and green	21·00	11·00

DESIGNS: 1d. Out Island regatta; 1½d. Hospital; 2d. High School; 3d. Greater flamingo; 4d. R.M.S. *Queen Elizabeth*; 6d. "Development"; 8d. Yachting; 10d. Public square; 1s. Sea garden; 2s. Old cannons at Fort Charlotte; 2s.6d. Sikorsky S-38 flying boat, 1929, and Boeing 707 airliner; 5s. Williamson film project, 1914, and undersea post office, 1939; 10s. Queen or pink conch; £1 Columbus's flagship.

1965. Centenary of I.T.U. As T **36** of Antigua.

262	1d. red and orange	15	10
263	2s. purple and olive	65	45

1965. No. 254 surch **9d.**

264	9d. on 8d. purple, blue & bronze	30	15

1965. I.C.Y. As T **37** of Antigua.

265	½d. purple and turquoise	10	1·10
266	1s. green and lavender	30	40

1966. Churchill Commemoration. As T **38** of Antigua.

267	½d. blue	10	75
268	2d. green	50	30
269	10d. brown	85	85
270	1s. violet	85	1·40

1966. Royal Visit. As T **39** of Antigua but inscr "to the Caribbean" omitted.

271	6d. black and blue	1·00	50
272	1s. black and mauve	1·25	1·25

1966. Decimal currency. Nos. 247/61 surch.

273	49	1c. on ½d. multicoloured	10	30
274	-	2c. on 1d. slate, blue and orange	75	30
275	-	3c. on 2d. slate, green and blue	10	10
276	-	4c. on 3d. red, blue and purple	2·00	20
277	-	5c. on 4d. green, blue and brown	2·00	3·00
278	-	8c. on 6d. green, blue and red	20	20
279	-	10c. on 8d. purple, blue and bronze	30	75
280	-	11c. on 1½d. red, green and brown	15	30
281	-	12c. on 10d. brown, green and violet	15	10
282	-	15c. on 1s. multicoloured	25	10
283	-	22c. on 2s. brown, blue and green	60	1·25
284	-	50c. on 2s.6d. olive, blue and red	1·00	1·40
285	-	$1 on 5s. brown, blue and green	1·75	1·50
286	-	$2 on 10s. red, blue and brown	7·50	4·50
287	-	$3 on £1 brown, blue and red	7·50	4·50

1966. World Cup Football Championships. As T **40** of Antigua.

288	8c. multicoloured	35	15
289	15c. multicoloured	40	25

1966. Inauguration of W.H.O. Headquarters, Geneva. As T **41** of Antigua.

290	11c. black, green and blue	50	90
291	15c. black, purple and ochre	50	50

1966. 20th Anniv of UNESCO As T **54/6** of Antigua.

292	3c. multicoloured	10	10
293	15c. yellow, violet and olive	35	20
294	$1 black, purple and orange	1·10	2·00

1967. As Nos. 247/51, 253/9 and 261 but values in decimal currency, and new designs for 5c. and $2.

295	49	1c. multicoloured	10	3·25
296	-	2c. slate, blue and green	50	60
297	-	3c. slate, green and violet	10	10
298	-	4c. red, light blue and blue	4·75	50
299	-	5c. black, blue and purple	1·00	3·50
300	-	8c. green, blue and brown	2·75	10
301	-	10c. purple, blue and red	30	70
302	-	11c. red, green and blue	25	80
303	-	12c. brown, green and olive	25	10
304	-	15c. multicoloured	55	10
305	-	22c. brown, blue and red	70	65
306	-	50c. olive, blue and green	2·75	1·00
307	-	$1 maroon, blue and purple	2·00	60
308	-	$2 multicoloured	13·00	3·00
309	-	$3 brown, blue and purple	3·75	2·00

NEW DESIGNS: 5c. *Oceanic*; $2 Conch shell (different).

69 Bahamas Crest

1967. Diamond Jubilee of World Scouting. Multicoloured.

310	3c. Type **69**	35	15
311	15c. Scout badge	40	15

71 Globe and Emblem

1968. Human Rights Year. Multicoloured.

312	3c. Type **71**	10	10
313	12c. Scales of Justice and emblem	20	10
314	$1 Bahamas Crest and emblem	70	80

74 Golf

1968. Tourism. Multicoloured.

315	5c. Type **74**	1·75	1·75
316	11c. Yachting	1·25	50
317	15c. Horse-racing	1·75	55
318	50c. Water-skiing	2·50	7·00

78 Racing Yacht and Olympic Monument

1968. Olympic Games, Mexico City.

319	78	5c. brown, yellow and green	40	75
320	-	11c. multicoloured	40	25
321	-	50c. multicoloured	60	1·25
322	78	$1 grey, blue and violet	2·00	2·25

DESIGNS: 11c. Long jumping and Olympic Monument; 50c. Running and Olympic Monument.

81 Legislative Building

1968. 14th Commonwealth Parliamentary Conference. Multicoloured.

323	3c. Type **81**	10	30
324	10c. Bahamas Mace and Westminster Clock Tower (vert)	15	30
325	12c. Local straw market (vert)	15	25
326	15c. Horse-drawn surrey	20	35

85 Obverse and reverse of $100 Gold Coin

1968. Gold Coins commemorating the first General Election under the New Constitution.

327	85	3c. red on gold	40	40
328	-	12c. green on gold	45	50
329	-	15c. purple on gold	50	60
330	-	$1 black on gold	1·25	4·50

OBVERSE AND REVERSE OF: 12c. $50 gold coin; 15c. $20 gold coins; $1, $10 gold coin.

89 First Flight Postcard of 1919

1969. 50th Anniv of Bahamas Airmail Services.

331	89	12c. multicoloured	50	50
332	-	15c. multicoloured	60	1·75

DESIGN: 15c. Sikorsky S-38 flying boat of 1929.

91 Game-fishing Boats

1969. Tourism. One Millionth Visitor to Bahamas. Multicoloured.

333	3c. Type **91**	25	10
334	11c. Paradise Beach	35	15
335	12c. "Sunfish" sailing boats	35	15
336	15c. Rawson Square and parade	45	25
MS337	130×96 mm. Nos. 333/6	2·75	4·00

92 *The Adoration of the Shepherds (Louis le Nain)*

1969. Christmas. Multicoloured.

338	3c. Type **92**		20	20
339	11c. *The Adoration of the Shepherds* (Poussin)		30	30
340	12c. *The Adoration of the Kings* (Gerard David)		30	20
341	15c. *The Adoration of the Kings* (Vincenzo Foppa)		30	65

93 *Badge of Girl Guides*

1970. Diamond Jubilee of Girl Guides' Association. Multicoloured.

342	3c. Type **93**	30	30
343	12c. Badge of Brownies	45	40
344	15c. Badge of Rangers	50	50

94 *New U.P.U. Headquarters and Emblem*

1970. New U.P.U. Headquarters Building.

345	**94**	3c. multicoloured	10	40
346	**94**	15c. multicoloured	20	60

95 *Coach and Globe*

1970. "Goodwill Caravan". Multicoloured.

347	3c. Type **95**	85	20
348	11c. Diesel train and globe	1·60	60
349	12c. *Canberra* (liner), yacht and globe	1·60	60
350	15c. B.A.C. One Eleven airliner and globe	1·60	1·75
MS351	165×125 mm. Nos. 347/50	9·50	17·00

96 *Nurse, Patients and Greater Flamingo*

1970. Centenary of British Red Cross. Multicoloured.

352	3c. Type **96**	1·00	50
353	15c. Hospital and blue marlin	1·00	1·75

97 *The Nativity (detail, Pittoni)*

1970. Christmas. Multicoloured.

354	3c. Type **97**	15	15
355	11c. *The Holy Family* (detail, Anton Raphael Mengs)	20	25
356	12c. *The Adoration of the Shepherds* (detail, Giorgione)	20	20
357	15c. *The Adoration of the Shepherds* (detail, School of Seville)	30	75
MS358	114×140 mm. Nos. 354/7	1·40	4·25

98 *International Airport*

1971. Multicoloured.

359	1c. Type **98**	10	30
360	2c. Breadfruit	15	35
361	3c. Straw market	15	30
362	4c. Hawksbill turtle	1·75	11·00
363	5c. Nassau grouper	60	60
364	6c. As 4c.	45	1·25
365	7c. Hibiscus	2·00	5·00
366	8c. Yellow elder	60	1·50
367	10c. Bahamian sponge boat	55	30
368	11c. Greater flamingos	2·50	3·25
369	12c. As 7c.	2·00	3·00
370	15c. Bonefish	55	55
466	16c. As 7c.	1·25	35
371	18c. Royal poinciana	65	65
467a	21c. As 2c.	80	1·25
372	22c. As 18c.	2·75	16·00
468	25c. As 4c.	90	40
469	40c. As 10c.	8·00	75
470	50c. Post Office, Nassau	1·50	1·75
471	$1 Pineapple (vert)	1·50	2·50
399	$2 Crawfish (vert)	1·50	6·00
473	$3 Junkanoo (vert)	1·50	9·50

99 *Snowflake*

1971. Christmas.

377	**99**	3c. purple, orange and gold	10	10
378	-	11c. blue and gold	20	15
379	-	15c. multicoloured	20	20
380	-	18c. blue, ultram & gold	25	25
MS381	126×95 mm. Nos. 377/80		1·25	1·50

DESIGNS: 11c. *Peace on Earth* (doves); 15c. *Arms of Bahamas and holly*; 18c. *Starlit lagoon*.

100 *High Jumping*

1972. Olympic Games, Munich. Multicoloured.

382	10c. Type **100**	35	60
383	11c. Cycling	1·75	75
384	15c. Running	60	75
385	18c. Sailing	95	1·25
MS386	127×95 mm. Nos. 382/5	3·25	3·00

101 *Shepherd*

1972. Christmas. Multicoloured.

387	3c. Type **101**	10	10
388	6c. Bells	10	10
389	15c. Holly and Cross	15	20
390	20c. Poinsettia	25	45
MS391	108×140 mm. Nos. 387/90	80	3·00

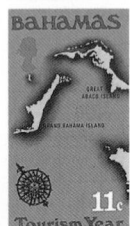

102 *Northerly Bahama Islands*

1972. Tourism Year of the Americas. Sheet 133×105 mm, containing T **102**.

MS392 11, 15, 18 and 50c. multicoloured
4·00 3·25

The four designs are printed, *se-tenant* in **MS**392, forming a composite map design of the Bahamas.

1972. Royal Silver Wedding. As T **52** of Ascension, but with mace and galleon in background.

393	11c. pink	15	15
394	18c. violet	15	20

104 *Weather Satellite*

1973. Centenary of I.M.O./W.M.O. Multicoloured.

410	15c. Type **104**	50	25
411	18c. Weather radar	60	35

105 *C. A. Bain (national hero)*

1973. Independence. Multicoloured.

412	3c. Type **105**	10	10
413	11c. Coat of arms	15	10
414	15c. Bahamas flag	20	15
415	$1 Governor-General, M. B. Butler	65	1·00
MS416	86×121 mm. Nos. 412/15	2·00	2·00

106 *The Virgin in Prayer (Sassoferrato)*

1973. Christmas. Multicoloured.

417	3c. Type **106**	10	10
418	11c. *Virgin and Child with St. John* (Filippino Lippi)	15	15
419	15c. *A Choir of Angels* (Simon Marmion)	15	15
420	18c. *The Two Trinities* (Murillo)	25	25
MS421	120×99 mm. Nos. 417/20	1·75	1·40

107 *"Agriculture and Sciences"*

1974. 25th Anniv of University of West Indies. Multicoloured.

422	15c. Type **107**	20	25
423	18c. "Arts, Engineering and General Studies"	25	30

108 *U.P.U. Monument, Berne*

1974. Centenary of U.P.U.

424	**108**	3c. multicoloured	10	15
425	-	13c. multicoloured (vert)	20	25
426	-	14c. multicoloured	20	30
427	-	18c. multicoloured (vert)	25	40
MS428	128×95 mm. Nos. 424/7		80	1·60

DESIGNS—As Type **108** but showing different arrangements of the U.P.U. Monument.

109 *Roseate Spoonbills*

1974. 15th Anniv of Bahamas National Trust. Multicoloured.

429	13c. Type **109**	1·40	90
430	14c. White-crowned pigeon	1·40	65
431	21c. White-tailed tropic birds	1·75	1·00
432	36c. Cuban amazon ("Bahamian parrot")	1·75	4·50
MS433	123×120 mm. Nos. 429/32	8·00	12·00

110 *The Holy Family (Jacques de Stella)*

1974. Christmas. Multicoloured.

434	8c. Type **110**	10	10
435	10c. *Madonna and Child* (16th-century Brescian School)	15	15
436	12c. *Virgin and Child with St. John the Baptist and St. Catherine* (Previtali)	15	15
437	21c. *Virgin and Child with Angels* (Previtali)	25	30
MS438	126×105 mm. Nos. 434/7	1·00	1·40

111 *Anteos maerula*

1975. Butterflies. Multicoloured.

439	3c. Type **111**	25	15
440	14c. *Eurema nicippe*	80	50
441	18c. *Papilio andraemon*	95	65
442	21c. *Euptoieta hegesia*	1·10	85
MS443	194×94 mm. Nos. 439/42	7·50	6·50

112 *Sheep Husbandry*

1975. Economic Diversification. Multicoloured.

444	3c. Type **112**	10	10
445	14c. Electric-reel fishing (vert)	20	15
446	18c. Farming	25	20
447	21c. Oil refinery (vert)	80	35
MS448	127×94 mm. Nos. 444/7	1·25	1·50

113 *Rowena Rand (evangelist)*

1975. International Women's Year.

449	**113**	14c. brown, lt blue & bl	20	50
450	-	18c. yellow, grn & brn	25	75

DESIGN: 18c. I.W.Y. symbol and harvest symbol.

114 *Adoration of the Shepherds (Perugino)*

1975. Christmas. Multicoloured.

451	3c. Type **114**	15	60
452	8c. *Adoration of the Magi* (Ghirlandaio)	20	10
453	18c. As 8c.	55	90
454	21c. Type **114**	60	95
MS455	142×107 mm. Nos. 451/4	2·25	4·50

115 *Telephones, 1876 and 1976*

1976. Centenary of Telephone. Multicoloured.

456	3c. Type **115**	20	50
457	16c. Radio-telephone link, Deleporte	40	50
458	21c. Alexander Graham Bell	50	65
459	25c. Satellite	60	1·00

116 Map of North America

1976. Bicentenary of American Revolution. Multicoloured.
475	16c. Type **116**		30	30
476	$1 John Murray, Earl of Dunmore		1·50	1·75
MS477	127×100 mm. Nos. 476×4		6·00	7·50

117 Cycling

1976. Olympic Games, Montreal.
478	**117**	8c. mauve, blue and light blue	1·60	20
479	–	16c. orange, brown and light blue	35	30
480	–	25c. blue, mauve and light blue	45	50
481	–	40c. brown, orange and blue	55	1·60
MS482	100×126 mm. Nos. 478/81		3·00	3·25

DESIGNS: 16c. Jumping; 25c. Sailing; 40c. Boxing.

118 Virgin and Child (detail, Lippi)

1976. Christmas. Multicoloured.
483	3c. Type **118**		10	10
484	21c. *Adoration of the Shepherds* (School of Seville)		30	15
485	25c. *Adoration of the Kings* (detail, Foppa)		30	20
486	40c. *Virgin and Child* (detail, Vivarini)		40	40
MS487	107×127 mm. Nos. 483/6		1·00	2·00

119 Queen beneath Cloth of Gold Canopy

1977. Silver Jubilee. Multicoloured.
488	8c. Type **119**		10	10
489	16c. The Crowning		15	10
490	21c. Taking the Oath		15	15
491	40c. Queen with sceptre and orb		25	30
MS492	122×90 mm. Nos. 488/91		80	1·25

120 Featherduster

1977. Marine Life. Multicoloured.
493	3c. Type **120**		40	15
494	8c. Porkfish and cave		60	20
495	16c. Elkhorn coral		70	40
496	21c. Soft coral and sponge		80	55
MS497	119×93 mm. Nos. 493/6		2·75	4·50

121 Scouts around Campfire and Home-made Shower

1977. Sixth Caribbean Scout Jamboree. Multicoloured.
498	16c. Type **121**		75	30
499	21c. Boating scenes		85	35

1977. Royal Visit. Nos. 488/91 optd **Royal Visit October 1977.**
500	8c. Type **119**		15	10

501	16c. The Crowning		20	15
502	21c. Taking the Oath		25	25
503	40c. Queen with sceptre and orb		30	40
MS504	122×90 mm. Nos. 500/3		1·25	1·50

123 Virgin and Child

1977. Christmas. Multicoloured.
505	3c. Type **123**		10	10
506	16c. The Magi		30	25
507	21c. Nativity scene		30	40
508	25c. The Magi and star		40	45
MS509	136×74 mm. Nos. 505/8		1·00	1·75

124 Public Library, Nassau (Colonial)

1978. Architectural Heritage.
510	**124**	3c. black and green	10	10
511	–	8c. black and blue	15	10
512	–	16c. black and mauve	20	20
513	–	18c. black and pink	25	30
MS514	91×91 mm. Nos. 510/13		70	1·60

DESIGNS: 8c. St. Matthew's Church (Gothic); 16c. Government House (Colonial); 18c. Hermitage, Cat Island (Spanish).

125 Sceptre, St. Edward's Crown and Orb

1978. 25th Anniv of Coronation. Multicoloured.
515	16c. Type **125**		15	10
516	$1 Queen in Coronation regalia		50	65
MS517	147×96 mm. Nos. 515/16		1·25	1·00

126 Coat of Arms within Wreath and Three Ships

1978. Christmas.
532	**126**	5c. gold, lake and red	15	10
533	–	21c. gold, deep blue and blue	30	25
MS534	95×95 mm. Nos. 532/3		1·75	5·50

DESIGN: 21c. Three angels with trumpets.

127 Child reaching for Adult

1979. International Year of the Child. Multicoloured.
535	5c. Type **127**		20	15
536	16c. Boys playing leapfrog		40	45
537	21c. Girls skipping		50	60
538	25c. Bricks with I.Y.C. emblem		50	75
MS539	101×125 mm. Nos. 535/8		1·40	3·25

128 Sir Rowland Hill and Penny Black

1979. Death Centenary of Sir Rowland Hill. Multicoloured.
540	10c. Type **128**		30	10
541	21c. Printing press, 1840, and 6d. stamp of 1862		40	30
542	25c. Great Britain 1856 6d. with "A 05" (Nassau) cancellation, and 1840 2d. Blue		40	50
543	40c. Early mailboat and 1d. stamp of 1859		45	70
MS544	115×80 mm. Nos. 540/3		2·00	3·25

129 Commemorative Plaque and Map of Bahamas

1979. 250th Anniv of Parliament. Multicoloured.
545	16c. Type **129**		35	10
546	21c. Parliament buildings		40	15
547	25c. Legislative Chamber		40	15
548	$1 Senate Chamber		80	1·00
MS549	116×89 mm. Nos. 545/8		2·50	3·75

130 Goombay Carnival Headdress

1979. Christmas.
550	**130**	5c. multicoloured	10	10
551	–	10c. multicoloured	15	10
552	–	16c. multicoloured	20	10
553	–	21c. multicoloured	20	20
554	–	25c. multicoloured	25	20
555	–	40c. multicoloured	30	45
MS556	50×88 mm. Nos. 550/5		2·00	3·00

DESIGNS: 10c. to 40c. Various Carnival costumes.

131 Landfall of Columbus, 1492

1980. Multicoloured.
557	1c. Type **131**		1·25	2·50
558	3c. Blackbeard the pirate		30	2·50
559	5c. Eleutheran Adventurers (Articles and Orders, 1647)		30	1·25
560	10c. Ceremonial mace		20	40
561	12c. The Loyalists, 1783–88		30	2·50
562	15c. Slave trading, Vendue House		5·50	1·25
563	16c. Wrecking in the 1800s		1·75	1·25
564	18c. Blockade running (American Civil War)		2·50	2·50
565	21c. Bootlegging, 1919–29		60	2·50
566	25c. Pineapple cultivation		40	2·50
567	40c. Sponge clipping		70	1·50
568	50c. Tourist development		75	1·50
569	$1 Modern agriculture		75	4·25
570	$2 Boeing 737 and sea transport		4·25	5·50
571	$3 Banking (Central Bank)		1·25	4·00
572	$5 Independence, 10 July 1973		1·50	6·00

132 Virgin and Child

1980. Christmas. Straw-work. Multicoloured.
573	5c. Type **132**		10	10
574	21c. Three Kings		25	10
575	25c. Angel		25	15
576	$1 Christmas tree		75	85
MS577	168×105 mm. Nos. 573/6		1·25	2·25

133 Disabled Persons with Walking Stick

1981. International Year of Disabled People. Multicoloured.
578	5c. Type **133**		10	10
579	$1 Disabled person in wheelchair		1·25	1·25
MS580	120×60 mm. Nos. 578/9		1·40	2·50

134 Grand Bahama Tracking Site

1981. Space Exploration. Multicoloured.
581	10c. Type **134**		30	15
582	20c. Satellite view of Bahamas (vert)		60	50
583	25c. Satelite view of Eleuthera		65	60
584	50c. Satellite view of Andros and New Province (vert)		1·00	1·25
MS585	115×99 mm. Nos. 581/4		2·25	2·25

135 Prince Charles and Lady Diana Spencer

1981. Royal Wedding. Multicoloured.
586	30c. Type **135**		1·50	30
587	$2 Prince Charles and Prime Minister Pindling		1·50	1·25
MS588	142×120 mm. Nos. 586/7		5·00	1·25

136 Bahamas Pintail ("Bahama Duck")

1981. Wildlife (1st series). Birds. Multicoloured.
589	5c. Type **136**		1·25	60
590	20c. Reddish egret		1·75	60
591	25c. Brown booby		1·75	65
592	$1 Black-billed whistling duck ("West Indian Tree Duck")		3·50	7·50
MS593	100×74 mm. Nos. 589/92		8·50	8·50

See also Nos. 626/30, 653/7 and 690/4.

1981. Commonwealth Finance Ministers' Meeting. Nos. 559/60, 566 and 568 optd **COMMONWEALTH FINANCE MINISTERS' MEETING 21–23 SEPTEMBER 1981.**
594	5c. Eleutheran Adventures (Articles and Orders, 1647)		15	15
595	10c. Ceremonial mace		20	20
596	25c. Pineapple cultivation		50	60
597	50c. Tourist development		85	1·50

138 Poultry

1981. World Food Day. Multicoloured.
598	5c. Type **138**		20	10
599	20c. Sheep		35	35
600	30c. Lobsters		45	50
601	50c. Pigs		75	1·50
MS602	115×63 mm. Nos. 598/601		1·50	3·25

139 Father Christmas

1981. Christmas. Multicoloured.
603	5c. Type **139**		55	85
604	5c. Mother and child		55	85
605	5c. St. Nicholas, Holland		55	85

606	25c. Lussilbruden, Sweden	70	95
607	25c. Mother and child (different)	70	95
608	25c. King Wenceslas, Czechoslovakia	70	95
609	30c. Mother with child on knee	70	95
610	30c. Mother carrying child	70	95
611	$1 Christkindl Angel, Germany	1·00	1·50

140 Robert Koch

1982. Centenary of Discovery of Tubercle Bacillus by Robert Koch.

612	**140**	5c. black, brown and lilac	75	50
613	-	16c. black, brown & orge	1·40	50
614	-	21c. multicoloured	1·60	55
615	-	$1 multicoloured	3·00	7·50
MS616	94×97 mm. Nos. 612/15		6·00	7·50

DESIGNS: 16c. Stylised infected person; 21c. Early and modern microscopes; $1 Mantoux test.

141 Greater Flamingo (male)

1982. Greater Flamingos. Multicoloured.

617	25c. Type **141**	1·60	1·00
618	25c. Female	1·60	1·00
619	25c. Female with nestling	1·60	1·00
620	25c. Juvenile	1·60	1·00
621	25c. Immature bird	1·60	1·00

142 Lady Diana Spencer at Ascot, June, 1981

1982. 21st Birthday of Princess of Wales. Multicoloured.

622	16c. Bahamas coat of arms	20	10
623	25c. Type **142**	45	15
624	40c. Bride and Earl Spencer arriving at St. Paul's	60	20
625	$1 Formal portrait	1·00	1·25

1982. Wildlife (2nd series). Mammals. As T **136**. Multicoloured.

626	10c. Buffy flower bat	1·00	15
627	16c. Bahamian hutia	1·25	25
628	21c. Common racoon	1·50	55
629	$1 Common dolphin	3·00	1·90
MS630	115×76 mm. Nos. 626/9	6·00	3·50

143 House of Assembly Plaque

1982. 28th Commonwealth Parliamentary Association Conference. Multicoloured.

631	5c. Type **143**	15	10
632	25c. Association coat of arms	50	35
633	40c. Coat of arms	80	60
634	50c. House of Assembly	1·10	75

144 Wesley Methodist Church, Baillou Hill Road

1982. Christmas. Churches. Multicoloured.

635	5c. Type **144**	10	20
636	12c. Centreville Seventh Day Adventist Church	15	20
637	15c. The Church of God of Prophecy, East Street	15	30
638	21c. Bethel Baptist Church, Meeting Street	15	30
639	25c. St. Francis Xavier Catholic Church, Highbury Park	15	50
640	$1 Holy Cross Anglican Church, Highbury Park	60	3·00

145 Prime Minister Lyndon O. Pindling

1983. Commonwealth Day. Multicoloured.

641	5c. Type **145**	10	10
642	25c. Bahamian and Commonwealth flags	50	40
643	35c. Map showing position of Bahamas	50	50
644	$1 Ocean liner	1·10	1·40

1983. Nos. 562/5 surch.

645	20c. on 15c. Slave trading, Vendue House	50	35
646	31c. on 21c. Bootlegging, 1919–29	60	55
647	35c. on 16c. Wrecking in the 1800s	70	60
648	80c. on 18c. Blockade running (American Civil War)	80	1·40

147 Customs Officers and *Queen Elizabeth 2* (liner)

1983. 30th Anniv of Customs Co-operation Council. Multicoloured.

649	31c. Type **147**	1·50	45
650	$1 Customs officers and Lockheed L.1329 JetStar airliner	3·50	2·75

148 Raising the National Flag

1983. Tenth Anniv of Independence. Multicoloured.

651	**148**	$1 multicoloured	1·00	1·40
MS652	105×65 mm. No. 651		1·00	1·40

1983. Wildlife (3rd series). Butterflies. As T **136**.

653	5c. multicoloured	1·25	20
654	25c. multicoloured	2·00	40
655	31c. black, yellow and red	2·00	55
656	50c. multicoloured	2·00	85
MS657	120×80 mm. Nos. 653/6	6·50	6·00

DESIGNS: 5c. *Atalopedes carteri*; 25c. *Ascia monuste*; 31c. *Phoebis agarithe*; 50c. *Dryas julia*.

149 *Loyalist Dreams*

1983. Bicentenary of Arrival of American Loyalists in the Bahamas. Multicoloured.

658	5c. Type **149**	10	10
659	31c. New Plymouth, Abaco (horiz)	30	50
660	35c. New Plymouth Hotel (horiz)	40	70
661	50c. *Island Hope*	45	90
MS662	111×76 mm. Nos. 658/61	1·25	2·50

150 Consolidated PBY-5 Catalina flying boatf

1983. Air. Bicentenary of Manned Flight. Multicoloured.

663	10c. Type **150**	55	15
664	25c. Avro Tudor IV "Star Lion"	75	30
665	31c. Avro Lancastrian	85	45
666	35c. Consolidated Commodore flying boat	1·00	50

For these stamps without the Manned Flight logo, see Nos. 699/702.

151 "Christmas Bells" (Monica Pinder)

1983. Christmas. Children's Paintings. Multicoloured.

667	5c. Type **151**	15	10
668	20c. *Flamingo* (Cory Bullard)	35	30
669	25c. *Yellow Hibiscus with Christmas Candle* (Monique Bailey)	45	40
670	31c. *Santa goes-a-sailing* (Sabrina Seiler) (horiz)	55	45
671	35c. *Silhouette scene with Palm Trees* (James Blake)	60	50
672	50c. *Silhouette scene with Pelicans* (Erik Russell) (horiz)	70	70

152 1861 4d. Stamp

1984. 125th Anniv of First Bahamas Postage Stamp. Multicoloured.

673	5c. Type **152**	25	10
674	$1 1859 1d. stamp	1·75	1·50

153 *Trent I* (paddle-steamer)

1984. 250th Anniv of *Lloyd's List* (newspaper). Multicoloured.

675	5c. Type **153**	50	10
676	31c. *Orinoco II* (mail ship), 1886	1·00	60
677	35c. Cruise liners in Nassau harbour	1·10	75
678	50c. *Oropesa* (container ship)	1·40	1·60

154 Running

1984. Olympic Games, Los Angeles.

679	**154**	5c. green, black and gold	15	20
680	-	25c. blue, black and gold	50	50
681	-	31c. red, black and gold	55	60
682	-	$1 brown, black and gold	6·00	7·00
MS683	115×80 mm. Nos. 679/82		6·50	8·00

DESIGNS: 25c. Shot-putting; 31c. Boxing; $1 Basketball.

155 Bahamas and Caribbean Community Flags

1984. Fifth Conference of Caribbean Community Heads of Government.

684	**155**	50c. multicoloured	1·00	1·00

156 Bahama Woodstar

1984. 25th Anniv of National Trust. Multicoloured.

685	31c. Type **156**	3·75	3·75
686	31c. Belted kingfishers, greater flamingos and *Eleutherodactylus planirostris* (frog)	3·75	3·75
687	31c. Black-necked stilts, greater flamingos and *Phoebis sennae* (butterfly)	3·75	3·75
688	31c. *Urbanus proteus* (butterfly) and *Chelonia mydas* (turtle)	3·75	3·75
689	31c. Osprey and greater flamingos	3·75	3·75

Nos. 685/9 were printed together in horiz strips of 5 forming a composite design.

1984. Wildlife (4th series). Reptiles and Amphibians. As T **136**. Multicoloured.

690	5c. Allens' Cay iguana	85	20
691	25c. Curly-tailed lizard	1·75	60
692	35c. Greenhouse frog	2·00	85
693	50c. Atlantic green turtle	2·25	3·50
MS694	112×82 mm. Nos. 690/3	6·25	7·50

157 *The Holy Virgin with Jesus and Johannes* (19th-century porcelain plaque after Titian)

1984. Christmas. Religious Paintings. Multicoloured.

695	5c. Type **157**	30	10
696	31c. *Madonna with Child in Tropical Landscape* (aquarelle, Anais Colin)	1·00	60
697	35c. *The Holy Virgin with the Child* (miniature on ivory, Elena Caula)	1·25	65
MS698	116×76 mm. Nos. 695/7	2·50	4·25

1985. Air. As Nos. 663/6, but without Manned Flight logo.

699	10c. Type **150**	80	50
700	25c. Avro Tudor IV "Star Lion"	95	50
701	31c. Avro Lancastrian	95	60
702	35c. Consolidated Commodore flying boat	1·40	1·10

158 Brownie Emblem and Queen or Pink Conch

1985. International Youth Year. 75th Anniv of Girl Guide Movement. Multicoloured.

703	5c. Type **158**	60	50
704	25c. Tents and coconut palm	1·25	1·00
705	31c. Guide salute and greater flamingos	1·90	1·50
706	35c. Ranger emblem and marlin	1·90	1·50
MS707	95×74 mm. Nos. 703/6	5·50	7·50

159 Killdeer Plover

1985. Birth Bicent of John J. Audubon (ornithologist). Multicoloured.

708	5c. Type **159**	1·00	60
709	31c. *Mourning dove* (vert)	2·25	60
710	35c. *Mourning dove* (John J. Audubon) (vert)	2·25	65
711	$1 *Killdeer Plover* (John J. Audubon)	4·00	4·50

160 The Queen Mother at Christening of Peter Phillips, 1977

1985. Life and Times of Queen Elizabeth the Queen Mother. Multicoloured.

712	5c. Visiting Auckland, New Zealand, 1927	45	20
713	25c. Type **160**	70	40
714	35c. The Queen Mother attending church	75	55
715	50c. With Prince Henry at his christening (from photo by Lord Snowdon)	1·50	2·00
MS716	91×73 mm. $1.25, In horse-drawn carriage, Sark	2·75	1·90

161 Ears of Wheat and Emblems

1985. 40th Anniv of U.N.O. and F.A.O.

717	**161**	25c. multicoloured	1·25	70

162 Queen Elizabeth II

1985. Commonwealth Heads of Government Meeting, Nassau. Multicoloured.

718	31c. Type **162**	3·00	3·75
719	35c. Bahamas Prime Minister's flag and Commonwealth emblem	3·00	3·75

163 *Grandma's Christmas Bouquet* (Alton Roland Lowe)

1985. Christmas. Paintings by Alton Roland Lowe. Multicoloured.

736	5c. Type **163**	60	40
737	25c. *Junkanoo Romeo and Juliet* (vert)	1·50	1·00
738	31c. *Bunce Gal* (vert)	1·75	1·50
739	35c. *Home for Christmas*	1·75	3·25
MS740	110×68 mm. Nos. 736/9	2·75	3·25

1986. 60th Birthday of Queen Elizabeth II. As T **110** of Ascension. Multicoloured.

741	10c. Princess Elizabeth aged one, 1927	15	15
742	25c. The Coronation, 1953	30	30
743	35c. Queen making speech at Commonwealth Banquet, Bahamas, 1985	35	40
744	40c. In Djakova, Yugoslavia, 1972	35	45
745	$1 At Crown Agents Head Office, London, 1983	80	1·40

164 1980 1c. and 18c. Definitive Stamps

1986. "Ameripex '86" International Stamp Exn, Chicago.

746	**164**	5c. multicoloured	85	50
747	-	25c. multicoloured	2·00	50
748	-	31c. multicoloured	2·25	60
749	-	50c. multicoloured	3·00	5·00
750	-	$1 black, green and blue	3·25	6·00
MS751	80×80 mm. No. 750		4·00	4·00

DESIGNS—HORIZ: (showing Bahamas stamps)—25c. 1969 50th Anniv of Bahamas Airmail Service pair; 31c. 1976 Bicentenary of American Revolution 16c., 50c. 1981 Space Exploration miniature sheet. VERT: $1 Statue of Liberty.

No. 750 also commemorates the Centenary of the Statue of Liberty.

1986. Royal Wedding. As T **112** of Ascension. Multicoloured.

756	10c. Prince Andrew and Miss Sarah Ferguson	20	20
757	$1 Prince Andrew	1·25	2·10

165 Rock Beauty (juvenile)

1986. Fish. Multicoloured.

758A	5c. Type **165**	75	75
759A	10c. Stoplight parrotfish	80	1·00
760A	15c. Jackknife-fish	1·50	1·50
761A	20c. Flamefish	1·25	1·25
762A	25c. Peppermint basslet ("Swissguard basslet")	1·50	1·50
763A	30c. Spot-finned butterflyfish	1·10	1·50
764A	35c. Queen triggerfish	1·10	2·75
765B	40c. Four-eyed butterflyfish	1·10	1·60
766A	45c. Royal gramma ("Fairy basslet")	1·50	1·25
767A	50c. Queen angelfish	2·00	3·75
797	60c. Blue chromis	2·25	6·00
769B	$1 Spanish hogfish	4·50	3·00
799	$2 Harlequin bass	3·00	9·50
771A	$3 Black-barred soldierfish	6·00	7·00
772A	$5 Cherub angelfish ("Pygmy angelfish")	6·50	8·00
773A	$10 Red hind	20·00	27·00

166 Christ Church Cathedral, Nassau, 1861

1986. 125th Anniv of City of Nassau. Diocese and Cathedral. Multicoloured.

774	10c. Type **166**	30	20
775	40c. Christ Church Cathedral, 1986	70	80
MS776	75×100 mm. Nos. 774/5	4·25	6·50

167 Man and Boy looking at Crib

1986. Christmas. International Peace Year. Multicoloured.

777	10c. Type **167**	35	20
778	40c. Mary and Joseph journeying to Bethlehem	85	75
779	45c. Children praying and Star of Bethlehem	95	1·00
780	50c. Children exchanging gifts	1·00	2·50
MS781	95×90 mm. Nos. 777/80	8·50	11·00

168 Great Isaac Lighthouse

1987. Lighthouses. Multicoloured.

782	10c. Type **168**	3·00	85
783	40c. Bird Rock lighthouse	6·00	1·75
784	45c. Castle Island lighthouse	6·00	2·00
785	$1 "Hole in the Wall" lighthouse	9·00	12·00

169 Anne Bonney

1987. Pirates and Privateers of the Caribbean. Multicoloured.

786	10c. Type **169**	4·00	1·50
787	40c. Edward Teach ("Blackbeard")	7·00	4·00
788	45c. Captain Edward England	7·00	4·00
789	50c. Captain Woodes Rogers	7·50	8·00
MS790	75×95 mm. $1.25, Map of Bahamas and colonial coat of arms	14·00	7·50

170 Boeing 737

1987. Air. Aircraft. Multicoloured.

800	15c. Type **170**	3·50	1·50
801	40c. Boeing 757-200	4·50	2·25
802	45c. Airbus Industrie A300 B4-200	4·50	2·25
803	50c. Boeing 747-200	5·00	4·50

171 *Norway* (liner) and Catamaran

1987. Tourist Transport. Multicoloured.

804	40c. Type **171**	2·25	2·25
805	40c. Liners and speedboat	2·25	2·25
806	40c. Game fishing boat and cruising yacht	2·25	2·25
807	40c. Game fishing boat and racing yachts	2·25	2·25
808	40c. Fishing boat and schooner	2·25	2·25
809	40c. Hawker Siddeley H.S.748 airliner	2·25	2·25
810	40c. Boeing 737 and Boeing 727-200 airliners	2·25	2·25
811	40c. Beech 200 Super King Air aircraft and radio beacon	2·25	2·25
812	40c. Aircraft and Nassau control tower	2·25	2·25
813	40c. Helicopter and parked aircraft	2·25	2·25

Nos. 804/8 and 809/13 were each printed together, se-tenant, forming composite design.

172 *Cattleyopsis lindenii*

1987. Christmas. Orchids. Multicoloured.

814	10c. Type **172**	1·75	60
815	40c. *Encyclia lucayana*	3·00	1·50
816	45c. *Encyclia hodgeana*	3·00	1·50
817	50c. *Encyclia lleidae*	3·00	3·00
MS818	120×92 mm. Nos. 814/17	12·00	13·00

173 King Ferdinand and Queen Isabella of Spain

1988. 500th Anniv (1992) of Discovery of America by Columbus (1st issue). Multicoloured.

819	10c. Type **173**	85	60
820	40c. Columbus before Talavera Committee	1·75	1·75
821	45c. Lucayan village	1·90	1·90
822	50c. Lucayan potters	2·00	3·50
MS823	65×50 mm. $1.50, Map of Antilles, c. 1500	6·00	3·75

See also Nos. 844/8, 870/4, 908/12 and 933/7.

174 Whistling Ducks in Flight

1988. Black-billed Whistling Duck. Multicoloured.

824	5c. Type **174**	2·25	1·75
825	10c. Whistling duck in reeds	2·25	1·75
826	20c. Pair with brood	4·00	2·75
827	45c. Pair wading	6·00	3·25

175 Grantstown Cabin, c.1820

1988. 150th Anniv of Abolition of Slavery. Multicoloured.

828	10c. Type **175**	50	30
829	40c. Basket-making, Grantstown	1·25	95

176 Olympic Flame, High Jumping, Hammer throwing, Basketball and Gymnastics

1988. Olympic Games, Seoul. Designs taken from painting by James Martin. Multicoloured.

830	10c. Type **176**	90	50
831	40c. Athletics, archery, swimming, long jumping, weightlifting and boxing	90	60
832	45c. Javelin throwing, gymnastics, hurdling and shot put	90	60
833	$1 Athletics, hurdling, gymnastics and cycling	3·50	5·00
MS834	113×85 mm. Nos. 830/3	6·00	3·25

1988. 300th Anniv of Lloyd's of London. As T **123** of Ascension. Multicoloured.

835	10c. *Lloyd's List* of 1740	30	20
836	40c. Freeport Harbour (horiz)	2·00	60
837	45c. Space shuttle over Bahamas (horiz)	2·00	60
838	$1 *Yarmouth Castle* (freighter) on fire	3·50	3·00

177 "Oh Little Town of Bethlehem"

1988. Christmas. Carols. Multicoloured.

839	10c. Type **177**	55	30
840	40c. *Little Donkey*	1·50	75
841	45c. *Silent Night*	1·50	90
842	50c. *Hark the Herald Angels Sing*	1·60	2·25
MS843	88×108 mm. Nos. 839/42	2·75	2·25

1989. 500th Anniv (1992) of Discovery of America by Columbus (2nd issue). As T **173**. Multicoloured.

844	10c. Columbus drawing chart	2·25	85
845	40c. Types of caravel	3·25	1·75
846	45c. Early navigational instruments	3·25	1·75
847	50c. Arawak artefacts	3·25	5·00
MS848	64×64 mm. $1.50, Caravel under construction (from 15th-cent *Nuremburg Chronicles*)	2·50	2·50

178 Cuban Emerald

1989. Hummingbirds. Multicoloured.

849	10c. Type **178**	1·75	1·25
850	40c. Ruby-throated hummingbird	3·00	2·00

851	45c. Bahama woodstar	3·00	2·00
852	50c. Rufous hummingbird	3·25	4·50

179 Teaching Water Safety

1989. 125th Anniv of Int Red Cross. Multicoloured.

853	10c. Type **179**	1·75	50
854	$1 Henri Dunant (founder) and Battle of Solferino	3·75	5·50

1989. 20th Anniv of First Manned Landing on Moon. As T **126** of Ascension. Multicoloured.

855	10c. "Apollo 8" Communications Station, Grand Bahama	1·25	50
856	40c. Crew of "Apollo 8" (30×30 mm)	2·00	90
857	45c. "Apollo 8" emblem (30×30 mm)	2·00	90
858	$1 The Earth seen from "Apollo 8"	2·75	5·00
MS859	100×83 mm. $2 "Apollo 11" astronauts in training, Manned Spacecraft Centre, Houston	5·00	6·00

180 Church of the Nativity, Bethlehem

1989. Christmas. Churches of the Holy Land. Multicoloured.

860	10c. Type **180**	1·50	30
861	40c. Basilica of the Annunciation, Nazareth	2·50	70
862	45c. Tabgha Church, Galilee	2·50	70
863	$1 Church of the Holy Sepulchre, Jerusalem	4·50	7·00
MS864	92×109 mm. Nos. 860/3	10·00	11·00

181 1974 U.P.U. Centenary 13c. Stamp and Globe

1989. "World Stamp Expo '89" International Stamp Exhibition, Washington. Multicoloured.

865	10c. Type **181**	70	40
866	40c. New U.P.U. Headquarters Building 3c. and building	1·40	85
867	45c. 1986 "Ameripex '86" $1 and Capitol, Washington	1·40	90
868	$1 1949 75th anniv of U.P.U. 2½d. and Boeing 737 airliner	5·50	7·00
MS869	107×80 mm. $2 Map showing route of Columbus, 1492 (30×38 mm)	10·00	14·00

1990. 500th Anniv (1992) of Discovery of America by Columbus (3rd issue). As T **173**. Multicoloured.

870	10c. Launching caravel	1·75	80
871	40c. Provisional ship	2·75	2·00
872	45c. Shortening sail	2·75	2·00
873	50c. Lucayan fisherman	2·75	4·00
MS874	70×61 mm. $1.50, Departure of Columbus, 1492	5·50	7·00

182 Bahamas Flag, O.A.S. Headquarters and Centenary Logo

1990. Centenary of Organization of American States.

875	**182** 40c. multicoloured	2·00	2·25

183 Supermarine Spitfire Mk I "Bahamas I"

1990. "Stamp World London 90" International Stamp Exhibition, London. Presentation Fighter Aircraft. Sheet 107×78 mm. containing T **183**. Multicoloured.

MS876	$1 Type **183**; $1 Hawker Hurricane Mk IIC "Bahamas V"	10·00	8·50

184 Teacher with Boy

1990. International Literacy Year. Multicoloured.

877	10c. Type **184**	1·00	50
878	40c. Three boys in class	1·75	1·25
879	50c. Teacher and children with books	1·75	5·00

1990. 90th Birthday of Queen Elizabeth the Queen Mother. As T **134** of Ascension.

880	40c. multicoloured	1·50	50
881	$1.50 black and ochre	2·75	6·00

DESIGNS—21×36 mm: 40c. *Queen Elizabeth 1938* (Sir Gerald Kelly); 29×37 mm: $1.50, Queen Elizabeth at garden party, France, 1938.

185 Cuban Amazon preening

1990. Cuban Amazon ("Bahamian Parrot"). Multicoloured.

882	10c. Type **185**	1·25	85
883	40c. Pair in flight	2·25	1·50
884	45c. Cuban amazon's head	2·25	1·50
885	50c. Perched on branch	2·50	3·75
MS886	73×63 mm. $1.50, Feeding on berries	8·00	10·00

186 The Annunciation

1990. Christmas. Multicoloured.

887	10c. Type **186**	65	50
888	40c. The Nativity	1·25	70
889	45c. Angel appearing to Shepherds	1·25	70
890	$1 The Three Kings	3·00	6·00
MS891	94×110 mm. Nos. 887/90	14·00	14·00

187 Green-backed Heron ("Green Heron")

1991. Birds. Multicoloured.

892	5c. Type **187**	80	1·50
893	10c. Turkey vulture	1·50	2·25
976	15c. Osprey	1·00	1·00
895	20c. Clapper rail	1·00	80
978	25c. Royal tern	1·00	70
979	30c. Key West quail dove	6·50	1·25
898	40c. Smooth-billed ani	1·75	55
899	45c. Burrowing owl	3·00	80
900	50c. Hairy woodpecker	2·50	80
983	55c. Mangrove cuckoo	2·00	1·00
902	60c. Bahama mockingbird	2·50	1·75
903	70c. Red-winged blackbird	2·50	1·75
904	$1 Thick-billed vireo	3·00	1·50
905	$2 Bahama yellowthroat	6·00	7·00
988	$5 Stripe-headed tanager	6·50	9·00
907	$10 Greater Antillean bullfinch	16·00	18·00

1991. 500th Anniv (1992) of Discovery of America by Columbus (4th issue). As T **173**. Multicoloured.

908	15c. Columbus navigating by stars	1·75	85
909	40c. Fleet in mid-Atlantic	2·50	2·25
910	55c. Lucayan family worshipping at night	2·50	2·50
911	60c. Map of First Voyage	3·25	5·00
MS912	56×61 mm. $1.50, *Pinta* lookout sighting land	6·00	7·00

1991. 65th Birthday of Queen Elizabeth II and 70th Birthday of Prince Philip. As T **139** of Ascension. Multicoloured.

913	15c. Prince Philip	1·00	1·50
914	$1 Queen Elizabeth II	1·75	2·00

188 Radar Plot of Hurricane Hugo

1991. International Decade for Natural Disaster Reduction. Multicoloured.

915	15c. Type **188**	1·50	65
916	40c. Diagram of hurricane	2·00	1·50
917	55c. Flooding caused by Hurricane David, 1979	2·25	2·25
918	60c. U.S. Dept of Commerce weather reconnaissance Lockhead WP-3D Orion	3·00	4·00

189 The Annunciation

1991. Christmas. Multicoloured.

919	15c. Type **189**	1·25	30
920	55c. Mary and Joseph travelling to Bethlehem	2·25	1·00
921	60c. Angel appearing to the shepherds	2·25	1·50
922	$1 Adoration of the kings	3·75	4·50
MS923	92×108 mm. Nos. 919/22	10·00	11·00

190 First Progressive Liberal Party Cabinet

1992. 25th Anniv of Majority Rule. Multicoloured.

924	15c. Type **190**	75	40
925	40c. Signing of Independence Constitution	1·60	1·10
926	55c. Prince of Wales handing over Constitutional Instrument (vert)	1·75	1·50
927	60c. First Bahamian Governor-General, Sir Milo Butler (vert)	2·00	3·50

1992. 40th Anniv of Queen Elizabeth II's Accession. As T **143** of Ascension. Multicoloured.

928	15c. Queen Elizabeth with bouquet	60	30
929	40c. Queen Elizabeth with flags	1·10	70
930	55c. Queen Elizabeth at display	1·10	90
931	60c. Three portraits of Queen Elizabeth	1·25	1·50
932	$1 Queen Elizabeth II	1·50	2·50

1992. 500th Anniv of Discovery of America by Columbus (5th issue). As T **173**. Multicoloured.

933	15c. Lucayans sighting fleet	2·00	1·00
934	40c. *Santa Maria* and dolphins	2·75	1·75
935	55c. Lucayan canoes approaching ships	2·75	2·25
936	60c. Columbus giving thanks for landfall	3·25	4·25
MS937	61×57 mm. $1.50, Children at Columbus Monument	3·50	6·00

191 Templeton, Galbraith and Hansberger Ltd Building

1992. 20th Anniv of Templeton Prize for Religion.

938	**191** 55c. multicoloured	1·50	1·75

192 Pole Vaulting

1992. Olympic Games, Barcelona. Multicoloured.

939	15c. Type **192**	60	50

193 Arid Landscape and Starving Child

1992. International Conference on Nutrition, Rome. Multicoloured.

944	15c. Type **193**	1·25	75
945	55c. Seedling, cornfield and child	2·00	2·00

1992. 500th Anniv of Discovery of America by Columbus (6th issue). Sheet 65×65 mm, containing vert design as T **173**. Multicoloured.

MS946	$2 Columbus landing in Bahamas	7·50	8·00

194 Mary visiting Elizabeth

1992. Christmas. Multicoloured.

947	15c. Type **194**	40	20
948	55c. The Nativity	1·10	1·00
949	60c. Angel and shepherds	1·25	1·50
950	70c. Wise Men and star	1·40	2·50
MS951	95×110 mm. Nos. 947/50	7·50	8·50

1992. Hurricane Relief. No. MS876 showing each stamp surch **HURRICANE RELIEF+$1**.

MS952	$1+$1 Type **183**; $1+$1 Hawker Hurricane Mk IIc "Bahamas V"	12·00	15·00

196 Flags of Bahamas and U.S.A. with Agricultural Worker

1993. 50th Anniv of The Contract (U.S.A.–Bahamas farm labour programme). Each including national flags. Multicoloured.

953	15c. Type **196**	1·75	75
954	55c. Onions	2·25	1·50
955	60c. Citrus fruit	2·50	2·50
956	70c. Apples	2·75	3·25

1993. 75th Anniv of Royal Air Force. As T **149** of Ascension. Multicoloured.

957	15c. Westland Wapiti IIA	1·75	85
958	40c. Gloster Gladiator I	2·25	1·00
959	55c. de Havilland Vampire F.3	2·50	1·75
960	70c. English Electric Lightning F.3	3·00	5·00
MS961	110×77 mm. 60c. Avro Shackleton M.R.2; 60c. Fairey Battle; 60c. Douglas Boston III; 60c. de Havilland D.H.9a	8·75	7·75

197 1978 Coronation Anniversary Stamps

1993. 40th Anniv of Coronation. Multicoloured.

962	15c. Type **197**	70	50
963	55c. Two examples of 1953 Coronation stamp	1·75	1·75
964	60c. 1977 Silver Jubilee 8c. and 16c. stamps	1·75	2·00
965	70c. 1977 Silver Jubilee 21c. and 40c. stamps	2·00	2·75

198 *Lignum vitae* (national tree)

1993. 20th Anniv of Independence. Multicoloured.

966	15c. Type **198**	30	20
967	55c. Yellow elder (national flower)	90	90
968	60c. Blue marlin (national fish)	1·25	1·25
969	70c. Greater flamingo (national bird)	2·00	3·00

199 Cordia

1993. Environment Protection (1st series). Wild-flowers. Multicoloured.

970	15c. Type **199**	1·50	50
971	55c. Seaside morning glory	3·00	1·25
972	60c. Poinciana	3·25	2·25
973	70c. Spider lily	3·75	4·50

See also Nos. 1017/21, 1035/8, 1084/7, 1121/4, 1149/53 and 1193/6.

200 The Annunciation

1993. Christmas. Multicoloured.

990	15c. Type **200**	75	50
991	55c. Angel and shepherds	2·25	1·75
992	60c. Holy Family	2·25	2·00
993	70c. Three Kings	2·75	3·75
MS994	86×106 mm. $1 Virgin Mary and Child	5·50	7·50

201 Family

1994. "Hong Kong '94" International Stamp Exhibition. International Year of the Family. Multicoloured.

995	15c. Type **201**	1·50	40
996	55c. Children doing homework	2·50	1·25
997	60c. Grandfather and grandson fishing	2·75	1·75
998	70c. Grandmother teaching grandchildren the Lord's Prayer	3·25	5·00

202 Flags of Bahamas and Great Britain

1994. Royal Visit. Multicoloured.

999	15c. Type **202**	1·50	50
1000	55c. Royal Yacht *Britannia*	2·75	1·75
1001	60c. Queen Elizabeth II	2·75	1·75
1002	70c. Queen Elizabeth and Prince Philip	2·75	4·50

203 Yachts

1994. 40th Anniv of National Family Island Regatta. Multicoloured.

1003	15c. Type **203**	80	40
1004	55c. Dinghies racing	1·75	1·25
1005	60c. Working boats	1·75	1·75
1006	70c. Sailing sloop	2·25	4·00
MS1007	76×54 mm. $2 Launching sloop (vert)	8·00	9·00

204 Logo and Bahamas 1968 Olympic Games Stamp

1994. Centenary of International Olympic Committee. Multicoloured.

1008	15c. Type **204**	1·75	50
1009	55c. 1976 Olympic Games stamps (vert)	2·75	1·25
1010	60c. 1984 Olympic Games stamps	2·75	2·25
1011	70c. 1992 Olympic Games stamps (vert)	3·00	4·50

205 Star of Order

1994. First Recipients of Order of the Caribbean Community. Sheet 90×69 mm.

MS1012	**205** $2 multicoloured	5·50	6·50

206 *Calpodes ethlius* and Canna

1994. Butterflies and Flowers. Multicoloured.

1013	15c. Type **206**	1·10	55
1014	55c. *Phoebis sennae* and cassia	2·00	1·50
1015	60c. *Anartia jatrophae* and passion flower	2·25	2·25
1016	70c. *Battus devilliersi* and calico flower	2·25	3·00

207 Spot-finned Hogfish and Spanish Hogfish

1994. Environment Protection (2nd series). Marine Life. Multicoloured.

1017	40c. Type **207**	1·00	1·25
1018	40c. Tomate and long-spined squirrelfish	1·00	1·25
1019	40c. French angelfish	1·00	1·25
1020	40c. Queen angelfish	1·00	1·25
1021	40c. Rock beauty	1·00	1·25
MS1022	57×55 mm. $2 Rock beauty, Queen angelfish and windsurfer	6·00	7·00

Nos. 1017/21 were printed together, *se-tenant*, with the backgrounds forming a composite design.

208 Angel

1994. Christmas. Multicoloured.

1023	15c. Type **208**	30	30
1024	55c. Holy Family	90	1·10
1025	60c. Shepherds	1·10	1·40
1026	70c. Wise Men	1·25	2·50
MS1027	73×85 mm. Jesus in manger	3·50	5·00

209 Lion and Emblem

1995. 20th Anniv of the College of the Bahamas. Multicoloured.

1028	15c. Type **209**	30	30
1029	70c. Queen Elizabeth II and College building	1·25	1·75

1995. 50th Anniv of End of Second World War. As T **161** of Ascension. Multicoloured.

1030	15c. Bahamian infantry drilling	75	50
1031	55c. Consolidated PBY-5A Catalina flying boat	2·00	1·25
1032	60c. Bahamian women in naval operations room	2·00	2·25
1033	70c. Consolidated B-24 Liberator bomber	2·50	3·75
MS1034	75×85 mm. $2 Reverse of 1939–45 War Medal (vert)	2·50	4·00

210 Kirtlands Warbler on Nest

1995. Environment Protection (3rd series). Endangered Species. Kirtland's Warbler. Mult.

1035	15c. Type **210**	55	75
1036	15c. Singing on branch	55	75
1037	25c. Feeding chicks	55	75
1038	25c. Catching insects	55	75
MS1039	73×67 mm. $2 On branch	7·50	8·50

No. MS1039 does not show the W.W.F. Panda emblem.

211 Eleuthera Cliffs

1995. Tourism. Multicoloured.

1040	15c. Type **211**	1·50	50
1041	55c. Clarence Town, Long Island	2·50	1·25
1042	60c. Albert Lowe Museum	2·75	2·50
1043	70c. Yachts	3·00	5·00

212 Pigs and Chick

1995. 50th Anniv of F.A.O. Multicoloured.

1044	15c. Type **212**	1·50	50
1045	55c. Seedling and hand holding seed	2·00	1·10
1046	60c. Family with fruit and vegetables	2·50	2·25
1047	70c. Fishes and crustaceans	3·50	4·50

213 Sikorsky S-55 Helicopter, Sinai, 1957

1995. 50th Anniv of United Nations. Multicoloured.

1048	15c. Type **213**	70	50
1049	55c. Ferret armoured car, Sinai, 1957	1·25	1·25
1050	60c. Fokker F.27 Friendship (airliner), Cambodia, 1991–93	1·50	2·00
1051	70c. Lockheed C-130 Hercules (transport)	1·60	2·75

214 St. Agnes Anglican Church

1995. Christmas. Churches. Multicoloured.

1052	15c. Type **214**	30	25
1053	55c. Church of God, East Street	90	90
1054	60c. Sacred Heart Roman Catholic Church	95	1·25
1055	70c. Salem Union Baptist Church	1·10	1·75

215 Microscopic View of AIDS Virus

1995. World AIDS Day. Multicoloured.

1056	25c. Type **215**	60	50
1057	70c. Research into AIDS	1·00	1·50

216 Sunrise Tellin

1996. Sea Shells. Multicoloured.

1058	5c. Type **216**	50	1·50
1059	10c. Queen conch	55	1·50
1060	15c. Angular triton	75	55
1061	20c. True tulip	1·00	1·00
1062	25c. Reticulated cowrie-helmet	1·00	80
1063	30c. Sand dollar	1·25	80
1063a	35c. As 30c.	1·50	80
1064	40c. Lace short-frond murex	1·50	80
1065	45c. Inflated sea biscuit	1·75	80
1066	50c. West Indian top shell	1·75	1·00
1067	55c. Spiny oyster	1·75	1·00
1068	60c. King helmet	1·75	1·25
1068a	65c. As 45c.	2·50	1·25
1069	70c. Lion's paw	2·00	1·50
1069a	80c. As 55c.	2·50	1·50
1070	$1 Crown cone	3·00	2·25
1071	$2 Atlantic partridge tun	4·50	5·50
1072	$5 Wide-mouthed purpura	9·00	13·00
1073	$10 Atlantic trumpet triton	25·00	24·00

217 East Goodwin Lightship with Marconi Apparatus on Mast

1996. Centenary of Radio. Multicoloured.

1074	15c. Type **217**	1·75	80
1075	55c. Newspaper headline concerning Dr. Crippen	2·50	1·25
1076	60c. *Philadelphia* (liner) and first readable transatlantic message	2·50	2·00
1077	70c. Guglielmo Marconi and *Elettra* (yacht)	2·75	3·50
MS1078	80×47 mm. $2 *Titanic* and *Carpathia* (liners)	8·50	8·50

218 Swimming

1996. Centenary of Modern Olympic Games. Multicoloured.

1079	15c. Type **218**	40	35
1080	55c. Running	90	90
1081	60c. Basketball	2·00	1·75
1082	70c. Long jumping	1·40	2·50
MS1083	73×86 mm. $2 Javelin throwing	3·00	4·00

219 Green Anole

1996. Environment Protection (4th series). Reptiles. Multicoloured.

1084	15c. Type **219**	55	50
1085	55c. Little Bahama bank boa	1·10	1·00
1086	60c. Inagua freshwater turtle	1·50	1·75
1087	70c. Acklins rock iguana	1·75	2·75
MS1088	85×105 mm. Nos. 1084/7	5·50	6·50

220 The Annunciation

1996. Christmas. Multicoloured.

1089	15c. Type **220**	1·25	40
1090	55c. Joseph and Mary travelling to Bethlehem	2·50	1·00
1091	60c. Shepherds and angel	2·50	1·50
1092	70c. Adoration of the Magi	2·75	4·00
MS1093	70×87 mm. $2 Presentation in the Temple	4·00	4·50

221 Department of Archives Building

1996. 25th Anniv of Archives Department.

| 1094 | **221** | 55c. multicoloured | 1·50 | 1·00 |
| MS1095 | 83×54 mm. $2 multicoloured | | 4·75 | 6·50 |

1997. "HONG KONG '97" International Stamp Exhibition. Sheet 130×90 mm, containing design as No. 1070, but with "1997" imprint date. Multicoloured.

| MS1096 | $1 Crown cone | 3·25 | 3·50 |

1997. Return of Hong Kong to China. Sheet 130×90 mm, containing design as No. 1069, but with "1997" imprint date.

| MS1097 | 70c. Lion's paw | 2·00 | 2·50 |

1997. Golden Wedding of Queen Elizabeth and Prince Philip. As T **173** of Ascension. Multicoloured.

1114	50c. Queen Elizabeth II in Bonn, 1992	2·00	2·25
1115	50c. Prince Philip and Prince Charles at Trooping the Colour	2·00	2·25
1116	60c. Prince Philip	2·00	2·25
1117	60c. Queen at Trooping the Colour	2·00	2·25
1118	70c. Queen Elizabeth and Prince Philip at polo, 1970	2·00	2·25
1119	70c. Prince Charles playing polo	2·00	2·25
MS1120	110×70 mm. $2 Queen Elizabeth and Prince Philip in landau (horiz)	6·50	7·00

222 Underwater Scene

1997. Environment Protection (5th series). International Year of the Reefs.

1121	**222**	15c. multicoloured	1·25	60
1122	-	55c. multicoloured	2·25	1·00
1123	-	60c. multicoloured	2·25	1·75
1124	-	70c. multicoloured	2·50	3·00

DESIGNS: 55c. to 70c. Different children's paintings of underwater scenes.

223 Angel

1997. Christmas. Multicoloured.

1125	15c. Type **223**	1·50	40
1126	55c. Mary and Baby Jesus	2·25	80
1127	60c. Shepherd	2·25	1·25
1128	70c. King	2·75	3·75
MS1129	74×94 mm. $2 Baby Jesus wrapped in swaddling-bands.	8·00	8·50

223a Wearing Grey Jacket, 1988

1998. Diana, Princess of Wales Commemoration.

| 1130 | **223a** | 15c. multicoloured | 50 | 50 |
| MS1131 | 145×70 mm. 15c. As No. 1130; 55c. Wearing striped jacket, 1983; 60c. In evening dress, 1983; 70c. Meeting crowds, 1993 | | 2·00 | 2·75 |

1998. 80th Anniv of the Royal Air Force. As T **178** of Ascension. Multicoloured.

1132	15c. Handley Page Hyderabad	55	40	
1133	55c. Hawker Demon	1·00	85	
1134	60c. Gloster Meteor F8	1·10	1·25	
1135	70c. Lockheed P2 Neptune	1·40	2·25	
MS1136	110×76 mm. 50c. Sopwith Camel; 50c. Short 184 (seaplane); 50c. Supermarine Spitfire PR.19; 50c. North American Mitchell III		4·00	4·25

224 Newsletters

1998. 50th Anniv of Organization of American States. Multicoloured.

| 1137 | 15c. Type **224** | 30 | 30 |
| 1138 | 55c. Headquarters building and flags, Washington | 70 | 80 |

225 Start of Declaration and Birds

1998. 50th Anniv of Universal Declaration of Human Rights.

| 1139 | **225** | 55c. blue and black | 1·75 | 1·00 |

226 University Arms and Graduates

1998. 50th Anniv of University of the West Indies.

| 1140 | **226** | 55c. multicoloured | 1·50 | 1·00 |

227 Supreme Court Building

1998. 25th Anniv of Independence. Multicoloured.

1141	15c. Type **227**	1·00	50
1142	55c. Nassau Library	1·75	1·00
1143	60c. Government House	1·90	1·50
1144	70c. Gregory Arch	2·00	3·00
MS1145	70×55 mm. $2 Island Regatta, George Town	3·50	5·00

228 *Disney Magic* (cruise liner) at Night

1998. Disney Cruise Line's Castaway Cay Holiday Development. Multicoloured.

| 1146 | 55c. Type **228** | 2·00 | 2·00 |
| 1147 | 55c. *Disney Magic* by day | 2·00 | 2·00 |

229 *Ryndam* (cruise liner)

1998. Holland America Line's Half Moon Cay Holiday Development.

| 1148 | **229** | 55c. multicoloured | 2·75 | 1·25 |

230 Barrel Pink Rose

1998. Environment Protection (6th series). Roses. Multicoloured.

1149	55c. Type **230**	1·50	1·60
1150	55c. Yellow cream	1·50	1·60
1151	55c. Seven sisters	1·50	1·60
1152	55c. Big red	1·50	1·60
1153	55c. Island beauty	1·50	1·60
MS1154	100×70 mm. No. 1153	1·50	1·75

231 The Annunciation

1998. Christmas. Multicoloured.

1155	15c. Type **231**	50	30
1156	55c. Shepherds	1·00	70
1157	60c. Three Kings	1·25	1·10
1158	70c. The Flight into Egypt	1·50	2·75
MS1159	87×67 mm. The Nativity	3·00	4·00

232 Killer Whale and other Marine Life

1998. International Year of the Ocean. Multicoloured.

| 1160 | 15c. Type **232** | 65 | 50 |
| 1161 | 55c. Tropical fish | 85 | 90 |

233 Timothy Gibson (composer)

1998. 25th Anniv of *March on Bahamaland* (national anthem).

| 1162 | **233** | 60c. multicoloured | 1·00 | 1·25 |

234 Head of Greater Flamingo and Chick

1999. 40th Anniv of National Trust (1st issue). Inagua National Park. Multicoloured.

1163	55c. Type **234**	1·50	1·60
1164	55c. Pair with two chicks	1·50	1·60
1165	55c. Greater flamingos asleep or stretching wings	1·50	1·60
1166	55c. Greater flamingos feeding	1·50	1·60
1167	55c. Greater flamingos in flight	1·50	1·60

Nos. 1163/7 were printed together, *se-tenant*, with the backgrounds forming a composite design.
See also Nos. 1173/7, 1198/1202 and 1207/11.

235 Arawak Indian Canoe

1999. "Australia '99" World Stamp Exhibition, Melbourne. Maritime History. Multicoloured.

1168	15c. Type **235**	55	30
1169	55c. *Santa Maria* (Columbus), 1492	2·25	1·40
1170	60c. *Queen Anne's Revenge* (Blackbeard), 1716	2·25	1·75
1171	70c. *The Banshee* (Confederate paddle-steamer) running blockade	2·50	3·50

| MS1172 | 110×66 mm. $2 Firing on American ships, 1776 | 5·50 | 5·50 |

1999. 40th Anniv of National Trust (2nd issue). Exuma Cays Land and Sea Park. As T **234**. Multicoloured.

1173	55c. Dolphin	1·60	1·75
1174	55c. Angelfish and parrotfish	1·60	1·75
1175	55c. Queen triggerfish	1·60	1·75
1176	55c. Turtle	1·60	1·75
1177	55c. Lobster	1·60	1·75

Nos. 1173/7 were printed together, *se-tenant*, with the backgrounds forming a composite design.

236 Society Headquarters Building

1999. 40th Anniv of Bahamas Historical Society.

| 1178 | **236** | $1 multicoloured | 1·50 | 2·25 |

1999. 30th Anniv of First Manned Landing on Moon. As T **186** of Ascension. Multicoloured.

1179	15c. Constructing ascent module	45	40
1180	65c. Diagram of command and service module	1·25	1·25
1181	70c. Lunar module descending	1·25	1·75
1182	80c. Lunar module preparing to dock with service module	1·25	2·50
MS1183	90×80 mm. $2 Earth as seen from Moon (circular, 40 mm diam)	3·25	4·25

1999. "Queen Elizabeth the Queen Mother's Century". As T **187** of Ascension. Multicoloured.

1184	15c. Visiting Herts Hospital, 1940	60	35
1185	65c. With Princess Elizabeth, Hyde Park, 1944	1·50	1·00
1186	70c. With Prince Andrew, 1997	1·50	1·50
1187	80c. With Irish Guards' mascot, 1997	1·50	1·75
MS1188	145×70 mm. $2 Lady Elizabeth Bowes-Lyon with her brother David, 1904, and England World Cup team celebrating, 1966.	4·50	5·00

237 *Delaware* (American mail ship), 1880

1999. 125th Anniv of U.P.U. Ships. Multicoloured.

1189	15c. Type **237**	1·50	50
1190	65c. *Atlantis* (liner), 1923	2·50	1·25
1191	70c. *Queen of Bermuda 2* (liner), 1937	2·50	2·25
1192	80c. U.S.S. *Saufley* (destroyer), 1943	3·00	3·25

238 *Turtle Pond* (Green Turtle)

1999. Environment Protection (7th series). Marine Life Paintings by Ricardo Knowles. Multicoloured.

1193	15c. Type **238**	50	35
1194	65c. *Turtle Cliff* (Loggerhead turtle)	1·25	1·00
1195	70c. *Barracuda*	1·40	1·40
1196	80c. *Coral Reef*	1·50	2·25
MS1197	90×75 mm. $2 *Atlantic Bottle-nosed Dolphins*	4·50	5·50

The 65c. is inscribed "GREEN TURTLES" in error.

1999. 40th Anniv of National Trust (3rd issue). Birds. As T **234**. Multicoloured.

1198	65c. Bridled tern and white-tailed tropic bird	1·75	1·75
1199	65c. Louisiana heron	1·75	1·75
1200	65c. Bahama woodstar	1·75	1·75
1201	65c. Black-billed whistling duck	1·75	1·75
1202	65c. Cuban amazon	1·75	1·75

Nos. 1198/1202 were printed together, *se-tenant*, with the backgrounds forming a composite design.

239 Man on Elephant Float

1999. Christmas. Junkanoo Festival. Multicoloured.

1203	15c. Type **239**	50	30
1204	65c. Man in winged costume	1·00	1·00
1205	70c. Man in feathered mask	1·25	1·25
1206	80c. Man blowing conch shell	1·50	2·00

1999. 40th Anniv of National Trust (4th issue). Flora and Fauna. As T 234. Multicoloured.

1207	65c. Foxglove	2·25	2·25
1208	65c. Vole	2·25	2·25
1209	65c. Cuban amazon	2·25	2·25
1210	65c. Lizard	2·25	2·25
1211	65c. Red hibiscus	2·25	2·25

Nos. 1207/11 were printed together, *se-tenant*, with the backgrounds forming a composite design.

240 New Plymouth

2000. Historic Fishing Villages. Multicoloured.

1212	15c. Type **240**	1·25	40
1213	65c. Cherokee Sound	2·25	2·25
1214	70c. Hope Town	2·50	2·00
1215	80c. Spanish Wells	2·75	3·25

241 Gold Medal Winning Bahamas Women's Relay Team

2000. "The Golden Girls" winners of 4×100 metre Relay at I.A.A.F. World Track and Field Championship '99, Spain. Sheet 100×55 mm.

MS1216	**241** $2 multicoloured	3·00	3·75

242 Prickly Pear

2000. Medicinal Plants (1st series). Multicoloured.

1217	15c. Type **242**	35	30
1218	65c. Buttercup	1·25	1·25
1219	70c. Shepherd's needle	1·25	1·50
1220	80c. Five fingers	1·40	2·25

See also Nos. 1282/5 and 1324/7.

243 Re-arming and Re-fuelling Supermarine Spitfire

2000. "The Stamp Show 2000" International Stamp Exhibition, London. 60th Anniv of Battle of Britain. Multicoloured.

1221	15c. Type **243**	70	45
1222	65c. Sqdn. Ldr. Stanford-Tuck's Hurricane Mk I	1·40	1·40
1223	70c. Dogfight between Spitfires and Heinkel IIIs	1·60	1·75
1224	80c. Flight of Supermarine Spitfires attacking	1·60	2·25
MS1225	90×70 mm. $2 Presentation Spitfire Bahamas	3·50	4·00

244 Teachers' and Salaried Workers' Co-operative Credit Union Building

2000. Co-operatives Movement in Bahamas. Sheet 90×50 mm.

MS1226	**244** $2 multicoloured	3·50	4·25

245 Swimming

2000. Olympic Games, Sydney. Each inscribed with details of previous Bahamian participation. Multicoloured.

1227	15c. Type **245**	50	30
1228	65c. Triple jump	1·40	1·25
1229	70c. Women's 4×100 m relay	1·40	1·40
1230	80c. Sailing	1·50	2·25

246 Encyclia cochleata

2000. Christmas. Orchids. Multicoloured.

1231	15c. Type **246**	85	30
1232	65c. Encyclia plicata	1·75	1·40
1233	70c. Bletia purpurea	1·90	1·75
1234	80c. Encyclia gracilis	2·25	2·50

247 Cuban Amazon and Primary School Class

2000. Bahamas Humane Society. Multicoloured.

1235	15c. Type **247**	1·75	50
1236	65c. Cat and Society stall	2·75	1·40
1237	70c. Dogs and veterinary surgery	3·25	2·75
1238	80c. Goat and animal rescue van	3·25	4·00

248 Meadow Street, Inagua

2001. Early Settlements. Paintings by Ricardo Knowles. Multicoloured.

1239	15c. Type **248**	40	30
1240	65c. *Bain Town*	1·25	1·00
1241	70c. *Hope Town, Abaco*	1·40	1·40
1242	80c. *Blue Hills*	1·50	2·25

249 Lynden Pindling presenting Independence Constitution, 1972

2001. Sir Lynden Pindling (former Prime Minister) Commemoration. Multicoloured.

1243	15c. Type **249**	50	40
1244	65c. Sir Lynden Pindling with Bahamas flag	1·40	1·50

250 Cocoaplum

2001. Edible Wild Fruits. Paintings by Alton Roland Lowe. Multicoloured.

1245	15c. Type **250**	35	25
1246	65c. *Guana Berry*	1·25	1·10
1247	70c. *Mastic*	1·25	1·25
1248	80c. *Seagrape*	1·50	2·25

251 Reddish Egret

2001. Birds and their Eggs. Multicoloured.

1249	5c. Type **251**	75	1·50
1250	10c. American purple gallinule	75	1·50
1251	15c. Antillean nighthawk	1·00	55
1252	20c. Wilson's plover	1·25	1·00
1253	25c. Killdeer plover	1·25	70
1254	30c. Bahama woodstar	1·40	1·00
1255	40c. Bahama swallow	1·40	1·25
1256	50c. Bahama mockingbird	1·75	1·25
1257	60c. Black-cowled oriole	2·00	1·50
1258	65c. Great lizard cuckoo	2·00	1·25
1259	70c. Audubon's shearwater	2·25	1·50
1260	80c. Grey kingbird	2·25	1·50

1261	$1 Bananaquit	3·25	3·00
1262	$2 Yellow warbler	6·00	6·00
1263	$5 Greater Antillean bullfinch	13·00	14·00
1264	$10 Roseate spoonbill	22·00	24·00

252 H.M.S. *Norfolk* (cruiser), 1933

2001. Royal Navy Ships connected to Bahamas. Multicoloured.

1265	15c. Type **252**	1·50	50
1266	25c. H.M.S. *Scarborough* (sloop), 1930s	1·75	70
1267	50c. H.M.S. *Bahamas* (frigate), 1944	2·25	1·75
1268	65c. H.M.S. *Battleaxe* (frigate), 1979	2·50	1·75
1269	70c. H.M.S. *Invincible* (aircraft carrier), 1997	2·50	2·25
1270	80c. H.M.S. *Norfolk* (frigate), 2000	2·50	3·00

253 Adoration of the Shepherds

2001. Christmas. Paintings by Rubens. Multicoloured.

1271	15c. Type **253**	55	25
1272	65c. "*Adoration of the Magi* (with Van Dyck)	1·40	1·10
1273	70c. *Holy Virgin in Wreath of Flowers* (with Breughel)	1·50	1·40
1274	80c. *Holy Virgin adored by Angels*	1·60	2·00

2002. Golden Jubilee. As T 200 of Ascension.

1275	15c. black, green and gold	45	25
1276	65c. multicoloured	1·25	1·00
1277	70c. multicoloured	1·40	1·50
1278	80c. multicoloured	1·40	2·00
MS1279	162×95 mm. Nos. 1275/8 and $2 multicoloured	6·50	6·50

DESIGNS—HORIZ: 15c. Princess Elizabeth; 65c. Queen Elizabeth in Bonn, 1992; 70c. Queen Elizabeth with Prince Edward, 1965; 80c. Queen Elizabeth at Sandringham, 1996. VERT (38×51 mm)—$2 Queen Elizabeth after Annigoni.

254 Avard Moncur (athlete)

2002. Award of BAAA Most Outstanding Male Athlete Title to Avard Moncur. Sheet 65×98 mm.

MS1280	**254** $2 multicoloured	3·25	3·75

255 Statue of Liberty with U.S. and Bahamas Flags

2002. In Remembrance. Victims of Terrorist Attacks on U.S.A. (11 September 2001).

1281	**255** $1 multicoloured	3·00	3·00

2002. Medicinal Plants (2nd series). As T 242. Multicoloured.

1282	15c. Wild sage	50	35
1283	65c. Seaside maho	1·40	1·10
1284	70c. Sea ox-eye	1·50	1·60
1285	80c. Mexican poppy	1·50	2·00

2002. Queen Elizabeth the Queen Mother Commemoration. As T 202 of Ascension.

1286	15c. brown, gold and purple	75	40
1287	65c. multicoloured	1·75	1·50
MS1288	145×70 mm. 70c. black and gold; 80c. multicoloured	3·75	3·75

DESIGNS: 15c. Queen Elizabeth at American Red Cross Club, London, 1944; 65c. Queen Mother at Remembrance Service, 1989; 70c. Queen Elizabeth, 1944; 80c. Queen Mother at Cheltenham Races, 2000.

256 Rice Bird and Rice

2002. Illustrations from *The Natural History of Carolina, Florida and the Bahama Islands* by Mark Catesby (1747). Multicoloured.

1289	15c. Type **256**	85	45
1290	25c. Alligator and red mangrove	1·00	60
1291	50c. Parrot fish	1·40	1·10
1292	65c. Ilathera duck and sea ox-eye	1·75	1·50
1293	70c. Flamingo and gorgonian coral	1·90	2·00
1294	80c. Crested bittern and inkberry	2·00	2·25

257 *While Shepherds watched their Flocks*

2002. Christmas. Scenes from Carols. Multicoloured.

1295	15c. Type **257**	60	25
1296	65c. *We Three Kings*	1·40	1·10
1297	70c. *Once in Royal David's City*	1·50	1·50
1298	80c. *I saw Three Ships*	1·60	2·25

258 Flamingo on Nest

2003. Inagua National Park Wetlands. Flamingos. Multicoloured.

1299	15c. Type **258**	70	45
1300	25c. Flock of flamingos feeding	95	65
1301	50c. Group of flamingos	1·50	1·10
1302	65c. Group of flamingos walking	1·75	1·50
1303	70c. Flamingos taking-off	1·90	1·90
1304	80c. Flamingos in flight	2·00	2·25

259 Captain Edward Teach ("Blackbeard")

2003. Pirates. Multicoloured.

1305	15c. Type **259**	85	45
1306	25c. Captain "Calico Jack" Rackham	1·25	65
1307	50c. Anne Bonney	2·00	1·40
1308	65c. Captain Woodes Rogers	2·25	1·75
1309	70c. Sir John Hawkins	2·25	2·25
1310	80c. Captain Bartholomew Roberts ("Black Bart")	2·50	2·50

260 Dinghies

2003. 50th Anniv of Family Island Regatta. Multicoloured.

1311	15c. Type **260**	75	40
1312	65c. *New Courageous* (racing sloop)	2·00	1·50
1313	70c. *New Susan Chase* (racing sloop)	2·25	2·00
1314	80c. *Tida Wave* (racing sloop)	2·40	2·75

2003. 50th Anniv of Coronation. As T 206 of Ascension. Multicoloured.

1315	65c. Queen with crown, orb and sceptre	1·50	1·40
1316	80c. Royal family on Buckingham Palace balcony	2·00	2·25
MS1317	95×115 mm. 15c. As 65c.; 70c. As 80c.	2·25	2·50

Nos. 1315/16 have red frame; stamps from **MS**1317 have no frame and country name in mauve panel.

2003. Medicinal Plants (3rd series). As T **242**.

1318	15c. *Asystasia*	40	25
1319	65c. *Cassia*	1·40	1·25
1320	70c. *Lignum vitae*	1·50	1·60
1321	80c. Snowberry	1·60	2·00

2003. Centenary of Powered Flight. As T **209** of Ascension. Multicoloured.

1322	15c. Piper Cub	90	60
1323	25c. de Havilland Tiger Moth	1·25	90
1324	50c. Lockheed SR-71A Blackbird	1·75	1·60
1325	65c. Supermarine S6B	2·00	1·90
1326	70c. North American P-51D Mustang "Miss America"	2·00	2·00
1327	80c. Douglas DC-3 Dakota	2·25	2·50

261 Interior with Stained Glass Window

2003. Christmas. St. Matthew's Church, Nassau. Multicoloured.

1328	15c. Type **261**	60	25
1329	65c. Church interior (horiz)	1·50	1·10
1330	70c. St. Matthew's Church (horiz)	1·75	1·60
1331	80c. Church tower	2·00	2·00

262 *Crawfishin*

2003. "Waters of Life". Paintings by Alton Lowe. Multicoloured.

1332	15c. Type **262**	75	30
1333	65c. *Summer*	1·75	1·25
1334	70c. *The Whelkers*	2·00	1·75
1335	80c. *Annual Visit*	2·25	2·25

263 Egrets on Dead Tree

2004. Wetlands (2nd series). Harrold and Wilson Ponds, New Providence Island. Multicoloured.

1336	15c. Type **263**	60	40
1337	25c. Green-backed heron and duck	80	65
1338	50c. Birdwatchers in canoes	1·50	1·40
1339	65c. Egret and Bahama pintail ducks	1·75	1·60
1340	70c. Egret and Louisiana heron	2·00	2·00
1341	80c. Birdwatchers with binoculars and telescope	2·25	2·75

264 Methodist Church, Cupid's Cay, Governor's Harbour

2004. 300th Birth Anniv of John Wesley (founder of Methodist Church) (2003). Multicoloured.

1342	15c. Type **264**	70	40
1343	25c. Church, Grants Town, Nassau	90	55
1344	50c. Wooden Chapel, Marsh Harbour (vert)	1·60	1·50
1345	65c. Ebeneezer Methodist Church	1·90	1·75
1346	70c. Trinity Methodist Church	2·25	2·50
1346a	80c. Portrait by Antonius Roberts (vert)	2·50	3·00

265 Cattleya

2004. Bicentenary of the Royal Horticultural Society. Multicoloured.

1347	15c. Type **265**	90	40
1348	65c. Hibiscus	1·40	1·10
1349	70c. Canna	1·50	1·60
1350	80c. Thunbergia	2·00	2·25

266 Elbow Reef Lighthouse

2004. Lighthouses (1st series). Multicoloured.

1351	15c. Type **266**	1·00	50
1352	50c. Great Stirrup	1·75	1·25
1353	65c. Great Isaac	2·00	1·50
1354	70c. Hole in the Wall	2·25	2·00
1355	80c. Hog Island	2·50	2·50

See also Nos. 1396/1400.

267 Boxing

2004. Olympic Games, Athens. Multicoloured.

1356	15c. Type **267**	50	30
1357	50c. Swimming	1·25	1·10
1358	65c. Tennis	1·40	1·40
1359	70c. Relay racing	1·40	1·75

268 "Anticipation"

2004. Christmas. Junkanoo Festival. Multicoloured.

1360	15c. Type **268**	40	20
1361	25c. "First Time"	50	25
1362	50c. "On The Move" (vert)	1·00	60
1363	65c. "I'm Ready"	1·10	1·00
1364	70c. "Trumpet Player" (vert)	1·25	1·40
1365	80c. "Drummer Boy" (vert)	1·40	1·60

269 RMS *Mauretania*

2004. Merchant Ships. Multicoloured.

1366	15c. Type **269**	80	45
1367	25c. MV *Adonia*	1·10	65
1368	50c. MS *Royal Princess*	1·75	1·40
1369	65c. SS *Queen of Nassau*	1·90	1·50
1370	70c. RMS *Transvaal Castle*	2·00	2·00
1371	80c. SS *Norway*	2·25	2·50

2005. Medicinal Plants (4th series). As T **242**. Multicoloured.

1372	15c. Aloe vera	35	25
1373	25c. Red stopper	45	35
1374	50c. Blue flower	80	80
1375	65c. Bay lavender	1·10	1·25

270 Commando Squadron

2005. 25th Anniv of the Royal Bahamas Defence Force. Multicoloured.

1376	15c. Type **270**	60	40
1377	25c. HMBS *Abaco*	85	55
1378	50c. HMBS *Bahamas*	1·60	1·25
1379	65c. Officers and marines in uniform	1·75	1·75

2005. Bicentenary of Battle of Trafalgar. Multicoloured (except **MS**1386) designs as T **216** of Ascension.

1380	15c. Tower Sea Service pistols, 1801 RN Pattern (vert)	60	40
1381	25c. Royal Marine, 1805 (vert)	80	55
1382	50c. HMS *Boreas* off Bahamas, 1787	1·50	1·25

1383	65c. "Death of Nelson" (A. W. Devis)	1·60	1·40
1384	70c. HMS *Victory*	2·00	2·00
1385	80c. *Achille* surrendering to HMS *Polyphemus*	2·00	2·25

MS1386 120×78 mm. $1 Admiral Collingwood (brown, black and grey) (vert); $1 HMS *Polyphemus* (vert) — 8·00, 8·50

No. 1384 contains traces of powdered wood from HMS *Victory*.

271 William Curry

2005. Abaco—Key West Connections. Multicoloured.

1387	15c. Type **271**	45	35
1388	25c. Captain John Bartlum's House (horiz)	60	50
1389	50c. Captain John Bartlum	1·25	1·25
1390	65c. Captain Tuggy Roberts' House (horiz)	1·50	1·75

272 Flags of EU and Bahamas and Map

2005. 50th Anniv of First Europa Stamp. Designs, all showing flags of EU and Bahamas, outline Map of Western Europe and different seascapes. Multicoloured.

1391	15c. Type **272**	45	45
1392	25c. Seascape with bands of thin high cloud	65	65
1393	50c. Seascape with small island	1·25	1·40
1394	$5 Seascape with clouds	9·00	11·00

MS1395 120×77 mm. Nos. 1391/4 — 10·00, 12·00

2005. Lighthouses (2nd series). As T **266**. Multicoloured.

1396	15c. Bird Rock	90	50
1397	50c. Castle Island	2·00	1·25
1398	65c. San Salvador	2·25	1·50
1399	70c. Great Inagua	2·50	2·50
1400	80c. Cay Lobos	2·75	3·00

2005. Pope John Paul II Commemoration. As T **219** of Ascension.

1401	$1 multicoloured	2·75	2·75

273 College Entrance, Nassau

2005. 30th Anniv of the College of the Bahamas. Sheet 81×88 mm.

MS1402 **273** $2 multicoloured — 3·25, 3·75

2005. Christmas. Birth Bicentenary of Hans Christian Andersen (writer). As T **220** of Ascension. Multicoloured.

1403	15c. *The Little Fir Tree*	30	20
1404	25c. *The Princess and the Pea*	45	35
1405	50c. *The Tin Soldier*	90	90
1406	65c. *Thumbelina*	1·10	1·25

274 Bahama Nuthatch

2006. BirdLife International. Bahama Nuthatch (Sitta insularis). Multicoloured.

1407	15c. Type **274**	90	50
1408	25c. On thick branch (facing left)	1·40	70
1409	50c. On tree trunk (facing right)	2·00	1·40
1410	65c. On thin branch among pine needles	2·25	1·60
1411	70c. Nuthatch seen from underside	2·50	2·50
1412	80c. On tree trunk near hole (facing left)	2·75	3·00

MS1413 170×85 mm. Nos. 1407/12 — 10·50, 10·50

The stamps within No. **MS**1413 form a composite design showing nuthatches in Caribbean pine trees.

2006. 80th Birthday of Queen Elizabeth II. As T **223** of Ascension. Multicoloured.

1414	15c. Princess Elizabeth	70	35
1415	25c. Queen Elizabeth II, c. 1952	1·00	55
1416	50c. Wearing blue feathered hat	1·75	1·40
1417	65c. Wearing hat with brim raised at one side	2·00	2·00

MS1418 144×75 mm. $1·50 As No. 1415; $1·50 As No. 1416 — 8·00, 8·00

275 H. R. (Rusty) Bethel (Manager, ZNS Radio 1945–70)

2006. 70th Anniv of Broadcasting in the Bahamas. Multicoloured.

1419	15c. Type **275**	55	30
1420	25c. New Broadcasting Corporation of the Bahamas logo	75	40
1421	50c. National Headquarters of Broadcasting Corporation of the Bahamas	1·25	1·00
1422	65c. ZNS Nassau Radio stations building	1·50	1·25
1423	70c. Radio mast and map of Bahamas	1·75	1·75
1424	80c. "ZNS Radio" (70th anniv) and microphone	1·75	2·00

276 Amaryllis (*Hippeastrum puniceum*)

2006. Flowers of the Bahamas. Paintings by Alton Roland Lowe. Multicoloured.

1425	5c. Type **276**	50	75
1426	10c. *Barleria cristata*	55	1·00
1495a	15c. Yesterday, today, tomorrow (*Brunfelsia solanaceae*)	30	15
1427	25c. Desert rose (*Adenium obesum*)	40	20
1428	35c. Poor man's orchid (*Bauhinia* sp.)	55	25
1429	40c. Frangipani (*Plumeria* sp.)	1·25	65
1430	55c. Herald's trumpet (*Beaumontia grandiflora*)	1·75	1·25
1431	65c. Oleander (*Nerium oleander*)	1·90	1·25
1432	75c. Bird of Paradise (*Strelitzia reginae*)	2·00	1·50
1433	80c. *Plumbago capensis*	2·00	1·60
1434	90c. Rose (*Rosa* sp.)	2·50	2·00
1435	$1 Rubber vine (*Cryptostegia madagascariensis*)	2·75	2·25
1436	$2 Star of Bethlehem (*Jatropha integerrima*)	5·50	5·50
1437	$5 Angel's trumpet (*Brugmansia suaveolens*)	13·00	15·00
1438	$10 Wine lily (*Crinum* sp.)	24·00	26·00

277 *Centrosema virginianum* (blue pea)

2006. Wild Flowering Vines. Paintings by Alton Roland Lowe. Multicoloured.

1439	15c. Type **277**	60	35
1440	50c. *Urechites lutea* (allamanda)	1·40	1·00
1441	65c. *Ipomoea indica* (morning glory)	1·50	1·40
1442	70c. *Ipomoea microdactyla* (sky vine)	1·75	2·00

278 Christmas Sunday

2006. Christmas. Multicoloured.

1443	15c. Type **278**	40	25
1444	25c. Christmas dinner	60	30
1445	50c. Bay Street shopping	1·00	1·00
1446	65c. Boxing Day Junkanoo	1·25	1·00
1447	70c. Watch Night service	1·40	1·60
1448	80c. New Year's Day Junkanoo	1·50	2·25

279 Blainville's Beaked Whale

2007. Endangered Species. Blainville's Beaked Whale (*Mesoplodon densirostris*). Multicoloured.
1449	15c. Type **279**	60	40
1450	25c. Three whales	80	60
1451	50c. Whales just beneath surface	1·40	1·25
1452	60c. Two whales	1·50	1·40

280 Princess Elizabeth and Lt. Philip Mountbatten, 1949

2007. Diamond Wedding of Queen Elizabeth II and Prince Philip. Multicoloured.
1453	15c. Type **280**	50	25
1454	25c. Princess Elizabeth riding in carriage on her wedding day, 1949	75	45
1455	50c. Princess Elizabeth and Prince Philip waving from balcony on wedding day, 1949	1·40	1·25
1456	65c. Princess Elizabeth, Prince Philip and Queen Mary	1·60	1·75
MS1457	125×85 mm. $5 Wedding portrait (42×56 mm)	11·00	12·00

281 Bahamas Scouts at Church Service

2007. Centenary of Scouting. Multicoloured.
1458	15c. Type **281**	70	40
1459	25c. Scout in adventure playground	90	55
1460	50c. Scout barbecue	1·50	1·25
1461	65c. Bahamas girl scouts on parade	1·75	1·75
MS1462	90×65 mm. 70c. Scouts playing ball (*vert*); 80c. Lord Baden-Powell (*vert*)	2·50	3·00

282 Scouts repairing Causeway ('Service')

2007. 20th Anniv of Governor-General's Youth Award. Multicoloured.
1463	15c. Type **282**	30	20
1464	25c. Painting ('Skills')	45	30
1465	50c. Kayaking ('Physical Recreation')	90	90
1466	65c. Hiking ('Adventurous Journey')	1·25	1·25
1467	70c. Conch shell emblem	1·50	2·00

283 Flower Decoration

2007. Christmas. Tree Decorations. Multicoloured.
1468	15c. Type **283**	25	15
1469	25c. Sea shells decoration	40	25
1470	50c. Sea shells decoration (different)	90	70
1471	65c. Bow and sea shells decoration	1·25	90
1472	70c. Gold woven decoration	1·40	1·50
1473	80c. 'Angel' made from sea shells	1·60	2·00

284 Choir

2007. 300th Birth Anniv of Charles Wesley. Multicoloured.
1474	15c. Type **284**	40	25
1475	50c. Charles and John Wesley (evangelists) (*vert*)	1·00	80
1476	65c. Revd. Charles Wesley and *Hymns and Sacred Poems* (*vert*)	1·25	1·25
1477	70c. Harbour Island Methodist Church (*horiz*)	1·50	1·75

285 *Heliconius charitonius* (zebra longwing)

2008. Bahamas Butterflies. Multicoloured.
1478	15c. Type **285**	50	30
1479	25c. *Dryas julia carteri* (Julia)	70	45
1480	50c. *Phoebis sennae* (cloudless sulphur)	1·40	1·10
1481	65c. *Danaus gilippus berenice* (The Queen)	1·60	1·25
1482	70c. *Urbanus proteus* (long-tailed skipper)	1·75	2·00
1483	80c. *Dione vanillae insularis* (Gulf fritillary)	2·00	2·50
MS1484	170×75 mm. Nos. 1478/83	7·50	8·00

286 His Majesty's Independant Company

2008. Military Uniforms. Multicoloured.
1485	15c. Type **286**	50	30
1486	25c. 47th Regiment of Foot	70	45
1487	50c. 99th Regiment of Foot	1·40	1·25
1488	65c. Royal Artillery	1·50	1·50
1489	70c. Black Garrison Companies	1·75	2·00

287 Athlete breaking Finish Tape

2008. Olympic Games, Beijing. Multicoloured.
1490	15c. Type **287**	40	25
1491	50c. High jump	1·25	1·00
1492	65c. Javelin thrower	1·50	1·50
1493	70c. Triple jump	1·75	2·00

288 Centenary Emblem

2008. Centenary of the Royal Bank of Canada in the Bahamas. Multicoloured.
1506	15c. Type **288**	50	30
1507	25c. Regional Head Office	65	45
1508	50c. Main Branch, Bay Street, Nassau, early 1900s	1·40	1·00
1509	65c. Artist's rendering of new Carmichael Road Branch, Nassau	1·60	1·75
1510	70c. Ross McDonald, Head of Caribbean Banking, and Nathaniel Beneby Jr., Vice President and Country Head	1·75	2·25

289 Launch of Space Shuttle *Discovery* in STS-26 'Return to Flight' Mission

2008. 50th Anniv of NASA. Multicoloured.
1511	15c. Type **289**	50	30
1512	25c. Apollo 16 Command and Service Module over the Moon, 1972	70	45
1513	50c. *Skylab 3*, 1973	1·40	1·00
1514	65c. Hubble Space Telescope	1·60	1·50
1515	70c. Gasses in the Swan Nebula	1·75	1·90
1516	80c. Star forming region in the Carina Nebula	2·00	2·25

290 The Three Kings worshipping Jesus

2008. Christmas. Book Illustrations by Leonhard Diefenbach from *The First Christmas for Our Dear Little Ones* by Rosa Mulholland. Multicoloured.
1517	15c. Type **290**	45	15
1518	50c. The Three Kings at the court of King Herod	1·25	80
1519	65c. Shepherds telling the news of the birth of Jesus	1·60	1·50
1520	70c. The shepherds visit the Baby Jesus	1·75	2·00

291 Students

2008. 60th Anniv of the University of the West Indies. Multicoloured.
1521	15c. Type **291**	30	20
1522	25c. Plaque marking Bahamas Clinical Training Programme becoming part of University of the West Indies, 2007	50	40
1523	65c. Scroll	1·60	1·75

292 Battle of Lexington, 1775

2008. 225th Anniv of the Treaty of Paris (recognising US Independence). Multicoloured.
1524	15c. Type **292**	60	40
1525	50c. Washington crossing the Delaware, 1776	1·50	1·25
1526	65c. American signatories of Treaty of Paris, 1783 (Benjamin West)	1·75	1·75
1527	70c. Detail of Treaty of Paris showing signatures	2·00	2·25

293 Bahamas Oriole (*Icterus northropi*)

2009. Endangered Species–Resident Breeders. Multicoloured.
1528	15c. Type **293**	75	40
1529	50c. Rose throated parrot (*Amazona leucocephala bahamensis*)	1·75	1·25
1530	65c. Great lizard cuckoo (*Saurothera merlini bahamensis*)	2·00	1·75
1531	70c. Audubon's shearwater (*Puffinus lherminieri*)	2·25	2·25

294 Peony

2009. China 2009 World Stamp Exhibition and Peony Festival, Luoyang. Sheet 180×110 mm. Multicoloured; colours of right-hand borders given.
MS1532	Type **294**×8 (colours of right-hand borders cream, white, pale pink, pale blue, pale flesh, pale green, pale yellow and pale azure)	9·00	10·00

295 'Tripod'

2009. Potcake Dogs. Multicoloured.
1533	15c. Type **295**	70	40
1534	50c. 'Amigo'	1·75	1·25
1535	65c. 'Turtle'	2·00	1·75
1536	70c. 'Oreo'	2·25	2·50

296 Bahamas 1859 1d Stamp

2009. 150th Anniv of the First Bahamas Stamp. Multicoloured, background colour given.
1537	**296**	15c. pink	70	70
1538	**296**	15c. azure	70	70
1539	**296**	15c. dull green	70	70
1540	**296**	15c. dull reddish lilac	70	70
MS1541	130×100 mm. Nos. 1537/40		2·50	2·50

2009. Centenary of Naval Aviation. As T **87** of British Antarctic Territory. Multicoloured.
1542	15c. Hawker Sea Hurricane	65	40
1543	65c. Hawker Sea Fury	2·00	1·75
1544	70c. Fairey Gannet	2·25	2·25
1545	80c. de Havilland Sea Vampire	2·50	2·75
MS1546	110×70 mm. $2 Aircraft on deck of merchant aircraft carrier MV *Empire MacKendrick*	6·50	6·50

297 East Street Tabernacle of Church of God of Prophecy

2009. Christmas. Churches. Multicoloured.
1547	15c. Type **297**	35	15
1548	25c. The Mission Baptist Church	50	30
1549	50c. Grant's Town Seventh-Day Adventist Church	95	65
1550	65c. Wesley Methodist Church, Harbour Island	1·50	1·40
1551	70c. St. Francis Xavier Cathedral	1·60	1·75
1552	80c. St. Ambrose Anglican Church	1·75	2·25

298 The House of Assembly

2009. 60th Anniv of the Commonwealth. Sheet 120×85 mm.
MS1553	**298** $2 multicoloured	4·50	5·00

299 Dolphin and Whale

2010. Friends of the Environment. Multicoloured.
1554	15c. Type **299**	35	15
1555	50c. Parrot and island map	1·00	75
1557	70c. Bird and tree	1·60	2·00

300 Winston
Churchill

2010. 70th Anniv of the Battle of Britain. Multicoloured.

1558	15c. Type **300** ("...we shall never surrender...")		55	25
1559	25c. ..the Battle of Britain is about to begin...		75	35
1560	50c. "...never in the field of human conflict was so much owed by so many to so few..."		1·25	90
1561	65c. ...this was their finest hour...		1·75	1·50
1562	70c. ...upon this battle depends the survival of Christian civilization...		2·00	2·25
1563	80c. ...we shall fight on the beaches...		2·25	2·75
MS1563a 110×70 mm. $2 Sir Douglas Bader			6·50	6·50

301 Palm Trees in
High Wind

2010. Hurricane Awareness. Multicoloured.

1564	15c. Type **301**		80	40
1565	50c. Map tracking hurricane across Bahamas		1·60	1·40
1566	65c. Reconnaissance aircraft flying through storm to measure intensity		2·25	2·25
1567	70c. Hurricane and NEMA (National Emergency Management Agency) logo		2·75	3·00

302 Cruise Ship and
Fireworks

2010. Christmas. 'Tourist Winter Escapes'. Multicoloured.

1568	15c. Type **302**		75	40
1569	50c. Atlantis Hotel, Paradise Island and fireworks		1·75	1·25
1570	65c. Aircraft tailfin and fireworks		2·25	1·75
1571	70c. Fort Fincastle and Water Tower and fireworks		2·75	3·25

303 The Annual Heart Ball

2011. 50th Anniv of the Sir Victor Sassoon Heart Foundation. Multicoloured.

1572	15c. Type **303**		75	55
1573	50c. Doctor with young child		1·75	1·50
1574	65c. Doctor and young girl		2·25	3·25
1575	70c. Sir Victor Sassoon		2·75	3·00

2011. Queen Elizabeth II and Prince Philip. 'A Lifetime of Service'. Multicoloured.

1576	15c. Queen Elizabeth II, Balmoral, 6 February 1982		75	50
1577	50c. Queen Elizabeth II and Prince Philip, Windsor Castle, June 1959		1·75	1·40
1578	65c. Queen Elizabeth II and Prince Philip, Thames Valley University, London, 20 February 2009		2·25	1·90
1579	70c. Queen Elizabeth II and Prince Philip, Westminster Abbey, 8 March 2010		2·50	2·50
1580	$1 Queen Elizabeth II and Prince Philip, Buckingham Palace, 19 July 1957		4·00	4·25
1581	$2 Prince Philip, Balmoral, 6 February 1982		6·50	7·00
MS1582 175×164 mm. Nos. 1576/81 and three stamp-size labels			16·00	16·00
MS1583 110×70 mm. $2·50 Queen Elizabeth II and Prince Philip, Sandringham House, Norfolk, 1992			8·00	8·00

304 Prince William and Miss Catherine Middleton at Friend's Wedding, Austria, September 2008

2011. Royal Wedding. Multicoloured.

1584	15c. Type **304**		60	25
1585	50c. Engagement photograph, St. James's Palace, London, November 2010		1·75	1·50
1586	65c. Kissing on Buckingham Palace balcony after wedding		2·25	2·50
MS1587 94×64 mm. $5 Wedding in Westminster Abbey (vert)			16·00	16·00

305 Christ Church
Cathedral

2011. 150th Anniv of the Anglican Diocese and City of Nassau. Multicoloured.

1588	15c. Type **305**		75	50
1589	50c. Rawson Square, 1861		1·75	1·40
1590	65c. Government House, 1861		2·25	1·90
1591	70c. Bay Street, 1861		2·50	2·50
1592	$1 Dr. Charles Caulfield (first Bishop of Nassau), 1862		4·00	4·00
1593	$2 Royal Governor Charles Bayley, 1857-64		6·50	7·50

306 Angel Gabriel
appearing to Mary

2011. Christmas. Angels. Multicoloured.

1594	15c. Type **306**		75	30
1595	25c. Angel watching over Mary and Joseph on journey to Bethlehem		1·10	35
1596	50c. Angel guiding Wise Men		1·75	1·25
1597	65c. Angel watching over Infant Jesus in manger		2·25	2·00
1598	70c. Angel appearing to Shepherds		2·50	2·75
1599	80c. Angel watching over Mary and Infant Jesus		2·75	3·25

307 Common Sea Fan
(*Gorgonia ventalina*)

2012. Marine Life. Multicoloured.

1600	5c. Type **307**		25	25
1601	10c. Christmas tree worm (*Spirobranchus giganteus*)		35	35
1602	15c. Elkhorn coral (*Acropora palmata*)		65	35
1603	20c. Cushion sea star (*Oreaster reticulatus*)		75	40
1604	25c. Queen conch (*Strombus gigas*)		90	40
1605	30c. Hawksbill turtle (*Eretmochelys imbricata*)		1·00	55
1606	40c. Green moray eel (*Gymnothorax funebris*)		1·25	65
1607	50c. Bonefish (*Albula vulpes*)		1·50	80
1608	60c. Spider crab (*Mithrax spinosissimus*)		1·75	1·10
1609	65c. Spiny lobster (*Panulirus argus*)		1·90	1·10
1610	70c. Nassau grouper (*Epinephelus striatus*)		2·25	1·25
1611	80c. Yellowtail snapper (*Ocyurus chrysurus*)		2·75	2·50
1612	$1 Great barracuda (*Sphyraena barracuda*)		3·75	3·25
1613	$2 Spotted eagle ray (*Aetobatus narinari*)		6·50	6·00
1614	$5 Caribbean reef shark (*Carcharhinus perezi*)		14·00	15·00
1615	$10 Bottlenose dolphin (*Tursiops truncatus*)		26·00	28·00

308 Caribbean
Flamingo

2012. Endangered Species. Caribbean Flamingo (*Phoenicopterus ruber*). Multicoloured.

1616	15c. Type **308**		75	60
1617	50c. Chick and egg		1·75	1·25
1618	65c. Two flamingos feeding		2·50	2·25
1619	70c. Three flamingos in foreground		3·00	3·25
MS1620 90×70 mm. $5 Flamingos on beach			16·00	16·00

309 Boxer and
Houses of
Parliament

2012. Olympic Games, London. Olympic Sports and London Landmarks. Multicoloured.

1621	15c. Type **309**		75	30
1622	50c. High jump and Nelson's Column		1·75	1·25
1623	65c. Swimmer at start and Tower Bridge		2·25	2·00
1624	70c. Running athlete and Main Olympic Stadium		2·50	2·75

310 Prince Harry at
Thanksgiving
Service, Christ
Church Cathedral,
Nassau

2012. Diamond Jubilee and Visit of Prince Harry, March 2012. Multicoloured.

1625	15c. Type **310**		75	30
1626	50c. Prince Harry visiting Harbour Island, Eleuthera		1·75	1·25
1627	65c. Prince Harry at Youth Rally, Thomas A. Robinson National Stadium, Nassau		2·25	2·00
1628	70c. Queen Elizabeth II		2·50	2·75

311 Mary
Ingraham

2012. 50th Anniv of Women's Suffrage. Campaigners for Women's Suffrage. Multicoloured.

1629	15c. Type **311**		75	30
1630	25c. Georgianna Symonette		1·10	65
1631	50c. Mabel Walker		1·75	1·25
1632	65c. Eugenia Lockhart		2·25	2·00
1633	70c. Dame Alberta Isaacs		2·50	2·75
1634	80c. Dr. Doris Johnson		2·75	3·25

312 The Annunciation

2012. Christmas. Multicoloured.

1635	15c. Type **312**		65	55
1636	25c. Joseph and Mary find no room at the inn in Bethlehem		80	65
1637	50c. The Nativity		1·50	1·25

1638	65c. An Angel appears to the Shepherds		2·10	1·90
1639	70c. Three Wise Men carrying gifts of gold, frankincense and myrrh		2·50	2·75
1640	80c. Flight into Egypt		2·75	3·25

313 Queen Victoria

2013. 60th Anniv of Coronation. 'A Celebration of Coronation Commemoratives'

1641	65c. Type **313**		2·10	1·90
1642	70c. Coronation of King Edward VII and Queen Alexandra, 1902		2·50	2·25
1643	80c. King George V and Queen Mary		2·75	2·50
1644	$1 King George VI and Queen Elizabeth's tour of Canada and USA, 1939 (souvenir)		3·00	3·00
1645	$2 Crown, shamrock, thistle, daffodil, poppy and Union flag (souvenir of Coronation of Queen Elizabeth II)		6·00	7·00
MS1646 110×70 mm. $3 Queen Elizabeth II, c. 1953 (32×48 mm)			8·00	7·50

314 Sir William Murphy (Governor of the Bahamas) presenting Colonial Police Medal for Gallantry to Constable Fred Neville Seymour, 10 June 1948

2013. 120th Anniv of Royal Bahamas Police Force Band. Multicoloured.

1647	15c. Type **314**		65	55
1648	25c. Royal Bahamas Police Force Band performing as Queen Elizabeth II boards Royal Yacht *Britannia*, 1975		75	65
1649	50c. Royal Bahamas Police Force Band performing		1·50	1·25
1650	65c. Royal Bahamas Police Force Band and Atlantis Resort		2·10	1·90
1651	70c. Close-up of drum being played		2·50	2·25
1652	80c. Royal Bahamas Police Force Band marching down road		2·75	2·50

SPECIAL DELIVERY STAMPS

1916. Optd **SPECIAL DELIVERY**.

S2	**6**	5d. black and orange	60	10·00
S3	**6**	5d. black and mauve	40	4·00

Pt. 1

BAHAWALPUR

A former Indian Feudatory state which joined Pakistan in 1947 and continued to use its own stamps until 1953.

12 pies = 1 anna, 16 annas = 1 rupee.

(1)

1947. Nos. 265/8, 269a/77 and 259/62 of India optd with Type **1**.

1	**100a**	3p. slate		40·00
3	**100a**	9p. green		40·00
2	**100a**	½a. purple		40·00
4	**100a**	1a. red		40·00
5	**101**	1½a. violet		40·00
6	**101**	2a. red		40·00
7	**101**	3a. violet		40·00
8	**101**	3½a. blue		40·00
9	**102**	4a. brown		40·00
10	**102**	6a. green		40·00
11	**102**	8a. violet		40·00
12	**102**	12a. lake		40·00
13	–	14a. purple		85·00
14	**93**	1r. grey and brown		50·00
15	**93**	2r. purple and brown		£3750
16	**93**	5r. green and blue		£3750
17	**93**	10r. purple and red		£3750

2 Amir Muhammad
Bahawal Khan I
Abbasi

1948. Bicentenary Commemoration.

| 18 | **2** | ½a. black and red | 3·75 | 8·00 |

4 H. H. the Amir
of Bahawalpur

5 The Tombs of the Amirs

1948

19	**4**	3p. black and blue	3·00	20·00
21	**4**	9p. black and green	2·75	20·00
20	**4**	½a. black and red	2·75	20·00
22	**4**	1a. black and red	2·75	20·00
23	**4**	1½a. black and violet	4·00	16·00
24	**5**	2a. green and red	4·00	20·00
25	-	4a. orange and brown	4·00	20·00
26	-	6a. violet and blue	4·00	20·00
27	-	8a. red and green	5·50	20·00
28	-	12a. green and red	6·00	30·00
29	-	1r. violet and brown	19·00	45·00
35	-	1r. green and orange	1·75	20·00
30	-	2r. green and brown	55·00	80·00
36	-	2r. black and red	2·00	24·00
31	-	5r. black and violet	55·00	£100
37	-	5r. brown and blue	2·00	42·00
32	-	10r. red and black	32·00	£130
38	-	10r. brown and green	2·00	55·00

DESIGNS—HORIZ: 6a. Fort Derawar from the lake; 8a. Nur-Mahal Palace; 12a. Sadiq-Garh Palace. 46×32 mm: 10r. Three generations of Rulers. VERT (As Type **5**): 4a. Mosque in Sadiq-Garh; 1, 2, 5r. H.H. the Amir of Bahawalpur.

12 H.H. the Amir of
Bahawalpur and Mohammed
Ali Jinnah

1948. First Anniv of Union with Pakistan.

| 33 | **12** | 1½a. red and green | 1·75 | 7·00 |

13 Soldiers of
1848 and 1948

1948. Centenary of Multan Campaign.

| 34 | **13** | 1½a. black and red | 1·25 | 16·00 |

14 Irrigation

1949. Silver Jubilee of Accession of H.H. the Amir of Bahawalpur.

39	**14**	3p. black and blue	10	8·00
41	-	9p. black and green	10	8·00
40	-	½a. black and orange	10	8·00
42	-	1a. black and red	10	8·00

DESIGNS: ½a. Wheat; 9p. Cotton; 1a. Sahiwal bull.

18 UPU Monument,
Berne

1949. 75th Anniv of U.P.U.

43	**17**	9p. black and green	20	2·25
44	**17**	1a. black and mauve	20	2·25
45	**17**	1½a. black and orange	20	2·25
46	**17**	2½a. black and blue	20	2·25

OFFICIAL STAMPS

O4 Eastern White
Pelicans

1945. As Type O 4 with Arabic opt.

O1	-	½a. black and green	11·00	15·00
O2	-	1a. black and red	3·75	16·00
O7	-	1a. black and brown	95·00	85·00
O3	-	2a. black and violet	3·25	13·00
O4	**O 4**	4a. black and olive	16·00	28·00
O5	-	8a. black and brown	35·00	18·00
O6	-	1r. black and orange	35·00	18·00

DESIGNS: ½a. Panjnad Weir; 1a. (No. O2), Camel and calf; 1a. (No. O7), Baggage camels; 2a. Blackbuck antelopes; 8a. Friday Mosque, Fort Derawar; 1r. Temple at Pattan Munara.

(O8)

1945. Types as Nos. O1, etc., in new colours and without Arabic opt. (a) Surch as Type O 8.

O11		½a. on 8a. black and purple (as No. O5)	7·50	7·00
O12		1½a. on 5r. black and orange (as No. O6)	40·00	11·00
O13		1½a. on 2r. black and blue (as No. O1)	£140	8·50

1945. Optd SERVICE and Arabic inscription

O14		½a. black and red (as No. O1)	1·25	11·00
O15		1a. black and red (as No. O2)	2·00	13·00
O16		2a. black and orange (as No. O3)	3·50	55·00

1945. As Type 4 but inscr "SERVICE" at left.

| O17 | | 3p. black and blue | 8·00 | 16·00 |
| O18 | | 1½a. black and violet | 27·00 | 8·00 |

O11 Allied Banners

1946. Victory.

| O19 | **O11** | 1½a. green and grey | 5·50 | 4·50 |

1948. Stamps of 1948 with Arabic opt as in Type O 4.

O20	**4**	3p. black and blue	80	13·00
O21	**4**	1a. black and red	80	12·00
O22	**5**	2a. green and red	80	13·00
O23	-	4a. orange and brown	80	18·00
O24	-	1r. green and orange	80	20·00
O25	-	2r. black and red	80	26·00
O26	-	5r. chocolate and blue	80	42·00
O27	-	10r. brown and green	80	42·00

1949. 75th Anniv of U.P.U. optd as in Type O 4.

O28	**17**	9p. black and green	15	4·50
O29	**17**	1a. black and mauve	15	4·50
O30	**17**	1½a. black and orange	15	4·50
O31	**17**	2½a. black and blue	15	4·50

Pt. 1, Pt. 19

BAHRAIN

An archipelago in the Persian Gulf on the Arabian coast. An independent shaikhdom with Indian and later British postal administration. The latter was closed on 1 January 1966, when the Bahrain Post Office took over.

1933. 12 pies = 1 anna; 16 annas = 1 rupee.
1957. 100 naya paise = 1 rupee.

Stamps of India optd BAHRAIN.

1933. King George V.

1	**55**	3p. grey	3·50	45
3	**80**	9p. green	3·75	4·50
2	**56**	½a. green	8·00	4·25
15	**79**	½a. green	8·50	2·25
4	**57**	1a. brown	9·00	2·75
16	**81**	1a. brown	11·00	40
5	**82**	1a.3p. mauve	16·00	4·00
6	**70**	2a. orange	10·00	19·00
17	**59**	2a. orange	45·00	7·50
7	**62**	3a. blue	19·00	70·00
18	**62**	3a. red	4·75	60
8	**83**	3a.6p. blue	3·75	40
9	**71**	4a. green	18·00	70·00

19	**63**	4a. olive	5·00	40
10	**65**	8a. mauve	6·00	30
11	**66**	12a. red	7·50	2·25
12	**67**	1r. brown and green	16·00	15·00
13	**67**	2r. red and orange	32·00	40·00
14w	**67**	5r. blue and violet	£150	£170

1938. King George VI.

20	**91**	3p. slate	20·00	8·00
22	**91**	9p. green	16·00	14·00
21	**91**	½a. brown	9·00	20
23	**91**	1a. red	16·00	20
24	**92**	2a. red	5·00	6·50
26	-	3a. green (No. 253)	12·00	13·00
27	-	3a.6p. blue (No. 254)	6·00	10·00
28	-	4a. brown (No. 255)	£180	70·00
30	-	8a. violet (No. 257)	£300	35·00
31	-	12a. red (No. 258)	£160	50·00
32	**93**	1r. slate and brown	8·00	2·00
33	**93**	2r. purple and brown	19·00	11·00
34	**93**	5r. green and blue	15·00	13·00
35	**93**	10r. purple and red	90·00	60·00
36w	**93**	15r. brown and green	90·00	90·00
37	**93**	25r. slate and purple	£130	£110

1942. King George VI.

38	**100a**	3p. slate	3·50	2·50
40	**100a**	9p. green	18·00	23·00
39	**100a**	½a. mauve	4·75	4·50
41	**100a**	1a. red	8·00	1·00
42	**101**	1a.3p. bistre	10·00	24·00
43	**101**	1½a. violet	7·00	8·00
44	**101**	2a. red	7·00	1·50
45	**101**	3a. violet	22·00	7·50
46	**101**	3½a. blue	6·50	22·00
47	**102**	4a. brown	7·50	2·00
48	**102**	6a. green	20·00	12·00
49	**102**	8a. violet	12·00	7·00
50	**102**	12a. purple	17·00	7·00

Stamps of Great Britain surch **BAHRAIN** and new value in Indian currency.

1948. King George VI.

71	**128**	½a. on ½d. orange	2·50	3·75
51	**128**	½a. on 1d. green	50	1·25
52	**128**	1a. on 1d. red	50	3·50
72	**128**	1a. on 1d. blue	3·00	20
53	**128**	1½a. on 1½d. brown	50	5·00
73	**128**	1½a. on 1½d. green	3·50	13·00
54	**128**	2a. on 2d. orange	50	20
74	**128**	2a. on 2d. brown	1·50	30
55	**128**	2½a. on 2½d. blue	50	5·50
75	**128**	2½a. on 2½d. red	3·50	17·00
56	**128**	3a. on 3d. violet	50	10
76	**129**	4a. on 4d. blue	5·00	1·50
57	**129**	6a. on 6d. purple	50	10
58	**130**	1r. on 1s. brown	1·25	10
59	**131**	2r. on 2s.6d. green	5·50	5·50
60	**131**	5r. on 5s. red	5·50	5·50
60a	-	10r. on 10s. blue (No. 478a)	95·00	80·00

1948. Silver Wedding.

| 61 | **137** | 2½a. on 2½d. blue | 1·00 | 2·75 |
| 62 | **138** | 15r. on £1 blue | 32·00 | 50·00 |

1948. Olympic Games.

63	**139**	2½a. on 2½d. blue	1·50	4·75
64	**140**	3a. on 3d. violet	1·00	4·25
65	-	6a. on 6d. purple	1·50	4·25
66	-	1r. on 1s. brown	2·75	4·25

1949. U.P.U.

67	**143**	2½a. on 2½d. blue	60	2·75
68	**144**	3a. on 3d. violet	70	5·00
69	-	6a. on 6d. purple	60	3·00
70	-	1r. on 1s. brown	1·25	3·75

1951. Pictorial stamps (Nos. 509/11).

77	**147**	2r. on 2s.6d. green	40·00	16·00
78	-	5r. on 5s. red	15·00	6·50
79	-	10r. on 10s. blue	38·00	10·00

1952. Queen Elizabeth II.

97	**154**	½a. on ½d. orange	10	15
81	**154**	1a. on 1d. red	15	10
82	**154**	1½a. on 1½d. green	10	10
83	**154**	2a. on 2d. brown	30	10
84	**155**	2½a. on 2½d. red	20	1·75
85	**155**	3a. on 3d. lilac	3·00	10
86	**155**	4a. on 4d. blue	18·00	30
99	**157**	6a. on 6d. purple	50	75
88	**160**	12a. on 1s.3d. green	3·25	20
89	**160**	1r. on 1s.6d. blue	3·25	10

1953. Coronation.

90	**161**	2½a. on 2½d. red	1·25	75
91	-	4a. on 4d. blue	2·25	8·00
92	**163**	12a. on 1s.3d. green	6·00	6·50
93	-	1r. on 1s.6d. blue	7·50	50

1955. Pictorial stamps (Nos. 595a/598a).

| 94 | **166** | 2r. on 2s.6d. brown | 5·50 | 2·00 |

| 95 | - | 5r. on 5s. red | 17·00 | 2·75 |
| 96 | - | 10r. on 10s. blue | 20·00 | 2·75 |

1957. Queen Elizabeth II.

102	**157**	1n.p. on 5d. brown	10	10
103	**154**	3n.p. on ½d. orange	50	3·00
104	**154**	6n.p. on 1d. blue	50	3·00
105	**154**	9n.p. on 1½d. green	50	3·25
106	**154**	12n.p. on 2d. pale brown	30	70
107	**155**	15n.p. on 2½d. red	30	15
108	**155**	20n.p. on 3d. lilac	30	10
109	**155**	25n.p. on 4d. blue	1·25	2·50
110	**157**	40n.p. on 6d. purple	40	10
111	**157**	50n.p. on 9d. olive	3·75	4·50
112	**157**	75n.p. on 1s.3d. green	2·50	10

1957. World Scout Jubilee Jamboree.

113	**170**	15n.p. on 2½d. blue	35	35
114	**171**	25n.p. on 4d. blue	35	35
115	-	75n.p. on 1s.3d. green	40	45

16 Shaikh
Sulman bin
Hamed
al-Khalifa

1960

117	**16**	5n.p. blue	20	10
118	**16**	15n.p. orange	20	10
119	**16**	20n.p. violet	20	10
120	**16**	30n.p. bistre	20	10
121	**16**	40n.p. grey	20	10
122	**16**	50n.p. green	20	10
123	**16**	75n.p. brown	30	15
124	-	1r. black	3·00	30
125	-	2r. red	3·00	2·50
126	-	5r. blue	5·00	3·50
127	-	10r. green	14·00	6·00

The rupee values are larger, 27×32½ mm.

18 Shaikh Isa
bin Sulman
al-Khalifa

19 Air Terminal,
Muharraq

1964

128	**18**	5n.p. blue	10	10
129	**18**	15n.p. orange	15	1·00
130	**18**	20n.p. violet	15	10
131	**18**	30n.p. bistre	15	10
132	**18**	40n.p. slate	15	10
133	**18**	50n.p. green	15	1·50
134	**18**	75n.p. brown	25	10
135	**19**	1r. black	11·00	2·25
136	**19**	2r. red	11·00	5·00
137	-	5r. blue	15·00	20·00
138	-	10r. myrtle	15·00	20·00

DESIGN—As Type **19**: 5r., 10r. Deep water harbour.

21 Shaikh Isa
bin Sulman
al-Khalifa

22 Ruler and Bahrain
Airport

1966

139	**21**	5f. green	20	20
140	**21**	10f. red	20	20
141	**21**	15f. blue	20	20
142	**21**	20f. purple	30	20
143	**22**	30f. black and green	45	20
144	**22**	40f. black and blue	55	20
145	-	50f. black and red	75	30
146	-	75f. black and violet	95	45
147	-	100f. blue and yellow	3·25	1·30
148	-	200f. green and orange	2·75	
149	-	500f. brown and yellow	12·00	4·75
150	-	1d. multicoloured	21·00	10·50

DESIGNS—As Type **22**: 50f., 75f. Ruler and Mina Sulman deep-water harbour. VERT (26½×42½ mm): 100f. Pearl-diving; 200f. Lanner falcon and horse-racing; 500f. Serving coffee, and ruler's palace. LARGER (37×52½ mm): 1d. Ruler, crest, date palm, horse, dhow, pearl necklace, mosque, coffee-pot and Bab-al-Bahrain (gateway).

23 Produce

1966. Trade Fair and Agricultural Show.
151	**23**	10f. turquoise and red	55	10
152	**23**	20f. lilac and green	75	10
153	**23**	40f. blue and brown	2·10	55
154	**23**	200f. red and blue	10·00	4·75

24 W.H.O.
Emblem and
Map of Bahrain

1968. 20th Anniv of W.H.O.
155	**24**	20f. black and grey	95	65
156	**24**	40f. black and turquoise	3·25	1·70
157	**24**	150f. black and red	14·00	6·50

25 View of Isa Town

1968. Inauguration of Isa New Town. Multicoloured.
158		50f. Type **25**	4·75	1·40
159		80f. Shopping centre	7·00	2·75
160		120f. Stadium	10·50	5·00
161		150f. Mosque	13·00	6·50

26 Symbol of Learning

1969. 50th Anniv of School Education in Bahrain.
162	**26**	40f. multicoloured	1·90	1·20
163	**26**	60f. multicoloured	3·75	1·90
164	**26**	150f. multicoloured	10·00	5·00

27 Dish Aerial and Map of
Persian Gulf

1969. Opening of Satellite Earth Station, Ras Abu Jarjour.
Multicoloured.
165		20f. Type **27**	2·75	65
166		40f. Dish aerial and palms (vert)	6·00	1·10
167		100f. Type **27**	13·00	4·75
168		150f. As 40f.	21·00	7·00

28 Arms, Map and Manama
Municipality Building

1970. Second Arab Cities Organization Conf, Manama.
169	**28**	30f. multicoloured	2·75	2·75
170	**28**	150f. multicoloured	15·00	15·00

29 Copper Bull's Head,
Barbar

1970. Third International Asian Archaeology Conference,
Bahrain. Multicoloured.
171		60f. Type **29**	4·75	2·50
172		80f. Palace of Dilmun excava-tions	7·50	3·25
173		120f. Desert gravemounds	9·00	4·25
174		150f. Dilmun seal	10·50	5·25

30 Vickers Super VC-10
Airliner, Big Ben, London,
and Bahrain Minaret

1970. First Gulf Aviation Vickers Super VC-10 Flight,
Doha–London.
175	**30**	30f. multicoloured	3·25	95
176	**30**	60f. multicoloured	6·50	2·10
177	**30**	120f. multicoloured	12·00	6·50

31 I.E.Y. Emblem and Open
Book

1970. International Education Year. Multicoloured.
178		60f. Type **31**	5·25	5·25
179		120f. Emblem and Bahraini children	10·50	10·50

32 Allegory of
Independence

1971. Independence Day and Tenth Anniv of Ruler's
Accession. Multicoloured.
180		30f. Type **32**	2·40	1·30
181		60f. Government House	4·75	2·40
182		120f. Arms of Bahrain	12·00	6·00
183		150f. Arms of Bahrain (gold background)	16·00	8·00

33 Arab Dhow with Arab
League and U.N. Emblems

1972. Bahrain's Membership of Arab League and U.N.
Multicoloured.
184		30f. Type **33**	6·00	6·00
185		60f. Type **33**	9·75	9·75
186		120f. Dhow sails (vert)	13·00	13·00
187		150f. As 120f.	24·00	24·00

34 Human Heart

1972. World Health Day.
188	**34**	30f. multicoloured	6·00	6·00
189	**34**	60f. multicoloured	12·00	12·00

35 F.A.O. and U.N.
Emblems

1973. Tenth Anniv of World Food Programme.
190	**35**	30f. brown, red and green	5·25	5·25
191	**35**	60f. brown, lt brown & grn	10·00	10·00

36 "Races of the World"

1973. 25th Anniv of Declaration of Human Rights.
192	**36**	30f. blue, brown and black	6·50	6·50
193	**36**	60f. red, brown and black	9·75	9·75

38 Flour Mill

1973. National Day. "Progress in Bahrain". Mult.
195		30f. Type **38**	2·40	65
196		60f. Muharraq Airport	3·25	1·20
197		120f. Sulmaniya Medical Centre	6·50	3·50
198		150f. Aluminium Smelter	6·50	3·75

39 U.P.U. Emblem within Letters

1974. Admission of Bahrain to U.P.U. Multicoloured.
199		30f. Type **39**	2·40	2·40
200		60f. U.P.U. emblem on letters	4·00	4·00
201		120f. Ruler and emblem on dove with letter in beak (37×28 mm)	4·00	4·00
202		150f. As 120f. (37×28 mm)	6·00	6·00

40 Traffic Lights
and Directing
Hands

1974. International Traffic Day.
203	**40**	30f. multicoloured	4·75	4·75
204	**40**	60f. multicoloured	8·50	8·50

41 U.P.U. "Stamp" and Mail
Transport

1974. Centenary of U.P.U.
205	**41**	30f. multicoloured	1·30	1·30
206	**41**	60f. multicoloured	1·50	1·50
207	**41**	120f. multicoloured	4·00	4·00
208	**41**	150f. multicoloured	5·25	5·25

42 Emblem and
Sitra Power
Station

1974. National Day. Multicoloured.
209		30f. Type **42**	85	30
210		60f. Type **42**	2·75	1·40
211		120f. Emblem and Bahrain Dry Dock	4·50	2·75
212		150f. As 120f.	6·00	3·75

43 Costume and
Headdress

1975. Bahrain Women's Costumes.
213	**43**	30f. multicoloured	85	85
214	-	60f. multicoloured	2·00	2·00
215	-	120f. multicoloured	4·00	4·00
216	-	150f. multicoloured	4·75	4·75

DESIGNS: Nos. 214/16, Costumes as Type **43**.

44 Jewelled
Pendant

1975. Costume Jewellery. Multicoloured.
217		30f. Type **44**	1·10	1·10
218		60f. Gold crown	2·50	2·50
219		120f. Jewelled necklace	5·00	5·00
220		150f. Gold necklace	6·50	6·50

45 Women
planting "Flower"

1975. International Women's Year. Multicoloured.
221		30f. Type **45**	2·40	1·10
222		60f. Woman holding I.W.Y. emblem	6·50	2·40

46 Head of Horse

1975. Horses. Multicoloured.
223a		60f. Type **46**	7·50	7·50
223b		60f. Grey	7·50	7·50
223c		60f. Grey with foal (horiz)	7·50	7·50
223d		60f. Close-up of Arab with grey	7·50	7·50
223e		60f. Grey and herd of browns (horiz)	7·50	7·50
223f		60f. Grey and brown (horiz)	7·50	7·50
223g		60f. Arabs riding horses (horiz)	7·50	7·50
223h		60f. Arab leading grey beside sea (horiz)	7·50	7·50

47 National
Flag

48 Map of
Bahrain within
Cog and Laurel

1976
224	**47**	5f. red, pink and blue	30	30
225	**47**	10f. red, pink & green	30	30
226	**47**	15f. red, pink & black	30	30
227	**47**	20f. red, pink & brown	55	30
227b	**48**	25f. black and grey	65	30
228	**48**	40f. black and blue	65	45
228a	**48**	50f. green, black & olive	65	55
228b	**48**	60f. black and green	1·10	65
229	**48**	80f. black and mauve	1·70	75
229b	**48**	100f. black and red	1·70	95
230	**48**	150f. black and yellow	3·25	1·50
231	**48**	200f. black and yellow	3·75	1·80

49 Concorde Taking off

1976. First Commercial Flight of Concorde. Multicoloured.
232		80f. Type **49**	4·00	3·00
233		80f. Concorde landing	4·00	3·00
234		80f. Concorde en route	4·00	3·00
235		80f. Concorde on runway	4·00	3·00

MS236 154×115 mm. Nos. 232/5.
Imperf 18·00 18·00

50 Soldier, Crest
and Flag

1976. Defence Force Cadets' Day.
237 **50** 40f. multicoloured 3·00 3·00
238 **50** 80f. multicoloured 5·25 5·25

51 King Khalid of Saudi
Arabia and Shaikh of Bahrain
with National Flags

1976. Visit to Bahrain of King Khalid of Saudi Arabia.
239 **51** 40f. multicoloured 2·40 1·70
240 **51** 80f. multicoloured 4·75 3·75

52 Shaikh Isa
bin Sulman
al-Khalifa

1976
241 **52** 300f. green and pale
green 5·25 2·75
242 **52** 400f. purple and pink 7·50 3·75
243 **52** 500f. blue and pale blue 9·00 4·75
244 **52** 1d. black and grey 16·00 8·50
244a **52** 2d. violet and lilac 20·00 10·50
244b **52** 3d. brown and pink 48·00 32·00

53 Ministry of
Housing Emblem,
Designs for
Houses and
Mosque

1976. National Day.
245 **53** 40f. multicoloured 2·10 95
246 **53** 80f. multicoloured 4·75 1·90

54 A.P.U. Emblem

1977. 25th Anniv of Arab Postal Union.
247 **54** 40f. multicoloured 2·10 1·60
248 **54** 80f. multicoloured 4·75 3·25

55 Dogs on Beach

1977. Saluki Dogs. Multicoloured.
249a 80f. Type **55** 3·75 3·75
249b 80f. Dog and dromedaries 3·75 3·75
249c 80f. Dog and antelope 3·75 3·75
249d 80f. Dog on lawn of building 3·75 3·75
249e 80f. Head of dog 3·75 3·75
249f 80f. Heads of two dogs 3·75 3·75
249g 80f. Dog in scrubland 3·75 3·75
249h 80f. Dogs fighting 3·75 3·75

56 Arab Students and
Candle

1977. International Literacy Day.
250 **56** 40f. multicoloured 2·10 1·60
251 **56** 80f. multicoloured 4·75 3·25

57 Shipyard Installations
and Arab Flags

1977. Inauguration of Arab Shipbuilding and Repair Yard
Co.
252 **57** 40f. multicoloured 2·10 1·60
253 **57** 80f. multicoloured 4·75 3·25

58 Microwave Antenna

1978. Tenth World Telecommunications Day.
254 **58** 40f. multicoloured 2·10 1·60
255 **58** 80f. silver, dp blue
& blue 4·75 3·25

59 Child being
helped to Walk

1979. International Year of the Child. Multicoloured.
256 50f. Type **59** 2·10 1·50
257 100f. Hands protecting child 4·50 2·75

60 Boom Dhow

1979. Dhows. Multicoloured.
258 100f. Type **60** 6·50 6·50
259 100f. Baghla 6·50 6·50
260 100f. Shu'ai (horiz) 6·50 6·50
261 100f. Ghanja (horiz) 6·50 6·50
262 100f. Kotia 6·50 6·50
263 100f. Sambuk 6·50 6·50
264 100f. Jaliboot (horiz) 6·50 6·50
265 100f. Zarook (horiz) 6·50 6·50

61 Dome of
Mosque, Mecca

1980. 1400th Anniv of Hejira.
266 **61** 50f. multicoloured 1·10 55
267 **61** 100f. multicoloured 2·40 1·80
268 **61** 150f. multicoloured 2·75 1·90
269 **61** 200f. multicoloured 3·75 3·00
MS270 84×91 mm. No. 267 (sold at
200f.) 10·00 10·00

62 Arab with Gyr Falcon

1980. Falconry. Multicoloured.
271 100f. Type **62** 4·25 2·40
272 100f. Arab looking at Lanner
falcon on wrist 4·25 2·40
273 100f. Peregrine falcon resting
with outstretched wings 4·25 2·40
274 100f. Peregrine falcon in flight 4·25 2·40
275 100f. Gyr falcon on pillar (with
camels in background) (vert) 4·25 2·40
276 100f. Gyr falcon on pillar (closer
view) (vert) 4·25 2·40
277 100f. Close-up of gyr falcon
facing right (vert) 4·25 2·40
278 100f. Close-up of Lanner falcon
full-face (vert) 4·25 2·40

63 Map and I.Y.D.P. Emblem

1981. International Year for Disabled Persons.
279 **63** 50f. multicoloured 2·75 75
280 **63** 100f. multicoloured 5·25 2·75

64 Jubilee Emblem

1981. 50th Anniv of Electrical Power in Bahrain.
281 **64** 50f. multicoloured 1·90 85
282 **64** 100f. multicoloured 4·50 2·40

65 Carving

1981. Handicrafts. Multicoloured.
283 50f. Type **65** 1·60 65
284 100f. Pottery 2·10 1·20
285 150f. Weaving 2·75 2·10
286 200f. Basket-making 4·25 2·75

66 Mosque

1981. Mosques.
287 **66** 50f. multicoloured 1·60 65
288 - 100f. multicoloured 2·10 1·20
289 - 150f. multicoloured 2·75 2·10
290 - 200f. multicoloured 4·25 2·75
DESIGNS: 100f. to 200f. As Type **66** but showing different
mosques.

67 Shaikh Isa bin
Sulman al-Khalifa

1981. 20th Anniv of Coronation of Shaikh Isa bin Sulman
al-Khalifa.
291 **67** 15f. gold, grey and
mauve 75 75
292 **67** 50f. gold, grey and red 1·50 1·50
293 **67** 100f. gold, grey and
brown 2·50 2·50

294 **67** 150f. gold, grey and blue 4·00 4·00
295 **67** 200f. gold, grey and blue 4·75 4·75

68 Dorcas Gazelle

1982. Al-Areen Wildlife Park. Multicoloured.
296 100f. Goitred gazelle 2·75 2·75
297 100f. Type **68** 2·75 2·75
298 100f. Dhub lizard 2·75 2·75
299 100f. Brown hares 2·75 2·75
300 100f. Arabian oryx 2·75 2·75
301 100f. Addax 2·75 2·75

69 Flags and
Clasped Hands
encircling Emblem

1982. Third Supreme Council Session of Gulf Co-
operation Council.
302 **69** 50f. multicoloured 1·20 1·20
303 - 100f. multicoloured 3·25 3·25

70 Madinat Hamad

1983. Opening of Madinat Hamad New Town.
Multicoloured.
304 50f. Type **70** 2·10 65
305 100f. View of Madinat Hamad
(different) 3·75 2·10

71 Shaikh Isa bin Sulman
al-Khalifa

1983. Bicentenary of Al-Khalifa Dynasty. Multicoloured.
306 100f. Type **71** 1·30 1·30
307 100f. Cartouche of Ali bin
Khalifa al-Khalifa 1·30 1·30
308 100f. Isa bin Ali al-Khalifa 1·30 1·30
309 100f. Hamad bin Isa al-Khalifa 1·30 1·30
310 100f. Salman bin Hamad
al-Khalifa 1·30 1·30
311 100f. Cartouche of Ahmed bin
Mohammed al-Khalifa 1·30 1·30
312 100f. Cartouche of Salman bin
Ahmed al-Khalifa 1·30 1·30
313 100f. Cartouche of Abdullah bin
Ahmed al-Khalifa 1·30 1·30
314 100f. Cartouche of Mohammed
bin Khalifa al-Khalifa 1·30 1·30
MS315 109×83 mm. 500f. Type **71**
(60×38 mm) 8·50 8·50

72 G.C.C. and Traffic and
Licensing Directorate
Emblems

1984. Gulf Co-operation Council Traffic Week.
316 **72** 15f. multicoloured 55 20
317 **72** 50f. multicoloured 1·60 55
318 **72** 100f. multicoloured 2·40 1·10

73 Hurdling

1984. Olympic Games, Los Angeles. Multicoloured.
319 15f. Type **73** 30 30
320 50f. Show-jumping 1·10 1·10
321 100f. Swimming 2·10 2·10

322		150f. Fencing	2·75	2·75
323		200f. Shooting	4·50	4·50

74 Manama and Emblem

1984. Centenary of Postal Services.

324	74	15f. multicoloured	55	20
325	74	50f. multicoloured	1·60	55
326	74	100f. multicoloured	2·75	1·40

75 Narrow-barred Spanish Mackerel

1985. Fish. Multicoloured.

327		100f. Type **75**	2·10	2·10
328		100f. Crocodile needlefish (three fishes)	2·10	2·10
329		100f. Sombre sweetlips (fish swimming to left, blue and lilac background)	2·10	2·10
330		100f. White-spotted rabbitfish (two fishes, blue and lilac background)	2·10	2·10
331		100f. Grey mullet (two fishes, green and pink background)	2·10	2·10
332		100f. Two-banded seabream (green and grey background)	2·10	2·10
333		100f. River seabream (blue background)	2·10	2·10
334		100f. Malabar grouper (green background)	2·10	2·10
335		100f. Small-toothed emperor (pink anemone background)	2·10	2·10
336		100f. Golden trevally (fish swimming to right, blue and lilac background)	2·10	2·10

76 Hands cupping Emblem

1985. Arabian Gulf States Social Work Week.

337	76	15f. multicoloured	45	45
338	76	50f. multicoloured	1·30	1·30
339	76	100f. multicoloured	2·75	2·75

77 I.Y.Y. Emblem

1986. International Youth Year.

340	77	15f. multicoloured	45	45
341	77	50f. multicoloured	1·30	1·30
342	77	100f. multicoloured	2·75	2·75

78 Aerial View of Causeway

1986. Opening of Saudi–Bahrain Causeway. Multicoloured.

343	78	15f. Type **78**	45	45
344		50f. Aerial view of island	1·30	1·30
345		100f. Aerial view of road bridge	2·10	2·10

79 Shaikh Isa bin Sulman al-Khalifa

1986. 25th Anniv of Accession of Shaikh Isa bin Sulman al-Khalifa.

346	79	15f. multicoloured	45	45
347	79	50f. multicoloured	1·30	1·30
348	79	100f. multicoloured	2·10	2·10
MS349		148×110 mm. Nos. 346/8	8·50	8·50

80 Emblem

1988. 40th Anniv of W.H.O.

350	80	50f. multicoloured	75	75
351	80	150f. multicoloured	2·10	2·10

81 Centre

1988. Opening of Ahmed al-Fateh Islamic Centre.

352	81	50f. multicoloured	75	75
353	81	150f. multicoloured	2·10	2·10

82 Running

1988. Olympic Games, Seoul. Multicoloured.

354		50f. Type **82**	45	30
355		80f. Dressage	85	55
356		150f. Fencing	1·80	1·30
357		200f. Football	2·75	2·10

83 Emblem in "1988"

1988. Ninth Supreme Council Meeting of Gulf Co-operation Council.

358	83	50f. multicoloured	75	75
359	83	150f. multicoloured	2·10	2·10

84 Arab leading Camel

1989. Camels. Multicoloured.

360		150f. Type **84**	1·60	1·60
361		150f. Arab leading camel (different)	1·60	1·60
362		150f. Head of camel and pump-head	1·60	1·60
363		150f. Close-up of Arab on camel	1·60	1·60
364		150f. Arab riding camel	1·60	1·60
365		150f. Two Arab camel-riders	1·60	1·60
366		150f. Head of camel and camel-rider (horiz)	1·60	1·60
367		150f. Camels at rest in camp (horiz)	1·60	1·60
368		150f. Camels with calf (horiz)	1·60	1·60
369		150f. Heads of three camels (horiz)	1·60	1·60
370		150f. Camel in scrubland (horiz)	1·60	1·60
371		150f. Arab on camel (horiz)	1·60	1·60

85 Shaikh Isa bin Sulman al-Khalifa

1989. Multicoloured, colour of frame given.

372	85	25f. green	30	20
373	85	40f. grey	45	20
374	85	50f. pink	45	20
375	85	60f. brown	55	20
376	85	75f. mauve	75	20
377	85	80f. green	75	20
378	85	100f. orange	1·10	30
379	85	120f. violet	1·20	30
380	85	150f. grey	1·50	55
381	85	200f. blue	1·80	75
MS382		167×132 mm. Nos. 372/81	9·00	9·00

86 Houbara Bustards

1990. The Houbara Bustard. Multicoloured.

383		150f. Type **86**	1·50	1·50
384		150f. Two bustards (facing each other)	1·50	1·50
385		150f. Chicks and eggs	1·50	1·50
386		150f. Adult and chick	1·50	1·50
387		150f. Adult (vert)	1·50	1·50
388		150f. In flight	1·50	1·50
389		150f. Adult (facing right)	1·50	1·50
390		150f. Young bird (vert)	1·50	1·50
391		150f. Adult (facing left)	1·50	1·50
392		150f. Bird in display plumage	1·50	1·50
393		150f. Two bustards in display plumage	1·50	1·50
394		150f. Two bustards with bridge in background	1·50	1·50

87 Anniversary Emblem

1990. 40th Anniv of Gulf Air.

395	87	50f. multicoloured	55	30
396	87	80f. multicoloured	85	55
397	87	150f. multicoloured	1·60	1·10
398	87	200f. multicoloured	2·40	1·50

88 Anniversary Emblem

1990. 50th Anniv of Bahrain Chamber of Commerce and Industry.

399	88	50f. multicoloured	55	30
400	88	80f. multicoloured	75	55
401	88	150f. multicoloured	1·40	95
402	88	200f. multicoloured	1·80	1·30

89 I.L.Y. Emblem

1990. International Literacy Year.

403	89	50f. multicoloured	55	30
404	89	80f. multicoloured	75	55
405	89	150f. multicoloured	1·40	95
406	89	200f. multicoloured	1·90	1·30

90 Crested Lark

1991. Birds. Multicoloured.

407		150f. Type **90**	1·30	1·30
408		150f. Hoopoe (*Upupa epops*)	1·30	1·30
409		150f. White-cheeked bulbul (*Pycnonotus leucogenys*)	1·30	1·30
410		150f. Turtle dove (*Streptopelia turtur*)	1·30	1·30
411		150f. Collared dove (*Streptopelia decaocto*)	1·30	1·30
412		150f. Common kestrel (*Falco tinnunculus*)	1·30	1·30
413		150f. House sparrow (*Passer domesticus*) (horiz)	1·30	1·30
414		150f. Great grey shrike (*Lanius excubitor*) (horiz)	1·30	1·30
415		150f. Rose-ringed parakeet (*Psittacula krameri*)	1·30	1·30

91 Shaikh Isa bin Sulman al-Khalifa

1991. 30th Anniv of Amir's Coronation.

416	91	50f. multicoloured	45	30
417	A	50f. multicoloured	45	30
418	91	80f. multicoloured	65	45
419	A	80f. multicoloured	65	45
420	91	150f. multicoloured	1·40	85
421	A	150f. multicoloured	1·40	85
422	91	200f. multicoloured	1·80	1·10
423	A	200f. multicoloured	1·80	1·10
MS424		134×114 mm. **91** 500f. multicoloured; A 500f. multicoloured	10·50	10·50

DESIGN: A, The Amir and sunburst.

92 White Stork (*Ciconia ciconia*)

1992. Migratory Birds. Multicoloured.

425		150f. Type **92**	1·20	1·20
426		150f. European bee eater (*Merops apiaster*)	1·20	1·20
427		150f. Common starling (*Sturnus vulgaris*)	1·20	1·20
428		150f. Grey hypocolius (*Hypocolius ampelinus*)	1·20	1·20
429		150f. European cuckoo (*Cuculus canorus*)	1·20	1·20
430		150f. Mistle thrush (*Turdus viscivorus*)	1·20	1·20
431		150f. European roller (*Coracias garrulus*)	1·20	1·20
432		150f. Eurasian goldfinch (*Carduelis carduelis*)	1·20	1·20
433		150f. Red-backed shrike (*Lanius collurio*)	1·20	1·20
434		150f. Redwing (*Turdus iliacus*) (horiz)	1·20	1·20
435		150f. Pied wagtail (*Motacilla alba*) (horiz)	1·20	1·20
436		150f. Golden oriole (*Oriolus oriolus*) (horiz)	1·20	1·20
437		150f. European robin (*Erithacus rubecula*)	1·20	1·20
438		150f. Nightingale (*Luscinia luscinia*)	1·20	1·20
439		150f. Spotted flycatcher (*Muscicapa striata*)	1·20	1·20
440		150f. Barn swallow (*Hirundo rustica*)	1·20	1·20

93 Start of Race

1992. Horse-racing. Multicoloured.

441		150f. Type **93**	1·30	1·30
442		150f. Parading in paddock	1·30	1·30
443		150f. Galloping around bend	1·30	1·30
444		150f. Galloping past national flags	1·30	1·30
445		150f. Galloping past spectator stand	1·30	1·30
446		150f. Head-on view of horses	1·30	1·30
447		150f. Reaching winning post	1·30	1·30
448		150f. A black and a grey galloping	1·30	1·30

94 Show-jumping

1992. Olympic Games, Barcelona. Multicoloured.

449		50f. Type **94**	45	45
450		80f. Running	85	85
451		150f. Karate	1·60	1·60
452		200f. Cycling	2·10	2·10

95 Airport

1992. 60th Anniv of Bahrain International Airport.

453	95	50f. multicoloured	45	45
454	95	80f. multicoloured	85	85

| 455 | 95 | 150f. multicoloured | 1·60 | 1·60 |
| 456 | 95 | 200f. multicoloured | 2·10 | 2·10 |

96 Girl skipping

1992. Children's Paintings. Multicoloured.

457	50f. Type **96**	45	30
458	80f. Women	65	45
459	150f. Women preparing food (horiz)	1·30	85
460	200f. Pearl divers (horiz)	1·70	1·20

97 Cable-cars and Pylons

1992. Expansion of Aluminium Industry. Multicoloured.

461	50f. Type **97**	45	45
462	80f. Worker in aluminium plant	85	85
463	150f. Aerial view of aluminium plant	1·60	1·60
464	200f. Processed aluminium	2·10	2·10

98 Artillery Gun Crew

1993. 25th Anniv of Bahrain Defence Force. Multicoloured.

465	50f. Type **98**	45	45
466	80f. General Dynamics Fighting Falcon jet fighters, tanks and patrol boat	75	75
467	150f. "Ahmed al Fatah" (missile corvette) (horiz)	1·50	1·50
468	200f. Fighting Falcon over Bahrain (horiz)	1·90	1·90

99 Satellite View of Bahrain

1993. World Meteorological Day. Multicoloured.

469	50f. Type **99**	65	65
470	150f. Satellite picture of world (horiz)	1·60	1·60
471	200f. Earth seen from space	2·50	2·50

100 Purple Heron

1993. Water Birds. Multicoloured.

472	150f. Type **100**	1·60	1·60
473	150f. Moorhen (*Gallinula chloropus*)	1·60	1·60
474	150f. Socotra cormorant (*Phalacrocorax nigrogularis*)	1·60	1·60
475	150f. Crab plover (*Dromas ardeola*)	1·60	1·60
476	150f. River kingfisher (*Alcedo atthis*)	1·60	1·60
477	150f. Northern lapwing (*Vanellus vanellus*)	1·60	1·60
478	150f. Oystercatcher (*Haematopus ostralegus*) (horiz)	1·60	1·60
479	150f. Black-crowned night heron (*Nycticorax nycticorax*)	1·60	1·60
480	150f. Caspian tern (*Sterna caspia*) (horiz)	1·60	1·60

481	150f. Ruddy turnstone (*Arenaria interpres*) (horiz)	1·60	1·60
482	150f. Water rail (*Rallus aquaticus*) (horiz)	1·60	1·60
483	150f. Mallard (*Anas platyrhynchos*) (horiz)	1·60	1·60
484	150f. Lesser black-backed gull (*Larus fuscus*) (horiz)	1·60	1·60

101 Fawn

1993. The Goitered Gazelle. Multicoloured.

485	25f. Type **101**	1·20	1·20
486	50f. Doe walking	2·40	2·40
487	50f. Doe with ears pricked	2·40	2·40
488	150f. Male gazelle	7·00	7·00

102 *Lycium shawii*

1993. Wild Flowers. Multicoloured.

489	150f. Type **102**	1·10	1·10
490	150f. *Alhagi maurorum*	1·10	1·10
491	150f. Caper-bush (*Caparis spinosa*)	1·10	1·10
492	150f. *Cistanche phelypae*	1·10	1·10
493	150f. *Asphodelus tenuifolius*	1·10	1·10
494	150f. *Limonium axillare*	1·10	1·10
495	150f. *Cynomorium coccineum*	1·10	1·10
496	150f. *Calligonum polygonoides*	1·10	1·10

103 Children and Silhouettes of Parents' Heads

1994. International Year of the Family.

497	103	50f. multicoloured	45	45
498	103	80f. multicoloured	75	75
499	103	150f. multicoloured	1·50	1·50
500	103	200f. multicoloured	1·90	1·90

104 *Lepidochrysops arabicus*

1994. Butterflies. Multicoloured.

501	50f. Type **104**	30	30
502	50f. *Ypthima bolanica*	30	30
503	50f. Desert grass yellow (*Eurema brigitta*)	30	30
504	50f. *Precis limnoria*	30	30
505	50f. Small tortoiseshell (*Aglais urticae*)	30	30
506	50f. Protomedia (*Colotis protomedia*)	30	30
507	50f. Clouded mother-of-pearl (*Salamis anacardii*)	30	30
508	50f. *Byblia ilithyia*	30	30
509	150f. Swallowtail (*Papilio machaon*) (horiz)	95	95
510	150f. Blue (*Agrodiaetus loewii*) (horiz)	95	95
511	150f. Painted lady (*Vanessa cardui*) (horiz)	95	95
512	150f. Chequered swallowtail (*Papilio demoleus*) (horiz)	95	95
513	150f. Guineafowl (*Hamanumida daedalus*) (horiz)	95	95
514	150f. *Funonia orithya* (horiz)	95	95
515	150f. *Funonia chorimine* (horiz)	95	95
516	150f. *Colias croceus* (horiz)	95	95

105 Anniversary Emblem

1994. 75th Anniv of International Red Cross and Red Crescent.

517	105	50f. multicoloured	45	45
518	105	80f. multicoloured	75	75
519	105	150f. multicoloured	1·50	1·50
520	105	200f. multicoloured	1·90	1·90

106 Goalkeeper

1994. World Cup Football Championship, U.S.A. Multicoloured.

521	50f. Type **106**	55	55
522	80f. Players	85	85
523	150f. Players' legs	1·60	1·60
524	200f. Player on ground	2·10	2·10

107 Earth Station

1994. 25th Anniv of Ras Abu Jarjour Satellite Earth Station.

525	107	50f. multicoloured	45	45
526	107	80f. multicoloured	75	75
527	107	150f. multicoloured	1·50	1·50
528	107	200f. multicoloured	1·90	1·90

108 Children on Open Book, Pen as Torch and School

1994. 75th Anniv of Education in Bahrain.

529	108	50f. multicoloured	45	45
530	108	80f. multicoloured	75	75
531	108	150f. multicoloured	1·50	1·50
532	108	200f. multicoloured	1·90	1·90

109 Dove with "Olive Branch" of Members' Flags

1994. 15th Gulf Co-operation Council Supreme Council Session, Bahrain.

533	109	50f. multicoloured	45	45
534	109	80f. multicoloured	75	75
535	109	150f. multicoloured	1·40	1·40
536	109	200f. multicoloured	1·80	1·80

110 Date Palm in Bloom

1995. The Date Palm.

537	110	80f. Type **110**	75	75
538	100f. Date palm with unripened dates	85	85	
539	200f. Dates ripening	1·80	1·80	

| 540 | 250f. Date palm trees with ripened dates | 2·10 | 2·10 |
| **MS**541 | 134×126 mm. 500f. Dates, coffee pot, cups and date palms (65×47 mm) | 4·25 | 4·25 |

111 Campaign Emblem

1995. World Health Day. Anti-poliomyelitis Campaign.

542	111	80f. multicoloured	55	55
543	111	200f. multicoloured	1·50	1·50
544	111	250f. multicoloured	2·00	2·00

112 Exhibition Emblem

1995. First National Industries Exhibition.

545	112	80f. multicoloured	55	55
546	112	200f. multicoloured	1·50	1·50
547	112	250f. multicoloured	2·00	2·00

113 Crops

1995. 50th Anniv of F.A.O. Multicoloured.

548	80f. Type **113**	55	55
549	200f. Field of crops	1·50	1·50
550	250f. Field of cabbages	2·00	2·00

114 Headquarters, Cairo

1995. 50th Anniv of Arab League.

551	114	80f. multicoloured	55	55
552	114	200f. multicoloured	1·50	1·50
553	114	250f. multicoloured	2·00	2·00

115 U.N. Headquarters and Map of Bahrain

1995. 50th Anniv of U.N.O.

554	115	80f. multicoloured	55	55
555	115	100f. multicoloured	75	75
556	115	200f. multicoloured	1·60	1·60
557	115	250f. multicoloured	2·00	2·00

116 Tower

1995. Traditional Architecture. Multicoloured.

558	200f. Type **116**	1·30	1·30
559	200f. Balcony	1·30	1·30
560	200f. Doorway	1·30	1·30
561	200f. Multi-storied facade	1·30	1·30
562	200f. Entrance flanked by two windows	1·30	1·30
563	200f. Three arched windows	1·30	1·30

117 National Flag
and Shaikh Isa Bin
Sulman al-Khalifa

1995. National Day.

564	117	80f. multicoloured	55	55
565	117	100f. multicoloured	75	75
566	117	200f. multicoloured	1·60	1·60
567	117	250f. multicoloured	2·00	2·00

118 Bookcase and
Open Book

1996. 50th Anniv of Public Library.

568	118	80f. multicoloured	55	55
569	118	200f. multicoloured	1·60	1·60
570	118	250f. multicoloured	2·00	2·00

119 Divers on Dhow

1996. Pearl Diving. Multicoloured.

571		80f. Type **119**	55	55
572		100f. Divers	65	65
573		200f. Diver on sea-bed and dhow	1·30	1·30
574		250f. Diver with net	1·80	1·80
MS575		119×119 mm. 500f. Diving equipment (70×70 mm)	4·25	4·25

120 Globe, Ship and Olympic
Rings

1996. Olympic Games, Atlanta.

576	120	80f. multicoloured	55	55
577	120	100f. multicoloured	65	65
578	120	200f. multicoloured	1·30	1·30
579	120	250f. multicoloured	1·80	1·80

121 Interpol Emblem and
Map, Arms and Flag of
Bahrain

1996. 24th Anniv of Membership of International Criminal Police (Interpol).

580	121	80f. multicoloured	55	55
581	121	100f. multicoloured	75	75
582	121	200f. multicoloured	1·60	1·60
583	121	250f. multicoloured	2·00	2·00

122 Anniversary Emblems in
English and Arabic

1996. 25th Anniv of Aluminium Bahrain.

584	122	80f. multicoloured	45	45
585	122	100f. multicoloured	55	55
586	122	200f. multicoloured	1·30	1·30
587	122	250f. multicoloured	1·60	1·60

123 National Flag, Map and
Shaikh Isa bin Sulman
al-Khalifa

1996. 35th Anniv of Amir's Accession.

588	123	80f. multicoloured	55	55
589	123	100f. multicoloured	75	75
590	123	200f. multicoloured	1·60	1·60
591	123	250f. multicoloured	2·00	2·00

124 Tanker, Refinery and
Storage Tanks

1997. 60th Anniv of Bahrain Refinery.

592	124	80f. multicoloured	55	55
593	124	200f. multicoloured	1·40	1·40
594	124	250f. multicoloured	1·90	1·90

125 Kuheilaan Weld umm
Zorayr

1997. Arab Horses at Amiri Stud. Multicoloured.

595	200f. Musannaan (white horse), Al-Jellabieh and Rabdaan	1·40	1·40
596	200f. Type **125**	1·40	1·40
597	200f. Al-Jellaby	1·40	1·40
598	200f. Musannaan (brown horse)	1·40	1·40
599	200f. Kuheilaan Aladiyat	1·40	1·40
600	200f. Kuheilaan Aafas	1·40	1·40
601	200f. Al-Dhahma	1·40	1·40
602	200f. Mlolshaan	1·40	1·40
603	200f. Al-Kray	1·40	1·40
604	200f. Krush	1·40	1·40
605	200f. Al Hamdaany	1·40	1·40
606	200f. Hadhfaan	1·40	1·40
607	200f. Rabda	1·40	1·40
608	200f. Al-Suwaitieh	1·40	1·40
609	200f. Al-Obeyah	1·40	1·40
610	200f. Al-Shuwaimeh	1·40	1·40
611	200f. Al-Ma'anaghieh	1·40	1·40
612	200f. Al-Tuwaisah	1·40	1·40
613	200f. Wadhna	1·40	1·40
614	200f. Al-Saqlawieh	1·40	1·40
615	200f. Al-Shawafah	1·40	1·40

126 Championship Emblem

1997. Ninth World Men's Junior Volleyball Championship.

616	126	80f. multicoloured	55	55
617	126	100f. multicoloured	75	75
618	126	200f. multicoloured	1·40	1·40
619	126	250f. multicoloured	1·80	1·80

127 Emblem

1997. Tenth Anniv of Montreal Protocol (on reduction of use of chlorofluorocarbons).

620	127	80f. multicoloured	55	55
621	127	100f. multicoloured	75	75
622	127	200f. multicoloured	1·40	1·40
623	127	250f. multicoloured	1·80	1·80

128 Close-up of Support

1997. Inauguration of Shaikh Isa bin Salman Bridge between Manama and Muharraq. Multicoloured.

624		80f. Type **128**	55	55
625		200f. Distant view of middle section	1·50	1·50
626		250f. View of complete bridge (75×26 mm)	1·80	1·80
MS627		137×116 mm. 500f. As No. 626	3·75	3·75

129 Complex at Night

1998. Inauguration of Urea Plant at Gulf Petrochemical Industries Co Complex. Mult.

628		80f. Type **129**	55	55
629		200f. Refining towers	1·50	1·50
630		250f. Aerial view of complex	1·80	1·80

130 Map of Bahrain and
Anniversary Emblem

1998. 50th Anniv of W.H.O.

631	130	80f. multicoloured	55	55
632	130	200f. multicoloured	1·50	1·50
633	130	250f. multicoloured	1·80	1·80

131 Emblem

1998. World Cup Football Championship, France. Multicoloured.

634		80f. Type **131**	55	55
635		200f. Globes and football forming "98" (vert)	1·50	1·50
636		250f. Footballers and globe (vert)	1·80	1·80

132 Football

1998. 14th Arabian Gulf Cup Football Championship, Bahrain. Multicoloured.

637		80f. Type **132**	55	55
638		200f. Close-up of football	1·50	1·50
639		250f. As No. 638	1·80	1·80

133 Emblem and
Koran

1999. Holy Koran Reading Competition.

640	133	100f. multicoloured	75	75
641	133	200f. multicoloured	1·60	1·60
642	133	250f. multicoloured	1·80	1·80

134 Shaikh Isa bin
Sulman al-Khalifa and
State Flag

1999. Shaikh Isa bin Sulman al-Khalifa Commemoration. Multicoloured.

643		100f. Type **134**	75	75
644		200f. Shaikh and map of Bahrain (41×31 mm)	1·60	1·60
645		250f. Shaikh, map of Bahrain and state flag	1·80	1·80
MS646		125×170 mm. 500f. Type **134** (67×102 mm)	4·25	4·25

135 Emblem

1999. International Year of the Elderly. Multicoloured.

647		100f. Type **135**	75	75
648		200f. Emblem and flame	1·60	1·60
649		250f. Emblem (different)	1·80	1·80

136 Emblem

1999. Tenth Anniv of Bahrain Stock Exchange. Multicoloured.

650		100f. Type **136**	75	75
651		200f. Shaikh Isa bin Salman Bridge and emblem	1·60	1·60
652		250f. Globe and emblem	1·80	1·80

137 Shaikh Isa
bin Salman and
Shaikh Hamad
bin Isa holding
Flag

1999. National Day. Multicoloured.

653		100f. Type **137**	75	75
654		200f. Shaikh Hamad bin Isa and flag	1·60	1·60
655		250f. Shaikh Hamad bin Isa and globe	1·80	1·80
MS656		115×155 mm. 500f. As Type **137** (56×96 mm)	3·75	3·75

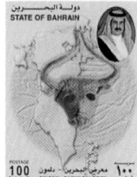

138 Map of Bahrain
and Animal Skull

2000. Dilmun Exhibition. Multicoloured.

657		100f. Type **138**	75	75
658		200f. Map of Bahrain superimposed over animal skull	1·60	1·60
659		250f. Map of Bahrain and artefact	1·80	1·80

139 Map of Bahrain and
Emblem

2000. 50th Anniv of Gulf Air. Multicoloured.

660	100f. Type **139**	1·20	1·20
661	200f. Map of Bahrain and emblem in circle	2·40	2·40
662	250f. Map of Bahrain, emblem and eagles	2·75	2·75

140 Emblem

2000. "Made in Bahrain 2000" Exhibition. Multicoloured.

663	100f. Type **140**	1·20	1·20
664	200f. Type **140**	2·40	2·40
665	250f. Oil refinery	2·75	2·75

141 Minarets and Fort

2000. Millennium. Multicoloured.

666	100f. Type **141**	1·30	1·30
667	100f. Dhows and factories	1·30	1·30
668	100f. Man harvesting dates	1·30	1·30
669	100f. Fort, globe and dish aerial	1·30	1·30
670	200f. Lake and bridge	1·80	1·80
671	200f. Modern building and woman	1·80	1·80
672	200f. Dhows, jug and wicker basket	1·80	1·80
673	200f. Horseman and falconer	1·80	1·80
674	250f. Pearl divers	2·20	2·20
675	250f. Opening clams	2·20	2·20
676	250f. Fishermen	2·20	2·20
677	250f. Man mending fishing nets	2·20	2·20

142 Emblem

2000. 21st Gulf Co-operation Council Supreme Council Session, Bahrain. Multicoloured.

678	100f. Type **142**	1·20	1·20
679	200f. Members' flags	2·40	2·40

143 Stained-glass Window

2001. Tenth Anniv of Beit Al Qur'an (Islamic institution). Multicoloured.

680	100f. Type **143**	75	75
681	200f. Beit Al Qur'an by night	1·50	1·50
682	250f. Facade	2·00	2·00

MS683 170×80 mm. 500f. Subjects as Nos. 680/2 but forming composite design. Imperf ... 3·75 3·75

144 Building

2001. 25th Anniv of Ministry of Housing and Agriculture. Multicoloured.

684	100f. Type **144**	75	75
685	150f. Sculpture and building	1·20	1·20
686	200f. Building viewed through arch	1·50	1·50
687	250f. Tall, arched building	2·00	2·00

145 Emblem and Stylized Figures

2001. International Year of Volunteers. Multicoloured.

688	100f. Type **145**	75	75
689	150f. Hands encircling emblem	1·20	1·20
690	200f. Star pattern and emblem	1·50	1·50
691	250f. Paper cut figures	2·00	2·00

146 Emblem

2002. Arab Women's Day. Multicoloured.

692	100f. Type **146**	75	75
693	200f. Elliptical shapes and emblem	1·60	1·60
694	250f. Women (horiz)	2·00	2·00

147 Football and Emblem

2002. World Cup Football Championship, Japan and South Korea. Sheet 124×64 mm containing T **147** and similar vert designs. Multicoloured.

MS695 100f. Type **147**; 200f. Earth, football and emblem; 250f. Football and white peaks ... 4·25 4·25

148 Shaikh Hamad Bin Isa Al Khalifa

2002. Multicoloured, background colour given. (a) Size 22×28 mm.

696	**148**	25f. brown	10	10
697	**148**	40f. purple	30	30
698	**148**	50f. grey	40	40
699	**148**	60f. blue	50	50
700	**148**	80f. blue	65	65
701	**148**	100f. orange	75	75
702	**148**	125f. mauve	95	95
703	**148**	150f. orange	1·10	1·10
704	**148**	200f. green	1·60	1·60
705	**148**	250f. pink	2·00	2·00
706	**148**	300f. brown	2·40	2·40
707	**148**	400f. green	3·25	3·25

(b) 26×36 mm.

708	500f. mauve	3·75	3·75
709	1d. orange	8·00	8·00
710	2d. blue	16·00	16·00
711	3d. brown	24·00	24·00

MS712 246×162 mm. Nos. 696/711 ... 65·00 65·00

149 Stylized Teacher, Child and Symbols of Communication

2002. World Teacher's Day.

713	**149**	100f. multicoloured	65	65
714	**149**	200f. multicoloured	1·30	1·30

150 Emblem

2002. Parliamentary Election, 2002. Multicoloured.

715	100f. Type **150**	65	65
716	200f. Hand posting voting slip (vert)	1·30	1·30

151 Shaikh Hamad Bin Isa Al Khalifa and Flag

2002. National Day. Multicoloured.

717	100f. Type **151**	65	65
718	200f. Shaikh Hamad Bin Isa and flag (different) (vert)	1·30	1·30
719	250f. As No. 718 but with maroon background (vert)	1·60	1·60

152 Bahrain

2003. Arab Summit Conference, Sharm el-Sheikh, Egypt. Designs representing landmarks from each state.

720	100f. Type **152**	65	65
721	100f. Sudan	65	65
722	100f. Saudi Arabia	65	65
723	100f. Djibouti	65	65
724	100f. Algeria	65	65
725	100f. Tunisia	65	65
726	100f. UAE	65	65
727	100f. Jordan	65	65
728	200f. Comoros	1·30	1·30
729	200f. Qatar	1·30	1·30
730	200f. Palestine	1·30	1·30
731	200f. Oman	1·30	1·30
732	200f. Iraq	1·30	1·30
733	200f. Somalia	1·30	1·30
734	200f. Syria	1·30	1·30
735	250f. Yemen	1·60	1·60
736	250f. Mauritania	1·60	1·60
737	250f. Egypt	1·60	1·60
738	250f. Libya	1·60	1·60
739	250f. Lebanon	1·60	1·60
740	250f. Kuwait	1·60	1·60

MS741 120×103 mm. 500f. Buildings surrounding Holy Kabba. Imperf ... 3·25 3·25

153 Children, Emblem and Flowers

2003. World Health Day. Multicoloured.

742	100f. Type **153**	75	75
743	200f. Stylized figures and emblem	1·60	1·60

154 Swan

2003. World Environment Day. Flora and Fauna. Multicoloured.

744	100f. Type **154**	75	75
745	100f. Peacock	75	75
746	100f. Flamingos	75	75
747	100f. Ostrich	75	75
748	200f. *Rumex vesicarius*	1·50	1·50
749	200f. *Arnebia hispidissima*	1·50	1·50
750	200f. *Capparis spinosa*	1·50	1·50
751	200f. *Cassia italica*	1·50	1·50
752	250f. Crab	1·80	1·80
753	250f. Turtle	1·80	1·80
754	250f. Sting ray	1·80	1·80
755	250f. Shark	1·80	1·80

155 Girl Writing

2003. Children's Day. Multicoloured.

756	100f. Type **155**	60	60
757	150f. Girl painting	80	80
758	200f. Children playing (horiz)	1·20	1·20
759	250f. School class (horiz)	1·40	1·40

156 Shaikh Hamad Bin Isa Al Khalifa on Horseback

2003. National Day.

760	**156**	100f. multicoloured	60	60
761	**156**	200f. multicoloured	1·20	1·20
762	**156**	250f. multicoloured	1·40	1·40

MS763 125×167 mm. **156** 500f. multicoloured (57×87 mm) ... 2·75 2·75

157 Mother and Baby

2004. Mothers' Day. Multicoloured.

764	100f. Type **157**	55	55
765	200f. Mother and child reading	1·10	1·10

158 Computer Model of Formula One Car (image scaled to 56% of original size)

2004. Bahrain Formula One Grand Prix. Sheet 180×180 mm containing T **158** and similar multicoloured designs.

MS766 100f. Type **158**; 150f. Model facing right; 200f. Side view; 250f. Rear view; 500f. Shakir tower, Bahrain International Circuit (40×40 mm) ... 6·50 6·50

159 Healthy Figures reaching for Drug Abuser

2004. International Day against Drug Abuse. Multicoloured.

767	100f. Type **159**	55	55
768	150f. Shrunken arm	70	70
769	200f. Needles and seated figure	1·10	1·10
770	250f. Healthy hands reaching to diseased hand	1·30	1·30

160 Running

2004. Olympic Games, Athens 2004. Sheet 211×65 mm containing T **160** and similar horiz designs. Multicoloured.

MS771 100f. Type **160**; 150f. Swimming; 200f. Windsurfing; 250f. Pistol Shooting ... 3·50 3·50

161 Hands holding Emblem

2004. 25th Session of Arabian Gulf States Co-operation Supreme Council. Multicoloured.

772	100f. Type **161**		55	55
773	200f. Emblem with flags as ribbons		1·10	1·10
774	250f. Emblem on background of flags		1·30	1·30
MS775	201×100 mm. 500f. Symbols of Gulf States (175×34 mm)		2·30	2·30

162 Amaryllis Flower and Fair Emblem

2005. Bahrain Garden Fair. Multicoloured.

776	100f. Type **162**	55	55
777	200f. Rose	1·10	1·10
778	250f. Jasmine	1·30	1·30

163 Scales and Court Building

2005. Inauguration of Constitutional Court.

779	**163**	100f. multicoloured	55	55
780	**163**	200f. multicoloured	1·10	1·10
791	**163**	250f. multicoloured	70	70

164 Statuette

2005. 50th Anniv of Discovery of Dilmon Civilization. Multicoloured.

782	100f. Type **164**	55	55
783	100f. Engraved seals	55	55
784	100f. Horseman (statue)	55	55
785	200f. pot spilling jewellery	1·10	1·10
786	200f. Two decorated pots	1·10	1·10
787	200f. Cylindrical vase and pot with lid	1·10	1·10
788	250f. Walls and gateway (horiz)	1·30	1·30
789	250f. Aerial view (horiz)	1·30	1·30
790	250f. Walls and steps (horiz)	1·30	1·30
MS791	Two sheets. (a) 195×155 mm. Nos. 782/90. (b) 140×105 mm. 500f. Sheikh Salman Bin Hamad Al Khalifa and archaeologists (88×58 mm)	10·50	10·50

165 King Hamad bin Isa Al Khalifa

2005. National Day. Multicoloured.

792	100f. Type **165**	55	55
793	200f. Flag and King Al Khalifa (vert)	1·10	1·10
794	250f. Towers and King Al Khalifa	1·30	1·30

166 Flag

2006. 25th Anniv of Gulf Co-operation Council. Multicoloured.

795	100f. Type **166**	1·00	1·00
MS796	165×105 mm. 500f. Flags of member states. Imperf	2·40	2·40

Stamps of similar designs were issued by Kuwait, Oman, Qatar, Saudi Arabia and United Arab Emirates.

167 Emblem

2006. World Cup Football Championship, Germany. Multicoloured.

797	100f. Type **167**	55	55
798	200f. Globe and balls	1·10	1·10
799	250f. Emblem (different)	1·30	1·30

168 King Hamad Bin Isa Al Khalifa

2006. National Day. Accession of King Hamad Bin Isa Al Khalifa. Multicoloured.

800	100f. Type **168**	55	55
801	200f. Facing front	1·10	1·10
802	250f. Facing left	1·30	1·30
803	500f. As Type **168** (40×54 mm)	2·40	2·40

169 Figures under Umbrella

2007. Consumer Protection Day. Multicoloured.

804	100f. Type **169**	50	50
805	200f. Flags as umbrella	1·00	1·00

170 King Hamad Bin Isa Al Khalifa

2007. National Day. Multicoloured.

806	100f. Type **170**	55	55
807	200f. Seated (horiz)	1·10	1·10
808	250f. King Hamad Bin Isa Al Khalifa and previous rulers (horiz)	1·30	1·30
MS809	125×201 mm. 100f.×2, No. 806×2; Horiz. 200f.×2, No. 807×2	2·75	2·75

171 Clay Carving and Basket Work

2008. Arab Productive Families Day. Multicoloured.

810	100f. Type **171**	50	50
811	200f. Stud work and embroi-derey	1·00	1·00

172 Operating Theatre

2008. International Nurses Day. Multicoloured.

812	100f. Type **172**	50	50
813	200f. Neo-natal nurses	1·00	1·00

173 Symbols of Bahrain and China

2008. Arab–Chinese Cooperation Forum Ministerial Meeting, Manama. Multicoloured.

814	100f. Type **173**	50	50
815	200f. Great Wall and Bahrain World Trade Centre towers	1·00	1·00

174 'BUSINESS friendly'

2008. Economic Developement Board. Multicoloured.

816	100f. Type **174**	60	60
817	200f. BUSINESS FRIENDLY	1·20	1·20

175 Athletics

2008. Olympic Games, Beijing. Sheet 145×64 mm containing T **175** and similar square design. Multicoloured.

MS818	100f. Type **175**; 200f. Show jumping	1·80	1·80

176 Dancers

2008. National Day. Bahraini Ardha (dance). Two sheets containing T **176** and similar horiz designs. Multicoloured.

MS819	210×151 mm. 100f.×8, Type **176**; Dancer with lowered sword and two rows of dancers facing each other; Dancer with out-stretched sword and four dancers wearing blue and yellow costumes; Dancer with raised sword and large square of dancers; Unarmed dancer and men with raised swords; Dancer with rifle and three others; Dancer with sword to his left and three men; Dancer with sword to his right and drummers	4·50	4·50
MS820	210×151 mm. Size 54×40 mm. 200f.×3, Dancer holding flag and sword and dancers with flag; Dancer holding scabard and dancers wearing blue and yellow costumes; Dancer with raised sword and dancers	2·75	2·75

177 Dhow

2009. First GCC–ASEAN Ministerial Meeting, Manama. Multicoloured.

821	100f. Type **177**	60	60
822	200f. As Type **177**	1·00	1·00

178 Pigeon

2009. Arab Post Day. Sheet 170×60 mm containing T **178** and similar horiz design. Multicoloured.

MS823	500f.×2, Type **178**; Camels	5·25	5·25

179 Emblems

2009. Palm Tree–Life and Civilization Symposium.

824	**179** 100f. multicoloured	60	60

180 Emblem

2009. National Women's Day. Multicoloured.

825	100f. Type **180**	60	60
826	200f. Emblem and flag	1·00	1·00

181 Students

2009. 90th Anniv of Education in Bahrain. Sheet 160×99 mm containing T **181** and similar horiz designs. Multicoloured.

MS827	100f. Type **181**; 100f. Classroom, teacher at whiteboard; 200f. Students in laboratory; 200f. Graduating students; 250f. Students, teacher wearing blue lab coat; 250f. Classroom, female teacher with student	6·25	6·25

182 King Hamad Bin Isa Al Khalifa

2009. National Day. 10th Anniv of Accession of King Hamad Bin Isa Al Khalifa. Multicoloured.

828	100f. Type **182**	60	60
829	200f. As Type **182**	1·00	1·00
830	250f. King Hamad Bin Isa Al Khalifa, Isa bin Salman Al Khalifa, Salman Bin Hamad Al Khalifa and Isa bin Ali Al Khalifa	1·50	1·50
MS831	126×101 mm. 500f. As No. 830. Imperf	5·25	5·25

183 King Hamad Bin Isa Al Khalifa and Jet Fighter Aircraft

2010. International Airshow, Bahrain. Multicoloured.

832	100f. Type **183**	65	65
833	200f. Emblem	1·10	1·10

184 Championship Emblem

2010. World Cup Football Championship, South Africa. Multicoloured.

834	100f. Type **184**	65	65
835	200f. Championship mascot	1·10	1·10
836	250f. Football, emblem and globe (39×29 mm)	1·50	1·50

185 Emblem

2010. World Post Day

837	**185** 250f. multicoloured	1·50	1·40

186 King Hamad bin Isa Al Khalifa, Dove and Ballot Box

2010. National Day. Multicoloured.

838	100f. Type **186**	60	55
839	200f. Dove and scales	1·00	90
840	250f. Dove, pen and paper (vert)	1·50	1·40

187 Anniversary Emblem

2011. Bahraini Women's Day. Bahraini Women in Economic Development. Tenth Anniv of Supreme Council of Women. Multicoloured.

841	100f. Type **187**	60	55
842	200f. Anniversary emblem (different)	1·00	90
MS843	140×70 mm.500f. Headquarter (90×35 mm)	5·25	5·00

188 Heart and Crowd

2011. National Day. Multicoloured.

844	100f. Type **188**	60	55
845	200f. Dove and map	1·10	1·00
846	250f. Emblem (vert)	1·50	1·40

WAR TAX STAMPS

T36 "War Effort"

1973

T192	**T36**	5f. blue and cobalt	£130	85·00

T37 "War Effort"

1973

T194a	**T37**	5f. blue	5·25	45

Pt. 1

BAMRA

A state in India. Now uses Indian stamps.

12 pies = 1 anna; 16 annas = 1 rupee.

1 (¼a.)

1888

1	1	¼a. black on yellow	£700	
2	1	½a. black on red	£120	
3	1	1a. black on blue	90·00	
4	1	2a. black on green	£130	£600
5	1	4a. black on yellow	£110	£600
6	1	8a. black on red	70·00	

8

1890. Imperf.

10	8	¼a. black on red	2·50	2·75
11	8	½a. black on green	6·00	6·00
30	8	1a. black on yellow	5·50	3·25
16	8	2a. black on red	6·00	6·00
19	8	4a. black on red	20·00	13·00
22	8	8a. black on red	14·00	22·00
25	8	1r. black on red	21·00	22·00

Pt. 1

BANGLADESH

Formerly the Eastern wing of Pakistan. Following a landslide victory at the Pakistan General Election in December 1970 by the Awami League party the National Assembly was suspended. Unrest spread throughout the eastern province culminating in the intervention of India on the side of the East Bengalis. The new state became effective after the surrender of the Pakistan army in December 1971.

1971. 100 paisa = 1 rupee.
1972. 100 paisa = 1 taka.

1 Map of Bangladesh

1971

1	1	10p. indigo, orange and blue	20	10
2	-	20p. multicoloured	20	10
3	-	50p. multicoloured	20	10
4	-	1r. multicoloured	30	10
5	-	2r. turquoise, blue and red	30	35
6	-	3r. light green, green and blue	30	65
7	-	5r. multicoloured	50	1·25
8	-	10r. gold, red and blue	1·00	2·25

DESIGNS: 20p. "Dacca University Massacre"; 50p. "75 Million People"; 1r. Flag of Independence; 2r. Ballot box; 3r. Broken chain; 5r. Shaikh Majibur Rahman; 10r. "Support Bangla Desh" and map.

1971. Liberation. Nos. 1 and 7/8 optd **BANGLADESH LIBERATED.**

9		10p. indigo, orange and blue	20	10
10		5r. multicoloured	2·00	2·25
11		10r. gold, red and blue	3·00	3·75

The remaining values of the original issue were also overprinted and placed on sale in Great Britian but were not issued in Bangladesh.

On 1 February 1972 the Agency placed on sale a further issue in the flag, map and Sheikh Mujib designs in new colours and new currency (100 paisa = 1 taka). This issue proved to be unacceptable to the Bangladesh authorities who declared them to be invalid for postal purposes, no supplies being sold within Bangladesh. The values comprise 1, 2, 3, 5, 7, 10, 15, 20, 25, 40, 50, 75p., 1, 2 and 5t.

3 "Martyrdom"

1972. In Memory of the Martyrs.

12	3	20p. green and red	30	50

4 Flames of Independence

1972. First Anniv of Independence.

13	4	20p. lake and red	25	10
14	4	60p. blue and red	40	45
15	4	75p. violet and red	45	55

5 Doves of Peace

1972. Victory Day.

16	5	20p. multicoloured	20	10
17	5	60p. multicoloured	30	55
18	5	75p. multicoloured	30	55

6 "Homage to Martyrs"

1973. In Memory of the Martyrs.

19	6	20p. multicoloured	15	10
20	6	60p. multicoloured	30	40
21	6	1t.35 multicoloured	65	1·75

7 Embroidered Quilt **8** Court of Justice

1973

22	7	2p. black	10	1·00
23	-	3p. green	30	1·00
24	-	5p. brown	30	10
25	-	10p. black	30	10
26	-	20p. green	50	10
27	-	25p. mauve	3·25	10
28	-	50p. purple	2·25	30
29	-	60p. grey	1·75	1·25
30	-	75p. orange	1·25	1·25
31	-	90p. brown	1·50	2·00
32	8	1t. violet	6·00	30
33	-	2t. green	6·00	1·00
34	-	5t. blue	7·50	2·50
35	-	10t. pink	10·00	5·00

DESIGNS—As Type **7**: 3p. Jute field; 5p. Jack fruit; 10p. Bullocks ploughing; 20p. Rakta jaba (flower); 25p. Tiger; 60p. Bamboo grove; 75p. Plucking tea; 90p. Handicrafts. (28×22 mm): 50p. Hilsa (fish). As Type **8**. VERT: 2t. Date tree. HORIZ: 5t. Fishing boat; 10t. Sixty-dome mosque, Bagerhat.

See also Nos. 49/51a, 64/75 and 711.

9 Flame Emblem

1973. 25th Anniv of Declaration of Human Rights.

36	9	10p. multicoloured	10	10
37	9	1t.25 multicoloured	20	20

10 Family, Map and Graph

1974. First Population Census.

38	10	20p. multicoloured	10	10
39	10	25p. multicoloured	10	10
40	10	75p. multicoloured	20	20

11 Copernicus and Heliocentric System

1974. 500th Birth Anniv of Copernicus.

41	11	25p. orange, violet and black	10	10
42	11	75p. orange, green and black	25	50

12 U.N. H.Q. and Bangladesh Flag

1974. Bangladesh's Admission to the U.N.

43	12	25p. multicoloured	10	10
44	12	1t. multicoloured	35	40

13 U.P.U. Emblem

1974. Centenary of Universal Postal Union. Multicoloured.

45	13	25p. Type **13**	10	10
46		1t.25 Mail runner	20	15
47		1t.75 Type **13**	20	25
48		5t. As 1t.25	80	1·60

14 Courts of Justice

1974. As Nos. 32/5 with revised inscriptions.

49	14	1t. violet	1·50	10
50	-	2t. olive	2·00	2·00
51	-	5t. blue	7·00	70
51a	-	10t. pink	23·00	15·00

For these designs redrawn to 32×20 mm or 20×32 mm, see Nos. 72/5 and, to 35×22 mm, see No. 711.

15 Tiger

1974. Wildlife Preservation. Multicoloured.

52	15	25p. Type **15**	70	10
53		50p. Tiger cub	1·00	70
54		2t. Tiger in stream	1·75	3·50

16 Symbolic Family

1974. World Population Year. "Family Planning for All". Multicoloured.

55	16	25p. Type **16**	15	10
56		70p. Village family	25	50
57		1t.25 Heads of family (horiz)	40	1·10

17 Radar Antenna

1975. Inauguration of Betbunia Satellite Earth Station.

58	17	25p. black, silver and red	10	10
59	17	1t. black, silver and blue	20	70

18 Woman's Head

1975. International Women's Year.

60	**18**	50p. multicoloured	10	10
61	**18**	2t. multicoloured	25	1·00

1976. As Nos. 24/31 and 49/51a but redrawn in smaller size.

(a) 23×18 mm (50p.) or 18×23 mm (others)

64	-	5p. green	20	10
65	-	10p. black	20	10
66	-	20p. green	1·50	10
67	-	25p. mauve	5·00	10
68	-	50p. purple	3·75	10
69	-	60p. grey	40	40
70	-	75p. green	1·75	3·25
71	-	90p. brown	40	60

(b) 20×32 mm (2t.) or 32×20 mm (others)

72	**14**	1t. violet	2·00	10
73	-	2t. green	9·00	10
74	-	5t. blue	3·25	3·00
75	-	10t. red	11·00	4·50

Nos. 64/71 are 23×18 mm (50p.) or 18×23 mm (others) and Nos. 72/75 are 20×32 mm (2t.) or 32×20 mm (others).
For the 10t. redrawn to 35×22 mm, see No. 711.

19 Telephones of 1876 and 1976

1976. Centenary of Telephone.

76	**19**	2t.25 multicoloured	25	20
77	-	5t. red, green and black	55	65

DESIGN: 5t. Alexander Graham Bell.

20 Eye and Nutriments

1976. Prevention of Blindness.

78	**20**	30p. multicoloured	50	10
79	**20**	2t.25 multicoloured	1·40	2·75

21 Liberty Bell

1976. Bicentenary of American Revolution. Multicoloured.

80	**21**	30p. Type **21**	10	10
81	-	2t.25 Statue of Liberty	20	25
82	-	5t. "Mayflower"	40	40
83	-	10t. Mount Rushmore	40	70
MS84	167×95 mm. No. 83		1·00	2·50

22 Industry, Science, Agriculture and Education

1976. 25th Anniv of Colombo Plan.

85	**22**	30p. multicoloured	15	10
86	**22**	2t.25 multicoloured	35	1·00

23 Hurdling

1976. Olympic Games, Montreal. Multicoloured.

87		25p. Type **23**	10	10
88		30p. Running (horiz)	10	10
89		1t. Pole vaulting	15	10
90		2t.25 Swimming (horiz)	30	45
91		3t.50 Gymnastics	55	1·25
92		5t. Football	1·00	2·00

24 The Blessing

1977. Silver Jubilee. Multicoloured.

93		30p. Type **24**	10	10
94		2t.25 Queen Elizabeth II	20	25
95		10t. Queen Elizabeth and Prince Philip	70	85
MS96	114×127 mm. Nos. 93/5		80	1·50

25 Qazi Nazrul Islam (poet)

1977. Qazi Nazrul Islam Commemoration.

97	**25**	40p. green and black	10	10
98	-	2t.25 brown, red & lt brn	50	30

DESIGN—HORIZ: 2t.25, Head and shoulders portrait.

26 Bird with Letter

1977. 15th Anniv of Asian–Oceanic Postal Union.

99	**26**	30p. red, blue and grey	10	10
100	**26**	2t.25 red, blue and grey	20	25

27 Sloth Bear

1977. Animals. Multicoloured.

101	**27**	40p. Type **27**	15	10
102		1t. Spotted deer	15	10
103		2t.25 Leopard (horiz)	30	20
104		3t.50 Gaur (horiz)	30	35
105		4t. Indian elephant (horiz)	80	50
106		5t. Tiger (horiz)	90	75

The Bengali numerals on the 40p. resemble "80", and that on the 4t. resembles "8".

28 Campfire and Tent

1978. First National Scout Jamboree.

107	**28**	40p. red, blue and pale blue	25	10
108	-	3t.50 lilac, green and blue	80	30
109	-	5t. green, blue and red	95	45

DESIGNS—HORIZ: 3t.50, Scout stretcher-team. VERT: 5t. Scout salute.

29 Michelia champaca

1978. Flowers. Multicoloured.

110	**29**	40p. Type **29**	20	20
111		1t. Cassia fistula	25	15
112		2t.25 Delonix regia	30	30

113		3t.50 Nymphaea nouchali	35	60
114		4t. Butea monosperma	35	80
115		5t. Anthocephalus indicus	35	85

30 St. Edward's Crown and Sceptres

1978. 25th Anniv of Coronation. Multicoloured.

116		40p. Type **30**	10	10
117		3t.50 Balcony scene	15	30
118		5t. Queen Elizabeth and Prince Philip	25	50
119		10t. Coronation portrait by Cecil Beaton	45	80
MS120	89×121 mm. Nos. 116/19		1·10	1·50

31 Sir Alan Cobham's de Havilland D.H.50

1978. 75th Anniv of Powered Flight.

121	**31**	40p. multicoloured	15	10
122	-	2t.25 brown and blue	25	45
123	-	3t.50 brown and yellow	25	65
124	-	5t. multicoloured	2·50	3·50

DESIGNS: 2t.25, Captain Hans Bertram's seaplane *Atlantis*; 3t.50, Wright brothers' Flyer III; 5t. Concorde.

32 Fenchuganj Fertiliser Factory

1978

125		5p. brown	10	10
126	**32**	10p. blue	10	10
127	-	15p. orange	10	10
128	-	20p. red	10	10
129	-	25p. blue	15	10
130	-	30p. green	3·00	10
131	-	40p. purple	30	10
132	-	50p. black	5·50	1·50
134	-	80p. brown	20	10
136	-	1t. violet	9·00	10
137	-	2t. blue	3·00	3·25

DESIGNS—HORIZ: 5p. Lalbag Fort; 25p. Jute on a boat; 40, 50p. Baitul Mukarram Mosque; 1t. Dotara (musical instrument); 2t. Karnaphuli Dam. VERT: 15p. Pineapple; 20p. Bangladesh gas; 30p. Banana tree; 80p. Mohastan Garh.

33 Tawaf-E-Ka'aba, Mecca

1978. Pilgrimage to Mecca. Multicoloured.

140		40p. Type **33**	20	10
141		3t. Pilgrims in Wuquf, Arafat (horiz)	60	45

34 Jasim Uddin

1979. Third Death Anniv of Jasim Uddin (poet).

142	**34**	40p. multicoloured	20	50

35 Moulana Abdul Hamid Khan Bhashani

1979. Third Death Anniv of Moulana Abdul Hamid Khan Bhashani (national leader).

143	**35**	40p. multicoloured	40	30

36 Sir Rowland Hill

1979. Death Centenary of Sir Rowland Hill.

144	**36**	40p. blue, red and light blue	10	10
145	-	3t.50 multicoloured	35	30
146	-	10t. multicoloured	80	1·00
MS147	176×96 mm. Nos. 144/6		2·25	2·75

DESIGNS: 3t.50, Sir Rowland Hill and first Bangladesh stamp; 10t. Sir Rowland Hill and Bangladesh U.P.U. stamp.

37 Children with Hoops

1979. International Year of the Child. Multicoloured.

148		40p. Type **37**	10	10
149		3t.50 Boy with kite	35	35
150		5t. Children jumping	50	50
MS151	170×120 mm. Nos. 148/50		1·50	2·75

38 Rotary International Emblem

1980. 75th Anniv of Rotary International.

152	**38**	40p. black, red and yellow	20	10
153	-	5t. gold and blue	65	1·00

DESIGN: 5t. Rotary emblem (different).

39 Canal Digging

1980. Mass Participation in Canal Digging.

154	**39**	40p. multicoloured	40	30

40 A. K. Fazlul Huq

1980. 18th Death Anniv of A. K. Fazlul Huq (national leader).

155	**40**	40p. multicoloured	30	30

41 Early Forms of Mail Transport

1980. "London 1980" International Stamp Exhibition. Multicoloured.

156	1t. Type **41**	15	10
157	10t. Modern forms of mail transport	1·25	1·40
MS158	140×95 mm. Nos. 156/7	1·40	2·00

42 Dome of the Rock

1980. Palestinian Welfare.

159	**42**	50p. lilac	1·00	30

43 Outdoor Class

1980. Education.

160	**43**	50p. multicoloured	40	30

44 Beach Scene

1980. World Tourism Conference, Manila. Multicoloured.

161	50p. Type **44**	35	50
162	5t. Beach scene (different)	65	1·10
MS163	140×88 mm. Nos. 161/2	1·00	1·60

45 Mecca

1980. Moslem Year 1400 A. H. Commemoration.

164	**45**	50p. multicoloured	50	20

46 Begum Roquiah

1980. Birth Centenary of Begum Roquiah (campaigner for women's rights).

165	**46**	50p. multicoloured	10	10
166	**46**	2t. multicoloured	35	20

47 Spotted Deer and Scout Emblem

1981. Fifth Asia–Pacific and Second Bangladesh Scout Jamboree.

167	**47**	50p. multicoloured	25	15
168	**47**	5t. multicoloured	1·00	2·00

1981. Second Population Census. Nos. 38/40 optd **2nd. CENSUS 1981.**

169	**10**	20p. multicoloured	10	10
170	**10**	25p. multicoloured	10	10
171	**10**	75p. multicoloured	20	30

49 Queen Elizabeth the Queen Mother

1981. 80th Birthday of the Queen Mother.

172	**49**	1t. multicoloured	15	15
173	**49**	15t. multicoloured	1·75	2·50
MS174	95×73 mm. Nos. 172/3		1·75	2·50

50 Revolutionary with Flag and Sub-machine-gun

1981. Tenth Anniv of Independence. Multicoloured.

175	50p. Type **50**	15	10
176	2t. Figures on map symbolizing Bangladesh life style	25	45

51 Bangladesh Village and Farm Scenes

1981. U.N. Conference on Least Developed Countries, Paris.

177	**51**	50p. multicoloured	45	15

52 Kemal Ataturk in Civilian Dress

1981. Birth Centenary of Kemal Ataturk (Turkish statesman).

178	50p. Type **52**	45	30
179	1t. Kemal Ataturk in uniform	80	1·25

53 Deaf People using Sign Language

1981. Int Year for Disabled Persons. Multicoloured.

180	50p. Type **53**	40	20
181	2t. Disabled person writing (horiz)	85	2·50

54 Farm Scene and Wheat Ear

1981. World Food Day.

182	**54**	50p. multicoloured	50	1·00

55 River Scene

1982. Tenth Anniv of Human Environment Conference.

183	**55**	50p. multicoloured	50	1·00

56 Dr. M. Hussain

1982. First Death Anniv of Dr. Motahar Hussain (educationist).

184	**56**	50p. multicoloured	50	1·00

57 Knotted Rope surrounding Bengali "75"

1982. 75th Anniv of Boy Scout Movement and 125th Birth Anniv of Lord Baden-Powell. Multicoloured.

185	50p. Type **57**	50	30
186	2t. Lord Baden-Powell (vert)	2·00	4·50

(58)

1982. Armed Forces' Day. No. 175 optd with T **58**.

187	50p. Type **50**	3·50	3·00

59 Captain Mohiuddin Jahangir

1983. Heroes and Martyrs of the Liberation. Multicoloured, background colour of commemorative plaque given.

188	50p. Type **59** (orange)	30	50
189	50p. Sepoy Hamidur Rahman (green)	30	50
190	50p. Sepoy Mohammed Mustafa Kamal (red)	30	50
191	50p. Muhammed Ruhul Amin (yellow)	30	50
192	50p. Flt. Lt. M. Matiur Rahman (brown)	30	50
193	50p. Lance-Naik Munshi Abdur Rob (brown)	30	50
194	50p. Lance-Naik Nur Mouhammad (green)	30	50

60 Metric Scales

1983. Introduction of Metric Weights and Measures. Multicoloured.

195	50p. Type **60**	40	30
196	2t. Weights, jug and tape measure (horiz)	1·40	2·75

61 Dr. Robert Koch

1983. Centenary (1982) of Robert Koch's Discovery of Tubercle Bacillus. Multicoloured.

197	50p. Type **61**	1·00	40
198	1t. Microscope, slide and X-ray	2·25	3·50

62 Open Stage Theatre

1983. Commonwealth Day. Multicoloured.

199	1t. Type **62**	10	15
200	3t. Boat race	20	30
201	10t. Snake dance	35	90
202	15t. Picking tea	50	1·50

63 Dr. Muhammed Shahidulla

1983. Dr. Muhammed Shahidulla (Bengali scholar) Commemoration.

203	**63**	50p. multicoloured	75	1·00

64 Magpie Robin

1983. Birds of Bangladesh. Multicoloured.

204	50p. Type **64**	75	40
205	2t. White-throated kingfisher (vert)	1·00	2·00
206	3t.75 Lesser flame-backed woodpecker (vert)	1·25	2·50
207	5t. White-winged wood duck	1·40	2·75
MS208	165×110 mm. Nos. 240/7 (sold at 13t.)	4·00	11·00

65 "Macrobrachium rosenbergii"

1983. Marine Life. Multicoloured.

209	50p. Type **65**	40	30
210	2t. White pomfret	60	1·50
211	3t.75 Rohu	75	1·75
212	5t. Climbing perch	90	2·50
MS213	119×98 mm. Nos. 209/12 (sold at 13t.)	2·50	6·00

1983. Visit of Queen Elizabeth II. No. 95 optd **Nov. '83 Visit of Queen**.

214	10t. Queen Elizabeth and Prince Philip	7·00	7·50

67 Conference Hall, Dhaka

1983. 14th Islamic Foreign Ministers' Conference, Dhaka. Multicoloured.

215	50p. Type **67**	35	30
216	5t. Old Fort, Dhaka	1·25	3·00

68 Early Mail Runner

1983. World Communications Year. Multicoloured.

217	50p. Type **68**	30	15
218	5t. Sailing ship, steam train and Boeing 707 airliner	2·00	1·50
219	10t. Mail runner and dish aerial (horiz)	2·75	4·50

69 Carrying
Mail by Boat

1983. Postal Communications.

220	**69**	5p. blue	10	40
221	-	10p. purple	10	40
222	-	15p. blue	20	40
223	-	20p. black	1·25	40
224	-	25p. grey	30	40
225	-	30p. brown	30	40
226	-	50p. brown	1·00	10
227	-	1t. blue	1·25	10
228	-	2t. green	1·25	10
228a	-	3t. brown	4·00	10
229	-	5t. purple	2·00	1·00

DESIGNS—HORIZ (22×17 mm): 10p. Counter, Dhaka G.P.O.; 15p. I.W.T.A. Terminal, Dhaka; 20p. Inside railway travelling post office; 30p. Emptying pillar box; 50p. Mobile post office van. (30×19 mm): 1t. Kamalapur Railway Station, Dhaka; 2t. Zia International Airport; 3t. Sorting mail by machine; 5t. Khulna G.P.O. VERT (17×22 mm): 25p. Delivering a letter.

(70)

1984. First National Stamp Exhibition (1st issue). Nos. 161/2 optd with T **70** (5t.) or First Bangladesh National Philatelic Exhibition—1984 (50p.).

230	**44**	50p. multicoloured	1·50	2·00
231	-	5t. multicoloured	2·00	2·75

71 Girl with Stamp Album

1984. First National Stamp Exhibition (2nd issue). Multicoloured.

232		50p. Type **71**	65	1·25
233		7t.50 Boy with stamp album	1·10	2·25
MS234	98×117 mm. Nos. 232/3 (sold at 10t.)		3·00	4·25

72 Sarus Crane and
Gavial

1984. Dhaka Zoo. Multicoloured.

235		1t. Type **72**	1·75	85
236		2t. Common peafowl and tiger	2·50	4·25

73 Eagle attacking
Hen with Chicks

1984. Centenary of Postal Life Insurance. Multicoloured.

237		1t. Type **73**	50	25
238		5t. Bangladesh family and postman's hand with insurance cheque	1·50	2·25

74 Abbasuddin
Ahmad

1984. Abbasuddin Ahmad (singer) Commemoration.

239	**74**	3t. multicoloured	1·00	1·25

(75)

1984. "Khulnapex-84" Stamp Exhibition. No. 86 optd with T **75**.

240	**22**	2t.25 multicoloured	1·00	1·75

76 Cycling

1984. Olympic Games, Los Angeles. Multicoloured.

241		1t. Type **76**	1·75	30
242		5t. Hockey	2·50	2·25
243		10t. Volleyball	2·75	4·25

77 Farmer with Rice and
Sickle

1985. Ninth Annual Meeting of Islamic Development Bank, Dhaka. Multicoloured.

244		1t. Type **77**	35	15
245		5t. Citizens of four races	1·25	2·25

78 Mother and Baby

1985. Child Survival Campaign. Multicoloured.

246		1t. Type **78**	30	10
247		10t. Young child and growth graph	2·00	3·25

উপজেলা নির্বাচন ১৯৮৫
(79)

1985. Local Elections. Nos. 110/15 optd with T **79**.

248		40p. Type **29**	40	50
249		1t. *Cassia fistula*	50	30
250		2t.25 *Delonix regia*	70	75
251		3t.50 *Nymphaea nouchali*	80	1·25
252		4t. *Butea monosperma*	80	1·25
253		5t. *Anthocephalus indicus*	85	1·50

80 Women working
at Traditional Crafts

1985. U.N. Decade for Women. Multicoloured.

254		1t. Type **80**	25	10
255		10t. Women with microscope, computer terminal and in classroom	1·25	2·25

81 U.N. Building, New York,
Peace Doves and Flags

1985. 40th Anniv of United Nations Organization and 11th Anniv of Bangladesh Membership. Multicoloured.

256		1t. Type **81**	10	10
257		10t. Map of world and Bangladesh flag	1·40	1·75

82 Head of Youth,
Flowers and
Symbols of
Commerce and
Agriculture

1985. International Youth Year. Multicoloured.

258		1t. Type **82**	10	10
259		5t. Head of youth, flowers and symbols of industry	40	60

83 Emblem and
Seven Doves

1985. First Summit Meeting of South Asian Association for Regional Co-operation, Dhaka. Multicoloured.

260		1t. Type **83**	10	10
261		5t. Flags of member nations and lotus blossom	1·75	1·25

84 Zainul Abedin

1985. Tenth Death Anniv of Zainul Abedin (artist).

262	**84**	3t. multicoloured	1·00	55

(85)

1985. Third National Scout Jamboree. No. 109 optd with T **85**.

263		5t. green, blue and red	2·50	3·50

86 "Fishing Net" (Safiuddin
Ahmed)

1986. Bangladesh Paintings. Multicoloured.

264		1t. Type **86**	15	10
265		5t. *Happy Return* (Quamrul Hassan)	40	50
266		10t. *Levelling the Ploughed Field* (Zainul Abedin)	70	80

87 Two Players competing
for Ball

1986. World Cup Football Championship, Mexico. Multicoloured.

267		1t. Type **87**	50	10
268		10t. Goalkeeper and ball in net	2·25	3·00
MS269	105×75 mm. 20t. Four players (60×44 mm) Imperf		5·50	6·50

88 General M. A. G.
Osmani

1986. General M. A. G. Osmani (army commander-in-chief) Commemoration.

270	**88**	3t. multicoloured	1·75	1·00

1986. South Asian Association for Regional Co-operation Seminar. No. 183 optd **SAARC SEMINAR '86**.

271	**55**	50p. multicoloured	3·25	3·75

90 Butterflies and
Nuclear Explosion

1986. International Peace Year. Multicoloured.

272		1t. Type **90**	50	25
273		10t. Flowers and ruined buildings	2·75	4·00
MS274	109×80 mm. 20t. Peace dove and soldier		1·50	2·00

1987. Conference for Development. Nos. 152/3 optd **CONFERENCE FOR DEVELOPMENT '87**, No. 275 also surch **TK. 1.00**.

275	**38**	1t. on 40p. black, red and yellow	10	20
276	-	5t. gold and blue	55	1·75

92 Demonstrators with
Placards

1987. 35th Anniv of Bangla Language Movement. Multicoloured.

277		3t. Type **92**	1·40	2·50
278		3t. Martyrs' Memorial	1·40	2·50

Nos. 277/8 were printed together, se-tenant, forming a composite design.

93 Nurse
giving Injection

1987. World Health Day.

279	**93**	1t. black and blue	1·75	2·00

See also No 295.

94 Pattern and
Bengali Script

1987. Bengali New Year Day. Multicoloured.

280		1t. Type **94**	10	10
281		10t. Bengali woman	40	60

95 Jute Shika

1987. Export Products. Multicoloured.

282		1t. Type **95**	10	10
283		5t. Jute carpet (horiz)	30	35
284		10t. Cane table lamp	45	70

96 Ustad Ayet Ali Khan and Surbahar

1987. 20th Death Anniv of Ustad Ayet Ali Khan (musician and composer).

285	**96**	5t. multicoloured	1·50	1·00

97 Palanquin

1987. Transport. Multicoloured.

286	2t. Type **97**		20	15
287	3t. Bicycle rickshaw		1·00	35
288	5t. River steamer		1·25	65
289	7t. Express diesel train		3·25	1·25
290	10t. Bullock cart		60	1·50

98 H. S. Suhrawardy

1987. Hossain Shadid Suhrawardy (politician) Commemoration.

291	**98**	3t. multicoloured	20	30

99 Villagers fleeing from Typhoon

1987. International Year of Shelter for the Homeless. Multicoloured.

292	5t. Type **99**		50	70
293	5t. Villagers and modern houses		50	70

100 President Ershad addressing Parliament

1987. First Anniv of Return to Democracy.

294	**100**	10t. multicoloured	65	1·00

1988. World Health Day. As T **93**.

295	25p. brown		60	20

DESIGN: 25p. Oral rehydration.

101 Woman planting Palm Saplings

1988. I.F.A.D. Seminar on Agricultural Loans for Rural Women. Multicoloured.

296	3t. Type **101**		15	25
297	5t. Village woman milking cow		20	75

102 Basketball

1988. Olympic Games, Seoul. Multicoloured.

298	5t. Type **102**		1·25	80
299	5t. Weightlifting		1·25	80
300	5t. Tennis		1·25	80
301	5t. Rifle-shooting		1·25	80
302	5t. Boxing		1·25	80

103 Interior of Shait Gumbaz Mosque, Bagerhat

1988. Historical Buildings. Multicoloured.

303	1t. Type **103**		40	10
304	4t. Paharpur Monastery		80	30
305	4t. Kantanagar Temple, Dinajpur		80	30
306	10t. Lalbag Fort, Dhaka		1·25	1·00

104 Henri Dunant (founder), Red Cross and Crescent

1988. 125th Anniv of International Red Cross and Red Crescent. Multicoloured.

307	5t. Type **104**		1·40	30
308	10t. Red Cross workers with patient		2·00	1·10

105 Dr. Qudrat-i-Khuda in Laboratory

1988. Dr. Qudrat-i-Khuda (scientist) Commem.

309	**105**	5t. multicoloured	50	40

106 Wicket-keeper

1988. Asia Cup Cricket. Multicoloured.

310	1t. Type **106**		80	90
311	5t. Batsman		1·00	1·25
312	10t. Bowler		1·75	2·25

107 Labourers, Factory and Technician

1988. 32nd Meeting of Colombo Plan Consultative Committee, Dhaka.

313	**107**	3t. multicoloured	10	10
314	**107**	10t. multicoloured	40	45

108 Dhaka G.P.O. Building

1988. 25th Anniv of Dhaka G.P.O. Building. Multicoloured.

315	1t. Type **108**		15	10
316	5t. Post Office counter		30	30

৫ম জাতীয় রোভার মুট
১৯৮৮-৮৯
(109)

1988. 5th National Rover Scout Moot. No. 168 optd with T **109**.

317	**47**	5t. multicoloured	3·50	3·00

110 Bangladesh Airport

1989. Bangladesh Landmarks.

318	**110**	3t. black and blue	40	10
318a	-	4t. blue	40	10
320	-	10t. red	4·00	35
321	-	20t. multicoloured	1·00	40

DESIGNS—VERT (22×33 mm): 5t. Curzon Hall. (19½×31½ mm): 10t. Fertiliser factory, Chittagong. HORIZ (33×23 mm): 4t. Chittagong port; 20t. Postal Academy, Rajshahi.

চতুর্থ দ্বিবার্ষিক এশীয়
চারুকলা প্রদর্শনী
বাংলাদেশ ১৯৮৯
(111)

1989. Fourth Biennial Asian Art Exhibition. No. 266 optd with T **111**.

322	10t. *Levelling the Ploughed Field* (Zainul Abedin)		75	1·00

112 Irrigation Methods and Student with Telescope

1989. 12th National Science and Technology Week.

323	**112**	10t. multicoloured	50	60

113 Academy Logo

1989. 75th Anniv of Police Academy, Sardah.

324	**113**	10t. multicoloured	75	60

114 Rejoicing Crowds, Paris, 1789

1989. Bicentenary of French Revolution. Multicoloured.

325	17t. Type **114**		70	75
326	17t. Storming the Bastille, 1789		70	75

MS327 125×125 mm 5t. Men with pickaxes; 10t. *Liberty guiding the People* (detail) (Delacroix); 10t. Crowd with cannon. P 14 ... 2·00 3·00

MS328 152×88 mm. 25t. Storming the Bastille. Imperf ... 2·00 3·00

The design of No. **MS**328 incorporates the three scenes featured on No. **MS**327.

115 Sowing and Harvesting

1989. Tenth Anniv of Asia–Pacific Integrated Rural Development Centre. Multicoloured.

329	5t. Type **115**		65	65
330	10t. Rural activities		65	65

Nos. 329/30 were printed together, *se-tenant*, forming a composite design.

116 Helper and Child playing with Baby

1989. 40th Anniv of S.O.S. International Children's Village. Multicoloured.

331	1t. Type **116**		15	10
332	10t. Foster mother with children		85	90

117 U.N. Soldier on Watch

1989. First Anniv of Bangladesh Participation in U.N. Peace-keeping Force. Multicoloured.

333	4t. Type **117**		50	30
334	10t. Two soldiers checking positions		1·00	70

118 Festival Emblem

1989. Second Asian Poetry Festival, Dhaka.

335	**118**	2t. red, deep red and green	15	10
336	-	10t. multicoloured	85	90

DESIGN: 10t. Festival emblem and hall.

119 State Security Printing Press

1989. Inauguration of State Security Printing Press, Gazipur.

337	**119**	10t. multicoloured	65	65

120 Water Lilies and T.V. Emblem

1989. 25th Anniv of Bangladesh Television. Multicoloured.

338	5t. Type **120**		35	30
339	10t. Central emblem and water lilies		65	80

121 Gharial in Shallow Water

1990. Endangered Wildlife. Gharial. Multicoloured.

340	50p. Type **121**		80	45
341	2t. Gharial feeding		1·00	60
342	4t. Gharials basking on sand bank		1·40	70
343	10t. Two gharials resting		1·75	95

122 Symbolic Family

1990. Population Day.
344 **122** 6t. multicoloured ... 55 35

123 Justice S. M. Murshed

1990. Tenth Death Anniv of Justice Syed Mahbub Murshed.
345 **123** 5t. multicoloured ... 2·25 1·25

124 Boy learning Alphabet

1990. International Literacy Year. Multicoloured.
346 6t. Type **124** ... 1·00 50
347 10t. Boy teaching girl to write ... 1·50 1·25

125 Penny Black with "Stamp World London 90" Exhibition Emblem

1990. 150th Anniv of the Penny Black. Multicoloured.
348 7t. Type **125** ... 1·50 2·00
349 10t. Penny Black, 1983 World Communications Year stamp and Bengali mail runner ... 1·75 2·50

126 Goalkeeper and Ball

1990. World Cup Football Championship, Italy. Multicoloured.
350 8t. Type **126** ... 1·75 1·75
351 10t. Footballer with ball ... 2·00 2·25
MS352 104×79 mm. 25t. Colosseum, Rome, with football. Imperf ... 12·00 12·00

127 Mango

1990. Fruit. Multicoloured.
353 1t. Type **127** ... 30 20
354 2t. Guava ... 30 20
355 3t. Water melon ... 35 25
356 4t. Papaya ... 40 30
357 5t. Bread fruit ... 65 65
358 10t. Carambola ... 1·25 1·50

128 Man gathering Wheat

1990. U.N. Conference on Least Developed Countries, Paris.
359 **128** 10t. multicoloured ... 1·25 1·25

129 Map of Asia with Stream of Letters

1990. 20th Anniv of Asia–Pacific Postal Training Centre. Multicoloured.
360 2t. Type **129** ... 1·75 1·75
361 6t. Map of Pacific with stream of letters ... 1·75 1·75
Nos. 360/1 were printed together, *se-tenant*, forming a composite map design.

130 Canoe Racing

1990. Asian Games, Beijing. Multicoloured.
362 2t. Type **130** ... 1·00 30
363 4t. Kabaddi ... 1·25 30
364 8t. Wrestling ... 1·75 1·50
365 10t. Badminton ... 3·00 2·00

131 Lalan Shah

1990. First Death Anniv of Lalan Shah (poet).
366 **131** 6t. multicoloured ... 1·50 1·00

132 U.N. Logo and "40"

1990. 40th Anniv of United Nations Development Programme.
367 **132** 6t. multicoloured ... 1·00 70

133 Baby

1990. Immunization.
368 **133** 1t. green ... 50 50
369 **133** 2t. brown ... 50 25

134 "Danaus chrysippus"

1990. Butterflies. Multicoloured.
370 6t. Type **134** ... 1·60 1·60
371 6t. *Precis almana* ... 1·60 1·60
372 10t. *Ixias pyrene* ... 1·75 1·75
373 10t. *Danaus plexippus* ... 1·75 1·75

135 Drugs attacking Bangladesh

1991. U.N. Anti-drugs Decade. Multicoloured.
374 2t. Type **135** ... 1·25 50
375 4t. "Drug" snake around globe ... 1·75 1·25

136 Salimullah Hall

1991
376 **136** 6t. blue and yellow ... 20 15

137 Silhouetted People on Map

1991. Third National Census.
382 **137** 4t. multicoloured ... 1·50 1·50

138 *Invincible Bangla* (statue)

1991. 20th Anniv of Independence. Multicoloured.
383 4t. Type **138** ... 85 1·00
384 4t. *Freedom Fighter* (statue) ... 85 1·00
385 4t. Mujibnagar Memorial ... 85 1·00
386 4t. Eternal flame ... 85 1·00
387 4t. National Martyrs' Memorial ... 85 1·00
Nos. 383/7 were issued together, *se-tenant*, forming a composite design.

139 President Rahman Seated

1991. Tenth Death Anniv of President Ziaur Rahman. Multicoloured.
388 50p. Type **139** ... 30 15
389 2t. President Rahman's head in circular decoration ... 1·00 1·10
MS390 146×75 mm. Nos. 388/9 (sold at 10t.) ... 1·90 2·75

140 Red Giant Flying Squirrel

1991. Endangered Species. Multicoloured.
391 2t. Type **140** ... 2·00 2·25
392 4t. Black-faced monkey (vert) ... 2·00 2·25
393 6t. Great Indian hornbill (vert) ... 2·00 2·25
394 10t. Armoured pangolin ... 2·00 2·25

141 Kaikobad

1991. 40th Death Anniv of Kaikobad (poet).
395 **141** 6t. multicoloured ... 1·60 1·25

142 Rabindranath Tagore and Temple

1991. 50th Death Anniv of Rabindranath Tagore (poet).
396 **142** 4t. multicoloured ... 1·00 65

143 Voluntary Blood Programme

1991. 14th Anniv of "Sandhani" (medical students' association).
397 **143** 3t. black and red ... 1·00 50
398 – 5t. multicoloured ... 2·00 2·25
DESIGN: 5t. Blind man and eye.

144 Shahid Naziruddin and Crowd

1991. First Death Anniv of Shahid Naziruddin Jahad (democrat).
399 **144** 2t. black, green and brown ... 1·00 60

145 Shaheed Noor Hossain with Slogan on Chest

1991. Fourth Death Anniv of Shaheed Noor Hossain (democrat).
400 **145** 2t. multicoloured ... 1·00 55

146 Bronze Stupa

1991. Archaeological Relics from Mainamati. Multicoloured.
401 4t. Type **146** ... 1·50 1·60
402 4t. Earthenware and bronze pitchers ... 1·50 1·60
403 4t. Remains of Salban Vihara Monastery ... 1·50 1·60
404 4t. Gold coins ... 1·50 1·60
405 4t. Terracotta plaque ... 1·50 1·60

147 Demostrators

1991. First Anniv of Mass Uprising.
406 **147** 4t. multicoloured ... 1·25 80

148 Munier Chowdhury

1991. 20th Anniv of Independence. Martyred Intellectuals (1st series). Each black and brown.
407 2t. Type **148** ... 50 55
408 2t. Ghyasuddin Ahmad ... 50 55
409 2t. Rashidul Hasan ... 50 55
410 2t. Muhammad Anwar Pasha ... 50 55
411 2t. Dr. Muhammad Mortaza ... 50 55
412 2t. Shahid Saber ... 50 55
413 2t. Fazlur Rahman Khan ... 50 55
414 2t. Ranada Prasad Saha ... 50 55
415 2t. Adhyaksha Joges Chandra Ghose ... 50 55

416	2t. Santosh Chandra Bhat-tacharyya	50	55
417	2t. Dr. Gobinda Chandra Deb	50	55
418	2t. A. Muniruzzaman	50	55
419	2t. Mufazzal Haider Chaudhury	50	55
420	2t. Dr. Abdul Alim Choudhury	50	55
421	2t. Sirajuddin Hossain	50	55
422	2t. Shahidulla Kaiser	50	55
423	2t. Altaf Mahmud	50	55
424	2t. Dr. Jyotirmay Guha Thakurta	50	55
425	2t. Dr. Muhammad Abul Khair	50	55
426	2t. Dr. Serajul Haque Khan	50	55
427	2t. Dr. Mohammad Fazle Rabbi	50	55
428	2t. Mir Abdul Quyyum	50	55
429	2t. Golam Mostafa	50	55
430	2t. Dhirendranath Dutta	50	55
431	2t. S. Mannan	50	55
432	2t. Nizamuddin Ahmad	50	55
433	2t. Abul Bashar Chowdhury	50	55
434	2t. Selina Parveen	50	55
435	2t. Dr. Abul Kalam Azad	50	55
436	2t. Saidul Hassan	50	55

See also Nos. 483/92, 525/40, 568/83, 620/35, 656/71, 691/706, 731/46 and 779/94.

149 "Penaeus monodon"

1991. Shrimps. Multicoloured.
437	6t. Type **149**	2·00	2·25
438	6t. *Metapenaeus monoceros*	2·00	2·25

150 Death of Raihan Jaglu

1992. Fifth Death Anniv of Shaheed Mirze Abu Raihan Jaglu.
439	**150**	2t. multicoloured	1·50	60

151 Rural and Urban Scenes

1992. World Environment Day. Multicoloured.
440	4t. Type **151**	75	25
441	10t. World Environment Day logo (horiz)	2·00	2·75

152 Nawab Sirajuddaulah

1992. 235th Death Anniv of Nawab Sirajuddaulah of Bengal.
442	**152**	10t. multicoloured	1·50	2·00

153 Syed Ismail Hossain Sirajee

1992. 61st Death Anniv of Syed Ismail Hossain Sirajee.
443	**153**	4t. multicoloured	1·25	60

154 Couple planting Seedling

1992. Plant Week. Multicoloured.
444	2t. Type **154**	1·00	80
445	4t. Birds on tree (vert)	2·00	1·25

155 Canoe Racing

1992. Olympic Games, Barcelona. Multicoloured.
446	4t. Type **155**	1·40	1·75
447	6t. Hands holding torch with Olympic rings	1·40	1·75
448	10t. Olympic rings and doves	1·40	1·75
449	10t. Olympic rings and multiracial handshake	1·40	1·75

1992. "Banglapex '92", National Philatelic Exhibition (1st issue). No. 290 optd **Banglapex '92** in English and Bengali.
450	10t. Bullock cart	2·25	2·75

See also Nos. 452/3.

157 Masnad-e-Ala Isa Khan

1992. 393rd Death Anniv of Masnad-e-Ala Isa Khan.
451	**157**	4t. multicoloured	1·00	60

158 Ceremonial Elephant (19th-century ivory carving)

1992. "Banglapex '92" National Philatelic Exhibition (2nd issue). Multicoloured.
452	10t. Type **158**	1·60	2·25
453	10t. Victorian pillarbox between early and modern postmen	1·60	2·25
MS454	145×92 mm. Nos. 452/3. Imperf (sold at 25t.)	4·50	5·00

159 Star Mosque

1992. Star Mosque, Dhaka.
455	**159**	10t. multicoloured	2·00	2·00

160 Meer Nisar Ali Titumeer and Fort

1992. 161st Death Anniv of Meer Nisar Ali Titumeer.
456	**160**	10t. multicoloured	1·75	1·75

161 Terracotta Head and Seal

1992. Archaeological Relics from Mahasthangarh. Multicoloured.
457	10t. Type **161**	1·75	1·90
458	10t. Terracotta panel showing swan	1·75	1·90
459	10t. Terracotta statue of Surya	1·75	1·90
460	10t. Gupta stone column	1·75	1·90

162 Young Child and Food

1992. Int Conference on Nutrition, Rome.
461	**162**	4t. multicoloured	1·00	55

163 National Flags

1992. Seventh South Asian Association for Regional Co-operation Summit Conference, Dhaka. Mult.
462	6t. Type **163**	1·40	75
463	10t. S.A.A.R.C. emblem	1·60	2·00

164 Syed Abdus Samad

1993. Syed Abdus Samad (footballer) Commem.
464	**164**	2t. multicoloured	1·50	70

165 Haji Shariat Ullah

1993. Haji Shariat Ullah Commemoration.
465	**165**	2t. multicoloured	1·50	70

166 People digging Canal

1993. Irrigation Canals Construction Project. Multicoloured.
466	2t. Type **166**	80	80
467	2t. Completed canal and paddy-fields	80	80

167 Accident Prevention

1993. World Health Day. Multicoloured.
468	6t. Type **167**	2·00	75
469	10t. Satellite photograph and symbols of trauma (vert)	2·25	2·75

168 National Images

1993. 1400th Year of Bengali Solar Calendar.
470	**168**	2t. multicoloured	1·00	50

169 Schoolchildren and Bengali Script

1993. Compulsory Primary Education. Multicoloured.
471	2t. Type **169**	80	80
472	2t. Books and slate (horiz)	80	80

170 Nawab Sir Salimullah and Palace

1993. 122nd Birth Anniv of Nawab Sir Salimullah.
473	**170**	4t. multicoloured	1·25	70

171 Fish Production

1993. Fish Fortnight.
474	**171**	2t. multicoloured	50	40

172 Sunderban

1993. Natural Beauty of Bangladesh. Multicoloured.
475	10t. Type **172**	1·00	1·40
476	10t. Kuakata beach	1·00	1·40
477	10t. Madhabkunda waterfall (vert)	1·00	1·40
478	10t. River Piyain, Jaflang (vert)	1·00	1·40
MS479	174×102 mm. Nos. 475/8. Imperf (sold at 50t.)	3·50	5·00

173 Exhibition Emblem

1993. Sixth Asian Art Biennale.
480	**173**	10t. multicoloured	80	1·00

174 Foy's Lake

1993. Tourism Month.
481	**174**	10t. multicoloured	1·00	1·25

175 Burdwan House

1993. Foundation Day, Bangla Academy.
482	**175**	2t. brown and green	1·25	40

1993. Martyred Intellectuals (2nd series). As T **148**. Each black and brown.
483	2t. Lt. Cdr. Moazzam Hussain	20	30
484	2t. Muhammad Habibur Rahman	20	30
485	2t. Khandoker Abu Taleb	20	30
486	2t. Moshiur Rahman	20	30
487	2t. Md. Abdul Muktadir	20	30
488	2t. Nutan Chandra Sinha	20	30
489	2t. Syed Nazmul Haque	20	30

490		2t. Dr. Mohammed Amin Uddin		20	30
491		2t. Dr. Faizul Mohee		20	30
492		2t. Sukha Ranjan Somaddar		20	30

176 Throwing the Discus

1993. Sixth South Asian Federation Games, Dhaka. Multicoloured.

493		2t. Type **176**	20	20
494		4t. Running (vert)	35	35

177 Tomb of Sultan Ghiyasuddin Azam Shah

1993. Muslim Monuments.

495	**177**	10t. multicoloured	75	1·00

178 Scouting Activities and Jamboree Emblem

1994. 14th Asian–Pacific and 5th Bangladesh National Scout Jamboree.

496	**178**	2t. multicoloured	40	30

179 Emblem and Mother giving Solution to Child

1994. 25th Anniv of Oral Rehydration.

497	**179**	2t. multicoloured	65	30

180 Interior of Chhota Sona Mosque, Nawabgonj

1994. Ancient Mosques. Multicoloured.

498		4t. Type **180**	40	20
499		6t. Exterior of Chhota Sona Mosque	50	65
500		6t. Exterior of Baba Adam's Mosque, Munshigonj	50	65

181 Agricultural Workers and Emblem

1994. 75th Anniv of I.L.O. Multicoloured.

501		4t. Type **181**	25	20
502		10t. Worker turning cog (vert)	1·00	1·00

182 Priest releasing Peace Doves

1994. 1500th Year of Bengali Solar Calendar.

503	**182**	2t. multicoloured	55	30

183 Scenes from Baishakhi Festival

1994. Folk Festivals. Multicoloured.

504		4t. Type **183**	35	35
505		4t. Scenes from Nabanna and Paush Parvana Festivals	35	35

184 Family, Globe and Logo

1994. International Year of the Family.

506	**184**	10t. multicoloured	1·00	1·50

185 People planting Saplings

1994. Tree Planting Campaign. Multicoloured.

507		4t. Type **185**	50	25
508		6t. Hands holding saplings	75	60

186 Player kicking Ball

1994. World Cup Football Championship, U.S.A. Multicoloured.

509		20t. Type **186**	2·25	3·00
510		20t. Player heading ball	2·25	3·00

187 Traffic on Bridge

1994. Inauguration of Jamuna Multi-purpose Bridge Project.

511	**187**	4t. multicoloured	2·00	60

188 Asian Black-headed Oriole

1994. Birds. Multicoloured.

512		4t. Type **188**	40	40
513		6t. Greater racquet-tailed drongo	60	80
514		6t. Indian tree pie	60	80
515		6t. Red junglefowl	60	80
MS516		165×110 mm. Nos. 512/15 (sold at 25t.)	2·00	2·75

189 Dr. Mohammad Ibrahim and Hospital

1994. Fifth Death Anniv of Dr. Mohammad Ibrahim (diabetes treatment pioneer).

517	**189**	2t. multicoloured	40	20

190 Nawab Faizunnessa Chowdhurani

1994. 160th Birth Anniv of Nawab Faizunnessa Chowdhurani (social reformer).

518	**190**	2t. multicoloured	50	20

191 Boxing

1994. Asian Games, Hiroshima, Japan.

519	**191**	4t. multicoloured	1·50	60

192 Pink and White Pearls with Windowpane Oysters

1994. Sea Shells. Multicoloured.

520		6t. Type **192**	1·40	1·60
521		6t. Tranquelous scallop and other shells	1·40	1·60
522		6t. Lister's conch, Asiatic Arabian cowrie, bladder moon and woodcock murex	1·40	1·60
523		6t. Spotted tun, spiny frog shell, spiral melongena and gibbous olive (vert)	1·40	1·60

193 Dr. Milon and Demonstrators

1994. Fourth Death Anniv of Dr. Shamsul Alam Khan Milon (medical reformer).

524	**193**	2t. multicoloured	25	20

1994. Martyred Intellectuals (3rd series). As T **148**. Each black and brown.

525		2t. Dr. Harinath Dey	25	30
526		2t. Dr. A. F. Ziaur Rahman	25	30
527		2t. Mamun Mahmud	25	30
528		2t. Mohsin Ali Dewan	25	30
529		2t. Dr. N. A. M. Jahangir	25	30
530		2t. Shah Abdul Majid	25	30
531		2t. Muhammad Akhter	25	30
532		2t. Meherunnesa	25	30
533		2t. Dr. Kasiruddin Talukder	25	30
534		2t. Fazlul Haque Choudhury	25	30
535		2t. Md. Shamsuzzaman	25	30
536		2t. A. K. M. Shamsuddin	25	30
537		2t. Lt. Mohammad Anwarul Azim	25	30
538		2t. Nurul Amin Khan	25	30
539		2t. Mohammad Sadeque	25	30
540		2t. Md. Araz Ali	25	30

194 *Diplazium esculentum*

1994. Vegetables. Multicoloured.

541		4t. Type **194**	70	50
542		4t. *Momordica charantia*	70	50
543		6t. *Lagenaria siceraria*	90	70
544		6t. *Trichosanthes dioica*	90	70
545		10t. *Solanum melongena*	1·40	2·00
546		10t. *Cucurbita maxima* (horiz)	1·40	2·00

195 Sonargaon

1995. 20th Anniv of World Tourism Organization.

547	**195**	10t. multicoloured	1·75	1·75

196 Exports

1995. Dhaka International Trade Fair '95. Multicoloured.

548		4t. Type **196**	20	20
549		6t. Symbols of industry	45	65

197 Soldiers of Ramgarh Battalion (1795) and of Bangladesh Rifles (1995)

1995. Bicentenary of Bangladesh Rifles. Multicoloured.

550		2t. Type **197**	1·25	50
551		4t. Riflemen on patrol	1·60	90

198 Surgical Equipment and Lightning attacking Crab (cancer)

1995. Campaign against Cancer.

552	**198**	2t. multicoloured	40	25

199 Fresh Food and Boy injecting Insulin

1995. National Diabetes Awareness Day.

553	**199**	2t. multicoloured	1·00	30

200 Munshi Mohammad Meherullah

1995. Munshi Mohammad Meherullah (Islamic educator) Commemoration.

554	**200**	2t. multicoloured	30	25

রাজশাহীপেক্স-৯৫
(201)

1995. "Rajshahipex '95" National Philatelic Exhibition. No. 499 optd with T **201**.

555		6t. Exterior of Chhota Sona Mosque	2·25	2·50

202 *Lagerstroemia speciosa*

1995. Flowers. Multicoloured.

556		6t. Type **202**	90	90
557		6t. *Bombax ceiba* (horiz)	90	90
558		10t. *Passiflora incarnata*	1·25	1·40
559		10t. *Bauhina purpurea*	1·25	1·40
560		10t. *Canna indica*	1·25	1·40
561		10t. *Gloriosa superba*	1·25	1·40

203 Aspects of Farming

1995. 50th Anniv of F.A.O.

562	**203**	10t. multicoloured	1·00	1·25

204 Anniversary Emblem, Peace Dove and U.N. Headquarters

1995. 50th Anniv of United Nations. Multicoloured.

563		2t. Type **204**	30	20
564		10t. Peace doves circling dates and Globe	90	1·40
565		10t. Clasped hands and U.N. Headquarters	90	1·40

205 Diseased Lungs, Microscope, Family and Map

1995. 18th Eastern Regional Conference on Tuberculosis, Dhaka.

566	**205**	6t. multicoloured	1·50	1·00

206 Peace Doves, Emblem and National Flags

1995. Tenth Anniv of South Asian Association for Regional Co-operation.

567	**206**	2t. multicoloured	1·40	55

1995. Martyred Intellectuals (4th series). As T **148**. Each black and brown.

568		2t. Abdul Ahad	25	30
569		2t. Lt. Col. Mohammad Qadir	25	30
570		2t. Mozammel Hoque Chowdhury	25	30
571		2t. Rafiqul Haider Chowdhury	25	30
572		2t. Dr. Azharul Haque	25	30
573		2t. A. K. Shamsuddin	25	30
574		2t. Anudwaipayan Bhattacharjee	25	30
575		2t. Lutfunnahar Helena	25	30
576		2t. Shaikh Habibur Rahman	25	30
577		2t. Major Naimul Islam	25	30
578		2t. Md. Shahidullah	25	30
579		2t. Ataur Rahman Khan Khadim	25	30

580		2t. A. B. M. Ashraful Islam Bhuiyan	25	30
581		2t. Dr. Md. Sadat Ali	25	30
582		2t. Sarafat Ali	25	30
583		2t. M. A. Sayeed	25	30

207 Aspects of COMDECA Projects

1995. Second Asia–Pacific Community Development Scout Camp.

584	**207**	2t. multicoloured	70	35

208 Volleyball Players

1995. Centenary of Volleyball.

585	**208**	6t. multicoloured	1·00	55

209 Man in Punjabi and Lungi

1995. Traditional Costumes. Multicoloured.

586		6t. Type **209**	1·00	1·00
587		6t. Woman in sari	1·00	1·00
588		10t. Christian bride and groom	1·40	1·50
589		10t. Muslim bride and groom	1·40	1·50
590		10t. Buddhist bride and groom (horiz)	1·40	1·50
591		10t. Hindu bride and groom (horiz)	1·40	1·50

210 Shaheed Amanullah Mohammad Asaduzzaman

1996. 27th Death Anniv of Shaheed Amanullah Mohammad Asaduzzaman (student leader).

592	**210**	2t. multicoloured	40	25

211 Bowler and Map

1996. World Cup Cricket Championship. Multicoloured.

593		4t. Type **211**	1·25	55
594		6t. Batsman and wicket keeper	1·50	80
595		10t. Match in progress (horiz)	2·00	2·25

212 Liberation Struggle, 1971

1996. 25th Anniv of Independence. Multicoloured.

596		4t. Type **212**	70	70
597		4t. National Martyrs Memorial	70	70

598		4t. Education	70	70
599		4t. Health	70	70
600		4t. Communications	70	70
601		4t. Industry	70	70

213 Michael Madhusudan Dutt

1996. Michael Madhusudan Dutt (poet) Commemoration.

602	**213**	4t. multicoloured	50	20

214 Gymnastics

1996. Olympic Games, Atlanta. Multicoloured.

603		4t. Type **214**	30	20
604		6t. Judo	40	35
605		10t. Athletics (horiz)	45	70
606		10t. High jumping (horiz)	45	70
MS607	165×110 mm. Nos. 603/6 (sold at 40t.)		1·50	2·00

1996. 25th Anniv of Bangladesh Stamps. No. **MS**234 optd **Silver Jubilee Bangladesh Postage Stamps 1971-96** on sheet margin.

MS608	98×117 mm. Nos. 232/3 (sold at 10t.)		1·40	1·75

215 Bangabandhu Sheikh Mujibur Rahman

1996. 21st Death Anniv of Bangabandhu Sheikh Mujibur Rahman.

609	**215**	4t. multicoloured	40	25

216 Maulana Mohammad Akrum Khan

1996. 28th Death Anniv of Maulana Mohammad Akrum Khan.

610	**216**	4t. multicoloured	40	20

217 Ustad Alauddin Khan

1996. 24th Death Anniv of Ustad Alauddin Khan (musician).

611	**217**	4t. multicoloured	70	30

218 *Kingfisher* (Mayeesha Robbani)

219 Syed Nazrul Islam

1996. 21st Death Anniv of Jail Martyrs. Multicoloured.

614		4t. Type **219**	30	40
615		4t. Tajuddin Ahmad	30	40
616		4t. M. Monsoor Ali	30	40
617		4t. A. H. M. Quamaruzzaman	30	40

220 Children receiving Medicine

1996. 50th Anniv of UNICEF Multicoloured.

618		4t. Type **220**	50	25
619		10t. Mother and child	1·10	1·40

1996. Martyred Intellectuals (5th series). As T **148**. Each black and brown.

620		2t. Dr. Jekrul Haque	45	45
621		2t. Munshi Kabiruddin Ahmed	45	45
622		2t. Md. Abdul Jabbar	45	45
623		2t. Mohammad Amir	45	45
624		2t. A. K. M. Shamsul Huq Khan	45	45
625		2t. Dr. Siddique Ahmed	45	45
626		2t. Dr. Soleman Khan	45	45
627		2t. S. B. M. Mizanur Rahman	45	45
628		2t. Aminuddin	45	45
629		2t. Md. Nazrul Islam	45	45
630		2t. Zahirul Islam	45	45
631		2t. A. K. Lutfor Rahman	45	45
632		2t. Afsar Hossain	45	45
633		2t. Abul Hashem Mian	45	45
634		2t. A. T. M. Alamgir	45	45
635		2t. Baser Ali	45	45

221 Celebrating Crowds

1996. 25th Anniv of Victory Day. Multicoloured.

636		4t. Type **221**	35	30
637		6t. Soldiers and statue (vert)	65	70

222 Paul P. Harris

1997. 50th Death Anniv of Paul Harris (founder of Rotary International).

638	**222**	4t. multicoloured	35	25

223 Shaikh Mujibur Rahman making Speech

1997. 25th Anniv of Shaikh Mujibur's Speech of 7 March (1996).

639	**223**	4t. multicoloured	35	25

224 Sheikh Mujibur
Rahman

1997. 77th Birth Anniv of Sheikh Mujibur Rahman (first
President).

| 640 | **224** | 4t. multicoloured | 50 | 25 |

225 Sheikh Mujibur Rahman and
Crowd with Banners

1997. 25th Anniv (1996) of Independence.

| 641 | **225** | 4t. multicoloured | 35 | 25 |

226 Heinrich von
Stephan

1997. Death Centenary of Heinrich von Stephan (founder
of U.P.U.).

| 642 | **226** | 4t. multicoloured | 35 | 25 |

227 Sheep

1997. Livestock. Multicoloured.

643	**227**	4t. Type **227**	75	75
644		4t. Goat	75	75
645		6t. Buffalo bull	90	90
646		6t. Cow	90	90

228 "Tilling the Field – 2" (S.
Sultan)

1997. Bangladesh Paintings. Multicoloured.

| 647 | | 6t. Type **228** | 40 | 30 |
| 648 | | 10t. *Three Women* (Quamrul Hassan) | 60 | 1·25 |

229 Trophy, Flag and Cricket
Ball

1997. Sixth International Cricket Council Trophy
Championship, Malaysia.

| 649 | **229** | 10t. multicoloured | 3·25 | 2·75 |

230 Kusumba Mosque,
Naogaon

1997. Historic Mosques. Multicoloured.

650		4t. Type **230**	65	35
651		6t. Atiya Mosque, Tangail	85	45
652		10t. Bagha Mosque, Rajshahi	1·25	1·75

231 Adul Karim
Sahitya Vishard

1997. 126th Birth Anniv of Abdul Karim Sahitya Vishard
(scholar).

| 653 | **231** | 4t. multicoloured | 40 | 25 |

232 River Moot
Emblem and Scouts
standing on top of
World

1997. Ninth Asia-Pacific and Seventh Bangladesh Rover
Moot, Lakkatura.

| 654 | **232** | 2t. multicoloured | 50 | 25 |

233 Officers and Flag

1997. 25th Anniv of Armed Forces.

| 655 | **233** | 2t. multicoloured | 1·50 | 60 |

1997. Martyred Intellectuals (6th series). As T **148**. Each
black and brown.

656		2t. Dr. Shamsuddin Ahmed	65	65
657		2t. Mohammad Salimullah	65	65
658		2t. Mohiuddin Haider	65	65
659		2t. Abdur Rahin	65	65
660		2t. Nitya Nanda Paul	65	65
661		2t. Abdel Jabber	65	65
662		2t. Dr. Humayun Kabir	65	65
663		2t. Khaja Nizamuddin Bhuiyan	65	65
664		2t. Gulam Hossain	65	65
665		2t. Ali Karim	65	65
666		2t. Md. Moazzem Hossain	65	65
667		2t. Rafiqul Islam	65	65
668		2t. M. Nur Husain	65	65
669		2t. Captain Mahmood Hossain Akonda	65	65
670		2t. Abdul Wahab Talukder	65	65
671		2t. Dr. Hasimoy Hazra	65	65

234 Mohammad
Mansooruddin

1998. Professor Mohammad Mansooruddin (folklorist)
Commemoration.

| 672 | **234** | 4t. multicoloured | 1·40 | 60 |

235 Standard-bearer and
Soldiers

1998. 50th Anniv of East Bengal Regiment.

| 673 | **235** | 2t. multicoloured | 1·00 | 55 |

236 Bulbul
Chowdhury

1998. Bulbul Chowdhury (traditional dancer)
Commemoration.

| 674 | **236** | 4t. multicoloured | 40 | 25 |

237 World Cup
Trophy

1998. World Cup Football Championship, France.
Multicoloured.

| 675 | | 6t. Type **237** | 75 | 30 |
| 676 | | 18t. Footballer and trophy | 2·00 | 2·50 |

238 Eastern Approach Road,
Bangabandhu Bridge

1998. Opening of Bangabandhu Bridge. Multicoloured.

677		4t. Type **238**	65	30
678		6t. Western approach road	75	40
679		8t. Embankment	95	1·40
680		10t. Main span, Bangabandhu Bridge	1·25	1·60

239 Diana, Princess
of Wales

1998. Diana, Princess of Wales Commemoration.
Multicoloured.

681		8t. Type **239**	1·40	1·40
682		18t. Wearing pearl choker	1·75	1·75
683		22t. Wearing pendant necklace	1·75	2·00

240 Means of
collecting Solar
Energy

1998. World Solar Energy Programme Summit.

| 684 | **240** | 10t. multicoloured | 1·50 | 1·50 |

241 World Habitat
Day Emblem and City
Scene

1998. World Habitat Day.

| 685 | **241** | 4t. multicoloured | 1·25 | 60 |

242 Farmworkers,
Sunflower and "20"

1998. 20th Anniv of International Fund for Agricultural
Development. Multicoloured.

| 686 | | 6t. Type **242** | 65 | 35 |
| 687 | | 10t. Farmworker with baskets and harvested crops | 1·10 | 1·40 |

243 Batsman

1998. Wills International Cricket Cup, Dhaka.

| 688 | **243** | 6t. multicoloured | 1·75 | 1·25 |

244 Begum Rokeya

1998. Begum Rokeya (campaigner for women's
education) Commemoration.

| 689 | **244** | 4t. multicoloured | 1·25 | 60 |

245 Anniversary Logo

1998. 50th Anniv of Universal Declaration of Human
Rights.

| 690 | **245** | 10t. multicoloured | 1·25 | 1·25 |

1998. Martyred Intellectuals (7th series). As T **148**. Each
black and brown.

691		2t. Md. Khorshed Ali Sarker	50	50
692		2t. Abu Yakub Mahfuz Ali	50	50
693		2t. S. M. Nural Huda	50	50
694		2t. Nazmul Hoque Sarker	50	50
695		2t. Md. Taslim Uddin	50	50
696		2t. Gulam Mostafa	50	50
697		2t. A. H. Nural Alam	50	50
698		2t. Timir Kanti Dev	50	50
699		2t. Altaf Hossain	50	50
700		2t. Aminul Hoque	50	50
701		2t. S. M. Fazlul Hoque	50	50
702		2t. Mozammel Ali	50	50
703		2t. Syed Akbar Hossain	50	50
704		2t. Sk. Abdus Salam	50	50
705		2t. Abdur Rahman	50	50
706		2t. Dr. Shyamal Kanti Lala	50	50

246 Dove of Peace
and U.N. Symbols

1998. 50th Anniv of U.N. Peace-keeping Operations.

| 707 | **246** | 10t. multicoloured | 1·25 | 1·50 |

247 Kazi Nazrul Islam

1998. Birth Centenary (1999) of Kazi Nazrul Islam (poet).

| 708 | **247** | 6t. multicoloured | 1·25 | 70 |

248 Jamboree
Emblem and Scout
Activities

1999. Sixth Bangladesh National Scout Jamboree.

| 709 | **248** | 2t. multicoloured | 1·00 | 50 |

1999. As No. 75 but redrawn. Size 35×22 mm.
711		10t. red	1·10	30
710	–	5t. black and brown	60	15

No. 711 has been redrawn so that "SIXTY-DOME MOSQUE" appears above the face value at bottom right instead of below the main inscription at top left.

249 Surjya Sen and Demonstrators

1999. Surjya Sen (revolutionary) Commemoration.
715	**249**	4t. multicoloured	1·25	60

250 Dr. Fazlur Rahman Khan and Sears Tower

1999. 70th Birth Anniv of Dr. Fazlur Rahman Khan (architect).
716	**250**	4t. multicoloured	1·00	55

251 National Team Badges

1999. Cricket World Cup, England. Multicoloured.
717		8t. Type **251**	1·75	2·00
718		10t. Bangladesh cricket team badge and flag	2·50	2·50
MS719	139×89 mm. Nos. 717/18 (sold at 30t.)		4·50	4·75

252 Mother Teresa

1999. Mother Teresa Commemoration.
720	**252**	4t. multicoloured	1·50	65

253 Sheikh Mujibur Rahman, New York Skyline and Dove

1999. 25th Anniv of Bangladesh's Admission to U.N.
721	**253**	6t. multicoloured	1·00	65

254 Shaheed Mohammad Maizuddin

1999. 15th Death Anniv of Shaheed Mohammad Maizuddin (politician).
722	**254**	2t. multicoloured	60	30

255 Faces in Tree

1999. International Year of the Elderly.
723	**255**	6t. multicoloured	1·00	60

256 Shanty Town and Modern Buildings between Hands

1999. World Habitat Day.
724	**256**	4t. multicoloured	1·00	50

257 Mobile Post Office

1999. 125th Anniv of U.P.U. Multicoloured.
725		4t. Type **257**	80	65
726		4t. Postman on motorcycle	80	65
727		6t. Postal motor launch	1·00	90
728		6t. Douglas DC-10 and Boeing 737	1·00	90
MS729	141×90 mm. Nos. 725/8 (sold at 25t.)		3·25	3·25

258 Sir Jagadis Chandra Bose

1999. Sir Jagadis Chandra Bose (physicist and botanist) Commemoration.
730	**258**	4t. multicoloured	1·50	60

1999. Martyred Intellectuals (8th series). As T **148**. Each black and brown.
731		2t. Dr. Mohammad Shafi	50	50
732		2t. Maulana Kasimuddin Ahmed	50	50
733		2t. Quazi Ali Imam	50	50
734		2t. Sultanuddin Ahmed	50	50
735		2t. A. S. M. Ershadullah	50	50
736		2t. Mohammad Fazlur Rahman	50	50
737		2t. Captain A. K. M. Farooq	50	50
738		2t. Md. Latafot Hossain Joarder	50	50
739		2t. Ram Ranjan Bhattacharjya	50	50
740		2t. Abani Mohan Dutta	50	50
741		2t. Sunawar Ali	50	50
742		2t. Abdul Kader Miah	50	50
743		2t. Major Rezaur Rahman	50	50
744		2t. Md. Shafiqul Anowar	50	50
745		2t. A. A. M. Mozammel Hoque	50	50
746		2t. Khandkar Abul Kashem	50	50

259 Bangladesh Flag and Monument

2000. New Millennium. Multicoloured.
747		4t. Type **259**	75	45
748		6t. Satellite, computer and dish aerial (vert)	1·00	1·10

260 Cub Scouts, Globe and Flag

2000. Fifth Bangladesh Cub Camporee.
749	**260**	2t. multicoloured	70	40

261 Jibananada Das

2000. Death Centenary (1999) of Jibananada Das (poet).
750	**261**	4t. multicoloured	70	40

262 Dr. Muhammad Shamsuzzoha

2000. 30th Death Anniv (1999) of Dr. Muhammad Shamsuzzoha.
751	**262**	4t. multicoloured	1·00	40

263 Shafiur Rahman

2000. International Mother Language Day. Multicoloured.
752		4t. Type **263**	65	75
753		4t. Abul Barkat	65	75
754		4t. Abdul Jabbar	65	75
755		4t. Rafiq Uddin Ahmad	65	75

264 Meteorological Equipment

2000. 50th Anniv of World Meteorological Organization.
756	**264**	10t. multicoloured	1·75	1·75

265 Cricket Week Logo and Web Site Address

2000. International Cricket Week.
757	**265**	6t. multicoloured	1·75	1·25

266 Wasp

2000. Insects. Multicoloured.
758		2t. Type **266**	50	30
759		4t. Grasshopper	70	35
760		6t. Bumble bee	90	65
761		10t. Silkworms	1·50	2·25

267 Gecko

2000. Native Fauna. Multicoloured.
762		4t. Type **267**	70	70
763		4t. Indian crested porcupine	70	70
764		6t. Indian black-tailed python	95	95
765		6t. Bengal monitor	95	95

268 Batsman

2000. Pepsi 7th Asia Cricket Cup.
766	**268**	6t. multicoloured	1·75	1·25

269 Water Cock

2000. Birds. Multicoloured.
767		4t. Type **269**	90	80
768		4t. White-breasted waterhen (*Amaurornis phoenicurus*)	90	80
769		6t. Javanese cormorant (*Phalacrocorax niger*) (vert)	1·25	1·10
770		6t. Indian pond heron (*Ardeola grayii*) (vert)	1·25	1·10

270 Women's Shotput

2000. Olympic Games, Sydney. Multicoloured.
771		6t. Type **270**	1·00	50
772		10t. Men's Shotput	1·50	1·75

271 Clasped Hands, Landmarks and Flags

2000. 25th Anniv of Diplomatic Relations with People's Republic of China.
773	**271**	6t. multicoloured	1·50	75

272 Idrakpur Fort, Munshigonj

2000. Archaeology. Multicoloured.
774		4t. Type **272**	75	40
775		6t. Statue of Buddha, Mainamati (vert)	1·25	1·00

273 Year Emblem

2000. International Volunteers' Year.
776	**273**	6t. multicoloured	1·25	65

274 Hason Raza

2000. 80th Death Anniv of Hason Raza (mystic poet).
777 **274** 6t. multicoloured 1·50 75

275 U.N.H.C.R. Logo

2000. 50th Anniv of United Nations High Commissioner for Refugees (U.N.H.C.R.).
778 **275** 10t. multicoloured 1·50 2·00

2000. Martyred Intellectuals (9th series). As T **148**. Each black and brown.
779 2t. M. A. Gofur 55 55
780 2t. Faizur Rahman Ahmed 55 55
781 2t. Muslimuddin Miah 55 55
782 2t. Sgt. Shamsul Karim Khan 55 55
783 2t. Bhikku Zinananda 55 55
784 2t. Abdul Jabber 55 55
785 2t. Sekander Hayat Chowdhury 55 55
786 2t. Chishty Shah Helalur Rahman 55 55
787 2t. Birendra Nath Sarker 55 55
788 2t. A. K. M. Nurul Haque 55 55
789 2t. Sibendra Nath Mukherjee 55 55
790 2t. Zahir Raihan 55 55
791 2t. Ferdous Dowla Bablu 55 55
792 2t. Capt A. K. M. Nurul Absur 55 55
793 2t. Mizanur Rahman Miju 55 55
794 2t. Dr. Shamshad Ali 55 55

276 Map of Faces

2001. Population and Housing Census.
795 **276** 4t. multicoloured 1·25 55

277 Producing Food

2001. "Hunger-free Bangladesh" Campaign.
796 **277** 6t. multicoloured 1·25 65

278 "Peasant Women" (Rashid Chowdbury)

2001. Bangladesh Paintings.
797 **278** 10t. multicoloured 2·00 2·00

279 Lalbagh Kella Mosque

2001. Historic Buildings. Multicoloured.
798 **279** 6t. Type **279** 85 85
799 6t. Uttara Ganabhavan, Natore 85 85
800 6t. Armenian Church, Ar-manitola 85 85
801 6t. Panam Nagar, Sonargaon 85 85

280 Smoking Accessories, Globe and Paper People

2001. World No Tobacco Day.
802 **280** 10t. multicoloured 1·75 1·75

281 Ustad Gul Mohammad Khan

2001. Artists. Multicoloured.
803 6t. Type **281** 80 80
804 6t. Ustad Khadem Hossain Khan 80 80
805 6t. Gouhar Jamil 80 80
806 6t. Abdul Alim 80 80

282 Begum Sufia Kamal

2001. Begum Sufia Kamal (poet) Commemoration.
807 **282** 4t. multicoloured 75 40

283 Hilsa

2001. Fish. Multicoloured.
808 10t. Type **283** 1·10 1·10
809 10t. Tengra 1·10 1·10
810 10t. Punti 1·10 1·10
811 10t. Khalisa 1·10 1·10

284 Parliament House, Dhaka

2001. Completion of First Full National Parliamentary Term.
812 **284** 10t. multicoloured 2·25 2·25

285 Parliament House, Dhaka

2001. Eighth Parliamentary Elections.
813 **285** 2t. multicoloured 70 45

286 "Children encircling Globe" (Urska Golob)

2001. U.N. Year of Dialogue among Civilizations.
814 **286** 10t. multicoloured 1·25 1·50
MS815 95×65 mm. **286** 10t. multicoloured (sold at 30t.) 1·75 3·00

287 Meer Mosharraf Hossain

2001. Meer Mosharraf Hossain (writer) Commemoration.
816 **287** 4t. black, red and crimson 65 40

288 Drop of Blood surrounded by Images

2001. World AIDS Day.
817 **288** 10t. multicoloured 1·75 1·75

289 Sreshto Medal

2001. 30th Anniv of Independence. Gallantry Medals. Multicoloured.
818 10t. Type **289** 1·25 1·50
819 10t. Uttom medal 1·25 1·50
820 10t. Bikram medal 1·25 1·50
821 10t. Protik medal 1·25 1·50

290 Publicity Poster

2002. Tenth Asian Art Biennale, Dhaka.
822 **290** 10t. multicoloured 1·00 1·25

291 Letters from Bengali Alphabet

2002. 50th Anniv of Amar Ekushey (language movement). International Mother Language Day.
823 **291** 10t. black, gold and red 80 1·10
824 - 10t. black, gold and red 80 1·10
825 - 10t. black, gold and red 80 1·10
MS826 96×64 mm. 30t. multicoloured 2·25 2·25
DESIGNS—HORIZ: No. 824, Language Martyrs' Monument, Dhaka; 825, Letters from Bengali alphabet ("INTERNATIONAL MOTHER LANGUAGE DAY" inscr at right). VERT: No. **MS**826, Commemorative symbol of Martyrs' Monument.

292 Rokuon-Ji Temple, Japan

2002. 30th Anniv of Diplomatic Relations with Japan.
827 **292** 10t. multicoloured 1·00 1·25

293 Silhouetted Goats

2002. Goat Production.
828 **293** 2t. multicoloured 45 25

294 Children

2002. U.N. Special Session on Children.
829 **294** 10t. multicoloured 1·25 1·25

295 Mohammad Nasiruddin

2002. Mohammad Nasiruddin (journalist) Commemoration.
830 **295** 4t. black and brown 75 40

296 National Flags (trophy at top right)

2002. World Cup Football Championship, Japan and Korea. Multicoloured.
831 10t. Type **296** 1·00 1·25
832 10t. Pitch markings on world map 1·00 1·25
833 10t. National flags (trophy at top left) 1·00 1·25

297 Children tending Saplings

2002. National Tree Planting Campaign. Multicoloured.
834 10t. Type **297** 90 1·00
835 10t. Citrus fruit 90 1·00
836 10t. Trees within leaf symbol (vert) 90 1·00

298 Children inside Symbolic House

2002. 30th Anniv of S.O.S. Children's Village in Bangladesh.
837 **298** 6t. multicoloured 80 45

299 Rural Family

2002. World Population Day.
838 **299** 6t. multicoloured 80 45

300 Ompook Pabda (fish)

2002. Fish. Multicoloured.
839	**300**	4t. Type 300	50	50
840		4t. *Labeo gonius*	50	50

301 Bangladesh–U.K. Friendship Bridge, Bhairab

2002. Opening of Bangladesh–U.K. Friendship Bridge, Bhairab.
841	**301**	4t. multicoloured	1·00	45

302 Dhaka City Centre

2002. World Habitat Day.
842	**302**	4t. multicoloured	70	35

303 Dariabandha (Tag)

2002. Rural Games. Multicoloured.
843	**303**	4t. Type 303	70	70
844		4t. Kanamachee (Blind-man's buff)	70	70

304 Jasimuddin

2003. Birth Centenary of Jasimuddin (poet).
845	**304**	5t. multicoloured	50	35

305 Books

2003. National Book Year.
846	**305**	6t. multicoloured	60	35

306 Footballers and Flags of Participating Countries

2003. Third SAFF Championship, Bangladesh.
847	**306**	10t. multicoloured	1·75	1·75

ইফাদ-এর ২৫ বছর
25 Years of IFAD
(307)

2003. 25th Anniv of International Fund for Agricultural Development. No. 687 optd with T **307**.
848		10t. Farmworker with baskets and harvested crops	1·75	1·75

308 Shefa-ul-Mulk Hakim Habib-ur-Rahman

2003. 56th Death Anniv of Shefa-ul-Mulk Hakim Habib-ur-Rahman.
849	**308**	4t. multicoloured	45	25

309 Ziaur Rahman

2003. 22nd Death Anniv of Ziaur Rahman (President 1977–1981).
850	**309**	4t. multicoloured	45	25

310 Sapling in Cupped Hands and Family

2003. National Tree Plantation Campaign. Multicoloured.
851	**310**	8t. Type 310	1·00	60
852		12t. Trees, plant, fruit and adult with children inside "petals"	1·25	1·50

311 Fruit

2003. Fruit Tree Plantation Fortnight.
853	**311**	6t. multicoloured	1·25	60

312 *Labeo Calbasu* (Orange-fin labeo)

2003. Fish Fortnight.
854	**312**	2t. multicoloured	60	30

313 Train on Jamuna Bridge and Signals

2003. Inauguration of Direct Train Communication between Rajshahi and Dhaka.
855	**313**	10t. multicoloured	1·50	1·50

314 Jatiya Sangsad Bhaban (Parliament House)

2003. 49th Commonwealth Parliamentary Conference.
856	**314**	10t. multicoloured	1·25	1·40

315 Mosque

2003. Eid Mubarak.
857	**315**	4t. multicoloured	1·00	65

316 Emblem

2003. International Centre for Diarrhoeal Disease Research, Bangladesh.
858	**316**	10t. multicoloured	1·25	1·40

317 Rajshahi University

2003. 50th Anniv of Rajshahi University.
859	**317**	4t. multicoloured	1·00	55

318 Books

2004. National Library Year (2003).
860	**318**	6t. multicoloured	1·00	70

319 Tents inside Emblem and Member Flags

2004. Seventh Bangladesh and Fourth South Asian Association for Regional Co-operation Jamboree.
861	**319**	2t. multicoloured	1·00	45

320 Runner with Olympic Torch

2004. Sport and Environment.
862	**320**	10t. multicoloured	1·00	1·00

321 Emblems

2004. 11th Asian Art Biennale.
863	**321**	5t. multicoloured	45	25

322 Ziaur Rahman

2004. 33rd Anniv of Independence and National Day.
864	**322**	5t. multicoloured	45	25

323 Road and Emblems

2004. World Health Day.
865	**323**	6t. multicoloured	45	25

2004. 25th Anniv of Bangladesh National Philatelic Association. No. 843 optd **Silver Jubilee Bangladesh National Philatelic Association** and emblem.
866		4t. Type 303	45	30

325 Stylized Tree, Fruits and Berries

2004. National Tree Plantation Campaign. Multicoloured.
867		10t. Type 325	65	70
868		10t. Trees and saplings	65	70

326 Hafez Shirazi, Iranian Flag and Banay-e Azadi (Freedom Monument), Tehran

2004. Commemoration of Diplomatic Relations with Iran. Multicoloured.
869		10t. Type 326	80	90
870		10t. Nazrul Islam, Bangladeshi flag and War memorial, Dhaka	80	90

327 Woman Planting Tree and Fruit

2004. Fruit Tree Plantation Campaign.
871	**327**	10t. multicoloured	75	75

328 Workers carrying Rice Harvest

2004. International Year of Rice.
872	**328**	5t. multicoloured	60	60

329 Man feeding Child and Two Women

2004. World Population Day.
873	**329**	6t. multicoloured	45	30

330 UN Headquarters and Flags

2004. 30th Anniv of United Nations Membership.
874	**330**	4t. multicoloured	30	20

331 Bhasani Novo Theatre, Dhaka

2004. Bhasani Novo Theatre, Dhaka.
875 **331** 4t. multicoloured 30 20

332 Centennial Bell

2004. Centenary of Rotary International.
876 **332** 4t. multicoloured 30 20

333 *Argemone mexicana*

2004. Wild Flowers. Multicoloured.
877 **333** 5t. Type **333** 70 75
878 5t. *Cyanotis axillaries* 70 70
879 5t. *Thevetia Peruvians* 70 70
880 5t. *Pentapetes phoenicea* 70 70
881 5t. *Aegle marmelos* 70 70
882 5t. *Datura stramonium* 70 70

2004. 13th SAARC (South Asian Association for Regional Co-operation) Summit, Dhaka (2005).
883 **334** 6t. multicoloured 40 25

335 *Sperata aor*

2004. Fish Fortnight. Multicoloured.
884 **335** 10t. Type **335** 80 95
885 10t. *Notopterus notepturus* 80 95

336 Cub in Sunflower

2004. Sixth National Cub Camporee.
886 **336** 6t. multicoloured 40 25

337 Woman Farmer and Microcredit Symbol

2005. United Nations International Year of Microcredit. Multicoloured.
887 **337** 4t. Type **337** 30 30
888 10t. Woman turning lever on coin and microcredit symbol pulley 70 80

338 Beach at Sunset

2005. South Asia Tourism Year.
889 **338** 4t. multicoloured 30 20

339 Major Ziaur Rahman and War Memorial, Dhaka

2005. Independence and National Day.
890 **339** 10t. multicoloured 75 75

340 Sewing Machinist, Fish in Net, Dairy Cattle, Hens and Goats

2005. Centenary of Co-operative Movement in Bangladesh.
891 **340** 5t. multicoloured 40 25

341 Family Planting Tree

2005. National Tree Plantation Campaign. Multicoloured.
892 6t. Type **341** 70 75
893 6t. Three types of different varieties 70 75

342 G. A. Mannan (choreographer)

2005. Talented Artists. Multicoloured.
894 6t. Type **342** 60 70
895 6t. Unstad Phuljhuri Khan (musician) 60 70
896 6t. Ustad Abed Hossian Khan (musician and composer) 60 70
897 6t. Ustad Munshi Raisuddin (musician) 60 70

343 *Nandus nandus*

2005. Fish Fortnight.
898 **343** 10t. multicoloured 1·00 75

344 Dr. Nawab Ali

2005. Dr. Nawab Ali (physician) Commemoration.
899 **344** 8t. multicoloured 60 60

345 Books, Compass and Dividers

2006. Science Book Year (2005).
900 **345** 10t. multicoloured 75 75

346 Emblems, Globe and Computer Screen

2006. World Summit on the Information Society, Tunis (2005).
901 **346** 10t. multicoloured 1·00 75

347 Verwaltungssitz, Vienna and Emblem

2006. 30th Anniv of OPEC Fund for International Development (2005).
902 **347** 10t. multicoloured 75 75

348 Palace of Heavenly Peace, Beijing

2006. 30th Anniv of Bangladesh–China Diplomatic Relations (2005). Multicoloured.
903 10t. Type **348** 70 70
904 10t. Parliament Building, Dhaka 70 70
905 10t. 5th Bangladesh–China Friendship Bridge over Gabkhan River 70 70
906 10t. Great Wall of China 70 70
MS907 140×90 mm. Nos. 903/6 2·50 2·50

349 Major Ziaur Rahman and War Memorial, Dhaka

2006. 35th Anniversary of Independence and National Day.
908 **349** 10t. multicoloured 1·00 75

350 Palm Tree

2006. National Tree Plantation Campaign and Tree Fair.
909 **350** 10t. multicoloured 1·00 75

351 Mother with Baby and Toddler

2006. World Health Day.
910 **351** 6t. multicoloured 1·25 1·00

352 Silhouette of Batsman

2006. ICC Under 19 Cricket World Cup (2004), Bangladesh.
911 **352** 10t. multicoloured 1·50 1·25

353 Peace Dove and Modern Buildings and Roads

2006. Five Years of Peace and Development.
912 **353** 10t. multicoloured 1·00 1·00

354 AIDS Ribbon and Globe

2006. World AIDS Day.
913 **354** 10t. multicoloured 1·00 1·00

355 Profiles

2006. International Women's Day.
914 **355** 10t. multicoloured 1·00 1·00

356 Family and Jar of Coins ('Invest in health')

2007. World Health Day.
915 **356** 6t. multicoloured 1·00 1·00

357 Falling Wicket

2007. World Cup Cricket, West Indies. Multicoloured.
916 10t. Type **357** 1·00 1·00
917 10t. Tiger, bowler and trophy (horiz) 1·00 1·00
918 10t. Bangladesh team and Cricket World Cup trophy 1·00 1·00
919 10t. Batsman and trophy (horiz) 1·00 1·00

358 House and Girls
in Plantation

2007. National Tree Plantation Campaign.
920　**358**　10t. multicoloured　　　1·00　1·00

359 Md. Habibullah
Bahar Choudhury

2007. Birth Centenary (2006) of Md. Habibullah Bahar Choudhury (politician and writer).
921　**359**　10t. multicoloured　　　1·00　1·00

360 Boy and Girl Scouts

2007. Centenary of World Scouting. Multicoloured.
922　10t. Type **360**　　　　　1·00　1·00
923　10t. Lord Baden-Powell
　　　(founder)　　　　　　　1·00　1·00

(361)

2007. 20th Anniv of Philatelic Association of Bangladesh. No. 768 optd with T **361**.
924　4t. White-breasted waterhen
　　　(*Amaurornis phoenicurus*)　1·50　1·00

362 Dr. Muhammad
Yunus and Peace
Medal

2007. Dr. Muhammad Yunus and Grameen Bank–winner of Nobel Peace Prize (2006).
925　**362**　10t. multicoloured　　　1·50　1·50

363 Children standing in
Flood Water

2008. In Charity of Flood Victims. Multicoloured.
926　2t. Type **363**　　　　　70　80
927　2t. Children and sheep in flood
　　　water　　　　　　　　　70　80
928　2t. People and goats taking ref-
　　　uge on corrugated iron roof　70　80
929　2t. Women queuing for food　70　80
930　2t. Woman and children with
　　　food bowls and flooded
　　　houses　　　　　　　　70　80

364 Cricket Match

2007. ICC World Twenty20 2007 Cricket Cup, South Africa. Multicoloured.
931　4t. Type **364**　　　　　80　80
932　4t. Cricketer and map of South
　　　Africa　　　　　　　　80　80

365 Emblem and Globe

2008. International Migrants Day.
933　**365**　10t. multicoloured　　　1·50　1·50

366 Soldiers with
Flag

2008. Independence and National Day.
934　**366**　10t. multicoloured　　　1·50　1·50

367 Melting Glacier and
Flooded Village

2008. World Health Day. 'Protecting Health From Climate Change'.
935　**367**　10t. multicoloured　　　1·50　1·50

368 Herd of Spotted Deer

2008. The Sundarbans World Heritage Site. Multicoloured.
936　10t. Type **368**　　　　　1·50　1·50
937　10t. Waterway and mangrove
　　　forest　　　　　　　　1·50　1·50
938　10t. Collecting bee nests for
　　　honey　　　　　　　　1·50　1·50
939　10t. Tiger　　　　　　　1·50　1·50
MS940　167×95 mm. Nos. 936/9　6·50　6·50
　No. **MS**940 also exists imperforate.

369 'CELEBRATING
50 YEARS' and
Pattern

2008. Golden Jubilee of the Aga Khan (2007).
941　**369**　3t. emerald and green　55　55
942　**369**　3t. red and rose　　　55　55
943　–　3t. gold pattern on
　　　　white　　　　　　　55　55
944　–　3t. white pattern on
　　　　gold　　　　　　　　55　55
　DESIGN: Nos. 943/4 'CELEBRATING 50 YEARS' in circle surrounded by pattern.

370 Athletes on Training
Run

2008. Olympic Games, Beijing. Multicoloured.
945　10t. Type **370**　　　　　1·00　1·00
946　15t. Rifle shooting　　　　1·25　1·25
947　20t. Olympic mascots Beibei,
　　　Jingjing, Huanhuan, Yingying
　　　and Nini　　　　　　　1·40　1·40
948　25t. Pierre de Coubertin
　　　(founder of modern
　　　Olympics) and Olympic
　　　stamps of Greece (1876) and
　　　Bangladesh (1976)　　　1·60　1·60

371 The First Stamps of Bangladesh,
1971

2008. Stamp Day. Sheet 140×90 mm.
MS949　**371**　50t. multicoloured　　3·75　4·50

372 Khepupara Radar
Station, Patuakhali

2008. Japanese International Cooperation Agency ('Friends from the Birth of Bangladesh'). Sheet 123×75 mm containing T **372** and similar horiz designs. Multicoloured.
MS950　3t. Type **372**; 7t. Vocational
　training programme; 10t. Jamuna
　Multi-purpose Bridge; 10t. Polio vac-
　cination programme　　　2·50　2·75

373 Emblem

2008. 50th Anniv of Dhaka Chamber of Commerce and Industry.
951　**373**　10t. multicoloured　　　1·50　1·50

374 Farmer and
Workers in Rice Field

2008. First National Agriculture Day.
952　**374**　4t. multicoloured　　　70　50

375 Nimtali Deuri (gateway
of Nimtali Palace)

2008. 400th Anniv of Dhaka.
953　**375**　6t. multicoloured　　　80　60

376 Cox's Bazar

2008. Cox's Bazar (world's longest unbroken sea beach).
954　**376**　10t. multicoloured　　　1·00　1·00

377 Disabled Man

2008. International Day of Persons with Disabilities.
955　**377**　3t. multicoloured　　　70　45

378 Women and
Child and Emblem

2008. International Year of Sanitation.
956　**378**　3t. multicoloured　　　70　45

379 1972 'In Memory
of the Martyrs' 20p.
Stamp

2009. International Mother Language Day. Sheet 180×119 mm.
MS957　**379**　50t. multicoloured　　6·00　6·00

380 Sheikh Mujibur Rahman and
Children

2009. Sheikh Mujibur Rahman Commemoration and National Children's Day.
958　**380**　10t. multicoloured　　　1·25　1·25

381 Ziaur Rahman,
National Flag and
Painting

2009. Independence and National Day.
959　**381**　3t. multicoloured　　　1·00　45

382 Doctors and
Nurses with Patients
and Hospital Building

2009. World Health Day.
960　**382**　3t. multicoloured　　　1·00　55

383 China 2009
Emblem

2009. China 2009 World Stamp Exhibition, Luoyang. Sheet 100×70 mm containing T **383** and similar horiz designs. Multicoloured.
MS961　10t. Type **383**; 10t. China 2009
　'Tree Peony Messenger' mascot;
　20t. Ox　　　　　　　　4·75　4·75
　No. **MS**5961 contains three stamps and a stamp size label.

384 Shamsun Nahar
Mahmud

2009. Birth Centenary (2008) of Shamsun Nahar Mahmud (writer).
962　**384**　4t. multicoloured　　　70　50

385 Couple holding Tree Seedlings

2009. National Tree Plantation Campaign and Tree Fair.

| 963 | 385 | 3t. multicoloured | 50 | 35 |

386 Clock

2009. Day Light Saving Time.

| 964 | 386 | 5t. multicoloured | 65 | 65 |

387 Silhouette of Family

2009. World Population Day.

| 965 | 387 | 6t. multicoloured | 70 | 70 |

388 Galilean Telescope, 1609

2009. International Year of Astronomy. Multicoloured.

| 966 | | 10t. Type 388 | 1·50 | 1·50 |
| 967 | | 10t. Andromeda Galaxy | 1·50 | 1·50 |

389 Begum Fazilatunnessa Mujib

2009. National Mourning Day. Sheikh Mujibur Rahman and his Family. Multicoloured.

968	389	3t. Type 389	35	35
969		3t. Sheikh Kamal	35	35
970		3t. Sheikh Jamal	35	35
971		3t. Sheikh Russel	35	35
972		3t. Sheikh Abu Naser	35	35
973		3t. Sultana Kamal Khuku	35	35
974		3t. Parveen Jamal Rosy	35	35
975		3t. Abdur Rab Serniabat	35	35
976		3t. Sheikh Fazlul Haque Moni	35	35
977		3t. Begum Arju Moni	35	35
978		3t. Colonel Jamiluddin Ahmed	35	35
979		3t. Baby Serniabat	35	35
980		3t. Arif Serniabat	35	35
981		3t. Sukanto Abdullah Babu	35	35
982		3t. Shahid Serniabat	35	35
983		3t. Abdul Nayeem Khan Rintu	35	35
984		15t. Sheikh Mujibur Rahman	35	35

390 Coin

2009. World Food Day. Multicoloured.

985		3t. Type 390	45	45
986		3t. Bread and agricultural produce	45	45
987		3t. Boat loaded with produce	45	45
988		3t. Fishermen with catch	45	45

391 Valerie Taylor with Patient

2009. 30th Anniv of Centre for the Rehabilitation of the Paralysed, Dhaka.

| 989 | 391 | 7t. Type 391 | 90 | 90 |
| 990 | | 7t. Rehabilitation | 90 | 90 |

392 Professor Abdul Moktader

2009. Birth Centenary of Professor Abdul Moktader.

| 991 | 392 | 4t. multicoloured | 50 | 50 |

393 Scouts saluting

2010. Eighth National Scout Jamboree

| 992 | 393 | 10t. multicoloured | 3·25 | 3·25 |

394 'Alec's Red'

2010. Roses: Cultivated Varieties in Bangladesh. Multicoloured.

993		10t. Type 394	2·75	2·75
994		10t. Royal Highness	2·75	2·75
995		10t. Queen Elizabeth	2·75	2·75
996		10t. Ballerina	2·75	2·75
997		10t. Alexander	2·75	2·75
998		10t. Blue Moon	2·75	2·75
999		10t. Papa Meilland	2·75	2·75
1000		10t. Double Delight	2·75	2·75
1001		10t. Iceberg	2·75	2·75
1002		10t. Sonia	2·75	2·75
1003		10t. Sunblest	2·75	2·75
1004		10t. Piccadilly	2·75	2·75
1005		10t. Pascali	2·75	2·75

395 'Alec's Red'

2010. Inauguration of International Mother Language Institute, Dhaka

| 1006 | 395 | 15t. multicoloured | 4·25 | 4·25 |

396 Women with Raised Fists

2010. Centenary of International Women's Day

| 1007 | 396 | 5t. multicoloured | 2·00 | 2·00 |

397 1997 4t. Sheikh Mujibur Rahman Stamp

2010. National Children's Day. Sheet 140×100 mm.

| MS1008 | 397 | 10t. multicoloured (sold at 25t.) | 8·50 | 8·50 |

398 Liberation Monument, Public Library Campus, Brahman Baria

2010. Independence and National Day. Multicoloured.

| MS1009 | | 5t.×4, Type 398; Liberation Monument, Shafipur, Gazipur; Liberation Monument, Jagannath Hall, Dhaka University; Liberation Monument, Vocational Training Institute, Rangpur | 7·00 | 7·00 |

399 Cricket Badges

2010. ICC World Twenty20 2010 Cricket Cup

| 1010 | 398 | 15t. multicoloured | 4·25 | 4·25 |

400 Emblem

2010. 12th Anniv of Bangabandhu Sheikh Mujib Medical University

| MS1011 | 400 | 20t. multicoloured | 7·25 | 7·25 |

401 City Park

2010. National Tree Plantation Campaign and Tree Fair

| 1012 | 401 | 6t. multicoloured | 1·50 | 1·50 |

402 Bara Katra (Mughal Dhaka)

2010. 400th Anniv (2008) of Dhaka (2nd issue). Multicoloured.

1013		10t. Type 402	3·00	3·00
1014		10t. Buriganga River and Buckland Bund (embankment) (British Dhaka)	3·00	3·00
1015		10t. Kamlapur Railway Station (Pakistan Period)	3·00	3·00
1016		10t. Dhaka City Corporation building and modern Dhaka	3·00	3·00

403 Anniversary Emblem

2010. 50th Anniv of ICDDR'B (International Centre for Diarrhoeal Disease Research, Bangladesh)

| 1017 | 403 | 5t. gold and black | 1·75 | 1·75 |

404 Two Players

2010. World Cup Football Championships, South Africa. Multicoloured.

1018		10t. Type 404	1·50	1·50
1019		10t. Three players pursuing headed ball	1·50	1·50
1020		20t. Zakumi mascot	3·00	3·00

405 Chakma Woman

2010. Indigenous Peoples in Bangladesh. Multicoloured.

1021		5t. Type 405	60	60
1022		5t. Marma woman wearing flower in hair	60	60
1023		5r. Mru woman (head and shoulders, wearing red)	60	60
1024		5r. Tripura (head and shoulders, wearing red)	60	60
1025		5r. Pangkhua woman	60	60
1026		5r. Chakma woman (full length portrait, wearing sash)	60	60
1027		5r. Marma woman holding bouquet of flowers	60	60
1028		5r. Mru woman (threequarter length portrait, bracelets on arms)	60	60
1029		5r. Tripura woman (head and shoulders, wearing white)	60	60
1030		5r. Pangkhua man and woman	60	60
1031		5r. Chakma woman weaving	60	60
1032		5r. Two Marma women gathering crops	60	60
1033		5r. Two Mru women poundng grain	60	60
1034		5r. Two Tripura women carrying firewood	60	60
1035		5r. Pangkhua man making basket	60	60
1036		5r. Two Chakma women	60	60
1037		5r. Two Marma women dancing	60	60
1038		5r. Mru man spearing pig in pen	60	60
1039		5r. Tripura woman dancing	60	60
1040		5r. Pangkhua man with bull's skull	60	60

406 Rajban Bihar Pagoda, ('Raj Banbihar'), Rangamati

2010. Bangkok 2010 25th Asian International Stamp Exhibition, Bangkok, Thailand. Sheet 140×90 mm containing T 406 and similar horiz design. Multicoloured.

| MS1041 | | 20t. Type 406; 20t. Buddha Dhatu Jadi, Bandarban | 5·50 | 5·50 |

407 Tiger

2010. 35th Anniv of Diplomatic Relations between Bangladesh and the People's Republic of China. Year of the Tiger

| 1042 | 407 | 50t. multicoloured | 6·00 | 6·00 |

408 Abu Nayem Mohammed
Nazibuddin Khan (Khurram)

2010. Abu Nayem Mohammed Nazibuddin Khan (Khurram) (1954-71) Commemoration

| 1043 | **408** | 3t. multicoloured | 35 | 35 |

409 Emblem

2011. Population and Housing Census

| 1044 | **409** | 3t. multicoloured | 35 | 35 |

410 Children

2011. Seventh National Cub Camporee

| 1045 | **410** | 10t. multicoloured | 1·50 | 1·50 |

411 Sheikh Mujibur
Rahman and Followers

2011. Return to Bangladesh of Sheikh Mujibur Rahman, 1972 (" Bangabandhu's Homecoming Day"). Multicoloured.

1046	5t. Type **411**		60	60
1047	5t. Sheikh Mujibur Rahman waving to crowd		60	60
1048	10t. Sheikh Mujibur Rahman (1920-75, first President of Bangladesh)		1·50	1·50

412 Mahatma Gandhi at
Laksham Railway Station

2011. Indipex 2011 World Philatelic Exhibition, New Delhi. Mahatma Gandhi's Visit to Noakhali, 1946. Multicoloured.

1049	10t. Type **412**		1·50	1·50
1050	15t. Mahatma Gandhi and others at Noakhali, 1946		2·25	2·25
1051	20t. Mahatma Gandhi at Noakhali, 1946		3·00	3·00

413 Bowler

2011. ICC Cricket World Cup, Bangladesh. Multicoloured.

1052	20t. Type **413**		3·00	3·00
1053	20t. Batsman		3·00	3·00
1054	20t. Wicket-keeper		3·00	3·00
1055	20t. Fielder		3·00	3·00

MS1056 127×91 mm. 50t. Umpire, batsman and players. Imperf | | | 6·00 | 6·00 |

414 Emblem

2011. Anti-Corruption Day (9 December 2010)

| 1057 | **414** | 5t. multicoloured | 60 | 60 |

415 Bangabandhu
Square Fountain,
Dhaka

2011. 40th Anniv of Independence. Multicoloured.

MS1058 10t. Type **415**; 10t. Victory of Bangla Monument, Chittagong; 10t. Memorial of Liberation War, Rajarbagh Police Line, Dhaka; 10t. Invincible Bhoirab, Kishoreganj; 20t. Sheikh Mujibur Rahman (32×84 mm) | | 7·25 | 7·25 |

416 Probashi Kallyan Bank,
Banknotes and Globe

2011. Inauguration of Probashi Kallyan Bank

| 1059 | **416** | 10t. multicoloured | 1·50 | 1·50 |

417 Rabindranath Tagore and
Shlaidaha, Kushtia

2011. 150th Birth Anniv of Rabindranath Tagore (poet). Multicoloured.

1060	10t. Type **417**		1·50	1·50
1061	10t. Rabindranath Tagore and Shahjadpur, Sirajganj		1·50	1·50
1062	10t. Rabindranath Tagore and Dakkhindihi, Khulna		1·50	1·50
1063	10t. Rabindranath Tagore and Patishar, Naogaon		1·50	1·50

418 Planting Sapling

2011. National Tree Plantation Campaign

| 1064 | **418** | 10t. multicoloured | 1·50 | 1·50 |

419 Kazi Nazrul Islam

2011. International Nazrul Conference. 90th Anniv of Publication of Poem *Bidrohi* (*The Rebel*) by Kazi Nazrul Islam (1899-1976, Bengali poet and musician). Multicoloured.

1065	10t. Type **419**		1·50	1·50
1066	10t. Kazi Nazrul Islam and Nazrul Academy, Trishal		1·50	1·50
1067	10t. Kazi Nazrul Islam wearing hat and building with arches		1·50	1·50
1068	10t. Kazi Nazrul Islam as old man and sculpture at Nazrul Museum		1·50	1·50

420 *Hardella thurjii*

2011. Rare Species of Turtle. Multicoloured.

| 1069 | 10t. Type **420** | | 1·50 | 1·50 |
| 1070 | 10t. *Geoclemys hamiltonii* | | 1·50 | 1·50 |

421 *Heliopais personata*

2011. Birds of the Sundarbans. Multicoloured.

1071	10t. Type **421**		1·50	1·50
1072	10t. *Leptoptilos javanicus*		1·50	1·50
1073	10t. *Haliaeetus leucogaster*		1·50	1·50
1074	10t. *Bubo coromandus*		1·50	1·50
1075	10t. *Pelargopsis amauroptera*		1·50	1·50
1076	10t. *Halcyon coromanda*		1·50	1·50
1077	10t. *Alcedo meninting*		1·50	1·50
1078	10t. *Halcyon pileata*		1·50	1·50
1079	10t. *Todiramphus chloris*		1·50	1·50
1080	10t. *Treron bicincta*		1·50	1·50
1081	10t. *Gorsachius melanolophus*		1·50	1·50
1082	10t. *Pitta megarhyncha*		1·50	1·50

Nos. 1083/6, T **422** are left for Traditional Musical Instruments, issued 21 July 2011, not yet received

423 Coin of Sultan Fakhr al-Din Mubarak
Shah (1334-49)

2011. Coins of the Independent Sultans of Bengal (1st series). Multicoloured.

MS1087 10t. Type **423**; 10t. Coin of Sultan Shams al-Din Ilyas Shah (1342-57); 10t. Coin of Sultan Ghiyath al-Din Azam Shah (1389-1410); 10t. Coin of Sultan Jalal al-Din Muhammad Shah (1415-32) | | 5·50 | 5·50 |

424 Dhaka Club

2011. Centenary of Dhaka Club

| 1088 | **424** | 3t. multicoloured | 35 | 35 |

425 Emblem and Globe

2011. E Asia 2011 Conference, Dhaka

| 1089 | 10t. multicoloured | 1·50 | 1·50 |

426 Sheikh Mujibur Rahman
and National Memorial,
Savar

2011. 40th Anniv of Victory in War of Independence

| 1090 | **426** | 10t. multicoloured | 1·50 | 1·50 |

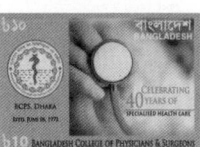

427 Emblem and Stethoscope

2011. 40th Anniv of Bangladesh College of Physicians and Surgeons

| 1091 | **427** | 10t. multicoloured | 1·50 | 1·50 |

OFFICIAL STAMPS

1973. Nos. 22, etc. optd **SERVICE**.

O1	**7**	2p. black	10	1·50
O2	-	3p. green	10	1·50
O3	-	5p. brown	20	10
O4	-	10p. black	20	10
O5	-	20p. green	1·75	10
O6	-	25p. mauve	4·00	10
O7	-	60p. grey	4·00	2·25
O8	-	75p. orange	1·50	30
O9	**8**	1t. violet	17·00	6·50
O10	-	5t. blue	5·00	9·00

1974. Nos. 49/51 optd **SERVICE**.

O11	**14**	1t. violet	5·00	50
O12	-	2t. olive	7·00	2·25
O13	-	5t. blue	18·00	14·00

1976. Nos. 64/70 and 72/4 optd **SERVICE**.

O14		5p. green	1·50	1·00
O15		10p. black	3·00	1·00
O16		20p. green	3·25	1·25
O17		25p. mauve	3·50	1·00
O18		50p. purple	5·00	60
O19		60p. grey	30	3·00
O20		75p. olive	30	3·75
O21	**14**	1t. blue	3·25	70
O22	-	2t. green	35	2·50
O23	-	5t. blue	30	2·75

32
Fenchuganj
Fertiliser
Factory

1981. Nos. 125/37 optd **SERVICE**.

O24		5p. brown	2·75	2·50
O25	**32**	10p. blue	2·75	3·00
O26	-	15p. orange	2·75	2·75
O27	-	20p. red	1·50	2·75
O28	-	25p. blue	80	2·75
O29	-	30p. green	5·00	3·00
O30	-	40p. purple	2·75	2·75
O31	-	50p. black	30	10
O32	-	80p. brown	2·25	50
O33	-	1t. violet	30	10
O34	-	2t. blue	35	3·25

1983. Nos. 220/9, 318a and 710 (1989) optd **Service**.

O35	**69**	5p. blue	20	60
O36	-	10p. purple	20	30
O37	-	15p. blue	20	45
O38	-	20p. black	20	30
O39	-	25p. grey	20	40
O40	-	30p. brown	25	40
O41	-	50p. brown	25	20
O42	-	1t. blue	50	20
O43	-	2t. green	1·75	30
O44	-	3t. black and blue	50	50
O45	-	4t. blue	55	55
O46	-	5t. purple	2·25	1·00

সার্ভিস
(O5)

1989. Nos. 227 and 710 (1989) optd with Type **O5**.

| O47 | 1t. blue | 50 | 20 |
| O48 | 5t. black and brown | 1·00 | 1·00 |

সার্ভিস
(O6)

1990. Nos. 368/9 (Immunization) optd with Type **O6**.

| O49 | **133** | 1t. green | 25 | 50 |
| O50 | **133** | 2t. brown | 25 | 50 |

1992. No. 376 optd as Type **O6** but horiz.

| O51 | **136** | 6t. blue and yellow | 50 | 50 |

1995. No. 553 (National Diabetes Awareness Day) optd as Type **O6** but horiz.

| O52 | **199** | 2t. multicoloured | 1·00 | 1·00 |

সার্ভিস
(O7)

1996. Nos. 221 and 223 optd with Type **O7**.

| O53 | 10p. purple | 75 | 75 |
| O54 | 20p. black | 1·25 | 1·25 |

1999. No. 710 optd as Type **O5** but vert.

| O56 | 5t. black and brown | 1·00 | 1·00 |

Pt. 1

BARBADOS

An island in the Br. West Indies, E. of the Windward Islands, attained self-government on 16 October 1961 and achieved independence within the Commonwealth on 30 November 1966.

1852. 12 pence = 1 shilling; 20 shillings = 1 pound.
1950. 100 cents = 1 West Indian, later Barbados, dollar.

1 Britannia **2**

1852. Imperf.

8	1	(½d.) green	£180	£200
10	1	(1d.) blue	85·00	60·00
4a	1	(2d.) slate	£300	£1200
5	1	(4d.) red	£120	£275
11	2	6d. red	£750	£120
12a	2	1s. black	£225	75·00

1860. Perf.

21	1	(½d.) green	29·00	32·00
24	1	(1d.) blue	70·00	4·00
25	1	(4d.) red	£150	70·00
31	2	6d. red	£150	32·00
33	2	6d. orange	£190	50·00
35	2	1s. black	65·00	10·00

1873. Perf.

72		½d. green	22·00	50
74		1d. blue	£130	1·50
63		3d. brown	£325	£110
75		3d. mauve	£160	14·00
76		4d. red	£150	14·00
79		6d. yellow	£150	2·25
81		1s. purple	£160	8·00

3

1873

64	3	5s. red	£950	£300

1878. Half of No. 64 surch 1D.

86	1d. on half 5s. red	£5000	£650

4

1882

90	4	½d. green	30·00	2·00
92	4	1d. red	50·00	1·25
93	4	2½d. blue	£120	1·50
96	4	3d. purple	8·00	29·00
97	4	4d. grey	£350	4·50
99	4	4d. brown	15·00	2·00
100	4	6d. black	75·00	48·00
102	4	1s. brown	29·00	21·00
103	4	5s. bistre	£170	£200

1892. Surch HALF-PENNY.

104		½d. on 4d. brown	2·25	6·00

6 Seal of Colony

1892

105	6	¼d. grey and red	2·50	10
163	6	¼d. brown	10·00	30
106	6	½d. green	2·50	10
107	6	1d. red	4·75	10
108	6	2d. black and orange	10·00	75
166	6	2d. grey	9·50	20·00
139	6	2½d. blue	27·00	15
110	6	5d. olive	7·50	4·50
111	6	6d. mauve and red	16·00	2·00
168	6	6d. deep purple and purple	21·00	32·00
112	6	8d. orange and blue	4·25	30·00
113	6	10d. green and red	9·00	9·50
169	6	1s. black on green	16·00	17·00
114	6	2s.6d. black and orange	48·00	65·00
144	6	2s.6d. violet and green	65·00	£150

7

1897. Diamond Jubilee.

116	7	¼d. grey and red	9·00	60
117	7	½d. green	9·00	60
118	7	1d. red	10·00	60
119	7	2½d. blue	14·00	85
120	7	5d. brown	32·00	20·00
121	7	6d. mauve and red	42·00	25·00
122	7	8d. orange and blue	22·00	27·00
123	7	10d. green and red	65·00	55·00
124	7	2s.6d. black and orange	95·00	60·00

8 Nelson Monument

1906. Death Centenary of Nelson.

145	8	¼d. black and grey	16·00	1·75
146	8	½d. black and green	11·00	15
147	8	1d. black and red	12·00	15
148	8	2d. black and yellow	2·50	4·50
149	8	2½d. black and blue	4·00	1·25
150	8	6d. black and mauve	19·00	28·00
151	8	1s. black and red	23·00	50·00

9 Olive Blossom, 1650

1906. Tercentenary of Annexation of Barbados.

152	9	1d. black, blue and green	17·00	25

1907. Surch Kingston Relief Fund. 1d.

153	6	1d. on 2d. black and orange	6·50	13·00

11

1912

170	11	¼d. brown	1·75	1·50
171	11	½d. green	3·75	10
172	11	1d. red	11·00	10
173	11	2d. grey	6·50	20·00
174	11	2½d. blue	1·75	65
175	11	3d. purple on yellow	2·00	14·00
176	11	4d. black and red on yellow	4·25	24·00
177	11	6d. deep purple and purple	12·00	12·00

Larger type, with portrait at top centre.

178		1s. black on green	13·00	24·00
179		2s. purple and blue on blue	60·00	65·00
180		3s. green and violet	£110	£120

14

1916

181	14	¼d. brown	75	40
182	14	½d. green	3·25	15
183a	14	1d. red	2·50	15
184	14	2d. grey	12·00	35·00
185	14	2½d. blue	6·00	3·50
186	14	3d. purple on yellow	9·00	14·00
187	14	4d. red on yellow	1·25	14·00
199	14	4d. black and red	1·25	3·75
188	14	6d. purple	10·00	7·50
189	14	1s. black on green	12·00	12·00
190	14	2s. purple on blue	17·00	7·50
191	14	3s. violet	70·00	£170

1917. Optd WAR TAX.

197	11	1d. red	50	15
200	14	3s. green and violet	27·00	£110

16

1920. Victory. Inscr "VICTORY 1919".

201	16	¼d. black and brown	30	70
202	16	½d. black and green	1·75	15
203	16	1d. black and red	4·00	10
204	16	2d. black and grey	2·25	16·00
205	16	2½d. indigo and blue	2·75	27·00
206	16	3d. black and purple	3·25	6·50
207	16	4d. black and green	3·25	7·00
208	16	6d. black and orange	4·75	23·00
209	-	1s. black and green	19·00	50·00
210	-	2s. black and brown	50·00	75·00
211	-	3s. black and orange	55·00	95·00

The 1s. to 3s. show Victory full-face.

18

1921

217	18	¼d. brown	25	10
219	18	½d. green	1·50	10
220	18	1d. red	80	10
221	18	2d. grey	1·75	20
222	18	2½d. blue	1·50	9·00
213	18	3d. purple on yellow	2·00	9·00
214	18	4d. red on yellow	1·75	23·00
225	18	6d. purple	3·50	7·00
215	18	1s. black on green	5·50	22·00
227	18	2s. purple on blue	10·00	22·00
228	18	3s. violet	24·00	85·00

19

1925. Inscr "POSTAGE & REVENUE".

229	19	¼d. brown	25	10
230	19	½d. green	60	10
231	19	1d. red	60	10
231ca	19	1½d. orange	6·00	1·00
232	19	2d. grey	75	3·25
233	19	2½d. blue	50	80
234	19	3d. purple on yellow	1·00	45
235	19	4d. red on yellow	75	1·00
236	19	6d. purple	1·00	90
237	19	1s. black on green	2·00	8·00
238	19	2s. purple on blue	7·00	8·50
238a	19	2s.6d. red on blue	30·00	42·00
239	19	3s. violet	11·00	20·00

20 King Charles I and King George V

1927. Tercentenary of Settlement of Barbados.

240	20	1d. red	1·00	75

1935. Silver Jubilee. As T 13 of Antigua.

241		1d. blue and red	2·00	20
242		1½d. blue and grey	5·00	8·50
243		2½d. brown and blue	2·75	6·50
244		1s. grey and purple	24·00	35·00

1937. Coronation. As T 2 of Aden.

245		1d. red	30	15
246		1½d. brown	55	75
247		2½d. blue	1·25	75

21 Badge of the Colony

1938. "POSTAGE & REVENUE" omitted.

248	21	½d. green	6·00	15
248c	21	½d. bistre	15	30
249a	21	1d. red	16·00	10
249bc	21	1d. green	15	10
250	21	1½d. orange	15	40
250c	21	2d. purple	1·25	2·50
250d	21	2d. red	75	70
251	21	2½d. blue	1·00	60
252b	21	3d. brown	30	60
252c	21	3d. blue	1·00	1·75
253	21	4d. black	30	10
254	21	6d. violet	80	40
254a	21	8d. mauve	55	2·00
255a	21	1s. olive	2·00	10
256	21	2s.6d. purple	9·00	1·50
256a	21	5s. blue	9·00	13·00

22 Kings Charles I, George VI, Assembly Chamber and Mace

1939. Tercentenary of General Assembly.

257	22	½d. green	3·00	1·00
258	22	1d. red	3·00	1·25
259	22	1½d. orange	3·25	60
260	22	2½d. blue	5·00	8·50
261	22	3d. brown	5·00	5·50

1946. Victory. As T 9 of Aden.

262		1½d. orange	15	50
263		3d. brown	15	50

1947. Surch ONE PENNY.

264	17	1d. on 2d. red	2·25	5·00

1948. Silver Wedding. As T 10/11 of Aden.

265		1½d. orange	30	50
266		5s. blue	17·00	12·00

1949. U.P.U. As T 22/03 of Antigua.

267		1½d. orange	50	2·00
268		3d. blue	2·50	7·00
269		4d. grey	50	3·25
270		1s. olive	50	60

24 Dover Fort **35** Seal of Barbados

1950

271	24	1c. indigo	35	4·50
272	-	2c. green	15	3·00
273	-	3c. brown and green	1·25	4·00
274	-	4c. red	15	40
275	-	6c. blue	15	2·25
276	-	8c. blue and brown	1·50	3·75
277	-	12c. blue and olive	1·00	1·75
278	-	24c. red and black	1·00	50
279	-	48c. violet	9·00	7·00
280	-	60c. green and lake	10·00	13·00
281	-	$1.20 red and olive	13·00	4·50
282	35	$2.40 black	26·00	42·00

DESIGNS—As Type **24**: HORIZ: 2c. Sugar cane breeding; 3c. Public buildings; 6c. Casting net; 8c. "Frances W. Smith" (schooner); 12c. Four-winged flyingfish; 24c. Old Main Guard Garrison; 60c. Careenage. VERT: 4c. Statue of Nelson; 48c. St. Michael's Cathedral; $1.20, Map and wireless mast.

1951. Inauguration of B.W.I. University College. As T 24/25 of Antigua.

283		3c. brown and blue	30	40
284		12c. blue and olive	1·25	2·25

36 King George VI and Stamp of 1852

1952. Centenary of Barbados Stamps.

285	36	3c. green and slate	40	40
286	36	4c. blue and red	40	1·00
287	36	12c. slate and green	40	1·00
288	36	24c. brown and sepia	50	55

37 Harbour Police

1953. As 1950 issue but with portrait or cypher (No. 301) of Queen Elizabeth II as in T 37.

289	24	1c. indigo	10	80
290	-	2c. orange and turquoise	15	1·50
291	-	3c. black and green	1·00	1·00
292	-	4c. black and orange	20	20
293	37	5c. blue and red	1·00	60
294	-	6c. brown	3·00	60
314	-	8c. black and blue	70	35

296	–	12c. blue and olive	1·00	10
297	–	24c. red and black	1·00	10
317	–	48c. violet	5·00	1·50
318	–	60c. green and purple	10·00	4·00
300	–	$1.20 red and olive	19·00	6·50
319	**35**	$2.40 black	1·25	1·75

1953. Coronation. As T **13** of Aden.

302		4c. black and orange	1·00	20

1958. British Caribbean Federation. As T **28** of Antigua.

303		3c. green	45	20
304		6c. blue	60	2·25
305		12c. red	60	30

38 Deep Water Harbour, Bridgetown

1961. Opening of Deep Water Harbour.

306	**38**	4c. black and orange	45	50
307	**38**	8c. black and blue	45	60
308	**38**	24c. red and black	50	60

39 Scout Badge and Map of Barbados

1962. Golden Jubilee of Barbados Boy Scout Association.

309	**39**	4c. black and orange	85	15
310	**39**	12c. blue and brown	1·25	15
311	**39**	$1.20 red and green	1·90	3·75

1965. Centenary of I.T.U. As T **36** of Antigua.

320		2c. lilac and red	20	40
321		48c. yellow and drab	45	1·00

40 Deep Sea Coral

1965

342	**40**	1c. black, pink and blue	10	20
323	–	2c. brown, yell & mve	20	15
324	–	3c. brown and orange	45	60
344	–	3c. brown and orange	30	2·75
325	–	4c. blue and green	15	20
326	–	5c. sepia, red and lilac	30	20
327	–	6c. multicoloured	45	20
328	–	8c. multicoloured	25	10
329	–	12c. multicoloured	35	10
330	–	15c. black, yellow and red	4·00	30
331	–	25c. blue and ochre	1·00	30
332	–	35c. red and green	1·50	15
333	–	50c. blue and green	2·00	40
334	–	$1 multicoloured	3·50	2·00
335	–	$2.50 multicoloured	2·75	7·00
355a	–	$5 multicoloured	21·00	16·00

DESIGNS—HORIZ: 2c. Lobster; 3c. (No. 324) Lined seahorse (wrongly inscribed "Hippocanpus"); 3c. (No. 344) (correctly inscribed "Hippocampus"); 4c. Sea urchin; 5c. Staghorn coral; 6c. Spot-finned butterflyfish; 8c. Rough file shell; 12c. Porcupinefish ("Balloon fish"); 15c Grey angel-fish; 25c. Brain coral; 35c. Brittle star; 50c. Four-winged flyingfish; $1 Queen or pink conch shell; $2.50, Fiddler crab. VERT: $5 Dolphin.

1966. Churchill Commemoration. As T **38** of Antigua.

336		1c. blue	10	3·50
337		4c. green	55	10
338		25c. brown	1·25	50
339		35c. violet	1·25	70

1966. Royal Visit. As T **39** of Antigua.

340		3c. black and blue	75	1·00
341		35c. black and mauve	1·75	1·00

54 Arms of Barbados

1966. Independence. Multicoloured.

356		4c. Type **54**	10	10
357		25c. Hilton Hotel (horiz)	15	10
358		35c. G. Sobers (Test cricketer)	1·50	65
359		50c. Pine Hill Dairy (horiz)	70	1·10

1967. 20th Anniv of U.N.E.S.C.O. As T **54/56** of Antigua.

360		4c. multicoloured	20	10
361		12c. yellow, violet and olive	45	50
362		25c. black, purple and orange	75	1·25

58 Policeman and Anchor

1967. Centenary of Harbour Police. Multicoloured.

363		4c. Type **58**	25	10
364		25c. Policeman and telescope	40	15
365		35c. "BPI" (police launch) (horiz)	45	15
366		50c. Policeman outside H.Q.	60	1·60

62 Governor-General Sir Winston Scott G.C.M.G

1967. Firstt Anniv of Independence. Multicoloured.

367		4c. Type **62**	15	10
368		25c. Independence Arch (horiz)	25	10
369		35c. Treasury Building (horiz)	30	10
370		50c. Parliament Building (horiz)	40	90

66 U.N. Building, Santiago, Chile

1968. 20th Anniv of Economic Commission for Latin America.

371	**66**	15c. multicoloured	10	10

67 Radar Antenna

1968. World Meteorological Day. Multicoloured.

372		3c. Type **67**	10	10
373		25c. Meteorological Institute (horiz)	25	10
374		50c. Harp Gun and Coat of Arms	30	90

70 Lady Baden-Powell and Guide at Campfire

1968. Golden Jubilee of Girl Guiding in Barbados.

375	**70**	3c. blue, black and gold	20	60
376	–	25c. blue, black and gold	30	60
377	–	35c. yellow, black and gold	35	60

DESIGNS: 25c. Lady Baden-Powell and Pax Hill; 35c. Lady Baden-Powell and Guides' Badge.

73 Hands breaking Chain, and Human Rights Emblem

1968. Human Rights Year.

378	**73**	4c. violet, brown and green	10	20
379	–	25c. black, blue and yellow	10	25
380	–	35c. multicoloured	15	25

DESIGNS: 25c. Human Rights emblem and family enchained; 35c. Shadows of refugees beyond opening fence.

76 Racehorses in the Paddock

1969. Horse Racing. Multicoloured.

381		4c. Type **76**	25	15
382		25c. Starting-gate	25	15
383		35c. On the flat	30	15
384		50c. The winning-post	35	2·40
MS385		117×85 mm. Nos. 381/4	2·00	2·75

80 Map showing "CARIFTA" Countries

1969. First Anniv of "CARIFTA". Multicoloured.

386		5c. Type **80**	10	10
387		12c. "Strength in Unity" (horiz)	10	10
388		25c. Type **80**	10	10
389		50c. As 12c.	15	20

82 I.L.O. Emblem and "1919–1969"

1969. 50th Anniv of I.L.O.

390	**82**	4c. black, green and blue	10	10
391	**82**	25c. black, mauve and red	20	10

1969. No. 363 surch **ONE CENT**.

392	**58**	1c. on 4c. multicoloured	10	10

84 National Scout Badge

1969. Independence of Barbados Boy Scouts Association and 50th Anniv of Barbados Sea Scouts. Multicoloured.

393		5c. Type **84**	15	10
394		25c. Sea Scouts rowing	45	10
395		35c. Scouts around campfire	55	10
396		50c. Scouts and National Scout H.Q.	80	1·25
MS397		155×115 mm. Nos. 393/6	15·00	13·00

1970. No. 326 surch **4**.

398		4c. on 5c. sepia, red and lilac	10	10

89 Lion at Gun Hill

1970. Multicoloured.. Multicoloured..

399		1c. Type **89**	10	2·50
400		2c. Trafalgar Fountain	30	1·25
401		3c. Montefiore Drinking Fountain	60	1·00
402a		4c. St. James' Monument	30	10
403		5c. St. Ann's Fort	10	10
404		6c. Old Sugar Mill, Morgan Lewis	35	3·00
405		8c. The Cenotaph	10	10
406a		10c. South Point Lighthouse	1·25	15
407		12c. Barbados Museum (horiz)	1·75	10

408		15c. Sharon Moravian Church (horiz)	30	15
409		25c. George Washington House (horiz)	25	15
410		35c. Nicholas Abbey (horiz)	30	85
411		50c. Bowmanston Pumping Station (horiz)	40	1·00
412		$1 Queen Elizabeth Hospital (horiz)	70	2·50
413		$2.50 Suger Factory (horiz)	1·50	4·00
467		$5 Seawell International Airport (horiz)	7·50	5·50

105 Primary Schoolgirl

1970. 25th Anniv of U.N. Multicoloured.

415		4c. Type **105**	10	10
416		5c. Secondary schoolboy	10	10
417		25c. Technical student	35	10
418		50c. University building	55	1·50

106 Minnie Root

1970. Flowers of Barbados. Multicoloured.

419		1c. Barbados Easter lily (vert)	10	2·50
420		5c. Type **106**	40	10
421		10c. Eyelash orchid	1·75	30
422		25c. Pride of Barbados (vert)	1·25	75
423		35c. Christmas hope	1·25	85
MS424		162×101 mm. Nos. 419/23. Imperf	2·00	6·50

107 "Via Dolorosa" Window, St. Margaret's Church, St. John

1971. Easter. Multicoloured.

425		4c. Type **107**	10	10
426		10c. *The Resurrection* (Benjamin West)	10	10
427		35c. Type **107**	15	10
428		50c. As 10c.	30	1·50

108 "Sailfish" Dinghy

1971. Tourism. Multicoloured.

429		1c. Type **108**	10	50
430		5c. Tennis	40	10
431		12c. Horse-riding	60	10
432		25c. Water-skiing	40	20
433		50c. Scuba-diving	50	90

109 S. J. Prescod (politician)

1971. Death Centenary of Samuel Jackman Prescod.

434	**109**	3c. multicoloured	10	15
435	**109**	35c. multicoloured	15	15

110 Arms of Barbados

1971. Fifth Anniv of Independence. Multicoloured.

436		4c. Type **110**	20	10

437	15c. National flag and map	45	10
438	25c. Type **110**	45	10
439	50c. As 15c.	90	1·60

111 Transmitting "Then and Now"

1972. Centenary of Cable Link. Multicoloured.

440	4c. Type **111**	10	10
441	10c. Cable Ship "Stanley Angwin"	20	10
442	35c. Barbados Earth Station and "Intelsat 4"	35	20
443	50c. Mt. Misery and Tropo-spheric Scatter Station	50	1·75

112 Map and Badge

1972. Diamond Jubilee of Scouts. Multicoloured.

444	5c. Type **112**	15	10
445	15c. Pioneers of scouting (horiz)	15	10
446	25c. Scouts (horiz)	30	15
447	50c. Flags (horiz)	60	1·00

113 Mobile Library

1972. International Book Year. Multicoloured.

448	4c. Type **113**	20	10
449	15c. Bedford mobile cinema truck	25	10
450	25c. Public library	25	10
451	$1 Codrington College	1·00	1·50

114 Potter's Wheel

1973. Pottery in Barbados. Multicoloured.

468	5c. Type **114**	10	10
469	15c. Kilns	20	10
470	25c. Finished products	25	10
471	$1 Market scene	90	1·10

115 Wright Type B First Flight, 1911

1973. Aviation.

472	**115** 5c. multicoloured	30	10
473	– 15c. multicoloured	90	10
474	– 25c. blue, blk & cobalt	1·25	20
475	– 50c. multicoloured	2·00	1·90

DESIGNS: 15c. de Havilland Cirrus Moth on first flight to Barbados, 1928; 25c. Lockheed 14 Super Electra, 1939; 50c. Vickers Super VC-10 airliner, 1973.

116 University Chancellor

1973. 25th Anniv of University of West Indies. Multicoloured.

476	5c. Type **116**	10	10
477	25c. Sherlock Hall	25	15
478	35c. Cave Hill Campus	30	25

1974. No. 462 surch **4c.**

479	4c. on 25c. multicoloured	15	15

118 Old Sail Boat

1974. Fishing Boats of Barbados. Multicoloured.

480	15c. Type **118**	30	15
481	35c. Rowing-boat	55	25
482	50c. Motor fishing-boat	70	70
483	$1 *Calamar* (fishing boat)	1·10	1·40
MS484	140×140 mm. Nos. 480/3	3·50	3·00

119 *Cattleya gaskelliana alba*

1974. Orchids. Multicoloured.

510	1c. Type **119**	15	1·25
511	2c. *Renanthera storiei* (vert)	15	1·25
512	3c. *Dendrobium* "Rose Marie" (vert)	15	1·00
488	4c. *Epidendrum ibaguense* (vert)	1·75	90
514	5c. *Schomburgkia humboldtii* (vert)	35	15
490	8c. *Oncidium ampliatum* (vert)	1·75	90
515	10c. *Arachnis maggie oei* (vert)	35	10
492	12c. *Dendrobium aggregatum* (vert)	45	2·75
517	15c. *Paphiopedilum puddle* (vert)	70	15
493b	20c. *Spathoglottis* "The Gold"	6·00	4·75
518	25c. *Epidendrum ciliare* (Eyelash)	70	10
550	35c. *Bletia patula* (vert)	2·00	1·75
519	45c. *Phalaenopsis schilleriana* "Sunset Glow" (vert)	60	15
496	50c. As 45c. (vert)	7·00	4·50
497	$1 *Ascocenda* "Red Gem" (vert)	10·00	3·25
498	$2.50 *Brassolaeliocattleya* "Nugget"	2·50	7·00
499	$5 *Caularthron bicornutum*	2·50	6·00
500	$10 *Vanda* "Josephine Black" (vert)	2·75	14·00

120 4d. Stamp of 1882, and U.P.U. Emblem

1974. Centenary of Universal Postal Union.

501	**120** 8c. mauve, orange & grn	10	10
502	– 35c. red, orge & brown	20	10
503	– 50c. ultram, bl & silver	25	35
504	– $1 blue, brown & black	75	1·00
MS505	126×101 mm. Nos. 501/4	1·75	2·50

DESIGNS: 35c. Letters encircling the globe; 50c. U.P.U. emblem and arms of Barbados; $1 Map of Barbados, sailing ship and Boeing 747 airliner.

121 Royal Yacht *Britannia*

1975. Royal Visit. Multicoloured.

506	8c. Type **121**	85	30
507	25c. Type **121**	1·40	30
508	35c. Sunset and palms	60	35
509	$1 As 35c.	1·75	5·00

122 St. Michael's Cathedral

1975. 150th Anniv of Anglican Diocese. Multicoloured.

526	5c. Type **122**	10	10
527	15c. Bishop Coleridge	15	10
528	50c. All Saints' Church	45	50
529	$1 "Archangel Michael and Satan" (stained glass window, St. Michael's Cathedral, Bridgetown)	70	80
MS530	95×96 mm. Nos. 526/9	1·40	2·00

123 Pony Float

1975. Crop-over Festival. Multicoloured.

531	8c. Type **123**	10	10
532	25c. Man on stilts	15	10
533	35c. Maypole dancing	20	10
534	50c. Cuban dancers	40	80
MS535	127×85 mm. Nos. 531/4	1·00	1·60

124 Barbados Coat of Arms

1975. Coil Definitives.

536	**124** 5c. blue	15	1·00
537	**124** 25c. violet	25	1·10

125 17th-Century Sailing Ship

1975. 350th Anniv of First Settlement. Multicoloured.

538	4c. Type **125**	50	20
539	10c. Bearded fig tree and fruit	30	15
540	25c. Ogilvy's 17th-century map	1·00	30
541	$1 Captain John Powell	1·00	5·00
MS542	105×115 mm. Nos. 538/41	2·50	7·00

126 Map of Caribbean

1976. West Indian Victory in World Cricket Cup.

559	**126** 25c. multicoloured	1·25	1·00
560	– 45c. black and purple	1·25	2·00

DESIGN—VERT: 45c. The Prudential Cup.

127 Flag and Map of South Carolina

1976. Bicentenary of American Revolution. Multicoloured.

561	15c. Type **127**	75	15
562	25c. George Washington and map of Bridgetown	75	15
563	50c. Independence Declaration	60	1·00
564	$1 Prince Hall	75	3·00

128 Early Postman

1976. 125th Anniv of Post Office Act. Multicoloured.

565	8c. Type **128**	10	10
566	35c. Modern postman	25	10
567	50c. Early letter	30	75
568	$1 Delivery van	50	1·75

129 Coast Guard *Commander Marshall* and *T. T. Lewis* launches

1976. Tenth Anniv of Independence. Multicoloured.

569	5c. Type **129**	30	20
570	15c. Reverse of currency note	30	10
571	25c. Barbados national anthem	30	20
572	$1 Independence Day parade	1·10	3·00
MS573	90×125 mm. Nos. 569/72	2·75	3·75

130 Arrival of Coronation Coach at Westminster Abbey

1977. Silver Jubilee. Multicoloured.

574	15c. Queen knighting Garfield Sobers, 1975	30	25
575	50c. Type **130**	30	40
576	$1 Queen entering Abbey	30	70

131 Underwater Park

1977. Natural Beauty of Barbados. Multicoloured.

577	5c. Type **131**	20	10
578	35c. Royal palms (vert)	35	10
579	50c. Underwater caves	50	50
580	$1 Stalagmite in Harrison's Cave (vert)	90	1·10
MS581	138×92 mm. Nos. 577/80	2·50	2·75

132 Maces of the House of Commons

1977. 13th Regional Conference of Commonwealth Parliamentary Association.

582	**132** 10c. orange, yellow & brn	10	10
583	– 25c. green, orge & dp grn	10	10
584	– 50c. multicoloured	20	20
585	– $1 blue, orange and dp bl	55	75

DESIGNS—VERT: 25c. Speaker's Chair; 50c. Senate Chamber. HORIZ: $1 Sam Lord's Castle.

133 The Charter Scroll

1977. 350th Anniv of Granting of Charter to Earl of Carlisle. Multicoloured.

586	12c. Type **133**	15	10
587	25c. The earl receiving charter	15	10
588	45c. The earl and Charles I (horiz)	30	35
589	$1 Ligon's map, 1657 (horiz)	75	1·00

1977. Royal Visit. As Nos. 574/6 but inscr "SILVER JUBILEE ROYAL VISIT".

590	15c. Garfield Sobers being knighted, 1975	60	50
591	50c. Type **130**	20	75
592	$1 Queen entering Abbey	30	1·25

134 Gibson's Map of Bridgtown, 1766

1978. 350th Anniv of Founding of Bridgetown.

593	**134** 12c. multicoloured	15	10
594	– 25c. black, green & gold	15	10
595	– 45c. multicoloured	20	15
596	– $1 multicoloured	30	60

DESIGNS: 25c. *A Prospect of Bridgetown in Barbados* (engraving by S. Copens, 1695); 45c. *Trafalgar Square, Bridgetown* (drawing by J. M. Carter, 1835); $1 The Bridges, 1978.

135 Brown Pelican

1978. 25th Anniv of Coronation.

597	50c. olive, black & blue	25	50
598	50c. multicoloured	25	50
599	**135** 50c. olive, black & blue	25	50

DESIGNS: No. 597, Griffin of Edward III. No. 598, Queen Elizabeth II.

136 Barbados Bridge League Logo

1978. Seventh Regional Bridge Tournament, Barbados. Multicoloured.

600	5c. Type **136**	10	10
601	10c. Emblem of World Bridge Federation	15	10
602	45c. Central American and Caribbean Bridge Federation emblem	25	10
603	$1 Playing cards on map of Caribbean	60	85
MS604	134×83 mm. Nos. 600/3	2·00	2·75

137 Camp Scene

1978. Diamond Jubilee of Guiding. Multicoloured.

605	12c. Type **137**	25	15
606	28c. Community work	40	15
607	50c. Badge and "60" (vert)	55	30
608	$1 Guide badge (vert)	75	1·00

138 Garment Industry

1978. Industries of Barbados. Multicoloured.

609	12c. Type **138**	15	10
610	28c. Cooper (vert)	25	25
611	45c. Blacksmith (vert)	35	1·25
612	50c. Wrought iron working	40	1·50

139 *Forth* (early mail steamer)

1979. Ships. Multicoloured.

613	12c. Type **139**	35	10
614	25c. *Queen Elizabeth 2* in Deep Water Harbour	55	15
615	50c. *Ra II* nearing Barbados	75	1·00
616	$1 Early mail paddle-steamer	1·00	2·50

140 1953 1c. Definitive Stamp

1979. Death Cent of Sir Rowland Hill. Multicoloured.

617	12c. Type **140**	15	15
618	28c. 1975 350th anniv of first settlement 25c. commemorative (vert)	20	30
619	45c. Penny Black with Maltese Cross postmark (vert)	30	45
MS620	137×90 mm. 50c. Unissued "Brittannia" blue	55	50

1979. St. Vincent Relief Fund. No. 495 surch **28c+4c ST. VINCENT RELIEF FUND**.

621	28c.+4c. on 35c. "Bletia patula"	50	60

142 Grassland Yellow Finch ("Grass Canary")

1979. Birds. Multicoloured.

622	1c. Type **142**	10	1·25
623	2c. Grey kingbird ("Rainbird")	10	1·25
624	5c. Lesser Antillean bullfinch ("Sparrow")	10	70
625	8c. Magnificent frigate bird ("Frigate Bird")	75	2·25
626	10c. Cattle egret	10	40
627	12c. Green-backed heron ("Green Gaulin")	1·00	1·50
627a	15c. Carib grackle ("Blackbird")	4·50	5·00
628	20c. Antillean crested hummingbird ("Humming Bird")	20	55
629	25c. Scaly-breasted ground dove ("Ground Dove")	20	60
630	28c. As 15c.	2·00	2·00
631	35c. Green-throated carib	70	70
631b	40c. Red-necked pigeon ("Ramier")	4·50	5·50
632	45c. Zenaida dove ("Wood Dove")	1·75	1·50
633	50c. As 40c.	1·50	2·00
633a	55c. American golden plover ("Black breasted Plover")	4·00	3·50
633b	60c. Bananaquit ("Yellow Breasted")	4·50	6·00
634	70c. As 60c.	2·25	3·75
635	$1 Caribbean elaenia ("Peer whistler")	2·00	1·50
636	$2.50 American redstart ("Christmas Bird")	2·00	6·00
637	$5 Belted kingfisher ("Kingfisher")	3·25	9·00
638	$10 Moorhen ("Red-seal Coot")	4·50	14·00

143 Unloading H.A.R.P. Gun on Railway Wagon at Foul Bay

1979. Space Projects Commemorations. Multicoloured.

639	10c. Type **143**	30	10
640	12c. H.A.R.P. gun on railway wagon under tow (vert)	30	15
641	20c. Firing launcher (vert)	30	20
642	28c. Bath Earth Station and "Intelsat"	30	30
643	45c. "Intelsat" over Caribbean	35	50
644	50c. "Intelsat" over Atlantic (vert)	35	60
MS645	118×90 mm. $1 Lunar module descending on to Moon	1·50	1·00

144 Family

1979. International Year of the Child. Multicoloured.

646	12c. Type **144**	10	10
647	28c. Ring of children and map of Barbados	15	15
648	45c. Child with teacher	20	20
649	50c. Children playing	20	20
650	$1 Children and kite	35	45

145 Map of Barbados

1980. 75th Anniv of Rotary International. Multicoloured.

651	12c. Type **145**	15	10
652	28c. Map of Caribbean	15	15
653	50c. Rotary anniversary emblem	20	35
654	$1 Paul P. Harris (founder)	30	95

146 Private, Artillery Company, Barbados Volunteer Force, c.1909

1980. Barbados Regiment. Multicoloured.

655	12c. Type **146**	30	10
656	35c. Drum Major, Zouave uniform	45	15
657	50c. Sovereign's and Regimental Colours	50	30
658	$1 Barbados Regiment Women's Corps	60	70

147 Early Postman

1980. "London 1980" International Stamp Exhibition. Two sheets each 122×125 mm containing T **147** or similar vert design. Multicoloured.

MS659	(a) 28c.×6, Type **147**. (b) 50c.×6, Modern postwoman and Inspector Set of 2 sheets	1·00	1·25

148 Yellow-tailed Snapper

1980. Underwater Scenery. Multicoloured.

660	12c. Type **148**	20	10
661	28c. Banded butterflyfish	35	15
662	50c. Male and female blue-headed wrasse and princess parrotfish	45	25
663	$1 French grunt and French angelfish	70	70
MS664	136×110 mm. Nos. 660/3	2·50	3·75

149 Bathsheba Railway Station

1981. Early Transport. Multicoloured.

665	12c. Type **149**	30	10
666	28c. Cab stand at The Green	20	15
667	45c. Animal-drawn tram	30	30
668	70c. Horse-drawn bus	45	60
669	$1 Railway Station, Fairchild Street	70	95

150 The Blind at Work

1981. Int Year for Disabled Persons. Multicoloured.

670	10c. Type **150**	20	10
671	25c. Sign Language (vert)	25	15
672	45c. "Be alert to the white cane" (vert)	40	25
673	$2.50 Children at play	80	3·00

151 Prince Charles dressed for Polo

1981. Royal Wedding. Multicoloured.

674	28c. Wedding bouquet from Barbados	15	10
675	50c. Type **151**	20	15
676	$2.50 Prince Charles and Lady Diana Spencer	55	1·25

152 Landship Manoeuvre

1981. Carifesta (Caribbean Festival of Arts), Barbados. Multicoloured.

677	15c. Type **152**	15	15
678	20c. Yoruba dancers	15	15
679	40c. Tuk band	20	25
680	55c. Sculpture by Frank Collymore	25	35
681	$1 Harbour scene	50	75

1981. Nos. 630, 632 and 634 surch.

682	15c. on 28c. Carib grackle	30	15
683	40c. on 45c. Zenaida dove	30	35
684	60c. on 70c. Bananaquit	30	45

154 Satellite View of Hurricane

1981. Hurricane Season.

685	**154** 35c. black and blue	35	20
686	- 50c. multicoloured	45	35
687	- 60c. multicoloured	70	50
688	- $1 multicoloured	85	90

DESIGNS: 50c. Hurricane *Gladys* from "Apollo 7"; 60c. Police Department on hurricane watch; $1 McDonnell Banshee "hurricane chaser" aircraft.

155 Twin Falls

1981. Harrison's Cave. Multicoloured.

689	10c. Type **155**	10	10
690	20c. Stream in Rotunda Room	20	15
691	55c. Formations in Rotunda Room	25	30
692	$2.50 Cascade Pool	60	2·25

156 Black Belly Ram

1982. Black Belly Sheep. Multicoloured.

693	40c. Type **156**	15	20
694	50c. Black belly ewe	15	20
695	60c. Ewe with lambs	20	45
696	$1 Ram and ewe, with map of Barbados	35	1·50

157 Barbados Coat of Arms and Flag

1982. President Reagan's Visit. Multicoloured.

697	20c. Type **157**	30	1·00
698	20c. U.S.A. coat of arms and flag	30	1·00
699	55c. Type **157**	40	1·25
700	55c. As No. 698	40	1·25

158 Lighter

1982. Early Marine Transport. Multicoloured.

701	20c. Type **158**	20	15
702	35c. Rowing boat	35	25
703	55c. Speightstown schooner	50	40
704	$2.50 Inter-colonial schooner	1·75	2·50

159 Bride and Earl Spencer Proceeding up the Aisle

1982. 21st Birthday of Princess of Wales. Mult.

705	20c. Barbados coat of arms	20	15
706	60c. Princess at Llanelwedd, October, 1981	45	50
707	$1.20 Type **159**	75	1·10
708	$2.50 Formal portrait	1·25	1·90

160 "To Help other People"

1982. 75th Anniv of Boy Scout Movement. Multicoloured.

709	15c. Type **160**	50	10
710	40c. "I Promise to do my Best" (horiz)	80	30
711	55c. "To do my Duty to God, the Queen and my Country" (horiz)	90	65
712	$1 National and Troop flags	1·40	1·75
MS713	119×93 mm. $1.50, The Scout Law	2·75	3·00

161 Arms of George Washington

1982. 250th Birth Anniv of George Washington. Multicoloured.

714	10c. Type **161**	10	10
715	55c. Washington House, Barbados	25	30
716	60c. Washington with troops	25	35
717	$2.50 Washington taking Oath	75	1·60

162 *Agraulis vanillae*

1983. Butterflies. Multicoloured.

718	20c. Type **162**	1·00	40
719	40c. *Danaus plexippus*	1·50	40
720	55c. *Hypolimnas misippus*	1·50	45
721	$2.50 *Hemiargus hanno*	3·25	3·75

163 Map of Barbados and Satellite View

1983. Commonwealth Day. Multicoloured.

722	15c. Type **163**	20	10
723	40c. Tourist beach	25	20
724	60c. Sugar cane harvesting	35	40
725	$1 Cricket match	1·25	1·10

164 U.S. Navy "M" Class Airship M-20

1983. Bicentenary of Manned Flight.

726	20c. Type **164**	40	15
727	40c. Douglas DC-3	45	40
728	55c. Vickers Viscount 837	45	50
729	$1 Lockheed TriStar 500	65	2·50

165 Nash 600, 1934 (inscr "1941")

1983. Classic Cars. Multicoloured.

730	25c. Type **165**	40	20
731	45c. Dodge D-8 coupe, 1938	50	30
732	75c. Ford Model A tourer, 1930	80	1·50
733	$2.50 Dodge Four tourer, 1918	1·25	4·50

166 Game in Progress

1983. Table Tennis World Cup Competition. Multicoloured.

734	20c. Type **166**	25	20
735	65c. Map of Barbados	50	55
736	$1 World Table Tennis Cup	75	1·00

167 Angel playing Lute (detail *The Virgin and Child*) (Masaccio)

1983. Christmas. 50th Anniv of Barbados Museum.

737	**167** 10c. multicoloured	30	10
738	- 25c. multicoloured	60	20
739	- 45c. multicoloured	90	40
740	- 75c. black and gold	1·40	1·60
741	- $2.50 multicoloured	4·50	6·00
MS742	59×98 mm. $2 multicoloured	1·75	2·00

DESIGNS—HORIZ: 45c. *The Barbados Museum* (Richard Day); 75c. *St. Ann's Garrison* (W. S. Hedges); $2.50, Needham's Point, Carlisle Bay. VERT: 25c., $2 Different details from *The Virgin and Child* (Masaccio).

168 Track and Field Events

1984. Olympic Games, Los Angeles.

745	**168** 50c. green, black and brown	60	45
746	- 65c. orange, blk & brn	80	60
747	- 75c. blue, black & dp bl	1·00	85
748	- $1 brown, black and yellow	2·50	2·00
MS749	115×97 mm. Nos. 745/8	8·00	9·00

DESIGNS: 65c. Shooting; 75c. Sailing; $1 Cycling.

169 Global Coverage

1984. 250th Anniv of *Lloyd's List* (newspaper). Multicoloured.

750	45c. Type **169**	80	40
751	65c. Bridgetown harbour	90	50
752	75c. "Philosopher" (full-rigged ship), 1857	1·40	1·00
753	$1 "Sea Princess" (liner), 1984	1·40	1·40

170 U.P.U. 1943 3d. Stamp and Logo

1984. Universal Postal Union Congress, Hamburg. Sheet 90×75 mm.

MS754	**170** $2 multicoloured	2·50	2·50

171 Local Junior Match

1984. 60th Anniv of International Chess Federation. Multicoloured.

755	25c. Type **171**	1·50	30
756	45c. Staunton and 19th-century knights	1·75	50
757	65c. Staunton queen and 18th-century queen from Macao	2·00	1·75
758	$2 Staunton and 17th-century rooks	3·75	6·50

172 Poinsettia

1984. Christmas. Flowers. Multicoloured.

759	50c. Type **172**	1·75	90
760	65c. Snow-on-the-Mountain	2·00	1·75
761	75c. Christmas Candle	2·25	3·25
762	$1 Christmas Hope	2·50	3·75

173 Pink-tipped Anemone

1985. Marine Life. Multicoloured.

794A	1c. Bristle worm	30	2·75
795B	2c. Spotted trunkfish	30	2·75
796A	5c. Coney	1·00	1·50
797B	10c. Type **173**	30	30
798B	20c. Christmas tree worm	30	40
799B	25c. Hermit crab	40	40
800A	35c. Animal flower	1·50	1·50
801B	40c. Vase sponge	50	50
802B	45c. Spotted moray	60	50
803B	50c. Ghost crab	60	60
804B	55c. Flamingo tongue snail	65	70
805B	75c. Sergeant major	1·25	75
806B	$1 Caribbean warty anemone	1·00	85
807B	$2.50 Green turtle	1·25	6·00
808B	$5 Rock beauty (fish)	1·50	8·00
809B	$10 Elkhorn coral	2·00	8·00

174 The Queen Mother at Docks

1985. Life and Times of Queen Elizabeth the Queen Mother. Multicoloured.

779	25c. In the White Drawing Room, Buckingham Palace, 1930s	50	20
780	65c. With Lady Diana Spencer at Trooping the Colour, 1981	2·50	1·00
781	75c. Type **174**	80	1·00
782	$1 With Prince Henry at his christening (from photo by Lord Snowdon)	85	1·25
MS783	91×73 mm. $2 In Land Rover Series I opening Syon House Garden Centre	2·50	1·50

175 Peregrine Falcon

1985. Birth Bicentenary of John J. Audubon (ornithologist). Designs showing original paintings. Multicoloured.

784	45c. Type **175**	2·25	80
785	65c. Prairie warbler (vert)	2·50	2·25
786	75c. Great blue heron (vert)	2·75	3·00
787	$1 Yellow warbler (vert)	3·00	4·00

176 Intelsat Satellite orbiting Earth

1985. 20th Anniv of Intelsat Satellite System.

788	**176** 75c. multicoloured	1·00	70

177 Traffic Policeman

1985. 150th Anniv of Royal Barbados Police. Multicoloured.

789	25c. Type **177**	80	20
790	50c. Police band on bandstand	1·40	80
791	65c. Dog handler	1·60	1·40
792	$1 Mounted policeman in ceremonial uniform	1·75	2·00
MS793	85×60 mm. $2 Police Band on parade (horiz).	1·50	2·75

1986. 60th Birthday of Queen Elizabeth II. As T **110** of Ascension. Multicoloured.

810	25c. Princess Elizabeth aged two, 1928	40	20
811	50c. At University College of West Indies, Jamaica, 1953	50	40
812	65c. With Duke of Edinburgh, Barbados, 1985	70	50
813	75c. At banquet in Sao Paulo, Brazil, 1968	70	60
814	$2 At Crown Agents Head Office, London, 1983	1·10	1·50

178 Canadair DC-4M2 North Star of Trans-Canada Airlines

1986. "Expo '86" World Fair, Vancouver. Multicoloured.

815	50c. Type **178**	75	50
816	$2.50 "Lady Nelson" (cargo liner)	2·00	2·50

1986. "Ameripex '86" International Stamp Exhibition, Chicago. As T **164** of Bahamas, showing Barbados stamps. Multicoloured.

817	45c. 1976 Bicentenary of American Revolution 25c.	70	35
818	50c. 1976 Bicentenary of American Revolution 50c.	80	55
819	65c. 1981 Hurricane Season $1	90	1·00
820	$1 1982 Visit of President Reagan 55c.	1·00	1·75
MS821	90×80 mm. $2 Statue of Liberty and liner "Queen Elizabeth 2"	10·00	12·00

No. **MS**821 also commemorates the Centenary of the Statue of Liberty.

1986. Royal Wedding. As T **112** of Ascension. Multicoloured.

822	45c. Prince Andrew and Miss Sarah Ferguson	75	35
823	$1 Prince Andrew in midshipman's uniform	1·25	75

179 Transporting Electricity Poles, 1923

1986. 75th Anniv of Electricity in Barbados. Multicoloured.

824	10c. Type **179**	15	10
825	25c. Heathman Ladder, 1935 (vert)	25	20
826	65c. Transport fleet, 1941	60	60
827	$2 Bucket truck, 1986 (vert)	1·60	2·00

180 *Alpinia purpurata* and Church Window

1986. Christmas. Multicoloured.

828	25c. Type **180**	20	20
829	50c. *Anthurium andraeanum*	45	45
830	75c. *Heliconia rostrata*	75	80
831	$2 *Heliconia × psittacorum*	1·50	4·25

181 Shot Putting

1987. Tenth Anniv of Special Olympics. Multicoloured.

832	15c. Type **181**	25	15
833	45c. Wheelchair racing	45	30
834	65c. Long jumping	60	65
835	$2 Logo and slogan	1·25	2·50

182 Barn Swallow

1987. "Capex '87" International Stamp Exhibition, Toronto. Birds. Multicoloured.

836	25c. Type **182**	2·00	50
837	50c. Yellow warbler	2·25	1·75
838	65c. Audubon's shearwater	2·25	1·75
839	75c. Black-whiskered vireo	2·50	3·25
840	$1 Scarlet tanager	2·75	4·00

183 Sea Scout saluting

1987. 75th Anniv of Scouting in Barbados. Multicoloured.

841	10c. Type **183**	20	10
842	25c. Scout jamboree	30	20
843	65c. Scout badges	65	45
844	$2 Scout band	1·60	1·75

184 Bridgetown Synagogue

1987. Restoration of Bridgetown Synagogue. Multicoloured.

845	50c. Type **184**	2·00	1·75
846	65c. Interior of Synagogue	2·25	2·25
847	75c. Ten Commandments (vert)	2·50	2·50
848	$1 Marble laver (vert)	2·75	3·75

185 Arms and Colonial Seal

1987. 21st Anniv of Independence. Multicoloured.

849	25c. Type **185**	50	20

850	45c. Flags of Barbados and Great Britain	1·25	35
851	65c. Silver dollar and one penny coins	1·25	55
852	$2 Colours of Barbados Regiment	2·50	2·75
MS853	94×56 mm. $1.50, Prime Minister E. W. Barrow (vert)	1·50	1·75

186 Herman C. Griffith

1988. West Indian Cricket. Each showing portrait, cricket equipment and early belt buckle. Multicoloured.

854	15c. E. A. (Manny) Martindale	2·75	75
855	45c. George Challenor	3·50	75
856	50c. Type **186**	3·75	2·25
857	75c. Harold Austin	4·00	3·50
858	$2 Frank Worrell	5·00	11·00

187 *Kentropyx borckianus*

1988. Lizards of Barbados. Multicoloured.

859	10c. Type **187**	1·75	50
860	50c. *Hemidactylus mabouia*	3·00	70
861	65c. *Anolis extremus*	3·25	1·25
862	$2 *Gymnophthalmus under-woodii*	6·50	10·00

188 Cycling

1988. Olympic Games, Seoul. Multicoloured.

863	25c. Type **188**	1·75	40
864	45c. Athletics	70	30
865	75c. Relay swimming	85	65
866	$2 Yachting	2·00	2·75
MS867	114×63 mm. Nos. 863/6	4·75	3·00

1988. 300th Anniv of Lloyd's of London. As T **123** of Ascension.

868	40c. multicoloured	55	30
869	50c. multicoloured	65	35
870	65c. multicoloured	1·50	45
871	$2 blue and red	7·00	4·00

DESIGNS—VERT: 40c. Royal Exchange, 1774; $2 Sinking of *Titanic*, 1912. HORIZ: 50c. Early sugar mill; 65c. *Author* (container ship).

189 Harry Bayley and Observatory

1988. 25th Anniv of Harry Bayley Observatory. Multicoloured.

872	25c. Type **189**	75	20
873	65c. Observatory with North Star and Southern Cross constellations	1·60	75
874	75c. Andromeda galaxy	1·75	90
875	$2 Orion constellation	3·25	6·00

190 L.I.A.T. Hawker Siddeley H.S.748

1989. 50th Anniv of Commercial Aviation in Barbados. Multicoloured.

876	25c. Type **190**	2·50	40
877	65c. Pan Am Douglas DC-8-62	3·25	1·25
878	75c. British Airways Concorde at Grantley Adams Airport	3·75	1·75
879	$2 Caribbean Air Cargo Boeing 707-351C	6·00	9·50

191 Assembly Chamber

1989. 350th Anniv of Parliament.

880	**191** 25c. multicoloured	40	20
881	- 50c. multicoloured	60	35
882	- 75c. blue and black	1·00	50
883	- $2.50 multicoloured	2·50	2·25

DESIGNS: 50c. The Speaker; 75c. Parliament Buildings, c. 1882; $2.50, Queen Elizabeth II and Prince Philip in Parliament.

192 Brown Hare

1989. Wildlife Preservation. Multicoloured.

884	10c. Type **192**	80	30
885	50c. Red-footed tortoise (horiz)	2·00	70
886	65c. Savanna ("Green") monkey	2·25	1·25
887	$2 "Bufo marinus" (toad) (horiz)	4·00	8·00
MS888	87×97 mm. $1 Small Indian mongoose	1·25	1·50

1989. 35th Commonwealth Parliamentary Conference. Square design as T **191**. Multicoloured.

MS889	108×69 mm. $1 Barbados Mace	1·00	1·50

193 Bread 'n Cheese

1989. Wild Plants. Multicoloured.

921	2c. Type **193**	50	1·75
891	5c. Scarlet cordia	50	1·00
892	10c. Columnar cactus	50	30
893	20c. Spiderlily	50	30
925	25c. Rock balsam	65	20
895	30c. Hollyhock	70	25
895a	35c. Red sage	1·25	1·00
927	45c. Yellow shak-shak	75	35
928	50c. Whitewood	80	40
898	55c. Bluebell	1·00	55
930	65c. Prickly sage	90	55
900	70c. Seaside samphire	1·25	1·25
901	80c. Flat-hand dildo	1·75	1·40
901a	90c. Herringbone	1·75	2·25
902	$1.10 Lent tree	1·50	2·25
934	$2.50 Rodwood	2·50	4·25
935	$5 Cowitch	3·75	7·00
936	$10 Maypole	7·00	10·00

194 Water Skiing

1989. "World Stamp Expo '89" International Stamp Exhibition, Washington. Watersports. Multicoloured.

906	25c. Type **194**	1·50	40
907	50c. Yachting	2·50	1·00
908	65c. Scuba diving	2·50	1·75
909	$2.50 Surfing	6·50	11·00

195 Barbados 1852 1d. Stamp

1990. 150th Anniv of the Penny Black and "Stamp World London '90" International Stamp Exn.

910	**195** 25c. green, black and yellow	1·50	40
911	- 50c. multicoloured	2·00	1·00
912	- 65c. multicoloured	2·00	1·50
913	- $2.50 multicoloured	5·00	9·00
MS914	90×86 mm. 50c. multicoloured; 50c. multicoloured	1·75	2·75

DESIGNS: 50c. 1882 1d. Queen Victoria stamp; 65c. 1899 2d. stamp; $2.50, 1912 3d. stamp; miniature sheet, 50c. Great Britain Penny Black, 50c. Barbados "1906" Nelson Centenary 1s.

196 Bugler and Jockeys

1990. Horse Racing. Multicoloured.

915	25c. Type **196**	60	30
916	45c. Horse and jockey in parade ring	85	50
917	75c. At the finish	1·25	85
918	$2 Leading in the winner (vert)	2·75	6·00

1990. 90th Birthday of Queen Elizabeth the Queen Mother. As T **134** of Ascension.

919	75c. multicoloured	75	60
920	$2.50 black and green	2·25	3·25

DESIGNS—21×36 mm: 75c. Lady Elizabeth Bowes-Lyon, April 1923 (from painting by John Lander). 29×37 mm: $2.50, Lady Elizabeth Bowes-Lyon on her engagement, January 1923.

197 *Orthemis ferruginea* (dragonfly)

1990. Insects. Multicoloured.

937	50c. Type **197**	1·50	80
938	65c. *Ligyrus tumulosus* (beetle)	1·75	1·00
939	75c. *Neoconocephalus* sp. (grasshopper)	2·00	1·25
940	$2 *Bostra maxwelli* (stick-insect)	3·50	5·50

1990. Visit of the Princess Royal. Nos. 925, 901 and 903 optd **VISIT OF HRH THE PRINCESS ROYAL OCTOBER 1990.**

941	25c. Rock balsam	2·25	50
942	80c. Flat-hand dildo	3·50	2·00
943	$2.50 Rodwood	8·50	12·00

199 Star

1990. Christmas. Multicoloured.

944	20c. Type **199**	65	20
945	50c. Figures from crib	1·00	50
946	$1 Stained glass window	2·00	1·50
947	$2 Angel (statue)	3·00	5·50

200 Adult Male Yellow Warbler

1991. Endangered Species. Yellow Warbler. Multicoloured.

948	10c. Type **200**	1·40	80
949	25c. Pair feeding chicks in nest	2·00	80
950	45c. Female feeding chicks in nest	2·50	80
951	$1 Male with fledgeling	4·00	5·50

201 Sorting Daily
Catch

1991. Fishing in Barbados. Multicoloured.

952	5c. Type **201**	50	50
953	50c. Line fishing (horiz)	1·75	90
954	75c. Fish cleaning (horiz)	2·25	1·25
955	$2.50 Game fishing	4·50	6·50

202 Masonic
Building, Bridgetown

1991. 250th Anniv of Freemasonry in Barbados (1990).

956	**202**	25c. multicoloured	1·75	50
957	–	65c. multicoloured	2·50	1·25
958	–	75c. black, yellow & brn	2·50	1·25
959	–	$2.50 multicoloured	5·00	7·00

DESIGNS: 65c. Compass and square (masonic symbols); 75c. Royal Arch jewel; $2.50, Ceremonial apron, columns and badge.

203 Battus polydamus

1991. "Phila Nippon '91" International Stamp Exhibition, Tokyo. Butterflies. Multicoloured.

960	20c. Type **203**	1·00	40
961	50c. Urbanus proteus (vert)	1·50	65
962	65c. Phoebis sennae	1·60	95
963	$2.50 Junonia evarete (vert)	4·00	6·00
MS964	87×86 mm. $4 Vanessa cardui	9·00	10·00

204 School Class

1991. 25th Anniv of Independence. Multicoloured.

965	10c. Type **204**	30	20
966	25c. Barbados Workers' Union Labour College	45	30
967	65c. Building a house	1·00	90
968	75c. Sugar cane harvesting	1·00	1·00
969	$1 Health clinic	1·75	2·00
MS970	123×97 mm. $2.50, Gordon Greenidge and Desmond Haynes (cricketers) (vert)	12·00	12·00

205 Jesus carrying
Cross

1992. Easter. Multicoloured.

971	35c. Type **205**	80	30
972	50c. Crucifixion	1·40	90
973	90c. Descent from the Cross	1·50	1·25
974	$3 Risen Christ	4·00	6·50

206 Cannon Ball

1992. Conservation. Flowering Trees. Multicoloured.

975	10c. Type **206**	75	40
976	30c. Golden shower tree	1·25	50
977	80c. Frangipani	2·75	2·50
978	$1.10 Flamboyant	3·00	3·00

207 Epidendrum "Costa
Rica"

1992. Orchids. Multicoloured.

979	55c. Type **207**	1·25	65
980	65c. Cattleya guttaca	1·40	1·00
981	70c. Laeliacattleya "Splashing Around"	1·40	1·00
982	$1.40 Phalaenopsis "Kathy Saegert"	2·50	3·00

208 Mini Moke and Gun
Hill Signal Station, St.
George

1992. Transport and Tourism. Multicoloured.

983	5c. Type **208**	70	70
984	35c. Tour bus and Bathsheba Beach, St. Joseph	1·75	30
985	90c. B.W.I.A. McDonnell Douglas MD-83 over Grantley Adams Airport	3·50	2·50
986	$2 Festivale (liner) and Bridgetown harbour	5·00	7·50

209 Barbados
Gooseberry

1993. Cacti and Succulents. Multicoloured.

987	10c. Type **209**	55	30
988	35c. Night-blooming cereus	1·25	35
989	$1.40 Aloe	3·00	3·50
990	$2 Scrunchineel	3·50	5·50

1993. 75th Anniv of Royal Air Force. As T 149 of Ascension. Multicoloured.

991	10c. Hawker Hunter F.6	75	40
992	30c. Handley Page Victor K2	1·50	40
993	70c. Hawker Typhoon IB	2·00	1·50
994	$3 Hawker Hurricane Mk I	4·00	6·50
MS995	110×77 mm. 50c. Armstrong Whitworth Siskin IIIA; 50c. Supermarine S6B; 50c. Supermarine Walrus Mk I; 50c. Hawker Hart	2·75	2·75

1993. 14th World Orchid Conference, Glasgow. Nos. 979/82 optd WORLD ORCHID CONFERENCE 1993.

996	55c. Type **207**	1·25	1·25
997	65c. Cattleya guttaca	1·40	1·40
998	70c. Laeliacattleya "Splashing Around"	1·40	1·40
999	$1.40 Phalaenopsis "Kathy Saegert"	2·25	3·50

211 18 pdr Culverin of
1625, Denmark Fort

1993. 17th-century English Cannon. Multicoloured.

1000	5c. Type **211**	30	50
1001	45c. 6 pdr of 1649–60, St. Ann's Fort	85	50
1002	$1 9 pdr demi-culverin of 1691, The Main Guard	1·75	2·00
1003	$2.50 32 pdr demi–cannon of 1693–94, Charles Fort	2·75	4·50

212 Sailor's
Shell-work Valentine
and Carved
Amerindian

1993. 60th Anniv of Barbados Museum. Multicoloured.

1004	10c. Type **212**	50	50

1005	75c. "Barbados Mulatto Girl" (Agostino Brunias)	1·50	1·50
1006	90c. Morris Cup and soldier of West India Regiment, 1858	2·25	2·50
1007	$1.10 Ogilby's map of Barbados, 1679, and Ashanti gold weights	2·75	3·25

213 Plesiosaurus

1993. Prehistoric Aquatic Animals. Multicoloured.

1008	90c. Type **213**	2·25	3·00
1009	90c. Ichthyosaurus	2·25	3·00
1010	90c. Elasmosaurus	2·25	3·00
1011	90c. Mosasaurus	2·25	3·00
1012	90c. Archelon	2·25	3·00

Nos. 1008/12 were printed together, se-tenant, with the background forming a composite design.

214 Cricket

1994. Sports and Tourism. Multicoloured.

1013	10c. Type **214**	1·25	75
1014	35c. Rally driving	1·40	50
1015	50c. Golf	2·50	1·75
1016	70c. Long distance running	1·75	2·50
1017	$1.40 Swimming	2·00	3·50

215 Whimbrel

1994. "Hong Kong '94" Int Stamp Exhibition. Migratory Birds. Multicoloured.

1018	10c. Type **215**	50	50
1019	35c. Pacific golden plover ("American Golden Plover")	1·00	50
1020	70c. Ruddy turnstone	1·50	1·50
1021	$3 Louisiana heron ("Tricoloured Heron")	3·50	5·50

216 Bathsheba Beach and Logo

1994. First United Nations Conference of Small Island Developing States. Multicoloured.

1022	10c. Type **216**	25	15
1023	65c. Pico Tenneriffe	1·00	70
1024	90c. Ragged Point Lighthouse	6·00	2·50
1025	$2.50 Consett Bay	3·00	5·50

217 William Demas

1994. First Recipients of Order of the Caribbean Community. Multicoloured.

1026	70c. Type **217**	70	1·00
1027	70c. Sir Shridath Ramphal	70	1·00
1028	70c. Derek Walcott	70	1·00

218 Dutch Flyut, 1695

1994. Ships. Multicoloured.

1075	5c. Type **218**	3·50	3·00
1076	10c. Geestport (freighter), 1994	1·00	50

1031B	25c. H.M.S. Victory (ship of the line), 1805	1·25	40
1078	30c. Royal Viking Queen (liner), 1994	50	30
1079	35c. H.M.S. Barbados (frigate), 1945	50	35
1080	45c. Faraday (cable ship), 1924	50	30
1081	50c. U.S.C.G. Hamilton (coast-guard cutter), 1974	7·50	75
1082	65c. H.M.C.S. Saguenay (destroyer), 1939	80	1·25
1083	70c. Inanda (cargo liner), 1928	80	70
1084	80c. H.M.S. Rodney (battleship), 1944	80	1·50
1085	90c. U.S.S. John F. Kennedy (aircraft carrier), 1982	80	70
1086	$1.10 William and John (immigrant ship), 1627	1·50	1·00
1087	$5 U.S.C.G. Champlain (coast-guard cutter), 1931	4·50	5·00
1042B	$10 Artist (full-rigged ship), 1877	8·50	9·00

219 Private, 2nd
West India Regt,
1860

1995. Bicentenary of Formation of West India Regiment. Multicoloured.

1043	30c. Type **219**	75	35
1044	50c. Light Company private, 4th West India Regt, 1795	90	55
1045	70c. Drum Major, 3rd West India Regt, 1860	1·25	1·40
1046	$1 Privates in undress and working dress, 5th West India Regt, 1815	1·40	1·50
1047	$1.10 Troops from 1st and 2nd West India Regts in Review Order, 1874	1·60	1·90

1995. 50th Anniv of End of Second World War. As T 161 of Ascension. Multicoloured.

1048	10c. Barbadian Bren gun crew	60	50
1049	35c. Avro Type 683 Lancaster bomber	90	50
1050	55c. Supermarine Spitfire	1·25	75
1051	$2.50 Davisian (cargo liner)	3·00	4·75
MS1052	75×85 mm. $2 Reverse of 1939–45 War Medal (vert)	1·50	2·25

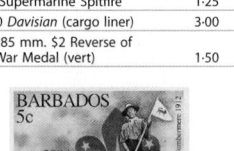

220 Member of 1st Barbados
Combermere Scout Troop,
1912

1995. 300th Anniv of Combermere School. Multicoloured.

1053	5c. Type **220**	25	40
1054	20c. Violin and sheet of music	45	30
1055	35c. Sir Frank Worrell (cricketer) (vert)	1·50	55
1056	$3 Painting by pupil	2·25	4·50
MS1057	174×105 mm. Nos. 1053/6 and 90c. 1981 Carifesta 55c. stamp.	4·00	4·75

1995. 50th Anniv of United Nations. As T 213 of Bahamas. Multicoloured.

1058	30c. Douglas C-124 Globemaster (transport), Korea, 1950–53	70	40
1059	45c. Royal Navy Sea King helicopter	1·00	50
1060	$1.40 Westland Wessex helicopter, Cyprus, 1964	1·50	2·00
1061	$2 Sud Aviation SA 341 Gazelle helicopter, Cyprus, 1964	1·50	2·75

221 Blue Beauty

1995. Water Lilies. Multicoloured.

1062	10c. Type **221**	45	30
1063	65c. White water lily	1·25	60
1064	70c. Sacred lotus	1·25	60
1065	$3 Water hyacinth	3·00	5·00

222 Magnifying Glass, Tweezers and 1896 Colony Seal ¼d. Stamp

1996. Centenary of Barbados Philatelic Society. Each showing magnifying glass, tweezers and stamp. Multicoloured.

1066	10c. Type **222**	30	30
1067	55c. 1906 Tercentenary of Annexation 1d.	65	45
1068	$1.10 1920 Victory 1s.	1·25	1·40
1069	$1.40 1937 Coronation 2½d.	1·60	2·50

223 Football

1996. Cent of Modern Olympic Games. Multicoloured.

1070	20c. Type **223**	40	30
1071	30c. Relay running	45	30
1072	55c. Basketball	1·60	60
1073	$3 Rhythmic gymnastics	2·25	4·00
MS1074	68×89 mm. $2.50, "The Discus Thrower" (Myron)	2·00	3·25

224 Douglas DC-10 of Canadian Airlines

1996. "CAPEX '96" International Stamp Exhibition, Toronto. Aircraft. Multicoloured.

1089	10c. Type **224**	80	30
1090	90c. Boeing 767 of Air Canada	1·75	80
1091	$1 Airbus Industrie A320 of Air Canada	1·75	1·25
1092	$1.40 Boeing 767 of Canadian Airlines	2·25	3·50

225 Chattel House

1996. Chattel Houses.

1093	**225** 35c. multicoloured	40	25
1094	- 70c. multicoloured	70	60
1095	- $1.10 multicoloured	90	1·10
1096	- $2 multicoloured	1·60	3·25

DESIGNS: 70c. to $2, Different houses.

226 Going to Church

1996. Christmas. 50th Anniv of U.N.I.C.E.F. Children's Paintings. Multicoloured.

1097	10c. Type **226**	35	15
1098	30c. *The Tuk Band*	55	25
1099	55c. *Singing carols*	70	40
1100	$2.50 *Decorated house*	1·75	3·50

227 Doberman Pinscher

1997. "HONG KONG '97" International Stamp Exhibition. Dogs. Multicoloured.

1101	10c. Type **227**	1·00	50
1102	30c. German shepherd	1·75	40
1103	90c. Japanese akita	2·25	1·25
1104	$3 Irish red setter	4·75	7·00

228 Barbados Flag and State Arms

1997. Visit of President Clinton of U.S.A. Multicoloured.

1105	35c. Type **228**	1·00	75
1106	90c. American flag and arms	1·00	1·25

229 Measled Cowrie

1997. Shells. Multicoloured.

1107	5c. Type **229**	30	30
1108	35c. Trumpet triton	75	25
1109	90c. Scotch bonnet	1·40	90
1110	$2 West Indian murex	2·00	3·50
MS1111	71×76 mm. $2.50, Underwater scene	2·50	3·75

230 Lucas Manuscripts

1997. 150th Anniv of the Public Library Service. Multicoloured.

1112	10c. Type **230**	25	15
1113	30c. Librarian reading to children	50	25
1114	70c. Mobile library van	1·10	60
1115	$3 Man using computer	2·50	4·50

231 Barbados Cherry

1997. Local Fruits. Multicoloured.

1116	35c. Type **231**	55	30
1117	40c. Sugar apple	60	30
1118	$1.15 Soursop	1·25	1·25
1119	$1.70 Pawpaw	2·00	3·25

232 Arms of former British Caribbean Federation

1998. Birth Centenary of Sir Grantley Adams (statesman). Sheet 118×74 mm, containing T **232** and similar vert designs. Multicoloured.

MS1120	$1 Type **232**; $1 Sir Grantley Adams; $1 Flag of former British Caribbean Federation	7·00	8·00

1998. Diana, Princess of Wales Commemoration. Sheet 145×70 mm, containing vert designs as T **177** of Ascension. Multicoloured.

MS1121	$1.15, Wearing blue hat, 1985; $1.15, Wearing red jacket, 1981; $1.15, Wearing tiara, 1987; $1.15, Wearing black jacket	2·50	3·75

233 Environment Regeneration

1998. 50th Anniv of Organization of American States. Multicoloured.

1122	15c. Type **233**	20	15
1123	$1 Stilt dancing	70	80
1124	$2.50 Judge and figure of Justice	1·75	3·25

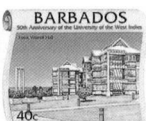

234 Frank Worrell Hall

1998. 50th Anniv of University of West Indies. Multicoloured.

1125	40c. Type **234**	50	30
1126	$1.15 Student graduating	1·25	1·25
1127	$1.40 50th anniversary plaque	1·50	2·00
1128	$1.75 Quadrangle	2·75	4·00

235 Catamaran

1998. Tourism. Multicoloured.

1129	10c. Type **235**	50	30
1130	45c. *Jolly Roger* (tourist schooner) (horiz)	1·25	35
1131	70c. *Atlantis* (tourist submarine) (horiz)	1·75	1·10
1132	$2 *Harbour Master* (ferry)	3·50	4·50

236 Racing Yacht

1999. "Australia '99" World Stamp Exhibition, Melbourne. Sheet 90×90 mm.

MS1133	**236** $4 multicoloured	3·50	5·00

237 Juvenile Piping Plover in Shallow Water

1999. Endangered Species. Piping Plover. Multicoloured.

1134	10c. Type **237**	30	30
1135	45c. Female with eggs	65	55
1136	50c. Male and female with fledglings	65	75
1137	70c. Male in shallow water	80	1·25

1999. 30th Anniv of First Manned Landing on Moon. As T **186** of Ascension. Multicoloured.

1138	40c. Astronaut in training	55	45
1139	45c. 1st stage separation	55	45
1140	$1.15 Lunar landing module	1·40	1·25
1141	$1.40 Docking with service module	1·50	2·25
MS1142	90×80 mm. $2.50, Earth as seen from Moon (circular, 40 mm diam)	2·25	3·25

238 Hare running

1999. "China '99" International Stamp Exhibition, Beijing. Hares. Multicoloured.

1143	70c. Type **238**	1·40	1·50
1144	70c. Head of hare	1·40	1·50
1145	70c. Baby hares suckling	1·40	1·50
1146	70c. Hares boxing	1·40	1·50
1147	70c. Two leverets	1·40	1·50

Nos. 1143/7 were printed together, *se-tenant*, forming a composite background design.

239 Horse-drawn Mail Cart

234 Frank Worrell Hall

1999. 125th Anniv of U.P.U. Multicoloured.

1148	10c. Type **239**	1·50	45
1149	45c. Mail van	2·00	50
1150	$1.75 Sikorsky S42 flying boat	2·25	2·50
1151	$2 Computer and fax machine	2·25	2·75

240 Globe and Barbados Flag

2000. New Millennium. Sheet 90×80 mm.

MS1152	**240** $3 multicoloured	4·00	4·50

241 Drax Hall House

2000. Pride of Barbados. Multicoloured.

1153	5c. Type **241**	20	30
1154	10c. Reaping sugar cane (vert)	20	30
1155	40c. Needham's Point Light-house (vert)	1·50	60
1156	45c. Port St. Charles	60	30
1157	65c. Interior of Jewish synagogue	1·75	1·00
1158	70c. Bridgetown Port (I)	2·00	3·00
1158a	70c. Bridgetown Port (II)	2·00	2·25
1159	90c. Harrison's Cave	1·00	60
1160	$1.15 Villa Nova	1·10	85
1161	$1.40 Cricket at Kensington Oval	3·25	1·60
1162	$1.75 Sunbury House	1·50	1·75
1163	$2 Bethel Methodist Church	1·75	2·00
1164	$3 Peacock, Barbados Wildlife Reserve (vert)	2·75	3·50
1165	$5 Royal Westmoreland Golf Course (vert)	6·00	7·50
1166	$10 Grantley Adams International Airport	9·00	12·00

Two types of 70c.:
I. Central design reversed. The bows of three of the four liners shown point to the right.
II. Design corrected. The bows of three of the four liners point to the left.

242 Sir Conrad Hunte batting

2000. West Indies Cricket Tour and 100th Test Match at Lord's. Multicoloured.

1167	45c. Type **242**	1·25	50
1168	90c. Malcolm Marshall bowling	2·00	1·00
1169	$2 Sir Garfield Sobers batting	3·50	4·00
MS1170	121×104 mm. $2.50, Lord's Cricket Ground (horiz)	2·75	3·50

243 Golf Clubs, Flag and Ball on Tee Peg

2000. "EXPO 2000" World Stamp Exhibition, Anaheim, U.S.A. Golf. Multicoloured.

1171	25c. Type **243**	70	35
1172	40c. Golfer teeing off on top of giant ball	90	35
1173	$1.40 Golfer on green	1·75	1·90
1174	$2 Golfer putting	2·25	3·50

244 Bentley Mk VI Drophead Coupe, 1947

2000. Vintage Cars. Multicoloured.

1175	10c. Type **244**	35	15
1176	30c. Vanden Plas Princess Limousine, 1964	65	25
1177	90c. Austin Atlantic, 1952	1·25	70
1178	$3 Bentley Special, 1950	3·25	5·00

245 Thread Snake

2001. "HONG KONG 2001" Stamp Exhibition. Sheet 125×80 mm.
MS1179 **245** $3 multicoloured 4·25 4·50

246 Lizardfish

2001. Deep Sea Creatures. Multicoloured.

1180	45c. Type **246**	65	75
1181	45c. Golden-tailed moray	65	75
1182	45c. Black-barred soldierfish	65	75
1183	45c. Golden zoanthid	65	75
1184	45c. Sponge brittle star	65	75
1185	45c. Magnificent feather duster	65	75
1186	45c. Bearded fireworm	65	75
1187	45c. Lima shell	65	75
1188	45c. Yellow tube sponge	65	75

247 Octagonal, Fish and Butterfly Kites

2001. "Philanippon '01" International Stamp Exhibition, Tokyo. Kites. Multicoloured.

1189	10c. Type **247**	20	15
1190	65c. Hexagonal, bird and geometric kites	60	55
1191	$1.40 Policeman, Japanese and butterfly kites	1·40	1·50
1192	$1.75 Anti-drug, geisha and eagle kites	1·60	2·25

248 George Washington on the Quay, 1751

2001. 250th Anniv of George Washington's Visit to Barbados. Multicoloured.

1193	45c. Type **248**	75	50
1194	50c. George Washington in Barbados	75	50
1195	$1.15 George Washington superimposed on Declaration of Independence, 1776	1·50	1·00
1196	$2.50 Needham's Point Fort, 1750	3·00	4·00
MS1197	110×90 mm. $3 George Washington as President of U.S.A.	2·50	3·25

249 Shaggy Bear (Traditional Carnival Character)

2001. 35th Anniv of Independence. Multicoloured.

1198	25c. Type **249**	40	20
1199	45c. Tuk band	70	30
1200	$1 Landship Dancers	1·25	1·00
1201	$2 Guitar, saxophone and words of National Anthem	2·25	3·25

2002. Golden Jubilee. As T **200** of Ascension.

1202	10c. black, violet and gold	45	20
1203	70c. multicoloured	1·00	60
1204	$1 black, violet and gold	1·25	1·00
1205	$1.40 multicoloured	1·50	2·00
MS1206	162×95 mm. Nos. 1202/5 and $3 multicoloured	4·75	5·50

DESIGNS—HORIZ: 10c. Princess Elizabeth; 70c. Queen Elizabeth in cerise hat; $1 Queen Elizabeth wearing Imperial State Crown, Coronation, 1953; $1.40, Queen Elizabeth in purple feathered hat. VERT (38×51 mm)—$3 Queen Elizabeth after Annigoni.

Designs as Nos. 1202/5 in MS1206 omit the gold frame around each stamp and "Golden Jubilee 1952–2002" inscription.

250 1852 (½d.) Britannia Stamp and Map

2002. 150th Anniv of Inland Postal Service. Multicoloured.

1207	10c. Type **250**	30	15
1208	45c. Early twentieth-century postman delivering letter	60	35
1209	$1.15 *Esk* (mail steamer)	1·50	1·25
1210	$2 B.W.I.A. Tri-Star airliner	2·00	3·00

251 *Alpinia purpurata*

2002. Flowers. Multicoloured.

1211	10c. Type **251**	20	20
1212	40c. *Heliconia caribaea*	40	30
1213	$1.40 *Polianthes tuberosa* (horiz)	1·50	1·40
1214	$2.50 *Anthurium* (horiz)	2·00	3·00

252 Drax Hall Windmill, St. George

2002. 375th Anniv of First Settlement.

1215	**252** 10c. brown, agate and blue	35	15
1216	– 45c. brown, agate and blue	1·00	35
1217	– $1.15 multicoloured	1·50	1·40
1218	– $3 multicoloured	3·25	4·50

DESIGNS: 45c. Donkey cart; $1.15, Cattle Mill ruins, Gibbons; $3, Morgan Lewis windmill, St. Andrew.

253 Traditional Christmas Fare

2002. Christmas. Multicoloured.

1219	45c. Type **253**	60	35
1220	$1.15 Christmas morning in the park	1·25	1·25
1221	$1.40 Nativity scene from float parade	1·40	1·50

254 AIDS Ribbon

2002. Centenary of Pan American Health Organization. Multicoloured.

1222	10c. Type **254**	40	15
1223	70c. Amateur athletes	85	50
1224	$1.15 Sir George Alleyne (Director-General of P.A.H.O.)	1·25	1·10
1225	$2 Pregnant woman	1·75	2·50

255 H.M.S. *Tartar*, 1764

2003. Royal Navy Connections. Multicoloured.

1226	10c. Type **255**	65	25
1227	70c. H.M.S. *Barbadoes*, 1803	1·25	65
1228	$1.15 H.M.S. *Valerian*, 1926	1·60	1·25
1229	$2.50 H.M.S. *Victorious*, 1941	2·75	4·00

256 Broad Street, c. 1900

2003. 375th Anniv of the Settlement of Bridgetown. Multicoloured.

1230	10c. Type **256**	55	20
1231	$1.15 Swan Street, 1900	1·40	1·00
1232	$1.40 Roebuck Street, c. 1880	1·60	1·40
1233	$2 Chamberlain Bridge	2·25	3·50
MS1234	160×120 mm. Nos. 1230/3	5·50	6·50

2003. Centenary of Powered Flight. As T **209** of Ascension. Multicoloured.

1235	10c. McDonnell F2H-2P Banshee	55	25
1236	45c. Vickers Viscount 700	80	40
1237	50c. Douglas DC-9-30	90	40
1238	$1.15 Short Sunderland Mk II	1·40	80
1239	$1.40 North American P-51D Mustang	1·50	1·25
1240	$2.50 Concorde	3·25	4·00

257 Fishermen (Oistins Fish Festival)

2003. Barbados Festivals. Multicoloured.

MS1241	127×105 mm. 45c. Type **257**; 45c. Saxophone player (Barbados Jazz Festival); 45c. Man and woman in traditional costume (Crop Over Festival); 45c. Actresses (National Independence Festival of Creative Arts); 45c. School choir (National Independence Festival of Creative Arts); 45c. Carnival dancers (Crop Over Festival); 45c. Bass player (Barbados Jazz Festival); 45c. Competitor in fish boning competition (Oistins Fish Festival)	6·00	7·00

258 Cadet Corps Banner

2004. Centenary of the Cadet Corps. Multicoloured.

1242	10c. Type **258**	35	20
1243	25c. The Regular band marching	60	25
1244	50c. The Toy Soldier band	80	35
1245	$1 The Sea Cadets	1·25	80
1246	$3 Map reading	2·50	4·50

259 Swimming

2004. Olympic Games, Athens. Multicoloured.

1247	10c. Type **259**	40	20
1248	70c. Shooting	80	45
1249	$1.15 Running	1·25	1·10
1250	$2 Judo	2·00	3·25

260 Football Player

2004. Centenary of FIFA (Federation Internationale de Football Association). Multicoloured.

1251	5c. Type **260**	20	40
1252	90c. Player in blue strip	1·15	70
1253	$1.40 Goal keeper	1·40	1·25
1254	$2.50 Player in yellow strip	2·00	3·00

261 Brain Coral

2004. Coral. Multicoloured.

1255	$1 Type **261**	2·00	2·00
1256	$1 Pillar coral	2·00	2·00
1257	$1 Pillar coral (different)	2·00	2·00
1258	$1 Fan coral	2·00	2·00
1259	$1 Yellow pencil coral	2·00	2·00
MS1260	85×85 mm. $3.50 Maze coral (36×36 mm)	4·25	4·75

262 White Peacock

2005. Pacific Explorer 2005 World Stamp Expo, Sydney, Australia. Butterflies. Multicoloured.

1261	50c. Type **262**	90	40
1262	$1 Great southern white	1·50	1·00
1263	$1.40 Orion	2·00	1·50
1264	$2.50 Mimic	3·00	4·00
MS1265	85×85 mm. $8 Monarch	8·00	10·00

263 Baobab

2005. Flowering Trees. Multicoloured.

1266	5c. Type **263**	30	60
1267	10c. African tulip tree	35	25
1268	25c. Rose of Sharon	65	25
1269	45c. Black willow	1·00	30
1270	50c. Black pearl tree	1·00	35
1271	75c. Seaside mahoe	1·25	65
1272	90c. Quickstick	1·40	75
1273	$1 Jerusalem Thorn	1·50	80
1274	$1.15 Pink cassia	1·75	80
1275	$1.40 Orchid tree	2·00	90
1276	$1.75 Yellow poui	2·50	1·75
1277	$2.10 Lignum vitae	3·00	2·75
1278	$3 Wild cinnamon	4·50	5·50
1279	$5 Pride of India	7·00	8·00
1280	$10 Immortelle	11·00	13·00

264 Firemen, c. 1955

2005. 50th Anniv of the Barbados Fire Service. Multicoloured.

1281	5c. Type **264**	55	55
1282	10c. Fire Officers marching, Fire Service Headquarters, Bridgetown, 2003	55	55
1283	90c. Rosenbauer-Panther FL 6×6 Airport Rescue and Fire Fighting tender	1·75	85
1284	$1.15 Fire Service parade with Dennis Pump Escape, Garrison Savannah, 1975	2·00	1·25
1285	$2.50 Scania 94G Water and Foam Tender	4·75	6·00

265 Three Anoles

2005. Extreme Anole (*Anolis extremus*). Multicoloured.

1286	10c. Type **265**	50	50
1287	50c. Two anoles	1·00	45
1288	$1.75 One anole	2·75	3·25
1289	$2 Young anole hatching	2·75	3·25

266 Queen Triggerfish and Diver

2006. Endangered Species. Queen Triggerfish (*Balistes vetula*). Multicoloured.

1290	10c. Type **266**	40	30
1291	$1.15 Pair at edge of coral reef	1·40	1·00
1292	$1.40 Queen Triggerfish above sandy sea floor	1·75	1·25
1293	$2.10 Queen Triggerfish on coral reef	2·50	3·50

267 Girls reading

2006. Washington 2006 International Stamp Exhibition. "Children – they are the future". Multicoloured.

1294	10c. Type **267**	40	20
1295	50c. Wheelchair basketball	1·25	55
1296	$2 Three children using computer	2·25	2·75
1297	$2.50 Two children playing violins	2·50	3·00

268 Cave Shepherd, c. 1911

2006. Centenary of Cave Shepherd Store, Bridgetown. Multicoloured.

1298	10c. Type **268**	40	20
1299	50c. Cave Shepherd, c. 2000	75	35
1300	$1.75 Cave Shepherd, c. 1975	2·25	2·50
1301	$2 Cave Shepherd, c. 1920	2·50	3·00

269 Old Town Hall, Bridgetown

2006. 175th Anniv of the Enfranchisement of Free Coloured and Black Barbadians. Multicoloured.

1302	10c. Type **269**	40	20
1303	50c. Samuel Jackman Prescod, 1806–71 (campaigner for enfranchisement)	75	35
1304	$1.40 Voting in ballot box (introduced 1885)	1·50	1·40
1305	$2.50 Sir James Lyon (Governor of Barbados, 1829–33)	2·50	4·00

270 Joel 'Big Bird' Garner

2007. World Cup Cricket, West Indies. Multicoloured.

1306	$1.75 Type **270**	2·25	2·00
1307	$2.10 Old Kensington Oval, Barbados (horiz)	2·75	2·75
1308	$3 New Kensington Oval, Barbados (horiz)	3·50	4·00
MS1309 161×121 mm. $10 World Cup Cricket trophy		9·00	10·00

271 Emancipation (Bussa) Statue

2007. Bicentenary of the Abolition of the Slave Trade Act. Multicoloured (except **MS**1314).

1310	10c. Type **271**	15	15
1311	$1 William Wilberforce (abolitionist)	1·00	1·00
1312	$1.75 Slave hut (horiz)	1·25	1·50
1313	$2 Freedom celebrations, 1838 (horiz)	1·60	2·00
MS1314 115×80 mm. $3 Slave ship (black and violet)		3·00	3·50

272 Interior of Nidhe Israel Synagogue, Bridgetown

2007. Opening of Nidhe Israel Museum, Bridgetown. Multicoloured.

1315	5c. Type **272**	25	35
1316	10c. Nidhe Israel Museum (adjacent to synagogue)	25	20
1317	$1.40 Hanukiah (candelabra)	1·50	1·10
1318	$2.50 Stained glass window in synagogue	2·50	3·25

273 Green Turtle

2007. Turtles. Multicoloured.

1319	10c. Type **273**	25	15
1320	50c. Loggerhead turtle	65	45
1321	$1 Hawksbill turtle	1·00	1·00
1322	$2.50 Leatherback turtle	2·50	3·00

274 *Padina gymnospora*

2008. Algae. Multicoloured.

1323	10c. Type **274**	20	15
1324	50c. *Ulva lactuca*	60	45
1325	$1.75 *Sargassum platycarpum*	1·50	2·00
1326	$2 *Udotea conglutinata*	2·00	2·50

275 The Second Barbados Contingent of Volunteers for Armed Forces, 1940

2008. Airmen and Aircraft. Multicoloured.

1327	10c. Type **275**	20	15
1328	50c. Warren Alleyne (Telegraphist 1) and Supermarine Spitfire Mk IX, 1944	90	45
1329	$1.75 Wing Commander Aubrey Inniss and Bristol Beaufighter Mk VIC, 1943	2·50	2·50
1330	$2 Flying Officer Errol Barrow and Avro Lancaster B Mk 1, 1945	2·75	3·00
MS1331 100×73 mm. $6 Concorde over Barbados		7·50	8·00

Nos. 1327/30 commemorate the 90th anniversary of the Royal Air Force.

276 *Christmas Moon* (Alison Chapman-Andrews)

2008. Christmas. Designs showing paintings. Multicoloured.

1332	10c. Type **276**	25	20
1333	50c. *Preparing for Christmas* (Virgil Broodhagen)	75	45
1334	$1.40 *Christmas Candles* (Darla Trotman)	1·50	85
1335	$3 *Poinsettia and Snow on the Mountain* (Darla Trotman)	3·50	4·50

277 Mop making

2009. Birth Bicentenary of Louis Braille (inventor of Braille writing for the blind) and Barbados Association for the Blind and Deaf. Multicoloured.

1336	50c. Type **277**	75	45
1337	$1.40 Chair caning	1·50	1·25
1338	$1.75 Girl using Braille typewriter	1·75	1·75
1339	$2 Louis Braille	2·25	2·50

278 New Court House

2009. 300th Anniv of the Restructured Criminal Court. Multicoloured.

1340	10c. Type **278**	20	15
1341	50c. Handcuffs and seal of the Court	75	45
1342	$1.40 Judge's robe, wig and gavel	1·50	1·00
1343	$2.50 Old Court House	2·25	3·00

279 Queen's Park Fountain

2010. Centenary (2009) of Queen's Park, Bridgetown. Multicoloured.

1344	90c. Type **279**	1·00	90
1345	$1 The Boaba Tree (baobab *Adansonia digitata*)	1·00	95
1346	$1.40 Queen's Park House	1·50	1·60
1347	$2 The Band Stand	2·25	2·50
MS1348 140×91 mm. $4 Queen's Park in 1909		4·75	5·50

280 J 24 Keelboats flying Spinnakers

2010. Fireball International World Championships, Carlisle Bay. Multicoloured.

1349	10c. Type **280**	20	10
1350	50c. J24 keelboats	55	50
1351	90c. J24 keelboats	1·00	90
1352	$1.75 Laser dinghies	2·25	2·25
1353	$2 Racing keelboats	2·50	2·75

2010. As Nos. 1266/7, 1270 and 1274/6 but W w **18** (sideways) and with imprint date "2010"

281 Guides camping

2010. Centenary of Girl Guiding. Multicoloured.

1354	10c. Type **281**	20	10
1355	50c. Guides saluting ('The Promise')	60	50
1356	$1 Brownies and guides ('Guiding Uniforms')	1·25	1·25
1357	$2.50 Parade of guides	2·75	3·25
MS1358 94×64 mm. $3.50 Emblem		4·50	5·00

282 Golden Apple (*Spondias cytherea*)

2011. Local Fruits. Multicoloured.

1359	5c. Type **282**	15	15
1360	10c. Coconut (*Cocos nucifera*)	25	25
1361	35c. Cashew (*Anacardium occidentale*)	55	45
1362	40c. Mammy apple (*Mammea americana*)	55	50
1363	60c. Barbados cherry (*Malpighia emarginata*)	80	75
1364	65c. Sugar apple (*Annona squamosa*)	85	80
1365	80c. Sea grape (*Coccoloba uvifera*)	1·00	95
1366	$1 Tamarind (*Tamarindus indica*)	1·25	1·00
1367	$1.25 Carambola (*Averrhoa carambola*)	1·50	1·25
1368	$1.50 Mango (*Mangifera indica*)	1·75	1·60
1369	$1.80 Banana (*Musa X*)	2·25	1·90
1370	$2.20 Guava (*Psidium guajava*)	2·50	2·25
1371	$2.75 Avocado (*Persea americana*)	3·00	2·50
1372	$3 Gooseberry (*Phyllanthus acidus*)	3·50	3·00
1373	$5 Soursop (*Annona muricata*)	6·50	6·00
1374	$10 Pomegranate (*Punica granatum*)	10·00	10·00

283 'Sailors' Valentine' from 1800s

2011. 'Sailors' Valentines' (collages of sea shells within octagonal wooden frames). Multicoloured.

1375	10c. Type **283**	25	25
1376	65c. Modern 'sailors' valentine' by Daphne Hunte	80	65
1377	$2.20 'Sailors' valentine' with 'Live Today Hope Tomorrow' inscription	2·75	2·75
1378	$2.75 Modern 'sailors' valentine' by Pamela Boynton	3·00	3·50

284 Miss Catherine Middleton and Maid of Honour Pippa Middleton arriving at Westminster Abbey

2011. Royal Wedding. Multicoloured.

1379	15c. Type **284**	55	40
1380	65c. Duke and Duchess of Cambridge in State Landau	1·10	80
1381	$1.80 Duke and Duchess of Cambridge at Westminster Abbey after wedding ceremony (vert)	2·50	2·25
1382	$2.20 Duke and Duchess of Cambridge waving from Buckingham Palace balcony (vert)	2·75	3·25

285 Queen Elizabeth II leaving 350th Anniversary Assembly of Parliament, Barbados, 1989

2012. Diamond Jubilee. Multicoloured.

1383	10c. Type **285**	40	35
1384	$1.40 Queen Elizabeth II wearing tiara on way to opening session of Parliament, London, 4 November 1952	1·75	1·75
1385	$2.10 Queen Elizabeth II inspecting Barbados Defence Force, 31 October 1977	2·25	2·75
1386	$2.50 Queen Elizabeth II at NASA's Goddard Space Flight Center, Maryland, USA, 8 May 2007	3·25	3·50
MS1387 162×94 mm. $4 Queen Elizabeth II and Prince Philip at opening of the 350th anniversary Parliament, Barbados, March 1989 (60×40 mm)		5·00	5·50

286 Gun Hill Signal Station

2012. Barbados Garrison. Multicoloured.

1388	10c. Type **286**	40	35
1389	65c. The Main Guard, Clock Tower	1·00	85
1390	$2 St. Mary's Church (horiz)	2·50	2·50
1391	$2.75 The Public Library (horiz)	3·25	3·75

287 Pelican Island

2012. 50th Anniv (2011) of Bridgetown Port. Black and grey (10c.) or multicoloured (others).

1392	10c. Type **287**	40	35
1393	65c. Lighters delivering cargo	1·00	85
1394	$1.75 *Barbados II* (tug)	2·25	2·25
1395	$2.80 Aerial view of cruise liners in Bridgetown port	3·25	3·75

POSTAGE DUE STAMPS

D1

1934
D1	D1	½d. green	1·25	8·50
D2	D1	1d. black	1·75	1·25
D3	D1	3d. red	20·00	23·00

1950. Values in cents.
D4a	1c. green	30	3·00
D8	2c. black	30	5·00
D9	6c. red	50	7·00

D2

1976
D14a	D2	1c. mauve and pink	10	10
D15a	-	2c. blue and light blue	10	10
D16a	-	5c. brown and yellow	10	15
D17a	-	10c. blue and lilac	15	20
D18a	-	25c. deep green and green	20	30
D19	-	$1 red and deep red	75	1·25

DESIGNS: Nos. D15/19 show different floral backgrounds.

Pt. 1

BARBUDA

One of the Leeward Is., Br. W. Indies. Dependency of Antigua. Used stamps of Antigua and Leeward Is. concurrently. The issues from 1968 are also valid for use in Antigua. From 1971 to 1973 the stamps of Antigua were again used.

1922. 12 pence = 1 shilling; 20 shillings = 1 pound.
1951. 100 cents = 1 West Indian dollar.

1922. Stamps of Leeward Islands optd **BARBUDA.**
1	11	½d. green	1·50	13·00
2	11	1d. red	1·50	13·00
3	11	2d. grey	1·50	7·00
4	11	2½d. blue	1·50	7·50
9	11	3d. purple on yellow	1·75	13·00
5	11	6d. purple	2·00	18·00
10	11	1s. black on green	1·50	8·00
6	11	2s. purple and blue on blue	14·00	55·00
7	11	3s. green and violet	35·00	80·00
8	11	4s. black and red	42·00	80·00
11	11	5s. green and red on yellow	65·00	£130

2 Map of Barbuda **3** Greater Amberjack

1968
12	2	½c. brown, black and pink	55	3·50
13	2	1c. orange, black and flesh	1·50	35
14	2	2c. brown, red and rose	2·25	1·25
15	2	3c. brown, yellow and lemon	1·75	55
16	2	4c. black, green & lt green	3·00	3·50
17	2	5c. turquoise and black	2·25	20
18	2	6c. black, purple and lilac	1·25	3·25
19	2	10c. black, blue and cobalt	1·75	1·25
20	2	15c. black, green & turq	2·00	3·75
20a	-	20c. multicoloured	1·50	2·00
21	3	25c. multicoloured	1·00	25
22		35c. multicoloured	3·00	25
23	-	50c. multicoloured	1·00	2·00
24	-	75c. multicoloured	1·00	80
25	-	$1 multicoloured	50	1·50
26	-	$2.50 multicoloured	55	2·00
27	-	$5 multicoloured	65	2·25

DESIGNS: As T **3**—20c. Great barracuda; 35c. French angelfish; 50c. Porkfish; 75c. Princess parrotfish; $1, Longspined squirrelfish; $2.50, Bigeye; $5, Blue chromis.

10 Sprinting and Aztec Sun-stone

1968. Olympic Games. Mexico. Multicoloured.
28	25c. Type **10**	50	35
29	35c. High-jumping and Aztec statue	55	35
30	75c. Dinghy-racing and Aztec lion mask	60	1·25
MS31	87×76 mm. $1 Football and engraved plate	2·00	3·25

14 "The Ascension" (Orcagna)"

1969. Easter Commemoration.
32	14	25c. black and blue	15	45
33	14	35c. black and red	15	50
34	14	75c. black and lilac	15	55

15 Scout Enrolment Ceremony

1969. Third Caribbean Scout Jamboree. Multicoloured.
35	25c. Type **15**	35	55
36	35c. Scouts around camp fire	45	65
37	75c. Sea Scouts rowing boat	55	1·40

18 *Sistine Madonna* (Raphael).

1969. Christmas.
38	18	½c. multicoloured	10	30
39	18	25c. multicoloured	10	15
40	18	35c. multicoloured	10	20
41	18	35c. multicoloured	20	35

19 William I (1066–87)

1970. English Monarchs. Multicoloured.
42	35c. Type **19**	30	15
43	35c. William II (1087–1100)	10	15
44	35c. Henry I (1100–35)	10	15
45	35c. Stephen (1135–54)	10	15
46	35c. Henry II (1154–89)	10	15
47	35c. Richard I (1189–99)	10	15
48	35c. John (1199–1216)	10	15
49	35c. Henry III (1216–72)	10	15
50	35c. Edward I (1272–1307)	10	15
51	35c. Edward II (1307–27)	10	15
52	35c. Edward III (1327–77)	10	15
53	35c. Richard II (1377–99)	10	15
54	35c. Henry IV (1399–1413)	10	15
55	35c. Henry V (1413–22)	10	15
56	35c. Henry VI (1422–61)	10	15
57	35c. Edward IV (1462–83)	10	15
58	35c. Edward V (April–June 1483)	10	15
59	35c. Richard III (1483–85)	10	15
60	35c. Henry VII (1485–1509)	35	15
61	35c. Henry VIII (1509–47)	35	15
62	35c. Edward VI (1547–53)	35	15
63	35c. Lady Jane Grey (1553)	35	15
64	35c. Mary I (1553–8)	35	15
65	35c. Elizabeth I (1558–1603)	35	15
66	35c. James I (1603–25)	35	15
67	35c. Charles I (1625–49)	35	15
68	35c. Charles II (1649–1685)	35	15
69	35c. James II (1685–1688)	35	15
70	35c. William III (1689–1702)	35	15
71	35c. Mary II (1689–1694)	35	15
72	35c. Anne (1702–1714)	35	15
73	35c. George I (1714–1727)	35	15
74	35c. George II (1727–1760)	35	15
75	35c. George III (1760–1820)	35	15
76	35c. George IV (1820–1830)	35	15
77	35c. William IV (1830–1837)	35	60
78	35c. Victoria (1837–1901)	35	60

See also Nos. 710/5.

1970. No. 12 surch **20c.**
| 79 | 2 | 20c. on ½c. brn, blk & pink | 20 | 20 |

21 *The Way to Calvary* (Ugolino)

1970. Easter. Paintings. Multicoloured.
80	25c. Type **21**	15	30
81	35c. *The Deposition from the Cross* (Ugolino)	15	30
82	75c. *Crucifix* (The Master of St. Francis)	15	35

22 Oliver is introduced to Fagin (*Oliver Twist*)

1970. Death Centenary of Charles Dickens. Multicoloured.
83	20c. Type **22**	45	35
84	75c. Dickens and scene from *The Old Curiosity Shop*	80	90

23 *Madonna of the Meadows* (G. Bellini)

1970. Christmas. Multicoloured.
85	20c. Type **23**	10	25
86	50c. *Madonna, Child and Angels* (from Wilton diptych)	15	30
87	75c. *The Nativity* (della Francesca)	15	35

24 Nurse with Patient in Wheelchair

1970. Centenary of British Red Cross. Multicoloured.
88	20c. Type **24**	15	30
89	35c. Nurse giving patient magazines (horiz)	20	40
90	75c. Nurse and mother weighing baby (horiz)	25	70

25 Angel with Vases

1971. Easter. *Mond Crucifixion* by Raphael. Multicoloured.
91	35c. Type **25**	15	85
92	50c. *Christ crucified*	15	95
93	75c. Angel with vase	15	1·00

26 Martello Tower

1971. Tourism. Multicoloured.
94	20c. Type **26**	15	35
95	25c. "Sailfish" dinghy	25	40
96	50c. Hotel bungalows	25	45
97	75c. Government House and Mystery Stone	25	55

27 *The Granducal Madonna* (Raphael)

1971. Christmas. Multicoloured.
98	½c. Type **27**	10	10
99	35c. *The Ansidei Madonna* (Raphael)	10	20
100	50c. *The Madonna and Child* (Botticelli)	15	25
101	75c. *The Madonna of the Trees* (Bellini)	15	30

1973. Royal Wedding. Nos. 370/1 of Antigua optd **BARBUDA** twice.
102	106	25c. multicoloured	3·25	2·00
103	106	$2 multicoloured	1·25	1·25

Four stamps to commemorate the 500th Birth Anniv of Durer were prepared in late 1971, but their issue was not authorised by the Antigua Government.

1973. Ships. Nos. 269/85 of Antigua optd **BARBUDA.**
116	92	½c. multicoloured	15	20
104	-	1c. multicoloured	15	30
105	-	2c. multicoloured	25	30
117	-	3c. multicoloured	25	25
106	-	4c. multicoloured	30	30
107	-	5c. multicoloured	40	40
108	-	6c. multicoloured	40	40
109	-	10c. multicoloured	45	45
118	-	15c. multicoloured	45	50
110	-	20c. multicoloured	55	60
111	-	25c. multicoloured	55	60
112	-	35c. multicoloured	55	70
113	-	50c. multicoloured	55	70
114	-	75c. multicoloured	55	70
119	-	$1 multicoloured	55	70
115	-	$2.50 multicoloured	75	1·50
121	-	$5 multicoloured	1·10	2·50

1973. Commemorative stamps of Antigua optd

(a) Military Uniforms. Nos. 353, 355 and 357 of Antigua optd **BARBUDA.**
122	½c. multicoloured	10	10
123	20c. multicoloured	15	10
124	75c. multicoloured	40	15
MS125	127×145 mm. Nos. 353/7 of Antigua	2·00	3·50

(b) Carnival. Nos 360/3 of Antigua optd **BARBUDA**
126	20c. multicoloured	10	10
127	35c. multicoloured	10	10
128	75c. multicoloured	20	25
MS129	134×95 mm. Nos. 359/62 of Antigua	1·00	2·25

1973. Christmas. Nos. 364/69 of Antigua optd **BARBUDA.**
130	105	3c. multicoloured	10	10
131	-	5c. multicoloured	10	10
132	-	20c. multicoloured	10	10
133	-	35c. multicoloured	15	15
134	-	$1 multicoloured	30	30
MS135	130×128 mm. Nos. 130/4	2·25	9·00	

1973. Honeymoon Visit. Nos. 373/4 of Antigua additionally optd **BARBUDA.**
136	35c. multicoloured	30	20
137	$2 multicoloured	70	60
MS138	78×100 mm. Nos. 136/7	1·10	1·00

1974. University of West Indies. Nos. 376/9 of Antigua optd **BARBUDA.**
139	5c. multicoloured	10	10
140	20c. multicoloured	10	10
141	35c. multicoloured	15	15
142	75c. multicoloured	15	15

1974. Military Uniforms. Nos. 380/4 of Antigua optd **BARBUDA.**
143	½c. multicoloured	10	10
144	10c. multicoloured	20	10
145	20c. multicoloured	30	10
146	35c. multicoloured	35	10
147	75c. multicoloured	50	25

1974. Centenary of U.P.U. (1st issue). Nos. 386/92 of Antigua optd with either a or b. (a) **BARBUDA 13 JULY 1992**; (b) **BARBUDA 15 SEPT. 1874 G.P.U** ("General Postal Union")

148	½c. multicoloured (a)		10	10
149	½c. multicoloured (b)		10	10
150	1c. multicoloured (a)		10	10
151	1c. multicoloured (b)		10	10
152	2c. multicoloured (a)		20	15
153	2c. multicoloured (b)		20	15
154	5c. multicoloured (a)		50	15
155	5c. multicoloured (b)		50	15
156	20c. multicoloured (a)		40	70
157	20c. multicoloured (b)		40	70
158	35c. multicoloured (a)		80	1·50
159	35c. multicoloured (b)		80	1·50
160	$1 multicoloured (a)		1·75	4·00
161	$1 multicoloured (b)		1·75	4·00
MS162	141×164 mm. No. **MS393** of Antigua optd **BARBUDA**		3·50	6·00

1974. Antiguan Steel Bands. Nos. 394/98 of Antigua optd **BARBUDA**.

163	5c. deep red, red and black		10	10
164	20c. brown, lt brown & blk		10	10
165	35c. light green, green and black		10	10
166	75c. deep blue, blue and black		20	20
MS167	115×108 mm. Nos. 163/6		65	80

39 Footballers

1974. World Cup Football Championships (1st issue).

168	**39**	35c. multicoloured	10	10
169	-	$1.20 multicoloured	25	35
170	-	$2.50 multicoloured	35	50
MS171	70×128 mm. Nos. 168/70		85	90

DESIGNS: $1.20, $2.50, Footballers in action similar to Type **39**.

1974. World Cup Football Championships (2nd issue). Nos. 399/403 of Antigua optd **BARBUDA**.

172	**111**	35c. multicoloured	10	10
173	-	35c. multicoloured	20	10
174	-	75c. multicoloured	25	15
175	-	$1 multicoloured	25	25
MS176	135×130 mm. Nos. 172/5		75	1·25

41 Ship Letter of 1833

1974. Cent of Universal Postal Union (2nd issue). Multicoloured.

177	35c. Type **41**		10	10
178	$1.20 Stamps and postmarks of 1922		25	50
179	$2.50 Britten Norman Islander mailplane over map of Barbuda		35	75
MS180	128×97 mm. Nos. 177/9		1·00	2·00

42 Greater Amberjack

1974. Multicoloured.

181	½c. Oleander, Rose Bay (vert)		10	40
182	1c. Blue petrea (vert)		15	40
183	2c. Poinsettia (vert)		15	40
184	3c. Cassia tree (vert)		15	40
185	4c. Type **42**		1·75	40
186	5c. Holy Trinity School		15	15
187	6c. Snorkeling		15	30
188	10c. Pilgrim Holiness Church		15	20
189	15c. New Cottage Hospital		15	20
190	20c. Post Office and Treasury		15	20
191	25c. Island jetty and boats (vert)		30	30
192	35c. Martello Tower		30	30
193	50c. Warden's House		30	30
194	75c. Britten Norman Islander aircraft		3·50	1·00
195	$1 Tortoise		70	80
196	$2.50 Spiny lobster		80	1·75
197	$5 Magnificent frigate bird		4·00	2·50
197b	$10 Hibiscus (vert)		1·50	4·50

The 50c. to $1 are 39×25 mm, $2.50 and $5 45×29 mm, $10 34×48 mm.

1974. Birth Centenary of Sir Winston Churchill (1st issue). Nos. 408/12 of Antigua optd **BARBUDA**.

198	**113**	5c. multicoloured	15	10
199	-	35c. multicoloured	25	15
200	-	75c. multicoloured	40	45
201	-	$1 multicoloured	75	70
MS202	107×82 mm. Nos. 198/201		7·00	14·00

43 Churchill making Broadcast

1974. Birth Centenary of Sir Winston Churchill (2nd issue). Multicoloured.

203	5c. Type **43**		10	10
204	35c. Churchill and Chartwell		10	10
205	75c. Churchill painting		20	20
206	$1 Churchill making "V" sign		25	30
MS207	146×95 mm. Nos. 203/6		75	2·50

1974. Christmas. Nos. 413/21 of Antigua optd **BARBUDA**.

208	**114**	½c. multicoloured	10	10
209	-	1c. multicoloured	10	10
210	-	2c. multicoloured	10	10
211	-	3c. multicoloured	10	10
212	-	5c. multicoloured	10	10
213	-	20c. multicoloured	10	10
214	-	35c. multicoloured	15	15
215	-	75c. multicoloured	30	30
MS216	139×126 mm. Nos. 208/15		80	1·40

1975. Nelson's Dockyard. Nos. 427/32 of Antigua optd **BARBUDA**.

217	**116**	5c. multicoloured	15	15
218	-	15c. multicoloured	35	25
219	-	35c. multicoloured	40	35
220	-	50c. multicoloured	45	50
221	-	$1 multicoloured	50	80
MS222	130×134 mm. As Nos. 217/21, but larger format; 43×28 mm		1·75	2·75

45 Ships of the Line

1975. Sea Battles. Battle of the Saints, 1782. Multicoloured.

223	35c. Type **45**		40	65
224	50c. H.M.S. *Ramillies*		40	75
225	75c. *Bonhomme Richard* (American frigate) firing broadside		50	90
226	95c. *L'Orient* (French ship of the line) burning		50	1·25

1975. "Apollo–Soyuz" Space Project. No. 197 optd **U.S.A.-U.S.S.R SPACE COOPERATION 1975** with **APOLLO** (No. 227) or **SOYUZ** (No. 228).

227	$5 multicoloured		3·25	6·00
228	$5 multicoloured		3·25	6·00

47 Officer, 65th Foot, 1763

1975. Military Uniforms. Multicoloured.

229	35c. Type **47**		60	60
230	50c. Grenadier, 27th Foot 1701–14		75	75
231	75c. Officer, 21st Foot, 1793–6		80	80
232	95c. Officer, Royal Regiment of Artillery, 1800		90	90

1975. 25th Anniv of United Nations. Nos. 203/6 optd **30TH ANNIVERSARY UNITED NATIONS 1945–1975**.

233	**43**	5c. multicoloured	10	10
234	-	35c. multicoloured	10	15
235	-	75c. multicoloured	15	20
236	-	$1 multicoloured	20	30

1975. Christmas. Nos. 457/65 of Antigua optd **BARBUDA**.

237	**121**	½c. multicoloured	10	15
238	-	1c. multicoloured	10	15
239	-	2c. multicoloured	10	15
240	-	3c. multicoloured	10	15
241	-	5c. multicoloured	10	15
242	-	10c. multicoloured	10	15
243	-	35c. multicoloured	15	20
244	-	$2 multicoloured	60	1·00
MS245	138×119 mm. Nos. 241/4		1·10	2·25

1975. World Cup Cricket Winners. Nos. 466/8 of Antigua optd **BARBUDA**.

246	**122**	5c. multicoloured	1·50	1·75
247	-	35c. multicoloured	2·75	2·00
248	-	$2 multicoloured	4·25	5·50

51 Surrender of Cornwallis at Yorktown (Trumbull)

1976. Bicentenary of American Revolution.

249	**51**	15c. multicoloured	10	15
250	-	15c. multicoloured	10	15
251	-	15c. multicoloured	10	15
252	-	35c. multicoloured	10	15
253	-	35c. multicoloured	10	15
254	-	35c. multicoloured	10	15
255	-	$1 multicoloured	15	25
256	-	$1 multicoloured	15	25
257	-	$1 multicoloured	15	25
258	-	$2 multicoloured	25	40
259	-	$2 multicoloured	25	40
260	-	$2 multicoloured	25	40
MS261	140×70 mm. Nos. 249/54 and 255/60 (two sheets)		1·40	9·00

DESIGNS—As Type **51**: Nos. 249/51; 252/4, The Battle of Princeton; 255/7, Surrender of General Burgoyne at Saratoga; 258/60, Jefferson presenting Declaration of Independence. Type **51** shows the left-hand stamp of the 15c. design.

52 Bananaquits

1976. Birds. Multicoloured.

262	35c. Type **52**		20	25
263	50c. Blue-hooded euphonia		20	40
264	75c. Royal tern		20	50
265	95c. Killdeer plover ("Killdeer")		25	55
266	$1.25 Shiney-headed cowbird ("Glossy Cowbird")		25	70
267	$2 American purple gallinule ("Purple Gallinule")		30	85

1976. Royal Visit to the U.S.A. Nos. 249/60 additionally inscr **H.M. QUEEN ELIZABETH ROYAL VISIT 6TH JULY 1976 H.R.H. DUKE OF EDINBURGH**.

268	15c. multicoloured		10	15
269	15c. multicoloured		10	15
270	15c. multicoloured		10	15
271	35c. multicoloured		10	20
272	35c. multicoloured		10	20
273	35c. multicoloured		10	20
274	$1 multicoloured		15	50
275	$1 multicoloured		15	50
276	$1 multicoloured		15	50
277	$2 multicoloured		25	70
278	$2 multicoloured		25	70
279	$2 multicoloured		25	70
MS280	143×81 mm. Nos. 268/73 and 274/9 (two sheets)		1·50	9·00

1976. Christmas. Nos. 514/18 of Antigua optd **BARBUDA**.

281	**128**	8c. multicoloured	10	10
282	-	10c. multicoloured	10	10
283	-	10c. multicoloured	10	10
284	-	50c. multicoloured	15	10
285	-	$1 multicoloured	25	30

1976. Olympic Games, Montreal. Nos. 495/502 of Antigua optd **BARBUDA**.

286	**125**	½c. brown, yellow and black	10	10
287	-	1c. violet and black	10	10
288	-	2c. green and black	10	10
289	-	15c. blue and black	10	10
290	-	30c. brown, yellow & blk	10	10
291	-	$1 orange, red and black	20	20
292	-	$2 red and black	35	35
MS293	88×138 mm. Nos. 289/92		1·75	2·40

55 P.O. Tower, Telephones and Alexander Graham Bell

1977. Cent of First Telephone Transmission. Multicoloured.

294	75c. Type **55**		15	35
295	$1.25 T.V. transmission by satellite		20	55
296	$2 Globe showing satellite transmission scheme		30	75
MS297	96×144 mm. Nos. 294/6		70	2·00

56 St. Margaret's Church, Westminster

1977. Silver Jubilee (1st issue). Multicoloured.

298	75c. Type **56**		10	15
299	75c. Street decorations		10	15
300	75c. Westminster Abbey		10	15
301	$1.25 Household Cavalry		15	20
302	$1.25 Coronation Coach		15	20
303	$1.25 Postillions		15	20
MS304	148×83 mm. As Nos. 298/303, but with silver borders.		75	1·50

Nos. 298/300 and 301/3 were printed together, se-tenant, forming composite designs.
See also Nos. 323/30 and 375/8.

1977. Nos. 469/86 of Antigua optd **BARBUDA**.

305	½c. Antillean crested hummingbird		1·00	75
306	1c. Imperial amazon ("Imperial Parrot")		1·00	75
307	2c. Zenaida dove		1·00	75
308	3c. Loggerhead kingbird		1·00	75
309	4c. Red-necked pigeon		1·00	75
310	5c. Rufous throated solitaire		1·00	75
311	6c. Orchid tree		50	50
312	10c. Bougainvillea		30	20
313	15c. Geiger tree		30	25
314	20c. Flamboyant		30	25
315	25c. Hibiscus		30	25
316	35c. Flame of the Wood		35	30
317	50c. Cannon at Fort James		40	40
318	75c. Premier's Office		40	40
319	$1 Potworks Dam		50	60
320	$2.50 Irrigation scheme		75	1·60
321	$5 Government House		1·25	3·25
322	$10 Coolidge Airport		3·50	7·50

1977. Silver Jubilee (2nd issue). Nos. 526/31 of Antigua optd **BARBUDA**

(a) Ordinary gum.

323	10c. Royal Family		10	15
324	30c. Royal visit, 1966		10	20
325	50c. The Queen enthroned		15	30
326	90c. The Queen after Coronation		15	40
327	$2.50 The Queen and Prince Charles		45	1·25
MS328	116×78 mm. $5 Queen Elizabeth and Prince Philip		80	1·25

(b) Self-adhesive.

329	50c. Queen after Coronation		40	70
330	$5 The Queen and Prince Philip		3·00	9·00

1977. Caribbean Scout Jamboree, Jamaica. Nos. 534/40 of Antigua optd **BARBUDA**.

331	½c. Type **131**		10	10
332	1c. Hiking		10	10
333	2c. Rock-climbing		10	10
334	10c. Cutting logs		10	10
335	30c. Map and sign reading		25	40
336	50c. First aid		25	65
337	$2 Rafting		55	2·25
MS338	127×114 mm. Nos. 335/7		1·75	4·00

1977. 21st Anniv of Carnival. Nos. 542/47 of Antigua optd **BARBUDA**.

339	10c. Type **312**		10	10
340	30c. Carnival Queen		10	10
341	50c. Butterfly costume		15	20
342	90c. Queen of the Band		20	35
343	$1 Calypso King and Queen		25	45
MS344	140×120 mm. Nos. 339/43		1·00	1·75

61 Royal Yacht *Britannia*

1977. Royal Visit (1st issue). Multicoloured.
345	50c. Type **61**	10	20
346	$1.50 Jubilee emblem	25	35
347	$2.50 Union Jack and flag of Antigua	35	55
MS348	77×124 mm. Nos. 345/7	85	2·25

1977. Royal Visit (2nd issue). Nos. 548/53 of Antigua optd **BARBUDA**.
349A	10c. Royal Family	35	35
350B	30c. Queen Elizabeth and Prince Philip in car	10	15
351B	50c. Queen enthroned	15	20
352B	90c. Queen after Coronation	20	30
353B	$2.50 The Queen and Prince Charles	45	80
MS354A	116×78 mm. $5 Queen and Prince Philip	1·50	4·00

1977. Christmas. Nos. 554/61 of Antigua optd **BARBUDA**.
355	½c. Type **134**	10	10
356	1c. Crivelli	10	10
357	2c. Lotto	10	10
358	8c. Pontormo	10	10
359	10c. Tura (different)	10	10
360	25c. Lotto (different)	15	10
361	$2 Crivelli (different)	45	45
MS362	144×118 mm. Nos. 358/61	1·00	1·75

64 Airship LZ-1

1977. Special Events, 1977. Multicoloured.
363	75c. Type **64**	30	30
364	75c. German battleship and German Navy airship L-31	30	30
365	75c. *Graf Zeppelin* in hangar	30	30
366	75c. Gondola of military airship	30	30
367	95c. Sputnik 1	35	35
368	95c. Vostok rocket	35	35
369	95c. Voskhod rocket	35	35
370	95c. Space walk	35	35
371	$1.25 Fuelling for flight	40	45
372	$1.25 Leaving New York	40	45
373	$1.25 *Spirit of St. Louis*	40	45
374	$1.25 Welcome to England	40	45
375	$2 Lion of England	50	70
376	$2 Unicorn of Scotland	50	70
377	$2 Yale of Beaufort	50	70
378	$2 Falcon of Plantagenets	50	70
379	$5 *Daniel in the Lion's Den* (Rubens)	50	1·25
380	$5 Different detail of painting	50	1·25
381	$5 Different detail of painting	50	1·25
382	$5 Different detail of painting	50	1·25
MS383	132×156 mm. Nos. 362/82	6·00	17·00

EVENTS: 75c. 75th anniv of navigable airships; 95c. 20th anniv of U.S.S.R. space programme; $1.25, 50th anniv of Lindbergh's transatlantic flight; $2 Silver Jubilee of Queen Elizabeth II; $5 400th birth anniv of Rubens.
Nos. 379/82 form a composite design.

1978. Tenth Anniv of Statehood. Nos. 562/7 of Antigua optd **BARBUDA**.
384	10c. Type **135**	10	10
385	15c. State flag	15	10
386	50c. Police band	1·25	80
387	90c. Premier V. C. Bird	20	40
388	$2 State Coat of Arms	40	1·00
MS389	122×99 mm. Nos. 385/88	7·00	4·00

66 *Pieta* (sculpture) (detail)

1978. Easter. Paintings and Sculptures by Michelangelo. Multicoloured.
390	75c. Type **66**	15	15
391	95c. *The Holy Family*	15	20
392	$1.25 *Libyan sibyl* (from the Sistine Chapel)	15	35
393	$2 *The Flood* (from the Sistine Chapel)	20	45
MS394	117×85 mm. Nos. 390/3	1·90	2·00

1978. 75th Anniv of Powered Flight. Nos. 568/75 of Antigua optd **BARBUDA**.
395	½c. Wright Glider No. III, 1902	10	10
396	1c. Wright Flyer I, 1903	10	10

397	2c. Launch system and engine	10	10
398	10c. Orville Wright (vert)	10	10
399	50c. Wright Flyer III, 1905	25	20
400	90c. Wilbur Wright (vert)	35	25
401	$2 Wright Type B, 1910	60	45
MS402	90×75 mm. $2.50, Wright Flyer I on launch system	1·50	2·50

1978. Sailing Week. Nos. 576/80 of Antigua optd **BARBUDA**.
403	10c. Sunfish regatta	20	10
404	50c. Fishing and work boat race	40	25
405	90c. Curtain Bluff race	55	35
406	$2 Power boat rally	85	75
MS407	110×77 mm. $2.50, Guadeloupe–Antigua race	1·25	1·60

68 St. Edward's Crown

1978. 25th Anniv of Coronation (1st issue). Multicoloured.
408	75c. Type **68**	15	20
409	75c. Imperial State Crown	15	20
410	$1.50 Queen Mary's Crown	20	30
411	$1.50 Queen Mother's Crown	20	30
412	$2.50 Queen Consort's Crown	35	50
413	$2.50 Queen Victoria's Crown	35	50
MS414	123×117 mm. Nos. 408/13	1·10	1·75

1978. 25th Anniv of Coronation (2nd issue). Nos. 581/5 of Antigua optd **BARBUDA**.

(a) Sheet stamps
415	10c. Queen Elizabeth and Prince Philip	10	10
416	30c. The Crowning	10	10
417	50c. Coronation procession	10	15
418	90c. Queen seated in St. Edward's Chair	15	20
419	$2.50 Queen wearing Imperial State Crown	30	60
MS420	114×103 mm. $5 Queen Elizabeth and Prince Philip	1·00	1·50

(b) Booklet stamps
421	25c. Glass Coach	30	70
422	50c. Irish State Coach	30	70
423	$5 Coronation Coach	1·00	2·25

1978. World Cup Football Championship, Argentina. Nos. 590/3 of Antigua optd **BARBUDA**.
424	10c. Player running with ball	10	10
425	15c. Players in front of goal	10	10
426	$3 Referee and player	1·25	1·25
MS427	126×88 mm. 25c. Player crouching with ball; 30c. Players heading ball; 50c. Players running with ball; $2 Goalkeeper diving	80	90

1978. Flowers. As Nos. 594/7 of Antigua optd **BARBUDA**.
428	25c. Petrea	15	20
429	50c. Sunflower	25	40
430	90c. Frangipani	35	45
431	$2 Passion flower	60	90
MS432	118×85 mm. $2.50, Hibiscus	1·00	1·50

1978. Christmas. As Nos. 599/601 of Antigua optd **BARBUDA**.
433	8c. St. Ildefonso receiving the Chasuble from the Virgin	10	10
434	25c. *The Flight of St. Barbara*	15	15
435	$2 *Madonna and Child, with St. Joseph, John the Baptist and Donor*	60	1·25
MS436	170×113 mm. $4 *The Annuciation*	1·00	2·25

70 Black-barred Soldierfish

1978. Flora and Fauna. Multicoloured.
437	25c. Type **70**	75	1·50
438	50c. *Cynthia cardui* (butterfly)	1·50	2·25
439	75c. Dwarf poinciana	80	2·25
440	95c. *Heliconius charithonia* (butterfly)	1·50	2·50
441	$1.25 Bougainvillea	90	2·50

71 Footballers and World Cup

1978. Anniversaries and Events.
442	75c. Type **71**	30	30
443	95c. Wright Brothers and Flyer I (horiz)	30	40
444	$1.25 Balloon "Double Eagle II" and map of Atlantic (horiz)	55	45
445	$2 Prince Philip paying homage to the Queen	55	60
MS446	122×90 mm. Nos. 442/5. Imperf	5·00	6·00

EVENTS: 75c. Argentina—Winners of World Cup Football Championship; 95c. 75th anniv of powered flight; $1.25, First Atlantic crossing by balloon; $2 25th anniv of Coronation.

72 Sir Rowland Hill

1979. Death Centenary of Sir Rowland Hill (1st issue). Multicoloured.
447	75c. Type **72**	25	45
448	95c. Mail coach, 1840 (horiz)	25	50
449	$1.25 London's first pillar box, 1855 (horiz)	30	60
450	$2 Mail leaving St. Martin's Le Grand Post Office, London	45	85
MS451	129×104 mm. Nos. 447/50. Imperf	1·40	2·25

1979. Death Centenary of Sir Rowland Hill (2nd issue). Nos. 603/6 of Antigua optd **BARBUDA**.
452	25c. 1d. Stamp of 1863	15	15
453	50c. Penny Black	20	20
454	$1 Stage-coach and woman posting letter, c. 1840	35	30
455	$2 Modern mail transport	80	60
MS456	108×82 mm. $2.50, Sir Rowland Hill	75	80

1979. Easter. Works of Durer. Nos. 608/11 of Antigua optd **BARBUDA**.
457	10c. multicoloured	10	10
458	50c. multicoloured	20	20
459	$4 black, mauve and yellow	90	1·10
MS460	114×99 mm. $2.50, multicoloured	55	75

74 Passengers alighting from British Airways Boeing 747

1979. 30th Anniv of International Civil Aviation Organization. Multicoloured.
461	75c. Type **74**	25	50
462	95c. Air traffic control	25	50
463	$1.25 Ground crew-man directing Douglas DC-8 on runway	25	50

1979. International Year of the Child (1st issue). Nos. 612/15 of Antigua optd **BARBUDA**.
464	25c. Yacht	20	15
465	50c. Rocket	30	25
466	90c. Car	40	35
467	$2 Toy train	80	60
MS468	80×112 mm. $5 Airplane	1·10	1·10

1979. Fish. Nos. 617/21 of Antigua optd **BARBUDA**.
469	30c. Yellow jack	20	15
470	50c. Blue-finned tuna	25	20
471	90c. Sailfish	30	30
472	$3 Wahoo	65	1·10
MS473	122×75 mm. $2.50, Great barracuda	1·00	1·25

1979. Death Bicentenary of Captain Cook. Nos. 622/6 of Antigua optd **BARBUDA**.
474	25c. Cook's Birthplace, Marton	25	25
475	50c. H.M.S. *Endeavour*	70	35
476	90c. Marine chronometer	70	40
477	$3 Landing at Botany Bay	1·50	1·00
MS478	110×85 mm. $2.50, H.M.S. *Resolution*	1·25	1·50

77 Virgin with the Pear

1979. International Year of the Child (2nd issue). Paintings by Durer. Multicoloured.
479	25c. Type **77**	15	15
480	50c. *Virgin with the Pink* (detail)	20	25
481	75c. *Virgin with the Pear* (different detail)	25	30
482	$1.25 *Nativity* (detail)	25	40
MS483	86×118 mm. Nos. 479/82	1·00	1·75

1979. Christmas. Nos. 627/31 of Antigua optd **BARBUDA**.
484	8c. The Holy Family	10	10
485	25c. Mary and Jesus on donkey	15	10
486	50c. Shepherd looking at star	25	15
487	$4 The Three Kings	85	80
MS488	113×94 mm. $3 Angel with trumpet	80	1·10

1980. Olympic Games, Moscow. Nos. 632/6 of Antigua optd **BARBUDA**.
489	10c. Javelin	10	10
490	25c. Running	15	10
491	$1 Pole vault	35	20
492	$2 Hurdles	55	40
MS493	127×96 mm. $3 Boxing	70	1·10

1980. "London 1980" International Stamp Exhibition. Nos. 452/5 optd **LONDON 1980**.
494	25c. 1d. stamp of 1863	35	20
495	50c. Penny Black	45	40
496	$1 Stage-coach and woman posting letter, c. 1840	85	65
497	$2 Modern mail transport	2·75	1·50

80 "Apollo 11" Crew Badge

1980. Tenth Anniv of "Apollo 11" Moon Landing. Multicoloured.
498	75c. Type **80**	60	25
499	95c. Plaque left on Moon	60	30
500	$1.25 Rejoining the mother-ship	70	50
501	$2 Lunar module	90	75
MS502	118×84 mm. Nos. 498/501	1·60	2·25

81 American Wigeon ("American Widgeon")

1980. Birds. Multicoloured.
503	1c. Type **81**	70	1·50
504	2c. Snowy plover	70	80
505	4c. Rose-breasted grosbeak	75	80
506	6c. Mangrove cuckoo	75	80
507	10c. Adelaide's warbler	75	70
508	15c. Scaly-breasted thrasher	80	70
509	20c. Yellow-crowned night heron	80	70
510	25c. Bridled quail dove	80	70
511	35c. Carib grackle	85	1·50
512	50c. Northern pintail	90	55
513	75c. Black-whispered vireo	1·00	55
514	$1 Blue-winged teal	1·25	80
515	$1.50 Green-throated carib (vert)	1·50	80
516	$2 Red-necked pigeon (vert)	2·25	1·25
517	$2.50 Wied's crested flycatcher ("Stolid Flycatcher") (vert)	2·75	1·50
518	$5 Yellow-bellied sapsucker (vert)	3·50	3·75
519	$7.50 Caribbean elaenia (vert)	4·00	6·50
520	$10 Great egret (vert)	4·00	5·00

1980. Famous Works of Art. Nos. 651/8 of Antigua optd **BARBUDA**.
521	10c. *David* (statue, Donatello)	10	10
522	30c. *The Birth of Venus* (painting, Sandro Botticelli)	15	15
523	50c. *Reclining Couple* (sarcophagus), Cerveteri	15	20
524	90c. *The Garden of Earthly Delights* (painting, Hieronymus Bosch)	20	25

525	$1 *Portinari Altarpiece* (painting, Hugo van der Goes)	20	25
526	$4 *Eleanora of Toledo and her Son Giovanni de'Medici* (painting, Agnolo Bronzino)	60	80
MS527	99×124 mm. $5 *The Holy Family* (painting, Rembrandt)	1·50	1·75

1980. 75th Anniv of Rotary International. Nos. 658/62 of Antigua optd **BARBUDA.**

528	30c. Rotary Headquarters	15	15
529	50c. Antigua Rotary banner	20	20
530	90c. Map of Antigua	25	25
531	$3 Paul P. Harris (founder)	65	65
MS532	102×77 mm. $5 Antigua flags and Rotary emblems	1·50	2·25

1980. 80th Birthday of the Queen Mother. Nos. 663/5 of Antigua optd **BARBUDA.**

533	10c. multicoloured	50	15
534	$2.50 multicoloured	1·25	1·50
MS535	68×88 mm. $3 multicoloured	2·00	1·75

1980. Birds. Nos. 666/70 of Antigua optd **BARBUDA.**

536	10c. Ringed kingfisher	3·25	1·00
537	30c. Plain pigeon	3·75	1·10
538	$1 Green-throated carib	5·00	3·00
539	$2 Black necked stilt	6·00	6·00
MS540	73×73 mm. $2.50, Roseate tern	6·50	2·75

1981. Sugar Cane Railway Locomotives. Nos. 681/5 of Antigua optd **BARBUDA.**

541	25c. Diesel locomotive No. 15	1·00	25
542	50c. Narrow-gauge steam locomotive	1·25	35
543	90c. Diesel locomotive Nos. 1 and 10	1·75	45
544	$3 Steam locomotive hauling sugar cane	3·25	1·40
MS545	82×111 mm. $2.50, Antigua sugar factory, railway yard and sheds	1·50	1·75

84 Florence Nightingale

1981. Famous Women.

546	**84**	50c. multicoloured	15	30
547	-	90c. multicoloured	40	55
548	-	$1 multicoloured	35	60
549	-	$4 black, brown and lilac	50	1·75

DESIGNS: 90c. Marie Curie; $1 Amy Johnson; $4 Eleanor Roosevelt.

85 Goofy in Motor-boat

1981. Walt Disney Cartoon Characters. Multicoloured.

550	10c. Type **85**	90	15
551	20c. Donald Duck reversing car into sea	1·25	20
552	25c. Mickey Mouse asking tug-boat to take on more than it can handle	1·40	30
553	30c. Porpoise turning tables on Goofy	1·40	35
554	35c. Goofy in sailing boat	1·40	35
555	40c. Mickey Mouse and boat being lifted out of water by fish	1·40	40
556	75c. Donald Duck fishing for flying-fish with butterfly net	2·00	60
557	$1 Minnie Mouse in brightly decorated sailing boat	2·00	80
558	$2 Chip and Dale on floating ship-in-bottle	2·50	1·40
MS559	127×101 mm. $2.50, Donald Duck	4·50	3·00

1981. Birth Centenary of Picasso. Nos. 697/701 of Antigua optd with **BARBUDA.**

560	10c. "Pipes of Pan"	10	10
561	50c. Seated Harlequin	25	15
562	90c. *Paulo as Harlequin*	35	30
563	$4 Mother and Child	90	1·00
MS564	115×140 mm. $5 *Three Musicians* (detail)	1·40	1·40

87/8 Buckingham Palace

1981. Royal Wedding (1st issue). Buildings. Each printed in black on either pink, green or lilac backgrounds.

565	$1 Type **87**	25	40
566	$1 Type **88**	25	40
567	$1.50 Caernarvon Castle (right)	30	50
568	$1.50 Caernarvon Castle (left)	30	50
569	$4 Highgrove House (right)	55	90
570	$4 Highgrove House (left)	55	90
MS571	75×90 mm. $5 black and yellow (St. Paul's Cathedral—26×32 mm)	80	1·25

Same prices for any background colour. The two versions of each value form composite designs.

1981. Royal Wedding (2nd issue). Nos. 702/5 of Antigua optd **BARBUDA.**

572	25c. Prince Charles and Lady Diana Spencer	15	15
573	50c. Glamis Castle	25	25
574	$4 Prince Charles skiing	75	1·00
MS575	95×85 mm. $5 Glass coach	90	90

89 "Integration and Travel"

1981. International Year of Disabled Persons (1st issue).

576	**89**	50c. multicoloured	25	20
577	-	90c. black, orange and green	25	25
578	-	$1 black, blue and green	30	30
579	-	$4 black, yellow and brown	45	85

DESIGNS: 90c. Braille and sign language; $1 "Helping hands"; $4 "Mobility aids for disabled".
See also Nos. 603/6.

1981. Royal Wedding (3rd issue). Nos. 706/12 of Antigua optd **BARBUDA.**

580	25c. Prince of Wales at Investiture, 1969	40	70
581	25c. Prince Charles as baby, 1948	40	70
582	$1 Prince Charles at R.A.F. College, Cranwell, 1971	50	85
583	$1 Prince Charles attending Hill House School, 1956	50	85
584	$2 Prince Charles and Lady Diana Spencer	75	1·00
585	$2 Prince Charles at Trinity College, 1967	75	1·00
586	$5 Prince Charles and Lady Diana	4·25	6·50

1981. Independence. No. 686/96 of Antigua additionally optd **BARBUDA.**

587	6c. Orchid tree	50	15
588	10c. Bougainvillea	55	15
589	20c. Flamboyant	70	20
590	25c. Hibiscus	80	25
591	35c. Flame of the wood	90	30
592	50c. Cannon at Fort James	1·10	45
593	75c. Premier's Office	1·25	75
594	$1 Potworks Dam	1·50	80
595	$2.50 Irrigation scheme, Diamond Estate	2·50	2·75
596	$5 Government House and Gardens	2·75	3·75
597	$10 Coolidge International Airport	4·50	6·00

1981. 50th Anniv of Antigua Girl Guide Movement. Nos. 713/16 of Antigua optd **BARBUDA.**

598	10c. Irene Joshua (founder)	55	10
599	50c. Campfire sing-song	1·25	30
600	90c. Sailing	1·75	45
601	$2.50 Animal tending	3·00	1·40
MS602	170×113 mm. $4 "The Annunciation" (Rubens)	3·50	3·50

1981. International Year of Disabled Persons (2nd issue). Sport for the Disabled. Nos. 728/32 of Antigua optd **BARBUDA.**

603	10c. Swimming	15	15
604	50c. Discus throwing	20	25
605	90c. Archery	45	45
606	$2 Baseball	60	1·50
MS607	108×84 mm. $4 Basketball	2·00	1·75

1981. Christmas. Paintings. Nos. 723/7 of Antigua optd **BARBUDA.**

608	8c. *Holy Night* (Jacques Stella)	10	10
609	30c. *Mary with Child* (Julius Schnorr von Carolfeld)	20	20
610	$1 *Virgin and Child* (Alsono Cano)	40	40
611	$3 *Virgin and Child* (Lorenzo di Credi)	1·10	1·10

MS612	77×111 mm. $5 *Holy Family* (Pieter von Avon)	1·75	2·25

93 Princess of Wales

1982. Birth of Prince William of Wales (1st issue).

613	**93**	$1 multicoloured	75	50
614	**93**	$2.50 multicoloured	1·00	1·10
615	**93**	$5 multicoloured	1·60	1·75
MS616		88×108 mm. $4 multicoloured	2·00	2·10

1982. South Atlantic Fund. Nos. 580/6 surch **S. Atlantic Fund + 50c.**

617	25c.+50c. +50c. Prince of Wales at Investiture, 1969	30	50
618	25c.+50c. +50c. Prince Charles as baby, 1948	30	50
619	$1+50c. +50c. Prince Charles at R.A.F. College, Cranwell, 1971	50	75
620	$1+50c. +50c. Prince Charles attending Hill House School, 1956	50	75
621	$2+50c. +50c. Prince Charles and Lady Diana Spencer	75	1·10
622	$2+50c. +50c. Prince Charles at Trinity College, 1967	75	1·10
623	$5+50c. +50c. Prince Charles and Lady Diana Spencer	3·00	4·25

1982. 21st Birthday of Princess of Wales (1st issue). As Nos. 613/16 but inscr "Twenty First Birthday Greetings to H.R.H. The Princess of Wales".

624	$1 multicoloured	1·50	45
625	$2.50 multicoloured	2·25	1·25
626	$5 multicoloured	3·00	2·40
MS627	88×108 mm. $4 multicoloured	2·75	2·25

1982. 21st Birthday of Princess of Wales (2nd issue). Nos. 748/51 of Antigua optd **BARBUDA MAIL.**

628	90c. Queen's House, Greenwich	80	45
629	$1 Prince and Princess of Wales	1·25	50
630	$4 Princess of Wales	3·00	1·50
MS631	114×94 mm. $3 Angel with trumpet	1·75	2·00

1982. Birth of Prince William of Wales (2nd issue). Nos. 757/60 of Antigua further optd **BARBUDA MAIL.**

632	90c. Queen's House, Greenwich	80	45
633	$1 Prince and Princess of Wales	1·50	50
634	$4 Princess of Wales	3·25	2·00
MS635	102×75 mm. $5 Princess of Wales (different)	4·50	2·50

1982. Birth Centenary of Franklin D. Roosevelt and 250th Birth Anniv of George Washington. Nos. 761/8 of Antigua optd **BARBUDA MAIL.**

636	10c. Roosevelt in 1940	10	10
637	25c. Washington as blacksmith	15	15
638	45c. Churchill, Roosevelt and Stalin at Yalta Conference	2·00	25
639	60c. Washington crossing Delaware	20	25
640	$1 *Roosevelt Special* train	2·00	40
641	$3 Portrait of Roosevelt	60	90
MS642	92×87 mm. $4 Roosevelt and wife	1·00	1·75
MS643	92×87 mm. $4 Portrait of Washington	1·00	1·75

1982. Christmas. Religious Paintings by Raphael. Nos. 769/73 of Antigua optd **BARBUDA MAIL.**

644	10c. *Annunciation*	10	10
645	30c. *Adoration of the Magi*	15	15
646	$1 *Presentation at the Temple*	40	40
647	$4 *Coronation of the Virgin*	1·00	1·00
MS648	95×142 mm. $5 *Marriage of the Virgin*	1·25	2·00

1983. 500th Birth Anniv of Raphael. Details from *Galatea* Fresco. Nos. 774/8 of Antigua optd **BARBUDA MAIL.**

649	45c. Tritons and dolphins	20	20
650	50c. Sea Nymph carried off by Triton	20	20
651	60c. Winged angel steering dolphins (horiz)	25	25
652	$4 Cupids shooting arrows	1·00	1·00
MS653	101×102 mm. $5 Galatea pulled along by dolphins	1·25	2·00

1983. Commonwealth Day. Nos. 779/82 of Antigua optd **BARBUDA MAIL.**

654	25c. Pineapple produce	45	55
655	45c. Carnival	55	70
656	60c. Tourism	70	1·25
657	$3 Airport	1·50	3·50

1983. World Communications Year. Nos. 783/6 of Antigua optd **BARBUDA MAIL.**

658	15c. T.V. satellite coverage of Royal Wedding	2·00	1·00
659	50c. Police communications	5·00	90
660	60c. House-to-diesel train telephone call	3·00	90

661	$3 Satellite earth station with planets Jupiter and Saturn	4·25	2·50
MS662	100×90 mm. $5 "Comsat" satellite over West Indies	1·50	2·25

97 Vincenzo Lunardi's Balloon Flight, London, 1785

1983. Bicent of Manned Flight (1st issue). Multicoloured.

663	$1 Type **97**	35	35
664	$1.50 Montgolfier brothers' balloon flight, Paris, 1783	50	55
665	$2.50 Blanchard and Jeffries' Cross-Channel balloon flight, 1785	70	90
MS666	111×111 mm. $5 Maiden flight of airship LZ-127 *Graf Zeppelin*, 1928	2·00	2·75

See also Nos. 672/6.

1983. Whales. Nos. 788/93 of Antigua optd **BARBUDA MAIL.**

667	15c. Bottlenose dolphin	1·25	40
668	50c. Finback whale	4·00	1·60
669	90c. Bowhead whale	4·50	1·75
670	$3 Spectacled porpoise	5·50	4·25
MS671	122×101 mm. $5 Narwhal	6·00	4·50

1983. Bicentenary of Manned Flight (2nd issue). Nos. 811/15 of Antigua optd **BARBUDA MAIL.**

672	30c. Dornier Do-X flying boat	1·50	35
673	50c. Supermarine S6B seaplane	1·75	60
674	60c. Curtiss Sparrowhawk biplane and airship U.S.S. *Akron*	2·25	70
675	$4 Hot-air balloon *Pro-Juventute*	5·50	4·00
MS676	0×105 mm. $5 Airship LZ-127 *Graf Zeppelin*	3·75	4·25

1983. Nos. 565/70 surch.

677	45c. on $1 Type **87**	25	45
678	45c. on $1 Type **88**	25	45
679	50c. on $1.45 Caernarvon Castle (right)	25	45
680	50c. on $1.45 Caernarvon Castle (left)	25	45
681	60c. on $4 Highgrove House (left)	25	45
682	60c. on $4 Highgrove House (right)	25	45

1983. Nos. 793/810 of Antigua optd **BARBUDA MAIL.**

683	1c. Cashew nut	10	40
684	2c. Passion fruit	15	40
685	3c. Mango	15	40
686	5c. Grapefruit	15	40
687	10c. Pawpaw	20	30
688	15c. Breadfruit	40	20
689	20c. Coconut	50	30
690	25c. Oleander	50	20
691	30c. Banana	55	20
692	40c. Pineapple	65	25
693	45c. Cordia	70	30
694	50c. Cassia	80	30
695	60c. Poui	80	30
696	$1 Frangipani	1·10	50
697	$2 Flamboyant	1·75	1·50
698	$2.50 Lemon	2·00	2·00
699	$5 Lignum vitae	3·00	3·25
700	$10 National flag and coat of arms	4·50	6·00

1983. Christmas. 500th Birth Anniv of Raphael. Nos. 816/20 of Antigua optd **BARBUDA MAIL.**

701	10c. multicoloured	10	10
702	30c. multicoloured	10	20
703	$1 multicoloured	30	50
704	$4 multicoloured	1·00	1·50
MS705	101×131 mm. $5 multicoloured	1·40	2·50

1983. Bicentenary (1984) of Methodist Church. Nos. 821/4 of Antigua optd **BARBUDA MAIL.**

706	15c. Type **181**	20	15
707	50c. Nathaniel Gilbert (founder in Antigua)	30	25
708	60c. St. John Methodist Church steeple	30	30
709	$3 Ebenezer Methodist Church, St John's	80	1·00

100 Edward VII

1984. Members of British Royal Family. Multicoloured.

710	$1 Type **100**	70	1·50
711	$1 George V	70	1·50
712	$1 George VI	70	1·50
713	$1 Elizabeth II	70	1·50
714	$1 Charles, Prince of Wales	70	1·50
715	$1 Prince William of Wales	70	1·50

1984. Olympic Games, Los Angeles (1st issue). Nos. 825/9 of Antigua optd **BARBUDA MAIL.**

716	25c. Discus	25	20
717	50c. Gymnastics	40	40
718	90c. Hurdling	50	60
719	$3 Cycling	2·75	1·50
MS720	82×67 mm. $5 Volleyball	2·00	3·25

1984. Ships. Nos. 830/4 of Antigua optd **BARBUDA MAIL.**

721	45c. *Booker Vanguard* (freighter)	1·50	45
722	50c. *Canberra* (liner)	1·50	50
723	60c. Yachts	1·75	60
724	$4 *Fairwind* (cargo liner)	4·25	2·75
MS725	101×80 mm. $5 18th-century British man-o-war (vert)	4·50	4·25

1984. Universal Postal Union Congress, Hamburg. Nos. 835/8 of Antigua optd **BARBUDA MAIL.**

726	15c. Chenille	25	15
727	50c. Shell flower	30	30
728	60c. Anthurium	40	40
729	$3 Angels trumpet	75	1·25
MS730	100×75 mm. $5 Crown of Thorns	2·00	2·50

101 Olympic Stadium, Athens, 1896

1984. Olympic Games, Los Angeles (2nd issue). Multicoloured.

731	$1.50 Type **101**	40	90
732	$2.50 Olympic stadium, Los Angeles, 1984	60	1·50
733	$5 Athlete carrying Olympic torch	95	2·25
MS734	121×95 mm. No. 733	1·50	2·50

1984. Presidents of the United States of America. Nos. 856/63 of Antigua optd **BARBUDA MAIL.**

735	10c. Abraham Lincoln	10	10
736	20c. Harry Truman	15	15
737	30c. Dwight Eisenhower	20	25
738	40c. Ronald Reagan	25	30
739	90c. Gettysburg Address, 1863	40	55
740	$1.10 .10 Formation of N.A.T.O., 1949	40	65
741	$1.50 Eisenhower during Second World War	45	70
742	$2 Reagan and Caribbean Basin Initiative	50	1·00

1984. Abolition of Slavery. Nos. 864/8 of Antigua optd **BARBUDA MAIL.**

743	40c. View of Moravian Mission	30	30
744	50c. Antigua Courthouse, 1823	40	40
745	60c. Planting sugar-cane, Monks Hill	45	45
746	$3 Boiling house, Delaps' Estate	1·40	1·40
MS747	95×70 mm. $5 Loading sugar, Willoughby Bay	2·00	2·50

1984. Songbirds. Nos. 869/74 of Antigua optd **BARBUDA MAIL.**

748	40c. Rufous-sided towhee	2·25	55
749	50c. Parula warbler	2·25	70
750	60c. House wren	2·25	75
751	$2 Ruby-crowned kinglet	3·25	2·00
752	$3 Common flicker ("Yellow-shafted Flicker")	3·50	2·75
MS753	76×76 mm. $5 Yellow-breasted chat	4·00	4·50

1984. 450th Death Anniv of Correggio (painter). Nos. 878/82 of Antigua optd **BARBUDA MAIL.**

754	25c. *The Virgin and Infant with Angels and Cherubs*	15	20
755	60c. *The Four Saints*	40	45
756	90c. *St. Catherine*	50	55
757	$3 *The Campori Madonna*	1·25	1·75
MS758	90×60 mm. $5 *St. John the Baptist*	1·75	3·25

1984. "Ausipex" International Stamp Exibition Melbourne. Australian Sports. Nos. 875/7 of Antigua optd **BARBUDA MAIL.**

759	$1 Grass-skiing	50	40
760	$5 Australian Football	1·50	2·25
MS761	108×78 mm. Boomerang-throwing	1·50	2·75

1984. 150th Birth Anniv of Edgar Degas (painter). Nos. 883/7 of Antigua optd **BARBUDA MAIL.**

762	15c. *The Blue Dancers*	10	10
763	50c. *The Pink Dancers*	30	40
764	70c. *Two Dancers*	45	55
765	$4 *Dancers at the Bar*	1·25	3·50
MS766	90×60 mm. $5 *The Folk Dancers* (40×27 mm)	1·75	2·75

1985. Famous People. Nos. 888/96 of Antigua optd **BARBUDA MAIL.**

767	60c. Winston Churchill	7·00	3·00
768	60c. Mahatma Gandhi	7·00	3·00
769	60c. John F. Kennedy	7·00	3·00
770	60c. Mao Tse-tung	7·00	3·00
771	$1 Churchill with General De Gaulle, Paris, 1944 (horiz)	7·00	3·00
772	$1 Gandhi leaving London by train, 1931 (horiz)	7·00	3·00
773	$1 Kennedy with Chancellor Adenauer and Mayor Brandt, Berlin, 1963 (horiz)	7·00	3·00
774	$1 Mao Tse-tung with Lin Piao, Peking, 1969 (horiz)	7·00	3·00
MS775	114×80 mm. $5 Flags of Great Britain, India, the United States and China	12·00	8·50

103 Lady Elizabeth Bowes-Lyon, 1907, and Camellias

1985. Life and Times of Queen Elizabeth the Queen Mother. Multicoloured.

776	15c. Type **103**	35	20
777	45c. Duchess of York, 1926, and "Elizabeth of Glamis" roses	45	25
778	50c. The Queen Mother after the Coronation, 1937	45	25
779	60c. In Garter robes, 1971, and dog roses	45	30
780	90c. Attending Royal Variety Show, 1967, and red Hibiscus	60	45
781	$1 The Queen Mother in 1982, and blue plumbago	75	1·10
782	$3 Receiving 82nd birthday gifts from children, and morning glory	95	2·50

104 Roseate Tern

1985. Birth Bicentenary of John J. Audubon (ornithologist) (1st issue). Designs showing original paintings. Multicoloured.

783	45c. Type **104**	20	30
784	50c. Mangrove cuckoo	20	30
785	60c. Yellow-crowned night heron	20	40
786	$5 Brown pelican	80	3·50

See also Nos. 794/7 and 914/17.

1985. Centenary (1986) of Statue of Liberty (1st issue). Nos. 907/13 of Antigua optd **BARBUDA MAIL.**

787	25c. Torch from statue in Madison Square Park, 1885	20	20
788	30c. Statue of Liberty and scaffolding ("Restoration and Renewal") (vert)	20	20
789	50c. Frederic Bartholdi (sculpture) supervising construction, 1876	30	30
790	90c. Close-up of Statue	55	55
791	$1 Statue and sailing ship ("Operation Sail", 1976) (vert)	80	60
792	$3 Dedication ceremony, 1886 (vert)	1·75	1·75
MS793	110×80 mm. $5 Port of New York	5·75	4·75

See also Nos. 987/96.

1985. Birth Bicentenary of John J. Audubon (ornithologist) (2nd issue). Nos. 924/8 of Antigua optd **BARBUDA MAIL.**

794	90c. Slavonian grebe ("Horned Grebe")	10·00	4·25

1985. "Ausipex" International Stamp Exibition Melbourne. Nos. 875/7 ...

795	$1 British storm petrel ("Least Petrel")	10·00	4·50
796	$1.50 Great blue heron	11·00	8·50
797	$3 Double-crested cormorant (white phase)	16·00	13·00
MS798	103×72 mm. $5 White-tailed tropic bird (vert)	28·00	11·00

1985. Butterflies. Nos. 929/33 of Antigua optd **BARBUDA MAIL.**

799	25c. *Anaea cyanea*	7·00	1·25
800	60c. *Leodonta dysoni*	9·00	2·00
801	90c. *Junea doraete*	10·00	2·50
802	$4 *Prepona pylene*	19·00	19·00
MS803	132×105 mm. $5 *Caervois gerdtrudtus*	17·00	9·00

1985. Centenary of Motorcycle. Nos. 919/23 of Antigua optd **BARBUDA MAIL.**

804	10c. Triumph 2hp "Jap", 1903	1·25	40
805	30c. Indian "Arrow", 1949	1·75	45
806	60c. BMW "R100RS", 1976	2·25	70
807	$4 Harley Davidson "Model II", 1916	5·75	5·00
MS808	90×93 mm. $5 Laverda "Jota", 1975	7·00	4·00

1985. 85th Birthday of Queen Elizabeth the Queen Mother. Nos. 776/82 optd **4TH AUG 1900–1985.**

809	15c. Type **103**	75	50
810	45c. Duchess of York, 1926 and "Elizabeth of Glamis" roses	1·10	60
811	50c. The Queen Mother after the Coronation, 1937	1·10	60
812	60c. In Garter robes, 1971, and dog roses	1·25	1·00
813	90c. Attending Royal Variey Show, 1967, and red hibiscus	1·25	1·25
814	$2 The Queen Mother in 1982, and blue plumbago	1·40	3·75
815	$3 Receiving 82nd birthday gifts from children, and morning glory	1·50	3·75

1985. Native American Artefacts. Nos. 914/18 of Antigua optd **BARBUDA MAIL.**

816	15c. Arawak pot sherd and Indians making clay utensils	15	10
817	50c. Arawak body design and Arawak Indians tattooing	25	25
818	60c. Head of the god "Yocahu" and Indians harvesting manioc	35	35
819	$3 Carib war club and Carib Indians going into battle	1·25	1·50
MS820	97×68 mm. $5 Taino Indians worshiping stone idol	2·00	3·00

1985. 40th Anniv of International Civil Aviation Organization. Nos. 934/8 of Antigua optd **BARBUDA MAIL.**

821	30c. Cessna Skyhawk	2·75	75
822	90c. Fokker D.VII	3·75	1·25
823	$1.50 SPAD VII	4·75	6·00
824	$3 Boeing 747	6·50	9·00
MS825	97×83 mm. De Havilland D.H.C.6 Twin Otter	3·25	3·50

1985. Life and Times of Queen Elizabeth the Queen Mother (2nd series). Nos. 946/9 of Antigua optd **BARBUDA MAIL.**

826	$1 The Queen Mother attending church	6·00	2·50
827	$1.50 Watching children playing in London garden	7·00	3·00
828	$2.50 The Queen Mother in 1979	8·00	3·50
MS829	56×85 mm. $5 With Prince Edward at Royal Wedding, 1981	17·00	11·00

1985. 850th Birth Anniv of Maimonides (physician philosopher and scholar). Nos. 939/40 of Antigua optd **BARBUDA MAIL.**

830	$2 green	4·50	4·50
MS831	70×84 mm. $5 brown	4·25	4·50

1985. Marine Life. Nos. 950/4 of Antigua optd **BARBUDA MAIL.**

832	15c. Magnificent frigate bird	7·00	1·25
833	45c. Brain coral	7·00	80
834	60c. Cushion star	7·00	1·25
835	$3 Spotted moray	15·00	5·50
MS836	110×80 mm. $5 Elkhorn coral	18·00	6·50

1986. International Youth Year. Nos. 941/5 of Antigua optd **BARBUDA MAIL.**

837	25c. Young farmers with produce	15	15
838	50c. Hotel management trainees	25	30
839	60c. Girls with goat and boys with football ("Environment")	30	35
840	$3 Windsurfing ("Leisure")	1·50	1·60
MS841	102×72 mm. $5 Young people with Antiguan flag	2·75	3·25

1986. Royal Visit. Nos. 965/8 of Antigua optd **BARBUDA MAIL.**

842	60c. Flags of Great Britain and Antigua	3·75	50
843	$1 Queen Elizabeth II (vert)	3·00	65
844	$4 Royal Yacht *Britannia*	8·50	2·50
MS845	110×83 mm. $5 Map of Antigua	12·00	4·00

1986. 75th Anniv of Girl Guide Movement. Nos. 955/9 of Antigua optd **BARBUDA MAIL.**

846	15c. Girl Guides nursing	1·50	80
847	45c. Open-air Girl Guide meeting	2·75	1·75
848	60c. Lord and Lady Baden-Powell	2·75	2·50
849	$3 Girl Guides gathering flowers	7·50	9·50
MS850	67×96 mm. $5 Barn swallow (Nature study)	35·00	23·00

1986. 300th Birth Anniv of Johann Sebastian Bach (composer). Nos. 960/4 of Antigua optd **BARBUDA MAIL.**

851	25c. multicoloured	3·50	70
852	50c. multicoloured	3·75	1·40
853	$1 multicoloured	5·00	2·00
854	$3 multicoloured	8·50	9·00
MS855	104×73 mm. $5 black and grey	27·00	12·00

1986. Christmas. Religious Paintings. Nos. 985/8 of Antigua optd **BARBUDA MAIL.**

856	10c. *Madonna and Child* (De Landi)	40	30
857	25c. *Madonna and Child* (Berlinghiero)	80	50
858	60c. *The Nativity* (Fra Angelico)	1·50	1·00
859	$4 *Presentation in the Temple* (Giovanni di Paolo)	4·00	7·00
MS860	113×81 mm. $5 *The Nativity* (Antoniazzo Romano)	4·25	5·50

108 Queen Elizabeth II meeting Members of Legislature

1986. 60th Birthday of Queen Elizabeth II (1st issue). Multicoloured.

861	$1 Type **108**	50	1·00
862	$2 Queen with Headmistress of Liberta School	60	1·10
863	$2.50 Queen greeted by Governor-General of Antigua	60	1·25
MS864	95×75 mm. $5 Queen Elizabeth in 1928 and 1986 (33×27 mm)	6·50	8·50

See also Nos. 872/5.

109 Halley's Comet over Barbuda Beach

1986. Appearance of Halley's Comet (1st issue). Multicoloured.

865	$1 Type **109**	60	1·25
866	$2.50 Early telescope and dish aerial (vert)	80	2·25
867	$5 Comet and world map	1·40	3·75

See also Nos. 886/9.

1986. 40th Anniv of United Nations Organization. Nos. 981/4 of Antigua optd **BARBUDA MAIL.**

868	40c. Benjamin Franklin and U.N. (New York) 1953 U.P.U. 5c. stamp	1·50	1·00
869	$1 George Washington Carver (agricultural chemist) and 1982 Nature Conservation 28c. stamp	2·25	2·25
870	$3 Charles Lindbergh (aviator) and 1978 I.C.A.O. 25c. stamp	4·00	5·00
MS871	101×77 mm. $5 Marc Chagell (artist) (vert)	13·00	14·00

1986. 60th Birthday of Queen Elizabeth II (2nd issue). Nos. 1005/8 of Antigua optd **BARBUDA MAIL.**

872	60c. black and yellow	2·50	1·25
873	$1 multicoloured	3·00	2·00
874	$4 multicoloured	4·75	4·50
MS875	120×85 mm. $5 black and brown	8·00	9·00

1986. World Cup Football Championship, Mexico. Nos. 995/9 of Antigua optd **BARBUDA MAIL.**

876	30c. Football, boots and trophy	4·00	1·00
877	60c. Goalkeeper (vert)	5·50	2·00
878	$1 Referee blowing whistle (vert)	6·00	2·25
879	$4 Ball in net	13·00	7·00
MS880	87×76 mm. $5 Two players competing for ball	24·00	15·00

1986. "Ameripex '86" International Stamp Exhibition, Chicago. Famous American Trains. Nos. 1014/18 of Antigua optd **BARBUDA MAIL.**

881	25c. *Hiawatha* express	2·00	1·50
882	50c. *Grand Canyon* express	2·75	2·25
883	$1 *Powhattan Arrow* express	3·50	3·00
884	$3 *Empire State* express	6·00	7·00
MS885	117×87 mm. $5 *Southern Pacific Daylight* express	9·00	9·50

1986. Appearance of Halley's Comet (2nd issue). Nos. 1000/4 of Antigua optd **BARBUDA MAIL.**

886	5c. Edmond Halley and Old Greenwich Observatory	2·75	1·00
887	10c. Messerschmitt Me 163B Komet (fighter aircraft), 1944	2·75	1·00
888	60c. Montezuma (Aztec Emperor) and Comet in 1517 (from "Historias de las Indias de Neuva Espana")	3·75	2·00
889	$4 Pocahontas saving Capt. John Smith and Comet in 1607	13·00	8·00
MS890	101×70 mm. $5 Halley's Comet over English Harbour, Antigua	7·00	5·00

1986. Royal Wedding. Nos. 1019/22 of Antigua optd **BARBUDA MAIL.**

891	45c. Prince Andrew and Miss Sarah Ferguson	75	50
892	60c. Prince Andrew	90	65
893	$4 Prince Andrew with Prince Philip	3·50	4·00
MS894	88×88 mm. $5 Prince Andrew and Miss Sarah Ferguson (different)	8·00	8·00

1986. Sea Shells. Nos. 1023/7 of Antigua optd **BARBUDA MAIL.**

895	15c. Fly-specked cerith	2·50	2·00
896	45c. Smooth Scotch bonnet	2·75	2·25
897	60c. West Indian crown conch	3·50	2·75
898	$3 Criboney murex	8·00	12·00
MS899	109×75 mm. $5 Colourful Atlantic moon (horiz)	20·00	18·00

1986. Flowers. Nos. 1028/36 of Antigua optd **BARBUDA MAIL.**

900	10c. Nymphaea ampla (water lily)	50	50
901	15c. Queen of the night	60	50
902	50c. Cup of gold	1·00	70
903	60c. Beach morning glory	1·10	70
904	70c. Golden trumpet	1·25	90
905	$1 Air plant	1·50	90
906	$3 Purple wreath	3·00	4·00
907	$4 Zephyr lily	3·50	4·25
MS908	Two sheets, each 102×72 mm. (a) $4 Dozakie. (b) $5 Four o'clock flower Set of 2 sheets	27·00	24·00

1986. Mushrooms. Nos. 1042/6 of Antigua optd **BARBUDA MAIL.**

909	10c. Hygrocybe occidentalis var scarletina	90	50
910	50c. Trogia buccinalis	3·25	1·75
911	$1 Collybia subpruinosa	4·75	2·75
912	$4 Leucocoprinus brebissonii	9·50	8·00
MS913	102×82 mm. $5 Pyrrhoglossum pyrrhum	27·00	18·00

1986. Birth Bicentenary of John J. Audubon (ornithologist) (3rd issue). Nos. 990/3 of Antigua optd **BARBUDA MAIL.**

914	60c. Mallard	7·50	2·50
915	90c. North American black duck ("Dusky Duck")	9·50	2·75
916	$1.50 American pintail ("Common Pintail")	13·00	8·50
917	$3 American wigeon ("Wigeon")	19·00	14·00

1987. Local Boats. Nos. 1009/13 of Antigua optd **BARBUDA MAIL.**

918	30c. Tugboat	1·50	1·50
919	60c. Game fishing boat	1·75	80
920	$1 Yacht	2·25	1·25
921	$4 Lugger with auxiliary sail	4·50	6·00
MS922	108×78 mm. $5 Boats under construction	24·00	17·00

1987. Centenary of First Benz Motor Car. Nos. 1052/60 of Antigua optd **BARBUDA MAIL.**

923	10c. Auburn "Speedster" (1933)	1·25	45
924	15c. Mercury "Sable" (1986)	1·50	50
925	50c. Cadillac (1959)	2·00	70
926	60c. Studebaker (1950)	2·00	70
927	70c. Lagonda "V-12" (1939)	2·25	1·00
928	$1 Adler "Standard" (1930)	2·50	1·00
929	$3 DKW (1956)	3·25	4·00
930	$4 Mercedes "500K" (1936)	3·25	4·00
MS931	Two sheets, each 99×70 mm. (a) $5 Daimler (1896). (b) $5 Mercedes "Knight" (1921) Set of 2 sheets	27·00	15·00

1987. World Cup Football Championship Winners, Mexico. Nos. 1037/40 of Antigua optd **BARBUDA MAIL.**

932	30c. Football, boots and trophy	4·50	1·00
933	60c. Goalkeeper (vert)	5·00	1·50
934	$1 Referee blowing whistle (vert)	6·00	2·25
935	$4 Ball in net	13·00	12·00

1987. America's Cup Yachting Championship. Nos. 1072/6 of Antigua optd **BARBUDA MAIL.**

936	30c. Canada I (1981)	90	40
937	60c. Gretel II (1970)	1·25	50
938	$1 Sceptre (1958)	1·60	80
939	$3 Vigilant (1893)	2·25	3·50
MS940	113×84 mm. $5 Australia II defeating Liberty (1983) (horiz)	4·75	5·00

1987. Marine Life. Nos. 1077/85 of Antigua optd **BARBUDA MAIL.**

941	15c. Bridled burrfish	7·00	1·50
942	30c. Common noddy ("Brown Noddy")	12·00	1·50
943	40c. Nassau grouper	9·00	1·50
944	50c. Laughing gull	14·00	2·25
945	60c. French angelfish	10·00	1·75
946	$1 Porkfish	10·00	2·50
947	$2 Royal tern	22·00	10·00
948	$3 Sooty tern	22·00	11·00
MS949	Two sheets, each 120×94 mm. (a) $5 Banded butterflyfish. (b) $5 Brown booby Set of 2 sheets	60·00	24·00

1987. Milestones of Transportation. Nos. 1100/9 of Antigua optd **BARBUDA MAIL.**

950	10c. Spirit of Australia (fastest powerboat), 1978	3·50	1·50
951	15c. Werner von Siemens's electric locomotive, 1879	4·50	1·25
952	30c. U.S.S. Triton (first submerged circumnavigation), 1960	4·50	1·25
953	50c. Trevithick's steam carriage (first passenger-carrying vehicle), 1801	5·00	2·00
954	60c. U.S.S. New Jersey (battleship), 1942	6·50	2·00
955	70c. Draisine bicycle, 1818	7·50	2·75
956	90c. United States (liner) (holder of the Blue Riband), 1952	7·50	2·25
957	$1.50 Cierva C.4 (first autogyro), 1923	7·50	7·00
958	$2 Curtiss NC-4 flying boat (first transatlantic flight), 1919	8·00	8·00
959	$3 Queen Elizabeth 2 (liner), 1969	12·00	10·00

110 Shore Crab

1987. Marine Life. Multicoloured.

960	5c. Type **110**	10	20
961	10c. Sea cucumber	10	20
962	15c. Stop-light parrotfish	10	20
963	25c. Banded coral shrimp	15	20
964	35c. Spotted drum	15	20
965	60c. Thorny starfish	20	40
966	75c. Atlantic trumpet triton	20	60
967	90c. Feather star and yellow beaker sponge	20	65
968	$1 Blue gorgonian (vert)	20	65
969	$1.25 Slender filefish (vert)	20	85
970	$5 Barred hamlet (vert)	45	3·50
971	$7.50 Royal gramma ("Fairy basslet") (vert)	60	4·50
972	$10 Fire coral and banded butterflyfish (vert)	75	5·00

1987. Olympic Games, Seoul (1988). Nos. 1086/90 of Antigua optd **BARBUDA MAIL.**

973	10c. Handball	1·00	50
974	60c. Fencing	2·25	80
975	$1 Gymnastics	2·75	1·40
976	$3 Football	4·50	5·50
MS977	100×77 mm. $5 Boxing gloves	9·00	4·75

1987. Birth Centenary of Marc Chagall (artist). Nos. 1091/9 of Antigua optd **BARBUDA MAIL.**

978	10c. The Profile	25	40
979	30c. Portrait of the Artist's Sister	35	20
980	40c. Bride with Fan	40	30
981	60c. David in Profile	45	30
982	90c. Fiancee with Bouquet	60	50
983	$1 Self Portrait with Brushes	70	55
984	$3 The Walk	2·00	2·50
985	$4 Three Candles	2·25	2·75
MS986	Two sheets, each 110×95 mm. (a) $5 Fall of Icarus (104×89 mm). (b) $5 Myth of Orpheus (104×89 mm) Set of 2 sheets	7·00	8·00

1987. Centenary (1986) of Statue of Liberty (2nd issue). Nos. 1110/19 of Antigua optd **BARBUDA MAIL.**

987	15c. Lee Iacocoa at unveiling of restored statue	20	20
988	30c. Statue at sunset (side view)	30	20
989	45c. Aerial view of head	45	25
990	50c. Lee Iacocoa and torch	50	30
991	60c. Workmen inside head of statue (horiz)	55	30
992	90c. Restoration work (horiz)	70	50
993	$1 Head of statue	80	75
994	$2 Statue at sunset (front view)	1·25	1·75
995	$3 Inspecting restoration work (horiz)	1·60	2·50
996	$5 Statue at night	2·50	3·50

1987. Entertainers. Nos. 1120/7 of Antigua optd **BARBUDA MAIL.**

997	15c. Grace Kelly	2·00	70
998	30c. Marilyn Monroe	5·00	1·25
999	45c. Orson Welles	2·00	75
1000	50c. Judy Garland	2·00	1·00
1001	60c. John Lennon	15·00	2·50
1002	$1 Rock Hudson	2·75	1·75
1003	$1 John Wayne	4·50	3·50
1004	$3 Elvis Presley	26·00	11·00

1987. "Capex '87" International Stamp Exhibition, Toronto. Reptiles and Amphibians. Nos. 1133/7 of Antigua optd **BARBUDA MAIL.**

1005	30c. Whistling frog	7·00	2·00
1006	60c. Croaking lizard	8·00	2·00
1007	$1 Antiguan anole	9·00	3·00
1008	$3 Red-footed tortoise	18·00	17·00
MS1009	106×76 mm. $5 Ground lizard	30·00	12·00

1988. Christmas. Religious Paintings. Nos. 1144/8 of Antigua optd **BARBUDA MAIL.**

1010	45c. Madonna and Child (Bernardo Daddi)	2·00	30
1011	60c. St. Joseph (detail, The Nativity (Sano di Pietro))	2·00	55
1012	$1 Virgin Mary (detail, The Nativity (Sano di Pietro))	2·25	1·25
1013	$4 Music-making Angel (Melozzo da Forli)	6·50	8·50
MS1014	90×70 mm. $5 The Flight into Egypt (Sano di Pietro)	9·00	6·50

1988. Salvation Army's Community Service. Nos. 1163/71 of Antigua optd **BARBUDA MAIL.**

1015	25c. First aid at daycare centre, Antigua	2·25	1·00
1016	30c. Giving penicillin injection, Indonesia	2·25	1·00
1017	40c. Children at daycare centre, Bolivia	2·25	1·00
1018	45c. Rehabilitation of the handicapped, India	2·25	1·00
1019	50c. Training blind man, Kenya	2·75	1·50
1020	60c. Weighing baby, Ghana	2·75	1·50
1021	$1 Training typist, Zambia	3·25	2·50
1022	$2 Emergency food kitchen, Sri Lanka	3·75	4·00
MS1023	152×83 mm. $5 General Eva Burrows	28·00	25·00

1988. Bicentenary of U.S. Constitution. Nos. 1139/43 of Antigua optd **BARBUDA MAIL.**

1024	15c. House of Burgesses, Virginia ("Freedom of Speech")	10	15
1025	45c. State Seal, Connecticut	20	25
1026	60c. State Seal, Delaware	25	40
1027	$4 Gouverneur Morris (Pennsylvania delegate) (vert)	1·75	3·25
MS1028	105×75 mm. $5 Roger Sherman (Connecticut delegate) (vert)	2·75	3·25

1988. Royal Ruby Wedding. Nos. 1149/53 of Antigua optd **BARBUDA MAIL.**

1029	25c. brown, black and blue	2·75	40
1030	60c. multicoloured	3·25	65
1031	$2 brown, black and green	7·00	2·50
1032	$3 multicoloured	8·00	3·00
MS1033	102×77 mm. $5 multicoloured	17·00	6·50

1988. Birds of Antigua. Nos. 1154/62 of Antigua optd **BARBUDA MAIL.**

1034	10c. Great blue heron	4·00	1·75
1035	15c. Ringed kingfisher (horiz)	4·25	1·75
1036	50c. Bananaquit (horiz)	6·00	1·75
1037	60c. American purple gallinule ("Purple Gallinule") (horiz)	6·00	1·75
1038	70c. Blue-hooded euphonia (horiz)	6·50	2·75
1039	$1 Brown-throated concure ("Caribbean Parakeet") (horiz)	7·50	2·75
1040	$3 Troupial (horiz)	13·00	8·50
1041	$4 Purple-throated carib (horiz)	13·00	8·50
MS1042	Two sheets, each 115×86 mm. (a) $5 Greater flamingo. (b) $5 Brown pelican Set of 2 sheets	40·00	19·00

1988. 500th Anniv (1992) of Discovery of America by Columbus (1st issue). Nos. 1172/80 of Antigua optd **BARBUDA MAIL.**

1043	10c. Columbus's second fleet, 1493	3·50	80
1044	30c. Painos Indian village and fleet	3·50	80
1045	45c. Santa Mariagalante (flagship) and Painos village	4·25	80
1046	60c. Painos Indians offering Columbus fruit and vegetables	3·00	85
1047	90c. Painos Indian and Columbus with scarlet macaw	7·50	1·75
1048	$1 Columbus landing on island	6·00	1·75
1049	$3 Spanish soldier and fleet	7·50	4·50
1050	$4 Fleet under sail	7·50	4·50
MS1051	Two sheets, each 110×80 mm. (a) $5 Queen Isabella's cross. (b) $5 Gold coin of Ferdinand and Isabella Set of 2 sheets	20·00	14·00

See also Nos. 1112/16, 1177/85, 1285/93, 1374/80 and 1381/2.

1988. 500th Birth Anniv of Titian. Nos. 1181/9 of Antigua optd **BARBUDA MAIL.**

1052	30c. Bust of Christ	1·00	20
1053	40c. Scourging of Christ	1·25	25
1054	45c. Madonna in Glory with Saints	1·25	25
1055	50c. The Averoldi Polyptych (detail)	1·40	30
1056	$1 Christ Crowned with Thorns	2·00	50
1057	$2 Christ Mocked	2·75	1·50
1058	$3 Christ and Simon of Cyrene	3·25	2·75
1059	$4 Crucifixion with Virgin and Saints	3·25	3·00
MS1060	Two sheets, each 110×95 mm. (a) $5 Ecce Homo (detail). (b) $5 Noli me Tangere (detail) Set of 2 sheets	11·00	8·00

1988. 16th World Scout Jamboree, Australia. Nos. 1128/32 of Antigua optd **BARBUDA MAIL.**

1061	10c. Scouts around campfire and red kangaroo	2·50	1·00
1062	60c. Scouts canoeing and blue-winged kookaburra	8·50	1·50
1063	$1 Scouts on assault course and ring-tailed rock wallaby	4·00	1·75
1064	$3 Field kitchen and koala	7·50	6·50
MS1065	103×78 mm. $5 Flags of Antigua, Australia and Scout Movement	10·00	6·50

1988. Sailing Week. Nos. 1190/4 of Antigua optd **BARBUDA MAIL.**

1066	30c. Two yachts rounding buoy	60	35
1067	60c. Three yachts	1·00	70
1068	$1 British yacht under way	1·25	1·10
1069	$3 Three yachts (different)	2·25	2·75
MS1070	103×92 mm. $5 Two yachts	7·50	4·50

1988. Flowering Trees. Nos. 1213/21 of Antigua optd **BARBUDA MAIL.**

1071	10c. Jacaranda	15	20
1072	30c. Cordia	30	20
1073	50c. Orchid tree	40	25
1074	90c. Flamboyant	60	45
1075	$1 African tulip tree	70	60
1076	$2 Potato tree	1·25	1·50
1077	$3 Crepe myrtle	1·50	2·00
1078	$4 Pitch apple	1·75	2·50
MS1079	Two sheets, each 106×76 mm. (a) $5 Cassia. (b) $5 Chinaberry Set of 2 sheets	6·00	6·50

1988. Olympic Games, Seoul. Nos. 1222/6 of Antigua optd **BARBUDA MAIL.**

1080	40c. Gymnastics	1·50	40
1081	60c. Weightlifting	1·75	55
1082	$1 Water polo (horiz)	2·00	1·00
1083	$3 Boxing (horiz)	2·75	3·00
MS1084	114×80 mm. $5 Runner with Olympic torch	3·00	2·40

1988. Caribbean Butterflies. Nos. 1227/44 of Antigua optd **BARBUDA MAIL.**

1085	1c. Danaus plexippus	50	1·00
1086	2c. Greta diaphanus	50	1·00
1087	3c. Calisto archebates	60	1·00
1088	5c. Hamadryas feronia	60	1·00
1089	10c. Mestra dorcas	75	1·00
1090	15c. Hypolimnas misippus	1·00	60
1091	20c. Dione juno	1·25	60
1092	25c. Heliconius charithonia	1·25	60
1093	30c. Eurema pyro	1·25	60
1094	40c. Papilio androgeus	1·50	60
1095	45c. Anteos maerula	1·50	60
1096	50c. Aphrissa orbis	1·75	85
1097	60c. Astraptes xagua	1·75	70
1098	$1 Heliopetes arsalte	2·50	1·00
1099	$2 Polites baracoa	4·25	4·50
1100	$2.50 Phocides pigmalion	4·50	4·75
1101	$5 Prepona amphitoe	6·00	7·00
1102	$10 Oarisma nanus	9·00	10·00
1102a	$20 Parides lycimenes	16·00	17·00

1989. 25th Death Anniv of John F. Kennedy (American statesman). Nos. 1245/53 of Antigua optd **BARBUDA MAIL.**

1103	1c. President Kennedy and family	10	75
1104	2c. Kennedy commanding PT109	10	75
1105	3c. Funeral cortege	10	75
1106	4c. In motorcade, Mexico	10	75
1107	30c. As 1c.	1·50	50
1108	60c. As 4c.	3·50	60
1109	$1 As 3c.	3·50	1·50
1110	$4 As 2c.	9·00	11·00
MS1111	105×75 mm. $5 Kennedy taking presidential oath of office	4·50	6·00

1989. 500th Anniv (1992) of Discovery of America by Columbus (2nd issue). Pre-Columbian Arawak Society. Nos. 1267/71 of Antigua optd **BARBUDA MAIL.**

1112	$1.50 Arawak warriors	4·50	4·50
1113	$1.50 Whip dancers	4·50	4·50
1114	$1.50 Whip dancers and chief with pineapple	4·50	4·50
1115	$1.50 Family and camp fire	4·50	4·50
MS1116	71×84 mm. $6 Arawak chief	5·50	6·50

1989. 50th Anniv of First Jet Flight. Nos. 1272/80 of Antigua optd **BARBUDA MAIL**.

1117	10c. Hawker Siddeley Comet 4 airliner	3·50	2·00
1118	30c. Messerschmitt Me 262 fighter	4·50	1·50
1119	40c. Boeing 707 airliner	4·75	2·25
1120	60c. Canadair CL-13 Sabre fighter	6·00	1·25
1121	$1 Lockheed Starfighters	7·00	2·50
1122	$2 Douglas DC-10 airliner	9·00	8·00
1123	$3 Boeing 747-300/400 airliner	10·00	11·00
1124	$4 McDonnell Douglas Phantom II fighter	10·00	11·00

MS1125 Two sheets, each 114×83 mm. (a) $7 Grumman F-14 Tomcat fighter. (b) $7 Concorde airliner Set of 2 sheets 55·00 40·00

1989. Caribbean Cruise Ships. Nos. 1281/9 of Antigua optd **BARBUDA MAIL**.

1126	25c. *Festivale*	4·00	1·50
1127	45c. *Southward*	4·25	1·50
1128	50c. *Sagafjord*	4·25	1·75
1129	60c. *Daphne*	4·25	1·75
1130	75c. *Cunard Countess*	4·50	2·75
1131	90c. *Song of America*	4·50	2·75
1132	$3 *Island Princess*	12·00	10·00
1133	$4 *Galileo*	12·00	10·00

MS1134 (a) 113×87 mm. $6 *Norway*. (b) 111×82 mm. $6 *Oceanic* Set of 2 sheets 55·00 38·00

1989. Japanese Art. Paintings by Hiroshige. Nos. 1290/8 of Antigua optd **BARBUDA MAIL**.

1135	25c. *Fish swimming by Duck half-submerged in Stream*	4·50	1·00
1136	45c. *Crane and Wave*	5·50	1·00
1137	50c. *Sparrows and Morning Glories*	5·50	1·50
1138	60c. *Crested Blackbird and Flowering Cherry*	5·50	1·50
1139	$1 *Great Knot sitting among Water Grass*	6·50	1·75
1140	$2 *Goose on a Bank of Water*	8·50	4·25
1141	$3 *"Black Paradise Fly-catcher and Blossoms*	10·00	5·00
1142	$4 *Sleepy Owl perched on a Pine Branch*	11·00	5·50

MS1143 Two sheets, each 102×75 mm. (a) $5 *Bullfinch flying near a Clematis Branch*. (b) $5 *Titmouse on a Cherry Branch* Set of 2 sheets 50·00 23·00

1989. World Cup Football Championship, Italy (1990). Nos. 1308/12 of Antigua optd **BARBUDA MAIL**.

1144	15c. Goalkeeper	2·00	65
1145	25c. Goalkeeper moving towards ball	2·00	65
1146	$1 Goalkeeper reaching for ball	5·00	2·00
1147	$4 Goalkeeper saving goal	8·00	10·00

MS1148 Two sheets, each 75×105 mm. (a) $5 Three players competing for ball (horiz). (b) $5 Ball and players' legs (horiz) Set of 2 sheets 38·00 32·00

1989. Christmas. Paintings by Raphael and Giotto. Nos. 1351/9 of Antigua optd **BARBUDA MAIL**.

1149	10c. *The Small Cowper Madonna* (Raphael)	40	30
1150	25c. *Madonna of the Goldfinch* (Raphael)	50	20
1151	30c. *The Alba Madonna* (Raphael)	50	20
1152	50c. *Saint* (detail, *Bologna Altarpiece*) (Giotto)	80	30
1153	60c. *Angel* (detail, *Bologna Altarpiece*) (Giotto)	85	45
1154	70c. *Angel slaying serpent* (detail, *Bologna Altarpiece*) (Giotto)	90	60
1155	$4 *Evangelist* (detail, *Bologna Altarpiece*) (Giotto)	3·00	4·50
1156	$5 *Madonna of Foligno* (Raphael)	3·00	4·50

MS1157 wo sheets, each 71×96 mm. (a) $5 *"The Marriage of the Virgin* (detail) (Raphael). (b) $5 Madonna and Child (detail, *Bologna Altarpiece*) (Giotto) Set of 2 sheets 13·00 15·00

1990. Fungi. Nos. 1313/21 of Antigua optd **BARBUDA MAIL**.

1158	10c. *Mycena pura*	2·50	1·50
1159	25c. *Psathyrella turberculata* (vert)	2·75	65
1160	50c. *Psilocybe cubenis*	3·25	1·00
1161	60c. *Leptonia caeruleocapitata* (vert)	3·25	1·00
1162	75c. *Xeromphalina tenuipes* (vert)	3·25	1·40
1163	$1 *Chlorophyllum molybdites* (vert)	3·50	1·40
1164	$3 *Marasmius haematocephalus*	6·00	7·50
1165	$4 *Cantharellus cinnabarinus*	6·00	7·50

MS1166 Two sheets, each 88×62 mm. (a) $6 *Leucopaxillus gracillimus* (vert). (b) $6 *Volvariella volvacea* Set of 2 sheets 38·00 23·00

1990. Local Fauna. Nos. 1322/6 optd **BARBUDA MAIL**.

1167	25c. Desmarest's hutia	1·00	60
1168	45c. Caribbean monk seal	2·50	1·25

1169	60c. Mustache bat (vert)	1·75	1·25
1170	$4 American manatee (vert)	4·25	6·50

MS1171 113×87 mm. $5 West Indian giant rice rat 22·00 22·00

1990. 20th Anniv of First Manned Landing on Moon. Nos. 1346/50 optd **BARBUDA MAIL**.

1172	10c. Launch of "Apollo 11"	3·25	1·50
1173	45c. Aldrin on Moon	6·00	80
1174	$1 Module "Eagle" over Moon (horiz)	7·50	2·75
1175	$4 Recovery of "Apollo 11" crew after splashdown (horiz)	13·00	13·00

MS1176 107×77 mm. $5 Astronaut Neil Armstrong 24·00 23·00

1990. 500th Anniv (1992) of Discovery of America by Columbus (3rd issue). New World Natural History – Marine Life. Nos. 1360/8 of Antigua optd **BARBUDA MAIL**.

1177	10c. Star-eyed hermit crab	1·75	1·75
1178	20c. Spiny lobster	2·25	1·25
1179	25c. Magnificent banded fanworm	2·25	1·75
1180	45c. Cannonball jellyfish	3·25	1·00
1181	60c. Red-spiny sea star	3·50	1·00
1182	$2 Peppermint shrimp	4·75	5·00
1183	$3 Coral crab	5·00	6·00
1184	$4 Branching fire coral	5·00	6·00

MS1185 Two sheets, each 101×69 mm. (a) $5 Common sea fan. (b) $5 Portuguese man-o-war Set of 2 sheets 28·00 27·00

1990. "EXPO 90" International Gardens and Greenery Exhibition, Osaka. Orchids. Nos. 1369/77 of Antigua optd **BARBUDA MAIL**.

1186	15c. *Vanilla mexicana*	2·00	80
1187	45c. *Epidendrum ibaguense*	2·50	80
1188	50c. *Epidendrum secundum*	2·50	90
1189	60c. *Maxillaria conferta*	2·75	1·10
1190	$1 *Onicidium altissimum*	3·00	1·75
1191	$2 *Spiranthes lanceolata*	5·00	5·00
1192	$3 *Tonopsis utricularioides*	5·50	6·50
1193	$5 *Epidendrum nocturnum*	7·00	8·50

MS1194 Two sheets, each 101×69 mm. (a) $6 *Octomeria graminifolia*. (b) $6 *Rodriguezia lanceolata* Set of 2 sheets 38·00 23·00

1990. Reef Fishes. Nos. 1386/94 of Antigua optd **BARBUDA MAIL**.

1195	10c. Flamefish	2·50	1·75
1196	15c. Coney	2·50	1·75
1197	50c. Long-spined squirrelfish	3·50	1·50
1198	60c. Sergeant major	3·50	1·50
1199	$1 Yellow-tailed snapper	4·25	2·50
1200	$2 Rock beauty	7·00	7·00
1201	$3 Spanish hogfish	9·00	10·00
1202	$4 Striped parrotfish	9·00	10·00

MS1203 Two sheets, each 99×70 mm. (a) $5 Black-barred soldierfish. (b) $5 Four-eyed butterflyfish Set of 2 sheets 38·00 32·00

1990. First Anniv of Hurricane Hugo. Nos. 971/2 surch **1st Anniversary Hurricane Hugo 16th September, 1989-1990** and new value.

1204	$5 on $7.50 Fairy basslet (vert)	12·00	15·00
1205	$7.50 on $10 on $10 Fire coral and butterfly fish (vert)	13·00	17·00

1990. 90th Birthday of Queen Elizabeth the Queen Mother. Nos. 1415/19 of Antigua optd **BARBUDA MAIL**.

1206	15c. multicoloured	8·00	1·75
1207	35c. multicoloured	11·00	1·50
1208	75c. multicoloured	17·00	3·25
1209	$3 multicoloured	30·00	19·00

MS1210 67×98 mm. $6 multicoloured 55·00 26·00

1990. Achievements in Space. Nos. 1395/414 of Antigua optd **BARBUDA MAIL**.

1211	45c. "Voyager 2" passing Saturn	3·75	3·25
1212	45c. "Pioneer 11" photographing Saturn	3·75	3·25
1213	45c. Astronaut in transporter	3·75	3·25
1214	45c. Space shuttle *Columbia*	3·75	3·25
1215	45c. "Apollo 10" command module on parachutes	3·75	3·25
1216	45c. "Skylab" space station	3·75	3·25
1217	45c. Astronaut Edward White in space	3·75	3·25
1218	45c. "Apollo" spacecraft on joint mission	3·75	3·25
1219	45c. "Soyuz" spacecraft on joint mission	3·75	3·25
1220	45c. "Mariner 1" passing Venus	3·75	3·25
1221	45c. "Gemini 4" capsule	3·75	3·25
1222	45c. "Sputnik 1"	3·75	3·25
1223	45c. Hubble space telescope	3·75	3·25
1224	45c. North American X-15 rocket plane	3·75	3·25
1225	45c. Bell XS-1 airplane	3·75	3·25
1226	45c. "Apollo 17" astronaut and lunar rock formation	3·75	3·25
1227	45c. Lunar rover	3·75	3·25
1228	45c. "Apollo 14" lunar module	3·75	3·25
1229	45c. Astronaut Buzz Aldrin on Moon	3·75	3·25

1230	45c. Soviet "Lunokhod" lunar vehicle	3·75	3·25

1990. Christmas. Paintings by Renaissance Masters. Nos. 1457/65 of Antigua optd **BARBUDA MAIL**.

1231	25c. *Madonna and Child with Saints* (detail, Sebastiano del Piombo)	2·25	60
1232	30c. *Virgin and Child with Angels* (detail, Grunewald) (vert)	2·25	60
1233	40c. *The Holy Family and a Shepherd* (detail, Titian)	2·25	60
1234	60c. *Virgin and Child* (detail, Lippi) (vert)	3·00	1·10
1235	$1 *Jesus, St. John and Two Angels* (Rubens)	3·75	3·25
1236	$2 *Adoration of the Shepherds* (detail, Vincenzo Catena)	5·50	6·00
1237	$4 *Adoration of the Magi* (detail, Giorgione)	8·50	9·50
1238	$5 *Virgin and Child adored by Warriors* (detail, Vincenzo Catena)	8·50	9·50

MS1239 Two sheets, each 71×101 mm. (a) $6 *Allegory of the Blessings of Jacob* (detail, Rubens) (vert). (b) $6 *Adoration of the Magi* (detail, Fra Angelico) (vert) Set of 2 sheets 27·00 28·00

1991. 150th Anniv of the Penny Black. Nos. 1378/81 of Antigua optd **BARBUDA MAIL**.

1240	45c. green	5·00	5·00
1241	60c. mauve	5·00	1·10
1242	$5 blue	15·00	15·00

MS1243 102×80 mm. $6 purple 20·00 15·00

1991. "Stamp World London 90" International Stamp Exhibition. Nos. 1382/4 of Antigua optd **BARBUDA MAIL**.

1244	50c. green and red	5·00	1·00
1245	75c. brown and red	5·00	1·50
1246	$4 blue and red	15·00	15·00

MS1247 104×81 mm. $6 black and red 22·00 23·00

BARBUDA

60c

119 Troupial

1991. Wild Birds. Multicoloured.

1248	60c. Type **119**	2·25	65
1249	$2 Adelaide's warbler ("Christmas Bird")	3·75	3·00
1250	$4 Rose-breasted grosbeak	5·50	6·50
1251	$7 Wied's crested flycatcher ("Stolid Flycatcher")	7·50	11·00

1991. Olympic Games, Barcelona (1992). Nos. 1429/33 of Antigua optd **BARBUDA MAIL**.

1252	50c. Men's 20 kilometres walk	2·75	90
1253	75c. Triple jump	3·00	1·00
1254	$1 Men's 10,000 metres	3·25	1·75
1255	$5 Javelin	12·00	14·00

MS1256 100×70 mm. $6 Athlete lighting Olympic flame at Los Angeles Olympics 16·00 18·00

1991. Birds. Nos. 1448/56 of Antigua optd **BARBUDA MAIL**.

1257	10c. Pearly-eyed thrasher	3·00	1·75
1258	25c. Purple-throated carib	4·00	1·00
1259	50c. Common yellowthroat	5·00	1·25
1260	60c. American kestrel	5·00	1·25
1261	$1 Yellow-bellied sapsucker	5·50	2·00
1262	$2 American purple gallinule ("Purple Gallinule")	7·50	7·00
1263	$3 Yellow-crowned night heron	8·00	9·00
1264	$4 Blue-hooded euphonia	8·00	9·00

MS1265 Two sheets, each 76×60 mm. (a) $6 Brown pelican. (b) Magnificent frigate bird Set of 2 sheets 32·00 25·00

1991. 350th Death Anniv of Rubens. Nos. 1466/74 of Antigua optd **BARBUDA MAIL**.

1266	25c. *Rape of the Daughters of Leucippus* (detail)	2·50	80
1267	45c. *Bacchanal* (detail)	3·00	80
1268	50c. *Rape of the Sabine Women* (detail)	3·00	85
1269	60c. *Battle of the Amazons* (detail)	3·25	90
1270	$1 *Rape of the Sabine Women* (different detail)	3·75	1·75
1271	$2 *Bacchanal* (different detail)	6·00	6·50
1272	$3 *Rape of the Sabine Women* (different detail)	8·50	10·00
1273	$4 *Bacchanal* (different detail)	8·50	10·00

MS1274 Two sheets, each 111×71 mm. (a) $6 *Rape of Hippodameia* (detail). (b) *Battle of the Amazons* (different detail) Set of 2 sheets 30·00 32·00

1991. 50th Anniv of Second World War. Nos. 1475/88 of Antigua optd **BARBUDA MAIL**.

1275	10c. U.S. troops cross into Germany, 1944	3·25	2·25
1276	15c. Axis surrender in North Africa, 1943	3·75	2·00
1277	25c. U.S. tanks invade Kwala-jalein, 1944	4·00	1·50
1278	45c. Roosevelt and Churchill meet at Casablanca, 1943	12·00	2·50
1279	50c. Marshall Badoglio, Prime Minister of Italian anti-facist government, 1943	3·75	1·75
1280	$1 Lord Mountbatten, Supreme Allied Commander South-east Asia, 1943	15·00	4·75
1281	$2 Greek victory at Koritza, 1940	10·00	10·00
1282	$4 Anglo-Soviet mutual assistance pact, 1941	12·00	13·00
1283	$5 Operation Torch landings, 1942	13·00	13·00

MS1284 Two sheets, each 108×80 mm. (a) $6 Japanese attack on Pearl Harbor, 1941. (b) $6 U.S.A.A.F. daylight raid on Schweinfurt, 1943 Set of 2 sheets 60·00 40·00

1991. 500th Anniv (1992) of Discovery of America by Columbus (4th issue). History of Exploration. Nos. 1503/11 of Antigua optd **BARBUDA MAIL**.

1285	10c. multicoloured	2·25	2·00
1286	15c. multicoloured	2·50	2·00
1287	45c. multicoloured	3·50	1·00
1288	60c. multicoloured	3·75	1·25
1289	$1 multicoloured	4·00	2·00
1290	$2 multicoloured	6·50	6·00
1291	$4 multicoloured	10·00	11·00
1292	$5 multicoloured	10·00	11·00

MS1293 Two sheets, each 106×76 mm. (a) $6 black and red. (b) $6 black and red Set of 2 sheets 35·00 28·00

1991. Butterflies. Nos. 1494/502 of Antigua optd **BARBUDA MAIL**.

1294	10c. *Heliconius charithonia*	3·25	2·25
1295	35c. *Marpesia petreus*	4·50	1·25
1296	50c. *Anartia amathea*	5·00	1·40
1297	75c. *Siproeta stelenes*	6·00	2·25
1298	$1 *Battus polydamas*	6·00	2·50
1299	$2 *Historis odius*	9·00	8·50
1300	$4 *Hypolimnas misippus*	11·00	12·00
1301	$5 *Hamadryas feronia*	11·00	12·00

MS1302 Two sheets. (a) 73×100 mm. $6 *Vanessa cardui* (caterpillar) (vert). (b) 100×73 mm. $6 *Danaus plexippus* (caterpillar) (vert) Set of 2 sheets 40·00 35·00

1991. 65th Birthday of Queen Elizabeth II. Nos. 1534/8 of Antigua optd **BARBUDA MAIL**.

1303	15c. Queen Elizabeth and Prince Philip in 1976	6·00	1·50
1304	20c. The Queen and Prince Philip in Portugal, 1985	6·00	1·00
1305	$2 Queen Elizabeth II	17·00	8·00
1306	$4 The Queen and Prince Philip at Ascot, 1986	26·00	17·00

MS1307 68×90 mm. $4 The Queen at National Theatre, 1986 and Prince Philip 50·00 20·00

1991. Tenth Wedding Anniv of Prince and Princess of Wales. Nos. 1539/43 of Antigua optd **BARBUDA MAIL**.

1308	10c. Prince and Princess of Wales at party, 1986	5·50	2·50
1309	40c. Separate portraits of Prince, Princess and sons	11·00	1·75
1310	$1 Prince Henry and Prince William	13·00	4·50
1311	$5 Princess Diana in Australia and Prince Charles in Hungary	27·00	19·00

MS1312 68×90 mm. $4 Prince Charles in Hackney and Princess and sons in Majorca, 1987 50·00 20·00

1991. Christmas. Religious Paintings by Fra Angelico. Nos. 1595/1602 of Antigua optd **BARBUDA MAIL**.

1313	10c. *The Annunciation*	2·50	1·50
1314	30c. *Nativity*	3·00	70
1315	40c. *Adoration of the Magi*	3·00	70
1316	60c. *Presentation in the Temple*	3·75	70
1317	$1 *Circumcision*	5·00	1·75
1318	$3 *Flight into Egypt*	8·50	9·00
1319	$4 *Massacre of the Innocents*	8·50	10·00
1320	$5 *Christ teaching in the Temple*	8·50	10·00

1992. Death Centenary (1990) of Vincent van Gogh (artist). Nos. 1512/24 of Antigua optd **BARBUDA MAIL**.

1321	5c. *Camille Roulin*	2·00	2·00
1322	10c. *Armand Roulin*	2·25	2·00
1323	15c. *Young Peasant Woman with Straw Hat sitting in the Wheat*	2·50	2·00
1324	25c. *Adeline Ravoux*	2·50	2·00
1325	30c. *The Schoolboy*	2·50	1·25
1326	40c. *Doctor Gachet*	2·75	1·50
1327	50c. *Portrait of a Man*	2·75	1·75
1328	75c. *Two Children*	4·25	2·25
1329	$2 *The Postman Joseph Roulin*	8·00	7·50
1330	$3 *The Seated Zouave*	9·00	9·00

1331	$4 *L'Arlesienne*	9·50	10·00
1332	$5 *Self-Portrait, November/December 1888*	9·50	10·00

MS1333 Three sheets, each 102×76 mm. (a) $5 *Farmhouse in Provence* (horiz). (b) $5 *Flowering Garden* (horiz). (c) $6 *The Bridge at Trinquetaille* (horiz). Imperf Set of 3 sheets 45·00 42·00

1992. Birth Centenary of Charles de Gaulle (French statesman). Nos. 1562/70 of Antigua optd **BARBUDA MAIL**.

1334	10c. Pres. De Gaulle and Kennedy, 1961	3·00	2·00
1335	15c. General De Gaulle with Pres. Roosevelt, 1945 (vert)	3·00	2·00
1336	45c. President De Gaulle with Chancellor Adenauer, 1962 (vert)	3·75	80
1337	60c. De Gaulle at Arc de Triomphe, Liberation of Paris, 1944 (vert)	4·00	1·00
1338	$1 General De Gaulle crossing the Rhine, 1945	4·75	2·25
1339	$2 General De Gaulle in Algiers, 1944	8·00	8·00
1340	$4 Presidents De Gaulle and Eisenhower, 1960	10·00	13·00
1341	$5 De Gaulle returning from Germany, 1968 (vert)	10·00	13·00

MS1342 Two sheets. (a) 76×106 mm. $6 De Gaulle with crowd. (b) 106×76 mm. $6 De Gaulle and Churchill at Casablanca, 1943 Set of 2 sheets 42·00 35·00

1992. Easter. Religious Paintings. Nos. 1627/35 of Antigua optd **BARBUDA MAIL**.

1343	10c. *Supper at Emmaus* (Caravaggio)	1·75	1·50
1344	15c. *The Vision of St. Peter* (Zurbaran)	2·00	1·50
1345	30c. *Christ driving the Money-changers from the Temple* (Tiepolo)	2·25	80
1346	40c. *Martyrdom of St. Bartholomew* (detail) (Ribera)	2·25	80
1347	$1 *Christ driving the Money-changers from the Temple* (detail) (Tiepolo)	4·00	2·25
1348	$2 *Crucifixion* (detail) (Altdorfer)	6·00	6·50
1349	$4 *The Deposition* (detail) (Fra Angelico)	8·50	10·00
1350	$5 *The Deposition* (different detail) (Fra Angelico)	8·50	10·00

MS1351 Two sheets. (a) 102×71 mm. $6 *The Last Supper* (detail) (Masip). (b) 71×102 mm. $6 *Crucifixion* (detail) (vert) (Altdorfer) Set of 2 sheets 30·00 27·00

1992. Anniversaries and Events. Nos. 1573/83 of Antigua optd **BARBUDA MAIL**.

1352	25c. Germans celebrating Reunification	1·00	70
1353	75c. Cubs erecting tent	2·25	1·50
1354	$1.50 *Don Giovanni* and Mozart	12·00	4·25
1355	$2 Chariot driver and Gate at night	3·00	3·50
1356	$2 Lord Baden-Powell and members of the 3rd Antigua Methodist cub pack (vert)	3·00	3·50
1357	$2 Lilienthal's signature and glider *Flugzeug Nr. 5*	3·00	3·50
1358	$2.50 Driver in Class P36 steam locomotive (vert)	9·00	4·50
1359	$3 Statues from podium	3·00	4·50
1360	$3.50 Cubs and campfire	4·50	5·50
1361	$4 St. Peter's Cathedral, Salzburg	15·00	11·00

MS1362 Two sheets. (a) 100×72 mm. $4 Detail of chariot and helmet. (b) 89×117 mm. $5 Antiguan flag and Jamboree emblem (vert) Set of 2 sheets 45·00 35·00

1992. 50th Anniv of Japanese Attack on Pearl Harbor. Nos. 1585/94 of Antigua optd **BARBUDA MAIL**.

1364	$1 *Nimitz* class carrier and *Ticonderoga* class cruiser	7·00	4·00
1365	$1 Tourist launch	7·00	4·00
1366	$1 U.S.S. *Arizona* memorial	7·00	4·00
1367	$1 Wreaths on water and aircraft	7·00	4·00
1368	$1 White tern	7·00	4·00
1369	$1 Japanese torpedo bombers over Pearl City	7·00	4·00
1370	$1 Zeros attacking	7·00	4·00
1371	$1 Battleship Row in flames	7·00	4·00
1372	$1 U.S.S. *Nevada* (battleship) underway	7·00	4·00
1373	$1 Zeros returning to carriers	7·00	4·00

1992. 500th Anniv of Discovery of America by Columbus (5th issue). World Columbian Stamp "Expo '92", Chicago. Nos. 1654/60 of Antigua optd **BARBUDA MAIL**.

1374	15c. Memorial cross and huts, San Salvador	1·25	1·25
1375	30c. Martin Pinzon with telescope	1·50	90
1376	40c. Christopher Columbus	2·50	1·00
1377	$1 *Pinta*	7·00	3·00
1378	$2 *Nina*	9·00	8·00
1379	$4 *Santa Maria*	13·00	15·00

MS1380 Two sheets, each 108×76 mm. (a) $6 Ship and map of West Indies. (b) $6 Sea monster Set of 2 sheets 35·00 38·00

1992. 500th Anniv of Discovery of America by Columbus (6th issue). Organization of East Caribbean States. Nos. 1670/1 of Antigua optd **BARBUDA MAIL**.

1381	$1 Columbus meeting Amerindians	8·50	2·50
1382	$2 Ships approaching island	8·50	9·50

1992. Postage Stamp Mega Event, New York. No. MS1690 of Antigua optd **BARBUDA MAIL**.

MS1383 $6 multicoloured 15·00 17·00

1992. 40th Anniv of Queen Elizabeth II's Accession. Nos. 1604/8 of Antigua optd **BARBUDA MAIL**.

1384	10c. Queen Elizabeth II and bird sanctuary	8·00	2·25
1385	30c. Nelson's Dockyard	9·00	1·25
1386	$1 Ruins on Shirley Heights	13·00	2·75
1387	$5 Beach and palm trees	26·00	17·00

MS1388 Two sheets, each 75×98 mm. (a) $6 Beach. (b) $6 Hillside foliage Set of 2 sheets 55·00 29·00

1992. Prehistoric Animals. Nos. 1618/26 of Antigua optd **BARBUDA MAIL**.

1389	10c. Pteranodon	2·25	2·00
1390	15c. Brachiosaurus	2·75	2·00
1391	30c. Tyrannosaurus Rex	3·25	1·50
1392	50c. Parasaurolophus	3·25	2·50
1393	$1 Deinonychus (horiz)	4·00	2·50
1394	$2 Triceratops (horiz)	6·50	6·00
1395	$4 Protoceratops hatching (horiz)	7·50	9·50
1396	$5 Stegosaurus (horiz)	7·50	9·50

MS1397 Two sheets, each 100×70 mm. (a) $6 Apatosaurus (horiz). (b) $6 Allosaurus (horiz) Set of 2 sheets 45·00 38·00

1992. Christmas. Nos. 1691/9 of Antigua optd **BARBUDA MAIL**.

1398	10c. Virgin and Child with Angels (School of Piero della Francesca)	2·00	1·25
1399	25c. Madonna degli Alberelli (Giovanni Bellini)	2·00	1·00
1400	30c. Madonna and Child with St. Anthony Abbot and St. Sigismund (Neroccio)	2·00	85
1401	40c. Madonna and the Grand Duke (Raphael)	2·25	85
1402	60c. The Nativity (Georges de la Tour)	2·50	1·00
1403	$1 Holy Family (Jacob Jordaens)	3·25	1·50
1404	$4 Madonna and Child Enthroned (Magaritone)	7·50	9·50
1405	$5 Madonna and Child on a Curved Throne (Byzantine school)	7·50	9·50

MS1406 Two sheets, each 76×102 mm. (a) $6 Madonna and Child (Domenco Ghirlando). (b) $6 The Holy Family (Pontormo) Set of 2 sheets 27·00 30·00

1993. Fungi. Nos. 1645/53 of Antigua optd **BARBUDA MAIL**.

1407	10c. Amanita caesarea	1·75	1·75
1408	15c. Collybia fusipes	2·00	1·75
1409	30c. Boletus aereus	2·25	1·50
1410	40c. Laccaria amethystina	2·25	1·50
1411	$1 Russula virescens	3·25	2·00
1412	$2 Tricholoma equestre ("Tricholoma auratum")	4·50	4·00
1413	$4 Calocybe gambosa	5·50	7·00
1414	$5 Lentinus tigrinus ("Panus tigrinus")	5·50	7·00

MS1415 Two sheets, each 100×70 mm. (a) $6 Clavariadelphus truncatus. (b) $6 Auricularia auricula-judae Set of 2 sheets 28·00 26·00

1993. "Granada '92" International Stamp Exhibition, Spain. Spanish Paintings. Nos. 1636/44 of Antigua optd **BARBUDA MAIL**.

1416	10c. The Miracle at the Well (Alonzo Cano)	1·50	1·50
1417	15c. The Poet Luis de Goingora y Argote (Velazquez)	1·75	1·50
1418	30c. The Painter Francisco Goya (Vincente Lopez Portana)	2·00	1·00
1419	40c. Maria de las Nieves Michaela Fourdinier (Luis Paret y Alcazar)	2·00	1·00
1420	$1 Carlos III eating before his Court (Alcazar) (horiz)	3·50	2·25
1421	$2 Rain Shower in Granada (Antonio Munoz Degrain) (horiz)	5·50	5·50
1422	$4 Sarah Bernhardt (Santiago Ruisnol i Prats)	7·50	9·00
1423	$5 The Hermitage Garden (Joaquin Mir Trinxet)	7·50	9·00

MS1424 Two sheets, each 120×95 mm. (a) $6 *The Ascent of Monsieur Boucle's Montgolfier Balloon in the Gardens of Aranjuez* (Antonio Carnicero) (112×87 mm). (b) $6 *Olympus: Battle with the Giants* (Francisco Bayeu y Subias) (112×87 mm). Imperf Set of 2 sheets 22·00 25·00

1993. "Genova '92" International Thematic Stamp Exhibition. Hummingbirds and Plants. Nos. 1661/9 of Antigua optd **BARBUDA MAIL**.

1425	10c. Antillean crested hummingbird and wild plantain	2·75	2·00
1426	25c. Green mango and parrot's plantain	3·00	1·50
1427	45c. Purple-throated carib and lobster claws	3·50	1·25
1428	60c. Antillean mango and coral plant	3·50	1·50
1429	$1 Vervain hummingbird and cardinal's guard	4·50	2·25
1430	$2 Rufous-breasted hermit and heliconia	6·00	5·50
1431	$4 Blue-headed hummingbird and reed ginger	7·50	9·00
1432	$5 Green-throated carib and ornamental banana	7·50	9·00

MS1433 Two sheets, each 100×70 mm. (a) $6 Bee humming-bird and jungle flame. (b) $6 Western streamertail and bignonia Set of 2 sheets 35·00 25·00

1993. Inventors and Inventions. Nos. 1672/80 of Antigua optd **BARBUDA MAIL**.

1434	10c. Ts'ai Lun and paper	65	1·10
1435	25c. Igor Sikorsky and *Bolshoi Baltiskii* (first four-engined airplane)	4·00	1·00
1436	30c. Alexander Graham Bell and early telephone	1·50	80
1437	40c. Johannes Gutenberg and early printing press	1·50	80
1438	60c. James Watt and stationary steam engine	11·00	2·25
1439	$1 Anton van Leeuwenhoek and early microscope	3·50	2·75
1440	$4 Louis Braille and hands reading braille	10·00	11·00
1441	$5 Galileo and telescope	10·00	11·00

MS1442 Two sheets, each 100×71 mm. (a) $6 Edison and Latimer's phonograph. (b) $6 *Clermont* (first commercial paddle-steamer) Set of 2 sheets 32·00 35·00

1993. Anniversaries and Events. Nos. 900/14 of Antigua optd **BARBUDA MAIL**.

1443	10c. Russian cosmonauts	2·00	1·75
1444	40c. *Graf Zeppelin* (airship), 1929	3·50	1·00
1445	45c. Bishop Daniel Davis	1·00	70
1446	75c. Konrad Adenauer making speech	1·25	1·00
1447	$1 Bus Mosbacher and *Weatherly* (yacht)	2·50	1·75
1448	$1.50 Rain forest	3·50	3·25
1449	$2 Tiger	12·00	6·00
1450	$2 National flag, plant and emblem (horiz)	7·00	4·00
1451	$2 Members of Community Players company (horiz)	4·00	4·00
1452	$2.25 Women carrying pots	4·00	4·25
1453	$3 Lions Club emblem	4·25	4·75
1454	$4 Chinese rocket on launch tower	7·00	8·00
1455	$4 West German and N.A.T.O. flags	7·00	8·00
1456	$6 Hugo Eckener (airship pioneer)	7·50	8·50

MS1457 Four sheets, each 100×71 mm. (a) $6 Projected European space station. (b) $6 Airship LZ-129 *Hindenburg*, 1936. (c) $6 Brandenburg Gate on German flag. (d) $6 *Danaus plexippus* (butterfly) Set of 4 sheets 60·00 45·00

1993. Flowers. Nos. 1733/41 of Antigua optd **BARBUDA MAIL**.

1458	15c. Cardinal's guard	1·75	1·25
1459	25c. Giant granadilla	1·90	1·10
1460	30c. Spider flower	2·00	1·25
1461	40c. Gold vine	2·25	1·40
1462	$1 Frangipani	3·50	2·25
1463	$2 Bougainvillea	4·50	4·50
1464	$4 Yellow oleander	6·00	7·00
1465	$5 Spicy jatropha	6·00	7·00

MS1466 Two sheets, each 100×70 mm. (a) $6 Bird lime tree. (b) $6 Fairy lily Set of 2 sheets 32·00 32·00

1993. World Bird Watch. Nos. 1248/51 optd **WORLD BIRDWATCH 9-10 OCTOBER 1993**.

1467	60c. Type **119**	4·00	1·75
1468	$2 Adelaide's warbler	7·00	4·50
1469	$4 Rose-breasted grosbeak	9·50	10·00
1470	$7 Wied's crested flycatcher	12·00	13·00

1993. Endangered Species. Nos. 1759/71 of Antigua optd **BARBUDA MAIL**.

1471	$1 St. Lucia amazon ("St. Lucia Parrot")	5·50	4·00
1472	$1 Cahow	5·50	4·00
1473	$1 Swallow-tailed kite	5·50	4·00
1474	$1 Everglade kite ("Everglades Kite")	5·50	4·00
1475	$1 Imperial amazon ("Imperial Parrot")	5·50	4·00
1476	$1 Humpback whale	5·50	4·00
1477	$1 Plain pigeon ("Puerto Rican Plain Pigeon")	5·50	4·00
1478	$1 St. Vincent amazon ("St. Vincent Parrot")	5·50	4·00
1479	$1 Puerto Rican amazon ("Puerto Rican Parrot")	5·50	4·00
1480	$1 Leatherback turtle	5·50	4·00
1481	$1 American crocodile	5·50	4·00
1482	$1 Hawksbill turtle	5·50	4·00

MS1483 Two sheets, each 100×70 mm. (a) $6 As No. 1476. (b) $6 West Indian manatee Set of 2 sheets 50·00 35·00

1994. Bicentenary of the Louvre, Paris. Paintings by Peter Paul Rubens. Nos. 1742/9 and MS1758 of Antigua optd **BARBUDA MAIL**.

1484	$1 *The Destiny of Marie de' Medici* (upper detail)	4·75	3·50
1485	$1 *The Birth of Marie de' Medici*	4·75	3·50
1486	$1 *The Education of Marie de' Medici*	4·75	3·50
1487	$1 *The Destiny of Marie de' Medici* (lower detail)	4·75	3·50
1488	$1 *Henry VI receiving the Portrait of Marie*	4·75	3·50
1489	$1 *The Meeting of the King and Marie at Lyons*	4·75	3·50
1490	$1 *The Marriage by Proxy*	4·75	3·50
1491	$1 *The Birth of Louis XIII*	4·75	3·50

MS1492 70×100 mm. $6 *Helene Fourment with a Coach* (52×85 mm) 22·00 23·00

1994. World Cup Football Championship, 1994, U.S.A. (1st Issue). Nos. 1816/28 of Antigua optd **BARBUDA MAIL**.

1493	$2 Paul Gascoigne	3·50	2·50
1494	$2 David Platt	3·50	2·50
1495	$2 Martin Peters	3·50	2·50
1496	$2 John Barnes	3·50	2·50
1497	$2 Gary Lineker	3·50	2·50
1498	$2 Geoff Hurst	3·50	2·50
1499	$2 Bobby Charlton	3·50	2·50
1500	$2 Bryan Robson	3·50	2·50
1501	$2 Bobby Moore	3·50	2·50
1502	$2 Nobby Stiles	3·50	2·50
1503	$2 Gordon Banks	3·50	2·50
1504	$2 Peter Shilton	3·50	2·50

MS1505 Two sheets, each 135×109 mm. (a) $6 Bobby Moore holding World Cup. (b) $6 Gary Lineker and Bobby Robson Set of 2 sheets 30·00 23·00

See also Nos. 1573/9.

1994. Anniversaries and Events. Nos. 1829/38, 1840 and 1842/7 of Antigua optd **BARBUDA MAIL**.

1506	10c. Grand Inspector W.Heath	5·00	2·50
1507	15c. Rodnina and Oulanov (U.S.S.R.) (pairs figure skating) (horiz)	2·00	2·00
1508	30c. Present Masonic Hall, St. John's (horiz)	6·50	2·50
1509	30c. Willy Brandt with Helmut Schmidt and George Leber (horiz)	1·50	1·50
1510	30c. *Cat and Bird* (Picasso) (horiz)	1·50	1·50
1511	40c. Previous Masonic Hall, St. John's (horiz)	6·50	2·50
1512	40c. *Fish on a Newspaper* (Picasso) (horiz)	1·50	1·50
1513	40c. Early astronomical equipment	1·50	1·50
1514	40c. Prince Naruhito and engagement photographs (horiz)	1·50	1·50
1515	60c. Grand Inspector J.Jeffery	7·50	2·50
1516	$3 Masako Owada and engagement photographs (horiz)	3·00	4·25
1517	$4 Willy Brandt and protest march (horiz)	4·50	5·50
1518	$4 Galaxy	4·50	5·50
1519	$5 Alberto Tomba (Italy) (giant slalom) (horiz)	4·50	5·50
1520	$5 *Dying Bull* (Picasso) (horiz)	4·50	5·50
1521	$5 Pres. Clinton and family (horiz)	4·50	5·50

MS1522 Six sheets. (a) 106×75 mm. $5 Copernicus. (b) 106×75 mm. $6 Womens' 1500 metre speed skating medallists (horiz). (c) 106×75 mm. $6 Willy Brandt at Warsaw Ghetto Memorial (horiz). (d) 106×75 mm. $6 *Woman with a Dog* (detail) (Picasso) (horiz). (e) 106×75 mm. $6 Masako Owada. (f) 106×75 mm. $6 Pres. Clinton taking the Oath (42½×57 mm) Set of 6 sheets 60·00 55·00

1994. Aviation Anniversaries. Nos. 1848/55 of Antigua optd **BARBUDA MAIL**.

1523	30c. Hugo Eckener and Dr. W. Beckers with airship *Graf Zeppelin* over Lake George, New York	3·25	1·75
1524	40c. Chicago World's Fair from *Graf Zeppelin*	3·25	1·75
1525	40c. Gloster Whittle E28/39, 1941	3·25	1·75
1526	40c. George Washington writing balloon mail letter (vert)	3·25	1·75
1527	$4 Pres. Wilson and Curtiss *Jenny*	10·00	11·00
1528	$5 Airship LZ-129 *Hindenburg* over Ebbets Field baseball stadium, 1937	10·00	11·00

1529　　$5 Gloster Meteor in dogfight　10·00　11·00

MS1530 Three sheets. (a) 86×105 mm. $6 Hugo Eckener (vert). (b) 105×86 mm. $6 Consolidated Catalina PBY-5 flying boat (57×42½ mm). (c) 105×86 mm. $6 Alexander Hamilton, Washington and John Jay watching Blanchard's balloon, 1793 (horiz) Set of 3 sheets　42·00　35·00

1994. Centenaries of Henry Ford's First Petrol Engine (Nos. 1531, 1533, 1533a) and Karl Benz's First Four-wheeled Car (others). Nos. 1856/60 of Antigua optd **BARBUDA MAIL.**

1531	30c. Lincoln Continental	2·50	1·50
1532	40c. Mercedes racing car, 1914	2·50	1·50
1533	$4 Ford "GT40", 1966	7·50	8·50
1534	$5 Mercedes Benz "gull-wing" coupe, 1954	7·50	8·50

MS1535 Two sheets. (a) 114×87 mm. $6 Ford's Mustang emblem. (b) 87×114 mm. $6 Germany 1936 12pf. Benz and U.S.A. 1968 12c. Ford stamps Set of 2 sheets　24·00　21·00

1994. Famous Paintings by Rembrandt and Matisse. Nos. 1881/9 of Antigua optd **BARBUDA MAIL.**

1536	15c. Hannah and Samuel (Rembrandt)	2·50	2·00
1537	15c. Guitarist (Matisse)	2·50	2·00
1538	30c. The Jewish Bride (Rembrandt)	2·75	1·10
1539	40c. Jacob wrestling with the Angel (Rembrandt)	2·75	1·10
1540	60c. Interior with a Goldfish Bowl (Matisse)	3·25	1·25
1541	$1 Mlle. Yvonne Landsberg (Matisse)	4·00	1·75
1542	$4 The Toboggan (Matisse)	8·00	9·00
1543	$5 Moses with the Tablets of the Law (Rembrandt)	8·00	9·00

MS1544 Two sheets. (a) 124×99 mm. $6 The Blinding of Samson by the Philistines (detail) (Rembrandt). (b) 99×124 mm. $6 The Three Sisters (detail) (Matisse) Set of 2 sheets　23·00　23·00

1994. "Polska '93" International Stamp Exhibition, Poznan. Nos. 1839, 1841 and **MS**1847f of Antigua optd **BARBUDA MAIL.**

| 1545 | $1 Woman Combing her Hair (W. Slewinski) (horiz) | 5·00 | 2·50 |
| 1546 | $3 Artist's Wife with Cat (Konrad Kryzanowski) (horiz) | 9·00 | 10·00 |

MS1547 70×100 mm. $6 General Confusion (S. I. Witkiewicz)　10·00　12·00

1994. Orchids. Nos. 1949/56 of Antigua optd **BARBUDA MAIL.**

1548	10c. Spiranthes lanceolata	3·50	2·25
1549	20c. Ionopsis utricularioides	4·50	2·25
1550	30c. "Tetramicra canaliculata	5·00	1·50
1551	50c. Oncidium picturatum	5·50	1·50
1552	$1 Epidendrum difforme	6·50	2·50
1553	$2 Epidendrum ciliare	8·00	6·50
1554	$4 Epidendrum ibaguense	9·00	10·00
1555	$5 Epidendrum nocturnum	9·00	10·00

MS1556 Two sheets, each 100×73 mm. (a) $6 Rodriguezia lanceolata. (b) $6 Encyclia cochleata Set of 2 sheets　35·00　27·00

1994. Centenary of Sierra Club (environmental protection society) (1992). Endangered Species. Nos. 1907/22 of Antigua optd **BARBUDA MAIL.**

1557	$1.50 Sumatran rhinoceros lying down	3·00	2·50
1558	$1.50 Sumatran rhinoceros feeding	3·00	2·50
1559	$1.50 Ring-tailed lemur on ground	3·00	2·50
1560	$1.50 Ring-tailed lemur on branch	3·00	2·50
1561	$1.50 Red-fronted brown lemur on branch	3·00	2·50
1562	$1.50 Head of red-fronted brown lemur	3·00	2·50
1563	$1.50 Head of red-fronted brown lemur in front of trunk	3·00	2·50
1564	$1.50 Sierra Club Centennial emblem	1·75	1·60
1565	$1.50 Head of bactrian camel	3·00	2·50
1566	$1.50 Bactrian camel	3·00	2·50
1567	$1.50 African elephant drinking	3·00	2·50
1568	$1.50 Head of African elephant	3·00	2·50
1569	$1.50 Leopard sitting upright	3·00	2·50
1570	$1.50 Leopard in grass (emblem at right)	3·00	2·50
1571	$1.50 Leopard in grass (emblem at left)	3·00	2·50

MS1572 Four sheets. (a) 100×70 mm. $1.50, Sumatran rhinoceros (horiz). (b) 70×100 mm. $1.50, Ring-tailed lemur (horiz). (C) 70×100 mm. $1.50, Bactrian camel (horiz) (d) 100×70 mm. $1.50, African elephant (horiz) Set of 4 sheets　22·00　20·00

1995. World Cup Football Championship, U.S.A. (2nd issue). Nos. 2039/45 of Antigua optd **BARBUDA MAIL.**

| 1573 | 15c. Hugo Sanchez (Mexico) | 2·25 | 1·25 |
| 1574 | 35c. Jurgen Klinsmann (Germany) | 2·75 | 1·25 |

1575	65c. Antiguan player	3·00	1·25
1576	$1.20 Cobi Jones (U.S.A.)	4·00	2·75
1577	$4 Roberto Baggio (Italy)	8·00	8·50
1578	$5 Bwalya Kalusha (Zambia)	8·00	8·50

MS1579 Two sheets. (a) 72×105 mm. $6 Maldive Islands player (vert). (b) 107×78 mm. $6 World Cup trophy (vert) Set of 2 sheets　22·00　17·00

1995. Christmas. Religious Paintings. Nos. 2058/66 of Antigua optd **BARBUDA MAIL.**

1580	15c. Virgin and Child by the Fireside (Robert Campin)	1·75	1·00
1581	35c. The Reading Madonna (Giorgione)	2·25	70
1582	40c. Madonna and Child (Giovanni Bellini)	2·25	70
1583	45c. The Little Madonna (Da Vinci)	2·25	70
1584	65c. The Virgin and Child under the Apple Tree (Lucas Cranach the Elder)	2·75	1·00
1585	75c. Madonna and Child (Master of the Female Half-lengths)	2·75	1·25
1586	$1.20 An Allegory of the Church (Alessandro Allori)	4·25	4·00
1587	$5 Madonna and Child wreathed with Flowers (Jacob Jordaens)	8·50	13·00

MS1588 Two sheets. (a) 123×88 mm. $6 Madonna and Child with Commissioners (detail) (Palma Vecchio). (b) 88×123 mm. $6 The Virgin Enthroned with Child (detail) (Bohemian master) Set of 2 sheets　20·00　18·00

1995. "Hong Kong '94" International Stamp Exhibition (1st issue). Nos. 1890/1 of Antigua optd **BARBUDA MAIL.**

| 1589 | 40c. Hong Kong 1981 $1 Fish stamp and sampans, Shau Kei Wan | 4·00 | 2·50 |
| 1590 | 40c. Antigua 1990 $2 Reef fish stamp and sampans, Shau Kei Wan | 4·00 | 2·50 |

See also Nos. 1591/6.

1995. "Hong Kong '94" International Stamp Exhibition (2nd issue). Nos. 1892/7 of Antigua optd **BARBUDA MAIL.**

1591	40c. Terracotta warriors	1·25	1·00
1592	40c. Cavalryman and horse	1·25	1·00
1593	40c. Warriors in armour	1·25	1·00
1594	40c. Painted bronze chariot and team	1·25	1·00
1595	40c. Pekingese dog	1·25	1·00
1596	40c. Warriors with horses	1·25	1·00

1995. Centenary of International Olympic Committee. Nos. 1990/2 of Antigua optd **BARBUDA MAIL.**

| 1597 | 50c. Edwin Moses (U.S.A.) (400 metres hurdles), 1984 | 1·00 | 75 |
| 1598 | $1.50 Steffi Graf (Germany) (tennis), 1988 | 8·50 | 4·25 |

MS1599 79×110 mm. $6 Johann Olav Koss (Norway) (500, 1500 and 10,000 metre speed skating), 1994　10·00　11·00

1995. Dogs of the World. Chinese New Year ("Year of the Dog"). Nos. 1923/47 of Antigua optd **BARBUDA MAIL.**

1600	50c. West Highland white terrier	1·60	1·10
1601	50c. Beagle	1·60	1·10
1602	50c. Scottish terrier	1·60	1·10
1603	50c. Pekingese	1·60	1·10
1604	50c. Dachshund	1·60	1·10
1605	50c. Yorkshire terrier	1·60	1·10
1606	50c. Pomeranian	1·60	1·10
1607	50c. Poodle	1·60	1·10
1608	50c. Shetland sheepdog	1·60	1·10
1609	50c. Pug	1·60	1·10
1610	50c. Shih tzu	1·60	1·10
1611	50c. Chihuahua	1·60	1·10
1612	50c. Mastiff	1·60	1·10
1613	50c. Border collie	1·60	1·10
1614	50c. Samoyed	1·60	1·10
1615	50c. Airedale terrier	1·60	1·10
1616	50c. English setter	1·60	1·10
1617	50c. Rough collie	1·60	1·10
1618	50c. Newfoundland	1·60	1·10
1619	50c. Weimarana	1·60	1·10
1620	50c. English springer spaniel	1·60	1·10
1621	50c. Dalmatian	1·60	1·10
1622	50c. Boxer	1·60	1·10
1623	50c. Old English sheepdog	1·60	1·10

MS1624 Two sheets, each 93×58 mm. (a) $6 Welsh corgi. (b) $6 Labrador retriever Set of 2 sheets　35·00　23·00

1995. Centenary of First English Cricket Tour to the West Indies (1995). Nos. 1994/7 of Antigua optd **BARBUDA MAIL.**

1625	35c. Mike Atherton (England) and Wisden Trophy	4·00	1·50
1626	75c. Viv Richards (West Indies) (vert)	6·00	2·75
1627	$1.20 Richie Richardson (West Indies) and Wisden Trophy	8·00	4·75

MS1628 80×100 mm. $3 English team, 1895 (black and brown)　13·00　11·00

1995. "Philakorea '94" International Stamp Exhibition (1st issue). Nos. 1998/2009 of Antigua optd **BARBUDA MAIL.**

1629	40c. Entrance bridge, Song-gwangsa Temple	1·00	80
1630	75c. Long-necked ware	1·25	1·50
1631	75c. Punch'ong ware jar with floral decoration	1·25	1·50
1632	75c. Punch'ong ware jar with blue dragon pattern	1·25	1·50
1633	75c. Ewer in shape of bamboo shoot	1·25	1·50
1634	75c. Punch'ong ware green jar	1·25	1·50
1635	75c. Pear-shaped bottle	1·25	1·50
1636	75c. Porcelain jar with brown dragon pattern	1·25	1·50
1637	75c. Porcelain jar with floral pattern	1·25	1·50
1638	90c. Song-op Folk Village, Cheju	1·25	1·25
1639	$3 Port Sogwipo	3·00	3·75

MS1640 104×71 mm. $4 Ox herder playing flute (vert)　4·75　6·50

1995. First Recipients of Order of the Caribbean Community. Nos. 2046/8 of Antigua optd **BARBUDA MAIL.**

1641	65c. Sir Shridath Ramphal	60	75
1642	90c. William Demas	90	1·00
1643	$1.20 Derek Walcott	4·50	4·25

1995. 25th Anniv of First Moon Landing. Nos. 1977/89 of Antigua optd **BARBUDA MAIL.**

1644	$1.50 Edwin Aldrin (astronaut)	4·25	2·75
1645	$1.50 First lunar footprint	4·25	2·75
1646	$1.50 Neil Armstrong (astronaut)	4·25	2·75
1647	$1.50 Aldrin stepping onto Moon	4·25	2·75
1648	$1.50 Aldrin and equipment	4·25	2·75
1649	$1.50 Aldrin and U.S.A. flag	4·25	2·75
1650	$1.50 Aldrin at Tranquility Base	4·25	2·75
1651	$1.50 Moon plaque	4·25	2·75
1652	$1.50 "Eagle" leaving Moon	4·25	2·75
1653	$1.50 Command module in lunar orbit	4·25	2·75
1654	$1.50 First day cover of U.S.A. 1969 10c. First Man on Moon stamp	4·25	2·75
1655	$1.50 Pres. Nixon and astronauts	4·25	2·75

MS1656 72×102 mm. $6 Armstrong and Aldrin with postal official　23·00　16·00

1995. International Year of the Family. No. 1993 of Antigua optd **BARBUDA MAIL.**

| 1657 | 90c. Antiguan family | 1·75 | 1·50 |

1995. 50th Anniv of D-Day. Nos. 2010/13 of Antigua optd **BARBUDA MAIL.**

1658	40c. Short S.25 Sunderland flying boat	4·50	1·25
1659	$2 Lockheed P-38 Lightning fighters attacking train	13·00	6·50
1660	$3 Martin B-26 Marauder bombers	13·00	8·00

MS1661 108×78 mm. $6 Hawker Typhoon fighter bomber　21·00　19·00

122 Queen Elizabeth the Queen Mother (95th birthday)

1995. Anniversaries. Multicoloured.

1662	$7.50 Type **122**	12·00	13·00
1663	$8 German bombers over St. Paul's Cathedral, London (horiz) (50th anniv of end of Second World War)	27·00	18·00
1664	$8 New York skyline with U.N. and national flags (horiz) (50th anniv of United Nations)	16·00	18·00

1995. Hurricane Relief. Nos. 1662/4 surch **HURRICANE RELIEF** and premium.

1665	$7.50+$1 +$1 Type **122** (90th birthday)	8·00	11·00
1666	$8+$1 +$1 German bombers over St. Paul's Cathedral, London (horiz) (50th anniv of end of Second World War)	20·00	16·00
1667	$8+$1 +$1 New York skyline with U.N. and national flags (horiz) (50th anniv of United Nations)	8·00	11·00

1996. Marine Life. Nos. 1967/76 of Antigua optd **BARBUDA MAIL.**

1668	50c. Bottlenose dolphin	1·50	1·50
1669	50c. Killer whale	1·50	1·50
1670	50c. Spinner dolphin	1·50	1·50

1671	50c. Oceanic sunfish	1·50	1·50
1672	50c. Caribbean reef shark and short fin pilot whale	1·50	1·50
1673	50c. Copper-banded butterflyfish	1·50	1·50
1674	50c. Mosaic moray	1·50	1·50
1675	50c. Clown triggerfish	1·50	1·50
1676	50c. Red lobster	1·50	1·50

MS1677 Two sheets, each 106×76 mm. (a) $6 Seahorse. (b) $6 Swordfish ("Blue Marlin") (horiz) Set of 2 sheets　21·00　21·00

1996. Christmas. Religious Paintings. Nos. 2267/73 of Antigua optd **BARBUDA MAIL.**

1678	15c. Rest on the Flight into Egypt (Paolo Veronese)	65	60
1679	35c. Madonna and Child (Van Dyck)	75	50
1680	65c. Sacred Conversation Piece (Veronese)	1·00	70
1681	75c. Vision of St. Anthony (Van Dyck)	1·25	80
1682	90c. Virgin and Child (Van Eyck)	1·40	90
1683	$6 The Immaculate Conception (Giovanni Tiepolo)	4·75	9·00

MS1684 Two sheets. (a) 101×127 mm. $5 Christ appearing to his Mother (detail) (Van der Weyden). (b) 127×101 mm. $6 The Infant Jesus and the Young St. John (Murillo) Set of 2 sheets　18·00　20·00

1996. Stars of Country and Western Music. Nos. 2014/38 of Antigua optd **BRBAUDA MAIL.**

1685	75c. Travis Tritt	80	80
1686	75c. Dwight Yoakam	80	80
1687	75c. Billy Ray Cyrus	80	80
1688	75c. Alan Jackson	80	80
1689	75c. Garth Brooks	80	80
1690	75c. Vince Gill	80	80
1691	75c. Clint Black	80	80
1692	75c. Eddie Rabbit	80	80
1693	75c. Patsy Cline	80	80
1694	75c. Tanya Tucker	80	80
1695	75c. Dolly Parton	80	80
1696	75c. Anne Murray	80	80
1697	75c. Tammy Wynette	80	80
1698	75c. Loretta Lynn	80	80
1699	75c. Reba McEntire	80	80
1700	75c. Skeeter Davis	80	80
1701	75c. Hank Snow	80	80
1702	75c. Gene Autry	80	80
1703	75c. Jimmie Rodgers	80	80
1704	75c. Ernest Tubb	80	80
1705	75c. Eddy Arnold	80	80
1706	75c. Willie Nelson	80	80
1707	75c. Johnny Cash	80	80
1708	75c. George Jones	80	80

MS1709 Three sheets. (a) 100×70 mm. $6 Hank Williams Jr. (b) 100×70 mm. $6 Hank Williams Sr. (c) 70×100 mm. $6 Kitty Wells (horiz) Set of 3 sheets　17·00　17·00

1996. Birds. Nos. 2067/81 of Antigua optd **BARBUDA MAIL.**

1710	15c. Magnificent frigate bird	1·50	1·25
1711	25c. Antillean euphonia ("Blue-hooded Euphonia")	1·60	1·25
1712	35c. Eastern meadowlark ("Meadowlark")	1·75	1·00
1713	40c. Red-billed tropic bird	1·75	1·00
1714	45c. Greater flamingo	1·75	1·00
1715	60c. Yellow-faced grassquit	2·00	1·50
1716	65c. Yellow-billed cuckoo	2·00	1·50
1717	70c. Purple-throated carib	2·00	2·00
1718	75c. Bananaquit	2·00	1·25
1719	90c. Painted bunting	2·25	1·25
1720	$1.20 Red-legged honeycreeper	2·50	2·25
1721	$2 Northern jacana ("Jacana")	3·50	3·50
1722	$5 Greater Antillean bullfinch	5·50	7·50
1723	$10 Caribbean elaenia	8·50	13·00
1724	$20 Brown trembler ("Trembler")	13·00	19·00

1996. Birds. Nos. 2050, 2052 and 2054/7 of Antigua optd **BARBUDA MAIL.**

1725	15c. Bridled quail dove	2·00	1·50
1726	40c. Purple-throated carib (vert)	2·50	1·00
1727	$1 Broad-winged hawk ("Antigua Broad-winged Hawk") (vert)	3·75	2·50
1728	$4 Yellow warbler	6·00	8·00

MS1729 Two sheets. (a) 70×100 mm. $6 Female magnificent frigate bird (vert). (b) 100×70 mm. $6 Black-billed whistling duck ducklings Set of 2 sheets　17·00　18·00

1996. Prehistoric Animals. Nos. 2082/100 of Antigua optd **BARBUDA MAIL.**

1730	15c. Head of pachycephalosaurus	2·00	2·00
1731	20c. Head of afrovenator	2·00	2·00
1732	40c. Centrosaurus	2·00	2·00
1733	75c. Kronosaurus (horiz)	2·00	2·00
1734	75c. Ichthyosaurus (horiz)	2·00	2·00
1735	75c. Plesiosaurus (horiz)	2·00	2·00
1736	75c. Archelon (horiz)	2·00	2·00

1737	75c. Pair of tyrannosaurus (horiz)	2·00	2·00
1738	75c. Tyrannosaurus (horiz)	2·00	2·00
1739	75c. Parasaurolophus (horiz)	2·00	2·00
1740	75c. Pair of parasaurolophus (horiz)	2·00	2·00
1741	75c. Oviraptor (horiz)	2·00	2·00
1742	75c. Protoceratops with eggs (horiz)	2·00	2·00
1743	75c. Pteranodon and protoceratops (horiz)	2·00	2·00
1744	75c. Pair of protoceratops (horiz)	2·00	2·00
1745	90c. Pentaceratops drinking	2·25	1·50
1746	$1.20 Head of tarbosaurus	2·75	2·00
1747	$5 Head of styracosaurus	6·50	7·50

MS1748 Two sheets, each 101×70 mm. (a) $6 Head of Corythosaurus (horiz). (b) $6 Head of Carnotaurus (horiz). Set of 2 sheets — 20·00, 23·00

1996. Olympic Games, Atlanta (1st issue). Previous Gold Medal Winners. Nos. 2101/7 of Antigua optd **BARBUDA MAIL**.

1749	15c. Al Oerter (U.S.A.) (discus – 1956, 1960, 1964, 1968)	1·50	1·00
1750	20c. Greg Louganis (U.S.A.) (diving – 1984, 1988)	1·50	1·00
1751	65c. Naim Suleymanoglu (Turkey) (weightlifting – 1988)	2·00	1·50
1752	90c. Louise Ritter (U.S.A.) (high jump – 1988)	2·50	1·25
1753	$1.20 Nadia Comaneci (Rumania) (gymnastics – 1976)	4·00	2·75
1754	$5 Olga Bondarenko (Russia) (10,000 m – 1988)	6·00	8·50

MS1755 Two sheets, each 106×76 mm. (a) $6 United States crew (eight-oared shell – 1964). (b) $6 Lutz Hessilch (Germany) (cycling – 1988) (vert) Set of 2 sheets — 18·00, 16·00

See also Nos. 1922/44.

1996. 18th World Scout Jamboree, Netherlands. Tents. Nos. 2203/9 of Antigua optd **BARBUDA MAIL**.

1756	$1.20 The Explorer Tent	1·25	1·50
1757	$1.20 Camper tent	1·25	1·50
1758	$1.20 Wall tent	1·25	1·50
1759	$1.20 Trail tent	1·25	1·50
1760	$1.20 Miner's tent	1·25	1·50
1761	$1.20 Voyager tent	1·25	1·50

MS1762 Two sheets, each 76×106 mm. (a) $6 Scout and camp fire. (b) $6 Scout with back pack Set of 2 sheets — 8·00, 10·00

1996. Centenary of Nobel Prize Trust Fund. Nos. 2226/44 of Antigua optd **BARBUDA MAIL**.

1763	$1 Dag Hammarskjold (1961 Peace)	1·60	1·25
1764	$1 Georg Wittig (1979 Chemistry)	1·60	1·25
1765	$1 Wilhelm Ostwold (1909 Chemistry)	1·60	1·25
1766	$1 Robert Koch (1905 Medicine)	1·60	1·25
1767	$1 Karl Ziegler (1963 Chemistry)	1·60	1·25
1768	$1 Alexander Fleming (1945 Medicine)	1·60	1·25
1769	$1 Hermann Staudinger (1953 Chemistry)	1·60	1·25
1770	$1 Manfred Eigen (1967 Chemistry)	1·60	1·25
1771	$1 Arno Penzias (1978 Physics)	1·60	1·25
1772	$1 Shumal Agnon (1966 Literature)	1·60	1·25
1773	$1 Rudyard Kipling (1907 Literature)	1·60	1·25
1774	$1 Aleksandr Solzhenitsyn (1970 Literature)	1·60	1·25
1775	$1 Jack Steinburger (1988 Physics)	1·60	1·25
1776	$1 Andrei Sakharov (1975 Peace)	1·60	1·25
1777	$1 Otto Stern (1943 Physics)	1·60	1·25
1778	$1 John Steinbeck (1962 Literature)	1·60	1·25
1779	$1 Nadine Gordimer (1991 Literature)	1·60	1·25
1780	$1 William Faulkner (1949 Literature)	1·60	1·25

MS1781 Two sheets, each 100×70 mm. (a) $6 Elie Wiesel (1986 Peace) (vert). (b) $6 Dalai Lama (1989 Peace) (vert) Set of 2 sheets — 14·00, 17·00

1996. 70th Birthday of Queen Elizabeth II. Nos. 2355/8 of Antigua optd **BARBUDA MAIL**.

1782	$2 Queen Elizabeth II in blue dress	3·25	2·75
1783	$2 With bouquet	3·25	2·75
1784	$2 In Garter robes	3·25	2·75

MS1785 96×111 mm. $6 Wearing white dress — 8·50, 7·50

1997. Christmas. Religious Paintings by Filippo Lippi. Nos. 2377/83 of Antigua optd **BARBUDA MAIL**.

1786	60c. *Madonna Enthroned*	60	35
1787	90c. *Adoration of the Child and Saints*	85	55
1788	$1 *The Annunciation*	1·00	80
1789	$1.20 *Birth of the Virgin*	1·25	1·10
1790	$1.60 *Adoration of the Child*	1·60	2·00
1791	$1.75 *Madonna and Child*	1·75	2·25

MS1792 Two sheets, each 76×106 mm. (a) $6 *Madonna and Child* (different). (b) $6 *The Circumcision* Set of 2 sheets — 12·00, 15·00

1997. 50th Anniv of F.A.O. Nos. 2121/4 of Antigua optd **BARBUDA MAIL**.

1793	75c. Woman buying produce from market	1·00	1·00
1794	90c. Women shopping	1·10	1·10
1795	$1.20 Women talking	1·40	1·75

MS1796 100×70 mm. $6 Tractor — 5·50, 7·00

1997. 90th Anniv of Rotary International (1995). No. 2126 of Antigua optd **BARBUDA MAIL**.

1797	75c. Beach and rotary emblem	3·25	4·25

MS1798 74×104 mm. $6 National flag and emblem — 4·50, 5·50

1997. 50th Anniv of End of Second World War in Europe and the Pacific. Nos. 2108/16 and 2132/8 of Antigua optd **BARBUDA MAIL**.

1799	$1.20 Map of Berlin showing Russian advance	1·50	1·50
1800	$1.20 Russian tank and infantry	1·50	1·50
1801	$1.20 Street fighting in Berlin	1·50	1·50
1802	$1.20 German tank exploding	1·50	1·50
1803	$1.20 Russian air raid	1·50	1·50
1804	$1.20 German troops surrendering	1·50	1·50
1805	$1.20 Hoisting the Soviet flag on the Reichstag	1·50	1·50
1806	$1.20 Captured German standards	1·50	1·50
1807	$1.20 Gen. Chiang Kai-shek and Chinese guerrillas	1·50	1·50
1808	$1.20 Gen. Douglas MacArthur and beach landing	1·50	1·50
1809	$1.20 Gen. Claire Chennault and U.S. fighter aircraft	1·50	1·50
1810	$1.20 Brig. Orde Wingate and supply drop	1·50	1·50
1811	$1.20 Gen. Joseph Stilwell and U.S. supply plane	1·50	1·50
1812	$1.20 Field-Marshal Bill Slim and loading cow onto plane	1·50	1·50

MS1813 Two sheets, each 100×70 mm. (a) $3 Admiral Nimitz and aircraft carrier. (b) $6 Gen. Konev (vert) Set of 2 sheets — 14·00, 15·00

1997. Bees. Nos. 2172/6 of Antigua optd **BARBUDA MAIL**.

1814	90c. Mining bees	1·00	50
1815	$1.20 Solitary bee	1·25	80
1816	$1.65 Leaf-cutter bee	1·60	1·75
1817	$1.75 Honey bees	1·75	2·00

MS1818 110×80 mm. $6 Solitary mining bird — 5·50, 6·50

1997. Flowers. Nos. 2177/89 of Antigua optd **BARBUDA MAIL**.

1819	75c. Narcissus	75	85
1820	75c. Camellia	75	85
1821	75c. Iris	75	85
1822	75c. Tulip	75	85
1823	75c. Poppy	75	85
1824	75c. Peony	75	85
1825	75c. Magnolia	75	85
1826	75c. Oriental lily	75	85
1827	75c. Rose	75	85
1828	75c. Pansy	75	85
1829	75c. Hydrangea	75	85
1830	75c. Azaleas	75	85

MS1831 80×110 mm. $6 Calla lily — 6·50, 8·00

1997. Cats. Nos. 2190/202 of Antigua optd **BARBUDA MAIL**.

1832	45c. Somali	70	70
1833	45c. Persian and butterflies	70	70
1834	45c. Devon rex	70	70
1835	45c. Turkish angora	70	70
1836	45c. Himalayan	70	70
1837	45c. Maine coon	70	70
1838	45c. Ginger non-pedigree	70	70
1839	45c. American wirehair	70	70
1840	45c. British shorthair	70	70
1841	45c. American curl	70	70
1842	45c. Black non-pedigree and butterfly	70	70
1843	45c. Birman	70	70

MS1844 104×74 mm. $6 Siberian kitten (vert) — 9·00, 10·00

1997. 95th Birthday of Queen Elizabeth the Queen Mother. Nos. 2127/31 of Antigua optd **BARBUDA MAIL**.

1845	$1.50 brown, lt brown & black	5·00	3·50
1846	$1.50 multicoloured	5·00	3·50
1847	$1.50 multicoloured	5·00	3·50
1848	$1.50 multicoloured	5·00	3·50

MS1849 102×27 mm. $6 multicoloured — 14·00, 11·00

1997. 50th Anniv of United Nations. Nos. 2117/18 of Antigua optd **BARBUDA MAIL**.

1850	75c. Signatures and Earl of Halifax	80	80
1851	90c. Virginia Gildersleeve	90	90
1852	$1.20 Harold Stassen	1·25	1·50

MS1853 100×70 mm. $6 Pres. Franklin D. Roosevelt — 4·50, 6·00

1997. Trains of the World. Nos. 2210/25 of Antigua optd **BARBUDA MAIL**.

1854	35c. Trans-Gabon diesel-electric train	90	30
1855	65c. Canadian Pacific diesel-electric locomotive	1·00	40
1856	75c. Santa Fe Railway diesel-electric locomotive, U.S.A.	1·00	50
1857	90c. High Speed Train, Great Britain	1·00	60
1858	$1.20 TGV express train, France	1·00	1·25
1859	$1.20 Diesel-electric locomotive, Australia	1·00	1·25
1860	$1.20 Pendolino "ETR 450" electric train, Italy	1·00	1·25
1861	$1.20 Diesel-electric locomotive, Thailand	1·00	1·25
1862	$1.20 Pennslyvania Railroad Type 4 steam locomotive, U.S.A.	1·00	1·25
1863	$1.20 Beyer-Garratt steam locomotive, East African Railways	1·00	1·25
1864	$1.20 Natal Govt steam locomotive	1·00	1·25
1865	$1.20 Rail gun, American Civil War	1·00	1·25
1866	$1.20 Locomotive *Lion* (red livery), Great Britain	1·00	1·25
1867	$1.20 William Hedley's *Puffing Billy* (green livery), Great Britain	1·00	1·25
1868	$6 Amtrak high speed diesel locomotive, U.S.A.	3·50	4·50

MS1869 Two sheets, each 110×80 mm. (a) $6 Locomotive *Iron Rooster* China (vert). (b) $6 *Indian-Pacific* diesel-electric locomotive, Australia (vert) Set of 2 sheets — 13·00, 16·00

1997. Golden Wedding of Queen Elizabeth II and Prince Philip (1st issue). Nos. 1662/3 optd **Golden Wedding of H.M. Queen Elizabeth II and Prince Philip 1947-1997**.

1870	$7.50 Type **122**	7·50	8·00
1871	$8 German bombers over St. Paul's Cathedral, London (horiz)	9·50	10·00

See also Nos. 1925/30.

1997. Fungi. Nos. 2274/82 of Antigua optd **BARBUDA MAIL**.

1872	75c. *Hygrophoropsis aurantiaca*	1·50	1·50
1873	75c. *Hygrophorus bakerensis*	1·50	1·50
1874	75c. *Hygrophorus conicus*	1·50	1·50
1875	75c. *Hygrophorus miniatus* ("Hygrocybe miniata")	1·50	1·50
1876	75c. *Suillus brevipes*	1·50	1·50
1877	75c. *Suillus luteus*	1·50	1·50
1878	75c. *Suillus granulatus*	1·50	1·50
1879	75c. *Suillus caerulescens*	1·50	1·50

MS1880 Two sheets, each 106×76 mm. (a) $6 *Conocybe filaris*. (b) $6 *Hygrocybe flavescens* Set of 2 sheets — 13·00, 15·00

1997. Birds. Nos. 2140/64 of Antigua optd **BARBUDA MAIL**.

1881	75c. Purple-throated carib	90	90
1882	75c. Antilean crested hummingbird	90	90
1883	75c. Bananaquit	90	90
1884	75c. Mangrove cuckoo	90	90
1885	75c. Green-throated carib	90	90
1886	75c. Troupial	90	90
1887	75c. Yellow warbler	90	90
1888	75c. Antillean euphonia ("Blue-hooded Euphonia")	90	90
1889	75c. Scaly-breasted thrasher	90	90
1890	75c. Burrowing owl	90	90
1891	75c. Carib grackle	90	90
1892	75c. Adelaide's warbler	90	90
1893	75c. Ring-necked duck	90	90
1894	75c. Ruddy duck	90	90
1895	75c. Green-winged teal	90	90
1896	75c. Wood duck	90	90
1897	75c. Hooded merganser	90	90
1898	75c. Lesser scaup	90	90
1899	75c. Black-billed whistling duck ("West Indian Tree Duck")	90	90
1900	75c. Fulvous whistling duck	90	90
1901	75c. Bahama pintail	90	90
1902	75c. Northern shoveler ("Shoveler")	90	90
1903	75c. Masked duck	90	90
1904	75c. American wigeon	90	90

MS1905 Two sheets, each 104×74 mm. (a) $6 Head of purple gallinule. (b) $6 Heads of blue-winged teals Set of 2 sheets — 14·00, 13·00

1997. Sailing Ships. Nos. 2283/301 of Antigua optd **BARBUDA MAIL**.

1906	15c. H.M.S. "Resolution" (Cook)	1·25	1·00
1907	25c. "Mayflower" (Pilgrim Fathers)	1·00	50
1908	45c. "Santa Maria" (Columbus)	1·25	60
1909	75c. "Aemilia" (Dutch galleon)	1·00	60
1910	75c. "Sovereign of the Seas" (English galleon)	1·00	60
1911	90c. H.M.S. "Victory" (Nelson)	1·25	1·00
1912	$1.20 As No. 1909	1·25	1·25
1913	$1.20 As No. 1910	1·25	1·25
1914	$1.20 "Royal Louis" (French galleon)	1·25	1·25
1915	$1.20 H.M.S. "Royal George" (ship of the line)	1·25	1·25
1916	$1.20 "Le Protecteur" (French frigate)	1·25	1·25
1917	$1.20 As No. 1911	1·25	1·25
1918	$1.50 As No. 1908	1·25	1·40
1919	$1.50 "Victoria" (Magellan)	1·25	1·40
1920	$1.50 "Golden Hind" (Drake)	1·25	1·40
1921	$1.50 As No. 1907	1·25	1·40
1922	$1.50 "Griffin" (La Salle)	1·25	1·40
1923	$1.50 As No. 1906	1·25	1·40

MS1924 (a) 102×72 mm. $6 U.S.S. "Constitution" (frigate). (b) 98×67 mm. $6 "Grande Hermine" (Cartier) Set of 2 sheets — 10·00, 12·00

1997. Golden Wedding of Queen Elizabeth and Prince Philip (2nd issue). Nos. 2474/80 of Antigua optd **BARBUDA MAIL**.

1925	$1 Queen Elizabeth II	2·50	2·00
1926	$1 Royal coat of arms	2·50	2·00
1927	$1 Queen Elizabeth and Prince Philip at reception	2·50	2·00
1928	$1 Queen Elizabeth and Prince Philip in landau	2·50	2·00
1929	$1 Balmoral	2·50	2·00
1930	$1 Prince Philip	2·50	2·00

MS1931 100×71 mm. $6 Queen Elizabeth with Prince Philip in naval uniform — 14·00, 13·00

1997. Christmas. Religious Paintings. Nos. 2566/72 of Antigua optd **BARBUDA MAIL**.

1932	15c. "The Angel leaving Tobias and his Family" (Rembrandt)	80	60
1933	25c. "The Resurrection" (Martin Knoller)	90	60
1934	60c. "Astronomy" (Raphael)	1·25	75
1935	75c. "Music-making Angel" (Melozzo da Forli)	1·40	1·25
1936	90c. "Amor" (Parmigianino)	1·60	1·25
1937	$1.20 "Madonna and Child with Saints" (Rosso Fiorentino)	1·75	2·00

MS1938 Two sheets, each 105×96 mm. (a) $6 "The Wedding of Tobias" (Gianantonio and Francesco Guardi) (horiz). (b) $6 "The Portinari Altarpiece" (Hugo van der Goes) (horiz) Set of 2 sheets — 9·00, 11·00

1998. Sea Birds. Nos. 2325/33 of Antigua optd **BARBUDA MAIL**.

1939	75c. Black skimmer	1·50	1·50
1940	75c. Black-capped petrel	1·50	1·50
1941	75c. Sooty tern	1·50	1·50
1942	75c. Royal tern	1·50	1·50
1943	75c. Pomarine skua ("Pomarine Jaegger")	1·50	1·50
1944	75c. White-tailed tropic bird	1·50	1·50
1945	75c. Northern gannet	1·50	1·50
1946	75c. Laughing gull	1·50	1·50

MS1947 Two sheets, each 105×75 mm. (a) $5 Great frigate bird. (b) $6 Brown pelican Set of 2 sheets — 9·00, 11·00

1998. Centenary of Radio. Entertainers. Nos. 2372/6 of Antigua optd **BARBUDA MAIL**.

1948	75c. Kate Smith	90	65
1949	75c. Dinah Shore	1·00	85
1950	90c. Rudy Vallee	1·25	90
1951	$1.20 Bing Crosby	1·50	2·25

MS1952 72×104 mm. $6 Jo Stafford (28×42 mm) — 5·50, 7·50

1998. Olympic Games, Atlanta (2nd issue). Previous Medal Winners. Nos. 2302/23 of Antigua optd **BARBUDA MAIL**.

1953	65c. Florence Griffith Joyner (U.S.A.) (Gold – track, 1988)	85	75
1954	75c. Olympic Stadium, Seoul (1988) (horiz)	85	75
1955	90c. Allison Jolly and Lynne Jewell (U.S.A.) (Gold – yachting, 1988) (horiz)	1·00	1·00
1956	90c. Wolfgang Nordwig (Germany) (Gold – pole vaulting, 1972)	1·00	1·00
1957	90c. Shirley Strong (Great Britain) (Silver – 100 m hurdles, 1984)	1·00	1·00
1958	90c. Sergei Bubka (Russia) (Gold – pole vault, 1988)	1·00	1·00
1959	90c. Filbert Bayi (Tanzania) (Silver – 3000 m steeplechase, 1980)	1·00	1·00
1960	90c. Victor Saneyev (Russia) (Gold – triple jump, 1968, 1972, 1976)	1·00	1·00
1961	90c. Silke Renk (Germany) (Gold – javelin, 1992)	1·00	1·00
1962	90c. Daley Thompson (Great Britain) (Gold – decathlon, 1980, 1984)	1·00	1·00

1963	90c. Robert Richards (U.S.A.) (Gold – pole vault, 1952, 1956)	1·00	1·00
1964	90c. Parry O'Brien (U.S.A.) (Gold – shot put, 1952, 1956)	1·00	1·00
1965	90c. Ingrid Kramer (Germany) (Gold – Women's platform diving, 1960)	1·00	1·00
1966	90c. Kelly McCormick (U.S.A.) (Silver – Women's spring-board diving, 1984)	1·00	1·00
1967	90c. Gary Tobian (U.S.A.) (Gold – Men's springboard diving, 1960)	1·00	1·00
1968	90c. Greg Louganis (U.S.A.) (Gold – Men's diving, 1984 and 1988)	1·00	1·00
1969	90c. Michelle Mitchell (U.S.A.) (Silver – Women's platform diving, 1984 and 1988)	1·00	1·00
1970	90c. Zhou Jihong (China) (Gold – Women's platform diving, 1984)	1·00	1·00
1971	90c. Wendy Wyland (U.S.A.) (Bronze – Women's platform diving, 1984)	1·00	1·00
1972	90c. Xu Yanmei (China) (Gold – Women's platform diving, 1988)	1·00	1·00
1973	90c. Fu Mingxia (China) (Gold – Women's platform diving, 1992)	1·00	1·00
1974	$1.20 2000 m tandem cycle race (horiz)	3·25	3·00
MS1975	Two sheets, each 106×76 mm. (a) $5 Bill Toomey (U.S.A.) (Gold – decathlon, 1968) (horiz). (b) $6 Mark Lenzi (U.S.A.) (Gold – Men's springboard diving, 1992) Set of 2 sheets	9·00	11·00

1998. World Cup Football Championship, France. Nos. 2525/39 of Antigua optd **BARBUDA MAIL**.

1976	60c. multicoloured	75	60
1977	75c. brown	75	60
1978	90c. multicoloured	80	65
1979	$1 brown	80	80
1980	$1 brown	80	80
1981	$1 brown	80	80
1982	$1 black	80	80
1983	$1 brown	80	80
1984	$1 brown	80	80
1985	$1 brown	80	80
1986	$1 brown	80	80
1987	$1.20 multicoloured	1·00	1·10
1988	$1.65 multicoloured	1·25	1·40
1989	$1.75 multicoloured	1·40	1·60
MS1990	Two sheets, each 102×127 mm. (a) $6 multicoloured. (b) $6 multicoloured Set of 2 sheets	9·00	11·00

1998. Cavalry through the Ages. Nos. 2359/63 of Antigua optd **BARBUDA MAIL**.

1991	60c. Ancient Egyptian cavalry-man	1·50	1·25
1992	60c. 13th-century English knight	1·50	1·25
1993	60c. 16th-century Spanish lancer	1·50	1·25
1994	60c. 18th-century Chinese cavalryman	1·50	1·25
MS1995	100×70 mm. $6 19th-century French cuirassier (vert)	6·50	8·00

1998. 50th Anniv of UNICEF Nos. 2364/7 of Antigua optd **BARBUDA MAIL**.

1996	75c. Girl in red sari	90	90
1997	90c. South American mother and child	1·10	1·10
1998	$1.20 Nurse with child	1·40	2·00
MS1999	114×74 mm. $6 Chinese child	4·75	6·50

1998. 3000th Anniv of Jerusalem. Nos. 2368/71 of Antigua optd **BARBUDA MAIL**.

2000	75c. Tomb of Zachariah and "Verbascum sinuatum"	2·00	1·10
2001	90c. Pool of Siloam and "Hyacinthus orientalis"	2·25	1·10
2002	$1.20 Hurva Synagogue and "Ranunculus asiaticus"	2·50	2·75
MS2003	66×80 mm. $6 Model of Herod's Temple and "Cercis siliquastrum"	7·00	7·00

1998. Diana, Princess of Wales Commemoration. Nos. 2573/85 of Antigua optd **BARBUDA MAIL**.

2004	$1.65 Diana, Princess of Wales	1·25	1·10
2005	$1.65 Wearing hoop earrings (red and black)	1·25	1·10
2006	$1.65 Carrying bouquet	1·25	1·10
2007	$1.65 Wearing floral hat	1·25	1·10
2008	$1.65 With Prince Harry	1·25	1·10
2009	$1.65 Wearing white jacket	1·25	1·10
2010	$1.65 In kitchen	1·25	1·10
2011	$1.65 Wearing black and white dress	1·25	1·10
2012	$1.65 Wearing hat (brown and black)	1·25	1·10
2013	$1.65 Wearing floral print dress (brown and black)	1·25	1·10
2014	$1.65 Dancing with John Travolta	1·25	1·10
2015	$1.65 Wearing white hat and jacket	1·25	1·10
MS2016	Two sheets, each 70×100 mm. (a) $6 Wearing red jumper. (b) $6 Wearing black dress for Papal audience (brown and black) Set of 2 sheets	9·00	11·00

1998. Broadway Musical Stars. Nos. 2384/93 of Antigua optd **BARBUDA MAIL**.

2017	$1 Robert Preston (The Music Man)	1·50	1·50
2018	$1 Michael Crawford (Phantom of the Opera)	1·50	1·50
2019	$1 Zero Mostel (Fiddler on the Roof)	1·50	1·50
2020	$1 Patti Lupone (Evita)	1·50	1·50
2021	$1 Raul Julia (Threepenny Opera)	1·50	1·50
2022	$1 Mary Martin (South Pacific)	1·50	1·50
2023	$1 Carol Channing (Hello Dolly)	1·50	1·50
2024	$1 Yul Brynner (The King and I)	1·50	1·50
2025	$1 Julie Andrews (My Fair Lady)	1·50	1·50
MS2026	106×76 mm. $6 Mickey Rooney (Sugar Babies)	7·00	8·50

1998. 20th Death Anniv of Charlie Chaplin (film star). Nos. 2404/13 of Antigua optd **BARBUDA MAIL**.

2027	$1 Charlie Chaplin as young man	1·50	1·50
2028	$1 Pulling face	1·50	1·50
2029	$1 Looking over shoulder	1·50	1·50
2030	$1 In cap	1·50	1·50
2031	$1 In front of star	1·50	1·50
2032	$1 In The Great Dictator	1·50	1·50
2033	$1 With movie camera and megaphone	1·50	1·50
2034	$1 Standing in front of camera lens	1·50	1·50
2035	$1 Putting on make-up	1·50	1·50
MS2036	76×106 mm. $6 Charlie Chaplin	9·00	10·00

1998. Butterflies. Nos. 2414/36 of Antigua optd **BARBUDA MAIL**.

2037	90c. Charaxes porthos	1·00	70
2038	$1.10 Charaxes protoclea protoclea	1·00	1·00
2039	$1.10 Byblia ilithyia	1·00	1·00
2040	$1.10 Black-headed tchagra (bird)	1·00	1·00
2041	$1.10 Charaxes nobilis	1·00	1·00
2042	$1.10 Pseudacraea boisduvali trimeni	1·00	1·00
2043	$1.10 Charaxes smaragdalis	1·00	1·00
2044	$1.10 Charaxes lasti	1·00	1·00
2045	$1.10 Pseudacraea poggei	1·00	1·00
2046	$1.10 Graphium antheus	1·00	1·00
2047	$1.10 Carmine bee eater (bird)	1·00	1·00
2048	$1.10 Pseudacraea eurytus	1·00	1·00
2049	$1.10 Hypolimnas monteironis	1·00	1·00
2050	$1.10 Charaxes anticlea	1·00	1·00
2051	$1.10 Graphium leonidas	1·00	1·00
2052	$1.10 Graphium illyris	1·00	1·00
2053	$1.10 Nephronia argia	1·00	1·00
2054	$1.10 Graphium policenes	1·00	1·00
2055	$1.10 Papilio dardanus	1·00	1·00
2056	$1.20 Aethiopana honorius	1·00	1·10
2057	$1.60 Charaxes hadrianus	1·25	1·40
2058	$1.75 Precis westermanni	1·40	1·60
MS2059	Three sheets, each 107×76 mm. (a) $6 Charaxes lactincus (horiz). (b) $6 Eupheadra reophron. (c) $6 Euxantha tiberius (horiz) Set of 3 sheets	19·00	22·00

1998. Christmas. Dogs. Nos. 2771/8 of Antigua optd **BARBUDA MAIL**.

2060	15c. Border collie	65	60
2061	25c. Dalmatian	75	60
2062	65c. Weimaraner	1·40	80
2063	75c. Scottish terrier	1·40	85
2064	90c. Long-haired dachshund	1·50	85
2065	$1.20 Golden retriever	1·75	1·75
2066	$2 Pekingese	2·25	2·75
MS2067	Two sheets, each 75×66 mm. (a) $6 Dalmatian. (b) $6 Jack Russell terrier Set of 2 sheets	13·00	12·00

1999. Lighthouses of the World. Nos. 2612/20 of Antigua optd **BARBUDA MAIL**.

2068	45c. Europa Point Lighthouse, Gibraltar	1·50	65
2069	65c. Tierra del Fuego, Argentina (horiz)	1·75	75
2070	75c. Point Loma, California, U.S.A. (horiz)	1·75	90
2071	90c. Groenpoint, Cape Town, South Africa	1·75	90
2072	$1 Youghal, Cork, Ireland	1·75	1·25
2073	$1.20 Launceston, Tasmania, Australia	1·90	1·50
2074	$1.65 Point Abino, Ontario, Canada (horiz)	2·25	2·75
2075	$1.75 Great Inagua, Bahamas (horiz)	2·25	2·75
MS2076	99×70 mm. $6 Cape Hatteras, North Carolina, U.S.A.	11·00	11·00

1999. Endangered Species. Nos. 2457/69 of Antigua optd **BARBUDA MAIL**.

2077	$1.20 Red bishop	2·00	2·00
2078	$1.20 Yellow baboon	2·00	2·00
2079	$1.20 Superb starling	2·00	2·00
2080	$1.20 Ratel	2·00	2·00
2081	$1.20 Hunting dog	2·00	2·00
2082	$1.20 Serval	2·00	2·00
2083	$1.65 Okapi	2·25	2·25
2084	$1.65 Giant forest squirrel	2·25	2·25
2085	$1.65 Lesser masked weaver	2·25	2·25
2086	$1.65 Small-spotted genet	2·25	2·25
2087	$1.65 Yellow-billed stork	2·25	2·25
2088	$1.65 Red-headed agama	2·25	2·25
MS2089	Three sheets, each 106×76 mm. (a) $6 South African crowned crane. (b) $6 Bat-eared fox. (c) $6 Malachite kingfisher Set of 3 sheets	19·00	22·00

1999. "Pacific 97" International Stamp Exhibition, San Francisco. Death Centenary of Heinrich von Stephan (founder of the U.P.U.). Nos. 2481/4 of Antigua optd **BARBUDA MAIL**.

2090	$1.75 blue	2·50	2·50
2091	$1.75 brown	2·50	2·50
2092	$1.75 mauve	2·50	2·50
MS2093	82×119 mm. $6 violet	4·75	6·00

DESIGNS: No. 2090, Kaiser Wilhelm I and Heinrich von Stephan; 2091, Von Stephan and Mercury; 2092, Carrier pigeon and loft; **MS**2093 Von Stephan and 15th-century Basel messenger.

1999. 175th Anniv of Brothers Grimm's Third Collection of Fairy Tales. Cinderella. Nos. 2485/8 of Antigua optd **BARBUDA MAIL**.

2094	$1.75 The Ugly Sisters and their Mother	2·75	2·75
2095	$1.75 Cinderella and her Fairy Godmother	2·75	2·75
2096	$1.75 Cinderella and the Prince	2·75	2·75
MS2097	124×96 mm. $6 Cinderella trying on slipper	6·00	7·50

1999. Orchids of the World. Nos. 2502/24 of Antigua optd **BARBUDA MAIL**.

2098	45c. Odontoglossum cervantesii	1·50	45
2099	65c. Phalaenopsis Medford Star	1·75	35
2100	75c. Vanda Motes Resplendent	1·75	85
2101	90c. Odontonia Debutante	2·00	1·00
2102	$1 Iwanagaara Apple Blossom	2·25	1·10
2103	$1.65 Cattleya Sophia Martin	2·25	2·00
2104	$1.65 Dogface Butterfly	2·25	2·00
2105	$1.65 Laeliocattleya Mini Purple	2·25	2·00
2106	$1.65 Cymbidium Showgirl	2·25	2·00
2107	$1.65 Brassolaeliocattleya Dorothy Bertsch	2·25	2·00
2108	$1.65 Disa blackii	2·25	2·00
2109	$1.65 Paphiopedilum leeanum	2·25	2·00
2110	$1.65 Paphiopedilum macra-nthum	2·25	2·00
2111	$1.65 Brassocattleya Angel Lace	2·25	2·00
2112	$1.65 Saphrolae liocattleya Pre-cious Stones	2·25	2·00
2113	$1.65 Orange Theope Butterfly	2·25	2·00
2114	$1.65 Promenaea xanthina	2·25	2·00
2115	$1.65 Lycaste macrobulbon	2·25	2·00
2116	$1.65 Amestella philippinensis	2·25	2·00
2117	$1.65 Masdevallia Machu Picchu	2·25	2·00
2118	$1.65 Phalaenopsis Zuma Urchin	2·25	2·00
2119	$2 Dendrobium victoria-reginae	2·75	2·75
MS2120	Two sheets, each 76×106 mm. (a) $6 Miltonia Seine. (b) $6 Paphio-pedilum gratrixanum Set of 2 sheets	15·00	15·00

1999. 50th Death Anniv of Paul Harris (founder of Rotary International). No. 2472/3 of Antigua optd **BARBUDA MAIL**.

2121	$1.65 Paul Harris and James Grant	2·50	3·25
MS2122	78×107 mm. $6 Group study exchange, New Zealand	5·00	7·00

1999. Royal Wedding. Nos. 2912/16 of Antigua optd **BARBUDA MAIL**.

2123	$3 Sophie Rhys-Jones	2·50	2·75
2124	$3 Sophie and Prince Edward	2·50	2·75
2125	$3 Prince Edward	2·50	2·75
MS2126	108×78 mm. $6 Prince Edward with Sophie Rhys-Jones and Windsor Castle	6·00	7·50

1999. Fungi. Nos. 2489/501 of Antigua optd **BARBUDA MAIL**.

2127	45c. Marasmius rotula	1·00	35
2128	65c. Cantharellus cibarius	1·25	55
2129	70c. Lepiota cristata	1·25	60
2130	90c. Auricularia mesenterica	1·40	70
2131	$1 Pholiota alnicola	1·40	1·00
2132	$1.75 Leccinum aurantiacum	1·40	1·75
2133	$1.75 Entoloma serrulatum	1·40	1·75
2134	$1.75 Panaeolus sphinctrinus	1·40	1·75
2135	$1.75 Volvariella bombycina	1·40	1·75
2136	$1.75 Conocybe percincta	1·40	1·75
2137	$1.75 Pluteus cervinus	1·40	1·75
2138	$1.75 Russula foetens	1·40	1·75
MS2139	Two sheets, each 106×76 mm. (a) $6 Amanita cothurnata. (b) $6 Panellus serotinus Set of 2 sheets	12·00	14·00

1999. First Death Anniv of Diana, Princess of Wales. No. 2753 of Antigua optd **BARBUDA MAIL**.

2140	$1.20 Diana, Princess of Wales	1·50	1·50

1999. Railway Locomotives of the World. Nos. 2553/65 of Antigua optd **BARBUDA MAIL**.

2141	$1.65 Original drawing by Richard Trevithick, 1803	1·75	1·75
2142	$1.65 William Hedley's Puffing Billy, (1813–14)	1·75	1·75
2143	$1.65 Crampton locomotive of French Nord Railway, 1858	1·75	1·75
2144	$1.65 Lawrence Machine Shop locomotive, U.S.A., 1860	1·75	1·75
2145	$1.65 Natchez and Hamburg Railway steam locomotive Mississippi, 1834	1·75	1·75
2146	$1.65 Bury "Coppernob" locomotive, Furness Railway, 1846	1·75	1·75
2147	$1.65 David Joy's Jenny Lind, 1847	1·75	1·75
2148	$1.65 Schenectady Atlantic locomotive, U.S.A., 1899	1·75	1·75
2149	$1.65 Kitson Class 1800 tank locomotive, Japan, 1881	1·75	1·75
2150	$1.65 Pennsylvania Railroad express freight	1·75	1·75
2151	$1.65 Karl Golsdorf's 4 cylinder locomotive, Austria	1·75	1·75
2152	$1.65 Series "E" locomotive, Russia, 1930	1·75	1·75
MS2153	Two sheets, each 72×100 mm. (a) $6 George Stephenson's "Patentee" Type locomotive, 1843. (b) $6 Brunel's trestle bridge over River Lynher, Cornwall	11·00	12·00

1999. 175th Anniv of Cedar Hall Moravian Church. Nos. 2605/11 of Antigua optd **BARBUDA MAIL**.

2154	20c. First Church and Manse, 1822–40	45	50
2155	45c. Cedar Hall School, 1840	55	40
2156	75c. Hugh A. King, minister, 1945–53	75	60
2157	90c. Present Church building	85	60
2158	$1.20 Water tank, 1822	1·25	1·25
2159	$2 Former Manse, demolished 1978	1·75	3·00
MS2160	100×70 mm. $6 Present church building (different) (50×37 mm)	4·75	6·50

1999. Christmas. Religious Paintings. Nos. 2945/51 of Antigua optd **BARBUDA MAIL**.

2161	15c. multicoloured	35	40
2162	25c. black, stone and yellow	40	30
2163	45c. multicoloured	55	30
2164	60c. multicoloured	80	35
2165	$2 multicoloured	1·75	2·50
2166	$4 black, stone and yellow	2·75	4·50
MS2167	76×106 mm. $6 multicoloured	4·50	6·00

1999. Centenary of Thomas Oliver Robinson Memorial School. Nos. 2634/40 of Antigua optd **BARBUDA MAIL**.

2168	20c. green and black	35	40
2169	45c. multicoloured	55	30
2170	65c. green and black	75	45
2171	75c. multicoloured	80	65
2172	90c. multicoloured	90	65
2173	$1.20 brown, green and black	1·10	1·60
MS2174	106×76 mm. $6 brown	4·50	6·00

2000. Cats and Dogs. Nos. 2540/52 of Antigua optd **BARBUDA MAIL**.

2175	$1.65 Scottish fold kitten	2·25	2·25
2176	$1.65 Japanese bobtail	2·25	2·25
2177	$1.65 Tabby manx	2·25	2·25
2178	$1.65 Bicolor American shorthair	2·25	2·25
2179	$1.65 Sorel Abyssinian	2·25	2·25
2180	$1.65 Himalayan blue point	2·25	2·25
2181	$1.65 Dachshund	2·25	2·25
2182	$1.65 Staffordshire terrier	2·25	2·25
2183	$1.65 Shar-pei	2·25	2·25
2184	$1.65 Beagle	2·25	2·25
2185	$1.65 Norfolk terrier	2·25	2·25
2186	$1.65 Golden retriever	2·25	2·25
MS2187	Two sheets, each 107×77 mm. (a) $6 Red tabby (vert). (b) $6 Siberian husky (vert)	15·00	17·00

2000. Fish. Nos. 2586/604 of Antigua optd **BARBUDA MAIL**.

2188	75c. Yellow damselfish	75	50
2189	90c. Barred hamlet	80	55
2190	$1 Yellow-tailed damselfish ("Jewellfish")	90	70
2191	$1.20 Blue-headed wrasse	1·10	1·00
2192	$1.50 Queen angelfish	1·25	1·25
2193	$1.65 Jackknife-fish	1·25	1·25
2194	$1.65 Spot-finned hogfish	1·25	1·25
2195	$1.65 Sergeant major	1·25	1·25
2196	$1.65 Neon goby	1·25	1·25
2197	$1.65 Jawfish	1·25	1·25
2198	$1.65 Flamefish	1·25	1·25
2199	$1.65 Rock beauty	1·25	1·25
2200	$1.65 Yellow-tailed snapper	1·25	1·25
2201	$1.65 Creole wrasse	1·25	1·25

2202		$1.65 Slender filefish	1·25	1·25
2203		$1.65 Long-spined squirrelfish	1·25	1·25
2204		$1.65 Royal gramma ("Fairy Basslet")	1·25	1·25
2205		$1.75 Queen triggerfish	1·40	1·40
MS2206		Two sheets, each 80×110 mm. (a) $6 Porkfish. (b) $6 Black-capped basslet	20·00	20·00

2000. Ships of the World. Nos. 2679/85 of Antigua optd **BARBUDA MAIL.**

2207		$1.75 Savannah (paddle-steamer)	1·75	1·75
2208		$1.75 Viking longship	1·75	1·75
2209		$1.75 Greek galley	1·75	1·75
2210		$1.75 Sailing clipper	1·75	1·75
2211		$1.75 Dhow	1·75	1·75
2212		$1.75 Fishing catboat	1·75	1·75
MS2213		Three sheets, each 100×70 mm. (a) $6 13th-century English warship (41×22 mm). (b) $6 Sailing dory (22×41 mm). (c) $6 Baltimore clipper (41×22 mm)	14·00	16·00

2000. Modern Aircraft. Nos. 2700/12 of Antigua optd **BARBUDA MAIL.**

2214		$1.65 Lockheed-Boeing General Dynamics Yf-22	1·75	1·75
2215		$1.65 Dassault-Breguet Rafale BO 1	1·75	1·75
2216		$1.65 MiG 29	1·75	1·75
2217		$1.65 Dassault-Breguet Mirage 2000D	1·75	1·75
2218		$1.65 Rockwell B-1B "Lancer"	1·75	1·75
2219		$1.65 McDonnell-Douglas C-17A	1·75	1·75
2220		$1.65 Space Shuttle	1·75	1·75
2221		$1.65 SAAB "Grippen"	1·75	1·75
2222		$1.65 Eurofighter EF-2000	1·75	1·75
2223		$1.65 Sukhoi SU 27	1·75	1·75
2224		$1.65 Northrop B-2	1·75	1·75
2225		$1.65 Lockheed F-117 "Nighthawk"	1·75	1·75
MS2226		Two sheets, each 110×85 mm. (a) $6 F18 Hornet. (b) $6 Sukhoi SU 35	13·00	15·00

2000. Classic Cars. Nos. 2687/MS2699 of Antigua optd **BARBUDA MAIL.**

2227		$1.65 Ford (1896)	1·75	1·75
2228		$1.65 Ford A (1903)	1·75	1·75
2229		$1.65 Ford T (1928)	1·75	1·75
2230		$1.65 Ford T (1922)	1·75	1·75
2231		$1.65 Ford Blackhawk (1929)	1·75	1·75
2232		$1.65 Ford Sedan (1934)	1·75	1·75
2233		$1.65 Torpedo (1911)	1·75	1·75
2234		$1.65 Mercedes 22 (1913)	1·75	1·75
2235		$1.65 Rover (1920)	1·75	1·75
2236		$1.65 Mercedes Benz (1956)	1·75	1·75
2237		$1.65 Packard V-12 (1934)	1·75	1·75
2238		$1.65 Opel (1924)	1·75	1·75
MS2239		Two sheets, each 70×100 mm. (a) $6 Ford (1908) (60×40 mm). (b) $6 Ford (1929) (60×40 mm) Set of 2 sheets	12·00	13·00

2000. 19th World Scout Jamboree, Chile. Nos. 2739/ **MS**2742 of Antigua optd **BARBUDA MAIL.**

2240		90c. Scout handshake	1·50	1·00
2241		$1 Scouts hiking	1·75	1·25
2242		$1.20 Scout salute	2·25	2·50
MS2243		68×98 mm. $6 Lord Baden-Powell	7·50	8·50

2000. 50th Anniv of Organisation of American States (1998). No. 2730 of Antigua optd **BARBUDA MAIL.**

2244		$1 Stylized Americas	1·25	1·50

2000. International Year of the Ocean (1998). Nos. 2641/ **MS**2678a/b of Antigua optd **BARBUDA MAIL.**
2245/69 40c.×25 Spotted eagle ray; Manta ray; Hawksbill turtle; Jellyfish; Queen angelfish; Octopus; Emperor angelfish; Regal angelfish; Porkfish; Racoon butterflyfish; Atlantic barracuda; Sea horse; Nautilus; Trumpetfish; White tip shark; Sunken Spanish galleon; Black tip shark; Long-nosed butterflyfish; Green moray eel; Captain Nemo; Treasure chest; Hammerhead shark; Divers; Lionfish; Clownfish ... 14·00 15·00

2270/81 75c.×12 Maroon-tailed conure; Cocoi heron; Common tern; Rainbow loriket; Saddleback butterflyfish; Goatfish and cat shark; Blue shark and stingray; Majestic snapper; Nassau grouper; Black-cap gramma and blue tang; Stingrays; Stingray and giant starfish ... 18·00 20·00

MS2282		Two sheets. (a) $6 68×98 mm. $6 Humpback whale. (b) $6 98×68 mm. $6 Fiddler ray Set of 2 sheets	15·00	16·00

Nos. 2245/69 and 2270/81 were each printed together, *se-tenant*, with the backgrounds forming composite designs.

2000. Olympic Games, Sydney. Nos. 3109/12 of Antigua optd **BARBUDA MAIL.**

2283		$2 Marcus Latimer Hurley (cycling), St Louis (1904)	4·50	3·75
2284		$2 Diving	4·50	3·75
2285		$2 Flaminio Stadium, Rome (1960) and Italian flag	4·50	3·75
2286		$2 Ancient Greek javelin thrower	4·50	3·75

2000. West Indies Cricket Tour and 100th Test Match at Lord's. Nos. 3113/**MS**3115 of Antigua optd **BARBUDA MAIL.**

2287		90c. Richie Richardson	2·25	1·60
2288		$5 Viv Richards	8·00	9·00
MS2289		121×104 mm. $6 Lord's Cricket Ground	9·00	10·00

2000. Satellites and Spacecraft. Nos. 2835/40 and **MS**2847b of Antigua optd **BARBUDA MAIL.**

2290		$1.65 "Luna 2" moon probe	2·50	2·50
2291		$1.65 "Mariner 2" space probe	2·50	2·50
2292		$1.65 Giotto space probe	2·50	2·50
2293		$1.65 Rosat satellite	2·50	2·50
2294		$1.65 International Ultraviolet Explorer	2·50	2·50
2295		$1.65 Ulysses space probe	2·50	2·50
MS2296		106×76 mm. $6 "MIR" space station	8·50	9·50

2000. No. **MS**3233 of Antigua optd **BARBUDA MAIL.**

MS2313		Two Sheets, each 90×60 mm. (a) $6 Junkers 87B (dive bomber). (b) $6 Supermarine Spitfires at dusk	17·00	18·00

BARWANI

A State of Central India. Now uses Indian stamps.

12 pies = 1 anna; 16 annas = 1 rupee.

1 Rana Ranjit Singh **2**

1921

5	1	¼a. green	25·00	£140
18	1	¼a. pink	3·75	19·00
19	1	¼a. blue	2·00	11·00
37B	1	¼a. black	6·00	50·00
4	1	½a. blue	24·00	£325
29	1	½a. green	3·00	22·00
10	2	1a. red	4·00	28·00
39B	2	1a. brown	15·00	40·00
11	2	2a. purple	2·75	35·00
41B	2	2a. red	42·00	£180
31	2	4a. orange	£100	£350
42B*a*		4a. green	18·00	65·00

DESIGN: 4a. Another portrait of Rana Ranjit Singh.

4 Rana Devi Singh

1932

32A	4	¼a. slate	4·25	29·00
33A	4	½a. green	5·50	29·00
34A	4	1a. brown	6·00	27·00
35A	4	2a. purple	4·25	60·00
36A	4	4a. olive	6·00	50·00

5

1938

43	5	1a. brown	55·00	90·00

BASUTOLAND

An African territory under British protection, N.E. of Cape Province. Self-Government introduced on 1 April 1965. Attained independence on 4 October 1966, when the country was renamed Lesotho.

1933. 12 pence = 1 shilling; 20 shillings = 1 pound.
1961. 100 cents = 1 rand.

1 King George V, Nile Crocodile and Mountains

1933

1	1	½d. green	1·00	1·75
2	1	1d. red	75	1·25
3	1	2d. purple	1·00	80
4	1	3d. blue	75	1·25
5	1	4d. grey	2·00	7·00
6	1	6d. yellow	2·25	1·75
7	1	1s. orange	3·50	4·50
8	1	2s.6d. brown	35·00	55·00
9	1	5s. violet	65·00	85·00
10	1	10s. olive	£190	£200

1935. Silver Jubilee. As T **13** of Antigua.

11		1d. blue and red	75	3·50
12		2d. blue and grey	1·00	3·50
13		3d. brown and blue	4·00	8·00
14		6d. grey and purple	4·25	8·00

1937. Coronation. As T **2** of Aden.

15		1d. red	35	1·25
16		2d. purple	50	1·25
17		3d. blue	60	1·25

1938. As T **1**, but portrait of King George VI.

18		½d. green	30	1·25
19		1d. red	1·25	70
20		1½d. blue	60	50
21		2d. purple	50	60
22		3d. blue	50	1·25
23		4d. grey	2·50	3·75
24		6d. yellow	3·25	1·50
25		1s. orange	3·25	1·00
26		2s.6d. brown	19·00	8·50
27		5s. violet	45·00	9·50
28		10s. olive	45·00	23·00

1945. Victory. Stamps of South Africa optd **Basutoland.** Alternate stamps inscr in English or Afrikaans.

29	**55**	1d. brown and red	50	10
30	**55**	2d. blue and violet	50	10
31	**55**	3d. blue	50	15

Prices are for bi-lingual pairs.

5 King George VI and Queen Elizabeth

1947. Royal Visit.

32	-	1d. red	10	10
33	**5**	2d. green	10	10
34	-	3d. blue	10	10
35	-	1s. mauve	15	10

DESIGNS—VERT: 1d. King George VI. HORIZ: 3d. Queen Elizabeth II as Princess and Princess Margaret; 1s. The Royal Family.

1948. Silver Wedding. As T **10/11** of Aden.

36		1½d. blue	20	10
37		10s. green	48·00	50·00

1949. U.P.U. As T **20/23** of Antigua.

38		1½d. blue	20	1·50
39		3d. blue	2·00	2·00
40		6d. orange	1·00	5·50
41		1s. brown	50	1·40

1953. Coronation. As T **13** of Aden.

42		2d. black and purple	65	40

8 Qiloane **18** Mohair (Shearing Goats)

1954

43	**8**	½d. black and sepia	65	10
44	-	1d. black and green	60	10

45	-	2d. blue and orange	1·25	10
46	-	3d. sage and red	2·25	30
47	-	4½d. indigo and blue	1·50	15
48	-	6d. brown and green	2·25	15
49	-	1s. bronze and purple	2·25	30
50	-	1s.3d. brown and turquoise	28·00	9·00
51	-	2s.6d. blue and red	28·00	12·00
52	-	5s. black and red	12·00	12·00
53	**18**	10s. black and purple	38·00	27·00

DESIGNS—HORIZ: 1d. Orange River; 2d. Mosuto horseman; 3d. Basuto household; 4½d. Maletsunyane Falls; 6d. Herd-boy playing lesiba; 1s. Pastoral scene; 1s.3d. De Havilland Comet 1 airplane over Lancers' Gap; 2s.6d. Old Fort, Leribe; 5s. Mission cave house.

1959. No. 45 Surch ½d. and bar.

54		½d. on 2d. blue and orange	35	20

20 "Chief Moshoeshoe I" (engraving by Delangle)

1959. Inauguration of National Council.

55	**20**	3d. black and olive	60	10
56	-	1s. red and green	60	20
57	-	1s.3d. blue and orange	1·00	45

DESIGNS: 1s. Council house; 1s.3d. Mosuto horseman.

1961. Nos. 43/53 surch.

58	**8**	½c. on ½d. black and sepia	10	30
59	-	1c. on 1d. black and green	30	10
60	-	2c. on 2d. blue and orange	1·50	1·50
61	-	2½c. on 3d. green and red	15	10
62	-	3½c. on 4½d. indigo and blue	45	10
63a	-	5c. on 6d. brown and green	50	10
64	-	10c. on 1s. green and purple	50	10
65a	-	12½c. on 1s.3d. brown and turquoise	6·50	2·50
66	-	25c. on 2s.6d. blue and red	2·25	75
67a	-	50c. on 5s. black and red	5·00	5·50
68b	**18**	1r. on 10s. black and purple	29·00	26·00

26 Basuto Household

1961. As 1954 but value in new currency as in T **26**.

69	**8**	½c. black and brown	20	20
70	-	1c. black and green (as 1d.)	25	40
71	-	2c. blue and orange (as 2d.)	3·00	1·40
86	**26**	2½c. green and red	25	25
73	-	3½c. indigo and blue (as 4½d.)	55	1·50
88	-	5c. brown and green (as 6d.)	40	50
75	-	10c. green and purple (as 1s.)	50	40
90	-	12½c. brown & grn (as 1s.3d.)	11·00	1·50
77	-	25c. blue and red (as 2s.6d.)	6·50	6·50
92	-	50c. black and red (as 5s.)	7·25	14·00
79	**18**	1r. black and purple	55·00	26·00

1963. Freedom from Hunger. As T **28** of Aden.

80		12½c. violet	40	15

1963. Centenary of Red Cross. As T **33** of Antigua.

81		2½c. red and black	30	10
82		12½c. red and blue	1·10	60

28 Mosotho Woman and Child

1965. New Constitution. Inscr "SELF GOVERNMENT 1965". Multicoloured.

94		2½c. Type **28**	30	10
95		3½c. Maseru border post	45	20
96		5c. Mountain scene	45	20
97		12½c. Legislative Buildings	60	70

1965. Centenary of I.T.U. As T **36** of Antigua.

98	1c. red and purple	15	10
99	20c. blue and brown	50	30

1965. I.C.Y. As T **37** of Antigua.

100	½c. purple and turquoise	10	1·25
101	12½c. green and lavender	45	35

1966. Churchill Commemoration. As T **38** of Antigua.

102	1c. blue	15	1·50
103	2½c. green	60	10
104	10c. brown	1·00	50
105	22½c. violet	1·25	1·50

OFFICIAL STAMPS

1934. Nos. 1/3 and 6 optd **OFFICIAL**.

O1	1	½d. green	£14000	£7500
O2	1	1d. red	£5000	£3750
O3	1	2d. purple	£5500	£1200
O4	1	6d. yellow	£14000	£5000

POSTAGE DUE STAMPS

1933. As Type D **1** of Barbados.

D1b	1d. red	2·00	8·00
D2a	2d. violet	30	25·00

D 2

1956

D3	D2	1d. red	30	3·00
D4	D2	2d. violet	30	6·00

1961. Surch.

D5	1c. on 1d. red	10	35	
D6	1c. on 2d. violet	10	1·25	
D7	5c. on 2d. violet	15	45	
D8	-	5c. on 2d. violet (No. D2a)	1·00	7·00

1964. As Type D **2**, but value in decimal currency.

D9	1c. red	4·75	26·00
D10	5c. violet	4·75	26·00

For later issues see **LESOTHO**.

Pt. 1

BATUM

Batum, a Russian port on the Black Sea, had been taken by Turkish troops during the First World War. Following the Armistice, British Forces occupied the town on 1 December 1918. Batum was handed over to the National Republic of Georgia on 7 July 1920.

100 kopeks = 1 rouble.

1 Aloe Tree

1919. Imperf.

1	1	5k. green	7·50	25·00
2	1	10k. blue	8·50	25·00
3	1	50k. yellow	8·00	13·00
4	1	1r. brown	11·00	9·00
5	1	3r. violet	11·00	19·00
6	1	5r. brown	10·00	38·00

БАТУМ. ОБ.

РУб 10 РУб

(2)

1919. Arms types of Russia surch as T **2**. Imperf (Nos. 7/8), perf (Nos. 9/10).

7	10r. on 1k. orange	75·00	85·00
8	10r. on 3k. red	30·00	38·00
9	10r. on 5k. purple	£425	£475
10	10r. on 10 on 7k. blue	£500	£550

1919. T **1** optd **BRITISH OCCUPATION**.

11	5k. green	28·00	18·00
12	10k. blue	16·00	21·00
13	25k. yellow	27·00	21·00
14	1r. blue	8·00	21·00
15	2r. pink	1·00	8·50
16	3r. violet	1·00	8·50
17	5r. brown	1·25	8·50
18	7r. red	6·00	12·00

1919. Arms types of Russia surch with Russian inscr, **BRITISH OCCUPATION** and new value.

19	10r. on 3k. red	27·00	29·00
20a	15r. on 1k. orange	75·00	80·00
29	25r. on 5k. purple	50·00	70·00
30a	25r. on 10 on 7k. blue	85·00	95·00
31	25r. on 20 on 14k. red and blue	95·00	£120

32a	25r. on 25k. purple and green	£110	£140
33a	25r. on 50k. green and purple	90·00	£120
21	50r. on 1k. orange	£600	£700
34	50r. on 2k. green	£130	£160
35	50r. on 3k. red	£130	£160
36	50r. on 4k. red	£120	£140
37	50r. on 5k. purple	95·00	£120
27	50r. on 10k. blue	£2500	£2500
28	50r. on 15k. blue and brown	£750	£900

1920. Romanov type of Russia surch with Russian inscr, **BRITISH OCCUPATION** and new value.

41	50r. on 4k. red	£110	£130

1920. Nos. 11, 13 and 3 surch with new value (50r. with **BRITISH OCCUPATION** also).

42	25r. on 5k. green	50·00	55·00
43	25r. on 25k. yellow	40·00	42·00
44a	50r. on 50k. yellow	21·00	23·00

1920. T **1** optd **BRITISH OCCUPATION**.

45	1r. brown	2·25	16·00
46	2r. blue	2·25	16·00
47	3r. pink	2·25	16·00
48	5r. black	2·25	16·00
49	7r. yellow	2·25	16·00
50	10r. green	2·25	16·00
51	15r. violet	2·75	21·00
52	25r. red	2·50	20·00
53	50r. blue	2·75	23·00

Pt. 7

BAVARIA

In S. Germany. A kingdom till 1918, then a republic. Incorporated into Germany in 1920.

1849. 60 kreuzer = 1 gulden.
1874. 100 pfennig = 1 mark.

1

1849. Imperf.

1	1k. black	£1300	£2000

2 (Circle cut)

1849. Imperf. Circle cut by labels.

3	2	3k. blue	£325	5·25
23	2	3k. red	70·00	8·75
7	2	6k. brown	£9500	£325

1850. Imperf. As T **2**, but circle not cut.

8a	1k. red	£400	49·00
21	1k. yellow	£100	27·00
11	6k. brown	65·00	13·00
25	6k. blue	£100	55·00
16	9k. green	£275	22·00
28	9k. brown	£160	22·00
18	12k. red	£200	£190
31	12k. green	£130	85·00
19	18k. yellow	£190	£275
32	18k. red	£200	£650

3 **6**

1867. Imperf.

34	3	1k. green	90·00	16·00
37	3	3k. red	95·00	3·25
39	3	6k. blue	60·00	27·00
41	3	6k. brown	£110	65·00
43	3	7k. blue	£550	22·00
46	3	9k. brown	60·00	49·00
48	3	12k. mauve	£500	£130
50	3	18k. red	£190	£250
65	6	1m. mauve	£900	£110

1870. Perf.

51A	3	1k. green	17·00	2·20
69	3	3k. red	1·10	11·00
55A	3	6k. brown	45·00	44·00
56A	3	7k. blue	5·00	6·00
59A	3	9k. brown	7·75	5·50
60A	3	10k. yellow	9·00	22·00
61A	3	12k. mauve	£1800	£6500
63A	3	18k. red	20·00	22·00

8

1876. Perf.

120	8	2pf. grey	3·25	75
103	8	3pf. green	14·50	2·75
121	8	3pf. brown	45	85
107	8	5pf. mauve	29·00	13·00
122	8	5pf. green	45	85
123	8	10pf. red	55	1·10
124	8	20pf. blue	55	1·10
114	8	25pf. brown	45·00	11·00
125	8	25pf. orange	65	1·30
126	8	30pf. olive	1·10	1·10
127	8	40pf. yellow	1·10	1·50
86	8	50pf. red	80·00	9·75
117	8	50pf. brown	85·00	11·00
128	8	50pf. purple	65	2·20
129	8	80pf. mauve	4·50	5·50
100	6	1m. mauve	6·75	5·50
101a	6	2m. orange	7·75	11·00
136	6	3m. brown	12·50	49·00
137	6	5m. green	12·50	60·00

11 **13** Prince Luitpold

1911. Prince Regent Luitpold's 90th Birthday.

138c	11	3pf. brown on drab	45	1·10
139c	11	5pf. green on green	45	1·10
140d	11	10pf. red on buff	45	1·10
141b	11	20pf. blue on blue	2·75	1·70
142a	11	25pf. deep brown on buff	4·50	3·25
143a		30pf. orange on buff	2·75	2·50
144a		40pf. olive on buff	4·50	2·50
145a		50pf. red on drab	4·50	4·25
146		60pf. green on buff	4·50	4·25
147a		80pf. violet on drab	13·50	14·00
148a	13	1m. brown on drab	4·50	5·50
149a	13	2m. green on drab	6·75	16·00
150a	13	3m. red on buff	18·00	£100
151	13	5m. blue on buff	36·00	65·00
152	13	10m. orange on yellow	60·00	95·00
153	13	20m. brown on yellow	36·00	50·00

The 30 pf. to 80 pf. values are similar to Type **11**, but larger.

14

1911. 25th Anniv of Regency of Prince Luitpold.

154	14	5pf. yellow, green & black	1·10	2·00
155	14	10pf. yellow, red & black	1·70	3·25

 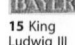

15 King Ludwig III **16**

1914. Imperf or perf.

171A	15	2pf. slate	35	2·75
172A	15	2½ on 2pf. slate	35	2·75
173A	15	3pf. brown	35	2·75
175A	15	5pf. green	35	2·75
176A	15	7½pf. green	35	2·75
178A	15	10pf. red	35	2·75
179A	15	15pf. red	35	2·75
182A	15	20pf. blue	35	2·75
183A	15	25pf. grey	35	2·75
184A	15	30pf. orange	1·00	2·75
185A	15	40pf. olive	35	2·75
186A	15	50pf. brown	35	2·75
187A	15	60pf. green	1·70	2·75
188A	15	80pf. violet	35	2·75
189A	16	1m. brown	35	2·75
190A	16	2m. violet	45	4·00
191A	16	3m. red	60	7·75
192A	-	5m. blue	80	29·00
193A	-	10m. green	2·50	80·00
194A	-	20m. brown	4·50	£110

The 5, 10 and 20m. are larger.

1919. Peoples' State Issue. Overprinted **Volksstaat Bayern**. Imperf or perf.

195A	15	3pf. brown	35	2·75
196A	15	5pf. green	35	2·75
197A	15	7½pf. green	35	2·75
198A	15	10pf. lake	35	2·75
199A	15	15pf. red	35	2·75
200A	15	20pf. blue	35	2·75
201A	15	25pf. grey	35	2·75
202A	15	30pf. orange	35	2·75
203A	15	35pf. orange	35	3·25
204A	15	40pf. olive	35	2·75
205A	15	50pf. brown	35	2·75
206A	15	60pf. turquoise	35	2·75
207A	15	75pf. brown	35	2·75
208A	15	80pf. violet	35	2·75
209A	16	1m. brown	35	2·75
210A	16	2m. violet	45	6·75
211A	16	3m. red	70	6·75
212A	-	5m. blue (No. 192)	1·40	17·00
213A	-	10m. green (No. 193)	2·10	75·00
214A	-	20m. brown (No. 194)	3·50	80·00

1919. First Free State Issue. Stamps of Germany (inscr "DEUTSCHES REICH") optd **Freistaat Bayern**.

215	24	2½pf. grey	35	2·75
216	10	3pf. brown	35	2·75
217	10	5pf. green	35	2·75
218	24	7½pf. orange	35	2·75
219	10	10pf. red	35	2·75
220	24	15pf. violet	35	2·75
221	10	20pf. blue	35	2·75
222	10	25pf. black & red on yell	35	2·75
223	24	35pf. brown	35	2·75
224	10	40pf. black and red	60	2·75
225	10	75pf. black and green	80	3·25
226	10	80pf. black & red on rose	80	4·50
227	12	1m. red	1·80	6·75
228	13	2m. blue	2·30	16·00
229	14	3m. black	2·30	18·00
230	15	5m. red and black	2·30	18·00

1919. Second Free State Issue. Stamps of Bavaria overprinted **Freistaat Bayern**. Imperf or perf.

231A		3pf. brown	35	2·75
232A		5pf. green	35	2·75
233A		7½pf. green	35	22·00
234A		10pf. lake	35	2·75
235A		15pf. red	35	2·75
236A		20pf. blue	35	2·75
237A		25pf. grey	35	2·75
238A		30pf. orange	35	2·75
239A		40pf. olive	35	20·00
240A		50pf. brown	35	2·75
241A		60pf. turquoise	35	20·00
242A		75pf. brown	60	20·00
243A		80pf. violet	35	5·00
244A	16	1m. brown	35	4·00
245A	16	2m. violet	35	7·75
246A	16	3m. red	90	10·00
247A	-	5m. blue (No. 192)	1·60	25·00
248A	-	10m. green (No. 193)	3·00	50·00
249A	-	20m. brown (No. 194)	3·50	85·00

1919. War Wounded. **Surch 5 Pf. fur Kriegs-beschadigte Freistaat Bayern**. Perf.

250	15	10pf.+5pf. lake	60	2·75
251	15	15pf.+5pf. red	60	2·75
252	15	20pf.+5pf. blue	60	3·25

1920. Surch **Freistaat Bayern** and value. Imperf or perf.

253A	16	1m.25pf. on 1m. green	35	3·25
254A	16	1m.50pf. on 1m. orange	35	4·50
255A	16	2m.50pf. on 1m. slate	70	9·00

1920. No. 121 surch **20** in four corners.

256	8	20 on 3pf. brown	35	2·75

26 **27** **28**

29 **30**

1920

257	26	5pf. green	25	3·25
258	26	10pf. orange	25	3·25
259	26	15pf. red	25	3·25
260	27	20pf. violet	25	4·50
261	27	30pf. blue	25	4·50
262	27	40pf. brown	25	3·25
263	28	50pf. red	25	3·25

264	28	60pf. turquoise	25	3·25
265	28	75pf. red	25	3·25
266	29	1m. red and grey	45	3·25
267	29	1¼m. blue and brown	35	3·25
268	29	1½m. green and grey	35	4·50
269	29	2½m. black and grey	35	45·00
270	30	3m. blue	1·00	20·00
271	30	5m. orange	1·00	20·00
272	30	10m. black	1·60	33·00
273	30	20m. black	2·20	47·00

OFFICIAL STAMPS

O18

1916

O195	O18	3pf. brown	35	1·10
O196	O18	5pf. green	35	1·10
O197	O18	7½pf. green on green	35	65
O198	O18	7½pf. green	35	1·70
O199	O18	10pf. red	35	1·70
O200	O18	15pf. red on buff	90	1·10
O201	O18	15pf. red	35	1·70
O202	O18	20pf. blue on blue	3·00	2·75
O203	O18	20pf. blue	35	1·70
O204	O18	25pf. grey	35	90
O205	O18	30pf. orange	35	90
O206	O18	60pf. turquoise	35	1·70
O207	O18	1m. purple on buff	1·40	4·00
O208	O18	1m. purple	4·00	£650

1919. Optd **Volksstaat Bayern.**

O215		3pf. brown	35	19·00
O216		5pf. green	35	2·75
O217		7½pf. green	35	18·00
O218		10pf. red	35	3·00
O219		15pf. red	35	3·00
O220		20pf. blue	35	3·00
O221		25pf. grey	35	3·00
O222		30pf. orange	35	3·00
O223		35pf. orange	35	3·00
O224		50pf. olive	35	3·25
O225		60pf. turquoise	45	19·00
O226		75pf. brown	45	5·00
O227		1m. purple on buff	1·60	20·00
O228		1m. purple	5·75	£550

O31 **O32** **O33**

1920

O274	O31	5pf. green	35	9·00
O275	O31	10pf. orange	35	9·00
O276	O31	15pf. red	35	9·00
O277	O31	20pf. violet	35	9·00
O278	O31	30pf. blue	35	10·00
O279	O31	40pf. brown	35	10·00
O280	O32	50pf. red	35	31·00
O281	O32	60pf. green	35	13·50
O282	O32	70pf. lilac	35	40·00
O283	O32	75pf. grey	35	50·00
O284	O32	80pf. blue	35	50·00
O285	O32	90pf. olive	35	80·00
O286	O33	1m. brown	35	65·00
O287	O33	1¼m. green	35	90·00
O288	O33	1½m. red	35	90·00
O289	O33	2½m. blue	35	£100
O290	O33	3m. lake	80	£140
O291	O33	5m. green	3·50	£170

POSTAGE DUE STAMPS

D6

1862. Inscr "Bayer. Posttaxe" at top. Imperf.

D34	D6	3k. black	£180	£425

1870. As Type D **6**, but inscr "Bayr. Posttaxe" at top. Perf.

D65B		1k. black	17·00	£1100
D66B		3k. black	17·00	£650

1876. Optd **Vom Empfanger zahlbar.**

D130a	8	2pf. grey	1·10	3·25
D131a	8	3pf. grey	1·10	5·50
D132a	8	5pf. grey	1·60	5·00
D133a	8	10pf. grey	1·10	2·75

1895. No. D131a surch **2** in each corner.

D134		2 on 3pf. grey	†	£65000

1908. Stamps of 1876 optd **E.**

R133		3pf. brown	1·10	6·00

R134		5pf. green	35	55
R135		10pf. red	35	55
R136		20pf. blue	65	1·10
R137		50pf. purple	6·25	9·75

Pt. 1

BECHUANALAND

A colony and protectorate in Central S. Africa. British Bechuanaland (colony) was annexed to Cape of Good Hope in 1895. Internal Self-Government in the protectorate was introduced on 1 March 1965. Attained independence on 30 September 1966, when the country was renamed Botswana.

1885. 12 pence = 1 shilling; 20 shillings = 1 pound.
1961. 100 cents = 1 rand.

A. BRITISH BECHUANALAND

1885. Stamps of Cape of Good Hope ("Hope" seated) optd **British Bechuanaland.**

4	6	½d. black	12·00	25·00
38	6	1d. red	3·50	2·25
32	6	2d. bistre	5·50	2·25
2	6	3d. red	50·00	60·00
3	6	4d. blue	85·00	80·00
7	6	6d. purple	£170	38·00
8	6	1s. green	£325	£170

1887. Stamp of Great Britain (Queen Victoria) optd **BRITISH BECHUANALAND.**

9	71	½d. red	1·50	1·50

3 **4**

1887

10	3	1d. lilac and black	23·00	3·50
11	3	2d. lilac and black	£100	2·25
12	3	3d. lilac and black	8·00	7·00
13	3	4d. lilac and black	55·00	2·50
14	3	6d. lilac and black	70·00	2·50
15	4	1s. green and black	30·00	9·50
16	4	2s. green and black	60·00	55·00
17	4	2s.6d. green and black	70·00	75·00
18	4	5s. green and black	£110	£160
19	4	10s. green and black	£225	£375
20	-	£1 lilac and black	£850	£750
21	-	£5 lilac and black	£4000	£1700

Nos. 20/1 are as Type **4** but larger, 23×39½ mm.

1888. Surch.

22	3	"1d." on 1d. lilac and black	7·50	7·00
23	3	"2d." on 2d. lilac and black	55·00	4·00
25	3	"4d." on 4d. lilac and black	£425	£550
26	3	"6d." on 6d. lilac and black	£140	12·00
28		"1s." on 1s. green and black	£200	85·00

1888. Surch **ONE HALF PENNY** and bars.

29	3	½d. on 3d. lilac and black	£250	£300

1891. Stamps of Great Britain (Queen Victoria) optd **BRITISH BECHUANALAND.**

33	57	1d. lilac	7·00	1·50
34	73	2d. green and red	21·00	4·00
35	76	4d. green and brown	3·75	60
36	79	6d. purple on red	7·50	2·00
37	82	1s. green	13·00	17·00

B. BECHUANALAND PROTECTORATE

1888. No. 9 to 19 optd **Protectorate** or surch also.

40	71	½d. red	12·00	50·00
41	3	1d. on 1d. lilac and black	17·00	15·00
42	3	2d. on 2d. lilac and black	38·00	17·00
43	3	3d. on 3d. lilac and black	£180	£225
51	3	4d. on 4d. lilac and black	£120	50·00
45	3	6d. on 6d. lilac and black	£100	50·00
46	4	1s. green and black	£120	55·00
47	4	2s. green and black	£700	£1100
48	4	2s.6d. green and black	£600	£950
49	4	5s. green and black	£1300	£2250
50	4	10s. green and black	£4750	£7000

1889. Stamp of Cape of Good Hope ("Hope" seated) optd **Bechuanaland Protectorate.**

52	6	½d. black	6·00	55·00

1889. No. 9 surch **Protectorate Fourpence.**

53	71	4d. on ½d. red	40·00	6·00

1897. Stamp of Cape of Good Hope ("Hope" seated) optd **BRITISH BECHUANALAND.**

56	6	½d. green	2·50	19·00

1897. Queen Victoria stamps of Great Britain optd **BECHUANALAND PROTECTORATE.**

59	71	½d. red	1·75	2·25
60	71	1d. red	1·40	3·50
61	57	1d. lilac	4·00	75
62	73	2d. green and red	11·00	3·50
63	75	3d. purple on yellow	6·00	10·00
64	76	4d. brown and green	24·00	23·00
65	79	6d. purple on red	24·00	12·00

1904. King Edward VII stamps of Great Britain optd **BECHUANALAND PROTECTORATE.**

66	83	½d. turquoise	2·75	3·25
68	83	1d. red	10·00	30
69	83	2½d. blue	12·00	8·00
70	-	1s. green and red (No. 314)	55·00	£160

1912. King George V stamps of Great Britain optd **BECHUANALAND PROTECTORATE.**

73	105	½d. green	1·25	1·50
72	102	1d. red	3·50	60
92	104	1d. red	2·00	70
75	105	1½d. brown	7·00	2·50
93	104	2d. orange	2·25	1·00
78	104	2½d. blue	3·50	27·00
79	106	3d. violet	6·00	14·00
80	106	4d. grey	6·50	32·00
81	107	6d. purple	9·50	25·00
82	108	1s. brown	20·00	38·00
88	109	2s.6d. brown	90·00	£160
89	109	5s. red	£110	£275

22 King George V, Baobab Tree and Cattle drinking

1932

99	22	½d. green	2·75	50
100	22	1d. red	1·75	40
101	22	2d. brown	1·75	45
102	22	3d. blue	4·00	4·25
103	22	4d. orange	4·00	10·00
104	22	6d. purple	5·50	7·50
105	22	1s. black and olive	4·00	7·50
106	22	2s. black and orange	24·00	70·00
107	22	2s.6d. black and red	24·00	50·00
108	22	3s. black and purple	48·00	60·00
109	22	5s. black and blue	£100	£120
110	22	10s. black and brown	£250	£275

1935. Silver Jubilee. As T **13** of Antigua.

111		1d. blue and red	1·75	7·00
112		2d. blue and black	2·75	6·50
113		3d. brown and blue	4·25	9·00
114		6d. grey and purple	9·50	9·50

1937. Coronation. As T **2** of Aden.

115		1d. red	45	40
116		2d. brown	60	1·00
117		3d. blue	60	1·25

1938. As T **22**, but portrait of King George VI.

118		½d. green	4·25	3·75
119		1d. red	75	50
120a		1½d. blue	1·00	1·00
121		2d. brown	75	50
122		3d. blue	1·00	2·50
123		4d. orange	2·00	3·50
124a		6d. purple	5·50	2·50
125		1s. black and olive	5·50	9·50
126		2s.6d. black and red	14·00	20·00
127		5s. black and blue	48·00	32·00
128		10s. black and brown	30·00	38·00

1945. Victory. Stamps of South Africa optd **Bechuanaland.** Alternate stamps inscr in English or Afrikaans.

129	55	1d. brown and red	75	1·50
130	55	2d. blue and violet (No. 109)	50	1·50
131	55	2d. blue (No. 110)	50	1·75

Prices for bi-lingual pairs.

1947. Royal Visit. As Nos. 32/5 of Basutoland.

132		1d. red	10	10
133		2d. green	10	10
134		3d. blue	10	10
135		1s. mauve	10	10

1948. Silver Wedding. As T **10/11** of Aden.

136		1½d. blue	30	10
137		10s. grey	42·00	50·00

1949. U.P.U. As T **20/23** of Antigua.

138		1½d. blue	30	1·25
139		3d. blue	1·50	2·50

140		6d. mauve	60	4·75
141		1s. olive	60	1·50

1953. Coronation. As T **13** of Aden.

142		2d. black and brown	1·50	30

1955. As T **22** but portrait of Queen Elizabeth II, facing right.

143		½d. green	50	30
144		1d. red	80	10
145		2d. brown	1·25	30
146		3d. blue	3·00	2·50
146b		4d. orange	13·00	14·00
147		4½d. blue	1·50	35
148		6d. purple	1·25	60
149		1s. black and olive	1·25	1·00
150		1s.3d. black and lilac	15·00	9·50
151		2s.6d. black and red	12·00	10·00
152		5s. black and blue	18·00	18·00
153		10s. black and brown	40·00	19·00

26 Queen Victoria. Queen Elizabeth II and Landscape

1960. 75th Anniv of Protectorate.

154	26	1d. sepia and black	50	50
155	26	3d. mauve and black	50	30
156	26	6d. blue and black	55	50

1961. Stamps of 1955 surch.

157		1c. on 1d. red	30	10
158		2c. on 2d. brown	30	10
159		2½c. on 2d. brown	30	10
160		2½c. on 3d. blue	8·00	11·00
161d		3½c. on 4d. orange	20	60
162a		5c. on 6d. purple	20	10
163		10c. on 1s. black and olive	20	10
164		12½c. on 1s.3d. black and lilac	65	20
165		25c. on 2s.6d. black and red	1·50	50
166		50c. on 5s. black and blue	2·00	2·25
167b		1r. on 10s. black and brown	20·00	15·00

28 African Golden Oriole ("Golden Oriole")

1961

168	28	1c. multicoloured	1·50	50
169	-	2c. orange, black and olive	2·00	4·50
170	-	2½c. multicoloured	1·75	10
171	-	3½c. multicoloured	2·50	5·00
172	-	5c. multicoloured	3·25	1·00
173	-	7½c. multicoloured	2·25	2·25
174	-	10c. multicoloured	2·25	60
175	-	12½c. multicoloured	18·00	6·00
176	-	20c. brown and drab	4·00	4·50
177	-	25c. sepia and lemon	2·00	1·50
178	-	35c. blue and orange	4·50	5·00
179	-	50c. sepia and olive	3·50	2·75
180	-	1r. black and brown	11·00	2·75
181	-	2r. brown and turquoise	30·00	15·00

DESIGNS—VERT: 2c. Hoopoe ("African Hoopoe"); 2½c. Scarlet-chested sunbird; 3½c. Yellow-rumped bishop ("Cape Widow-bird"); 5c. Swallow-tailed bee eater; 7½c. African grey hornbill ("Grey Hornbill"); 10c. Red-headed weaver; 12½c. Brown-hooded kingfisher; 20c. Woman musician; 35c. Woman grinding maize; 1r. Lion; 2r. Police camel patrol. HORIZ: 25c. Baobab tree; 50c. Bechuana ox.

1963. Freedom from Hunger. As T **28** of Aden.

182		12½c. green	30	15

1963. Centenary of Red Cross. As T **33** of Antigua.

183		2½c. red and black	30	10
184		12½c. red and blue	70	50

1964. 400th Birth Anniv of Shakespeare. As T **34** of Antigua.

185		12½c. brown	15	15

C. BECHUANALAND

42 Map and Gaberones Dam

1965. New Constitution.

186	42	2½c. red and gold	30	10

187	**42**	5c. blue and gold	30	40
188	**42**	12½c. brown and gold	40	40
189	**42**	25c. green and gold	45	55

1965. Centenary of I.T.U. As T **36** of Antigua.

190		2½c. red and yellow	20	10
191		12½c. mauve and brown	45	30

1965. I.C.Y. As T **37** of Antigua.

192		1c. purple and turquoise	10	45
193		12½c. green and lavender	60	55

1966. Churchill Commemoration. As T **38** of Antigua.

194		1c. blue	30	2·75
195		2½c. green	40	10
196		12½c. brown	75	35
197		20c. violet	75	55

43 Haslar Smoke Generator

1966. Bechuanaland Royal Pioneer Corps.

198	**43**	2½c. blue, red and green	25	10
199	-	5c. brown and blue	30	20
200	-	15c. blue, red and green	1·50	25
201	-	35c. multicoloured	30	1·00

DESIGNS: 5c. Bugler; 15c. Gun-site; 35c. Regimental cap badge.

POSTAGE DUE STAMPS

1926. Postage Due stamps of Great Britain optd **BECHUANALAND PROTECTORATE**.

D1	**D1**	½d. green	13·00	£130
D2	**D1**	1d. red	13·00	80·00
D3	**D1**	2d. black	13·00	90·00

D 3

1932.

D4	**D3**	½d. green	6·00	60·00
D5a	**D3**	1d. red	1·50	29·00
D6c	**D3**	2d. violet	1·75	22·00

1961. Surch.

D7		1c. on 1d. red	25	50
D8		2c. on 2d. violet	25	1·50
D9		5c. on ½d. green	20	60

1961. As Type D **3** but value in decimal currency.

D10		1c. red	30	2·00
D11		2c. violet	30	2·00
D12		5c. green	50	2·00

For later issues see **BOTSWANA**.

Pt. 10

BELARUS

Formerly a constituent republic of the Soviet Union, Belarus became independent in 1991.

100 kopeks = 1 rouble.
2000. Currency Revaluation.

1 12th-century Cross

1992

1	**1**	1r. multicoloured	1·30	75

2 Shyrma

1992. Birth Cent of R. R. Shyrma (composer).

2	**2**	20k. lt blue, blue and black	50	30

3 Arms of Polotsk

1992

3	**3**	2r. multicoloured	80	55

See also Nos. 63 and 89/90.

4 Flag and Map

1992

4	**4**	5r. multicoloured	1·30	95
5	-	5r. black, yellow and red	1·30	95

DESIGN: No. 5, State arms.

(5)

1992. Millenary of Orthodox Church in Belarus. (a) No. 1 optd with T **5**.

6	**1**	1r. multicoloured	1·00	75

(b) Sheet 91×66 mm.

MS7	5r. multicoloured	2·00	1·90

DESIGN: 24×36 mm—5r. Cross of Polotsk.

6 Kamen Tower

1992. Ancient Buildings and Monuments. Multicoloured.

8		2r. Type **6**	50	30
9		2r. Calvinist church, Zaslavl	50	30
10		2r. St. Euphrosyne's church, Polotsk	50	30
11		2r. St. Boris Gleb church, Grodno (horiz)	50	30
12		2r. Mir castle (horiz)	50	30
13		2r. Nesvizh castle (horiz)	50	30

7 State Arms

1992

14	**7**	30k. blue	20	15
15	**7**	45k. green	25	15
16	**7**	50k. green	25	15
17	**7**	1r. brown	25	15
18	**7**	2r. brown	25	15
19	**7**	3r. yellow	35	20
20	**7**	5r. blue	40	20
21	**7**	10r. red	95	55
22	**7**	15r. violet	55	35
23	**7**	25r. green	80	45
24	**7**	50r. mauve	25	20
25	**7**	100r. red	55	35
26	**7**	150r. purple	80	45
27	**7**	200r. green	20	20
28	**7**	300r. red	20	20
29	**7**	600r. mauve	25	20
30	**7**	1000r. red	45	20
31	**7**	3000r. blue	1·20	65

8 Jug and Bowl

1992. Pottery. Multicoloured.

40		1r. Type **8**	40	30
41		1r. Vases and jug on jug tree	40	30
42		1r. Flagon	40	30
43		1r. Jugs	40	30

9 Chickens

1993. Corn Dollies. Multicoloured.

44		5r. Type **9**	20	10
45		10r. Woman and gunman (vert)	30	20
46		15r. Woman (vert)	50	40
47		25r. Man and woman (vert)	1·00	75

10 Harezki

1993. Birth Centenary of M. I. Harezki (author).

48	**10**	50r. purple	60	35

11 Emblem

1993. World Belarussian Congress, Minsk.

49	**11**	50r. red, gold and black	2·00	1·60

12 Man Over Vitebsk

1993. Europa. Contemporary Art. Paintings by Marc Chagall. Multicoloured.

50		1500r. Type **12**	8·00	7·50
51		1500r. Promenade (vert)	8·00	7·50
MS52	142×103 mm. 2500r. Allegory (50×37 mm)		70·00	65·00

(13) **(14)**

1993. Sports Events. Nos. 4/5 variously surch. (a) Winter Olympic Games, Lillehammer, Norway (1994). Surch **Winter Pre-Olympic Games Lillehammer, Norway 1500** (in capitals on No. 44) or in Cyrillic as T **13**.

53	**4**	1500r. on 5r. mult (in Cyrillic)	5·00	4·75
54	**4**	1500r. on 5r. mult (in English)	5·00	4·75
55	-	1500r. on 5r. black, yellow and red (in Cyrillic)	5·00	4·75
56	-	1500r. on 5r. black, yellow and red (in English)	5·00	4·75
MS57	Two sheets. (a) 1500r. on 5r. multicoloured (in Cyrillic); (b) 1500r. on 5r. (in English)		20·00	19·00

(b) World Cup Football Championship, U.S.A. (1994). Surch WORLD CUP USA 94 1500 or in Cyrillic as T **14**.

58	**4**	1500r. on 5r. mult (in Cyrillic)	5·00	4·75
59	**4**	1500r. on 5r. mult (in English)	5·00	4·75
60	-	1500r. on 5r. black, yellow and red (in Cyrillic)	5·00	4·75
61	-	1500r. on 5r. black, yellow and red (in English)	5·00	4·75
MS62	Two sheets. (a) 1500r. on 5r. multicoloured (in Cyrillic); (b) 1500r. on 5r. multicoloured (in English)		20·00	19·00

1993. Town Arms. As T **3** . Multicoloured.

63		25r. Minsk	50	30

15 St. Stanislav's Church, Mogilev

1993

64	**15**	150r. multicoloured	80	60

16 Kastus Kalinowski (leader)

1993. 130th Anniv of Peasants' Uprising.

65	**16**	50r. multicoloured	40	30

17 Princess Ragneda

1993. Tenth century Rulers of Polotsk. Multicoloured.

66	**17**	75r. Type **17**	50	30
67		75r. Prince Ragvalod and map	50	30

18 Statue of Budny

1993. 400th Death Anniv of Simon Budny (poet).

68	**18**	100r. multicoloured	70	65

19 Golden Eagle

1994. Birds in the Red Book. Multicoloured.

69		20r. Type **19**	20	20
70		40r. Mute swan (Cygnus olor)	30	30
71		40r. River kingfisher (Alcedo atthis)	30	30

1994. Nos. 14/16 surch.

72	**7**	15r. on 30k. blue	20	10
73	**7**	25r. on 45k. green	30	20
74	**7**	50r. on 50k. green	50	30

See also Nos. 86/8.

21 Map and Rocket Launchers (Liberation of Russia)

1994. 50th Anniv of Liberation. Multicoloured.

75		500r. Type **21**	60	45
76		500r. Map and Ilyushin 11-2 Shturmovick airplanes (Ukraine)	60	45
77		500r. Map, tank and soldiers (Byelorussia)	60	45

22 Yasev Drazdovich and "Persecution"

1994. Artists and Paintings. Multicoloured.

78		300r. Type **22**	30	20
79		300r. Pyotr Sergievich and The Path through Life	30	20
80		300r. Ferdinand Rushchyts and The Land	30	20

23 Figure Skating

1994. Winter Olympic Games, Lillehammer, Norway. Multicoloured.

81		1000r. Type **23**	40	30
82		1000r. Biathlon	40	30
83		1000r. Cross-country skiing	40	30
84		1000r. Speed skating	40	30
85		1000r. Ice hockey	40	30

1994. Birds in the Red Book. As Nos. 69/71 but values changed. Multicoloured.

86		300r. As Type **19**	50	30
87		400r. As No. 70	60	40
88		400r. As No. 71	60	40

1994. Town Arms. As T **3**. Multicoloured.

89		700r. Grodno	30	20
90		700r. Vitebsk	30	20

25 Church, Synkavichai (16th-century)

1994. Religious Buildings. Multicoloured.

91		700r. Type **25**	30	20
92		700r. Sts. Peter and Paul's Cathedral, Gomel (19th-century)	30	20

26 Belarus

1994. 150th Birth Anniv of Ilya Repin (painter). Multicoloured.

93		1000r. Type **26**	50	30
94		1000r. Repin Museum	50	30

Nos. 93/4 were issued together, se-tenant, forming a composite design.

27 Tomasz Wojshezki and Battle Scene

1995. Bicentenary (1994) of Polish Insurrection. Multicoloured.

95		600r. Type **27**	45	35
96		600r. Jakub Jasinski	45	35
97		1000r. Mikhail Aginski	60	45
98		1000r. Tadeusz Kosciuszko	60	45

28 Memorial

1995. 50th Anniv of End of Second World War. Multicoloured.

99		180r. Type **28**	20	15
100		600r. Clouds and memorial	30	20

29 Aleksandr Stepanovich Popov (radio pioneer)

1995. Centenary of First Radio Transmission (by Guglielmo Marconi).

101	**29**	600r. multicoloured	50	40

30 Obelisk to the Fallen of the Red Army, Minsk

1995

102	**30**	180r. bistre and red	20	15
103	**30**	200r. green and bistre	30	20
104	**30**	280r. green and blue	40	30
107	**30**	600r. purple and bistre	50	40

31 Cherski

1995. 150th Birth Anniv of Ivan Cherski (explorer).

115	**31**	600r. multicoloured	50	40

32 Motal

1995. Traditional Costumes (1st series). Multiccoloured.

116		180r. Type **32**	20	15
117		600r. Vaukavysk-Kamyanets	40	30
118		1200r. Pukhavits	70	55

See also Nos. 188/190, 256/8 and 460/1.

33 Head of Beaver

1995. The Eurasian Beaver. Multicoloured.

119		300r. Type **33**	30	20
120		450r. Beaver gnawing branch	40	30
121		450r. Beaver (horiz)	40	30
122		800r. Beaver swimming	75	45

34 Writer and Script

1995. Writers' Day.

123	**34**	600r. multicoloured	50	40

35 Arms

1995. National Symbols. Multicoloured.

124		600r. Type **35**	40	30
125		600r. Flag over map and arms	40	30

36 Anniversary Emblem

1995. 50th Anniv of U.N.O.

126	**36**	600r. blue, black and gold	50	40

37 Mstislavl Church

1995. Churches. Multicoloured.

127		600r. Type **37**	40	30
128		600r. Kamai Church	40	30

See also Nos. 227/8.

1995

125 год

з дня нараджэння

(38)

1995. 125th Birth Anniv of Ferdinand Rushchyts (artist). No. 80 optd with T **38**.

129		300r. multicoloured	1·00	95

39 Sukhoi and Aircraft

1995. Birth Centenary of P. V. Sukhoi (aircraft designer).

130	**39**	600r. multicoloured	40	30

40 Red Deer (Cervus elaphus)

1995. Nature. Sheet 100×64 mm. Imperf.

MS131	**40**	10000r. multicoloured	4·00	3·75

41 Leu Sapega (statesman)

1995. 17th-century Belarussians. Multicoloured.

132		600r. Type **41**	35	20
133		1200r. Kazimir Semyanovich (military scholar)	50	30
134		1800r. Simyaon Polatski (writer)	70	45

42 Lynx

1996. Mammals. Multicoloured.

135		1000r. Type **42**	45	30
136		2000r. Roe deer (vert)	75	45
137		2000r. Brown bear	75	45
138		3000r. Elk (vert)	95	75
139		5000r. European bison	1·50	1·30

1996. Nos. 17 and 23 optd with capital letter.

140	**7**	B (200r.) on 1r. brown	30	20
141	**7**	A (400r.) on 25r. green	30	20

44 Krapiva

1996. Birth Centenary of Kandrat Krapiva (writer).

142	**44**	1000r. multicoloured	50	30

45 Beaver

1996. The Eurasian Beaver (Castor fiber). Sheet 90×70 mm.

MS143	**45**	1200r. multicoloured	70	45

46 Purple Emperor (Apatura iris)

1996. Butterflies and Moths. Multicoloured.

144		300r. Type **46**	1·20	95
145		300r. Lopinga achine	1·20	95
146		300r. Scarlet tiger moth (Callimorpha dominula)	1·20	95
147		300r. Clifden's nonpareil (Catocala fraxini)	1·20	95
148		300r. Swallowtail (Papilio machaon)	1·20	95
149		300r. Apollo (Parnassius apollo)	1·20	95
150		300r. Ammobiota hebe	1·20	95
151		300r. Palaeno sulphur yellow (Colias palaeno)	1·20	95

MS152	Two sheets, each 100×70 mm. (a) 1000r. Vacciniina optilete; (b) 1000r. Willow-herb hawk moth (Proserpinus proserpina)	16·00	15·00

47 Radioactivity Symbol within Eye

1996. Tenth Anniv of Chernobyl Nuclear Disaster. Multicoloured.

153		300r. Type **47**	30	20
154		1000r. Radioactivity symbol on diseased leaf	30	20
155		1000r. Radioactivity symbol on boarded-up window	30	20

48 State Arms

1996. Arms and value in black, background colours given.

159	**48**	100r. blue	15	10
160	**48**	200r. grey	30	25
161	**48**	400r. brown	20	15
162	**48**	500r. green	15	10
163	**48**	600r. red	15	10
164	**48**	800r. blue	20	15
165	**48**	1000r. orange	20	10
166	**48**	1500r. mauve	25	15
167	**48**	1500r. blue	25	25
168	**48**	1800r. violet	25	15
169	**48**	2000r. green	35	30
170	**48**	2200r. mauve	30	20
171	**48**	2500r. blue	35	30
172	**48**	3000r. brown	30	30
173	**48**	3300r. yellow	40	25
174	**48**	5000r. blue	50	40
175	**48**	10000r. green	1·00	75
176	**48**	30000r. brown	3·00	2·30
177	**48**	50000r. purple	5·25	3·75

49 Russian and Belarussian Flags

1996. Russian–Belarussian Treaty.

182	**49**	1500r. multicoloured	70	45

50 Gymnastics

1996. Olympic Games, Atlanta. Multicoloured.

183		3000r. Type **50**	90	65
184		3000r. Throwing the discus	90	65
185		3000r. Weightlifting	90	65
186		3000r. Wrestling	90	65

MS187	100×71 mm. 5000r. Rifle-shooting. Imperf	1·50	1·10

51 Kapyl-Kletski

1996. Traditional Costumes (2nd series). Multicoloured.

188	1800r. Type **51**	40	30
189	2200r. David-Garadots Turau	60	40
190	3300r. Kobryn	70	45
MS191	95×71 mm. 5000r. Naraulyanski. Imperf	1·50	1·10

See also Nos. 256/8 and 460/1.

52 Acorus calamus

1996. Medicinal Plants. Multicoloured.

192	1500r. Type **52**	40	30
193	1500r. Sanguisorba officinalis	40	30
194	2200r. Potentilla erecta	60	40
195	3300r. Frangula alnus	70	45
MS196	96×71 mm. 5000r. Menyanthes trifoliate. Imperf	1·50	1·10

53 Grey Heron (*Ardea cinerea*)

1996. Birds. Multicoloured.

197	400r. Type **53**	60	40
198	400r. Black storks (*Ciconia nigra*)	60	40
199	400r. Great cormorant (*Phalacrocorax carbo*)	60	40
200	400r. White stork (*Ciconia ciconia*)	60	40
201	400r. Black-headed gulls (*Larus ridibundus*)	60	40
202	400r. Common snipe (*Gallinago gallinago*)	60	40
203	400r. White-winged black tern (*Chlidonias leucopterus*)	60	40
204	400r. Penduline tit (*Remiz pendulinus*)	60	40
205	400r. Eurasian bittern (*Botaurus stellaris*)	60	40
206	400r. Black coot (*Fulica atra*)	60	40
207	400r. Little bittern (*Ixobrychus minutus*)	60	40
208	400r. River kingfisher (*Alcedo atthis*)	60	40
209	400r. Green-winged teals (*Anas crecca*)	60	40
210	400r. Gadwalls (*Anas strepera*)	60	40
211	400r. Northern pintails (*Anas acuta*)	60	40
212	400r. Mallards (*Anas platyrhynchos*)	60	40
213	400r. Greater scaups (*Aythya marila*)	60	40
214	400r. Long-tailed duck (*Clangula hyemalis*)	60	40
215	400r. Northern shovelers (*Anas clypeata*)	60	40
216	400r. Garganeys (*Anas querquedula*)	60	40
217	400r. European wigeon (*Anas penelope*)	60	40
218	400r. Ferruginous ducks (*Aythya nyroca*)	60	40
219	400r. Common goldeneyes (*Bucephala clangula*)	60	40
220	400r. Goosander (*Mergus merganser*)	60	40
221	400r. Smew (*Mergus albellus*)	60	40
222	400r. Tufted duck (*Aythya fuligula*)	60	40
223	400r. Red-breasted merganser (*Mergus serrator*)	60	40
224	400r. Common pochard (*Aythya ferina*)	60	40
MS225	Two sheets, each 100×70 mm. (a) 1000r. Common snipe (*Gallinago gallinago*); (b) 1000r. European pochards (*Aythya farina*)	10·00	9·50

54 Title Page

1996. 400th Anniv of Publication of First Belarussian Grammar.

226	**54** 1500r. multicoloured	80	55

1996. Churches. As T **37**. Multicoloured.

227	3300r. St. Nicholas's Church, Mogilev	1·00	70
228	3300r. Franciscan church, Pinsk	1·00	70

55 Shchakatsikhin

1996. Birth Centenary of Mikola Shchakatsikhin (artist).

229	**55** 2000r. multicoloured	75	45

56 Old and New Telephones

1996. Cent of Telephone Service in Minsk.

230	**56** 2000r. multicoloured	75	45

57 Lukashenka

1996. President Alyaksandr Rygoravich Lukashenka.

231	**57** 2500r. multicoloured	60	45

58 Kiryla Turovski (12th-century Bishop of Turov)

1996. Multicoloured.

232	3000r. Type **58**	65	45
233	3000r. Mikolaj Radziwill (16th-century Chancellor of Lithuania)	65	45
234	3000r. Mikola Gusovski (15th-16th century writer)	65	45

59 Decorated Tree, Minsk

1996. New Year. Multicoloured.

235	1500r. Type **59**	30	20
236	2000r. Winter landscape (horiz)	50	40

60 Paraskeva

1996. Icons in National Museum, Minsk. Multicoloured.

237	3500r. Type **60**	60	45
238	3500r. *Illya* (17th-century)	60	45
239	3500r. *Three Holy Men* (Master of Sharashov)	60	45
240	3500r. *Madonna of Smolensk*	60	45
MS241	70×100 mm. 5000r. *Birth of the Madonna* (Patr Yavseevich)	1·50	1·10

61 Zhukov

1997. Birth Cent of Marshal G. K. Zhukov.

242	**61** 2000r. black, gold and red	50	40

62 Theatre

1997. Kupala National Theatre, Minsk.

243	**62** 3500r. black and gold	70	55

63 Byalnitsky-Birulya

1997. 125th Birth Anniv of W. K. Byalnitsky-Birulya (painter).

244	**63** 2000r. black and brown	50	40

(64)

1997. 105th Birth Anniv of R. R. Shyrma (composer). No. 2 surch with T **64**.

245	**2** 3500r. on 20k. light blue, blue and black	60	55

65 Salmon

1997. Fish. Multicoloured.

246	2000r. Type **65**	40	30
247	3000r. Vimba	60	45
248	4500r. Barbel (*Barbus barbus*)	80	65
249	4500r. European grayling (*Thymallus thymallus*)	80	65
MS250	90×60 mm. 5000r. Sterlet (*Acipenser ruthenus*)	1·50	1·10

66 "SOS" on Globe

1997. International Conference on Developing Countries, Minsk. Multicoloured.

251	3000r. Type **66**	50	40
252	4500r. Protective hand over ecosystem	70	55

Nos. 251/2 were issued together, *i se-tenant*, with intervening label showing the Conference emblem, the whole strip forming a composite design.

67 Emblem

1997. 50th Anniv of Belarussian Membership of Universal Postal Union.

253	**67** 3000r. multicoloured	60	45

1997. No. 18 surch **100 1997**.

254	**7** 100r. on 2r. brown	30	20

69 Map, National Flag and Monument to the Fallen of Second World War, Minsk

1997. Independence Day.

255	**69** 3000r. multicoloured	75	55

1997. Traditional Costumes (3rd series). As T **51**. Multicoloured.

256	2000r. Dzisensk	35	35
257	3000r. Navagrydsk	60	55
258	4500r. Bykhaisk	85	80

70 Page from Skorina Bible and Vilnius

1997. 480th Anniv of Printing in Belarus. Each red, black and grey.

259	3000r. Type **70**	60	55
260	3000r. Page from Skorina Bible and Prague	60	55
261	4000r. Franzisk Skorina and Polotsk	60	55
262	7500r. Skorina and Cracow	1·30	1·20

71 Jesuit College

1997. 900th Anniv of Pinsk.

263	**71** 3000r. multicoloured	60	55

72 Books and Entrance

1997. 75th Anniv of National Library.

264	**72** 3000r. multicoloured	60	55

73 Dark Glasses reflecting Hands reading Braille

1997. Centenary of Schools for the Blind in Belarus.

265	**73** 3000r. multicoloured	50	45

74 Child in Hand "Flower"

1997. World Children's Day.

266	**74** 3000r. multicoloured	60	55

75 Red Ribbon and Crowd

1997. Red Ribbon AIDS Solidarity Campaign.

267	**75** 4000r. multicoloured	70	65

76 Model 1221

1997. Belarussian Tractors. Multicoloured.

268		3300r. Type **76**	60	55
269		4400r. First Belarussian tractor, 1953	75	70
270		7500r. Model 680	1·20	1·10
271		7500r. Model 952	1·20	1·10

(77)

1997. Restoration of Cross of St. Ephrosina of Polotsk. No. 1 surch with T **77**.

272	**1**	3000r. on 1r. multicoloured	50	40

78 St. Nicholas hang-gliding over Houses (New Year)

1997. Greetings Stamps. Multicoloured.

273		1400r. Type **78**	30	20
274		4400r. Procession of musicians (Christmas)	60	45

79 Cross-country Skiing

1998. Winter Olympic Games, Nagano, Japan. Multicoloured.

275		2000r. Type **79**	40	30
276		3300r. Ice hockey	50	40
277		4400r. Biathlon	70	55
278		7500r. Freestyle skiing	90	75

80 Mashcherov

1998. 80th Birth Anniv of P. M. Mashcherov (writer).

279	**80**	2500r. multicoloured	50	40

81 MAZ-205 Lorry, 1947

1998. Tipper Trucks. Multicoloured.

280		1400r. Type **81**	30	20
281		2000r. MAZ-503, 1968	35	25
282		3000r. MAZ-5549, 1977	40	30
283		4400r. MAZ-5551, 1985	60	45
284		7500r. MAZ-5516, 1994	85	70

82 Entrance to Nyasvizh Castle

1998. Europa. National Festivals.

285	**82**	15000r. multicoloured	1·00	95

83 Mickiewicz

1998. Birth Bicentenary of Adam Mickiewicz (political writer).

286	**83**	8600r. multicoloured	65	65

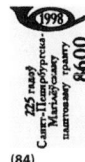

(84)

1998. 225th Anniv of Postal Service between Mogilov and St. Petersburg. No. 64 surch with T **84**.

287	**15**	8600r. on 150r. mult	65	65

85 Bluethroat

1998. Birds. Multicoloured.

288		1500r. Type **85**	20	10
289		3200r. Penduline tit	30	30
290		3800r. Aquatic warbler	40	35
291		5300r. Savi's warbler	50	45
292		8600r. Azure tit	85	80

86 Watermill

1998

293	**86**	100r. black and green	20	15
294	-	200r. black and brown	20	15
295	-	500r. black and blue	20	15
296	-	800r. black and violet	20	15
297	-	1000r. black and green	20	15
298	-	1500r. black and brown	30	30
299	-	2000r. black and blue	20	15
300	-	3000r. black and yellow	20	20
301	-	3200r. black and green	30	20
302	-	5000r. black and blue	25	30
303	-	5300r. black and blue	30	30
304	-	10000r. black and orange	45	40
305	**86**	30000r. black and blue	50	45
306	-	50000r. black, orange and deep orange	60	55
308	-	100000r. black and mauve	80	75
309	-	500000r. black and brown	4·00	3·75

DESIGNS—VERT: 200, 50000r. Windmill; 500r. Stork; 800r. Cathedral of the Holy Trinity, Ishkold; 1000r. Bison; 1500, 3200r. Dulcimer; 2000r. Star; 3000, 5300r. Lute; 5000r. Church; 10000r. Flaming wheel; 500000r. Lyavoniha (folk dance). HORIZ: 100000r. Exhibition centre, Minsk.

87 Bulldozer Model 7821

1998. 50th Anniv of Belaz Truck Works. Multicoloured.

310		1500r. Type **87**	20	15
311		3200r. Tipper Model 75131	25	20
312		3800r. Tipper Model 75303	30	25
313		5300r. Tipper Model 75483	35	30
314		8600r. Tipper Model 7555	40	40

88 Common Morel

1998. Fungi. Multicoloured.

315		2500r. Type **88**	20	15
316		3800r. *Morchella conica*	25	20
317		4600r. Shaggy parasol	30	25
318		5800r. Parasol mushroom	35	30
319		9400r. Shaggy ink cap	65	50

89 Lion's Head

1998. Wood Sculptures. Multicoloured.

320		3400r. Type **89**	30	25
321		3800r. Archangel Michael	35	30
322		5800r. Prophet Zacharias	40	35
323		9400r. Madonna and Child	60	55

90 Emblem and Belarussian Stamps

1998. World Post Day.

324	**90**	5500r. multicoloured	60	45

91 *Kalozha* (V. K. Tsvirka)

1998. Paintings. Multicoloured.

325		3000r. Type **91**	20	20
326		3500r. *Hotel Lounge* (S. Yu. Zhukoiski)	20	20
327		5000r. *Winter Sleep* (V. K. Byalynitski-Birulya)	25	20
328		5500r. *Portrait of a Girl* (I. I. Alyashkevich) (vert)	25	20
329		10000r. *Portrait of an Unknown Woman* (I. F. Khrutski) (vert)	40	40

92 Anniversary Emblem

1998. 50th Anniv of Universal Declaration of Human Rights.

330	**92**	7100r. multicoloured	50	40

93 Girl, Rabbit and Fir Trees

1998. Christmas and New Year. Multicoloured.

331		5500r. Type **93**	25	25
332		5500r. Girl, rabbit and house	25	25

94 Pushkin and Adam Mickiewicz Monument, St. Petersburg (A. Anikeichyk)

1999. Birth Bicentenary of Aleksandr Pushkin (writer).

333	**94**	15300r. multicoloured	80	75

95 MAZ Model 8007 Truck and Excavator

1999. Minsk Truck and Military Works. Multicoloured.

334		10000r. Type **95**	25	20
335		15000r. MAZ model 543M and Smerch rocket system	30	25
336		30000r. MAZ model 7907 crane	45	40
337		30000r. MAZ model 543M Rubezh missile launcher	45	40

MS338 175×120 mm. Nos. 334/7; 5000r. Model 7917 and Topol missile; 150000r. Model 74135 low-loader 6·00 5·75

96 Dish, Jar and Vase

1999. Glasswork. Multicoloured.

339		30000r. Type **96**	50	45
340		30000r. Chalice	50	40
341		100000r. Oil lamp	1·00	95

(97)

1999. "iBRA '99" International Stamp Exhibition, Nuremberg. No. 69 surch with T **97**.

342		150000r. on 20r. multicoloured (Type 19)	2·00	1·90

98 Belavezhskaya Pushcha Reserve

1999. Europa. Parks and Gardens. Multicoloured.

345		150000r. Type **98**	1·50	1·40
346		150000r. Beaver in Byarezinski Reserve	1·50	1·40

99 Well

1999. Wooden Buildings. Multicoloured.

347		50000r. Type **99**	70	45
348		50000r. Public house	70	45
349		100000r. Windmill	1·10	95

100 *Portrait of Yu. M. Pen* (A. M. Brazer)

1999. Vitebsk Art School. Paintings. Multicoloured.
350		30000r. Type **100**	30	20
351		60000r. *St. Anthony's Church, Vitebsk* (S. B.Yudovin)	70	45
352		100000r. *Street in Vitebsk* (Yu. M. Pen)	1·20	85
353		100000r. *Kryvaya Street, Vitebsk* (M. P. Mikhalap) (horiz)	1·20	85
MS354		104×82 mm. 200000r. *The World is a River without Banks* (Marc Chagall)	2·00	1·90

101 Karvat

1999. Third Death Anniv of Wing Commander Karvat.
355	**101**	25000r. multicoloured	1·20	95

102 Main Post Office, Minsk, 1954

1999. 125th Anniv of Universal Postal Union. Multicoloured.
356		150000r. Type **102**	1·80	1·60
357		150000r. First post office in Minsk, 1800	1·80	1·60

103 Golden Mushroom

1999. Fungi. Multicoloured.
358		30000r. Type **103**	30	20
359		50000r. Changeable agaric	55	40
360		75000r. *Lyophyllum connatum*	90	55
361		100000r. *Lyophyllum decastes*	1·20	85
MS362		97×79 mm. 150000r. Boot-lace fungus (*Armillariella mellea*)	1·80	1·60

104 East and West Belarussians Embracing

1999. 60th Anniv of Re-unification of Republic of Byelorussia.
363	**104**	29000r. multicoloured	40	30

105 MAZ MA3-6430, 1998

1999. Minsk Truck and Military Works. Lorries. Multicoloured.
364		51000r. Type **105**	50	30
365		86000r. Lorry Model MAZ MA3-4370	70	45

106 Landscape (Olya Smantser)

1999. Children's Painting Competition Winners. Multicoloured.
366		32000r. Type **106**	30	20
367		59000r. Girl (Masha Dudarenko) (vert)	50	30

107 Teddybear in Snow (Mitya Kutas)

1999. Christmas and New Year. Children's Paintings. Multicoloured.
368		30000r. Type **107**	40	30
369		30000r. Children building snow-man and ice-skating (Yulya Yakubovich)	40	30

108 Spasa-Praabrazhenskaya Church, Polatsk

2000. Birth Bimillenary of Jesus Christ (1st issue). Multicoloured.
370		50r. Type **108**	40	30
371		75r. St. Atsistratsiga Cathedral, Slutsk	70	45
372		100r. The Reverend Serafim Sa-rovskaga Church, Belaazersk	90	65

109 Our Lady Oranta (mosaic, Spohia Catherdral, Kiev, Ukraine)

2000. Birth Bimillenary of Jesus Christ (2nd issue). Sheet 150×100 mm containing T **109** and similar vert designs. Multicoloured.
MS373		100r. Type **109**; 100r. Jesus Christ (fresco, Spasa-Praabrazhen-skaya Church, Polatsk); 100r. Our Lady Volodimirska (icon, National Tretyakov Gallery, Moscow, Russia)	3·00	2·75

110 Bison

2000
374	**110**	1r. black and green	20	10
375	-	2r. black and blue	20	10
376	-	3r. black and yellow	20	10
377	-	5r. black and blue	20	10
378	-	10r. black and orange	20	10
380	-	20r. black and mauve	30	15
382	-	30r. black and green	40	20
383	-	50r. black and yellow	60	40
387	-	100r. black and mauve	80	55

DESIGNS—VERT: 2r. Star; 3r. Lyre; 5r. Synkovichy Church; 10r. Flaming wheel; 20r. Type **111**; 30r. Watermill; 50r. Windmill. HORIZ: 100r. Exhibition Centre.

111 Kryzhachok (folk dance)

2000. Self-adhesive.
391	**111**	20r. black and red	30	15

112 Su-24 Bomber

2000. 25th Death Anniv of Pavel Sukhoi (aircraft designer). Multicoloured.
392		50r. Type **112**	80	60
393		50r. Su-27 fighter	80	60
394		50r. Su-25 battle fighter	80	60
MS395		120×83 mm. 150r. Type **112**; 150r. As No. 394; 150r. As No. 393	2·50	2·30

113 Kupala Holiday

2000
396	**113**	A black and blue	40	30

No. 396 was for Inland Letter Post rate.

114 Stone-Curlew

2000. Birds in the Red Book. Multicoloured.
397		50r. Type **114**	60	40
398		50r. Smew (*Mergellus albellus*)	60	40
399		75r. Willow grouse	70	45
400		100r. Lesser spotted eagle (vert)	90	65

115 *The Partisan Madonna of Minsk* (M. Savitsky)

2000. 55th Anniv of End of Second World War.
401	**115**	100r. multicoloured	90	65

116 "Building Europe"

2000. Europa.
402	**116**	250r. multicoloured	3·00	2·75

117 Scene from *Creation of the World*

2000. National Ballet Company. Multicoloured.
403		100r. Type **117**	1·00	75
MS404		77×73 mm. 150r. Scene from *Passions*	1·80	1·60

118 Hands holding Lifebelt

2000. 50th Anniv of United Nations High Commission for Refugees.
405	**118**	50r. multicoloured	45	35

119 Head of Lynx

2000. Endangered Species. The Lynx. Multicoloured.
406		100r. Type **119**	80	65
407		100r. On branch	80	65
408		150r. Walking through woodland	1·20	95
409		150r. Adult and cub	1·20	95

120 People wearing National Costumes

2000. International Year of Culture.
410	**120**	100r. multicoloured	80	65

121 Rings

2000. Olympic Games, Sydney. Multicoloured.
411		100r. Type **121**	80	65
412		100r. Kayaking	80	65
413		100r. Rhythmic gymnastics	80	65
MS414		77×74 mm. 400r. Athletes	3·00	2·75

122 Amber

2000. Minerals. Multicoloured.
415		200r. Type **122**	1·30	1·10
416		200r. Galit	1·30	1·10
417		200r. Flint	1·30	1·10
418		200r. Silvin	1·30	1·10

123 People around decorated Tree

2000. New Year.
419	**123**	200r. multicoloured	1·50	1·30

124 Nativity Scene

2000. Christmas.
420	**124**	100r. multicoloured	1·20	95

125 *Connection of Times* (Roman Zabello)

2000. New Millennium. Children's Paintings. Multicoloured.
421		100r. Type **125**	80	65
422		100r. *Festival of Life* (Alena Emeliyanova)	80	65

126 Euphrosiniya Polotskaya and Church (image scaled to 52% of original size)

2001. 900th Birth Anniv of St. Euphrosiniya Polotskaya (Saint Euphrosyne). Imperf.

423	**126**	500r. multicoloured	2·30	2·10

127 Brest

2001. Town Arms. Multicoloured.

424	160r. Dubrovna		50	30
424a	200r. Type **127**		60	40
425	200r. Gomel		60	40
426	200r. Borisov		60	40
427	300r. Minsk		75	45
428	300r. David-Gorodok		75	45
429	350r. Kamjanets		80	55
430	460r. Slonim		90	65
431	500r. Novogrudok		95	75
432	500r. Turov		95	75
433	780r. Zaslavl		1·00	85
434	900r. Magilev		1·20	95

128 Runner

2001. Byelorussian Medal Winners, Olympic Games, Sydney. Sheet 78×75 mm.

MS435	**128**	1000r. multicoloured	4·00	3·75

No. **MS**435 is as No. **MS**414 but with face value changed and design altered to include list of winners.

129 Tupolev ANT-25 RD

2001. 25th Death Anniv of Pavel Sukhoy (aircraft designer). Multicoloured.

436	250r. Type **129**		1·20	95
437	250r. Tupolev ANT-37 Rodina		1·20	95

2001. As T **86**.

438	1r. black and green (inscr "2002")		20	10
439	2r. black and blue (inscr "2002")		20	10
440	3r. black and yellow "2002")		20	10
441	5r. black and blue (inscr "2002")		20	10
442	10r. black and brown (inscr "2002")		20	10
442a	20r. black and mauve (inscr "2002")		30	15
442b	30r. black and green (inscr "2002")		40	20
442c	50r. black and yellow (inscr "2002")		60	40
442d	100r. black and mauve (inscr "2002")		80	55
442e	100r. black and brown (inscr "2003")		80	55
443	200r. black and green		80	55
444	500r. black and brown		1·80	1·40

DESIGNS: 1r. Bison; 2r. Star; 3r. Lyre; 5r. Synkovichy Church; 10r. Flaming wheel; 20r. Dancers; 50r. Windmill; 100r. Exhibition centre; 100r. (442e), Layavoniha folk dance; 200r. 18th-century town house, Vitebsk; 500r. As No. 309.

130 Stag Beetle (*Lucanus cervus*)

2001. Beetles. Multicoloured.

445	300r. Type **130**		1·50	1·20
446	300r. European rhinoceros beetle (*Oryctes nasicornis*)		1·50	1·20

2001. As T **110**. Self-adhesive.

447	100r. black and mauve		60	40
448	200r. black and green (vert)		80	65

DESIGNS: 100r. As No. 387; 200r. As No. 438.

131 *Nymphaea alba*

2001. Endangered Species. Flowers. Multicoloured.

455	200r. Type **131**		80	65
456	400r. *Cypripedium calceolus*		1·70	1·40

132 Swans and Lake, Narochanskyi Nature Reserve

2001. Europa. Water Resources. Multicoloured.

457	400r. Geese and lake, Pripjatiskyi Nature Reserve		2·00	1·40
458	1000r. Type **132**		5·00	4·25

133 Eye and Tear

2001. 15th Anniv of Chernobyl Nuclear Disaster.

459	**133**	50r. black and rose	50	30

2001. Traditional Costumes (4th series). As T **51**. Multicoloured.

460	200r. 19th-century, Slutsk region		70	55
461	1000r. 19th-century, Pinsk region		3·50	3·25

134 National Arms

2001. Tenth Anniv of State Sovereignty.

462	**134**	500r. multicoloured	2·00	1·90

135 Union Emblem

2001. Tenth Anniv of Union of Independent States.

463	**135**	195r. multicoloured	80	55

2001. No. 166 surch **400**.

464	400r. on 1500r. mauve		1·20	95

137 King and Courtier (*The blue suit made inside out*)

2001. Folk Tales. Multicoloured.

465	100r. Type **137**		50	30
466	200r. Horse-drawn coach (*Okh and the golden snuff-box*)		90	65

138 Figures encircling Globe

2001. United Nations Year of Dialogue among Civilizations.

467	**138**	400r. multicoloured	1·20	95

139 Otto Schmidt

2001. 110th Birth Anniv of Otto Yulievich Schmidt (scientist and Arctic explorer). Sheet 78×74 mm.

MS468	**139**	3000r. multicoloured	8·00	7·50

2001. Surch.

469	400r. on 100r. blue (No. 159)		1·10	85
470	400r. on 600r. red (No. 163)		1·10	85
471	400r. on 1500r. blue (No. 167)		1·10	85
472	400r. on 3300r. yellow (No. 173)		1·10	85
473	1000r. on 100r. black and green (No. 293)		2·50	2·10
474	1000r. on 180r. brown and red (No. 102)		2·50	2·10
475	1000r. on 280r. green and blue (No. 104)		2·50	2·10

141 Wind-surfer

2001. Aquatic Sports. Multicoloured.

476	200r. Type **141**		70	45
MS477	102×66 mm. 1000r. Water-skier		3·00	2·75

142 Arms of Francisk Skorina

2001. Architecture and Arms. Multicoloured.

478	1000r. Type **142**		2·20	1·90
479	2000r. City Hall, Minsk		4·25	3·75
480	3000r. City Hall, Nesvizh		6·25	5·75
481	5000r. City Hall, Cherchersk		10·00	9·50

143 Building Facade

2001. House of Mercy (Orthodox Church humanitarian centre), Minsk.

495	**143**	200r. multicoloured	70	55

144 Calligraphy

2001. Christmas (496) and New Year (497). Multicoloured.

496	100r. Type **144**		50	30
497	100r. Snowy scene contained in bauble		50	30

145 E. V. Klumov

2001. 125th Birth Anniv of E. V. Klumov (surgeon and resistance worker).

498	**145**	100r. multicoloured	50	30

146 Ski Slalom

2002. Winter Olympics, Salt Lake City, USA (1st issue). Multicoloured.

499	300r. Type **146**		90	65
500	300r. Figure skating		90	65
501	500r. Biathlon		1·30	1·00
502	500r. Ski jumping		1·30	1·00

See also No. **MS**507.

147 *Formica rufa*

2002. Ants. Multicoloured.

503	200r. Type **147**		70	45
504	1000r. Grubs and worker ants (vert)		2·10	1·90
MS505	100×72 mm. 1000r. No. 504 plus label (vert) forming a composite design		2·50	1·90

148 Woman carrying Corn (Dozhinki Feast)

2002

506	**148**	B (55r.) black and yellow	30	20

149 Ice Hockey Player

2002. Winter Olympic Games, Salt Lake City, USA (2nd issue). Sheet 100×70 mm.

MS507	**149**	2000r. multicoloured	5·00	4·75

2002. As T **113** but inscr "2002".

508	**113**	A black and blue	40	30

No. 508 was for use on inland letters.

150 Clown riding Unicycle

2002. Europa. Circus. Multicoloured.

509	400r. Type **150**		1·50	1·40
510	500r. Horse		1·80	1·60

151 Yanka Kupala

2002. 120th Birth Annivs of Poets. Multicloured.

511	100r. Type **151**		30	20
512	100r. Yacub Kolas		30	20
MS513	100×70 mm. 500r.×2 Nos. 511/12		2·20	2·10

152 Church, Polotsk

2002. No value expressed. Multicoloured.

514	H (236r.) Type **152**		60	40
515	C (314r.) Railway Station, Brest		80	55

No. 514 was for use on letters up to 20 grams to Russia, Lithuania, Latvia, Uzbekistan, Tadjikistan and Turkmenistan.

No. 515 was for use on airmail letters up to 20 grams to the same countries.

153 Clover *Trifolium*

2002. Flowers. Multicoloured. Self-adhesive gum.

516	30r. Type **153**		30	15
517	50r. Matricaria		35	20
518	B (75r.) Flax (*Linium*)		20	10

519	A (90r.) Cornflower (*Centaurea cyanus*)	30	20
520	100r. Pasque flower (*Pulsatilla patens*)	40	25
521	200r. Yellow water lily (*Nuphar lutea*)	50	30
522	H (236r.) Campanula	70	45
523	C (314r.) Rhododendron	70	45
524	500r. Fireweed (*Chamaenerion angustifolium*)	90	65

No. 518 was for use on post cards within Belarus.

No. 519 was for use on letters up to 20 grams within Belarus.

No. 522 was for use on letters up to 20 grams to Russia, Lithuania, Latvia, Uzbekistan, Tadjikistan and Turkmenistan.

No. 523 was for use on airmail letters up to 20 grams to Russia, Lithuania, Latvia, Uzbekistan, Tadjikistan and Turkmenistan.

154 Go-Kart

2002. Children's Activities. Multicoloured.

525	90r. Type **154**	30	15
526	239r. Model aircraft	70	45

155 White Stork (*Ciconia ciconia*)

2002. Birds. Sheet 94×72 mm containing T **155** and similar horiz design. Multicoloured.

MS527 200r. Type **155**; 200r. Golden oriole (*Oriolus oriolus*); 200r. Pied wagtail (*Matacilla alba*) 1·50 1·40

156 Bridge over River Svisloch, Minsk

2002. Bridges.

528	**156** 200r. black, mauve and blue	40	30
529	- 300r. multicoloured	70	55
530	- 500r. black, blue and green	1·00	85

DESIGNS: 200r. Type **156**; 300r. Bridge over River Sozh, Gomel; 500r. Bridge over River Zapadnaja Dvina, Vitebsk.

157 Lake, Braslav

2002. International Year of Eco-Tourism.

531	**157** 300r. multicoloured	1·00	95

158 *By the Church* (F. Rushchits)

2002. Art. Multicoloured.

532	**158** 300r. multicoloured	75	55
533	300r. *Battle at Nemiga* (M. Philippovich) (horiz)	75	55

159 V. V. Kovalyonok and P. I. Klimuk (cosmonauts)

2002. 45th Anniv of Space Exploration. Sheet 131×71 mm.

MS534 **159** 3000r. multicoloured 5·50 5·25

160 Father Christmas

2002. Christmas and New Year. Multicoloured.

535	300r. Type **160**	75	55
536	300r. Angel	75	55

161 Ksimir Malevich and *Black Square*

2003. 125th Birth Anniv of Kasimir Malevich (artist). Sheet 82×54 mm.

MS537 **161** 3000r. multicoloured 6·00 5·75

162 Smooth Snake (*Coronella austriaca*)

2003. Reptiles. Multicoloured.

538	300r. Type **162**	60	40
539	600r. European pond turtle (*Emys orbicularis*)	1·00	75

163 Glass containing Land and Water

2003. International Year of Freshwater.

540	**163** 370r. multicoloured	80	55

164 House Sparrow

2003

541	**164** 630r. multicoloured	1·20	95

165 In-line Skates

2003. Children's Sports. Multicoloured.

542	300r. Type **165**	60	40
543	300r. Scooter (vert)	60	40

166 "Europa"

2003. Europa. Poster Art. Multicoloured.

544	400r. Type **166**	80	55
545	700r. Painted wooden panels	1·30	1·00

167 Globeflower (*Trollius europaeus*)

2003. Endangered Flora. Multicoloured.

546	270r. Type **167**	60	40
547	740r. Siberian iris (*Iris sibirica*)	1·30	1·00

168 Women's Costumes, Polesye

2003. Traditional Costumes. Multicoloured.

548	380r. Type **168**	70	55
549	430r. Men and women's costumes, Mogilyov	80	65

See also Nos. 636/7.

169 470 Class Sailing Dinghy

2003. Dinghy Sailing. Sheet 128×78 mm, containing T 169 and similar multicoloured design.

MS550 1000r. Type **169**; 1000r. Laser dinghy (vert) 3·25 3·00

170 Bronze Age Axe Head

2003. National Museum of Natural History and Culture, Minsk. Three sheets, each 82×52 mm, containing T **170** and similar multicoloured designs.

MS551 (a) 1000r. Type **170**; (b) 1500r. Bronze age pot (28×30 mm); (c) 1500r. 14th-century bowl (28×30 mm) 7·00 6·50

171 Horse Stall, Povitie (19th-century)

2003. Architecture. Multicoloured.

552	270r. Type **171**	50	30
553	430r. Church, Sinkevichi (1724)	80	55
554	740r. Watermill, Volma (19th-century)	1·10	85
MS555	97×112 mm. Nos. 552/4	2·50	2·30

172 Golden Retriever

2003. Dogs. Multicoloured.

556	270r. Type **172**	60	40
557	380r. Great dane	70	50
558	430r. German shepherd	80	65

173 Young Player holding Ball

2003. Centenary of FIFA (Federation Internationale de Football Association). Multicoloured.

559	380r. Type **173**	70	50
560	380r. Five players (horiz)	70	50
561	460r. Three players (horiz)	80	65
562	780r. Player holding ball	1·30	1·00

174 Angel

2003. Christmas. Multicoloured.

563	380r. Type **174**	50	40
564	780r. Grandfather Frost	1·10	85

175 "Arrival of Spring" (Pavel Maslennikov)

2004

565	**175** 290r. multicoloured	60	40

176 Blackthorn (*Prunus spinosa*)

2004. Fruit. Multicoloured.

566	5r. Type **176**	30	15
567	10r. Lingonberry (*Vaccinium vitis idaea*)	30	15
568	20r. Bilberry (*Vaccinium myrtillus*)	30	15
569	30r. Cranberry (*Oxycoccus palustris*)	30	15
570	50r. Bog blueberry (*Vaccinium uliginosum*)	30	15
571	100r. Raspberry (*Rubus idaeus*)	30	15
572	B (100r.) Strawberry (*Fragaria ananassa*)	30	15
573	A (120r.) Red currant (*Ribes rubrum*)	30	15
574	200r. Dewberry (*Rubus caesius*)	30	15
575	H (290r.) Black currant (*Ribes nigrum*)	50	30
576	300r. Stone bramble (*Rubus saxatilis*)	50	30
577	C (420r.) Gooseberry (*Grossularia reclinata*)	60	40
578	500r. Wild strawberry (*Fragaria*)	70	50
579	P (780r.) Sea buckthorn (*Hippophae rhamnoides*)	1·00	75
580	1000r. Sour cherry (*Cerasus vulgaris*)	1·30	90

177 Queen and King of Hearts

2004. St. Valentine's Day.

581	**177** H (290r.) black, scarlet and yellow	75	50

178 Alder (*Alnus incana*)

2004. Trees. Multicoloured. Self-adhesive gum.

582	100r. Type **178**	30	15
583	B (100r.) Birch (*Betula pendula*)	30	15
584	A (120r.) Scots pine (*Pinus sylvestris*)	30	15
585	200r. *Viburnum opulus*	30	15
586	H (290r.) Ash (*Fraxinus excelsior*)	50	30
587	300r. Lime (*Tillia cordata*)	50	30
588	400r. Hazel (*Corylus avellana*)	60	40
589	C (420r.) Rowan (*Sorbus aucuparia*)	60	40
590	500r. Oak (*Quercus robur*)	75	50
591	P (780r.) Hornbeam (*Carpinus betulus*)	1·00	85
592	1000r. Elm (*Ulmus laevis*)	1·30	1·00

179 Swallow

2004
593	**179**	870r. multicoloured	1·30	1·00

180 Player

2004. International Ice Hockey Federation World Under-18 Championships, Minsk.
594	**180**	320r. multicoloured	75	50

181 Forest and Walker

2004. Europa. Holidays. Multicoloured.
595		320r. Type **181**	60	40
596		870r. Fisherman	1·40	1·10

182 Mount of Glory Monument

2004. 60th Anniv of the Liberation of Minsk. Sheet 121×81 mm containing T **182** and similar multicoloured design.
MS597 500r. Type **182**; 1000r. *The Parade of Partisans* (Y. Zaitsev) (52×30 mm)	2·30 2·10

183 Class 130 Series D Locomotive and Early 20th-century Station, Mosty

2004. Railways. Multicoloured.
598		320r. Type **183**	70	45
599		870r. Class 230 series A locomotive and 19th-century station, Vitebsk	1·20	1·00

184 *Polistes gallicus*

2004. Insects. Multicoloured.
600		320r. Type **184**	60	40
601		505r. *Bombus lucorum*	80	65
MS602 75×102 mm. 2000r. *Apis mellifera* (40×30 mm)			3·00	2·75

185 *Self Portrait*

2004. 150th Birth Anniv of Yury Pan (artist). Sheet 115×75 mm containing T **185** Multicoloured.
MS603 1000m.×2, Type **185**; *Watchmaker* (horiz)	3·00 2·75

186 Cycling

2004. Olympic Games, Athens (1st issue). Multicoloured.
604		320r. Type **186**	60	40
605		505r. Hammer throwing	80	65
606		870r. Tennis	1·30	1·00
See also No. **MS611**.

187 *Euphydryas matuma*

2004. Butterflies. Multicoloured.
607		300r. Type **187**	50	30
608		500r. *Pericallia matronula*	70	50
609		800r. *Zerynthia polyxena*	1·00	75
610		1200r. *Eudia pavonia*	1·60	1·30

188 Yuiya Nesterenko

2004. Olympic Games, Athens (2nd issue). Gold Medal Winners. Sheet 103×73 mm containing T **188** and similar vert design. Multicoloured.
MS611 500r.×2, Type **188** (100 metres); Igor Makarov (judo)	2·00 1·90
The stamps and margin of No. **MS611** form a composite design.

189 Byelorussian Harness Horse

2004. Horses. Sheet 120×100 mm containing T **189** and similar horiz designs. Multicoloured.
MS612 500r.×4, Type **89**; Andalusian horse; Head of Byelorussian horse; Head of Andalusian horse	3·00 2·75
The stamps and margin of No. **MS612** form a composite design.

190 Black Persian

2004. Cats. Sheet 103×115 mm containing T **190** and similar horiz designs. Multicoloured.
MS613 300r. Type **190**; 500r. Siamese seal-point; 500r. Red Persian; 800r. Tortoiseshell Persian; 800r. British shorthair	4·50 4·25
The stamps and margin of No. **MS613** form a composite design.

191 Father Christmas

2004. Christmas and New Year.
614	**191**	320r. multicoloured	75	50

192 Train in Station

2004. Minsk Underground Railway. Multicoloured.
615		560r. Type **192**	75	55

616		560r. Locomotive, decorated pillar and passengers	75	55

193 Gerasim Bogomolov

2005. Birth Centenary of Gerasim Vasilievich Bogomolov (hydrologist).
617	**193**	350r. black and vermilion	75	55

194 Madonna and Child (Protoierej Povnyji)

2005. 21st Century Icons. Sheet 151×101 mm containing T **194** and similar vert designs.
MS618 1500r.×3, Type **194**; Nativity (George Sutulin and Olga Belaja); Archangel Michael (Andrey Kosikov)	6·50 6·00

195 Great Grey Owl (*Strix nebulosa*)

2005
619	**195**	900r. multicoloured	1·00	85

196 Partisans

2005. 60th Anniv of the End of World War II. Multicoloured.
620		A (160r.) Type **196**	30	15
621		H (360r.) Liberation	50	30
622		H (360r.) Woman, bells and monument, Khatyn	50	30
623		P (930r.) Victory flag	1·00	80
MS624 150×74 mm. 1000r.×2, Signing treaty (40×30 mm); Victory parade (52×30 mm)			3·00	2·75

197 Greater Spotted Eagle (*Aquila clanga*)

2005. Fauna. Sheet 133×68 mm containing T **197** and similar horiz designs. Multicoloured.
MS625 500r. Type **197**; 500r. *Catocala sponsa*; 1000r. Beaver (*Castor fiber*); 1000r. Badger (*Meles meles*)	4·25 4·00
The stamps and margin of No. **MS625** form a composite design. Stamps of the same design were issued by Russia.

198 Vegetables

2005. Europa. Gastronomy. Multicoloured.
626		500r. Type **198**	75	50
627		1000r. Bread and hat	1·30	95

199 Stefaniya Stanyuta

2005. Birth Centenary of Stanyuta Stefaniya Mikhailovna (Stefaniya Stanyuta) (actress).
628	**199**	160r. black and vermilion	40	20

200 Hans Christian Andersen

2005. Birth Bicentenary of Hans Christian Andersen (writer). Sheet 120×80 mm.
MS629	**200**	2000r. multicoloured	3·00 2·75

201 Black Stork

2005. Endangered Species. Black Stork (Ciconia nigra). Multicoloured.
630		500r. Type **201**	75	55
631		500r. In flight	75	55
632		1000r. Facing left	1·30	1·00
633		1000r. Nestlings	1·30	1·00

202 *Harvesting* (Mikhail Sevryuk)

2005. National Art Museum. Birth Centenary of Mikhail Sevryuk (artist).
634	**202**	360r. multicoloured	50	30

203 Emblem

2005. World Information Society Summit, Tunis.
635	**203**	360r. multicoloured	60	40

2005. Traditional Costumes. As T **168**. Multicoloured
636		380r. Women, Mosty	60	40
637		570r. Women, Lepel	80	65

204 Runner and Hockey Players

2005. International Year of Sports and Physical Education.
638	**204**	570r. multicoloured	80	65

205 Arms and Town

2005. Volkvoysk Millenary.
639	**205**	360r. multicoloured	70	45

206 Kiril Turovsky Monument

2005. Turov Diocese Millenary.
640	**206**	360r. gold and vermilion	60	40

207 Early Chess
Players

2005. Chess. Background colour given.
641	**207**	500r. multicoloured (chestnut)	70	55
642	**207**	500r. multicoloured (red)	70	55

208 Vytautas Castle

2005. Architecture. Sheet 113×72 mm containing T **208** and similar horiz design. Multicoloured.
MS643 500r. Type **208**; 1000r. Lida
Castle 1·80 1·60

209 Tree and Town

2005. Christmas and New Year.
644	**209**	360r. silver, ultramarine and emerald	60	40

210 Snowboarding

2005. Winter Olympic Games, Turin. Multicoloured.
645	**210**	500r. Type **210**	75	55
MS646 117×76 mm. 2000r. Freestyle
skiing (30×40 mm) 2·30 2·10

211 Lapwing (*Vanellus vanellus*)

2006
647	**211**	930r. multicoloured	1·30	1·00

212 Atomic Symbol and Flowers

2006. 20th Anniv of Chernobyl Nuclear Disaster.
648	**212**	360r. multicoloured	60	40

213 Penguins (Lina Filippoch)

2006. Europa. Integration. Winning Designs in Children's Painting Competition. Multicoloured.
649	**213**	500r. Type **213**	75	55
650		1000r. Pegasus (Daria Buneeva) (horiz)	1·30	1·00

214 Ivan Shamyakin

2006. 85th Birth Anniv of Ivan Shamyakin (writer).
651	**214**	360r. multicoloured	60	40

215 Wheatear

2006. Birds. Multicoloured.
652		10r. Type **215**	20	10
653		20r. Blue tit	20	10
654		30r. Pied flycatcher	20	10
655		50r. Linnet	20	10
656		100r. Lesser whitethroat	25	15
657		B (160r.) Robin	30	20
658		A (190r.) Black redstart	35	20
659		200r. Chaffinch	40	25
660		300r. Tree sparrow	50	30
661		H (360r.) Great tit	55	35
662		500r. Greenfinch	70	50
663		1000r. Hawfinch	1·10	95

216 *Myotis dasycneme*

2006. Bats. Multicoloured.
664		500r. Type **216**	75	55
665		500r. *Vespertilio murinus*	75	55
666		500r. *Barbastella barbastellus*	75	55
MS667 97×115 mm. 1000r.×3, As
Nos. 664/6 4·00 3·75

217 Silver Medals

2006. Free-style Ski Team and Dmitri Daschinski—Silver Medal Winners—Winter Olympic Games, Turin. Sheet 102×72 mm.
MS668 **217** 2000r. multicoloured 2·50 2·30

218 Canoeists

2006. Avgustovo Channel. Sheet 113×74 mm.
MS669 **218** 2000r. multicoloured 2·50 2·30

219 Series E Steam
Locomotive, Railway
Station, Molodechno

2006. Railways. Multicoloured.
670		1000r. Type **219**	1·40	1·30
671		1000r. Series O steam locomotive, railway station, Brest	1·40	1·30

220 *Cephalanthera rubra*

2006. Orchids. Multicoloured.
672		1000r. Type **220**	1·40	1·30
673		1000r. *Dactylorhiza majalis*	1·40	1·30
674		1000r. As Type **220** but with design reversed	1·40	1·30

221 Wind Turbines

2006. Renewable Energy. Multicoloured.
675		210r. Type **221**	30	30
676		970r. Hydro-electric dam	1·20	1·10

222 Emblem

2006. 15th Anniv of Regional Concord of Communication (RCC).
677	**222**	410r. multicoloured	70	65

2006. Fifth National Philatelic Exhibition (BelFILA 2006). No. MS131 surch. Sheet 100×70 mm. Imperf.
MS678 3500r. on 1000r. multicoloured 4·50 4·25

224 Red Discus

2006. Fish. Discus (*Symphysodon discus*). Multicoloured.
679		500r. Type **224**	75	70
680		500r. Violet	75	70
681		500r. Green striped	75	70
682		500r. Yellow, pink striped and green	75	70

225 Decorated
Tree

2006. Happy New Year.
684	**225**	500r. ultramarine and blue	75	70
685	**225**	500r. blue	75	70

226 Napoleon
Orda

2007. Birth Bicentenary of Napoleon Orda (artist).
686	**226**	2000r. multicoloured	5·25	5·00

2007. As T **152**. Multicoloured.
687		2000r. Minsk City Hall	2·50	2·30

227 Thrush Nightingale

2007
688	**227**	1000r. multicoloured	1·30	1·20

228 Reef Knot

2007. Europa. Centenary of Scouting. Multicoloured.
689	**228**	500r. Type **228**	65	40
690		1000r. Emblem	1·30	80

229 *Mustela putorius*
(polecat)

2007. Fauna. Multicoloured.
691		B (190r.) Type **229**	20	15
692		B (190r.) *Vulpes vulpes* (red fox)	20	15
693		A (220r.) *Sciurus vulgaris* (red squirrel)	35	20
694		A (220r.) *Dryomys nitedula* (forest dormouse)	35	20

230 Map of Belarus

2007. World Heritage. Points of Struve Geodetic Arc (points where measurements were taken to determine the shape and size of Earth) in Belarus. Sheet 112×79 mm.
MS695 **230** 5000r. multicoloured 6·25 6·25

231 *Gallinago media*
(snipe)

2007. Cepkeliai and Kotra Nature Reserves. Multicoloured.
696		1000r. Type **231**	1·20	70
697		1000r. *Crex crex* (corncrake)	1·20	70

Nos. 696/7 were issued together, *se-tenant*, forming a composite design. Stamps of a similar design were issued by Lithuania.

232 *Nyctea
scandiaca* (snowy
owl)

2007. Owls. Multicoloured.
698		500r. Type **232**	55	35
699		500r. *Surnia ulula* (northern hawk owl)	55	35
700		1000r. *Asio flammeus* (short eared owl)	1·20	70
701		1000r. *Athene noctua* (little owl)	1·20	70

233 *Alexandra Marianna
Veselovskaya* (1640)

2007. Paintings from National Art Museum. Multicoloured.
702		1050r. Type **233**	2·40	1·40
703		1050r. *Griesel Sapega* (1632)	2·40	1·40
704		1050r. *Kshishtof Veselovsky* (1636)	2·40	1·40

234 Children and
Snowman

2007. Christmas and New Year. Multicoloured.
705		240r. Type **234**	40	25
706		240r. Children and parcel	40	25
707		1050r. Candle	2·10	1·30
708		1050r. Christmas tree	2·10	1·30
MS709 100×94 mm. 240r. As No. 705; 240r. As No. 706; 1500r. Child wearing Santa outfit; 1500r. Girl holding star 3·25 3·25

The stamps and margins of **MS**709 form a composite design.

235 Blagovest Bell (1937)

2007. Bells. Multicoloured.
710		600r. Type **235**	35	20
711		1000r. Blagovest bell (19th century)	1·40	85
712		1200r. Sub chime bell (1928)	1·75	1·00
MS713 106×79 mm. 2500r. Sub chime bell (18th century) 3·00 3·00

The stamps and margins of **MS**713 form a composite design.

236 Blacksmith and Armour

2007. Traditional Crafts. Multicoloured.
714	600r. Type **236**		75	45
715	600r. Weaver and cloth		75	45

237 Lamb, Sheep and Sheepdog

2007. Domestic Animals. Multicoloured.
716	240r. Type **237**		30	20
717	440r. Ram, sheep and sheepdog		60	35
718	500r. Piglets		70	40
719	1050r. Cattle		1·50	90
720	1500r. Goats		1·90	1·20

238 Medieval Falconers

2008. Hunting. Multicoloured.
721	440r. Type **238**		60	35
722	1050r. Deer hunting (horiz)		1·30	80

239 Vincent Dunin-Marcinkevich

2008. Birth Bicentenary of Vincent Dunin-Marcinkevich (writer and social activist).
723	**239**	440r. multicoloured	1·00	60

240 Konstantin Ostrozhsky

2008. 400th Death Anniv of Konstanty Wasyl Ostrogski (Konstantin Ostrozhsky) (Lithuanian prince). Sheet 93×78 mm.
MS724	**240**	2500r. multicoloured	1·70	1·70

241 Egretta alba (great white egret)

2008. Great White Egret.
725	**241**	1050r. multicoloured	1·30	80

242 Symbols of Information

2008. TIBO International Exhibition and Congress, Minsk.
726	**242**	H (440r.) multicoloured	60	35

243 Birch Parchment and Styli

2008. Europa. The Letter. Multicoloured.
727	1000r. Type **243**		1·20	75
728	1000r. Envelope, keyboard and '@'		1·20	75

244 Nyctereutes procyonoides (raccoon dog)

2008. Animals. Multicoloured.
729	10r. Type **244**		10	10
730	200r. Mustela lutreola (European mink)		20	10
731	300r. Lepus europaeus (hare)		25	15
732	400r. Canis lupus (wolf)		40	25
733	1000r. Martes martes (pine martin)		1·30	80

245 Paeonia lactiflora

2008. Garden Flowers. Multicoloured.
734	20r. Type **245**		10	10
735	30r. Petunia hybrida		10	10
736	50r. Narcissus hybridus		15	10
737	100r. Tulipa gesneriana		20	15
738	B (200r.) Dahlia cultorum		30	20
739	A (240r.) Rosa hybrida		35	20
740	H (440r.) Zinnia elegans		45	30
741a	500r. Lilium hybrida		50	30

No. 739 was for use on domestic postcards and was originally on sale for 200r., No. 740 was for use on domestic mail and was originally on sale for 240r. and No. 741 was for use on mail to Russia, Lithuania and Turkmenistan, weighing up to 20 grams.

246 Cantharellus cibarius

2008. Fungi. Multicoloured.
741	1000r. Type **246**		1·50	90
742	1500r. Boletus edulis		2·00	1·20

247 Rowers

2008. Olympic Games, Beijing.
743	**247**	1000r. multicoloured	4·75	2·75

248 Order For Exceptional Courage

2008. State Medals. Multicoloured.
744	1000r. Type **248**		1·20	75
745	1000r. Order of Military Glory		1·20	75
746	1000r. Order of the Motherland classes I, II and III		1·20	75
747	1000r. Order For Service to Motherland classes I, II and III		1·20	75
748	1000r. Order of Friendship of Peoples		1·20	75
749	1000r. Order of Honour		1·20	75
750	1000r. Order of Francysk Skaryna		1·20	75
751	1000r. Order of Mothers		1·20	75
752	1000r. Military Service Medal		1·20	75
753	1000r. Hero of Belarus Medal		1·20	75
754	1000r. Medal For Bravery		1·20	75
755	1000r. Medal For Labor Achievements		1·20	75
756	1000r. Medal For Perfect Service classes I, II and III		1·20	75
757	1000r. Guarding Civil Order Medal		1·20	75
758	1000r. Guarding State Border Medal		1·20	75
759	1000r. Medal of Francysk Skaryna (different)		1·20	75

2008. Town Arms. As T 127. Multicoloured.
760	600r. Vitsebsk		1·00	60

2008. Town Arms. As T 127. Multicoloured.
761	500r Orsha		1·00	60
762	1000r. Nesvizh		1·00	60

249 Barbed Wire

2008. Holocaust Remembrance.
763	**249**	500r. multicoloured	1·20	75

250 Holy Virgin of Iljinsk and Chernigov

2008. 1020th Anniv of the Christianization of the Rus. Sheet 140×96 mm containing T 250 and similar vert designs showing icons. Multicoloured.
MS764	1500r.×3, Type **250**; Christ Pantocrator; Grand Prince Vladimir		5·75	5·75

251 Nesvizh

2008. 425th Anniv of Nesvizh Castle. Sheet 70×77 mm. Multicoloured.
MS765	**251**	multicoloured	4·00	4·00

252 Angel

2008. Christmas.
766	**252**	500r. multicoloured	1·00	60

253 Signs of the Zodiac

2008. New Year.
767	**253**	1000r. multicoloured	1·25	75

254 Bison bonasus (European bison)

2008. Animals.
768	**254**	5000r. multicoloured	5·75	3·30

255 Bubo bubo (Eurasian eagle owl)

2008. Owls. Multicoloured.
769	500r. Type **255**		65	35
770	500r. Athene noctua (little owl)		65	35
771	1000r. Otus scops (common Scops owl)		1·25	75
772	1000r. Strix uralensis (Ural owl)		1·25	75

256 Hands reading and Louis Braille

2009. Birth Bicentenary of Louis Braille (inventor of Braille writing for the blind).
773	**256**	700r. multicoloured	1·00	60

257 Vladimir Muliavin

2009. Vladimir Muliavin (founder of Pesnyary folk-rock band) Commemoration.
774	**257**	1000r. multicoloured	1·25	75

258 Tanks

2009. 20th Anniv of Withdrawal of Troops.
775	**258**	400r. multicoloured	1·00	60

259 Executive Committee Building

2009
776	**259**	500r. multicoloured	1·00	60

260 Kaljady (winter holiday (7th–19th January))

2009. Holidays and Celebrations. Sheet 122×93 mm containing T 260 and similar vert designs. Multicoloured.
MS777	500r.×4, Type **260**; Invitation to Spring (pagan festival); Dozhinki (rye harvest); Kupalle (7th July)		2·40	2·40

261 Anser anser (grey goose)

2009. Grey Goose.
778	**261**	1000r. multicoloured	1·25	75

262 Symbols of Early Astronomy

2009. Europa. Astronomy. Multicoloured.
779	1000r. Type **262**	1·25	75
780	1000r. Symbols of modern astronomy	1·25	75

263 Globe and Butterflies

2009. Year of Native Land. Sheet 72×50 mm.
MS781 multicoloured 2·75 2·75

264 Ducks

2009. Poultry. Multicoloured.
782	1000r. Type **264**	1·50	90
783	1000r. Geese	1·50	90
MS784	69×91 mm. 3000r. Chickens (horiz)	4·00	4·00

265 *Scorzonera glabra*

2009. Endangered Flora. Multicoloured.
785	1500r. Type **265**	1·50	90
786	1500r. *Anemone sylvestris*	1·50	90

266 Monument and Fireworks

2009. 65th Anniv of Liberation. Sheet 81×66 mm. Multicoloured.
MS786 500r.×2 Type **266**; Women
soldiers 1·00 1·00

267 Antonov An-2 and Parachutist

2009. Air Sports. Multicoloured.
787	1500r. Type **267**	1·50	90
788	1500r. Yakovlev Yak-52	1·50	90

268 Andrei Gromyko

2009. Birth Centenary of Andrei Andreyevich Gromyko (Soviet Union Minister for Foreign Affairs (1957–85) and Presidium of the Supreme Soviet Chairman (1985–88)).
789	**268**	800r. multicoloured	1·00	60

269 Holy Virgin of Borkolabovo

2009. 350th Anniv of Holy Virgin of Borkolabovo (icon).
790	**269**	1380r. multicoloured	1·50	90

2008. Arms. As T **127**. Multicoloured.
791	1000r. Smorgon	1·00	60

2008. Arms. As T **127**. Multicoloured.
792	1000r Kobrin	1·00	60

270 Red Deer

2009. 600th Anniv of the Nature Reserve—Belovezhskaya Puscha. Sheet 142×60 mm containing T **270** and similar horiz designs. Multicoloured.
MS793 1500r.×3, Type **270**; Bison;
Wild boar 4·75 4·75

271 Telegraph Machine

2009. 150th Anniv of Minsk-Bobruisk Telegraph Line.
794	**271**	1380r. multicoloured	1·50	90

272 Galina Makarova

2009. 90th Birth Anniv of Galina Makarova (actress).
795	**272**	800r. multicoloured	75	45

273 *The Azure Day* (V.K. Tsvirko)

2009. 70th Anniv of National Museum. Multicoloured.
796	1000r. Type **273**	1·00	90
797	1000r. *Evening in Minsk Province* (A.G. Goravsky)	1·00	90

274 Decorated Tree

2009. Christmas and New Year. Bateleika–Christmas Puppet Show. Sheet 110×97 mm mm containing T **274** and similar vert design. Multicoloured.
MS798 1500r.×2, Type **274**; Angel 3·75 3·75
No. **MS**798 also contains a central stamp size label which, with the stamps and margins forms a composite design of a puppet theatre.

275 Kittens

2009. Russian Blue Cats. Sheet 131×101 mm containing T **275** and similar horiz designs. Multicoloured.
MS799 2500r.×3, Type **275**; Three kit-
tens seated; Head of mother cat 3·25 3·25

276 Soccer Stadium, Minsk

2009. Sports Stadiums. Multicoloured.
800	1500r. Type **276**	1·90	90
801	1500r. MCSC, Minsk	1·90	90

277 Anniversary Emblem

2009. Tenth Anniv of Creation of Union State. Sheet 113×70 mm.
MS802 multicoloured 4·75 4·75

278 Games Emblem

2010. Winter Olympic Games, Vancouver. Sheet 132×71 mm.
MS803 multicoloured 3·00 3·00

No. 804 and Type **279** are left for Birth Bicentenary of I. Khrutski, issued on 8 February 2010, not yet received.

280 Ivan Naumenko

2010. 85th Birth Anniv of Ivan Naumenko (writer).
805	**280**	800r. multicoloured	1·00	60

281 *Falco tinnunculus* (kestrel)

2010. Birds.
806	**281**	1000r. multicoloured	1·00	90

282 Iosif Zhagel

2010. Slutsk Sashes. Sheet 138×67 mm containing T **282** and similar horiz designs. Multicoloured.
MS807 1000r.×3, Type **282**; Slutsk gate,
Nesvizh; Slutsk sash (18th century) 2·50 2·50
The stamps and margin of **MS**807 form a composite design.

283 Boy reading

2010. Europa. Children's Books. Multicoloured.
808	1000r. Type **283**	1·00	90
809	1000r. Girl reading	1·00	90

284 Liberating Soldiers

2010. 65th Anniv of End of World War II. Multicoloured
810	500r. Type **284**	50	30
MS811	104×100 mm. 500r. Celebrating-soldiers in Berlin; 1500r. Monument to Liberation, Berlin	3·00	3·00

285 Bears

2010. International Year of Biodiversity. Sheet 132×49 mm. Multicoloured
MS812 300r. Type **285**; 300r. Fish;
2400r. Emblem 4·00 4·00

286 Emblem

2010. Expo 2010, Shanghai
813	**286**	500r. multicoloured	2·20	1·30

287 Arms

2010. First Anniv of Belarus Sovereign Military Order of Malta Postal Agreement
814	**287**	H (920r.) multicoloured	1·10	65
No. 814 was for international surface mail weighing 20g. or less.

288 Optimist

2010. Yachts. Multicoloured.
815	920r. Type **288**	1·10	65
816	1420r. *Luch*	1·70	1·00

289 Knights

2010. 600th Anniv of Battle of Grunwald
817	**289**	1500r. multicoloured	1·80	1·10

290 Darya Domracheva (Bronze medal winner (biathlon))

2010. Winter Olympic Games Medal Winners. Multicoloured.
818	A (290r.) Type **290**	55	35
819	H (920r.) Sergei Novikov (Silver medal winner (biathlon))	95	60
820	P (1420r.) Aleksei Grishin (Olympic champion (freestyle skier))	1·50	90
MS820a	100×135 mm. Nos. 818/20, each×2	2·10	1·60

291 Andrei Bahdanovich and Aliaksandr Bahdanovich (C2 1000m)

2010. Olympic Games Gold Medallists
MS821 1000r.×4, Type **291**; Aksana
Miankova (women's hammer throw);
Andrei Aramnau (weight lifter);
Raman Piatrushenka, Aliaksei Abal-
masau, Artur Litvinchuk and Vadzim
Makhneu (K-4 1000m) 4·50 4·50

292 Locomotive S Class, Vilenski Station, Minsk

2010. Early 20th-century Locomotives and Stations. Multicoloured.
822 1000r. Type **292** 1·30 70
823 1000r. Locomotive Sch class, Mogilyov Station 1·30 70

293

2010. Endangered Species. Green Snaketail Dragonfly (*Ophiogomphus cecilia*). Multicoloured.
824 900r. Type **293** 95 60
825 1000r. Larva and adult 1·10 70
826 1400r. Adult facing left front 1·60 95
827 1500r. Facing left rear 1·80 1·10

294
Clavariadelphus pistillaris

2010. Endangered Species. Fungi. Multicoloured.
828 Type **294** 45 30
829 500r. *Langermannia gigantea* 45 30
830 500r. *Hericium coralloides* 45 30
831 1000r. *Sparassis laminosa* 1·30 80
832 1000r. *Polyporus umbellatus* 1·30 80

2010. Arms. Multicoloured.
833 900r. Khoiniki 1·00 60

295 Trade Union Headquarters

2010. Sixth Trade Union Congress of Belarus
MS834 **295** 2000r. multicoloured 2·30 2·40

2010. Arms. Multicoloured.
835 1400r Lida 1·50 90

296 Dove, Globe, '65' and Emblem

2010. 65th Anniv of United Nations
836 **296** 1000r. multicoloured 1·30 80

297 Spaniel

2010. Hunting dogs. Multicoloured.
837 1000r. Type **297** 1·20 75
838 1000r. Irish setter 1·20 75
839 1000r. Russian laika 1·20 75

298 Star, Angels and Snow-covered Bethlehem (Merry Christmas)

2010. Christmas and New Year. Multicoloured.
840 1000r. Type **298** 2·30 1·40
841 1000r. Children, snowman, Christmas tree and Santa Claus (Happy New Year) 2·30 1·40
MS841a 138×156 mm. Nos. 840/1, each×2 9·00 5·50

2010. Arms. Multicoloured.
842 900r Gantsevichi 1·00 60

299 Competition Emblem and Children

2010. Junior Eurovision Song Contest, Minsk
843 **299** H (1010r.) multicoloured 1·30 80

300 Castle Façade

2010. Mirsky Castle
844 **300** 5000r. multicoloured 5·75 5·75

301 *Primula elatior*

2011. Endangered Flora. Multicoloured.
845 H (1010r.) Type **301** 1·00 60
846 P (1560r.) *Orchis ustulata* 1·60 95
MS846a 107×103 mm. Nos. 845/6, each×2 5·25 2·10

302 Emperor Penguins and Ice Cap

2011. Preserve Polar Regions and Glaciers. Multicoloured.
847 1500r. Type **302** 1·10 65
848 2500r. Polar bear 2·50 1·50

303 Curlew

2011. Birds
849 **303** 1500r. multicoloured 1·60 95

304 Cross (detail)

2011. 800th Anniv of Cross of St. Euphrosyne of Polotsk
MS850 5000r. Type **304** 1·00 60
MS851 10000r. As Type **304** (with colours reversed) 1·60 95

305 Yuri Gagarin

2011. 50th Anniv of the First Manned Space Flight
852 **305** H (1160r.) multicoloured 1·30 80

306 Deer in forest

2011. Europa. Forests. Multicoloured.
853 2000r. Type **306** 1·80 1·10
854 2500r. Bison 2·20 1·40

307 Tower and Flowers

2011. 25th Anniv of Chernobyl Nuclear Accident
855 **307** H (1330r.) multicoloured 1·20 75

308 Hands enclosing Ribbon

2011. 30th Anniv of AIDS Prevention Campaign
856 **308** H (1330r.) multicoloured 1·20 75

309 Tar

2011. Musical Instruments. Multicoloured.
857 H (1330r.) Type **309** 1·20 75
858 H (1330r.) Wheel Lyra 1·20 75

310 Minsk

2011. Capital Cities. Multicoloured.
859 H (1330r.) Type **310** 1·40 90
860 H (1330r.) Erevan 1·40 90

311 Anniversary Emblem

2011. 20th Anniv of Commonwealth of Independent States
861 **311** H (1330r.) multicoloured 1·40 90

312 Belarus and Venezuela Flags

2011. 15th Anniv of Friendship and Cooperation between Belarus and Venezuela. Sheet 93×62 mm
MS862 **312** 3000r. multicoloured 3·75 2·30

313 Summer Amphitheatre

2011. Slavianski Bazaar in Vitebsk, International Festival of Arts. Multicoloured.
863 A (360r.) Type **313** 45 30
864 H (1400r.) Vitebsk Town Hall 1·40 90
Nos. 863/4 were printed, *se-tenant*, forming a composite design.

314 Horse Racing

2011. Equestrian Sport
865 H (1400r.) Type **314** 1·40 90
866 H (1400r.) Jumping 1·40 90
867 H (1400r.) Dressage 1·40 90

MS868 90×60 mm. P (2160r.) Dressage, half-pass (vert) 2·75 1·90

315 Dove and Olive Branch

2011. 50th Anniv of Non-Aligned Movement
869 **315** H (1400r.) multicoloured 1·40 90

316 *Lota lota* (burbot)

2011. Fish. Multicoloured.
870 H (1400r.) Type **316** 1·40 90
871 P (2160r.) *Esox lucius* (northern pike) 2·75 1·90

317 Emblem

2011. 20th Anniv of Regional Communication Community (RCC)
872 **317** H (1540r.) multicoloured 1·30 80

318 Mir Castle (UNESCO World Heritage Site)

2011. Architecture. Multicoloured.
MS873 P (2380r.)×2, Type **318**; Karim-khani Citadel, Shiraz (prospective UNESCO World Heritage Site) 5·75 4·25

2011. Arms. Multicoloured.
874 H (1620r.) Molodechno 1·50 95

319 Malorita Region

2011. Traditional Costumes. Multicoloured.
875 H (1620r.) Type **319** 1·50 95
876 P (2500r.) Kalinkovichi region 3·00 2·20

320 Christmas Bells

2011. Christmas and New Year. Multicoloured.
877 H (2450r.) Type **320** 2·30 1·50
878 P (3750r.) Angel 2·50 1·80

321 Pigeons

2011. Pigeons. Multicoloured.
879 5000r. Type **321** 4·50 3·25
880 5000r. Carrier pigeons 4·50 3·25
881 5000r. Fancy pigeons (white with pale brown ruff and base of tail) 4·50 3·25

322 Arms of
Belarus and China

2012. 20th Anniv of Belarus - China Diplomatic Relations.
Sheet 100×55 mm
MS882 **322** 15000r. multicoloured 18·00 18·00

323 Textile

2012. Textile
883 **323** N (1100r.) multicoloured
(grey country name,
vermilion value) 1·40 1·40
884 **323** M (1650r.) multicoloured
(vermilion name,
vermilion value) 1·90 1·90

324 St. Sophia
Cathedral, Polotsk

2012. Architecture. Orthodox Temples of Belarus.
Multicoloured.
MS885 10000r.×2, Type **324**; All Saints'
Monument Church, Minsk 1·70 1·70

325
Mogilev
Town Hall

2012. Architecture. Architectural Monuments.
Multicoloured.

(a) Ordinary gum
886 50r. Type **325** 10 10
887 100r. Tower, Kamenets 15 10
888 200r. Nesvizh Castle 20 10
889 500r. Church in Polatsk 50 30
890 1000r. Palace of Rumyantsev-
Paskevich, Gomel 1·10 65
891 2000r. Mirski Castle 1·90 1·10
892 5000r. Main post office, Minsk 4·00 2·40
893 10000r. Lida Castle 4·50 4·75
894 20000r. Budslav Monastrey 7·00 4·25
895 A (500r.) Kossov's Palace 50 30
896 H (2450r.) Red Castle, Minsk 2·00 1·20
897 P (3750r.) Church-fortress,
Murovanka 2·50 1·50

(b) Self-adhesive
898 50r. Type **325** (As No.
886) 10 10
899 - 100r. Tower, Kamenets
(As No. 887) 15 10
900 - 200r. Nesvizh Castle (As
No. 888) 20 15
901 - 500r. Church in Polatsk
(As No. 889) 50 30
902 - 1000r. Palace of Rumy-
antsev-Paskevich,
Gomel (As No. 890) 1·10 65
903 - 2000r. Mirski Castle (As
No. 891) 1·90 1·10
904 - 5000r. Main post office,
Minsk (As No. 892) 4·00 2·40
905 - 10000r. Lida Castle (As
No. 893) 4·50 2·75
906 - 20000r. Budslav Monast-
rey (As No. 894) 7·00 4·25
907 - A (500r.) Kossov's Palace
(As No. 895) 50 30
908 - H (2450r.) Red Castle,
Minsk (As No. 896) 2·00 1·20
909 - P (3750r.) Church-
fortress, Murovanka
(As No. 897) 2·50 1·50

326 Couple
presenting Hen
and Basket of
Fruit

2012. Europa. Visit Belarus. Multicoloured.
910 5000r. Type **326** 1·00 60
911 5000r. Couple, facing left,
presenting bread and jug
of wine 1·00 60
Nos. 910/11 were printed, *se-tenant*, forming a com-
posite design.

327 Swift

2012. Birds. *Apus apus* (swift)
912 **327** P (3750r.) multicoloured 1·40 1·40

328 Turov and
Mozyr Region

2012. Traditional Costumes. Multicoloured.
913 H (2750r.) Type **328** 95 95
914 P (4250r.) Liahovichi region 2·30 2·30

329 *Polypodium vulgare*

2012. Endangered Species. Ferns. Multicoloured.
915 H (2750r.) Type **329** 95 95
916 P (4250r.) *Salvinia natans* 2·30 2·30

330 Arms of
Belarus and Cuba

2012. 20th Anniversary of Belarus - Cuba Diplomatic
Relations. Sheet 100×55 mm
MS917 **330** 15000r. multicoloured 5·25 5·25

331 *Hemiechinus auritus*

2012. Hedgehogs. Multicoloured.
918 H (3300r.) Type **331** 1·40 1·40
919 P (5100r.) *Erinaceus concolor* 1·80 1·80

332 *Trititrus cristatus*

2012. Newts. Multicoloured.
920 H (3300r.) Type **332** 1·40 1·80
921 P (5100r.) *Lissotriton vulgaris* 1·80 1·80

333 Mark Chagall
(Yehuda (Yuri) Pen)

2012. 125th Birth Anniv of Mark Chagall (artist). Sheet
70×75 mm
MS922 **333** 15000r. multicoloured 5·25 5·25

334 Infantry

2012. Bicentenary of Patriotic War (French invasion of
Russia) of 1812
923 **334** P (5100r.) multicoloured 1·80 1·80

335 Symbols of 'Innovative
Biotechnologies'

2012. Eurasian Economic Community
924 **335** H (3000r.) multicoloured 2·00 1·20

336 Early Steam and Modern
Locomotives

2012. 150th Anniv of Belarusian Railways
925 **336** P (5100r.) multicoloured 50 30

2012. Arms. Multicoloured.
926 H (4800r.) Glubokoye 3·75 3·50
927 P (5800r.) Gorki 4·75 4·50

337 Competitior

2012. 75th Anniv of Fire and Rescue Sports
928 **337** 5000r. multicoloured 4·00 3·75

338 Maksim Tank

2012. Birth Centenary of Yevgeniy Skurko (Maksim Tank)
(poet)
929 **338** H (4800r.) multicoloured 3·75 3·50

339

2012. Christmas and New Year. Multicoloured.
930 N (3000r.) Type **339** 1·85 1·85
931 M (4500r.) Christmas tree 2·50 2·50

340 Arms of
Belarus and Israel

2012. 20th Anniv of Belarus - Israel Diplomatic Relations.
Sheet 100×55 mm
MS932 **340** 15000r. multicoloured 7·00 7·00

341 Gymnastics, Canoeing,
Tennis and Weightlifting

2012. Olympic Games, London
933 M (4500r.) bronze and black 4·50 3·25
934 N (5500r.) silver and black 4·50 3·25
935 P (5800r.) gold and black 4·50 3·25
Designs: Type **341** (Belarus bronze medals); Conoeing,
gymnastics and swimming (Belarus silver medals); Tennis
and shooting (Belarus gold medals)

342 Emblem

2013. UCI Track Cycling World Championships, Minsk,
Belarus
936 **342** H (5500r.) multicoloured 2·85 2·85

343 *Botrychium
matricariifolium*

2013. Endangered Species. Flora and Fauna.
Multicoloured.
937 H (5500r.) Type **343** 2·85 2·85
938 P (5800r.) *Coracias garrulus*
(European Roller) 3·00 3·00
MS939 94×78 mm. Nos. 937/8 6·00 6·00

344 Embroidered
Flowers

2013. Embroidery. Multicoloured.
940 N (3000r.) Type **344** 1·85 1·85
941 M (4500r.) Cockerel 2·50 2·50
942 H (5500r.) Red embroidered
edging 2·85 2·85

345 Hoopoe

2013. Birds. *Upupa epops* (Hoopoe)
943 **345** P (5800r.) multicoloured 3·00 3·00

346 Khatyn
Memorial (Yuzif
Kaminsky carrying
his dying son)

2013. 70th Anniv of Massacre at Khatyn
944 **346** M (4500r.) multicoloured 2·50 2·50

Pt. 4

BELGIAN CONGO

A Belgian colony in Central Africa. Became independent in July 1960. for later issues see Congo, Zaire, Democratic Republic of Congo, Katanga, and South Kasai.

100 centimes = 1 franc.

INDEPENDENT STATE OF THE CONGO

The Independent State of the Congo was established in 1885, with King Leopold II of the Belgians as ruler.

1 Leopold II

1886. Various frames.

1	1	5c. green	21·00	24·00
2	1	10c. red	7·50	9·50
3	1	25c. blue	50·00	26·00
4	1	50c. green	13·00	13·00
5	1	5f. lilac	£325	£180

1887. Surch COLIS-POSTAUX Fr. 3.50.

6		3f.50 on 5f. lilac	£900	£650

5 Leopold II

1887

7	5	5c. green	45	1·10
8	5	10c. red	1·70	85
9	5	25c. blue	2·30	1·40
10	5	50c. brown	65·00	15·00
11	5	50c. grey	5·00	12·00
12	5	5f. lilac	£900	£350
13	5	5f. grey	£110	90·00
14	5	10f. orange	£400	£225

1887. Surch COLIS-POSTAUX Fr. 3.50.

15		3f.50 on 5f. violet	£800	£450

1889. Surch COLIS-POSTAUX Fr. 3.50 in frame.

16		3f.50 on 5f. violet	£600	£300
17		3f.50 on 5f. grey	£120	£120

7 Port of Matadi **8** Stanley Falls

13 Oil Palms **14** Native Canoe

1894. Inscr "ETAT INDEPENDANT DU "CONGO".

18	7	5c. black and blue	30·00	42·00
24	7	5c. black and brown	3·25	1·90
30	7	5c. black and green	1·30	60
19	8	10c. black and brown	36·00	50·00
25	8	10c. black and blue	1·70	1·00
31	8	10c. black and red	2·75	75
26	13	15c. black and brown	11·00	70
20	-	25c. black and orange	5·75	3·25
32	-	25c. black and blue	5·75	1·80
27	14	40c. black and green	18·00	3·50
21	-	50c. black and green	4·50	1·80
33	-	50c. black and brown	20·00	2·30
22	-	1f. black and violet	48·00	23·00
35	-	1f. black and red	£225	5·00
28	-	3f.50 black and red	£130	80·00
23	-	5f. black and red	75·00	20·00
29	-	10f. black and green	£120	18·00

DESIGNS—HORIZ: 25c. Inkissi Falls; 50c. Railway Bridge over the M'pozo; 1f. African elephant hunt; 3f.50 Congo village; 10f. *Deliverance* (stern wheel paddle-steamer). VERT: 5f. Bangala Chief Morangi and wife.

BELGIAN CONGO

The Congo was annexed to Belgium in 1908 and was renamed the Belgian Congo.

1909. Nos. 23, 26/29 and 30/33 optd CONGO BELGE.

36A	7	5c. black and green	4·50	3·50
37A	8	10c. black and red	7·50	2·75
38A	13	15c. black and brown	8·25	2·75
49	-	25c. black and blue	3·75	2·00
50	14	40c. black and green	10·00	6·75
51	-	50c. black and brown	16·00	3·75
52	-	1f. black and red	55·00	7·50

53	-	3f.50 black and red	60·00	18·00
54	-	5f. black and red	70·00	34·00
55b	-	10f. black and green	£120	40·00

1909. As 1894 issue but inscr "CONGO BELGE".

56	7	5c. black and green	2·75	3·75
57	8	10c. black and red	1·00	2·75
58	13	15c. black and brown	40·00	25·00
59	-	50c. black and bistre	4·50	5·75

1910. As 1894 issue but inscr "CONGO BELGE BELGISCH-CONGO" with values in French and Flemish.

60	7	5c. black and green	1·60	20
61	8	10c. black and red	1·30	20
62	13	15c. black and brown	40	10
63	-	25c. black and blue	3·50	90
64	14	40c. black and green	3·50	4·25
65	-	50c. black and bistre	5·75	3·25
66	-	1f. black and red	10·50	3·75
68	-	3f. black and red	28·00	34·00
67	-	5f. black and red	23·00	36·00
69	-	10f. black and green	50·00	46·00

32 Port of Matadi **33** Stanley Falls

34 Inkissi Falls

1915. New types as 32 to 34 (with value in words at top) and other types as 1910 all inscr "CONGO BELGE" and "BELGISCH-CONGO".

70	32	5c. black and green	90	1·00
71	33	10c. black and red	3·25	2·75
72b	13	15c. black and green	1·50	55
73	34	25c. black and blue	3·25	1·10
74	14	40c. black and red	9·50	4·50
75	-	50c. black and red	15·00	3·75
76	-	1f. black and olive	8·00	1·30
77	-	5f. black and orange	4·00	2·50

1918. Types as before, surch with red cross and premium.

78	32	5c.+10c. blue and green	30	5·50
79	33	10c.+15c. blue and red	70	5·50
80	13	15c.+20c. blue and green	50	4·50
81	34	25c.+25c. blue	1·50	6·00
82	14	40c.+40c. blue and red	1·30	7·75
83	-	50c.+50c. black and red	60	7·50
84	-	1f.+1f. blue and olive	6·50	10·00
85	-	5f.+5f. blue and orange	17·00	40·00
86	-	10f.+10f. blue and green	£110	£120

38 Congo Wharf

1920. Air.

87	38	50c. black and orange	60	55
88	-	1f. black and violet	85	30
89	-	2f. black and blue	95	85
90	-	5f. black and green	2·50	75

DESIGNS—HORIZ: 1f. District stores; 2f. Native canoes on beach. VERT: 5f. Provinicial prison.

1921. Stamps of 1910 surch.

91	14	5c. on 40c. black and green	1·70	7·00
92	-	10c. on 5c. black and green	1·00	40
93	-	15c. on 50c. black and olive	40	2·75
94	13	25c. on 15c. black & yellow	4·25	1·10
95	8	30c. on 10c. black and red	85	1·10
96	-	50c. on 25c. black and blue	2·50	75

1921. Stamps of 1910 optd 1921.

97	-	1f. black and red	1·40	1·40
98	-	3f. black and red	2·50	3·75
99	-	5f. black and lake	13·00	24·00
100	-	10f. black and green	14·00	11·50

1922. Stamps of previous issues variously surch without bars.

101	-	5c. on 50c. black and lake (No. 75)	45	1·90
102	32	10c. on 5c. black and green (No. 70)	55	25
103	14	25c. on 40c. black and lake (No. 74)	4·75	40
104	33	30c. on 10c. black and red (No. 71)	1·10	1·30

105	34	50c. on 25c. black and blue (No. 73)	45	35
114	8	0.25 on 30c. on 10c. black and red (No. 95)	23·00	50·00
115	33	0.25 on 30c. on 10c. black and red (No. 104)	10·00	48·00

1922. Stamps of 1915 surch with new value and two bars through old values.

108	32	10c. on 5c. black & green	6·75	7·75
110	-	10c. on 1f. black & olive	3·25	7·25
112	14	25c. on 40c. black & lake	1·40	60
113	-	25c. on 5f. blk & orange	5·25	11·00

46 Wood Carver **56** Native Cattle

1923

117	A	5c. yellow	35	85
118	B	10c. green	50	10
119	C	15c. brown	15	10
120	D	20c. olive	15	1·90
121	E	20c. green	85	1·40
122	F	25c. brown	15	10
123	46	30c. red	50	4·25
124	46	30c. olive	60	2·30
125	46	35c. green	8·00	6·00
142	56	45c. purple	70	1·20
126	D	50c. purple	50	10
127	G	50c. blue	55	1·00
128	G	50c. orange	70	10
143	56	60c. red	35	25
129	E	75c. orange	20	45
130	E	75c. blue	95	2·50
131	46	75c. red	1·00	15
132	H	1f. brown	60	95
133	H	1f. blue	30	10
134	H	1f. red	1·10	10
135	D	1f.25 blue	45	1·70
136	D	1f.50 blue	1·10	10
137	D	1f.75 blue	3·75	3·00
138	I	3f. brown	8·00	5·25
139	J	5f. grey	10·50	12·50
140	K	10f. black	22·00	21·00

DESIGNS: A, Ubangi woman; B, Baluba woman; C, Babuende woman; D, Ubangi man; E, Weaver; F, Basket-maker; G. Archer; H, Potter; I, Rubber worker; J, Palm oil; K, African elephant.

55 Native Canoe

1925. Great War Colonial Memorial Fund. Inscr in French or in Flemish.

141a	55	25c.+25c. black and red	1·30	12·00

1927. No. 136 surch 1.75.

144		1.75 on 1f. 50 blue	45	35

58 H. M. Stanley

1928. 50th Anniv of Stanley's Exploration of the Congo.

145	58	5c. olive	10	35
146	58	10c. violet	10	10
147	58	20c. red	55	75
148	58	35c. green	2·30	3·25
149	58	40c. brown	1·60	1·90
150	58	60c. sepia	1·80	1·10
151	58	1f. red	45	10
152	58	1f.60 grey	6·75	6·00
153	58	1f.75 blue	1·40	1·00
154	58	2f. brown	90	45
155	58	2f.75 purple	4·50	1·80
156	58	3f.50 red	1·40	1·30
157	58	5f. turquoise	85	2·00
158	58	10f. blue	1·20	2·00
159	58	20f. red	7·50	5·25

59 Nurse weighing Children **60** Doctor and Tent Surgery

1930. Congo Natives Protection Fund.

160	59	10c.+5c. red	95	12·00
161	-	20c.+10c. brown	1·80	12·50
162	60	35c.+15c. green	3·50	19·00
163	-	60c.+30c. purple	3·25	18·00
164	-	1f.+50c. red	6·75	24·00
165	-	1f.75+75c. blue	6·00	36·00
166	-	3f.50+1f.50 green	9·50	60·00
167	-	5f.+2f.50 brown	10·00	65·00
168	-	10f.+5f. black	13·00	65·00

DESIGNS—VERT: 20c. Missionary and child; 1f. Dispenser attending patients. HORIZ: 60c. View of local hospital; 1f.75, Nurses and patients; 3f.50, Nurse bathing baby; 5f. Operating theatre in local hospital; 10f. Children in school.

61 Native Kraal

1930. Air.

169	61	15f. black and sepia	8·75	4·25
170	-	30f. black and purple	15·00	9·75

DESIGN: 30f. Native porters.

1931. Surch.

171		40c. on 35c. grn (No. 148)	1·80	2·75
177		40c. on 35c. green (125)	5·50	11·00
178		50c. on 45c. purple (142)	2·30	1·30
172		1f.25 on 1f. red (151)	2·00	10
173		2f. on 1f.60 grey (152)	75	15
174		2f. on 1f.75 blue (153)	90	20
179		2f. on 1f.75 blue (137)	10·00	9·75
175		3f.25 on 2f.75 purple (155)	2·50	1·60
180		3f.25 on 3f. brown (138)	11·00	20·00
176		3f.25 on 3f.50 red (156)	4·50	7·00

67 Sankuru River **68** Flute Players

1931

181	67	10c. brown	1·00	1·40
182	-	15c. grey	1·00	20
183	-	20c. mauve	1·20	1·10
184	-	25c. blue	70	35
185	68	40c. green	1·00	2·30
186	-	50c. violet	1·00	10
187	-	60c. purple	1·30	2·30
188	-	75c. red	50	35
189	-	1f. red	4·25	55
190	-	1f.25 brown	3·25	10
190b	-	1f.50 black	6·25	2·50
191	-	2f. blue	3·25	1·30
191a	-	2f.50 blue	5·00	5·00
192	-	3f.25 grey	3·75	6·75
193	-	4f. lilac	3·00	1·60
194	-	5f. purple	6·50	1·60
195	-	10f. orange	5·50	5·75
196	-	20f. sepia	6·25	5·75

DESIGNS—HORIZ: 15c., 25c. Native kraals (different views); 20c. Waterfall; 50c. Native musicians (seated); 1f.50, 2f., Riverside dwellings; 2f.50, 3f.25, Okapi; 4f. Canoes on river shore. VERT: 60c. Native musicians (standing); 75c. Mangbethu woman; 1f. Elephant transport; 1f.25., Native chief; 5f. Pressing out tapioca; 10f. Witch doctor; 20f. Woman carrying latex.

69 Fokker F.VIIb/3m over Congo

1934. Air.

197	69	50c. black	3·50	2·50
198	69	1f. red	2·30	1·30
199	69	1f.50 green	85	15
200	69	3f. brown	75	75
201	69	4f.50 blue	3·00	50
202	69	5f. red	1·70	95
203	69	15f. purple	5·50	5·50
204	69	30f. red	9·25	10·00
205	69	50f. violet	9·25	6·00

70 King Albert I

1934. Death of King Albert.
206	**70**	1f.50 black	95	55

71 The Kings of Belgium

1935. 50th Anniv of Independent State of the Congo.
207	**71**	50c. green	1·80	3·25
208	**71**	1f.25 red	1·10	60
209	**71**	1f.50 purple	1·10	20
210	**71**	2f.40 orange	6·50	6·50
211	**71**	2f.50 blue	3·50	2·75
212	**71**	4f. violet	5·25	3·50
213	**71**	5f. brown	5·75	6·00

1936. Air. Surch **3.50F.**
214	**69**	3f.50 on 3f. brown	70	10

1936. King Albert Memorial Fund. Surch **+ 50** c.
215	**71**	1f.50+50c. purple	4·50	12·50
216	**71**	2f.50+50c. blue	2·30	21·00

74 Queen Astrid and Congo Children

1936. Queen Astrid Fund for Congo Children.
217	**74**	1f.25+5c. brown	1·30	3·75
218	**74**	1f.50+10c. red	1·60	5·25
219	**74**	2f.50+25c. blue	1·80	11·50

75 Mitumba Forest **76** R. Molindi

1937. Promotion of National Parks. (a) Sheet (140×111 mm) comprising block of four.
MS219a	**75**	4f.50 black and red	11·00	27·00

(b) As T **76.**
220	**76**	5c. black and violet	10	10
221	-	90c. brown and red	2·00	2·75
222	-	1f.50 black and purple	45	1·30
223	-	2f.40 brown and grey	65	1·50
224	-	2f.50 black and blue	95	55
225	-	4f.50 brown and green	2·50	2·30

DESIGNS—VERT: 90c. Bamboo-canes; 1f.50, R. Suza; 2f.40, R. Rutshuru. HORIZ: 2f.50, Mt. Karisimbi; 4f.50, Mitumba Forest.

1938. Tourism Congress, Costermansville. Sheet 140×120 mm containing Nos. 220/5 but all printed in brown and blue.
MS225a	**5c.** to 4f.50		50·00	65·00

77 Marabou Stork and Ruppels Griffon

1939. Leopoldville Zoological Gardens.
226	**77**	1f.+1f. purple	13·50	21·00
227	-	1f.25+1f.25 red	10·00	20·00
228	-	1f.50+1f.50 violet	13·50	44·00
229	-	4f.50+4f.50 green	9·25	36·00
230	-	5f.+5f. brown	11·00	36·00

DESIGNS: 1f.25, Kob; 1f.50, Young chimpanzees; 4f.50, Crocodiles; 5f. Lioness.

78 King Albert Memorial, Leopoldville

1941
231	**78**	10c. grey	4·75	6·25
232	**78**	15c. brown	1·00	1·80
233	**78**	25c. blue	20	80
234	**78**	50c. lilac	2·75	1·30
235	**78**	75c. pink	4·00	2·00
236	**78**	1f.25 brown	3·00	2·30
237	**78**	1f.75 orange	8·00	11·00
238	**78**	2f.50 red	3·50	20
239	**78**	2f.75 blue	6·25	2·30
240	**78**	5f. olive	5·00	2·30
241	**78**	10f. red	9·50	7·00

1941. Surch.
242	-	5c. on 1f.50 black & purple (No. 222) (postage)	35	3·25
243	**78**	75c. on 1f.75 orange	10·50	14·00
244	-	2f.50 on 2f.40 brown and grey (No. 223)	2·00	2·50
245	**69**	50c. on 1f.50 green (air)	2·30	5·00

81 "Belgium Shall Rise Again"

1942. War Relief Fund.
246	**81**	10f.+40f. green	9·00	13·00
247	**81**	10f.+40f. blue	8·75	13·00

82 Oil Palms **84** Leopard

1942. (a) Inscr "BELGISCH CONGO BELGE".
248	**82**	5c. red	10	10
249	-	50f. black and blue	9·75	2·50
250	-	100f. black and red	19·00	1·80

(b) Inscr "CONGO BELGE BELGISCH CONGO", or vice versa.
251a	**82**	10c. olive	10	10
252a	**82**	15c. brown	10	50
253a	**82**	20c. blue	10	10
254a	**82**	25c. purple	10	10
255a	**82**	30c. blue	10	10
256	**82**	50c. green	1·50	10
257a	**82**	60c. brown	80	40
258	-	75c. black and violet	1·90	10
259a	-	1f. black and brown	1·70	10
260	-	1f.25 black and red	1·30	10
261	**84**	1f.75 brown	2·75	2·75
262a	**84**	2f. yellow	3·75	10
263a	**84**	2f.50 red	1·60	10
264a	-	3f.50 olive	1·60	10
265a	-	5f. orange	1·80	10
266a	-	6f. blue	2·00	10
267	-	7f. black	2·30	10
268	-	10f. brown	1·10	10
269a	-	20f. black and red	8·50	4·25

DESIGNS—As Type **82**: 75c. to 1f.25, Head of a native woman; 3f.50 to 10f. Askari sentry. As Type **84**: 20f. Okapi; 28×33 mm: 50 f. Head of woman; 100f. Askari sentry.

1944. Red Cross Fund. Surch **Au profit de la Croix Rouge Ten voordeele van het Roode Kruis** (or with French and Flemish reversed) and additional value.
269aa	**82**	50c.+50f. green	20·00	55·00
269b	-	1f.25+100f. black and red (No. 260)	19·00	55·00
269c	**84**	1f.75+100f. brown	20·00	55·00
269d	-	3f.50+100f. green (No. 264)	16·00	55·00

87 Driving Slaves to Market **88** Leopold II

1947. 50th Anniv of Abolition of Slavery in Belgian Congo.
270	**87**	1f.25 brown	60	15
270a	-	1f.50 violet	5·00	2·75
270b	-	3f. brown	2·75	45
271	-	3f.50 blue	35	10
272	**88**	10f. orange	80	1·30

PORTRAITS—As Type **88**: 1f.50, Lavigerie. 3f. Dhanis. 3f.50, Lambermont.

89 Seated Figure

1947. Native masks and carvings as T **89**.
273	**89**	10c. orange	35	10
274	**A**	15c. blue	10	10
275	**B**	20c. blue	35	35
276	**C**	25c. red	60	10
277	**D**	40c. purple	1·20	10
278	**89**	50c. brown	2·75	10
279	**A**	70c. green	35	50
280	**B**	75c. purple	85	10
281	-	1f. purple and orange	2·50	10
281a	**A**	1f.20 brown and grey	5·00	2·75
282	**D**	1f.25 purple and green	1·00	50
282a	**E**	1f.50 red and green	25·00	12·50
282b	**B**	1f.60 blue and grey	3·75	2·50
283	**89**	2f. red and orange	3·25	10
283a	**C**	2f.40 green and turquoise	2·00	60
284	**A**	2f.50 green and brown	60	10
284a	**E**	3f. indigo and blue	9·75	10
285	**B**	3f.50 green and blue	5·75	25
286	**C**	5f. purple and bistre	4·25	10
287	**D**	6f. green and orange	2·30	10
287a	**F**	6f.50 brown and red	5·50	10
287b	**D**	8f. green and blue	4·00	25
288	**E**	10f. brown and violet	20·00	15
289	**F**	20f. brown and red	3·50	10
290	**E**	50f. black and brown	5·25	80
291	**F**	100f. black and red	7·50	2·75

DESIGNS: A, Seated figure (different); B, Kneeling figure; C, Double mask; D, Mask; E, Mask with tassels; F, Mask with horns.

90 Railway Train and Map

1948. 50th Anniv of Matadi–Leopoldville Railway.
292	**90**	2f.50 green and blue	2·30	55

91 Globe and 19th-century Full-rigged Ship

1949. 75th Anniv of U.P.U.
293	**91**	4f. blue	80	1·40

92 Allegorical Figure and Map

1950. 50th Anniv of "Comite Special du Katanga" (Chartered Company).
294	**92**	3f. slate and blue	2·30	4·00
295	**92**	6f.50 sepia and red	2·30	1·90

93 "Littonia"

1952. Flowers. Multicoloured.
296	10c. "Dissotis"		35	10
297	15c. "Protea"		10	10
298	20c. "Vellozia"		10	10
299	25c. Type **93**		10	10
300	40c. "Ipomoea"		25	35
301	50c. "Angraecum"		80	10
302	60c. "Euphorbia"		60	60
303	75c. "Ochna"		1·10	20
304	1f. "Hibiscus"		1·20	10
305	1f.25 "Protea"		4·50	4·00
306	1f.50 "Schizoglossum"		1·20	85
307	2f. "Ansellia"		1·50	10
308	3f. "Costus"		1·00	10
309	4f. "Nymphaea"		2·30	10
310	5f. "Thunbergia"		1·90	10
311	6f.50 "Thonningia"		2·30	10
312	7f. "Gerbera"		2·20	10
313	8f. "Gloriosa"		5·75	60
314	10f. "Silene"		5·00	25
315	20f. "Aristolochia"		7·25	25
316	50f. "Eulophia"		18·00	1·40
317	100f. "Cryptosepalum"		22·00	7·50

SIZES: Nos. 296/315, 21×25½ mm. Nos. 316/17, 22½×32½ mm.

94 St. Francis Xavier

1953. 400th Death Anniv of St. Francis Xavier.
318	**94**	1f.50c. black and blue	4·00	1·40

95 Lake Kivu

1953. Kivu Festival.
319	**95**	3f. black and red	3·50	1·20
320	**95**	7f. brown and blue	4·75	30

96 Medallion

1954. 25th Anniv of Belgian Royal Colonial Institute. No. 322 has different frame.
321	**96**	4f.50 grey and blue	90	40
322	**96**	6f.50 brown and green	65	20

97 King Baudouin and Mountains

1955. Inscr "CONGO BELGE . BELGISCH CONGO" or vice versa.
323	**97**	1f.50 black and red	9·50	3·25
324	-	3f. black and green	6·50	90
325	-	4f.50 black and blue	7·25	1·00
326	-	6f.50 black & purple	9·50	3·00

DESIGNS: 3f. Forest; 4f.50, River; 6f.50, Grassland.

98 Badge and Map

1955. Fifth International Congress of African Tourism. Inscr in Flemish or French.
327	**98**	6f.50 brown	4·50	3·00

1956. Birth Bicentenary of Mozart. As T **316/17** of Belgium.
328	**316**	4f.50+1f.50 violet	9·75	14·50
329	**317**	6f.50+2f.50 blue	9·25	10·00

99 Nurse with Children

1957. Red Cross Fund. Cross in red.

330	99	3f.+50c. blue	5·00	10·50
331	-	4f.50+50c. green	8·00	11·50
332	-	6f.50+50c. brown	5·50	11·50

DESIGNS—HORIZ: 4f.50, Doctor inoculating patient; 6f.50, Nurse in tropical kit bandaging patient.

100 Belgian Monarchs

1958. 50th Anniv of Belgian Annexation of the Congo.

333	100	1f. red	60	10
334	100	1f.50 blue	70	10
335	100	3f. red	2·00	1·00
336	100	5f. green	3·00	85
337	100	6f.50 brown	2·30	25
338	100	10f. violet	2·00	1·20

101 Roan Antelope

1959. Wild Animals.

339	101	10c. brown, sepia & blue	20	95
340	-	20c. blue and red	10	3·25
341	-	40c. brown and blue	80	2·75
342	-	50c. multicoloured	1·30	95
343	-	1f. black, green & brown	1·90	1·30
344	-	1f.50 black and yellow	2·30	1·30
345	-	2f. black, brown and red	3·50	1·80
346	-	3f. black, purple & slate	2·75	2·00
347	-	5f. brown, green & sepia	3·25	2·30
348	-	6f.50 brn, yellow & blue	1·90	1·20
349	-	8f. bistre, violet & brown	3·75	2·50
350	-	10f. multicoloured	4·50	5·50

DESIGNS—HORIZ: 20c. White rhinoceros; 50c. Demidoff's galago; 1f.50, African buffaloes; 3f. African elephants; 6f.50, Impala; 10f. Eland and common zebras. VERT: 40c. Giraffe; 1f. Gorilla; 2f. Eastern Black and White Colobus monkey; 5f. Okapis; 8f. Giant ground pangolin.

102 Madonna and Child

1959. Christmas.

351	102	50c. brn, ochre & chestnut	15	15
352	102	1f. brown, violet & blue	15	15
353	102	2f. brown, blue and grey	25	55

103 "African Resources"

1960. Tenth Anniv of African Technical Co-operation Commission. Inscr in French or Flemish.

354	103	3f. orange and grey	1·20	3·00

104 High Jumping

1960. Child Welfare Fund.

355	104	50c.+25c. blue and red	1·50	7·50
356	-	1f.50+50c. red & green	1·30	7·50
357	-	2f.+1f. green and red	1·50	9·25
358	-	3f.+1f.25 purple & bl	3·25	12·50
359	-	6f.50+3f.50 brn & red	2·75	16·00

DESIGNS: 1f.50, Hurdling; 2f. Football; 3f. Throwing the javelin; 6f.60, Throwing the discus.

For later issues see **CONGO (KINSHASA)**, **ZAIRE REPUBLIC** and **DEMOCRATIC REPUBLIC OF CONGO**.

Pt. 7

BELGIAN OCCCUPATION OF GERMANY

Stamps used in German territory occupied by Belgian Forces at the end of the War of 1914/18, and including the districts of Eupen and Malmedy, now incorporated in Belgium.

100 centimes = 1 Belgian franc.

1919. Stamps of Belgium optd **ALLEMAGNE DUITSCHLAND.**

1	51	1c. orange	45	95
2	51	2c. brown	45	95
3	51	3c. grey	45	3·50
4	51	5c. green	95	1·80
5	51	10c. red	1·80	3·50
6	51	15c. violet	95	1·80
7	51	20c. purple	1·40	1·80
8	51	25c. blue	1·80	3·00
9	63	25c. blue	6·00	18·00
10	52	35c. black and brown	1·80	1·80
11	-	40c. black and green	1·80	3·50
12	-	50c. black and red	8·75	17·00
13	-	65c. black and red	4·75	18·00
14	55	1f. violet	33·00	29·00
15	-	2f. grey	60·00	70·00
16	-	5f. blue (FRANK, No. 194)	13·00	18·00
17	-	10f. sepia	70·00	95·00

1920. Stamps of Belgium surch **EUPEN & MALMEDY** and value.

18	51	5pf. on 5c. green	45	60
19	51	10pf. on 10c. red	45	60
20	51	15pf. on 15c. violet	85	70
21	51	20pf. on 20c. purple	85	1·70
22	51	30pf. on 25c. blue	1·20	1·70
23	-	75pf. on 50c. black and red	24·00	29·00
24	55	1m.25 on 1f. violet	33·00	31·00

1920. Stamps of Belgium optd **Eupen.**

25	51	1c. orange	60	60
26	51	2c. brown	60	60
27	51	3c. grey	85	2·40
28	51	5c. green	85	1·40
29	51	10c. red	1·40	2·00
30	51	15c. violet	2·00	2·00
31	51	20c. purple	2·40	2·40
32	51	25c. blue	2·00	3·00
33	63	25c. blue	7·00	15·00
34	52	35c. black and brown	3·00	3·00
35	-	40c. black and green	3·50	3·50
36	-	50c. black and red	9·50	12·00
37	-	65c. black and red	5·25	18·00

POSTAGE DUE STAMPS

D54

1923

D141	D54	5c. sepia	10	4·50
D142a	D54	10c. red	35	5·50
D143	D54	15c. violet	35	5·25
D144	D54	30c. green	50	1·60
D145	D54	50c. blue	35	2·00
D146	D54	1f. grey	40	65

D86

1943

D270a	D86	10c. olive	30	4·50
D271a	D86	20c. blue	15	2·75
D272a	D86	50c. green	20	4·75
D273a	D86	1f. brown	35	3·75
D274a	D86	2f. orange	15	3·50

D99

1957

D330	D99	10c. brown	90	3·00
D331	D99	20c. purple	1·00	3·00
D332	D99	50c. green	1·50	3·00
D333	D99	1f. blue	1·60	4·50
D334	D99	2f. red	2·00	4·50
D335	D99	4f. violet	2·30	5·00
D336	D99	6f. blue	3·00	5·50

38	55	1f. violet	38·00	29·00
39	-	2f. grey	65·00	55·00
40	-	5f. blue (FRANK, No. 194)	20·00	18·00
41	-	10f. sepia	85·00	75·00

1920. Stamps of Belgium optd **Malmedy.**

42	51	1c. orange	40	60
43	51	2c. brown	40	60
44	51	3c. grey	70	2·40
45	51	5c. green	95	1·40
46	51	10c. red	1·40	2·00
47	51	15c. violet	2·40	2·40
48	51	20c. purple	3·00	3·00
49	51	25c. blue	2·40	3·00
50	63	25c. blue	7·00	14·00
51	52	35c. black and brown	3·00	3·50
52	-	40c. black and green	3·00	3·50
53	-	50c. black and red	12·00	12·00
54	-	65c. black and red	5·25	18·00
55	55	1f. violet	38·00	29·00
56	-	2f. grey	65·00	55·00
57	-	5f. blue (FRANK, No. 194)	20·00	26·00
58	-	10f. sepia	85·00	90·00

POSTAGE DUE STAMPS

1920. Postage Due stamps of Belgium, 1919. (a) Optd **Eupen.**

D1		5c. green	1·40	1·80
D2		10c. red	3·00	3·00
D3		20c. green	7·00	8·25
D4		30c. blue	6·00	7·00
D5		50c. grey	29·00	24·00

(b) Optd **Malmedy.**

D6		5c. green	3·00	1·80
D7		10c. red	6·00	3·00
D8		20c. green	24·00	24·00
D9		30c. blue	12·00	13·00
D10		50c. grey	24·00	21·00

Pt. 4

BELGIUM

An independent Kingdom of N.W. Europe.

1849. 100 centimes = 1 franc.
2002. 100 cents = 1 euro.

1 "Epaulettes"

1849. Imperf.

1	1	10c. brown	£3500	£100
2a	1	20c. blue	£4000	70·00

3 "Medallions"

1861. Imperf.

12	3	1c. green	£300	£160
13	3	10c. brown	£650	11·50
14	3	20c. blue	£700	11·50
15	3	40c. red	£5500	£100

1863. Perf.

24		1c. green	85·00	35·00
25		10c. brown	£110	4·75
26		20c. blue	£110	4·75
27		40c. red	£600	32·00

5 **8**

1865. Various frames.

34	5	10c. grey	£250	3·00
35	5	20c. blue	£400	2·50
36	5	30c. brown	£850	13·50
37	8	40c. red	£1100	26·00
38	5	1f. lilac	£2750	£140

10 "Small Lion"

1866

43	10	1c. grey	£140	16·00
44	10	2c. blue	£500	£110
45	10	5c. brown	£600	£100

11 **13** **14**

15 **20**

1869. Various frames.

46	11	1c. green	11·50	60
59a	11	2c. blue	27·00	4·00
60	11	5c. buff	75·00	1·70
49	11	8c. lilac	£100	70·00
50	13	10c. green	38·00	60
51b	14	20c. blue	£190	1·70
62	15	25c. bistre	£130	4·00
53a	13	30c. buff	£110	4·25
54b	13	40c. red	£190	8·75
55a	15	50c. grey	£375	14·50
56	13	1f. mauve	£550	21·00
57a	20	5f. brown	£2250	£1900

Types **13** to **20** and all later portraits to Type **38** are of Leopold II.

21

1883. Various frames.

63	21	10c. red	35·00	3·50
64	-	20c. grey	£250	14·00
65	-	25c. blue	£500	46·00
66	-	50c. violet	£475	46·00

25

1884. Various frames.

67	11	1c. olive	22·00	85
68	11	1c. grey	5·75	60
69	11	2c. brown	19·00	2·30
70	11	5c. green	50·00	60
71	25	10c. red	17·00	60
72	-	20c. olive	£275	2·30
73	-	25c. blue on red	21·00	3·50
74	-	35c. brown	26·00	3·50
75	-	50c. bistre	17·00	2·50
76	-	1f. brown on green	£1000	21·00
77	-	2f. lilac	80·00	44·00

32 **33**

1893

78a	32	1c. grey	95	35
79	32	2c. yellow	85	1·50
80	32	2c. brown	2·30	60
81	32	5c. green	13·00	60
82	33	10c. brown	3·75	25
83	33	10c. red	3·25	60
84	33	20c. olive	20·00	85
85	33	25c. blue	14·00	60
86a	33	35c. brown	29·00	1·70
87	33	50c. brown	75·00	25·00
88	33	50c. grey	85·00	3·75
89	33	1f. red on green	£110	29·00
90	33	1f. orange	£140	7·50
91	33	2f. mauve	95·00	75·00

The prices for the above and all following issues with the tablet are for stamps with the tablet attached. Without tablet, the prices will be about half those quoted.
See also Nos. 106/8.

34 Arms of Antwerp

1894. Antwerp Exhibition.

93	**34**	5c. green on red	7·00	4·75
94	**34**	10c. red on blue	3·50	3·00
95	**34**	25c. blue on red	1·20	1·20

35 St. Michael encountering Satan **36**

1896. Brussels Exhibition of 1897.

96	**35**	5c. violet	85	85
97	**36**	10c. red	8·75	5·25
98	**36**	10c. brown	30	30

37 **38**

1905. Various frames.

99	**37**	10c. red	1·70	85
100	**37**	20c. olive	39·00	1·50
101	**37**	25c. blue	17·00	1·20
102	**37**	35c. purple	41·00	3·00
103	**38**	50c. grey	£140	3·00
104	**38**	1f. orange	£190	14·00
105	**38**	2f. mauve	£130	29·00

1907. As T **32** but no scroll pattern between stamps and labels.

106		1c. grey	2·00	30
107		2c. red	23·00	8·75
108		5c. green	20·00	85

40 St. Martin and the Beggar (from altarpiece by Van Dyck)

1910. Brussels Exhibition. A. Unshaded background. B. Shaded background. A.

109	**40**	1c. (+1c.) grey	1·20	1·20
110	**40**	2c. (+2c.) purple	13·00	13·00
111	**40**	5c. (+5c.) green	3·50	3·50
112	**40**	10c. (+5c.) red	3·50	3·50

B.

113		1c. (+1c.) green	3·50	3·50
114		2c. (+2c.) purple	9·25	9·25
115		5c. (+5c.) green	3·50	3·50
116		10c. (+5c.) red	3·50	3·50

1911. Nos. 109/16 optd **1911**. A.

117		1c. (+1c.) grey	42·00	29·00
118		2c. (+2c.) purple	£200	£100
119		5c. (+5c.) green	13·00	11·50
120		10c. (+5c.) red	13·00	11·50

B.

121		1c. (+1c.) grey	65·00	41·00
122		2c. (+2c.) purple	£100	46·00
123		5c. (+5c.) green	13·00	11·50
124		10c. (+5c.) red	13·00	11·50

1911. Charleroi Exhibition. Nos. 109/16 optd **CHARLEROI–1911**. A.

125		1c. (+1c.) grey	8·25	4·25
126		2c. (+2c.) purple	21·00	17·00
127		5c. (+5c.) green	11·50	11·50
128		10c. (+5c.) red	11·50	11·50

B.

129		1c. (+1c.) grey	8·25	4·25
130		2c. (+2c.) purple	21·00	17·00
131		5c. (+5c.) green	11·50	11·50
132		10c. (+5c.) red	11·50	11·50

42 **43** **44**

45 Albert I

1912

133	**42**	1c. orange	25	25
134	**43**	2c. brown	35	35
135	**44**	5c. green	25	25
136	**45**	10c. red	70	60
137	**45**	20c. olive	22·00	5·75
138	**45**	35c. brown	1·20	85
139	**45**	40c. green	23·00	21·00
140	**45**	50c. grey	1·20	85
141	**45**	1f. orange	5·00	4·25
142	**45**	2f. violet	38·00	26·00
143	-	5f. purple	£120	38·00

The 5f. is as Type **45** but larger (23×35 mm).

46 (Larger head)

1912. Large head.

148	**46**	10c. red	25	25
145	**46**	20c. olive	35	45
150	**46**	25c. blue	35	35
147	**46**	40c. green	75	75

47 Merode Monument

1914. Red Cross.

151	**47**	5c. (+5c.) red & green	4·75	4·75
152	**47**	10c. (+10c.) red & pink	7·00	7·00
153	**47**	20c. (+20c.) red & vio	75·00	75·00

48 Albert I

1914. Red Cross.

154	**48**	5c. (+5c.) red and green	5·75	5·75
155	**48**	10c. (+10c.) red	60	60
156	**48**	20c. (+20c.) red & violet	18·00	18·00

49 Albert I

1915. Red Cross.

157	**49**	5c. (+5c.) red and green	13·00	3·00
158	**49**	10c. (+10c.) red and pink	37·00	14·50
159	**49**	20c. (+20c.) red & violet	65·00	23·00

51 Albert I **52** Cloth Hall, Ypres

55 Freeing of the Scheldt

1915

170	**51**	1c. orange	25	25
171	**51**	2c. brown	25	25
179	**51**	3c. grey	60	45
172	**51**	5c. green	1·50	25
173	**51**	10c. red	1·40	25
174	**51**	15c. violet	2·20	25
187	**51**	20c. purple	3·50	40
176	**51**	25c. blue	60	45
188	**52**	35c. black and brown	60	35
189	-	40c. black and green	60	35
190	-	50c. black and red	6·50	35
191	**55**	1f. violet	49·00	1·20
192	-	2f. grey	31·00	2·30
193	-	5f. blue (FRANKEN)	£500	£190
194	-	5f. blue (FRANK)	1·70	1·20
195	-	10f. brown	28·00	27·00

DESIGNS: As T **52**: 40c. Dinant; 50c. Louvain. As T **55**: 2f. Annexation of the Congo; 5f. King Albert at Furnes; 10f. The Kings of Belgium.

1918. Red Cross. Surch with new value and cross. Some colours changed.

222	**51**	1c.+1c. orange	30	30
223	**51**	2c.+2c. brown	30	30
224	**51**	5c.+5c. green	1·70	1·50
225	**51**	10c.+10c. red	3·50	3·25
226	**51**	15c.+15c. purple	7·00	7·00
227	**51**	20c.+20c. brown	14·50	13·00
228	**51**	25c.+25c. blue	29·00	29·00
229	**52**	35c.+35c. black & violet	14·00	13·50
230	-	40c.+40c. black & brown	14·00	13·50
231	-	50c.+50c. black and blue	14·50	13·50
232	**55**	1f.+1f. grey	46·00	45·00
233	-	2f.+2f. green	£100	£100
234	-	5f.+5f. brn (FRANKEN)	£250	£250
235	-	10f.+10f. blue	£850	£750

63 "Perron" at Liege

1919

236a	**63**	25c. blue	3·50	50

64 Albert I

1919

237	**64**	1c. brown	25	25
238	**64**	2c. olive	25	25
239	**64**	5c. green	25	25
240	**64**	10c. red	35	35
241	**64**	15c. violet	45	45
242	**64**	20c. sepia	1·70	1·70
243	**64**	25c. blue	2·30	2·30
244	**64**	35c. brown	2·50	2·50
245	**64**	40c. red	9·25	8·75
246	**64**	50c. brown	15·00	14·50
247	**64**	1f. orange	60·00	55·00
248	**64**	2f. purple	£550	£500
249	**64**	5f. red	£130	£130
250	**64**	10f. red	£170	£170

SIZES: 1c., 2c., 18½×21½ mm. 5c. to 2f., 22½×26½ mm. 5f., 10f., 27½×33 mm.

67 Discus thrower **68** Charioteer

1920. Olympic Games, Antwerp.

256	**67**	5c. (+5c.) green	2·50	2·30
257	**68**	10c. (+5c.) red	2·00	1·70
258	-	15c. (+5c.) brown	3·00	2·30

DESIGN—VERT: 15c. Runner.

73 Hotel de Ville, Termonde

1920

308b	**73**	65c. black and purple	85	45

1921. Nos. 256/8 surch **20c. 20c.**

309	**67**	20c. on 5c. green	85	30
310	**68**	20c. on 10c. red	60	30
311	-	20c. on 15c. brown	85	30

76 Albert I

1921

313	**76**	50c. blue	30	10
314	**76**	75c. red	40	35
315	**76**	75c. blue	50	10
316	**76**	1f. sepia	60	10
317	**76**	1f. blue	50	30
318	**76**	2f. green	1·20	30
319	**76**	5f. purple	19·00	18·00
320	**76**	5f. brown	11·50	11·50
321	**76**	10f. red	13·00	9·25

1921. Surch **55c 55c.**

322	**73**	55c. on 65c. black & pur	3·50	45

80

1922. War Invalids Fund.

348	**80**	20c.+20c. brown	1·70	1·70

81 Albert I

1922

349	**81**	1c. orange	10	10
350	**81**	2c. olive	30	30
351	**81**	3c. brown	10	10
352	**81**	5c. slate	10	10
353	**81**	10c. green	25	25
354	**81**	15c. plum	25	25
355	**81**	20c. brown	25	25
356	**81**	25c. purple	30	15
357	**81**	25c. violet	60	15
358	**81**	30c. red	45	25
359	**81**	30c. mauve	35	25
360	**81**	35c. brown	45	45
361	**81**	35c. green	60	30
362	**81**	40c. red	60	25
363	**81**	50c. bistre	65	30
364	**81**	60c. olive	4·25	15
365	**81**	75c. violet	1·30	85
366	**81**	1f. yellow	60	60
367	**81**	1f. red	1·50	30
368	**81**	1f.25 blue	1·70	1·50
369	**81**	1f.50 blue	3·00	60
370	**81**	1f.75 blue	2·00	25
371	**81**	2f. blue	4·25	60
372	**81**	5f. green	60·00	3·00
373	**81**	10f. brown	£100	13·00

83 Wounded Soldier

1923. War Invalids Fund.

374	**83**	20c.+20c. slate	1·70	1·70

87 Leopold I and Albert I

1925. 75th Anniv of 1st Belgian Stamps.

410	**87**	10c. green	11·00	11·00

411	87	15c. violet	4·25	4·25
412	87	20c. brown	4·25	4·25
413	87	25c. slate	4·25	4·25
414	87	30c. red	4·25	4·25
415	87	35c. blue	4·25	4·25
416	87	40c. sepia	4·25	4·25
417	87	50c. brown	4·25	4·25
418	87	75c. blue	4·25	4·25
419	87	1f. purple	9·25	9·25
420	87	2f. blue	5·75	5·75
421	87	5f. black	4·75	4·75
422	87	10f. red	9·75	9·75

88

1925. Anti-T.B. Fund.

423	88	15c.+5c. red and mauve	30	30
424	88	30c.+5c. red and grey	30	30
425	88	1f.+10c. red and blue	1·50	1·50

1926. Flood Relief. Type of 1922 surch Inondations 30 c Watersnood.

426	81	30c.+30c. green	1·20	1·20

90

1926. Flood Relief Fund. A. Shaded background. B. Solid background. A.

427	90	1f.+1f. blue	7·50	7·50

B.

428		1f.+1f. blue	1·70	1·70

91 / 92 Queen Elisabeth and King Albert

1926. War Tuberculosis Fund.

429	91	5c.+5c. brown	10	10
430	91	20c.+5c. brown	60	60
431	91	50c.+5c. violet	25	25
432	92	1f.50+25c. blue	80	80
433	92	5f.+1f. red	7·50	7·50

1927. Stamps of 1922 surch.

434	81	3c. on 2c. olive	25	25
435	81	10c. on 15c. plum	25	25
436	81	35c. on 40c. red	25	10
437	81	1f.75 on 1f.50 blue	1·60	1·20

94 Rowing Boat

1927. Anti-T.B. Fund.

438	94	25c.+10c. brown	1·20	1·20
439	94	35c.+10c. green	1·20	1·20
440	94	60c.+10c. violet	30	30
441	94	1f.75+25c. blue	1·50	1·50
442	94	5f.+1f. purple	5·25	5·25

96 Ogives / 97 Ruins of Orval Abbey

1928. Orval Abbey Restoration Fund. Inscr "ORVAL 1928" or "ORVAL".

461	96	5c.+5c. red and gold	30	30
462	-	25c.+5c. violet and gold	45	45
463	-	35c.+10c. green	1·30	1·30
464	-	60c.+15c. brown	85	30
465	-	1f.75+25c. blue	3·50	2·30
466	-	2f.+40c. purple	29·00	24·00
467	-	3f.+1f. red	26·00	23·00
468	97	5f.+5f. lake	19·00	17·00
469	-	10f.+10f. sepia	19·00	17·00

DESIGNS—VERT: 35c., 2f. Cistercian monk stone-carving; 60c., 1f.75, 3f. Duchess Matilda retrieving her ring.

99 Mons Cathedral / 101 Malines Cathedral

1928. Anti-T.B. Fund.

472	99	5c.+5c. red	30	30
473	-	25c.+15c. sepia	30	30
474	101	35c.+10c. green	1·50	1·50
475	-	60c.+15c. brown	60	60
476	-	1f.75+25c. violet	10·00	10·00
477	-	5f.+5f. purple	23·00	28·00

DESIGNS—As Type **99**: 25c. Tournai Cathedral. As Type **101**: 60c. Ghent Cathedral; 1f.75, St. Gudule Cathedral, Brussels; 5f. Louvain Library.

1929. Surch BRUXELLES 1929 BRUSSEL 5 c in frame.

478	81	5c. on 30c. mauve	15	15
479	-	5c. on 75c. violet	25	25
480	81	5c. on 1f.25c. blue	15	15

The above cancellation, whilst altering the original face value of the stamps, also constitutes a precancel, although stamps also come with additional ordinary postmark. The unused prices are for stamps with full gum and the used prices are for stamps without gum, with or without postmarks. We do not list precancels where there is no change in face value.

104 The Belgian Lion / 105 Albert I

1929

487	104	1c. orange	25	25
488	104	2c. green	60	30
489	104	3c. brown	25	10
490	104	5c. green	25	10
491	104	10c. bistre	25	10
492	104	20c. mauve	1·40	40
493	104	25c. red	60	10
494	104	35c. green	60	10
495	104	40c. purple	45	15
496	104	50c. blue	45	10
497	104	60c. mauve	3·00	30
498	104	70c. brown	1·70	25
499	104	75c. blue	3·00	25
500	104	75c. brown	8·25	30
501	105	10f. brown	23·00	5·75
502	105	20f. green	£120	35·00
503a	105	50f. purple	29·00	29·00
504a	105	100f. red	35·00	35·00

1929. Laying of first Stone towards Restoration of Orval Abbey. Nos. 461/9 optd with crown over ornamental letter "L" and 19-8-29.

543		5c.+5c. red and gold	£100	95·00
544		25c.+5c. violet and gold	£100	95·00
545		35c.+10c. green	£100	95·00
546		60c.+15c. brown	£100	95·00
547		1f.75+25c. blue	£100	95·00
548		2f.+40c. purple	£120	£100
549		3f.+1f. red	£100	95·00
550		5f.+5f. lake	£100	95·00
551		10f.+10f. sepia	£100	95·00

109 Canal and Belfry, Bruges

1929. Anti-T.B. Fund.

552	-	5c.+5c. brown	30	30
553	-	25c.+15c. grey	2·00	2·00
554	-	35c.+10c. green	1·70	1·70
555	-	60c.+15c. lake	60	60
556	-	1f.75+25c. blue	8·75	8·75
557	109	5f.+5f. purple	42·00	42·00

DESIGNS—HORIZ: 5c. Waterfall at Coo; 35c. Menin Gate, Ypres; 60c. Promenade d'Orleans, Spa; 1f.75, *Aquitania* and *Dinteldyk* (liners), Antwerp Harbour. VERT: 25c. Bayard Rock, Dinant.

110 Paul Rubens / 111 Zenobe Gramme

1930. Antwerp and Liege Exns.

558	110	35c. green	60	30
559	111	35c. green	60	30

112 Fokker F. VIIa/m I-BOEO over Ostend

1930. Air.

560	112	50c. blue	60	30
561	-	1f.50 brown (St. Hubert)	3·50	3·50
562	-	2f. green (Namur)	2·30	1·20
563	-	5f. red (Brussels)	2·30	1·50
564	-	5f. violet (Brussels)	38·00	38·00

113 *Leopold II* by Jef Lempoels

1930. Centenary of Independence.

565		60c. purple	30	30
566	113	1f. red	1·20	85
567	-	1f.75 blue	3·00	1·70

PORTRAITS: 60c. *Leopold I* by Lievin de Winne. 1f.75, King Albert I.

114 Antwerp City Arms

1930. International Philatelic Exhibition, Antwerp. Sheet 138×136 mm.

MS568	114	4f. (+6f.) green	£350	£350

1930. I.L.O. Congress. Nos. 565/7 optd B.I.T. OCT. 1930.

569		60c. purple	3·00	3·00
570		1f. red	11·50	11·50
571		1f.75 blue	20·00	20·00

116 Wynendaele / 117 Gaesbeek

1930. Anti-T.B. Fund.

572	-	10c.+5c. mauve	45	45
573	116	25c.+15c. sepia	1·30	1·30
574	-	40c.+10c. purple	1·20	1·20
575	-	70c.+15c. slate	1·20	1·20
576	-	1f.+25c. red	9·75	9·75
577	-	1f.75+25c. blue	6·50	6·50
578	117	5f.+5f. green	49·00	49·00

DESIGNS: 10c. Bornhem; 40c. Beloeil; 70c. Oydonck, 1f. Ghent; 1f.75, Bouillon.

1931. Surch 2c.

579	104	2c. on 3c. brown	15	15

1931. Surch BELGIQUE 1931 BELGIE 10c.

580	104	10c. on 60c. mauve	70	30

See note below No. 480.

121 Albert I / 123

1931

582	121	75c. brown (18×22 mm)	1·70	10
583	121	1f. lake (21×23½ mm)	35	30
584	123	1f.25 black	80	60
585	123	1f.50 purple	1·70	60
586	123	1f.75 blue	60	10
587	123	2f. brown	1·20	30

588	123	2f.45 violet	3·50	60
589	123	2f.50 sepia	13·50	60
590	123	5f. green	37·00	1·60
591	123	10f. red	70·00	19·00

See also No. 654.

124 Prince Leopold

1931. Disabled Soldiers' Relief Fund. Brussels National Philatelic Exhibition. Sheet 123×161 mm.

MS592	124	2f.45+55c. red (sold at 5f.)	£250	£225

125 Queen Elisabeth

1931. Anti-Tuberculosis Fund.

593	125	10c.+5c. brown	30	30
594	125	25c.+15c. violet	1·50	60
595	125	50c.+10c. green	85	60
596	125	75c.+15c. sepia	60	30
597	125	1f.+25c. lake	11·50	9·75
598	125	1f.75+25c. blue	8·50	5·75
599	125	5f.+5f. purple	75·00	75·00

1932. Surch BELGIQUE 1932 BELGIE 10c.

600	104	10c. on 40c. mauve	4·00	40
601	104	10c. on 70c. brown	4·00	15

See Note below No. 480.

126 Reaper / 127 Mercury

1932

602	126	2c. green	50	50
603	127	5c. red	10	10
604	126	10c. green	15	10
605	127	20c. lilac	1·50	30
606	126	25c. red	85	25
607	127	35c. green	3·50	10

129 Cardinal Mercier

1932. Cardinal Mercier Memorial Fund.

609	129	10c.+10c. purple	60	60
610	129	50c.+30c. mauve	3·00	3·00
611	129	75c.+25c. brown	3·00	3·00
612	129	1f.+2f. red	11·00	11·00
613	-	1f.75+75c. blue	85·00	85·00
614	-	2f.50+2f.50 brown	85·00	85·00
615	-	3f.+4f.50 green	85·00	85·00
616	-	5f.+20f. purple	£120	£120
617	-	10f.+40f. red	£250	£225

DESIGNS: 1f.75, 3f. Mercier protecting refugees at Malines; 2f.50, 5f. Mercier with busts of Aristotle and Thomas Aquinas; 10f. Mercier when Professor at Louvain University.

132

1932. Infantry Memorial.

618	132	75c.+3f.25 red	95·00	95·00
619	132	1f.75+4f.25 blue	95·00	95·00

133 Prof Piccard's Stratosphere Balloon *F.N.R.S.*, 1931

1932. Scientific Research Fund.

621	**133**	75c. brown	3·50	30
622	**133**	1f.75 blue	20·00	3·25
623	**133**	2f.50 violet	23·00	17·00

134 Hulpe-Waterloo Sanatorium

1932. Anti-T.B. Fund.

624	**134**	10c.+5c. violet	30	30
625	**134**	25c.+15c. mauve	3·25	2·00
626	**134**	50c.+10c. red	3·00	85
627	**134**	75c.+15c. brown	1·70	30
628	**134**	1f.+25c. red	20·00	14·50
629	**134**	1f.75+25c. blue	13·00	11·00
630	**134**	5f.+5f. green	£110	£110

1933. Lion type surch **BELGIQUE 1933 BELGIE 10c.**

631	**104**	10c. on 40c. mauve	21·00	4·00
632	**104**	10c. on 70c. brown	19·00	1·70

See note below No. 480.

135 The Transept

1933. Orval Abbey Restoration Fund. Inscr "ORVAL".

633	-	5c.+5c. green	75·00	75·00
634	-	10c.+15c. green	75·00	75·00
635	-	25c.+15c. brown	55·00	50·00
636	**135**	50c.+25c. lake	55·00	50·00
637	-	75c.+50c. green	55·00	50·00
638	-	1f.+1f.25 lake	55·00	50·00
639	-	1f.25+1f.75 sepia	55·00	50·00
640	-	1f.75+2f.75 blue	85·00	85·00
641	-	2f.+3f. mauve	85·00	85·00
642	-	2f.50+5f. brown	85·00	85·00
643	-	5f.+20f. purple	85·00	85·00
644	-	10f.+40f. blue	£350	£350

DESIGNS—VERT: 10c. Abbey Ruins; 75c. Belfry, new abbey; 1f. Fountain, new abbey. HORIZ: 5c. The old abbey; 25c. Guests' Courtyard, new abbey; 1f.25, Cloister, new abbey; 1f.75, Foundation of Orval Abbey in 1131; 2f. Restoration of the abbey, XVI and XVII centuries; 2f.50, Orval Abbey, XVIII century; 5f. Prince Leopold laying foundation stone of new abbey; 10f. The Virgin Mary (30×45 mm).

138 Anti-T.B. Symbol

1933. Anti-tuberculosis Fund.

646	**138**	10c.+5c. grey	85	85
647	**138**	25c.+15c. mauve	3·75	3·75
648	**138**	50c.+10c. brown	3·00	3·00
649	**138**	75c.+15c. sepia	60	60
650	**138**	1f.+25c. red	23·00	21·00
651	**138**	1f.75+25c. blue	36·00	35·00
652	**138**	5f.+5f. purple	£160	£160

1934. Lion type surch **BELGIQUE 1934 BELGIE 10c.**

653	**104**	10c. on 40c. mauve	19·00	1·70

See note below No. 480.

1934. King Albert's Mourning Stamp.

654	**121**	75c. black	30	10

140 Peter Benoit

1934. Benoit Centenary Memorial Fund.

658	**140**	75c.+25c. brown	7·00	7·00

141 Brussels Palace

1934. International Exhibition, Brussels.

659	-	35c. green	85	45
660	**141**	1f. red	1·50	60
661	-	1f.50 brown	7·00	1·40
662	-	1f.75 blue	7·00	45

DESIGNS: 35c. Congo Palace; 1f.50, Old Brussels; 1f.75, Grand Palace of the Belgian section.

142 King Leopold III

1934. War Invalids' Fund. (a) Size 18×22 mm. (b) Size 21×24 mm. (i) Exhibition Issue.

663	**142**	75c.+25c. green (a)	20·00	20·00
664	**142**	1f.+25c. purple (b)	17·00	17·00

(ii) Ordinary postage stamps.

665		75c.+25c. purple (a)	5·25	5·25
666		1f.+25c. red (b)	8·75	8·75

143 King Leopold III

1934

667		70c. green	45	10
668		75c. brown	70	35
669	**143**	1f. red	3·50	40

144 Health Crusader

1934. Anti-tuberculosis Fund. Cross in red.

670	**144**	10c.+5c. black	25	25
671	**144**	25c.+15c. brown	4·50	4·50
672	**144**	50c.+10c. green	2·30	2·00
673	**144**	75c.+15c. purple	1·50	1·50
674	**144**	1f.+25c. red	14·50	14·50
675	**144**	1f.75+25c. blue	11·50	11·50
676	**144**	5f.+5f. purple	£150	£150

145 The Royal Children

1935. Queen Astrid's Appeal.

680	**145**	35c.+15c. green	1·20	1·20
681	**145**	70c.+30c. purple	1·20	1·20
682	**145**	1f.75+50c. blue	5·75	5·75

146 "Mail-diligence"

1935. Brussels Int Exn.

683	**146**	10c.+10c. olive	60	60
684	**146**	25c.+25c. brown	2·50	2·50
685	**146**	35c.+25c. green	3·75	3·75

1935. Air. Surch with new value twice.

686	**112**	1f. on 1f.50 brown	60	60
687	**112**	4f. on 5f. red	11·00	11·00

148 Francis of Taxis

1935. Brussels Philatelic Exhibition (SITEB). Sheet 93×118 mm.

MS688	**148**	5f.+5f. grey	£170	£170

151 Queen Astrid

1935. Death of Queen Astrid. Mourning Stamp.

713	**151**	70c.+5c. black	25	25

1935. Anti-tuberculosis Fund. Black borders.

714		10c.+5c. olive	25	25
715		25c.+15c. brown	45	45
716		35c.+5c. green	25	25
717		50c.+10c. mauve	60	60
718		1f. +25c. red	1·50	1·50
719		1f.75+25c. blue	2·00	2·00
720		2f.45+55c. violet	4·00	4·00

152 State arms

1936

727	**152**	2c. green	10	10
728	**152**	5c. orange	10	10
729	**152**	10c. olive	10	10
730	**152**	15c. blue	10	10
731	**152**	20c. violet	10	10
732	**152**	25c. red	10	10
733	**152**	25c. yellow	30	10
734	**152**	30c. brown	25	10
735	**152**	35c. green	10	10
736	**152**	40c. lilac	30	30
737	**152**	50c. blue	60	10
738	**152**	60c. grey	15	10
739	**152**	65c. mauve	4·25	45
740	**152**	70c. green	40	30
741	**152**	75c. mauve	1·00	10
742	**152**	80c. green	15·00	35
743	**152**	90c. violet	75	15
744	**152**	1f. brown	70	15

153

1936. Various frames. (a) Size 17½×22 mm.

745	**153**	70c. brown	30	10
746	**153**	75c. olive	30	30
747	**153**	1f. red	35	10

(b) Size 21×24 mm.

748		1f. red	35	10
749		1f.20 brown	2·50	15
750		1f.50 mauve	60	45
751		1f.75 blue	30	30
752		1f.75 red	30	10
753		2f. violet	1·70	1·70
754		2f.25 black	30	30
755		2f.50 red	10·50	40
756		3f.25 brown	30	30
757		5f. green	1·70	70

Nos. 746/7, 751/2, 754/5 and 757 are inscribed "BELGIE BELGIQUE".

155 King Leopold III

1936

760	**155**	1f.50 mauve	85	50
761	**155**	1f.75 blue	30	30
762	**155**	2f. violet	60	35
763	**155**	2f.25 violet	65	65
764	**155**	2f.45 black	60·00	85
765	**155**	2f.50 black	4·75	30
770	**155**	3f. brown	2·00	25
766	**155**	3f.25 brown	40	25
771	**155**	4f. blue	5·00	15
767	**155**	5f. green	3·50	60
772	**155**	6f. red	18·00	45
768	**155**	10f. purple	60	30
769	**155**	20f. red	1·20	60

See also No. 2775.

156 Borgerhout Town Hall

1936. Borgerhout Philatelic Exhibition. Sheet 95×119 mm.

MS775	**156**	70c.+30c. brown	£100	95·00

157 Charleroi Town Hall

1936. Charleroi Philatelic Exhibition. Sheet 95×119 mm.

MS776	**157**	2f.45+55c. blue	75·00	75·00

158 Prince Baudouin

1936. Anti-tuberculosis Fund.

777	**158**	10c.+5c. brown	30	30
778	**158**	25c.+5c. violet	30	30
779	**158**	35c.+5c. green	35	35
780	**158**	50c.+5c. brown	60	60
781	**158**	70c.+5c. olive	25	25
782	**158**	1f.+25c. red	1·70	1·70
783	**158**	1f.75+25c. blue	2·30	2·30
784	**158**	2f.45+2f.55 purple	5·75	5·75

1937. Stamp of 1929 surch **BELGIQUE 1937 BELGIE 10c.**

785	**104**	10c. on 40c. purple	30	30

See note below No. 480.

1937. International Stamp Day.

786	**158**	2f.45.+2f.55c. slate	3·00	3·00

159 Queen Astrid and Prince Baudouin

1937. Queen Astrid Public Utility Fund.

787	**159**	10c.+5c. purple	30	30
788	**159**	25c.+5c. olive	30	30
789	**159**	35c.+5c. green	30	30
790	**159**	50c.+5c. violet	60	60
791	**159**	70c.+5c. black	30	30
792	**159**	1f.+25c. red	1·70	1·70
793	**159**	1f.75c.+25c. blue	4·00	4·00
794	**159**	2f.45c.+1f.55c. brown	8·75	8·75

160 Queen Elisabeth

1937. Eugene Ysaye Memorial Fund.

795	**160**	70c.+5c. black	35	35
796	**160**	1f.75+5c. blue	80	80
MS797		113×146 mm. **160** 1f.50+2f.50 red (2); 2f.45+3f.55, violet (2)	44·00	20·00

See also **MS**1963.

161 Princess Josephine Charlotte

1937. Anti-tuberculosis Fund.

798	**161**	10c.+5c. green	35	35
799	**161**	25c.+5c. brown	40	40

800	161	35c.+5c. green	35	35
801	161	50c.+5c. olive	40	40
802	161	70c.+5c. purple	30	30
803	161	1f.+25c. red	2·00	2·00
804	161	1f.75+25c. blue	2·00	2·00
805	161	2f.45+2f.55 purple	5·75	5·75

163 King Albert Memorial, Nieuport

1938. King Albert Memorial Fund. Sheet 138×115 mm.
MS809 163 2f.45+7f.55 red 23·00 23·00

164 King Leopold

1938. Aeronautical Propaganda.

810	164	10c.+5c. purple	35	35
811	164	35c.+5c. green	50	50
812	164	70c.+5c. black	60	60
813	164	1f.75+25c. blue	3·75	3·75
814	164	2f.45+2f.55 violet	5·25	5·25

165 Basilica of the Sacred Heart, Koekelberg

1938. Building (Completion) Fund.

815	165	10c.+5c. brown	35	35
816	-	35c.+5c. green	35	35
817	165	70c.+5c. grey	35	35
818	-	1f.+25c. red	50	50
819	165	1f.75+25c. blue	50	50
820	-	2f.45+2f.55 red	5·50	5·50
821	165	5f.+5f. green	11·50	11·50

MS822 95×120 mm. 5f.+5f. violet (as 821) 19·00 17·00
DESIGNS—HORIZ: 35c., 1f., 2f.45, Front view of Basilica. VERT: 5f. Interior view.

1938. Surch. **2F50**.
823 155 2f.50 on 2f.45 black 14·50 30

167 Exhibition Pavilion

1938. International Exhibition, Liege (1939). Inscr "LIEGE 1939 LUIK".

824	-	35c. green	25	25
825	167	1f. red	25	35
826	-	1f.50 brown	1·50	60
827	-	1f.75 blue	1·50	30

DESIGNS—VERT: 35c. View of Liege. HORIZ: 1f.50, R. Meuse at Liege; 1f.75, Albert Canal and King Albert.

1938. Koekelberg Basilica Completion Fund. Surch.

828		40c. on 35c.30 green (No. 816)	85	85
829	165	75c. on 70c.30 grey	60	60
830	-	2f.50+2f.50 on 2f.45+2f.55 red (No. 820)	7·75	7·75

170 Prince Albert of Liege

1938. Anti-tuberculosis Fund.

831	170	10c.+5c. brown	35	35
832	170	30c.+5c. purple	35	35
833	170	40c.+5c. olive	35	35
834	170	75c.+5c. grey	35	35
835	170	1f.+25c. red	1·60	1·60
836	170	1f.75+25c. blue	1·40	1·40
837	170	2f.50+2f.50 green	7·25	7·25
838	170	5f.+5f. purple	16·00	16·00

171 King Leopold and Royal Children

1939. Fifth Anniv of Int Red Cross Society.

839	-	10c.+5c. brown	30	30
840	-	30c.+5c. red	35	35
841	-	40c.+5c. olive	35	35
842	171	75c.+5c. black	35	35
843	-	1f.+25c. red	2·10	2·10
844	171	1f.75+25c. blue	1·50	1·50
845	-	2f.50+2f.50 violet	2·00	2·00
846	-	5f.+5f. green	9·25	9·25

DESIGNS—VERT: 10c. H. Dunant; 30c. Florence Nightingale; 40c. and 1f. Queen Elisabeth and Royal children; 2f.50, Queen Astrid. HORIZ: 5f. Queen Elisabeth and wounded soldier (larger).

173 Rubens's House (after engraving by Harrewijn)

1939. Rubens's House Restoration Fund.

847	173	10c.+5c. brown	35	35
848	-	40c.+5c. purple	35	35
849	-	75c.+5c. green	45	45
850	-	1f.+25c. red	2·30	2·30
851	-	1f.50+25c. brown	3·00	3·00
852	-	1f.75+25c. blue	4·75	4·75
853	-	2f.50+2f.50 purple	18·00	18·00
854	-	5f.+5f. grey	23·00	23·00

DESIGNS—As Type 173: VERT: 40c. Rubens's Sons, Albert and Nicholas; 1f. Helene Fourment (2nd wife) and Children; 1f.50, Rubens and Isabella Brant (1st wife); 1f.75, Rubens (after engraving by Pontius); 2f.50, Straw Hat (Suzanne Fourment). HORIZ: 75c. Arcade of Rubens's house. 35 ×45 mm: 5f. The Descent from the Cross.

175 Portrait by Memling

1939. Exn of Memling's Paintings, Bruges.
855 175 75c.+75c. olive 2·30 2·30

177 Orval Abbey Cloisters and Belfry

1939. Orval Abbey Restoration Fund. Inscr "ORVAL".

861	-	75c.+75c. olive	5·25	5·25
862	177	1f.+1f. red	2·50	2·50
863	-	1f.50+1f.50 brown	2·50	2·50
864	-	1f.75+1f.75 blue	3·50	3·50
865	-	2f.50+2f.50 mauve	9·75	9·75
866	-	5f.+5f. purple	11·00	11·00

DESIGNS—As Type 177: VERT: 75c. Monks in laboratory. HORIZ: 1f.50, Monks harvesting; 1f.75, Aerial view of Orval Abbey; 52½×35½ mm: 2f.50, Cardinal Van Roey, Statue of the Madonna and Abbot of Orval; 5f. Kings Albert and Leopold III and shrine.

180 Thuin

1939. Anti-tuberculosis Fund. Belfries.

868	-	10c.+5c. olive	35	35
869	180	30c.+5c. brown	35	35
870	-	40c.+5c. purple	35	35
871	-	75c.+5c. grey	35	35
872	-	1f.+25c. red	1·50	1·50
873	-	1f.75+25c. blue	1·20	1·20
874	-	2f.50+2f.50 brown	11·00	11·00
875	-	5f.+5f. violet	13·00	13·00

DESIGNS—As Type 180: 10c. Bruges; 40c. Lier; 75c. Mons. LARGER (21½×34 mm): 1f. Furnes; 1f.75, Namur; 2f.50, Alost; 5f. Tournai.

182 Arms of Mons

1940. Winter Relief Fund.

901	182	10c.+5c. black, red and green	35	35
902	-	30c.+5c. multicoloured	35	35
903	-	40c.+10c. multicoloured	35	35
904	-	50c.+10c. multicoloured	35	35
905	-	75c.+15c. multicoloured	35	35
906	-	1f.+25c. multicoloured	45	45
907	-	1f.75+50c. mult	70	70
908	-	2f.50+2f.50c. olive, red and black	1·30	1·30
909	-	5f.+5f. multicoloured	1·60	1·60

MS910 103×145 mm. Nos. 901/9 each in first colour given, together with red 14·00 14·00
DESIGNS: 30c. to 5f. Arms of Ghent, Arlon, Bruges, Namur, Hasselt, Brussels, Antwerp and Liege, respectively.

183 Painting

184 Monks studying Plans of Orval Abbey

1941. Orval Abbey Restoration Fund.

935	183	10c.+15c. brown	50	50
936	-	30c.+30c. grey	50	50
937	-	40c.+60c. brown	50	50
938	-	50c.+65c. violet	50	50
939	-	75c.+1f. mauve	50	50
940	-	1f.+1f.50 red	50	50
941	183	1f.25+1f.75 green	50	50
942	-	1f.75+2f.50 blue	50	50
943	-	2f.+3f.50 mauve	50	50
944	-	2f.50+4f.50 brown	50	50
945	-	3f.+5f. green	50	50
946	184	5f.+10f. brown	1·80	1·80

MS947 183×165 mm. 5f.+15f. blue (as 946) 10·00 9·25
DESIGNS—As Type 183. 30c., 1f., 2f.50, Sculpture; 40c., 2f. Goldsmiths (Monks carrying candlesticks and cross); 50c., 1f.75 Stained glass (Monk at prayer); 75c., 3f. Sacred music.

1941. Surch.

955	152	10c. on 30c. brown	10	10
956	152	10c. on 40c. lilac	10	10
957	153	10c. on 70c. brown	10	10
958	153	50c. on 75c. olive	30	30
959	155	2f.25 on 2f.50 black	65	65

189 Maria Theresa

1941. Soldiers' Families Relief Fund.

960	189	10c.+5c. black	25	25
961	-	35c.+5c. green	25	25
962	-	50c.+10c. brown	25	25
963	-	60c.+10c. violet	25	25
964	-	1f.+15c. red	25	25
965	-	1f.50+1f. mauve	25	25
966	-	1f.75+1f.75 blue	25	25
967	-	2f.25+2f.25 brown	30	30
968	-	3f.25+3f.25 brown	50	50
969	-	5f.+5f. green	1·00	1·00

PORTRAITS: 35c. to 5f. Charles of Lorraine, Margaret of Parma, Charles V, Johanna of Castile, Philip the Good, Margaret of Austria, Charles the Bold, Archduke Albert and Archduchess Isabella respectively.

190 St. Martin, Dinant

1941. Winter Relief Fund. Statues.

970	190	10c.+5c. brown	30	30
971	-	35c.+5c. green	30	30
972	-	50c.+10c. violet	30	30
973	-	60c.+10c. brown	30	30
974	-	1f.+15c. red	30	30
975	190	1f.50+25c. green	30	30
976	-	1f.75+50c. blue	35	35
977	-	2f.25+2f.25 mauve	35	35
978	-	3f.25+3f.25 brown	45	45
979	-	5f.+5f. green	85	85

MS980 105×139 mm. 5f.+20f. purple (as 979) 27·00 27·00
DESIGNS (Statues of St. Martin in churches)—As Type 190: 35c., 1f. Lennick, St. Quentin; 50c., 3f. Beck, Limberg; 60c., 2f.25, Dave on the Meuse; 1f.75, Hal, Brabant. 35×50 mm: 5f. St. Trond.

192 Concert Hall, Argenteuil

1941. Fund for Queen Elisabeth's Concert Hall. Two sheets, each 103×133 mm.
MS981 192 10f.+15f. green 8·25 7·50
MS982 As last with perforated crown and monogram with violet control number on back 8·25 7·50

193 Mercator

1942. Anti-tuberculosis Fund. Portraits.

986	-	10c.+5c. brown	10	10
987	-	35c.+5c. green	10	10
988	-	50c.+10c. brown	10	10
989	-	60c.+10c. green	10	10
990	-	1f.+15c. red	10	10
991	193	1f.75+50c. blue	10	10
992	-	3f.25+3f.25 purple	10	10
993	-	5f.+5f. violet	25	25
994	-	10f.+30f. orange	1·70	1·70

MS995 77×59 mm. 3f.25+6f.75 green (as 968); 5f.+10f. red (as 969) 14·00 14·00
SCIENTISTS—As T 193: 10c. Bolland. 35c. Versale. 50c. S. Stevin. 60c. Van Helmont. 1f. Dodoens. 3f.25, Oertell. 5f. Juste Lipse. 25½×28½ mm: 10f. Plantin.

198 Prisoner writing Letter

1942. Prisoners of War Fund.
1000 198 5f.+45f. grey 8·75 8·75

199 St. Martin **200** St. Martin sharing his cloak

1942. Winter Relief Fund.

1001	199	10c.+5c. orange	25	25
1002	-	35c.+5c. green	25	25
1003	-	50c.+10c. brown	25	25
1004	-	60c.+10c. black (horiz)	25	25
1005	-	1f.+15c. green	25	25
1006	-	1f.50+25c. green	30	30
1007	-	1f.75+50c. blue	30	35
1008	-	2f.25+2f.25 brn (horiz)	35	35

1009	-	3f.25+3f.25 purple (horiz)	60	60
1010	200	5f.+10f. brown	1·60	1·60
1011	200	10f.+20f. brown & vio	1·70	1·70
1012	200	10f.+20f. red & violet	1·50	1·50

201 Soldiers and Vision of Home

1943. Prisoners of War Relief Fund.

1013	201	1f.+30f. red	3·50	3·50
1014	-	1f.+30f. brown	2·30	2·30

DESIGN: No. 1014, Soldiers emptying parcel of books and vision of home.

202 Tiler

1943. Anti-tuberculosis Fund. Trades.

1015	202	10c.+5c. brown	25	25
1016	-	35c.+5c. green	25	25
1017	-	50c.+10c. brown	25	25
1018	-	60c.+10c. green	25	25
1019	-	1f.+15c. red	30	25
1020	-	1f.75+75c. blue	25	25
1021	-	3f.25+3f.25 purple	35	35
1022	-	5f.+20f. violet	1·20	1·20

DESIGNS: 35c. Blacksmith; 50c. Coppersmith; 60c. Gunsmith; 1f. Armourer; 1f.75, Goldsmith; 3f.25, Fishmonger; 5f. Clockmaker.

203 Ornamental Letter

204 Ornamental Letter

1943. Orval Abbey Restoration Fund. Designs showing single letters forming "ORVAL".

1023	203	50c.+1f. black	45	45
1024	-	60c.+1f.90 violet	35	35
1025	-	1f.+3f. red	35	35
1026	-	1f.75+5f.25 blue	35	35
1027	-	3f.25+16f.75 green	65	65
1028	204	5f.+30f. brown	1·10	1·10

205 St. Leonard's Church, Leon, and St. Martin

206 Church of Notre Dame, Hal, and St. Martin

207 St. Martin and River Scheldt

1943. Winter Relief Fund.

1029	205	10c.+5c. brown	30	30
1030	-	35c.+5c. green	30	30
1031	-	50c.+15c. green	30	30
1032	-	60c.+20c. purple	30	30
1033	-	1f.+1f. red	35	35
1034	-	1f.75+4f.25 blue	80	80
1035	-	3f.25+11f.75 mauve	1·60	1·60
1036	206	5f.+25f. blue	2·40	2·40
1037	207	10f.+30f. green	1·90	1·90
1038	-	10f.+30f. brown	1·90	1·90

DESIGNS: (Various churches and statues of St. Martin sharing his cloak). As Type 205: HORIZ: 35c. Dion-le-Val; 50c. Alost; 60c. Liege; 3f.25, Loppem. VERT: 1f. Courtrai; 1f.75, Angre. As Type 207: 10f. brown Meuse landscape.

208 "Daedalus and Icarus"

1944. Red Cross.

1039	208	35c.+1f.65 green	40	40
1040	-	50c.+2f.50 grey	40	40
1041	-	60c.+3f.40 brown	40	40
1042	-	1f.+5f. red	60	60
1043	-	1f.75+8f.25 blue	60	60
1044	-	5f.+30f. brown	95	95

DESIGNS: 50c. *The Good Samaritan* (Jacob Jordsen); 60c. *Christ healing the Paralytic* (detail); 1f. *Madonna and Child*; 1f.75, *Self-portrait*; 5f. *St. Sebastian*.
Nos. 1039 and 1041/4 depict paintings by Anthony van Dyck.

209 Jan van Eyck

1944. Prisoners of War Relief Fund.

1045	209	10c.+15c. violet	35	35
1046	-	35c.+15c. green	35	35
1047	-	50c.+25c. brown	35	35
1048	-	60c.+40c. olive	35	35
1049	-	1f.+50c. red	35	35
1050	-	1f.75+4f.25 blue	35	35
1051	-	2f.25+8f.25 slate	80	80
1052	-	3f.25+11f.25 brown	40	40
1053	-	5f.+35f. grey	85	85

PORTRAITS: 35c. "Godefroid de Bouillon". 50c. "Jacob van Maerlant". 60c. "Jean Joses de Dinant". 1f. "Jacob van Artevelde". 1f.75, "Charles Joseph de Ligne". 2f.25, "Andre Gretry". 3f.25, "Jan Moretus-Plantin". 5f. "Ruusbroeck".

210 "Bayard and Four Sons of Aymon", Namur

1944. Anti-tuberculosis Fund. Provincial legendary types.

1054	210	10c.+5c. brown	10	10
1055	-	35c.+5c. green	10	10
1056	-	50c.+10c. violet	10	10
1057	-	60c.+10c. brown	10	10
1058	-	1f.+15c. red	10	10
1059	-	1f.75+5f.25 blue	10	10
1060	-	3f.25+11f.75 green	35	35
1061	-	5f.+25f. blue	45	45

DESIGNS—VERT: 35c. "Brabo severing the giant's hand", Antwerp; 60c. "Thyl Ulenspiegel" and "Nele", Flanders; 1f. "St. George and the Dragon", Hainaut; 1f.75, "Genevieve of Brabant, with the Child and the Hind", Brabant. HORIZ: 50c. "St. Hubert encounters the Hind with the Cross", Luxemburg; 3f.25, "Tchantches wrestling with the Saracen", Liege; 5f. "St. Gertrude rescuing the Knight with the cards", Limburg.

211 Lion Rampant

1944. Inscr "BELGIQUE-BELGIE" or "BELGIE-BELGIQUE".

1062A	211	5c. brown	10	10
1063A	211	10c. green	10	10
1064A	211	25c. blue	10	10
1065A	211	35c. brown	10	10
1066A	211	60c. green	10	10
1067B	211	75c. violet	10	10
1068B	211	1f. red	10	10
1069B	211	1f.25 brown	25	25
1070B	211	1f.50 orange	40	40
1071A	211	1f.75 blue	10	10
1072B	211	2f. blue	1·70	1·70
1073A	211	2f.75 mauve	10	10
1074B	211	3f. red	25	25
1075B	211	3f.50 grey	15	10
1076B	211	5f. brown	3·50	3·50
1077B	211	10f. black	85	85

1944. Overprinted with large V.

1078	152	2c. green	10	10
1079	152	15c. blue	10	10
1080	152	20c. violet	10	10
1081	152	60c. grey	10	10

213 King Leopold III and "V"

1944

1082	213	1f. red	15	10
1083	213	1f.50 mauve	15	10
1084	213	1f.75 blue	45	45
1085	213	2f. violet	60	35
1086	213	2f.25 green	45	45
1087	213	3f.25 brown	30	15
1088	213	5f. green	1·20	35

214 War Victims 215 Rebuilding Homes

1945. War Victims' Relief Fund.

1114	214	1f.+30f. red	1·90	1·00
1115	215	1¾f.+30f. blue	1·90	1·00

Nos. 1114/15 measure 50×35 mm.

1945. Post Office Employers' Relief Fund.

1119	214	1f.+9f. red	40	25
1120	215	1f.+9f. red	45	25

217 Resister 218 Group of Resisters

1945. Prisoners of War Relief Fund.

1121	217	10c.+15c. orange	25	25
1122	-	20c.+20c. violet	25	25
1123	-	60c.+25c. brown	25	25
1124	-	70c.+30c. green	25	25
1125	217	75c.+50c. brown	25	25
1126	-	1f.+75c. green	30	25
1127	-	1f.50+1f. red	30	25
1128	-	3f.50+3f.50 blue	2·00	1·30
1129	218	5f.+40f. brown	2·50	1·50

DESIGNS—VERT: 20c., 1f. Father and child; 60c., 1f.50, Victim tied to stake. HORIZ: 70c., 3f.50, Rifleman.

219 West Flanders

1945. Anti-tuberculosis Fund.

1130	219	10c.+15c. green	60	30
1131	-	20c.+20c. red	35	30
1132	-	60c.+25c. brown	35	30
1133	-	70c.+30c. green	35	30
1134	-	75c.+50c. brown	35	30
1135	-	1f.+75c. violet	35	30
1136	-	1f.50+1f. green	35	30
1137	-	3f.50+1f.50 blue	75	75
1138	-	5f.+45f. mauve	4·25	2·40

ARMS DESIGNS—VERT: 20c. to 5f. Arms of Luxemburg, East Flanders, Namur, Limburg Hainaut, Antwerp, Liege and Brabant respectively.

222 Douglas DC-400-DAA

1946. Air.

1165	222	6f. blue	40	30
1166	222	8f.50 red	75	60
1167	222	50f. green	7·00	1·20
1168	222	100f. grey	11·50	9·50

1946. Surch -10%, reducing the original value by 10%.

1171	213	"-10%" on 1f.50 mauve	85	30
1172	213	"-10%" on 2f. violet	2·30	85
1173	213	"-10%" on 5f. green	2·00	30

224 *Marie Henriette* (paddle-steamer)

1946. Ostend–Dover Mail-boat Service Centenary.

1174a		1f.35 blue	45	25
1175	224	2f.25 green	60	40
1176	-	3f.15 grey	65	30

DESIGNS—21½×18½ or 21×17 mm: 1f.35, *Prince Baudouin* (mail steamer). As T 224: 3f.15, *Diamant* (paddle-steamer), formerly *Le Chemin de Fer*.

225 Paratrooper

1946. Air. Bastogne Monument Fund.

1177	225	17f.50+62f.50 green	1·90	85
1178	225	17f.50+62f.50 purple	1·90	85

226 Father Damien 227 E. Vandervelde

228 Francois Bovesse

1946. Belgian Patriots. (a) Father Damien.

1179	226	65c.+75c. blue	2·30	1·50
1180	-	1f.35+2f. brown	2·30	1·50
1181	-	1f.75+18f. lake	2·30	1·50

DESIGNS—HORIZ: 1f.35, Molokai Leper Colony. VERT: 1f.75, Damien's statue.

(b) Emile Vandervelde.

1182	227	65c.+75c. green	2·30	1·50
1183	-	1f.35+2f. blue	2·30	1·50
1184	-	1f.75+18f. red	2·30	1·50

DESIGNS—HORIZ: 1f.35, Vandervelde, miner, mother and child. VERT: 1f.75, Sower.

(c) Francois Bovesse.

1185	-	65c.+75c. violet	2·30	1·50
1186	228	1f.35+2f. brown	2·30	1·50
1187	-	1f.75+18f. red	2·30	1·50

DESIGNS—VERT: 65c. Symbols of Patriotism and Learning; 1f.75, Draped memorial figures holding wreath and torch.

229 Pepin d'Herstal

1946. War Victims' Relief Fund.

1188	229	75c.+25c. green	60	25
1189	-	1f.+50c. blue	85	35
1190	-	1f.50+1f. purple	85	45
1191	-	3f.50+1f.50 blue	1·20	70
1192	-	5f.+45f. mauve	15·00	14·00
1194	-	5f.+45f. orange	13·00	13·00

DESIGNS: 1f. Charlemagne; 1f.50, Godfrey of Bouillon; 3f.50, Robert of Jerusalem; 5f. Baudouin of Constantinople.
 See also Nos. 1207/11, 1258/9 and 1302/6.

230 Allegory of "Flight"

1946. Air.
1193 **230** 2f.+8f. violet 65 60

231 Malines

1946. Anti-tuberculosis Fund. No date.
1195 **231** 65c.+35c. red 70 25
1196 - 90c.+60c. olive 80 25
1197 - 1f.35+1f.15 green 80 25
1198 - 3f.15+1f.85 blue 1·20 45
1199 - 4f.50+45f.50 brown 19·00 16·00
DESIGNS—(Arms and Industries): 90c. Dinant; 1f.35, Ostend; 3f.15, Verviers; 4f.50, Louvain.
 See also Nos. 1212/16.

1947. Air. "Cipex" International Stamp Exhibition, New York. Nos. 1179/87 surch LUCHTPOST POSTE AERIENNE or POSTE AERIENNE LUCHTPOST and new value. (a) Father Damien.
1199a 1f.+2f. on 65c. +75c. blue 95 60
1199b 1f.50+2f.50 on 1f.35+2f. brown 95 60
1199c 2f.+45f. on 1f.75+18f. red 95 60

(b) Emile Vandervelde.
1199d 1f.+2f. on 65c.+75c. green 95 60
1199e 1f.50+2f.50 on 1f.35+2f. blue 95 60
1199f 2f.+45f. on 1f.75+18f. red 95 60

(c) Francois Bovesse.
1199g 1f.+2f. on 65c.+75c. vio 95 60
1199h 1f.50+2f.50 on 1f.35+2f. brown 95 60
1199i 2f.+45f. on 1f.75+18f. red 95 60

232 Joseph Plateau

1947. Int Film and Belgian Fine Arts Festival.
1200 **232** 3f.15 blue 1·50 30

233 Adrien de Gerlache **234** Explorers landing from *Belgica*

1947. 50th Anniv of Belgian Antarctic Expedition.
1201 **233** 1f.35 red 30 10
1202 **234** 2f.25 grey 4·75 70

1947. War Victims' Relief Fund. Mediaeval Princes as T 229.
1207 65c.+35c. blue 1·30 60
1208 90c.+60c. brown 1·90 85
1209 1f.35+1f.15 red 3·75 1·20
1210 3f.15+1f.85 blue 4·75 1·50
1211 20f.+20f. purple 60·00 48·00
DESIGNS: 65c. John II, Duke of Brabant; 90c. Philippe of Alsace; 1f.35, William the Good; 3f.15, Notger, Bishop of Liege; 20f. Philip the Noble.

1947. Anti-Tuberculosis Fund. Arms designs as T 231, but dated "1947".
1212 65c.+35c. orange 70 60
1213 90c.+60c. purple 80 70
1214 1f.35+1f.15 brown 95 75
1215 3f.15+1f.85 blue 3·25 1·50
1216 20f.+20f. green 31·00 20·00
DESIGNS (Arms and Industries): 65c. Nivelles; 90c. St. Truiden; 1f.35, Charleroi; 3f.15, St. Nicholas; 20f. Bouillon.

237 Chemical Industry **240** Textile Machinery

239 Antwerp Docks

1948. National Industries.
1217 **237** 60c. blue 15 15
1218 **237** 1f.20 brown 3·00 30
1219 - 1f.35 brown 15 15
1220 - 1f.75 green 70 30
1221 - 1f.75 red 30 25
1222 **239** 2f.25 grey 85 60
1223 - 2f.50 mauve 9·50 65
1224 **239** 3f. purple 15·00 60
1225 **240** 3f.15 blue 1·40
1226 **240** 4f. blue 14·50 45
1227 - 6f. blue 36·00 65
1228 - 6f.30 purple 3·50 2·75
DESIGNS—As Type 237: 1f.35, 1f.75 green, Woman making lace; 1f.75 red, 2f.50, Agricultural produce. As Type 239: 6f., 6f.30, Steel works.

242 St. Benedict and King Totila

1948. Achel Abbey Fund. Inscr "ACHEL".
1232 **242** 65c.+65c. brown 1·20 85
1233 - 1f.35+1f.35 green 1·70 1·20
1234 - 3f.15+2f.85 blue 4·00 1·50
1235 - 10f.+10f. purple 14·00 11·50
DESIGNS—HORIZ: 1f.35, Achel Abbey. VERT: 3f.15, St. Benedict as Law-Giver; 10f. Death of St. Benedict.

243 St. Bega and Chevremont Castle

1948. Chevremont Abbey Fund. Inscr "CHEVREMONT".
1236 **243** 65c.+65c. blue 1·20 85
1237 - 1f.35+1f.35 red 1·70 1·20
1238 - 3f.15+2f.85 blue 3·50 1·50
1239 - 10f.+10f. brown 13·50 10·50
DESIGNS—HORIZ: 1f.35, Chevremont Basilica and Convent. VERT: 3f.15, Madonna of Chevremont and Chapel; 10f. Monk and Madonna of Mt. Carmel.

244 Statue of Anseele **245** Ghent and E. Anseele

1948. Inauguration of Edward Anseele (Socialist Leader) Statue.
1245 **244** 65c.+35c. red 3·00 1·70
1246 **245** 90c.+60c. grey 4·00 2·30
1247 - 1f.35+1f.15 brn 3·00 1·70
1248 - 3f.15+1f.85 blue 5·75 5·75
MS1249 82×145 mm. Nos. 1245/8 £250 £110
DESIGNS: 1f.35, Statue and Ed. Anseele; 3f.15, Reverse side of statue.

247 "Liberty" **248** "Resistance"

1948. Antwerp and Liege Monuments Funds.
1253 **247** 10f.+10f. green 60·00 29·00
1254 **248** 10f.+10f. brown 26·00 14·50

249 Cross of Lorraine

1948. Anti-tuberculosis Fund.
1255 **249** 20c.+5c. green 60 30
1256 **249** 1f.20+30c. purple 2·00 60
1257 **249** 1f.75+25c. red 2·30 85
1258 - 4f.+3f.25 blue 9·50 5·75
1259 - 20f.+20f. green 50·00 35·00
DESIGNS—As Type 229: 4f. Isabel of Austria; 20f. Albert, Archduke of Austria.

250 'Madonna and Child'

1949. Social and Cultural Funds. Sheets 140×90 mm sold at 50f. each incl premium (a) Paintings by R. van der Weyden.
MS1260 90c. brown (T 250 *Madonna and Child*); 1f.75 purple (*Crucifixion*); 4f. blue (*Mary Magdalene*) £225 £200

(b) Paintings by J. Jordaens.
MS1261 90c. violet (*Woman Reading*); 1f.75 red (*Flute-player*); 4f. blue (*Old Woman and Letter*) £225 £200

1949. Surch 1-1-49 at top, 31-XII-49 and value at bottom with posthorn in between. (a) Arms type.
1262 **152** 5c. on 15c. blue 10 10
1263 **152** 5c. on 30c. brown 10 10
1264 **152** 5c. on 40c. lilac 10 10
1265 **152** 20c. on 70c. green 10 10
1266 **152** 20c. on 75c. mauve 10 10

(b) Anseele Statue.
1267 **244** 10c. on 65c.+35c. red 3·00 3·00
1268 **245** 40c. on 90c.+60c. grey 1·70 1·70
1269 - 80c. on 1f.35+1f.15 brown 85 90
1270 - 1f.20 on 3f.15+1f.85 blue 1·50 1·50

251 King Leopold I **252** Forms of Postal Transport

1949. Belgian Stamp Centenary.
1271 **251** 90c. green (postage) 75 40
1272 **251** 1f.75 brown 40 30
1273 **251** 3f. red 11·00 3·50
1274 **251** 4f. blue 7·00 1·00
1275 **252** 50f. brown (air) 60·00 23·00

253 St. Madeleine from *The Baptism of Christ*

1949. Exhibition of Paintings by Gerard David, Bruges.
1276 **253** 1f.75 brown 85 30

255 Hemispheres and Allegorical Figure

1949. 75th Anniv of U.P.U.
1295 **255** 4f. blue 5·50 2·50

256 Guido Gezelle

1949. 50th Death Anniv of Gezelle (poet).
1297 **256** 1f.75+75c. green 2·00 1·50

257 Arnica

1949. Anti-tuberculosis and other Funds. (a) Flowers.
1298 **257** 20c.+5c. black, yellow and green 35 30
1299 - 65c.+10c. black, green and buff 1·40 45
1300 - 90c.+10c. black, blue and red 2·00 1·00
1301 - 1f.20+30c. mult 2·50 1·30
FLOWERS: 65c. Thistle. 90c. Periwinkle. 1f.20, Poppy.

(b) Portraits as T 229.
1302 1f.75+25c. orange 1·20 40
1303 3f.+1f.50 red 13·00 8·25
1304 4f.+2f. blue 13·50 8·25
1305 6f.+3f. brown 23·00 11·50
1306 8f.+4f. green 27·00 15·00
PORTRAITS: 1f.75, Philip the Good. 3f. Charles V. 4f. Maria Christina. 6f. Charles of Lorraine. 8f. Maria Theresa.

260 Anglo-Belgian Monument, Hertain

1950. Anglo-Belgian Union and other Funds.
1307 - 80c.+20c. green 1·50 60
1308 - 2f.50+50c. red 6·75 4·00
1309 **260** 4f.+2f. blue 10·50 7·00
DESIGNS—HORIZ: 80c. Arms of Great Britain and Belgium; 2f.50, British tanks at Tournai.

261 Allegory of Saving

1950. National Savings Bank Centenary.
1310 **261** 1f.75 sepia 60 30

262 Hurdling

1950. European Athletic Championships. Inscr "HEYSEL 1950".
1311 **262** 20c.+5c. green 60 30
1312 - 90c.+10c. purple 4·75 2·30
1313 - 1f.75+25c. red 9·25 2·50
1314 - 4f.+2f. blue 44·00 23·00
1315 - 8f.+4f. green 46·00 30·00
MS1316 70×119 mm. 1f.75+25c. (+18f.) (No. 1313) 95·00 60·00
DESIGNS—HORIZ: 1f.75, Relay racing. VERT: 90c. Javelin throwing; 4f. Pole vaulting; 8f. Sprinting.

263 Sikorsky S-51 Helicopter and Douglas DC-4 leaving Melsbroeck Airport

1950. Air. Inauguration of Helicopter Airmail Services and Aeronautical Committee's Fund.
1317 **263** 7f.+3f. blue 9·75 5·75

265 Gentian **266** Sijsele Sanatorium

1950. Anti-tuberculosis and other Funds. Cross in red.
1326 **265** 20c.+5c. blue, green and purple 35 30

1327	-	65c.+10c. green and brown	1·40	45
1328	-	90c.+10c. light green and green	1·70	1·20
1329	-	1f.20+30c. blue, green and ultramarine	2·00	1·30
1330	266	1f.75+25c. red	2·50	1·70
1331	-	4f.+2f. blue	23·00	1·70
1332	-	8f.+4f. green	31·00	10·50

DESIGNS—Flowers as Type **265**: 65c. Rushes; 90c. Foxglove; 1f.20, Sea lavender. Sanatoria as Type **266**: HORIZ: 4f. Jauche. VERT: 8f. Tombeek.

267 The Belgian Lion

1951. (a) 17½×20½ mm.

1334	267	2c. brown	10	10
1335	267	3c. violet	10	10
1336	267	5c. lilac	10	10
1336a	267	5c. pink	10	10
1337	267	10c. orange	10	10
1338	267	15c. mauve	10	10
1333	267	20c. blue	30	10
1339	267	20c. red	10	10
1340	267	25c. green	1·70	15
1341	267	25c. blue	10	10
1342	267	30c. green	10	10
1343	267	40c. brown	10	10
1344a	267	50c. blue	15	25
1345	267	60c. mauve	10	10
1346	267	65c. purple	13·50	60
1347	267	75c. lilac	10	10
1348	267	80c. green	85	35
1349	267	90c. blue	1·30	35
1350	267	1f. red	10	10
1351	267	1f.50 grey	10	10
1353	267	2f. green	25	10
1354	267	2f.50 brown	25	10
1355	267	3f. mauve	25	10
1355a	267	4f. purple	35	10
1355b	267	4f.50 blue	25	10
1355c	267	5f. purple	15	10

(b) 20½×24½ mm.

1356		50c. blue	25	15
1357		60c. purple	80	65
1358a		1f. red	10	10

(c) Size 17½×22 mm.

1359		50c. blue	10	10
1360		1f. pink	1·30	75
1361		2f. green	50	25

268 "Science"

1951. UNESCO Fund. Inscr "UNESCO".

1365	268	80c.+20c. rose	1·70	60
1366	-	2f.50+50c. brown	12·00	7·00
1367	-	4f.+2f. blue	15·00	8·75

DESIGNS—HORIZ: 2f.50, "Education". VERT: 4f. "Peace".

269 Fairey Tipsy Belfair Trainer I00-TIC

1951. Air. 50th Anniv of National Aero Club.

1368		6f. blue	38·00	20·00
1369	269	7f. red	38·00	20·00

DESIGN: 6f. Arsenal Air 100 glider.

1951. Air.

1370	-	6f. brown (glider)	7·25	30
1371	269	7f. green	7·25	85

270 Monument

1951. Political Prisoners' National Monument Fund.

1372	270	1f.75+25c. brown	3·50	60
1373	-	4f.+2f. blue	37·00	20·00
1374	-	8f.+4f. green	38·00	23·00

DESIGNS—HORIZ: 4f. Breendonk Fort. VERT: 8f. Side view of monument.

272 Queen Elisabeth

1951. Queen Elisabeth Medical Foundation Fund.

1376	272	90c.+10c. grey	5·25	1·20
1377	272	1f.75+25c. red	11·50	2·50
1378	272	3f.+1f. green	38·00	17·00
1379	272	4f.+2f. blue	41·00	19·00
1380	272	8f.+4f. sepia	49·00	23·00

273 Lorraine Cross and Dragon **274** Beersel Castle

1951. Anti-tuberculosis and other Funds.

1381	273	20c.+5c. red	45	30
1382	273	65c.+10c. blue	70	35
1383	273	90c.+10c. brown	85	40
1384	273	1f.20+30c. violet	1·70	60
1385	274	1f.75+75c. brown	5·25	1·70
1386	-	3f.+1f. green	16·00	9·50
1387	-	4f.+2f. blue	20·00	11·50
1388	-	8f.+4f. black	30·00	16·00

CASTLES—As Type **274**: VERT: 3f. Horst Castle. 8f. Veves Castle. HORIZ: 4f. Lavaux St. Anne Castle.

For stamps as Type **273** but dated "1952" see Nos. 1416/19 and for those dated "1953" see Nos. 1507/10.

276 Consecration of the Basilica

1952. 25th Anniv of Cardinalate of Primate of Belgium and Koekelberg Basilica Fund.

1389		1f.75+25c. brown	1·70	60
1390		4f.+2f. blue	19·00	9·25
1391	276	8f.+4f. purple	28·00	13·50

MS1392 120×72 mm. Nos. 1389/91
(10f.) £475 £200

DESIGNS—24×35 mm: 1f.75, Interior of Koekelberg Basilica; 4f. Exterior of Koekelberg Basilica.

277 King Baudouin **278** King Baudouin

1952

1393	277	1f.50 grey	1·70	25
1394	277	2f. red	60	25
1395	277	4f. blue	8·75	30
1396a	278	50f. purple	4·00	25
1397a	278	100f. red	20·00	70

279 Francis of Taxis

1952. 13th U.P.U. Congress, Brussels. Portraits of Members of the House of Thurn and Taxis.

1398	279	80c. green	35	30
1399	-	1f.75 orange	35	30
1400	-	2f. brown	70	45
1401	-	2f.50 red	1·40	45
1402	-	3f. olive	1·40	35
1403	-	4f. blue	1·50	30
1404	-	5f. brown	3·75	45
1405	-	5f.75 violet	5·25	1·50
1406	-	8f. black	23·00	4·00
1407	-	10f. purple	29·00	9·25

1408	-	20f. grey	£120	55·00
1409	-	40f.+10f. turquoise	£180	£150

DESIGNS—VERT: 1f.75, John Baptist; 2f. Leonard; 2f.50, Lamoral; 3f. Leonard Francis; 4f. Lamoral Claud; 5f. Eugene Alexander; 5f.75, Anselm Francis; 8f. Alexander Ferdinand; 10f. Charles Anselm; 20f. Charles Alexander; 40f. Beaulieu Chateau.

281 A. Vermeylen

1952. Culture Fund. Writers.

1410	281	65c.+30c. lilac	7·25	3·00
1411	-	80c.+40c. green	7·75	3·50
1412	-	90c.+45c. olive	8·25	4·00
1413	-	1f.75+75c. lake	17·00	5·75
1414	-	4f.+2f. blue	46·00	21·00
1415	-	8f.+4f. sepia	49·00	24·00

PORTRAITS: 80c. K. van de Woestijne. 90c. C. de Coster. 1f.75, M. Maeterlinck. 4f. E. Verhaeren. 8f. H. Conscience.

A 4f. blue as No. 1414 and an 8f. lake as No. 1415 each se-tenant with a label showing a laurel wreath and bearing a premium "+ 9 fr." were put on sale by subscription only.

282 Arms, Malmedy

1952. Anti-tuberculosis and other Funds. As T **273** but dated "1952" and designs as T **282**.

1416	273	20c.+5c. brown	35	30
1417	273	80c.+20c. green	80	40
1418	273	1f.20+30c. purple	2·00	1·20
1419	273	1f.50+50c. olive	2·30	1·50
1420	282	3f.+75c. red	3·25	1·50
1421	-	3f.+1f.50 brown	27·00	16·00
1422	-	4f.+2f. blue	25·00	15·00
1423	-	8f.+4f. purple	27·00	17·00

DESIGNS—HORIZ: 3f. Ruins, Burgreuland. VERT: 4f. Dam, Eupen; 8f. Saint and lion, St. Vith.

284 Dewe and Monument at Liege

1953. Walthere Dewe Memorial Fund.

1435	284	2f.+1f. lake	3·25	2·00

285 Princess Josephine Charlotte

1953. Red Cross National Disaster Fund. Cross in red.

1436	285	80c.+20c. green	4·00	1·70
1437	285	1f.20+30c. brown	3·75	1·50
1438	285	2f.+50c. lake	3·25	1·50
1439	285	2f.50+50c. red	20·00	11·50
1440	285	4f.+1f. blue	22·00	10·50
1441	285	5f.+2f. black	22·00	10·50

286 Fishing Boats *Marcel, De Meeuw* and *Jacqueline Denise*

1953. Tourist Propaganda and Cultural Funds.

1442	286	80c.+20c. green	2·30	1·20
1443	-	1f.20+30c. brown	7·00	3·25
1444	-	2f.+50c. sepia	8·25	3·25
1445	-	2f.50+50c. mauve	19·00	9·25
1446	-	4f.+2f. blue	30·00	15·00

1447	-	8f.+4f. green	38·00	18·00

DESIGNS—HORIZ: 1f.20, Bridge Bouillon; 2f. Antwerp. VERT: 2f.50, Namur; 4f. Ghent; 8f. Freyr Rocks and River Meuse.

289 King Baudouin

1953. (a) 21×24½ mm.

1453	289	1f.50 black	30	10
1454	289	2f. red	9·25	30
1455	289	2f. green	30	10
2188	289	2f.50 brown	25	10
1457	289	3f. purple	1·20	10
1458	289	3f.50 green	60	10
1459	289	4f. blue	4·00	25
2188A	289	4f.50 brown	80	50
1462	289	5f. violet	1·50	10
1463	289	6f. mauve	2·50	10
1464	289	6f.50 grey	£120	19·00
2189	289	7f. blue	50	25
1466	289	7f.50 brown	£110	21·00
1467	289	8f. blue	60	15
1468	289	8f.50 purple	26·00	60
1469	289	9f. olive	£120	2·30
1470	289	12f. turquoise	17·00	60
1471	289	30f. orange	14·50	35

(b) 17½×22 mm.

1472		1f.50 black	35	35
1473		2f.50 brown	7·50	6·50
1474		3f. mauve	25	10
1475		3f.50 green	35	10
1476		4f.50 brown	1·70	80

290

1953. European Child Welfare Fund.

1482	290	80c.+20c. green	5·75	3·50
1483	290	2f.50+1f. red	35·00	23·00
1484	290	4f.+1f.50 blue	37·00	26·00

293 Ernest Malvoz

1953. Anti-tuberculosis and other Funds. As T **273** but dated "1953" and portraits as T **293**.

1507	273	20c.+5c. blue	70	35
1508	273	80c.+20c. purple	1·90	80
1509	273	1f.20+30c. brown	3·00	1·20
1510	273	1f.50+50c. slate	3·50	1·50
1511	293	2f.+75c. green	4·25	2·00
1512	-	3f.+1f.50 red	20·00	10·50
1513	-	4f.+2f. blue	23·00	13·00
1514	-	8f.+4f. brown	29·00	16·00

PORTRAITS—VERT: 3f. Carlo Forlanini. 4f. Albert Calmette. HORIZ: 8f. Robert Koch.

1954. Surch **20c** and **I-I-54** at top, **31-XII-54** at bottom and bars in between.

1515	267	20c. on 65c. purple	1·70	15
1516	267	20c. on 90c. blue	1·70	15

See note below No. 480.

296 King Albert Statue

1954. King Albert Memorial Fund.

1520	296	2f.+50c. brown	11·50	4·75
1521	-	4f.+2f. green	38·00	17·00
1522	-	9f.+4f.50 black	31·00	17·00

DESIGNS—HORIZ: 4f. King Albert Memorial. VERT: 9f. Marche-les-Dames Rocks and medallion portrait.

298 Monument **299** Breendonk Camp and Fort

1954. Political Prisoners' National Monument Fund.

1531	298	2f.+1f. red	27·00	24·00
1532	299	4f.+2f. brown	55·00	26·00
1533	-	9f.+4f.50 green	65·00	32·00

DESIGN—VERT: 9f. As Type **298** but viewed from different angle.

300 Entrance to Beguinal House

1954. Beguinage of Bruges Restoration Fund.

1534	300	80c.+20c. green	1·20	60
1535	-	2f.+1f. red	16·00	8·25
1536	-	4f.+2f. violet	21·00	11·50
1537	-	7f.+3f.50 purple	44·00	24·00
1538	-	8f.+4f. brown	44·00	24·00
1539	-	9f.+4f.50 blue	80·00	38·00

DESIGNS—HORIZ: 2f. River scene. VERT: 4f. Convent Buildings; 7f. Cloisters; 8f. Doorway; 9f. Statue of our Lady of the Vineyard (larger, 35×53 mm).

302 Map of Europe and Rotary Symbol

1954. 50th Anniv of Rotary International and Fifth Regional Conference, Ostend.

1540	302	20c. red	25	25
1541	-	80c. green	35	25
1542	-	4f. blue	1·70	35

DESIGNS: 80c. Mermaid, "Mercury" and Rotary symbol; 4f. Rotary symbol and hemispheres.

303 Child **304** "The Blind Man and the Paralytic" (after Anto-Carte)

1954. Anti-T.B. and other Funds.

1543	303	20c.+5c. green	30	30
1544	303	80c.+20c. black	85	35
1545	303	1f.20+30c. brown	2·30	1·40
1546	303	1f.50+50c. violet	4·75	2·50
1547	304	2f.+75c. red	9·25	4·75
1548	304	4f.+1f. blue	35·00	15·00

305 Begonia and the Rabot

1955. Ghent Flower Show.

1549	305	80c. red	60	60
1550	-	2f.50 sepia	10·50	3·00
1551	-	4f. lake	6·00	80

DESIGNS—VERT: 2f.50, Azaleas and Chateau des Comtes; 4f. Orchid and the "Three Towers".

 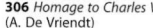

306 Homage to Charles V (A. De Vriendt) **307** Charles V (Titian)

1955. Emperor Charles V Exhibition, Ghent.

1552	306	20c. red	25	25
1553	307	2f. green	95	25
1554	-	4f. blue	5·25	1·50

DESIGN—As Type **306**: 4f. Abdication of Charles V (L. Gallait).

308 Emile Verhaeren (after C. Montald)

1955. Birth Centenary of Verhaeren (poet).

1555	308	20c. black	25	25

309 "Textile Industry"

1955. Second Int Textile Exhibition, Brussels.

1556	309	2f. purple	1·30	30

310 The Foolish Virgin (R. Wouters)

1955. Third Biennial Sculpture Exn, Antwerp.

1557	310	1f.20 green	1·20	40
1558	310	2f. violet	2·00	30

311 "The Departure of the Liege Volunteers in 1830" (Soubre)

1955. Liege Exn. 125th Anniv of 1830 Revolution.

1559	311	20c. green	30	30
1560	311	2f. brown	85	30

312 Ernest Solvay

1955. Cultural Fund. Scientists.

1561	312	20c.+5c. brown	35	35
1562	-	80c.+20c. violet	1·40	50
1563	-	1f.20+30c. blue	7·50	4·00
1564	-	2f.+50c. red	7·00	3·75
1565	-	3f.+1f. green	16·00	9·75
1566	-	4f.+2f. brown	16·00	9·75

PORTRAITS—VERT: 80c. Jean-Jacques Dony. 2f. Leo H. Baekeland. 3f. Jean-Etienne Lenoir. HORIZ: 1f.20, Egide Walschaerts. 4f. Emile Fourcault and Emile Gobbe.

313 The Joys of Spring (E. Canneel) **314** E. Holboll (Danish postal official)

1955. Anti-T.B. and other Funds.

1567	313	20c.+5c. mauve	35	35
1568	313	80c.+20c. green	70	45
1569	313	1f.20+30c. brown	3·25	1·20
1570	313	1f.50+50c. violet	3·75	1·50
1571	314	2f.+50c. red	12·00	5·75
1572	-	4f.+2f. blue	30·00	14·50
1573	-	8f.+4f. sepia	31·00	18·00

PORTRAITS—As Type **314**: 4f. J. D. Rockefeller (philanthropist). 8f. Sir R. W. Philip (physician).

315 Blood Donors Emblem

1956. Blood Donors.

1574	315	2f. red	35	30

316 Mozart when a Child

317 Queen Elisabeth and Mozart Sonata

1956. Birth Bicentenary of Mozart. Inscr as in T **316**.

1575	-	80c.+20c. green	60	30
1576	316	2f.+1f. purple	4·75	3·00
1577	317	4f.+2f. lilac	10·50	5·50

DESIGN—As Type **316**: 80c. Palace of Charles de Lorraine, Brussels.

318

1956. "Scaldis" Exhibitions in Tournai, Ghent and Antwerp.

1578	318	2f. blue	30	30

319 Queen Elisabeth Medallion (Courtens)

1956. 80th Birthday of Queen Elisabeth and Foundation Fund.

1579	319	80c.+20c. green	60	40
1580	319	2f.+1f. lake	4·75	2·40
1581	319	4f.+2f. sepia	6·50	3·75

320

1956. Europa.

1582	320	2f. green	3·50	25
1583	320	4f. violet	13·00	35

321 Electric Train Type 122 and Railway Bridge

1956. Electrification of Brussels–Luxembourg Railway Line.

1584	321	2f. blue	30	25

322 E. Anseele

1956. Birth Centenary of Anseele (statesman).

1588	322	20c. purple	25	25

323 Medieval Ship **324** Weighing a Baby

1956. Anti-tuberculosis and other Funds.

1589	323	20c.+5c. brown	30	30
1590	323	80c.+20c. green	60	40
1591	323	1f.20+30c. purple	1·20	70
1592	323	1f.50+50c. slate	1·50	95
1593	324	2f.+50c. green	3·75	2·30
1594	-	4f.+2f. green	15·00	9·25
1595	-	8f.+4f. red	17·00	11·50

DESIGNS—As Type **324**: HORIZ: 4f. X-ray examination. VERT: 8f. Convalescence and rehabilitation.

325 "Atomium" and Exhibition Emblem

1957. Brussels International Exhibition.

1596	325	2f. red	30	30
1597	325	2f.50 green	35	30
1598	325	4f. violet	70	25
1599	325	5f. purple	1·60	70

327 Emperor Maximilian I, with Messenger

1957. Stamp Day.

1603	327	2f. red	40	30

328 Charles Plisnier and Albrecht Rodenbach (writers)

1957. Cultural Fund. Belgian Celebrities.

1604	328	20c.+5c. violet	30	30
1605	-	80c.+20c. brown	40	30
1606	-	1f.20+30c. sepia	95	70
1607	-	2f.+50c. red	2·40	1·60
1608	-	3f.+1f. green	3·50	2·30
1609	-	4f.+2f. blue	4·00	3·00

DESIGNS—80c. Professors Emiel Vliebergh and Maurice Wilmotte; 1f.20, Paul Pastur and Julius Hoste; 2f. Lodewijk de Raet and Jules Destree (politicians); 3f. Constantin Meunier and Constant Permeke (artists); 4f. Lieven Gevaert and Edouard Empain (industrialists).

329 Sikorsky S-58 Helicopter

1957. Conveyance of 100,000th Passenger by Belgian Helicopter Service.

1610	329	4f. blue, green and grey	95	45

330 Steamer entering Zeebrugge Harbour

1957. 50th Anniv of Completion of Zeebrugge Harbour.
1611	**330**	2f. blue	40	30

331 King Leopold I entering Brussels (after Simonau)

1957. 126th Anniv of Arrival of King Leopold I in Belgium.
1612	**331**	20c. green	30	30
1613	-	2f. mauve	70	30

DESIGN—HORIZ: 2f. King Leopold I at frontier (after Wappers).

332 Scout and Guide Badges

1957. 50th Anniv of Boy Scout Movement and Birth Centenary of Lord Baden-Powell.
1614	**332**	80c. brown	30	30
1615	-	4f. green	1·50	50

DESIGN—VERT: 4f. Lord Baden-Powell.

333 Kneeling Woman (after Lehmbruck)

1957. Fourth Biennial Sculpture Exn, Antwerp.
1616	**333**	2f.50 green	1·20	60

334 "Agriculture and Industry"

1957. Europa.
1617	**334**	2f. purple	1·20	30
1618	**334**	4f. blue	3·75	45

335 Sledge-dog Team

1957. Belgian Antarctic Expedition, 1957–58.
1619	**335**	5f.+2f.50 orange, brown and grey	4·00	3·00

MS1620 115×83 mm. Block of four of No. 1619 in new colours, brown, red and blue £200 £160

336 General Patton's Grave at Hamm

1957. General Patton Memorial Issue.
1621	**336**	1f.+50c. black	2·30	1·20
1622	-	2f.50+50c. green	3·50	1·70
1623	-	3f.+1f. brown	4·75	2·30
1624	-	5f.+2f.50 slate	10·50	6·50
1625	-	6f.+3f. red	14·00	9·25

DESIGNS—HORIZ: 2f.50, Patton Memorial project at Bastogne; 3f. Gen. Patton decorating Brig.-General A. MacAuliffe; 6f. (51×35½ mm) Tanks in action. VERT: 5f. General Patton.

337 Adolphe Max

1957. 18th Death Anniv of Burgomaster Adolphe Max (patriot).
1626	**337**	2f.50+1f. blue	1·50	65

338 Queen Elisabeth with Doctors Depage and Debaisieux at a surgical operation

1957. 50th Anniv of "Edith Cavell-Marie Depage" and "St. Camille" Nursing Schools.
1627	**338**	30c. red	30	30

339 Carnival Kings of Fosses (Namur)　**340** Infanta Isabella with Crossbow (Brussels)

1957. Anti-tuberculosis and other Funds. Provincial Legends.
1628	**339**	30c.+20c. pur & yell	30	30
1629	-	1f.+50c. sepia & blue	35	35
1630	-	1f.50+50c. grey & red	70	40
1631	-	2f.+1f. black & green	1·00	45
1632	**340**	2f.50+1f. grn & mve	2·30	1·70
1633	-	5f.+2f. black & blue	4·75	3·75
1634	-	6f.+2f.50 lake & red	5·75	4·75

DESIGNS: As Type **339**—HORIZ: 1f.50, "St. Remacle and the Wolf" (Liege). VERT: 1f. "Op Signoorken" (Antwerp); 2f. "The Long Man and the Pea Soup" (Limburg). As Type **340**—HORIZ: 6f. "Carnival Kings of Binche" (Hainaut). VERT: 5f. "The Virgin with the Inkwell" (West Flanders).

341 Posthorn and Postillon's Badges

1958. Postal Museum Day.
1635	**341**	2f.50 grey	30	30

342 Benelux Gate

1958. Inauguration of Brussels International Exhibition. Inscr as in T 342.
1636	**342**	30c.+20c. sepia, brown and violet	30	30
1637	-	1f.+50c. purple, slate and green	30	30
1638	-	1f.50+50c. violet, turquoise and green	35	30
1639	-	2f.50+1f. red, blue and vermilion	35	30
1640	-	3f.+1f.50 blue, black and red	85	60
1641	-	5f.+3f. mauve, black and blue	1·90	1·50

DESIGNS—HORIZ: 1f. Civil Engineering Pavilion; 1f.50, Belgian Congo and Ruanda-Urundi Pavilion; 2f.50, "Belgium, 1900"; 3f. Atomium; 5f. (49×33½ mm) Telexpo Pavilion.

343 "Food and Agriculture Organization"

1958. United Nations Commemoration.
1642		50c. grey (postage)	3·00	2·75
1643	**343**	1f. red	35	35
1644	-	1f.50 blue	40	35
1645	-	2f. purple	60	50
1646	-	2f.50 green	40	35
1647	-	3f. turquoise	65	60
1648	-	5f. mauve	40	35
1649	-	8f. brown	75	60
1650	-	11f. lilac	1·60	1·50
1651	-	20f. red	3·25	2·75

1652	-	5f. blue (air)	30	30
1653	-	6f. green	35	30
1654	-	7f.50 violet	45	35
1655	-	8f. sepia	50	40
1656	-	9f. red	60	45
1657	-	10f. brown	70	50

DESIGNS (Emblems and symbols)—HORIZ: 50c. I.L.O. 2f.50, UNESCO 3f. U.N. Pavilion, Brussels Int Exn; 6f. World Meteorological Organization; 8f. (No. 1649), Int Monetary Fund; 8f. (No. 1655), General Agreement on Tariffs and Trade; 10f. Atomic Energy Agency; 11f. W.H.O. 20f. U.P.U. VERT: 1f.50, U.N.O. 2f. World Bank; 5f. (No. 1648), I.T.U. 5f. (No. 1652), I.C.A.O. 7f.50, Protection of Refugees; 9f. UNICEF.

344 Eugene Ysaye

1958. Birth Centenary of Ysaye (violinist).
1658	**344**	30c. blue and red	30	25

345 "Europa"

1958. Europa.
1659	**345**	2f.50 blue and red	3·50	25
1660	**345**	5f. red and blue	7·75	35

346 Marguerite Van Eyck (after Jan Van Eyck)

1958. Cultural Relief Funds. Paintings as T **346**. Frames in brown and yellow.
1661	**346**	30c.+20c. myrtle	60	30
1662	-	1f.+50c. lake	85	60
1663	-	1f.50+50c. blue	1·50	85
1664	-	2f.50+1f. sepia	3·00	2·00
1665	-	3f.+1f.50 red	4·00	2·50
1666	-	5f.+3f. blue	5·00	5·25

PAINTINGS—HORIZ: 1f. Carrying the Cross (Hieronymus Bosch). 3f. The Rower (James Ensor). VERT: 1f.50, St. Donatien (Jan Gossaert). 2f.50, Self-portrait (Lambert Lombard). 5f. Henriette with the Large Hat (Henri Evenepoel).

347 "Hoogstraten"　**348** Pax—"Creche vivante"

1958. Anti-tuberculosis and other Funds. Provincial Legends.
1667	**347**	40c.+10c. blue & grn	30	30
1668	-	1f.+50c. sepia & yell	35	35
1669	-	1f.50+50c. pur & grn	65	35
1670	-	2f.+1f. brown & red	70	45
1671	**348**	2f.50+1f. red and green	2·10	1·20
1672	-	5f.+2f. purple & blue	4·75	3·25
1673	-	6f.+2f. blue & red	5·75	4·75

DESIGNS: As Type **347**—VERT: 1f. "Jean de Nivelles"; 1f.50, "Jeu de Saint Evermare a Russon". HORIZ: 2f. "Les penitents de Furnes". As Type **348**—HORIZ: "Marches de l'Entre Sambre et Meuse". VERT: 6f. "Pax—Vierge".

349 "Human Rights"

1958. Tenth Anniv of Human Rights Declaration.
1674	**349**	2f.50 slate	40	25

350 "Europe of the Heart"

1959. "Heart of Europe". Fund for Displaced Persons.
1675	**350**	1f.+50c. purple	45	35
1676	**350**	2f.50+1f. green	1·00	80
1677	**350**	5f.+2f.50 brown	1·70	1·20

351 J. B. de Taxis taking the oath at the hands of Charles V (after J.-E. Van den Bussche)

1959. Stamp Day.
1680	**351**	2f.50 green	50	30

352 N.A.T.O. Emblem

1959. Tenth Anniv of N.A.T.O.
1681	**352**	2f.50 blue and red	45	30
1682	**352**	5f. blue and green	1·30	60

On the 5f. value the French and Flemish inscriptions are transposed.
For similar design but inscr "1969", see No. 2112.

353 "Blood Transfusion"

354 J. H. Dunant and battle scene at Solferino, 1859

1959. Red Cross Commem. Inscr "1859 1959".
1683	**353**	40c.+10c. red & grey	35	35
1684	**353**	1f.+50c. red & sepia	1·30	50
1685	**353**	1f.50+50c. red and lilac	3·75	2·00
1686	-	2f.50+1f. red & grn	4·25	2·30
1687	-	3f.+1f.50 red and blue	7·75	4·75
1688	**354**	5f.+3f. red and sepia	14·50	7·00

DESIGN—As Type **353**—HORIZ: 2f.50, 3f. Red Cross and broken sword ("Aid for the wounded").

355 Philip the Good　**356** Arms of Philip the Good

1959. Royal Library of Belgium Fund. Multicoloured.
1689		40c.+10c. Type **355**	30	30
1690		1f.+50c. Charles the Bold	45	45
1691		1f.50+50c. Maximillian of Austria	1·60	1·00
1692		2f.50+1f. Philip the Fair	2·75	2·30
1693		3f.+1f.50 Charles V	5·00	3·50
1694		5f.+3f. Type **356**	6·75	5·00

358 Town Hall, Oudenarde

1959. Oudenarde Town Hall Commem.

1699	358	2f.50 purple	40	30

359 Pope Adrian VI

1959. 500th Birth Anniv of Pope Adrian VI.

1700	359	2f.50 red	30	30
1701	359	5f. blue	40	30

360 "Europa"

1959. Europa.

1702	360	2f.50 red	85	30
1703	360	5f. turquoise	1·50	40

361 Boeing 707

1959. Inauguration of Boeing 707 Airliners by SABENA.

1704	361	6f. blue, grey and red	2·10	75

362 Antwerp fish (float) **363** Stavelot "Blancs Moussis" (carnival figures)

1959. Anti-tuberculosis and other Funds. Carnival scenes.

1705	362	40c.+10c. green, red and bistre	30	30
1706	-	1f.+50c. green, violet and olive	40	30
1707	-	2f.+50c. yellow, purple and brown	50	35
1708	363	2f.50+1f. blue, violet and grey	85	35
1709	-	3f.+1f. purple, yellow and grey	2·30	1·20
1710	-	6f.+2f. blue, red and olive	5·00	4·50
1711	-	7f.+3f. blk, yell, & bl	6·50	5·25

DESIGNS—As Type **362**—HORIZ: 1f. Mons dragon (float); 2f. Eupen and Malmedy clowns in chariot. As Type **363**—VERT: 3f. Ypres jester. HORIZ: 6f. Holy Family; 7f. Madonna and child.

364 Countess Alexandrine of Taxis (tapestry)

1960. Stamp Day.

1712	364	3f. blue	70	30

365 Indian Azalea

1960. Ghent Flower Show. Inscr as in T 365.

1713	365	40c. red and purple	30	30
1714	-	3f. yellow, red and green	70	30
1715	-	6f. red, green and blue	1·70	60

FLOWERS: 3f. Begonia. 6f. Anthurium and bromelia.

366 Refugee

1960. World Refugee Year. Inscr as in T 366.

1716		40c.+10c. purple	30	30
1717	366	3f.+1f.50 sepia	65	30
1718	-	6f.+3f. blue	1·40	1·20

MS1719 121×93 mm. Nos. 1716/18 in new colours, violet, brown and red respectively £100 85·00

DESIGNS: 40c. Child refugee; 6f. Woman refugee.

367 "Labour" (after Meunier)

1960. 75th Anniv of Belgian Socialist Party. Inscr as in T 367.

1720	367	40c. purple and red	30	30
1721	-	3f. brown and red	60	30

DESIGN—HORIZ: 3f. "Workers" (after Meunier).

369 Parachutist on ground

1960. Parachuting. Designs bearing emblem of National Parachuting Club.

1726		40c.+10c. black & blue	35	30
1727		1f.+50c. black & blue	1·90	85
1728		2f.+50c. black, blue and green	4·00	2·30
1729		2f.50+1f. black, turquoise and green	7·00	3·75
1730	369	3f.+1f. black, blue and green	7·00	3·75
1731	369	6f.+2f. black, blue and green	7·75	4·75

DESIGNS—HORIZ: 40c., 1f., Parachutists dropping from Douglas DC-4 aircraft. VERT: 2f., 2f.50, Parachutists descending.

370 Ship's Officer and Helmsman

1960. Congo Independence.

1732	370	10c. brown	30	30
1733	-	40c. red	30	30
1734	-	1f. purple	70	25
1735	-	2f. green	70	30
1736	-	2f.50 blue	1·30	30
1737	-	3f. blue	1·30	35
1738	-	6f. violet	3·25	80
1739	-	8f. brown	10·50	6·75

DESIGNS—As Type **370**: 40c. Doctor and nurses with patient; 1f. Tree-planting; 2f. Sculptors; 2f.50, Sport (putting the shot); 3f. Broadcasting from studio. (52×35½ mm): 6f. Children with doll; 8f. Child with globe.

371 Refugee Airlift

1960. Congo Refugees Relief Fund.

1740	371	40c.+10c. turquoise	30	30
1741	-	3f.+1f.50 red	3·00	1·70
1742	-	6f.+3f. violet	6·00	4·25

DESIGNS—As Type **371**: 3f. Mother and child. 35×51½ mm: 6f. Boeing 707 airplane spanning map of aircraft route.

1960. Surch.

1743	267	15c. on 30c. green	10	10
1744	267	15c. on 50c. blue	10	10
1745	267	20c. on 30c. green	10	10

373 Conference Emblem

1960. First Anniv of E.P.T. Conference.

1746	373	3f. lake	1·00	35
1747	373	6f. green	1·60	60

374 Young Stamp Collectors

1960. "Philately for the Young" Propaganda.

1748	374	40c. black and bistre	30	30

375 Pouring Milk for Child

1960. United Nations Children's Fund.

1749	375	40c.+10c. yellow, green and brown	30	30
1750	-	1f.+50c. red, blue and drab	85	60
1751	-	2f.+50c. bistre, green and violet	2·30	1·70
1752	-	2f.50+1f. sepia, blue and red	2·50	1·70
1753	-	3f.+1f. violet, orange and turquoise	3·25	2·00
1754	-	6f.+2f. brown, green and blue	5·25	3·00

DESIGNS: 1f. Nurse embracing children; 2f. Child carrying clothes, and ambulance; 2f.50, Nurse weighing baby; 3f. Children with linked arms; 6f. Refugee worker and child.

376 Frere Orban (founder)

1960. Centenary of Credit Communal (Co-operative Bank).

1755	376	10c. brown and yellow	30	30
1756	376	40c. brown and green	35	30
1757	376	1f.50 brown and violet	1·00	75
1758	376	3f. brown and red	1·00	30

377 Tapestry

1960. Anti-T.B. and other Funds. Arts and Crafts.

1759	377	40c.+10c. ochre, brown and blue	30	30
1760	-	1f.+50c. blue, brown and indigo	95	85
1761	-	2f.+50c. green, black and brown	1·70	1·20
1762	-	2f.50+1f. yellow and brown	3·75	2·50
1763	-	3f.+1f. black, brown and blue	4·25	3·00
1764	-	6f.+2f. lemon and black	6·25	3·75

DESIGNS—VERT: 1f. Crystalware; 2f. Lace. HORIZ: 2f.50, Brassware; 3f. Diamond-cutting; 6f. Ceramics.

378 King Baudouin and Queen Fabiola

1960. Royal Wedding.

1765	378	40c. sepia and green	35	30
1766	378	3f. sepia and purple	1·00	30
1767	378	6f. sepia and blue	2·75	35

1961. Surch in figs and 1961 at top, 1962 at bottom and bars in between.

1768	267	15c. on 30c. green	1·20	25
1769	267	20c. on 30c. green	2·40	1·20

See note below No. 480.

379 Nicolaus Rockox (after Van Dyck)

1961. 400th Birth Anniv of Nicolaus Rockox (Burgomaster of Antwerp).

1770	379	3f. black, bistre & brn	45	30

380 Seal of Jan Bode

1961. Stamp Day.

1771	380	3f. sepia and brown	45	30

381 K. Kats (playwright) and Father N. Pietkin (poet)

1961. Cultural Funds. Portrait in purple.

1772		40c.+10c. lake and pink	60	35
1773		1f.+50c. lake and brown	2·50	1·40
1774		2f.+50c. red and yellow	4·50	3·50
1775		2f.50+1f. myrtle and sage	4·75	3·50
1776		3f.+1f. blue and light blue	5·00	3·50
1777		6f.+2f. blue and lavender	7·00	4·75

PORTRAITS—As Type **381**. 1f. A. Mockel and J. F. Willems (writers). 2f. J. van Rijswijck and X. Neujean (politicians). 2f.50, J. Demarteau (journalist) and A. van de Perre (politician). 3f. J. David (litterateur) and A. du Bois (writer). 6f. H. Vieuxtemps (violinist) and W. de Mol (composer).

382 White Rhinoceros

1961. Philanthropic Funds. Animals of Antwerp Zoo.

1778		40c.+10c. dp brown & brn	35	35
1779		1f.+50c. brown and green	1·30	80
1780		2f.+50c. sepia, red and black	2·00	1·60
1781		2f.50+1f. brown and red	2·20	1·70
1782		3f.+1f. brown and orange	2·50	1·90
1783		6f.+2f. ochre and blue	3·25	2·30

ANIMALS—VERT: 40c. Type **382**; 1f. Wild horse and foal; 2f. Okapi. HORIZ: 2f.50, Giraffe; 3f. Lesser panda; 6f. Elk.

383 Cardinal A.P. de Granville (first Archbishop)

1961. 400th Anniv of Archbishopric of Malines.

1784	383	40c.+10c. brown, red and purple	35	35

| 1785 | - | 3f.+1f.50 mult | 95 | 80 |
| 1786 | - | 6f.+3f. bistre, violet and purple | 1·60 | 1·50 |

DESIGNS: 3f. Cardinal's Arms; 6f. Symbols of Archbishopric and Malines.

385 "Interparliamentary Union"

1961. 50th Interparliamentary Union Conference, Brussels.

| 1791 | **385** | 3f. brown and turquoise | 70 | 30 |
| 1792 | **385** | 6f. purple and red | 1·00 | 60 |

386 Doves

1961. Europa.

| 1793 | **386** | 3f. black and olive | 45 | 30 |
| 1794 | **386** | 6f. black and brown | 95 | 45 |

387 Reactor BR 2, Mol

1961. Euratom Commemoration.

1795	**387**	40c. green	30	30
1796	-	3f. mauve	35	30
1797	-	6f. blue	50	45

DESIGNS—VERT: 3f. Heart of reactor BR 3, Mol. HORIZ: 6f. View of reactor BR 3, Mol.

388 *The Mother and Child* (after Paulus)

1961. Anti-T.B. and other Funds. Belgian paintings of mothers and children. Frames in gold.

1798	**388**	40c.+10c. sepia	30	30
1799	-	1f.+50c. blue	75	70
1800	-	2f.+50c. red	1·30	1·30
1801	-	2f.50+1f. lake	1·40	1·30
1802	-	3f.+1f. violet	1·30	1·20
1803	-	6f.+2f. myrtle	1·90	1·60

PAINTINGS: 1f. *Maternal Love* (Navez). 2f. *Maternity* (Permeke). 2f.50, *The Virgin and the Child* (Van der Weyden). 3f. *The Virgin with the Apple* (Memling), 6f. *The Myosotis Virgin* (Rubens).

389 Horta Museum

1962. Birth Cent of Victor Horta (architect).

| 1804 | **389** | 3f. brown | 40 | 30 |

390 Male Castle

1962. Cultural and Patriotic Funds. Buildings.

1805	**390**	40c.+10c. green	30	30
1806	-	90c.+10c. mauve	35	35
1807	-	1f.+50c. lilac	50	50
1808	-	2f.+50c. violet	1·00	1·00
1809	-	2f.50+1f. brown	1·40	1·40
1810	-	3f.+1f. turquoise	1·50	1·50
1811	-	6f.+2f. red	2·40	2·40

BUILDINGS—HORIZ: 90c. Royal Library, Brussels. 1f. Collegiate Church, Soignies. 6f. Ypres Halls. VERT: 1f. Notre-Dame Basilica, Tongres. 2f.50, Notre-Dame Church, Hanswijk, Malines. 3f. St. Denis-en-Broqueroie Abbey.

391 16th-Century Postilion

1962. Stamp Day.

| 1812 | **391** | 3f. brown and green | 40 | 30 |

See also No. 1997.

392 G. Mercator (after F. Hogenberg)

1962. 450th Birth Anniv of Mercator (geographer).

| 1813 | **392** | 3f. sepia | 40 | 30 |

393 Brother A. M. Gochet (scholar)

1962. Gochet and Triest Commemoration.

| 1814 | **393** | 2f. blue | 30 | 30 |
| 1815 | - | 3f. brown | 35 | 30 |

PORTRAIT: 3f. Canon P.-J. Triest (benefactor of the aged).

394 Guianan Cock of the Rock ("Coq de Roch, Rotshann")

1962. Philanthropic Funds. Birds of Antwerp Zoo. Birds, etc., in natural colours; colours of name panel and inscription given.

1816	**394**	40c.+10c. blue	35	35
1817	-	1f.+50c. blue and red	60	60
1818	-	2f.+50c. mauve & blk	1·00	95
1819	-	2f.50+1f. turq & red	1·30	1·30
1820	-	3f.+1f. brown & grn	1·70	1·60
1821	-	6f.+2f. blue and red	2·00	1·90

BIRDS: 1f. Red lory ("Rode Lori, Lori Rouge"); 2f. Green turaco ("Touracou du Senegal, Senegal Toerakoe"); 2f.50, Keel-billed toucan ("Kortbek Toecan, Toucan a Bec Court"); 3f. Greater bird of paradise ("Grand Paradijsier, Grosse Paradisvogel"); 6f. Congo peafowl ("Kongo Pauw, Paon du Congo").

395 Europa "Tree"

1962. Europa.

| 1822 | **395** | 3f. black, yellow & red | 75 | 30 |
| 1823 | **395** | 6f. black, yellow & olive | 1·30 | 45 |

396 *Captive Hands* (after sculpture by lanchelivici)

1962. Concentration Camp Victims.

| 1824 | **396** | 40c. blue and black | 30 | 30 |

397 Reading Braille

1962. Handicapped Children Relief Funds.

1825	**397**	40c.+10c. brown	35	30
1826	-	1f.+50c. red	60	60
1827	-	2f.+50c. mauve	1·30	1·20
1828	-	2f.50+1f. green	1·30	1·20
1829	-	3f.+1f. blue	1·30	1·20
1830	-	6f.+2f. sepia	1·60	1·50

DESIGNS—VERT: 1f. Girl solving puzzle; 2f.50, Crippled child with ball; 3f. Girl walking with crutches. HORIZ: 2f. Child with earphones; 6f. Crippled boys with football.

398 *Adam* (after Michelangelo)

1962. *The Rights of Man.*

| 1831 | **398** | 3f. sepia and green | 35 | 30 |
| 1832 | **398** | 6f. sepia and brown | 60 | 40 |

399 Queen Louise-Marie

1962. Anti-tuberculosis and other Funds. Belgian Queens in green and gold.

1833		40c.+10c. Type **399**	30	30
1834		40c.+10c. As T **399** but inscr "ML"	30	30
1835		1f.+50c. Marie-Henriette	75	65
1836		2f.+1f. Elisabeth	1·50	1·40
1837		3f.+1f.50 Astrid	2·10	1·90
1838		8f.+2f.50 Fabiola	2·30	2·00

400 Menin Gate, Ypres

1962. Ypres Millenary.

| 1839 | **400** | 1f.+50c. multicoloured | 45 | 45 |
| MS1840 | | 113×137 mm. Block of eight | 7·00 | 7·00 |

401 H. Pirenne

1963. Birth Cent of Henri Pirenne (historian).

| 1841 | **401** | 3f. blue | 40 | 30 |

402 "Peace Bell"

1963. Cultural Funds and Installation of "Peace Bell" in Koekelberg Basilica. Bell in yellow; "PAX" in black.

1842	**402**	3f.+1f.50 green & bl	1·90	1·90
1843	**402**	6f.+3f. chestnut & brn	1·00	1·00
MS1844		82×116 mm. No. 1842 (block of four)	9·25	9·25

403 *The Sower* (after Brueghel)

1963. Freedom from Hunger.

1845	**403**	2f.+1f. brown, black and green	35	35
1846	-	3f.+1f. brown, black and purple	40	40
1847	-	6f.+2f. yellow, black and brown	70	70

PAINTINGS—HORIZ: 3f. *The Harvest* (Brueghel). VERT: 6f. *The Loaf* (Anto Carte).

404 17th-century Duel

1963. 350th Anniv of Royal Guild and Knights of St. Michael.

1848	**404**	1f. red and blue	30	30
1849	-	3f. violet and green	35	30
1850	-	6f. multicoloured	80	45

DESIGNS—HORIZ: 3f. Modern fencing. VERT: 6f. Arms of the Guild.

405 19th-century Mail-coach

1963. Stamp Day.

| 1851 | **405** | 3f. black and ochre | 35 | 30 |

See also No. 1998.

406 Hotel des Postes, Paris, and Belgian 1c. Stamp of 1863

1963. Centenary of Paris Postal Conference.

| 1852 | **406** | 6f. sepia, mauve & grn | 70 | 40 |

407 Child in Wheatfield

1963. "8th May" Peace Movement.

| 1853 | **407** | 3f. multicoloured | 40 | 30 |
| 1854 | **407** | 6f. multicoloured | 1·00 | 40 |

408 "Transport"

1963. European Transport Ministers' Conference, Brussels.

| 1855 | **408** | 6f. black and blue | 70 | 40 |

409 Town Seal

1963. Int Union of Towns Congress, Brussels.

| 1856 | **409** | 6f. multicoloured | 70 | 40 |

410 Racing
Cyclists

1963. Belgian Cycling Team's Participation in Olympic
Games, Tokyo (1964).

1857	**410**	1f.+50c. multicoloured	30	30
1858	-	2f.+1f. multicoloured	35	35
1859	-	3f.+1f.50 mult	40	40
1860	-	6f.+3f. multicoloured	70	70

DESIGNS—HORIZ: 2f. Group of cyclists; 3f. Cyclists rounding bend. VERT: 6f. Cyclists being paced by motorcyclists.

411 Sud Aviation SE 210
Caravelle

1963. 40th Anniv of SABENA Airline.

1861	**411**	3f. black and turquoise	40	30

412 "Co-operation"

1963. Europa.

1862	**412**	3f. black, brown & red	1·30	30
1863	**412**	6f. black, brown & blue	2·40	45

No. 1863 is inscr with "6 F" on the left, "BELGIE" at foot and "BELGIQUE" on right.

413 Princess
Paola with
Princess Astrid

1963. Centenary of Red Cross and Belgian Red Cross Fund. Cross in red.

1864	-	40c.+10c. red & yell	25	25
1865	**413**	1f.+50c. grey & yellow	30	30
1866	-	2f.+50c. mauve & yell	40	40
1867	-	2f.50+1f. blue & yell	50	50
1868	-	3f.+1f. brown & yell	80	80
1869	-	3f.+1f. bronze & yell	2·50	2·50
1870	-	6f.+2f. green & yellow	2·10	2·10

DESIGNS—As T **413**: 40c. Prince Philippe; 2f. Princess Astrid; 2f.50, Princess Paola; 6f. Prince Albert; 46×35 mm: 3f. (2), Prince Albert and family.

414 J. Destree (writer)

1963. Jules Destree and H. Van de Velde Commems.

1871	**414**	1f. purple	25	25
1872	-	1f. green	25	25

DESIGN: No. 1872, H. Van de Velde (architect).

415 Bas-reliefs from
Facade of Postal Cheques
Office (after O. Jespars)

1963. 50th Anniv of Belgian Postal Cheques Office.

1873	**415**	50c. black, blue & red	25	25

416 Balthasar
Gerbier's Daughter

1963. T.B. Relief and Other Funds. Rubens's Drawings. Background buff; inscr in black: designs colour given.

1874	**416**	50c.+10c. blue	30	30
1875	-	1f.+40c. red	35	35
1876	-	2f.+50c. violet	40	40
1877	-	2f.50+1f. green	80	80
1878	-	3f.+1f. brown	70	70
1879	-	6f.+2f. black	1·20	1·20

DRAWINGS—VERT: Rubens's children—1f. Nicolas (aged 2). 2f. Franz (aged 4). 2f.50, Nicolas (aged 6). 3f. Albert (aged 3). HORIZ: (46½×35½ mm): 6f. Infant Jesus, St. John and two angels.

417 Dr. G. Hansen and
Laboratory

1964. Leprosy Relief Campaign.

1880	**417**	1f. black and brown	30	30
1881	-	2f. brown and black	30	30
1882	-	5f. black and brown	60	45
MS1883	135×98 mm. Nos. 1880/2 (+4f.)		3·50	3·50

DESIGNS: 2f. Leprosy hospital; 5f. Father Damien.

418 A. Vesale
(anatomist) with
Model of Human
Arm

1964. Belgian Celebrities.

1884	**418**	50c. black and green	30	30
1885	-	1f. black and green	30	30
1886	-	2f. black and green	30	30

DESIGNS—HORIZ: 1f. J. Boulvin (engineer) and internal combustion engine; 2f. H. Jaspar (statesman) and medallion.

419 Postilion

1964. Stamp Day.

1887	**419**	3f. grey	35	30

420 Admiral Lord Gambier and
U.S. Ambassador J. Q. Adams
after signing treaty (from
painting by Sir A. Forestier)

1964. 150th Anniv of Signing of Treaty of Ghent.

1888	**420**	6f.+3f. blue	70	70

421 Arms of Ostend

1964. Millenary of Ostend.

1889	**421**	3f. multicoloured	35	30

422 Ida of Bure
(Calvin's wife)

1964. "Protestantism in Belgium".

1890	-	1f.+50c. blue	30	30
1891	**422**	3f.+1f.50 red	35	35
1892	-	6f.+3f. brown	65	65

PORTRAITS: 1f. P. Marnix of St. Aldegonde (Burgomaster of Antwerp). 6f. J. Jordaens (painter).

423 Globe,
Hammer and
Flame

1964. Centenary of Socialist International.

1893	**423**	50c. red and blue	30	30
1894	-	1f. red and blue	30	30
1895	-	2f. red and blue	30	30

DESIGNS: 1f. "SI" on Globe; 2f. Flames.

424 Infantryman
of 1918

1964. 50th Anniv of German Invasion of Belgium. Multicoloured.

1896	**424**	1f.+50c. Type **424**	30	30
1897	-	2f.+1f. Colour sergeant of the Guides Regt, 1914	30	30
1898	-	3f.+1f.50 Trumpeter of the Grenadiers & Drummers of the Infantry and Carabiniers, 1914	45	45

425 Soldier at
Bastogne

1964. "Liberation–Resistance". Multicoloured.

1899	-	3f.+1f. Type **425**	35	35
1900	-	6f.+3f. Soldier at estuary of the Scheldt	70	70

426 Europa
"Flower"

1964. Europa.

1901	**426**	3f. grey, red and green	1·70	35
1902	**426**	6f. blue, green and red	4·00	45

427 "Philip the
Good"

428 Descent from the Cross

1964. Cultural Funds. 500th Death Anniv of R. van der Weyden. Two sheets each 153×114 mm showing paintings by Van der Weyden.

MS1903	1f. Type **427**; 2f. Portrait of a Lady; 3f. The Man with the Arrow (+8f.)	5·00	5·00
MS1904	**428** 8f. (+8f.) brown	4·75	4·75

429 Pand Abbey, Ghent

1964. Pand Abbey Restoration Fund.

1905	**429**	2f.+1f. bl, turq & blk	35	30
1906	-	3f.+1f. brown, blue and purple	35	35

DESIGN: 3f. Waterside view of Abbey.

430 King Baudouin, Queen
Juliana and Grand Duchess
Charlotte

1964. 20th Anniv of "BENELUX".

1907	**430**	3f. purple, blue and olive	50	30

431 One of
Charles I's Children
(Van Dyck)

1964. T.B. Relief and Other Funds. Paintings of Royalty.

1908	**431**	50c.+10c. purple	30	30
1909	-	1f.+40c. red	30	30
1910	-	2f.+1f. purple	30	30
1911	-	3f.+1f. grey	35	35
1912	-	4f.+2f. violet	40	40
1913	-	6f.+3f. violet	50	50

DESIGNS—VERT: 1f. "William of Orange and his fiancee, Marie" (Van Dyck); 2f. "Portrait of a Little Boy" (E. Quellin and Jan Fyt); 3f. "Alexander Farnese at the age of 12 Years" (A. Moro); 4f. "William II, Prince of Orange" (Van Dyck). HORIZ—LARGER (46×35 mm): 6f. "Two Children of Cornelis De Vos" (C. de Vos).

432 "Diamonds"

1965. "Diamantexpo" (Diamonds Exn) Antwerp.

1914	**432**	2f. multicoloured	30	25

433 "Textiles"

1965. "Textirama" (Textile Exn), Ghent.

1915	**433**	1f. black, red and blue	30	25

434 Vriesia

1965. Ghent Flower Show. Inscr "FLORALIES GANTOISES", etc. Multicoloured.

1916	**434**	1f. Type **434**	30	30
1917	-	2f. Echinocactus	30	30
1918	-	3f. Stapelia	30	30

435 Paul Hymans

1965. Birth Cent of Paul Hymans (statesman).

1919	**435**	1f. violet	30	30

436 Rubens

1965. Centenary of General Savings and Pensions Funds. Painters.

1920	**436**	1f. sepia and mauve	30	30
1921	-	2f. sepia and turquoise	30	30
1922	-	3f. sepia and purple	30	30
1923	-	6f. sepia and red	60	35
1924	-	8f. sepia and blue	75	60

PAINTERS: 2f. Franz Snyders. 3f. Adam van Noort. 6f. Anthony van Dyck. 8f. Jakob Jordaens.

437 *Sir Rowland Hill with Young Collectors* (detail from mural by J. Van den Bussche)

1965. "Philately for the Young".

1925	**437**	50c. green	30	30

438 19th-century Postmaster

1965. Stamp Day.

1926	**438**	3f. green	30	30

1965. U.N.W.R.A. Commemoration. Sheet 123×89 mm. Nos. 1916/18 in new colours.

MS1927	1f., 2f., 3f. (+14f.)		1·70	1·70

439 Globe and Telephone

1965. Centenary of I.T.U.

1928	**439**	2f. black and purple	30	30

440 Handclasp

1965. 20th Anniv of Liberation of Prison Camps.

1929	**440**	50c.+50c. purple, black and bistre	30	30
1930	-	1f.+50c. multicoloured	30	30
1931	-	3f.+1f.50 black, purple and green	40	35
1932	-	8f.+5f. multicoloured	95	95

DESIGNS—VERT: 1f. Hand reaching for barbed wire. HORIZ: 3f. Tank entering prison camp; 8f. Rose within broken wall.

441 Abbey Staircase

1965. Affligem Abbey.

1933	**441**	1f. blue	30	30

442 St. Jean Berchmans, Birthplace and Residence

1965. St. Jean Berchmans.

1934	**442**	2f. brown and purple	30	30

443 Toc H Lamp and Arms of Poperinge

1965. 50th Anniv of Founding of Toc H Movement at Talbot House, Poperinge.

1935	**443**	3f. multicoloured	35	30

444 Maison Stoclet, Brussels

1965. Josef Hoffman (architect) Commemoration.

1936	**444**	3f.+1f. grey and drab	45	45
1937	-	6f.+3f. brown	70	70
1938	-	8f.+4f. purple & drab	1·00	1·00

DESIGNS—Maison Stoclet: VERT: 6f. Entrance hall. HORIZ: 8f. Rear of building.

445 Tractor ploughing

1965. 75th Anniv of Boerenbond (Belgian Farmers' Association). Multicoloured.

1939		50c. Type **445**	30	30
1940		3f. Horse-drawn plough	35	30

446 Europa "Sprig"

1965. Europa.

1941	**446**	1f. black and pink	40	30
1942	**446**	3f. black and green	75	30

447 Jackson's Chameleon

1965. Philanthropic Funds. Reptiles of Antwerp Zoo. Multicoloured.

1943		1f.+50c. Type **447**	30	30
1944		2f.+1f. Iguana	30	30
1945		3f.+1f.50 Nile lizard	40	35
1946		6f.+3f. Komodo lizard	65	60

MS1947	118×98 mm. 8f.+4f. Soft-shelled turtle (larger)		1·20	1·20

448 J. Lebeau (after A. Schollaert)

1965. Death Cent of Joseph Lebeau (statesman).

1948	**448**	1f. multicoloured	30	30

449 Leopold I (after 30c. and 1f. Stamps of 1865)

1965. Death Centenary of King Leopold I.

1949	**449**	3f. sepia	35	30
1950	-	6f. violet	70	45

DESIGN: 6f. As 3f. but with different portrait frame.

450 Huy

1965. Tourist Publicity. Multicoloured.

1951	**450**	50c. Type **450**	10	10
1952	-	50c. Hoeilaart (vert)	10	10

See also Nos. 1995/6, 2025/6, 2083/4, 2102/3, 2123/4, 2159/60, 2240/1 and 2250/1.

451 Guildhouse

1965. T.B. Relief and Other Funds. Public Buildings, Brussels.

1953	**451**	50c.+10c. blue	30	30
1954	-	1f.+40c. turquoise	30	30
1955	-	2f.+1f. purple	30	30
1956	-	3f.+1f.50 violet	35	35
1957	-	10f.+4f.50 sepia and grey	95	95

BUILDINGS—HORIZ: 1f. Brewers' House; 2f. Builders' House; 3f. House of the Dukes of Brabant. VERT: (24½×44½ mm): 10f. Tower of Town Hall.

452 Queen Elisabeth (from medallion by A. Courtens)

1965. Queen Elisabeth Commem.

1958	**452**	3f. black	35	30

453 "Peace on Earth"

1966. 75th Anniv of *Rerum Novarum* (papal encyclical). Multicoloured.

1959		50c. Type **453**	30	30
1960		1f. "Building for Tomorrow" (family and new building)	30	30
1961		3f. Arms of Pope Paul VI (vert 24½×45 mm)	35	30

1966. Queen Elisabeth. Sheets 82×116 mm incorporating old designs, each with se-tenant label showing Crown over "E". (a) In brown, blue, gold and grey.

MS1962	3f. T **125** and 3f. T **317** (sold at 20f.)		1·60	1·60

(b) In brown, myrtle and green.

MS1963	3f. T **160** and 3f. T **172** (sold at 20f.)		1·60	1·60

454 Rural Postman

1966. Stamp Day.

1964	**454**	3f. black, lilac & buff	35	30

455 High Diving

1966. Swimming.

1965	**455**	60c.+40c. brown, green and blue	30	30
1966	-	10f.+4f. brown, purple and green	1·00	1·00

DESIGN: 10f. Diving from block.

456 Iguanodon Fossil (Royal Institute of Natural Sciences)

1966. National Scientific Institutions.

1967	**456**	1f. black and green	30	30
1968	-	2f. black, orge & cream	30	30
1969	-	2f. multicoloured	30	30
1970	-	3f. multicoloured	30	30
1971	-	3f. gold, black and red	30	30
1972	-	6f. multicoloured	40	30
1973	-	8f. multicoloured	65	60

DESIGNS—HORIZ: No. 1968, Kasai head (Royal Central African Museum); No. 1969, Snow crystals (Royal Meteorological Institute). VERT: No. 1970, *Scholar* (Royal Library); No. 1971, Seal (General Archives); No. 1972, Arend-Roland comet and telescope (Royal Observatory); No. 1973, Satellite and rocket (Space Aeronomy Inst.).

457 Eurochemic Symbol

1966. European Chemical Plant, Mol.

1974	**457**	6f. black, red and drab	45	35

458 A. Kekule

1966. Centenary of Professor August Kekule's Benzene Formula.

1975	**458**	3f. brown, black & blue	35	30

1966. 19th World I.P.T.T. Congress, Brussels. Optd XIXe CONGRES IPTT and emblem.

1976	**454**	3f. black, lilac and buff	35	30

460 Rik Wouters (self-portrait)

1966. 50th Death Anniv of Rik Wouters (painter).

1977	**460**	60c. multicoloured	10	10

461 Minorites Convent, Liege

1966. Cultural Series.

1978	**461**	60c.+40c. purple, blue and brown	30	30
1979	-	1f.+50c. blue, purple and turquoise	30	30
1980	-	2f.+1f. red, purple and brown	30	30
1981	-	10f.+4f.50 purple, turquoise and green	85	85

DESIGNS: 1f. Val-Dieu Abbey, Aubel; 2f. Huy and town seal; 10f. Statue of Ambiorix and castle, Tongres.

463 Europa "Ship"

1966. Europa.

1989	**463**	3f. green	45	25
1990	**463**	6f. purple	1·00	40

464 Surveying

1966. Antarctic Expeditions.

1991	**464**	1f.+50c. green	30	30
1992	-	3f.+1f.50 violet	30	30
1993	-	6f.+3f. red	60	60
MS1994	130×95 mm. 10f.+5f. multi-coloured		1·20	1·20

DESIGNS: 3f. Commander A. de Gerlache and *Belgica* (polar barque); 6f. *Magga Dan* (Antarctic supply ship) and meteorological operations. 52×35½ mm.—10f. *Magga Dan* and emperor penguins.

1966. Tourist Publicity. As T **450**. Multicoloured.

1995	2f. Bouillon	10	10
1996	2f. Lier (vert)	10	10

1966. 75th Anniv of Royal Federation of Belgian Philatelic Circles. Stamps similar to Nos. 1812 and 1851 but incorporating "1890 1996" and F.I.P. emblem.

1997	**391**	60c. purple and green	30	30
1998	**405**	3f. purple and ochre	30	30

466 Children with Hoops

1966. "Solidarity" (Child Welfare).

1999	-	1f.+1f. black & pink	30	30
2000	-	2f.+1f. black & green	30	30
2001	-	3f.+1f.50 black & lav	30	30
2002	**466**	6f.+3f. brown & flesh	60	60
2003	-	8f.+3f.50 brown & grn	70	70

DESIGNS—VERT: 1f. Boy with ball and dog; 2f. Girl with skipping-rope; 3f. Boy and girl blowing bubbles. HORIZ: 8f. Children and cat playing "Follow My Leader".

467 Lions Emblem

1967. Lions International.

2004	**467**	3f. sepia, blue and olive	30	30
2005	**467**	6f. sepia, violet and green	45	40

468 Part of Cleuter Pistol

1967. Arms Museum, Liege.

2006	**468**	2f. black, yellow & red	30	30

469 I.T.Y. Emblem

1967. International Tourist Year.

2007	**469**	6f. blue, red and black	60	35

470 Young Refugee

1967. European Refugee Campaign Fund. Sheet 110×77 mm comprising T **470** and similar vert designs.

MS2008	1f. black and yellow (Type **470**); 2f. black and blue; 3f. black and orange (sold at 20f.)		1·20	1·20

471 Woodland and Trientalis (flowers), Hautes Fagnes

1967. Nature Conservation. Multicoloured.

2009	1f. Type **471**	30	30
2010	1f. Dunes and eryngium (flowers), Westhoek	30	30

472 Paul-Emile Janson (statesman)

1967. Janson Commemoration.

2011	**472**	10f. blue	85	60

473 19th-century Postman

1967. Stamp Day.

2012	**473**	3f. purple and red	30	30

474 Cogwheels

1967. Europa.

2013	**474**	3f. black, red and blue	60	30
2014	**474**	6f. black, yellow & green	1·20	45

475 Flax Plant and Shuttle

1967. Belgian Linen Industry.

2015	**475**	6f. multicoloured	45	35

476 Kursaal in 19th Century

1967. 700th Anniv of Ostend's Rank as Town.

2016	**476**	2f. sepia, buff and blue	30	30

478 With F.I.T.C.E. Emblem

1967. European Telecommunications Day. "Stamp Day" design of 1967 incorporating F.I.T.C.E. emblem as T **478** in green.

2021	**478**	10f. sepia and blue	30	30

"F.I.T.C.E." "Federation des Ingenieurs des Tele-communications de la Communaute Europeenne."

479 Robert Schuman (statesman)

1967. Charity.

2022	**479**	2f.+1f. green	30	30
2023	-	5f.+2f. brown, yellow and black	50	50
2024	-	10f.+5f. multicoloured	1·00	1·00

DESIGNS—HORIZ: 5f. Kongolo Memorial, Gentinnes (Congo Martyrs). VERT: 10f. "Colonial Brotherhood" emblem (Colonial Troops Memorial).

1967. Tourist Publicity. As T **450**. Multicoloured.

2025	1f. Ypres	10	10
2026	1f. Spontin	10	10

480 *Caesar Crossing the Rubicon* (Tournai Tapestry)

1967. Charles Plisnier and Lodewijk de Raet Foundations.

2028	**480**	1f. multicoloured	30	30
2029	-	1f. multicoloured	30	30

DESIGN No. 2029, "Maximilian hunting boar" (Brussels tapestry).

481 "Jester in Pulpit" (from Erasmus's *Praise of Folly*)

1967. Cultural Series. "Erasmus and His Time".

2030	1f.+50c. multicoloured	30	30
2031	2f.+1f. multicoloured	30	30
2032	3f.+1f.50 multicoloured	35	35
2033	5f.+2f. black, red & carmine	60	60
2034	6f.+3f. multicoloured	70	70

DESIGNS—VERT: 1f. Type **481**. 2f. "Jester declaiming" (from Erasmus' *Praise of Folly*); 3f. Erasmus; 6f. Pierre Gilles ("Aegidius" from painting by Metzijs). HORIZ: 5f. *Sir Thomas More's Family* (Holbein).

482 Princess Margaret of York (from miniature)

1967. "British Week".

2035	**482**	6f. multicoloured	55	40

483 Arms of Ghent University

1967. Universities of Ghent and Liege. Multicoloured.

2036	3f. Type **483**	30	30
2037	3f. Liege	30	30

484 Emblem of "Pro-Post" Association

1967. "Postphila" Stamp Exhibition, Brussels. Sheet 110×77 mm.

MS2038	**484**	10f.+5f. black, green, red and brown	1·20	1·20

485 Our Lady of Virga Jesse, Hasselt

1967. Christmas.

2039	**485**	1f. blue	30	30

486 *Children's Games* (section of Brueghel's painting)

1967. "Solidarity".

2040	**486**	1f.+50c. multicoloured	30	30
2041	-	2f.+50c. multicoloured	30	30
2042	-	3f.+1f. multicoloured	40	30
2043	-	6f.+3f. multicoloured	65	60
2044	-	10f.+4f. multicoloured	1·00	90
2045	-	13f.+6f. multicoloured	1·25	1·25

Nos. 2040/5 together form the complete painting.

487 Worker in Protective Hand

1968. Industrial Safety Campaign.

2046	**487**	3f. multicoloured	30	30

489 Army Postman (1916)

1968. Stamp Day.

2068	**489**	3f. purple, brown & blue	30	30

490 Belgian 1c. "Small Lion" Stamp of 1866

1968. Cent of State Printing Works, Malines.

2069	**490**	1f. olive	30	30

491 Grammont and Seal of Baudouin VI

1968. "Historical Series". Multicoloured.

2070	2f. Type **491**	35	30
2071	3f. Theux-Franchimont Castle and battle emblems	35	30
2072	6f. Archaeological discoveries, Spiennes	55	35
2073	10f. Roman oil lamp and town crest, Wervik	85	60

492 Europa "Key"

1968. Europa.

2074	**492**	3f. gold, black & green	90	30
2075	**492**	6f. silver, black and red	1·80	50

493 Queen Elisabeth and Dr. Depage

1968. Belgian Red Cross Fund. Cross in red.

2076	**493**	6f.+3f. sepia, black and green	85	70
2077	-	10f.+5f. sepia, black and green	1·20	1·10

DESIGN: 10f. Queen Fabiola and baby.

494 Gymnastics

1968. Olympic Games, Mexico. Multicoloured.

2078	1f.+50c. Type **494**	30	30
2079	2f.+1f. Weightlifting	30	30
2080	3f.+1f.50 Hurdling	35	30
2081	6f.+2f. Cycling	70	60
2082	13f.+5f. Sailing (vert 24½x45 mm)	1·30	1·20

Each design includes the Olympic "rings" and a Mexican cultural motif.

1968. Tourist Publicity. As Type **450**.

2083	2f. multicoloured	10	10
2084	2f. black, blue and green	10	10

DESIGNS: No. 2083, Farm-house and windmill, Bokrijk; No. 2084, Bath-house and fountain, Spa.

495 "Explosion"

1968. Belgian Disasters. Victims Fund. Multicoloured.

2085	10f.+5f. Type **495**	90	70
2086	12f.+5f. "Fire"	1·20	1·10
2087	13f.+5f. "Typhoon"	1·50	1·20

496 St. Laurent Abbey, Liege

1968. "National Interest".

2088	**496**	2f. black, bistre & blue	30	30
2089	-	3f. brown, grey & lt brn	35	30
2090	-	6f. black, blue & dp bl	70	35
2091	-	10f.	95	40

DESIGNS: 3f. Church, Lissewege; 6f. *Mineral Seraing* and *Gand* (ore carriers), canal-lock, Zandvliet; 10f. Canal-lift, Ronquieres.

497 Undulate Triggerfish

1968. "Solidarity" and 125th Anniv of Antwerp Zoo. Designs showing fish. Multicoloured.

2092	1f.+50c. Type **497**	25	25
2093	3f.+1f.50 Ear-spotted angelfish	35	30
2094	6f.+3f. Lionfish	70	55
2095	10f.+5f. Diagonal butterflyfish	1·10	85

498 King Albert in Bruges (October, 1918)

1968. Patriotic Funds.

2096	**498**	1f.+50c. multicoloured	30	30
2097	-	3f.+1f.50 mult	35	30
2098	-	6f.+3f. multicoloured	60	55
2099	-	10f.+5f. multicoloured	90	85

DESIGNS—HORIZ: 3f. King Albert entering Brussels (November, 1918); 6f. King Albert in Liege (November, 1918). LARGER (46x35 mm): 10f. Tomb of the Unknown Soldier, Brussels.

499 Lighted Candle

1968. Christmas.

2100	**499**	1f. multicoloured	30	30

500 *Mineral Seraing* (ore carrier) in Ghent Canal

1968. Ghent Maritime Canal.

2101	**500**	6f. black brown, & blue	55	30

1969. Tourist Publicity. As Type **450**.

2102	1f. black, blue & pur (vert)	10	10
2103	1f. black, olive and blue	10	10

DESIGNS. No. 2102, Town Hall, Louvain; No. 2103, Valley of the Ourthe.

501 Albert Magnis (detail of wood carving by Quellin, Confessional, St. Paul's Church, Antwerp)

1969. St. Paul's Church, Antwerp, and Aulne Abbey Commemoration.

2104	**501**	2f. sepia	30	30
2105	-	3f. black and mauve	30	30

DESIGN: 3f. Aulne Abbey.

502 The Travellers (sculpture, Archaeological Museum, Arlon)

1969. 2,000th Anniv of Arlon.

2106	**502**	2f. purple	30	30

503 Broodjes Chapel, Antwerp

1969. "150 Years of Public Education in Antwerp".

2107	**503**	3f. black and grey	30	30

504 Mail Train

1969. Stamp Day.

2108	**504**	3f. multicoloured	30	30

505 Colonnade

1969. Europa.

2109	**505**	3f. multicoloured	50	30
2110	**505**	6f. multicoloured	85	35

506 The painter and the Amateur (detail, Brueghel)

1969. "Postphila 1969" Stamp Exhibition, Brussels. Sheet 91x124 mm.

MS2111	**506**	10f.+5f. brown	1·40	1·20

507 NATO Emblem

1969. 20th Anniv of N.A.T.O.

2112	**507**	6f. blue and brown	55	40

508 The Builders (F. Leger)

1969. 50th Anniv of I.L.O.

2113	**508**	3f. multicoloured	35	30

509 Houses (I. Dimitrova)

1969. UNICEF "Philanthropy" Funds. Multicoloured.

2114	1f.+50c. Type **509**	30	30
2115	3f.+1f.50 "My Art" (C. Patric)	35	30
2116	6f.+3f. "In the Sun" (H. Rejchova)	70	60
2117	10f.+5f. "Out for a Walk" (P. Sporn) (horiz)	1·10	85

510 Racing Cyclist

1969. World Championship Cycle Races, Zolder.

2118	**510**	6f. multicoloured	60	30

511 Mgr. V. Scheppers

1969. Monseigneur Victor Scheppers (founder of "Brothers of Mechlin") Commemoration.

2119	**511**	6f.+3f. purple	85	60

512 National Colours

1969. 25th Anniv of BENELUX Customs Union.

2120	**512**	3f. multicoloured	35	30

513 Pascali Rose and Annevoie Gardens

1969. Flowers and Gardens. Multicoloured.

2121	2f. Type **513**	25	30
2122	2f. Begonia and Lochristi Gardens	30	30

1969. Tourist Publicity. As Type **450**.

2123	2f. brown, red and blue	25	10
2124	2f. black, green and blue	25	10

DESIGNS: No. 2123, Veurne Furnes; No. 2124, Vielsalm.

514 "Feats of Arms" from *History of Alexander the Great* (Tournai, 15th century)

1969. "Cultural Works" Tapestries. Multicoloured.

2125	1f.+50c. Type **514**	30	30
2126	3f.+1f.50 "The Violinist" from "Festival" (David Teniers II, Oudenarde, c.1700)	50	40
2127	10f.+4f. "The Paralytic", from "The Acts of the Apostles" (Brussels, c.1517)	1·20	1·10

515 Astronauts and Location of Moon Landing

1969. First Man on the Moon.

2128	**515**	6f. sepia	50	35
MS2129	95x130 mm. 20f.+10f. blue		3·50	3·00

DESIGN: MS2129 is as T **515**, but in vert format.

516 Wounded Soldier

1969. 50th Anniv of National War Invalids Works (O.N.I.G.).

2130	**516**	1f. green	30	30

517 "The Postman" (Daniella Sainteney)

1969. "Philately for the Young".
2131 517 1f. multicoloured 30 30

518 John F. Kennedy Motorway Tunnel, Antwerp

1969. Completion of Belgian Road-works. Multicoloured.
2132 3f. Type **518** 35 30
2133 6f. Loncin flyover, Wallonie motorway 55 50

519 Count H. Carton de Wiart (from painting by G. Geleyn)

1969. Birth Centenary of Count Henry Carton de Wiart (statesman).
2134 519 6f. sepia 65 50

520 *Barbu d'Anvers* (Cockerel)

1969. "The Poultry-yard" (poultry-breeding).
2135 520 10f.+5f. multicoloured 1·30 1·10

521 *Le Denombrement de Bethleem* (detail, Brueghel)

1969. Christmas.
2136 521 1f.50 multicoloured 30 30

522 Emblem, "Coin" and Machinery

1969. 50th Anniv of National Credit Society (S.N.C.I.).
2137 522 3f.50 brown and blue 35 30

523 Window, St. Waudru Church, Mons

1969. "Solidarity". Musicians in Stained-glass Windows. Multicoloured.
2138 1f.50+50c. Type **523** 30 30
2139 3f.50+1f.50 s-Hereneldern Church 35 30
2140 7f.+3f. St. Jacques Church, Liege 80 70

2141 9f.+4f. Royal Museum of Art and History, Brussels 1·20 1·10
No. 2141 is larger, 36×52 mm.

524 Camellias

1970. Ghent Flower Show. Multicoloured.
2142 1f.50 Type **524** 30 30
2143 2f.50 Water-lily 30 30
2144 3f.50 Azaleas 35 30
MS2145 122×92 mm. Nos. 2142/4 in slightly different shades 2·40 2·20

525 Beech Tree in National Botanical Gardens

1970. Nature Conservation Year. Multicoloured.
2146 3f.50 Type **525** 30 30
2147 7f. Birch 60 35

526 Young "Postman"

1970. "Philately for the Young".
2148 526 1f.50 multicoloured 30 30

527 New U.P.U. Headquarters Building

1970. New U.P.U. Headquarters Building.
2149 527 3f.50 green 35 30

528 "Flaming Sun"

1970. Europa.
2150 528 3f.50 cream, blk & lake 80 30
2151 528 7f. flesh, black and blue 1·20 4·75

529 Open-air Museum, Bokrijk

1970. Cultural Works. Multicoloured.
2152 1f.50+50c. Type **529** 30 30
2153 3f.50+1f.50 Relay Post-house, Courcelles 30 30
2154 7f.+3f. *The Reaper of Trevires* (bas-relief, Virton) 65 60
2155 9f.+4f. Open-air Museum, Mid-delheim, (Antwerp) 90 85

530 Clock-tower, Virton

1970. Historic Towns of Virton and Zelzate.
2156 530 2f.50 violet and ochre 30 30
2157 2f.50 black and blue 30 30
DESIGN—HORIZ: No. 2157, *Skaustand* (freighter), canal bridge, Zelzate.

531 Co-operative Alliance Emblem

1970. 75th Anniv of Int Co-operative Alliance.
2158 531 7f. black and orange 60 30

1970. Tourist Publicity, As Type **450**.
2159 1f.50 green, blue and black 20 20
2160 1f.50 buff, blue & deep blue 20 20
DESIGNS—HORIZ: No. 2159, Kasterlee. VERT: No. 2160, Nivelles.

532 Allegory of Resistance Movements

1970. 25th Anniv of Prisoner of War and Concentration Camps Liberation.
2161 532 3f.50+1f.50 black, red and green 40 30
2162 — 7f.+3f. black, red and mauve 80 60
DESIGN: 7f. Similar to Type **532**, but inscr "LIBERATION DES CAMPS", etc.

533 King Baudouin

1970. King Baudouin's 40th Birthday.
2163 533 3f.50 brown 30 10
See also Nos. 2207/23c and 2335/9b.

534 Fair Emblem

1970. 25th International Ghent Fair.
2164 534 1f.50 multicoloured 30 30

535 U.N. Headquarters, New York

1970. 25th Anniv of United Nations.
2165 535 7f. blue and black 60 35

536 Queen Fabiola

1970. Queen Fabiola Foundation.
2166 536 3f.50 black and blue 30 30

537 Angler's Rod and Reel

1970. Sports. Multicoloured.
2167 3f.50+1f.50 Type **537** 35 35
2168 9f.+4f. Hockey stick and ball (vert) 85 70

538 Belgian 8c. Stamp of 1870

1970. "Belgica 72" Stamp Exhibition, Brussels (1st issue).
MS2169 1f.50+50c. violet and black; 3f.50+1f.50 lilac and black; 9f.+4f. brown and black 4·25 3·50
DESIGNS: 3f.50, Belgian 1f. stamp of 1870; 9f. Belgian 5f. stamp of 1870.

539 "The Mason" (sculpture by G. Minne)

1970. 50th Anniv of National Housing Society.
2170 539 3f.50 brown & yell 30 30

540 Man, Woman and Hillside Town

1970. 25th Anniv of Belgian Social Security.
2171 540 2f.50 multicoloured 30 30

541 *Madonna and Child* (Jan Gossaert)

1970. Christmas.
2172 541 1f.50 brown 30 30

542 C. Huysmans (statesman)

1970. Cultural Works. Famous Belgians.
2173 542 1f.50+50c. brown and red 30 30
2174 — 3f.50+1f.50 brown and purple 30 30
2175 — 7f.+3f. brown & green 65 60
2176 — 9f.+4f. brown & blue 1·90 1·80
PORTRAITS: 3f.50, Cardinal J. Cardijn. 7f. Maria Baers (Catholic social worker). 9f. P. Pastur (social reformer).

543 Arms of Eupen, Malmedy and St. Vith

1970. 50th Anniv of Annexation of Eupen, Malmedy and St. Vith.
2177 543 7f. brown and sepia 50 35

544 *The Uneasy Town* (detail, Paul Delvaux)

1970. "Solidarity". Paintings. Multicoloured.
| 2178 | | 3f.50+1f.50 Type **544** | 35 | 35 |
| 2179 | | 7f.+3f. *The Memory* (Rene Magritte) | 35 | 60 |

545 Telephone

1971. Inaug of Automatic Telephone Service.
| 2183 | **545** | 1f.50 multicoloured | 30 | 30 |

546 "Auto" Car

1971. 50th Brussels Motor Show.
| 2184 | **546** | 2f.50 black and red | 30 | 30 |

547 Touring Club Badge

1971. 75th Anniv of Royal Touring Club of Belgium.
| 2185 | **547** | 3f.50 gold, red & blue | 30 | 30 |

548 Tournai Cathedral

1971. 800th Anniv of Tournai Cathedral.
| 2186 | **548** | 7f. blue | 50 | 40 |

549 *The Letter-box* (T. Lobrichon)

1971. "Philately for the Young".
| 2187 | **549** | 1f.50 brown | 30 | 30 |

550 Notre-Dame Abbey, Marche-les-Dames

1971. Cultural Works.
| 2190 | **550** | 3f.50+1f.50 black, green and brown | 35 | 30 |
| 2191 | - | 7f.+3f. black, red and yellow | 70 | 65 |

DESIGN: 7f. Convent, Turnhout.

552 King Albert I, Jules Destree and Academy

1971. 50th Anniv of Royal Academy of French Language and Literature.
| 2201 | **552** | 7f. black and grey | 30 | 10 |

553 Postman of 1855 (from lithograph, J. Thiriar)

1971. Stamp Day.
| 2202 | **553** | 3f.50 multicoloured | 30 | 30 |

554 Europa Chain

1971. Europa.
| 2203 | **554** | 3f.50 brown and black | 90 | 30 |
| 2204 | **554** | 7f. green and black | 1·50 | 50 |

555 Satellite Earth Station

1971. World Telecommunications Day.
| 2205 | **555** | 7f. multicoloured | 60 | 50 |

556 Red Cross

1971. Belgian Red Cross.
| 2206 | **556** | 10f.+5f. red & black | 1·00 | 70 |

1971. As T **533**, but without dates.
2207		1f.75 green	70	60
2208		2f.25 green	30	10
2208a		2f.50 green	25	10
2209		3f. green	30	10
2209a		3f.25 plum	30	25
2210		3f.50 brown	50	10
2211		4f. blue	40	10
2212		4f.50 purple	95	10
2212a		4f.50 blue	40	10
2213		5f. violet	50	10
2214		6f. red	50	10
2214b		6f.50 violet	50	10
2215		7f. red	65	10
2215ba		7f.50 mauve	40	10
2216a		8f. black	70	10
2217		9f. sepia	95	10
2217a		9f. brown	90	10
2218a		10f. mauve	70	10
2218b		11f. sepia	1·00	10
2219		12f. blue	3·00	30
2219b		13f. blue	1·20	10
2219c		14f. green	1·40	10
2220		15f. violet	1·20	10
2220b		16f. green	2·10	10
2220c		17f. purple	1·40	10
2221		18f. blue	1·40	10
2221a		18f. turquoise	2·10	25
2222		20f. blue	1·60	10
2222b		22f. black	2·10	1·80
2222c		22f. turquoise	1·90	50
2222d		25f. purple	2·10	10
2223a		30f. orange	2·40	10
2223b		35f. turquoise	4·00	30
2223c		40f. blue	4·75	30
2223d		45f. brown	5·75	55

See also Nos. 2335/9.

557 Scientist, Adelie Penguins and "Erika Dan" (polar vessel)

1971. TEnth Anniv of Antarctic Treaty.
| 2230 | **557** | 10f. multicoloured | 80 | 60 |

558 *The Discus thrower* and Munich Cathedral

1971. Olympic Games, Munich (1972) Publicity.
| 2231 | **558** | 7f.+3f. black & blue | 80 | 70 |

559 G. Hubin (statesman)

1971. Georges Hubin Commemoration.
| 2232 | **559** | 1f.50 violet and black | 30 | 30 |

560 Notre-Dame Abbey, Orval

1971. 900th Anniv of Notre-Dame Abbey, Orval.
| 2233 | **560** | 2f.50 brown | 30 | 30 |

561 Processional Giants, Ath

1971. Historic Towns.
| 2234 | **561** | 2f.50 multicoloured | 30 | 30 |
| 2235 | - | 2f.50 brown | 30 | 30 |

DESIGN—HORIZ (46×35 mm): No. 2235, View of Ghent.

562 Test-tubes and Diagram

1971. 50th Anniv of Discovery of Insulin.
| 2236 | **562** | 10f. multicoloured | 85 | 60 |

563 Flemish Festival Emblem

1971. Cultural Works. Festivals. Multicoloured.
| 2237 | | 3f.50+1f.50 Type **563** | 35 | 35 |
| 2238 | | 7f.+3f. Walloon Festival emblem | 85 | 70 |

564 Belgian Family and "50"

1971. 50th Anniv of "League of Large Families".
| 2239 | **564** | 1f.50 multicoloured | 30 | 30 |

1971. Tourist Publicity. Designs similar to T **450**.
| 2240 | | 2f.50 black, brown and blue | 25 | 10 |
| 2241 | | 2f.50 black, brown and blue | 25 | 10 |

DESIGNS: No. 2240, St. Martin's Church, Alost; No. 2241, Town Hall and belfry, Mons.

565 Dr. Jules Bordet (medical scientist)

1971. Belgian Celebrities.
| 2242 | **565** | 3f.50 green | 35 | 30 |
| 2243 | - | 3f.50 brown | 35 | 30 |

DESIGN: No. 2242, Type **565** (10th death anniv); No. 2243, "Stijn Streuvels" (Frank Lateur, writer, birth cent.).

566 Achaemenid Tomb, Buzpar

1971. 2500th Anniv of Persian Empire.
| 2244 | **566** | 7f. multicoloured | 60 | 50 |

567 Elewijt Chateau

1971. "Belgica 72" Stamp Exhibition, Brussels (2nd issue).
2245	-	3f.50+1f.50 green	35	35
2246	**567**	7f.+3f. brown	85	85
2247	-	10f.+5f. blue	1·20	1·20

DESIGNS—HORIZ. (52×35½ mm): 3f. Attre Chateau; 10f. Royal Palace, Brussels.

568 F.I.B./V.B.N. Emblem

1971. 25th Anniv of Federation of Belgian Industries.
| 2248 | **568** | 3f.50 gold, black & blue | 35 | 30 |

569 *The Flight into Egypt* (15th-century Dutch School)

1971. Christmas.
| 2249 | **569** | 1f.50 multicoloured | 30 | 30 |

1971. Tourist Publicity. Designs similar to T **450**.
| 2250 | | 1f.50 blue and buff | 10 | 10 |
| 2251 | | 2f.50 blue and buff | 25 | 10 |

DESIGNS—HORIZ: 1f.50, Town Hall, Malines. VERT: 2f.50, Basilica, St. Hubert.

570 *Actias luna*

1971. "Solidarity". Insects in Antwerp Zoo. Multicoloured.
2252		1f.50+50c. Type **570**	30	30
2253		3f.50+1f.50 *Tabanus bromius* (horiz)	35	35
2254		7f.+3f. *Polistes gallicus* (horiz)	85	85
2255		9f.+4f. *Cicindela campestris*	95	95

572 Road Signs
and Traffic
Signals

1972. 20th Anniv of "Via Secura" Road Safety
Organization.
2263 **572** 3f.50 multicoloured 30 30

573 Book Year
Emblem

1972. International Book Year.
2264 **573** 7f. blue, brown & black 60 40

574 Coins of
Belgium and
Luxembourg

1972. 50th Anniv of Belgo–Luxembourgeoise Economic
Union.
2265 **574** 1f.50 silver, black and
orange 30 30

576 "Auguste
Vermeylen" (I.
Opsomer)

1972. Birth Centenary of Auguste Vemeylen (writer).
2267 **576** 2f.50 multicoloured 30 30

577 "Belgica 72" Emblem

1972. "Belgica 72" Stamp Exn, Brussels (3rd Issue).
2268 **577** 3f.50 purple, blue & brn 35 30

578 Heart Emblem

1972. World Heart Month.
2269 **578** 7f. multicoloured 60 40

579 Astronaut
cancelling Letter
on Moon

1972. Stamp Day.
2270 **579** 3f.50 multicoloured 35 30

580 "Communications"

1972. Europa.
2271 **580** 3f.50 multicoloured 75 30
2272 **580** 7f. multicoloured 1·20 60

581 Quill Pen and
Newspaper

1972. "Liberty of the Press". 50th Anniv of Belga
News Agency and 25th Congress of International
Federation of Newspaper Editors (F.I.E.J.).
2273 **581** 2f.50 multicoloured 30 30

582 "UIC" on Coupled
Wagons

1972. 50th Anniv of Int Railways Union (U.I.C.).
2274 **582** 7f. multicoloured 60 40
See also No. P2266.

583 Couvin

1972. Tourist Publicity.
2275 **583** 2f.50 purple, blue & grn 25 25
2276 – 2f.50 brown and blue 25 25
DESIGN—VERT: No. 2276, Aldeneik Church, Maaseik.

584 Leopold I
10c. "Epaulettes"
Stamp of 1849

1972. "Belgica 72" Stamp Exn, Brussels (4th issue).
2277 **584** 1f.50+50c. brown, black
and gold 30 30
2278 – 2f.+1f. red, brown and
gold 35 35
2279 – 2f.50+1f. red, brown
and gold 40 40
2280 – 3f.50+1f.50 lilac, black
and gold 45 45
2281 – 6f.+3f. violet, black and
gold 60 60
2282 – 7f.+3f. red, black and
gold 70 70
2283 – 10f.+5f. blue, black and
gold 1·00 1·00
2284 – 15f.+7f.50 green, tur-
quoise and gold 1·60 1·60
2285 – 20f.+10f. chestnut,
brown and gold 2·10 2·10
DESIGNS: 2f. Leopold I 40c. "Medallion" of 1849; 2f.50,
Leopold II 10c. of 1883. 3f.50, Leopold II 50c. of 1883;
6f. Albert I; 2f. "Tin Hat" of 1919; 7f. Albert I 50f. of 1929;
10f. Albert I 1f.75 of 1931; 15f. Leopold III 5f. of 1936; 20f.
Baudouin 3f.50 of 1970.

585 Beatrice (G.
de Smet)

1972. "Philately for the Young".
2287 **585** 3f. multicoloured 35 30

586 Emblem of
Centre

1972. Inauguration of William Lennox Epileptic Centre,
Ottignies.
2288 **586** 10f.+5f. multicoloured 1·20 1·20

587 Dish Aerial
and "Intelstat 4"
Satellite

1972. Inaug of Satellite Earth Station, Lessive.
2289 **587** 3f.50 black, silver & bl 35 30

588 Frans
Masereel
(wood-carver and
painter)

1972. Masereel Commem.
2290 **588** 4f.50 black and green 40 30

589 "Adoration of
the Magi" (F.
Timmermans)

1972. Christmas.
2291 **589** 3f.50 multicoloured 35 30

590 Empress Maria
Theresa (unknown artist)

1972. Bicentenary of Belgian Royal Academy of Sciences,
Letters and Fine Arts.
2292 **590** 2f. multicoloured 30 30

591 Greylag
Goose

1972. "Solidarity". Birds from Zwin Nature Reserve.
Multicoloured.
2293 2f.+1f. Type **591** 35 35
2294 4f.50+2f. Northern lapwing 60 60
2295 8f.+4f. White stork 70 95
2296 9f.+4f.50 Common kestrel
(horiz) 1·00 1·00

592 "Fire"

1973. Industrial Buildings Fire Protection Campaign.
2297 **592** 2f. multicoloured 30 30

593 W.M.O. Emblem and
Meteorological
Equipment

1973. Centenary of World Meteorological Organization.
2298 **593** 9f. multicoloured 80 45

594 Bijloke Abbey and Museum,
Ghent

1973. Cultural Works. Religious Buildings.
2299 **594** 2f.+1f. green 40 40
2300 – 4f.50+2f. brown 50 50
2301 – 8f.+4f. red 95 95
2302 – 9f.+4f.50 blue 1·20 1·20
DESIGNS: 4f.50, Collegiate Church of St. Ursmer, Lobbes;
8f. Park Abbey, Heverlee; 9f. Floreffe Abbey.

595 W.H.O.
Emblem as Man's
"Heart"

1973. 25th Anniv of W.H.O.
2303 **595** 8f. black, yellow & red 60 45

596 Ball in Hands

1973. First World Basketball Championships for the
Handicapped, Bruges.
2304 **596** 10f.+5f. multicoloured 1·20 1·20

597 Europa "Posthorn"

1973. Europa.
2305 **597** 4f.50 blue, yellow & brn 1·30 35
2306 **597** 8f. blue, yellow & green 2·50 35

598 Thurn and
Taxis Courier
(17th-cent)

1973. Stamp Day.
2307 **598** 4f.50 brown and red 40 30

599 Fair Emblem

1973. 25th International Fair, Liege.
2308 **599** 4f.50 multicoloured 40 30

600 Arrows encircling Globe

1973. Fifth World Telecommunications Day.

2309	**600**	3f.50 multicoloured	35	30

601 *Sport* (poster for Ghent Exhibition, 1913)

1973. 60th Anniv of Workers' International Sports Organization.

2310	**601**	4f.50 multicoloured	40	30

602 Douglas DC-10-30CF and De Havilland D.H.9

1973. 50th Anniv of SABENA.

2311	**602**	8f. black, blue and grey	70	45

603 Ernest Tips's Biplane, 1908

1973. 35th Anniv (1972) of "Les Vieilles Tiges de Belgique" (pioneer aviators' association).

2312	**603**	10f. black, blue & green	85	50

604 15th-Century Printing-press

1973. Historical Events and Anniversaries.

2313	**604**	2f.+1f. blk, brn & red	40	40
2314	-	3f.50+1f.50 mult	40	40
2315	-	4f.50+2f. mult	45	45
2316	-	8f.+4f. multicoloured	85	85
2317	-	9f.+4f.50 mult	1·00	1·00
2318	-	10f.+5f. multicoloured	1·30	1·30

DESIGNS—VERT (As Type **604**): 2f. (500th anniv of first Belgian printed book, produced by Dirk Martens); 3f.50, Head of Amon (Queen Elisabeth Egyptological Foundation. 50th anniv.); 4f.50, *Portrait of a Young Girl* (Petrus Christus, 500th death anniv). HORIZ (36×25 mm): 8f. Gold coins of Hadrian and Marcus Aurelius (Discovery of Roman treasure at Luttre-Liberchies); (52×35 mm); 9f. *Members of the Great Council* (Coessaert) (Great Council of Malines, 500th anniv.). 10f. *Jong Jacob* (East Indiaman) (Ostend Merchant Company, 250th anniv.).

605 *Woman Bathing* (fresco by Lemaire)

1973. Thermal Treatment Year.

2319	**605**	4f.50 multicoloured	40	30

606 Adolphe Sax and Tenor Saxophone

1973. Belgian Musical Instrument Industry.

2320	**606**	9f. multicoloured	70	40

607 St. Nicholas Church, Eupen

1973. Tourist Publicity.

2321	**607**	2f. multicoloured	30	30

See also Nos. 2328/9, 2368/70, 2394/5, 2452/5, 2508/11, 2535/8, 2573/6, 2595/6 and 2614.

608 *Little Charles* (Evenepoel)

1973. "Philately for the Young".

2322	**608**	3f. multicoloured	35	30

609 J. B. Moens (philatelist) and Perforations

1973. 50th Anniv of Belgian Stamp Dealers Association.

2323	**609**	10f. multicoloured	80	60

610 *Adoration of the Shepards* (H. van der Goes)

1973. Christmas.

2324	**610**	4f. blue	40	30

611 Motorway and Emblem

1973. 50th Anniv of "Vlaamse Automobilistenbond" (VAB) (motoring organization).

2325	**611**	5f. multicoloured	45	30

612 L. Pierard (after sculpture by Ianchelevici)

1973. 21st Death Anniv of Louis Pierard (politician and writer).

2326	**612**	4f. red and cream	40	40

613 Early Microphone

1973. 50th Anniv of Belgium Radio.

2327	**613**	4f. black and blue	40	30

1973. Tourist Publicity. As T **607**.

2328		3f. grey, brown and blue	30	30
2329		4f. grey and green	40	30

DESIGNS—HORIZ: 3f. Town Hall, Leau; 4f. Chimay Castle.

614 F. Rops (self-portrait)

1973. 75th Death Anniv of Felicien Rops (artist and engraver).

2330	**614**	7f. black and brown	60	35

615 Jack of Diamonds

1973. "Solidarity". Old Playing Cards. Multicoloured.

2331		5f.+2f.50 Type **615**	60	60
2332		5f.+2f.50 Jack of Spades	60	60
2333		5f.+2f.50 Queen of Hearts	60	60
2334		5f.+2f.50 King of Clubs	60	60

1973. As Nos. 2207/23 but smaller, 22×17 mm.

2335	**583**	3f. green	30	10
2336	**583**	4f. blue	35	25
2337	**583**	4f.50 blue	40	10
2338	**583**	5f. mauve	40	25
2338c	**583**	6f. red	50	30
2339	**583**	6f.50 violet	50	30
2339b	**583**	8f. grey	65	30

616 King Albert (Baron Opsomer)

1974. 40th Death Anniv of King Albert I.

2340	**616**	4f. blue and black	35	30

617 "Blood Donation"

1974. Belgian Red Cross. Multicoloured.

2341		4f.+2f. Type **617**	45	45
2342		10f.+5f. "Traffic Lights" (Road Safety)	1·20	1·20

618 "Protection of the Environment"

1974. Robert Schuman Association for the Protection of the Environment.

2343	**618**	3f. multicoloured	35	30

619 Armand Jamar (Self-portrait)

1974. Belgian Cultural Celebrities. Multicoloured.

2344		4f.+2f. Type **619**	40	40
2345		5f.+2f.50 Tony Bergmann (author) and view of Lier	45	45
2346		7f.+3f.50 Henri Vieuxtemps (violinist) and view of Verviers	70	70
2347		10f.+5f. "James Ensor" (self-portrait with masks) (35×52 mm)	1·00	1·00

620 N.A.T.O. Emblem

1974. 25th Anniv of North Atlantic Treaty Organization.

2348	**620**	10f. blue and light blue	85	50

621 Hubert Krains (Belgian postal administrator)

1974. Stamp Day.

2349	**621**	5f. black and grey	40	30

622 "Destroyed Town" (O. Zadkine)

1974. Europa. Sculptures.

2350	**622**	5f. black and red	80	30
2351	-	10f. black and blue	1·60	50

DESIGN: 10f. *Solidarity* (G. Minne).

623 Heads of Boy and Girl

1974. Tenth Lay Youth Festival.

2352	**623**	4f. multicoloured	40	30

625 New Planetarium, Brussels

1974. Historical Buildings.

2354	**625**	3f. brown and blue	35	30
2355	-	4f. brown and red	45	30
2356	-	5f. brown and green	50	30
2357	-	7f. brown and yellow	65	35
2358	-	10f. brown, orange & bl	80	35

DESIGNS—As T **625**. HORIZ: 4f. Pillory, Braine-le-Chateau. VERT: 10f. Belfry, Bruges. 45×25 mm: 5f. Ruins of Soleilmont Abbey; 7f. *Procession* (fountain sculpture, Ghent).

626 "BENELUX"

1974. 30th Anniv of Benelux Customs Union.

2359	**626**	5f. blue, green & lt blue	40	30

627 *Jan Vekemans at the Age of Five* (Cornelis de Vos)

1974. "Philately for the Young".
2360 **627** 3f. multicoloured ... 35 ... 30

628 Self-portrait and Van Gogh House, Cuesmes

1974. Opening of Vincent Van Gogh House, Cuesmes.
2361 **628** 10f.+5f. multicoloured ... 1·20 ... 85

629 Corporal Tresignies and Brule Bridge

1974. 60th Death Anniv of Corporal Leon Tresignies (war hero).
2362 **629** 4f. green and brown ... 40 ... 30

630 Montgomery Blair and U.P.U. Emblem

1974. Centenary of U.P.U.
2363 **630** 5f. black and green ... 45 ... 30
2364 - 10f. black and red ... 80 ... 50
DESIGN: 10f. H. von Stephan and U.P.U. Monument.

631 Graph within Head

1974. 25th Anniv of Central Economic Council.
2365 **631** 7f. multicoloured ... 65 ... 40

632 Rotary Emblem on Belgian Flag

1974. 50th Anniv of Rotary Int in Belgium.
2366 **632** 10f. multicoloured ... 80 ... 45

633 Wild Boar

1974. 40th Anniv of Granting of Colours to Ardennes Regiment of Chasseurs.
2367 **633** 3f. multicoloured ... 35 ... 30

1974. Tourist Publicity. As T **607**.
2368 3f. brown and yellow ... 40 ... 30
2369 4f. green and blue ... 40 ... 35
2370 4f. green and blue ... 40 ... 35
DESIGNS—VERT: No. 2368, Aarschot. HORIZ: No. 2369, Meeting of three frontiers, Gemmenich; 2370, Nassogne.

634 "Angel" (detail, "The Mystic Lamb", Brothers Van Eyck)

1974. Christmas.
2371 **634** 4f. purple ... 40 ... 30

635 Gentian

1974. "Solidarity". Flora and Fauna. Multicoloured.
2372 **635** 4f.+2f. Type **635** ... 45 ... 45
2373 5f.+2f.50 Eurasian badger (horiz) ... 65 ... 65
2374 7f.+3f.50 *Carabus auratus* (beetle) (horiz) ... 75 ... 75
2375 10f.+5f. Spotted cat's-ear ... 1·20 ... 1·20

636 Adolphe Quetelet (after J. Odevaere)

1974. Death Centenary of Adolphe Quetelet. (scientist).
2376 **636** 10f. black and brown ... 80 ... 50

637 Exhibition Emblem

1975. "Themabelga" Stamp Exhibition, Brussels (1st issue).
2377 **637** 6f.50 orange, blk & grn ... 45 ... 30
See also Nos. 2411/16.

638 *Neoregelia carolinae*

1975. Ghent Flower Show. Multicoloured.
2378 4f.50 Type **638** ... 40 ... 35
2379 5f. *Tussilago petasites* ... 45 ... 30
2380 6f.50 *Azalea japonica* ... 50 ... 30

639 Student and Young Boy

1975. Cent of Charles Buls Normal School.
2381 **639** 4f.50 multicoloured ... 40 ... 30

640 Foundation Emblem

1975. Centenary of Davids Foundation (Flemish cultural organisation).
2382 **640** 5f. multicoloured ... 40 ... 30

641 King Albert I

1975. Birth Centenary of King Albert I.
2383 **641** 10f. black and purple ... 80 ... 45

642 Pesaro Palace, Venice

1975. Cultural Works.
2384 **642** 6f.50+2f.50 brown ... 65 ... 65
2385 - 10f.+4f.50 purple ... 1·00 ... 1·00
2386 - 15f.+6f.50 blue ... 1·50 ... 1·50
DESIGNS—HORIZ: 10f. Sculpture Museum, St. Bavon Abbey, Ghent. VERT: 15f. *Virgin and Child* (Michelangelo, 500th Birth Anniv.).

643 *Postman of 1840* (J. Thiriar)

1975. Stamp Day.
2387 **643** 6f.50 purple ... 50 ... 30

644 "An Apostle" (detail, *The Last Supper*, Dirk Bouts)

1975. Europa. Paintings.
2388 **644** 6f.50 black, blue & grn ... 80 ... 30
2389 - 10f. black, red & orange ... 1·70 ... 60
DESIGN: 10f. "The Suppliant's Widow" (detail, *The Justice of Otho*, Dirk Bouts).

645 Prisoners' Identification Emblems

1975. 30th Anniv of Concentration Camps' Liberation.
2390 **645** 4f.50 multicoloured ... 40 ... 30

646 St John's Hospice, Bruges

1975. European Architectural Heritage Year.
2391 **646** 4f.50 purple ... 45 ... 30
2392 - 5f. green ... 50 ... 30
2393 - 10f. blue ... 1·00 ... 45
DESIGNS—VERT: 5f. St. Loup's Church, Namur. HORIZ: 10f. Martyrs Square, Brussels.

1975. Tourist Publicity. As T **607**.
2394 4f.50 brown, buff and red ... 40 ... 30
2395 5f. multicoloured ... 50 ... 30
DESIGN—VERT: 4f.50, Church, Dottignies. HORIZ: 5f. Market Square, Saint Truiden.

647 G. Ryckmans and L. Cerfaux (founders), and Louvain University Library

1975. 25th Anniv of Louvain Colloquium Biblicum (Biblical Scholarship Association).
2396 **647** 10f. sepia and blue ... 85 ... 45

648 *Metamorphosis* (P. Mara)

1975. Queen Fabiola Foundation for the Mentally Ill.
2397 **648** 7f. multicoloured ... 60 ... 35

649 Marie Popelin (women's rights pioneer) and Palace of Justice

1975. International Women's Year.
2398 **649** 6f.50 purple and green ... 65 ... 30

650 *Assia* (Charles Despiau)

1975. 25th Anniv of Middelheim Open-air Museum, Antwerp.
2399 **650** 5f. black and green ... 40 ... 30

651 Dr. Hemerijckx and Leprosy Hospital, Zaire

1975. Dr. Frans Hemerijckx (treatment of leprosy pioneer) Commemoration.
2400 **651** 20f.+10f. mult ... 2·10 ... 2·10

652 Canal Map

1975. Opening of Rhine–Scheldt Canal.
2401 **652** 10f. multicoloured ... 85 ... 40

653 *Cornelia Vekemans at the Age of Seven* (Cornelis de Vos)

1975. "Philately for the Young".
2402 **653** 4f.50 multicoloured ... 45 ... 30

654 National Bank and F. Orban (founder)

1975. 125th Anniv of Belgian National Bank.
2403 **654** 25f. multicoloured ... 2·20 ... 60

655 Edmond Thieffry (pilot) and Hadley Page H.P.26 W.8e Hamilton OË-BAHO "Princess Marie-Jose"

1975. 50th Anniv of First Flight, Brussels–Kinshasa.
2404	**655**	7f. purple and black	60	40

656 University Seal

1975. 550th Anniv of Louvain University.
2405	**656**	6f.50 black, green & bl	60	30

657 "Angels", (detail, *The Nativity*, R. de le Pasture)

1975. Christmas.
2406	**657**	5f. multicoloured	40	25

658 Emile Moyson (Flemish Leader)

1975. "Solidarity".
2407	**658**	4f.50+2f. purple	45	45
2408		6f.50+3f. green	70	70
2409	-	10f.+5f. vio, blk & bl	1·00	1·00
2410	-	13f.+6f. multicoloured	1·30	1·30

DESIGNS—VERT: 6f.50, Dr. Augustin Snellaert (Flemish literature scholar); 13f. Detail of retable, St. Dymphne Church, Geel. HORIZ: 10f. Eye within hand, and Braille characters (150th anniv of introduction of Braille).

659 Cheese Seller

1975. "Themabelga" International Thematic Stamp Exhibition, Brussels (2nd issue). Traditional Belgian Trades. Multicoloured.
2411	4f.50+1f.50 Type **659**	45	45
2412	6f.50+3f. Potato seller	70	70
2413	6f.50+3f. Basket-carrier	70	70
2414	10f.+5f. Prawn fisherman and pony (horiz)	1·00	1·00
2415	10f.+5f. Knife-grinder and cart (horiz)	1·00	1·00
2416	30f.+15f. Milk-woman with dog-cart (horiz)	2·75	2·75

660 "African" Collector

1976. Centenary of "Conservatoire Africain" (Charity Organization).
2417	**660**	10f.+5f. multicoloured	1·20	1·20

661 Owl Emblem and Flemish Buildings

1976. 125th Anniv of Wilhems Foundation (Flemish cultural organization).
2418	**661**	5f. multicoloured	40	30

662 Bicentennial Symbol

1976. Bicentenary of American Revolution.
2419	**662**	14f. multicoloured	1·20	65

663 Cardinal Mercier

1976. 50th Death Anniv of Cardinal Mercier.
2420	**663**	4f.50 purple	40	30

664 "Vlaams Ekonomisch Verbond"

1976. 50th Anniv of Flemish Economic Federation.
2421	**664**	6f.50 multicoloured	50	30

665 Swimming

1976. Olympic Games, Montreal. Multicoloured.
2422	4f.50+1f.50 Type **665**	45	45
2423	5f.+2f. Running (vert)	45	45
2424	6f.50+2f.50 Horse jumping	70	70

666 Money Centre Building, Brussels

1976. Stamp Day.
2425	**666**	6f.50 brown	50	30

667 Queen Elisabeth playing Violin

1976. 25th Anniv of Queen Elisabeth International Music Competitions.
2426	**667**	14f.+6f. red & black	1·40	1·40

668 Basket-making

669 Truck on Motorway

1976. Europa. Traditional Crafts. Multicoloured.
2427	6f.50 Type **668**	95	25
2428	14f. Pottery (horiz)	2·10	60

1976. 14th Congress of International Road Haulage Union, Brussels.
2429	**669**	14f. black, red & yellow	1·30	50

670 Queen Elisabeth

1976. Birth Centenary of Queen Elisabeth.
2430	**670**	14f. green	1·20	50

672 Jan Olieslagers (aviator), Bleriot XI Monoplane and club Badge

1976. 75th Anniv of Belgian Royal Aero Club. Sheet 82×116 mm.
MS2435	**672**	25f.+10f. black, yellow and blue	2·50	2·50

673 Ardennes Horses

1976. 50th Anniv of Ardennes Draught Horses Society.
2436	**673**	5f. multicoloured	45	35

674 King Baudouin

1976. 25th Anniv of King Baudouin's Accession. Two sheets each 110×62 mm containing stamps as T **674**.
MS2437	(a) 4f.50 grey; 6f.50 yellow; 10f. red (sold at 30f.). (b) 20f. green; 30f. blue (sold at 70f.)	7·50	7·50

675 *Madonna and Child* (detail)

1976. 400th Birth Anniv of Peter Paul Rubens (artist) (1st issue). Multicoloured.
2438	4f.50+1f.50 *Descent from the Cross* (detail)	60	60
2439	6f.50+3f. *Adoration of the Shepherds* (detail) (24½×35 mm)	70	60
2440	6f.50+3f. *Virgin of the Parrot* (detail) (24½×35 mm)	70	70
2441	10f.+5f. *Adoration of the Kings* (detail) (24½×35 mm)	1·20	1·20
2442	10f.+5f. *Last Communion of St. Francis* (detail) (24½×35 mm)	1·20	1·20
2443	30f.+15f. Type **675**	3·00	3·00

See also Nos. 2459 and 2497.

676 William the Silent, Prince of Orange

1976. 400th Anniv of Pacification of Ghent.
2444	**676**	10f. green	85	45

678 Underground Train

1976. Opening of Brussels Metro (Underground) Service.
2446	**678**	6f.50 multicoloured	65	30

679 *The Young Musician* (W. C. Duyster)

1976. "Philately for the Young" and Young Musicians' Movement.
2447	**679**	4f.50 multicoloured	40	30

680 Charles Bernard (writer, birth cent)

1976. Cultural Anniversaries.
2448	**680**	5f. purple	45	30
2449	-	5f. red	45	30
2450	-	6f.50 brown	65	30
2451	-	6f.50 green	65	30

DESIGNS—VERT: No. 2449, Fernand Toussaint van Boelaere (writer, birth cent 1975); No. 2450, *St. Jerome in Mountain Landscape* (J. le Patinier) (25th anniv of Charles Plisnier Foundation). HORIZ: No. 2451,*Story of the Blind* (P. Brueghel) (25th anniv of *Vereniging voor Beschaafde Omgangstaal* (Dutch language organisation)).

1976. Tourist Publicity. As T **607**.
2452	4f.50 multicoloured	45	35
2453	4f.50 multicoloured	45	35
2454	5f. brown and blue	45	35
2455	5f. brown and olive	45	35

DESIGNS—HORIZ: No. 2452, Hunnegem Priory, Grammont; No. 2454, River Lys, Sint-Martens-Latem; No. 2455, Chateau. Ham-sur-Heure. VERT: No. 2453, Remouchamps Caves.

681 *Child with Impediment* (Velasquez)

1976. National Association for Aid to the Mentally Handicapped.
2456	**681**	14f.+6f. multicoloured	1·60	1·60

682 *The Nativity* (detail, Master of Flemalle)

1976. Christmas.
2457	**682**	5f. violet	45	30

683 Monogram

1977. 400th Birth Anniv of Peter Paul Rubens (2nd issue).
2459 **683** 6f.50 black and lilac 60 30

684 Belgian Lion

1977. (a) Size 17×20 mm.
2460 **684** 50c. brown 10 10
2461 **684** 65c. red 10 10
2462 **684** 1f. mauve 10 10
2463 **684** 1f.50 grey 10 10
2464a **684** 2f. orange 10 10
2465 **684** 2f.50 green 35 25
2466 **684** 2f.75 blue 35 35
2467a **684** 3f. violet 25 10
2468 **684** 4f. brown 25 10
2469 **684** 4f.50 blue 45 25
2470 **684** 5f. green 35 10
2471 **684** 6f. red 45 10
2472 **684** 7f. red 60 10
2473 **684** 8f. blue 35 10
2474 **684** 9f. orange 1·20 10

(b) 17×22 mm.
2475 1f. mauve 25 25
2476 2f. orange 45 35
2477 3f. violet 50 40

685 Dr. Albert Hustin (pioneer of blood transfusion)

1977. Belgian Red Cross.
2478 **685** 6f.50+2f.50 red and black 75 75
2479 - 14f.+7f. red, blue and black 1·40 1·40
DESIGN: 14f.+7f. Knee joint and red cross (World Rheumatism Year).

686 "50 Years of F.A.B.I."

1977. 50th Anniv of Federation of Belgian Engineers.
2480 **686** 6f.50 multicoloured 60 30

687 Jules Bordet School, Brussels (bicent)

1977. Cultural Anniversaries.
2481 **687** 4f.50+1f. mult 40 40
2482 - 4f.50+1f. mult 40 40
2483 - 5f.+2f. multicoloured 50 45
2484 - 6f.50+2f. mult 60 60
2485 - 6f.50+2f. red & black 60 60
2486 - 10f.+5 slate 1·00 1·00
DESIGNS—VERT: 24×37 mm: No. 2482, Marie-Therese College, Herve (bicentenary); 2483, Detail from *La Grande Pyramide Musicale* (E. Tytgat) (50th anniv of Brussels Philharmonic Society). 35×45 mm: No. 2486, Camille Lemonnier (75th anniv of Society of Belgian Authors writing in French). HORIZ: 35×24 mm: No. 2484, Lucien van Obbergh and stage scene (50th anniv of Union of Artists). 37×24 mm: No. 2485, Emblem of Humanist Society (25th anniv).

688 Gulls in Flight

1977. 25th Anniv of District 112 of Lions International.
2487 **688** 14f. multicoloured 1·20 35

689 Footballers

1977. 30th International Youth Tournament of European Football Association.
2488 **689** 10f.+5f. multicoloured 1·20 1·20

690 Pillar Box, 1852

1977. Stamp Day.
2489 **690** 6f.50 olive 65 30

691 Gileppe Dam, Jalhay

1977. Europa. Multicoloured.
2490 6f.50 Type **691** 1·20 30
2491 14f. The Yser, Nieuport 2·00 60

692 "Mars and Mercury Association Emblem"

1977. 50th Anniv of Mars and Mercury Association of Reserve and Retired Officers.
2492 **692** 5f. green, black & brown 40 30

693 De Hornes Coat of Arms

1977. Historical Anniversaries.
2493 **693** 4f.50 lilac 40 30
2494 - 5f. red 45 30
2495 - 6f.50 brown 45 30
2496 - 14f. green 1·20 60
DESIGNS AND EVENTS—VERT: 4f.50, Type **693** (300th anniv of creation of principality of Overijse under Eugene-Maximilien de Hornes); 6f.50, Miniature (600th anniv of Froissart's *Chronicles*); 14f. *The Conversion of St. Hubert* (1250th death anniv). HORIZ: (45×24 mm): 5f. Detail from *Oxford Chest* (675th anniv of Battle of Golden Spurs).

694 Self-Portrait

1977. 400th Birth Anniv of Peter Paul Rubens (3rd issue).
2497 **694** 5f. multicoloured 45 30
MS2498 100×152 mm. As No. 2497 but larger (24×37 mm) ×3 (sold at 20f.) 1·40 1·40

695 The Mystic Lamb (detail, Brothers Van Eyck)

1977. 50th Anniv of International Federation of Library Associations and Congress, Brussels.
2499 **695** 10f. multicoloured 80 45

696 Gymnast and Footballer

1977. Sports Events and Anniversaries.
2500 **696** 4f.50 red, black & grn 45 30
2501 - 6f.50 black, violet and brown 50 30
2502 - 10f. turquoise, black and salmon 85 45
2503 - 14f. green, blk & ochre 1·30 60
DESIGNS—VERT: 4f.50, Type **696** (50th anniv of Workers' Central Sports Association); 10f. Basketball (20th European Championships); 14f. Hockey (International Hockey Cup competition). HORIZ: 6f.50, Disabled fencers (Rehabilitation through sport).

697 Festival Emblem

1977. "Europalia '77" Festival.
2504 **697** 5f. multicoloured 45 30

699 The Egg-seller (Gustave de Smet)

1977. Promoting Belgian Eggs.
2506 **699** 4f.50 black and ochre 40 30

700 The Stamp Collectors (detail, Constant Cap)

1977. "Philately for the Young".
2507 **700** 4f.50 sepia 40 30

1977. Tourist Publicity. As T **607**.
2508 4f.50 multicoloured 40 30
2509 4f.50 black, blue and green 40 30
2510 5f. multicoloured 40 30
2511 5f. multicoloured 40 30
DESIGNS—VERT: No. 2508, Bailiff's House, Gembloux; No. 2509, St. Aldegone's Church. HORIZ: No. 2510, View of Liege and statue of Mother and Child; No. 2511, View and statue of St. Nicholas.

701 Nativity (detail, R. de la Pasture)

1977. Christmas.
2512 **701** 5f. red 40 35

702 Albert-Edouard Janssen (financier)

1977. "Solidarity".
2513 **702** 5f.+2f.50 black 45 45
2514 - 5f.+2f.50 red 45 45
2515 - 10f.+5f. purple 1·00 1·00
2516 - 10f.+5f. grey 1·00 1·00
DESIGNS: No. 2514, Joseph Wauters (politician); No. 2516, Jean Capart (egyptologist); No. 2515, August de Boeck (composer).

703 Distressed Girl (Deserted Children)

1978. Philanthropic Works. Multicoloured.
2517 4f.50+1f.50 Type **703** 40 40
2518 6f.+3f. Blood pressure measurement (World Hypertension Month) 60 60
2519 10f.+5f. De Mick Sanatorium, Brasschaat (Anti-tuberculosis) (horiz) 1·00 1·00

704 Railway Signal as Arrows on Map of Europe

1978. "European Action". Multicoloured.
2520 10f. Type **704** (25th anniv of European Conference of Transport Ministers) 85 35
2521 10f. European Parliament Building, Strasbourg (first direct elections) 85 35
2522 14f. Campidoglio Palace, Rome and map of EEC countries (20th anniv of Treaties of Rome) (horiz) 1·20 50
2523 14f. Paul Henri Spaak (Belgian Prime Minister) (horiz) 1·20 50

705 Grimbergen Abbey

1978. 850th Anniv of Premonstratensian Abbey, Grimbergen.
2524 **705** 4f.50 brown 40 30

706 Emblem

1978. 175th Anniv of Ostend Chamber of Commerce and Industry.
2525 **706** 8f. multicoloured 60 30

707 5f. Stamp of 1878

1978. Stamp Day.
2526 **707** 8f. brown, blk & drab 60 30

708 Antwerp Cathedral

1978. Europa. Multicoloured.
2527 8f. Type **708** 1·20 35
2528 14f. Pont des Trous, Tournai (horiz) 2·30 60

709 Theatre and
Characters from
*The Brussels Street
Singer*

1978. Cultural Anniversaries.

2529	**709**	6f.+3f. multicoloured	60	60
2530	-	6f.+3f. multicoloured	60	60
2531	-	8f.+4f. brown	75	75
2532	-	10f.+5f. brown	1·00	1·00

DESIGNS AND EVENTS: No. 2529, (Type **709**) (Royal Flemish Theatre Cent.); 2530, Arquebusier with standard, arms and Company Gallery, Vise (Royal Company of Crossbowmen of Vise 400th anniv); 2531, Karel van de Woestijne (poet) (birth cent); 2532, Don John of Austria (signing of Perpetual Edict, 400th anniv).

710 "Education"

1978. Teaching. Multicoloured.

2533	6f. Type **710** (Municipal education in Ghent, 150th anniv)		45	35
2534	8f. Paul Pastur Workers' University, Charleroi (75th anniv)		70	30

1978. Tourist Publicity. As T 607.

2535	4f.50 sepia, buff and blue	40	35
2536	4f.50 multicoloured	40	35
2537	6f. multicoloured	50	35
2538	6f. multicoloured	50	35

DESIGNS—VERT: No. 2535, Jonathas House, Enghien. HORIZ: No. 2536, View of Wetteren and couple in local costume; 2537, Brussels tourist hostess; 2538, Carnival Prince and church tower.

711 "K.V.I."

1978. 50th Anniv of Royal Flemish Association of Engineers.

2539	**711**	8f. black and red	60	30

712 Young Stamp Collector

1978. "Philately for the Young".

2540	**712**	4f.50 violet	40	30

713 Mountain Scenery

1978. Olympic Games (1980) Preparation.

2541	**713**	6f.+2f.50 mult	65	65
2542	-	8f.+3f.50 green, brown and black	75	75
MS2543	150×100 mm. 7f. + 3f., 14f.+6f. multicoloured		2·30	2·30

DESIGNS: 7f. Ancient Greek athletes; 8f. Kremlin Towers, Moscow; 14f. Olympic flame.

714 *The Nativity* (detail, Bethlehem Door, Notre Dame, Huy)

1978. Christmas.

2544	**714**	6f. black	50	35

715 Tabernacle, Brussels Synagogue (centenary)

1978. "Solidarity". Anniversaries.

2545	**715**	6f.+2f. brown, grey and black	65	65
2546	-	8f.+3f. multicoloured	80	80
2547	-	14f.+7f. multicoloured	1·50	1·50

DESIGNS—HORIZ: (36×24 mm): 8f. Dancing figures (Catholic Students Action, 50th anniv); 14f. Father Dominique-Georges Pire and African Village (Award of Nobel Peace Prize, 20th anniv).

716 Relief Workers giving First Aid

1978. Belgian Red Cross. Multicoloured.

2548	8f.+3f. Type **716**		85	85
2549	16f.+8f. Skull smoking, bottle and syringe ("Excess kills")		1·70	1·70

717 "Till Eulenspiegel" (legendary character)

1979. Tenth Anniv of Lay Action Centres.

2550	**717**	4f.50 multicoloured	40	30

718 "European Dove"

1979. First Direct Elections to European Assembly.

2551	**718**	8f. multicoloured	70	30

719 Millenary Emblem

1979. Brussels Millenary (1st issue).

2552	**719**	4f.50 brown, blk & red	35	30
2553	**719**	8f. turquoise, blk & grn	80	30

See also Nos. 2559/62.

720 Sculpture at N.A.T.O. Headquarters and Emblem

1979. 30th Anniv of North Atlantic Treaty Organization.

2554	**720**	30f. blue, gold and light blue	2·30	60

721 Drawing of Monument

1979. 25th Anniv of Breendonk Monument.

2555	**721**	6f. orange and black	45	35

722 Railway Parcels Stamp, 1879

1979. Stamp Day.

2556	**722**	8f. multicoloured	65	30

723 Mail Coach and Renault R4 Post Van

1979. Europa. Multicoloured.

2557	8f. Type **723**		1·70	30
2558	14f. Semaphore posts, satellite and dish aerial		3·00	60

724 *Legend of Our Lady of Sablon* (detail of tapestry, Town Museum of Brussels)

1979. Brussels Millenary (2nd issue). Multicoloured.

2559	6f.+2f. Type **724**		60	60
2560	8f.+3f. Different detail of tapestry		70	70
2561	14f.+7f. *Legend of Our Lady of Sablon* (tapestry)		1·50	1·50
2562	20f.+10f. Different detail of tapestry		2·20	2·20
MS2563	100×150 mm. 20f.+10f. Different detail of Town Museum tapestry (48×37 mm)		2·30	2·30

The tapestry shown on Nos. 2559/60 is from Brussels Town Museum and that on Nos. 2561/2 from the Royal Museum of Art and History.

725 Caduceus and Factory

1979. 175th Anniv of Verviers Chamber of Commerce.

2564	**725**	8f. multicoloured	60	30

726 "50" and Bank Emblem

1979. 50th Anniv of Professional Credit Bank.

2565	**726**	4f.50 blue and gold	40	30

727 Bas-relief

1979. 50th Anniv of Chambers of Trade and Commerce.

2566	**727**	10f. crimson, orange and red	75	40

728 Cambre Abbey

1979. Cultural Anniversaries.

2567	**728**	6f.+2f. multicoloured	60	60
2568	-	8f.+3f. multicoloured	70	75
2569	-	14f.+7f. black, orange and green	1·50	1·50
2570	-	20f.+10f. brown, red and grey	2·20	2·20

DESIGNS: 6f. Type **728** (50th anniv of restoration); 8f. Beauvoorde Chateau; 14f. Barthelemy Dumortier (founder) and newspaper "Courrier de L'Escaut" (150th anniv); 20f. Crypt, shrine and Collegiate Church of St. Hermes, Renaix (850th anniv of consecration).

729 "Tintin" with Dog, Stamps and Magnifier

1979. "Philately for the Young".

2571	**729**	8f. multicoloured	2·30	70

730 Le Grand-Hornu

1979. Le Grand-Hornu Industrial Archaeological Site.

2572	**730**	10f.+5f. black & grey	1·00	1·00

1979. Tourist Publicity. As T 607.

2573	5f. multicoloured	45	35
2574	5f. multicoloured	45	35
2575	6f. black, turquoise & green	60	35
2576	6f. multicoloured	60	35

DESIGNS—HORIZ: No. 2573, Royal African Museum, Tervuren, and hunters with hounds; 2575, St. John's Church, Poperinge, and statue of Virgin Mary. VERT: No. 2574, Belfry, Thuin, and men carrying religious image; 2576, St. Nicholas's Church and cattle market, Ciney.

731 Francois Auguste Gevaert

1979. Music. Each brown and ochre.

2577	5f. Type **731** (150th birth anniv)	45	35
2578	6f. Emmanuel Durlet	65	35
2579	14f. Grand piano and string instruments (40th anniv of Queen Elisabeth Musical Chapel)	1·00	60

732 Madonna and Child, Foy-Notre-Dame Church

1979. Christmas.

2580	**732**	6f. black and blue	40	30

733 H. Heyman (politician, birth centenary)

1979. "Solidarity".

2581	**733**	8f.+3f. brown, green and black	60	60
2582	-	10f.+5f. multicoloured	95	95
2583	-	16f.+8f. black, green and yellow	1·60	1·60

DESIGNS—VERT: As Type **733**. 10f. War Invalids Organization medal (50th anniv). HORIZ: (44×24 mm): 16f. Child's head and International Year of the Child emblem.

734 "1830–1980"

1980. 150th Anniv of Independence (1st issue).
2584 **734** 9f. mauve & lt mauve 70 30
See also Nos. 2597/2601.

735 Frans Van
Cauwelaert

1980. Birth Centenary of Frans Van Cauwelaert
(politician).
2585 **735** 5f. black 45 30

736 Spring
Flowers

1980. Ghent Flower Show. Multicoloured.
2586 5f. Type **736** 45 35
2587 6f.50 Summer flowers 60 35
2588 9f. Autumn flowers 70 35

737 Telephone and
Diagram of Satellite Orbit

1980. 50th Anniv of Telegraph and Telephone Office.
2589 **737** 10f. multicoloured 80 35

738 5f. Airmail Stamp of
1930

1980. Stamp Day.
2590 **738** 9f. multicoloured 75 30

739 St. Benedict
of Nursia

1980. Europa. Multicoloured.
2591 9f. Type **739** 1·40 30
2592 14f. Marguerite of Austria 2·10 70

740 Ivo van
Damme

1980. Ivo van Damme (athlete) Commemoration.
2593 **740** 20f.+10f. mult 2·10 2·10

741 Palais de la
Nation

1980. Fourth Interparliamentary Conference on European
Co-operation and Security, Brussels.
2594 **741** 5f. blue, lilac and black 40 35

742 Golden Carriage,
Mons

1980. Tourist Publicity. Multicoloured.
2595 6f.50 Type **742** 50 35
2596 6f.50 Damme 50 35

743 King Leopold I and Queen
Louise-Marie

1980. 150th Anniv of Belgian Independence (2nd issue).
2597 **743** 6f.50+1f.50 pur & blk 65 65
2598 - 9f.+3f. blue & black 75 75
2599 - 14f.+6f. green & blk 1·40 1·40
2600 - 17f.+8f. orange. & blk 1·70 1·70
2601 - 25f.+10f. green & blk 2·40 2·40
MS2602 100×150 mm. 50f. black (sold
at 75f.) 5·25 5·25
DESIGNS: 9f. King Leopold II and Queen Marie-Henriette;
14f. King Albert I and Queen Elisabeth; 17f. King Leopold
III and Queen Astrid; 25f. King Baudouin and Queen Fa-
biola; 50f. Royal Mint Theatre, Brussels.

744 King
Baudouin

1980. King Baudouin's 50th Birthday.
2603 **744** 9f. red 75 25

745 Brewer
(detail, Reliquary
of St. Lambert)

1980. Millenary of Liège. Multicoloured.
2604 9f.+3f. Type **745** 75 75
2605 17f.+6f. The Miner (sculpture by
Constantin Meunier) (horiz) 1·70 1·70
2606 25f.+10f. Seat of Wisdom
(Madonna, Collegiate Church
of St. John, Liège) 2·40 2·40
MS2607 150×100 mm. 20f.+10f. Seal of
Prince Bishop Notger (43×24 mm) 4·25 4·25

746 Chiny

1980. Tourist Publicity.
2608 **746** 5f. multicoloured 45 30

747 Emblem of
Cardiological League of
Belgium

1980. Heart Week.
2609 **747** 14f. light blue, red and
blue 1·20 60

748 Rodenbach
(statue at
Roulers)

1980. Death Cent of Albrecht Rodenbach (poet).
2610 **748** 9f. brown, blue and
deep blue 75 30

749 "Royal Procession" (children of
Thyl Uylenspiegel Primary School)

1980. "Philately for the Young".
2611 **749** 5f. multicoloured 40 35

750 Emblem

1980. 50th Anniv of Belgian Broadcasting Corporation.
2612 **750** 10f. black and grey 80 45

751 "Garland of Flowers
and Nativity" (attr. D.
Seghers)

1980. Christmas.
2613 **751** 6f.50 multicoloured 50 35

752 Gateway,
Diest

1980. Tourist Publicity.
2614 **752** 5f. multicoloured 45 35
See also Nos. 2648/51 and 2787/92.

754 Brain

1981. International Year of Disabled Persons.
Multicoloured.
2637 10f.+5f. Type **754** 1·20 1·20
2638 25f.+10f. Eye (horiz) 2·50 2·50

755 Baron de
Gerlache (after F.
J. Navez)

1981. Historical Anniversaries.
2639 **755** 6f. multicoloured 45 30
2640 - 9f. multicoloured 70 30
2641 - 50f. brown & yellow 3·75 70
DESIGNS—As T **755**: 6f. Type **755** (1st President of Cham-
ber of Deputies) (150th anniv of Chamber); 9f. Baron de
Stassart (1st President of Senate) (after F. J. Navez) (150th
anniv of Senate). 35×51 mm: 50f. Statue of King Leopold
I by Geefs (150th anniv of royal dynasty).

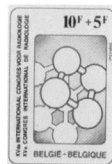

756 Emblem of
15th
International
Radiology
Convention

1981. Belgian Red Cross.
2642 **756** 10f.+5f. bl, blk & red 1·00 1·00
2643 - 25f.+10f. blue, red and
black 2·40 2·40
DESIGN: 25f. Dove and globe symbolizing international
emergency assistance.

757 Tchantches and
Op-Signoorke (puppets)

1981. Europa. Multicoloured.
2644 9f. Type **757** 1·50 30
2645 14f. D'Artagnan and Woltje
(puppets) 2·50 85

758 Stamp
Transfer-roller
depicting A. de
Cock (founder of
Postal Museum)

1981. Stamp Day.
2646 **758** 9f. multicoloured 75 30

759 Ovide Decroly

1981. 110th Birth Anniv of Dr. Ovide Decroly
(educational psychologist).
2647 **759** 35f.+15f. brown & bl 3·50 2·30

1981. Tourist Publicity. As T **752**. Multicoloured.
2648 6f. Statue of our Lady of Tongre 60 35
2649 6f. Egmont Castle, Zottegem 60 35
2650 6f.50 Dams on Eau d'Heure
(horiz) 60 35
2651 6f.50 Tongerlo Abbey, Antwerp
(horiz) 60 35

760 Footballer

1981. Cent of Royal Antwerp Football Club.
2652 **760** 6f. red, brown & black 60 30

761 Edouard
Remouchamps
(Walloon
dramatist)

1981. 125th Anniv of Society of Walloon Language and
Literature.
2653 **761** 6f.50 brown and stone 50 30

762 French Horn

1981. Centenary of De Vredekring Band, Antwerp.

| 2654 | **762** | 6f.50 blue, mve & blk | 50 | 30 |

763 Audit Office

1981. 150th Anniv of Audit Office.

| 2655 | **763** | 10f. purple | 80 | 30 |

764 Pietà

1981. 25th Anniv of Bois du Cazier Mining Disaster. Sheet 150×100 mm.

| MS2656 | **764** | 20f. multicoloured (sold at 30f.) | 2·30 | 2·30 |

765 Tombs of Marie of Burgundy and Charles the Bold

1981. Relocation of Tombs of Marie of Burgundy and Charles the Bold in Notre-Dame Church, Bruges.

| 2657 | **765** | 50f. multicoloured | 3·75 | 85 |

766 Boy holding Globe in Tweezers

1981. "Philately for Youth".

| 2658 | **766** | 6f. multicoloured | 45 | 30 |

767 King Baudouin

1981

2659	**767**	50f. light blue and blue	5·50	30
2660	**767**	65f. mauve and black	7·00	95
2661	**767**	100f. brown and blue	11·50	60

768 Max Waller (founder)

1981. Cultural Anniversaries.

2672	**768**	6f. multicoloured	45	30
2673	-	6f.50 multicoloured	50	30
2674	-	9f. multicoloured	70	30
2675	-	10f. multicoloured	80	30
2676	-	14f. lt brn & brn	1·30	60

DESIGNS: 6f. Type **768** (centenary of literary review *La Jeune Belgique*); 6f.50," Liqueur Drinkers" (detail, Gustave van de Woestijne (inscr "Woestyne") (birth centenary); 9f. Fernand Severin (poet, 50th death anniv); 10f. Jan van Ruusbroec (mystic, 600th death anniv); 14f. Owl (La Pensee et les Hommes organization, 25th anniv).

769 Nativity (miniature from *Missale ad usum d. Leodensis*)

1981. Christmas.

| 2677 | **769** | 6f.50 brown and black | 45 | 30 |

770 Mounted Gendarme, 1832

1981. "Solidarity". Multicoloured.

2678	**770**	9f.+4f. Type **770**	1·00	1·00
2679		20f.+7f. Carabinier	2·00	2·00
2680		40f.+20f. Mounted Guide, 1843	4·00	4·00

771 Cellist and Royal Conservatory of Music, Brussels

1982. 150th Anniversaries. Multicoloured.

| 2681 | **771** | 6f.50 Type **771** | 45 | 30 |
| 2682 | | 9f. Front of former Law Court, Brussels (anniv of judiciary) | 70 | 30 |

772 Sectional View of Cyclotron

1982. Science. Multicoloured.

2683	**772**	6f. Type **772** (Installation of cyclotron at National Radio-elements Institute, Fleurus)	45	35
2684		14f. Telescope and galaxy (Royal Observatory)	1·00	45
2685		50f. Dr. Robert Koch and tubercle bacillus (centenary of discovery)	3·50	80

773 Billiards

1982. Sports. Multicoloured.

2686	**773**	6f.+2f. Type **773**	95	95
2687		9f.+4f. Cycling	1·30	1·30
2688		10f.+5f. Football	1·40	1·40
2689		50f.+14f. *Treaty of Rome* (yacht)	4·00	4·00
MS2690	105×100 mm. 25f. multicoloured (Type **773**); 25f. brown, yellow and black (as No. 2687); 25f. red, yellow and black (as No. 2688); 25f. multicoloured (as No. 2689)		8·75	8·25

774 Joseph Lemaire (after Jean Maillard)

1982. Birth Centenary of Joseph Lemaire (Minister of State and social reformer).

| 2691 | **774** | 6f.50 multicoloured | 50 | 30 |

775 Voting (Universal Suffrage)

1982. Europa.

| 2692 | **775** | 10f. multicoloured | 2·30 | 35 |
| 2693 | - | 17f. green, black and grey | 4·00 | 60 |

DESIGN: 17f. Portrait and signature of Emperor Joseph II (Edict of Toleration).

1982. Surch **1 F**.

| 2694 | **684** | 1f. on 5f. green | 10 | 10 |

777 17th-century Postal Messenger

1982. Stamp Day.

| 2695 | **777** | 10f. multicoloured | 75 | 30 |

778 *Tower of Babel* (Brueghel the Elder)

1982. World Esperanto Congress, Antwerp.

| 2696 | **778** | 12f. multicoloured | 95 | 45 |

1982. Tourist Publicity. As T **752**.

2697		7f. blue and light blue	65	35
2698		7f. black and green	65	35
2699		7f.50 brown and light brown	65	35
2700		7f.50 violet and lilac	65	35
2701		7f.50 black and grey	65	35
2702		7f.50 black and pink	65	35

DESIGNS—VERT: No. 2697, Gosselies Tower; 2698, Zwijveke Abbey, Termonde; 2701, Entrance gate, Grammont Abbey; 2702, Beveren pillory. HORIZ: No. 2699, Stavelot Abbey; 2700, Abbey ruins, Villers-la-Ville.

780 Louis Paul Boon (writer)

1982. Cultural Anniversaries.

2707	**780**	7f. black, red and grey	45	30
2708	-	10f. multicoloured	70	30
2709	-	12f. multicoloured	95	45
2710	-	17f. multicoloured	1·70	45

DESIGNS: 7f. Type **780** (70th birth anniv); 10f. *Adoration of the Shepherds* (detail of Portinari retable) (Hugo van der Goes, 500th death anniv); 12f. Michel de Ghelderode (dramatist, 20th death anniv); 17f. *Motherhood* (Pierre Paulus, birth centenary (1981)).

781 Abraham Hans

1982. Birth Centenary of Abraham Hans (writer).

| 2711 | **781** | 17f. black, turquoise and blue | 1·10 | 35 |

782 Children playing Football

1982. "Philately for the Young". Scout Year.

| 2712 | **782** | 7f. multicoloured | 65 | 35 |

783 Masonic Emblems

1982. 150th Anniv of Belgium Grand Orient (Freemasonry Lodge).

| 2713 | **783** | 10f. yellow and black | 75 | 30 |

784 Star over Village

1982. Christmas.

| 2714 | **784** | 10f.+1f. multicoloured | 80 | 30 |

785 Cardinal Cardijn

1982. Birth Centenary of Cardinal Joseph Cardijn.

| 2715 | **785** | 10f. multicoloured | 80 | 10 |

786 King Baudouin **787** King Baudouin

1982

2716	**786**	10f. blue	95	10
2717	**786**	11f. brown	1·20	10
2718	**786**	12f. green	3·00	60
2719	**786**	13f. red	1·30	10
2720	**786**	14f. black	1·20	10
2721	**786**	15f. red	2·00	35
2722	**786**	20f. blue	2·00	10
2723	**786**	22f. purple	3·00	1·20
2724	**786**	23f. green	3·00	60
2725	**786**	24f. grey	2·30	35
2726	**786**	25f. blue	2·50	30
2727	**786**	30f. brown	2·40	10
2728	**786**	40f. red	4·00	10
2729	**787**	50f. light brown, brown and black	5·75	10
2730	**787**	100f. blue, deep blue and black	16·00	25
2731	**787**	200f. light green, green and deep green	34·00	85

788 St. Francis preaching to the Birds

1982. 800th Birth Anniv of St. Francis of Assisi.

| 2736 | **788** | 20f. multicoloured | 1·50 | 60 |

789 Messenger handing Letter to King in the Field

1982. "Belgica 82" Postal History Exhibition. Multicoloured.

2737		7f.+2f. Type **789**	60	60
2738		7f.50+2f.50 Messenger, Basel (vert)	70	70
2739		10f.+3f. Messenger, Nuremburg (vert)	85	85
2740		17f.+7f. Imperial courier, 1750 (vert)	1·60	1·60
2741		20f.+9f. Imperial courier, 1800	1·90	1·90
2742		25f.+10f. Belgian postman, 1886	2·20	2·20
MS2743	123×89 mm. 50f.+25f. Mail coach (48×37 mm)		5·25	5·25

790 Emblem

1983. 50th Anniv of Caritas Catholica Belgica.
2744 **790** 10f.+2f. red and grey 95 95

791 Horse Tram

1983. Trams. Multicoloured.
2745 7f.50 Type **791** 80 40
2746 10f. Electric tram 1·20 35
2747 50f. Tram with trolley (invented by K. van de Poele) 4·50 70

792 Mountaineer

1983. Belgian Red Cross. Multicoloured.
2748 12f.+3f. Type **792** 1·20 1·20
2749 20f.+5f. Walker 2·00 2·00

793 Brussels Buildings, Open Periodicals and Globe

1983. 24th International Periodical Press Federation World Congress, Brussels.
2750 **793** 20f. multicoloured 1·50 60

794 Woman at Work

1983. Women.
2751 **794** 8f. multicoloured 80 35
2752 – 11f. multicoloured 95 30
2753 – 20f. yellow, brown & bl 1·70 60
DESIGNS: 11f. Woman at home; 20f. Woman manager.

795 Graphic Representation of Midi Railway Station, Brussels

1983. Stamp Day. World Communications Year.
2754 **795** 11f. black, red and blue 95 30

796 Procession of the Holy Blood

1983. Procession of the Holy Blood, Bruges.
2755 **796** 8f. multicoloured 65 35

797 The Man in the Street

1983. Europa. Paintings by Paul Delvaux. Multicoloured.
2756 11f. Type **797** 1·70 35
2757 20f. Night Trains (horiz) 3·50 70

798 Hot-air Balloon over Town

1983. Bicentenary of Manned Flight. Multicoloured.
2758 11f. Type **798** 80 30
2759 22f. Hot-air balloon over countryside 1·70 70

799 Church of Our Lady, Hastiere

1983. Tourist Publicity. Multicoloured.
2760 8f. Type **799** 75 35
2761 8f. Tumulus, Landen 75 35
2762 8f. Park, Mouscron 75 35
2763 8f. Wijnendale Castle, Torhout 75 35

800 Milkmaid

1983. Tineke Festival, Heule.
2764 **800** 8f. multicoloured 65 35

801 Plaque on Wall

1983. European Small and Medium-sized Industries and Crafts Year.
2765 **801** 11f. yellow, black & red 85 30

802 Rainbow and Child

1983. "Philately for the Young". 20th Anniv of Queen Fabiola Village No. 1 (for handicapped people).
2766 **802** 8f. multicoloured 65 30

803 Textiles

1983. Belgian Exports (1st series). Multicoloured.
2767 10f. Type **803** 95 35
2768 10f. Steel beams (metallurgy) 95 35
2769 10f. Diamonds 95 35
See also Nos. 2777/80.

804 Conscience (after wood engraving by Nelly Degouy)

1983. Death Centenary of Hendrik Conscience (writer).
2770 **804** 20f. black and green 1·60 45

805 "Madonna" (Jef Wauters)

1983. Christmas.
2771 **805** 11f.+1f. multicoloured 95 95

806 2nd Foot Regiment

1983. "Solidarity". Military Uniforms. Multicoloured.
2772 8f.+2f. Type **806** 85 85
2773 11f.+2f. Lancer 1·50 1·50
2774 50f.+12f. Grenadier 4·25 4·25

1983. King Leopold III Commemoration.
2775 **155** 11f. black 85 30

807 Free University of Brussels

1984. 150th Anniv of Free University of Brussels.
2776 **807** 11f. multicoloured 95 25

1984. Belgian Exports (2nd series). As T **803**. Multicoloured.
2777 11f. Retort and test tubes (chemicals) 95 35
2778 11f. Combine harvester (agricultural produce) 95 35
2779 11f. Ship, coach and electric commuter train (transport) 95 35
2780 11f. Atomic emblem and computer terminal (new technology) 95 35

808 Albert I

1984. 50th Death Anniv of King Albert I.
2781 **808** 8f. black and stone 70 35

809 Judo

1984. Olympic Games, Los Angeles. Multicoloured.
2782 8f.+2f. Type **809** 70 70
2783 12f.+3f. Windsurfing (vert) 1·20 1·20
MS2784 125×90 mm. 10f. Archery; 24f. Dressage 2·50 2·50

810 Releasing Doves

1984. 25th Anniv of Movement without a Name.
2785 **810** 12f. multicoloured 95 30

811 Clasped Hands

812 St. John Bosco with Children

1984. 50th Anniv of National Lottery.
2786 **811** 12f.+3f. multicoloured 1·20 1·20

1984. 50th Anniv of Canonization of St. John Bosco (founder of Salesians).
2787 **812** 8f. multicoloured 70 30

813 Bridge

1984. Europa. 25th Anniv of European Posts and Telecommunications Conference.
2788 **813** 12f. red and black 1·50 30
2789 **813** 22f. blue and black 3·25 60

814 Leopold II 1884 10c. Stamp

1984. Stamp Day.
2790 **814** 12f. multicoloured 1·00 30

815 Dove and Pencils

1984. Second European Parliament Elections.
2791 **815** 12f. multicoloured 1·00 30

816 Shako

1984. 150th Anniv of Royal Military School.
2792 **816** 22f. multicoloured 1·70 50

817 Church of Our Lady of the Chapel, Brussels

1984. Tourist Publicity. Multicoloured.
2793 10f. Type **817** 85 40
2794 10f. St. Martin's Church and lime tree, Montigny-le-Tilleul 85 40
2795 10f. Belfry and Town Hall, Tielt (vert) 85 40

818 Curious Masks (detail, James Ensor)

1984. Inaug of Brussels Modern Art Museum.
2796 **818** 8f.+2f. multicoloured 85 85
2797 – 12f.+3f. multicoloured 1·50 1·50
2798 – 22f.+5f. multicoloured 2·00 2·00
2799 – 50f.+13f. grn, bl & blk 4·75 4·75
DESIGNS: 12f. The Empire of Lights (detail, Rene Magritte); 22f. The End (detail, Jan Cox); 50f. Rhythm No. 6 (Jo Delahaut).

819 Symbolic Design

1984. 50th Anniv of Chirojeugd (Christian youth movement).
2800 **819** 10f. yellow, violet & bl 85 40

820 Averbode Abbey

1984. Abbeys.
2801 **820** 8f. green and brown 65 40
2802 – 22f. brown & dp brown 1·70 65
2803 – 24f. green & light green 1·70 65
2804 – 50f. lilac and brown 4·00 85
DESIGNS—VERT: 22f. Chimay; 24f. Rochefort. HORIZ: 50f. Affligem.

821 Smurf as Postman

1984. "Philately for the Young".
2805 **821** 8f. multicoloured 1·50 45

822 Child collecting Flowers

1984. Children.
2806 **822** 10f.+2f. Type **822** 95 95
2807 – 12f.+3f. Children with globe 1·20 1·20
2808 – 15f.+3f. Child on merry-go-round 1·40 1·40

823 Meulemans

1984. Birth Cent of Arthur Meulemans (composer).
2809 **823** 12f. black and orange 1·00 30

824 Three Kings

1984. Christmas.
2810 **824** 12f.+1f. multicoloured 1·20 1·20

825 St. Norbert

1985. 850th Death Anniv of St. Norbert.
2811 **825** 22f. brown & lt brown 1·80 60

826 Virgin of Louvain (attr. Jan Gossaert)

1985. "Europalia 85 Espana" Festival.
2812 **826** 12f. multicoloured 1·00 30

827 Press Card in Hatband

1985. Cent of Professional Journalists Association.
2814 **827** 9f. multicoloured 75 30

828 Blood System as Tree

1985. Belgian Red Cross. Blood Donations.
2815 **828** 9f.+2f. multicoloured 95 95
2816 – 23f.+5f. red, blue and black 2·20 2·20
DESIGN: 23f. Two hearts.

829 *Sophrolaelio cattleya* "Burlingama"

1985. Ghent Flower Festival. Orchids. Multicoloured.
2817 12f. Type **829** 95 30
2818 12f. Phalaenopsis "Malibu" 95 30
2819 12f. Tapeu orchid ("Vanda coerulea") 95 30

830 Pope John Paul II

1985. Visit of Pope John Paul II.
2820 **830** 12f. multicoloured 95 30

831 Rising Sun behind Chained Gates

1985. Centenary of Belgian Workers' Party.
2821 **831** 9f. Type **831** 70 40
2822 12f. Broken wall, flag and rising sun 95 30

832 Jean de Bast (engraver)

1985. Stamp Day.
2823 **832** 12f. blue 95 30

834 Class 18 Steam Locomotive, 1896

1985. Public Transport Year. Multicoloured.
2826 9f. Type **834** 80 35
2827 12f. Locomotive *Elephant*, 1835 95 30
2828 23f. Class 23 tank engine, 1904 1·90 70
2829 24f. Class I Pacific locomotive, 1935 1·90 70
MS2830 150×100 mm. 50f. Class 27 electric locomotive, 1979 4·75 4·75

835 Cesar Franck and Score

1985. Europa. Music Year. Multicoloured.
2831 12f. Type **835** 2·30 30
2832 23f. Queen and King with viola dressed in music score (Queen Elisabeth International Music Competition) 4·00 70

836 Planned Canal Lock, Strepy-Thieu

1985. Permanent International Navigation Congress Association Centenary Congress, Brussels. Multicoloured.
2833 23f. Type **836** 1·90 70
2834 23f. Aerial view of Zeebrugge harbour 1·90 70

837 Church of Our Lady's Assumption, Avernas-le-Bauduin

1985. Tourist Publicity. Multicoloured.
2835 12f. Type **837** 95 35
2836 12f. Saint Martin's Church, Marcinelle (horiz) 95 35
2837 12f. Roman tower and Church of old beguinage, Tongres 95 35
2838 12f. House, Wachtebeke (horiz) 95 35

838 Queen Astrid

1985. 50th Death Anniv of Queen Astrid.
2839 **838** 12f. lt brown & brown 1·00 30

839 Baking Matton Tart, Grammont

1985. Traditional Customs. Multicoloured.
2840 12f. Type **839** 1·00 30
2841 24f. Young people dancing on trumpet filled with flowers (cent of Red Youths, St. Lambert Cultural Circle, Hermalle-sous-Argenteau) 1·90 60

840 Dove and Concentration Camp

1985. 40th Anniv of Liberation. Multicoloured.
2842 9f. Type **840** 80 35
2843 23f. Battle of the Ardennes 1·90 70
2844 24f. Troops landing at Scheldt estuary 1·90 70

841 Hawfinch ("Appelvink – Gros Bec")

1985. Birds (1st series). Multicoloured.
2845 1f. Lesser spotted woodpecker ("Pic epeichette") 35 10
2846 2f. Eurasian tree sparrow ("Moineau friquet") 30 10
2847 3f. Type **841** 60 10
2847a 3f.50 European robin ("Rouge-gorge") 35 10
2848 4f. Bluethroat ("Gorge-bleue") 45 10
2848a 4f.50 Common stonechat ("Traquet patre") 50 25
2849 5f. Eurasian nuthatch ("Sittelle torche-pot") 45 10
2850 6f. Northern bullfinch ("Bou-vreuil") 70 10
2851 7f. Blue tit ("Mesange bleue") 70 25
2852 8f. River kingfisher ("Martin-pecheur") 80 10
2853 9f. Eurasian goldfinch ("Char-donneret") 1·20 10
2854 10f. Chaffinch ("Pinson") 85 10
See also Nos. 3073/86 and 3306/23.

842 Claes and Fictional Character

1985. Birth Centenary of Ernest Claes (writer).
2855 **842** 9f. multicoloured 75 30

843 Youth

1985. "Philately for the Young". International Youth Year.
2856 **843** 9f. multicoloured 75 30

844 Trazegnies Castle

1985. "Solidarity". Castles. Multicoloured.
2857 9f.+2f. Type **844** 95 95
2858 12f.+3f. Laarne 1·20 1·20
2859 23f.+5f. Turnhout 2·00 2·00
2860 50f.+12f. Colonster 4·00 4·00

845 Miniature from *Book of Hours of Duc de Berry*

1985. Christmas.
2861 **845** 12f.+1f. multicoloured 1·00 1·00

846 King Baudouin and Queen Fabiola

1985. Royal Silver Wedding.
2862 **846** 12f. grey, blue and deep blue 1·20 30

847 Map and 1886 25c. Stamp

1986. Centenary of First Independent State of Congo Stamp.
2863 **847** 10f. blue, grey & dp blue 1·60 35

848 Giants and Belfry, Alost

1986. Carnivals. Multicoloured.
2864	9f. Type **848**	70	40
2865	12f. Clown, Binche	1·00	30

849 Dove as Hand holding Olive Twig

1986. International Peace Year.
2866	**849** 23f. multicoloured	2·00	60

850 Emblem

1986. Tenth Anniv of King Baudouin Foundation.
2867	**850** 12f.+3f. blue, light blue and grey	1·50	1·50

851 Virgin Mary

1986. *The Mystic Lamb* (altarpiece, Brothers Van Eyck). Multicoloured.
2868	9f.+2f. Type **851**	90	90
2869	13f.+3f. Christ in Majesty	1·30	1·30
2870	24f.+6f. St. John the Baptist	2·30	2·30
MS2871	92×150 mm. 50f.+12f. The Lamb (central panel) (48×37 mm)	9·00	9·00

852 Exhibits

1986. Stamp Day. 50th Anniv of Postal Museum, Brussels.
2872	**852** 13f. multicoloured	1·10	30

853 Living and Dead Fish and Graph

1986. Europa. Multicoloured.
2873	13f. Type **853**	1·90	30
2874	24f. Living and dead trees and graph	3·75	65

854 Malinois Shepherd Dog

1986. Belgian Dogs. Multicoloured.
2875	9f. Type **854**	85	40
2876	13f. Tervuren shepherd dog	1·30	30
2877	24f. Groenendael cattle dog	2·20	60
2878	26f. Flanders cattle dog	2·30	60

855 St. Ludger Church, Zele

1986. Tourist Publicity.
2879	**855**	9f. brown and flesh	70	35
2880	-	9f. red and pink	70	35
2881	-	13f. green & light green	1·10	35
2882	-	13f. black and green	1·10	35
2883	-	13f. blue and azure	1·10	35
2884	-	13f. brown & lt brown	1·10	35

DESIGNS—VERT: No. 2880, Town Hall, Wavre; 2882, Chapel of Our Lady of the Dunes, Bredene. HORIZ: 2881, Water-mills, Zwalm; 2883, Chateau Licot, Viroinval; 2884, Chateau d'Eynebourg, La Calamine.

856 Boy, Broken Skateboard and Red Triangle

1986. "Philately for the Young". 25th International Festival of Humour, Knokke.
2885	**856** 9f. black, green & red	70	40

857 Constant Permeke (artist)

1986. Celebrities. Multicoloured.
2886	Type **857** (birth centenary)	70	35
2887	13f. Michael Edmond de Selys-Longchamps (naturalist)	1·20	35
2888	24f. Felix Timmermans (writer) (birth cent)	2·10	60
2889	26f. Maurice Careme (poet)	2·20	60

858 Academy Building, Ghent

1986. Centenary of Royal Academy for Dutch Language and Literature.
2890	**858** 9f. blue	70	35

859 Hops, Glass of Beer and Barley

1986. Belgian Beer.
2891	**859** 13f. multicoloured	1·20	30

860 Symbols of Provinces and National Colours

1986. 150th Anniv of Provincial Councils.
2892	**860** 13f. multicoloured	1·10	30

861 Lenoir Hydrocarbon Carriage, 1863

1986. "Solidarity". Cars. Multicoloured.
2893	9f.+2f. Type **861**	90	90
2894	13f.+3f. Pipe de Tourisme saloon, 1911	1·30	1·30

2895	24f.+6f. Minerva 22 h.p. coupe, 1930	2·40	2·40
2896	26f.+6f. FN 8 cylinder saloon, 1931	2·50	2·50

862 Snow Scene

1986. Christmas.
2897	**862** 13f.+1f. multicoloured	1·20	1·20

863 Tree and "100"

1986. Centenaries. Multicoloured.
2898	9f. Type **863** (Textile Workers Christian Union)	70	40
2899	13f. Tree and "100" (Christian Unions)	1·10	30

864 Corneel Heymans

1987. Belgian Red Cross. Nobel Physiology and Medicine Prize Winners. Each black, red and stone.
2900	13f.+3f. Type **864**	1·50	1·50
2901	24f.+6f. Albert Claude	2·75	2·75

865 Emblem

1987. "Flanders Technology International" Fair.
2902	**865** 13f. multicoloured	1·10	30

866 Bee Orchid

1987. European Environment Year. Multicoloured.
2903	9f.+2f. Type **866**	1·10	1·10
2904	24f.+6f. Small horse-shoe bat	2·40	2·40
2905	26f.+6f. Peregrine falcon (Slech-tvalk–Faucan Pelerin)	2·75	2·75

867 *Waiting* (detail of mural, Gustav Klimt)

1987. "Europalia 87 Austria" Festival.
2906	**867** 13f. multicoloured	1·10	30

868 Jakob Wiener (engraver)

1987. Stamp Day.
2907	**868** 13f. deep green and green	1·10	30

869 Penitents' Procession, Furnes

1987. Folklore Festivals. Multicoloured.
2908	9f. Type **869**	70	40
2909	13f. "John and Alice" (play), Wavre	1·10	30

870 Louvain-la-Neuve Church (Jean Cosse)

1987. Europa. Architecture. Multicoloured.
2910	13f. Type **870**	2·40	30
2911	24f. St.-Maartensdal (Regional Housing Association tower block), Louvain (Braem, de Mol and Moerkerke)	4·25	90

871 Statue of Gretry and Stage Set

1987. 20th Anniv of Wallonia Royal Opera.
2912	**871** 24f. multicoloured	2·10	70

872 Virelles Lake

1987. Tourist Publicity. Multicoloured.
2913	13f. St. Christopher's Church, Racour	1·10	30
2914	13f. Type **872**	1·10	30
2915	13f. Heimolen windmill, Keerbergen	1·10	30
2916	13f. Boondael Chapel	1·10	30
2917	13f. Statue of Jan Breydel and Pieter de Coninck, Bruges	1·10	30

873 Rowing

1987. Centenary of Royal Belgian Rowing Association (2918) and European Volleyball Championships (2919). Multicoloured.
2918	9f. Type **873**	70	40
2919	13f. Volleyball (27×37 mm)	1·10	30

874 Emblem

1987. Foreign Trade Year.
2920	**874** 13f. multicoloured	1·10	30

875 *Leisure Time* (P. Paulus)

1987. Centenary of Belgian Social Law.
2921	**875** 26f. multicoloured	2·10	65

876 Willy and Wanda (comic strip characters)

1987. "Philately for the Young".

| 2922 | **876** | 9f. multicoloured | 2·10 | 60 |

878 Rixensart Castle

1987. "Solidarity". Castles. Multicoloured.

2928		9f.+2f. Type **878**	90	90
2929		13f.+3f. Westerlo	1·20	1·20
2930		26f.+5f. Fallais	2·40	2·40
2931		50f.+12f. Gaasbeek	4·50	4·50

879 *Madonna and Child* (Remi Lens)

1987. Christmas.

| 2932 | **879** | 13f.+1f. multicoloured | 1·20 | 1·20 |

880 Cross and Road

1987. 50th Anniv of Yellow and White Cross (home nursing organization).

| 2933 | **880** | 9f.+2f. multicoloured | 1·20 | 1·20 |

881 Newsprint ("Le Soir")

1987. Newspaper Centenaries.

| 2934 | **881** | 9f. multicoloured | 85 | 35 |
| 2935 | - | 9f. black and brown | 85 | 35 |

DESIGN—VERT: No. 2935, Type characters (*Het Laatste Nieuws* (1988)).

882 Lighthouse, *Snipe* (trawler) and Horse Rider in Sea

1988. The Sea. Multicoloured.

2936		10f. Type **882**	85	70
2937		10f. *Asannot* (trawler) and people playing on beach	85	70
2938		10f. Cross-channel ferry, yacht and bathing huts	85	70
2939		10f. Container ship, spotted redshank and oystercatcher	85	70

Nos. 2936/9 were issued together, *se-tenant*, forming a composite design.

883 *Flanders Alive* (cultural activities campaign)

1988. Regional Innovations.

| 2940 | **883** | 13f. multicoloured | 1·10 | 30 |
| 2941 | - | 13f. black, yellow & red | 1·10 | 30 |

DESIGN: No. 2941, "Operation Athena" emblem (technological advancement in Wallonia).

884 19th-century Postman (after James Thiriar)

1988. Stamp Day.

| 2942 | **884** | 13f. brown and cream | 1·10 | 30 |

885 *Bengale Triomphant*

1988. Philatelic Promotion Fund. Illustrations from *60 Roses for a Queen* by Pierre-Joseph Redouté (1st series). Multicoloured.

2943		13f.+3f. Type **885**	1·50	1·50
2944		24f.+6f. *Centfeuille cristata*	2·40	2·40
MS2945	150×100 mm. 50f.+12f. White tea rose		8·50	8·50

See also Nos. 2979/**MS**2981, 3009/**MS**3011 and **MS**3025.

886 Non-polluting Motor

1988. Europa. Transport and Communications. Multicoloured.

| 2946 | | 13f. Dish aerial | 2·40 | 30 |
| 2947 | | 24f. Type **886** | 4·75 | 90 |

887 Table Tennis

1988. Olympic Games, Seoul. Multicoloured.

2948		9f.+2f. Type **887**	1·30	1·30
2949		13f.+3f. Cycling	1·50	1·50
MS2950	125×85 mm. 50f.+12f. Running		8·50	8·50

888 Amay Tower

1988. Tourist Publicity.

2951	**888**	9f. black and brown	85	35
2952	-	9f. black and blue	85	35
2953	-	9f. black, green and pink	85	35
2954	-	13f. black and pink	1·10	30
2955	-	13f. black and grey	1·10	30

DESIGNS—VERT: No. 2952, Lady of Hanswijk Basilica, Malines; 2954, Old Town Hall and village pump, Peer. HORIZ: No. 2953, St. Sernin's Church, Waimes; 2955, Basilica of Our Lady of Bon Secours, Peruwelz.

889 Monnet

1988. Birth Centenary of Jean Monnet (statesman).

| 2956 | **889** | 13f. black and cream | 1·10 | 30 |

890 Tapestry (detail) and Academy Building

1988. 50th Annivs of Royal Belgian Academy of Medicine (2957) and Royal Belgian Academy of Sciences, Literature and Fine Arts (2958). Multicoloured.

| 2957 | | 9f. Type **890** | 70 | 35 |
| 2958 | | 9f. Symbols of Academy and building | 70 | 35 |

891 Antwerp Ethnographical Museum Exhibits

1988. Cultural Heritage. Multicoloured.

2959		9f. Type **891**	85	35
2960		13f. Tomb of Lord Gilles Othon and Jacqueline de Lalaing, St. Martin's Church, Trazegnies	1·10	30
2961		24f. Organ, St. Bartholomew's Church, Geraardsbergen	2·10	70
2962		26f. St. Hadelin's reliquary, St. Martin's Church, Vise	2·30	70

892 Spirou (comic strip character) and Stamp

1988. "Philately for the Young". 50th Anniv of "Spirou" (comic).

| 2963 | **892** | 9f. multicoloured | 1·80 | 60 |

893 Jacques Brel (songwriter)

1988. "Solidarity". Death Anniversaries. Multicoloured.

2964		9f.+2f. Type **893** (10th)	1·50	1·50
2965		13f.+3f. Jef Denyn (carilloner) (47th)	1·50	1·50
2966		26f.+6f. Fr. Ferdinand Verbiest (astronomer) (300th)	2·40	2·40

894 "75"

1988. 75th Anniv of Belgian Giro Bank.

| 2967 | **894** | 13f. multicoloured | 1·20 | 30 |

895 Winter Scene

1988. Christmas.

| 2968 | **895** | 9f. multicoloured | 80 | 35 |

896 Standard Bearer and Guards of Royal Mounted Escort

1988. 50th Anniv of Royal Mounted Escort.

| 2969 | **896** | 13f. multicoloured | 1·10 | 30 |

897 Wooden Press, 1600

1988. Printing Presses.

2970	**897**	9f. black, pink and blue	85	30
2971	-	24f. brown, pink and deep brown	1·90	65
2972	-	26f. green, pink and light green	2·10	60

DESIGNS—VERT: 24f. 18th-cent Stanhope metal letterpress. HORIZ: 26f. 19th-cent Krause lithographic press.

898 *Crucifixion of Christ* (detail, Rogier van der Weyden)

1989. Belgian Red Cross. Paintings. Multicoloured.

2973		9f.+2f. Type **898**	1·20	1·20
2974		13f.+3f. "Virgin and Child" (Gerard David)	1·70	1·70
2975		24f.+6f. "The Good Samaritan" (detail, Denis van Alsloot)	2·50	2·50

899 Marche en Famenne

1989. Lace-making Towns.

2976	**899**	9f. green, black & brown	85	40
2977	-	13f. blue, black & grey	1·10	30
2978	-	13f. red, black & grey	1·10	30

DESIGNS: No. 2977, Bruges; 2978, Brussels.

1989. Philatelic Promotion Fund. *60 Roses for a Queen* by Pierre-Joseph Redouté (2nd series). As T **885**. Multicoloured.

2979		13f.+5f. *Centfeuille unique melee de rouge*	1·50	1·50
2980		24f.+6f. *Bengale a grandes feuilles*	2·40	2·40
MS2981	150×100 mm. 50f.+17f. *Aime vibere*		8·50	8·50

900 Post-chaise and Mail Coach

1989. Stamp Day.

| 2982 | **900** | 13f. yellow, black & brn | 1·00 | 30 |

901 Marbles

1989. Europa. Children's Games and Toys. Multicoloured.

| 2983 | | 13f. Type **901** | 2·20 | 30 |
| 2984 | | 24f. Jumping-jack | 3·75 | 70 |

902 Palette on Column

1989. 325th Anniv of Royal Academy of Fine Arts, Antwerp.

| 2985 | **902** | 13f. multicoloured | 1·00 | 30 |

903 Brussels

1989. Third Direct Elections to European Parliament.
2986 **903** 13f. multicoloured 1·00 30

904 Hand (detail, "Creation of Adam", Michelangelo)

1989. Bicentenary of French Declaration of Rights of Man.
2987 **904** 13f. black, red and blue 1·00 30

905 St. Tillo's Church, Izegem

1989. Tourist Publicity. Multicoloured.
2988 9f. Type **905** 85 35
2989 9f. Logne Castle, Ferrieres (vert) 85 35
2990 13f. Antoing Castle (vert) 1·20 30
2991 13f. St. Laurentius's Church, Lokeren (vert) 1·20 30

906 Mallard

1989. Ducks. Multicoloured.
2992 13f. Type **906** 1·50 60
2993 13f. Green-winged teal ("Sarcelle d'Hiver") 1·50 60
2994 13f. Common shoveler ("Canard Souchet") 1·50 60
2995 13f. Pintail ("Canard Pilet") 1·50 60

907 Shogun Uesugi Shigefusa (Kamakura period wood figure)

1989. "Europalia 89 Japan" Festival.
2996 **907** 24f. multicoloured 1·90 70

908 Profiles

1989. 125th Anniv of League of Teaching and Permanent Education.
2997 **908** 13f. multicoloured 1·00 30

909 Map

1989. 150th Anniv of Division of Limburg between Netherlands and Belgium.
2998 **909** 13f. multicoloured 1·00 30

910 Nibbs (comic strip character)

1989. "Philately for the Young".
2999 **910** 9f. multicoloured 1·50 50

911 Flower Beds in Greenhouse

1989. "Solidarity". Royal Greenhouses, Laeken. Multicoloured.
3000 9f.+3f. Statue and greenhouses (horiz) 1·20 1·20
3001 13f.+4f. Type **911** 1·60 1·60
3002 24f.+5f. External view of greenhouse 2·30 2·30
3003 26f.+6f. Trees in greenhouse 2·50 2·50

912 Treble Clef

1989. 50th Anniv of Queen Elisabeth Musical Chapel, Waterloo.
3004 **912** 24f.+6f. multicoloured 2·40 2·40

913 Army Musicians

1989. Christmas. Centenary of Salvation Army in Belgium.
3005 **913** 9f. multicoloured 80 30

914 Fr. Damien and Church

1989. Death Cent of Fr. Damien (missionary).
3006 **914** 24f. multicoloured 2·10 65

915 Fr. Daens

1989. 150th Birth Anniv of Fr. Adolf Daens (social reformer).
3007 **915** 9f. turquoise and green 70 30

916 Courier (Albrecht Durer)

1990. 500th Anniv of Regular European Postal Services.
3008 **916** 14f. chocolate, buff and brown 1·10 30

1990. Philatelic Promotion Fund. 60 Roses for a Queen by Pierre-Joseph Redoute (3rd series). As T **885**. Multicoloured.
3009 14f.+7f. Bengale Desprez 1·80 1·80
3010 25f.+12f. Bengale Philippe 3·00 3·00
MS3011 151×100 mm. 50f.+20f. Maria Leonida 8·50 8·50

917 Iris florentina

1990. Ghent Flower Show. Multicoloured.
3012 10f. Type **917** 85 50
3013 14f. Cattleya harrisoniana 1·20 35
3014 14f. Lilium bulbiferum 1·20 35

918 Emilienne Brunfaut (women's rights activist)

1990. International Women's Day.
3015 **918** 25f. red and black 2·10 85

919 Special Olympics

1990. Sporting Events. Multicoloured.
3016 10f. Type **919** 80 50
3017 14f. Football (World Cup football championship, Italy) 1·20 35
3018 25f. Disabled pictogram and ball (Gold Cup wheelchair basketball championship, Bruges) 1·90 70

920 Water, Tap and Heart

1990. 75th Anniv of Foundation of National Water Supply Society (predecessor of present water-supply companies).
3019 **920** 14f. multicoloured 1·10 30

921 Postman Roulin (Vincent van Gogh)

1990. Stamp Day.
3020 **921** 14f. multicoloured 1·10 30

922 Worker and Crowd

1990. Centenary of Labour Day.
3021 **922** 25f. brown, pink & black 2·10 85

923 Liege I Post Office

1990. Europa. Post Office Buildings.
3022 – 14f. black and blue 2·40 35
3023 **923** 25f. black and red 4·50 85
DESIGN—HORIZ: 14f. Ostend I Post Office.

924 Monument of the Lys, Courtrai

1990. 50th Anniv of the 18 Days Campaign (resistance to German invasion).
3024 **924** 14f. black, yellow & red 1·20 30

1990. "Belgica 90" International Stamp Exhibition, Brussels. 60 Roses for a Queen by Pierre-Joseph Rerdoute (4th series). Sheet 189×120 mm containing vert designs as T **885**. Multicoloured.
MS3025 14f. Tricoloured rose; 14f. Belle Rubanee; 14f. Mycrophylla; 25f. Amelie; 25f. Adelaide; 25f. Helene (sold at 220f.) 36·00 36·00

925 Battle Scene

1990. 175th Anniv of Battle of Waterloo.
3026 **925** 25f. multicoloured 2·10 1·80

926 Berendrecht Lock, Antwerp

1990. Tourist Publicity. Multicoloured.
3027 10f. Type **926** 95 50
3028 10f. Procession of Bayard Steed, Termonde 95 50
3029 14f. St. Rolende's March, Gerpinnes (vert) 1·10 35
3030 14f. Lommel (1000th anniv) 1·10 35
3031 14f. St. Clement's Church, Watermael 1·10 35

927 King Baudouin

1990
3032 **927** 14f. multicoloured 1·30 25

928 Eurasian Perch

1990. Fishes. Multicoloured.
3033 14f. Type **928** 2·10 70
3034 14f. Eurasian minnow ("Vairon") 2·10 70
3035 14f. European bitterling ("Bouviere") 2·10 70
3036 14f. Three-spined stickle-back ("Epinoche") 2·10 70

929 Orchestra and Children

1990. "Solidarity". Multicoloured.
3037 10f.+2f. Type **929** (50th anniv of Jeunesses Musicales) 2·20 2·20
3038 14f.+3f. Count of Egmont (16th-century campaigner for religious tolerance) and Beethoven (composer of "Egmont" overture) 2·75 2·75
3039 25f.+6f. Jozef Cantre (sculptor) and sculptures (birth centenary) 3·75 3·75

930 Lucky Luke (comic strip character)

1990. "Philately for the Young".
| 3040 | **930** | 10f. multicoloured | 1·80 | 60 |

931 St. Bernard

1990. 900th Birth Anniv of St. Bernard (Abbot of Clairvaux and Church mediator).
| 3041 | **931** | 25f. black and flesh | 2·10 | 70 |

932 *Pepingen, Winter 1977* (Jozef Lucas)

1990. Christmas.
| 3042 | **932** | 10f. multicoloured | 85 | 30 |

933 *Self-portrait*

1990. 300th Death Anniv of David Teniers, the Younger (painter). Multicoloured.
3043		10f. Type **933**	85	35
3044		14f. *Dancers*	1·20	35
3045		25f. *Peasants playing Bowls outside Village Inn*	2·20	70

934 King Baudouin and Queen Fabiola (photograph by Valeer Vanbeckbergen)

1990. Royal 30th Wedding Anniversary.
| 3046 | **934** | 50f.+15f. mult | 8·50 | 8·50 |

935 *Temptation of St. Anthony* (detail, Hieronymus Bosch)

1991. Belgian Red Cross. Paintings. Multicoloured.
| 3047 | | 14f.+3f. Type **935** | 2·75 | 2·75 |
| 3048 | | 25f.+6f. *The Annunciation* (detail, Dirck Bouts) | 4·00 | 4·00 |

936 "The Sower" (detail of *Monument to Labour*, Brussels) (Constantin Meunier)

1991. 19th-Century Sculpture.
| 3049 | **936** | 14f. black & cinnamon | 1·10 | 35 |
| 3050 | - | 25f. black and blue | 1·80 | 70 |
DESIGN: 25f. Detail of Brabo Fountain, Antwerp (Jef Lambeaux).

937 Rhythmic Gymnastics (European Youth Olympic Days, Brussels)

1991. Sports Meetings.
| 3051 | **937** | 10f. grey, mauve & blk | 80 | 30 |
| 3052 | - | 10f. grey, green & black | 80 | 30 |
DESIGN: No. 3052, Korfball (Third World Championship, Belgium).

938 New Stamp Printing Office, Malines (Hugo van Hoecke)

1991. Stamp Day.
| 3053 | **938** | 14f. multicoloured | 1·10 | 35 |

939 Cogwheels

1991. Centenary of Liberal Trade Union.
| 3054 | **939** | 25f. blue, light blue and deep blue | 1·90 | 70 |

940 "Olympus 1" Communications Satellite

1991. Europa. Europe in Space. Multicoloured.
| 3055 | | 14f. Type **940** | 2·40 | 30 |
| 3056 | | 25f. "Ariane 5" rocket carrying space shuttle *Hermes* | 4·00 | 80 |

941 Leo XIII's Arms and Standard, and Christian Labour Movement Banners

1991. Centenary of "Rerum Novarum" (encyclical letter from Pope Leo XIII on workers' rights).
| 3057 | **941** | 14f. multicoloured | 1·10 | 30 |

942 *Isabella of Portugal and Philip the Good* (anon)

1991. "Europalia 91 Portugal" Festival.
| 3058 | **942** | 14f. multicoloured | 1·10 | 30 |

943 Neptune Grottoes, Couvin

1991. Tourist Publicity. Multicoloured.
3059		14f. Type **943**	1·10	35
3060		14f. Dieleghem Abbey, Jette	1·10	35
3061		14f. Niel Town Hall (vert)	1·10	35
3062		14f. Hautes Fagnes nature reserve	1·10	35
3063		14f. Giant Rolarius, Roeselare (vert)	1·10	35

944 King Baudouin (photograph by Dimitri Ardelean)

1991. 60th Birthday (1990) and 40th Anniv of Accession to Throne of King Baudouin.
| 3064 | **944** | 14f. multicoloured | 2·20 | 30 |

945 Academy Building, Caduceus and Leopold I

1991. 150th Anniv of Royal Academy of Medicine.
| 3065 | **945** | 10f. multicoloured | 80 | 35 |

946 "The English Coast at Dover"

1991. 61st Death Anniv of Alfred Finch (painter and ceramic artist).
| 3066 | **946** | 25f. multicoloured | 2·00 | 70 |

947 Death Cap

1991. Fungi. Multicoloured.
3067		14f. Type **947**	2·10	85
3068		14f. The Blusher (inscr "Gol-motte")	2·10	85
3069		14f. Flaky-stemmed witches' mushroom (inscr "Bolet a pied rouge")	2·10	85
3070		14f. "Hygrocybe persistens" (inscr "Hygrophore jaune conique")	2·10	85

948 Hands reaching through Bars

1991. 30th Anniv of Amnesty International (3071) and 11th Anniv of Belgian Branch of Medecins sans Frontieres (3072). Multicoloured.
| 3071 | | 25f. Type **948** | 2·00 | 70 |
| 3072 | | 25f. Doctor examining baby | 2·00 | 70 |

1991. Birds (2nd series). As T **841**. Multicoloured.
3073		50c. Goldcrest ("Roitelet Huppe")	15	15
3074		1f. Redpoll ("Sizerin Flamme")	25	15
3075		2f. Blackbird ("Merle Noir")	25	15
3076		3f. Reed bunting ("Bruant des Roseaux")	50	15
3077		4f. Pied wagtail ("Bergeronette Grise")	45	15
3078		5f. Barn swallow ("Hirondelle de Cheminee")	45	15
3079		5f.50 Jay ("Geai des Chenes")	65	25
3080		6f. White-throated dipper ("Cincle Plongeur")	65	15
3081		6f.50 Sedge-warbler ("Phragmite des Jones")	65	25
3082		7f. Golden oriole ("Loriot")	75	15
3083		8f. Great tit ("Mesange Charbonniere")	75	15
3084		9f. Song thrush ("Grive Musicienne")	90	25
3085		10f. Western greenfinch ("Verdier")	95	25
3086		11f. Winter wren ("Troglodyte Mignon")	1·00	15
3087		13f. House sparrow ("Moineau Domestique")	1·30	15
3088		14f. Willow warbler ("Pouillot Fitis")	1·30	25
3088a		16f. Bohemian waxwing ("Jaseur Boreal")	1·60	15

949 Exhibition Emblem

1991. "Telecom 91" International Telecommunications Exhibition, Geneva.
| 3089 | **949** | 14f. multicoloured | 1·10 | 30 |

950 Blake and Mortimer in *The Yellow Mark* (Edgar P. Jacobs)

1991. "Philately for the Young". Comic Strips. Multicoloured.
3090		14f. Type **950**	2·00	1·30
3091		14f. Cori the ship boy in "The Ill-fated Voyage" (Bob de Moor)	2·00	1·30
3092		14f. *Cities of the Fantastic* (Francois Schuiten)	2·00	1·30
3093		14f. *Boule and Bill* (Jean Roba)	2·00	1·30

951 Charles Dekeukeleire

1991. "Solidarity". Film Makers.
3094	**951**	10f.+2f. black, brown and green	1·30	1·30
3095	-	14f.+3f. black, orange and brown	1·90	1·90
3096	-	25f.+6f. black, ochre and brown	3·50	3·50
DESIGNS: 14f. Jacques Ledoux; 25f. Jacques Feyder.

952 Printing Press forming "100" ("Gazet van Antwerpen")

1991. Newspaper Centenaries. Multicoloured.
| 3097 | **952** | 10f. black, lt grn & grn | 80 | 30 |
| 3098 | - | 10f. yellow, blue & blk | 80 | 30 |
DESIGN: No. 3098, Cancellation on "stamp" ("Het Volk").

953 *Our Lady rejoicing in the Child* (icon, Chevetogne Abbey)

1991. Christmas.
| 3099 | **953** | 10f. multicoloured | 75 | 40 |

954 Mozart and Score

1991. Death Bicentenary of Wolfgang Amadeus Mozart (composer).
| 3100 | **954** | 25f. purple, bl & ultram | 2·10 | 1·00 |

955 Speed
Skating

1992. Olympic Games, Albertville and Barcelona. Multicoloured.
3101	10f.+2f.	Type **955**	1·40	1·40
3102	10f.+2f.	Baseball	1·40	1·40
3103	14f.+3f.	Tennis (horiz)	1·90	1·90
3104	25f.+6f.	Clay-pigeon shooting	3·50	3·50

956 Fire Hose
and Service
Emblem

1992. Fire Service.
3105	**956**	14f. multicoloured	1·10	30

957 Flames and
Silhouette of Man

1992. The Resistance.
3106	**957**	14f. yellow, black & red	1·10	30

958 Tapestry and
Carpet

1992. Prestige Occupations. Multicoloured.
3107	10f. Type **958**		75	45
3108	14f. Chef's hat and cutlery (10th anniv (1991) of Association of Belgian Master Chefs)		1·10	30
3109	27f. Diamond and "100" (centenary (1993) of Antwerp Diamond Club)		2·20	70

959 Belgian Pavilion and
Exhibition Emblem

1992. "Expo '92" World's Fair, Seville.
3110	**959**	14f. multicoloured	1·10	30

960 King **961**
Baudouin

1992
3111	**960**	15f. red	1·10	15
3115	**960**	28f. green	2·50	70
3120	**961**	100f. green	9·50	65

962 Van Noten at
Work

1992. Stamp Day. Tenth Death Anniv of Jean van Noten (stamp designer).
3124	**962**	15f. black and red	1·10	30

963 White Magic No. VI

1992. Original Art Designs for Stamps. Multicoloured.
3125	15f. Type **963**		1·10	40
3126	15f. Colours (horiz)		1·10	40

964 Compass Rose, Setting Sun
and Harbour

1992. Europa. 500th Anniv of Discovery of America. Multicoloured.
3127	15f. Type **964**		2·50	45
3128	28f. Globe and astrolabe forming "500"		5·00	95

965 Faces of
Different Colours

1992. Anti-racism.
3129	**965**	15f. grey, black & pink	1·10	30

966 The Hamlet (Jacob Smits)

1992. Belgian Paintings in Orsay Museum, Paris. Multicoloured.
3130	11f. Type **966**		80	40
3131	15f. The Bath (Alfred Stevens)		1·40	30
3132	30f. Man at the Helm (Theo van Rysselberghe)		2·50	90

967 Proud Margaret

1992. Folk Tales. Multicoloured.
3133	11f.+2f. Type **967**		1·60	1·60
3134	15f.+3f. Witches (Les Macrales)		2·20	2·20
3135	28f.+6f. Reynard the fox		3·75	3·75

968 Mannekin-Pis,
Brussels

1992. Tourist Publicity. Multicoloured.
3136	15f. Type **968**		1·10	30
3137	15f. Former Landcommandery of Teutonic Order, Alden Biesen (now Flemish cultural centre) (horiz)		1·10	30
3138	15f. Andenne (1300th anniv)		1·10	30
3139	15f. Carnival revellers on Fools' Monday, Renaix (horiz)		1·10	30
3140	15f. Great Procession (religious festival), Tournai (horiz)		1·10	30

969 European Polecat

1992. Mammals. Multicoloured.
3141	15f. Type **969**		1·90	80
3142	15f. Eurasian red squirrel		1·90	80
3143	15f. Eurasian hedgehog		1·90	80
3144	15f. Common dormouse		1·90	80

970 Henri van der Noot, Jean
van der Meersch and Jean Vonck

1992. 203rd Anniv of Brabant Revolution.
3145	**970**	15f. multicoloured	1·10	30

971 Arms of
Thurn and Taxis

1992. 500th Anniv of Mention of Thurn and Taxis Postal Services in Lille Account Books.
3146	**971**	15f. multicoloured	1·10	30

972 Gaston Lagaffe
(cartoon character)

1992. "Philately for the Young".
3147	**972**	15f. multicoloured	1·50	45

973 Star, "B" and Map

1992. European Single Market.
3148	**973**	15f. multicoloured	1·10	40

974 Okapi

1992. 150th Anniv of Antwerp Zoo. Multicoloured.
3149	15f. Type **974**		1·10	40
3150	30f. Golden-headed tamarin		2·30	50

975 Place Royale in Winter
(Luc de Decker)

1992. Christmas.
3151	**975**	11f. multicoloured	75	30

976 Man with Pointed Hat
(Adriaen Brouwer)

1993. Belgian Red Cross. Paintings. Multicoloured.
3152	15f.+3f. Type **976**		2·40	2·40
3153	28f.+7f. Nereid and Triton (Peter Paul Rubens) (horiz)		4·75	4·75

977 Council of Leptines,
743

1993. Historical Events. Multicoloured.
3154	11f. Type **977**		75	40
3155	15f. Queen Beatrix and King Matthias I Corvinus of Hungary (detail of "Missale Romanum") (77×24 mm)		1·30	40
3156	30f. Battle scene (Battles of Neerwinden, 1673 and 1773)		2·50	75
MS3157	105×155 mm. 28f. Illustration from Matthias I Corvinus's Missale Romanum, 1485 (54×39 mm)		2·50	2·50

978 Town Hall

1993. Antwerp, European City of Culture. Multicoloured.
3158	15f. Panorama of Antwerp (76×24 mm)		1·30	30
3159	15f. Type **978**		1·30	30
3160	15f. "Study of Women's Heads and Male Torso" (Jacob Jordaens)		1·30	30
3161	15f. St. Job's altarpiece, Schoonbroek		1·30	30
3162	15f. "Angels" (stained glass window by Eugeen Yoors, Mother of God Chapel, Marie-Josee Institute, Elisa-bethville) (vert)		1·30	30

979 1893 2f. Stamp

1993. Stamp Day.
3163	**979**	15f. multicoloured	1·10	30

980 "Florence
1960" (Gaston
Bertrand)

1993. Europa. Contemporary Art. Multicoloured.
3164	15f. Type **980**		1·30	30
3165	28f. The Gig (Constant Permeke)		2·50	75

981 Red Admiral (Vanessa
atalanta)

1993. Butterflies. Multicoloured.
3166	15f. Type **981**		1·10	40
3167	15f. Purple emperor (Apatura iris)		1·10	40

3168		15f. Peacock (*Inachis io*)	1·10	40
3169		15f. Small tortoiseshell (*Aglais urticae*)	1·10	40

982 Knot

1993. 150th Anniv of Alumni of Free University of Brussels Association.

3170	**982**	15f. blue and black	1·10	30

983 Mayan Warrior (statuette)

1993. "Europalia 93 Mexico" Festival.

3171	**983**	15f. multicoloured	1·10	30

984 Ommegang, Brussels

1993. Folklore Festivals. Multicoloured.

3172		11f. Type **984**	95	45
3173		15f. Royale Moncrabeau, Namur	1·10	30
3174		28f. Stilt-walkers, Merchtem (vert)	1·90	75

985 La Hulpe Castle

1993. Tourist Publicity.

3175	**985**	15f. black and blue	1·10	30
3176	-	15f. black and lilac	1·10	30
3177	-	15f. black and grey	1·10	30
3178	-	15f. black and pink	1·10	30
3179	-	15f. black and green	1·10	30

DESIGNS—HORIZ: No. 3176, Cortewalle Castle, Beveren; 3177, Jehay Castle; 3179, Raeren Castle. VERT: No. 3178, Arenberg Castle, Heverlee.

986 Emblem

1993. Second International Triennial Textile Exhibition, Tournai.

3180	**986**	15f. blue, red and black	1·10	30

987 Presidency Emblem

1993. Belgian Presidency of European Community Council.

3181	**987**	15f. multicoloured	1·10	30

988 Magritte

1993. 25th Death Anniv (1992) of Rene Magritte (artist).

3182	**988**	30f. multicoloured	2·20	90

989 King Baudouin

1993. King Baudouin Commemoration.

3183	**989**	15f. black and blue	1·30	25

990 Red and White Cat

1993. Cats. Multicoloured.

3184		15f. Type **990**	1·40	75
3185		15f. Tabby and white cat standing on rock	1·40	75
3186		15f. Silver tabby lying on wall	1·40	75
3187		15f. Tortoiseshell and white cat sitting by gardening tools	1·40	75

991 Highlighted Cancer Cell

1993. Anti-cancer Campaign.

3188	**991**	15f.+3f. multicoloured	1·90	1·90

992 Frontispiece

1993. 450th Anniv of *De Humani Corporis Fabrica* (treatise on human anatomy) by Andreas Vesalius.

3189	**992**	15f. black, brown & red	1·10	30

993 Natacha (cartoon character)

1993. "Philately for the Young".

3190	**993**	15f. multicoloured	1·40	50

994 Sun's Rays

1993. 50th Anniv of Publication of *Le Faux Soir* (resistance newspaper).

3191	**994**	11f. multicoloured	80	50

995 *Madonna and Child* (statue, Our Lady of the Chapel, Brussels)

1993. Christmas.

3192	**995**	11f. multicoloured	75	30

996 Child looking at Globe

1993. Children's Town Councils.

3193	**996**	15f. multicoloured	1·10	30

997 King Albert II **998** King Albert II

1993

3194	**997**	16f. multicoloured	1·70	15
3195	**997**	16f. turquoise and blue	1·30	20
3196	**997**	20f. brown and stone	1·70	25
3197	**997**	30f. purple and mauve	1·90	25
3198	**997**	32f. orange and yellow	2·20	15
3199	**997**	40f. red and mauve	3·00	15
3200	**997**	50f. myrtle and green	5·25	25
3201	**998**	100f. multicoloured	7·50	45
3202	**998**	200f. multicoloured	16·00	65

999 *Ma Toute Belle* (Serge Vandercam)

1994. Painters' Designs. Multicoloured.

3210		16f. Type **999**	1·10	40
3211		16f. *The Malleable Darkness* (Octave Landuyt) (horiz)	1·10	40

1000 Olympic Flames and Rings

1994. Sports. Multicoloured.

3212		16f.+3f. Type **1000** (cent of International Olympic Committee)	2·20	2·20
3213		16f.+3f. Footballers (World Cup Football Championship, U.S.A.)	2·20	2·20
3214		16f.+3f. Skater (Winter Olympic Games, Lillehammer, Norway)	2·20	2·20

1001 Hanriot HD-1

1994. Biplanes. Multicoloured.

3215		13f. Type **1001**	1·10	45
3216		15f. Spad XIII	1·30	40
3217		30f. Schrenck FBA.H flying boat	2·20	75
3218		32f. Stampe SV-4B biplane	2·30	65

1002 Masthead of *Le Jour-Le Courrier* (centenary)

1994. Newspaper Anniversaries. Multicoloured.

3219		16f. Type **1002**	1·10	40
3220		16f. Masthead of *La Wallonie* (75th anniv) (horiz)	1·10	40

1003 *Fall of the Golden Calf* (detail, Fernand Allard l'Olivier)

1994. Centenary of Charter of Quaregnon (social charter).

3221	**1003**	16f. multicoloured	1·10	45

1004 1912 5f. Stamp

1994. Stamp Day. 60th Death Anniv of King Albert I.

3222	**1004**	16f. purple, mauve & bl	1·10	40

1005 Reconciliation of Duke John I and Arnold, Squire of Wezemaal

1994. 700th Death Anniv of John I, Duke of Brabant. Illustrations from 15th-century *Brabantse Yeesten*. Multicoloured.

3223		13f. Type **1005**	95	45
3224		16f. Tournament at wedding of his son John to Margaret of York, 1290	1·10	40
3225		30f. Battle of Woeringen (77×25 mm)	2·40	90

1006 Georges Lemaitre (formulator of expanding Universe and of "big bang" theory)

1994. Europa. Discoveries and Inventions. Multicoloured.

3226		16f. Type **1006**	1·30	40
3227		30f. Gerardus Mercator (inventor of Mercator projection in cartography)	2·50	90

1007 Father Damien (missionary and leprosy worker)

1994. Visit of Pope John Paul II. Multicoloured.

3228		16f. Type **1007** (beatification)	1·10	30
3229		16f. St. Mutien-Marie (5th anniv of canonization)	1·10	30

1008 St. Peter's Church, Bertem

1994. Tourist Publicity. Multicoloured.

3230		16f. Type **1008**	1·10	40
3231		16f. St. Bavo's Church, Kanegem (vert)	1·10	40
3232		16f. Royal St. Mary's Church, Schaarbeek	1·10	40
3233		16f. St. Gery's Church, Aubechies	1·10	40
3234		16f. Sts. Peter and Paul's Church, St.-Severin en Condroz (vert)	1·10	40

1009 Tournai Porcelain Plate from Duke of Orleans Service (Mariemont Museum)

1994. Museum Exhibits. Multicoloured.

3235		16f.+3f. Type **1009**	1·90	1·90
3236		16f.+3f. Etterbeek porcelain coffee cup and saucer (Louvain Municipal Museum)	1·90	1·90
MS3237		125×90 mm. 50f.+11f. Delft containers (Pharmacy Museum, Maaseik)	9·50	9·50

1010 Guillame Lekeu (composer)

1994. Anniversaries. Multicoloured.

3238		16f. Type **1010** (death cent)	1·10	40

3239 16f. Detail of painting by Hans Memling (500th death anniv) 1·10 40

1011 Generals Crerar, Montgomery and Bradley and Allied Troops

1994. 50th Anniv of Liberation.
3240 **1011** 16f. multicoloured 1·30 40

1012 Marsh Marigold (*Caltha palustris*)

1994. Flowers. Multicoloured.
3241 16f. Type **1012** 1·60 75
3242 16f. White helleborine ("Cephalanthera damasonium") 1·60 75
3243 16f. Sea bindweed ("Calystegia soldanella") 1·60 75
3244 16f. Broad-leaved helleborine ("Epipactis helleborine") 1·60 75

1013 Cubitus (cartoon character)

1994. "Philately for the Young".
3245 **1013** 16f. multicoloured 1·60 50

1014 Simenon and Bridge of Arches, Liege

1994. Fifth Death Anniv of Georges Simenon (novelist).
3246 **1014** 16f. multicoloured 1·60 40

The depiction of the bridge alludes to Simenon's first novel Au Pont des Arches.

1015 Deaf Man and Butterfly

1994. "Solidarity".
3247 **1015** 16f.+3f. mult 1·50 1·50

1016 Santa Claus on Rooftop

1994. Christmas.
3248 **1016** 13f. multicoloured 95 40

1017 Field and Flax Knife (Flax Museum, Courtrai)

1995. Museums. Multicoloured.
3249 16f.+3f. Type **1017** 1·40 1·40
3250 16f.+3f. River and pump (Water and Fountain Museum, Genval) 1·40 1·40
MS3251 125×90 mm. 34f.+6f. Mask (International Carnival and Mask Museum, Binche) 3·75 3·75

The premium was for the promotion of philately.

1018 Emblem

1995. Anniversaries. Anniversary emblems.
3252 **1018** 16f. red, blue & black 1·10 40
3253 – 16f. multicoloured 1·10 40
3254 – 16f. multicoloured 1·10 40
3255 – 16f. red, black & brown 1·10 40
ANNIVERSARIES: No. 3252, 50th anniv of August Vermeylen Fund; 3253, Centenary of Touring Club of Belgium; 3254, Centenary of Federation of Belgian Enterprises; 3255, 50th anniv of Social Security in Belgium.

1019 "*ibiscus rosa-sinensis*"

1995. Ghent Flower Show. Multicoloured.
3256 13f. Type **1019** 95 50
3257 16f. Azalea 1·30 40
3258 30f. Fuchsia 2·20 75

1020 Crossword Puzzle

1995. Games and Pastimes. Multicoloured.
3259 13f. Type **1020** 95 45
3260 16f. King (chess piece) 1·10 40
3261 30f. Scrabble 2·20 75
3262 34f. Queen (playing cards) 2·30 95

1021 Frans de Troyer (promoter of thematic philately)

1995. Post Day.
3263 **1021** 16f. black, stone & orge 1·10 40

1022 Watch Tower and Barbed Wire Fence

1995. Europa. Peace and Freedom. Multicoloured.
3264 16f. Type **1022** (50th anniv of liberation of concentration camps) 2·50 90
3265 30f. Nuclear cloud (25th anniv of Non-Proliferation Treaty) 4·50 90

1023 Soldiers of the Irish Brigade and Memorial Cross

1995. 250th Anniv of Battle of Fontenoy.
3266 **1023** 16f. multicoloured 1·30 30

1024 U.N. Emblem

1995. 50th Anniv of U.N.O.
3267 **1024** 16f. multicoloured 1·10 40

1025 "Sauvagemont, Maransart" (Pierre Alechinsky)

1995. Artists' Philatelic Creations.
3268 **1025** 16f. red, black & yellow 1·10 40
3269 – 16f. multicoloured 1·10 40
DESIGN: No. 3269, "Telegram-style" (Pol Mara).

1026 Paul Cauchie (Brussels)

1995. Tourist Publicity. Art nouveau house facades by named architects. Multicoloured.
3270 16f. Type **1026** 1·10 40
3271 16f. Frans Smet-Verhas (Antwerp) 1·10 40
3272 16f. Paul Jaspar (Liege) 1·10 40

1027 Anniversary Emblem

1995. Cent of Royal Belgian Football Assn.
3273 **1027** 16f.+4f. mult 1·60 1·60

1028 Mercator (Belgian cadet barque)

1995. Sailing Ships. Multicoloured.
3274 16f. Type **1028** 1·40 75
3275 16f. "ruzenshern (Russian cadet barque) (inscr "Kruzenstern") 1·40 75
3276 16f. Sagres II (Portuguese cadet barque) 1·40 75
3277 16f. Amerigo Vespucci (Italian cadet ship) 1·40 75

1029 Princess Astrid and Globe

1995. Red Cross. Multicoloured.
3278 16f.+3f. Type **1029** (Chairwoman) 1·40 1·40
3279 16f.+3f. Wilhelm Rontgen (discoverer of X-rays) and X-ray of hand 1·40 1·40
3280 16f.+3f. Louis Pasteur (chemist) and microscope 1·40 1·40

1030 1908 Minerva

1995. Motorcycles. Multicoloured.
3281 13f. Type **1030** 95 50
3282 16f. 1913 FN (vert) 1·10 40
3283 30f. 1929 La Mondiale 2·00 75
3284 32f. 1937 Gillet (vert) 2·20 65

1031 Sammy (cartoon character)

1995. "Philately for the Young".
3285 **1031** 16f. multicoloured 1·40 45

1032 Couple and Condom in Wrapper

1995. "Solidarity". AIDS Awareness.
3286 **1032** 16f.+4f. mult 1·40 1·40

1033 King Albert II and Queen Paola (photograph by Christian Louis)

1995. King's Day.
3287 **1033** 16f. multicoloured 1·30 40

1034 Nativity (from 15th-century breviary)

1995. Christmas.
3288 **1034** 13f. multicoloured 95 40

1035 Puppets, Walloon Museum, Liege

1996. Museums. Multicoloured.
3289 16f.+4f. Type **1035** 1·40 1·40
3290 16f.+4f. National Gin Museum, Hasselt 1·40 1·40
MS3291 126×90 mm. 34f.+6f. Fall of Saul (detail of title panel), Butchers' Guild Hall Museum, Antwerp 3·75 3·75

The premium was used for the promotion of philately.

1036 Emile Mayrisch

1996. 70th Death Anniv of Theo van Rysselberghe (painter). No value expressed.
3292 **1036** A (16f.) mult 1·30 40

1037 "LIBERALISME"

1996. 150th Anniv of Liberal Party.
3293 **1037** 16f. dp blue, violet & bl 1·30 40

1038 Oscar Bonnevalle (stamp designer) and *Gelatenheid*

1996. Stamp Day.
3294	**1038**	16f. multicoloured	1·30	40

1039 Dragonfly (*Sympetrum sanguineum*)

1996. 150th Anniv of Royal Institute of Natural Sciences of Belgium. Insects. Multicoloured.
3295	16f. Type **1039**	90	70
3296	16f. Buff-tailed bumble bee (*Bombus terrestris*)	90	70
3297	16f. Stag beetle (*Lucanus cervus*)	90	70
3298	16f. May beetle (*Melolontha melolontha*)	90	70
3299	16f. European field cricket (*Gryllus campestris*)	90	70
3300	16f. Seven-spotted ladybird (*Coccinella septempunctata*)	90	70

1040 Yvonne Nevejean (rescuer of Jewish children)

1996. Europa. Famous Women. Multicoloured.
3301	16f. Type **1040**	1·00	40
3302	30f. Marie Gevers (poet)	2·10	90

1996. Birds (3rd series). As T 841. Multicoloured.
3303	1f. Crested tit ("Mesange Huppee")	25	15
3304	2f. Redwing ("Grive mauvis")	30	25
3305	3f. Eurasian skylark ("Alouette des champs")	30	25
3306	4f. Pied flycatcher ("Goremouche noir")	45	40
3307	5f. Common starling ("Etourneau sansonnet")	45	25
3308	6f. Spruce siskin ("Tarin des aulnes")	50	30
3309	7f. Yellow wagtail ("Bergeronnette printaniere")	45	15
3310	7f.50 Great grey shrike ("Pie-Grienche Grise")	50	40
3311	9f. Green woodpecker ("Pic Vert")	65	50
3312	10f. Turtle dove ("Tourterelle des Bois")	65	40
3313	15f. Willow tit ("Mesange boreale")	1·20	25
3314	16f. Coal tit ("Mesange noire")	1·00	30
3315	21f. Fieldfare ("Grive Litorne") (horiz)	1·40	80
3316	150f. Black-billed magpie ("Pie bavarde") (35×25 mm)	10·50	25

1042 King Albert II

1996. 62nd Birthday of King Albert II.
3327	**1042**	16f. multicoloured	1·40	25

1043 Han sur Lesse Grottoes

1996. Tourist Publicity. Multicoloured.
3328	16f. Type **1043**	1·20	40
3329	16f. Statue of beguine, Begijnendijk (vert)	1·20	40

1044 Royal Palace

1996. Brussels, Heart of Europe. Multicoloured.
3330	16f. Type **1044**	1·30	40
3331	16f. St. Hubert Royal Galleries	1·30	40
3332	16f. Le Petit Sablon, Egmont Palace (horiz)	1·30	40
3333	16f. Jubilee Park (horiz)	1·30	40

1045 1900 Germain 6CV Voiturette

1996. Cent of Motor Racing at Spa. Multicoloured.
3334	16f. Type **1045**	1·20	40
3335	16f. 1925 Alfa Romeo P2	1·20	40
3336	16f. 1939 Mercedes Benz W154	1·20	40
3337	16f. 1967 Ferrari 330P	1·20	40

1046 Table Tennis

1996. Olympic Games, Atlanta. Multicoloured.
3338	16f.+4f. Type **1046**	1·60	1·60
3339	16f.+4f. Swimming	1·60	1·60
MS3340	125×90 mm. 34f.+6f. High jumping (41×34 mm)	3·50	3·50

1996
3341	16f. blue	1·20	30
3342	17f. blue	1·40	15
3343	18f. green	1·30	50
3344	19f. lilac	1·60	20
3344a	20f. brown	1·40	20
3345	25f. brown	1·70	40
3346	28f. brown	2·40	50
3347	32f. violet	2·10	20
3348	34f. blue	1·90	40
3349	36f. blue	2·30	25
3350	50f. green	4·00	30

1047 *The Straw Hat* (Peter Paul Rubens)

1996. Paintings by Belgian Artists in the National Gallery, London. Multicoloured.
3351	14f. *St. Ivo* (Rogier van der Weyden)	1·20	40
3352	16f. Type **1047**	1·40	40
3353	30f. *Man in a Turban* (Jan van Eyck)	2·75	65

1048 Philip the Fair

1996. 500th Anniv of Marriage of Philip the Fair and Joanna of Castile and Procession into Brussels. Details of triptych by the Master of Affligem Abbey at Zierikzee Town Hall. Multicoloured.
3354	16f. Type **1048**	4·00	40
3355	16f. Joanna of Castile	1·30	40

1049 Cloro (cartoon character)

1996. "Philately for the Young".
3356	**1049**	16f. multicoloured	1·40	40

1050 Title of First Issue and Charles Letellier (founder)

1996. 150th Anniv of "Mons Almanac".
3357	**1050**	16f. black, yell & mve	1·30	40

1051 Arthur Grumiaux (violinist, 10th death anniv)

1996. Music and Literature Anniversaries.
3358	**1051**	16f. multicoloured	1·30	40
3359	-	16f. multicoloured	1·30	40
3360	-	16f. black and brown	1·30	40
3361	-	16f. multicoloured	1·30	40

DESIGNS: No. 3359, Flor Peeters (organist, 10th death anniv); 3360, Christian Dotremont (poet, 5th death anniv); 3361, Paul van Ostaijen (writer, birth centenary) and cover drawing by Oscar Jespers for "Bezette Stad".

1052 Globe and Children of Different Races

1996. "Solidarity". 50th Anniv of UNICEF.
3362	**1052**	16f.+4f. mult	1·40	1·40

1053 Christmas Trees

1996. Christmas. Sheet 185×145 mm containing T 1053 and similar horiz designs. Multicoloured.
MS3363 14f. Type **1053**; 14f. "Happy Christmas" in Flemish, German and French; 14f. Church; 14f. Cake stall; 14f. Stall with cribs; 14f. Meat stall; 14f. Father Christmas; 14f. Crowd including man smoking pipe; 14f. Crowd including man carrying holly	9·25 9·25

1054 Students

1997. Centenary of Catholic University, Mons.
3364	**1054**	17f. multicoloured	1·30	30

1055 Barbed Wire and Buildings

1997. Museums. Multicoloured.
3365	17f.+4f. Type **1055** (Deportation and Resistance Museum, Dossin Barracks, Malines)	1·60	1·60
3366	17f.+4f. Foundryman pouring molten metal (Fourneau Saint-Michel Iron Museum)	1·60	1·60

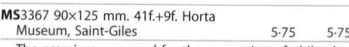

MS3367	90×125 mm. 41f.+9f. Horta Museum, Saint-Giles	5·75	5·75

The premium was used for the promotion of philately.

1056 Deer and Landscape

1997. "Cantons of the East" (German-speaking Belgium).
3368	**1056**	17f. black and brown	1·30	40

1057 Marie Sasse

1997. Opera Singers. Multicoloured.
3369	17f. Type **1057**	1·20	40
3370	17f. Ernest van Dijck	1·20	40
3371	17f. Hector Dufranne	1·20	40
3372	17f. Clara Clairbert	1·20	40

1058 Soldier on Duty

1997. Belgian Involvement in United Nations Peacekeeping Forces.
3373	**1058**	17f. multicoloured	1·20	40

1059 The Goat Riders

1997. Europa. Tales and Legends. Multicolourd.
3374	17f. Type **1059**	1·40	40
3375	30f. Jean de Berneau	2·50	90

1060 Spinoy working on Recess Plate

1997. Stamp Day. Fourth Death Anniv of Constant Spinoy (engraver).
3376	**1060**	17f. brown, yell & blk	1·20	40

1061 *The Man in the Street* (detail)

1997. Birth Centenary of Paul Delvaux (artist). Multicoloured.
3377	15f. Type **1061**	1·00	50
3378	17f. *The Public Voice* (horiz)	1·30	40
3379	32f. *The Messenger of the Night*	2·50	80

1062 Flower Arrangement

1997. Second International Flower Show, Liege.
3380	**1062**	17f. multicoloured	1·30	40

judo

17+4 BELGIË BELGIQUE

1063 Men's Judo

1997. Judo. Each black and red.

3381	17f.+4f. Type **1063**		1·40	1·30
3382	17f.+4f. Women's judo (showing female symbol)		1·40	1·30

1064 Queen Paola and Belvedere Villa

1997. 60th Birthday of Queen Paola.

3383	**1064**	17f. multicoloured	1·30	40

1065 Jommeke, Flip and Filiberke (comic strip characters)

1997. "Philately for the Young".

3384	**1065**	17f. multicoloured	1·60	45

1066 *Rosa damascena* "Coccinea"

1997. Roses. Illustrations by Pierre-Joseph Redoute. Multicoloured.

3385	17f. Type **1066**		1·30	40
3386	17f. *Rosa sulfurea*		1·30	40
3387	17f. *Rosa centifolia*		1·30	40

1067 St. Martin's Cathedral, Hal

1997. Tourist Publicity. Multicoloured.

3388	17f. Type **1067**		1·30	40
3389	17f. Notre-Dame Church, Laeken (horiz)		1·30	40
3390	17f. St. Martin's Cathedral, Liege		1·30	40

1068 Stonecutter

1997. Trades. Multicoloured.

3391	17f. Type **1068**		1·30	30
3392	17f. Bricklayer		1·30	30
3393	17f. Carpenter		1·30	30
3394	17f. Blacksmith		1·30	30

1069 Queen amidst Workers

1997. Centenary of Apimondia (International Apicultural Association) and 35th Congress, Antwerp. Bees. Multicoloured.

3395	17f. Type **1069**		1·30	90
3396	17f. Development of egg		1·30	90
3397	17f. Bees emerging from cells		1·30	90
3398	17f. Bee collecting nectar from flower		1·30	90

3399	17f. Bee fanning at hive entrance and worker arriving with nectar		1·30	90
3400	17f. Worker feeding drone		1·30	90

1070 *Belgica* (polar barque) ice-bound

1997. Cent of Belgian Antarctic Expedition.

3401	**1070**	17f. multicoloured	1·30	50

1071 Mask

1997. Centenary of Royal Central Africa Museum, Tervuren. Multicoloured.

3402	17f. Type **1071**		1·30	40
3403	17f. Museum (74×24 mm)		1·30	40
3404	34f. Statuette		2·50	1·00

1073 *Fairon* (Pierre Grahame)

1997. Christmas.

3408	**1073**	15f. multicoloured	1·20	40

1074 Disjointed Figure

1997. "Solidarity". Multiple Sclerosis.

3409	**1074**	17f.+4f. black & blue	1·60	1·60

1997. Willow Tit. As No. 3318 but horiz.

3410		15f. multicoloured	1·50	1·40

1075 Azalea "Mrs. Haerens A"

1997. Self-adhesive.

3411	**1075**	(17f.) multicoloured	1·30	20

1076 Female Symbol

1998. 50th Anniv of Women's Suffrage in Belgium.

3412	**1076**	17f. red, brown & sepia	1·20	40

1077 Thalys High Speed Train on Antoing Viaduct

1998. Paris-Brussels-Cologne-Amsterdam High Speed Rail Network.

3413	**1077**	17f. multicoloured	1·30	40

1078 Gerard Walschap

1998. Writers' Birth Centenaries. Multicoloured.

3414	17f. Type **1078**		1·20	40
3415	17f. Norge (Georges Mogin)		1·20	40

1079 King Leopold III

1998. Kings of Belgium (1st series).

3416	**1079**	17f.+8f. green	1·70	1·70
3417	-	32f.+15f. brown	3·00	3·00
MS3418	125×90 mm. 50f.+25f. red		7·00	7·00

KINGS: 32f. Baudouin I; 50f. Albert II.
The premium was used for the promotion of philately.
See also Nos. 3466/8 and **MS**3508.

1080 Black Magic

1998. Birth Centenary of Rene-Ghislain Magritte (artist) (1st issue). Multicoloured.

3419	17f. Type **1080**		1·30	40
3420	17f. *The Sensitive Chord* (horiz)		1·30	40
3421	17f. *The Castle of the Pyrenees*		1·30	40

See also No. 3432.

1081 *La Foire aux Amours* (Felicien Rops)

1998. Art Anniversaries. Multicoloured.

3422	17f. Type **1081** (death cent)		1·20	1·00
3423	17f. *Hospitality for the Strangers* (Gustave van de Woestijne) (bicentenary of Museum of Fine Arts, Ghent)		1·20	1·00
3424	17f. *Man with Beard* (self-portrait of Felix de Boeck, birth centenary)		1·20	1·00
3425	17f. *black writing mixed with colours...* (Karel Appel and Christian Dotremont) (50th anniv of Cobra art movement)		1·20	1·00

1082 Anniversary Emblem

1998. 75th Anniv of Belgian Postage Stamp Dealers' Association.

3426	**1082**	17f. multicoloured	1·20	40

1083 Avro RJ85 Airplane

1998. 75th Anniv of Sabena Airlines.

3427	**1083**	17f. multicoloured	1·30	40

1084 Fox

1998. Wildlife of the Ardennes. Multicoloured.

3428	17f. Type **1084**		1·30	50
3429	17f. Red deer ("Cervus elaphus")		1·30	50
3430	17f. Wild boar ("Sus scrofa")		1·30	50
3431	17f. Roe deer ("Capreolus capreolus")		1·30	50

1085 The Return (Magritte)

1998. Birth Centenary of Rene-Ghislain Magritte (artist) (2nd issue).

3432	**1085**	17f. multicoloured	1·30	50

1086 Struyf

1998. Stamp Day. Second Death Anniv of Edmond Struyf (founder of Pro-Post (organization for promotion of philately)).

3433	**1086**	17f. black, red & yellow	1·20	40

1087 Guitarist (Torhout and Werchter Festival)

1998. Europa. National Festivals.

3434	**1087**	17f. violet and yellow	1·40	40
3435	-	17f. violet and mauve	1·40	40

DESIGN: No. 3435, Music conductor (Wallonie Festival).

1088 Pelote

1998. Sports. Multicoloured.

3436	17f.+4f. Type **1088**		1·50	1·50
3437	17f.+4f. Handball		1·50	1·50
MS3438	123×88 mm. 30f.+7f. Goalkeeper (World Cup Football Championship, France)		3·00	3·00

1089 Emblem

1998. European Heritage Days. Multicoloured.

3439	17f. Type **1089**		1·20	50
3440	17f. Bourla Theatre, Antwerp		1·20	50
3441	17f. La Halle, Durbuy		1·20	50
3442	17f. Halletoren, Kortrijk		1·20	50
3443	17f. Louvain Town Hall		1·20	50
3444	17f. Perron, Liege		1·20	50
3445	17f. Royal Theatre, Namur		1·20	50
3446	17f. Aspremont-Lynden Castle, Rekem		1·20	50
3447	17f. Neo-Gothic kiosk, Saint Nicolas		1·20	50

3448		17f. Saint-Vincent's Chapel, Tournai	1·20	50
3449		17f. Villers-la-Ville Abbey	1·20	50
3450		17f. Saint-Gilles Town Hall	1·20	50

1090 Marnix van Sint-Aldegonde

1998. 400th Death Anniv of Philips van Marnix van St. Aldegonde (writer).

3451	**1090**	17f. multicoloured	1·20	40

1091 Face

1998. Bicentenary of "Amis Philanthropes" (circle of free thinkers).

3452	**1091**	17f. black and blue	1·20	40

1092 Mniszech Palace

1998. Belgium Embassy, Warsaw, Poland.

3453	**1092**	17f. multicoloured	1·20	40

1093 King Albert II

1998

3454	**1093**	19f. lilac	1·70	1·60

No. 3454 was for use on direct mail by large companies.

1094 The Eighth Day (dir. Jaco van Dormael)

1998. 25th Anniv of Brussels and Ghent Film Festivals. Multicoloured.

3455		17f. Type **1094**	1·30	40
3456		17f. Daens (dir. Stijn Coninx)	1·30	40

1096 Chick Bill and Ric Hochet

1998. "Philately for the Young". Comic Strip Characters.

3460	**1096**	17f. multicoloured	1·30	50

1097 "Youth and Space"

1998. 14th World Congress of Association of Space Explorers.

3461	**1097**	17f. multicoloured	1·30	45

1098 Universal Postal Union Emblem

1998. World Post Day.

3462	**1098**	34f. blue & ultramarine	2·50	1·30

1099 "The Three Kings" (Michel Provost)

1998. Christmas. No value indicated.

3463	**1099**	(17f.) multicoloured	1·20	40

1100 Detail of Triptych by Constant Dratz

1998. Cent of General Belgium Trade Union.

3464	**1100**	17f. multicoloured	1·20	40

1101 Blind Man with Guide Dog

1998. "Solidarity". Guide Dogs for the Blind.

3465	**1101**	17f.+4f. multicoloured	1·60	1·60

The face value is embossed in Braille.

1999. Kings of Belgium (2nd series). As T **1079**.

3466		17f.+8f. deep green & green	1·90	1·90
3467		32f.+15f. black	3·25	3·25
MS3468	125×90 mm. 50f.+25f. brown and purple		5·75	5·75

KINGS: 17f. Albert I; 32f. Leopold II; 50f. Leopold I. The premium was used for the promotion of philately.

1102 Candle ("Happy Birthday")

1999. Greetings stamps. No value expressed. Multicoloured.

3469		(17f.) Type **1102**	1·20	50
3470		(17f.) Stork carrying heart ("Welcome" (new baby))	1·20	50
3471		(17f.) Wristwatch ("Take your Time" (retirement))	1·20	50
3472		(17f.) Four-leafed clover ("For your pleasure")	1·20	50
3473		(17f.) White doves ("Congratulations" (marriage))	1·20	50
3474		(17f.) Arrow through heart ("I love you")	1·20	50
3475		(17f.) Woman with heart as head ("Happy Mother's Day")	1·20	50
3476		(17f.) Man with heart as head ("Happy Father's Day")	1·20	50

1103 Barn Owl

1999. Owls. Multicoloured.

3477		17f. Type **1103**	1·30	40
3478		17f. Little owl ("Athene noctua")	1·30	40
3479		17f. Tawny owl ("Strix aluco")	1·30	40
3480		17f. Long-eared owl ("Asio otus")	1·30	40

1104 Leopard Tank (Army)

1999. 50th Anniv of North Atlantic Treaty Organization. Multicoloured.

3481		17f. Type **1104**	1·20	40
3482		17f. Lockhead Martin F-16 Fighting Falcon (Air Force)	1·20	40
3483		17f. "De Wandelaar" (frigate) (Navy)	1·20	40
3484		17f. Field hospital (Medical Service)	1·20	40
3485		17f. Display chart of military operations (General Staff)	1·20	40

1105 Envelopes and World Map

1999. 125th Anniv of U.P.U.

3486	**1105**	34f. multicoloured	2·30	65

1106 De Bunt Nature Reserve, Hamme

1999. Europa. Parks and Gardens. Multicoloured.

3487		17f. Type **1106**	1·40	40
3488		17f. Harchies Marsh	1·40	40

1107 1849 10c. "Epaulettes" Stamp

1999. Stamp Day. 150th Anniv of First Belgian Postage Stamp. Multicoloured.

3489		17f. Type **1107**	1·10	30
3490		17f. 1849 20c. "Epaulettes" stamp	1·10	30

1108 Racing

1999. Sport. Belgian Motor Cycling. Multicoloured.

3491		17f.+4f. Type **1108**	1·60	1·60
3492		17f.+4f. Trial (vert)	1·60	1·60
MS3493	90×125 mm. 30f.+7f. Motocross (vert)		3·25	3·25

1109 My Favourite Room

1999. 50th Death Anniv of James Ensor (artist) (1st issue).

3494	**1109**	17f. mullticoloured	1·10	40

See also Nos. 3501/3.

1110 Giant Family, Geraardsbergen

1999. Tourist Publicity. Multicoloured.

3495		17f. Type **1110**	1·10	40
3496		17f. Members of Confrerie de la Misericorde in Car d'Or procession, Mons (horiz)	1·10	40

1111 Harvesting of Cocoa Beans

1999. Belgian Chocolate. Multicoloured.

3497		17f. Type **1111**	1·10	40
3498		17f. Chocolate manufacture	1·10	40
3499		17f. Selling product	1·10	40

1112 Photographs of 1959 and 1999

1999. 40th Wedding Anniv of King Albert and Queen Paola.

3500	**1112**	17f. multicoloured	1·30	40

1113 Woman eating Oysters

1999. 50th Death Anniv of James Ensor (artist) (2nd issue).

3501	**1113**	17f. multicoloured	1·10	40
3502	-	30f. black, brown and grey	1·90	80
3503	-	32f. multicoloured	2·10	80

DESIGNS—30f. Triumph of Death; 32f. Old Lady with Masks.

1999. "Bruphila '99" National Stamp Exhibition, Brussels. Kings of Belgium (3rd series). Sheet 191×121 mm containing vert designs as T **1079**. Each deep blue and blue.

MS3508	17f. As No. 3466; 17f. Type **1079**; 32f. As No. 3467; 32f. As No. 3417; 50f. As No. **MS**3468; 50f. As No. **MS**3418		26·00	26·00

1115 Henri la Fontaine (President of International Peace Bureau), 1913

1999. Belgian Winners of Nobel Peace Prize.

3509	**1115**	17f. red and gold	1·10	40
3510	-	21f. blue and gold	1·30	80

DESIGNS: 3510, Auguste Beernaert (Prime Minister 1884–94), 1909.

DENOMINATION. From No. 3511 Belgian stamps are denominated both in Belgian francs and in euros.

1116 King Albert II **1116a** King Albert II

1999

3511	**1116**	17f. multicoloured	1·20	15
3512	**1116**	17f. blue	1·20	15
3513	**1116**	19f. purple	1·30	40
3514	**1116**	20f. brown	1·30	30
3515	**1116**	25f. brown	2·50	2·30
3516	**1116**	30f. purple	2·10	25
3517	**1116**	32f. green	1·90	25
3518	**1116**	34f. blue	2·30	65
3519	**1116**	36f. brown	2·30	15
3520	**1116a**	50f. blue	3·25	65
3521	**1116a**	200f. lilac	13·00	1·60

1117 "Corentin" (Paul Cuvelier)

1999. "Philately for the Young". Comic Strips. Sheet 185×145 mm containing T **1117** and similar horiz designs. Multicoloured.
MS3525 17f. Type **1117**; 17f. "Jerry Spring" (Jije); 17f. "Gil Jourdan" (Maurice Tillieux); 17f. "Beaver Patrol" (Mitacq); 17f. Entrance Hall, Belgian Comic Strip Centre; 17f. "Hassan and Kadour" (Jacques Laudy); 17f. "Buck Danny" (Victor Hubinon); 17f. "Tif and Tondu" (Fernand Dineur); 17f. "Les Timour" (Sirius) 11·50 .. 11·50

1118 Geranium "Matador"

1999. Flowers. No value expressed (geranium) or inscr "ZONE A PRIOR" (tulip). Multicoloured. Self-adhesive.
3528 (17f.) Type **1118** 1·60 .. 45
3529 (21f.) Tulip (21×26 mm) 1·20 .. 40
The geranium design was for use on inland letters up to 20g. and the tulip design for letters within the European Union up to 20g.

1119 Reindeer holding Glass of Champagne

1999. Christmas.
3530 **1119** 17f. multicoloured 1·20 .. 40

1120 Child bandaging Teddy Bear

1999. "Solidarity". Red Cross. Multicoloured.
3531 17f.+4f. Type **1120** 1·50 .. 1·50
3532 17f.+4f. Child and teddy bear cleaning teeth (vert) 1·50 .. 1·50

1121 Prince Philippe and Mathilde d'Udekem d'Acoz

1999. Engagement of Prince Philippe and Mathilde d'Udekem d'Acoz.
3533 17f. Type **1121** 1·60 .. 50
MS3534 120×89 mm. 21f. Prince Philippe and Mathilde d'Udekem d'Acoz (different) 1·80 .. 1·80

1122 Pope John Paul XXIII

1999. The Twentieth Century (1st issue). Personalities, Sports and Leisure. Sheet 166×200 mm containing T **1122** and similar vert designs. Multicoloured.
MS3535 17f. Type **1122**; 17f. King Baudouin; 17f. Willy Brandt (German statesman); 17f. John F. Kennedy (U.S. President, 1961–3); 17f. Mahatma Gandhi (Indian leader); 17f. Martin Luther King (civil rights leader); 17f. Vladimir Lenin (Prime Minister of Russia, 1917–24; 17f. Che Guevara (revolutionary); 17f. Golda Meir (Prime Minister of Israel, 1969–74); 17f. Nelson Mandela (Prime Minister of South Africa, 1994–99); 17f. Jesse Owens (American athlete) (modern Olympics); 17f. Football; 17f. Eddy Merckx (racing cyclist) (Tour de France); 17f. Edith Piaf (French singer); 17f. The Beatles (English pop band); 17f. Charlie Chaplin (English film actor and director); 17f. Postcards (tourism); 17f. Children around campfire (youth movements); 17f. Tintin and Snowy (comic strip); 17f. Magnifying glass over stamp (hobbies) 23·00 .. 23·00
See also Nos. **MS**3613 and **MS**3656.

1123 Fireworks and Streamer forming "2000"

2000. New Year.
3536 **1123** 17f. multicoloured 1·30 .. 25

1124 Red-backed Shrike

2000. Birds. Multicoloured.
3537 50c. Goldcrest ("Roitelet Huppe") 15 .. 25
3538 1f. Red crossbill ("Beccroisé des Sapins") 25 .. 15
3539 2f. Short-toed treecreeper ("Grimpereau des Jardins") 25 .. 15
3540 3f. Meadow pipit ("Pipit Farlouse") 25 .. 15
3541 5f. Brambling ("Pinson du Nord") 30 .. 15
3542 7f.50 Great grey shrike ("Pie-Grieche Grise") 50 .. 50
3543 8f. Great tit ("Mesange Charbonniere") 65 .. 30
3544 10f. Wood warbler ("Pouillot Siffleur") 65 .. 40
3545 16f. Type **1124** 1·10 .. 40
3546 16f. Common tern ("Sterne Pierregarin") 1·10 .. 25
3547 21f. Fieldfare ("Grive Litorne") (horiz) 1·30 .. 50
3548 150f. Black-billed magpie ("Pie Bavarde") (36×25 mm) 9·75 .. 65

1125 Brussels Skyline and Group of People

2000. Brussels, European City of Culture. Multicoloured.
3555 17f. Type **1125** 1·10 .. 50
3556 17f. Toots Tielmans (jazz musician), Anne Teresa de Keersmaeker (gymnast) and skyline 1·10 .. 50
3557 17f. Lockheed L-1011 Tristar, train and skyline 1·10 .. 50
Nos. 3555/7 were issued together, se-tenant, forming a composite design showing the Brussels skyline.

1126 Queen Astrid

2000. Queens of Belgium (1st series).
3558 **1126** 17f.+8f. green and deep green 1·90 .. 1·90

3559 - 32f.+15f. brown and black 3·25 .. 3·25
MS3560 125×89 mm. 50f.+25f. deep purple and purple 4·75 .. 4·75
DESIGNS: 32f. Queen Fabiola; 50f. Queen Paola. The premium was used for the promotion of philately. See also Nos. 3615/**MS**3617 and **MS**3618.

1127 Mathematical Formulae

2000. World Mathematics Year.
3561 **1127** 17f. multicoloured 1·10 .. 40

1128 Globe and Technology (Joachim Beckers)

2000. "Stampin' the Future". Winning Entries in Children's International Painting Competition.
3562 **1128** 17f. multicoloured 1·10 .. 40

1129 Charles V as Sovereign Master of the Order of the Golden Fleece (anon)

2000. 500th Birth Anniv of Charles V, Holy Roman Emperor. Paintings of Charles V. Multicoloured.
3563 17f. Type **1129** 1·10 .. 40
3564 21f. Charles V (Corneille de la Haye) 1·30 .. 75
MS3565 125×88 mm. 34f. Charles V on Horseback (Titian) 2·50 .. 2·50

1130 Common Adder

2000. Amphibians and Reptiles. Multicoloured.
3566 17f. Type **1130** 1·10 .. 40
3567 17f. Sand lizard (Lacerta agilis) (vert) 1·10 .. 40
3568 17f. Common tree frog (Hyla arborea) (vert) 1·10 .. 40
3569 17f. Spotted salamander (Salamander salamander) 1·10 .. 40

1131 Children flying Kites

2000. Red Cross and Red Crescent Movements.
3570 **1131** 17f.+4f. multicoloured 1·50 .. 1·50

1132 Players Celebrating

2000. European Football Championship, Belgium and The Netherlands. Multicoloured. (a) With face value. Size 26×38 mm.
3571 17f. Type **1132** 1·30 .. 25
3572 21f. Football 1·60 .. 40

(b) Size 20×26 mm. Self-adhesive.
3573 (17f.) As Type **1132** 1·60 .. 40
Nos. 3571/3 were printed together, se-tenant, with the backgrounds forming the composite design of a crowd of spectators and the Belgian flag.

1133 Cat and Rabbit reading Book

2000. Stamp Day. Winning Entry in Stamp Design Competition.
3574 **1133** 17f. black, blue and red 1·10 .. 40

1134 Francois de Tassis (detail of tapestry)

2000. "Belgica 2001" Int Stamp Exhibition, Brussels, (1st issue).
3575 **1134** 17f. multicoloured 1·10 .. 50
See also Nos. 3629/33.

1135 Iris spuria

2000. Ghent Flower Show. Multicoloured.
3576 16f. Type **1135** 1·30 .. 50
3577 17f. Rhododendron (horiz) 1·50 .. 40
3578 21f. Begonia (vert) 1·60 .. 75

1136 Prince Philippe

2000. Second Anniv of Prince Philippe (cultural organization).
3579 **1136** 17f. brn, grey & sil 1·10 .. 40

1137 Harpsichord

2000. 250th Death Anniv of Johann Sebastian Bach. No value expressed. Multicoloured.
3580 (17f.) Type **1137** 1·30 .. 1·00
3581 (17f.) Violin 1·30 .. 1·00
3582 (17f.) Two tenor lutes 1·30 .. 1·00
3583 (17f.) Treble viol 1·30 .. 1·00
3584 (17f.) Three trumpets 1·30 .. 1·00
3585 (17f.) Bach 1·30 .. 1·00

1138 Belgium Team Emblem and Olympic Rings

2000. Olympic Games, Sydney. Multicoloured.
3586 17f. Type **1138** 1·00 .. 50
3587 17f.+4f. Tae-kwon-do 1·40 .. 1·40
3588 17f.+4f. Paralympic athlete (horiz) 1·40 .. 1·40
MS3589 125×90 mm. 30f.+7f. Swimmer (horiz) 2·50 .. 2·50

1139 "Building Europe"

2000. Europa.

3590	**1139**	21f. multicoloured	1·50	75

1140 Flemish Beguinages

2000. UNESCO World Heritage Sites in Belgium. Multicoloured.

3591		17f. Type **1140**	1·10	30
3592		17f. Grand-Place, Brussels	1·10	30
3593		17f. Four lifts, Centre Canal, Wallonia	1·10	30

1141 Baroque Organ, Norbertine Abbey Church, Grimbergen

2000. Tourism. Churches and Church Organs. Multicoloured.

3594		17f. Type **1141**	1·10	40
3595		17f. St. Wandru Abbey, Mons	1·10	40
3596		17f. O.-L.-V. Hemelvaartkerk (former abbey church), Ninove	1·10	40
3597		17f. St. Peter's Church, Bastogne	1·10	40

1142 Red-backed Shrike ("Pie grieche ecorcheur")

2000

3598	**1142**	16f. multicoloured	2·20	1·60
3599	–	17f. mult (51×21 mm)	3·50	2·50
3600	–	23f. lilac	2·50	2·00

DESIGNS: 17f. Francois de Tassis (detail of tapestry) and Belgica 2001 emblem; 23f. King Albert II.

1143 Marcel, Charlotte, Fanny and Konstantinopel

2000. "Philately for the Young". Kiekeboe (cartoon series created by Robert Merhottein).

3601	**1143**	17f. multicoloured	1·10	50

1144 "Springtime"

2000. Hainaut Flower Show.

3602	**1144**	17f. multicoloured	1·10	40

1145 Pansies

2000. Flowers. No value expressed. Self-adhesive.

3603	**1145**	(17f.) multicoloured	1·30	25

1147 "Bing of the Ferro Lusto X" (Panamarenko)

2000. Modern Art. Multicoloured.

3608		17f. Type **1147**	1·10	65
3609		17f. "Construction" (Anne-Mie van Kerckhoven) (vert)	1·10	65
3610		17f. "Belgique eternelle" (Jacques Charlier)	1·10	65
3611		17f. "Les Belles de Nuit" (Marie Jo Lafontaine)	1·10	65

1148 Postman

2000. Christmas.

3612	**1148**	17f. multicoloured	1·10	40

1149 Soldiers at Yser Front, West Flanders (First World War, 1914–18)

2000. The Twentieth Century (2nd issue). War, Peace and Art. Sheet 200×166 mm containing T 1149 and similar horiz designs. Multicoloured.

MS3613 17f. Type **1149**; 17f. German concentration camp and prisoners (black and scarlet); 17f. Atomic cloud and Hiroshima (atomic bomb, 1945); 17f. Winston Churchill, Franklin D. Roosevelt and Joseph Stalin (Yalta conference, 1945); 17f. Headquarters (United Nations established, 1945); 17f. Joseph Kasavubu (first President) and map of Africa (independence of Belgian Congo, 1960); 17f. American soldiers and Boeing CH-14 Chinook(Vietnam War); 17f. Collapse of Berlin Wall, 1989; 17f. Campaign for Nuclear Disarmament emblem and crowd; 17f. Dome of the Rock (Middle East conflict); 17f. Rene Magritte (artist); 17f. Le Corbusier (architect) and building; 17f. Bertolt Brecht (dramatist and poet) and actors; 17f. James Joyce (novelist); 17f. Anne Teresa de Keersmaeker (choreographer); 17f. Bila Bartok (composer); 17f. Andy Warhol (artist); 17f. Maria Callas (opera singer); 17f. Henry Moore (sculptor) and sculpture; 17f. Charlie Parker (alto saxophonist and composer) and Toots Thielemans (composer and jazz musician) 23·00 23·00

1150 Stars

2000. New Year.

3614	**1150**	17f. gold, blue & blk	1·30	50

2001. Queens of Belgium (2nd series). As T 1126.

3615		17f.+8f. green & dp green	1·90	1·90
3616		32f.+15f. black and green	3·25	3·25

MS3617 126×91 mm. 50f.+25f. deep brown and brown 4·75 4·75
DESIGNS: 17f. Queen Elisabeth; 32f. Queen Marie-Henriette; 50f. Queen Louise-Marie.
The premium was used for the promotion of philately.

2001. Queens of Belgium (3rd series). Vert designs as T 1126. Each blue, deep blue and ochre.

MS3618 190×121 mm. 17f. As No. 3615; 17f. As Type 1126; 32f. As No. 3616; 32f. As No. 3559; 50f. As No. MS3617; 50f. As No. MS3560 23·00 23·00

1151 Movement of a Dynamo

2001. Death Centenary of Zenobe Gramme (physicist).

3619	**1151**	17f. black, red & black	1·10	40

1152 Virgin and Child (statue)

2001. 575th Anniv of Louvain Catholic University.

3620	**1152**	17f. multicoloured	1·10	40

2001. As T 998 but with face value expressed in francs and euros.

3621		100f. multicoloured	6·25	55

1153 Willem Elsschot (poet)

2001. Music and Literature.

3622	**1153**	17f. brown and black	1·10	40
3623	–	17f. grey and black	1·10	40

MS3624 125×90 mm. 21f. orange and brown 1·50 1·50
DESIGNS—VERT: No. 3623, Albert Ayguesparse (poet). HORIZ: MS3624 21f. Queen Elisabeth and emblem (50th anniv of Queen Elisabeth International Music Competition).

1154 Boy washing Hands

2001. Europa. Water Resources.

3625	**1154**	21f. multicoloured	1·40	75

1155 Type 12 Steam Locomotive

2001. 75th Anniv of National Railway Company. Multicoloured.

3626		17f. Type **1155**	1·10	65
3627		17f. Series 06 dual locomotive No. 671	1·10	65
3628		17f. Series 03 locomotive No. 328	1·10	65

Nos. 3626/8 were issued together, se-tenant, forming a composite design.

1156 16th-century Postman on horseback

2001. "Belgica 2001" International Stamp Exhibition, Brussels (2nd issue). 500th Anniv of European Post. Multicoloured.

3629		17f. Type **1156**	1·40	65
3630		17f. 17th-century postman with walking staff (vert)	1·40	65
3631		17f. 18th-century postman and hand using quill (vert)	1·40	65
3632		17f. Steam locomotive and 19th-century postman (vert)	1·40	65
3633		17f. 20th-century forms of communication (vert)	1·40	65

MS3634 190×120 mm. 150f. Female postal worker (35×46 mm) 20·00 20·00

1157 Hassan II Mosque, Casablanca

2001. Places of Worship. Multicoloured.

3635		17f. Type **1157**	1·10	40
3636		34f. Koekelberg Basilica	2·30	1·00

1158 Winter Landscape with Skaters (Pieter Bruegel the Elder)

2001. Art. Multicoloured.

3637		17f. Type **1158**	1·10	95
3638		17f. *Heads of Negros* (Peter Paul Rubens)	1·10	95
3639		17f. *Sunday* (Frits van den Berghe)	1·10	95
3640		17f. *Mussels* (Marcel Broodthaers)	1·10	95

1159 Pottery Vase

2001. Chinese Pottery. Multicoloured.

3641		17f. Type **1159**	1·10	30
3642		34f. Teapot	2·30	80

1160 Luc Orient

2001. "Philately for the Young". Cartoon Characters.

3643	**1160**	17f. multicoloured	1·10	50

1161 Cyclists (World Cycling Championship, Antwerp)

2001. Sports. Multicoloured.

3644		17f.+4f. Type **1161**	1·40	1·40
3645		17f.+4f. Gymnast (World Gymnastics Championships, Ghent)	1·40	1·40

1162 Emblem

2001. Belgian Presidency of European Union.

3646	**1162**	17f. multicoloured	1·10	50

1163 Binche

2001. Town Hall Belfries.
| 3647 | 1163 | 17f. mauve and black | 1·10 | 40 |
| 3648 | - | 17f. blue, mauve & blk | 1·10 | 40 |

DESIGN: No. 3648, Diksmuide.

1164 Damme

2001. Large Farmhouses. Multicoloured.
3649		17f. Type **1164**	1·10	40
3650		17f. Beauvechain	1·10	40
3651		17f. Louvain	1·10	40
3652		17f. Honnelles	1·10	40
3653		17f. Hasselt	1·10	40

1165 Red Cross and Doctor

2001. Red Cross.
| 3654 | 1165 | 17f.+4f. multicoloured | 1·40 | 1·40 |

1166 Stam and Pilou

2001. Stamp Day. No value expressed. Self-adhesive.
| 3655 | 1166 | (17f.) multicoloured | 1·40 | 50 |

No. 3655 was for use on inland standard letters up to 20g.

1167 Ovide Decroly (educational psychologist) and Road Sign

2001. The Twentieth Century. Science and Technology. Sheet 166×200 mm. Multicoloured.

MS3656 17f. Type **1167**; 17f. Dandelion and windmills (alternative energy sources); 17f. Globe, signature and map (first solo non-stop crossing of North Atlantic by Charles Lindbergh); 17f. Man with head on lap (Sigmund Freud, founder of psychoanalysis); 17f. Astronaut and foot print on moon surface (Neil Armstrong, first man on the moon, 1969); 17f. Claude Levi-Strauss (anthropologist); 17f. DNA double helix and athletes (human genetic code); 17f. Pierre Teilhard de Chardin (theologian palaeontologist and philosopher); 17f. Max Weber (sociologist) and crowd; 17f. Albert Einstein (physicist) (Theory of Relativity); 17f. Knight and jacket of pills (discovery of Penicillin, 1928); 17f. Ilya Prigogine (theoretical chemist and clock face; 17f. Text and Roland Barthes (writer and critic); 17f. Simone de Beauvoir (feminist writer); 17f. Globe and technology highway (computer science); 17f. John Maynard Keynes (economist) and folded paper; 17f. Marc Bloch (historian) and photographs; 17f. Tools and Julius Robert Oppenheimer (nuclear physicist); 17f. Marie and Pierre Curie, discoverers of radioactivity, 1896); 17f. Caricature of Ludwig Josef Wittgenstein (philosopher) 23·00 23·00

1168 Nativity

2001. Christmas.
| 3657 | 1168 | 15f. multicoloured | 1·10 | 45 |

1169 Sunset

2001. Bereavement. No value expressed.
| 3658 | 1169 | (17f.) multicoloured | 1·60 | 40 |

See also Nos. 3732 and 3856.

1170 Daffodil

2001. Flowers. No value expressed. Self-adhesive. (a) Without service indicator. Multicoloured.
| 3659 | | (17f.) Type **1170** | 1·30 | 40 |

(b) Inscr "ZONE A PRIOR".
| 3660 | | (21f.) Tulip "Darwin" (vert) | 1·40 | 50 |

No. 3659 was for use on inland letters up to 20g. and No. 3660 was for use on letters within the European Union up to 20g.

1171 Tintin

2001. 70th Anniv of Tintin in Congo (cartoon strip). Multicoloured.
| 3661 | | 17f. Type **1171** | 1·30 | 65 |
| MS3662 | 123×88 mm. 34f. Tintin, Snowy and guide in car (48×37 mm) | | 3·25 | 3·25 |

1172 King Albert II **1173** King Albert II

2002
3663	1173	7c. blue and red (postage)	25	15
3666	1172	42c. red	1·10	40
3667	1172	47c. green	1·30	50
3668	1173	49c. red	1·30	50
3669	1173	52c. blue	1·40	50
3670	1172	59c. blue	1·80	55
3671	1172	60c. blue	1·20	90
3672	1173	79c. blue and red	2·50	65
3674	1173	€4.21 brown and red	10·00	2·50
3674a	1172	70c. blue (air)	1·50	65
3674b	1172	80c. blue	1·80	65
3674c	1172	80c. purple and red	2·00	65

Nos. 3663, 3668 and 3672 are inscribed "PRIOR" at left.

1174 Female Tennis Player

2002. Centenary of Royal Belgian Tennis Federation. Multicoloured.
| 3675 | | 42c. Type **1174** | 1·30 | 50 |
| 3676 | | 42c. Male tennis player | 1·30 | 50 |

1175 Cyclist

2002. International Cycling Events held at Circuit Zolder. Multicoloured.
| 3677 | | 42c. Type **1175** (World Cyclo-Cross Championships) | 1·30 | 50 |
| 3678 | | 42c. Cyclist with hand raised (Road Cycling Championships) | 1·30 | 50 |

1176 Dinosaur

2002. Winning Entry in Children's Stamp Design Competition at "Belgica 2001".
| 3679 | 1176 | 42c.+10c. mult | 1·50 | 1·50 |

The premium was used for the promotion of philately.

1177 Antwerp from River

2002. 150th Anniv of Antwerp University.
| 3680 | 1177 | 42c. blue and black | 1·10 | 45 |

1178 Buildings and Architectural Drawing

2002. "Bruges 2002", European City of Culture. Multicoloured.
3681		42c. Type **1178**	1·30	45
3682		42c. Organ pipes and xylophone	1·30	45
3683		42c. Octopus	1·30	45

1179 16th-century Manuscript (poem, Anna Bijns)

2002. Women and Art. Multicoloured.
| 3684 | | 42c. Type **1179** | 1·30 | 45 |
| 3685 | | 84c. *Woman writing* (painting, Anna Boch) (vert) | 2·10 | 1·00 |

1180 Fountain Pen and Writing

2002. Stamp Day.
| 3686 | 1180 | 47c. multicoloured | 1·40 | 55 |

1181 Papillon

2002. Centenary of Flanders Canine Society. Multicoloured.
3687		42c. Type **1181**	1·30	65
3688		42c. Brussels griffon	1·30	65
3689		42c. Bloodhounds	1·30	65
3690		42c. Bouvier des Ardennes	1·30	65
3691		42c. Schipperke	1·30	65

1182 Stock Dove ("Pigeon Colombin-Holenduif")

2002. Birds. Multicoloured.
3692		1c. Nightingale ('Rossignol philomele') (postage)	15	15
3692a		1c. Black Woodpecker ('Pic noir')	15	15
3693		2c. Snipe ('Becassine des Marais')	20	15
3693a		3c. Marsh Tit ('Mesange Nonnette')	25	15
3693b		5c. Cirl Bunting ('Bruant Zizi')	25	15
3693ba		5c. Little Grebe ('Grebe castagneux') (24×28mm)	25	15
3693c		5c. Teal ('Sarcelle D'Hiver')	25	15
3693d		6c. Burrowing Owl ('Chouette Cheveche')	25	15
3694		7c. Type **1182**	30	20
3694a		8c. Pintail Duck ('Canard Pilet')	30	20
3694b		10c. Hedge Sparrow ('Accentor Maichet') (AIRPRIOR)	30	20
3694ba		10c. Tengmalm's Owl ('Chouette De Tengmalm')	30	20
3694c		10c. Tawny Owl ('Chouette Hulotte')	30	20
3695		15c. Spotted Nutcracker ('Cassenoix Mouchete') (AIRPRIOR)	30	20
3697		20c. Mediterranean Gull ('Mouette Melanocephale')	40	25

3697a		23c. Black-necked Grebe ('Greb a Cou Noir')	40	25
3697b		23c. Jackdaw ('Choucas des Tours')	40	25
3698		25c. Oystercatcher ("Scholekster-Huîtrier Pie")	65	40
3698a		27c. Woodcock ('Bécasse des bois')	65	40
3699		30c. Corncrake ('Rale des Genets')	75	40
3700		35c. Spotted Woodpecker ('Pic Epeiche')	75	40
3700a		40c. Spotted Flycatcher ('Gobemouche gris')	1·00	50
3700b		40c. Long-eared owl ('Hibou Moyen')	1·00	50
3700c		V-A (40c.) Black Grouse ('Tétras Lyre') (24×33 mm)	1·00	50
3701		41c. Collared Dove ('Tourterelle Turque')	1·30	65
3701a		44c. Housemartin ('Hirondelle de fenetre')	1·30	65
3701b		44c. Wood pigeon ('Pigeon Ramier')	1·30	65
3701c		46c. Avocet ('Avocette')	1·30	70
3701d		52c. Hoopoe ('Huppe Fasciee')	1·40	75
3701e		55c. Plover ('Petit gravelot')	1·40	80
3702		57c. Black Tern ('Guifette Noire')	1·50	90
3702a		60c. Partridge ('Perdrix Crise')	1·50	1·00
3703		65c. Black-headed gull ('Mouette rieuse')	1·60	1·10
3704		70c. Redshank ('Chevalier Gambette')	1·90	1·20
3704a		70c. Swift ('Martinet noir')	1·90	1·20
3704aa		75c. Golden Plover ('Pluvier doré')	1·90	1·20
3704b		75c. Firecrest ('Roitelet Triple-Bandeau')	1·90	1·20
3704ba		75c. Kestrel ('Faucon Crécerelle')	1·90	1·20
3704c		78c. Black-tailed godwit ('Barge A Queue Noir')	2·00	1·30
3705		€1 Wheatear ('Traquet Motteux') (38×27 mm)	3·00	1·50
3706		€2 Ringed Plover ('Grand Gravelot') (38×27 mm)	4·00	2·50
3707		€3.72 Moorhen ('Poule d'eau') (38×27 mm)	11·50	3·25
3708		€4 Eagle Owl ('Hibou grand-duc-Oehoe') (38×27 mm)	13·00	5·25
3708a		€4.09 Pheasant ('Faisan de Colchide') (32×24 mm)	13·50	5·25
3708aa		€4.30 Grebe ('Grèbe Huppé')	14·00	5·75
3708ab RP		(€4.35) Short-eared Owl ('Hibou des marais')	13·50	5·25
3708b		€4.40 Peregrine Falcon ('Faucon Pélerin') (38×28 mm)	14·50	6·00
3708c		€ 4.60 White-tailed Eagle ('Pyrargueà queue blanche') (33×28 mm)	15·00	6·25
3708ca		€ 4.60 Barn owl ('Chouette effraie')	15·00	6·25
3708cb R-A		(€ 4.90) Osprey ('Chouette effraie')	15·00	6·25
3709		€5 Ruff ('Combattant Varie') (38×27 mm)	16·00	7·00
3709a R-A		(€5.03) Arctic Tern ('Sterne Arctique')	16·00	7·00

1183 Big Top, Ringmaster, Seal and Clown

2002. Europa. Circus. Winning Entry in Children's Drawing Competition.
| 3710 | 1183 | 52c. multicoloured | 2·50 | 1·00 |

1184 Paramedic, Patient and Damaged Buildings

2002. Red Cross.
| 3711 | 1184 | 84c.+12c. multicoloured | 2·50 | 2·50 |

1185 Abbey Buildings

2002. 850th Anniv of Leffe Abbey.
| 3712 | 1185 | 42c. multicoloured | 1·50 | 50 |

1186 Loppem Castle

2002. Tourism. Castles. Sheet 161×141 mm containing T **1186** and similar horiz designs showing castles. Multicoloured.

MS3713 42c. Type **1186**; 42c. Horst;
42c. Wissekerke; 42c. Chimay; 42c.
Ecaussinnes-Lalaing; 42c. Reinhard-
stein; 42c. Modave; 42c. Ooidonk;
42c. Corroy-le-Chateau; 42c. Alden
Biesen 11·50 11·50

1187 Show Jumping

2002. Horses. Designs showing equestrian events. Multicoloured.

3714 40c. Type **1187** 1·00 45
3715 42c. Carriage driving (vert) 1·10 50
MS3716 126×91 mm. 52c. Two Brabant
draught horses' heads (Centenary of
St. Paul's horse procession, Opwijk)
(37×48 mm) 1·60 1·60

1188 Golden
Spur and Battle
Scene

2002. 700th Anniv of Battle of the Golden Spurs (Flemish--French battle), Kortrijk. Multicoloured.

3717 42c. Type **1188** 1·10 40
3718 52c. Broel towers 1·30 75
MS3719 126×91 mm. 57c. Flemish and
French soldiers, river and knight on
horseback (48×38 mm) 1·60 1·60

1189
Onze-Lieve-Vrouw-
Lombeek,
Roosdaal

2002. Windmills. Multicoloured.

3720 42c. Type **1189** 1·10 40
3721 52c. Faial Island, Azores,
Portugal 1·40 75

Stamps of a similar design were issued by Portugal.

1190 Liedekerke
Lacework and
Statue of
Lace-maker

2002. Lace-making. Multicoloured.

3722 42c. Type **1190** 1·10 40
3723 74c. Pag lacework 2·00 90

Stamps of a similar design were issued by Croatia.

1191 Bakelandt, Red Zita
and Stagecoach

2002. "Philately for the Young". Bakelandt (comic strip created by Hec Leemans). Multicoloured.

3724 **1191** 42c. multicoloured 1·30 65

1192 Teddy Bear

2002. "The Rights of the Child".

3725 **1192** 42c. multicoloured 1·30 40

1193 Rey

2002. Birth Centenary of Jean Rey (politician).

3726 **1193** 52c. blue and cobalt 1·60 75

1194 Princess
Elisabeth

2002. First Birthday of Princess Elisabeth. Multicoloured.

3727 49c. Type **1194** 1·60 50
3728 59c. Princess Elisabeth with
parents (horiz) 1·90 75
MS3729 123×88 mm 84c. Princess
Elisabeth (different) (59×38 mm) 2·75 2·75

No. 3727 was issued with a se-tenant label inscribed "PRIOR".

1195 Church, Ice
Cream Van and
Family

2002. Christmas. Sheet 166×40 mm containing T **1195** and similar vert designs. Multicoloured.

MS3730 41c. Type **1195**; 41c. Skier in
snowy fir tree; 41c. Tobogganist and
bird wearing hat; 41c. Skier wearing
kilt; 41c. Skiers holding candles;
41c. Boy holding snowman-shaped
ice cream; 41c. Children throwing
snowballs; 41c. Children, snowman,
and elderly man; 41c. Brazier, re-
freshment hut and people; 41c. Hut,
robbers, cow and policeman 12·50 12·50

1196 Bricks

2002. The Twentieth Century. Society. Sheet 200×166 mm containing T **1196**.

MS3731 41c. purple, red and pink
(Type **1196** (social housing)); 41c.
deep purple, orange and purple
("MEI/MAI 68" and rubble (student
protests)); 41c. slate, grey and green
(telephone telecommunications));
41c. red, orange and brown (slabs
(gap between wealth and poverty));
41c. brown, bistre and blue (broken
crucifix (secularization of society));
41c. multicoloured (towers of blocks
(urbanization)); 41c. pink, violet and
purple (combined female and male
symbols (universal suffrage)); 41c.
blue, orange and grey (enclosed
circle (social security)); 41c. grey,
green and bistre (schoolbag
(equality in education)); 41c. grey,
purple and deep purple (elderly
man (ageing population)); 41c. blue,
green and emerald ("E" (European
Union)); 41c. chestnut, brown and
yellow (stylized figure (declaration of
Human Rights)); 41c. bistre, orange
and light orange (pyramid of blocks
(growth of consumer society)); 41c.
blue, mauve and green (female
symbol (feminism)); 41c. brown,
sepia and light brown (mechanical
arm (de-industrialization)); 41c.
brown and green (dripping nozzle
(oil crises)); 41c. multicoloured
(vehicle (transportation)); 41c. lilac,
brown and purple (sperm and egg
(contraception)); 41c. green, red and
grey (television (growth of television
and radio)); 41c. pink, violet and
blue (electric plug (increase in home
appliances)) 25·00 25·00

1197 Sunset

2002. Bereavement. No value expressed.

3732 **1197** (49c.) multicoloured 1·50 65

1198 Crocus

2002. Flowers. No value expressed. Ordinary or self-adhesive gum.

3733 **1198** (49c.) multicoloured 1·50 65

No. 3733 was for use on inland letters up to 50 g.

1199 Nero and
Adhemar
(cartoon
characters)

2003. 80th (2002) Birth Anniv of Marc Sleen (cartoonist). Multicoloured.

3735 49c. Type **1199** 1·60 60
MS3736 121×91 mm 82c. Nero and
Marc Sleen (49×38 mm) 2·75 2·75

1200 Firefighters, Engine
and Ladders

2003. Public Services (Nos. 3737/41) and St. Valentine (3742). Multicoloured.

3737 49c. Type **1200** 1·60 60
3738 49c. Traffic police men and
policewoman 1·60 60
3739 49c. Civil defence workers
mending flood defences 1·60 60
3740 49c. Elderly woman wearing
breathing mask, hand
holding syringe and theatre
nurse 1·60 60
3741 49c. Postman riding bicycle
and obtaining signature
for parcel 1·60 60
3742 49c. Hearts escaping from
birdcage 1·60 60

1201 Van de Velde and
New House, Tervuren

2003. 140th Birth Anniv of Henry van de Velde (architect). Multicoloured.

3743 49c. Type **1201** 1·60 60
3744 59c. Van de Velde and Belgian
pavilion, Paris International
Exhibition, 1937 (vert) 1·90 70
3745 59c. Van de Velde and Book
Tower, Central Library, Ghent
University (vert) 1·90 70
MS3746 91×125 mm 84c. Woman and
Art Nouveau newel post 2·75 2·75

1202 Bowls

2003. Traditional Sports. Multicoloured.

3747 49c. Type **1202** 1·80 65
3748 49c. Archery 1·80 65
MS3749 91×126 mm. 82c. Pigeon
racing 3·00 3·00

1203 Berlioz

2003. Birth Bicentenary of Hector Berlioz (composer).

3750 **1203** 59c. multicoloured 2·10 75

1204 Statue of
Men Conversing

2003. Anniversaries. Multicoloured.

3751 49c. Type **1204** (150th anniv of
engineers' association) 1·80 65
3752 49c. Statue of seated man
(centenary of Solvay Business
School) 1·80 65

1205 Papy
Ferdinand

2003. Red Cross. Cartoon characters in rescue attempt. Multicoloured.

3753 41c. + 9c. Type **1205** 2·10 1·30
3754 41c. + 9c. Pilou holding light 2·10 1·30
3755 41c. + 9c. Stam running for
help 2·10 1·30

Nos. 3753/5 were issued together, se-tenant, forming a composite design.

1206 Bouquet

2003. Third International Flower Show, Liege.

3756 **1206** 49c. multicoloured 2·00 65

1207 "Maigret"
(film poster)

2002. Birth Centenary of Georges Simenon (writer). Multicoloured.

3757 49c. Type **1207** 2·00 65
3758 59c. "Le chat" (film poster) 2·40 80
MS3759 91×126 mm. 84c. Simenon
(38×49 mm) 3·25 3·25

1208 Bells of St. Rumbold's
Cathedral, Maline

2003. 150th Anniv of Belgium–Russia Diplomatic Relations. Multicoloured.

3760 59c. Type **1208** 2·40 80
3761 59c. Bells of St. Peter and Paul's
Cathedral, St. Petersburg 2·40 80

1209 Eternity Symbol and "Mail Art"

2003. Stamp Day. Mail Art.

3762 **1209** 49c. multicoloured 2·10 65

1210 Roland on Horseback

2003. "Philately for the Young". *The Valiant Knight* (comic strip created by Francois Craenhals).

3763	**1210**	49c. multicoloured	2·10	65

1211 Calcite

2003. Minerals. Multicoloured.

3764	49c. Type **1211**	2·10	65
3765	49c. Quartz	2·10	65
3766	49c. Barytes	2·10	65
3767	49c. Galena	2·10	65
3768	49c. Turquoise	2·10	65

1212 "Belgium, The Coast" (Leo Marfut)

2003. Europa. Poster Art.

3769	**1212**	59c. multicoloured	2·75	1·40

1213 *La Robe de Mariee* (Paul Delvaux, Koksijde)

2003. "This is Belgium" (1st series). Sheet 167×200 mm containing T **1213** and similar vert designs showing sites from smaller Belgian towns. Multicoloured.

MS3770 41c. Type **1213**; 41c. Mural, Town Hall, Oudenaarde; 41c. *De vius* (sculpture, Rik Poot) and Town Hall, Vilvoorde; 41c. Turnhout chateau; 41c. Ambiorix (sculpture), Gallo-Roman museum, Tongeren; 41c. Fountain (sculpture, Pol Bury), La Louviere; 41c. Town Hall, Braine; 52c. Mardasson Memorial, Bastogne; 52c. Tower and snow scene, Sankt Vith; 57c. Saxophone and Citadel, Dinant 20·00 11·00

See also Nos. MS3809, MS3943 and MS4033.

1214 *Monument to the Seasonal Worker, Rillaar* (Jan Peirelinck)

2003. Tourism. Statues. Multicoloured.

3771	49c. Type **1214**	2·20	70
3772	49c. *La Tionade, Treignes* (Yves and Claude Rahir)	2·20	70
3773	49c. *Textile Teut, Town Hall, Hamont-Achel* (Teo Groenen)	2·20	70
3774	49c. *The Canal Guy,* Brussels (Tom Frantzen)	2·20	70
3775	49c. *The Maca,* Wavre (Jean Godart)	2·20	70

1215 King Baudouin and Prince Albert

2003. Tenth Anniv of the Accession of King Albert. Multicoloured.

3776	49c. Type **1215**	2·20	70
MS3777 90×125 mm. 59c. King Baudouin (38×48 mm); 84c. King Albert (38×48 mm)		6·75	5·50

1216 *Argenteuil* (Edouard Manet)

2003. Art.

3778	**1216**	49c. + 11c. multicoloured	2·75	1·80

No. 3778 was issued with a se-tenant label inscribed "PRIOR".

1217 *Still Life* (Giorgio Morandi)

2003. "Europhalia 2003 Italy" Festival. Italian Presidency of European Union. Multicoloured.

3779	49c. Type **1217**	2·20	75
3780	59c. Cistalia 202 (1947)	2·75	90

No. 3779 was issued with a se-tenant label inscribed "PRIOR".

Stamps of the same design were issued by Italy.

1218 Elderly Couple, Family and Young People

2003. Social Cohesion.

3781	**1218**	49c. multicoloured	2·20	80

No. 3781 was issued with a se-tenant label inscribed "PRIOR".

1219 St. Nicholas

2003. Christmas.

3782	**1219**	49c. multicoloured	2·20	80

No. 3782 was issued with a se-tenant label inscribed "PRIOR".

1220 King Albert II

2003

3783	**1220**	49c. red	2·20	80
3784	**1220**	50c. red	2·20	80
3785	**1220**	79c. blue and red	3·50	1·30
3786	**1220**	80c. violet and red	3·50	1·30

Nos. 3783/6 are inscribed "PRIOR" at left.

1221 Woman holding Cat ("Jardin extraordinaire")

2003. 50th Anniv of Belgian Television. Sheet 166×140 mm containing T **1221** and similar vert designs. Multicoloured.

MS3795 41c.×5 Type **1221**; Cameraman and camera; Broadcasting tower; Brothers Cassiers and Jef Burm; Scene from "Schipper naast Mathide" 9·00 6·50

1222 Man leaning against Pile of Books

2003. The Book. Multicoloured.

3796	49c. Type **1222**	2·20	80
3797	49c. Man rolling through printing machine (horiz)	2·20	80
3798	49c. Books on shelves	2·20	80

Nos. 3796/8 were each issued with an attached label inscribed "Prior".

1223 Maurice Gilliams

2003. Writers.

3799	**1223**	49c. brown, sepia and light brown	2·20	80
3800	-	59c. brown and orange	2·75	95

DESIGN: 59c. Marguerite Yourcenar (Maguerite de Crayencour).

No. 3799 was issued with an attached label inscribed "Prior".

1224 Tulip

2003. Flowers. No value expressed. Self-adhesive.

3801	**1224**	(59c.) multicoloured	2·50	95

No. 3801 was for use on inland letters up to 50g.

1225 Herbeumont Church

2003. Christmas and New Year.

3802	**1225**	41c. multicoloured	1·70	65

1226 Justin Henin Hardenne

2003. Belgian Tennis Champions. Multicoloured.

3803	49c. Type **1226** (2003 Roland Garros and U.S. Open champion)	2·30	80
3804	49c. Kim Clijsters (2002 Masters Cup and 2003 WTA No. 1 champion) (horiz)	2·30	80

Nos. 3803/4 were each issued with an attached label inscribed "Prior", either at top or bottom (vert) or left or right (horiz).

1227 XIII and Lighthouse

2004. "Philately for the Young". XIII (comic strip created by Jean van Damme and William Vance).

3805	**1227**	41c. multicoloured	1·80	65

1228 *Portrait of Marguerite Khonopff*

2004. Fernand Khnopff (artist) Commemoration. Sheet 160×140 mm containing T **1228** and similar multicoloured designs.

MS3806 41c.×4, Type **1228**; *Caresses* (55×24 mm); *The Abandoned City; Brown Eyes and a Blue Flower* (55×24 mm) 5·25 4·75

1229 Carnation

2004. Flowers. No value expressed. Self-adhesive.

3807	**1229**	(49c.) multicoloured	1·80	80

No. 3807 was for use on inland letters up to 50g.

1230 Profile, Stamp and Kiss

2004. Stamp Day.

3808	**1230**	41c. multicoloured	1·40	65

1231 Peter Piot (AIDS agency director)

2004. "This is Belgium" (2nd series). Sheet 166×200 mm containing T **1231** and similar vert designs showing Belgian personalities. Multicoloured.

MS3809 57c.×10, Type **1231**; Nicole Van Goethem (film maker); Dirk Frimout and Frank de Winnie (astronaut and cosmonaut); Jaques Rogge (president, International Olympic Committee); Christian de Duve (winner, Nobel Prize for Medicine); Gabrielle Petit (war heroine); Catherine Verfaillie (director, Stem Cell Institute, Minnesota) and Christine Van Broeckhoven (director, Molecular Biology Laboratory, University of Antwerp); Jaques Stilbe (philatelist); Queen Fabiola; Adrien van der Burch (organizer, Brussels Exhibition, 1935) 18·00 14·50

1232 Herg and Models of Rocket and Tintin

2004. 75th Anniv of Tintin (cartoon character created by Georges Remi (Herge)). Sheet 163×126 mm containing T **1232** and similar vert designs. Multicoloured.

MS3810 41c.×5, Type **1232**; Technical sketch for Destination Moon; Tintin and Snowy (Bobbie); Tintin climbing up rocket (*Explorers on the Moon*); Tintin, Captain Haddock and Snowy on the moon (cover illustration, *Explorers on the Moon*) 7·25 6·50

1233 Sugar Beet

2004. Sugar Industry. Multicoloured.

3811	**49c.**	Type **1233**	1·60	70

3812	**49c.**	49c. Sugar refinery	1·60	70
3813	**49c.**	49c. Tienen city	1·60	70

Nos. 3811/13 were each issued with a *se-tenant* label inscribed "Prior".

1234 Stars

2004. European Elections.

3814	**1234**	22c. cobalt, ultramarine and yellow	80	35

1235 *Temptation* (Salvador Dali)

2004. Birth Centenary of Salvador Dali (artist).

3815	**1235**	49c.+11c. multicoloured	2·10	1·90

No. 3815 was issued with a *se-tenant* label inscribed "Prior".

1236 Chapel, Buggenhout

2004. Tourism. Places of Pilgrimage.

3816	**1236**	49c. green	1·60	70
3817	-	49c. agate	1·60	70
3818	-	49c. purple	1·60	70
3819	-	49c. indigo	1·60	70

DESIGNS: No. 3817, Banneux; 3818, Scherpenheuvel; 3819, Beauraing (horiz).

Nos. 3816/19 were each issued with a *se-tenant* label inscribed "Prior".

1237 New Member's Flags and EU Emblem

2004. Enlargement of European Union (1st issue). Sheet 125×90 mm containing T **1237** and similar horiz designs. Multicoloured.

MS3820	50c.×2 Type **1237**×2; 60c.×2 Parliament building; As No. 3814		8·00	7·25

See also Nos. 3835/44.

1238 *Le Faune Mordu* (sculpture) (Jef Lambeaux), Boverie Park

2004. Liege ("Lidje todi"). Multicoloured.

3821	**1238**	49c. Type **1238**	1·40	65
3822		49c. Bridge (Santiago Calatrava)	1·40	65
MS3823	90×125 mm. 75c. Blast furnace, Seraing (38×49 mm)		2·50	2·30

1239 Earth showing Clouds and Ozone Layer (climate and CO_2)

2004. Climatology. Multicoloured.

3824	**1239**	50c. Type **1239**	1·60	65
3825		65c. Sun and earth (earth–sun relationship)	2·00	85
3826		80c. Earth showing continent and viewed from space (earth)	2·50	1·00
3827		80c. Sun viewed through tel- escope and showing spots	2·50	1·00

Nos. 3824 and 3826 were each issued with a *se-tenant* label inscribed "Prior".

1240 Edgar Jacobs

2004. Birth Centenary of Edgar Pierre Jacobs (creator of Blake and Mortimer (comic strip)). Black and yellow (60c.) or multicoloured (other).

3828	**60c.**	Type **1240**	2·20	90
MS3829	125×90 mm. €1.20 Blake and Mortimer (45×36 mm)		3·75	3·00

Stamps of a similar design were issued by France.

1241 Django Reinhardt

2004. Jazz Musicians. Multicoloured.

3830	**50c.**	Type **1241** (guitarist)	1·60	65
3831	50c.	Fud Candrix (saxophonist)	1·60	65
3832	50c.	Rene Thomas (guitarist)	1·60	65
3833	50c.	Jack Sels (composer and saxophonist)	1·60	65
3834	50c.	Bobby Jaspar (flautist and saxophonist)	1·60	65

Nos. 3830/4 were each issued with a *se-tenant* label inscribed "Prior".

1242 EU Emblem and Cyprus Flag

2004. Enlargement of European Union (2nd issue). Designs showing emblem and new member flag. Multicoloured. Self-adhesive.

3835	**44c.**	Type **1242**	1·60	65
3836	44c.	Estonia	1·60	65
3837	44c.	Hungary	1·60	65
3838	44c.	Latvia	1·60	65
3839	44c.	Lithuania	1·60	65
3840	44c.	Malta	1·60	65
3841	44c.	Poland	1·60	65
3842	44c.	Czech Republic	1·60	65
3843	44c.	Slovakia	1·60	65
3844	44c.	Slovenia	1·60	65

1243 King Albert II

2004. 70th Birthday of King Albert II. Each black and gold.

3845	**50c.**	Type **1243**	1·60	65
MS3846	90×125 mm. 80c. As No. 3845 (38×48 mm)		2·50	2·10

No. 3845 was issued with a *se-tenant* label inscribed "Prior".

1244 Wind Break (Belgian Coast)

2004. Europa. Holidays. Winning Designs in Photographic Competition. Multicoloured.

3847	**55c.**	Type **1244** (Muriel Vekemans)	1·70	1·40
3848	55c.	Semois valley (Belgian Ardennes) (Freddy Deburgh- graeve)	1·70	1·40

1245 Female Basketball Player

2004. Olympic Games, Athens 2004. Multicoloured.

3849	**50c.**	Type **1245**	1·70	65
3850	55c.	Cyclist (horiz)	1·80	75
3851	60c.	Pole vaulter (horiz)	2·00	80
MS3852	136×90 mm. 80c. Olympic flame		2·75	2·10

No. 3849 was issued with a *se-tenant* label inscribed "Prior".

1246 Red Cross Workers

2004. Red Cross.

3853	**1246**	50c.+11c. multicoloured	2·00	1·60

No. 3853 was issued with a *se-tenant* label inscribed "Prior".

1247 *L'appel*

2004. Tenth Death Anniv of Idel Ianchelevici (sculptor). Multicoloured.

3854	**1247**	50c. Type **1247**	1·70	65
3855		55c. "Perennis perdurat poeta"	1·80	75

No. 3854 was issued with a *se-tenant* label inscribed "Prior".

Stamps of the same design were issued by Romania.

2004. Mourning Stamp. As T **1197**.

3856	**1197**	50c. multicoloured	1·70	65

1248 Squirrel and Blackcap

2004. Forest Week. Sheet 90×125 mm containing T **1248** and similar vert designs. Multicoloured.

MS3857	44c.×4, Type **1248**; Nightin- gale, robin and red admiral butterfly; Bee, vole and weasel; Jay and pea- cock butterfly		6·50	5·25

The stamps and margin of MS3857 form a composite design of a forest scene.

1249 Volunteer Medal

2004. War Volunteers.

3858	**1249**	50c. multicoloured	1·70	65

1250 Impatiens

2004. Flowers. No value expressed. Self-adhesive.

3859	**1250**	(50c.) multicoloured	1·70	65

No. 3859 was for use on inland letters up to 50g.

1251 Foal

2004. Belgica 2006 International Stamp Exhibition, Brussels (1st issue). Sheet 166×140 mm containing T **1251** and similar vert designs. Multicoloured.

MS3860	44c.×5, Type **1251**; Robin; Cat; Puppy; Fish		17·00	14·50

See also Nos. 3892/MS3897.

1252 Jack O' Lantern

2004. Halloween. Self-adhesive. Multicoloured.

3861	**1252**	44c. Type **1252**	1·70	65
3862		44c. Witch, cat and bats	1·70	65

1253 Raymond Jean de Kramer

2004. Writers' Death Anniversaries. Multicoloured.

3863	**1253**	50c. Type **1253** (writing as Jean Ray or John Flanders) (40th)	1·70	65
3864		75c. Johan Daisne (26th)	2·50	1·00
3865		80c. Thomas Owen (2nd) (vert)	2·75	1·10

Nos. 3863 and 3865 were issued with a *se-tenant* label inscribed "Prior".

1254 Soldiers, Mother and Child on Snow-covered Street

2004. 60th Anniv of Attack on Bastogne. Multicoloured.

3866		44c. Type **1254**	1·70	65
3867		55c. Soldiers assisting wounded (vert)	1·80	75
3868		65c. Soldiers amongst trees	2·10	85

1255 *Flight into Egypt*

2004. Christmas (1st issue). Paintings by Peter Paul Rubens. Multicoloured.

3869	**1255**	44c. Type **1255**	1·70	65
3870		44c. *Adoration of the Magi*	1·70	65

Stamps of the same design were issued by Germany. See also No. 3872.

1256 Rene Baeten

2004. Belgian International Motocross Champions. Sheet 151×166 mm containing T **1256** and similar horiz designs.

MS3871	50c.×12, (23bis a, d, e, f, g, i, j, k and l) multicoloured; (23bis b) green and brown; (23bis c) brown, lemon and deep brown; (23bis h) blue and brown		20·00	16·00

DESIGNS: Type **1256**; Jacky Martens; Georges Jobe; Joel Roberts; Eric Geboers; Roger de Coster; Stefan Everts; Gaston Rahier; Joel Smets; Harry Everts; Andre Malherbe and Steve Ramon.

The stamps of MS3871 were arranged around a central label, showing a motocross rider, each with a *se-tenant* label inscribed "Prior" attached at either left or right. The Belgium Post identification number is given in brackets to assist identification.

2004. Christmas (2nd issue). Paintings by Peter Rubens. Self-adhesive.

3872		44c. As No. 3870 (22×22 mm)	1·70	65

1257 Stylized Posthorn

2005

3873	**1257**	6c. scarlet	35	15
3874	**1257**	10c. blue	85	40
3877	**1257**	1 (52c.) scarlet	1·00	90

1258 Woman's Legs

2005. Centenary of Women's Council.

3882	**1258**	50c. multicoloured	1·70	65

No. 3882 was issued with a *se-tenant* label inscribed "Prior".

1259 Michel Vaillant

2005. "Philately for the Young". Michel Vaillant (comic strip created by Jean Graton).
3883	**1259**	50c. multicoloured	1·70	65

No. 3883 was issued with a *se-tenant* label inscribed "Prior".

1260 The Violinist (Kees van Dongen)

2005. "Promotion of Philately".
3884	**1260**	50c.+12c. multicoloured	2·10	1·70

1261 "www.175-25. be"

2005. 175th Anniv of Independence (1st issue). 25th Anniv of Federal State. No value expressed. Self-adhesive.
3885	**1261**	(50c.) multicoloured	1·70	65

See also No. **MS**3889 and **MS**3891.

1262 Johan Hendrick van Dale and *van Dale* (Dutch dictionary)

2005. Language. Multicoloured.
3886	**1262**	55c. Type **1262**	1·80	75
3887		55c. Maurice Grevisse and "le bon usage" (French grammar)	1·80	75

1263 Child receiving Polio Vaccine

2005. Centenary of Rotary International (charitable organization). Polio Eradication Campaign.
3888	**1263**	80c. multicoloured	2·75	1·30

1264 First Railway Journey from Brussels to Malines (1835)

2005. 175th Anniv of Independence (2nd issue). Sheet 166×200 mm containing T **1264** and similar horiz designs. Multicoloured.
MS3889	44c.×10, Type **1264** (transport); Bakuba dancers, Congo; Early school children (education); Factory workers (industrialization); Family (social development); Bombardment of Edingen, 1940; Brussels Expo, 1958 (trade); Rue de la Loi, Wetstraat (federalization); Berlaymont building, Brussels (Europe); "The Shadow and its Shadow" (Rene Mgritte) (art)	15·00 13·50

1265 "TSUNAMI" and Sea

2005. Red Cross. Support for Victims of Tsunami Disaster.
3890	**1265**	50c.+12c. multicoloured	2·10	1·70

No. 3890 was issued with a *se-tenant* label inscribed "Prior".

1266 King Albert II and Queen Paola

2005. 175th Anniv of Independence (3rd issue). Sheet 126×90 mm.
MS3891	**1266**	75c. multicoloured	2·50	2·00

1267 Go-Kart

2005. Belgica 2006 International Stamp Exhibition, Brussels (2nd issue). Multicoloured. (a) Self-adhesive.
3892	44c. Type **1267**		1·50	60
3893	44c. Motor boat		1·50	60
3894	44c. Train		1·50	60
3895	44c. Airplane		1·50	60
3896	44c. Spacecraft		1·50	60

(b) Size 27×39 mm. Miniature Sheet. Ordinary gum.
MS3897	166×131 mm. Nos. 3892/5	17·00	13·50

1268 Rose "Belinda"

2005. Ghent Flower Show. Multicoloured.
3898	44c. Type **1268**		1·50	60
3899	70c. Rose "Pink Iceberg" (vert)		2·30	95
3900	80c. Rose "Old Master"		2·75	1·10

Nos. 3898/3900 were impregnated with the scent of roses.

No. 3900 was issued with a *se-tenant* label inscribed "Prior".

1269 The Children's Table (Gustave van de Woestijne)

2005. Europa. Gastronomy. Multicoloured.
3901	60c. Type **1269**		2·00	1·60
3902	60c. *Still Life with Oysters, Fruit and Pastry*		2·00	1·60

1270 Black Stork

2005. Stamp Day.
3903	**1270**	€4 multicoloured	13·00	5·25

1271 Soldiers

2005. 55th Anniv of Korean War.
3904	**1271**	44c. multicoloured	1·50	60

1272 Celebration

2005. 60th Anniv of End of World War II. Multicoloured.
3905	**1272**	44c. Type **1272**	1·50	60
3906		44c. Camp prisoner	1·50	60
3907		44c. Returning service men and prisoners	1·50	60

1273 Zimmer Tower, Lier, Flanders

2005. Tourism. Clock Towers.
3908	**1273**	44c. black	1·50	60
3909	-	44c. agate	1·50	60
3910	-	44c. chocolate	1·50	60

DESIGNS: No. 3908 Type **1273**; 3909 Belfry, Mons, Wallonia; 3910 Mont des Arts Clock, Brussels.

1274 Hiker (Ardennes)

2005. Holidays. Multicoloured.
3911	50c. Type **1274**		1·70	65
3912	50c. Sunbather		1·70	65

Nos. 3911/12 were each issued with a se-tenant label inscribed "Prior".

1275 Hearts

2005. Greetings Stamps. Multicoloured. Self-adhesive.
3913	(50c.) Type **1275**		1·70	65
3914	80c. Doves (wedding)		2·75	1·10
3915	80c. Two rings (wedding)		2·75	1·10
3916	80c. Boy (birth)		2·75	1·10
3917	80c. Girl (birth)		2·75	1·10

No. 3913 was for use on inland letters up to 50g.

1276 Tulip

2005. Air. Flowers. No value expressed. Multicoloured. Self-adhesive.
3918	**1276**	(70c.) multicoloured	2·30	95

1277 *L'humanitie assaillie par les sept Peches capiteux* (Seven Deadly Sins) (16th-century tapestry, Brussels)

2005. Carpets and Tapestries. Multicoloured.
3919	44c. Type **1277**		1·50	60
3920	60c. Carpet, Hereke, Turkey		2·00	80

Stamps of a similar design were issued by Turkey.

1278 Radio Waves

2005. 75th Anniv of Radio.
3921	**1278**	50c. magenta and black	1·70	65

No. 3921 was issued with a *se-tenant* label inscribed "Prior".

1279 Robert Van de Walle

2005. Belgian International Judo Champions. Sheet 100×167 mm containing T **1279** and similar horiz designs. Multicoloured.
MS3922	50c.×6, Type **1279**; Ingrid Berghmans; Ulla Werbrouck; Gella Vandecaveye; Christel Deliege; Johan Laats	10·00 8·00

The stamps of **MS**3922 were each issued with a *se-tenant* label inscribed "Prior" attached at either left or right.

1280 King Albert II

2005
3923	**1280**	50c. multicoloured (postage)	1·00	85
3923a	**1280**	52c. multicoloured	1·00	70
3928	**1280**	70c. blue and light (air)	2·30	95
3928a	**1280**	80c. blue, grey and black	95	65
3928b	**1280**	83c. multicoloured	1·00	70
3929	**1280**	90c. blue, grey and black	2·75	1·10

Nos. 3923 and 3928/9 were inscribed "Prior".

1281 *Buccinum undatum*

2005. Molluscs. Sheet 161×130 mm containing T **1281** and similar designs. Multicoloured. Self-adhesive.
MS3933	44c.×6, Type **1281**; *Epitonium clathrus*; *Cepea nemoralis* and *Arion rufus*; *Donax vittatus*; *Anodonta cygnea*; *Anodonta cygnea* (different)	9·00 7·25

1282 Centre for Comic Strip Art, Brussels

2005. Architecture. Multicoloured.
3934	44c. Type **1282**		1·50	60
3935	44c. Museum of Musical Instruments, Brussels		1·50	60
3936	65c. Bukit Pasoh Road, Singapore		2·10	85
3937	65c. Kandahar Street, Singapore		2·10	85

Stamps of the same design were issued by Singapore.

1283 Chrysanthemum

2005. Flowers. No value expressed. Self-adhesive.
3938	**1283**	(50c.) multicoloured	1·70	65

No. 3938 was for use on inland letters up to 50g.

1284 The Reaper (Kasimir Malevich)

2005. "Europhalia 2005—Russia" Festival. Multicoloured.
3939	50c. Type **1284**		1·70	65
3940	70c. "Allegory" (Sergei Sudeikin)		2·30	95

No. 3939 was issued with a *se-tenant* label inscribed "Prior".

1285 Shrine of Our Lady, Tournai

2005. 800th Anniv of Shrine of Our Lady by Nicolas of Verdun.

3941	**1285**	75c. bronze and gold	2·50	1·00

1286 Asterix

2005. Asterix (comic strip written by Rene Goscinny and illustrated by Albert Uderzo). Sheet 161×130 mm containing T **1286** and similar designs showing characters. Multicoloured.

MS3942 60c.×6, Type **1286**; Cacofonix (27×41 mm.); Getafix (41×27 mm.); Obelix (41×27 mm.); Abraracourcix (27×41 mm.); Asterix feasting (39×34 mm.) 11·50 10·50

1287 "Objet" (Joelle Tuerlinckx)

2005. "This is Belgium" (3rd series). Art. Sheet 166×201 mm containing T **1287** and similar designs.

MS3943 44c.×10, black and claret (Type **1287**); multicoloured (*ABC* (Jef Geys)); multicoloured (*La Traviata* (Lili Dujourie)); multicoloured (*Representation d'un corps rond* (Ann Veronica Janssens)); black (*Portrait of an Artist by Himself (XIII)* (Jan Vercuysse)); multicoloured (*Donderwolk* (Panamarenko)); multicoloured (*Tournus* (Marthe Wery)); multicoloured (*Figuur op de rug gezien (la nuque)* (I Luc Tuymans)); black and bright carmine (*Jeu de mains* (Michel Francois)); *Mur de la montee des Anges* (Jan Fabre)) 13·00 12·00

The stamps of No. MS3943 form a composite design.

1288 *The Princess and the Pea*

2005. Birth Bicentenary of Hans Christian Andersen (writer). Multicoloured. (a) Ordinary gum.

3944	50c. Type **1288b**		1·70	65
3945	50c. *The Ugly Duckling*		1·70	65
3946	50c. *Thumbelina*		1·70	65
3947	50c. *The Little Mermaid*		1·70	65
3948	50c. *The Emperor's New Clothes*		1·70	65

(b) Size 28×22 mm. Self-adhesive.

3949	50c. As No. 3944		1·70	65
3950	50c. As No. 3945		1·70	65
3951	50c. As No. 3946		1·70	65
3952	50c. As No. 3947		1·70	65
3953	50c. As No. 3948		1·70	65

Nos. 3944/8 each have a label inscribed "Prior" attached at left.

1289 Father Christmas

2005. Christmas. (a) Ordinary gum.

3954	**1289**	44c. multicoloured	1·50	60

(b) Size 23×28 mm. Self-adhesive.

3955		44c. multicoloured	1·50	60

1290 Maurits Sabbe

2005. Popular Literature. Writers. Multicoloured.

3956	44c. Type **1290**		1·50	60
3957	44c. Arthur Masson		1·50	60

1291 Queen Astrid

2005. Birth Centenary of Queen Astrid. Each black and gold.

3958	44c. Type **1291**		1·50	60

MS3959 90×125 mm. 80c. Queen Astrid and Prince Albert (38×49 mm) 2·75 2·10

1292 Drum

2005. Music. Brass Bands. Multicoloured.

3960	50c. Type **1292**		1·70	70
3961	50c. Cornet		1·70	70
3962	50c. Sousaphone		1·70	70
3963	50c. Clarinet		1·70	70
3964	50c. Tuba		1·70	70

Nos. 3960/4 each have a label inscribed "Prior" attached at foot.

1293 Donkey

2006. Farm Animals. Multicoloured. Self-adhesive.

3965	46c. Type **1293**		1·40	65
3966	46c. Hens		1·40	65
3967	46c. Ducks		1·40	65
3968	46c. Pigs		1·40	65
3969	46c. Cow		1·40	65
3970	46c. Goat		1·40	65
3971	46c. Rabbits		1·40	65
3972	46c. Horses		1·40	65
3973	46c. Sheep		1·40	65
3974	46c. Geese		1·40	65

1294 Michel de Ghelderode

2006. Writers Commemorations.

3975	**1294**	52c. black and blue	1·60	70
3976	-	78c. black and magenta	1·90	85

DESIGN: 78c. Herman Terlinck.

No. 3975 has a label inscribed "Prior" attached at left.

1295 Guillaume Dufay and Gilles Binchois

2006. Renaissance Polyphonists (part song writers). Multicoloured.

3977	60c. Type **1295**		1·80	75
3978	60c. Johannes Ockeghem		1·80	75
3979	60c. Jacob Obrecht		1·80	75

3980	60c. Adriaan Willaert		1·80	75
3981	60c. Orlandus Lassus		1·80	75

1296 Musical Score and Mozart

2006. 250th Birth Anniv of Wolfgang Amadeus Mozart.

3982	**1296**	70c. multicoloured	2·30	1·00

1297 Cross Bowman **1298** Cross Bowman

2006. Cross Bowmen. (a) Ordinary gum.

3983	**1297**	46c. multicoloured	1·50	65

(b) Size 24×32 mm. Self-adhesive gum.

3984	**1298**	(52c.) multicoloured	1·70	70

1299 Senate

2006. 175th Anniv of Democracy. Sheet 200×83 mm containing T **1299** and similar multicoloured designs.

MS3985 46c.×3, Type **1299**; King Leopold (vert); Chamber of representatives 4·50 3·75

1300 Head with Open Mouth

2006. Freedom of the Press. Sheet 197×100 mm containing T **1300** and similar multicoloured designs.

MS3986 52c.×5, Type **1300** ×3; Blue sky ×2 (horiz) 8·25 7·25

The stamps of MS3986 each have a label inscribed "Prior" attached at foot. The stamp depicting a blue sky shows a woman's face when tilted.

1301 Mouth and Script **1302** Mouth and Script

2006. Stamp Festival. Winning Entry in Design a Stamp Competition. (a) Ordinary gum.

3987	**1301**	46c. multicoloured	1·50	65

(b) Size 29×25 mm. Self-adhesive gum.

3988	**1302**	(52c.) multicoloured	1·70	70
3988a	**1302**	(52c.) As Type **1302** but design reversed	1·70	70

Nos. 3988/a were each issued with a se-tenant label inscribed "Prior".

1303 Justus Lipsius

2006. 400th Death Anniv of Justus Lipsius (writer and scientist).

3989	**1303**	70c. brown and cinnamon	2·30	1·00

1304 Winner and Trophy

2006. First Four Stages—Giro Italia (cycle race), Wallonia.

3990	**1304**	52c. multicoloured	1·70	70

1305 John Walker

2006. 30th Anniv of Memorial Van Damme Track and Field Event. Sheet 167×100 mm containing T **1305** and similar vert designs. Multicoloured.

MS3991 52c.×5, Type **1305**; Alberto Juantorena; Ivo Van Damme; Sebastian Coe; Steve Ovett 8·25 7·25

The stamps of MS3991 were each issued with a label inscribed "Prior" at foot.

1306 Clement Van Hassel

2006. Belgian World Champions—Billiards. Sheet 153×167 mm containing T **1306** and similar horiz designs. Multicoloured.

MS3992 52c.×12, Type **1306**; Tony Schrauwen; Leo Corin; Emile Wafflard; Ludo Dielis; Jos Vervest; Frederic Caudron; Laurent Boulanger; Paul Stroobants; Eddy Leppens and Peter De Backer; Raymond Ceulemans; Raymond Steylaerts; Jozef Philipoom 18·00 16·00

The stamps of MS3992 were each issued with a label inscribed "Prior" at either left or right.

The stamps of MS3992 were not for sale separately.

1307 *L'offrande de Joachim Refusee* (Lambert Lombard)

2006. Art. 500th Birth Anniv of Lambert Lombard (3393/4) or 150th Birth Anniv of Leon Spilliaert (3395/6). Multicoloured.

3993	65c. Type **1307**		2·10	90
3994	65c. *August et la Sybille de Tibur* (Lambert Lombard)		2·10	90
3995	65c. *Duizeling* (Leon Spilliaert)		2·10	90
3996	65c. *De Dame met de Hoed* (Leon Spilliaert)		2·10	90

1308 Ostend Lighthouse

2006. Lighthouses. Multicoloured.

3997	46c. Type **1308**		1·50	65
3998	46c. Blankenberge		1·50	65
3999	46c. Nieuwport		1·50	65
4000	46c. Heist		1·50	65

1309 Dogfish

2006. North Sea Fish. Sheet 146×124 mm containing T **1309** and similar multicoloured designs.

MS4001 46c.×5, Type **1309**; Cod (47×26 mm); Thornback skate; Plaice (33×26 mm); Herring (33×26 mm) 7·50 6·50

The stamps and margins of **MS**4001 form a composite design.

1310 Emblem **1311** Emblem

2006. Belgica 2006 International Stamp Exhibition. (a) Ordinary Gum.

4002	**1310**	46c. multicoloured	1·50	65

(b) Size 24×28 mm. Self-adhesive gum.

4003	**1311**	(52c.) multicoloured	1·50	65

1312 Nurse, Patients and Bandages **1313** Nurse, Patients and Bandages

2006. Red Cross. Benjamin Secouriste (children's Red Cross certificate scheme). (a) Ordinary Gum.

4004	**1312**	52c.+12c. multicoloured	2·00	85

(b) Size 24×28 mm. Self-adhesive gum.

4005	**1313**	(52c.) multicoloured	1·70	70
4005a	**1313**	(52c.) As Type **1313** but design reversed	1·70	70

No. 4005/a were issued with a *se-tenant* label inscribed "Prior".

1314 Emblem

2006. Centenary of BOIC (Belgian Olympic and Interfederal Committee).

4006	**1314**	52c. multicoloured	1·70	70

No. 4006 was issued with a *se-tenant* label inscribed "Prior".

1315 Deigne

2006. Tourism. Wallonia. Showing village scenes. Multicoloured.

4007	52c. Type **1315**	1·70	70
4008	52c. Mein	1·70	70
4009	52c. Celles	1·70	70
4010	52c. Lompret	1·70	70
4011	52c. Ny	1·70	70

Nos. 4007/11 were each issued with a *se-tenant* label inscribed "Prior".

1316 Part of Football

2006. World Cup Football Championship, Germany. Sheet 126×90 mm.

MS4012	**1316**	€1.30 multicoloured	4·25	3·75

1317 *Centauria*

2006. Flowers. No value expressed. Self-adhesive.

4013	**1317**	(52c.) multicoloured	1·70	70

No. 4013 was for use on inland letters up to 50g.

1318 Miner

2006. 50th Anniv of Marcinelle Mine Disaster.

4014	**1318**	70c. multicoloured	2·30	1·00

1319 Tulip

2006. Air. Flowers. No value expressed. Self-adhesive. Multicoloured.

4015	**1319**	(70c.) multicoloured	2·30	1·00

No. 4015 was for use on letters of up to 50g. within Europe.

1320 *Oosterlinghuis* (beguinage (religious community), Bruges) (painting)

2006. 650th Anniv of Hanseatic League. Multicoloured.

4016	70c. Type **1320**	2·30	1·00
4017	80c. *Oosters Huis* (Bremen town hall) (painting)	2·50	1·10

1321 Institute Building

2006. Centenary of the Institute of Tropical Medicine.

4018	**1321**	80c. multicoloured	2·50	1·10

1322 "ABA"

2006. Academie de Philatelie de Belgique.

4019	**1322**	52c. multicoloured	1·60	70

No. 4019 was issued with a *se-tenant* label inscribed "Prior" attached at top.

1323 *Le Kleptomane* (Theodore Gericault)

2006. Foreign Masterpieces in Belgian Collections.

4020	**1323**	52c.+12c. multicoloured	2·10	95

No. 4020 was issued with a label inscribed "Prior" attached at left. The premium was for the promotion of philately.

1324 Ying Yang Symbol

2006. Belgica 2006 International Stamp Exhibition. Young Philatelist World Championship. Two sheets containing T **1324** and similar vert designs. Multicoloured.

MS4021	(a) 166×133 mm. 46c.×5, Type **1324**; Tulips as wine glasses; Butterflies as four leaf clover; Tent at night; Comic page containing all designs. (b) 190×120 mm. €1.95 Emblem (38×49 mm)	29·00	26·00

Nos. **MS**4021a/b were each sold for €5, the premium for the promotion of philately.

1325 Animals (Nassira Tadmiri)

2006. Europa. Integration. Multicoloured.

4022	52c. Type **1325**	1·60	70
4023	52c. Children of many nations and rainbow (Lize-Maria Verhaeghe)	1·60	70

1326 *New Skin* (Pierre Alechinsky) **1327** *New Skin* (Pierre Alechinsky)

2006. CoBrA (artistic movement). Multicoloured. (a) Miniature sheet. Ordinary gum.

MS4024	125×90 mm. 46c. Type **1326**; 70c. "Untitled" (Asger Jorn)	3·75	3·25

(b) Size 28×25 mm. No value expressed. Self-adhesive gum.

4025	(52c.) Type **1327**	1·60	70

Stamps of similar design were issued by Denmark.

1328 Rock and Roll **1329** Rock and Roll

2006. Dance. Multicoloured.

(a) Size 30×26 mm. No value expressed. Self-adhesive gum.

4026	(52c.) Type **1329**	1·60	70
4027	(52c.) Waltz	1·60	70
4028	(52c.) Tango	1·60	70
4029	(52c.) Cha-cha-cha	1·60	70
4030	(52c.) Samba	1·60	70

(b) Miniature sheet. Ordinary gum.

MS4031	166×125 mm. 60c.×5, Type **1328**; Waltz; Tango; Cha-cha-cha; Samba	8·75	8·75

1330 Kramikske

2006. Youth Philately. Kramikske Briochon, cartoon character created by Jean-Pol Vandenbroek.

4032	**1330**	46c. multicoloured	1·50	70

1331 Tomato and Shrimps

2006. "This is Belgium" (4th series). Food. Sheet 154×186 mm containing T **1331** and similar multicoloured designs.

MS4033	46c.×10, Type **1331**; Trappist beer (vert); Jenever (spirit) (vert); Chicory au gratin; Ham and sausages (vert); Waffles (vert); Stewed eels in chervil sauce; Chocolate; Mussels and fries (vert); Gueuze (beer) (vert)	13·50	13·00

1332 Angel playing Psaltery (detail) **1333** Angel playing Psaltery (detail)

2006. Christmas. Altarpiece by Hans Memling. Showing angel musicians. Multicoloured. (a) Ordinary gum.

4034	46c. Type **1332**	1·50	70
4035	46c. Tromba marina	1·50	70
4036	46c. Lute	1·50	70
4037	46c. Trumpet	1·50	70
4038	46c. Shawn	1·50	70

(b) Size 25×29 mm. Self-adhesive.

4039	46c. Type **1333**	1·50	70
4040	46c. Tromba marina	1·50	70
4041	46c. Lute	1·50	70
4042	46c. Trumpet	1·50	70
4043	46c. Shawn	1·50	70

Nos. 4034/8 were issued together, se-tenant, forming a composite design.

1334 "HAPPY BIRTHDAY TO YOU"

2006. Greetings Stamps. Self-adhesive. Multicoloured. No value expressed.

4044	(52c.) Type **1334**	1·50	70
4045	(52c.) Birthday cake (Prior at right)	1·50	70
4046	(52c.) As No. 4045 (Prior at left)	1·50	70
4047	(52c.) As No. 4044 (Prior at right)	1·50	70

1335 Cycle Wheel (cyclocross)

2007. Sport. Multicoloured. (a) Ordinary gum.

4048	46c. Type **1335**	1·40	65
4049	60c. Ball and skittles (bowling)	1·80	85
4050	65c. Club and ball (golf)	2·00	95

(b) Size 25×29 mm. Self-adhesive. No Value Expressed.

4051	(52c.) As Type **1335**	1·50	70
4052	(52c.) As No. 4049	1·50	70
4053	(52c.) As No. 4050	1·50	70

1336 *Nu Assis* (Amedo Modigliani)

2007. Sheet 90×125 mm.

MS4054	**1336**	60c.+30c. multicoloured	2·75	2·50

The premium was for the promotion of philately.

1337 Alix

2007. "Philately for the Young". Alix (comic strip created by Jacques Martin).

4055	**1337**	52c. multicoloured	1·70	80

1338 Piano Accordion

2007. Bellows-driven Aerophones. Sheet 166×100 mm containing T 1338 and similar vert designs. Multicoloured.

MS4056 52c.×5 Type **1338**; Concertina; Button accordion; Melodeon; Melodeon (different) 7·50 7·25

The stamps of **MS4056** each have a se-tenant label inscribed "Prior" attached at foot.

The stamps of **MS4056** were not for sale separately.

1339 Julia Tulkens

2007. Women in Literature. Sheet 166×100 mm containing T **1339** and similar vert designs. Multicoloured.

MS4057 52c.×5 Type **1339**; Madeleine Bourdhouxhe; Christine d'Haen; Jacqueline Harpman; Maria Rosseels 7·50 7·25

The stamps of **MS4057** each have a se-tenant label inscribed "Prior" attached at foot and form a composite background design.

1340 Hospital Librarian and Patient **1341** Hospital Librarian and Patient

2007. Red Cross. Multicoloured. (a) Self-adhesive gum.

| 4058 | (52c.) Type **1340** | 1·50 | 70 |
| 4059 | (52c.) As No. 4058 but with "Prior" at right | 1·50 | 70 |

(b) Size 39×27 mm. Ordinary gum.

| 4060 | 52c.+25c. Type **1341** | 2·40 | 1·10 |

No. 4060 has a label inscribed "Prior" attached at right.

1342 *Tati l'periki* (Tati the hairdresser) (Edouard Remouchamps)

2007. Belgian Popular Theatre. Sheet 198×83 mm containing T **1342** and similar multicoloured designs.

MS4061 46c.×3, Type **1342**; Romain DeConinck (vert); *Le Mariage de Melle Beulemans* (Jean-Francois Fonson and Fernand Wicheler) 4·50 4·25

The stamps of **MS4061** form a composite design.

1343 Stoclet Palace (interior) (Josef Hoffman)

2007. Architecture. Multicoloured.

| 4062 | 46c. Type **1343** | 1·70 | 80 |
| 4063 | 80c. Stoclet Palace (exterior) | 2·40 | 1·10 |

No. 4063 has a label inscribed "Prior" attached at top. Stamps of a similar design were issued by Czech Republic.

1344 Robert Baden-Powell (founder)

2007. Europa. Centenary of Scouting. Multicoloured.

| 4064 | 52c. Type **1344** | 1·60 | 80 |

MS4065 90×125 mm. 75c. Scouts (38×48 mm) 2·50 2·50

The stamp and margins of **MS4065** form a composite background design.

1345 Country Identification Letters of Signatories

2007. 50th Anniv of Treaty of Rome.

| 4066 | **1345** | 80c. multicoloured | 2·50 | 1·30 |

1346 'Tintin au pays de Soviets' (Tintin in the land of Soviets) (French)

2007. Birth Centenary of Georges Remi (Herge) (creator of Tintin). Designs showing Tintin book covers in different languages. Multicoloured.

4067	46c. Type **1346**	1·60	80
4068	46c. Tintin in the Congo (Danish)	1·60	80
4069	46c. Tintin in America	1·60	80
4070	46c. Cigars of the Pharaoh (Luxembourg)	1·60	80
4071	46c. The Blue Lotus (Chinese)	1·60	80
4072	46c. The Broken Ear (Portuguese)	1·60	80
4073	46c. The Black Island (Bengali)	1·60	80
4074	46c. King Ottokar's Sceptre (Slovakian)	1·60	80
4075	46c. The Crab with the Golden Claws (Russian)	1·60	80
4076	46c. The Shooting Star (Icelandic)	1·60	80
4077	46c. The Secret of the Unicorn (Polish)	1·60	80
4078	46c. Red Rackham's Treasure (Afrikaans)	1·60	80
4079	46c. Herge	1·60	80
4080	46c. The Seven Crystal Balls (Arabic)	1·60	80
4081	46c. Prisoners of the Sun (Spanish)	1·60	80
4082	46c. Land of Black Gold (German)	1·60	80
4083	46c. Destination Moon (Finnish)	1·60	80
4084	46c. Explorers of the Moon (Swedish)	1·60	80
4085	46c. The Calculus Affair (Japanese)	1·60	80
4086	46c. The Red Sea Sharks (Turkish)	1·60	80
4087	46c. Tintin in Tibet (Tibetan)	1·60	80
4088	46c. The Castifiore Emerald (Italian)	1·60	80
4089	46c. Flight 714 (Indonesian)	1·60	80
4090	46c. Tintin and the Picaros (Greek)	1·60	80
4091	46c. Tintin and the Alph-Art (Dutch)	1·60	80

1347 Dress (Museum of Fashion, Hasselt)

2007. Small Museums. Multicoloured.

4092	46c. Type **1347**	1·60	80
4093	75c. Skeleton and woman (Notre-Dame a la Rose Hospital Cultural Museum, Lessines)	2·40	1·20
4094	92c. Beaker (Jewish Museum, Brussels)	3·00	1·50

1348 Men carrying Canoe **1349** Men carrying Canoe

2007. Summer Stamps. No Value Expressed. Multicoloured. (a) Self-adhesive.

| 4095 | (52c.) Type **1348** | 1·60 | 80 |

4096	(52c.) As No. 4095 but with "Prior" at left	1·60	80
4097	(52c.) Couple with kite	1·60	80
4098	(52c.) As No. 4097 but with "Prior" at left	1·60	80

(b) Ordinary gum.

| 4099 | 52c. Type **1349** | 1·60 | 80 |
| 4100 | 52c. As No. 4098 | 1·60 | 80 |

1350 Building

2007. 50th Anniv of King Baudouin Antarctic Base (1st Belgian Antarctic research station). Sheet 90×125 mm.

MS4101 75c. multicoloured 2·50 2·50

1351 Cyclists

2007. Tour de France Cycle Race.

| 4102 | **1351** | 52c. multicoloured | 1·70 | 85 |

1352 Ship in Port **1353** Ship in Port

2007. Centenary of Zeebrugge. No Value Expressed. Multicoloured. (a) Self-adhesive.

| 4103 | (52c.) Type **1352** | 1·70 | 85 |
| 4104 | (52c.) As No. 4103 but with 'Prior' at left | 1·70 | 85 |

(b) Ordinary gum.

| 4105 | €1.04 Type **1353** but with 'Prior' at left | 3·50 | 1·80 |

1354 Athenee Royal Francois Bovesse, Namur

2007. Tourism. Multicoloured.

4106	52c. Type **1354**	1·90	1·10
4107	52c. Saint Michel College, Brussels	1·90	1·10
4108	52c. Heilig Hart College	1·90	1·10

1355 Scene from *Misere au Borinage* (film by Henri Storck)

2007. Belgium Cinema. Birth Centenary of Henri Storck (filmmaker). Sheet 98×167 mm containing T **1355** and similar horiz designs. Multicoloured.

MS4109 52c.×5, Type **1355**; Boy sleeping (*Les Fils* by Luc and Jean-Pierre Dardenne); Haircut (*L'homme au crane rase* (Man who had his hair cut short) by Andre Delvaux); Bedside scene (*Malpertius* by Harry Kumel); Seated woman (*Dust* by Marion Hansel) 8·50 8·50

1356 Tombeau du Geant, Botassart

2007. Luxembourg European Capital of Culture–2007. Multicoloured.

| 4110 | 52c. Type **1356** | 1·90 | 1·10 |

| 4111 | 80c. Rotunda, Luxembourg Train Station | 3·00 | 1·70 |

Stamp of a similar design was issued by Luxembourg.

1357 Queen Paola

2007. 70th Birth Anniv of Queen Paola. Sheet 125×90 mm.

MS4112 **1357** €1.04 multicoloured 3·75 3·75

1358 King Albert II

2007

4113	**1358**	1 (52c.) red and vermilion	1·80	1·10
4114	**1358**	2 (€1.04) olive, green and slate	3·50	2·10
4115	**1358**	3 (€1.56) blue, indigo and slate	5·25	3·25
4116	**1358**	5 (€2.60) violet, purple and slate	9·00	5·25
4117	**1358**	7 (€3.64) brown, deep brown and slate	12·50	7·50

This set is to introduce the new franking system which is in multiples of base price (currently 52c.). 1 (52c.) is for use on standard domestic mail from 0–50 grams, 2 (€1.04 ie twice base rate of 52c.)) is for use on non-standard domestic mail from 0–100 grams, 3 (€1.56) is for use on non-standard domestic mail from 100–350 grams, 5 (€2.60) is for use on non-standard domestic mail from 350 grams–1 kilo, 7 (€3.64) is for use on non-standard domestic mail from 1–2 kilos.

1359 Pears

2007. Fruit. Multicoloured. Self-adhesive.

4118	1 (52c.) Type **1359**	1·80	1·10
4119	1 (52c.) Strawberries	1·80	1·10
4120	1 (52c.) Red currants	1·80	1·10
4121	1 (52c.) Apples	1·80	1·10
4122	1 (52c.) Grapes	1·80	1·10
4123	1 (52c.) Cherries	1·80	1·10
4124	1 (52c.) Raspberries	1·80	1·10
4125	1 (52c.) Peaches	1·80	1·10
4126	1 (52c.) Plums	1·80	1·10
4127	1 (52c.) Blackberries	1·80	1·10

1360 Remington (20th-century) **1361** Remington (20th-century)

2007. Stamp Festival. Typewriters. Multicoloured. (a) Self-adhesive.

4128	1 (52c.) Type **1360**	1·80	1·10
4129	1 (52c.) Royal (1925)	1·80	1·10
4130	1 (52c.) Olympia (1950)	1·80	1·10
4131	1 (52c.) Olivetti (1972)	1·80	1·10
4132	1 (52c.) Laptop word processor	1·80	1·10

(b) Ordinary gum.

MS4133 100×165 mm. 1 (52c.)×5, Type **1361**; As No. 4129; As No. 4130; As No. 4131; As No. 4132 9·00 9·00

1362 Dahlia

2007. Flowers. Multicoloured. Self-adhesive.

| 4134 | 1 (52c.) Type **1362** | 1·80 | 1·10 |
| 4135 | 2 (€1.04) Petunia | 3·50 | 2·10 |

1363 Marc Van Montagu (molecular genetics)

2007. This Belgium. Science. Sheet 166×193 mm containing T **1363** and similar circular designs. Multicoloured. Self-adhesive.
MS4136 70c.×9, Type **1363**; Paul Janssen (medicine); Lise Thirly (microbiology/virology); Chris Van den Wyngaert (international criminal law); Peter Carmeliet (molecular medicine); Philippe Van Parijs (social philosophy); Marie-Claire Foblets (anthropology); Andre Berger (climate studies); Pierre Rene Deligne (mathematics) 18·00 18·00

1364 Tulip 'Peach Blossom'

2007. Self-adhesive.
4137 **1364** A (80c.) multicoloured 2·75 1·70

1365 Sunset

2007. Bereavement. No value expressed.
4138 **1365** 1 (52c.) multicoloured 1·80 1·10

1366 Les chemins de la liberte (Le voyage) (Thierry Merget)

2007. Postal Art.
4139 **1366** 1 (52c.) multicoloured 1·80 1·10

1367 Couple in Wedding Outfits

2007. Greetings Stamps. Multicoloured. Self-adhesive.
4140 1 (52c.) Type **1367** 1·80 1·10
4141 1 (52c.) Father holding boy baby 1·80 1·10
4142 1 (52c.) Mother holding girl baby 1·80 1·10

2007. Belgian Billiards World Champions. Sheet 80×140 mm containing horiz designs as T **1306**. Multicoloured.
MS4143 1 (52c.)×9, Piet J. Van Duppen; Albert Collette; Gustaaf Van Belle; Piet Sels; Gaston De Doncker; Theo Moons; Rene Gabriels; Victor Luypaerts; Rene Vingerhoerdt 14·50 14·50
See also MS**3992.**

1368 Christmas Tree

2007. Christmas and New Year. (a) Ordinary gum.
4144 **1368** 1 (52c.) multicoloured (postage) 1·80 1·10

1369 Christmas Tree

(b) Self-adhesive.
4145 **1369** 1 (52c.) multicoloured 1·80 1·10

1370 Christmas Tree

(c) Self-adhesive.
4146 **1370** A (80c.) multicoloured (air) 2·75 1·70

1371 The Man From the Sea

2008. Rene Magritte (artist) Commemoration. Sheet 80×140 mm containing T **1371** and similar multicoloured designs.
MS4147 1 (52c.)×5, Type **1371**; Scheherazade; The Midnight Marriage; Georgette (32×41 mm); The Ignorant Fairy (49×37 mm) 9·00 9·00

1372 Give Blood

2008. Red Cross. Give Blood Campaign. (a) Self-adhesive.
4148 **1372** 1 (52c.) multicoloured 1·80 1·10

1373 Give Blood

(b) Ordinary gum.
4149 **1373** 1 (52c.)+25c. multicoloured 2·75 1·70

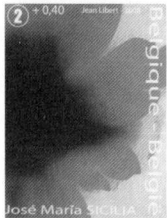

1374 La Luz que se Apaga (Jose Maria Sicilia)

2008. Art. Sheet 90×125 mm.
MS4150 **1374** 2 (€1.04)+40c. multicoloured 5·25 5·25

1375 Jeremiah and Kurdy Malloy

2008. 'Philately for the Young'. Jeremiah (comic strip created by Hermann Huppen (Hermann)).
4151 **1375** 1 (52c.) multicoloured 2·10 1·30

1376 Car

2008. Toys. Self-adhesive. Multicoloured.
4152 1 (52c.) Type **1376** 2·10 1·30

4153	1 (52c.) Pram	2·10	1·30
4154	1 (52c.) Doll	2·10	1·30
4155	1 (52c.) Airplane	2·10	1·30
4156	1 (52c.) Horse	2·10	1·30
4157	1 (52c.) Tram	2·10	1·30
4158	1 (52c.) Diablo	2·10	1·30
4159	1 (52c.) Teddy	2·10	1·30
4160	1 (52c.) Top	2·10	1·30
4161	1 (52c.) Wooden scooter	2·10	1·30

1377 Flowers

2008. Bicentenary of Ghent Flower Show. Sheet 90×125 mm.
MS4162 **1377** 80c. multicoloured 3·00 3·00

1378 Suzy Delair as Mila Malou and Pierre Fresnay as Wens (scene from film L'assassin habite au 21)

2008. Detective Novels. Multicoloured.
4163 1 (52c.) Type **1378** (novel by Stanislas–Andre Steeman) 2·10 1·30
4164 1 (52c.) Jan Decleir as Angelo Ledda (scene from film De zaak Alzheimer) (novel by Jef Geeraerts) 2·10 1·30

1379 Menorah

2008. Bicentenary of Belgian Jewish Community.
4165 **1379** 90c. blue and black 3·50 2·10

1380 Central Station

2008. Antverpia 2010 European Philatelic Championship, Antwerp. 120th Anniv of Royal National Association of Stamp Collectors. Sheet 161×141 mm containing T **1380** and similar vert designs. Multicoloured.
MS4166 1 (54c.)×5, Type **1380**; Cathedral of Our Lady and Pieter Paul Rubens memorial; Port; Fashion; Diamond necklace by Reena Ahluwalia 17·00 17·00
No. MS4166 was sold for €5.

1381 Comte de Champignac

2008. 70th Anniv of Spirou (cartoon character drawn by Andre Franquin). Sheet 166×100 mm containing T **1381** and similar vert designs. Multicoloured.
MS4167 1 (54c.)×5, Type **1381**; Fantasio; Spirou and Spip; Seccotine; Zorglub 10·50 10·50

1382 Coastal Route

2008. Trams. Trams enroute. Multicoloured.
4168 1 (54c.) Type **1382** 2·10 1·30
4169 80c. Charleroi 3·00 1·90
4170 90c. Brussels 3·50 2·10

1383 Mickey Mouse

2008. 80th Anniv of Mickey Mouse (cartoon character created by Walt Disney).
4171 **1383** 1 (54c.) multicoloured 2·10 1·30

1384 Letterbox and Envelope **1385** Letterbox and Envelope

2008. Europa. The Letter. (a) Self-adhesive gum.
4172 **1384** 1 (54c.) multicoloured 2·10 1·30

(b) Size 40×27 mm. Ordinary gum.
4173 **1385** 80c. multicoloured 3·00 1·90

1386 Tagetes portula

2008. Flowers. Multicoloured. Self-adhesive.
4174 1 (54c.) Type **1386** (postage) 2·10 1·30

No value expressed.
4175 (80c.) Tulip 'Orange Favourite' (air) 3·00 1·90

1387 Artificial Hand and Hands of Many Nations

2008. Diversity in the Workplace.
4176 **1387** 2 (€1.08) multicoloured 4·25 2·50

1388

2008. Freemasonry. Sheet 125×90 mm.
MS4177 **1388** 3 multicoloured 6·25 6·25

1389 Family hiking **1390** Family hiking

2008. Summer Stamps. Multicoloured. (a) Ordinary gum.
4178 1 (52c.) Type **1389** 2·10 1·30
4179 1 (52c.) Family cycling 2·10 1·30

(b) Size 30×25 mm. Self-adhesive.
4180 1 (52c.) Type **1390** 2·10 1·30
4181 1 (52c.) Family cycling 2·10 1·30

1391 Queen Fabiola and King Baudouin

2008. 80th Birth Anniv of Queen Fabiola. Sheet 170×120 mm containing T **1391** and similar vert designs. Multicoloured.

MS4182 1 (52c.)×3, Type **1391**; Portrait of Queen Fabiola; Queen Fabiola and King Baudouin, older, wearing casual dress 6·25 6·25

1392 Woman (George Grard), Musee George Grard, Gijverinkhove

2008. Tourism. Multicoloured.
4183	1 (52c.)	Type **1392**	2·20	1·40
4184	80c.	*Imago* (Emile Desmedt), Musee en Plein Air du Sart-Tilman, Liege	3·25	2·00
4185	90c.	*Autoportrait* (Gerald Dederen), Jardin de sculptures de l'UCL, Brussels	3·50	2·30

1393 USSR Pavilion

2008. 50th Anniv of EXPO'58, Brussels. Multicoloured.
MS4186 1 (54c.)×5, Type **1393**; Thailand pavilion; Hostesses carrying flags; Expo logo as lighting; Atomium 10·50 10·50

The stamps of **MS**4186 were not for sale individually.

1394 Planting of May Tree (tree of joy), Brussels (700th anniv)

2008. Folklore and Traditions. Multicoloured.
4187	1 (54c.)	Type **1394**	2·20	1·40
4188	1 (54c.)	Hops, beer barrel, bonfire and hop devil, Asse (Hopduvelfeesten) (horiz)	2·20	1·40
4189	1 (54c.)	Jugglers (Eupen carnival)	2·20	1·40
4190	1 (54c.)	Men on stage (centenary (2007) of *La Royale Compagnie du Cabaret Wallon Tournaisien*) (philanthropic and literary company)	2·20	1·40

1395 BMX

2008. Olympic Games, Beijing. Multicoloured.
4191	1 (54c.)	Type **1395**	2·30	1·50
4192	90c.	Relay (horiz)	3·75	2·40

MS4193 125×90 mm. (2) €1.08 Tennis (49×38 mm) 4·50 4·50

1396 Angel Gabriel

2008. Stamp Day. 50th Anniv of Cercle St-Gabriel. 50th Anniv of Thematic Philately in Belgium.
4194 **1396** 1 (54c.) multicoloured 2·30 1·50

1397 Marten **1398** Marten

2008. Nature. Mustelidae. Multicoloured. (a) Self-adhesive gum.
4195	1 (54c.)	Type **1397**	2·30	1·50
4196	1 (54c.)	Stone marten	2·30	1·50
4197	1 (54c.)	Polecat	2·30	1·50
4198	1 (54c.)	Otter	2·30	1·50
4199	1 (54c.)	Badger	2·30	1·50

(b) Ordinary gum. Sheet 178×146 mm.
MS4200 1 (54c.)×6, Type **1398** (48×38 mm); Ermine (38×42 mm); Stone marten (48×38 mm); Polecat (38×42 mm); Otter (38×48 mm); Badger (48×38 mm) 12·00 12·00

1399 Smurf **1400** Smurf and Smurfette

2008. The Smurfs (characters created by Peyo (Pierre Culliford)). Multicoloured. (a) Self-adhesive gum.
4201	1 (54c.)	Type **1399**	2·30	1·50
4202	1 (54c.)	Smurfette	2·30	1·50
4203	1 (54c.)	Papa Smurf	2·30	1·50
4204	1 (54c.)	Smurf and drum (horiz)	2·30	1·50
4205	1 (54c.)	Poet Smurf	2·30	1·50
4206	1 (54c.)	Jokey Smurf	2·30	1·50
4207	1 (54c.)	Smurf carrying bag and envelope	2·30	1·50
4208	1 (54c.)	Brainy Smurf	2·30	1·50
4209	1 (54c.)	Gargamel	2·30	1·50
4210	1 (54c.)	Harmony Smurf (horiz)	2·30	1·50

(b) Ordinary gum. Sheet 186×153 mm.
MS4211 1 (54c.)×5, Type **1400** (42×33 mm); Smurf in party hat (42×33 mm); Two smurfs (42×33 mm); Smurf carrying cake (42×33 mm); Smurf eating cake (38×42 mm) 12·00 12·00

1401 Mothers and Children (Tim Driven)

2008. Belgian Photographers. Sheet 100×166 mm containing **1401** and similar horiz designs. Multicoloured.
MS4212 80c.×5, Type **1401**; Jars (Paul Ausloos); Woman carrying pail (Leonard Misonne); Coloured lights in trees (Harry Gruyaert); Woman cycling (Stephan Vanfleteren) 16·00 16·00

1402 1909 Belgian Congo 1f. Stamp (As No. 40B)

2008. Centenary of Belgian Congo.
4213 **1402** 1 (54c.) multicoloured 2·30 1·50

1403 National Museum of Shoes, Izegem

2008. Museums. Multicoloured.
4214	1 (54c.)	Type **1403**	2·30	1·50
4215	80c.	Picornue Museum (religious museum), Bastogne	3·25	2·10
4216	80c.	David and Alice van Buren Museum , Brussels	3·25	2·10

1404 Menin Gate, Ypres

2008. 90th Anniv of End of First World War. Sheet 201×85 mm containing T **1404** and similar vert designs. Multicoloured.
MS4217 90c.×3, Type **1404**; King Albert I (statue); Poppies 10·50 10·50

1405 The Nativity **1406** The Nativity

2008. Christmas. Multicoloured. (a) Self-adhesive.
4218	1 (54c.)	Type **1405**	2·40	1·70
4219	1 (80c.)	Type **1406**	3·50	2·40

(b) Ordinary gum. Sheet 127×124 mm.
MS4220 1 (54c.)×5, Type **1407**; St. Francis; Mary and Joseph; Friar; Infant Jesus 12·00 12·00

No. 4219 was inscribed 'INTERNATIONAL' and was originally on sale for 80c.

No. **MS**4220 includes four labels which, with the stamps form a composite design of a stained glass window.

1407 Cardinal Mercier

1408 Queen Elisabeth (Concours Reine Elisabeth (Queen Elisabeth International Music Competition))

2008. This Belgium. Music. Sheet 166×200 mm containing T **1408** and similar square designs. Multicoloured.
MS4221 80c.×10, Type **1408**; Jose van Dam (bass-baritone); Rock Werchter Festival; Philippe Herreweghe and Collegium Vocale Gent (music ensemble); dEus (rock band); Il Novecento (orchestra) and Robert Groslot (conductor); Philip Catherine (jazz guitarist); Dani Klein (singer with Vaya con Dios); Salvatore Adamo (composer and ballad singer); Jaques Brel (singer–songwriter) 32·00 32·00

The stamps of **MS**4136 were not for sale separately.

1409 Face

2008. Universal Declaration of Human Rights.
4222 **1409** 90c. multicoloured 4·25 3·00

1410 *Tulipa bakeri*

2009. Air. Flowers. Self-adhesive.
4223 **1410** 1 (90c.) multicoloured 4·25 3·00

1411 King Albert II

2009. Air.
4224	**1411**	1 (90c.) multicoloured	4·25	3·00
4225	**1411**	1 (€1.05) multicoloured	5·00	3·00
4226	**1411**	3 (€2.40) multicoloured	11·00	7·75
4227	**1411**	3 (€2.70) multicoloured	12·00	8·50

No. 4224 and 4225 were for use on airmail within Europe, Nos. 4226 and 4227 for use on international airmail.
See also 4113/17.

1412 '€'

2009. Tenth Anniv of European Union. Self-adhesive.
4228 **1412** 1 (59c.) multicoloured 2·75 2·00

1413 Monument

2009. Regions. German Community. Sheet 150×183 mm containing T **1413** and similar multicoloured designs.
MS4229 1 (90c.)×5, Type **1413**; Three handled pitcher; Lake Butgenbach; Eupen sanatorium (33×40 mm); Shooting (49×37 mm) 19·00 19·00

The stamps of **MS**4229 were not for sale separately.

1414 Hands 'reading' Braille

2009. Birth Bicentenary of Louis Braille (inventor of Braille writing for the blind).
4230 **1414** 1 (59c.) multicoloured 2·75 2·00

1415 Child and Tap

2009. Red Cross. Water.
4231 **1415** 1 (59c.) + 25c. black and vermillion 4·00 2·75

1416 Barge

2009. Transportation. Inland Waterways.
4232 **1416** 2 (€1.18) multicoloured 5·50 4·00

1417 Figure and Postbox (Emitis Mohsenin)

2009. Post Day.
4233 **1417** 1 (59c.) multicoloured 2·75 2·00

1418 Marthe Boel (promoter of women's issues)

2009. Women in Action. Multicoloured.
4234	1 (59c.)	Type **1418**	2·75	2·00
4235	1 (59c.)	Lily Boeykens (lawyer and journalist)	2·75	2·00

1419 Penguins

2009. Preserve Polar Regions and Glaciers. Sheet 120×80 mm containing T **1419** and similar multicoloured design.
MS4236 2 (€1.05)×2, Type **1419**; Polar bear 9·25 9·25

The stamps of **MS**4236 were for use on international priority mail and not for sale separately.

1420 Bob

2009. Bob and Bobette (comic series created by Willy Vandersteen) in *Les Diables du Texas* (animated film). Showing characters from the film. Multicoloured. Self-adhesive.

4237	1 (59c.) Type **1420**		2·75	2·00
4238	1 (59c.) Bobette		2·75	2·00
4239	1 (59c.) Jerome		2·75	2·00
4240	1 (59c.) Lambik		2·75	2·00
4241	1 (59c.) Aunt Sidonie		2·75	2·00

1421 Telescope and Globe

2009. Europa. Astronomy. Sheet 125×90mm.
MS4242 **1421** 1 (59c.) multicoloured 4·25 4·25
No. MS4242 was for use on mail within Europe.

1422 Neolithic Flint Mines, Spiennes

2009. World Heritage Sites. Sheet 166×100 mm containing T **1422** and similar vert designs. Multicoloured.
MS4243 1 (€1.05)×5, Type **1422**; Notre Dame Cathedral, Tournai; Plantin-Moretus Museum, Antwerp; Historic Centre, Bruges; Maison de Maitre (Victor Horta), Brussels 23·00 23·00
No. MS4243 was for use on International mail.

1423 Girl with Camera

2009. Summer Stamps. Holidays in Wallonia and Flanders. Multicoloured. Self-adhesive.

4244	1 (59c.) Type **1423**		2·75	2·00
4245	1 (59c.) Boy with camera		2·75	2·00

1424 Muhka and *Flemish Village* (Luc Tuymans)

2009. Antverpia 2010–International Stamp Exhibition, Antwerp. Artistic Antwerp (1st series). Sheet 180×64 mm containing T **1424** and similar vert designs. Multicoloured.
MS4246 1 (59c.)×5, Type **1424**; *Orbino* (Luc Deleu), Middelheim Sculpture Museum;Bourla Theater and Toneelhuis theatre company; *Hollywood on the Scheldt*, Robbe De Hert, Roma Cinema; *Willem Elschot* (writer) (sculpture by Wilfred Pas) and manuscript of *Kaas* 23·00 23·00
See also Nos. MS4290.

1425 Henry Purcell (350th birth anniv)

2009. Composers Anniversaries. Sheet 180×64 mm containing T **1425** and similar vert designs. Multicoloured.
MS4247 1 (90c.)×5, Type **1425**; George Frideric Handel (250th death anniv); Franz Joseph Haydn (death bicentenary); Jakob Ludwig Felix Mendelssohn Bartholdy (birth bicentenary); Clara Schumann (nee Clara Josephine Wieck) (190th birth anniv) 21·00 21·00
The stamps and margins of MS4247 form a composite design.
The stamps of MS4247 were for use on mail within Europe

1426 Low Energy Lightbulb

2009. Green Stamps. Environmental Preservation. Multicoloured. Self-adhesive.

4248	1 (59c.) Type **1426**		2·75	2·00
4249	1 (59c.) Wind turbine		2·75	2·00
4250	1 (59c.) Shared transport		2·75	2·00
4251	1 (59c.) Solar panels		2·75	2·00
4252	1 (59c.) Insulated house		2·75	2·00

1427 International Space Station, 2009

2009. Aviation, From Bleriot to De Winne. Multicoloured.

4253	1 (59c.) Type **1427** (Frank de Winne, first European Space Agency astronaut to command mission)		2·75	2·00
4254	1 (59c.) Apollo 11, 1969 (first men on the moon)		2·75	2·00
4255	1 (59c.) Concorde, 1969 (first supersonic flight)		2·75	2·00
4256	1 (59c.) LZ 127 Graf Zeppelin, 1929 (flight around the world)		2·75	2·00
4257	1 (59c.) *Bleriot XI*, 1909 (first flight over English Channel)		2·75	2·00

1428 Yoko Tsuno

2009. Youth Philately. Yoko Tsuno (comic created by Roger Leloup).
4258 **1428** 1 (59c.) multicoloured 2·75 2·00

1429 King Albert and Queen Paola

2009. 50th Anniv of Wedding of King Albert and Queen Paola. Sheet 209×104 mm.
MS4259 **1429** 3 multicoloured 7·25 7·25

1430 Citroen 2CV Delivery Van, c. 1959

2009. Postal Vehicles. Multicoloured.

4260	1 (59c.) Type **1430**		2·75	2·00
4261	1 (59c.) Bedford van, c. 1960		2·75	2·00
4262	1 (59c.) Large Renault van, c. 1970		2·75	2·00
4263	1 (59c.) Renault 4 Fourgonnette van, c. 1980		2·75	2·00
4264	1 (59c.) Modern Citroen van		2·75	2·00

1431 Orchestra

2009. The Circus. Multicoloured. Self-adhesive.

4265	1 (59c.) Type **1431**		2·75	2·00
4266	1 (59c.) Highwire artistes		2·75	2·00
4267	1 (59c.) Illusionist		2·75	2·00
4268	1 (59c.) Acrobat pyramid		2·75	2·00
4269	1 (59c.) Trapeze artiste		2·75	2·00
4270	1 (59c.) Clowns		2·75	2·00
4271	1 (59c.) Acrobats balancing		2·75	2·00
4272	1 (59c.) Illusionist with tophat, rabbit and doves		2·75	2·00
4273	1 (59c.) Equestrian artiste		2·75	2·00
4274	1 (59c.) Clown juggling on uni-cycle		2·75	2·00

1432 Maurice Bejart

2009. Maurice Bejart (dancer) Commemoration.
4275 **1432** 1 (90c.) multicoloured 4·00 3·00

1433 Archives of Belgium

2009. Monts des Arts. Sheet 200×166 mm containing T **1433** and similar multicoloured designs.
MS4276 1 (59c.)×10, Type **1433**; Royal Museum of Fine Arts; Royal Library; Square Meeting Centre; Brussels Palace (38×49 mm); Saint Jaques sur Coudenberg Church and Protestant Chapel (49×38 mm); Palace of Fine Arts; Royal Belgian Filmarchive (Cinematheque Royale de Belgique); Belvue Museum; Musical Instruments Museum 25·00 25·00

1434 Seven Sacraments Altarpiece (detail)

2009. Master of Passions
4277 **1434** 2 (€1.18) multicoloured 5·00 4·00

1435 Lion Mask

2009. Europalia International Arts Festival, China. Self-adhesive.
4278 **1435** 1 (59c.) multicoloured 2·75 2·00

1436 Mettoy Streamline Train, 1950

2009. Miniature Trains. Sheet 160×200 mm containing T **1436** and similar square designs. Multicoloured.
MS4279 1 (59c.)×10, Type **1436**; Bavarian locomotive *Aloisus*; Locomotive tender; Diesel locomotive; Locomotive tender *Storchenbein*; Locomotive Type 16; Tin toy train; ICE Deutsche Bahn; Wooden toy train with waggon; Blue and red wooden toy train 28·00 28·00

1437 Pine Tree

2009. La Foret de Soignes (Sonian Forest). Sheet 166×100 mm containing T **1437** and similar vert designs. Multicoloured.
MS4280 2 (€2.18)×5, Type **1437**; Beech; Birch; Larch; Oak 25·00 25·00

1438 Father Damien

2009. Canonization of Father Damien (Jozef De Veuster) (Roman Catholic missionary who ministered to lepers on the Hawaiian island of Molokai).
4281 **1438** 1 Europe (90c.) multicoloured 4·00 3·00

1439 Emblem

2009. 20th Anniv of Comic Strip Art Museum. Sheet 90×120 mm.
MS4282 **1439** 1 (59c.) multicoloured 4·50 3·25

1440 Tom Lanoye

2009. This is Belgium. Literature. Sheet 160×200 mm containing T **1440** and similar multicoloured designs.
MS4283 1 (59c.)×10, Type **1440**; Hugo Claus; Anne Provoost; Poeziezomers, Watou (summer poetry festival) (vert); Redu, Book Village (vert); Book Fair, Antwerp (vert); Book Fair, Brussels (vert); Pierre Mertens; Amelie Northomb; Henri Vernes 25·00 25·00

1441 Gold Baubles

2009. Christmas. Multicoloured. Self-adhesive.

4284	1 (59c.) Type **1441**		2·75	2·00
4285	1 (90c.) Blue baubles		2·75	2·00

No. 4284 were for use on domestic mail and were originally on sale for 59c.
No. 4285 were for use on international mail were originally on sale for 90c.

1442 1920 65c. Stamp (As No. 308b)

2009. Monacophil 2009. Promotion of Philately. Sheet 120×170 mm.
MS4286 **1442** 1 multicoloured 5·75 4·25
The premium was for the promotion of philately.

1443 Sunset

2010. Bereavement. Self-adhesive.
4288 **1443** (59c.) multicoloured 2·75 2·00

1468 Leisure Centre, Rotselar (de Mena Brewery)

2010. Breweries, Change of Use. Multicoloured.

4336	1 (90c.) Type **1468**	3·25	2·25
4337	1 (€1.05) Telematics Support Centre, Marche-en-Famenne (Carmelite monastery and brewery)	4·00	2·75
4338	2 (€1.18) Weils Contemporary Art Centre, Brussels	5·25	3·50

1469 Shoe Making

2010. Craft Trades. Multicoloured.

4339	1 (59c.) Type **1469**	2·50	1·70
4340	1 (59c.) Clog making	2·50	1·70
4341	1 (59c.) Blacksmithing	2·50	1·70
4342	1 (59c.) Spinning	2·50	1·70
4343	1 (59c.) Laundry	2·50	1·70

FOLON

1470 *Voyage dans la lune*

2010. Tenth Anniv of Folon Foundation. Multicoloured.

4344	1 (59c.) Type **1470**	2·50	1·70
4345	1 (59c.) *Pays de connaissance*	2·50	1·70
4346	1 (59c.) *Un cri* (horiz)	2·50	1·70
4347	1 (59c.) *La mer ce grand sculpteur* (Knokke) (horiz)	2·50	1·70
4348	1 (59c.) *L'étranger* (horiz)	2·50	1·70
4349	1 (59c.) *Oiseau* (horiz)	2·50	1·70
4350	1 (59c.) *Pluie* (La Hulpe)	2·50	1·70
4351	1 (59c.) Stained glass window, Eglise de Waha (Marche-en-Famenne)	2·50	1·70
4352	1 (59c.) *L'aube*	2·50	1·70
4353	1 (59c.) *Un monde*	2·50	1·70

1471 Virgin and Child (Caen)

2010. Flemish Primitive Art in French and Belgian Collections. Multicoloured.

MS4354 3 (€2.07)×2, Type **1471**; *Portrait of Laurent Froimont* (Brussels) ... 18·00 18·00

Stamps of a similar design were issued by France.

1472 Santa in his Sleigh

2010. . Multicoloured.

| 4355 | 1 (59c.) Type **1472** | 2·75 | 2·00 |
| 4356 | 1 (90c.) Santa in his sleigh (different) | 5·25 | 3·50 |

1473 '1-1-11'

2011. Liberalization of Postal Market from 1st January 2011

| 4357 | **1473** 1 (59c.) multicoloured | 2·75 | 2·00 |

1474

2011. International Year of Chemistry

| 4358 | **1474** 1 (71c.) multicoloured | 3·00 | 1·75 |

1475

2011. Western Zodiac

| 4359 | **1475** 1 (71c.) multicoloured | 3·00 | 1·75 |

1476

2011. Writer's Houses. Multicoloured.

4360	1 (71c.) Type **1476**	3·00	1·75
4361	1 (€1.03) Domus Erasmi (Desiderius Erasmus)	4·50	2·75
4362	2 (€1.42) Het Lijsternest (Stijn Streuvels)	6·00	3·00

1477

2011. Luc Tuymans (artist) Retrospective Exhibition

| 4363 | **1477** 1 (71c.) multicoloured | 3·00 | 1·75 |

1478

2011. Voluntary Work. Booklet Stamp

| 4364 | **1478** 1 (71c.) multicoloured | 3·00 | 1·75 |

1479

2011. AIR. Highlights of Belgium. Booklet Stamps. Multicoloured.

4365	1 (€1.20) Type **1479**	5·50	2·75
4366	1 (€1.20) Chateau and cathedral belfries	5·50	2·75
4367	1 (€1.20) Atomium and Manneken Pis	5·50	2·75
4368	1 (€1.20) Mardasson Memorial, Bastogne	5·50	2·75
4369	1 (€1.20) Lion Mound Monument, on site of Battle of Waterloo, Braine-l'Alleud	5·50	2·75

1480

2011. Dead Rat's Ball (Bal du Rat Mort), Ostend. 150th Anniv of Le Royal Cercle Cœcilia (founder)

| 4370 | **1480** 1 (71c.) multicoloured | 3·00 | 1·75 |

1481

2011. Vegetables of Yore. Multicoloured.

MS4371 1 (71c.)×5, Type **1481**; White squash; Violet carrot and parsnip; Swiss chard; Cardoon ... 27·00 27·00

1482

2011. Fairground Attractions. Booklet Stamps. Multicoloured.

4372	1 (71c.) Type **1482**		1·75
4373	1 (71c.) Fortune telling		1·75
4374	1 (71c.) Carousel		1·75
4375	1 (71c.) Switchback ride		1·75
4376	1 (71c.) Big wheel		1·75
4377	1 (71c.) Shooting range		1·75
4378	1 (71c.) Candyfloss stall		1·75
4379	1 (71c.) Dodgems		1·75
4380	1 (71c.) Children's Carousel		1·75
4381	1 (71c.) Haunted House		1·75

1483

2011. The Mining Country of Campine. Multicoloured.

MS4382 1 (€1.20)×5, Type **1483**; Coal; Station and tower where first coal was found; Forested slag heap, Zolder (33×40 mm); Grassed slag heap, Eisden (49×37 mm) ... 20·00 20·00

1484

2011. Stamp Festival. Letterboxes. Multicoloured.

4383	1 (71c.) Type **1484**	3·00	1·75
4384	1 (71c.) Rectangular wall-mounted rural letterbox	3·00	1·75
4385	1 (71c.) 1930's free-standing letterbox with pointed top	3·00	1·75
4386	1 (71c.) Napoleonic-style letterbox with curved lid	3·00	1·75
4387	1 (71c.) Modern wall-mounted letterbox	3·00	1·75

1485

2011. The Art of Graffitii. De Wand Tram Station, Laeken, Brussels (largest graffitii installation in Europe). Multicoloured.

MS4388 1 (€1.20)×5, Type **1485**; Tram (abstract); Figures and letters; Yellow buildings and pylons; Infant's face and letters ... 20·00 20·00

1486

2011. Art. Paintings/Posters by Henri Toulouse-Lautrec in Ixelles Museum. Booklet Stamps. Multicoloured.

4389	1 (71c.) Type **1486**	3·00	1·75
4390	1 (71c.) *Aristide Bruant dans Cabaret*	3·00	1·75
4391	1 (71c.) *Mary Milton*	3·00	1·75
4392	1 (71c.) *Divan Japonais*	3·00	1·75
4393	1 (71c.) *Reine de Joie*	3·00	1·75
4394	1 (71c.) *Le Salon des Cent Exposition Internationale d'Affiches*	3·00	1·75
4395	1 (71c.) *Caudieux*	3·00	1·75
4396	1 (71c.) *Jane Avril*	3·00	1·75
4397	1 (71c.) *Eldorado. Aristide Bruant dans Cabaret*	3·00	1·75
4398	1 (71c.) *Moulin Rouge. La Goulue*	3·00	1·75

1487

2011. This is Belgium. Power through Humour. Multicoloured.

MS4399 1 (71c.)×10, Type **1487**; Zak (Jaques Moeraert); K (Kamagurka) (Luc Zeebroek); duBus (Frédéric du Bus); Clou (Christian Louis); GAL (Gerard Alsteens); Kroll (Pierre Kroll); Vadot (Nicolas Vadot); Zaza (Klaas Storme); cecile bertrand (Cécile Bertrand) ... 30·00 30·00

1488

2011. Women's Team Sports. Multicoloured.

MS4400 1 (€1.20)×5, Type **1488**, Football; Basketball; Volleyball; Handball ... 20·00 20·00

1489

2011. Courthouses, Old and New. Multicoloured.

MS4401 2 (€1.34)×5, Type **1489**; Ghent; Bergen; Anvers (Antwerp); Charleroi ... 22·00 22·00

1490

2011. Youth Philately. The Adventures of Tintin on Screen (characters created by Georges Remi (Hergé)). Multicoloured.

MS4402 1 (71c.)×10, Type **1490**; Tintin and the Crab with the Golden Claws (comic book, 1941);The Black Island (animated film, 1961); The Black Island (comic book, 1938); Tintin and the Mystery of the Golden Fleece (film, 1961); Tintin and the Blue Oranges (film, 1964); Tintin and the Temple of the Sun (animated film, 1969); Tintin and the Temple of the Sun (comic book, 1949); Tintin and the Blue Lotus (animated film, 1991); Tintin and the Blue Lotus (comic book, 1936) ... 22·00 22·00

1491

2011. Personal Stamp

	(a) Ordinary gum		
4403	**1491** 1 (71c.) scarlet and slate-grey	3·00	1·75
	(b) Self-adhesive		
4403a	**1491** 1 (71c.) scarlet and slate-grey	3·00	1·75

1492

2011. Promotion of Philately. Grand-Place, Brussels (UNESCO world heritage site). Multicoloured.
MS4404 1 (71c.)×5, Type **1492**; Maison de l'Étoile, Maison du Cygne and La Maison de l'Arbre d'Or; Maison La Renommée, Maison L'Ermitage, Maison Le Moulin à vent, Maison Le Pot d'étain,Maison La Colline and Maison La Bourse (horiz); Maison Le Roi d'Espagne, Maison La Brouette, Maison Le Sac and Maison La Louve (horiz); Maison du Roi 15·00 15·00

1493

2011. Europa. Forests. Multicoloured.
MS4405 3 (€3.09)×2, Type **1493**; Fawn 22·00 22·00

1494

2011. Queen Paola's Youth Inititatives
4406 **1494** 1 (71c.) multicoloured 3·00 1·75

1495

2011. Belgian Candies. Multicoloured.
MS4407 1 (€1.03)×5, Type **1495**; Babelutten (25×33 mm); Caramels (25×33 mm); Guimauves (26×51 mm); Gommen (26×51 mm) 18·00 18·00

1496

2011. Christmas. Multicoloured.
4408 1 (71c.) Type **1496** 3·00 1·75
4409 1 (€1.03) Angel 5·00 2·75

1497

2011. Europalia International Arts Festival - Brazil. Multicoloured.
MS4410 3 (€2.13)×2, Type **1497**; Girl with ritual makeup 20·00 20·00

1498 Mermaid

2012. Mythical Creatures. Booklet Stamps. Multicoloured.
4411 1 (71c.) Type **1498** 3·00 1·75
4412 1 (71c.) Werewolf 3·00 1·75
4413 1 (71c.) Unicorn 3·00 1·75
4414 1 (71c.) Dragon 3·00 1·75

4415 1 (71c.) Amphiptere 3·00 1·75
4416 1 (71c.) Pegasus 3·00 1·75
4417 1 (71c.) Griffon 3·00 1·75
4418 1 (71c.) Centaur 3·00 1·75
4419 1 (71c.) Sphinx 3·00 1·75
4420 1 (71c.) Harpy 3·00 1·75

1499 Achel

2012. Trappist Beers. Multicoloured.
MS4421 1 (€1.03)×6, Type **1499**; Chimay; Orval; Rochefort; Westmalle; Westvleteren 19·00 19·00

1500 Mayan Calendar (detail)

2012. Mayan Calendar Prediction. 21 December 2012 End of World
4422 **1500** 1 (€1.24) multicoloured 5·75 5·00

1501 Latin (Brody Neuenschwander)

2012. Write! Calligraphy. Booklet Stamps. Multicoloured.
4423 1 (€1.24) Type **1501** 5·75 5·00
4424 1 (€1.24) Arab (Wassam Shawkat) 5·75 5·00
4425 1 (€1.24) Chinese (Jianing Wang) 5·75 5·00
4426 1 (€1.24) Hindi (Dharmesh Jadeja) 5·75 5·00
4427 1 (€1.24) Greek (Georgia Angelopoulos) 5·75 5·00

1502 Atomium and Symbols of Belgium

2012. Europa. Visit Belgium. Multicoloured.
MS4428 3 (€3.09)×2, Type **1502**; Atomium and symbols of Belgium (right) 22·00 22·00

2012. Personal Stamp

(a) Ordinary gum
4429 1 (71c.) As Type **1491** 3·00 1·75

(b) Self-adhesive
4430 1 (71c.) As Type **1491** 3·00 1·75

1503 Cirque du Soleil (Las Vegas, 1998)

2012. Franco Dragone Entertainment Group. Booklet Stamps. Multicoloured.
4431 1 (€1.03) Type **1503** 4·75 3·25
4432 1 (€1.03) Décroucher la lune (La Louvière, 2000 - 2002 - 2006 - 2009) 4·75 3·25
4433 1 (€1.03) A New Day (Las Vegas, 2005) 4·75 3·25
4434 1 (€1.03) La Rêve (Las Vegas, 2005) 4·75 3·25
4435 1 (€1.03) The House of Dancing Water (Macau, 2010) 4·75 3·25

Nos. 4431/35 have wavy edges (simulating perforations) on two or three sides depending on position.

1054 Gerard Mercator

2012. Cartography. 500th Birth Anniv of Gerardus Mercator. Multicoloured.
MS4436 160×112 mm. 3 (€3.09)×2, Type **1504**; Jodocus Hondius 22·00 22·00

1505 Canaries

2012. Pets. Booklet Stamps. Multicoloured.
4437 1 (77c.) Type **1505** 3·00 1·75
4438 1 (77c.) Guinea Pig 3·00 1·75
4439 1 (77c.) Cat 3·00 1·75
4440 1 (77c.) Goldfish 3·00 1·75
4441 1 (77c.) Two Budgerigars 3·00 1·75
4442 1 (77c.) Pony 3·00 1·75
4443 1 (77c.) Chihuahua 3·00 1·75
4444 1 (77c.) Two Gerbils 3·00 1·75
4445 1 (77c.) Two Dwarf Rabbits 3·00 1·75
4446 1 (77c.) Collie 3·00 1·75

1506 Titanic and Lifeboat

2012. Centenary of Sinking of Titanic. Multicoloured.
MS4447 146×105 mm. 3 (€3.09)×2, Type **1506**×2 22·00 22·00

Jef Geys
1507 Floristan

2012. Jef Geys Exhibition, Royal Museums of Fine Arts of Belgium
4448 **1507** 1 (71c.) multicoloured 3·00 1·75

1508 Relay Handover

2012. Olympic Games, London
4449 **1508** 1 (€1.24) multicoloured 5·75 5·00

1509 Drum

2012. 50th Anniv of Burundi and Rwanda Independence. Multicoloured.
4450 1 (€1.24) Type **1509** 5·75 5·00
4451 1 (€1.24) Woven pot 5·75 5·00

1510 Volcan ensorcelé

2012. Art. Pierre Alechinsky (artist and founder of CoBrA). Booklet Stamps. Multicoloured.
4452 1 (71c.) Type **1510** 3·00 1·75
4453 1 (71c.) A propos de Binche 3·00 1·75
4454 1 (71c.) Sans espoir de bâtiment pour Anvers ni même pour l'Escaut 3·00 1·75
4455 1 (71c.) Parfois c'est l'inverse 3·00 1·75
4456 1 (71c.) A la ligne (vert) 3·00 1·75

4457 1 (71c.) Aquarelle estampillée (vert) 3·00 1·75
4458 1 (71c.) Labyrinthe d'apparat (vert) 3·00 1·75
4459 1 (71c.) Encreur (vert) 3·00 1·75
4460 1 (71c.) Nuages en pantalons 3·00 1·75
4461 1 (71c.) Le dernier jour 3·00 1·75

1511 Cabaret au Bord de la Rivière (Jan Brueghel the Younger)

2012. Philately without Frontiers. Philatelic Collection of Prince Albert II of Monaco Exhibition, Bruges, 2012
4462 **1511** 1 (71c.) multicoloured 3·00 1·75

1512 Pieris brassicae (Large White)

2012. Butterflies (1st issue). Booklet Stamp
4463 **1512** 1 (71c.) multicoloured 3·00 1·75

1513 Papilio machaon (Old World Swallowtail)

2012. AIR. Butterflies (2nd issue). Booklet Stamps
4464 **1513** 1 (€1.20) multicoloured 5·50 4·75

1514 Gil&Jo (by Jef Nys)

2012. This is Belgium. Tenth Anniversary. Multicoloured.
MS4465 1 (71c.)×10, Type **1514**; Bob de Moor (28×41 mm); André Franquin (28×41 mm); Marc Sleen (28×41 mm); SU (Willy Vandersteen) (38×24 mm); Hergé (32×36 mm); Lucky Comics (Morris) (28×41 mm); Jije (Jerry Spring) (41×28 mm); Studio Jacobs (E. P. Jacobs) (41×28 mm); Peyo (41×28 mm) 30·00 30·00

1515 Zenobe Gramme (Training Ship)

2012. 50th (2011) Anniv of Launch of Zenobe Gramme. Temsifil 2012 Exhibition
4466 **1515** 1 (71c.) multicoloured 3·00 1·75

1516 Acer macrophyllum

2012. Tree Leaves. Booklet Stamps. Multicoloured.
4467 1 (71c.) Type **1516** 3·00 1·75
4468 1 (71c.) Acer palmatum 3·00 1·75
4469 1 (71c.) Morus nigra 3·00 1·75
4470 1 (71c.) Sorbus alinifolia 3·00 1·75
4471 1 (71c.) Ginkgo biloba 3·00 1·75
4472 1 (71c.) Betula pendula 3·00 1·75
4473 1 (71c.) Fagus sylvatica 3·00 1·75
4474 1 (71c.) Aesculus hippocastanum 3·00 1·75
4475 1 (71c.) Euonymus europaeus 3·00 1·75
4476 1 (71c.) Quercus 'pondaim' 3·00 1·75

Jacob Jordaens

1517 *Hommage à Céres*

2012. Art. Jacob Jordaens Exhibition, Royal Museum of Fine Art, Brussels
4477 **1517** 1 (71c.) multicoloured — 3·00 — 1·75

1518 St. Martin's Festival

2012. St. Martin's Day
4478 **1518** 1 (71c.) multicoloured — 3·00 — 1·75

1519 Bales of Hay

2012. Regions. Condroz. Multicoloured.
MS4479 152×185 mm. 1 (€1.20)×5, Type **1519**; Fontaine Castle; Glasses of beer; Belgian Blue cattle (33×40 mm);Collegiate Church of Notre-Dame and view of Dinant from Meuse River (49×37 mm) — 20·00 — 20·00

1520 *Apatura ilia*

2012. Butterflies (3rd issue). Coil Stamp
4480 **1520** 1 (71c.) multicoloured — 3·00 — 1·75

1521 Statue of Jan Breydel and Pieter de Coninck

2012. Promotion of Philately. Grand-Place, Bruges (UNESCO world heritage site)
MS4481 160×184 mm. 1 (71c.)×5, Type **1521**; Belfrey; Maison Boechoute, Craenenburg, Die Maene and Pathe Cinema (horiz); Le Panier d'Or; Provincial Court (horiz) — 15·00 — 15·00

1522 Saint Martin's Church, Kessenich

2011. Christmas. Multicoloured.
4482 1 (71c.) Type **1522** — 3·00 — 1·75
4483 1 (€1.03) Saint Mard Church, Vieux-Virton — 4·75 — 3·25
No. 4484 is vacant.

1523 Princess Mathilde

2013. 50th Birth Anniv of Princess Mathilde
4485 **1523** 1 (71c.) multicoloured — 3·00 — 1·75

1524 Kid Paddle

2013. Youth Philately. Kid Paddle
4486 **1524** 1 (71c.) multicoloured — 3·00 — 1·75

1525 Devil

2013. Characters from Fairy Tales. Booklet Stamps. Multicoloured.
4487	1 (71c.) Type **1525**	3·00	1·75	
4488	1 (71c.) Troll	3·00	1·75	
4489	1 (71c.) Ghost	3·00	1·75	
4490	1 (71c.) Wizard	3·00	1·75	
4491	1 (71c.) Witch	3·00	1·75	
4492	1 (71c.) Gnome	3·00	1·75	
4493	1 (71c.) Fairy	3·00	1·75	
4494	1 (71c.) Giant	3·00	1·75	
4495	1 (71c.) Prince	3·00	1·75	
4496	1 (71c.) Elf	3·00	1·75	

EXPRESS LETTER STAMPS

E107 Ghent

1929
E530	-	1f.75 blue	70	35
E531	**E107**	2f.35 red	2·20	50
E581		2f.45 green	23·00	3·00
E532		3f.50 purple	14·00	14·00
E533		5f.25 olive	13·50	13·00

DESIGNS: 1f.75, Town Hall, Brussels; 2f.45, Eupen; 3f.50, Bishop's Palace, Liege; 5f.25, Antwerp Cathedral.

1932. No. E581 surch **2 Fr 50** and cross.
E608 2f.50 on 2f.45 green — 16·00 — 2·30

MILITARY STAMPS

1967. As T **289** (Baudouin) but with letter "M" within oval at foot.
M2027 1f.50 green — 25 — 20

1971. As Nos. 2207/8a and 2209a but with letter "M" within oval at foot.
M2224	1f.75 green	35	35
M2225	2f.25 green	30	40
M2226	2f.50 green	25	25
M2227	3f.25 plum	30	30

NEWSPAPER STAMPS

1928. Railway Parcels stamps of 1923 optd **JOURNAUX DAGBLADEN 1928.**
N443	**P 84**	10c. red	60	35
N444	**P 84**	20c. green	60	35
N445	**P 84**	40c. olive	60	35
N446	**P 84**	60c. orange	85	35
N447	**P 84**	70c. brown	85	35
N448	**P 84**	80c. violet	1·20	60
N449	**P 84**	90c. slate	10·50	3·50
N450	-	1f. blue	2·30	60
N451	-	2f. olive	4·75	85
N452	-	3f. red	4·75	85
N453	-	4f. red	4·75	85
N454	-	5f. violet	4·75	85
N455	-	6f. brown	7·25	2·00
N456	-	7f. orange	20·00	3·50
N457	-	8f. brown	14·50	2·30
N458	-	9f. purple	41·00	10·50
N459	-	10f. green	14·50	3·50
N460	-	20f. pink	41·00	14·50

1929. Railway Parcels stamps of 1923 optd **JOURNAUX DAGBLADEN** only.
N505	**P 84**	10c. red	1·20	60
N506	**P 84**	20c. green	60	60
N507	**P 84**	40c. olive	60	60
N508	**P 84**	60c. orange	85	60
N509	**P 84**	70c. brown	60	60
N510	**P 84**	80c. violet	1·20	1·20
N511	**P 84**	90c. slate	7·75	6·50
N512	-	1f. blue	1·70	60
N513	-	1f.10 brown	5·75	1·70
N514	-	1f.50 blue	5·75	1·70
N515	-	2f. olive	3·75	1·20
N516	-	2f.10 slate	17·00	12·00
N517	-	3f. red	3·75	1·20
N518	-	4f. red	3·75	1·20
N519	-	5f. violet	3·75	1·20
N520	-	6f. brown	8·75	1·70
N521	-	7f. orange	26·00	1·70
N522	-	8f. brown	17·00	1·70
N523	-	9f. purple	35·00	19·00
N524	-	10f. green	20·00	4·75
N525	-	20f. pink	49·00	17·00

PARCEL POST STAMPS

1928. Optd **COLIS POSTAL POSTCOLLO.**
B470	81	4f. brown	8·75	2·00
B471	81	5f. bistre	8·75	2·00

B106 G.P.O., Brussels

1929
B526	**B106**	3f. sepia	1·50	30
B527	**B106**	4f. slate	1·50	30
B528	**B106**	5f. red	1·50	30
B529	**B106**	6f. purple	36·00	36·00

1933. Surch **X4 4X.**
B645 4f. on 6f. purple — 32·00 — 45

POSTAGE DUE STAMPS

D21

1870
D63	**D21**	10c. green	4·75	3·00
D64	**D21**	20c. blue	95·00	5·75

D35

1895
D96a	**D35**	5c. green	15	15
D97	**D35**	10c. brown	26·00	2·30
D101	**D35**	10c. red	15	10
D98a	**D35**	20c. green	15	15
D102	**D35**	30c. blue	20	15
D99	**D35**	50c. brown	26·00	7·00
D103	**D35**	50c. grey	45	45
D100	**D35**	1f. red	23·00	13·00
D104	**D35**	1f. yellow	5·75	5·75

1919. As Type **D35**, but value in colour on white background.
D251	5c. green	60	30	
D323	5c. grey	10	10	
D252b	10c. red	1·70	30	
D324	10c. green	10	10	
D253b	20c. green	8·75	1·50	
D325	20c. brown	10	10	
D254	30c. blue	4·75	60	
D326	30c. red	80	60	
D327	35c. green	25	15	
D328	40c. brown	25	15	
D329	50c. blue	1·50	25	
D330	50c. grey	25	10	
D331	60c. red	30	15	
D1146	65c. green	7·50	3·50	
D332	70c. brown	30	15	
D333	80c. grey	30	15	
D334	1f. violet	50	25	
D335	1f. purple	60	30	
D336	1f.20 olive	65	25	
D337	1f.40 green	65	60	
D338	1f.50 olive	65	60	
D1147	1f.60 mauve	14·50	7·00	
D1148	1f.80 red	16·00	5·75	
D339	2f. mauve	65	30	
D1149	2f.40 lavender	9·25	3·50	
D1150	3f. red	1·70	60	
D340	3f.50 blue	65	30	
D1151	4f. blue	11·00	60	
D1152	5f. brown	3·50	30	
D1153	7f. violet	3·50	1·70	
D1154	8f. purple	13·00	10·50	
D1155	10f. violet	7·50	3·25	

D218

1945. Inscr "A PAYER" at top and "TE BETALEN" at bottom, or vice versa.
D1130A	**D218**	10c. olive	10	10
D1131A	**D218**	20c. blue	10	10
D1132A	**D218**	30c. blue	10	10
D1133A	**D218**	40c. blue	10	10
D1134A	**D218**	50c. green	10	10
D1135A	**D218**	1f. brown	10	10
D1136A	**D218**	2f. orange	10	10

D462

1966
D2812	**D462**	1f. mauve	10	10
D2813	**D462**	2f. green	10	10
D2814	**D462**	3f. blue	1·40	25
D2815	**D462**	4f. green	25	25
D1985ab	**D462**	5f. purple	30	30
D2816	**D462**	5f. lilac	30	30
D1986	**D462**	6f. brown	85	15
D1987	**D462**	7f. red	70	†
D2818	**D462**	7f. orange	45	45
D2819	**D462**	8f. grey	45	45
D2820	**D462**	9f. red	50	50
D2821	**D462**	10f. brown	60	60
D1988	**D462**	20f. green	1·30	50
D2822	**D462**	20f. green	1·20	1·20

On No. D1988 the "F" is outside the shield; on No. D2822 it is inside.

RAILWAY PARCELS STAMPS

P21

1879
P63	**P21**	10c. brown	£160	10·50
P64	**P21**	20c. blue	£400	29·00
P65	**P21**	25c. green	£550	17·00
P66	**P21**	50c. red	£2750	14·50
P67	**P21**	80c. yellow	£3000	85·00
P68	**P21**	1f. grey	£400	†

In Belgium the parcels service is largely operated by the Belgian Railways for which the following stamps were issued.

Certain stamps under this heading were also on sale at post offices in connection with a "small parcels" service. These show a posthorn in the design except for Nos. P1116/18.

P22

1882
P69	**P22**	10c. brown	35·00	3·00
P73	**P22**	15c. grey	14·50	10·50
P75	**P22**	20c. blue	£100	5·75
P77	**P22**	25c. green	£100	6·00
P78	**P22**	50c. red	£100	1·20
P81	**P22**	80c. yellow	£110	3·00
P84	**P22**	80c. brown	£110	3·00
P86	**P22**	1f. grey	£600	4·75
P87	**P22**	1f. purple	£650	5·75
P88	**P22**	2f. buff	£350	£100

P35

1895. Numerals in black except 1f. and 2f.
P96	**P35**	10c. brown	14·50	1·20
P97	**P35**	15c. slate	14·50	11·50
P98	**P35**	20c. blue	23·00	2·30
P99	**P35**	25c. green	23·00	3·50
P100	**P35**	30c. orange	28·00	2·50
P101	**P35**	40c. green	41·00	2·50
P102	**P35**	50c. red	41·00	1·20
P103	**P35**	60c. lilac	75·00	1·20
P104	**P35**	70c. brown	75·00	2·00
P105	**P35**	80c. yellow	75·00	2·00
P106	**P35**	90c. red	£110	3·00
P107	**P35**	1f. purple	£300	4·75
P108	**P35**	2f. buff	£350	23·00

P37 Winged Railway Wheel

1902

P109a	10c. slate and brown	30	30	
P110	15c. purple and slate	30	30	
P111	20c. brown and blue	30	30	
P112	25c. red and green	30	30	
P113	30c. green and orange	30	30	
P114	35c. green and brown	30	30	
P115	40c. mauve and green	30	30	
P116	50c. mauve and pink	30	30	
P117	55c. blue and purple	30	30	
P118	60c. red and lilac	30	30	
P119	70c. red and blue	30	30	
P120	80c. purple and yellow	30	30	
P121	90c. green and red	30	30	
P122	**P37**	1f. orange and purple	30	30
P123	**P37**	1f.10 black and red	30	30
P124	**P37**	2f. green and bistre	30	30
P125	**P37**	3f. blue and black	30	30
P126	**P37**	4f. red and green	2·00	2·00
P127	**P37**	5f. green and orange	1·20	1·20
P128	**P37**	10f. purple and yellow	1·20	1·20

1915. Stamps of 1912–14 optd **CHEMINS DE FER SPOORWEGEN** and Winged Railway Wheel.

P160	**44**	5c. green	£225
P161	**46**	10c. red	£250
P162	**46**	20c. green	£300
P163	**46**	25c. blue	£300
P164	**45**	35c. brown	£400
P165	**46**	40c. green	£350
P166	**45**	50c. grey	£375
P167	**45**	1f. orange	£350
P168	**45**	2f. violet	£2000
P169	-	5f. purple (No. 143)	£4000

P59 Winged Railway Wheel

P60 Steam Locomotive

1915

P196	**P59**	10c. blue	1·20	60
P197	**P59**	15c. olive	2·00	2·00
P198	**P59**	20c. red	1·70	1·20
P199	**P59**	25c. brown	1·70	1·20
P200	**P59**	30c. mauve	1·70	1·20
P201	**P59**	35c. grey	2·00	1·20
P202	**P59**	40c. orange	3·25	3·00
P203	**P59**	50c. bistre	3·00	1·20
P204	**P59**	55c. brown	3·50	3·25
P205	**P59**	60c. lilac	3·00	1·20
P206	**P59**	70c. green	2·00	1·20
P207	**P59**	80c. brown	2·00	1·20
P208	**P59**	90c. blue	3·00	1·50
P209	**P60**	1f. grey	2·00	1·20
P210	**P60**	1f.10 bl (FRANKEN)	44·00	33·00
P211	**P60**	1f.10 blue (FRANK)	3·00	1·20
P212	**P60**	2f. red	65·00	1·70
P213	**P60**	3f. violet	65·00	1·70
P214	**P60**	4f. green	75·00	3·25
P215	**P60**	5f. brown	£150	4·25
P216	**P60**	10f. orange	£200	3·75

P69 Winged Railway Wheel

P70 Steam Train

1920

P259	**P69**	10c. green	2·30	1·20
P280	**P69**	10c. red	60	30
P281	**P69**	15c. green	60	30
P261	**P69**	20c. red	2·30	1·20
P282	**P69**	20c. green	2·00	30
P262	**P69**	25c. brown	3·50	1·20
P283	**P69**	25c. blue	85	30
P263	**P69**	30c. mauve	38·00	34·00
P284	**P69**	30c. brown	85	30
P285	**P69**	35c. brown	85	45
P264	**P69**	40c. orange	85	30
P265	**P69**	50c. bistre	11·50	2·00
P287	**P69**	50c. red	85	30
P266	**P69**	55c. brown	13·00	9·50
P288	**P69**	55c. yellow	7·00	5·75
P267	**P69**	60c. purple	15·00	1·70
P289	**P69**	60c. red	85	30
P290	**P69**	70c. green	4·00	60
P269	**P69**	80c. brown	65·00	2·00
P291	**P69**	80c. violet	3·00	45
P270	**P69**	90c. blue	17·00	1·70
P292	**P69**	90c. yellow	46·00	43·00
P293	**P69**	90c. purple	8·75	45
P271	**P70**	1f. grey	£120	2·00
P272	**P70**	1f.10 blue	38·00	2·00
P273	**P70**	1f.20 green	23·00	†
P274	**P70**	1f.40 brown	23·00	1·70
P275	**P70**	2f. red	£170	1·70
P276	**P70**	3f. mauve	£200	1·20
P277	**P70**	4f. green	£200	1·70
P278	**P70**	5f. brown	£200	1·20
P279	**P70**	10f. orange	£200	1·70

On Nos. P271/9 the engine has one head lamp.

1920. Three head lamps on engine.

P294	**P70**	1f. brown	8·75	30
P296	**P70**	1f.10 blue	3·00	30
P297	**P70**	1f.20 orange	3·75	30
P298	**P70**	1f.40 yellow	21·00	3·50
P299	**P70**	1f.60 green	38·00	70
P300	**P70**	2f. red	41·00	30
P301	**P70**	3f. red	41·00	30
P302	**P70**	4f. green	41·00	30
P303	**P70**	5f. violet	41·00	30
P304	**P70**	10f. yellow	£225	23·00
P305	**P70**	10f. brown	50·00	30
P306	**P70**	15f. red	50·00	30
P307	**P70**	20f. blue	£600	3·75

P75

1921

P312	**P75**	2f. black	11·50	95
P313	**P75**	3f. brown	£100	95
P314	**P75**	4f. green	26·00	95
P315	**P75**	5f. red	26·00	95
P316	**P75**	10f. brown	26·00	95
P317	**P75**	15f. red	26·00	1·50
P318	**P75**	20f. blue	£190	3·75

P84

1923

P375	**P84**	5c. brown	25	25
P376	**P84**	10c. red	10	10
P377	**P84**	15c. blue	30	30
P378	**P84**	20c. green	15	10
P379	**P84**	30c. purple	15	10
P380	**P84**	40c. olive	15	10
P381	**P84**	50c. red	15	10
P382	**P84**	60c. orange	15	10
P383	**P84**	70c. brown	15	10
P384	**P84**	80c. violet	15	10
P385	**P84**	90c. slate	1·00	10

Similar type, but horiz.

P386	1f. blue	30	15
P388	1f.10 orange	2·30	85
P389	1f.50 green	2·30	60
P390	1f.70 brown	60	60
P391	1f.80 red	3·50	85
P392	2f. olive	30	30
P393	2f.10 green	6·50	1·70
P394	2f.40 violet	4·00	1·70
P395	2f.70 grey	45·00	1·70
P396	3f. red	30	25
P397	3f.30 brown	70·00	1·70
P398	4f. red	30	25
P399	5f. violet	60	25
P400	6f. brown	30	25
P401	7f. orange	60	25
P402	8f. brown	60	25
P403	9f. purple	2·00	85
P404	10f. green	85	25
P405	20f. pink	1·20	85
P406	30f. green	4·00	60
P407	40f. slate	55·00	1·70
P408	50f. bistre	7·75	60

See Nos. P911/34.

1924. No. P394 surch **2F 30.**

P409	2f.30 on 2f.40 violet	5·75	85

P139 Type 5 Steam locomotive "Goliath", 1930

1934

P655	**P139**	3f. green	14·50	2·50
P656	**P139**	4f. mauve	5·75	30
P657	**P139**	5f. red	80·00	30

P149 Diesel Locomotive

1935. Centenary of Belgian Railway.

P689	**P149**	10c. red	35	30
P690	**P149**	20c. violet	35	30
P691	**P149**	30c. brown	60	30
P692	**P149**	40c. blue	60	30
P693	**P149**	50c. orange	60	30
P694	**P149**	60c. green	65	30
P695	**P149**	70c. blue	65	30
P696	**P149**	80c. black	65	30
P697	**P149**	90c. red	1·20	60

Horiz type. Locomotive *Le Belge*, 1835.

P698	1f. purple	85	30
P699	2f. black	2·30	30
P700	3f. orange	3·25	30
P701	4f. purple	3·25	30
P702	5f. purple	4·75	30
P703	6f. green	6·50	30
P704	7f. violet	26·00	30
P705	8f. black	26·00	35
P706	9f. blue	29·00	35
P707	10f. red	29·00	35
P708	20f. green	55·00	35
P709	30f. violet	£150	5·75
P710	40f. brown	£150	5·75
P711	50f. red	£200	5·25
P712	100f. blue	£375	85·00

P162 Winged Railway Wheel and Posthorn

1938

P806	**P162**	5f. on 3f.50 green	26·00	25
P807	**P162**	5f. on 4f.50 purple	30	10
P808	**P162**	6f. on 5f.50 red	60	10
P1162	**P162**	8f. on 5f.50 brown	60	15
P1163	**P162**	10f. on 5f.50 blue	85	15
P1164	**P162**	12f. on 5f.50 violet	1·50	25

P176 Seal of the International Railway Congress

1939. International Railway Congress, Brussels.

P856	**P176**	20c. brown	5·25	5·25
P857	**P176**	50c. blue	5·25	5·25
P858	**P176**	2f. red	5·25	5·25
P859	**P176**	9f. green	5·25	5·25
P860	**P176**	10f. purple	5·25	5·25

1939. Surch **M. 3Fr.**

P867	**P162**	3f. on 5f.50 red	30	25

1940. Optd **B** in oval and two vert bars.

P878	**P84**	10c. red	10	10
P879	**P84**	20c. green	10	10
P880	**P84**	30c. purple	10	10
P881	**P84**	40c. olive	10	10
P882	**P84**	50c. red	10	10
P883	**P84**	60c. orange	75	70
P884	**P84**	70c. brown	10	10
P885	**P84**	80c. violet	10	10
P886	**P84**	90c. slate	30	30
P887	**P84**	1f. blue	15	15
P888	**P84**	2f. olive	25	25
P889	**P84**	3f. red	25	25
P890	**P84**	4f. red	25	25
P891	**P84**	5f. violet	25	25
P892	**P84**	6f. brown	30	25
P893	**P84**	7f. orange	30	25
P894	**P84**	8f. brown	30	25
P895	**P84**	9f. purple	30	25
P896	**P84**	10f. green	30	25
P897	**P84**	20f. pink	75	45
P898	**P84**	30f. green	1·20	1·20
P899	**P84**	40f. slate	3·00	2·50
P900	**P84**	50f. bistre	1·70	1·70

1940. As Type **P84** but colours changed.

P911		10c. olive	10	10
P912		20c. violet	10	10
P913		30c. red	10	10
P914		40c. blue	10	10
P915		50c. green	10	10
P916		60c. grey	10	10
P917		70c. green	10	10
P918		80c. orange	30	10
P919		90c. lilac	3·00	10

Similar design, but horizontal.

P920	1f. green	30	10
P921	2f. brown	35	10
P922	3f. grey	35	10
P923	4f. olive	40	10
P924	5f. lilac	45	10
P925	5f. black	85	10
P926	6f. red	85	10
P927	7f. violet	85	10
P928	8f. green	85	10
P929	9f. blue	1·20	10
P930	1f. mauve	1·20	25
P931	20f. blue	3·50	30
P932	30f. yellow	5·75	1·00
P933	40f. red	7·25	1·00
P934	50f. red	11·50	85

No. P925 was for use as a railway parcels tax stamp.

P195 Engine Driver

1942. Various designs.

P1090	**P195**	10c. grey	30	25
P1091	**P195**	20c. violet	30	25
P1092	**P195**	30c. red	30	25
P1093	**P195**	40c. blue	30	25
P1094	**P195**	50c. blue	30	25
P1095	**P195**	60c. black	30	25
P1096	**P195**	70c. green	45	25
P1097	**P195**	80c. orange	45	25
P1098	**P195**	90c. brown	45	25
P1099	-	1f. green	30	25
P1100	-	2f. purple	30	25
P1101	-	3f. black	1·50	30
P1102	-	4f. blue	30	25
P1103	-	5f. brown	30	25
P1104	-	6f. green	1·50	60
P1105	-	7f. violet	30	25
P1106	-	8f. red	30	25
P1107	-	9f. blue	60	25
P996	-	9f.20 red	60	60
P1108	-	10f. red	3·25	35
P1109	-	10f. brown	2·30	45
P997	**P195**	12f.30 green	60	60
P998	-	14f.30 green	60	60
P1110	-	20f. green	1·20	25
P1111	-	30f. violet	1·20	25
P1112	-	40f. red	1·20	25
P1113	-	50f. blue	20·00	1·20
P999	-	100f. blue	24·00	24·00

DESIGNS—As Type P **195**: 1f. to 9f.20, Platelayer; 10f. and 14f.30 to 50f. Railway porter; 24½×34½ mm: 100f. Electric train.

No. P1109 was for use as a railway parcels tax stamp.

P216 Mercury

1945. Inscribed "BELGIQUE-BELGIE" or vice-versa.

P1116A	**P216**	3f. green	30	15
P1117A	**P216**	5f. blue	30	15
P1118A	**P216**	6f. red	30	15

P224 Level Crossing

1947
P1174 **P224** 100f. green | 7·25 | 30

P230 Archer

1947
P1193 **P230** 8f. brown | 1·20 | 40
P1194 **P230** 10f. blue and black | 1·20 | 30
P1195 **P230** 12f. violet | 1·70 | 30

1948. Surch.
P1229 9f. on 8f. brown | 1·50 | 25
P1230 11f. on 10f. blue and black | 1·50 | 40
P1231 13f.50 on 12f. violet | 2·00 | 25

P246 "Parcel Post"

1948
P1250 **P246** 9f. brown | 8·75 | 35
P1251 **P246** 11f. red | 7·50 | 25
P1252 **P246** 13f.50 black | 13·00 | 25

P254 Type 1 Locomotive, 1867 (dated 1862)

1949. Locomotives.
P1277 - ½f. brown | 35 | 25
P1278 **P254** 1f. red | 60 | 25
P1279 - 2f. blue | 80 | 25
P1280 - 3f. red (1884) | 2·50 | 25
P1281 - 4f. green (1901) | 1·70 | 25
P1282 - 5f. red (1902) | 1·70 | 25
P1283 - 6f. purple (1904) | 2·50 | 25
P1284 - 7f. green (1905) | 4·00 | 25
P1285 - 8f. blue (1906) | 5·25 | 25
P1286 - 9f. brown (1909) | 5·75 | 25
P1287 - 10f. olive (1910) | 14·00 | 3·50
P1288 - 10f. black and red (1905) | 7·00 | 25
P1289 - 20f. orange (1920) | 13·00 | 25
P1290 - 30f. blue (1928) | 23·00 | 25
P1291 - 40f. red (1930) | 41·00 | 25
P1292 - 50f. mauve (1935) | 70·00 | 25
P1293 - 100f. red (1939) | £120 | 30
P1294 - 300f. violet (1951) | £170 | 60
DESIGNS: 50c. Locomotive Le Belge, 1835; 2f. Type 29 locomotive, 1875; 3f. Type 25 locomotive, 1884; 4f. Type 18 locomotive, 1901; 5f. Type 22 locomotive, 1902; 6f. Type 53 locomotive, 1904; 7f. Type 8 locomotive, 1905; 8f. Type 16 locomotive, 1906; 9f. Type 10 locomotive, 1909; 10f. (P1287) Type 36 locomotive, 1910; 10f. (P 1288) Type 38 locomotive, 1905; 20f. Type 38 locomotive, 1920; 30f. Type 48 locomotive, 1928; 40f. Type 5 locomotive, 1935; 50f. Type 1 Pacific locomotive, 1935; 100f. Type 12 locomotive, 1939; 300f. Two-car electric train, 1951.
 The 300f. is larger (37½×25 mm).

1949. Electrification of Charleroi–Brussels Line. As Type P254.
P1296 60f. brown | 2·00 | 1·50
DESIGN: 60f. Type 101 electric locomotive, 1945.

P258 Loading Parcels

1950
P1307 - 11f. orange | 5·75 | 25
P1308 - 12f. purple | 22·00 | 2·00
P1309 - 13f. green | 7·50 | 25
P1310 - 15f. blue | 16·00 | 30
P1311 **P258** 16f. grey | 5·75 | 25
P1312 - 17f. brown | 7·50 | 25
P1313 **P258** 18f. red | 16·00 | 25
P1314 **P258** 20f. orange | 7·50 | 30
DESIGNS—HORIZ: 11, 12, 17f. Dispatch counter; 13, 15f. Sorting compartment.

P271 Mercury

1951. 25th Anniv of National Belgian Railway Society.
P1375 **P271** 25f. blue | 15·00 | 13·00

1953. Nos. P1307, P1310 and P1313 surch.
P1442 - 13f. on 15f. blue | 65·00 | 5·75
P1443 - 17f. on 11f. orange | 32·00 | 1·20
P1444 **P258** 20f. on 18f. red | 17·00 | 3·50

P288 Electric Train and Brussels Skyline

1953. Inauguration of Nord-Midi Junction.
P1451 **P288** 200f. green | £250 | 85
P1452 **P288** 200f. green & brown | £275 | 3·75

P291 Nord Station | **P292** Central Station

1953. Brussels Railway Stations.
P1485 **P291** 1f. ochre | 30 | 25
P1486 **P291** 2f. black | 45 | 25
P1487 **P291** 3f. green | 60 | 30
P1488 **P291** 4f. orange | 85 | 40
P1489 **P291** 5f. brown | 3·00 | 25
P1490 - 5f. brown | 10·50 | 25
P1491 **P291** 6f. purple | 1·20 | 25
P1492 **P291** 7f. green | 1·20 | 25
P1493 **P291** 8f. red | 1·50 | 25
P1494 **P291** 9f. blue | 2·00 | 25
P1495 - 10f. green | 2·40 | 25
P1496 - 10f. black | 1·50 | 30
P1497 - 15f. red | 14·50 | 45
P1498 - 20f. blue | 4·00 | 25
P1498a - 20f. green | 2·30 | 45
P1499 - 30f. purple | 6·50 | 25
P1500 - 40f. mauve | 8·75 | 25
P1501 - 50f. mauve | 10·50 | 25
P1501a - 50f. blue | 3·50 | 70
P1502 - 60f. violet | 22·00 | 25
P1503 - 80f. purple | 35·00 | 25
P1504 **P292** 100f. green | 20·00 | 50
P1505 **P292** 200f. blue | £120 | 1·00
P1506 **P292** 300f. mauve | £200 | 1·70
DESIGNS—VERT: 5f. (P1490), 10f. (P1496), 15, 20f. (P1498a), 50f. (P1501a), Congress Station; 10f. (P1495), 20f. (P1498) to 50f. (P1501), Midi Station. HORIZ: 60, 80f. Chapelle Station.
 Nos. P1490, P1496/7, P1498a and P1501a were for use as railway parcels tax stamps.

P295 Electric Train Type 121 and Nord Station, Brussels

1953
P1517 **P295** 13f. brown | 23·00 | 30
P1518 **P295** 18f. blue | 23·00 | 30
P1519 **P295** 21f. mauve | 23·00 | 30

1956. Surch in figures.
P1585 14f. on 13f. brown | 8·25 | 30
P1586 19f. on 18f. blue | 8·25 | 30
P1587 22f. on 21f. mauve | 8·25 | 30

P326 Mercury and Railway Winged Wheel

1957
P1600 **P326** 14f. green | 8·25 | 25
P1601 **P326** 19f. sepia | 8·25 | 25
P1602 **P326** 22f. red | 8·25 | 40

1959. Surch **20 F.**
P1678 20f. on 19f. sepia | 29·00 | 30
P1679 20f. on 22f. red | 29·00 | 70

P357 Brussels Nord Station, 1861–1954

1959
P1695 **P357** 20f. olive | 14·50 | 25
P1696 - 24f. red | 5·75 | 30
P1697 - 26f. red | 5·75 | 30
P1698 - 28f. purple | 5·75 | 3·50
DESIGNS—VERT: 24f. Brussels Midi station, 1869–1949. HORIZ: 26f. Antwerp Central station, 1905; 28f. Ghent St. Pieter's station.

P368 Congress Seal, Type 202 Diesel and Type 125 Electric Locomotives

1960. 75th Anniv of Int Railway Congress Assn.
P1722 **P368** 20f. red | 50·00 | 35·00
P1723 **P368** 50f. blue | 50·00 | 35·00
P1724 **P368** 60f. purple | 50·00 | 35·00
P1725 **P368** 70f. green | 50·00 | 35·00

1961. Nos. P1695/8 surch.
P1787 **P357** 24f. on 20f. olive | 60·00 | 30
P1788 - 26f. on 24f. red | 5·75 | 30
P1789 - 28f. on 26f. blue | 5·75 | 30
P1790 - 35f. on 28f. purple | 5·75 | 30

P477 Arlon Station

1967
P2017 **P477** 25f. ochre | 9·25 | 45
P2018 **P477** 30f. green | 2·30 | 45
P2019 **P477** 35f. blue | 3·00 | 45
P2020 **P477** 40f. red | 26·00 | 70

P488 Type 122 Electric Train

1968
P2047 **P488** 1f. bistre | 30 | 30
P2048 **P488** 2f. green | 30 | 30
P2049 **P488** 3f. green | 60 | 30
P2050 **P488** 4f. orange | 60 | 30
P2051 **P488** 5f. brown | 60 | 30
P2052 **P488** 6f. plum | 60 | 30
P2053 **P488** 7f. green | 60 | 30
P2054 **P488** 8f. red | 90 | 30
P2055 **P488** 9f. blue | 1·50 | 30
P2056 - 10f. green | 3·00 | 30
P2057 - 20f. blue | 1·80 | 30
P2058 - 30f. lilac | 5·50 | 30
P2059 - 40f. violet | 6·00 | 30
P2060 - 50f. purple | 7·50 | 30
P2061 - 60f. violet | 11·00 | 30
P2062 - 70f. brown | 48·00 | 30
P2063 - 80f. purple | 7·50 | 30
P2063a - 90f. green | 7·25 | 50
P2064 - 100f. green | 12·00 | 30
P2065 - 200f. violet | 15·00 | 60
P2066 - 300f. mauve | 27·00 | 1·50
P2067 - 500f. yellow | 42·00 | 2·10
DESIGNS: 10f. to 40f. Type 126 electric train; 50, 60, 70, 80, 90f. Type 160 electric train; 100, 200, 300f. Type 205 diesel-electric train; 500f. Type 210 diesel-electric train.

1970. Surch.
P2180 **P477** 37f. on 25f. ochre | 65·00 | 7·75
P2181 **P477** 48f. on 35f. blue | 6·00 | 6·00
P2182 **P477** 53f. on 40f. red | 6·00 | 6·00

P551 Ostend Station

1971. Figures of value in black.
P2192 **P551** 32f. ochre | 1·80 | 1·50
P2193 **P551** 37f. grey | 16·00 | 15·00
P2194 **P551** 42f. blue | 2·40 | 1·80

P2195 **P551** 44f. mauve | 2·40 | 1·80
P2196 **P551** 46f. violet | 2·75 | 1·80
P2197 **P551** 50f. red | 2·40 | 1·80
P2198 **P551** 52f. brown | 17·00 | 16·00
P2199 **P551** 54f. green | 6·75 | 6·00
P2200 **P551** 61f. blue | 3·50 | 2·75

1972. Nos. P2192/5 and P2198/200 surch in figures.
P2256 - 34f. on 32f. ochre | 2·75 | 1·20
P2257 - 40f. on 37f. grey | 2·75 | 1·20
P2258 - 47f. on 44f. mauve | 3·00 | 1·20
P2259 - 53f. on 46f. violet | 3·50 | 1·20
P2260 - 56f. on 52f. brown | 3·50 | 1·20
P2261 - 59f. on 54f. green | 4·00 | 1·20
P2262 - 66f. on 61f. blue | 4·25 | 1·20

P575 Emblems within Bogie Wheels

1972. 50th Anniv of Int Railways Union (U.I.C.).
P2266 **P575** 100f. black, red and green | 9·00 | 2·40
See also No. 2274.

P624 Global Emblem

1974. Fourth International Symposium of Railway Cybernetics, Washington.
P2353 **P624** 100f. black, red and yellow | 7·00 | 2·30

P671 Railway Junction

1976
P2431 **P671** 20f. black, bl & lilac | 1·50 | 1·50
P2432 **P671** 50f. black, green and turquoise | 2·50 | 1·50
P2433 **P671** 100f. black & orange | 5·25 | 2·00
P2434 **P671** 150f. black, mauve and deep mauve | 8·25 | 2·00

P677 Modern Electric Train

1976. 50th Anniv of National Belgian Railway Company.
P2445 **P677** 6f.50 multicoloured | 50 | 15

P698 Railway Station at Night

1977
P2505 **P698** 1000f. mult | 60·00 | 29·00

P753 Goods Wagon, Type 2216 A8

1980. Values in black.
P2615 **P753** 1f. ochre | 30 | 30
P2616 **P753** 2f. red | 30 | 30
P2617 **P753** 3f. blue | 30 | 30
P2618 **P753** 4f. blue | 30 | 30
P2619 **P753** 5f. brown | 30 | 30
P2620 **P753** 6f. orange | 45 | 45
P2621 **P753** 7f. violet | 60 | 60
P2622 **P753** 8f. black | 60 | 60
P2623 **P753** 9f. green | 60 | 60
P2624 - 10f. brown | 60 | 60
P2625 - 20f. blue | 1·50 | 60
P2626 - 30f. ochre | 2·30 | 60
P2627 - 40f. mauve | 2·75 | 60
P2628 - 50f. purple | 3·25 | 80

P2629	-	60f. olive	3·75	80
P2630	-	70f. blue	5·00	3·50
P2631	-	80f. purple	6·00	1·20
P2632	-	90f. mauve	6·50	4·00
P2633	-	100f. red	7·25	1·70
P2634	-	200f. brown	15·00	2·00
P2635	-	300f. olive	21·00	9·00
P2636	-	500f. purple	37·00	5·00

DESIGNS: 10f. to 40f. Packet wagon, Type 3614 A5; 50f. to 90f. Self-discharging wagon, Type 1000 D; 100f. to 500f. Tanker wagon, Type 2000 G.

P833 Electric Train entering Station

1985. 150th Anniv of Belgian Railways. Paintings by P. Delvaux. Multicoloured.

P2824	250f. Type P **833**	17·00	11·50
P2825	500f. Electric trains in station	41·00	20·00

RAILWAY PARCEL TAX STAMPS

1940. As Nos. P399 and P404 but colours changed.

P876	**P84**	5f. brown	60	60
P877	**P84**	10f. black	6·50	6·50

P779 Electric Locomotive at Station

1982

P2703	**P779**	10f. red & black	2·00	30
P2704	**P779**	20f. green & blk	2·30	1·50
P2705	**P779**	50f. brown & blk	4·25	85
P2706	**P779**	100f. blue & blk	7·50	1·20

P877 Buildings and Electric Locomotive

1987

P2923	**P877**	10f. red	1·20	60
P2924	**P877**	20f. green	1·80	1·50
P2925	**P877**	50f. brown	5·50	2·10
P2926	**P877**	100f. purple	9·75	4·25
P2927	**P877**	150f. brown	15·00	5·50

RAILWAY OFFICIAL STAMPS

1929. Stamps of 1922 optd with winged wheel.

O481	81	5c. slate	35	30
O482	81	10c. green	35	30
O483	81	35c. brown	45	30
O484	81	60c. olive	60	30
O485	81	1f.50 blue	19·00	9·25
O486	81	1f.75 blue	2·30	1·20

For use on the official mail of the Railway Company.

1929. Stamps of 1929 optd with winged wheel.

O534	104	5c. green	30	15
O535	104	10c. bistre	30	15
O536	104	25c. red	2·50	45
O537	104	35c. green	80	25
O538	104	40c. purple	80	25
O539	104	50c. blue	40	25
O540	104	60c. mauve	23·00	11·50
O541	104	70c. brown	4·00	1·40
O542	104	75c. blue	8·25	1·20

1932. Stamps of 1931–34 optd with winged wheel.

O620	126	10c. green	85	60
O677	127	35c. green	17·00	65
O678	142	70c. green	5·75	40
O679	121	75c. brown	2·50	50

1936. Stamps of 1936 optd with winged wheel.

O721	152	10c. olive	15	15
O722	152	35c. green	15	15
O723	152	40c. lilac	25	25
O724	152	50c. blue	60	60
O725	152	70c. brown	4·75	4·75
O726	153	75c. olive	60	60

1941. Optd B in oval frame.

O948	152	10c. green	15	15
O949	152	40c. lilac	15	15
O950	152	50c. blue	25	25
O951	153	1f. red (No. 747)	30	30
O952a	153	1f. red (No. 748)	60	60
O953	153	2f.25 black	70	70
O954	155	2f.25 violet	35	35

1942. Nos. O722, O725 and O726 surch.

O983	152	10c. on 35c. green	10	15
O984	153	50c. on 70c. brown	10	15
O985	153	50c. on 75c. olive	25	25

O221

1946. Designs incorporating letter "B".

O1156	**O 221**	10c. green	10	10
O1157	**O 221**	20c. violet	3·75	1·20
O1158	**O 221**	50c. blue	10	10
O1159	**O 221**	65c. purple	5·25	1·50
O1160	**O 221**	75c. mauve	25	15
O1161	**O 221**	90c. violet	6·00	35
O1240	-	1f.35 brn (as 1219)	3·00	60
O1241	-	1f.75 green (as 1220)	7·50	60
O1242	239	3f. purple	35·00	10·50
O1243	240	3f.15 blue	14·00	8·75
O1244	240	4f. blue	28·00	11·50

O283

1952

O1424	**O 283**	10c. orange	40	15
O1425	**O 283**	20c. red	4·25	85
O1426	**O 283**	30c. green	1·70	60
O1427	**O 283**	40c. brown	40	15
O1428	**O 283**	50c. blue	35	15
O1429	**O 283**	60c. mauve	85	30
O1430	**O 283**	65c. purple	35·00	29·00
O1431	**O 283**	80c. green	5·75	1·50
O1432	**O 283**	90c. blue	8·75	1·50
O1433	**O 283**	1f. red	60	15
O1433a	O 283	1f.50 grey	25	25
O1434	**O 283**	2f.50 brown	30	15

1954. As T **289** (King Baudouin) but with letter "B" incorporated in design.

O1523	1f.50 black		40	15
O1524	2f. red		46·00	40
O1525	2f. green		45	15
O1526	2f.50 brown		37·00	85
O1527	3f. mauve		2·00	15
O1528	3f.50 green		85	15
O1529	4f. blue		1·20	35
O1530	6f. red		2·00	60

1971. As Nos. 2209/20 but with letter "B" incorporated in design.

O2224	3f. green	1·30	90
O2225	3f.50 brown	50	30
O2226	4f. blue	1·50	60
O2227	4f.50 purple	40	30
O2228	4f.50 blue	30	30
O2229	5f. violet	30	30
O2230	6f. red	50	30
O2231	6f.50 violet	60	30
O2232a	7f. red	35	25
O2233	8f. black	60	30
O2233a	9f. brown	60	30
O2234	10f. red	60	30
O2235	15f. violet	60	30
O2236	25f. purple	1·80	60
O2237	30f. brown	1·90	90

1977. As T **684** but with letter "B" incorporated in design.

O2455	50c. brown	25	25
O2456	1f. mauve	25	25
O2457	2f. orange	25	25
O2458	4f. brown	30	30
O2459	5f. green	30	30

BELIZE

British Honduras was renamed Belize on 1 June 1973 and the country became independent within the Commonwealth on 21 September 1981.

100 cents = 1 dollar.

1973. Nos. 256/66 and 277/8 of British Honduras optd **BELIZE** and two stars.

347		½c. multicoloured	10	20
348	63	1c. black, brown and yellow	10	20
349	-	2c. black, green and yellow	10	20
350	-	3c. black, brown and lilac	10	10
351	-	4c. multicoloured	10	30
352	-	5c. black and red	10	30
353	-	10c. multicoloured	15	15
354	-	15c. multicoloured	20	20
355	-	25c. multicoloured	35	35
356	-	50c. multicoloured	65	75
357	-	$1 multicoloured	75	1·50
358	-	$2 multicoloured	1·25	2·75
359	-	$5 multicoloured	1·40	5·25

1973. Royal Wedding. As T **47** of Anguilla. Background colours given. Multicoloured.

360	26c. blue	15	10
361	50c. brown	15	20

82 Mozambique Mouthbrooder

1974. As Nos. 256/66 and 276/78 of British Honduras. Multicoloured.

362	½c. Type **82**	10	50
363	1c. Spotted jewfish	10	30
364	2c. White-lipped peccary ("Waree")	10	30
365	3c. Misty grouper	10	30
366	4c. Collared anteater	10	30
367	5c. Bonefish	10	30
368	10c. Paca ("Gibnut")	15	15
369	15c. Dolphin	20	20
370	25c. Kinkajou ("Night Walker")	35	35
371	50c. Mutton snapper	60	70
372	$1 Tayra ("Bush Dog")	75	1·50
373	$2 Great barracuda	1·25	2·50
374	$5 Puma	1·50	5·50

83 Deer

1974. Mayan Artefacts (1st series). Pottery Motifs. Multicoloured.

375	3c. Type **83**	10	10
376	6c. Jaguar deity	10	10
377	16c. Sea monster	15	10
378	26c. Cormorant	25	10
379	50c. Scarlet macaw	40	40

See also Nos. 398/402.

84 "Parides arcas"

1974. Butterflies of Belize. Multicoloured.

380	½c. Type **84**	1·00	5·00
381	1c. *Evenus regalis*	1·00	1·75
405	2c. *Colobura dirce*	50	70
406	3c. *Catonephele numilia*	1·25	70
407	4c. *Battus belus*	3·00	30
408	5c. *Callicore patelina*	3·25	30
386	10c. *Diaethria astala*	1·50	70
410	15c. *Nessaea aglaura*	75	70
388	16c. *Prepona pseudojoiceyi*	5·00	9·00
412	25c. *Papilio thoas*	6·50	40
390	26c. *Hamadryas arethusa*	2·00	4·25
413	35c. Type **84**	13·00	4·50
391	50c. *Panthiades bathildis*	3·25	65
392	$1 *Caligo uranus*	6·50	7·00
393	$2 *Heliconius sapho*	4·00	1·25
394	$5 *Eurytides philolaus*	5·50	6·00
395	$10 *Philaethria dido*	10·00	4·00

85 Churchill when Prime Minister, and Coronation Scene

1974. Birth Centenary of Sir Winston Churchill. Multicoloured.

396	50c. Type **85**	20	20
397	$1 Churchill in stetson, and Williamsburg Liberty Bell	30	30

86 The Actun Balam Vase

1975. Mayan Artefacts (2nd series). Multicoloured.

398	3c. Type **86**	10	10
399	6c. Seated figure	10	10
400	16c. Costumed priest	25	15
401	26c. Head with headdress	35	20
402	50c. Layman and priest	45	1·75

87 Musicians

1975. Christmas. Multicoloured.

435	6c. Type **87**	10	10
436	26c. Children and "crib"	20	10
437	50c. Dancer and drummers (vert)	30	55
438	$1 Family and map (vert)	55	1·60

88 William Wrigley Jr. and Chicle Tapping

1976. Bicent of American Revolution. Multicoloured.

439	10c. Type **88**	10	10
440	35c. Charles Lindbergh	20	40
441	$1 J. L. Stephens (archaeologist)	50	1·50

89 Cycling

1976. Olympic Games, Montreal. Multicoloured.

442	35c. Type **89**	55	10
443	45c. Running	20	15
444	$1 Shooting	35	1·40

1976. No. 390 surch **20c.**

445	20c. on 26c. multicoloured	1·50	1·75

1976. West Indian Victory in World Cricket Cup. As Nos. 559/60 of Barbados.

446	35c. multicoloured	40	50
447	$1 black and purple	60	2·00

1976. No. 426 surch **5c.**

448	5c. on 15c. multicoloured	1·50	2·75

92 Queen and Bishops

1977. Silver Jubilee. Multicoloured.

449	10c. Royal Visit, 1975	10	10
450	35c. Queen and Rose Window	15	15
451	$2 Type **92**	45	90

93 Red-capped Manakin

1977. Birds (1st series). Multicoloured.

452	8c. Type **93**	75	55
453	10c. Hooded oriole	90	30
454	25c. Blue-crowned motmot	1·25	55
455	35c. Slaty-breasted tinamou	1·50	75
456	45c. Ocellated turkey	1·75	1·25
457	$1 White hawk	3·00	5·50
MS458 110×133 mm. Nos. 452/7		8·25	11·00

See also Nos. 467/78, 488/94 and 561/7.

94 Laboratory Workers

1977. 75th Anniv of Pan-American Health Organization. Multicoloured.

459	35c. Type **94**	20	20
460	$1 Mobile medical unit	40	65
MS461 126×95 mm. Nos. 459/60		85	1·40

1978. Nos. 386 and 413 optd BELIZE DEFENCE FORCE 1ST JANUARY 1978.

462	10c. "Diaethria astala"	75	1·50
463	35c. Type **84**	1·50	2·25

96 White Lion of Mortimer

1978. 25th Anniv of Coronation.

464	**96**	75c. brown, red and silver	20	30
465	-	75c. multicoloured	20	30
466	-	75c. brown, red and silver	20	30

DESIGNS: No. 465, Queen Elizabeth II; 466, Jaguar (Maya god of Day and Night).

1978. Birds (2nd series). As T 93. Multicoloured.

467	10c. White-capped parrot("White-crowned Parrot")	55	30
468	25c. Crimson-collared tanager	80	45
469	35c. Black-headed trogon (*Citreoline Trogon*)	1·10	55
470	45c. American finfoot ("Sun-grebe")	1·25	1·75
471	50c. Muscovy duck	1·40	2·50
472	$1 King vulture	2·00	6·50
MS473 111×133 mm. Nos. 467/72		8·00	11·00

97 "Russelia sarmentosa"

1978. Christmas. Wild Flowers and Ferns. Multicoloured.

474	10c. Type **97**	15	10
475	15c. *Lygodium polymorphum*	20	15
476	35c. *Heliconia aurantiaca*	20	20
477	45c. *Adiantum tetraphyllum*	20	40
478	50c. *Angelonia ciliaris*	35	50
479	$1 *Thelypteris obliterata*	50	1·25

98 Fairchild Monoplane of Internal Airmail Service, 1937

1979. Centenary of U.P.U. Membership. Multicoloured.

480	5c. Type **98**	25	30
481	10c. *Heron H* (mail boat), 1949	25	10
482	35c. Internal mail service, 1920 (canoe)	25	20
483	45c. Steam Creek Railway mail, 1910	45	55
484	50c. Mounted mail courier, 1882	45	60
485	$2 *Eagle* (mail boat), 1856	80	2·50

1979. No. 413 surch 15c.

487	**84**	15c. on 35c. multicoloured	2·25	1·75

1979. Birds (3rd series). As T 93. Multicoloured.

488	10c. Boat-billed heron	50	30
489	25c. Grey-necked wood rail	75	30
490	35c. Lineated woodpecker	85	55
491	45c. Blue-grey tanager	90	70
492	50c. Laughing falcon	90	1·25
493	$1 Long-tailed hermit	1·40	4·50
MS494 113×136 mm. Nos. 488/93		4·75	7·00

101 Paslow Building, Belize G.P.O.

1979. 25th Anniv of Coronation. Multicoloured.

495	25c. Type **101**	1·50	10
496	50c. Houses of Parliament	2·00	10
497	75c. Coronation State Coach	2·50	15
498	$1 Queen on horseback (vert)	3·25	20
499	$2 Prince of Wales (vert)	3·25	35
500	$3 Queen and Duke of Edinburgh (vert)	3·25	35
501	$4 Portrait of Queen (vert)	3·25	40
502	$5 St. Edward's Crown (vert)	3·50	40
MS503 Two sheets, both 126×95 mm: (a) $5 Princess Anne on horseback at Montreal Olympics (vert); $10 Queen at Montreal Olympics (vert). (b) $15 As Type **101** Set of 2 sheets		26·00	

102 Mortimer and Vaughan "Safety" Airplane, 1910

1979. Death Centenary of Sir Rowland Hill. 60th Anniv of I.C.A.O. (International Civil Aviation Organization), previously Int Commission for Air Navigation. Multicoloured.

504	4c. Type **102**	50	10
505	25c. Boeing 720	1·50	20
506	50c. Concorde	4·25	30
507	75c. Handley Page H.P.18 W.8b (1922)	2·00	30
508	$1 Avro Type F (1912)	2·00	30
509	$1.50 Samuel Cody's biplane (1910)	2·75	30
510	$2 A.V. Roe Triplane I (1909)	2·75	40
511	$3 Santos Dumont's biplane "14 bis" (1906)	2·75	45
512	$4 Wright Type A	3·00	65
MS513 Two sheets: (a) 115×95 mm. $5 Dunne D-5 (1910), $5 G.B. 1969 Concorde stamp; (b) 130×95 mm. $10 Boeing 720 (different) Set of 2 sheets		22·00	

103 Handball

1979. Olympic Games, Moscow (1980). Multicoloured.

514	25c. Type **103**	45	10
515	50c. Weightlifting	65	10
516	75c. Athletics	90	15
517	$1 Football	1·25	20
518	$2 Yachting	1·75	25
519	$3 Swimming	2·00	30
520	$4 Boxing	2·50	30
521	$5 Cycling	11·00	1·25
MS522 Two sheets: (a) 126×92 mm. $5 Athletics (different), $10 Boxing (different); (b) 92×126 mm. $15 As $5 Set of 2 sheets		16·00	

104 Olympic Torch

1979. Winter Olympic Games, Lake Placid (1980). Multicoloured.

523	25c. Type **104**	20	10
524	50c. Giant slalom	45	15
525	75c. Figure-skating	65	15
526	$1 Downhill skiing	80	15
527	$2 Speed-skating	1·60	20
528	$3 Cross-country skiing	2·50	30
529	$4 Shooting	3·00	40
530	$5 Gold, Silver and Bronze medals	3·50	45
MS531 Two sheets: (a) 127×90 mm. $5 Lighting the Olympic Flame, $10 Gold, Silver and Bronze medals (different); (b) 90×127 mm. $15 Olympic Torch (different) Set of 2 sheets		20·00	

105 Measled Cowrie

1980. Shells. Multicoloured.

532	1c. Type **105**	75	10
533	2c. Callico clam	90	10
534	3c. Altantic turkey wing (vert)	1·00	10
535	4c. Leafy jewel box (vert)	1·00	10
536	5c. Trochlear latirus	1·00	10
537	10c. Alphabet cone (vert)	1·50	10
538	15c. Cabrits murex (vert)	2·00	10
539	20c. Stiff pen shell	2·00	10
540	25c. Little knobbed scallop (vert)	2·00	10
541	35c. Glory of the Atlantic cone (vert)	2·50	10
542	45c. Sunrise tellin (vert)	2·75	10
543	50c. *Leucozonia nassa leucozonalis*	2·75	10
544	85c. Triangular typhis	4·50	10
545	$1 Queen or pink conch (vert)	4·75	10
546	$2 Rooster-tail conch (vert)	7·00	30
547	$5 True tulip	9·50	50
548	$10 Tent arene	11·00	90
MS549 Two sheets, each 125×90 mm. (a) Nos. 544 and 547. (b) Nos. 546 and 548		45·00	15·00

106 Girl and Flower Arrangement

1980. International Year of the Child (1st issue). Multicoloured.

550	25c. Type **106**	45	10
551	50c. Boy holding football	70	10
552	75c. Boy with butterfly	1·00	10
553	$1 Girl holding doll	1·00	10
554	$1.50 Boy carrying basket of fruit	1·50	15
555	$2 Boy holding reticulated cowrie-helmet shell	1·75	20
556	$3 Girl holding posy	2·25	25
557	$4 Boy and girl wrapped in blanket	2·50	30
MS558 130×95 mm. $5 Three children of different races. $5 "Madonna with Cat" (A. Dürer) (each 35×53 mm)		9·00	
MS559 111×151 mm. $10 Children and Christmas tree (73×110 mm).		9·00	

See also Nos. 583/91.

1980. No. 412 surch 10c.

560	10c. on 25c. "Papilio thoas"	1·25	1·25

108 Jabiru

1980. Birds (4th series). Multicoloured.

561	10c. Type **108**	7·00	2·75
562	25c. Barred antshrike	8·00	2·75
563	35c. Northern royal flycatcher ("Royal Flycatcher")	8·00	2·75
564	45c. White-necked puffbird	8·00	3·00
565	50c. Ornate hawk-eagle	8·00	3·00
566	$1 Golden-masked tanager	8·50	3·75
MS567 85×90 mm. $2 Type **108**, $3 As $1		32·00	18·00

109 Speed Skating

1980. Winter Olympic Games, Lake Placid. Medal Winners. Multicoloured.

568	25c. Type **109**	45	20
569	50c. Ice-hockey	75	20
570	75c. Figure-skating	80	20
571	$1 Alpine-skiing	1·10	20
572	$1.50 Giant slalom (women)	1·50	30
573	$2 Speed-skating (women)	1·75	40
574	$3 Cross-country skiing	2·25	50
575	$5 Giant slalom	3·50	65
MS576 Two sheets: (a) 126×91 mm. $5 Type **109**; $10 Type **109**; (b) 91×126 mm. $10 As 75 c. Set of 2 sheets		16·00	

1980. "ESPAMER" International Stamp Exhibition, Madrid. Nos. 561/5 optd BELIZE ESPAMER '80 MADRID 3-12 OCT 1980 and emblem (Nos. 577/9) or surch also.

577	10c. Type **108**	8·00	2·75
578	25c. Barred antshrike	8·50	3·00
579	35c. Northern royal flycatcher	8·50	3·00
580	40c. on 45c. White-necked puffbird	9·00	3·25
581	40c. on 50c. Ornate hawk eagle	9·00	3·25
582	40c. on $1 Golden-masked tanager	9·00	3·25

111 Witch in Sky

1980. International Year of the Child (2nd issue). "Sleeping Beauty".

583	**111**	25c. multicoloured	2·25	15
584	-	40c. multicoloured	2·50	15
585	-	50c. multicoloured	2·75	15
586	-	75c. multicoloured	3·00	20
587	-	$1 multicoloured	3·00	25
588	-	$1.50 multicoloured	3·75	40
589	-	$3 multicoloured	4·75	50
590	-	$4 multicoloured	4·75	55
MS591 Two sheets: (a) 82×110 mm. $8 "Paumgartner Altar-piece" (Dürer); (b) 110×82 mm. $5 Marriage ceremony, $5 Sleeping Beauty and Prince on horseback Set of 2 sheets		24·00		

DESIGNS: 40c. to $4, Illustrations from the story.

112 H.M. Queen Elizabeth the Queen Mother

1980. 80th Birthday of H.M. Queen Elizabeth the Queen Mother.

592	**112**	$1 multicoloured	2·50	65
MS593 82×110 mm, $5 As Type **112** (41×32 mm)		14·00	4·75	

113 The Annunciation

1980. Christmas. Multicoloured.

594	25c. Type **113**	65	10
595	50c. Bethlehem	1·25	10
596	75c. The Holy Family	1·50	10
597	$1 The Nativity	1·60	15
598	$1.50 The Flight into Egypt	1·75	25
599	$2 Shepherds following the Star	2·00	35
600	$3 Virgin, Child and Angel	2·25	40
601	$4 Adoration of the Kings	2·25	45

MS602 Two sheets, each 82×111 mm: (a) $5 As $1: (b) $10 As $3 Set of 2 sheets ... 14·00

1981. "WIPA" International Stamp Exhibition, Vienna. Nos. 598 and 601 surch.

603	$1 on $1.50 The Flight into Egypt	11·00	2·00
604	$2 on $4 Adoration of the Kings	12·00	3·00

MS605 82×111 mm. $2 on $10 Virgin, Child and Angel ... 20·00 ... 6·00

115 Paul Harris (founder)

1981. 75th Anniv of Rotary International. Multicoloured.

606	25c. Type **115**	2·50	25
607	50c. Emblems of Rotary activities	3·00	35
608	$1 75th Anniversary emblem	3·50	65
609	$1.50 Educational scholarship programme (horiz)	4·25	1·00
610	$2 "Project Hippocrates"	4·75	1·40
611	$3 Emblems	6·50	2·00
612	$5 Emblems and handshake (horiz)	7·50	3·25

MS613 Two sheets: (a) 95×130 mm. $10 As 50c. (b) 130×95 mm, $5 As $1, $10 As $2 Set of 2 sheets ... 45·00

116 Coat of Arms of Prince of Wales

1981. Royal Wedding. Multicoloured

(a) Size 22×38 mm

614	50c. Type **116**	45	50
615	$1 Prince Charles in military uniform	80	90
616	$1.50 Royal couple	1·25	1·50

(b) Size 25×42 mm, with gold borders.

617	50c. Type **116**	45	30
618	$1 As No. 615	80	50
619	$1.50 As No. 616	1·25	70

MS620 145×85 mm. $3×3 As Nos 614/16, but 30×47 mm. P 14 ... 2·50 ... 4·25

1981. No. 538 surch **10c.**

621	10c. on 15c. "Murex cabritii"	3·50	3·75

1522 Saint Martin's Church, Kessenich

2011. Christmas. Multicoloured.

4482	1 (71c.) Type **1522**	3·00	1·75

118 Athletics

1981. History of the Olympics. Multicoloured.

622	85c. Type **118**	2·75	30
623	$1 Cycling	9·50	50
624	$1.50 Boxing	3·50	50
625	$2 1984 Games–Los Angeles and Sarajevo	4·50	50
626	$3 Baron de Coubertin	5·50	60
627	$5 Olympic Flame	6·50	70

MS628 Two sheets, each 175×123 mm: (a) $5 As $3, $10 As $5 (each 35×53 mm). P13½; (b) $15 As $2 (45×67 mm). P 14½. Set of 2 sheets ... 48·00

1981. Independence Commemoration (1st issue). Optd **Independence 21 Sept., 1981**

(a) On Nos. 532/44 and 546/8.

629	1c. Type **105**	1·25	20
630	2c. Callico clam	1·25	20
631	3c. Atlantic turkey wing (vert)	1·25	20
632	4c. Leafy jewel box (vert)	1·25	20
633	5c. Trochlear latirus	1·50	20
634	10c. Alphabet cone (vert)	2·00	20
635	15c. Cabrits murex (vert)	2·75	20
636	20c. Stiff pen shell	2·75	25
637	25c. Little knobbed scallop (vert)	3·00	25
638	35c. Glory of the Atlantic cone (vert)	3·00	30
639	45c. Sunrise tellin (vert)	3·50	40
640	50c. *Leucozonia nassa leucozonalis*	3·50	40
641	85c. Triangular typhis	5·50	90
642	$2 Rooster-tail conch (vert)	10·00	3·50
643	$5 True tulip	12·00	6·50
644	$10 Star arene	14·00	12·00

MS645 Two sheets, each 126×91 mm; (a) Nos. 641 and 643; (b) Nos. 642 and 644 Set of 2 sheets ... 45·00

(b) On Nos. 606/12.

646	25c. Type **115**	2·75	25
647	50c. Emblems of Rotary activities	3·00	35
648	$1 75th Anniversary emblem	3·50	65
649	$1.50 Educational scholarship programme (vert)	4·25	1·25
650	$2 Project Hippocrates	5·00	1·60
651	$3 Emblems	7·00	2·50
652	$5 Emblems and hand-shake	8·00	3·75

MS653 Two sheets: (a) 95×130 mm. $10 As 50c.; (b) 130×95 mm. $5 As $1, $10 As $2 Set of 2 sheets ... 40·00

See also Nos. 657/63.

1981. "ESPAMER" International Stamp Exhibition, Buenos Aires. No. 609 surch **$1 ESPAMER 81 BUENOS AIRES 13-22 NOV** and emblem.

654	$1 on $1.50 Educational scholarship programme	14·00	3·75

MS655 95×130 mm. $1 on $5 75th anniversary emblem, $1 on $10 *Project Hippocrates* ... 20·00 ... 9·50

(121)

1981. "Philatelia 81" International Stamp Exhibition, Frankfurt. No. **MS**549 surch with T **121**.

MS656 Two sheets, each 125×90 mm: (a) $1 on 85c. *Triprerotyphis triangularis*, $1 on $5 *Fasciolaria tulipa*; (b) $1 on $2 *Strombus gallus*, $1 on $10 *Arene cruentata* Set of 2 sheets ... 70·00

122 Black Orchid

1981. Independence Commemoration (2nd issue). Multicoloured.

657	10c. Belize Coat of Arms (horiz)	3·00	40
658	35c. Map of Belize	7·00	75
659	50c. Type **122**	10·00	1·50

660	85c. Baird's tapir (horiz)	3·25	1·50
661	$1 Mahogany tree	2·75	50
662	$2 Keel-billed toucan (horiz)	15·00	4·50

MS663 130×98 mm. $5 As 10c. ... 20·00 ... 7·50

123 Uruguayan Footballer

1981. World Cup Football Championship, Spain (1st issue). Multicoloured.

664	10c. Type **123**	2·25	20
665	25c. Italian footballer	3·25	20
666	50c. German footballer	4·00	45
667	$1 Brazilian footballer	5·00	70
668	$1.50 Argentinian footballer	6·50	1·50
669	$2 English footballer	7·00	1·75

MS670 Two sheets: (a) 145×115 mm. $2 "SPAIN '82" logo; (b) 155×115 mm. $3 Footballer (46×76 mm) Set of 2 sheets ... 30·00 ... 7·50

See also Nos. 721/7.

124 H.M.S. *Centurion* (frigate)

1981. Sailing Ships. Multicoloured.

671	10c. Type **124**	3·50	40
672	25c. Madagascar (1837)	5·00	50
673	35c. Brig *Whitby* (1838)	6·00	55
674	55c. China (1838)	7·00	85
675	85c. Swiftsure (1850)	8·50	1·25
676	$2 Windsor Castle (1857)	12·00	3·00

MS677 110×87 mm. $5 Ships in battle ... 38·00 ... 9·50

1982. "ESSEN '82" Int Stamp Exn, West Germany. Nos. 662 and 669 surch **$1 ESSEN 82.**

678	$1 on $2 Keel-billed toucan	12·00	3·00
679	$1 on $2 English footballer	12·00	3·00

126 Princess Diana

1982. 21st Birthday of Princess of Wales

(a) Size 22×38 mm

680	**126**	50c. multicoloured	1·60	45
681	-	$1 multicoloured	2·00	75
682	-	$1.50 multicoloured	2·00	1·50

(b) Size 25×43 mm.

683	**126**	50c. multicoloured	1·60	30
684	-	$1 multicoloured	2·00	60
685	-	$1.50 multicoloured	2·00	1·10

MS686 145×85 mm. $3×3 As Nos. 680/2, but 30×47 mm. ... 2·75 ... 3·00

DESIGNS: Portraits of Princess of Wales with different backgrounds.

127 Lighting Campfire

1982. 125th Birth Anniv of Lord Baden-Powell. Multicoloured.

687	10c. Type **127**	1·75	20
688	25c. Bird watching	5·00	30
689	35c. Three scouts, one playing guitar	2·75	30
690	50c. Hiking	3·25	55
691	85c. Scouts with flag	4·50	1·00
692	$2 Saluting	5·00	2·50

MS693 Two sheets: each 85×115 mm: (a) $2 Scout with flag; (b) $3 Portrait of Lord Baden-Powell Set of 2 sheets ... 35·00 ... 13·00

128 *Gorgonia ventalina*

1982. First Anniv of Independence. Marine Life. Multicoloured.

694	10c. Type **128**	2·50	30
695	35c. *Carpiuis corallinus*	4·00	30
696	50c. *Plexaura flexuasa*	4·25	55
697	85c. *Condylactis gigantea*	4·50	70
698	$1 *Stenopus hispidus*	6·00	1·00
699	$2 Sergeant major	7·50	2·00

MS700 130×98 mm. $5 *Schyllarides aequinoclialis* ... 32·00 ... 10·00

1982. "BELGICA 82" International Stamp Exhibition, Brussels. Nos. 687/92 optd **BELGICA 82 INT. YEAR OF THE CHILD SIR ROWLAND HILL 1795 1879** Picasso **CENTENARY OF BIRTH** and emblems.

701	10c. Type **127**	3·25	70
702	25c. Bird watching	8·00	1·50
703	35c. Three scouts, one playing guitar	4·25	1·25
704	50c. Hiking	4·75	1·75
705	85c. Scouts with flag	12·00	3·00
706	$2 Saluting	13·00	8·50

1982. Birth of Prince William of Wales (1st issue). Nos. 680/5 optd **BIRTH OF H.R.H. PRINCE WILLIAM ARTHUR PHILIP LOUIS 21ST JUNE 1982**

(a) Size 22×38 mm

707	50c. multicoloured	45	45
708	$1 multicoloured	55	60
709	$1.50 multicoloured	75	85

(b) Size 25×43 mm.

710	50c. multicoloured	45	45
711	$1 multicoloured	55	60
712	$1.50 multicoloured	75	85

MS713 145×85 mm. $3×3 as Nos. 707/9, but 30×477mm ... 7·50 ... 7·00

1982. Birth of Prince William of Wales (2nd issue). Nos. 614/19 optd **BIRTH OF H.R.H. PRINCE WILLIAM ARTHUR PHILIP LOUIS 21ST JUNE 1982**

(a) Size 22×38 mm

714	50c. Type **116**	3·25	1·00
715	$1 Prince Charles in military uniform	6·00	2·00
716	$1.50 Royal couple	8·50	3·00

(b) Size 25×42 mm.

717	50c. Type **116**	50	50
718	$1 As No. 715	70	70
719	$1.50 As No. 716	1·10	1·10

MS720 145×85 mm. $3×3 As Nos. 714/16 but 30×47 mm ... 7·50 ... 7·00

131 Scotland v New Zealand

1982. World Cup Football Championship, Spain (2nd issue). Multicoloured.

721	20c. +10c. Type **131**	2·75	1·50
722	30c. +15c. Scotland v New Zealand (different)	2·75	1·50
723	40c. +20c. Kuwait v France	3·00	1·50
724	60c. +30c. Italy v Brazil	3·50	1·75
725	$1 +50c. France v Northern Ireland	4·25	2·00
726	$1.50 +75c. Austria v Chile	5·00	2·50

MS727 Two sheets: (a) 91×137 mm. $1+50c. Germany v Italy (50×70 mm); (b) 122×116 mm. $2+$1 England v France (50×70 mm) Set of 2 sheets ... 20·00 ... 9·50

133 Belize Cathedral

1983. Visit of Pope John Paul II.

729	133	50c. multicoloured	2·75	1·50

MS730 135×110 mm. $2.50, Pope John Paul II (30×47 mm) ... 25·00 ... 9·00

4483	1 (€1.03) Saint Mard Church, Vieux-Virton	4·75	3·25

No. 4484 is vacant.

134 Map of Belize

1983. Commonwealth Day. Multicoloured.

731	35c. Type **134**	35	35
732	50c. *Maya Stella* from Lamanai Indian church (horiz)	40	50
733	85c. Supreme Court Building (horiz)	50	75
734	$2 University Centre, Belize (horiz)	85	2·50

1983. No. 658 surch 10c.

735	10c. on 35c. Map of Belize	35·00	10·00

136 De Lana-Terzis *Aerial Ship*, 1670

1983. Bicentenary of Manned Flight. Multicoloured.

736	10c. Type **136**	2·75	65
737	25c. De Gusmao's *La Passarole*, 1709	3·50	70
738	50c. Guyton de Morveau's balloon with oars, 1784	3·75	1·10
739	85c. Airship	4·50	1·25
740	$1 Airship "Clement Bayard"	5·00	1·60
741	$1.50 Beardmore airship R-34	5·50	3·25
MS742	Two sheets: (a) 125×84 mm. $3 Charles Green's balloon *Royal Vauxhall*; (b) 115×128 mm. $3 Montgolfier balloon, 1783 (vert) Set of 2 sheets	35·00	7·00

1983. Nos. 662 and 699 surch $1.25.

743	$1.25 on $2 Keel-billed toucan	21·00	14·00
744	$1.25 on $2 Sergeant major	7·00	9·50

1983. No. 541 surch 10c.

746	10c. on 35c. Glory of the Atlantic cone	60·00	15·00

141 Altun Ha

1983. Maya Monuments. Multicoloured.

747	10c. Type **141**	10	10
748	15c. Xunantunich	10	10
749	75c. Cerros	30	40
750	$3 Lamanal	70	1·75
MS751	102×72 mm. $3 Xunantunich (different)	1·00	1·75

142 Belmopan Earth Station

1983. World Communications Year. Multicoloured.

752	10c. Type **142**	20	10
753	15c. "Telstar 2"	30	25
754	75c. U.P.U. logo	45	1·75
755	$2 M.V. "Heron H" mail service	1·00	4·50

143 Jaguar Cub

1983. The Jaguar. Multicoloured.

756	5c. Type **143**	30	75
757	10c. Adult jaguar	35	45
758	85c. Jaguar in river	1·40	3·00
759	$1 Jaguar on rock	1·50	3·25
MS760	102×72 mm. $3 Jaguar in tree (44×28 mm). P 13½×14	1·50	2·50

144 Pope John Paul II

1983. Christmas.

761	**144** 10c. multicoloured	25	10
762	**144** 15c. multicoloured	25	10
763	**144** 75c. multicoloured	50	60
764	**144** $2 multicoloured	80	1·40
MS765	**144** 102×72 mm. $3 multicoloured	1·50	4·00

145 Four-eyed Butterflyfish

1984. Marine Life of the Belize Coral Reef. Multicoloured.

766	1c. Type **145**	45	1·50
767	2c. Cushion star	50	1·50
768	3c. Flower coral	50	1·50
769	4c. Royal gramma ("Fairy basslet")	65	1·50
770	5c. Spanish hogfish	70	1·50
771	6c. Star-eyed hermit crab	70	1·75
772a	10c. Sea fans and fire sponge	70	35
773a	15c. Blue-headed wrasse	1·00	60
774a	25c. Blue-striped grunt	1·00	80
775a	50c. Coral crab	1·00	1·75
776a	60c. Tube sponge	1·00	2·00
777	$1 Brain coral	1·00	1·50
778	$1 Yellow-tailed snapper	1·00	1·25
779	$1 Common lettuce slug	1·00	55
780	$5 Three-spotted damselfish	1·25	70
781	$10 Rock beauty	1·50	1·10

1984. Visit of the Archbishop of Canterbury. Nos. 772a and 775a optd VISIT OF THE LORD ARCHBISHOP OF CANTERBURY 8th–11th MARCH 1984.

782	10c. Sea fans and fire sponge	1·00	50
783	50c. Coral crab	1·75	2·00

147 Shooting

1984. Olympic Games, Los Angeles. Multicoloured

(a) Sheet stamps

784	25c. Type **147**	30	25
785	75c. Boxing	50	70
786	$1 Marathon	60	90
787	$2 Cycling	2·75	2·75
MS788	101×72 mm. $3 Statue of discus thrower	1·60	3·00

(b) Similar designs to T 147 but Royal cypher replaced by Queen's Head.

789	5c. Marathon	20	90
790	20c. Sprinting	25	90
791	25c. Shot-putting	25	90
792	$2 Olympic torch	35	1·25

148 British Honduras 1866 1s. Stamp

1984. "Ausipex" International Stamp Exhibition, Melbourne. Multicoloured.

793	15c. Type **148**	25	15
794	30c. British mail coach, 1784	35	25
795	65c. Sir Rowland Hill and Penny Black	65	65
796	75c. British Honduras railway locomotive, 1910	70	75
797	$2 Royal Exhibition Buildings, Melbourne (46×28 mm)	1·00	2·25
MS798	103×73 mm. $3 Australia 1932 Sydney Harbour Bridge 5s. and British Honduras 1866 1s. stamps (44×28 mm). P 13½×14	1·10	2·00

149 Prince Albert

1984. 500th Anniv (1985) of British Royal House of Tudor. Multicoloured.

799	50c. Type **149**	25	45
800	50c. Queen Victoria	25	45
801	75c. King George VI	30	55
802	75c. Queen Elizabeth the Queen Mother	30	55
803	$1 Princess of Wales	40	75
804	$1 Prince of Wales	40	75
MS805	147×97 mm. $1.50, Prince Philip; $1.50, Queen Elizabeth II	1·25	2·00

150 White-fronted Amazon ("White-fronted Parrot")

1984. Parrots. Multicoloured.

806	$1 Type **150**	1·75	2·25
807	$1 White-capped parrot (horiz)	1·75	2·25
808	$1 Mealy amazon ("Mealy Parrot") (horiz)	1·75	2·25
809	$1 Red-lored amazon ("Red-lored Parrot")	1·75	2·25
MS810	102×73 mm. $3 Scarlet macaw	3·25	4·00

Nos. 806/9 were issued together, se-tenant, forming a composite design.

151 Effigy Censer, 1450 (Santa Rita Site)

1984. Maya Artefacts. Multicoloured.

811	25c. Type **151**	30	25
812	75c. Vase, 675 (Actun Chapat)	60	80
813	$1 Tripod vase, 500 (Santa Rita site)	65	1·00
814	$2 Sun god Kinich Ahau, 600 (Altun Ha site)	90	2·50

152 Governor-General inspecting Girl Guides

1985. International Youth Year and 75th Anniv of Girl Guides Movement. Multicoloured.

815	25c. Type **152**	30	15
816	50c. Girl Guides camping	45	40
817	90c. Checking map on hike	60	55
818	$1.25 Students in laboratory	70	80
819	$2 Lady Baden-Powell (founder)	90	1·40

153 White-tailed Kite

1985. Birth Bicentenary of John J. Audubon (ornithologist). Designs showing original paintings. Multicoloured.

820	10c. Type **153**	50	60
821	15c. Ruby-crowned kinglet ("Cuvier's Kinglet") (horiz)	50	60
822	25c. Painted bunting	60	60
822a	60c. As 25c.	27·00	9·00
823	75c. Belted kingfisher	60	1·40
824	$1 Common cardinal ("Northern Cardinal")	60	2·25
825	$3 Long-billed curlew (horiz)	1·00	3·00
MS826	139×99 mm. $5 "John James Audubon" (John Syme)	2·50	2·00

154 The Queen Mother with Princess Elizabeth, 1928

1985. Life and Times of Queen Elizabeth the Queen Mother. Multicoloured.

827	10c. Type **154**	10	10
828	15c. The Queen Mother, 1980	10	10
829	75c. Waving to the crowd, 1982	40	40
830	$5 Four generations of Royal Family at Prince William's Christening	1·50	2·75
MS831	Two sheets, each 138×98 mm. (a) $2 The Queen Mother with Prince Henry (from photo by Lord Snowdon) (38×50 mm): (b) $5 The Queen Mother, 1984 (38×50 mm) Set of 2 sheets	3·75	4·50

1985. Inauguration of New Government. Nos. 772/3 and 775 optd INAUGURATION OF NEW GOVERNMENT – 21st. DECEMBER 1984.

832	10c. Sea fans and fire sponge	1·50	60
833	15c. Blue-headed wrasse	1·50	60
834	50c. Coral crab	2·00	3·50

156 British Honduras 1935 Silver Jubilee 25c. stamp and King George V with Queen Mary in Carriage

1985. 50th Anniv of First Commonwealth Omnibus Issue. Designs showing British Honduras/Belize stamps. Multicoloured.

835	50c. Type **156**	55	85
836	50c. 1937 Coronation 3c., and King George VI and Queen Elizabeth in Coronation robes	55	85
837	50c. 1946 Victory 3c. and Victory celebrations	55	85
838	50c. 1948 Royal Silver Wedding 4c. and King George VI and Queen Elizabeth at Westminster Abbey service	55	85
839	50c. 1953 Coronation 4c. and Queen Elizabeth II in Coronation robes	55	85
840	50c. 1966 Churchill 25c., Sir Winston Churchill and fighter aircraft	55	85
841	50c. 1972 Royal Silver Wedding 50c. and 1948 Wedding photograph	55	85
842	50c. 1973 Royal Wedding 50c. and Princess Anne and Capt. Mark Phillips at their Wedding	55	85
843	50c. 1977 Silver Jubilee $2 and Queen Elizabeth II during tour	55	85
844	50c. 1978 25th anniversary of Coronation 75c. and Imperial Crown	55	85
MS845	138×98 mm. $5 Queen Elizabeth in Coronation robes (38×50 mm)	4·50	4·50

157 Mounted Postboy and Early Letter to Belize

1985. 350th Anniv of British Post Office. Multicoloured.

846	10c. Type **157**	50	25
847	15c. "Hinchinbrook II" (sailing packet) engaging "Grand Turk" (American privateer)	70	25
848	25c. "Duke of Marlborough II" (sailing packet)	85	30
849	75c. "Diana" (packet)	1·40	1·50
850	$1 Falmouth packet ship	1·40	2·00
851	$3 "Conway" (mail paddle-steamer)	2·25	5·50

1985. Commonwealth Heads of Government Meeting, Nassau, Bahamas. Nos. 827/**MS**831 optd **COMMONWEALTH SUMMIT CONFERENCE, BAHAMAS 16th-22nd OCTOBER 1985.**

852	10c. Type **154**	30	30
853	15c. The Queen Mother, 1980	40	35
854	75c. Waving to the crowd, 1982	80	80
855	$4 Four generations of Royal Family at Prince William's christening	2·00	3·75

MS856 Two sheets, each 138×98 mm.
(a) $2 The Queen Mother with Prince Henry (from photo by Lord Snowdon) (38×50 mm): (b) $5 The Queen Mother, 1984 (38×50 mm)

Set of 2 sheets	2·75	3·50

1985. 80th Anniv of Rotary International. Nos. 815/19 optd **80TH ANNIVERSARY OF ROTARY INTERNATIONAL.**

857	25c. Type **152**	70	40
858	50c. Girl Guides camping	1·25	75
859	90c. Checking map on hike	1·75	90
860	$1.25 Students in laboratory	2·25	2·75
861	$2 Lady Baden-Powell (founder)	2·75	3·50

160 Royal Standard and Belize Flag

1985. Royal Visit. Multicoloured.

862	25c. Type **160**	1·00	95
863	75c. Queen Elizabeth II	1·25	2·00
864	$4 Royal Yacht "Britannia" (81×39 mm)	4·50	4·00

MS865 138×98 mm. $5 Queen Elizabeth II (38×50 mm) 5·00 5·50

161 Mountie in Canoe (Canada)

1985. Christmas. 30th Anniv of Disneyland, U.S.A. Designs showing dolls from "It's a Small World" exhibition. Multicoloured.

866	1c. Type **161**	10	15
867	2c. Indian chief and squaw (U.S.A.)	10	15
868	3c. Incas climbing Andes (South America)	10	15
869	4c. Africans beating drums (Africa)	10	15
870	5c. Snake-charmer and dancer (India and Far East)	10	15
871	6c. Boy and girl with donkey (Belize)	10	15
872	50c. Musician and dancer (Balkans)	1·75	1·50
873	$1.50 Boys with camel (Egypt and Saudi Arabia)	2·75	3·50
874	$3 Woman and girls playing with kite (Japan)	3·75	5·00

MS875 127×102 mm. $4 Beefeater and castle (Great Britain). P 13½×14 5·50 8·00

1985. World Cup Football Championship, Mexico (1986) (1st issue). Nos. 835/44 optd **PRE "WORLD CUP FOOTBALL" MEXICO 1986** and trophy.

876	50c. Type **156**	75	90
877	50c. 1937 Coronation 3c., and King George VI and Queen Elizabeth in Coronation robes	75	90
878	50c. Victory 3c., and Victory celebrations	75	90
879	50c. 1948 Royal Silver Wedding 4c., and King George VI and Queen Elizabeth at Westminster Abbey service	75	90
880	50c. 1953 Coronation 4c., and Queen Elizabeth II in Coronation robes	75	90
881	50c. 1966 Churchill 25c., Sir Winston Churchill and fighter aircraft	75	90
882	50c. 1972 Royal Silver Wedding 50c. and 1948 wedding photograph	75	90
883	50c. 1973 Royal Wedding 5c., and Princess Anne and Capt. Mark Phillips at their Wedding	75	90

884	50c. 1977 Silver Jubilee $2 and Queen Elizabeth II during tour	75	90
885	50c. 1978 25th anniv of Coronation 75c. and Imperial Crown	75	90

MS886 138×98 mm. $5 Queen Elizabeth II in Coronation robes 4·25 4·25

See also Nos. 936/40.

163 Indian Costume

1986. Costumes of Belize. Multicoloured.

887	5c. Type **163**	75	30
888	10c. Maya	80	30
889	15c. Garifuna	1·00	35
890	25c. Creole	1·25	35
891	50c. Chinese	1·75	1·25
892	75c. Lebanese	2·00	2·00
893	$1 European c. 1900	2·00	2·50
894	$2 Latin	2·75	3·75

MS895 139×98 mm. Amerindian (38×50 mm) 6·00 7·00

164 Pope Pius X

1986. Easter. 20th-century Popes. Multicoloured.

896	50c. Type **164**	1·40	1·50
897	50c. Benedict XV	1·40	1·50
898	50c. Pius XI	1·40	1·50
899	50c. Pius XII	1·40	1·50
900	50c. John XXIII	1·40	1·50
901	50c. Paul VI	1·40	1·50
902	50c. John Paul I	1·40	1·50
903	50c. John Paul II	1·40	1·50

MS904 147×92 mm. $4 Pope John Paul II preaching (vert). 12·00 10·00

165 Princess Elizabeth aged Three

1986. 60th Birthday of Queen Elizabeth II. Multicoloured.

905	25c. Type **165**	40	55
906	50c. Queen wearing Imperial State Crown	60	75
907	75c. At Trooping the Colour	75	85
908	$3 Queen wearing diadem	1·40	2·25

MS909 147×93 mm. $4 Queen Elizabeth II (37×50 mm) 3·25 4·50

166 Halley's Comet and Japanese "Planet A" Spacecraft

1986. Appearance of Halley's Comet. Multicoloured.

910	10c. Type **166**	55	80
911	15c. Halley's Comet, 1910	65	90
912	50c. Comet and European "Giotto" spacecraft	70	1·00
913	75c. Belize Weather Bureau	90	1·00
914	$1 Comet and U.S.A. space telescope	1·25	1·40
915	$2 Edmond Halley	1·60	1·90

MS916 147×93 mm. $4 Computer enhanced photograph of Comet (37×50 mm) 6·50 8·50

167 George Washington

1986. United States Presidents. Multicoloured.

917	10c. Type **167**	35	60
918	20c. John Adams	35	65
919	30c. Thomas Jefferson	40	70
920	50c. James Madison	50	70
921	$1.50 James Monroe	80	1·25
922	$2 John Quincy Adams	1·00	1·50

MS923 147×93 mm. $4 George Washington (different) 3·75 5·50

168 Auguste Bartholdi (sculptor) and Statue's Head

1986. Centenary of Statue of Liberty. Multicoloured.

924	25c. Type **168**	40	65
925	50c. Statue's head at U.S. Centennial Celebration, Philadelphia, 1876	55	85
926	75c. Unveiling ceremony, 1886	55	90
927	$4 Statue of Liberty and flags of Belize and U.S.A.	1·50	2·50

MS928 147×92 mm. $4 Statue of Liberty and New York skyline (37×50 mm) 3·75 5·50

169 British Honduras 1866 1s. Stamp

1986. "Ameripex" International Stamp Exhibition, Chicago. Multicoloured.

929	10c. Type **169**	40	55
930	15c. 1981 Royal Wedding $1.50 stamps	55	75
931	50c. U.S.A. 1918 24c. airmail inverted centre error	75	80
932	75c. U.S.S. "Constitution" (frigate)	75	1·10
933	$1 Liberty Bell	80	1·40
934	$2 White House	90	1·60

MS935 147×93 mm. $4 Capitol, Washington (37×50 mm) 3·25 4·50

170 English and Brazilian Players

1986. World Cup Football Championship, Mexico (2nd issue). Multicoloured.

936	25c. Type **170**	1·50	1·75
937	50c. Mexican player and Maya statues	1·75	2·00
938	75c. Two Belizean players	2·00	2·25
939	$3 Aztec stone calendar	2·25	2·50

MS940 147×92 mm. $4 Flags of competing nations on two footballs (37×50 mm) 6·50 8·00

171 Miss Sarah Ferguson

1986. Royal Wedding. Multicoloured.

941	25c. Type **171**	65	40
942	75c. Prince Andrew	1·00	90
943	$3 Prince Andrew and Miss Sarah Ferguson (92×41 mm)	1·75	2·75

MS944 155×106 mm. $1 Miss Sarah Ferguson (different). $3 Prince Andrew (different) 4·25 6·00

1986. World Cup Football Championship Winners, Mexico. Nos. 936/9 optd **ARGENTINA – WINNERS 1986.**

945	25c. Type **170**	1·75	2·00
946	50c. Mexican player and Maya statues	2·00	2·25
947	75c. Two Belizean players	2·25	2·50
948	$3 Aztec stone calendar	3·25	3·50

MS949 147×92 mm. $4 Flags of competing nations on two footballs (37×50 mm) 8·00 10·00

1986. "Stockholmia '86" International Stamp Exhibition, Sweden. Nos. 929/34 optd **STOCKHOLMIA 86** and emblem.

950	10c. Type **169**	50	75
951	15c. 1981 Royal Wedding $1.50 stamp	65	90
952	50c. U.S.A. 1918 24c. airmail inverted centre error	80	1·10
953	75c. U.S.S. "Constitution"	1·00	1·50
954	$1 Liberty Bell	1·25	1·60
955	$2 White House	1·60	1·90

MS956 147×93 mm. $4 Capitol, Washington (37×50 mm) 5·00 7·00

174 American Indian Girl

1986. International Peace Year. Multicoloured.

957	25c. Type **174**	65	80
958	50c. European boy and girl	80	1·10
959	75c. Japanese girl	1·00	1·60
960	$3 Indian boy and European girl	1·75	2·75

MS961 132×106 mm. $4 As 25c. but vert (35×47 mm) 5·50 7·00

175 Amanita lilloi

1986. Fungi and Toucans. Multicoloured.

962	5c. Type **175**	1·50	1·25
963	10c. Keel-billed toucan	1·75	1·60
964	20c. *Boletellus cubensis*	2·00	1·75
965	25c. Collared aracari	2·00	1·75
966	75c. *Psilocybe caerulescens*	2·25	2·00
967	$1 Emerald toucanet	2·25	2·00
968	$1.25 Crimson-rumped toucanet ("Crimson-rumped Toucan")	2·50	2·25
969	$2 *Russula puiggarii*	2·50	2·50

176 Jose Carioca

1986. Christmas. Designs showing Walt Disney cartoon characters in scenes from "Saludos Amigos". Multicoloured.

970	2c. Type **176**	20	20
971	3c. Jose Carioca, Panchito and Donald Duck	20	20
972	4c. Daisy Duck as Rio Carnival dancer	20	20
973	5c. Mickey and Minnie Mouse as musician and dancer	20	20
974	6c. Jose Carioca using umbrella as flute	20	20
975	50c. Donald Duck and Panchito	1·00	1·75
976	65c. Joe Carioca and Donald Duck playing hide and seek	1·25	2·00
977	$1.35 Donald Duck playing maracas	2·00	3·25
978	$2 Goofy as matador	2·75	3·75

MS979 131×111 mm. $4 Donald Duck 9·00 11·00

177 Princess Elizabeth in Wedding Dress, 1947

1987. Royal Ruby Wedding. Multicoloured.

980	25c. Type **177**	25	20
981	75c. Queen and Duke of Edinburgh, 1972	45	50
982	$1 Queen on her 60th birthday	50	60
983	$4 In Garter robes	1·00	2·00
MS984	171×112 mm. $6 Queen and Duke of Edinburgh (44×50 mm)	6·50	7·50

178 America II, 1983

1987. America's Cup Yachting Championship. Multicoloured.

985	25c. Type **178**	30	25
986	75c. Stars and Stripes, 1987	40	50
987	$1 Australia II, 1983	50	60
988	$4 White Crusader	1·00	2·00
MS989	171×112 mm. $6 Sails of Australia II (44×50 mm.)	5·00	7·50

179 "Mother and Child"

1987. Wood Carvings by George Gabb. Multicoloured.

990	25c. Type **179**	15	25
991	75c. Standing Form	35	50
992	$1 Love-doves	40	60
993	$4 Depiction of Music	1·10	2·00
MS994	173×114 mm. $6 African Heritage (44×50 mm.)	4·25	7·00

180 Black-handed Spider Monkey

1987. Primates. Multicoloured.

995	25c. Type **180**	25	20
996	75c. Black howler monkey	40	55
997	$1 Spider monkeys with baby	45	65
998	$4 Two black howler monkeys	1·10	2·25
MS999	171×112 mm. $6 Young spider monkey (44×50 mm.)	5·50	8·00

181 Guides on Parade

1987. 50th Anniv of Girl Guide Movement in Belize. Multicoloured.

1000	25c. Type **181**	45	20
1001	75c. Brownie camp	80	1·00
1002	$1 Guide camp	1·00	1·25
1003	$4 Olave, Lady Baden-Powell	3·00	5·00
MS1004	173×114 mm. $6 As $4 but vert (44×50 mm)	4·25	7·00

182 Indian Refugee Camp

1987. Int Year of Shelter for the Homeless. Multicoloured.

1005	25c. Type **182**	50	25
1006	75c. Filipino family and slum	90	90
1007	$1 Family in Middle East shanty town	1·10	1·25
1008	$4 Building modern house in Belize	2·00	4·50

183 "Laelia euspatha"

1987. Christmas. Orchids. Illustrations from Sander's *Reichenbachia*. Multicoloured.

1009	1c. Type **183**	95	95
1010	2c. Cattleya citrina	95	95
1011	3c. Masdevallia backhousiana	95	95
1012	4c. Cypripedium tautzianum	95	95
1013	5c. Trichopilia suavis alba	95	95
1014	6c. Odontoglossum hebraicum	95	95
1015	7c. Cattleya trianaei schroederiana	95	95
1016	10c. Saccolabium giganteum	95	95
1017	30c. Cattleya warscewiczii	1·25	1·25
1018	50c. Chysis bractescens	1·50	1·50
1019	70c. Cattleya rochellensis	1·75	1·75
1020	$1 Laellia elegans schilleriana	1·90	1·90
1021	$1.50 Laelia anceps percivaliana	2·00	2·00
1022	$3 Laelia gouldiana	2·50	2·50
MS1023	Two sheets, each 171×112 mm. (a) $3 Odontoglossum roezlii (40×47 mm). (b) $5 Cattleya dowiana aurea (40×47 mm) Set of 2 sheets	12·00	13·00

184 Christ condemned to Death

1988. Easter. The Stations of the Cross. Multicoloured.

1024	40c. Type **184**	35	60
1025	40c. Christ carrying the Cross	35	60
1026	40c. Falling for the first time	35	60
1027	40c. Christ meets Mary	35	60
1028	40c. Simon of Cyrene helping to carry the Cross	35	60
1029	40c. Veronica wiping the face of Christ	35	60
1030	40c. Christ falling a second time	35	60
1031	40c. Consoling the women of Jerusalem	35	60
1032	40c. Falling for the third time	35	60
1033	40c. Christ being stripped	35	60
1034	40c. Christ nailed to the Cross	35	60
1035	40c. Dying on the Cross	35	60
1036	40c. Christ taken down from the Cross	35	60
1037	40c. Christ being laid in the sepulchre	35	60

185 Basketball

1988. Olympic Games, Seoul. Multicoloured.

1038	10c. Type **185**	3·00	1·00
1039	25c. Volleyball	1·00	30
1040	60c. Table tennis	1·00	60
1041	75c. Diving	1·00	70
1042	$1 Judo	1·25	1·10
1043	$2 Hockey	7·00	5·00
MS1044	76×106 mm. $3 Gymnastics	6·00	6·50

186 Public Health Nurse, c. 1912

1988. 125th Anniv of Int Red Cross. Multicoloured.

1045	60c. Type **186**	3·25	1·25
1046	75c. "Aleda E. Lutz" (hospital ship) and ambulance launch, 1937	3·50	1·50
1047	$1 Ambulance at hospital tent, 1956	4·00	2·00
1048	$2 Auster ambulance plane, 1940	5·50	6·00

187 Collared Anteater ("Ants Bear")

1989. Small Animals of Belize. Multicoloured.

1049	10c. Paca ("Gibnut")	2·75	2·50
1050	25c. Four-eyed opossum (vert)	2·75	1·75
1051	50c. Type **187**	3·25	2·25
1052	60c. As 10c.	3·25	2·50
1053	75c. Red brocket	3·25	2·50
1054	$1 Collared peccary	4·50	6·50

1989. 20th Anniv of First Manned Landing on Moon. As T **126** of Ascension. Multicoloured.

1055	25c. Docking of "Apollo 9" modules	2·00	30
1056	50c. "Apollo 9" command service module in Space (30×30 mm)	2·50	75
1057	75c. "Apollo 9" emblem (30×30 mm)	2·75	1·25
1058	$1 "Apollo 9" lunar module in space	3·00	2·25
MS1059	83×100 mm. $5 "Apollo II" command service module undergoing test	11·00	10·00

1989. No. 771 surch **5c.**

1060	5c. on 6c. Star-eyed hermit crab	20·00	2·75

1989. "World Stamp Expo '89" International Stamp Exhibition, Washington. No. MS1059 optd **WORLD STAMP EXPO '89, United States Postal Service Nov 17—20 and Nov 24—Dec 3. 1989 Washington Convention Center Washington, DC** and emblem.

MS1061	83×100 mm. $5 "Apollo II" command service module undergoing tests	9·50	10·00

190 Wesley Church

1989. Christmas. Belize Churches.

1062	**190**	10c. black, pink and brown	20	10
1063	-	25c. black, lilac and mauve	25	20
1064	-	60c. black, turq & bl	50	70
1065	-	75c. black, grn & grn	65	90
1066	-	$1 black, lt yell & yell	80	1·25

DESIGNS: 25c. Baptist Church; 60c. St. John's Anglican Cathedral; 75c. St. Andrew's Presbyterian Church; $1 Holy Redeemer Roman Catholic Cathedral.

191 White-winged Tanager and *Catonephele numilia*

1990. Birds and Butterflies. Multicoloured.

1067A	5c. Type **191**	60	1·25
1068A	10c. Keel-billed Toucan and *Nessaea aglaura*	80	80
1069A	15c. Magnificent frigate bird and *Eurytides philolaus*	80	40
1070A	25c. Jabiru and *Heliconius sapho*	80	40

1071A	30c. Great blue heron and *Colobura dirce*	80	50
1072A	50c. Northern oriole and *Hamadyras arethusia*	1·00	60
1073A	60c. Scarlet macaw and *Evenus regalis*	1·25	70
1074A	75c. Red-legged honey-creeper and *Callicore patelina*	1·25	75
1075A	$1 Spectacled owl and *Caligo uranus*	2·25	1·60
1076A	$2 Green jay and *Philaethria dido*	2·75	3·50
1077A	$5 Turkey vulture and *Battus belus*	4·50	6·50
1078A	$10 Osprey and *Papilio thoas*	8·50	12·00

1990. First Belize Dollar Coin. No. 1075 optd **FIRST DOLLAR COIN 1990.**

1079	$1 Spectacled owl and "Caligo uranus"	4·75	2·75

193 Green Turtle

1990. Turtles. Multicoloured.

1080	10c. Type **193**	65	40
1081	25c. Hawksbill turtle	1·00	40
1082	60c. Saltwater loggerhead turtle	1·50	1·50
1083	75c. Freshwater loggerhead turtle	1·60	1·60
1084	$1 Bocatora turtle	2·00	2·00
1085	$2 Hicatee turtle	2·75	5·50

194 Fairey Battle

1990. 50th Anniv of the Battle of Britain. Multicoloured.

1086	10c. Type **194**	1·25	50
1087	25c. Bristol Type 152 Beaufort	1·75	50
1088	60c. Bristol Type 142 Blenheim Mk IV	2·25	2·00
1089	75c. Armstrong-Whitworth Whitley	2·25	2·00
1090	$1 Vickers-Armstrong Wellington Mk 1c	2·25	2·00
1091	$1 Handley Page Hampden	2·75	4·00

195 *Cattleya bowringiana*

1990. Christmas. Orchids. Multicoloured.

1092	25c. Type **195**	85	20
1093	50c. Rhyncholaelia digbyana	1·25	50
1094	60c. Sobralia macrantha	1·50	1·00
1095	75c. Chysis bractescens	1·50	1·00
1096	$1 Vanilla planifolia	1·75	1·75
1097	$2 Epidendrum polyanthum	2·50	4·00

196 Common Iguana

1991. Reptiles and Mammals. Multicoloured.

1098	25c. Type **196**	80	35
1099	50c. Morelet's crocodile	1·25	90
1100	60c. American manatee	1·50	1·50
1101	75c. Boa constrictor	1·75	1·75
1102	$1 Baird's tapir	2·00	2·00
1103	$2 Jaguar	2·75	3·75

1991. 65th Birthday of Queen Elizabeth II and 70th Birthday of Prince Philip. As T **139** of Ascension. Multicoloured.

1104	$1 Queen Elizabeth II wearing tiara	1·00	1·50
1105	$1 Prince Philip wearing panama	1·00	1·50

197 Weather Radar

1991. International Decade for Natural Disaster Reduction.

1106	**197**	60c. multicoloured	1·50	1·25
1107	-	75c. multicoloured	1·60	1·40
1108	-	$1 blue and black	1·75	1·75
1109	-	$2 multicoloured	2·50	3·25

DESIGNS: 75c. Weather station; $1 Floods in Belize after Hurricane Hattie, 1961; $2 Satellite image of Hurricane Gilbert.

198 Thomas Ramos and Demonstration

1991. Tenth Anniv of Independence. Famous Belizeans (1st series). Multicoloured.

1110	25c. Type **198**		60	30
1111	60c. Sir Isaiah Morter and palm trees		1·25	1·50
1112	75c. Antonio Soberanis and political meeting		1·25	1·75
1113	$1 Santiago Ricalde and cutting sugar-cane		1·50	2·00

See also Nos. 1126/9 and 1148/51.

199 "Anansi the Spider"

1991. Christmas. Folklore. Multicoloured.

1114	25c. Type **199**		1·75	20
1115	50c. "Jack-o-Lantern"		2·25	55
1116	60c. "Tata Duende" (vert)		2·50	1·25
1117	75c. "Xtabai"		2·50	1·25
1118	$1 "Warrie Massa" (vert)		2·75	2·25
1119	$2 "Old Heg"		4·00	7·00

200 Gongora quinquenervis

1992. Easter. Orchids. Multicoloured.

1120	25c. Type **200**		1·50	20
1121	50c. Oncidium sphacelatum		2·00	75
1122	60c. Encyclia bratescens		2·25	1·75
1123	75c. Epidendrum ciliare		2·25	1·75
1124	$1 Psygmorchis pusilla		2·50	2·25
1125	$2 Galeandra batemanii		4·00	5·50

1992. Famous Belizeans (2nd series). As T **198**, but inscr "EMINENT BELIZEANS" at top. Multicoloured.

1126	25c. Gwendolyn Lizarraga (politician) and High School		75	30
1127	60c. Rafael Fonseca (civil servant) and Government Offices, Belize		1·50	1·50
1128	75c. Vivian Seay (health worker) and nurses		1·75	1·75
1129	$1 Samuel Haynes (U.N.I.A. worker) and words of National Anthem		2·00	2·50

201 Xunantunich and National Assembly

1992. 500th Anniv of Discovery of America by Columbus. Mayan sites and modern buildings. Multicoloured.

1130	25c. Type **201**		1·00	25
1131	60c. Altun Ha and Supreme Court		1·50	1·00
1132	75c. Santa Rita and Tower Hill Sugar Factory		1·60	1·25
1133	$5 Lamanai and Citrus Company works		8·00	11·00

202 Hashishi Pampi

1992. Christmas. Folklore. Multicoloured.

1134	25c. Type **202**		30	20
1135	60c. Cadejo		60	60
1136	$1 La Sucia (vert)		90	1·00
1137	$5 Sisimito		4·00	7·00

1993. 75th Anniv of Royal Air Force. As T **149** of Ascension. Multicoloured.

1138	25c. Sud Aviation SA 330L Puma helicopter		1·25	60
1139	50c. Hawker Siddeley Harrier GR3		1·50	80
1140	60c. de Havilland DH98 Mosquito Mk XVIII		1·60	1·10
1141	75c. Avro Type 683 Lancaster		1·60	1·10
1142	$1 Consolidated Liberator I		1·75	1·40
1143	$3 Short Stirling Mk I		3·50	6·00

203 Lycaste aromatica

1993. 14th World Orchid Conference, Glasgow. Multicoloured.

1144	25c. Type **203**		40	25
1145	60c. Sobralia decora		75	80
1146	$1 Maxillaria alba		1·00	1·25
1147	$2 Brassavola nodosa		1·75	3·00

1993. Famous Belizeans (3rd series). As T **198**, but inscr "EMINENT BELIZEANS" at top. Multicoloured.

1148	25c. Herbert Watkin Beaumont, Post Office and postmark		40	25
1149	60c. Dr. Selvyn Walford Young and score of National Anthem		75	85
1150	75c. Cleopatra White and health centre		90	1·25
1151	$1 Dr. Karl Heusner and early car		1·10	1·40

204 Boom and Chime Band

1993. Christmas. Local Customs. Multicoloured.

1152	25c. Type **204**		1·00	20
1153	60c. John Canoe dance		2·00	75
1154	75c. Cortez dance		2·00	80
1155	$2 Maya musical group		4·50	7·00

1994. "Hong Kong '94" International Stamp Exhibition. No. 1075 optd **HONG KONG '94** and emblem.

1156	$1 Spectacled owl and "Caligo uranus"		3·00	2·50

1994. Royal Visit. As T **202** of Bahamas. Multicoloured.

1157	25c. Flags of Belize and Great Britain		1·75	55
1158	60c. Queen Elizabeth II in yellow coat and hat		2·25	1·25
1159	75c. Queen Elizabeth in evening dress		2·50	1·50
1160	$1 Queen Elizabeth, Prince Philip and Yeomen of the Guard		2·75	2·50

205 Lonchorhina aurita (bat)

1994. Bats. Multicoloured.

1161	25c. Type **205**		45	20
1162	60c. Vampyrodes caraccioli		75	65
1163	75c. Noctilio leporinus		90	80
1164	$2 Desmodus rotundus		2·00	3·50

1994. 75th Anniv of I.L.O. No. 1074 surch **10c** and anniversary emblem.

1165	10c. on 75c. multicoloured		2·25	2·00

207 "Cycnoches chlorochilon"

1994. Christmas. Orchids. Multicoloured.

1166	25c. Type **207**		45	20
1167	60c. Brassavola cucullata		75	70
1168	75c. Sobralia mucronata		90	90
1169	$1 Nidema boothii		1·10	1·50

208 Ground Beetle

1995. Insects. Multicoloured.

1170A	5c. Type **208**		55	1·00
1171A	10c. Harlequin beetle		65	1·00
1172A	15c. Giant water bug		70	1·00
1173A	25c. Peanut-head bug		85	30
1174A	30c. Coconut weevil		85	35
1175A	50c. Mantis		90	40

1995. 50th Anniv of End of Second World War. As T **161** of Ascension. Multicoloured.

1182	25c. War memorial		35	25
1183	60c. Remembrance Day parade		1·00	1·00
1184	75c. British Honduras forestry unit		1·10	1·10
1185	$1 Vickers Type **271** Wellington bomber		1·40	1·75

(209)

1995. "Singapore '95" International Stamp Exhibition. Nos. 1166/9 optd with T **209**.

1186	25c. Type **207**		1·00	30
1187	60c. Brassavola cucullata		1·50	90
1188	75c. Sobralia mucronata		1·75	1·25
1189	$1 Nidema boothii		2·00	2·25

1995. 50th Anniv of United Nations. As T **213** of Bahamas. Multicoloured.

1190	25c. M113-light reconnaisance vehicle		25	20
1191	60c. Sultan armoured command vehicle		60	65
1192	75c. Leyland-Daf 8×4 drop truck		75	80
1193	$2 Warrior infantry combat vehicle		1·50	2·50

210 Male and Female Blue Ground Dove

1995. Christmas. Doves. Multicoloured.

1194	25c. Type **210**		35	20
1195	60c. White-fronted doves		70	70
1196	75c. Pair of ruddy ground doves		85	90
1197	$1 White-winged doves		1·25	1·50

1996. "CHINA '96" Ninth Asian International Stamp Exhibition, Peking. Nos. 1172, 1174/5 and 1179 optd **'96 CHINA** and emblem.

1198	15c. Giant water bug		20	15
1199	30c. Coconut weevil		40	30
1200	50c. Mantis		55	50
1201	$2 Dobson fly		1·75	2·50

212 Unloading Banana Train, Commerce Bight Pier

1996. "CAPEX '96" International Stamp Exhibition, Toronto. Railways. Multicoloured.

1202	25c. Type **212**		1·50	55
1203	60c. Locomotive No. 1 Stann Creek station		2·00	1·25
1204	75c. Locomotive No. 4 pulling mahogany log train		2·00	1·40
1205	$3 L.M.S. No. 5602 British Honduras locomotive		3·75	6·00

213 Epidendrum stamfordianum

1996. Christmas. Orchids. Multicoloured.

1206	25c. Type **213**		60	20
1207	60c. Oncidium cartha- genense		90	70
1208	75c. Oerstedella verrucosa		1·00	90
1209	$1 Coryanthes speciosa		1·40	1·50

214 Red Poll

1997. "HONG KONG '97" International Stamp Exhibition. Chinese New Year ("Year of the Ox"). Cattle Breeds. Multicoloured.

1210	25c. Type **214**		60	25
1211	60c. Brahman		95	1·00
1212	75c. Longhorn		1·25	1·40
1213	$1 Charbray		1·40	1·90

215 Coral Snake

1997. Snakes. Multicoloured.

1214	25c. Type **215**		45	20
1215	60c. Green vine snake		70	70
1216	75c. Yellow-jawed tommygoff		80	80
1217	$1 Speckled racer		95	1·25

216 Adult Male Howler Monkey

1997. Endangered Species. Howler Monkey. Multicoloured.

1218	10c. Type **216**		35	25
1219	25c. Female feeding		55	25
1220	60c. Female with young		90	90
1221	75c. Juvenile monkey feeding		1·10	1·40

217 Maxillaria elatior

1997. Christmas. Orchids. Multicoloured.

1222	25c. Type **217**		75	25
1223	60c. Dimmerandra emarginata		1·25	75
1224	75c. Macradenia brassavolae		1·40	1·25
1225	$1 Ornithocephalus gladiatus		1·75	2·00

1998. Diana, Princess of Wales Commemoration. Sheet, 145×70 mm, containing vert designs as T **177** of Ascension. Multicoloured.

MS1226	$1 Wearing floral dress, 1988; $1 In evening dress, 1981; $1 Wearing pearl drop earrings, 1988; $1 Carrying bouquet, 1983	2·50	3·25

218 School Children using the Internet

1998. 50th Anniv of Organization of American States. Multicoloured.
| 1227 | 25c. Type **218** | 25 | 20 |
| 1228 | $1 Map of Central America | 2·00 | 1·75 |

219 University Arms

1998. 50th Anniv of University of West Indies.
| 1229 | **219** | $1 multicoloured | 1·50 | 1·25 |

220 Baymen Gun Flats

1998. Bicentenary of Battle of St. George's Cay. Multicoloured.
1230	10c. Boat moored at quayside (vert)	50	70
1231	10c. Three sentries and cannon (vert)	50	70
1232	10c. Cannon and rowing boats (vert)	50	70
1233	25c. Type **220**	70	25
1234	60c. Baymen sloops	1·00	85
1235	75c. British schooners	1·10	90
1236	$1 H.M.S. *Merlin* (sloop)	1·25	1·25
1237	$2 Spanish flagship	2·00	2·50

221 *Brassia maculata*

1998. Christmas. Orchids. Multicoloured.
1238	25c. Type **221**	35	20
1239	60c. *Encyclia radiata*	50	40
1240	75c. *Stanhopea ecornuta*	50	55
1241	$1 *Isochilus carnosiflorus*	60	80

222 *Eucharis grandiflora*

1999. Easter. Flowers. Multicoloured.
1242	10c. Type **222**	20	10
1243	25c. *Hippeastrum puniceum*	30	20
1244	60c. *Zephyranthes citrina*	50	50
1245	$1 *Hymenocallis littoralis*	60	80

223 Postman on Bicycle

1999. 125th Anniv of UPU. Multicoloured.
1246	25c. Type **223**	70	40
1247	60c. Postal truck	85	70
1248	75c. "Dee" (mail ship)	1·10	90
1249	$1 Modern airliner	1·40	1·60

224 Holy Family with Jesus and St. John (School of Rubens)

1999. Christmas. Religious Paintings. Multicoloured.
| 1250 | 25c. Type **224** | 40 | 20 |
| 1251 | 60c. Holy Family with St. John (unknown artist) | 75 | 60 |

| 1252 | 75c. *Madonna and Child with St. John and Angel* (unknown artist) | 85 | 80 |
| 1253 | $1 *Madonna with Child and St. John* (Andrea del Salerno) | 1·25 | 1·40 |

225 Iguana

2000. Wildlife. Multicoloured.
A. Without imprint date at foot
1254A	5c. Type **225**	30	70
1255A	10c. Gibnut	30	70
1256A	15c. Howler monkey	40	70
1257A	25c. Collared anteater	55	25
1258A	30c. Hawksbill turtle	55	25
1259A	50c. Red brocket antelope	90	40
1260A	60c. Jaguar	1·10	45
1261A	75c. American manatee	1·25	60
1262A	$1 Crocodile	1·75	1·00
1263A	$2 Baird's tapir	3·00	3·25
1264A	$5 Collared peccary	7·00	8·00
1265A	$10 Boa constrictor	13·00	16·00

226 Mango

2000. Fruits. Multicoloured.
1266	25c. Type **226**	50	25
1267	60c. Cashew	90	75
1268	75c. Papaya	1·25	1·10
1269	$1 Banana	1·50	2·00

227 Meeting in Battlefield Park and Supreme Court, 1950

2000. 50th Anniv of People's United Party. Multicoloured.
1270	10c. Type **227**	20	20
1271	25c. Voters queuing, 1954	30	25
1272	60c. Legislative Council and Mace, 1964	55	60
1273	75c. National Assembly Building (under construction and completed), Belmopan, 1967–70	70	90
1274	$1 Belizean flag in searchlights, Independence, 1981	2·25	2·00

228 *Bletia purpurea*

2000. Christmas. Orchids. Multicoloured.
1275	25c. Type **228**	75	25
1276	60c. *Cyrtopodium punctatum*	1·25	65
1277	75c. *Cycnoches egertonianum*	1·50	1·10
1278	$1 *Catasetum integerrimum*	2·00	2·50

229 Children at Computers

2001. 20th Anniv of Independence. Multicoloured.
1279	25c. Type **229**	35	25
1280	60c. Shrimp farm	60	50
1281	75c. Privassion Cascade (vert)	75	60
1282	$2 Map of Belize (vert)	3·50	4·00

230 *Sobralia fragrans*

2001. Christmas. Orchids. Multicoloured.
1283	25c. Type **230**	75	25
1284	60c. *Encyclia cordigera*	1·25	75
1285	75c. *Maxillaria fulgens*	1·50	1·25
1286	$1 *Epidendrum nocturnum*	2·00	2·25

2002. Golden Jubilee. As T **200** of Ascension.
1287	25c. black, violet and gold	45	25
1288	60c. multicoloured	75	60
1289	75c. black, violet and gold	90	80
1290	$1 multicoloured	1·10	1·25
MS1291	162×95 mm. Nos. 1287/90 and $5 multicoloured	6·50	7·50

DESIGNS—Horiz: 25c. Princess Elizabeth in pantomime, Windsor, 1943; 60c. Queen Elizabeth in floral hat; 75c. Queen Elizabeth in garden with Prince Charles and Princess Anne, 1952; $1 Queen Elizabeth in South Africa, 1995. VERT (38×51 mm)—$5 Queen Elizabeth after Annigoni.

231 *Dichaea neglecta*

2002. Christmas. Orchids. Multicoloured.
1292	25c. Type **231**	70	25
1293	50c. *Epinendrum hawkesii*	1·00	55
1294	60c. *Encyclia belizensis*	1·10	60
1295	75c. *Eriopsis biloba*	1·25	70
1296	$1 *Harbenaria monorrhiza*	1·40	1·60
1297	$2 *Mormodes buccinator*	2·50	4·00

232 B.D.F. Emblem

2003. 25th Anniv of Belize Defence Force.
| 1298 | **232** | 25c. multicoloured | 50 | 35 |

233 Avro Shackleton MK 3

2003. Centenary of Powered Flight. Multicoloured.
1299	25c. Type **233**	85	45
1300	60c. Lockheed L-749 Constellation	1·25	70
1301	75c. Sepecat Jaguar GR. 1	1·40	80
1302	$3 British Aerospace Harrier GR. 3	3·25	4·75
MS1303	116×66 mm. $5 Ryan NYP *Spirit of St. Louis*, Belize, 1927	5·00	6·00

234 Head of Scarlet Macaw

2003. Christmas. Scarlet Macaw. Multicoloured.
1304	25c. Type **234**	90	45
1305	60c. Pair on tree	1·50	65
1306	75c. Three macaws feeding on clay	1·75	75
1307	$5 Pair in flight	6·00	8·00

235 Whale Shark

2004. Whale Shark. Multicoloured.
1308	25c. Type **235**	65	30
1309	60c. Near surface of water	1·10	65
1310	75c. Whale shark and diver	1·25	75
1311	$5 Near coral reef	5·00	7·00

2004. Wildlife. Nos. 1259/1261 surch.
1312	10c. on 50c. Red brocket antelope	75	1·00
1313	10c. on 60c. Jaguar	75	1·00
1314	15c. on 75c. American manatee	1·00	1·00

237 Woolly Opossum

2005. Endangered Species. Woolly Opossum. Showing the Woolly Opossum with the country name in different colours. Multicoloured.
1315	25c. Type **237**	85	30
1316	60c. Bright new blue	1·40	70
1317	75c. Dull orange (horiz)	1·60	90
1318	$5 Magenta (horiz)	5·00	7·00

2005. No. 1300 surch.
| 1318a | 10c. on 60c. Lockheed L-749 Constellation | 1·00 | 1·00 |

2005. No. 1305 surch.
| 1318b | 10c. on 60c. Pair (of scarlet macaws) on tree | 1·00 | 1·00 |

2005. Pope John Paul II Commemoration. As T **219** of Ascension.
| 1319 | $1 multicoloured | 2·25 | 2·00 |

239 Blue-crowned Motmot and Flower, Guanacaste National Park, Cayo District

2005. Ecological and Cultural Heritage. Multicoloured.
1320	5c. Type **239**	1·00	1·00
1321	10c. Government House of Culture, Belize City	25	40
1322	15c. Lubaantun Archaeological Reserve and ball court warriors, Toledo District	35	40
1323	25c. Altun Ha Archaeological Reserve and jade head, Belize District	1·00	30
1324	30c. Nohoch Che'n Archaeological Reserve and jar, Cayo District	50	30
1325	50c. Goff's Caye, Belize District	75	50
1326	60c. Blue Hole Natural Monument and diver, Belize District	85	60
1327	75c. Lamanai Archaeological Reserve and crocodile effigy, Orange Walk District	1·00	75
1328	$1 Half Moon Caye, lighthouse and red footed booby (bird), Belize District	2·50	1·75
1329	$2 Beach and starfish, Placencia Peninsula, Stann Creek District	3·00	3·50
1330	$5 Museum of Belize, Belize City	7·00	8·00
1331	$10 Cerros Archaeological Reserve and Olmec jade pendant, Corozal District	11·00	13·00

240 25c. Postman on Bicycle Stamp

2006. 50th Anniv of First Europa Stamp. Designs showing Belize 1999 125th Anniv of Universal Postal Union stamps. Multicoloured.
1332	25c. Type **240**	1·25	40
1333	75c. 60c. Postal truck stamp	2·00	75
1334	$3 75c. Mail ship *Dee* stamp	4·25	5·00
1335	$5 $1 Airliner stamp	7·00	9·00
MS1336	Nos. 1332/5	13·00	14·00

241 George Price (Independence negotiator and first Prime Minister)

2006. 25th Anniv of Independence. Multicoloured.
| 1337 | 25c. Type **241** | 60 | 30 |
| 1338 | 30c. Black orchid, Baird's tapir, keel-billed toucan and mahogany tree (national symbols) (horiz) | 1·75 | 60 |

1339	60c. Map of Belize	2·50	1·00
1340	$1 1981 Independence logo	2·00	1·50
1341	$5 The Constitution of Belize (horiz)	6·50	8·50

242 Roman Goddess Diana reaching for Arrow

2006. Breast Cancer Research.

| 1342 | **242** | $1 multicoloured | 2·00 | 1·75 |

A similar stamp was issued by the USA on 29 July 1998.

243 *Sleeping Giant* sculpture (George Gabb)

2007. Belizean Artists. Multicoloured.

1343	25c. Type **243**	20	10
1344	30c. *Market Scene* (Louis Belisle) (horiz)	25	20
1345	60c. *The Original Turtle Shell Band* (Pen Cayetano) (horiz)	60	45
1346	75c. *Have Some Coconut Water* (Benjamin Nicholas)	75	65
1347	$2 Woodcarving by Reuben Miguel	1·75	2·00
1348	$3 Mural of Corozal Town (Manuel Villamor)	2·40	3·25

244 Slave

2007. Bicentenary of the Abolition of the Slave Trade Act.

| 1349 | **244** | $2 multicoloured | 2·40 | 3·25 |

245 Scroll

2008. 60th Anniv of the University of the West Indies.

| 1350 | **245** | $1 multicoloured | 1·25 | 1·25 |

2009. As No. 1323

| 1351 | 25c. Altun Ha Archaeological Reserve and jade head, Belize District | 30 | 30 |

Nos. 1352/62 are left for possible additions.

246 Yellow-headed Parrot (*Amazona oratrix*)

2009. Endangered Birds. Multicoloured.

1363	25c. Type **246**	1·00	50
1364	60c. Harpy eagle (*Harpia harpyja*)	1·40	90
1365	$1 Slate-colored seedeater (*Sporophila schistacea*)	1·60	1·50
1366	$2 Green honeycreeper (*Chlorophanes spiza*)	2·25	2·50
1367	$5 Great curassow (*Crax rubra*)	4·00	5·00

247 Encyclia polybulbon

2010. Christmas. Orchids. Multicoloured.

1368	25c. Type **247**	1·25	20
1369	60c. *Oncidium ensatum*	1·75	65
1370	$2 *Encyclia livida*	2·50	2·50
1371	$5 *Epidendrum difforme*	4·50	5·00

248 Queen Elizabeth II

2012. Diamond Jubilee. Multicoloured.

1372	25c. Type **248**	1·25	45
1373	60c. Queen Elizabeth II wearing pale grey hat, c. 2005	1·75	80
1374	75c. Queen Elizabeth II, c. 1970	2·00	1·00
1375	$1 Queen Elizabeth II wearing blue, c. 1990	2·25	1·75
1376	$2 Queen Elizabeth II wearing tiara, c. 1952	2·75	2·75
1377	$5 Queen Elizabeth II, c. 1980	4·50	5·50
MS1378	174×163 mm. Nos. 1372/7 and three stamp-size labels	13·00	13·00
MS1379	110×70 mm. $10 Queen Elizabeth II, c. 2005	8·50	9·00

POSTAGE DUE STAMPS

D2

1976

D6	**D2**	1c. red and green	10	1·00
D7	-	2c. purple and violet	15	1·00
D8	-	5c. green and brown	20	1·25
D9	-	15c. green and red	30	1·50
D10	-	25c. orange and green	40	1·75

DESIGNS: Nos. D7/10 as Type D **2** but with different frames.

Pt. 6, Pt. 12

BENIN

A French possession on the west coast of Africa incorporated, in 1899, into the colony of Dahomey.

100 centimes = 1 franc.

A. FRENCH COLONY

1892. Stamps of French Colonies. "Commerce" type, optd **BENIN.**

1	J	1c. black on blue	£140	£140
2	J	2c. brown on yellow	£130	£130
3	J	4c. brown on grey	75·00	75·00
4	J	5c. green on light green	18·00	16·00
5	J	10c. black on lilac	£100	80·00
6	J	15c. blue on light blue	60·00	26·00
7	J	20c. red on green	£225	£200
8	J	25c. black on red	£120	70·00
9	J	30c. brown on drab	£180	£160
10	J	35c. black on orange	£180	£160
11	J	40c. red on yellow	£160	£150
12	J	75c. red on pink	£300	£275
13	J	1f. green	£325	£275

1892. Nos. 4 and 6 surch.

14	01 on 5c. green on lt green	£275	£225
15	40 on 15c. blue on lt blue	£170	£120
16	75 on 15c. blue on lt blue	£750	£450

1893. "Tablet" key-type inscr "GOLFE DE BENIN" in red (1, 5, 15, 25, 75c., 1f.) or blue (others).

17	D	1c. black on blue	3·00	8·75
18	D	2c. brown on buff	3·75	4·50
19	D	4c. brown on grey	3·25	8·50
20	D	5c. green on light green	10·00	12·50
21	D	10c. black on lilac	10·50	15·00
22	D	15c. blue	40·00	50·00
23	D	20c. red on green	7·25	11·00
24	D	25c. black on red	40·00	19·00
25	D	30c. brown on drab	14·50	15·00
26	D	40c. red on yellow	2·75	7·00
27	D	50c. red on pink	3·75	5·50
28	D	75c. brown on orange	11·50	22·00
29	D	1f. green	75·00	80·00

1894. "Tablet" key-type inscr "BENIN" in red (1, 5, 15, 25, 75c., 1f.) or blue (others).

33	1c. black on blue	2·75	3·25
34	2c. brown on buff	3·75	4·25
35	4c. brown on grey	2·75	4·25
36	5c. green on light green	7·25	8·75
37	10c. black on lilac	6·00	8·25
38	15c. blue	18·00	3·25
39	20c. red on green	14·00	17·00
40	25c. black on pink	11·00	4·50
41	30c. brown on drab	7·25	12·00
42	40c. red on yellow	17·00	18·00

43	50c. red on pink	25·00	29·00
44	75c. brown on orange	18·00	8·75
45	1f. green	7·00	12·50

POSTAGE DUE STAMPS

1894. Postage Due stamps of French Colonies optd **BENIN.** Imperf.

D46	U	5c. black	£150	85·00
D47	U	10c. black	£150	85·00
D48	U	20c. black	£150	85·00
D49	U	30c. black	£150	85·00

B. PEOPLE'S REPUBLIC

The Republic of Dahomey was renamed the People's Republic of Benin on 30 November 1975.

185 Celebrations

1976. Republic of Benin Proclamation. Multicoloured.

603	50f. Type **185**	75	30
604	60f. President Kerekou making Proclamation	1·10	40
605	100f. Benin arms and flag	1·80	70

186 Skiing

1976. Air. Winter Olympic Games, Innsbruck. Multicoloured.

606	60f. Type **186**	1·30	70
607	150f. Bobsleighing (vert)	2·30	1·20
608	300f. Figure-skating	4·75	2·30

1976. Various Dahomey stamps surch **POPULAIRE DU BENIN** and new value (609/11) or surch only (617/18).NIN

609	-	135f. brown, purple and blue (No. 590) (air)	2·00	90
610	-	210f. on 300f. brown, red and blue (No. 591)	2·75	1·30
611	-	380f. on 500f. brown, red and green (No. 592)	4·75	2·20
617	**108**	50f. on 1f. multicoloured (postage)	70	30
618	-	60f. on 2f. multicoloured (No. 415)	95	45

188 Alexander Graham Bell, Early Telephone and Satellite

1976. Telephone Centenary.

| 612 | **188** | 200f. red, violet & brown | 3·25 | 1·70 |

189 Basketball

1976. Air. Olympic Games, Montreal. Multicoloured.

613	60f. Long jump (horiz)	1·00	45
614	150f. Type **189**	2·00	95
615	200f. Hurdling (horiz)	2·50	1·70
MS616	150×120 mm. Nos. 613/15	7·50	6·75

191 Scouts and Camp-fire

1976. African Scout Jamboree, Jos, Nigeria.

| 619 | **191** | 50f. purple, brown & blk | 75 | 35 |
| 620 | - | 70f. brown, green & blk | 1·00 | 55 |

DESIGN: 70f. "Comradeship".

192 Konrad Adenauer

1976. Air. Birth Centenary of Konrad Adenauer (German statesman).

| 621 | **192** | 90f. slate, blue and red | 1·50 | 65 |
| 622 | - | 250f. blue, red & lt blue | 4·00 | 1·50 |

DESIGN—HORIZ: 250f. Adenauer and Cologne Cathedral.

193 Benin 1c. Stamp, 1893, and Lion Cub

1976. Air. "Juvarouen 76" Youth Stamp Exhibition, Rouen.

| 623 | 60f. blue and turquoise | 1·00 | 50 |
| 624 | **193** | 210f. red, brown & olive | 3·25 | 1·50 |

DESIGN—HORIZ: 60f. Dahomey 60f. Stamp of 1965, and children's silhouettes.

194 Blood Bank, Cotonou

1976. National Days of Blood Transfusion Service. Multicoloured.

625	5f. Type **194**	20	10
626	50f. Casualty and blood clinic	70	40
627	60f. Donor, patient and ambulance	1·10	55

195 Manioc

1976. National Products Campaign Year. Multicoloured.

628	20f. Type **195**	50	15
629	50f. Maize cultivation	75	25
630	60f. Cocoa trees	1·00	40
631	150f. Cotton plantation	2·30	80

196 "Apollo" Emblem and Rocket

1976. Air. Fifth Anniv of "Apollo 14" Space Mission.

| 632 | **196** | 130f. lake, brown & blue | 1·50 | 70 |
| 633 | - | 270f. blue, turquoise & red | 3·00 | 1·50 |

DESIGN: 270f. Landing on Moon.

197 Classroom

1976. Third Anniv of Bariba Periodical "Kparo".
| 634 | 197 | 50f. multicoloured | 1·00 | 55 |

198 Roan Antelope

1976. Mammals in Pendjari National Park. Multicoloured.
635		10f. Type **198**	45	25
636		30f. African buffalo	80	50
637		50f. Hippopotamus (horiz)	1·60	85
638		70f. Lion	1·80	1·00

199 "Freedom"

1976. First Anniv of Proclamation of Republic.
Multicoloured.
| 639 | | 40f. Type **199** | 60 | 25 |
| 640 | | 150f. Maize cultivation | 1·80 | 85 |

200 The Annunciation
(Master of Jativa)

1976. Air. Christmas. Multicoloured.
641		50f. Type **200**	80	40
642		60f. The Nativity (David)	90	50
643		270f. Adoration of the Magi (Dutch school)	3·75	1·80
644		300f. The Flight into Egypt (Fabriano) (horiz)	4·00	2·30

201 Table Tennis and Games
Emblem

1976. West African University Games, Cotonou.
Multicoloured.
| 645 | | 10f. Type **201** | 55 | 10 |
| 646 | | 50f. Sports Hall, Cotonou | 80 | 25 |

202 Loser with Ticket and Winner
with Money

1977. Air. Tenth Anniv of National Lottery.
| 647 | **202** | 50f. multicoloured | 75 | 45 |

203 Douglas
DC-10 crossing
Globe

1977. Europafrique.
| 648 | **203** | 200f. multicoloured | 3·00 | 2·10 |

204 Chateau Sassenage, Grenoble

1977. Air. Tenth Anniv of International French Language
Council.
| 649 | **204** | 200f. multicoloured | 2·50 | 1·10 |

205 Adder

1977. Reptiles and Domestic Animals. Multicoloured.
650		2f. Type **205**	45	10
651		3f. Tortoise	45	10
652		5f. Zebus	45	10
653		10f. Cats	85	25

206 Concorde

1977. Air. Aviation.
654	**206**	80f. red and blue	95	40
655	-	150f. red, violet & green	2·10	90
656	-	300f. violet, red & mauve	3·00	1·60
657	-	500f. red, blue & green	6·25	3·25

DESIGNS: 150f. *Graf Zeppelin*; 300f. Charles Lindbergh and
Spirit of St. Louis; 500f. Charles Nungesser and Francois
Coli with *L'Oiseau Blanc*.

207 Footballer
heading Ball

1977. Air. World Football Cup Eliminators. Multicoloured.
| 658 | **207** | 60f. Type **207** | 80 | 35 |
| 659 | | 200f. Goalkeeper and players | 2·30 | 1·30 |

208 Rheumatic Patients

1977. World Rheumatism Year.
| 660 | **208** | 100f. multicoloured | 1·50 | 75 |

209 Karate

1977. Second African Games, Lagos.
661	**209**	90f. multicoloured	1·40	70
662	-	100f. multicoloured	1·40	90
663	-	150f. multicoloured	2·30	1·10
MS664		144×92 mm. Nos. 661/3	6·75	6·50

DESIGNS—HORIZ: 100f. Javelin. VERT: 150f. Hurdles.

210 Mao
Tse-tung

1977. First Death Anniv of Mao Tse-tung.
| 665 | **210** | 100f. multicoloured | 2·75 | 1·40 |

211 Sterilising
Scalpels

1977. 150th Birth Anniv of Joseph Lister.
| 666 | **211** | 150f. grey, red & carmine | 2·00 | 90 |
| 667 | - | 210f. olive, green & red | 2·50 | 1·30 |

DESIGN: 210f. Lister and antiseptic spray.

212 Miss Haverfield
(Gainsborough)

1977. Air. Paintings.
668	**212**	100f. green and brown	2·40	60
669	-	150f. brown, bistre & red	3·50	1·30
670	-	200f. red and bistre	4·75	1·80

DESIGNS: 150f. *Self-Portrait* (Rubens); 200f. *Study of an Old
Man* (da Vinci).

213 Jarre Trouee
Emblem of King
Ghezo (D'Abomey
Museum)

1977. Historic Museums of Benin. Multicoloured.
671		50f. Type **213**	75	40
672		60f. Mask (Porto-Novo Museum) (horiz)	1·30	55
673		210f. D'Abomey Museum	2·75	1·20

214 Atacora
Waterfall

1977. Tourism. Multicoloured.
674		50f. Type **214**	70	40
675		60f. Stilt houses, Ganvie (horiz)	95	55
676		150f. Hut village, Savalou	2·30	1·10
MS677		144×92 mm. Nos. 674/6	5·25	5·25

1977. Air. First Commercial Concorde Flight. Paris–New
York. No. 654 optd **1er VOL COMMERCIAL 22.11.77
PARIS NEW-YORK.**
| 678 | **206** | 80f. red and blue | 1·70 | 85 |

216 "Viking" on Mars ("Operation
Viking", 1977)

1977. Air. Space Conquest Anniversaries.
679	**216**	100f. brown, olive & red	1·00	60
680	-	150f. blue, turq & mve	1·80	85
681	-	200f. brown, blue & red	2·75	1·10
682	-	500f. blue, brn & olive	6·50	3·00

DESIGNS AND EVENTS: 150f. Sir Isaac Newton, apple and
stars (250th death anniv); 200f. Komarov and "Soyuz 2"
over Moon (10th death anniv); 500f. Space dog "Laika"
and rocket (20th anniv of ascent into Space).

217 Monument, Red Flag
Square, Cotonou

1977. Air. First Anniv of Inauguration of Red Flag Square
Monument.
| 683 | **217** | 500f. multicoloured | 6·25 | 2·75 |

218 Mother and
Child with Owl of
Wisdom

1977. Fight against Witchcraft. Multicoloured.
| 684 | | 60f. Type **218** | 1·30 | 55 |
| 685 | | 150f. Felling the tree of sorcery | 2·50 | 1·10 |

219 Suzanne Fourment

1977. Air. 400th Birth Anniv of Rubens.
| 686 | **219** | 200f. brown, red & green | 3·25 | 1·30 |
| 687 | - | 380f. orange and brown | 5·50 | 2·20 |

DESIGN: 380f. *Albert Rubens.*

220 Battle Scene

1978. "Victory over Imperialism".
| 688 | **220** | 50f. multicoloured | 1·20 | 45 |

221 Benin Houses
and Map of Heads

1978. General Population Census.
| 689 | **221** | 50f. multicoloured | 80 | 35 |

222 Sir Alexander Fleming,
Microscope and Drugs

1978. 50th Anniv of Discovery of Antibiotics.
| 690 | **222** | 300f. multicoloured | 4·50 | 2·10 |

223 Abdoulaye Issa

1978. First Death Anniv of Abdoulaye Issa.
| 691 | **223** | 100f. multicoloured | 1·00 | 50 |

224 El Hadj Omar

1978. Heroes of Anti-colonial Resistance.
| 692 | - | 90f. multicoloured | 1·30 | 45 |
| 693 | **224** | 100f. green, grey & blue | 1·30 | 65 |

DESIGN: 90f. Samory Toure.

225 "Communications"

1978. Tenth World Telecommunications Day.
| 694 | **225** | 100f. multicoloured | 1·50 | 75 |

226 Footballer and Stadium

1978. World Cup Football Championship, Argentina.
Multicoloured.
695	**226**	200f. Type **226**	2·30	1·00
696	-	300f. Tackling (vert)	3·00	1·60
697	-	500f. Footballer and world map	5·50	2·50
MS698		190×121 mm. Nos. 695/7 in different colours	12·00	9·00

1978. Argentina's Victory in World Cup Football
Championship. Nos. 695/7 optd.
699	**226**	200f. multicoloured	2·00	1·10
700	-	300f. multicoloured	3·00	1·90
701	-	500f. multicoloured	5·50	3·25
MS702		190×121 mm. Nos. 699/701 multicoloured	13·50	12·50

OPTS: 200f. **FINALE ARGENTINE: 3 HOLLANDE: 1**; 300f.
CHAMPION 1978 ARGENTINE; 500f. **3e BRESIL 4e
ITALIE**.

228 Map, Olympic Flag and
Basketball Players

1978. Third African Games, Algiers. Multicoloured.
703	**228**	50f. Type **228**	55	25
704	-	60f. African map and Volleyball	95	45
705	-	80f. Cyclists and map of Algeria	1·00	55
MS706		208×80 mm. Nos. 703/5 in different colours	4·00	3·75

229 Martin Luther
King

1978. Tenth Anniv of Martin Luther King's Assassination.
| 707 | **229** | 300f. multicoloured | 3·50 | 1·70 |

230 Bicycle Taxi (Oueme)

1978. Benin Provinces. Multicoloured.
708	**230**	50f. Type **230**	1·20	40
709	-	60f. Leather work (Borgou)	1·10	40
710	-	70f. Drums (Oueme)	1·20	45
711	-	100f. Calabash with burnt-work ornamentation (Zou)	1·50	55

231 "Stamps" and Magnifying Glass

1978. Philatelic Exhibition, Riccione, Italy.
| 712 | **231** | 200f. multicoloured | 2·30 | 1·10 |

232 Parthenon and Frieze
showing Horsemen

1978. Air. UNESCO Campaign for the Preservation of the
Acropolis. Multicoloured.
713		70f. Acropolis and Frieze showing Procession	80	25
714		250f. Type **232**	2·50	1·20
715		500f. The Parthenon (horiz)	5·00	2·20

235 Turkeys

1978. Domestic Poultry. Multicoloured.
722		10f. Type **235**	35	10
723		20f. Ducks	60	25
724		50f. Chickens	1·70	50
725		60f. Helmeted guineafowl	1·90	70

236 Post Runner
and Boeing 747

1978. Centenary of UPU. Paris Congress. Multicoloured.
726		50f. Messenger of the Dahomey Kings (horiz)	1·00	40
727		60f. Pirogue oarsman, boat and post car	1·10	40
728		90f. Type **236**	1·30	55

237 Red-breasted Merganser and
Baden 1851 1k. Stamp

1978. Air. "Philexafrique" Exhibition, Libreville (Gabon)
(1st issue) and International Stamp Fair, Essen, West
Germany. Multicoloured.
| 729 | | 100f. Type **237** | 4·00 | 1·50 |
| 730 | | 100f. African Buffalo and Dahomey 1966 50f. African Pygmy Goose stamp | 4·00 | 1·50 |

See also Nos. 747/8.

238 Raoul Follereau

1978. First Death Anniv of Raoul Follereau (leprosy
pioneer).
| 731 | **238** | 200f. multicoloured | 2·00 | 95 |

239 Wilbur and Orville Wright and
Wright Flyer 1

1978. Air. 75th Anniv of First Powered Flight.
| 732 | **239** | 500f. blue, yellow & brn | 6·00 | 3·00 |

240 I.Y.C. Emblem

1979. International Year of the Child. Multicoloured.
733	**240**	10f. Type **240**	15	10
734	-	20f. Children in balloon	30	10
735	-	50f. Children dancing around globe	45	30

241 Hydrangea

1979. Flowers. Multicoloured.
736	**241**	20f. Type **241**	20	25
737	-	25f. Assangokan	45	25
738	-	30f. Geranium	70	35
739	-	40f. Water Lily (horiz)	90	40

242 Flags around Map of
Africa

1979. OCAM Summit Meeting, Cotonou (1st series).
Multicoloured.
740	**242**	50f. Type **242**	55	40
741	-	60f. Flags and map of Benin	85	45
742	-	80f. OCAM flag and map of member countries	1·20	60

See also Nos. 754/6.

1979. Various stamps surch.
743	**205**	50f. on 2f. multicoloured (postage)	£190	2·75
743a	-	50f. on 3f. multicoloured (651)	95·00	2·75
743b	-	50f. on 70f. brown, green and black (620)	95·00	2·75
744	**207**	50f. on 60f. mult (air)	95·00	2·75
745	**192**	50f. on 90f. blue, deep blue and red	95·00	2·75
746	-	50f. on 150f. mult (607)	95·00	2·75
747	**189**	50f. on 150f. mult	95·00	2·75

244 Antenna, Satellite
and Wave Pattern

1979. World Telecommunications Day.
| 748 | **244** | 50f. multicoloured | 80 | 45 |

245 Headquarters
Building

1979. West African Savings Bank Building Opening.
| 749 | **245** | 50f. multicoloured | 75 | 40 |

246 Resolution and Discovery in
Karakakoa Bay, Hawaii

1979. Air. Death Bicentenary of Capt. James Cook.
| 750 | **246** | 20f. blue, green & brown | 1·30 | 40 |
| 751 | - | 50f. brown, green & blue | 1·00 | 45 |

DESIGN: 50f. Cook's death at Kowrowa.

247 Guelede Mask, Abomey
Tapestry and Fiery-breasted Bush
Shrike

1979. "Philexafrique" Stamp Exhibition, Gabon (2nd
issue).
| 752 | **247** | 15f. multicoloured | 1·50 | 55 |
| 753 | - | 50f. orange, yellow & turq | 2·00 | 95 |

DESIGN: 50f. Lockheed L-1011 Tristar 500, satellite, U.P.U.
emblem and canoe post.

1979. Common African and Mauritian Organization
Summit Conference, Cotonou (2nd issue). Nos. 740/2
optd **26 Au 28 Juin 1979**.
754	**242**	50f. Type **242**	80	40
755	-	60f. Map of Benin and flags of members	95	50
756	-	80f. OCAM flag and map showing member countries	1·10	55

249 Olympic Flame, Benin
Flags and Pictograms

1979. Pre-Olympic Year. Multicoloured.
| 757 | **249** | 10f. Type **249** | 30 | 10 |
| 758 | - | 50f. High jump | 1·00 | 45 |

250 Roan Antelope

1979. Endangered Animals. Multicoloured.
759	**250**	5f. Type **250**	40	20
760	-	10f. Giraffes (vert)	55	35
761	-	20f. Chimpanzee	85	50
762	-	50f. African elephants (vert)	1·80	75

Benin 513

251 Emblem, Concorde and Map of Africa

1979. 20th Anniv of ASECNA (African Air Safety Organization). Multicoloured.
| 763 | 50f. Type **251** | 50 | 25 |
| 764 | 60f. As No. 763 but emblem at bottom right and without dates | 55 | 25 |

252 Post Offices, Antenna, Telephone and Savings Book

1979. 20th Anniv of Posts and Telecommunications Office. Multicoloured.
| 765 | 50f. Type **252** | 50 | 25 |
| 766 | 60f. Collecting, sorting and delivering mail | 55 | 25 |

253 Rotary Emblem, Symbols of Services and Globe

1980. 75th Anniv of Rotary International. Multicoloured.
| 767 | 90f. Cotonou Rotary Club banner (vert) | 95 | 45 |
| 768 | 200f. Type **253** | 1·80 | 95 |

254 Copernicus and Planetary System

1980. 50th Anniv of Discovery of Planet Pluto. Multicoloured.
| 769 | 70f. Kepler and astrolabe | 80 | 45 |
| 770 | 100f. Type **254** | 1·20 | 55 |

255 Pharaonic Capital

1980. 20th Anniv of Nubian Monuments Preservation Campaign. Multicoloured.
771	50f. Type **255**	55	30
772	60f. Rameses II, Abu Simbel	95	45
773	150f. Temple, Abu Simbel (horiz)	1·50	85

256 Lenin in Library

1980. 110th Birth Anniv of Lenin. Multicoloured.
| 774 | 50f. Lenin and globe | 75 | 25 |
| 775 | 150f. Type **256** | 2·00 | 85 |

257 Monument

1980. Martyrs Square, Cotonou.
776	**257**	50f. multicoloured	45	10
777	-	60f. multicoloured	55	25
778	-	70f. multicoloured	75	25
779	-	100f. multicoloured	1·20	40
DESIGNS—HORIZ: 60f. to 100f. Different views of the monument.

258 Farmer using Telephone

1980. World Telecommunications Day. Multicoloured.
| 780 | 50f. Type **258** | 45 | 25 |
| 781 | 60f. Telephone | 55 | 30 |

259 Assan

1980. Traditional Musical Instruments. Multicoloured.
782	5f. Type **259**	25	10
783	10f. Tinbo (horiz)	25	10
784	15f. Tam-tam sato	55	25
785	20f. Kora (horiz)	55	25
786	30f. Gangan (horiz)	85	40
787	50f. Sinhoun (horiz)	1·60	55

260 Monument

1980. King Gbehanzin Monument.
| 788 | **260** | 1000f. multicoloured | 13·00 | 8·50 |

261 Dieudonne Costes, Maurice Bellonte and *Point d'Interrogation*

1980. 50th Anniv of First Paris–New York Non-stop Flight.
| 789 | - | 90f. red, lt blue and blue | 1·00 | 45 |
| 790 | **261** | 100f. red, blue and flesh | 1·20 | 55 |
DESIGN: 90f. Airplane *Point d'Interrogation* and scenes of New York and Paris.

262 "Lunokhod I"

1980. Tenth Anniv of "Lunokhod I".
| 791 | - | 90f. brown, blue and violet (postage) | 95 | 55 |
| 792 | **262** | 210f. purple, blue and yellow (air) | 2·75 | 1·30 |

DESIGN (48×36 mm): 90f. Rocket and "Lunokhod I".

263 Show-jumping

1980. Olympic Games, Moscow. Multicoloured.
793	50f. Olympic Flame, running track, emblem and mascot Mischa the bear (horiz)	50	25
794	60f. Type **263**	55	40
795	70f. Judo (horiz)	95	45
796	200f. Olympic flag and globe surrounded by sports pictogram	2·00	90
797	300f. Weightlifting	3·00	1·50

264 OCAM Building

1980. Common African and Mauritian Organization Village, Cotonou. Multicoloured.
798	50f. Entrance to OCAM village	60	25
799	60f. View of village	75	25
800	70f. Type **264**	95	55

265 Dancers

1980. Agbadja Dance. Multicoloured.
801	30f. Type **265**	55	25
802	50f. Singer and musicians	95	45
803	60f. Dancers and musicians	95	55

266 Casting a Net

1980. Fishing. Multicoloured.
804	5f. Type **266**	10	10
805	10f. Fisherman with catch (vert)	30	10
806	15f. Line fishing	30	25
807	20f. Fisherman emptying eel-pot	35	25
808	50f. Hauling in a net	95	45
809	60f. Fish farm	95	45

267 Philippines under Magnifying Glass

1980. World Tourism Conference, Manila. Multicoloured.
| 810 | 50f. Type **267** | 55 | 25 |
| 811 | 60f. Conference flag on globe | 95 | 30 |

268 "Othreis materna"

1980. Insects. Multicoloured.
812	40f. Type **268**	80	35
813	50f. *Othreis fullonia* (butterfly)	1·20	45
814	200f. *Oryctes* sp. (beetle)	3·75	1·60

269 Map of Africa and Posthorn

1980. Fifth Anniv of African Posts and Telecommunications.
| 815 | **269** | 75f. multicoloured | 75 | 25 |

270 Hands freed from Chains

1980. 30th Anniv of Signing of Human Rights Convention. Multicoloured.
816	30f. Type **270**	30	10
817	50f. African pushing through bars	50	25
818	60f. Figure holding Human Rights flame	75	25

271 *Self-portrait*

1980. 90th Death Anniv of Van Gogh (artist). Multicoloured.
| 819 | 100f. Type **271** | 2·00 | 70 |
| 820 | 300f. *The Postman Roulin* | 5·00 | 2·20 |

272 Offenbach and Scene from *Orpheus in the Underworld*

1980. Death Centenary of Jacques Offenbach (composer).
| 821 | **272** | 50f. black, red and green | 1·30 | 50 |
| 822 | - | 60f. blue, brown & dp brn | 1·90 | 75 |
DESIGN: 60f. Offenbach and scene from *La Vie Parisienne*.

273 Kepler and Astronomical Diagram

1980. 30th Death Anniv of Johannes Kepler (astronomer).
| 823 | **273** | 50f. red, blue and grey | 75 | 25 |
| 824 | - | 60f. blue, black and green | 95 | 45 |
DESIGN: 60f. Kepler, satellite and dish aerials.

274 Footballers

1981. Air. World Cup Football Championship. Multicoloured.
825 200f. Football and globe 1·80 70
826 500f. Type **274** 5·00 1·90

275 Disabled Person holding Flower

1981. International Year of Disabled People.
827 **275** 115f. multicoloured 1·20 50

276 Yuri Gagarin

1981. 20th Anniv of First Man in Space.
828 **276** 500f. multicoloured 5·50 2·75

277 ITU and WHO Emblems and Ribbons forming Caduceus

1981. World Telecommunications Day.
829 **277** 115f. multicoloured 1·20 45

278 Amaryllis

1981. Flowers. Multicoloured.
830 10f. Type **278** 20 15
831 20f. *Eischornia crassipes* 45 30
832 80f. *Parkia biglobosa* 1·50 50

279 Hotel and Map

1981. Opening of Benin Sheraton Hotel.
833 **279** 100f. multicoloured 1·00 45

1981. Surch **50F.**
834 **216** 50f. on 100f. brown, green and red 85 25
835 **193** 50f. on 210f. red, brown and green 85 25

281 Prince Charles, Lady Diana Spencer and Tower Bridge

1981. Air. British Royal Wedding.
836 **281** 500f. multicoloured 4·50 2·00

282 Guinea Pig

1981. Domestic Animals. Multicoloured.
837 5f. Type **282** 35 25
838 60f. Cat 1·00 45
839 80f. Dogs 1·40 70

283 Heinrich von Stephan (founder of UPU)

1981. World Universal Postal Union Day.
840 **283** 100f. slate and red 95 45

284 Heads, Quill, Paper Darts and U.P.U. Emblem

1981. International Letter Writing Week.
841 **284** 100f. blue and purple 95 45

285 The Dance

1981. Air. Birth Centenary of Pablo Picasso. Multicoloured.
842 300f. Type **285** 3·00 1·20
843 500f. *The Three Musicians* 5·50 2·00

286 Globe, Map of Member Countries and Communication Symbols

1981. Fifth Anniv of ECOWAS (Economic Community of West African States).
844 **286** 60f. multicoloured 75 25

287 St. Theodore Stratilates (tile painting)

1981. Air. 1300th Anniv of Bulgarian State.
845 **287** 100f. multicoloured 95 45

288 Tractor and Map

1981. Tenth Anniv of West African Rice Development Association.
846 **288** 60f. multicoloured 75 25

289 Pope John Paul II

1982. Air. Papal Visit.
847 **289** 80f. multicoloured 2·00 90

290 John Glenn

1982. Air. 20th Anniv of First United States Manned Space Flight.
848 **290** 500f. multicoloured 5·50 2·20

291 Dr. Robert Koch

1982. Centenary of Discovery of Tubercle Bacillus.
849 **291** 115f. multicoloured 1·80 70

292 Washington, U.S. Flag and Map

1982. 250th Birth Anniv of George Washington.
850 **292** 200f. multicoloured 2·30 85

1982. Red Cross. Surch **Croix Rouge 8 Mai 1982 60f.**
851 **266** 60f. on 5f. multicoloured 75 25

294 Map of Member Countries and Torch

1982. Fifth Economic Community of West African States Summit, Cotonou.
852 **294** 60f. multicoloured 60 25

295 Scouts round Campfire

1982. Air. 75th Anniv of Boy Scout Movement.
853 **295** 105f. multicoloured 1·20 60

296 Footballers

1982. World Cup Football Championship, Spain. Multicoloured.
854 90f. Type **296** 95 40
855 300f. Leg with sock formed from flags of participating countries and globe/football 3·00 1·20

1982. African Posts and Telegraph Union. Surch **UAPT 1982 60f.**
856 **282** 60f. on 5f. multicoloured 75 25

298 Stamp of Map of France and Magnifying Glass

1982. "Philexfrance 82" International Stamp Exhibition, Paris.
857 **298** 90f. multicoloured 95 45

1982. World Cup Football Championship Results. Nos. 854/5 optd.
858 90f. Type **296** 1·20 45

859 300f. Leg with flags of participating countries and football "globe" 3·75 1·30
OVERPRINTS: 90f. **COUPE 82 ITALIE bat RFA 3-1**; 300f. **COUPE 82 1 ITALIE 2 RFA 3 POLOGNE.**

1982. Riccione Stamp Exhibition. Optd **RICCIONE 1982.**
860 **231** 200f. multicoloured 1·80 80

301 Laughing Kookaburra (*Dacelo Gigas*)

1982. Birds. Multicoloured.
861 5f. Type **301** 65 30
862 10f. Bluethroat ("La Gorge Bleue") (horiz) 1·00 30
863 15f. Barn swallow ("L'Hirondelle") 1·00 35
864 20f. Woodland kingfisher ("Martin-Pecheur") and Village weaver ("Tisserin") 1·60 40
865 30f. Reed warbler ("La Rousserolle") (horiz) 2·20 50
866 60f. Warbler sp. ("Faurette Commoune") (horiz) 3·00 75
867 80f. Eagle owl ("Hibou Grand Doc") 5·50 1·40
868 100f. Sulphur-crested cockatoo ("Cacatoes") 6·50 1·80

302 World Map and Satellite

1982. I.T.U. Delegates' Conference, Nairobi.
869 **302** 200f. turq, blue & blk 2·00 80

303 UPU Emblem and Heads

1982. UPU Day.
870 **303** 100f. green, blue & brown 1·00 45

305 *Claude Monet in his Studio*

1982. Air. 150th Birth Anniv of Edouard Manet (artist).
876 **305** 300f. multicoloured 6·75 2·40

306 "irgin and Child (Grunewald)

1982. Air. Christmas. Multicoloured.
877 200f. Type **306** 2·20 1·10
878 300f. *Virgin and Child with Angels and Cherubins* (Correggio) 3·25 1·40

307 Pres. Mitterrand and Pres. Kerekou

1983. Visit of President Mitterrand.
879	**307**	90f. multicoloured	1·50	70

1983. Various stamps surch.
880	-	60f. on 50f. multicoloured (No. 798) (postage)	1·20	45
881	-	60f. on 70f. multicoloured (No. 778)	1·20	45
882	**279**	60f. on 100f. mult	47·00	2·75
883	-	75f. on 80f. multicoloured (No. 832)	1·40	55
884	-	75f. on 80f. multicoloured (No. 839)	1·50	85
885	**262**	75f. on 210f. red, blue and yellow (air)	1·50	85

309 *Tender Benin* (tug) and *Amazone* (oil rig)

1983. Seme Oilfield.
886	**309**	125f. multicoloured	1·50	60

1983. Various stamps surch.
887	**267**	5f. on 50f. multicoloured	3·00	50
888	**284**	10f. on 100f. blue & pur	3·00	50
889	-	10f. on 200f. mult (No. 659)	3·00	50
890	-	15f. on 200f. red and bistre (No. 670)	3·00	50
891	-	15f. on 200f. mult (No. 796)	3·00	50
892	-	15f. on 210f. green, deep green and red (No. 667)	3·00	50
893	-	15f. on 270f. mult (No. 643)	3·00	50
894	**219**	20f. on 200f. brown, red and olive	3·00	50
895	-	25f. on 70f. mult (No. 795)	3·00	60
896	-	25f. on 210f. mult (No. 673)	3·00	60
897	-	25f. on 270f. blue, turq & red (No. 633)	3·00	50
898	-	25f. on 380f. brown and red (No. 687)	3·00	50
899	-	30f. on 200f. brown, blue and red (No. 681)	3·00	60
900	**290**	40f. on 500f. mult	3·00	60
901	**282**	75f. on 5f. multicoloured	3·25	65
902	-	75f. on 100f. red, blue and pink (No. 790)	3·25	65
903	-	75f. on 150f. mult (No. 631)	3·25	65
904	-	75f. on 150f. violet, red and green (No. 655)	3·25	65
905	**211**	75f. on 150f. grey, orange and red	3·25	65
906	-	75f. on 150f. dp brown, brown & red (No. 669)	3·25	65

311 WCY Emblem

1983. World Communications Year.
907	**311**	185f. multicoloured	1·80	80

312 Stamps of Benin and Thailand and World Map

1983. Air. "Bangkok 1983" International Stamp Exhibition.
908	**312**	300f. multicoloured	3·00	1·40

313 Hand with Tweezers and Stamp

1983. "Riccione 83" Stamp Fair, San Marino.
909	**313**	500f. multicoloured	4·50	2·00

314 First Aid

1983. 20th Anniv of Benin Red Cross.
910	**314**	105f. multicoloured	1·20	60

315 Carved Table and Chairs

1983. Benin Woodwork. Multicoloured.
911		75f. Type **315**	1·00	25
912		90f. Rustic table and chairs	1·10	40
913		200f. Monkeys holding box	2·00	75

316 Boeing 747, World Map and UPU Emblem

1983. UPU Day.
914	**316**	125f. green, blue & brown	1·20	60

317 Egoun

1983. Religious Cults. Multicoloured.
915		75f. Type **317**	1·00	45
916		75f. Zangbeto	1·00	45

318 Rockcoco

1983. Hair-styles. Multicoloured.
917		30f. Type **318**	30	15
918		75f. Serpent	75	45
919		90f. Songas	1·30	55

319 Alfred Nobel

1983. 150th Birth Anniv of Alfred Nobel.
920	**319**	300f. multicoloured	3·00	1·50

320 *Madonna of Lorette* (Raphael)

1983. Air. Christmas.
921	**320**	200f. multicoloured	2·75	1·20

1984. Various stamps surch.
922	-	5f. on 150f. mult (No. 685) (postage)	3·25	75
923	**316**	5f. on 125f. green, blue and brown	3·25	75
924	**292**	10f. on 200f. mult	3·25	75
925	-	10f. on 200f. mult (No. 913)	3·25	75
926	-	15f. on 300f. mult (No. 820)	3·25	80
927	-	25f. on 300f. mult (No. 644)	3·25	80
928	**276**	40f. on 500f. mult	3·25	80
929	**314**	75f. on 105f. mult	3·50	1·00
930	**275**	75f. on 115f. mult	3·50	90
931	**277**	75f. on 115f. mult	3·50	90
932	**291**	75f. on 115f. mult	3·50	90
933	**311**	75f. on 185f. mult	3·50	1·00
934	**302**	75f. on 200f. turquoise, blue and black	3·50	1·00
935	**320**	15f. on 200f. mult (air)	3·25	75
936	**285**	15f. on 300f. mult	3·25	75
937	**312**	25f. on 300f. mult	3·25	80
938	**281**	40f. on 500f. mult	3·50	90
939	**295**	75f. on 105f. mult	3·50	90
940	**306**	90f. on 200f. mult	3·75	95
941	**305**	90f. on 300f. mult	3·75	95

322 Flags, Agriculture and Symbol of Unity and Growth

1984. 25th Anniv of Council of Unity.
942	**322**	75f. multicoloured	75	25
943	**322**	90f. multicoloured	95	40

323 UPU Emblem and Magnifying Glass

1984. 19th Universal Postal Union Congress, Hamburg.
944	**323**	90f. multicoloured	95	45

324 Abomey-Calavi Ground Station

1984. Inauguration of Abomy-Calavi Ground Station.
945	**324**	75f. multicoloured	75	45

325 Koumboro (Borgou)

1984. Traditional Costumes. Multicoloured.
946		5f. Type **325**	15	10
947		10f. Taka (Borgou)	30	25
948		20f. Toko (Atacora Province)	30	25

326 Olympic Mascot

1984. Air. Olympic Games, Los Angeles.
949	**326**	300f. multicoloured	3·00	1·40

327 Plant and Starving Child

1984. World Food Day.
950	**327**	100f. multicoloured	95	45

328 Anatosaurus

1984. Prehistoric Animals. Multicoloured.
951		75f. Type **328**	3·75	65
952		90f. Brontosaurus	4·00	90

329 *Virgin and Child* (detail, Murillo)

1984. Air. Christmas.
953	**329**	500f. multicoloured	5·50	2·20

1984. Various stamps surch.
954	**203**	75f. on 200f. mult (post)	6·00	1·30
955	**226**	75f. on 200f. mult	6·00	1·30
956	-	75f. on 300f. mult (No. 696)	6·00	1·30
957	**229**	75f. on 300f. mult	6·00	1·30
958	-	90f. on 300f. mult (No. 855)	6·25	1·40
959	-	90f. on 300f. mult (No. 697)	6·25	1·40
960	-	90f. on 300f. mult (No. 701)	6·75	1·40
961	**204**	75f. on 200f. mult (air)	4·50	1·30
962	-	75f. on 200f. mult (No. 825)	4·50	1·30
963	-	75f. on 300f. violet, red and mauve (No. 656)	4·50	1·30
964	-	75f. on 300f. mult (No. 878)	4·50	1·30
965	**239**	90f. on 500f. blue, yellow and brown	4·50	1·40
966	-	90f. on 500f. mult (No. 715)	4·50	1·40
967	-	90f. on 500f. mult (No. 843)	4·50	1·40

331 Sidon Merchant Ship (2nd century)

1984. Air. Ships.
968	**331**	90f. black, green & blue	1·30	60
969	-	125f. multicoloured	2·00	85

DESIGN—VERT: 125f. Sail merchantman *Wavetree*, 1895.

332 Emblem on Globe and Hands reaching for Cultural Symbols

1985. 15th Anniv of Cultural and Technical Co-operation Agency.
970 **332** 300f. multicoloured 3·25 1·20

333 Benin Arms

1985. Air. Postal Convention between Benin and Sovereign Military Order of Malta. Multicoloured.
971 75f. Type **333** 75 25
972 75f. Arms of Sovereign Military Order 75 25

334 Soviet Flag, Soldier and Tank

1985. 40th Anniv of End of Second World War.
973 **334** 100f. multicoloured

335 Teke Dance, Borgou

1985. Traditional Dances. Multicoloured.
974 75f. Type **335** 1·00 40
975 100f. Tipen ti dance, Atacora 1·30 60

1985. Various Dahomey Stamps optd **POPULAIRE DU BENIN** (985/6) or **REPUBLIQUE POPULAIRE DU BENIN** (others), Nos. 976/7 and 979/85 surch also.
976 **174** 15f. on 40f. mult (post) 2·75 60
977 **182** 25f. on 40f. brown, blue and violet (air) 1·20 60
978 **115** 40f. black, purple & bl 1·30 70
978a – 75f. on 85f. brown, blue and green (No. 468) 48·00 1·60
979 – 75f. on 85f. brown, blue and green (No. 482) 3·00 75
980 **135** 75f. on 100f. purple, violet and green 3·00 75
981 – 75f. on 125f. green, blue and purple (No. 509) 3·00 75
982 **127** 90f. on 20f. brown, blue and green 3·00 80
983 – 90f. on 150f. purple, blue & brown (No. 456) 3·00 80
984 – 90f. on 200f. green, red and blue (No. 438) 3·00 80
985 – 90f. on 200f. mult (No. 563) 3·00 80
986 – 150f. mult (No. 562) 3·50 1·00

338 Oil Rig

1985. Air. "Philexafrique" International Stamp Exhibition, Lome, Togo (1st issue). Multicoloured.
987 200f. Type **338** 2·30 1·50
988 200f. Footballers 2·30 1·50
See also Nos. 999/1000.

339 Emblem

1985. International Youth Year.
989 **339** 150f. multicoloured 1·40 75

340 Football between Globes

1985. World Cup Football Championship, Mexico (1986) (1st issue).
990 **340** 200f. multicoloured 1·80 95
See also No. 1015.

341 Boeing 727, Map and Emblem

1985. 25th Anniv of Aerial Navigation Security Agency for Africa and Malagasy.
991 **341** 150f. multicoloured 1·80 75

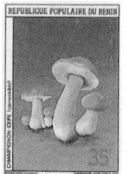

342 Boletus edulis

1985. Fungi. Multicoloured.
992 35f. Type **342** 1·50 45
993 40f. Amanita phalloides 1·80 75
994 100f. Paxillus involutus 4·50 1·70

343 Audubon and Arctic Skua ("Labbe Parasite")

1985. Birth Bicentenary of John J. Audubon (ornithologist). Multicoloured.
995 150f. Type **343** 3·00 1·50
996 300f. Audubon and oyster-catcher ("Huitrier Pie") 7·00 2·20

344 Emblem, Hands and Dove

1985. 40th Anniv of United Nations Organization and 25th Anniv of Benin's Membership.
997 **344** 250f. multicoloured 2·30 1·10

345 Stamps and Globe

1985. "Italia '85" International Stamp Exhibition, Rome.
998 **345** 100f. multicoloured 1·80 95

1985. "Philexafrique" International Stamp Exhibition, Lome, Togo (2nd issue). As Type **338**. Multicoloured.
999 250f. Forest and hand holding tools 4·25 1·80

1000 250f. Magnifying glass over judo stamp 3·00 1·50

1985. Various Dahomey stamps optd **Republique Populaire du Benin**. Nos. 1001/9 and 1011 surch also.
1001 – 75f. on 35f. mult (No. 596) (postage) 2·50 60
1002 – 90f. on 70f. mult-oured (No. 419) 2·50 65
1003 – 90f. on 140f. multicol-oured (No. 446) 2·50 65
1004 **113** 100f. on 40f. red, brown and green 1·90 65
1005 – 150f. on 45f. multicol-oured (No. 597) 2·10 80
1006 – 75f. on 70f. multicol-oured (No. 342) (air) 4·25 90
1007 – 75f. on 100f. multicol-oured (No. 251) 4·25 90
1008 **59** 75f. on 200f. mult 4·25 90
1009 – 90f. on 250f. multicol-oured (No. 272) 4·25 90
1010 **110** 100f. multicoloured 2·75 90
1011 – 150f. on 500f. multicol-oured (No. 252) 2·75 90
No. 1010 is surcharged on the unoverprinted unissued stamp subsequently issued as No. 422.

349 Church, Children playing and Nativity Scene

1985. Air. Christmas.
1012 **349** 500f. multicoloured 5·25 2·30

350 Emblem

1986. Tenth Anniv of African Parliamentary Union and Ninth Conference, Cotonou.
1013 **350** 100f. multicoloured 95 50

351 Halley, Comet and "Giotto" Space Probe

1986. Appearance of Halley's Comet.
1014 **351** 205f. multicoloured 3·00 1·50

352 Footballers

1986. World Cup Football Championship, Mexico (2nd issue). Multicoloured.
1015 **352** 500f. Footballers 4·50 2·30

353 Dead and Healthy Trees

1986. Anti-desertification Campaign.
1016 **353** 150f. multicoloured 1·50 70

354 Amazone

1986
1017 **354** 100f. blue 75 30
1018 **354** 150f. purple 1·30 50

355 Haemanthus

1986. Flowers. Multicoloured.
1019 100f. Type **355** 1·10 70
1020 205f. Hemerocallis 2·75 1·20

356 "Inachis io, Aglais urticae and Nymphalis antiopa

1986. Butterflies. Multicoloured.
1021 150f. Type **356** 3·00 1·30
1022 150f. Anthocharis cardamines, Papilio machaon and Cynthia cardui 3·00 1·30

1986. Various stamps of Dahomey surch **Republique Populaire du** Benin and new value.
1024 – 150f. on 100f. mult (444) (postage) 55·00 2·75
1025 – 15f. on 85f. mult (600) (air) 33·00 2·75
1026 – 25f. on 200f. mult (432) 55·00 2·75
1027 **150** 25f. on 200f. deep green, violet and green 55·00 2·75
1030 **175** 100f. purple, indigo & bl 55·00 2·75
1031 **128** 150f. on 100f. blue, violet and red

358 Statue and Buildings

1986. Centenary of Statue of Liberty.
1032 **358** 250f. multicoloured 3·00 1·20

359 Bust of King Behanzin

1986. King Behanzin.
1033 **359** 440f. multicoloured 5·00 2·20
For design in smaller size, see Nos. 1101/4.

360 Family with Crib, Church and Nativity Scene

1986. Air. Christmas.
1034 **360** 300f. multicoloured 5·25 1·80

361 Rainbow and Douglas DC-10

1986. Air. 25th Anniv of Air Afrique.
1035 **361** 100f. multicoloured 1·00 50

362 Emblem around Map in Cog

1987. Brazil Culture Week, Cotonou.
1036	**362**	150f. multicoloured	1·40	65

363 Cotonou Centre for the Blind and Partially Sighted

1987. Rotary International 910 District Conference, Cotonou.
1037	**363**	300f. multicoloured	3·25	1·40

1987. Various stamps of Dahomey optd **Republique Populaire du Benin**. Nos. 1038/9 and 1042/53 surch also.
1038	**129**	10f. on 65f. black, violet and red (postage)		
1039	-	15f. on 100f. red, blue and green (434)	43·00	1·80
1040	**98**	40f. green, blue and brown	55·00	2·75
1042	-	150f. on 200f. mult (560)		
1043	**144**	10f. on 65f. black, yellow & purple (air)		
1046	-	25f. on 150f. mult (487)	55·00	2·75
1047	-	30f. on 300f. mult (602)		
1048	**140**	40f. on 15f. purple, green and blue	47·00	2·75
1049	-	40f. on 100f. mult (453)	43·00	2·75
1051	-	50f. on 140f. mult (601)	55·00	2·75
1052	-	50f. on 500f. mult (252)	55·00	2·75
1053	-	70f. on 250f. mult (462)	55·00	2·75
1054	-	80f. mult (286)	55·00	2·75
1055	-	100f. mult (429)	55·00	2·75
1055a	-	100f. mult (447)	55·00	2·75

365 De Dion-Bouton and Trepardoux Steam Tricycle and Ford Coupe

1987. Centenary of Motor Car. Multicoloured.
1058	150f. Type **365**		1·50	70
1059	300f. Daimler motor carriage, 1886 and Mercedes Benz W124 series saloon		3·25	1·40

366 Baptism in the Python Temple

1987. Ritual Ceremonies.
1060	**366**	100f. multicoloured	1·50	70

367 Shrimp

1987. Shellfish. Multicoloured.
1061	100f. Type **367**		1·30	75
1062	150f. Crab		2·00	1·00

368 G. Hansen and R. Follereau (leprosy pioneers) and Patients

1987. Anti-leprosy Campaign.
1063	**368**	200f. multicoloured	2·50	1·20

369 Crop-spraying and Locusts

1987. Anti-locust Campaign.
1064	**369**	100f. multicoloured	1·20	65

370 Fisherman and Farmer

1987. Air. Tenth Anniv of International Agricultural Development Fund.
1065	**370**	500f. multicoloured	4·50	2·40

371 Nativity Scene in Moon and Father Christmas giving Sweets to Crowd

1987. Christmas.
1066	**371**	150f. multicoloured	1·50	85

372 Rally

1988. 15th Anniv (1987) of Start of Benin Revolution.
1067	**372**	100f. multicoloured	£100	2·75

1988. Various stamps surch. (a) Stamps of Dahomey surch **Populaire du Benin** (1081c) or **Republique Populaire du Benin** (others).
1068	-	5f. on 3f. black and blue (173) (postage)	55·00	2·75
1069	-	20f. on 100f. mult (506)	55·00	2·75
1071	-	25f. on 100f. mult (576)	55·00	2·75
1073	-	50f. on 45f. mult (320)	65·00	2·75
1074	**178**	55f. on 200f. olive, brown and green	95·00	2·75
1075a	**178**	125f. on 100f. mult (557)		
1076	**116**	10f. on 50f. black, orange and blue (air)	55·00	2·75
1077	**161**	15f. on 150f. red and black	55·00	2·75
1078	-	25f. on 100f. mult (526)	75·00	2·75
1079	**156**	25f. on 100f. blue, brown and violet	75·00	2·75
1079a	**153**	40f. on 35f. mult	55·00	2·75
1080	-	40f. on 100f. mult (495)	55·00	
1081	**162**	40f. on 10f. red, brown and blue	55·00	2·75
1081a	**148**	100f. brown and green	55·00	2·75
1081b	**181**	125f. on 75f. lilac, red and green	45·00	2·75
1081c	-	125f. on 150f. blue and purple (541)		2·75
1082	-	125f. on 250f. mult (491)	55·00	2·75
1082a	-	125f. red and brown (540)	55·00	2·75

1083	-	190f. on 250f. brown, green and red (594)	90·00	
1084	-	1000f. on 150f. multicoloured (545)	55·00	2·75

(b) No. 618 of Benin surch **Republique Populaire du Benin**.
1085		10f. on 60f. on 2f. mult	55·00	2·75

(c) Stamps of Benin surch only.
1086	**359**	125f. on 440f. mult (postage)		
1087	**338**	125f. on 200f. mult (air)		
1088	-	190f. on 250f. mult (999)	90·00	
1089	-	190f. on 250f. mult (1000)		

375 Hands holding Pot Aloft

1988. 25th Anniv of Organization of African Unity.
1094	**375**	125f. multicoloured	1·20	50

376 Resuscitation of Man pulled from River

1988. 125th Anniv of Red Cross Movement.
1095	**376**	200f. multicoloured	3·25	1·60

377 King

1988. 20th Death Anniv of Martin Luther King (Civil Rights leader).
1096	**377**	200f. multicoloured	2·00	95

378 Scout and Camp

1988. First Benin Scout Jamboree, Savalou.
1097	**378**	125f. multicoloured	1·20	55

379 Healthy Family and Health Care

1988. 40th Anniv of W.H.O. and Tenth Anniv of "Health for All by 2000" Declaration.
1098	**379**	175f. multicoloured	1·50	80

380 Dugout Canoes and Houses

1988. Ganvie (lake village). Multicoloured.
1099	125f. Type **380**		1·20	55
1100	190f. Boatman and houses		1·80	85

1988. As T **359** but smaller (17×24 mm).
1101	**359**	40f. black	30	15
1102	**359**	125f. red	1·00	45
1103	**359**	190f. blue	1·50	65
1104	**359**	220f. green	1·80	80

381 Adoration of the Magi

1988. Air. Christmas.
1105	**381**	500f. multicoloured	4·50	2·20

382 Offering to Hebiesso, God of Thunder

1988. Ritual Ceremony.
1106	**382**	125f. multicoloured	1·20	55

383 Roseate Tern

1989. Endangered Animals. Roseate Tern. Multicoloured.
1107	10f. Type **383**		1·10	70
1108	15f. Tern with fish		1·10	70
1109	50f. Tern on rocks		2·50	1·40
1110	125f. Tern flying		5·00	2·75

384 Eiffel Tower

1989. Centenary of Eiffel Tower.
1111	**384**	190f. multicoloured	2·50	1·10

386 Tractor, Map and Pump

1989. 30th Anniv of Agriculture Development Council.
1113	**386**	75f. multicoloured	95·00	

387 Symbols of Revolution and France 1950 National Relief Fund Stamps

1989. Bicentenary of French Revolution and "Philexfrance 89" International Stamp Exhibition, Paris.
1114	**387**	190f. multicoloured	2·50	1·50

388 Burbot

1989. Fish. Multicoloured.
1115	125f. Type **388**		1·30	60
1116	190f. Northern pike and Atlantic salmon		2·00	95

389 Circuit Breaker,
Illuminated Road and
Solar Energy Complex

1989. 20th Anniv of Benin Electricity Community.
1117 **389** 125f. multicoloured 1·30 60

390 Lion within
Wreath

1989. Death Centenary of King Glele.
1118 **390** 190f. multicoloured 1·70 90

391 Nativity

1989. Christmas.
1119 **391** 200f. multicoloured 1·80 95

392 Anniversary Emblem
and Means of
Communications

1990. Centenary of Postal and Telecommunications
Ministry (1st issue).
1120 **392** 125f. multicoloured 1·30 60
See also No. 1127.

393 Oranges

1990. Fruit and Flowers. Multicoloured.
1121 60f. Type **393** 75 40
1122 190f. Kaufmannia tulips (vert) 2·00 95
1123 250f. Cashew nuts (vert) 2·50 1·30

394 Launch of "Apollo 11"
and Footprint on Moon

1990. 21st Anniv of First Manned Moon Landing.
1124 **394** 190f. multicoloured 1·70 85

395 Footballers

1990. World Cup Football Championship, Italy.
Multicoloured.
1125 125f. Type **395** 1·20 60
1126 190f. Mascot holding torch and
 pennant (vert) 1·90 85

396 Balloons,
Emblem and Means
of Communication

1990. Centenary of Postal and Telecommunications
Ministry (2nd issue).
1127 **396** 150f. multicoloured 1·40 65

1990. World Cup Finalists. No. 1125 optd **FINALE R.F.A.-
ARGENTINE 1-0.**
1128 **395** 125f. multicoloured 1·20 60

398 De Gaulle

1990. Birth Centenary of Charles de Gaulle (French
statesman) (1st issue).
1129 **398** 190f. multicoloured 2·00 1·20
See also No. 1160.

399 "Galileo" Space Probe
orbiting Jupiter

1990. Space Exploration.
1130 **399** 100f. multicoloured 1·00 60

400 Nativity

1990. Christmas.
1131 **400** 200f. multicoloured 1·90 1·20

401 Hands
pointing to Scales
of Justice

1990. National Conference of Active Forces.
1132 **401** 125f. multicoloured

406 Different Cultures and
Emblem

1991. African Tourism Year.
1150 **406** 190f. multicoloured 1·90 1·20

407 Tennis Player

1991. Cent of French Open Tennis Championships.
1151 **407** 125f. multicoloured 1·50 95

408 Flag and Arms

1991. 31st Anniv of Independence.
1152 **408** 125f. multicoloured 1·30 50

1991. "Riccione 91" Stamp Fair. No. 1130 optd "**Riccione
91**".
1153 **399** 100f. multicoloured 95 70

410 Adoration of the Magi

1991. Christmas.
1154 **410** 125f. multicoloured 1·30 60

411 Guelede Dancer

1991
1155 **411** 190f. multicoloured 2·00 80

412 Mozart

1991. Death Bicentenary of Wolfgang Amadeus Mozart
(composer).
1156 **412** 1000f. multicoloured 10·00 5·75

413 Slave in Chains and
Route Map

1992. 500th Anniv of Discovery of America by Columbus.
1157 **413** 500f. black, brown & bl 4·50 3·00
1158 - 1000f. multicoloured 9·00 5·75
MS1159 133×93 mm. Nos. 1157/8 15·00 14·00
DESIGN—HORIZ: 1000f. Columbus landing at Guanahami,
Bahamas.

1992. Birth Centenary (1990) of Charles de Gaulle (French
statesman) (2nd issue). As No. 1129 but value
changed.
1160 **398** 300f. multicoloured 3·00 1·60

414 Child, Produce
and Emblems

1992. International Nutrition Conference, Rome.
1161 **414** 190f. multicoloured 1·80 1·20

415 Pope John
Paul II

1993. Papal Visit.
1162 **415** 190f. multicoloured 2·00 1·10

416 Emblem and
Voodoo Culture

1993. "Ouidah 92" Voodoo Culture Festival.
1163 **416** 125f. multicoloured 1·20 60

417 Well and
Blue-throated Roller

1993. Possotome Artesian Well.
1164 **417** 125f. multicoloured 2·20 1·40

418 Map, Clasped Hands and
Flags of Member Countries

1993. 30th Anniv of Organization of African Unity.
1165 **418** 125f. multicoloured 1·20 70

419 John F. Kennedy (President of
United States, 1961–63)

1993. Death Anniversaries. Multicoloured.
1166 190f. Type **419** (30th anniv) 1·90 1·10
1167 190f. Dr. Martin Luther King
 (American civil rights cam-
 paigner, 25th anniv) (vert) 2·00 1·10

1993. Stamps of Dahomey variously optd or surch. (a)
REPUBLIQUE DU BENIN.
1167a **139** 5f. multicoloured
 (postage) 80·00 2·75
1170 **108** 50f. on 1f. multicoloured
 (617) 55·00 2·75
1171 **113** 80f. on 40f. red, brown
 and green 43·00 2·75
1173 **113** 135f. on 20f. black, green
 and red (190) 95·00
1175 **113** 135f. on 30f. black,
 brown and violet
 (472) 55·00
1177 **107** 135f. on 40f. mult 38·00
1179 - 135f. on 60f. olive, red
 and purple (181) 55·00 2·75
1181 - 200f. on 100f. mult (322) 65·00 2·75
1186 - 15f. on 40f. mult (458)
 (air) 47·00 2·75
1190 **126** 100f. multicoloured 55·00 2·75
1190a **119** 125f. on 40f. mult 23·00 2·75

1191	-	125f. on 65f. red and blue (552)	55·00	2·75
1201	-	200f. on 250f. mult (569)	47·00	

(b) DU BENIN.

1207	60	5f. on 1f. multicoloured (postage)	65·00	2·75
1208	-	10f. on 3f. black and blue (173)	55·00	
1211	-	25f. multicoloured (441)	47·00	2·75
1220	-	135f. on 3f. mult (274)	80·00	
1223	-	20f. on 200f. mult (451) (air)	55·00	
1225	-	25f. on 85f. mult (600)	47·00	2·75
1227	140	30f. on 15f. purple, green and blue	38·00	
1231	-	125f. on 70f. mult (383)	65·00	2·75
1235	-	150f. purple, blue and brown (456)	80·00	
1236	-	150f. multicoloured (527)	55·00	2·75
1239	150	200f. green, violet and emerald	65·00	2·75
1242	-	200f. on 150f. mult (562)	95·00	
1243	179	300f. multicoloured	55·00	2·75

(c) BENIN.

1257	-	25f. on 500f. brown, red and green (592) (air)	47·00	2·75
1258	-	30f. on 200f. mult (528)	24·00	2·75
1260a	-	100f. brown, green and blue (522)	55·00	2·75
1261	116	125f. on 50f. black, orange and blue	43·00	2·75
1263a	-	190f. on 200f. mult (478)	£190	2·75
1266	-	300f. brn, red & bl (591)	70·00	2·75

422 Conference Emblem

1994. UNESCO Conference on the Slave Route, Ouidah.

1275	**422**	300f. multicoloured	47·00	2·75

423 World Map

1994. International Year of the Family.

1276	**423**	200f. multicoloured	75·00	2·75

425 Water Polo

1995. Olympic Games, Atlanta (1996) (1st issue). Multicoloured.

1278	**425**	45f. Type **425**	20	20
1279		50f. Throwing the javelin (vert)	30	25
1280		75f. Weightlifting (vert)	45	35
1281		100f. Tennis (vert)	60	50
1282		135f. Baseball (vert)	75	55
1283		200f. Synchronised swimming (vert)	1·30	1·00
MS1284 60×79 mm. 300f. Diving (31×39 mm)			2·40	2·20

See also Nos. 1347/**MS**1353.

426 Paddle-steamer

1995. Ships. Multicoloured.

1285	**426**	40f. Type **426**	25	15
1286		50f. *Charlotte* (paddle steamer)	30	15
1287		75f. *Citta di Catania* (Italian liner)	45	20
1288		100f. *Mountbatten* SR-N4 (hovercraft)	45	25
1289		135f. *Queen Elizabeth 2* (liner)	85	30
1290		200f. *Matsu-Nef* (Japanese nuclear-powered freighter)	1·30	60
MS1291 72×58 mm. 300f. *Savannah* (sail/paddle-steamer) (39×31 mm)			2·40	2·40

427 Chimpanzee

1995. Primates. Multicoloured.

1292		50f. Type **427**	30	15
1293		75f. Mandrill	45	20
1294		100f. Colobus	60	25
1295		135f. Barbary ape	85	30
1296		200f. Hamadryas baboon	1·30	70
MS1297 93×72 mm. 300f. Yellow baboons (31×39 mm)			2·50	2·10

428 Tabby Shorthair

1995. Cats. Multicoloured.

1298		40f. Type **428**	25	15
1299		50f. Sorrel Abyssinian ("Ruddy red")	30	15
1300		75f. White Persian long-hair	45	20
1301		100f. Seal colourpoint	60	25
1302		135f. Tabby point	85	30
1303		200f. Black shorthair	1·30	60
MS1304 82×86 mm. 300f. Kitten climbing out of basket (38×31 mm)			2·50	2·50

429 German Shepherd

1995. Dogs. Multicoloured.

1305		40f. Type **429**	25	15
1306		50f. Beagle	30	15
1307		75f. Great dane	45	20
1308		100f. Boxer	60	25
1309		135f. Pointer	85	30
1310		200f. Long-haired fox terrier	1·30	60
MS1311 80×70 mm. 300f. Schnauzer			2·50	2·50

430 Arms

1995

1312	**430**	135f. multicoloured	85	25
1313	**430**	150f. multicoloured	95	55
1314	**430**	200f. multicoloured	1·30	55

See also Nos. 1458 and 1480/2.

431 Lion

1995. Mammals. Multicoloured.

1315		50f. Type **431**	30	15
1316		75f. African buffalo	45	20
1317		100f. Chimpanzee	65	25
1318		135f. Impala	85	30
1319		200f. Cape ground squirrel (horiz)	1·30	70
MS1320 80×60 mm. 300f. African elephant (31×39 mm)			2·50	2·50

432 Hawfinches

1995. Birds and their Young. Multicoloured.

1321		40f. Type **432**	25	15
1322		50f. Spotted-necked doves	30	15
1323		75f. Peregrine falcons	45	20
1324		100f. Blackburnian warblers	60	25
1325		135f. Black-headed gulls	80	30
1326		200f. Eastern white pelican	1·20	60

433 *Dracunculus vulgaris*

1995. Flowers. Multicoloured.

1327		40f. Type **433**	25	15
1328		50f. Daffodil	30	15
1329		75f. Amaryllis	45	20
1330		100f. Water-lily	60	25
1331		135f. *Chrysanthemum carinatum*	80	30
1332		200f. Iris	1·20	60

434 Lynx

1995. Big Cats and their Young. Multicoloured.

1333		40f. Type **434**	25	15
1334		50f. Pumas	30	15
1335		75f. Cheetahs	45	20
1336		100f. Leopards	60	25
1337		135f. Tigers	80	30
1338		200f. Lions	1·30	60

435 *Angraecum sesquipedale*

1995. Orchids. Multicoloured.

1339		40f. Type **435**	25	15
1340		50f. *Polystachya virgínea*	30	15
1341		75f. *Disa uniflora*	45	20
1342		100f. *Ansellia africana*	60	25
1343		135f. *Angraecum eichlerianum*	95	30
1344		200f. *Jumellea confusa*	1·30	60

436 Emblem

1995. Sixth Francophone Summit, Cotonou.

1345	**436**	150f. multicoloured	85	55
1346	**436**	200f. multicoloured	1·10	80

437 Diving

1996. Olympic Games, Atlanta (2nd issue). Multicoloured.

1347		40f. Type **437**	30	25
1348		50f. Tennis	35	30
1349		75f. Running	45	35
1350		100f. Gymnastics	60	50
1351		135f. Weightlifting	90	65
1352		200f. Shooting	1·30	1·00
MS1353 65×65 mm. 1000f. Water polo (31×39 mm)			5·25	4·00

438 Player with Ball

1996. World Cup Football Championship, France (1998) (1st issue).

1354	**438**	40f. multicoloured	25	20
1355	-	50f. multicoloured	25	20
1356	-	75f. multicoloured	50	40
1357	-	100f. multicoloured	60	50
1358	-	135f. multicoloured	1·00	65
1359	-	200f. multicoloured	1·30	1·10
MS1360 88×63 mm. 1000f. Tackle (31×39 mm)			4·75	4·00

DESIGNS: 50f. to 1000f. Different players. See also Nos. 1614/**MS**1620.

439 Small Striped Swallowtail

1996. Butterflies. Multicoloured.

1361		40f. Type **439**	25	20
1362		50f. Red admiral	25	20
1363		75f. Common blue	45	35
1364		100f. African monarch	55	45
1365		135f. Painted lady	95	60
1366		200f. *Argus celbulina ortbitulus*	1·30	1·00
MS1367 60×70 mm. 1000f. Foxy charaxes (*Charaxes jasius*) (31×39 mm)			4·50	4·00

440 Dancer

1996. "China '96" International Stamp Exhibition, Peking. Multicoloured.

1368		40f. Type **440**	35	30
1369		50f. Exhibition emblem	40	35
1370		75f. Water-lily	60	50
1371		100f. Temple of Heaven, Peking	85	75

Nos. 1368/71 were issued together, *se-tenant*, forming a composite design.

441 Emblem

1996. 15th Convention of Lions Club International, Cotonou.

1372	**441**	135f. multicoloured	1·10	75
1373	**441**	150f. multicoloured	1·10	80
1374	**441**	200f. multicoloured	1·50	1·10
1457	**441**	100f. multicoloured	55	25

442 Holy Family of Rouvre (Raphael)

1996. Christmas. Multicoloured.

1375		40f. Type **442**	25	20
1376		50f. *The Holy Family* (Raphael)	25	20
1377		75f. *St. John the Baptist* (Bartolome Murillo)	50	40
1378		100f. *The Virgin of the Scales* (Leonardo da Vinci)	65	50
1379		135f. *The Virgin and Child* (Gerhard David)	90	65
1380		200f. *Adoration of the Magi* (Juan Mayno)	1·30	1·10

MS1381 99×74 mm. 1000f. *Rest during the Flight into Egypt* (Murillo) (39×31 mm) 5·25 3·75

443 *Thermopylae* (clipper) (inscr "Thermopyles")

1996. Ships. Multicoloured.
1382	40f. Type **443**	20	15
1383	50f. Barque	25	20
1384	75f. *Nightingale* (full-rigged ship)	45	30
1385	100f. Opium clipper	50	40
1386	135f. *Torrens* (full-rigged ship)	80	60
1387	200f. English tea clipper	1·20	1·00

MS1388 78×58 mm. 1000f. Opium clipper (31×39 mm) 5·25 4·00

444 Serval

1996. Big Cats. Multicoloured.
1389	40f. Type **444**	25	20
1390	50f. Golden cat	25	20
1391	75f. Ocelot	45	35
1392	100f. Bobcat	55	45
1393	135f. Leopard cat	95	60
1394	200f. "Felis euptilura"	1·30	1·00

MS1395 80×64 mm. 1000f. Clouded leopard (*Neofelis nebulosa*) (31×39 mm) 5·25 4·00

445 Hurdler and Gold Medal

1996. Centenary of Issue by Greece of First Olympic Stamps. Multicoloured.
1396	40f. Type **445**	35	30
1397	50f. Hurdler and Olympic flames	40	35
1398	75f. Pierre de Coubertin (founder of modern Olympics) and map showing south-west U.S.A.	60	50
1399	100f. Map showing south-east U.S.A.	85	75

Nos. 1396/9 were issued together, *se-tenant*, forming a composite design.

446 Running

1996. "Olymphilex '96" Olympics and Sports Stamp Exhibition, Atlanta. Multicoloured.
1400	40f. Type **446**	25	20
1401	50f. Canoeing	25	20
1402	75f. Gymnastics	50	40
1403	100f. Football	60	50
1404	135f. Tennis	1·00	65
1405	200f. Baseball	1·40	1·10

MS1406 65×95 mm. 1000f. Basketball (31×39 mm) 5·25 4·00

447 *Parodia subterranea*

1996. Flowering Cacti. Multicoloured.
1407	40f. Type **447**	25	20
1408	50f. Astrophytum senile	25	20
1409	75f. Echinocereus melanocentrus	50	40
1410	100f. Turbinicarpus klinkerianus	60	50
1411	135f. Astrophytum capricorne	1·00	65
1412	200f. Nelloydia grandiflora	1·40	1·10

448 Chestnut Horse

1996. Horses. Multicoloured.
1413	40f. Type **448**	25	20
1414	50f. Horse on hillside	25	20
1415	75f. Foal by fence	45	35
1416	100f. Mother and foal	55	45
1417	135f. Pair of horses	95	60
1418	200f. Grey horse (horiz)	1·30	1·00

449 Longisquama

1996. Prehistoric Animals. Multicoloured.
1419	40f. Type **449**	25	20
1420	50f. Dimorphodon	25	20
1421	75f. Dunkleosteus (horiz)	45	35
1422	100f. Eryops (horiz)	55	45
1423	135f. Peloneustes (horiz)	85	60
1424	200f. Deinonychus (horiz)	1·30	1·00

450 Ivory-billed Woodpecker

1996. Birds. Multicoloured.
1425	40f. Type **450**	25	20
1426	50f. Grey-necked bald crow	25	20
1427	75f. Kakapo	45	35
1428	100f. Puerto Rican amazon	55	45
1429	135f. Japanese crested ibis	95	60
1430	200f. California condor	1·30	1·00

MS1431 65×91 mm. 1000f. Blue bird of paradise (*Paradisaea rudolphi*) (31×39 mm) 5·25 4·00

451 Golden Tops

1996. Fungi. Multicoloured.
1432	40f. Type **451**	25	20
1433	50f. Psilocybe zapotecorum	25	20
1434	75f. Psilocybe mexicana	55	40
1435	100f. Conocybe siligineoides	65	50
1436	135f. Psilocybe caerulescens mazatecorum	1·00	65
1437	200f. Psilocybe caerulescens nigripes	1·40	1·10

MS1438 93×71 mm. 1000f. *Psilocybe aztecorum* (39×31 mm) 5·25 4·00

452 Impala

1996. Mammals. Multicoloured.
1439	40f. Type **452**	25	20
1440	50f. Waterbuck	25	20
1441	75f. African buffalo	45	35
1442	100f. Blue wildebeest	55	45
1443	135f. Okapi	85	60
1444	200f. Greater kudu	1·30	1·00

453 White Whale

1996. Marine Mammals. Multicoloured.
1445	40f. Type **453**	25	20
1446	50f. Bottle-nosed dolphin	25	20
1447	75f. Blue whale	45	35
1448	100f. "Eubalaena australis"	55	45
1449	135f. "Gramphidelphis griseus"	95	60
1450	200f. Killer whale	1·30	1·00

454 Grey Angelfish

1996. Fish. Multicoloured.
1451	50f. Type **454**	30	25
1452	75f. Sail-finned tang (horiz)	40	35
1453	100f. Golden trevally (horiz)	60	45
1454	135f. Pyramid butterflyfish (horiz)	85	60
1455	200f. Racoon butterflyfish (horiz)	1·30	1·00

MS1456 80×61 mm. 1000f. Parrotfish (horiz) 5·25 4·00

1996. Arms. Dated "1996".
1458	**430**	100f. multicoloured	65	25

1996. Stamps of Benin variously surch.
1469	**311**	15f. on 185f. mult (postage)	65·00	2·75
1470	**379**	25f. on 175f. mult		
1473	**359**	50f. on 220f. green (1104)	65·00	2·75
1479	**414**	150f. on 190f. mult		
1480	**415**	150f. on 190f. mult		
1484	**412**	250f. on 1000f. mult	65·00	2·75
1494	**193**	40f. on 210f. red, brown and green (air)	65·00	2·75
1495	–	40f. on 210f. purple, blue and yellow (792)		
1499	–	150f. on 500f. red, ultramarine and green (657)		

1996. Stamps of Dahomey variously optd or surch. (a) **Republique de Benin** (1510, 1516, 1519, 1522, 1526/9, 1535, 1544, 1556, 1558 and 1568) or **REPUBLIQUE DU BENIN** (others).
1510		35f. on 85f. brown, orange and green (493) (postage)		
1511		125f. on 100f. violet, red and black (510)		
1516	**85**	150f. on 30f. mult		
1519	**113**	150f. on 40f. red, brown and green		
1522	–	150f. on 45f. mult (597)		
1526	–	35f. on 100f. deep blue and blue (326) (air)		
1527	–	35f. on 100f. on 200f. multicoloured (409)		
1528	–	35f. on 125f. green, blue and light blue (553)		
1529	–	35f. on 300f. brown, red and blue (591)		
1535	–	150f. multicoloured (527)		
1544	**112**	150f. on 40f. multicoloured		
1556	–	150f. on 110f. mult (386)		
1558	–	150f. on 120f. mult (404)		
1568	–	200f. on 500f. mult (252)		

		(b) **DU BENIN**.		
1578		35f. on 125f. brown and green (540) (air)		
1579		125f. on 65f. mult (465)		
1580	**168**	135f. on 35f. mult		
		(c) **BENIN**.		
1587	**68**	150f. on 30f. mult (post)	75·00	2·75
1591	**68**	25f. on 85f. mult (600) (air)		

455 Grenadier, Glassenapps Regiment

1997. Military Uniforms. Multicoloured.
1600	135f. Type **455**	60	30
1601	150f. Officer, Von Groben's Regiment	80	35
1602	200f. Private, Dohna's Regiment	1·00	60
1603	270f. Artilleryman	1·30	70
1604	300f. Cavalry trooper	1·60	90
1605	400f. Trooper, Mollendorf's Dragoons	2·10	1·30

MS1606 90×108 mm. 1000f. Standard bearer (31×39 mm) 5·25 4·00

456 Reid Macleod Gas-turbine Locomotive, 1920

1997. Railway Locomotives. Multicoloured.
1607	135f. Type **456**	60	30
1608	150f. Class O5 steam locomotive, 1935, Germany	80	40
1609	200f. Locomotive "Silver Fox", Great Britain	1·00	55
1610	270f. Class "Merchant Navy" locomotive, 1941, Great Britain	1·30	75
1611	300f. Diesel locomotive, 1960, Denmark	1·60	80
1612	400f. GM Type diesel locomotive, 1960	2·10	1·10

MS1613 94×64 mm. 1000f. "Coronation", 1937 (39×31 mm) 5·25 4·00

No. 1607 is wrongly inscr "Reid Maclead 1920".

457 Footballer and Map

1997. World Cup Football Championship, France (1998) (2nd issue).
1614	**457**	135f. multicoloured	60	30
1615	–	150f. multicoloured	80	35
1616	–	200f. multicoloured	1·00	60
1617	–	270f. multicoloured	1·30	70
1618	–	300f. mult (horiz)	1·60	90
1619	–	400f. mult (horiz)	2·10	1·30

MS1620 107×83 mm. 1000f. multicoloured (39×31 mm) 5·25 4·00

DESIGNS: 135f. to 1000f. Each showing map of France and player.

458 Arms

1997. T **430** redrawn as T **458**. Dated "1997".
1621	**458**	135f. multicoloured	70	25
1622	**458**	150f. multicoloured	1·00	60
1623	**458**	200f. multicoloured	1·20	60

459 Horse's Head

1997. Horses. Multicoloured.

1624	135f. Type **459**	70	30
1625	150f. Bay horse	80	45
1626	200f. Chestnut horse looking forward	1·00	55
1627	270f. Chestnut horse looking backwards	1·30	70
1628	300f. Black horse	1·70	80
1629	400f. Profile of horse	2·10	1·00
MS1630 84×109 mm. 1000f. Bay horse with white nose		5·25	4·00

460 Irish Setter

1997. Dogs. Multicoloured.

1631	135f. Type **460**	60	30
1632	150f. Saluki	80	45
1633	200f. Dobermann pinscher	1·00	55
1634	270f. Siberian husky	1·60	70
1635	300f. Basenji	1·60	80
1636	400f. Boxer	2·30	1·00
MS1637 110×90 mm. 1000f. Rhodesian ridgeback (31×39 mm)		5·25	4·00

461 Phalaenopsis penetrate

1997. Orchids. Multicoloured.

1638	135f. Type **461**	70	35
1639	150f. Phalaenopsis "Golden Sands"	80	45
1640	200f. Phalaenopsis "Sun Spots"	1·00	55
1641	270f. Phalaenopsis fuscata	1·70	70
1642	300f. Phalaenopsis christi floyd	1·70	85
1643	400f. Phalaenopsis cayanne	2·50	1·10
MS1644 99×99 mm. 1000f. Phalaenopsis "Janet Kuhn" (31×39 mm)		5·25	4·00

462 Buick Model C Tourer, 1905

1997. Motor Cars. Multicoloured.

1645	135f. Type **462**	70	30
1646	150f. Ford model A tonneau, 1903	80	45
1647	200f. Stanley steamer tourer, 1913	1·00	60
1648	270f. Stoddar-Dayton tourer, 1911	1·30	70
1649	300f. Cadillac convertible sedan, 1934	1·70	85
1650	400f. Cadillac convertible sedan, 1931	2·10	1·10
MS1651 112×85 mm. 1000f. Ford, 1928 (39×31 mm)		5·25	4·00

463 Northern Bullfinch

1997. Birds. Multicoloured.

1652	135f. Type **463**	60	30
1653	150f. Spruce siskin	80	40
1654	200f. Ring ousel	1·00	55
1655	270f. Crested tit	1·30	70
1656	300f. Spotted nutcracker	1·60	80
1657	400f. Nightingale	2·10	1·10
MS1658 107×87 mm. 1000f. Yellow wagtail (31×39 mm)		5·25	4·00

464 Faucaria lupina

1997. Cacti. Multicoloured.

1659	135f. Type **464**	60	30
1660	150f. Conophytum bilobun	80	45
1661	200f. Lithops aucampiae	1·00	60
1662	270f. Lithops helmutii	1·30	75
1663	300f. Stapelia grandiflora	1·60	80
1664	400f. Lithops fulviceps	2·10	1·20
MS1665 109×90 mm. 1000f. Pleiospilos willowmorensis (31×38 mm)		5·25	4·00

465 Egyptian Merchant Ship

1997. Ancient Sailing Ships. Multicoloured.

1666	135f. Type **465**	60	30
1667	150f. Greek merchant ship	80	40
1668	200f. Phoenician galley	1·00	55
1669	270f. Roman merchant ship	1·30	70
1670	300f. Norman knarr	1·60	80
1671	400f. Mediterranean sailing ship	2·10	1·00
MS1672 109×89 mm. 1000f. English kogge of Richard II's reign (28×36 mm)		5·25	4·00

466 Black-tipped Grouper

1997. Fish. Multicoloured.

1673	135f. Type **466**	60	30
1674	150f. Cardinal fish	75	40
1675	200f. Indo-Pacific humpheaded parrotfish	1·00	55
1676	270f. Regal angelfish	1·30	70
1677	300f. Wrasse	1·60	80
1678	400f. Hawkfish	2·10	1·00
MS1679 109×90 mm. 1000f. Hogfish (39×31 mm)		5·25	4·00

467 Emblem

1997. Tenth Anniv of African Petroleum Producers' Association.

1680	**467** 135f. multicoloured	60	30
1681	**467** 200f. multicoloured	1·00	55
1682	**467** 300f. multicoloured	1·50	80
1683	**467** 500f. multicoloured	2·75	1·40

468 Caesar's Mushroom

1997. Fungi. Multicoloured.

1684	135f. Type **468**	60	30
1685	150f. Slimy-banded cort	80	40
1686	200f. Amanita bisporigera	1·00	55
1687	270f. The blusher	1·30	70
1688	300f. Cracked green russula	1·60	80
1689	400f. Strangulated amanita	2·10	1·00
MS1690 90×110 mm. 1000f. Fly agaric (31×37 mm)		5·25	4·00

469 Puffing Billy, 1813

1997. Steam Railway Locomotives. Multicoloured.

1691	135f. Type **469**	60	30
1692	150f. Rocket, 1829	80	40
1693	200f. Royal George, 1827	1·00	55
1694	270f. Novelty, 1829	1·30	70
1695	300f. Locomotion, 1825 (vert)	1·60	80
1696	400f. Sans Pareil, 1829 (vert)	2·10	1·00
MS1697 110×89 mm. 1000f. Richard Trevithick's locomotive, 1803 (39×31 mm)		5·25	4·00

470 Tephrocybe carbonaria

1998. Fungi. Multicoloured.

1698	135f. Type **470**	55	30
1699	150f. Butter mushroom	75	40
1700	200f. Oyster fungus	95	55
1701	270f. Hohenbuehelia geogenia	1·20	70
1702	300f. Bitter bolete	1·50	80
1703	400f. Lepiota leucothites	2·00	1·00
MS1704 108×90 mm. 1000f. Gymnoplius junonius		4·75	3·75

471 Philadelphia or "Double Deck", 1885

1998. Fire Engines. Multicoloured.

1705	135f. Type **471**	55	30
1706	150f. Veteran, 1850	75	40
1707	200f. Merryweather, 1894	95	55
1708	270f. 19 19th-century Hippomobile	1·20	70
1709	300f. Jeep Willy, 1948	1·50	80
1710	400f. Chevrolet 6400	2·00	1·00
MS1711 110×89 mm. 1000f. Foamite, 1952 (38×30 mm)		4·75	3·75

472 Uranite

1998. Minerals. Multicoloured.

1712	135f. Type **472**	55	30
1713	150f. Quartz	75	40
1714	200f. Aragonite	95	55
1715	270f. Malachite	1·20	70
1716	300f. Turquoise	1·50	80
1717	400f. Corundum	2·00	1·00
MS1718 89×109 mm. 1000f. Marble (short side as base)		4·75	3·75

473 Locomotive

1998. Steam Railway Locomotives. Multicoloured.

1719	135f. Type **473**	55	30
1720	150f. Green locomotive	75	40
1721	200f. Brown locomotive	95	55
1722	270f. Lilac locomotive	1·20	70
1723	300f. Toledo Furnace Co No. 1	1·50	80
1724	400f. No. 1 Helvetia	2·00	1·00
MS1725 109×86 mm. Shelby Steel Tube Co. Locomotive (39×31 mm)		4·75	3·75

474 Diana, Princess of Wales

1998. First Death Anniv of Diana, Princess of Wales. Multicoloured.

1726	135f. Type **474**	55	35
1727	150f. Wearing pink dress	75	40
1728	200f. Wearing beige jacket	95	55
1729	270f. Wearing white jacket with revers	1·20	75
1730	300f. Making speech	1·50	80
1731	400f. Wearing collarless single-breasted white jacket	2·00	1·10
1732	500f. Wearing red jacket	2·40	1·40
1733	600f. Wearing black jacket	2·75	1·70
1734	700f. Wearing double-breasted white jacket	3·25	2·00

475 Sordes

1998. Prehistoric Animals. Multicoloured.

1735	135f. Type **475**	55	35
1736	150f. Scaphognatus	70	40
1737	200f. Dsungaripterus	95	55
1738	270f. Brontosaurus	1·20	75
1739	300f. Diplodocus	1·50	80
1740	400f. Coelurus and baryonyx	2·00	1·10
1741	500f. Kronosaurus and ichthyosaurus	2·40	1·40
1742	600f. Ceratosaurus	2·75	1·70
1743	700f. Yangchuansaurus	3·25	2·00

Nos. 1735/43 were issued together, *se-tenant*, forming a composite design.

476 Beagle

1998. Dogs. Multicoloured.

1744	135f. Type **476**	55	30
1745	150f. Dalmatians	70	40
1746	200f. Dachshund	95	55
1747	270f. Cairn terrier	1·20	70
1748	300f. Shih-tzus	1·50	80
1749	400f. Pug	2·00	1·00
MS1750 110×90 mm. 1000f. Springer spaniels (39×31 mm)		4·75	3·75

477 Abyssinian

1998. Cats. Multicoloured.

1751	135f. Type **477**	55	30
1752	150f. Striped silver tabby	70	40
1753	200f. Siamese	95	55
1754	270f. Red tabby (horiz)	1·20	70
1755	300f. Wild cat (horiz)	1·50	80
1756	400f. Manx (horiz)	2·00	1·00
MS1757 110×89 mm. 1000f. Tortoiseshell and white (39×31 mm)		4·75	3·75

478 Bugatti 13 Torpedo, 1910

1998. Motor Cars. Multicoloured.

1758	135f. Type **478**	55	30

1759	150f. Clement voiturette, 1903	70	40
1760	200f. Stutz Bearcat speedster, 1914	95	55
1761	270f. Darracq phaeton, 1907	1·20	70
1762	300f. Napier delivery car, 1913	1·50	80
1763	400f. Pierce Arrow roadster, 1911	2·00	1·00
MS1764	109×91 mm. 1000f. Piccolo, 1904 (31×39 mm)	4·75	3·75

479 Apollo

1998. Butterflies. Multicoloured.

1765	135f. Type **479**	55	30
1766	150f. Orange-tip	70	40
1767	200f. Camberwell beauty	95	55
1768	250f. Speckled wood	1·20	70
1769	300f. Purple-edged copper	1·50	80
1770	400f. Chequered skipper	2·00	1·10
MS1771	106×76 mm. 1000f. Small tortoiseshell (39×31 mm)	4·75	3·75

480 Gouldian Finch

1999. Birds. Multicoloured.

1772	135f. Type **480**	55	30
1773	150f. Saffron finch	70	40
1774	200f. Red-billed quelea	95	55
1775	270f. Golden bishop	1·20	70
1776	300f. Red-crested cardinal	1·50	80
1777	400f. Golden-breasted bunting	2·00	1·10
MS1778	110×89 mm. 1000f. Green-backed twin-spot (31×39 mm)	4·75	3·75

481 Boat, Ceylon

1999. Sailing Boats. Multicoloured.

1779	135f. Type **481**	55	30
1780	150f. Tanka-Tim, Canton, Macao	70	40
1781	200f. Sampan, Hong Kong	95	55
1782	270f. Outrigger sailing canoe, Polynesia	1·20	70
1783	300f. Junk, Japan	1·50	80
1784	400f. Dacca-Pulwar, Bengal	2·00	1·10
MS1785	84×109 mm. 1000f. Junk, China (39×31 mm)	4·75	3·75

482 White Rhinoceros

1999. Mammals.

1786	**482**	50f. grey	15	10
1787	-	100f. violet	45	25
1788	-	135f. green	50	25
1789	-	135f. black	50	25
1790	-	150f. blue	65	30
1791	-	150f. green	65	30
1792	-	200f. blue	85	45
1793	-	200f. brown	85	45
1794	-	300f. brown	1·40	70
1795	-	300f. red	1·40	70
1796	-	400f. brown	1·80	90
1797	-	500f. brown	2·20	1·10

DESIGNS: No. 1787, Sable antelope; 1788, Warthog (*Phacochoerus aethiopicus*); 1789, Brown hyena (*Hyaena brunnea*); 1790, Eastern black-and-white colobus (*Colobus guereza*); 1791, Hippopotamus (*Hippopotamus amphibius*); 1792, Mountain zebra (*Equus zebra*); 1793, African buffalo (*Syncerus caffer*) (wrongly inscr "Cyncerus"); 1794, Lion (*Panthera leo*); 1795, Cheetah (*Acinonyx jubatus*); 1796, Hunting dog; 1797, Potto.

483 Mikhail Tal

1999. Chess Players. Multicoloured.

1798	135f. Type **483**	55	30
1799	150f. Emanuel Lasker	70	40
1800	200f. Jose Raul Capablanca	95	55
1801	270f. Aleksandr Alekhine	1·20	70
1802	300f. Max Euwe	1·50	80
1803	400f. Mikhail Botvinnik	2·00	1·10
MS1804	85×109 mm. 1000f. Wilhelm Steinitz (29×36 mm)	4·75	3·75

484 *Brassocattleya cliftonii*

1999. Orchids. Multicoloured.

1805	50f. Type **484**	25	10
1806	100f. Wilsonara	45	25
1807	150f. *Cypripedium paeony*	70	40
1808	300f. *Cymbidium babylon*	1·50	80
1809	400f. Cattleya	2·00	1·10
1810	500f. *Miltonia minx*	2·40	1·50
MS1811	87×110 mm. 1000f. "Isis miltonia" (28×36 mm)	4·75	3·75

485 Royal Python

1999. Snakes. Multicoloured.

1812	135f. Type **485**	55	35
1813	150f. Royal python (different)	70	40
1814	200f. African rock python	95	55
1815	2000f. Head of African rock python	9·50	6·75

486 Clown Knifefish

1999. Fish. Multicoloured.

1816	135f. Type **486**	55	30
1817	150f. *Puntius filamentosus*	70	40
1818	200f. *Epalzeorhynchos bicolor*	95	55
1819	270f. Spotted rasbora	1·20	70
1820	300f. Tigernander	1·50	80
1821	400f. Siamese fighting fish	2·00	1·10
MS1822	96×86 mm. 1000f. Three-spotted gourami (39×31 mm)	4·75	3·75

487 A. Murdock's Steam Tricycle, 1786

1999. Steam-powered Vehicles. Multicoloured.

1823	135f. Type **487**	55	30
1824	150f. Richard Trevithick's loco-motive, 1800	70	40
1825	200f. Trevithick's locomotive, 1803	95	55
1826	270f. John Blenkinsop's locomo-tive, 1811	1·20	70
1827	300f. Foster and Rastik's Stour-bridge Lion, 1829	1·50	80
1828	400f. Peter Cooper's *Tom Thumb*, 1829	2·00	1·10
MS1829	110×85 mm. 1000f. Isaac New-ton's locomotive, 1760 (36×28 mm)	4·75	3·75

488 Aesculapian Snake

1999. Snakes. Multicoloured.

1830	135f. Type **488**	55	30
1831	150f. Common pine snake	70	40
1832	200f. Grass snake	95	55
1833	270f. Green whip snake	1·20	70
1834	300f. Jamaica boa	1·50	80
1835	400f. Diamond-back rattlesnake	2·00	1·10
MS1836	109×86 mm. 1000f. Common European adder (39×29 mm)	4·75	3·75

489 Testing Chinese Lantern (14th-century)

1999. "China 1999" International Stamp Exhibition, Peking. Multicoloured.

1837	50f. Type **489**	15	10
1838	100f. Satellite launching centre, Jiuquan	45	25
1839	135f. DFH-3 communications satellite	55	40
1840	150f. Satellite launch	70	45
1841	200f. Launch of *Long March* (rocket)	95	60
1842	300f. *Yuan Wang* (passenger ferry) at sea	1·50	90
1843	400f. Dish aerial	2·00	1·20
1844	500f. Items of space post	2·40	1·80

Nos. 1837/44 were issued together, *se-tenant*, with the backgrounds forming a composite design of the Earth.

490 Cheetah

1999. Big Cats. Multicoloured.

1845	135f. Type **490**	55	30
1846	150f. Jaguar	70	40
1847	200f. Snow leopard	95	55
1848	270f. Leopard	1·20	55
1849	300f. Puma	1·50	65
1850	400f. Tiger	2·00	90
MS1851	110×85 mm. 2000f. Lion	4·75	3·75

490a *Mammillaria lenta*

1999. Cacti. Multicoloured.

1856	135f. Type **490a**		
1857	150f. *Oehmea nelsonii*		
1858	200f. *Neobesseya rosiflora*		
1859	270f. *Opuntia gosseliniana*		
1860	300f. *Parodia nivosa*		
1861	400f. *Rebutia senilis*		
MS1862	90×110 mm. 1000f. *Opuntia retrorsa*		

492 Team Members

1999. Manchester United—Triple Cup Winners. Sheet 180×132 mm containing T **492** and similar horiz designs. Multicoloured.

MS1867	135f. Type **492**; 200f. Winning goal; 300f. Celebrating; 400f. Old Trafford football ground; 500f. Champions League, FA Cup and European Cup trophies; 1000f. Alex Ferguson (manager) and Champions League trophy		

493 Inscr 'Estrilda locustella'

1999. Birds. Multicoloured.

1868	135f. Type **493**		
1869	150f. *Estrilda melanotis*		
1870	200f. Inscr 'Pyrelia melba'		
1871	270f. *Uraeginthus bengalensis*		
1872	300f. *Pyromelana orix*		
1873	400f. *Ploceus cucullatus*		
MS1874	90×110 mm. 1000f. *Steganura paradisea*		

PARCEL POST STAMPS

1982. Optd or surch Colis Postaux.

P871	-	100f. multicoloured (No. 779) (postage)	95	50
P872	256	150f. mult	95	50
P873	-	300f. mult (No. 797)	2·75	1·40
P874	260	1000f. multicoloured	8·25	4·00
P875	274	5000f. on 500f. mult (air)	41·00	19·00

1988. No. 543 of Dahomey surch **Republique Populaire du Benin** colis postaux.

P1089	174	5f. on 40f. multicoloured (postage)		
P1092	-	300f. on 200f. blue, yel-low & brown (air)		
P1093	-	500f. on 200f. mult	5·25	2·30

POSTAGE DUE STAMPS

D 233 Pineapples

1978. Fruits. Multicoloured.

D716	10f. Type **D 233**	30	25
D717	20f. Cashew nuts (vert)	45	25
D718	40f. Oranges	95	55
D719	50f. Breadfruit	1·10	75

D234 Village Postman on Bicycle

1978. Rural Post.

D720	**D234**	60f. brown, grn & red	95	45
D721	-	80f. blue, brn & red	95	55

DESIGN: 80f. River village and postman in canoe.

APPENDIX

The following stamps have either been issued in ex-cess of postal needs, or have not been available to the public in reasonable quantities at face value. Such stamps may later be given full listings if there is evidence of reg-ular postal use. Miniature sheets and imperforate stamps are excluded from this listing.

2000

Year of the Dragon. 135, 150, 200, 270, 300, 400f.
Dogs. 135, 150, 200, 270, 300, 400f.
Insects. 135, 150, 200, 270, 300, 400f.
Birds. 135×2, 150×2, 200×2, 270×2, 300×2, 400f.×2

BERGEDORF

A German city on the Elbe, governed by Hamburg and Lubeck until 1867 when it was purchased by the former. In 1868 became part of North German Confederation.

16 schilling = 1 Hamburg mark.

1

1861. Various sizes. Imperf.

1	1	½s. black on lilac		£600
2	1	½s. black on blue	60·00	£1100
4	1	1s. black on white	60·00	£600
5	1	1½s. black on yellow	28·00	£2000
6	1	3s. black on red		£900
7	1	3s. blue on red	33·00	£3000
8	1	4s. black on brown	33·00	£3250

BERMUDA

A group of islands in the W. Atlantic, E. of N. Carolina. Usually regarded by collectors as part of the Br. W. Indies group, though this is not strictly correct.

1865. 12 pence = 1 shilling; 20 shillings = 1 pound.
1970. 100 cents = 1 dollar (U.S.).

9 Queen Victoria

1865. Portrait. Various frames.

19	9	½d. stone	7·50	4·75
21a	9	½d. green	4·50	80
24a	9	1d. red	17·00	20
25	9	2d. blue	70·00	80
26a	9	2d. purple	4·75	2·00
27b	9	2½d. blue	16·00	40
10	9	3d. yellow	£180	60·00
28	9	3d. grey	23·00	9·50
20	9	4d. red	18·00	1·75
28a	9	4d. brown	35·00	60·00
7	9	6d. mauve	23·00	12·00
11	9	1s. green	16·00	£120
29b	9	1s. brown	14·00	21·00

1874. Surch in words.

15		1d. on 2d. blue	£700	£375
16		1d. on 3d. yellow	£450	£350
17		1d. on 1s. green	£500	£250
12		3d. on 1d. red	£18000	
14		3d. on 1s. green	£1500	£650

1901. Surch **ONE FARTHING** and bar.

30		¼d. on 1s. grey	5·00	75

13 Dry Dock

1902

34	13	¼d. brown and violet	1·75	1·50
31	13	½d. black and green	13·00	3·75
36	13	½d. green	21·00	4·25
32	13	1d. brown and red	8·00	10
38	13	1d. red	22·00	10
39	13	2d. grey and orange	7·50	10·00
40	13	2½d. brown and blue	28·00	7·00
41	13	2½d. blue	24·00	9·50
33	13	3d. mauve and green	5·00	2·25
42	13	4d. blue and brown	3·00	16·00

14 Badge of the Colony **15**

1910

44a	14	¼d. brown	2·00	1·50
77	14	½d. green	1·50	3·00
78	14	1d. red	17·00	60
79b	14	1½d. brown	10·00	35
80	14	2d. grey	1·50	1·50
81a	14	2½d. green	3·25	1·50
82b	14	2½d. blue	1·75	70
83	14	3d. blue	19·00	26·00
84	14	3d. purple on yellow	4·00	1·00
85	14	4d. red on yellow	2·25	1·00
86	14	6d. purple	1·50	80
51	14	1s. black on green	6·00	4·50
51b		2s. purple and blue on blue	21·00	55·00
52	15	2s.6d. black and red on blue	35·00	80·00
52b	15	4s. black and red	60·00	£160
53d	15	5s. green and red on yellow	60·00	£120
92	15	10s. green and red on green	£140	£250
93	15	12s.6d. black and orange	£250	£375
55	15	£1 purple and black on red	£325	£550

1918. Optd **WAR TAX.**

56	14	1d. red	50	1·25

18 **19**

1920. Tercentenary of Representative Institutions. (a) 1st Issue.

59	18	¼d. brown	3·50	26·00
60	18	½d. green	9·50	18·00
65	18	1d. red	4·50	30
61	18	2d. grey	17·00	55·00
66	18	2½d. blue	19·00	20·00
62	18	3d. purple on yellow	12·00	55·00
63	18	4d. black and red on yellow	12·00	40·00
67	18	6d. purple	29·00	95·00
64	18	1s. black on green	17·00	48·00

(b) 2nd Issue.

74	19	¼d. brown	4·25	3·75
75	19	½d. green	3·50	8·50
76	19	1d. red	9·00	35
68	19	2d. grey	11·00	50·00
69	19	2½d. blue	14·00	6·00
70	19	3d. purple on yellow	5·50	18·00
71	19	4d. red on yellow	19·00	32·00
72	19	6d. purple	19·00	65·00
73	19	1s. black on green	25·00	65·00

1935. Silver Jubilee. As T **13** of Antigua.

94	1d. blue and red	1·00	2·25
95	1½d. blue and grey	1·00	3·50
96	2½d. brown and blue	1·50	2·50
97	1s. grey and purple	22·00	50·00

20 Hamilton Harbour **22** "Lucie" (yacht)

1936

98	20	½d. green	10	10
99	-	1d. black and red	65	30
100	-	1½d. black and brown	1·00	50
101	22	2d. black and blue	5·00	1·50
102	-	2½d. blue	1·00	25
103	-	3d. black and red	4·50	2·75
104	-	6d. red and violet	80	10
105	-	1s. green	15·00	19·00
106	20	1s.6d. brown	50	10

DESIGNS—HORIZ: 1d., 1½d. South Shore, near Spanish Rock; 3d. Point House, Warwick Parish. VERT: 2½d., 1s. Grape Bay, Paget Parish; 6d. House at Par-la-Ville, Hamilton.

The 1d., 1½d., 2½d. and 1s. values include a portrait of King George V.

1937. Coronation. As T **2** of Aden.

107	1d. red	90	1·50
108	1½d. brown	60	1·75
109	2½d. blue	70	1·75

26 Ships in Hamilton Harbour **28** White-tailed Tropic Bird, Arms of Bermuda and Native Flower

1938

110	26	1d. black and red	2·75	20
111b	26	1½d. blue and brown	2·25	2·00
112	22	2d. brown and blue	50·00	10·00
112a	22	2d. blue and red	2·25	2·25
113	-	2½d. blue and deep blue	11·00	1·25
113b	-	2½d. blue and black	4·00	3·50
114	-	3d. black and red	42·00	6·00
114a	-	3d. black and blue	2·50	40
114bc	28	7½d. black, blue and green	8·00	2·75
115	-	1s. green	2·00	50

DESIGNS—VERT: 3d. St. David's Lighthouse. The 2½d. and 1s. are as 1935, but with King George VI portrait.

1938. As T **15**, but King George VI portrait.

116c		2s. purple and blue on blue	11·00	1·50
117d		2s.6d. black and red on blue	16·00	22·00
118f		5s. green and red on yellow	35·00	30·00
119e		10s. green and red on green	48·00	50·00
120b		12s.6d. grey and orange	£110	55·00
121d		£1 purple and black on red	55·00	85·00

1940. Surch **HALF PENNY.**

122	26	½d. on 1d. black and red	1·25	3·25

1946. Victory. As T **9** of Aden.

123	1½d. brown	15	15
124	3d. blue	40	65

1948. Silver Wedding. As T **10/11** of Aden.

125	1½d. brown	30	50
126	£1 red	45·00	55·00

31 Postmaster Perot's Stamp

1949. Centenary of Postmaster Perot's Stamp.

127	31	2½d. blue and brown	35	35
128	31	3d. black and blue	35	15
129	31	6d. violet and green	40	15

1949. U.P.U. As T **20/23** of Antigua.

130		2½d. black	30	2·00
131		3d. blue	1·75	1·25
132		6d. purple	40	75
133		1s. green	40	1·50

1953. Coronation. As T **13** of Aden.

134	1½d. black and blue	1·25	40

34 Easter Lily **43** Hog Coin

1953

135a	-	½d. olive	40	2·25
136	-	1d. black and red	2·00	50
137	34	1½d. green	30	10
138	-	2d. blue and red	50	40
139	-	2½d. red	2·00	50
140	-	3d. purple	30	10
141	-	4d. black and blue	55	1·75
142	-	4½d. green	1·50	1·00
143	-	6d. black and turquoise	6·50	60
156	-	6d. black and mauve	1·50	15
143a	-	8d. black and red	3·25	30
143b	-	9d. violet	12·00	2·50
144	-	1s. orange	50	15
145	-	1s.3d. blue	3·75	30
146	-	2s. brown	4·00	85
147	-	2s.6d. red	10·00	45
148	43	5s. red	22·00	85
149	-	10s. blue	19·00	9·00
150	-	£1 multicoloured	45·00	21·00

DESIGNS—HORIZ: ½d. Easter lilies; 1d., 4d. Postmaster Perot's stamp; 2d. *Victory II* (racing dinghy); 2½d. Sir George Somers and *Sea Venture*; 3d., 1s.3d. Map of Bermuda; 4½d. *Sea Venture* (galleon), coin and Perot stamp; 6d. (No. 143), 8d. White-tailed tropic bird; 6d. (No. 156), Perot's Post Office; 9d. Early Bermuda coins; 2s. Arms of St. George's 10s. Obverse and reverse of hog coin; £1 Arms of Bermuda. VERT: 2s.6d. Warwick Fort.

No. 156 commemorates the restoration and reopening of Perot's Post Office.

1953. Royal Visit. As No. 143a but inscr "ROYAL VISIT 1953".

151	6d. black and turquoise	1·00	20

1953. Three Power Talks. Nos. 140 and 145 optd **Three Power Talks December, 1953.**

152	3d. purple	20	10
153	1s.3d. blue	20	10

1956. 50th Anniv of United States-Bermuda Yacht Race. Nos. 143a and 145 optd **50TH ANNIVERSARY US – BERMUDA OCEAN RACE 1956.**

154	8d. black and red	30	45
155	1s.3d. blue	30	55

49 Arms of King James I and Queen Elizabeth II

1959. 350th Anniv of Settlement. Arms in red, yellow and blue. Frame colours given.

157	49	1½d. blue	35	10
158	49	3d. grey	40	50
159	49	4d. purple	45	55
160	49	8d. violet	45	15
161	49	9d. olive	45	1·25
162	49	1s.3d. brown	45	30

50 The Old Rectory, St George's, c.1730

1962

163	50	1d. purple, black and orange	10	75
164	-	2d. multicoloured	1·00	35
165	-	3d. brown and blue	10	10
166	-	4d. brown and mauve	20	40
167	-	5d. blue and red	75	3·00
168	-	6d. blue, green & lt blue	30	30
169	-	8d. blue, green and orange	30	35
170	-	9d. blue and brown	30	60
197	-	10d. violet and ochre	75	60
171	-	1s. multicoloured	30	10
172	-	1s.3d. lake, grey and bistre	75	15
173	-	1s.6d. violet and ochre	75	1·00
199	-	1s.6d. blue and red	1·00	30
200	-	2s. brown and orange	1·00	60
175	-	2s.3d. sepia and green	1·00	7·00
176	-	2s.6d. sepia, green & yell	55	50
177	-	5s. purple and green	1·25	1·50
178	-	10s. mauve, green and buff	5·00	7·00
179	-	£1 black, olive and orange	14·00	14·00

DESIGNS: 2d. Church of St. Peter, St. George's; 3d. Government House, 1892; 4d. The Cathedral, Hamilton, 1894; 5d., 1s.6d. (No. 199) H.M. Dockyard, 1811; 6d. Perot's Post Office, 1848; 8d. G.P.O., Hamilton, 1869; 9d. Library, Par-la-Ville; 10d., 1s.6d. (No. 173) Bermuda cottage, c. 1705; 1s. Christ Church, Warwick, 1719; 1s.3d. City Hall, Hamilton, 1960; 2s. Town of St. George; 2s.3d. Bermuda house, c. 1710; 2s.6d. Bermuda house, early 18th century; 5s. Colonial Secretariat, 1833; 10s. Old Post Office, Somerset, 1890; £1 The House of Assembly, 1815.

1963. Freedom from Hunger. As T **28** of Aden.

180	1s.3d. sepia	60	40

1963. Centenary of Red Cross. As T **33** of Antigua.

181	3d. red and black	50	25
182	1s.3d. red and blue	1·00	2·50

67 *Tsotsi in the Bundu* (Finn class yacht)

1964. Olympic Games, Tokyo.

183	67	3d. red, violet and blue	10	10

1965. Centenary of ITU. As T **36** of Antigua.

184	3d. blue and green	35	25
185	2s. yellow and blue	65	1·50

68 Scout Badge and St. Edward's Crown

1965. 50th Anniv of Bermuda Boy Scouts Association.

186	68	2s. multicoloured	50	50

1965. ICY. As T **37** of Antigua.

187	4d. purple and turquoise	40	20
188	2s.6d. green and lavender	60	80

1966. Churchill Commemoration. As T **38** of Antigua.

189	3d. blue	30	20

190	6d. green	70	1·00
191	10d. brown	1·00	75
192	1s.3d. violet	1·25	2·50

1966. World Cup Football Championship. As T **40** of Antigua.

193	10d. multicoloured	1·00	15
194	2s.6d. multicoloured	1·25	1·25

1966. 20th Anniv of UNESCO. As T **54/56** of Antigua.

201	4d. multicoloured	45	15
202	1s.3d. yellow, violet and olive	75	50
203	2s. black, purple and orange	1·00	1·10

69 GPO Building

1967. Opening of New General Post Office.

204	**69**	3d. multicoloured	10	10
205	**69**	1s. multicoloured	15	10
206	**69**	1s.6d. multicoloured	30	25
207	**69**	2s.6d. multicoloured	35	70

70 *Mercury* (cable ship) and Chain Links

1967. Inauguration of Bermuda–Tortola Telephone Service. Multicoloured.

208		3d. Type **70**	15	10
209		1s. Map, telephone and microphone	25	10
210		1s.6d. Telecommunications media	25	25
211		2s.6d. "Mercury" (cable ship) and marine fauna	40	70

74 Human Rights Emblem and Doves

1968. Human Rights Year.

212	**74**	3d. indigo, blue and green	10	10
213	**74**	1s. brown, blue and light blue	10	10
214	**74**	1s.6d. black, blue and red	10	15
215	**74**	2s.6d. green, blue and yellow	15	25

75 Mace and Queen's Profile

1968. New Constitution.

216	**75**	3d. multicoloured	10	10
217	**75**	1s. multicoloured		
218	-	1s.6d. yellow, black and blue	10	20
219	-	2s.6d. lilac, black and yellow	15	75

DESIGNS: 1s.6d., 2s.6d., Houses of Parliament, and House of Assembly, Bermuda.

77 Football, Athletics and Yachting

1968. Olympic Games, Mexico.

220	**77**	3d. multicoloured	15	10
221	**77**	1s. multicoloured	25	10
222	**77**	1s.6d. multicoloured	50	30
223	**77**	2s.6d. multicoloured	50	1·40

78 Brownie and Guide

1969. 50th Anniv of Girl Guides. Multicoloured.

224	3d. Type **78**	10	10
225	1s. Type **78**	20	10
226	1s.6d. Guides and Badge	25	40
227	2s.6d. As 1s.6d.	35	1·40

80 Emerald-studded Gold Cross and Seaweed

1969. Underwater Treasure. Multicoloured.

228	4d. Type **80**	20	10
229	1s.3d. Emerald-studded gold cross and sea-bed	35	15
230	2s. As Type **80**	45	90
231	2s.6d. As 1s.3d.	45	1·75

1970. Decimal Currency. Nos. 163/79 surch.

232	1c. on 1d. purple, black & orge	10	1·75
233	2c. on 2d. multicoloured	10	10
234	3c. on 3d. brown and blue	10	30
235	4c. on 4d. brown and mauve	10	10
236	5c. on 8d. blue, green & orge	15	2·25
237	6c. on 6d. blue, green & lt blue	15	1·75
238	9c. on 9d. blue and brown	30	2·75
239	10c. on 10d. violet and ochre	30	25
240	12c. on 1s. multicoloured	30	1·25
241	15c. on 1s.3d. lake, grey & bis	2·00	1·75
242	18c. on 1s.6d. blue and red	80	65
243	24c. on 2s. brown and orange	85	4·00
244	30c. on 2s.6d. sepia, grn & yell	1·00	3·00
245	36c. on 2s.3d. sepia and green	1·75	8·00
246	60c. on 5s. purple and green	2·25	4·00
247	$1.20 on 10s. mve, grn & buff	5·50	12·00
248	$2.40 on £1 black, ol & orge	6·50	15·00

83 Spathiphyllum

1970. Flowers. Multicoloured.

249	1c. Type **83**	10	20
250	2c. Bottlebrush	20	25
251	3c. Oleander (vert)	15	10
252	4c. Bermudiana	15	10
253	5c. Poinsettia	2·50	20
254	6c. Hibiscus	30	30
255	9c. Cereus	20	45
256	10c. Bougainvillea (vert)	20	15
257	12c. Jacaranda	60	60
258	15c. Passion flower	90	1·00
258a	17c. As 15c.	2·75	5·00
259	18c. Coralita	2·25	1·00
259a	20c. As 18c.	2·75	4·00
260	24c. Morning glory	1·50	5·00
260a	25c. As 24c.	2·75	4·50
261	30c. Tecoma	1·00	1·00
262	36c. Angel's trumpet	1·25	1·25
262a	40c. As 36c.	2·75	5·50
263	60c. Plumbago	1·75	1·25
263a	$1 As 60c.	3·25	6·50
264	$1.20 Bird of paradise flower	2·25	1·25
264a	$2 As $1.20	9·00	10·00
265	$2.40 Chalice cup	4·50	1·50
265a	$3 As $2.40	11·00	11·00

84 The State House, St. George's

1970. 350th Anniv of Bermuda Parliament. Multicoloured.

266	4c. Type **84**	10	10
267	15c. The Sessions House, Hamilton	30	20
268	18c. St. Peter's Church, St. George's	30	25
269	24c. Town Hall, Hamilton	40	1·00
MS270	131×95 mm. Nos. 266/9	1·00	1·50

85 Street Scene, St. George's

1971. "Keep Bermuda Beautiful". Multicoloured.

271	4c. Type **85**	20	10
272	15c. Horseshoe Bay	65	65
273	18c. Gibbs Hill Lighthouse	1·50	2·25
274	24c. Hamilton Harbour	1·25	2·50

86 Building of the *Deliverance*

1971. Voyage of the "Deliverance". Multicoloured.

275	4c. Type **86**	60	20
276	15c. *Deliverance* and *Patience* at Jamestown (vert)	1·50	1·75
277	18c. Wreck of the *Sea Venture* (vert)	1·50	2·25
278	24c. *Deliverance* and *Patience* on high seas	1·75	2·50

87 Green overlooking Ocean View

1971. Golfing in Bermuda. Multicoloured.

279	4c. Type **87**	70	10
280	15c. Golfers at Port Royal	1·25	65
281	18c. Castle Harbour	1·25	1·00
282	24c. Belmont	1·50	2·00

1971. Anglo-American Talks. Nos. 252, 258, 259 and 260 optd **HEATH-NIXON DECEMBER 1971.**

283	4c. Bermudiana	10	10
284	15c. Passion flower	10	20
285	18c. Coralita	15	65
286	24c. Morning glory	20	1·00

89 Bonefish

1972. World Fishing Records. Multicoloured.

287	4c. Type **89**	30	10
288	15c. Wahoo	30	50
289	18c. Yellow-finned tuna	35	75
290	24c. Greater amberjack	40	1·25

1972. Silver Wedding. As T **52** of Ascension, but with "Admiralty Oar" and Mace in background.

291	4c. violet	15	10
292	15c. red	15	50

91 Palmetto

1973. Tree Planting Year. Multicoloured.

293	4c. Type **91**	25	10
294	15c. Olivewood bark	65	75
295	18c. Bermuda cedar	70	1·25
296	24c. Mahogany	75	1·60

1973. Royal Wedding. As T **47** of Anguilla, background colour given. Multicoloured.

297	15c. mauve	15	15
298	18c. blue	15	15

92 Bernard Park, Pembroke, 1973

1973. Centenary of Lawn Tennis. Multicoloured.

299	4c. Type **92**	30	10
300	15c. Clermont Court, 1873	40	65

301	18c. Leamington Spa Court, 1872	45	1·75
302	24c. Staten Island Courts, 1874	50	2·00

93 Weather Vane, City Hall

1974. 50th Anniv of Rotary in Bermuda. Multicoloured.

320	5c. Type **93**	15	10
321	17c. St. Peter's Church, St. George's	45	35
322	20c. Somerset Bridge	50	1·50
323	25c. Map of Bermuda, 1626	60	2·25

94 Jack of Clubs and "good bridge hand"

1975. World Bridge Championships, Bermuda. Multicoloured.

324	5c. Type **94**	20	10
325	17c. Queen of Diamonds and Bermuda Bowl	35	50
326	20c. King of Hearts and Bermuda Bowl	40	1·75
327	25c. Ace of Spades and Bermuda Bowl	40	2·50

95 Queen Elizabeth II and the Duke of Edinburgh

1975. Royal Visit.

328	**95**	17c. multicoloured	60	65
329	**95**	20c. multicoloured	65	2·10

96 Short S.23 Flying Boat *Cavalier*, 1937

1975. 50th Anniv of Air-mail Service to Bermuda. Multicoloured.

330	5c. Type **96**	40	10
331	17c. U.S. Navy airship *Los Angeles*, 1925	1·25	85
332	20c. Lockheed Constellation, 1946	1·40	2·75
333	25c. Boeing 747-100, 1970	1·50	3·50
MS334	128×85 mm. Nos. 330/3	11·00	15·00

97 Supporters of American Army raiding Royal Magazine

1975. Bicentenary of Gunpowder Plot, St. George's. Multicoloured.

335	5c. Type **97**	15	10
336	17c. Setting off for raid	30	40
337	20c. Loading gunpowder aboard American ship	35	1·40
338	25c. Gunpowder on beach	35	1·50
MS339	165×138 mm. Nos. 335/8	2·75	7·00

98 Launching *Ready* (bathysphere)

139 Morgan's Island

1989. 150 Years of Photography. Multicoloured.
578	18c. Type **139**		85	25
579	30c. Front Street, Hamilton		1·10	45
580	50c. Waterfront, Front Street, Hamilton		1·60	1·25
581	60c. Crow Lane from Hamilton Harbour		1·75	1·40
582	70c. Shipbuilding, Hamilton Harbour		1·90	2·50
583	$1 Dockyard		2·25	3·50

1989. Old Garden Roses (2nd series). As T **136**. Multicoloured.
584	18c. "Agrippina" (vert)	90	25
585	30c. "Smith's Parish" (vert)	1·25	60
586	50c. "Champney's Pink Cluster"	1·75	1·40
587	60c. "Rosette Delizy"	1·75	1·60
588	$1.50 *Rosa bracteata*	2·75	6·00

1989. Old Garden Roses (3rd series). Designs as Nos. 561/5 and 584/8, but with royal cypher at top left instead of Queen's head. Multicoloured.
589	50c. As No. 565 (vert)	1·75	2·25
590	50c. As No. 563 (vert)	1·75	2·25
591	50c. Type **136**	1·75	2·25
592	50c. As No. 562	1·75	2·25
593	50c. As No. 564	1·75	2·25
594	50c. As No. 585 (vert)	1·75	2·25
595	50c. As No. 584 (vert)	1·75	2·25
596	50c. As No. 586	1·75	2·25
597	50c. As No. 587	1·75	2·25
598	50c. As No. 588	1·75	2·25

140 Main Library, Hamilton

1989. 150th Anniv of Bermuda Library. Multicoloured.
599	18c. Type **140**	60	25
600	50c. The Old Rectory, St. George's	1·25	65
601	60c. Somerset Library, Springfield	1·25	85
602	$2 Cabinet Building, Hamilton	3·25	4·50

141 1865 1d. Rose

1989. Commonwealth Postal Conference. Multicoloured.
603	**141**	18c. grey, pink and red	1·50	25
604	-	50c. grey, blue & lt blue	2·00	75
605	-	60c. grey, purple and mauve	2·25	1·25
606	-	$2 grey, green and emerald	3·75	5·00

DESIGNS: 50c. 1866 2d. blue; 60c. 1865 6d. purple; $2 1865 1s. green.

142 Fairylands, c. 1890 (Ross Turner)

1990. Bermuda Paintings (2nd series). Multicoloured.
607	18c. Type **142**	75	25
608	50c. *Shinebone Alley, c. 1953* (Ogden Pleissner)	1·25	1·25
609	60c. *Salt Kettle, 1916* (Prosper Senat)	1·25	1·50
610	$2 *St. George's, 1934* (Jack Bush)	3·25	7·00

1990. "Stamp World London 90" International Stamp Exhibition. Nos. 603/6 optd **Stamp World London 90** and logo.
611	18c. grey, pink and red		1·25	25
612	50c. grey, blue and light blue		1·75	1·50
613	60c. grey, purple and mauve		2·00	1·75
614	$2 grey, green and emerald		3·50	6·00

1990. Nos. 511, 516 and 519 surch.
615	30c. on 12c. "Warwick" (galleon), (1619)	1·75	1·50
616	55c. on 50c. "Mark Antonie" (Spanish privateer), 1777	2·25	2·50
617	80c. on $1.50 "Caesar" (brig), 1818	2·50	5·00

145 The Halifax and Bermudas Cable Company Office, Hamilton

1990. Centenary of Cable and Wireless in Bermuda.
618	**145**	20c. brown and black	70	25
619	-	55c. brown and black	2·00	1·25
620	-	70c. multicoloured	2·00	2·75
621	-	$2 multicoloured	4·75	7·50

DESIGNS: 55c. "Westmeath" (cable ship), 1890; 70c. Wireless transmitter station, St. George's, 1928; $2 "Sir Eric Sharp" (cable ship).

1991. President Bush–Prime Minister Major Talks, Bermuda. Nos. 618/19 optd **BUSH-MAJOR 16 MARCH 1991.**
622	**145**	20c. brown and black	2·00	1·50
623	-	55c. brown and black	3·00	3·50

147 Two-seater Pony Cart, 1805

1991. Transport (4th series). Horse-drawn Carriages. Multicoloured.
624	20c. Type **147**	80	30
625	30c. Varnished rockaway, 1830	90	60
626	55c. Vis-a-Vis victoria, 1895	1·60	1·10
627	70c. Semi-formal phaeton, 1900	2·25	2·50
628	80c. Pony runabout, 1905	2·50	3·75
629	$1 Ladies phaeton, 1910	2·75	4·50

148 *Bermuda, 1916* (Prosper Senat)

1991. Bermuda Paintings (3rd series). Multicoloured.
630	20c. Type **148**	1·00	30
631	55c. *Bermuda Cottage* 1930 (Frank Allison) (horiz)	2·00	1·40
632	70c. *Old Maid's Lane, 1934* (Jack Bush)	2·50	3·25
633	$2 *St. George's, 1953* (Ogden Pleissner) (horiz)	5·00	8·50

1991. 65th Birthday of Queen Elizabeth II and 70th Birthday of Prince Philip. As T **139** of Ascension. Multicoloured.
634	55c. Prince Philip in tropical naval uniform	1·25	1·75
635	70c. Queen Elizabeth II in Bermuda	1·25	1·75

149 H.M.S. *Argonaut* (cruiser) in Floating Dock

1991. 50th Anniv of Second World War. Multicoloured.
636	20c. Type **149**	1·50	40
637	55c. Kindley Airfield	2·25	1·40
638	70c. Boeing 314A flying boat and map of Atlantic route	2·75	3·25
639	$2 Censored trans-Atlantic mail	4·50	7·50

1992. 40th Anniv of Queen Elizabeth II's Accession. As T **143** of Ascension. Multicoloured.
640	20c. Old fort on beach	60	30
641	30c. Public gardens	75	55
642	55c. Cottage garden	1·25	90
643	70c. Beach and hotels	1·60	2·25
644	$1 Queen Elizabeth II	1·90	2·75

150 Rings and Medallion

1992. 500th Anniv of Discovery of America by Columbus. Spanish Artifacts. Multicoloured.
645	25c. Type **150**	1·25	35
646	35c. Ink wells	1·40	75
647	60c. Gold ornaments	2·25	2·00
648	75c. Bishop buttons and crucifix	2·50	3·25
649	85c. Earrings and pearl buttons	2·75	3·75
650	$1 Jug and bowls	3·00	4·25

151 "Wreck of 'Sea Venture' "

1992. Stained Glass Windows. Multicoloured.
651	25c. Type **151**	1·75	40
652	60c. "Birds in tree"	3·00	2·00
653	75c. "St. Francis feeding bird"	3·50	3·00
654	$2 "Shells"	7·50	11·00

152 German Shepherd

1992. Seven World Congress of Kennel Clubs. Multicoloured.
655	25c. Type **152**	1·50	40
656	35c. Irish setter	1·75	70
657	60c. Whippet (vert)	2·50	2·25
658	75c. Border terrier (vert)	2·50	3·25
659	85c. Pomeranian (vert)	3·00	4·25
660	$1 Schipperke (vert)	3·00	4·75

153 Policeman, Cyclist and Cruise Liner

1993. Tourism Posters by Adolph Treidler. Multicoloured.
679	25c. Type **153**	2·25	80
680	60c. Seaside golf course	3·00	2·75
681	75c. Deserted beach	2·50	2·75
682	$2 Dancers in evening dress and cruise liner	4·50	7·00

154 "Duchesse de Brabant" and Bee

1993. Garden Roses (4th series).
683	**154**	10c. multicoloured	75	1·40
684	**154**	25c. multicoloured	75	60
685	**154**	50c. multicoloured	2·75	4·00
686	**154**	60c. multicoloured	1·25	1·75

1993. 75th Anniv of Royal Air Force. As T **149** of Ascension. Multicoloured.
687	25c. Consolidated PBY-5 Catalina	85	35
688	60c. Supermarine Spitfire Mk IX	2·00	2·00
689	75c. Bristol Type 156 Beaufighter Mk X	2·25	2·25
690	$2 Handley Page Halifax Mk III	3·75	6·00

155 Hamilton from the Sea

1993. Bicentenary of Hamilton. Multicoloured.
691	25c. Type **155**	1·25	35
692	60c. Waterfront	2·25	2·00
693	75c. Barrel warehouse	2·25	2·50
694	$2 Sailing ships off Hamilton	6·00	8·00

156 *Queen of Bermuda* (liner) at Hamilton

1994. 75th Anniv of Furness Line's Bermuda Cruises. Adolphe Treidler Posters. Multicoloured.
695	25c. Type **156**	65	35
696	60c. *Queen of Bermuda* entering port (horiz)	1·50	1·60
697	75c. *Queen of Bermuda* and *Ocean Monarch* (liners) (horiz)	1·60	1·75
698	$2 Passengers on promenade deck at night	3·50	6·50

157 Queen Elizabeth II in Bermuda

1994. Royal Visit. Multicoloured.
699	25c. Type **157**	1·00	35
700	60c. Queen Elizabeth and Prince Philip in open carriage	2·50	1·75
701	75c. Royal Yacht "Britannia"	5·50	3·50

158 Peach

1994. Flowering Fruits. Multicoloured.
792	5c. Type **158**	50	1·50
703A	7c. Fig	40	1·75
704A	10c. Calabash (vert)	35	35
795	15c. Natal plum	75	60
796	18c. Locust and wild honey	80	60
797	20c. Pomegranate	80	75
798	25c. Mulberry (vert)	80	75
709A	35c. Grape (vert)	70	55
710A	55c. Orange (vert)	1·00	80
711A	60c. Surinam cherry	3·00	2·00
802	75c. Loquat	2·25	1·75
803	90c. Sugar apple	2·50	2·50
804	$1 Prickly pear (vert)	2·75	3·75
715A	$2 Paw paw	5·50	6·50
716A	$3 Bay grape	6·00	7·50
717A	$5 Banana (vert)	7·50	8·00
718A	$8 Lemon	11·00	12·00

159 Nurse with Mother and Baby

1994. Centenary of Hospital Care. Multicoloured.
719	25c. Type **159**	1·00	35
720	60c. Patient on dialysis machine	2·00	1·90
721	75c. Casualty on emergency trolley	2·25	2·25
722	$2 Elderly patient in wheelchair with physiotherapists	4·75	7·00

160 Gombey Dancers

1994. Cultural Heritage (1st series). Multicoloured.
723	25c. Type **160**	70	35
724	60c. Christmas carol singers	1·40	1·50
725	75c. Marching band	2·50	2·00
726	$2 National Dance Group performers	4·75	7·50

See also Nos. 731/4.

161 Bermuda 1970 Flower
1c. Stamps and 1c. Coin

1995. 25th Anniv of Decimal Currency. Multicoloured.

727	25c. Type **161**	75	35
728	60c. 1970 5c. stamps and coin	1·40	1·50
729	75c. 1970 10c. stamps and coin	1·75	2·00
730	$2 1970 25c. stamps and coin	4·50	6·50

1995. Cultural Heritage (2nd series). As T **160**. Multicoloured.

731	25c. Kite flying	75	35
732	60c. Majorettes	1·50	1·50
733	75c. Portuguese dancers	1·75	2·00
734	$2 Floral float	4·00	6·00

162 Bermuda
Coat of Arms

1995. 375th Anniv of Bermuda Parliament.

735	**162**	25c. multicoloured	1·25	35
736	**162**	$1 multicoloured	2·50	3·25

For design as No. 736 but inscr "Commonwealth Finance Ministers Meeting", see No. 765.

163 U.S. Navy Ordnance
Island Submarine Base

1995. Military Bases. Multicoloured.

737	20c. Type **163**	90	60
738	25c. Royal Naval Dockyard	90	35
739	60c. U.S.A.F. Fort Bell and Kindley Field	1·75	1·25
740	75c. R.A.F. Darrell's Island flying boat base	2·00	2·00
741	90c. U.S. Navy operating base	2·25	3·00
742	$1 Canadian Forces Communications Station, Daniel's Head	2·25	3·00

164 Triple Jump

1996. Olympic Games, Atlanta. Multicoloured.

743	25c. Type **164**	70	35
744	30c. Cycling	3·50	1·00
745	65c. Yachting	2·00	2·00
746	80c. Show jumping	2·00	3·00

165 Jetty and Islets,
Hamilton

1996. Panoramic Paintings of Hamilton (Nos. 747/51) and St. George's (Nos. 752/6) by E. J. Holland. Multicoloured.

747	60c. Type **165**	1·75	2·25
748	60c. End of island and buildings	1·75	2·25
749	60c. Yachts and hotel	1·75	2·25
750	60c. Islet, hotel and cathedral	1·75	2·25
751	60c. Cliff and houses by shore	1·75	2·25
752	60c. Islet and end of main island	1·75	2·25
753	60c. Yacht and houses on hillside	1·75	2·25
754	60c. Yacht and St. George's Hotel on hilltop	1·75	2·25
755	60c. Shoreline and fishing boats	1·75	2·25
756	60c. Entrance to harbour channel	1·75	2·25

166 Somerset Express Mail
Cart, c. 1900

1996. "CAPEX '96" International Stamp Exhibition, Toronto. Local Transport. Multicoloured.

757	25c. Type **166**	1·25	35
758	60c. Victoria carriage and railcar, 1930s	2·75	1·75
759	75c. First bus, 1946	2·75	2·00
760	$2 Sightseeing bus, c. 1947	5·00	7·50

167 Hog Fish
Beacon

1996. Lighthouses. Multicoloured.

761	30c. Type **167**	1·75	50
762	65c. Gibbs Hill Lighthouse	2·25	1·25
763	80c. St. David's Lighthouse	2·75	2·00
764	$2 North Rock Beacon	4·75	7·00

See also Nos. 770/3.

1996. Commonwealth Finance Ministers' Meeting. As No. 736, but inscr "Commonwealth Finance Ministers Meeting" at top and with wider gold frame.

765	$1 multicoloured	2·50	3·00

168 Waterville

1996. Architectural Heritage. Multicoloured.

766	30c. Type **168**	1·25	45
767	65c. Bridge House	1·60	1·50
768	80c. Fannie Fox's Cottage	2·00	2·00
769	$2.50 Palmetto House	4·25	7·00

1997. "HONG KONG '97" International Stamp Exhibition. Designs as Nos. 761/4, but incorporating "HONG KONG '97" logo and with some values changed.

770	30c. As Type **167**	2·25	65
771	65c. Gibbs Hill Lighthouse	3·00	1·50
772	80c. St David's Lighthouse	3·25	2·25
773	$2.50 North Rock Beacon	6·00	10·00

169 White-tailed Tropic Bird

1997. Bird Conservation. Multicoloured.

774	30c. Type **169**	75	50
775	60c. White-tailed tropic bird and chick (vert)	1·50	1·25
776	80c. Cahow and chick (vert)	2·00	2·00
777	$2.50 Cahow	4·00	6·50

170 Queen Elizabeth II
with Crowd

1997. Golden Wedding of Queen Elizabeth and Prince Philip. Multicoloured.

778	30c. Type **170**	50	40
779	$2 Queen Elizabeth and Prince Philip	3·25	4·50
MS780	90×56 mm. Nos. 778/9	3·75	4·50

171 Father playing with
Children

1997. Education. Multicoloured.

781	30c. Type **171**	60	40
782	40c. Teacher and children with map	70	55
783	60c. Boys holding sports trophy	95	1·25

784	65c. Pupils outside Berkeley Institute	1·00	1·25
785	80c. Scientific experiments	1·40	2·00
786	90c. New graduates	1·60	2·50

1998. Diana, Princess of Wales Commemoration. Sheet, 145×170 mm, containing vert designs as T **177** of Ascension. Multicoloured.

MS787	30c. Wearing black hat, 1983; 40c. Wearing floral dress, 1996; 65c. Wearing blue evening dress, 1996; 80c. Carrying bouquets, 1993 (sold at $2.15 + 25c. charity premium)	3·00	4·00

172 Fox's Cottage, St.
Davids (Ethel Tucker)

1998. Paintings by Catherine and Ethel Tucker. Multicoloured.

788	30c. Type **172**	1·25	40
789	40c. East Side, Somerset	1·40	70
790	65c. Long Bay Road, Somerset	2·25	1·25
791	$2 Flatts Village	5·00	7·50

173 Horse and Carriage

1998. Hospitality in Bermuda. Multicoloured.

809	25c. Type **173**	1·25	40
810	30c. Golf club desk	1·75	75
811	65c. Chambermaid preparing room	1·50	1·25
812	75c. Kitchen staff under training	1·50	2·00
813	80c. Waiter at beach hotel	1·75	2·25
814	90c. Nightclub bar	2·00	3·00

174 Agave attenuata

1998. Centenary of Botanical Gardens. Multicoloured.

815	30c. Type **174**	1·25	40
816	65c. Bermuda palmetto tree	2·25	90
817	$1 Banyan tree	2·75	2·75
818	$2 Cedar tree	4·00	7·00

175 Lizard with
Fairy Lights (Claire
Critchley)

1998. Christmas. Children's Paintings. Multicoloured.

819	25c. Type **175**	1·25	35
820	40c. Christmas stairway (Cameron Rowling) (horiz)	1·50	1·25

176 Shelly Bay

1999. Bermuda Beaches. Multicoloured.

821	30c. Type **176**	90	40
822	60c. Catherine's Bay	1·25	1·00
823	65c. Jobson's Cove	1·40	1·10
824	$2 Warwick Long Bay	3·75	6·50

177 Tracking Station

1999. 30th Anniv of First Manned Landing on Moon. Multicoloured.

825	30c. Type **177**	1·00	40
826	60c. Mission launch (vert)	1·50	90
827	75c. Aerial view of tracking station, Bermuda	1·75	1·25
828	$2 Astronaut on Moon (vert)	3·75	6·00

MS829	90×80 mm. 65c. Earth as seen from Moon (circular, 40 mm diam)	3·25	4·00

178 Theodolite and Map,
1901

1999. Centenary of First Digital Map of Bermuda.

830	**178** 30c. multicoloured	1·50	40
831	- 65c. black, stone & silver	2·25	1·50
832	- 80c. multicoloured	2·75	2·50
833	- $1 multicoloured	2·75	4·00

DESIGNS: 65c. Street map, 1901; 80c. Street plan and aerial photograph, 1999; $1 Satellite and Bermuda from Space, 1999.

179 Victorian
Pillar Box and
Bermuda 1865 1s.
Stamp

1999. Bermuda Postal History. Multicoloured.

834	30c. Type **179**	1·00	40
835	75c. King George V pillar box and 1920 2s. stamp	2·25	1·50
836	95c. King George VI wall box and 1938 3d. stamp	2·50	3·25
837	$1 Queen Elizabeth II pillar box and 1953 Coronation 1½d. stamp	2·50	3·25

180 Sir Henry
Tucker and
Meeting of House
of Assembly

2000. Pioneers of Progress (1st series). Each brown, black and gold.

838	30c. Type **180**	1·10	1·25
839	30c. Gladys Morrell and suffragettes	1·10	1·25
840	30c. Dr. E. F. Gordon and workers	1·10	1·25

See also Nos. 988/92 and 1018/1019.

181 Amerigo
Vespucci
(full-rigged ship)

2000. Tall Ships Race. Multicoloured.

841	30c. Type **181**	1·50	50
842	60c. Europa (barque)	2·00	1·50
843	80c. Juan Sebastian de Elcano (schooner)	2·25	2·50

182 Prince William

2000. Royal Birthdays. Multicoloured.

844	35c. Type **182**	1·50	55
845	40c. Duke of York	1·50	65
846	50c. Princess Royal	1·60	1·10
847	70c. Princess Margaret	2·00	2·75
848	$1 Queen Elizabeth the Queen Mother	2·50	3·50
MS849	169×90 mm. Nos. 844/8	9·00	9·50

183 Santa Claus with Smiling Vegetable (Meghan Jones)

2000. Christmas. Children's Paintings. Multicoloured.

850	30c. Type **183**	1·00	45
851	45c. *Christmas tree and presents* (Carlita Lodge)	1·25	80

2001. Endangered Species. Bird Conservation. Designs as Nos. 774/7, but with different face values, inscriptions redrawn and WWF panda emblem added. Multicoloured.

852	15c. As Type **169**	1·00	1·25
853	15c. Cahow	1·00	1·25
854	20c. White-tailed tropic bird with chick (vert)	1·00	1·25
855	20c. Cahow with chick (vert)	1·00	1·25
MS856	200×190 mm. Nos. 852/5 each × 4	12·00	14·00

No. **MS**856 includes the "HONG KONG 2001" logo on the margin.

184 King's Castle

2001. Historic Buildings, St. George's. Multicoloured.

857	35c. Type **184**	1·10	55
858	50c. Bridge House	1·50	75
859	55c. Whitehall	1·60	1·00
860	70c. Fort Cunningham	1·90	2·25
861	85c. St. Peter's Church	2·50	3·25
862	95c. Water Street	2·50	3·25

185 Boer Prisoners on Boat and Plough

2001. Centenary of Anglo-Boer War. Multicoloured.

863	35c. Type **185**	85	55
864	50c. Prisoners in shelter and boot	1·10	75
865	70c. Elderly Boer with children and jewellery	1·60	1·75
866	95c. Bermuda residents and illustrated envelope of 1902	2·00	3·00

186 Girl touching Underwater Environment

2001. 75th Anniv of Bermuda Aquarium. Multicoloured.

867	35c. Type **186**	90	55
868	50c. Museum exhibits (horiz)	1·25	75
869	55c. Feeding giant tortoise (horiz)	1·25	95
870	70c. Aquarium building (horiz)	1·75	1·75
871	80c. Lesson from inside tank	1·75	2·25
872	95c. Turtle	2·25	3·00

187 *Fishing Boats* (Charles Lloyd Tucker)

2001. Paintings of Charles Lloyd Tucker. Multicoloured.

873	35c. Type **187**	1·40	55
874	70c. *Bandstand and City Hall, Hamilton*	2·00	1·50
875	85c. *Hamilton Harbour*	2·25	2·50
876	$1 *Train in Front Street, Hamilton*	3·00	4·25

2002. Golden Jubilee. As T **200** of Ascension.

877	10c. black, violet and gold	60	60
878	35c. multicoloured	1·50	1·10
879	70c. black, violet and gold	2·00	1·60
880	85c. multicoloured	2·25	2·25
MS881	162×95 mm. Nos. 887/80 and $1 multicoloured	7·00	7·50

DESIGNS—HORIZ: 10c. Princess Elizabeth with corgi; 35c. Queen Elizabeth in evening dress, 1965; 70c. Queen Elizabeth in car, 1952; 85c. Queen Elizabeth on Merseyside, 1991. VERT (38×51 mm)—$2 Queen Elizabeth after Annigoni.

Designs as Nos. 877/80 in No. **MS**881 omit the gold frame around each stamp and the "Golden Jubilee 1952–2002" inscription.

188 Fantasy Cave

2002. Caves. Multicoloured.

882	35c. Type **188**	1·60	55
883	70c. Crystal Cave	2·25	1·75
884	80c. Prospero's Cave	2·50	2·75
885	$1 Cathedral Cave	3·00	4·50

189 Fielder and Somerset Club Colours

2002. Centenary of Bermuda Cup Cricket Match.

886	35c. Type **189**	1·50	1·50
887	35c. Batsman and wicket-keeper with St. George's Club colours	1·50	1·50
MS888	110×85 mm. $1 Batsman (48×31 mm)	3·50	4·00

2002. Queen Elizabeth the Queen Mother Commemoration. As T **202** of Ascension.

889	30c. brown, gold and purple	1·00	45
890	$1.25 multicoloured	2·50	3·00
MS891	145×70 mm. Nos. 889/90	4·50	4·75

DESIGNS: 30c. Duchess of York, 1923; $1.25, Queen Mother on her birthday, 1995.

Designs as Nos. 889/90 in No. **MS**891 omit the "1900–2002" inscription and the coloured frame.

190 Slit Worm-shell

2002. Shells. Multicoloured.

892	5c. Type **190**	15	10
893	10c. Netted olive	20	40
894	20c. Angular triton (horiz)	50	60
895	25c. Frog shell (horiz)	60	60
896	30c. Colourful atlantic moon (horiz)	70	65
897	35c. Noble wentletrap	1·00	45
898	40c. Atlantic trumpet triton (horiz)	1·00	50
899	45c. Zigzag scallop	1·10	55
900	50c. Bermuda cone	1·25	65
901	75c. Very distorted distorsio (horiz)	2·00	1·10
902	80c. Purple sea snail (horiz)	2·25	1·40
903	90c. Flame helmet (horiz)	2·25	1·75
904	$1 Scotch bonnet (horiz)	2·50	2·00
905	$2 Gold mouth triton (horiz)	4·75	4·25
906	$3 Bermuda's slit shell (horiz)	6·50	6·00
907	$4 Reticulated cowrie-helmet (horiz)	7·50	8·00
908	$5 Dennison's morum (horiz)	8·50	9·50
909	$8 Sunrise tellin (horiz)	13·00	16·00

191 Dove of Peace

2002. World Peace Day.

910	**191**	35c. multicoloured	1·25	50
911	–	70c. multicoloured	2·00	2·25

DESIGN: 70c. Dove.

192 Research Station and *Weatherbird II* (research ship)

2003. Centenary of Bermuda Biological Research Station. Multicoloured.

912	35c. Type **192**	1·50	50
913	70c. Spotfin butterflyfish (horiz)	2·50	1·75
914	85c. Collecting coral (horiz)	2·75	3·00
915	$1 Krill	3·25	3·75

193 Costume Dolls

2003. Heritage "Made in Bermuda". (1st Series). Multicoloured.

916	35c. Type **193**	1·00	40
917	70c. Model sailing ship	1·75	1·40
918	80c. Abstract sculpture in wood	2·00	2·25
919	$1 Silverware	2·50	3·00

See also Nos. 934/7, 952/5 and 980/3.

2003. 50th Anniv of Coronation. As T **206** of Ascension. Multicoloured.

920	35c. Queen in Coronation Coach	75	40
921	70c. Queen in Coronation chair, flanked by bishops of Durham and Bath & Wells	1·25	1·50
MS922	95×115 mm. $1.25 As 35c.; $2 As 70c.	5·00	6·00

Nos. 920/1 have red frame; stamps from **MS**922 have no frame and country name in mauve panel.

194 Red Poinsettias

2003. Christmas Greetings. Poinsettias. Multicoloured.

925	30c. Type **194**	75	35
926	45c. White poinsettias	1·10	55
927	80c. Pink poinsettias	2·00	2·75

195 Gateway

2004. Royal Naval Dockyard, Bermuda. Multicoloured.

928	25c. Type **195**	65	50
929	35c. Fountain and Clock Tower	90	80
930	70c. Waterside seat and Clock Tower	1·75	1·50
931	85c. Marina	1·90	2·25
932	95c. Window in ramparts	2·25	2·75
933	$1 Boats moored at pontoon and Clocktower Centre	2·40	3·25

2004. Heritage "Made in Bermuda" (2nd series). As T **193**. Multicoloured.

934	35c. Carver chair	65	45
935	70c. Ceramic jug and plate	1·10	90
936	80c. Glass fish and glass plate with shell design	1·25	1·40
937	$1.25 Quilt	1·75	2·50

196 Bluefin Tuna

2004. Endangered Species. Bluefin Tuna. Multicoloured.

938	10c. Type **196**	30	50
939	35c. Five bluefin tuna	85	50
940	85c. Bluefin tuna near surface of water	1·90	1·90
941	$1.10 Bluefin tuna swimming left	2·25	2·50

197 Yellow Oncydium Orchids

2004. 50th Anniv of the Orchid Society. Multicoloured.

942	35c. Type **197**	1·10	55
943	45c. *Encyclia radiate*	1·25	65
944	85c. Purple and white orchids	2·50	2·50
945	$1.10 *Paphiopedilum spicerianum*	3·00	3·25

198 1940 Map of Bermuda and Compass

2005. 500th Anniv of Discovery of Bermuda by Juan de Bermudez (Spanish navigator). Multicoloured.

946	25c. Type **198**	1·50	65
947	35c. 1846 map and sextant	1·75	65
948	70c. 1764 map and box compass	2·75	1·75
949	$1.10 1692 map and telescope	4·00	4·50
950	$1.25 1548 map and calipers	4·00	5·00
MS951	115×95 mm. $5 Aerial view of Bermuda	16·00	17·00

2005. Heritage "Made in Bermuda" (3rd series). As T **193**. Multicoloured.

952	35c. Picture of Bermuda Gombey dancers	80	45
953	70c. Papier-mache sculpture of parrotfish on tube coral	1·50	1·40
954	85c. Stained glass picture of lion and lamb	2·00	2·50
955	$1 Earrings and pendant of silver, pearls and garnets	2·25	3·00

2005. Bicentenary of Battle of Trafalgar. As T **216** of Ascension but horiz. Multicoloured.

956	10c. HMS *Victory*	80	80
957	35c. HMS *Pickle* under construction in Bermuda	1·50	60
958	70c. HMS *Pickle* picking up survivors from burning *Achille*	2·00	2·00
959	85c. HMS *Pickle* racing back to England with news of victory	2·25	2·75

No. 956 contains traces of powdered wood from HMS *Victory*.

199 Ruddy Turnstone and Semipalmated Sandpiper

2005. Bermuda Habitats. Scenes from dioramas in Bermuda Natural History Museum. Multicoloured.

960	10c. Type **199**	75	80
961	25c. Least bittern in reeds	1·40	60
962	35c. White-tailed tropic bird	1·60	50
963	70c. Eastern bluebird	2·25	1·75
964	85c. Saw-whet owl	2·75	3·00
965	$1 Yellow-crowned night heron	3·00	3·50

200 Christmas Tree with Lights

2005. Christmas Greetings. Festival of Lights. Multicoloured.

966	30c. Type **200**	60	50
967	45c. Dolphin	80	60
968	80c. Snowman	1·50	2·00

201 Man working on Overhead Power Cables

2006. Centenary of the Bermuda Electric Light Company Ltd. Multicoloured.

969	35c. Type **201**	80	45
970	70c. Engineer, power lines and vehicle	1·60	1·40
971	85c. Power plant	2·00	2·50
972	$1 Office block	2·25	3·00

2006. 80th Birthday of Queen Elizabeth II. As T **223** of Ascension. Multicoloured.

973	35p. Princess Elizabeth with corgi	1·40	60
974	70p. Queen wearing tiara (black/white photo)	2·00	1·40
975	85p. Wearing tiara and drop earrings (colour photo)	2·25	2·25
976	$1.25 Wearing blue hat	3·25	4·00
MS977	144×75 mm. $1.25 As No. 974; $2 As No. 975	7·50	8·50

202 Map of Bermuda, 1747

2006. Washington 2006 International Stamp Exhibition.

978	**202**	$1.10 multicoloured	2·50	2·75
MS979	82×65 mm. No. 978		2·50	2·75

2006. Heritage "Made in Bermuda" (4th series). As T **193**. Multicoloured.

980	35c. Bees, honeycomb and honey	1·40	55
981	70c. Stonecutters (detail) (Sharon Wilson)	2·00	1·50
982	85c. I've Caught Some Whoppers (sculpture) by Desmond Fountain	2·50	2·75
983	$1.25 Flower and perfume (Bermuda Perfumery)	3·50	4·00

203 Advent Wreath

2006. Christmas. Greetings. Advent Wreaths.

984	203	30c. multicoloured	1·00	50
985	-	35c. multicoloured	1·10	30
986	-	45c. multicoloured	1·40	50
987	-	80c. multicoloured	2·75	3·00

DESIGNS: 35c. to 80c. Showing different advent wreaths.

204 Francis L. Patton

2007. Pioneers of Progress (2nd series). Educators. Multicoloured.

988	35c. Type **204**	75	85
989	35c. Adele Tucker	75	85
990	35c. Edith and Matilda Crawford	75	85
991	35c. Millie Neversen	75	85
992	35c. May Francis	75	85

205 Hull under Construction at Rockport, Maine, USA

2007. Spirit of Bermuda. Sail training schooner. Multicoloured.

993	10c. Type **205**	60	60
994	35c. Close-up view	1·25	40
995	70c. Spirit of Bermuda at sea	2·00	1·25
996	85c. Off coast of Bermuda	2·25	2·00
997	$1.10 At Hamilton, Bermuda	2·50	2·75
998	$1.25 Spirit of Bermuda seen from stern	2·75	3·25

206 Deliverance off Building Bay

2007. 400th Anniv of Jamestown, Virginia, USA. Voyage of the Deliverance from Bermuda to Jamestown, 1610. Multicoloured.

999	35c. Type **206**	1·75	75
1000	$1.10 Deliverance sailing from Building Bay, St. George's, Bermuda	4·00	4·50

2007. Centenary of World Scouting. As T **281** of Bahamas. Multicoloured.

1001	35c. Bishop's Own Cubs, Government House, 22 February 1930	1·00	40
1002	70c. Lord Baden-Powell inspecting the Cubs, Hamilton, February 1930	1·75	1·40
1003	85c. Scout parade, Front Street, Hamilton, 25 February 1930	2·00	2·25
1004	$1.10 Dance of Kaa, Government House, 25 February 1930	2·25	2·50
MS1005	90×65 mm. $1.25 Bermuda Scouts emblem; $2 Lord Baden-Powell inspecting the Cubs, Hamilton, February 1930 (both vert)	7·00	8·00

207 Celeste & Al Harris

2008. Bermuda Calypso Music. Designs showing album covers. Multicoloured.

1006	35c. Type **207**	1·00	40
1007	70c. Bermuda Calypsos	1·75	1·40
1008	85c. Calypso Varieties from Bermuda	2·00	2·25
1009	$1.10 The Talbot Brothers of Bermuda	2·25	2·50

208 Perot Stamp, 1848

2008. 160th Anniv of the Perot Stamp (stamps prepared and issued by W. B. Perot, postmaster at Hamilton).

1010	**208**	35c. brown and black	1·25	55
1011	**208**	70c. blue and black	2·25	1·60
1012	**208**	85c. sepia and black	2·75	2·75
1013	**208**	$1.25 silver and black	4·00	4·50

209 Deep Bay, West Pembroke

2008. Bermuda Scenes. Multicoloured. Self-adhesive.

1014	(35c.) Type **209**	1·25	1·00
1015	(70c.) Spanish Point Park	1·60	1·75
1016	(85c.) Flatts Inlet	1·75	2·00
1017	(95c.) Tucker's Town Bay	1·90	2·50

No. 1014 is inscribed 'Postage Paid Local', No. 1015 'Postage Paid Zone 1', No. 1016 'Postage Paid Zone 2' and No. 1017 'Postage Paid Zone 3'.

210 Dame Lois Browne-Evans

2008. Pioneers of Progress (3rd series). Multicoloured.

1018	35c. Type **210** (barrister and PLP leader 1968–72, 1976–85)	1·25	1·25
1019	35c. Dr. Pauulu Roosevelt Brown Kamarakafego (civil rights campaigner and rural technologist)	1·25	1·25

211 Sprinter at Start

2008. Olympic Games, Beijing. Multicoloured.

1020	10c. Type **211**	60	60
1021	35c. Swimmer diving from start	1·40	40
1022	70c. Horse and rider jumping	2·50	2·25
1023	85c. Yachting	2·75	3·25

212 Reindeer Lights outside Houses

2008. Christmas. Greetings. Designs showing Christmas lights. Multicoloured.

1024	30c. Type **212**	70	40
1025	35c. Lights on balcony and across street	75	35
1026	45c. Horse and carriage and street lamp lights on roof	1·00	45
1027	80c. Single storey house with lights around roof and verandah and in garden	1·60	2·25

213 Hamilton in 1930s and Modern Photographs

2009. 400th Anniv of Settlement of Bermuda. Each showing scene from past and modern photograph. Multicoloured.

1028	35c. Type **213**	1·10	50
1029	70c. St. George's in 1830s painting by Thomas Driver and modern photograph	2·00	1·60
1030	85c. Flatts Village in 1797 watercolour by Capt. George Tobin and modern photograph	2·50	2·50
1031	$1.25 17th-century map and aerial photograph of Bermuda	3·75	4·75

214 Aerial View of Cooper's Island

2009. International Year of Astronomy. 40th Anniv of First Moon Landing. Multicoloured.

1032	35c. Type **214**	1·00	45
1033	70c. Tracking Station, Cooper's Island	2·00	1·50
1034	85c. Apollo 11 Lunar Landing Module, 1969	2·25	2·25
1035	$1.25 STS 126, 2008	2·50	2·75
1036	$1.25 International Space Station	3·25	3·75
MS1037	100×80 mm. $1.10 Lunar Landing Module on Moon (39×59 mm)	2·75	3·25

215 Winner and Trophy

2009. Centenary of Bermuda Marathon Derby.

1038	**215**	35c. black, brown-red and brown	85	35
1039	–	70c. black, orange-yellow and brown	1·50	1·40
1040	–	85c. black, orange-yellow and brown	1·90	2·00
1041	–	$1.10 black, brown-red and brown	2·25	3·00

DESIGNS: 70c. Winner with trophy (different); 85c. Runners and motorcycle; $1.10 Runners.

216 Concordia

2009. Tall Ships Atlantic Challenge 2009. Multicoloured.

1042	35c. Type **216**	1·00	35
1043	70c. Picton Castle	1·75	1·25
1044	85c. Jolie Brise (horiz)	2·00	1·50
1045	95c. Tecla	2·50	2·25
1046	$1.10 Europa	2·75	2·75
1047	$1.25 Etoile (horiz)	3·25	3·75

217 Theatre Boycott, Upstairs Right, 1959 (Robert Barritt)

2009. 50th Anniv of Theatre Boycott (ended segregation in public buildings). Multicoloured.

1048	35c. Type **217**	70	35
1049	70c. Storm in a Teacup (Charles Lloyd Tucker) (vert)	1·40	1·25
1050	85c. Bronze statue of boycott leaders by Chesley Trott (vert)	1·75	1·75
1051	$1.25 Scene from documentary When Voices Rise	2·75	3·50

218 Basket with Berries and Red Bow

2009. Christmas Greetings. Tree Decorations. Multicoloured.

1052	30c. Type **218**	60	45
1053	35c. Angel	65	45
1054	70c. Circular basket with red bow	1·25	1·00
1055	85c. Gold bow and tassels	1·60	1·75

219 Guides and Leaders

2010. Centenary of Girlguiding. Multicoloured.

1056	35c. Type **219**	90	55
1057	70c. Guide camp	1·40	1·25
1058	85c. Parade of guides and brownies	1·75	1·75
1059	$1.10 Guides with carnival float carrying model galleon	2·50	3·00
MS1060	127×89 mm. $1.25 1st and 2nd Excelsior Gudies (Bermuda's first Black Unit)	2·75	3·25

220 Cobbs Hill Methodist Church

2010. African Diaspora Heritage Trail. Multicoloured.

1061	35c. Type **220**	1·10	60
1062	70c. The Bermudian Heritage Museum	1·75	1·40
1063	85c. St. Peter's Church	2·25	2·25
1064	$1.10 Barr's Bay Park	3·25	3·50

221 Lined
Seahorse

2010. Endangered Species. Multicoloured.
1065		35c. Type **221**	1·00	60
1066		70c. Pair of seahorses	1·75	1·40
1067		85c. Pair hiding in seaweed	2·25	2·25
1068		$1.25 Adults and young	3·25	3·50

222 HMS *Urgent* in
Floating Dock,
c.1880

2010. Pioneers of Progress (4th series). Dockyard Apprentices. Multicoloured.
1069	35c. Type **222**	1·00	30
1070	70c. Dockyard Gate and part of dockyard gate	1·75	1·25
1071	85c. George Dixon (senior shipfitter) in front of power saw	2·00	2·25
1072	$1.10 Workmen outside chief constructor's shipfitting shop and tools	3·00	3·50

2011. Queen Elizabeth II and Prince Philip 'A Lifetime of Service'. Multicoloured.
1073	10c. Queen Elizabeth II, c. 1952	35	35
1074	35c. Queen Elizabeth II and Prince Philip (black and white photo)	1·00	40
1075	70c. Queen Elizabeth II (wearing red) and Prince Philip (in white uniform)	1·75	1·25
1076	85c. Queen Elizabeth II (wearing blue) and Prince Philip	2·25	2·25
1077	$1.10 Princess Elizabeth and Prince Philip (in uniform)	2·50	2·75
1078	$1.25 Prince Philip, c. 1952	2·50	3·00
MS1079	174×164 mm. Nos. 1073/8 and three stamp-size labels	9·00	9·50
MS1080	110×70 mm. $2.50 Queen Elizabeth II (wearing pale blue) and Prince Philip	5·50	6·00

223 Piloting Crew
bringing Gig
ashore and the
Heathers Chart

2011. Pioneers of Progress (5th series). Piloting. Multicoloured.
1081	35c. Type **223**	1·00	30
1082	70c. Painting of pilot sloop *Gibbs Hill*	1·75	1·25
1083	85c. Pilot sloop and portrait of pilot Jacob Miners	2·00	2·25
1084	$1.10 Photographs of gig in rough seas and pilot crew at leisure	3·00	3·50

224 Bermuda Dockyard and
Casemates Barracks, 1857

2011. Casemates Barracks, Bermuda Dockyard. Multicoloured.
1085	35c. Type **224**	1·00	30
1086	70c. Watercolour of western warehouse of Victualling Yard and construction of main Dockyard buildings, 1857	1·75	1·25
1087	85c. Casemates Barracks and Great Eastern Storehouse, late 1850s	2·00	2·25
1088	$1.25 Casemates Barracks complex, late 1800s	3·25	3·75

2011. Royal Wedding. Multicoloured.
MS1089 35c. Duke and Duchess of Cambridge at Westminster Abbey after Wedding ceremony (vert); 70c. Waving from State Landau; 85c. Leaving Buckingham Palace in car with 'JU5T WED' numberplate; $1.25 Kissing on Buckingham Palace balcony (vert) 7·25 7·25

225 Queen Elizabeth II, c. 1955

2012. Diamond Jubilee. Multicoloured.
1090	10c. Type **225**	50	50
1091	35c. At State Opening of Parliament, c. 2005	1·25	55
1092	70c. Queen Elizabeth II wearing headscarf, c. 1970	2·00	1·50
1093	85c. Queen Elizabeth II wearing bright pink, c. 2005	2·50	2·25
1094	$1.10 Queen Elizabeth II wearing blue dress, jacket and hat, c. 1955	3·25	3·50
1095	$1.25 Queen Elizabeth II wearing pearl and diamond earrings and necklace, c. 1970	3·75	4·00
MS1096	174×164 mm. Nos. 1090/5 and three stamp-size labels	12·00	12·00
MS1097	110×70 mm. $2.50 Coronation photograph, 1953	6·00	6·00

226 William Perot and Cancellation
of 1848

2012. Bicentenary of Bermuda Postal Service. Multicoloured.
1098	25c. Type **226**	1·25	60
1099	35c. Bermuda Queen Victoria 1d. red stamp and 19th-century mail ferry	1·40	60
1100	70c. Bermuda 1920 Tercentenary of Representative Institutions ½d. stamp and mail carriage, 1920s	2·25	1·75
1101	95c. Bermuda 1940 2d. ultramarine and scarlet yacht stamp and Imperial Airways Cavalier flying boat, 1930s	3·00	3·00
1102	$1.10 Bermuda 1968 2s.6d. Constitution stamp and mail van, 1960s	3·25	3·25
1103	$1.25 Stylised letters ('R-Post 2000s')	3·50	4·00

227 *South Shore, Bermuda*
(Thomas Anschutz)

2012. 25th Anniv of Masterworks Museum of Bermuda Art. Multicoloured.
1104	35c. Type **227**	1·00	30
1105	70c. *St. George's* (Ogden Pleissner)	1·75	1·25
1106	80c. *Front Street* (André Biéler)	2·00	2·00
1107	$1.10 *Street Scene, Bermuda* (Elliott Street) (Dorothy Austen Stevens)	2·75	2·75
1108	$1.25 *La Maison du Gouverneur* (Albert Gleizes) (vert)	3·00	3·25
1109	$1.65 *The Welcoming Smile* (Frank Small) (vert)	4·00	4·50

228 Clock Tower

2012. 400th Anniv of St. Peter's Church, St. George's. Multicoloured.
1110	35c. Type **228**	75	25

1111		95c. Chandelier and part of roof	2·50	2·00
1112		$1.10 Bronze plaque	2·75	2·50
1113		$1.25 Entrance and steps	3·00	3·50

EXPRESS LETTER STAMP

E1 Queen
Elizabeth II

1996.
E1	**E1**	$22 orange and blue	30·00	35·00

2003. As T **207** of Ascension.
E2	$25 black, blue and violet	29·00	30·00

Pt. 1

BHOPAL

A state of C. India. Now uses Indian stamps.

12 pies = 1 anna; 16 annas = 1 rupee.

3 (¼a.)

1876. Imperf.
5	**3**	¼a. black	8·00	22·00
2		½a. red	20·00	70·00

4 (¼a.)

1878. Imperf or perf.
7		¼a. green	13·00	25·00
15		¼a. red	7·00	5·50
8	**5**	½a. red	7·00	23·00
9		½a. brown	40·00	65·00

1881. As T **3**, but larger. Imperf or perf.
29	¼a. black	2·25	3·00
37	½a. red	2·00	3·75
46	½a. black	2·50	1·75
30	1a. brown	2·50	4·75
31	2a. blue	2·25	3·25
32	4a. yellow	2·50	3·75

1884. Perf
49	**13**	¼a. green	6·00	25·00
76	**13**	¼a. black	2·25	1·50

15 (½a.)

1884. Imperf or perf.
64	**15**	¼a. green	80	70
65	**15**	¼a. black	75	50
53	**15**	½a. black	1·00	3·50
56	**15**	½a. red	75	1·75

17 (8a.)

1890. Imperf or perf
71	**17**	8a. greenish black	23·00	23·00

1902. Imperf.
90	**19**	¼a. red	1·25	7·00
91	**19**	½a. black	1·25	5·00
92	**19**	1a. brown	5·00	11·00
94	**19**	2a. blue	11·00	32·00
96	**19**	4a. yellow	20·00	65·00
97	**19**	8a. lilac	70·00	£160
98	**19**	1r. red	£110	£300

20 State
Arms

1908. Perf.
100	**20**	1a. green	3·75	6·50

OFFICIAL STAMPS

1908. As T **20** but inscr "H.H. BEGUM'S SERVICE" optd **SERVICE**.
O301		½a. green	2·25	10
O302		1a. red	4·25	40
O307		2a. blue	4·00	60
O304		4a. brown	15·00	55

(O 4)

1930. Type **O4** optd **SERVICE**.
O309	**O4**	½a. green	15·00	1·75
O310	**O4**	1a. red	16·00	15
O311	**O4**	2a. blue	10·00	45
O312	**O4**	4a. brown	15·00	90

1932. As T **20**
(a) BHOPAL STATE" at right
O313	¼a. orange	2·50	1·00

(b) "BHOPAL GOVT" at right
O314	½a. green	9·00	10
O315	1a. green	11·00	15
O316	2a. blue	16·00	45
O317	4a. brown	13·00	1·00

1935. Nos. O314, etc, surch.
O319	3p. on ½a. on ½a. green	4·00	4·00
O321	3p. on 2a. on 2a. blue	4·50	5·50
O325	3p. on 4a. on 4a. brown	2·50	3·50
O318	¼a. on ½a. on ½a. green	45·00	18·00
O320	¼a. on 2a. on 2a. blue	45·00	26·00
O323	¼a. on 4a. on 4a. brown	£120	38·00
O326	1a. on ½a. on ½a. green	5·00	1·50
O328	1a. on 2a. on 2a. blue	70	2·50
O329	1a. on 4a. on 4a. brown	7·50	5·50

(O 8)

1935

(a) Inscr "BHOPAL GOVT POSTAGE". Optd "SERVICE"
O330	**O8**	1a.3p. blue and red	3·50	2·00

(b) Inscr "BHOPAL STATE POSTAGE". Optd "SERVICE"
O331	**O8**	1a.6p. blue and red	2·50	1·50
O332	**O8**	1a.6p. red	6·00	2·75

Nos. O331/2 are similar to Type O **8**, but inscr "BHOPAL STATE POSTAGE".

(O 9)

1936. Type **O9** optd **SERVICE**.
O333	**O9**	¼a. yellow	90	60
O335	**O9**	1a. red	1·50	10

O 10 The Moti Mahal

1936. As Type **O4** optd **SERVICE**.
O336d			70	50
O337	-	2a. brown and blue	2·00	1·00
O338	-	2a. green and violet	17·00	30
O339	-	4a. blue and brown	3·75	50
O340	-	8a. purple and blue	5·50	2·50

DESIGNS: 2a. The Moti Masjid; 4a. Taj Mahal and Be-Nazir Palaces; 8a. Ahmadabad Palace; 1r. Rait Ghat.

Nos. O336 is inscr "BHOPAL GOVT" below the arms, other values have "BHOPAL STATE".

1940. Animal designs, as Type **O10** but inscr "SERVICE" in bottom panel.
O344		¼a. blue (Tiger)	6·50	1·75
O345		1a. purple (Spotted deer)	42·00	4·25

1941. As Type **O8** but "SERVICE" inscr instead of optd.

O346	**O8**	1a.3p. green	3·00	3·00

1944. Palaces as Type **O 10** but smaller.

O347		½a. green (Moti Mahal)	1·00	1·00
O348c		2a. violet (Moti Masjid)	4·75	3·75
O349		4a. brown (Be-Nazir)	11·00	2·25

The 2a. and 4a. are inscr "BHOPAL STATE", and the other "BHOPAL GOVT".

O20 Arms of Bhopal

1944

O350	**O14**	3p. blue	1·00	1·00
O351b	**O14**	9p. brown	2·25	5·00
O352	**O14**	1a. purple	9·00	1·75
O353	**O14**	1½a. red	3·00	1·25
O354	**O14**	3a. yellow	23·00	22·00
O355	**O14**	6a. red	28·00	70·00

1949. Surch 2 As. and bars.

O356		2a. on 1½a. on 1½a. red	2·50	9·50

1949. Surch 2 As. and ornaments.

O357		2a. on 1½a. on 1½a. red	£1900	£1900

Pt. 1

BHOR

A state of W. India, Bombay district. Now uses Indian stamps.

12 pies = 1 anna; 16 annas = 1 rupee.

1

1879. Imperf.

1	**1**	½a. red	5·00	7·50
2		1a. red	7·00	10·00

3 Pandit Shankar Rao

1901. Imperf.

3	**3**	½a. red	19·00	45·00

Pt. 21

BHUTAN

An independent territory in treaty relations with India and bounded by India, Sikkim and Tibet.

100 chetrum = 1 ngultrum.

1 Postal Runner

1962

1	**1**	2ch. red and grey	30	25
2	-	3ch. red and blue	50	40
3	-	5ch. brown and green	1·10	95
4	-	15ch. yellow, black and red	60	50
5	**1**	33ch. green and violet	50	40
6	-	70ch. ultramarine and blue	75	65
7	-	1n.30 black and blue	2·40	2·10

DESIGNS—HORIZ: 3, 70ch. Archer. 5ch., 1n.30, Yak. 15ch. Map of Bhutan, Maharaja Druk Gyalpo and Paro Dzong (fortress and monastery).

2 "Uprooted Tree" Emblem and Crest of Bhutan

1962. World Refugee Year.

8	**2**	1n. red and blue	3·75	3·25
9	**2**	2n. violet and green	5·75	5·00

3 Accoutrements of Ancient Warrior

1962. Membership of Colombo Plan.

10	**3**	33ch. multicoloured	95	85
11	**3**	70ch. multicoloured	1·20	1·00
12	**3**	1n.30 red, brown & yellow	1·80	1·60

4 "Boy filling box" (with grain)

1963. Freedom from Hunger.

13	**4**	20ch. brown, blue & yellow	95	85
14	**4**	1n.50 purple, brown & blue	1·90	1·70

1964. Winter Olympic Games, Innsbruck, and Bhutanese Winter Sports Committee Fund. Nos. 10/12 surch **INNSBRUCK 1964 +50 ch**, Olympic rings and emblem.

15	**3**	33ch.+50ch. multicoloured	3·75	3·25
16	**3**	70ch.+50ch. multicoloured	3·75	3·25
17	**3**	1n.30+50ch. multicoloured	3·75	3·25

6 Dancer with upraised hands

1964. Bhutanese Dancers. Multicoloured.

18		2ch. Standing on one leg (vert)	10	10
19		3ch. Type **6**	10	10
20		5ch. With tambourine (vert)	15	15
21		20ch. As 2ch.	20	15
22		33ch. Type **6**	25	20
23		70ch. With sword	30	25
24		1n. With tasselled hat (vert)	55	50
25		1n.30 As 5ch.	1·20	1·00
26		2n. As 70ch.	1·90	1·70

7 Bhutanese Athlete

1964. Olympic Games, Tokyo. Multicoloured.

27		2ch. Type **7**	10	10
28		5ch. Boxing	25	20
29		15ch. Type **7**	30	25
30		33ch. As 5ch.	40	35
31		1n. Archery	70	65
32		2n. Football	1·30	1·20
33		3n. As 1n.	2·40	2·10
MS33a		85×118 mm. Nos. 31/2	19·00	17·00

8 Flags at Half-mast

1964. Pres. Kennedy Commemoration.

34	**8**	33ch. multicoloured	50	40
35	**8**	1n. multicoloured	95	85
36	**8**	3n. multicoloured	1·40	1·30
MS36a		82×119 mm. Nos. 35/6	5·75	5·00

9 Primula

1965. Flowers. Multicoloured.

37		2ch. Type **9**	10	10
38		5ch. Gentian	20	15
39		15ch. Type **9**	30	25
40		33ch. As 5ch.	40	35
41		50ch. Rhododendron	50	40
42		75ch. Peony	65	60
43		1n. As 50ch.	85	75
44		2n. As 75ch.	2·20	1·90

1965. Churchill Commemoration. Optd **WINSTON CHURCHILL 1874 1965**.

45	**1**	33ch. green and violet	75	65
46	**8**	1n. multicoloured	1·20	1·00
47	-	1n. multicoloured (No. 43)	1·20	1·00
48	-	2n. multicoloured (No. 44)	1·70	1·50
49	**8**	3n. multicoloured	2·50	2·20

11 Pavilion and Skyscrapers

1965. New York World's Fair. Multicoloured.

50		1ch. Type **11**	10	10
51		10ch. Buddha and Michelangelo's "Pieta"	30	25
52		20ch. Bhutan houses and New York skyline	40	35
53		33ch. Bhutan and New York bridges	50	40
54		1n.50 Type **11**	1·20	1·10
55		2n. As 10ch.	2·10	1·80
MS55a		120×86 mm. Nos. 54/5	7·75	6·75

1965. Surch.

56	**2**	5ch. on 1n. (No. 8)	55·00	50·00
57	**2**	5ch. on 2n. (No. 9)	55·00	50·00
58	-	10ch. on 70ch. (No. 23)	16·00	14·00
59	-	10ch. on 2n. (No. 26)	16·00	14·00
60	-	15ch. on 70ch. (No. 6)	14·50	12·50
61	-	15ch. on 1n.30 (No. 7)	14·50	12·50
62	-	20ch. on 1n. (No. 24)	19·00	17·00
63	-	20ch. on 1n.30 (No. 25)	19·00	17·00

13 "Telstar" and Portable Transmitter

1966. Centenary of I.T.U. Multicoloured.

64		35ch. Type **13**	30	25
65		2n. "Telstar" & morse key	50	40
66		3n. "Relay" and headphones	1·20	1·00
MS67		118×78 mm. Nos. 65/6	5·75	5·00

14 Asiatic Black Bear

1966. Animals. Multicoloured.

68		1ch. Type **14**	10	10
69		2ch. Snow leopard	10	10
70		4ch. Pygmy hog	15	15
71		8ch. Tiger	20	15
72		10ch. Dhole	25	20
73		75ch. As 8ch.	40	35
74		1n. Takin	50	40
75		1n.50 As 10ch.	95	85
76		2n. As 4ch.	1·20	1·00
77		3n. As 2ch.	1·70	1·50
78		4n. Type **14**	2·40	2·10
79		5n. As 1n.	3·25	3·00

15 Simtoke Dzong (fortress)

1966

80		5c. brown	4·75	2·50
81	**15**	15ch. brown	4·75	3·25
82	**15**	20ch. green	4·75	3·25

DESIGN: 5ch. Rinpung Dzong (fortress).

16 King Jigme Dorji Wangchuck (obverse of 50n.p. coin)

1966. 40th Anniv of King Jigme Wangchuck's Accession (father of King Jigme Dorji Wangchuck). Circular designs, embossed on gold foil, backed with multicoloured patterned paper. Imperf. Sizes: (a) Diameter 38 mm; (b) Diameter 50 mm; (c) Diameter 63 mm. (i) 50n.p. Coin.

83	**16**	10ch. green (a)	50	40

(ii) 1r. Coin.

84		25ch. green (b)	75	65

(iii) 3r. Coin.

85		50ch. green (c)	95	85

(iv) 1 sertum Coin.

86		1n. red (a)	1·50	1·30
87	-	1n.30 red (a)	2·30	2·00

(v) 2 sertum Coin.

88	**16**	2n. red (b)	3·25	3·00
89	-	3n. red (b)	5·25	4·50

(vi) 5 sertum Coin.

90	**16**	4n. red (c)	5·75	5·00
91	-	5n. red (c)	6·75	5·75

Nos. 87, 89 and 91 show the reverse side of the coins (Symbol).

17 "Abominable Snowman"

1966. "Abominable Snowman". Various triangular designs.

92	**17**	1ch. multicoloured	10	10
93	-	2ch. multicoloured	10	10
94	-	3ch. multicoloured	10	10
95	-	4ch. multicoloured	10	10
96	-	5ch. multicoloured	10	10
97	-	15ch. multicoloured	15	15
98	-	30ch. multicoloured	20	15
99	-	40ch. multicoloured	25	20
100	-	50ch. multicoloured	30	25
101	-	1n.25 multicoloured	50	40
102	-	2n.50 multicoloured	70	65
103	-	3n. multicoloured	80	70
104	-	5n. multicoloured	95	85
105	-	6n. multicoloured	1·20	1·00
106	-	7n. multicoloured	1·30	1·20

1967. Air. Optd **AIR MAIL** and Sikorsky S-55 helicopter.

107	**6**	33ch. multicoloured	30	25
108	-	50ch. mult (No. 41)	40	35
109	-	70ch. mult (No. 23)	50	40
110	-	75ch. mult (No. 42)	60	50
111	-	1n. mult (No. 24)	65	60
112	-	1n.50 mult (No. 75)	85	75
113	-	2n. mult (No. 76)	1·20	1·10
114	-	3n. mult (No. 77)	1·70	1·50
115	**14**	4n. multicoloured	3·00	2·50
116	-	5n. mult (No. 79)	3·25	3·00

20 "Lilium sherriffiae"

1967. Flowers. Multicoloured.

117		3ch. Type **20**	10	10
118		5ch. "Meconopsis"	10	10
119		7ch. "Rhododendron dhwoju"	15	15

120		10ch. "Pleione hookeriana"	20	20
121		50ch. Type **20**	30	25
122		1n. As 5ch.	50	45
123		2n.50 As 7ch.	1·30	1·10
124		4n. As 10ch.	1·50	1·20
125		5n. "Rhododendron giganteum"	1·90	1·60

21 Scouts planting Sapling

1967. Bhutanese Boy Scouts. Multicoloured.

126		5ch. Type **21**	10	10
127		10ch. Scouts preparing meal	20	20
128		15ch. Scout mountaineering	30	25
129		50ch. Type **21**	50	45
130		1n.25. As 10ch.	1·30	1·10
131		4n. As 15ch.	2·75	2·30
MS132		93×93 mm. Nos. 130/1	10·50	8·75

1967. World Fair, Montreal. Nos. 53/5 optd expo67 and emblem.

133	-	33ch. multicoloured	1·00	85
134	**11**	1n.50 multicoloured	1·10	90
135	-	2n. multicoloured	1·30	1·10
MS136		120×86 mm. Nos. 134/5	4·50	3·75

23 Avro Type **683**
Lancaster

1967. Churchill and Battle of Britain Commemoration. Multicoloured.

137		45ch. Type **23**	40	35
138		2n. Supermarine Spitfire Mk IIB	75	60
139		4n. Hawker Hurricane Mk IIC	1·50	1·20
MS140		118×75 mm. Nos. 138/9	4·25	3·50

1967. World Scout Jamboree, Idaho. Nos. 126/31 optd **WORLD JAMBOREE IDAHO, U.S.A. AUG. 1-9/67.**

141	**21**	5ch. multicoloured	30	25
142	-	10ch. multicoloured	40	35
143	-	15ch. multicoloured	50	45
144	-	50ch. multicoloured	75	60
145	-	1n.25 multicoloured	1·40	1·10
146	-	4n. multicoloured	3·00	2·50
MS147		93×93 mm. Nos. 145/6	8·25	7·00

25 Painting

1967. Bhutan Girl Scouts. Multicoloured.

148		5ch. Type **25**	10	10
149		10ch. Playing musical instrument	15	15
150		15ch. Picking fruit	20	20
151		1n.50 Type **25**	75	60
152		2n.50 As 10ch.	1·90	1·60
153		5n. As 15ch.	4·50	3·75
MS154		93×93 mm. Nos. 152/3	9·50	8·00

26 Astronaut in Space

1967. Space Achievements. With laminated prismatic-ribbed plastic surface. Multicoloured.

155		3ch. Type **26** (postage)	30	25
156		5ch. Space vehicle and astronaut	40	35
157		7ch. Astronaut and landing vehicle	65	55
158		10ch. Three astronauts in space	80	65
159		15ch. Type **26**	95	80
160		30ch. As 5ch.	1·10	95

161		50ch. As 7ch.	2·00	1·70
162		1n.25 As 10ch.	4·25	4·00
163		2n.50 Type **26** (air)	2·50	2·40
164		4n. As 5ch.	4·25	4·00
165		5n. As 7ch.	5·25	4·75
166		9n. As 10ch.	9·50	8·50
MS167		Three sheets, each 130×111 mm. Nos. 155/8, 159/62 and 163/6. Imperf	47·00	44·00

The laminated plastic surface gives the stamps a three-dimensional effect.

27 Tashichho Dzong

1968

168	**27**	10ch. purple and green	5·25	4·50

28 Elephant

1968. Mythological Creatures.

169	**28**	2ch. red, blue and brown (postage)	10	10
170	-	3ch. pink, blue & green	10	10
171	-	4ch. orange, green & blue	10	10
172	-	5ch. blue, yellow & pink	10	10
173	-	15ch. green, purple & blue	10	10
174	**28**	20ch. brown, blk & orge	15	15
175	-	30ch. yellow, black & blue	20	20
176	-	50ch. bistre, green & black	25	20
177	-	1n.25 black, green & red	35	30
178	-	2n. yellow, violet & black	50	45
179	**28**	1n.50 green, purple and yellow (air)	40	35
180	-	2n.50 red, black & blue	65	55
181	-	4n. orange, green & black	1·10	95
182	-	5n. brown, grey & orange	1·60	1·30
183	-	10n. violet, grey & black	2·75	2·40

DESIGNS: 3, 30ch., 2n.50, Garuda; 4, 50ch., 4n. Tiger; 5ch., 1n.25, 5n. Wind horse; 15ch., 2, 10n. Snow lion.

29 Tongsa Dzong

1968

184	**29**	50ch. green	2·50	2·20
185	-	75ch. brown and blue	4·25	3·50
186	-	1n. blue and violet	4·25	3·50

DESIGNS: 75ch. Daga Dzong; 1n. Lhuntsi Dzong.

30 Ward's Trogon

1968. Rare Birds.

187		2ch. Red-faced liocichla ("Crimson-winged Laughing Thrush") (horiz) (postage)	10	10
188		3ch. Type **30**	10	10
189		4ch. Burmese ("Grey") Peacock-pheasant	10	10
190		5ch. Rufous-necked hornbill	15	15
191		15ch. Fire-tailed 'myzornis' ("Myzornis") (horiz)	20	20
192		20ch. As No. 187	25	20
193		30ch. Type **30**	30	25
194		50ch. As No. 189	35	30
195		1n.25 As No. 190	50	45
196		2n. As No. 191	80	65
197		1n.50 As No. 187 (air)	65	55
198		2n.50 Type **30**	1·00	90
199		4n. As No. 189	1·30	1·10

200		5n. As No. 190	1·80	1·50
201		10n. As No. 191	3·50	2·75

31 Mahatma Gandhi

1969. Birth Centenary of Mahatma Gandhi.

202	**31**	20ch. brown and blue	65	55
203	**31**	2n. brown and yellow	2·50	2·20

1970. Various stamps surch **5 CH** or **20 CH**. (a) Freedom from Hunger (No. 14).

223		20ch. on 1n.50 purple, brown and blue	4·75	4·25

(b) Animals (Nos. 75/9).

224		20ch. on 1n.50 multicoloured	4·75	4·25
225		20ch. on 2n. multicoloured	4·75	4·25
204		20ch. on 3n. multicoloured	4·25	3·75
205		20ch. on 4n. multicoloured	4·25	3·75
206		20ch. on 5n. multicoloured	4·25	3·75

(c) Abominable Snowmen (Nos. 101/6).

226		20ch. on 1n.25 multicoloured	4·75	4·25
227		20ch. on 2n.50 multicoloured	4·75	4·25
207		20ch. on 3n. multicoloured	4·00	3·50
208		20ch. on 5n. multicoloured	4·25	3·75
209		20ch. on 6n. multicoloured	4·75	4·25
210		20ch. on 7n. multicoloured	4·75	4·25

(d) Flowers (Nos. 124/5).

211		20ch. on 4n. multicoloured	4·25	3·75
212		20ch. on 5n. multicoloured	4·50	4·00

(e) Boy Scouts (Nos. 130/1).

228		20ch. on 1n.25 multicoloured	4·75	4·25
213		20ch. on 4n. multicoloured	21·00	18·00

(f) Churchill (Nos. 138/9).

229		20ch. on 2n. multicoloured	4·75	4·25
230		20ch. on 4n. multicoloured	4·75	4·25

(g) 1968 Pheasants (Appendix).

231		20ch. on 2n. multicoloured	5·25	4·50
214		20ch. on 4n. multicoloured	4·25	3·75
232		20ch. on 7n. multicoloured	5·25	4·50

(h) Mythological Creatures (Nos. 175/80 and 182/3).

215		20ch. on 2n. yellow, violet and black	4·25	3·75
216		20ch. on 5n. brown, grey and orange	4·50	4·00
217		20ch. on 10n. violet, grey and black	4·25	3·75
233		5ch. on 30ch. yellow, black and blue (postage)	2·10	1·90
234		5ch. on 50ch. bistre, green and black	2·10	1·90
235		5ch. on 1n.25 black, green and red	2·10	1·90
236		5ch. on 2n. yellow, vio & blk	2·10	1·90
237		5ch. on 1n.50 green, purple and brown (air)	2·10	1·90
238		5ch. on 2n.50 red, black and blue	2·10	1·90

(i) Rare Birds (Nos. 193/201).

218		20ch. on 2n. multicoloured	4·75	4·25
219		20ch. on 2n.50. multicoloured	4·75	4·25
220		20ch. on 4n. multicoloured	4·25	3·75
221		20ch. on 5n. multicoloured	4·50	4·00
222		20ch. on 10n. multicoloured	5·25	4·50
239		20ch. on 30ch. mult (postage)	5·25	4·50
240		20ch. on 50ch. multicoloured	5·25	4·50
241		20ch. on 1n. 25. multicoloured	5·25	4·50
242		20ch. on 1n.50. mult (air)	5·25	4·50

(j) 1969 U.P.U. (Appendix).

243		20ch. on 1n.05. multicoloured	4·75	4·25
244		20ch. on 1n.40. multicoloured	4·75	4·25
245		20ch. on 4n. multicoloured	4·75	4·25

For stamps surcharged with 55 or 90ch. values, see Nos. 253/65 and for 25ch. surcharges see Nos. 385/410.

33
Wangdiphodrang
Dzong and Bridge

1971

246	**33**	2ch. grey	1·50	1·20
247	**33**	3ch. mauve	1·70	1·40
248	**33**	4ch. violet	1·80	1·50
249	**33**	5ch. green	70	55
250	**33**	10ch. brown	95	80
251	**33**	15ch. blue	1·30	1·10
252	**33**	20ch. purple	1·80	1·50

1971. Various stamps surch **55 CH** or **90 CH**. I. Dancers (Nos. 25/6).

253		55ch. on 1n.30 multicoloured	2·50	2·40
254		90ch. on 2n. multicoloured	2·50	2·40

II. Animals (Nos. 77/8).

255		55ch. on 3n. multicoloured	2·50	2·40
256		90ch. on 4n. multicoloured	2·50	2·40

III. Boy Scouts (No. 131).

257		90ch. on 4n. multicoloured	3·25	2·75

IV. 1968 Pheasants (Appendix).

258		55ch. on 5n. multicoloured	4·25	3·75
259		90ch. on 9n. multicoloured	4·25	3·75

V. Air. Mythological Creatures (No. 181).

260		55ch. on 4n. orange, green and black	2·30	2·20

VI. 1968 Mexico Olympics (Appendix).

261		90ch. on 1n.05 multicoloured	2·75	2·75

VII. Rare Birds (No. 196).

262		90ch. on 2n. multicoloured	4·25	3·75

VIII. 1969 UPU (Appendix).

263		55ch. on 60ch. multicoloured	2·50	2·40

IX. 1970 New UPU Headquarters (Appendix).

264		90ch. on 2n.50 gold and red	3·75	3·25

X. 1971 Moon Vehicles (plastic-surfaced) (Appendix).

265		90ch. on 1n.70 multicoloured	9·50	8·25

34 Book Year Emblem

1972. International Book Year.

266	**34**	2ch. green and blue	20	20
267	**34**	3ch. brown and yellow	30	25
268	**34**	5ch. brown, orange & red	40	35
269	**34**	20ch. brown and blue	50	45

35 Dochi

1972. Dogs. Multicoloured.

270		5ch. Apsoo standing on hind legs (vert)	10	10
271		10ch. Type **35**	15	15
272		15ch. Brown and white damci	20	20
273		25ch. Black and white damci	30	25
274		55ch. Apsoo lying down	40	35
275		8n. Two damci	3·25	2·75
MS276		100×119 mm. Nos. 274/5	6·25	5·25

36 King and Royal Crest

1974. Coronation of King Jigme Singye Wangchuck. Multicoloured.

277		10ch. Type **36**	40	35
278		25ch. Bhutan Flag	50	45
279		1n.25 Good Luck signs	75	60
280		2n. Punakha Dzong	95	80
281		3n. Royal Crown	1·00	90
MS282		Two sheets, each 177×127 mm. (a) 5ch. As 10ch.; 5ch. As 3n.; (b) 90ch. As 1n.25; 4n. As 2n. Perf or imperf	8·25	7·00

37 Mail Delivery
by Horse

1974. Centenary of UPU. Multicoloured.

283		1ch. Type **37** (postage)	10	10
284		2ch. Early and modern locomotives	15	15

285	3ch. "Hindoostan" (paddle-steamer) and "Iberia" (liner)		20	20
286	4ch. Vickers FB-27 Vimy and Concorde aircraft		30	25
287	25ch. Mail runner and four-wheel drive post car		50	45
288	1n. As 25ch. (air)		75	60
289	1n.40 As 2ch.		85	70
290	2n. As 4ch.		1·90	1·60
MS291	91×78 mm. 10n. As 4 ch		6·00	5·25

38 Family and WPY Emblem

1974. World Population Year.

292	**38**	25ch. multicoloured	20	20
293	**38**	50ch. multicoloured	30	25
294	**38**	90ch. multicoloured	40	35
295	**38**	2n.50 multicoloured	95	80
MS296	116×79 mm. **38** 10n. multi-coloured		3·75	3·25

39 Eastern Courtier

1975. Butterflies. Multicoloured.

297	**39**	1ch. Type **39**	10	10
298		2ch. Bamboo forester	10	10
299		3ch. Tailed labyrinth	15	15
300		4ch. Blue duchess	20	20
301		5ch. Cruiser	25	20
302		10ch. Bhutan glory	40	35
303		3n. Bi-coloured commodore	1·10	95
304		5n. Red-breasted jezebel	2·50	2·10
MS305	116×91 mm. 10n. Brown gorgon (*Dabasa gyas*)		4·25	3·75

40 King Jigme Singye Wangchuck

1976. King Jigme's 20th Birthday. Imperf. (a) Diameter 39 mm.

306	**40**	15ch. green on gold	55	50
307	**40**	1n. red on gold	1·60	1·30
308	-	1n.30 red on gold	2·00	1·70

(b) Diameter 50 mm.

309	**40**	25ch. green on gold	1·00	90
310	**40**	2n. red on gold	2·20	1·80
311	-	3n. red on gold	2·75	2·40

(c) Diameter 63 mm.

312	**40**	90ch. green on gold	1·50	1·20
313	**40**	4n. red on gold	5·00	4·25
314	-	5n. red on gold	6·25	5·25

DESIGN: 1n.30, 3, 5n. Decorative motif.

41 "Apollo"

1976. "Apollo"–"Soyuz" Space Link. Multicoloured.

315	**41**	10n. "Apollo"	3·75	3·00
316		10n. "Soyuz"	3·75	3·00
MS317	130×89 mm. 15n. Type **41**; 15n. As No. 316		10·50	9·25

42 Jewellery

1976. Handicrafts and Craftsmen. Multicoloured.

318	**42**	1ch. Type **42**	10	10
319		2ch. Coffee-pot, hand bell and sugar dish	10	10
320		3ch. Powder horns	10	10
321		4ch. Pendants and inlaid box	10	10

322		5ch. Painter	10	10
323		15ch. Silversmith	20	20
324		20ch. Wood carver with tools	25	20
325		1n.50 Textile printer	85	70
326		10n. Printer	2·50	2·20
MS327	105×79 mm. 5n. As No. 326		3·00	2·50

43 *Rhododendron cinnabarinum*

1976. Rhododendrons. Multicoloured.

328		1ch. Type **43**	10	10
329		2ch. R. campanulatum	10	10
330		3ch. R. fortunei	10	10
331		4ch. R. arboreum	15	15
332		5ch. R. arboreum (different)	25	20
333		1n. R. falconeri	30	25
334		3n. R. hodgsonii	75	60
335		5n. R. keysii	1·60	1·30
MS336	105×79 mm. 10n. R. cinnabarinum (different)		4·25	3·75

44 Skiing

1976. Winter Olympic Games, Innsbruck. Multicoloured.

337		1ch. Type **44**	10	10
338		2ch. Bobsleighing	10	10
339		3ch. Ice hockey	10	10
340		4ch. Cross-country skiing	15	15
341		5ch. Women's figure skating	25	20
342		2n. Downhill skiing	50	45
343		4n. Speed skating	95	80
344		10n. Pairs figure skating	3·00	2·50
MS345	78×104 mm. 6n. Ski jumping		2·50	2·40

45 Dragon Mask

1976. Ceremonial Masks. Laminated prismatic-ribbed plastic surface.

346	**45**	5ch. mult (postage)	40	35
347	-	10ch. multicoloured	50	45
348	-	15ch. multicoloured	65	55
349	-	20ch. multicoloured	75	60
350	-	25ch. multicoloured	85	70
351	-	30ch. multicoloured	95	80
352	-	35ch. multicoloured	1·00	90
353	-	1n. multicoloured (air)	2·50	2·10
354	-	2n. multicoloured	2·75	2·40
355	-	2n.50 multicoloured	3·25	2·75
356	-	3n. multicoloured	3·50	3·00
MS357	Two sheets, each 119×160 mm. (a) 5n. As No. 348; (b) 10n. As No. 351		29·00	26·00

DESIGNS: 10ch. to 10n. Similar Bhutanese masks.

46 Orchid

1976. Flowers. Multicoloured.

358		1ch. Type **46**	10	10
359		2ch. Orchid (different)	10	10
360		3ch. Orchid (different)	10	10
361		4ch. Primula denticulata	15	15
362		5ch. Arum	25	20
363		2n. Orchid (different)	90	75
364		4n. Leguminosa	1·60	1·30
365		6n. Rhododendron	2·50	2·20
MS366	106×80 mm. 10n. Arum (different)		6·25	5·50

47 Double Carp Emblem

1976. 25th Anniv of Colombo Plan.

367		3ch. Type **47**	10	10
368		4ch. Vase emblem	10	10
369		5ch. Geometric design	10	10
370		25ch. Design incorporating animal's face	20	20
371		1n.25 Ornamental design	40	35
372		2n. Floral design	65	55
373		2n.50 Carousel design	85	70
374		3n. Wheel design	1·10	95

48 Bandaranaike Conference Hall

1976. Fifth Non-aligned Countries Summit Conference, Colombo.

375	**48**	1n.25 multicoloured	75	60
376	**48**	2n.50 multicoloured	1·60	1·30

49 Liberty Bell

1978. Anniversaries and Events. Multicoloured.

377		20n. Type **49** (bicentenary of U.S. independence)	5·50	4·75
378		20n. Alexander Graham Bell early telephone (telephone centenary)	5·50	4·75
379		20n. Archer (Olympic Games, Montreal)	5·50	4·75
380		20n. Alfred Nobel (75th anniv of Nobel Prizes)	5·50	4·75
381		20n. "Spirit of St. Louis" (50th anniv of Lindbergh's transat-lantic flight)	7·00	6·00
382		20n. Airship LZ3 (75th anniv of Zeppelin)	7·00	6·00
383		20n. Queen Elizabeth II (25th anniv of Coronation)	5·50	4·75
MS384	Seven sheets, each 103×79 mm. (a) 25n. Flags of Bhutan and United States; (b) 25n. "Syncom II" communications satellite; (c) 25n. Shot putter; (d) 25n. Nobel medal; (e) 25n. "Spirit of St. Louis" landing at Le Bourget; (f) 25n. Airship "Viktoria Luise"; (g) 25n. Westminster Abbey		55·00	48·00

1978. Provisionals. Various stamps surch **25 Ch** (385, 394) or **25 CH** (others). I. Girl Scouts (No. 153).

385		25ch. on 5n. mult (postage)	13·00	11·50

II. Air. 1968 Mythological Creatures (Nos. 181 and 183).

386		25ch. on 4n. orange, green and black	2·50	2·20
387		25ch. on 10n. violet, grey and black	2·50	2·20

III. 1971 Admission to U.N. (Appendix).

388		25ch. on 3n. mult (postage)	2·20	1·80
389		25ch. on 5n. mult (air)	2·20	1·80
390		25ch. on 6n. multicoloured	2·20	1·80

IV. Boy Scouts Anniv (Appendix).

391		25ch. on 6n. multicoloured	13·50	12·00

V. 1972 Dogs (No. 275).

392		25ch. on 8n. multicoloured	4·00	3·50

VI. 1973 Dogs (Appendix).

393		25ch. on 8n. multicoloured	4·00	3·50

VII. 1973 "Indipex 73" (Appendix).

394		25ch. on 3n. mult (postage)	3·50	3·00
395		25ch. on 5n. mult (air)	3·50	3·00
396		25ch. on 6n. multicoloured	3·50	3·00

VIII. U.P.U. (Nos. 289/90).

397		25ch. on 1n. 40 multicoloured	3·25	2·75
398		25ch. on 2n. multicoloured	3·25	2·75

IX. World Population Year (No. 295).

399		25ch. on 2n.50 multicoloured	5·25	4·50

X. Butterflies (Nos. 303/4).

400		25ch. on 3n. multicoloured	5·25	4·50
401		25ch. on 5n. multicoloured	5·25	4·50

XI. "Apollo"–"Soyuz" (Nos. 315/16).

402		25ch. on 10n. mult (315)	13·00	11·50
403		25ch. on 10n. mult (316)	13·00	11·50

XII. Handicrafts (No. 326).

404		25ch. on 10n. multicoloured	2·50	2·20

XIII. Rhododendrons (No. 335).

405		25ch. on 5n. multicoloured	4·50	4·00

XIV. Winter Olympics (Nos. 343/4).

406		25ch. on 4n. multicoloured	6·00	5·25
407		25ch. on 10n. multicoloured	6·00	5·25

XV. Flowers (Nos. 364/5).

408		25ch. on 4n. multicoloured	2·20	1·80
409		25ch. on 6n. multicoloured	2·20	1·80

XVI. Colombo Plan (No. 373).

410		25ch. on 2n.50 multicoloured	2·50	2·20

50 Mother and Child

1979. International Year of the Child. Multicoloured.

411		2n. Type **50**	95	80
412		5n. Mother carrying two children	1·70	1·40
413		10n. Children at school	2·75	2·40
MS414	131×103 mm. Nos. 411/13		4·75	4·25

51 Conference Emblem and Dove

1979. Sixth Non-Aligned Countries Summit Conference, Havana. Multicoloured.

415		25ch. Type **51**	30	25
416		10n. Emblem and Bhutanese symbols	3·50	3·00

52 Dorji (rattle)

1979. Antiquities. Multicoloured.

417		5ch. Type **52**	10	10
418		10ch. Dilbu (hand bell) (vert)	20	20
419		15ch. Jadum (cylindrical pot) (vert)	30	25
420		25ch. Jamjee (teapot)	40	35
421		1n. Kem (cylindrical container) (vert)	50	45
422		1n.25 Jamjee (different)	65	55
423		1n.70 Sangphor (ornamental vessel) (vert)	1·00	90
424		2n. Jamjee (different) (vert)	1·30	1·10
425		3n. Yangtho (pot with lid) (vert)	1·50	1·20
426		4n. Battha (circular case)	1·90	1·60
427		5n. Chhap (ornamental flask) (vert)	2·50	2·20

53 Rinpiang Dzong, Bhutan Stamp and Rowland Hill Statue

1980. Death Cent of Sir Rowland Hill. Multicoloured.

428		1n. Type **53**	50	45
429		2n. Dzong, Bhutan stamp and statue	1·00	90
430		5n. Ounsti Dzong, Bhutan stamp and statue	2·10	1·80
431		10n. Lingzi Dzong and British 1912 1d. stamp	4·00	3·50
MS432	102×103 mm. 20n. Rope bridge, British 1d. black stamp and statue		10·00	9·50

54 Dungtse Lhakhang,
Paro

1981. Monasteries. Multicoloured.

433	1n. Type **54**	50	45
434	2n. Kich Lhakhang, Paro (horiz)	75	60
435	2n.25 Kurjey Lhakhang (horiz)	1·00	90
436	3n. Tangu, Thimphu (horiz)	1·30	1·10
437	4n. Cheri, Thimphu (horiz)	1·70	1·40
438	5n. Chorten, Kora (horiz)	2·50	2·20
439	7n. Tak-Tsang, Paro	3·75	3·00

55 St. Paul's
Cathedral

1981. Wedding of Prince of Wales. Multicoloured.

440	1n. Type **55**	20	20
441	5n. Type **55**	1·40	1·10
442	20n. Prince Charles and Lady Diana Spencer	4·75	4·25
443	25n. As No. 442	6·25	5·50
MS444	69×90 mm. 20n. Wedding procession	5·25	4·50

56 Orange-bellied
Leafbird
("Orange-billed
Chiropsis")

1982. Birds. Multicoloured.

445	2n. Type **56**	1·30	1·10
446	3n. Himalayan monal pheasant ("Monal Pheasant")	1·90	1·60
447	5n. Ward's trogon	3·75	3·25
448	10n. Mrs. Gould's sunbird	5·75	5·00
MS449	95×101 mm. 25n. Maroon oriole (*Oriolus trailii*)	10·50	9·25

57 Footballers

1982. World Cup Football Championship, Spain.

450	**57**	1n. multicoloured	30	25
451	-	2n. multicoloured	65	55
452	-	3n. multicoloured	95	80
453	-	20n. multicoloured	4·50	4·00
MS454		79×108 mm. 25n. multicoloured (horiz)	12·50	11·00

DESIGNS: 2n. to 25n. Various football scenes.
No. MS454 exists in two versions, differing in the list of qualifying countries in the border.

58 St. James's
Palace

1982. 21st Birthday of Princess of Wales. Multicoloured.

455	1n. Type **58**	1·00	90
456	10n. Prince and Princess of Wales	3·75	3·00
457	15n. Windsor Castle	6·25	5·50

458	25n. Princess in wedding dress	10·00	8·50
MS459	102×76 mm. 20n. Princess of Wales	16·00	13·00

59 Lord
Baden-Powell
(founder)

1982. 75th Anniv of Boy Scout Movement. Multicoloured.

460	3n. Type **59**	85	70
461	5n. Scouts around campfire	1·70	1·40
462	15n. Map reading	4·00	3·50
463	20n. Pitching tents	6·00	5·25
MS464	91×70 mm. 25n. Scout	7·75	7·00

60 Rama finds Mowgli

1982. *The Jungle Book* (cartoon film). Multicoloured.

465	1ch. Type **60**	10	10
466	2ch. Bagheera leading Mowgli to Man-village	10	10
467	3ch. Kaa planning attack on Bagheera and Mowgli	10	10
468	4ch. Mowgli and elephants	10	10
469	5ch. Mowgli and Baloo	10	10
470	10ch. Mowgli and King Louie	10	10
471	30ch. Kaa and Shere Khan	25	20
472	2n. Mowgli, Baloo and Bagheera	1·00	90
473	20n. Mowgli carrying jug for girl	6·25	5·25
MS474	Two sheets, each 127×102 mm. (a) 20n. Mowgli and Baloo; (b) 20n. Mowgli and Baloo floating down river	14·50	12·50

1982. Birth of Prince William of Wales. Nos. 455/MS459 optd **ROYAL BABY 21.6.82**.

475	1n. multicoloured	65	55
476	10n. multicoloured	2·10	1·80
477	15n. multicoloured	4·75	4·25
478	25n. multicoloured	7·25	6·25
MS479	102×76 mm. 20n. multicoloured	12·50	11·00

62 Washington surveying

1982. 250th Birth Anniv of George Washington and Birth Centenary of Franklin D. Roosevelt. Multicoloured.

480	50ch. Type **62**	10	10
481	1n. Roosevelt and Harvard University	20	10
482	2n. Washington at Valley Forge	50	45
483	3n. Roosevelt's mother and family	65	55
484	4n. Washington at Battle of Monmouth	85	70
485	5n. Roosevelt and the White House	1·30	1·10
486	15n. Washington and Mount Vernon	3·75	3·00
487	20n. Churchill, Roosevelt and Stalin at Yalta	5·25	4·50
MS488	Two sheets, each 102×73 mm. (a) 25n. Washington (vert); (b) 25n. Roosevelt (vert)	12·50	11·00

1983. "Druk Air" Bhutan Air Service. Various stamps optd **DRUK AIR** (491) or **Druk Air** (others), No. 489 surch also.

489	**42**	30ch. on 1n. multicoloured (postage)	3·25	2·75
490	-	5n. multicoloured (Scouts, Appendix)	5·25	4·50
491	-	8n. mult (No. 275)	6·25	5·50
492	-	5n. mult ("Indipex 73", Appendix) (air)	8·25	7·25
493	-	7n. mult (Munich Olympics, Appendix)	10·50	9·25

64 *Angelo Doni*

1983. 500th Birth Anniv of Raphael (artist). Multicoloured.

494	1n. Type **64**	40	35
495	4n. *Maddalena Doni*	1·00	90
496	5n. *Baldassare Castiglione*	1·60	1·30
497	20n. *Woman with Veil*	6·25	5·50
MS498	Two sheets, each 127×101 mm. (a) 25n. Self-portrait (detail from *Mass of Bolsena*); (b) 25n. Self-portrait (detail from *Expulsion of Heliodorus*)	19·00	17·00

65 Ta-Gyad-Boom-Zu
(the eight
luck-bringing
symbols)

1983. Religious Offerings. Multicoloured.

499	25ch. Type **65**	25	10
500	50ch. Doeyun Nga (the five sensory symbols)	40	25
501	2n. Norbu Chadun (the seven treasures) (47×41 mm)	75	60
502	3n. Wangpo Nga (the five sensory organs)	1·00	90
503	8n. Sha Nga (the five kinds of flesh)	2·10	1·80
504	9n. Men-Ra-Tor Sum (the sacrificial cake) (47×41 mm)	2·50	2·20
MS505	180×135 mm. Nos. 499/504	8·25	7·25

66 Dornier Wal Flying Boat
Boreas

1983. Bicentenary of Manned Flight. Multicoloured.

506	50ch. Type **66**	25	10
507	3n. Savoia-Marchetti S.66 flying boat	95	80
508	10n. Hawker Osprey biplane	3·25	2·75
509	20n. Astra airship *Ville de Paris*	6·25	5·50
MS510	106×80 mm. 25n. Henri Giffard's balloon *Le Grand Ballon Captif*	7·25	6·25

67 Mickey Mouse as
Caveman

1984. World Communications Year. Multicoloured.

511	4ch. Type **67**	10	10
512	5ch. Goofy as printer	10	10
513	10ch. Chip 'n' Dale with morse key	10	10
514	20ch. Pluto talks to girlfriend on telephone	10	10
515	25ch. Minnie Mouse pulling record from bulldog	10	10
516	50ch. Morty and Ferdie with microphone and loudhailers	25	15
517	1n. Huey, Dewey, and Louie listening to radio	65	55
518	5n. Donald Duck watching television on buffalo	2·00	1·70
519	20n. Daisy Duck with computers and abacus	6·75	5·75
MS520	Two sheets, each 127×102 mm. (a) 20n. Mickey Mouse on television (horiz); (b) 20n. Donald Duck and satellite (horiz)	13·50	12·00

68 Golden Langur

1984. Endangered Species. Multicoloured.

521	50ch. Type **68**	65	55
522	1n. Golden langur family in tree (horiz)	1·00	90
523	2n. Male and female Golden langurs with young (horiz)	2·50	2·20
524	4n. Group of langurs	4·75	4·25
MS525	Three sheets. (a) 88×121 mm. 20n. Snow leopard; (b) 121×88 mm. 25n. Yak; (c) 121×88 mm. 25n. Bharal (horiz)	25·00	22·00

69 Downhill
Skiing

1984. Winter Olympic Games, Sarajevo. Multicoloured.

526	50ch. Type **70**	35	20
527	1n. Cross-country skiing	50	25
528	3n. Speed skating	1·30	1·10
529	20n. Four-man bobsleigh	5·50	4·75
MS530	108×76 mm. 25n. Ice hockey	7·25	6·25

70 *Sans Pareil*,
1829

1984. Railway Locomotives. Multicoloured.

531	50ch. Type **70**	10	10
532	1n. *Planet*, 1830	30	20
533	3n. *Experiment* 1832	1·00	90
534	4n. *Black Hawk*, 1835	1·50	1·20
535	5n. *Jenny Lind*, 1847 (horiz)	1·90	1·60
536	8n. *Bavaria*, 1851 (horiz)	2·50	2·20
537	10n. Great Northern locomotive No. 1, 1870 (horiz)	3·25	2·75
538	25n. Steam locomotive Type 110, Prussia, 1880 (horiz)	7·75	6·75
MS539	Four sheets, each 92×65 mm. (a) 20n. Crampton's locomotive, 1846 (horiz); (b) 20n. *Erzsebet*, 1870 (horiz); (c) 20n. Sondermann freight, 1896 (horiz); (d) 20n. Darjeeling–Himalaya railway (horiz)	25·00	22·00

71 Riley Sprite Sports Car,
1936

1984. Cars. Multicoloured.

540	50ch. Type **71**	10	10
541	1n. Lanchester Forty saloon, 1919	30	20
542	3n. Itala 35/45 racer, 1907	85	70
543	4n. Morris Oxford (Bullnose) tourer, 1913	1·30	1·10
544	5n.50 Lagonda LG6 drophead coupe, 1939	1·60	1·30
545	6n. Wolseley four seat tonneau, 1903	1·90	1·60
546	8n. Buick Super convertible, 1952	2·30	1·90
547	20n. Maybach Zeppelin limousine, 1933	6·25	5·50
MS548	Two sheets, each 126×99 mm. (a) 25n. Renault (1901); (b) 25n. Simplex (1912)	16·00	14·00

72 Women's Archery

1984. Olympic Games, Los Angeles. Multicoloured.
549	15ch. Type **72**		10	10
550	25ch. Men's archery		30	15
551	2n. Table tennis		65	55
552	2n.25 Basketball		85	70
553	5n.50 Boxing		1·60	1·30
554	6n. Running		1·90	1·60
555	8n. Tennis		3·00	2·50
MS556	115×82 mm. 25n. Couple practising archery (72×43 mm)		6·75	6·00

73 Domkhar Dzong

1984. Monasteries.
557	**73**	10ch. blue	10	10
558	–	25ch. red	30	15
559	–	50ch. violet	50	45
560	–	1n. brown	75	60
561	–	2n. red	95	80
562	–	5n. green	2·10	1·80

DESIGNS: 25ch. Shemgang Dzong; 50ch. Chapcha Dzong; 1n. Tashigang Dzong; 2n. Pungthang Dzong; 5n. Dechenphoda Dzong.

74 "Magician Mickey"

1984. 50th Anniv of Donald Duck. Scenes from films. Multicoloured.
563	4ch. Type **74**	10	10
564	5ch. "Slide, Donald, Slide"	10	10
565	10ch. "Donald's Golf Game"	10	10
566	20ch. "Mr. Duck Steps Out"	10	10
567	25ch. "Lion Around"	10	10
568	50ch. "Alpine Climbers"	20	10
569	1n. "Flying Jalopy"	40	25
570	5n. "Frank Duck brings 'Em Back Alive"	1·50	1·20
571	20n. "Good Scouts"	6·25	5·50
MS572	Two sheets, each 128×101 mm. (a) 20n. "Sea Scouts"; (b) 20n. "The Three Caballeros"	14·50	12·50

1984. Various stamps surch. (a) World Cup Football Championship, Spain (Nos. 450/3).
573	5n. on 1n. multicoloured	2·75	2·40
574	5n. on 2n. multicoloured	2·75	2·40
575	5n. on 3n. multicoloured	2·75	2·40
576	5n. on 20n. multicoloured	2·75	2·40
MS577	79×108 mm. 20n. on 25n. multicoloured	17·00	15·00

No. **MS**577 exists in two versions, differing in the list of qualifying countries in the border.

(b) 21st Birthday of Princess of Wales (Nos. 455/8).
578	5n. on 1n. multicoloured	2·75	2·40
579	5n. on 10n. multicoloured	2·75	2·40
580	5n. on 15n. multicoloured	2·75	2·40
581	40n. on 25n. multicoloured	21·00	18·00
MS582	102×76 mm. 25n. on 20n. multicoloured	13·50	12·00

(c) Birth of Prince William of Wales (Nos. 475/8).
583	5n. on 1n. multicoloured	2·75	2·40
584	5n. on 10n. multicoloured	2·75	2·40
585	5n. on 15n. multicoloured	2·75	2·40
586	40n. on 25n. multicoloured	21·00	18·00
MS587	102×76 mm. 25n. on 20n. multicoloured	13·50	12·00

(d) Wedding of Prince of Wales (Nos. 440/3).
588	10n. on 1n. multicoloured	4·50	3·75
589	10n. on 10n. multicoloured	4·50	3·75
590	10n. on 20n. multicoloured	4·50	3·75
591	10n. on 25n. multicoloured	4·50	3·75
MS592	69×90 mm. 30n. on 20n. multicoloured	14·50	12·50

On Nos. 588/**MS**592 the new value is surcharged twice.

(e) 75th Anniv of Boy Scout Movement (Nos. 460/3).
593	10n. on 3n. multicoloured	4·50	3·75
594	10n. on 5n. multicoloured	4·50	3·75
595	10n. on 15n. multicoloured	4·50	3·75
596	10n. on 20n. multicoloured	4·50	3·75
MS597	91×70 mm. 20n. on 25n. multicoloured	13·50	12·00

76 Shinje Choegyel

1985. The Judgement of Death Mask Dance. Multicoloured.
598	5ch. Type **76**	10	10
599	35ch. Raksh Lango	20	10
600	50ch. Druelgo	30	15
601	2n.50 Pago	85	70
602	3n. Telgo	1·00	90
603	4n. Due Nakcung	1·50	1·20
604	5n. Lha Karpo	1·70	1·40
605	5n.50 Nyalbum	2·00	1·70
606	6n. Khimda Pelkyi	2·20	1·80
MS607	90×135 mm. Nos. 598/9 and 603/4	4·75	3·75

77 Bhutan and UN Flags

1985. 40th Anniv of UNO.
608	**77**	50ch. multicoloured	30	20
609	–	15n. multicoloured	2·75	2·40
610	–	20n. black and blue	4·00	3·25
MS611	65×80 mm. 25n. black, yellow and scarlet		5·75	5·00

DESIGNS—VERT: 15n. UN building, New York; 25n. 1945 charter; HORIZ: 20n. Veterans' War Memorial Building San Francisco (venue of signing charter, 1945).

78 Mickey Mouse tramping through Black Forest

1985. 150th Birth Anniv of Mark Twain (writer) and International Youth Year. Multicoloured.
612	50ch. Type **78**	10	10
613	2n. Mickey Mouse, Donald Duck and Goofy on steamboat trip on Lake Lucerne	50	25
614	5n. Mickey Mouse, Donald Duck and Goofy climbing Rigi-Kulm	1·40	1·10
615	9n. Mickey Mouse and Goofy rafting to Heidelberg on River Neckar	2·50	2·20
616	20n. Mickey Mouse leading Donald Duck on horse back up the Riffelberg	5·75	5·00
MS617	126×101 mm. 25n. Mickey Mouse and Goofy	7·25	6·25

Nos. 612/**MS**617 show scenes from "A Tramp Abroad" (cartoon film of Twain novel).

79 Prince sees Rapunzel

1985. Birth Bicentenaries (1985 and 1986) of Grimm Brothers (folklorists). Multicoloured.
618	1n. Type **79**	40	15
619	4n. Rapunzel (Minnie Mouse) in tower	85	55
620	7n. Mother Gothel calling to Rapunzel to let down her hair	1·90	1·60
621	8n. Prince climbing tower using Rapunzel's hair	2·50	2·20
622	15n. Prince proposing to Rapunzel	4·25	3·50
MS623	126×101 mm. 25n. Prince riding away with Rapunzel	8·25	7·25

80 Brewers Duck (mallard)

1985. Birth Bicentenary of John J. Audubon (ornithologist). Audubon illustrations. Multicoloured.
624	50ch. Type **80**	20	10
625	1n. "Willow Ptarmigan" (Willow/ red Grouse)	30	20
626	2n. "Mountain Plover"	50	45
627	3n. "Red-throated Loon" (Red-throated Diver)	85	70
628	4n. "Spruce Grouse"	1·40	1·10
629	5n. "Hooded Merganser"	1·70	1·40
630	15n. "Trumpeter Swan" (Whooper Swan)	4·75	4·00
631	20n. Common goldeneye	6·00	5·25
MS632	75×105 mm. 25n. "Sharp-shinned Hawk"	7·75	6·75
MS633	75×105 mm. 25n. "Tufted Titmouse"	7·75	6·75

81 Members' Flags around Buddhist Design

1985. South Asian Regional Co-operation Summit, Dhaka, Bangladesh.
634	**81**	50ch. multicoloured	50	25
635	**81**	5n. multicoloured	1·80	1·50

82 Precious Wheel

1986. The Precious Symbols. Multicoloured.
636	30ch. Type **82**	15	10
637	50ch. Precious Gem	20	10
638	1n.25 Precious Queen	30	20
639	2n. Precious Minister	50	40
640	4n. Precious Elephant	85	70
641	6n. Precious Horse	1·30	1·10
642	8n. Precious General	1·90	1·60

1986. Olympic Games Gold Medal Winners. Nos. 549/50 and 552/5 optd.
643	**72**	15ch. **GOLD HYANG SOON SEO SOUTH KOREA**	10	10
644	–	25ch. **GOLD DARRELL PACE USA**	20	10
645	–	2n.25 **GOLD MEDAL USA**	65	55
646	–	5n.50 **GOLD MARK BRELAND USA**	1·00	90
647	–	6n. **GOLD DALEY THOMPSON ENGLAND**	1·30	1·10
648	–	8n. **GOLD STEFAN EDBERG SWEDEN**	1·90	1·60
MS649	Two sheets, each 115×82 mm. (a) 25n. **HYANG SOON SEO, SOUTH KOREA**; (b) 25n. **DARRELL PACE, U.S.A.**		12·50	11·00

1986. "Ameripex 86" International Stamp Exhibition, Chicago. Various stamps optd **AMERIPEX 86**. (a) Nos. 615/**MS**617.
650	8n. multicoloured	3·25	2·75
651	20n. multicoloured	6·75	6·00
MS652	126×101 mm. 25n. multicoloured	7·75	6·75

(b) Nos. 621/**MS**623.
653	8n. multicoloured	2·50	2·20
654	15n. multicoloured	4·25	3·50
MS655	126×101 mm. 25n. multicoloured	7·75	6·75

85 Mandala of Phurpa (Ritual Dagger)

1986. Kilkhor Mandalas of Mahayana Buddhism. Multicoloured.
656	10ch. Type **85**	10	10
657	25ch. Mandala of Amitayus in Wrathful Form	20	10
658	50ch. Mandala of Overpowering Deities	25	10
659	75ch. Mandala of the Great Wrathful One	30	15
660	1n. Type **85**	40	25
661	3n. As 25ch.	85	70
662	5n. As 50ch.	1·30	1·10
663	7n. As 75ch.	1·70	1·40

1986. 75th Anniv of Girl Guides. Nos. 460/3 optd **75th ANNIVERSARY GIRL GUIDES**.
664	3n. multicoloured	1·90	1·60
665	5n. multicoloured	3·75	3·25
666	15n. multicoloured	10·00	8·75
667	20n. multicoloured	13·50	11·50
MS668	91×70 mm. 25n. multicoloured	16·00	13·50

87 Babylonian Tablet and Comet over Noah's Ark

1986. Appearance of Halley's Comet. Multicoloured.
669	50ch. Type **87**	20	10
670	1n. 17th-century print	25	10
671	2n. 1835 French silhouette	30	25
672	3n. Bayeux tapestry	50	45
673	4n. Woodblock from *Nuremburg Chronicle*	85	70
674	5n. Illustration of Revelation 6, 12–13 from 1650 Bible	1·30	1·10
675	15n. Comet in constellation of Cancer	3·50	3·00
676	20n. Decoration on Delft plate	4·75	4·00
MS677	Two sheets, each 109×79 mm. (a) 25n. Comet over dzong in Himalayas; (b) 25n. Comet over shrine	12·50	11·00

88 Statue and *Libertad* (Argentine full-rigged cadet ship)

1986. Centenary of Statue of Liberty. Multicoloured.
678	50ch. Type **88**	20	10
679	1n. "Shalom" (Israeli liner)	25	10
680	2n. "Leonardo da Vinci" (Italian liner)	30	25
681	3n. "Mircea" (Rumanian cadet barque)	50	45
682	4n. "France" (French liner)	85	70
683	5n. S.S. *United States* (American liner)	1·30	1·10
684	15n. "Queen Elizabeth 2" (British liner)	3·50	3·00
685	20n. "Europa" (West German liner)	4·75	4·00
MS686	Two sheets, each 114×83 mm. (a) Statue (27×41 mm); (b) Statue and tower blocks (27×41 mm)	11·50	10·00

The descriptions of the ships on Nos. 678 and 681 were transposed in error.

89 "Santa Maria"

1987. 500th Anniv (1992) of Discovery of America by Columbus. Multicoloured.
687	20ch. Type **89**	55	50
688	25ch. Queen Isabella of Spain	55	50
689	50ch. Flying fish	55	50
690	1n. Columbus's coat of arms	95	80
691	2n. Christopher Columbus	1·60	1·40

692	3n. Columbus landing with Spanish soldiers	2·30	2·00

MS693 Seven sheets, each 97×65 mm. (a) 20ch. Pineapple; (b) 25ch. Indian hammock (horiz); (c) 50ch. Tobacco plant; (d) 1n. Greater flamingo; (e) 2n. Astrolabe; (f) 3n. Lizard (horiz); (g) 5n. Iguana (horiz)
| | | 22·00 | 19·00 |

MS694 170×144 mm. As Nos. 687/92 but with white backgrounds
| | | 26·00 | 24·00 |

90 Canadian National Class "U1-f" Steam Locomotive No. 6060

1987. "Capex '87" International Stamp Exhibition, Toronto. Canadian Railways. Multicoloured.

695	50ch. Type **90**	15	10
696	1n. Via Rail "L.R.C." electric locomotive No. 6903	25	10
697	2n. Canadian National GM "GF30t" diesel locomotive No. 5341	50	45
698	3n. Canadian National steam locomotive No. 6157	75	60
699	8n. Canadian Pacific steam locomotive No. 2727	2·10	1·80
700	10n. Via Express diesel locomotive No. 6524	2·50	2·10
701	15n. Canadian National "Turbotrain"	3·75	3·00
702	20n. Canadian Pacific diesel-electric locomotive No. 1414	4·75	4·00

MS703 Two sheets, each 102×75 mm. (a) 25n. Cab and tender of Royal Hudson steam locomotive (27×41 mm); (b) 25n. Canadian National steam locomotive (27×41 mm)
| | | 11·50 | 10·00 |

91 Two Faces (sculpture)

1987. Birth Centenary of Marc Chagall (artist). Multicoloured.

704	50ch. Type **91**	20	20
705	1n. At the Barber's	30	25
706	2n. Old Jew with Torai	50	45
707	3n. Red Maternity	85	70
708	4n. Eve of Yom Kippur	1·30	1·10
709	5n. The Old Musician	1·50	1·20
710	6n. The Rabbi of Vitebsk	1·70	1·40
711	7n. Couple at Dusk	1·90	1·60
712	9n. The Artistes	2·30	1·90
713	10n. Moses breaking the Tablets	2·50	2·10
714	12n. Bouquet with Flying Lovers	3·00	2·50
715	20n. In the Sky of the Opera	5·00	4·25

MS716 12 sheets, each 95×110 mm (e) or 110×95 mm (others). Imperf. (a) 25n. The Red Gateway. (b) 25n. Romeo and Juliet. (c) 25n. Maternity. (d) 25n. The Carnival for Aleko, Scene II. (e) 25n. Magician of Paris. (f) 25n. Visit to the Grandparents. (g) 25n. Cow with Parasol. (h) 25n. Russian Village. (i) 25n. Still Life. (j) 25n. Composition with Goat. (k) 25n. The Smolensk Newspaper. (l) 25n. The Concert
| | | 75·00 | 65·00 |

92 Goofy (slalom)

1988. Winter Olympic Games, Calgary. Multicoloured.

717	50ch. Type **92**	20	10
718	1n. Donald Duck pushing Goofy at start (downhill skiing)	40	25
719	2n. Goofy in goal (ice hockey)	50	35
720	4n. Goofy (biathlon)	1·00	90
721	7n. Goofy and Donald Duck (speed skating)	1·80	1·50
722	8n. Minnie Mouse (figure skating)	2·20	1·80
723	9n. Minnie Mouse (free-style skating)	2·50	2·10
724	20n. Goofy and Mickey Mouse (two-man bobsleigh)	5·25	4·50

MS725 Two sheets, each 127×101 mm. (a) 25n. Goofy (ski jumping); (b) 25n. Donald and Daisy Duck (ice skating)
| | | 12·50 | 11·00 |

93 Stephenson's Railway Locomotive Rocket, 1829

1988. Transport. Multicoloured.

726	50ch. Pullman "Pioneer" sleeper, 1985	10	10
727	1n. Type **93**	30	20
728	2n. Pierre Lallement's Veloci-pede, 1866	40	35
729	3n. Benz Patent Motor Wagon, 1866	65	55
730	4n. Volkswagen Beetle	85	70
731	5n. Mississippi paddle-steamers Natchez and Robert E. Lee, 1870	95	80
732	6n. American La France motor fire engine, 1910	1·10	95
733	7n. Frigate U.S.S. Constitution, 1797 (vert)	1·40	1·10
734	9n. Bell rocket belt, 1961 (vert)	1·80	1·50
735	10n. Trevithick's railway loco-motive, 1804	2·00	1·70

MS736 Four sheets, each 118×89 mm. (a) 25n. Steam locomotive Mallar" (27×41 mm); (b) 25n. French "TGV" express train (41×27 mm); (c) 25n. Japanese Shinkansen Tokaido bullet train (41×27 mm); (d) 25n. Concorde supersonic airplane (41×27 mm)
| | | 29·00 | 26·00 |

No. 731 is wrongly inscribed "Natches" and No. 733 is wrongly dated "1787".

94 Dam and Pylon

1988. Chhukha Hydro-electric Project.

737	**94** 50ch. multicoloured	1·00	90

1988. World Aids Day. Nos. 411/13 optd **WORLD AIDS DAY**.

738	**50** 2n. multicoloured	65	55
739	— 5n. multicoloured	1·50	1·20
740	— 10n. multicoloured	3·25	2·75

96 Diana and Actaeon (detail)

1989. 500th Birth Anniv of Titian (painter). Multicoloured.

741	50ch. Gentleman with a Book	10	10
742	1n. Venus and Cupid, with a Lute Player (detail)	30	20
743	2n. Type **96**	50	45
744	3n. Cardinal Ippolito dei Medici	85	70
745	4n. Sleeping Venus (detail)	1·30	1·10
746	5n. Venus risen from the Waves (detail)	1·60	1·30
747	6n. Worship of Venus (detail)	2·10	1·80
748	7n. Fete Champetre (detail)	2·50	2·20
749	10n. Perseus and Andromeda (detail)	3·25	2·75
750	15n. Danae (detail)	4·75	4·00
751	20n. Venus at the Mirror	6·25	5·50
752	25n. Venus and the Organ Player (detail)	7·75	6·75

MS753 12 sheets, each 109×94 (a/d) or 94×109 mm (others). (a) 25n. Bacchus and Ariadne; (b) 25n. Danae with the Shower of Gold (horiz); (c) 25n. The Pardo Venus (horiz); (d) 25n. Venus and Cupid with an Organist; (e) 25n. Diana and Callisto; (f) 25n. Mater Dolorosa with Raised Hands; (g) 25n. Miracle of the Irascible Son; (h) 25n. Portrait of Johann Friedrich; (i) 25n. Portrait of Laura Dianti; (j) 25n. St. John the Almsgiver; (k) 25n. Venus blindfolding Cupid; (l) 25n. Venus of Urbino
| | | 75·00 | 65·00 |

97 Volleyball

1989. Olympic Games, Seoul (1988). Multicoloured.

754	50ch. Gymnastics	10	10
755	1n. Judo	20	10
756	2n. Putting the shot	40	35
757	4n. Type **97**	85	70
758	7n. Basketball (vert)	1·40	1·10
759	8n. Football (vert)	1·60	1·30
760	9n. High jumping (vert)	1·90	1·60
761	20n. Running (vert)	4·00	3·25

MS762 Two sheets. (a) 109×79 mm. 25n. Fencing. (b) 79×109 mm. 25n. Archery (vert)
| | | 10·50 | 9·25 |

1989. "Fukuoka '89" Asia-Pacific Exhibition. Nos. 598/606 optd **ASIA-PACIFIC EXPOSITION FUKUOKA '89.**

763	5ch. multicoloured	10	10
764	35ch. multicoloured	15	10
765	50ch. multicoloured	20	10
766	2n.50 multicoloured	65	55
767	3n. multicoloured	80	65
768	4n. multicoloured	1·00	85
769	5n. multicoloured	1·30	1·10
770	5n.50 multicoloured	1·50	1·20
771	6n. multicoloured	1·60	1·30

99 Mickey Mouse

1989. 60th Anniv of Mickey Mouse. Film Posters. Multicoloured.

772	1ch. Type **99**	20	15
773	2ch. "Barnyard Olympics"	20	15
774	3ch. "Society Dog Show"	20	15
775	4ch. "Fantasia"	20	15
776	5ch. "The Mad Dog"	20	15
777	10ch. "A Gentleman's Gentle-man"	20	15
778	50ch. "Symphony hour"	30	20
779	10n. "The Moose Hunt"	2·10	1·80
780	15n. "Wild Waves"	3·25	2·75
781	20n. "Mickey in Arabia"	4·25	3·50
782	25n. "Tugboat Mickey"	5·50	4·75
783	30n. "Building a Building"	6·75	6·00

MS784 12 sheets, each 127×101 mm. (a) 25n. The Klondike Kid; (b) 25n. "The Mad Doctoe" (c) 25n. "The Meller Drammer"; (d) 25n. "Mickey's Good Deed"; (e) 25n. "Mickey's Nightmare"; (f) 25n. "Mickey's Pal Pluto"; (g) 25n. "Steamboat Willie"; (h) 25n. "Touchdown Mickey"; (i) 25n. "Trader Mickey"; (j) 25n. "The Wayward Canary"; (k) 25n. "The Whoopee Party"; (l) 25n. "Ye Olden Days"
| | | 70·00 | 60·00 |

100 Tricholoma pardalotum

1989. Fungi. Multicoloured.

785	50ch. Type **100**	10	10
786	1n. Suillus placidus	20	10
787	2n. Royal boletus	40	35
788	3n. Gomphidius glutinosus	65	55
789	4n. Scarlet-stemmed boletus	85	70
790	5n. Elegant boletus	1·00	90
791	6n. Boletus appendiculatus	1·40	1·10
792	7n. Griping toadstool	1·70	1·40
793	10n. Macrolepiota rhacodes	2·10	1·80
794	15n. The blusher	3·25	2·75
795	20n. Death cap	4·25	3·50
796	25n. False death cap	5·25	4·50

MS797 12 sheets, each 97×68 mm. (a) 25n. Boletus rhodoxanthus; (b) 25n. Chanterelle Chanterelle repdandum; (c) 25n. Dentinum repandum; (d) 25n. Chestnut boletus (Gyroporus castaneus); (e) 25n. Indigo boletus (Gyroporus cyanescens); (f) 25n. Hydnum imbricatum; (g) 25n. Blue leg (Lepista nuda); (h) 25n. Lepista saeva; (i) 25n. Brown roll-rim (Paxillus involutus); (j) 25n. Golden russula (Russula aurata); (k) 25n. Russula olivacea; (l) 25n. Downy boletus (Xerocomus subtomentosus)
| | | 70·00 | 60·00 |

101 La Reale (Spanish galley), 1680

1989. 30th Anniv of International Maritime Organization. Multicoloured.

798	50ch. Type **101**	20	10
799	1n. Turtle (submarine), 1776	40	20
800	2n. Charlotte Dundas (steam-ship), 1802	80	65
801	3n. Great Eastern (paddle-steamer), 1858	1·00	90
802	4n. H.M.S. Warrior (armoured ship), 1862	1·30	1·10
803	5n. Mississippi river steamer, 1884	1·50	1·20
804	6n. Preussen (full-rigged ship), 1902	1·90	1·60
805	7n. U.S.S. Arizona (battleship), 1915	2·10	1·80
806	10n. Bluenose (fishing schooner), 1921	2·50	2·20
807	15n. Steam trawler, 1925	4·00	3·25
808	20n. Liberty freighter, 1943	5·25	4·50
809	25n. United States (liner), 1952	6·25	5·50

MS810 12 sheets, each 100×70 mm. (a) 25n. Chinese junk, 1988; (b) 25n. U.S.S. Constitution (frigate); (c) 25n. VIIC type U-boat, 1942; (d) 25n. Cutty Sark (clipper), 1869; (e) 25n. H.M.S. Dreadnought (battleship), 1906; (f) 25n. U.S.S. Monitor (ironclad), 1862; (g) 25n. Moran Company tug, 1950; (h) 25n. Normandie (French liner), 1933; (i) 25n. H.M.S. Resolution (Capt. Cook); (j) 25n. Titanic (liner), 1912; (k) 25n. H.M.S. Victory (ship of the line), 1805; (l) 25n. Yamato (Japanese battleship), 1944
| | | 70·00 | 60·00 |

102 Nehru

1989. Birth Centenary of Jawaharlal Nehru (Indian statesman).

811	**102** 1n. brown	65	55

No. 811 is erroneously inscribed "ch".

103 Greater Flamed-backed Woodpecker

1989. Birds. Multicoloured.

812	50ch. Type **103**	20	10
813	1n. Black-naped blue monarch ("Black-naped Monarch")	40	20
814	2n. White-crested laughing thrush	80	65
815	3n. Blood pheasant	1·00	90
816	4n. Plum-headed ("Blossom-headed") parakeet	1·30	1·10
817	5n. Rosy minivet	1·50	1·20
818	6n. Chestnut-headed fulvetta ("Tit-Babbler") (horiz)	1·90	1·60
819	7n. Blue pitta (horiz)	2·10	1·80
820	10n. Black-naped oriole (horiz)	2·50	2·20
821	15n. Green magpie (horiz)	4·00	3·25
822	20n. Three-toed kingfisher ("Indian Three-toed Kingfisher") (horiz)	5·25	4·50
823	25n. Ibis bill (horiz)	6·25	5·50

MS824 12 sheets, each 76×104 mm (vert designs) or 104×76 mm (horiz). (a) 25n. Fire-tailed sunbird; (b) 25n. Crested tree swift (inscr "Indian Crested Swift"); (c) 25n. Greater (inscr "Large") racket-tailed drongo; (d) 25n. Little spider hunter; (e) 25n. Blue-backed fairy bluebird (horiz); (f) 25n. Great Indian (inscr "Pied") hornbill (horiz); (g) 25n. Red-legged (inscr "Himalayan Redbreasted") falconet (horiz); (h) 25n. Lammergeier (horiz); (i) 25n. Satyr tragopan (horiz); (j) 25n. Spotted forktail (horiz); (k) 25n. Wallcreeper (horiz); (l) 25n. White eared-pheasant (wrongly inscr "White-eared") (horiz)
| | | 75·00 | 65·00 |

104 *Best Friend of Charleston, 1830, U.S.A.*

1990. Steam Railway Locomotives. Multicoloured.

825	50ch. Type **104**	10	10
826	1n. Class U locomotive, 1948, France	20	10
827	2n. Consolidation locomotive, 1866, U.S.A.	40	35
828	3n. Luggage engine, 1843, Great Britain	65	55
829	4n. Class 60-3 Shay locomotive No. 18, 1913, U.S.A.	85	70
830	5n. "John Bull", 1831, U.S.A.	1·00	90
831	6n. "Hercules", 1837, U.S.A.	1·40	1·10
832	7n. Locomotive No. 947, 1874, Great Britain	1·70	1·40
833	10n. "Illinois", 1852, U.S.A.	2·10	1·80
834	15n. Class O5 locomotive, 1935, Germany	3·25	2·75
835	20n. Standard locomotive, 1865, U.S.A.	4·25	3·50
836	25n. Class Ps-4 locomotive, 1936, U.S.A.	5·25	4·50

MS837 12 sheets, each 74×100 mm (horiz designs) or 100×74 mm (vert). (a) 25n. "The Cumberland" (U.S.A., 1845); (b) 25n. "Ariel" (U.S.A., 1877); (c) 25n. No. 22 Baldwin locomotive (U.S.A., 1873); (d) 25n. Class "A" (U.S.A., 1935) (vert); (e) 25n. Class "K-36" (U.S.A., 1923); (f) 25n. No. 999 "Empire State Express" (U.S.A., 1893); (g) 25n. "John Stevens" (U.S.A., 1849) (vert); (h) 25n. Class "A4" (Great Britain, 1935) (vert); (i) 25n. "Puffing Billy" (Great Britain, 1814) (vert); (j) 25n. "The Rocket" (Great Britain, 1829) (vert); (k) 25n. Class "P-1" (U.S.A., 1943) (vert); (l) 25n. No. 1301 Webb compound engine (Great Britain, 1889) ... 70·00 60·00

105 *Charaxes harmodius*

1990. Butterflies. Multicoloured.

838	50ch. Type **105**	10	10
839	1n. *Prioneris thestylis*	35	10
840	2n. Eastern courtier	55	45
841	3n. *Penthema lisarda* (horiz)	75	65
842	4n. Golden birdwing	1·00	85
843	5n. Great nawab	1·30	1·10
844	6n. *Polyura dolon* (horiz)	1·60	1·40
845	7n. Tailed labyrinth (horiz)	2·00	1·70
846	10n. *Delias descombesi*	2·50	2·20
847	15n. *Childreni childrena* (horiz)	3·75	3·25
848	20n. Leaf butterfly (horiz)	5·00	4·25
849	25n. *Elymnias malelas* (horiz)	6·00	5·25

MS850 12 sheets, each 110×80 mm. (a) 25n. Bhutan glory; (b) 25n. Blue (inscr "Blue Banded") peacock; (c) 25n. Camberwell beauty; (d) 25n. Chequered swallowtail; (e) 25n. Chestnut tiger; (f) 25n. Common birdwing; (g) 25n. Common map butterfly; (h) 25n. Common (inscr "Great") eggfly; (i) 25n. Jungle glory; (j) 25n. Kaiser-i-hind; (k) 25n. Red lacewing; (l) 25n. Swallowtail ... 80·00 75·00

106 *Renanthera monachica*

1990. "Expo '90" International Garden and Greenery Exposition, Osaka. Orchids. Multicoloured.

851	10ch. Type **106**	10	10
852	50ch. *Vanda coerulea*	20	10
853	1n. *Phalaenopsis violacea*	35	20
854	2n. *Dendrobium nobile*	55	45
855	5n. *Vandopsis lissochiloides*	85	75
856	6n. *Paphiopedilum rothschildianum*	1·30	1·10
857	7n. *Phalaenopsis schilleriana*	1·60	1·40
858	9n. *Paphiopedilum insigne*	2·00	1·70
859	10n. *Paphiopedilum bellatulum*	2·20	1·80
860	20n. *Doritis pulcherrima*	4·25	3·75

861	25n. *Cymbidium giganteum*	5·50	4·75
862	35n. *Phalaenopsis mariae*	7·50	6·75

MS863 12 sheets, each 111×84 mm. (a) 30n. *Dendrobium aphyllum*; (b) 30n. *Dendrobium loddigesii*; (c) 30n. *Dendrobium margaritaceum*; (d) 30n. *Paphiopedilum haynaldianum*; (e) 30n. *Paphiopedilum niveum*; (f) 30n. *Phalaenopsis amabilis*; (g) 30n. *Phalaenopsis cornu-cervi*; (h) 30n. *Phalaenopsis equestris*; (i) 30n. *Vanda alpine*; (j) 30n. *Vanda coerulescens*; (k) 30n. *Vanda cristata*; (l) 30n. *Vandopsis parishi* ... 80·00 75·00

107 *Plum Estate, Kameido*

1990. Death of Emperor Hirohito and Accession of Emperor Akihito of Japan. *100 Famous Views of Edo* by Ando Hiroshige. Multicoloured.

864	10ch. Type **107**	10	10
865	20ch. *Yatsumi Bridge*	10	10
866	50ch. *Ayase River and Kanegafuchi*	15	10
867	75ch. *View of Shiba Coast*	20	15
868	1n. *Grandpa's Teahouse, Meguro*	35	25
869	2n. *Inside Kameido Tenjin Shrine*	45	35
870	6n. *Yoroi Ferry, Koami-cho*	1·40	1·20
871	7n. *Sakasai Ferry*	1·70	1·50
872	10n. *Fukagawa Lumberyards*	2·50	2·10
873	15n. *Suido Bridge and Surugadai*	3·75	3·25
874	20n. *Meguro Drum Bridge and Sunset Hill*	5·00	4·25
875	25n. *Atagoshita and Yabu Lane*	6·00	5·25

MS876 12 sheets, each 102×76 mm. (a) 25n. *The City Flourishing, Tanabata Festival*; (b) 25n. *Fukagawa Susaki and Jumantsubo*; (c) 25n. *Horikiri Iris Garden*; (d) 25n. *Komakata Hall and Azuma Bridge*; (e) 25n. *Minowa, Kanasugi, Mikawashima*; (f) 25n. *New Year's Eve Foxfires at the Changing Tree, Oji*; (g) 25n. *Nihonbashi, Clearing after Snow*; (h) 25n. *Sudden Shower over Shin-Ohashi Bridge and Atake*; (i) 25n. *Suijin Shrine and Massaki on the Sumida River*; (j) 25n. *"Suruga-cho"*; (k) 25n. *Towboats along the Yotsugidori Canal*; (l) 25n. *View to the North from Asukayama* ... 65·00 60·00

108 *Thimphu Post Office*

1990

877	**108**	1n. multicoloured	80	70

109 *Giant Panda*

1990. Mammals. Multicoloured.

878	50ch. Type **109**	10	10
879	1n. Giant panda in tree	35	20
880	2n. Giant panda with cub	55	45
881	3n. Giant panda (horiz)	85	75
882	4n. Giant panda eating (horiz)	1·10	90
883	5n. Tiger (horiz)	1·40	1·20
884	6n. Giant pandas pulling up bamboo (horiz)	1·70	1·50
885	7n. Giant panda and cub resting (horiz)	2·20	1·80
886	10n. Indian elephant (horiz)	2·75	2·30
887	15n. Giant panda beside fallen tree	4·00	3·50
888	20n. Indian muntjac (inscr "Barking deer") (horiz)	5·50	4·75
889	25n. Snow leopard (horiz)	6·50	5·75

MS890 12 sheets, each 100×73 mm. (a) 25n. Asiatic black bear; (b) 25n. Dhole (inscr "Asiatic wild dog"); (c) 25n. Clouded leopard; (d) 25n. Gaur; (e) 25n. Giant panda; (f) 25n. Golden cat; (g) 25n. Siberian musk deer (inscr "Himalayan"); (h) 25n. Redd deer (inscr "Himalayan shou"); (i) 25n. Pygmy hog; (j) 25n. Indian rhinoceros; (k) 25n. Sloth bear; (l) 25n. Wolf ... 80·00 75·00

110 *Roim*

1990. Religious Musical Instruments. Multicoloured.

891	10ch. Dungchen (large trumpets)	10	10
892	20ch. Dungkar (Indian chank shell)	10	10
893	30ch. Type **110**	10	10
894	50ch. Tinchag (cup cymbals)	10	10
895	1n. Dradu and drilbu (pellet drum and hand bell)	35	15
896	2n. Gya-ling (oboes)	45	35
897	2n.50 Nga (drum)	65	55
898	3n.50 Kang-dung (trumpets)	80	70

MS899 Two sheets, each 92×135 mm. (a) Nos. 891, 893, 895 and 898; (b) Nos. 892, 894 and 896/7 ... 11·00 9·75

111 *Penny Black and Bhutan 1962 2ch. Stamp*

1990. "Stamp World London 90" International Stamp Exhibition. 150th Anniv of the Penny Black. Multicoloured.

900	50ch. Type **111**	10	10
901	1n. Oldenburg 1852½oth. stamp	25	20
902	2n. Bergedorf 1861 1½s. stamp	45	35
903	4n. German Democratic Republic 1949 50pf. stamp	85	75
904	5n. Brunswick 1852 1 sgr. stamp	1·10	90
905	6n. Basel 1845 2½r. stamp	1·40	1·10
906	8n. Geneva 1843 5c.+5c. stamp	1·70	1·50
907	10n. Zurich 1843 4r. stamp	2·20	1·80
908	15n. France 1849 20c. stamp	3·25	2·75
909	20n. Vatican City 1929 5c. stamp	4·25	3·75
910	25n. Israel 1948 3m. stamp	5·50	4·75
911	30n. Japan 1871 48m. stamp	6·50	5·75

MS912 12 sheets, each 106×76 mm. (a) 15n. Baden 1851 1k. stamp, 15n. Wurttemberg 1851 1k. stamp; (b) 15n. Germany 1872 3k. and 2g. stamps, 15n. Prussia 1850 6pf. stamp; (c) 15n. Hamburg 1859 ½s. stamp, 15n. North German Confederation 1868 ¼g. and 1k. stamps; (d) 15n. Heligoland 1867 ½ch. stamp, 15n. Hanover 1850 1ggr. stamp; (e) 15n. Schleswig-Holstein 1850 1s. stamp, 15n. Lubeck 1859 4s. stamp; (f) 15n. Mecklenburg-Schwerin 1856 4/4s. stamp, 15n. Mecklenburg-Strelitz 1864 ¼sgr. stamp; (g) 15n. Thurn and Taxis (Northern District) 1852 ½sgr. stamp, 15n. Thurn and Taxis (Southern District) 1852 1k. stamp; (h) 30n. Bavaria 1849 1k. stamp; (i) 30n. West Berlin 1948 2pf. stamp; (j) 30n. Great Britain 1840 Penny Black; (k) 30n. Saxony 1850 3pf. stamp; (l) 30n. United States 1847 5c. stamp ... 70·00 65·00

Each value also depicts the Penny Black. No. 901 is wrongly inscribed "Oldenberg".

112 *Girls*

1990. South Asian Association for Regional Co-operation Girl Child Year. Multicoloured.

913	50ch. Type **112**	45	35
914	20n. Girl	4·25	3·75

113 *Temple of Artemis, Ephesus*

1991. Wonders of the World. Designs featuring Walt Disney cartoon characters. Multicoloured.

915	1ch. Type **113**	10	10
916	2ch. Statue of Zeus, Olympia	10	10
917	3ch. Pyramids of Egypt	10	10
918	4ch. Lighthouse of Alexandria, Egypt	10	10
919	5ch. Mausoleum, Halicarnassus	10	10
920	10ch. Colossus of Rhodes	10	10
921	50ch. Hanging Gardens of Babylon	15	10
922	5n. Mauna Loa Volcanoes, Hawaii (horiz)	1·50	1·30
923	6n. Carlsbad Caverns, New Mexico (horiz)	1·90	1·60
924	10n. Rainbow Bridge National Monument, Utah (horiz)	2·50	2·10
925	15n. Grand Canyon, Colorado (horiz)	3·25	2·75
926	20n. Old Faithful, Yellowstone National Park, Wyoming (horiz)	4·50	4·00
927	25n. Sequoia National Park, California (horiz)	6·00	5·25
928	30n. Crater Lake and Wizard Island, Oregon (horiz)	7·00	6·25

MS929 14 sheets, each 127×101 mm. (a) 25n. Alcan Highway, Alaska and Canada (horiz); (b) 25n. Catacombs of Alexandria; (c) 25n. Sears Tower, Chicago, Illinois (horiz); (d) 25n. Great Wall of China (horiz); (e) 25n. St. Sophia's Mosque, Constantinople; (f) 25n. Porcelain Tower, Nanking, China (horiz); (g) 25n. Hoover Dam, Nevada; (h) 25n. Empire State Building, New York City; (i) 25n. Panama Canal (horiz); (j) 25n. Leaning Tower of Pisa; (k) 25n. Colosseum Rome; (l) 25n. Gateway Arch, St. Louis, Missouri (horiz); (m) 25n. Golden Gate Bridge, San Francisco (horiz); (n) 25n. Stonehenge ... 70·00 65·00

114 *Atalanta and Meleager (detail)*

1991. 350th Death Anniv (1990) of Peter Paul Rubens (painter). Multicoloured.

930	10ch. Type **114**	10	10
931	50ch. *The Fall of Phaeton* (detail)	15	10
932	1n. *Feast of Venus Verticordia* (detail)	35	30
933	2n. *Achilles slaying Hector* (detail)	65	55
934	3n. *Arachne punished by Minerva* (detail)	1·10	90
935	4n. *Jupiter receives Psyche on Olympus* (detail)	1·50	1·30
936	5n. *Atalanta and Meleager* (different detail)	1·90	1·60
937	6n. *Atalanta and Meleager* (different detail)	2·10	1·70
938	7n. *Venus in Vulcan's Furnace* (detail)	2·40	2·00
939	10n. *Atalanta and Meleager* (different detail)	3·25	2·75
940	20n. *Briseis returned to Achilles* (detail)	6·00	5·25
941	30n. *Mars and Rhea Sylvia* (detail)	7·50	6·75

MS942 12 sheets, each 72×101 mm (a/e) or 101×72 mm (f/l). (a) 25n. *Atlanta and Meleager*; (b) 25n. *Feast of Venus Verticordia*; (c) 25n. *Ganymede and the Eagle*; (d) 25n. *Jupiter receives Psyche on Olympus*; (e) 25n. *Venus shivering*; (f) 25n. *Adonis and Venus* (horiz); (g) 25n. *Arachne punished by Minerva* (horiz); (h) 25n. *Briseis returned to Achilles* (horiz); (i) 25n. *The Fall of the Titans* (horiz); (j) 25n. *Hero and Leander* (horiz); (k) 25n. *Mars and Rhea Sylvia* (horiz); (l) 25n. *The Origin of the Milky Way* (horiz) ... 80·00 75·00

115 Cottages,
Reminiscence of the North

1991. Death Centenary (1990) of Vincent van Gogh (painter). Multicoloured.

943	10ch. Type **115**	10	10
944	50ch. *Head of a Peasant Woman with Dark Cap*	15	10
945	1n. *Portrait of a Woman in Blue*	35	20
946	2n. *Head of an Old Woman with White Cap (the Midwife)*	75	65
947	8n. *Vase with Hollyhocks*	1·80	1·60
948	10n. *Portrait of a Man with a Skull Cap*	2·30	1·90
949	12n. *Agostina Segatori sitting in the Cafe du Tambourin*	2·75	2·30
950	15n. *Vase with Daisies and Anemones*	3·50	3·00
951	18n. *Fritillaries in a Copper Vase*	4·25	3·75
952	20n. *Woman sitting in the Grass*	4·50	4·00
953	25n. *On the Outskirts of Paris (horiz)*	5·50	4·75
954	30n. *Chrysanthemums and Wild Flowers in a Vase*	6·50	5·75
MS955	12 sheets, each 76×101 mm (a/h) or 101×76 mm (i/l). (a) 30n. *Le Moulin de Blute-Fin*; (b) 30n. *Le Moulin de la Galette*; (c) 30n. *Le Moulin de la Galette* (with man in foreground); (d) 30n. *Poppies and Butterflies*; (e) 30n. *Trees in the Garden of St. Paul Hospital*; (f) 30n. *Vase with Peonies*; (g) 30n. *Vase with Red Poppies*; (h) 30n. *Vase with Zinnias*; (i) 30n. *Bowl with Sunflowers, Roses and Other Flowers* (horiz); (j) 30n. *Fishing in the Spring, Pont de Clichy* (horiz); (k) 30n. *Vase with Zinnias and Other Flowers* (horiz); (l) 30n. *Village Street in Auvers* (horiz)	90·00	85·00

116 Winning Uruguay Team, 1930

1991. World Cup Football Championship. Multicoloured.

956	50ch. Type **116**	10	10
957	1n. *Italy, 1934*	25	20
958	2n. *Italy, 1938*	35	25
959	3n. *Uruguay, 1950*	65	55
960	5n. *West Germany, 1954*	1·10	90
961	10n. *Brazil, 1958*	2·20	1·80
962	20n. *Brazil, 1962*	4·25	3·75
963	25n. *England, 1966*	5·50	4·50
964	29n. *Brazil, 1970*	6·00	5·25
965	30n. *West Germany, 1974*	6·25	5·50
966	31n. *Argentina, 1978*	6·50	5·75
967	32n. *Italy, 1982*	6·75	6·00
968	33n. *Argentina, 1986*	6·75	6·00
969	34n. *West Germany, 1990*	7·00	6·25
970	35n. *Stadium, Los Angeles (venue for 1994 World Cup)*	7·00	6·25
MS971	6 sheets, each 105×120 mm. (a) 30n. *Roberto Baggio, Italy* (vert); (b) 30n. *Claudio Canniggia, Argentina* (vert); (c) 30n. *Paul Gascoigne, England* (vert); (d) 30n. *Lothar Matthaus, West Germany* (vert); (e) 30n. *Salvatore Schillaci, Italy* (vert); (f) 30n. *Peter Shilton, England*	50·00	46·00

117 Bhutan and Japan
State Flags

1991. "Phila Nippon '91" International Stamp Exhibition, Tokyo.

972	**117** 15n. multicoloured	3·75	3·25

118 Teachers, Pupils and
Hemisphere

1992. "Education for All by Year 2000".

973	**118** 1n. multicoloured	55	45

119 Hurdler

1992. Olympic Games, Barcelona. Multicoloured.

974	25n. Type **119**	4·25	3·75
975	25n. *Body of hurdler*	4·25	3·75
MS976	110×75 mm. 25n. *Archery*	6·00	5·25

Nos. 974/5 were issued together, *se-tenant*, forming a composite design.

120 Santa Maria

1992. 500th Anniv of Discovery of America by Columbus. Multicoloured.

977	15n. Type **120**	2·75	2·30
978	20n. *Columbus*	3·50	3·00
MS979	78×118 mm. 25n. As No. 978 but without inscription at top (27×43 mm)	4·25	3·75

121 Brandenburg Gate and
rejoicing Couple

1992. Second Anniv of Reunification of Germany. Multicoloured.

980	**121** 25n. multicoloured	3·25	2·75
MS981	110×82 mm. 25n. As No. 980 but without inscription at top (43×27 mm)	3·50	3·00

122 British Aerospace BAe
146 and Post Van

1992. 30th Anniv of Bhutan Postal Organization. Multicoloured.

982	1n. Type **122**	35	30
983	3n. *Rural letter courier*	55	45
984	5n. *Emptying post box*	80	70

123 Industry and
Agriculture

1992. 20th Anniv of Accession of King Jigme Singye Wangchuck. Multicoloured.

985	1n. Type **123**	35	30
986	5n. *British Aerospace RJ70 of National Airline*	55	45
987	10n. *House with water-pump*	1·10	90
988	15n. *King Jigme Singye Wangchuk*	1·80	1·60
MS989	94×62 mm. 20n. *King, flag and Bhutanese people* (43×26 mm)	3·25	3·00

Nos. 985/8 were issued together, *se-tenant*, each horizontal pair within the block forming a composite design.

124 Dragon

1992. International Volunteer Day.

990	**124** 1n.50 multicoloured	55	45
991	**124** 9n. multicoloured	1·10	90
992	**124** 15n. multicoloured	2·75	2·30

125 *Meconopsis grandis*

1993. Medicinal Flowers. Designs showing varieties of the Asiatic Poppy. Multicoloured.

993	1n.50 Type **125**	45	35
994	7n. *Meconopsis* sp.	1·20	1·00
995	10n. *Meconopsis wallichii*	1·50	1·30
996	12n. *Meconopsis horridula*	2·10	1·70
997	20n. *Meconopsis discigera*	3·50	3·00
MS998	74×107 mm. 25n. *Meconopsis horridula* (different) (27×43 mm)	6·50	5·75

126 Rooster and Chinese Signs of the Zodiac

1993. New Year. Year of the Water Rooster. Sheet 89×89 mm.

MS999	**126** 25n. multicoloured	7·50	6·75

127 *The Love Letter*
(Jean Honore
Fragonard)

1993. Paintings. Multicoloured.

1000	1ch. Type **127** (postage)	15	15
1001	2ch. *The Writer* (Vittore Carpaccio)	15	15
1002	3ch. *Mademoiselle Lavergne* (Jean Etienne Liotard)	15	15
1003	5ch. *Portrait of Erasmus* (Hans Holbein)	15	15
1004	10ch. *Woman writing a Letter* (Gerard Terborch)	15	15
1005	15ch. Type **127**	15	15
1006	25ch. As No. 1001	15	15
1007	50ch. As No. 1002	15	15
1008	60ch. As No. 1003	15	15
1009	80ch. As No. 1004	20	15
1010	1n. Type **127**	25	20
1011	1n.25 As No. 1001	35	30
1012	2n. As No. 1002 (air)	45	35
1013	3n. As No. 1003	65	55
1014	6n. As No. 1004	1·10	90
MS1015	135×97 mm. As Nos. 1012/14 but with copper borders	5·75	5·00

128 Lesser Panda

1993. Environmental Protection. Multicoloured.

1016	7n. Type **128**	1·10	90
1017	10n. *One-horned rhinoceros*	1·50	1·30
1018	15n. *Black-necked crane and blue poppy*	2·30	1·90
1019	20n. *Takin*	2·75	2·30

Nos. 1016/19 were issued together, se-tenant, forming a composite design.

1993. "Taipei'93" International Stamp Exhibition, Taiwan. No. **MS999** surch **TAIPEI'93 NU 30**.

MS1020	**126** 30n. on 25n. multicoloured	6·00	5·25

130 Namtheo-say

1993. Door Gods. Multicoloured.

1021	1n.50 Type **130**	45	35
1022	5n. *Pha-ke-po*	1·10	90
1023	10n. *Chen-mi Jang*	2·40	2·00
1024	15n. *Yul-khor-sung*	3·75	3·00

131 *Rhododendron mucronatum*

1994. Flowers. Multicoloured.

1025	1n. Type **131**	20	15
1026	1n.50 *Anemone rupicola*	20	15
1027	2n. *Polemonium coeruleum*	20	15
1028	2n.50 *Rosa marophylla*	25	20
1029	4n. *Paraquilegia microphylla*	45	35
1030	5n. *Aquilegia nivalis*	1·10	90
1031	6n. *Geranium wallichianum*	1·30	1·10
1032	7n. *Rhododendron campanulatum* (wrongly inscr "Rhodendron")	1·50	1·30
1033	9n. *Viola suavis*	2·00	1·70
1034	10n. *Cyananthus lobatus*	2·40	2·00
MS1035	126×86 mm. 13n. *Lily* (horiz)	3·75	3·25

132 Dog

1994. New Year. Year of the Dog. "Hong Kong '94" International Stamp Exhibition.

1036	**132** 11n.50 multicoloured	1·90	1·60
MS1037	118×178 mm. **132** 20n. multicoloured	4·50	4·00

133 Trophy and Mascot

1994. World Cup Football Championship, U.S.A.

1038	**133** 15n. multicoloured	2·20	1·80

134 Tagtshang Monastery (image scaled to 57% of original size)

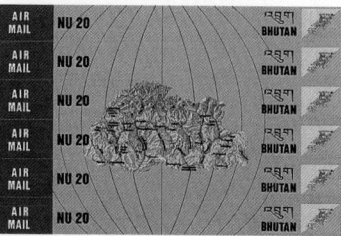

135 Relief Map of Bhutan (image scaled to 58% of original size)

1994. Air. Self-adhesive.

1039	134	16n. multicoloured	10·00	85
1040	135	20n. multicoloured	11·00	1·00

The individual stamps are peeled directly from the card backing. Each card contains six different designs with the same face value forming the composite designs illustrated. Each stamp is a horizontal strip with a label indicating the main class of mail covered by the rate at the left, separated by a vertical line of rouletting. The outer edges of the cards are imperforate.

136 Tower Bridge, London
(centenary)

1994. Bridges. Sheet 160×101 mm containing T **136** and similar horiz design. Multicoloured.
MS1041 15n. Type **136**; 16n. *Wangdur Bridge, Bhutan* (Samuel Davies)
(250th anniv) 5·00 4·25

137 Astronaut on Moon

1994. 25th Anniv of First Manned Moon Landing. Sheet 114×57 mm containing T **137** and similar horiz design. Multicoloured.
MS1042 30n. Type **137**; 36n. Space
shuttle 9·75 8·50

138 Horseman with raised Sword

1994. 350th Anniv of Victory over Tibet-Mongol Army. Multicoloured.

1043	15n. Type **138**	1·60	1·40
1044	15n. Archers and hand-to-hand sword fighting	1·60	1·40
1045	15n. Horseman with insignia on helmet amongst infantry	1·60	1·40
1046	15n. Drummer, piper and troops	1·60	1·40

Nos. 1043/6 were issued together, *se-tenant*, forming a composite design of a battle scene and the Drugyel Dzong.

139 Paro Valley

1995. World Tourism Year. Sheet 111×92 mm containing T **139** and similar horiz designs. Multicoloured.
MS1047 1n.50 Type **139**; 5n. Chorton Kora; 10n. Thimphu Tshechu; 15n. Wangdue Tshechu 6·50 5·75

140 Lunar Rat

1995. New Year. Year of the Boar. Multicoloured.

1048	10ch. Type **140**	20	15
1049	20ch. Lunar ox	20	15
1050	30ch. Lunar tiger	20	15
1051	40ch. Lunar rabbit	20	15
1052	1n. Lunar dragon	25	20
1053	2n. Lunar snake	45	25
1054	3n. Lunar horse	50	30
1055	4n. Lunar sheep	55	35
1056	5n. Lunar monkey	1·10	90
1057	7n. Lunar rooster	1·40	1·20
1058	8n. Lunar dog	1·60	1·40
1059	9n. Lunar boar	2·00	1·70
MS1060 111×92 mm. 10n. Wood hogs 3·25 2·75

141 *Pleione praecox*

1995. Flowers. Multicoloured.

1061	9n. Type **141**	65	55
1062	10n. *Primula calderina*	75	65
1063	16n. *Primula whitei*	1·30	1·10
1064	18n. *Notholirion macrophyllum*	1·40	1·20

142 Human Resources Development

1995. 50th Anniv of UNO. Multicoloured.

1065	1n.50 Type **142**	20	20
1066	5n. Transport and Communications	45	35
1067	9n. Health and Population	65	55
1068	10n. Water and Sanitation	75	65
1069	11n.50 UN in Bhutan	85	75
1070	16n. Forestry and Environment	1·20	1·00
1071	18n. Peace and Security	1·30	1·10

143 Greater Pied Kingfisher
("Himalayan Pied Kingfisher")

1995. "Singapore '95" International Stamp Exhibition. Birds. Multicoloured.

1072	1n. Type **143**	20	15
1073	2n. Blyth's tragopan	25	15
1074	3n. Long-tailed minivets	35	20
1075	10n. Red junglefowl	75	65
1076	15n. Black-capped sibia	1·10	90
1077	20n. Red-billed chough	1·30	1·10
MS1078 73×97 mm. 20n. Black-necked
crane 2·75 2·30

144 Making Paper

1995. Traditional Crafts. Multicoloured.

1079	1n. Type **144**	20	15
1080	2n. Religious painting	25	15
1081	3n. Clay sculpting	35	20
1082	10n. Weaving	75	65
1083	15n. Making boots	1·10	90
1084	20n. Carving wooden bowls	1·30	1·10
MS1085 121×82 mm. 20n. Decorative
carvings on wooden buildings 2·40 2·10

145 Golden Langer

1996. New Year. Year of the Rat. Sheet 111×176 mm containing T **145** and similar square designs. Multicoloured.
MS1086 10n. Type **145**; 10n. Rat; 10n. Dragon 4·25 4·00

146 *The White Bird*

1996. Folk Tales. Multicoloured.

1087	1n. Type **146**	20	15
1088	2n. *Sing Sing Lhamo and the Moon*	25	15
1089	3n. *The Hoopoe*	35	20
1090	5n. *The Cloud Fairies*	45	35
1091	10n. *The Three Wishes*	85	75
1092	20n. *The Abominable Snowman*	1·40	1·20
MS1093 109×75 mm. 25n. As No. 1090 3·25 2·75

147 Blue Pansy

1996. Butterflies. Multicoloured.

1094	2n. Type **147**	25	15
1095	3n. Blue peacock	35	20
1096	5n. Great mormon	55	45
1097	10n. Fritillary	1·00	85
1098	15n. Blue duke	1·30	1·10
1099	25n. Brown gorgon	2·00	1·70
MS1100 Two sheets, each 108×75 mm.
(a) 30n. Fivebar swordtail; (b) 30n.
Xanthomelas 8·75 7·50

148 300n. Football Coin

1996. Olympic Games, Atlanta. Multicoloured.

1101	5n. Type **148**	55	45
1102	7n. 300n. basketball coin	1·10	90
1103	10n. 5s. judo coin	1·60	1·40
MS1104 102×80 mm. 15n. Archery 2·20 1·90

149 Standard Goods Locomotive, India

1996. Trains. Multicoloured.

1105	20n. Type **149**	1·40	1·20
1106	20n. Diesel-electric locomotive, Finland	1·40	1·20
1107	20n. Shunting tank locomotive, Russia	1·40	1·20
1108	20n. Alco PA-1 diesel-electric locomotive, U.S.A.	1·40	1·20
1109	20n. Class C11 passenger tank locomotive, Japan	1·40	1·20
1110	20n. Settebello high speed electric train, Italy	1·40	1·20
1111	20n. Tank locomotive No. 191, Chile	1·40	1·20
1112	20n. Pacific locomotive, France	1·40	1·20
1113	20n. Steam locomotive No. 10, Norway	1·40	1·20
1114	20n. Atlantic express locomotive, Germany	1·40	1·20
1115	20n. Express steam locomotive, Belgium	1·40	1·20
1116	20n. Type 4 diesel-electric locomotive, Great Britain	1·40	1·20
MS1117 Two sheets, each 96×66 mm.
(a) 70n. *Hikari* express train, Series
200, Japan; (b) Class KD steam
goods locomotive, Sweden 11·00 9·75

150 Penny Black

1996

1118	150	140n. gold and black	11·00	9·75

151 Vegard Ulvang, Norway

1997. Winter Olympic Gold Medallists. Multicoloured. (a) Without frame.

1119	10n. Type **151** (30km. cross-country skiing, 1992)	75	65
1120	15n. Kristi Yamaguchi, U.S.A. (women's figure skating, 1992)	1·10	90
1121	25n. Markus Wasmeier, Germany (men's super giant slalom, 1994)	2·00	1·70
1122	30n. Georg Hackl, Germany (luge, 1992)	2·20	1·80

(b) As T **151** but with black frame around design.

1123	15n. Andreas Ostler, West Germany (two-man bob-sleighing, 1952)	1·10	90
1124	15n. East German team (four-man bobsleighing, 1984)	1·10	90
1125	15n. Stein Eriksen, Norway (men's giant slalom, 1952)	1·10	90
1126	15n. Alberto Tomba, Italy (men's giant slalom, 1988)	1·10	90
MS1127 Two sheets, each 106×76 mm.
(a) 70n. Henri Oreiller, France (men's
downhill skiing, 1948); (b) 70n. Swiss
team (four-man bobsleighing, 1924) 11·00 9·75

152 Bee

1997. Insects and Arachnidae. Multicoloured.

1128	1ch. Type **152**	10	10
1129	2ch. *Neptunides polychromus* (beetle)	10	10
1130	3ch. *Conocephalus maculctus* (grasshopper)	10	10
1131	4ch. *Blattidae sp.* (beetle)	10	10
1132	5ch. Great diving beetle	10	10
1133	10ch. Hercules beetle	10	10
1134	15ch. Ladybird	10	10
1135	20ch. *Sarcophaga haemor-rhoidalis* (fly)	10	10
1136	25ch. Stag beetle	10	10
1137	30ch. Caterpillar	10	10
1138	35ch. *Lycia hirtaria* (moth)	10	10
1139	40ch. *Clytarius pennatus* (beetle)	10	10
1140	45ch. *Ephemera denica* (mayfly)	10	10
1141	50ch. European field cricket	10	10
1142	60ch. Elephant hawk moth	10	10
1143	65ch. *Gerris sp.* (beetle)	10	10
1144	70ch. Banded agrion	10	10
1145	80ch. *Tachyta nana* (beetle)	10	10
1146	90ch. *Eurydema pulchra* (shieldbug)	10	10
1147	1n. *Hadrurus hirsutus* (scorpion)	10	10
1148	1n.50 *Vespa germanica* (wasp)	15	10
1149	2n. *Pyrops sp.* (beetle)	15	10
1150	2n.50 Praying mantis	20	15
1151	3n. *Araneus diadematus* (spider)	25	15
1152	3n.50 *Atrophaneura sp.* (but-terfly)	35	20
MS1153 76×111 mm. 15n. Cockchafer
(*Melolontha sp.*) 2·10 1·80

153 Polar Bears

1997. "Hong Kong '97" International Stamp Exhibition. Multicoloured.

1154	10n. Type **153**	1·10	90
1155	10n. Koalas (*Phascolarctos cinereus*)	1·10	90
1156	10n. Asiatic black bear (*Selenarctos thibetanus*)	1·10	90
1157	10n. Lesser panda (*Ailurus fulgens*)	1·10	90
MS1158	107×75 mm. 20n. Giant panda (*Ailuropoda melanoleuca*)	2·75	2·50

154 Rat

1997. New Year. Year of the Ox. Multicoloured.

1159	1ch. Type **154**	15	15
1160	2ch. Ox	15	15
1161	3ch. Tiger	15	15
1162	4ch. Rabbit	15	15
1163	90ch. Monkey	20	15
1164	5n. Dragon	45	35
1165	6n. Snake	55	45
1166	7n. Horse	65	55
1167	8n. Ram	85	75
1168	10n. Cock	1·10	90
1169	11n. Dog	1·20	1·00
1170	12n. Boar	1·30	1·10
MS1171	70×66 mm. 20n. Ox	2·40	2·10

155 Lynx

1997. Endangered Species. Multicoloured.

1172	10n. Type **155**	1·10	90
1173	10n. Lesser ("Red") panda (*Ailurus fulgens*)	1·10	90
1174	10n. Takin (*Budorcas taxicolor*)	1·10	90
1175	10n. Forest musk deer (*Moschus chrysogaster*)	1·10	90
1176	10n. Snow leopard (*Panthera uncia*)	1·10	90
1177	10n. Golden langur (*Presbytis geei*)	1·10	90
1178	10n. Tiger (*Pnthera tigris*)	1·10	90
1179	10n. Indian muntjac (*Muntiacus muntjak*)	1·10	90
1180	10n. Bobak marmot (*Marmota bobak*)	1·10	90
1181	10n. Dhole (*Cuon alpinis*) running	1·10	90
1182	10n. Dhole walking	1·10	90
1183	10n. Mother dhole nursing cubs	1·10	90
1184	10n. Two dhole	1·10	90
MS1185	Two sheets, each 106×76 mm. (a) 70n. Bharal (*Pseudois nayaur*); (b) 70n. Asiatic black bear (*Ursus thibetanus*)	14·00	12·50

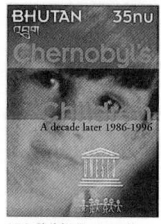

156 Child's Face and UNESCO Emblem

1997. Tenth Anniv of Chernobyl Nuclear Disaster.

1186	**156** 35n. multicoloured	4·25	3·75

157 Mount Huangshah, China

1997. 50th Anniv of UNESCO World Heritage Sites. Multicoloured.

1187	10n. Type **157**	1·10	90
1188	10n. Statue of Emperor Qin, China	1·10	90
1189	10n. Imperial bronze dragon, China	1·10	90
1190	10n. Pyramids, Tikal National Park, Guatemala	1·10	90
1191	10n. Fountain, Evora, Portugal	1·10	90
1192	10n. Forest path, Shirakami-Sanchi, Japan	1·10	90
1193	10n. View from Eiffel Tower, Paris, France	1·10	90
1194	10n. Wooden walkway, Valley Below the Falls, Croatia	1·10	90
1195	15n. Bamberg Cathedral, Germany	1·60	1·40
1196	15n. Aerial view of Bamberg	1·60	1·40
1197	15n. St. Michael's Church, Hildesheim, Germany	1·60	1·40
1198	15n. Potsdam Palace, Germany	1·60	1·40
1199	15n. Church, Potsdam	1·60	1·40
1200	15n. Waterfront, Lubeck, Germany	1·60	1·40
1201	15n. Quedlinberg, Germany	1·60	1·40
1202	15n. Benedictine church, Lorsch, Germany	1·60	1·40
MS1203	Two sheets, each 126×102 mm. (a) 60n. House, Goslar, Germany (horiz); (b) 60n. Comenzada Cathedral, Portugal (horiz)	11·00	9·75

158 Turkish Angora

1997. Domestic Animals. Mult. (a) Cats.

1204	10n. Type **158**	1·10	90
1205	15n. Oriental shorthair	1·60	1·40
1206	15n. Japanese bobtail	1·60	1·50
1207	15n. Ceylon	1·60	1·40
1208	15n. Exotic	1·60	1·40
1209	15n. Rex	1·60	1·40
1210	15n. Ragdoll	1·60	1·40
1211	15n. Russian blue	1·60	1·40
1212	20n. British shorthair	1·70	1·50
1213	25n. Burmese	1·80	1·60

(b) Dogs.

1214	10n. Dalmatian	1·10	90
1215	15n. Siberian husky	1·60	1·40
1216	20n. Saluki	1·70	1·50
1217	20n. Dandie Dinmont terrier	1·70	1·50
1218	20n. Chinese crested	1·70	1·50
1219	20n. Norwich terrier	1·70	1·50
1220	20n. Basset hound	1·70	1·50
1221	20n. Cardigan Welsh corgi	1·70	1·50
1222	20n. French bulldog	1·70	1·50
1223	25n. Shar-Pei	1·80	1·60
MS1224	Two sheets, each 76×106 mm. (a) 60n. Tokinese (cat); (b) 60n. Hovawart (dog)	5·00	4·25

Nos. 1206/11 and 1217/22 respectively were issued together, *se-tenant*, forming composite designs.

159 Stuart Pearce (England)

1997. World Cup Football Championship, France (1998). Black (Nos. 1225, 1231, 1235, 1237, 1241, 1243) or multicoloured (others).

1225	5n. Type **159**	55	45
1226	10n. Paul Gascoigne (England)	1·10	90
1227	10n. Diego Maradona (Argentina 1986) (horiz)	1·10	90
1228	10n. Carlos Alberto (Brazil 1970) (horiz)	1·10	90
1229	10n. Dunga (Brazil 1994) (horiz)	1·10	90
1230	10n. Bobby Moore (England 1966) (horiz)	1·10	90
1231	10n. Fritz Walter (West Germany 1954) (horiz)	1·10	90
1232	10n. Walter Matthaus (Germany 1990) (horiz)	1·10	90
1233	10n. Franz Beckenbauer (West Germany 1974) (horiz)	1·10	90
1234	10n. Daniel Passarella (Argentina 1978) (horiz)	1·10	90
1235	10n. Italy team, 1938 (horiz)	1·10	90
1236	10n. West Germany team, 1954 (horiz)	1·10	90
1237	10n. Uruguay team, 1958 (horiz)	1·10	90
1238	10n. England team, 1966 (horiz)	1·10	90
1239	10n. Argentina team, 1978 (horiz)	1·10	90
1240	10n. Brazil team, 1962 (horiz)	1·10	90
1241	10n. Italy team, 1934 (horiz)	1·10	90
1242	10n. Brazil team, 1970 (horiz)	1·10	90
1243	10n. Uruguay team, 1930 (horiz)	1·10	90
1244	10n. David Beckham (England)	1·60	1·40
1245	20n. Steve McManaman (England)	1·70	1·50
1246	25n. Tony Adams (England)	2·00	1·70
1247	30n. Paul Ince (England)	2·50	2·10
MS1248	Two sheets, each 102×127 mm. (a) 35n. Salvatore "Toto" Schillaci (Italy) (horiz); (b) 35n. Philippe Albert (Belgium)	8·75	7·50

160 Buddha in Lotus Position

1997. "Indepex '97" International Stamp Exhibition, New Delhi. 50th Anniv of Independence of India. Multicoloured.

1249	3n. Type **160**	35	20
1250	7n. Mahatma Gandhi with hands together	55	45
1251	10n. Gandhi (three-quarter face portrait)	75	65
1252	15n. Buddha with feet on footstool	1·10	90
MS1253	Two sheets, each 75×106 mm. (a) 15n. Buddha with right hand raised; (b) 15n. Gandhi carrying stick	3·75	3·50

161 Jawaharlal Nehru and King Jigme Dorji Wangchuck

1997. Int Friendship between India and Bhutan.

1254	**161** 3n. black and pink	45	20
MS1256	100×70 mm. 20n. multicoloured	2·20	1·90

DESIGNS: 10n. Prime Minister Rajiv Gandhi of India and King Jigme Singye Wangchuck. 76×34 mm—20n. President R Venkataraman of India and King Jigme Singye Wangchuck.

162 Tiger

1998. New Year. Year of the Tiger. T **162** and similar square designs. Multicoloured.

1257	3n. Type **162**	45	20
MS1258	Two sheets. (a) 95×95 mm. 3n. Type **162**; 5n. Lying down; 15n. Hunting; 17n. On rocky outcrop; (b) 114×81 mm. 20n. Head of tiger	4·00	3·75

163 Safe Motherhood and Anniversary Emblems

1998. 50th Anniv of WHO.

1259	**163** 3n. multicoloured	20	10
1260	**163** 10n. multicoloured	75	65

164 Mother Teresa

1998. Mother Teresa (founder of Missionaries of Charity) Commemoration. Multicoloured.

1262	10n. Type **164**	1·10	90
1263	10n. With Diana, Princess of Wales	1·10	90
1264	10n. Holding child	1·10	90
1265	10n. Holding baby	1·10	90
1266	10n. With Sisters	1·10	90
1267	10n. Smiling	1·10	90
1268	10n. Praying	1·10	90
1269	10n. With Pope John Paul II	1·10	90
1270	10n. Close-up of face	1·10	90
MS1271	150×122 mm. 25n. As No. 1263 but 39×46 mm; 25n. As No. 1269 but different colour background and 39×46 mm	3·25	3·00

MS1261 100×60 mm. 15n. Safe Motherhood emblem (134×34 mm) — 1·30 1·20

165 Red-billed Chough

1998. Birds. Multicoloured.

1272	10ch. Type **165**	20	20
1273	30ch. Great Indian hornbill ("Great Hornbill")	20	20
1274	50ch. Western Singing bush lark ("Singing Lark")	20	20
1275	70ch. Chestnut-flanked white-eye	20	20
1276	90ch. Magpie robin (wrongly inscr "Megpie-robin")	20	20
1277	1n. Mrs. Gould's sunbird	20	20
1278	2n. Long-tailed tailor bird ("Tailorbird")	20	20
1279	3n. Mallard ("Duck")	35	30
1280	5n. Great spotted cuckoo ("Spotted Cuckoo")	55	45
1281	7n. Severtzov's tit warbler ("Goldcrest")	75	65
1282	9n. Common mynah	1·00	85
1283	10n. Green cochoa	1·10	90
MS1284	75×118 mm. 15n. Turtle dove (40×29 mm)	2·20	1·90

166 Rabbit

1999. New Year. Year of the Rabbit. Multicoloured.

1285	4n. Type **166**	65	55
1286	16n. Rabbit on hillock	1·10	90
MS1287	83×114 mm. 20n. Rabbit beneath tree (34×34 mm)	2·40	2·10

167 Nuremberg

1999. "iBRA '99" International Stamp Exhibition, Nuremberg. Sheet 75×94 mm containing T **167** and similar square design. Multicoloured.

MS1288	35n. Type **167**; 40n. Exhibition emblem	5·00	4·25

168 King Wangchuck

1999. 25th Anniv of Coronation of King Jigme Singye Wangchuck. Multicoloured.

1289	25n. Type **168**	2·00	1·70
1290	25n. Facing left (yellow background)	2·00	1·70
1291	25n. Facing forwards (orange background)	2·00	1·70
1292	25n. With arm raised (green background)	2·00	1·70
MS1293	180×140 mm. 25n. King Wangchuk (magenta background)	2·10	1·80

169 Early German Steam Locomotive

1999. Trains. Multicoloured.

1294	5n. Type **169**	35	30
1295	10n. Electric locomotive	85	75
1296	10n. *Hikari* express train, Japan	85	75
1297	10n. Steam locomotive, South Africa, 1953	85	75
1298	10n. Super Chief locomotive, U.S.A., 1946	85	75
1299	10n. Magleus Magnet train, Japan, 1991	85	75
1300	10n. *Flying Scotsman*, Great Britain, 1992	85	75
1301	10n. Kodama locomotive, Japan, 1958	85	75
1302	10n. *Blue Train*, South Africa, 1969	85	75
1303	10n. Intercity train, Germany, 1960	85	75
1304	10n. ET 403 high speed electric locomotive, Germany, 1973	85	75
1305	10n. 4-4-0 steam locomotive, U.S.A., 1855	85	75
1306	10n. Beyer-Garratt steam locomotive, South Africa, 1954 (wrongly inscr "BAYER GARRATT")	85	75
1307	10n. Settebello locomotive, Italy, 1953	85	75
1308	15n. Pacific Class 01 steam locomotive, Germany	1·20	1·00
1309	15n. Neptune Express, Germany	1·20	1·00
1310	15n. 4-6-0 steam locomotive, Great Britain	1·20	1·00
1311	15n. Shovelnose Streamliner diesel locomotive, U.S.A.	1·20	1·00
1312	15n. Electric locomotive, Germany	1·20	1·00
1313	15n. Early steam locomotive, Germany	1·20	1·00
1314	15n. Union Pacific diesel locomotive, U.S.A.	1·20	1·00
1315	15n. 1881 Borsig steam locomotive, Germany	1·20	1·00
1316	15n. Borsig 4-6-4 diesel locomotive, Germany	1·20	1·00
1317	15n. Diesel-electric locomotive, France	1·20	1·00
1318	15n. Pennsylvania Railroad locomotive, U.S.A.	1·20	1·00
1319	15n. Steam locomotive, Germany	1·20	1·00
1320	15n. Amtrak locomotive, U.S.A.	1·20	1·00
1321	15n. 2-2-2 steam locomotive, Great Britain	1·20	1·00
1322	15n. P class steam locomotive, Denmark	1·20	1·00
1323	15n. Electric locomotive, France	1·20	1·00
1324	15n. First Japanese locomotive	1·20	1·00
1325	15n. 2-8-2 steam locomotive, Germany	1·20	1·00
1326	20n. Steam locomotive	1·50	1·30
1327	30n. Electric locomotive	2·20	1·80
MS1328	Two sheets, each 110×85 mm. (a) 80n. City of Los Angeles, U.S.A.; (b) 80n. Great Northern diesel-electric Streamliner locomotive, U.S.A	13·00	11·50

170 *Festive Dancers*

1999. 150th Death Anniv of Katsushika Hokusai (artist). Multicoloured.

1329	15n. Type **170**	1·10	90
1330	15n. *Drawings of Women* (woman reading)	1·10	90
1331	15n. *Festive Dancers* (man wearing pointed hat)	1·10	90
1332	15n. *Festive Dancers* (man looking up)	1·10	90

1333	15n. *Drawings of Women* (woman sitting on ground)	1·10	90
1334	15n. *Festive Dancers* (woman)	1·10	90
1335	15n. *Suspension Bridge between Hida and Etchu*	1·10	90
1336	15n. *Drawings of Women* (woman dressing hair)	1·10	90
1337	15n. *Exotic Beauty*	1·10	90
1338	15n. *The Poet Nakamaro in China*	1·10	90
1339	15n. *Drawings of Women* (woman rolling up sleeve)	1·10	90
1340	15n. *Chinese Poet in Snow*	1·10	90
1341	15n. *Mount Fuji seen above Mist on the Tama River* (horiz)	1·10	90
1342	15n. *Mount Fuji seen from Shichirigahama* (horiz)	1·10	90
1343	15n. *Sea Life* (turtle) (horiz)	1·10	90
1344	15n. *Sea Life* (fish) (horiz)	1·10	90
1345	15n. *Mount Fuji reflected in a Lake* (horiz)	1·10	90
1346	15n. *Mount Fuji seen through the Piers of Mannenbashi* (horiz)	1·10	90
MS1347	Three sheets (a) 100×71 mm 80n. *Peasants leading Oxen*; (b) 71×100 mm 80n. *The lotus Pedestal.* (c) 71×100 mm 870n. *Kusunoki Masahige*	20·00	17·00

171 Tyrannosaurus Rex

1999. Prehistoric Animals. Multicoloured.

1348	10n. Type **171**	75	65
1349	10n. Dimorphodon	75	65
1350	10n. Diplodocus	75	65
1351	10n. Pterodaustro	75	65
1352	10n. Tyrannosaurus Rex (different)	75	65
1353	10n. Edmontosaurus	75	65
1354	10n. Apatosaurus	75	65
1355	10n. Deinonychus	75	65
1356	10n. Hypsilophodon	75	65
1357	10n. Oviraptor	75	65
1358	10n. Stegosaurus beside lake	75	65
1359	10n. Head of Triceratops	75	65
1360	10n. Pterodactylus and Brachiosaurus	75	65
1361	10n. Pteranodon	75	65
1362	10n. Anurognathus and Tyrannosaurus Rex	75	65
1363	10n. Brachiosaurus	75	65
1364	10n. Corythosaurus	75	65
1365	10n. Iguanodon	75	65
1366	10n. Lesothosaurus	75	65
1367	10n. Allosaurus	75	65
1368	10n. Velociraptor	75	65
1369	10n. Triceratops in water	75	65
1370	10n. Stegosaurus in water	75	65
1371	10n. Compsognathus	75	65
1372	20n. Moeritherium	1·50	1·30
1373	20n. Platybelodon	1·50	1·30
1374	20n. Woolly mammoth	1·50	1·30
1375	20n. African elephant	1·50	1·30
1376	20n. Deinonychus	1·50	1·30
1377	20n. Dimorphodon	1·50	1·30
1378	20n. Archaeopteryx	1·50	1·30
1379	20n. Common pheasant ("Ring-necked Pheasant")	1·50	1·30
MS1380	Four sheets, each 110×85 mm. (a) 80n. Hoatzin (vert); (b) 80n. Icthyosaurus (wrongly inscr "Present Day Dolphin") (vert); (c) 80n. Triceratops (vert); (d) 80n. Pteranodon (wrongly inscr "Triceratops")	24·00	21·00

Nos. 1348/59 and 1360/71 were issued together, *se-tenant*, with the backgrounds forming a composite design.

172 Siberian Musk Deer

1999. "China '99" World Philatelic Exhibition, Peking. Animals. Multicoloured.

1381	20n. Type **172**	1·70	1·50
1382	20n. Takin (*Budorcas taxicolor*)	1·70	1·50
1383	20n. Bharal ("Blue sheep") (*Pseudois nayur*) (wrongly inscr "nayour")	1·70	1·50
1384	20n. Yak (*Bos gunniens*)	1·70	1·50
1385	20n. Common goral (*Nemorhaedus goral*)	1·70	1·50

173 Sara Orange-tip

1999. Butterflies. Multicoloured.

1386	5n. Type **173**	45	35
1387	10n. Pipe-vine swallowtail	75	65
1388	15n. Longwings	1·10	90
1389	20n. Viceroy	1·40	1·20
1390	20n. Frosted skipper	1·40	1·20
1391	20n. Fiery skipper	1·40	1·20
1392	20n. Banded hairstreak	1·40	1·20
1393	20n. Cloudless ("Clouded") sulphur	1·40	1·20
1394	20n. Milbert's tortoiseshell	1·40	1·20
1395	20n. Eastern tailed blue	1·40	1·20
1396	20n. Jamaican kite ("Zebra") swallowtail	1·40	1·20
1397	20n. Colorado hairstreak	1·40	1·20
1398	20n. Pink-edged sulphur	1·40	1·20
1399	20n. Barred sulphur (wrongly inscr "Fairy Yellow")	1·40	1·20
1400	20n. Red-spotted purple	1·40	1·20
1401	20n. Aphrodite	1·40	1·20
1402	25n. Silver-spotted skipper (vert)	1·80	1·60
1403	30n. Great spangled fritillary (vert)	2·20	1·80
1404	35n. Little copper (vert)	2·50	2·20
MS1405	Four sheets, each 98×68 mm. (a) 80n. Monarch (vert); (b) 80n. Checkered white; (c) 80n. Gulf fritillary (vert); (d) 80n. Grey hairstreak (vert)	24·00	21·00

Nos. 1390/95 and 1396/1401 were issued together, *se-tenant*, forming a composite design.

174 Chestnut-breasted Chlorophonia

1999. Birds. Multicoloured.

1406	15n. Type **174**	1·10	90
1407	15n. Yellow-faced amazon	1·10	90
1408	15n. White ibis	1·10	90
1409	15n. Parrotlet sp. ("Caique")	1·10	90
1410	15n. Green jay	1·10	90
1411	15n. Tufted coquette	1·10	90
1412	15n. Troupial	1·10	90
1413	15n. American purple gallinule ("Purple Gallinule")	1·10	90
1414	15n. Copper-rumped hummingbird	1·10	90
1415	15n. Great egret ("Common egret")	1·10	90
1416	15n. Rufous-browed pepper shrike	1·10	90
1417	15n. Glittering-throated emerald	1·10	90
1418	15n. Great kiskadee	1·10	90
1419	15n. Cuban green woodpecker	1·10	90
1420	15n. Scarlet ibis	1·10	90
1421	15n. Belted kingfisher	1·10	90
1422	15n. Barred antshrike	1·10	90
1423	15n. Brown-throated conure ("Caribbean Parakeet")	1·10	90
1424	15n. Rufous-tailed jacamar (vert)	1·10	90
1425	15n. Scarlet macaw (vert)	1·10	90
1426	15n. Channel-billed toucan (vert)	1·10	90
1427	15n. Louisiana heron ("Tri-colored heron") (vert)	1·10	90
1428	15n. St. Vincent amazon ("St. Vincent Parrot") (vert)	1·10	90
1429	15n. Blue-crowned motmot (vert)	1·10	90
1430	15n. Horned screamer (vert)	1·10	90
1431	15n. Grey plover ("Black-billed Plover") (vert)	1·10	90
1432	15n. Eastern meadowlark ("Common meadowlark") (vert)	1·10	90
MS1433	Three sheets, each 85×110 mm. (a) 80n. Military macaw (vert); (b) 80n. Toco toucan; (c) 80n. Red-billed scythebill (vert)	18·00	16·00

Nos. 1406/14, 1415/23 and 1424/32 were issued together, *se-tenant*, forming a composite design.

175 Yuri Gagarin (first person in space, 1961)

1999. 30th Anniv of First Manned Moon Landing. Multicoloured.

1434	20n. Type **175**	1·50	1·30
1435	20n. Alan Shepard (first American in space, 1961)	1·50	1·30
1436	20n. John Glenn (first American to orbit Earth, 1962)	1·50	1·30
1437	20n. Valentina Tereshkova (first woman in space, 1963)	1·50	1·30
1438	20n. Edward White (first American to walk in space, 1965)	1·50	1·30
1439	20n. Neil Armstrong (first person to set foot on Moon, 1969)	1·50	1·30
1440	20n. Neil Armstrong (wearing N.A.S.A. suit)	1·50	1·30
1441	20n. Michael Collins	1·50	1·30
1442	20n. Edwin (Buzz) Aldrin	1·50	1·30
1443	20n. *Columbia* (pointing upwards)	1·50	1·30
1444	20n. *Eagle* on lunar surface	1·50	1·30
1445	20n. Edwin Aldrin on lunar surface	1·50	1·30
1446	20n. North American X-15 rocket (1960)	1·50	1·30
1447	20n. Gemini 8 (1966)	1·50	1·30
1448	20n. Saturn V rocket (1969)	1·50	1·30
1449	20n. *Columbia* (pointing downwards)	1·50	1·30
1450	20n. *Eagle* above Moon	1·50	1·30
1451	20n. Edwin Aldrin descending ladder	1·50	1·30
MS1452	Three sheets. (a) 111×85 mm. 80n. Neil Armstrong (different); (b) 111×85 mm. 80n. Gemini 8 docking with Agena target vehicle (56×41 mm); (c) 85×111 mm. 80n. Apollo 11 command module landing in Pacific Ocean (vert)	18·00	16·00

Nos. 1434/9, 1440/5 and 1446/51 were issued together, *se-tenant*, forming a composite design.

176 Tortoiseshell Cat

1999. Animals. Multicoloured.

1453	5n. Type **176**	1·00	85
1454	5n. Man watching blue and white cat	1·00	85
1455	10n. Chinchilla golden longhair adult and kittens	1·80	1·60
1456	12n. Russian blue adult and kitten	85	75
1457	12n. Birman	85	75
1458	12n. Devon rex	85	75
1459	12n. Pewter longhair	85	75
1460	12n. Bombay	85	75
1461	12n. Sorrel somali	85	75
1462	12n. Red tabby manx	85	75
1463	12n. Blue smoke longhair	85	75
1464	12n. Oriental tabby shorthair adult and kitten	85	75
1465	12n. Australian silky terrier	85	75
1466	12n. Samoyed	85	75
1467	12n. Basset bleu de Gascogne	85	75
1468	12n. Bernese mountain dog	85	75
1469	12n. Pug	85	75
1470	12n. Bergamasco	85	75
1471	12n. Basenji	85	75
1472	12n. Wetterhoun	85	75
1473	12n. Drever	85	75
1474	12n. Przewalski horse	85	75
1475	12n. Shetland pony	85	75
1476	12n. Dutch gelderlander horse	85	75
1477	12n. Shire horse	85	75
1478	12n. Arab	85	75
1479	12n. Boulonnais	85	75
1480	12n. Falabella	85	75
1481	12n. Orlov trotter	85	75
1482	12n. Suffolk punch	85	75
1483	15n. Lipizzaner	1·60	1·40
1484	20n. Andalusian	2·20	1·80
1485	25n. Weimaraner (dog)	2·75	2·30
1486	30n. German shepherd dog	3·75	3·25
MS1487	Three sheets, each 115×91 mm. (a) 70n. Labrador retriever; (b) 70n. Norwegian forest cat; (c) 70n. Connemara horse	16·00	14·50

177 Bharal

1999. Animals and Birds of the Himalayas. Multicoloured.
(a) Animals.

1489	20n. Type **177**		1·60	1·40
1490	20n. Lynx		1·60	1·40
1491	20n. Rat snake		1·60	1·40
1492	20n. Indian elephant		1·60	1·40
1493	20n. Langur		1·60	1·40
1494	20n. Musk deer		1·60	1·40
1495	20n. Otter		1·60	1·40
1496	20n. Tibetan wolf		1·60	1·40
1497	20n. Himalayan black bear		1·60	1·40
1498	20n. Snow leopard		1·60	1·40
1499	20n. Flying squirrel		1·60	1·40
1500	20n. Red fox		1·60	1·40
1501	20n. Ibex		1·60	1·40
1502	20n. Takin		1·60	1·40
1503	20n. Agama lizard		1·60	1·40
1504	20n. Marmot		1·60	1·40
1505	20n. Red panda		1·60	1·40
1506	20n. Leopard cat		1·60	1·40

MS1507 Three sheets, each 78×118 mm. (a) 100n. Cobra; (b) 100n. Tiger; (c) 100n. Rhinoceros (wrongly inscr "Rhinoerous") ... 21·00 19·00

(b) Birds.

1508	20n. Red-crested pochard		1·60	1·40
1509	20n. Satyr tragopan		1·60	1·40
1510	20n. Lammergeier ("Lammer-geier Vulture")		1·60	1·40
1511	20n. Kalij pheasant		1·60	1·40
1512	20n. Great Indian hornbill		1·60	1·40
1513	20n. White stork ("Stork")		1·60	1·40
1514	20n. Rufous-necked hornbill (wrongly inscr "Rofous")		1·60	1·40
1515	20n. Black drongo ("Drongo")		1·60	1·40
1516	20n. Himalayan monal pheasant		1·60	1·40
1517	20n. Black-necked crane		1·60	1·40
1518	20n. Little green bee-eater		1·60	1·40
1519	20n. Oriental ibis ("Ibis")		1·60	1·40
1520	20n. Crested lark		1·60	1·40
1521	20n. Ferruginous duck		1·60	1·40
1522	20n. Blood pheasant		1·60	1·40
1523	20n. White-crested laughing thrush ("Laughing Thrush")		1·60	1·40
1524	20n. Golden eagle		1·60	1·40
1525	20n. Siberian rubythroat		1·60	1·40

MS1526 Three sheets, each 78×118 mm. (a) 100n. Siberian rubythroat (different); (b) 100n. Black-naped monarch; (c) 100n. Mountain peacock pheasant ... 21·00 19·00

178 Elephant, Monkey, Rabbit and Bird (Four Friends)

1999. Year 2000.

1527	**178**	10n. multicoloured	75	65
1528	**178**	20n. multicoloured	1·40	1·20

179 Elegant Stink Horn

1999. Fungi. Multicoloured.

1529	20n. Type **179**		1·60	1·40
1530	20n. Pholiota squarrosoides		1·60	1·40
1531	20n. Scaly inky cap (Coprinus quadrifidus)		1·60	1·40
1532	20n. Golden spindles (Clavulinopsis fusiformis)		1·60	1·40
1533	20n. Spathularia velutipes		1·60	1·40
1534	20n. Ganoderma lucidum		1·60	1·40
1535	20n. Microglossum rufum		1·60	1·40

1536	20n. Lactarius hygrophoroides		1·60	1·40
1537	20n. Lactarius speciosus complex		1·60	1·40
1538	20n. Calostoma cinnabarina		1·60	1·40
1539	20n. Clitocybe clavipes		1·60	1·40
1540	20n. Microstoma floccosa		1·60	1·40
1541	20n. Frost's bolete (Boletus frostii)		1·60	1·40
1542	20n. Common morel (Morchella esculenta) (wrongly inscr "estculena")		1·60	1·40
1543	20n. Hypomyces lactifuorum		1·60	1·40
1544	20n. Polyporus auricularius		1·60	1·40
1545	20n. Cantharellus lateritius		1·60	1·40
1546	20n. Volvariella pusilla		1·60	1·40

MS1547 Three sheets, each 78×118 mm. (a) 100n. Pholiota aurivella; (b) 100n. Ramarai grandis; (c) 100n. Oudemansiella lucidum ... 21·00 19·00

180 Green Dragon with Red Flames

2000. New Year. Year of the Dragon. Multicoloured.

1548	3n. Type **180**		35	30
1549	5n. Green dragon encircling moon		45	35
1550	8n. Dragon and symbols of Chinese zodiac		75	65
1552	12n. Brown dragon encircling moon		1·20	1·00

MS1553 90×130 mm. 15n. Dragon head (29×40 mm) ... 1·60 1·50

181 LZ-1 (first flight), 1900

2000. Centenary of First Zeppelin Flight. Multicoloured.

1554	25n. Type **181**		1·80	1·60
1555	25n. LZ-2, 1906		1·80	1·60
1556	25n. LZ-3 over hills (first flight, 1906)		1·80	1·60
1557	25n. LZ-127 Graf Zeppelin (first flight, 1928)		1·80	1·60
1558	25n. LZ-129 Hindenberg (first flight, 1936)		1·80	1·60
1559	25n. LZ-130 Graf Zeppelin II (first flight, 1938)		1·80	1·60
1560	25n. LZ-1 over hill with tree		1·80	1·60
1561	25n. LZ-2 over mountains		1·80	1·60
1562	25n. LZ-3 against sky		1·80	1·60
1563	25n. LZ-4 (first flight, 1908)		1·80	1·60
1564	25n. LZ-5 (first flight, 1909)		1·80	1·60
1565	25n. LZ-6 (formation of Deutsche Liftschiffahrts Aktien Gesallschaft (DELAG) (world's first airline), 1909)		1·80	1·60
1566	25n. LZ-1 over grassy hills, 1900		1·80	1·60
1567	25n. Z11 Ersatz, 1913		1·80	1·60
1568	25n. LZ-6 exiting hangar, 1909		1·80	1·60
1569	25n. LZ-10 Schwabein (first flight, 1911)		1·80	1·60
1570	25n. LZ-7 Deutschland (inscr "Ersatz Deutschland")		1·80	1·60
1571	25n. LZ-11 Viktoria Luise		1·80	1·60

MS1572 Three sheets, each 106×80 mm. (a) 80n. Ferdinand von Zeppelin wearing white cap (vert); (b) 80n. Zeppelin wearing cap (vert); (c) 80n. Zeppelin (vert) ... 18·00 16·00

182 Lunix III

2000. "WORLD STAMP EXPO 2000" International Stamp Exhibition, Anaheim, California. Space. Multicoloured.

1573	25n. Type **182**		1·80	1·60
1574	25n. Ranger 9		1·80	1·60
1575	25n. Lunar Orbiter		1·80	1·60
1576	25n. Lunar Prospector spacecraft		1·80	1·60
1577	25n. Apollo 11 spacecraft		1·80	1·60
1578	25n. Selen satellite		1·80	1·60
1579	25n. Space shuttle Challenger		1·80	1·60
1580	25n. North American X-15 experimental rocket aircraft		1·80	1·60
1581	25n. Space shuttle Buran		1·80	1·60
1582	25n. Hermes (experimental space plane)		1·80	1·60
1583	25n. X-33 Venturi Star (reusable launch vehicle)		1·80	1·60

1584	25n. Hope (unmanned experimental spacecraft)		1·80	1·60
1585	25n. Victor Patsayev (cosmonaut)		1·80	1·60
1586	25n. Yladisloav Volkov (cosmonaut)		1·80	1·60
1587	25n. Georgi Dobrvolski (cosmonaut)		1·80	1·60
1588	25n. Virgil Grissom (astronaut)		1·80	1·60
1589	25n. Roger Chaffee (astronaut)		1·80	1·60
1590	25n. Edward White (astronaut)		1·80	1·60

MS1591 Three sheets. (a) 76×111 mm. 80n. Launch of space shuttle Challenger (vert); (b) 76×111 mm. 80n. Launch of space shuttle Buran (vert); (c) 116×85 mm. 80n. Edwin E. Aldrin on moon (first manned Moon landing, 1969) (vert) ... 18·00 16·00

183 Trashigang Dzong

2000. "EXPO 2000" World's Fair, Hanover, Germany (1st issue). Monasteries. Multicoloured.

1592	3n. Type **183**		20	20
1593	4n. Lhuentse Dzong		25	25
1594	6n. Gasa Dzong		45	35
1595	7n. Punakha Dzong		55	45
1596	10n. Trashichhoe Dzong		65	55
1597	20n. Paro Dzong		1·30	1·10

MS1598 157×98 mm. 15n. Roof (29×40 mm) ... 2·00 1·70

184 Snow Leopard

2000. "EXPO 2000" World's Fair, Hanover, Germany (2nd issue). Wildlife. Multicoloured.

1599	10n. Type **184**		75	65
1600	10n. Common raven ("Raven")		75	65
1601	10n. Golden langur		75	65
1602	10n. Rhododendron		75	65
1603	10n. Black-necked crane		75	65
1604	10n. Blue poppy		75	65

185 Jesse Owens (U.S.A.) (Berlin, 1936)

2000. Olympic Games, Sydney. Multicoloured.

1605	20n. Type **185**		1·40	1·20
1606	20n. Kayaking (modern games)		1·40	1·20
1607	20n. Fulton County Stadium, Atlanta, Georgia (1996 games)		1·40	1·20
1608	20n. Ancient Greek athlete		1·40	1·20

186 G. and R. Stephenson's Rocket (first steam locomotive)

2000. 175th Anniv of Opening of Stockton and Darlington Railway. Multicoloured.

1609	50n. Type **186**		3·75	3·00
1610	50n. Steam locomotive (opening of London and Birmingham railway, 1828)		3·75	3·00
1611	50n. Northumbrian locomotive, 1825		3·75	3·00

MS1612 118×79 mm. 100n. Inaugural run on Stockton and Darlington Railway, 1825 (56×42 mm) ... 7·00 6·25

187 Laird Commercial (biplane), 1929

2000. Airplanes. Multicoloured.

1613	25n. Type **187**		1·80	1·60

1614	25n. Ryan B-5 Brougham, 1927 (wrongly inscr "Broughm")		1·80	1·60
1615	25n. Cessna AW, 1928		1·80	1·60
1616	25n. Travel Air 4000 biplane, 1927		1·80	1·60
1617	25n. Fairchild F-71, 1927		1·80	1·60
1618	25n. Command Aire biplane, 1928		1·80	1·60
1619	25n. Waco YMF biplane, 1935		1·80	1·60
1620	25n. Piper J-4 Cub Coupe, 1938		1·80	1·60
1621	25n. Ryan ST-A, 1937		1·80	1·60
1622	25n. Spartan Executive, 1939		1·80	1·60
1623	25n. Luscombe 8, 1939		1·80	1·60
1624	25n. Stinson SR5 Reliant seaplane, 1935		1·80	1·60
1625	25n. Cessna 195 seaplane, 1949		1·80	1·60
1626	25n. Waco SRE biplane, 1940		1·80	1·60
1627	25n. Erco Ercope, 1948		1·80	1·60
1628	25n. Boeing Stearman biplane, 1941		1·80	1·60
1629	25n. Beech Staggerwing biplane, 1944		1·80	1·60
1630	25n. Republic Seabee, 1947		1·80	1·60

MS1631 Three sheets, each 77×108 mm. (a) 100n. Waco CSO seaplane, 1929; (b) 100n. Curtiss-Wright 19W, 1936; (c) 100n. Grumman G-44 Widgeon flying boat, 1941 ... 21·00 20·00

188 A Kind of Loving, 1962

2000. Berlin Film Festival. Winners of Golden Bear Award. Multicoloured.

1632	25n. Type **188**		1·80	1·60
1633	25n. Bushido Zankoku Monogatari, 1963		1·80	1·60
1634	25n. Hobson's Choice, 1954		1·80	1·60
1635	25n. El Lazarillo de Tormes, 1960		1·80	1·60
1636	25n. In the Name of the Father, 1997		1·80	1·60
1637	25n. Les Cousins, 1959		1·80	1·60

MS1638 96×102 mm. 100n. Die Ratten, 1962 ... 7·00 6·50

189 Einstein

2000. Albert Einstein—Time Magazine Man of the Century. Sheet 113×83 mm.
MS1639 **189** 100n. multicoloured ... 8·75 8·00

190 Aquinas

2000. 775th Birth Anniv of Thomas Aquinas (Catholic philosopher and theologian). Sheet 136×76 mm.
MS1640 **190** 25n.×4 multicoloured ... 1·80 1·60

191 Pierre de Coubertin

2000. New Millennium. Multicoloured. (a) Centenary of the Modern Olympic Games.

1641	25n. Type **191** (founder of modern games)		1·80	1·60
1642	25n. Hand holding baton (first modern Games, Athens, 1896)		1·80	1·60
1643	25n. Jesse Owen (Berlin, 1936)		1·80	1·60
1644	25n. Handprint and white dove (Munich, 1972)		1·80	1·60
1645	25n. Sydney Opera House (Sydney, 2000)		1·80	1·60
1646	25n. Children wearing T-shirts (Greece, 2004)		1·80	1·60

(b) Breakthroughs in Modern Medicine.

1647	25n. Albert Calmette (bacteriologist, joint discoverer of B.C.G. vaccine)	1·80	1·60
1648	25n. Camillo Colgi and S. Ramon y Cajal (discovery of the neurone)	1·80	1·60
1649	25n. Alexander Fleming (bacteriologist, discoverer of penicillin)	1·80	1·60
1650	25n. Jonas Salk (virologist, developer of polio vaccine)	1·80	1·60
1651	25n. Christiaan Barnard (surgeon, performed first human heart transplant)	1·80	1·60
1652	25n. Luc Mantagnier (A.I.D.S. research)	1·80	1·60

192 Paro Taktsang

2000. Sheet 86×49 mm.

MS1653 **192** 100n. multicoloured 7·00 6·50

193 Christopher Columbus

2000. Explorers. Two sheets, each 66×83 mm. Multicoloured.

MS1654 (a) 100n. Type **193**; (b) 100n. Captain James Cook 14·00 13·00

194 *Crinum amoenum*

2000. Flowers of the Himalayan Mountains. Multicoloured.

1655	25n. Type **194**	1·80	1·60
1656	25n. *Beaumontia grandiflora*	1·80	1·60
1657	25n. *Trachelospermum lucidum*	1·80	1·60
1658	25n. *Curcuma aromatica*	1·80	1·60
1659	25n. *Barleria cristata*	1·80	1·60
1660	25n. *Holmskioldia sanguinea*	1·80	1·60
1661	25n. *Meconopsis villosa*	1·80	1·60
1662	25n. *Salva hians*	1·80	1·60
1663	25n. *Caltha palustris*	1·80	1·60
1664	25n. *Anemone polyanthes*	1·80	1·60
1665	25n. *Cypripedium cordigerum*	1·80	1·60
1666	25n. *Cryptochilus luteus*	1·80	1·60
1667	25n. *Androsace globifera*	1·80	1·60
1668	25n. *Tanacetum atkinsonii*	1·80	1·60
1669	25n. *Aster stracheyi*	1·80	1·60
1670	25n. *Arenaria glanduligera*	1·80	1·60
1671	25n. *Sibbaldia purpurea*	1·80	1·60
1672	25n. *Saxifraga parnassifolia*	1·80	1·60

MS1673 Three sheets, each 68×98 mm. (a) 100n. *Dendrobium densiflorum* (vert); (b) 100n. *Rhododendron arboreum* (vert); (c) 100n. *Gypsophila cerastioides* 21·00 20·00

Nos. 1655/60, 1661/6 and 1667/72 respectively were issued together, se-tenant, forming a composite design.

195 *The Duke and Duchess of Osuna with their Children* (detail, Francisco de Goya)

2000. "Espana 2000" International Stamp Exhibition, Madrid. Prado Museum Exhibits. Multicoloured.

1674	25n. Type **195**	1·80	1·60
1675	25n. Young child (detail from *The Duke and Duchess of Osuna with their Children*)	1·80	1·60

1676	25n. Duke (detail from *The Duke and Duchess of Osuna with their Children*)	1·80	1·60
1677	25n. *Isidoro Maiquez* (Francisco de Goya)	1·80	1·60
1678	25n. *Dona Juana Galarza de Goicoechea* (Francisco de Goya)	1·80	1·60
1679	25n. *Ferdinand VII in an Encampment* (Francisco de Goya)	1·80	1·60
1680	25n. *Portrait of an Old Man* (Joos van Cleve)	1·80	1·60
1681	25n. *Mary Tudor* (Anthonis Mor)	1·80	1·60
1682	25n. *Portrait of a Man* (Jan van Scorel)	1·80	1·60
1683	25n. *The Court Jester Pejeron* (Anthonis Mor)	1·80	1·60
1684	25n. *Elizabeth of France* (Frans Pourbus the Younger)	1·80	1·60
1685	25n. *King James I* (Paul van Somer)	1·80	1·60
1686	25n. *The Empress Isabella of Portugal* (Titian)	1·80	1·60
1687	25n. *Lucrecia di Baccio del Fede, the Painter's Wife* (Andrea del Sarto)	1·80	1·60
1688	25n. *Self-Portrait* (Titian)	1·80	1·60
1689	25n. *Philip II* (Sofonisba Anguisciola)	1·80	1·60
1690	25n. *Portrait of a Doctor* (Lucia Anguisciola)	1·80	1·60
1691	25n. *Anna of Austria* (Sofonisba Anguisciola)	1·80	1·60

MS1692 Three sheets (a) 90×110 mm. 100n. Duchess and Duke (detail from *The Duke and Duchess of Osuna with their Children* (Francisco de Goya) (horiz); (b) 90×110 mm. 100n. *Charles V at Mühlberg* (Titian); (c) 110×90 mm. 100n. *The Relief of Genoa* (Antonio de Pereda) Set of 3 sheets 21·00 20·00

196 Butterfly

2000. "Indepex Asiana 2000" International Stamp Exhibition, Calcutta. Multicoloured.

1693	5n. Type **196**	30	25
1694	8n. Red jungle fowl	60	50
1695	10n. *Zinnia elegans*	70	65
1696	12n. Tiger	80	75

MS1697 144×84 mm. 15n. Spotted deer (28×34 mm) 2·20 2·10

197 Snake

2001. New Year. Year of the Snake. Multicoloured.

1698	3n. Type **197**	25	20
1699	20n. Snake	1·50	1·40

MS1700 135×135 mm. 3, 10n. As Type **197**; 15, 20n. As No. 1699 3·50 3·50

198 Snow Leopard (*Uncia uncia*)

2001. "Hong Kong 2001" International Stamp Exhibition. Nature Protection. Sheet 195×138 mm containing T **198** and similar horiz designs. Multicoloured.

MS1701 15n. Type **198**; 15n. Rufous-necked hornbill (*Aceros nipalensis*); 15n. Black-necked crane (*Grus nigricollis*); 15n. Tiger (*Panthera tigris*) 5·50 5·25

199 Working in Fields

2001. International Year of Volunteers. Multicoloured.

1702	3n. Type **199**	35	30
1703	4n. Planting crops	45	40
1704	10n. Children and bucket	95	85
1705	15n. Planting seeds and making compost	1·30	1·10

MS1706 170×120 mm. Nos. 1702/5 3·50 3·25

200 Chenrezig

2001. Buddhist Art, Taksang Monastery. Sheet 120×147 mm containing T **200** and similar vert designs. Multicoloured.

MS1707 10n. Type **200**; 15n. Guru Rimpoche; 20n. Sakyamuni 3·75 3·50

2001. Nos. 557/60 surch.

1708	4n. on 10ch. blue	60	50
1709	10n. on 25ch. red	1·20	1·00
1710	15n. on 50ch. violet	1·80	1·60
1711	20n. on 1n. brown	2·30	2·10

202 Snow Leopard's Head

2001. Snow Leopard (*Uncia uncia*). Sheet 172×140 mm containing T **202** and similar multicoloured design.

MS1712 10n.×4, each ×2, Type **202**; Two adults; Three juveniles; Crouched adult 7·50 7·00

203 Horse carrying Treasure Vase (Buddhist symbol)

2002. Year of the Horse. Multicoloured.

1713	20n. Type **203**	1·50	1·40
1714	20n. White horse	1·50	1·40

MS1715 94×94 mm. 25n. Horse and Dharma Wheel (horiz) 1·80 1·70

Nos. 1713/14 were issued together, se-tenant forming a composite design.

204 Teri gang

2002. International Year of Mountains. Sheet 144×105 mm containing T **204** and similar horiz designs. Multicoloured.

MS1716 20n. Type **204**; 20n. Tsenda gang; 20n. Jomolhari; 20n. Gangeheytag; 20n. Jitchudrake; 20n. Tse-rim Gang 10·00 9·25

205 *Rhomboda lanceolata*

2002. Orchids. Sheet 162×131 mm containing T **205** and similar vert designs. Multicoloured.

MS1717 10n. Type **205**; 10n. *Odontochilus lanceolatus*; 10n. *Zeuxine glandulosai*; 10n. *Goodyera schlechtendaliana*; 10n. *Anoectochilus lanceolatus*; 10n. *Goodyera hispida* 5·75 5·25

206 Rhododendron niveum

2002. Rhododendrons. Sheet 132×132 mm containing T **206** and similar square designs. Multicoloured.

MS1718 15n. Type **206**; 15n. *Rhododendron glaucophyllum*; 15n. *Rhododendron arboretum*; 15n. *Rhododendron grande*; 15n. *Rhododendron dalhousiae*; 15n. *Rhododendron barbatum* 9·50 8·75

207 Kapok Tree (*Bombax ceiba*)

2002. Medicinal Plants. Multicoloured.

1719	10n. Type **207**	1·00	90
1720	10n. Angel's trumpet (*Brugmansia suaveolens*)	1·00	90
1721	10n. Himalayan mayapple (*Podophyllum hexandrum*)	1·00	90
1722	10n. Himalayan pokeberry (*Photlacca acinosa*)	1·00	90

MS1723 85×106 mm. 10n.×4, Nos. 1719/22 4·50 4·25

208 Fireman and Flags

2002. "United We Stand".

1724	**208** 25n. multicoloured	2·40	2·10

209 Zinedine Zidane

2002. World Cup Football Championships, Japan and South Korea. Two sheets containing T **209** and similar vert designs. Multicoloured.

MS1725 (a) 167×118 mm. 25n. Type **209**; 25n. Michael Owen; 25n. Miyagi stadium, Japan; 25n. Cuauhtemoc Blanco (inscr "Cuahutemoc"); 25n. Gabriel Batistuta; 25n. Incheon stadium, South Korea; (b) 97×112 mm. 150n. Roberto Carlos 18·00 16·00

210 Queen Elizabeth

2002. Golden Jubilee of Queen Elizabeth II. Two sheets containing T **210** and similar square designs. Multicoloured.

MS1726 (a) 133×101 mm. 40n. Type **210**; 40n. Wearing green floral hat; 40n. With Duke of Edinburgh; 40n. Wearing white hat; (b) 79×108 mm. 90n. Wearing tiara 16·00 14·50

211 Ski Jumping

2002. Winter Olympic Games, Salt Lake City, USA. Sheet 89×120 mm containing T **211** and similar vert design. Multicoloured.

MS1727 50n. Type **211**; 50n. Cross
country skiing 6·25 6·00

212 Lotus Flower

2002. United Nations Year of Eco-Tourism. Two sheets containing T **212** and similar vert designs. Multicoloured.

MS1728 (a) 117×75 mm. 50n. Type
212; 50n. Northern jungle queen
butterfly; 50n. Bengal tiger; (b)
72×95 mm. 90n. Peacock 18·00 16·00

213 Cub Scout

2002. World Scout Jamboree, Thailand. Two sheets containing T **213** and similar multicoloured designs.

MS1729 (a) 182×142 mm. 50n. Type
213; 50n. Scouts of different nation-
alities; 50n. 1908 Scout; (b) 90×120
mm. 90n. Dan Beard (founder of
American Boy Scouts) (vert) 18·00 16·00

214 Charles
Lindbergh and *The
Spirit of St Louis*

2002. 75th Anniv of First Solo Trans-Atlantic Flight. Two sheets containing T **214** and similar vert designs. Multicoloured.

MS1730 (a) 171×134 mm. 75n. Type
214; 75n. Lindbergh; (b) 123×89
mm. 90n. Lindbergh (different) 18·00 16·00

215 Guar

2002. Flora and Fauna. Twelve sheets containing T **215** and similar horiz designs. Multicoloured.

MS1731 (a) 132×155 mm. 25n. Type
215; 25n. Hog badger; 25n. Indian
cobra; 25n. Leopard gecko; 25n.
Gavial; 25n. Hispid hare; (b) 132×155
mm. 25n. Yellow-legged gull; 25n.
Sand martin; 25n. Asian open-bill
stork; 25n. White stork; 25n.
Eurasian oystercatcher; 25n. Indian
pitta; (c) 132×155 mm. 25n. Blue
oak-leaf butterfly (inscr "Dead leaf
butterfly") (Kalima horsfieldi); 25n.
Golden birdwing (*Troides aeacus*);
25n. *Atrophaneura latrellei*; 25n.
Kaiser-I-Hind (*Teinopalpus imperialis*);
25n. *Zeuxidia aurelius*; 25n. *Euploea
dufresne*; (d) 137×158 mm. 25n.
Primula cawdoriana; 25n. *Meconopsis
aculeate*; 25n. *Primula wigramiana*;
25n. *Primula stuartii*; 25n. *Saxifraga
andersonii*; 25n. *Rheum nobile*; (e)
133×153 mm. 25n. *Russula integra*;
25n. *Hydgrophorus marzuolus*; 25n.
Tricholoma fulvum; 25n. *Hypholoma
fasciculare*; 25n. *Tricholoma pop-
ulinum*; 25n. *Cortinarius orellanus*;
(f) 136×161 mm. 25n. *Coelogyne
rhodeana*; 25n. *Coelogyne virescens*;
25n. *Phalanopsis schilleriana*; 25n.
Angraecum eburneum; 25n. *Dend-
robium aureum*; 25n. *Dendrobium
Ceasar*; (g) 89×92 mm. 90n. Esturine
crocodile; (h) 89×94 mm. 90n.
Mandarin duck; (i) 93×94 mm. 90n.
Portia philota; (j) 103×101 mm. 90n.
Paris polyphylla; (k) 101×101 mm.
90n. *Clathrus archeri*; (l) 99×100 mm.
90n. *Dendrobium chrysotoxum* £110 £100

216 Elvis Presley

2003. Anniversaries in 2002. 25th Death Anniv of Elvis Presley (entertainer) (MS1732a/b). 85th Birth Anniv of John Fitzgerald Kennedy (president USA, 1961–1963) (MS1732c/d). 5th Death Anniv of Diana, Princess of Wales (MS1732e/f). Six sheets containing T **216** and similar vert designs. Multicoloured.

MS1732 Six sheets (a) 110×178 mm.
25n.×4, Type **216**; Holding guitar
at waist; Singing into microphone;
Seated holding guitar to side; (b)
195×131 mm. 25n.×6, Wearing
shirt and kerchief; (c) 132×146 mm.
25n.×6, College graduate, 1935;
Walking with John F. Kennedy
Jr.; As Congressman, 1946; At the
White House, 1961; With Jacqueline
Kennedy on tennis court; Jacqueline
Kennedy and children at John
F. Kennedy's funeral; (d) 76×108
mm. 90n. Head and shoulders; (e)
134×118 mm. 25n.×4, Wearing
earrings and red dress; Wearing ball-
gown; Wearing jacket and blouse;
Wearing tiara; (f) 65×98 mm. 90n.
Wearing hat with feathers 55·00 50·00

2003. No. 659 surch **8NU**.
1733 8n. on 75ch. multicoloured 1·30 1·10

218 Lamb

2003. Chinese New Year. ("Year of the Sheep"). Sheet 120×80 mm containing T **218** and similar multicoloured design.

MS1734 15n. Type **218**; 20n. Sheep's
head (vert) 3·75 3·50

219 *Egret and
Willow* (Suzuki
Kitsu)

2003. Japanese Paintings. Six sheets containing T **219** and similar multicoloured designs.

MS1735 (a) 135×210 mm. 25n.×6, Type
219; White Cranes (Ito Jakuchu);
Cranes (Suzuki Kitsu); "andarin Ducks
amid Snow-covered Reeds (Ito Jaku-
chu); Rooster, Hen and Hydrangea
(Ito Jakuchu); Hawk on Snow-covered
Branch (Shibara Zeshin); (b) 135×210
mm. 25n.×6, Beauty reading Letter
(Utagawa Kunisada); Two Beauties
(Katsukawa Shunsho); Beauty arrang-
ing her Hai" (Kaigetsudo Doshin);
Dancing (Suzuki Kitsu); Two Beauties
(Kitagawa Kikumaro); Kambun
Beauty; (c) 159×140 mm. 25n.×6,
Two seated men and one lying
down (38×51 mm); Man holding fan,
man holding lute and man facing
left (38×51 mm); Man with raised
arm and woman facing left (38×51
mm); Two men talking and two fac-
ing left (38×51 mm); Man wearing
blue robe facing right and bald man
(38×51 mm); Man with beard and
two women (38×51 mm); (d) 90×90
mm. 90n. Heads of Nine Beauties in a
Roundel with Plum Blossom (Hosoda
Eishi); (e) 90×90 mm. Hawk carrying
Monkey (Shibata Zeshin); (f) 92×92
mm. Chrysanthemums by a Stream,
with Rocks (Ito Jakuchu) 50·00 46·00

The stamps of No. MS1735c form a composite design of "Thirty six Poets".

220 Lyonpo
Sangay Ngedup

2003. Move for Health Walk (walk by Lyonpo Sangay Ngedup (Health Minister) from Trashigang to Thimphu). Sheet 120×80 mm.

MS1736 220 50n. multicoloured 3·25 3·00

221 Girl and Parrot

2003. Education for All. Sheet 70×109 mm containing T **221** and similar vert designs. Multicoloured.

MS1737 25n. Type **221**; 5n. Girl reading;
10n. Boy and girl carrying books;
20n. Girl holding football 2·75 2·50

222 Kalij Pheasant
(*Lophura
leucomelana*) (inscr
"leucomelanus")

2003. Endangered Species. Birds. Sheet 69×100 mm containing T **222** and similar vert designs. Multicoloured.

MS1738 2n. Type **222**; 5n. Blyth's
tragopan (*Tragopan blythii*); 8n.
Satyr tragopan (*Tragopan satyra*);
15n. Himalayan monal pheasant
(*Lophophorus impeyanus*) (inscr
"impejanus") 3·75 3·50

223 Monkey

2004. New Year. Year of the Monkey. Sheet 95×130 mm containing T **223** and similar vert designs. Multicoloured.

MS1739 10n.×4, Type **223**; Facing left;
With raised back legs; Family 5·00 4·50

The stamps and margin of No. MS1739 were issued to-gether, se-tenant, forming a composite design.

224 Brazil World Cup
Champions Team, 2002

2004. Centenary of FIFA (Federation Internationale de Football Association). Multicoloured.
1740 10n. Type **224** 1·00 90
1741 10n. France World Cup Champi-
ons team, 1998 1·00 90

2004. No. 421 surch **5n**.
1742 5n. on 1n. multicoloured 1·30 90

226 Traditional Ploughing

2004. 20th Anniv of Continuing Japanese Assistance with Food Production. Two sheets containing T **226** and similar multicoloured designs.

MS1743 (a) 155×105 mm. 5n.×6, Type
225; Women transplanting; Tradi-
tional threshing; Modern ploughing;
Modern transplanting; Modern
threshing. (b) 130×85 mm. 30n. King
Jigme Singe Wangchuk ploughing 6·25 5·50

The stamps and margin of No. MS1743a were issued together, se-tenant, forming a composite design.

227 Jungle Fowl

2005. New Year. "Year of the Rooster". Sheet 155×110 mm containing T **227** and similar horiz design. Multicoloured.

MS1744 15n. Type **227**; 20n. Domestic
fowl 3·50 3·25

228 Dancer

2005. EXPO 2005 World Exposition, Aichi, Japan. Two sheets containing T **228** and similar vert designs. Multicoloured.

MS1745 126×201 mm. 10n. Type **228**;
10n. Dancer wearing skull mask; 20n.
Dancer holding drum; 20n. Dancer
wearing horned mask 5·00 4·50
MS1746 124×80 mm. 30n. Buddha
(25×35 mm) 2·50 2·30

229 Pope John
Paul II

2005. Pope John Paul II Commemoration. Multicoloured.
1747 15n. Type **229** 1·30 1·10
1747a 15n. As No. 1747 2·50 2·30
1747b 15n. As No. 1747 2·50 2·30
1747c 15n. As No. 1747 2·50 2·30

230 Locomotive P36 N 0097

2005. Bicentenary of Steam Locomotives (2004). Multicoloured.
1748 30n. Type **230** 3·00 3·00
1749 30n. Diesel locomotive VAI F
40 6428 3·00 3·00
1750 30n. InterRegio electric train 3·00 3·00
1751 30n. Amtrak 464 3·00 3·00
MS1752 100×71 mm. 85n. Locomotive
P36N0032 (vert) 9·50 8·50

231 Guido Buchwald

2005. 75th Anniv of World Cup Football Championships. Multicoloured.
1753 40n. Type **231** 3·75 3·75
1754 40n. Mario Basler 3·75 3·75
1755 40n. Torsten Frings 3·75 3·75
MS1756 124×105 mm. 85n. Fredi Bobic 9·50 8·50

232 Linked Hands and
Emblem

2005. Centenary of Rotary International. Sheet 95×113 mm.
MS1757 **232** 85n. multicoloured 9·50 8·50

232a Wachy Zam,
Wangduephodrang

2005. Bridges. Sheet 200×160 mm containing T **232a** and similar horiz designs. Multicoloured.

MS1758 10n. Type **232a**; 10n. Chain bridge, Doksam; 10n. Wooden canti-levered bridge, Mishi, Paro; 20n. Mo Chu bridge, Punakha; 20n. Langjo bridge, Thimphu; 20n. Punatshang Chu bridge, Wangduephodrang 10·00 9·00

233 Children from Many Nations

2005. "My Dream of Peace One Day". Winning Designs in Children's Painting Competition. Multicoloured.

1759	10n. Type **233**	1·10	90
1760	10n. Candle of flags	1·10	90
1761	10n. Children holding jigsaw of family	1·10	90
1762	10n. Dove and light and dark hands holding globe	1·10	90
1763	10n. Hands holding children and dark globe releasing doves	1·10	90
1764	10n. Globe holding umbrella of flags	1·10	90

234 King Jigme Singye Wangchuck

2005. 50th Birth Anniv of King Jigme Singye Wangchuck. Sheet 216×163 mm containing T **234** and similar vert designs. Multicoloured.

MS1765 20n.×5 Type **234**; Standing on podium (inauguration) (39×87 mm); Speaking with microphone; Seated on throne; With women 10·50 9·50

The stamps of **MS**1765 share a composite background design.

234a Raven

2005. National Symbols. Sheet 200×160 mm containing T **234a** and similar square designs. Multicoloured.

MS1766 10n. Takin (*Budorcas taxicolor*); 20n. Cypress tree; 20n. Blue poppy 3·75 3·50

235 St. Bernard

2006. New Year. Year of the Dog. Multicoloured.

1767	5n. Type **235**	40	35
1768	10n. Lhasa Apso (inscr 'Apsoo')	65	55
1769	15n. Maltese terrier (inscr 'Maltese')	1·00	90
1770	20n. Papillion (inscr 'Papillon')	1·30	1·10

MS1771 125×105 mm. 5n. As No. 1767; 10n. As No. 1768; 15n. As No. 1769; 20n. As No. 1770; 25n. Husky (36×70 mm) 4·75 4·25

236 Jakur
Dzong

2006. 50th Anniv of Europa Stamps. Multicoloured.

1772	150n. Type **236**	8·75	8·00
1773	250n. Archery	14·00	12·50

MS1774 100×72 mm. Nos. 1772/3 24·00 21·00

237 Female Fire
Hog

2007. New Year. Year of the Pig. Multicoloured.

1775	20n. Type **237**	1·30	1·10

MS1776 93×120 mm. 25n. Pig (35×33 mm) 1·60 1·50

Nos. 1777/8 and Type **238** have been left for 'Year of the Rat', issued on 8 February 2008, not yet received.

No. **MS**1778 consists of a sleeve containing a CD ROM.

239 Ugyen Wangchuck
(1907–1926)

2008. Centenary of Monarchy. Two sheets containing T **239** and similar multicoloured designs. Self-adhesive (**MS**1780) or ordinary gum (**MS**1779).

MS1779 170×122 mm. 5n. Type **239**; 10n. Jigme Wangchuck (1926–52); 15n. Jigme Dorji Wangchuck (1952–72); 20n. Jigme Singye Wangchuck (1972–2006); 25n. Jigme Khesar Namgyel Wangchuck (2006–) 5·50 5·00

MS1780 97×97 mm. 225n. Kings of Wangchuck dynasty 19·00

240 (Illustration reduced. Actual size 97×97 mm) (image scaled to 50% of original size)

2008. In Harmony with Nature. Sheet 97×97 mm. Self-adhesive.

MS1781 225n. **240** multicoloured 19·00

No. **MS**1781 consists of a sleeve containing a CD ROM.

241 Archer

2008. Olympic Games, Beijing. Sheet 130×130 mm containing T **241** and similar diamond shaped designs. Multicoloured.

MS1782 10n. Type **241**; 15n. Archer with leg raised; 25n. Auspicious symbols; 25n. Garuda in flight 5·50 4·75

242 Masked Dancers

2008. Bhutan's Participation at Smithsonian Folklife Festival. Three sheets containing T **242** and similar multicoloured designs.

MS1783 230×168 mm. 20n.×5, Type **242**; Archer; Ploughing; Dancers; Wood carving 7·50 6·75

MS1784 100×90 mm. 50n. Pavillion (38×50 mm) 3·75 3·50

MS1785 100×90 mm. 50n. Fireworks (50×38 mm) 3·75 3·50

243 Ox

2009. Chinese New Year

1786	20n. Type **243**	1·90	1·70

MS1787 162×210 mm. 30n. As Type **243** (40×30 mm) 2·50 2·30

244 Cantilever Bridge

2009. Punakha Dzong Bridge. Multicoloured.

1788	20n. Type **244**	1·50	1·40

MS1789 170×118 mm. 25n.×2, Bridge, left; Bridge, right 3·75 3·50

The stamps and margins of **MS**1789 form a composite design of the bridge and environs.

245 Eclipse (diamond ring effect)

2009. International Year of Astronomy. Multicoloured.

MS1790 25n.×2, Type **245**; Musicians and partial eclipse 3·75 3·50

246 Child leading Yaks carrying Gifted Rice from Japan

2009. 35th Anniv of World Food Programme in Bhutan

MS1791 20n.×6, Type **246**; 10n.Yaks carrying gifted rice from Saudi Arabia; 10n. Gifted rice in store; 10n. Cultivating hillside; 10n. People on track; 10n. New dwelling; 20n. Mother and child; 20n. Feeding children; 20n. Children studying 7·50 6·75

MS1792 100×75mm. 25n. Children holding red 'fill the cup' mugs (46×46mm) 1·90 1·70

247 Kushuthara

2009. Textiles. Multicoloured.

MS1793 20n.×4, Type **247**; Mentse Mathra; Lungserma; Yathra 4·50 4·00

248 Red Panda and Cub

2009. Red Panda (*Ailurus fulgens*). Multicoloured.

1794	20n. Type **248**	1·10	1·00
1795	20n. Facing left	1·10	1·00
1796	25n. Two pandas sleeping	1·50	1·40
1797	25n. Eating bamboo shoots	1·50	1·40

249 Tiger

2010. Chinese New Year. Year of the Tiger–Save the Tiger Campaign. Multicoloured.

MS1798 30n.×2, Type **249**; Laying facing right 5·00 4·50

MS1799 50n. Head and shoulders (vert) 4·25 3·75

250 National Memorial Chorten (stupa)

2010. World Health Day, 2010. Urbanization, a Challenge for Public Health. Multicoloured.

MS1800 10n.×6, Type **250**; Main street, Thimpu; Aerial view of Thimpu; Golf; New roadway; Clock tower and central square of Thimpu 5·25 4·75

MS1801 25n. New urban housing (50×38 mm) 2·50 2·30

251 Afghanistan

2010. 16th SAARC (South Asian Association for Regional Cooperation) Summit 2010, Bhutan. Multicoloured.

MS1802 200×150 mm. 10n.×8, Type **251**; Bangladesh; Bhutan; India; Maldives; Nepal; Pakistan; Sri Lnka 7·00 6·25

MS1803 148×100 mm. 25n. All members flags (51×40 mm) 2·50 2·30

252 King Jigme Dorji Wangchuck with Bow

2010. King Jigme Khesar Namgyel Wangchuck

MS1804 210×148 mm. 10n.×6, Type **252**; Throwing dart; Playing football with children; Playing basketball with children; In water, playing waterpolo; Riding mountain bike 5·25 4·75

MS1805 210×148 mm. 10n.×6, Greeting school children outside school; Seated in doorway with four children; Seated amongst children all with arms raised; Talking to children wearing grey; Greeting children from podium; With mother and child 5·25 4·75

MS1806 210×148 mm. 10n.×6, Clasping hands with monk; Crouched writing in book by firelight; Seated in doorway with family of four; Performing Namaste amongst crowd; Seated with family of five; Seated on earth bank with crowd 9·75 8·75

MS1807 101×145 mm. 20n. King Jigme Khesar Namgyel Wangchuck, head and shoulders (40×50 mm.) 1·90 1·70

MS1808 190×128 mm. 30n.×3, King Jigme Khesar Namgyel Wang-chuck×3 (with gold, silver or bronze backgrounds) (38 mm (circular)) 7·50 6·75

253 Desi Jigme Namgyel

2010. Wangchuck Dynasty. Multicoloured.
MS1809 15n.×6, Type **253**; Ugyen Wangchuck (1st king) (1907 - 1926); Jigme Wangchchuck (1926 - 1952); King Jigme Khesar Namgyel Wangchuck (2006 - present) (30×76 mm); Jigme Dorji Wangchuck (1952 - 1972) (45×30 mm); Jigme Singe Wangchuck (1972 - 2006) (45×30 mm) 7·50 6·75

254 Ashi Tsendu Lhamo Wangchuck

2010. Queens of Bhutan. Multicoloured.
MS1810 15n.n×8, Type **254**; Ashi Phuntsho Choden Wangchuck; Ashi Pema Dechen Wangchuck; Ashi Kezang Choden Wangchuck; Ashi Dorji Wangma Wangchuck; Ashi Tshering Pem Wangchuck; Ashi Tshering Yangdon Wangchuck; Ashi Sangay Choden Wangchuck 10·00 9·00

255 Rabbit

2011. Chinese New Year. Year of the Rabbit. Sheet 100×150 mm.
MS1811 **255** 25n. multicoloured 2·50 2·30

256 Cherry Blossom and *Meconopsis*

2011. 25th Anniv of Bhutan - Japan Diplomatic Relations. Multicoloured.
MS1812 20n.×4, Type **256**; Bridge; Cultivators; Apple orchard 6·50 5·75

257 King Jigme Dorji Wangchuck greeting Jawaharlal Nehru (prime minister of India)

2011. First Visit of Indian Prime Minister (Jawaharlal Nehru) to Bhutan. Multicoloured.
MS1813 120n×170 mm. 10n.×4, Type **257**; Inspecting troops; Prime Minister Nehru and royal family; 3·50 3·25
MS1814 120n×80 mm. 25n. Prime Minister Nehru riding yak (50×40 mm) 2·50 2·30

258 King Jigme Khesar Namgyel Wangchuck and Queen Jetsun Pema

2011. Wedding of King Jigme Khesar Namgyel Wangchuck to Jetsun Pema. Multicoloured.
MS1815 150×225 mm. 25n.×4, Type **258**; Jetsun Pema; As Type **258**, with trees as background; Jetsun Pema, with dark background 6·50 60·00
MS1816 122×82 mm. 50n. As Type **258** , orange-brown background (31×31 mm) 3·25 3·00
MS1817 115×77 mm. 50n. King Jigme Khesar Namgyel Wangchuck and Queen Jetsun Pema (44×65 mm) 3·25 3·00
MS1818 131×171 mm. 50n. Queen Jetsun Pema (41×65 mm) 3·25 3·00
MS1819 85×130 mm. 100n. King Jigme Khesar Namgyel Wangchuck and Queen Jetsun Pema with meconopsis and lotus flowers (50×72 mm) 6·50 5·75
MS1820 108×173 mm. 225n. King Jigme Khesar Namgyel Wangchuck and Queen Jetsun Pema (gold) (42×60 mm) 15·00 13·50

APPENDIX

The following stamps have either been issued in excess of postal needs or have not been available to the public in reasonable quantities at face value. Such stamps may later be given full listing if there is evidence of regular postal use.

1968

Bhutan Pheasants. 1, 2, 4, 8, 15ch., 2, 4, 5, 7, 9n.
Winter Olympic Games, Grenoble. Optd on 1966 Abominable Snowmen issue. 40ch., 1n.25, 3, 6n.
Butterflies (plastic-surfaced). Postage 5, 50ch., 1n.25, 2n.; Air 3, 4, 5, 6n.
Paintings (relief-printed). Postage 2, 5, 10, 45, 80ch., 1n.05, 1n.40, 2, 3, 4, 5n.; Air 1n.50, 2n.50, 6, 8n.
Olympic Games, Mexico. 5, 45, 60, 80ch., 1n.05, 2, 3, 5n.
Human Rights Year. Die-stamped surch on unissued "Coins". 15ch. on 50n.p., 33ch. on 1r., 9n. on 3r.75.

1969

Flood Relief. Surch on 1968 Mexico Olympics issue. 5ch.+5ch., 80ch.+25ch., 2n.+50ch.
Fish (plastic-surfaced). Postage 15, 20, 30ch.; Air 5, 6, 7n.
Insects (plastic-surfaced). Postage 10, 75ch., 1n.25, 2n.; Air 3, 4, 5, 6n.
Admission of Bhutan to Universal Postal Union. 5, 10, 15, 45, 60ch., 1n.05, 1n.40, 4n.
5000 Years of Steel Industry. On steel foil. Postage 2, 5, 15, 45, 75ch., 1n.50, 1n.75, 2n.; Air 3, 4, 5, 6n.
Birds (plastic-surfaced). Postage 15, 50ch., 1n.25, 2n.; Air 3, 4, 5, 6n.
Buddhist Prayer Banners. On silk rayon. 15, 75ch., 2, 5, 6n.
Moon Landing of "Apollo 11" (plastic-surfaced). Postage 3, 5, 15, 20, 25, 45, 50ch., 1n.75; Air 3, 4, 5, 6n.

1970

Famous Paintings (plastic-surfaced). Postage 5, 10, 15ch., 2n.75; Air 3, 4, 5, 6n.
New U.P.U. Headquarters Building, Berne. 3, 10, 20ch., 2n.50.
Flower Paintings (relief-printed). Postage 2, 3, 5, 10, 15, 75ch., 1n., 1n.40; Air 80, 90ch., 1n.10, 1n.40, 1n.60, 1n.70, 3n., 3n.50.
Animals (plastic-surfaced). Postage 10, 20, 25, 30, 40, 65, 75, 85ch.; Air 2, 3, 4, 5n.
Conquest of Space (plastic-surfaced). Postage 2, 5, 15, 25, 30, 50, 75ch., 1n.50; Air 2, 3, 6, 7n.

1971

History of Sculpture (plastic-moulded). Postage 10, 75ch., 1n.25, 2n.; Air 3, 4, 5, 6n.
Moon Vehicles (plastic-surfaced). Postage 10ch., 1n.70; Air 2n.50, 4n.
History of the Motor Car (plastic-surfaced). Postage 2, 5, 10, 15, 20, 30, 60, 75, 85ch., 1n., 1n.20, 1n.55, 1n.80, 2n., 2n.50; Air 4, 6, 7, 9, 10n.
Bhutan's Admission to United Nations. Postage 5, 10, 20ch., 3n.; Air 2n.50, 5, 6n.
60th Anniv of Boy Scout Movement. 10, 20, 50, 75ch., 2, 6n.
World Refugee Year. Optd on 1971 United Nations issue. Postage 5, 10, 20ch., 3n.; Air 2n.50, 5, 6n.

1972

Famous Paintings (relief-printed). Postage 15, 20, 90ch., 2n.50; Air 1n.70, 4n.60, 5n.40, 6n.
Famous Men (plastic-moulded). Postage 10, 15, 55ch.; Air 2, 6, 8n.
Olympic Games, Munich. Postage 10, 15, 20, 30, 45ch.; Air 35ch., 1n.35, 7n.
Space Flight of "Apollo 16" (plastic-surfaced). Postage 15, 20, 90ch., 2n.50; Air 1n.70, 4n.60, 5n.40, 6n.

1973

Dogs. 2, 3, 15, 20, 30, 99ch., 2n.50, 4n.
Roses (on scent-impregnated paper). Postage 15, 25, 30ch., 3n.; Air 6, 7n.
Moon Landing of "Apollo 17" (plastic-surfaced). Postage 10, 15, 55ch. 2n.; Air 7, 9n.
"Talking Stamps" (miniature records). Postage 10, 25ch., 1n.25, 7, 8n.; Air 3, 9n.
Death of King Jigme Dorji Wangchuck. Embossed on gold foil. Postage 10, 25ch., 3n.; Air 6, 8n.
Mushrooms. 15, 25, 30ch., 4n.
"Indipex 73" Stamp Exhibition, New Delhi. Postage 5, 10, 15, 25ch., 1n.25, 3n.; Air 5, 6n.

BIAFRA

The Eastern Region of Nigeria declared its Independence on 30 May 1967 as the Republic of Biafra. Nigerian military operations against the breakaway Republic commenced in July 1967.

The Biafran postal service continued to use Nigerian stamps when supplies of these became low. In July 1967 "Postage Paid" cachets were used pending the issue of Nos. 1/3.

12 pence = 1 shilling; 20 shillings = 1 pound.

1 Map of Republic

1968. Independence. Multicoloured.

1		2d. Type **1**	10	70
2		4d. Arms, flag and date of Independence	10	70
3		1s. Mother and child (17×22 mm)	15	2·00

1968. Nos. 172/5 and 177/85 of Nigeria optd SOVEREIGN BIAFRA and arms.

4	½d. multicoloured (No. 172)	2·25	5·50
5	1d. multicoloured (No. 173)	3·50	8·50
6	1½d. multicoloured (No. 174)	12·00	17·00
7	2d. multicoloured (No. 175)	35·00	50·00
8	4d. multicoloured (No. 177)	19·00	50·00
9	6d. multicoloured (No. 178)	9·00	16·00
10	9d. blue and red (No. 179)	3·50	3·75
11	1s. multicoloured (No. 180)	65·00	£120
12	1s.3d. multicoloured (No. 181)	35·00	55·00
13	2s.6d. multicoloured (No. 182)	4·00	17·00
14	5s. multicoloured (No. 183)	3·75	16·00
15	10s. multicoloured (No. 184)	10·00	42·00
16	£1 multicoloured (No. 185)	10·00	42·00

The overprint on No. 15 does not include **SOVEREIGN**.

5 Flag and Scientist

1968. First Anniv of Independence. Multicoloured.

17	4d. Type **5**		25	20
18	1s. Victim of atrocity		25	30
19	2s.6d. Nurse and refugees		70	5·50
20	5s. Biafran arms and banknote		80	6·00
21	10s. Orphaned child		1·10	6·50

16 Child in Chains, and Globe

1969. Second Anniv of Independence. Multicoloured; frame colours given.

35	16	2d. orange	1·25	4·25
36	16	4d. red	1·25	4·25
37	16	1s. blue	1·75	7·50
38	16	2s.6d. green	2·00	15·00

17 Pope Paul VI, Africa, and Papal Arms

1969. Visit of Pope Paul to Africa. Multicoloured; background colours given.

39	**17**	4d. orange	85	3·00
40	-	6d. blue	1·10	7·00
41	-	9d. green	1·40	8·50
42	-	3s. mauve	3·00	15·00

DESIGNS: Pope Paul VI, map of Africa and 6d. Arms of Vatican; 9d. St. Peter's Basilica; 3s. Statue of St. Peter.

BIJAWAR

A state of Central India. Now uses Indian stamps.

12 pies = 1 anna; 16 annas = 1 rupee.

1 Maharaja Sarwant Singh

1935

6	1	3p. brown	7·50	11·00
2	1	6p. red	9·00	7·00
3	1	9p. violet	13·00	7·50
4	1	1a. blue	15·00	7·00
5	1	2a. green	13·00	7·00

2 Maharaja Sarwant Singh

1937

11	2	4a. orange	22·00	£160
12	2	6a. lemon	22·00	£160
13	2	8a. green	24·00	£200
14	2	12a. blue	24·00	£225
15	2	1r. violet	48·00	£275

BOHEMIA AND MORAVIA

Following the proclamation of Slovak Independence on 14 March, 1939, the Czech provinces of Bohemia and Moravia became a German Protectorate. The area was liberated in 1945 and returned to Czechoslovakia.

100 haleru = 1 koruna.

1939. Stamps of Czechoslovakia optd BOHMEN u. MAHREN CECHY a MORAVA.

1	34	5h. blue	55	5·00
2	34	10h. brown	55	5·00
3	34	20h. red	70	5·00
4	34	25h. green	35	8·25
5	34	30h. purple	55	5·00
6	59	40h. blue	4·50	20·00
7	35	50h. green	35	5·00
8	60a	60h. violet	4·50	23·00
9	61	1k. purple (No. 348)	80	8·25
10	61	1k. purple (No. 395)	70	5·00
11	-	1k.20 purple (No. 354)	4·00	20·00
12	64	1k.50 red	3·50	26·00
13	-	1k.60 green (No. 355a)	5·00	29·00
14	-	2k. green (No. 356)	1·60	26·00
15	-	2k.50 blue (No. 357)	4·00	20·00
16	-	3k. brown (No. 358)	4·00	26·00
17	65	4k. violet	6·25	29·00
18	-	5k. green (No. 361)	6·25	37·00
19	-	10k. blue (No. 362)	6·75	55·00

2 Linden Leaves and Buds **3** Karluv Tyn Castle **5** Zlin

1939

20	2	5h. blue	20	45
21	2	10h. brown	20	55
22	2	20h. red	20	45
23	2	25h. green	20	45
24	2	30h. purple	20	45
25	-	40h. blue	20	45
26	3	50h. green	20	45
27	-	60h. violet	20	45
28	-	1k. red	20	45
29	-	1k.20 purple	40	80
30	-	1k.50 red	20	45
31	-	2k. green	20	70
32	-	2k.50 blue	20	45
33	5	3k. mauve	20	45
34	-	4k. grey	20	55
35	-	5k. green	65	1·10
36	-	10k. blue	55	1·40
37	-	20k. brown	1·60	2·75

DESIGNS—As Type **3**: 40h. Svikov Castle; 60h. St. Barbara's Church, Kutna Hora; 1k. St. Vitus's Cathedral, Prague. As Type **5**—VERT: 1k.20, 1k.50, Brno Cathedral; 2k., 2k.50, Olomouc. HORIZ: 4k. Ironworks, Moravska-Ostrava; 5k., 10k., 20k. Karlsburg, Prague.

1940. As 1939 issue, but colours changed and new values.

No.	Type	Description		
38	2	30h. brown	20	30
39	2	40h. orange	20	30
40	2	50h. green	20	30
44	-	60h. violet	30	35
41	2	60h. violet	20	30
42	2	80h. orange	30	35
45	-	80h. blue	20	45
43	2	1k. brown	30	35
46	-	1k.20 brown	40	35
47	-	1k.20 red	30	35
48	-	1k.50 pink	30	45
49	-	2k. green	30	35
50	-	2k. blue	30	45
51	-	2k.50 blue	65	80
52	-	3k. green	85	1·10
53	-	5k. green	30	35
54	-	6k. brown	30	80
55	-	8k. green	30	45
56	-	10k. blue	65	45
57	-	20k. brown	1·30	3·50

DESIGNS—As Type **3**: 50h. (No. 44), Neuhaus Castle; 80h. (No. 45), 3k. Pernstyn Castle; 1k.20 (No. 46), 2k.50, Brno Cathedral; 1k.20 (No. 47), St. Vitus's Cathedral, Prague; 1k.50 St. Barbara's Church, Kutna Hora; 2k. Pardubitz Castle. As Type **5**—HORIZ: 5k. Bridge at Beching; 6k. Samson Fountain, Budweis; 8k. Kremsier; 10k. Wallenstein Palace, Prague; 20k. Karlsburg, Prague.

6 Red Cross Nurse and Wounded Soldier

1940. Red Cross Relief Fund.

58	6	60h.+40h. blue	70	1·70
59	6	1k.20+80h. plum	70	1·70

7 Patient in Hospital

1941. Red Cross Relief Fund.

60	7	60h.+40h. blue	40	1·50
61	7	1k.20+80h. plum	40	1·50

8 Anton Dvorak

1941. Birth Centenary of Dvorak (composer).

62	8	60h. violet	40	80
63	8	1k.20 brown	40	80

9 Harvesting **10** Blast furnace, Pilsen

1941. Prague Fair.

64	9	30h. brown	25	55
65	9	60h. green	25	55
66	10	1k.20 plum	25	55
67	10	2k.50 blue	25	1·50

11 "Ständetheater", Prague **12** Mozart

1941. 150th Death Anniv of Mozart.

68	11	30h.+30h. brown	25	45
69	11	60h.+60h. green	25	45
70	12	1k.20+1k.20 red	25	45
71	12	2k.50+2k.50 blue	45	90

15. III. 1939
18. III. 1942
(13)

1942. Third Anniv of German Occupation. Optd with T **13**

72		1k.20 red (No. 47)	55	1·50
73		2k.50 blue (No. 51)	55	1·50

14 Adolf Hitler

1942. Hitler's 53rd Birthday.

74	14	30h.+20h. brown	20	45
75	14	60h.+40h. green	20	45
76	14	1k.20+80h. purple	20	45
77	14	2k.50+1k.50 blue	35	1·50

15 Adolf Hitler

1942. Various sizes.

78	15	10h. black	20	35
79	15	30h. brown	20	35
80	15	40h. blue	20	35
81	15	50h. green	20	35
82	15	60h. violet	20	35
83	15	80h. orange	20	35
84	15	1k. brown	20	35
85	15	1k.20 red	25	45
86	15	1k.50 red	25	45
87	15	1k.60 green	25	45
88	15	2k. blue	25	45
89	15	2k.40 brown	25	45
90	15	2k.50 blue	25	45
91	15	3k. olive	25	45
92	15	4k. purple	25	45
93	15	5k. green	25	45
94	15	6k. brown	25	55
95	15	8k. blue	25	55
96	15	10k. green	25	1·10
97	15	20k. violet	25	1·10
98	15	30k. red	55	2·75
99	15	50k. blue	1·10	3·50

SIZES—17½×21½ mm: 10h. to 80h.; 18½×21 mm: 1k. to 2k.40; 19×24 mm: 2k.50 to 8k.; 24×30 mm: 10k. to 50k.

16 Nurse and Patient

1942. Red Cross Relief Fund.

100	16	60h.+40h. blue	20	45
101	16	1k.20+80h. red	20	45

17 Mounted Postman

1943. Stamp Day.

102	17	60h. purple	25	80

18 Peter Parler

1943. Winter Relief Fund.

103	-	60h.+40h. violet	20	35
104	18	1k.20+80h. red	20	35
105	-	2k.50+1k.50 blue	25	35

DESIGNS: 60h. Charles IV; 2k.50, King John of Luxembourg.

19 Adolf Hitler

1943. Hitler's 54th Birthday.

106	19	60h.+1k.40 violet	25	90
107	19	1k.20+3k.80 red	25	90

20 Scene from "The Mastersingers of Nuremberg" **21** Richard Wagner

1943. 130th Birth Anniv of Wagner.

108	20	60h. violet	10	55
109	21	1k.20 red	10	55
110		2k.50 blue	10	55

DESIGN: 2k.50, Blacksmith scene from *Siegfried*.

22 Reinhard Heydrich

1943. First Death Anniv of Reinhard Heydrich (German Governor).

111	22	60h.+4k.40 black	50	2·30

23 Arms of Bohemia and Moravia and Red Cross

1943. Red Cross Relief Fund.

112	23	1k.20+8k.80 blk & red	35	70

24 National Costumes **25** Arms of Bohemia and Moravia

1944. Fifth Anniv of German Occupation.

113	24	1k.20+3k.80 red	25	45
114	25	4k.20+18k.80 brown	25	45
115	24	10k.+20k. blue	25	45

26 Adolf Hitler

1944. Hitler's 55th Birthday.

116	26	60h.+1k.40 red	25	45
117	26	1k.20+3k.80 green	25	45

27 Smetana

1944. 60th Death Anniv of Bedrich Smetana (composer).

118	27	60h.+1k.40 green	25	45
119	27	1k.20+3k.80 red	25	45

28 St. Vitus's Cathedral, Prague

1944

120	28	1k.50 purple	25	45
121	28	2k.50 violet	25	55

29 Adolf Hitler

1944

122	29	4k.20 green	35	80

NEWSPAPER STAMPS

N6 Dove

1939. Imperf.

N38	N6	2h. brown	35	45
N39	N6	5h. blue	35	45
N40	N6	7h. red	35	45
N41	N6	9h. green	35	45
N42	N6	10h. red	35	45
N43	N6	12h. blue	35	45
N44	N6	20h. green	35	45
N45	N6	50h. brown	35	55
N46	N6	1k. green	55	1·10

1940. For bulk postings. No. N42 optd **GD-OT**.

N60		10h. red	30	90

N19 Dove

1943. Imperf.

N106	N19	2h. brown	10	25
N107	N19	5h. blue	10	25
N108	N19	7h. red	10	25
N109	N19	9h. green	10	25
N110	N19	10h. red	10	25
N111	N19	12h. blue	10	25
N112	N19	20h. green	10	25
N113	N19	50h. brown	10	25
N114	N19	1k. green	10	25

OFFICIAL STAMPS

O7 Numeral and Laurel Wreath

1941

O60	O7	30h. brown	20	25
O61	O7	40h. blue	20	25
O62	O7	50h. green	20	25
O63	O7	60h. green	20	25
O64	O7	80h. red	55	25
O65	O7	1k. brown	25	25
O66	O7	1k.20 red	30	25
O67	O7	1k.50 purple	40	25
O68	O7	2k. blue	40	25
O69	O7	3k. green	40	25
O70	O7	4k. green	55	70
O71	O7	5k. yellow	1·30	1·40

O19 Eagle and Numeral

1943

O106	O19	30h. brown	10	55
O107	O19	40h. blue	10	55
O108	O19	50h. green	10	55
O109	O19	60h. violet	10	55
O110	O19	80h. red	10	55
O111	O19	1k. brown	10	55
O112	O19	1k.20 red	10	55
O113	O19	1k.50 purple	10	55
O114	O19	2k. blue	10	55
O115	O19	3k. green	10	55
O116	O19	4k. purple	10	70
O117	O19	5k. green	10	70

PERSONAL DELIVERY STAMPS

P6

1939

P38	P6	50h. blue	3·25	4·00
P39	P6	50h. red	2·10	4·50

POSTAGE DUE STAMPS

D6

1939

D38	D 6	5h. red	35	45
D39	D 6	10h. red	35	45
D40	D 6	20h. red	35	45
D41	D 6	30h. red	35	45
D42	D 6	40h. red	35	45
D43	D 6	50h. red	35	45
D44	D 6	60h. red	35	45
D45	D 6	80h. red	35	45
D46	D 6	1k. blue	35	55
D47	D 6	1k.20 blue	45	55
D48	D 6	2k. blue	1·40	1·70
D49	D 6	5k. blue	1·60	2·30
D50	D 6	10k. blue	2·30	2·75
D51	D 6	20k. blue	4·00	4·50

Pt. 20

BOLIVAR

One of the states of the Granadine Confederation. A department of Colombia from 1886, now uses Colombian stamps.

1863. 100 centavos = 1 peso.

1

1863. Imperf.

1	1	10c. green	£1700	£800
2	1	10c. red	39·00	37·00
3	1	1p. red	11·00	10·50

2 **3**

1872. Various frames. Imperf.

4	2	5c. blue	10·00	9·50
5	3	10c. mauve	10·00	9·50
6	-	20c. green	44·00	43·00
7	-	80c. red	90·00	85·00

6 **7** **8**

1874. Imperf.

8	6	5c. blue	33·00	18·00
9	7	5c. blue	11·00	9·50
10	8	10c. mauve	5·50	4·75

9 Simon Bolivar

1879. Various frames. Dated "1879". White or blue paper. Perf.

14	9	5c. blue	45	45
12	9	10c. mauve	35	30
13	9	20c. red	45	45

1880. Various frames. Dated "1880". White or blue paper.

19	9	5c. blue	45	45
20		10c. mauve	55	55
21		20c. red	55	55
22		80c. green	3·25	3·25
23		1p. orange	3·50	3·50

10 Simon Bolivar

1882

30	10	5p. red and blue	1·00	85
31	10	10p. blue and purple	2·20	2·10

11 Simon Bolivar

1882. Various frames. Dated "1882".

32A	11	5c. blue	45	45
33A	11	10c. mauve	35	30
34A	11	20c. red	45	45
35A	11	80c. green	90	85
36A	11	1p. orange	90	85

1883. Various frames. Dated "1883".

37B		5c. blue	35	30
38B		10c. mauve	45	45
39B		20c. red	45	45
40B		80c. green	45	45
41A		1p. orange	3·00	3·00

1884. Various frames. Dated "1884".

42B		5c. blue	45	45
43B		10c. mauve	35	30
44B		20c. red	35	30
45B		80c. green	45	45
46B		1p. orange	45	45

1885. Various frames. Dated "1885".

47B		5c. blue	20	20
48B		10c. mauve	20	20
49B		20c. red	20	20
50B		80c. green	35	30
51B		1p. orange	45	45

12 Simon Bolivar

1891

56	12	1c. black	45	45
57	12	5c. orange	45	45
58	12	10c. red	45	45
59	12	20c. blue	90	85
60	12	50c. green	1·30	1·30
61	12	1p. violet	1·30	1·30

13 Simon Bolivar

1903. Various sizes and portraits. Imperf or perf. On paper of various colours.

63A	13	50c. green	90	85
64Ab	13	50c. blue	75	75
65A	13	50c. violet	6·00	6·00
67A	-	1p. red	90	85
68A	-	1p. green	2·20	2·20
69A	-	5p. red	90	85
70Ab	-	10p. blue	1·90	1·80
71A	-	10p. violet	4·00	4·75

PORTRAITS: 1p. Fernandez Madrid. 5p. Rodriguez Torices. 10p. Garcia de Toledo.

20 J. M. del Castillo

1904. Various portraits. Imperf or perf.

77A	20	5c. black	35	30
78A	-	10c. brown (M. Anguiano)	35	30
80A	-	20c. red (P.G. Ribon)	45	45

23

1904. Figures in various frames. Imperf.

81	23	½c. black	45	45
82	23	1c. blue (horiz)	75	75
83	23	2c. violet	90	85

ACKNOWLEDGEMENT OF RECEIPT STAMPS

AR19

1903. Imperf. On paper of various colours.

AR75A	AR19	20c. orange	1·90	1·80
AR76A	AR19	20c. blue	2·75	2·75

AR27

1904. Imperf.

AR85	AR27	2c. red	1·40	1·40

LATE FEE STAMPS

L18

1903. Imperf. On paper of various colours.

L73A	L18	20c. red	90	85
L74A	L18	20c. violet	90	85

REGISTRATION STAMPS

1879. As T **9** but additionally inscr "CERTIFICADA".

R17	9	40c. brown	45	45

1880. As previous issue dated "1880".

R28		40c. brown	45	45

1882. As T **11**, but additionally inscr "CERTIFICADA". Dated as shown.

R52B	11	40c. brown ("1882")	45	45
R53B	11	40c. brown ("1883")	45	45
R54B	11	40c. brown ("1884")	45	45
R55B	11	40c. brown ("1885")	45	45

R17

1903. Imperf. On paper of various colours.

R72A	R17	20c. orange	3·50	3·50

R26

1904. Imperf.

R84	R26	5c. black	2·30	2·30

Pt. 20

BOLIVIA

A republic of Central South America.

1867. 100 centavos = 1 boliviano.
1963. 100 centavos = 1 peso boliviano.
1963. Currency reform. 1000 (old) pesos = 1 (new) peso
1987. 100 centavos = 1 boliviano.

1 Condor

1867. Imperf.

3a	1	5c. green	2·50	5·00
10	1	5c. mauve	£200	£150
7	1	10c. brown	£180	£160
8	1	50c. yellow	28·00	39·00
11	1	50c. blue	£400	£350
9	1	100c. blue	43·00	95·00
12	1	100c. green	£170	£180

4 (9 Stars)

1868. Nine stars below Arms. Perf.

32	4	5c. green	22·00	12·50
33	4	10c. red	39·00	15·00
34	4	50c. blue	47·00	28·00
35	4	100c. orange	55·00	28·00
36	4	500c. black	£750	£750

1871. Eleven stars below Arms. Perf.

37		5c. green	15·00	7·50
38		10c. red	25·00	12·50
39		50c. blue	39·00	22·00
40		100c. orange	43·00	22·00
41		500c. black	£2250	£2250

7

1878. Perf.

42	7	5c. blue	9·50	3·25
43	7	10c. orange	8·75	2·40
44	7	20c. green	24·00	4·75
45	7	50c. red	£120	20·00

1887. Eleven stars below Arms. Roul.

46	4	1c. red	3·25	3·00
47	4	2c. violet	3·25	3·00
48	4	5c. blue	10·50	5·25
49	4	10c. orange	10·50	5·25

1890. Nine stars below Arms. Perf.

50	1c. red		2·75	1·30
58	2c. violet		7·00	4·00
52	5c. blue		5·75	1·40
53	10c. orange		14·00	1·40
54	20c. green		20·00	2·75
55	50c. red		9·00	2·50
56	100c. yellow		18·00	5·25

1893. Eleven stars below Arms. Perf.

59		5c. blue	8·50	2·75

11

1894

63	11	1c. bistre	2·00	1·80
64	11	2c. red	2·75	2·50
65	11	5c. green	2·00	1·80
66	11	10c. brown	2·00	1·80
67	11	20c. blue	8·00	5·75
68	11	50c. red	17·00	11·50
69	11	100c. red	40·00	29·00

12 Frias **13**

1897

77	12	1c. green	2·10	1·50
78	-	2c. red (Linares)	3·00	2·50
79	-	5c. green (Murillo)	2·00	90
80	-	10c. purple (Monteagudo)	2·30	1·50
81	-	20c. black and red (J. Ballivian)	4·25	2·20
82	-	50c. orange (Sucre)	6·50	3·75
83	-	1b. blue (Bolivar)	8·00	5·25
84	13	2b. multicoloured	48·00	75·00

18 Sucre

1899

92	18	1c. blue	2·75	1·70
93	18	2c. red	4·00	1·70
94	18	5c. green	4·00	1·70
95	18	5c. red	2·75	90
96	18	10c. orange	3·75	1·70
97	18	20c. red	4·25	2·20
98	18	50c. brown	10·00	3·75
99	18	1b. lilac	3·25	3·50

19 A. Ballivian **24**

1901

100	19	1c. red	45	25
101	-	2c. green (Camacho)	55	35
102	-	5c. red (Campero)	55	35
103	-	10c. blue (J. Ballivian)	2·30	50
104	-	20c. black and purple (Santa Cruz)	1·30	30
105	24	2b. brown	7·00	4·00

25 **26** Murillo

1909. Issued in La Paz. Centenary of Revolution of July, 1809. Centres in black.

110	25	5c. blue	16·00	12·50
111	26	10c. green	16·00	12·50
112	-	20c. orange (Lanza)	16·00	12·50
113	-	2b. red (Montes)	16·00	12·50

37 P. D.
Murillo

1909. Centenary of Beginning of War of Independence, 1809–25.

115		1c. black and brown	65	40
116		2c. black and green	1·10	55
117	37	5c. black and red	1·10	45
118	-	10c. black and blue	1·30	35
119	-	20c. black and violet	1·30	55
120	-	50c. black and bistre	1·40	70
121	-	1b. black and brown	1·80	50
122	-	2b. black and brown	1·90	1·50

PORTRAITS: 1c. M. Betanzos. 2c. I. Warnes. 10c. B. Monteagudo. 20c. E. Arze. 50c. A. J. Sucre. 1b. S. Bolivar. 2b. M. Belgrano.

1910. Centenary of Liberation of Santa Cruz, Potosi and Cochabamba. Portraits as T **37**.

123		5c. black and green	55	25
124		10c. black and red	55	35
125		20c. black and blue	1·10	55

PORTRAITS: 5c. I. Warnes. 10c. M. Betanzos. 20c. E. Arze.

1911. Nos. 101 and 104 surch **5 Centavos 1911.**

127		5c. on 2c. green	65	35
128		5c. on 20c. black & purple	23·00	25·00

F8 Figure of
Justice

1912. Stamps similar to Type **F8** optd **CORREOS 1912.** or surch also.

130	F8	2c. green	45	35
131	F8	5c. orange	75	55
132	F8	10c. red	1·50	70
129	F8	10c. on 1c. blue	75	35

1913. Portraits as 1901 and new types.

133	19	1c. pink	30	25
134	-	2c. red	30	25
135	-	5c. green	45	25
136	-	8c. yellow (Frias)	1·30	45
137	-	10c. grey	75	25
139	-	50c. purple (Sucre)	1·90	55
140	-	1b. blue (Bolivar)	3·25	1·50
141	24	2b. black	8·00	5·25

46 Monolith **47** Mt. Potosi

1916. Various sizes.

142	46	½c. brown	35	30
143	47	1c. green	45	30
144	-	2c. black and red	50	30
145	-	5c. blue	65	35
147	-	10c. blue and orange	1·60	25

DESIGNS—HORIZ: 2c. Lake Titicaca; 5c. Mt. Illimani; 10c. Parliament Building, La Paz.

51

1919

158a	51	1c. lake	30	15
158b	51	2c. violet	45	15
151	51	5c. green	65	10
152	51	10c. red	65	10
179	51	15c. blue	1·20	35

180	51	20c. blue	95	35
154	51	22c. blue	1·60	1·50
155	51	24c. violet	1·60	90
162	51	50c. orange	3·50	80
163	51	1b. brown	95	45
164	51	2b. brown	65	45

See also Nos. 194/206.

1923. Surch Habilitada and value.

165		5c. on 1c. lake	55	25
169		15c. on 10c. red	1·30	45
168		15c. on 22c. blue	95	45

54 Morane
Saulnier Type P
Airplane

1924. Air. Establishment of National Aviation School.

170	54	10c. black and red	55	45
171	54	15c. black and lake	2·10	1·70
172	54	25c. black and blue	1·10	80
173	54	50c. black and orange	1·80	1·40
174	-	1b. black and brown	2·30	1·90
175	-	2b. black and brown	4·50	4·00
176	-	5b. black and violet	6·50	6·25

Nos. 174/6 have a different view.

57 Andean Condor

1925. Centenary of Independence.

184		5c. red on green	1·10	90
185		10c. red on yellow	1·20	1·10
186		15c. red	85	45
187	57	25c. blue	1·90	80
188	-	50c. purple	1·60	80
189	-	1b. red	3·75	1·90
190	-	2b. yellow	4·75	2·75
191	-	5b. brown	5·00	3·00

DESIGNS—VERT: 5c. Torch of Freedom; 10c. Kantuta (national flower); 15c. Pres. B. Saavedra; 50c. Head of Liberty; 1b. Mounted archer; 5b. Marshal Sucre. HORIZ: 2b. Hermes.

1927. Surch **1927** and value.

192	51	5c. on 1c. lake	4·50	3·25
193	51	10c. on 24c. violet	4·50	3·25

1928

194		2c. yellow	55	35
195		3c. pink	75	70
196		4c. red	55	50
197		20c. olive	95	35
198		25c. blue	95	45
199		30c. violet	1·20	1·00
200		40c. orange	2·10	1·90
201		50c. brown	2·10	1·90
202		1b. red	2·50	1·90
203		2b. purple	3·75	3·25
204		3b. green	4·25	3·75
205		4b. lake	5·75	4·75
206		5b. brown	7·00	6·00

1928. Optd Octubre **1927** and star.

207		5c. green	35	20
208		10c. grey	45	20
209		15c. red	60	35

1928. Surch **15 cts. 1928.**

211		15c. on 20c. blue	13·00	13·00
213		15c. on 24c. violet	2·30	1·30
216		15c. on 50c. orange	1·80	1·00

66 "L.A.B." (Lloyd
Aereo Boliviano)

1928. Air.

217	66	15c. green	3·25	2·10
218	66	20c. blue	5·25	4·25
219	66	35c. red	4·25	3·25

68 Andean
Condor

1928

221	68	5c. green	2·30	30
222	-	10c. blue	45	20

223	-	15c. red	75	20

DESIGNS: 10c. Pres. Siles; 15c. Map of Bolivia.

1930. Stamps of 1913 and 1916 surch **R. S. 21-4 1930** and value.

224		0.01c. on 2c. (No. 134)	1·30	1·30
225		0.03c. on 2c. (No. 144)	1·60	1·40
226	46	25c. on ½c. brown	1·70	1·10
227	-	25c. on 2c. (No. 144)	1·80	1·10

1930. Air. Optd **CORREO AEREO R. S. 6-V-1930** or surch **5 Cts.** also.

228	54	5c. on 10c. black & red	11·50	13·00
229	54	10c. black and red	11·50	13·00
231	54	15c. black and lake	11·50	13·00
232	54	25c. black and blue	11·50	13·00
233	54	50c. black and orange	11·50	13·00
235	54	1b. black and brown	£225	£225

1930. *Graf Zeppelin* Air stamps. Stamps of 1928 surch **Z 1930** and value.

241	66	1b.50 on 15c. green	75·00	85·00
242	66	3b. on 20c. blue	75·00	85·00
243	66	6b. on 35c. red	£120	£130

75 Junkers F-13
over Bullock Cart

1930. Air.

244	75	5c. violet	1·90	1·10
245	-	15c. red	1·90	1·10
246	-	20c. yellow	1·50	95
247	75	35c. green	1·20	70
248	-	50c. blue	2·30	1·60
249	75	1b. brown	3·50	2·40
250	-	2b. red	4·50	3·25
251	75	3b. grey	7·00	4·50

DESIGN: 15, 20, 50c., 2b. Junkers F-13 seaplane over river boat.

77 Pres. Siles **78** Map of **79** Marshal Sucre
 Bolivia

1930

252	77	1c. brown	45	45
253	-	2c. green (Potosi)	2·10	75
254	-	5c. blue (Illimani)	2·10	30
255	-	10c. red (E. Abaroa)	2·10	30
256	78	15c. violet	2·10	30
257	78	35c. red	3·25	1·30
258	78	45c. orange	3·25	1·30
259	79	50c. slate	1·30	60
260	-	1b. brown (Bolivar)	1·90	1·50

80 Symbols of Revolution

1931. First Anniv of Revolution.

263	80	15c. red	3·75	65
264	80	50c. lilac	1·60	85

81

1932. Air.

265	81	5c. blue	3·50	2·75
266	81	10c. grey	1·90	1·50
267	81	15c. red	2·30	1·80
268	81	25c. orange	2·30	1·80
269	81	30c. green	1·60	90
270	81	50c. purple	3·50	2·75
271	81	1b. brown	3·50	2·75

1933. Surch **Habilitada D. S. 13-7-1933** and value.

273	51	5c. on 1b. red	95	55
274	78	15c. on 35c. red	55	55
275	78	15c. on 45c. orange	95	45
276	51	15c. on 50c. brown	1·90	45
277	51	25c. on 40c. orange	55	55

83

1933

278	83	2c. green	45	30
279	83	5c. blue	35	25
280	83	10c. red	75	45
281	83	15c. violet	55	30
282	83	25c. blue	1·10	85

84 M. Baptista

1935. Ex-President Baptista Commemoration.

283	84	15c. violet	75	30

85 Map of
Bolivia

1935

284	85	2c. blue	45	20
285	85	3c. yellow	45	20
286	85	5c. green	45	20
287	85	5c. red	45	20
288	85	10c. brown	45	20
289	85	15c. blue	45	20
290	85	15c. red	45	20
291	85	20c. green	55	20
292	85	25c. blue	55	20
293	85	30c. red	1·10	45
294	85	40c. orange	1·10	30
295	85	50c. violet	1·10	20
296	85	1b. yellow	1·10	75
297	85	2b. brown	2·30	1·40

86 Fokker
Super Universal

1935. Air.

298	86	5c. brown	20	20
299	86	10c. green	20	20
300	86	20c. violet	20	20
301	86	30c. blue	20	20
302	86	50c. orange	30	20
303	86	1b. brown	30	45
304	86	1½b. yellow	1·10	20
305	86	2b. red	1·10	20
306	86	5b. brown	1·80	55
307	86	10b. brown	3·75	1·30

1937. Surch **Comunicaciones D.S. 25-2-37** and value in figures.

308	83	5c. on 2c. green	30	30
310	83	15c. on 25c. blue	45	45
311	83	30c. on 25c. blue	75	75
312	51	45c. on 1b. brown	85	85
313	51	1b. on 2b. purple	1·10	1·10
314	83	2b. on 25c. blue	1·10	1·10
315	80	3b. on 50c. lilac	1·50	1·50
316	80	5b. on 50c. lilac	2·30	2·30

1937. Air. Surch **Correo Aereo D. S. 25-2-37** and value in figures.

321	75	5c. on 35c. green	45	30
322	66	20c. on 35c. red	55	45
323	66	50c. on 35c. red	1·10	1·30
324	66	1b. on 35c. red	1·10	95
325	54	2b. on 50c. black & orge	1·70	1·40
317	-	3b. on 50c. pur (No. 188)	2·30	1·40
318	-	4b. on 1b. red (No. 189)	2·75	1·80
319	57	5b. on 2b. orange	3·75	2·10
320	57	10b. on 5b. sepia (No. 191)	7·00	4·50
326	54	12b. on 10c. black & red	9·00	6·50
327	54	15b. on 10c. black & red	9·00	3·75

89 Native School **92** Junkers Ju52/3m over
 Cornfield

1938

328	89	2c. red (postage)	85	65
329	-	10c. orange	95	45
330	-	15c. green	1·40	45
331	-	30c. yellow	1·70	55
332	-	45c. red	3·25	1·30
333	-	60c. violet	2·50	65
334	-	75c. blue	3·50	55
335	-	1b. brown	5·00	55
336	-	2b. buff	4·50	1·20

DESIGNS—VERT: 10c. Oil Wells; 15c. Industrial buildings; 30c. Pincers and torch; 75c. Indian and condor. HORIZ: 45c. Sucre-Camiri railway map; 60c. Natives and book; 1b. Machinery; 2b. Agriculture.

337		20c. red (air)	30	25
338		30c. grey	30	25
339		40c. yellow	30	25
340	92	50c. green	65	25
341	-	60c. blue	65	25
342	-	1b. red	85	25
343	-	2b. buff	1·60	30
344	-	3b. brown	1·60	30
345	-	5b. violet	2·30	55

DESIGNS—VERT: 20c. Mint, Potosi; 30c. Miner; 40c. Symbolical of women's suffrage; 1b. Pincers, torch and slogan; 3b. New Government emblem; 5b. Junkers aircraft over map of Bolivia. HORIZ: 60c. Airplane and monument; 2b. Airplane over river.

102 Llamas 103 Arms

1939

346	102	2c. green	75	55
347	102	4c. orange	75	55
348	102	5c. mauve	75	45
349	-	10c. black	95	55
350	-	15c. green	95	60
351	-	20c. green	95	45
352	103	25c. yellow	1·10	45
353	-	30c. blue	95	45
354	-	40c. red	2·10	55
355	-	45c. black	2·10	55
356	-	60c. red	2·10	85
357	-	75c. slate	3·25	85
358	-	90c. orange	3·75	85
359	-	1b. blue	3·75	85
360	-	2b. red	4·50	85
361	-	3b. violet	5·75	1·30
362	-	4b. brown	6·50	1·80
363	-	5b. purple	8·00	2·10

DESIGNS—HORIZ: 10, 15, 20c. Vicuna; 60, 75c. Mountain viscacha; 90c., 1b. Toco toucan; 2, 3b. Andean condor; 4, 5b. Jaguar. VERT: 40, 45c. Cocoi herons.

107 Virgin of Copacabana

1939. Air. Second National Eucharistic Congress. Inscr "IIº CONGRESO EUCARISTICO NACIONAL".

364		5c. violet	75	45
365	107	30c. green	1·10	30
366	-	45c. blue	1·10	30
367	-	60c. red	1·10	50
368	-	75c. red	1·10	75
369	-	90c. blue	1·10	30
370	-	2b. brown	1·60	35
371	-	4b. mauve	2·75	55
372	107	5b. blue	6·50	1·10
373	-	10b. yellow	9·00	1·60

DESIGNS—TRIANGULAR: 5c., 10b. Allegory of the Light of Religion. VERT: 45c., 4b. The "Sacred Heart of Jesus"; 75c., 90c. S. Anthony of Padua. HORIZ: 60c., 2b. Facade of St. Francis's Church, La Paz.

111 Workman

1939. Obligatory Tax. Workers' Home Building Fund.

374	111	5c. violet	1·20	30

112 Flags of 21 American Republics

1940. 50th Anniv of Pan-American Union.

375	112	9b. red, blue & yellow	2·40	1·20

114 Urns of Murillo and Sagarnaga

1941. 130th Death Anniv of P. D. Murillo (patriot).

376		10c. purple	20	10
377	114	15c. green	30	10
378	-	45c. red	30	20
379	-	1b.05 blue	65	30

DESIGNS—VERT: 10c. Murillo statue; 1b.05 Murillo portrait. HORIZ: 45c. "Murillo dreaming in Prison".

117 Shadow of Aeroplane on Lake Titicaca

1941. Air.

380	117	10b. green	4·50	55
381	117	20b. blue	5·25	85
382	-	50b. mauve	10·50	1·40
383	-	100b. brown	24·00	8·50

DESIGN: 50, 100b. Andean condor over Mt. Illimani.

119 1867 and 1941 Issues

1942. First Students' Philatelic Exn, La Paz.

384	119	5c. mauve	75	65
385	119	10c. orange	75	65
386	119	20c. green	1·60	1·10
387	119	40c. red	2·00	1·30
388	119	90c. blue	3·75	1·60
389	119	1b. violet	4·75	2·50
390	119	10b. brown	16·00	13·00

120 "Union is Strength"

1942. Air. Chancellors' Meeting, Rio de Janeiro.

391	120	40c. red	45	30
392	120	50c. blue	45	30
393	120	1b. brown	1·70	1·10
394	120	5b. mauve	1·10	45
395	120	10b. purple	3·50	1·70

121 Mt. Potosi 122 Chaquiri Dam

1943. Mining Industry.

396	121	15c. brown	30	20
397	-	45c. blue	65	30
398	-	1b.25 purple	1·10	55
399	-	1b.50 green	80	55
400	-	2b. brown	1·10	55
401	122	2b.10 blue	85	75
402	-	3b. orange	3·50	1·40

DESIGNS—VERT: 45c. Quechisla (at foot of Mt. Choroloque); 1b.25, Miner Drilling. HORIZ: 1b.50, Dam; 2b. Truck Convoy; 3b. Entrance to Pulacayo Mine.

125 Gen. Ballivian leading Cavalry Charge

1943. Centenary of Battle of Ingavi.

403	125	2c. green	30	10
404	125	3c. orange	30	10
405	125	25c. purple	45	15
406	125	45c. blue	55	20
407	125	3b. red	95	55
408	125	4b. purple	1·30	65
409	125	5b. sepia	1·50	85
MS409a		Two sheets each 139×100 mm. Nos. 403/6 and Nos. 407/9	14·00	18·00
MS409b		Do. Imperf	14·00	18·00

126 Gen. Ballivian and Trinidad Cathedral

1943. Centenary of Founding of El Beni. Centres in brown.

410	126	5c. green (postage)	30	15
411	126	10c. purple	35	20
412	126	30c. red	35	20
413	126	45c. blue	45	30
414	126	2b.10 orange	75	55
415	-	10c. violet (air)	30	15
416	-	20c. green	35	15
417	-	30c. red	45	20
418	-	3b. blue	65	30
419	-	5b. black	95	55

DESIGN: Nos. 415/19, Gen. Ballivian and mule convoy crossing bridge below airplane.

127 Trans. "Honour-Work-Law/All for the Country" 129 Allegory of "Flight"

1944. Revolution of 20th December, 1943.

420	127	20c. orange (postage)	20	10
421	127	20c. green	20	10
422	127	90c. blue	20	10
423	127	90c. red	20	10
424	-	1b. purple	25	10
425	-	2b.40 brown	30	20

DESIGN—VERT: 1b., 2b.40, Clasped hands and flag.

131 Posthorn and Envelope

1944. Obligatory Tax.

430	131	10c. red	1·10	30
432	131	10c. blue	1·10	30

Smaller Posthorn and Envelope.

469		10c. red	2·30	75
470		10c. yellow	2·30	75
471		10c. green	2·30	75
472		10c. brown	2·30	75

132 Douglas DC-2 and National Airways Route Map

1945. Air. Panagra Airways, 10th Anniv of First La Paz–Tacna Flight.

433	132	10c. red	20	15
434	132	50c. orange	25	15
435	132	90c. green	30	20
436	132	5b. blue	55	30
437	132	20b. brown	1·90	65

133 Lloyd-Aereo Boliviano Air Routes

1945. Air. 20th Anniv of First National Air Service.

438	133	20c. blue, orange & vio	20	10
439	133	30c. blue, orange & brn	20	10
440	133	50c. blue, orange & grn	20	10
441	133	90c. blue, orange & pur	20	10
442	133	2b. blue and orange	25	10
443	133	3b. blue, orange & red	30	20
444	133	4b. blue, orange & bistre	55	30

134 L. B. Vincenti and J. I. de Sanjines, Composers of National Anthem

1946. Centenary of National Anthem.

445	134	5c. black and mauve	10	10
446	134	10c. black and blue	10	10
447	134	15c. black and green	10	10
448	134	30c. brown and red	20	15
449	134	90c. brown and blue	20	15
450	134	2b. brown and black	75	55
MS450a		Two sheets each 86×131 mm. (a) No. 448; (b) No. 450. Imperf. Each sold at 4b	7·00	7·00

1947. Surch **1947 Habilitada Bs. 1.40**.

451		1b.40 on 75c. blue (No. 334) (postage)	25	15
452		1b.40 on 75c. slate (No. 357)	25	15
455		1b.40 on 75c. red (No. 368) (air)	30	20

136 Seizure of Government Palace 137 Mt. Illimani

1947. Popular Revolution of 21 July 1946.

456	136	20c. green (postage)	10	10
457	136	50c. purple	10	10
458	136	1b.40 blue	10	10
459	136	3b.70 orange	20	10
460	136	4b. violet	30	10
461	136	10b. olive	95	45
462	137	1b. red (air)	10	10
463	137	1b.40 green	10	10
464	137	2b.50 blue	20	15
465	137	3b. orange	30	20
466	137	4b. mauve	45	20

138 Arms of Bolivia and Argentina

1947. Meeting of Presidents of Bolivia and Argentina.

467	138	1b.40 orange (postage)	45	25
468	138	2b.90 blue (air)	55	45

140 Cross and Child

1948. Third Inter-American Catholic Education Congress.

473	-	1b.40 bl & yell (postage)	45	10
474	140	2b. green and orange	55	20
475	-	3b. green and orange	85	25
476	-	5b. violet and orange	1·10	30
477	-	5b. brown and green	1·50	30
478	-	2b.50 orange & yell (air)	65	45
479	140	3b.70 red and buff	75	45
480	-	4b. mauve and blue	75	30
481	-	4b. blue and orange	75	25
482	-	13b.60 blue and green	95	45

DESIGNS—1b.40, 2b.50, Christ the Redeemer, Monument; 3b., 4b. (No. 480), Don Bosco; 5b. (No. 476), 4b. (No. 481), Virgin of Copacabana; 5b. (No. 477), 13b.60, Pope Pius XII.

141 Map of S. America and Bolivian Auto Club Badge

1948. Pan-American Motor Race.

483	**141**	5b. blue & pink (postage)	2·30	75
484	**141**	10b. green & cream (air)	2·10	30

142 Posthorn, Globe and Pres. G. Pacheco

1950. 75th Anniv of U.P.U.

485	**142**	1b.40 blue (postage)	25	10
486	**142**	4b.20 red	30	10
487	**142**	1b.40 brown (air)	25	10
488	**142**	2b.50 orange	30	10
489	**142**	3b.30 purple	25	10

1950. Air. Surch **XV ANIVERSARIO PANAGRA 1935–1950** and value.

490	**132**	4b. on 10c. red	20	10
491	**132**	10b. on 20b. brown	55	35

1950. No. 379 surch **Bs. 2.- Habilitada D.S.6.VII.50.**

492		2b. on 1b.05 blue	45	20

145 Apparition at Potosi

1950. 400th Anniv of Apparition at El Potosi.

493	**145**	20c. violet	30	15
494	**145**	30c. orange	30	15
495	**145**	50c. purple	30	15
496	**145**	1b. red	30	15
497	**145**	2b. blue	35	15
498	**145**	6b. brown	45	15

146 Douglas DC-2

1950. Air. 25th Anniv of Lloyd Aereo Boliviano.

499	**146**	20c. orange	20	10
500	**146**	30c. violet	20	10
501	**146**	50c. green	20	10
502	**146**	1b. yellow	20	10
503	**146**	3b. blue	20	10
504	**146**	15b. red	65	20
505	**146**	50b. brown	1·90	65

1950. Air. Surch **Triunfo de la Democracia 24 de Sept. 49 Bs. 1.40.**

506	**137**	1b.40 on 3b. orange	30	30

148 UN Emblem and Globe

1950. Fith Anniv of UNO.

507	**148**	60c. blue (postage)	1·60	20
508	**148**	2b. green	2·10	30
509	**148**	3b.60 red (air)	75	20
510	**148**	4b.70 brown	95	20

150 St. Francis Gate **149** Gate of the Sun, Tiahuanacu

1951. Fourth Centenary of Founding of La Paz. Centres in black.

511	**149**	20c. green (postage)	20	10
512	**150**	30c. orange	20	10
513	**A**	40c. brown	20	10
514	**B**	50c. red	20	10
515	**C**	1b. purple	20	10
516	**D**	1b.40 violet	30	15
517	**E**	2b. purple	30	15
518	**F**	3b. mauve	45	20
519	**G**	5b. red	55	30
520	**H**	10b. sepia	1·10	45
MS520a		Three sheets each 150×100 mm. Nos. 511/12, 520; 513, 516, 519; 514/15, 517/18	8·50	8·50
MS520b		Do. Imperf	8·50	8·50
521	**149**	20c. red (air)	20	10
522	**150**	30c. violet	20	10
523	**A**	40c. slate	20	10
524	**B**	50c. green	20	10
525	**C**	1b. red	30	20
526	**D**	2b. orange	55	45
527	**E**	3b. blue	75	65
528	**F**	4b. red	80	65
529	**G**	5b. green	85	75
530	**H**	10b. brown	90	85
MS530a		Three sheets each 150×100 mm. Nos. 521/2, 530; 523, 527, 529; 524/5, 526, 528	8·25	8·25
MS530b		Do. Imperf	8·25	8·25

DESIGNS—HORIZ: As Type **149**: A, Camacho Avenue; B, Consistorial Palace; C, Legislative Palace; D, G.P.O. E, Arms; F, Pedro de la Casca authorizes plans of City; G, Founding the City; H, City Arms and Captain A. de Mendoza.

151 Tennis

1951. Sports. Centres in black.

531	-	20c. blue (postage)	20	10
532	**151**	50c. red	20	10
533	-	1b. purple	25	10
534	-	1b.40 yellow	30	20
535	-	2b. red	65	45
536	-	3b. brown	1·30	1·10
537	-	4b. blue	1·60	1·40
MS537a		Two sheets each 150×100 mm. Nos. 531/2, 535/6; 533/4, 537	6·50	6·50
MS537b		Do. Imperf	6·50	6·50
538		20c. violet (air)	30	10
539		30c. purple	45	15
540		50c. orange	75	20
541		1b. brown	75	20
542		2b.50 orange	1·20	45
543		3b. sepia	1·60	1·20
544		5b. red	3·25	2·30
MS544a		130×80 mm. Nos. 741/3	18·00	18·00
MS544b		Do. Imperf	18·00	18·00

DESIGNS—Postage: 20c. Boxing; 1b. Diving; 1b.40, Football; 2b. Skiing; 3b. Pelota; 4b. Cycling. Air: 20c. Horsejumping; 30c. Basketball; 50c. Fencing; 1b. Hurdling; 2b.50, Javelin; 3b. Relay race; 5b. La Paz Stadium.

152 Andean Condor and Flag

1951. 100th National Flag Anniv. Flag in red, yellow and green.

545	**152**	2b. green	10	10
546	**152**	3b.50c. blue	10	10
547	**152**	5b. violet	10	15
548	**152**	7b.50c. grey	55	20
549	**152**	15b. red	75	45
550	**152**	30b. brown	1·80	95

153 Posthorn and Envelope

1951. Obligatory Tax.

551	-	20c. orange	75	30
551b	-	20c. green	75	30
552	-	20c. blue	75	30
553	**153**	50c. green	85	30
553d	**153**	50c. red	85	30
553e	**153**	3b. green	85	30
553f	**153**	3b. bistre	95	75
553g	**153**	5b. violet	1·10	75

DESIGN: 20c. Condor over posthorn and envelope.

154 E. Abaroa

1952. 73rd Death Anniv of Abaroa (patriot).

554	**154**	80c. red (postage)	10	10
555	**154**	1b. orange	10	10
556	**154**	2b. green	20	10
557	**154**	5b. blue	65	20
558	**154**	10b. mauve	1·90	45
559	**154**	20b. brown	3·25	75
560	**154**	70c. red (air)	20	10
561	**154**	2b. yellow	45	20
562	**154**	3b. green	30	20
563	**154**	5b. blue	65	20
564	**154**	50b. purple	1·90	75
565	**154**	100b. black	3·25	1·60

155 Isabella the Catholic

1952. 500th Birth Anniv of Isabella the Catholic.

566	**155**	2b. blue (postage)	30	20
567	**155**	6b.30 red	55	25
568	**155**	50b. green (air)	95	30
569	**155**	100b. brown	45	35

156 Columbus Lighthouse

1952. Columbus Memorial Lighthouse. On tinted papers.

570	**156**	2b. blue (postage)	30	20
571	**156**	5b. red	85	65
572	**156**	9b. green	1·50	85
573	**156**	2b. purple (air)	25	20
574	**156**	3b.70 turquoise	25	20
575	**156**	4b.40 orange	30	20
576	**156**	20b. brown	65	30

157 Miner

1953. Nationalization of Mining Industry.

577	**157**	2b.50c. red	20	10
578	**157**	8b. violet	30	15

158 Villarroel, Paz Estenssoro and Siles Zuazo **159** Revolutionaries

1953. First Anniv of Revolution of April 9th, 1952.

579	**158**	50c. mauve (postage)	20	10
580	**158**	1b. red	20	10
581	**158**	2b. blue	20	10
582	**158**	3b. green	20	10
583	**158**	4b. yellow	20	10
584	**158**	5b. violet	30	10
585	**158**	3b.70 brown (air)	30	10
586	**158**	9b. red	30	10
587	**158**	10b. turquoise	30	10
588	**158**	16b. orange	30	20
589	**158**	40b. grey	65	20
590	**159**	6b. mauve	30	10
591	**159**	22b.50 brown	1·10	85

1953. Obligatory Tax. No. 551b and similar stamp surch 50 cts.

592	**158**	50c. on 20c. mauve	55	30
593	**158**	50c. on 20c. green	45	20

161

1954. Obligatory Tax.

594	**161**	1b. lake	1·30	30
595	**161**	1b. brown	30	30

162 Ear of Wheat and Map

1954. First National Agronomical Congress.

596	**162**	25b. blue	30	10
597	**162**	85b. brown	65	25

163 Pres. Paz Estenssoro embracing Indian

1954. Air. Third Inter-American Indigenous Congress.

598	**163**	20b. brown	20	10
599	**163**	100b. turquoise	80	10

1954. First Anniv of Agrarian Reform. As T **162**, but designs inscr "REFORMA AGRARIA".

600		5b. red (postage)	10	10
601		17b. turquoise	15	10
602		27b. mauve (air)	20	15
603		30b. orange	30	20
604		45b. purple	55	20
605		300b. green	2·30	45

DESIGNS—5b., 17b. Cow's head and map; 27b. to 300b. Indian peasant woman.

1955. Obligatory Tax. Nos. 553e and 553f surch **Bs. 5.— D. S. 21-IV-55.**

606	**153**	5b. on 3b. green	55	20
607	**153**	5b. on 3b. bistre	1·40	20

166 Refinery **167** Derricks

1955. Development of Petroleum Industry.

608	**166**	10b. blue (postage)	10	10
609	**166**	35b. red	15	10
610	**166**	40b. green	20	15
611	**166**	50b. purple	30	20
612	**166**	80b. brown	55	30
613	**166**	55b. blue (air)	20	10
614	**167**	70b. black	45	10
615	**167**	90b. green	55	15
616	**167**	500b. mauve	1·90	95
617	**167**	1000b. brown	3·25	1·90

168 Control Tower **169** Douglas DC-6B Aircraft

1957. Obligatory Tax. Airport Building Fund.

618	**168**	5b. blue	55	20
619	**169**	10b. brown	45	20
620	**168**	5b. red	9·50	9·50
620b	**169**	20b. brown	55	30

DESIGNS: 5b. (No. 620), Douglas DC-6B over runway; 20b. Lockheed Constellation in flight.

1957. Currency revaluation. Founding of La Paz stamps of 1951 surch. Centres in black.

621	**F**	50b. on 3b. mauve (post)	10	10
622	**E**	100b. on 2b. purple	15	10
623	**C**	200b. on 1b. purple	20	10
624	**D**	300b. on 1b.40 violet	30	10
625	**149**	350b. on 20c. green	45	15

626	A	400b. on 40c. brown	45	15
627	150	600b. on 30c. orange	65	20
628	B	800b. on 50c. red	75	20
629	H	1000b. on 10b. sepia	75	25
630	G	2000b. on 5b. red	1·30	55
631	E	100b. on 3b. blue (air)	10	10
632	D	200b. on 2b. orange	15	10
633	F	500b. on 4b. red	20	10
634	C	600b. on 1b. red	25	15
635	149	700b. on 20c. red	55	20
636	A	800b. on 40c. slate	65	30
637	150	900b. on 30c. violet	75	20
638	B	1800b. on 50c. green	1·30	65
639	G	3000b. on 5b. green	1·70	1·20
640	H	5000b. on 10b. brown	3·25	2·10

172 Congress Buildings (Santiago de Chile and La Paz)
173 "Latin America" on Globe

1957. Seventh Latin-America Economic Congress, La Paz.

641	172	150b. bl & grey (postage)	10	10
642	172	350b. grey and brown	20	10
643	172	550b. sepia and blue	25	10
644	172	750b. green and red	35	15
645	172	900b. brown and green	55	20
646	173	700b. violet & lilac (air)	65	35
647	173	1200b. brown	70	45
648	173	1350b. red and mauve	1·10	65
649	173	2700b. olive and turq	1·90	90
650	173	4000b. violet and blue	3·75	1·50

174 Steam Train and Presidents of Bolivia and Argentina

1957. Yacuiba-Santa Cruz Railway Inauguration.

651	174	50b. orange (postage)	35	35
652	174	350b. blue and light blue	85	40
653	174	1000b. brown & cinna	1·90	60
654	174	600b. purple & pink (air)	80	40
655	174	700b. violet and blue	1·40	60
656	174	900b. green	1·90	45

175 Presidents and Flags of Bolivia and Mexico

1960. Visit of Mexican President to Bolivia.

657	175	350b. olive (postage)	30	10
658	175	600b. brown	45	20
659	175	1,500b. sepia	95	30
660	175	400b. red (air)	95	10
661	175	800b. blue	1·30	30
662	175	2,000b. green	1·90	75

The President's visit to Bolivia did not take place.

176 Indians and Mt. Illimani
177 "Gate of the Sun", Tiahuanacu

1960. Tourist Publicity.

663	176	500b. bistre (postage)	75	30
664	176	1000b. blue	1·40	45
665	176	2000b. sepia	3·25	75
666	176	4000b. green	5·75	75
667	177	3000b. grey (air)	3·25	1·70
668	177	5000b. orange	4·75	1·80
669	177	10,000b. purple	7·50	4·25
670	177	15,000b. violet	10·50	7·00

178 Refugees
179 "Uprooted Tree"

1960. World Refugee Year.

671	178	50b. brown (postage)	10	10
672	178	350b. purple	20	10
673	178	400b. blue	30	15
674	178	1000b. sepia	85	55
675	178	3000b. green	1·90	1·20
676	179	600b. blue (air)	55	20
677	179	700b. brown	55	30
678	179	900b. turquoise	65	35
679	179	1800b. violet	1·30	85
680	179	2000b. black	1·80	1·30

180 Jaime Laredo (violinist)
181 Jaime Laredo (violinist)

1960. Jaime Laredo Commem.

681	180	100b. green (postage)	30	10
682	180	350b. lake	65	10
683	180	500b. blue	75	15
684	180	1000b. brown	95	20
685	180	1500b. violet	1·80	55
686	180	3000b. black	5·75	1·60
687	181	600b. plum (air)	1·30	45
688	181	700b. olive	1·50	55
689	181	800b. brown	1·50	55
690	181	900b. blue	2·00	55
691	181	1800b. turquoise	2·30	1·60
692	181	4000b. grey	5·75	2·30

182 Rotary Emblem and Nurse with Children

1960. Founding of Children's Hospital by La Paz Rotary Club. Wheel in blue and yellow, foreground in yellow; background given.

693	182	350b. green (postage)	30	10
694	182	500b. sepia	45	10
695	182	600b. violet	65	15
696	182	1000b. grey	75	25
697	182	600b. brown (air)	75	45
698	182	1000b. olive	1·10	45
699	182	1800b. purple	1·50	75
700	182	5000b. black	4·75	2·10

183

1960. Air. Unissued stamp, surch as in T **183**.

701	183	1200b. on 10b. orange	1·30	95

184 Design from Gate of the Sun

1960. Unissued Tiahuanacu Excavation stamps surch as in T **184**. Gold backgrounds.

702	50b. on ½c. red	85	55
703	100b. on 1c. red	55	20
704	200b. on 2c. black	1·50	20
705	300b. on 5c. green	30	20
706	350b. on 10c. green	30	1·20
707	400b. on 15c. blue	55	20
708	500b. on 20c. red	55	20
709	500b. on 50c. red	65	20
710	600b. on 22½c. green	85	45
711	600b. on 60c. violet	95	55
712	700b. on 25c. violet	1·40	30
713	700b. on 1b. green	1·90	1·20
714	800b. on 30c. red	95	30

715	900b. on 40c. green	85	45
716	1000b. on 2b. blue	95	55
717	1800b. on 3b. grey	9·50	6·50
718	4000b. on 4b. grey	75·00	65·00
719	5000b. on 5b. grey	19·00	14·00

DESIGNS: Various gods, motifs and ornaments. SIZES: Nos. 702/6, As Type **184**. Nos. 707/17, As Type **184** but horiz. No. 718, 49×23 mm. No. 719, 50×52½ mm.

185 Flags of Argentina and Bolivia

1961. Air. Visit of Pres. Frondizi of Argentina.

720	185	4000b. multicoloured	1·40	1·30
721	-	6000b. sepia and green	2·10	1·70

DESIGN: 6000b. Presidents of Argentina and Bolivia.

186 Miguel de Cervantes (First Mayor of La Paz)

1961. M. de Cervantes Commem and 4th Centenary of Santa Cruz de la Sierra (1500b.).

722	186	600b. violet and ochre (postage)	65	30
723	-	1500b. blue and orange	1·20	45
724	-	1400b. brown & green (air)	85	30

DESIGNS: 1400b. Portrait as Type **186** (diamond shape, 30½×30½ mm); 1500b. Nuflo de Chaves (vert: as Type **186**).
See also Nos. 755/6.

187 "United in Christ"

1962. Fourth National Eucharistic Congress, Santa Cruz.

725	187	1000b. yellow, red and green (postage)	85	45
726	-	1400b. yellow, pink and brown (air)	85	45

DESIGN: 1400b. Virgin of Cotoca.

1962. Nos. 671/80 surch.

727	178	600b. on 50b. brown (postage)	55	20
728	178	900b. on 350b. purple	60	20
729	178	1000b. on 400b. blue	65	25
730	178	2000b. on 1000b. brown	75	55
731	178	3500b. on 3000b. green	1·30	1·10
732	179	1200b. on 600b. blue (air)	1·20	55
733	179	1300b. on 700b. brown	1·20	55
734	179	1400b. on 900b. green	1·20	55
735	179	2800b. on 1800b. violet	1·90	75
736	179	3000b. on 2000b. black	1·90	1·10

189 Hibiscus

1962. Flowers in actual colours; background colours given.

737	189	200b. green (postage)	85	20
738	-	400b. brown	1·30	20
739	-	600b. deep blue	2·10	15
740	-	1000b. violet	3·00	45
741	-	100b. blue (air)	75	20
742	-	800b. green	1·40	30
743	-	1800b. violet	3·00	75
744	-	10,000b. deep blue	9·00	4·50
MS744a	130×80 mm. Nos. 741/3. Imperf		13·00	13·00

FLOWERS: Nos. 738, 740 Orchids; 739, St. James' lily; 741/4, Types of Kantuta (national flowers).

190 Infantry

1962. Armed Forces Commemoration.

745	190	400b. mult (postage)	10	10
746	-	500b. multicoloured	20	10
747	-	600b. multicoloured	30	15
748	-	2000b. multicoloured	85	55
749	-	600b. mult (air)	55	20
750	-	1200b. multicoloured	65	30
751	-	2000b. multicoloured	95	55
752	-	5000b. multicoloured	2·10	1·40

DESIGNS: No. 746, Cavalry; 747, Artillery; 748, Engineers; 749, Parachutists and aircraft; 750, 752, "Overseas Flights" (Lockheed Super Electra airplane over oxen-cart); 751, "Aerial Survey" (Douglas DC-3 airplane photographing ground).

191 Campaign Emblem

1962. Malaria Eradication.

753	191	600b. yellow, violet and lilac (postage)	65	45
754	-	2000b. yellow, green and blue (air)	2·00	95

DESIGN: 2000b. As No. 753 but with laurel wreath and inscription encircling emblem.

1962. Spanish Discoverers. As T **186** but inscribed "1548–1962".

755		600b. mauve on blue (postage)	45	20
756		1200b. brown on yellow (air)	65	30

PORTRAITS: 600b. A. de Mendoza. 1200b. P. de la Gasca.

192 Goal-Keeper diving to save Goal

1963. 21st South American Football Championships, La Paz. Multicoloured.

757	192	60c. Type **192** (postage)	75	15
758	192	1p. Goalkeeper saving ball (vert)	1·20	30
759	192	1p.40 Andean condor on football (vert) (air)	1·90	1·30
760	192	1p.80 Ball in corner of net (vert)	2·00	1·40

193 Globe and Emblem

1963. Freedom from Hunger.

761	193	60c. yellow, blue and indigo (postage)	55	15
762	-	1p.20 yellow, blue and myrtle (air)	1·30	1·20

DESIGN: 1p.20, Ear of wheat across Globe.

194 Alliance Emblem

1963. Air. "Alliance for Progress".

763	194	1p.20 green, blue & bis	1·30	1·20

195 Oil Derrick

1963. Tenth Anniv of Revolution (1962).

764	195	10c. grn & brn (postage)	20	10
765	-	60c. sepia and orange	30	15

766	-	1p. yellow, violet & green	45	25
767	-	1p.20 pink, brown and grey (air)	65	30
768	-	1p.40 green and ochre	75	35
769	-	2p.80 buff and slate	1·60	1·40

DESIGNS: 60c. Map of Bolivia; 1p. Students; 1p.20, Ballot box and voters; 1p.40, Peasant breaking chain; 2p.80, Miners.

196 Flags of Bolivia and Peru

197 Marshal Santa Cruz

1966. Death Centenary of Marshal Santa Cruz.

770	**196**	10c. mult (postage)	20	10
771	**196**	60c. multicoloured	30	15
772	**196**	1p. multicoloured	55	30
773	**196**	2p. multicoloured	75	55
774	**197**	20c. blue (air)	20	10
775	**197**	60c. green	30	15
776	**197**	1p.20 brown	75	55
777	**197**	2p.80 black	1·30	1·10

198 Generals Barrientos and Ovando, Bolivian Map and Flag

1966. Co-Presidents Commemoration.

778	**198**	60c. mult (postage)	55	10
779	**198**	1p. multicoloured	65	15
780	**198**	2p.80 mult (air)	1·70	1·10
781	**198**	10p. multicoloured	3·75	1·40

MS782 136×83 mm. Nos. 778/81. Imperf — 10·00 10·00

199 Needy Children

1966. Aid for Poor Children.

783	**199**	30c. brown, sepia and ochre (postage)	55	20
784	-	1p.40 black & blue (air)	2·50	65

DESIGN: 1p.40, Mother and needy children.

1966. Commemorative Issues. Various stamps surch with inscr (as given below) and value. (i) Red Cross Centenary. Surch Centenario de la Cruz Roja Internacional.

785		20c. on 150b. (No. 641) (post)	30	10
786		4p. on 4000b. (No. 650) (air)	2·10	1·60

(ii) General Azurduy de Padilla. Surch **Homenaje a la Generala J. Azurduy de Padilla.**

787		30c. on 550b. (No. 643)	45	20
788		2p.80 on 750b. (No. 644)	1·20	75

(iii) Air. Tupiza Cent. Surch **Centenario de Tupiza.**

789		60c. on 1350b. (No. 648)	75	30

(iv) Air. 25th Anniv of Bolivian Motor Club. Surch **XXV Aniversario Automovil Club Boliviano.**

790		2p.80 on 2700b. (No. 649)	3·25	2·30

(v) Air. Cochabamba Philatelic Society Anniv. Surch **Aniversario Centro Filatelico Cochabamba.**

791		1p.20 on 800b. (No. 742)	1·60	30
792		1p.20 on 1800b. (No. 743)	1·60	30

(vi) Rotary Help for Children's Hospital. Surch with value only. (a) Postage.

793		1p.60 on 350b. (No. 693)	1·20	75
794		2p.40 on 500b. (No. 694)	1·60	1·20

(b) Air.

795		1p.40 on 1000b. (No. 698)	85	75
796		1p.40 on 1800b. (No. 699)	85	75

(vii) 150th Anniv of Coronilla Heroines. Surch **CL Aniversario Heroinas Coronilla.** (a) Postage.

797		60c. on 350b. (No. 682)	75	20

(b) Air.

798		1p.20 on 800b. (No. 689)	1·20	75

(viii) Air. Centenary of Hymn La Paz. Surch **Centenario Himno Paceno.**

799		1p.40 on 4000b. (No. 692)	1·20	75

(ix) Air. 12th Anniv of Agrarian Reform. Surch **XII Aniversario Reforma Agraria.**

800		10c. on 27b. (No. 602)	30	20

(x) Air. 25th Anniv of Chaco Peace Settlement. Surch **XXV Aniversario Paz del Chaco.**

801		10c. on 55b. (No. 613)	30	20

(xi) Centenary of Rurrenabaque. Surch **Centenario de Rurrenabaque.**

802		1p. on 10b. brown	75	30

(xii) 25th Anniv of Busch Government. Surch **XXV Aniversario Gobierno Busch.**

803		20c. on 5b. red	30	20

(xiii) 20th Anniv of Villarroel Government. Surch **XX Aniversario Gob. Villarroel.**

804		60c. on 2b. green	45	20

(xiv) 25th Anniv of Pando Department. Surch **XXV Aniversario Dpto. Pando.** (a) Postage.

805		1p.60 on 50c. violet	75	30

(b) Air. Surch Aereo also.

806		1p.20 on 1b. blue	85	45

201 Sower

1967. 50th Anniv of Lions International. Multicoloured.

807	**201**	70c. Type **201** (postage)	55	20
808	**201**	2p. Lions emblem and Inca obelisks (horiz) (air)	1·30	95

MS809 129×80 mm. Nos. 807/8. Imperf — 5·75 5·75

202 "Macheteros"

1968. Ninth Congress of the UPAE (Postal Union of the Americas and Spain). Bolivian Folklore. Designs showing costumed figures. Multicoloured.

810	**202**	30c. Type **202** (postage)	30	10
811	**202**	60c. "Chunchos"	45	20
812	**202**	1p. "Wiphala"	65	25
813	**202**	2p. "Diablada"	95	30
814	**202**	1p.20 "Pujllay" (air)	55	20
815	**202**	1p.40 "Ujusiris"	65	25
816	**202**	2p. "Morenada"	1·30	45
817	**202**	3p. "Auki-aukis"	1·70	55

MS818 Two sheets each 132×80 mm. Nos. 810/13 and 814/17. Imperf — 27·00 27·00

203 Arms of Tarija

1968. 150th Anniv of Battle of the Tablada (1817).

819	**203**	20c. mult (postage)	20	10
820	**203**	30c. multicoloured	20	10
821	**203**	40c. multicoloured	30	10
822	**203**	60c. multicoloured	45	15
823	-	1p. multicoloured (air)	55	20
824	-	1p.20 multicoloured	65	20
825	-	2p. multicoloured	1·20	55
826	-	4p. multicoloured	1·70	85

DESIGNS: Nos. 823/6, Moto Mendez.

204 President G. Villarroel

1968. 400th Anniv of Cochabamba.

827	**204**	20c. brn & orge (postage)	80	20
828	**204**	30c. brown & turquoise	80	20
829	**204**	40c. brown and purple	80	20
830	**204**	50c. brown and green	80	20
831	**204**	1p. brown and bistre	95	20
832	-	1p.40 black & red (air)	1·10	45
833	-	3p. black and blue	1·50	55
834	-	4p. black and red	1·90	65

835	-	5p. black and green	2·40	65
836	-	10p. black and violet	4·25	1·30

DESIGN—HORIZ: 1p.40 to 10p. Similar portrait of President.

205 Painted Clay Cup

1968. 20th Anniv of UNESCO (1966).

837	**205**	20c. mult (postage)	40	10
838	**205**	60c. multicoloured	75	45
839	**205**	1p.20 black & blue (air)	75	45
840	**205**	2p.80 black and green	1·40	95

DESIGNS: Nos. 839/40, UNESCO emblem.

206 President J. F. Kennedy

1968. Fifth Death Anniv of John F. Kennedy (U.S. President).

841	**206**	10c. black & grn (postage)	30	10
842	**206**	4p. black and violet	2·10	2·10
843	**206**	1p. black and green (air)	40	20
844	**206**	10p. black and red	4·25	4·25

MS845 Two sheets each 131×80 mm. (a) No. 842; (b) No. 843. Imperf — 9·50 9·50

207 ITU Emblem

1968. Centenary (1965) of ITU.

846	**207**	10c. black grey and yellow (postage)	30	10
847	**207**	60c. black, orange & bistre	55	30
848	**207**	1p.20 black, grey and yellow (air)	75	40
849	**207**	1p.40 black, blue & brn	85	30

208 Tennis Player

1968. South American Tennis Championships, La Paz.

850	**208**	10c. black, brown and grey (postage)	40	15
851	**208**	20c. black, brown & yell	40	15
852	**208**	30c. black, brown & blue	40	15
853	**208**	1p.40 black, brown and orange (air)	1·30	45
854	**208**	2p.80 black, brown & bl	2·40	95

MS855 Two sheets each 132×81 mm. (a) Nos. 850/2; (b) No. 853. Imperf — 17·00 17·00

209 Unofficial 1r. Stamp of 1863

1963. Stamp Centenary.

856	**209**	10c. brown, black and green (postage)	90	15
857	**209**	30c. brown, black & blue	90	15
858	**209**	2p. brown, black & drab	90	15
859	-	1p.40 green, black and yellow (air)	1·30	70
860	-	2p.80 green, blk & pink	2·40	1·40
861	-	3p. green, black & lilac	2·40	1·40

MS862 Two sheets each 132×83 mm. (a) Nos. 856/8; (b) Nos. 859/61. Imperf — 11·00 11·50

DESIGN: Nos. 859/61, First Bolivian stamp.

210 Rifle-shooting

1969. Olympic Games, Mexico (1968).

863	**210**	40c. black, red and orange (postage)	55	25
864	-	50c. black, red and green	55	25
865	-	60c. black, blue & green	55	25
866	-	1p.20 black, green and ochre	70	50
867	-	2p.80 black, red & yell	1·40	1·00
868	-	5p. multicoloured	2·20	2·10

MS869 Two sheets each 131×81 mm. (a) Nos. 863/5; (b) Nos. 866/8 — 17·00 17·00

DESIGNS—HORIZ: 50c. Horse-jumping; 60c. Canoeing; 5p. Hurdling. VERT: 1p.20, Running; 2p.80, Throwing the discus.

211 F. D. Roosevelt

1969. Air. Franklin D. Roosevelt Commem.

870	**211**	5p. black, orange & brown	2·00	1·50

212 Temensis laothoe violetta

1970. Butterflies. Multicoloured.

871	**212**	5c. Type **212** (postage)	90	80
872	-	10c. Papilio crassus	1·80	1·60
873	-	20c. Catagramma cynosura	1·80	1·60
874	-	30c. Eunica eurota flora	1·80	1·60
875	-	80c. Ituna phenarete	1·80	1·60
876	-	1p. Metamorpha dido wernichei (air)	2·00	1·70
877	-	1p.80 Heliconius felix	2·75	2·40
878	-	2p.80 Morpho casica	3·75	3·50
879	-	3p. Papilio yuracares	4·00	3·50
880	-	4p. Heliconsus melitus	5·00	4·50

MS881 Two sheets each 132×80 mm. (a) Nos. 871/3; (b) Nos. 876/8. Imerf — 29·00 29·00

213 Scout mountaineering

1970. Bolivian Scout Movement. Multicoloured.

882	**213**	5c. Type **213** (postage)	25	10
883	**213**	10c. Girl-scout planting shrub	25	10
884	**213**	50c. Scout laying bricks (air)	25	15
885	**213**	1p.20 Bolivian scout badge	55	45

214 President A. Ovando and Revolutionaries

1970. Obligatory Tax. Revolution and National Day.

886	**214**	20c. blk & red (postage)	65	25
887	**214**	30c. black & green (air)	65	25

DESIGN: 30c. Pres. Ovando, oil derricks and laurel sprig.

1970. "Exfilca 70" Stamp Exhibition, Caracas, Venezuela. No. 706 further surch **EXFILCA 70** and new value.

888		30c. on 350b. on 10c.	45	30

1970. Provisionals. Various stamps surch.

889	**178**	60c. on 900b. on 350b.	35	10
890	-	1p.20 on 1500b. (No. 723)	65	15
891	**185**	1p.20 on 4000b. (air)	45	15

217 Pres. G. Busch and Oil Derrick

1971. 32nd Death Anniv of President G. Busch and 25th Death Anniv of Pres. Villarroel.

892	**217**	20c. blk & lilac (postage)	65	25
893	-	30c. black and blue (air)	65	25

DESIGN: 30c. Pres. Villarroel and oil refinery.

218 Amaryllis escobar uriae

1971. Bolivian Flora. Multicoloured.

894		30c. Type **218** (postage)	35	15
895		40c. Amaryllis evansae	35	15
896		50c. Amaryllis yungacensis (vert)	55	25
897		2p. Gymnocalycium chiquitanum (vert)	1·40	55
898		1p.20 Amaryllis pseudopardina (air)	80	55
899		1p.40 Rebutia kruegeri (vert)	1·20	70
900		2p.80 Lobivia pentlandii	2·00	1·00
901		4p. Rebutia tunariensis (vert)	2·75	1·70

MS902 Two sheets each 130×80 mm. (a) Nos. 894/5, 898 and 900; (b) Nos. 896/7, 899 and 901. Imperf ... 27·00 ... 27·00

219 Sica Sica Cathedral

1971. "Exfilima" Stamp Exhibition, Lima, Peru.

903	**219**	20c. multicoloured	45	25

220 Pres. H. Banzer

1972. "Bolivia's Development".

904	**220**	1p.20 multicoloured	1·80	25

221 Chiriwano de Achocalla Dance

1972. Folk Dances. Multicoloured.

905		20c. Type **221** (postage)	25	10
906		40c. Rueda Chapaca	45	15
907		60c. Kena-Kena	65	25
908		1p. Waca Thokori	80	30
909		1p.20 Kusillo (air)	70	25
910		1p.40 Taquirari	90	25

222 Virgin and Child (B. Bitti)

1972. Bolivian Paintings. Multicoloured.

911		10c. The Washerwoman (M. P. Holguin) (postage)	35	10
912		50c. Coronation of the Virgin (G. M. Berrio)	45	10
913		70c. Arquebusier (anon.)	65	10
914		80c. St. Peter of Alcantara (M. P. Holguin)	70	15
915		1p. Type **222**	1·00	20
916		1p.40 Chola Pacena (G. de Rojas) (air)	70	10
917		1p.50 Adoration of the Kings (G. Gamarra)	70	10
918		1p.60 Pachamama Vision (A. Borda)	70	10
919		2p. Idol's Kiss (G. de Rojas)	1·10	30

223 Tarija Cathedral

1972. "EXFILIBRA 72" Stamp Exhibition, Rio de Janeiro.

920	**223**	30c. multicoloured	45	15

224 National Arms

1972. Air.

921	**224**	4p. multicoloured	2·75	65

225 Santos Dumont and "14 bis"

1973. Air. Birth Centenary of Alberto Santos Dumont (aviation pioneer).

922	**225**	1p.40 black and yellow	90	40

226 Echinocactus notocactus

1973. Cacti. Multicoloured.

923		20c. Type **226** (postage)	55	25
924		40c. Echinocactus lenninghaussii	55	25
925		50c. Mammillaria bocasana	60	25
926		70c. Echinocactus lenninghaussii (different)	65	40
927		1p.20 Mammillaria bocasana (different) (air)	70	25
928		1p.90 Opuntia cristata	1·10	30
929		2p. Echinocactus rebutia	1·80	45

227 Power Station, Santa Isabel

1973. Bolivian Development Multicoloured.

930		20c. Type **227** (postage)	1·30	25
931		20c. Tin foundry	1·30	25
932		90c. Bismuth plant	1·50	30
933		1p. Gas plant	1·50	30
934		1p.40 Road bridge, Highways 1 and 4 (air)	2·50	40
935		2p. Inspection car crossing bridge, Al Beni	3·75	45

228 Cattleya nobilior

1974. Orchids. Multicoloured.

936		20c. Type **228** (postage)	1·30	25
937		50c. Zygopetalum bolivianum	1·30	25
938		1p. Huntleya melagris	1·30	25
939		2p.50 Cattleya luteola (horiz) (air)	2·30	40
940		3p.80 Stanhopaea	2·75	55
941		4p. Catasetum (horiz)	3·00	70
942		5p. Maxillaria	5·00	80

1974. Philatelic Exhibitions, 1975, 1976 and 1977. Four sheets each 130×80 mm showing reproductions of various stamps.

MS943 (a) Nos. 36, 911 and 942; (b) Nos. 36, 912 and 941; (c) Nos. 36, 914 and 939; (d) Nos. 36 and 921 ... 16·00 ... 16·00

See also No. **MS**954.

229 Morane Saulnier Type P and Emblem

1974. Air. 50th Anniv of Bolivian Air Force. Multicoloured.

944		3p. Type **229**	80	65
945		3p.80 Douglas DC-3 crossing Andes	1·30	80
946		4p.50 Triplane trainer and Morane Saulnier Paris I aircraft	1·30	80
947		8p. Col. Rafael Pabon and biplane fighter	2·00	1·60
948		15p. Jet airliner on "50"	4·25	2·50

230 General Sucre (after J. Wallpher)

1974. 150th Anniv of Battle of Avacucho.

949	**230**	5p. multicoloured	1·30	65

231 UPU and Exhibition Emblems

1974. Centenary of UPU and Expo UPU (Montevideo) and Prenfil UPU (Buenos Aires) Stamp Exhibitions.

950	**231**	3p.50 green, black & bl	1·20	45

232 Lions Emblem and Steles

1975. 50th Anniv of Lions International in Bolivia.

951	**232**	30c. multicoloured	45	40

233 Exhibition Emblem

1975. "Espana 75" International Stamp Exhibition, Madrid.

952	**233**	4p.50 multicoloured	95	40

234 Emblem of Meeting

1975. Cartagena Agreement. First Meeting of Postal Ministers, Quito, Ecuador.

953	**234**	2p.50 silver, violet & blk	80	30

1975. Philatelic Exhibitions 1975, 1976 and 1977. Four sheets as MS943.

MS954 (a) Nos. 36 and 950; (b) Nos. 36 and 951; (c) Nos. 36 and 952; (d) Nos. 36 and 953 ... 17·00 ... 17·00

235 Arms of Pando

1975. 150th Anniv of Republic (1st issue). Provincial Arms. Multicoloured.

955		20c. Type **235** (postage)	40	15
956		2p. Chuzuisaca	85	45
957		3p. Cochabamba	1·10	65

958	20c. Beni (air)	40	15
959	30c. Tarija	40	15
960	50c. Potosi	55	25
961	1p. Oruro	1·10	65
962	2p.50 Santa Cruz	2·00	1·30
963	3p. La Paz	2·00	1·30

See also Nos. 965/78.

236 Presidents Perez and Banzer

1975. Air. Visit of Pres. Perez of Venezuela.

964	**236**	3p. multicoloured	85	65

237 Pres. Victor Paz Estenssoro

1975. 150th Anniv of Republic (2nd issue).

965		30c. Type **237** (postage)	10	10
966		60c. Pres. Thomas Frias	15	10
966a		1p. Ismael Montes	25	15
967		2p.50 Aniceto Arce	65	25
968		7p. Bautista Saavedra	1·60	80
969		10p. Jose Manuel Pando	2·50	1·30
970		15p. Jose Maria Linares	3·25	1·60
971		50p. Simon Bolivar	12·50	8·75
972		50c. Rene Barrientos Ortuno (air)	15	10
973		2p. Francisco B. O'Connor	80	25
973a		3p.80 Gualberto Villaroel	80	65
974		4p.20 German Busch	1·30	80
975		4p.50 Pres. Hugo Banzer Suarez	1·30	80
976		20p. Jose Ballivian	5·00	3·25
977		30p. Pres. Andres de Santa Cruz	6·00	4·25
978		40p. Pres. Antonio Jose de Sucre	7·75	5·50

Nos. 965/70, 972/4 and 976/78 are smaller, 24×33 mm.

238 Laurel Wreath and LAB Emblem

1975. Air. 50th Anniv of Lloyd-Aereo Boliviano (national airline). Multicoloured.

979		1p. Type **238**	45	25
980		1p.50 Douglas DC-9 and L.A.B. route map (horiz)	70	35
981		2p. Guillermo Kyllmann (founder) and Junkers F-13 aircraft (horiz)	95	45

1975. Obligatory Tax. As No. 893 but inscr "XXV ANIVERSARIO DE SU GOBIERNO".

982	30c. black and blue	3·50	3·25

239 "EXFIVIA"

1975. "Exfivia 75". Stamp Exhibition.

983	**239**	3p. multicoloured	95	70

240 UPU Emblem

1975. Air. Centenary (1974) of UPU.

984	**240**	25p. multicoloured	3·50	3·25

241 Chiang Kai-shek

1976. First Death Anniv of President Chiang Kai-shek.
985 **241** 2p.50 multicoloured 3·50 1·30

242 Geological Hammer, Lamp and Map

1976. Bolivian Geological Institute.
986 **242** 4p. multicoloured 1·00 45

243 Naval Insignia

1976. Navy Day.
987 **243** 50c. multicoloured 45 30

244 Douglas DC-10 and Divided Roundel

1976. 50th Anniv of Lufthansa Airline.
988 **244** 3p. multicoloured 1·20 45

245 Bolivian Boy Scout and Badge

1976. 60th Anniv of Bolivian Boy Scouts.
989 **245** 1p. multicoloured 65 40

246 Battle Scene

1976. Bicentenary of American Revolution.
990 **246** 4p.50 multicoloured 1·70 80
MS991 130×81 mm. No. 990 20·00 20·00

247 Brother Vicente Bernedo (missionary)

1976. Brother Vincente Bernedo Commemoration.
992 **247** 1p.50 multicoloured 40 25

248 Rainbow over La Paz, Police Handler with Dog

1976. 150th Anniv of Police Service.
993 **248** 2p.50 multicoloured 70 55

249 Bolivian Family

1976. National Census.
994 **249** 2p.50 multicoloured 65 45

250 Pedro Poveda (educator)

1976. Poveda Commemoration.
995 **250** 1p.50 multicoloured 45 25

251 Arms, Bolivar and Sucre

1976. International Bolivarian Societies Congress.
996 **251** 1p.50 multicoloured 80 40

252 "Numeral"

1976
997 **252** 20c. brown 30 10
998 **252** 1p. blue 55 25
999 **252** 1p.50 green 95 65

253 Boy and Girl

1977. Christmas 1976 and 50th Anniv of Inter-American Children's Institute.
1000 **253** 50c. multicoloured 30 10

254 Caduceus

1977. National Seminar on "Chagas Disease".
1001 **254** 3p. multicoloured 85 25

255 Court Buildings, La Paz

1977. 150th Anniv of Bolivian Supreme Court. Multicoloured.
1002 **255** 2p.50 Type **255** 40 10
1003 4p. Dr. Manuel M. Urcullu, first President 55 10
1004 4p.50 Dr. Pantaleon Dalence, President, 1883–89 80 15

256 Tower and Map

1977. 90th Anniv of Oruro Club.
1005 **256** 3p. multicoloured 65 25

257 Newspaper Mastheads

1977. Bolivian Newspapers. Multicoloured.
1006 1p.50 Type **257** 30 10
1007 2p.50 *Ultima Hora* and Alfredo Alexander (horiz) 40 15
1008 3p. *El Diaro* and Jose Carrasco (horiz) 45 25
1009 4p. *Los Tiempos* and Demetrio Canelas 65 30
1010 5p.50 *Presencia* 80 25

258 Games Poster

1977. Eighth Bolivarian Games, La Paz.
1011 **258** 5p. multicoloured 85 30

259 Tin Miner and Mining Corporation Emblem

1977. 25th Anniv of Bolivian Mining Corporation.
1012 **259** 3p. multicoloured 85 25

260 Miners, Globe and Chemical Symbol for Tin

1977. International Tin Symposium, La Paz.
1013 **260** 6p. multicoloured 1·20 45

261 Map of Bolivia and Radio Masts

1977. 50th Anniv of Bolivian Radio.
1014 **261** 2p.50 multicoloured 65 40

1977. "Exfivia 77" Philatelic Exhibition, Cochabamba. No. 719 surch EXFIVIA — 77 $b. 5.—.
1015 5p. on 5,000b. on $b. 5 grey and gold 2·40 1·60

263 "Eye", Compass, Key and Law Book

1978. 50th Anniv of Audit Department.
1016 **263** 5p. multicoloured 85 25

264 Aesculapius Staff and Map of Andean Countries

1978. Fifth Meeting of Andean Countries' Health Ministers.
1017 **264** 2p. orange and black 45 25

265 Map of the Americas

1978. World Rheumatism Year (1977).
1018 **265** 2p.50 blue and red 65 25

266 Mt. Illimani

1978
1019 **266** 50c. green and blue 25 10
1020 - 1p. yellow and brown 25 10
1021 - 1p.50 grey and red 40 20
DESIGNS—HORIZ: 1p.50, Mt. Cerro de Potosi. VERT: 1p. Pre-Columbian monolith.

267 Central Bank

1978. 50th Anniv of Bank of Bolivia.
1022 **267** 7p. multicoloured 1·20 30

268 Jesus with Children

1979. International Year of the Child.
1023 **268** 8p. multicoloured 1·20 40

269 Antofagasta Cancellation **270** Antofagasta

1979. Centenary of Loss of Litoral Department to Chile.
1024 **269** 50c. brown and black 30 10
1025 - 1p. mauve and black 55 10
1026 - 1p.50 green and black 55 10
1027 **270** 5p.50 multicoloured 80 15
1028 - 6p.50 multicoloured 95 30
1029 - 7p. multicoloured 95 30
1030 - 8p. multicoloured 1·10 35
1031 - 10p. multicoloured 1·50 40
DESIGNS—HORIZ: 1p. La Chimba cancel; 1p.50, Mejillonos cancel. VERT: (As Type **270**). 6p.50, Woman in chains; 7p. Eduardo Arbaroa; 8p. Map of Department, 1876; 10p. Arms of Litoral.

271 Map and Radio Club Emblem

1979. Radio Club of Bolivia.
1032 **271** 3p. multicoloured 95 55

1987. "Exfivia 87" Stamp Exhibition, Potosi. Multicoloured.
1139	40c. Type 333	80	45
1140	50c. 18th-century engraving of Potosi	1·90	55

334 *Nina* and Stern of *Santa Maria*

1987. "Espamer '87" Stamp Exhibition, La Coruna. Multicoloured.
1141	20c. Type 334	45	25
1142	20c. *Pinta* and bow of *Santa Maria*	45	25

Nos. 1141/2 were printed together, *se-tenant*, forming a composite design.

335 Pan-pipes and Indian Flute

1987. Musical Instruments. Multicoloured.
1143	50c. Type 335	1·10	45
1144	1b. Indian guitars	1·90	1·00

336 Carabuco Church

1988. Visit of Pope John Paul II. Multicoloured.
1145	20c. Type 336	45	25
1146	20c. Tihuanacu church	45	25
1147	20c. Cathedral of the Kings, Beni	45	25
1148	30c. St. Joseph church, Chiquitos	70	25
1149	30c. St. Francis's church, Sucre	70	25
1150	40c. Cobija chapel (vert)	85	35
1151	50c. Cochabamba cathedral (vert)	1·10	35
1152	50c. Jayu Kcota church	1·10	35
1153	60c. St. Francis's Basilica, La Paz (vert)	1·30	45
1154	70c. Church of Jesus, Machaca	1·50	45
1155	70c. St. Lawrence's church, Potosi (vert)	1·50	45
1156	80c. Vallegrande church	1·70	65
1157	80c. Copacabana Virgin (vert)	1·70	65
1158	80c. "The Holy Family" (Peter Paul Rubens) (vert)	1·70	65
1159	1b.30 Concepcion church	2·75	1·10
1160	1b.30 Tarija cathedral (vert)	2·75	1·10
1161	1b.50 Pope and Arms of John Paul II and Bolivia	3·00	1·40

337 Handshake and Flags

1988. Visit of President Jose Sarney of Brazil.
1162	337	50c. multicoloured	85	45

338 St. John Bosco

1988. Death Centenary of St. John Bosco (founder of Salesian Brothers).
1163	338	30c. multicoloured	50	25

339 La Paz–Beni Steam Locomotive

1988. Centenary of Bolivian Railways.
1164	339	1b. multicoloured	2·30	80

340 Aguirre

1988. Death Cent of Nataniel Aguirre (writer).
1165	340	1b. black and brown	1·90	80

341 "Column of the Future" (Battle of Bahia Monument)

1988. 50th Anniv of Pando Department. Multicoloured.
1166	40c. Type 341	75	25
1167	60c. Rubber production	1·00	45

342 Athlete

1988. Olympic Games, Seoul.
1168	342	1b.50 multicoloured	2·75	2·30

343 Mother Rosa Gattorno

1988. 88th Death Anniv of Mother Rosa Gattorno (Founder of the Daughters of St. Anne).
1169	343	80c. multicoloured	1·50	65

344 Bernardino de Cardenas

1988. 220th Death Anniv of Br. Bernardino de Cardenas (first Bishop of La Paz).
1170	344	70c. black and brown	1·30	60

345 Ministry Building

1988. Ministry of Transport and Communications.
1171	345	2b. black, green & red	3·50	1·70

346 Arms

1988. 50th Anniv of Army Communications Corps.
1172	346	70c. multicoloured	1·40	65

347 Rally Car

1988. 50th Anniv of Bolivian Automobile Club.
1173	347	1b.50 multicoloured	2·50	1·20

348 Microphone and Emblem

1989. 50th Anniv of Radio Fides.
1174	348	80c. multicoloured	1·30	65

349 Obverse and Reverse of 1852 Gold Cuartillo

1989. Coins.
1175	349	1b. multicoloured	1·80	70

350 "Bulgaria 89" Stamp Exhibition Emblem and Orchid

1989. Events and Plants. Multicoloured.
1176	50c. Type 350	1·60	35
1177	60c. "Italia '90" World Cup football championship emblem and kantuta (national flower) (horiz)	1·90	45
1178	70c. "Albertville 1986" emblem and *Heliconia humilis*	2·30	55
1179	1b. Olympic Games, Barcelona emblem and *Hoffmanseggia*	3·00	80
1180	2b. Olympic Games, Seoul emblem and bromeliad	6·25	1·50

351 Birds

1989. Bicentenary of French Revolution.
1181	351	70c. multicoloured	1·40	55

352 Clock Tower and Steam Locomotive

1989. Centenary of Uyuni.
1182	352	30c. grey, black & blue	85	25

353 Federico Ahlfeld Waterfall, River Pauserna

1989. Noel Kempff Mercado National Park. Multicoloured.
1183	1b.50 Type 353	3·00	1·20
1184	3b. Pampas deer	6·25	2·00

354 Making Metal Articles

1989. America. Tiahuanacu Culture. Multicoloured.
1185	50c. Type 354	1·40	35
1186	1b. Kalasasaya Temple	2·75	70

355 Dr. Carlos Perez and Jaime Zamora

1989. Meeting of Presidents of Bolivia and Venezuela.
1187	355	2b. multicoloured	3·00	1·10

356 Cobija Arch

1989. World Heritage Site, Potosi. Multicoloured.
1188	60c. Type 356	70	45
1189	80c. Mint	95	65

357 *Andean Lake* (Arturo Borda)

1989. Christmas. Paintings. Multicoloured.
1190	40c. Type 357	85	25
1191	60c. *Virgin of the Roses* (anon)	1·30	35
1192	80c. *Conquistador* (Jorge de la Reza)	1·80	55
1193	1b. *Native Harmony* (Juan Rimsa)	2·40	65
1194	1b.50 *Woman with Pitcher* (Cecilio Guzman de Rojas)	3·25	1·10
1195	2b. *Flower of Tenderness* (Gil Imana)	4·25	1·40

358 Foot crushing Syringe

1990. Anti-drugs Campaign.
1196	358	80c. multicoloured	1·20	70

359 Map of Americas

1990. Centenary of Organization of American States.
1197	359	80c. blue and deep blue	1·20	45

360 Colonnade

1990. 450th Anniv of White City.
1198	360	1b.20 multicoloured	1·80	80

361 Penny Black, Sir Rowland Hill and Bolivian 5c. Condor Stamp

1990. 150th Anniv of the Penny Black.
1199	361	4b. multicoloured	6·25	2·40

362 Giuseppe Meaza
Stadium, Milan

1990. World Cup Football Championship, Italy. Multicoloured.

1200	2b. Type **362**		2·50	1·40
1201	6b. Match scene		8·00	3·50

363 Emblem

1990. Cent of Bolivian Chamber of Commerce.

1202	**363**	50c. black, blue & gold	85	55

364 Satellite, Map
and Globe

1990. Telecommunications Development Year.

1203	**364**	70c. multicoloured	1·00	70

365 Hall

1990. Centenary of Cochabamba Social Club.

1204	**365**	40c. multicoloured	65	35

366 Chipaya Village,
Oruro

1990. America. Multicoloured.

1205	80c. Type **366**		4·00	45
1206	1b. Nevado Huayna, Cordillera Real (mountain) (vert)		4·75	65

367 Emblem

1990. "Meeting of Two Worlds. United towards Progress". 500th Anniv (1992) of Discovery of America by Columbus.

1207	**367**	2b. multicoloured	2·50	1·20

368 Trees and
Mountains

1990. 400th Anniv of Larecaja District.

1208	**368**	1b.20 multicoloured	1·50	70

369 Dove and
German National
Colours

1990. Unification of Germany.

1209	**369**	2b. multicoloured	2·75	1·10

370 Boys playing
Football (Omar
Espana)

1990. Christmas. Rights of the Child.

1210	**370**	50c. multicoloured	65	25

371 Arms of Bolivia
and Ecuador

1990. Visit of Pres. Rodrigo Borja Cevallos of Ecuador.

1211	**371**	80c. multicoloured	1·50	55

372 Flags and Andes

1990. Fourth Andean Presidents' Council, La Paz.

1212	**372**	1b.50 multicoloured	2·10	70

373 Andes

1990. "Exfivia 90" National Stamp Exhibition.

1213	**373**	40c. blue	55	25

374 Arms of Bolivia
and Mexico

1990. Visit of Pres. Carlos Salinas de Gortari of Mexico.

1214	**374**	60c. multicoloured	1·30	55

375 Emblem, Globe and
Flags

1990. Express Mail Service.

1215	**375**	1b. multicoloured	1·30	45

376 Emblem

1991. 50th Anniv of Bolivian Radio Club.

1216	**376**	2b.40 multicoloured	2·75	1·10

377 Head of Bear

1991. The Spectacled Bear. Multicoloured.

1217	30c. Type **377**		1·90	45
1218	30c. Bear on branch		1·90	45
1219	30c. Bear and cub at water's edge		1·90	45
1220	30c. Bear and cubs on branches		1·90	45

378 National
Museum of
Archaeology

1991. "Espamer '91" Spain–Latin America Stamp Exhibition, Buenos Aires. Multicoloured.

1221	50c. Type **378**		55	20
1222	50c. National Art Museum		55	20
1223	1b. National Museum of Ethnography and Folklore		1·20	45

379 Map

1991. 56th Anniv of Ending of Chaco War and Beginning of Construction of "Heroes of Chaco" Road.

1224	**379**	60c. multicoloured	75	35

380 Statue of Our
Lady of La Paz and
Cathedral

1991. La Paz Cathedral.

1225	**380**	1b.20 multicoloured	1·90	65

381 Presidents Lacalle and
Paz Zamora

1991. Meeting of Uruguayan and Bolivian Presidents.

1226	**381**	1b. multicoloured	1·10	45

382 Presidents Paz Zamora
and Menem

1991. Meeting of Bolivian and Argentine Presidents.

1227	**382**	1b. multicoloured	1·10	45

383 "Exfivia 83", "87"
and "90" Stamps

1991. 20th Anniv of Bolivian Philatelic Federation.

1228	**383**	70c. multicoloured	1·00	35

384 Presidents Fujimori and
Paz Zamora

1991. Presidential Summit of Bolivia and Peru.

1229	**384**	50c. multicoloured	65	20

385 Route Map,
Motor Cycle and
Rally Car

1991. Pres. Jaime Paz Zamora National Grand Prix Motor Rally, Tarija-Cobija.

1230	**385**	50c. multicoloured	65	20

386 Data Retrieval Systems

1991. "Ecobol" Postal Security.

1231	**386**	1b.40 multicoloured	1·80	65

387 "First Discovery of
Chuquiago" (Arturo
Reque)

1991. America. Voyages of Discovery. Multicoloured.

1232	60c. Type **387**		2·10	35
1233	1b.20 "Foundation of City of Our Lady of La Paz" (J. Rimsa) (vert)		4·25	65

388 Stylized Figures
and City Skyline

1991. National Population and Housing Census.

1234	**388**	50c. multicoloured	65	20

389 "Landscape" (Daniel
Pena y Sarmiento)

1991. Christmas. Multicoloured.

1235	2b. Type **389**		2·50	80
1236	5b. "Fruit Seller" (Cecilio Guzman de Rojas)		6·25	2·00
1237	15b. "Native Mother" (Crespo Gastelu)		18·00	5·50

390 Camp-site and Emblem

1992. 75th Anniv (1990) of Bolivian Scout Movement and Los Andes Jamboree, Cochabamba.

1238	**390**	1b.20 multicoloured	1·60	80

391 Simon Bolivar

1992. "Exfilbo 92" National Stamp Exhibition, La Paz.
| 1239 | **391** | 1b.20 deep brown, brown and stone | 1·60 | 80 |

392 Raising Flag

1992. Creation of Bolivian Free Zone in Ilo, Peru. Multicoloured.
1240		1b.20 Type **392**	1·40	80
1241		1b.50 Presidents Fujimori (Peru) and Paz Zamora (horiz)	1·60	90
1242		1b.80 Beach at Ilo (horiz)	2·10	1·00

393 Logotype of Pavilion

1992. "Expo '92" World's Fair, Seville, and "Granada '92" Int Stamp Exhibition. Multicoloured.
| 1243 | | 30c. Type **393** | 40 | 30 |
| 1244 | | 50c. Columbus's fleet | 70 | 40 |

394 Rotary International Emblem and Prize

1992. Rotary Club Miraflores District 4690 "Illimani de Oro" Prize.
| 1245 | **394** | 90c. gold, blue & black | 1·20 | 70 |

395 School and Perez

1992. Birth Centenary of Elizardo Perez (founder of Ayllu School, Warisata).
| 1246 | **395** | 60c. blue, black & yellow | 80 | 40 |

396 Government Palace

1992. UNESCO World Heritage Site, Sucre.
| 1247 | **396** | 50c. multicoloured | 1·30 | 30 |

397 Mario Martinez Guzman

1992. Olympic Games, Barcelona.
| 1248 | **397** | 1b.50 multicoloured | 2·00 | 1·00 |

398 Front Page

1992. 25th Anniv of *Los Tiempos* (newspaper).
| 1249 | **398** | 50c. multicoloured | 70 | 40 |

399 Canoeing

1992. First International River Bermejo Canoeing Championship.
| 1250 | **399** | 1b.20 multicoloured | 2·00 | 90 |

400 Columbus leaving Palos (after Bejarano)

1992. America. 500th Anniv of Discovery of America by Columbus.
| 1251 | **400** | 60c. brown and black | 1·20 | 50 |
| 1252 | - | 2b. multicoloured | 4·25 | 1·50 |
DESIGN—HORIZ: 2b. "Columbus meeting the Caribisis Tribe" (Luis Vergara).

401 Football Match

1992. World Cup Football Championship, U.S.A. (1994).
| 1253 | **401** | 1b.20 multicoloured | 2·50 | 1·00 |

402 "Chenopodium quinoa"

1992. 50th Anniv of Interamerican Institute for Agricultural Co-operation.
| 1254 | **402** | 1b.20 multicoloured | 1·90 | 90 |

403 University Arms and Minerals

1992. Cent of Oruro Technical University.
| 1255 | **403** | 50c. multicoloured | 70 | 40 |

404 Mascots

1992. 12th Bolivarian Games, Cochabamba and Santa Cruz (1st issue).
| 1256 | **404** | 2b. multicoloured | 2·75 | 1·20 |
See also No. 1271.

405 Cayman

1992. Ecology and Conservation. Multicoloured.
1257		20c. Type **405**	20	10
1258		50c. Spotted cavy	70	20
1259		1b. Chinchilla	1·40	60
1260		2b. Anteater	2·75	1·20
1261		3b. Jaguar	4·25	1·80
1262		4b. Long-tailed sylph ("Picaflor") (vert)	5·75	2·50
1263		5b. Piranhas	7·75	3·25
Each stamp also bears the emblem of an anniversary or event.

406 Battle Scene

1992. 150th Anniv of Battle of Ingavi.
| 1264 | **406** | 1b.20 brown and black | 2·75 | 70 |

407 Man following Star in Boat

1992. Christmas. Multicoloured.
1265		1b.20 Type **407**	1·60	60
1266		2b.50 Star over church	3·50	1·30
1267		6b. Infant in manger and church	8·25	3·25

408 Nicolas Copernicus (450th death anniv)

1993. Astronomy.
| 1268 | | 50c. multicoloured | 70 | 40 |
| 1269 | **408** | 2b. black | 2·75 | 1·00 |
DESIGN—HORIZ: 50c. Santa Ana International Astronomical Observatory, Tarija (10th anniv (1992)).

409 Mother Nazaria (after Victor Eusebio Choque)

1993. Beatification (1992) of Mother Nazaria Ignacia March Meza.
| 1270 | **409** | 60c. multicoloured | 1·10 | 40 |

410 Pictograms and Flags of Ecuador, Venezuela, Peru, Bolivia, Colombia and Panama

1993. 12th Bolivarian Games, Cochabamba and Santa Cruz (2nd issue).
| 1271 | **410** | 2b.30 multicoloured | 2·75 | 1·20 |

411 Bolivia 1962 10000b. Kantuta and Brazil 90r. "Bull's Eye" Stamps

1993. 150th Anniv of First Brazilian Stamps.
| 1272 | **411** | 2b.30 multicoloured | 2·75 | 1·20 |

412 *Morpho* sp.

1993. Butterflies. Multicoloured.
1273		60c. Type **412**	1·10	30
1274		60c. *Archaeoprepona demophon*	1·10	30
1275		80c. *Papilio* sp.	1·50	40
1276		80c. Orion (*Historis odius*)	1·50	40
1277		80c. Mexican fritillary (*Euptoieta hegesia*)	1·50	40
1278		1b.80 *Morpho deidamia*	3·25	90
1279		1b.80 Orange swallowtail (*Papilio thoas*)	3·25	90
1280		1b.80 Monarch (*Danaus plexippus*)	3·25	90
1281		2b.30 Scarlet emperor (*Anaea marthesia*)	4·25	1·20
1282		2b.30 *Caligo* sp.	4·25	1·20
1283		2b.30 *Rothschildia* sp.	4·25	1·20
1284		2b.70 *Heliconius* sp.	5·00	1·40
1285		2b.70 *Marpesia corinna*	5·00	1·40
1286		2b.70 *Prepona chromus*	5·00	1·40
1287		3b.50 Rusty-tipped page (*Siproeta epaphus*)	6·75	1·90
1288		3b.50 *Heliconius* sp.	6·75	1·90

413 "Eternal Father" (wood statuette, Gaspar de la Cueva)

1993
| 1289 | **413** | 1b.80 multicoloured | 2·75 | 90 |

414 "Virgin of Urkupina"

1993. 400th Anniv of Quillacollo.
| 1290 | **414** | 50c. multicoloured | 1·10 | 40 |

415 Student, Machinery and Emblem

1993. 50th Anniv (1992) of Pedro Domingo Murillo Technical College.
| 1291 | **415** | 60c. multicoloured | 70 | 30 |

416 Owl (painting, Chuquisaca)

1993. Cave Art. Multicoloured.
1292		80c. Type **416**	2·30	40
1293		80c. Animals (painting, Cochabamba)	2·30	40
1294		80c. Geometric patterns (engraving, Chuquisaca) (vert)	2·30	40
1295		80c. Sun (engraving, Beni) (vert)	2·30	40
1296		80c. Llama (painting, Oruro)	2·30	40
1297		80c. Human figure (engraving, Potosi)	2·30	40
1298		80c. Church and tower (painting, La Paz) (vert)	2·30	40
1299		80c. Warrior (engraving, Tarija) (vert)	2·30	40
1300		80c. Religious mask (engraving, Santa Cruz) (vert)	2·30	40

417 Common Squirrel-monkeys

1993. America. Endangered Animals. Multicoloured.
| 1301 | | 80c. Type **417** | 1·40 | 40 |
| 1302 | | 2b.30 Ocelot | 3·25 | 1·20 |

418 Emblems and Map

1993. 90th Anniv (1992) of Pan-American Health Organization. Anti-AIDS Campaign.

1303	**418**	80c. multicoloured	1·00	40

419 Yolanda Bedregal (poet)

1993. Personalities. Each brown.

1304		50c. Type **419**	50	30
1305		70c. Simon Martinic (President of Cochabamba Philatelic Centre)	80	40
1306		90c. Eugenio von Boeck (politician and President of Bolivian Philatelic Federation)	1·00	45
1307		1b. Marina Nunez del Prado (sculptor)	1·10	50

420 *Virgin with Child and Saints* (anonymous)

1993. Christmas. Multicoloured.

1308		2b.30 *Adoration of the Shepherds* (Leonardo Flores)	5·00	1·20
1309		3b.50 Type **420**	8·25	1·80
1310		6b. *Virgin of the Milk* (Melchor Perez de Holguin)	13·50	3·00

421 Riberalta Square

1994. Centenary of Riberalta.

1311	**421**	2b. multicoloured	2·40	1·00

422 *Population and Our World* (Mayari Rodriguez)

1994. Second Prize-winning Design (6–8 year group) in United Nations Fund for Population Activities International Design Contest.

1312	**422**	2b.30 multicoloured	3·75	1·20

423 Sanchez de Lozada

1994. Presidency of Gonzalo Sanchez de Lozada.

1313	**423**	2b. multicoloured	2·40	1·00
1314	**423**	2b.30 multicoloured	2·75	1·20

424 Mascot

1994. World Cup Football Championship, U.S.A. Multicoloured.

1315		80c. Type **424**	1·00	40
1316		1b.80 Bolivia v Uruguay	2·20	90
1317		2b.30 Bolivia v Venezuela	2·75	1·20
1318		2b.50 Bolivian team (left half)	2·75	1·30
1319		2b.50 Bolivian team (right half)	2·75	1·30
1320		2b.70 Bolivia v Ecuador	3·00	1·40
1321		3b.50 Bolivia v Brazil	4·50	1·80

Nos. 1318/19 were issued together, se-tenant, forming a composite design.

425 Child

1994. S.O.S. Children's Villages.

1322	**425**	2b.70 multicoloured	3·00	1·30

426 St. Peter's Church and Mgr. Jorge Manrique Hurtado (Archbishop, 1967–87)

1994. 50th Anniv (1993) of Archdiocese of La Paz. Multicoloured.

1323		1b.80 Type **426**	2·75	90
1324		2b. Church of the Sacred Heart of Mary and Mgr. Abel Antezana y Rojas (first Archbishop, 1943–67) (vert)	3·25	1·00
1325		3b.50 Santo Domingo Church and Mgr. Luis Sainz Hinojosa (Archbishop since 1987) (vert)	6·00	1·70

427 *Buddleja coriacea*

1994. Environmental Protection. Trees. Multicoloured.

1326		60c. Type **427**	65	30
1327		1b.80 *Bertholletia exelsa*	1·90	90
1328		2b. *Schinus molle* (horiz)	2·20	1·00
1329		2b.70 *Polylepis racemosa*	2·75	1·30
1330		3b. *Tabebuia chrysantha*	3·25	1·50
1331		3b.50 *Erythrina falcata* (horiz)	3·75	1·70

428 Paz

1994. Dr. Victor Paz Estenssoro (former President).

1332	**428**	2b. multicoloured	2·20	90

429 Tramcar and Mail Van

1994. America. Postal Transport. Multicoloured.

1333		1b. Type **429**	1·10	40
1334		5b. Boeing 747 and ox cart	5·50	2·30

430 Coral Tree

1994. 300th Anniv of San Borja.

1335	**430**	1b.60 multicoloured	1·70	70

431 Diagram of Eclipse

1994. Solar Eclipse.

1336	**431**	3b.50 multicoloured	3·75	1·50

432 1894 100c. Stamp

1994. Centenary of Arms Issue of 1894.

1337	**432**	1b.80 multicoloured	1·90	80

433 Col. Marzana and Soldiers

1994. 62nd Anniv of Defence of Fort Boqueron.

1338	**433**	80c. multicoloured	90	30

434 *Delicate Flower of Tarija*

1994. Christmas. Pastels of children by Maria Susana Castillo. Multicoloured.

1339		2b. Type **434**	3·50	90
1340		5b. "Child of the High Plateau"	8·75	2·30
1341		20b. "Shoot of the Bolivian East"	25·00	9·25

435 Emblem

1994. Pan-American Scout Jamboree, Cochabamba.

1342	**435**	1b.80 multicoloured	1·90	90

436 Sucre

1995. Birth Bicentenary of General Antonio Jose de Sucre. Multicoloured.

1343		1b.80 Type **436**	2·30	90
1344		3b.50 Sucre and national colours	4·75	1·70

437 Santa Ana Cathedral

1995. Centenary (1994) of Yacuma Province, Beni Department.

1345	**437**	1b.90 multicoloured	2·40	1·00
1346	**437**	2b.90 multicoloured	3·50	1·50

438 "Holy Virgin of Copacabana", Sanctuary and Franciscans

1995. Centenary of Franciscan Presence at Copacabana Sanctuary.

1347	**438**	60c. multicoloured	1·00	35
1348	**438**	80c. multicoloured	1·40	55

439 Anniversary Emblem

1995. 25th Anniv of Andean Development Corporation.

1349	**439**	2b.40 multicoloured	2·75	1·30

440 Paraguay and Bolivia Flags (Chaco Peace Treaty, 1938)

1995. Visit of President Juan Carlos Wasmosy of Paraguay and 169th Anniv (1994) of Republic of Bolivia.

1350	**440**	2b. multicoloured	2·00	1·10

441 Montenegro

1995. 50th Anniv of Publication of "Nationalism and Colonialism" by Carlos Montenegro.

1351	**441**	1b.20 black and pink	2·75	65

442 Digging Potatoes

1995. 50th Anniv of FAO.

1352	**442**	1b. multicoloured	2·00	55

443 Anniversary Emblem

1995. 50th Anniv of UNO.

1353	**443**	2b.90 dp blue, gold & bl	2·40	1·70

444 Andean Condor ("Condor")

1995. America. Endangered Species. Multicoloured.

1354		5b. Type **444**	4·50	2·75
1355		5b. Llamas	4·50	2·75

Nos. 1354/5 were issued together, *se-tenant*, forming a composite design.

445 Airbus Industrie
A320

1995. 50th Anniv (1994) of ICAO.
1356 **445** 50c. multicoloured 90 45

446 Stone Head

1995. Archaeology. Samaipata Temple, Florida. Multicoloured.
1357 1b. Type **446** 90 55
1358 1b.90 Stone head (different) 1·70 1·10
1359 2b. Excavation and stone head 1·70 1·10
1360 2b.40 Entrance and animal-
shaped vessel 2·00 1·30
Nos. 1357/60 were issued together, *se-tenant*, forming a composite design.

447 Brewery Complex

1995. Centenary of Taquina Brewery.
1361 **447** 1b. multicoloured 2·40 55

448 *The Annunciation*
(Cima da Conegliano)

1995. Christmas. Multicoloured.
1362 1b.20 Type **448** 1·30 65
1363 3b. "The Nativity" (Hans
Baldung) 3·25 1·70
1364 3b.50 "Adoration of the Wise
Men" (altarpiece, Rogier van
der Weyden) 4·00 2·00

449 Jose de Sanjines
(lyricist)

1995. 150th Anniv of National Anthem. Multicoloured.
1365 1b. Type **449** 90 55
1366 2b. Benedetto Vincenti
(composer) 1·70 1·10
Nos. 1365/6 were issued together, *se-tenant*, forming a composite design.

450 Flats, Villarroel,
Factories, Road and
Railway

1996. 50th Anniv of Decree for Abolition of Enforced Amerindian Labour. Multicoloured.
1367 1b.90 Type **450** 1·70 1·10
1368 2b.90 Pres. Gualberto Villarroel
addressing Congress and
freed workers 2·40 1·70

Nos. 1367/8 were issued together, *se-tenant*, forming a composite design.

1996. Various stamps surch.
1369 - 50c. on 3000000p. mul-
ticoloured (No. 1126)
(postage) 45 35
1370 265 60c. on 2p.50 blue
and red 90 40
1371 313 60c. on 5000000p. on
2000p. blue and red
(No. 1116) 55 35
1372 319 60c. on 1400000p. mult 55 35
1373 319 1b. on 2500000p. green
and yellow (No. 1120) 90 55
1374 311 1b.50 on 11000p. blue 1·30 90
1375 312 2b.50 on 23000p. brown
and sepia 2·20 1·40
1376 316 3b. on 1000000p. blue
and gold 2·40 1·70
1377 272 3b.50 on 6p.50 mult 3·25 2·00
1378 279 3b.50 on 9p. mult 3·25 2·00
1379 323 3b.50 on 2000000p.
brown 3·25 2·00
1380 298 20b. on 10p. black,
purple and bronze 19·00 11·00
1381 299 20b. on 13p. mult 19·00 11·00
1382 - 3b.80 on 3p.80 mult (No.
945) (air) 3·25 2·10
1383 - 20b. on 3p.80 mult (No.
973a) 19·00 11·00

452 Summit Emblem

1996. Tenth Rio Group Summit Meeting, Cochabamba. Multicoloured.
1384 2b.50 Type **452** 2·10 1·30
1385 3b.50 Rio Group emblem 2·75 2·00

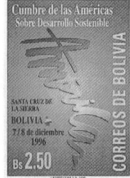

453 Summit Emblem

1996. Summit of the Americas on Sustainable Development, Santa Cruz de la Sierra.
1386 **453** 2b.50 multicoloured 2·10 1·30
1387 **453** 5b. multicoloured 4·25 2·75

454 Facade

1996. National Bank.
1388 **454** 50c. black and blue 55 35

455 De Lemoine

1996. 220th Birth Anniv of Jose Joaquin de Lemoine (first postal administrator).
1389 **455** 1b. brown and stone 1·20 65

456 Family

1997. CARE (Co-operative for American Relief Everywhere). Multicoloured.
1390 60c. Type **456** (20th anniv in
Bolivia) 55 35
1391 70c. Hands cradling globe (50th
anniv) (vert) 65 45

457 Musicians
playing Piccolo and
Saxophone

1997. 50th Anniv of National Symphony Orchestra. *Overture* by G. Rodo Boulanger. Multicoloured.
1392 1b.50 Type **457** 1·40 1·00
1393 2b. Musicians playing violin
and cello 1·90 1·20
Nos. 1392/3 were issued together, *se-tenant*, forming a composite design of the complete painting.

458 Casa Dorada
(cultural centre)

1997. Tarija. Multicoloured.
1394 50c. Type **458** 45 35
1395 60c. Entre Rios Church and
musician 55 40
1396 80c. Narrows of San Luis (horiz) 85 60
1397 1b. Memorial to the Fallen of
the Chaco War (territorial dis-
pute with Paraguay) (horiz) 1·10 90
1398 3b. Virgin and shrine of
Chaguaya (horiz) 3·25 2·75
1399 20b. Birthplace and statue
of Jose Eustaquio Mendez
(Independence hero), San
Lorenzo (horiz) 20·00 18·00

459 La Glorieta, Sucre

1997. Chuquisaca. Multicoloured.
1400 60c. Type **459** 55 45
1401 1b. Government Palace, Sucre
(vert) 90 75
1402 1b.50 Footprints and drawing
of dinosaur 1·40 1·20
1403 1b.50 Interior of House of
Freedom 1·40 1·20
1404 2b. Man playing traditional
wind instrument (vert) 2·00 1·50
1405 3b. Statue of Juana Azurduy
de Padilla (Independence
heroine) (vert) 2·75 2·50

460 Miners' Monument

1997. Oruro. Multicoloured.
1406 50c. Type **460** 55 45
1407 60c. Demon carnival mask 85 55
1408 1b. Vigin of the Cave (statue) 1·10 90
1409 1b.50 Sajama (volcano) (horiz) 1·40 1·10
1410 2b.50 Chipaya child and belfry 2·40 2·20
1411 3b. Moreno (Raul Shaw) (singer
and musician) (horiz) 2·75 2·50

461 Pres. Gonzalo Sanchez
de Lozada of Bolivia and
Pres. Chirac

1997. Visit to Bolivia of President Jacques Chirac of France.
1412 **461** 4b. multicoloured 4·00 3·25

462 Children playing
(Pamela G. Villarroel)

1997. 50th Anniv of UNICEF Children's Drawings. Multicoloured.
1413 50c. Type **462** 55 45
1414 90c. Boy leaping across clifftop
(Lidia Acapa) 1·00 90
1415 1b. Children of different races
on top of world (Gabriela
Philco) 1·20 1·00
1416 2b.50 Children and swing (Jes-
sica Grundy) 2·75 2·40

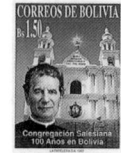

463 St. John
Bosco (founder)

1997. Centenary of Salesian Brothers in Bolivia. Multicoloured.
1417 1b.50 Type **463** 1·40 1·20
1418 2b. Church and statue of Bosco
with child 2·00 1·70

464 Chulumani

1997. La Paz. Multicoloured.
1419 50c. Type **464** 45 35
1420 80c. Inca stone monolith 75 65
1421 1b.50 La Paz and Mt. Illimani 1·40 1·30
1422 2b. Gate of the Sun, Tiahuanaco
(horiz) 2·00 1·90
1423 2b.50 Dancers 2·40 2·30
1424 10b. *Virgin of Copacabana* and
balsa raft on Lake Titicaca
(horiz) 10·00 9·75

465 Emblem

1997. Football Events. Multicoloured.
1425 3b. Type **465** (America Cup
Latin-American Football
Championship, Bolivia) 2·75 2·75
1426 5b. Eiffel Tower and trophy
(World Cup Football
Championship, France (1998)
Eliminating Rounds) 5·00 4·75

466 Parliamentary
Session and Building

1997. National Congress.
1427 **466** 1b. multicoloured 90 75

467 Valley

1997. America. Traditional Costumes. Multicoloured.
1428 5b. Type **467** 5·00 4·75
1429 15b. Eastern region 14·50 14·00

468 Members Flags
and Southern Cross

1997. Sixth Anniv of Mercosur (South American Common
Market).
| 1430 | **468** | 3b. multicoloured | 2·75 | 2·75 |

469 "Virgin of the
Hill" (anon)

1997. Christmas. Multicoloured.
1431		2b. Type **469**	2·40	2·20
1432		5b. "Virgin of the Milk" (anon)	5·50	5·00
1433		10b. "Holy Family" (Melchor Perez Holguin)	11·00	10·00

470 Diana, Princess
of Wales

1997. Diana, Princess of Wales Commemoration.
Multicoloured.
| 1434 | | 2b. Type **470** | 2·20 | 2·00 |
| 1435 | | 3b. Diana, Princess of Wales beside minefield warning sign (horiz) | 2·75 | 2·50 |

471 Presidents of Boliva and
Spain

1998. State Visit of Prime Minister Jose Maria Aznar of
Spain.
| 1436 | **471** | 6b. multicoloured | 5·50 | 5·00 |

472 Juan Munoz Reyes
(President) and
Medallion

1998. 75th Anniv of Bolivian Engineers' Association.
| 1437 | **472** | 3b.50 multicoloured | 3·25 | 2·75 |

473 Linked Arms
and Globe

1998. 70th Anniv of Rotary International in Bolivia.
| 1438 | **473** | 5b. multicoloured | 4·75 | 4·25 |

474 Delivering
Letter, 1998

1998. America. The Postman. Multicoloured.
| 1439 | | 3b. Type **474** | 2·75 | 2·50 |
| 1440 | | 4b. Postmen on parade, 1942 (horiz) | 3·75 | 3·25 |

475 Werner Guttentag
Tichauer (35th anniv
of his bibliography)

1998. Anniversaries.
1441	**475**	1b.50 brown	1·30	1·10
1442	-	2b. green	1·90	1·60
1443	-	3b.50 black	3·25	2·75
DESIGNS—VERT: 2b. Martin Cardenas Hermosa (botanist,
birth centenary (1999)); 3b. Adrian Patino Carpio (com-
poser, 47th death anniv).

476 Amazon Water-lily

1998. Beni. Multicoloured.
1444		50c. Type **476**	35	30
1445		1b. *Callandria* sp.	90	75
1446		1b.50 White tajibo tree (vert)	1·30	1·10
1447		3b.50 Ceremonial mask	3·25	2·75
1448		5b. European otter	4·75	4·00
1449		7b. King vulture ("Tropical Condor")	6·50	5·75

477 River Acre

1998. Pando. Multicoloured.
1450		50c. Type **477**	45	40
1451		1b. Pale-throated sloth (vert)	90	75
1452		1b.50 Arroyo Bahia (vert)	1·30	1·10
1453		4b. Boa constrictor	3·50	3·00
1454		5b. Capybara with young	4·50	3·75
1455		7b. Palm trees, Cobija (vert)	6·00	5·25

478 Rural Activities
and First Lady

1998. America. Women. Multicoloured.
| 1456 | | 1b.50 Type **478** | 1·30 | 1·10 |
| 1457 | | 2b. First Lady, girl at blackboard and woman using computer | 1·80 | 1·50 |
Nos. 1456/7 were issued together, *se-tenant*, forming a
composite design.

479 Town Arms and Church

1998. 450th Anniv of La Paz.
| 1458 | **479** | 2b. multicoloured | 2·10 | 1·80 |

480 Emblem

1998. 50th Anniv of Organization of American States.
| 1459 | **480** | 3b.50 blue and yellow | 3·00 | 2·75 |

481 Magnifying Glass
and 1998 7b. Stamp

1998. "Espamer 98" Stamp Exhibition, Buenos Aires and
25th Anniv of Bolivian Philatelic Federation.
| 1460 | **481** | 2b. multicoloured | 1·80 | 1·50 |

482 "People going to
Church" (Kathia Lucuy
Saenz)

1998. Christmas. Multicoloured.
1461		2b. Type **482**	1·70	1·40
1462		6b. Pope John Paul II (vert)	4·75	4·00
1463		7b. Pope John Paul II with Mother Teresa (vert)	5·50	4·75

483 U.P.U. Monument,
Berne

1999. 125th Anniv of Universal Postal Union.
| 1464 | **483** | 3b.50 multicoloured | 2·75 | 2·50 |

484 Statue of
Football Player

1999. 75th Anniv of Cochabamba Football Association.
| 1465 | **484** | 5b. multicoloured | 4·75 | 4·25 |

485 Red Cross Lorries
at Earthquake Site

1999. 50th Anniv of Geneva Conventions.
| 1466 | **485** | 5b. multicoloured | 4·00 | 3·50 |

486 Bernardo Guarachi and
Mt. Everest

1999. First Ascent (1998) of Mt. Everest by a Bolivian.
| 1467 | **486** | 6b. multicoloured | 5·50 | 4·75 |

487 Winners on
Podium

1999. 30th Anniv of First Special Olympics. Multicoloured.
| 1468 | | 2b. Type **487** | 1·70 | 1·40 |
| 1469 | | 2b.50 Athletes on race track and winners on podium | 2·00 | 1·70 |

488 Golden Palace

1999. Centenary of Japanese Immigration to Bolivia.
Multicoloured.
| 1470 | | 3b. Type **488** | 2·40 | 2·10 |
| 1471 | | 6b. View over lake and flags (vert) | 5·00 | 4·25 |

489 Children dancing

1999. Anti-drugs Campaign.
| 1472 | **489** | 3b.50 multicoloured | 2·75 | 2·40 |

490 Route Map and
Presidents Hugo Banzer
Suarez of Bolivia and
Fernando Cardoso of Brazil

1999. Inauguration of Gas Pipeline from Santa Cruz,
Bolivia, to Campinas, Brazil. Multicoloured.
| 1473 | | 3b. Type **490** | 2·40 | 2·10 |
| 1474 | | 6b. Presidents Hugo Banzer Suarez and Fernando Cardoso embracing | 4·75 | 3·75 |

491 Village
Scene

1999. 50th Anniv of SOS Children's Villages.
| 1475 | **491** | 3b.50 multicoloured | 2·75 | 2·40 |

492 *Hacia la Gloria*
(directed Rau Duran,
Mario Camacho and
Jose Jimenez)

1999. Centenary of Motion Pictures in Bolivia.
Multicoloured.
1476		50c. Type **492**	35	30
1477		50c. *Jonah and the Pink Whale* (dir. J. Carlos Valdivia)	35	30
1478		1b. *Wara Wara* (dir. Jose Velasco)	65	55
1479		1b. *Vuelve Sebastiana* (dir. Jorge Ruiz)	65	55
1480		3b. *The Chaco Campaign* (dir. Juan Penaranda, Jose Velasco and Mario Camacho)	2·10	1·80
1481		3b. *The Watershed* (dir. Jorge Ruiz)	2·10	1·80
1482		6b. *Yawar Mallku* (dir. Jorge Sanjines)	4·25	3·50
1483		6b. *Mi Socio* (dir. Paolo Agazzi)	4·25	3·50
MS1484		180×80 mm. Nos. 1476/83	14·50	14·00

493 International
Lions Emblem

1999. 50th Anniv (1998) of La Paz Lions Club.
| 1485 | **493** | 3b.50 multicoloured | 2·75 | 2·40 |

494 Mt. Tunari

1999. Cochabamba. Multicoloured.
1486		50c. Type **494**	35	30
1487		1b. Forest, Cochabamba Valley	65	55
1488		2b. Omereque vase and fertility goddess (vert)	1·40	1·20
1489		3b. Totora	2·10	1·80
1490		5b. Teofilo Vargas Candia (composer) and music score (vert)	3·50	3·00
1491		6b. "Christ of Harmony" (mountain-top statue) (vert)	4·25	3·50

495 Tarapaya
Lagoon (Inca spa)

1999. Potosi. Multicoloured.
| 1492 | | 50c. Type **495** | 35 | 30 |

1493	1b. First republican coins, minted in 1827 (horiz)	65	55
1494	2b. Mt. Chorolque (horiz)	1·40	1·20
1495	3b. Green Lagoon (horiz)	2·10	1·80
1496	5b. "The Mestizo sitting on a Trunk" (Teofilo Loaiza)	3·50	3·00
1497	6b. Alfredo Dominguez Romeo (Tupiceno singer)	4·25	3·50

496 Globe with Children, Fish, Flower, Pencil, Heart and Stars

1999. America. A New Millennium without Arms. Multicoloured.

1498	3b.50 Type **496**	2·40	2·10
1499	3b.50 Globe emerging from flower	2·40	2·10

497 Children from S.O.S. Childrens Village

1999. Christmas. Multicoloured.

1500	2b. Type **497**	1·30	1·10
1501	6b. "The Birth of Jesus" (Gaspar Miguel de Berrios) (vert)	4·00	3·50
1502	7b. "Our Family in the World" (Omar Medina) (vert)	5·00	4·25

498 Ugarte

2000. Fifth Death Anniv of Victor Agustin Ugarte (football player).

1503	**498**	3b. grey, green and yellow	2·20	1·90

499 El Arenal Park

2000. Santa Cruz. Multicoloured.

1504	50c. Type **499**	35	30
1505	1b. Ox cart	75	65
1506	2b. Raul Otero Reiche, Gabriel Rene Moreno and Hernando Sanabria Fernandez (writers)	1·50	1·30
1507	3b. Cotoca Virgin (statue) (vert)	2·20	1·90
1508	5b. Anthropomorphic vase (vert)	4·00	3·50
1509	6b. Bush dog	4·75	4·00

500 "The Village of Serinhaem in Brazil" (Frans Post)

2000. 500th Anniv of Discovery of Brazil.

1510	**500**	5b. multicoloured	3·75	3·25

501 Granado

2000. Javier del Granado (poet) Commemoration.

1511	**501**	3b. grey, blue and red	3·00	2·75

502 Cyclists

2000. "Double Copacabana" Cycle Race.

1512	**502**	1b. multicoloured	65	55
1513	-	3b. multicoloured	2·20	1·90
1514	-	5b. multicoloured	3·75	3·25
1515	-	7b. multicoloured	5·00	4·25

DESIGNS: 3b. to 7b. Various race scenes.

503 Oriental Clay Figure

2000. National Archaeology Museum Exhibits. Each brown and gold.

1516	50c. Type **503**	35	30
1517	50c. Clay figure, Potosi	35	30
1518	70c. Oriental clay head, Beni	55	45
1519	90c. Clay vase, Tarija	65	55
1520	1b. Clay head, Oruro	70	60
1521	1b. Yampara clay urn	70	60
1522	3b. Inca wood carving	2·20	1·90
1523	5b. Oriental anthropomorphic vase	3·75	3·25
1524	20b. Tiwanaku clay mask	15·00	14·00

504 Male and Female Symbols in Red Vortex

2000. America. Anti-AIDS Campaign. Multicoloured.

1525	3b.50 Type **504**	2·75	2·50
1526	3b.50 Couple walking through wall	2·75	2·50

505 Soldier's Head and Bird on Laurel Wreath

2000. Centenary of Maximiliano Parades Military School.

1527	**505**	2b.50 multicoloured	2·20	1·90

506 Self-portrait

2000. Birth Centenary of Cecilio Guzman de Rojas (artist). Showing paintings. Multicoloured.

1528	1b. Type **506**	75	65
1529	2b.50 Triumph of Nature (horiz)	2·20	1·90
1530	5b. Andina	4·50	3·75
1531	6b. Students Quarrel (horiz)	5·00	4·25

507 Crowd and Brandenburg Gate

2000. 50th Anniv of German Federal Republic.

1532	**507**	6b. multicoloured	5·00	4·25

508 San Francisco Basilica, La Paz

2000. Holy Year 2000. Bolivian Episcopal Conference. Multicoloured.

1533	4b. Type **508**	3·25	2·75
1534	6b. Stalks of grain breaking through barbed-wire	5·00	4·25

509 Waterfall and Statue

2000. New Millennium.

1535	**509**	5b. multicoloured	4·00	3·50

510 Archangel Gabriel

2000. Christmas. Showing 17th-century paintings of Angels from Calamarca Church. Multicoloured.

1536	3b. Type **510**	2·20	1·90
1537	5b. Angel of Virtue	4·50	3·75
1538	10b. Angel with ear of corn	7·75	6·50

511 Painting of John the Baptist and Emblem

2000. 900th Anniv of Sovereign Military Order of St. John.

1539	**511**	6b. multicoloured	4·75	4·00

512 Lobster Claw (Heliconia rostrata)

2001. Patriotic Symbols. Multicoloured.

1540	10b. Type **512** (designated national flower, 1990)	7·75	6·50
1541	20b. Periphrangus dependens (designated national flower 1924)	15·00	13·00
1542	30b. First Bolivian coat of arms (adopted 1825)	22·00	19·00
1543	50b. Second Bolivian coat of arms (adopted 1826)	40·00	34·00
1544	100b. Present day Bolivian coat of arms (adopted 1851)	75·00	65·00

513 Map and Stars of European Union and Map of Bolivia

2001. 25th Anniv of Co-operation between Bolivia and European Union.

1550	**513**	6b. multicoloured	4·75	4·00

514 Statue of Justice, Lion and Portico

2001. 171st Anniv of Faculty of Law and Political Sciences, Universidad de Mayor de San Andres, La Paz.

1551	**514**	6b. multicoloured	4·75	4·00

515 Temple of San Francisco, Potosi

2001. America. UNESCO World Heritage Sites. Multicoloured.

1552	1b.50 Type **515**	1·20	1·00
1553	5b. "Fraile" and "Ponce" (monoliths) (horiz)	4·25	3·50

516 Man carrying Envelopes up Stairs

2001. Philately. Each green.

1554	50c. Type **516**	35	30
1555	1b. Boy with six stamps	75	65
1556	1b.50 Man with glasses and stamp album	1·20	1·00
1557	2b. Child wearing hat, and three stamps	1·50	1·30
1558	2b.50 Humanized stamp lying in tray	2·00	1·70

517 Devil's Molar (mountain)

2001

1559	**517**	1b.50 multicoloured	1·20	1·00

518 Family

2001. National Census. Multicoloured.

1560	1b. Type **518**	90	75
1561	1b.50 People surrounding wheelchair user	1·20	1·00
1562	1b.50 Aboriginal woman and people of different races	1·20	1·00
1563	2b.50 People of different races	2·00	1·70
1564	3b. Children	2·40	2·10

519 Silver Spot (Dione juno)

2001. Butterflies and Insects. Multicoloured.

1565	1b. Type **519**	75	65
1566	1b. Orthoptera sp.	75	65
1567	1b.50 Bamboo page (Philaethria dido)	1·20	1·00
1568	2b.50 Jewel butterfly (Diaethria clymena) (inscr "Diathria clymene")	2·00	1·70
1569	2b.50 Mantis religiosa	2·00	1·70
1570	3b. Tropidacris latreillei	2·40	2·10
1571	4b. Hercules beetle (Dynastes hercules) (inscr "Escarabajo Hercule")	3·25	2·75
1572	5b. Arctiidae sp.	4·25	3·50
1573	5b. Acrocinus longimanus	4·25	3·50
1574	5b. Lucanidae sp.	4·25	3·50
1575	6b. Morpho godarti	4·75	4·25
1576	6b. Caligo idomeneus ("inscr idomineus")	4·75	4·25

520 Map of Americas and Emblem

2001. 21st Inter-America Scout Conference, Cochabamba.
| 1577 | **520** | 3b.50 multicoloured | 2·75 | 2·50 |

521 Woman and
Emblem

2001. Breast Cancer Prevention Campaign.
| 1578 | **521** | 1b.50 multicoloured | 1·20 | 1·00 |

522 St. Mary
Magdalen

2001. Christmas. Showing sculptures by Gaspar of
La Cueva from Convent of San Francisco, Potosí.
Multicoloured.
1579	3b. Type **522**	2·40	2·10
1580	5b. St. Apolonia	4·25	3·50
1581	10b. St. Teresa de Avila	8·25	7·00

523 Portrait and
Casa La Laertad,
Sucre

2001. Joaquin Gantier Valda Commemoration.
| 1582 | **523** | 4b. multicoloured | 3·25 | 2·75 |

524 Flags and Hands
enclosing Farmer,
Mother, Child and
Doctor

2001. 25th Anniv of Co-operation between Bolivia and
Belgium.
| 1583 | **524** | 6b. multicoloured | 4·75 | 4·25 |

525 Aerial
Photograph and
Bridge

2002. Bolivia–Peru Presidential Summit. Multicoloured.
| 1584 | 50c. Type **525** | 45 | 40 |
| 1585 | 3b. Aerial photograph and bridge (different) | 2·40 | 2·10 |

526 Charangos
(guitars) and Musical
Score

2001. Birth Centenary of Mauro Nunez (musician).
Multicoloured.
| 1586 | 1b. Type **526** | 90 | 75 |
| 1587 | 6b. Mauro Nunez | 4·75 | 4·25 |

527 Dancers with
Horned Head-dresses
(Diablada)

2001. Cultural Heritage. Oruro Carnival. Multicoloured.
| 1588 | 50c. Type **527** | 45 | 40 |

1589	1b.50 Female dancer (Morenada)	1·10	95
1590	2b.50 Female dancers and man in embroidered clothes (Caporales)	1·80	1·50
1591	5b. Male dancers in multicoloured head-dresses (Tobas)	3·50	3·00
1592	7b. Woman dancer in elaborate hat and yellow skirt (Suri Sikuri) (vert)	5·00	4·25
1593	7b. Dancers wearing bonnets (Pujllay) (vert)	5·00	4·25

2002. Butterflies and Insects (2nd series). As T **519**.
Multicoloured.
1594	3b. White-tailed page (*Urania leilus*)	2·40	2·10
1595	3b. *Tropidacris latreilli*	2·40	2·10
1596	3b. *Papilio cresphontes macho*	2·40	2·10
1597	3b. Longhorn beetle (*Acrocinus longimanus*)	2·40	2·10
1598	3b. *Prepona buckleyana*	2·40	2·10
1599	3b. *Thysannia agripyna cramer* (left wings)	2·40	2·10
1600	3b. *Thysannia agripyna cramer* (right wings)	2·40	2·10
1601	3b. *Lucanus verde* (inscr "Lucano")	2·40	2·10
1602	3b. Butterfly (inscr "Nymphalidae")	2·40	2·10
1603	3b. *Escarabajo hercule*	2·40	2·10
1604	3b. Butterfly (different) (inscr "Heliconinae")	2·40	2·10
1605	3b. Grasshopper (inscr "Orthopterdae")	2·40	2·10

Nos. 1599/1600 were issued in se-tenant pairs within
the sheet, each pair forming a composite design.

528 "El Kusillo" (folk
character)

2002. Third International Theatre Festival, La Paz.
| 1606 | **528** | 3b. multicoloured | 2·40 | 2·10 |

529 Mountain
Viscachas (rodent),
Potosi

2002. International Year of Mountains and Eco-tourism.
Multicoloured.
1607	80c. Type **529**	65	55
1608	1b. Polylepis (tree), Cochabamba (vert)	90	75
1609	1b.50 Huayna Potosi mountains, La Paz	1·30	1·10
1610	2b.50 Payachatas mountains, Oruro	2·20	1·90
1611	2b.50 Sajama mountain, Oruro (vert)	2·20	1·90

530 Anniversary Emblem
and Rainbow

2002. Centenary of Pan-American Health Organization.
| 1612 | **530** | 3b. multicoloured | 2·40 | 2·10 |

531 Gunnar Mendoza

2002. Dr. Gunnar Mendoza (scientist) Commemoration.
| 1613 | **531** | 4b. multicoloured | 3·00 | 2·75 |

532 Gates Learget 25
over Mountains

2002. 50th Anniv of Military Aviation College, Gemán
Busch. Multicoloured.
| 1614 | 4b. Type **532** | 3·00 | 2·75 |

| 1615 | 5b. Acrobatic aeroplanes (vert) | 4·00 | 3·50 |
| 1616 | 6b. Three helicopters | 4·75 | 4·00 |

533 Orinoco
Goose (*Neochen
jubata*)

2002. Day of Natural Resources. Multicoloured.
1617	50c. Type **533** (CEFILCO philatelic association)	45	40
1618	4b. Orange-breasted falcon (*Falco deiroleucus*) (30th anniv of Bolivian philatelic federation)	3·25	2·75
1619	6b. Black-bodied woodpecker (*Dryocopus schulzi*) (PHILAKOREA 2002)	4·75	4·25

534 Thousand Year
old Cedar Tree and
Church Tower

2002. 400th Anniv of Sucre Monastery.
| 1620 | **534** | 4b. multicoloured | 3·00 | 2·75 |

535 Indian
Madonna

2002. Twentieth-century Art. Multicoloured.
1621	70c. Type **535** (sculpture, Marina Nunez del Prado)	55	45
1622	70c. Mountain (painting, Maria Luisa Pachero)	55	45
1623	80c. Indian mother (sculpture, Marina Nunez del Prado)	65	55
1624	80c. *Cordillera* (painting, Maria Luisa Pachero)	65	55
1625	5b. Venus Negra (sculpture, Marina Nunez del Prado)	4·00	3·50
1626	5b. *Cerros* (painting, Maria Luisa Pachero) (horiz)	4·00	3·50

536 Potosi and
Armando Alba
Zambrana

2002. Birth Centenary (2001) of Armando Alba Zambrana
(historian).
| 1627 | **536** | 3b. multicoloured | 2·40 | 2·10 |

537 Couple wearing
Traditional Costume

2002. Birth Bicentenary of Alcide d'Orbigny (naturalist
and palaeontologist). Multicoloured.
1628	1b. Type **537**	75	65
1629	4b. Boat on river (horiz)	3·00	2·75
1630	6b. Alcide d'Orbigny	4·75	4·00

538 Teacher and Pupils

2002. America. Education and Literacy Campaign.
Multicoloured.
| 1631 | 1b. Type **538** | 65 | 55 |

| 1632 | 2b.50 Indigenous children and computer | 1·50 | 1·30 |

539 Mary and
Jesus

2002. Christmas. Multicoloured.
1633	3b. Type **539**	1·70	1·40
1634	5b. Nativity	2·75	2·40
1635	6b. *The Adoration of the Kings* (painting, 18th-century)	3·25	2·75

540 Apolinar
Camacho

2003. First Death Anniv of Apolinar Camacho (composer).
| 1636 | **540** | 2b.50 multicoloured | 1·40 | 1·20 |

541 Soldier
(statue)

2003. Centenary of Battle of Bahia. Multicoloured.
| 1637 | 50c. Type **541** | 35 | 30 |
| 1638 | 1b. Three soldiers (statue) | 55 | 45 |

542 Anniversary
Emblem

2003. 25th Anniv of Culture of Peace Month (UN peace
initiative). Bolivian Permanent Assembly of Human
Rights.
| 1639 | **542** | 6b. ultramarine | 3·25 | 2·75 |

543 Currency and
Bank Emblem

2003. 75th Anniv of Central Bank.
| 1640 | **543** | 4b. multicoloured | 2·20 | 1·90 |

544 Court Emblem

2003. Fifth Anniv of Sucre Constitutional Court.
| 1641 | **544** | 1b.50 multicoloured | 90 | 75 |

545 Quinoa
(*Chenopodium quinoa*)

2003. America. Flora and Fauna Multicoloured.
| 1642 | 50c. Type **545** | 3·25 | 2·75 |
| 1643 | 1b. Llama | 3·75 | 3·25 |

546 Anniversary Emblem

2003. Centenary of Panama Republic.
| 1644 | **546** | 7b. multicoloured | 3·75 | 3·25 |

547 Porfirio Diaz Machicao, Rosendo Villalobos and Monsignor Juan Quiros (writers)

2003. 75th Anniv of Language Academy.
| 1645 | **547** | 6b. multicoloured | 3·25 | 2·75 |

548 Flags and Latin America

2003. Latin American, Spanish and Portuguese Heads of Government Conference, Santa Cruz. Multicoloured.
| 1646 | | 6b. Type **548** | 3·25 | 2·75 |
| 1647 | | 6b. Eastern globe and flags | 3·25 | 2·75 |

Nos. 1646/7 were issued together, se-tenant, forming a composite design.

549 Virgin of Guadelupe (Brother Diego de Ocana)

2003. 450th Anniv of La Plata Archdiocese.
| 1648 | **549** | 6b. multicoloured | 3·25 | 2·75 |

550 Adoration of the Shepherds (Leonardo Flores) (Templo de Calamarca, La Paz)

2003. Christmas. Multicoloured.
1649		1b.50 Type **550**	90	75
1650		6b. Adoration of the Shepherds (Bernardo Bitti) (Cathedral museum, Sucre)	3·25	2·75
1651		7b. Adoration of the Shepherds (Melchor Perez de Holguin) (Santa Teresa museum, Potosi) (horiz)	3·75	3·25

551 Pope John Paul II

2004. 25th Anniv of Pontificate of Pope John Paul II. Multicoloured.
1652		1b. Type **551**	55	45
1653		1b.50 Seated facing right (painting)	90	75
1654		5b. Giving blessing to native Bolivians	2·75	2·40
1655		6b. Wearing gold cope	3·25	2·75
1656		7b. Seated facing left	3·75	3·25
MS1657	150×110 mm. 10b.×2, Mary of Copacabana and balsa boat on the Lake Titicaca; Santa Tersa de Avila (statue) (Gaspar de la Cueva)		11·00	10·50

552 Girl and Rainbow

2004. Tenth Anniv of ARCO IRIS Foundation (street children's charitable organization).
| 1658 | **552** | 1b.80 multicoloured | 1·40 | 1·20 |

553 Battle Scene (painting)

2004. 25th Anniv of Military History Academy.
| 1659 | **553** | 1b. multicoloured | 55 | 45 |

554 Athens, 2004 Emblem, Rifle Shooting, Gymnastics and Judo

2004. Olympic Games, Athens. Multicoloured.
| 1660 | | 1b.50 Type **554** | 90 | 75 |
| 1661 | | 7b. Emblem, running and swimming | 3·75 | 3·25 |

555 Holy Family

2004. Christmas. Multicoloured.
1662		1b.50 Type **555**	90	75
1663		3b. Child praying	2·40	2·10
1664		6b. Candle	3·25	2·75

556 Typewriter on Wheels

2004. 75th Anniv of La Paz Journalists' Association.
| 1665 | **556** | 1b.50 multicoloured 2015 | 90 | 75 |

557 Palm

2004. America. Environmental Protection. Multicoloured.
| 1666 | | 5b. Type **557** | 2·75 | 2·40 |
| 1667 | | 6b. Parrots (Gilka Wara Libermann) | 3·25 | 2·75 |

558 Map of Bolivia and Emblems

2005. Centenary of Rotary International (charitable organization). Multicoloured.
| 1668 | | 3b. Type **558** | 2·40 | 2·10 |
| 1669 | | 3b. Paul Harris (founder), "100" and emblem | 2·40 | 2·10 |

Nos. 1668/9 were issued together, se-tenant, forming a composite design.

559 Water Pipe Outflow and Beach

2005. Environmental Projects. Multicoloured.
| 1670 | | 5b. Type **559** (Pras Pando (water project)) | 2·75 | 2·40 |
| 1671 | | 6b. Seedling, European Union and Bolivian Flags (PRAEDAC (programme to support alternate development)) (vert) | 3·25 | 2·75 |

560 Striped Cloth

2005. Cultural Heritage. Textiles. Multicoloured.
1672		50c. Type **560**	45	40
1673		1b. Horizontal stripes and dark bands	55	45
1674		1b.50 Vertical decorated stripes and red bands	90	75
1675		6b. Wide black bands	3·25	2·75
1676		6b. Two decorated squares (horiz)	3·25	2·75

561 Otto Felipe Braun

2005. 80th Anniv of Colegio Mariscal Braun, La Paz.
| 1677 | **561** | 6b. multicoloured | 3·25 | 2·75 |

562 Harpia harpyja

2005. Birds. Multicoloured.
1678		1b. Type **562** (Interexpo '05, Dominican Republic)	55	45
1679		1b.50 Penelope dabbenei (35th anniv of Filatelica Boliviana)	90	75
1680		7b. Aulacorhynchus coeruleicinctus (Washington 2006)	3·75	3·25

563 Pope John Paul II and Children

2005. Pope John Paul II Commemoration (1681) and Inauguration of Pope Benedict XVI (1682). Multicoloured.
| 1681 | | 5b. Type **563** | 2·75 | 2·40 |
| 1682 | | 5b. Pope Benedict XVI (vert) | 2·75 | 2·40 |

564 Sail Ship

2005. The Pacific War of 1879–1884.
| 1683 | **564** | 5b. multicoloured | 2·75 | 2·40 |

565 Don Quixote riding Rocinante

2005. 400th Anniv of the Publication of Don Quixote de la Mancha by Miguel de Cervantes.
| 1684 | **565** | 4b. multicoloured | 2·20 | 1·90 |

566 Mother and Child

2005. America. Struggle against Poverty. Multicoloured.
| 1685 | | 6b. Type **566** | 3·25 | 2·75 |
| 1686 | | 7b. Fisherman and fleshless fish | 3·75 | 3·25 |

567 Idelfonso Murguia

2005. 184th Anniv of Infanteria Colorado Regiment (presidential escort).
| 1687 | **567** | 2b. multicoloured | 1·50 | 1·30 |

568 Flamingos in Flight

2005. Tourism.
| 1688 | **568** | 6b. multicoloured | 3·25 | 2·75 |

569 Two-toed Sloth

2005. 20th Anniv of LIDEMA (conservation group).
| 1689 | **569** | 6b. multicoloured | 3·25 | 2·75 |

570 1863 Un-issued 2r. Stamps

2005. Stamp Day. Sheet 91×110 mm containing T **570** and similar horiz designs. Multicoloured.
| **MS**1690 | 2r.×3, Type **570**; 1924 5b. stamp; British 1840 Penny Black (1st stamp) and Brazil 1843 30r. ("Olho de Boi" ("Bull's Eye")) stamp; 4r.×3, 1867 5c. stamps (1st Bolivian stamps); 1930 3b. surch on 20c. ("Graf Zeppelin") stamp; 1987 60c. stamp | | 14·50 | 14·00 |

571 Three Wise Men

2005. Christmas. Multicoloured.

1691	1b.50 Type **571**	90	75
1692	3b. Holy family	1·70	1·40

2006. Nos. 1119, 1115 and No. 1119 surch.

1693	1b. on 1000000p. black and green	65	55
1694	2b. on 550000 multicoloured	1·40	1·20
1695	2b.50 on 1000000 multicoloured	2·30	2·00

575 School Building, 1906

2006. Centenary of Engineering University.

1696	**575**	6b. multicoloured	3·25	2·75

576 President Morales

2006. Election of President Juan Evo Morales Ayma (Evo Morales) (first indigenous South American President. Multicoloured.

1697	1b.50 Type **576**	90	75
1698	5b. At inauguration	2·75	2·40
1699	6b. Wearing tribal dress	3·25	2·75

577 Red Cross Worker

2006. Bolivian Red Cross.

1700	**577**	5b. multicoloured	2·75	2·40

578 Inca Messenger and Envelopes

2006. 15th Anniv of ECOBOL.

1701	**578**	1b. green	55	45
1702	**578**	1b.50 ultramarine	90	75

579 Boy Scouts at Exfivia 75

2006. Stamp Collectors' Day. Sheet 90×105 mm containing T **579** and similar horiz designs. Multicoloured.

MS1703 1b.50 Type **579**; 1b.50 Stamp album; 1b.50 Bird stamps of Boliva and Honduras; 6b. Exfilmar 80; 6b. Ship stamps of Bolivia and Iceland; 6b. Floral stamps of Bolivia and Dominican Republic 15·00 14·00

580 Legislative Palace and Second Adapted National Flag of 1851

2006. Flags. Multicoloured.

1704	1b.50 Type **580**	55	45
1705	5b. Liberty House and first adapted national flag of 1826	2·75	2·40
1706	6b. Liberty House and first national flag of 1825	3·25	2·75

581 Friar and Donkey

2006. 400th Anniv of Franciscan Order in Tarija. Multicoloured.

1707	2b. Type **581**	1·40	1·20
1708	2b. Early church	1·40	1·20
1709	6b. Basilica interior (vert)	3·25	2·75
1710	6b. "La Inmaulada" (vert)	3·25	2·75

582 14-bis

2006. Centenary of First Flight by Alberto Santos Dumont.

1711	**582**	1b.50 multicoloured	90	75

583 Sajama National Park

2006. 400th Anniv of Oruro.

1712	**583**	4b. multicoloured	2·20	1·90

584 9 February Avenue

2006. Centenary of Bahia Harbour. Multicoloured.

1713	1b. Type **584**	55	45
1714	1b.50 German Busch Plaza	90	75
1715	2b.50 Tree (vert)	2·20	1·90
1716	3b. Potosi Plaza	2·40	2·10
1717	4b. Bahia Pando river	2·75	2·30
1718	6b. Friendship Bridge	3·25	2·75
1719	7b. Port Avenue (vert)	3·75	3·25

585 Vicuna

2006. Endangered Species. Multicoloured.

1720	1b. Type **585**	55	45
1721	1b.50 Head of Yacare caiman (Caiman yacare) (horiz)	90	75
1722	5b. Yacare caiman (horiz)	2·75	2·40
1723	7b. Vicuna (horiz)	3·75	3·25

586 Area damaged by Mining

2006. International Year of Deserts and Desertification. Multicoloured.

1724	1b.50 Type **586**	90	75
1725	2b. Erosion, Tolomosa river basin	1·40	1·20
1726	3b. Terraces	2·40	2·10
1727	4b. Erosion, Caranavi	2·75	2·30

587 Low Energy Bulb as Flower

2006. America. Energy Conservation. Multicoloured.

1728	3b. Type **587**	2·40	2·10
1729	4b. Light bulb containing cash	2·75	2·30

588 Virgin of Roses

2006. Christmas. Multicoloured.

1730	4b. Type **588**	2·75	2·30
1731	5b. Adoration of the Magi	3·00	2·50
1732	6b. Adoration of the shepherds	3·25	2·75

589 Rocks (astronomical observatory)

2006. Manco Kapac. Multicoloured.

1733	5b. Type **589**	3·00	2·50
1734	6b. Copacabana Temple	3·25	2·75
1735	7b. Boat on lake	3·75	3·25

590 Toucan

2006. Birds of Pando. Multicoloured.

1736	2b.50 Type **590**	1·40	1·20
1737	6b. Inscr "Pajaro azul"	3·25	2·75

591 Helmeted Curassow (inscr "Pavichi cresta azul")

2006. Birds of Santa Cruz. Multicoloured.

1738	3b.50 Type **591**	2·75	2·40
1739	7b. Harpy eagle (inscr "Aguila arpia")	3·75	3·25

592 Miniature Schnauzer

2006. Dogs. Multicoloured.

1740	1b. Type **592**	90	75
1741	2b. Husky	1·40	1·20
1742	3b. American boxer	2·40	2·10
1743	4b. Inscr "Criollo"	2·75	2·40

593 14 September Plaza

2007. 'Latin America and Caribbean Lions' Forum, Cochabamba, Bolivia.

1744	**593**	6b. multicoloured	3·25	2·75

594 Map of Europe

2007. 50th Anniv of Treaty of Rome. Multicoloured.

1745	3b.50 Type **594**	2·75	2·30
1746	7b. Flag of stars	3·75	3·25

Nos. 1745/6 were issued together, *se-tenant*, forming a composite design.

595 Philatelic Magazines

2007. 50th Anniv of Philatelic Association. Multicoloured.

1747	50c. Type **595**	45	40
1748	1b. Arnold Glaeser (first president) and overprinted stamp	90	75
1749	2b.50 Simon Martinic and stamp catalogue	2·00	1·70
1750	3b. Franz Steimbach and Oscar Roca	2·40	2·10
1751	3b.50 Cathedral and 'Heroinas de la Coronilla' monument	2·75	2·30
1752	6b. 'Christ of the Concord' (statue) and Cathedral, Cochabamba	3·25	2·75

Nos. 1751/2 were issued together, se-tenant, forming a composite design.

596 Charango

2007. Cultural Heritage. Multicoloured.

1753	4b. Type **596**	2·75	2·40
1754	6b. Charango (different)	3·25	2·75

597 Emblem and '90'

2007. 90th Anniv of Bolivian Red Cross.

1755	**597**	2b.50 multicoloured	2·00	1·70

598 Francis Harrington (missionary and institute founder)

2007. Centenary of American Institute.

1756	**598**	7b.50 multicoloured	4·25	3·50

599 Cog, Map and Emblems

2007. 75th Anniv of Chamber of Commerce. Multicoloured.

1757	9b. Type **599**	5·00	4·25
1758	12b. '75 Anos', emblems and cog	6·50	5·75

599a *Ara ararauna* (blue and gold macaw)

2007. Birds. Multicoloured.

1758a	5b.50 Type **599a**	3·00	2·75
1758b	7b.50 *Porphyrula martinica* (purple gallinule)	4·25	3·50

600 Jaguar

2007. Santa Cruz Zoo. Multicoloured.
| 1759 | 6b. Type **600** | 3·25 | 2·75 |
| 1760 | 9b. Puma | 5·00 | 4·25 |

601 Emblems

2007. Heads of the American Air Force Conference, Santa Cruz, Bolivia.
| 1761 | **601** | 10b.50 multicoloured | 6·00 | 5·25 |

602 Andean Condor (inscr 'Opisthocomus hoazin')

2007. Birds of La Paz. Multicoloured.
| 1762 | 4b. Type **602** | 2·75 | 2·40 |
| 1763 | 5b.50 Andean cock-of-the rock (*Rupicola peruviana*) (inscr "Tunqui") (horiz) | 3·00 | 2·75 |

603 Robert Baden Powell (founder)

2007. Centenary of World Scouting. Multicoloured.
| 1764 | 7b.50 Type **603** | 4·25 | 3·50 |
| 1765 | 8b.50 Emblem (vert) | 4·75 | 4·00 |

604 *Cyclarhis guyannensis*

2007. Birds. Multicoloured.
1766	3b.50 Type **604**	2·75	2·30
1767	4b. *Egretta alba* (vert)	2·75	2·40
1767a	5b.50 *Ramphastos toco*	3·00	2·75
1769	6b.50 *Bubo virgianus* (vert)	3·50	3·00
1770	6b.50 *Trogon melanurus* (vert)	3·50	3·00
1771	6b.50 *Falco sparverius*	3·50	3·00
1772	6b.50 *Hymantopus mexicanus* (vert)	3·50	3·00
1774	7b.50 *Platalea ajaja*	4·25	3·50
1774a	7b.50 *Opisthocomus hoazin*	4·25	3·50
1775	8b.50 *Sarcoramphus papa*	4·75	4·00
1776	8b.50 *Momotus momta*	4·75	4·00
1777	9b. *Tinamotis pentlandii* (vert)	5·00	4·25
1778	9b. *Chlorostilbon aureoventris* (vert)	5·00	4·25
1779	10b.50 *Ardea cocoi* (vert)	5·75	5·00

Nos. 1768 and 1773 have been left for stamps not yet received.

605 Signature

2007. 40th Death Anniv of Ernesto (Che) Guevara (resistance fighter). Multicoloured.
| 1780 | 30b. Type **605** | 22·00 | 19·00 |
| 1781 | 50b. Images of Che Guevara (vert) | 40·00 | 34·00 |

606 North American F-86 Sabres on Runway

2007. 50th Anniv of Bolivian Airforce. Multicoloured.
| 1782 | 7b.50 Type **606** | 4·25 | 3·50 |
| 1783 | 9b. Aircraft in flight | 5·00 | 4·25 |

607 Globe and Aircraft

2007. International Day of Civil Aviation. Multicoloured
| 1784 | 6b.50 Type **607** | 3·50 | 3·00 |
| 1785 | 8b.50 Map and aircraft | 4·75 | 4·00 |

608 School Pupils

2007. America. Education for All. Multicoloured.
1786	3b. Type **608**	2·40	2·10
1787	5b. Siembra, siembra no import que otro.....etc	3·00	2·50
1788	6b. Mother and child reading	3·25	2·75
1789	9b. Girl and flowers	5·00	4·25

609 Syncline, Maragua

2007. Tourism. Multicoloured.
1790	2b. Type **609**	1·40	1·20
1791	2b.50 Fescue, Pasto Iro	2·00	1·70
1792	3b.50 Trees in lake	2·75	2·30
1793	5b. Beni river lake	3·00	2·50
1794	5b.50 Manuripi river	3·25	2·75
1795	5b.50 Serranias de Tarija valley	3·25	2·75
1796	5b.50 Zongo valley	3·25	2·75
1797	7b.50 Orthon river	4·25	3·50
1798	7b.50 Tornado in Sajama valley (vert)	4·25	3·50
1799	9b. Bridge over Pilcomayo river	5·00	4·25
1800	9b. Cactus, Isla del Pescador (vert)	5·00	4·25
1801	10b. Chapare river valley	5·50	4·75
1802	10b.50 Salar de Uyuni (world's largest salt flat)	5·75	5·00
1803	10b.50 *Trichocereus camarguensis*	5·75	5·00
1804	20b. Caiman lake	10·00	8·50
1805	30b. Zongo (vert)	12·00	10·50
1806	50b. Plaza Sucre	17·00	14·00
1807	100b. Acoiris waterfall (vert)	22·00	19·00

610 *Holy Family* (Luca Cambiasso)

2007. Christmas. Multicoloured.
1808	3b.50 Type **610**	2·75	2·30
1809	4b. *Adoration of the Shepherds* (Pieter Aersten)	2·75	2·40
1810	6b.50 *The Nativity* (Gregoria Gamarra)	3·50	3·00

611 Globe as Post Box

2008. World Post Day.
| 1811 | **611** | 1b. multicoloured | 90 | 75 |

612 Christ, Map and People

2008. 50th Anniv of ECOBOL (Episcopal social welfare commission). Multicoloured.
| 1812 | 10b. Type **612** | 5·50 | 4·75 |
| 1813 | 15b. Indigenous inhabitants (vert) | 8·25 | 7·00 |

613 Church

2008. Jesuit Church, Santa Cruz. Multicoloured.
| 1814 | 5b. Type **613** | 3·00 | 2·50 |
| 1815 | 9b. Church, veranda and tower | 5·00 | 4·25 |

614 '80' enclosing Emblem

2008. 80th Anniv (2007) of Rotary Club, Cochabamba.
| 1816 | **614** | 20b. multicoloured | 10·00 | 8·50 |

615 Justice and Court Building

2008. 150th Anniv (2005) of High Court of Justice.
| 1817 | **615** | 20b. multicoloured | 10·00 | 8·50 |

616 Centenary Emblem

2008. Centenary of 'The Strongest' Football Club. Multicoloured.
1818	1b.50 Type **616**	1·20	1·00
1819	2b.50 Arms	2·00	1·70
1820	5b.50 Model of *Quinteros*	3·25	2·75
1821	6b.50 Founding team	3·50	3·00

617 Pope Benedict XVI

2008. Pope Benedict XVI. Multicoloured.
| 1822 | 12b. Type **617** | 6·50 | 5·75 |
| 1823 | 15b. Wearing cope | 8·25 | 7·00 |

618 Stadium and Football

2008. Football—No Veto for Altitude.
| 1824 | **618** | 3b. multicoloured | 2·40 | 2·10 |

619 Clock Tower

2008. Sucre 2009–Bicentenary of Independence. Multicoloured.
1825	1b.50 Type **619**	1·20	1·00
1826	5b.50 Bell tower	3·25	2·75
1827	7b.50 Clock tower and '25 de Mayo'	4·25	3·50
1828	9b. White tower	5·00	4·25

620 Emblem

2008. 80th Anniv of Supervision of Banks and Financial Institutions. Multicoloured.
| 1829 | 3b. Type **620** | 2·40 | 2·10 |
| 1830 | 7b. Building facade (vert) | 3·75 | 3·25 |

621 MA 60 in Flight

2008. Air Force—Incorporation of Xian Y7-MA 60. Multicoloured.
| 1831 | 1b.50 Type **621** | 1·20 | 1·00 |
| 1832 | 9b. On ground | 5·00 | 4·25 |

622 Luk'i Negra

2008. International Year of the Potato. Multicoloured.
1833	1b.50 Type **622**	1·20	1·00
1834	5b.50 Sani Imilla	3·25	2·75
1835	7b.50 Saq'ampaya	4·25	3·50
1836	10b.50 Waych'a	5·75	4·50

623 Emblem

2009. First Anniv of Nationalization of ENTEL (telecom company). Multicoloured.
| 1837 | 2b. Type **623** | 1·10 | 85 |
| 1838 | 3b. Men and women (horiz) | 2·40 | 2·10 |

624 Children and Rainbow

2009. 15th Anniv of Fundacion Arcoiris (Rainbow Foundation) (charity for abandoned children).
| 1839 | **624** | 5b. multicoloured | 2·75 | 2·20 |

625 Building Facade

2009. Centenary of Mariscal Sucre National University.
| 1840 | **625** | 3b. multicoloured | 2·40 | 2·10 |

626 Detainees

2009. Freedom for Cuban Five.
1841 **626** 7b.50 multicoloured 4·25 3·50

627 Children

2009. 50th Anniv of Inter–American Development Bank (IDB).
1842 **627** 5b. multicoloured 3·25 2·75

628 Rebels

2009. Bicentenary of Bolivian Liberation.
1843 **628** 2b. multicoloured 1·10 85

629 Building Facade

2009. 80th (2011) Anniv of School for Indigenous Pupils, Warisate.
1844 **629** 2b.50 multicoloured 2·00 1·70

630 Institute of Bacteriology Building

2009. Centenary of National Institute of Health Laboratories (INLASA).
1845 **630** 1b.50 multicoloured 1·20 1·00

631 Building Facade

2009. Centenary of Venezuela National High School.
1846 **631** 3b. multicoloured 2·40 2·10

632 Palm Tree and Building

2009. 50th Anniv of Enrique Lindemann B Educational Unit.
1847 **632** 3b.50 multicoloured 2·50 2·20

633 Bernardo Guarachi

2009. Tenth Anniv of Bernardo Guarachi's Ascent of Mount Everest (first Bolivian ascent). Multicoloured.
1848 50c. Type **633** 40 30
1849 7b. Wearing mountain equip-
 ment (horiz) 3·75 3·25

634 Elderly Couple

2009. Centenary of San Ramon Nursing Home.
1850 **634** 2b. multicoloured 1·10 85

635 Games Emblem

2009. Sucre 2009. Multicoloured.
1851 1b.50 Type **635** 1·20 1·10
1852 9b. Emblem (different) 4·75 4·50

636 Jacks

2009. America. Games. Multicoloured.
1853 1b. Type **636** 80 75
1854 7b. Kite flying 3·75 3·50

637 Bromeliad

2009. 38th Anniv of Philatelic Federation.
1855 **637** 3b.50 multicoloured 2·50 2·20

638 Holy Family

2009. Christmas. Multicoloured.
1856 7b. Type **638** 3·75 3·50
1857 9b. Infant Jesus 4·75 4·50

639 Pres Evo Morales Ayma

2010. Second Term of President Evo Morales Ayma. Multicoloured.
1858 1b.50 Type **639** 80 60
1859 9b. Wearing presidential sash
 and formal dress 1·40 1·20

640 Bi-plane (Potez 25 F-AJDZ) and Part of Envelope

2010. 80th Anniv of First Aeropostale Flight from the Pyrenees to Andes
1860 **640** 9b. multicoloured 2·00 1·80

641 Nevado Chacaltaya Glacier showing Ice Shrinkage

2010. Global Warming Awareness Campaign. Multicoloured.
1861 2b.50 Type **641** 95 70
1862 10b. Nevado Chacaltaya before
 ice shrinkage 1·90 1·70

642 Tupac Katari and Bartolina Sisa

2010. Tupac Katari and his Wife, Bartolina Sisa (Aymara anti-colonial rebels) Commemoration
1863 **642** 1b.50 reddish brown 45 30

643 Pepino

2010. Folklore. Multicoloured.
1864 1b. Type **643** 35 20
1865 2b. Moreno 80 60
1866 9b. Chuncho 3·25 2·75
1867 10b. Kusillo 4·00 3·50

644 Table set with Food for the Dead (All Saints)

2010. Traditions. Multicoloured.
1868 1b.50 Type **644** 80 60
1869 10b.50 Ekeko, God of Abun-
 dance and Wealth 1·40 1·20

645 Flowers

2010. Flowers. Multicoloured.
1870 1b.50 Type **645** 70 50
1871 1b.50 Flowers, butterfly on pink
 flower at right 70 50
Nos. 1870/1 were printed, *se-tenant*, each pair forming a composite design.

646 Rainer and José Luis Ibsen

2010. Rainer Ibsen Cárdenas and José Luis Ibsen Peña (disappeared) Commemoration
1872 **646** 3b. multicoloured 70 50

647 Tank, Modern Military Equipment and Soldiers

2010. Bicentenary of National Army. Multicoloured.
1873 3b.50 Type **647** 1·30 1·00
1874 9b. Personalities and scene
 from early battle 3·25 2·75

648 Footballer, Cyclist and Games Emblem

2010. Youth Olympic Games, Singapore. Multicoloured.
1875 2b. Type **648** 80 60
1876 9b. Swimmer, runner and
 games emblem 3·25 2·75

649 Revolutionary Statue, Cochabamba and Grupo Bicentenario Emblem

2010. Bicentenary of Latin American Freedom from Colonialism (1st issue)
1877 **649** 9b. multicoloured 3·25 2·75

650 Oxen, Basílica Menor de San Lorenzo, Santa Cruz and Grupo Bicentenario Emblem

2010. Bicentenary of Latin American Freedom from Colonialism (2nd issue)
1878 **650** 5b. multicoloured 2·10 1·80

651 Andean Condor (national bird)

2010. America. Multicoloured.
1879 2b.50 Type **651** 1·30 1·00
1880 5b. Patuju (national flower) 2·00 1·80
Nos. 1879/80 were printed, *se-tenant*, each pair forming a composite design.

652 EMI Building

2010. 60th Anniv of Military School of Engineering (EMI)
1881 **652** 7b. multicoloured 2·60 2·40

638a Adult Education

2009. 30th Anniv of JICA (Japan International Co-operation Agency) in Bolivia. Multicoloured.
1855a 1b. Type **638a** 35 25
1855b 1b.50 Children and teacher 50 30
1855c 3b. Drilling for water and
 children at stand pipe 1·30 1·00
1855d 9b. Martial arts class 3·25 2·75

654 Building

2010. Bicentenary of Potosinos
1886 **654** 3b.50 multicoloured 1·40 1·10

655 *Puya raimondii*

2010. Endangered Species. Multicoloured.

1887	1b. Type **655**		35	25
1888	2b. *Leopardus jacobita* (Andean mountain cat) (horiz)		70	50
1889	2b.50 *Atelopus tricolor* (three-coloured harlequin toad) (horiz)		1·00	75
1890	3b.50 *Anairetes alpinus* (ash-breasted tit-tyrant) (horiz)		1·40	1·10

656 Pan Pipe Players (wooden carving)

2010. Birth Centenary of Fausto Aoiz Vilaseca (artist)

1891	**656**	2b. multicoloured	75	55

657 Angel (Baroque sculpture)

2010. Christmas. Multicoloured.

1892	3b. Type **657**		1·10	90
1893	9b. The Nativity (18th century painting) (horiz)		3·25	2·75

658 Jaime Gutierrez

2011. Jaime Alfonso Escalante Gutierrez (educator) Commemoration

1894	**658**	2b. multicoloured	70	50

659 Orange

2011. Fruit. Multicoloured.

1895	1b.50 Type **659**		45	35
1896	5b.50 Mango		1·60	1·40
1897	7b.50 Papaya		2·75	2·40
1898	9b. Avocado		3·25	2·75
1899	10b.50 Banana		3·50	3·00

660 *Chenopodium quinoa*

2011. Cereals. Multicoloured.

1900	1b. Type **660**		35	25
1901	2b. *Amaranthus*		70	50
1902	2b.50 *Chenopodium pallidicaule*		80	70
1903	5b. *Lupinus mutabilis*		1·50	1·30

661 BOA Airliner

2011. BOA Aviation (Boliviana de Aviacion) (state-owned airline)

1904	**661**	3b. multicoloured	1·10	90

662 Eye Test (health)

2011. Bolivia - Cuba Cooperation. Multicoloured.

1905	2b. Type **662**		70	50
1906	2b.50 Dove and faces (solidarity with Cuba) (vert)		80	70
1907	3b. Indigenous woman and Cuban teacher (education)		1·10	90

663 Container Transport (Paraguay Waterway Paraná)

2011. Tenth Anniv of RIBB (Bolivian International Registration of Ships). Multicoloured.

1908	1b.50 Type **663**		45	35
1909	9b. Multi-purpose naval ship		3·25	2·75

664 Emblem

2011. Blood Donation Day

1910	**664**	3b. multicoloured	1·30	1·10

665 Anniversary Emblem

2011. Centenary of UPAEP

1911	**665**	9b. multicoloured	3·25	2·75

666 *Orestias agssii*

2011. Endangered Species. Fish. Multicoloured.

1912	1b. Type **666**		35	25
1913	1b.50 *Cichla pleiozona*		45	35
1914	3b. *Colossoma macropomum*		1·10	90
1915	9b. *Orestias luteus*		3·25	2·75

667 Graph, Equation and Stylised People

2011. 75th Anniv of National Institute of Statistics

1916	**667**	9b. multicoloured	3·25	2·75

668 UPAEP Emblem and Mailbox from 'Jose Joaquin Lemoine' Postal Museum

2011. America. Mailboxes. Multicoloured.

1917	1b.50 Type **668**		45	35
1918	9b. Emblem and mailbox from 'Jose Joaquin Lemoine' Postal Museum (different)		3·25	2·76

669 Star, Girl and Christmas Tree (Sarah Laura Zalles Azeñas)

2011. Christmas. Children's Drawings. Multicoloured.

1919	1b. Type **669**		35	25
1920	9b. Children, Christmas tree and map of South America (Adriana Nahir Peñaloza Cusi) (horiz)		3·25	2·75

670 Symbols of Human Rights

2011. Human Rights Day

1921	**670**	9b. multicoloured	3·25	2·75

671 *Bertholletia excelsa* (Brazil nut tree)

2011. International Year of Forests. Multicoloured.

1922	2b.50 Type **671**		80	70
1923	3b. *Swietenia macrophylla*		1·10	90

672 Saice Tarajeno

2011. Gastronomy. Multicoloured.

1924	1b. Type **672**		35	25
1925	1b.50 Majao camba		45	35
1926	2b.50 Silpancho cochabambino		80	70
1927	9b. Plato paceno		3·25	2·75

673 Coca Leaf Products

2011. Coca Leaf. Multicoloured.

1928	50c. Type **673**		20	15
1929	9b. Coca leaves on plant (vert)		3·25	2·75

674 Workers carrying Pipeline

2011. 75th Anniv of Yacimientos Petroliferos Fiscales Bolivianos (YPFB) (state owned petroleum corporation). Multicoloured.

1930	50c. Type **674**		20	15
1931	9b. Dionisio Foianini (founder) and oil drill (vert)		3·25	2·75

675 Disputed Area

2012. Atacama Border Dispute

1932	**675**	5b. multicoloured	2·00	1·80

676 Children

2012. Year of Non-violence Against Children and Adolescents

1933	**676**	3b.50 multicoloured	1·40	1·10

677 Harvesting

2012. Professions. Multicoloured.

1934	50c. Type **677**		20	10
1935	1b. Using sewing machines (Fabrication)		35	25
1936	3b. Two miners at rockface		1·10	90
1937	5b. Wiping stick on rag (Petro-leum) (vert)		2·00	1·80

No. 1937a and Type **678** are left for OEA Assembly, issued on 7 May 2012, not yet received.

Nos. 1938/9 and Type **679** are left for Tupac Katari, issued on 15 May 2012, not yet received.

680 '@' on Globe

2012. International Day of the Internet. Multicoloured.

1940	1b. Type **680**		35	25
1941	1b.50 Mouse pointer and pixelated globe		55	35
1942	3b. Multicoloured '@' enclosing internet addresses		1·10	90

681 Bicentenary Emblem

2012. Bicentenary of Courage

1943	**681**	1b.50 multicoloured	55	30

Nos. 1944/7 and Type **682** are left for Domestic Animals, issued on 28 May 2012, not yet received.

682 Theropod and Footprints, Niñu Mayu-Sucre

2012. Paleontological Deposits of Chuquisaca. Multicoloured.

1948	50c. Type **683**		20	10
1949	1b.50 Ankylosaur		35	25
1950	3b. Sauropod		1·10	90
1951	5b. Stegosaurus		2·00	1·80

POSTAGE DUE STAMPS

D81

1931

D265	**D81**	5c. blue	1·60	2·30
D266	**D81**	10c. red	1·80	2·50
D267	**D81**	15c. yellow	2·75	3·50
D268	**D81**	30c. green	2·75	3·50
D269	**D81**	40c. violet	4·00	5·50
D270	**D81**	50c. sepia	5·75	7·00

D93 "Youth"

1938. Triangular designs.

D346	**D93**	5c. red	75	75
D347	-	10c. green	75	75
D348	-	30c. blue	75	75

DESIGNS: 10c. Torch of Knowledge; 30c. Date and Symbol of 17 May 1936 Revolution.

129 Allegory of "Flight"

1944

426	**129**	40c. mauve (air)	20	10
427	-	1b. violet	25	10
428	-	1b.50 green	25	10
429	-	2b.50 blue	65	30

DESIGN—HORIZ: 1b.50, 2b.50, Lockheed 10 Electra airplane and sun.

Pt. 1

BOPHUTHATSWANA

The republic of Bophuthatswana was established on 6 December 1977 as one of the "black homelands" constructed from the territory of the Republic of South Africa.

Although this independence did not receive international political recognition we are satisfied that the stamps had "de facto" acceptance as valid for the carriage of mail outside Bophuthatswana.

Bophuthatswana was formally re-incorporated into South Africa on 27 April 1994.

100 cents = 1 rand.

1 Hand releasing Dove

1977. Independence. Multicoloured.

1	4c. Type **1**	25	25
2	10c. Leopard (national emblem)	50	40
3	15c. Coat of arms	75	1·00
4	20c. National flag	1·25	1·40

2 African Buffalo

1977. Tribal Totems. Multicoloured.

5a	1c. Type **2**	15	20
6a	2c. Bush pig	25	20
7a	3c. Chacma baboon	15	20
8a	4c. Leopard	20	10
9a	5c. Crocodile	20	10
10	6c. Savanna monkey	20	10
11a	7c. Lion	30	15
12a	8c. Spotted hyena	20	15
13	9c. Cape porcupine	20	15
14	10c. Aardvark	20	10
15	15c. Tilapia (fish)	1·00	15
16	20c. Hunting dog	25	20
17	25c. Common duiker	30	30
18	30c. African elephant	1·00	35
19	50c. Python	50	40
20	1r. Hippopotamus	1·00	1·00
21	2r. Greater kudu	70	1·50

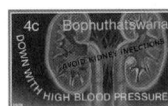

3 Infected Kidney

1978. World Hypertension Month. Multicoloured.

22	4c. Type **3**	50	25
23	10c. Heart and spoon of salt	70	70
24	15c. Spoon reflecting skull, knife and fork	1·25	1·25

4 Skull behind Steering Wheel of Car

1978. Road Safety. Multicoloured.

25	4c. Type **4**	70	40
26	10c. Child knocked off tricycle	90	80
27	15c. Pedestrian stepping in front of car	1·00	1·10
28	20c. Cyclist ignoring stop sign	1·40	1·75

5 Cutting slabs of Travertine

1978. Semi-precious Stones. Multicoloured.

29	4c. Type **5**	65	25
30	10c. Polishing travertine	1·25	85
31	15c. Sorting semi-precious stones	1·50	1·25
32	20c. Factory at Taung	2·25	1·60

6 Wright Flyer I

1978. 75th Anniv of First Powered Flight by Wright Brothers.

33	**6**	10c. black, blue and red	1·00	1·00
34	-	15c. black, blue and red	1·40	1·50

DESIGN: 15c. Orville and Wilbur Wright.

7 Pres. Lucas M. Mangope

1978. 1st Anniv of Independence. Multicoloured.

35	4c. Type **7**	25	20
36	15c. Full face portrait of President	75	60

8 Drying Germinated Wheat Sorghum

1978. Sorghum Beer-making. Multicoloured.

37	4c. Type **8**	20	20
38	15c. Cooking the ground grain	50	70
39	20c. Sieving the liquid	60	75
40	25c. Drinking the beer	65	1·00

9 Kallie Knoetze (South Africa)

1979. Knoetze–Tate Boxing Match. Multicoloured.

41	15c. Type **9**	55	75
42	15c. John Tate (U.S.A.)	55	75

10 Emblem and Drawing of Local Fable (Hendrick Sebapo)

1979. International Year of the Child. Children's Drawings of Local Fables. Multicoloured.

43	4c. Type **10**	20	20
44	15c. Family with animals (Daisy Morapedi)	25	25
45	20c. Man's head and landscape (Peter Tladi)	35	35
46	25c. Old man, boy and donkey (Hendrick Sebapo)	45	60

11 Miner and Molten Platinum

1979. Platinum Industry.

47	**11**	4c. multicoloured	25	10
48	-	15c. multicoloured	35	30
49	-	20c. multicoloured	45	45
50	-	25c. black and grey	60	65

DESIGNS: 15c. Platinum granules and industrial use; 20c. Telecommunications satellite; 25c. Jewellery.

12 Cattle

1979. Agriculture. Multicoloured.

51	5c. Type **12**	20	20
52	15c. Picking cotton	25	25
53	20c. Scientist examining maize	30	30
54	25c. Catch of fish	35	35

13 Cigarettes forming Cross

1979. Anti-smoking Campaign.

55	**13**	5c. multicoloured	40	20

14 Landolphia capensis

1980. Edible Wild Fruits. Multicoloured.

56	5c. Type **14**	15	15
57	10c. *Vangueria infausta*	30	30
58	15c. *Bequaertiodendron magalismontanum*	40	40
59	20c. *Sclerocarya caffra*	55	55

15 Pied Babbler

1980. Birds. Multicoloured.

60	5c. Type **15**	25	20
61	10c. Carmine bee eater	35	35
62	15c. Shaft-tailed whydah	50	60
63	20c. Brown parrot ("Meyer's Parrot")	55	65

16 Sun City Hotel

1980. Tourism. Sun City. Multicoloured.

64	5c. Type **16**	10	15
65	10c. Gary Player Country Club	40	30
66	15c. Casino	45	50
67	20c. Extravaganza	50	70

17 Deaf Child

1981. Int Year of Disabled Persons. Multicoloured.

68	5c. Type **17**	15	10
69	15c. Blind child	30	20
70	20c. Archer in wheelchair	45	35
71	25c. Tuberculosis X-ray	60	60

18 "Behold the Lamb of God …"

1981. Easter. Multicoloured.

72	5c. Type **18**	10	10
73	15c. Bread ("I am the bread of life")	25	25
74	20c. Shepherd ("I am the good shepherd")	35	35
75	25c. Wheatfield ("Unless a grain of wheat falls into the earth and dies …")	45	45

19 Siemens and Halske Wall Telephone, 1885

1981. History of the Telephone (1st series). Multicoloured.

76	5c. Type **19**	10	10
77	15c. Ericsson telephone, 1895	25	25
78	20c. Hasler telephone, 1900	35	35
79	25c. Mix and Genest wall telephone, 1904	45	45

See also Nos. 92/5, 108/11 and 146/9.

20 Themeda triandra

1981. Indigenous Grasses (1st series). Multicoloured.

80	5c. Type **20**	10	10
81	15c. "Rhynchelytrum repens"	20	25
82	20c. "Eragrostis capensis"	20	30
83	25c. "Monocymbium ceresiiforme"	30	45

See also Nos. 116/19.

21 Boy Scout

1982. 75th Anniv of Boy Scout Movement. Multicoloured.

84	5c. Type **21**	15	10
85	15c. Mafeking siege stamps	30	35
86	20c. Original cadet	30	40
87	25c. Lord Baden-Powell	35	45

22 Jesus arriving at Bethany (John 12:1)

1982. Easter. Multicoloured.

88	15c. Type **22**	25	25
89	20c. Jesus sending disciples for donkey (Matthew 21:1,2)	25	30
90	25c. Disciples taking donkey (Mark 11:5,6)	30	40
91	30c. Disciples with donkey and foal (Matthew 21:7)	30	45

23 Ericsson Telephone, 1878

1982. History of the Telephone (2nd series). Multicoloured.

92	8c. Type **23**	15	10
93	15c. Ericsson telephone, 1885	20	20
94	20c. Ericsson telephone, 1893	20	20
95	25c. Siemens and Halske telephone, 1898	30	30

24 Old Parliament Building

1982. Fifth Anniv of Independence. Multicoloured.

96	8c. Type **24**	10	10
97	15c. New government offices	20	20
98	20c. University, Mmabatho	25	25
99	25c. Civic Centre, Mmabatho	30	30

25 White Rhinoceros

1983. Pilanesberg Nature Reserve. Multicoloured.

100	8c. Type **25**	30	10
101	20c. Common zebras	40	30
102	25c. Sable antelope	40	35
103	40c. Hartebeest	60	60

26 Disciples bringing Donkeys to Jesus (Matthew 21:7)

1983. Easter. Palm Sunday. Multicoloured.

104	8c. Type **26**	10	10
105	20c. Jesus stroking colt (Mark 11:7)	30	30
106	25c. Jesus enters Jerusalem on donkey (Matthew 21:8)	35	35
107	40c. Crowd welcoming Jesus (Mark 11:9)	60	60

1983. History of the Telephone (3rd series). As T 19. Multicoloured.

108	10c. A.T.M. table telephone c. 1920	15	10
109	20c. A/S Elektrisk wall telephone, c. 1900	25	30
110	25c. Ericsson wall telephone c. 1900	30	35
111	40c. Ericsson wall telephone c. 1900 (different)	40	60

27 Kori Bustard

1983. Birds of the Veld. Multicoloured.

112	10c. Type **27**	30	20
113	20c. Black bustard ("Black Korhaan")	45	45
114	25c. Crested bustard ("Red-crested Korhaan")	55	55
115	40c. Denhan's ("Stanley Bustard")	70	80

1984. Indigenous Grasses (2nd series). As T 20. Multicoloured.

116	10c. *Panicum maximum*	15	10
117	20c. *Hyparrhenia dregeana*	20	20
118	25c. *Cenchrus ciliaris*	25	35
119	40c. *Urochloa brachyura*	50	70

28 Money-lenders in the Temple (Mark 11:11)

1984. Easter. Multicoloured.

120	10c. Type **28**	15	10
121	20c. Jesus driving the money-lenders from the Temple (Mark 11:15)	25	20
122	25c. Jesus and fig tree (Matthew 21:9)	30	35
123	40c. The withering of the fig tree (Matthew 21:9)	40	70

29 Car Upholstery, Ga-Rankuwa

1984. Industries. Multicoloured.

124	1c. Textile mill	10	10
125	2c. Sewing sacks, Selosesha	10	10
126	3c. Ceramic tiles, Babelegi	10	10
127	4c. Sheepskin car seat covers	10	10
128	5c. Crossbow manufacture	15	10
129	6c. Automobile parts, Babelegi	15	10
130	7c. Hosiery, Babelegi	15	10
131	8c. Specialised bicycle factory, Babelegi	30	10
132	9c. Lawn mower assembly line	30	15
133	10c. Dress factory, Thaba 'Nchu	20	10
134	11c. Molten platinum	60	20
135	12c. Type **29**	40	15
136	14c. Maize mill, Mafeking	50	15
137	15c. Plastic bags, Babelegi	25	15
137b	16c. Brick factory, Mmabatho	60	15
137c	18c. Cutlery manufacturing, Mogwase	60	15
138	20c. Men's clothing, Babelegi	25	15
138b	21c. Welding bus chassis	50	50
138c	21c. Fitting engine to bus chassis	50	50
138d	21c. Bus body construction	50	50
138e	21c. Spraying and finishing bus	50	50
138f	21c. Finished bus	50	50
139	25c. Chromium plating pram parts	30	20
140	30c. Spray painting metal beds	40	25
141	50c. Milk processing plant	50	40
142	1r. Modern printing works	60	75
143	2r. Industrial complex, Babelegi	1·00	2·50

1984. History of the Telephone (4th series). As T 19. Multicoloured.

146	11c. Schuchhardt table telephone, 1905	15	10
147	20c. Siemens wall telephone, 1925	25	20
148	25c. Ericsson table telephone, 1900	30	30
149	30c. Oki table telephone, 1930	40	50

30 Yellow-throated Plated Lizard

1984. Lizards. Multicoloured.

150	11c. Type **30**	20	10
151	25c. Transvaal girdled lizard	25	30
152	30c. Ocellated sand lizard	25	40
153	45c. Bibron's thick-toed gecko	40	60

31 Giving Oral Vaccine against Polio

1985. Health. Multicoloured.

154	11c. Type **31**	40	10
155	25c. Vaccinating against measles	50	30
156	30c. Examining child for diphtheria	55	40
157	50c. Examining child for whooping cough	80	90

32 Chief Montshiwa of Barolong booRatshidi

1985. Centenary of Mafeking.

158	**32**	11c. black, grey and orange	20	10
159	–	25c. black, grey and blue	40	30

DESIGN: 25c. Sir Charles Warren.

33 The Sick flock to Jesus in the Temple (Matthew, 21:41)

1985. Easter. Multicoloured.

160	12c. Type **33**	20	10
161	25c. Jesus cures the sick (Matthew 21:14)	30	20
162	30c. Children praising Jesus (Matthew 21:15)	35	10
163	50c. Community leaders discussing Jesus's acceptance of praise (Matthew 21:15, 16)	50	60

34 "Faurea saligna" and planting Sapling

1985. Tree Conservation. Multicoloured.

164	12c. Type **34**	20	10
165	25c. "Boscia albitrunca" and kudu	25	20
166	30c. "Erythrina lysistemon" and mariqua sunbird	35	30
167	50c. "Bequaertiondendron magalismontanum" and bee	55	50

35 Jesus at Mary and Martha's, Bethany (John 12:2)

1986. Easter. Multicoloured.

168	12c. Type **35**	25	10
169	20c. Mary anointing Jesus's feet (John 12:3)	30	20
170	25c. Mary drying Jesus's feet with her hair (John 12:3)	35	25
171	30c. Disciple condemns Mary for anointing Jesus's head with oil (Matthew 26:7)	45	50

36 Wesleyan Mission Station and Residence of Moroka, Chief of the Barolong, 1834 (C. D. Bell)

1986. Paintings of Thaba 'Nchu. Multicoloured.

172	14c. Type **36**	40	15
173	20c. *James Archbell's Congregation, 1834* (Charles Davidson Bell)	60	60
174	25c. *Mission Station at Thaba 'Nchu, 1850* (Thomas Baines)	65	80

37 Farmer using Tractor (agricultural development)

1986. Temisano Development Project. Multicoloured.

175	14c. Type **37**	20	10

176	20c. Children at school (community development)	30	20
177	25c. Repairing engine (training)	35	30
178	30c. Grain elevator (secondary industries)	50	50

38 Stewardesses and Cessna Citation II

1986. "B.O.P." Airways. Multicoloured.

179	14c. Type **38**	25	10
180	20c. Passengers disembarking from Boeing 707	40	20
181	25c. Mmabatho International Airport	50	35
182	30c. Cessna Citation II	60	50

39 Netball

1987. Sports. Multicoloured.

183	14c. Type **39**	20	15
184	20c. Tennis	30	30
185	25c. Football	30	30
186	30c. Athletics	45	50

40 *Berkheya zeyheri*

1987. Wild Flowers. Multicoloured.

187	16c. Type **40**	25	15
188	20c. *Plumbago auriculata*	35	35
189	25c. *Pterodiscus speciosus*	35	35
190	30c. *Gazania krebsiana*	40	50

41 E. M. Mokgoko Farmer Training Centre

1987. Tertiary Education. Multicoloured.

191	16c. Type **41**	20	15
192	20c. Main lecture block, University of Bophuthatswana	30	35
193	25c. Manpower Centre	30	35
194	30c. Hotel Training School	30	50

42 Posts

1987. Tenth Anniv of Independence. Communications. Multicoloured.

195	16c. Type **42**	25	15
196	30c. Telephone	35	35
197	40c. Radio	35	35
198	50c. Television	40	50

43 Jesus entering Jerusalem on Donkey (John 12:12–14)

1988. Easter. Multicoloured.

199	16c. Type **43**	25	15
200	30c. Judas negotiating with chief priests (Mark 14:10–11)	35	35
201	40c. Jesus washing the disciples' feet (John 13:5)	35	35
202	50c. Jesus handing bread to Judas (John 13:26)	40	50

44 Environment Education

1988. National Parks Board. Multicoloured.
203	16c. Type **44**	25	15
204	30c. Rhinoceros (Conservation)	40	40
205	40c. Catering workers	40	40
206	50c. Cheetahs (Tourism)	55	65

45 Sunflowers

1988. Crops. Multicoloured.
207	16c. Type **45**	25	15
208	30c. Peanuts	35	35
209	40c. Cotton	45	45
210	50c. Cabbages	60	60

46 Ngotwane Dam

1988. Dams. Multicoloured.
211	16c. Type **46**	30	20
212	30c. Groothoek Dam	50	50
213	40c. Sehujwane Dam	50	50
214	50c. Molatedi Dam	70	70

47 The Last Supper
(Matthew 26:26)

1989. Easter. Multicoloured.
215	16c. Type **47**	40	20
216	30c. Jesus praying in Garden of Gethsemane (Matthew 26:39)	60	55
217	40c. Judas kissing Jesus (Mark 14:45)	70	70
218	50c. Peter severing ear of High Priest's slave (John 18:10)	85	1·00

48 Cock (Thembi Atong)

1989. Children's Art. Designs depicting winning entries in National Children's Day Art Competition.
219	18c. Type **48**	30	20
220	30c. Traditional thatched hut (Muhammad Mahri)	40	40
221	40c. Airplane, telephone wires and houses (Tshepo Mashokwi)	45	45
222	50c. City scene (Miles Brown)	50	60

49 Black-shouldered Kite

1989. Birds of Prey. Paintings by Claude Finch-Davies. Multicoloured.
223	18c. Type **49**	1·25	30
224	30c. Pale chanting goshawk	1·40	75
225	40c. Lesser kestrel	1·60	1·10
226	50c. Short-toed eagle	1·75	1·50

50 Bilobial House

1989. Traditional Houses. Multicoloured.
227	18c. Type **50**	25	20
228	30c. House with courtyards at front and side	35	35
229	40c. House with conical roof	35	35
230	50c. House with rounded roof	40	50

51 Early Learning Schemes

1990. Community Services. Multicoloured.
231	18c. Type **51**	25	20
232	30c. Clinics	35	35
233	40c. Libraries	35	35
234	50c. Hospitals	40	45

52 Lesser Climbing Mouse

1990. Small Mammals. Multicoloured.
235	21c. Type **52**	30	20
236	30c. Zorilla	40	40
237	40c. Transvaal elephant shrew	60	60
238	50c. Large-toothed rock hyrax	80	85

53 Variegated Sandgrouse

1990. Sandgrouse. Paintings by Claude Finch-Davies. Multicoloured.
239	21c. Type **53**	90	30
240	35c. Double-banded sand-grouse	1·10	75
241	40c. Namaqua sandgrouse	1·10	90
242	50c. Yellow-throated sand-grouse	1·40	1·40

54 Basketry

1990. Traditional Crafts. Multicoloured.
243	21c. Type **54**	40	20
244	35c. Training	60	60
245	40c. Beer making	60	65
246	50c. Pottery	65	75

55 Sud Aviation SE3130 Alouette II Helicopter

1990. Bophuthatswana Air Force. Multicoloured.
247	21c. Type **55**	1·40	1·10
248	21c. MBB-Kawasaki BK-117 helicopter	1·40	1·10
249	21c. Pilatus PC-7 turbo trainer	1·40	1·10
250	21c. Pilatus PC-6	1·40	1·10
251	21c. CASA C-212 Aviocar	1·40	1·10

56 Wild Custard Apple

1991. Edible Wild Fruit. Multicoloured.
252	21c. Type **56**	50	25
253	35c. Spine-leaved monkey orange	65	70
254	40c. Sycamore fig	70	75
255	50c. Kei apple	85	95

57 Arrest of Jesus (Mark 14:46)

1991. Easter. Multicoloured.
256	21c. Type **57**	45	25
257	35c. First trial by the Sanhedrin (Mark 14:53)	60	55
258	40c. Assault and derision of Jesus after sentence (Mark 14:65)	70	70
259	50c. Servant girl recognizing Peter (Mark 14:67)	75	90

58 Class 7A Locomotive No. 350, 1897

1991. Steam Locomotives. Multicoloured.
260	25c. Class 6A locomotive No. 194, 1897, trucks and caboose (71×25 mm)	95	55
261	40c. Type **58**	1·25	85
262	50c. Double-boiler Class 6Z locomotives pulling Cecil Rhodes's funeral train (71×25 mm)	1·40	1·25
263	60c. Class 8 locomotive at Mafeking station, 1904	1·50	1·75

59 Caneiro Chart, 1502

1991. Old Maps (1st series). Multicoloured.
264	25c. Type **59**	1·10	40
265	40c. Cantino Chart, 1502	1·50	95
266	50c. Giovanni Contarini's map, 1506	1·75	1·40
267	60c. Martin Waldseemuller's map, 1507	1·75	1·90

See also Nos. 268/71 and 297/300.

60 Fracanzano Map, 1508

1992. Old Maps (2nd series). Multicoloured.
268	27c. Type **60**	1·10	40
269	45c. Martin Waldseemuller's map (from edition of Ptolemy), 1513	1·50	95
270	65c. Section of Waldseemuller's woodcut "Carta Marina Navigatora Portugallan Navigationes", 1516	1·75	1·50
271	85c. Map from Laurent Fries's *Geographia*, 1522	1·75	2·00

61 Delivery of Jesus to Pilate (Mark 15:1)

1992. Easter. Multicoloured.
272	27c. Type **61**	25	20
273	45c. Scourging of Jesus (Mark 15:15)	40	40
274	65c. Placing crown of thorns on Jesus's head (Mark 15:17–18)	50	70
275	85c. Soldiers mocking Jesus (Mark 15:19)	60	90

62 Sweet Thorn

1992. Acacia Trees. Multicoloured.
276	35c. Type **62**	30	25
277	70c. Camel thorn	50	60

278	90c. Umbrella thorn	60	80
279	1r.05 Black thorn	70	1·00

63 View of Palace across Lake

1992. The Lost City Complex, Sun City. Multicoloured.
280	35c. Type **63**	40	45
281	35c. Palace facade	40	45
282	35c. Palace porte cochere	40	45
283	35c. Palace lobby	40	45
284	35c. Tusk Bar, Palace	40	45

64 Light Sussex

1993. Chickens. Multicoloured.
285	35c. Type **64**	40	25
286	70c. Rhode Island red	55	50
287	90c. Brown leghorn	60	80
288	1r.05 White leghorn	70	1·10

65 Pilate offering Release of Barabbas (Luke 23:25)

1993. Easter. Multicoloured.
289	35c. Type **65**	60	30
290	70c. Jesus falling under cross (John 19:17)	95	75
291	90c. Simon of Cyrene carrying cross (Mark 15:21)	1·25	1·25
292	1r.05 Jesus being nailed to cross (Mark 15:23)	1·40	1·75

66 Mafeking Locomotive Shed, 1933

1993. Steam Locomotives (2nd series). Multicoloured.
293	45c. Type **66**	65	55
294	65c. Rhodesian Railways steam locomotive No. 5, 1901 (34×25 mm)	75	65
295	85c. Class 16B locomotive pulling "White Train" during visit of Prince George, 1934	95	95
296	1r.05 Class 19D locomotive, 1923 (34×25 mm)	1·25	1·40
MS297	127×113 mm. Nos. 293/6	2·75	3·25

67 Sebastian Munster's Map (from edition of Ptolemy), 1540

1993. Old Maps (3rd series). Multicoloured.
298	45c. Type **67**	50	50
299	65c. Jacopo Gastaldi's map, 1564	65	65
300	85c. Map from Mercator's "Atlas", 1595	75	90
301	1r.05 Map from Ortelius's "Theatrum Orbis Terrarum", 1570	90	1·25

68 Crucifixion (Luke 23:33)

1994. Easter. Multicoloured.
302	35c. Type **68**	65	45
303	65c. Soldiers and Jews mocking Jesus (Luke 23:35–36)	95	80
304	85c. Soldier offering Jesus vinegar (Luke 23:36)	1·10	1·25
305	1r.05 Jesus on cross and charge notice (Luke 23:38)	1·60	1·75

Pt. 2, Pt. 3

BOSNIA AND HERZEGOVINA

Turkish provinces administered by Austria from 1878 and annexed by her in 1908. In 1928 it became part of Yugoslavia.

In 1992 Bosnia and Herzegovina declared itself independent. Hostilities subsequently broke out between the Croat, Moslem and Serbian inhabitants, which ultimately led to the establishment of three de facto administrations: the mainly Moslem Bosnian government, based in Sarajevo ; the Croats in Mostar; and the Serbian Republic in Pale. Under the Dayton Agreement in November 1995 the Republic was split between a Moslem-Croat Federation and the Serbian Republic.

A. Austro-Hungarian Military Post.
1879. 100 kreuzer = 1 gulden.
1900. 100 heller = 1 krone.
1993. 100 paras = 1 dinar.
2002. 100 cents = 1 euro.

B. Independent Republic.
I. Sarajevo Government.
1993. 100 paras = 1 dinar.
1997. 100 fennig = 1 mark.

II. Croatian Posts.
1993. 100 paras = 1 Croatian dinar.
1994. 100 lipa = 1 kuna.
1999. 100 feninga (f) = 1 marka (m).

Republika Srpska.
1992. 100 paras = 1 dinar.
1998. 100 fennig = 1 mark.

A. AUSTRO-HUNGARIAN MILITARY POST

1 Value at top

1879

106	1	½k. black	28·00	30·00
135	1	1k. grey	6·50	1·50
136	1	2k. yellow	4·00	65
137	1	3k. green	6·50	1·60
146	1	5k. red	6·50	80
139	1	10k. blue	9·25	1·20
140	1	15k. brown	8·25	4·50
141	1	20k. green	9·00	5·25
142	1	25k. purple	10·50	8·50

2 Value at bottom

1900

148	2	1h. black	45	15
149	2	2h. grey	45	15
151	2	3h. yellow	45	15
152	2	5h. green	40	10
154	2	6h. brown	60	20
155	2	10h. red	40	10
156	2	20h. pink	£225	11·00
158	2	25h. blue	1·70	40
160	2	40h. orange	£325	16·00
161	2	50h. purple	1·20	80
173	2	30h. brown	£325	11·00

Larger stamps with value in each corner.

162	1k. red	1·50	60
163	2k. blue	2·40	1·90
164	5k. green	5·00	5·75

1901. Black figures of value.

177	20h. pink and black	75	55
178	30h. brown and black	75	55
180	35h. blue and black	1·20	85
181	40h. orange and black	85	85
182	45h. turquoise and black	95	85

4 View of Doboj **5** In the Carshija (business quarter) Sarajevo

1906

186A	4	1h. black	15	15
187A	-	2h. violet	15	15
188A	-	3h. yellow	15	15
189A	-	5h. green	40	10
190A	-	6h. brown	25	30
191A	-	10h. red	45	10

192A	-	20h. brown	95	45
193A	-	25h. blue	2·30	1·60
194A	-	30h. green	2·30	80
195A	-	35h. green	2·30	80
196A	-	40h. orange	2·30	80
197A	-	45h. red	2·30	1·60
198A	-	50h. brown	2·30	1·60
199A	5	1k. red	7·00	3·75
200A	-	2k. green	7·75	16·00
201A	-	5k. blue	6·25	9·75

DESIGNS—As Type **4**: 2h. Mostar; 3h. The old castle, Jajce; 5h. Naretva pass and Prenz Planina; 6h. Valley of the Rama; 10h. Valley of the Vrbas; 20h. Old Bridge, Mostar; 25h. The Begova Djamia (Bey's Mosque), Sarajevo; 30h. Post by beast of burden; 35h. Village and lake, Jezero; 40h. Mail wagon; 45h. Bazaar at Sarajevo; 50h. Post car. As Type **5**: 2k. St. Luke's Campanile at Jajce; 5k. Emperor Francis Joseph I.
See also Nos. 359/61.

1910. 80th Birthday of Francis Joseph I. As stamps of 1906 but with date-label at foot.

343	1h. black		70	40
344	2h. violet		70	40
345	3h. yellow		70	40
346	5h. green		75	40
347	6h. brown		1·00	40
348	10h. red		80	15
349	20h. brown		2·50	2·30
350	25h. blue		4·25	3·75
351	30h. green		4·00	3·75
352	35h. green		4·00	3·75
353	40h. orange		4·00	4·50
354	45h. red		6·00	7·25
355	50h. brown		7·25	7·25
356	1k. red		7·50	7·75
357	2k. green		31·00	29·00
358	5k. blue		3·25	9·75

1912. As T **4** (new values and views).

359	12h. blue	5·50	6·50
360	60h. grey	3·00	5·50
361	72h. red	14·50	27·00

DESIGNS: 12h. Jajce; 60h. Konjica; 72h. Vishegrad.

25 Francis Joseph I **26** Francis Joseph I

1912. Various frames. Nos. 378/82 are larger (27×22 mm).

362	25	1h. olive	40	15
363	25	2h. blue	40	15
364	25	3h. lake	40	15
365	25	5h. green	40	15
366	25	6h. black	40	15
367	25	10h. red	40	15
368	25	12h. green	55	35
369	25	20h. brown	5·00	20
370	25	25h. blue	2·50	20
371	25	30h. red	2·50	20
372	26	35h. green	2·50	20
373	26	40h. violet	8·00	20
374	26	45h. brown	5·00	35
375	26	50h. blue	3·50	20
376	26	60h. brown	5·00	20
377	26	72h. blue	5·00	5·25
378	25	1k. brown on cream	15·00	65
379	25	2k. blue on blue	9·00	85
380	26	3k. red on green	12·00	11·50
381	26	5k. lilac and grey	25·00	29·00
382	26	10k. blue on grey	£100	£130

1914. Nos. 189 and 191 surch **1914**. and new value.

383	7h. on 5h. green	60	75
384	12h. on 10h. red	60	75

1915. Nos. 189 and 191 surch **1915**. and new value.

385	7h. on 5h. green	11·00	16·00
386	12h. on 10h. red	40	55

1915. Surch **1915**. and new value.

387	25	7h. on 5h. green	85	1·20
388	25	12h. on 10h. red	1·90	3·50

1916. Surch **1916**. and new value.

389	7h. on 5h. green	80	80
390	12h. on 10h. red	80	1·00

31

1916. War Invalids' Fund.

391	31	5h. (+2h.) green	1·10	1·80
392	-	10h. (+2h.) purple	1·70	2·40

DESIGN: 10h. Blind soldier and girl. See also Nos. 434/5.

33 Francis Joseph I **34** Francis Joseph I

1916

393	33	3h. black	45	35
394	33	5h. olive	60	60
395	33	6h. violet	60	60
396	33	10h. bistre	2·50	3·00
397	33	12h. grey	75	95
398	33	15h. red	50	25
399	33	20h. brown	90	90
400	33	25h. blue	80	95
401	33	30h. green	80	95
402	33	40h. red	80	95
403	33	50h. green	80	95
404	33	60h. lake	80	95
405	33	80h. brown	2·00	80
406	33	90h. purple	2·00	1·40
407	34	2k. red on yellow	1·20	2·75
408	34	3k. green on blue	1·60	4·00
409	34	4k. red on green	7·00	16·00
410	34	10k. violet on grey	28·00	38·00

1917. War Widows' Fund. Optd **WITWEN-UND WAISENWOCHE 1917**.

411	33	10h. (+2h.) bistre	25	35
412	33	15h. (+2h.) pink	25	35

36 Design for Memorial Church, Sarajevo

1917. Assassination of Archduke Ferdinand. Fund for Memorial Church at Sarajevo.

413	36	10h. (+2h.) black	25	40
414	-	15h. (+2h.) red	25	40
415	-	40h. (+2h.) blue	25	40

PORTRAITS—HORIZ: 40h. Francis Ferdinand and Sophie. VERT: 15h. Archduke Francis Ferdinand.

39 Emperor Charles

1917

416	39	3h. grey	40	30
417	39	5h. olive	25	25
418	39	6h. violet	1·00	90
419	39	10h. brown	40	15
420	39	12h. blue	1·10	90
421	39	15h. red	25	15
422	39	20h. brown	50	25
423	39	25h. blue	1·60	80
424	39	30h. green	70	40
425	39	40h. bistre	60	40
426	39	50h. green	1·60	80
427	39	60h. red	1·60	80
428	39	80h. blue	90	55
429	39	90h. lilac	2·00	1·80
430	-	2k. red on yellow	1·50	80
431	-	3k. green on blue	21·00	29·00
432	-	4k. red on green	8·00	20·00
433	-	10k. violet on grey	4·00	21·00

The kronen values are larger (25×25 mm) and with different border.

1918. War Invalids' Fund.

434		10h. (+2h.) green (as No. 392)	1·30	1·70
435	31	15h. (+2h.) brown	1·30	1·70

40 Emperor Charles

1918. Emperor's Welfare Fund.

436	40	10h. (+10h.) green	80	1·20
437	-	15h. (+10h.) brown	80	1·20
438	40	40h. (+10h.) purple	80	1·20

DESIGN—15h. Empress Zita.

1918. Optd **1918**.

439	-	2h. violet (No. 344)	90	2·30
440	25	2h. blue	90	1·80

NEWSPAPER STAMPS

N27 Girl in Bosnian Costume

1913. Imperf.

N383	N27	2h. blue	65	1·10
N384	N27	6h. mauve	2·30	3·50
N385	N27	10h. red	2·75	3·50
N386	N27	20h. green	3·00	3·75

For these stamps perforated see Yugoslavia, Nos. 25 to 28.

N35 Mercury

1916. For Express.

N411	N35	2h. green	55	65
N412	N35	5h. green	80	1·00

POSTAGE DUE STAMPS

D4

1904. Imperf. or perf.

D183	D4	1h. black, red & yellow	1·20	30
D184	D4	2h. black, red & yellow	1·20	30
D185	D4	3h. black, red & yellow	1·20	30
D186	D4	4h. black, red & yellow	1·20	30
D187	D4	5h. black, red & yellow	5·75	30
D188	D4	6h. black, red & yellow	1·20	30
D189	D4	7h. black, red & yellow	8·25	4·00
D190	D4	8h. black, red & yellow	8·25	1·90
D191	D4	10h. black, red & yellow	1·60	30
D192	D4	15h. black, red & yellow	1·60	30
D193	D4	20h. black, red & yellow	11·00	40
D194	D4	50h. black, red & yellow	5·50	80
D195	D4	200h. black, red & grn	27·00	2·75

D35

1916

D411	D35	2h. red	60	1·20
D412	D35	4h. red	75	1·20
D413	D35	5h. red	1·20	1·20
D414	D35	6h. red	55	1·40
D415	D35	10h. red	80	1·20
D416	D35	15h. red	6·25	9·00
D417	D35	20h. red	80	1·40
D418	D35	25h. red	2·30	3·50
D419	D35	30h. red	2·75	3·50
D420	D35	40h. red	31·00	22·00
D421	D35	50h. red	70·00	65·00
D422	D35	1k. red	4·00	11·50
D423	D35	3k. blue	16·00	43·00

B. Independent Republic.
I. SARAJEVO GOVERNMENT

The following issues were used for postal purposes in those areas controlled by the Sarajevo government.

50 State Arms

1993. Imperf.

450	50	100d. blue, lemon & yellow	10	10
451	50	500d. blue, yellow & pink	15	15
452	50	1000d. ultramarine, yellow and blue	20	20
453	50	5000d. blue, yellow & grn	85	85
454	50	10000d. blue, lemon & yell	1·70	1·70

455	**50**	20000d. blue, yellow & bis	3·25	3·25
456	**50**	50000d. blue, yellow & grey	8·75	8·75

51 Games Emblem

1994. Tenth Anniv of Winter Olympic Games, Sarajevo. Imperf.

457	**51**	50000d. black and orange	1·20	1·20

MS458 78×65 mm. 100000d. black, orange and lilac; 200000d. black, orange and lilac ... 9·75 9·75
DESIGNS: 45×27 mm—100000d. Four-man bobsleigh; 200000d. Ice hockey.

52 Koran Illustration

1995. Bairam Festival. Sheet 105×50 mm containing T **52** and similar horiz design. Multicoloured.
MS459 400d. Type **52**; 600d. Koran illustration (different) ... 11·00 11·00

53 Facade

1995. Sarajevo Head Post Office. Multicoloured.

460	10d.	Type **53**	10	10
461	20d.	Interior	20	20
462	30d.	As No. 461	25	25
463	35d.	Before conflict	35	35
464	50d.	As No. 463	55	55
465	100d.	Present day	1·20	1·20
466	200d.	As No. 465	2·40	2·40

54 Historical Map, 10th–15th Centuries

1995. Bosnian History. Multicoloured.

467	35d.	Type **54**	55	55
468	100d.	15th-century Bogomil tomb, Oplicici (vert)	1·30	1·30
469	200d.	Arms of Kotromanic Dynasty (14th-15th centuries) (vert)	2·40	2·40
470	300d.	Charter by Ban Kulin of Bosnia, 1189	3·50	3·50

55 Postman and Globe

1995. World Post Day.

471	**55**	100d. multicoloured	1·10	1·10

56 Dove with Olive Branch

1995. Europa. Peace and Freedom.

472	**56**	200d. multicoloured	3·50	3·50

57 Children and Buildings (A. Softic)

1995. Children's Week.

473	**57**	100d. multicoloured	1·40	1·40

58 Tramcar, 1895

1995. Centenary of Sarajevo Electric Tram System.

474	**58**	200d. multicoloured	2·75	2·75

59 Simphyandra hofmannii

1995. Flowers. Multicoloured.

475	100d.	Type **59**	1·60	1·60
476	200d.	Turk's-head lily	2·75	2·75

60 Dalmatian Barbel Gudgeon

1995. Fish. Multicoloured.

477	100d.	Type **60**	1·60	1·60
478	200d.	Adriatic minnow	2·75	2·75

61 Kozija Bridge, Sarajevo

1995. Bridges. Multicoloured.

479	20d.	Type **61**	20	20
480	30d.	Arslanagica Bridge, Trebinje	35	35
481	35d.	Latinska Bridge, Sarajevo	45	45
482	50d.	Old bridge, Mostar	55	55
483	100d.	Visegrad	1·10	1·10

62 Visiting Friends

1995. Christmas. Multicoloured.

484	100d.	Type **62**	1·10	1·10
485	200d.	Madonna and Child (vert)	2·20	2·20

63 Queen Jelena of Bosnia and Tomb (600th death anniv)

1995. Multicoloured.

486	30d.	Type **63**	35	35
487	35d.	Husein Kapetan Gradascevic "Dragon of Bosnia" (leader of 1831 uprising against Turkey)	45	45
488	100d.	Mirza Safvet Basagic (125th death anniv) (horiz)	1·10	1·10

64 Places of Worship and Graveyards

1995. Religious Pluralism.

489	**64**	35d. multicoloured	80	80

65 Stadium and Sports

1995. Destruction of Olympic Stadium, Sarajevo. Multicoloured.

490	35d.	Type **65**	45	45
491	100d.	Stadium ablaze (vert)	1·60	1·60

66 Bahrija Hadzic (opera singer)

1996. Europa. Famous Women. Multicoloured.

492	80d.	Type **66**	1·30	1·30
493	120d.	Nasiha Hadzic (children's writer and radio presenter)	2·00	2·00

67 Child's Handprint

1996. 50th Anniv of UNICEF. Multicoloured.

494	50d.	Child stepping on landmine (P. Mirna and K. Princes)	55	55
495	150d.	Type **67**	1·60	1·60

68 Bobovac Castle

1996

496	**68**	35d. black, blue and violet	60	60

69 Roofed Fountain and Extract from Holy Koran

1996. Bairam Festival.

497	**69**	80d. multicoloured	1·10	1·10

70 Town Hall

1996. Centenary of Sarajevo Town Hall.

498	**70**	80d. multicoloured	1·10	1·10

71 Hands on Computer Keyboard and Title Page of *Bosanki Prijatelj*

1996. 150th Anniv of Journalists' Association.

499	**71**	100d. multicoloured	1·30	1·30

72 Essen

1996. Essen 96, International Stamp Fair, Essen.

500	**72**	200d. multicoloured	2·50	2·50

73 Running

1996. Centenary of Modern Olympic Games and Olympic Games, Atlanta. Multicoloured.

501	30d.	Type **73**	35	35
502	35d.	Games emblem	40	40
503	80d.	Torch bearer and Olympic flag	85	85
504	120d.	Pierre de Coubertin (founder)	1·30	1·30

Nos. 501/4 were issued together, *se-tenant*, with the backgrounds forming a composite design of athletes.

74 Campanula hercegovina

1996. Flowers. Multicoloured.

505	30d.	Type **74**	40	40
506	35d.	*Iris bosniaca*	45	45

75 Barak

1996. Dogs. Multicoloured.

507	35d.	Type **75**	45	45
508	80d.	Tornjak	85	85

76 Globe, Telephone and Alexander Bell

1996. Anniversaries. Multicoloured.

509	80d.	Type **76** (120th anniv of Bell's invention of telephone)	1·00	1·00
510	120d.	1910 50h. stamp (cent of post car in Bosnia and Herzegovina)	1·40	1·40

77 Charter with Seal

1996. Granting of Privileges to Dubrovnik by Ban Stepan II Kotromanic, 1333.

511	**77**	100d. multicoloured	1·20	1·20

78 Hot-air Balloons

1996. SOS Children's Village, Sarajevo.

512	**78**	100d. multicoloured	1·20	1·20

79 Muslim Costume of Bjelasnice

1996. Traditional Costumes. Multicoloured.

513	50d.	Type **79**	55	55
514	80d.	Croatian	1·10	1·10
515	100d.	Muslim costume of Sarajevo	1·60	1·60

80 Bogomil Soldier

1996. Military Uniforms. Multicoloured.
516	35d. Type **80**		45	45
517	80d. Austro-Hungarian rifleman		85	85
518	100d. Turkish light cavalryman		1·10	1·10
519	120d. Medieval Bosnian king		1·40	1·40

81 Mosque

1996. Winter Festival, Sarajevo.
520	**81**	100d. multicoloured	1·20	1·20

82 Map and State Arms

1996. Bosnia Day.
521	**82**	120d. multicoloured	1·40	1·40

83 Crowd around Baby Jesus

1996. Christmas.
522	**83**	100d. multicoloured	1·30	1·30

84 Pope John Paul II

1996. Papal Visit.
523	**84**	500d. multicoloured	7·25	7·25

85 Palaeolithic Rock Carving, Badanj

1997. Archaeological Finds. Multicoloured.
524	35d. Type **85**		45	45
525	50d. Neolithic ceramic head, Butmir		65	65
526	80d. Bronze Age "birds" wagon, Glasinac		1·10	1·10
MS527	100×72 mm. 100, 120d. Walls of Illyrian town of Daorson (composite design)		2·75	2·75

86 Ferhad Pasha Mosque, Banja Luka

1997. Bairam Festival.
528	**86**	200d. multicoloured	2·50	2·50

87 Clown (Martina Nokto)

1997. Children's Week.
529	**87**	100d. multicoloured	1·20	1·20

88 Komadina

1997. 72nd Death Anniv of Mujaga Komadina (developer and Mayor of Mostar).
530	**88**	100d. multicoloured	1·20	1·20

89 Trojan Warriors and Map

1997. Europa. Tales and Legends. Multicoloured.
531	100d. Type **89** (theory of Roberto Prays)		1·60	1·60
532	120d. Man on prayer-mat and castle (*The Miraculous Spring of Ajvatovica*)		1·70	1·70

90 Rainbow Warrior

1997. 26th Anniv of Greenpeace (environmental organization). Designs showing the *Rainbow Warrior*. Multicoloured.
533	35d. Type **90**		45	45
534	80d. inscr "Dorreboom"		85	85
535	100d. inscr "Beltra"		1·20	1·20
536	120d. inscr "Morgan"		1·40	1·40

91 Open Air Cinema, Sarajevo

1997. Third International Film Festival, Sarajevo.
537	**91**	110d. multicoloured	1·20	1·20

92 Games Emblem

1997. Mediterranean Games, Bari. Multicoloured.
538	40d. Type **92**		45	45
539	130d. Boxing, basketball and kick boxing		1·40	1·40

93 Diagram of Electrons

1997. Anniversaries and Event. Multicoloured.
540	40d. Type **93** (centenary of discovery of electrons)		75	75
541	110d. Vasco da Gama (navigator) and map (500th anniv of science of navigation) (vert)		1·60	1·60

542	130d. Airmail envelope and airplane (Stamp Day)		1·80	1·80
543	150d. Steam locomotive "Bosna" (125th anniv of railway in Bosnia and Herzegovina)		2·00	2·00

94 Vole

1997. Flora and Fauna. Multicoloured.
544	40d. Type **94**		55	55
545	40d. *Oxytropis prenja*		55	55
546	80d. Alpine newt		1·10	1·10
547	110d. *Dianthus freynii*		1·60	1·60

95 Map and Flags

1997. International Peace Day. Multicoloured.
548	50d. Type **95**		55	55
549	60d. Flags and right half of globe showing Europe and Africa		65	65
550	70d. Flags and left half of globe showing the Americas		75	75
551	110d. Map and flags (including U.S.A. and U.K.)		1·20	1·20

Nos. 548/51 were issued together, *se-tenant*, Nos. 549/50 forming a composite design.

96 House with Attic

1997. Architecture. Multicoloured.
552	40d. Type **96**		45	45
553	50d. Tiled stove and door		55	55
554	130d. Three-storey house		1·40	1·40

97 Sarajevo in 1697 and 1997

1997. 300th Anniv of Great Fire of Sarajevo.
555	**97**	110d. multicoloured	2·40	2·40

98 Augustin Tin Ujevic

1997. Personalities. Multicoloured.
556	1m.30 Type **98** (lyricist and essayist)		1·30	1·30
557	2m. Zaim Imanovic (singer) (vert)		2·20	2·20

99 Sarajevo and Corps Emblem

1997. Contribution of Italian Pioneer Corps in Reconstruction of Sarajevo.
558	**99**	1m.40 multicoloured	1·60	1·60

100 Diana, Princess of Wales, and Roses

1997. Diana, Princess of Wales, Commem.
559	**100**	2m.50 multicoloured	5·50	5·50

101 Gnijezdo (Fikret Libovac)

1997. Art. Multicoloured.
560	35f. Type **101**		35	35
561	80f. *Sarajevo Library* (sculpture, Nusret Pasic)		85	85

102 Youth Builders Emblem attached to Route Map

1997. 50th Anniv of Samac-Sarajevo Railway.
562	**102**	35f. multicoloured	45	45

103 Nativity (icon)

1997. Religious Events. Multicoloured.
563	50f. Type **103** (Orthodox Christmas)		65	65
564	1m.10 Wreath on door (Christmas)		1·30	1·30
565	1m.10 Pupils before teacher (14th-century miniature) (Haggadah)		1·30	1·30

104 Giant Slalom, Luge, Two-man Bobsleigh and Speed Skating

1998. Winter Olympic Games, Nagano, Japan. Sheet 78×60 mm containing T **104** and similar vert design. Multicoloured.
MS566	35f. Type **104**; 1m. Games emblem		1·60	1·60

105 Mosque Fountain

1998. Bairam Festival.
567	**105**	1m. multicoloured	1·10	1·10

106 Zvornik

1998. Old Fortified Towns. Multicoloured.
568	35f. Type **106**		55	55
569	70f. Bihac		1·10	1·10
570	1m. Pocitelj		1·40	1·40
571	1m.20 Gradacac		1·60	1·60

107 Muradbegovic

1998. Birth Centenary of Ahmed Muradbegovic (dramatist and actor-director).
572	**107**	1m.50 multicoloured	1·60	1·60

108 Branislav Djurdjev

1998. Former Presidents of the University of Arts and Science. Multicoloured.
573	40f. Type **108**		45	45
574	70f. Alojz Benac		75	75
575	1m.30 Edhem Camo		1·40	1·40

109 White Storks

1998. Endangered Species. The White Stork. Multicoloured.
576	70f. Type **109**		1·10	1·10
577	90f. Two storks flying		1·40	1·40
578	1m.10 Two adult storks on nest		1·50	1·50
579	1m.30 Adult stork with young		1·60	1·60

110 International Theatre Festival, Sarajevo

1998. Europa. National Festivals.
580	**110**	1m.10 multicoloured	2·75	2·75

111 Footballs

1998. World Cup Football Championship, France. Multicoloured.
581	50f. Type **111**		55	55
582	1m. Map of Bosnia and ball		1·10	1·10
583	1m.50 Asim Ferhatovic Hase (footballer)		1·60	1·60

112 Emblem

1998. International League of Humanists World Congress, Sarajevo. Sheet 104×61 mm containing T **112** and two labels.
MS584	**112**	2m. multicoloured	2·20	2·20

113 Common Morel

1998. Fungi. Multicoloured.
585	50f. Type **113**		55	55
586	80f. Chanterelle		85	85
587	1m.10 Edible mushroom		1·20	1·20
588	1m.35 Caesar's mushroom		1·40	1·40

114 Tunnel

1998. Fifth Anniv of Sarajevo's Supply Tunnels.
589	**114**	1m.10 multicoloured	1·10	1·10

115 Eiffel Tower and Underground Train

1998. Paris Metro.
590	**115**	2m. multicoloured	2·20	2·20

116 Henri Dunant (founder of Red Cross)

1998. Anti-tuberculosis Week.
591	**116**	50f. multicoloured	55	55

117 Vesna Misanovic

1998. Bosnian and Herzegovina Chess Teams. Sheet 109×88 mm containing T **117** and similar horiz designs. Multicoloured.
MS592	20f. Type **117** (silver medal, tenth European Team championship, Debrecen, 1992); 40f. Men's team (silver medal winners, 31st Chess Olympiad, Moscow, 1994); 60f. Women's team (32nd Chess Olympiad, Yerevan, 1996); 80f. National team (11th European Team championship, Pula, 1997)			2·20	2·20

118 Travnik

1998. Old Towns.
593	**118**	5f. black and green	10	10
597	-	38f. black and brown	45	45

DESIGN: 38f. Sarajevo.

119 Postal Workers in New Uniforms

1998. World Post Day.
605	**119**	1m. multicoloured	1·10	1·10

120 Lutes

1998. Musical Instruments.
606	**120**	80f. multicoloured	85	85

121 *The Creation of Adam* (detail of fresco on ceiling of Sistine Chapel, Michelangelo)

1998. World Disabled Day.
607	**121**	1m. multicoloured	1·60	1·60

122 Bjelasnica Mountain Range

1998
608	**122**	1m. multicoloured	1·10	1·10

123 People

1998. 50th Anniv of Universal Declaration of Human Rights.
609	**123**	1m.35 multicoloured	1·60	1·60

124 Christmas Tree (Lamija Pehilj)

1998. Christmas and New Year. Multicoloured.
610	1m. Type **124**		1·10	1·10
611	1m.50 Father Andeo Zvizdovic		1·60	1·60

125 Sarajevo University and *Proportion of Man* (Leonardo da Vinci)

1999. Anniversaries. Multicoloured.
612	40f. Type **125** (50th anniv)		45	45
613	40f. Sarajevo High School (120th anniv) (horiz)		45	45

126 Feral Rock Pigeons

1999. Flora and Fauna. Multicoloured.
614	80f. Type **126**		1·10	1·10
615	1m.10 *Knautia sarajevensis*		1·60	1·60

127 Astronaut, Earth and Moon

1999. 30th Anniv of First Manned Moon Landing.
616	**127**	2m. multicoloured	2·20	2·20

128 Slapovi Une

1999. Europa. Parks and Gardens.
617	**128**	2m. multicoloured	3·25	3·25

129 Gorazde

1999
618	**129**	40f. multicoloured	45	45

130 Children playing Football in Sun (Pranjkovic Nenad)

1999. Children's Week.
619	**130**	50f. multicoloured	55	55

131 House

1999. World Environment Day.
620	**131**	80f. multicoloured	85	85

132 Church, Mosque and Emblem

1999. Philexfrance 99, International Stamp Exhibition, Paris, France.
621	**132**	2m. multicoloured	2·20	2·20

133 Sarajevo on Stamp

1999. 120th Anniv of First Bosnia and Herzegovina Stamps.
622	**133**	1m. multicoloured	1·10	1·10

134 Letters encircling Globe and Telephones

1999. 125th Anniv of Universal Postal Union.
623	**134**	1m.50 multicoloured	1·60	1·60

135 Tuzlait from Tuoanj

1999. Minerals. Multicoloured.
624	40f. Type **135**		45	45
625	60f. Siderit from Vitez		65	65
626	1m.20 Hijelofan from Busovaca		1·30	1·30
627	1m.80 Quartz from Srebrenica (vert)		2·00	2·00

136 Dove and Cathedral

1999. Southern Europe Stability Pact, Sarajevo.
628	136	2m. multicoloured	2·20	2·20

137 Kursum Medresa, Sarajevo, 1537 (site of library)

1999. Gazi-Husref Library. Multicoloured.
629	1m. Type **137**		1·10	1·10
630	1m.10 Miniature from Hval Codex, 1404		1·20	1·20

138 Koran, 1550

1999
631	138	1m.50 multicoloured	1·60	1·60

139 X-Ray and Thermal Image of Hands

1999. Centenary of Radiology in Bosnia and Herzegovina.
632	139	90f. multicoloured	1·00	1·00

140 Kresevljakovic

1999. 40th Death Anniv of Hamdija Kresvljakovic (historian).
633	140	1m.30 multicoloured	1·40	1·40

141 Chess Emblems and Stars

1999. 15th European Chess Clubs Championship Final, Bugojno.
634	141	1m.10 multicoloured	1·20	1·20

142 Twipsy (exhibition mascot)

1999. Expo 2000, World's Fair, Hanover, Germany.
635	142	1m. multicoloured	1·10	1·10

143 Painting (Afan Ramic)

1999
636	143	1m.20 multicoloured	1·30	1·30

144 Globe and Baby

1999. Birth of World's Six Billionth Inhabitant in Sarajevo.
637	144	2m.50 multicoloured	2·75	2·75

145 Bjelasnica Observatory

1999. 105th Anniv of Bjelsnica Meteorological Observatory. Sheet 100×60 mm.
MS638	145	1m.10 multicoloured	1·20	1·20

146 Philharmonic Orchestra Building, Sarajevo

1999. International Music Festival, Sarajevo.
639	146	40f. black and red	45	45
640	-	1m.10 multicoloured	1·20	1·20

DESIGN: 1m.10, Festival poster.

147 Woman

2000. Bairam Festival.
641	147	1m.10 multicoloured	1·20	1·20

148 Map of Bosnia and Herzegovina and Emblem

2000. Olympic Games, Sydney. Sheet 104×72 mm containing T **148** and similar horiz design. Multicoloured.
MS642	1m.30 Type **148**; 1m.70 Map of Australia and stylised sailing boats		3·25	3·25

149 Spaho

2000. 60th (1999) Death Anniv of Mehmed Spaho (politician).
643	149	1m. multicoloured	1·10	1·10

150 Morse Apparatus

2000. 50th Anniv of Amateur Radio in Bosnia and Herzegovina.
644	150	1m.50 multicoloured	1·60	1·60

151 Illuminated Manuscript

2000. 50th Anniv of Institute of Oriental Studies, Sarajevo University.
645	151	2m. multicoloured	2·20	2·20

152 Boracko River

2000. 15th Anniv of Emerald River Nature Protection Organization. Multicoloured.
646	40f. Type **152**		65	65
647	1m. Figure of woman and river (vert)		1·70	1·70

153 Scorpionfish

2000. Greenpeace (environmental organization). Sheet 100×72 mm containing T **153** and similar horiz design. Multicoloured.
MS648	50f. Type **153**; 60f. Crayfish; 90f. Crimson anemone; 1m.50 Wreck of *Rainbow Warrior* (campaign ship)		3·75	3·75

154 Griffon Vulture

2000. Birds. Multicoloured.
649	1m. Type **154**		1·10	1·10
650	1m.50 White spoonbill		1·60	1·60

155 "Building Europe"

2000. Europa.
651	155	2m. multicoloured	3·00	3·00

156 Count Ferdinand von Zeppelin and *LZ-1*

2000. Centenary of 1st Zeppelin Flight.
652	156	1m.50 multicoloured	1·60	1·60

157 Zenica

2000. Towns. Multicoloured.
653	50f. Type **157**		55	55
654	1m. Mostar		1·10	1·10

655	1m.10 Bihac		1·20	1·20
656	1m.50 Tuzla (vert)		1·60	1·60

158 Millennium

2000. New Millennium. Sheet 100×72 mm containing T **158** and similar multicoloured design.
MS657	80f. Type **158**; 1m.20, Millennium (57×57 mm)		2·20	2·20

159 Vranduk

2000. Towns. Multicoloured.
658	1m.30 Type **159**		1·50	1·50
659	1m.50 Franciscan Abbey, Kraljeva Sutjeska		1·70	1·70

160 Tom Sawyer, Huckleberry Finn (characters) and Twain

2000. *The Adventures of Tom Sawyer* (children's book by Mark Twain).
660	160	1m.50 multicoloured	1·60	1·60

161 *People walking* (Ismet Mujezinovic)

2000. Paintings. Multicoloured.
661	60f. Type **161**		65	65
662	80f. *Trees* (Ivo Seremet)		85	85

162 Children and Globe

2000. International Children's Week.
663	162	1m.60 multicoloured	1·70	1·70

163 Refugees

2000. 50th Anniv of United Nations Commissioner for Refugees.
664	163	1m. multicoloured	1·10	1·10

164 Tesanj

2001. Towns. Multicoloured.
665	10f. Type **164**		10	10
666	20f. Bugojno (horiz)		20	20
667	30f. Konjic (horiz)		35	35
668	35f. Zivinice (horiz)		45	45
669	2m. Cazin (horiz)		2·20	2·20

165 Horse wearing Skirt

2001. Thelma (cartoon character). Sheet 125×170 mm containing T **165** and similar vert designs. Multicoloured.
MS670 30f. Type **165**; 30f. Bear chased by bees; 30f. Cat and boot; 30f. Thelma wet from watering can; 30f. Roast turkey 1·60 1·60

166 Kingfisher (*Alcedo athinis*)

2001. Fauna. Multicoloured.
671	90f. Type **166**	1·30	1·30
672	1m.10 Bohemian waxwing (*Bombycilla garrulous*)	1·40	1·40
673	1m.10 Serbian work horse (*Equus caballus*)	1·40	1·40
674	1m.90 Head of Serbian horse	2·40	2·40

167 Disney

2001. Birth Centenary of Walt Disney (film maker).
| 675 | **167** | 1m.10 multicoloured | 1·20 | 1·20 |

168 Sea Snail

2001. Fossils. Multicoloured.
| 676 | 1m.30 Type **168** | 1·40 | 1·40 |
| 677 | 1m.80 Ammonite | 1·80 | 1·80 |

169 Land and Sea Sports

2001. 14th Mediterranean Games, Tunis.
| 678 | **169** | 1m.30 multicoloured | 1·40 | 1·40 |

170 Swans on Lake

2001. Europa. Water Resources. Sheet 60×81 mm.
MS679 **170** 2m. multicoloured 3·25 3·25

171 Building

2001. Adil Zulfikarpasic Foundation Bosniak Institute (inter-denominational foundation). Sheet 81×50 mm.
MS680 **171** 1m.10 multicoloured 1·20 1·20

172 Balic

2001. Emir Balic (bridge diving competition winner). Sheet 66×47 mm.
MS681 **172** 2m. multicoloured 2·20 2·20

173 Ferrari 625 F1 (1954)

2001. Ferrari Racing Cars. Multicoloured.
682	40f. Type **173**	45	45
683	60f. Ferrari 312 B (1970)	65	65
684	1m.30 Ferrari 312 T3 (1978)	1·40	1·40
685	1m.70 Ferrari 126 C3 (1983)	1·80	1·80

174 Zeljeznicar, Sarajevo Football Team

2001. National Football Champions, 2001.
| 686 | **174** | 1m. multicoloured | 1·20 | 1·20 |

175 Ink Well, Quill Pen, Medal and Dove

2001. Centenary of First Nobel Prize.
| 687 | **175** | 1m.50 multicoloured | 1·70 | 1·70 |

176 Charlie Chaplin

2001. Charlie Chaplin Commemoration.
| 688 | **176** | 1m.60 multicoloured | 1·90 | 1·90 |

177 *Traces* (Edin Numankadic)

2001. Art. Multicoloured.
| 689 | 80f. Type **177** | 1·20 | 1·20 |
| 690 | 2m. *David* (detail) (sculpture) | 2·30 | 2·30 |

178 Feeding Bottle enclosed in Stop Sign and Baby at Breast

2001. International Breastfeeding Week.
| 691 | **178** | 1m.10 multicoloured | 1·40 | 1·40 |

179 Acropolis, Castle and Pyramid

2001. United Nations Year of Dialogue Among Civilizations.
| 692 | **179** | 1m.30 multicoloured | 1·60 | 1·60 |

180 Horse-drawn Tram

2001. Posteurop Plenary, Sarajevo.
| 693 | **180** | 1m.10 multicoloured | 1·40 | 1·40 |

181 Alija Bejtic and Monument

2001. 20th Death Anniv of Alija Bejtic (cultural historian).
| 694 | **181** | 80f. multicoloured | 95 | 95 |

182 Albert Einstein and Formula

2001. 80th Anniv of Albert Einstein's Nobel Prize for Physics (photoelectric effect).
| 695 | **182** | 1m.50 multicoloured | 1·70 | 1·70 |

183 Davorin Popovic

2002. First Death Anniv of Davorin Popovic (musician).
| 696 | **183** | 38f. multicoloured | 60 | 60 |

184 Bridge, Figure and Books

2002. 350th Birth Anniv of Mustafa Ejubovic (Sejh Jujo) (writer).
| 697 | **184** | 1m. multicoloured | 1·20 | 1·20 |

185 Juraj Neidhardt

2002. Birth Centenary (2001) of Juraj Neidhardt (architect).
| 698 | **185** | 1m. multicoloured | 1·20 | 1·20 |

186 Sevala Zidzic

2002. Birth Centenary (2003) of Sevala Zidzic (first female Bosnian doctor).
| 699 | **186** | 1m.30 multicoloured | 1·70 | 1·70 |

187 Skier

2002. Sarajevo's Candidacy for Winter Olympic Games, 2010.
| 700 | **187** | 1m.50 multicoloured | 1·80 | 1·80 |

188 Trees

2002. International Earth Day.
| 701 | **188** | 2m. multicoloured | 2·40 | 2·40 |

189 Scout Camp

2002. 80th Anniv of Bosnian Scouts.
| 702 | **189** | 1m. multicoloured | 1·20 | 1·20 |

190 Gentian (*Gentiana dinarica*)

2002. Flora. Multicoloured.
| 703 | 1m. Type **190** | 1·40 | 1·40 |
| 704 | 1m.50 Aquilegia (*Aquilegia dinarica*) | 2·20 | 2·20 |

191 *War and Peace* (Asad Nuhanovic)

2002. Tenth Anniv of Independence.
| 705 | **191** | 2m.50 multicoloured | 3·50 | 3·50 |

192 Apollo (*Parnassius Apollo*)

2002. Butterflies. Multicoloured.
| 706 | 1m.50 Type **192** | 1·80 | 1·80 |
| 707 | 2m.50 Scarce swallowtail (*Iphiclides podalirius*) | 3·50 | 3·50 |

193 Firemen fighting Fire

2002. 120th Anniv of Sarajevo Fire Brigades. Sheet 68×48 mm.
MS708 **193** 2m.20 multicoloured 3·00 3·00

194 Clown

2002. Europa. Circus.
709 **194** 2m.50 multicoloured 3·50 3·50

195 Boy wearing Gag

2002. Letter Writing Campaign. Sheet 120×105 mm containing T **195** and similar vert designs showing scenes from *Young Philatelists* (animated film). Multicoloured.
MS710 40f. Type **195**; 40f. Boy with burnt face; 40f. Boy hit by frying pan; 40f. Boy hit by hammer; 40f. Boy hit with saucepan lids 3·25 3·25

196 Cevapcici (traditional dish)

2002
711 **196** 1m.10 multicoloured 1·70 1·70

197 Galley

2002. Roman Ships. Sheet 90×54 mm containing T **197** and similar horiz design. Multicoloured.
MS712 1m.20 Type **197**; 1m.80 Galleon 4·00 4·00

198 White Water Rafting

2002. 30th Anniv of Una International Regatta.
713 **198** 1m.30 multicoloured 1·90 1·90

199 Association Emblem

2002. Centenary of Napredak (Croatian cultural association).
714 **199** 1m. multicoloured 1·50 1·50

200 Mountaineer and Hut

2002. 110th Anniv of Mountaineering Association.
715 **200** 1m. multicoloured 1·50 1·50

201 Synagogue

2002. Centenary of Ashkenazi Synagogue, Sarajevo.
716 **201** 2m. multicoloured 3·00 3·00

202 Metal Worker

2002. Traditional Crafts. Sheet 110×75 mm containing T **202** and similar horiz designs. Multicoloured.
MS717 80f. Type **202**; 1m.10 Leather worker; 1m 20 Filigree jewellery; 1m.30 Lace work 6·50 6·50

203 Bosnia and Herzegovina Flag

2002
718 **203** 1m. multicoloured 1·50 1·50

204 Coin and Map of Europe

2002. "The Euro" (European currency).
719 **204** 2m. multicoloured 3·00 3·00

205 Tvrtka I Coin (1376-1391)

2002. Old Coins.
720 **205** 20f. grey, red and black 25 25
721 — 30f. green, red and black 40 40
722 — 50f. blue, red and black 65 65
DESIGNS: 20f. Type **205**; 30f. Stepana Tomasa coin (1443-1461); 50f. Stepana Tomasevita coin (1461-1463).

206 Mother and Child Institute, Sarajevo

2002
723 **206** 38f. multicoloured 65 65

207 Horse's Head

2002. Art. Multicoloured.
724 **207** 40f. Type **207** 65 65
725 1m.10 Portrait of a woman (25×42 mm) 1·70 1·70
726 1m.50 Sculpture and portrait of two women (42×25 mm) 2·30 2·30

208 Mak Dizdar

2002. 85th Birth Anniv of Mak Dizdar (poet).
727 **208** 1m. multicoloured 1·50 1·50

209 Emaciated Man

2002. Anti-Drugs Campaign.
728 **209** 1m. multicoloured 25 25

210 Josip Stadler

2003. 160th Birth Anniv of Josip Stadler (first archbishop).
729 **210** 50f. multicoloured 65 65
A stamp of the same design was issued by Bosnia and Herzegovina Croatian Posts.

211 Musician

2003. Centenary of Bosnian Cultural Union "Preporod".
730 **211** 1m. multicoloured 1·30 1·30

212 Stylized Skier

2003. European Nordic Skiing Competition, Sarajevo (2006).
731 **212** 1m. multicoloured 1·30 1·30

213 "Mother and Child"

2003. Birth Centenary of Omer Mujadzic (artist).
732 **213** 70f. multicoloured 1·10 1·00

214 Svetozar Zimonjic

2003. 75th Birth Anniv of Svetozar Zimonjic (president of Sciences and Arts Academy).
733 **214** 90f. multicoloured 1·30 1·30

215 Edelweiss (*Leontopodium alpinium*)

2003. Flowers. Multicoloured.
734 90f. Type **215** 1·30 1·30
735 90f. Yellow gentian (*Gentiana symphyandra*) 1·30 1·30

216 Team Members

2003. National Volleyball Team—World Champions, 2002.
736 **216** 1m. multicoloured 1·70 1·50

217 Butterflies

2003. Europa. Poster Art.
737 **217** 1m. multicoloured 4·25 3·75

218 Pope John Paul II and Ivan Merz

2003. Second Visit of Pope John Paul II.
738 **218** 1m.50 multicoloured 2·50 2·30
A stamp of the same design was issued by Bosnia and Herzegovina Croatian Posts.

219 Stylized DNA

2003. 50th Anniv of the Discovery of DNA (genetic material).
739 **219** 50f. multicoloured 75 65

220 Man on Rooftop

2003. Letter Writing Campaign. Sheet 116×73 mm containing T **220** and similar horiz designs showing scenes from *The Sleep of Monsters* (graphic novel by Enki Bilal). Multicoloured.
MS740 50f.×4, Type **220**; Flying taxi; Man and woman (37×25 mm); Faces (37×25 mm) 3·00 2·75

221 Arches, Cekrelci Muslihudin Mosque

2003. Architecture. Multicoloured.
741 1m. Type **221** 2·30 2·30
742 2m. Hajji Sinan Dervish Convent, Sarajevo (30×30 mm) 4·75 4·75

222 *Skakavac Waterfall* (Helena Skec)

2003
743	**222**	1m.50 multicoloured	3·50	3·50

223 Children

2003. Children's Week. Ordinary gum or Self-adhesive gum.
744	**223**	50f. multicoloured	1·00	1·00

224 *Alija Izetbegovic*

2003. Alija Izetbegovic (first president) Commemoration. Sheet 68×52 mm.
MS746	**224**	2m. multicoloured	4·75	4·75

225 Lamps and Clock

2003. 90th Anniv of Post Building, Sarajevo. Sheet 80×65 mm.
MS747	**225**	3m. multicoloured	7·00	7·00

226 *Chamois* (*Rupicapra rupicapra*)

2003. Fauna. Multicoloured.
748	**226**	30f. Type **226**	80	80
749		50f. Grizzly bear (*Ursus arctos*)	1·20	1·20

227 *Plemenitas II* (Dzevad Hozo)

2003
750	**227**	10f. multicoloured	1·00	1·00

228 Sleigh and Hands holding Present

2003. Christmas.
751	**228**	20f. multicoloured	1·00	1·00

229 Orville and Wilbur Wright and Wright *Flyer I*

2003. Centenary of Powered Flight.
752	**229**	1m. multicoloured	2·40	2·40

230 Allegorical Painting

2003. 65th Birth Anniv of Ibrahim Ljubovic (artist).
753	**230**	1m.50 multicoloured	3·75	3·75

231 Bird

2004. Bayram Festival.
754	**231**	50f. multicoloured	1·30	1·30

232 Kulin on Horseback

2004. 800th Anniv of Reign of Kulin Ban (king).
755	**232**	50f. multicoloured	1·20	1·20

233 Aries

2004. Western Zodiac. Multicoloured. (a) Self-adhesive.
756		50f. Type **233**	95	95
757		50f. Taurus	95	95
758		50f. Gemini	95	95
759		50f. Cancer	95	95
760		50f. Leo	95	95
761		50f. Virgo	95	95
762		50f. Libra	95	95
763		50f. Scorpio	95	95
764		50f. Sagittarius	95	95
765		50f. Capricorn	95	95
766		50f. Aquarius	95	95
767		50f. Pisces	95	95

(b) Ordinary gum.
MS768	200×130 mm. 50f.×12, Nos. 756/67		14·00	14·00

234 Hearts

2004. St. Valentine's Day.
769	**234**	2m. multicoloured	4·75	4·75

235 Gloved Hand holding Torch

2004. 20th Anniv of Winter Olympics, Sarajevo.
770	**235**	1m.50 multicoloured	3·50	3·50

236 Jajce

2004. Towns. Multicoloured.
770a		10f. Breko (horiz)	40	40
771		20f. Type **236**	60	60
771a		20f. Livno (horiz)	60	60
771b		30f. Vissoko	80	80
772		50f. Jablanica (horiz)	1·20	1·20
771c		1m. Sanski Most	2·30	2·30
773		2m. Stolac (horiz)	4·75	4·75
774		4m. Gradacac	9·25	9·25
775		5m. Fojinca (horiz)	11·50	11·50

237 *Cattleya intermedia*

2004. Orchids. Multicoloured.
780	**237**	1m.50 Type **237**	4·00	4·00
781		2m. *Brassavola*	5·00	5·00

Nos. 780/1 were issued in *se-tenant* pairs within the sheet and were impregnated with the scent of orchid.

238 *Aloe barbardensis*

2004. Succulents. Multicoloured.
782		1m.50 Type **238**	4·00	4·00
783		2m. *Carnegiea gigantean*	5·00	5·00

239 Centenary Emblem

2004. Centenary of FIFA (Federation Internationale de Football Association).
784	**239**	2m. multicoloured	4·75	4·75

240 Alarm Clock on Skis

2004. Europa. Holidays. Multicoloured.
785		1m. Type **240**	2·30	2·30
786		1m.50 Alarm clocks on beach	3·50	3·50

241 Speech Bubbles

2004. European Youth Peace Conference, Sarajevo.
787	**241**	1m.50 multicoloured	3·75	3·75

242 Clown holding Balloons

2004. Greetings Stamps. Multicoloured.
788	**242**	50f. Type **242** (birthday)	95	95
789		1m. Bride and bridegroom (wedding)	3·25	3·25

243 Bee on Flower

2004. Bees. Sheet 100×50 mm containing T **243** and similar horiz design. Multicoloured.
MS790		2m.×2, Type **243**; Flying bee	8·75	8·75

244 *Old Bridge, Mostar* (painting)

2004. Reconstruction of Mostar Bridge. Multicoloured.
791		50f. Type **244**	1·20	1·20
792		100f. Bridge (different)	2·30	2·30
MS793		287×110 mm. Nos. 791/2	3·50	3·50

245 Athlete and Horses' Heads

2004. Olympic Games, Athens. Sheet 101×71 mm.
MS794	**245**	2m. multicoloured	4·75	4·75

246 "10" in Lights

2004. Tenth International Film Festival, Sarajevo.
795	**246**	1m.50 vermilion, yellow and black	3·50	3·50

247 Abstract

2004. New Year.
796	**247**	1m. multicoloured	2·30	2·30

248 Svrzo House (18th-century Ottoman house)

2004. Cultural Heritage. Houses. Multicoloured.
797		1m. Type **248**	2·40	2·40
798		1m. Despic house (Serbian merchant's house)	2·40	2·40

249 Emblem, "50" and "@"

2004. 50th Anniv of European Cultural Convention.
799	**249**	1m.50 multicoloured	3·50	3·50

250 *Prozori* (window) (Safet Zec)

2004. Art.
800 **250** 2m. multicoloured 4·75 4·75

251 Nikola Sop

2004. Birth Centenary of Nikola Sop (writer).
801 **251** 3m. multicoloured 7·00 7·00

252 Auditorium

2005. 50th Anniv of Chamber Theatre 55.
802 **252** 40f. multicoloured 1·00 1·00

253 Dam

2005. 50th Anniv of Jablanica Hydroelectric Power Plant.
803 **253** 60f. multicoloured 1·40 1·40

254 Electric Tram

2005. 110th Anniv of Electrification and First Electric Tram.
804 **254** 2m. multicoloured 4·75 4·75

255 Izet Sarajlic

2005. 75th Birth Anniv of Izet Sarajlic (writer).
805 **255** 1m. multicoloured 2·30 2·30

256 Hasan Kickic

2005. Birth Centenary of Hasan Kickic (writer).
806 **256** 1m.50 multicoloured 3·50 3·50

257 *Rosa damascene*

2005. Roses. Multicoloured.
807 80f. Type **257** 1·60 1·60
808 1m.20 *Rosa alba* 2·30 2·30

258 Baklava

2005. Europa. Gastronomy. Multicoloured.
809 **258** 2m. Type **258** 3·50 3·50
810 2m. Sogon Dolma (stuffed
 onions) 3·50 3·50
MS811 115×88 mm. Nos. 809/10 7·00 7·00
 The stamps and margin of No. **MS**811 form a compos-
ite design of a table laid with food.

259 Partridge (inscr "Tatro urogallus")

2005. Fauna. Multicoloured.
812 2m. Type **259** 3·50 3·50
813 3m. Beaver (*Castor fiber*) 5·25 5·25

260 Sportsmen

2005. Mediterranean Games, Almeria.
814 **260** 1m. multicoloured 1·80 1·80

261 Composers and Building Facade

2005. 50th Anniv of Sarajevo Music Academy.
815 **261** 1m. multicoloured 1·80 1·80

262 Grieving Women

2005. Tenth Anniv of Srebrenica Massacre.
816 **262** 1m. multicoloured 1·80 1·80

263 Sarajevo and Doha

2005
817 **263** 2m. multicoloured 3·50 3·50
 A stamp of the same design was issued by Qatar.

264 Emblem and Post Van (EMS)

2005. Postal Service. Multicoloured.
818 10f. Type **264** 45 45
819 20f. Emblem and sorter (hybrid
 mail) 60 60
820 30f. Emblem and "IZBOR JE
 VAS!" (door to door) 75 75
821 50f. Emblem and pigeons
 (philately) 1·00 1·00

265 *Pyrus communis*

2005. Fruit. Multicoloured.
822 1m. Type **265** 2·10 2·10
823 1m.50 Orange (inscr "Orange
 carica") 3·25 3·25
824 2m. *Ficus carica* 4·25 4·25
825 2m.50 *Prunus domestica* 5·25 5·25
826 5m. Cherry (inscr "Prunus
 avium") 10·50 10·50

266 Column and Garden (Hakija Kulenovic)

2005. Birth Centenary of Hakija Kulenovic (artist).
827 **266** 2m. multicoloured 4·75 4·75

267 Dogs and Girl

2005. Youth Stamps. Sheet 96×72 mm containing T **267**
 and similar vert design. Multicoloured.
MS828 50f.×2, Type **267**; Hedgehog
windsurfing 2·40 2·40

268 Trade Union Building

2005. Centenary of Trade Unions.
829 **268** 1m. multicoloured 2·40 2·40

269 Stylized Buildings

2005. Plehan Monastery.
830 **269** 1m. multicoloured 2·40 2·40

270 Aladza Mosque, Foca

2005. Cultural Heritage. Multicoloured.
831 1m. Type **270** 2·40 2·40
832 1m. Zitomislici Monastery 2·40 2·40

271 King Tvrtko Kotromanic

2005. History. Bogomils. Multicoloured.
833 50f. Type **271** 1·20 1·20
834 50f. Kulin Ban 1·20 1·20
835 1m. Burning man (Inquisition)
 (stone plaque) 2·30 2·30
836 2m. Eugene IV's Papal Bull
 (1439) 4·75 4·75

272 Decorated Salon

2005. Bosnia Institute. Multicoloured.
837 70f. Type **272** 1·60 1·60
838 4m. Exhibition 9·25 9·25

273 Flowers over map

2005. 10th Anniv of Dayton Agreement.
839 **273** 1m.50 multicoloured 3·50 3·50

274 Emblem

2005. 60th Anniv of End of World War II.
840 **274** 1m. multicoloured 2·40 2·40

275 Members' Flags and Globe (left)

2005. 50th Anniv of Europa Stamps. Multicoloured.
841 3m. Type **275** 5·00 5·00
842 3m. Globe (right) and members
 flags 5·00 5·00
843 3m. Euro coin and map of
 Europe 5·00 5·00
844 3m. Stars and 1999 chess
 championships emblem 5·00 5·00
MS845 104×76 mm. Nos. 841/4 19·00 19·00
 Nos. 841/2 were issued together, *se-tenant*, forming a
composite design.

276 Faces

2005. World Vision. People with Special Needs Week.
846 **276** 50f. multicoloured 1·60 1·60

277 Slalom Skier

2006. Winter Olympic Games, Turin. Sheet 88×77
 mm containing T **277** and similar horiz design.
 Multicoloured.
MS847 1m. Type **277**; 2m. Speed
skaters 7·00 7·00

278 Treskavica Mountains, Trnovo

2006. Tourism. Multicoloured.
848 1m. Type **278** 2·30 2·30
849 1m. Rafting, Goradzde (vert) 2·30 2·30

279 Mercedes Benz 500K Cabriolet B, 1935

2006. Cars. Sheet 104×76 mm containing T **279** and similar horiz designs. Multicoloured.
MS850 50f.×2 Type **279**; Dodge D11 Graber Cabriolet, 1939; 1m. Mercedes Benz SS Schwarzer, 1929; 2m. Bugatti T 57 Ventoux, 1939 9·50 9·50

280 Crowd

2006. Europa. Integration. Multicoloured.
851 2m. Type **280** 5·00 5·00
852 2m. Crowd (different) 5·00 5·00
MS853 115×87 mm. 2m.×2, As Type **280**; As No. 852 16·00 16·00

281 *Formica rufa*

2006. Fauna and Flora. Multicoloured.
854 1m.50 Type **281** 3·50 3·50
855 3m. *Sarcosphaera crassa* 7·00 7·00

282 Prisoners and Barbed Wire

2006. Prisoner of War Day.
856 **282** 1m. multicoloured 2·40 2·40

283 Gallery Facade

2006. 60th Anniv of National Art Gallery.
857 **283** 1m. multicoloured 2·40 2·40

284 Illustration from *Zenidba nosaca Samuela*

2006. Isak Samokovlija (writer) Commemoration.
858 **284** 1m. multicoloured 2·40 2·40

284a Mohamed Kadic

2006. Birth Centenaries. Multicoloured.
858a 1m. Type **284a** 2·40 2·40
858b 1m. Mustafa Kamaric 2·40 2·40

285 Team Members

2006. Football Event and Anniversary. Multicoloured.
859 1m. Type **285** (60th anniv of Sarajevo Football Club) 2·40 2·40
860 3m. Player, globe and flags (World Cup Football Championship, Germany) 7·00 7·00

286 Potatoes

2006. Vegetables. Multicoloured.
861 10f. Type **286** 60 60
862 20f. Cauliflower 80 80

863 30f. Savoy cabbage 95 95
864 40f. Green cabbage 1·20 1·20
865 1m. Carrots 2·50 2·50

286a *Lepus europaeus*

2006. Fauna. Multicoloured.
866 1m.50 Type **286a** 3·50 3·50
867 2m. *Capreolus capreolus* 4·75 4·75
868 2m.50 *Anas* (mallard) (horiz) 5·75 5·75
869 4m. *Vulpes vulpes* 9·25 9·25
870 5m. *Canis lupus* (horiz) 11·50 11·50

287 Emblem

2006. European Junior Table Tennis Championship.
871 **287** 1m. multicoloured 2·40 2·40

288 Basilica, Breza

2006. Cultural and Historical Heritage. Multicoloured.
872 1m. Type **288** 2·40 2·40
873 1m. Semiz Ali Pasha's Mosque, Praca (vert) 2·40 2·40

289 Orange Bird

2006. Youth Philately. Sheet 115×88 mm containing T **289** and similar vert design. Multicoloured.
MS874 50f.×2, Type **289**; Yellow bird 4·75 4·75

290 Girl

2006. Children's Week. Stop Violence against Children Campaign. Self-adhesive.
875 **290** 50f. multicoloured 1·20 1·20

291 School Building

2006. 300th Anniv of Muslim Secondary School, Travnik.
876 **291** 1m. multicoloured 2·40 2·40

292 Vladimir Prelog (Chemistry, 1975)

2006. Nobel Prize Winners. Multicoloured.
877 1m. Type **292** 2·40 2·40
878 2m.50 Iro Andric (Literature, 1961) 5·75 5·75

293 Emblem

2006. 30th Anniv of Tuzli University.
879 **293** 1m. multicoloured 2·40 2·40

294 Museum Exhibits

2006
880 **294** 1m. multicoloured 2·40 2·40

295 Steam Locomotive

2006. Railways. Multicoloured.
881 50f. Type **295** 1·20 1·20
882 1m. Modern locomotive 2·40 2·40

296 Sheep

2007. Domestic Animals. Multicoloured.
883 10f. Type **296** 60 60
884 20f. Goat 80 80
885 30f. Cow 95 95
886 40f. Donkey 1·20 1·20
887 70f. Horse (42×35 mm) 1·90 1·90
888 1m. Cat (42×35 mm) 2·40 2·40

297 Arms

2007. 60th Anniv of National Opera Theatre.
889 **297** 50f. multicoloured 1·30 1·30

298 Scouts

2007. Europa. Centenary of Scouting. Multicoloured.
890 2m. Type **298** 4·75 4·75
891 2m. Scouts by campfire 4·75 4·75

299 Prokos Lake

2007. Tourism.
892 **299** 2m.50 multicoloured 6·00 6·00

300 *Knautia travnicensis*

2007. Fauna and Flora. Multicoloured.
893 80f. Type **300** 1·70 1·70
894 1m.20 *Sciurus vulgaris* (squirrel) (horiz) 3·00 3·00

301 Kozarac

2007. Tourism.
895 **301** 1m. multicoloured 2·40 2·40

302 Building Facade

2007. 140th Anniv of Cazin Madrasah (Islamic school).
896 **302** 2m. multicoloured 4·75 4·75

302a Fountain, Tuzla

2007. Fountains. Multicoloured.
897 1m.50 Type **302a** 3·50 3·50
898 2m. Mostar 4·75 4·75
899 2m.50 Sanski Most 5·75 5·75
900 4m. Sebilj, Sarajevo (horiz) 9·25 9·25
901 5m. Fountain, Bey's Mosque 11·50 11·50

303 Masthead

2007. Centenary of Gajret Periodical.
902 **303** 1m. multicoloured 2·40 2·40

304 Courtyard

2007. 30th Anniv of Islamic Science Faculty, Sarajevo.
903 **304** 2m. multicoloured 4·75 4·75

305 Front Elevation

2007. Gazi Husrev-Begova Library.
904 **305** 1m.50 multicoloured 3·50 3·50

306 *Landscape* (Ismet Rizvic)

2007. Art. Multicoloured.
905 1m. Pocitelj Visual Art Colony 2·40 2·40
906 1m.50 Type **306** 3·50 3·50

307 '140' and Stylised Building

2007. 140th Anniv of Abdulah Nakas Hospital.
907 **307** 1m.50 red and silver 3·50 3·50

308 Bear Figurine

2007. Museum Exhibit.
908 **308** 1m. multicoloured 2·40 2·40

309 Buildings and Karel Parik

2007. 150th Birth Anniv of Karel Parik (architect).
909 **309** 2m.50 multicoloured 6·00 6·00

310 Combatants

2007. Karate.
910 **310** 1m. multicoloured 2·40 2·40

311 *Self Portrait* (Zuko Dzumhur)

2007. Zuko Dzumhur (artist, writer and caricaturist).
911 **311** 1m. multicoloured 2·40 2·40

312 Building Facade

2007. 60th Anniv of Medical Faculty of Sarajevo University.
912 **312** 1m. multicoloured 2·40 2·40

313 Joseph Blatter

2007. Honorary Ambassadors for Sport and Culture of Peace. Multicoloured.
913 2m. Type **313** 4·50 4·50
914 2m. Juan Antonio Samaranch (41×27 mm) 4·50 4·50

314 Heart (Amira Halilovic)

2007. Ecology. Children's Drawings. Multicoloured.
915 50f. Type **314** 1·30 1·30
916 50f. Couple holding globe (Maida Hasanic) 1·30 1·30
MS916a 75×95 mm. Nos. 915/16 2·50 2·50

315 Fortress, Samobor

2007. Cultural Heritage.
917 **315** 1m. multicoloured 2·40 2·40

316 Meat Pie

2007. Gastronomy.
918 **316** 2m. multicoloured 4·75 4·75

317 Stegosaurus

2007. Pre-History. Dinosaurs.
919 **317** 2m. multicoloured 5·00 5·00

318 Laika

2007. 50th Anniv of Space Exploration.
920 **318** 3m. multicoloured 7·00 7·00

319 Emblem

2007. 60th Anniv of University Sports Association.
921 **319** 50f. multicoloured 1·40 1·40

320 Player

2007. 60th Anniv of Bosnia Handball Club.
922 **320** 50f. multicoloured 1·30 1·30

321 Emblem

2008. 95th Anniv of Merhamet (Muslim charitable society).
923 **321** 70f. multicoloured 1·80 1·80

321a College Campus (image scaled to 56% of original size)

2008. 35th Anniv of College of Pharmacy.
923a **321a** 2m. multicoloured 4·75 4·75

322 Bosanska Krupa

2008. Tourism. Multicoloured.
924 70f. Type **322** 4·75 4·75
925 1m. Velika Kladusa (horiz) 7·00 7·00

323 Shish-Kebab

2008. Gastronomy. Multicoloured.
926 1m. Type **323** 2·40 2·40
927 2m. Stuffed apple 4·75 4·75

324 Building Facade

2008. 50th Anniv of Blood Transfusion Service.
928 **324** 1m.50 multicoloured 3·50 3·50

325 Woman

2008. Centenary of International Women's Day.
929 **325** 2m. multicoloured 4·75 4·75

326 Candle, Quill and Letter

2008. Europa. The Letter. Multicoloured.
930 2m. Type **326** 4·75 4·75
931 3m. Postcard and hand holding pen 7·00 7·00
MS932 88×115 mm. Nos. 930/1 11·50 11·50

327 Emblem

2008. Centenary of Esperanto.
933 **327** 1m.50 multicoloured 3·50 3·50

328 Anniversary Emblem

2008. 60th Anniv of Shooting Club, Sarajevo.
934 **328** 1m.50 multicoloured 3·50 3·50

329 Judo

2008. Olympic Games, Beijing. Multicoloured.
935 1m. Type **329** 1·80 1·80
936 1m.50 Shot put and athletics 3·50 3·50

330 Oural-3 (M-66)

2008. Motorcycles. Multicoloured.
937 1m.50 Type **330** 3·50 3·50
938 1m.50 Jawa Trail 90 3·50 3·50

331 Vjetrenica Cave

2008. World Heritage Site.
939 **331** 1m. multicoloured 2·40 2·40

332 Signing

2008. Bosnia Hergovina–European Union Stabilization and Association Agreement.
940 **332** 70f. multicoloured 1·80 1·80

333 *Nymphaea alba*

2008. Flora and Fauna. Multicoloured.
941 1m.50 Type **333** 3·50 3·50
942 2m. *Rana esculenta* 4·75 4·75

334 Krivaja Villa, Zavidovici

2008. Cultural Heritage (1st issue).
943 **334** 2m.50 multicoloured 5·75 5·75

335 Musalla (place of prayer), Kamengrad

2008. Cultural Heritage (2nd issue). Multicoloured.
944 1m. Type **335** 2·40 2·40
945 1m.50 Ostrovica (horiz) 3·50 3·50

336 Turritella turris

2008. Fossils.

| 946 | **336** | 1m.50 multicoloured | 3·50 | 3·50 |

337 Stylized Symbols of Kuwait and Bosnia Herzgovina (image scaled to 54% of original size)

2008. Bosnia Herzgovina–Kuwait Relations.

| 947 | **337** | 3m. multicoloured | 7·00 | 7·00 |

338 Skier

2008. 80th Anniv of Sarajevo Ski Club.

| 948 | **338** | 2m. multicoloured | 4·75 | 4·75 |

339 Lynx

2008. Flora and Fauna. Multicoloured.

949	5f. Type **339**		1·30	1·30
950	70f. Goshawk (*Accipiter gentilis*)		1·80	1·80
951	70f. Conifer and fields (horiz)		1·80	1·80
952	70f. Birch grove (horiz)		1·80	1·80
953	70f. Conifers and snow-covered chalet (horiz)		1·80	1·80
954	5m. Owl		11·50	11·50

340 Family

2009. International Day of Missing Persons.

| 955 | **340** | 20f. black and scarlet | 45 | 45 |

341 *Hirundo rustica* (barn swallow)

2009

| 956 | **341** | 70f. multicoloured | 1·80 | 1·80 |

342 Documents (image scaled to 37% of original size)

2009. Cultural Heritage. Historical Archives.

| 957 | **342** | 70f. multicoloured | 1·80 | 1·80 |

343 Building Facade

2009. 60th Anniv of Arkus–Seljo Academic Cultural Centre, University of Sarajevo.

| 958 | **343** | 1m. multicoloured | 2·40 | 2·40 |

344 Emblem

2009. 60th Anniv Council of Europe.

| 959 | **344** | 1m. multicoloured | 2·40 | 2·40 |

345 Coffee

2009. Bosnian Gastronomy.

| 960 | **345** | 1m. multicoloured | 2·40 | 2·40 |

346 Museum Emblem

2009. 60th Anniv of Sarajevo Museum.

| 961 | **346** | 1m. multicoloured | 2·40 | 2·40 |

347 Runners

2009. IAAF World Athletics Championships–Berlin 2009. Multicoloured.

962	1m.50 Type **347**	3·50	3·50
963	2m. Stylized figures	4·50	4·50
MS964	106×50 mm. Nos. 962/3	8·00	8·00

348 Charles Darwin and Progression of Humanoids

2009. Birth Bicentenary of Charles Darwin (naturalist and evolutionary theorist).

| 965 | **348** | 2m. multicoloured | 4·50 | 4·50 |

349 Planets

2009. Europa. Astronomy. Multicoloured.

966	2m. Type **349**	4·50	4·50
967	3m. Satellite	7·00	7·00
MS968	114×90 mm. Nos. 966/7	11·50	11·50

350 Family Group

2009. Children's Week.

| 969 | **350** | 70f. multicoloured | 1·80 | 1·80 |

350a Building Facade and Justice

2009. 130th Anniv of Canton Tribunal, Sarajevo.

| 969a | **350a** | 1m. multicoloured | 2·40 | 2·40 |

351 *Viola wittrockiana*

2009. Pansy.

| 970 | **351** | 1m. multicoloured | 2·40 | 2·40 |

352 Gazi Husrev-beg Mosque, Sarajevo and Selimiye Mosque, Edirne

2009. BH Post Sarajevo and Turkish Post Co-operation.

| 971 | **352** | 2m. multicoloured | 5·00 | 5·00 |

353 Strawberries

2009. Days of Berrylike Fruits Festival, Celic.

| 972 | **353** | 5m. multicoloured | 11·50 | 11·50 |

354 Hands

2009. Sign Language.

| 973 | **354** | 1m.50 multicoloured | 3·50 | 3·50 |

355 St Francis of Assisi

2009. 800th Anniv of Franciscan Order.

| 974 | **355** | 1m.50 multicoloured | 3·50 | 3·50 |

356 Building Facade

2009. Centenary of Franciscan Theology Study Centre.

| 975 | **356** | 1m. multicoloured | 2·40 | 2·40 |

357 Speed Skater and Athletes

2010. Winter Olympic Games, Vancouver. Multicoloured.

| **MS**976 | 1m.50 Type **357**; 2m. Bobsleigh and other athletes | 8·50 | 8·50 |

358 Old Town, Srebrenik

2010. Cultural Heritage. Multicoloured.

| 977 | 1m. Old Town and Castle, Ostrozac | 2·20 | 2·20 |
| 978 | 70f. Type **358** | 2·75 | 2·75 |

359 *Taxus baccata* (yew)

2010. Trees. Multicoloured.

| 979 | 1m. Type **359** | 3·50 | 3·50 |
| 980 | 1m. *Aesculus hippocastanum* (horse chestnut) | 4·50 | 4·50 |

360 *Cynus olor* (mute swan)

2010. Water Bird

| **MS**981 | **360** | 2m. multicoloured | 5·50 | 5·50 |

361 Wounded Chief watched over by his Sisters

2010. Ballad of Hasanaginica

| 982 | **361** | 1m. multicoloured | 2·75 | 2·75 |

362 Noch the little Dragon

2010. Europa. Multicoloured.

983	1m. Type **362**	3·00	3·00
984	1m.50 Little Blu	4·00	4·00
MS985	67×103 mm. Nos. 982/3	7·00	7·00

Nos. 983/4 were printed, *se-tenant*, forming a composite design.

363 Knight on Horseback (image scaled to 55% of original size)

2010. 500th Anniv of Ajvatovica (Prusac)

| 986 | **363** | 1m.50 multicoloured | 3·50 | 3·50 |

364 Robert Alexander Schumann

2010. Composers' Birth Bicentenaries. Multicoloured.

| 987 | 1m. Type **364** | 3·00 | 3·00 |
| 988 | 1m.50 Fryderyk Franciszek (Frédéric) Chopin | 3·50 | 3·50 |

365 Branches

2011. Europa. Forests. Multicoloured.

989	2m.50 Type **365**	9·00	9·00
990	2m.50 Tree trunk	9·00	9·00
MS991	73×115 mm. Nos. 989/90	18·00	18·00

366 *Gentiana jasnae*

2011. Flora. Gentian
992 366 2m. multicoloured 6·00 6·00

367 Yuri Gagarin

2011. 50th Anniv of First Manned Space Flight. Sheet 80×60 mm
MS993 367 2m. multicoloured 6·00 6·00

368 368 Virgin Mary (statue), St James Church, Hand holding Rose and Christ (image scaled to 55% of original size)

2011. Medjugorje
994 368 2m.50 multicoloured 9·00 9·00

369 *Passer domesticus* (House Sparrow)

2011. Birds. House Sparrow. Sheet 80×60 mm
MS995 369 2m.50 multicoloured 9·00 9·00

370 Coat of Arms

2011. Herceg Stjepan's Coat of Arms
996 370 1m. multicoloured 3·00 3·00

371 AIDS Ribbon

2011. 30th Anniv of AIDS Prevention Campaign
997 371 70f. scarlet-vermilion and black 2·75 2·75

372 Boats (image scaled to 55% of original size)

2011. Hutovo Blato Nature Reserve
998 372 70f. multicoloured 2·75 2·75

373 *Astacus astacus*

Fauna. European Crayfish
999 373 1m.50 multicoloured 4·00 4·00

374 Skender Kulenović

2011. Personalities. Writers. Multicoloured.
1000 1m. Type 374 3·00 3·00
1001 1m.50 Meša Selimović 4·00 4·00

375 Fridtjof Nansen

2011. 150th Birth Anniv of Fridtjof Nansen (Norwegian explorer, scientist and winner of 1922 Nobel Peace Prize)
1002 375 1m.50 multicoloured 4·00 4·00

376 Locomotive 55-99

2012. Steam Locomotives. Multicoloured.
MS1003 1m. Type 376; 1m.50 Locomotive 83-180 4·00 4·00

377 Titanic

2012. Centenary of Sinking of *Titanic*. Sheet 80×60 mm
MS1004 377 2m.50 multicoloured 9·00 9·00

378 Minaret and Fountain, Baščaršija Square and Coffee Pot

2012. Europa. Visit Bosnia Herzegovina. Multicoloured.
1005 2m.50 Type 365 9·00 9·00
1006 2m.50 Kravice waterfall and boat on lake 9·00 9·00
MS1007 102×91 mm. Nos. 1005/6 18·00 18·00

379 *Viola odorata*

2012. Flora. Multicoloured.
MS1008 70f.x10, Type 379; *Primula veris*; Green flowered hellebore ('Helleborus'); Snowdrop ('Galanthus'); *Crocus sativus*; *Viola odorata* (different); *Primula veris* (different); Hellebore (different); Snowdrop (different); *Crocus sativa* (different) 18·00 18·00

380 Rustempasic, near Bugojno

2012. Cultural Heritage. Castles
1009 380 2m. multicoloured 6·00 6·00

381 Bužim

2012. Cultural Heritage. Old Cities. Multicoloured.
1010 20f. Type 381 3·00 3·00
1011 20f. Tešanj 4·00 4·00

II. CROATIAN POSTS
Issues made by the Croat administration in Mostar.

C1 Statue and Church

1993. Sanctuary of Our Lady Queen of Peace Shrine, Medugorje.
C1 C1 2000d. multicoloured 1·20 1·20

C2 Silvije Kranjcevic (poet)

1993. Multicoloured.. Multicoloured..
C2 200d. Type C2 20 20
C3 500d. Jajce 35 35
C4 1000d. Mostar (horiz) 75 75

C3 Medieval Gravestone

1993. 250th Anniv of Census in Bosnia and Herzegovina.
C5 C3 100d. multicoloured 40 40

C4 "Madonna of the Grand Duke" (Raphael)

1993. Christmas.
C6 C4 6000d. multicoloured 2·30 2·30

C5 Uplands in Bloom

1993. Europa. Contemporary Art. Paintings by Gabrijel Jurkic. Multicoloured.
C7 3500d. Type C5 4·75 4·75
C8 5000d. *Wild Poppy* 5·25 5·25

C6 Kravica Waterfall

1993
C9 C6 3000d. multicoloured 1·30 1·30

C7 Hrvoje (from *Hrvoje's Missal* by Butko)

1993. 577th Death Anniv of Hrvoje Vukcic Hrvatinic, Duke of Split, Viceroy of Dalmatia and Croatia and Grand Duke of Bosnia.
C10 C7 1500d. multicoloured 80 80

C8 Plehan Monastery

1993
C11 C8 2200d. multicoloured 85 85

C9 Arms

1994. Proclamation (August 1993) of Croatian Community of Herceg Bosna.
C12 C9 10000d. multicoloured 4·00 4·00

C10 Bronze Cross, Rama-Scit (Mile Blazevic)

1994
C13 C10 2m.80 multicoloured 1·20 1·20

C 11 *Campanula hercegovina*

1994. Flora and Fauna. Multicoloured.
C14 3m.80 Type C11 1·60 1·60
C15 4m. Mountain dog 1·70 1·70

C 12 Hutova Swamp

1994
C16 C12 80f. multicoloured 45 45

C 13 Penny Farthing Bicycles

1994. Europa. Discoveries and Inventions. Multicoloures.
C17 8m. Type C13 4·75 4·75
C18 10m. Mercedes cars, 1901 5·75 5·75

C14 Views of Town and Fortress

1994. 550th Anniv of First Written Record of Ljubuski.
C19 C14 1m. multicoloured 50 50

C15 Hospital and Christ

1994. Second Anniv of Dr. Nikolic Franciscan Hospital, Nova Bila.
C20 C15 5m. multicoloured 2·00 2·00

C16 Anniversary Emblem

1995. 50th Anniv of UNO. Self-adhesive. Rouletted.
C21 **C16** 1m.50 blue, red & black 60 60

C17 Crib

1995. Christmas.
C22 **C17** 5m.40 multicoloured 2·20 2·20

C18 Franciscan Monastery, Kraljeva Sutjeska

1995
C23 **C18** 3m. multicoloured 1·20 1·20

C 19 Srebrenica

1995. Towns. Multicoloured.
C24 **C19** 2m. Type **C19** 70 70
C25 4m. Franciscan Monastery, Mostar 1·40 1·40

C20 Christ on the Cross

1995. Europa. Peace and Freedom.
C26 **C20** 6m.50 multicoloured 23·00 23·00

C21 Statue and Church

1996. 15th Anniv of Sanctuary of Our Lady Queen of Peace Shrine, Medugorje.
C27 **C21** 10m. multicoloured 4·75 4·75

C22 Queen Katarina Kosaca Kotromanic

1996. Europa. Famous Women.
C28 **C22** 2m.40 multicoloured 1·90 1·90

C23 Monastery

1996. 150th Anniv of Franciscan Monastery and Church, Siroki Brijeg.
C29 **C23** 1m.40 multicoloured 55 55

C24 Virgin Mary

1996. Self-adhesive.
C30 **C24** 2m. mult (postage) 60 60
C31 **C24** 9m. multicoloured (air) 3·00 3·00

1996. Taipeh '96, International Stamp Exn. Nos. C30/1 surch **1.10** and emblem.
C32 1m.10 on 2m. mult (postage) 45 45
C33 1m.10 on 9m. mult (air) 45 45

C26 Madonna and Child (anon)

1996. Christmas.
C34 **C26** 2m.20 multicoloured 90 90

C 27 St. George and the Dragon

1997. Europa. Tales and Legends. Mult.
C35 2m. Type **C27** 95 95
C36 5m. Zeus as bull and Europa (39×34 mm) 2·10 2·10

C28 Pope John Paul II

1997. Papal Visit.
C37 **C28** 3m.60 multicoloured 1·50 1·50
MSC38 90×100 mm. No. 37×4 6·00 6·00

C29 Chapel, Samatorje, Gorica

1997
C39 **C29** 1m.40 multicoloured 55 55

C30 Purple Heron

1997. Flora and Fauna. Multicoloured.
C40 1m. Type **C30** 60 60
C41 2m.40 Symphyandra hofmannii (orchid) 1·00 1·00

C31 Birth of Christ (fresco, Giotto)

1997. Christmas.
C42 **C31** 1m.40 multicoloured 55 55

C32 Cats

1998. Europa. Animated Film Festival.
C43 **C32** 6m.50 multicoloured 4·50 4·50

C33 Seal

1998. 550th Anniv of Herzegovina.
C44 **C33** 2m.30 red, black and gold 90 90

C34 Livno

1998. 1100th Anniv of Livno.
C45 **C34** 1m.20 multicoloured 55 55

C35 Sibiraea croatica

1998
C46 **C35** 1m.40 multicoloured 80 80

C36 Griffon Vulture

1998
C47 **C36** 2m.40 multicoloured 1·10 1·10

C37 Adoration of the Wise Men

1998. Christmas.
C48 **C37** 5m.40 multicoloured 2·20 2·20

C38 Woman, Posavina Region

1999. Regional Costumes.
C49 **C38** 40f. multicoloured 55 55

C39 Ruins of Bobovac

1999. Old Towns.
C50 **C39** 10f. multicoloured 25 25

C40 Simic

1999. Birth Centenary (1998) of Antun Simic (writer).
C51 **C40** 30f. multicoloured 55 55

C41 Blidinje Nature Park

1999. Europa. Parks and Gardens.
C52 **C41** 1m.50 multicoloured 4·00 4·00

C42 Dianthus freynii

1999
C53 **C42** 80f. multicoloured 1·30 1·30

C43 Pine Marten

1999
C54 **C43** 40f. multicoloured 55 55

C44 Gradina Osanici, Stolac

1999. Archaeology.
C55 **C44** 10f. multicoloured 25 25

C45 The Nativity (mosaic)

1999. Christmas.
C56 **C45** 30f. multicoloured 55 55

C46 Sop

2000. 96th Birth Anniv of Nikola Sop (poet).
C57 **C46** 40f. multicoloured 60 60

C47 Emblem

2000. World Health Day.
C58 **C47** 40f. multicoloured 60 60

C48 Ceramic Doves

2000. Europa.
C59 **C48** 1m.80 multicoloured 4·00 4·00

C49 Chess Board and Emblem

2000. 40th Anniv of Bosnian Chess Association. Chess Events in 2000. Multicoloured.
C60 80f. Type **C49** (30th Chess Olympiad, Sarajevo) 1·30 1·30

C61 80f. Octopus holding pawn
 and emblem (16th European
 Chess Club Cup, Neum) 1·30 1·30

C50 Brother
Karaula

2000. Birth Bicentenary of Brother Lovro Karaula.
C62 **C50** 80f. multicoloured 1·30 1·30

C51 Oak Tree
(*Quercus sessilis*)

2000. Chestnut Oak of Siroki Brijeg.
C63 **C51** 1m.50 multicoloured 2·20 2·20

C52 European Eel
(*Anguilla anguilla*)

2000
C64 **C52** 80f. multicoloured 1·30 1·30

C53 Franciscan
Monastery, Tomislavgrad

2000
C65 **C53** 1m.50 multicoloured 2·20 2·20

C54 Woman and
Patterned Cloth

2000. Traditional Costume from Kraljeve Sutjeske.
C66 **C54** 40f. multicoloured 80 80

C55 Man and
Reflection

2000. A.I.D.S. Awareness Campaign.
C67 **C55** 80f. multicoloured 1·30 1·30

C56 Nativity

2000. Christmas.
C68 **C56** 40f. multicoloured 65 65

C57 *Chondrostoma
phoxinus*

2001. Fishes. Multicoloured.
C69 30f. Type **C57** 40 40
C70 1m.50 *Salmo marmoratus* 2·20 2·20

C58 Tihaljina
Spring

2001. Europa. Water Resources. Multicoloured.
C71 1m.10 Type **C58** 2·00 2·00
C72 1m.80 Pliva Waterfall 3·25 3·25

C59 Petar Zrinski

2001. 330th Death Anniversaries. Multicoloured.
C73 40f. Type **C59** 60 60
C74 40f. Fran Krsto Frankopan 60 60

C60 16th-century Galley
Ship

2001
C75 **C60** 1m.80 multicoloured 2·75 2·75

C61 Boat, Neretva River
Valley

2001
C76 **C61** 80f. multicoloured 1·30 1·30

C62 Queen of
Peace of
Medugorje

2001. 20th Anniv of Medugorje. Sheet 90×65 mm.
MSC77 **C62** 3m.80 multicoloured 5·25 5·25

C63 Our Lady of
Kondzilo
(17th-century
painting)

2001
C78 **C63** 80f. multicoloured 1·30 1·30

C64 Binary Digits

2001. 50th Anniv of Computers. Each black and red.
C79 40f. Type **C64** 65 65
C80 40f. Binary forming "50" 65 65

C65 Mars, Globe and
Sisyphus pushing Stone

2001. Millennium.
C81 **C65** 1m.50 multicoloured 2·00 2·00

C66 Father Slavko
Barbaric

2001. First Death Anniv of Father Slavko Barbaric.
C82 **C66** 80f. multicoloured 1·30 1·30

C67 Minnie and Mickey
Mouse (Danijela Nedic)

2001. Birth Centenary of Walt Disney (film maker).
C83 **C67** 1m.50 multicoloured 2·40 2·40

C68 Nativity

2001. Christmas.
C84 **C68** 40f. multicoloured 65 65

C69 Alfred Nobel

2001. Centenary of the Nobel Prize.
C85 **C69** 1m.80 multicoloured 3·00 3·00

C70 Skier

2002. Winter Olympic Games, Salt Lake City, U.S.A.
C86 **C70** 80f. multicoloured 1·40 1·40

C71 Vran Mountain

2002. International Year of Mountains.
C87 **C71** 40f. multicoloured 70 70

C72 Bridge over River
Neretva, Mostar

2002. 550th Anniv of First Written Record of Mostar.
C88 **C72** 30f. multicoloured 55 55

C73 Clown, Lion and
Mouse

2002. Europa. Circus. Multicoloured.
C89 80f. Type **C73** 2·10 2·00
C90 1m.50 Big Top and clowns 3·50 3·50

C74 Leonardo da
Vinci and
Designs

2002. 550th Birth Anniv of Leonardo da Vinci (artist and
 designer).
C91 **C74** 40f. brown and agate 70 70

C75 Players and
Football

2002. World Cup Football Championships, Japan and
 South Korea.
C92 **C75** 1m.50 multicoloured 2·50 2·40

C76 Father
Buntic and
Children

2002. 60th Death Anniv of Father Didak Buntic
 (humanitarian).
C93 **C76** 80f. multicoloured 1·40 1·40

C77 Inscribed Tablet

2002. 11th-century Inscribed Tablet, Humac.
C94 **C77** 40f. multicoloured 70 70

C78 Marilyn Monroe

2002. 40th Death Anniv of Marilyn Monroe (actor).
C95 **C78** 40f. multicoloured 70 70

C79 Elvis Presley

2002. 25th Death Anniv of Elvis Presley (entertainer).
C96 **C79** 1m.50 multicoloured 2·50 2·40

C80 Transmitter
Tower

2002. 50th Anniv of Television.
C97 **C80** 1m.50 multicoloured 2·50 2·40

C81 1905 Postcard

2002. Stamp Day.
C98 **C81** 80f. multicoloured 1·40 1·40

C82 1929
Calendar

2002. Centenary of "Naprodak" (cultural association).
C99 **C82** 40f. multicoloured 70 70

C83 Stylized Player

2002. European Bowling Championships, Grude.
C100 **C83** 1m.50 multicoloured 2·50 2·40

C84 *Viola beckiana*

2002. Flowers.
C101 **C84** 30f. multicoloured 55 55

C85 Red Admiral (*Vanessa atalanta*)

2002. Butterflies.
C102 **C85** 80f. multicoloured 1·40 1·40

C86 Madonna and Child (painting, Bernardino Luini)

2002. Christmas.
C103 **C86** 40f. multicoloured 70 70

C87 School Buildings

2002. 120th Anniv of Society of Jesuits High School, Travnik.
C104 **C87** 80f. multicoloured 1·40 1·40

C88 Josip Stadler

2003. 160th Birth Anniv of Josip Stadler (first archbishop of Vrhbosna).
C105 **C88** 50f. multicoloured 85 85

C89 Sirokom Brijegu High School

2003.
C106 **C89** 40f. multicoloured 80 80

C90 Key Box and Letter Holder

2003. Europa. Poster Art.
C107 **C90** 1m.80 multicoloured 4·75 4·75

C91 Figures

2003. 800th Anniv of the Abjuration at Bilino Polje.
C108 **C91** 50f. multicoloured 95 95

C92 Mary and Angels

2003. Tenth Anniv of HP Mostar.
C109 **C92** 980f. multicoloured 1·60 1·60

C93 Corkscrews

2003. World Wine Day.
C110 **C93** 1m.50 multicoloured 2·75 2·75

C94 *Oxytropis prenja*

2003. Flora and Fauna. Multicoloured.
C111 50f. Type **C94** 95 95
C112 2m. Rock partridge (*Alectoris graeca*) 3·75 3·75

C95 Pope John Paul II and Ivan Merz

2003. 2nd Visit of Pope John Paul II.
C113 **C95** 1m.50 multicoloured 2·75 2·75

C96 Crucifix

2003. 440th Birth Anniv of Matija Divkovic (writer).
C114 **C96** 3m.80 multicoloured 7·00 7·00

C97 Woman wearing Folk Costume, Rama

2003. Cultural Heritage. Multicoloured.
C115 50f. Type **C97** 95 95
C116 70f. Jewellery, Neum (horiz) 1·20 1·20

C98 Summit Cross

2003. 70th Anniv of Summit Cross on Krizevac Mountain.
C117 **C98** 80f. multicoloured 1·60 1·60

C99 Stjepan Kotromanic

2003. 650th Death Anniv of Stjepan Kotromanic (King of Bosnia).
C118 **C99** 20f. multicoloured 45 45

C100 Tele-printer

2003. World Post Day.
C119 **C100** 1m.50 black and red 3·25 3·25

C101 Quill and Inkwell

2003. Birth Bicentenary of Alberto Fortis (writer).
C120 **C101** 50f. multicoloured 1·00 1·00

C102 Car and Bicycle

2003. Children.
C121 **C102** 1m. multicoloured 2·10 2·10

C103 Nativity

2003. Christmas.
C122 **C103** 50f. multicoloured 1·00 1·00

C104 "100"

2003. Centenary of Powered Flight.
C123 **C104** 2m. multicoloured 4·25 4·25

C105 Emblem

2004. International Investment Conference.
C124 **C105** 5m. silver 11·50 11·50

C106 Hearts

2004. St. Valentine's Day.
C125 **C106** 10f. multicoloured 1·00 1·00

C107 Albert Einstein

2004. 125th Birth Anniv of Albert Einstein (physicist).
C126 **C107** 50f. multicoloured 1·30 1·30

C108 Decorated Hand

2004. Tattooing.
C127 **C108** 50f. multicoloured 1·30 1·30

C109 *Aquilegia dinarica*

2004. Flora and Fauna.
C128 1m. Type **C109** 2·40 2·40
C129 1m.50 *Salamandra atra prenjensis* (horiz) 3·50 3·50

C110 Skis and Snow Scene

2004. Europa. Holidays. Multicoloured.
C130 1m.50 Type **C110** 3·75 3·75
C131 2m. Flippers and Beach Scene 4·75 4·75

C111 Andrije Kacica Miosica

2004. 300th Birth Anniv of Andrije Kacica Miosica (writer and theologian).
C132 **C111** 70f. yellow and brown 1·80 1·80

C112 Ball and Boots

2004. European Football Championship 2004, Portugal.
C133 **C112** 2m. multicoloured 5·00 5·00

C113 Kocerin Tablet (carved stone), Siroki Brijeg (c.1404)

2004.
C134 **C113** 70f. multicoloured 1·50 1·50

C114 Footprint

2004. 35th Anniv of First Landing on Moon.
C135 **C114** 1m. multicoloured 2·50 2·50

C115 Old Bridge, Mostar

2004. Reconstruction of Mostar Bridge.
C136 **C115** 50f. multicoloured 1·30 1·30

C116 Water Wheel, Buna

2004
C137 **C116** 1m. Multicoloured 2·50 2·50

C117 Envelope and
Earth

2004. World Post Day.
C138 **C117** 1m.50 multicoloured 3·75 3·75

C118 Money Box and
Hippopotamus

2004. World Savings Day.
C139 **C118** 50f. multicoloured 1·30 1·30

C119 Karl Friedrich Benz

2004. 160th Birth Anniv of Karl Friedrich Benz (German
motor pioneer).
C140 **C119** 1m.50 multicoloured 3·75 3·75

C120 Mary and Joseph

2004. Christmas. Multicoloured.
C141 50f. Type **C120** 1·30 1·30
C142 1m. Postman carrying present 2·50 2·50

C121 Woman
wearing Folk
Costume,
Kupres

2005. Cultural Heritage.
C143 **C121** 1m.50 multicoloured 3·75 3·75

C122 *Gentiana
dinarica*

2005. Flora. Multicoloured.
C144 50f. Type **C122** 1·30 1·30
C145 50f. *Petteria ramentacea* 1·30 1·30

C123 Little Egret
(*Egretta garzetta*)

2005. Birds. Multicoloured.
C146 1m. Type **C123** 2·50 2·50
C147 1m. Black-winged stilt (*Himan-
 topus himantopus*) 2·50 2·50
C148 1m. Kingfisher (*Alcedo atthis*) 2·50 2·50
C149 1m. European bee eater
 (*Merops apiaster*) 2·50 2·50

C124 Early Footballers

2005. Centenary of CSC Zrinjski Sports Club.
Multicoloured.
C150 3m. Type **C124** 7·25 7·25
C151 3m. Modern footballers 7·25 7·25

C125 Figure
holding Flag

2005. Easter.
C152 **C125** 50f. multicoloured 1·30 1·30

C126 *Thumbelina*
(Hans Christian
Andersen)

2005. Writers Anniversaries. Multicoloured.
C153 20f. Type **C126** (birth bicen-
 tenary) 50 50
C154 20f. *Tintilinic* (Ivana Brlic
 Mazuranic) (130th (2004)
 birth anniv) 50 50

C127 Bread, Grapes, Wine, Nuts
and Soft Cheese

2005. Europa. Gastronomy. Multicoloured.
C155 2m. Type **C127** 5·00 5·00
C156 2m. Bread, garlic, meats, glass
 and flagon 5·00 5·00

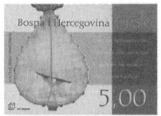

C128 Gusle

2005. Musical Instruments.
C157 **C128** 5m. multicoloured 12·50 12·50

C129 Vjetrenica Cave

2005. International Day of Water.
C158 **C129** 1m. multicoloured 2·50 2·50

C130 Steam Locomotive

2005. 120th Anniv of Metkovic—Mostar Railway.
C159 **C130** 50f. multicoloured 1·30 1·30

C131 Virgin Mary
(statue) and Crowds

2005. Medjugorje Youth Festival.
C160 **C131** 1m. multicoloured 2·50 2·50

C132 Father
Grgo Martic

2005. Birth Centenary of Father Grgo Martic.
C161 **C132** 1m. multicoloured 2·50 2·50

C133 Trumpet

2005. International Music Day.
C162 **C133** 50f. multicoloured 1·00 1·00

C134 Flowers over
map

2005. Tenth Anniv of Dayton Agreement.
C163 **C134** 1m.50 multicoloured 3·75 3·75

C135 Slavko
Barbaric

2005. Fifth Death Anniv of Slavko Barbaric (writer).
C164 **C135** 1m. multicoloured 2·50 2·50

C136 Mary and
Jesus

2005. Christmas. Multicoloured.
C165 50f. Type **C136** 1·30 1·30
C166 50f. Tree 1·30 1·30

C137 "50"

2005. 50th Anniv of Europa Stamps. Multicoloured.
C167 2m. Type **C137** 3·75 3·75
C168 2m. Sunflowers and envelope 3·75 3·75
C169 2m. Map and 2003 1k.80 stamp
 (No. C107) 3·75 3·75
C170 2m. European flags 3·75 3·75
MSC171 90×100 mm. Nos. 167/70 20·00 20·00

C138 Lake and Bearded
Tit

2006. International Swamp Protection Day.
C172 **C138** 1m. multicoloured 2·50 2·50

C139 Faces

2006. Europa. Integration. Multicoloured.
C173 2m. Type **C139** 5·00 5·00
C174 2m. "Integration" 5·00 5·00

C140 Sunflower and
Globe

2006. Earth Day.
C175 **C140** 1m. multicoloured 2·50 2·50

C141 Paper Birds

2006. World Press Freedom Day.
C176 **C141** 50f. multicoloured 1·30 1·30

C142 Cable

2006. World Telecommunications Day.
C177 **C142** 1m. multicoloured 2·50 2·50

C143 Queen of
Peace (statue) and
Church

2006. 25th Anniv of Medugorje. Multicoloured.
C178 1m. Type **C143** 2·40 2·40
C179 1m. Statue with multicoloured
 halo amongst rocks 2·40 2·40
C180 1m. Cross, Krizevac Hill and
 statue 2·40 2·40
C181 1m. Statue (detail) and church 2·40 2·40
C182 1m. Stylized church and crowd 2·40 2·40

C144 Church

2006. 150th Anniv of Uzdol Parish.
C183 **C144** 50f. multicoloured 1·30 1·30

C145 Nikola Tesla

2006. 150th Birth Anniv of Nikola Tesla (engineer).
C184 **C145** 2m. multicoloured 5·00 5·00

C146 Archer and Stag

2006. Stecci (medieval tombstones).
C185 **C146** 20f. multicoloured 1·00 1·00

C147 Car

2006. Car Free Day.
C186	**C147**	1m. black, vermilion and yellow	2·50	2·50

C148 Crucifix from Woman's Rosary, Franciscan Monastery, Humac

2006
C187	**C148**	5m. multicoloured	12·50	12·50

C149 *Upupa epops* (hoopoe)

2006. Birds of Hutovo. Multicoloured.
C188	70f. Type **C149**		1·80	1·80
C189	70f. *Alauda arvensis* (skylark)		1·80	1·80

Nos. C190/1 have been left for additions to this set.

C150 *Papaver kerneri*

2006. Flora. Multicoloured.
C192	20f. Type **C150**		50	50
C193	20f. *Cerastium dinaricum*		50	50

C151 Door with Wreath

2006. Christmas and New Year. Multicoloured.
C194	50f. Type C **151**		1·30	1·30
C195	1m. Grass and candles		2·50	2·50

C152 Hearts and Birds

2007. St. Valentine's Day.
C196	**C152**	10f. multicoloured	1·00	1·00

C153 Head of Dog

2007. Dogs. Tornjak. Multicoloured.
C197	70f. Type **C153**		1·70	1·70
C198	70f. Head of dog, black markings		1·70	1·70
C199	70f. Dog with black markings		1·70	1·70
C200	70f. Dog with brown markings		1·70	1·70

C154 Mak Dizdar

2007. 90th Birth Anniv of Mehmedalija Mak Dizdar (poet).
C201	**C154**	1m. multicoloured	2·50	2·50

C155 Clasped Hands

2007. Europa. Centenary of Scouting. Multicoloured.
C202	3m. Type **C155**		6·75	6·75
C203	3m. Reef knot		6·75	6·75

C156 *Sorbus domestica*

2007. Tree Day. Sheet 68×91 mm.
MSC204	**C156**	2k.10 multicoloured	5·25	5·25

C157 Lion (bas relief) and Map

2007. Gabela Archaeological Site, Capljina.
C205	**C157**	1m.50 multicoloured	3·75	3·75

C158 Iris

2007. *Iris Illyrica.* Multicoloured.
C206	2m. Type **C158**		5·00	5·00
MSC207	61×80 mm. 3k. Iris and trireme (24×58 mm)		7·75	7·75

C159 Virgin Mary (statue)

2007. Medugorje. Multicoloured.
C208	1m. Type **C159**		2·40	2·40
C209	1m. Hands holding rosary		2·40	2·40
C210	1m. Virgin Mary and pilgrims		2·40	2·40
C211	1m. Bronze statue of Friar		2·40	2·40
C212	1m. Virgin Mary (statue) and tower		2·40	2·40

C160 Friar Marko Dobretic

2007. 300th Birth Anniv of Friar Marko Dobretic.
C213	**C160**	60f. multicoloured	1·50	1·50

C161 Duke Vlatko's Tombstone, Boljuni Necropolis

2007. Cultural Heritage Day.
C214	**C161**	20f. multicoloured	1·00	1·00

C162 Emblem

2007. World Bowling Championship, Grude.
C215	**C162**	5m. black and scarlet	12·50	12·50

C163 Hemp and Spindle

2007. Ethnological Treasures.
C216	**C163**	70f. multicoloured	1·80	1·80

C164 *Fulica atra* (coot)

2007. Birds. Multicoloured.
C217	2m. Type **C164**		3·75	3·75
C218	2m. *Anas platyrhynchos* (mallard)		3·75	3·75
C219	2m. *Anas crecca* (common teal)		3·75	3·75
C220	2m. *Streptopella turtur* (turtle dove)		3·75	3·75

C165 *Gentiana lutea*

2007. Flora of Blidinje Park. Multicoloured.
C221	3m. Type **C165**		7·75	7·75
MSC222	80×60 mm. 3k. *Vaccinium vitis-idaea*		7·75	7·75

The stamp and margins **MS**C222 form a composite design.

C166 Candles

2007. Christmas. Multicoloured.
C223	50f. Type **C166**		1·30	1·30
C224	70f. Decorated trees and doorway		1·90	1·90

C167 Friar Andeo Kraljevic

2007. Birth Bicentenary of Friar Ivan (Andeo) Kraljevic.
C225	**C167**	1m. multicoloured	2·75	2·75

C168 Chick and Flowers

2008. Easter.
C226	**C168**	70f. multicoloured	1·90	1·90

C169 Piano Keys

2008. Tenth Anniv of Matica Hrvatska (cultural institution)'s Festival Week.
C227	**C169**	10f. black and vermilion	1·00	1·00

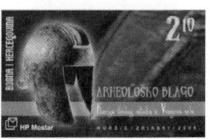

C170 Hand holding Envelope as Paper Aeroplane

2008. Europa. The Letter. Multicoloured.
C228	3m. Type **C170**		7·00	7·00
C229	3m. Pen nib		7·00	7·00

C171 Illyrian Warrior's Helmet, Vranjevo Selo

2008. Archaeology.
C230	**C171**	2m.10 multicoloured	6·00	6·00

C172 Grave of Mosha Danon, Rabbi of Sarajevo

2008. International Day of Diversity.
C231	**C172**	1m.50 multicoloured	4·25	4·25

C173 *Achillea millefolium* (milfoil)

2008. Myth and Flora. Andrija Simic and Milfoil. Sheet 80×60 mm.
MSC232	**C173**	multicoloured	8·25	8·25

C174 Virgin Mary, Girl and Dove

2008. Medugorje. Multicoloured.
C233	1m. Type **C174**		2·75	2·75
C234	1m. Church of St. Jacob		2·75	2·75
C235	1m. Page, crucified Christ and praying hands		2·75	2·75
C236	1m. Virgin Mary (statue)		2·75	2·75
C237	1m. Summit Cross		2·75	2·75

C175 Grapes

2008. Vintage Days in Brotnjo, 2008. Multicoloured.
C238	50f. Type **C175**		1·30	1·30
C239	70f. White grapes		2·20	2·20

C176 Building

2008. Zaostrog Monastery.
C240	**C176**	1m. multicoloured	3·00	3·00

C177 Tobacco Cutter

2008. Cultural Heritage. Ethnological Treasures. Avan (tobacco cutter).
C241 **C177** 2m. multicoloured 3·75 3·75

C178 Zepce

2008. 550th Anniv of Zepce.
C242 **C178** 1m.50 multicoloured 4·50 4·50

C179 Tubers

2008. International Year of the Potato. Multicoloured.
C243 50f. Type **C179** 1·75 1·75
MSC244 80×60 mm. 5m. Flowers 14·00 14·00

C180 Falco tinnunculus (Kestrel)

2008. Birds. Multicoloured.
C245 1m.50 Type **C180** 90 90
C246 1m.50 Circactus gallicus (short-toed eagle) 90 90
C247 1m.50 Bubo bubo (eagle owl) 90 90
C248 1m.50 Accipiter gentilis (goshawk) 90 90

C181 Leo Petrovic

2008. Father Leo Petrovic (professor of theology) Commemoration.
C249 **C181** 1m. multicoloured 9·25 9·25

C182 Gingerbread Man

2008. Christmas. Multicoloured.
C250 70f. Type **C182** 6·50 6·50
C251 70f. Bow 6·50 6·50

C183 Early Players

2008. 60th Anniv of Siroki Brijeg Football Club. Multicoloured.
C252 70f. Type **C183** 6·50 6·50
MSC253 80×60 mm. 2m.10 Modern players (35×30 mm) 18·00 18·00

C184 Woman holding Daffodil

2009. Daffodil Day (breast cancer awareness day).
C254 **C184** 20f. magenta and chrome yellow 1·00 1·00

C185 Waterfall, River Pliva

2009. International Water Day. Watermills in Pliva Lakes. Multicoloured.
C255 70f. Type **C185** 1·70 1·70
C256 70f. Watermills 1·70 1·70

C186 '60'

2009. 60th Anniv of Council of Europe and European Court of Human Rights. Each new blue and lemon.
C257 1m.50 Type **C186** 4·50 4·50
C258 1m.50 Court of Human Rights building (horiz) 4·50 4·50

C187 Earth and Planets

2009. Europa. Astronomy. Multicoloured.
C259 3m. Type **C187** 9·00 9·00
C260 3m. Telescope and planets 9·00 9·00

C188 Arms of Herzeg Stipan Vukcic Kosaca

2009. Archaeology.
C261 **C188** 1m.50 multicoloured 4·50 4·50

C189 Tanacetum balsamita (costamary)

2009. Myths and Flora. Multicoloured.
C262 2m.10 Type **C189** 4·00 4·00
MSC263 80×60 mm. 2m.10 Girl and flowers 4·00 4·00

C190 Building Facade

2009. 150th Anniv of Franciscan Monastery, Guca Gora.
C264 **C190** 70f. multicoloured 1·70 1·70

C191 Church of St. Jacob

2009. Medjugorje. Multicoloured.
C265 1m. Type **C191** 90 90
C266 1m. Summit Cross 90 90
C267 1m. Crucified Christ 90 90
C268 1m. Virgin Mary and Church of St. Jacob 90 90
C269 1m. Virgin Mary 90 90

C192 Festival Emblem

2009. Tenth Mediterranean Film Festival.
C270 **C192** 70f. multicoloured 1·70 1·70

C193 Chapel Entrance

2009. 800th Anniv of Franciscan Order.
C271 1m. multicoloured 1·20 1·20
C272 – 1m. deep brown 1·20 1·20
DESIGNS: Type C **193**; C272 Franciscan waist cord.

C194 Decorated Chest

2009. Stamp Day. Ethnological Treasures.
C273 **C194** 70f. multicoloured 1·70 1·70

C195 Monastery

2009. 150th Anniv Franciscan Monastery, Gorica Livno.
C274 **C195** 60f. multicoloured 1·70 1·70

C196 Nycticorax nycticorax (black-crowned night heron)

2009. Birds of Hutovo Blato. Multicoloured.
C275 1m.50 Type **C196** 1·20 1·20
C276 1m.50 Cuculus canorus (cuckoo) 1·20 1·20
C277 1m.50 Coturnix coturnix (quail) 1·20 1·20
C278 1m.50 Rallus aquaticus (water rail) 1·20 1·20

C197 Flowers and Fruit

2009. Prunus domestica (plum). Multicoloured.
C279 5m. multicoloured 11·50 11·50
MSC280 65×65 mm. 5m. Fruit 11·50 11·50

C198 Candles

2009. Christmas. Multicoloured.
C281 70f. Type **C198** 1·70 1·70
C282 70f. Heart shaped cushion and parcels 1·70 1·70

C199 Maple Leaf

2010. Winter Olympic Games, Vancouver. Multicoloured.
C283 70f. multicoloured 1·60 1·70
C284 1m.50 bright scarlet, black and gold 2·10 2·10
Designs: 70f. Type **C199**; 1m.50 Stylized maple leaf on skis

C200 Carnations

2010. Centenary of International Women's Day
C284a **C200** 20f. multicoloured 1·00 1·00

C201 Friar Martin Nedic

2010. Birth Bicentenary of Friar Martin Nedić (builder of monastery and church in Tolisa)
C285 **C201** 2m.10 multicoloured 4·25 4·25

C202 Open Book, Stylized Child standing on Rainbow and Kite

2010. Europa. Multicoloured.
C286 3m. Type **C202** 5·75 5·75
C287 3m. Stylized child standing on open book holding windmill 5·75 5·75

C203 Cave Entrance and Pintadera

2010. Archeological Heritage
C288 **C203** 1m.50 multicoloured 3·25 3·25

C204 Linden Flower and Leaf

2010. Myths and Flora. Sheet 80×60 mm
MSC289 **C204** 5m. multicoloured 8·25 8·25

C205 Virgin Mary

2010. Medjugorje. Multicoloured.
C290 1m. Type **C205** 2·10 2·10
C291 1m. Summit Cross 2·10 2·10
C292 1m. Hand holding rosary 2·10 2·10
C293 1m. Virgin Mary (head and shoulders) 2·10 2·10
C294 1m. Pilgrims and flags 2·10 2·10

C206 Lighthouse
and Emblem

2010. General Assembly of Matrix Croatica
C295 **C206** 1m. scarlet-vermilion
 and black 2·10 2·10

C207 Mother Teresa and
Child

2010. Birth Centenary of Agnes Gonxha Bojaxhiu (Mother
Teresa) (founder of Missionaries of Charity in
Calcutta)
C296 **C207** 2m.10 bright ultramarine 4·25 4·25

C208 Prokoško Lake

2010. Environmental Protection. Multicoloured.
C297 1m. Type **C208** 2·10 2·10
C298 1m. *Triturus alpestris reiseri*
 (newt) 2·10 2·10

C209 Peasant
Shoes

2010. Ethnological Treasures
C299 **C209** 70f. multicoloured 1·60 1·60

C210 Balkan Green
Lizard

2010. Balkan Green Lizard (*Lacerta trilineata*).
Multicoloured.
C300 50f. Type **C210** 1·40 1·40
C301 50f. Basking on rock 1·40 1·40
C302 50f. Climbing tree 1·40 1·40
C303 50f. Juvenile (brown striped) 1·40 1·40

C211 Fly Agaric
(*Amanita muscaria*)

2010. Fungi. Multicoloured.
C304 2m.10 Type **C211** 4·25 4·25
C305 2m.10 Puffball (*Lycoperdon
 perlatum*) 4·25 4·25

C212 Slavko
Barbaric

2010. Tenth Death Anniv of Fr. Slavko Barbaric
C306 **C212** 1m. multicoloured 2·10 2·10

C213 Rocking Horse
Tree Decoration

2010. Christmas and New Year. Multicoloured.
C307 70f. Type **C213** 1·70 1·70
C308 70f. Angel 1·70 1·70

C214 Text and Book

2011. 400th Anniv of First Printed Book in National
Language
C309 **C214** 70f. multicoloured 1·70 1·70

C215 Wind sock

2011. World Meteorological Day
C310 **C215** 20f. multicoloured 60 60

C216 Symbols of Easter

2011. Easter
C311 **C216** 70f. brown and black 1·80 2·80

C217 Coniferous Forest

2011. Europa. Forests. Multicoloured.
C312 3m. Type **C217** 5·75 5·75
C313 3m. Deciduous forest in
 autumn 5·75 5·75

C218 Yuri Gagarin

2011. 50th Anniv of First Manned Space Flight
C314 **C218** 10f. multicoloured 1·00 1·00

C219 Floor Plan

2011. Archaeological Treasures. Early Christian Basilica in
Cim
C315 **C219** 1m.50 multicoloured 2·25 2·25

C220 Symbols of
Science

2011. 300th Birth Anniv of Josip Rudjer Boskovic
(physicist, mathematician, astronomer, geodesist,
poet, philosopher, engineer and diplomat)
C316 **C220** 2m.10 multicoloured 4·25 4·25

C221 Hawthorn

2011. Myths and Flora. Sheet 80×60 mm
MSC317 **C221** 5m. multicoloured 10·25 19·25

C222 Virgin Mary (head
and shoulders)

2011. Medjugorje. Multicoloured.
C318 1m. Type **C222** 2·10 2·10
C319 1m. Crucified Christ 2·10 2·10
C320 1m. Virgin Mary and Church of
 St. Jacob 2·10 2·10
C321 1m. Summit Cross and rosary 2·10 2·10

C223 St. Anthony

2011. St. Anthony of Padua Commemoration
C322 **C223** 1m. multicoloured 2·10 2·10

C224 Cyclist

2011. World Bicycle Day
C323 **C224** 70f. green 1·70 1·70

C225 Parish Church

2011. Centenary of Skopaljska Gracanica Parish
C324 **C225** 50f. multicoloured 1·50 1·50

C226 Martyrs of
Drina

2011. Martyrs of Drina
C325 **C226** 70f. multicoloured 1·70 1·70

C227 Golinjevo Fibulae
(clasps)

2011. Post Day. Fibulae
C326 **C227** 1m. black and carmine-
 vermilion 2·10 2·10

C228 Fridtjof
Nansen

2011. 150th Birth Anniv of Fridtjof Nansen (polar
explorer, politician and diplomat)
C327 **C228** 1m.50 multicoloured 4·50 4·50

C229 Pomegranate
(*Punica granatum*)

2011. Fruit. Multicoloured.
C328 2m.10 Type **C229** 4·25 4·25
C329 2m.10 Figs (*Ficus carica*) 4·25 4·25

C230 Lynx

2011. Lynx (*Lynx lynx*). Multicoloured.
C330 3m. Type **C230** 2·10 2·10
C331 3m. Facing left 2·10 2·10
C332 3m. Mother and cub 2·10 2·10
C333 3m. In snow facing right 2·10 2·10

C231 Holy Family

2011. Christmas. Multicoloured.
C334 70f. Type **C231** 2·10 2·10
C335 70f. Decorated tree 2·10 2·10

C232 Title and
Monastery

2012. 300th Anniv of Toma Babic's Grammar
C336 **C232** 70f. multicoloured 1·70 1·70

C233 Trappist Cheese
and Maria Stern
Monastery, Banja Luka

2012. Gastronomy. Trappist Cheese
C337 **C233** 2m.50 multicoloured 6·50 6·50

C234 The Old Bridge,
Mostar

2012. Europa. Visit Mostar. Multicoloured.
C338 3m. Type **C234** 4·25 4·25
C339 3m. Herceg Stjepan Kosaca
 Lodge 4·25 4·25

C235 Nurse

2012. World Red Cross Day
C340 **C235** 1m. multicoloured 2·10 2·10

C236 Stone Frieze

2012. Archeological Treasures. Cult of the God Mithra
C341 **C236** 70f. multicoloured 1·70 1·70

C237 Hornbeam
(*Carpinus betulus*)

2012. Myths and Flora. Diva Grabovceva and Hornbeam.
Sheet 80×60 mm
MSC342 **C236** 3m. multicoloured 8·25 8·25

C238 Vladimir Prelog and Ivo Andric

2012. Bosnia and Herzegovina Nobel Laureates. Ivo Andric (Nobel Prize for Literature, 1961) and Vladimir Prelog (Nobel prize for Chemistry, 1973)

C343	**C238**	1m.50 multicoloured	4·50	4·50

III. REPUBLIKA SRPSKA

Issued by the Serb administration based in Pale.

Република
Српска
(S1)

1992. Nos. 2587/98 of Yugoslavia surch as Type B.

S1	5d. on 10p. violet and green	1·10	1·10
S2	30d. on 3d. blue and red	£140	£140
S3a	50d. on 40p. green & purple	1·10	1·10
S4	60d. on 20p. red and yellow	1·20	1·20
S5	60d. on 30p. green & orange	1·20	1·20
S6	100d. on 1d. blue and purple	1·20	1·20
S7a	100d. on 2d. blue and red	1·20	1·20
S8	100d. on 3d. blue and red	1·20	1·20
S9a	300d. on 5d. ultram & blue	1·50	1·50
S10	500d. on 50p. green & violet	1·50	1·50
S11	500d. on 60p. mauve & red	1·50	1·50

S2 Stringed Instrument

1993. Dated "1992".

S12	**S2**	10d. black and yellow	4·50	4·50
S13	**S2**	20d. black and blue	20	20
S14	**S2**	30d. black and pink	50	50
S15	-	50d. black and red	60	60
S16	-	100d. black and red	1·50	1·50
S17	-	500d. black and blue	3·00	3·00

DESIGNS—VERT: 50, 100d. Coat of arms. HORIZ: 500d. Monastery.

1993. Dated "1993".

S18	**S2**	5000d. black and lilac	10	10
S19	**S2**	6000d. black and yellow	20	20
S20	**S2**	10000d. black and blue	3·50	3·50
S21	-	20000d. black and red	95	95
S22	-	30000d. black and red	1·50	1·50
S23	-	50000d. black and lilac	1·50	1·50

DESIGNS—VERT: 20000, 30000d. Coat of arms. HORIZ: 50000d. Monastery.

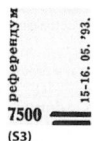

референдум
15-16. 05. '93.

7500
(S3)

1993. Referendum. Nos. S15/16 surch as Type S3.

S24	7500d. on 50d. black and red	2·00	2·00
S25	7500d. on 100d. black and red	2·00	2·00
S26	9000d. on 50d. black and red	2·75	2·75

S4 Symbol of St. John the Evangelist

1993. No value expressed.

S27	**S4**	A red	70	70

No. S27 was sold at the rate for internal letters.

S5 Icon of St. Stefan

1994. Republic Day.

S28	**S5**	1d. multicoloured	7·00	7·00

S6 King Petar I

1994. 150th Birth Anniv of King Petar I of Serbia.

S29	**S6**	80p. sepia and brown	3·50	3·50

S7 Banja Luka

1994. 500th Anniv of Banja Luka.

S30	**S7**	1d.20 multicoloured	4·00	4·00

1994. Issued at Doboj. Surch with letter. (a) On Nos. S13/16.

S31	**S2**	A on 20d. black and blue		
S32	**S2**	R on 20d. black and blue		
S33	**S2**	R on 30d. black and pink		
S34	-	R on 50d. black and red		
S35	-	R on 100d. black and red		

(b) On Nos. S18/19 and S21/2.

S36	**S2**	R on 5000d. black and lilac		
S37	**S2**	R on 6000d. black and yellow		
S38	-	A on 20000d. black and red		
S39	-	R on 20000d. black and red		
S40	-	R on 30000d. black and red		

Stamps surcharged "A" were sold at the current rate for internal letters and those surcharged "R" at the rate for internal registered letters. The "R" on No. S32 is reversed.

S9 Madonna and Child (icon)

1994. Cajnicka Church.

S41	**S9**	1d. multicoloured	3·50	3·50

1994. Nos. S18/20 and S23 surch (Nos. 542/3 with letter).

S42	**S2**	A on 5000d. black & lilac	2·00	2·00
S43	**S2**	R on 6000d. black & yell	2·00	2·00
S44	**S2**	40p. on 10000d. blk & bl	2·00	2·00
S45	-	2d. on 50000d. black and lilac	2·00	2·00

No. S42 was sold at the current rate for internal letters and No. S43, which shows the surcharge as the cyrillic letter resembling "P", at the rate for internal registered letters.

S11 Tavna Monastery

1994. Monasteries. Multicoloured.

S46	60p. Type S 11	2·00	2·00
S47	1d. Mostanica (horiz)	3·00	3·00
S48	1d.20 Zitomislic	3·50	3·50

S12 Aquilegia dinarica

1996. Nature Protection. Multicoloured.

S49	1d.20 Type S12	2·00	2·00
S50	1d.20 Edraianthus niveus (plant)	2·00	2·00
S51	1d.20 Shore lark	2·00	2·00
S52	1d.20 Dinaromys bogdanovi (dormouse)	2·00	2·00

S6 King Petar I

1996. Nos. S14/16, S19 and S22 surch.

S53	**S2**	70p. on 30d. black and pink	60	60
S54	-	1d. on 100d. black & red	70	70
S55	-	2d. on 30000d. blk & red	1·30	1·30
S56	-	3d. on 50d. black and red	1·90	1·90
S57	**S2**	5d. on 6000d. black and yellow	3·25	3·25

S14 Relay Station, Mt. Kozara

1996

S58	**S14**	A green and bistre	25	25
S59	-	R purple and brown	60	60
S60	-	1d.20 violet and blue	65	65
S61	-	2d. lilac and mauve	1·30	1·30
S62	-	5d. purple and blue	2·75	2·75
S63	-	10d. brown and sepia	5·75	5·75

DESIGNS—VERT: R, Kraljica relay station, Mt. Ozren; 2d. Relay station, Mt. Romanija; 5d. Stolice relay station, Mt. Maljevica. HORIZ: 1d.20, Bridge over river Drina at Srbinje; 10d. Bridge at Visegrad.

No. S58 was sold at the current rate for an internal letter and No. S59 at the rate for an internal registered letter.

S15 Orthodox Church, Bascarsiji

1997

S64	**S15**	2d.50 multicoloured	1·40	1·40

S16 Pupin

1997. 62nd Death Anniv of Michael Pupin (physicist and inventor).

S65	**S16**	2d.50 multicoloured	1·40	1·40

S17 Primula kitaibeliana

1997. Flowers. Multicoloured.

S66	3d.20 Type S17	1·50	1·50
S67	3d.20 Pedicularis hoermanniana	1·50	1·50
S68	3d.20 Knautia sarajevensis	1·50	1·50
S69	3d.20 Oxytropis campestris	1·50	1·50

S18 Robert Koch

1997. Obligatory Tax. Anti-tuberculosis Week. Self-adhesive.

S70	**S18**	15f. red and blue	45	45

S19 Branko Copic

1997. Writers. Each mauve and yellow.

S71	A (60p.) Type **S19**	35	35
S72	R (90p.) Jovan Ducic	60	60
S73	1d.50 Mesa Selimovic	60	60
S74	3d. Aleksa Santic	1·40	1·40
S75	5d. Petar Kocic	2·30	2·30
S76	10d. Ivo Andric	4·75	4·75

S20 European Otter

1997. Nature Protection. Multicoloured.

S77	2d.50 Type S20	60	60
S78	4d.50 Roe deer	1·70	1·70
S79	6d.50 Brown bear	3·50	3·50

S21 Two Queens

1997. Europa. Tales and Legends. Multicoloured.

S80	2d.50 Type **S21**	9·25	9·25
S81	6d.50 Prince on horseback	20·00	20·00

S22 Diana, Princess of Wales

1998. Diana, Princess of Wales Commemoration.

S82	**S22**	3d.50 multicoloured ("DIANA" in Roman alphabet)	5·75	5·75
S83	**S22**	3d.50 multicoloured ("DIANA" in Cyrillic alphabet)	5·75	5·75

S23 Cross and Globe

1998. Obligatory Tax. Red Cross. Self-adhesive.

S84	**S23**	90f. red, blue and ultram	1·20	1·20

S24 Brazil

1998. World Cup Football Championship, France. Showing flags and players of countries in final rounds. Multicoloured.

S85	90f. Type **S24**	1·90	1·90
S86	90f. Morocco	1·90	1·90
S87	90f. Norway	1·90	1·90
S88	90f. Scotland	1·90	1·90
S89	90f. Italy	1·90	1·90
S90	90f. Chile	1·90	1·90
S91	90f. Austria	1·90	1·90
S92	90f. Cameroun	1·90	1·90
S93	90f. France	1·90	1·90
S94	90f. Saudi Arabia	1·90	1·90
S95	90f. Denmark	1·90	1·90
S96	90f. South Africa	1·90	1·90
S97	90f. Spain	1·90	1·90
S98	90f. Nigeria	1·90	1·90
S99	90f. Paraguay	1·90	1·90
S100	90f. Bulgaria	1·90	1·90
S101	90f. Netherlands	1·90	1·90
S102	90f. Belgium	1·90	1·90
S103	90f. Mexico	1·90	1·90
S104	90f. South Korea	1·90	1·90
S105	90f. Germany	1·90	1·90
S106	90f. United States of America	1·90	1·90
S107	90f. Yugoslavia	1·90	1·90
S108	90f. Iran	1·90	1·90
S109	90f. Romania	1·90	1·90
S110	90f. England (U.K. flag)	1·90	1·90
S111	90f. Tunisia	1·90	1·90
S112	90f. Colombia	1·90	1·90
S113	90f. Argentina	1·90	1·90
S114	90f. Jamaica	1·90	1·90
S115	90f. Croatia	1·90	1·90
S116	90f. Japan	1·90	1·90

S25 Couple and Musical Instrument

1998. Europa. National Festivals. Multicoloured.

S117	7m.50 Type **S25**		9·25	9·25
S118	7m.50 Couple from Neretva and musical instrument		9·25	9·25

S26 Family walking in Countryside

1998. Obligatory Tax. Anti-tuberculosis Week.

S119	**S26**	75f. multicoloured	1·20	1·20

S27 St. Pantelejmon

1998. 800th Anniv of Hilandar Monastery. Icons. Multicoloured.

S120	50f. Type **S27**		80	80
S121	70f. Jesus Christ		1·20	1·20
S122	1m.70 St. Nikola		2·50	2·50
S123	2m. St. John of Rila		3·00	3·00

S28 Bijeljina

1999. Towns. Multicoloured. (a) With face value.

S124	15f. Type **S28**		25	25
S125	20f. Sokolac		35	35
S126	75f. Prijedor		1·20	1·20
S127	2m. Brcko		3·00	3·00
S128	4m.50 Zvornik		6·50	6·50
S129	10m. Doboj		15·00	15·00

(b) Face value expressed by letter.

S130	A (50f.) Banja Luka		70	70
S131	R (1m.) Trebinje		1·50	1·50

No. S130 was sold at the current rate for an internal letter and No. S131 at the rate for an internal registered letter.

S29 Avions de Transport Regional ATR 72 over Lake

1999. Founding of Air Srpska (state airline). Multicoloured.

S132	50f. Type **S29**		70	70
S133	50f. Airliner above clouds		70	70
S134	75f. Airliner over beach		1·20	1·20
S135	1m.50 Airliner over lake (different)		2·20	2·20

S30 Table Tennis Ball as Globe

1999. International Table Tennis Championships, Belgrade. Multicoloured.

S136	1m. Type **S30**		1·70	1·70
S137	2m. Table tennis table, bat and ball		3·50	3·50

S31 Kozara National Park

1999. Europa. National Parks. Multicoloured.

S138	1m.50 Type **S31**		75·00	75·00
S139	2m. Perucica National Park		75·00	75·00

S32 Open Hands

1999. Obligatory Tax. Red Cross.

S140	**S32**	10f. multicoloured	45	45

S33 Manuscript

1999. 780th Anniv of Bosnia and Herzegovina Archbishopric (S142, S144/8) and 480th Anniv of Garazole Printing Works (S141, S143). Mult.

S141	50f. Type **S33**		70	70
S142	50f. Dobrun Monastery		70	70
S143	50f. "G"		70	70
S144	50f. Zhitomislib Monastery		70	70
S145	50f. Gomionitsa Monastery		70	70
S146	50f. Madonna and Child with angels and prophets (icon, 1578)		70	70
S147	50f. St. Nicolas (icon)		70	70
S148	50f. Wise Men (icon)		70	70

S34 Brown Trout

1999. Fish. Multicoloured.

S149	50f. Type **S34**		6·75	1·20
S150	50f. Lake trout (*Salmo trutta morpha lacustris*)		1·20	1·20
S151	75f. Huchen		1·70	1·70
S152	1m. European grayling		2·30	2·30

S35 Lunar Module on Moon's Surface

1999. 30th Anniv of First Manned Landing on Moon. Multicoloured.

S153	1m. Type **S35**		1·90	1·90
S154	2m. Astronaut on Moon		3·00	3·00

S36 Pencil and Emblem

1999. 125th Anniv of Universal Postal Union. Multicoloured

S155	75f. Type **S36**		1·20	1·20
S156	1m.25 Earth and emblem		2·00	2·00

S36a Roadway to '2000'

1999. Obligatory Tax. Tuberculosis Week. Ordinary or self adhesive gum.

S156a	10f. Type **S36a**			

S37 Madonna and Child

1999. Art. Icons. Multicoloured.

S157	50f. Type **S37**		75	75
S158	50f. Madonna, Cajnice		75	75
S159	50f. Madonna Pelagonitisa		75	75
S160	50f. Holy Kirjak Otselnik		75	75
S161	50f. Pieta		75	75
S162	50f. Entry of Christ into Jerusalem		75	75
S163	50f. St. Jovan		75	75
S164	50f. Sava and Simeon		75	75

S38 Ancient Egyptians

1999. Millennium (1st series). Sheet 137×86 mm containing Type **S38** and similar horiz designs. Multicoloured.

MS S170	50f.×5, Type **S38**; Inventions for time keeping; Iron working; Invention of steam engines; Transport; 1m. Space exploration.		10·00	10·00

S39 Postal Stage-Coach during Austro-Hungarian Occupation

1999. 135th Anniv of Postal Service. Multicoloured.

S171	50f. Type **S39**		75	75
MS S172	55×70 mm. 3m. Tatar postmen crossing bridge during Turkish regency		80·00	80·00

S40 Fresco of St. Simeon (Stefan Nemanja) holding Studenica Monastery

2000. 800th Death Anniv of Stefan Nemanja (Stephen II).

S173	**S40**	1m.50 multicoloured	2·20	2·20

S41 *Prunus domestica* (plum)

2000. Trees. Multicoloured.

S174	1m. Type **S41**		1·50	1·50
S175	2m. *Corylus avellana* (hazel)		3·00	3·00

S42 Bridge, Sepk

2000. Bridges on Drina River. Multicoloured.

S176	1m. Type **S42**		1·60	1·60
S177	1m. Pavlovica Bridge, Bijeljina		1·60	1·60
S178	1m. Stag and iron bridge, Bratunac		1·60	1·60
S179	1m. Train crossing bridge, Zvornik		1·60	1·60

S43 Jovan Ducic

2000. Jovan Ducic (writer) Commemoration.

S180	**S43**	20f. multicoloured	35	35

S44 Construction of Europe

2000. Europa. Construction of Europe. Multicoloured.

S181	1m.50 Type **S44**		70·00	70·00
S182	2m.50 Children and stars		80·00	80·00

S45 Girl

2000. Obligatory Tax. Red Cross Week. Multicoloured. (a) Ordinary gum.

S183	10f. Type **S45**		50	50
S183a	10f. Symbols of care (30×41 mm)		50	50

(b) Self-adhesive.

S183b	50f. As No. 183a (20×30 mm)		50	50

S46 Basilica, Banja Luka (destroyed in 1941)

2000. Centenary of Banja Luka Province.

S184	**S46**	1m.50 multicoloured	2·20	2·20

S47 Footballers

2000. Euro 2000–European Football Championships, Belgium and the Netherlands. Multicoloured.

S185	1m. Type **S47**		1·50	1·50
S186	2m. Footballers (different)		3·00	3·00
MS S187	66×83 mm. 6m. Netherlands and Belgium flags as map and footballers (35×42 mm)		12·50	12·50

S48 Leaders of Herzegovina Uprising

2000. 125th Anniv of Herzegovina Rebellion (Nevesinje uprising).

S188	**S48**	1m.50 multicoloured	2·40	2·40

S49 Outline of Australia and Hurdling

2000. Olympic Games, Sydney. Multicoloured.

S189	50f. Type **S49**		75	75
S190	50f. Australia and volleyball		75	75
S191	50f. Australia and basketball		75	75
S192	50f. Australia and handball		75	75

MSS193 71×98 mm. 2m. Australia, emu
and kangaroo 3·00 3·00

No. MSS193 also contains a stamp size label showing Sydney Opera House and Olympic Stadium, the whole forming a composite design.

S50 Toddler

2000. Obligatory Tax. Tuberculosis Week. Multicoloured.
(a) Ordinary gum.
S194 10f. Type **S50** 50 50

(b) Self-adhesive.
S195 1m. As Type **S50** (20×30 mm) 50 50

S51 Locomotive, 1848

2000. 175th Anniv of Railways. Multicoloured.
S196 50f. Type **S51** 2·50 2·50
S197 50f. Steam locomotive, 1865 2·50 2·50
S198 50f. Steam locomotive, 1930 2·50 2·50
S199 1m. Electric locomotive, 1990 3·75 3·75

S52 *Leontopodium alpinum* (edelweiss)

2000. European Nature Protection. Multicoloured.
S200 1m. Type **S52** 1·50 1·50
S201 2m. *Proteus anguinus* (olm)
(horiz) 3·00 3·00

S53 Columbus discovering America

2000. Millennium (2nd series). Two sheets, each 140×86 mm containing Type **S53** and similar horiz designs. Multicoloured.
MSS202 (a) 50f.×6, Type **S53**; Discovery of glass, iron and steel; First printing press; Industrial revolution; James Watt and steam engine; Hubble telescope and satellite (space exploration). (b) 3m. Exploration by sea (105×55 mm) 9·25 9·25
Nos. MSS202a/b were issued in a folder.

S54 The Assumption of Mary (fresco)

2000. Icons and Frescoes. Multicoloured.
S203 50f. Type **S54** 75 75
S204 50f. Entry of Christ into Jerusalem (icon) 75 75
S205 1m. Madonna with Child and Angels (icon) 1·50 1·50
S206 1m. Christos Pantocrator (ceiling fresco) 1·50 1·50

S55 Alexander Graham Bell and Development of Telephones

2001. 125th Anniv of Telephony.
S207 **S55** 1m. multicoloured 1·50 1·50

S56 Yuri Gagarin and *Vostok 1*

2001. 40th Anniv of First Manned Space Flight. Multicoloured.
S208 1m. Type **S56** 1·50 1·50
MSS209 86×66 mm. 3m. Yuri Gagarin, take off and first flight orbit (53×34 mm) 8·75 8·75

S57 Vlado Milosevic

2001. Birth Centenary of Vlado Milosevic (composer and ethnomusicologist).
S210 **S57** 50f. multicoloured 75 75

S58 Waterfall, Sutjeska River

2001. Europa. Water Conservation. Multicoloured.
S211 1m. Type **S58** 2·75 2·75
S212 2m. Turjanica river 5·50 5·50

59 *Maniola jurtina*

2001. Butterflies. Multicoloured.
S213 50f. Type **S59** 75 75
S214 50f. *Pyrgus malvae* 75 75
S215 1m. *Papilio machaon* 1·50 1·50
S216 1m. *Lycaena phlaeas* inscr 'Lycaena pylaeas ' 1·50 1·50

S60 Women's Costumes, Popovo

2001. Traditional Costumes. Multicoloured.
S217 50f. Type **S60** 75 75
S218 50f. Bridal costume, Zmijanje 75 75
S219 1m. Woman's costume, Bileca mountains 1·50 1·50
S220 1m. Two women, Lijevce 1·50 1·50

S61 Combatants

2001. Republic of Srpska–Karate World Champion, 2001.
S221 **S61** 1m.50 multicoloured 2·20 2·20

S62 Old Castle, Kostajnica

2001. Towns. Multicoloured.
S222 25f. Type **S62** 35 35
S223 A (50f.) As No. S130 (24×22 mm) 75 75
S224 1m. Square with monument dedicated to war victims, Srbinje 1·50 1·50

No. S225 is vacant.

S63 Emblem

2001. Obligatory Tax. Anti-Tuberculosis Week.
S226 **S63** 10f. multicoloured 50 50

S64 Rastusa Cave, Teslic

2001. Caves. Multicoloured.
S227 50f. Type **S64** 75 75
S228 50f. Vagan cave, Vitorog 75 75
S229 50f. Pavlova cave, Petrovo 75 75
S230 50f. Orlovaca cave, Pale 75 75
S231 50f. Ledana cave, Bobija 75 75
S232 50f. Hole, Podovi plateau 75 75

S65 Alfred Nobel (founder)

2001. Centenary of Nobel Prizes. Multicoloured.
S233 1m. Type **S65** 1·50 1·50
S234 2m. Ivo Andric (winner of Nobel prize for Literature, 1961) 3·00 3·00

S66 Klinje Lake, Gacko

2001. European Nature Protection. Multicoloured.
S235 1m. Type **S66** 1·50 1·50
S236 1m. Bardaca Lake, Srbac 1·50 1·50

S67 *Still Life with Parrot* (Jovan Bijelic)

2001. Art. Multicoloured.
S237 50f. Type **S67** 75 75
S238 50f. *Djerdap* (Todor Svrakic) 75 75
S239 50f. *Suburb of Belgrade* (Kosta Hakman) 75 75
S240 50f. *Adela* (Miodrag Vujacic Mirski) (vert) 75 75

S68 Birth of Christ (icon, Studenica Monastery)

2001. Christmas.
S 241 **S68** 1m. multicoloured 1·50 1·50

S69 Player and Club Badge

2001. 75th Anniv of Borac Football Club.
S242 **S69** 1m.50 multicoloured 2·20 2·20

S70 National Arms

2002. Tenth Anniv of Republic Srpska. Multicoloured.
S243 50f. Type **S70** 80 80
S243a 1m. National flag (horiz) 1·60 1·60
MSS243b 71×64 mm. 2m. Map (42×35 mm) 3·25 3·25

S71 Hand gripping Cobra

2002. Fight against Terrorism. Multicoloured.
S244 1m. Type **S71** 1·60 1·60
MSS244a 68×76 mm. 2m. Eyes enclosed in globe 3·25 3·25

S72 Ski Jump

2002. Winter Olympic Games, Salt Lake City. Multicoloured.
S245 50f. Type **S72** 80 80
S246 1m. Two man bobsleigh 1·60 1·60

S73 Seated Woman with Cultural Symbols

2002. Centenary of Prosvjeta Cultural Association.
S247 **S73** 1m. multicoloured 1·60 1·60

S74 Vasilije Ostroski Church, Sarajevo

2002. Towns. Multicoloured.
S248 50f. Type **S74** 80 80
S249 2m. Oil Refinery, Srpski Brod (horiz) 3·25 32·00

NOTE: Due to the time lapse since Republika Srpska was last listed and the lack of stamps, several numbers have been left pending.

S75 Charles Lindbergh and *Spirit of St. Louis*

2002. 75th Anniv of First Trans-Atlantic Flight.
S250 **S75** 1m. multicoloured 1·60 1·60

S76 Horses and Clown

2002. Europa. Circus. Multicoloured.
S251 1m. Type **S76** 1·60 1·60
S252 1m.50 Elephants 2·40 2·40

S76a Rescue Workers

2002. Obligatory Tax. Red Cross Week. Multicoloured. (a) Ordinary gum.
S252a 10f. Type **S76a** 55 55

(b) Self-adhesive.
S252b 50f. As Type **S76a** plus emblem 55 55

S77 Footballers

2002. World Cup Football Championships, Japan and South Korea.Multicoloured.
S253 50f. Type **S77** 80 80
S254 1m. Footballers (different) 1·60 1·60

S78 Slatina

2002. Spas. Multicoloured.
S255 25f. Type **S78** 40 40
S256 50f. Mljecanica 80 80
S257 75f. Vilina Vlas 1·30 1·30
S258 1m. Laktasi 1·70 1·70
S259 1m.50 Vrucica 2·50 2·50
S260 5m. Dvorovi 8·75 8·75

S79 Greek-Illyrian Helmet (4th—5th century BC)

2002. Museum Exhibits. Multicoloured.
S261 50f. Type **S79** 85 85
S262 50f. Murano glass cup 85 85
S263 1m. Headstone of Grd (12th century parish priest) (horiz) 1·70 1·70
S264 1m. Silver bracelet (4th–5th century BC) (horiz) 1·70 1·70

S79a Waterfall and Lungs as Forest

2002. Obligatory Tax. Tuberculosis Week. Multicoloured. (a) Ordinary gum.
S264a 10f. Type **S79a** 55 55

(b) Self-adhesive.
S264b 50f. As Type **S79a** (20×30 mm) 55 55

S80 Boletus regius

2002. Fungi. Multicoloured.
S265 50f. Type **S80** 85 85
S266 50f. Macrolepiota procera 85 85
S267 1m. Amanita caesarea 1·70 1·70
S268 1m. Craterellus cornucopoides 1·70 1·70

S81 Magic Mountain

2002. European Nature Protection. Multicoloured.
S269 50f. Type **S81** 85 85
S269a 1m. Klekovaca Mountain 1·70 1·70

S82 Petar Popovic Pecija (Spiro Bocaric) (1933)

2002. Art. Multicoloured.
S270 50f. Type **S82** 85 85
S271 50f. Black Lake beneath Durmitor (Lazar Drljaca) (1935) (horiz) 85 85
S272 1m. Zembilj Street (Branko Sotra) (1937) (horiz) 1·70 1·70
S273 1m. Birds and Landscape (Milan Sovilj) (2000) (horiz) 1·70 1·70

S83 Vrbas Canyon (scene from film by Spiro Bocaric) (1937)

2003. Centenary of First Film shown in Republic Srpska. Sheet 92×73 mm.
MSS274 **S83** 3m. multicoloured 5·00 5·00

S84 Alekse Santic

2003. 135th Birth Anniv of Alekse Santic (writer).
S275 **S84** 1m. multicoloured 1·80 1·80

S85 Crucifixion, Sretenje Monastery

2003. Easter. Multicoloured.
S276 50f. Type **S85** 90 90
S277 1m. Resurrection (painting, Altarpiece, Eisenheim by Matias Greenwald) 1·80 1·80

S86 Everest Peaks

2003. 50th Anniv of First Ascent of Mount Everest. Sheet 82×58 mm containing Type **S86** and similar vert design. Multicoloured.
MSS278 1m.50 Type **S86**; 1m.50 Mountaineer through magnifying glass 7·25 7·25
The stamps and margin of MSS278 form a composite design.

S87 Aviation Poster

2003. Europa. Poster Art. Multicoloured.
S279 1m. Type **S87** 1·80 1·80
S280 1m.50 Naval poster 2·75 2·75

S87a Transfusion Equipment and Family

2003. Obligatory Tax. Red Cross Week.
S280a **S87a** 10f. multicoloured 60 60

S88 Arab

2003. Horses. Multicoloured.
S281 50f. Type **S88** 90 90
S282 50f. Lipizzaner 90 90
S283 1m. Inscr 'Bosanko' 1·80 1·80
S284 1m. Inscr 'Posavatz' 1·80 1·80

S89 Pope John Paul II

2003. Second Visit of Pope John Paul II to Bosnia Hercegovina. Multicoloured.
S285 1m.50 Type **S89** 8·25 8·25
S285a 1m.50 Pope John Paul II and Ivan Merz (Croatian lay academic, beatified by Pope John-Paul II on Sunday, June 22, 2003 at Banja Luka) (horiz) 3·00 3·00
Stamps of the same design as No. S285a were issued by Bosnia Herzegovina (Sarajevo) and Bosnia Herzegovina (Croatia).

S90 Medal of Honour

2003. Medals. Multicoloured.
S286 50f. Type **S90** 1·00 1·00
S287 1m. Njegos I medal 2·00 2·00

S91 Dagger piercing Globe

2003. Fight against Terrorism.
S288 **S91** 1m. multicoloured 2·00 2·00

S91a 'Stop TB'

2003. Obligatoery Tax. Tuberculosis Week. (a) Ordinary gum.
S288a **S91a** 10f. multicoloured 65 65

(b) Self-adhesive.
S288b 50f. As No. S288a (30×20 mm) 65 65

S92 Leo Tolstoy

2003. 175th Birth Anniv of Count Lev Nikolayevich (Leo) Tolstoy (writer, pacifist, Christian anarchist and educational reformer).
S289 **S92** 1m. multicoloured 2·10 2·10

S93 Ugar River Canyon

2003. European Nature Protection. Multicoloured.
S290 50f. Type **S93** 1·10 1·10
S291 1m. Drina River canyon 2·10 2·10

S94 St. Sava and Martyr Varvara (Radul)

2003. Religious Art. Multicoloured.
S292 50f. Type **S94** 1·30 1·30
S293 50f. St. Lazar (Andrej Raicevic) 1·30 1·30
S294 1m. Coronation of Madonna with Saints (Dimitrije Bacevic) 2·75 2·75
S295 1m. Deisis (intercession of Madonna and Jovan Pretaca) 2·75 2·75

S95 Child and Snowman

2003. Christmas and New Year. Multicoloured.
S296 50f. Type **S95** 1·30 1·30
S297 1m. Santa Claus and reindeer 2·75 2·75

S96 Wright Brothers and Wright Flyer I

2003. Centenary of Powered Flight. Multicoloured.
S298 50f. Type **S96** 1·30 1·30
S299 1m. Ferdinand von Zeppelin and air ship LZ 127 Graf Zeppelin 2·75 2·75

S97 Oath of Rebels (bas relief, memorial fountain, Orasac)

2004. Bicentenary of First Serbian Uprising. Sheet 78×62 mm containing Type **S97** and similar vert design. Multicoloured.
MSS300 1m.50×2, Type **S97**; Oath of Rebels (right) 8·00 8·00
The stamps of MSS300 form a composite design.

S98 Early Greek Chariot Race

2004. Olympic Games, Athens. Sheet 100×60 mm containing Type **S98** and similar vert design. Multicoloured.
MSS301 1m.50×2, Type **S98**; Early Greek chariot race (right) 8·50 8·50
The stamps of MSS301 form a composite design.

S99 Albert Einstein

2004. 125th Birth Anniv of Albert Einstein (physicist and 1921–Nobel Prize winner).

S302	**S99**	1m.50 multicoloured	4·25	4·25

S100 Risen Christ

2004. Easter. Multicoloured.

S303	50f. Type **S100**		1·40	1·40
S304	1m. Risen Christ (different)		2·75	2·75

S101 Canoeing

2004. Europa. Holidays. Multicoloured.

S305	50f. Type **S101**	2·75	2·75
S306	1m. Hang-gliding	4·25	4·25

S102 Hands holding Blood Droplet as Gift

2004. Obligatory Tax. Red Cross.

S307	**S102**	10f. multicoloured	1·00	1·00

S103 Kulasi

2004. Spas.

S308	**S103**	20f. multicoloured	1·00	1·00

S104 Milutina Milankovica

2004. 125th Birth Anniv of Milutina Milankovica (scientist).

S309	**S104**	1m. multicoloured	2·75	2·75

S105 Football and Map

2004. European Football Championships, Portugal.

S310	**S105**	1m.50 multicoloured	4·25	4·25

S106 Discus Thrower, Games Emblem and Temple Ruins

2004. Olympic Games, Greece. Multicoloured.

S311	50f. Type **S106**	1·40	1·40
S312	50f. Hurdler, ruins and early runners	1·40	1·40
S313	1m. Early and modern runners and temple ruins	2·75	2·75
S314	1m. Runners and charioteers	2·75	2·75

S107 *Arctostaphylos uva* (bear ears)

2004. European Nature Protection. Multicoloured.

S315	50f. Type **S107**	1·40	1·40
S316	1m. *Monticola saxatilis* (rufous-tailed rock thrush)	2·75	2·75

S107a Stylized Lung

2004. Obligatory Tax. Tuberculosis Week. (a) Ordinary gum.

S316a	**S107a**	10f. multicoloured	1·00	1·00

(b) Self-adhesive.

S316b	10f. As Type **S107a** (20×30 mm)	1·00	1·00

S108 Antimonite

2004. Minerals. Multicoloured.

S317	50f. Type **S108**	1·40	1·40
S318	50f. Pyrites	1·40	1·40
S319	1m. Sphalerite	2·75	2·75
S320	1m. Quartz	2·75	2·75

S109 Mihajlo Pupin

2004. 150th Birth Anniv of Mihajlo Pupin (scientist).

S321	**S109**	1m. multicoloured	2·75	2·75

S110 Child, Grenade and Pigeons

2004. Struggle against Terrorism.

S322	**S110**	1m. multicoloured	2·75	2·75

S110a *Digitalis grandiflora*

2004. Flora. Multicoloured.

S322a	50f. Type **S110a**	1·40	1·40
S322b	50f. *Arnica montana*	1·40	1·40
S322c	1m. *Rosa pendulina*	2·75	2·75
S322d	1m. *Gentiana lutea*	2·75	2·75

S111 Mljecanica near Kozarska Dubica

2004. Spas. Multicoloured.

S323	50f. Type **S111**	1·40	1·40
S324	1m. Laktasi	2·75	2·75

S112 The Nativity (icon)

2004. Christmas.

S325	**S112**	1m. multicoloured	2·75	2·75

S113 *Serbian Peasant from Semberija*

2005. Art. Paintings by Milenko Atanackovic. Multicoloured.

S326	50f. Type **S113**	1·40	1·40
S327	1m. *Beledija–Old Community* (horiz)	2·75	2·75

S114 Janj River

2005. International Day of Water Protection.

S328	**S114**	1m. multicoloured	2·75	2·75

S115 Traditional Hearth

2005. Europa. Gastronomy. Multicoloured.

S329	1m. Type **S115**	2·75	2·75
S330	1m.50 Table laid with food	4·25	4·25

S116 *The Christ Guardian* (icon), Church of Madonna, Ljeviska

2005. Easter.

S331	**S116**	50f. multicoloured	1·50	1·50

S117 Pope John Paul II

2005. Pope John Paul II Commemoration. Multicoloured.

S332	1m.50 Type **S117**	4·25	4·25
MSS333	56×49 mm. 5m. St. Peters Basilica and Pope John Paul II	14·00	14·00

S118 Emblem

2005. Obligatory Tax. Red Cross. Self-adhesive.

S334	10f. vermilion and black	1·00	1·00

S119 *Vipera berus berus*

2005. Snakes. Multicoloured.

S335	50f. Type **S119**	1·40	1·40

S336	50f. *Vipera ursinii*	1·40	1·40
S337	1m. *Vipera berus bosniensis*	2·75	2·75
S338	1m. *Vipera ammodytes*	2·75	2·75

S120 Castle

2005. 50th Anniv of Disneyland Theme Park, Florida. Multicoloured.

S339	50f. Type **S120**	1·40	1·40
S340	1m. houses	2·75	2·75

S121 Fighting Bulls, Grmec

2005. Traditions.

S341	**S121**	1m.50 multicoloured	4·25	4·25

S122 *Prasuma Perucica*

2005. 50th Anniv of Europa Stamps. Multicoloured.

S342	1m.95 Type **S122**	5·50	5·50
S343	1m.95 Rafting, Odmor	5·50	5·50
S344	1m.95 Mostar bridge	5·50	5·50
S345	1m.95 Drina river	5·50	5·50

S123 Landscape and Lungs

2005. Obligatory Tax. Anti-Tuberculosis Week.

S346	**S123**	10f. multicoloured	1·00	1·00

S124 Balls and Belgrade Arena

2005. European Basketball Championship, Belgrade. Multicoloured, colour wash given.

S347	**S124**	50f. lilac	1·40	1·40
S348	**S124**	50f. yellow	1·40	1·40
S349	**S124**	50f. green	1·40	1·40
S350	**S124**	50f. lilac	1·40	1·40
S351	**S124**	50f. blue	1·40	1·40

S125 National Museum

2005. 75th Anniversaries. Multicoloured.

S352	1m. Type **S125**	2·75	2·75
S353	1m. National Theatre (horiz)	2·75	2·75

S126 Tunnel, Sargan

2005. Tourism. Makra Gora Railway, Visegard. Sheet 101×54 mm containing Type **S126** and similar vert design. Multicoloured.

MSS354	50f. Type **S126**; 1m. Station, Makra Gora	4·25	4·25

The stamps and margin of **MS**S354 form a composite design.

S127 *Bleriot XI*

2005. Centenary of International Aviation Federation (FAI).
S355 **S127** 1m.50 multicoloured 4·25 4·25

S128 Flowers over map

2005. Tenth Anniv of Dayton Agreement.
S356 **S128** 1m.50 multicoloured 4·25 4·25

S129 Guber

2005. Spas.
S357 **S129** 50f. multicoloured 1·40 1·40

S130 *Crex crex* (corncrake)

2005. European Nature Protection. Birds. Multicoloured.
S358 50f. Type **S130** 1·40 1·40
S359 1m. *Platalea leucorodia* (spoonbill) 2·75 2·75

S131 Monument to Victims

2005. 60th Anniv of Liberation of Jasenovac Concentration Camp.
S360 **S131** 50f. multicoloured 1·40 1·40

S132 Mozart

2006. 250th Birth Anniv of Wolfgang Amadeus Mozart (composer and musician).
S361 **S132** 1m.50 multicoloured 4·25 4·25

S133 Branke Sotre

2006. Birth Centenary of Branke Sotre (artist).
S362 **S133** 1m. multicoloured 2·75 2·75

S134 Biathlete

2006. Winter Olympic Games, Turin. Multicoloured.
S363 50f. Type **S134** 1·40 1·40
S364 1m. Alpine skier 2·75 2·75

S135 Kulasi

2006. Spas.
S365 **S135** 20f. multicoloured 1·00 1·00
No. S365 is as No. S308 but redrawn.

S136 Inscr "Saxifraga prenja"

2006. Flora. Multicoloured.
S366 50f. Type **S136** 1·40 1·40
S367 50f. *Asperula hercegovina* 1·40 1·40
S368 1m. *Campanula hercegovina* 2·75 2·75
S369 1m. Inscr "Oxtropis prenja" 2·75 2·75

S137 Basket of Eggs

2006. Easter.
S370 **S137** 70f. multicoloured 2·10 2·10

S138 Tear (Luja Kajkut)

2006. Europa. Integration. Multicoloured.
S371 1m. Type **S138** 2·75 2·75
S372 1m.50 "Country Dance" (Milica Popic) 4·25 4·25

S139 Emblem

2005. Obligatory Tax. Red Cross.
S373 **S139** 20f. multicoloured 1·00 1·00

S140 Legs and Ball

2006. World Cup Football Championship, Germany. Multicoloured.
S374 50f. Type **S140** 1·40 1·40
S375 1m. Stadium and ball 2·75 2·75
MSS376 65×49 mm. 3m.German player and ball 8·25 8·25

S141 Runner

2006. Tenth Anniv of Vidovdan Road Race.
S377 **S141** 1m. multicoloured 2·75 2·75

S142 Nikola Tesla

2006. 150th Birth Anniv of Nikola Tesla (engineer) (1st issue). Sheet 66×60 mm.
MSS378 1m.50 multicoloured 4·25 4·25
The stamps and margin of **MS**S378 form a composite design.
See also No. S385.

S143 "CTON TB"

2006. Obligatory Tax. Anti-Tuberculosis Week.
S379 **S143** 20f. multicoloured 1·00 1·00

S144 *Tetrao urogallus* (capercaille)

2006. European Nature Protection. Multicoloured.
S380 50f. Type **S144** 1·40 1·40
S381 1m. *Rupicapra rupicapra* (chamois) 2·75 2·75

No. S382 and Type S 145 have been left for "50th Anniv of Children's Theatre", issued on 14 October 2006, not yet received.

S146 Buckle

2006. Museum Exhibits. Multicoloured.
S383 1m. Type **S146** 2·75 2·75
S384 1m. Curved buckle with red stones 2·75 2·75

S147 Nikola Tesla

2006. 150th Birth Anniv of Nikola Tesla (engineer) (2nd issue).
S385 **S147** 70f. multicoloured 2·10 2·10

S148 Johann von Goethe

2007. 175th Birth Anniv of Johann Wolfgang von Goethe (polymath).
S386 **S148** 1m.50 multicoloured 4·25 4·25

S149 Decorated Egg

2007. Easter.
S387 **S149** 70f. multicoloured 2·10 2·10

S150 Study for Isabella d'Este

2007. 555th Birth Anniv of Leonardo da Vinci (artist and polymath). Multicoloured.
S388 70f. Type **S150** 2·10 2·10
S389 1m. Study for The Last Supper 2·75 2·75

S151 Campsite

2007. Europa. Centenary of Scouting. Multicoloured. (a) 26×41 mm.
S390 1m. Type **S151** 2·75 2·75
S391 1m.50 Scouts 4·25 4·25

 (b) Size 35×45 mm.
S392 1m. As Type **S151**, with pink upper edge 2·75 2·75
S393 1m. As Type S 151, with pink lower edge 'EUROPA 100 JAHRE PFADFINDERBEWE-GUNG' 2·75 2·75
S394 1m. As Type S **151** with pink lower edge 'EUROPA 100 ANS DU SCOUTISME' 2·75 2·75
S395 1m.50 As No. S 391, with pink upper edge 4·25 4·25
S396 1m.50 As No. S 391, with pink upper edge 'EUROPA 100 YEARS OF SCOUTING' 4·25 4·25
S397 1m.50 As No. S 391, with pink lower edge 4·25 4·25

S152 Clasped Hands

2007. Obligatory Tax. Red Cross.
S398 **S152** 20f. multicoloured 1·00 1·00

S153 Liplje Monastery

2007. Monasteries. Multicoloured.
S399 70f. Type **S153** 1·90 1·90
S400 1m. Dobricevo 2·75 2·75

S154 Koarac

2007. Cities. Multicoloured.
S401 20f. Type **S154** 70 70
S402 20f. Derventa 70 70
S403 20f. Prjedor 70 70
S404 20f. Laktasi 70 70
S405 20f. Foca 70 70
S406 20f. Bijelijina 70 70
S407 70f. Srebrenica 2·10 2·10
S408 1m.50 Sipovo 4·25 4·25
S409 1m.50 Mrkonjic Grad 4·25 4·25
S410 2m. Trebinje 5·50 5·50
S411 5m. Zvornik 14·00 14·00

S155 Serbian Tri-colour Hound

2007. Dogs. Multicoloured.
S412 70f. Type **S155** 2·10 2·10
S413 70f. Istarski Ostrodlaki gonic (rough coated scent hound) 2·10 2·10
S414 70f. Srpski odbrambeni pas (Serbian guard dog) 2·10 2·10
S415 70f. Tornak (sheep dog) 2·10 2·10

S156 Orthodox Church and Old Post Office

2007. Centenary of Post Office, Obudovac.
S416 **S156** 10f. multicoloured 1·00 1·00

S157 Ban Milosavljevic (statue)

2007. 125th Birth Anniv of Ban Svetislav Milosavljevic (leader 1930–33).
S417 **S157** 1m.50 multicoloured 4·25 4·25

S158 Apple containing People

2007. Obligatory Tax. Anti-Tuberculosis Week.
S418 **S158** 20f. multicoloured 1·20 1·20

S159 Early Racquet and Balls

2007. Centenary of Banja Luca Tennis Club. Sheet 83×58 mm containing Type **S159** and similar horiz design. Multicoloured.
MSS419 1m.×2 Type **S159**; Modern racquet and ball 5·50 5·50

The stamps and margin of **MS**S419 form a composite design.

S160 Sputnik and Globe

2007. 50th Anniv of Space Exploration.
S420 **S160** 1m.50 multicoloured 4·25 4·25

S161 *Picea abies*

2007. European Nature Protection. Conifers. Multicoloured.
S421 70f. Type **S161** 1·90 1·90
S422 1m. *Picea omorica* 2·75 2·75

S162 Post Office Building

2008. 125th Anniv of Samac Post Office.
S422a **S162** 1m.40 multicoloured 4·25 4·25

S163 *Self Portrait*

2008. 155th Birth Anniv of Vincent Van Gogh (artist).
S423 **S163** 1m.50 multicoloured 4·25 4·25

S164 Player's Foot and Ball

2008. Euro 2008–European Football Championships, Austria and Switzerland. Sheet 82×60 mm containing Type **S164** and similar vert design. Multicoloured.
MSS424 1m.40×2, Type **S164**; Ball and red and white boot 8·25 8·25

The stamps and margins of **MS**S424 form a composite design.

S165 Quill and Ink Pot

2008. Europa. The Letter. Multicoloured.
S425 1m. Type **S165** 2·75 2·75
S426 2m. Hand holding pencil 5·50 5·50
MSS427 108×82 mm. Nos. S425/6, each×3 26·00 26·00

S166 Hands

2008. Obligatory Tax. Red Cross.
S428 **166** 20f. multicoloured 1·20 1·20

S167 Children and Microphone

2008. 15th Children's Song Festival, Djurdjerdan.
S429 **S167** 1m.50 multicoloured 4·25 4·25

S168 Post Van

2008. Personal Stamps. Multicoloured. Self-adhesive.
S430 70f. Type **S168** 2·10 2·10
S431 70f. Post box (vert) 2·10 2·10
S432 70f. Hand stamp (vert) 2·10 2·10
S433 70f. Post horn 2·10 2·10

S169 Festival Mascot as Postman

2008. Banja Luka International Festival.
S434 **S169** 1m.50 multicoloured 4·25 4·25

S170 *Gyromitra esculenta*

2008. Poisonous Fungi. Multicoloured.
S435 70f. Type **S170** 2·10 2·10
S436 70f. *Amanita muscaria* 2·10 2·10
S437 70f. *Amanita pantherina* 2·10 2·10
S438 70f. *Amanita phalloides* 2·10 2·10

S171 Charles Darwin

2008. 150th Anniv of Publication of *On the Origin of Species* by Charles Darwin.
S439 **S171** 1m.50 multicoloured 4·25 4·25

S172 *Gentiana verna*

2008. Flowers. Multicoloured.
S440 50f. Type **S172** 1·60 1·60
S441 1m.50 *Galanthus nivalis* (vert) 4·75 4·75
S442 2m. *Viola odorata* 6·25 6·25
S443 5m. *Centaurea cyanus* 16·00 16·00

S173 High Jump and National Stadium

2008. Olympic Games, Beijing. Multicoloured.
S444 70f. Type **S173** 2·40 2·40
S445 2m.10 Swimmer and National Aquatic Center, Beijing 6·50 6·50
MSS446 3m.10 Gymnast 10·00 10·00

No. S447 is vacant.

S174 *Ciconia ciconia* (white stork)

2008. European Nature Protection. Birds. Multicoloured.
S448 1m. Type **S174** 3·25 3·25
S449 1m. *Strix aluco* (Eurasian tawny owl) 3·25 3·25

S175 Tvrdos

2008. Monasteries. Multicoloured.
S450 1m. Type **S175** 3·25 3·25
S451 1m. Gracanica 3·25 3·25

S175a Flowers

2008. Obligatory Tax. Tuberculosis Week.
S451a **S175a** 20f. multicoloured 1·20 1·20

S176 Milan Jelic

2008. Milan Jelic (president 2006–7) Commemoration. Sheet 87×63 mm.
MSS452 multicoloured 6·50 6·50

S177 Train and Travellers

2008. 125th Anniv of Orient Express.
S453 **S177** 1m.40 multicoloured 4·20 4·25

S178 Alfred Nobel

2008. 175th Birth Anniv of Alfred Nobel (chemist, engineer, inventor of dynamite and instituted Nobel Prizes).
S454 **S178** 1m.50 multicoloured 4·75 4·75

S179 Jovan Zmaj

2008. 125th Birth Anniv of Jovan Jovanovic Zmaj (writer).
S455 **S179** 1m.50 multicoloured 4·25 4·25

S180 Celebratory Loaf of Bread

2008. Christmas.
S456 **S180** 1m. multicoloured 3·00 3·00

S181 Vucko (games mascot)

2009. 25th Anniv of Winter Olympic Games, Sarajevo.
S457 **S181** 1m.50 multicolured 4·75 4·75

S182 Amerigo Vespucci

2009. Explorers. Multicoloured.
S458 70f. Type **S182** 2·10 2·10
S459 1m.50 Marco Polo 4·75 4·75

S183 Triceratops

2009. Dinosaurs. Multicoloured.
S460 70f. Type **S183** 2·10 2·10
S461 1m.50 Diplodocus 4·75 4·75

S184 Court of Human Rights Building

2009. 50th Anniv of European Court of Human Rights (S462) or 60th Anniv of Council of Europe (S463). Multicoloured.
S462 1m. Type **S184** 3·75 3·75
S463 1m.50 Council of Europe Building 4·75 4·75

Nos. S464/6 and Type S **185** are left for Animals, issued on 15 April 2009, not yet received.

Nos. S467/9 and Type S **186** are left for Europa. Astronomy, issued on 23 April 2009, not yet received.

S187 Globe and Red Cross Flag

2009. Obligatory Tax.150th Anniv of Red Cross.
S470 **S187** 20f. multicoloured 1·00 1·00

Nos. S471 and Type S **188** are left for World Rafting Championship, issued on 15 May 2009, not yet received.

S189 Paje Jovanovic

2009. 150th Birth Anniv of Paje Jovanovic (artist).
S472 **S189** 1m.50 multicoloured 4·25 4·25

S190 Self and Other Portraits

2009. 125th Birth Anniv of Amedeo Clemente Modigliani (artist).
S473 **S190** 1m.50 multicoloured 4·25 4·25

S191 Siamese

2009. Cats. Multicoloured.
S474 70f. Type **S191** 2·10 2·10
S475 70f. Tabby 2·10 2·10
S476 70f. Russian Blue 2·10 2·10
S477 70f. Persian 2·10 2·10

S192 Dragonfly

2009. Insects. Multicoloured.
S478 1m. Type **S192** 2·75 2·75
S479 1m. Ladybird 2·75 2·75
S480 1m. Staghorn beetle 2·75 2·75

S193 Robert Koch (bacteriologist, Nobel Prize Winner for Physiology or Medicine, 1905)

2009. Obligatory Tax. Tuberculosis Week.
S481 **S193** 20f. multicoloured 4·75 4·75

S194 Zvornik

2009. Castles. Multicoloured.
S482 70f. Type **S194** 2·10 2·10
S483 1m. Banja Luka 3·25 3·25

S195 Locomotive SKODA 1937

2009. Narrow Gauge. Multicoloured.
S484 70f. Type **S195** 2·10 2·10
S485 70f. Locomotive RAMA 2·10 2·10
S486 80f. Locomotive JZ 83-057 2·75 2·75
S487 80f. Locomotive UNRRA 22 2·75 2·75

S196 Citroen 2 CV

2009. Classic Cars. Multicoloured.
S488 70f. Type **S196** 2·10 2·10
S489 70f. Fiat Cinquecento 2·10 2·10
S490 80f. Volkswagen Beetle 2·75 2·75

S197 Snowman

2009. Christmas and New Year. Multicoloured.
S491 60f. Type **S197** 1·70 1·70
S492 60f. Santa Claus 1·70 1·70

S198 Badger

2009. Fauna.
S493 **S198** 20f. multicoloured 75 75

S199 Bridge and Tower

2010. 600th Anniv of Zvornik
S494 **S199** 70f. multicoloured

S200 Games Emblem and Luge

2010. Winter Olympic Games, Vancouver. Multicoloured.
S495 70f. Type **S200** 1·60 1·60
S496 1m.50 Ice dance 3·25 3·25

S201 Frédéric Chopin

2010. Birth Bicentenary of Frédéric François Chopin (composer)
S497 **S201** 1m.50 multicocloured 4·75 4·75

No. S498 and Type S **202** are left for Birth Centenary of Mesa Selimovic, issued on 26 April 2010, not yet received.
Nos. S499/501 and Type S **203** are left for Europa, issued on 7 May 2010, not yet received.

204 Player's Legs

2010. World Cup Football Championships, South Africa. Multicoloured.
S502 1m.50 Type **S204** 4·25 4·25
S503 1m.50 No. 11 player with arms wide spread 4·25 £425

S205 Hedgehog

2010. Fauna. Multicoloured.
S504 10f. Type **S205** 2·10 2·10
S505 50f. Wild boar 2·10 2·10
S506 90f. Wolf 2·10 2·10
S507 1m. Brown bear 2·10 2·10

S206 Sword (yataghan)

2010. Weaponry. Multicoloured.
S508 1m.80 Type **S206** 6·25 6·25
S509 2m. Flintlock pistol 6·50 6·50
S510 5m. Iron mace 14·50 14·50

S207 Rhododendron hirsutum

2010. Flora. Multicoloured.
S511 70f. Type **S207** 2·30 2·30
S512 70f. *Edraianthus sutjeski* (inscr 'Edrainthus Sutjeski') 2·30 2·30
S513 70f. *Trollius europaeus* 2·30 2·30
S514 70f. *Pancicia serbica* 2·30 2·30

S208 Figures (bas-relief)

2010. Cultural Heritage. Multicoloured.
S515 70f. Type **S208** 1·60 1·60
S516 1m.50 Inscribed tablet 3·25 3·25

S209 Trumpets and Trumpeter

2010. 50th Anniv of Trumpet Festival, Guca
S517 **S209** 1m.50 multicoloured 4·75 4·75

S210 Empty Silhouette

2010. Day of Missing and Fallen Persons
S518 **S210** 90f. scarlet-vermilion and black 2·75 2·75

Nos. S519/20 and Type S **211** are left for Nature Protection, issued on 23 September 2010, not yet received.

S212 '80' wearing Hats

2010. 80th Anniv of National Museum
S521 **S212** 90f. multicoloured 6·25 6·25

S213 St. Nicholas and Stocking

2010. Christmas
S522 **S213** 1m. multicoloured 3·25 3·25

No. S523 and Type **S214** are left for 400th Birth Anniv of St. Vasilije, issued on 28 December 2010, not yet received.
No. S524/5 and Type **S215** are left for Museum Exhibits, issued on 24 January 2011, not yet received.
No. S526 and Type **S216** are left for 120th Birth Anniv of Milan Budmir, issued on 11 February 2011, not yet received.

S217 Marie Curie and Chemistry Equipment

2011. Centenary of Marie Curie's Nobel Prize for Chemistry
S527 **S217** 1m.50 multicoloured 2·10 2·10

S213 Woodpecker, Deer, Fawn and Hare

2011. Europa. Forests. Multicoloured.
S528 1m. Type **S218** 2·10 2·10
S529 2m. Owl, fox and bear in coniferous woodland 4·25 4·25
MSS530 131×90 mm. 1m. As Type S**218** (35×45 mm) (imperf at foot); 1m. As Type S**218** (35×45 mm) (imperf at top); 1m. As Type S**218** (47×45 mm) (imperf at foot and right vertical side); 2m. As No. S529 (35×45 mm) (imperf at top); 2m. As S529 (35×45 mm) (imperf at foot); 2m. As S529 (47×45 mm) (imperf at top and right vertical side) 20·00 20·00

No. S531/4 and Type **S2**19 are left for Fauna, issued on 20 April 2011, not yet received.

S220 Red Cross

2011. OBLIGATORY TAX. Red Cross Week

(a) Sheet stamp
S535 **S220** 20f. multicoloured 80 80

(b) Coil Stamp
S535a **S220** 20f. multicoloured 80 80

Nos. S536/9 and Type **S221** are left for Birds, issued on 10 May 2011, not yet received.

S222 Books

2011. 75th Anniv of National Library and University
S540 **S222** 90f. multicoloured 2·75 2·75

No. S541 and Type **S223** are left for Canoeing Championship, issued on 7 June 2011, not yet received.

S224 Crown and Saint

2011. Illuminated Letters from Miroslav's Gospel. Multicoloured.
S542 1m.50 Type S**224** 3·75 3·75
S543 2m.30 Figure leading multicoloured animal 4·75 4·75
S544 5m. Two birds 14·00 14·00

S225 Emblem

2011. International Year of Youth
S545 **S225** 90f. multicoloured 2·75 2·75

S226 Locomotive DHL 720-001

2011. Locomotives. Multicoloured.
SS546 90f. Type S**226** 2·75 2·75
SS547 90f. DHL 740-108 2·75 2·75
SS548 90f. DIVIV 801 2·75 2·75
SS549 90f. DIVIV 802 2·75 2·75
MSSS550 80×58 mm. 3m. DHL L45H-096 8·25 8·25

Pt. 1

BOTSWANA

Formerly Bechuanaland Protectorate, attained independence on 30 September 1966, and changed its name to Botswana.

1966. 100 cents = 1 rand.
1976. 100 thebe = 1 pula.

47 National Assembly Building

1966. Independence. Multicoloured.

202	2½c. Type **47**		15	10
203	5c. Abattoir, Lobatsi		20	10
204	15c. National Airways Douglas DC-3		65	20
205	35c. State House, Gaberones		40	30

1966. Nos. 168/81 of Bechuanaland optd REPUBLIC OF BOTSWANA.

206	**28**	1c. multicoloured	25	10
207	-	2c. orange, black and olive	30	1·75
208	-	2½c. multicoloured	30	10
209	-	3½c. multicoloured	1·50	40
210	-	5c. multicoloured	1·75	1·50
211	-	7½c. multicoloured	50	1·75
212	-	10c. multicoloured	1·00	90
213	-	12½c. multicoloured	2·00	3·25
214	-	20c. brown and drab	20	1·00
215	-	25c. sepia and lemon	20	2·00
216	-	35c. blue and orange	30	2·75
217	-	50c. sepia and olive	20	70
218	-	1r. black and brown	40	1·25
219	-	2r. brown and turquoise	60	3·00

52 Golden Oriole

1967. Multicoloured.

220	1c. Type **52**		30	15
221	2c. Hoopoe ("African Hoopoe")		60	70
222	3c. Groundscraper thrush		55	10
223	4c. Cordon-bleu ("Blue Waxbill")		55	10
224	5c. Secretary bird		55	10
225	7c. Southern yellow-billed hornbill ("Yellow-billed Hornbill")		60	1·00
226	10c. Burchell's gonolek ("Crimson-breasted Shrike")		60	15
227	15c. Malachite kingfisher		8·00	3·00
228	20c. African fish eagle ("Fish Eagle")		8·00	2·00
229	25c. Go-away bird ("Grey Loerie")		4·00	1·50
230	35c. Scimitar-bill		6·00	3·00
231	50c. Comb duck ("Knob-Billed Duck")		2·75	2·75
232	1r. Levaillant's barbet ("Crested Barbet")		5·00	3·50
233	2r. Didric cuckoo ("Diederick Cuckoo")		7·00	17·00

66 Students and University

1967. First Conferment of University Degrees.

234	**66**	3c. sepia, blue and orange	10	10
235	**66**	7c. sepia, blue and turquoise	10	10
236	**66**	15c. sepia, blue and red	10	10
237	**66**	35c. sepia, blue and violet	20	20

67 Bushbuck

1967. Chobe Game Reserve. Multicoloured.

238	3c. Type **67**		10	20
239	7c. Sable Antelope		15	30
240	35c. Fishing on the Chobe River		90	1·10

70 Arms of Botswana and Human Rights Emblem

1968. Human Rights Year.

241	**70**	3c. multicoloured	10	10
242	-	15c. multicoloured	25	45
243	-	25c. multicoloured	25	60

The designs of Nos. 242/3 are similar, but are arranged differently.

73 Eland and Giraffe Rock Paintings, Tsodilo Hills

1968. Opening of National Museum and Art Gallery. Multicoloured.

244	3c. Type **73**		20	20
245	7c. Girl wearing ceremonial beads (31×48 mm)		25	40
246	10c. "Baobab Trees" (Thomas Baines)		25	30
247	15c. National Museum and art gallery (72×19 mm)		40	1·50
MS248	132×82 mm. Nos. 244/7		1·00	2·25

77 African Family, and Star over Village

1968. Christmas.

249	**77**	1c. multicoloured	10	10
250	**77**	2c. multicoloured	10	10
251	**77**	5c. multicoloured	10	10
252	**77**	25c. multicoloured	15	50

78 Scout, Lion and Badge in frame

1969. 22nd World Scout Conference, Helsinki. Multuicoloured.

253	3c. Type **78**		35	30
254	15c. Scouts cooking over open fire (vert)		35	1·00
255	25c. Scouts around camp fire		40	1·00

81 Woman, Child and Christmas Star

1969. Christmas.

256	**81**	1c. blue and brown	10	10
257	**81**	2c. olive and brown	10	10
258	**81**	4c. yellow and brown	10	10
259	**81**	35c. brown and violet	20	20
MS260	86×128 mm. Nos. 256/9		70	1·10

82 Diamond Treatment Plant, Orapa

1970. Developing Botswana. Multicoloured.

261	3c. Type **82**		80	20
262	7c. Copper-nickel mining		1·00	20
263	10c. Copper-nickel mine, Selebi-Pikwe (horiz)		1·25	15
264	35c. Orapa Diamond mine and diamonds (horiz)		3·00	1·25

83 Mr. Micawber (*David Copperfield*)

1970. Death Centenary of Charles Dickens. Multicoloured.

265	3c. Type **83**		25	10
266	7c. Scrooge (*A Christmas Carol*)		25	10
267	15c. Fagin (*Oliver Twist*)		45	40
268	25c. Bill Sykes (*Oliver Twist*)		70	60
MS269	114×81 mm. Nos. 265/8		2·75	4·00

84 U.N. Building and Emblem

1970. 25th Anniv of United Nations.

270	**84**	15c. blue, brown and silver	70	30

85 Crocodile

1970. Christmas. Multicoloured.

271	1c. Type **85**		10	10
272	2c. Giraffe		10	10
273	7c. Elephant		15	15
274	25c. Rhinoceros		60	80
MS275	128×90 mm. Nos. 271/4		1·00	3·00

86 Sorghum

1971. Important Crops. Multicoloured.

276	3c. Type **86**		15	10
277	7c. Millet		20	10
278	10c. Maize		20	10
279	35c. Groundnuts		70	1·00

87 Map and Head of Cow

1971. Fifth Anniv of Independence.

280	**87**	3c. black, brown and green	10	10
281	-	4c. black, light blue and blue	10	10
282	-	7c. black and orange	20	15
283	-	10c. multicoloured	20	15
284	-	20c. multicoloured	55	2·50

DESIGNS: 4c. Map and cogs; 7c. Map and common zebra; 10c. Map and sorghum stalk crossed by tusk; 20c. Arms and map of Botswana.

88 King bringing Gift of Gold

1971. Christmas. Multicoloured.

285	2c. Type **88**		10	10
286	3c. King bringing frankincense		10	10
287	7c. King bringing myrrh		10	10
288	20c. Three Kings behold the star		35	65
MS289	85×128 mm. Nos. 285/8		1·00	3·50

89 Orion

1972. "Night Sky".

290	**89**	3c. blue, black and red	1·00	40
291	-	7c. blue, black and yellow	1·25	85
292	-	10c. green, black and orange	1·40	1·00
293	-	20c. blue, black and green	2·00	3·50

CONSTELLATIONS: 7c. The Scorpion; 10c. The Centaur; 20c. The Cross.

90 Postmark and Map

1972. Mafeking-Gubulawayo Runner Post. Multicoloured.

294	3c. Type **90**		30	10
295	4c. Bechuanaland stamp and map		30	35
296	7c. Runners and map		45	50
297	20c. Mafeking postmark and map		1·10	1·50
MS298	84×216 mm. Nos. 294/7 vertically *se-tenant*, forming a composite map design		11·00	15·00

For these designs with changed inscription see Nos. 652/5.

91 Cross, Map and Bells

1972. Christmas. Each with Cross and Map. Multicoloured.

299	2c. Type **91**		10	75
300	3c. Cross, map and candle		10	10
301	7c. Cross, map and Christmas tree		15	25
302	20c. Cross, map, star and holly		40	85
MS303	96×119 mm. Nos. 299/302		1·25	3·50

92 Thor

1973. Centenary of I.M.O./W.M.O. Norse Myths. Multicoloured.

304	3c. Type **92**		20	10
305	4c. Sun God's chariot (horiz)		25	15
306	7c. Ymir, the frost giant		30	15
307	20c. Odin and Sleipnir (horiz)		75	70

93 Livingstone and River Scene

1973. Death Centenary of Dr. Livingstone. Multicoloured.

308	3c. Type **93**		20	10
309	20c. Livingstone meeting Stanley		90	90

94 Donkey and
Foal at Village
Trough

1973. Christmas. Multicoloured.
310	3c. Type **94**	10	10
311	4c. Shepherd and flock (horiz)	10	10
312	7c. Mother and Child	10	10
313	20c. Kgotla meeting (horiz)	40	85

95 Gaborone Campus

1974. Tenth Anniv of University of Botswana, Lesotho and Swaziland. Multicoloured.
314	3c. Type **95**	10	10
315	7c. Kwaluseni Campus	10	10
316	20c. Roma Campus	15	20
317	35c. Map and flags of the three countries	20	35

96 Methods of Mail Transport

1974. Centenary of U.P.U. Multicoloured.
318	2c. Type **96**	55	35
319	3c. Post Office, Palapye, circa 1889	55	35
320	7c. Bechuanaland Police Camel Post, circa 1900	95	70
321	20c. Hawker Siddeley H.S.748 and de Havilland D.H.9 mail planes of 1920 and 1974	2·75	2·50

97 Amethyst

1974. Botswana Minerals. Multicoloured.
322	1c. Type **97**	60	2·50
323	2c. Agate–"Botswana Pink"	60	2·50
324	3c. Quartz	65	80
325	4c. Copper nickel	70	60
326	5c. Moss agate	70	1·00
327	7c. Agate	80	1·25
328	10c. Stilbite	1·60	65
329	15c. Moshaneng banded marble	2·00	4·00
330	20c. Gem diamonds	4·00	4·50
331	25c. Chrysotile	5·00	2·50
332	35c. Jasper	5·00	5·50
333	50c. Moss quartz	4·50	7·00
334	1r. Citrine	7·50	10·00
335	2r. Chalcopyrite	20·00	20·00

98 *Stapelia variegata*

1974. Christmas. Multicoloured.
336	2c. Type **98**	20	40
337	7c. *Hibiscus lunarifolius*	30	20
338	15c. *Ceratotheca triloba*	45	1·00
339	20c. *Nerine laticoma*	60	1·25
MS340	85×130 mm. Nos. 336/9	2·00	4·25

99 President Sir Seretse Khama

1975. Tenth Anniv of Self-Government.
341	**99** 4c. multicoloured	10	10
342	**99** 10c. multicoloured	15	10
343	**99** 20c. multicoloured	25	25
344	**99** 35c. multicoloured	45	50
MS345	93×130 mm. Nos. 341/4	1·00	1·50

100 Ostrich

1975. Rock Paintings, Tsodilo Hills. Multicoloured.
346	4c. Type **100**	60	10
347	10c. White rhinoceros	1·00	10
348	25c. Spotted hyena	2·00	55
349	35c. Scorpion	2·00	1·10
MS350	150×150 mm. Nos. 346/9	12·00	7·50

101 Map of British Bechuanaland, 1885

1975. Anniversaries. Multicoloured.
351	6c. Type **101**	30	20
352	10c. Chief Khama, 1875	40	15
353	25c. Chiefs Sebele, Bathoen and Khama, 1895 (horiz)	80	75

EVENTS: 6c. 90th anniv of Protectorate; 10c. Centenary of Khama's accession; 25c. 80th anniv of Chiefs' visit to London.

102 *Aloe marlothii*

1975. Christmas. Aloes. Multicoloured.
354	3c. Type **102**	20	10
355	10c. *Aloe lutescens*	40	20
356	15c. *Aloe zebrina*	60	1·50
357	25c. *Aloe littoralis*	75	2·50

103 Drum

1976. Traditional Musical Instruments. Multicoloured.
358	4c. Type **103**	15	10
359	10c. Hand piano	20	10
360	15c. Segankuru (violin)	25	50
361	25c. Kudu signal horn	30	1·25

104 One Pula Note

1976. First National Currency. Multicoloured.
362	4c. Type **104**	15	10
363	10c. Two pula note	20	10
364	15c. Five pula note	35	20
365	25c. Ten pula note	45	45
MS366	163×107 mm. Nos. 362/5	1·00	3·50

1976. Nos. 322/35 surch in new currency.
367	1t. on 1c. multicoloured	2·00	70
368	2t. on 2c. multicoloured	2·00	1·75
369	3t. on 3c. multicoloured	1·50	60
370	4t. on 4c. multicoloured	2·50	40
371	5t. on 5c. multicoloured	2·50	40
372	7t. on 7c. multicoloured	1·25	2·75
373	10t. on 10c. multicoloured	1·25	80
374	15t. on 15c. multicoloured	4·25	3·25
375	20t. on 20c. multicoloured	7·50	80
376	25t. on 25c. multicoloured	5·00	1·25
377	35t. on 35c. multicoloured	4·00	5·00
378	50t. on 50c. multicoloured	5·50	9·00
379	1p. on 1r. multicoloured	6·00	9·50
380	2p. on 2r. multicoloured	8·00	11·00

106 Botswana Cattle

1976. Tenth Anniv of Independence. Multicoloured.
381	4t. Type **106**	15	10
382	10t. Antelope, Okavango Delta (vert)	20	10
383	15t. School and pupils	20	40
384	25t. Rural weaving (vert)	20	50
385	35t. Miner (vert)	75	85

107 *Colophospermum mopane*

1976. Christmas. Trees. Multicoloured.
386	3t. Type **107**	15	10
387	4t. *Baikiaea plurijuga*	15	10
388	10t. *Sterculia rogersii*	20	10
389	25t. *Acacia nilotica*	45	50
390	40t. *Kigelia africana*	75	1·25

108 Coronation Coach

1977. Silver Jubilee. Multicoloured.
391	4t. The Queen and Sir Seretse Khama	10	10
392	25t. Type **108**	20	15
393	40t. The Recognition	35	90

109 African Clawless Otter

1977. Diminishing Species. Multicoloured.
394	3t. Type **109**	4·25	40
395	4t. Serval	4·25	40
396	10t. Bat-eared fox	4·75	40
397	25t. Temminck's ground pangolin	11·00	2·00
398	40t. Brown hyena	13·00	7·50

110 Cwihaba Caves

1977. Historical Monuments. Multicoloured.
399	4t. Type **110**	20	10
400	5t. Khama Memorial	20	10
401	15t. Green's Tree	30	40
402	20t. Mmajojo Ruins	30	45
403	25t. Ancient morabaraba board	30	50
404	35t. Matseng's footprint	40	60
MS405	154×105 mm. Nos. 399/404	2·50	3·25

111 *Hypoxis nitida*

1977. Christmas. Lilies. Multicoloured.
406	3t. Type **111**	15	10
407	5t. *Haemanthus magnificus*	15	10
408	10t. *Boophane disticha*	20	10
409	25t. *Vellozia retinervis*	40	55
410	40t. *Ammocharis coranica*	55	1·25

112 Black Bustard

1978. Birds. Multicoloured.
411	1t. Type **112**	70	1·25
412	2t. Marabou stork	90	1·25
413	3t. Green wood hoopoe ("Red Billed Hoopoe")	70	85
414	4t. Carmine bee eater	2·00	1·00
415	5t. African jacana	1·00	40
416	7t. African paradise flycatcher ("Paradise Flycatcher")	1·00	3·00
417	10t. Bennett's woodpecker	2·00	60
418	15t. Red bishop	1·50	3·00
419	20t. Crowned plover	1·75	2·00
420	25t. Giant kingfisher	70	3·00
421	30t. White-faced whistling duck ("White-faced Duck")	70	70
422	35t. Green-backed heron	70	3·25
423	45t. Black-headed heron	1·00	3·00
424	50t. Spotted eagle owl	5·00	4·50
425	1p. Gabar goshawk	2·50	4·50
426	2p. Martial eagle	3·00	8·00
427	5p. Saddle-bill stork	5·50	16·00

113 Tawana making Kaross

1978. Okavango Delta. Multicoloured.
428	4t. Type **113**	10	30
429	5t. Tribe localities	10	10
430	15t. Bushman collecting roots	25	40
431	20t. Herero woman milking	35	70
432	25t. Yei poling "mokoro" (canoe)	40	60
433	35t. Mbukushu fishing	45	1·75
MS434	150×98 mm. Nos. 428/33	1·50	3·75

114 *Caralluma lutea*

1978. Christmas. Flowers. Multicoloured.
435	5t. Type **114**	35	10
436	10t. *Hoodia lugardii*	50	15
437	15t. *Ipomoea transvaalensis*	90	55
438	25t. *Ansellia gigantea*	1·10	70

115 Sip Well

1979. Water Development. Multicoloured.
439	3t. Type **115**	10	10
440	5t. Watering pit	10	10
441	10t. Hand dug well	15	10
442	22t. Windmill	20	30
443	50t. Drilling rig truck	40	55

116 Pottery

1979. Handicrafts. Multicoloured.
444	5t. Type **116**	10	10
445	10t. Clay modelling	10	10
446	25t. Basketry	20	25
447	40t. Beadwork	40	50
MS448	123×96 mm. Nos. 444/7	1·00	2·50

117 British Bechuanaland 1885 1d. Stamp and Sir Rowland Hill

1979. Death Centenary of Sir Rowland Hill. Multicoloured.
449	5t. Type **117**	20	10
450	25t. Bechuanaland Protectorate 1932 2d. stamp	45	50
451	45t. 1967 Hoopoe 2c. definitive stamp	55	1·25

118 Children Playing

1979. International Year of the Child. Multicoloured.
452	5t. Type **118**	20	10
453	10t. Child playing with doll (vert)	30	20

119 *Ximenia caffra*

1979. Christmas. Flowers. Multicoloured.
454	5t. Type **119**	10	10
455	10t. *Sclerocarya caffra*	20	20
456	15t. *Hexalobus monopetalus*	35	35
457	25t. *Ficus soldanella*	45	45

120 Flap-necked Chameleon

1980. Reptiles. Multicoloured.
458	5t. Type **120**	30	10
459	10t. Leopard tortoise	30	15
460	25t. Puff adder	50	65
461	40t. White-throated monitor	60	2·50

121 Rock Breaking

1980. Early Mining. Multicoloured.
462	5t. Type **121**	25	15
463	10t. Ore hoisting	30	15
464	15t. Ore transport	70	60
465	20t. Ore crushing	75	90
466	25t. Smelting	80	90
467	35t. Tool and products	1·00	1·75

122 "Chiwele and the Giant"

1980. Folktales. Multicoloured.
468	5t. Type **122**	10	10
469	10t. "Kgori is not deceived" (vert)	15	10
470	30t. "Nyambi's wife and Crocodile" (vert)	45	45
471	45t. "Clever Hare" (horiz)	60	60

The 10t. and 30t. are 28×37 mm and the 45t. 44×27 mm.

123 Game watching, Makgadikgadi Pans

1980. World Tourism Conference, Manila.
472	**123** 5t. multicoloured	45	20

124 *Acacia gerrardii*

1980. Christmas. Multicoloured.
473	6t. Type **124**	10	10
474	1t. *Acacia nilotica*	20	10
475	25t. *Acacia erubescens*	45	30
476	40t. *Dichrostachys cinerea*	70	70

125 Heinrich von Stephan and Botswana 3d. and 3c. U.P.U. Stamps

1981. 150th Birth Anniv of Heinrich von Stephan (founder of Universal Postal Union). Multicoloured.
477	6t. Type **125**	50	30
478	20t. 6d. and 7c. U.P.U. stamps	1·25	2·25

126 *Anax imperator* (dragonfly)

1981. Insects. Multicoloured.
479	6t. Type **126**	15	10
480	7t. *Sphodromantis gastrica* (mantid)	15	20
481	10t. *Zonocerus elegans* (grasshopper)	15	20
482	20t. *Kheper nigroaeneus* (beetle)	25	50
483	30t. *Papilio demodocus* (butterfly)	35	70
484	45t. *Acanthocampa belina* (moth larva)	40	1·10
MS485	180×89 mm. Nos. 479/84	3·00	8·50

127 Camphill Community Rankoromane, Otse

1981. International Year for Disabled Persons. Multicoloured.
486	6t. Type **127**	20	10
487	20t. Resource Centre for the Blind, Mochudi	55	35
488	30t. Tlamelong Rehabilitation Centre, Tlokweng	75	45

128 Woman reading Letter

1981. Literacy Programme. Multicoloured.
489	6t. Type **128**	20	10
490	7t. Man filling in form	20	15
491	20t. Boy reading newspaper	60	35
492	30t. Child being taught to read	80	45

129 Sir Seretse Khama and Building

1981. First Death Anniv of Sir Seretse Khama (former President). Multicoloured.
493	6t. Type **129**	15	10
494	10t. Seretse Khama and building (different)	25	15
495	30t. Seretse Khama and Botswana flag	40	45
496	45t. Seretse Khama and building (different)	55	70

1981. Nos. 417 and 422 surch.
497	25t. on 35t. Green-backed heron	2·50	2·00
498	30t. on 10t. Bennett's woodpecker	2·50	2·00

131 Traditional Ploughing

1981. Cattle Industry. Multicoloured.
499	6t. Type **131**	10	10
500	20t. Agricultural show	30	50
501	30t. Botswana Meat Commission	35	60
502	45t. Vaccine Institute, Botswana	50	1·00

132 *Nymphaea caerulea*

1981. Christmas. Flowers. Multicoloured.
503	6t. Type **132**	20	10
504	10t. *Nymphoides indica*	25	10
505	25t. *Nymphaea lotus*	60	90
506	40t. *Ottelia kunenensis*	80	2·25

133 *Cattle Post Scene* (Boitumelo Golaakwena)

1982. Children's Art. Multicoloured.
507	6t. Type **133**	40	10
508	10t. *Kgotla Meeting* (Reginald Klinck)	50	15
509	30t. *Village Water Supply* (Keronmemang Matswiri)	1·75	1·25
510	45t. *With the Crops* (Kennedy Balemoge)	1·75	3·00

134 Common Type

1982. Traditional House. Multicoloured.
511	6t. Type **134**	40	15
512	10t. Kgatleng type	50	15
513	30t. North Eastern type	2·00	1·10
514	45t. Sarwa type	2·00	3·00

135 African Masked Weaver

1982. Birds. Multicoloured.
515	1t. Type **135**	80	1·75
516	2t. Miombo double-collared sunbird ("Lesser double-collared Sunbird")	90	1·75
517	3t. Red-throated bee eater	1·00	1·75
518	4t. Ostrich	1·00	1·75
519	5t. Grey-headed gull	1·00	1·75
520	6t. African pygmy ("Pygmy Goose")	1·00	40
521	7t. Cattle egret	1·00	15
522	8t. Lanner falcon	2·50	1·75
523	10t. Yellow-billed stork	1·00	20
524	15t. Red-billed pintail ("Redbilled Teal") (horiz)	2·75	25
525	20t. Barn owl (horiz)	5·50	3·50
526	25t. Hammerkop ("Hammerkop") (horiz)	3·25	70
527	30t. South African stilt ("Stilt") (horiz)	3·75	90
528	35t. Blacksmith plover (horiz)	3·75	80
529	45t. Senegal wattled plover ("Watted Plover") (horiz)	3·75	1·75
530	50t. Helmeted guineafowl ("Crowned Guineafowl") (horiz)	4·75	2·50
531	1p. Cape vulture (horiz)	9·00	12·00
532	2p. Augur buzzard (horiz)	11·00	17·00

136 *Coprinus comatus*

1982. Christmas. Fungi. Multicoloured.
533	7t. Type **136**	2·50	20
534	15t. *Lactarius deliciosus*	3·75	65
535	35t. *Amanita pantherina*	6·00	2·00
536	50t. *Boletus edulis*	7·50	8·00

137 President Quett Masire

1983. Commonwealth Day. Multicoloured.
537	7t. Type **137**	10	10
538	15t. Native dancers	15	20
539	35t. Melbourne conference centre	45	55
540	45t. Meeting of Heads of State, Melbourne	55	80

138 Wattled Crane

1983. Endangered Species. Multicoloured.
541	7t. Type **138**	3·00	55
542	15t. *Aloe lutescens*	2·50	80
543	35t. Roan antelope	3·00	3·25
544	50t. Ivory palm	3·50	7·00

139 Wooden Spoons

1983. Traditional Artifacts. Multicoloured.
545	7t. Type **139**	25	10
546	15t. Personal ornaments	45	30
547	35t. Ox-hide milk bag	75	65
548	50t. Decorated knives	1·00	1·10
MS549	115×102 mm. Nos. 545×8	4·25	5·00

140 *Pantala flavescens*

1983. Christmas. Dragonflies. Multicoloured.
550	7t. Type **140**	85	10
551	15t. *Anax imperator*	1·75	50
552	25t. *Trithemis arteriosa*	2·00	85
553	45t. *Chlorolestes elegans*	2·75	4·75

141 Sorting
Diamonds

1984. Mining Industry. Multicoloured.

554	7t. Type **141**	2·00	50
555	15t. Lime kiln	2·00	75
556	35t. Copper-nickel smelter plant (vert)	3·25	3·25
557	60t. Stockpiled coal (vert)	3·75	10·00

142 Riding Cattle

1984. Traditional Transport. Multicoloured.

558	7t. Type **142**	20	10
559	25t. Sledge	65	60
560	35t. Wagon	85	1·50
561	50t. Two-wheeled donkey cart	1·25	4·50

143 Avro 504 Aircraft

1984. 40th Anniv of International Civil Aviation Organization. Multicoloured.

562	7t. Type **143**	75	20
563	10t. Westland Wessex trimotor	1·00	35
564	15t. Junkers Ju 52/3m	1·40	95
565	25t. de Havilland Dominie	2·00	1·75
566	35t. Douglas DC-3 *Wenala*	2·25	3·50
567	50t. Fokker Friendship	2·50	7·00

144 *Papilio demodocus*

1984. Christmas. Butterflies. Multicoloured.

568	7t. Type **144**	2·00	30
569	25t. *Byblia anvatara*	3·25	1·50
570	35t. *Danaus chrysippus*	3·50	3·00
571	50t. *Graphium taboranus*	4·75	11·00

No. 570 is incorrectly inscr "Hypolimnas misippus".

145 Seswaa (meat dish)

1985. Fifth Anniv of Southern African Development Co-ordination Conference. Traditional Foods. Multicoloured.

572	7t. Type **145**	50	10
573	15t. Bogobe (cereal porridge)	75	35
574	25t. Madila (soured coagulated cow's milk)	1·00	55
575	50t. Phane (caterpillars)	1·50	2·25
MS576	117×103 mm. Nos. 572/5	7·00	10·00

146 1885 British Bechuanaland Overprint on Cape of Good Hope ½d.

1985. Centenary of First Bechuanaland Stamps.

577	**146**	7t. black, grey and red	1·00	20
578	-	15t. black, brown yell	1·75	50
579	-	25t. black and red	2·25	80
580	-	35t. black, blue and gold	2·50	2·00
581	-	50t. multicoloured	2·75	3·75

DESIGNS—VERT: 15t. 1897 Bechuanaland Protectorate overprint on G.B. 3d.; 25t. Bechuanaland Protectorate 1932 1d. definitive. HORIZ: 35t. Bechuanaland 1965 Internal Self-Government 5c.; 50t. Botswana 1966 Independence 2½c.

147 Bechuanaland Border Police, 1885–95

1985. Centenary of Botswana Police. Multicoloured.

582	7t. Type **147**	2·25	50
583	10t. Bechuanaland Mounted Police, 1895–1902	2·50	50
584	25t. Bechuanaland Protectorate Police, 1903–66	3·50	2·00
585	50t. Botswana Police, from 1966	5·50	7·50

148 *Cucumis metuliferus*

1985. Christmas. Edible Wild Cucumbers. Multicoloured.

586	7t. Type **148**	1·25	10
587	15t. *Acanthosicyos naudinianus*	2·25	70
588	25t. *Coccinia sessifolia*	3·50	1·25
589	50t. *Momordica balsamina*	5·00	9·50

149 Mr. Shippard and Chief Gaseitsiwe of the Bangwaketse

1985. Centenary of Declaration of Bechuanaland Protectorate. Multicoloured.

590	7t. Type **149**	35	10
591	15t. Sir Charles Warren and Chief Sechele of the Bakwena	70	45
592	25t. Revd. Mackenzie and Chief Khama of the Bamangwato	1·25	85
593	50t. Map showing Protectorate	2·75	6·50
MS594	130×133 mm. Nos. 590/3	13·00	15·00

150 Halley's Comet over Serowe

1986. Appearance of Halley's Comet. Multicoloured.

595	7t. Type **150**	80	15
596	15t. Comet over Bobonong at sunset	1·50	70
597	35t. Comet over Gomare at dawn	2·00	1·50
598	50t. Comet over Thamaga and Letlhakeng	2·25	3·75

151 Milk Bag

1986. Traditional Milk Containers. Multicoloured.

599	8t. Type **151**	30	10
600	15t. Clay pot and calabashes	45	30
601	35t. Wooden milk bucket	75	65
602	50t. Milk churn	1·00	1·40

152 Map showing National Parks and Reserves

1986. 20th Anniv of Independence. Sheet 100×120 mm. Multicoloured.

MS603	20t. Type **152**; 20t. Morupule power station; 20t. Cattle breeding in Kgalagadi; 20t. National Assembly Building	3·75	2·50

153 *Ludwigia stogonifera*

1986. Christmas. Flowers of Okavango. Multicoloured.

604	8t. Type **153**	1·25	10
605	15t. *Sopubia mannii*	2·25	1·10
606	35t. *Commelina diffusa*	3·50	3·00
607	50t. *Hibiscus diversifolius*	4·00	12·00

154 Divining

1987. Traditional Medicine. Multicoloured.

608	8t. Type **154**	80	10
609	15t. Lightning prevention	1·50	80
610	35t. Rain making	2·25	2·50
611	50t. Blood letting	2·75	8·50

1987. Nos. 520, 523 and 530 surch.

612	3t. on 6t. African pygmy goose	1·75	75
613	5t. on 10t. Yellow-billed stork	1·75	1·25
614	20t. on 50t. Helmeted guinea-fowl (horiz)	3·25	1·40

156 Oral Rehydration Therapy

1987. UNICEF Child Survival Campaign. Multicoloured.

615	8t. Type **156**	35	10
616	15t. Growth monitoring	60	55
617	35t. Immunization	1·25	2·00
618	50t. Breast feeding	1·50	5·00

157 Cape Fox

1987. Animals of Botswana. Multicoloured.

619	1t. Type **157**	10	1·25
620	2t. Lechwe	50	1·75
621	3t. Zebra	15	1·25
622	4t. Duiker	15	1·75
623	5t. Banded mongoose	20	1·75
624	6t. Rusty-spotted genet	20	1·75
625	8t. Hedgehog	30	10
626	10t. Scrub hare	30	10
627	12t. Hippopotamus	4·00	4·00
628	15t. Suricate	2·50	2·25
629	20t. Caracal	70	65
630	25t. Steenbok	70	1·50
631	30t. Gemsbok	1·50	1·50
632	35t. Square-lipped rhinoceros	2·50	3·00
633	40t. Mountain reedbuck	1·75	1·50
634	50t. Rock dassie	90	1·75
635	1p. Giraffe	2·50	4·00
636	2p. Tsessebe	2·50	5·50
637	3p. Side-striped jackal	3·75	8·00
638	5p. Hartebeest	6·00	9·00

158 *Cyperus articulatus*

1987. Christmas. Grasses and Sedges of Okavango. Multicoloured.

639	8t. Type **158**	40	10
640	15t. Broomgrass	60	40
641	30t. *Cyperus alopurcides*	1·25	75

642	1p. Bulrush sedge	2·50	5·75
MS643	88×99 mm. Nos. 639/42	4·25	5·75

159 Planting Seeds with Digging Stick

1988. Early Cultivation. Multicoloured.

644	8t. Type **159**	40	10
645	15t. Using iron hoe	60	35
646	35t. Wooden ox-drawn plough	1·00	1·00
647	50t. Villagers working in lesotlas communal field	1·40	2·00

160 Red Lechwe at Water-hole

1988. Red Lechwe. Multicoloured.

648	10t. Type **160**	90	15
649	15t. Red lechwe and early morning sun	1·75	65
650	35t. Female and calf	2·50	1·75
651	75t. Herd on the move	3·75	8·50

161 Gubulawayo Postmark and Route Southwards to Tati

1988. Cent of Mafeking–Gubalawayo Runner Post. Designs as Nos. 294/7, but redrawn smaller with changed inscriptions as in T **161**. Multicoloured.

652	10t. Type **161**	35	10
653	15t. Bechuanaland 1888 6d. on 6d. stamp and route from Tati southwards	55	30
654	30t. Runners and twin routes south from Shoshong	95	75
655	60t. Mafeking postmark and routes to Bechuanaland and Transvaal	1·60	2·75
MS656	81×151 mm. Nos. 652/5 vertically se-tenant, forming a composite map design	9·00	9·50

162 Pope John Paul II and Outline Map of Botswana

1988. Visit of Pope John Paul II. Multicoloured.

657	10t. Type **162**	2·00	20
658	15t. Pope John Paul II	2·25	30
659	30t. Pope giving blessing and outline map	2·75	70
660	80t. Pope John Paul II (different)	3·50	4·00

163 National Museum and Art Gallery, Gaborone

1988. 20th Anniv of National Museum and Art Gallery, Gaborone. Multicoloured.

661	8t. Type **163**	15	10
662	15t. Pottery	20	25
663	30t. Blacksmith's buffalo bellows	35	40
664	60c. Children and land rover mobile museum van	70	1·00

164 *Grewia flava*

1988. Flowering Plants of South-eastern Botswana. Multicoloured.

665	8t. Type **164**	20	10
666	15t. *Cienfuegosia digitata*	30	25
667	40t. *Solanum seaforthianum*	60	55
668	75t. *Carissa bispinosa*	1·00	1·40

165 Basket Granary

1989. Traditional Grain Storage. Multicoloured.

669	8t. Type **165**	75	10
670	15t. Large letlole granary	1·25	40
671	30t. Pot granary	2·00	60
672	60t. Two types of serala	2·75	2·25

166 Female with Eggs

1989. Slaty Egret. Multicoloured.

673	8t. Type **166**	55	15
674	15t. Chicks in nest	75	40
675	30t. In flight	1·00	75
676	60t. Pair building nest	1·40	2·25
MS677	119×89 mm. Nos. 673/6	3·25	3·75

167 My Work at Home (Ephraim Seeletso)

1989. Children's Paintings. Multicoloured.

678	10t. Type **167**	35	10
679	15t. *My Favourite Game* (hop-scotch) (Neelma Bhatia) (vert)	50	35
680	30t. *My Favourite Toy* (clay animals) (Thabo Habana)	75	70
681	1p. *My School Day* (Thabo Olesitse)	2·00	3·25

168 *Eulophia angolensis*

1989. Christmas. Orchids. Multicoloured.

682	8t. Type **168**	90	10
683	15t. *Eulophia hereroensis*	1·50	60
684	30t. *Eulophia speciosa*	2·00	1·00
685	60t. *Eulophia petersii*	3·50	7·00

169 Bechuanaland 1965 New Constitution 25c. Stamp (25th anniv of Self-Government)

1990. Anniversaries.

686	**169**	8t. multicoloured	70	15
687	-	15t. multicoloured	75	50
688	-	30t. multicoloured	3·75	1·60
689	-	60t. black, blue and yellow	3·75	7·00

DESIGNS: 15t. Casting vote in ballot box (25th anniv of First Elections); 30t. Outline map and flags of Southern Africa Development Co-ordination Conference countries (10th anniv); 60t. Penny Black (150th anniv of first postage stamp).

1990. Nos. 619, 624 and 627 surch.

690	10t. on 1t. Type **157**	60	20

691	20t. on 6t. Rusty-spotted genet	1·00	80
692	50t. on 12t. Hippopotamus	3·50	3·50

171 Telephone Engineer

1990. Stamp World London 90, International Stamp Exhibition. Multicoloured.

693	8t. Type **171**	35	10
694	15t. Transmission pylon	65	40
695	30t. Public telephone	1·00	75
696	2p. Testing circuit board	3·00	6·50

172 Young Children

1990. Traditional Dress. Multicoloured.

697	8t. Type **172**	45	10
698	15t. Young woman	80	40
699	30t. Adult man	1·40	70
700	2p. Adult woman	3·50	6·50
MS701	104×150 mm. Nos. 697/700	8·00	10·00

173 *Acacia nigrescens*

1990. Christmas. Flowering Trees. Multicoloured.

702	8t. Type **173**	60	10
703	15t. *Peltophorum africanum*	95	35
704	30t. *Burkea africana*	1·75	75
705	2p. *Pterocarpus angolensis*	3·75	7·50

174 Children running in front of Hatchback

1990. First National Road Safety Day. Multicoloured.

706	8t. Type **174**	2·50	30
707	15t. Careless overtaking	3·00	1·00
708	30t. Cattle on road	3·75	2·75

175 Cattle

1991. Rock Paintings. Multicoloured.

709	8t. Type **175**	2·25	40
710	15t. Cattle, drying frames and tree	2·75	85
711	30t. Animal hides	3·25	1·50
712	2p. Family herding cattle	6·00	10·00

176 Children

1991. National Census. Multicoloured.

713	8t. Type **176**	1·50	20
714a	15t. Village	2·00	55
715	30t. School	2·25	1·00
716	2p. Hospital	8·00	11·00

177 Tourists viewing Elephants

1991. African Tourism Year. Okavango Delta. Multicoloured.

717	8t. Type **177**	1·75	70
718	15t. Crocodiles basking on river bank	2·00	90
719	35t. Fish eagles and de Havil-land D.H.C.7 Dash Seven aircraft	4·25	3·25
720	2p. Okavango wildlife (26×44 mm)	6·00	9·00

178 *Harpagophytum procumbens*

1991. Christmas. Seed Pods. Multicoloured.

721	8t. Type **178**	60	10
722	15t. *Tylosema esculentum*	1·00	40
723	30t. *Abrus precatorius*	1·75	90
724	2p. *Kigelia africana*	4·50	8·50

1992. Nos. 621, 624 and 627 surch.

725	8t. on 12t. Hippopotamus	1·50	70
726	10t. on 12t. Hippopotamus	1·50	70
727	25t. on 6t. Rusty-spotted genet	1·25	1·50
728	40t. on 3t. Zebra	2·25	4·00

179 *Cacosternum boettgeri*

1992. Climbing Frogs. Multicoloured.

729	8t. Type **179**	75	30
730	10t. *Hyperolius marmoratus angolensis* (vert)	75	30
731	40t. *Bufo fenoulheti*	2·50	1·50
732	1p. *Hyperolius* sp. (vert)	5·00	7·00

180 Air-conditioned Carriages

1992. Deluxe Railway Service. Multicoloured.

733	10t. Type **180**	1·50	40
734	25t. Diesel locomotive No. BD001 (vert)	2·25	80
735	40t. Carriage interior (vert)	2·50	1·25
736	2p. Diesel locomotive No. BD028	3·75	7·50
MS737	127×127 mm. Nos. 733/6	13·00	13·00

181 Cheetah

1992. Animals. Multicoloured.

738	1t. Type **181**	40	2·00
739	2t. Spring hare	40	2·00
740	4t. Blackfooted cat	50	2·00
741	5t. Striped mouse	50	1·75
742	10t. Oribi	65	10
743	12t. Pangolin	1·25	3·00
744	15t. Aardwolf	1·25	40
745	20t. Warthog	1·25	40
746	25t. Ground squirrel	1·25	20
747	35t. Honey badger	1·50	30
748	40t. Common mole rat	1·50	30
749	45t. Wild dog	1·50	30
750	50t. Water mongoose	1·50	35
751	80t. Klipspringer	2·50	2·50
752	1p. Lesser bushbaby	2·50	2·50
753	2p. Bushveld elephant shrew	3·50	4·50
754	5p. Zorilla	5·50	8·00
755	10p. Vervet monkey	8·00	12·00

182 Boxing

1992. Olympic Games, Barcelona. Multicoloured.

756	10t. Type **182**	60	10
757	50t. Running	1·50	50
758	1p. Boxing (different)	2·00	2·50
759	2p. Running (different)	2·50	5·00
MS760	87×117 mm. Nos. 756/9	6·00	8·00

183 *Adiantum incisum*

1992. Christmas. Ferns. Multicoloured.

761	10t. Type **183**	40	10
762	25t. *Actiniopteris radiata*	70	35
763	40t. *Ceratopteris cornuta*	1·00	55
764	1p.50 *Pellaea calomelanos*	3·00	7·00

184 Helping Blind Person (Lions Club International)

1993. Charitable Organizations in Botswana. Multicoloured.

765	10t. Type **184**	80	20
766	15t. Nurse carrying child (Red Cross Society) (horiz)	90	40
767	25t. Woman watering seedling (Ecumenical Decade)	90	50
768	35t. Deaf children (Round Table) (horiz)	1·25	1·50
769	40t. Crowd of people (Rotary International)	1·25	1·75
770	50t. Hands at prayer (Botswana Christian Council) (horiz)	1·50	2·50

185 Bechuanaland Railways Class "6" Locomotive No. 1

1993. Railway Centenary. Multicoloured.

771	10t. Type **185**	75	40
772	40t. Class "19" locomotive No. 317	1·40	75
773	50t. Class "12" locomotive No. 256	1·40	90
774	1p.50 Class "7" locomotive No. 71	2·00	5·00
MS775	190×100 mm. Nos. 771/4	5·00	7·00

186 Long-crested Eagle

1993. Endangered Eagles. Multicoloured.

776	10t. Type **186**	70	35
777	25t. Short-toed eagle ("Snake eagle")	1·25	65
778	50t. Bateleur ("Bateleur Eagle")	1·60	1·75
779	1p.50 Secretary bird	2·50	6·50

187 *Aloe zebrina*

1993. Christmas. Flora. Multicoloured.

780	12t. Type **187**	40	10
781	25t. *Croton megalobotrys*	60	25
782	50t. *Boophane disticha*	85	70
783	1p. *Euphoria davyi*	1·25	3·50

188 Boy with String Puppet

1994. Traditional Toys. Multicoloured.

784	10t. Type **188**	20	10
785	40t. Boys with clay cattle	45	30
786	50t. Boy with spinner	50	50
787	1p. Girls playing in make-believe houses	1·10	3·00

189 Interior of Control Tower, Gaborone Airport

1994. 50th Anniv of I.C.A.O. Multicoloured.

788	10t. Type **189**	40	10
789	25t. Crash fire tender	75	40
790	40t. Loading supplies onto airliner (vert)	1·00	85
791	50t. Control tower, Gaborone (vert)	1·00	1·75

1994. No. 743 surch **10t.**

792	10t. on 12t. Pangolin	8·50	75

191 Lesser Flamingos at Sua Pan

1994. Environment Protection. Makgadikgadi Pans. Multicoloured.

793	10t. Type **191**	1·00	40
794	35t. Baobab trees (horiz)	50	40
795	50t. Zebra and palm trees	65	80
796	2p. Map of area (horiz)	3·00	6·00

192 *Ziziphus mucronata*

1994. Christmas. Edible Fruits. Multicoloured.

797	10t. Type **192**	25	10
798	25t. *Strychnos cocculoides*	40	30
799	40t. *Bauhinia petersiana*	60	70
800	50t. *Schinziphyton rautoneii*	70	1·40

193 Fisherman with Bow and Arrow

1995. Traditional Fishing. Multicoloured.

801	15t. Type **193**	35	20
802	40t. Men in canoe and boy with fishing rod	60	45
803	65t. Fisherman with net	80	90
804	80t. Fisherman with basket fish trap	1·00	2·00

194 Boys watering Horses (FAO)

1995. 50th Anniv of United Nations. Multicoloured.

805	20t. Type **194**	20	10

806	50t. Schoolchildren queueing for soup (WFP)	35	30
807	80t. Policeman conducting census (UNDP)	1·00	1·00
808	1p. Weighing baby (UNICEF)	70	2·00

195 Brown Hyena

1995. Endangered Species. Brown Hyena. Multicoloured.

809	20t. Type **195**	45	60
810	50t. Pair of hyenas	65	75
811	80t. Hyena stealing ostrich eggs	1·10	1·50
812	1p. Adult hyena and cubs	1·25	2·25

196 *Adenia glauca*

1995. Christmas. Plants. Multicoloured.

813	20t. Type **196**	35	10
814	50t. *Pterodiscus ngamicus*	60	30
815	80t. *Sesamothamnus lugardii*	1·00	1·00
816	1p. *Fockea multiflora*	1·10	2·00

1996. Nos. 738/40 surch.

817	20t. on 2t. Spring hare	1·00	30
818	30t. on 1t. Type **181**	1·25	30
819	70t. on 4t. Blackfooted cat	2·00	3·25

198 Spears

1996. Traditional Weapons. Multicoloured.

820	20t. Type **198**	20	10
821	50t. Axes	35	30
822	80t. Shield and knobkerries	55	65
823	1p. Knives and sheaths	60	1·50

199 Child with Basic Radio

1996. Centenary of Radio. Multicoloured.

824	20t. Type **199**	25	10
825	50t. Radio Botswana's mobile transmitter	40	30
826	80t. Police radio control	1·50	1·10
827	1p. Listening to radio	70	1·75

200 Olympic Flame, Rings and Wreath

1996. Centenary of Modern Olympic Games. Multicoloured.

828	20t. Type **200**	40	10
829	50t. Pierre de Coubertin (founder of modern Olympics)	60	30
830	80t. Map of Botswana with flags and athletes	1·50	1·00
831	1p. Ruins of ancient stadium at Olympia	1·00	1·60

201 Family Planning Class (Botswana Family Welfare Association)

1996. Local Charities. Multicoloured.

832	20t. Type **201**	20	10
833	30t. Blind workers (Pudulogong Rehabilitation Centre)	20	15
834	50t. Collecting seeds (Forestry Association of Botswana)	30	30
835	70t. Secretarial class (YWCA)	40	70
836	80t. Children's day centre (Botswana Council of Women)	50	80
837	1p. Children's village, Tlokweng (S.O.S. Children's village)	60	1·50

202 *Adansonia digitata* Leaf and Blossom

1996. Christmas. Parts of Life Cycle for *Adansonia digitata*. Multicoloured.

838	20t. Type **202**	25	10
839	50t. Fruit	40	25
840	80t. Tree in leaf	60	75
841	1p. Tree with bare branches	70	1·60

203 Tati Hotel

1997. Francistown Centenary. Multicoloured.

842	20t. Type **203**	15	10
843	50t. Railway Station	75	35
844	80t. Company Manager's House	60	80
845	1p. Monarch Mine	1·00	1·60

204 Steam Locomotive, Bechuanaland Railway, 1897

1997. Railway Centenary. Multicoloured.

846	35t. Type **204**	40	20
847	50t. Elephants crossing railway line	60	35
848	80t. First locomotive in Bechuanaland, 1897	70	45
849	1p. Beyer-Garratt type steam locomotive No. 352	75	75
850	2p. Diesel locomotive No. BD339	1·00	1·75
851	2p.50 Fantuzzi container stacker	1·25	2·25

205 Pel's Fishing Owl

1997. Birds. Multicoloured.

852	5t. Type **205**	70	1·25
853	10t. African harrier hawk ("Gymnogene") (horiz)	70	1·25
854	15t. Brown parrot ("Meyer's Parrot")	75	1·25
855	20t. Harlequin quail (horiz)	80	1·25
856	25t. Mariqua sunbird ("Marico Sunbird") (horiz)	80	1·25
857	30t. Kurrichane thrush (horiz)	85	1·25
858	40t. Paradise sparrow ("Redheaded Finch")	90	80
859	50t. Red-billed buffalo weaver ("Buffalo Weaver")	1·00	50
860	60t. Sacred ibis (horiz)	1·25	1·00

861	70t. Cape shoveler (horiz)	1·25	1·00
862	80t. Black-throated honeyguide ("Greater Honeyguide") (horiz)	1·25	1·00
863	1p. Woodland kingfisher (horiz)	1·50	1·00
864	1p.25 Purple heron	2·00	1·75
865	1p.50 Yellow-billed oxpecker (horiz)	2·00	2·25
866	2p. Shaft-tailed whydah	2·25	2·50
867	2p.50 White stork	2·75	3·00
868	5p. Ovampo sparrow hawk ("Sparrowhawk")	4·00	4·50
869	10p. Spotted crake	6·50	8·00

No. 861 is inscribed "Shoveller" in error.

1997. Golden Wedding of Queen Elizabeth and Prince Philip. As T **173** of Ascension. Multicoloured.

870	35t. Prince Philip with carriage	20	55
871	35t. Queen Elizabeth with binoculars	20	55
872	2p. Queen Elizabeth with horse team	90	1·50
873	2p. Prince Philip and horse	90	1·50
874	2p.50 Queen Elizabeth and Prince Philip	1·10	1·50
875	2p.50 Princess Anne and Prince Edward	1·10	1·50

MS876 110×70 mm. 10p. Queen Elizabeth and Prince Philip in landau (horiz) 4·00 5·50

206 *Combretum zeyheri*

1997. Christmas. Plants. Multicoloured.

877	35t. Type **206**	45	10
878	1p. *Combretum apiculatum*	1·00	35
879	2p. *Combretum molle*	1·75	1·90
880	2p.50 *Combretum imberbe*	2·00	2·75

207 Baobab Trees

1998. Tourism (1st series). Multicoloured.

881	35t. Type **207**	25	15
882	1p. Crocodile	50	45
883	2p. Stalactites (vert)	95	1·10
884	2p.50 Tourists and rock paintings (vert)	1·25	1·60

See also Nos. 899/902.

1998. Diana, Princess of Wales Commemoration. As T **223a** of Bahamas. Multicoloured.

885	35t. Princess Diana, 1990	25	15
886	1p. In green hat, 1992	40	35
887	2p. In white blouse, 1993	75	1·10
888	2p.50 With crowd, Cambridge, 1993	90	1·50

MS889 145×70 mm. As Nos. 885/8, but each with a face value of 2p.50 3·00 3·75

208 *Village Life* (tapestry)

1998. Botswana Weavers. Multicoloured.

890	35t. Type **208**	30	15
891	55t. Weaver dyeing threads	40	20
892	1p. *African Wildlife* (tapestry)	1·40	1·00
893	2p. Weaver at loom	1·50	2·25

MS894 68×58 mm. 2p.50, *Elephants* (tapestry) (horiz) 3·00 3·75

209 *Ficus ingens*

1998. Christmas. Plants. Multicoloured.

895	35t. Type **209**	45	10
896	55t. *Ficus pygmaea*	65	20
897	1p. *Ficus abutilifolia*	1·25	55
898	2p.50 *Ficus sycomorus*	2·00	3·00

1999. Tourism (2nd series). As T 207. Multicoloured.

899	35t. Rock painting of men and cattle	85	25
900	55t. Expedition at Salt Pan	1·25	30
901	1p. Rock painting of elephant and antelope (vert)	1·50	1·40
902	2p. Tourists under Baobab tree (vert)	1·60	2·50

210 Road Map

1999. Southern African Development Community Day. Sheet 77×84 mm.

MS903	210 5p. multicoloured	3·75	4·00

211 Modern Post Office

1999. 125th Anniv of Universal Postal Union.

904	211 2p. multicoloured	2·00	2·00

212 Mpule Kwelagobe winning contest

1999. Mpule Kwelagobe ("Miss Universe 1999"). Multicoloured.

905	35t. Type 212	35	10
906	1p. In traditional dress (horiz)	75	30
907	2p. In traditional dancing costume with lion	1·10	60
908	2p.50 Wearing "Botswana" sash (horiz)	1·25	75
909	15p. With leopard in background (horiz)	7·00	12·00
MS910	175×80 mm. Nos. 905/9	9·50	12·00

213 Saddle-bill Stork and Limpopo River

2000. Scenic Rivers. Multicoloured.

911	35t. Type 213	60	20
912	1p. Hippopotamuses in water lilies (vert)	1·00	60
913	2p. African skimmer and makoro (dugout canoe)	1·75	1·75
914	2p.50 African elephant at sunset, Chobe River (vert)	2·00	2·50

214 Mopane Moth

2000. Moths. Multicoloured.

915	35t. Type 214	15	10
916	70t. Wild silk moth	25	20
917	1p. Crimson speckled footman ("Tiger Moth")	35	30
918	2p. African lunar moth	65	60
919	15p. Speckled emperor moth	4·75	9·00
MS920	175×135 mm. Nos. 915/19	7·50	10·00

No. **MS**920 is in the shape of a moth.

215 Mother reading Medicine Label with Child ("Protect Your Children")

2000. United Nations Literacy Decade. Multicoloured.

921	35t. Type 215	20	10
922	70t. Adult literacy class ("Never Too Old To Learn")	30	20
923	2p. Man smoking next to petrol pump ("Be Aware Of Danger")	75	1·10
924	2p.50 Man at Automatic Teller Machine ("Be Independent")	90	2·00

216 Pres. Sir Seretse Khama

2000. Chiefs and Presidents.

925	216	35t. black, red and gold	50	10
926	-	1p. multicoloured	75	40
927	-	2p. multicoloured	1·25	1·40
928	-	2p.50 multicoloured	1·50	2·25

DESIGNS—HORIZ (60×40 mm): 35t. Chiefs Sebele I of Bakwena, Bathoen I of Bangwaketse and Khama III of Bangato, 1895. VERT (as T **216**): 2p. Pres. Sir Ketumile Masire; 2p.50, Pres. Festus Mogae.

217 Doctor giving Eye Test

2000. Airborne Medical Service. Multicoloured.

929	35t. Type 217	30	10
930	1p. Medical team and family	65	40
931	2p. Aircraft over canoes	1·25	1·40
932	2p.50 Donkeys and mule cart on airstrip	1·50	2·25

218 Hippopotamus

2000. Wetlands (1st series). Okavango Delta. Multicoloured.

933	35t. Type 218	50	20
934	1p. Tiger fish and tilapia	55	30
935	1p.75 Painted reed frog and wattled crane (vert)	1·50	1·50
936	2p. Pels fishing owl and vervet monkey (vert)	1·75	1·75
937	2p.50 Nile crocodile, Sitatunga and red lechwe	1·75	1·75
MS938	175×80 mm. Nos. 933/7	6·50	6·50

See also Nos. 958/62, 994/**MS**999 and 1009/**MS**1014.

2001. HONG KONG 2001 Stamp Exhibition. No. MS938 overprinted with exhibition logo on sheet margin.

MS939	175×80 mm. Nos. 933/7	6·00	7·00

219 Diamonds

2001. Diamonds. Multicoloured. Self-adhesive.

940	35t. Type 219	70	35
941	1p.75 J.C.B. in open-cast mine	1·75	2·00
942	2p. Quality inspector	2·00	2·25
943	2p.50 Diamonds in jewellery	2·50	3·00

220 African Pygmy Falcon

2001. Kgalagadi Transfrontier Wildlife Park. Joint Issue with South Africa. Multicoloured.

944	35t. Type 220	1·50	45
945	1p. Leopard	1·00	75
946	2p. Gemsbok	1·60	2·25
947	2p.50 Bat-eared fox	1·60	2·25
MS948	115×80 mm. Nos. 945 and 947	2·50	3·00

221 Shallow Basket

2001. Traditional Baskets. Multicoloured.

949	35t. Type 221	20	15
950	1p. Tall basket	35	25
951	2p. Woman weaving basket	60	85
952	2p.50 Spherical basket	65	95
MS953	177×92 mm. Nos. 949/52	2·00	3·50

222 Boys by River at Sunset

2001. Scenic Skies. Multicoloured.

954	50t. Type 222	35	15
955	1p. Woman with baby at sunset	60	25
956	2p. Girls carrying firewood at sunset	90	75
957	10p. Traditional village at sunset near huts	3·50	4·50

2001. Wetlands (2nd series). Chobe River. As T 218. Multicoloured.

958	50t. Water monitor and carmine bee-eater	65	20
959	1p.75 Buffalo	75	60
960	2p. Savanna baboons (vert)	90	1·00
961	2p.50 Lion (vert)	1·10	1·40
962	3p. African elephants in river	2·25	2·25
MS963	175×80 mm. Nos. 958/62	5·00	5·00

223 Black Mamba

2002. Snakes. Multicoloured.

964	50t. Type 223	45	15
965	1p.75 Spitting cobra (vert)	70	45
966	2p.50 Puff adder	80	1·40
967	3p. Boomslang (vert)	1·00	1·75

224 Mbukushu Pots

2002. Botswana Pottery. Multicoloured.

968	50t. Type 224	45	10
969	2p. Sekgatla pots	80	75
970	2p.50 Setswana pots	90	1·10
971	3p. Kalanga pots	1·10	1·50

225 Queen Elizabeth in Evening Dress and Commonwealth Emblem

2002. Golden Jubilee. Multicoloured.

972	55t. Type 225	65	15
973	2p.75 Queen Elizabeth with bouquet (vert)	1·75	2·00

226 Tree Squirrel

2002. Mammals. Multicoloured.

974	5t. Type 226	10	30
975	10t. Black-backed jackal	15	30
976	20t. African wild cat	20	40
977	30t. Slender mongoose (horiz)	30	40
978	40t. African civet (horiz)	50	50
979	55t. Elephant	1·75	50
980	90t. Reedbuck	60	50
981	1p. Kudu	70	50
982	1p.45 Waterbuck	1·00	1·00

983	1p.95 Sable (horiz)	1·50	1·50
984	2p.20 Sitatunga (horiz)	1·50	1·50
985	2p.75 Porcupine (horiz)	1·50	1·50
986	3p.30 Serval (horiz)	1·60	1·75
987	4p. Antbear (horiz)	2·00	2·50
988	5p. Bushpig (horiz)	2·25	2·75
989	15p. Chakma baboon	5·00	7·00

227 Tebelopele (counselling and testing centres) Symbol

2002. AIDS Awareness. Multicoloured.

990	55t. Type 227	60	15
991	1p.10 AIDS ribbon and mother and baby badge	1·10	40
992	2p.75 Hands and male gender symbol	1·75	2·25
993	3p.30 Orphans with foster parent	1·90	2·50

2002. Wetlands (3rd series). The Makgadikgadi Pans. As T 218. Multicoloured.

994	55t. Aardwolf	50	15
995	1p.10 Blue wildebeest and zebra	1·00	30
996	2p.50 Zebra (vert)	1·75	1·40
997	2p.75 Flamingo (vert)	2·25	2·50
998	3p.30 Pelican in flight	2·50	3·00
MS999	175×80 mm. Nos. 994/8	7·25	8·00

228 Lentswe la Baratani ("Hill of Lovers")

2003. Natural Places of Interest. Multicoloured.

1000	55t. Type 228	35	15
1001	2p.20 Sand dunes	1·00	90
1002	2p.75 Moremi Waterfalls (vert)	1·50	2·00
1003	3p.30 Gcwihaba Cave	1·75	2·50

229 Ngwale

2003. Beetles. Multicoloured.

1004	55t. Type 229	40	15
1005	2p.20 Kgomo-ya-buru	1·10	80
1006	2p.75 Kgomo-ya-pula	1·40	1·75
1007	3p.30 Lebitse	1·75	2·25
MS1008	69×59 mm. 5p.50 Kgaladuwa	5·00	5·50

2003. Wetlands (4th series). The Limpopo River. As Type 218. Multicoloured.

1009	55t. Giraffe	70	35
1010	1p.45 Black eagle and Nile crocodile (vert)	1·50	85
1011	2p.50 Ostrich (vert)	2·00	1·50
1012	2p.75 Klipspringer (vert)	1·60	1·75
1013	3p.30 Serval cat	1·90	2·25
MS1014	175×80 mm. Nos. 1010/13	7·00	8·00

230 San People with Birds (Cg'Ose Ntcox'o)

2004. Kuru Art Project. Multicoloured.

1015	55t. Type 230	35	20
1016	1p.45 Tree with gum (Nxaedom Qhomatca)	75	55
1017	2p.75 Tree with berries (Nxaedom Qhomatca)	1·10	1·60
1018	3p.30 Snake (Qgoma Ncokg'o)	1·50	2·00

231 Masimo (working the land)

2004. Traditional Life Styles. Multicoloured.
1019	80t. Type **231**	50	25
1020	2p.10 Kgotla (village meeting place)	1·25	85
1021	3p.90 Moraka (cattle post)	1·75	2·25
1022	4p.70 Legae (compound within village)	2·25	3·00

232 Child posting Letter

2004. World Post Day. Multicoloured.
1023	80t. Type **232**	45	25
1024	2p.10 Children sharing a letter	1·00	85
1025	3p.90 Post man	1·60	2·25
1206	4p.70 Woman reading letter	2·00	2·50

233 Peregrine Falcon (Angola)

2004. First Joint Issue of Southern Africa Postal Operators Association Members. Sheet 170×95 mm containing T **233** and similar hexagonal designs showing national birds of Association members. Multicoloured.
MS1027 40t. Type **233**; 50t. Two African Fish Eagles in flight (Zambia); 60t. Two African fish eagles perched (Zimbabwe); 70t. Bar-tailed trogon (Malawi) (inscribed "apaloderma vittatum"); 80t. Purple-crested turaco ("Lourie") (Swaziland); 1p. African fish eagle (Namibia); 2p. Stanley ("Blue") crane (South Africa); 5p. Cattle egret (Botswana) 13·00 14·00
The 70t. value stamp is not inscribed with the country of which the bird is a national symbol. Miniature sheets of similar designs were also issued by Namibia, Zimbabwe, Angola, Swaziland, South Africa, Malawi and Zambia.

234 *Pterodiscus speciosus*

2004. Christmas. Flowers. Multicoloured.
1028	80t. Type **234**	50	25
1029	2p.10 *Bulbine narcissifolia*	95	60
1030	3p.90 *Bulbiana hypogea*	1·75	2·25
1031	4p.70 *Hibiscus micranthus*	2·25	3·00

235 Blackbeard's Store, Phalatswe

2005. Historical Buildings. Multicoloured.
1032	80t. Type **235**	45	25
1033	2p.10 Primary School	85	60
1034	3p.90 Telegraph Office, Phalatswe	1·60	2·25
1035	4p.70 Magistrate's Court, Phalatswe	2·00	3·00

236 Cowpeas ("beans")

2005. Edible Crops. Multicoloured.
1036	80t. Type **236**	40	20
1037	2p.10 Pearl millet	80	55
1038	3p.90 Sorghum	1·40	2·25
1039	4p.70 Watermelon	1·75	3·00

237 Black-footed Cat with Prey

2005. Endangered Species. Black-footed Cat (*Felis nigripes*). Multicoloured.
1040	80t. Type **237**	45	20
1041	2p.10 Black-footed cat	85	60
1042	3p.90 With cub	1·60	2·00
1043	4p.70 In close-up	2·00	2·75
MS1044	160×185 mm. Nos. 1040/3, ×2	7·00	8·50

238 Namaqua Dove

2005. Christmas. Doves and Pigeons. Multicoloured.
1045	80t. Type **238**	50	20
1046	2p.10 Red-eyed dove	95	60
1047	3p.90 Laughing doves (pair)	1·75	2·25
1048	4p.70 Green pigeons (pair)	2·25	3·00

2006. Nos. 690 and 693 surch
1048a	80t. on 90t. Reedbuck	75	35
1048b	2p.10 on 1p.95 Sable (horiz)	1·25	1·25

239 Nembwe

2006. Okavango Fish. Multicoloured.
1049	80t. Type **239**	50	40
1050	2p.10 Tiger fish	1·25	80
1051	3p.90 Pike	1·75	2·00
1052	4p.70 Spotted squeaker	2·25	2·75

240 Oxen

2006. Tswana Cattle. Multicoloured.
1053	1p.10 Type **240**	40	35
1054	2p.60 Cows and calves	85	75
1055	4p.10 Bulls	1·25	2·00
1056	4p.90 Horn shapes	1·50	2·25

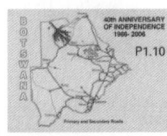

241 Road Map

2006. 40th Anniv of Independence. Showing maps of Botswana. Multicoloured.
1057	1p.10 Type **241**	75	45
1058	2p.60 Population distribution	95	90
1059	4p.10 Mines and coal resources	2·50	2·50
1060	4p.90 National parks and game reserves	2·75	3·00

242 *Hyphaene petersiana*

2006. Christmas. Trees. Multicoloured.
1062	1p.10 Type **242**	45	30
1063	2p.60 *Phoenix reclinata*	1·00	70
1064	4p.10 *Hyphaene petersiana*	1·50	2·00
1065	4p.90 *Phoenix reclinata*	1·75	2·50

243 Pied Kingfisher

2007. Kingfishers. Multicoloured.
1066	1p.10 Type **243**	60	45
1067	2p.60 Malachite kingfisher	1·40	1·00
1068	4p.10 Woodland kingfisher	2·00	2·25
1069	4p.90 Brown-hooded kingfisher	2·50	3·00

244 *Chlorophyllum molybdites* (false parasol)

2007. Fungi. Multicoloured.
1070	1p.10 Type **244**	40	30
1071	2p.60 *Phlebopus sudanicus* (bushveld bolete)	90	80
1072	4p.10 *Ganoderma lucidum* (laquered bracket fungus)	1·50	1·75
1073	4p.90 *Geastrum triplex* (collared earthstar)	1·75	2·00

245 Nyala (pair) (Malawi)

2007. Second Joint Issue of Southern Africa Postal Operators Association Members. Designs showing national animals of association members. Multicoloured.
1074	1p.10 Type **245**	40	30
1075	2p.60 Nyala (Zimbabwe)	90	80
1076	4p.10 Oryx (Namibia)	1·50	1·75
1077	4p.90 African buffalo (Zambia)	1·75	2·00
1078	5p.50 Burchell's zebra (Botswana)	2·25	2·50
MS1079	135×170 mm. Nos. 1074/9	7·00	7·50

Miniature sheets containing similar designs were also issued by Malawi, Namibia, Zambia and Zimbabwe. Zambia also issued sheet stamps.

246 Students and Tutor (University of Botswana Library)

2007. 25th Anniv of University of Botswana. Multicoloured.
1080	1p.10 Type **246**	35	30
1081	2p.60 Farmers and Sir Seretse Khama (first Botswana President) (BUCA campus appeal)	75	70
1082	4p.10 Researcher, village and wetland (Okavango Research)	1·25	1·50
1083	4p.90 Students and university buildings ('Infrastructure; old and new')	1·75	2·00

247 Mimosa Sapphire (*Iolaus mimosae mimosae*)

2007. Butterflies. Multicoloured.
1084	10t. Type **247**	10	10
1085	20t. Bushveld orange-tip (*Colotis pallene*)	10	10
1086	30t. African monarch (*Danaus chrysippus aegyptius*)	10	10
1087	40t. Common black-eye (*Gonatomyrina gorgias gorgias*)	15	20
1088	50t. Brown playboy (*Virachola antalus*)	25	30
1089	1p. Sapphire (*Iolaus silas*)	50	55
1090	(1p.10) Scarlet tip (*Colotis* (C) *danae annae*)	55	60
1091	2p. Large blue emperor (*Charaxes bohemani*)	65	70
1092	(2p.60) Dwarf blue (*Oraidium barberae*))	70	75
1093	3p. Apricot playboy (*Virachola dinochares*)	80	85
1094	4p. Blue pansy (*Junonia oenone oenone*)	90	95
1095	5p. Black-striped hairtail (*Anthene amarah amarah*)	1·10	1·25
1096	10p. Natal barred blue (*Spindasis natalensis*)	2·25	2·40
1097	20p. Foxy charaxes (*C. jasius saturnus*)	4·50	4·75

No. 1090 was inscr 'Standard Postage A' and sold for 1p.10. No. 1092 was inscr 'Standard Postage B' and sold for 2p.60.

248 Traditional Dancer (Boitshepo Lesego)

2008. Artists in Botswana. Designs showing winning entries in stamp design competition. Multicoloured.
1098	1p.10 Type **248**	35	30
1099	2p.60 Baobab tree (Philip Huebsch)	75	70
1100	4p.10 Girl playing with dolls (Giel Kgamane)	1·25	1·40
1101	4p.90 Donkeys tired after hard work (Tineni Kepaletswe) (horiz)	1·60	2·00
1102	5p.50 Donkeys in the city (Andrew Jones) (horiz)	1·90	2·40

249 Hunter and Guide facing Bull Elephant

2008. Elephants in Botswana. Multicoloured.
1103	1p.10 Type **249**	75	45
1104	2p.60 Tourists photographing female elephant with baby from dugout canoe	1·50	90
1105	4p.10 Villagers chasing crop raiding elephant	2·25	2·25
1106	4p.90 Elephant-back safari in Okavango Delta	2·50	2·75

250 Athletes

2008. Olympic Games, Athens. Multicoloured.
1107	1p.10 Type **250**	45	40
1108	2p.60 Boxers	80	85

251 Pitse Ya Naga
Launch

2008. 40th Anniv of Botswana National Museum.
Multicoloured.

1109	1p.10 Type 251	35	30
1110	2p.60 Botanical Garden (vert)	65	60
1111	4p.10 New Museum Galleries	1·25	1·25
1112	4p.90 Rock painting, Tsodilo Hills	1·60	2·00
1113	5p.50 Official opening (vert)	1·75	2·25

252 Address Plaque for
The No. 1 Ladies
Detective Agency and
Precious Ramotswe

2008. Events of Botswana 2008. Multicoloured.

1114	4p.10 Type 252 (Botswana Movie Premiere of *The No. 1 Ladies Detective Agency*)	1·25	1·25
1115	4p.90 Heart within heart (launch of Heart Foundation) (vert)	1·60	1·75
1116	5p.50 DTC Building (launch of Diamond Trading Company Botswana)	1·90	2·25

253 *Gymnopleurus humanus* (small green
dung beetle)

2008. Beetles of Botswana. Multicoloured.

1117	1p.10 Type 253	60	40
1118	2p.60 *Cheilomenes lunata* (lunate ladybird)	1·25	90
1119	4p.10 *Pachnoda sinuata* (garden fruit chafer)	1·75	1·90
1120	4p.90 *Eleodes* sp. (darkling beetle)	2·00	2·25

254 Lesser
Flamingo

2009. Endangered Birds of Botswana. Multicoloured.

1121	1p.10 Type 254	55	40
1122	2p.60 Grey crowned crane (horiz)	1·25	90
1123	4p.10 Wattled crane (horiz)	1·60	1·75
1124	4p.90 Blue crane (horiz)	1·90	2·25

255 Boy and Girl reading
('Education')

2009. Children of Botswana. Multicoloured.

1125	1p.10 Type 255	45	40
1126	2p.60 Boy washing hands under tap ('Sanitation') (vert)	90	80
1127	4p.10 Giving girl oral vaccine ('Inoculation') (vert)	1·50	1·60
1128	4p.90 Woman with children ('Orphan Care')	1·75	2·00

256 Southern Cross over Tsodilo
World Heritage Site and Giraffes

2009. Night Skies. Multicoloured.

1129	1p.10 Type 256	45	40
1130	2p.60 Meteorite over Okavango Delta and Ju/'hoansi firing arrows	90	80

1131	4p.10 Moon, Jupiter and Venus over central Kalahari and three Setswana women	1·50	1·60
1132	4p.90 Solar eclipse over Setswana village and trickster lion from Naro story	1·75	2·00

257 Honey Bee alighting
on Flower

2010. Honey Bees. Multicoloured.

1133	1p.10 Type 257	35	30
1134	2p.60 Two bees on honeycomb	75	70
1135	4p.10 Bee's nest in tree	1·25	1·40
1136	4p.90 Bee gathering pollen from flower	1·60	1·75

258 Player, Football,
Botswana Flag and
Zakumi Mascot

2010. Third Joint Issue of Southern Africa Postal Operators Association Members. World Cup Football Championship, South Africa. Multicoloured.

1137	1p.10 Type 258	10	10
1138	2p.60 Namibia	70	75
1139	3p. South Africa	80	85
1140	4p. Zimbabwe	90	95
1141	4p.10 Malawi	1·00	1·10
1142	4p.90 Swaziland	1·40	1·50
1143	5p.50 Mauritius	1·50	1·75
1144	6p.60 Lesotho	1·75	1·90
1145	8p.20 Zambia	2·25	2·40
MS1146	188×167 mm. As Nos. 1137/45 but with gold foil background	9·25	10·00

Stamps from **MS**1146 have a shiny gold background; the sheet stamps have a matt gold background.

Similar designs were issued by Lesotho, Malawi, Mauritius, Namibia, South Africa, Swaziland, Zambia and Zimbabwe.

259 Family
watching Television
('Coal for National
Power Grid')

2010. Energy Sources and Uses. Multicoloured.

1147	2p.60 Type 259	70	75
1148	4p.10 Woman using mobile phone and solar panel ('Solar Power Voltaic Panels')	1·00	1·10
1149	5p.50 Diesel locomotive	1·50	1·75
1150	6p.10 Compact fluorescent light bulb ('CFLs Save Money and Energy') (horiz)	1·75	1·90

Nos. 1151/6, T **260** are left for Night Animals, issued 1 December 2010, not yet received.

261 Motantanyane
(*Ipomoea obscura*)

2011. Flowers. Multicoloured.

1157	2p.60 Type 261	70	75
1158	4p.10 Ledelele (*Xenostegia tridentata*)	1·00	1·10
1159	5p.50 Tsebe-tsankuku (*Ipomoea magnusiana*)	1·50	1·75
1160	6p.10 Kgane (*Ipomoea bolusiana*)	1·75	1·90

POSTAGE DUE STAMPS

1967. Nos. D10/12 of Bechuanaland optd **REPUBLIC OF BOTSWANA**.

D13	D1	1c. red	15	1·75
D14	D1	2c. violet	15	1·75
D15	D1	5c. green	20	1·75

D 5 African
Elephant

1971

D16	D5	1c. red	1·10	3·25
D17	D5	2c. violet	1·40	3·50
D18	D5	6c. brown	1·75	5·50
D19	D5	14c. green	2·00	7·50

D 6 Common
Zebra

1977

D25a	D6	1t. black and red	60	1·25
D26a	D6	2t. black and green	60	1·25
D27a	D6	4t. black and red	60	1·25
D28a	D6	10t. black and blue	60	1·25
D29a	D6	16t. black and brown	70	1·50

Pt. 20

BOYACA

One of the states of the Granadine Confederation. A Department of Colombia from 1886, now uses Colombian stamps.

100 centavos = 1 peso.

1 Mendoza
Perez

1899. Imperf or perf.

1	1	5c. green	1·20	1·20

2　　**6** Battle of Boyaca
Monument

1903. Imperf or perf.

3A	2	10c. grey	35	30
4B	2	10c. blue	4·00	3·75
12	-	10c. orange	35	30
5A	2	20c. brown	45	45
5Aa	2	20c. lake	45	45
6B	-	50c. turquoise	45	45
8A	-	1p. red	45	45
9B	-	1p. red	4·00	3·75
10B	6	5p. black on red	1·50	1·50
11A	-	10p. black on buff	1·50	1·50

DESIGNS—As Type **2**: 10c. orange, Building; 50c. Gen. Pinzon; 1p. Figure of value. As Type **6**: 10p. Pres. Marroquin.

Pt. 20

BRAZIL

A country in the N.E. of S. America. Portuguese settlement, 1500. Kingdom, 1815. Empire, 1822. Republic from 1889.

1843. 1000 reis = 1 milreis.
1942. 100 centavos = 1 cruzeiro.
1986. 100 centavos = 1 cruzado.
1990. 100 centavos = 1 cruzeiro.
1994. 100 centavos = 1 real.
2008. 1st PCC = 1st porte Commercials.

1 "Bull's Eye"

1843. Imperf.

4	1	30r. black	£1900	£275
5	1	60r. black	£375	£150
6	1	90r. black	£1800	£750

2

1844. Imperf.

10B	2	10r. black	70·00	13·50
11B	2	30r. black	90·00	20·00
12B	2	60r. black	70·00	13·50
13B	2	90r. black	£550	70·00
14B	2	180r. black	£2500	£900
15B	2	300r. black	£3750	£1200
16B	2	600r. black	£3500	£1400

3

1850. Imperf.

17A	3	10r. black	28·00	38·00
18A	3	20r. black	85·00	£110
19A	3	30r. black	11·00	3·25
20A	3	60r. black	11·00	2·75
21A	3	90r. black	95·00	13·00
22A	3	180r. black	95·00	60·00
23A	3	300r. black	£375	65·00
24A	3	600r. black	£425	£100

4

1854. Imperf.

25		10r. blue	13·50	13·00
26		30r. blue	37·00	55·00
27	4	280r. red	£160	£110
28	4	430r. yellow	£250	£150

5　　**6**　　**17** Emperor
Dom Pedro II

1866. Various frames, but in T **5** the Emperor has a dark beard. Perf or roul.

43	5	10r. red	13·50	5·50
44a	6	20r. purple	24·00	3·25
45	5	50r. blue	34·00	2·75
46a	5	80r. purple	£170	19·00
47	5	100r. green	£534	1·70
55	6	200r. black	95·00	8·50
56	5	500r. orange	£225	40·00
67	17	300r. green and orange	95·00	23·00

12　　**13**

1878. Various frames, but in T **13** the Emperor's beard is white. Roulette.

57	12	10r. red	13·50	3·25
58	13	20r. mauve	19·00	2·75
59	12	50r. blue	30·00	5·00
60	12	80r. red	32·00	11·00
61	12	100r. green	22·00	1·40
62	12	200r. black	£160	19·00
63	12	260r. brown	95·00	25·00
64	12	300r. brown	95·00	6·50
65	12	700r. red	£190	90·00
66	12	1000r. grey	£200	42·00

21

1881. Various frames. Perf.

71	21	10r. black	15·00	32·00
72	21	10r. orange	3·75	4·75
73	21	50r. blue	46·00	4·75
74	21	100r. olive	55·00	4·50
77a	21	100r. lilac	70·00	7·00
75a	21	200r. red	60·00	15·00

No. 77 is inscr "CORREIO".

27 Pedro II

1884

81	27	100r. lilac	£110	3·75

25 **26** **29**

30 Southern **31** **32**
Cross

33 Entrance
to Bay of Rio
de Janeiro

1884

78	25	20r. green	46·00	4·50
80	26	50r. blue	44·00	6·50
83	29	100r. lilac	95·00	2·30
84	30	300r. blue	£325	37·00
85a	31	500r. olive	£180	18·00
86	32	700r. lilac	£100	£150
87	33	1000r. blue	£375	£150

35 Southern
Cross

1890

97a	35	20r. green	3·00	1·80
89	35	50r. green	6·00	1·70
110a	35	100r. purple	50·00	2·00
91	35	200r. violet	13·00	2·30
92	35	200r. blue	£120	15·00
100	35	300r. slate	£120	8·00
93	35	500r. buff	20·00	13·00
94	35	500r. grey	20·00	10·50
95	35	700r. brown	28·00	32·00
96	35	1000r. yellow	24·00	4·75

37 Head of
Liberty

1891

111d	37	100r. red and blue	39·00	1·70

38 Head of
Liberty

1893

114	38	100r. red	70·00	1·50

39 Sugar-loaf **41** Head of **43** Head of
Mountain Liberty Mercury

1894

124	39	10r. blue and red	2·40	85
125	39	20r. blue and orange	1·60	55
126	39	50r. blue	9·50	2·75
232	39	50r. green	17·00	95
127	41	100r. black and red	8·00	60
239	41	100r. red	17·00	55
128	41	200r. black and orange	1·20	45
234	41	200r. blue	20·00	55
129	41	300r. black and green	17·00	70
153	41	500r. black and mauve	35·00	2·50
131a	41	700r. black and mauve	20·00	2·20
132	43	1000r. mauve and green	65·00	2·00
133	43	2000r. purple and grey	75·00	18·00

1897. As T **39** but inscr "REIS REIS" instead of "DEZ REIS".

165	43	10r. blue and red	1·40	55

1898. Newspaper stamps of 1889 surch 1898 between
value twice in figures.

168	N34	100r. on 50r. orange	2·40	50·00
169	N34	200r. on 100r. mauve	4·25	1·40
170	N34	300r. on 200r. black	4·25	1·40
171	N34	500r. on 300r. red	7·50	5·50
172	N34	700r. on 500r. orange	7·75	11·50
173	N34	700r. on 500r. green	9·50	2·30
174	N34	1000r. on 700r. orange	39·00	32·00
175	N34	1000r. on 700r. blue	27·00	17·00
176	N34	2000r. on 1000r. orange	33·00	17·00
177	N34	2000r. on 1000r. brown	24·00	6·75

1898. Newspaper stamp of 1890 surch **200** over 1898.

181	N37	200r. on 100r. mauve	11·00	5·00

1898. Newspaper stamps of 1890 surch **1898** over new
value.

182	N38	20r. on 10r. blue	3·25	6·00
183	N38	50r. on 20r. green	8·50	10·00
184	N38	100r. on 50r. green	18·00	20·00

1899. Postage stamps of 1890 surch **1899** over new
value.

194	35	50r. on 20r. green	1·40	2·00
195	35	100r. on 50r. green	1·40	2·00
196	35	300r. on 200r. violet	5·25	8·00
190	35	500r. on 300r. blue	12·50	5·00
190b	35	500r. on 300r. slate	12·50	5·00
191	35	700r. on 500r. buff	17·00	4·00
192a	35	1,000r. on 700r. brown	12·50	4·00
193	35	2,000r. on 1,000r. yellow	42·00	3·00

50 Discovery of Brazil **52** Emancipation of
Slaves

1900. 400th Anniv of Discovery of Brazil.

226	50	100r. red	7·25	5·75
227	-	200r. green and yellow	7·25	5·75
228	52	500r. blue	7·25	5·75
229	-	700r. green	7·25	5·75

DESIGNS—HORIZ: 200r. Declaration of Independence.
VERT: 700r. Allegory of Republic.

56 Pan-American
Congress

1906

259a	56	100r. red	39·00	23·00
259b	56	200r. blue	95·00	10·50

57 Aristides **61** Liberty
Lobo

1906

260	57	10r. grey	1·10	25
261	-	20r. violet	65	15
262	-	50r. green	1·10	25
264	-	100r. red	1·40	15
265	-	200r. blue	2·40	25
267	-	300r. brown	3·75	75
268	-	400r. olive	35·00	2·30
269	-	500r. violet	7·00	65
272	-	600r. olive	1·10	35
273	-	700r. brown	7·00	3·50
274	61	1000r. red	39·00	1·10
275	-	1000r. green	4·75	45
276	-	1000r. grey	28·00	75
277a	61	2000r. green	7·00	70
278	61	2000r. blue	14·00	45
279	61	5000r. pink	10·00	1·90
280	-	5000r. brown	55·00	8·50
281	-	10000r. brown	9·50	2·30

PORTRAITS: 20r. B. Constant. 50r. A. Cabral. 100r. Wan-
dendkolk. 200r. D. da Fonseca. 300r. F. Peixoto. 400r.,
600r. P. de Moraes. 500r. C. Salles. 700r., 5000r. (No. 280)
R. Alves. 1000r. (Nos. 275/6) B. do Rio Branco. 10000r. N.
Pecanha.

64 King Carlos and Pres.
Affonso Penna and
Emblems of
Portuguese-Brazilian
Amity

1908. Centenary of Opening of Brazilian Ports to Foreign
Commerce.

282	64	100r. red	10·50	1·10

65 Emblems of
Peace,
Commerce and
Industry

1908. National Exhibition, Rio de Janeiro.

283	65	100r. red	23·00	1·70

66 Bonifacio,
San Martin,
Hidalgo,
Washington,
O'Higgins,
Bolivar

1909. Pan-American Congress, Rio de Janeiro.

284	66	200r. blue	10·50	1·00

67 Cape Frio

1915. 300th Anniv of Discovery of Cape Frio.

285	67	100r. turquoise on yellow	4·75	3·75

69 Bay of Guajara

1916. 300th Anniv of City of Belem.

286	69	100r. red	10·50	5·25

70 Revolutionary Flag

1917. Centenary of Pernambuco Revolution.

287	70	100r. blue	17·00	7·50

71 Liberty **72** Liberty **74** Inscr
"BRAZIL"

1918. Various frames.

288A	71	10r. brown	60	30
289A	71	20r. violet	60	30
290A	71	25r. grey	60	30
291B	71	50r. green	1·70	60
292A	72	100r. red	2·00	30
293B	72	200r. blue	7·25	60
294A	72	300r. orange	23·00	3·75
295A	72	500r. purple	23·00	3·75
296B	72	600r. orange	3·00	9·50
297	74	1000r. blue	8·00	30
298	74	2000r. brown	35·00	8·50
299	74	5000r. lilac	10·00	8·50
300a	74	10,000r. red	11·00	1·10

77 Steam
Locomotive **78** "Industry" **79** "Agriculture"

80 "Aviation" **81** Mercury **82** "Shipping"

1920. T **74** inscr "BRASIL".

317	77	10r. purple	35	25
387A	80	10r. brown	20	15
318	77	20r. grey	35	25
388A	80	20r. violet	20	15
389A	78	25r. purple	20	15
354	79	40r. brown	60	35
306	78	50r. green	1·10	45
355	78	50r. brown	90	35
390	80	50r. purple	20	15
391	80	50r. green	20	15
308	79	80r. green	35	2·20
309	80	100r. red	3·75	45
367	80	100r. green	45	20
392A	80	100r. orange	35	15
420	80	100r. yellow	2·00	30
335	80	150r. violet	1·30	25
312	80	200r. blue	6·00	45
330	80	200r. red	30	10
383	80	200r. orange	3·25	85
333	81	300r. red	25	15
394A	81	300r. green	70	15
405	81	300r. grey	20	15
335	81	400r. orange	55	40
406	81	400r. blue	25	20
385	81	500r. blue	1·70	25
407	81	500r. brown	4·00	15
341	82	600r. orange	2·50	45
397	81	600r. brown	4·00	15
422	81	600r. orange	6·00	30
409	81	700r. violet	4·25	15
342	82	1000r. purple	6·75	30
410	81	1000r. blue	12·00	35
362d	74	2000r. blue	7·00	40
411	74	2000r. violet	32·00	1·40
363	74	5000r. brown	20·00	5·25
364	74	10000r. purple	21·00	1·00

93 King Albert and Pres.
Pessoa

1920. Visit of King of the Belgians.

431	93	100r. red	90	85

94 Declaration of
Ypiranga

1922. Centenary of Independence.

432	94	100r. blue	3·75	75
433	-	200r. red	6·50	50
434	-	300r. green	6·50	50

DESIGNS: 200r. Dom Pedro I and J. Bonifacio; 300r. Na-
tional Exn. and Pres. Pessoa.

97 Brazilian Army
entering Bahia

1923. Centenary of Capture of Bahia from the
Portuguese.

435	97	200r. red	10·50	6·50

98 Arms of the
Confederation

1924. Centenary of Confederation of the Equator.

436	98	200r. multicoloured	4·00	2·50

99 Ruy
Barbosa

1927

438a	99	1000r. red	2·75	55

100 "Justice"

1927. Centenary of Law Courses.

439	100	100r. blue	1·00	55
440	-	200r. red	90	40

DESIGN: 200r. Map and Balances.

1928. Air. Official stamps of 1913, Type O67, surch SERVICO AEREO and new value. Centres in black.

441	50r. on 10r. grey	45	30
442	200r. on 1000r. brown	2·40	4·75
443	200r. on 2000r. brown	1·40	11·00
444	200r. on 5000r. brown	1·60	1·40
445	200r. on 500r. yellow	1·60	2·30
446	300r. on 600r. purple	85	85
447	500r. on 50r. grey	1·60	75
448	1000r. on 20r. olive	1·20	25
449	2000r. on 100r. red	2·75	1·90
450	2000r. on 200r. blue	3·50	1·90
451	2000r. on 10,000r. black	3·25	70
452	5000r. on 20,000r. blue	9·25	4·25
453	5000r. on 50,000r. green	9·25	4·25
454	5000r. on 100,000r. red	31·00	32·00
455	10,000r. on 500,000r. brown	35·00	23·00
456	10,000r. on 1,000,000r. sepia	33·00	30·00

104 Liberty holding Coffee Leaves

1928. Bicent of Introduction of the Coffee Plant.

457	104	100r. orange	1·60	65
458	104	200r. red	1·00	50
459	104	300r. black	8·75	40

1928. Official stamps of 1919 surch.

460	O77	700r. on 500r. orange	7·50	7·00
461	O77	1000r. on 100r. red	4·50	50
462	O77	2000r. on 200r. blue	6·25	1·90
463	O77	5000r. on 50r. green	7·25	1·50
464	O77	10,000r. on 10r. brown	27·00	1·90

106 Ruy Barbosa

1929

465	106	5000r. blue	19·00	90

108 Santos Dumonts Airship 'No. 6' **109** Santos Dumont

1929. Air.

469	-	50r. green	30	25
470	108	200r. red	1·40	15
471	-	300r. blue	2·00	15
472	-	500r. purple	2·50	15
473	-	1000r. brown	8·50	30
479	-	2000r. green	12·50	50
480	-	5000r. red	14·50	1·30
481a	109	10,000r. grey	9·00	1·30

DESIGNS: 50r. De Gusmao's monument; 300r. A. Severo's airship "Pax"; 500r. Santos Dumont's biplane 14 bi"; 1000r. R. de Barros's flying boat Jahu; 2000r. De Gusmao; 5000r. A. Severo.

110

1930. Air.

486	110	3000r. violet	2·20	1·80

112

1930. Fourth Pan-American Architectural Congress.

487	-	100r. turquoise	2·40	1·30
488	112	200r. grey	4·25	95
489	-	300r. red	6·50	1·70

DESIGNS: 100r. Sun rays inscr "ARCHITECTOS"; 300r. Architrave and Southern Cross.

113 G. Vargas and J. Pessoa – "Redemption of Brazil"

114 O. Aranha – "What is the matter?"

1931. Charity. Revolution of 3 October 1930.

490	113	10r.+10r. blue	20	10·00
491	113	20r.+20r. brown	20	7·50
492	114	50r.+50r. green, red and yellow	20	35
493	113	100r.+50r. orange	45	40
494	113	200r.+100r. green	45	40
495	-	300r.+150r. mult	45	40
496	113	400r.+200r. red	1·50	1·20
497	113	500r.+250r. blue	1·40	90
498	113	600r.+300r. purple	90	10·50
499	113	700r.+350r. mult	1·70	85
500	114	1$+500r. green, red and yellow	3·00	45
501	-	2$+1$ grey and red	12·50	80
502	-	5$+2$ 500r. black & red	31·00	12·00
503	-	10$+5$ green & yellow	75·00	22·00

DESIGNS: 300r., 700r. as Type 113, but portraits in circles and frames altered. Milreis values as Type 114 with different portraits and frames.

1931. No. 333 surch 1931 200 Reis.

507	81	200r. on 300r. red	45	25

1931. Zeppelin Air Stamps. Surch ZEPPELIN and value.

508	108	2$500 on 200r. red (No. 470)	27·00	24·00
511	106	3$500 on 5000r. blue (No. 468b)	28·00	27·00
509	-	5$000 on 300r. blue (No. 471)	35·00	32·00
512	74	7$000 on 10,000r. red (No. 364)	28·00	27·00

1931. Air. No. 486 surch 2.500 REIS.

510	110	2500r. on 3000r. violet	24·00	23·00

121 Brazil

1932. 400th Anniv of Colonization of Sao Vicente.

513	121	20r. purple	25	40
514	-	100r. black	55	45
515	-	200r. violet	1·10	25
516	-	600r. brown	1·90	1·90
517	-	700r. blue	3·50	2·75

DESIGNS: 100r. Natives; 200r. M. Afonso de Souza; 600r. King John III of Portugal; 700r. Founding of Sao Vicente.

125 Soldier and Flag

130 "Justice"

1932. Sao Paulo Revolutionary Government issue.

518	-	100r. brown	55	2·75
519	125	200r. red	45	95
520	-	300r. green	2·75	5·00
521	-	400r. blue	9·25	10·50
522	-	500r. sepia	11·00	10·50
523	-	600r. red	11·00	10·50
524	125	700r. violet	5·00	10·50
525	-	1000r. orange	2·40	10·50
526	-	2000r. brown	21·00	28·00
527	-	5000r. green	24·00	48·00
528	130	10,000r. purple	29·00	55·00

DESIGNS—As Type 125: 100, 500r. Map of Brazil; 300r., 600r. Symbolical of freedom, etc., 400, 1000r. Soldier in tin helmet. As Type 130: 2000r. "LEX" and sword; 5000r. "Justice" and soldiers with bayonets.

131 Campo Bello Square and Memorial. Vassouras

1933. Centenary of Vassouras.

529	131	200r. red	1·30	1·10

132 Flag and Dornier Wal Flying Boat

1933. Air.

532	132	3500r. blue, green & yell	4·00	2·00

1933. Surch 200 REIS.

536	81	200r. on 300r. red	55	50

134 Flag of the Race

1933. 441st Anniv of Departure of Columbus from Polos.

537	134	200r. red	1·00	90

135 Christian Symbols

1933. First Eucharistic Congress, Sao Salvador.

538	135	200r. red	1·00	90

136 From Santos Dumont Statue, St. Cloud

1933. Obligatory Tax for Airport Fund.

539	136	100r. purple	75	25

137 Faith and Energy

1933

540	137	200r. red	60	20
543	137	200r. violet	1·40	30

138 "Republic" and Flags

1933. Visit of Pres. Justo of Argentina.

545	138	200r. blue	55	55
546	138	400r. green	1·80	1·70
547	138	600r. red	6·50	9·00
548	138	1000r. violet	9·25	6·50

139 Santos Dumont Statue, St. Cloud

1934. First National Aviation Congress, Sao Paulo.

549	139	200r. blue	1·10	1·00

140 Exhibition Building

1934. Seventh International Sample Fair, Rio de Janeiro.

550	140	200r. brown	65	55
551	140	400r. red	2·75	2·75
552	140	700r. blue	2·75	1·90
553	140	1000r. orange	7·75	1·30

141 Brazilian Stamp of 1844

1934. National Philatelic Exhibition, Rio. Imperf.

555	141	200r.+100r. purple	1·80	5·50
556	141	300r.+100r. red	1·80	5·50
557	141	700r.+100r. blue	10·50	46·00
558	141	1000r.+100r. black	10·50	46·00

142 Christ of Mt. Corcovado

1934. Visit of Cardinal Pacelli.

559	142	300r. red	5·50	5·50
560	142	700r. blue	22·00	22·00

143 Jose de Anchieta

1934. 400th Anniv of Founding of Sao Paulo by Anchieta.

561	143	200r. brown	90	75
562	143	300r. violet	65	55
563	143	700c. blue	4·00	4·00
564	143	1000r. green	7·75	1·70

145 "Brazil" and "Uruguay"

1935. Visit of President Terra of Uruguay.

565	-	200r. orange	1·30	75
566	145	300r. yellow	1·70	1·40
567	145	700r. blue	6·50	8·75
568	-	1000r. violet	17·00	8·75

DESIGN—HORIZ: 200, 1000r. Female figures as in Type 145 and bridge.

146 Town of Igarassu

1935. 400th Anniv of Founding of Pernambuco.

569	146	200r. brown and red	2·00	1·30
570	146	300r. olive and violet	2·00	1·10

147 Nurse and Patient

1935. Third Pan-American Red Cross Conference.

571	147	200r.+100r. violet	2·40	2·40
572	147	300r.+100r. brown	2·40	2·00
573	147	700r.+100r. blue	17·00	14·50

149 Gen. da Silva

1935. Cent of Farroupilha "Ragged Revolution".

574	-	200r. black	1·80	1·80
575	-	300r. red	1·80	1·10
576	149	700r. blue	5·00	8·75
577	-	1000r. violet	6·00	5·50

DESIGNS: 200, 300r. Mounted Gaucho; 1000r. Marshal Caxias.

151 Gavea

1935. Children's Day.

578	151	300r. violet and brown	3·50	2·75
579	151	300r. turquoise and black	3·50	2·75
580	151	300r. blue and green	3·50	2·75
581	151	300r. black and red	3·50	2·75

152 Federal District Coat of Arms

1935. Eighth International Fair.
582 **152** 200r. blue 5·00 5·25

153 Coutinho's ship *Gloria*, 1535

1935. 400th Anniv of Colonization of State of Espirito Santo.
583 **153** 300r. red 3·25 1·40
584 - 700r. blue 7·25 4·25
DESIGN—VERT: 700r. Arms of Coutinho.

154a
Viscount Cairu

1936. Death Centenary of Cairu.
585 **154a** 1200r. violet 12·00 8·75

155 Cameta

1936. Tercentenary of Founding of Cameta.
586 **155** 200r. buff 2·20 2·00
587 **155** 500r. green 2·20 1·10

156 Coin Press

1936. Numismatic Congress, Sao Paulo.
588 **156** 300r. brown 2·00 2·00

157 Scales of Justice

1936. First National Juridical Congress, Rio.
589 **157** 300r. red 2·40 90

158 A. Carlos Gomes

159 *Il Guarany*

1936. Birth Centenary of C. Gomes (composer).
590 **158** 300r. red 1·10 1·10
591 **158** 300r. brown 1·10 1·10
592 **159** 700r. blue 4·50 2·75
593 **159** 700r. buff 5·00 4·00

1936. Ninth International Sample Fair, Rio. As T **152** with inscription and date altered.
594 **152** 200r. red 1·50 90

160 Congress Seal

1936. Second National Eucharistic Congress, Belo Horizonte.
595 **160** 300r. multicoloured 1·40 90

161 Botafogo Bay

1937. Birth Centenary of Dr. Francisco Pereira Passos.
596 **161** 700r. blue 1·80 1·20
597 **161** 700r. black 1·80 1·20

162 Esperanto Star and National Flags

1937. Ninth Brazilian Esperanto Congress, Rio de Janeiro.
598 **162** 300r. green 1·90 1·00

163 Bay of Rio de Janeiro

1937. Second S. American Radio Conference.
599 **163** 300r. black and orange 1·10 1·10
600 **163** 700r. brown and blue 3·00 1·10

164 Globe

1937. Golden Jubilee of Esperanto.
601 **164** 300r. green 1·80 1·00

166 Iguazu Falls

1937. Tourist Propaganda.
602 - 200r. blue and brown 1·30 1·30
603 - 300r. green and orange 1·30 1·30
604 **166** 1000r. brown and sepia 4·00 2·75
605 - 2000r. red and green 17·00 18·00
606 **166** 5000r. green and black 33·00 33·00
607 - 10,000r. blue and red 65·00 65·00
DESIGNS—HORIZ: 200, 2000r. Monroe Palace, Rio. VERT: 300, 10,000r. Botanical Gardens, Rio.

168 J. Da Silva Paes

1937. Bicent of Founding of Rio Grande do Sul.
608 **168** 300r. blue 1·30 65

169 Eagle and Shield

1937. 150th Anniv of U.S. Constitution.
609 **169** 400r. blue 1·90 90

170 Coffee

1938. Coffee Propaganda.
610 **170** 1200r. multicoloured 7·75 65

171 "Grito" Memorial

1938. Commemoration of Abortive Proclamation of Republic.
611 **171** 400r. brown 1·30 65

172 Arms of Olinda

1938. Fourthth Centenary of Olinda.
612 **172** 400r. violet 1·10 55

173 Couto de Magalhaes

1938. Birth Centenary of De Magalhaes.
613 **173** 400r. green 1·00 55

174 National Archives

1938. Centenary of Founding of National Archives.
614 **174** 400r. brown 1·00 55

174a
Rowland Hill

1938. Brazilian International Philatelic Exhibition (BRAPEX), Rio de Janeiro. T **174a** repeated ten times in sheet together with exhibition emblem.
MS614a 117×118 mm. 400r. green 30·00 35·00

174b
President Vargas

1938. First Anniv of Constitution issued by President Vargas. T **174b** repeated ten times in sheet together with star emblem.
MS614b 115×138 mm. 400r. blue 33·00 33·00

175 Rio de Janeiro

1939
615 **175** 1200r. purple 2·75 20

176 Santos

1939. Centenary of Santos City.
616 **176** 400r. blue 65 45

177 Chalice-vine and Cup-of-gold Blossoms

1939. First S. American Botanical Congress, Rio.
617 **177** 400r. green 2·10 45

178 Seal of Congress

1939. Third National Eucharistic Congress, Recife.
618 **178** 400r. red 65 65

179 Duke of Caxias

1939. Soldiers' Day.
619 **179** 400r. blue 65 65

180 Washington

1939. New York World's Fair. Inscr "FEIRA MUNDIAL DE NOVA YORK".
620 **180** 400r. orange 90 45
621 - 800r. green 45 35
622 - 1200r. red 1·00 35
623 - 1600r. blue 1·00 45
DESIGNS—HORIZ: 1200r. Grover Cleveland. VERT: 800r. Dom Pedro II; 1m. Water lily; 1600r. Statue of Liberty, Rio de Janeiro; 5m. Bust of Pres. Vargas; 10m. Relief map of Brazil.

184 Benjamin Constant

1939. 50th Anniv of Constitution.
624 **184** 400r. green 1·10 75
625 - 800r. black 75 65
626 - 1200r. brown 1·20 75
DESIGNS—VERT: 800r. Marshal da Fonseca. HORIZ: 1200r. Marshal da Fonseca and Pres. Vargas.

188 Child and Southern Cross

1940. Child Welfare.
627 100r.+100r. violet 1·30 1·30
628 200r.+100r. blue 1·80 1·80
629 **188** 400r.+200r. olive 1·30 1·10
630 - 1200r.+400r. red 5·50 2·40
DESIGNS: 100r. Three Wise Men; 200r. Angel and Child; 1200r. Mother and Child.

189 Roosevelt, Vargas and American Continents

1940. 50th Anniv of Pan-American Union.
631 **189** 400r. blue 1·30 75

190 Map of
Brazil

1940. Ninth National Geographical Congress, Florianopolis.

632	**190**	400r. red	65	65

191 Water Lily **192** Map of
Brazil

1940. New York World's Fair (2nd issue). No gum.

633	**191**	1m. violet	1·80	1·80
634	—	5m. red (Pres. Vargas)	13·00	10·50
635	**192**	10m. blue	15·00	5·00
MS635a	Three sheets each 127×147 mm. Nos. 633/5 each in block of ten		£375	£500

1940. Birth Centenary of Machado de Assis (poet and novelist). As T **173** but portrait of de Assis, dated "1839–1939".

636		400r. black	90	45

193 Two Workers

1940. Bicentenary of Colonization of Porto Alegre.

637	**193**	400r. green	75	45

194 Acclaiming King John
IV of Portugal

1940. Centenaries of Portugal (1140–1640-1940) (1st issue).

638	**194**	1200r. grey	3·25	55

See also Nos. 642/5.

195 Brazilian
Flags and Head
of Liberty

1940. Tenth Anniv of Govt. of President Vargas.

639B	**195**	400r. purple	90	35

196 Date of Fifth **197** Globe showing
Census Spotlight on Brazil

1941. Fifth General Census.

640a	**196**	400r. blue & red (post-age)	45	20
641	**197**	1200r. brown (air)	4·75	90

199 Father
Antonio Vieira

1941. Centenaries of Portugal (2nd issue).

642B	-	200r. pink	35	20
643B	**199**	400r. blue	35	10
644B	-	800r. violet	55	35
645B	-	5400r. green	2·75	75

DESIGNS—VERT: 200r. Alfonso Henriques; 800r. Governor-Gen. Benevides. HORIZ: 5,400r. Carmona and Vargas.

202 Father
Jose Anchieta

1941. 400th Anniv of Order of Jesuits.

646	**202**	1m. violet	2·20	1·30

205 Oil **210** Count
Wells of Porto
 Alegre

1941. Value in reis.

647A	**205**	10r. orange	55	40
648A	**205**	20r. olive	55	40
649A	**205**	50r. brown	55	40
650A	**205**	100r. turquoise	65	40
651B	-	200r. brown	2·00	65
652A	-	300r. red	65	40
653B	-	400r. blue	65	45
654A	-	500r. red	75	40
655B	-	600r. violet	90	55
656A	-	700r. red	65	40
657B	-	1000r. grey	3·25	65
658B	-	1200r. blue	4·00	65
659A	-	2000r. purple	6·00	65
660B	-	5000r. blue	7·75	65
661B	**210**	10,000r. red	17·00	2·75
662A	-	20,000r. brown	20·00	2·00
663D	-	50m. red	29·00	5·50
664D	-	100m. blue	2·00	6·50

DESIGNS: 200r. to 500r. Wheat harvesting machinery; 600r. to 1200r. Smelting works; 2000r. "Commerce"; 5000r. Marshal F. Peixoto; 20,000r. Admiral Maurity; 50m. "Armed Forces"; 100m. Pres. Vargas.

For stamps with values in centavos and cruzeiros see Nos. 751, etc.

213 Amador
Bueno

1941. 300th Anniv of Amador Bueno as King of Sao Paulo.

665	**213**	400r. black	1·10	65

214 Brazilian Air Force
Emblem

1941. Aviation Week.

666	**214**	5400r. green	6·00	4·50

1941. Air. Fourth Anniv of President Vargas's New Constitution. Optd **AEREO "10 Nov." 937-941**.

667a		5400r. green (No. 645)	3·75	1·75

215 Indo-Brazilian Cow

1942. Second Agriculture and Cattle Show, Uberaba.

668	**215**	200r. blue	1·00	65
669	**215**	400r. brown	90	60

216
Bernardino
de Campos

1942. Birth Centenaries of B. de Campos and P. de Morais (lawyers and statesmen).

670	**216**	1000r. red	2·20	1·40
671	-	1200r. blue	7·25	65

PORTRAIT: 1200r. Prudente de Morais.

217 Torch of
Learning

1942. 8th National Education Congress, Goiania.

672	**217**	400r. brown	90	55

218 Map of
Brazil showing
Goiania

1942. Founding of Goiania City.

673	**218**	400r. violet	90	55

219 Congressional
Seal

1942. Fourth National Eucharistic Congress, Sao Paulo.

674	**219**	400r. brown	1·10	40

1942. Air. Fifth Anniv of President Vargas's New Constitution. No. 645 surch **AEREO "10 Nov." 937-942** and value.

675a		5cr.40 on 5400r. green	4·50	2·40

221 Tributaries of R.
Amazon

1943. 400th Anniv of Discovery of River Amazon.

676	**221**	40c. brown	75	70

222 Early
Brazilian Stamp

1943. Centenary of Petropolis.

677	**222**	40c. violet	1·10	60

223 Memorial Tablet

1943. Air. Visit of Pres. Morinigo of Paraguay.

678	**223**	1cr.20 blue	3·25	2·20

224 Map of S.
America showing
Brazil and Bolivia

1943. Air. Visit of President Penaranda of Bolivia.

679	**224**	1cr.20 multicoloured	2·75	1·70

225 "Bulls-eye"

1943. Centenary of First Brazilian Postage Stamps. (a) Postage. Imperf.

680	**225**	30c. black	1·10	1·00
681	**225**	60c. black	1·20	45
682	**225**	90c. black	75	75
MS682a	127×95 mm. Nos. 680/2. No gum. Imperf		29·00	33·00

226

(b) Air. Perf.

683	**226**	1cr. black and yellow	4·50	3·25
684	**226**	2cr. black and green	6·00	3·25
685	**226**	5cr. black and red	7·25	4·50
MS685a	155×155 mm. Nos. 683/5. Imperf. No gum		75·00	75·00

227 Book of the
Law

1943. Air. Inter-American Advocates Conference.

686	**227**	1cr.20 red and brown	1·70	65

228 Ubaldino
do Amaral

1943. Birth Centenary of Ubaldino do Amaral.

687	**228**	40c. grey	1·00	20

229 Indo-Brazilian
Cow

1943. Ninth Cattle Show, Bahia.

688	**229**	40c. brown	1·40	90

230 Justice and
Seal

1943. Centenary of Institute of Brazilian Lawyers.

689a	**230**	2cr. red	1·50	90

231 Santa Casa de
Misericordia Hospital

1943. 400th Anniv of Santa Casa de Misericordia de Santos.

690	**231**	1cr. blue	90	65

232 Barbosa Rodrigues

1943. Birth Centenary of B. Rodrigues (botanist).

691	**232**	40c. green	90	45

233 Pedro
Americo

1943. Birth Centenary of Pedro Americo (artist and author).

692	**233**	40c. brown	1·10	45

1944. Air. No. 629 surch. **AEREO** and value.

693	188	20c. on 400r.+200r.	1·80	1·00
694	188	40c. on 400r.+200r.	2·75	1·00
695	188	60c. on 400r.+200r.	4·00	70
696	188	1cr. on 400r.+200r.	6·25	1·00
697	188	1cr.20 on 400r.+200r.	6·00	65

235 Gen. Carneiro and Defenders of Lapa

1944. 50th Anniv of Siege of Lapa.
| 698 | 235 | 1cr.20c. red | 1·50 | 75 |

236 Baron do Rio Branco

1944. Inauguration of Monument to Baron do Rio Branco.
| 699 | 236 | 1cr. blue | 1·00 | 65 |

237 Duke of Caxias

1944. Centenary of Pacification of Revolutionary Uprising of 1842.
| 700 | 237 | 1cr.20 green and yellow | 1·60 | 65 |

238 Emblems of YMCA

1944. Centenary of YMCA.
| 701 | 238 | 40c. blue, red and yellow | 65 | 35 |

239 Rio Grande Chamber of Commerce

1944. Centenary of Founding of Rio Grande Chamber of Commerce.
| 702 | 239 | 40c. brown | 70 | 35 |

240 Bartolomeo de Gusmao and the Aerostat (Bernardino de Souza Pereira)

1944. Air. Air Week.
| 703 | 240 | 1cr.20 red | 75 | 45 |

241 Ribeiro de Andrada

1945. Death Centenary of M. de Andrada (statesman).
| 704 | 241 | 40c. blue | 90 | 20 |

242 Meeting between Caxias and Canabarro

1945. Centenary of Pacification of Rio Grande do Sul.
| 705 | 242 | 40c. blue | 90 | 20 |

244 L. L. Zamenhof

1945. Tenth Brazilian Esperanto Congress, Rio de Janeiro.
| 706 | - | 40c. green (postage) | 1·20 | 65 |
| 707 | 244 | 1cr.20 brown (air) | 90 | 55 |

DESIGN: 40c. Woman and map.

247 Baron do Rio Branco (statesman)

1945. Birth Centenary of Baron do Rio Branco.
708	-	40c. blue (postage)	1·20	55
709	-	1cr.20 purple (air)	75	55
710	247	5cr. purple	2·10	90

DESIGNS—HORIZ: 40c. Bookplate. VERT: 1cr.20, S. America.

248 "Glory" **250** "Co-operation"

1945. Victory of Allied Nations in Europe. Roul.
711	-	20c. violet	55	20
712	248	40c. red	55	20
713	-	1cr. orange	1·10	55
714	-	2cr. blue	2·75	65
715	250	5cr. green	5·50	90

SYMBOLICAL DESIGNS—VERT: 20c. Tranquility (inscr "SAUDADE"). HORIZ: 1cr. "Victory" (inscr "VITORIA"); 2cr. "Peace" (inscr "PAZ").

251 F. M. da Silva

1945. 150th Birth Anniv of Francisco Manoel da Silva (composer of Brazilian National Anthem).
| 716 | 251 | 40c. red | 1·30 | 60 |

252 Bahia Institute

1945. 50th Anniv of Founding of Bahia Institute of Geography and History.
| 717 | 252 | 40c. blue | 2·00 | 35 |

253 Shoulder Flash **255** "V" Sign and Flashes

1945. Return of Brazilian Expeditionary Force.
718	253	20c. blue, red and green	55	45
719	-	40c. multicoloured	55	45
720	-	1cr. multicoloured	1·50	90
721	-	2cr. multicoloured	2·20	1·30
722	255	5cr. multicoloured	6·50	1·50

DESIGNS (embodying shoulder flashes) As Type **253**: 40c. B.E.F. flash. As Type **255**. HORIZ: 1cr. U.S.A. flag; 2cr. Brazilian flag.

256 Wireless Mast and Map

1945. Third Inter-American Radio Communication Conference.
| 723 | 256 | 1cr.20 black | 1·40 | 20 |

257 Admiral Saldanha da Gama

1946. Birth Centenary of Admiral S. da Gama.
| 724 | 257 | 40c. grey | 90 | 1·40 |

258 Princess Isabel d'Orleans-Braganza

1946. Birth Centenary of Princess Isabel d'Orleans-Braganza.
| 725 | 258 | 40c. black | 90 | 1·90 |

260 Lockheed 14 Super Electra over Bay of Rio de Janeiro **261** P.O., Rio de Janeiro

1946. Fifth Postal Union. Congress of the Americas and Spain.
726	-	40c. orange and black	55	45
727	260	1cr.30 orange and green	75	75
728	260	1cr.70 orange and red	75	75
729	261	2cr. blue and slate	1·10	45
730	260	2cr.20 orange and blue	1·10	1·10
731	261	5cr. blue and brown	5·50	1·90
732	261	10cr. blue and violet	6·00	1·10

DESIGN (25×37 mm): 40c. Post-horn, V and envelope.

262 Proposed Columbus Lighthouse

1946. Construction of Columbus Lighthouse, Dominican Republic.
| 733 | 262 | 5cr. blue | 17·00 | 3·75 |

263 "Liberty"

1946. New Constitution.
| 734 | 263 | 40c. grey | 55 | 35 |

264 Orchid

1946. Fourth National Exn of Orchids, Rio de Janeiro.
| 735 | 264 | 40c. blue, red and yellow | 1·20 | 35 |

265 Gen. A. E. Gomes Carneiro

1946. Birth Centenary of Gen. A. E. Gomes Carneiro.
| 736 | 265 | 40c. green | 55 | 10 |

266 Academy of Arts

1946. 50th Anniv of Brazilian Academy of Arts.
| 737 | 266 | 40c. blue | 65 | 45 |

267 Antonio de Castro Alves

1947. Birth Centenary of Castro Alves (poet).
| 738 | 267 | 40c. turquoise | 55 | 10 |

268 Pres. Gonzalez

1947. Visit of Chilean President.
| 739 | 268 | 40c. brown | 55 | 10 |

269 "Peace and Security" **270** "Dove of Peace"

1947. Inter-American Defence Conference, Rio de Janeiro.
| 740 | 269 | 1cr.20 (postage) | 55 | 45 |
| 741 | 270 | 2cr.20 green (air) | 75 | 55 |

271 Pres. Truman, Map of S. America and Statue of Liberty

1947. Visit of President Truman.
| 742 | 271 | 40c. blue | 65 | 10 |

272 Pres. Enrico Gaspar Dutra

1947. Commemorating Pres. Dutra.
743	272	20c. green (postage)	20	10
744	272	40c. red	35	10
745	272	1cr.20 blue	65	10

MS746a 130×75 mm. Nos. 743/5. No gum. Imperf (air) £110 £130

273 Woman and Child

1947. Children's Week. First Brazilian Infant Welfare Convention and Paediatrics.
| 747 | 273 | 40c. blue | 65 | 10 |

274 Icarus

1947. Obligatory Tax. "Week of the Wing" Aviation Fund.
748 **274** 40c.+10c. orange 75 20

275 Santos Dumont Monument, St. Cloud, France

1947. Air. Homage to Santos Dumont (aviation pioneer).
749 **275** 1cr.20c. brown & green 1·10 55

276 Arms of Belo Horizonte

1947. 50th Anniv of Founding of City of Belo Horizonte.
750 **276** 1cr.20c. red 90 10

1947. As postage stamps of 1941, but values in centavos or cruzeiros.
751 **205** 2c. olive 35 10
752 **205** 5c. brown 35 10
753 **205** 10c. turquoise 45 10
754 - 20c. brown (No. 651) 55 10
755 - 30c. red (No. 652) 1·40 20
756 - 40c. blue (No. 653) 55 10
757 - 50c. red (No. 654) 1·40 20
758 - 60c. violet (No. 655) 2·20 20
759 - 70c. red (No. 656) 1·00 20
760 - 1cr. grey (No. 657) 4·50 20
761 - 1cr.20 blue (No. 658) 5·50 20
762 - 2cr. purple (No. 659) 7·75 20
763 - 5cr. blue (No. 660) 19·00 20
764 **210** 10cr. red 14·50 20
765 - 20cr. brown (No. 662) 26·00 20
766a - 50cr. red (No. 663) 31·00 5·50

277 Rio de Janeiro and Rotary Emblem

1948. Air. 39th Rotary Congress Rio de Janeiro.
769 **277** 1cr.20 red 1·10 90
770 **277** 3cr.80 violet 2·20 95

278 Globe **279** Quitandinha Hotel

1948. International Industrial and Commercial Exhibition, Quitandinha.
771 **278** 40c. grn & mve (postage) 65 30
772 **279** 1cr.20 brown (air) 55 55
773 **279** 3cr.80 violet 1·40 65

280 Arms of Paranagua

1948. Tercentenary of Founding of Paranagua.
774 **280** 5cr. brown 4·50 1·10

281 Girl Reading

1948. National Children's Campaign.
775 **281** 40c. green 55 20

282 Three Muses (after Henrique Bernardelli)

1948. Air. Centenary of National School of Music.
776 **282** 1cr.20 blue 1·40 35

283 President Berres

1948. Air. Visit of Uruguayan President.
777 **283** 1cr.70 blue 75 35

284 Merino Ram

1948. Air. International Livestock Show, Bage.
778 **284** 1cr.20 orange 1·70 65

285 Congress Seal

1948. Air. Fifth National Eucharistic Congress, Porto Alegre.
779 **285** 1cr.20 purple 75 35

286 "Tiradentes" (trans. "Tooth-puller")

1948. Birth Bicentenary of A. J. J. da Silva Xavier (patriot).
780 **286** 40c. orange 55 20

287 Crab and Globe

1948. Anti-cancer Campaign.
781 **287** 40c. purple 55 55

288 Adult Student

1949. Campaign for Adult Education.
782 **288** 60c. purple 55 10

289 Battle of Guararapes

1949. 300th Anniv of Second Battle of Guararapes.
783 **289** 60c. blue (postage) 2·20 1·10
784 - 1cr.20 pink (air) 3·25 1·70
DESIGN: 1cr.20, View of Guararapes.

290 St. Francis of Paula Church

1949. Bicentenary of Ouro Fino.
785 **290** 60c. brown 65 35
MS785a 70×89 mm. No. 785. Imperf 75·00 65·00

291 Father Nobrega **292** De Souza meeting Indians

1949. Fourth Centenary of Founding of Bahia. (a) Postage. Imperf.
786 **291** 60c. violet 65 35

(b) Air. Perf.
787 **292** 1cr.20 blue 75 40

293 Franklin D. Roosevelt

1949. Air. Homage to Franklin D. Roosevelt. Imperf.
788 **293** 3cr.80 brown 2·20 1·50
MS788a 85×110 mm. No. 788. 39·00 46·00

294 Douglas DC-3 and Air Force Badge

1949. Homage to Brazilian Air Force. Imperf.
789 **294** 60c. violet 55 10

295 Joaquim Nabuco

1949. Air. Birth Centenary of J. Nabuco (lawyer and author).
790 **295** 3cr.80 purple 1·70 45

296 "Revelation"

1949. First Sacerdotal Vocational Congress, Bahia.
791 **296** 60c. purple 65 20

297 Globe

1949. 75th Anniv of UPU.
792 **297** 1cr.50 blue 90 10

298 Ruy Barbosa

1949. Birth Centenary of Ruy Barbosa (statesman).
793 **298** 1cr.20 red 1·40 45

299 Cardinal Arcoverde

1950. Birth Centenary of Cardinal Joaquim Arcoverde.
794 **299** 60c. pink 75 15

300 "Agriculture and Industry"

1950. 75th Anniv of Arrival of Italian Immigrants.
795 **300** 60c. red 65 10

301 Virgin of the Globe

1950. Centenary of Establishment of Daughters of Charity of St. Vincent de Paul.
796 **301** 60c. blue and black 55 10

302 Globe and Footballers **303** Stadium

1950. Fourth World Football Championship, Rio de Janeiro.
797 **302** 60c. grey & bl (postage) 1·90 55
798 **303** 1cr.20 orange and blue (air) 2·10 90
799 - 5cr.80 yellow, green and blue 6·50 1·10
DESIGN—VERT: 5cr.80 Linesman and flag.

304 Three Heads, Map and Graph **305** Line of People and Map

1950. Sixth Brazilian Census, 1950.
800 **304** 60c. red (postage) 55 10
801 **305** 1cr.20 brown (air) 85 20

306 Oswaldo Cruz

1950. Fifth International Microbiological Congress. Rio de Janeiro.
802 **306** 60c. brown 90 10

307 Blumenau and Itajai River

1950. Centenary of Founding of Blumenau.
| 803 | **307** | 60c. pink | 90 | 10 |

308 Government Offices

1950. Centenary of Amazon Province.
| 804 | **308** | 60c. red | 65 | 10 |

309 Arms

1950. Centenary of Juiz de Fora City.
| 805 | **309** | 60c. red | 75 | 35 |

310 P.O. Building, Recife

1951. Inauguration of Head Post Office, Pernambuco Province.
| 806 | **310** | 60c. red | 65 | 10 |
| 807 | **310** | 1cr.20 red | 70 | 10 |

311 Arms of Joinville

1951. Centenary of Founding of Joinville.
| 808 | **311** | 60c. brown | 70 | 15 |

312 S. Romero

1951. Birth Centenary of Sylvio Romero (poet).
| 809 | **312** | 60c. brown | 90 | 10 |

313 De La Salle

1951. Birth Tricentenary of Jean-Baptiste de la Salle (educational reformer).
| 810 | **313** | 60c. blue | 65 | 10 |

314 Heart and Flowers

1951. Mothers' Day.
| 811 | **314** | 60c. purple | 1·00 | 55 |

315 J. Caetano and Stage

1951. First Brazilian Theatrical Congress.
| 812 | **315** | 60c. blue | 65 | 10 |

316 O. A. Derby

1951. Birth Centenary of Derby (geologist).
| 813 | **316** | 2cr. slate | 1·00 | 55 |

317 Crucifix and Congregation

1951. Fourth Inter-American Catholic Education Congress, Rio de Janeiro.
| 814 | **317** | 60c. brown and buff | 65 | 10 |

318 E. P. Martins and Map

1951. 29th Anniv of First Rio–New York Flight.
| 815 | **318** | 3cr.80 brown & lemon | 3·75 | 75 |

319 Penha Convent

1951. 400th Anniv of Founding of Vitoria.
| 816 | **319** | 60c. brown and buff | 75 | 15 |

320 Santos Dumont and Boys with Model Aircraft

1951. "Week of the Wing" and 50th Anniv of Santos Dumont's Flight over Paris.
| 817 | **320** | 60c. brn & orge (postage) | 1·00 | 35 |
| 818 | - | 3cr.80 violet (air) | 3·25 | 45 |
DESIGN: 3cr.80, "Ballon No. 6" airship over Eiffel Tower.

321 Wheat Harvesters

1951. Wheat Festival, Bage.
| 819 | **321** | 60c. green and grey | 90 | 75 |

322 Bible and Map

1951. Bible Day.
| 820 | **322** | 1cr.20 brown | 1·30 | 65 |

323 Isabella the Catholic

1952. 500th Birth Anniv of Isabella the Catholic.
| 821 | **323** | 3cr.80 blue | 1·60 | 55 |

324 Henrique Oswald

1952. Birth Centenary of Henrique Oswald (composer).
| 822 | **324** | 60c. brown | 65 | 10 |

325 Map and Symbol of Labour

1952. Fifth Conf of American Members of I.L.O.
| 823 | **325** | 1cr.50 red | 65 | 10 |

326 Dr. L. Cardoso

1952. Birth Centenary of Cardoso (scientist) and 4th Brazilian Homoeopathic Congress, Porto Alegre.
| 824 | **326** | 60c. blue | 75 | 35 |

327 Gen. da Fonseca

1952. Centenary of Telegraphs in Brazil.
825	**327**	2cr.40 red	1·00	20
826	-	5cr. blue	5·00	35
827	-	10cr. turquoise	5·00	35
PORTRAITS—VERT: 5cr. Baron de Capanema. 10cr. E. de Queiros.

328 L. de Albuquerque

1952. Bicentenary of Mato Grosso City.
| 828 | **328** | 1cr.20 violet | 65 | 10 |

329 Olympic Flame and Athletes

1952. 50th Anniv of Fluminense Football Club.
| 829 | **329** | 1cr.20 blue | 1·50 | 75 |

330 Councillor J. A. Saraiva

1952. Centenary of Terezina City.
| 830 | **330** | 60c. mauve | 65 | 10 |

331 Emperor Dom Pedro II

1952. Stamp Day and Second Philatelic Exhibition, Sao Paulo.
| 831 | **331** | 60c. black and blue | 65 | 10 |

332 Globe, Staff and Rio de Janeiro Bay

1952. Second American Congress of Industrial Medicine.
| 832 | **332** | 3cr.80 green and brown | 1·90 | 65 |

333 Dove, Globe and Flags

1952. United Nations Day.
| 833 | **333** | 3cr.80 blue | 2·10 | 65 |

334 Compasses and Modern Buildings, Sao Paulo

1952. City Planning Day.
| 834 | **334** | 60c. yellow, green & blue | 65 | 10 |

335 D. A. Feijo (Statesman)

1952. Homage to D. A. Feijo.
| 835 | **335** | 60c. brown | 75 | 10 |

336 Father Damien

1952. Obligatory Tax. Leprosy Research Fund.
| 836 | **336** | 10c. brown | 90 | 35 |
| 837 | **336** | 10c. green | 40 | 15 |

337 R. Bernardelli

1952. Birth Centenary of Bernardelli (sculptor).
| 838 | **337** | 60c. blue | 65 | 10 |

338 Arms of Sao Paulo and Settler **339** "Expansion"

1953. 400th Anniv of Sao Paulo (1st issue).
839	**338**	1cr.20 black and brown	2·20	55
840	-	2cr. green and yellow	4·50	55
841	-	2cr.80 brown and orange	3·25	35
842	**339**	3cr.80 brown and green	3·25	35
843	**339**	5cr.80 blue and green	2·10	35

DESIGNS—VERT: (Inscr as Type **339**): 2cr. Coffee blossom and berries; 2cr.80, Monk planting tree.
 See also Nos. 875/9.

340

1953. Sixth Brazilian Accountancy Congress, Port Alegre.
844	**340**	1cr.20 brown	65	10

341 J. Ramalho

1953. Fourth Centenary of Santo Andre.
845	**341**	60c. blue	65	10

342 A. Reis and Plan of Belo Horizonte

1953. Birth Centenary of A. Reis (engineer).
846	**342**	1cr.20 brown	65	10

343 *Almirante Saldanha* (cadet ship)

1953. Fourth Voyage of Circumnavigation by Training Ship *Almirante Saldanha*.
847	**343**	1cr.50 blue	1·00	35

344 Viscount de Itaborahy

1953. Centenary of Bank of Brazil.
848	**344**	1cr.20 violet	65	10

345 Lamp and Rio-Petropolis Highway

1953. Tenth Int Nursing Congress, Petropolis.
849	**345**	1cr.20 grey	65	10

346 Bay of Rio de Janeiro

1953. Fourth World Conference of Young Baptists.
850	**346**	3cr.80c. turquoise	1·00	35

347 Ministry of Health and Education

1953. Stamp Day and First National Philatelic Exhibition of Education, Rio de Janeiro.
851	**347**	1cr.20 turquoise	65	10

348 Arms and Map

1953. Centenary of Jau City.
852	**348**	1cr.20 violet	65	10

349 Maria Quiteria de Jesus

1953. Death Centenary of Maria Quiteria de Jesus.
853	**349**	60c. blue	40	10

350 Pres. Odria

1953. Visit of President of Peru.
854	**350**	1cr.40 purple	65	10

351 Caxias leading Troops

1953. 150th Birth Anniv of Duke of Caxias.
855	**351**	60c. turquoise	40	15
856	-	1cr.20 purple	90	15
857	-	1cr.70 blue	90	15
858	-	3cr.80 brown	2·10	20
859	-	5cr.80 violet	1·30	20

DESIGNS: 1cr.20, Tomb; 1cr.70, 5cr.80, Portrait of Caxias; 3cr.80, Coat of arms.

352 Quill-pen and Map

1953. Fifth National Congress of Journalists, Curitiba.
860	**352**	60c. blue	65	20

353 H. Hora

1953. Birth Centenary of H. Hora (painter).
861	**353**	60c. purple and orange	65	10

354 President Somoza

1953. Visit of President Somoza of Nicaragua.
862	**354**	1cr.40 purple	65	20

355 A. de Saint-Hilaire

1953. Death Centenary of A. de Saint-Hilaire (explorer and botanist).
863	**355**	1cr.20 lake	75	30

356 J. do Patrocinio and "Spirit of Emancipation" (after R. Amoedo)

1953. Death Centenary of J. do Patrocinio (slavery abolitionist).
864	**356**	60c. slate	65	20

357 Clock Tower, Crato

1953. Centenary of Crato City.
865	**357**	60c. green	65	20

358 C. de Abreu

1953. Birth Centenary of Abreu (historian).
866	**358**	60c. blue	40	10
867	**358**	5cr. violet	2·40	35

359 "Justice"

1953. 50th Anniv of Treaty of Petropolis.
868	**359**	60c. blue	65	10
869	**359**	1cr.20 purple	65	10

360 Harvesting

1953. Third National Wheat Festival, Erechim.
870	**360**	60c. turquoise	65	10

361 Teacher and Pupils

1953. First National Congress of Elementary Schoolteachers, Salvador.
871	**361**	60c. red	65	20

362 Porters with Trays of Coffee Beans

1953. Centenary of State of Parana.
872a	-	2cr. brown and black	1·90	55
873	**362**	5cr. orange and black	3·00	55

DESIGN: 2cr. Portrait of Z. de Gois e Vasconellos.

363 A. de Gusmao

1954. Death Bicentenary of Gusmao (statesman).
874	**363**	1cr.20 purple	75	30

364 Growth of Sao Paulo **365** Sao Paulo and Arms

1954. 400th Anniv of Sao Paulo (2nd issue).
875	**364**	1cr.20 brown	2·10	90
876	-	2cr. mauve	3·25	65
877	-	2cr.80 violet	3·75	55
878	**365**	3cr.80 green	4·50	55
879	**365**	5cr.80 red	4·50	55

DESIGNS—VERT: 2cr. Priest, pioneer and Indian; 2cr.80, J. de Anchieta.

366 J. F. Vieira, A. V. de Negreiros, A. F. Camarao and H. Dias

1954. 300th Anniv of Recovery from the Dutch of Pernambuco.
880	**366**	1cr.20 blue	90	35

367 Sao Paulo and Allegorical Figure

1954. Tenth International Congress of Scientific Organization, Sao Paulo.
881	**367**	1cr.50 purple	75	35

368 Grapes and Winejar

1954. Grape Festival, Rio Grande do Sul.
882	**368**	40c. lake	65	20

369 Immigrants' Monument

1954. Immigrants' Monument, Caxias do Sul.
883 **369** 60c. violet 65 20

370 "Baronesa", 1852 (first locomotive used in Brazil)

1954. Centenary of Brazilian Railways.
884 **370** 40c. red 1·30 40

371 Pres. Chamoun

1954. Visit of President of Lebanon.
885 **371** 1cr.50 lake 75 30

372 Sao Jose College, Rio de Janeiro **373** Vel Marcelino Champagnat

1954. 50th Anniv of Marists in Brazil.
886 **372** 60c. violet 50 20
887 **373** 1cr.20 blue 50 20

374 Apolonia Pinto

1954. Birth Centenary of Apolonia Pinto (actress).
888 **374** 1cr.20 green 65 20

375 Admiral Tamandare

1954. Portraits.
889 **375** 2c. blue 35 20
890 **375** 5c. red 35 10
891 **375** 10c. green 35 10
892 – 20c. red 35 15
893 – 30c. slate 55 10
894 – 40c. red 1·00 20
895 – 50c. lilac 1·30 20
896 – 60c. turquoise 50 15
897 – 90c. salmon 1·00 20
904a – 1cr. brown 1·90 55
899 – 1cr.50 blue 35 10
904b – 2cr. green 2·75 55
904c – 5cr. purple 8·50 35
902 – 10cr. green 2·50 30
903 – 20cr. red 2·50 30
904 – 50cr. blue 15·00 30

PORTRAITS—20, 30, 40c. O. Cruz; 50c. to 90c. J. Murtinho; 1cr., 1cr.50, 2cr. Duke of Caxias; 5, 10cr., R. Barbosa; 20, 50cr. J. Bonifacio.

376 Boy Scout

1954. International Scout Encampment, Sao Paulo.
905 **376** 1cr.20 blue 1·60 35

377 B. Fernandes

1954. Tercentenary of Sorocaba City.
906 **377** 60c. red 75 20

378 Cardinal Piazza

1954. Visit of Cardinal Piazza (Papal Legate).
907 **378** 4cr.20 red 1·60 35

379 Virgin and Map

1954. Marian Year. Inscr "ANO MARIANO".
908 **379** 60c. lake 90 30
909 – 1cr.20 blue 1·10 45
DESIGN: 1cr.20, Virgin and globe.
 No. 909 also commemorates the Centenary of the Proclamation of the Dogma of the Immaculate Conception.

380 Benjamin Constant and Braille Book

1954. Centenary of Education for the Blind in Brazil.
910 **380** 60c. green 65 15

381 River Battle of Riachuelo **382** Admiral Barroso

1954. 150th Birth Anniv of Admiral Barroso.
911 **381** 40c. brown 75 20
912 **382** 60c. violet 50 20

383 S. Hahnemann (physician)

1954. First World Congress of Homoeopathy.
913 **383** 2cr.70 green 75 35

384 Nisia Floresta (suffragist)

1954. Removal of Ashes of Nisia Floresta (suffragist) from France to Brazil.
914 **384** 60c. mauve 75 20

385 Ears of Wheat

1954. Fourth Wheat Festival, Carazinho.
915 **385** 60c. olive 75 35

386 Globe and Basketball Player

1954. Second World Basketball Championship.
916 **386** 1cr.40 red 1·00 45

387 Girl, Torch and Spring Flowers

1954. Sixth Spring Games.
917 **387** 60c. brown 75 35

388 Father Bento

1954. Obligatory Tax. Leprosy Research Fund.
918 **388** 10c. blue 40 10
919 **388** 10c. mauve 40 10
919a **388** 10c. salmon 40 10
919b **388** 10c. green 40 10
919c **388** 10c. lilac 40 10
919d **388** 10c. brown 40 10
919e **388** 10c. slate 40 10
919f **388** 2cr. lake 40 10
919g **388** 2cr. lilac 40 10
919h **388** 2cr. orange 40 10
 See also Nos. 1239/40.

389 Sao Francisco Power Station

1955. Inauguration of Sao Francisco Hydro-electric Station.
920 **389** 60c. orange 65 15

390 Itutinga Power Plant

1955. Inauguration of Itutinga Hydro-electric Station.
921 **390** 40c. blue 65 15

391 Rotary Symbol and Rio Bay

1955. 50th Anniv of Rotary International.
922 **391** 2cr.70 green and black 3·25 55

392 Aviation Symbols

1955. Third Aeronautical Congress, Sao Paulo.
923 **392** 60c. grey and black 65 15

393 Fausto Cardoso Palace

1955. Centenary of Aracaiu.
924 **393** 40c. brown 65 20

394 Arms of Botucatu

1955. Centenary of Botucatu.
925 **394** 60c. brown 50 10
926 **394** 1cr.20 green 65 15

395 Young Athletes

1955. Fifth Children's Games, Rio de Janeiro.
927 **395** 60c. brown 75 15

396 Marshal da Fonseca

1955. Birth Centenary of Marshal da Fonseca.
928 **396** 60c. violet 65 15

397 Congress Altar, Sail and Sugar-loaf Mountain

1955. 36th International Eucharistic Congress.
929 **397** 1cr.40 green 50 10
930 – 2cr.70 lake (St. Pascoal) 65 15

398 Cardinal Masella

1955. Visit of Cardinal Masella (Papal Legate) to Eucharistic Congress.
931 **398** 4cr.20 blue 75 20

399 Gymnasts

1955. Seventh Spring Games.
932 **399** 60c. mauve 65 15

400 Monteiro Lobato

1955. Honouring M. Lobato (author).
933 **400** 40c. green 65 15

401 A. Lutz

1955. Birth Centenary of A. Lutz (public health pioneer).
934 **401** 60c. green 65 15

402 Lt.-Col. T. C. Vilagran Cabrita

1955. Centenary of First Battalion of Engineers.
935 **402** 60c. blue 65 15

403 Salto Grande Dam

1956. Salto Grande Dam.
936 **403** 60c. red 65 15

404

1956. 18th International Geographical Congress, Rio de Janeiro.
937 **404** 1cr.20 blue 1·60 20

405 Arms of Mococa

1956. Centenary of Mococa, Sao Paulo.
938 **405** 60c. red 65 15

406 Girls Running

1956. Sixth Children's Games.
939 **406** 2cr.50 blue 1·00 15

407 Douglas DC-3 and Map

1956. 25th Anniv of National Air Mail.
940 **407** 3cr.30 blue 1·10 45

408 Rescue Work

1956. Centenary of Firemen's Corps, Rio de Janeiro.
941 **408** 2cr.50 red 1·10 55

409 Franca Cathedral

1956. Centenary of City of Franca.
942 **409** 2cr.50 blue 75 20

410 Open book with Inscription and Map

1956. 50th Anniv of Arrival of Marist Brothers in N. Brazil.
943 **410** 2cr.50 blue (postage) 75 20
944 - 3cr.30 purple (air) 75 35
DESIGN—VERT: 3cr.30, Father J. B. Marcelino Champagnat.

411 Hurdler

1956. Eighth Spring Games.
945 **411** 2cr.50 red 1·50 20

412 Forest and Map of Brazil

1956. Afforestation Campaign.
946 **412** 2cr.50 green 75 15

413 Baron da Bocaina and Express Letter

1956. Birth Centenary of Baron da Bocaina.
947 **413** 2cr.50 brown 75 15

414 Commemorative Stamp from Panama

1956. Pan-American Congress. Panama.
948 **414** 3cr.30 black and green 1·40 45

415 Santos Dumont's Biplane *14 bis*

1956. Air. 50th Anniv of Dumont's First Heavier-than-air Flight.
MS948a 125×156 mm. 415 3cr. red (in block of four) 18·00 15·00

1956. Air. Alberto Santos Dumont (aviation pioneer) Commemoration.
949 **415** 3cr. green 2·50 35
950 **415** 3cr.30 blue 25 10
951 **415** 4cr. purple 1·50 10
952 **415** 6cr.50 brown 25 10
953 **415** 11cr.50 orange 4·00 35

416 Volta Redonda Steel Mill, and Molten Steel

1957. Nat Steel Company's Expansion Campaign.
955 **416** 2cr.50 brown 75 10

417 J. E. Gomes da Silva (civil engineer)

1957. Birth Centenary of Gomes da Silva.
956 **417** 2cr.50 green 75 10

418 Allan Kardec, Code and Globe

1957. Centenary of Spiritualism Code.
957 **418** 2cr.50 brown 65 15

419 Young Gymnast

1957. Seventh Children's Games.
958 **419** 2cr.50 lake 1·50 20

420 Gen. Craveiro Lopes

1957. Visit of President of Portugal.
959 **420** 6cr.50 blue 1·50 20

421 Stamp of 1932

1957. 25th Anniv of Sao Paulo Revolutionary Government.
960 **421** 2cr.50 red 75 10

422 Lord Baden-Powell

1957. Air. Birth Centenary of Lord Baden-Powell.
961 **422** 3cr.30 lake 1·50 20

423 Convent of Santo Antonio

1957. 300th Anniv of Emancipation of Santo Antonio Province.
962 **423** 2cr.50 purple 65 15

424 Volleyball

1957. Ninth Spring Games.
963 **424** 2cr.50 brown 1·50 20

425 Basketball

1957. Second Women's World Basketball Championships.
964 **425** 3cr.30 green and brown 1·50 20

426 U.N. Emblem, Map of Suez Canal and Soldier

1957. Air. United Nations Day.
965 **426** 5cr.30 blue 75 15

427 Count of Pinhal (founder), Arms and Locomotive

1957. Centenary of City of San Carlos.
966 **427** 2cr.50 red 90 15

428 Auguste Comte (philosopher)

1957. Death Centenary of Auguste Comte.
967 **428** 2cr.50 brown 75 15

429 Sarapui Radio Station

1957. Inauguration of Sarapui Radio Station.
968 **429** 2cr.50 myrtle 75 15

430 Admiral Tamandare (founder) and *Almirante Tamandare* (cruiser)

1957. 150th Anniv of Brazilian Navy.
969	**430**	2cr.50 blue	90	15
970	-	3cr.30 green	1·80	45

DESIGN: 3cr.30, Aircraft-carrier *Minas Gerais*.

431 Coffee Beans and Emblem

1957. Centenary of City of Ribeirao Preto.
971a	**431**	2cr.50 red	1·40	15

432 King John VI of Portugal and Sail Merchantman

1958. 150th Anniv of Opening of Ports to Foreign Trade.
972	**432**	2cr.50 purple	1·00	20

433 Bugler

1958. 150th Anniv of Corps of Brazilian Marines.
973	**433**	2cr.50 red	1·00	35

434 Locomotive *Baronesa*, 1852, and Dom Pedro II Station, Rio de Janeiro

1958. Centenary of Central Brazil Railway.
974	**434**	2cr.50 brown	1·00	35

435 High Court Building

1958. 150th Anniv of Military High Courts.
975	**435**	2cr.50 green	75	15

436 Brazilian Pavilion

1958. Brussels International Exhibition.
976	**436**	2cr.50 blue	90	35

437 Marshal C. M. da Silva Rondon

1958. Rondon Commemoration and "Day of the Indian".
977	**437**	2cr.50 purple	75	20

438 Jumping

1958. Eighth Children's Games, Rio de Janeiro.
978	**438**	2cr.50 red	75	20

439 Hydro-electric Station

1958. Inauguration of Salto Grande Hydro-electric Station.
979	**439**	2cr.50 purple	75	20

440 National Printing Works

1958. 150th Anniv of National Printing Works.
980	**440**	2cr.50 brown	75	20

441 Marshal Osorio

1958. 150th Birth Anniv of Marshal Osorio.
981	**441**	2cr.50 violet	75	20

442 Pres. Morales of Honduras

1958. Visit of President of Honduras.
982	**442**	6cr.50 green	5·00	1·90

443 Botanical Gardens, Rio de Janeiro

1958. 150th Anniv of Botanical Gardens, Rio de Janeiro.
983	**443**	2cr.50 green	75	20

444 Hoe, Rice and Cotton

1958. 50th Anniv of Japanese Immigration.
984	**444**	2cr.50 red	75	20

445 Prophet Joel

446 Brazil on Globe

1958. Bicentenary of Basilica of the Good Jesus, Matosinhos.
985	**445**	2cr.50 blue	75	20

1958. Int Investments Conference, Belo Horizonte.
986	**446**	2cr.50 brown	75	20

447 Tiradentes Palace, Rio de Janeiro

1958. 47th Inter-Parliamentary Union Conf.
987	**447**	2cr.50 brown	75	20

448 J. B. Brandao (statesman)

1958. Centenary of Julio Buend Brandão.
988	**448**	2cr.50 brown	75	20

449 Dawn Palace, Brasilia

1958. Construction of Presidential Palace.
989	**449**	2cr.50 blue	75	20

450 Freighters

1958. Govt Aid for Brazilian Merchant Navy.
990	**450**	2cr.50 blue	75	20

451 J. C. da Silva

1958. Birth Centenary of J. C. Da Silva (author).
991	**451**	2cr.50 brown	75	20

452 Pres. Gronchi

1958. Visit of President of Italy.
992	**452**	7cr. blue	1·50	45

453 Archers

1958. Tenth Spring Games, Rio de Janeiro.
993	**453**	2cr.50 orange	1·10	35

454 Old People within Hour-glass

1958. Old People's Day.
994	**454**	2cr.50 lake	75	20

455 Machado de Assis (writer)

1958. 50th Death Anniv of Machado de Assis.
995	**455**	2cr.50 brown	75	20

456 Pres. Vargas with oily Hand

1958. Fifth Anniv of State Petroleum Law.
996	**456**	2cr.50 blue	75	20

457 Globe showing Brazil and the Americas

1958. Seventh Inter-American Municipalities Congress, Rio de Janeiro.
997	**457**	2cr.50 blue	75	20

458 Gen. L. Sodre

1958. Birth Centenary of L. Sodre.
998	**458**	3cr.30 green	75	20

459 UN Emblem

1958. Tenth Anniv of Human Rights Declaration.
999	**459**	2cr.50 blue	75	20

460 Footballer

1959. World Football Cup Victory, 1958.
1000	**460**	3cr.30 brown & green	1·10	45

461 Map and Railway Line

1959. Centenary of Opening of Patos-Campina Grande Railway.
1001	**461**	2cr.50 brown	75	20

462 Pres. Sukarno

1959. Visit of President of Indonesia.
1002	**462**	2cr.50 blue	75	20

463 Basketball Player

1959. Air. World Basketball Championships 1959.
1003	**463**	3cr.30 brown & blue	1·00	20

464 King John VI of Portugal

1959
1004	**464**	2cr.50 red	75	20

465 Polo Players

1959. Children's Games.
1005	**465**	2cr.50 brown	75	20

466 Dockside Scene

1959. Rehabilitation of National Ports Law.
1006	**466**	2cr.50 green	75	20

467 Church Organ, Diamantina

1959. Bicentenary of Carmelite Order in Brazil.
1007	**467**	3cr.30 lake	75	20

468 Dom J. S. de Souza (First Archbishop)

1959. Birth Centenary of Archbishop of Diamantina.
1008	**468**	2cr.50 brown	75	20

469 Sugar-loaf Mountain and Road

1959. 11th International Roads Congress.
1009	**469**	3cr.30 blue and green	75	20

470 Londrina and Parana

1959. 25th Anniv of Londrina.
1010	**470**	2cr.50 green	75	20

471 Putting the Shot

1959. Spring Games.
1011	**471**	2cr.50 mauve	75	20

472 Daedalus

1959. Air. Aviation Week.
1012	**472**	3cr.30 blue	75	20

473 Globe and "Snipe" Class Yachts

1959. World Sailing Championships, Porto Alegre.
1013	**473**	6cr.50 green	75	20

474 Lusignan Cross and Arms of Salvador, Bahia

1959. Fourth International Brazilian–Portuguese Study Conference, Bahia University.
1014	**474**	6cr.50 blue	75	20

475 Gunpowder Factory

1959. 50th Anniv of President Vargas Gunpowder Factory.
1015	**475**	3cr.30 brown	75	20

476

1959. Thanksgiving Day.
1016	**476**	2cr.50 blue	75	20

477 Sud Aviation SE 210 Caravelle

1959. Air. Inauguration of "Caravelle" Airliners by Brazilian National Airlines.
1017	**477**	6cr.50 blue	75	20

478 Burning Bush

1959. Centenary of Presbyterian Work in Brazil.
1018	**478**	3cr.30 green	75	20

479 P. da Silva and *Schistosoma mansoni*

1959. 50th Anniv of Discovery and Identification of *Schistosoma mansoni* (fluke).
1019	**479**	2cr.50 purple	1·50	45

480 L. de Matos and Church

1960. Birth Centenary of Luiz de Matos (Christian evangelist).
1020	**480**	3cr.30 brown	75	20

481 Pres. Lopez Mateos of Mexico

1960. Air. Visit of Mexican President.
1021	**481**	6cr.50 brown	75	20

482 Pres. Eisenhower

1960. Air. Visit of United States President.
1022	**482**	6cr.50 brown	75	20

483 Dr. L. Zamenhof

1960. Birth Centenary of L. Zamenhof (inventor of Esperanto).
1023	**483**	6cr.50 green	75	20

484 Adel Pinto (engineer)

1960. Birth Centenary of Adel Pinto.
1024	**484**	11cr.50 red	1·00	35

485 "Care of Refuges"

1960. Air. World Refugee Year.
1025	**485**	6cr.50 blue	75	20

486 Plan of Brasilia

1960. Inauguration of Brasilia as Capital.
1026	-	2cr.50 green (postage)	75	35
1027	-	3cr.30 violet (air)	50	20
1028	-	4cr. blue	2·10	45
1029	-	6cr.50 mauve	50	20
1030	**486**	11cr.50 brown	50	20

1960. Birthday of Pres. Kubitschek.
MS1031	110×52 mm. 27cr. Orange (postage)		2·20	1·90

DESIGNS—Outlines representing: HORIZ: 2cr.50 President's Palace of the Plateau; 3cr.30 Parliament Buildings; 4cr. Cathredral; 11cr.50, 27cr. T **486**. VERT: 6cr.50 Tower.

487 Congress Emblem

1960. Air. Seventh Nat Eucharistic Congress, Curitiba.
1032	**487**	3cr.30 mauve	75	20

488 Congress Emblem, Sugar-loaf Mountain and Cross

1960. Air. Tenth Baptist World Alliance Congress, Rio de Janeiro.
1033	**488**	6cr.50 blue	75	20

489 Boy Scout

1960. Air. 50th Anniv of Scouting in Brazil.
1034	**489**	3cr.30 orange	75	20

490 "Agriculture"

1960. Cent of Brazilian Ministry of Agriculture.
1035	**490**	2cr.50 brown	75	20

491 Caravel

1960. Air. Fifth Death Centenary of Prince Henry the Navigator.
1036	**491**	6cr.50 black	75	20

492 P. de
Frontin

1960. Birth Centenary of Paulo de Frontin (engineer).
1037 **492** 2cr.50 orange 75 20

493
Locomotive
Piston Gear

1960. Tenth Pan-American Railways Congress.
1038 **493** 2cr.50 blue 1·50 55

494 Athlete

1960. 12th Spring Games.
1039 **494** 2cr.50 turquoise 75 20

495

1960. World Volleyball Championships.
1040 **495** 11cr. blue 25 10

496 Maria Bueno in play

1960. Air. Maria Bueno's Wimbledon Tennis Victories,
1959–60.
1041 **496** 6cr. brown 75 20

497 Exhibition Emblem

1960. International Industrial and Commercial Exhibition,
Rio de Janeiro.
1042 **497** 2cr.50 brown & yellow 75 20

498 War Memorial, Rio de
Janeiro

1960. Air. Return of Ashes of World War II Heroes from
Italy.
1043 **498** 3cr.30 lake 75 20

499 Pylon and
Map

1961. Air. Inauguration of Tres Marias Hydro-electric
Station.
1044 **499** 3cr.30 mauve 75 20

500 Emperor
Haile Selassie

1961. Visit of Emperor of Ethiopia.
1045 **500** 2cr.50 brown 75 20

501 Sacred Book and Map
of Brazil

1961. 50th Anniv of Sacre-Coeur de Marie College.
1046 **501** 2cr.50 blue 75 20

502 Map of Guanabara
State

1961. Promulgation of Guanabara Constitution.
1047 **502** 7cr.50 brown 75 20

503 Arms of
Academy

1961. 150th Anniv of Agulhas Negras Military Academy.
1048 **503** 2cr.50 green 65 15
1049 - 3cr.30 red 65 15
DESIGN: 3cr.30, Military cap and sabre.

504 "Spanning
the Atlantic
Ocean"

1961. Visit of Foreign Minister to Senegal.
1050 **504** 27cr. blue 90 35

505 View of Ouro Preto

1961. 250th Anniv of Ouro Preto.
1051 **505** 1cr. orange 75 20

506 Arsenal, Rio de Janeiro

1961. 150th Anniv of Rio de Janeiro Arsenal.
1052 **506** 5cr. brown 75 20

507 Coffee
Plant

1961. Int Coffee Convention, Rio de Janeiro.
1053 **507** 20cr. brown 3·00 30

508 Tagore

1960. Birth Centenary of Rabindranath Tagore (poet).
1054 **508** 10cr. mauve 75 10

509 280r. Stamp of 1861
and Map of France

1961. "Goat's Eyes" Stamp Centenary.
1055 **509** 10cr. red 2·00 10
1056 - 20cr. orange 6·25 10
DESIGN: 20cr. 430r. stamp and map of the Netherlands.

510 Cloudburst

1962. World Meteorological Day.
1057 **510** 10cr. brown 2·30 55

511 Pinnacle,
Rope and
Haversack

1962. 50th Anniv of First Ascent of "Finger of God"
Mountain.
1058 **511** 8cr. green 80 25

512 Dr. G. Vianna and
parasites

1962. 50th Anniv of Vianna's Cure for Leishman's Disease.
1059 **512** 8cr. blue 70 25

513 Campaign
Emblem

1962. Air. Malaria Eradication.
1060 **513** 21cr. blue 70 25

514 Henrique Dias (patriot)

1962. 300th Death Anniv of Henrique Dias.
1061 **514** 10cr. purple 80 30

515 Metric
Measure

1962. Cent of Brazil's Adoption of Metric System.
1062 **515** 100cr. red 1·40 10

516 "Snipe"
Sailing-boats

1962. 13th "Snipe" Class Sailing Championships, Rio de
Janeiro.
1063 **516** 8cr. turquoise 70 25

517 J. Mesquita and
Newspaper *O Estado de Sao
Paulo*

1962. Birth Centenary of J. Mesquita (journalist and
founder of *O Estado de Sao Paulo*).
1064 **517** 8cr. bistre 95 25

518 Empress
Leopoldina

1962. 140th Anniv of Independence.
1065 **518** 8cr. mauve 70 25

519 Brasilia

1962. 51st Interparliamentary Conference, Brasilia.
1066 **519** 10cr. orange 80 40

520 Foundry
Ladle

1962. Inauguration of "Usiminas" (national iron and steel
foundry).
1067 **520** 8cr. orange 70 25

521 UPAE Emblem

1962. 50th Anniv of Postal Union of the Americas and
Spain.
1068 **521** 8cr. mauve 70 25

522 Emblems
of Industry

1962. Tenth Anniv of National Bank.
1069 **522** 10cr. turquoise 70 25

523 Q. Bocaiuva

1962. 50th Death Anniv of Q. Bocaiuva (journalist and patriot).
1070 **523** 8cr. brown 80 40

524 Footballer

1962. Brazil's Victory in World Football Championships, 1962.
1071 **524** 10cr. turquoise 1·30 15

525 Carrier Pigeon

1962. Tercentenary of Brazilian Posts.
1072 **525** 8cr. multicoloured 70 25
MS1072a 145×58 mm. **525** 100cr.
 multicoloured 4·75 4·25

526 Dr. S. Neiva (first Brazilian P.M.G.)

1963
1073 **526** 8cr. violet 70 15
1073a - 30cr. turquoise (Euclides
 da Cunha) 3·75 15
1073b - 50cr. brown (Prof. A.
 Moreira da Costa
 Lima) 2·75 15
1073c - 100cr. blue (G. Dias) 1·10 15
1073d - 200cr. red (Tiradentes) 5·75 15
1073e - 500cr. brown (Emperor
 Pedro I) 40·00 40
1073f - 1000cr. blue (Emperor
 Pedro II) £100 1·00

527 Rockets and Dish Aerial

1963. Int Aeronautics and Space Exn, Sao Paulo.
1074 **527** 21cr. blue 70 15

528 Cross

1963. Ecumenical Council, Vatican City.
1075 **528** 8cr. purple 70 25

529 "abc" Symbol

1963. National Education Week.
1076 **529** 8cr. blue 70 25

530 Basketball

1963. Fourth World Basketball Championships.
1077 **530** 8cr. mauve 70 10

531 Torch Emblem

1963. Fourth Pan-American Games, Sao Paulo.
1078 **531** 10cr. red 90 15

532 "OEA" and Map

1963. 15th Anniv of Organization of American States.
1079 **532** 10cr. orange 90 40

533 J. B. de Andrada e Silva

1963. Birth Bicentenary of Jose B. de Andrada e Silva ("Father of Independence").
1080 **533** 8cr. bistre 70 15

534 Campaign Emblem

1963. Freedom from Hunger.
1081 **534** 10cr. blue 90 40

535 Centenary Emblem

1963. Red Cross Centenary.
1082 **535** 8cr. red and yellow 70 15

536 J. Caetano

1963. Death Centenary of Joao Caetano (actor).
1083 **536** 8cr. black 70 15

537 "Atomic" Development

1963. First Anniv of National Nuclear Energy Commission.
1084 **537** 10cr. mauve 70 10

538 Throwing the Hammer

1963. International Students' Games, Porto Alegre.
1085 **538** 10cr. black and grey 1·40 40

539 Pres. Tito

1963. Visit of President Tito of Yugoslavia.
1086 **539** 80cr. drab 1·70 55

540 Cross and Map

1963. Eigth Int Leprology Congress, Rio de Janeiro.
1087 **540** 8cr. turquoise 70 15

541 Petroleum Installations

1963. Tenth Anniv of National Petroleum Industry.
1088 **541** 8cr. green 70 15

542 "Jogos da Primavera"

1963. Spring Games.
1089 **542** 8cr. yellow 70 15

543 A. Borges de Medeiros

1963. Birth Centenary of A. Borges de Medeiros (politician).
1090 **543** 8cr. brown 70 15

544 Bridge of Sao Joao del Rey

1963. 250th Anniv of Sao Joao del Rey.
1091 **544** 8cr. blue 70 15

545 Dr. A. Alvim

1963. Birth Cent of Dr. Alvaro Alvim (scientist).
1092 **545** 8cr. slate 70 15

546 Viscount de Maua

1963. 150th Birth Anniv of Viscount de Maua (builder of Santos–Jundiai Railway).
1093 **546** 8cr. mauve 70 15

547 Cactus

1964. Tenth Anniv of North-East Bank.
1094 **547** 8cr. green 70 15

548 C. Netto

1964. Birth Centenary of Coelho Netto (author).
1095 **548** 8cr. violet 70 15

549 L. Muller

1964. Birth Cent of Lauro Muller (patriot).
1096 **549** 8cr. red 70 15

550 Child with Spoon

1964. Schoolchildren's Nourishment Week.
1097 **550** 8cr. yellow and brown 70 15

551 "Chalice" (carved rock), Vila Velha, Parana

1964. Tourism.
1098 **551** 80cr. red 90 15

552 A. Kardec (author)

1964. Cent of Spiritual Code, "O Evangelho".
1099 **552** 30cr. green 1·60 40

553 Pres. Lubke

1964. Visit of Pres. Lubke of West Germany.
1100 **553** 100cr. brown 1·70 45

554 Pope John XXIII

1964. Pope John Commemoration.
1101 **554** 20cr. lake 70 15

555 Pres. Senghor

1964. Visit of Pres. Senghor of Senegal.
1102 **555** 20cr. sepia 70 15

556 "Visit Rio de Janeiro"

1964. 400th Anniv (1965) of Rio de Janeiro.
1103 **556** 15cr. blue and orange 90 45
1104 - 30cr. red and blue 80 15
1105 - 30cr. black and blue 80 40
1106 - 35cr. black and orange 55 30
1107 - 100cr. brn & grn on yell 70 30
1108 - 200cr. red and green 5·75 25
MS1109 Two sheets 129×76 mm. containing stamps similar to Nos. 1103, 1107/8 each in brown (sold at 320cr.) and 132×78 mm containing stamps similar to Nos. 1104/6 each in orange (sold at 100cr.) 22·00 24·00
DESIGNS: As Type **556**—HORIZ: 30cr. (No. 1105), Tramway viaduct; 200cr. Copacabana Beach. VERT: 35cr. Estacio de Sa's statue; 100cr. Church of Our Lady of the Rock. SMALLER (24½×37 mm): 30cr. (No. 1104), Statue of St. Sebastian.

558 Pres. De Gaulle

1964. Visit of Pres. De Gaulle.
1110 **558** 100cr. brown 1·00 15

559 Pres. Kennedy

1964. Pres. Kennedy Commemoration.
1111 **559** 100cr. black 70 30

560 Nahum (statue)

1964. 150th Death Anniv of A. F. Lisboa (sculptor).
1112 **560** 10cr. black 70 15

561 Cross and Sword

1965. Fisrst Anniv of Democratic Revolution.
1113 **561** 120cr. grey 80 30

562 V. Brazil (scientist)

1965. Birth Cent of Vital Brazil.
1114 **562** 120cr. orange 80 30

563 Shah of Iran

1965. Visit of Shah of Iran.
1115 **563** 120cr. red 70 15

564 Marshal Rondon and Map

1965. Birth Cent of Marshal C. M. da S. Rondon.
1116 **564** 30cr. purple 70 15

565 Lions Emblem

1965. Brazilian Lions Clubs National Convention, Rio de Janeiro.
1117 **565** 35cr. black and lilac 70 15

566 I.T.U. Emblem and Symbols

1965. I.T.U. Centenary.
1118 **566** 120cr. green and yellow 90 15

567 E. Pessoa

1965. Birth Centenary of Epitacio Pessoa.
1119 **567** 35cr. slate 70 15

568 Barrosos Statue

1965. Centenary of Naval Battle of Riachuelo.
1120 **568** 30cr. blue 70 15

569 Author and Heroine

1965. Centenary of Publication of Jose de Alencar's *Iracema*.
1121 **569** 30cr. purple 70 15

570 Sir Winston Churchill

1965. Winston Churchill Commemoration.
1122 **570** 200cr. slate 1·80 25

571 Scout Badge and Emblem of Rio's 400th Anniv

1965. First Pan-American Scout Jamboree, Rio de Janeiro.
1123 **571** 30r. multicoloured 80 30

572 ICY Emblem

1965. International Co-operation Year.
1124 **572** 120cr. black and blue 70 15

573 L. Correia

1965. Birth Centenary of Leoncia Correia (poet).
1125 **573** 35cr. green 70 15

574 Exhibition Emblem

1965. Sao Paulo Biennale (Art Exn).
1126 **574** 30cr. red 70 15

575 President Saragat

1965. Visit of President of Italy.
1127 **575** 100cr. green on pink 70 15

576 Grand Duke and Duchess of Luxembourg

1965. Visit of Grand Duke and Duchess of Luxembourg.
1128 **576** 100cr. brown 70 15

577 Curtiss Fledgling on Map

1965. Aviation Week and Third Philatelic Exn.
1129 **577** 35cr. blue 70 15

578 OEA Emblem

1965. Inter-American Conference, Rio de Janeiro.
1130 **578** 100cr. black and blue 70 15

579 King Baudouin and Queen Fabiola

1965. Visit of King and Queen of the Belgians.
1131 **579** 100cr. slate 80 15

580 Coffee Beans

1965. Brazilian Coffee.
1132 **580** 30cr. brown on cream 90 15

581 F. A. Varnhagen

1965. Air. 150th Birth Anniv of Francisco Varnhagen (historian).
1133 **581** 45cr. brown 70 15

582 Emblem and Map

1966. Air. Fifth Anniv of "Alliance for Progress".
1134 **582** 120cr. blue & turquoise 1·40 15

583 Sister and
Globe

1966. Air. Centenary of Dorothean Sisters Educational
Work in Brazil.
1135 **583** 35cr. violet 70 15

584 Loading Ore at
Quayside

1966. Inauguration of Rio Doce Iron-ore Terminal
Tubarao, Espirito Santo.
1136 **584** 110cr. black and bistre 80 30

585 "Steel"

1966. Silver Jubilee of National Steel Company.
1137 **585** 30cr. black on orange 70 15

586 Prof. Rocha
Lima

1966. 50th Anniv of Professor Lima's Discovery of the
Characteristics of *Rickettsia prowazeki* (cause of
typhus fever).
1138 **586** 30cr. turquoise 1·10 40

587 Battle Scene

1966. Centenary of Battle of Tuiuti.
1139 **587** 30cr. green 90 15

588 "The Sacred
Face"

1966. Air. "Concilio Vaticano II".
1140 **588** 45cr. brown 70 15

589 Mariz e
Barros

1966. Air. Death Centenary of Commander Mariz e
Barros.
1141 **589** 35cr. brown 70 15

590 Decade
Symbol

1966. International Hydrological Decade.
1142 **590** 100cr. blue and brown 90 15

591 Pres. Shazar

1966. Visit of President Shazar of Israel.
1143 **591** 100cr. blue 80 40

592 Youth

1966. Air. Birth Centenary of Eliseu Visconti (painter).
1144 **592** 120cr. brown 1·10 40

593 Imperial Academy of
Fine Arts

1966. 150th Anniv of French Art Mission's Arrival in Brazil.
1145 **593** 100cr. brown 2·20 25

594 Military Service Emblem

1966. New Military Service Law.
1146 **594** 30cr. blue and yellow 70 15
MS1147 111×53 mm. No. 1146. No
gum (sold at 100cr.) 2·30 2·40

595 R. Dario

1966. 50th Death Anniv of Ruben Dario (Nicaraguan
poet).
1148 **595** 100cr. purple 70 15

596 Santarem Candlestick

1966. Centenary of Goeldi Museum.
1149 **596** 30cr. brown on salmon 70 15

597 Arms of
Santa Cruz do
Sul

1966. First National Tobacco Exn, Santa Cruz.
1150 **597** 30cr. green 70 15

598 UNESCO Emblem

1966. 20th Anniv of UNESCO.
1151 **598** 120cr. black 2·20 45
MS1152 110×52 mm. No. 1151. No
gum (sold at 150cr.) 5·75 5·50

599 Capt. A. C.
Pinto and Map

1966. Bicentenary of Arrival of Captain A. C. Pinto.
1153 **599** 30cr. red 70 15

600 Lusigan
Cross and
Southern Cross

1966. Lubrapex 1966 Stamp Exn, Rio de Janeiro.
1154 **600** 100cr. green 80 30

601 Madonna
and Child

1966. Christmas.
1155 **601** 30cr. green 70 15
1156 - 35cr. blue and orange 70 15
1157 - 150cr. pink and blue 6·75 6·75
DESIGN—DIAMOND(34×34 mm). 35cr. Madonna and
child (different). VERT (46×103 mm). 150cr. As 35cr. inscr
"Pax Hominibus" but not "Brazil Correio".

602 Arms of Laguna

1967. Centenary of Laguna Postal and Telegraphic
Agency.
1158 **602** 60cr. sepia 70 15

603 Grota Funda Viaduct
and 1866 Viaduct

1967. Centenary of Santos–Jundiai Railway.
1159 **603** 50cr. orange 1·50 25

604 Polish Cross and "Black
Madonna"

1967. Polish Millennium.
1160 **604** 50cr. red, blue & yellow 1·30 30

605 Research
Rocket

1967. World Meteorological Day.
1161 **605** 50cr. black and blue 1·70 25

606 Anita
Garibaldi

1967
1162 - 1c. blue 55 10
1163 - 2c. red 55 10
1164 - 3c. green 55 10
1165 **606** 5c. black 1·00 15
1166 - 6c. brown 1·00 15
1167 - 10c. green 3·00 40
PORTRAITS: 1c. Mother Angelica. 2c. Marilia de Dirceu. 3c.
Dr. R. Lobato. 6c. Ana Neri. 10c. Darci Vargas.

607 "VARIG 40
Years"

1967. 40th Anniv of Varig Airlines.
1171 **607** 6c. black and blue 80 25

608 Lions Emblem and
Globes

1967. 50th Anniv of Lions International.
1172 **608** 6c. green 80 25
MS1173 130×80 mm. No. 1172. Imperf
(sold at 15c.) 7·50 7·50

609 "Madonna
and Child"

1967. Mothers' Day.
1174 **609** 5c. violet 80 25
MS1175 130×76 mm. **609** 15c. violet.
Imperf 7·50 7·50

610 Prince Akihito and
Princess Michiko

1967. Visit of Crown Prince and Princess of Japan.
1176 **610** 10c. black and red 80 25

611 Radar
Aerial and
Pigeon

1967. Inauguration of Communications Ministry, Brasilia.
1177 **611** 10c. black and mauve 70 15

612 Brother Vicente do Salvador

1967. 400th Birth Anniv of Brother Vicente do Salvador (founder of Franciscan Brotherhood, Rio de Janeiro).
1178	**612**	5c. brown	70	15

613 Emblem and Members

1967. National 4-S ("4-H") Clubs Day.
1179	**613**	5c. green and black	70	15

614 Mobius Symbol

1967. Sixth Brazilian Mathematical Congress. Rio de Janeiro.
1180	**614**	5c. black and blue	70	15

615 Dorado (fish) and "Waves"

1967. Bicentenary of Piracicaba.
1181	**615**	5c. black and blue	80	25

616 Papal Arms and "Golden Rose"

1967. Pope Paul VI's "Golden Rose" Offering to Our Lady of Fatima.
1182	**616**	20c. mauve and yellow	2·75	80

617 General A. de Sampaio

1967. Gen. Sampaio Commemoration.
1183	**617**	5c. blue	70	15

618 King Olav of Norway

1967. Visit of King Olav.
1184	**618**	10c. brown	70	15

619 Sun and Rio de Janeiro

1967. Meeting of International Monetary Fund, Rio de Janeiro.
1185	**619**	10c. black and red	70	15

620 N. Pecanha (statesman)

1967. Birth Centenary of Nilo Pecanha.
1186	**620**	5c. purple	70	15

621 Our Lady of the Apparition and Basilica

1967. 250th Anniv of Discovery of Statue of Our Lady of the Apparition.
1187	**621**	5c. blue and ochre	80	25

MS1188 80×130 mm. **621** 5c. and 10c. each blue and ochre. Imperf 10·50 10·50

No. **MS**1188 was issued for Christmas.

622 "Song Bird"

1967. International Song Festival.
1189	**622**	20c. multicoloured	1·40	80

623 Balloon, Rocket and Airplane

1967. Aviation Week.
1190	**623**	10c. blue	1·40	55

MS1191 131×76 mm. **623** 15c. blue. Imperf 17·00 17·00

624 Pres. Venceslau Braz

1967
1192	-	10c. blue	70	15
1193	-	20c. brown	2·20	15
1195	**624**	50c. black	11·00	40
1198	-	1cr. purple	17·00	40
1199	-	2cr. green	3·50	25

Portraits of Brazilian Presidents: 10c. Arthur Bernardes. 20c. Campos Salles. 1cr. Washington Luiz. 2cr. Castello Branco.

625 Rio Carnival

1967. International Tourist Year.
1200	**625**	10c. multicoloured	80	25

MS1201 76×130 mm. **625** 15c. multi-coloured. Imperf 10·50 11·00

626 Sailor, Anchor and *Almirante Tamandare* (cruiser)

1967. Navy Week.
1202	**626**	10c. blue	80	25

627 Christmas Decorations

1967. Christmas.
1203	**627**	5c. multicoloured	70	15

628 O. Bilac (poet), Aircraft, Tank and Aircraft Carrier *Minas Gerais*

1967. Reservists Day.
1204	**628**	5c. blue and yellow	80	25

629 J. Rodrigues de Carvalho

1967. Birth Centenary of Jose Rodrigues de Carvalho (jurist and writer).
1205	**629**	10c. green	70	15

630 O. Rangel

1968. Birth Centenary of Orlando Rangel (chemist).
1206	**630**	5c. black and blue	1·00	45

631 Madonna and Diver

1968. 250th Anniv of Paranagua Underwater Exploration.
1207	**631**	10c. green and slate	1·00	45

632 Map of Free Zone

1968. Manaus Free Zone.
1208	**632**	10c. red, green and yellow	1·00	45

633 Human Rights Emblem

1968. 20th Anniv of Declaration of Human Rights.
1209	**633**	10c. red and blue	1·00	45

634 Paul Harris

1968. Birth Centenary of Paul Harris (founder of Rotary International).
1210	**634**	20c. brown and green	3·00	1·40

GUM. All the following issues to No.1425 are without gum, except where otherwise stated.

635 College Arms

1968. Centenary of St. Luiz College. With gum.
1211	**635**	10c. gold, blue and red	1·60	70

636 Cabral and his Fleet, 1500

1968. 500th Birth Anniv of Pedro Cabral (discoverer of Brazil).
1212	**636**	10c. multicoloured	2·30	85
1213	-	20c. multicoloured	2·50	1·20

DESIGN: 20c. *The First Mass* (C. Portinari).

637 *Maternity* (after H. Bernardeli)

1968. Mother's Day.
1214	**637**	5c. multicoloured	1·00	45

638 Harpy Eagle

1968. 150th Anniv of National Museum. With gum.
1215	**638**	20c. black and blue	9·75	1·20

639 Women of Brazil and Japan

1968. Inauguration of "VARIG" Brazil–Japan Air Service.
1216 **639** 10c. multicoloured 1·70 80

640 Horse-racing

1968. Centenary of Brazilian Jockey Club.
1217 **640** 10c. multicoloured 1·00 45

641 Musician Wren

1968. Birds.
1218 - 10c. multicoloured 2·30 55
1219 **641** 20c. brown, green & bl 2·50 55
1220 - 50c. multicoloured 5·75 1·10
DESIGNS—VERT: 10c. Red-crested cardinal; 50c. Royal fly-catcher.

642 Ancient Post-box

1968. Stamp Day. With gum.
1221 **642** 5c. black, green & yellow 70 15

643 Marshal E.
Luiz Mallet

1968. E. Luiz Mallet Commemoration. With gum.
1222 **643** 10c. lilac 70 15

644 Map of
South America

1968. Visit of Chilean President. With gum.
1223 **644** 10c. orange 70 15

645 Lyceum
Badge

1968. Centenary of Portuguese Literacy Lyceum (High School). With gum.
1224 **645** 5c. green and pink 70 15

646 Map and Telex Tape

1968. "Telex Service for 25th City (Curitiba)". With gum.
1225 **646** 20c. green and yellow 1·40 45

647 "Cock" shaped as
Treble Clef

1968. Third Int Song Festival, Rio de Janeiro.
1227 **647** 6c. multicoloured 80 30

648 Soldiers on
Medallion

1968. Eighth American Armed Forces Conference.
1226 **648** 5c. black and blue 1·40 55

649 "Petrobras" Refinery

1968. 15th Anniv of National Petroleum Industry.
1228 **649** 6c. multicoloured 1·30 80

650 Boy
walking
towards Rising
Sun

1968. UNICEF.
1229 **650** 5c. black and blue 90 45
1230 - 10c. black, red & blue 1·10 45
1231 - 20c. multicoloured 1·40 45
DESIGNS—HORIZ: 10c. Hand protecting child. VERT: 20c. Young girl in plaits.

651 Children with Books

1968. Book Week.
1232 **651** 5c. multicoloured 80 25

652 WHO Emblem and Flags

1968. 20th Anniv of WHO.
1233 **652** 20c. multicoloured 1·70 70

653 J. B. Debret (painter)

1968. Birth Bicentenary of Jean Baptiste Debret (1st issue).
1234 **653** 10c. black and yellow 1·00 45
See Nos. 1273/4.

654 Queen Elizabeth II

1968. State Visit of Queen Elizabeth II.
1235 **654** 70c. multicoloured 4·50 2·00

655 Brazilian Flag

1968. Brazilian Flag Day.
1236 **655** 10c. multicoloured 1·10 55

656 F. Braga
and part of
"Hymn of
National Flag"

1968. Birth Cent of Francisco Braga (composer).
1237 **656** 5c. purple 1·10 45

657 Clasped Hands

1968. Blood Donors' Day.
1238 **657** 5c. red, black and blue 70 25

1968. Obligatory Tax. Leprosy Research Fund. Revalued currency. With gum.
1239 **388** 5c. green 2·10 85
1240 **388** 5c. red 80 25

658 Steam Locomotive No. 1 *Maria Fumaca*, 1868

1968. Centenary of Sao Paulo Railway.
1241 **658** 5c. multicoloured 2·75 95

659 Angelus
Bell

1968. Christmas. Multicoloured.
1242 5c. Type **659** 80 25
1243 6c. Father Christmas giving present 80 25

660 F.A.V.
Caldas Jr

1968. Birth Centenary of Francisco Caldas Junior (founder of *Correio do Povo* newspaper).
1244 **660** 10c. black, pink & red 70 20

661 Reservists Emblem and
Memorial

1968. Reservists' Day. With gum.
1245 **661** 5c. green and brown 1·00 40

662 Dish Aerial

1969. Inauguration of Satellite Communications System.
1246 **662** 30c. black and blue 2·10 1·10

663 Viscount
do Rio Branco

1969. 150th Birth Anniv of Viscount do Rio Branco.
1247 **663** 5c. sepia and drab 80 30

664 St. Gabriel

1969. St. Gabriel's Day (Patron Saint of Telecommunications).
1248 **664** 5c. multicoloured 1·10 40

665 Shoemaker's Last and
Globe

1969. Fourth Int Shoe Fair, Novo, Hamburgo.
1249 **665** 5c. multicoloured 70 30

666 Kardec and Monument

1969. Death Centenary of "Allan Kardec" (Professor H. Rivail) (French educationalist and spiritualist).
1250 **666** 5c. brown and green 80 30

667 Men of Three Races and
Arms of Cuiaba

1969. 250th Anniv of Cuiaba (capital of Mato Grosso state).
1251 **667** 5c. multicoloured 80 30

668 Mint and Banknote Pattern

1969. Opening of New State Mint Printing Works.
1252 **668** 5c. bistre and orange 1·30 70

669 Society Emblem and Stamps

1969. 50th Anniv of Sao Paulo Philatelic Society.
1253	**669**	5c. multicoloured	80	30

670 "Our Lady of Santana" (statue)

1969. Mothers' Day.
1254	**670**	5c. multicoloured	1·40	80

671 ILO Emblem

1969. 50th Anniv of ILO. With gum.
1255	**671**	5c. gold and red	70	25

672 Diving Platform and Swimming Pool

1969. 40th Anniv of Cearense Water Sports Club, Fortaleza.
1256	**672**	20c. black, green & brn	1·70	85

673 *Mother and Child at Window* (after Di Cavalcanti)

1969. Tenth Art Exhibition Biennale, Sao Paulo. Multicoloured.
1257	**673**	10c. Type **673**	1·80	45
1258		20c. Modern sculpture (F. Leirner)	1·80	1·00
1259		50c. *Sunset in Brasilia* (D. di Prete)	4·50	2·50
1260		1cr. *Angelfish* (A. Martins)	4·00	2·00

No. 1258 is square, size 33×33 mm and Nos. 1259/60 vertical, size 33×53 mm.

674 Freshwater Angelfish

1969. ACAPI Fish Preservation and Development Campaign.
1261		20c. Type **674**	1·70	80
MS1262 134×100 mm. Four designs each 38×22 mm. 10c. Tetra; 15c. Piranha; 20c. *Megalamphodus mega-lopterus*; 30c. Black tetra			17·00	17·00

675 I. O. Teles de Manezes (founder)

1969. Centenary of Spiritualist Press. With gum.
1263	**675**	50c. green and orange	3·00	2·00

676 Postman delivering Letter

1969. Stamp Day. With gum.
1264	**676**	30c. blue	2·75	1·70

677 General Fragoso

1969. Birth Centenary of General Tasso Fragoso. With gum.
1265	**677**	20c. green	2·30	95

678 Map of Army Bases

1969. Army Week. Multicoloured.
1266		10c. Type **678**	1·40	60
1267		20c. Monument and railway bridge (39×22 mm)	2·30	1·00

679 Jupia Dam

1969. Inauguration of Jupia Dam.
1268	**679**	20c. multicoloured	1·70	1·00

680 Mahatma Gandhi and Spinning-wheel

1969. Birth Centenary of Mahatma Gandhi.
1269	**680**	20c. black and yellow	1·20	60

681 Alberto Santos Dumont, Balloon No. 6, Eiffel Tower and Moon Landing

1969. First Man on the Moon and Santos Dumont's Flight (1906). Commemoration.
1270	**681**	50c. multicoloured	4·25	1·90

682 Smelting Plant

1969. Expansion of USIMINAS Steel Consortium.
1271	**682**	20c. multicoloured	1·30	85

683 Steel Furnace

1969. 25th Anniv of ACESITA Steel Works.
1272	**683**	10c. multicoloured	1·30	85

684 *The Water Cart* (after Debrot)

1969. Birth Centenary of J. B. Debret (painter) (2nd issue). Multicoloured. No. 1274 dated "1970".
1273		20c. Type **684**	3·00	95
1274		30c. *Street Scene*	3·00	1·90

685 Exhibition Emblem

1969. "Abuexpo 69" Stamp Exn.
1275	**685**	10c. multicoloured	1·10	35

686 Embraer Bandeirante Airplane

1969. Brazilian Aeronautical Industry Expansion Year.
1276	**686**	50c. multicoloured	7·00	2·50

687 Pele scoring Goal

1969. Footballer Pele's 1,000th Goal.
1277	**687**	10c. multicoloured	1·30	95
MS1278 81×120 mm. **687** 75c. multi-coloured. Imperf			12·00	7·00

688 *Madonna and Child* (painted panel)

1969. Christmas.
1279	**688**	10c. multicoloured	1·20	35
MS1280 137×102 mm. **688** 75c. multi-coloured. Imperf			32·00	30·00

689 *Pernambuco* (destroyer) and *Bahia* (submarine)

1969. Navy Day. With gum.
1281	**689**	5c. blue	1·10	45

690 Dr. H. Blumenau

1969. 150th Birth Anniv of Dr. Hermann Blumenau (German immigrant leader). With gum.
1282	**690**	20c. green	2·20	80

691 Carnival Dancers

1969. Carioca Carnival, Rio de Janeiro (1970). Multicoloured.
1283		5c. Type **691**	1·10	60
1284		10c. Samba dancers (horiz)	1·10	60
1285		20c. Clowns (horiz)	1·30	80
1286		30c. Confetti and mask	7·00	5·25
1287		50c. Tambourine-player	7·00	4·75

692 Carlos Gomes conducting

1970. Centenary of Opera *O. Guarani* by A. Carlos Gomes.
1288	**692**	20c. multicoloured	1·70	80

693 Monastery

1970. 400th Anniv of Penha Monastery, Vilha Velha.
1289	**693**	20c. multicoloured	85	35

694 National Assembly Building

1970. Tenth Anniv of Brasilia. Multicoloured.
1290		20c. Type **694**	2·50	1·40
1291		50c. Reflecting Pool	6·00	3·50
1292		1cr. Presidential Palace	6·00	3·50

695 Emblem on Map

1970. Rondon Project (students' practical training scheme).

1293	**695**	50c. multicoloured	6·50	7·00

696 Marshal Osorio and Arms

1970. Opening of Marshal Osorio Historical Park.

1294	**696**	20c. multicoloured	4·25	1·90

697 *Madonna and Child* (San Antonio Monastery)

1970. Mothers' Day.

1295	**697**	20c. multicoloured	1·20	80

698 Brasilia Cathedral (stylized)

1970. Eighth National Eucharistic Congress, Brasilia. With gum.

1296	**698**	20c. green	85	45

699 Census Symbol

1970. Eigth National Census.

1297	**699**	20c. yellow and green	1·70	1·70

700 Jules Rimet Cup, and Map

1970. World Cup Football Championships Mexico.

1298	**700**	50c. black, gold & blue	2·40	2·20

701 Statue of Christ

1970. Marist Students. Sixth World Congress.

1299	**701**	50c. multicoloured	7·00	6·50

702 Bellini and Swedish Flag (1958)

1970. Brazil's Third Victory in World Cup Football Championships. Multicoloured.

1300	1cr. Type **702**		4·75	3·50
1301	2cr. Garrincha and Chilean flag (1962)		9·25	3·50
1302	3cr. Pele and Mexican flag (1970)		7·75	2·50

703 Pandia Calogeras

1970. Birth Centenary of Pandia Calogeras (author and politician).

1303	**703**	20c. green	1·40	95

704 Brazilian Forces Badges and Map

1970. 25th Anniv of World War II. Victory.

1304	**704**	20c. multicoloured	1·30	95

705 *The Annunciation* (Cassio M'Boy)

1970. St. Gabriel's Day (Patron Saint of Telecommunications).

1305	**705**	20c. multicoloured	3·00	1·90

706 Boy in Library

1970. Book Week.

1306	**706**	20c. multicoloured	3·00	1·90

707 U.N. Emblem

1970. 25th Anniv of United Nations.

1307	**707**	50c. blue, silver & ultram	3·00	2·30

708 *Rio de Janeiro, circa 1820*

1970. Third Brazilian–Portuguese Stamp Exhibition Lubrapex 70, Rio de Janeiro.

1308	**708**	20c. multicoloured	3·00	1·50
1309	-	50c. brown and black	7·00	3·00
1310	-	1cr. multicoloured	7·25	4·50
MS1311	60×80 mm. **708** 1cr. multicoloured. Imperf		24·00	26·00

DESIGNS: 50c. Post Office Symbol; 1cr. Rio de Janeiro (modern view).

709 *The Holy Family* (C. Portinari)

1970. Christmas.

1312	**709**	50c. multicoloured	3·00	3·00
MS1313	107×52 mm. **709** 1cr. multicoloured. Imper		42·00	45·00

710 *Graca Aranha* (destroyer)

1970. Navy Day.

1314	**710**	20c. multicoloured	3·00	1·70

711 Congress Emblem

1971. Third Inter-American Housing Congress, Rio de Janeiro.

1315	**711**	50c. red and black	3·75	4·00

712 Links and Globe

1971. Racial Equality Year.

1316	**712**	20c. multicoloured	1·80	1·10

713 *Morpho melacheilus*

1971. Butterflies. Multicoloured.

1317	20c. Type **713**		2·40	1·40
1318	1cr. *Papilio thoas brasiliensis*		10·50	7·50

714 Madonna and Child

1971. Mothers' Day.

1319	**714**	20c. multicoloured	2·10	90

715 Hands reaching for Ball

1971. Sixth Women's Basketball World Championships.

1320	**715**	70c. multicoloured	4·25	2·20

716 Eastern Part of Highway Map

1971. Trans-Amazon Highway Project. Multicoloured.

1321	40c. Type **716**		12·00	6·00
1322	1cr. Western part of Highway Map		12·00	9·75

Nos. 1321/2 were issued together *se-tenant*, forming a composite design.

717 *Head of Man* (V. M. Lima)

1971. Stamp Day. Multicoloured.

1323	40c. Type **717**		4·25	1·80
1324	1cr. *Arab Violinist* (Pedro Americo)		9·50	3·75

718 General Caxias and Map

1971. Army Week.

1325	**718**	20c. red and green	1·30	1·40

719 Anita Garibaldi

1971. 150th Birth Anniv of Anita Garibaldi.

1326	**719**	20c. multicoloured	1·30	90

720 Xavante and Santos Dumont's Biplane *14 bis*

1971. First Flight of Embraer Xavante Jet Fighter.

1327	**720**	40c. multicoloured	4·25	1·70

721 Flags of Central American Republics

1971. 150th Anniv of Central American Republics' Independence.

1328	**721**	40c. multicoloured	3·00	1·40

722 Exhibition Emblem

1971. Franca 71 Industrial, Technical and Scientific Exhibition, Sao Paulo.

| 1329 | **722** | 1cr.30 multicoloured | 4·25 | 2·50 |

723 *The Black Mother* (L. de Albuquerque)

1971. Centenary of Slaves Emancipation Law.

| 1330 | **723** | 40c. multicoloured | 2·00 | 1·10 |

724 *Archangel Gabriel*

1971. St. Gabriel's Day (Patron Saint of Communications).

| 1331 | **724** | 40c. multicoloured | 1·90 | 1·50 |

725 *Couple on Bridge* (Marisa da Silva Chaves)

1971. Children's Day. Multicoloured.

1332		35c. Type **725**	1·40	1·00
1333		45c. *Couple on Riverbank* (Mary Rosa e Silva)	3·00	1·00
1334		60c. *Girl in Hat* (Teresa A. P. Ferreira)	1·40	1·00

726 *Laelia purpurata Werkhauserii superba*

1971. Brazilian Orchids.

| 1335 | **726** | 40c. multicoloured | 5·25 | 2·30 |

727 *Eunice Weaver*

1971. Obligatory Tax. Leprosy Research Fund.

| 1336 | **727** | 10c. green | 1·70 | 55 |
| 1337 | **727** | 10c. purple | 60 | 20 |

728 *"25 Senac"*

1971. 25th Anniv of SENAC (apprenticeship scheme) and SESC (workers' social service).

| 1338 | **728** | 20c. blue and black | 3·00 | 2·30 |
| 1339 | **728** | 40c. orange and black | 3·00 | 2·30 |

DESIGN: 40c. As Type **728**, but inscribed "25 SESC".

729 *Parati* (gunboat)

1971. Navy Day.

| 1340 | **729** | 20c. multicoloured | 2·00 | 1·20 |

730 *Cruciform Symbol*

1971. Christmas.

1341	**730**	20c. lilac, red and blue	1·00	80
1342	**730**	75c. black on silver	2·10	6·25
1343	**730**	1cr.30 multicoloured	10·50	4·75

731 *Washing Bomfim Church*

1972. Tourism. Multicoloured.

1344		20c. Type **731**	3·75	1·70
1345		40c. Cogwheel and grapes (Grape Festival, Rio Grande do Sul)	5·75	1·20
1346		75c. Nazareth Festival procession, Belem	6·00	5·50
1347		1cr.30 Street scene (Winter Festival of Ouro Preto)	13·00	5·75

732 *Pres. Lanusse*

1972. Visit of President Lanusse of Argentina.

| 1348 | **732** | 40c. multicoloured | 4·75 | 5·75 |

733 *Presidents Castello Branco, Costa e Silva and Medici*

1972. Eighth Anniv of 1964 Revolution.

| 1349 | **733** | 20c. multicoloured | 3·00 | 1·40 |

734 *Post Office Symbol*

1972

| 1350 | **734** | 20c. brown | 4·75 | 30 |

735 *Pres. Tomas*

1972. Visit of Pres. Tomas of Portugal.

| 1351 | **735** | 75c. multicoloured | 4·75 | 3·75 |

736 *Exploratory Borehole (C.P.R.M.)*

1972. Mineral Resources. Multicoloured.

1352		20c. Type **736**	3·00	1·20
1353		40c. Oil rig (PETROBRAS) (vert)	7·25	1·90
1354		75c. Power station and dam (ELECTROBRAS)	3·25	3·25
1355		1cr.30 Iron ore production (Vale do Rio Doce Co.)	7·25	3·25

737 *Female Nude* (1922 Catalogue cover by Di. Cavalcanti.)

1972. 50th Anniv of First Modern Art Week, Sao Paulo. Sheet 79×111 mm. With gum.

| MS1356 | **737** | 1cr. black and carmine | 70·00 | 65·00 |

738 *Postman and Map (Post Office)*

1972. Communications. Multicoloured.

1357	**738**	35c. Type **738**	3·25	85
1358		45c. Microwave Transmitter (Telecommunications) (vert)	3·50	3·50
1359		60c. Symbol and diagram of Amazon microwave system	3·50	2·75
1360		70c. Worker and route map (Amazon Basin development)	4·50	2·75

739 *Motor Cars*

1972. Major Industries.

1361	**739**	35c. orange, red & black	2·50	1·20
1362	-	45c. multicoloured	2·50	1·40
1363	-	70c. multicoloured	2·50	1·20

DESIGNS—HORIZ: 45c. Three hulls (Shipbuilding); 70c. Metal Blocks (Iron and Steel Industry).

740 *Footballer (Independence Cup Championships)*

1972. Sports and Pastimes.

1364	**740**	20c. black and brown	2·40	1·20
1365	-	75c. black and red	4·25	6·50
1366	-	1cr.30 black and blue	8·00	6·50

DESIGNS: 75c. Treble clef in open mouth ("Popular Music"); 1cr.30, Hand grasping plastic ("Plastic Arts").

741 *Diego Homem's Map of Brazil, 1568*

1972. EXFILBRA 72 Fourth International Stamp Exhibition, Rio de Janeiro. Multicoloured.

1367	**741**	70c. Type **741**	1·30	1·20
1368		1cr. Nicolau Visscher's Map of Americas, c. 1652	18·00	2·30
1369		2cr. Lopo Homem's World Map, 1519	8·75	3·50
MS1370	125×89 mm. 1cr. *Declaration of Ypiranga* (Pedro Americo) (horiz)		10·50	11·00

742 *Figurehead, Sao Francisco River*

1972. Brazilian Folklore. Multicoloured.

1371		45c. Type **742**	2·10	85
1372		60c. Fandango, Rio Grande do Sul	3·25	2·75
1373		75c. Capoeira (game), Bahia	70	65
1374		1cr.15 Karaja statuette	1·40	1·30
1375		1cr.30 *Bumba-Meu-Boi* (folk play)	10·00	3·75

743 *Institution of Brazilian Flag*

1972. 150th Anniv of Independence.

1376	**743**	30c. green and yellow	3·00	2·75
1377	-	70c. mauve and pink	2·40	1·80
1378	-	1cr. red and brown	14·50	2·75
1379	-	2cr. black and brown	7·50	2·75
1380	-	3cr.50 black and grey	14·00	7·00

DESIGNS—HORIZ: 70c. *Proclamation of Emperor Pedro I* (lithograph after Debret); 2cr. Commemorative gold coin of Pedro I; 3cr.50, Declaration of Ypiranga monument. VERT: 1cr. *Emperor Pedro I* (H. J. da Silva).

744 Numeral and P.T.T. Symbol **745** Scroll

1972

1383	**744**	5c. orange	55	20
1384	**744**	10c. brown	80	20
1394	**744**	15c. blue	45	10
1385	**744**	20c. blue	80	20
1396	**744**	25c. brown	55	30
1386	**744**	30c. red	90	20
1387	**744**	40c. green	45	20
1388	**744**	50c. green	70	20
1398	**744**	70c. purple	70	10
1389	**745**	1cr. purple	1·00	20
1390	**745**	2cr. blue	1·60	20
1391	**745**	4cr. orange and lilac	3·50	20
1392	**745**	5cr. brown, cinnamon and red	5·25	20
1393	**745**	10cr. green, brown & blk	11·00	65

Nos. 1392/3 have a background of multiple P.T.T. symbols.

746 *Fittipaldi in Racing Car*

1972. Emerson Fittipaldi's Victory in Formula 1 World Motor-racing Championship. Sheet 122×87 mm.

| MS1411 | **746** | 2cr. multicoloured | 22·00 | 25·00 |

747 *Writing Hand and People ("Mobral" Literacy Campaign)*

1972. Social Development. Multicoloured.

1412	**747**	10c. Type **747**	45	55
1413		20c. Graph and people (National Census Cent)	2·50	1·70
1414		1cr. House in hand (Pension Fund system)	17·00	65
1415		2cr. Workers and factory (Gross National Product)	4·75	1·70

748 Legislative Building, Brasilia

1972. National Congress Building, Brasilia.
| 1416 | 748 | 1cr. black, orange & bl | 20·00 | 11·00 |

749 Pottery Crib

1972. Christmas.
| 1417 | 749 | 20c. black and brown | 2·10 | 1·20 |

750 Farm-worker and Pension Book (Rural Social Security Scheme)

1972. Government Services.
1418	750	10c. black, orange & bl	1·30	1·20
1419	-	10c. multicoloured	2·50	2·30
1420	-	70c. black, brown & red	18·00	7·00
1421	-	2cr. multicoloured	29·00	12·50

DESIGNS—VERT: 70c. Dr. Oswald Cruz, public health pioneer (birth cent.). HORIZ: 10c. (No. 1419), Children and traffic lights (Transport system development); 2cr. Bull, fish and produce (Agricultural exports).

751 Brazilian Expeditionary Force Monument

1972. Armed Forces' Day.
1422	751	10c. black, purple & brn	3·75	2·50
1423	-	30c. multicoloured	3·75	2·50
1424	-	30c. multicoloured	3·75	2·50
1425	-	30c. black, brn & lilac	3·75	2·50

DESIGNS: No. 1423, Sail-training ship (Navy); No. 1424, Trooper (Army); No. 1425, Dassault Mirage IIIC jet fighter (Air Force).

GUM. All the following issues are with gum, except where otherwise stated.

752 Emblem and Cogwheels

1973. 50th Anniv of Rotary in Brazil.
| 1426 | 752 | 1cr. blue, lt blue & yell | 4·00 | 3·50 |

753 Swimming

1973. Sporting Events.
1427	753	40c. brown and blue	80	75
1428	-	40c. red and green	5·50	2·10
1429	-	40c. brown and purple	1·70	1·60

DESIGNS AND EVENTS—HORIZ: No. 1427, ("Latin Cup" Swimming Championships); No. 1428, Gymnast (Olympic Festival of Gymnastics, Rio de Janeiro). VERT: No. 1429, Volleyball player (Internation Volleyball Championships, Rio de Janeiro).

754 Paraguayan Flag

1973. Visit of Pres. Stroessner of Paraguay.
| 1430 | 754 | 70c. multicoloured | 4·00 | 2·75 |

755 "Communications"

1973. Inauguration of Ministry of Communications Building, Brasilia.
| 1431 | 755 | 70c. multicoloured | 1·90 | 1·60 |

756 Neptune and Map

1973. Inauguration of "Bracan I" Underwater Cable, Recife to Canary Islands.
| 1432 | 756 | 1cr. multicoloured | 9·75 | 7·00 |

757 Congress Emblem

1973. 24th Int Chamber of Commerce Congress.
| 1433 | 757 | 1cr. purple and orange | 9·50 | 7·00 |

758 Swallow-tailed Manakin and *Acacia decurrens*

1973. Tropical Birds and Plants. Multicoloured.
1434	758	20c. Type 758	2·75	75
1435		20c. Troupial and *Cereus peruvianus*	2·75	75
1436		20c. Brazilian ruby and *Tecoma umbellata*	2·75	75

759 "Tourism"

1973. National Tourism Year.
| 1437 | 759 | 70c. multicoloured | 2·50 | 1·90 |

760 "Caboclo" Festival Cart

1973. Anniversaries. Multicoloured.
1438	760	20c. Type 760	1·80	75
1439		20c. Arariboia (Indian chief)	1·80	75
1440		20c. Convention delegates	1·80	75
1441		20c. *The Graciosa Road*	1·80	75

EVENTS: No. 1438, 150th anniv of Liberation Day; 1439, 400th anniv of Niteroi; 1440, Cent of Itu Convention; 1441, Cent of Nhundiaquara highway.

761 "Institute of Space Research"

1973. Scientific Research Institute. Multicoloured.
1442		20c. Type 761	90	65
1443		70c. "Federal Engineering School", Itajuba	6·25	2·30
1444		1cr. "Institute for Pure and Applied Mechanics"	8·00	2·30

762 Santos Dumont and Biplane *14 bis*

1973. Birth Centenary of Alberto Santos Dumont (aviation pioneer).
1445	762	20c. brown, grn & lt grn	2·20	55
1446	-	70c. brown, red & yellow	4·50	2·75
1447	-	2cr. brown, ultram & bl	5·25	2·75

DESIGNS: 70c. Airship *No. 6*; 2cr. Monoplane No. 20 *Demoiselle*.

763 Map of the World

1973. Stamp Day.
| 1448 | 763 | 40c. black and red | 5·75 | 4·75 |
| 1449 | - | 40c. black and red | 5·75 | 4·75 |

The design of No. 1449 differs from Type 763 in that the red portion is to the top and right, instead of to the top and left.

764 G. Dias

1973. 150th Birth Anniv of Goncalves Dias (poet).
| 1450 | 764 | 40c. black and violet | 2·10 | 85 |

See also Nos. 1459 and 1477.

765 Copernicus and "Sun-god"

1973. 500th Birth Anniv of Nicholas Copernicus (astronomer). Sheet 125×87 mm.
| MS1451 | 765 | 1cr. multicoloured | 14·00 | 13·00 |

766 Festival Banner

1973. National Folklore Festival.
| 1452 | 766 | 40c. multicoloured | 2·10 | 1·20 |

767 Masonic Emblems

1973. 150th Anniv of Masonic Grand Orient Lodge of Brazil.
| 1453 | 767 | 1cr. blue | 6·75 | 4·25 |

768 Fire Protection

1973. National Protection Campaign. Multicoloured.
1454	768	40c. Type 768	1·80	85
1455		40c. Cross and cornice (cultural protection)	1·80	85
1456		40c. Winged emblem (protection in flight)	1·80	85
1457		40c. Leaf (protection of nature)	1·80	85

769 St. Gabriel and Papal Bull

1973. First National Exhibition of Religious Philately, Rio de Janeiro. Sheet 125×87 mm.
| MS1458 | 769 | 1cr. black and ochre | 17·00 | 18·00 |

1973. Birth Centenary of St. Theresa of Lisieux. As T 764.
| 1459 | | 2cr. brown and orange | 8·50 | 5·75 |

DESIGN: Portrait of St. Theresa.

770 M. Lobato and *Emilia*

1973. Monteiro Lobato's Children's Stories. Multicoloured.
1460		40c. Type 770	1·90	1·20
1461		40c. "Aunt Nastasia"	1·90	1·20
1462		40c. "Nazarinho", "Pedrinho" and "Quindim"	1·90	1·20
1463		40c. "Visconde de Sabugosa"	1·90	1·20
1464		40c. "Dona Benta"	1·90	1·20

771 Father J. M. Nunes Garcia

1973. "The Baroque Age". Multicoloured.
1465		40c. Wood carving, Church of St. Francia, Bahia	70	65
1466		40c. *Prophet Isaiah* (detail, sculpture by Aleijadinho)	70	65
1467		70c. Type 771	3·75	3·25
1468		1cr. Portal, Church of Conceicao da Praia	16·00	7·00
1469		2cr. *Glorification of Holy Virgin*, ceiling, St. Francis Assisi Church, Ouro Preto	8·50	7·00

772 Early Telephone and Modern Instruments

1973. 50th Anniv of Brazilian Telephone Company.
| 1470 | 772 | 40c. multicoloured | 80 | 65 |

773 Angel (J. Kopke)

1973. Christmas.
| 1471 | 773 | 40c. multicoloured | 80 | 65 |

774 *Gailora* (river steamboat)

1973. Brazilian Boats. Multicoloured.
1472	774	40c. Type 774	80	65
1473		70c. *Regatao* (river trading boat)	2·75	2·50
1474		1cr. *Jangada* (coastal raft)	9·75	4·50
1475		2cr. *Saveiro* (passenger boat)	9·75	4·50

775 Scales of Justice

1973. Judiciary Power.
1476	**775**	40c. violet and mauve	1·40	65

1973. Birth Centenary of Placido de Castro. As T **764**.
1477	40c. black and red	1·70	85
DESIGN: Portrait of Castro.

776 Scarlet Ibis and "Victoria Regia" Lilies

1973. Brazilian Flora and Fauna. Multicoloured.
1478	40c. Type **776**	2·50	45
1479	70c. Jaguar and Indian tulip	7·50	3·75
1480	1cr. Scarlet macaw and palm	9·75	45
1481	2cr. Greater rhea and mulunga plant	16·00	6·00

777 Saci Perere (goblin)

1974. Brazilian Folk Tales. Multicoloured.
1482	40c. Type **777**	90	55
1483	80c. Zumbi (warrior)	1·80	1·30
1484	1cr. Chico Rei (African king)	4·00	1·10
1485	1cr.30 Little black boy of the pasture (32×33 mm)	6·25	1·90
1486	2cr.50 Iara, queen of the waters (32×33 mm)	21·00	5·75

778 View of Bridge

1974. Inauguration of President Costa e Silva (Rio de Janeiro–Niteroi) Bridge.
1487	**778**	40c. multicoloured	1·70	65

779 "Press"

1974. Brazilian Communications Pioneers.
1488	**779**	40c. red, blue & bistre	1·10	65
1489	-	40c. brown, blue & bistre	1·10	65
1490	-	40c. blue, pink & brown	1·10	65
DESIGNS AND EVENTS: No. 1488, Birth bicentenary of Hipolito da Costa (founder of newspaper *Correio Brasiliense*, 1808); 1489, *Radio waves* (Edgar R. Pinto, founder of Radio Sociedade do Rio de Janeiro, 1923); 1490, *Television screen* (F. de Assis Chateaubriand, founder of first T.V. station, Sao Paulo, 1950).

780 "Construction"

1974. Tenth Anniv of March Revolution.
1491	**780**	40c. multicoloured	1·70	95

781 Christ of the Andes

1974. Birth Cent of G. Marconi (radio pioneer).
1492	**781**	2cr.50 multicoloured	11·50	6·50

782 Heads of Three Races

1974. Ethnical Origins and Immigration. Multicoloured.
1493	40c. Type **782**	80	65
1494	40c. Heads of many races	45	45
1495	2cr.50 German immigration	8·50	3·50
1496	2cr.50 Italian immigration	12·50	3·50
1497	2cr.50 Japanese immigration	3·00	2·10

783 Artwork and Stamp-printing Press

1974. State Mint.
1498	**783**	80c. multicoloured	2·50	45

784 Sete Cidades National Park

1974. Tourism. Multicoloured.
1499	40c. Type **784**	1·80	1·20
1500	80c. Ruins of church of St. Michael of the Missions	1·80	1·20

785 Footballer

1974. World Cup Football Championship, West Germany. Sheet 125×87 mm.
MS1501	**785**	2cr.50 multicoloured	9·75	9·75
See also No. 1506.

786 Caraca College

1974. Bicentenary of Caraca College.
1502	**786**	40c. multicoloured	1·30	85

787 Wave Pattern

1974. Third Brazilian Telecommunications Congress, Brasilia.
1503	**787**	40c. black and blue	70	65

788 Fernao Dias Paes

1974. 300th Anniv of Paes Expedition.
1504	**788**	20c. multicoloured	70	65

1974. Visit of President Alvarez of Mexico. As T **754**. Multicoloured.
1505	80c. Mexican Flag	6·25	2·30

789 Flags and Crowd in Stadium

1974. World Cup Football Championship, West Germany (2nd issue).
1506	**789**	40c. multicoloured	1·30	1·20

790 Braille "Eye" and Emblem

1974. Fifth General Assembly of World Council for Welfare of the Blind. Sheet 127×90 mm.
MS1507	**790**	1cr.30 multicoloured	2·30	3·25

791 Pederneiras (after J. Carlos)

1974. Birth Centenary of Raul Pederneiras (lawyer, author and artist).
1508	**791**	40c. black & yell on brn	70	65

792 Emblem and Seascape

1974. 13th Int Union of Building Societies and Savings Associations Congress, Rio de Janeiro.
1509	**792**	1cr.30 multicoloured	3·50	2·00

793 Five Women of Guaratingueta (E di Cavalcanti)

1974. Lubrapex 74 Stamp Exhibition, Sao Paulo (1st issue). Sheet 87×126 mm.
MS1510	**793**	2cr. multicoloured	6·75	10·50
See also No. 1522.

794 "UPU" on World Map

1974. Centenary of UPU.
1511	**794**	2cr.50 black and blue	11·50	3·75

795 Aruak Hammock

1974. "Popular Culture".
1512	**795**	50c. purple	4·50	85
1513	-	50c. light blue and blue	5·75	85
1514	-	50c. brown, red & yellow	1·40	85
1515	-	50c. brown and yellow	1·80	85

DESIGNS—SQUARE: No. 1513, Bilro Lace. VERT: (24×37 mm), No. 1514, Guitar player (folk literature); 1515, Horseman (statuette by Vitalino).

796 Coffee Beans

1974. Bicentenary of City of Campinas.
1516	**796**	50c. multicoloured	2·30	1·30

797 Hornless Tabapua

1974. Domestic Animals. Multicoloured.
1517	80c. Type **797**	2·50	1·50
1518	1cr.30 Creole horse	2·40	1·50
1519	2cr.50 Brazilian mastiff	16·00	4·50

798 Ilha Solteira Dam

1974. Ilha Solteira Hydro-electric Power Project.
1520	**798**	50c. brown, grey & yell	3·50	1·20

799 Herald Angel

1974. Christmas.
1521	**799**	50c. multicoloured	1·70	65

800 The Girls (Carlos Reis)

1974. Lubrapex 74 Stamp Exhibition, Sao Paulo (2nd issue).
1522	**800**	1cr.30 multicoloured	1·70	1·20

801 "Justice for Juveniles"

1974. 50th Anniv of Brazilian Juvenile Court.
1523	**801**	90c. multicoloured	70	65

802 Athlete

1974. 50th Anniv of Sao Silvestre Long-distance Race.
1524	**802**	3cr.30 multicoloured	1·80	1·70

803 Mounted Newsvendor and Newspaper Masthead

1975. Centenary of Newspaper *O Estado de S. Paulo*.
1525	**803**	50c. multicoloured	3·00	1·70

804 Industrial Complex, Sao Paulo

1975. Economic Resources.
1526	**804**	50c. yellow and blue	3·25	85
1527	-	1cr.40 yellow & brown	1·40	85
1528	-	4cr.50 yellow & black	11·00	85

DESIGNS: 1cr.40 Rubber industry, Acre; 4cr.50, Manganese industry, Amapa.

805 Santa Cruz Fortress, Rio de Janeiro

1975. Colonial Forts. Each brown on yellow.
1529		50c. Type **805**	70	45
1530		50c. Reis Magos Fort, Rio Grande do Norte	1·30	55
1531		50c. Monte Serrat Fort, Bahia	2·30	55
1532		90c. Nossa Senhora dos Remedios Fort, Fernando de Noronha	70	45

806 "Palafita" House, Amazonas

1975. Brazilian Architecture. Multicoloured.
1533		50c. Modern Architecture, Brasilia	2·75	2·50
1534		50c. Modern Architecture, Brasilia (yellow line at left)	19·00	11·50
1535		1cr. Type **806**	1·90	45
1536		1cr.40 Indian hut, Rondonia (yellow line at left)	4·25	4·00
1537		1cr.40 As No. 1536 but yellow line at right	1·10	1·00
1538		3cr.30 "Enxaimel" house, Santa Catarina (yellow line at right)	1·80	1·70
1539		3cr.30 As No. 1538 but yellow line at left	8·00	7·50

807 Oscar (*Astronotus ocellatus*)

1975. Freshwater Fish. Multicoloured.
1540		50c. Type **807**	3·75	45
1541		50c. South American pufferfish (*Colomesus psitacus*)	90	85
1542		50c. Tail-spot livebearer (*Phallocerus caudimaculatus*)	90	85
1543		50c. Red discus (*Symphysodon discus*)	1·40	55

808 Flags forming Serviceman's Head

1975. Honouring Ex-Servicemen of Second World War.
1544	**808**	50c. multicoloured	90	65

809 Brazilian Pines

1975. Fauna and Flora Preservation. Multicoloured.
1545		70c. Type **809**	4·00	75
1546		1cr. Giant otter (vert)	2·50	1·10
1547		3cr.30 Marsh cayman	2·50	1·10

810 Inga Carved Stone, from Paraiba

1975. Archaeology. Multicoloured.
1548		70c. Type **810**	1·40	85
1549		1cr. Marajoara pot from Para	80	75
1550		1cr. Fossilized garfish from Ceara (horiz)	80	75

811 Statue of the Virgin Mary

1975. Holy Year. 300th Anniv of Franciscan Province of Our Lady of the Immaculate Conception.
1551	**811**	3cr.30 multicoloured	2·50	1·60

812 Ministry of Communications Building, Rio de Janeiro

1975. Stamp Day.
1552	**812**	70c. red	1·70	65

813 "Congada" Sword Dance, Minas Gerais

1975. Folk Dances. Multicoloured.
1553		70c. Type **813**	90	75
1554		70c. "Frevo" umbrella dance, Pernambuco	90	75
1555		70c. "Warrior" dance, Alagoas	90	75

814 Stylized Trees

1975. Tree Festival.
1556	**814**	70c. multicoloured	70	55

815 Dish Aerial and Globe

1975. Inauguration of Tangua Satellite Telecommunications Station.
1557	**815**	3cr.30 multicoloured	1·70	1·60

816 Woman holding Globe

1975. International Women's Year.
1558	**816**	3cr.30 multicoloured	2·50	1·40

817 Tile, Balcony Rail and Memorial Column, Alcantara

1975. Historic Towns. Multicoloured.
1559		70c. Type **817**	1·50	95
1560		70c. Belfry, weather vane and jug, Goias (26×38 mm)	1·50	95
1561		70c. Sao Francisco Convent, Sao Cristovao (40×22 mm)	1·50	95

818 Crowd welcoming Walking Book

1975. Day of the Book.
1562	**818**	70c. multicoloured	55	55

819 ASTA Emblem and Arrows

1975. 45th American Society of Travel Agents Congress.
1563	**819**	70c. multicoloured	55	55

820 Two Angels

1975. Christmas.
1564	**820**	70c. brown and red	55	45

821 Aerial, and Map of America

1975. Second International Telecommunications Conference, Rio de Janeiro.
1565	**821**	5cr.20 multicoloured	7·50	4·50

822 Friar Nicodemus

1975. Obligatory Tax. Leprosy Research Fund.
1566	**822**	10c. brown	35	30

823 People in front of Cross

1975. Thanksgiving Day.
1567	**823**	70c. turquoise and blue	90	85

824 Emperor Pedro II in Naval Uniform (after P. P. da Silva Manuel)

1975. 150th Birth Anniv of Emperor Pedro II.
1568	**824**	70c. brown	2·10	95

825 Sal Stone Beach, Piaui

1975. Tourism. Multicoloured.
1569		70c. Type **825**	70	65
1570		70c. Guarapari Beach, Espirito Santo	70	65
1571		70c. Torres Cliffs Rio Grande do Sul	70	65

826 Triple Jump

1975. Seventh Pan-American Games, Santo Domingo, Dominican Republic.
1572	**826**	1cr.60 turquoise & black	70	65

827 UN Emblem and HQ Building, New York

1975. 30th Anniv of United Nations.
1573	**827**	1cr.30 violet on blue	55	55

828 Light Bulbs and House

1976. "Preservation of Fuel Resources". Multicoloured.
1574		70c. Type **828**	70	45
1575		70c. Drops of petrol and car	70	45

829 Concorde

1976. Concorde's First Commercial Flight, Paris–Rio de Janeiro.
1576	**829**	5cr.20 black and grey	1·30	75

830 Pinheiro's Nautical Map of 1776

1976. Centenary of Hydrographical and Navigational Directorate. Sheet 88×124 mm.
MS1577	**830**	70c. multicoloured	2·75	2·75

831 Early and Modern Telephone Equipment

1976. Telephone Centenary.
1578	**831**	5cr.20 black & orange	1·90	1·20

832 "Eye"-part of Exclamation Mark

1976. World Health Day.
1579	**832**	1cr. red, brown & violet	1·30	1·20

833 Kaiapo
Body-painting

1976. Brazil's Indigenous Culture. Multicoloured.
1580		1cr. Type **833**	45	30
1581		1cr. Bakairi ceremonial mask	45	30
1582		1cr. Karaja feather head-dress	45	30

834 Itamaraty Palace,
Brasilia

1976. Diplomats' Day.
1583	**834**	1cr. multicoloured	1·90	1·40

835 *The Sprinkler* (3D
composition by J.
Tarcisio)

1976. Modern Brazilian Art. Multicoloured.
1584		1cr. Type **835**	55	45
1585		1cr. *Beribboned Fingers* (P. Chec- cacci) (horiz)	55	45

836 Basketball

1976. Olympic Games, Montreal.
1586	**836**	1cr. black and green	45	45
1587		1cr.40 black and blue	45	45
1588		5cr.20 black and orange	1·60	1·30

DESIGNS: 1cr.40, Olympic yachts; 5cr.20, Judo.

837 Golden
Lion-Tamarin

1976. Nature Protection. Multicoloured.
1589		1cr. Type **837**	1·40	45
1590		1cr. Orchid (*Acacallis cyanea*)	1·40	45

838 Cine
Camera on
Screen

1976. Brazilian Cinematograph Industry.
1591	**838**	1cr. multicoloured	55	55

839 Ox-cart
Driver

1976
1592	**839**	10c. red	45	20
1593	-	15c. brown	70	30
1594	-	20c. blue	45	10
1595	-	30c. red	45	10
1596	-	40c. orange	55	20

1597a	-	50c. brown	45	20
1598	-	70c. black	55	20
1599	-	80c. green	1·90	30
1600a	-	1cr. black	45	20
1601	-	1cr.10 purple	45	10
1602	-	1cr.30 red	55	10
1603a	-	1cr.80 violet	55	20
1604a	-	2cr. brown	1·10	30
1605	-	2cr.50 brown	55	20
1605a	-	3cr.20 blue	55	20
1606a	-	5cr. lilac	4·50	55
1607	-	7cr. violet	8·00	30
1608a	-	10cr. green	4·50	55
1609	-	15cr. green	2·75	30
1610	-	20cr. blue	6·75	30
1611	-	21cr. purple	1·60	30
1612	-	27cr. brown	1·60	55

DESIGNS—HORIZ: 20c. Pirogue fisherman; 40c. Cowboy; 3cr.20, Sao Francisco boatman; 27cr. Muleteer. VERT: 15c. Bahia woman; 30c. Rubber gatherer; 50c. Gaucho; 70c. Women breaking Babacu chestnuts; 80c. Gold-washer; 1cr. Banana gatherer; 1cr.10, Grape harvester; 1cr.30, Coffee harvester; 1cr.80, Carnauba cutter; 2cr. Potter; 2cr.50, Basket maker; 5cr. Sugar-cane cutter; 7cr. Salt worker; 10cr. Fisherman; 15cr. Coconut vendor; 20cr. Lace maker; 21cr. Ramie cutter.

840 Neon Tetra
(*Paracheirodon innesi*)

1976. Brazilian Freshwater Fish. Multicoloured.
1613		1cr. Type **840**	1·40	85
1614		1cr. Splash tetra (*Copeina arnold*)	1·40	85
1615		1cr. Prochilodus (*Prochilodus insignis*)	1·40	85
1616		1cr. Spotted pike cichlid (*Crenicichla lepidota*)	1·40	85
1617		1cr. Bottle-nosed catfish (*Ageneiosus* sp.)	1·40	85
1618		1cr. Reticulated corydoras (*Corydoras reticulatus*)	1·40	85

841 Santa Marta
Lighthouse

1976. 300th Anniv of Laguna.
1619	**841**	1cr. blue	45	20

842 Postage Stamps as
Magic Carpet

1976. Stamp Day.
1620	**842**	1cr. multicoloured	55	30

843 Oil Lamp and Profile

1976. 50th Anniv of Brazilian Nursing Assn.
1621	**843**	1cr. multicoloured	55	30

844 Puppet
Soldier

1976. Mamulengo Puppet Theatre. Multicoloured.
1622	**844**	1cr. Type **844**	45	20
1623		1cr.30 Puppet girl	45	20
1624		1cr.60 Finger puppets (horiz)	45	20

845 Winner's
Medal

1976. 27th International Military Athletics Championships, Rio de Janeiro.
1625	**845**	5cr.20 multicoloured	1·70	1·20

846 Family within
"House"

1976. SESC and SENAC National Organizations for Appenticeship and Welfare.
1626	**846**	1cr. blue	55	20

847 Rotten Tree

1976. Conservation of the Environment.
1627	**847**	1cr. multicoloured	55	20

848 Electron Orbits and
Atomic Agency Emblem

1976. 20th International Atomic Energy Conference, Rio de Janeiro.
1628	**848**	5cr.20 multicoloured	1·70	1·20

849 Underground Train

1976. Inauguration of Sao Paulo Underground Railway.
1629	**849**	1cr.60 multicoloured	80	30

850 St. Francis

1976. 750th Death Anniv of St. Francis of Assisi.
1630	**850**	5cr.20 multicoloured	1·70	85

851 School
Building

1976. Centenary of Ouro Preto Mining School.
1631	**851**	1cr. violet	90	1·10

852 *Three Kings* (J. A. da
Silva)

1976. Christmas. Multicoloured.
1632		80c. Type **852**	70	45

1633		80c. *Father Christmas* (T. Onivaldo Cogo)	70	45
1634		80c. *Nativity Scene* (R. Yabe)	70	45
1635		80c. *Angels* (E. Folchini)	70	45
1636		80c. *Nativity* (A.L. Cintra)	70	45

853 Section of Brazilian
30,000-reis Banknote

1976. Opening of Bank of Brazil's Thousandth Branch at Barra do Bugres. Sheet 125×88 mm.
MS1637	**853**	80c. multicoloured	1·70	2·75

854 *Our Lady of Monte
Serrat* (Friar A. da
Piedade)

1976. Brazilian Sculpture. Multicoloured.
1638		80c. Type **854**	45	45
1639		5cr. *St. Joseph* (unknown artist) (25×37 mm)	1·60	85
1640		5cr.60 *The Dance* (J. Bernardelli) (square)	1·60	85
1641		6cr.50 *The Caravel* (B. Giorgi) (As 5cr.)	1·60	85

855 Hands in Prayer

1976. Thanksgiving Day.
1642	**855**	80c. multicoloured	70	45

856 Sailor of
1840

1976. Brazilian Navy Commemoration. Multicoloured.
1643		80c. Type **856**	70	30
1644		2cr. Marine of 1808	90	55

857 "Natural Resources"

1976. Brazilian Bureau of Standards.
1645	**857**	80c. multicoloured	55	30

858 *Wheel of Life*
(wood-carving, G.
T. de Oliveira)

1977. Second World Black and African Festival of Arts and Culture, Lagos (Nigeria). Multicoloured.
1646		5cr. Type **858**	1·40	75
1647		5cr.60 *The Beggar* (wood-carving, A. dos Santos)	1·40	75
1648		6cr.50 Benin pectoral mask	2·75	85

859 Airport Layout

1977. Inauguration of Operation of International Airport, Rio de Janeiro.
1649	**859**	6c.50 multicoloured	2·10	1·40

860 Seminar Emblem

1977. Sixth InterAmerican Budget Seminar.
1650	**860**	1cr.10 turq, bl & stone	1·90	45

861 Salicylic Acid Crystals

1977. World Rheumatism Year.
1651	**861**	1cr.10 multicoloured	70	30

862 Emblem of Lions Clubs

1977. 25th Anniv of Brazilian Lions Clubs.
1652	**862**	1cr.10 multicoloured	70	30

863 H. Villa-Lobos and Music

1977. Brazilian Composers. Multicoloured.
1653	**863**	1cr.10 Type **863**	45	10
1654		1cr.10 Chiquinha Gonzaga and guitar	45	10
1655		1cr.10 Noel Rosa and guitar	45	10

864 Rural and Urban Workers

1977. Industrial Protection and Safety. Multicoloured.
1656	**864**	1cr.10 Type **864**	45	10
1657		1cr.10 Laboratory vessels	45	10

865 Memorial, Porto Seguro

1977. Centenary of UPU Membership. Views of Porto Seguro. Multicoloured.
1658	**865**	1cr.10 Type **865**	35	10
1659		5cr. Beach	2·75	65
1660		5cr.60 Old houses	1·50	65
1661		6cr.50 Post Office	2·00	65

866 Newspaper Title in Linotype and Print

1977. 150th Anniv of Brazilian Newspaper *Diario de Porto Allegre.*
1662	**866**	1cr.10 black & purple	55	30

867 Blue Whale

1977. Fauna Preservation.
1663	**867**	1cr.30 multicoloured	3·50	45

868 "Cell System"

1977. 25th Anniv of National Economic Development Bank.
1664	**868**	1cr.30 multicoloured	55	30

869 Locomotive leaving Tunnel

1977. Centenary of Rio de Janeiro–Sao Paulo Railway.
1665	**869**	1c.30 black	1·10	45

870 Goliath Conch

1977. Brazilian Molluscs. Multicoloured.
1666	**870**	1cr.30 Type **870**	1·40	45
1667		1cr.30 Thin-bladed murex (*Murex tenuivaricosus*)	1·40	45
1668		1cr.30 Helmet vase (*Vasum cassiforme*)	1·40	45

871 Caduceus

1977. Third International Congress of Odontology.
1669	**871**	1cr.30 brown, bis & orge	45	20

872 Masonic Symbols

1977. 50th Anniv of Brazilian Grand Masonic Lodge.
1670	**872**	1cr.30 blue, dp bl & blk	55	30

873 "Sailboat"

1977. Stamp Day.
1671	**873**	1cr.30 multicoloured	45	20

874 Law Proclamation

1977. 150th Anniv of Juridical Courses.
1672	**874**	1cr.30 multicoloured	55	30

875 "Cavalhada" (horsemen)

1977. Folklore. Multicoloured.
1673		1cr.30 Type **875**	45	20
1674		1cr.30 Horseman with flag	45	20
1675		1cr.30 Jousting (horiz)	45	20

876 Doubloon

1977. Brazilian Colonial Coins. Multicoloured.
1676		1cr.30 Type **876**	45	20
1677		1cr.30 Pataca	45	20
1678		1cr.30 Vintem	45	20

877 Toy Windmill

1977. National Day.
1679	**877**	1cr.30 multicoloured	55	30

878 *Neoregelia carolinae*

1977. Nature Conservation.
1680	**878**	1cr.30 multicoloured	55	30

879 Pen, Pencil and Writing

1977. 150th Anniv of Official Elementary Schooling.
1681	**879**	1cr.30 multicoloured	55	30

880 Observatory and Electrochromograph of Supernova

1977. 150th Anniv of National Observatory.
1682	**880**	1cr.30 multicoloured	70	35

881 Airship *Pax*

1977. Aviation Anniversaries. Multicoloured.
1683		1cr.30 Type **881**	80	55
1684		1cr.30 Savoia Marchetti flying boat *Jahu*	80	55

ANNIVERSARIES: No. 1683, 75th anniv of *Pax* flight; 1684, 50th anniv of *Jahu* South Atlantic crossing.

882 Text from *O Guarani* and Ceci

1977. Day of the Book and Jose de Alencar Commemoration.
1685	**882**	1cr.30 multicoloured	55	20

883 Radio Waves

1977. Amateur Radio Operators' Day.
1686	**883**	1cr.30 multicoloured	55	20

884 Nativity (in carved gourd)

1977. Christmas. Multicoloured.
1687		1cr.30 Type **884**	55	20
1688		2cr. The Annunciation	70	30
1689		5cr. Nativity	1·50	45

885 Emerald

1977. Portucale 77 Thematic Stamp Exhibition. Multicoloured.
1690		1cr.30 Type **885**	70	45
1691		1cr.30 Topaz	70	45
1692		1cr.30 Aquamarine	70	45

886 Angel holding Cornucopia

1977. Thanksgiving Day.
1693	**886**	1cr.30 multicoloured	55	30

887 Curtiss Fledgling Douglas DC-3 and Badge (National Airmail Service)

1977. National Integration. Multicoloured.
1694		1cr.30 Type **887**	70	45
1695		1cr.30 Amazon River naval patrol boat and badge (Amazon Fleet)	70	45

1696 1cr.30 Train crossing bridge and badges (Engineering Corps and Railway Battalion) 70 45

888 Douglas DC-10 and Varig Airline Emblems

1977. 50th Anniv of Varig State Airline.
1697 **888** 1cr.30 black, lt bl & bl 55 30

889 Sts. Cosmus and Damian Church, Igaracu

1977. Regional Architecture, Churches. Multicoloured.
1698 2cr.70 Type **889** 70 30
1699 7cr.50 St. Bento Monastery Church, Rio de Janeiro 2·10 75
1700 8cr.50 St. Francis Assisi Church, Ouro Preto 2·20 85
1701 9cr.50 St. Anthony Convent Church, Joao Pessoa 2·75 95

890 Woman with Wheat Sheaf

1977. Diplomats' Day.
1702 **890** 1cr.30 multicoloured 55 30

891 Scene from *Fosca* and Carlos Gomes (composer)

1978. Bicentenary of La Scala Opera House, Milan, and Carlos Gomes Commemoration.
1703 **891** 1cr.80 multicoloured 45 20

892 Foot kicking Ball

1978. World Cup Football Championship, Argentina. Multicoloured.
1704 1cr.80 Type **892** 70 20
1705 1cr.80 Ball in net 70 20
1706 1cr.80 Stylized player with cup 70 20

893 "Postal Efficiency"

1978. Postal Staff College.
1707 **893** 1cr.80 multicoloured 55 30

894 Electrocardiogram

1978. World Hypertension Month.
1708 **894** 1cr.80 multicoloured 55 30

895 World Map and Antenna

1978. World Telecommunications Day.
1709 **895** 1cr.80 multicoloured 55 30

896 Saffron Finch

1978. Birds. Multicoloured.
1710 7cr.50 Type **896** 2·30 85
1711 8cr.50 Banded cotinga 2·40 1·10
1712 9cr.50 Seven-coloured tanager 2·75 1·30

897 *Discussing the Opening Speech* (G. Mondin)

1978. 85th Anniv of Union Court of Audit.
1713 **897** 1cr.80 multicoloured 55 30

898 Post and Telegraph Headquarters, Brasilia

1978. Opening of Post and Telegraph Headquarters.
1714 **898** 1cr.80 multicoloured 55 45

1978. Brapex III Third Brazilian Philatelic Exhibition. Sheet 70×90 mm.
MS1715 **898** 7cr. 50 multicoloured 2·30 3·25

899 President Geisel

1978. President Geisel Commemoration.
1716 **899** 1cr.80 olive 55 30

900 Savoia Marchetti S-64 and Map

1978. 50th Anniv of South Atlantic Flight by del Prete and Ferrarin.
1717 **900** 1cr.80 multicoloured 55 30

901 "Smallpox"

1978. Global Eradication of Smallpox.
1718 **901** 1cr.80 multicoloured 55 30

902 10r. Pedro II "White Beard" Stamp of 1878

1978. Stamp Day.
1719 **902** 1cr.80 multicoloured 45 20

903 *Jangadeiros*

1978. Birth Centenary of Helios Seelinger (painter).
1720 **903** 1cr.80 multicoloured 55 30

904 Musicians with Violas

1978. Folk Musicians. Multicoloured.
1721 1cr.80 Type **904** 45 20
1722 1cr.80 Two fife players 45 20
1723 1cr.80 Berimbau players 45 20

905 Children playing Football

1978. National Week.
1724 **905** 1cr.80 multicoloured 55 30

906 Patio de Colegio Church

1978. Restoration of Patio de Colegio Church, Sao Paulo.
1725 **906** 1cr.80 brown 55 30

907 *Justice* (A. Ceschiatti)

1978. 150th Anniv of Federal Supreme Court.
1726 **907** 1cr.80 black and bistre 55 30

908 Ipe (flowering tree)

1978. Environment Protection. Iguacu Falls National Park. Multicoloured.
1727 1cr.80 Type **908** 55 30
1728 1cr.80 Iguacu Falls 55 30

909 Stages of Intelsat Assembly

1978. Third Assembly. Users of Intelsat Telecommunications Satellite.
1729 **909** 1cr.80 multicoloured 55 30

910 Flag of the Order of Christ

1978. Lubrapex 78 Stamp Exhibition. Flags. Multicoloured.
1730 1cr.80 Type **910** 1·30 1·10
1731 1cr.80 Principality of Brazil 1·30 1·10
1732 1cr.80 United Kingdom of Brazil 1·30 1·10
1733 8cr.50 Empire of Brazil 1·30 1·10
1734 8cr.50 National Flag of Brazil 1·30 1·10

911 Postal Tramcar

1978. 18th U.P.U. Congress, Rio de Janeiro.
1735 **911** 1cr.80 brown, blk & bl 1·50 65
1736 - 1cr.80 brown, blk & bl 1·50 65
1737 - 1cr.80 grey, blk & rose 1·50 65
1738 - 1cr.80 brown, blk & rose 1·80 85
1739 - 8cr.50 brown, blk & grn 2·10 95
1740 - 9cr.50 brown, blk & grn 2·30 1·10

DESIGNS: No. 1736, Post container truck; 1737, Post van, 1914; 1738, Travelling post office; 1739, Mail coach; 1740, Mule caravan.

912 Gaucho

1978. Day of the Book and J. Guimaraes Rosa Commemoration.
1741 **912** 1cr.80 multicoloured 45 30

913 *Morro de Santo Antonio* (Nicolas Antoine Taunay)

1978. Landscape Paintings. Multicoloured.
1742 1cr.80 Type **913** 45 30
1743 1cr.80 *View of Pernambuco* (Frans Post) 45 30
1744 1cr.80 *Morro de Castelo* (Victor Meirelles) 45 30
1745 1cr.80 *Landscape at Sabara* (Alberto da Veiga Guignard) 45 30

914 Angel with Lute

1978. Christmas. Multicoloured.
1746 1cr.80 Type **914** 45 30
1747 1cr.80 Angel with lyre 45 30
1748 1cr.80 Angel with trumpet 45 30

915 "Thanksgiving"

1978. Thanksgiving Day.
1749 **915** 1cr.80 ochre, blk & red 55 30

916 Red Cross Services

1978. 70th Anniv of Brazilian Red Cross.
1750 **916** 1cr.80 red and black 55 30

917 Peace Theatre, Belem

1978. Brazilian Theatres. Multicoloured.
1751 10cr.50 Type **917** 1·50 55
1752 12cr. Jose de Alencar Theatre, Fortaleza 1·60 65
1753 12cr.50 Rio de Janeiro Municipal Theatre 1·90 75

918 Underground Trains

1979. Inauguration of Rio de Janeiro Underground Railway.
1754	**918**	2cr.50 multicoloured	1·10	45

919 Old and New Post Offices

1979. Tenth Anniv of Post & Telegraph Department and 18th U.P.U. Congress (2nd issue). Multicoloured.
1755	2cr.50 Type **919**	55	30
1756	2cr.50 Mail boxes	55	30
1757	2cr.50 Mail sorting	55	30
1758	2cr.50 Mail planes	55	30
1759	2cr.50 Telegraph and telex machines	55	30
1760	2cr.50 Postmen	55	30

920 "O'Day 23" Class Yacht

1979. Brasiliana 79 3rd World Thematic Stamp Exhibition (1st issue). Multicoloured.
1761	2cr.50 Type **920**	70	55
1762	10cr.50 "Penguin" class dinghy	1·40	75
1763	12cr. "Hobie Cat" class catamaran	1·60	65
1764	12cr.50 "Snipe" class dinghy	1·90	75

See Nos. 1773/6 and 1785/90.

921 Joao Bolinha (characters from children's story)

1979. Children's Book Day.
1765	**921**	2cr.50 multicoloured	55	30

922 Victoria amazonica

1979. 18th U.P.U. Congress (3rd issue). Amazon National Park. Multicoloured.
1766	10cr.50 Type **922**	1·60	85
1767	12cr. Amazon manatee	1·80	1·10
1768	12cr.50 Tortoise	1·90	1·20

923 Bank Emblem

1979. 25th Anniv of Northeast Bank of Brazil.
1769	**923**	2cr.50 multicoloured	55	30

924 Physicians and Patient (15th cent woodcut)

1979. 150th Anniv of National Academy of Medicine.
1770	**924**	2cr.50 yellow and black	55	30

925 Clover with Hearts as Leaves

1979. 35th Brazilian Cardiology Congress.
1771	**925**	2cr.50 multicoloured	55	30

926 Hotel Nacional, Rio de Janeiro

1979. Brasiliana 79 (2nd issue). Sheet 87×124 mm.
MS1772	**926**	12cr.50 multicoloured	2·30	2·50

927 Cithaerias aurora

1979. Brasiliana 79 (2nd issue). Butterflies. Multicoloured.
1773	2cr.50 Type **927**	45	20
1774	10cr.50 Evenus regalis	1·70	45
1775	12cr. Caligo eurilochus	1·70	65
1776	12cr.50 Diaethria clymena janeira	1·90	75

928 Embraer Xingu

1979. Tenth Anniv of Brazilian Aeronautical Industry.
1777	**928**	2cr.50 dp blue and blue	55	30

929 Globe illuminating Land

1979. National Week.
1778	**929**	3cr.20 blue, green & yell	55	30

930 Our Lady Aparecida

1979. 75th Anniv of Coronation of Our Lady Aparecida.
1779	**930**	2cr.50 multicoloured	55	30

931 Envelope and Transport

1979. 18th UPU Congress, Rio de Janeiro (4th issue). Multicoloured.
1780	2cr.50 Type **931**	55	30
1781	2cr.50 Post Office emblems	55	30
1782	10cr.50 Globe	1·10	95
1783	12cr. Flags of Brazil and UPU	1·60	1·30
1784	12cr.50 UPU emblem	1·80	1·50

932 Igreja da Gloria

1979. Brasiliana 79 Third World Thematic Stamp Exhibition (3rd issue). Paintings by Leandro Joaquim. Multicoloured.
1785	2cr.50 Type **932**	45	30
1786	12cr. Fishing on Guanabara Bay	1·40	1·10
1787	12cr. Boqueirao Lake and Carioca Arches	1·60	1·30

933 Pyramid Fountain, Rio de Janeiro

1979. Brasiliana 79 (4th issue). 1st International Exhibition of Classical Philately. Fountains.
1788	**933**	2cr.50 black, grn & emer	45	30
1789	-	10cr.50 black, turq & bl	1·00	75
1790	-	12cr. black, red and pink	1·40	1·10

DESIGNS—VERT: 12cr. Boa Vista, Recife. HORIZ: 10cr.50, Marilia Fountain, Ouro Preto.

934 World Map

1979. Third World Telecommunications Exhibition, Geneva.
1791	**934**	2cr.50 multicoloured	55	30

935 "UPU" and Emblem

1979. UPU Day.
1792	**935**	2cr.50 multicoloured	55	45
1793	**935**	10cr.50 multicoloured	1·30	1·10
1794	**935**	12cr. multicoloured	1·40	1·20
1795	**935**	12cr.50 multicoloured	1·60	1·30

936 "Peteca" (shuttlecock)

1979. International Year of the Child. Multicoloured.
1796	2cr.50 Type **936**	55	45
1797	3cr.20 Spinning top	70	55
1798	3cr.20 Jumping Jack	70	55
1799	3cr.20 Rag doll	70	55

937 The Birth of Jesus

1979. Christmas. Tiles from the Church of Our Lady of Health and Glory, Salvador. Multicoloured.
1800	3cr.20 Type **937**	55	30
1801	3cr.20 Adoration of the Kings	55	30
1802	3cr.20 The Boy Jesus among the Doctors	55	30

938 Hands reading Braille

1979. 150th Anniv of First Braille Publication. Sheet 127×88 mm.
MS1803	**938**	3cr.20 multicoloured	1·10	1·10

939 Woman with Wheat

1979. Thanksgiving Day.
1804	**939**	3cr.20 multicoloured	55	30

940 Steel Mill

1979. 25th Anniv of Cosipa Steel Works, Sao Paulo.
1805	**940**	3cr.20 multicoloured	55	30

941 Plant within Raindrop

1980. Energy Conservation. Multicoloured.
1806	3cr.20 Type **941**	55	30
1807	17cr.+7cr. Sun and lightbulb	2·75	1·30
1808	20cr.+8cr. Windmill and lightbulb	3·50	1·60
1809	21cr.+9cr. Dam and lightbulb	4·75	1·70

942 Coal Trucks

1980. Coal Industry.
1810	**942**	4cr. black, orge & red	55	30

943 Coconuts

1980
1811	**943**	2cr. brown	25	10
1812	-	3cr. red	35	10
1813	-	4cr. orange	55	10
1814	-	5cr. violet	25	10
1815	-	7cr. orange	55	20
1816	-	10cr. green	25	10
1817	-	12cr. green	45	20
1818	-	15cr. brown	25	10
1819	-	17cr. red	55	20
1820	-	20cr. brown	25	10
1821	-	24cr. orange	2·30	20
1822	-	30cr. black	2·50	30
1823	-	34cr. brown	9·75	1·50
1824	-	38cr. red	3·50	85
1825	-	42cr. green	17·00	1·70
1825a	-	45cr. brown	25	10
1826	-	50cr. orange	55	20
1826a	-	57cr. brown	2·50	1·80
1826b	-	65cr. purple	45	20
1827	-	66cr. violet	13·50	1·90
1827a	-	80cr. red	1·10	95
1828	-	100cr. brown	4·75	30
1828a	-	120cr. blue	1·30	30
1829	-	140cr. red	8·00	95

1829a	-	150cr. green	70	20
1830	-	200cr. green	2·30	30
1830a	-	300cr. purple	2·50	45
1831	-	500cr. brown	2·50	45
1832	-	800cr. green	2·75	45
1833	-	1000cr. olive	2·75	45
1834	-	2000cr. orange	2·75	55

DESIGNS: 3cr. Mangoes; 4cr. Corn; 5cr. Onions; 7cr. Oranges; 10cr. Passion fruit; 12cr. Pineapple; 15cr. Bananas; 17cr. Guarana; 20cr. Sugar cane; 24cr. Bee and honeycomb; 30cr. Silkworm and mulberry; 34cr. Cocoa beans; 38cr. Coffee; 42cr. Soya bean; 45cr. Manioc; 50cr. Wheat; 57cr. Peanuts; 65cr. Rubber; 66cr. Grapes; 80cr. Brazil nuts; 100cr. Cashews; 120cr. Rice; 140cr. Tomatoes; 150cr. Eucalyptus; 200cr. Castor-oil bean; 300cr. Parana pine; 500cr. Cotton; 800cr. Carnauba palm; 1000cr. Babassu palm; 2000cr. Sunflower.

944 Banknote with Development Symbols

1980. 21st Inter-American Bank of Development Directors' Annual Assembly Meeting, Rio de Janeiro.

1836	**944**	4cr. blue, brown & blk	55	30

945 Tapirape Mask

1980. Indian Art. Ritual Masks. Multicoloured.

1837		4cr. Type **945**	55	30
1838		4cr. Tukuna mask (vert)	55	30
1839		4cr. Kanela mask (vert)	55	30

946 Geometric Head

1980. 30th Anniv of Brazilian Television.

1840	**946**	4cr. multicoloured	55	30

947 *Duke of Caxias* (after Miranda Junior)

1980. Death Centenary of Duke de Caxias (General and statesman).

1841	**947**	4cr. multicoloured	55	30

948 *The Labourer* (Candido Portinari)

1980. Art in Brazilian Museums. Multicoloured.

1842		24cr. Type **948**	2·50	1·20
1843		28cr. *Mademoiselle Pogany* (statuette, Constantin Brancusi)	2·75	1·30
1844		30cr. *The Glass of Water* (A. de Figueiredo)	4·00	1·50

MUSEUMS. 24cr. Sao Paulo Museum of Art. 28cr. Rio de Janeiro Museum of Modern Art. 30cr. Rio de Janeiro Museum of Fine Art.

949 *Graf Zeppelin* flying through "50"

1980. 0th Annivs of "*Graf Zeppelin* and First South Atlantic Air Mail Flight.

1845	**949**	4cr. black, blue & violet	1·00	45
1846	-	4cr. multicoloured	1·00	45

DESIGN: No. 1846, Latecoere seaplane *Comte de la Vaulx*.

950 Sail and Bone-lace "Sun"

1980. Brapex IV National Stamp Exhibition, Fortaleza. Sheet 125×87 mm.

MS1847 **950**	30cr. multicoloured	2·30	3·25

951 Pope John Paul II and Fortaleza Cathedral

1980. Papal Visit and 10th National Eucharistic Congress. Pope John Paul II and cathedrals. Multicoloured.

1848		4cr. Type **951**	55	30
1849		4cr. St. Peter's, Rome (horiz)	55	30
1850		24cr. Apericida (horiz)	1·90	75
1851		28cr. Rio de Janeiro (horiz)	2·10	85
1852		30cr. Brasilia (horiz)	3·75	95

952 Shooting

1980. Olympic Games, Moscow. Multicoloured.

1853		4cr. Type **952**	55	30
1854		4cr. Cycling	55	30
1855		4cr. Rowing	55	30

953 Classroom

1980. Rondon Project (voluntary student work in rural areas).

1856	**953**	4cr. multicoloured	55	30

954 Helen Keller and Anne Sullivan

1980. Birth Centenary of Helen Keller, and 4th Brazilian Congress on Prevention of Blindness, Belo Horizonte.

1857	**954**	4cr. multicoloured	55	30

955 Sao Francisco River Canoe

1980. Stamp Day. Sheet 125×86 mm.

MS1858 **955**	24cr. multicoloured	2·30	2·40

956 Houses and Microscope

1980. National Health Day. Campaign against Chagas Disease (barber bug fever).

1859	**956**	4cr. multicoloured	55	30

957 Communications Equipment

1980. 15th Anniv of National Telecommunications System.

1860	**957**	5cr. stone, blue & green	55	30

958 Hands with Lily

1980. Sixth World Union of St. Gabriel (Religious Philately Federation) Congress, Sao Paulo. Sheet 124×86 mm.

MS1861 **958**	30cr. multicoloured	2·30	2·30

959 *Cattleya amethysto-glossa*

1980. Espamer 80 International Stamp Exhibition, Madrid. Orchids. Multicoloured.

1862		5cr. Type **959**	55	30
1863		5cr. *Laelia cinnabarina*	55	30
1864		24cr. *Zygopetalum crinitum*	2·30	1·20
1865		28cr. *Laelia tenebrosa*	2·30	1·20

960 Vinaceous Amazon

1980. Lubrapex 80 Portuguese–Brazilian Stamp Exhibition, Lisbon. Parrots. Multicoloured.

1866		5cr. Type **960**	80	50
1867		5cr. Red-tailed amazon	80	50
1868		28cr. Red-spectacled amazon	5·25	2·10
1869		28cr. Brown backed parrotlet	5·25	2·10

961 Captain Rodrigo (fictional character)

1980. Book Day and Erico Verissimo (writer). Commemoration.

1870	**961**	5cr. multicoloured	55	30

962 Flight into Egypt

1980. Christmas.

1871	**962**	5cr. multicoloured	55	30

963 Wave-form

1980. Inauguration of Telecommunications Centre for Research and Development, Campanas City.

1872	**963**	5cr. multicoloured	70	30

964 Carvalho Viaduct, Paranagua–Curitiba Railway Line

1980. Centenary of Engineering Club.

1873	**964**	5cr. multicoloured	80	35

965 Postal Chessboard

1980. Postal Chess.

1874	**965**	5cr. multicoloured	70	45

966 Sun and Wheat

1980. Thanksgiving Day.

1875	**966**	5cr. multicoloured	55	30

967 Father Anchieta writing Poem in Sand

1980. Beatification of Father Jose de Anchieta.

1876	**967**	5cr. multicoloured	55	30

968 Christ on the Mount of Olives

1980. 250th Birth Anniv of Antonio Lisboa (Aleijadinho) (sculptor). Wood sculptures of Christ's head. Multicoloured.

1877		5cr. Type **968**	70	45
1878		5cr. The Arrest in the Garden	70	45
1879		5cr. Flagellation	70	45
1880		5cr. Wearing Crown of Thorns	70	45
1881		5cr. Carrying the cross	70	45
1882		5cr. Crucifixion	70	45

969 Agricultural Produce

1981. Agricultural Development. Multicoloured.

1883		30cr. Type **969**	2·75	65
1884		35cr. Shopping	2·30	65
1885		40cr. Exporting	2·30	65

970 Scout sitting by Camp Fire

1981. Fourth Pan-American Jamboree. Multicoloured.

1886		5cr. Type **970**	55	10
1887		5cr. Troop cooking	55	10
1888		5cr. Scout with totem pole	55	10

971 First-class
Mailman
(Empire period)

1981. 50th Anniv of Integrated Post Office and Telegraph
Department (DCT). Sheet 99×70 mm containing T
971 and similar vert designs. Multicoloured.
MS1889 30cr. Type **971**; 35cr. DCT
mailman; 40cr. Telegraph messenger
(first republic) 8·50 8·50

972 The Hunter and the
Jaguar

1981. Death Centenary of Felix Emile, Baron of Tauny
(artist). Sheet 70×90 mm.
MS1890 **972** 30cr. multicoloured 3·00 3·25

973 Lima Barreto and Rio
de Janeiro Street Scene

1981. Birth Centenary of Lima Barreto (author).
1891 **973** 7cr. multicoloured 60 25

974 Tupi-Guarani
Ceramic Funeral Urn

1981. Artefacts from Brazilian Museums. Multicoloured.
1892 7cr. Type **974** (Archaeology
and Popular Arts Museum,
Paranagua) 60 25
1893 7cr. Marajoara "tanga" ceramic
loincloth (Emilio Goeldi Mu-
seum, Para) 60 25
1894 7cr. Maraca tribe funeral urn
(National Museum, Rio de
Janeiro) 60 25

975 Ruby-topaz
Hummingbird

1981. Hummingbirds. Multicoloured.
1895 7cr. Type **975** 1·70 55
1896 7cr. Horned sungem 1·70 55
1897 7cr. Frilled coquette 1·70 55
1898 7cr. Planalto hermit 1·70 55

976 Hands and
Cogwheels

1981. 72nd Int Rotary Convention, Sao Paulo.
1899 **976** 7cr. red and black 45 45
1900 - 35cr. multicoloured 2·20 1·60
DESIGN: 35cr. Head and cogwheels.

977 "Protection of the
Water"

1981. Environment Protection. Multicoloured.
1901 7cr. Type **977** 70 20
1902 7cr. "Protection of the forests" 70 20

1903 7cr. "Protection of the air" 70 20
1904 7cr. "Protection of the soil" 70 20

978 Curtiss Fledgling

1981. 50th Anniv of National Air Mail Service.
1905 **978** 7cr. multicoloured 1·00 45

979 Locomotive Colonel
Church and Map of Railway

1981. 50th Anniv of Madeira–Mamore Railway
Nationalization.
1906 **979** 7cr. multicoloured 1·40 55

980 Esperanto Star and
Arches of Alvorada
Governmental Palace,
Brasilia

1981. 66th World Esperanto Congress, Brasilia.
1907 **980** 7cr. green, grey & black 45 20

981 Pedro II and 50r.
"Small Head" Stamp

1981. Centenary of Pedro II "Small Head" Stamps.
1908 **981** 50cr. brown, blk & bl 2·75 55
1909 - 55cr. mauve and green 2·75 55
1910 - 60cr. blue, black & orge 2·75 55
DESIGNS: 55cr. Pedro II and 100r. "Small Head" stamp; 60r.
Pedro II and 200r. "Small Head" stamp.

982 Military Institute of
Engineering

1981. 50th Anniv of Military Institute of Engineering.
1911 **982** 12cr. multicoloured 45 30

983 Caboclinhos
Folkdance

1981. Festivities. Multicoloured.
1912 50cr. Type **983** 1·90 55
1913 55cr. Marujada folk festival 1·90 55
1914 60cr. Resado parade 1·90 55

984 Sun and Erect,
Drooping, and
Supported Flowers

1981. International Year of Disabled Persons.
1915 **984** 12cr. multicoloured 45 10

985 Dalechampia
capero-niodes

1981. Flowers of the Central Plateau. Multicoloured.
1916 12cr. Type **985** 1·10 45

1917 12cr. Palicourea rigida 1·10 45
1918 12cr. Eremanthus sphaerocepha-
lus (vert) 1·10 45
1919 12cr. Cassia clausseni (vert) 1·10 45

986 Image of Our
Lady of Nazareth

1981. Festival of Our Lady of Nazareth, Belem.
1920 **986** 12cr. multicoloured 45 30

987 Christ the
Redeemer
Monument

1981. 50th Anniv of Christ the Redeemer Monument, Rio
de Janeiro.
1921 **987** 12cr. multicoloured 45 30

988 Farmhands seeding
the Land

1981. World Food Day.
1922 **988** 12cr. multicoloured 45 30

989 Santos Dumont and
Biplane 14 bis landing at
Paris

1981. 75th Anniv of Santos Dumont's First Powered
Flight.
1923 **989** 60cr. multicoloured 2·20 65

990 Friar Santos Rita Durao,
Title Page and Scene from
Caramuru

1981. Book Day and Bicentenary of Publication of Epic
Poem Caramuru.
1924 **990** 12cr. multicoloured 45 30

991 Crib, Juazeiro de
Norte (Cica)

1981. Christmas. Various designs showing Cribs.
Multicoloured.
1925 12cr. Type **991** 45 30
1926 50cr. Caruaru (Vitalino Filho) 2·75 45
1927 55cr. Sao Jose dos Campos
(Eugenia) (vert) 2·75 45
1928 60cr. Taubate (Candida) (vert) 2·75 55

992 Alagoas

1981. State Flags (1st series). Multicoloured.
1929 12cr. Type **992** 55 55
1930 12cr. Bahia 55 55
1931 12cr. Federal District 55 55
1932 12cr. Pernambuco 55 55
1933 12cr. Sergipe 55 55
See also Nos. 1988/92, 2051/5, 2113/17, 2204/7 and
3043/4.

993 Girls with
Wheat

1981. Thanksgiving Day.
1934 **993** 12cr. multicoloured 45 30

994 Heads and Symbols
of Occupations

1981. 50th Anniv of Ministry of Labour.
1935 **994** 12cr. multicoloured 55 30

995 Federal Engineering
School, Itajuba

1981. Birth Centenary of Theodomiro Carneiro Santiago
(founder of Federal Engineering School).
1936 **995** 15cr. green and mauve 90 45

996 Musician of
Police Military
Band and
Headquarters

1981. 150th Anniv of Sao Paulo Military Police.
Multicoloured.
1937 12cr. Type **996** 45 10
1938 12cr. Lancers of Ninth of July
Regiment, Mounted Police 45 10

997 Army Library "Ex
Libris"

1981. Centenary of Army Library.
1939 **997** 12cr. multicoloured 45 30

998 Envelope and "Bull's Eye"
Stamp

1981. 50th Anniv of Philatelic Club of Brazil. Sheet 89×69
mm.
MS1940 **998** 180cr. bistre, blue and
black 9·75 9·75

999 Brigadier Eduardo
Gomes

1982. Brigadier Eduardo Gomes Commem.
1941 **999** 12cr. blue and black 70 45

1000 Lage, Coal Trucks,
Ita freighter and HL-1
Airplane

1981. Birth Cent of Henrique Lage (industrialist).
1942 **1000** 17cr. multicoloured 1·60 45

1001 Tackle

1982. World Cup Football Championship, Spain. Multicoloured.

1943	75cr. Type **1001**	2·30	65
1944	80cr. Kicking ball	2·30	65
1945	85cr. Goalkeeper	2·30	65
MS1946	125×87 mm. 100cr.×3. As Nos. 1943/5. Imperf	8·00	8·00

1002 Microscope, Bacillus and Lung

1982. Centenary of Robert Koch's Discovery of Tubercle Bacillus. Multicoloured.

1947	90cr. Type **1002**	5·25	1·90
1948	100cr. Flasks, tablets, syringe, bacillus and lung	5·25	1·90

1003 *Laelia purpurata*

1982. Brapex V National Stamp Exhibition, Santa Catarina. Sheet 100×70 mm containing T **1003** and similar vert designs showing orchids. Multicoloured.

MS1949	75cr. Type **1003**; 80cr. *Oncidium flexuosum*; 85cr. *Cleistes revolute*	13·50	13·50

1004 Oil Rig Workers

1982. Birth Centenary of Monteiro Lobato (writer).

1950	**1004** 17cr. multicoloured	55	30

1005 St. Vincent de Paul

1982. 400th Birth Anniv of St. Vincent de Paul.

1951	**1005** 17cr. multicoloured	55	30

1006 Fifth Fall

1982. Guaira's Seven Falls. Multicoloured.

1952	17cr. Type **1006**	55	30
1953	21cr. Seventh fall	70	45

1007 Envelope, Telephone, Antenna and Postcode

1982. 15th Anniv of Ministry of Communications.

1954	**1007** 21cr. multicoloured	65	35

1008 The Old Arsenal (National Historical Museum)

1982. 50th Anniv of Museology Course.

1955	**1008** 17cr. black and pink	65	35

1009 Cogwheels and Ore Mountains

1982. 40th Anniv of Vale do Rio Doce Company.

1956	**1009** 17cr. multicoloured	65	35

1010 Martim Afonso de Souza proclaiming Sao Vicente a Town

1982. 450th Anniv of Sao Vicente.

1957	**1010** 17cr. multicoloured	70	45

1011 Giant Anteater

1982. Animals. Multicoloured.

1958	17cr. Type **1011**	1·30	45
1959	21cr. Maned wolf	1·40	50
1960	30cr. Pampas deer	3·75	55

1012 Film and "Golden Palm"

1982. 20th Anniv of "Golden Palm" Film Award to "The Given World".

1961	**1012** 17cr. multicoloured	55	30

1013 Obelisk with Reliefs illustrating Verses by Guilherme de Almeida

1982. 50th Anniv of Sao Paulo Revolutionary Government. Sheet 70×100 mm.

MS1962	**1013** 140cr. black and blue	5·25	5·25

1014 Church of Our Lady of O, Sabara

1982. Baroque-style Architecture in Minas Gerais. Multicoloured.

1963	17cr. Type **1014**	90	20
1964	17cr. Church of Our Lady of Carmo, Mariana (horiz)	90	20
1965	17cr. Church of Our Lady of Rosary, Diamantina (horiz)	90	20

1015 St. Francis of Assisi

1982. 800th Birth Anniv of St. Francis of Assisi.

1966	**1015** 21cr. multicoloured	55	30

1016 "Large Head" Stamp of 1882

1982. Centenary of Pedro II "Large Head" Stamps.

1967	**1016** 21cr. yellow, brn & blk	55	30

1017 Amazon River and Hands holding Seedling, Screw and Coin

1982. Manaus Free Trade Zone.

1968	**1017** 75cr. multicoloured	2·10	65

1018 Lord Baden-Powell

1982. 125th Birth Anniv of Lord Baden Powell and 75th Anniv of Boy Scout Movement. Sheet 100×70 mm containing T **1018** and similar vert design. Multicoloured.

MS1969	85cr. Type **1018**; 185cr. Scout saluting	10·50	10·50

1019 Xango

1982. Orixas Religious Costumes. Multicoloured.

1970	20cr. Type **1019**	50	10
1971	20cr. Iemanja	50	10
1972	20cr. Oxumare	50	10

1020 XII Florin

1982. Tenth Anniv of Brazilian Central Bank Values Museum. Multicoloured.

1973	25cr. Type **1020**	55	30
1974	25cr. Pedro I Coronation piece	55	30

1021 *Ipiranga Cry* (Dom Pedro proclaiming independence)

1982. Independence Week.

1975	**1021** 25cr. multicoloured	90	55

1022 St. Theresa of Jesus

1982. 400th Death Anniv of St. Theresa of Jesus.

1976	**1022** 85cr. multicoloured	2·40	55

1023 Musical Instrument Maker

1982. Lubrapex 82 Brazilian–Portuguese Stamp Exhibition, Curitiba. The Paranaense Fandango. Multicoloured.

1977	75cr. Type **1023**	2·00	1·10
1978	80cr. Dancers	2·00	1·10
1979	85cr. Musicians	2·00	1·10
MS1980	100×70 mm. Nos. 1977/9	8·00	8·00

1024 Embraer Tucano Trainers

1982. Aeronautical Industry Day.

1981	**1024** 24cr. multicoloured	55	25

1025 Bastos Tigre and Verse from *Saudade*

1982. Day of the Book and Birth Centenary of Bastos Tigre (poet).

1982	**1025** 24cr. multicoloured	55	30

1026 Telephone Dial on Map of Brazil

1982. TEnth Anniv of Telebras (Brazilian Telecommunications Corporation).

1983	**1026** 24cr. multicoloured	55	30

1027 Nativity (C.S. Miyaba)

1982. Christmas. Children's Paintings. Multicoloured.

1984	24cr. Type **1027**	2·10	10
1985	24cr. Choir of Angels (N. N. Aleluia)	2·10	10
1986	30cr. Holy Family (F. T. Filho)	2·10	20
1987	30cr. "ativity with Angel (N. Arand)	2·10	20

1982. State Flags (2nd series). As T **992**. Multicoloured.

1988	24cr. Ceara	2·30	65
1989	24cr. Espirito Santo	2·30	65
1990	24cr. Paraiba	2·30	65
1991	24cr. Rio Grande do Norte	2·30	65
1992	24cr. Rondonia	2·30	65

1028 "Germination"

1982. Thanksgiving Day.

1993	**1028** 24cr. multicoloured	90	20

1029 *Efeta* (S. Tempel)

1982. The Hard of Hearing.
1994 1029 24cr. multicoloured 70 45

1030 *Benjamin Constant*
(cadet ship)

1982. Bicentenary of Naval Academy. Multicoloured.
1995 24cr. Type **1030** 1·10 45
1996 24cr. *Almirante Saldanha* (cadet ship) 1·10 45
1997 24cr. *Brasil* (training frigate) 1·10 45

1031 300r.
Stamp of 1845

1982. Brasiliana 83 International Stamp Exhibition, Rio de Janeiro (1st issue). Sheet 99×69 mm.
MS1998 **1031** 200cr. black, ochre and blue 8·50 8·50
See Also Nos. 1999/2002, 2029/**MS**2032 and **MS**2033.

1032 Samba Parade
Drummers

1983. Brasiliana 83 International Stamp Exhibition, Rio de Janeiro. Carnival. Multicoloured.
1999 24cr. Type **1032** 1·10 45
2000 130cr. Masked clowns 4·00 1·10
2001 140cr. Dancer 4·00 1·10
2002 150cr. Indian 4·00 1·10

1033 Support Ship *Barao de Teffe* in Antarctic

1983. First Brazilian Antarctic Expedition.
2003 1033 150cr. multicoloured 4·50 1·20

1034 Woman
with Ballot Paper

1983. 50th Anniv of Women's Suffrage in Brazil.
2004 **1034** 130cr. multicoloured 2·75 95

1035 Itaipu Dam

1983. Itaipu Brazilian–Paraguayan Hydro-electric Project.
2005 1035 140cr. multicoloured 4·50 85

1036 Luther

1983. 500th Birth Anniv of Martin Luther (Protestant reformer).
2006 1036 150cr. deep green, green and black 3·50 65

1037 Microscope
and Crab

1983. Cancer Prevention. 30th Anniv of Antonio Prudente Foundation and A.C. Camargo Hospital. Multicoloured.
2007 30cr. Type **1037** 50 45
2008 38cr. Antonio Prudente, hospital and crab 50 45

1038 Tissue Culture

1983. Agricultural Research. Multicoloured.
2009 30cr. Type **1038** 50 10
2010 30cr. Brazilian wild chestnut tree 50 10
2011 38cr. Tropical soya beans 55 15

1039 Friar
Rogerio
Neuhaus before
Altar

1983. Cent of Ordination of Friar Rogerio Neuhaus.
2012 **1039** 30cr. multicoloured 50 10

1040 Council Emblem and
World Map

1983. 30th Anniv of Customs Co-operation Council.
2013 **1040** 30cr. multicoloured 50 10

1041 Satellite

1983. World Communications Year.
2014 **1041** 250cr. multicoloured 4·75 1·40

1042 Toco Toucan

1983. Toucans. Multicoloured.
2015 30cr. Type **1042** 1·10 35
2016 185cr. Red-billed toucan 4·00 1·10
2017 205cr. Red-breasted toucan 4·25 1·20
2018 215cr. Channel-billed toucan 4·50 1·30

1043 *The Resurrection*

1983. 500th Birth Anniv of Raphael (artist). Sheet 70×90 mm.
MS2019 **1043** 250cr. multicoloured 6·75 7·00

1044 Baldwin Locomotive
No. 1, 1881

1983. Locomotives. Multicoloured.
2020 30cr. Type **1044** 95 55
2021 30cr. Hohenzollern locomotive No. 980, 1875 95 55
2022 38cr. Locomotive No. 1 *Maria Fumaca*, 1868 95 55

1045 Basketball
Players

1983. Ninth Women's World Basketball Championship, Sao Paulo.
2023 30cr. Type **1045** 45 10
2024 30cr. Basketball players (different) 45 10

1046 *Bolivar* (after Tito
Salas)

1983. Birth Bicentenary of Simon Bolivar.
2025 **1046** 30cr. multicoloured 45 10

1047 Boy with Kite and
Boy waiting for Polio
Vaccination

1983. Polio and Measles Vaccination Campaign. Multicoloured.
2026 30cr. Type **1047** 50 20
2027 30cr. Girl on bicycle and girl receiving measles vaccination 50 20

1048 Minerva
and Computer
Punched Tape

1983. 20th Anniv of Post-graduate Master's Programmes in Engineering.
2028 **1048** 30cr. light brown, blue and brown 50 20

1049 30r. "Bulls
Eye" Stamp and
Rio de Janeiro
Bay

1983. Brasiliana 83 International Stamp Exhibition, Rio de Janeiro. 140th Anniv of "Bull's Eye" Stamps.
2029 **1049** 185cr. black and blue 2·50 85
2030 - 205cr. black and blue 2·50 85
2031 - 215cr. black and violet 2·50 85
MS2032 100×70 mm. 185cr., 205cr., 215cr. each black and blue 20·00 21·00
DESIGNS: Nos. 2030/1, As Type **1049** but showing 60r. and 90r. "Bull's-Eye" stamp respectively; No. **MS**2032, "Bull's-Eye" stamp on each value as for Nos. 2029/31, and composite design of Rio de Janeiro Bay across the three.

1050 Montgolfier
Balloon

1983. Brasiliana 83 International Stamp Exhibition, Rio de Janeiro (4th issue). Five sheets 105×149 mm (a, d) or 149×105 mm (others), each containing design as T **1050**. Multicoloured.
MS2033 Five sheets (a) 2000cr. Type **1050** (Bicentary of manned flight); (b) 2000cr. Racing car (Formula 1 champions 1972, 1974, 1981); (c) 2000cr. "Tornado" and "Class 470" sailing dinghies (Olympic sailing champion, 1980); (d) 2000cr. Triple jumper (Olympic triple jump champions, 1952, 1956); (e) 2000cr. World Cup and footballer (World Cup champions, 1958, 1962, 1970) £225 £225

1051 *The First
Mass in Brazil*

1983. 150th Birth Anniv (1982) of Victor Meireles (artist). Sheet 100×70 mm.
MS2034 **1051** 250cr. multicoloured 7·00 7·00

1052 Embracer EMB-120
Brasilia

1983. Brazilian Aeronautics Industry.
2035 **1052** 30cr. multicoloured 50 20

1053 Bosco and State
Departments Esplanade,
Brasilia

1983. Dom Bosco's Dream of Brazil.
2036 **1053** 130cr. multicoloured 1·60 45

1054 Council of State
decides on Independence
(detail, Georgina de
Albuquerque)

1983. National Week.
2037 **1054** 50cr. multicoloured 75 35

1055 Iron and Steel
Production

1983. Tenth Anniv of Siderbras (Brazilian Steel Corporation).
2038 **1055** 45cr. multicoloured 65 15

1056 *Pilosocereus
gounellei*

1983. Cacti. Multicoloured.

2039	45cr. Type **1056**	1·30	35
2040	45cr. *Melocactus bahiensis*	1·30	35
2041	57cr. *Cereus jamacari*	1·50	35

1057 Monstrance

1983. 50th Anniv of National Eucharistic Congress.

| 2042 | **1057** | 45cr. multicoloured | 1·00 | 35 |

1058 Mouth and Wheat

1983. 20th Anniv of World Food Programme. Fishery Resources. Multicoloured.

| 2043 | 45cr. Type **1058** | 1·30 | 20 |
| 2044 | 57cr. Fish and fishing pirogue | 2·50 | 45 |

1059 Telegraph Key and Praca da Republica, Rio de Janeiro

1983. Death Centenary of Louis Breguet (telegraph pioneer). Sheet 70×99 mm.

| MS2045 | **1059** | 376cr. multicoloured | 11·50 | 11·50 |

1060 *Our Lady of Angels* (wood, Franisco Xavier de Brito)

1983. Christmas. Statues of the Madonna. Multicoloured.

2046	45cr. Type **1060**	1·30	35
2047	315cr. *Our Lady of Birth*	3·50	1·20
2048	335cr. *Our Lady of Joy* (fired clay, Agostinho de Jesus)	3·50	1·30
2049	345cr. *Our Lady of Presentation*	3·50	1·40

1061 Moraes and Map of Italian Campaign

1983. Birth Centenary of Marshal Mascarenhas de Moraes.

| 2050 | **1061** | 45cr. pink, green & pur | 50 | 20 |

1983. State Flags (3rd series). As Type **992**. Multicoloured.

2051	45cr. Amazonas	1·00	55
2052	45cr. Goias	1·00	55
2053	45cr. Rio de Janeiro	1·00	55
2054	45cr. Mato Grosso do Sul	1·00	55
2055	45cr. Parana	1·00	55

1062 Praying Figure and Wheat

1983. Thanksgiving Day.

| 2056 | **1062** | 45cr. multicoloured | 75 | 35 |

1063 Friar Vincente Borgard

1983. Obligatory Tax. Anti-leprosy Week.

| 2057 | **1063** | 10cr. brown | 3·25 | 1·60 |

1064 Montgolfier Balloon

1983. Bicentenary of Manned Flight.

| 2058 | **1064** | 345cr. multicoloured | 10·00 | 3·00 |

1065 Indian, Portuguese Navigator and Negro

1984. 50th Anniv of Publication of *Masters and Slaves* by Gilberto Freyre.

| 2059 | **1065** | 45cr. multicoloured | 50 | 35 |

1066 Crystal Palace

1984. Centenary of Crystal Palace, Petropolis.

| 2060 | **1066** | 45cr. multicoloured | 50 | 35 |

1067 *Monument of the Flags*, Sao Paulo

1984. 90th Birth Anniv of Victor Brecheret (sculptor). Sheet 100×70 mm.

| MS2061 | **1067** | 805cr. multicoloured | 4·50 | 4·50 |

1068 *Don Afonso* (sail/steam warship) and Figurehead

1984. Cent of Naval Oceanographic Museum.

| 2062 | **1068** | 620cr. multicoloured | 3·25 | 1·10 |

1069 Manacled Hands and Beached Fishing Pirogue

1984. Centenary of Abolition of Slavery in Ceara and Amazonas. Multicoloured.

| 2063 | 585cr. Type **1069** | 2·30 | 60 |
| 2064 | 610cr. Emancipated slave | 2·40 | 65 |

1070 King Carl XVI Gustaf and Pres. Figueiredo

1984. Visit of King of Sweden. Sheet 98×69 mm.

| MS2065 | **1070** | 2105cr. multicoloured | 8·25 | 8·25 |

1071 Long Jumping

1984. Olympic Games, Los Angeles. Multicoloured.

2066	65cr. Type **1071**	1·30	45
2067	65cr. 100 metres	1·30	45
2068	65cr. Relay	1·30	45
2069	585cr. Pole vaulting	1·50	75
2070	610cr. High jumping	1·50	75
2071	620cr. Hurdling	1·50	75

1072 Oil Rigs and Blast Furnace

1984. Birth Cent (1983) of Getulio Vargas (President 1930–45 and 1951–54). Multicoloured.

2072	65cr. Type **1072**	50	10
2073	65cr. Ballot boxes and symbols of professions and trades	50	10
2074	65cr. Sugar refinery and electricity pylons	50	10

1073 Pedro Alvares Cabral

1984. Espana 84 International Stamp Exhibition, Madrid. Explorers. Multicoloured.

| 2075 | 65cr. Type **1073** | 75 | 20 |
| 2076 | 610cr. Christopher Columbus | 3·25 | 65 |

1074 Heads and Map of Americas

1984. Eighth Pan-American Surety Association General Assembly.

| 2077 | **1074** | 65cr. multicoloured | 50 | 35 |

1075 Chinese Painting

1984. Lubrapex 84 Brazilian-Portuguese Stamp Exhibition, Lisbon.

2078	**1075**	65cr. multicoloured	50	35
2079	-	585cr. multicoloured	2·00	75
2080	-	610cr. multicoloured	2·10	1·00
2081	-	620cr. multicoloured	2·30	1·00

DESIGNS: 585 to 620cr. Chinese paintings from Mariana Cathedral.

1076 FIFA Emblem

1984. 80th Anniv of International Federation of Football Associations. Sheet 98×68 mm.

| MS2082 | **1076** | 2115cr. mult | 7·50 | 7·50 |

1077 Marsh Deer and Great Egret

1984. Mato Grosso Flood Plain. Multicoloured.

2083	65cr. Type **1077**	1·30	45
2084	65cr. Jaguar, capybara and roseate spoonbill	1·30	45
2085	80cr. Alligator, jabiru and red-cowled cardinals	1·40	55

1078 *The First Letter Sent from Brazil* (Guido Mondin)

1079 Route Map and Dornier Wal Flying Boat

1984. First Anniv of Postal Union of the Americas and Spain H.Q., Montevideo, Uruguay.

| 2086 | **1078** | 65cr. multicoloured | 50 | 20 |

1984. 50th Anniv of First Trans-Oceanic Air Route. Multicoloured.

| 2087 | 610cr. Type **1079** | 2·50 | 1·00 |
| 2088 | 620cr. Support ship "Westfalen" and Dornier Wal | 2·75 | 1·10 |

1080 Mother and Baby

1984. Wildlife Preservation. Woolley Spider Monkey. Multicoloured.

| 2089 | 65cr. Type **1080** | 2·50 | 75 |
| 2090 | 80cr. Monkey in tree | 1·90 | 75 |

1081 Murrah Buffaloes

1984. Marajo Island Water Buffaloes. Designs showing different races. Multicoloured.

2091	65cr. Type **1081**	1·30	35
2092	65cr. Carabao buffaloes	1·30	35
2093	65cr. Mediterranean buffaloes	1·30	35

Nos. 2091/3 were issued together, *se-tenant*, forming a composite design.

1082 Headquarters, Salvador

1984. 150th Anniv of Economic Bank.

| 2094 | **1082** | 65cr. multicoloured | 25 | 10 |

1083 Da Luz Station, Sao Paulo

1984. Preservation of Historic Railway Stations. Multicoloured.

2095	65cr. Type **1083**	1·30	35
2096	65cr. Japeri station Rio de Janeiro	1·30	35
2097	80cr. Sao Joao del Rei station, Minas Gerais	1·30	35

1084 Girl Guide

1984. 65th Anniv of Girl Guides Movement in Brazil. Sheet 99×69 mm.

| MS2098 | **1084** | 585cr. multicoloured | 6·25 | 6·25 |

1086 Pedro I (Solano Peixoto Machado)

1984. 20th Anniv of National Housing Bank.
2099 **1085** 65cr. multicoloured 50 20

1085 Roof
protecting
Couple

1984. National Week. Designs showing children's
paintings. Multicoloured.
2100 100cr. Type **1086** 40 10
2101 100cr. Girl painting word
"BRASIL" (Juruce Maria Klein) 40 10
2102 100cr. Children of different
races under rainbow (Priscela
Barreto da Fonseca Bara) 40 10
2103 100cr. Caravels (Carlos Peixoto
Mangueira) 40 10

1087 Headquarters,
Mercury and Cogwheel

1984. 150th Anniv of Rio de Janeiro Commercial
Association.
2104 **1087** 100cr. multicoloured 50 20

1088 Pedro I

1984. 150th Death Anniv of Emperor Pedro I.
2105 **1088** 1000cr. multicoloured 4·50 2·40

1089 *Pycnoporus
sanguineus*

1984. Fungi. Multicoloured.
2106 120cr. Type **1089** 75 30
2107 1050cr. *Calvatia* sp. 3·25 1·00
2108 1080cr. *Pleurotus* sp. (horiz) 3·25 1·00

1090 Child
stepping from
Open Book

1984. Book Day. Children's Literature.
2109 **1090** 120cr. multicoloured 65 10

1091 New State
Mint and
17th-century
Minter

1984. Inauguration of New State Mint, Santa Cruz, Rio de
Janeiro.
2110 **1091** 120cr. blue & deep blue 65 10

1092 Computer Image of
Eye

1984. Informatica 84 17th National Information Congress
and Fourth International Informatics Fair, Rio de
Janeiro.
2111 **1092** 120cr. multicoloured 65 10

1093 Sculpture
by Bruno Giorgi
and Flags

1984. 14th General Assembly of Organization of
American States, Brasilia.
2112 **1093** 120cr. multicoloured 65 10

1984. State Flags (4th series). As T **992**.
2113 120cr. red, black & buff 1·00 65
2114 120cr. multicoloured 1·00 65
2115 120cr. multicoloured 1·00 65
2116 120cr. multicoloured 1·00 65
2117 120cr. multicoloured 1·00 65
DESIGNS: No. 2113, Minas Gerais; 2114, Mato Grosso;
2115, Piaui; 2116, Maranhao; 2117, Santa Catarina.

1094 Brasilia
Cathedral and
Wheat

1984. Thanksgiving Day.
2118 **1094** 120cr. multicoloured 65 10

1095
Father
Bento Dias
Pacheco

1984. Obligatory Tax. Anti-leprosy Week.
2119 **1095** 30cr. blue 75 35
See also Nos. 2208, 2263 and 2291.

1096 *Nativity* (Djanira da
Mota e Silva)

1984. Christmas. Paintings from Federal Savings Bank
collection. Multicoloured.
2120 120cr. Type **1096** 45 20
2121 120cr. *Virgin and Child* (Glauco
Rodrigues) 45 20
2122 1050cr. *Flight into Egypt* (Paul
Garfunkel) 2·50 75
2123 1080cr. *Nativity* (Emiliano
Augusto di Cavalcanti) 2·50 75

1097 Airbus Industrie
A300

1984. 40th Anniv of I.C.A.O.
2124 **1097** 120cr. multicoloured 65 20

1098 Symbols of
Agriculture and Industry
on Hat

1984. 25th Anniv of North-east Development Office.
2125 **1098** 120cr. multicoloured 50 20

1099 *Virgin of Safe
Journeys Church* (detail)

1985. 77th Death Anniv of Emilio Rouede (artist).
2126 **1099** 120cr. multicoloured 50 20

1100 "Brasilsat" over Brazil

1985. Launch of "Brasilsat" (first Brazilian
telecommunications satellite).
2127 **1100** 150cr. multicoloured 50 20

1101 Electric Trains and Plan
of Port Alegre Station

1985. Inauguration of Metropolitan Surface Railway,
Recife and Porto Alegre.
2128 **1101** 200cr. multicoloured 1·30 35

1102 Butternut Tree

1985. Opening of Botanical Gardens, Brasilia.
2129 **1102** 200cr. multicoloured 75 10

1103 Parachutist

1985. 40th Anniv of Military Parachuting.
2130 **1103** 200cr. multicoloured 75 10

1104 Map, Temperature Graph and
Weather Scenes

1985. National Climate Programme.
2131 **1104** 500cr. multicoloured 80 20

1105 Campolina

1985. Brazilian Horses. Multicoloured.
2132 1000cr. Type **1105** 2·10 55
2133 1500cr. Marajoara 2·75 65
2134 1500cr. Mangalarga pacer 2·75 65

1106 Ouro Preto

1985. UNESCO World Heritage Sites. Multicoloured.
2135 220cr. Type **1106** 40 10
2136 220cr. Sao Miguel das Missoes 40 10
2137 220cr. Olinda 40 10

1107
Polyvolume
(Mary Vieira)

1985. 40th Anniv of Rio-Branco Institute (diplomatic
training academy).
2138 **1107** 220cr. multicoloured 50 10

1108 National Theatre

1985. 25th Anniv of Brasilia. Multicoloured.
2139 220cr. Type **1108** 50 10
2140 220cr. Catetinho (home of
former President Juscelino
Keubitschek) and memorial 50 10

1109 Rondon and Morse
Telegraph

1985. 120th Birth Anniv of Marshal Candido Mariano da
Silva Rondon (military engineer and explorer).
2141 **1109** 220cr. multicoloured 50 10

1110 Fontoura
and
Pharmaceutical
Equipment

1985. Birth Centenary of Candido Fontoura (pharmacist).
2142 **1110** 220cr. multicoloured 50 10

1111 Lizards

1985. Rock Paintings. Multicoloured.
2143 300cr. Type **1111** 40 20
2144 300cr. Deer 40 20
2145 2000cr. Various animals 1·80 1·00
MS2146 100×70 mm. Nos. 2143/5 4·00 4·00
Nos. **MS**2146 is inscribed for Brapex VI national stamp
exhibition, Belo Horizonte.

1112 Numeral **1113** Numeral

1985
2147 **1112** 50cr. red 30 10
2148 **1112** 100cr. purple 30 10
2149 **1112** 150cr. lilac 30 10
2150 **1112** 200cr. blue 30 10
2151 **1112** 220cr. green 1·10 55
2152 **1112** 300cr. blue 30 10
2153 **1112** 500cr. black 40 20
2154 **1113** 1000cr. brown 30 10
2155 **1113** 2000cr. green 40 20
2156 **1113** 3000cr. lilac 45 20
2157 **1113** 5000cr. brown 2·20 20

1114 Common Noddies

1985. National Marine Park, Abrolhos. Multicolured.
2168 220cr. Type **1114** 1·20 40
2169 220cr. Magnificent frigate birds
and blue-faced booby 1·20 40
2170 220cr. Blue-faced boobies and
red-billed tropic bird 1·20 40
2171 2000cr. Grey plovers 3·50 75

1115
Breast-feeding

1985. United Nations Children's Fund Child Survival Campaign. Multicoloured.

2172	220cr. Type **1115**		35	15
2173	220cr. Growth chart and oral rehydration		35	15

1116 Bell 47J Ranger Helicopter rescuing Man, *Brasil* (corvette) and Diver

1985. International Sea Search and Rescue Convention, Rio de Janeiro.

2174	**1116**	220cr. multicoloured	60	40

1117 World Cup and Ball

1985. World Cup Football Championship, Mexico (1986) (1st issue). Sheet 70×99 mm.

MS2175	**1117**	2000cr. mult	8·25	8·25

See also No.**MS**2213.

1118 Children holding Hands

1985. International Youth Year.

2176	**1118**	220cr. multicoloured	45	25

1119 Hands holding Host

1985. 11th Nat Eucharistic Congress, Aparecida.

2177	**1119**	2000cr. multicoloured	1·70	75

1120 Scene from *Mineiro Blood*, Camera and Mauro

1985. 60th Anniv of Humberto Mauro's Cataguases Cycle of Films.

2178	**1120**	300cr. multicoloured	45	25

1121 Escola e Sacro Museum

1985. 400th Anniv of Paraiba State.

2179	**1121**	330cr. multicoloured	45	25

1122 Inconfidencia Museum, Ouro Preto

1985. Museums. Multicoloured.

2180	300cr. Type **1122**		35	15
2181	300cr. Historical and Diplomatic Museum Itamaraty		35	15

1123 *Cabano* (Guido Mondin)

1985. 150th Anniv of Cabanagem Insurrection, Belem City.

2182	**1123**	330cr. multicoloured	45	25

1124 Aeritalia/Aermacchi AM-X Fighter

1985. AM-X (military airplane) Project.

2183	**1124**	330cr. multicoloured	45	25

1125 Captain and Crossbowman (early 16th century)

1985. Military Dress. Multicoloured.

2184	300cr. Type **1125**		45	25
2185	300cr. Arquebusier and sergeant (late 16th cent)		45	25
2186	300cr. Musketeer and pikeman (early 17th century)		45	25
2187	300cr. Mulatto fusilier and pikeman with scimitar (early 17th century)		45	25

1126 *Farroupilha Rebels* (Guido Mondin)

1985. 150th Anniv of Farroupilha Revolution.

2188	**1126**	330cr. multicoloured	45	25

1127 Itaimbezinho Canyon

1985. Aparados da Serra National Park. Multicoloured.

2189	3100cr. Type **1127**		2·00	55
2190	3320cr. Mountain range		2·00	55
2191	3480cr. Pine forest		2·00	55

1128 Neves and Brasilia Buildings

1985. Tancredo Neves (President-elect) Commem.

2192	**1128**	330cr. black & orange	45	25

1129 "FEB" on Envelope

1985. 40th Anniv (1984) of Brazilian Expeditionary Force Postal Service.

2193	**1129**	500cr. multicoloured	45	25

1130 *Especuladora*, 1835

1985. 150th Anniv of Rio de Janeiro–Niteroi Ferry Service. Multicoloured.

2194	500cr. Type **1130**		60	30
2195	500cr. *Segunda*, 1862		60	30
2196	500cr. *Terceira*, 1911		60	30
2197	500cr. *Urca*, 1981		60	30

1131 Muniz M-7

1985. 50th Anniv of Muniz M-7 Biplane's Maiden Flight.

2198	**1131**	500cr. multicoloured	45	25

1132 Dove Emblem and Stylized Flags

1985. 40th Anniv of UNO.

2199	**1132**	500cr. multicoloured	45	25

1133 Front Page of First Edition

1985. 160th Anniv of *Pernambuco Daily News*.

2200	**1133**	500cr. multicoloured	45	25

1134 Adoration

1985. Christmas. Multicoloured.

2201	500cr. Type **1134**		45	25
2202	500cr. Adoration of the Magi		45	25
2203	500cr. Flight into Egypt		45	25

1985. State Flags (5th series). As T **992**. Multicoloured.

2204	500cr. Para		55	25
2205	500cr. Rio Grande do Sul		55	25
2206	500cr. Acre		55	25
2207	500cr. Sao Paulo		55	25

1985. Obligatory Tax. Anti-leprosy Week.

2208	**1095**	100cr. red	55	35

1135 Child holding Wheat

1985. Thanksgiving Day.

2209	**1135**	500cr. multicoloured	45	25

1136 Transport, Mined Ore and Trees

1985. Carajas Development Programme.

2210	**1136**	500cr. multicoloured	45	25

1137 Gusmao and Balloons

1985. 300th Birth Anniv of Bartolomeu Lourenco de Gusmao (inventor).

2211	**1137**	500cr. multicoloured	45	25

1138 The Trees

1985. Birth Centenary of Antonio Francisco da Costa e Silva (poet).

2212	**1138**	500cr. multicoloured	45	25

1139 Footballers

1986. World Cup Football Championship, Mexico (2nd issue) and Lubrepex 86 Brazilian—Portuguese Stamp Exhibition, Rio de Janeiro (1st issue). Sheet 69×99 mm.

MS2213	**1139**	10000cr. multicoloured	6·00	6·00

See also Nos. 2260/**MS**2262.

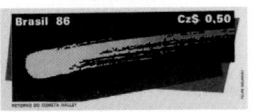

1140 Comet

1986. Appearance of Halley's Comet.

2214	**1140**	50c. multicoloured	45	25

1141 Flags and Station

1986. Second Anniv of Commander Ferraz Antarctic Station.

2215	**1141**	50c. multicoloured	45	25

1142 Symbols of Industry, Agriculture and Commerce

1986. Labour Day.

2216	**1142**	50c. multicoloured	45	25

1143 Maternity

1986. 50th Death Anniv of Henrique Bernardelli (artist).

2217	**1143**	50c. multicoloured	45	25

1144 Broken Chain Links as Birds

1986. 25th Anniv of Amnesty International.

2218	**1144**	50c. multicoloured	45	25

1145 *Pyrrhopyge ruficauda*

1986. Butterflies. Multicoloured.

2219	50c. Type **1145**	85	35
2220	50c. *Pierriballia mandela molione*	85	35
2221	50c. *Prepona eugenes diluta*	85	35

1146 Gomes Peri, and Score of *O Guarani*

1986. 150th Birth Anniv of Antonio Carlos Gomes (composer).

| 2222 | **1146** | 50c. multicoloured | 45 | 25 |

1147 Man in Safety Harness

1986. Prevention of Industrial Accidents.

| 2223 | **1147** | 50c. multicoloured | 45 | 25 |

1148 "Black Beard" 10r. Stamp

1986. Stamp Day. 120th Anniv of Pedro II Black Beard Stamps and 75th Anniv of Brazilian Philatelic Society. Sheet 69×99 mm.

| MS2224 **1148** 5cz. red and ochre | 2·00 | 2·00 |

1149 Garcia D'Avilas House Chapel, Nazare de Mata

1986

2225	**1149**	10c. green	35	10
2226	-	20c. blue	35	10
2228	-	50c. orange	1·10	25
2230	-	1cz. brown	35	10
2231	-	2cz. red	45	10
2233	-	5cz. green	1·30	25
2235	-	10cz. blue	1·10	25
2236	-	20cz. red	1·50	25
2238	-	50cz. orange	2·75	25
2240	-	100cz. green	2·75	25
2241	-	200cz. blue	2·75	25
2242	-	500cz. brown	3·50	80

DESIGNS—HORIZ: 20c. Church of Our Lady of the Assumptiom, Anchieta; 50c. Reis Magos Fortress, Natal; 1cz. Pelourinho, Alcantara; 2cz. St. Francis's Monastery, Olinda; 5cz. St. Anthony's Chapel, Sao Roque; 10cz. St Lawrence of the Indians Church, Niteroi; 20cz. Principe da Beira Fortress, Costa Marques, Rondobua; 100cz. Church of Our Lady of Sorrows, Campanha; 200cz. Counting House, Ouro Preto; 500cz. Customs building, Belem. VERT: 50cz. Church of the Good Jesus, Matasinhos.

1150 Kubitschek and Alvorada Palace

1986. Tenth Death Anniv of Juscelino Kubitschek (President 1956–61).

| 2244 | **1150** | 50c. multicoloured | 45 | 25 |

1151 Mangabeira and Itamaraty Palace, Rio de Janeiro

1986. Birth Cent of Octavio Mangabeira (politician).

| 2245 | **1151** | 50c. multicoloured | 45 | 25 |

1152 Congress Emblem and Sao Paulo

1986. Eighth World Gastroenterology Congress, Sao Paulo.

| 2246 | **1152** | 50c. multicoloured | 45 | 25 |

1153 Microphone and Radio Waves

1986. 50th Annivs. of National Radio and Education and Culture Ministry Radio.

| 2247 | **1153** | 50c. multicoloured | 45 | 25 |

1154 *Peace* (detail, Candido Portinari)

1986. International Peace Year.

| 2248 | **1154** | 50c. multicoloured | 45 | 25 |

1155 *Urera mitis*

1986. Flowers. Multicoloured.

2249	50c. Type **1155**	35	15
2250	6cz.50 *Couroupita guyanensis*	1·70	45
2251	6cz.90 Mountain ebony (horiz)	1·80	45

1156 Simoes Filho and Newspaper

1986. Birth Centenary of Ernesto Simoes Filho (politician and founder of *A Tarde*).

| 2252 | **1156** | 50c. multicoloured | 45 | 25 |

1157 Title Page of Gregorio de Matto's MS

1986. Book Day. Poets' Birth Anniversaries.

| 2253 | **1157** | 50c. brown & lt brown | 45 | 25 |
| 2254 | - | 50c. green and red | 45 | 25 |

DESIGNS: No. 2253, Type **1157** (350th anniv); 2254, Manuel Bandeira and last verse of *I'll Return to Pasargada* (centenary).

1158 Head Office, Brasilia

1986. 125th Anniv of Federal Savings Bank.

| 2255 | **1158** | 50c. multicoloured | 45 | 25 |

1159 Birds around Baby lying in Nest

1986. Christmas. Multicoloured.

2256	50c. Type **1159**	60	25
2257	6cz.50 Birds around tree with Christmas decorations	2·20	55
2258	7cz.30 Birds wearing Santa Claus caps	2·20	70

1160 Rocha on Strip of Film

1986. Fifth Death Anniv of Glauber Rocha (film producer).

| 2259 | **1160** | 50c. multicoloured | 45 | 25 |

1161 *History of Empress Porcina*

1986. Lubrapex 86 Brazilian–Portuguese Stamp Exhibition, Rio de Janeiro. Design showing scenes from Cordel Literature. Multicoloured.

2260	6cz.90 Type **1161**	1·40	70
2261	6cz.90 *Romance of the Mysterious Peacock*	1·40	70
MS2262 70×100 mm. Nos. 2260/2	4·25	4·25	

1986. Obligatory Tax. Anti-leprosy Week.

| 2263 | **1095** | 10c. brown | 35 | 25 |

1162 Lieutenant Commander, 1930

1986. Military Uniforms. Multicoloured.

| 2264 | 50c. Type **1162** | 35 | 25 |
| 2265 | 50c. Military Aviation flight lieutenant, 1930 | 35 | 25 |

1163 *Graf Zeppelin* over Hangar

1986. 50th Anniv of Bartolomeu de Gusmao Airport, Santa Cruz.

| 2266 | **1163** | 1cz. multicoloured | 45 | 35 |

1164 Museum

1165 Villa-Lobos conducting and Musical Motifs

1987. 50th Anniv of National Fine Arts Museum, Rio de Janeiro.

| 2267 | **1164** | 1cz. multicoloured | 45 | 35 |

1987. Birth Cent of Heitor Villa-Lobos (composer).

| 2268 | **1165** | 1cz.50 multicoloured | 55 | 35 |

1166 Flag, Lockheed C-130 Hercules Aircraft and Antarctic Landscape

1987. Air Force Participation in Brazilian Antarctic Programme.

| 2269 | **1166** | 1cz. multicoloured | 95 | 25 |

1167 Landscape on Open Envelope (Rural Post Office Network)

1987. Special Mail Services. Multicoloured.

| 2270 | 1cz. Type **1167** | 45 | 35 |
| 2271 | 1cz. Satchel and globe (International Express Mail Service) | 45 | 35 |

1168 "Brasilsat" Satellite, Radio Wave and Globe

1987. Telecom 87 World Telecommunications Exhibition, Geneva.

| 2272 | **1168** | 2cz. multicoloured | 45 | 35 |

1169 Modern Pentathlon

1987. Tenth Pan-American Games, Indianapolis, U.S.A.

| 2273 | **1169** | 18cz. multicoloured | 3·00 | 1·10 |

1170 Hawksbill Turtle

1987. Endangered Animals. Multicoloured.

| 2274 | 2cz. Type **1170** | 85 | 45 |
| 2275 | 2cz. Right whale | 85 | 45 |

1171 Old and New Court Buildings and Symbol of Justice

1987. 40th Anniv of Federal Appeal Court.

| 2276 | **1171** | 2cz. multicoloured | 45 | 35 |

1172 Arms

1987. Centenary of Military Club.
2277 **1172** 3cz. multicoloured 60 35

1173 Institute and Foodstuffs

1987. Centenary of Agronomic Institute, Campinas.
2278 **1173** 2cz. multicoloured 45 35

1174 *Fulgora servillei*

1987. 50th Anniv of Brazilian Entomology Society. Multicoloured.
2279 3cz. Type **1174** 85 35
2280 3cz. *Zoolea lopiceps* 85 35

1175 Features of Northern and North-east Regions

1987. National Tourism Year. Multicoloured.
2281 3cz. Type **1175** 45 35
2282 3cz. Features of mid-west,
 south-east and south regions 45 35

1176 Main Tower

1987. 150th Anniv of Royal Portuguese Reading Cabinet, Rio de Janeiro.
2283 **1176** 30cz. green and red 2·20 1·70

1177 International Sport Club (1975, 1976, 1979)

1987. Brazilian Football Championship Gold Cup Winners (1st series). Designs showing footballers and Club emblems.
2284 **1177** 3cz. red, black & yellow 45 25
2285 - 3cz. red, yellow & black 45 25
2286 - 3cz. multicoloured 45 25
2287 - 3cz. red, black & yellow 45 25
DESIGNS: No. 2285, Sao Paulo Football Club (1977, 1986); 2286, Guarani Football Club (1978); 2287, Regatas do Flamengo Club (1980, 1982, 1983).
 See also Nos. 2322/5, 2398 and 2408.

1178 St. Francis's Church and Tiled Column

1987. 400th Anniv of St. Francis's Monastery, Salvador.
2288 **1178** 4cz. multicoloured 45 35

1179 Almeida and Scenes from *A Bagaceira*

1987. Birth Centenary of Jose Americo de Almeida (writer).
2289 **1179** 4cz. multicoloured 35 25

1180 Barra do Picao

1987. 450th Anniv of Recife.
2290 **1180** 5cz. multicoloured 35 10

1987. Obligatory Tax. Anti-leprosy Week.
2291 **1095** 30cz. green 35 25

1181 Rainbow, Dove and Open Hands

1987. Thanksgiving Day.
2292 **1181** 5cz. multicoloured 35 25

1182 Angels

1987. Christmas. Multicoloured.
2293 6cz. Type **1182** 45 35
2294 6cz. Dancers on stage 45 35
2295 6cz. Shepherd playing flute 45 35

1183 Bernardo Pereira de Vasconcelos (founder) and Pedro II

1987. 150th Anniv of Pedro II School, Rio de Janeiro.
2296 **1183** 6cz. yellow, blk & red 45 35

1184 *Cattleya guttata*

1987. 50th Anniv of Brazilian Orchid Growers Society. Multicoloured.
2297 6cz. Type **1184** 85 25
2298 6cz. *Laelia lobata* 85 25

1185 Statue and Fatima Basilica, Portugal

1987. Marian Year. Visit to Brazil of Statue of Our Lady of Fatima.
2299 **1185** 50cz. multicoloured 3·00 2·30

1186 Sousa, Indians and Fauna

1987. 400th Anniv of *Descriptive Treaties of Brazil* by Gabriel Soares de Sousa.
2300 **1186** 7cz. multicoloured 45 35

1187 Page from Book of Gregorian Chants and Computer Terminal

1988. 150th Anniv of National Archives.
2301 **1187** 7cz. multicoloured 45 35

1188 National Colours, Caravel and Modern Ship

1988. 180th Anniv of Opening of Brazilian Ports to Free Trade.
2302 **1188** 7cz. multicoloured 45 35

1189 Microscope and Map

1988. Antarctic Research. Sheet 99×69 mm.
MS2303 **1189** 80cz. multicoloured 4·25 4·25

1190 Petrol Droplet

1988. Energy Conservation. Multicoloured.
2304 **1190** 14cz. Type **1190** 45 35
2305 14cz. Flash of electricity 45 35

1191 Williams-Honda Racing Car and Flag

1988. Nelson Piquet's Third Formula 1 Motor Racing World Championship Title (1987). Sheet 99×69 mm.
MS2306 **1191** 300cz. multicoloured 9·50 9·50

1192 Bonifacio and Emblems of his Life

1988. 150th Death Anniv of Jose Bonifacio de Andrada e Silva (scientist, writer and *Patriarch of the Independence*).
2307 **1192** 20cz. multicoloured 60 45

1193 Quill Pen on Page of Aurea Law

1988. Centenary of Abolition of Slavery. Multicoloured.
2308 **1193** 20cz. Type **1193** 45 35
2309 50cz. Norris map of Africa,
 1773, slave ship and plan of
 trading routes 1·30 1·00

1194 Church of the Good Jesus of Matosinhos

1988. UNESCO World Heritage Sites. Multicoloured.
2310 20cz. Type **1194** 45 35

2311 50cz. Brasilia 1·30 90
2312 100cz. Pelourinho, Salvador 2·40 1·80

1195 Concentric Circles on Map of Americas

1988. Americas Telecom 88 Telecommunications Exhibition, Rio de Janeiro.
2313 **1195** 50cz. multicoloured 1·90 90

1196 *Kasato Maru* (first immigrant ship) and Japanese Family

1988. 80th Anniv of Japanese Immigration into Brazil.
2314 **1196** 100cz. multicoloured 1·90 1·00

1197 Postal Authority Emblem

1988. No value expressed.
2315 **1197** (–) blue 1·40 25
 No. 2315 was valid for use at the current first class inland letter rate. It could not be used to pay postage to foreign countries.

1198 Judo

1988. Olympic Games, Seoul.
2316 **1198** 20cz. multicoloured 1·10 25

1199 Giant Anteater

1988. Endangered Mammals. Multicoloured.
2317 20cz. Type **1199** 60 35
2318 50cz. Thin-spined porcupine 95 45
2319 100cz. Bush dog 2·00 1·10

1200 *Motherland* (Pedro Bruno)

1988. Stamp Day. Brasiliana 89 International Stamp Exhibition. Sheet 98×69 mm.
MS2320 **1200** 250cz. multicoloured 6·50 6·50

1201 Industrial Symbols

1988. 50th Anniv of National Confederation of Industry.
2321 **1201** 50cz. multicoloured 60 35

1988. Brazilian Football Championship Gold Cup Winners (2nd series). As T **1177**. Multicoloured.

2322	50cz. Sport Club do Recife (1987)	45	25
2323	50cz. Coritiba Football Club (1985)	45	25
2324	100cz. Gremio Football Porto Alegrense (1981)	70	35
2325	200cz. Fluminense Football Club (1984)	1·20	80

1202 Congress, Brasilia

1988. Promulgation of 1998 Consitution. Sheet 99×69 mm.

MS2326	**1202** 550cz. multicoloured	5·00	5·00

1203 Raul Pompeia and Lines from *O Ateneu*

1988. Book Day. Centenaries of Publication of *O Ateneu* and *Verses*. Multicoloured.

2327	50cz. Type **1203**	40	25
2328	100cz. Olavo Bilac and lines from "Verses"	55	30

1204 Church

1988. Christmas. Origami by Marcia Bloch. Multicoloured.

2329	50cz. Type **1204**	60	35
2330	100cz. Nativity	70	35
2331	200cz. Santa Claus and parcels	1·40	80

1205
Father
Santiago
Uchoa

1988. Obligatory Tax. Anti-leprosy Week.

2332	**1205** 1cz.30 brown	45	25

See also Nos. 2614 and 2686.

1206 Mate and Rodeo Rider

1988. Abrafex Argentine–Brazilian Stamp Exhibition, Buenos Aires.

2333	**1206** 400cz. multicoloured	3·00	1·00

1207 Hatchetfish (*Gasteropelecus* sp.)

1988. Freshwater Fish. Multicoloured.

2334	55cz. Type **1207**	35	35
2335	55cz. Black arawana (*Osteoglossum ferreira*)	35	35
2336	55cz. Green moenkhausia (*Moenkhausia* sp.)	35	35
2337	55cz. Pearlfish (*Xavantei*)	35	35
2338	55cz. Armoured bristlemouth catfish (*Ancistrus hoplogenys*)	35	35
2339	55cz. Emerald catfish (*Brochis splendens*)	35	35

1208 Red-tailed Amazon

1988. Brapex VII National Stamp Exhibition, Sao Paulo. Conservation of Jurelia. Sheet 99×68 mm containing T **1208** and similar vert designs. Multicoloured.

MS2340	100cz. Type **1208**; 250cz.		
	Vriesia ensiformis (bromelia); 400cz.		
	Great egret	17·00	17·00

1209 Dish Aerials

1988. Tenth Anniv of Ansat 10 (first Brazilian dish aerial), Macapa.

2341	**1209** 70cz. multicoloured	35	35

1210 "Four Arts"

1988. Establishment of National Foundation of Scenic Arts.

2342	**1210** 70cz. multicoloured	45	35

1211 Court Building

1989. 380th Anniv of Bahia Court of Justice.

2343	**1211** 25c. multicoloured	95	55

1212 Library Building and Detail of Main Door

1989. Public Library Year. 178th Anniv of First Public Library, Bahia.

2344	**1212** 25c. multicoloured	95	55

1213 Facsimile Machine

1989. 20th Anniv of Post and Telegraph Department. Postal Services. Multicoloured.

2345	25c. Type **1213**	85	55
2346	25c. Hand holding parcel (Express Mail Service)	85	55
2347	25c. Airbus Industrie 300 airplane on runway (SEDEX express parcel service)	85	55
2348	25c. Putting coin in savings box (CEF postal savings)	85	55

1214 Senna

1989. Aryton Senna's Formula 1 Motor Racing World Championship Title (1988). Sheet 99×69 mm.

MS2349	**1214** 2cz. multicoloured	15·00	15·00

1215 Emblem

1989. "Our Nature" Programme.

2350	**1215** 25c. multicoloured	70	45

1216 Hand reaching for Symbol of Freedom

1989. Bicentenary of Inconfidencia Mineira (independence movement). Multicoloured.

2351	30c. Type **1216**	60	35
2352	30c. Man's profile and colonial buildings	60	35
2353	40c. Baroque buildings in disarray	95	45

1217 School

1989. Centenary of Rio de Janeiro Military School.

2354	**1217** 50c. multicoloured	1·10	70

1218 *Pavonia alnifolia*

1989. Endangered Plants. Multicoloured.

2355	50c. Type **1218**	1·40	1·00
2356	1cz. *Worsleya rayneri* (vert)	3·00	2·20
2357	1cz.50 *Heliconia farinosa* (vert)	4·25	3·50

1219 Barreto and Pedro II Square, Recife Law School

1989. 150th Birth Anniv of Tobias Barreto (writer).

2358	**1219** 50c. multicoloured	1·50	90

1220
Quiabentia zehntneri

1989. Flowers. Currency expressed as "NCz $". Multicoloured.

2359	10c. *Dichorisandra* sp.	35	25
2360	20c. Type **1220**	45	25
2361	50c. *Bougainvillea glabra*	95	30
2363	1cz. *Impatiens* sp.	2·10	40
2364	2cz. *Chorisia crispiflora* (vert)	70	25
2366	5cz. *Hibiscus trilineatus*	70	30

See also Nos. 2413/24.

1221 Shooting of "Revistinha"

1989. 20th Anniv of TV Cultura.

2371	**1221** 50c. multicoloured	1·40	90

1222 Postal Authority Emblem

1989. No value expressed.

2372	**1222** (–) blue and orange	1·40	30

No. 2372 was sold at the current rate for first class internal postage.

1223 Brasilia T.V. Tower and Microlight

1989. Aerosports and 80th Anniv of Santos Dumont's Flight in *Demoiselle*. Multicoloured.

2373	50c. Type **1223**	95	80
2374	1cz.50 Eiffel Tower and *Demoiselle*	3·25	2·20

1224 Largo da Carioca (detail, Nicolas Antoine Taunay)

1989. Philexfrance 89 International Stamp Exhibition, Paris and Bicentenary of French Revolution. Sheet 99×69 mm.

MS2375	**1224** 3cz. multicoloured	6·00	6·00

1225 Tourmaline

1989. Precious Stones. Multicoloured.

2376	50c. Type **1225**	95	55
2377	1cz.50 Amethyst	2·40	1·80

1226 Imperial Palace, Rio de Janeiro

1989. Stamp Day. Brasiliana 89 International Stamp Exhibition, Rio de Janeiro. Sheet 99×69 mm.

MS2378	**1226** 5cz. multicoloured	7·75	7·75

1227 Rainbow and Association H.Q. Mercury

1989. 150th Anniv of Pernambuco Trade Assn.

2379	**1227** 50c. multicoloured	85	55

1228 Pioneers' Names and 19th-century to Modern Photographs

1989. International Photography Year.

2380	**1228** 1cz.50 multicoloured	2·40	1·70

1229 Power Station

1989. Centenary of Marmelos-o Power Station (first South American hydro-electric power station).

2381	**1229** 50c. multicoloured	70	45

1230 Hebrew Volute

1989. Molluscs. Multicoloured.

2382	50c. Type **1230**	35	25
2383	1cz. Matthew's morum	85	45
2384	1cz.50 Travasso's ancilla	1·20	70

1231 Muiraquita

1989. America. Pre-Columbian Artefacts. Multicoloured.

2385	1cz. Type **1231**	95	6·75
2386	4cz. Caryatid vase (horiz)	3·75	2·75

1232 Limoes
(Danilo di Prete)

1989. 20th International Biennial Art Exhibition, Sao Paulo. Sheet 99×79 mm containing T **1232** and similar vert designs. Multicoloured.

MS2387	2cz. Type **1232**; 3cz. O Indio e a Suacuaoara (sculpture, Brecheret); 5cz. Francisco Matarazzo (exhibition founder)	7·75	7·75

1233 Casimiro de Abreu

1989. Book Day. Writers' Birth Annivs. Multicoloured.

2388	1cz. Type **1233** (150th anniv)	1·10	80
2389	1cz. Machado de Assis (150th anniv)	1·10	80
2390	1cz. Cora Coralina (cent)	1·10	80

1234 Postal Authority Emblem

1989. No value expressed. Burelage in second colour.

2391	**1234** (–) red and orange	4·50	1·90

No. 2391 was sold at the current rate for first class international postage.

1235 Police Emblem

1989. 25th Anniv of Federal Police Department.

2392	**1235** 1cz. multicoloured	60	35

1238 Candle Flame as Dove

1989. Thanksgiving Day.

2396	**1238** 1cz. multicoloured	45	35

1236 Deodoro presents the Flag of the Republic (detail, anon)

1989. Centenary of Proclamation of Republic. Sheet 98×68 mm.

MS2393	**1236** 15cz. multicoloured	8·75	8·75

1237 Angel

1989. Christmas. Multicoloured.

2394	70c. Type **1237**	35	35
2395	1cz. Nativity	45	35

1239 Fr. Damien de Veuster

1989. Obligatory Tax. Anti-leprosy Week.

2397	**1239** 2c. red	35	25

See also Nos. 2458, 2509 and 2565.

1989. Football Clubs. As T **1177**. Multicoloured.

2398	50c. Bahia Sports Club	45	35

1240 The Yellow Man

1989. Birth Cent of Anita Malfatti (painter).

2399	**1240** 1cz. multicoloured	45	35

1241 Archive and Proclamation by Bento Goncalves

1990. Cent of Bahia State Public Archive.

2400	**1241** 2cz. multicoloured	60	35

1242 Mimosa caesalpiniifolia

1990. 40th Anniv of Brazilian Botanical Society. Multicoloured.

2401	2cz. Type **1242**	45	35
2402	13cz. Caesalpinia echinata	2·75	2·20

1243 Cathedral of St. John the Baptist, Santa Cruz do Sul

1990. Churches. Multicoloured.

2403	2cz. Type **1243**	35	25
2404	3cz. Our Lady of Victory Church, Oeiras (horiz)	60	35
2405	5cz. Our Lady of the Rosary Church, Ouro Preto	85	55

1244 Sailing Barque and Modern Container Ship

1990. Cent of Lloyd Brasileiro Navigation Company.

2406	**1244** 3cz. multicoloured	45	25

1245 Chinstrap Penguins and Map

1990. Brazilian Antarctic Programme. Sheet 98×68 mm.

MS2407	**1245** 20cz. multicoloured	3·75	3·75

1990. Brazilian Football Clubs As T **1177**. Multicoloured.

2408	10cz. Vasco da Gama Regatas Club	95	80

1246 Collor and Newspaper Mastheads

1990. Birth Cent of Lindolfo Collor (journalist).

2409	**1246** 20cz. multicoloured	1·90	1·40

1247 Sarney

1990. Tribute to Jose Sarney (retiring President).

2410	**1247** 20cz. blue	2·00	1·40

1248 Gold Coin, Anniversary Emblem and Bank Headquarters, Brasilia

1990. 25th Anniv of Brazil Central Bank.

2411	**1248** 20cr. multicoloured	1·80	90

1249 Hearts sprouting in Flask

1990. World Health Day. Anti-AIDS Campaign.

2412	**1249** 20cr. multicoloured	1·90	90

1990. Flowers. As T **1220** but with currency expressed as "Cr$".

2413	1cr. Impatiens sp.	25	10
2414	2cr. Chorisia crispiflora (vert)	25	10
2415	5cr. Hibiscus trilineatus	25	10
2417	10cr. Tibouchina granulosa (vert)	35	25
2418	20cr. Cassia micranthera (vert)	60	35
2419	50cr. Tibouchina mutabillis (vert)	70	45
2420	50cr. Clitoria fairchildiana (vert)	70	45
2421	50cr. Tibouchina mutabilis (vert)	60	35
2422	100cr. Erythrina crista-galli (vert)	1·30	55
2423	200cr. Jacaranda mimosifolia (vert)	2·20	1·10
2424	500cr. Caesalpinia peltophoroides (vert)	3·50	1·80
2424a	1000cr. Pachira aquatica (vert)	45	25
2424b	2000cr. Hibiscus pernambucensis (vert)	60	25
2424c	5000cr. Triplaris surinamensis (vert)	1·40	60
2424d	10000cr. Tabebuia heptaphylia (vert)	3·00	1·20
2424e	20000cr. Erythrina speciosa (vert)	3·75	1·40

1250 Amazon Post Launch

1990. River Post Network.

2425	**1250** 20cr. multicoloured	1·90	1·00

1251 Emperor Pedro LL and 30r. "Bull's-Eye"

1990. Stamp World London 90 International Stamp Exhibition and 150th Anniv of Penny Black. Sheet 100×70 mm containing T **1251** and similar vert design, each black and lemon.

MS2426	20cr. Type **1251**; 100cr. Queen Victoria and Penny Black	8·25	8·25

1252 Map and Emblem

1990. World Cup Football Championship, Italy. Sheet 69×99 mm.

MS2427	**1252** 120cr. multicoloured	8·75	8·75

1253 Truck and Coach

1990. 22nd World Congress of Int Road Transport Union, Rio de Janeiro. Multicoloured.

2428	20cr. Type **1253**	1·30	90
2429	80cr. Volkswagen transporter van and car	1·90	1·40

Nos. 2428/29 were printed together, se-tenant, forming a composite design.

1254 Imperial Crown (Imperial Museum, Petropolis)

1990. Museum 50th Anniversaries. Multicoloured.

2430	20cr. Type **1254**	1·40	90
2431	20cr. Our Lady of the Immaculate Conception (woodcarving) (Missionary Museum, Sao Miguel das Missoes)	1·40	90

1990. Creation of State of Tocantins. As T **992**, showing state flag.

2432	20cr. yellow, blue and black	1·40	90

1255 Service Building. Hildebrand Theodolite and Map of Rio de Janeiro

1990. Centenary of Army Geographic Service.

2433	**1255** 20cr. multicoloured	1·40	90

1256 Adhemar Gonzaga (producer)

1990. Brazilian Film Industry. Each maroon and purple.

2434	25cr. Type **1256**	1·20	70
2435	25cr. Carmen Miranda (actress)	1·20	70
2436	25cr. Carmen Santos (actress)	1·20	70
2437	25cr. Oscarito (actor)	1·20	70

1257 Aerial View of House

1990. Fifth Anniv of France–Brazil House, Rio de Janeiro.

2438	**1257** 50cr. multicoloured	3·00	2·50

1258 Ball and Net

1990. 12th World Men's Volleyball Championship, Brazil.
2439 **1258** 10cr. multicoloured 85 45

1259 Embraer/FMA Vector

1990. Aeronautics Industry.
2440 **1259** 10cr. multicoloured 85 45

1260 Globe, Pencil and Alphabet

1990. International Literacy Year.
2441 **1260** 10cr. multicoloured 85 45

1261 Institute

1990. Cent of Granbery Institute, Juiz de Fora.
2442 **1261** 13cr. multicoloured 95 55

1262 Map, Track and Diesel Locomotive

1990. 18th Pan-American Railways Congress, Rio de Janeiro.
2443 **1262** 95cr. multicoloured 4·25 2·75

1263 Satellite and Computer Communication

1990. 25th Anniv of Embratel (Telecommunications Enterprise).
2444 **1263** 13cr. multicoloured 95 55

1264 "Bathers" (Alfredo Ceschiatti)

1990. Lubrapex 90 Brazilian–Portuguese Stamp Exhibition, Brasilia. Brasilia Sculptures. Multicoloured.
2445 25cr. Type **1264** 1·20 90
2446 25cr. *Warriors* (Bruno Giorgi) 1·20 90
2447 100cr. *St. John* (Ceschiatti) 2·50 1·80
2448 100cr. *Justice* (Ceschiatti) 2·50 1·80
MS2449 150×89 mm. Nos. 2445/8 12·00 12·00

1265 *Bromelia antiacantha*

1990. America. 500th Anniv of Discovery of America by Columbus. Praia do Sul Nature Reserve. Multicoloured.
2450 15cr. Type **1265** 95 55
2451 105cr. Wooded shoreline of Lagoa do Sul 4·75 3·50
Nos. 2450/1 were printed together, *se-tenant*, forming a composite design.

1266 Oswald de Andrade (birth centenary) and Illustration from *Anthropophagic Manifesto*

1990. Book Day. Anniversaries. Multicoloured.
2452 15cr. Type **1266** 85 55
2453 15cr. Guilherme de Almeida (birth cent) and illustration of *Geek Songs* 85 55
2454 15cr. National Library (180th anniv) and illuminated book 85 55

1267 Emblem and Tribunal Offices, Brasilia

1990. Centenary of National Accounts Tribunal.
2455 **1267** 15cr. multicoloured 85 55

1268 National Congress Building

1990. Christmas. Brasilia Lights. Multicoloured.
2456 15cr. Type **1268** 85 55
2457 15cr. Television Tower 85 55

1990. Obligatory Tax. Anti-Leprosy Week. As No. 2397 but value and colour changed.
2458 **1239** 50c. blue 35 25

1269 Fingers touching across Map of Americas

1990. Centenary of Organization of American States.
2459 **1269** 15cr. multicoloured 45 25

1270 "Nike Apache" Rocket on Launch Pad

1990. 25th Anniv of Launch of "Nike Apache" Rocket.
2460 **1270** 15cr. multicoloured 45 25

1271 Sao Cristovao City

1990. 400th Anniv of Colonization of Sergipe State.
2461 **1271** 15cr. multicoloured 45 25

1272 Gymnasts

1991. World Congress on Physical Education, Sports and Recreation, Foz do Iguacu.
2462 **1272** 17cr. multicoloured 55 25

1273 Cazuza

1991. "Rock in Rio" Concert. Multicoloured.
2463 25cr. Type **1273** 95 55
2464 185cr. Raul Seixas 3·50 90
Nos. 2463/4 were printed together, *se-tenant*, forming a composite design.

1274 Aeritalia/Aermacchi AM-X and Republic Thunderbolt

1991. 50th Anniv of Aeronautics Ministry.
2465 **1274** 17cr. multicoloured 55 35

1275 Effigies of Day Woman and Midnight Man, Olinda

1991. Carnival. Multicoloured.
2466 25cr. Type **1275** 35 30
2467 30cr. Electric trio on truck, Salvador 40 35
2468 280cr. Samba dancers, Rio de Janeiro 5·25 4·00

1276 Antarctic Wildlife

1991. Visit of President Collor to Antarctica.
2469 **1276** 300cr. multicoloured 4·25 2·30

1277 Hang-gliders

1991. Eighth World Free Flight Championships, Governador Valadares.
2470 **1277** 36cr. multicoloured 85 55

1278 Yachting

1991. 11th Pan-American Games, Cuba, and Olympic Games, Barcelona (1992). Mult.
2471 36cr. Type **1278** 70 45
2472 36cr. Rowing 70 45
2473 300cr. Swimming 4·75 3·75

1279 Cross over Bottle (alcoholism)

1991. Anti-addiction Campaign. Multicoloured.
2474 40cr. Type **1279** 85 55
2475 40cr. Cross over cigarette (smoking) 85 55
2476 40cr. Cross over syringe (drug abuse) 85 55

1280 Old and Present Offices and Mastheads

1991. Cent of *Jornal do Brasil* (newspaper).
2477 **1280** 40cr. multicoloured 85 55

1281 Yanomami Youth in Ceremonial Paint

1991. Indian Culture. The Yanomami. Multicoloured.
2478 40cr. Type **1281** 70 55
2479 400cr. Hunter (horiz) 7·00 5·25

1282 Orinoco Goose

1991. United Nations Conference on Environment and Development.
2480 **1282** 45cr. multicoloured 85 55

1283 Jararaca

1991. 90th Anniv of Butantan Institute (2481/2) and 173rd Anniv of National Museum (others). Multicoloured.
2481 45cr. Type **1283** 70 45
2482 45cr. Green tree boa 70 45
2483 45cr. Theropoda (dinosaurs) 70 45
2484 350cr. Sauropoda (dinosaurs) 4·25 3·00

1284 National Flag

1991. No value expressed.
2485a **1284** (–) multicoloured 45 25

1285 Early Steam Pump and Santos City 6th Fire Group's Headquarters

1991. Fire Fighting.
2486 **1285** 45cr. multicoloured 60 45

1286 Pedra Pintada, Boa Vista, Roraima

1991. Tourism. Centenaries of Boa Vista (1990) and Teresopolis. Multicoloured.

2487	45cr. Type **1286**		60	45
2488	350cr. God's Finger, Teresopolis, Rio de Janeiro		2·75	2·10

1287 Welder, "Justice" and Farmer

1991. 50th Anniv of Labour Justice Legal System.

2489	**1287**	45cr. multicoloured	60	45

1288 Folklore Characters, Singers and Mota

1991. Fifth International Festival of Folklore and Birth Centenary of Leonardo Mota (folklorist).

2490	**1288**	45cr. red, ochre & black	60	45

1289 Jose Basilio da Gama (poet)

1991. Writers' Birth Anniversaries. Multicoloured.

2491	45cr. Type **1289** (250th anniv)		55	40
2492	50cr. Luis Nicolau Fagundes Varela (poet, 150th anniv)		60	45
2493	50cr. Jackson de Figueiredo (essayist and philosopher, centenary)		60	45

1290 Pope John Paul II

1991. Papal Visit and 12th National Eucharistic Congress, Natal. Multicoloured.

2494	50cr. Type **1290**		60	45
2495	400cr. Congress emblem		1·80	1·10

Nos. 2494/5 were issued together, *se-tenant*, forming a composite design.

1291 *The Constitutional Commitment* (Aurelio de Figueiredo)

1991. Centenary of 1891 Constitution.

2496	**1291**	50cr. multicoloured	85	35

1292 Exhibition Emblem and dish Aerial

1991. Telecom 91 International Telecommunications Exhibition, Geneva.

2497	**1292**	50cr. multicoloured	85	35

1293 Ferdinand Magellan

1991. America. Voyages of Discovery. Multicoloured.

2498	50cr. Type **1293**		85	35
2499	400cr. Francisco de Orellana on River Amazon		2·75	2·10

1294 White-vented Violetear and *Cattleya warneri*

1991. Brapex 91 National Stamp Exhibition, Vitoria. Humming Birds and Orchids in Mata Atlantica Forest. Multicoloured.

2500	50cr. Type **1294**		60	35
2501	65cr. Glittering-bellied emerald and *Rodriguezia venusta*		70	45
2502	65cr. Brazilian ruby and *Zygopetalum intermedium*		70	45
MS2503	99×69 mm. 50cr. White-vented violetear and *Cattleya warneri*; 50cr. Glittering-bellied emerald and tree trunk; 500cr. *Rodriguezia venusta* and Brazilian ruby		12·00	12·00

1295 *Self-portrait III*

1991. Birth Centenary of Lasar Segall (artist).

2504	**1295**	400cr. multicoloured	1·80	75

1296 Agricultural Projects

1991. Centenary of Bureau of Agriculture and Provision, Sao Paulo.

2505	**1296**	70cr. multicoloured	60	35

1297 Dr. Manuel Ferraz de Campos Salles (President, 1898–1902)

1991. 150th Birth Anniversaries. Multicoloured.

2506	70cr. Type **1297**		60	35
2507	90cr. Dr. Prudente de Moraes (President, 1894–98) and Catete Palace, Rio de Janeiro (former Executive Headquarters)		70	45

Nos. 2506/7 were issued together, *se-tenant*, forming a composite design.

1298 Madonna and Child

1991. Christmas.

2508	**1298**	70cr. multicoloured	1·20	35

1991. Obligatory Tax. Anti-leprosy Week.

2509	**1239**	3cr. green	35	25

1299 Hand holding Prayer Book

1991. Thanksgiving Day.

2510	**1299**	70cr. multicoloured	60	35

1300 Pedro II

1991. 150th Anniv of Coronation and Death Centenary of Emperor Pedro II. Sheet 99×69 mm containing T **1300** and similar vert design. Multicoloured.

MS2511	80cr. Type **1300**; 800cr. Pedro II at coronation		4·75	4·75

1301 Policeman in Historic Uniform and Tobias de Aguiar Battalion Building, Sao Paulo

1991. Military Police.

2512	**1301**	80cr. multicoloured	60	35

1302 First Baptist Church, Niteroi (centenary)

1992. Church Anniversaries. Multicoloured.

2513	250cr. Type **1302**		1·30	45
2514	250cr. Presbyterian Cathedral, Rio de Janeiro (130th anniv)		1·30	45

1303 Afranio Costa (silver, free pistol)

1992. Olympic Games, Barcelona (1st issue). 1920 Olympics Shooting Medal Winners. Multicoloured.

2515	300cr. Type **1303**		1·80	85
2516	2500cr. Guilherme Paraense (gold, 30 m revolver)		14·00	3·50

See also No. 2526.

1304 Old and Modern Views of Port

1992. Centenary of Port of Santos.

2517	**1304**	300cr. multicoloured	1·10	55

1305 White-tailed Tropic Birds

1992. Second United Nations Conference on Environment and Development, Rio de Janeiro (1st issue). Multicoloured.

2518	400cr. Type **1305**		1·20	55
2519	2500cr. Spinner dolphins		4·25	2·00

See also Nos. 2532/5, 2536/8, 2539/42 and 2543/6.

1306 Ipe

1992. No value expressed.

2520	**1306**	(–) multicoloured	2·30	25

No. 2520 was valid for use at the second class inland letter rate.

1307 Hunting using Boleadeira

1992. Abrafex '92 Argentinian–Brazilian Stamp Exhibition, Porto Alegre. Multicoloured.

2521	250cr. Type **1307**		70	55
2522	250cr. Traditional folk dancing		70	55
2523	250cr. Horse and cart		70	55
2524	1000cr. Rounding-up cattle		1·40	1·10
MS2525	150×89 mm. 250cr. As No. 2522; 250cr. As No. 2523; 500cr. Type **1307**; 1500cr. As No. 2524		8·75	8·75

1308 Sportsmen on Globe

1992. Olympic Games, Barcelona (2nd issue).

2526	**1308**	300cr. multicoloured	60	35

1309 Tiradentes (sculpture, Bruno Giorgi)

1992. Death Bicentenary of Joaquim Jose da Silvaxavier (Independence fighter). Sheet 98×68 mm.

MS2527	**1309**	3500cr. mult	6·50	6·50

1310 Columbus's Fleet

1992. America. 500th Anniv of Discovery of America by Columbus. Multicoloured.

2528	500cr. Type **1310**		70	45
2529	3500cr. Columbus, route map and quadrant		3·75	2·30

Nos. 2528/9 were issued together, *se-tenant*, forming a composite design.

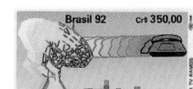

1311 Dish Aerial, Telephone and City

1992. Installation of 10,000,000th Telephone Line in Brazil.

2530	**1311**	350cr. multicoloured	70	35

1312 Sailing Canoes

1992. Lubrapex 92 Brazilian--Portuguese Stamp Exhibition, Lisbon. Bicentenary of *Philosophical Journey* by Alexandre Rodrigues Ferreira. Sheet 148×88 mm containing T **1312** and similar horiz designs.

MS2531 500cr., 1000cr., 2500cr. Composite design of watercolour by Jose Freire showing arrival of expedition's ship at Vila de Cameta ... 6·75 ... 6·75

1313 Hercule Florence (botanist)

1992. Second UN Conference on Environment and Development (2nd issue). 170th Anniv of Langsdorff Expedition. Multicoloured.

2532	500cr. Type **1313**	60	45
2533	500cr. Aime-Adrien Taunay (ethnographer) and Amerindians	60	45
2534	500cr. Johann Moritz Rugendas (zoologist)	60	45
2535	3000cr. Gregory Ivanovich Langsdorff and route map	3·75	2·50

1314 Urban and Rural Symbols

1992. Second UN Conference on Environment and Development (3rd issue). Multicoloured.

2536	450cr. Type **1314**	45	35
2537	450cr. Flags of Sweden (host of first conference) and Brazil around globe	45	35
2538	3000cr. Globe, map, flora and fauna	3·75	2·50

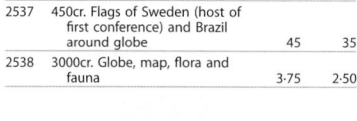

1315 Monica sitting by Waterfall

1992. Second UN Conference on Environment and Development (4th issue). Ecology. Designs showing cartoon characters. Multicoloured.

2539	500cr. Type **1315**	70	35
2540	500cr. Cebolinha in canoe	70	35
2541	500cr. Cascao photographing wildlife	70	35
2542	500cr. Magali picking wild fruit	70	35

Nos. 2539/42 were issued together, *se-tenant*, forming a composite design.

1316 Nidularium innocentii

1992. Second UN Conference on Environment and Development (5th issue). 3rd Anniv of Margaret Mee Brazilian Botanical Foundation. Flower paintings by Margaret Mee. Multicoloured.

2543	600cr. Type **1316**	85	55
2544	600cr. *Canistrum exiguum*	85	55
2545	700cr. *Nidularium rubens*	90	65
2546	700cr. *Canistrum cyathiforme*	90	65

1317 Humming-bird's Wings forming Flower

1992. National Diabetes Day.

2547	**1317**	600cr. multicoloured	85	35

1318 Training Tower and First Manual Pump

1992. Centenary of Joinville Volunteer Fire Service.

2548	**1318**	550cr. multicoloured	60	35

1319 Animals, Cave Paintings and Map of Piaui State

1992. 13th Anniv of Capivara Mountain National Park. Multicoloured.

2549	550cr. Type **1319**	60	35
2550	550cr. Canyons and map of Brazil	60	35

Nos. 2549/50 were issued together, *se-tenant*, forming a composite design.

1320 Projects within Flask

1992. 24th Anniv of Financing Agency for Studies and Projects.

2551	**1320**	550cr. multicoloured	60	35

1321 Students at Work

1992. 50th Anniv of National Industrial Training Service.

2552	**1321**	650cr. multicoloured	60	55

1322 Santa Cruz Fortress, Anhatomirim Island

1992. Santa Catarina Fortresses. Multicoloured.

2553	650cr. Type **1322**	60	45
2554	3000cr. Santo Antonio Fort, Ratones Grande island	2·20	1·80

1323 Masonic Emblem and Palace, Brasilia

1992. 170th Anniv of Grande Oriente (Federation of Brazil's Freemasonry Lodges).

2555	**1323**	650cr. multicoloured	60	35

1324 Profiles of Child and Man forming Hourglass

1992. 50th Anniv of Brazilian Legion of Assistance.

2556	**1324**	650cr. multicoloured	60	35

1325 Medical Equipment and Patients

1992. Sarah Locomotor Hospital, Brasilia.

2557	**1325**	800cr. multicoloured	60	45

1326 Menotti del Picchia

1992. Book Day. Writers' Birth Centenaries. Multicoloured.

2558	900cr. Type **1326**	60	45
2559	900cr. Graciliano Ramos	60	45
2560	1000cr. Assis Chateaubriand (journalist) (horiz)	65	50

1327 Meridian Circle, Map, Cruls and Tent

1992. Centenary of Luiz Cruls's Exploration of Central Plateau.

2561	**1327**	900cr. multicoloured	60	45

1328 Productivity Graph on Flag

1992. Second Anniv of Brazilian Quality and Productivity Programme.

2562	**1328**	1200cr. multicoloured	55	35

1329 Pepino Beach, Rio de Janeiro

1992. Year of Tourism in the Americas. Sheet 70×100 mm containing T **1329** and similar horiz design. Multicoloured.

MS2563 1200cr. Type **1329**; 9000cr. Sugar Loaf, Rio de Janeiro ... 3·75 ... 3·75

1330 Father Christmas

1992. Christmas. No value expressed.

2564	**1330**	(–) multicoloured	75	45

1992. Obligatory Tax. Anti-leprosy Week.

2565	**1239**	30cr. brown	65	55

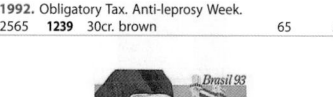

1331 Sister Dulce, Patients and Lacerda Lift, Salvador

1993. Sister Dulce (founder of Santo Antonio Hospital and Simoes Filho Educational Centre) Commemoration.

2566	**1331**	3500cr. multicoloured	40	25

1332 Diving

1993. South American Water Sports Championships, Goiania. Sheet 69×99 mm containing T **1332** and similar horiz designs. Multicoloured.

MS2567 3500cr. Type **1332**; 3500cr. Synchronized swimming; 25000cr. Water polo ... 5·25 ... 3·25

1333 Tube Station, Pine Trees and Church of the Third Order of St. Francis of Assisi and Stigmata

1993. 300th Anniv of Curitiba.

2568	**1333**	4500cr. multicoloured	75	70

1334 Heart dripping Blood onto Flowers

1993. Health and Preservation of Life. Multicoloured.

2569	4500cr. Type **1334** (blood donation)	50	35
2570	4500cr. Crab attacking healthy cell (anti-cancer campaign)	50	35
2571	4500cr. Rainbow, head and encephalogram (mental health)	50	35

1335 Night with the Geniuses of Study and Love

1993. 150th Birth Anniv of Pedro Americo (painter). Multicoloured.

2572	5500cr. Type **1335**	65	45
2573	36000cr. *David and Abizag* (horiz)	4·50	2·75
2574	36000cr. *A Carioca*	4·50	2·75

1336 Flag

1993. No value expressed. Self-adhesive. Die-cut.

2575	**1336**	(–) blue, yellow & grn	2·10	55

No. 2575 was valid for use at the current first class inland letter rate. It could not be used to pay postage to foreign countries.

1337 Dynastes hercules

1993. World Environment Day. Beetles. Multicoloured.

2576	8000cr. Type **1337**	65	45
2577	55000cr. *Batus barbicornis*	3·00	2·75

1338 Map, Flags and Discussion Themes

1993. Third Iberian–American Summit Conference, Salvador.

2578	**1338**	12000cr. multicoloured	75	35

1339 Lake, Congress Building and *Os Candangos* (statue), Brasilia

1993. Union of Portuguese-speaking Capital Cities. Multicoloured.

2579	15000cr. Type **1339**	40	25
2580	71000cr. Copacabana beach and "Christ the Redeemer" (statue), Rio de Janeiro	2·10	1·30

Nos. 2579/80 were issued together, *se-tenant*, forming a composite design.

1340 30r. "Bulls Eye" Stamp

1993. 150th Anniv of First Brazilian Stamps (1st issue) and Brasiliana 93 International Stamp Exhibition, Rio de Janeiro. Each black, red and yellow.

2581	30000cr. Type **1340**	90	45
2582	60000cr.60r. "Bull's Eye" stamp	1·90	1·10
2583	90000cr.90r. "Bull's Eye" stamp	2·50	1·60

MS2584 132×99 mm. As Nos. 2581/3 but without engraver's name and commemorative inscription | 15·00 | 15·00

See also Nos. 2585/8.

1341 Cebolinha designing Stamp

1993. 150th Anniv of First Brazilian Stamps (2nd issue). No value expressed. Cartoon characters. Multicoloured.

2585	(–) Type **1341**	75	25
2586	(–) Cascao as King and 30r. "Bull's Eye" stamp	75	25
2587	(–) Monica writing letter and 60r. "Bull's Eye" stamp	75	25
2588	(–) Magali receiving letter and 90r. "Bull's Eye" stamp	75	25

Nos. 2585/8 were issued together, *se-tenant*, forming a composite design.

Nos. 2585/8 were valid for use at the current first class inland letter rate. They could not be used to pay postage to other countries.

1342 Imperial Palace (former postal H.Q.), Rio de Janeiro

1993. 330th Anniv of Postal Service. Multicoloured.

2589	20000cr. Type **1342**	65	35
2590	20000cr. Petropolis post office	65	35
2591	20000cr. Main post office, Rio de Janeiro	65	35
2592	20000cr. Niteroi post office	65	35

1343 Polytechnic School, Sao Paulo University

1993. Engineering Schools. Multicoloured.

2593	17cr. Type **1343** (centenary, 1994)	90	55
2594	17cr. Old and new engineering schools, Rio de Janeiro Federal University (bicent, 1992)	90	55

1344 Forest Mound and Tools

1993. Preservation of Archaeological Sites. Mult.

2595	17cr. Type **1344**	65	45
2596	17cr. Coastal mound, shells and tools	65	45

1345 Guimaraes and National Congress

1993. Ulysses Guimaraes (politician).

2597	**1346** 22cr. Multicoloured.	65	55

1346 Hands holding Candles and Rope around Statue

1993. Bicentenary of Procession of "Virgin of Nazareth", Belem.

2598	22cr. multicoloured	65	55

1347 Hyacinth Macaw, Glaucous Macaw and Indige Macaw

1993. America. Endangered Macaws. Multicoloured.

2599	22cr. Type **1347**	75	45
2600	130cr. Spix's macaw	2·50	75

1348 Vinicius de Moraes

1993. Composers' Anniversaries. Multicoloured.

2601	22cr. Type **1348** (80th birth anniv)	40	25
2602	22cr. Alfredo da Rocha Vianna (pseud. Pixinguinha) and score of *Carinhoso* (20th death anniv)	40	25

1349 Liberty

1993. No value expressed.

2603	**1349** (–) blue, turq & yell	5·00	4·50

No. 2603 was sold at the current rate for first class international postage.

1350 Mario de Andrade

1993. Book Day. Writers' Birth Centenaries. Multicoloured.

2604	30cr. Type **1350**	40	25
2605	30cr. Alceu Amoroso Lima (pseud. Tristao de Athayde)	40	25
2606	30cr. Gilka Machado (poet)	40	25

1351 Knot

1993. 40th Anniv of Brazil–Portugal Consultation and Friendship Treaty.

2607	**1351** 30cr. multicoloured	50	25

1352 Nho-Quim

1993. Second International Comic Strip Biennial. No value expressed. Multicoloured.

2608	(–) Type **1352**	1·00	35
2609	(–) Benjamin (Louneiro)	1·00	35
2610	(–) Lamparina	1·00	35
2611	(–) Reco-Reco, Bolao and Azeitona (Luiz Sa)	1·00	35

See note below Nos. 2585/8.

1353 Diagram and *Tamoio* (submarine)

1993. Launch of First Brazilian-built Submarine.

2612	**1353** 240cr. multicoloured	3·25	2·75

1354 Nativity

1993. Christmas. No value expressed.

2613	**1354** (–) multicoloured	1·30	85

See note below Nos. 2585/8.

1993. Obligatory Tax. Anti-leprosy Week.

2614	**1205** 50c. blue	40	25

1355 Republic P-47 Thunderbolt Fighters over Tarquinia Camp, Italy

1993. 50th Anniv of Formation of 1st Fighter Group, Brazilian Expeditionary Force.

2615	**1355** 42cr. multicoloured	90	55

1356 Flag

1994. No value expressed. Self-adhesive. Imperf.

2616	**1356** (–) blue, yellow & green	1·20	70

See note below Nos. 2585/8.

1357 Foundation of Republican Memory, Convent and Cloisters

1994. 340th Anniv of Convent of Merces (now Cultural Centre), Sao Luis.

2617	**1357** 58cr. multicoloured	65	35

1358 "Mae Menininha"

1994. Birth Centenary of Mae Menininha do Gantois (Escolastica Maria da Conceiao Nazare).

2618	**1358** 80cr. multicoloured	75	70

1359 Olympic Rings and Rower

1994. Centenaries of International Olympic Committee and Rowing Federation, Rio Grande do Sul. No value expressed.

2619	**1359** (–) multicoloured	4·00	2·30

See note below No. 2603.

1360 Blue and White Swallow

1994. Birds. Multicoloured.

2620	10cr. Type **1360**	65	10
2621	20cr. Roadside hawk	65	10
2622	50cr. Rufous-bellied thrush	65	10
2623	100cr. Ruddy ground dove	65	10
2624	200cr. Southern lapwing	65	10
2625	500cr. Rufous-collared sparrow	1·90	35

See after Nos. 2649/61.

1361 Map and Prince Henry

1994. 600th Birth Anniv of Prince Henry the Navigator.

2626	**1361** 635cr. multicoloured	5·00	2·50

1362 Bicycle

1994. America. Postal Vehicles. Multicoloured.

2627	110cr. Type **1362**	65	35
2628	635cr. Post motor cycle	5·75	1·70

1363 Statue, Grain Store and Chapel of Help, Juazeiro do Norte

1994. 150th Anniv of Birth of Father Cicero Romao Batista. With service indicator.

2629	**1363** (–) multicoloured	1·20	85

See note below Nos. 2585/8.

1364 Sabin and Children

1994. First Death Anniv of Albert Sabin (developer of oral polio vaccine).

2630	**1364** 160cr. multicoloured	1·00	55

1365 Castello Branco and Brasilia

1994. Carlos Castello Branco (journalist).

2631	**1365** 160cr. multicoloured	1·00	55

1366 *Euterpe oleracea*

1994. Birth Bicentenary of Karl Friedrich Phillip von Martius (botanist). With service indicator. Multicoloured. (a) Inscr "1. PORTE NACIONAL".
| 2632 | (–) Type 1366 | 1·30 | 55 |
| 2633 | (–) *Jacaranda paucifoliolata* | 1·30 | 55 |

(b) Inscr "1. PORTE INTERNACIONAL TAXE PERCUE".
| 2634 | (–) *Barbacenia tomentosa* | 3·50 | 1·70 |

Nos. 2632/3 were for use at the current first class inland letter rate and Nos. 2634 for first class international postage.

1367 "Brazil"

1994. With service indicator. (a) Size 21×28 mm. Self-adhesive. Rouletted. (i) PRINTED MATTER. Inscr "1. PORTE IMPRESSO CATEGORIA II".
| 2635 | 1367 | (–) blue | 55 | 45 |

(ii) INLAND POSTAGE. Inscr "3. PORTE NACIONAL".
| 2636 | (3rd) red | 1·00 | 75 |

(b) INLAND POSTAGE. Inscr "PORTE NACIONAL". Size 26×35 mm.
| 2637 | (4th) green | 2·00 | 1·50 |
| 2638 | (5th) red | 4·00 | 2·75 |

Nos. 2635/8 were valid for internal use in the category described.

1368 Brazilian Player wearing "100"

1994. Centenary of Football in Brazil and World Cup Football Championship, U.S.A. With service indicator.
| 2639 | 1368 | (–) multicoloured | 3·75 | 2·50 |

See note below No. 2603.

1369 Emperor Tamarin (*Saguinus imperator*)

1994. Endangered Mammals. With service indicator. Multicoloured.
2640	(–) Type 1369	1·10	50
2641	(–) Bare-faced tamarin (*Saguinus bicolor*)	1·10	50
2642	(–) Golden lion tamarin (*Leontopithecus rosalia*)	1·10	50

See note below Nos. 2585/8.

1370 Book and Disks

1994. 46th International Book Fair, Frankfurt, Germany. Sheet 99×69 mm.
| MS2643 | 1370 | (–) multicoloured | 4·25 | 4·25 |

No. MS2643 was sold at the currant rate for first class international postage.

1371 Pencils Crossing over Fingerprint

1994. Ten Year Education Plan. With service indicator. Multicoloured.
2644	(–) Type 1371 (literacy campaign)	1·20	55
2645	(–) PRONAICA pencil and school (National Programme of Integral Care to Children and Teenagers)	1·20	55
2646	(–) Lecture scene and graph (increase in qualified teachers)	1·20	55
2647	(–) Pencil and "lecturers" on television (distance learning by video)	1·20	55

See note below Nos. 2585/8.

1372 Map of the Americas (Bartholomeu Velho, 1561) and Treaty Boundaries

1994. 500th Anniv of the Treaty of Tordesillas (defining Portuguese and Spanish spheres of influence). Sheet 67×99 mm.
| MS2648 | 1372 | (–) multicoloured | 4·00 | 4·00 |

No. MS2648 was sold at the currant rate for first class international postage.

1994. Birds. As T 1360 but with value expressed as "R$". Multicoloured.
2649	1c. Type 1360	45	15
2650	2c. As No. 2621	45	15
2652	5c. As No. 2622	45	15
2654	10c. As No. 2623	45	15
2655	15c. Saffron finch	80	45
2656	20c. As No. 2624	1·00	50
2657	22c. Fork-tailed fly-catcher	80	50
2658	50c. As No. 2625	3·00	1·30
2661	1r. Rufous hornero	5·25	2·50

1373 Edgard Santos (founder of Bahia University)

1994. Anniversaries. With service indicator. Multicoloured.
2662	(–) Type 1373 (birth centenary)	1·30	65
2663	(–) Oswaldo Aranha (politician, birth centenary)	1·30	65
2664	(–) Otto Lara Resende (author and journalist, 2nd death anniv)	1·30	65

See note below Nos. 2585/8.

1374 *Petrobras X* (drilling platform), Campos Basin. Rio de Janeiro

1994. 40th Anniv of Petrobras (state oil company).
| 2665 | 1374 | 12c. multicoloured | 80 | 50 |

1375 17th century Coin Production

1994. 300th Anniv of Brazilian Mint.
| 2666 | 1375 | 12c. multicoloured | 80 | 65 |

1376 Loaf of Bread

1994. Campaign against Famine and Misery. With service indicator.
| 2667 | 1376 | (–) multicoloured | 1·20 | 65 |
| 2668 | - | (–) black and blue | 1·20 | 65 |

DESIGN: No. 2668, Fish.
See note below Nos. 2585/8.

1377 Writing with Quill and Scales of Justice

1994. 150th Anniv of Brazilian Lawyers Institute.
| 2669 | 1377 | 12c. multicoloured | 80 | 65 |

1378 Family within Heart

1994. International Year of the Family.
| 2670 | 1378 | 84c. multicoloured | 5·25 | 4·00 |

1379 Hospital, White Stork and Babies forming "1000000"

1994. Centenary of Sao Paulo Maternity Hospital. Its Millionth Birth.
| 2671 | 1379 | 12c. multicoloured | 85 | 65 |

1380 Celestino performing and "Maternal Heart" (record sleeve)

1994. Birth Centenary of Vicente Celestino (singer).
| 2672 | 1380 | 12c. multicoloured | 1·30 | 50 |

1381 Fernando de Azevedo (educationist)

1994. Writers' Birth Anniversaries. Multicoloured.
| 2673 | 12c. Type 1381 (cent) | 65 | 40 |
| 2674 | 12c. Tomas Antonio Gonzaga (poet, 250th) | 65 | 40 |

1382 "Joao and Maria" (*Hansel and Gretel*)

1994. Centenary of Publication of *Fairy Tales* by Alberto Figueiredo Pimentel (first Brazilian children's book). Multicoloured.
2675	12c. Type 1382	85	65
2676	12c. "Dona Baratinha" (*Little Mrs Cockroach*)	85	65
2677	84c. *Puss in Boots*	3·50	2·40
2678	84c. *Tom Thumb*	3·50	2·40

1383 St. Clare, St. Damian's Convent and Statue of St. Francis

1994. 800th Birth Anniv of St. Clare of Assisi (founder of order of Poor Clares).
| 2679 | 1383 | 12c. multicoloured | 65 | 40 |

1384 McLaren–Honda F1 Racing Car and Brazilian Flag

1994. Ayrton Senna (racing driver) Commemoration. Multicoloured.
2680	12c. Type 1384	1·10	60
2681	12c. Senna and crowd waving farewell	1·10	60
2682	84c. Brazilian and chequered flags, racing cars and Senna giving victory salute	3·50	2·20

Nos. 2680/2 were issued together, *se-tenant*, forming a composite design.

1385 Books and Globe

1994. Centenary of Historical and Geographical Institute, Sao Paulo.
| 2683 | 1385 | 12c. multicoloured | 65 | 50 |

1386 Adoniran Barbosa and "11 o'Clock Train"

1994. Composers. Multicoloured.
| 2684 | 12c. Type 1386 | 65 | 50 |
| 2685 | 12c. Score of "The Sea" (Dorival Caymmi) | 65 | 50 |

1994. Obligatory Tax. Anti-Leprosy Week.
| 2686 | 1205 | 1c. purple | 40 | 25 |

1387 Maggot wearing Santa Claus Hat in Apple

1994. Christmas. Multicoloured.
2687	12c. Type 1387	55	40
2688	12c. Carol singers	55	40
2689	12c. Boy smoking pipe and letter in boot	55	40
2690	84c. Boy wearing saucepan on head and Santa Claus cloak	3·75	2·30

1388 Trophy

1994. Brazil, World Cup Football Championship (U.S.A.) Winners. Sheet 100×69 mm.
| MS2691 | 1388 | 2r.14 multicoloured | 10·50 | 10·00 |

1389 Pasteur

1995. Death Centenary of Louis Pasteur (chemist).
| 2692 | 1389 | 84c. multicoloured | 4·00 | 3·25 |

1390 Duke of Caxias and Soldiers

1995. 150th Anniv of Peace of Ponche Verde (pacification of Farroupilha Revolution) (2693) and 50th Anniv of Battle of Monte Castello (2694). Multicoloured.
| 2693 | 12c. Type 1390 | 65 | 40 |
| 2694 | 12c. Soldier, Brazilian flag and battle scene | 65 | 40 |

1391 Pres. Franco

1995. Itamar Franco (President 1992–94).
| 2695 | 1391 | 12c. multicoloured | 65 | 40 |

1392 Meal
before Child

1995. 50th Anniv of F.A.O.
2696 **1392** 84c. multicoloured 4·00 3·25

1393 Alexandre de
Gusmao (diplomat)

1995. Birth Anniversaries. Multicoloured.
2697 12c. Type **1393** (300th anniv) 65 40
2698 12c. Visconde (Viscount) de
 Jequitinhonha (lawyer, bicent
 (1994)) 65 40
2699 15c. Barao (Baron) do Rio
 Branco (diplomat, 150th
 anniv) 65 40

1394 Guglielmo Marconi
and his Transmitter

1995. Centenary of First Radio Transmission.
2700 **1394** 84c. multicoloured 4·00 3·25

1395 Ipe-amarelo and
Cherry Blossom

1995. Centenary of Brazil–Japan Friendship Treaty.
2701 **1395** 84c. multicoloured 4·00 3·25

1396 Solitary
Tinamou (Tinamus
solitarius)

1995. Birds. Multicoloured.
2702 12c. Type **1396** 1·00 50
2703 12c. Razor-billed curassow
 (Mitu mitu) 1·00 50

1397 St. John's Party, Campina Grande

1995. June Festivals. Multicoloured.
2704 12c. Type **1397** 65 40
2705 12c. Country wedding, Caruaru 65 40

1398 St. Antony holding
Child Jesus (painting,
Vieira Lusitano)

1995. 800th Birth Anniv of St. Antony of Padua.
2706 **1398** 84c. multicoloured 4·25 3·25

1399 Lumiere Brothers and
Early Projection Equipment

1995. Centenary of Motion Pictures. Sheet 99×70 mm.
MS2707 **1399** 2r.14 multicoloured 10·50 10·00

1400 Laurel and
"Republic"

1995. First Anniv of Real Currency.
2708 **1400** 12c. brown, green & blk 65 40

1401 Player, Net
and Anniversary
Emblem

1995. Centenary of Volleyball.
2709 **1401** 15c. multicoloured 1·10 65

1402 Angaturama limai

1995. 14th Brazilian Palaeontology Society Congress, Uberaba. Dinosaurs. Multicoloured.
2710 15c. Type **1402** 65 45
2711 1r.50 Titanosaurus 3·25 3·00

1403 Crash Test Dummies
in Car

1995. Road Safety Campaign. Multicoloured.
2712 12c. Type **1403** 65 50
2713 71c. Car crashing into glass
 of whisky 4·00 2·75

1404 Calathea
burle-marxii

1995. Singapore '95 International Stamp Exhibition. Tenth Anniv of Donation to Nation by Roberto Burle Marx of his Botanical Collection. Multicoloured.
2714 15c. Type **1404** 20 15
2715 15c. "Vellozia burle-marxii" 20 15
2716 1r.50 "Heliconia aemygdiana" 2·00 1·75

1405 Paratroopers
and Lockheed
C-130 Hercules

1995. 50th Anniv of Parachutist Infantry Brigade.
2717 **1405** 15c. multicoloured 80 65

1406 Paulista Museum
and Fernao Dias Paes
Leme (statue, Luigi
Brizzolara)

1995. Centenary of Paulista Museum of the University of Sao Paulo.
2718 **1406** 15c. multicoloured 80 65

1407 Olinda

1995. Lighthouses. Multicoloured.
2719 15c. Type **1407** 80 65
2720 15c. Sao Joao 80 65
2721 15c. Santo Antonio da Barra 80 65

1408 Scarlet Ibis
and Stoat catching
Fish

1995. Lubrapex 95 Brazilian–Portuguese Stamp Exhibition, Sao Paulo. Fauna of the Tiete River Valley. Multicoloured.
2722 15c. Type **1408** 80 65
2723 84c. Great egret flying over
 canoe 4·00 2·50
MS2724 125×185 mm. 1r.50×2 Motifs
 as in Nos. 2722/3 forming a com-
 posite design 14·50 14·50

1409 X-Ray of Hand

1995. 150th Birth Anniv of Wilhelm Rontgen and Centenary of his Discovery of X-Rays.
2725 **1409** 84c. multicoloured 4·25 3·25

1410 Arms and Crowd

1995. Centenary of Flamengo Regatta Club.
2726 **1410** 15c. multicoloured 95 65

1411 Fungi and Alligator

1995. America. Environmental Protection. Multicoloured.
2727 15c. Type **1411** 80 65
2728 84c. Black-necked swans
 on lake 3·50 2·40
Nos. 2727/8 were issued together, se-tenant, forming a composite design.

1412 Dove over
World Map (left
detail)

1995. 50th Anniv of U.N.O. Multicoloured.
2729 1r.05 Type **1412** 4·50 4·25
2730 1r.05 Dove over world map
 (right detail) 4·50 4·25
Nos. 2729/30 were issued together, se-tenant, forming a composite design.

1413 Jose Maria
Eca de Queiroz

1995. Book Day. Writers' Anniversaries. Multicoloured.
2731 15c. Type **1413** (150th birth) 65 50
2732 15c. Rubem Braga (5th death) 65 50
2733 23c. Carlos Drummond de
 Andrade (8th death) 1·10 65

1414 Zumbi

1995. 300th Death Anniv of Zumbi (leader of Palmares (autonomous state formed by rebelled slaves)). Sheet 100×69 mm.
2734 **1414** 1r.05 multicoloured 5·00 5·00

1415 Front Crawl
(Freestyle)

1995. 11th World Short-course Swimming Championships, Rio de Janeiro. Multicoloured.
2735 23c. Type **1415** 95 65
2736 23c. Backstroke 95 65
2737 23c. Butterfly 95 65
2738 23c. Breaststroke 95 65
Nos. 2735/8 were issued together, se-tenant, forming a composite design of a swimming pool.

1416 Cherub

1995. Christmas. Multicoloured.
2739 15c. Type **1416** 80 50
2740 23c. Cherub (different) 95 65
Nos. 2739/40 were issued together, se-tenant, forming a composite design.

1417 Flag, Former
Headquarters and
Manequinho (statue)

1995. Centenary (1994) of Botafogo Football and Regatta Club.
2741 **1417** 15c. multicoloured 80 65

1418 Computer,
Mouse and
Masthead

1995. 170th Anniv of Diario de Pernambuco (newspaper).
2742 **1418** 23c. multicoloured 95 65

1419 Theatre Dome

1996. Centenary of Amazon Theatre, Manaus. Sheet 98×69 mm.
MS2743 **1419** 1r.23 multicoloured 6·00 6·00

1420 Prestes Maia and
Sao Paulo

1996. Birth Centenary of Francisco Prestes Maia (Mayor of Sao Paulo).

2744	**1420**	18c. multicoloured	80	40

1421 Bornhausen and Santa Catarina

1996. Birth Centenary of Irineu Bornhausen (Governor of State of Santa Catarina).

2745	**1421**	27c. multicoloured	1·00	65

1422 *Ouro Preto Landscape* (Alberto da Veiga Guignard)

1996. Artists' Birth Centenaries. Multicoloured.

2746	**1422**	15c. Type **1422**	60	40
2747		15c. *Boat with Little Flags and Birds* (Alfredo Volpi)	60	40

1423 Doll

1996. 50th Anniv of United Nations Children's Fund. Campaign against Sexual Abuse.

2748	**1423**	23c. multicoloured	1·00	50

1424 Anniversary Emblem

1996. 500th Anniv (2000) of Discovery of Brazil by the Portuguese.

2749	**1424**	1r.05 multicoloured	3·75	2·50

1425 Pinheiro da Silva and National Congress

1996. Birth Centenary of Israel Pinheiro da Silva (politician).

2750	**1425**	18c. multicoloured	85	50

1426 Pantanal

1996. Tourism. Multicoloured. Self-adhesive. Imperf (backing paper rouletted).

2751		23c. Amazon River	1·00	65
2752		23c. Type **1426**	1·00	65
2753		23c. Jangada raft	1·00	65
2754		23c. *The Sugarloaf*, Guanabara Bay	1·00	65
2755		23c. Iguazu Falls	1·00	65

1427 Crimson Topaz

1996. Espamer 96 Spanish and Latin-American Stamp Exhibition, Seville, Spain. Hummingbirds. Multicoloured.

2756		15c. Type **1427**	85	40
2757		1r.05 Black-breasted plover-crest	5·00	2·50
2758		1r.15 Swallow-tailed hummingbird	5·00	2·50

1428 Marathon Runners

1996. Cent of Modern Olympic Games. Multicoloured.

2759		18c. Type **1428**	60	40
2760		23c. Gymnastics	65	50
2761		1r.05 Swimming	2·75	2·50
2762		1r.05 Beach volleyball	2·75	2·50

1429 Cave Entrance

1996. National Heritage. Caverns. Sheet 99×68 mm.

MS2763	**1429**	2r.68 multicoloured	9·50	9·50

1430 Dish Aerial, Satellite over Earth and Sports

1996. Americas Telecom 96 International Telecommunications Exn, Rio de Janeiro.

2764	**1430**	1r.05 multicoloured	4·00	2·50

1431 Sun and Raindrop replenishing Dry Tree

1996. World Anti-desertification Day. Sheet 70×96 mm.

MS2765	**1431**	1r.23 multicoloured	5·50	5·50

1432 Addict and Drugs

1996. Anti-drug Abuse Campaign.

2766	**1432**	27c. multicoloured	3·50	1·10

1433 Coloured Pencils

1996. Education Year.

2767	**1433**	23c. multicoloured	95	50

1434 Princess Isabel and Aurea Law

1996. 150th Birth Anniv of Princess Isabel the Redeemer.

2768	**1434**	18c. multicoloured	80	40

The Aurea Law abolished slavery in Brazil.

1435 Gomes and Peace Theatre

1996. Death Centenary of Carlos Gomes (opera composer).

2769	**1435**	50c. multicoloured	2·10	1·10

1436 *Cattleya eldorado*

1996. 15th International Orchid Conference, Rio de Janeiro. Multicoloured.

2770		15c. Type **1436**	1·30	45
2771		15c. *Cattleya loddigesii*	1·30	45
2772		15c. *Promenaea stapellioides*	1·30	45

1437 Melania and Maximino and Virgin Mary

1996. 150th Anniv of Apparition of Our Lady at La Salette, France.

2773	**1437**	1r. multicoloured	3·25	2·75

1438 Cuca

1996. BRAPEX 96 National Stamp Exhibition, Recife. Folk Legends. Sheet 72×100 mm containing T **1438** and similar horiz designs. Multicoloured.

MS2774		23c. Type **1438**; 1r.05 Boitata; 1r.15 Caipora	7·50	7·50

1439 *Marilyn Monroe* (Andy Warhol)

1996. 23rd International Biennale, Sao Paulo. Paintings. Multicoloured.

2775		55c. Type **1439**	1·40	1·00
2776		55c. *The Scream* (Edvard Munch)	1·40	1·00
2777		55c. *Mirror for the red Room* (Louise Bourgeois)	1·40	1·00
2778		55c. *Lent* (Pablo Picasso)	1·40	1·00

1440 Emblem

1996. Defenders of Nature (environmental organization).

2779	**1440**	10r. multicoloured	14·50	12·00

1441 Vaqueiro

1996. America. Traditional Costumes. Multicoloured.

2780		50c. Type **1441**	1·60	1·10
2781		1r. Baiana (seller of beancakes)	3·25	2·30

1442 Poinsettia and Lighted Candle

1996. Christmas.

2782	**1442**	(–) multicoloured	1·40	50

See second note below No. 2588.

1443 *Melindrosa* (cover of 1931 *O Cruzeiro* magazine)

1996. 46th Death Anniv of Jose Carlos (caricaturist).

2783	**1443**	(–) multicoloured	1·40	50

See second note below No. 2588.

1444 Ipiranga Monument

1996. Tourism. Multicoloured. Self-adhesive. Imperf (backing paper rouletted).

2784		(–) Type **1444**	80	55
2785		(–) Hercilio Luz Bridge	80	55
2786		(–) National Congress building	80	55
2787		(–) Pelourinho	80	55
2788		(–) Ver-o-Peso market	80	55

Nos. 2784/8 were valid for use at the current first stage inland letter rate.

1445 Campaign Emblem and Guanabara Bay

1997. Bid by Rio de Janeiro for 2004 Olympic Games.

2789	**1445**	(–) multicoloured	4·25	2·75

No. 2789 was valid for use at the current first stage international letter rate.

1446 Postman and Letter Recipients

1997. America. The Postman.

2790	**1446**	(–) multicoloured	1·30	60

No. 2790 was valid for use at the current first stage inland letter rate.

1447 Alves, Flogging and Salvador Harbour

1997. 150th Birth Anniv of Antonio de Castro Alves (poet).

2791	**1447**	15c. multicoloured	65	40

1448 *Tamandare* (after Miranda Junior) and *Rescue of 'Ocean Monarch'* by Don Afonso (Samuel Walters)

1997. Death Centenary of Marquis of Tamandare (naval reformer).
2792 **1448** 23c. multicoloured 65 50

1449 "Joy, Joy"

1997. Winning Entry in "Art on Stamps" Competition.
2793 **1449** 15c. multicoloured 4·25 65

1450 Globe in Glass of Water

1997. World Water Day.
2794 **1450** 1r.05 multicoloured 3·25 2·50

1451 Embraer EMB-145

1997. Brazilian Aircraft. Multicoloured. Self-adhesive. Imperf (backing paper rouletted).
2795 15c. Type **1451** 40 25
2796 15c. Aeritalia/Aermacchi AM-X jet fighter 40 25
2797 15c. Embraer EMB-312 H Super Tucano 40 25
2798 15c. Embraer EMB-120 Brasilia 40 25
2799 15c. Embraer EMB-312 Tucano trainer 40 25

1452 Red Ribbon inside Condom

1997. Family Health Association (A.S.F.) Anti-AIDS Campaign.
2810 **1452** 23c. multicoloured 75 45

1453 Traditional Weapons and Tribesmen

1997. Indian Cultures. Sheet 70×100 mm.
MS2811 **1453** 1r.15 multicoloured 3·50 3·25

1454 Emblem

1997. 500th Anniv (2000) of Discovery of Brazil by the Portuguese.
2812 **1454** 1r.05 multicoloured 3·25 2·50

1455 Pixinguinha

1997. Birth Centenary of Pixinguinha (musician).
2813 **1455** 15c. multicoloured 45 40

1456 Landmark

1997. Centenary of Brazilian Sovereignty of Trinidade Island. Sheet 99×68 mm.
MS2814 **1456** 1r.23 multicoloured 4·00 3·75

1457 Inscription

1997. "Human Rights, Rights of All".
2815 **1457** 18c. black and red 65 40

1458 Map

1997. Brazilian Antarctic Programme. Sheet 69×99 mm.
MS2816 **1458** 2r.68 multicoloured 8·75 8·25

1459 Melon

1997. Fruits. Self-adhesive. (a) Imperf (backing paper rouletted). (i) With service indicator.
2817 **1459** (–) red and green 55 50

(ii) With face values.
2818 1c. yellow, orange & grn 15 15
2819 2c. yellow, brown & blk 15 15
2820 5c. orange, yellow & blk 15 15
2821 10c. yellow, brown & grn 25 25
2822 20c. yellow, red & green 55 50

(b) Die-cut wavy edge.
2823 1c. yellow, orange & grn 15 15
2824 10c. yellow, brown & grn 15 15
2825 20c. lt green, grn & blk 55 50
2826 22c. red, purple & green 55 40
2827 27c. orange, brown and green 65 65
2828 40c. multicoloured 80 75
2829 50c. multicoloured 80 75
2830 51c. green, lt grn & brn 1·30 1·30
2831 80c. red, green & yellow 2·10 2·00
2832 82c. lt grn, grn & dp grn 2·10 2·00
2833 1r. red, green & yellow 2·75 1·60

DESIGNS—HORIZ: Nos. 2818, 2823, Oranges; 2819, Bananas; 2820, Mango. VERT: Nos. 2821, 2824, Pineapple; 2822, Cashew nuts; 2825, Sugar-apple; 2826, Grapes; 2827, Cupuacu; 2828, Soursop; 2829, Suriname cherry ("Pitanga"); 2830, Coconut; 2831, Apples; 2832, Limes; 2833, Strawberries.
No. 2817 was valid for use at the current first stage inland letter rate.

1460 Mahogany (*Swietenia macropylla*)

1997. World Environment Day. Amazon Flora and Fauna. Multicoloured.
2836 27c. Type **1460** 80 65
2837 27c. Arapaima (55×22 mm) 80 65

1461 Antonio Vieira in Pulpit

1997. Death Anniversaries of Missionaries to Brazil. Multicoloured.
2838 1r.05 Type **1461** (300th) 2·75 2·50
2839 1r.05 Indian children and Jose de Auchieta (400th) 2·75 2·50

1462 Parnaiba Delta and Sculpture (Mestre Dezinho)

1997. Tourism. With service indicator. Mult.
2840 (–) Type **1462** 2·75 2·50
2841 (–) Lencois Maranhenses National Park and costume 2·75 2·50
Nos. 2840/1 were valid for use at the current rate for first class international postage.

1463 Blue-black Grassquit

1997. Birds. Multicoloured. Self-adhesive. Imperf (backing paper rouletted). (a) With service indicator.
2842 (–) Type **1463** 95 90

(b) With face value.
2843 22c. Social flycatcher ("Vermilion-crowned Flycatcher") 55 50
No. 2842 was valid for use at the current first stage inland letter rate.

1464 Academy

1998. Centenary of Brazilian Literature Academy.
2850 **1464** 22c. multicoloured 95 50

1465 *Gipsies* (Di Cavalcanti)

1997. Birth Centenary of Emiliano di Cavalcanti (artist).
2851 **1465** 31c. multicoloured 85 75

1466 Pope John Paul II, "Christ the Redeemer" and Family

1997. Second World Meeting of Pope with Families, Rio de Janeiro.
2852 **1466** 1r.20 multicoloured 4·75 3·00

1467 Flags of Member Countries

1997. Mercosur (South American Common Market).
2853 **1467** 80c. multicoloured 2·75 1·90

1468 Antonio Conselheiro (religious leader)

1997. Centenary of End of Canudos War.
2854 **1468** 22c. multicoloured 70 50

1469 Mercosur Members starred on Map of South America

1997. 25th Anniv of Telebras.
2855 **1469** 80c. multicoloured 3·25 1·90

1470 Lorenzo Fernandez and Score of *Sonata Breve*

1997. Composers' Birth Centenaries. Each black and gold.
2856 22c. Type **1470** 70 50
2857 22c. Francisco Mignone and score of *Second Brazilian Fantasia* 70 50

1471 "Our Good Mother" and Blackboard with Marist Motto

1997. Centenary of Marist Brothers in Brazil.
2858 **1471** 22c. multicoloured 70 50

1472 Angel playing Trumpet

1997. Christmas.
2859 **1472** 22c. multicoloured 70 50

1473 'Equality' (Gian Calvi)

1997. Children and Citizenship. Multicoloured.
2860 22c.+8c. Type **1473** 85 75
2861 22c.+8c. "Love and Tenderness" (Alcy Linares) 85 75
2862 22c.+8c. "Admission to School" (Ziraldo) 85 75
2863 22c.+8c. "Healthy Pregnancy" (Claudio Martins) 85 75
2864 22c.+8c. "Being Happy" (Cica Fittipaldi) 85 75
2865 22c.+8c. "Work for Parents, School for Children" (Roger Mello) 85 75
2866 22c.+8c. "Breast-feeding" (Angela Lago) 85 75
2867 22c.+8c. "Civil Registration" (Mauricio de Sousa) 85 75
2868 22c.+8c. "Integration of the Handicapped" (Nelson Cruz) 85 75
2869 22c.+8c. "Presence of Parents during Illness" (Eliardo Franca) 85 75
2870 22c.+8c. "Quality of Teaching" (Graca Lima) 85 75
2871 22c.+8c. "Safe Delivery" (Eva Furnari) 85 75
2872 22c.+8c. "Family and Community Life" (Gerson Conforti) 85 75

2873	22c.+8c. "Music playing" (Ana Raquel)	85	75
2874	22c.+8c. "Respect and Dignity" (Helena Alexandrino)	85	75
2875	22c.+8c. "Summary of Children's Statute" (Darlan Rosa)	85	75

1474 Children and Globe

1997. Education and Citizenship.

2876	**1474**	31c. blue and yellow	1·00	75

1475 Belo Horizonte at Night

1997. Centenary of Belo Horizonte.

2877	**1475**	31c. multicoloured	1·00	75

1476
Outline Map
and Books
(Education)

1997. Citizens' Rights. Multicoloured. Self-adhesive.

2878	22c. Type **1476**		1·40	50
2879	22c. Map and hand holding labour card (work)		1·40	50
2880	22c. Map and fruit (agriculture)		1·40	50
2881	22c. Map and stethoscope (health)		1·40	50
2882	22c. Clapper-board and paint brush (culture)		1·40	50

1477 Alexandrite

1998. Minerals. Multicoloured.

2883	22c. Type **1477**	85	50
2884	22c. Chrysoberyl cat's-eye	85	50
2885	22c. Indicolite	85	50

1478 Elis Regina (singer)

1998. America. Famous Women. Multicoloured.

2886	22c. Type **1478**	70	50
2887	22c. Clementina de Jesus (singer)	70	50
2888	22c. Dulcina de Moraes (actress)	70	50
2889	22c. Clarice Lispector (writer)	70	50

1479 Pupils

1998. Education. Multicoloured.

2890	31c. Type **1479** (universal schooling)	85	75
2891	31c. Teacher (teacher appraisal)	85	75

Nos. 2390/1 were issued together, *se-tenant*, forming a composite design of a classroom.

1480 Cruze Sousa

1998. Death Centenary of Joao da Cruze Sousa (poet).

2892	**1480**	36c. multicoloured	1·10	90

1481 Map, 1519

1998. 500th Anniv (2000) of Discovery of Brazil by the Portuguese. Multicoloured.

2893		1r.05 Type **1481**	2·75	2·50
2894		1r.05 Galleon	2·75	2·50

Nos. 2893/4 were issued together, *se-tenant*, forming a composite design.

1482 Woman Caring for Elderly Man

1998. Voluntary Work. Multicoloured.

2895	31c. Type **1482**	85	75
2896	31c. Woman caring for child	85	75
2897	31c. Fighting forest fire	85	75
2898	31c. Adult's and child's hands	85	75

Nos. 2895/8 were issued together, *se-tenant*, forming a composite design.

1483 Clown

1998. Circus. Multicoloured.

2899	31c. Type **1483**	85	75
2900	31c. Clown resting on stick	85	75
2901	31c. Clown (left half) and outside of Big Top	85	75
2902	31c. Clown (right half) and inside of Big Top	85	75

Nos. 2899/2902 were issued together, *se-tenant*, forming a composite design.

1484 Turtle

1998. Expo '98 World's Fair, Lisbon. International Year of the Ocean. Multicoloured.

2903	31c. Type **1484**	85	75
2904	31c. Tail of whale	85	75
2905	31c. Barracuda	85	75
2906	31c. Jellyfish and fishes	85	75
2907	31c. Diver and school of fishes	85	75
2908	31c. Two dolphins	85	75
2909	31c. Angelfish (brown spotted fish)	85	75
2910	31c. Two whales	85	75
2911	31c. Two long-nosed butterflyfishes (with black stripe across eye)	85	75
2912	31c. Sea perch (red and yellow fish)	85	75
2913	31c. Manatee	85	75
2914	31c. Seabream (blue, yellow and white fish)	85	75
2915	31c. Emperor angelfish and coral	85	75
2916	31c. School of snappers (blue and yellow striped fishes)	85	75
2917	31c. Flying gurnard	85	75
2918	31c. Manta ray	85	75
2919	31c. Two butterflyfishes (black and green fishes)	85	75
2920	31c. Pipefish	85	75
2921	31c. Moray eel	85	75
2922	31c. Angelfish (blue, yellow and black) and coral	85	75
2923	31c. Red and yellow fish, starfish and coral	85	75
2924	31c. Crab and coral	85	75
2925	31c. Snapper and coral	85	75
2926	31c. Seahorse and coral	85	75

Nos. 2903/26 were issued together, *se-tenant*, forming a composite design.

1485 Ball breaking Net (Antonio Henrique Amaral)

1998. World Cup Football Championship, France. Designs depicting football art by named artists. Multicoloured.

2927	22c. Type **1485**	55	50
2928	22c. Aldemir Martins	55	50
2929	22c. Glauco Rodrigues	55	50
2930	22c. Marcia Grostein	55	50
2931	22c. Claudio Tozzi	55	50
2932	22c. Zelio Alves Pinto	55	50
2933	22c. Guto Lacaz	55	50
2934	22c. Antonio Peticov	55	50
2935	22c. Cildo Meireles	55	50
2936	22c. Mauricio Nogueira Lima	55	50
2937	22c. Roberto Magalhaes	55	50
2938	22c. Luiz Zerbine	55	50
2939	22c. Maciej Babinski (horiz)	55	50
2940	22c. Wesley Duke Lee (horiz)	55	50
2941	22c. Joao Camara (horiz)	55	50
2942	22c. Jose Zaragoza (horiz)	55	50
2943	22c. Mario Gruber (horiz)	55	50
2944	22c. Nelson Leirner (horiz)	55	50
2945	22c. Carlos Vergara (horiz)	55	50
2946	22c. Tomoshige Kusuno (horiz)	55	50
2947	22c. Gregorio Gruber (horiz)	55	50
2948	22c. Jose Roberto Aguilar (horiz)	55	50
2949	22c. Ivald Granato (horiz)	55	50
2950	22c. Leda Catunda (horiz)	55	50

1486 Bean Casserole and Vegetables

1998. Cultural Dishes.

2951	**1486**	31c. multicoloured	1·00	75

1487 *Araucaria angustifolia*

1998. Environmental Protection. Multicoloured.

2952	22c. Type **1487**	95	50
2953	22c. Azure jay (*Cyanocorax caeruleus*)	95	50

Nos. 2952/3 were issued together, *se-tenant*, forming a composite design.

1488 *Tapajo*

1998. Launching of Submarine *Tapajo*.

2954	**1488**	51c. multicoloured	1·40	1·30

1489 Bust of Queiroz and College Building

1998. Death Centenary of Luiz de Queiroz (founder of Agricultural College, Piracicaba).

2955	**1489**	36c. multicoloured	1·00	90

1490 Statue of St. Benedict and Monastery

1998. 400th Anniv of St. Benedict's Monastery, Sao Paulo.

2956	**1490**	22c. multicoloured	85	50

1491 Santos-Dumont and his First Balloon "Brasil"

1998. Aviation. Aircraft Designs by Alberto Santos-Dumont (aviator). Multicoloured.

2957	31c. Type **1491**	85	75
2958	31c. Santos-Dumont and Dirigible *No. 1*	85	75

1492 Early Film of Guanabara Bay

1998. Centenary (1997) of Brazilian Cinema. Multicoloured.

2959	31c. Type **1492**	85	75
2960	31c. Taciana Reis (actress) in *Limite* (dir. Mario Peixoto, 1912)	85	75
2961	31c. Grande Otela and Oscarito in *A Dupla do Barulho* (dir. Carlos Manga, 1953) (inscr "Chanchada")	85	75
2962	31c. Mazzaropi (actor) and film titles (Vera Cruz film company)	85	75
2963	31c. Glauber Rocha (director) (*New Cinema*)	85	75
2964	31c. Titles of prize-winning films, 1962–98	85	75

1493 Andrade, Entrance to St. Antony's Church (Tiradentes) and Church of Our Lady of the Rosary (Ouro Preto)

1998. Birth Centenary of Rodrigo Melo Franco de Andrade (founder of Federal Institution for Preservation of the National Historic and Artistic Patrimony).

2965	**1493**	51c. multicoloured	1·40	1·10

1494 Cascudo and Folk Characters

1998. Birth Centenary of Luis da Camara Cascudo (writer).

2966	**1494**	22c. multicoloured	90	50

1495 Fencing

1998. 42nd World Aeronautical Pentathlon Championships, Natal. Multicoloured.

2967	22c. Type **1495**	90	50
2968	22c. Running	90	50
2969	22c. Swimming	90	50
2970	22c. Shooting	90	50
2971	22c. Basketball	90	50

1496 Missionary Cross and St. Michael of the Missions Church

1998. Mercosur. Missions.

2972	**1496**	80c. multicoloured	2·30	1·50

1497 *Untitled Work* (Jose Leonilson) (Biennale emblem)

1998. 24th Art Biennale, Sao Paulo. Paintings. Multicoloured.

2973	31c. Type **1497**	85	65
2974	31c. *Tapuia Dance* (Albert von Eckhout)	85	65
2975	31c. *The Schoolboy* (Vincent van Gogh) (vert)	85	65
2976	31c. *Portrait of Michel Leiris* (Francis Bacon) (vert)	85	65
2977	31c. *The King's Museum* (Rene Magritte) (vert)	85	65
2978	31c. *Urutu* (Tarsila do Amaral)	85	65
2979	31c. *Facade with Arcs, Circle and Fascia* (Alfredo Volpi) (vert)	85	65
2980	31c. *The Raft of the Medusa* (Asger Jorn)	85	65

1498 "Citizenship" (Erika Albuquerque)

1998. Child and Citizenship.

2981	**1498**	22c. multicoloured	85	40

1499 Mail Coach and *Postilhao da America* (brigantine)

1998. Bicentenary of Reorganization of Maritime Mail Service between Portugal and Brazil.

2982	**1499**	1r.20 multicoloured	2·75	2·50

1500 *D. Pedro I* (Simplicio Rodrigues da Sa), Crown and Sceptre

1998. Birth Bicentenary of Emperor Pedro I.

2983	**1500**	22c. multicoloured	80	40

1501 Mangoes and Glasses of Juice

1998. Frisco (fruit juice) Publicity Campaign. Self-adhesive.

2984	**1501**	36c. multicoloured	4·00	2·75

1502 *Solanum lycocarpum*

1998. Cerrado Flowers. Multicoloured.

2985	31c. Type **1502**	80	65
2986	31c. *Cattleya walkeriana*	80	65
2987	31c. *Kielmeyera coriacea*	80	65

1503 Mother Teresa (founder of Missionaries of Charity)

1998. Peace and Fraternity. Multicoloured.

2988	31c. Type **1503**	80	65
2989	31c. Friar Galvao (first Brazilian to be beatified, 1998)	80	65
2990	31c. Betinho (Herbert Jose de Souza)	80	65
2991	31c. Friar Damiao	80	65

Nos. 2988/91 were issued together, *se-tenant*, forming a central composite design of the Earth.

1504 Sergio Motta and Headquarters, Brasilia

1998. First Anniv of National Telecommunications Agency.

2992	**1504**	31c. multicoloured	95	65

Motta was Minister of Communications when the agency was established.

1505 Tiles and Church of Our Lady of Fatima, Brasilia

1998. Christmas.

2993	**1505**	22c. multicoloured	90	40

1506 Moxoto Goat

1998. Domestic Animals. Mult. Self-adhesive.

2994	22c. Type **1506**	60	35
2995	22c. North-eastern donkey	60	35
2996	22c. Junqueira ox	60	35
2997	22c. Brazilian terrier (vert)	60	35
2998	22c. Brazilian shorthair (vert)	60	35

1507 Man casting Winged Shadow

1998. 50th Anniv of Universal Declaration of Human Rights.

2999	**1507**	1r.20 multicoloured	4·00	1·90

1508 Mother Luiza Lighthouse, Natal

1999. 400th Annivs of Natal (1999) and of Wise Men's Fortress (1998). Multicoloured.

3000	31c. Type **1508**	1·00	40
3001	31c. Wise Men's Fortress, Natal (horiz)	1·00	40

1509 Extent of Economic Zone, Satellite and Belmonte Lighthouse

1999. Evaluation Programme of Sustainable Potential of Living Resources in the Exclusive Economic Zone (REVIZEE). Multicoloured.

3002	31c. Type **1509** (Sao Pedro and Sao Paulo Archipelago Research Programme)	65	40
3003	31c. Blue-faced booby on buoy	65	40
3004	31c. *Riobaldo* (research ship)	65	40
3005	31c. Turtle	65	40
3006	31c. Dolphin	65	40
3007	31c. Diver	65	40

Nos. 3002/7 were issued together, *se-tenant*, forming a composite design.

No. 3004 includes the emblem of Australia 99 International Stamp Exhibition, Melbourne.

1510 Stamp Vending Machines of 1940s and 1998

1999. 125th Anniv of Universal Postal Union. Multicoloured.

3008	31c. Type **1510**	65	40
3009	31c. Postal products vending machines of 1906 and 1998	65	40
3010	31c. Postboxes of 1870 and 1973	65	40
3011	31c. Brazilian Quality and Productivity Programme silver award to Rio Grande postal region, 1998	65	40

Nos. 3008/11 were issued together, *se-tenant*, forming a composite design of the U.P.U. emblem.

1511 Lacerda Lift, Barra Lighthouse and Church of Our Lady of the Rosary

1999. 450th Anniv of Salvador.

3012	**1511**	1r.05 multicoloured	3·50	1·60

1512 Footprint, Iguanodon, Stegosaurus and Allosaurus

1999. iBRA 99 International Stamp Exhibition, Nuremberg, Germany. Valley of the Dinosaurs, Sousa.

3013	**1512**	1r.05 multicoloured	2·75	1·90

1513 Fortress

1999. 415th Anniv of St. Amaro of Barra Grande Fortress, Guaruja.

3014	**1513**	22c. multicoloured	75	40

1514 Children of Various Races

1999. 500th Anniv (2000) of Discovery of Brazil (4th issue). Sheet 69×99 mm.

MS3015	**1514**	2r.68 multicoloured	6·25	6·25

1515 Embracer EMB-110 Bandeirante, Emblem, Dove and Globe

1999. 30th Anniv of 6th Air Transportation Squadron.

3016	**1515**	51c. multicoloured	1·60	90

1516 Banner and Revellers

1999. Feast of the Holy Spirit, Planaltina.

3017	**1516**	22c. multicoloured	70	40

1517 Ouro Preto

1999. Philexfrance 99 International Stamp Exhibition. World Heritage Sites. Sheet 70×110 containing T **1517** and similar horiz designs. Multicoloured.

MS3018	1r.05 Type **1517**; 1r.05 Olinda; 1r.05 Sao Lius	7·00	7·00

1518 Symbols of Computer Science, Chemistry, Engineering, Metallurgy and Geology

1999. Centenary of Institute for Technological Research, Sao Paulo.

3019	**1518**	36c. multicoloured	95	50

1519 Santos-Dumont and Ballon No. 3

1999. Centenary of Flight of Alberto Santos-Dumont's Airship Ballon No. 3.

3020	**1519**	1r.20 multicoloured	3·50	1·80

1520 Anteater and Emblem

1999. National Campaign for Prevention and Combat of Forest Fires (PREVFOGO). Mult. Self-adhesive.

3021	51c. Type **1520**	1·10	75
3022	51c. Flower and IBAMA emblem	1·10	75
3023	51c. Leaf and IBAMA emblem	1·10	75
3024	51c. Burnt tree trunk and PREVFOGO emblem	1·10	75

Nos. 3021/4 were issued together, *se-tenant*, forming a composite design of a map and flames.

Nos. 3021/4 are also impregnated with the scent of burnt wood.

1521 Hands drawing Dove

1999. America. A New Millennium without Arms. Sheet 109×69 mm containing T **1521** and similar vert design. Multicoloured.

MS3025	90c. Type **1521**; 90c. Overturned tank	4·25	4·25

1522 Stitched Heart

1999. 20th Anniv of Political Amnesty in Brazil.

3026	**1522**	22c. multicoloured	65	25

1523 Joaquim Nabuco (politician)

1999. 150th Birth Anniversaries. Multicoloured.

3027	22c. Type **1523**	65	25
3028	31c. Rui Barbosa (politician)	80	40

1524 Dorado

1999. China '99 International Stamp Exhibition, Peking. Fishes. Multicoloured.

3029	22c. Type **1524**	30	25
3030	31c. *Brycon microlepis*	45	40
3031	36c. *Acestrorhynchus pantaneiro*	65	50
3032	51c. Tetra "*Hyphessobrycon eques*"	95	75
3033	80c. *Rineloricaria* sp.	1·40	1·10
3034	90c. *Leporinus macrocephalus*	1·60	1·30
3035	1r.05 *Abramites* sp.	1·90	1·50
3036	1r.20 Bristle-mouthed catfish	2·20	1·80

Nos. 3029/36 were issued together, *se-tenant*, with the backgrounds forming a composite design.

No. 3036 also includes a hologram of the exhibition emblem.

1525 Open Book and Flags of Member Countries

1999. Mercosur. The Book.

3037	**1525**	80c. multicoloured	2·50	1·30

1526 Aguas Emendadas Ecological Station

1999. Water Resources. Multicoloured.

3038	31c. Type **1526**	50	40
3039	31c. House and jetty	50	40
3040	31c. Cedro Dam	50	40
3041	31c. Oros Dam	50	40

Nos. 3038/41 were issued together, *se-tenant*, forming a composite design of a whirlpool.

1527 "Ex Libris" (Eliseu Visconti)

1999. National Library, Rio de Janeiro.

3042	**1527**	22c. multicoloured	55	25

1999. State Flags (6th series). As T **992**.

3043	31c. Amapa	65	50
3044	36c. Roraima	65	50

1528 Piano and Woman

1999. Fifth Death Anniv of Antonio Carlos Jobim (composer).

3045	**1528**	31c. multicoloured	65	50

1529 The Annunciation

1999. Christmas. Birth Bimillenary of Jesus Christ. Multicoloured.

3046	22c. Type **1529**	35	25
3047	22c. Adoration of the Magi	35	25
3048	22c. Presentation of Jesus in the Temple	35	25
3049	22c. Baptism of Jesus by John the Baptist	35	25
3050	22c. Jesus and the Twelve Apostles	35	25
3051	22c. Death and resurrection of Jesus	35	25

1530 Open Book and Globe

1999. New Middle School Education Programme.

3052	**1530**	31c. multicoloured	70	50

1531 Itamaraty Palace, Rio de Janeiro

1999. Centenary of Installation of Ministry of Foreign Relations Headquarters in Itamaraty Palace, Rio de Janeiro.

3053	**1531**	1r.05 brown and stone	2·75	1·60

1532 Buildings and Trees (Milena Karoline Ribeiro Reis)

2000. "Stampin the Future". Winning Entries in Children's International Painting Competition. Multicoloured.

3054	22c.+8c. Type **1532**	65	50
3055	22c.+8c. Globe, sun, trees, children and whale (Caio Ferreira Guimaraes de Oliveira)	65	50
3056	22c.+8c. Woman with globe on dress (Clarissa Cazane)	65	50
3057	22c.+8c. Children hugging globe (Jonas Sampaio de Freitas)	65	50

1533 "2000"

2000. New Millennium.

3058	**1533**	90c. multicoloured	2·00	1·50

1534 Map of South America and Children holding Books

2000. National School Book Programme.

3059	**1534**	31c. multicoloured	85	65

1535 Ada Rogato

2000. Women Aviators. Multicoloured.

3060	22c. Type **1535**	50	40
3061	22c. Thereza de Marzo	50	40
3062	22c. Anesia Pinheiro	50	40

1536 Moqueca Capixaba

2000. Cultural Dishes. Multicoloured.

3063	1r.05 Type **1536**	2·75	2·10
3064	1r.05 Moqueca baiana	2·75	2·10

1537 Freyre and Institute Facade

2000. Birth Centenary of Gilberto Freyre (writer).

3065	**1537**	36c. multicoloured	1·00	75

1538 Painting and Emblem

2000. 500th Anniv of the Discovery of Brazil.

3066	**1538**	51c. multicoloured	1·30	1·00

1539 Natives

2000. 500th Anniv of the Discovery of Brazil. Multicoloured.

3067	31c. Type **1539**	85	65
3068	31c. Natives watching ships	85	65
3069	31c. Sailors in rigging	85	65
3070	31c. Ships sails and natives	85	65

1540 Sailing Ship and Brazilian Flag

2000. 500th Anniv of the Discovery of Brazil. Multicoloured.

3071	45c. Type **1540**	1·30	1·00
3072	45c. Man dressed in red suit, pineapple and telephone dial	1·30	1·00
3073	45c. Red-spectacled amazon and silhouettes of sailing ships	1·30	1·00
3074	45c. Four babies	1·30	1·00
3075	45c. Go-kart, Formula 1 racing car and Ayrton Senna	1·30	1·00
3076	45c. Sloth, Toco toucan, crocodile, penguin and tiger	1·30	1·00
3077	45c. Outline of Brazil and compass roses	1·30	1·00
3078	45c. Peace dove	1·30	1·00
3079	45c. Child with decorated face	1·30	1·00
3080	45c. "500" emblem	1·30	1·00
3081	45c. Man wearing feather headdress	1·30	1·00
3082	45c. Man in boat, sails and town (Nataly M. N. Moriya)	1·30	1·00
3083	45c. Wristwatch, balloon, Alberto Santos-Dumont and his biplane *14 bis*	1·30	1·00
3084	45c. Sailing ship and document (first report of discovery)	1·30	1·00
3085	45c. Jules Rimet Cup and World Cup trophies, player, football and year dates (Brazilian victories in World Cup Football Championship)	1·30	1·00
3086	45c. Hand writing, street lights and fireworks	1·30	1·00
3087	45c. Banners and Brazilian flag forming cow	1·30	1·00
3088	45c. Golden conure perched on branch	1·30	1·00
3089	45c. Bakairi masks	1·30	1·00
3090	45c. Globe, ship and emblem	1·30	1·00

1541 Globe and Map of Brazil

2000. Second Anniv of BrazilTradeNet (business information web site).

3091	**1541**	27c. multicoloured	65	50

1542 Turtle, Scarlet Macaw and Map

2000. National Coastal Management Programme (GERCO).

3092	**1542**	40c. multicoloured	1·00	75

1543 Waterfall and Detail of Map

2000. EXPO 2000 World's Fair, Hanover, Germany and 31st International Geologic Congress, Rio de Janeiro. Sheet 109×69 mm containing T **1543** and similar vert design. Multicoloured.

MS3093	1r.30 Type **1543**; 1r.30 Map of Brazil; 1r.30 Gold ingot and minerals	10·00	10·00

1544 Cruz, Students and Building Facade

2000. Centenary of the Oswaldo Cruz Foundation (medical research institution).

3094	**1544**	40c. multicoloured	1·00	75

1545 Mask, Musical Instruments and Jewellery

2000. Africa Day.

3095	**1545**	1r.10 multicoloured	2·75	2·10

1546 Klink in Rowing Boat and Portion of Globe showing Route

2000. Voyages by Amyr Klink (navigator). Multicoloured.

3096	1r. Type **1546** (first South Atlantic crossing by rowing boat (1984))	2·75	2·00
3097	1r. *Paratii* (polar sailing boat) in Antarctica and portion of globe showing route (first single-handed circumnavigation of Antarctica (1999))	2·75	2·00

Nos. 3096/7 were issued together, *se-tenant*, forming a composite design.

1547 Flag, Buildings, Map and City Arms

2000. 150th Anniv of Juiz de Fora.

3098	**1547**	60c. multicoloured	1·70	1·30

1548 Hang Gliding

2000. Outdoor Pursuits. Multicoloured. Self-adhesive.

3099	27c. Type **1548**	65	50
3100	27c. Surfing	65	50
3101	40c. Rock climbing	1·00	75
3102	40c. Skateboarding	1·00	75

1549 Forest

2000. Environmental Protection. Multicoloured.

3103	40c. Type **1549**	1·20	90
3104	40c. Oncilla standing on branch in forest	1·20	90
3105	40c. Vegetation, adult oncilla and head of kitten	1·20	90
3106	40c. Vegetation, adult oncilla and body of kitten	1·20	90

Nos. 3103/6 were issued together, *se-tenant*, forming a composite design.

1550 Cisne Branco (full-rigged cadet ship)

2000. Brazilian Navy. Cadet Ships. Multicoloured.

3107	27c. Type **1550**	85	65
3108	27c. *Brasil* (cadet frigate)	85	65

1551 *Oswaldo Cruz* (hospital ship) and Birds

2000. Environment Protection. Sheet 137×84 mm.

MS3109	**1551** 1r.50 multicoloured	4·25	4·25

1552 Emblem

2000. America. Health Campaigns. Sheet 84×137 mm containing T **1552** and similar vert design. Multicoloured.

MS3110	1r.10 Type **1552** (anti-AIDS); 1r.10 Glasses, pills, needles and Marijuana leaves (national anti-drugs week)	6·00	6·00

1553 Teixeira, Carneiro Ribeiro Education Center, Salvador and Pupils

2000. Birth Centenary of Anisio Teixeira (education reformer).

3111	**1553** 45c. multicoloured	1·30	1·00

1554 Child walking to School

2000. Tenth Anniv of the Children and Teenagers Statute (3112) and 15th Anniv of National Movement of Street Boys and Girls (3113). Multicoloured.

3112	27c. Type **1554**	85	65
3113	40c. Rainbow with girl and boy holding star	1·20	90

1555 Capanema

2000. Birth Centenary of Gustavo Capanema Filho (politician).

3114	**1555** 60c. multicoloured	1·70	1·30

1556 Television and Hand writing in Notebook

2000. Fifth Anniv of Telecourse 2000 (educational television programme).

3115	**1556** 27c. multicoloured	85	65

1557 Campos

2000. Birth Centenary of Milton Campos (politician and lawyer).

3116	**1557** 1r. multicoloured	2·75	2·10

1558 Hand protecting Globe

2000. World Day for Protection of the Ozone Layer.

3117	**1558** 1r.45 multicoloured	3·75	3·00

1559 Archery

2000. Olympic Games, Sydney. Multicoloured.

3118	40c. Type **1559**	1·00	75
3119	40c. Beach volleyball	1·00	75
3120	40c. Boxing	1·00	75
3121	40c. Football	1·00	75
3122	40c. Canoeing	1·00	75
3123	40c. Handball	1·00	75
3124	40c. Diving	1·00	75
3125	40c. Rhythmic gymnastics	1·00	75
3126	40c. Badminton	1·00	75
3127	40c. Swimming	1·00	75
3128	40c. Hurdling	1·00	75
3129	40c. Pentathlon	1·00	75
3130	40c. Basketball	1·00	75
3131	40c. Tennis	1·00	75
3132	40c. Marathon	1·00	75
3133	40c. High-jump	1·00	75
3134	40c. Long-distance running	1·00	75
3135	40c. Triple jump	1·00	75
3136	40c. Triathlon	1·00	75
3137	40c. Sailing	1·00	75
3138	40c. Pommel horse (gymnastics)	1·00	75
3139	40c. Weightlifting	1·00	75
3140	40c. Discus	1·00	75
3141	40c. Rings (gymnastics)	1·00	75
3142	40c. Athletics	1·00	75
3143	40c. Javelin	1·00	75
3144	40c. Artistic gymnastics	1·00	75
3145	40c. Hockey	1·00	75
3146	40c. Volleyball	1·00	75
3147	40c. Synchronized swimming	1·00	75
3148	40c. Judo	1·00	75
3149	40c. Wrestling	1·00	75
3150	40c. Cycling	1·00	75
3151	40c. Rowing	1·00	75
3152	40c. Parallel bars (gymnastics)	1·00	75
3153	40c. Horse riding	1·00	75
3154	40c. Pole vault	1·00	75
3155	40c. Fencing	1·00	75
3156	40c. Rifle shooting	1·00	75
3157	40c. Taekwondo	1·00	75

1560 Surgeon and Electrocardiogram Graph

2000. Organ Donation. Multicoloured.

3158	1r.50 Type **1560**	4·00	3·00
3159	1r.50 Hands holding heart	4·00	3·00

Nos. 3158/9 were issued together, *se-tenant*, each pair forming a composite design.

1561 Brazilian Clovis Mask

2000. Brazil–China Joint Issue. 25th Anniv of Diplomatic Relations between Brazil and China. Multicoloured.

3160	27c. Type **1561**	65	50
3161	27c. Chinese Monkey King puppet	65	50

1562 Chico Landi and Ferrari 125 Formula 1 Racing Car

2000. Motor Racing Personalities. Multicoloured.

3162	1r.30 Type **1562**	3·25	2·40
3163	1r.45 Ayrton Senna and Formula 1 racing car	3·50	2·75

1563 Embraer EMB 145 AEW

2000. Brazilian Aircraft. Multicoloured. Self-adhesive.

3164	27c. Type **1563**	65	50
3165	27c. Super Tucano	65	50
3166	27c. Embraer AMX-T	65	50
3167	27c. Embraer ERJ 135	65	50
3168	27c. Embraer ERJ 170	65	50
3169	27c. Embraer ERJ 145	65	50
3170	27c. Embraer ERJ 190	65	50
3171	27c. Embraer EMB 145 RS/MP	65	50
3172	27c. Embraer EMB 140	65	50
3173	27c. Embraer EMB 120	65	50

1564 Hand reaching for Star

2000. Christmas. Multicoloured.

3174	27c. Type **1564**	65	50
3175	27c. Mary and Jesus	65	50
3176	27c. Family and fishes	65	50
3177	27c. Jesus pointing to his heart	65	50
3178	27c. Trees, Globe and open hand	65	50
3179	27c. Jesus and Globe	65	50

Nos. 3174/5, 3176/7 and 3178/9 respectively were issued together, *se-tenant*, forming a composite design.

1565 Conductor's Baton and Music Score

2000. Light and Sound Shows.

3180	**1565** 1r.30 multicoloured	3·25	2·50

1566 Maps and Baron Rio Branco

2000. Centenary of Arbitration Ruling setting Boundary between Brazil and French Guiana.

3181	**1566** 40c. multicoloured	1·00	75

1567 Three Wise Men, Chalice and Dove

2001. New Millennium. Multicoloured.

3182	40c. Type **1567**	1·00	75
3183	1r.30 Star of David, Menorah, scroll and stone tablets	3·25	2·50
3184	1r.30 Minaret, dome and Holy Kaaba	3·25	2·50
MS3185	68×113 mm. As Nos. 3182/4	7·50	7·50

No. **MS**3185 also has a barcode at the bottom of the sheet, separated from the miniature sheet by a line of rouletting.

1568 Map of Americas, Flags, Emblems and Waterfall

2001. 11th Pan American Scout Jamboree, Foz do Iguacu. Multicoloured.

3186	1r.10 Type **1568**	2·75	2·10
3187	1r.10 Waterfall, canoeists and emblems	2·75	2·10

Nos. 3186/7 were issued together, se-tenant, forming a composite design.

1569 Snake and Chinese Zodiac

2001. HONG KONG 2001 Stamp Exhibition. New Year. Year of the Snake.

3188	**1569** 1r.45 multicoloured	3·75	3·00

1570 *Dirphya* sp. and Institute

2001. Centenary of Butantan Institute (vaccine research centre), Sao Paulo. Venomous Animals. Sheet 115×155 mm containing T **1570** and similar horiz designs showing Institute building. Multicoloured.

3189	40c. Type **1570**	1·00	85
3190	40c. Puss caterpillar (*Megalopyge* sp.)	1·00	85
3191	40c. *Phoneutria* sp.	1·00	85
3192	40c. Brown scorpion (*Tityus bahiensis*)	1·00	85
3193	40c. Brazilian rattle snake (*Crotalus durissus*)	1·00	85
3194	40c. Coral snake (*Micrurus corallinus*)	1·00	85
3195	40c. Bushmaster (*Lachesis muta*)	1·00	85
3196	40c. Jararaca (*Bothrops jacaraca*)	1·00	85

1571 Old and Modern Printing Methods

2001. Publishing.

3197	**1571** 27c. multicoloured	65	55

1572 McDonnell Douglas DC-10, World Map and Ship

2001. Exports.

3198	**1572** 1r.30 multicoloured	3·00	2·50

1573 Books and Library Facade

2001. 190th Anniv of National Library, Rio de Janeiro.

3199	**1573** 27c. multicoloured	65	55

1574 Man, Microscope and Emblem

2001. Brazilian Council for Scientific and Technological Development (CNPq).

3200	**1574** 40c. blue	85	70

1575 Footballer and Emblem

2001. 89th Anniv of Santos Football Club.

3201	**1575** 1r. multicoloured	2·20	1·80

1576 Children

2001. International Decade for a Culture of Peace.
3202 **1576** 1r.10 multicoloured 2·50 2·10

1577 Mendes and Halfeld Street

2001. Birth Centenary of Muriles Mendes (poet).
3203 **1577** 40c. multicoloured 85 70

1578 Building Facade and View of Town

2001. Centenary of Minas Gerais Trade Association.
3204 **1578** 40c. multicoloured 85 70

1579 Sunflower and No-Smoking Signs

2001. World No-Smoking Day.
3205 **1579** 40c. multicoloured 85 70

1580 Do Rego and Illustrations from his Novels

2001. Birth Centenary of Jose Lins do Rego (writer).
3206 **1580** 60c. multicoloured 1·20 1·00

1581 Hyacinth Macaw (*Anodorhynchus hyacinthinus*)

2001. Birds. Sheet 106×149 mm containing T **1581** and similar vert designs. Multicoloured.
MS3207 1r.30 Type **1581**; 1r.30 Sun conure (*Aratinga solititialis auricapilla*); 1r.30 Blue-throated conure (*Pyrrhura cruentata*); 1r.30 Yellow-faced amazon (*Amazona xanthops*) 10·00 10·00

1582 Sobrinho

2001. First Death Anniv of Alexandre Jose Barbosa Lima Sobrinho (journalist).
3208 **1582** 40c. multicoloured 85 70

1583 Jericoacoara Beach, Ceara

2001. Beaches. Multicoloured.
3209 40c. Type **1583** 85 70

3210 40c. Ponta Negra beach, Rio Grande do Norte 85 70
3211 40c. Rosa beach, Santa Catarina 85 70

1584 Romi-Isetta, 1959 (½-size illustration)

2001. Cars. Sheet 159×115 mm containing T **1584** and similar horiz designs. Multicoloured.
MS3212 1r.10 Type **1584**; 1r.10 DKW-Vemag, 1965; 1r.10 Renault Gordini, 1962; 1r.10 Fusca-Volkswagen 1200, 1959; 1r.10 Simca Chambord, 1964; 1r.10 Aero Willys, 1961 13·00 13·00

1585 Sayao

2001. Birth Centenary of Bernado Sayao (politician and construction pioneer).
3213 **1585** 60c. multicoloured 1·20 1·00

1586 Eleazar de Carvalho, Musical Notation and Musicians

2001. Eleazar de Carvalho (composer and conductor) Commemoration.
3214 **1586** 45c. multicoloured 1·00 85

1587 Racquet and Ball

2001. Roland Garros Tennis Championship. Sheet 70×112 mm.
MS3215 **1587** 1r.30 multicoloured 2·75 2·75

1588 Emblem

2001. 50th Anniv of CAPES (training fund).
3216 **1588** 40c. multicoloured 85 70

1589 Buildings, Symbols of Justice and Pedro Alexio

2001. Birth Centenary of Pedro Alexio (Judge and politician).
3217 **1589** 55c. multicoloured 1·20 1·00

1590 Player and Ball

2001. Vasco da Gama Football Club.
3218 **1590** 70c. multicoloured 1·50 1·30

1591 Figure enclosing Map of Brazil (½-size illustration)

2001. Fifth Anniv of Solidarity Council. Multicoloured.
3219 55c. Type **1591** 1·20 1·00
3220 55c. Map enclosing figure 1·20 1·00
Nos. 3219/20 were issued together, *se-tenant*, forming a composite design.

1592 Player and Ball

2001. Palmeiras Football Club.
3221 **1592** 70c. multicoloured 1·50 1·30

1593 Emblem

2001. World Conference on Racism, Durban, South Africa.
3222 **1593** 1r.30 multicoloured 2·75 2·30

1594 Player and Ball

2001. Gremio Football Porto Algrense (football club).
3223 **1594** 70c. multicoloured 1·50 1·30

1595 Tambourine

2001. Musical Instruments. Multicoloured. Self-adhesive.
3224 1c. Type **1595** 15 15
3224a 1c. Conga drum 15 15
3225 5c. Saxophone 15 15
3225a 5c. Snare drum 15 15
3226 10c. Cavaquinho (guitar) 15 15
3226a 10c. Trumpet 15 15
3227 20c. Clarinet 35 30
3228 40c. Flute 85 70
3229 45c. Mandolin 90 80
3230 50c. Fiddle 1·00 85
3230a 50c. Tambourine 1·00 85
3231 55c. Viola (guitar) 1·20 1·00
3232 60c. Zabumba 1·30 1·10
3233 70c. Viola Caipira (guitar) 1·50 1·30
3234 70c. Rattle 1·50 1·30
3235 80c. Xylophone 1·70 1·40
3236 1r. Trombone 2·20 1·80
3236a 1r. Berimbau 2·20 1·80

1596 Clóvis Beviláqua

2001. Clóvis Beviláqua (lawyer) Commemoration.
3250 **1596** 55c. multicoloured 1·20 1·00

1597 Children encircling Globe

2001. United Nations Year of Dialogue among Civilizations.
3251 **1597** 1r.30 multicoloured 2·75 2·30

1598 Map of Brazil and Jewish and Dutch Flags

2001. 365th Anniv of First Jewish Synagogue in Recife.
3252 **1598** 1r.30 multicoloured 2·75 2·30

1599 Junkers F13 Passenger Aircraft

2001. Commercial Aircraft. Sheet 107×149 mm containing T **1599** and similar horiz designs. Multicoloured.
MS3253 55c. Type **1599**; 55c. Douglas DC-3/C47; 55c. Dornier Do-J Wal flying boat; 55c. Lockheed Constellation; 55c. Convair CV 340; 55c. Caravelle V1-R jet airliner 6·50 6·50

1600 Cecíla Meireles

2001. Birth Centenary of Cecíla Meireles (writer).
3254 **1600** 55c. multicoloured 1·20 1·00

1601 Aleijadinho (sculptor) and Bom Jesus de Matosinhos Sanctuary

2001. America. UNESCO World Heritage Sites.
3255 **1601** 1r.30 multicoloured 2·75 2·30

1602 Madalena Caramuru and Page

2001. Madalena Caramuru (first literate Brazilian woman) Commemoration.
3256 **1602** 55c. multicoloured 1·20 1·00

1603 Face, Gavel, Book and Dove

2001. National Black Awareness Day.
3257 **1603** 40c. multicoloured 85 70

1604 Caiman (*Caiman crocodilus*) and Roseate Spoonbill (*Platalea ajaja*) (inscr "*Plataleia*")

2001. Flora and Fauna. Multicoloured. Self-adhesive.
3258 55c. Type **1604** 1·20 1·00
3259 55c. American darter (*Anhinga anhinga*) 1·20 1·00
3260 55c. Cocoi heron (*Ardea cocoi*) 1·20 1·00
3261 55c. Jabiru (*Ephippiorhynchus mycteria*) (inscr "Jabiru") 1·20 1·00

3262	55c. *Pseudoplatystoma fascia-tum* (fish)	1·20	1·00
3263	55c. *Leporinus macrocephalus* (fish)	1·20	1·00
3264	55c. Capybara (*Hydrochoerus hydrochaeris*) (inscr "hydro-choeris")	1·20	1·00
3265	55c. Southern coati (*Nasua nasua*)	1·20	1·00
3266	55c. Water hyacinth (*Eichornia crassipes*)	1·20	1·00
3267	55c. Purple gallinule (*Porphyrula martinica*)	1·20	1·00

1605 Three Kings and Holy Family

2001. Christmas.

3268	**1605**	40c. multicoloured	85	70

1606 Emblem, Player and Football

2001. Libertadores da America Football Championship Winners (1st issue). Flamengo Football Club (1981).

3269	**1606**	1r. multicoloured	2·00	1·70

See also No. 3275.

1607 Imperial Topaz Necklace and Earrings

2001. Jewellery. Sheet 101×70 mm containing T **1607** and similar vert design. Multicoloured.

MS3270	1r.30 Type **1607**; 1r.30 Garnet ring	5·50	5·50

No. **MS**3270 was issued with a strip containing a bar-code separated by a line of rouletting.

1608 Stylized Eye, Mouth, Hand and Ear

2001. International Day of the Disabled.

3271	**1608**	1r.45 multicoloured	3·00	2·50

1609 Cup of Coffee and Beans

2001. Coffee.

3272	**1609**	1r.30 multicoloured	2·75	2·40

1610 Copacabana

2001. Merchant Ships. Multicoloured.

3273	**1610**	55c. Type **1610**	1·20	1·00
3274		55c. Flamengo	1·20	1·00

Nos. 3273/4 were issued together, *se-tenant*, forming a composite design.

1611 Emblem, Player and Football

2001. Libertadores da America Football Championship Winners (2nd issue). Sao Paulo Football Club (1992 and 1993).

3275	**1611**	70c. multicoloured	1·50	1·30

1612 Water Hyacinth (*Eichornia crassipes*)

2001. Mercosur. Flora.

3276	**1612**	1r. multicoloured	2·00	1·70

1613 Chinese Zodiac and Horse

2002. New Year. Year of the Horse.

3277	**1613**	1r.45 multicoloured	3·00	2·50

1614 Alpine skier

2002. Winter Olympic Games, Salt Lake City, USA. Multicoloured.

3278		1r.10 Type **1614**	2·30	2·00
3279		1r.10 Cross country skier	2·30	2·00
3280		1r.10 Luge	2·30	2·00
3281		1r.10 Bobsled	2·30	2·00

Nos. 3278/81 were issued together, *se-tenant*, forming a composite design.

1615 Brasilia and Lucio Costa

2002. Birth Centenary of Lucio Costa (architect).

3282	**1615**	55c. multicoloured	1·20	1·00

1616 Women encircling Globe

2002. International Women's Day.

3283	**1616**	40c. multicoloured	85	70

1617 View of City from River

2002. 150th Anniv of Sao Jose do Rio Preto.

3284	**1617**	40c. multicoloured	85	70

1618 Brasilia and Juscelino Kubitschek

2002. Birth Centenary of Juscelino Kubitschek (president, 1956–61).

3285	**1618**	55c. multicoloured	1·20	1·00

1619 Winners' Flags and Football

2002. World Cup Football Championship, Japan and South Korea. Multicoloured.

3286	**1619**	55c. Type **1619**	1·00	85
3287		55c. Footballer	1·00	85

1620 School Children and Alphabet

2002. Education. Multicoloured.

3288		40c. Type **1620**	85	70
3289		40c. Computer, globe and alphabet	85	70

1621 Josemaria Escriva

2002. Birth Centenary of Josemaria Escriva de Balaguer (founder of Opus Dei (religious organization)).

3290	**1621**	55c. multicoloured	1·20	1·00

1622 North American T6

2002. Smoke Air Squadron (air force display team). Sheet 105×150 mm containing T **1622** and similar horiz designs. Multicoloured.

MS3291	55c. ×6, Type **1622**; T-24 Fouga Magister; Neiva T-25 Universal (inscr "T-25 Universal"); Two Embraer EMB-312 Tucano (inscr "T-27 Tucano") and plateau; T-27 Tucano and heart-shape; T-27 Tucano over forest	6·50	6·50

1623 Boy wearing Crown, Girls carrying Banners and Boy with Sword

2002. Cavalhadinha (children's festival). Multicoloured.

3292		40c. Type **1623**	85	70
3293		40c. Boys riding hobby horses	85	70
3294		40c. Children wearing masks	85	70
3295		40c. Musicians and drinks vendor	85	70

1624 Cannonball Tree (*Couroupita guianensis*)

2002. Self-adhesive.

3296	**1624**	55c. multicoloured	1·00	85

1625 Coral and Fish

2002. Coral Reefs. Sheet 105×150 mm containing T **1625** and similar square designs. Multicoloured.

MS3297	40c. ×4, Type **1625**; Seahorse; Corals and fish; Fish and starfish	2·75	2·75

1626 Building Facade

2002. 150th Anniv of Sisterhood of Charity Hospital, Curitiba.

3298	**1626**	70c. multicoloured	1·00	85

1627 Jules Rimet and World Cup Trophies

2002. Brasil, Football World Cup Championship Winners (1958, 1962, 1970, 1994, 2002).

3299	**1627**	55c. multicoloured	1·20	1·00

1628 White-browed Guan (*Penelope jacucaca*)

2002. Conservation of North Eastern Caatinga Region. Sheet 70×111 mm.

MS3300	**1628**	1r.10 multicoloured	1·50	1·60

1629 Footballer and Emblem

2002. Centenary of Santos Football Club.

3301	**1629**	55c. multicoloured	65	55

1630 House Facade

2002. "The Enchanted House" Museum (house of Alberto Santos Dumont (aviation pioneer)), Rio De Janeiro. Sheet containing T **1630** and similar square design. Multicoloured.

MS3302	1r. ×2, Type **1630**; Alberto Santos Dumont	2·75	2·75

1631 Radar, Airplane, Boy, Animals and Birds

2002. SIVAM (environmental monitoring of Amazon project).

3303	**1631**	1r.10 multicoloured	1·50	1·30

1632 Families enclosed in Wheel

2002. Crianca Esperanca (Hope of the Child) Awareness Campaign. Multicoloured.

3304		(1st Porto) Type **1632** (child development)	85	70
3305		(1st Porto) Children playing (eradication of child labour)	85	70

1633 Jorge Amado

2002. First Death Anniv of Jorge Amado (writer).

3306	**1633**	40c. multicoloured	50	45

1634 Rio Branco Palace, Xapuri Village and Placido de Castro (revolutionary leader)

2002. Centenary of Acre River Revolution.

3307 **1634** 50c. multicoloured 65 55

1635 Whale and Calf

2002. Southern Right Whale Habitat Protection Project. Sheet 71×112 mm.

MS3308 **1635** 1r.30. multicoloured 1·70 1·70

1636 Rivers

2002. Watershed of Negro and Solimoes Rivers, Manaus.

3309 **1636** 45c. multicoloured 50 45

1637 Adhelmar Ferreira da Silva

2002. First Death Anniv of Adhelmar Ferreira da Silva (Olympic triple jump champion).

3310 **1637** 40c. multicoloured 50 45

1638 Yamaha 125cc. (1974) and YZF-R1

2002. Motorcycles. Sheet 105×149 mm containing T **1638** and similar horiz designs. Multicoloured.

MS3311 60c.×6 Type **1638**; Honda CB100 (1976) and CG125 Titan; Suzuki 1952 model and GSX-R1000; First Triumph model (1902) and Datona 955i; BMW R32 and R 1200C; First Harley Davidson model (1903) and V-Rod 4·25 4·25

1639 Steam Locomotive Baroneza (1852)

2002. Trains. Multicoloured.

3312 55c. Type **1639** 65 55
3313 55c. Locomotive Zeze Leoni (1922) 65 55

1640 Birds, Fish and Waterfall

2002. Mercosur (South American Common Market).

3314 **1640** 1r. multicoloured 1·40 1·20

1641 Itabira, Carlos Drummond de Andrade and Rio de Janeiro

2002. Birth Centenary of Carlos Drummond de Andrade (writer).

3315 **1641** 55c. multicoloured 80 70

1642 Fingerprint, Book, Globe and Figure Child

2002. America. Education and Literacy Campaign.

3316 **1642** 1r.30 multicoloured 1·80 1·60

1643 Map and Building

2002. National Archives.

3317 **1643** 40c. multicoloured 60 50

1644 Sergio Motta (founder) and Centre Building

2002. Sergio Motta Cultural Centre.

3318 **1644** 45c. multicoloured 60 50

1645 Nativity (Candido Portinari)

2002. Christmas.

3319 **1645** 45c. multicoloured 60 50

1646 "80"

2002. 80th Anniv of Social Security.

3320 **1646** 45c. multicoloured 60 50

1647 Dancing Tapuia

2002. Art. Paintings by Albert Eckhout. Paintings. Multicoloured.

3321 45c. Type **1647** 80 70
3322 45c. Mameluca 80 70
3323 45c. Tapuia Man 80 70
3324 45c. Tupi Man 80 70
3325 45c. Negro 80 70
3326 45c. Tupi Woman 80 70
3327 45c. West African Woman and Child 80 70
3328 45c. Mestizo Man 80 70

1648 Marajoara Pots, Brazil

2002. Centenary of Brazil–Iran Diplomatic Relations. Multicoloured.

3329 60c. Type **1648** 1·00 85
3330 60c. Iranian decorated pots 1·00 85

Stamps of a similar design were issued by Iran.

1649 Anniversary Emblem

2003. 80th Anniv of Rotary Club (charitable organization).

3331 **1649** 60c. multicoloured 1·00 85

1650 Salto do Itiquira, Formosa

2003. International Day of Freshwater. Waterfalls. Multicoloured.

3332 45c. Type **1650** 80 70
3333 45c. Salto do Rio Preto, Alto Paraiso 80 70

1651 Winnowing and Building

2003. Coffee Production. Sheet 70×110 mm containing T **1651** and similar square design. Multicoloured.

MS3334 1r.×2, Type **1651**; Buildings, planting and picking 3·25 3·25

1652 Flag, Hands, Dove and Map

2003. Timor Leste Independence.

3335 **1652** 1r.45 multicoloured 2·40 2·10

1653 Macrosiphonia velame

2003. America. Flora and Fauna. Sheet 107×150 mm containing T **1653** and similar square designs. Multicoloured.

MS3336 60c.×6, Type **1653**; Lychnophora ericoides; Lafoensia pacari; Tabebuia impetignosa;Xylopia aromatica; Himatanthus obovatus 5·00 5·00

1654 Decorated Bottles

2003. Mercosur. Recycling. Multicoloured.

3337 60c. Type **1654** 1·00 85
3338 60c. Paper dolls 1·00 85
3339 60c. Plastic flower pot 1·00 85
3340 60c. Decorated metal box 1·00 85

1655 Saint Inacio, College Building and Students

2003. Centenary of St. Inacio College, Rio de Janeiro.

3341 **1655** 60c. multicoloured 1·00 85

1656 Pluft and Maribel

2003. Pluft (cartoon character created by Maria Clara Machado).

3342 **1656** 80c. multicoloured 1·20 1·00

1657 Sail Boat on Beach

2003. Centenary of Ceara State.

3343 **1657** 70c. multicoloured 1·20 1·00

1658 Album, Tweezers and Stamps

2003. Philately. Sheet 110×71 mm containing T **1658** and similar square design. Multicoloured.

MS3344 1r.30×2, Type **1658**; Portuguese 25r. stamp 4·25 4·25

1659 Dolphins

2003. 500th Anniv of Fernando de Noronha Island. Sheet 69×100 mm.

MS3345 **1659** 2r.90 multicoloured 4·50 4·50

1660 Emblem, Buildings and Antonio Maria Zaccaria (founder)

2003. Centenary of Barnabite Priests in Brazil.

3346 **1660** 45c. multicoloured 80 70

1661 Duke of Caxias and Battle Scene

2003. Birth Bicentenary of Luis Alves de Lima y Silva, Duke of Caxias.

3347 **1661** 60c. multicoloured 1·00 85

1662 Self-Portrait

2003. Birth Centenary of Candido Potinari (artist).

3348 **1662** 80l. multicoloured 1·40 1·20

1663 Stop Sign enclosing Bottle

2003. Traffic Code Awareness. Multicoloured. Self-adhesive.

3349 (50c.) Type **1663** 80 70
3350 (74c.) Triangular traffic sign enclosing dove 1·20 1·00

1664 Club Emblem

2003. Centenary of Gremio Football Porto Alegrense.
3351 **1664** 60c. multicoloured 90 80

1665 Locomotive

2003. Preservation of Railways.
3352 **1665** 74c. multicoloured 1·20 1·00

1666 Kite Flying

2003. Children's Games. Multicoloured.
3353 50c. Type **1666** 80 70
3354 50c. Ball games 80 70
3355 50c. Skipping 80 70
3356 50c. Hula hoop 80 70

1667 Campaign Emblem

2003. Zero Hunger Campaign.
3357 **1667** 50c. multicoloured 80 70

1668 Grapes, Bridge and Mask

2003. Export Campaign. Sheet 110×69 mm.
MS3358 **1668** 1r.30 multicoloured 2·00 2·00

1669 Decorated Tree

2003. Christmas. Self-adhesive.
3359 **1669** 50c. multicoloured 80 70
3360 **1669** 50c. multicoloured 80 70

Sao Paulo Art Critcs Trophy and Auditing Court (building)

2003. Marcantonio Vilaca Cultural Space.
3361 **1670** 74c. multicoloured 1·20 1·00

1671 Ary Barroso and Maracana Stadium

2003. Birth Centenary of Ary Barroso (conductor and sports commentator).
3362 **1671** 1r.50 multicoloured 2·40 2·10

1672 Palacio des Arcos, Cadeia Velha and New Congress Building, Rio de Janeiro

2003. 180th Anniv of National Congress.
3363 **1672** 74c. multicoloured 1·20 1·00

1673 Para-glider over Sao Conrado, Rio de Janeiro

2003. Adventurous Sports.
3364 **1673** 75c. multicoloured 1·20 1·00

1674 Cedar Lebanon

2003. 60th Anniv of Diplomatic Relations with Lebanon.
3365 **1674** 1r.75 multicoloured 2·75 2·40

1675 Heart-shaped Ribbon and Hands

2003. AIDS Awareness Campaign.
3366 **1675** 74c. multicoloured 1·20 1·00

2003. Birth Centenary of Candido Potinari. Lost Paintings (1st issue). As T **1662**. Black. Self-adhesive.
3367 74c. *Menino de Brodoski* 1·20 1·00
3368 75c. *Cangaceiro* 1·20 1·00
See also Nos. 3382/6.

1676 Capistrano de Abreu

2003. 150th Birth Anniv of Capistrano de Abreu (historian and ethnographer).
3369 **1676** 50c. multicoloured 80 70

1677 Fernando Henrique Cardoso

2003. Fernando Henrique Cardoso (38th president).
3370 **1677** 74c. multicoloured 1·20 1·00

1678 Archangel St. Michael Chapel, Sao Paulo

2004. Cultural Heritage. Sheet 100×70 mm. Litho.
MS3371 **1678** 1r.50 multicoloured 2·20 2·20

1679 Faces

2004. 450th Anniv of Sao Paulo. Multicoloured.
3372 74c. Type **1679** 1·20 1·00
3373 74c. Buildings surrounding roadway 1·20 1·00
3374 74c. Park and city buildings 1·20 1·00
3375 74c. "450" 1·20 1·00

1680 Dom Vicente Scherer

2004. Birth Centenary of Cardinal Vicente Scherer.
3376 **1680** 50c. multicoloured 80 70

1681 Musicians and Dancers

2004. Lapa District, Rio de Janeiro.
3377 **1681** 75c. multicoloured 1·20 1·00

1682 Scarlet Ibis (*Eudocimus ruber*)

2004
3378 **1682** 74c. multicoloured 1·20 1·00

1683 Figure holding Water Droplet

2004. Mercosur. Water Conservation Campaign.
3379 **1683** 1r.20 multicoloured 1·80 1·60

1684 Orlando Villas Boas

2004. 90th Birth Anniv of Orlando Villas Boas (joint founder Xingu National Park and Nobel Peace Prize winner).
3380 **1684** 74c. multicoloured 1·20 1·00

1685 Anniversary Emblem

2004. Centenary of FIFA (Federation Internationale de Football Association).
3381 **1685** 1r.60 multicoloured 2·50 2·30

2004. Birth Centenary of Candido Potinari. Lost Paintings (2nd issue). As T **1662**. Self-adhesive.
3382 55c. multicoloured 90 80
3383 80c. multicoloured 1·20 1·00
3384 95c. multicoloured 1·50 1·30
3385 1r.15 black 1·70 1·50
3386 1r.50 multicoloured 2·40 2·10
DESIGNS: 55c. *Negrinha*; 80c. *Duas Criancas*; 95c. *Menino Sentado e Carneiro*; 1r.15 *Comosicao*; 1r.50 *Marcel Gontrau*.

1686 Emblem

2004. 92nd International Labour Conference (ILO).
3387 **1686** 50c. multicoloured 80 70

1687 Roseate Spoonbill (*Ajaia ajaja*)

2004. Mangrove Swamps and Tidal Zones Preservation. Sheet 149×105 mm containing T **1687** and similar horiz designs. Multicoloured.
MS3388 1r.60×5, Type **1687**; Great kiskadee (*Pitangus sulphuratus*); *Chasmagnathus granulate*; *Aramides mangle*; *Goniopsis cruentata* 10·50 10·50

1688 Runner holding Olympic Torch

2004. Olympic Games, Athens. Multicoloured
3389 1r.60 Type **1688** 2·50 2·30
3390 1r.60 Athens 2004 emblem 2·50 2·30
3391 1r.60 Dinghies and catamarans 2·50 2·30
3392 1r.60 Runner 2·50 2·30

1689 Senhor Bom Jesus do Bonfim Church, Salvador

2004. Cultural Heritage.
3393 **1689** 74c. multicoloured 1·20 1·00

1690 Caprichoso Bull

2004. Parintins Festival. Multicoloured.
3394 74c. Type **1690** 1·20 1·00
3395 74c. Garantido bull 1·20 1·00
Nos. 3394/5 were issued together, *se-tenant*, forming a composite design.

1691 Dura-Mater Artificial Heart Valve

2004. Brazilian Inventions. Multicoloured.
3396 50c. Type **1691** 80 70
3397 50c. Telephone caller identification (BINA) 80 70
3398 50c. Telephone cards 80 70

1692 Map of South America, Satellite and Brazilian and Chinese Flags as Clasped Hands

2004. CBER-2 (Brazilian—Chinese satellite).
3399 **1692** 1r.75 multicoloured 2·75 2·40

1693 Columns, Square and Compass

2004. Masonic Philatelic Association.

3400	50c. Type **1693**	80	70
3401	50c. Stone mason	80	70
3402	50c. Jacob's ladder	80	70
3403	50c. Masonic tools	80	70

1694 Nelson Rodrigues

2004. Nelson Rodrigues (writer) Commemoration.

3404	**1694**	50c. multicoloured	80	70

1695 FAB Emblem, Republic P-47 Thunderbolt and Campaign Medals

2004. World War II. Multicoloured.

3405	50c. Type **1695** (Italian air campaign)	80	70
3406	50c. Navy emblem, destroyer and campaign medals (South Atlantic campaign)	80	70
3407	50c. FEB emblem, soldiers and campaign medals (Italian land campaign)	80	70
3408	50c. Soldier reading letter	80	70

1696 Crowned Halo enclosing Statue

2004. Centenary of Coronation of Our Lady of Immaculate Conception ("Aparecida").

3409	**1696**	74c. multicoloured	1·20	1·00

1697 Allan Kardec

2004. Birth Bicentenary of Allan Kardec (writer).

3410	**1697**	1r.60 multicoloured	2·50	2·30

1698 Father Christmas

2004. Christmas. Self-adhesive.

3411	**1698**	1st class (50c.) multi-coloured	80	70

No. 3406 was for use on internal non-commercial mail weighing 20 grams or less.

1699 Post Office Building (museum)

2004. Porto Alegre Museum and Archive.

3412	**1699**	50c. multicoloured	80	70

1700 Cyperus articulatus

2004. Aromatic Plants.

3413	**1700**	1r.60 multicoloured	2·50	2·30

1701 Buildings and Statue

2004. Pampulha Architectural Complex.

3414	**1701**	80c. multicoloured	1·30	1·10

1702 Cat, Art, Textiles and Nise da Silveira

2005. Birth Centenary of Nise da Silveira (psychiatrist).

3415	**1702**	55c. multicoloured	90	80

1703 Rotary Emblem and Faces

2005. Centenary of Rotary International (charitable organization).

3416	**1703**	1r.45 multicoloured	2·40	2·10

1704 Fruit on Tree

2005. Cupacu (*Theobrome grandiflorum*). Sheet 70×111 mm containing T **1704** and similar square design. Multicoloured.

MS3417 1r.90×2, Type **1704**; Open fruit 6·00 6·00

1705 Brazilian and Lebanese Trees and Flags

2005. Lebanese Immigration to Brazil.

3418	**1705**	1r.75 multicoloured	2·75	2·40

1706 Museum Building

2005. Oscar Niemeyer Museum.

3419	**1706**	80c. multicoloured	1·30	1·10

1707 Pope John Paul II

2005. Pope John Paul II Commemoration.

3420	**1707**	80c. multicoloured	1·30	1·10

1708 Circle and Arrows

2005. World Information Society Summit, Tunis. Sheet 86×128 mm containing T **1708** and similar horiz designs. Multicoloured.

MS3421 80c.×3, Type **1708**; Figure enclosed in circle; Envelope contained in circle 3·50 3·50

The stamps and margins of No. **MS**3421 form a composite design.

1709 Dancers (contemporary dance)

2005. Brazil Year in France. Multicoloured.

3422	80c. Type **1709**	1·30	1·10
3423	80c. Pankaranu Indians (indigenous art)	1·30	1·10
3424	80c. Pato no Tucupi (gastronomy)	1·30	1·10
3425	80c. Choro musicians (music)	1·30	1·10
3426	80c. String of pages (literature)	1·30	1·10
3427	80c. Vivaldo Lima Stadium (architecture)	1·30	1·10

1710 Erico Verissimo

2005. Birth Centenary of Erico Verissimo (writer).

3428	**1710**	1r.25 multicoloured	1·90	1·60

1711 Mario Quintana

2005. Birth Centenary (2006) of Mario Quintana (writer).

3429	**1711**	80c. green	1·30	1·10

1712 Woman, Water Barrel, Cistern, Boy and Workmen

2005. America. Water Cisterns.

3430	**1712**	80c. multicoloured	1·30	1·10

1713 Emblem

2005. 19th Congress of America, Spain and Portugal Postal Union. Self-adhesive.

3431	**1713**	(80c.) multicoloured	1·30	1·10

1714 Gold panning, Route and Caravan

2005. Tourism. Estrada Real (road from Diamantina to Parati and Rio De Janeiro). Multicoloured.

3432	80c. Type **1714**	1·30	1·10
3433	80c. Hikers	1·30	1·10
3434	80c. Horse riders	1·30	1·10

Nos. 3432/4 were issued together, *se-tenant*, forming a composite design.

1715 Dancer

2005. Samba (dance).

3435	**1715**	55c. multicoloured	90	80

1716 Brazilian Flag and Samba Dancers

2005. National Dances. Multicoloured.

3436	80c. Type **1716**	1·30	1·10
3437	80c. Cuban flag and Son dancers	1·30	1·10

Stamps of a similar design were issued by Cuba.

1717 Sao Francisco River

2005

3438	**1717**	80c. multicoloured	1·30	1·10

1718 School Building

2005. Centenary of Command and General Staff School.

3439	**1718**	80c. multicoloured	1·30	1·10

1719 "ABC"

2005. Teachers' Day. Self-adhesive.

3440	**1719**	(1st porte) multicoloured	90	80

1720 Bell

2005. Christmas (1st issue). Self-adhesive.

3441	**1720**	(1st porte) multicoloured	90	80

See also No. **MS**3444.

1721 Referee and Players

2005. Women's Football.

3442	**1721**	85c. multicoloured	1·40	1·20

1722 Fish Leaping (*Salminus maxillosus*)

2005. Piracema (fish reproduction). Sheet 101×71 mm.
MS3443 **1722** 3r.10 multicoloured 5·00 5·00

1723 *Adoration of Shepherds* (Oscar Pereira da Silva)

2005. Christmas (2nd issue). Sheet 71×111 mm.
MS3444 **1723** 2r.90 multicoloured 4·50 4·50

1724 Light *Luna* (Fernando Prado)

2005. Brazilian Design. Multicoloured.
3445	85c.	Type **1724**	1·40	1·20
3446	85c.	Ventilator "Spirit" (Indio da Costa design)	1·40	1·20
3447	85c.	Chair "Corallo" (Hemberto and Fernando Corallo)	1·40	1·20
3448	85c.	Table "Bandeirola" (Ivan Rezende)	1·40	1·20

1725 Hans Christian Andersen and *The Ugly Duckling*

2005. Birth Bicentenary of Hans Christian Andersen (writer).
3449	**1725**	55c. multicoloured	90	80

1726 Dressmaker

2005. Professions. Multicoloured. Self-adhesive.
3450	5c.	Type **1726**	20	15
3451	20c.	Cobbler	40	35
3452	85c.	Shoe shine	1·40	1·20

1727 Sambista

2005. Urban Art. Multicoloured.
3453	55c.	Type **1727**	90	80
3454	55c.	Boy in pipe	90	80
3455	55c.	Graffiti artist (horiz)	90	80

1728 Santos-Dumont Biplane *14 bis*

2005. Centenarian Mission (Brazilian astronaut, Marcos Pontes's flight on Soyuz rocket to International Space Station). Multicoloured.
3456	**1728**	85c. Type **1728**	1·40	1·20
3457		85c. "Soyuz"	1·40	1·20
3458		85c. International Space Station	1·40	1·20

Nos. 3456/8 were issued together, *se-tenant*, forming a composite design.

1729 Emblem

2006. World Cup Football Championship, Germany.
3459	**1729**	85c. multicoloured	1·40	1·20

1730 Bidu Sayao

2006. Balduina de Oliveira Sayao (Bidu Sayao) (opera singer) Commemoration.
3460	**1730**	55c. multicoloured	90	80

1731 World Map and Faces

2006. International Day of Cultural Diversity.
3461	**1731**	1r.90 multicoloured	3·25	2·75

1732 Emblem

2006. RIO 2007—15th Pan American Games. Self-adhesive.
3462	**1732**	(1st Porte) multicoloured	1·40	1·20

1733 Stylized Athlete

2006. Brazilian Paralympics Committee.
3463	**1733**	1r.35 multicoloured	2·00	1·70

1734 Viola de Cocho

2006. Mercosur. Musical Instruments.
3464	**1734**	55c. multicoloured	90	80

1735 Rhea, Emas National Park

2006. National Parks. Multicoloured. Self-adhesive.
3465		85c. Type **1735**	1·40	1·20
3466		85c. Uakari monkey, Sustainable Development Reserve, Mamiraua	1·40	1·20
3467		85c. Maned wolf, Chapada dos Veadeiros National Park	1·40	1·20
3468		85c. Squirrel, Itaiaia National Park	1·40	1·20

2006. Urban Art (2nd issue). Sheet 111×70 mm containing vert designs as T **1727**. Multicoloured.
MS3468a 1r.60×2, As No. 3454; As No. 3455 5·00 5·00

1735a Leaves and Fruit

2006. Cajueiro (cashew nut tree). Sheet 111×70 mm.
MS3468b **1735a** 2r.90 multicoloured 4·50 4·50

No. **MS**3468b was cut round in the shape of a tree.

1736 Fernando de Noronha Archipelago

2006. Tourism.
3469	**1736**	2r.50 multicoloured	3·50	3·00

1737 Santos-Dumont *14-bis*

2006. Centenary of Flight of Santos-Dumont 14-bis.
3470	**1737**	(90c.) multicoloured	1·40	1·20

1738 Star, House and Mail Box

2006. Christmas (1st issue). Self-adhesive.
3471	**1738**	(1st Porte) multicoloured	1·00	85

2006. Professions. As T **1726**. Multicoloured. Self-adhesive.
3471a	1c.	Popcorn seller	20	15
3471b	1r.	Manicurist	1·75	1·75

1739 The Magi

2006. Christmas (2nd issue). Sheet 111×70 mm containing T **1739** and similar multicoloured designs.
MS3472 1r.60×3, Type **1739** Angel (36×40 mm) (arched): Holy family 7·00 7·00

1740 Hydro-electric Dam and Street Lighting

2006. America. Energy Conservation.
3473	**1740**	1r.75 multicoloured	2·75	2·40

1741 *Isurus oxyrinchus* and *Sphyrna lewini*

2006. Sharks. Sheet 70×111 mm containing T **1741** and similar square design. Multicoloured.
MS3474 1r.90×2, Type **1741** *Mustelus schmitti* 6·00 6·00

1742 Diving

2007. Pan American Games, Rio de Janeiro. Multicoloured. Self-adhesive.
3477		(1° Porte Carta Comercial) Type **1742**	1·20	1·00
3478		(1° Porte Carta Comercial) Swimming	1·20	1·00
3479		(1° Porte Carta Comercial) Synchronised Swimming	1·20	1·00
3480		(1° Porte Carta Comercial) Futsal	1·20	1·00
3481		(1° Porte Carta Comercial) Water polo	1·20	1·00

1743 Carimbo

2007. Dances. Multicoloured.
3482		(1° Porte Carta Comercial) Type **1743**	90	80
3483		(1° Porte Carta Comercial) Frevo	90	80

1744 Research Vessel

2007. International Polar Year. Multicoloured.
3484		(1° Porte Carta Comercial) Type **1744**	1·40	1·20
3485		(1° Porte Carta Comercial) Ferraz research station	1·40	1·20
3486		(1° Porte Carta Comercial) Penguin and map of Antarctica	1·40	1·20

Nos. 3484/6 were issued together, *setenant*, forming a composite design.

1745 First Church of Our Lady of Assumption

2007. Jose de Anchieta (Jesuit missionary) Commemoration. Multicoloured.
3487		90c. Type **1745**	1·40	1·20
3488		90c. Founding of Espirito Santo	1·40	1·20
3489		90c. Metropolitan Cathedral of Vitoria	1·40	1·20

Nos. 3487/9 were issued together, setenant, forming a composite design.

1746 Estadio Olimpico Edgard Proenca (Mangueirao), Belem

2007. Stadia. Multicoloured.
3490		60c. Type **1746**	1·00	85
3491		60c. Estadio Municipal Paulo Machado de Carvalho, Pacaembu	1·00	85
3492		90c. Estadio Serra Dourada, Goiania	1·50	1·30
3493		2r.60 Estadio Jornalista Mario Filho (Maracana), Rio de Janeiro	4·00	3·50

1747 JK Bridge

2007. Mercosul. National Architecture.
3494 **1747** (1° porte Carta Comer-
cial) mult 1·50 1·30

1748 Robert
Baden-Powell

2007. Centenary of Scouting.
3495 **1748** 2r. multicoloured 3·25 3·00

1749 Pope Benedict XVI

2007. Pope Benedict XVI Visit to Brazil.
3496 **1749** 90c. multicoloured 1·50 1·30

1750 *Cochlespira
elongate*

2007. Shells. Sheet 126×84 mm containing T **1750** and
similar vert designs. Multicoloured.
MS3497 2r.×3, Type **1750** *Charonia
variegata; Chicoreus* 9·75 9·75
The stamps and margins of **MS**3497 form a composite
design of a seashore.

1751 *My New
Accordion*
(Napachie
Pootoogook)

2007. 140th Anniv of Brazil–Canada Diplomatic Relations.
3498 **1751** 90c. multicoloured 1·50 1·30

1752 *Rio Pardo* and
Giuseppe Garibaldi

2007. Birth Bicentenary of Giuseppe Garibaldi (soldier
and nationalist). Multicoloured.
3499 **1752** 1r.40 Type **1752** 2·20 1·90
3500 1r.40 On horseback 2·20 1·90
Stamps of a similar design were issued by Uruguay.

1753 Metro Locomotive

2007. Transport. Multicoloured.
3501 1r.40 Type **1753** 2·20 1·90
3502 1r.45 Steam locomotive No. 1
Baroneza 2·30 2·00
3503 1r.90 Tram, Bonde Santa Teresa 3·25 2·75

1754 Teofilo Ottoni

2007. Birth Bicentenary of Teofilo Benedict Ottoni
(politician and journalist).
3504 **1754** 60c. multicoloured 1·00 85

1755 Children, Computers
and 'abc'

2007. America. Education for All.
3505 **1755** 60c. multicoloured 1·00 85

1756 Inscr 'High &;
Magic'

2007. Roses. Sheet 85×128 mm containing T **1756** and
similar vert designs.
MS3506 2r.60×3, Type **1756**; Inscr
'Caballero'; Inscr 'Avalanche' 12·00 12·00
The stamps and margins of **MS**3506 form a composite
design.

1757 Giraffes

2007. Zoological Fauna. Multicoloured.
3507 60c. Type **1757** 1·00 85
3508 60c. Tiger 1·00 85
3509 60c. Elephant 1·00 85
3510 60c. Lion 1·00 85
3511 60c. Chimpanzees 1·00 85
3512 60c. Macaw 1·00 85

1758 Candles

2007. Christmas. Multicoloured. Self-adhesive.
3513 1st (porte nao-Comercial)
Type **1758** 1·50 1·30
3514 1st (porte Comercial) The
Nativity 1·50 1·30

1759 King Joao VI

2008. Bicentenary of Portuguese Royal Family's Arrival in
Brazil (1st issue). Multicoloured.
3515 2r. Type **1759** 3·25 2·75
3516 2r. Royal Family and Entourage 3·25 2·75
Nos. 3515/16 were issued together, *se-tenant*, forming
a composite design.
Stamps of the same design were issued by Portugal.

1760 Ships (opening of
ports to friendly nations)

2008. Bicentenary of Portuguese Royal Family's Arrival in
Brazil (2nd issue). Bicentenary of External Relations.
Multicoloured.
3517 1st Porte Carta Comercial
Type **1760** 3·00 2·50
3518 1st Porte Carta Comercial Globe
(foreign trade) 3·00 2·50
No. 3519 is left for stamp not yet received.

1761 Dancer and
Musicians (Tambor
de Crioula)

2008. America. National Festivals. Self-adhesive.
3520 **1761** 1st Porte Carta Nao
Comercial multicol-
oured 3·00 2·50

1762 UFRJ Faculty of
Medicine

2008. Bicentenary of Portuguese Royal Family's Arrival
in Brazil (3rd issue). Bicentenary of Faculties of
Medicine. Multicoloured.
3521 1st Porte Carta Nao Comercial
Type **1762** 3·00 2·50
3522 1st Porte Carta Nao Comercial
Bahia Faculty of Medicine 3·00 2·50

1763 Stylized
figures and
Map as Jigsaw

2008. National Conference on Youth. Self-adhesive.
3523 **1763** 1st Porte Carta Nao
Comercial multicol-
oured 3·00 2·50

1764 Transport Ship,
Helicopter and Soldiers

2008. Bicentenary of Portuguese Royal Family's Arrival
in Brazil (4th issue). Bicentenary of Naval Fusiliers
Corps.
3524 **1764** 1st Porte Carta Comer-
cial multicoloured 3·00 2·50

1765 Museum of
Contemporary Art,
Niteroi

2008. Designs by Oscar Niemeyer (architect). Sheet
112×72 mm containing T **1765** and similar vert
design. Black, ultramarine and vermilion.
MS3525 2r.60×2, Type **1765**; Latin
America Memorial 7·75 7·75

1766 Building and
A Justica (Alfredo
Ceschiatti)

2008. Bicentenary of Portuguese Royal Family's Arrival
in Brazil (5th issue). Bicentenary of Independent
Judiciary.
3526 **1766** 1st Porte Carta Comer-
cial multicoloured 3·00 2·50

1767 Flag and 'Justice'

2008. Bicentenary of Portuguese Royal Family's Arrival in
Brazil (6th issue). Bicentenary of Supreme Military
Court.
3527 **1767** 1st Porte Carta Comer-
cial multicoloured 3·00 2·50

1768 Headquarters and
Gustavo de Lacerda
(founder)

2008. Centenary of Press Association.
3528 **1768** 1st Porte Carta Comer-
cial multicoloured 3·00 2·50

1769 Dom Pedro I
(first ruler of
independent
Brazil)

2008. National Heroes. Multicoloured.
3529 1st Porte Carta Comercial
Type **1769** 3·00 2·50
3530 1st Porte Carta Comercial Mare-
chal Deodoro da Foncesca
(first president of Republic
of Brazil) 3·00 2·50
3531 1st Porte Carta Comercial
Luís Alves de Lima e Silva,
Duke of Caxias (military
leader, statesman and Prime
Minister) 3·00 2·50
3532 1st Porte Carta Comercial
Admiral Francisco Manuel
Barroso da Silva (commander
of victorious Brazilian Navy
at Battle of Riachuelo) 3·00 2·50
3533 1st Porte Carta Comercial
Joaquim Marques Lisbon,
Admiral Tamandare 3·00 2·50
3534 1st Porte Carta Comercial Jose
Bonifacio de Andrada e Silva
(statesman and naturalist) 3·00 2·50
3535 1st Porte Carta Comercial
Alberto Santos-Dumont
(aviation pioneer) 3·00 2·50
3536 1st Porte Carta Comercial
Zumbi dos Palmares (last
leaders of Quilombo dos
Palmares (runaway and
free-born Black African slaves
community)) 3·00 2·50
3537 1st Porte Carta Comercial
Joaquim Jose da Silva Xavier
(Triadentes) (nationalist) 3·00 2·50
3538 1st Porte Carta Comercial
Placido de Castro 3·00 2·50

1770 Policeman

2008. Bicentenary of Portuguese Royal Family's Arrival in
Brazil (7th issue). Bicentenary of Civil Police (horiz)
or bicentenary of Dragoons (vert). Multicoloured.
3539 1st Porte Carta Comercial
Type **1770** 3·00 2·50
3540 1st Porte Carta Comercial
Cavalry (vert) 3·00 2·50

1771 Printing
Press, Print and
Building

2008. Bicentenary of Portuguese Royal Family's Arrival in
Brazil (8th issue). Bicentenary of National Press.
3541 **1771** 1st Porte Carta Comer-
cial multicoloured 3·00 2·50

1772 *Tangara cayana*
(burnished-buff tanager)

2008. Serra do Japi–São Paulo Natural Heritage. Sheet
111×70 mm containing T **1772** and similar horiz
design. Multicoloured.
MS3542 2r.×2, Type **1772**; *Consul
fabius drurii* 5·50 5·50

The stamps and margins of **MS**3542 form a composite design.

1773 *Lippia alba* and *Copaifera lucens*

2008. Bicentenary of Portuguese Royal Family's Arrival in Brazil (9th issue). Bicentenary of Botanic Garden.

3543	**1773**	1st Porte Carta Comercial multicoloured	3·00	2·50

1774 Ship

2008. Centenary of Japanese Immigration. Sheet 128×86 mm containing T **1774** and similar vert design. Multicoloured.

MS3544	3r.50×2, Type **1774**; Flags and origami	14·00 14·00

The stamps and margins of **MS**3544 form a composite design.

1775 Mer de Glace

2008. Landscapes. Multicoloured.

3545	2r. Type **1775**		3·25	2·75
3546	2r. Serra do Araca		3·25	2·75

Nos. 3545/6 were issued together, *se-tenant*, forming a composite design.

Stamps of a similar design were issued by France.

1776 Joao Guimaraes Rosa and Scene from *Grande Sertão: Veredas*

2008. Birth Centenary of Joao Guimaraes Rosa (writer).

3547	**1776**	60c. multicoloured	1·00	85

No. 3547 is embossed with Braille characters.

1777 Headquarters

2008. Bicentenary of Portuguese Royal Family's Arrival in Brazil (10th issue). Bicentenary of Ministry of Finance.

3548	**1777**	1st Porte Carta Comercial multicoloured	3·00	2·50

1778 Gymnastics

2008. Olympic Games, Beijing. Multicoloured.

3549	65c. Type **1778**	1·10	90
3550	65c. Equestrian	1·10	90
3551	65c. Swimming	1·10	90
3552	65c. Games emblem	1·10	90

1779 Cozido Completo and Quindim

2008. Bicentenary of Portuguese Royal Family's Arrival in Brazil (11th issue). Brazilian Portuguese Cuisine.

3553	**1779**	90c. multicoloured	1·50	1·30

1780 *Lontra longicaudis* (American river otter)

2008. Endangered Species. Multicoloured.

3554	1r. Type **1780**	1·50	1·30
3555	1r. *Trichechus inunguis* (Amazonian manatee)	1·50	1·30
3556	1r. *Pteronura brasiliensis* (giant otter)	1·50	1·30

1781 *Strix virgata* (mottled owl)

2008. Mercosul. Birds. Multicoloured.

3557	1r.40 Type **1781**	2·20	1·90
3558	1r.40 *Celeus obrieni* (Kaempfer's woodpecker)	2·20	1·90

1782 Nativity

2008. Christmas. Multicoloured. Self adhesive.

3559	1st Porte Carta Nao Comercial Type **1782** (800th anniv of Franciscans)	3·00	2·50
3560	1st Porte Carta Comercial San Antonio (400th anniv of Santo Antonio convent)	3·00	2·50

Nos. 3559/60 were for use on mail up to 20g., No. 3559 was originally on sale for 65c. and No. 3560 for 1r.

1783 Map and Symbols of Post

2008. Bicentenary of Portuguese Royal Family's Arrival in Brazil (9th issue). Bicentenary of Postal Provision.

3561	**1783**	1r. multicoloured	2·75	2·20

1784 Louis Braille

2009. Birth Bicentenary of Louis Braille (inventor of Braille writing for the blind).

3562	**1784**	2r.20 multicoloured	3·25	2·50

No. 3562 is embossed with Braille writing.

1785 Globe as Green Fuel Pump

2009. Brazil–Leader in Renewable Fuel Production. Self-adhesive.

3563	**1785**	1r. multicoloured	1·50	1·20

1786 Ox

2009. Chinese New Year. Year of the Ox.

3564	**1786**	2r.35 multicoloured	3·50	2·75

1787 Sao Simao Dam, Paranaiba River

2009. Natural Heritage. Rivers. Centenary of Meteorological Office. Two sheets, 112×70 mm, containing T **1787** and similar horiz design. Multicoloured.

MS3565	2r.60 Type **1787**	4·00	3·25
MS3566	3r.85 *Cichla mirianae* (Amazon peacock bass)	5·75	4·50

1788 Dom Helder Camara

2009. Birth Centenary of Dom Helder Camara

3567	**1788**	1r. multicoloured	70	55

1789 *Hydrurga leptonyx* (leopard seal)

2009. Preserve Polar Regions and Glaciers. Multicoloured.

3568	1r. Type **1789**	1·50	1·20
3569	1r. *Ursus maritimus* (polar bear)	1·50	1·20

No. 3567 and Type **1788** are left for Birth Centenary of Dom Helder Camara, issued on 7 February 2009, not yet received.

Nos. 3568/9, were printed, *se-tenant*, each pair forming a composite design.

1789a Postman holding Letter

2009. Postal Services (1st issue). Multicoloured.

3569a	65c. Type **1789a**	1·20 90
3569b	1r. Hand holding telegram	1·70 1·20

1790 Emblem

2009. Centenary of Sports Club International.

3570	**1790**	1r. multicoloured	1·50	1·20

1791 *Aechmea disticantha*, Atlantic Forest and Sao Pedro de Alcantara Cathedral

2009. Brazil–Thailand Diplomatic Relations. Multicoloured.

3571	2r.35 Type **1791**		3·50	2·75
3572	2r.35 *Rhynchostylis gigantea* and Dusit Maha Prasat Palace (Grand Palace)		3·50	2·75

1792 Books, Tower Blocks and Kahlil Gibran (writer)

2009. Brazil–Lebanon Diplomatic Relations. Beirut–World Book Capital, 2009.

3573	**1792**	2r.35 multicoloured	3·50	2·75

1793 Musicians and Dancers

2009. Capoeira and Craft of the Masters of Capoeira. Self-adhesive.

3574	**1793**	65c. multicoloured	1·00	80

1794 Justice and Building Facade

2009. Escola Judicial Desembargador Edesio Fernandes (Judge Edesio Fernandes judicial school).

3575	**1794**	1r. multicoloured	1·50	1·20

1795 Soyuz

2009. Brazil–Russia Diplomatic Relations. Co-operation in Space.

3576	**1795**	2r.35 multicoloured	3·50	2·75

1796 Theatre Facade

2009. Centenary of Rio de Janeiro Municipal Theatre.

3577	**1796**	1st Porte Carta Comercial multicoloured	3·00	2·50

1797 Anniversary Emblem

2009. Bicentenary of Royal Charter.

3578	**1797**	1r. multicoloured	1·50	1·20

1798 *Vitis labrusca*

2009. Mercosul. Exports. Fruit. Multicoloured.

3579	1st PCC Type **1798**	3·50	2·50
3580	1st PCC *Prunus persica* (peach)	3·00	2·50
3581	1st PCC *Prunus salicina* (Japanese plum)	3·00	2·50
3582	1st PCC *Malpighia glabra* (Barbados cherry)	3·00	2·50
3583	1st PCC *Vitis labrusca* (white grapes)	3·00	2·50
3584	1st PCC *Fragaria×ananassa* (strawberry)	3·00	2·50
3585	1st PCC *Pasiflora edulis* (passion fruit)	3·00	2·50
3586	1st PCC *Vitis* (black grapes)	3·00	2·50
3587	1st PCC *Ficus carica* (fig)	3·00	2·50
3588	1st PCC *Diospyros kaki* (persimmon)	3·00	2·50

1st PCC=Porte Carte Comercial

1799 Mauricio de Nassau

2009. Dutch Presence in Brazil. Sheet 105×148 mm containing T **1799** and similar vert designs. Multicoloured.
MS3589 2r.20×6, Type **1799**; *Zutphen*; Dutch pipes; Palacio de Friburgo, Santo Antônio, Recife; Palacio do Campo das Princesas (state administrative headquarters), Santo Antônio, Recife; Rua Aurora 6·50 6·50

1800 Marbles

2009. America. Games. Multicoloured.
3590	1r. Type **1800**	1·50	1·20
3591	1r. Dominoes	1·50	1·20
3592	1r. Chess	1·50	1·20
3593	1r. Table tennis	1·50	1·20

1801 '100', Symbols of Education and Map showing Centres

2009. Centenary of Federal Network of Professional Technical Education.
3594	**1801** 1st PCC multicoloured	3·00	2·50

1802 Lookouts of Sao Luis

2009. Lookouts of Sao Luis
3595	**1802** 1st PCC multicoloured	3·00	2·50

1803 *Paroaria coronata* (red-crested cardinal)

2009. Brightly Coloured Birds. Multicoloured.
MS3596 1r.×6, Type **1803**; *Rupicola rupicola* (cock-of-the-rock); *Chlorophonia cyanea* (blue-naped chlorophonia); *Porphyrospiza caerulescens* (yellow-billed blue finch); *Tangara cyanocephala* (red-necked tanager); *Amblyramphus holosericeus* (scarlet-headed blackbird) 5·25 5·25

1804 Carmen Miranda

2009. Brazil–Portugal Diplomatic Relations
3597	**1804** 2r.20 multicoloured	2·20	1·70

Nos. 3599/600 and Type **1806** are left for Postal Services, issued on 9 October 2009, not yet received.

1805 Carmen Miranda

2009. Brazil–France Diplomatic Relations. Year of France in Brazil. Multicoloured.
MS3598 2r.20×2, Type **1805**; Amerindian (Claude Levi-Strauss (anthropologist)) 4·25 4·25
The stamps and margins of **MS**3598 form a composite design.

2009. Postal Services (2nd issue). Multicoloured.
3599	1st PCC Mail bag (inscr 'MALOTE') (vert)	1·10	80
3600	1st PCC Motorcycle delivery (inscr 'SEDEX')	1·10	80

1807 Club Emblem

2009. Centenary of Coritiba Football Club
3601	**1807** 1r.05 multicoloured	1·70	1·20

1808 Garland

2009. Christmas (1st issue).
3602	**1808** 1st PCC multicoloured	1·70	1·20

1809 Roadside Crib

2009. Christmas (2nd issue). Multicoloured.
3603	1st PCC Type **1809**	1·70	1·20
3604	1st PCC The Nativity	1·70	1·20
3605	1st PCC Crib festooned with lights, amongst trees	1·70	1·20
3606	1st PCC Ceramic crib showing The Nativity and Magi	1·70	1·20
3607	1st PCC Thatched crib showing Magi, Infant Jesus, Mary and sheep	1·70	1·20
3608	1st PCC Ceramic crib showing Holy Family, shepherd holding child, cow and donkey	1·70	1·20

1810 Angel

2009. Christmas (3rd issue). Multicoloured.
MS3609 2r.70×2, Type **1810**; Angel facing left 5·75 5·75
The stamps and margins of **MS**3609 form a composite design.

1811 Incheon Bridge, South Korea

2009. Brazil–South Korea Diplomatic Relations. Multicoloured.
3610	1r.05 Type **1811**	1·70	1·20
3611	1r.05 Octávio Frias de Oliveira bridge, Brazil	1·70	1·20
Nos. 3610/11 were printed, *se-tenant*, each pair forming a composite design.

1812 Brazil Player

2009. Brazil–Hong Kong Diplomatic Relations. Multicoloured.
3612	1r.05 Type **1812**	1·70	1·20
3613	1r.05 Brazilian player (different)	1·70	1·20
3614	1r.05 Hong Kong player	1·70	1·20
3615	1r.05 Hong Kong goalkeeper	1·70	1·70
Nos. 3612/15 were printed, *se-tenant*, forming a composite design.
Stamps of a similar design were issued by Hong Kong.

1813 Runners

2010. Race of Kings (road race from Cuiabá–Mato Grosso).
3616	**1813** 70c. multicoloured	1·10	80

1814 Pres. Tancredo Neves

2010. Birth Centenary of Tancredo de Almeida Neves (politician and president March–April 1985 (who died before inauguration))
3617	**1814** 1r.05 multicoloured	1·70	1·20

1815 Zilda Arns

2010. Mercosur. Decade of Culture of Peace. Zilda Arns (founder and worker of Children's Pastoral, Brazilian church-based organisation (who died Haitian earthquake, 2010)) Commemoration
3618	**1815** 1r.45 multicoloured	2·40	2·00

1816 Chico Xavier

2010. Birth Centenary of Francisco Cândido Xavier (Chico Xavier) (spiritism medium)
3619	**1816** 1st PCC multicoloured	3·00	2·50

1817 Memorial JK (memorial to President Juscelino Kubitschek)

2010. 50th Anniv of Brasilia as National Capital. Multicoloured.
3620	1st PCC Type **1817**	3·00	2·50
3621	1st PCC *Dois Candangos* (two labourers)	3·00	2·50
3622	1st PCC Cathedral of Brasília (horiz)	3·00	2·50
3623	1st PCC Igrejinha de Fátima (little chapel of Fatima) (horiz)	3·00	2·50
3624	1st PCC Sculpture (by Alfredo Ceschiatti), Palacio da Alvorada (Oscar Niemeyer, architect)	3·00	2·50
3625	1st PCC National Congress Building and Ipe Amarelo (national flower)	3·00	2·50

1818 Monastery Façade

2010. Religious Architecture and Festivals
3626	**1818** 1st PCC multicoloured	3·00	2·50

1819 Amerigo Vespucci and Caravel

2010. Brazil–Italy Diplomatic Relations. Multicoloured.
MS3627 2r.40×2, Type **1819**; In old age 4·25 4·25
The stamps and margins of **MS**3627 form a composite design.

1820 'RIO 2011' and Games Emblem

2010. Rio 2011, Fifth International Military Games, Rio de Janeiro
3628	**1820** 2r. multicoloured	3·00	2·50

1821 Cathedral of Brasilia, Congress Emblem and Dois Candangos (two labourers)

2010. 50th Anniv of Brasilia as National Capital. Multicoloured.
MS3629 2r.70×2, Type **1821**; *Dois Candangos* (two labourers), *Memorial JK* and *Catetinho* (first official residence of the President in new capital) 5·50 5·50
The stamps and margins of **MS**3629 form a composite design.

2010. Religious Architecture and Festivals
3630	**1822** 1r.10 multicoloured	1·70	1·20

1823 The Holy Trinity, Mary, Shrine of Divine Eternal Father Basilica and Ox Cart

2010. Religious Architecture and Festivals
3631	**1823** 70c. multicoloured	1·40	1·00

1824 Flags surrounding Stylized Players

2010. World Cup Football Championships, South Africa
3632	**1824** 2r.55 multicoloured	4·25	3·75

1825 Peter Lund and Cave at Lagoa Santa

2010. Peter Wilhelm Lund ('father' of Brazilian paleontology and discoverer of Pleistocene era remains at Lagoa Santa) Commemoration
3633	**1825** 1r.50 multicoloured	1·70	1·20

1826 Abu Simbel Temples, Nubia

2010. Brazil–Egypt Diplomatic Relationships
3634	**1826** 1r.05 multicoloured	1·70	1·20

1827 Rio de Janeiro, Brazil and Maalula, Syria

2010. Brazil–Syria Diplomatic Relationships

| 3635 | **1827** | 2r. multicoloured | 2·20 | 1·70 |

No. 3636 is vacant.

1828 *Nimbochromis venustrus*

2010. Brazil–Malawi Diplomatic Relationships. Multicoloured.

| MS3637 | 2r.×3, Type **1828**; *A. jacobfreibergi eureka*; *Cynotilapia* | | 6·50 | 6·50 |

1829 Clock Tower and Village Skyline

2010. Paranapiacaba, Santo André (company town for employees of São Paulo Railway, privately owned British company)

| 3638 | **1829** | 1r.05 multicoloured | 1·70 | 1·20 |

1830 '150 ANOS' and Stylized Fields

2010. 150th Anniv of Ministry of Agriculture

| 2639 | **1830** | 1r.05 multicoloured | 1·70 | 1·20 |

1831 Barao de Maua (transport pioneer)

2010. 150th Anniv of Ministry of Transport

| 3640 | **1831** | 1r.05 multicoloured | 1·70 | 1·20 |

1832 *Gossyplum hirsutum*

2010. Textile Plants. Multicoloured.

3641		2r. Type **1832**	2·20	1·70
3642		2r. *Cocos nucifera* (coir)	2·20	1·70
3643		2r. *Corchorus capsularis* (jute)	2·20	1·70
3644		2r. *Agave sisalana* (sisal)	2·20	1·70

1833 Player and Club Emblem

2010. Centenary of Corinthians Paulista Sports Club

| 3645 | **1833** | 8r.30 multicoloured | 5·25 | 4·25 |

No. 3645 and Type **1833** are left for Centenary of Sport Club issued on 1 September 2010, not yet received.

1834 Arms

2010. America. Patriotic Symbols. Multicoloured.

3646		1r.05 Type **1834**	1·70	1·20
3647		1r.05 Flag	1·70	1·20
3648		1r.05 Seal	1·70	1·20
3649		1r.05 National anthem score	1·70	1·20

1835 Symbols of Tourism

2010. Association of Government Printers Conference

| 3650 | **1835** | 2r. multicoloured | 2·10 | 1·70 |

1836 Tomatoes on the Vine

2010. International Year of Biodiversity

| MS3651 | 2r.40×2, Type **1836**; Growing salad vegetables | | 4·25 | 4·25 |

1837 Eye enclosing Tree, Presents and Star (Nadia Gabrielle Mukae Iqueuti)

2010. Christmas. Childrens' Drawings (Nos. 3652/3)

		(a) Self-adhesive		
3652		1st PCNC Type **1837**	65	50
3653		1st PCC The Nativity (Maria Elisa Alcántata da Cruz)	85	70

| | | (b) Ordinary gum | | |
| MS3654 | 70×110 mm. 2r.70 The Holy Family (38×38 mm) | | 2·20 | 2·20 |

1838 Leopard

2010. Brazil - Zambia Diplomatic Relations. Multicoloured.

3654a		1r.05 Type **1838**	85	70
3655		1r.05 Victoria Falls	85	70
3656		1r.05 Lion	85	70
3657		1r.05 Buffalo	85	70
3658		1r.05 Rhinoceros	85	70
3659		1r.05 Elephant	85	70

Nos. 3654a/9 were printed, *se-tenant*, in blocks of six stamps within the sheet, each block forming a composite design.

1839 *Lonchorhina aurita*

2010. Bats. Multicoloured.

3660		2r. Type **1839**	2·10	1·70
3661		2r. *Artibeus gnomus*	2·10	1·70
3662		2r. *Platyrrhinus helleri*	2·10	1·70
3663		2r. *Lonchophylla dekeyseri*	2·10	1·70

1840 Pres. Lula

2011. President Luiz Inácio Lula da Silva

| 3664 | **1840** | 2r. multicoloured | 2·10 | 1·70 |

1841 'CAIXA' and Map

2011. 150th Anniv of Federal Savings Bank (CAIXA)

| 3665 | **1841** | 1st PCC multicoloured | 3·00 | 3·25 |

1842 Father de Moura

2011. Father Roberto Landell de Moura (priest and inventor who demonstrated a radio broadcast of human voice on June 3, 1900) Commemoration

| 3666 | **1842** | 1st PCC multicoloured | 3·00 | 2·50 |

1843 Anniversary Emblem

2011. Centenary of Postal Union of the Americas, Spain and Portugal (UPAEP)

| 3667 | **1843** | 1r.25 multicoloured | 3·25 | 2·75 |

1844 Emblem

2011. Centenary of Guarani Football Club

| 3668 | **1844** | 1st PCC multicoloured | 85 | 70 |

1845 St. Francis of Assisi Church, Our Lady of Mount Carmel Church, Partial View of Mariana painted in Blue (in style of Mestre Athayde, painter born in Mariana), *Maria Smoke* (locomotive), Mariana Pillory and Town Hall

2011. Historic Cities. 300th Anniv of Mariana

| 3669 | **1845** | 1r.10 multicoloured | 85 | 70 |

1846 Gates of Military Academy of Agulhas Negras, Colours of Brazilian Flag, Coat of Arms, 'AMAN 200 Anos', Marlins Caxias and Shako

2011. Bicentenary of Military Academy (AMAN)

| 3670 | **1846** | 1r.10 multicoloured | 85 | 70 |

1847 Julio Prestes Station

2011. Railway Stations

		(a) Ordinary gum		
3671		1r.10 Type **1847**	85	70
3672		1r.10 Luz Station	85	70

| | | (b) Self-adhesive | | |
| 3673 | | 1r.10 Brazil Central Station, Rio de Janeiro (vert) | 85 | 70 |

1848 Itaipu Hydroelectric Plant, Parana River and Bicentenary of Paraguay Independence Emblem

2011. Brazil - Paraguay Diplomatic Relations. Bicentenary of Paraguay Independence

| 3674 | **1848** | 1r.10 multicoloured | 85 | 70 |

1849 *Pelagia* and *Phyllorhyza punctata* (jellyfish)

2011. Marine Fauna. Philanippon 2011, International Philatelic Exhibition, Yokohama. Multicoloured.

| MS3675 | 2r.70×4, Type **1849**; *Sepioteuthis sepioidea* (squid); *Octopus insularis*; *Oreaster reticulatus* (starfish) | | 7·50 | 7·50 |

1850 *Tangara seledon* (green-headed tanager) and *Hadrolaelia lobata*

2011. Tijuca National Park. Multicoloured.

| MS3676 | 5r.×2, Type **1850**; *Thalurania glaucopis* (violet-capped woodnymph (hummingbird)) and *Coendou insidiosus* (hedgehog) | | 3·75 | 3·75 |

1851 Elderly Couple sheltering under Umbrella

2011. International Network for the Prevention of Violence Against the Elderly Day

| 3677 | **1851** | 1r.10 multicoloured | 85 | 70 |

1852 Bowl (used for gold extraction), Gold Bar, Houses with Carmo Church, Itacolomi Peak, Joaquim Jose da Silva Xavier (statue), Tiradentes Monument and Town

2011. Historic Cities. 300th Anniv of Ouro Preto

| 3678 | **1852** | 1r.10 multicoloured | 85 | 70 |

1853 Bicentenary Emblem

2011. Bicentenary of Commercial Association of Bahia

| 3679 | **1853** | 1r.10 multicoloured | 85 | 70 |

1854 Paulo Gracindo

2011. Mercosur. Birth Centenary of Pelopidas Gracindo Brandao Guimaraes (Paulo Gracindo) (actor)

3680	**1854**	1r.85 multicoloured	1·50	1·20

1855 Gold Museum, Gold Exhibits, Interior of Municipal Theatre (blue), Nossa Senhora do Ô Church, Sculpture (Aleijadinho), Church of Our Lady of Mount Carmel and City Hall

2011. Historic Cities. 300th Anniv of Sabara

3681	**1855**	1r.10 multicoloured	85	70

No. **MS**3682 and Type **1856** are left for Folklore, issued on 23 July 2011, not yet received.

No. 3683 and Type **1857** are left for Brazil - Ukraine Diplomatic Relations, issued on 24 August 2011, not yet received.

1858 Spanish Soldiers, First and Third Order of Carmel Churches, Mogi das Cruzes (blue), Dove, Tea House, Cocuera (built by Kazuo Hanaoka), Obelisk and City Hall

2011. Historic Cities. 400th Anniv of Mogi das Cruzes

3684	**1858**	1r.10 multicoloured	85	70

1859 Theatre Façade

2011. Centenary of Municipal Theatre, São Paulo

3685	**1859**	2r. multicoloured	1·70	1·40

EXPRESS STAMP

1930. Surch 1000 REIS EXPRESSO and bars.

E490	**66**	1000r. on 200r. blue	6·25	2·30

NEWSPAPER STAMPS

N34

1889. Roul.

N88	**N34**	10r. orange	4·75	4·50
N89	**N34**	20r. orange	9·25	11·50
N90	**N34**	50r. orange	15·00	9·00
N91	**N34**	100r. orange	6·00	4·50
N92	**N34**	200r. orange	4·75	2·30
N93	**N34**	300r. orange	4·75	2·30
N94	**N34**	500r. orange	33·00	13·00
N95	**N34**	700r. orange	4·75	15·00
N96	**N34**	1000r. orange	4·75	15·00

1889. Roul.

N97	10r. green	2·20	80
N98	20r. green	2·20	80
N99	50r. buff	2·75	1·40
N100	100r. mauve	3·75	2·00
N101	200r. black	3·50	2·10
N102	300r. red	14·50	11·00
N103	500r. green	60·00	60·00
N104	700r. blue	32·00	37·00
N105	1000r. brown	14·50	34·00

N37

1890. Perf.

N111	**N37**	10r. blue	19·00	11·50
N112	**N37**	20r. green	60·00	18·00
N113	**N37**	100r. mauve	21·00	15·00

N38 Southern Cross and Sugar-loaf Mountain

1890. Perf.

N119	**N38**	10r. blue	6·25	2·75
N123a	**N38**	20r. green	5·00	80
N127	**N38**	50r. green	18·00	10·00

OFFICIAL STAMPS

O64 Pres. Affonso Penna

1906. Various frames.

O282	**O64**	10r. green & orange	1·00	30
O283	**O64**	20r. green & orange	1·20	30
O284	**O64**	50r. green & orange	1·70	30
O285	**O64**	100r. green & orange	1·00	30
O286	**O64**	200r. green & orange	1·20	30
O287	**O64**	300r. green & orange	3·75	65
O288	**O64**	400r. green & orange	8·00	2·75
O289	**O64**	500r. green & orange	4·25	1·70
O290	**O64**	700r. green & orange	5·00	4·00
O291	**O64**	1000r. green & orange	4·00	1·30
O292	**O64**	2000r. green & orange	6·50	2·30
O293	**O64**	5000r. green & orange	12·50	1·60
O294	**O64**	10000r. green & orange	12·50	1·50

O67 Pres. Hermes de Fonseca

1913. Various frames.

O295	**O67**	10r. black and grey	40	60
O296	**O67**	20r. black and olive	40	60
O297	**O67**	50r. black and green	40	60
O298	**O67**	100r. black and red	90	40
O299	**O67**	200r. black and blue	1·50	40
O300	**O67**	500r. black & yellow	3·50	50
O301	**O67**	600r. black & purple	4·25	2·75
O302	**O67**	1000r. black & brown	5·00	1·50
O303	**O67**	2000r. black & brown	7·50	1·50
O304	**O67**	5000r. black & bistre	9·75	3·75
O305	**O67**	10000r. black	16·00	8·50
O306	**O67**	20000r. black & blue	30·00	29·00
O307	**O67**	50000r. black & green	55·00	60·00
O308	**O67**	100000r. black & red	£200	£200
O309	**O67**	500000r. black & brn	£350	£350
O310	**O67**	1000000r. black & brn	£375	£375

O77 Pres. Wenceslao Braz

1919

O311	**O77**	10r. brown	45	4·50
O312	**O77**	50r. green	1·20	1·40
O313	**O77**	100r. red	2·10	90
O314	**O77**	200r. blue	3·50	90
O315	**O77**	500r. orange	9·25	24·00

POSTAGE DUE STAMPS

D34

1889. Roul.

D88	**D34**	10r. red	2·75	2·10
D89	**D34**	20r. red	4·50	2·75
D90	**D34**	50r. red	7·75	5·75
D91	**D34**	100r. red	2·75	2·10
D92	**D34**	200r. red	90·00	21·00
D93	**D34**	300r. red	9·25	11·50
D94	**D34**	500r. red	9·25	11·50
D95	**D34**	700r. red	15·00	21·00
D96	**D34**	1000r. red	15·00	15·00

1890. Roul.

D97	10r. orange	90	45
D98	20r. blue	90	45
D99	50r. olive	2·00	45
D100	200r. red	9·25	85
D101	300r. green	4·50	2·10
D102	500r. grey	6·00	4·25
D103	700r. violet	7·25	11·50
D104	1000r. purple	8·75	7·50

D45

1895. Perf.

D172	**D45**	10r. blue	2·10	1·40
D173	**D45**	20r. green	8·75	3·25
D174	**D45**	50r. green	11·00	6·00
D175	**D45**	100r. red	7·25	1·40
D176b	**D45**	200r. lilac	5·50	3·50
D177	**D45**	300r. blue	4·00	2·50
D178	**D45**	2000r. brown	18·00	17·00

D64

1906

D282	**D64**	10r. slate	25	25
D283	**D64**	20r. violet	25	25
D284	**D64**	50r. green	30	25
D285	**D64**	100r. red	2·00	65
D286	**D64**	200r. blue	1·10	30
D287	**D64**	300r. grey	40	65
D288	**D64**	400r. green	1·30	1·40
D289	**D64**	500r. lilac	40·00	38·00
D290	**D64**	600r. purple	1·40	3·25
D291	**D64**	700r. brown	35·00	32·00
D292	**D64**	1000r. red	1·60	3·50
D293	**D64**	2000r. green	5·25	6·00
D294	**D64**	5000r. brown	1·60	23·00

D77

1919

D345	**D77**	5r. brown	25	25
D403	**D77**	10r. mauve	15	15
D365	**D77**	20r. olive	45	5·00
D404	**D77**	20r. black	15	15
D405	**D77**	50r. green	20	15
D375	**D77**	100r. red	1·00	95
D407	**D77**	200r. blue	30	20
D408	**D77**	400r. brown	1·40	1·40
D350	**D77**	600r. orange	65	55
D401	**D77**	600r. violet	25	15
D409	**D77**	1000r. turquoise	50	40
D411	**D77**	5000r. blue	90	70
D439	**D77**	2000r. brown	1·60	1·50

Pt. 7

BREMEN

A free city of the Hanseatic League, situated on the R. Weser in northern Germany. Joined the North German Confederation in 1868.

72 grote = 1 thaler (internal).

22 grote = 10 silbergroschen (overseas mail)

1

1855. Imperf.

1	**1**	3g. black on blue	£300	£425

2 **3**

1856. Imperf.

3	**2**	5g. black on red	£225	£475
4	**2**	7g. black on yellow	£325	£1100
5	**3**	5sg. green	£225	£475

4 **5**

1861. Zigzag roulette or perf.

17	**4**	2g. orange	£130	£475
19	**1**	3g. black on blue	£110	£450
20	**2**	5g. black on red	£180	£450
21	**2**	7g. black on yellow	£200	£6500
22	**5**	10g. black	£275	£1600
24	**3**	5sg. green	£700	£300

Pt. 1

BRITISH ANTARCTIC TERRITORY

Constituted in 1962 comprising territories south of latitude 60°S., from the former Falkland Island Dependencies.

1963. 12 pence = 1 shilling; 20 shillings = 1 pound.
1971. 100 (new) pence = 1 pound.

1 M.V. *Kista Dan*

1963

1	**1**	½d. blue	1·25	1·75
2	-	1d. brown	1·25	80
3	-	1½d. red and purple	1·25	1·50
4	-	2d. purple	1·50	80
5	-	2½d. myrtle	3·25	1·25
6	-	3d. turquoise	3·75	1·50
7	-	4d. sepia	2·75	1·50
8	-	6d. olive and blue	4·75	2·50
9	-	9d. green	3·50	2·00
10	-	1s. turquoise	4·25	1·50
11	-	2s. violet and brown	20·00	10·00
12	-	2s.6d. blue	22·00	15·00
13	-	5s. orange and red	22·00	19·00
14	-	10s. blue and green	45·00	26·00
15	-	£1 black and blue	48·00	48·00
15a	-	£1 red and black	£130	£120

DESIGNS: 1d. Manhauling; 1½d. Muskeg (tractor); 2d. Skiing; 2½d. de Havilland D.H.C.2 Beaver (aircraft); 3d. R.R.S. *John Biscoe II* 4d. Camp scene; 6d. H.M.S. *Protector*; 9d. Sledging; 1s. de Havilland D.H.C.3 Otter (aircraft); 2s. Huskies; 2s.6d. Westland Whirlwind helicopter; 5s. Snocat (tractor); 10s. R.R.S. *Shackleton*; £1 (No. 15), Antarctic map; £1 (No. 15a), H.M.S. *Endurance I*.

1966. Churchill Commemoration. As T **38** of Antigua.

16	½d. blue	80	3·25
17	1d. green	3·25	3·25
18	1s. brown	23·00	6·50
19	2s. violet	25·00	7·00

17 Lemaire Channel and Icebergs

1969. 25th Anniv of Continuous Scientific Work.

20	**17**	3½d. black, blue and ultram	2·50	3·00
21	-	6d. multicoloured	1·00	2·50
22	-	1s. black, blue and red	1·00	2·00
23	-	2s. black, orange and turquoise	1·00	3·00

DESIGNS: 6d. Radio Sonde balloon; 1s. Muskeg pulling tent equipment; 2s. Surveyors with theodolite.

1971. Decimal Currency. Nos. 1/14 surch.

24	½p. on ½d. blue	60	3·00
25	1p. on 1d. brown	1·00	90
26	1½p. on 1½d. red and purple	1·25	75
27	2p. on 2d. purple	1·25	40
28	2½p. on 2½d. green	3·00	2·25
29	3p. on 3d. blue	2·50	75
30	4p. on 4d. brown	2·25	75
31	5p. on 6d. green and blue	4·75	3·50
32	6p. on 9d. green	14·00	8·50
33	7½p. on 1s. blue	14·00	8·50
34	10p. on 2s. violet and brown	14·00	12·00
35	15p. on 2s.6d. blue	15·00	12·00
36	25p. on 5s. orange and red	15·00	15·00
37	50p. on 10s. blue and green	18·00	25·00

19 Setting up Camp, Graham Land

1971. Tenth Anniv of Antarctic Treaty. Multicoloured.

38	1½p. Type **19**		6·00	5·50
39	4p. Snow petrels		16·00	8·00
40	5p. Weddell seals		9·50	8·00
41	10p. Adelie penguins		22·00	9·00

Nos. 38/41 each include Antarctic map and Queen Elizabeth in their design.

1972. Royal Silver Wedding. As T **52** of Ascension, but with Kerguelen fur seals and Emperor penguins in background.

42	5p. brown	2·00	3·00
43	10p. green	2·00	3·00

21 James Cook and H.M.S. *Resolution*

1973. Multicoloured.

64a	½p. Type **21**		1·00	2·50
65	1p. Thaddeus von Bellingshausen and *Vostok*		60	2·25
66	1½p. James Weddell and *Jane*		60	2·25
67	2p. John Biscoe and *Tula*		1·50	2·50
48	2½p. J. S. C. Dumont d'Urville and *L'Astrolabe*		1·50	1·75
49	3p. James Clark Ross and H.M.S. *Erebus*		1·00	1·75
50	4p. C. A. Larsen and *Jason*		1·00	1·75
51	5p. Adrien de Gerlache and *Belgica*		1·00	1·75
52	6p. Otto Nordenskjold and *Antarctic*		1·25	3·50
53	7½p. W. S. Bruce and *Scotia*		1·25	3·50
74a	10p. Jean-Baptiste Charcot and *Pourquoi Pas?* (11.12.79)		50	3·00
75	15p. Ernest Shackleton and *Endurance*		1·25	2·75
76	25p. Hubert Wilkins and Lockheed Vega *San Francisco*		1·00	1·50
77b	50p. Lincoln Ellsworth and Northrop Gamma *Polar Star* (11.12.79)		85	2·75
78	£1 John Rymill and *Penola*		2·75	2·00

The 25p. and 50p. show aircraft; the rest show ships.

1973. Royal Wedding. As T **47** of Anguilla. Background colour given. Multicoloured.

59	5p. brown	40	20
60	15p. blue	70	30

22 Churchill and Churchill Peninsula, B.A.T.

1974. Birth Centenary of Sir Winston Churchill. Multicoloured.

61	5p. Type **22**	1·75	1·75
62	15p. Churchill and *Trepassey*	2·00	2·25
MS63	114×88 mm. Nos. 61/2	8·50	8·50

23 Sperm Whale

1977. Whale Conservation. Multicoloured.

79	2p. Type **23**	5·50	3·00
80	8p. Fin whale	6·50	3·50
81	11p. Humpback whale	7·00	3·50
82	25p. Blue whale	7·50	4·50

24 The Queen before Taking the Oath

1977. Silver Jubilee. Multicoloured.

83	6p. Prince Philip's visit, 1956/7	70	40
84	11p. The Coronation Oath	80	50
85	33p. Type **24**	1·00	65

25 Emperor Penguin

1978. 25th Anniv of Coronation.

86	–	25p. green, deep green and silver	60	1·00
87	–	25p. multicoloured	60	1·00
88	**25**	25p. green, deep green and silver	60	1·00

DESIGNS: No. 86, Black Bull of Clarence; 87, Queen Elizabeth II.

26 Macaroni Penguins

1979. Penguins. Multicoloured.

89	3p. Type **26**	9·00	11·00
90	8p. Gentoo penguins	2·00	2·75
91	11p. Adelie penguins	2·50	3·25
92	25p. Emperor penguins	3·50	4·25

27 Sir John Barrow and *Tula*

1980. 150th Anniv of Royal Geographical Society. Former Presidents. Multicoloured.

93	3p. Type **27**	15	15
94	7p. Sir Clement Markham and *Discovery*	15	25
95	11p. Lord Curzon and whaleboat *James Caird*	20	30
96	15p. Sir William Goodenough	20	35
97	22p. Sir James Wordie	25	55
98	30p. Sir Raymond Priestley	30	65

28 Map of Antarctic

1981. 20th Anniv of Antarctic Treaty.

99	**28**	10p. black, blue and light blue	30	70
100	–	13p. black, blue and green	35	80
101	–	25p. black, blue and mauve	40	90
102	–	26p. black, brown and red	40	90

DESIGNS: 13p. Conservation research ("scientific co-operation"); 25p. Satellite image mapping ("technical co-operation"); 26p. Global geophysics ("scientific co-operation").

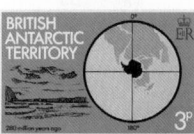

29 Map of Gondwana 280 million years ago and Contemporary Landscape Scene

1982. Gondwana – Continental Drift and Climatic Change. Maps of Gondwana showing position of continents, and contemporary landscapes. Multicoloured.

103	3p. Type **29**	20	40
104	6p. 260 million years ago	20	50
105	10p. 230 million years ago	25	60

106	13p. 175 million years ago	30	70
107	25p. 50 million years ago	35	75
108	26p. Present day	35	75

30 British Antarctic Territory Coat of Arms

1982. 21st Birthday of Princess of Wales. Multicoloured.

109	5p. Type **30**	15	30
110	17p. Princess of Wales (detail of painting by Bryan Organ)	35	60
111	37p. Wedding ceremony	50	90
112	50p. Formal portrait	90	1·25

31 Leopard Seal

1983. Tenth Anniv of Antarctic Seal Conservation Convention. Multicoloured.

113	5p. Type **31**	25	40
114	10p. Weddell seals	30	45
115	13p. Southern elephant seals	30	50
116	17p. Kerguelen fur seals	30	60
117	25p. Ross seals	30	70
118	34p. Crabeater seals	35	95

32 de Havilland Twin Otter 200/300

1983. Bicentenary of Manned Flight. Multicoloured.

119	5p. Type **32**	25	30
120	13p. de Havilland DHC-3 Twin Otter	35	45
121	17p. Consolidated PBY-5A Canso amphibian	45	60
122	50p. Lockheed Vega *San Francisco*	70	1·25

33 *Corethron criophilum*

1984. Marine Life. Multicoloured.

123	1p. Type **33**	60	1·75
124	2p. *Desmonema gaudichaudi*	65	1·75
125	3p. *Tomopteris carpenteri*	65	1·75
126	4p. *Pareuchaeta antarctica*	70	1·75
127	5p. *Antarctomysis maxima*	70	1·75
128	6p. *Antarcturus signiensis*	70	1·75
129	7p. *Serolis cornuta*	70	1·75
130	8p. *Parathemisto gaudichaudii*	70	1·75
131	9p. *Bovallia gigantea*	70	1·75
132	10p. *Euphausia superba*	70	1·75
133	15p. *Colossendeis australis*	70	1·75
134	20p. *Todarodes sagittatus*	75	1·75
135	25p. Antarctic rockcod	80	1·75
136	50p. Black-finned icefish	1·25	2·00
137	£1 Crabeater seal	1·75	2·50
138	£3 Antarctic marine food chain	5·00	6·50

34 M.Y. *Penola* in Stella Creek

1985. 50th Anniv of British Graham Land Expedition. Multicoloured.

139	7p. Type **34**	40	75
140	22p. Northern Base, Winter Island	70	1·40
141	27p. de Havilland DH.83 Fox Moth at Southern Base, Barry Island	80	1·60
142	54p. Dog Team, near Ablation Point, George VI Sound	1·50	2·25

35 Robert McCormick and South Polar Skua

1985. Early Naturalists. Multicoloured.

143	7p. Type **35**	80	1·25
144	22p. Sir Joseph Dalton Hooker and *Deschampsia antarctica*	1·25	2·50
145	27p. Jean Rene C. Quoy and hourglass dolphin	1·25	2·50
146	54p. James Weddell and Weddell seal	1·75	3·50

36 Dr. Edmond Halley

1986. Appearance of Halley's Comet. Multicoloured.

147	7p. Type **36**	75	1·25
148	22p. Halley Station, Antarctica	1·00	2·25
149	27p. *Halley's Comet, 1531* (from Peter Apian woodcut, 1532)	1·25	2·50
150	44p. "Giotto" spacecraft	2·25	4·50

37 Snow Crystal

1986. 50th Anniv of International Glaciological Society. Snow Crystals.

151	**37**	10p. light-blue and blue	40	75
152	–	24p. green and deep green	50	1·40
153	–	29p. mauve and deep mauve	60	1·50
154	–	58p. blue and violet	80	2·50

38 Captain Scott, 1904

1987. 75th Anniv of Captain Scott's Arrival at South Pole. Multicoloured.

155	10p. Type **38**	55	95
156	24p. Hut Point and *Discovery* Ross Island, 1902–4	90	2·00
157	29p. Cape Evans Hut, 1911–13	1·00	2·25
158	58p. Scott's expedition at South Pole, 1912	1·50	3·00

39 IGY Logo

1987. 30th Anniv of International Geophysical Year.

159	**39**	10p. black and green	30	75
160	–	24p. multicoloured	50	1·40
161	–	29p. multicoloured	60	1·75
162	–	58p. multicoloured	1·10	2·50

DESIGNS: 24p. Port Lockroy; 29p. Argentine Islands; 58p. Halley Bay.

40 Aurora over South Ice Plateau Station

1988. 30th Anniv of Commonwealth Trans-Antarctic Expedition. Multicoloured.

163	10p. Type **40**	30	75
164	24p. de Havilland Canada DHC-3 Otter at Theron Mountains	50	1·25
165	29p. Seismic ice-depth sounding	60	1·40
166	58p. "Sno-cat" over crevasse	1·00	2·00

41 Xanthoria elegans

1989. Lichens. Multicoloured.

167	10p. Type **41**	90	1·00
168	24p. Usnea aurantiaco-atra	1·60	2·00
169	29p. Cladonia chlorophaea	1·75	2·25
170	58p. Umbilicaria antarctica	2·50	3·25

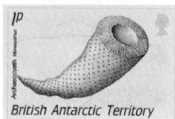

42 Monocyathus (archaeocyath)

1990. Fossils. Multicoloured.

171	1p. Type **42**	1·25	1·50
172	2p. Lingulella (brachiopod)	1·25	1·50
173	3p. Triplagnoslus (trilobite)	1·25	1·50
174	4p. Lyriaspis (trilobite)	1·50	1·50
175	5p. Glossopteris leaf (gymnosperm)	1·50	1·50
176	6p. Gonatosorus (fern)	1·50	1·60
177	7p. Belemnopsis aucklandica (belemnite)	1·50	1·60
178	8p. Sanmartinoceras africanum insignicostatum (ammonite)	1·50	1·60
179	9p. Pinna antarctica (mussel)	1·50	1·60
180	10p. Aucellina andina (mussel)	1·50	1·60
181	20p. Pterotrigonia malagninoi (mussel)	2·00	2·25
182	25p. Perissoptera (conch shell)	2·00	2·25
183	50p. Ainoceras sp. (ammonite)	2·75	3·50
184	£1 Gunnarites zinsmeisteri (ammonite)	3·75	4·75
185	£3 Hoploparia (crayfish)	7·50	8·50

1990. 90th Birthday of Queen Elizabeth the Queen Mother. As T **134** of Ascension.

186	26p. multicoloured	1·25	2·00
187	£1 black and brown	2·50	3·50

DESIGNS: 29×36 mm: 26p. Wedding of Prince Albert and Lady Elizabeth Bowes-Lyon, 1923. 29×37 mm: £1 The Royal Family, 1940.

43 Late Cretaceous Forest and Southern Beech Fossil

1991. Age of the Dinosaurs. Multicoloured.

188	12p. Type **43**	1·25	1·25
189	26p. Hypsilophodont dinosaurs and skull	2·00	2·25
190	31p. Frilled sharks and tooth	2·25	2·50
191	62p. Mosasaur, plesiosaur, and mosasaur vertebra	3·50	4·00

44 Launching Meteorological Balloon, Halley IV Station

1991. Discovery of Antarctic Ozone Hole. Multicoloured.

192	12p. Type **44**	90	1·75
193	26p. Measuring ozone with Dobson spectrophotometer	1·60	2·75
194	31p. Satellite map showing ozone hole	1·90	3·00
195	62p. Lockheed ER-2 aircraft and graph of chlorine monoxide and ozone levels	3·25	5·50

45 Researching Dry Valley

1991. 30th Anniv of Antarctic Treaty.

196	**45** 12p. multicoloured	90	90
197	- 26p. multicoloured	1·60	1·75
198	- 31p. black and green	1·75	1·90
199	- 62p. multicoloured	3·00	3·25

DESIGNS: 26p. Relief map of ice sheet; 31p. BIOMASS logo; 62p. Ross seal.

46 H.M.S. Erebus and H.M.S. Terror in the Antarctic (J. Carmichael)

1991. Maiden Voyage of James Clark Ross (research ship). Multicoloured.

200	12p. Type **46**	90	1·50
201	26p. Launch of James Clark Ross	1·60	2·50
202	31p. James Clark Ross in Antarctica	1·75	2·75
203	62p. Scientific research	3·00	3·75

1991. Birth Bicentenary of Michael Faraday (scientist). Nos. 200/3 additionally inscr "200th Anniversary M. Faraday 1791–1867".

204	12p. Type **46**	90	1·75
205	26p. Launch of James Clark Ross	1·60	2·75
206	31p. James Clark Ross in Antarctica	1·75	3·00
207	62p. Scientific research	3·00	4·50

47 Ross Seals

1992. Endangered Species. Seals and Penguins. Multicoloured.

208	4p. Type **47**	1·25	1·25
209	5p. Adelie penguins	1·25	1·25
210	7p. Weddell seal with pup	1·25	1·25
211	29p. Emperor penguins with chicks	2·50	2·25
212	34p. Crabeater seals with pup	1·75	2·25
213	68p. Bearded penguins ("Chinstrap Penguin") with young	2·50	2·75

48 Sun Pillar at Faraday

1992. Lower Atmospheric Phenomena. Multicoloured.

214	14p. Type **48**	80	1·50
215	29p. Halo over iceberg	1·40	1·90
216	34p. Lee Wave cloud	1·75	2·25
217	68p. Nacreous clouds	2·75	4·00

49 Fitzroy (mail and supply ship)

1993. Antarctic Ships. Multicoloured.

218	1p. Type **49**	2·25	2·75
219	2p. William Scoresby (research ship)	2·50	2·75
220	3p. Eagle (sealer)	2·50	2·75
221	4p. Trepassey (supply ship)	2·50	2·75
222	5p. John Biscoe I (research ship)	2·50	3·00
223	10p. Norsel (supply ship)	2·75	3·00
224	20p. H.M.S. Protector (ice patrol ship)	4·00	4·00
225	30p. Oluf Sven (supply ship)	4·50	4·50
226	50p. John Biscoe II and Shackleton (research ships)	5·50	6·00
227	£1 Tottan (supply ship)	7·00	8·00
228	£3 Perla Dan (supply ship)	11·00	12·00
229	£5 H.M.S. Endurance I (ice patrol ship)	15·00	16·00

1994. "Hong Kong '94", International Stamp Exhibition. Nos. 240/5 optd **HONG KONG '94** and emblem.

230	15p. Type **51**	1·10	1·50
231	24p. de Havilland Turbo Beaver III aircraft	1·60	2·00
232	31p. de Havilland Otter aircraft and dog team	1·75	2·50
233	36p. de Havilland Twin Otter 200/300 aircraft and dog team	1·90	2·75
234	62p. de Havilland Dash Seven aircraft over landing strip, Rothera Point	2·75	3·25
235	72p. de Havilland Dash Seven aircraft on runway	2·75	3·50

50 Bransfield House Post Office, Port Lockroy

1994. 50th Anniv of Operation Tabarin. Multicoloured.

236	15p. Type **50**	1·00	1·50
237	31p. Survey team, Hope Bay	1·60	2·00
238	36p. Dog team, Hope Bay	2·50	2·50
239	72p. Fitzroy (supply ship) and H.M.S. William Scoresby (minesweeper)	3·25	4·50

51 Huskies and Sledge

1994. Forms of Transportation. Multicoloured.

240	15p. Type **51**	70	80
241	24p. de Havilland Turbo Beaver III aircraft	90	1·00
242	31p. de Havilland Otter aircraft and dog team	1·00	1·10
243	36p. de Havilland Twin Otter 200/300 aircraft and dog team	1·10	1·40
244	62p. de Havilland Dash Seven aircraft over landing strip, Rothera Point	2·00	2·50
245	72p. de Havilland Dash Seven aircraft on runway	2·00	2·75

52 Capt. James Cook and H.M.S. Resolution

1994. Antarctic Heritage Fund. Multicoloured.

246	17p.+3p. +3p. Type **52**	2·50	3·25
247	35p.+15p. +15p. Sir James Clark Ross with H.M.S. Erebus and H.M.S. Terror	2·75	3·50
248	40p.+10p. +10p. Capt. Robert Falcon Scott and interior of hut	2·75	3·50
249	76p.+4p. +4p. Sir Ernest Shackleton and Endurance	3·75	4·75

53 Pair of Crabeater Seals

1994. Antarctic Food Chain. Multicoloured.

250	35p. Type **53**	2·25	3·00
251	35p. Blue whale	2·25	3·00
252	35p. Wandering albatross	2·25	3·00
253	35p. Mackerel icefish	2·25	3·00
254	35p. Krill	2·25	3·00
255	35p. Seven star flying squid	2·25	3·00

54 Hauberg Mountains

1995. Geological Structures. Multicoloured.

256	17p. Type **54**	1·75	2·00
257	35p. Arrowsmith Peninsula	2·50	2·75
258	40p. Colbert Mountains	2·75	3·00
259	76p. Succession Cliffs	4·00	5·75

55 World Map showing Member Countries

1996. 24th Meeting of Scientific Committee on Antarctic Research. Multicoloured.

260	17p. Type **55**	1·00	1·50
261	35p. Scientist analysing ice samples	1·75	2·00
262	40p. Releasing balloon	2·00	2·25
263	76p. Antarctic research ship catching marine life	2·75	4·00
MS264	100×90 mm. £1 S.C.A.R. logo	6·50	8·50

56 Killer Whales

1996. Whales. Multicoloured.

265	17p. Type **56**	80	1·25
266	35p. Sperm whales	1·40	1·75
267	40p. Minke whales	1·60	2·00
268	76p. Blue whale and calf	2·50	3·25
MS269	105×82 mm. £1 Humpback whale	4·00	4·25

1996. 70th Birthday of Queen Elizabeth II. As T **165** of Ascension, each incorporating a different photograph of the Queen. Multicoloured.

270	17p. At premiere of Chaplin, Leicester Square, 1992	1·00	1·25
271	35p. At Buckingham Palace dinner, 1991	1·50	1·60
272	40p. In Aberdeen, 1993	1·75	1·75
273	76p. At Royal Military School of Music, 1990	2·25	3·75

1997. "HONG KONG '97" International Stamp Exhibition. Sheet 130×90 mm, containing design as No. 226. Multicoloured.

MS274	50p. John Biscoe II and Shackleton (research ships)	1·75	2·25

1997. Return of Hong Kong to China. Sheet 130×90 mm containing design as No. 227, but with "1997" imprint date.

MS275	£1 Tottan	2·75	3·75

57 Chinstrap Penguins sledging

1997. Christmas. Multicoloured.

276	17p. Type **57**	2·25	1·50
277	35p. Emperor penguins carol singing	2·75	2·25
278	40p. Adelie penguins throwing snowballs	3·00	2·50
279	76p. Gentoo penguins ice-skating	4·25	5·50

1998. Diana, Princess of Wales Commemoration. Sheet 145×70 mm, containing vert designs as T **177** of Ascension. Multicoloured.

MS280	35p. Wearing sunglasses; 35p. Wearing round-necked white blouse, 1993; 35p. Wearing white blouse and jacket, 1990; 35p. Wearing green jacket, 1992 (sold at £1.40+20p. charity premium)	2·50	2·50

58 Chart of South Shetland Islands (Swedish South Polar Expedition, 1902–3)

1998. History of Mapping in Antarctica. Multicoloured.

281	16p. Type **58**	2·50	2·00
282	30p. Map of Antarctic Peninsula (1949)	3·00	2·50
283	35p. Map of Antarctic Peninsula (1964)	3·25	2·75
284	40p. Map of Antarctic Peninsula from Landsat (1981)	3·25	3·25
285	65p. Map of Antarctic Peninsula from satellite (1995)	4·50	6·00

59 Antarctic Explorer and H.M.S. *Erebus*, 1843

1998. Antarctic Clothing. Multicoloured.

286	30p. Type **59**	3·50	2·25
287	35p. Explorer with dog, and *Discovery I*, 1900	4·00	2·25
288	40p. Surveyor, and *Fitzroy*, 1943	4·00	2·50
289	65p. Scientist with Adelie penguins, and *James Clark Ross*, 1998	5·50	6·50

60 Snowy Sheathbill

1998. Antarctic Birds. Multicoloured.

290	1p. Type **60**	3·50	2·50
291	2p. Dove prion ("Antarctic Prion")	2·25	2·50
292	5p. Adelie penguin	2·25	2·50
293	10p. Emperor penguin	2·25	2·50
294	20p. Antarctic tern	2·50	2·50
295	30p. Black-bellied storm petrel	2·50	2·50
296	35p. Southern fulmar ("Antarctic Fulmar")	2·75	2·75
297	40p. Blue-eyed cormorant ("Blue-eyed Shag")	2·75	3·00
298	50p. South polar skua ("Mc-Cormick's Skua")	3·00	3·25
299	£1 Southern black-backed gull ("Kelp Gull")	5·00	6·00
300	£3 Wilson's storm petrel	9·50	11·00
301	£5 Antarctic skua ("Brown Skua")	13·00	15·00

61 Mackerel Icefish

1999. Fish of the Southern Ocean. Multicoloured.

302	10p. Type **61**	2·00	2·00
303	20p. Blenny rockcod ("Tooth-fish")	2·50	2·50
304	25p. Borch	2·50	2·50
305	50p. Marbled rockcod ("Marbled notothen")	4·00	4·00
306	80p. Bernacchi's rockcod ("Bernach")	6·50	7·50

62 Map showing Crustal Microplates of West Antarctica

1999. British Antarctic Survey Discoveries. Multicoloured.

307	15p. Type **62**	3·00	2·25
308	30p. Testing lead levels in ice	3·50	3·00
309	35p. Decolopodid sea spider (Gigantism in marine inverte-brates) (horiz)	3·50	3·00
310	40p. Scientist operating Dobson Spectrophotometer for test-ing ozone layer (horiz)	3·50	3·50
311	70p. Radar antenna (aurora electric field research) (horiz)	5·50	6·50

63 Wreck of *Endurance*

2000. Shackleton's Trans-Antarctic Expedition, 1914–17, Commemoration. Multicoloured.

312	35p. Type **63**	5·00	3·75
313	40p. Ocean Camp on ice	5·00	3·75
314	65p. Launching *James Caird* from Elephant Island	9·00	10·00

64 Iceberg and Opening Bars

2000. Composition of Antarctic Symphony by Sir Peter Maxwell Davies. Multicoloured.

315	37p. Type **64**	4·50	4·50
316	37p. Stern of *James Clark Ross* and pack ice	4·50	4·50
317	43p. de Havilland Canada DH-6 Twin Otter and camp on Jones Ice Self	5·00	5·00
318	43p. Frozen sea	5·00	5·00

65 Route of Commonwealth Trans-Atlantic Expedition, 1955-58

2000. "Heroic Age of Antarctica" (1st series). Commonwealth Trans-Antarctic Expedition, 1955–8. Multicoloured.

319	37p. Type **65**	8·50	7·00
320	37p. Expedition at South Pole, 1958	8·50	7·00
321	37p. *Magga Dan* (Antarctic supply ship)	8·50	7·00
322	37p. "Sno-cat" repair camp	8·50	7·00
323	37p. "Sno-cat" over crevasse	8·50	7·00
324	37p. Seismic explosion	8·50	7·00

See also Nos. 333/8 and 351/6.

66 *Bransfield* unloading "Sno-cat", Halley

2000. Survey Ships. Multicoloured.

325	20p. Type **66**	4·00	2·50
326	33p. *Ernest Shackelton* unload-ing supplies into *Tula*	6·00	4·00
327	37p. *Bransfield* in the ice (horiz)	6·00	4·00
328	43p. *Ernest Shackelton* with Westland Lynx helicopter (horiz)	7·50	7·00

67 Tourists at Port Lockroy

2001. Restoration of Port Lockroy Base. Multicoloured.

329	33p. Type **67**	4·00	2·50
330	37p. Port Lockroy and cruise ship	4·00	2·50
331	43p. Port Lockroy huts in 1945	4·50	2·75
332	65p. Interior of Port Lockroy laboratory in 1945	7·50	7·00

68 Map of Ross Sea Area

2001. "Heroic Age of Antarctica" (2nd series). Captain Scott's 1901–04 Expedition. Multicoloured.

333	33p. Type **68**	2·25	2·25
334	37p. Captain Robert F. Scott	2·50	2·50
335	43p. First Antarctic balloon ascent, 1902 (horiz)	3·00	3·00
336	65p. *Emperor Penguin* chick (drawing by Edward Wilson)	4·00	4·00
337	70p. Shackleton, Scott and Wilson and most southerly camp, 1902 (horiz)	4·00	4·00
338	80p. *Discovery I* trapped in ice off Hut Point (horiz)	4·50	4·50

2002. Golden Jubilee. As T **200** of Ascension.

339	20p. black, mauve and gold	1·50	1·50
340	37p. multicoloured	1·75	1·75
341	43p. black, mauve and gold	2·00	2·00
342	50p multicoloured	2·50	3·25
MS343	162×95 mm. Nos. 339/42 and 50p. multicoloured	8·50	10·00

DESIGNS—HORIZ: 20p. Princess Elizabeth and Princess Margaret making radio broadcast, 1940; 37p. Queen Elizabeth in Garter robes, 1998; 43p. Queen Elizabeth at Balmoral, 1952; 50p. Queen Elizabeth in London, 1996. VERT (38×51 mm)—50p. Queen Elizabeth after Annigoni.

Designs as Nos. 339/42 in No. **MS**343 omit the gold frame around each stamp and the "Golden Jubilee 1952–2002" inscription.

2002. Queen Elizabeth the Queen Mother Commemoration. As T **202** of Ascension.

344	40p. black, gold and purple	1·50	1·50
345	45p. multicoloured	1·50	1·50
MS346	145×70 mm. 70p. black and gold; 95p. multicoloured	7·50	7·50

DESIGNS: 40p. Lady Elizabeth Bowes-Lyon, 1913; 45p. Queen Mother on her birthday, 1996; 70p. Queen Elizabeth at niece's wedding, London, 1951; 95p. Queen Mother at Cheltenham Races, 1999.

Designs in No. **MS**346 omit the "1900–2002" inscription and the coloured frame.

69 Satellite and Antarctica

2002. 20th Anniv of Commission for Conservation of Antarctic Marine Living Resources (CCAMLR). Multicoloured.

347	37p. Type **69**	3·50	3·75
348	37p. Trawler and wandering albatross	3·50	3·75
349	37p. Icefish, toothfish and crabeater seal	3·50	3·75
350	37p. Krill and phytoplankton	3·50	3·75

2002. "Heroic Age of Antarctica" (3rd series). Scottish National Antarctic Expedition, 1902–04. As T **68** but horiz. Multicoloured.

351	30p. Map of Weddell Sea	4·00	3·25
352	40p. Piper Gilbert Kerr and emperor penguin (horiz)	4·50	4·00
353	45p. *Scotia* (expedition ship)	4·50	4·00
354	70p. Weather station and meteorologist (horiz)	5·00	5·50
355	95p. William Speirs Bruce	6·00	6·50
356	£1 Omond House, Laurie Island (horiz)	6·00	7·00

2003. 50th Anniv of Coronation. As T **206** of Ascension. Multicoloured.

357	40p. Coronation Coach in procession	2·50	2·00
358	45p. Queen Elizabeth II with Prince Charles on Bucking-ham Palace balcony	2·50	2·00
MS359	95×115 mm. 95p. As 40p.; 95p. As 45p.	8·50	7·50

Nos. 357/8 have scarlet frame; stamps from **MS**359 have no frame and country name in mauve panel.

2003. As T **207** of Ascension.

360	£2 multicoloured	6·00	6·00

70 Blue Whale

2003. Endangered Species. Blue Whale. Multicoloured.

361	40p. Type **70**	1·50	1·50
362	45p. Tail fluke	1·50	1·50
363	45p. Two blue whales	1·50	1·50
364	70p. Two blue whales at surface	2·00	2·00

71 Emperor Penguins

2003. Penguins of the Antarctic (1st series). Multicoloured.

365	(–) Type **71**	3·00	3·00
366	(–) Head of macaroni penguin	3·00	3·00
367	(–) Gentoo penguin	3·00	3·00
368	(–) Pair of adelie penguins	3·00	3·00
369	(–) Chinstrap penguin	3·00	3·00
370	(–) Gentoo penguin chick	3·00	3·00
371	(–) Emperor penguins (different)	3·00	3·00
372	(–) Chinstrap penguin chick	3·00	3·00
373	(–) Group of adelie penguins	3·00	3·00
374	(–) Gentoo penguin and chick	3·00	3·00
375	(–) Pair of macaroni penguins	3·00	3·00
376	(–) Emperor penguin chick	3·00	3·00

Nos. 365/76, inscribed "AIRMAIL POSTCARD", were initially sold at 40p.

See also Nos. 424/47 and 474/485.

72 Base G, Admiralty Bay

2003. Research Bases and Postmarks. Multicoloured.

377	1p. Type **72**	1·00	1·50
378	2p. Base B, Deception Island	1·00	1·50
379	5p. Base D, Hope Bay	1·25	1·75
380	22p. Base F, Argentine Islands	2·25	2·25
381	25p. Base E, Stonington Island	2·25	2·00
382	40p. Base A, Port Lockroy	2·75	2·50
383	45p. Base H, Signy	2·75	2·50
384	50p. Base N, Anvers Island	2·75	2·50
385	95p. Base P, Rothera	5·00	5·00
386	£1 Base T, Adelaide Island	5·00	5·00
387	£3 Base Y, Horseshoe Island	13·00	13·00
388	£5 Base Z, Halley Bay	18·00	18·00

73 Annual Temperature Trends since 1950

2004. Climate Change. Multicoloured.

389	24p. Type **73**	2·00	2·00
390	24p. Larsen ice shelf	2·00	2·00
391	42p. Ice core measurements	2·75	2·75
392	42p. Ice core drilling	2·75	2·75
393	50p. Rise in air temperatures at Faraday Station	3·50	3·50
394	50p. Antarctic pearlwort	3·50	3·50

74 Pintado ("Cape") Petrel

2005. Birdlife International. Petrels. Multicoloured.

395	25p. Type **74**	3·00	1·10
396	42p. Snow petrel	3·75	1·50
397	75p. Wilson's storm petrel	5·50	4·00
398	£1 Antarctic petrel	6·50	5·00
MS399	170×85 mm. 50p.×6 Southern giant petrel and glaciers; Southern giant petrel in flight (from side); Head of Southern giant petrel; Southern giant petrel standing over chick; Southern giant petrel roosting with chick; Southern giant petrel chick	22·00	20·00

75 *Endurance* 1914–15 (three masted barque)

2005. *Endurance*. Multicoloured.

400	42p. Type **75**	4·00	2·00
401	50p. HMS *Endurance*, 1968–90 (ice patrol and hydrographic survey ship)	5·50	3·25
402	£1 HMS *Endurance*, 1991 (class 1A1 ice-breaker ship)	9·00	6·50

76 Deception Island from the South East

2005. 50th Anniv of FIDASE (Falkland Islands and Dependencies Aerial Survey Expedition, 1955–7). Multicoloured.

403	45p. Type **76**	2·25	2·25
404	55p. Hunting Lodge, Deception Island	2·50	2·50
405	80p. Bell 47D helicopter with perspex bubble and flotation landing gear	6·00	6·00
406	£1 Canso flying boat	6·00	6·00

77 Samson, Shakespeare and
Surley

2005. Shackleton Expedition (1914—16) Dogs.
Multicoloured.

407	45p. Type **77**	4·00	3·00
408	45p. Tom Crean holding pup-pies (vert)	4·00	3·00
409	55p. Dogs outside ice kennels and HMS *Endurance*	5·00	3·25
410	£1 Sled dog team training on sea ice and HMS *Endurance* (vert)	8·00	8·50

78 Faber Maunsell's Winning
Concept Design

2005. Halley VI Research Station International Design
Competition. Multicoloured.

411	45p. Type **78**	2·50	2·50
412	45p. Buro Happold concept design	2·50	2·50
413	55p. Hopkins concept design	2·75	2·75
414	80p. Laws building at Halley V Research Station	5·00	6·00

79 Sea and
Icebergs (Erica
Currie)

2006. ATCM XXIX Edinburgh (Tristan da Cunha) 2006
Stamp Design Competition. Children's Paintings.
Multicoloured.

415	45p. Type **79**	2·00	2·00
416	45p. Penguins and icebergs (Meghan Joyce)	2·00	2·00
417	55p. Icebreaker (Lorna Mac-Donald)	2·25	2·25
418	£1 Penguin wearing Union Jack (Danielle Dalgleish)	4·25	5·00

2006. 80th Birthday of Queen Elizabeth II. As T **223** of
Ascension. Multicoloured.

419	45p. Princess Elizabeth	2·25	2·00
420	55p. Queen wearing diadem, c. 1952	2·50	2·25
421	80p. Wearing red hat	3·50	3·50
422	£1 In evening dress	3·75	3·75
MS423	144×75 mm. Nos. 420/1	5·50	5·50

Stamps from MS423 do not have white borders.

2006. Penguins of the Antarctic (2nd series). As T **71**.
Multicoloured

(a) Ordinary gum

424	(–) Chinstrap penguin chick	2·00	2·00
425	(–) Head of emperor penguin	2·00	2·00
426	(–) Adelie penguin with wings outstretched	2·00	2·00
427	(–) Head of chinstrap penguin	2·00	2·00
428	(–) Macaroni penguin	2·00	2·00
429	(–) Gentoo penguin feeding chick	2·00	2·00
430	(–) Emperor penguin chick	2·00	2·00
431	(–) Adelie penguin on nest	2·00	2·00
432	(–) Emperor penguin	2·00	2·00
433	(–) Gentoo penguin	2·00	2·00
434	(–) Adelie penguin feeding chick	2·00	2·00
435	(–) Two emperor penguin chicks	2·00	2·00

(b) Self-adhesive. Size 24×29 mm.

436	(–) As No. 424	1·75	2·25
437	(–) As No. 425	1·75	2·25
438	(–) As No. 426	1·75	2·25
439	(–) As No. 430	1·75	2·25
440	(–) As No. 431	1·75	2·25
441	(–) As No. 432	1·75	2·25
442	(–) As No. 427	1·75	2·25
443	(–) As No. 428	1·75	2·25
444	(–) As No. 429	1·75	2·25
445	(–) As No. 433	1·75	2·25
446	(–) As No. 434	1·75	2·25
447	(–) As No. 435	1·75	2·25

Nos. 424/47 are inscribed "AIRMAIL POSTCARD" and
were sold at 50p. each.

80 Elephant Seals

2006. Seals. Multicoloured.

448	25p. Type **80**	1·50	1·50
449	50p. Crabeater seals	2·25	2·25
450	60p. Weddell seals	2·50	2·75
451	£1.05 Leopard seal	4·00	5·00

81 *Marseniopsis molle* (sea
lemon)

2007. Marine Invertebrates. Multicoloured.

452	25p. Type **81**	1·75	1·50
453	50p. *Isotealia antarctica* (Antarc-tic sea anemone)	2·75	2·75
454	60p. *Decolopoda australis* (sea spider)	3·00	3·25
455	£1.05 *Odontaster validus* (sea star)	5·50	6·50

82 Pinnacle Iceberg

2007. Icebergs. Multicoloured.

456	25p. Type **82**	1·75	1·50
457	50p. Pinnacle and tabular icebergs and ice floes at sunset	2·75	2·75
458	60p. Wedge iceberg	3·00	3·25
459	£1.05 Tabular iceberg and ice floes	5·50	6·50

83 Aerial View of
Antarctica

2007. International Polar Year 2007–2008. Circular sheet
97×97 mm.

MS460	**83** £2 multicoloured	7·00	10·00

84 James Weddell, *Jane* and
Beaufoy

2008. Explorers and Ships. Multicoloured.

461	1p. Type **84**	20	30
462	2p. Sir James Clark Ross, *Erebus* and *Terror*	35	40
463	5p. Neil Alison Mackintosh and *Discovery II*	55	65
464	27p. Sir Douglas Mawson and *Discovery*	1·25	1·00
465	55p. Captain James Cook and *Resolution*	2·50	2·00
466	65p. Carsten Egeberg Borchgre-vink and *Southern Cross*	2·50	2·50
467	65p. Dr. William Speirs Bruce and *Scotia*	2·50	2·50
468	65p. Captain Robert Falcon Scott and *Discovery*	2·50	2·50
469	65p. Sir Ernest Shackleton and *Endurance*	2·50	2·50
470	£1.10 John Riddoch Rymill and *Penola*	4·25	4·50
471	£2.50 Captain Victor Marchesi and *William Scoresby*	8·25	8·50
472	£5 Sir Vivian Fuchs and *Magga Dan*	16·00	16·00
MS473	110×80 mm. As Nos. 466/9 but inscr 'AIRMAIL LETTER'	9·00	10·00

No. **MS**473 was sold for £2.60.

2008. Penguins of the Antarctic (3rd series). As T **71**.
Multicoloured.

474	(–) Head of chinstrap penguin	3·00	3·00
475	(–) Gentoo penguin and two chicks	3·00	3·00

476	(–) Head of macaroni penguin, calling with beak open	3·00	3·00
477	(–) Chinstrap penguin, calling, with beak open and wings and tail raised	3·00	3·00
478	(–) Two emperor penguins	3·00	3·00
479	(–) Adelie penguin	3·00	3·00
480	(–) Chinstrap penguin, walking with wings outstretched	3·00	3·00
481	(–) Head of gentoo penguin, calling with beak open	3·00	3·00
482	(–) Macaroni penguin	3·00	3·00
483	(–) Emperor penguin with chick	3·00	3·00
484	(–) Two adelie penguins	3·00	3·00
485	(–) Emperor penguin chick	3·00	3·00

Nos. 474/85, inscribed 'AIRMAIL POSTCARD' were
sold at 55p. each.

85 *Lophosoria cupulatus*,
Snow Island

2008. Fossil Ferns. Designs showing map of Antarctica
and fossil ferns. Multicoloured.

486	55p. Type **85**	3·00	2·00
487	65p. cf. *Cladophlebis oblonga*, Alexander Island	3·50	2·50
488	£1.10 *Pachypteris indica*, Snow Island	6·00	6·50
489	£1.10 *Aculea acicularis*, Alexan-der Island	6·00	6·50

86 Aurora Australis

2008. Aurora Australis. Multicoloured.

490	65p. Type **86**	3·50	3·50
491	65p. Blue aurora	3·50	3·50
492	65p. Red aurora	3·50	3·50
493	65p. Turquoise-blue aurora	3·50	3·50
494	65p. Green and white aurora	3·50	3·50

87 Fairey Seafox

2009. Centenary of Naval Aviation. Multicoloured.

495	10p. Type **87**	80	1·00
496	10p. Westland Lynx helicopter	80	1·00
497	90p. Supermarine Walrus	5·00	5·50
498	90p. Westland Wasp helicopter	5·00	5·50
MS499	110×70 mm. £2 HMA No. 1 *Mayfly* (airship)	8·50	10·00

88 Antarctic Fur Seal

2009. 50th Anniv of the Antarctic Treaty. Multicoloured. .
Multicoloured.

500	27p. Type **88**	1·10	1·25
501	27p. Humpback whale	1·10	1·25
502	55p. Southern giant petrel	2·00	1·75
503	55p. Gentoo penguin	2·00	1·55
504	65p. Giant squid	2·50	2·00
505	65p. Jellyfish	2·50	2·00

Nos. 500/1, 502/3 and 504/5 were each printed togeth-
er, *se-tenant*, as horizontal pairs in sheets of 24 (2 panes
2×6 with horizontal gutter), each pair forming a compos-
ite background design.

89 Crabeater Seal

2009. Endangered Species. Crabeater Seal (*Lobodon
carcinophaga*). Multicoloured.

506	27p. Type **89**	1·25	1·00
507	65p. Crabeater seal (close-up of head)	2·50	2·00
508	£1.10 Two crabeater seals	4·25	4·50
509	£1.50 Crabeater seal (swimming to right)	6·00	6·25

90 George VI Ice Shelf
(South)

2009. Climate Change. Sheet 165×130 mm containing
T **90** and similar vert designs showing the extent
of Antarctic ice shelves in 1950 and today.
Multicoloured.

MS510	£1.10×4 Type **90**; Larsen B Ice Shelf; Wilkins Ice Shelf; Larsen C Ice Shelf	18·00	18·00

91 Button Worm

2010. Marine Biodiversity. Multicoloured.

511	27p. Type **91**	90	90
512	27p. Amphipod	90	90
513	27p. Polychaete worm	90	90
514	27p. Sponge	90	90
MS515	140×95 mm. £1.15×4 Solitary coral; Amphipod (different); Comb jelly; Basket star (all 36×36 mm)	14·00	14·00

92 *Terra Nova* on the
Horizon

2010. Centenary of the British Antarctic Expedition
(1910–13). Each black and grey.

516	27p. Type **92**	90	90
517	27p. Expedition ponies	90	90
518	27p. Cavern in the iceberg	90	90
519	27p. The 'Tenements' bunks in Winterquarters Hut	90	90
520	27p. Captain Scott's birthday dinner	90	90
521	27p. Observing at the weather station	90	90
522	27p. Captain Scott writing in his journal	90	90
523	27p. *Terra Nova* in the ice	90	90
524	60p. *Terra Nova* in harbour	1·40	1·40
525	60p. Lieut. Rennick leading pony	1·40	1·40
526	60p. The Matterhorn Berg	1·40	1·40
527	60p. Nelson at work in the lab	1·40	1·40
528	60p. Captain Scott on skis	1·40	1·40
529	60p. Chris (dog) and the gramophone	1·40	1·40
530	60p. Motor and load passing Inaccessible Island	1·40	1·40
531	60p. The polar party at the South Pole	1·40	1·40

93 South Polar Skua

2010. Antarctic Birds. Multicoloured.

532	27p. Type **93**	90	90
533	27p. Adélie penguin	90	9·90
533	70p. Grey-headed albatross	2·10	2·10
535	70p. Emperor penguin	2·10	2·10
536	£1.15 Kelp gull	4·00	4·00
537	£1.15 Antarctic petrel	4·00	4·00

94 *James Clark Ross* en route to
Signy Research Station, South
Shetland Islands, 2007

2011. Research Ships. Multicoloured.

		(a) Ordinary paper		
538	(60p.) Type **94**		1·40	1·40
539	(60p.) RRS *Bransfield* loading outbound cargo from Halley Research Station		1·40	1·40
540	(60p.) RRS *Bransfield* alongside wharf at Rothera Research Station		1·40	1·40
541	(60p.) RRS *Ernest Shackleton* tied up against sea ice on the Brunt Ice Shelf		1·40	1·40
542	(60p.) RRS *Ernest Shackleton* (against Brunt Ice Shelf) and RRS *James Clark Ross*		1·40	1·40
543	(60p.) RRS *James Clark Ross* leaving Rothera Research Station, January 1998		1·40	1·40
MS544	100×80 mm. £1.15 Penguin and RRS *James Clark Ross* (20th anniv of maiden Antarctic voyage) (36×36 mm)		3·75	3·75

		(b) Self-adhesive coil stamps. Size 36×25 mm		
545	(60p.) As Type **94**		1·40	1·40
546	(60p.) As No. 539		1·40	1·40
547	(60p.) As No. 540		1·40	1·40
548	(60p.) As No. 541		1·40	1·40
549	(60p.) As No. 542		1·40	1·40
550	(60p.) As No. 543		1·40	1·40

Nos. 538/43 and 545/50 were all inscr 'AIRMAL POST-CARD' and originally sold for 60p. each.

95 Fur Seal

2011. BBC *Frozen Planet*. Multicoloured.

551	27p. Type **95**	90	90
552	27p. Elephant seal	90	90
553	27p. Crabeater seal	90	90
554	27p. Leopard seal	90	90
555	27p. Killer whale (dorsal fin and upper body above water)	90	90
556	27p. Killer whales (one with head above water)	90	90
557	27p. Humpback whales	90	90
558	27p. Two killer whales (dorsal fins and upper bodies above water)	90	90
559	60p. Gentoo penguin and chick	2·00	2·00
560	60p. Gentoo penguin and two chicks	2·00	2·00
561	60p. Adelie penguins adult and chicks	2·00	2·00
562	60p. Adelie penguin feeding chick	2·00	2·00
563	60p. Gentoo penguin chick	2·00	2·00
564	60p. Gentoo penguin moulting and boat	2·00	2·00
565	60p. Adelie penguins leaping onto ice	2·00	2·00
566	60p. Chinstrap penguin	2·00	2·00

96 Winterquarters Hut and Camp

2011. Antarctic Science. Multicoloured.
MS567 174×122 mm. 27p.×8 Type **96**; Bonner Laboratory at Rothera Research Station; Expedition members launching balloon with instruments to record temperature and pressure, 1910-13 (vert); Modern scientist launching helium filled balloon to take daily meteorological records, Halley Research Station (vert); Expedition members taking samples at stern of *Terra Nova* (vert); Sampling waters of Bellingshausen Sea from RRS *James Clark Ross* using CTD (conductivity, temperature, depth) device (vert); Expedition members on skiis; Divers on RIB (rigid inflatable boat), Rothera Research Station | 7·25 | 7·25

MS568 165×80 mm. 70p.×4 de Havilland Canada Dash-7 in flight; Geologist testing hot water drill on the Rutford Ice Stream; Meteorologist checking Met screen at Rothera Point; Piggott Space Science building, Halley Research Station (all 36×36 mm) | 9·50 | 9·50

MS569 165×80 mm. £1.15×4 Surgeon Dr. Edward Atkinson conducting experiments; Dr. George Simpson taking observations at weather station; Dr. Simpson's laboratory in Winterquarters Hut; Charles Wright (expedition physicist and glaciologist) with transit (instrument used for observation of star positions), (all British Antarctic Expedition 1910-13, all 36×36 mm) | 15·00 | 15·00

97 Expedition Members in Boat

2012. 75th Anniv of the British Graham Land Expedition (1934-7). Multicoloured.

570	40p. Type **97**	1·20	1·20
571	40p. Boat on shore, hut in background	1·20	1·20
572	40p. Husky	1·20	1·20
573	40p. Crew member with husky on board *Penola*	1·20	1·20
574	50p. Expedition plane on Graham Land	1·50	1·50
575	50p. Expedition seaplane	1·50	1·50
576	50p. *Penola* icebound	1·50	1·50
577	50p. *Penola* at anchor off Graham Land	1·50	1·50
MS578	110×70 mm. £1.20 *Penola* off ice shelf of Graham Land (48×32 mm)	3·50	3·50

98 Glacier

2012. Glaciers and Ice Sheets. Multicoloured.

579	65p. Type **98**	1·90	1·90
580	65p. Sea and edge of ice sheet (blue sky)	1·90	1·90
581	65p. Island	1·90	1·90
582	65p. Antarctic coast	1·90	1·90
583	65p. Edge of ice sheet (dark sky)	1·90	1·90
584	75p. Crevassed glacier	2·25	2·25
585	75p. Aerial view of landscape of mountains and icefields	2·25	2·25
586	75p. Aerial view of edge of ice with ice floes in sea	2·25	2·25
587	75p. Aerial view of mountains and glaciers	2·25	2·25
588	75p. Aerial view of ocean	2·25	2·25

99 HMS *Protector*

2012. HMS *Protector* (ice patrol ship). Sheet 85×118 mm
MS589 **99** £3.50 multicoloured | 10·00 | 10·00

<div align="right">Pt. 1</div>

BRITISH COLUMBIA AND VANCOUVER ISLAND

Former British colonies, now a Western province of the Dominion of Canada, whose stamps are now used.

1860. 12 pence = 1 shilling; 20 shillings = 1 pound.
1865. 100 cents = 1 dollar.

1

1860. Imperf or perf.

2	**1**	2½d. pink	£425	£200

VANCOUVER ISLAND

2

1865. Imperf or perf. Various frames.

13	**2**	5c. red	£350	£200
14	-	10c. blue	£250	£170

BRITISH COLUMBIA

4 Emblems of United Kingdom

1865

22	**4**	3d. blue	£110	85·00

1868. Surch in words or figures and words

28	2c. brown	£170	£140
29	5c. red	£250	£160
24	10c. red	£900	£700
31	25c. yellow	£250	£160
26	50c. mauve	£850	£700
27	$1 green	£1300	£1400

<div align="right">Pt. 1</div>

BRITISH COMMONWEALTH OCCUPATION FORCE (JAPAN)

Stamps used by British Commonwealth Occupation Forces, 1946–49.

12 pence = 1 shilling; 20 shillings = 1 pound.

1946. Stamps of Australia optd **B.C.O.F. JAPAN 1946**.

J1	**27**	½d. orange	7·50	12·00
J2	**46**	1d. purple	6·50	7·50
J3	**31**	3d. brown	2·75	4·75
J4	-	6d. brown (No. 189a)	27·00	21·00
J5	-	1s. green (No. 191)	18·00	23·00
J6	**1**	2s. red	45·00	65·00
J7a	**38**	5s. red	£110	£180

<div align="right">Pt. 1</div>

BRITISH EAST AFRICA

Now incorporated in Kenya and Uganda.

16 annas = 100 cents = 1 rupee.

1890. Stamps of Great Britain (1881) surch **BRITISH EAST AFRICA COMPANY** and value in annas.

1	**57**	½a. on 1d. lilac	£275	£200
2	**73**	1a. on 2d. green and red	£500	£275
3	**78**	4a. on 5d. purple and blue	£600	£325

3 Arms of the Company

1890. Nos. 16/19 are larger (24×25 mm).

4b	**3**	½a. brown	70	9·00
5	**3**	1a. green	9·00	13·00
6	**3**	2a. red	4·50	5·50
7c	**3**	2½a. black on yellow	4·75	7·00
8a	**3**	3a. black on red	2·75	14·00
9	**3**	4a. brown	2·50	12·00
11a	**3**	4½a. purple	2·50	18·00
29	**3**	5a. black on blue	1·25	11·00
30	**3**	7½a. black	1·25	17·00
12	**3**	8a. blue	5·50	9·50
13	**3**	8a. grey	£275	£225
14	**3**	1r. red	6·00	9·00
15	**3**	1r. grey	£225	£225
16	-	2r. red	14·00	50·00
17	-	3r. purple	10·00	55·00
18	-	4r. blue	12·00	55·00
19	-	5r. green	30·00	75·00

1891. With handstamped or pen surcharges. Initialled in black.

20	½a. on 2a. red	£10000	£1000	
31	½a. on 3a. black on red	£450	55·00	
32	1a. on 3a. black on red	£8000	£4500	
26	1a. on 4a. brown	£9000	£1800	

1894. Surch in words and figures.

27	5a. on 8a. blue	75·00	95·00
28	7½a. on 1r. red	75·00	95·00

1895. Optd **BRITISH EAST AFRICA.**

33	½a. brown	80·00	32·00
34	1a. green	£200	£120
35	2a. red	£200	£100
36	2½a. black on yellow	£200	60·00
37	3a. black on red	£100	55·00
38	4a. brown	65·00	42·00
39	4½a. purple	£225	£100
40	5a. black on blue	£300	£150
41	7½a. black	£140	85·00
42	8a. blue	£100	80·00
43	1r. brown	65·00	55·00
44	2r. red	£500	£325

45	-	3r. purple	£250	£160
46	-	4r. blue	£200	£180
47	-	5r. green	£450	£300

1895. Surch with large 2½.

48	**3**	2½a. on 4½a. purple	£225	85·00

1895. Stamps of India (Queen Victoria) optd **British East Africa.**

49	**23**	½a. turquoise	7·00	5·50
50	-	1a. purple	6·50	6·00
51	-	1½a. brown	4·25	4·00
52	-	2a. blue	8·50	3·00
53	-	2a.6p. green	13·00	2·50
54	-	3a. orange	22·00	11·00
55a	-	4a. green (No. 96)	28·00	26·00
56	-	6a. brown (No. 80)	50·00	50·00
57c	-	8a. mauve	30·00	55·00
58	-	12a. purple on red	22·00	38·00
59	-	1r. grey (No. 101)	£100	70·00
60	**37**	1r. green and red	50·00	£130
61	**38**	2r. red and orange	£120	£180
62	**38**	3r. brown and green	£140	£190
63	**38**	5r. blue and violet	£150	£200

1895. No. 51 surch with small 2½.

64	2½ on 1½a. brown	£120	50·00	

11

1896

65	**11**	½a. green	5·50	80
66	**11**	1a. red	14·00	40
67	**11**	2a. brown	11·00	7·50
68	**11**	2½a. blue	17·00	2·25
69	**11**	3a. grey	9·00	13·00
70	**11**	4a. green	8·50	4·25
71	**11**	4½a. yellow	16·00	17·00
72	**11**	5a. brown	8·50	7·50
73	**11**	7½a. mauve	10·00	24·00
74	**11**	8a. grey	10·00	7·00
75	**11**	1r. blue	80·00	27·00
76	**11**	2r. orange	70·00	32·00
77	**11**	3r. violet	70·00	38·00
78	**11**	4r. red	65·00	80·00
79	**11**	5r. brown	65·00	42·00

1897. Stamps of Zanzibar, 1896, optd **British East Africa.**

80	**13**	½a. green and red	60·00	50·00
81	**13**	1a. blue and red	£100	95·00
82	**13**	2a. brown and red	48·00	23·00
83	**13**	4½a. orange and red	60·00	30·00
84	**13**	5a. brown and red	65·00	45·00
85	**13**	7½a. mauve and red	70·00	48·00

1897. As last, surch 2½.

86	2½ on 1a. blue and red	£130	70·00	
89	2½ on 3a. grey and red	£130	65·00	

1897. As Type **11**, but larger.

92a	1r. blue	£100	50·00	
93	2r. orange	£130	£130	
94	3r. violet	£170	£180	
95	4r. red	£475	£550	
96	5r. brown	£425	£500	
97	10r. brown	£425	£550	
98	20r. green	£1100	£2250	
99	50r. mauve	£2250	£8000	

<div align="right">Pt. 1</div>

BRITISH FORCES IN EGYPT

SPECIAL SEALS AND STAMPS FOR THE USE OF BRITISH FORCES IN EGYPT

A. SEALS

A1

1932

A1	**A1**	1p. blue and red	95·00	4·75

		(b) Inscr "LETTER SEAL".		
A2	1p. blue and red	50·00	85	

A2

1932. Christmas Seals.

A3	**A2**	3m. black on blue	50·00	70·00

A4	**A2**	3m. lake	7·50	50·00
A5	**A2**	3m. blue	7·00	30·00
A6a	**A2**	3m. red	11·00	30·00

A3

1934

A8	**A3**	1p. green	6·00	5·50
A9	**A3**	1p. red	5·00	4·25

1935. Silver Jubilee. Optd **JUBILEE COMMEMORATION 1935.**

A10	1p. blue	£275	£180

1935. Provisional Christmas Seal. Surch **Xmas 1935 3 Milliemes.**

A11	3m. on 1p. on 1p. red	16·00	70·00

B. POSTAGE STAMPS

A6 King Fuad 1

1936

A12	**A6**	3m. green	1·00	2·50
A13	**A6**	10m. red	8·00	10

A7 King Farouk

1939

A14	**A7**	3m. green	7·00	9·50
A15	**A7**	10m. red	9·00	10

 Pt. 1

BRITISH GUIANA

Situated on the N.E. coast of S. America. A British colony granted full internal self-government in August 1951. Attained independence on 26 May 1966, when the country was renamed Guyana.

100 cents = 1 dollar.

1

1850. Imperf.

1	**1**	2c. black on red	—	£250000
2	**1**	4c. black on orange	£65000	£11000
4	**1**	8c. black on green	£45000	£11000
5	**1**	12c. black on blue	£20000	£7500

Prices are for used stamps cut round. Stamps cut square are worth much more.

2

1852. Imperf.

9	**2**	1c. black on magenta	£9500	£4250
10	**2**	4c. black on blue	£17000	£9000

3 Seal of the Colony

1853

12	**3**	1c. red	£4500	£1600
20	**3**	4c. blue	£1600	£600

6

1856. Imperf.

23	**6**	1c. black on magenta	†	
24	**6**	4c. black on magenta	—	£12000
25	**6**	4c. black on blue	£42000	£17000

7 **9**

1860. Perf.

29	**7**	1c. pink	£3250	£275
30	**7**	1c. brown	£450	£110
85	**7**	1c. black	22·00	8·00
87	**7**	2c. orange	55·00	4·75
89	**7**	4c. blue	£140	13·00
92	**9**	6c. blue	£190	35·00
95	**7**	8c. red	£275	35·00
98	**7**	12c. lilac	£275	24·00
99	**7**	12c. grey	£275	26·00
64	**7**	24c. green	£350	50·00
79	**9**	24c. green	£225	13·00
82	**9**	48c. red	£375	75·00

The prices quoted for Nos. 29/82 are for fine copies with four margins. Medium specimens can be supplied at much lower rates.

10

1862. Various borders. Roul.

116	**10**	1c. black on red	£5000	£800
119	**10**	2c. black on yellow	£5000	£425
122	**10**	4c. black on blue	£5500	£900

The above prices are for stamps signed in the centre by the Postmaster. Unsigned stamps are worth considerably less.

16

1876

126	**16**	1c. grey	2·75	1·40
171	**16**	2c. orange	48·00	15
172	**16**	4c. blue	£100	5·00
173	**16**	6c. brown	5·00	6·50
174	**16**	8c. red	£120	40
131	**16**	12c. violet	70·00	2·25
132	**16**	24c. green	75·00	3·50
133	**16**	48c. brown	£150	45·00
134	**16**	96c. olive	£475	£250

1878. Optd with thick horiz or horiz and vert bars

 (a) On postage stamps

137	**16**	1c. on 6c. brown	48·00	£130
141	**9**	1c. on 6c. blue	£225	75·00

 (b) On official stamps of 1875 and 1877

138	**7**	1c. black	£275	75·00
139	**16**	1c. grey	£200	70·00
140	**16**	2c. orange	£425	75·00
144	**16**	4c. blue	£400	£110
145	**16**	6c. brown	£600	£110
146	**7**	8c. red	£4500	£350
148	**16**	8c. red	£550	£130

1881. Surch with figure. Old value barred out in ink

 (a) On postage stamps

152	**9**	"1" on 48c. red	48·00	5·00
149		"1" on 96c. olive	5·50	9·50
150		"2" on 96c. olive	17·00	20·00

 (b) On stamps optd **OFFICIAL.**

153	**7**	"1" on 12c. lilac	£140	75·00
154	**16**	"1" on 48c. brown	£200	£130
155	**16**	"2" on 12c. violet	90·00	50·00
157	**16**	"2" on 24c. green	£100	60·00

26

1882

162	**26**	1c. black on red	70·00	30·00
165	**26**	2c. black on yellow	90·00	50·00

Each stamp is perforated with the word "SPECIMEN".

1888. T **16** without value in bottom tablet, surch **INLAND REVENUE** and value.

175	**16**	1c. purple	2·75	20
176	**16**	2c. purple	2·50	2·50
177	**16**	3c. purple	1·50	20
178	**16**	4c. purple	12·00	30
179	**16**	6c. purple	14·00	6·00
180	**16**	6c. purple	1·50	10
181	**16**	10c. purple	6·50	2·50
182	**16**	20c. purple	24·00	21·00
183	**16**	40c. purple	40·00	30·00
184	**16**	72c. purple	75·00	65·00
185	**16**	$1 green	£500	£600
186	**16**	$2 green	£250	£275
187	**16**	$3 green	£250	£275
188	**16**	$4 green	£600	£700
189	**16**	$5 green	£375	£400

1889. No. 176 surch with additional **2.**

192		"2" on 2c. purple	5·00	50

30

1889

193	**30**	1c. purple and grey	7·50	3·25
213	**30**	1c. green	1·00	10
194	**30**	2c. purple and orange	5·00	10
234	**30**	2c. purple and red	3·25	30
241a	**30**	2c. purple & black on red	5·00	10
253a	**30**	2c. red	8·50	10
195	**30**	4c. purple and blue	4·50	3·75
254	**30**	4c. brown and purple	3·25	1·25
214	**30**	5c. blue	3·50	10
243a	**30**	5c. purple & blue on blue	3·50	6·50
198	**30**	6c. purple and brown	7·50	23·00
236	**30**	6c. black and blue	7·50	11·00
256	**30**	6c. grey and black	13·00	7·00
199	**30**	8c. purple and red	17·00	3·75
215	**30**	8c. purple and black	7·00	2·00
200a	**30**	12c. purple and mauve	8·50	3·75
257	**30**	12c. orange and purple	4·00	6·00
246a	**30**	24c. purple and green	3·75	5·00
202	**30**	48c. purple and red	28·00	12·00
247a	**30**	48c. grey and brown	14·00	25·00
248a	**30**	60c. green and red	14·00	95·00
203	**30**	72c. purple and brown	28·00	50·00
205	**30**	96c. purple and red	65·00	70·00
250	**30**	96c. black & red on yellow	35·00	45·00

1890. Nos. 185/8 surch **ONE CENT.**

207	**16**	1 cent on $1 green	2·75	35
208	**16**	1 cent on $2 green	2·25	1·00
209	**16**	1 cent on $3 green	3·00	1·25
210	**16**	1 cent on $4 green	5·00	11·00

32 Mount Roraima **33** Kaieteur Falls

1898. Jubilee.

216	**32**	1c. black and red	8·50	2·25
217	**33**	2c. black and blue	32·00	4·25
219w	**32**	5c. green and brown	48·00	5·00
220	**33**	10c. black and red	26·00	29·00
221	**32**	15c. brown and blue	32·00	24·00

1899. Nos. 219/21 surch **TWO CENTS.**

222		2c. on 5c. green and brown	3·25	3·00
223	**33**	2c. on 10c. black and red	3·75	2·25
224	**32**	2c. on 15c. brown and blue	3·75	1·25

1905. T **30** but inscr "REVENUE", optd **POSTAGE AND REVENUE.**

251	**30**	$2.40 green and violet	£190	£450

37

1913

259a	**37**	1c. green	1·75	25
260	**37**	2c. red	1·50	10
274	**37**	2c. violet	2·50	10
261b	**37**	4c. brown and purple	3·75	25
262	**37**	5c. blue	1·75	1·00
263	**37**	6c. grey and black	3·50	2·50
276	**37**	6c. blue	3·00	30
264	**37**	12c. orange and violet	1·25	1·00
278	**37**	24c. purple and green	2·00	4·50
279	**37**	48c. grey and purple	9·50	3·50
280	**37**	60c. green and red	10·00	50·00
281	**37**	72c. purple and brown	35·00	75·00
269a	**37**	96c. black and red on yellow	27·00	50·00

1918. Optd **WAR TAX.**

271		2c. red	1·50	15

39 Ploughing a Rice Field **40** Indian shooting Fish

41 Kaieteur Falls **42** Public Buildings, Georgetown

1931. Centenary of County Union.

283	**39**	1c. green	2·50	1·25
284	**40**	2c. brown	2·00	10
285	**41**	4c. red	2·25	45
286	**42**	6c. blue	£250	1·25
287	**41**	$1 violet	50·00	60·00

43 Ploughing a Rice Field **44** Gold Mining

1934

288	**43**	1c. green	60	2·00
289	**40**	2c. brown	1·50	1·75
290	**44**	3c. red	30	10
291	**41**	4c. violet	2·00	3·50
292	-	6c. blue	5·00	7·00
293	-	12c. orange	20	20
294	-	24c. purple	3·50	11·00
295	-	48c. black	9·50	9·50
296	**41**	50c. green	14·00	21·00
297	-	60c. brown	26·00	29·00
298	-	72c. purple	1·50	2·25
299	-	96c. black	35·00	35·00
300	-	$1 violet	48·00	45·00

DESIGNS—HORIZ: 6c. Shooting logs over falls; 12c. Stabroek Market; 24c. Sugar canes in punts; 48c. Forest road; 60c. Victoria Regia lilies; 72c. Mount Roraima; $1 Botanical Gardens. VERT: 96c. Sir Walter Raleigh and his son.

The 2c., 4c. and 50c. are without the dates shown in Types **40/44** and the 12, 48, 72 and 96c. have no portrait.

1935. Silver Jubilee. As T **13** of Antigua.

301		2c. blue and grey	40	20
302		6c. brown and blue	2·00	5·00
303		12c. green and blue	9·00	8·50
304		24c. grey and purple	14·00	18·00

1937. Coronation. As T **2** of Aden.

305		2c. brown	15	10
306		4c. grey	60	60
307		6c. blue	75	2·00

53 South America

1938. Designs as for same values of 1934 issue (except where indicated) but with portrait of King George VI (as in T **53**) where portrait of King George V previously appeared.

308a	**43**	1c. green	30	10
309a		2c. violet (As 4c.)	55	10
310b	**53**	4c. red and black	1·00	15
311	-	6c. blue (As 2c.)	1·25	10
312a	-	24c. green	3·50	10
313a	-	36c. violet (As 4c.)	3·00	30
314	-	48c. orange	1·25	50
315	-	60c. brown (As 6c.)	19·00	9·50
316	-	96c. purple	11·00	2·75
317	-	$1 violet	25·00	35
318	-	$2 purple (As 72c.)	17·00	25·00
319	-	$3 brown	38·00	38·00

DESIGN—HORIZ: $3 Victoria Regia lilies.

1946. Victory. As T **9** of Aden.
320		3c. red	25	40
321		6c. blue	75	85

1948. Silver Wedding. As T **10/11** of Aden.
322		3c. red	10	40
323		$3 brown	22·00	26·00

1949. UPU. As T **20/23** of Antigua.
324		4c. red	10	50
325		6c. blue	1·75	1·75
326		12c. orange	15	50
327		24c. green	15	70

1951. Inauguration of BWI University College. As T **24/25** of Antigua.
328		3c. black and red	50	50
329		6c. black and blue	50	65

1953. Coronation. As T **13** of Aden.
330		4c. black and red	60	10

55 G.P.O., Georgetown

1954
331	**55**	1c. black	20	10
332	-	2c. myrtle	20	10
333	-	3c. olive and brown	3·50	20
334	-	4c. violet	1·75	10
335	-	5c. red and black	1·75	10
336	-	6c. green	1·25	10
337	-	8c. blue	65	20
338a	-	12c. black and brown	1·25	10
360	-	24c. black and orange	4·00	10
361	-	36c. red and black	1·00	60
341a	-	48c. blue and brown	1·00	1·00
342	-	72c. red and green	16·00	2·75
364	-	$1 multicoloured	8·00	90
344	-	$2 mauve	28·00	8·50
345	-	$5 blue and black	24·00	32·00

DESIGNS—HORIZ: 2c. Botanical Gardens; 3c. *Victoria Regia* lilies; 5c. Map of Caribbean; 6c. Rice combine-harvester; 8c. Sugar cane entering factory; 24c. Bauxite mining; 36c. Mount Roraima; $1 Channel-billed toucan; $2 Dredging gold. VERT: 4c. Amerindian shooting fish; 12c. Felling greenheart; 48c. Kaieteur Falls; 72c. Arapaima (fish); $5 Arms of British Guiana.

70

1961. History and Culture Week.
346	**70**	5c. sepia and red	20	10
347	**70**	6c. sepia and green	20	15
348	**70**	30c. sepia and orange	45	45

1963. Freedom from Hunger. As T **28** of Aden.
349		20c. violet	30	30

1963. Centenary of Red Cross. As T **33** of Antigua.
350		5c. red and black	20	20
351		20c. red and blue	55	35

71 Weightlifting

1964. Olympic Games, Tokyo.
367	**71**	5c. orange	10	10
368	**71**	8c. blue	15	35
369	**71**	25c. mauve	25	40

1965. Centenary of ITU. As T **36** of Antigua.
370		5c. green and olive	10	15
371		25c. blue and mauve	20	15

1965. ICY. As T **37** of Antigua.
372		5c. purple and brown	15	10
373		25c. green and lavender	30	20

72 St George's Cathedral, Georgetown

1966. Churchill Commemoration.
374	**72**	5c. black, red and gold	1·00	10
375	**72**	25c. black, blue and gold	2·25	50

1966. Royal Visit. As T **39** of Antigua.
376		3c. black and blue	75	15
377		25c. black and mauve	1·50	60

OFFICIAL STAMPS

1875. Optd **OFFICIAL**.
O1	**7**	1c. black	70·00	24·00
O2	**7**	2c. orange	£275	14·00
O3	**7**	8c. red	£350	£140
O4	**7**	12c. lilac	£3250	£500
O5	**9**	24c. green	£2500	£275

1877. Optd **OFFICIAL**.
O6	**16**	1c. grey	£325	65·00
O7	**16**	2c. orange	£150	15·00
O8	**16**	4c. blue	£130	25·00
O9	**16**	6c. brown	£5500	£600
O10	**16**	8c. red	£2000	£450

POSTAGE DUE STAMPS

1940. As Type D **1** of Barbados, but inscr "BRITISH GUIANA".
D1		1c. green	6·50	11·00
D2a		2c. black	4·50	8·00
D3		4c. blue	40	13·00
D4		12c. red	38·00	6·50

For later issues see **GUYANA**.

Pt. 1

BRITISH HONDURAS

A British colony on the East coast of Central America. Self-government was granted on 1 January 1964. The country was renamed Belize from 1 June 1973.

1866. 12 pence = 1 shilling; 20 shillings = 1 pound.
1888. 100 cents = 1 dollar.

1

1866
17	**1**	1d. blue	75·00	23·00
18	**1**	1d. red	23·00	14·00
13	**1**	3d. brown	£170	26·00
20	**1**	4d. mauve	95·00	4·75
21	**1**	6d. yellow	£275	£225
9	**1**	6d. red	£450	55·00
16	**1**	1s. green	£325	14·00
22	**1**	1s. grey	£250	£160

1888. Surch as **2 CENTS**.
36		1c. on 1d. green	80	1·50
37		2c. on 1d. red	60	2·25
25		2c. on 6d. red	£190	£170
38		3c. on 3d. brown	4·00	1·40
39		6c. on 3d. blue	5·50	24·00
40		10c. on 4d. mauve	25·00	50
41		20c. on 6d. yellow	19·00	14·00
42		50c. on 1s. grey	38·00	85·00

1888. No. 42 surch **TWO**.
35		"TWO" on 50c. on 1s. grey	60·00	£100

1891. No. 40 surch **6** and bar.
44		6c. on 10c. on 4d. mauve	2·25	1·50

1891. Nos. 38 and 39 surch
49		"FIVE" on 3c. on 3d. brown	1·25	1·40
50		"15" on 6c. on 3d. blue	14·00	28·00

8

1891
51	**8**	1c. green	2·50	1·25
52	**8**	2c. red	4·25	20
53	**8**	3c. brown	10·00	4·00
54	**8**	5c. blue	12·00	75
55	**8**	5c. black and blue on blue	20·00	3·00
56	**8**	6c. blue	14·00	2·00
57	**8**	10c. mauve and green (A)	14·00	16·00
58	**8**	10c. purple and green (B)	11·00	7·50
59	**8**	12c. lilac and green	2·50	3·25
60	**8**	24c. yellow and blue	6·50	22·00
61	**8**	25c. brown and green	90·00	£140
62	**8**	50c. green and red	29·00	65·00
63	**8**	$1 green and red	95·00	£150
64	**8**	$2 green and blue	£150	£200

65	**8**	$5 green and black	£325	£425

NOTE: 10c. (A) inscr "POSTAGE POSTAGE"; (B) inscr "POSTAGE & REVENUE".

1899. Optd **REVENUE**.
66		5c. blue	27·00	2·75
67		10c. mauve and green	17·00	19·00
68		25c. brown and green	4·00	38·00
69	**1**	50c. on 1s. on 1s. grey	£250	£400

14

1902
84a	**14**	1c. green	3·00	2·25
85a	**14**	2c. purple and black on red	2·00	20
96	**14**	2c. red	15·00	10
97	**14**	5c. black and blue on blue	2·00	20
97	**14**	5c. blue	2·50	10
87	**14**	10c. purple and green	4·00	17·00
83	**14**	20c. purple	13·00	17·00
89	**14**	25c. purple and orange	10·00	60·00
100	**14**	25c. black on green	7·50	48·00
90	**14**	50c. green and red	27·00	95·00
91	**14**	$1 green and red	75·00	£110
92	**14**	$2 green and blue	£160	£225
93	**14**	$5 green and black	£350	£400

16

1913
101	**16**	1c. green	4·50	1·50
102	**16**	2c. red	6·00	1·00
103	**16**	3c. orange	1·50	20
104	**16**	5c. blue	3·00	85
105	**16**	10c. purple and green	5·00	6·50
106	**16**	25c. black on green	1·25	12·00
107	**16**	50c. purple and blue on blue	28·00	15·00
108	**16**	$1 black and red	29·00	70·00
109	**16**	$2 purple and green	90·00	£110
110	**16**	$5 purple and black on red	£275	£325

1915. Optd with pattern of wavy lines.
111a		1c. green	50	20·00
112		2c. red	3·50	50
113		5c. blue	30	6·00

1916. Optd **WAR**.
114		1c. green (No. 111a)	10	2·75
119		1c. green (No. 101)	20	30
120		3c. orange (No. 103)	80	3·50

21

1921. Peace.
121	**21**	2c. red	5·00	50

1921. As No. 121 but without word "PEACE".
123		4c. grey	13·00	50

22

1922
126	**22**	1c. green	17·00	6·50
127	**22**	2c. brown	1·50	1·50
128	**22**	2c. red	11·00	1·50
129	**22**	3c. orange	35·00	4·00
130	**22**	4c. grey	21·00	85
131	**22**	5c. blue	1·50	55
132	**22**	10c. purple and olive	4·00	30
133	**22**	25c. black on green	2·50	8·50
134	**22**	50c. purple and blue on blue	7·00	16·00
136	**22**	$1 black and red	22·00	28·00
137	**22**	$2 green and purple	50·00	£130
125	**22**	$5 purple and black on red	£225	£300

1932. Optd **BELIZE RELIEF FUND PLUS** and value.
138		1c. +1c. green	2·75	15·00
139		2c. +2c. red	2·75	15·00
140		3c. +3c. orange	2·75	30·00

141		4c. +4c. grey	16·00	32·00
142		5c. +5c. blue	7·00	14·00

1935. Silver Jubilee. As T **13** of Antigua.
143		3c. blue and black	2·00	50
144		4c. green and blue	4·50	4·00
145		5c. brown and blue	2·00	2·50
146		25c. grey and purple	9·00	11·00

1937. Coronation. As T **2** of Aden.
147		3c. orange	30	30
148		4c. grey	70	30
149		5c. blue	80	1·90

24 Maya figures

1938
150	**24**	1c. purple and green	70	1·50
151	-	2c. black and red	1·25	1·00
152	-	3c. purple and brown	2·00	1·75
153	-	4c. black and green	1·50	70
154	-	5c. purple and blue	3·25	1·75
155	-	10c. green and brown	4·25	60
156	-	15c. brown and blue	7·50	1·50
157	-	25c. blue and green	4·50	2·00
158	-	50c. black and purple	28·00	4·50
159	-	$1 red and olive	48·00	10·00
160	-	$2 blue and purple	55·00	30·00
161	-	$5 red and brown	50·00	48·00

DESIGNS—VERT: 2c. Chicle tapping; 3c. Cohune palm; $1 Court House, Belize; $2 Mahogany felling; $5 Arms of Colony. HORIZ: 4c. Local products; 5c. Grapefruit; 10c. Mahogany logs in river; 15c. Sergeant's Cay; 25c. Dorey; 50c. Chicle industry.

1946. Victory. As T **9** of Aden.
162		3c. brown	10	20
163		5c. blue	10	20

1948. Silver Wedding. As T **10** and **11** of Aden.
164		4c. green	15	60
165		$5 brown	25·00	50·00

36 Island of Saint George's Cay

1949. 150th Anniv of Battle of Saint George's Cay.
166	**36**	1c. blue and green	20	1·25
167	**36**	3c. blue and brown	20	1·50
168	**36**	4c. olive and violet	20	1·75
169	-	5c. brown and blue	1·90	75
170	-	10c. green and brown	1·90	30
171	-	15c. green and blue	1·90	30

DESIGNS: 5, 10 and 15c. H.M.S. *Merlin*.

1949. U.P.U. As T **20/23** of Antigua.
172		4c. green	30	75
173		5c. blue	1·50	50
174		10c. brown	40	3·50
175		25c. blue	35	50

1951. Inauguration of B.W.I. University College. As T **24/25** of Antigua.
176		3c. violet and brown	45	1·50
177		10c. green and brown	45	30

1953. Coronation. As T **13** of Aden.
178		4c. black and green	75	30

39 Baird's Tapir　　**49** Mountain Orchid

1953
179		1c. green and black	10	40
180a	**39**	2c. brown and black	2·00	30
181a	-	3c. lilac and mauve	20	10
182	-	4c. brown and green	1·50	30
183	-	5c. olive and red	30	20
184a	-	10c. slate and blue	50	10
185	-	15c. green and violet	50	10
186	-	25c. blue and brown	7·00	3·75
187	-	50c. brown and purple	18·00	4·00
188	-	$1 slate and brown	10·00	5·00
189	-	$2 red and grey	10·00	4·50
190	**49**	$5 purple and slate	48·00	17·00

DESIGNS—HORIZ: 1c. Arms of British Honduras; 3c. Mace and Legislative Council Chamber; 4c. Pine industry; 5c. Spiny lobster; 10c. Stanley Field Airport; 15c. Maya frieze, Xunantunich; 25c. *Morpho peleides* (butterfly); $1 Nine-banded armadillo; $2 Hawkesworth Bridge. VERT: 50c. Maya indian.

50 *Belize from Fort George, 1842 (C. J. Hullmandel)*

1960. Post Office Centenary.

191	**50**	2c. green	55	1·25
192	-	10c. red	55	10
193	-	15c. blue	55	35

DESIGNS: 10c. Public seals, 1860 and 1960; 15c. Tamarind tree, Newtown Barracks.

1961. New Constitution. Stamps of 1953 optd **NEW CONSTITUTION 1960**.

194	**39**	2c. brown and black	25	40
195	-	3c. lilac and mauve	30	40
196	-	10c. slate and blue	30	10
197	-	15c. green and violet	30	20

1962. Hurricane Hattie Relief Fund. Stamps of 1953 optd **HURRICANE HATTIE**.

198	1c. green and black	10	65
199	10c. slate and blue	30	10
200	25c. blue and brown	1·75	80
201	50c. brown and purple	75	1·00

55 *Great Curassow*

1962. Birds in natural colours; portrait and inscr in black; background colours given.

239	**55**	1c. yellow	10	50
240	-	2c. grey	30	1·00
204	-	3c. green	4·25	3·25
241	-	4c. grey	2·50	2·00
242	-	5c. buff	60	10
243	-	10c. stone	40	10
244	-	15c. stone	40	10
209	-	25c. slate	4·50	30
210	-	50c. grey	6·00	35
211	-	$1 blue	9·00	2·00
212	-	$2 stone	23·00	5·50
213	-	$5 grey	28·00	16·00

BIRDS: 2c. Red-legged honeycreeper; 3c. Northern jacana ("American Jacana"); 4c. Great kiskadee; 5c. Scarlet-rumped tanager; 10c. Scarlet macaw; 15c. Slaty-tailed trogon ("Massena Trogon"); 25c. Red-footed booby; 50c. Keel-billed toucan; $1 Magnificent frigate bird; $2 Rufous-tailed jacamar; $5 Montezuma oropendola.

1963. Freedom from Hunger. As T **28** of Aden.

214	22c. green	30	15

1963. Centenary of Red Cross. As T **33** of Antigua.

215	4c. red and black	20	1·25
216	22c. red and blue	40	1·25

1964. New Constitution. Nos. 202, 204, 205, 207 and 209 optd **SELF GOVERNMENT 1964**.

217	**55**	1c. yellow	10	30
218	-	3c. green	45	30
219	-	4c. pale grey	45	30
220	-	10c. stone	45	10
221	-	25c. slate	55	30

1965. Centenary of I.T.U. As T **36** of Antigua.

222	2c. red and green	10	10
223	50c. yellow and purple	35	25

1965. I.C.Y. As T **37** of Antigua.

224	1c. purple and turquoise	10	15
225	22c. green and lavender	20	15

1966. Churchill Commemoration. As T **38** of Antigua.

226	1c. blue	10	75
227	4c. green	65	10
228	22c. brown	1·00	10
229	25c. violet	1·10	45

1966. Dedication of new Capital Site. Nos. 202, 204/5 207 and 209 optd **DEDICATION OF SITE NEW CAPITAL 9th OCTOBER 1965**.

230	**55**	1c. yellow	15	40
231	-	3c. green	60	40
232	-	4c. grey	60	40
233	-	10c. stone	60	10
234	-	25c. slate	85	35

58 *Citrus Grove*

1966. Stamp Centenary. Multicoloured.

235	5c. Type **58**	10	10
236	10c. Half Moon Cay	10	10
237	22c. Hidden Valley Falls	10	10
238	25c. Maya ruins, Xunantunich	15	45

59 *Sailfish*

1967. International Tourist Year.

246	**59**	5c. blue, black and yellow	20	30
247	-	10c. brown, black and red	20	10
248	-	22c. orange, black and green	35	10
249	-	25c. blue, black and yellow	35	60

DESIGNS: 10c. Red brocket; 22c. Jaguar; 25c. Atlantic tarpon.

60 *Schomburgkia tibicinis*

1968. 20th Anniv of Economic Commission for Latin America. Orchids. Multicoloured.

250	**60**	5c. Type **60**	20	15
251	-	10c. *Maxillaria tenuifolia*	25	10
252	-	22c. *Bletia purpurea*	30	10
253	-	25c. *Sobralia macrantha*	40	20

61 *Monument Belizean Patriots*

1968. Human Rights Year. Multicoloured.

254	22c. Type **61**	15	10
255	50c. Monument at site of new capital	15	20

63 *Spotted Jewfish*

1968. Wildlife

276	-	½c. multicoloured and blue	10	10
277	-	½c. multicoloured and yellow	2·50	1·50
256	**63**	1c. black, brown and yellow	30	10
257	-	2c. black, green and yellow	10	10
258	-	3c. black, brown and lilac	20	10
259	-	4c. multicoloured	15	1·25
260	-	5c. black and red	15	1·25
261	-	10c. multicoloured	15	10
262	-	15c. multicoloured	2·00	20
263	-	25c. multicoloured	30	20
264	-	50c. multicoloured	70	1·25
265	-	$1 multicoloured	2·50	1·25
266	-	$2 multicoloured	2·50	2·00
278	-	$5 multicoloured	2·50	10·00

DESIGNS: ½c. (Nos. 276 and 277) Mozambique mouth-brooder ("Crana"); 2c. White-lipped peccary; 3c. Misty grouper; 4c. Collared anteater; 5c. Bonefish; 10c. Paca; 15c. Dolphin; 25c. Kinkajou; 50c. Mutton snapper; $1 Tayra; $2 Great barracuda; $5 Puma.

64 *Rhyncholaelia digbyana*

1969. Orchids of Belize (1st series). Multicoloured.

268	5c. Type **64**	60	20
269	10c. *Cattleya bowringiana*	65	15
270	22c. *Lycaste cochleatum*	95	15
271	25c. *Coryanthes speciosum*	1·10	1·10

See also Nos. 287/90.

65 *Ziricote Tree*

1969. Indigenous Hardwoods (1st series). Multicoloured.

272	5c. Type **65**	10	20
273	10c. Rosewood	10	10
274	22c. Mayflower	20	10
275	22c. Mahogany	20	45

See also Nos. 291/4, 315/18 and 333/7.

66 *The Virgin and Child (Bellini)*

1969. Christmas. Paintings. Multicoloured.

279	5c. Type **66**	10	10
280	15c. Type **66**	10	10
281	22c. *The Adoration of the Magi* (Veronese)	10	10
282	25c. As No. 281	10	20

1970. Population Census. Nos. 260/3 optd **POPULATION CENSUS 1970**.

283	5c. multicoloured	10	10
284	10c. multicoloured	15	10
285	15c. multicoloured	20	10
286	25c. multicoloured	20	15

1970. Orchids of Belize (2nd series). As T **64**. Multicoloured.

287	5c. Black orchid	35	15
288	15c. White butterfly orchid	50	10
289	22c. Swan orchid	70	10
290	25c. Butterfly orchid	70	40

69 *Santa Maria*

1970. Indigenous Hardwoods (2nd series). Multicoloured.

291	5c. Type **69**	25	10
292	15c. Nargusta	40	10
293	22c. Cedar	45	10
294	25c. Sapodilla	45	35

70 *The Nativity (A. Hughes)*

1970. Christmas. Multicoloured.

295	½c. Type **70**	10	10
296	5c. *The Mystic Nativity* (Botticelli)	10	10
297	10c. Type **70**	15	10
298	15c. As 5c.	25	10
299	22c. Type **70**	30	10
300	50c. As 5c.	40	85

71 *Legislative Assembly House*

1971. Establishment of New Capital, Belmopan. Multicoloured.

301	5c. Old capital, Belize	10	10
302	10c. Government Plaza	10	10
303	15c. Type **71**	10	10
304	22c. Magistrates' Court	15	10
305	25c. Police H.Q	15	15
306	50c. New G.P.O	25	40

The 5c. and 10c. are larger, 60×22 mm.

72 *Tabebuia chrysantha*

1971. Easter. Flowers. Multicoloured.

307	½c. Type **72**	10	10
308	5c. *Hymenocallis littorallis*	10	10
309	10c. *Hippeastrum equestre*	10	10
310	15c. Type **72**	20	10
311	22c. As 5c.	20	10
312	25c. As 10c.	20	30

1971. Racial Equality Year. Nos. 261 and 264 optd **RACIAL EQUALITY YEAR–1971**.

313	10c. multicoloured	25	10
314	50c. multicoloured	55	20

74 *Tubroos*

1971. Indigenous Hardwoods (3rd series). Multicoloured.

315	5c. Type **74**	60	10
316	15c. Yemeri	80	30
317	26c. Billywebb	1·10	35
318	50c. Logwood	1·75	4·25
MS319	96×171 mm. Nos. 315/18	3·50	7·50

75 *Hawksworth and Belcan Bridges*

1971. Bridges of the World. Multicoloured.

320	½c. Type **75**	10	20
321	5c. Narrows Bridge, N.Y. and Quebec Bridge	30	15
322	26c. London Bridge (1871) and reconstructed, Arizona (1971)	80	15
323	50c. Belize Mexican Bridge and Swing Bridge	1·00	1·25

76 *Petrae volubis*

1972. Easter. Wild Flowers. Multicoloured.

324	6c. Type **76**	15	10
325	15c. Yemeri	30	30
326	26c. Mayflower	50	45
327	50c. Tiger's Claw	80	1·40

77 Seated
Figure

1972. Mayan Artefacts. Multicoloured.

328	3c. Type **77**	25	10
329	6c. Priest in "dancing" pose	25	10
330	16c. Sun God's head (horiz)	50	15
331	26c. Priest and Sun God	70	20
332	50c. Full-front figure	1·40	3·75

78 Banak

1972. Indigenous Hardwoods (4th series). Multicoloured.

333	3c. Type **78**	25	10
334	5c. Quamwood	25	10
335	16c. Waika Chewstick	55	15
336	26c. Mamee-Apple	75	25
337	50c. My Lady	1·60	3·25

1972. Royal Silver Wedding. As T **52** of Ascension, but with Orchids of Belize in background.

341	26c. green	25	10
342	50c. violet	40	65

80 Baron Bliss Day

1973. Festivals of Belize. Multicoloured.

343	3c. Type **80**	15	10
344	10c. Labour Day	15	10
345	26c. Carib Settlement Day	30	10
346	50c. Pan American Day	50	85

POSTAGE DUES

D1

1923

D1	**D1**	1c. black	2·25	13·00
D4	**D1**	2c. black	3·00	7·00
D5	**D1**	4c. black	1·50	7·00

For later issues see **BELIZE**.

Pt. 1

BRITISH INDIAN OCEAN TERRITORY

A Crown Colony, established 8 November 1965, comprising the Chagos Archipelago (previously administered by Mauritius) and Aldabra, Farquhar and Desroches, previously administered by Seychelles to which country they were returned on 29 June 1976.

The Chagos Archipelago has no indigenous population, but stamps were provided from 1990 for use by civilian workers at the U.S. Navy base on Diego Garcia.

1968. 100 cents = 1 rupee.
1990. 100 pence = 1 pound.

1968. Nos 196/200, 202/4 and 206/12 of Seychelles optd **B.I.O.T.**

1	**24**	5c. multicoloured	1·00	1·50
2	-	10c. multicoloured	10	15
3	-	15c. multicoloured	25	20
4	-	20c. multicoloured	20	15
5	-	25c. multicoloured	20	20
6	-	40c. multicoloured	20	20
7	-	45c. multicoloured	20	30
8	-	50c. multicoloured	20	30
9	-	75c. multicoloured	1·75	35
10	-	1r. multicoloured	1·75	35
11	-	1r.50 multicoloured	1·75	1·50
12	-	2r.25 multicoloured	3·00	3·75
13	-	3r.50 multicoloured	3·00	4·50
14	-	5r. multicoloured	10·00	6·50
15	-	10r. multicoloured	20·00	15·00

2 Lascar

1968. Marine Life. Multicoloured.

16	5c. Type **2**	1·00	2·25
17	10c. Smooth hammerhead (vert)	30	1·25
18	15c. Tiger shark	30	1·50
19	20c. Spotted eagle ray ("Bat ray")	30	1·00
20	25c. Yellow-finned butterflyfish and ear-spot angelfish (vert)	80	1·00
20a	30c. Robber crab	3·50	2·75
21	40c. Blue-finned trevalley ("Caranx")	2·25	40
22	45c. Crocodile needlefish ("Garfish") (vert)	2·25	2·50
23	50c. Pickhandle barracuda	2·25	30
23a	60c. Spotted pebble crab	3·50	3·50
24	75c. Indian Ocean steep-headed parrotfish	2·50	2·25
24a	85c. Rainbow runner ("Dorade")	4·50	3·00
25	1r. Giant hermit crab	1·75	35
26	1r.50 Parrotfish ("Humphead")	2·50	3·00
27	2r.25 Yellow-edged lyre-tail and Aredate grouper ("Rock cod")	12·00	10·00
28	3r.50 Black marlin	4·00	3·75
29	5r. black, green and blue (Whale shark) (vert)	21·00	15·00
30	10r. Lionfish	6·00	6·50

3 Sacred Ibis and Aldabra Coral Atoll

1969. Coral Atolls.

31	**3**	2r.25 multicoloured	1·75	1·00

4 Outrigger Canoe

1969. Ships of the Islands. Multicoloured.

32	45c. Type **4**	55	75
33	75c. Pirogue	55	80
34	1r. M.V. Nordvaer	60	90
35	1r.50 Isle of Farquhar	65	1·00

5 Giant Land Tortoise

1971. Aldabra Nature Reserve. Multicoloured.

36	45c. Type **5**	2·50	2·50
37	75c. Aldabra lily	3·00	2·50
38	1r. Aldabra tree snail	3·50	2·75
39	1r.50 Western reef heron ("Dimorphic Egrets")	12·00	10·00

6 Arms of Royal Society and White-throated Rail

1971. Opening of Royal Society Research Station, Aldabra.

40	**6**	3r.50 multicoloured	15·00	10·00

7 Staghorn Coral

1972. Coral. Multicoloured.

41	40c. Type **7**	3·50	4·00
42	60c. Brain coral	4·00	4·25
43	1r. Mushroom coral	4·00	4·25
44	1r.75 Organ pipe coral	5·00	6·50

1972. Royal Silver Wedding. As T **52** of Ascension, but with White-throated rail and Sacred ibis in background.

45	95c. green	50	40
46	1r.50 violet	50	40

9 Christ on the Cross

1973. Easter. Multicoloured.

47	45c. Type **9**	20	40
48	75c. Joseph and Nicodemus burying Jesus	30	55
49	1r. Type **9**	30	60
50	1r.50 As 75c.	30	70
MS51	126×110 mm. Nos. 47/50	1·00	4·00

10 Upsidedown Jellyfish

1973. Wildlife (1st series). Multicoloured.

53	50c. Type **10**	3·50	3·00
54	1r. Hypolimnas misippus and Belenois aldabrensis (butterflies)	4·00	3·00
55	1r.50 Nephila madagascarienis (spider)	4·25	3·00

See also Nos. 58/61, 77/80 and 86/9.

11 M.V. Nordvaer

1974. Fiifth Anniv of Nordvaer Travelling Post Office. Multicoloured.

56	85c. Type **11**	85	75
57	2r.50 Nordvaer off shore	1·40	1·25

12 Red-cloud Auger and Subulat Auger

1974. Wildlife (2nd series). Shells. Multicoloured.

58	45c. Type **12**	2·25	1·25
59	75c. Great green turban	2·50	1·50
60	1r. Strawberry drupe	2·75	1·75
61	1r.50 Bull-mouth helmet	3·00	2·00

13 Aldabra Drongo

1975. Birds. Multicoloured.

62	5c. Type **13**	1·25	2·75
63	10c. Black coucal ("Malagasy Coucal")	1·25	2·75
64	20c. Mascarene fody ("Red-Headed Forest Foddy")	1·25	2·75
65	25c. White tern	1·25	2·75
66	30c. Crested tern	1·25	2·75
67	40c. Brown booby	1·25	2·75
68	50c. Common noddy ("Noddy Tern") (horiz)	1·25	3·00
69	60c. Grey heron	1·25	3·00
70	65c. Blue-faced booby (horiz)	1·25	3·00
71	95c. Madagascar white eye ("Malagasy White-eye") (horiz)	1·25	3·00
72	1r. Green-backed heron (horiz)	1·25	3·00
73	1r.75 Lesser frigate bird (horiz)	2·00	5·00
74	3r.50 White-tailed tropic bird (horiz)	3·25	6·00
75	5r. Souimanga sunbird (horiz)	3·00	5·00
76	10r. Madagascar turtle dove ("Malagasy Turtle Dove") (horiz)	5·00	9·00

14 Grewia salicifolia

1975. Wildlife (3rd series). Seashore Plants. Multicoloured.

77	50c. Type **14**	50	1·25
78	65c. Cassia aldabrensis	55	1·40
79	1r. Hypoestes aldabrensis	65	1·50
80	1r.60 Euphorbia pyrifolia	80	1·60

15 Map of Aldabra

1975. Tenth Anniv of Territory. Maps. Multicoloured.

81	50c. Type **15**	80	65
82	1r. Desroches	95	85
83	1r.50 Farquhar	1·10	1·00
84	2r. Diego Garcia	1·25	1·25
MS85	147×147 mm. Nos. 81/4	7·00	14·00

16 Utetheisa pulchella (moth)

1976. Wildlife (4th series). Multicoloured.

86	65c. Type **16**	60	1·10
87	1r.20 Dysdercus fasciatus (bug)	75	1·25
88	1r.50 Sphex torridus (wasp)	80	1·40
89	2r. Oryctes rhinoceros (beetle)	85	1·40

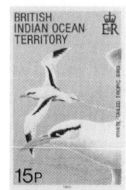

17 White-tailed Tropic Bird

1990. Birds. Multicoloured.

90	15p. Type **17**	1·10	2·00
91	20p. Madagascar turtle dove ("Turtle Dove")	1·25	2·00
92	24p. Great frigate bird ("Greater Frigate")	1·40	2·00
93	30p. Green-backed heron ("Little Green Heron")	1·50	2·25
94	34p. Great sand plover ("Greater Sand Plover")	1·60	2·25
95	41p. Crab plover	1·75	2·50
96	45p. Crested tern	4·50	2·50
97	54p. Lesser crested tern	2·25	3·00
98	62p. White tern ("Fairy Tern")	2·25	3·00
99	71p. Red-footed booby	2·25	3·00
100	80p. Common mynah ("Indian Mynah")	2·50	3·25
101	£1 Madagascar red fody ("Madagascar Fody")	3·25	3·50

18 1974 Wildlife 1r.50 Stamp

1990. "Stamp World London 90" International Stamp Exhibition. Multicoloured.

102	15p. Type **18**	4·50	3·25
103	20p. 1976 Wildlife 2r. stamp	5·00	3·50

104	34p. 1975 Diego Garcia map 2r. stamp	8·50	5·50
105	54p. 1969 "Nordvaer" 1r. stamp	10·00	7·50

1990. 90th Birthday of Queen Elizabeth the Queen Mother. As T **34** of Ascension.

106	24p. multicoloured	3·50	3·50
107	£1 black and ochre	6·50	6·50

DESIGNS—21×36 mm: Lady Elizabeth Bowes-Lyon, 1923. 29×37 mm: £1 Queen Elizabeth and her daughters, 1940.

19 Territory Flag

1990. 25th Anniv of British Indian Ocean Territory. Multicoloured.

108	20p. Type **19**	4·00	4·50
109	24p. Coat of arms	4·00	4·50
MS110	63×99 mm. £1 map of Chagos Archipelago	9·50	12·00

20 Postman emptying Pillar Box

1991. British Indian Ocean Territory Administration. Multicoloured.

111	20p. Type **20**	1·50	2·50
112	24p. Commissioner inspecting guard of Royal Marines	1·75	2·50
113	34p. Policeman outside station	3·50	4·50
114	54p. Customs officers boarding yacht	4·25	6·00

21 *Experiment* (E.I.C. survey brig), 1786

1991. Visiting Ships. Multicoloured.

115	20p. Type **21**	2·00	3·00
116	24p. *Pickering* (American brig), 1819	2·25	3·25
117	34p. *Emden* (German cruiser), 1914	3·00	4·25
118	54p. H.M.S. *Edinburgh* (destroyer), 1988	3·75	5·50

1992. 40th Anniv of Queen Elizabeth II's Accession. As T **143** of Ascension. Multicoloured.

119	15p. Catholic chapel, Diego Garcia	1·75	1·40
120	20p. Planter's house, Diego Garcia	2·00	1·60
121	24p. Railway tracks on wharf, Diego Garcia	4·50	2·25
122	34p. Three portraits of Queen Elizabeth	3·50	2·50
123	54p. Queen Elizabeth II	3·50	2·75

22 R.A.F. Consolidated PBY-5 Catalina (flying boat)

1992. Visiting Aircraft. Multicoloured.

124	20p. Type **22**	1·50	2·50
125	24p. R.A.F. Hawker Siddeley Nimrod M.R.2 (maritime reconnaissance aircraft)	1·75	2·50
126	34p. Lockheed P-3 Orion (transport aircraft)	2·50	3·25
127	54p. U.S.A.A.F. Boeing B-52 Stratofortress (heavy bomber)	3·00	4·50

23 The Mystical Marriage of St. Catherine (Correggio)

1992. Christmas. Religious Paintings. Multicoloured.

128	5p. Type **23**	70	80
129	24p. *Madonna* (anon)	1·25	1·60
130	34p. *Madonna* (anon) (different)	1·40	2·25
131	54p. *The Birth of Jesus* (Kaspar Jele)	1·75	3·50

24 Coconut Crab and Rock

1993. Endangered Species. Coconut Crab. Multicoloured.

132	10p. Type **24**	1·25	1·25
133	10p. Crab on beach	1·25	1·25
134	10p. Two crabs	1·25	1·25
135	15p. Crab climbing coconut tree	1·50	1·50

1993. 75th Anniv of Royal Air Force. As T **149** of Ascension. Multicoloured.

136	20p. Vickers Virginia Mk X	1·00	1·50
137	24p. Bristol Bulldog IIA	1·10	1·50
138	34p. Short S.25 Sunderland Mk III	1·25	2·00
139	54p. Bristol Blenheim Mk IV	2·00	3·25
MS140	110×77 mm. 20p. Douglas DC-3 Dakota; 20p. Gloster G.41 Javelin; 20p. Blackburn Beverley C1; 20p. Vickers VC-10	7·50	8·00

25 *Stachytarpheta urticifolia*

1993. Christmas. Flowers. Multicoloured.

141	20p. Type **25**	80	1·50
142	24p. *Ipomea pes-caprae*	80	1·50
143	34p. *Sida pusilla*	1·10	2·25
144	54p. *Catharanthus roseus*	1·75	3·50

1994. "Hong Kong '94" International Stamp Exhibition. Nos. 92 and 101 optd **HONG KONG '94** and emblem.

145	24p. Great frigate bird ("Greater Frigate")	5·00	3·00
146	£1 Madagascar red fody ("Madagascar Fody")	6·50	7·50

26 Forrest's Map of Diego Garcia, 1778

1994. 18th-century Maps. Each black and blue.

147	20p. Type **26**	70	1·50
148	24p. Blair's plan of Diego Garcia harbour, 1786–87	75	1·60
149	34p. Blair's chart of Chagos Archipelago, 1786–87	80	1·75
150	44p. Plan of part of Diego Garcia, 1774	90	1·90
151	54p. Fontaine's plan of Diego Garcia, 1770	1·10	2·00

27 *Junonia villida*

1994. Butterflies. Multicoloured.

152	24p. Type **27**	1·50	1·75

153	30p. *Petrelaea dana*	1·75	2·50
154	56p. *Hypolimnas misippus*	2·75	4·00

28 Short-tailed Nurse Sharks

1994. Sharks. Multicoloured.

155	15p. Type **28**	4·25	3·50
156	20p. Silver-tipped sharks	4·25	3·50
157	24p. Black-finned reef shark	4·25	3·50
158	30p. Oceanic white-tipped sharks	4·75	4·00
159	35p. Black-tipped shark	5·00	4·50
160	41p. Smooth hammerhead	5·00	4·50
161	46p. Sickle-finned lemon shark	5·00	4·50
162	55p. White-tipped reef shark	6·00	5·50
163	65p. Tiger sharks	6·50	5·50
164	74p. Indian sand tiger	6·50	6·00
165	80p. Great hammerhead	6·50	6·00
166	£1 Great white shark	7·50	7·00

1995. 50th Anniv of End of Second World War. As T **161** of Ascension. Multicoloured.

167	20p. Military cemetery	1·75	1·75
168	24p. Rusty 6-inch naval gun at Cannon Point	2·00	1·75
169	30p. Short S.25 Sunderland flying boat	2·25	2·25
170	56p. H.M.I.S. *Clive* (sloop)	3·50	3·75
MS171	75×85 mm. £1 Reverse of 1939–45 War Medal (vert)	2·50	3·00

29 Dolphin (fish)

1995. Gamefish. Multicoloured.

172	20p. Type **29**	1·75	1·60
173	24p. Sailfish	1·90	1·60
174	30p. Wahoo	2·50	2·50
175	56p. Striped marlin	3·50	3·75

30 *Terebra crenulata*

1996. Sea Shells. Multicoloured.

176	20p. Type **30**	1·25	1·50
177	24p. *Bursa bufonia*	1·25	1·50
178	30p. *Nassarius papillosus*	1·75	2·00
179	56p. *Lopha cristagalli*	3·00	3·25

1996. 70th Birthday of Queen Elizabeth II. As T **165** of Ascension, each incorporating a different photograph of the Queen. Multicoloured.

180	20p. View of lagoon from south	90	1·00
181	24p. Manager's House, Peros Banhos	1·00	1·00
182	30p. Wireless hut, Peros Banhos	1·25	1·40
183	56p. Sunset	1·75	2·00
MS184	64×66 mm. £1 Queen Elizabeth II	3·25	3·50

31 Loggerhead Turtle

1996. Turtles. Multicoloured.

185	20p. Type **31**	1·00	1·25
186	24p. Leatherback turtle	1·10	1·25
187	30p. Hawksbill turtle	1·40	1·60
188	56p. Green turtle	2·00	2·50

32 Commissioner's Representative (naval officer)

1996. Uniforms. Multicoloured.

189	20p. Type **32**	1·00	1·10

190	24p. Royal Marine officer	1·10	1·10
191	30p. Royal Marine in battle-dress	1·50	1·75
192	56p. Police officers	2·25	2·75

1997. "HONG KONG '97" International Stamp Exhibition. Sheet 130×90 mm, containing design as No. 163. Multicoloured.

MS193	65p. Tiger sharks	2·00	2·75

1997. Return of Hong Kong to China. Sheet 130×90 mm, containing design as No. 164, but with "1997" imprint date.

MS194	74p. Indian sand tiger	2·75	3·50

1997. Golden Wedding of Queen Elizabeth and Prince Philip. As T **173** of Ascension. Multicoloured.

195	20p. Queen Elizabeth at Bristol, 1994	1·60	1·75
196	20p. Prince Philip competing in Royal Windsor Horse Show, 1996	1·60	1·75
197	24p. Queen Elizabeth in phaeton, Trooping the Colour, 1987	1·60	1·75
198	24p. Prince Philip	1·60	1·75
199	30p. Queen Elizabeth and Prince Philip with Land Rover	1·60	1·75
200	30p. Queen Elizabeth at Balmoral	1·60	1·75
MS201	110×71 mm. £1.50, Queen Elizabeth and Prince Philip in landau (horiz)	9·00	9·50

Nos. 195/6, 197/8 and 199/20 respectively were printed together, *se-tenant*, with the backgrounds forming a composite design.

33 H.M.S. *Richmond* (frigate) and H.M.S. *Beaver* (frigate)

1997. Exercise Ocean Wave. Multicoloured.

202	24p. Type **33**	2·00	1·75
203	24p. H.M.S. *Illustrious* (aircraft carrier) launching BAe (Hawker) Sea Harrier	2·00	1·75
204	24p. H.M.S. *Beaver*	2·00	1·75
205	24p. Royal Yacht *Britannia*, R.F.A. *Sir Percival* and H.M.S. *Beaver*	2·00	1·75
206	24p. Royal Yacht *Britannia*	2·00	1·75
207	24p. H.M.S. *Richmond*, H.M.S. *Beaver* and H.M.S. *Gloucester* (destroyer)	2·00	1·75
208	24p. H.M.S. *Richmond*	2·00	1·75
209	24p. Aerial view of H.M.S. *Illustrious*	2·00	1·75
210	24p. H.M.S. *Gloucester* (wrongly inscr "Sheffield")	2·00	1·75
211	24p. H.M.S. *Trenchant* (submarine) and R.F.A. *Diligence*	2·00	1·75
212	24p. R.F.A. *Fort George* replenishing H.M.S. *Illustrious* and H.M.S. *Gloucester*	2·00	1·75
213	24p. Aerial view of H.M.S. *Richmond*, H.M.S. *Beaver* and H.M.S. *Gloucester*	2·00	1·75

1998. Diana, Princess of Wales Commemoration. Sheet 145×70 mm, containing vert designs as T **177** of Ascension. Multicoloured.

MS214	26p. Wearing patterned jacket, 1993; 26p. Wearing heart-shaped earrings, 1988; 34p. Wearing cream jacket, 1993; 60p. Wearing blue blouse, 1982 (sold at £1.46 + 20p. charity premium)	2·50	3·75

1998. 80th Anniv of the Royal Air Force. As T **178** of Ascension. Multicoloured.

215	26p. Blackburn Iris	1·25	1·10
216	34p. Gloster Gamecock	1·50	1·40
217	60p. North American SF-86 abre F.4	2·50	2·50
218	80p. Avro Type **694** Lincoln	3·00	3·00
MS219	110×77 mm. 34p. Sopwith Baby (seaplane); 34p. Martinsyde Elephant; 34p. de Havilland Tiger Moth; 34p. North American Mustang III	6·00	7·50

34 Bryde's Whale

1998. International Year of the Ocean. Multicoloured.

220	26p. Type **34**	2·50	2·50
221	26p. Striped dolphin	2·50	2·50
222	34p. Pilot whale	2·50	2·50
223	34p. Spinner dolphin	2·50	2·50

35 *Westminster* (East Indiaman), 1837

1999. Ships. Multicoloured.

224	2p. Type **35**	50	1·00
225	15p. *Sao Cristovao* (Spanish galleon), 1589	1·50	1·25
226	20p. *Sea Witch* (U.S. clipper), 1849	1·50	1·25
227	26p. H.M.S. *Royal George* (ship of the line), 1778	1·75	1·25
228	34p. *Cutty Sark* (clipper), 1883	2·75	1·75
229	60p. *Mentor* (East Indiaman), 1789	3·50	3·50
230	80p. H.M.S. *Trinculo* (brig), 1809	3·75	4·00
231	£1 *Enterprise* (paddle-steamer), 1825	4·75	5·00
232	£1.15 *Confiance* (French privateer), 1800	5·00	5·50
233	£2 *Kent* (East Indiaman), 1820	8·00	9·00

36 *Cutty Sark* (clipper)

1999. "Australia '99" World Stamp Exhibition, Melbourne. Sheet 150×75 mm, containing T **36** and similar horiz design. Multicoloured.

MS234	60p. Type **36**; 60p. *Thermopylae* (clipper)	6·00	8·00

37 Field Vole (Colin Sargent)

2000. "The Stamp Show 2000", International Stamp Exhibition, London. "Shoot a Stamp" Competition Winners. Sheet 150×100 mm, containing T **37** and similar vert designs. Multicoloured.

MS235	26p. Type **37**; 34p. Atlantic puffin (P. J. Royal); 55p. Red fox (Jim Wilson); £1 European robin ("Robin") (Harry Smith)	10·00	11·00

38 Satellite Image of Salomon Island

2000. New Millennium. Satellite Images of Islands. Multicoloured.

236	15p. Type **38**	1·60	1·60
237	20p. Egmont	1·75	1·75
238	60p. Blenheim Reef	2·75	3·00
239	80p. Diego Garcia	3·00	3·25

39 Queen Elizabeth the Queen Mother

2000. Queen Elizabeth the Queen Mother's 100th Birthday. Multicoloured.

240	26p. Type **39**	1·40	1·40
241	34p. Wearing green hat and outfit	1·40	1·40
MS242	113×88 mm. 55p. In blue hat and outfit	4·75	5·50

40 *Delonix regia*

2000. Christmas Flowers. Multicoloured.

243	26p. Type **40**	1·75	1·75
244	34p. *Barringtonia asiatica*	2·00	2·00
245	60p. *Zephyranthes rosea*	3·50	4·00

2000. "HONG KONG 2001" Stamp Exhibition. Sheet 150×90 mm, containing T **41** and similar design showing butterfly. Multicoloured.

MS246	26p. Type **41**; 34p. *Junonia villida chagoensis*	3·00	3·50

42 H.M.S. *Turbulent*

2001. Centenary of Royal Navy Submarine Service. Multicoloured (except Nos. 248 and 250).

247	26p. Type **42**	1·75	2·00
248	26p. H.M.S. *Churchill* (grey and black)	1·75	2·00
249	34p. H.M.S. *Resolution*	2·00	2·50
250	34p. H.M.S. *Vanguard*	2·00	2·50
251	60p. H.M.S. *Otter* (73×27 mm)	2·50	3·00
252	60p. H.M.S. *Oberon* (73×27 mm) (grey and black)	2·50	3·00

43 Cushion Star

2001. Endangered Species. Seastars. Multicoloured.

253	15p. Type **43**	1·25	1·25
254	26p. Azure sea star	1·75	1·50
255	34p. Crown-of-Thorns	1·90	1·75
256	56p. Banded bubble star	3·00	3·50

44 *Scadoxus multiflora*

2001. Plants (1st series). Flowers. Multicoloured.

257	26p. Type **44**	1·75	1·75
258	34p. *Striga asiatica*	2·00	2·00
MS259	173×78 mm. Nos. 257/8 and 10p. *Catharanthus roseus* (horiz); 60p. *Argusia argentea* (horiz); 70p. *Euphorbia cyathophora* (horiz)	5·50	6·50

In No. **MS259** the 60p. is inscribed "argentia" in error.

45 Crab Plovers on Beach

2001. Birdlife World Bird Festival. Crab Plovers. Sheet 175×80 mm, containing T **45** and similar multicoloured designs.

MS260	50p. Type **45**; 50p. Crab plover catching crab (vert); 50p. Head of crab plover (vert); 50p. Crab plovers in flight; 50p. Crab plover standing on one leg	7·50	8·50

2002. Golden Jubilee. As T **200** of Ascension.

261	10p. brown, blue and gold	1·00	1·00
262	25p. multicoloured	1·50	1·50
263	35p. black, blue and gold	1·75	1·75
264	55p. multicoloured	2·50	2·75
MS265	162×95 mm. Nos. 261/4 and 75p. multicoloured	6·50	7·00

DESIGNS—HORIZ: 10p. Princess Elizabeth in pantomime, Windsor, 1943; 25p. Queen Elizabeth in floral hat, 1967; 35p. Princess Elizabeth and Prince Philip on their engagement, 1947; 55p. Queen Elizabeth in evening dress. VERT (38×51 mm)—75p. Queen Elizabeth after Annigoni.

Designs as Nos. 261/4 in No. **MS265** omit the gold frame around each stamp and the "Golden Jubilee 1952–2002" inscription.

46 Adult Red-footed Booby

2002. Birdlife International. Red-footed Booby. Sheet 175×80 mm, containing T **46** and similar multicoloured designs.

MS266	50p. Type **46**; 50p. Head of dark morph red-footed booby; 50p. Adult bird in flight (vert); 50p. Dark morph on nest (vert); 50p. Fledgling on nest	8·50	10·00

2002. Queen Elizabeth the Queen Mother Commemoration. As T **202** of Ascension.

267	26p. brown, gold and purple	1·25	1·00
268	£1 multicoloured	2·75	3·00
MS269	145×70 mm. £1 black and gold; £1 multicoloured	7·00	8·00

DESIGNS: 26p. Lady Elizabeth Bowes-Lyon, 1921; £1 (No. 268) Queen Mother, 1986; £1 brownish black and gold (No. **MS269**) Queen Elizabeth at garden party, 1951; £1 multicoloured (No. **MS269**) Queen Mother at Cheltenham Races, 1994.

Designs in No. **MS269** omit the "1900–2002" inscription and the coloured frame.

47 Microgoby

2002. Tenth Anniv of Friends of Chagos (conservation association). Reef Fish. Multicoloured.

270	2p. Type **47**	45	70
271	15p. Angel fish	1·25	1·25
272	26p. Surgeonfish	1·50	1·50
273	34p. Trunkfish	1·75	1·75
274	58p. Soldierfish	2·75	3·25
275	£1 Chagos anemonefish	5·00	6·00

48 *Halgerda tesselata*

2003. Sea Slugs. Multicoloured.

276	2p. Type **48**	40	70
277	15p. *Notodoris minor*	90	90
278	26p. *Nembrotha lineolata*	1·10	1·10
279	50p. *Chromodoris quadricolor*	2·00	2·50
280	76p. *Glossodoris cincta*	2·75	3·50
281	£1.10 *Chromodoris cf leopardus*	3·50	4·50

2003. 50th Anniv of Coronation. As T **206** of Ascension. Multicoloured.

282	£1 Queen Elizabeth II wearing Imperial State Crown in Coronation Coach	3·50	3·75
283	£2 Queen with members of Royal Family in Coronation robes	6·50	7·50
MS284	95×115 mm. £1 As No. 282; £2 As No. 283	10·00	11·00

Nos. 282/3 have red frame; stamps from **MS284** have no frame and country name in mauve panel.

2003. As T **207** of Ascension.

285	£2.50 black, pink and red	7·00	7·50

2003. 21st Birthday of Prince William of Wales. As T **208** of Ascension. Multicoloured.

286	50p. Prince William at Cirencester Polo Club	2·25	2·25
287	£1 With Prince Charles on skiing holiday and at Cirencester Polo Club	3·75	3·00

2003. Centenary of Powered Flight. As Type **209** of Ascension. Multicoloured.

288	34p. Avro Type 683 Lancaster	2·00	2·00
289	34p. de Havilland D.H.98 Mosquito	2·00	2·00
290	58p. Hawker Hurricane	3·00	3·00
291	58p. Supermarine Spitfire	3·00	3·00
292	76p. Vickers-Armstrong Wellington	3·50	3·50
293	76p. Lockheed C-130 Hercules	3·50	3·50
MS294	233×85 mm. 26p. Boeing E-3A Sentry AWACS; 26p. Boeing B-17 Flying Fortress; 26p. Lockheed P-3 Orion; 26p. Consolidated B-24 Liberator; 26p. Lockheed C-141 StarLifter; 26p. Short S.25 Sunderland (flying boat); 26p. Supermarine Walrus; 26p. Short S.25 Sunderland (flying boat); 26p. Supermarine Stranraer; 26p. PBY Catalina; 26p. Supermarine Sea Otter	10·00	12·00

49 *Pacific Marlin* (fisheries patrol ship)

2004. Fisheries Patrol. Multicoloured.

MS295	150×110 mm. 34p. Type **49**; 34p. Marlin; 58p. Skipjack tuna; 58p. Yellowfin tuna; 76p. Swordfish; 76p. Bigeye tuna	12·00	13·00

50 Madagascar Red Fody ("Madagascar Fody")

2004. Birds. Multicoloured.

296	2p. Type **50**	50	85
297	14p. Zebra dove ("Barred Ground Dove")	1·25	1·25
298	20p. Common mynah ("Indian Mynah")	1·50	1·25
299	26p. Cattle egret	1·75	1·25
300	34p. White tern ("Fairy Tern")	2·00	1·40
301	58p. Blue-faced booby ("Masked Booby")	2·75	2·75
302	76p. Great frigate bird	4·00	4·00
303	80p. White-tailed tropic bird	4·00	4·00
304	£1.10 Green-backed heron ("Little Green Heron")	5·00	5·50
305	£1.34 Pacific golden plover	6·00	7·00
306	£1.48 Garganey ("Garganey Teal")	6·50	7·50
307	£2.50 Bar-tailed godwit	9·50	11·00

51 Coconut Crab

2004. Crabs. Multicoloured.

308	26p. Type **51**	1·10	80
309	34p. Land crab	1·40	1·00
310	76p. Rock crab	3·00	3·25
311	£1.10 Ghost crab	4·00	5·00

52 Two Hawksbill Turtle Babies

2005. Turtles. Multicoloured.

312	26p. Type **52**	1·50	1·50
313	26p. Baby Green turtle	1·50	1·50
314	34p. Adult Hawksbill turtle	2·00	2·00
315	34p. Adult Green turtle	2·00	2·00
316	76p. Hawksbill turtle swimming	3·50	3·50
317	£1.10 Green turtle swimming	4·50	4·50
MS318	90×63 mm. £1.70 As No. 317	6·50	7·50

No. **MS318** commemorates the Turtle Cove Clean-up operation sponsored by Cable and Wireless.

2005. Bicentenary of Battle of Trafalgar (1st issue). As T **216** of Ascension. Multicoloured.

319	26p. Tower Sea Service Pistol, 1796	1·40	1·40
320	26p. HMS *Phoebe*	1·40	1·40
321	34p. Boatswain RN, 1805	1·75	1·75
322	34p. HMS *Harrier*	1·75	1·75
323	76p. Portrait of Admiral Nelson	3·25	3·75
324	76p. HMS *Victory* (horiz)	3·25	3·75
MS325	120×79 mm. £1.10 HMS *Minotaur*; £1.10 HMS *Spartiate*	7·50	8·50

No. 324 contains traces of powdered wood from HMS *Victory*.

See also Nos. 344/6.

53 HMAS *Wollongong*, September 1942

2005. 60th Anniv of the End of World War II. "Route to Victory". As T **53**. Multicoloured.

326	26p. Type **53**	1·00	1·00
327	26p. *Ondina* (Dutch tanker) and HMS *Bengal* attacked by Japanese surface raiders, 11 November 1942	1·00	1·00
328	26p. HMS *Pathfinder* (arrived at Diego Garcia, 4 April 1944)	1·00	1·00
329	26p. HMS *Lossie* (rescued survivors from Australian freighter *Nellore*, 29 June 1944)	1·00	1·00
330	26p. US Liberty Ship *Jean Nicolet* (sunk by Japanese, 2 July 1944)	1·00	1·00
331	34p. General Douglas MacArthur and landing party wading ashore	1·40	1·40
332	34p. General Bernard Montgomery and tanks in North African desert	1·40	1·40
333	34p. General George Patton and tanks	1·40	1·40

334	34p. Winston Churchill and St. Paul's Cathedral	1·40	1·40
335	34p. US Pres. Franklin Roosevelt and steelworks	1·40	1·40

54 Blacktip Reef Shark

2005. Sharks and Rays. Multicoloured.

336	26p. Type **54**	1·00	1·00
337	26p. Grey reef shark	1·00	1·00
338	34p. Silvertip shark	1·40	1·40
339	34p. Tawny nurse shark	1·40	1·40
340	34p. Spotted eagle ray	1·40	1·40
341	34p. Manta ray	1·40	1·40
342	76p. Porcupine ray	2·75	3·00
343	£2 Feathertail stingray	7·00	8·00

2005. Bicentenary of the Battle of Trafalgar (2nd issue). As T **220** of Ascension. Multicoloured.

344	26p. HMS *Victory*	1·25	1·00
345	34p. Ships engaged in battle (horiz)	1·75	1·50
346	£2 Admiral Lord Nelson	7·00	8·50

55 Crab on Beach

2005. 40th Anniv of British Indian Ocean Territory. T **55** and similar vert designs. Multicoloured.

MS347 205×129 mm. 34p. Type **55**; 34p. Two hermit crabs on beach; 34p. Blue-faced boobies at nest; 34p. Outline map of Indian Ocean and lesser frigate bird; 34p. Pair of imperial angelfish; 34p. Pair of racoon butterflyfish; 34p. Moorish idol (fish); 34p. Outline map of British Indian Ocean Territory and turtle ... 12·00 14·00

The stamps within No. **MS347** form a composite background design showing a beach and coral reef.

2006. 80th Birthday of Queen Elizabeth II. As T **223** of Ascension. Multicoloured.

348	26p. Princess Elizabeth	1·25	1·00
349	26p. Queen Elizabeth II, c. 1952	1·75	1·50
350	76p. Wearing tiara	3·00	3·50
351	£1.10 Wearing headscarf	3·50	4·00

MS352 144×75 mm. £1 As No. 349; £1 As No. 350 ... 7·00 8·00

56 Dusky Angelfish

2006. Marine Life (1st series). Angelfish. Sheet 205×129 mm containing T **56** and similar horiz designs. Multicoloured.

MS353 26p. Type **56**; 26p. Two-spined angelfish; 26p. Bicolour angelfish; 34p. Orangeback angelfish; 34p. Emperor angelfish; £2 Threespot angelfish ... 14·00 15·00

The stamps and margins of No. MS353 form a composite design showing a coral reef.
See also Nos. MS354, MS356 and MS372.

2006. Marine Life (2nd series). Butterflyfish. Sheet 205×129 mm containing horiz designs as T **56**. Multicoloured.

MS354 26p. Melon butterflyfish; 26p. Raccoon butterflyfish; 26p. Scrawled butterflyfish; 34p. Longnose butterflyfish; 34p. Threadfin butterflyfish; £2 Masked bannerfish ... 14·00 15·00

The stamps and margins of No. MS354 form a composite design showing a coral reef.

57 Great Frigatebird

2006. BirdLife International. Barton Point Nature Reserve. Sheet 170×85 mm containing T **57** and similar horiz designs. Multicoloured.

MS355 26p. Type **57**; 26p. Black-naped tern; 26p. Yellow-billed tropicbird; 26p. White tern; 26p. Brown noddy; £2 Red-footed booby ... 14·00 15·00

The stamps within No. **MS355** form a composite design.

2007. Marine Life (3rd series). Parrotfish. Sheet 205×129 mm containing horiz designs as T **56**. Multicoloured.

MS356 54p. Common parrotfish; 54p. Daisy parrotfish; 54p. Bicolour parrotfish; 54p. Bridled parrotfish; 90p. Indian Ocean steephead parrotfish; 90p. Ember parrotfish ... 15·00 16·00

The stamps and margins of No. **MS356** form a composite design showing a coral reef.

58 Princess Elizabeth and Lt. Philip Mountbatten, c. 1947

2007. Diamond Wedding of Queen Elizabeth II and Duke of Edinburgh. Multicoloured.

357	54p. Type **58**	1·60	1·60
358	54p. Wedding procession and crowds, 1949	1·60	1·60
359	90p. Princess Elizabeth and Lt. Philip Mountbatten arm in arm, c. 1947	3·00	3·00
360	90p. Wedding ceremony, 1949	3·00	3·00

MS361 125×85 mm. £2.14 Princess Elizabeth and Lt. Philip Mountbatten, c. 1947 (42×56 mm) ... 8·00 8·50

59 Charles Darwin and Beach with Tropic Bird, Terns and Turtle

2007. 125th Death Anniv of Charles Darwin. Multicoloured.

362	54p. Type **59**	2·00	2·00
363	54p. HMS *Beagle*	2·00	2·00
364	90p. Turtles	3·75	3·75
365	90p. Coral reef	3·75	3·75

60 Pomarine Skua pursuing Tropic Bird

2007. BirdLife International. Pomarine Skua (*Stercorarius pomarinus*). Multicoloured.

366	54p. Type **60**	2·25	2·25
367	54p. Pomarine skua pursuing booby	2·25	2·25
368	54p. Pair of pomarine skuas in flight	2·25	2·25
369	54p. Pair of pomarine skuas on beach	2·25	2·25
370	90p. Pomarine skua pursuing terns	4·00	4·00
371	90p. Pomarine skua on sea	4·00	4·00

2008. Marine Life (4th series). Damselfish. Sheet 205×129 mm containing horiz designs as T **56**. Multicoloured.

MS372 54p. *Chrysiptera unimaculata* (onespot demoiselle); 54p. *Abudefduf septemfasciatus* (banded sergeant); 54p. *Plectroglyphidodon johnstonianus* (Johnston Island damsel); 54p. *Amphiprion chagosensis* (Chagos anemonefish); 90p. *Chromis atripectoralis* (black-axil chromis); 90p. *Pomacentrus caeruleus* (caerulean damsel) ... 9·50 10·00

The stamps and margins of No. **MS372** form a composite design showing a coral reef.

61 Royal Marines

2008. Military Uniforms. Multicoloured.

373	27p. Type **61**	1·40	1·40
374	27p. Royal Engineers	1·40	1·40
375	54p. Sepoys, East India Company Army	2·25	2·25
376	54p. Officer, East India Company Army	2·25	2·25
377	54p. Artillery Corps	2·25	2·25
378	54p. Sergeant, Royal Military Police	2·25	2·25

62 Avro 504

2008. 90th Anniv of the Royal Air Force. Multicoloured.

379	27p. Type **62**	1·25	1·25
380	27p. Short Sunderland	1·25	1·25
381	27p. de Havilland Mosquito	1·25	1·25
382	27p. Vickers VC10	1·25	1·25
383	54p. English Electric Canberra	2·00	2·00

MS384 70×110 mm. £1.72 King George V, Marshal of the RAF (vert). Wmk inverted ... 9·50 10·00

63 Pte Harry Lamin, 1918

2008. 90th Anniv of the End of World War I. Designs showing soldiers and their letters home. Multicoloured.

385	50p. Type **63**	2·00	2·25
386	50p. Second Lt. Eric Heaton, 1916	2·00	2·25
387	50p. Pte Dennis Harry Wilson, 1917	2·00	2·25
388	50p. Second Lt. Eric Rose, 1917	2·00	2·25
389	50p. Sgt.-Major Francis Proud, 1915	2·00	2·25
390	50p. Second Lt. Charles Roberts, 1917	2·00	2·25

MS391 110×70 mm. £1 UK Overseas Territories Wreath of Remembrance ... 3·75 4·25

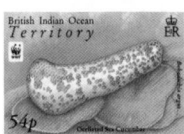

64 *Bohadschia argus* (ocellated sea cucumber)

2008. Endangered Species. Sea Cucumbers. Multicoloured.

392	54p. Type **64**	2·75	2·75
393	54p. *Thelenota ananas* (pineapple sea cucumber)	2·75	2·75
394	54p. *Pearsonothuria graeffei* (Graeffe's sea cucumber)	4·00	4·00
395	90p. *Stichopus chloronotus* (dark green sea cucumber)	4·00	4·00

65 HMS *Endeavour* (Cook)

2009. Seafaring and Exploration. Multicoloured.

396	54p. Type **65**	2·75	2·75
397	54p. HMS *Victory* (Nelson)	2·75	2·75
398	54p. HMS *Beagle* (Darwin)	2·75	2·75
399	54p. SS *Windsor Castle* (landing of Captain Raymond, Diego Garcia, 1884)	2·75	2·75
400	54p. SMS *Fürst Bismarck* (German armoured cruiser, 1900)	2·75	2·75
401	54p. HMS *Edinburgh* (1983)	2·75	2·75

MS402 110×70 mm. £1.30 Vasco da Gama (Portuguese navigator, sighted Chagos Archipelago, early 16th century) (vert) ... 6·00 6·50

2009. Centenary of Naval Aviation. Multicoloured (except MS407).

403	27p. Short S.38	1·75	1·75
404	27p. Sopwith Pup	1·75	1·75
405	54p. Supermarine Scimitar	3·00	3·00
406	54p. Westland Wessex helicopter	3·00	3·00

MS407 110×70 mm. £1.72 Sqn. Cdr. E. H. Dunning landing aircraft on HMS *Furious*, 1917 (black, deep ultramarine and rosine) ... 10·00 11·00

2009. International Year of Astronomy. 40th Anniv of First Moon Landing. Multicoloured.

408	54p. Development of early rockets *Corporal* and *Private*	2·50	2·50
409	54p. *Flying Bedstead*, 1964	2·50	2·50
410	54p. Apollo Launch Site, 1969	2·50	2·50
411	54p. Space Transportation System 71 launch, 1995	2·50	2·50
412	90p. ESA Columbus Laboratory STS 122, 2008	4·00	4·00

MS413 100×80 mm. £1.50 *Savoring the Moment* (astronaut Jack Schmitt on Moon) (Alan Bean) (39×59 mm) ... 6·50 7·00

66 Two Band Anemonefish (*Amphiprion bicinctus*)

2009. Fish, Fauna, Flora and Coves. Multicoloured.

414	1p. Type **66**	10	10
415	2p. Angelfish (*Centropyge bicolor*)	15	15
416	5p. Royal poinciana (*Delonix regia*)	25	25
417	12p. Beach morning glory (*Ipomoea pes-caprae*)	55	55
418	27p. Bay cedar (*Suriana maritima*)	1·25	1·25
419	45p. Scaevola bush (*Scaevola taccada*)	2·00	2·00
420	54p. Madagascan red fody (*Foudia madagascariensis*)	2·50	2·50
421	90p. Greater frigatebird (*Fregata minor*)	4·00	4·00
422	£1.30 Sharks Cove	5·00	5·00
423	£1.72 Turtle Cove	6·25	6·25
424	£2.64 Hawksbill turtle	8·75	8·75
425	£3.02 Sicklefin lemon shark (*Negaprion acutidens*)	11·00	11·00

MS426 194×134 mm. Nos. 414/25 ... 38·00 38·00

67 *Lentinus* sp.

2009. Fungi. Multicoloured.

427	54p. Type **67**	2·50	2·50
428	54p. *Entoloma* sp.	2·50	2·50
429	90p. *Leucocoprinus* sp.	4·00	4·00
430	90p. *Pycnoporus* sp.	4·00	4·00

68 Hugh Dowding

2010. 70th Anniv of the Battle of Britain. Aces and Leaders. Multicoloured.

431	50p. Type **68**	2·50	2·50
432	50p. Bob Stanford-Tuck	2·50	2·50
433	50p. Ginger Lacey	2·50	2·50
434	50p. Eric Lock	2·50	2·50
435	50p. Mike Crossley	2·50	2·50
436	50p. Bob Doe	2·50	2·50

MS437 110×70mm. $1.50 Sir Douglas Bader ... 6·00 6·50

69 Great Britain George V 1934 1½d. Stamp

2010. London 2010 Festival of Stamps and Centenary of Accession of King George V
MS438 **69** £1.50 multicoloured ... 6·00 6·50

70 Archer and Mounted Knight, Battle of Hastings, 1066

2010. Great Battles. Multicoloured.

439	50p. Type **70**		2·00	2·00
440	50p. Mounted knight carrying standard and archers, Battle of Agincourt, 1415		2·00	2·00
441	50p. Mounted knights, Battle of Bosworth, 1485		2·00	2·00
442	50p. Cavalry, Battle of Naseby, 1645		2·00	2·00
443	50p. Soldiers, Battle of Culloden, 1746		2·00	2·00
444	50p. Duke of Wellington on horseback and soldiers, Battle of Waterloo, 1815		2·00	2·00
445	50p. Soldiers and cavalryman, Battle of Alma, 1854		2·00	2·00
446	50p. British soldiers, Battle of Rorke's Drift, 1879		2·00	2·00
447	50p. Soldiers, Siege of Mafeking, 1899		2·00	2·00
448	50p. Soldiers, Battle of the Somme, 1916		2·00	2·00
449	50p. Soldiers, Battle of El Alamein, 1942		2·00	2·00
450	50p. Normandy Landings, 1944		2·00	2·00

Nos. 439/50 were each printed in sheetlets of six stamps with enlarged illustrated margins.

2011. Queen Elizabeth II and Prince Philip 'A Lifetime of Service'. Multicoloured.

451	54p. Queen Elizabeth II, c. 1952		1·80	1·80
452	54p. Queen Elizabeth II and Prince Philip (black/white photo), c. 1972		1·80	1·80
453	54p. Queen Elizabeth II and Prince Philip, c. 1955		1·80	1·80
454	54p. Queen Elizabeth II and Prince Philip (seen in profile), c. 2010		1·80	1·80
455	54p. Queen Elizabeth II and Prince Philip, c. 1970		1·80	1·80
456	54p. Prince Philip, c. 1955		1·80	1·80
MS457	174×163 mm. Nos. 451/6 and three stamp-size labels		10·50	10·50
MS458	110×70 mm. £3.02 Queen Elizabeth II and Prince Philip, c. 2007		10·50	10·50

71 Prince William and Miss Catherine Middleton

2011. Royal Wedding (1st issue)

MS459	**71** £3 multicoloured		11·00	11·00

2011. Royal Wedding (2nd issue). Multicoloured.

460	54p. Duke and Duchess of Cambridge waving from State Landau		1·90	1·90
461	54p. Duke and Duchess of Cambridge kissing on Buckingham Palace balcony (vert)		1·90	1·90
462	90p. Duke and Duchess of Cambridge at Westminster Abbey after wedding ceremony (vert)		2·75	2·75
463	90p. Leaving Buckingham Palace in car with 'JUST WED' numberplate		2·75	2·75

72 Field of Poppies, Flanders

2011. 90th Anniv of the Royal British Legion. Multicoloured.

464	50p. Type **72**		1·75	1·75
465	50p. Silhouette of soldier and war memorials		1·75	1·75
466	50p. War graves		1·75	1·75
467	50p. Poppy Appeal		1·75	1·75
468	50p. Aircraft dropping poppies		1·75	1·75
469	50p. Ex-servicemen wearing medals		1·75	1·75

470	50p. Wooden remembrance crosses with poppies		1·75	1·75
471	50p. Festival of Remembrance		1·75	1·75
MS472	94×64 mm. £1.50 Remembrance Day service		5·25	5·25

73 Queen Elizabeth II, c. 1970

2012. Diamond Jubilee. Multicoloured.

473	54p. Type **73**		1·90	1·90
474	54p. Queen Elizabeth II wearing blue hat, c. 1975		1·90	1·90
475	54p. Queen Elizabeth II wearing red, c. 1980		1·90	1·90
476	54p. Queen Elizabeth II wearing tiara, pendant and pearl earrings. c. 1955 (colour photo)		1·90	1·90
477	54p. Queen Elizabeth II wearing tiara, c. 1955 (black/white photo)		1·90	1·90
478	54p. Queen Elizabeth II, c. 2005		1·90	1·90
MS479	174×164 mm. Nos. 473/8 and three stamp-size labels		10·25	10·25
MS480	110×70 mm. £3.02 Queen Elizabeth II wearing red cardigan and pearl necklace, c. 1975		16·00	16·00

PARCEL POST STAMPS

2002. Tenth Anniv of Friends of Chagos (conservation association). Reef Fish. Sheet 115×95 mm, containing horiz design as T **47**. Multicoloured.

PMS1	£1.90 Parrotfish		11·00	12·00

Pt. 1

BRITISH LEVANT

Stamps used at British post offices in the Turkish Empire. These offices closed in 1914. The stamps were again in use after 1918, during the British Occupation of Turkey.

Stamps of Great Britain surcharged or overprinted.

40 paras = 1 piastre.

A. BRITISH POST OFFICES IN TURKISH EMPIRE I. TURKISH CURRENCY

1885. Queen Victoria stamps surch in **PARAS** or **PIASTRES**.

1	64	40pa. on 2½d. lilac	£130	1·25
4	74	40pa. on 2½d. purple on blue	16·00	10
7	71	40pa. on ½d. red	£425	£100
2	62	80pa. on 5d. green	£225	9·50
5	78	80pa. on 5d. purple & blue	18·00	30
6	81	4pi. on 10d. purple and red	45·00	8·00
3a	58	12pi. on 2s.6d. lilac	65·00	26·00

1902. King Edward VII stamps surch in **PARAS** or **PIASTRES**.

29	–	30pa. on 1½d. purple & grn	6·50	55
8	83	40pa. on 2½d. blue	23·00	10
9	–	80pa. on 5d. purple and blue	15·00	2·00
13	83	1pi. on 2½d. blue	27·00	10
30	–	2pi. on 5d. purple and blue	24·00	3·25
10	–	4pi. on 10d. purple and red	22·00	4·00
21	–	5pi. on 1s. green and red	4·25	16·00
11	–	12pi. on 2s.6d. purple	40·00	38·00
12	–	24pi. on 5s. red	32·00	42·00

1906. Surch **1 Piastre**.

15		1pi. on 2d. green and red	£1400	£650

1909. King Edward VII stamps surch in **PIASTRE PARAS**.

17	–	1pi. 10pa. on 3d. pur on yell	12·00	50·00
18	–	1pi. 30pa. on 4d. grn & brn	5·00	19·00
19	–	1pi. 30pa. on 4d. orange	22·00	70·00
20	83	2pi. 20pa. on 6d. purple	26·00	70·00

1910. King Edward VII stamps surch in **PIASTRES**.

22	–	1¼pi. on 3d. purple on yellow	75	1·00
23	–	1¼pi. on 4d. orange	50	60
24	83	2½pi. on 6d. purple	2·75	65

1913. King George V stamps surch.

35	105	30pa. on 1½d. brown	3·50	14·00
41	105	30pa. on ½d. green	75	17·00
36a	104	1pi. on 2½d. blue	13·00	15
37	106	1¼pi. on 3d. violet	8·00	4·25
42	104	1½pi. on 1d. red	1·75	1·50

38	106	1¾pi. on 4d. grey-green	3·50	8·00
43	104	3¼pi. on 2½d. blue	1·25	25
39	106	4pi. on 10d. blue	10·00	27·00
44	106	4½pi. on 3d. violet	2·00	3·75
40	108	5pi. on 1s. brown	42·00	65·00
45	107	7½pi. on 5d. brown	50	10
46	108	15pi. on 10d. blue	70	15
47	108	18¾pi. on 1s. brown	4·25	4·25
48	109	45pi. on 2s.6d. brown	21·00	45·00
49	109	90pi. on 5s. red	25·00	30·00
50	109	180pi. on 10s. blue	45·00	40·00

II. BRITISH CURRENCY

1905. King Edward VII stamps optd **LEVANT**.

L1	83	½d. green	8·50	15
L2	83	1d. red	14·00	15
L3	–	1½d. purple and green	6·00	2·25
L4a	–	2d. green and red	4·00	8·50
L5	83	2½d. blue	8·50	20·00
L6	–	3d. purple and yellow	7·00	12·00
L7	–	4d. green and brown	9·50	70·00
L8	–	5d. purple and blue	16·00	38·00
L9	83	6d. purple	12·00	25·00
L10	83	1s. green and red	42·00	50·00

1911. King George V stamps optd **LEVANT**.

L12	98	½d. green	2·50	3·25
L14	101	½d. green	2·75	20
L16	105	½d. green	2·00	3·50
L13	99	1d. red	60	8·50
L15	102	1d. red	2·50	1·60
L17	104	1d. red	40	7·50
L18	106	2d. orange	2·75	42·00
L19	106	3d. violet	7·50	10·00
L20	106	4d. green	5·00	22·00
L21	107	5d. brown	12·00	28·00
L22a	107	6d. purple	32·00	8·50
L23	108	1s. brown	19·00	8·50
L24	109	2s.6d. brown	38·00	95·00

B. BRITISH FIELD OFFICE IN SALONICA

1916. King George V stamps of Great Britain optd **Levant**.

S1	105	½d. green	70·00	£325
S2	104	1d. red	70·00	£325
S3	106	2d. orange	£200	£475
S4	106	3d. violet	£160	£475
S5	106	4d. green	£190	£475
S6	107	6d. purple	£110	£400
S7	108	9d. black	£400	£750
S8	108	1s. brown	£350	£650

The above stamps were optd at Salonica during the war of 1914–18.

Pt. 1

BRITISH OCCUPATION OF ITALIAN COLONIES

Issues for use in Italian colonies occupied by British Forces. Middle East Forces overprints were used in Cyrenaica, Dodecanese Islands, Eritrea, Italian Somaliland and Tripolitania.

Middle East Forces.
12 pence = 1 shilling; 20 shillings = 1 pound.

Cyrenaica.
10 milliemes = 1 piastre; 20 shillings = 1 pound.

Eritrea.
100 cents = 1 shilling.

MIDDLE EAST FORCES

1942. Stamps of Great Britain optd **M.E.F.**

M11	128	1d. red	1·50	10
M12	128	2d. orange	2·25	1·25
M13	128	2½d. blue	2·25	10
M4	128	3d. violet	2·25	30
M5	129	5d. brown	2·25	50
M16	129	6d. purple	65	10
M17	130	9d. olive	85	10
M18	130	1s. brown	50	10
M19	131	2s.6d. green	7·00	1·00
M20	131	5s. red	27·00	17·00
M21	131	10s. blue (No. 478a)	40·00	10·00

PRICES. Our prices for Nos. M1/21 in used condition are for stamps with identifiable postmarks of the territories in which they were issued. These stamps were also used in the United Kingdom with official sanction, from the summer of 1950 onwards, and with U.K. postmarks are worth about 25 per cent less.

POSTAGE DUE STAMPS

1942. Postage Due stamps of Great Britain optd **M.E.F.**

MD1	D1	½d. green	40	13·00
MD2	D1	1d. red	40	1·75
MD3	D1	2d. black	2·00	1·25
MD4	D1	3d. violet	50	4·25
MD5	D1	1s. blue	4·00	13·00

24 Mounted Warrior **25** Mounted Warrior

1950

136	24	1m. brown	4·25	8·00
137	24	2m. red	4·25	8·00
138	24	3m. yellow	4·25	7·00
139	24	4m. green	4·25	8·00
140	24	5m. grey	4·25	7·50
141	24	8m. orange	4·25	4·00
142	24	10m. violet	4·25	2·50
143	24	12m. red	4·25	3·50
144	24	20m. blue	4·25	2·50
145	25	50m. blue and brown	16·00	10·00
146	25	100m. red and black	25·00	12·00
147	25	200m. violet and blue	35·00	35·00
148	25	500m. yellow and green	60·00	85·00

POSTAGE DUE STAMPS

D26

1950

D149	D26	2m. brown	60·00	£110
D150	D26	4m. green	60·00	£110
D151	D26	8m. red	60·00	£120
D152	D26	10m. orange	60·00	£120
D153	D26	20m. yellow	60·00	£140
D154	D26	40m. blue	60·00	£180
D155	D26	100m. black	60·00	£200

ERITREA BRITISH MILITARY ADMINISTRATION

1948. Stamps of Great Britain surch **B.M.A. ERITREA** and value in cents or shillings.

E1	128	5c. on ½d. green	2·75	65
E2	128	10c. on 1d. red	2·00	2·50
E3	128	20c. on 2d. orange	3·00	2·25
E4	128	25c. on 2½d. blue	2·00	60
E5	128	30c. on 3d. violet	2·50	4·50
E6	129	40c. on 5d. brown	2·75	4·25
E7	129	50c. on 6d. purple	2·25	1·00
E7a	130	65c. on 8d. red	7·00	2·00
E8	130	75c. on 9d. olive	3·75	75
E9	130	1s. on 1s. brown	2·50	50
E10	131	2s.50 on 2s.6d. green	11·00	11·00
E11	131	5s. on 5s. red	13·00	24·00
E12	–	10s. on 10s. blue (No. 478a)	27·00	24·00

BRITISH ADMINISTRATION

1950. Stamps of Great Britain surch **B.A. ERITREA** and value in cents or shillings.

E13	128	5c. on ½d. green	1·50	8·00
E26	128	5c. on ½d. orange	2·00	3·50
E14	128	10c. on 1d. red	40	3·00
E27	128	10c. on 1d. blue	1·75	75
E15	128	20c. on 2d. orange	1·25	80
E28	128	20c. on 2d. brown	2·00	30
E16	128	25c. on 2½d. blue	1·00	60
E29	128	25c. on 2½d. red	2·00	30
E17	128	30c. on 3d. violet	40	2·25
E18	129	40c. on 5d. brown	2·75	1·75
E19	129	50c. on 6d. purple	40	20
E20	130	65c. on 8d. red	6·00	1·50
E21	130	75c. on 9d. olive	1·50	25
E22	130	1s. on 1s. brown	40	15
E23	131	2s.50 on 2s.6d. green	9·00	5·50
E24	131	5s. on 5s. red	9·00	12·00
E25	–	10s. on 10s. blue (No. 478a)	75·00	70·00

1951. Nos. 509/11 of Great Britain surch **B.A. ERITREA** and value in cents and shillings.

E30	147	2s.50 on 2s.6d. green	21·00	30·00
E31	–	5s. on 5s. red	23·00	32·00
E32	–	10s. on 10s. blue	28·00	32·00

POSTAGE DUE STAMPS

1948. Postage Due stamps of Great Britain surch **B.M.A ERITREA** and new value in cents and shillings.

ED1	D1	5c. on ½d. green	10·00	22·00
ED2	D1	10c. on 1d. red	10·00	24·00
ED3	D1	20c. on 2d. black	17·00	16·00
ED4	D1	30c. on 3d. violet	13·00	17·00
ED5	D1	1s. on 1s. blue	21·00	32·00

1950. Postage Due stamps of Great Britain surch **B.A. ERITREA** and new value in cents or shillings.

ED6	–	5c. on ½d. green	16·00	60·00
ED7	–	10c. on 1d. red	16·00	21·00
ED8	–	20c. on 2d. black	16·00	25·00

ED9		30c. on 3d. violet	20·00	45·00
ED10		1s. on 1s. blue	21·00	45·00

SOMALIA BRITISH OCCUPATION

1943. Stamps of Great Britain optd **E.A.F.** (East African Forces).

S1	128	1d. red	1·50	1·50
S2	128	2d. orange	1·75	1·75
S3	128	2½d. blue	2·00	3·50
S4	128	3d. violet	1·75	15
S5	129	5d. brown	2·50	40
S6	129	6d. purple	2·25	1·50
S7	130	9d. olive	2·75	3·75
S8	130	1s. brown	3·75	15
S9	131	2s.6d. green	32·00	14·00

PRICES. Our prices for Nos. S1/9 in used condition are for stamps with identifiable postmarks of the territories in which they were issued. These stamps were also used in the United Kingdom with official sanction, from the summer of 1950, and with U.K. postmarks are worth about 25 per cent less.

BRITISH MILITARY ADMINISTRATION

1948. Stamps of Great Britain surch **B.M.A. SOMALIA** and new value in cents and shillings.

S10	128	5c. on ½d. green	1·25	2·00
S11	128	15c. on 1½d. brown	1·75	15·00
S12	128	20c. on 2d. orange	3·00	5·00
S13	128	25c. on 2½d. blue	2·25	4·50
S14	128	30c. on 3d. violet	2·25	9·00
S15	129	40c. on 5d. brown	1·25	20
S16	129	50c. on 6d. purple	50	2·00
S17	130	75c. on 9d. olive	2·00	27·00
S18	130	1s. on 1s. brown	1·25	20
S19	131	2s.50 on 2s.6d. green	8·00	25·00
S20	131	5s. on 5s. red	19·00	60·00

BRITISH ADMINISTRATION

1950. Stamps of Great Britain surch **B.A. SOMALIA** and value in cents and shillings.

S21	128	5c. on ½d. green	20	3·00
S22	128	15c. on 1½d. brown	75	17·00
S23	128	20c. on 2d. orange	75	7·50
S24	128	25c. on 2½d. blue	50	13·00
S25	128	30c. on 3d. violet	1·25	8·50
S26	129	40c. on 5d. brown	55	1·50
S27	129	50c. on 6d. purple	50	1·00
S28	130	75c. on 9d. olive	2·00	11·00
S29	130	1s. on 1s. brown	60	1·50
S30	131	2s.50 on 2s.6d. green	7·50	32·00
S31	131	5s. on 5s. red	19·00	50·00

TRIPOLITANIA BRITISH MILITARY ADMINISTRATION

1948. Stamps of Great Britain surch **B.M.A. TRIPOLITANIA** and value in **M.A.L.** (Military Administration lire).

T1	128	1l. on ½d. green	1·00	3·75
T2	128	2l. on 1d. red	50	15
T3	128	3l. on 1½d. brown	50	50
T4	128	4l. on 2d. orange	50	70
T5	128	5l. on 2½d. blue	50	20
T6	128	6l. on 3d. violet	50	40
T7	129	10l. on 5d. brown	50	15
T8	129	12l. on 6d. purple	50	20
T9	130	18l. on 9d. olive	1·50	1·75
T10	130	24l. on 1s. brown	2·50	2·75
T11	131	60l. on 2s.6d. green	8·50	16·00
T12	131	120l. on 5s. red	27·00	28·00
T13	131	240l. on 10s. blue (No. 478a)	30·00	£140

BRITISH ADMINISTRATION

1950. As Nos. T1/13 but surch **B.A. TRIPOLITANIA** and value in **M.A.L.**

T14	128	1l. on ½d. green	6·00	13·00
T27	128	1l. on ½d. orange	40	9·50
T15	128	2l. on 1d. red	5·00	40
T28	128	2l. on 1d. blue	40	1·00
T16	128	3l. on 1½d. brown	3·75	13·00
T29	128	3l. on 1½d. green	40	8·00
T17	128	4l. on 2d. orange	4·25	4·50
T30	128	4l. on 2d. brown	40	1·25
T18	128	5l. on 2½d. blue	2·25	70
T31	128	5l. on 2½d. red	45	7·50
T19	128	6l. on 3d. violet	3·75	3·25
T20	129	10l. on 5d. brown	3·75	4·00
T21	129	12l. on 6d. purple	5·00	50
T22	130	18l. on 9d. olive	8·00	2·75
T23	130	24l. on 1s. brown	7·50	3·75
T25	131	120l. on 5s. red	35·00	38·00
T26	-	240l. on 10s. blue (No. 478a)	55·00	85·00

1951. Nos. 509/11 of Great Britain surch **B.A. TRIPOLITANIA** and value in **M.A.L.**

T32	147	60l. on 2s.6d. green	18·00	38·00
T33	-	120l. on 5s. red	18·00	38·00
T34	-	240l. on 10s. blue	50·00	80·00

POSTAGE DUE STAMPS

1948. Postage Due stamps of Great Britain surch **B.M.A. TRIPOLITANIA** and value in **M.A.L.**

TD1	D1	1l. on ½d. green	5·50	65·00
TD2	D1	2l. on 1d. red	2·50	55·00
TD3	D1	4l. on 2d. black	13·00	50·00
TD4	D1	6l. on 3d. violet	7·50	26·00
TD5	D1	24l. on 1s. blue	29·00	£110

1950. As Nos. TD1/5 but surch **B.A. TRIPOLITANIA** and value in **M.A.L.**

TD6		1l. on ½d. green	15·00	£100
TD7		2l. on 1d. red	9·50	30·00
TD8		4l. on 2d. black	11·00	48·00
TD9		6l. on 3d. violet	19·00	80·00
TD10		24l. on 1s. blue	55·00	£170

BRITISH POST OFFICES IN CHINA

Pt. 1

Stamps for use in Wei Hai Wei, and the neighbouring islands, leased to Great Britain from 1898 to 1 October 1930, when they were returned to China. The stamps were also used in the Treaty Ports from 1917 until 1922.

100 cents = 1 dollar.

1917. Stamps of Hong Kong (King George V) optd **CHINA**.

18	24	1c. brown	3·00	6·00
19	24	2c. green	7·00	2·25
3	24	4c. red	9·50	30
4	24	6c. orange	9·50	1·75
5	24	8c. grey	15·00	1·25
6	24	10c. blue	18·00	30
7	24	12c. purple on yellow	18·00	9·00
8	24	20c. purple and olive	25·00	1·50
9	24	25c. purple	12·00	15·00
11	24	30c. purple and orange	50·00	9·00
12b	24	50c. black on green	55·00	5·50
13	24	$1 purple and blue on blue	85·00	2·50
14	24	$2 red and black	£225	75·00
15	24	$3 green and purple	£1000	£250
16	24	$5 green and red on green	£375	£325
17	24	$10 purple and black on red	£950	£650

BRITISH POST OFFICES IN CRETE

Pt. 1

40 paras = 1 piastre.

B1

1898

B1	B1	20pa. violet	£450	£225

B2

1898

B2	B2	10pa. blue	10·00	24·00
B4	B2	10pa. brown	11·00	32·00
B3	B2	20pa. green	19·00	22·00
B5	B2	20pa. red	20·00	19·00

BRITISH POST OFFICES IN SIAM

Pt. 1

Used at Bangkok.

100 cents = 1 dollar.

1882. Stamps of Straits Settlements optd **B** on issue of 1867.

1	19	32c. on 2a. yellow	£35000

1882. On issues of 1867 to 1883.

14	5	2c. brown	£700	£400
15	5	2c. red	75·00	55·00
13	9	2c. on 32c. red (No. 60)	£3750	£3750
16	5	4c. red	£800	£375
17	5	4c. brown	£100	85·00
4	18	5c. brown	£450	£500
18	18	5c. blue	£350	£200
5	5	6c. lilac	£325	£150
20	5	8c. orange	£225	75·00
21	19	10c. grey	£225	95·00
8	5	12c. blue	£1200	£550
22	5	12c. purple	£375	£170
9	5	24c. green	£800	£170
10	8	30c. red	£45000	£30000
11	9	96c. grey	£7500	£3000

BRITISH POSTAL AGENCIES IN EASTERN ARABIA

Pt. 1

British stamps surcharged for use in parts of the Persian Gulf.

The stamps were used in Muscat from 1 April 1948 to 29 April 1966; in Dubai from 1 April 1948 to 6 January 1961; In Qatar: Doho from February 1956 to 31 March 1957; and in Abu Dhabi from 30 March 1963 (Das Island from December 1960) to 29 March 1964.

Nos 21/2 were placed on sale in Kuwait Post Offices in 1951 and from February to November 1953 due to shortages of stamps "KUWAIT" overprinted. Isolated examples of other values can be found comercially used from Bahrain and Kuwait.

1948. 12 pies = 1 anna; 16 annas = 1 rupee.
1957. 100 naya paise = 1 rupee.

Stamps of Great Britain surch in Indian currency.

1948. King George VI.

16	128	½a. on ½d. green	3·00	8·50
35	128	½a. on ½d. orange	1·00	9·00
17	128	1a. on 1d. red	3·00	30
36	128	1a. on 1d. blue	40	7·50
18	128	1½a. on 1½d. brown	17·00	8·00
37	128	1½a. on 1½d. green	19·00	42·00
19	128	2a. on 2d. orange	2·00	3·25
38	128	2a. on 2d. brown	40	8·50
20	128	2½a. on 2½d. blue	3·50	8·50
39	128	2½a. on 2½d. red	40	16·00
21	128	3a. on 3d. violet	3·50	10
40	129	4a. on 4d. blue	1·25	3·50
22	129	6a. on 6d. purple	4·25	10
23	130	1r. on 1s. brown	5·00	60
24	131	2r. on 2s.6d. green	12·00	50·00

1948. Royal Silver Wedding.

25	137	2½a. on 2½d. blue	2·75	5·00
26	138	15r. on £1 blue	25·00	35·00

1948. Olympic Games.

27	139	2½a. on 2½d. blue	45	2·50
28	140	3a. on 3d. violet	55	2·50
29	-	6a. on 6d. purple	65	2·75
30	-	1r. on 1s. brown	1·40	4·00

1949. 75th Anniv of U.P.U.

31	143	2½a. on 2½d. blue	60	3·00
32	144	3a. on 3d. violet	60	4·00
33	-	6a. on 6d. purple	60	2·75
34	-	1r. on 1s. brown	2·25	7·00

1951. Pictorial.

41	147	2r. on 2s.6d. green	45·00	7·50

1952. Queen Elizabeth.

42	154	½a. on ½d. orange	10	2·25
43	154	1a. on 1d. blue	10	2·25
44	154	1½a. on 1½d. green	10	2·25
45	154	2a. on 2d. brown	20	10
46	155	2½a. on 2½d. red	10	10
47	155	3a. on 3d. lilac	20	1·25
48	155	4a. on 4d. blue	2·75	4·00
49	157	6a. on 6d. purple	35	10
50	160	12a. on 1s.3d. green	8·50	30
51	160	1r. on 1s.6d. blue	2·25	10

1953. Coronation.

52	161	2½a. on 2½d. red	1·75	4·00
53	-	4a. on 4d. blue	1·75	1·00
54	163	12a. on 1s.3d. green	3·50	1·00
55	-	1r. on 1s.6d. blue	3·50	50

1955. Pictorials.

56	166	2r. on 2s.6d. green	10·00	70
57	-	5r. on 5s. red	10·00	2·25

1957. Value in naye paise. Queen Elizabeth II stamps surch **NP** twice (once only on 75n.p.) and value.

79	157	1n.p. on 5d. brown	10	20
80	154	3n.p. on ½d. orange	55	80
81	154	5n.p. on 1d. blue	1·75	4·00
67	154	6n.p. on 1d. red	20	2·75
68	154	9n.p. on 1½d. green	1·00	2·50
83	154	10n.p. on 1½d. green	1·00	2·75
69	154	12n.p. on 2d. brown	30	2·75
85	155	15n.p. on 2½d. red	25	10
71	155	20n.p. on 3d. lilac	20	10
72	155	25n.p. on 4d. blue	70	9·50
87	155	30n.p. on 4½d. green	40	50
73	157	40n.p. on 6d. purple	30	10
89	158	50n.p. on 9d. bronze	1·25	2·50
75	160	75n.p. on 1s.3d. green	3·25	40
91	159	1r. on 1s.6d. blue	30·00	9·50
92	166	2r. on 2s.6d. brown	15·00	55·00
93	166	5r. on 5s. red	30·00	65·00

DESIGN: No. 93 Caernarvon Castle.

1957. World Scout Jubilee Jamboree.

76	170	15n.p. on 2½d. red	35	85
77	171	25n.p. on 4d. blue	35	85
78	-	75n.p. on 3d. green	40	85

BRITISH VIRGIN ISLANDS

Pt. 1

A group of the Leeward Islands, Br. W. Indies. Used general issues for Leeward Islands concurrently with Virgin Islands stamps until 1 July 1956. A Crown Colony.

1951. 100 cents = 1 West Indian dollar.
1962. 100 cents = 1 U.S. dollar.

1 St. Ursula　2　3

4

1866

1	1	1d. green	48·00	60·00
16	3	4d. red	45·00	60·00
7	2	6d. red	60·00	90·00
11	4	1s. black and red	£275	£375

No. 11 has a double-lined frame.

1867. With heavy coloured border.

19	4	1s. black and red	75·00	85·00

6

1880

26	6	½d. yellow	85·00	85·00
27	6	½d. green	6·50	14·00
24	6	1d. green	75·00	90·00
29	6	1d. red	40·00	42·00
25	6	2½d. brown	£120	£130
31	6	2½d. blue	2·75	16·00

1887

32	1	1d. red	3·75	9·00
35	3	4d. brown	35·00	65·00
39	2	6d. violet	19·00	50·00
41	4	1s. brown	45·00	70·00

1888. No. 18 surch **4D**.

42		4d. on 1s. black and red	£140	£160

8

1899

43	8	½d. green	3·75	55
44	8	1d. red	5·50	2·50
45	8	2½d. blue	12·00	2·75
46	8	4d. brown	4·25	19·00
47	8	6d. violet	7·00	3·00
48	8	7d. green	13·00	6·00
49	8	1s. yellow	23·00	35·00
50	8	5s. blue	80·00	85·00

9

1904

54	9	½d. purple and green	1·00	40
55	9	1d. purple and red	2·50	35
56	9	2d. purple and brown	7·50	3·50
57	9	2½d. purple and blue	3·25	2·00
58	9	3d. purple and black	4·50	2·50
59	9	6d. purple and brown	3·50	2·50
60	9	1s. green and red	6·00	5·00
61	9	2s.6d. green and black	38·00	55·00
62	9	5s. green and blue	48·00	70·00

11

1913

69	11	½d. green	3·75	6·00
70a	11	1d. red	2·25	14·00
71	11	2d. grey	6·00	28·00

72	11	2½d. blue	7·50	9·00
73	11	3d. purple on yellow	2·75	6·50
74	11	6d. purple	8·50	18·00
75	11	1s. black on green	3·25	9·00
76	11	2s.6d. black and red on blue	50·00	55·00
77	11	5s. green and red on yellow	45·00	£130

1917. Optd WAR STAMP
| 78c | | 1d. red | 1·50 | 3·75 |
| 79a | | 3d. purple on yellow | 4·00 | 18·00 |

14

1922
86	14	½d. green	85	2·75
87	14	1d. red	60	60
88	14	1d. violet	1·25	5·50
91	14	1½d. red	2·00	1·50
92	14	2d. grey	1·25	6·00
94	14	2½d. orange	1·25	1·75
95	14	2½d. blue	13·00	3·50
96	14	3d. purple on yellow	2·25	11·00
97	14	5d. purple and olive	5·50	45·00
98	14	6d. purple	1·75	6·50
101	14	5s. green and red on yellow	19·00	70·00

1935. Silver Jubilee. As T 13 of Antigua.
103		1d. blue and red	1·25	8·50
104		1½d. blue and grey	1·25	7·50
105		2½d. brown and blue	3·75	7·00
106		1s. grey and purple	19·00	38·00

1937. Coronation. As T 2 of Aden.
107		1d. red	1·00	3·25
108		1½d. brown	75	3·00
109		2½d. blue	60	1·50

15 King George VI and Badge of Colony

1938
110a	15	½d. green	1·50	1·00
111a	15	1d. red	2·50	1·75
112a	15	1½d. brown	2·75	1·75
113a	15	2d. grey	2·75	1·75
114a	15	2½d. blue	3·50	2·75
115a	15	3d. orange	2·25	1·00
116a	15	6d. mauve	6·00	2·25
117a	15	1s. brown	4·50	2·25
118a	15	2s.6d. brown	17·00	5·50
119a	15	5s. red	17·00	6·50
120	15	10s. blue	9·00	10·00
121	15	£1 black	11·00	24·00

1946. Victory. As T 9 of Aden.
| 122 | | 1½d. brown | 10 | 10 |
| 123 | | 3d. orange | 10 | 60 |

1949. Silver Wedding. As T 10/11 of Aden.
| 124 | | 2½d. blue | 10 | 10 |
| 125 | | £1 grey | 16·00 | 21·00 |

1949. 75th Anniv of U.P.U. As T 20/23 of Antigua.
126		2½d. blue	30	2·50
127		3d. orange	1·50	2·50
128		6d. mauve	45	50
129		1s. olive	35	50

1951. Inauguration of B.W.I. University College. As T 24/25 of Antigua.
| 130 | | 3c. black and red | 40 | 2·50 |
| 131 | | 12c. black and violet | 60 | 1·75 |

16 Map

1951. Restoration of Legislative Council.
132	16	6c. orange	50	1·50
133	16	12c. purple	1·00	50
134	16	24c. olive	70	1·00
135	16	$1.20 red	2·75	1·00

18 Map of Jost Van Dyke

1952
136	-	1c. black	80	3·75
137	18	2c. green	70	30
138	-	3c. black and brown	80	2·50
139	-	4c. red	70	2·75
140	-	5c. red and black	1·50	50
141	-	8c. blue	1·00	2·00
142	-	12c. violet	1·00	2·00
143	-	24c. brown	70	50
144	-	60c. green and blue	5·00	11·00
145	-	$1.20 black and blue	5·50	12·00
146	-	$2.40 green and brown	16·00	18·00
147	-	$4.80 blue and red	20·00	20·00

DESIGNS—VERT: 1c. Sombrero lighthouse; 24c. Badge of Presidency. HORIZ—VIEWS: 3c. Sheep industry; 5c. Cattle industry; 60c. Dead Man's Chest (Is); $1.20, Sir Francis Drake Channel; $2.40, Road Town. HORIZ—MAPS: 4c. Anegada Island; 8c. Virgin Gorda Island; 12c. Tortola Island; $4.80, Virgin Islands.

1953. Coronation. As T 13 of Aden.
| 148 | | 2c. black and green | 30 | 1·25 |

29 Map of Tortola
30 Virgin Island Sloop

1956
149	29	½c. black and purple	1·25	30
150	-	1c. turquoise and slate	1·50	1·25
151	-	2c. red and black	30	10
152	-	3c. blue and olive	30	30
153	-	4c. brown and turquoise	70	30
154	-	5c. black	50	10
155	-	8c. orange and blue	2·00	40
156	-	12c. blue and red	4·00	75
157	-	24c. green and brown	1·00	65
158	-	60c. blue and orange	8·50	8·00
159	-	$1.20 green and red	4·50	10·00
160	30	$2.40 yellow and purple	45·00	14·00
161	-	$4.80 sepia and turquoise	45·00	14·00

DESIGNS—HORIZ: As Type 29: 1c. Virgin Islands sloop; 2c. Nelthrop Red Poll bull; 3c. Road Harbour; 4c. Mountain travel; 5c. Badge of the Presidency; 8c. Beach scene; 12c. Boat launching; 24c. White cedar tree; 60c. Skipjack tuna ("Bonito"); $1.20, Treasury Square Coronation celebrations. As Type 30: $4.80, Magnificent frigate bird ("Man-o'-War Bird").

1962. New Currency. Nos. 149/53, 155/61 surch in U.S. Currency.
162	29	1c. on ½c. black and purple	30	20
163	-	2c. on 1c. turq & vio	1·75	15
164	-	3c. on 2c. red and black	70	15
165	-	4c. on 3c. blue and olive	30	15
166	-	5c. on 4c. brown & turq	30	15
167	-	8c. on 8c. orange and blue	30	15
168	-	10c. on 12c. blue and red	2·00	15
169	-	12c. on 24c. green & brn	30	15
170	-	25c. on 60c. blue and orange	2·75	45
171	-	70c. on $1.20 green and red	35	45
172	30	$1.40 on $2.40 yellow and purple	9·50	4·50
173	-	$2.80 on $4.80 sepia & turq	9·50	4·50

1963. Freedom from Hunger. As T 28 of Aden.
| 174 | | 25c. violet | 20 | 10 |

1963. Centenary of Red Cross. As T 33 of Antigua.
| 175 | | 2c. red and black | 15 | 20 |
| 176 | | 25c. red and blue | 50 | 20 |

1964. 400th Birth Anniv of Shakespeare. As T 34 of Antigua.
| 177 | | 10c. blue | 20 | 10 |

43 Skipjack Tuna
44 Soper's Hole

1964
178	43	1c. blue and olive	30	2·00
179	44	2c. olive and red	15	30
180	44	3c. sepia and turquoise	4·75	2·50
181	-	4c. black and red	80	3·00

182	-	5c. black and green	1·75	2·25
183	-	6c. black and orange	30	85
184	-	8c. black and mauve	30	50
185	-	10c. lake and lilac	6·00	1·00
186	-	12c. green and blue	2·50	3·25
187	-	15c. green and black	1·50	2·75
188	-	25c. green and purple	11·00	2·50
189	-	70c. black and brown	4·25	8·50
190	-	$1 green and brown	3·00	2·50
191	-	$1.40 blue and red	24·00	12·00
192	-	$2.80 black and purple	26·00	13·00

DESIGNS—HORIZ (As Type 43): 2c. Soper's Hole; 3c. Brown pelican; 4c. Dead Man's Chest; 5c. Road Harbour; 6c. Fallen Jerusalem; 8c. The Baths, Virgin Gorda; 10c. Map of Virgin Islands; 12c. Youth of Tortola (Tortola–St Thomas ferry); 15c. The Towers, Tortola; 25c. Beef Island Airfield. VERT (As Type 44): $1 Virgin Gorda: $1.40, Yachts at anchor. (27½×37½ mm): $2.80, Badge of the Colony.

1965. Centenary of I.T.U. As T 36 of Antigua.
| 193 | | 4c. yellow and turquoise | 20 | 10 |
| 194 | | 25c. blue and buff | 45 | 20 |

1965. I.C.Y. As T 37 of Antigua.
| 195 | | 1c. purple and turquoise | 10 | 10 |
| 196 | | 25c. green and lavender | 30 | 15 |

1966. Churchill Commemoration. As T 38 of Antigua.
197		1c. blue	10	40
198		2c. green	40	40
199		10c. brown	90	10
200		25c. violet	1·40	25

1966. Royal Visit. As T 39 of Antigua.
| 201 | | 4c. black and blue | 40 | 10 |
| 202 | | 70c. black and mauve | 1·40 | 45 |

58 Atrato I (paddle-steamer), 1866

1966. Stamp Centenary. Multicoloured.
203		5c. Type 58	35	10
204		10c. 1d. and 6d. stamps of 1866	35	10
205		25c. Mail transport, Beef Island, and 6d. stamp of 1866	55	10
206		60c. Landing mail at Roadtown, 1866 and 1d. stamp of 1866	1·00	2·50

1966. Nos. 189 and 191/2 surch.
207	44	50c. on 70c. blk & brn	1·25	90
208	-	$1.50 on $1.40 blue and red	2·25	2·00
209	-	$3 on $2.80 black and purple	2·25	2·75

1966. 20th Anniv of UNESCO. As T 54/6 of Antigua.
210		2c. multicoloured	10	10
211		12c. yellow, violet and olive	30	10
212		60c. black, purple and orange	1·00	45

63 Map of Virgin Islands

1967. New Constitution.
213	63	2c. multicoloured	10	10
214	63	10c. multicoloured	15	10
215	63	25c. multicoloured	15	10
216	63	$1 multicoloured	55	40

64 Mercury (cable ship) and Bermuda–Tortola Link

1967. Inauguration of Bermuda–Tortola Telephone Service. Multicoloured.
217		4c. Type 64	30	10
218		10c. Chalwell Telecommunications Station	20	10
219		50c. Mercury (cable ship)	60	30

67 Blue Marlin

1968. Game Fishing. Multicoloured.
220		2c. Type 67	10	1·25
221		10c. Cobia	25	10
222		25c. Wahoo	55	10
223		40c. Fishing launch and map	85	85

1968. Human Rights Year. Nos. 185 and 188 optd 1968 INTERNATIONAL YEAR FOR HUMAN RIGHTS.
| 224 | | 10c. lake and lilac | 20 | 10 |
| 225 | | 25c. green and purple | 30 | 40 |

72 Dr. Martin Luther King, Bible, Sword and Armour Gauntlet

1968. Martin Luther King Commemoration.
| 226 | 72 | 4c. multicoloured | 25 | 20 |
| 227 | 72 | 25c. multicoloured | 40 | 40 |

73 de Havilland Canada DH-6 Twin Otter 100

1968. Opening of Beef Island Airport Extension. Multicoloured.
228		2c. Type 73	25	1·25
229		10c. Hawker Siddeley H.S.748 airliner	40	10
230		25c. de Havilland Canada DH-114 Heron 2 airplane	45	10
231		$1 Royal Engineers' cap badge	50	2·00

77 Long John Silver and Jim Hawkins

1969. 75th Death Anniv of Robert Louis Stevenson. Scenes from Treasure Island.
232	77	4c. blue, yellow and red	20	15
233	-	10c. multicoloured	20	10
234	-	40c. brown, black and blue	25	30
235	-	$1 multicoloured	45	1·00

DESIGNS—HORIZ: 10c. Jim Hawkins escaping from the pirates; $1 Treasure trove. VERT: 40c. The fight with Israel Hands.

82 Yachts in Road Harbour, Tortola

1969. Tourism. Multicoloured.
236		2c. Tourist and yellow-finned grouper (fish)	15	50
237		10c. Type 82	30	10
238		20c. Sun-bathing at Virgin Gorda National Park	40	20
239		$1 Tourist and Pipe Organ cactus at Virgin Gorda	90	1·50

Nos. 236 and 239 are vert.

85 Carib Canoe

1970
240	85	½c. buff, brown and sepia	10	1·50
241	-	1c. blue and green	15	75
242	-	2c. orange, brown and slate	40	1·00
243	-	3c. red, blue and sepia	30	1·25
244	-	4c. turquoise, blue & brn	30	50
245	-	5c. green, pink and black	30	10
246	-	6c. violet, mauve and green	40	2·25
247	-	8c. green, yellow and sepia	50	6·00
248	-	10c. blue and brown	50	15
249	-	12c. yellow, red and brown	65	1·50
250	-	15c. green, orange and brown	6·00	85
251	-	25c. green, blue and purple	4·00	1·75

252	-	50c. mauve, green and brown	3·25	1·50
253	-	$1 salmon, green and brown	4·00	3·75
254	-	$2 buff, slate and grey	8·50	7·00
255	-	$3 ochre, blue and sepia	2·75	4·50
256	-	$5 violet and grey	2·75	5·00

DESIGNS: 1c. *Santa Maria* (Columbus's flagship); 2c. *Elizabeth Bonaventure* (Drake's flagship); 3c. Dutch buccaneer, c. 1660; 4c. *Thetis*, 1827 (after etching by E. W. Cooke); 5c. Henry Morgan's ship (17th-century); 6c. H.M.S. *Boreas* (Captain Nelson, 1784); 8c. H.M.S. *Eclair*, 1804; 10c. H.M.S. *Formidable*, 1782; 12c. H.M.S. *Nymph*, 1778; 15c. *Windsor Castle* (sailing packet) engaging *Jeune Richard* (French brig), 1807; 25c. H.M.S. *Astrea*, 1808; 50c. Wreck of R.M.S. *Rhone*, 1867; $1 Tortola sloop; $2 H.M.S. *Frobisher*; $3 *Booker Viking* (cargo liner), 1967; $5 Hydrofoil *Sun Arrow*.

102 *A Tale of Two Cities*

1970. Death Centenary of Charles Dickens.

257	**102**	5c. black, red and grey	25	1·00
258	-	10c. black, blue and green	35	10
259	-	25c. black, green and yellow	50	25

DESIGNS: 10c. *Oliver Twist*; 25c. *Great Expectations*.

103 Hospital Visit

1970. Centenary of British Red Cross. Multicoloured.

260	4c. Type **103**	20	45
261	10c. First Aid class	20	10
262	25c. Red Cross and coat of arms	50	55

104 Mary Read

1970. Pirates. Multicoloured.

263	½c. Type **104**	10	15
264	10c. George Lowther	30	10
265	30c. Edward Teach (Blackbeard)	60	25
266	60c. Henry Morgan	80	1·00

105 Children and "UNICEF"

1971. 25th Anniv of UNICEF.

267	**105**	15c. multicoloured	10	10
268	**105**	30c. multicoloured	20	25

1972. Royal Visit of Princess Margaret. Nos 244 and 251 optd **VISIT OF H.R.H. THE PRINCESS MARGARET 1972 1972**.

269	4c. blue, light blue and brown	40	15
270	25c. green, blue and plum	60	45

107 Seaman of 1800

1972. "Interpex" Stamp Exhibition, New York. Naval Uniforms. Multicoloured.

271	½c. Type **107**	10	40
272	10c. Boatswain, 1787–1807	35	10
273	30c. Captain, 1795–1812	85	55
274	60c. Admiral, 1787–95	1·25	2·75

1972. Royal Silver Wedding. As T **52** of Ascension, but with sailfish and *Sir Winston Churchill* (cadet schooner) in background.

275	15c. blue	25	15
276	25c. blue	25	15

109 Blue Marlin

1972. Game Fish. Multicoloured.

277	½c. Type **109**	15	1·40
278	½c. Wahoo	15	1·40
279	15c. Yellow-finned tuna ("Allison tuna")	65	25
280	25c. White marlin	75	30
281	50c. Sailfish	1·25	1·50
282	$1 Dolphin	2·00	2·50
MS283	194×158 mm. Nos. 277/82	8·50	8·50

110 J. C. Lettsom

1973. "Interpex 1973" (Quakers). Multicoloured.

284	½c. Type **110**	10	15
285	10c. Lettsom House (horiz)	15	10
286	15c. Dr. W. Thornton	20	10
287	30c. Dr. Thornton and Capitol, Washington (horiz)	25	20
288	$1 William Penn (horiz)	60	1·10

111 Green-throated Carib and Antillean Crested Hummingbird

1973. First Issue of Coinage. Coins and local scenery. Multicoloured.

289	1c. Type **111**	10	30
290	5c. "Zenaida Dove" (5c. coin)	60	10
291	10c. "Ringed Kingfisher" (10c. coin)	75	10
292	25c. "Mangrove Cuckoo" (25c. coin)	95	15
293	50c. "Brown Pelican" (50c. coin)	1·10	1·00
294	$1 "Magnificent Frigate-bird ($1 coin)	1·40	2·00

1973. Royal Wedding. As T **47** of Anguilla. Multicoloured. Background colours given.

301	5c. brown	10	10
302	50c. blue	20	20

112 *Virgin and Child* (Pintoricchio)

1973. Christmas. Multicoloured.

303	½c. Type **112**	10	10
304	3c. Virgin and Child (Lorenzo di Credi)	10	10
305	25c. Virgin and Child (Crivelli)	15	10
306	50c. Virgin and Child with St. John (Luini)	30	40

113 Crest of the *Canopus* (French)

1974. "Interpex 1974". Naval Crests. Multicoloured.

307	5c. Type **113**	15	10
308	18c. U.S.S. *Saginaw*	25	25
309	25c. H.M.S. *Rothesay*	25	30
310	50c. H.M.C.S. *Ottawa*	45	60
MS311	196×128 mm. Nos. 307/10	1·25	4·50

114 Christopher Columbus

1974. Historical Figures.

312	**114**	5c. orange and black	20	10
313	-	10c. blue and black	20	10
314	-	25c. violet and black	25	25
315	-	40c. brown and deep brown	45	75
MS316		84×119 mm. Nos. 312/15	1·00	2·25

PORTRAITS: 10c. Sir Walter Raleigh; 25c. Sir Martin Frobisher; 40c. Sir Francis Drake.

115 Atlantic Trumpet Triton

1974. Seashells. Multicoloured.

317	5c. Type **115**	30	15
318	10c. West Indian murex	50	30
319	25c. Bleeding tooth	60	35
320	75c. Virgin Islands latirus	1·25	2·25
MS321	146×95 mm. Nos. 317/20	3·00	6·50

116 Churchill and St. Mary, Aldermanbury, London

1974. Birth Centenary of Sir Winston Churchill. Multicoloured.

322	10c. Type **116**	15	10
323	50c. St. Mary, Fulton, Missouri	35	50
MS324	141×108 mm. Nos. 322/3	80	1·40

117 H.M.S. *Boreas*

1975. "Interpex 1975" Stamp Exhibition, New York. Ships' Figure-heads. Multicoloured.

325	5c. Type **117**	20	10
326	18c. *Golden Hind*	50	15
327	40c. H.M.S. *Superb*	50	25
328	85c. H.M.S. *Formidable*	1·00	1·50
MS329	192×127 mm. Nos. 325/8	1·75	8·00

118 Rock Beauty

1975. Fish. Multicoloured.

330	½c. Type **118**	15	50
331	1c. Long-spined squirrelfish	40	2·75
332	3c. Queen triggerfish	1·00	2·75
333	5c. Blue angelfish	30	20
334	8c. Stoplight parrotfish	30	25
335	10c. Queen angelfish	30	25
336	12c. Nassau grouper	40	30
337	13c. Blue tang	40	30
338	15c. Sergeant major	40	35
339	18c. Spotted jewfish	80	1·50
340	20c. Bluehead wrasse	60	80
341	25c. Grey angelfish	1·00	60
342	50c. Glass-eyed snapper	1·25	2·25
343	$1 Blue chromis	1·75	1·75
344	$2.50 French angelfish	2·00	4·50
345	$3 Queen parrotfish	2·50	4·50
346	$5 Four-eyed butterflyfish	2·75	6·00

119 St. George's Parish School (first meeting-place, 1950)

1975. 25th Anniv of Restoration of Legislative Council. Multicoloured.

347	5c. Type **119**	10	10
348	25c. Legislative Council Building	20	10
349	40c. Mace and gavel	25	15
350	75c. Commemorative scroll	35	65

120 Copper Mine Point

1976. Historic Sites. Multicoloured.

351	5c. Type **120**	10	10
352	18c. Pleasant Valley	20	10
353	50c. Callwood Distillery	40	30
354	75c. The Dungeon	60	65

121 Massachusetts Brig *Hazard*

1976. Bicentenary of American Revolution. Multicoloured.

355	8c. Type **121**	30	15
356	22c. American privateer *Spy*	45	20
357	40c. *Raleigh* (American frigate)	55	60
358	75c. Frigate *Alliance* and H.M.S. *Trepassy*	80	1·25
MS359	114×89 mm. Nos. 355/8	2·25	11·00

122 Government House, Tortola

1976. Fifth Anniv of Friendship Day with U.S. Virgin Islands. Multicoloured.

360	8c. Type **122**	10	10
361	15c. Government House, St. Croix (vert)	10	10
362	30c. Flags (vert)	15	10
363	75c. Government seals	50	40

123 Royal Visit, 1966

1977. Silver Jubilee. Multicoloured.

364	8c. Type **123**	10	10
365	30c. The Holy Bible	15	15
366	60c. Presentation of Holy Bible	25	40

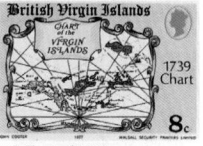

124 Chart of 1739

1977. 18th-century Maps. Multicoloured.

367	8c. Type **124**	40	10
368	22c. French map, 1758	55	30
369	30c. Map from English and Danish surveys, 1775	65	65
370	75c. Map of 1779	85	1·50

1977. Royal Visit. As Nos. 364/6 inscr "SILVER JUBILEE ROYAL VISIT".

371	5c. Type **123**	10	10
372	25c. The Holy Bible	20	10
373	50c. Presentation of Holy Bible	35	25

125 Divers
checking
Equipment

1978. Tourism. Multicoloured.
374	½c. Type **125**		10	10
375	5c. Cup coral on wreck of *Rhone*		20	10
376	8c. Sponge formation on wreck of *Rhone*		25	10
377	22c. Cup coral and sponges		45	15
378	30c. Sponges inside cave		60	20
379	75c. Marine life		90	85

126 Fire Coral

1978. Corals. Multicoloured.
380	8c. Type **126**		25	15
381	15c. Staghorn coral		40	30
382	40c. Brain coral		75	85
383	75c. Elkhorn coral		1·50	1·60

127 Iguana

1978. 25th Anniv of Coronation.
384	-	50c. brown, green and silver	20	40
385	-	50c. multicoloured	20	40
386	**127**	50c. brown, green and silver	20	40

DESIGNS: No. 384, Plantagenet Falcon; 385, Queen Elizabeth II.

128 Lignum Vitae

1978. Flowering Trees. Multicoloured.
387	8c. Type **128**		15	10
388	22c. Ginger Thomas		20	15
389	40c. Dog almond		30	20
390	75c. White cedar		45	70
MS391	131×95 mm. Nos. 387/90		1·00	3·00

129 *Eurema lisa*

1978. Butterflies. Multicoloured.
392	5c. Type **129**		25	10
393	22c. *Agraulis vanillae*		40	20
394	30c. *Heliconius charithonia*		1·10	30
395	75c. *Hemiargus hanno*		1·40	1·25
MS396	159×113 mm. No. 392×6 and No. 393×3		2·00	5·50

130 Spiny Lobster

1978. Wildlife Conservation. Multicoloured.
397	5c. Type **130**		15	10
398	15c. Large iguana (vert)		25	10
399	22c. Hawksbill turtle		40	15
400	75c. Black coral (vert)		75	90
MS401	130×153 mm. Nos. 397/400		1·40	3·75

131 Strawberry
Cactus

1979. Native Cacti. Multicoloured.
402	½c. Type **131**		10	10
403	5c. Snowy cactus		15	10
404	13c. Barrel cactus		20	20
405	22c. Tree cactus		25	35
406	30c. Prickly pear		30	40
407	75c. Dildo cactus		40	1·00

132 West Indian Girl

1979. International Year of the Child. Multicoloured.
408	5c. Type **132**		10	10
409	10c. African boy		10	10
410	13c. Asian girl		10	10
411	$1 European boy		50	85
MS412	91×114 mm. Nos. 408/11		70	1·50

133 1956 Road
Harbour 3c.
Definitive Stamp

1979. Death Centenary of Sir Rowland Hill.
413	**133**	5c. dp blue, blue & green	10	10
414	-	13c. blue and mauve	10	10
415	-	75c. blue and purple	45	50
MS416	37×91 mm. $1 blue and red		70	1·25

DESIGNS (39×27 mm)—13c. 1880 2½d. red-brown; 75c. Great Britain 1910 unissued 2d. Tyrian plum. (40×28 mm)—$1 1867 1s. "Missing Virgin" error.

134 Pencil Urchin

1979. Marine Life. Multicoloured.
417	½c. Calcified algae		40	2·75
418	1c. Purple-tipped sea anemone		55	2·75
419	3c. Common starfish		1·00	2·75
420	5c. Type **134**		1·25	2·25
421	8c. Atlantic trumpet triton		1·25	1·75
422	10c. Christmas tree worms		30	1·25
423a	13c. Flamingo Tongue snail		1·50	75
424	15c. Spider crab		40	1·00
425	18c. Sea squirts		2·00	4·25
426	20c. True tulip		55	1·50
427	25c. Rooster-tail conch		1·25	4·00
428	30c. West Indian fighting conch		2·50	1·50
429	60c. Mangrove crab		1·50	3·00
430	$1 Coral polyps		1·25	4·25
431	$2.50 Peppermint shrimp		1·25	4·00
432	$3 West Indian murex		1·25	4·50
433	$5 Carpet anemone		1·75	5·50

135 Rotary Athletics
Meeting, Tortola

1980. 75th Anniv of Rotary International. Multicoloured.
434	8c. Type **135**		10	10
435	22c. Paul P. Harris (founder)		15	10
436	60c. Mount Saga, Tortola ("Creation of National Park")		30	40

437	$1 Rotary anniversary emblem		55	75
MS438	149×148 mm. Nos. 434/7		1·00	3·75

136 Brown Booby

1980. "London 1980" International Stamp Exhibition. Birds. Multicoloured.
439	20c. Type **136**		20	20
440	25c. Magnificent frigate bird		25	25
441	50c. White-tailed tropic bird		40	40
442	75c. Brown pelican		55	55
MS443	152×130 mm. Nos. 439/42		1·25	2·25

1980. Caribbean Commonwealth Parliamentary Association Meeting, Tortola. Nos. 414/15 optd **CARIBBEAN COMMONWEALTH PARLIAMENTARY ASSOCIATION MEETING TORTOLA 11–19 JULY 1980.**
444	13c. blue and red		15	10
445	75c. deep blue and blue		40	40

138 Sir Francis
Drake

1980. Sir Francis Drake Commemoration. Multicoloured.
446	8c. Type **138**		60	10
447	15c. Queen Elizabeth I		80	15
448	30c. Drake receiving knighthood		1·00	30
449	75c. *Golden Hind* and coat of arms		1·90	1·25
MS450	171×121 mm. Nos. 446/9		3·75	6·50

139 Jost Van Dyke

1980. Island Profiles. Multicoloured.
451	2c. Type **139**		10	10
452	5c. Peter Island		10	10
453	13c. Virgin Gorda		15	10
454	22c. Anegada		20	10
455	30c. Norman Island		25	15
456	$1 Tortola		70	1·00
MS457	95×88 mm. No. 456		85	1·50

140 Dancing Lady

1981. Flowers. Multicoloured.
458	5c. Type **140**		10	10
459	20c. Love in the mist		15	15
460	22c. *Pitcairnia angustifolia*		15	15
461	75c. Dutchman's pipe		35	65
462	$1 Maiden apple		35	80

141 Wedding
Bouquet from
British Virgin
Islands

1981. Royal Wedding. Multicoloured.
463	10c. Type **141**		10	10
464	35c. Prince Charles and Queen Elizabeth the Queen Mother in Garter robes		20	15

465	$1.25 .25 Prince Charles and Lady Diana Spencer		60	80

142 Stamp
Collecting

1981. 25th Anniv of Duke of Edinburgh Award Scheme. Multicoloured.
466	10c. Type **142**		10	10
467	15c. Athletics		10	10
468	50c. Camping		25	25
469	$1 Duke of Edinburgh		40	45

143 "Development through
Education"

1981. International Year for Disabled Persons. Multicoloured.
470	15c. Type **143**		15	15
471	20c. Fort Charlotte Children's Centre		15	20
472	30c. "Developing cultural awareness"		20	30
473	$1 Fort Charlotte Children's Centre (different)		60	1·25

144 Detail from
*The Adoration of
the Shepherds*
(Rubens)

1981. Christmas.
474	**144**	5c. multicoloured	15	10
475	-	15c. multicoloured	25	10
476	-	30c. multicoloured	45	15
477	-	$1 multicoloured	1·10	1·10
MS478	117×90 mm. 50c. multicoloured (horiz)		2·00	1·00

DESIGNS: 15c. to $1 Further details from *The Adoration of the Shepherds* by Rubens.

145
Green-throated
Caribs and
Erythrina

1982. Hummingbirds. Multicoloured.
479	15c. Type **145**		50	15
480	30c. Green-throated carib and bougainvillea		60	45
481	35c. Antillean crested hummingbirds and *granadilla passiflora*		70	55
482	$1.25 Antillean crested hummingbirds and hibiscus		1·75	3·00

146 "People caring for People"

1982. Tenth Anniv of Lions Club of Tortola. Multicoloured.
483	10c. Type **146**		15	10
484	20c. Tortola Headquarters		20	15
485	30c. "We Serve"		25	15
486	$1.50 "Lions" symbol		60	1·00
MS487	124×102 mm. Nos. 483/6		1·75	4·25

147 Princess at Victoria and Albert Museum, November, 1981

1982. 21st Birthday of Princess of Wales. Multicoloured.

488	10c. British Virgin Islands coat of arms	15	10
489	35c. Type **147**	25	15
490	50c. Bride and groom proceeding into Vestry	35	35
491	$1.50 Formal portrait	80	1·10

148 Douglas DC-3

1982. Tenth Anniv of Air BVI. Multicoloured.

492	10c. Type **148**	45	15
493	15c. Britten-Norman BN-2 Islander	60	20
494	60c. Hawker Siddeley H.S.748	1·10	75
495	75c. Runway scene	1·25	90

149 Scouts raising Flag

1982. 75th Anniv of Boy Scout Movement and 50th Anniv of Scouting in B.V.I. Multicoloured.

496	8c. Type **149**	20	10
497	20c. Cub Scout	30	25
498	50c. Sea Scout	40	55
499	$1 First camp, Brownsea Island, and portrait of Lord Baden-Powell	70	1·50

150 Legislature in Session

1983. Commonwealth Day. Multicoloured.

500	10c. Type **150**	10	10
501	30c. Tourism	25	20
502	35c. Satellite view of Earth showing Virgin Islands	25	25
503	75c. B.V.I. and Commonwealth flags	70	90

151 Florence Nightingale

1983. Nursing Week. Multicoloured.

504	10c. Type **151**	60	15
505	30c. Staff nurse and assistant nurse	1·00	45
506	60c. Public Health nurses testing blood pressure (horiz)	1·90	1·25
507	75c. Peebles Hospital (horiz)	1·90	1·75

152 Frame Construction

1983. Traditional Boat-building. Multicoloured.

508	15c. Type **152**	25	25
509	25c. Planking	30	45
510	50c. Launching	50	80
511	$1 Maiden voyage	65	1·75
MS512	127×101 mm. Nos. 508/11	1·50	3·75

153 Grumman G21 Goose Amphibian

1983. Bicentenary of Manned Flight. Multicoloured.

513	10c. Type **153**	20	15
514	30c. Riley Turbo Skyliner	45	45
515	60c. Embraer EMB-110 Bandeirante	65	85
516	$1.25 Hawker Siddeley H.S.748	90	1·60

154 Madonna and Child with the Infant Baptist

1983. Christmas. 500th Birth Anniv of Raphael. Multicoloured.

517	8c. Type **154**	10	10
518	15c. La Belle Jardiniere	20	15
519	50c. Madonna del Granduca	50	60
520	$1 The Terranuova Madonna	90	1·10
MS521	108×101 mm. Nos. 517/20	2·25	3·50

155 Local Tournament

1984. 60th Anniv of International Chess Federation. Multicoloured.

522	10c. Type **155**	1·00	40
523	35c. Staunton king, rook and pawn (vert)	2·00	1·50
524	75c. Karpov's winning position against Jakobsen in 1980 Olympiad (vert)	3·75	4·25
525	$1 B.V.I. Gold Medal won by Bill Hook at 1980 Chess Olympiad	4·25	5·50

156 Port Purcell

1984. 250th Anniv of Lloyd's List (newspaper). Multicoloured.

526	15c. Type **156**	35	30
527	25c. Boeing 747-100	60	50
528	50c. Wreck of Rhone (mail steamer), 1867	1·00	95
529	$1 Booker Viking (cargo liner)	1·75	1·60

157 Mail Ship Boyne, Boeing 747-100 and U.P.U. Logo

1984. Universal Postal Union Congress, Hamburg. Sheet 90×69 mm.

MS530	**157** $1 blue and black	2·25	2·50

158 Running

1984. Olympic Games, Los Angeles. Multicoloured.

531	15c. Type **158**	40	40
532	15c. Runner	40	40
533	20c. Wind-surfing	40	45
534	20c. Surfer	40	45
535	30c. Sailing	45	65
536	30c. Yacht	45	65
MS537	97×69 mm. Torch-bearer	1·50	1·90

159 Steel Band

1984. 150th Anniv of Abolition of Slavery. Multicoloured.

538	10c. Type **159**	30	35
539	10c. Dancing girls	30	35
540	10c. Men in traditional costumes	30	35
541	10c. Girl in traditional costumes	30	35
542	10c. Festival Queen	30	35
543	30c. Green and yellow dinghies	45	50
544	30c. Blue and red dinghies	45	50
545	30c. White and blue dinghies	45	50
546	30c. Red and yellow dinghies	45	50
547	30c. Blue and white dinghies	45	50

DESIGNS: Various aspects of Emancipation Festival.
Nos. 543/7 form a composite design, the sail colours of the dinghies being described.

160 Sloop

1984. Boats. Multicoloured.

548	10c. Type **160**	40	20
549	35c. Fishing boat	60	65
550	60c. Schooner	75	1·25
551	75c. Cargo boat	75	1·60
MS552	125×90 mm. Nos. 548/51	1·50	4·00

161 One Cent Coin and Aerial View

1985. New Coinage. Coins and Local Scenery. Multicoloured.

553	1c. Type **161**	10	10
554	5c. Five cent coin and boulders on beach	10	10
555	10c. Ten cent coin and scuba diving	20	20
556	25c. Twenty-five cent coin and yachts	45	50
557	50c. Fifty cent coin and jetty	90	1·25
558	$1 One dollar coin and beach at night	1·75	2·25
MS559	103×159 mm. Nos. 553/8	3·00	7·00

162 Red-billed Tropic Bird

1985. Birds of the British Virgin Islands. Multicoloured.

560	1c. Type **162**	1·25	2·50
561	2c. Yellow-crowned night heron ("Night Gaulin")	1·25	2·50
562	5c. Mangrove cuckoo ("Rain Bird")	1·75	2·00
563	8c. Northern mockingbird ("Mockingbird")	1·75	3·00
564	10c. Grey kingbird ("Chinchary")	2·00	75
565	12c. Red-necked pigeon ("Wild Pigeon")	2·25	1·50
649	15c. Least bittern ("Bittlin")	2·75	1·50
567	18c. Smooth-billed ani ("Black Witch")	3·00	3·50
651	20c. Clapper rail ("Pond Shakey")	2·75	1·75
652	25c. American kestrel ("Killy-killy")	2·75	1·75
570	30c. Pearly-eyed thrasher ("Thrushie")	2·75	1·75
654	35c. Bridled quail dove ("Marmi Dove")	2·75	1·25
572	40c. Green-backed heron ("Little Gaulin")	3·25	1·75
573	50c. Scaly-breasted ground dove ("Ground Dove")	3·50	3·50
574	60c. Little blue heron ("Blue Gaulin")	4·00	5·00
658	$1 Audubon's shearwater ("Pimleco")	5·00	6·00

163 The Queen Mother at Festival of Remembrance

1985. Life and Times of Queen Elizabeth the Queen Mother. Multicoloured.

580A	10c. At Victoria Palace Theatre, 1984	10	20
582A	25c. Opening Celia Johnson Theatre, 1985	15	40
584A	50c. At the Tate Gallery, 1983	20	70
586A	75c. Unveiling Mountbatten Statue, 1983	25	1·00
MS587A	85×114 mm. $1 At Columbia University; $1 At a Wedding, St. Margaret's, Westminster, 1983	85	4·00
579B	10c. Type **163**	2·75	2·75
581B	25c. At the engagement of the Prince of Wales, 1981	2·75	2·75
583B	50c. The Queen Mother on her 82nd birthday	3·25	3·25
585B	75c. At the Royal Smithfield Show, 1983	3·25	3·25

164 Seaside Sparrow

1985. Birth Bicentenary of John J. Audubon (ornithologist). Designs showing original paintings. Multicoloured.

588	5c. Type **164**	30	20
589	30c. Passenger pigeon	40	70
590	50c. Yellow-breasted chat	45	1·75
591	$1 American kestrel	50	2·75

165 S.V. Flying Cloud

1986. Visiting Cruise Ships. Multicoloured.

592	35c. Type **165**	80	85
593	50c. M.V. Newport Clipper	1·10	1·50
594	75c. M.V. Cunard Countess	1·10	2·50
595	$1 M.V. Sea Goddess	1·25	3·00

1986. Inaugural Flight of Miami–Beef Island Air Service. Nos 581/2 and 585/6 optd **MIAMI B.V.I. INAUGURAL FLIGHT**.

596A	25c. At the engagement of the Prince of Wales, 1981	4·00	6·00
597A	25c. Opening Celia Johnson Theatre, 1985	40	50
598A	75c. At the Royal Smithfield Show, 1983	4·50	8·00
599A	75c. Unveiling Mountbatten statue, 1983	1·25	1·50

167 Queen Elizabeth II in 1958

1986. 60th Birthday of Queen Elizabeth II. Multicoloured.

600	12c. Type **167**	15	20
601	35c. At a Maundy Service	20	45
602	$1.50 Queen Elizabeth	45	1·75
603	$2 During a visit to Canberra, 1982 (vert)	60	2·25
MS604	85×115 mm. $3 Queen with bouquet	3·50	6·00

168 Miss Sarah Ferguson

1986. Royal Wedding. Multicoloured.

605	35c. Type **168**	30	70
606	35c. Prince Andrew and Miss Sarah Ferguson	30	70
607	$1 Prince Andrew in morning dress (horiz)	50	1·25
608	$1 Miss Sarah Ferguson (different) (horiz)	50	1·25
MS609	115×85 mm. $4 Duke and Duchess of York in carriage after wedding (horiz)	2·00	6·00

169 Harvesting Sugar Cane

1986. History of Rum Making. Multicoloured.

610	12c. Type **169**	1·50	45
611	40c. Bringing sugar cane to mill	1·75	1·25
612	60c. Rum distillery	2·25	3·50
613	$1 Delivering barrels of rum to ship	5·50	6·50
MS614	115×84 mm. $2 Royal Navy rum issue	6·50	8·50

170 Sentinel

1986. 20th Anniv of Cable and Wireless Caribbean Headquarters, Tortola. Cable Ships. Multicoloured.

615	35c. Type **170**	60	80
616	35c. Retriever (1961)	60	80
617	60c. Cable Enterprise (1964)	75	1·50
618	60c. Mercury (1962)	75	1·50
619	75c. Recorder (1955)	75	1·75
620	75c. Pacific Guardian (1984)	75	1·75
621	$1 Great Eastern (1860's)	80	2·00
622	$1 Cable Venture (1977)	80	2·00
MS623	Four sheets, each 102×131 mm. (a) 40c. × 2 As 35c. (b) 50c. × 2 As 60c. (c) 80c. × 2 As 75c. (d) $1.50 × 2 As $1 Set of 4 sheets	5·00	12·00

1986. Centenary of Statue of Liberty. T **17** and similar vert views of Statue in separate miniature sheets. Multicoloured.

MS624	Nine sheets, each 85×115 mm. 50c.; 75c.; 90c.; $1; $1.25; $1.50; $1.75; $2; $2.50 Set of 9 sheets	4·25	11·00

172 18th-century Spanish Galleon

1987. Shipwrecks. Multicoloured.

625	12c. Type **172**	2·50	55
626	35c. H.M.S. Astrea (frigate), 1808	3·75	1·40
627	75c. Rhone (mail steamer), 1867	5·50	4·50
628	$1.50 Captain Rokos (freighter), 1929	8·00	11·00
MS629	85×65 mm. $1.50, Volvart, 1819	16·00	15·00

173 Outline Map and Flag of Montserrat

1987. 11th Meeting of Organization of Eastern Caribbean States. Each showing map and flag. Multicoloured.

630	10c. Type **173**	70	70
631	15c. Grenada	80	75
632	20c. Dominica	85	80
633	25c. St. Kitts-Nevis	90	1·00
634	35c. St. Vincent and Grenadines	1·40	1·00
635	50c. British Virgin Islands	2·00	2·50
636	75c. Antigua and Barbuda	2·25	3·25
637	$1 St. Lucia	2·75	3·50

174 Spider Lily

1987. Opening of Botanical Gardens. Multicoloured.

638	12c. Type **174**	80	35
639	35c. Barrel cactus	1·75	1·00
640	$1 Wild plantain	2·75	3·25
641	$1.50 Little butterfly orchid	8·00	8·50
MS642	139×104 mm. $2.50, White cedar	3·75	6·00

175 Early Mail Packet and 1867 1s. Stamp

1987. Bicentenary of Postal Services. Multicoloured.

662	10c. Type **175**	1·75	80
663	20c. Map and 1899 1d. stamp	2·50	1·40
664	35c. Road Town Post Office and Customs House, c. 1913, and 1847 4d. stamp	2·50	1·75
665	$1.50 Piper PA-23 Apache mail plane and 1964 25c. definitive	8·00	11·00
MS666	70×60 mm. $2.50, Mail ship, 1880's, and 1880 1d.	6·00	9·50

1988. 500th Birth Anniv of Titian (artist). As T **238** of Antigua. Multicoloured.

667	10c. Salome	65	55
668	12c. Man with the Glove	70	60
669	20c. Fabrizio Salvaresio	90	80
670	25c. Daughter of Roberto Strozzi	1·00	90
671	40c. Pope Julius II	1·60	2·00
672	50c. Bishop Ludovico Beccadelli	1·75	2·00
673	90c. King Philip II	1·90	2·50
674	$1 Empress Isabella of Portugal	2·50	2·75
MS675	Two sheets, each 110×95 mm. (a) $2 Emperor Charles V at Muhlberg (detail). (b) $2 Pope Paul III and his Grandsons (detail) Set of 2 sheets	17·00	14·00

176 de Havilland Canada DHC-5 Transporter over Sir Francis Drake Channel and Staunton Pawn

1988. First British Virgin Islands Open Chess Tournament. Multicoloured.

676	35c. Type **176**	4·75	1·50
677	$1 Jose Capablanca (former World Champion) and Staunton king	9·50	8·50
MS678	109×81 mm. $2 Chess match	10·00	11·00

177 Hurdling

1988. Olympic Games, Seoul. Multicoloured.

679	12c. Type **177**	35	25
680	20c. Windsurfing	60	45
681	75c. Basketball	3·75	3·25
682	$1 Tennis	3·75	3·75
MS683	71×102 mm. $2 Athletics	3·00	4·50

178 Swimmer ("Don't Swim Alone")

1988. 125th Anniv of International Red Cross.

684	**178**	12c. black, red and blue	1·75	40
685	–	30c. black, red and blue	2·50	80
686	–	60c. black, red and blue	3·75	3·00
687	–	$1 black, red and blue	4·50	4·00
MS688	68×96 mm. 50c. × 4 black and red		5·00	6·50

DESIGNS—HORIZ: 30c. Swimmers ("No swimming during electrical storms"); 60c. Beach picnic ("Don't eat before swimming"); $1 Boat and equipment ("Proper equipment for boating"). VERT: 50c.×4 Recovery position, clearing airway, mouth-to-mouth resuscitation, cardiac massage.

179 Princess Alexandra

1988. Visit of Princess Alexandra. Designs showing different portraits.

689	**179**	40c. multicoloured	2·75	75
690	–	$1.50 multicoloured	6·00	4·75
MS691	102×98 mm. $2 multicoloured		5·50	6·50

180 Brown Pelican in Flight

1988. Wildlife (1st series). Aquatic Birds. Multicoloured.

692	10c. Type **180**	1·60	50
693	12c. Brown pelican perched on post	1·60	55
694	15c. Brown pelican	1·75	1·10
695	35c. Brown pelican swallowing fish	2·75	3·00
MS696	106×76 mm. $2 Common shoveler (horiz)	12·00	9·00

No. **MS**696 is without the W.W.F. logo.

181 Anegada Rock Iguana

1988. Wildlife (2nd series). Endangered Species. Multicoloured.

697	20c. Type **181**	1·50	75
698	40c. Virgin Gorda dwarf gecko	1·75	1·40
699	60c. Hawksbill turtle	2·75	3·50
700	$1 Humpback whale	7·50	8·00
MS701	106×77 mm. $2 Trunk turtle (vert)	7·00	8·50

182 Yachts at Start

1989. Spring Regatta. Multicoloured.

702	12c. Type **182**	45	40
703	40c. Yacht tacking (horiz)	1·00	1·00
704	75c. Yachts at sunset	1·60	2·50
705	$1 Yachts rounding buoy (horiz)	2·00	2·75
MS706	83×69 mm. $2 Yacht under full sail	5·50	7·00

1989. 500th Anniv (1992) of Discovery of America by Columbus (1st issue). Pre-Columbian Arawak Society. As T **247** of Antigua. Multicoloured.

707	10c. Arawak in hammock	70	45
708	20c. Making fire	1·00	50
709	25c. Making implements	1·00	60
710	$1.50 Arawak family	4·50	7·00
MS711	85×70 mm. $2 Religious ceremony	9·00	11·00

See also Nos. 741/5, 793/7 and 818/26.

183 "Apollo II" Emblem

1989. 20th Anniv of First Manned Landing on the Moon. Multicoloured.

712	15c. Type **183**	1·25	60
713	30c. Edwin Aldrin deploying scientific experiments	2·25	1·00
714	65c. Aldrin and U.S. flag on Moon	3·00	4·00
715	$1 "Apollo II" capsule after splashdown	4·00	4·25
MS716	102×77 mm. $2 Neil Armstrong (38×50 mm)	9·50	10·50

184 Black Harry and Nathaniel Gilbert preaching to Slaves

1989. Bicentenary of Methodist Church in British Virgin Islands. Multicoloured.

717	12c. Type **184**	1·00	50
718	25c. Methodist school exercise book	1·40	75
719	35c. East End Methodist Church, 1810	1·60	85
720	$1.25 Reverend John Wesley (founder of Methodism) and church youth choir	3·25	6·50
MS721	100×69 mm. $2 Dr. Thomas Cole	4·75	9·00

185 Player tackling

1989. World Cup Football Championship, Italy, 1990. Multicoloured.

722	5c. Type **185**	80	80
723	10c. Player dribbling ball	80	80
724	20c. Two players chasing ball	1·50	80
725	$1.75 Goalkeeper diving for ball	7·00	7·50
MS726	100×70 mm. $2 British Virgin Islands team captain	8·50	11·00

186 Princess Alexandra and Sunset House

1990. "Stamp World London 90" International Stamp Exhibition. Royal Visitors. Multicoloured.

727	50c. Type **186**	4·50	4·50
728	50c. Princess Margaret and Government House	4·50	4·50
729	50c. Hon. Angus Ogilvy and Little Dix Bay Hotel	4·50	4·50
730	50c. Princess Diana with Princes William and Henry and Necker Island Resort	4·50	4·50
MS731	89×80 mm. $2 Royal Yacht Britannia	15·00	15·00

187 Audubon's Shearwater

1990. Birds. Multicoloured.

732	5c. Type **187**	1·75	1·75
733	12c. Red-necked pigeon	2·25	60
734	20c. Moorhen ("Common Gallinule")	2·50	60
735	25c. Green-backed heron ("Green Heron")	2·50	60
736	40c. Yellow warbler	2·75	1·50
737	60c. Smooth-billed ani	3·00	2·75
738	$1 Antillean crested hummingbird	3·00	3·25
739	$1.25 Black-faced grassquit	3·00	4·50
MS740	Two sheets, each 98×70 mm. (a) $2 Royal tern egg (vert) (b) $2 Red-billed tropicbird egg (vert) Set of 2 sheets	11·00	7·00

1990. 500th Anniv (1992) of Discovery of America by Columbus (2nd issue). New World Natural History–Fishes. As T 260 of Antigua. Multicoloured.

741	10c. Blue tang (horiz)	1·50	60
742	35c. Glass-eyed snapper (horiz)	2·50	70
743	50c. Slippery dick (horiz)	3·00	3·50
744	$1 Porkfish (horiz)	4·50	4·75
MS745	100×70 mm. $2 Yellow-tailed snapper	5·00	6·50

188 Queen Elizabeth the Queen Mother

1990. 90th Birthday of Queen Elizabeth the Queen Mother.

746	**188**	12c. multicoloured	50	25
747	-	25c. multicoloured	90	55
748	-	60c. multicoloured	1·75	2·25
749	-	$1 multicoloured	2·00	2·50
MS750		75×75 mm. $2 multicoloured	2·75	2·75

DESIGNS: 25, 60c., $2 Recent photographs.

189 Footballers

1990. World Cup Football Championship, Italy.

751	**189**	12c. multicoloured	60	40
752	-	20c. multicoloured	90	50
753	-	50c. multicoloured	1·75	2·00
754	-	$1.25 multicoloured	2·50	3·75
MS755		91×76 mm. $2 multicoloured	4·50	4·50

DESIGNS: 20, 50c., $2, Footballers.

190 Judo

1990. Olympic Games, Barcelona (1992). Multicoloured.

756	12c. Type **190**	1·50	45
757	40c. Yachting	2·25	1·60
758	60c. Hurdling	2·75	3·75
759	$1 Show jumping	4·50	4·50
MS760	78×105 mm. $2 Windsurfing	4·50	4·00

191 Tree-fern, Sage Mountain National Park

1991. 30th Anniv of National Parks Trust. Multicoloured.

761	10c. Type **191**	1·00	1·25
762	25c. Coppermine ruins, Virgin Gorda (horiz)	1·75	80
763	35c. Ruined windmill, Mt. Healthy	1·75	80
764	$2 The Baths (rock formation), Virgin Gorda (horiz)	9·50	12·00

192 Haiti Haiti

1991. Flowers. Multicoloured.

765	1c. Type **192**	20	1·50
766	2c. Lobster claw	20	1·50
767	5c. Frangipani	20	1·50
887	10c. Autograph tree	50	1·40
768	12c. Yellow allamanda	40	30
889	15c. Lantana	65	40
771	20c. Jerusalem thorn	50	30
772	25c. Turk's cap	55	40
892	30c. Swamp immortelle	70	50
893	35c. White cedar	85	55
775	40c. Mahoe tree	75	65
895	45c. Pinguin	95	80
896	50c. Christmas orchid	2·25	2·00
778	70c. Lignum vitae	1·10	2·00
779	$1 African tulip tree	1·25	2·00
899	$2 Beach morning glory	3·00	5·50
781	$3 Organ pipe cactus	4·00	7·00
901	$5 Tall ground orchid	8·50	13·00
783	$10 Ground orchid	17·00	22·00

193 Phoebis sennae

1991. Butterflies. Multicoloured.

784	5c. Type **193**	1·00	1·50
785	10c. Dryas iulia	1·25	1·50
786	15c. Junonia evarete	1·75	75
787	20c. Dione vanillae	1·75	1·00
788	25c. Battus polydamus	1·75	1·00
789	30c. Eurema lisa	1·90	1·00
790	35c. Heliconius charitonius	1·90	1·10
791	$1.50 Siproeta stelenes	4·75	7·00
MS792	Two sheets. (a) 77×117 mm. $2 Danaus plexippus (horiz). (b) 117×77 mm. $2 Biblis hyperia (horiz) Set of 2 sheets	14·00	15·00

1991. 500th Anniv (1992) of Discovery of America by Columbus (3rd issue). History of Exploration. As T 277 of Antigua. Multicoloured.

793	12c. multicoloured	2·00	50
794	50c. multicoloured	3·75	2·00
795	75c. multicoloured	4·50	3·25
796	$1 multicoloured	5·00	4·00
MS797	105×76 mm. $2 black and orange	9·50	9·50

DESIGNS—HORIZ: 12c. Vitoria in Pacific (Magellan 1519–21); 50c. La Salle on the Mississippi, 1682; 75c. John Cabot landing in Nova Scotia, 1497–98; $1 Cartier discovering the St. Lawrence, 1534. VERT: $2 Santa Maria (woodcut).

1991. Death Centenary (1990) of Vincent Van Gogh (artist). As T 278 of Antigua. Multicoloured.

798	15c. Cottage with Decrepit Barn and Stooping Woman (horiz)	1·25	50
799	30c. Paul Gauguin's Armchair	1·75	80
800	75c. Breton Women (horiz)	3·00	3·00
801	$1 Vase with Red Gladioli	3·50	3·50
MS802	103×81 mm. $2 Dance Hall in Arles (detail) (horiz)	13·00	14·00

1991. Christmas. Religious Paintings by Quinten Massys. As T 291 of Antigua. Multicoloured.

803	15c. The Virgin and Child Enthroned (detail)	1·25	25
804	30c. The Virgin and Child Enthroned (different detail)	2·00	50
805	60c. Adoration of the Magi (detail)	3·50	3·75
806	$1 Virgin in Adoration	3·75	4·00
MS807	Two sheets, each 102×127 mm. (a) $2 The Virgin standing with Angels. (b) $2 The Adoration of the Magi Set of 2 sheets	16·00	18·00

194 Agaricus bisporus

1992. Fungi. Multicoloured.

808	12c. Type **194**	1·50	55
809	30c. Lentinula edodes (horiz)	2·25	85
810	45c. Hygocybe acutoconica	2·25	1·00
811	$1 Gymnopilus chrysopellus (horiz)	4·00	6·00
MS812	94×68 mm. $2 Pleurotous ostreatus (horiz)	12·00	13·00

1992. 40th Anniv of Queen Elizabeth II's Accession. As T 288 of Antigua. Multicoloured.

813	12c. Little Dix Bay, Virgin Gorda	1·25	30
814	25c. Deadchest Bay, Peter Island	2·75	90
815	60c. Pond Bay, Virgin Gorda	2·75	2·50
816	$1 Cane Garden Bay, Tortola	3·00	3·00
MS817	75×97 mm. $2 Long Bay, Beef Island	9·50	10·00

195 Queen Isabella of Spain

1992. 500th Anniv of Discovery of America by Columbus (4th issue). Multicoloured.

818	10c. Type **195**	90	1·00
819	15c. Fleet of Columbus (horiz)	1·60	1·00
820	20c. Arms awarded to Columbus	1·60	1·25
821	30c. Landing Monument, Watling Island and Columbus's signature (horiz)	1·60	1·00
822	45c. Christopher Columbus	2·25	1·40
823	50c. Landing in New World and Spanish royal standard (horiz)	2·25	2·25
824	70c. Convent at La Rabida	2·50	3·50
825	$1.50 Replica of Santa Maria and Caribbean Pavilion, New York World's Fair (horiz)	3·75	5·50
MS826	Two sheets. (a) 116×86 mm. $2 Ships of second voyage at Virgin, Gorda (horiz). (b) 86×116 mm. $2 De la Cosa's map of New World (horiz) Set of 2 sheets	15·00	17·00

196 Basketball

1992. Olympic Games, Barcelona. Multicoloured.

827	15c. Type **196**	2·50	75
828	30c. Tennis	2·50	90
829	60c. Volleyball	2·75	3·00
830	$1 Football	3·00	3·75
MS831	100×70 mm. $2 Olympic flame	12·00	14·00

197 Issuing Social Security Cheque

1993. 25th Anniv of Ministerial Government. Multicoloured.

832	12c. Type **197**	40	40
833	15c. Map of British Virgin Islands	1·25	70
834	45c. Administration building	80	70
835	$1.30 .30 International currency abbreviations	2·25	4·25

198 Cruising Yacht and Swimmers, The Baths, Virgin Gorda

1993. Tourism. Multicoloured.

836	15c. Type **198**	1·50	50
837	30c. Cruising yacht under sail (vert)	1·75	60
838	60c. Scuba diving	2·50	2·75
839	$1 Cruising yacht at anchor and snorklers (vert)	2·75	3·25
MS840	79×108 mm. $1 Promenade (trimaran) (vert); $1 Scuba diving (different) (vert)	7·50	8·50

1993. 40th Anniv of Coronation. As T 307 of Antigua.

841	12c. multicoloured	90	1·25
842	45c. multicoloured	1·25	1·50
843	60c. grey and black	1·40	1·75
844	$1 multicoloured	1·60	1·90

DESIGNS: 12c. Queen Elizabeth II at Coronation (photograph by Cecil Beaton); 45c. Orb; 60c. Queen with Prince Philip, Queen Mother and Princess Margaret, 1953; $1 Queen Elizabeth II on official visit.

200 Columbus with King Ferdinand and Queen Isabella

1993. 500th Anniv of Discovery of Virgin Islands by Columbus. Multicoloured.

846	3c. Type **200**	25	80
847	12c. Columbus's ship leaving port	70	40
848	15c. Blessing the fleet	75	45
849	25c. Arms and flag of B.V.I.	85	60
850	30c. Columbus and Santa Maria	1·00	70
851	45c. Ships of second voyage	1·25	95
852	60c. Columbus in ship's boat	1·75	2·50
853	$1 Landing of Columbus	2·25	2·75
MS854	Two sheets, each 120×80 mm. (a) $2 Amerindians sighting fleet. (b) $2 Christopher Columbus and ships Set of 2 sheets	13·00	14·00

201 Library Services Publications

1993. 50th Anniv of Secondary Education and Library Services. Multicoloured.

855	5c. Type **201**	65	1·50
856	10c. Secondary school sports	3·00	1·50
857	15c. Stanley Nibbs (school teacher) (vert)	1·25	80
858	20c. Mobile library	1·75	80
859	30c. Dr. Norwell Harrigan (adminstrator and lecturer) (vert)	1·75	80
860	35c. Children in library	1·75	80
861	70c. Commemorative inscription on book	2·50	3·50
862	$1 B.V.I. High School	2·75	3·50

202 Anegada Ground Iguana

1994. Endangered Species. Anegada Ground Iguana.

863	**202**	5c. multicoloured	90	1·25
864	-	10c. multicoloured	90	1·25
865	-	15c. multicoloured	1·00	75
866	-	45c. multicoloured	1·60	1·50
MS867		106×77 mm. $2 multicoloured	5·00	6·50

DESIGNS: 10c. to $2 Different iguanas.
No. MS867 does not carry the W.W.F. Panda emblem.

203 Loading Disaster Relief HS748 Aircraft

1994. Centenary of Rotary International in B.V.I. Multicoloured.

868	15c. Type **203**	35	35
869	45c. Training children in marine safety	85	85
870	50c. Donated operating table	90	1·00
871	90c. Paul Harris (founder) and emblem	1·60	2·50

1994. 25th Anniv of First Manned Moon Landing. As T 326 of Antigua. Multicoloured.

872	50c. Anniversary logo	2·00	2·25
873	50c. Lunar landing training vehicle	2·00	2·25
874	50c. Launch of "Apollo 11"	2·00	2·25
875	50c. Lunar module "Eagle" in flight	2·00	2·25
876	50c. Moon's surface	2·00	2·25
877	50c. Neil Armstrong (astronaut) taking first step	2·00	2·25
MS878	106×76 mm. $2 Signatures and mission logo	14·00	14·00

204 *Argentina v. Netherlands, 1978*

1994. World Cup Football Championship, U.S.A. Previous Winners. Multicoloured.

879	15c. Type **204**	1·25	50
880	35c. Italy v. West Germany, 1982	2·00	70
881	50c. Argentina v. West Germany, 1986	2·75	2·25
882	$1.30 .30 West Germany v. Argentina, 1990	4·50	6·50
MS883	74×101 mm. $2 U.S. flag and World Cup trophy (horiz)	12·00	14·00

1995. 50th Anniv of United Nations. As T **213** of Bahamas. Multicoloured.

903	15c. Peugeot P4 all-purpose field cars	45	40
904	30c. Foden medium road tanker	75	60
905	45c. SISU all-terrain vehicle	1·00	90
906	$2 Westland Lynx AH7 helicopter	3·75	5·50

205 *Pair of Juvenile Greater Flamingos*

1995. Anegada Flamingos Restoration Project. Multicoloured.

907	15c. Type **205**	85	50
908	20c. Pair of adults	85	55
909	60c. Adult feeding	1·40	2·00
910	$1.45 Adult feeding chick	2·50	4·00
MS911	80×70 mm. $2 Chicks	6·50	7·00

206 *Tortola House with Christmas Tree (Maureen Walters)*

1995. Christmas. Children's Paintings. Multicoloured.

912	12c. Type **206**	1·75	30
913	50c. Father Christmas in Rowing Boat (Collin Collins)	3·00	1·40
914	70c. Christmas Tree and Gifts (Clare Wassell)	3·25	2·75
915	$1.30 Peace Dove (Nicholas Scott)	4·50	6·50

207 *Seine Fishing*

1996. Island Profiles (1st series). Jost Van Dyke. Multicoloured.

916	15c. Type **207**	1·50	40
917	35c. Sandy Spit	1·75	55
918	90c. Map	4·00	3·50
919	$1.50 Foxy's Regatta	4·25	6·50

See also Nos. 1003/6 and 1105/10.

1996. 70th Birthday of Queen Elizabeth II. As T **165** of Ascension, each incorporating a different photograph of the Queen. Multicoloured.

920	10c. Government House, Tortola	30	20
921	30c. Legislative Council Building	65	55
922	45c. Liner in Road Harbour	1·50	70
923	$1.50 Map of British Virgin Islands	3·25	5·00
MS924	63×65 mm. $2 Queen Elizabeth II	3·00	3·75

208 *Hurdling*

1996. Centenary of Modern Olympic Games. Multicoloured.

925	20c. Type **208**	45	30
926	35c. Volley ball	70	60
927	50c. Swimming	1·10	1·75
928	$1 Yachting	2·00	2·75

209 *Mercedes-Benz 500 K A, Cabriolet 1934*

1996. "CAPEX '96" International Stamp Exhibition, Toronto. Early Motor Cars. Multicoloured.

929	15c. Type **209**	45	30
930	40c. Citroen 12 Traction saloon, 1934	1·00	70
931	60c. Cadillac V-8 Sport Phaeton, 1932	1·25	1·75
932	$1.35 .35 Rolls Royce Phantom II saloon, 1934	2·75	4·00
MS933	79×62 mm. $2 Ford Sport Coupe, 1932	3·25	4·25

210 *Children with Computer*

1996. 50th Anniv of UNICEF. Multicoloured.

934	10c. Type **210**	40	40
935	15c. Carnival costume	50	50
936	30c. Children on Scales of Justice	80	80
937	45c. Children on beach	1·25	1·25

211 *Young Rainbows in Art Class*

1996. 75th Anniv of Guiding in the British Virgin Islands. Multicoloured.

938	10c. Type **211**	20	20
939	15c. Brownies serving meals	30	25
940	30c. Guides around campfire	50	45
941	45c. Rangers on parade	65	60
942	$2 Lady Baden-Powell	2·75	4·00

212 *Spanish Mackerel*

1997. Game Fish. Multicoloured.

943	1c. Type **212**	10	50
944	10c. Wahoo	25	80
945	15c. Great barracuda	55	40
946	20c. Tarpon	90	40
947	25c. Tiger shark	90	50
948	35c. Sailfish	90	40
949	40c. Dolphin	1·50	75
950	50c. Black-finned tuna	1·50	90
951	60c. Yellow-finned tuna	1·50	90
952	75c. King mackerel ("Kingfish")	1·75	1·25
953	$1.50 White marlin	3·25	3·25
954	$1.85 Amberjack	4·00	3·50
955	$2 Atlantic bonito	4·50	4·50
956	$5 Bonefish	9·00	10·00
957	$10 Blue marlin	16·00	19·00

1997. "HONG KONG '97" International Stamp Exhibition. Sheet 130×90 mm, containing design as No. 953, but with "1997" imprint date. Multicoloured.

MS958	$1.50, White marlin	2·00	2·75

1997. Golden Wedding of Queen Elizabeth and Prince Philip. As T **173** of Ascension. Multicoloured.

959	30c. Prince Philip with horse	70	1·00
960	30c. Queen Elizabeth at Windsor, 1989	70	1·00
961	45c. Queen in phaeton, Trooping the Colour	90	1·25
962	45c. Prince Philip in Scots Guards uniform	90	1·25
963	70c. Queen Elizabeth and Prince Philip at the Derby, 1993	1·25	1·60
964	70c. Prince Charles playing polo, Mexico, 1993	1·25	1·60
MS965	110×70 mm. $2 Queen Elizabeth and Prince Philip in landau (horiz)	3·25	4·00

213 *Fiddler Crab*

1997. Crabs. Multicoloured.

966	12c. Type **213**	65	50
967	15c. Coral crab	70	50
968	35c. Blue crab	1·10	60
969	$1 Giant hermit crab	2·00	3·00
MS970	76×67 mm. $2 Arrow crab	3·50	4·50

214 *Psychilis macconnelliae*

1997. Orchids of the World. Multicoloured.

971	20c. Type **214**	1·25	1·25
972	50c. Tolumnia prionochila	1·40	1·40
973	60c. Tetramicra canaliculata	1·40	1·40
974	75c. Liparis elata	1·50	1·50
MS975	59×79 mm. $2 Dendrobium crumenatum (vert)	3·25	4·25

215 *Sir Francis Drake and Signature*

1997. 420th Anniv of Drake's Circumnavigation of the World. Multicoloured.

976	40c. Type **215**	1·75	1·75
977	40c. Drake's coat of arms	1·75	1·75
978	40c. Queen Elizabeth I and signature	1·75	1·75
979	40c. Christopher and Marigold	1·75	1·75
980	40c. Golden Hind	1·75	1·75
981	40c. Swan	1·75	1·75
982	40c. Cacafuego (Spanish galleon)	1·75	1·75
983	40c. Elizabeth	1·75	1·75
984	40c. Maria (Spanish merchant ship)	1·75	1·75
985	40c. Drake's astrolabe	1·75	1·75
986	40c. Golden Hind's figurehead	1·75	1·75
987	40c. Compass rose	1·75	1·75
MS988	96×76 mm. $2 Sir Francis Drake (ketch)	3·75	4·50

Nos. 976/87 were printed together, *se-tenant*, with the backgrounds forming a composite map of Drake's route.

1998. Diana, Princess of Wales Commemoration. Sheet 145×70 mm, containing vert designs as T **177** of Ascension. Multicoloured.

MS989	15c. Wearing pink jacket, 1992; 45c. Holding child, 1991; 70c. Laughing, 1991; $1 Wearing high-collared blouse, 1986 (sold at $2.30 + 20c. charity premium)	2·50	4·00

1998. 80th Anniv of Royal Air Force. As T **178** of Ascension. Multicoloured.

990	20c. Fairey IIIF (seaplane)	60	40
991	35c. Supermarine Scapa (flying boat)	85	50
992	50c. Westland Sea King H.A.R. (helicopter)	1·40	1·10
993	$1.50 BAe Harrier GR7	2·50	3·25
MS994	110×77 mm. 75c. Curtiss H.16 (flying boat); 75c. Curtiss JN-4A; 75c. Bell Airacobra; 75c. Boulton-Paul Defiant	6·50	7·00

216 *Fingerprint Cyphoma*

1998. Marine Life. Multicoloured.

995	15c. Type **216**	1·00	50
996	30c. Long-spined sea urchin	1·25	55
997	45c. Split crown feather duster worm	1·60	70
998	$1 Upside down jelly	2·50	3·75
MS999	77×56 mm. $2 Giant anemone	4·75	5·00

217 *Carnival Reveller (Rebecca Peck)*

1998. Festival. Children's Paintings. Multicoloured.

1000	30c. Type **217**	1·25	50
1001	45c. Leader of a Troupe (Jehiah Maduro)	1·50	65
1002	$1.30 .30 Steel Pans (Rebecca McKenzie) (horiz)	3·50	5·00

218 *Salt Pond*

1998. Island Profiles (2nd series). Salt Island. Multicoloured.

1003	12c. Type **218**	1·50	70
1004	30c. Wreck of "Rhone" (mail steamer)	2·00	75
1005	70c. Traditional house	1·75	2·25
1006	$1.45 Salt Island from the air	3·25	4·50
MS1007	118×78 mm. $2 Collecting salt	7·00	8·00

219 *Business Studies, Woodwork and Technology Students*

1998. Anniversaries. Multicoloured.

1008	5c. Type **219**	25	75
1009	15c. Comprehensive school band	45	40
1010	30c. Chapel, Mona Campus, Jamaica	60	50
1011	45c. Anniversary plaque and University arms	75	70
1012	50c. Dr. John Coakley Lettsom and map of Little Jost Van Dyke	1·00	1·25
1013	$1 The Medical Society of London building and arms	1·50	2·50

EVENTS: 5, 15c. 30th anniv of Comprehensive Education in B.V.I.; 30, 45c. 50th anniv of University of West Indies; 50c., $1 200th anniv of Medical Society of London.

220 *Rock Iguana*

1999. Lizards. Multicoloured.

1014	5c. Type **220**	30	65
1015	35c. Pygmy gecko	85	45
1016	60c. Slippery back skink	1·50	1·50
1017	$1.50 Wood slave gecko	2·25	3·50
MS1018	100×70 mm. 75c. Doctor lizard; 75c. Yellow-bellied lizard; 75c. Man lizard; 75c. Ground lizard	5·00	6·00

1999. Royal Wedding. As T **185** of Ascension. Multicoloured.

1019	20c. Photographs of Prince Edward and Miss Sophie Rhys-Jones	1·00	40
1020	$3 Engagement photograph	4·75	6·00

1999. 30th Anniv of First Manned Landing on Moon. As T **186** of Ascension. Multicoloured.

1021	10c. "Apollo 11" on launch pad	45	60
1022	40c. Firing of second stage rockets	1·00	65
1023	50c. Lunar module on Moon	1·10	1·00
1024	$2 Astronauts transfer to command module	3·00	4·50
MS1025	90×80 mm. $2.50, Earth as seen from moon (circular, 40 mm diam)	3·75	4·50

221 *Sunrise Tellin*

1999. Sea Shells. Multicoloured.

1026A	5c. Type **221**	65	90
1027A	10c. King helmet	65	90
1028A	25c. Measle cowrie	80	1·00
1029A	35c. West Indian top shell	85	1·00
1030A	75c. Zigzag scallop	1·25	1·50
1031A	$1 West Indian fighting conch	1·25	1·50

Nos. 1026A/31A were printed together, *se-tenant*, with the backgrounds forming a composite design.

222 Zion Hill Methodist Church

1999. Christmas. Church Buildings. Multicoloured.

1032	20c. Type **222**	45	35
1033	35c. Seventh Day Adventist Church, Fat Hogs Bay, 1982	60	45
1034	50c. Ruins of St. Phillip's Anglican Church, Kingstown	85	1·00
1035	$1 St. William's Catholic Church, Road Town	1·60	2·75

223 King Henry VII

2000. "Stamp Show 2000" International Stamp Exhibition, London. Kings and Queens of England. Multicoloured.

1036	60c. Type **223**	1·10	1·25
1037	60c. Lady Jane Grey	1·10	1·25
1038	60c. King Charles I	1·10	1·25
1039	60c. King William III	1·10	1·25
1040	60c. King George III	1·10	1·25
1041	60c. King Edward VII	1·10	1·25

2000. 18th Birthday of Prince William. As T **191** of Ascension. Multicoloured.

1042	20c. Prince William as baby (horiz)	60	35
1043	40c. Prince William playing with ball, 1984	90	60
1044	50c. Skiing in British Columbia, 1998	1·25	1·00
1045	$1 In evening dress, 1997 (horiz)	2·00	2·75
MS1046	175×95 mm. 60c. Prince William in 1999 (horiz) and Nos. 1042/5	8·50	8·50

224 Duchess of York, 1920s

2000. 100th Birthday of Queen Elizabeth the Queen Mother. Multicoloured.

1047	15c. Type **224**	50	25
1048	35c. As Queen Mother in 1957	1·00	1·50
1049	70c. In evening dress, 1970	1·50	1·75
1050	$1.50 With family on 99th birthday	2·50	3·25

225 Red Hibiscus

2000. Flowers. Multicoloured.

1051	10c. Type **225**	40	50
1052	15c. Pink oleander	45	50
1053	35c. Yellow bell	1·00	55
1054	50c. Yellow and white frangipani	1·25	1·00
1055	75c. Flamboyant	1·75	2·25
1056	$2 Bougainvillea	3·50	5·00

226 Sunday Morning Well (Site of Emancipation Proclamation)

2000. New Millennium. Multicoloured.

1057	5c. Type **226**	15	50
1058	20c. Nurse Mary Louise Davies M.B.E.	45	35
1059	30c. Cheyney University, U.S.A.	60	45
1060	45c. Enid Leona Scatliffe (former chief education officer)	80	70
1061	50c. H. Lavity Stoutt Community College	90	1·00
1062	$1 Sir J. Olva Georges	1·60	2·25
MS1063	69×59 mm. $2 Private Samuel Hodge's Victoria Cross (vert)	3·75	4·50

227 Dr. Q. William Osborne and Arnando Scatliffe

2000. 50th Anniv of Restoration of Legislative Council. Multicoloured.

1064	10c. Type **227**	25	50
1065	15c. H. Robinson O'Neal and A. Austin Henley	35	50
1066	20c. Wilfred W. Smith and John C. Brudenell-Bruce	45	50
1067	35c. Howard R. Penn and I. G. Fonseca	65	55
1068	50c. Carlton L. de Castro and Theodolph H. Faulkner	90	1·00
1069	60c. Willard W. Wheatley (Chief Minister, 1971–79)	1·25	1·50
1070	$1 H. Lavity Stoutt (Chief Minister, 1967–71, 1979–83 and 1986–95)	1·60	2·25

2001. "HONG KONG 2001" Stamp Exhibition. Sheet 150×90 mm, containing T **228** and similar horiz design showing dove. Multicoloured.

MS1071	50c. Type **41**; 50c. Bar-tailed cuckoo dove	3·50	4·50

229 H.M.S. *Wistaria* (sloop), 1923–30

2001. Royal Navy Ships connected to British Virgin Islands (1st series). Multicoloured.

1072	35c. Type **229**	1·50	55
1073	50c. H.M.S. *Dundee* (sloop), 1934–35	1·75	90
1074	60c. H.M.S. *Eurydice* (frigate), 1787	1·75	1·60
1075	75c. H.M.S. *Pegasus* (frigate), 1787	2·00	1·90
1076	$1 H.M.S. *Astrea* (frigate), 1807	2·75	2·75
1077	$1.50 Royal Yacht *Britannia*, 1966	4·00	5·00

See also Nos. 1101/4.

230 Fridtjof Nansen (Peace Prize, 1922)

2001. Centenary of Nobel Prize. Multicoloured.

1078	10c. Type **230**	70	1·00
1079	20c. Albert Einstein (Physics Prize,1921)	80	60
1080	25c. Sir Arthur Lewis (Economic Sciences Prize, 1979)	70	60
1081	40c. Saint-John Perse (Literature Prize, 1960)	80	80
1082	70c. Mother Teresa (Peace Prize, 1979)	6·00	3·50
1083	$2 Christian Lous Lange (Peace Prize, 1921)	3·75	5·00

2002. Golden Jubilee. As T **200** of Ascension.

1084	15c. brown, mauve and gold	70	70
1085	50c. multicoloured	1·25	1·00
1086	60c. multicoloured	1·25	1·40
1087	75c. multicoloured	1·50	1·75
MS1088	162×95 mm. Nos. 1084/7 and $1 multicoloured	8·00	9·00

DESIGNS—HORIZ: 15c. Princess Elizabeth in A.T.S. uniform, changing wheel; 50c. Queen Elizabeth in fur hat, 1977; 60c. Queen Elizabeth carrying bouquet; 75c. Queen Elizabeth at banquet, Prague, 1996. VERT (38×51 mm)—$1 Queen Elizabeth after Annigoni.

Designs as Nos. 1084/7 in No. MS1088 omit the gold frame around each stamp and the "Golden Jubilee 1952–2002" inscription.

231 Estuarine Crocodile

2002. Reptiles. Multicoloured.

1089	5c. Type **231**	30	75
1090	20c. Reticulated python	60	45
1091	30c. Komodo dragon	80	50
1092	40c. Boa constrictor	95	70
1093	$1 Dwarf caiman	2·25	2·50
1094	$2 *Sphaerodactylus partheno- pion* (gecko)	4·00	5·00
MS1095	89×68 mm. $1.50, Head of *Sphaerodactylus parthenopion* on finger	3·75	4·50

2002. Queen Elizabeth the Queen Mother Commemoration. As T **202** of Ascension.

1096	20c. brown, gold and purple	45	30
1097	60c. multicoloured	1·25	1·00
1098	$2 black, gold and purple	3·50	3·75
1099	$3 multicoloured	4·75	5·50
MS1100	145×70 mm. Nos. 1098/9	8·50	9·50

DESIGNS—20c. Duchess of York, 1920s; 60c. Queen Mother at Somerset House, 2000; $2 Lady Elizabeth Bowes-Lyon, 1920; $3 Queen Mother inspecting guard of honour.

Designs as Nos. 1098/9 in No. MS1100 omit the "1900–2002" inscription and the coloured frame.

2002. Royal Navy Ships connected to British Virgin Islands (2nd series). As T **229**. Multicoloured.

1101	20c. H.M.S. *Invincible* (ship of the line) re-capturing H.M.S. *Argo* (frigate), 1783	85	55
1102	35c. H.M.S. *Boreas* and H.M.S. *Solebay* (sailing frigates)	1·50	60
1103	50c. H.M.S. *Coventry* (frigate)	1·75	1·25
1104	$3 H.M.S. *Argyll* (frigate)	7·50	9·00

2002. Island Profiles (3rd series). Virgin Gorda. As T **218**. Multicoloured.

1105	5c. Spring Bay	30	75
1106	40c. Devils Bay	1·00	55
1107	60c. The Baths	1·40	1·00
1108	75c. St. Thomas Bay	1·50	1·50
1109	$1 Savannah and Pond Bay	1·75	2·00
1110	$2 Trunk Bay	3·50	5·00

232 Young West Indian Whistling Duck and Nest

2002. Birdlife International (1st series). West Indian Whistling Duck. Multicoloured.

1111	10c. Type **232**	40	65
1112	35c. Adult bird on rock (vert)	1·00	55
1113	40c. Adult bird landing on water (vert)	1·00	70
1114	50c. Two adult birds	1·50	2·00
MS1115	175×80 mm. Nos. 1111/14 and $2 Head of duck	6·00	7·00

See also Nos. 167/76.

233 200 Metres Race

2003. Anniversaries and Events. Multicoloured.

1116	10c. Type **233**	50	70
1117	10c. Indoor cycling	50	70
1118	35c. Laser class dinghy racing	75	75
1119	35c. Women's long-jumping	75	75
1120	50c. Bareboat class yachts	1·00	1·25
1121	50c. Racing cruiser class yachts	1·00	1·25
1122	$1.35 Carlos and Esme Downing (founders)	2·00	2·25
1123	$1.35 Copies of newspaper and anniversary logo	2·00	2·25

ANNIVERSARIES and EVENTS: 10c. Commonwealth Games, 2002; 35c. 20th anniv of British Virgin Islands' admission to Olympic Games; 50c. 30th anniv of Spring Regatta; $1.35, 40th anniv of *The Island Sun* (newspaper).

2003. 50th Anniv of Coronation. A T **206** of Ascension. Multicoloured.

1124	15c. Queen Elizabeth II	75	30
1125	$5 Queen and Royal Family on Buckingham Palace balcony	8·50	9·00
MS1126	95×115 mm. As Nos. 1124/5	8·00	8·50

Nos. 1124/5 have red frame; stamps from MS1126 have no frame and country name in mauve panel.

2003. As T **207** of Ascension.

1127	$5 black, bistre and brown	5·25	6·00

2003. 21st Birthday of Prince William of Wales. As T **208** of Ascension

(a) Multicoloured

1128	50c. Prince William at Tidworth and Beaufort Polo Clubs, 2002	1·00	75
1129	$2 Playing polo, 2002 and at Holyrood House, 2001	4·00	4·25

(b) As Nos. 1128/9 but with grey frame.

1130	50c. As No. 1128	1·00	75
1131	$2 As No. 1129	4·00	4·25

2003. Centenary of Powered Flight. As T **209** of Ascension. Multicoloured.

1132	15c. Douglas DC-4	70	50
1133	20c. Boeing Stearman Kaydet	75	50
1134	35c. North American B-25J Mitchell	1·00	50
1135	40c. McDonnell Douglas F-4B Phantom	1·10	60
1136	70c. Boeing-Vertol CH-47 Chinook helicopter	2·00	1·75
1137	$2 Hughes AH-64 Apache helicopter	4·25	5·50

234 Townsmen under Arcades

2003. Christmas. *Stories from the Life of St. Ursula: Arrival of the English Ambassadors* by Carpaccio. Multicoloured.

1138	20c. Type **234**	60	25
1139	40c. English ambassadors	1·00	50
1140	$2.50 King Maurus of Brittany	4·50	6·00
MS1141	172×87 mm. $1 King Maurus receiving English ambassadors (35×35 mm) and Nos. 1138/40	7·50	8·50

Nos. 1138/40 show details of the painting and No. MS1141 the complete painting.

2004. Game Fish. Designs as Nos. 945/6 and 948/9. Self-adhesive. Size 23×19 mm.

1142	15c. Great barracuda	15	20
1143	20c. Tarpon	25	30
1144	35c. Sailfish	40	45
1145	40c. Dolphin	45	50

235 Pomegranate

2004. Local Fruits. Multicoloured.

1146	1c. Hog plum	10	30
1147	10c. Coco plum	20	30
1148	15c. Type **235**	30	30
1149	20c. Cashew	40	30
1150	25c. Sugar apple	60	45
1151	35c. Tamarind	70	45
1152	40c. Soursop	75	50
1153	50c. Mango	85	65
1154	60c. Papaya	1·25	75
1155	75c. Custard apple	1·50	1·25
1156	$1 Otaheite gooseberry	2·00	2·00
1157	$1.50 Guava	3·00	3·25
1158	$2 Guavaberry	4·00	4·25
1159	$5 Mamee apple	8·50	10·00
1160	$10 Passion fruit	15·00	17·00

236 Festival Parade

2004. Golden Jubilee of Island Festival. Multicoloured.

1161	10c. Type **236**	30	50
1162	60c. Horse racing	1·75	1·00
1163	$1 Canoeing	2·00	2·00
1164	$2 Festival queen	3·75	4·75

237 Women's
Football

2004. Centenary of FIFA (Federation Internationale de
Football Association) and Olympic Games, Athens.
Multicoloured.

1165	75c. Type **237**	1·40	1·40
1166	$1 Sprinting	1·75	1·75

238 Black and White
Warbler

2005. Birdlife International (2nd series). Caribbean
Endemic Bird Festival. Multicoloured.

1167	5c. Type **238**	60	70
1168	10c. Prairie warbler	80	1·00
1169	15c. Yellow-rumped warbler	1·00	1·25
1170	25c. Worm-eating warbler	1·25	50
1171	35c. Yellow warbler	1·25	70
1172	40c. Black-throated warbler	1·50	2·00
1173	50c. Prothonotary warbler	1·50	1·50
1174	60c. Cape May warbler	2·25	3·00
1175	75c. Parula warbler (inscr "Northern Parula")	2·50	3·25
1176	$2.75 Palm warbler	5·50	6·50

2005. Pope John Paul II Commemoration. As T **219** of
Ascension.

1177	75c. multicoloured	2·25	2·00

239 Virgin Islands Tree Boa

2005. Endangered Species. Virgin Islands Tree Boa
(*Epicrates monensis granti*). Multicoloured.

1178	20c. Type **239**	75	55
1179	30c. Boa in plant (facing left)	1·00	60
1180	70c. On leafy branch	2·00	2·00
1181	$1.05 In foliage (facing right)	2·75	3·50

2005. Bicentenary of the Battle of Trafalgar. As T **220** of
Ascension. Multicoloured.

1182	5c. HMS *Colossus* in action before breaking the line	75	75
1183	25c. HMS *Boreas* off British Virgin Islands, 1787	1·75	75
1184	75c. HMS *Victory* (Francis Smitheman)	3·50	2·50
1185	$3 Admiral Lord Nelson (vert)	8·50	10·00
MS1186	120×79 mm. $2.50 HMS *Colossus* firing (44×44 mm)	9·00	10·00

240 Mr. Joshua
Smith (first director
of Social Security)

2005. Anniversaries. Multicoloured.

1187	20c. Type **240** (25th anniv of Social Security)	60	55
1188	40c. Transmitter on mast and world map (40th anniv of Radio Station ZBVI)	1·50	1·00
1189	50c. Control tower (25th anniv of Beef Island airstrip)	2·00	1·50
1190	$1 Emblem (Centenary of Rotary International)	2·50	3·50

241 Decorated
Century Plant

2005. Christmas. Plants and Flowers. Multicoloured.

1191	15c. Type **241**	65	30
1192	35c. Poinsettia (horiz)	1·25	70
1193	60c. Decorated ink-berry in pot	1·75	1·25
1194	$2.50 Snow-on-the-mountain (horiz)	5·50	7·50

2006. 80th Birthday of Queen Elizabeth II. As T **223** of
Ascension. Multicoloured.

1195	15c. Princess Elizabeth in Girl Guide uniform	75	30
1196	75c. Queen Elizabeth II wearing white hat and green and white jacket	2·00	1·25
1197	$1.50 Wearing drop earrings	3·50	4·25
1198	$2 Wearing pale mauve hat and jacket	4·75	6·00
MS1199	144×75 mm. $1.50 As No. 1196; $2 As No. 1197	8·00	9·00

Stamps from **MS**1199 do not have white borders.

242 New Red Cross
Headquarters, Virgin Gorda

2007. Red Cross Buildings. Multicoloured.

1200	20c. Type **242**	75	80
1201	$3 Former Red Cross building	4·50	5·00

2008. 90th Anniv of the Royal Air Force. As T **63** of
British Indian Ocean Territory. Multicoloured.

1202	18c. Supermarine Spitfire	60	50
1203	20c. Avro Lancaster	75	50
1204	35c. Douglas C-47 Dakota	1·25	55
1205	60c. Handley Page Halifax	2·25	1·75
1206	$1.75 Westland Lysander	4·75	6·00
MS1207	110×70 mm. $2.50 Spitfire patrolling D-Day beaches	6·00	6·50

243 Diana, Princess
of Wales

2008. Tenth Death Anniv of Diana, Princess of Wales.
Multicoloured.

1208	60c. Type **243**	1·00	1·00
MS1209	120×85 mm. $3.50 Wearing red sleeveless dress (42×57 mm)	6·00	7·00

244 Shield

2008. 300th Birth Anniv of Charles Wesley (2007).
Multicoloured.

1210	20c. Type **244**	60	40
1211	50c. Rev. Charles Wesley	1·25	1·25
1212	$1.75 Rev. Charles Wesley (in half profile)	3·00	4·00

245 Athlete running

2008. Olympic Games, Beijing. Multicoloured.

1213	15c. Type **245**	30	30
1214	18c. Yachting	35	35
1215	20c. Athlete in race	40	40
1216	$1 Dinghy sailing	2·25	2·75

246 Mace and Mace Head

2008. Ministerial Government. Multicoloured.

1217	18c. Type **246**	35	25
1218	35c. Facade and entrance of House of Assembly	70	55
1219	60c. Henry O. Creque and Ivan Dawson (legislators)	1·40	1·50
1220	$2 Paul Wattley and Terrance B. Lettsome (legislators)	3·75	5·00

247 Sanctuary
Wood Cemetery,
Ypres, Belgium

2008. 90th Anniv of the End of World War I.
Multicoloured.

1221	75c. Type **247**	1·60	1·75
1222	80c. Poppies growing on Somme Battlefield, France (horiz)	1·75	2·00
1223	90c. Lone Pine Cemetery, Gallipoli (horiz)	2·00	2·25
1224	$1 War Memorial, Vauquois, France	2·25	2·50
1225	$1.15 Thiepval Memorial, France (horiz)	2·50	2·75
1226	$1.25 Menin Gate, Ypres, Belgium (horiz)	2·50	2·75
MS1227	110×70 mm. $2 UK Overseas Territories Wreath of Remembrance	4·00	4·50

248 Climbing
Pandanus
(*Freycinetia
cumingiana*)

2009. J. R. O'Neal Botanic Gardens, Road Town, Tortola.
Multicoloured.

1228	20c. Type **248**	50	45
1229	35c. True aloe (*Aloe vera*)	85	65
1230	50c. Crown of thorns (*Euphorbia milii*)	1·50	1·50
1231	$1 Red-eared slider (*Trachemys scripta elegans*) (terrapin)	2·25	2·75
MS1232	64×90 mm. $2.50 Fountain and royal palms	4·50	5·50

2009. Seafaring and Exploration. As T **65** of British Indian
Ocean Territory. Multicoloured.

1233	15c. HMS *Ark Royal* (English galleon)	70	60
1234	20c. *Whydah* (three masted ship of galley design)	70	60
1235	60c. *Santa Maria* (Columbus)	1·75	1·40
1236	70c. RMS *Rhone* (steam packet)	1·90	1·90
1237	90c. *Golden Hind* (Drake)	2·50	2·25
1238	$1.95 HMY *Britannia* (royal yacht)	4·50	5·00
MS1239	110×70 mm. $2 Christopher Columbus	8·00	8·00

249 Lt. Robert Hampton Gray,
9 August 1945

2009. Centenary of Naval Aviation. Designs showing
Victoria Cross holders and aircraft. Multicoloured.

1240	18c. Type **249**	60	60
1241	35c. Lt. Cdr. (A) Eugene Esmonde, 12 February 1942	1·25	1·00
1242	60c. Flt. SLt. Rex Warneford, 7 June 1915	2·25	2·25
1243	90c. Sqn. Cdr. Richard Bell Davies, 19 November 1915	3·00	3·75
MS1244	110×70 mm. $2 Airplane on deck of HMS *Illustrious*, Taranto, 1940	5·50	6·00

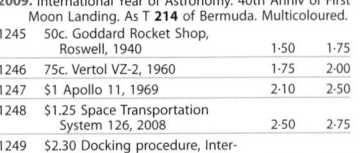

2009. International Year of Astronomy. 40th Anniv of First
Moon Landing. As T **214** of Bermuda. Multicoloured.

1245	50c. Goddard Rocket Shop, Roswell, 1940	1·50	1·75
1246	75c. Vertol VZ-2, 1960	1·75	2·00
1247	$1 Apollo 11, 1969	2·10	2·50
1248	$1.25 Space Transportation System 126, 2008	2·50	2·75
1249	$2.30 Docking procedure, International Space Station	3·00	3·50
MS1250	100×80 mm. $3 *Tuning in Earth* (Dave Scott pointing antenna at Earth and Jim Irwin loading Lunar Rover) (Alan Bean) (39×59 mm)	6·00	7·00

250 Turtle

2010. Coral Reefs.

1251	20c. Type **250**	50	50
1252	35c. Fish	65	55
1253	50c. Seahorse (vert)	1·50	1·50
1254	60c. Conch shell (vert)	1·60	1·60
1255	$1.50 Coral reef	3·75	4·50

251 Mr. John E.
George
(sub-postmaster)

2010. North Sound Post Office. Multicoloured.

1256	20c. Type **251**	90	90
1257	50c. New North Sound Sub Post Office (horiz)	1·60	1·60
1258	$2 Old North Sound Sub Post Office (horiz)	4·50	5·50

252 Church Bell

2010. Bicentenary of East End Methodist Church.
Multicoloured.

1259	20c. Type **252**	60	50
1260	50c. East End Methodist Church, 2010	1·75	1·60
1261	60c. East End Methodist Church, 1977	2·00	1·90
1262	$2 East End Methodist Church in early 19th century	5·00	6·00

253 Dinghy sailing

2011. Sailability BVI (sailing programme for the disabled).
Multicoloured.

1263	5c. Type **253**	15	25
1264	20c. Two sailors in dinghy with red sails	70	50
1265	25c. Two sailors in blue dinghy	75	65
1266	40c. Arrival of Geoff Holt (quad-riplegic transatlantic sailor) in Tortola, 2010	1·40	1·25
1267	50c. Geoff Holt on board yacht *Impossible Dream*, arm raised in triumph	1·60	1·60
1268	$1.50 Geoff Holt on board yacht *Impossible Dream*, arm raised in triumph	4·00	5·00

254 J24 Keel Boat racing,
2000

2011. 40th Anniv of British Virgin Islands Spring Regatta.
Multicoloured.

1269	15c. Type **254**	60	45
1270	35c. Mixed fleet (vert), 1980s	1·50	1·00
1271	50c. Yachts flying spinnakers, 1990s	1·90	1·90

1272		$2 Clubhouse and moored dinghies, 1970s	4·00	5·00

255 William and Miss Catherine Middleton

2011. Royal Wedding
MS1273	**255**	$5 multicoloured	7·50	8·00

OFFICIAL STAMPS

1985. Nos. 418/21 and 423/33 optd **OFFICIAL.**
O1		1c. Purple-tipped sea anemone	30	1·25
O2		3c. Common starfish	45	1·25
O3		5c. Type **134**	45	45
O4		8c. Triton's trumpet (shell)	55	60
O5		13c. Flamingo tongue snail	80	75
O6		15c. Spider crab	85	70
O7		18c. Sea squirts	90	1·75
O8		20c. True tulip (shell)	90	80
O9		25c. Rooster tail conch (shell)	1·25	2·00
O10		30c. Fighting conch (shell)	1·40	1·00
O11		60c. Mangrove crab	2·00	2·50
O12		$1 Coral polyps	3·00	3·75
O13		$2.50 Peppermint shrimp	4·50	9·00
O14		$3 West Indian murex (shell)	5·50	10·00
O15		$5 Carpet anemone	7·50	10·00

1986. Nos. 560/78 optd **OFFICIAL.**
O16		1c. Type **162**	60	1·75
O17		2c. Yellow-crowned night heron	40	1·75
O18		5c. Mangrove cuckoo	1·25	2·00
O19		8c. Northern mockingbird	55	2·75
O20		10c. Grey kingbird	1·25	2·00
O21		12c. Red-necked pigeon	1·50	40
O22		15c. Least bittern	1·50	40
O23		18c. Smooth-billed ani	70	75
O24		20c. Clipper rail	1·50	1·00
O25		25c. American kestrel	1·50	1·00
O26		30c. Pearly-eyed thrasher	1·50	1·00
O27		35c. Bridled quail dove	1·25	1·00
O28		40c. Green-backed heron	1·25	1·00
O29		50c. Scaly-breasted ground dove	1·40	1·75
O30		60c. Little blue heron	1·50	2·50
O31		$1 Audubon's shearwater	2·25	3·50
O32		$2 Blue-faced booby	2·50	4·00
O33		$3 Cattle egret	6·00	7·50
O34		$5 Zenaida dove	8·00	7·50

1991. Nos. 767/8, 771, 773/9 and 781 optd **OFFICIAL.**
O35		5c. Frangipani	60	1·50
O36		10c. Autograph tree	60	1·50
O37		20c. Jerusalem thorn	80	65
O38		30c. Swamp immortelle	1·00	65
O39		35c. White cedar	1·00	65
O40		40c. Mahoe tree	1·25	65
O41		45c. Pinguin	1·25	65
O42		50c. Christmas orchid	2·00	1·25
O43		70c. Lignum vitae	2·00	2·50
O44		$1 African tulip tree	2·00	2·75
O45		$3 Organ pipe cactus	5·00	7·50

Pt. 1

BRUNEI

A Sultanate on the North Coast of Borneo.

100 cents = 1 dollar.

1 Star and Local Scene

1895
1	**1**	½c. brown	6·00	20·00
2	**1**	1c. brown	5·50	15·00
3	**1**	2c. black	4·50	17·00
4	**1**	3c. blue	5·50	14·00
5	**1**	5c. green	6·50	18·00
6	**1**	8c. purple	6·50	48·00
7	**1**	10c. red	8·00	45·00
8	**1**	25c. green	80·00	£100
9	**1**	50c. green	26·00	£100
10	**1**	$1 green	28·00	£120

1906. Stamps of Labuan optd **BRUNEI.** or surch also.
11	**18**	1c. black and purple	48·00	55·00
12	**18**	2c. on 3c. black and brown	6·50	19·00
13	**18**	2c. on 8c. black and orange	27·00	80·00
14	**18**	3c. black and brown	38·00	85·00
15	**18**	4c. on 12c. black and yellow	7·00	5·00
16	**18**	5c. on 16c. green and brown	48·00	75·00
17	**18**	8c. black and orange	14·00	32·00
18	**18**	10c. on 16c. green and brown	6·50	22·00
19	**18**	25c. on 16c. green and brown	£110	£120
20	**18**	30c. on 16c. green and brown	£120	£130
21	**18**	50c. on 16c. green and brown	£120	£130
22	**18**	$1 on 8c. black and orange	£120	£130

5 View on Brunei River

1907
23	**5**	1c. black and green	2·25	11·00
24	**5**	2c. black and red	2·50	3·25
25	**5**	3c. black and brown	10·00	22·00
26	**5**	4c. black and mauve	7·50	7·00
27	**5**	5c. black and blue	50·00	95·00
28	**5**	8c. black and orange	7·50	23·00
29	**5**	10c. black and green	4·50	5·00
30	**5**	25c. blue and brown	32·00	48·00
31	**5**	30c. violet and black	29·00	22·00
32	**5**	50c. green and brown	15·00	22·00
33	**5**	$1 red and grey	60·00	90·00

1908
35		1c. green	60	2·00
60		1c. black	1·00	75
79		1c. brown	50	2·00
36		2c. black and brown	4·25	1·25
61		2c. brown	1·25	10·00
62		2c. green	2·00	1·00
80		2c. grey	60	8·00
37		3c. red	7·50	7·00
63		3c. green	1·75	6·50
64		4c. purple	1·50	1·25
65		4c. orange	2·00	1·00
40		5c. black and orange	7·00	7·00
67		5c. grey	22·00	12·00
68		5c. brown	22·00	1·00
82		5c. orange	80	2·00
41		8c. blue and indigo	7·00	11·00
71		8c. blue	6·00	5·00
72		8c. black	16·00	75
84		8c. red	50	2·25
42		10c. purple on yellow	6·50	1·75
85		10c. violet	2·25	30
86		15c. blue	1·75	70
87		25c. purple	2·75	2·25
44		30c. purple and yellow	14·00	16·00
88		30c. black and orange	2·50	1·00
77		50c. black on green	17·00	15·00
89		50c. black	6·00	1·25
46		$1 black and red on blue	27·00	48·00
90		$1 black and red	13·00	2·00
47		$5 red on green	£180	£325
91		$5 green and orange	20·00	25·00
92		$10 black and purple	95·00	30·00
48		$25 black on red	£650	£1300

1922. Optd **MALAYA- BORNEO EXHIBITION. 1922.**
51		1c. green	11·00	50·00
52		2c. black and brown	11·00	50·00
53		3c. red	12·00	55·00
54		4c. red	18·00	55·00
55		5c. orange	23·00	60·00
56		10c. purple on yellow	9·00	60·00
57		25c. lilac	14·00	80·00
58		50c. black on green	45·00	£150
59		$1 black and red on blue	75·00	£190

7 Native Houses, Water Village

1924
81	**7**	3c. green	1·50	7·00
70	**7**	6c. red	11·00	11·00
83	**7**	6c. black	1·25	5·00
74	**7**	12c. blue	4·50	9·00

8 Sultan Ahmed Tajudin and Water Village

1949. Silver Jubilee of H.H. the Sultan.
93	**8**	8c. black and red	1·25	1·25
94	**8**	25c. purple and orange	1·25	1·60
95	**8**	50c. black and blue	1·25	1·60

1949. 75th Anniv of UPU. As T **20/23** of Antigua.
96		8c. red	1·00	2·25
97		15c. blue	3·50	1·50
98		25c. mauve	1·00	1·50
99		50c. black	1·00	1·25

9 Sultan Omar Ali Saifuddin

1952. Dollar values as T **8**, but with arms instead of portrait inset.
100	**9**	1c. black	10	50
101	**9**	2c. black and orange	10	50
102	**9**	3c. black and lake	15	30
103	**9**	4c. black and green	20	20
104	**9**	6c. black and grey	1·50	10
123	**9**	8c. black and red	1·00	10
106	**9**	10c. black and sepia	20	10
125	**9**	12c. black and violet	1·50	10
126	**9**	15c. black and blue	55	10
109	**9**	25c. black and purple	2·50	10
110	**9**	50c. black and blue	5·50	10
111	**9**	$1 black and green (horiz)	2·00	1·40
112	**9**	$2 black and red (horiz)	5·50	3·00
113	**9**	$5 black and purple (horiz)	32·00	11·00

11 Brunei Mosque and Sultan Omar

1958. Opening of the Brunei Mosque.
114	**11**	8c. black and green	20	65
115	**11**	15c. black and red	25	15
116	**11**	35c. black and lilac	30	90

12 "Protein Foods"

1963. Freedom from Hunger.
117	**12**	12c. sepia	2·75	1·00

13 ITU Emblem

1965. Centenary of ITU.
132	**13**	4c. mauve and brown	35	10
133	**13**	75c. yellow and green	1·00	75

14 ICY Emblem

1965. International Co-operation Year.
134	**14**	4c. purple and turquoise	20	10
135	**14**	15c. green and lavender	55	35

15 Sir Winston Churchill and St. Paul's Cathedral in Wartime

1966. Churchill Commemoration. Designs in black, red and gold and with backgrounds in colours given.
136	**15**	3c. blue	30	2·25
137	**15**	10c. green	1·50	20
138	**15**	15c. brown	1·75	35
139	**15**	75c. violet	4·25	3·75

16 Footballer's Legs, Ball and Jules Rimet Cup

1966. World Cup Football Championships.
140	**16**	4c. multicoloured	20	15
141	**16**	75c. multicoloured	80	60

17 WHO Building

1966. Inauguration of WHO Headquarters, Geneva.
142	**17**	12c. black, green and blue	40	65
143	**17**	25c. black, purple and ochre	60	1·25

18 "Education"

1966. 20th Anniv of UNESCO.
144	**18**	4c. multicoloured	35	10
145	-	15c. yellow, violet and olive	75	50
146	-	75c. black, purple and orange	2·50	6·00

DESIGNS: 15c. "Science"; 75c. "Culture".

21 Religious Headquarters Building

1967. 1400th Anniv of Revelation of the Koran.
147	**21**	4c. multicoloured	10	10
148	**21**	10c. multicoloured	15	10
149	-	25c. multicoloured	20	30
150	-	75c. multicoloured	35	1·50

Nos. 149/50 have sprigs of laurel flanking the main design (which has a smaller circle) in place of flagpoles.

22 Sultan of Brunei, Mosque and Flags

1968. Installation of Y.T.M. Seri Paduka Duli Pengiran Temenggong. Multicoloured.
151		4c. Type **22**	15	80
152		12c. Sultan of Brunei, Mosque and Flags (different) (horiz)	40	1·60
153		25c. Type **22**	55	2·00

23 Sultan of Brunei

1968. Birthday of Sultan.

154	23	4c. multicoloured	10	50
155	23	12c. multicoloured	20	85
156	23	25c. multicoloured	30	1·40

24 Sultan of Brunei

1968. Coronation of Sultan of Brunei.

157		4c. multicoloured	15	25
158		12c. multicoloured	25	50
159		25c. multicoloured	40	75

25 New Building and Sultan's Portrait

1968. Opening of Hall of Language and Literature Bureau. Multicoloured.

160		10c. Type **25**	20	1·75
161		15c. New Building and Sultan's portrait (48½×22 mm)	20	35
162		30c. As 15c.	45	90

27 Human Rights Emblem and struggling Man

1968. Human Rights Year.

163	27	12c. black, yellow and green	10	20
164	27	25c. black, yellow and blue	15	25
165	27	75c. black, yellow and purple	45	1·75

28 Sultan of Brunei and WHO Emblem

1968. 20th Anniv of World Health Organization.

166	28	4c. yellow, black and blue	30	30
167	28	15c. yellow, black and violet	55	65
168	28	25c. yellow, black and olive	65	1·25

29 Deep Sea Oil-Rig, Sultan of Brunei and inset portrait of Pengiran Di-Gadong

1969. Installation (9th May, 1968) of Pengiran Shar-bandar as Y.T.M. Seri Paduka Duli Pengiran Di-Gadong Sahibol Mal.

169	29	12c. multicoloured	85	50
170	29	40c. multicoloured	1·25	2·00
171	29	50c. multicoloured	1·25	2·00

30 Aerial View of Parliament Buildings

1969. Opening of Royal Audience Hall and Legislative Council Chamber.

172	30	12c. multicoloured	20	25
173	30	25c. multicoloured	30	45
174	-	50c. red and violet	60	3·50

DESIGN: 50c. Elevation of new buildings.

32 Youth Centre and Sultan's Portrait

1969. Opening of New Youth Centre.

175	32	6c. multicoloured	20	1·00
176	32	10c. multicoloured	25	10
177	32	30c. multicoloured	70	1·00

33 Soldier, Sultan and Badge

1971. Tenth Anniv of Royal Brunei Malay Regiment. Multicoloured.

178	33	10c. Type **33**	80	30
179		15c. Bell 205 Iroquois helicopter, Sultan and badge (horiz)	1·75	70
180		75c. "Pahlawan" (patrol boat), Sultan and badge (horiz)	3·25	7·00

34 Badge, and Officer in Full-dress Uniform

1971. 50th Anniv of Royal Brunei Police Force. Multicoloured.

181	34	10c. Type **34**	50	30
182		15c. Badge and Patrol constable	60	90
183		50c. Badge and Traffic constable	1·10	6·00

35 Perdana Wazir, Sultan of Brunei and View of Water Village

1971. Installation of the Yang Teramat Mulia as the Perdana Wazir.

184	35	15c. multicoloured	40	50
185		25c. multicoloured	70	1·00
186	-	50c. multicoloured	1·40	5·00

Nos. 185/6 show various views of Brunei Town.

36 Pottery

1972. Opening of Brunei Museum. Multicoloured.

187		10c. Type **36**	30	10
188		12c. Straw-work	40	20
189		15c. Leather-work	45	20
190		25c. Gold-work	1·25	1·25
191		50c. Museum Building (58×21 mm)	2·25	5·50

37 Modern Building, Queen Elizabeth and Sultan of Brunei

1972. Royal Visit. Each design with portrait of Queen and Sultan. Multicoloured.

192		10c. Type **37**	70	20
193		15c. Native houses	95	55
194		25c. Mosque	2·00	1·60
195		50c. Royal Assembly Hall	3·75	7·00

38 Secretariat Building

1972. Renaming of Brunei Town as Bandar Seri Begawan.

196	38	10c. multicoloured	20	15
197	-	15c. green, yellow and black	25	15
198	-	25c. blue, yellow and black	45	50
199	-	50c. red, blue and black	75	2·25

VIEWS: 15c. Darul Hana Palace; 25c. Old Brunei Town; 50c. Town and Water Village.

39 Blackburn Beverley C1 parachuting Supplies

1972. Opening of R.A.F. Museum, Hendon. Multicoloured.

200		25c. Type **39**	1·75	1·25
201		75c. Blackburn Beverley C1 landing	3·25	4·75

1972. Royal Silver Wedding. As T **52** of Ascension, but with girl with traditional flower-pot, and boy with bowl and pipe in background.

210		12c. red	10	10
211		75c. green	20	50

41 Interpol H.Q., Paris

1973. 50th Anniv of Interpol.

212	41	25c. green, purple and black	1·50	1·25
213	-	50c. blue, ultram & red	1·50	1·25

DESIGN: 50c. Different view of the H.Q.

42 Sultan, Princess Anne and Captain Phillips

1973. Royal Wedding.

214	42	25c. multicoloured	15	10
215	42	50c. multicoloured	15	25

43 Churchill Painting

1973. Opening of Churchill Memorial Building. Multicoloured.

216		12c. Type **43**	10	20
217		50c. Churchill statue	30	1·40

44 Sultan Sir Hassanal Bolkiah Mu'izzaddin Waddaulah

1975. Multicoloured. Background colours given.

218	44	4c. green	20	20
219	44	5c. blue	20	30
220	44	6c. green	3·25	5·50
221	44	10c. lilac	30	10
222	44	15c. brown	2·50	40
223	44	20c. stone	30	20
224	44	25c. green	40	15
225	44	30c. blue	40	15
226	44	35c. grey	40	20
227	44	40c. purple	40	20
228	44	50c. brown	40	20
229	44	75c. green	60	3·50
256	44	$1 orange	1·50	3·50
231	44	$2 yellow	2·25	11·00
232	44	$5 silver	3·00	18·00
233	44	$10 gold	5·00	32·00

45 Aerial View of Airport

1974. Inauguration of Brunei International Airport. Multicoloured.

234		50c. Type **45**	1·25	1·00
235		75c. Sultan in Army uniform, and airport (48×36 mm)	1·50	1·50

46 U.P.U. Emblem and Sultan

1974. Centenary of Universal Postal Union.

236	46	12c. multicoloured	20	20
237	46	50c. multicoloured	40	1·40
238	46	75c. multicoloured	50	1·75

47 Sir Winston Churchill

1974. Birth Centenary of Sir Winston Churchill.

239	47	12c. black, blue and gold	25	20
240	-	75c. black, green and gold	45	1·40

DESIGN: 75c. Churchill smoking cigar (profile).

48 Boeing 737 and R.B.A. Crest

1975. Inauguration of Royal Brunei Airlines. Multicoloured.

241		12c. Type **48**	1·00	25
242		35c. Boeing 737 over Bandar Seri Begawan Mosque	1·75	1·50
243		75c. Boeing 737 in flight	2·50	3·00

1976. Surch **10 sen.**

263	44	10c. on 6c. brown	1·75	1·75

50 Royal Coat of Arms

1977. Silver Jubilee. Multicoloured.

264		10c. Type **50**	15	15
265		20c. Imperial State Crown	20	20

266		75c. Queen Elizabeth (portrait by Annigoni)	45	60

51 The Moment of Crowning

1978. 25th Anniv of Coronation. Multicoloured.

267		10c. Type **51**	15	10
268		20c. Queen in Coronation regalia	20	20
269		75c. Queen's departure from Abbey	55	80

52 Royal Crest

1978. Tenth Anniv of Coronation of Sultan.

270	**52**	10c. black, red and yellow	20	10
271	-	20c. multicoloured	40	25
272	-	75c. multicoloured	1·10	3·25
MS273		182×77 mm. Nos. 270/2	12·00	16·00

DESIGNS: 20c. Coronation; 75c. Sultan's Crown.

53 Human Rights Emblem and Struggling Man

1978. Human Rights Year.

274	**53**	10c. black, yellow and red	15	10
275	**53**	20c. black, yellow and violet	20	35
276	**53**	75c. black, yellow and bistre	40	2·50

Type **53** is similar to the design used for the previous Human Rights issue in 1968.

54 Smiling Children

1978. International Year of the Child.

277	**54**	10c. multicoloured	20	10
278	-	$1 black and green	80	2·50

DESIGN: $1 I.Y.C. emblem.

55 Earth Satellite Station

1979. Telisai Earth Satellite Station. Multicoloured.

279		10c. Type **55**	20	15
280		20c. Satellite and antenna	30	40
281		75c. Television camera, telex machine and telephone	60	2·75

56 Hegira Symbol

1979. Moslem Year 1400 A.H. Commemoration.

282	**56**	10c. black, yellow and green	10	15
283	**56**	20c. black, yellow and blue	15	30
284	**56**	75c. black, yellow and lilac	45	2·00
MS285		178×200 mm. Nos. 282/4	3·00	7·00

57 Installation Ceremony

1980. First Anniv of Prince Sufri Bolkiah's Installation as First Wazir. Multicoloured. Blue borders.

286		10c. Type **57**	15	10
287		75c. Prince Sufri	85	2·00

1980. First Anniv of Prince Jefri Bolkiah's Installation as Second Wazir. Designs similar to T **57**. Multicoloured. Green borders.

288		10c. Installation ceremony	15	10
289		75c. Prince Jefri	85	2·25

58 Royal Umbrella and Sash

1981. Royal Regalia (1st series). Multicoloured.

290		10c. Type **58**	20	15
291		15c. Sword and Shield	35	25
292		20c. Lance and Sheath	40	40
293		30c. Betel Leaf Container	60	1·25
294		50c. Coronation Crown (39×22 mm)	1·25	5·00
MS295		98×142 mm. Nos. 290/4	3·75	7·50

See Nos. 298/303, 314/19 and 320/5.

59 ITU and WHO Emblems

1981. World Telecommunications and Health Day.

296	**59**	10c. black and red	50	25
297	**59**	75c. black, blue and violet	2·25	5·00

60 Shield and Broadsword

1981. Royal Regalia (2nd series). Multicoloured.

298		10c. Type **60**	10	10
299		15c. Blunderbuss and Pouch	20	20
300		20c. Crossed Lances and Sash	30	30
301		30c. Sword, Shield and Sash	40	75
302		50c. Forked Lance	60	2·50
303		75c. Royal Drum (29×45 mm)	80	4·50

61 Prince Charles as Colonel of the Welsh Guards

1981. Royal Wedding. Multicoloured.

304		10c. Wedding bouquet from Brunei	15	15
305		$1 Type **61**	35	1·50

306		$2 Prince Charles and Lady Diana Spencer	50	2·50

62 Fishing

1981. World Food Day. Multicoloured.

307		10c. Type **62**	50	15
308		$1 Farm produce and machinery	4·50	7·50

63 Blind Man and Braille Alphabet

1981. International Year for Disabled Persons. Multicoloured.

309		10c. Type **63**	65	20
310		20c. Deaf people and sign language	1·50	80
311		75c. Disabled person and wheelchairs	3·00	6·75

64 Drawing of Infected Lungs

1982. Centenary of Robert Koch's Discovery of Tubercle Bacillus. Multicoloured.

312		10c. Type **64**	50	25
313		75c. Magnified tubercle bacillus and microscope	3·00	5·50

1982. Royal Regalia (3rd series). As T **60**. Multicoloured.

314		10c. Ceremonial Ornament	10	10
315		15c. Silver Betel Caddy	20	20
316		20c. Traditional Flowerpot	25	30
317		30c. Solitary Candle	50	90
318		50c. Golden Pipe	70	2·50
319		75c. Royal Chin Support (28×45 mm)	90	4·00

1982. Royal Regalia (4th series). As T **60**. Multicoloured.

320		10c. Royal Mace	25	10
321		15c. Ceremonial Shield and Spears	35	30
322		20c. Embroidered Ornament	45	40
323		30c. Golden-tasseled Cushion	75	1·50
324		50c. Ceremonial Dagger and Sheath	1·25	3·50
325		75c. Religious Mace (28×45 mm)	1·60	4·50

65 Brunei Flag

1983. Commonwealth Day.

326	**65**	10c. multicoloured	15	70
327	-	20c. blue, black and buff	20	80
328	-	75c. blue, black and buff	45	1·25
329	-	$2 blue, black and buff	1·10	1·75

DESIGNS: 20c. Brunei Mosque; 75c. Machinery; $2 Sultan of Brunei.

66 "Postal Service"

1983. World Communications Year.

330	**66**	10c. multicoloured	15	10
331	-	75c. yellow, brown and black	60	75
332	-	$2 multicoloured	1·75	2·25

DESIGNS: 75c. "Telephone Service"; $2 "Communications".

67 Football

1983. Official Opening of the National Hassanal Bolkiah Stadium. Multicoloured.

333		10c. Type **67**	55	15
334		75c. Athletics	2·25	1·50
335		$1 View of stadium (44×27 mm)	2·75	4·00

68 Fishermen and Crustacea

1983. Fishery Resources. Multicoloured.

336		10c. Type **68**	1·00	15
337		50c. Fishermen with net	3·25	1·50
338		75c. Fishing trawler	3·50	4·00
339		$1 Fishing with hook and tackle	3·75	4·50

69 Royal Assembly Hall

1984. Independence.

340	**69**	10c. brown and orange	20	10
341	-	20c. pink and red	30	20
342	-	35c. pink and purple	60	60
343	-	50c. light blue and blue	1·75	1·25
344	-	75c. light green and green	1·75	2·00
345	-	$1 grey and brown	2·00	2·50
346	-	$3 multicoloured	7·00	10·00
MS347		150×120 mm. Nos. 340/6	12·00	15·00

MS348 Two sheets, each 150×120 mm, containing 4 stamps (34×69 mm).
(a) 25c. × 4 grey-black and new blue (Signing of the Brunei Constitution).
(b) 25c. × 4 multicoloured (Signing of Brunei–U.K. Friendship Agreement). Set of 2 sheets 2·00 4·50

DESIGNS—34×25 mm: 20c. Government Secretariat Building; 35c. New Supreme Court; 50c. Natural gas well; 75c. Omar Ali Saifuddin Mosque; $1 Sultan's Palace. 68×24 mm: $3 Brunei flag and map of South-East Asia.

70 Natural Forests and Enrichment Planting

1984. Forestry Resources. Multicoloured.

349		10c. Type **70**	1·00	25
350		50c. Forests and water resources	2·50	2·25
351		75c. Recreation forests	3·25	4·50
352		$1 Forests and wildlife	4·75	6·00

71 Sultan Omar Saiffuddin 50c. Stamp of 1952

1984. "Philakorea" International Stamp Exhibition, Seoul. Multicoloured.

353		10c. Type **71**	50	15
354		75c. Brunei River view 10c. stamp of 1907	1·50	2·25
355		$2 Star and view ½c. stamp of 1895	2·50	6·50
MS356		Three sheets, 117×100 mm, each containing one stamp as Nos. 353/5 Set of 3 sheets	3·75	7·00

72 United Nations Emblem

1985. Admission of Brunei to World Organizations (1st issue).

357	**72**	50c. black, gold and blue	50	70
358	-	50c. multicoloured	50	70
359	-	50c. multicoloured	50	70
360	-	50c. multicoloured	50	70
MS361	110×151 mm. Nos. 357/60		2·25	3·00

DESIGNS: No. 358, Islamic Conference Organization logo; 359, Commonwealth logo; 360, A.S.E.A.N. emblem.
See also Nos. 383/7.

73 Young People and Brunei Flag

1985. International Youth Year. Multicoloured.

362	10c. Type **73**	1·25	20	
363	75c. Young people at work	5·00	7·00	
364	$1 Young people serving the community	6·00	7·50	

74 Palestinian Emblem

1985. International Palestinian Solidarity Day.

365	**74**	10c. multicoloured	2·00	20
366	**74**	50c. multicoloured	4·25	1·50
367	**74**	$1 multicoloured	5·25	3·00

75 Early and Modern Scout Uniforms

1985. National Scout Jamboree. Multicoloured.

368	10c. Type **75**	60	10	
369	20c. Scout on tower signalling with flag	90	40	
370	$2 Jamboree emblem	2·75	3·25	

76 Sultan Sir Hassanal Bolkiah Mu'izzaddin Waddaulah

1985

371	**76**	10c. multicoloured	30	10
372	**76**	15c. multicoloured	30	10
373	**76**	20c. multicoloured	40	10
374	**76**	25c. multicoloured	40	15
375	**76**	35c. multicoloured	55	20
376	**76**	40c. multicoloured	60	25
377	**76**	50c. multicoloured	70	35
378	**76**	75c. multicoloured	90	50
379	**76**	$1 multicoloured	1·25	70
380	**76**	$2 multicoloured	2·75	1·75
381	**76**	$5 multicoloured	4·25	5·00
382	**76**	$10 multicoloured	8·00	11·00

Nos. 379/82 are larger, size 32×39 mm.

1986. Admission of Brunei to World Organizations (2nd issue). As T **72**.

383	50c. black, gold and green	50	60	
384	50c. black, gold and mauve	50	60	
385	50c. black, gold and red	50	60	
386	50c. black, gold and blue	50	60	
MS387	105×155 mm. Nos. 383/6	1·50	4·00	

DESIGNS: No. 383, World Meteorological Organization emblem; 384, International Tele-communication Union emblem; 385, Universal Postal Union emblem; 386, International Civil Aviation Organization emblem.

78 Soldiers on Assault Course and Bell 205 UH-1H Iroquois Helicopter

1986. 25th Anniv of Brunei Armed Forces. Multicoloured.

388	10c. Type **78**	3·75	3·75	
389	20c. Operating computer	4·00	4·00	

390	50c. Anti-aircraft missile, MBB-Bolkow Bo 150L helicopter and missile boat	5·00	5·00	
391	75c. Army, commanders and parade	5·50	5·50	

Nos. 388/91 were printed together, se-tenant, forming a composite design.

79 Tunggul Charok Buritan, Alam Bernaga (Alam Besar), Pisang-Pisang and Sandaran

1986. Royal Ensigns (1st series).

392	**79**	10c. black, yellow and red	30	10
393	-	75c. multicoloured	1·10	1·10
394	-	$2 black, yellow and green	2·25	2·75

DESIGNS: 75c. Ula-Ula Besar, Sumbu Layang and Payong Haram; $2 Panji-Panji, Chogan Istiadat (Chogan Di-Raja) and Chogan Ugama.

1986. Royal Ensigns (2nd series). As T **79**.

395	10c. multicoloured	30	10	
396	75c. black, red and yellow	1·10	1·10	
397	$2 multicoloured	2·25	2·75	

DESIGNS: 10c. Dadap, Tunggul Kawan, Ambal, Payong Ubor-Ubor, Sapu-Sapu Ayeng and Rawai Lidah; 75c. Payong Tinggi and Payong Ubor-Ubor Tiga Ringkat; $2 Lambang Duli Yang Maha Mulia and Mahligai.

80 Stylized Peace Doves

1986. International Peace Year. Multicoloured.

398	50c. Type **80**	75	75	
399	75c. Stylized hands and "1986"	1·00	1·10	
400	$1 International Peace Year emblem and arms of Brunei	1·25	1·50	

81 Drug Addict in Cage and Syringe (poster by Othman bin Ramboh)

1987. National Anti-drug Campaign. Children's Posters. Multicoloured.

401	10c. Type **81**	1·25	35	
402	75c. Drug addict and noose (Arman bin Mohd. Zaman)	2·75	4·00	
403	$1 Blindfolded drug addict and noose (Abidin bin Hj. Rashid)	3·25	5·00	

82 Cannon ("badil")

1987. Brassware (1st series). Multicoloured.

404	50c. Type **82**	50	50	
405	50c. Lamp ("pelita")	50	50	
406	50c. Betel container ("languai")	50	50	
407	50c. Water jug ("kiri")	50	50	

See also Nos. 434/7.

83 Map showing Member Countries

84 Brunei Citizens

1987. 20th Anniv of Association of South East Asian Nations. Multicoloured.

408	20c. Type **83**	35	20	
409	50c. Dates and figures "20"	60	50	
410	$1 Flags of member states	1·25	1·25	

1987. 25th Anniv (1986) of Language and Literature Bureau. Multicoloured.

411	10c. Type **84**	30	30	
412	50c. Flame emblem and hands holding open book	60	60	
413	$2 Scenes of village life	1·50	1·50	

Nos. 411/13 were printed together, se-tenant, forming a composite design taken from a mural.

85 Artocarpus odoratissima

1987. Local Fruit (1st series). Multicoloured.

414	50c. Type **85**	45	55	
415	50c. Canarium odontophyllum mig	45	55	
416	50c. Litsea garciae	45	55	
417	50c. Mangifera foetida lour	45	55	

See also Nos. 421/4, 459/62, 480/2 and 525/8.

86 Modern House

1987. International Year of Shelter for the Homeless.

418	**86**	50c. multicoloured	40	50
419	-	75c. multicoloured	55	65
420	-	$1 multicoloured	80	90

DESIGNS: 75c., $1 Modern Brunei housing projects.

1988. Local Fruits (2nd series). As T **85**. Multicoloured.

421	50c. Durio spp	95	1·25	
422	50c. Durio oxleyanus	95	1·25	
423	50c. Durio graveolens (blue background)	95	1·25	
424	50c. Durio graveolens (white background)	95	1·25	

87 Wooden Lathe

1988. Opening of Malay Technology Museum. Multicoloured.

425	50c. Type **87**	15	10	
426	75c. Crushing sugar cane	55	70	
427	$1 Bird scarer	70	85	

88 Patterned Cloth

1988. Handwoven Material (1st series). Multicoloured.

428	10c. Type **88**	10	10	
429	20c. Jong Sarat cloth	15	15	
430	25c. Si Pugut cloth	20	25	
431	40c. Si Pugut Bunga Berlapis cloth	30	35	
432	75c. Si Lobang Bangsi Bunga Belitang Kipas cloth	55	80	
MS433	105×204 mm. Nos. 428/32	2·25	4·25	

See also Nos. 442/7.

1988. Brassware (2nd series). As T **82**. Multicoloured.

434	50c. Lidded two-handled pot ("periok")	40	50	
435	50c. Candlestick ("lampong")	40	50	
436	50c. Shallow circular dish with stand ("gangsa")	40	50	
437	50c. Repousse box with lid ("celapa")	40	50	

89 Sultan reading Proclamation

1988. 20th Anniv of Sultan's Coronation. Multicoloured.

438	20c. Type **89**	25	15	
439	75c. Sultan reading from Koran	80	60	
440	$2 In Coronation robes (26×63 mm)	2·00	1·60	
MS441	164×125 mm. Nos. 438/40	2·40	2·50	

1988. Handwoven Material (2nd series). As T **88**. Multicoloured.

442	10c. Beragi cloth	15	10	
443	20c. Bertabur cloth	20	20	
444	25c. Sukma Indra cloth	25	35	
445	40c. Si Pugut Bunga cloth	40	75	
446	75c. Beragi Si Lobang Bangsi Bunga Cendera Kesuma cloth	75	1·40	
MS447	150×204 mm. Nos. 442/6	3·00	4·25	

90 Malaria-carrying Mosquito

1988. 40th Anniv of WHO. Multicoloured.

448	25c. Type **90**	1·10	30	
449	35c. Man with insecticide spray and sample on slide	1·25	45	
450	$2 Microscope and magnified malaria cells	3·00	2·00	

91 Sultan and Council of Ministers

1989. Fifth Anniv of National Day. Multicoloured.

451	20c. Type **91**	15	10	
452	30c. Guard of honour	20	15	
453	60c. Firework display (27×55 mm)	45	40	
454	$2 Congregation in mosque	1·50	1·75	
MS455	164×124 mm. Nos. 451/4	2·25	2·75	

92 Dove escaping from Cage

1989. "Freedom of Palestine". Multicoloured.

456	20c. Type **92**	40	20	
457	75c. Map and Palestinian flag	1·50	1·00	
458	$1 Dome of the Rock, Jerusalem	2·25	1·40	

1989. Local Fruit (3rd series). As T **85**. Multicoloured.

459	60c. Daemonorops fissa	2·00	2·50	
460	60c. Eleiodoxa conferta	2·00	2·50	
461	60c. Salacca zalacca	2·00	2·50	
462	60c. Calamus ornatus	2·00	2·50	

93 Oil Pump

1989. 60th Anniv of Brunei Oil and Gas Industry. Multicoloured.

463	20c. Type **93**	2·00	30	
464	60c. Loading tanker	3·50	2·25	
465	90c. Oil well at sunset	3·75	3·00	
466	$1 Pipe laying	3·75	3·00	
467	$2 Oil terminal	7·00	8·00	

94 Museum Building and Exhibits

1990. 25th Anniv of Brunei Museum. Multicoloured.
468	30c. Type **94**	1·50	70
469	60c. Official opening, 1965	2·25	2·25
470	$1 Brunei Museum	3·00	3·75

95 Letters from Malay Alphabet

1990. International Literacy Year. Multicoloured.
471	15c. Type **95**	80	40
472	90c. English alphabet	3·50	4·25
473	$1 Literacy Year emblem and letters	3·50	4·25

96 Tarsier in Tree

1990. Endangered Species. Western Tarsier. Multicoloured.
474	20c. Western Tarsier on branch	1·25	45
475	60c. Western Tarsier feeding	2·50	3·00
476	90c. Type **96**	3·50	4·50

97 Symbolic Family

1990. Worldwide Campaign against AIDS. Multicoloured.
477	20c. Type **97**	2·25	60
478	30c. Sources of infection	3·00	2·00
479	90c. "AIDS" headstone surrounded by skulls	7·50	8·00

1990. Local Fruit (4th series). As T **85**. Multicoloured.
480	60c. *Willoughbea* sp. (brown fruit)	2·75	3·75
481	60c. Ripe *Willoughbea* sp. (yellow fruit)	2·75	3·75
482	60c. *Willoughbea angustifolia*	2·75	3·75

98 Proboscis Monkey on Ground

1991. Endangered Species. Proboscis Monkey. Multicoloured.
483	15c. Type **98**	1·50	60
484	20c. Head of monkey	1·60	70
485	50c. Monkey sitting on branch	3·00	3·25
486	60c. Female monkey with baby climbing tree	3·25	3·75

99 Junior School Classes

1991. Teachers' Day. Multicoloured.
487	60c. Type **99**	2·25	2·50
488	90c. Secondary school class	2·75	3·50

100 Young Brunei Beauty

1991. Fish. Brunei Beauty. Multicoloured.
489	30c. Type **100**	1·50	85
490	60c. Female fish	2·50	4·00
491	$1 Male fish	3·00	4·75

101 Graduate with Family

1991. Happy Family Campaign. Multicoloured.
492	20c. Type **101**	70	50
493	60c. Mothers with children	1·75	2·00
494	90c. Family	2·00	3·25

102 Symbolic Heart and Trace

1992. World Health Day.
495	102	20c. multicoloured	1·75	50
496	–	50c. multicoloured	3·25	2·50
497	–	75c. multicoloured	4·50	6·00

DESIGNS: 50c., 70c. (48×27 mm) Heart and heartbeat trace.

103 Map of Cable System

1992. Launching of Singapore–Borneo–Philippines Fibre Optic Submarine Cable System. Multicoloured.
498	20c. Type **103**	2·25	50
499	30c. Diagram of Brunei connection	2·25	1·50
500	90c. Submarine cable	4·75	6·00

104 Modern Sculptures

1992. Visit ASEAN Year. Multicoloured.
501	20c. Type **104**	2·00	2·25
502	60c. Traditional martial arts	2·25	2·75
503	$1 Modern sculptures (different)	2·50	3·00

Nos. 501/3 were printed together, *se-tenant*, the backgrounds forming a composite design.

105 "ASEAN 25" and Logo

1992. 25th Anniv of ASEAN (Association of South East Asian Nations). Multicoloured.
504	20c. Type **105**	1·25	65
505	60c. Headquarters building	2·75	2·75
506	90c. National landmarks	3·50	4·50

106 Sultan in Procession

1992. 25th Anniv of Sultan's Accession. Multicoloured.
507	25c. Type **106**	1·50	1·75
508	25c. Brunei International Airport	1·50	1·75
509	25c. Sultan's Palace	1·50	1·75
510	25c. Docks and Brunei University	1·50	1·75
511	25c. Mosque	1·50	1·75

Nos. 507/11 were printed together, *se-tenant*, forming a composite design.

107 Crested Wood Partridge

1992. Birds (1st series). Multicoloured.
512	30c. Type **107**	1·00	50
513	60c. Asiatic paradise flycatcher ("Asian Paradise Flycatcher")	2·00	2·25
514	$1 Great argus pheasant	2·25	3·00

See also Nos. 515/17, 518/20, 575/7 and 602/5.

1993. Birds (2nd series). As T **107**. Multicoloured.
515	30c. Long-tailed parakeet	1·00	50
516	60c. Magpie robin	2·00	2·25
517	$1 Blue-crowned hanging parrot ("Malay Lorikeet")	2·50	3·00

1993. Birds (3rd series). As T **107**. Multicoloured.
518	30c. Chesnut-breasted malkoha	1·25	50
519	60c. White-rumped shama	2·25	2·50
520	$1 Black and red broadbill (vert)	3·00	3·50

108 National Flag and "10"

1994. Tenth Anniv of National Day. Multicoloured.
521	10c. Type **108**	80	1·00
522	20c. Symbolic hands	85	85
523	30c. Previous National Day symbols	95	95
524	60c. Coat of arms	1·25	1·50

1994. Local Fruit (5th issue). As T **85**, but each 36×26 mm. Multicoloured.
525	60c. *Nephelium mutabile*	85	1·40
526	60c. *Nephelium xerospermoides*	85	1·40
527	60c. *Nephelium spp*	85	1·40
528	60c. *Nephelium macrophyllum*	85	1·40

109 Cigarette burning Heart and Deformed Baby in Womb

1994. World No Tobacco Day. Multicoloured.
529	10c. Type **109**	25	20
530	15c. Symbols of smoking over crowd of people	25	20
531	$2 Globe crushing cigarettes	2·75	4·50

110 Raja Isteri (wife of Sultan in Guide uniform)

1994. 40th Anniv of Brunei Girl Guides' Association. Multicoloured.
532	40c. Type **110**	1·40	1·50
533	40c. Guide receiving award	1·40	1·50
534	40c. Guide reading	1·40	1·50
535	40c. Group of guides	1·40	1·50
536	40c. Guides erecting tent	1·40	1·50

111 Fokker F-27 Friendship on Runway

1994. 20th Anniv of Royal Brunei Airlines. Multicoloured.
537	10c. Type **111**	55	30
538	20c. Boeing 757 on runway	85	35
539	$1 Boeing 757 in the air	2·00	3·50

112 Malay Family

1994. International Day against Drug Abuse and Trafficking. Multicoloured.
540	20c. Type **112**	80	1·40
541	60c. Chinese family	1·25	1·75
542	$1 Doctor, police officers and members of youth organizations	1·60	2·25

Nos. 540/2 were printed together, *se-tenant*, forming a composite design.

113 Aerial View of City, 1970

1995. 25th Anniv of Bandar Seri Begawan. Multicoloured.
543	30c. Type **113**	1·00	45
544	50c. City in 1980	1·50	1·50
545	$1 City in 1990	2·25	3·00

114 United Nations General Assembly

1995. 50th Anniv of United Nations. Multicoloured.
546	20c. Type **114**	40	25
547	60c. Security Council in session	75	80
548	90c. United Nations Building, New York (27×44 mm)	1·25	2·25

115 Students in Laboratory

1995. Tenth Anniv of University of Brunei. Multicoloured.
549	30c. Type **115**	45	35
550	50c. University building	70	70
551	90c. Sultan visiting University	1·25	2·25

116 Police Officers

1996. 75th Anniv of Royal Brunei Police Force. Multicoloured.

552	25c. Type **116**	85	40
553	50c. Aspects of police work	1·25	1·25
554	75c. Sultan inspecting parade	2·00	3·00

117 Telephones

1996. World Telecommunications Day. Children's Paintings. Multicoloured.

555	20c. Type **117**	50	30
556	35c. Telephone dial and aspects of telecommunications	65	45
557	$1 Globe and aspects of telecommunications	2·25	3·25

118 Sultan and Crowd

1996. 50th Birthday of Sultan Hassanal Bolkiah Mu'izzaddin Waddaulah. Multicoloured.

558	50c. Type **118**	85	1·25
559	50c. Sultan in ceremonial dress	85	1·25
560	50c. Sultan receiving dignitaries at mosque	85	1·25
561	50c. Sultan with subjects	85	1·25
MS562	152×100 mm. $1 Sultan in ceremonial dress (different)	1·75	2·50

119 Sultan Hassanal Bolkiah Mu'izzaddin Waddaulah

1996

563	**119**	10c. multicoloured	10	10
564	**119**	15c. multicoloured	10	15
565	**119**	20c. multicoloured	15	20
566	**119**	30c. multicoloured	20	25
567	**119**	50c. multicoloured	30	35
568	**119**	60c. multicoloured	40	45
569	**119**	75c. multicoloured	45	50
570	**119**	90c. multicoloured	55	60
571	–	$1 multicoloured	65	70
572	–	$2 multicoloured	1·25	1·40
573	–	$5 multicoloured	3·25	3·50
574	–	$10 multicoloured	6·25	6·50

DESIGN—27×39 mm: $1 to $10 Sultan in ceremonial robes.

121 Black-naped Tern

1996. Birds (4th series). Sea Birds. Multicoloured.

575	20c. Type **121**	75	50
576	30c. Roseate tern	75	50
577	$1 Bridled tern	1·75	2·75

No. 576 is inscr "ROSLATE TERN" in error.

122 *Acanthus ebracteatus*

1997. Mangrove Flowers. Multicoloured.

578	20c. Type **122**	45	25
579	30c. *Lumnitzera littorea*	50	35
580	$1 *Nypa fruticans*	1·40	2·50

123 *Heterocentrotus mammillatus*

1997. Marine Life. Multicoloured.

581	60c. Type **123**	60	85
582	60c. *Linckia laevigata* (starfish)	60	85
583	60c. *Oxycomanthus bennetti* (plant)	60	85
584	60c. *Bohadschia argus* (sea slug)	60	85

124 Children and Sign Language

1998. Asian and Pacific Decade of Disabled Persons, 1993–2002. Multicoloured.

585	20c. Type **124**	30	25
586	50c. Woman typing and firework display	60	75
587	$1 Disabled athletes	1·00	1·75

125 Sultan performing Ceremonial Duties

1998. 30th Anniv of Coronation of Sultan Hassanal Bolkiah Mu'izzaddin Waddaulah. Multicoloured.

588	60c. Type **125**	70	50
589	90c. Sultan on Coronation throne	1·10	1·40
590	$1 Coronation parade	1·25	1·40
MS591	150×180 mm. Nos. 588/90	2·75	3·50

126 A.S.E.A.N. Architecture and Transport

1998. 30th Anniv of Association of South-east Asian Nations. Multicoloured.

592	30c. Type **126**	90	90
593	30c. Map of Brunei and city scenes	90	90
594	30c. Flags of member nations	90	90

127 Crown Prince at Desk

1998. Proclamation of Prince Al-Muhtadee Billah as Crown Prince. Multicoloured.

595	$1 Type **127**	1·00	1·00
596	$2 Crown Prince in military uniform	1·75	2·75
597	$3 Crown Prince's emblem	2·25	3·75
MS598	175×153 mm. Nos. 595/7.	5·50	7·00

128 Koran, Civil Servants and Handshake

1998. Fifth Anniv of Civil Service Day. Multicoloured.

599	30c. Type **128**	40	30
600	60c. Symbols of progress	65	65
601	90c. Civil servants at work	95	1·25

129 Blue-eared Kingfisher

1998. Birds (5th series). Kingfishers. Multicoloured.

602	20c. Type **129**	70	50
603	30c. River kingfisher ("Common Kingfisher")	80	50
604	60c. White-collared kingfisher	1·25	95
605	$1 Stork-billed kingfisher	1·50	2·00

130 Water Village, Bandar Seri Begawan

1999. 15th Anniv of National Day. Multicoloured.

606	20c. Type **130**	30	20
607	60c. Modern telecommunications and Boeing 757	80	80
608	90c. Aspects of modern Brunei	1·25	1·50
MS609	118×85 mm. Nos. 606/8	2·00	2·75

131 Rifle-shooting

1999. 20th South-east Asia Games, Brunei. Multicoloured.

610	20c. Type **131**	45	50
611	20c. Golf and tennis	45	50
612	20c. Boxing and judo	45	50
613	20c. Squash and table tennis	45	50
614	20c. Swimming and canoe racing	45	50
615	20c. Hockey and cycling	45	50
616	20c. Basketball and football	45	50
617	20c. High jumping, shot putting and running	45	50
618	20c. Snooker	45	50
619	20c. Bowling	45	50
MS620	110×73 mm. $1 Various sports	1·60	2·40

132 Clasped Hands and Globe

1999. 125th Anniv of Universal Postal Union. Multicoloured.

621	20c. Type **132**	40	20
622	30c. "125" and logos	50	25
623	75c. Aspects of postal service	1·10	1·50

133 Modern Building and Children using Computer

2000. New Millennium. Multicoloured.

624	20c. Type **133**	45	50
625	20c. Royal Palace, tree and people using computer	45	50
626	20c. Aerial view of mosque and factory	45	50
627	20c. Plan of Parterre Gardens	45	50
628	20c. Container ships and Boeing 757	45	50
629	20c. Satellite dish aerials	45	50
MS630	221×121 mm. Nos. 624/9	1·75	2·25

Nos. 624/9 were printed together, *se-tenant*, with the backgrounds forming a composite design.

134 Sultan Mohamed Jemal-ul-Alam and Traditional Buildings, 1901–20

2000. Brunei in the 20th Century. Multicoloured.

631	30c. Type **134**	55	55
632	30c. Sultan Ahmed Tajudin, oil well and Brunei police, 1921–40	55	55
633	30c. Signing of the Constitution and Brunei Mosque, 1941–60	55	55
634	30c. Oil installation, satellite dish, Boeing 757 of Royal Brunei Airlines and bank note, 1961–80	55	55
635	30c. Sultan on throne, international organisation emblems and crowd with trophy, 1981–99	55	55

135 Sultan Hashim Jalil-ul-Alam, 1885–1906

2000. The Sultans of Brunei. Multicoloured.

636	60c. Type **135**	90	95
637	60c. Sultan Mohamed Jemal-ul-Alam, 1906–24	90	95
638	60c. Sultan Ahmed Tajudin, 1924–50	90	95
639	60c. Sultan Omar Ali Saifuddin, 1950–67	90	95
640	60c. Sultan Hassanal Bolkiah, 1967	90	95
MS641	190×99 mm. Nos. 636/40	3·50	5·00

136 *Rafflesia pricei*

2000. Local Flowers. Multicoloured.

642	30c. Type **136**	45	30
643	50c. *Rhizanthes lowi*	70	70
644	60c. *Nepenthes rafflesiana*	80	80

137 Information Technology

2000. Asia–Pacific Economic Cooperation. Heads of Government Meeting. Multicoloured.
645	20c. Type **137**	45	30
646	30c. Small and medium busi-nesses	55	35
647	60c. Tourism	1·00	1·10
MS648	150×108 mm. Nos. 645/7	1·75	2·25

138 Green Turtle

2000. Turtles. Multicoloured.
649	30c. Type **138**	60	65
650	30c. Hawksbill turtle	60	65
651	30c. Olive Ridley turtle	60	65

139 Tourist Canoe on River

2001. "Visit Brunei Year" (1st series). Multicoloured.
652	20c. Type **139**	60	45
653	30c. Traditional water village	70	45
654	60c. Carved building facade	1·50	1·50

See also Nos. 669/72.

140 Sultan in Army Uniform

2001. 55th Birthday of Sultan Hassanal Bolkiah Muizzaddin Waddaulah. Multicoloured.
655	55c. Type **140**	80	85
656	55c. Sultan in Air Force uniform	80	85
657	55c. Sultan in traditional dress	80	85
658	55c. Sultan in Army camouflage jacket	80	85
659	55c. Sultan in Navy uniform	80	85
MS660	100×75 mm. 55c. Sultan and Bandar Seri Begawan (40×71 mm)	1·25	1·50

141 First Aid Demonstration

2001. International Youth Camp. Multicoloured.
661	30c. Type **141**	60	65
662	30c. Brunei guides and tent demonstration	60	65
663	30c. Scouts with cooking pot	60	65
MS664	110×77 mm. Nos. 661/3	1·60	2·00

Nos. 661/3 were printed together, *se-tenant*, forming a composite design.

142 Islamic Regalia

2001. First Islamic International Exhibition, Brunei. Multicoloured.
665	20c. Type **142**	45	50
666	20c. Exhibition centre	45	50
667	20c. Computer communications	45	50
668	20c. Opening ceremony	45	50

143 Forest Walkway

2001. Visit Brunei (2nd series). Multicoloured.
669	20c. Type **143**	45	50
670	20c. Waterfall	45	50
671	20c. Jerudong Theme Park	45	50
672	20c. Footbridges across lake	45	50

144 "Children encircling Globe" (Urska Golob)

2001. U.N. Year of Dialogue among Civilisations. Multicoloured.
673	30c. Type **144**	50	55
674	30c. Quotation marks illustrated with faces	50	55
675	30c. Cubist portrait and Japanese girl	50	55
676	30c. Coloured leaves	50	55

145 Male and Female Bulwer's Pheasants

2001. Endangered Species. Bulwer's Pheasant. Multicoloured.
677	30c. Type **145**	50	55
678	30c. Male pheasant	50	55
679	30c. Female pheasant with chicks	50	55
680	30c. Female pheasant	50	55

146 Early and Modern Telephone Systems

2002. 50th Anniv of Department of Telecommunications (JTB). Multicoloured.
681	50c. Type **146**	65	70
682	50c. JTB Golden Jubilee emblem	65	70
683	50c. Computer networks	65	70

147 50th Anniversary Logo

2002. 50th Anniv of Survey Department. Multicoloured.
684	50c. Type **147**	65	70
685	50c. Survey Department Offices	65	70
686	50c. Theodolite and thermal map	65	70

148 Modern Housing, Water Village

2002. Tenth Anniv of Yayasan Sultan Haji Hassanal Bolkiah Foundation. Multicoloured.
687	10c. Type **148**	30	30
688	10c. Mosque and interior	30	30
689	10c. School and computer class	30	30
690	10c. University of Brunei	30	30

149 Anti-Corruption Bureau Headquarters

2002. 20th Anniv of Anti-Corruption Bureau. Multicoloured.
691	20c. Type **149**	45	50
692	20c. Skyscrapers and mosque	45	50
693	20c. Anti-Corruption Bureau posters	45	50

150 Melastoma malabathricum

2003. Flowering Medicinal Plants. Multicoloured.
694	20c. Type **150**	45	50
695	20c. Etlingera solaris	45	50
696	20c. Dillenia suffruticosa	45	50
697	20c. Costus speciosus	45	50

151 Drums and Musicians

2003. ASEAN—Japan Exchange Year. Multicoloured.
698	20c. Type **151**	25	30
699	20c. Woodworker and handicrafts	25	30
700	20c. Exchange Year logo	25	30

152 Sultan of Brunei and UN Emblem

2004. 20th Anniv of National Day. Multicoloured.
701	20c. Type **152**	25	30
702	20c. In military uniform	25	30
703	20c. Reading speech at National Day celebration	25	30
704	20c. Emblem	25	30
MS705	185×140 mm. Nos. 701/4	1·00	1·10

153 Brunei 1895 ½c. Stamp

2004. Brunei Darussalam National Philatelic Society. Multicoloured.
706	25c. Type **153**	25	30
707	25c. Magnifying glass, perfora-tion gauge, tweezers and stamps	25	30
708	25c. Postmarks, stamp cata-logue and first day covers	25	30

154 Crown Prince Al-Muhtadee Billah Bolkiah and Sarah Salleh

2004. Royal Wedding.
709	**154** 99c. multicoloured	1·60	1·75

155 Sultan of Brunei and Jame'Asr Hassanal Bolkiah Mosque

2006. 60th Birthday of Sultan Hassanal Bolkiah Muizzaddin Waddaulah. Designs showing montage of images, all with portrait of Sultan at top right. Multicoloured (except 60c), panel colours given.
710	60c. Type **155** (mauve)	1·00	1·00
711	60c. Sultan, palace and crowd with flags (red)	1·00	1·00
712	60c. Sultan and urban and agricultural scenes (yellow)	1·00	1·00
713	60c. Sultan speaking at 9th ASEAN–Japan Summit and at APEC 2000 (salmon)	1·00	1·00
714	60c. Sultan meeting woman (green)	1·00	1·00
715	60c. Sultan in military uniform (blue)	1·00	1·00
MS716	166×120 mm. Nos. 710/15	5·50	6·00
MS717	148×137 mm. $60 Montage of five black and white photographs of Sultan as young man, at Coronation, seated on throne and wearing crown and military uniform (black and grey) (99×90 mm)	42·00	48·00

156 General Post Office, Bandar Seri Begawan

157 Parcels and Letters travelling around Globe

2006. Centenary of Postal Services Department. Multicoloured

(a) As T **156**
718	100c. Type **156**	1·40	1·60
719	100c. Kuala Belait Post Office	1·40	1·60
720	100c. Tutong Post Office at the District Office, Tutong	1·40	1·60
721	100c. Bangar Post Office at the District Office, Temburong	1·40	1·60
MS722	115×115 mm. Nos. 718/21	5·00	5·75

(b) T **157** and similar vert designs showing children's drawings.
MS723	95×145 mm. 100s.×6 Type **157**; Postman; Globe, letter, house and aircraft; Air mail letters, postbox and post office; Letters, globe and fami-lies in Brunei and China; Globe and national flags ('EVERYONE REACHING EVERYWHERE')	7·00	8·00

158 Balistapus undulates (orangestriped triggerfish)

2007. Marine Life. Multicoloured.

724	60c. Type **158**		1·25	1·25
725	60c. *Taenionotis triacanthus* (leaf scorpionfish)		1·25	1·25
MS726	100×70 mm. $1 *Nautilus pompilus* (chambered nautilus); $1 *Ostracion meleagris* (spotted boxfish)		3·50	3·50

Stamps in similar designs were issued by Malaysia.

159 Sultan Hassanal Bolkiah Mu'izzaddin Waddaulah

2007. Multicoloured.

727	**159**	10c. multicoloured	10	10
728	**159**	15c. multicoloured	20	20
729	**159**	20c. multicoloured	25	25
730	**159**	30c. multicoloured	35	35
731	**159**	50c. multicoloured	60	60
732	**159**	60c. multicoloured	70	70
733	**159**	75c. multicoloured	90	90
734	**159**	90c. multicoloured	1·10	1·10
735	–	$1 multicoloured	1·25	1·25
736	–	$2 multicoloured	2·40	2·40
737	–	$5 multicoloured	6·00	6·00
738	–	$10 multicoloured	12·00	12·00

Nos. 735/8 are as Type **159** but larger, 27×40 mm.

160 Bubungan Dua Belas

2007. Centenary of Bubungan Dua Belas, Bukit Subok. Multicoloured.

739	30s. Type **160**		90	35
740	60s. Bubungan Dua Belas (seen from above)		1·60	1·25
741	$1 Bubungan Dua Belas, 1907		2·50	3·00
MS742	150×90 mm. Nos. 739/41		4·50	4·75

Bubungan Dua Belas—House of 12 Roofs was the British High Commissioner's Residence.

161 Public Works Department Headquarters

2007. Centenary (2006) of Public Works Department. Multicoloured.

743	75c. Type **161**		1·00	1·25
744	75c. Engineers Office, (PWD Headquarters), Subok, 1906		1·00	1·25
745	75c. 100		1·00	1·25

162 Secretariat Building, Brunei

2007. 40th Anniv of ASEAN (Association of South-east Asian Nations). Ancient and Modern Architecture. Multicoloured.

746	20c. Type **162**		1·10	1·10
747	20c. Yangon Post Office, Myanmar		1·10	1·10
748	20c. National Museum of Cambodia		1·10	1·10
749	20c. Malacañang Palace, Philippines		1·10	1·10
750	20c. Fatahillah Museum, Jakarta, Indonesia		1·10	1·10
751	20c. National Museum of Singapore		1·10	1·10
752	20c. Lao Typical House		1·10	1·10
753	20c. Vimanmek Mansion, Bangkok, Thailand		1·10	1·10
754	20c. Malayan Railway Headquarters Building, Kuala Lumpur, Malaysia		1·10	1·10
755	20c. Presidential Palace, Hanoi, Vietnam		1·10	1·10

Similar designs were issued by the ten member countries, Indonesia, Malaysia, Philippines, Singapore, Thailand, Vietnam, Laos, Myanmar and Cambodia.

163 Istana Majlis

2008. Centenary of Transition of the Capital City from Kampung Air to Mainland. Multicoloured.

756	20c. Type **163**		60	40
757	30c. Istana Kota		70	40
758	60c. Bandar Brunei Mula-Mula Dirona di Darat, 1906		1·40	1·25
759	100c. Modern city of Bandar Seri Begawan		2·25	2·75
MS760	130×130 mm. Nos. 756/9		4·50	4·50

164 Sultan saluting

2008. 40th Anniv of Coronation of Sultan Hassanal Bolkiah Mu'izzadin Waddaulah. Multicoloured.

761	40s. Type **164**		60	60
762	40s. Coronation ceremony		60	60
763	40s. Crowning of Sultan		60	60
764	40s. Crowned Sultan seated in chair		60	60
MS765	160×100 mm. Nos. 761/4		3·25	3·75
MS766	159×100 mm. $40 Crowned Sultan on throne and courtiers (44×69 mm)		35·00	40·00

165 Sultan Omar Ali Saifuddin outside Mosque, 1958

2008. 50th Anniv of Omar Ali Saifuddien Mosque. Multicoloured.

767	50c. Type **165**		85	95
768	50c. Sultan Hassanal Bolkiah Mu'izzaddin Waddaulah		85	95
769	50c. Sultan and courtiers inside Mosque		85	95
770	50c. Aerial view of Mosque		85	95
MS771	150×80 mm. Noc. 767/70		3·00	3·50
MS772	199×110 mm. $50 Omar Ali Saifuddin Mosque (44×71 mm)		40·00	45·00

166 Scanner and Medical Staff

2008. Centenary of Health Services in Brunei. Multicoloured.

773	10c. Type **166**		25	25
774	10c. Nurse with mother and baby		25	25
775	$1 First government hospital in Brunei town		1·75	2·00

167 Montage of Buildings

2009. National Day Silver Jubilee (25th Anniv of Independence). Multicoloured, background colours given.

776	25c. Type **167**		55	55
777	25c. Montage of buildings (different) (bright green)		55	55
778	25c. Military parade, helicopter (on ground) and buildings (cerise)		55	55
779	25c. Montage of buildings (different) (pale yellow)		55	55
780	25c. Oil refinery, oil well, storage tanks and docks (lavender)		55	55
781	25c. Dancers and processions with national flags (bright purple)		55	55
782	25c. Women using mobile phone and laptop computer, modern buildings and airliner (reddish-brown)		55	55
783	25c. Anniversary emblem		55	55
784	25c. As Type **167** but blue border		55	55
785	25c. As No. 777 but blue border		55	55
786	25c. As No. 778 but blue border		55	55
787	25c. As No. 779 but blue border		55	55
788	25c. As No. 780 but blue border		55	55
789	25c. As No. 781 but blue border		55	55
790	25c. As No. 782 but blue border		55	55
791	25c. As No. 783 but blue border		55	55
MS792	180×140 mm. $25 Sultan Hassanal Bolkiah Mu'izzadin Waddaulah, Sultan Omar Ali Saifuddin and Bandar Seri Begawan city (101×71 mm)		27·00	29·00

168 Dendrobium secundum

2009. Wild Orchids of Brunei (1st series). Multicoloured.

793	10c. Type **168**		15	15
794	20c. *Bulboplllum* sp.		45	45
795	$1 *Phaleonopsis cornucervi* Bred		1·40	1·40

2009. Wild Orchids of Brunei (2nd series). As T **168**. Multicoloured.

796	10c. *Bulbophyllum beccarii*		15	15
797	20c. *Vanda hastifera* rchb. f. var. *hastifera*		45	45
798	$1 *Corybas pictus*		1·40	1·40

169 Land Administration Office

2010. Centenary (2009) of Modern Land Administration. Multicoloured.

799	10c. Type **169**		15	15
800	20c. Surveyors at construction site		45	45
801	$1 Man receiving land title		1·40	1·40

170 Tanker in Harbour

2010. 40th Anniv (2009) of Brunei LNG (liquid natural gas). Multicoloured.

802	40c. Type **170**		65	65
803	40c. Control rooms		65	65
804	40c. Brunei LNG staff and pipeline		65	65

171 Sultan of Brunei

2011. 65th Birthday of Sultan Hassanal Bolkiah Mu'izzadin Waddaulah. Multicoloured.

805	65c. Type **171**		1·10	1·10
806	65c. Sultan wearing black hat		1·10	1·10
807	65c. Sultan wearing grey uniform		1·10	1·10
808	65c. Sultan wearing blue jacket		1·10	1·10
809	65c. Sultan wearing turban		1·10	1·10
810	65c. Sultan with children		1·10	1·10
MS812	168×127 mm. $65 Sultan of Brunei (68×120 mm)		60·00	60·00

No. **MS811** is left for a miniature sheet containing Nos. 805/10, not yet received.

172 Malay Books

2011. 50th Anniv of Dewan Bahasa dan Pustaka (Institute of Language and Literature). Multicoloured.

813	20c. Type **172**		40	40
814	50c. Institute building and library buildings		85	85
815	$1 Founding of Dewan Bahasa dan Pustaka		1·75	1·75
MS816	145×105 mm. Nos. 813/15		3·00	3·00

173 Fishermen

2011. Farmers' and Fishermens' Day. Multicoloured.

817	20c. Type **173**		45	45
818	20c. Produce		45	45

174 Growing Rice and '20%'

2011. Towards Self-Sufficiency in Rice Production 20%. Multicoloured.

819	20c. Type **174**		45	45
820	20c. Sultan of Brunei		45	45
821	20c. Sultan in rice field holding up sheaf of rice		45	45

175 Rice Farmers with Machinery

2011. Large Scale Rice Planting. Multicoloured.

822	20c. Type **175**		45	45
823	20c. Rice field		45	45
824	20c. Two workers in rice padi		45	45

176 Sultan Hassanal Bolkiah Mu'izzadin Waddaulah, Badges and Emblem

2012. 50th Anniv (2011) of Royal Brunei Armed Forces. Multicoloured.

825	50c. Type **176**		85	85
826	50c. Sultan in army uniform, emblem and badges		85	85
827	50c. Sultan in army uniform and inspecting troops		85	85
828	50c. Sultan in Royal Brunei Navy uniform and parade		85	85
829	50c. Sultan in Royal Brunei Air Force uniform and officers raising flag		85	85
MS830	190×110 mm. $50 Sultan and armed forces on parade (40×72 mm)		85·00	85·00

177 *Ipomoea pescaprae* (plant) (2007 $20 note), Omar Ali Saifuddien Mosque (1967 banknotes), Rain Forest Floor (1966 $5 Notes) and Vendor in Boat (1989 banknote)

2012. 45th Anniv of Currency Interchangeability Agreement between Singapore and Brunei. Multicoloured.

831	$1 Type **177**		1·75	1·75

832 $2 Singapore scene and Omar Ali Saifuddien Mosque from back of 40th anniversary commemorative note, 2007 ... 3·50 3·50

A stamp design as No. 832 was issued by Singapore.

178 *Trogonoptera triodes brookiana*

2012. Butterflies (1st series). Multicoloured.
833 10s. Type **178** ... 15 15
834 20s. *Graphium macareus* ... 45 45
835 $1 *Graphium delesserti* ... 1·75 1·75
MS836 101×70 mm. $2 *Graphium agamemnon* ... 3·50 3·50

JAPANESE OCCUPATION OF BRUNEI
These stamps were valid throughout British Borneo (i.e. in Brunei, Labuan, North Borneo and Sarawak).

(1) ("Imperial Japanese Government")

1942. Stamps of Brunei optd with T **1**.
J1 5 1c. black ... 9·50 23·00
J2 5 2c. green ... 50·00 £110
J3 5 2c. orange ... 6·00 9·00
J4 5 3c. green ... 30·00 75·00
J5 5 4c. orange ... 4·00 13·00
J6 5 5c. brown ... 6·00 13·00
J7 7 6c. grey ... 40·00 £300
J8 7 6c. red ... £600 £600
J9 5 8c. black ... £800 £900
J10 7 8c. red ... 9·00 12·00
J11 5 10c. purple on yellow ... 10·00 26·00
J12 5 12c. blue ... 32·00 26·00
J13 7 15c. blue ... 24·00 26·00
J14 5 25c. lilac ... 26·00 50·00
J15 5 30c. purple and orange ... 95·00 £180
J16 5 50c. black on green ... 38·00 60·00
J17 5 $1 black and red on blue ... 55·00 70·00
J18 5 $5 red on green ... £950 £3250
J19 5 $25 black on red ... £950 £3250

(2) ("Imperial Japanese Postal Service $3")

1944. No. J1 surch with T **2**.
J20 $3 on 1c. on 1c. black ... £9000 £9500

BRUNSWICK Pt. 7
Formerly a duchy of N. Germany. Joined North German Confederation in 1868.

30 silbergroschen = 1 thaler.

1

1852. Imperf.
1 1 1sg. red ... £3000 £450
2 1 2sg. blue ... £2000 £375
3 1 3sg. red ... £2000 £375

1853. Imperf.
4 1 ¼gg. black on brown ... £1100 £375
5 1 ½gg. black ... £200 £500
15 1 ½sg. black on green ... 33·00 £350
7 1 1sg. black on buff ... £550 95·00
8 1 2sg. black on blue ... £450 95·00
11 1 3sg. black on red ... £800 £250

3

1857. Imperf.
12 3 ¾gg. black on brown ... 55·00 £140

1864. Rouletted.
22 1 ½gg. black ... £650 £3250

23 1 ½sg. black on green ... £275 £4750
24 1 1sg. black on yellow ... £4500 £2250
25 1 1sg. yellow ... £550 £200
26 1 2sg. black on blue ... £550 £500
27 1 3sg. pink ... £1100 £750

4

1865. Roul.
28 4 ⅓g. black ... 39·00 £550
29 4 1g. red ... 3·25 75·00
32 4 2g. blue ... 12·50 £190
34 4 3g. brown ... 11·00 £225

BUENOS AIRES Pt. 20
A province of the Argentine Republic. Issued its own stamps from 1858 to 1862.

8 reales = 1 peso.

P1 Paddle Steamer

1858. Imperf.
P13 P1 4r. brown ... £225 £170
P17 P1 1 (IN) p. brown ... £300 £250
P20 P1 1 (IN) p. blue ... £120 £100
P25 P1 1 (TO) p. blue ... £500 £250
P1 P1 2p. blue ... £180 £100
P4 P1 3p. green ... £1200 £650
P7 P1 4p. red ... £3250 £1700
P10 P1 5p. yellow ... £2500 £1100

P2 Head of Liberty

1859. Imperf.
P37 P2 4r. green on blue ... £180 £100
P38 P2 1p. blue ... 15·00 9·00
P45 P2 1p. red ... £140 65·00
P43 P2 2p. red ... £200 £120
P48 P2 2p. blue ... £225 55·00

BULGARIA Pt. 3
Formerly a Turkish province; a principality under Turkish suzerainty from 1878 to 1908, when an independent kingdom was proclaimed. A People's Republic since 1946.

1879. 100 centimes = 1 franc.
1881. 100 stotinki = 1 lev.

1 Large Lion

1879. Value in centimes and franc.
1 1 5c. black and yellow ... £225 75·00
3 1 10c. black and green ... £1000 £200
5 1 25c. black and purple ... £600 50·00
7 1 50c. black and blue ... £850 £170
8 1 1f. black and red ... £130 50·00

2 Large Lion

1881. Value in stotinki.
10 2 3s. red and grey ... 43·00 8·25
11 2 5s. black and yellow ... 43·00 8·25
14 2 10s. black and green ... £250 26·00
15 2 15s. red and green ... £250 26·00
18 2 25s. black and purple ... £1000 £130
19 2 30s. blue and brown ... 43·00 21·00

See also No. 275/9.

A B C D

1882
46 1s. violet (Type A) ... 38·00 12·50
48 1s. violet (Type C) ... 2·75 50
47 2s. green (Type B) ... 37·00 11·50
49 2s. green (Type D) ... 2·75 50
21 3s. orange and yellow ... 2·20 1·00
23 5s. green ... 16·00 1·60
26 10s. red ... 22·00 1·60
28 15s. purple and mauve ... 22·00 1·30
31 25s. blue ... 20·00 2·10
33 30s. lilac and green ... 21·00 1·90
34 50s. blue and red ... 21·00 1·90
50 1l. black and red ... 75·00 9·50

1884. Surch with large figure of value.
38 3 on 10s. red ... £110 £100
43 5 on 30s. blue and brown ... £110 £100
45 15 on 25s. blue ... £200 £140
40 50 on 1f. black and red ... £750 £475

7

1889
85 7 1s. mauve ... 20 20
88 7 2s. grey ... 1·30 1·00
89 7 3s. brown ... 55 50
90 7 5s. green ... 20 20
94 7 10s. red ... 1·60 1·00
96 7 15s. orange ... 1·10 50
100 7 25s. blue ... 1·10 50
58 7 30s. brown ... 18·00 1·00
59 7 50s. green ... 1·10 50
60 7 1l. red ... 1·10 1·00
83 7 2l. red and pink ... 4·25 3·25
84 7 3l. black and buff ... 6·50 7·25

1892. Surch **15**.
61 15 on 30s. brown ... 55·00 2·10

1895. Surch **01**.
74 2a 01 on 2s. green (No. 49) ... 1·60 50

11 Arms of Bulgaria

1896. Baptism of Prince Boris.
78 11 1s. green ... 55 30
79 11 5s. blue ... 55 30
81 11 15s. violet ... 65 50
82 11 25s. red ... 9·25 3·25

1901. Surch in figures.
101 7 5 on 3s. brown ... 2·75 2·10
103 7 10 on 50s. green ... 2·75 2·30

13 Cherry wood Cannon used against the Turks

1901. 25th Anniv of Uprising against Turkey.
104 13 5s. red ... 2·20 1·60
105 13 15s. green ... 2·20 1·60

14 Prince Ferdinand

1901
106 14 1s. black and purple ... 35 15
107 14 2s. blue and green ... 55 15
108 14 3s. black and orange ... 55 15
109 14 5s. brown and green ... 2·20 20
110 14 10s. brown and red ... 3·25 20
113 14 15s. black and lake ... 1·60 30
114 14 25s. black and blue ... 1·60 15
116 14 30s. black and brown ... 49·00 1·00

117 14 50s. brown and blue ... 2·20 30
118 14 1l. green and red ... 5·50 40
120 14 2l. black and red ... 11·00 1·60
123 14 3l. red and grey ... 16·00 7·25

16 Fighting at Shipka Pass

1902. 25th Anniv of Battle of Shipka Pass.
124 16 5s. red ... 3·25 1·00
125 16 10s. green ... 3·25 1·00
126 16 15s. blue ... 13·00 5·25

1903. Surch.
140 15 5 on 15s. black and red ... 3·25 2·10
141 15 10 on 15s. black and red ... 5·50 1·00
143 15 25 on 30s. black & brown ... 18·00 2·10

18 Ferdinand I in 1887 and 1907

1907. 20th Anniv of Prince Ferdinand's Accession.
132 18 5s. green ... 22·00 2·10
134 18 10s. brown ... 33·00 2·30
137 18 25s. blue ... 75·00 4·25

1909. Optd 1909.
146 7 1s. mauve ... 2·20 95
149 7 5s. green ... 2·20 95

1909. Surch **1909** and new value.
151 5 on 30s. brown ... 3·75 65
153 10 on 15s. orange ... 3·75 1·30
156 10 on 50s. green ... 3·75 1·30

1910. Surch **1910** and new value.
157 14 1 on 3s. black and orange ... 8·75 2·10
158 14 5 on 15s. black and lake ... 2·20 1·60

23 King Asen Tower **24** Tsar in General's Uniform **25** Veliko Turnovo

1911
159 23 1s. green ... 35 15
182a 23 1s. slate ... 20 15
160 24 2s. black and red ... 35 15
161 25 3s. black and lake ... 85 15
162 - 5s. black and green ... 1·60 15
181 - 5s. purple and green ... 4·25 20
163 - 10s. black and red ... 2·75 20
181a - 10s. sepia and brown ... 20 15
164 - 15s. bistre ... 8·25 30
183 - 15s. olive ... 70 15
165 - 25s. black and blue ... 55 30
166 - 30s. black and blue ... 8·25 30
182 - 30s. brown and olive ... 55 20
167 - 50s. black and yellow ... 43·00 50
168 - 1l. brown ... 20·00 30
169 - 2l. black and purple ... 3·75 1·30
170 - 3l. black and violet ... 22·00 75

DESIGNS—VERT: 5, 10, 25s., 1l. Portraits of Tsar Ferdinand. HORIZ: 15s. R. Isker; 30s. Rila Monastery; 50s. Tsars and Princes (after Ya. Veshin); 2l. Monastery of the Holy Trinity, Veliko Turnovo; 3l. Varna.
See also Nos. 229/30 and 236/7.

35 Tsar Ferdinand

1912. Tsar's Silver Jubilee.
171 35 5s. grey ... 5·50 2·10
172 35 10s. red ... 7·50 3·75
173 35 25s. blue ... 11·00 5·75

ОСВОБ. ВОЙНА

1912-1913
(36) "War of Liberation" 1912–13

1913. Victory over Turks. Stamps of 1911 optd as T **36**.

174	23	1s. green	55	20
175	24	2s. black and red	55	20
176	25	3s. black and lake	2·20	50
177	-	5s. black and green	55	20
178	-	10s. black and red	55	20
179	-	15s. bistre	3·25	1·60
180	-	25s. black and blue	8·75	2·50

1915. No. 165 surch **10 CT.** and bar.

180a		10s. on 25s. blk & blue	1·30	30

3

СТОТИНКИ

(37a)

1916. Red Cross Fund. Surch with T **37a**.

185	7	3s. on 1s. mauve	13·00	12·50

38

39 Bulgarian Peasant

45 Veles

46 Bulgarian Ploughman

1917. Liberation of Macedonia.

193	45	1s. grey	20	10
194	46	1s. green	20	10
186	38	5s. green	55	40
195	-	5s. green	20	10
187	39	15s. grey	20	20
188	-	25s. blue	20	20
189	-	30s. orange	20	30
190	-	50s. violet	1·10	85
191	-	2l. brown	1·10	85
192	-	3l. red	1·60	1·40

DESIGNS—As Type **45**: 5s. Monastery of St. John, Ohrid. As Type **38**: 25s. Soldier and Mt. Sonichka; 50s. Ohrid and Lake. As Type **39**: 30s. Nish. 2l. Demir Kapija; 3l. Gevgeli.

48 Tsar Ferdinand

1918. 30th Anniv of Tsar's Accession.

196	48	1s. slate	20	15
197	48	2s. brown	20	15
198	48	3s. blue	55	50
199	48	10s. red	55	50

49 Parliament Building

1919

201	49	1s. black	20	15
202	49	2s. olive	20	15

50 King Boris III

1919. First Anniv of Enthronement of King Boris III.

203	50	3s. red	20	15
204	50	5s. green	20	15
205	50	10s. red	20	15
206	50	15s. violet	20	15
207	50	25s. blue	20	15
208	50	30s. brown	20	15
209	50	50s. brown	20	15

(52) **(53)**

1920. Prisoners of War Fund. Surch as T **52/53**.

210	49	1 on 2s. olive	20	15
211	50	2½ on 5s. green	20	15
212	50	5 on 10s. red	20	15
213	50	7½ on 15s. violet	20	15
214	50	12½ on 25s. blue	20	15
215	50	15 on 30s. brown	20	15
216	50	25 on 50s. brown	20	15
217	-	50 on 1l. brown (No. 168)	55	30
218	-	1 on 2l. brown (No. 191)	55	50
219	-	1½ on 3l. red (No. 192)	1·60	1·00

54 Vazov's Birthplace at Sopot and Cherry-wood Cannon

55 "The Bear-fighter", character from *Under the Yoke*

1920. 70th Birth Anniv of Ivan Vazov (writer).

220	54	30s. red	20	15
221	55	50s. green	45	20
222	-	1l. sepia	75	50
223	-	2l. brown	2·20	1·30
224	-	3l. violet	2·75	1·80
225	-	5l. blue	3·75	2·30

DESIGNS—HORIZ: 1l. Ivan Vazov in 1870 and 1920; 3l. Vazov's Houses in Plovdiv and Sofia. VERT: 2l. Vazov; 5l. Father Paisii Khilendarski (historian).

59 Aleksandr Nevski Cathedral, Sofia

62 King Boris III

1921

226	59	10s. violet	20	15
227	-	20s. green	20	15
228	62	25s. blue	20	15
229	25	50s. orange	45	20
230	25	50s. blue	9·25	3·50
231	-	75s. violet	20	15
232	-	75s. blue	55	20
233	62	1l. red	55	20
234	62	1l. blue	45	15
235	-	2l. brown	1·60	20
236	-	3l. purple	1·60	20
237	-	5l. blue	8·75	40
238	62	10l. red	22·00	4·75

DESIGNS—HORIZ: 20s. Alexander II "The Liberator" Monument, Sofia; 75s. Shipka Pass Monastery; 5l. Rila Monastery. VERT: 2l. Harvester; 3l. King Asen Tower.

66 Tsar Ferdinand and Map

68 Mt. Shar

1921

239	66	10s. red	20	15
240	-	10s. red	20	15
241	68	10s. red	20	15
242	-	10s. mauve	20	15
243	-	20s. blue	85	20

DESIGNS—VERT: No. 240, Tsar Ferdinand. HORIZ: No. 242, Bridge over Vardar, at Skopje; 243, St. Clement's Monastery, Ohrid.

71 Bourchier in Bulgarian Costume

72 J. D. Bourchier

73 Rila Monastery, Bourchier's Resting-place

1921. James Bourchier ("Times" Correspondent) Commemoration.

244	71	10s. red	20	20
245	71	20s. orange	20	20
246	72	30s. grey	20	20
247	72	50s. lilac	20	20
248	72	1l. purple	55	20
249	73	1½l. green	55	40
250	73	2l. green	55	30
251	73	3l. blue	1·30	50
252	73	5l. red	2·40	1·20

1924. Surch.

253	49	10s. on 1s. black	20	15
254	D 37	10s. on 20s. orange	20	15
255	D 37	20s. on 5s. green	27·00	26·00
256	D 37	20s. on 10s. violet	8·25	7·75
257	D 37	20s. on 30s. orange	20	15
258	50	1l. on 5s. green	35	15
259	25	3l. on 50s. blue	1·10	30
260	62	6l. on 1l. red	2·20	65

77 **78** **79** King Boris III

81 Aleksandr Nevski Cathedral, Sofia

82 Harvesters

1925

261	77	10s. blue & red on rose	35	20
262	77	15s. orange & red on blue	35	20
263	77	30s. buff and black	35	20
264	78	50s. brown on green	35	20
265	79	1l. olive	1·00	20
266	79	1l. green	1·20	20
267	81	2l. green and buff	4·25	20
267a	79	2l. brown	1·60	20
268	82	4l. red and yellow	4·25	20

83 Proposed Rest-home, Verona

1925. Sunday Delivery Stamps.

268b	83	1l. black on green	11·00	30
268c	83	1l. brown	11·00	30
268d	83	1l. orange	16·00	50
268e	83	1l. pink	14·00	50
268f	83	1l. violet on red	16·00	50
268g	-	2l. green	1·60	30
268h	-	2l. violet	1·60	30
268i	-	5l. blue	17·00	1·30
268j	-	5l. red	17·00	1·30

DESIGN: 2, 5l., Proposed Sanatorium, Bankya.

85 St. Nedelya's Cathedral, Sofia after Bomb Outrage

1926

269	85	50s. black	35	20

86 C. Botev (poet)

1926. Botev Commemoration.

270	86	1l. green	1·30	50
271	86	2l. blue	2·75	50
272	86	4l. red	3·75	2·50

87

1926

273	87	6l. olive and blue	2·20	30
274	87	10l. brown and sepia	16·00	4·00

1927. As T **2** in new colours.

275		10s. red and green	20	20
276		15s. black and yellow	20	20
277		30s. slate and buff	20	20
278		30s. blue and buff	20	20
279		50s. black and red	20	20

1927. Air. Various stamps optd with Albatros biplane and No. 281 surch **1l** also.

281		1l. on 6l. green and blue	2·20	2·10
282	79	2l. brown	2·20	2·10
283	82	4l. red and yellow	3·25	2·10
284	87	10l. orange and brown	85·00	50·00

89 King Boris III

1928

285	89	1l. green	3·25	20
286	89	2l. brown	4·25	20

90 Saint Clement of Ohrid

1929. 50th Anniv of Liberation of Bulgaria and Millenary of Tsar Simeon.

287	90	10s. violet	30	10
288	-	15a. purple	30	10
289	-	30s. red	30	10
290	-	50s. green	75	20
291	-	1l. red	1·90	20
292	-	2l. blue	2·10	20
293	-	3l. green	5·25	1·00
294	-	4l. brown	9·50	40
295	-	5l. brown	7·25	1·00
296	-	6l. blue	9·25	2·50

PORTRAITS—23½×33½ mm: 15s. Konstantin Miladinov (poet and folklorist); 1l. Father Paisii Khilendarski (historian); 2l. Tsar Simeon; 4l. Vasil Levski (revolutionary); 5l. Georgi Benkovski (revolutionary); 6l. Tsar Alexander II of Russia, "The Liberator". 19×28½ mm: 30s. Georgi Rakovski (writer). 19×26 mm: 3l. Lyuben Karavelov (journalist).

98 Convalescent Home, Varna

1930. Sunday Delivery stamps.

297	98	1l. green and purple	18·00	30
298	98	1l. yellow and green	2·10	30
299	98	1l. brown and red	2·10	30

99

1930. Wedding of King Boris and Princess Giovanna of Italy.

300	99	1l. green	50	40
301	-	2l. purple	85	50
302	-	4l. red	85	50
303	-	6l. blue	1·00	55

DESIGN: 2, 6l. Portraits in separate ovals.

101 King Boris III

1931

304a	101	1l. green (A)	1·30	20
305	101	2l. red (A)	1·30	20
306	101	4l. orange (A)	1·80	20
308a	101	4l. orange (B)	1·00	20
307	101	6l. blue (A)	1·30	20
308b	101	6l. blue (B)	2·75	20
308c	101	7l. blue (B)	40	20
308d	101	10l. slate (B)	42·00	2·50
308	101	12l. brown (A)	1·00	30
308e	101	14l. brown (B)	95	50
308f	-	20l. brown & pur (B)	2·50	1·00

(A) Without coloured frame-lines at top and bottom; (B) with frame-lines.
The 20l. is 24½×33½ mm.

103 Gymnastics

1931. Balkan Olympic Games.

309	103	1l. green	3·25	1·50
326	103	1l. turquoise	4·25	4·00
310	-	2l. red	4·25	2·00
327	-	2l. blue	6·25	4·50
311	-	4l. red	9·50	2·50
328	-	4l. purple	10·50	5·50
312	-	6l. blue	21·00	6·00
329	-	6l. red	21·00	10·00
313	-	10l. orange	42·00	15·00
330	-	10l. brown	£160	65·00
314	-	12l. blue	£130	40·00
331	-	12l. orange	£250	£100
315	-	50l. brown	£140	85·00
332	-	50l. red	£750	£750

DESIGNS—VERT (23×28 mm): 2l. Footballer; 4l. Horse-riding. As Type **103**—HORIZ: 6l. Fencing; 10l. Cycling. VERT: 12l. Diving; 50l. Spirit of Victory.

108

1931. Air.

316	108	1l. green	85	30
316a	108	1l. purple	50	20
317	108	2l. purple	85	30
317a	108	2l. green	65	30
318	108	6l. blue	1·00	50
318a	108	6l. red	1·60	60
319	108	12l. red	2·10	50
319a	108	12l. blue	1·80	70
320	108	20l. violet	2·10	1·00
321	108	30l. orange	4·25	2·00
322	108	50l. brown	5·75	3·50

109 Rila Monastery

1932. Air.

323	109	18l. green	£140	70·00
324	109	24l. red	95·00	45·00
325	109	28l. blue	50·00	35·00

1934. Surch 2.

333	101	2 on 3l. olive	13·50	1·00

111 Defending the Pass

1934. Unveiling of Shipka Pass Memorial.

334A	111	1l. green	2·10	1·00
340A	111	1l. green	2·10	1·00
335A	-	2l. red	1·60	50
341A	-	2l. orange	1·60	50
336A	-	3l. brown	5·25	3·00
342A	-	3l. yellow	5·25	3·00
337A	-	4l. green	3·75	1·00
343A	-	4l. red	3·75	1·00
338A	-	7l. blue	7·25	3·50
344A	-	7l. light blue	7·25	3·50

339A	-	14l. purple	27·00	18·00
345	-	14l. bistre	27·00	18·00

DESIGNS—VERT: 2l. Shipka Memorial; 3, 7l. Veteran standard-bearer; 14l. Widow showing memorial to orphans. HORIZ: 4l. Bulgarian veteran.

113 Convalescent Home, Troyan

1935. Sunday Delivery stamps.

346	113	1l. red and brown	2·10	30
347	113	1l. blue and green	2·10	30
348	-	5l. blue and red	6·75	1·50

DESIGN: 5l. Convalescent Home, Bakya.

114 Capt. Georgi Mamarchef

1935. Centenary of Turnovo Insurrection.

349	-	1l. blue	3·25	80
350	114	2l. purple	3·25	1·20

DESIGN: 1l. Velcho Atanasov Dzhamdzhiyata.

115 Aleksandr Nevski Cathedral, Sofia

1935. Fifth Balkan Football Tournament.

351	-	1l. green	8·25	6·00
352	115	2l. grey	12·50	8·00
353	-	4l. red	16·00	10·00
354	-	7l. blue	29·00	20·00
355	-	14l. orange	26·00	20·00
356	-	50l. brown	£475	£400

DESIGNS—HORIZ: 1l. Match in progress at Yunak Stadium, Sofia; 4l. Footballers. VERT: 7l. Herald and Balkan map; 14l. Footballer and trophy; 50l. Trophy.

116 Girl Gymnast

1935. Eighth Bulgarian Gymnastic Tournament. Dated "12–14. VII. 1935".

357	-	1l. green	9·50	8·00
358	-	2l. blue	10·50	9·00
359	116	4l. red	13·50	11·00
360	-	7l. blue	16·00	16·00
361	-	14l. brown	16·00	15·00
362	-	50l. orange	£325	£250

DESIGNS—VERT: 1l. Parallel bars; 2l. Male gymnast in uniform; 7l. Pole vault; 50l. Athlete and lion. HORIZ: 14l. Yunak Stadium, Sofia.

117 Janos Hunyadi

1935. Unveiling of Monument to Ladislas III of Poland at Varna. Inscr "WARNEN CZYK(A)", etc.

363A	117	1l. orange	3·25	1·00
364B	-	2l. red	5·00	1·50
365A	-	4l. red	26·00	7·00
366A	-	7l. blue	4·75	1·00
367A	-	14l. green	4·75	1·80

DESIGNS—VERT: 2l. King Ladislas of Hungary enthroned (22×32 mm); 7l. King Ladislas in armour (20×31 mm). HORIZ: 4l. Varna Memorial (33×24 mm); 14l. Battle scene (30×25 mm).

118 Dimitur

1935. 67th Death Anniv of Khadzhi Dimitur (revolutionary).

368A	-	1l. green	3·25	1·00
369A	118	2l. brown	5·25	2·00
370A	-	4l. red	14·50	5·00
371A	-	7l. blue	21·00	9·00
372A	-	14l. orange	26·00	10·00

DESIGNS—VERT: 1l. Dimitur's monument at Sliven; 7l. Revolutionary group (dated 1868). HORIZ: 4l. Dimitur and Stefan Karadzha (revolutionary); 14l. Dimitur's birthplace at Sliven.

119 **120**

1936

373	119	10s. red	20	15
373a	119	15s. green	20	15
374	120	30s. red	30	15
374a	120	30s. brown	20	15
374b	120	30s. blue	20	15
375	120	50s. blue	30	15
375a	120	50s. red	30	15
375b	120	50s. green	20	15

121 Nesebur

1936. Slav Geographical and Ethnographical Congress, Sofia.

376	-	1l. violet	4·25	2·00
377	-	2l. blue	4·25	2·00
378	121	7l. blue	8·25	4·00

DESIGNS—25×34 mm: 1l. Meteorological Bureau, Mt. Musala; 23×34 mm: 2l. Peasant girl.

122 St. Cyril and St. Methodius

1937. Millenary of Introduction of Cyrillic Alphabet and Slavonic Liturgy.

379	122	1l. green	75	30
380	122	2l. purple	75	30
381	-	4l. red	85	30
382	122	7l. blue	4·25	2·20
383	-	14l. red	4·25	2·30

DESIGN: 4., 14l. The Saints Preaching.

124 Princess Marie Louise

1937.

384	124	1l. green	75	20
385	124	2l. red	85	20
386	124	4l. red	85	50

125 King Boris III

1937. 19th Anniv of Accession.

387	125	2l. red	1·00	50
MS387a	76×115 mm. 125	2l. (+18l.) ultramarine. Imperf.	10·50	20·00

126 Harvesting

1938. Agricultural Products.

388	126	10s. orange	20	10
389	126	10s. red	20	10
390	-	15s. red	50	10
391	-	15s. purple	50	10
392	-	30s. brown	40	10
393	-	30s. brown	45	10
394	-	50s. blue	95	10
395	-	50s. black	95	10
396	-	1l. green	1·00	10
397	-	1l. green	1·00	10
398	-	2l. red	1·00	20
399	-	2l. brown	1·00	20
400	-	3l. purple	2·10	1·00
401	-	3l. purple	2·10	1·00
402	-	4l. brown	1·60	50
403	-	4l. purple	1·60	50
404	-	7l. violet	3·25	1·00
405	-	7l. blue	3·25	1·00
406	-	14l. brown	5·25	2·00
407	-	14l. brown	5·25	2·00

DESIGNS—VERT: 15s. Sunflower; 30s. Wheat; 50s. Chickens and eggs; 1l. Grapes; 3l. Strawberries; 4l. Girl carrying grapes; 7l. Roses; 14l. Tobacco leaves. HORIZ: 2l. "Attar of Roses".

129 Prince Simeon

1938. First Birthday of Heir Apparent.

408	129	1l. green	30	20
409	129	2l. red	30	20
410	-	4l. red	40	25
411	129	7l. blue	1·60	80
412	-	14l. brown	1·60	80

DESIGN: 4, 14l. Another portrait.

131 King Boris III

1938. 20th Anniv of King's Accession. Portraits of King in various uniforms.

413	131	1l. green	25	20
414	-	2l. red	1·30	30
415	-	4l. brown	40	30
416	-	7l. blue	65	50
417	-	14l. mauve	65	50

132 Class 01 Steam Locomotive

1939. 50th Anniv of Bulgarian State Railways. Locomotive types dated "1888–1938".

418	-	1l. green	50	40
419	132	2l. brown	50	40
420	-	4l. orange	3·25	1·50
421	-	7l. blue	9·50	5·50

DESIGNS: 1l. First Locomotive in Bulgaria, 1866; 4l. Train crossing viaduct; 7l. King Boris as engine-driver.

133 P.O. Emblem

1939. 60th Anniv of Bulgarian P.O. Inscr "1879 1939".

422	133	1l. green	40	10
423	-	2l. red (G.P.O., Sofia)	50	15

135 Gymnast

1939. Yunak Gymnastic Society's Rally, Sofia.

424	**135**	1l. green	50	40
425	-	2l. red	50	40
426	-	4l. brown	1·00	50
427	-	7l. blue	3·25	1·50
428	-	14l. mauve	16·00	12·00

DESIGNS: 2l. Yunak badge; 4l. *The Discus-thrower* (statue by Miron); 7l. Rhythmic dancer; 14l. Athlete holding weight aloft.

Наводнението
1939
1+1
лева
(136)
("Inundation 1939")

1939. Sevlievo and Turnovo Floods Relief Fund. Surch as T 136 and value.

429	**39**	1l.+1l. on 15s. grey	20	45
430	**73**	2l.+1l. on 1½l. olive	30	50
431	**73**	4l.+2l. on 2l. green	35	60
432	**73**	7l.+4l. on 3l. blue	1·00	1·50
433	**73**	14l.+7l. on 5l. red	1·60	2·50

137 Mail Plane

1940. Air.

434	**137**	1l. green	20	15
435	-	2l. red	2·50	15
436	-	4l. orange	20	15
437	-	6l. blue	40	20
438	-	10l. brown	75	30
439	-	12l. brown	1·00	50
440	-	16l. violet	1·60	80
441	-	19l. blue	1·70	1·00
442	-	30l. mauve	2·50	1·50
443	-	45l. violet	6·75	3·75
444	-	70l. red	5·25	4·00
445	-	100l. blue	21·00	14·00

DESIGNS—VERT: Aircraft over: King Asen's Tower (2l.), Bachovo Monastery (4l.), Aleksandr Nevski Cathedral, Sofia (45l.), Shipka Pass Memorial (70l.). 10l. Airplane, mail train and express motor cycle; 30l. Airplane and swallow; 100l. Airplane and Royal cypher. HORIZ: 6l. Loading mails at aerodrome. Aircraft over: Sofia Palace (12l.), Mt. El Tepe (16l.), Rila Lakes and mountains (19l.).

138 King Boris III

1940

445a	**138**	1l. green	40	20
446	**138**	2l. red	50	20

139 First Bulgarian Postage Stamp

1940. Cent of First Adhesive Postage Stamp.

447	**139**	10l. olive	3·25	2·50
448	-	20l. blue	3·25	2·50

DESIGN: 20l. has scroll dated "1840–1940".

140 Grapes **141** Ploughing **142** King Boris III

1940

449	**140**	10s. orange	20	15
450	-	15s. blue	20	15
451	**141**	30s. brown	20	15
452	-	50s. violet	20	15
452a	-	50s. green	20	15
453	**142**	1l. green	20	15
454	**142**	2l. red	30	15
455	**142**	4l. orange	30	15
456	**142**	6l. violet	50	20
457	**142**	7l. green	30	15
458	**142**	10l. green	50	20

DESIGNS—VERT: 15s. Beehive. HORIZ: 50s. Shepherd and flock.

143 Peasant Couple and King Boris **144** King Boris and Map of Dobrudja

1940. Recovery of Dobrudja from Rumania. Designs incorporating miniature portrait of King Boris.

464	**143**	1l. green	20	15
465	-	2l. red	30	20
466	**144**	4l. brown	50	30
467	**144**	7l. blue	1·00	80

DESIGN—VERT: 2l. Bulgarian flags and wheat-field.

145 Bee-keeping

1940. Agricultural Scenes.

468	-	10s. purple	20	15
469	-	10s. blue	20	15
470	-	15s. green	20	15
471	-	15s. olive	20	15
472	**145**	30s. orange	20	15
473	**145**	30s. green	20	15
474	-	50s. violet	20	15
475	-	50s. purple	20	15
476	-	3l. brown	85	20
477	-	3l. black	1·90	1·00
478	-	5l. brown	1·60	80
479	-	5l. blue	2·10	1·50

DESIGNS: 10s. Threshing; 15s. Ploughing with oxen; 50s. Picking apples; 3l. Shepherd; 5l. Cattle.

146 Pencko Slaveikov (poet) **147** St. Ivan Rilski

1940. National Relief.

480	**146**	1l. green	20	15
481	-	2l. red	20	15
482	**147**	3l. brown	25	20
483	-	4l. orange	30	20
484	-	7l. blue	2·10	1·50
485	-	10l. brown	3·25	2·00

DESIGNS: 2l. Bishop Sofronii of Vratsa; 4l. Marin Drinov (historian); 7l. Chernorisets Khratur (monk); 10l. Kolo Ficheto (writer).

148 Johannes Gutenberg **149** Nikola Karastoyanov

1940. 500th Anniv of Invention of Printing and Centenary of Bulgarian Printing.

486	**148**	1l. green	40	20
487	**149**	2l. brown	50	20

150 Botev **151** Arrival in Koslodui

1941. 65th Death Anniv of Khristo Botev (poet and revolutionary).

488	**150**	1l. green	20	15
489	**151**	2l. red	50	30
490	-	3l. brown	1·40	1·00

DESIGN—VERT: 3l. Botev Memorial Cross.

152 National History Museum

1941. Buildings in Sofia.

491	**152**	14l. brown	75	40
492	-	20l. green	85	50
493	-	50l. blue	3·75	2·00

DESIGNS: 20l. Tsarita Icanna Workers' Hospital; 50l. National Bank.

153 Thasos Island **154** Ohrid

1941. Reacquisition of Macedonia.

494	-	1l. green	20	15
495	**153**	2l. orange	20	15
496	-	2l. red	20	15
497	-	4l. brown	20	15
498	**154**	7l. blue	95	70

DESIGNS—VERT: 1l. Macedonian girl. HORIZ: 2l. (No. 496) King Boris and map dated "1941"; 4l. Poganovski Monastery.

155 Children on Beach

1942. Sunday Delivery. Inscr as in T 155.

499	-	1l. green	20	15
500	**155**	2l. orange	30	20
501	-	5l. blue	1·00	40

DESIGNS: 1l. St. Konstantin Sanatorium, Varna; 5l. Sunbathing terrace, Bankya.

156 Bugler at Camp **157** Folk Dancers

1942. "Work and Joy". Inscr as at foot of T 157.

502	-	1l. green	20	15
503	-	2l. red	30	15
504	-	4l. black	40	20
505	**156**	7l. blue	50	30
506	**157**	14l. brown	65	40

DESIGNS—VERT: 1l. Guitarist and accordion player; 2l. Camp orchestra; 4l. Hoisting the flag.

158 Wounded Soldier **159** Queen visiting Wounded

1942. War Invalids. Inscr as T 158/9.

507	**158**	1l. green	20	15
508	-	2l. red	20	15
509	-	4l. orange	20	15
510	-	7l. blue	20	15
511	-	14l. brown	30	15
512	**159**	20l. black	65	20

DESIGNS—HORIZ: 2l. Soldier and family; 4l. First aid on battlefield; 7l. Widow and orphans at grave; 14l. Unknown Soldiers Memorial.

160 Khan Kubrat (ruled 595–642)

1942. Historical series.

513	**160**	10s. black	20	15
514	-	15s. blue	20	15
515	-	30s. mauve	20	15
516	-	50s. blue	20	15
517	-	1l. green	20	15
518	-	2l. red	20	15
519	-	3l. brown	20	15
520	-	4l. orange	20	15
521	-	5l. green	20	15
522	-	7l. blue	20	15
523	-	10l. black	20	15
524	-	14l. olive	40	20
525	-	20l. brown	1·00	70
526	-	30l. black	2·10	1·00

DESIGNS: 15s. Cavalry charge (Khan as parukh, 680–701); 30s. Equestrian statue of Khan Krum (803–814); 50s. Baptism of King Boris I; 1l. St. Naum's School; 2l. King Boris crowns his son, Tsar Simeon; 3l. Golden Era of Bulgarian literature; 4l. Trial of Bogomil Vasilii; 5l. Proclamation of Second Bulgarian Empire; 7l. Ivan Asen II (1214–81) at Tebizond; 10l. Expulsion of Eutimil Patriarch of Turnovo; 14l. Wandering minstrels; 20l. Father Paisii Khilendarski (historian); 30l. Shipka Pass Memorial.

161 King Boris III

1944. King Boris Mourning Issue. Portraits dated "1894–1943". Perf or imperf.

527A	**161**	1l. olive	20	20
528A	-	2l. brown	25	25
529A	-	4l. brown	30	30
530A	-	5l. violet	85	85
531A	-	7l. blue	1·00	1·00

163 King Simeon II

1944

532A	**163**	3l. orange	20	10

ВСИЧКО ЗА ФРОНТА
(164)

1945. "All for the Front". Parcel Post stamps optd as T 164 or surch also.

533	P163	3l. brown	20	15
534	P163	4l. on 1l. red	20	15
535	P163	7l. purple	20	15
536	P163	20l. brown	30	15
537	P163	30l. purple	40	20
538	P163	50l. orange	75	50
539	P163	100l. blue	1·80	1·00

1945. Air. Optd with airplane or surch also.

540	**142**	1l. green	20	15
541	**142**	4l. orange	20	15
542	P 163	10l. on 100l. yellow	30	15
543	P 163	45l. on 100l. yellow	40	20
544	P 163	75l. on 100l. yellow	1·00	60
545	P 163	100l. yellow	1·30	90

Nos. 540/1 are perf; the rest imperf.

167

1945. Slav Congress. Perf or imperf.

546	**167**	4l. red	15	10
547	**167**	10l. blue	15	10
548	**167**	50l. red	40	30

СЪБИРАЙТЕ ВСЯКАКВИ ПАРЦАЛИ (168) "Collect All Rags" СЪБИРАЙТЕ СТАРО ЖЕЛЯЗО (169) "Collect Old Iron" СЪБИРАЙТЕ ХАРТИЕНИ ОТПАДЪЦИ (170) "Collect Wastepaper"

1945. Salvage Campaign. Nos. 457/9 optd with T 168/70.

549B	**142**	1l. green	30	40
550C	**142**	2l. red	1·30	40
551A	**142**	4l. orange	1·00	40

Prices are the same for these stamps with any one of the overprints illustrated.

171 Lion Rampant

172

1945. Lion Rampant, in various frames.

552	-	30s. green	25	15
553	-	50s. blue	25	15
554	171	1l. green	25	15
555	-	2l. brown	25	15
556	-	4l. blue	25	15
557	-	5l. violet	25	15
558	172	9l. grey	25	15
559	-	10l. blue	25	15
560	-	15l. brown	25	15
561	-	20l. black	50	15
562	-	20l. red	50	15

173 Chain-breaker

1945. Liberty Loan. Imperf.

563	173	50l. orange	30	15
564	173	50l. lake	30	15
565	-	100l. blue	40	20
566	-	100l. brown	40	20
567	-	150l. red	1·00	60
568	-	150l. green	1·00	60
569	-	200l. olive	1·30	80
570	-	200l. blue	1·30	80

MS570a Two blocks 88×123 mm, with
the four values imperf (a) in brown-
red and (b) in violet. Pair | 16·00 | 24·00

DESIGNS: 100l. Hand holding coin; 150l. Water-mill; 200l. Coin and symbols of industry and agriculture.

174 "VE Day"

1945. "Victory in Europe".

571	174	10l. green and brown	20	15
572	174	50l. green and red	65	30

175

176

1945. First Anniv of Fatherland Front Coalition.

573	175	1l. olive	20	15
574	175	4l. blue	20	15
575	175	5l. mauve	20	15
576	176	10l. blue	20	15
577	176	20l. red	20	20
578	175	50l. green	1·00	60
579	175	100l. brown	1·30	1·00

177 Refugee Children

178 Red Cross Train

1946. Red Cross. Cross in red.

580	177	2l. olive	20	15
645d	177	2l. brown	15	15
581	-	4l. violet	20	15
645e	-	4l. black	15	15
582	177	10l. purple	20	15
645f	177	10l. brown	20	20
583	-	20l. dark blue	20	15
645g	-	20l. light blue	50	50
584	-	30l. brown	30	20
645h	-	30l. green	65	60
585	178	35l. black	50	40
645i	178	35l. green	75	70
586	-	50l. purple	65	50
645j	-	50l. lake	1·00	1·00

587	178	100l. brown	2·10	1·80
645k	178	100l. blue	1·70	1·60

DESIGNS—HORIZ: 4l., 20l. Soldier on stretcher. VERT: 30l., 50l. Nurse and wounded soldier.

179 Postal Savings Emblem

180 Savings Bank-Note

1946. 50th Anniv of Savings Bank.

588	179	4l. red	20	15
589	180	10l. olive	20	15
590	-	20l. blue	20	15
591	-	50l. black	1·60	1·40

DESIGNS—VERT: 20l. Child filling money-box; 50l. Postal Savings Bank.

181 Arms of Russia and Bulgaria and Spray of Oak

1946. Bulgo-Russian Congress.

592	181	4l. red	10·00	10·00
593	181	4l. orange	20	20
594	181	20l. blue	10·00	10·00
595	181	20l. green	40	40

182 Lion Rampant

1946. Stamp Day. Imperf.

596	182	20l. blue	85	40

183

190

1946. Air. Inscr "PAR AVION".

597	183	1l. purple	25	15
598	183	2l. grey	25	15
599	-	4l. black	25	15
600	-	6l. blue	25	15
601	-	10l. green	25	15
602	-	12l. brown	25	15
603	-	16l. purple	25	15
604	-	19l. red	25	15
605	-	30l. orange	30	20
606	-	45l. green	65	25
607	-	75l. brown	95	30
608	190	100l. red	1·70	50
609	-	100l. grey	1·70	50

DESIGNS—23×18 mm: 4l. Bird carrying post; 100l. (No. 609), Airplane. 18×23 mm: 6l. Airplane and envelope; 10, 12, 19l. Wings and posthorn; 16l. Wings and envelope; 30l. Airplane; 45, 75l. Dove and posthorn.

192 Stamboliiski

1946. 23rd Death Anniv of Aleksandur Stamboliiski (Prime Minister 1919–23).

610	192	100l. orange	9·50	9·50

193 Flags of Albania, Bulgaria, Yugoslavia and Rumania

1946. Balkan Games.

611	193	100l. brown	1·80	1·80

195 Junkers Ju87B "Stuka" Dive Bombers

196 Artillery

1946. Military and Air Services.

612	-	2l. red	20	15
613	-	4l. grey	20	15
614	196	5l. red	20	15
615	195	6l. brown	20	15
616	-	9l. mauve	20	15
617	-	10l. violet	20	15
618	-	20l. blue	50	20
619	-	30l. orange	65	30
620	-	40l. olive	75	40
621	-	50l. green	95	70
622	-	60l. brown	1·30	80

DESIGNS—HORIZ: 2, 20l. Grenade thrower and machine-gunner; 9l. Building pontoon-bridge; 10, 30l. Cavalry charge; 40l. Supply column; 50l. Motor convoy; 60l. Tanks. VERT: 4l. Grenade thrower.

203 St. Ivan Rilski

1946. Death Millenary of St. Ivan Rilski.

623	203	1l. brown	20	15
624	-	4l. sepia	20	15
625	-	10l. green	30	20
626	-	20l. blue	50	25
627	-	50l. red	1·10	1·10

DESIGNS—HORIZ: 4l. Rila Monastery; 10l. Monastery entrance; 50l. Cloistered courtyard. VERT: 20l. Aerial view of Monastery.

208 "New Republic"

1946. Referendum.

628	208	4l. red	20	15
629	208	20l. blue	20	15
630	208	50l. brown	50	40

209 Assault

210 Ambuscade

1946. Partisan Activities.

631	209	1l. purple	20	15
632	210	4l. green	20	15
633	-	5l. brown	20	15
634	210	10l. red	20	15
635	209	20l. blue	50	20
636	-	30l. brown	65	30
637	-	50l. black	85	70

DESIGNS—VERT: 5l., 50l. Partisan riflemen; 30l. Partisan leader.

211 Nurse and Children

1947. Winter Relief.

638	211	1l. violet	20	15
639	-	4l. red	20	15
640	-	5l. olive	20	15
641	211	10l. grey	20	15
642	-	20l. blue	20	15
643	-	30l. brown	40	20

644	-	40l. red	50	40
645	211	50l. green	95	70

DESIGNS: 4l., 9l. Child carrying gifts; 20l., 40l. Hungry child; 30l. Destitute mother and child.

212a Partisans

1947. Anti-fascists of 1923, 1941 and 1944 Commem.

645a	-	10l. brown and orange	75	70
645b	212a	20l. dp blue & lt blue	75	70
645c	-	70l. brown and red	47·00	45·00

DESIGNS—HORIZ: 10l. Group of fighters; 70l. Soldier addressing crowd.

213 Olive Branch

214 Dove of Peace

1947. Peace.

646	213	4l. olive	20	15
647	214	10l. brown	20	20
648	-	20l. blue	50	50

"BULGARIA" is in Roman characters on the 20l.

215 "U.S.A." and "Bulgaria"

1947. Air. Stamp Day and New York International Philatelic Exhibition.

649	215	70l.+30l. brown	2·10	2·00

216 Esperanto Emblem and Map of Bulgaria

1947. 30th Esperanto Jubilee Congress, Sofia.

650	216	20l.+10l. purple & green	1·00	1·00

217 G.P.O., Sofia

218 National Theatre, Sofia

219 Parliament Building

220 President's Palace

221 G.P.O., Sofia

1947. Government Buildings. (a) T **217**.

651		1l. green	20	15

(b) T **218**.

652		50s. green	20	15
653		2l. red	20	15
654		4l. blue	20	15
655		9l. red	65	20

(c) T **219**.

656		50s. green	20	15
657		2l. blue	20	15
658		4l. blue	20	15
659		20l. blue	1·60	1·00

(d) T **220**.

660		1l. green	20	15

(e) T **221**.

661		1l. green	20	15
662		2l. red	20	15
663		4l. blue	20	15

222 Hydro-electric Power Station and Dam

223 Emblem of Industry

1947. Reconstruction.

664	**222**	4l. green	20	15
665	-	9l. brown (Miner)	30	25
666	**223**	20l. blue	40	35
667	-	40l. green (Motor plough)	1·30	1·20

224 Exhibition Building

225 Former Residence of the French Poet Lamartine

226 Rose and Grapes

1947. Plovdiv Fair. (a) Postage.

668	**224**	4l. red	15	10
669	**225**	9l. red	20	10
670	**226**	20l. blue	40	40

227 Airplane over City

(b) Air. Imperf.

671	**227**	40l. green	1·60	1·50

228 Cycle Racing

229 Basketball

1947. Balkan Games.

672	**228**	2l. lilac	75	40
673	**229**	4l. green	85	50
674	-	9l. brown	1·60	60
675	-	20l. blue	2·10	70
676	-	60l. red	4·75	3·25

DESIGNS—VERT: 9l. Chess; 20l. Football; 60l. Balkan flags.

231 V. E. Aprilov

1947. Death Cent of Vasil Aprilov (educationist).

677	**231**	40l. blue	85	50
678	-	4l. red	30	15

DESIGN: 4l. Another portrait of Aprilov.

233 Postman

1947. Postal Employees' Relief Fund.

679	**233**	4l.+2l. olive	15	15
680	-	10l.+5l. red	20	20
681	-	20l.+10l. blue	30	30
682	-	40l.+20l. brown	1·60	1·50

DESIGNS: 10l. Linesman; 20l. Telephonists; 40l. Wireless masts.

235 Geno Kirov

1947. Theatrical Artists' Benevolent Fund.

683	**235**	50s. brown	10	10
684	-	1l. green	10	10
685	-	2l. green	10	10
686	-	3l. blue	10	10
687	-	4l. red	10	10
688	-	5l. purple	10	10
689	-	9l.+5l. blue	20	15
690	-	10l.+6l. red	20	20
691	-	15l.+7l. violet	50	35
692	-	20l.+15l. blue	75	60
693	-	30l.+20l. purple	1·60	1·30

PORTRAITS: 1l. Zlotina Nedeva; 2l. Ivan Popov; 3l. Atanas Kirchev; 4l. Elena Snezhina; 5l. Stoyan Buchvarov; 9l. Khristo Ganchev; 10l. Adriana Budevska; 15l. Vasil Kirkov; 20l. Save Orgnyanov; 30l. Krustyn Sarafov.

236 "Rodina" (freighter)

1947. National Shipping Revival.

694	**236**	50l. blue	1·00	80

237 Worker and Flag

238 Worker and Globe

1948. Second General Workers' Union Congress.

695	**237**	4l. blue (postage)	20	10
696	**238**	60l. brown (air)	85	70

239

240

1948. Leisure and Culture.

697	**239**	4l. red	20	15
698	**240**	20l. blue	40	20
699	-	40l. green	75	40
700	-	60l. brown	1·30	80

DESIGNS—VERT: 40l. Workers' musical interlude; 60l. Sports girl.

241 Kikola Vaptsarov

1948. Poets.

701	**241**	4l. red on cream	20	15
702	-	9l. brown on cream	25	20
703	-	15l. purple on cream	30	25
704	-	20l. blue on cream	40	35
705	-	45l. green on cream	1·00	90

PORTRAITS: 9l. Peya Yavorov; 15l. Khristo Smirnenski; 20l. Ivan Vazov; 45l. Petko Slaveikov.

242 Petlyakov Pe-2 Bomber over Baldwin's Tower

1948. Air. Stamp Day.

706	**242**	50l. brown on cream	2·10	2·00

243 Soldier

244 Peasants and Soldiers

1948. Soviet Army Monument.

707	**243**	4l. red on cream	20	15
708	**244**	10l. green on cream	25	20
709	-	20l. blue on cream	50	40
710	-	60l. olive on cream	1·30	1·00

DESIGNS—HORIZ: 20l. Soldiers of 1878 and 1944. VERT: 60l. Stalin and Spassky Tower, Kremlin.

245 Malyovitsa Peak

1948. Bulgarian Health Resorts.

711		2l. red	20	15
712		3l. orange	20	15
713		4l. blue	20	15
714		10l. purple	40	20
715	**245**	20l. blue	1·60	30
716	-	20l. blue	2·30	60
717	**245**	5l. brown	75	15
718	-	15l. olive	1·00	15

DESIGNS: 2l. Bath, Gorna Banya; 3, 10l. Bath, Bankya; 4, 20l. (No. 716), Mineral bath, Sofia; 15l. Malyovitsa Peak.

246 Lion Emblem

1948

719	**246**	50s. orange	20	15
719a	**246**	50s. brown	20	15
720	**246**	1l. green	20	15
721	**246**	9l. black	50	30

247 Dimitur Blagoev

248 Youths marching

1948. 25th Anniv of September Uprising.

722	**247**	4l. brown	20	15
723	-	9l. brown	30	30
724	-	20l. blue	30	30
725	**248**	60l. brown	1·60	1·20

DESIGNS—VERT: 9l. Gabrit Genov. HORIZ: 20l. Bishop Andrei Monument.

249 Khristo Smirnenski

1948. 500th Birth Anniv of Smirnenski (poet and revolutionary).

726	**249**	4l. blue	15	
727	**249**	16l. brown	40	20

250 Miner

1948

728	**250**	4l. blue	40	20

251 Battle of Grivitsa

1948. Treaty of Friendship with Rumania.

729	**251**	20l. blue (postage)	30	20
730	-	40l. black (air)	50	40
731	-	100l. mauve	1·30	1·20

DESIGNS: 40l. Parliament Buildings in Sofia and Bucharest; 100l. Projected Danube Bridge.

252 Botev's House, Kalofer

253 Botev

1948. Birth Centenary of Khristo Botev (poet and revolutionary).

732	**252**	1l. green	20	15
733	**253**	4l. brown	20	15
734	**253**	4l. purple	20	15
735	-	9l. violet	20	15
736	-	15l. brown	20	15
737a	-	20l. blue	40	20
738	-	40l. brown	75	50
739	-	50l. black	1·00	70

DESIGNS—HORIZ: 9l. River paddle-steamer "Radetski"; 15l. Village of Kalofer; 40l. Botev's mother and verse of poem. VERT: 20l. Botev in uniform; 50l. Quill, pistol and laurel wreath.

254 Lenin

1949. 25th Death Anniv of Lenin. Inscr "1924–1949".

740	**254**	4l. brown	30	20
741	-	75l. red	75	60

DESIGN—(27×37 mm): 20l. Lenin as an orator.

255 Road Construction

1949. National Youth Movement.

742	**255**	4l. red	20	15
743	-	5l. brown	40	20
744	-	9l. green	1·00	50
745	-	10l. violet	65	40
746	-	20l. blue	1·30	1·00
747	-	40l. brown	1·20	1·20

DESIGNS—HORIZ: 5l. Tunnel construction; 9l. Class 10 steam locomotive; 10l. Textile workers; 20l. Girl driving tractor; 40l. Workers in lorry.

256 Lisunov Li-2 over Pleven Mausoleum

1949. Air. Seventh Philatelic Congress, Pleven.

748	**256**	50l. bistre	5·75	5·00

257 G. Dimitrov

258 G. Dimitrov

1949. Death of Georgi Dimitrov (Prime Minister 1946–49).

749	**257**	4l. red	30	30
750	**258**	20l. blue	1·60	60

259 Hydro-electric Power Station

260 Symbols of Agriculture and Industry

1949. Five Year Industrial and Agricultural Plan.

751	**259**	4l. olive (postage)	20	15
752	-	9l. red	30	25
753	-	15l. violet	50	30

754	-	20l. blue	1·60	90
755	**260**	50l. brown (air)	4·50	2·00

DESIGNS—VERT: 9l. Cement works; 15l. Tractors in garage. HORIZ: 20l. Tractors in field.

261 Javelin and Grenade Throwing **262** Motor-cyclist and Tractor

1949. Physical Culture Campaign.

756	**261**	4l. red	75	40
757	-	9l. olive	2·10	90
758	**262**	20l. blue	3·25	1·70
759	-	50l. red	7·75	4·25

DESIGNS—HORIZ: 9l. Hurdling and leaping barbed-wire. VERT: 50l. Two athletes marching.

263 Globe

1949. Air. 75th Anniv of Universal Postal Union.

760	**263**	50l. blue	3·25	1·70

265 Guardsman with Dog **264** Guardsman and Peasant

1949. Frontier Guards.

761	**264**	4l. brown (postage)	50	40
762	-	20l. blue	1·60	1·40
763	**265**	60l. green (air)	4·75	4·00

DESIGN—VERT: 20l. Guardsman on coast.

266 Georgi Dimitrov (Prime Minister 1946–49) **267** "Unanimity"

1949. Fatherland Front.

764	**266**	4l. brown	20	15
765	**267**	9l. violet	85	50
766	-	20l. blue	95	60
767	-	50l. red	1·30	1·00

DESIGNS: 20l. Man and woman with wheelbarrow and spade; 50l. Young people marching with banners.

268 Zosif Stalin

1949. 70th Birthday of Stalin.

768	**268**	4l. orange	50	20
769	-	40l. red	1·60	1·10

DESIGN—VERT: (25x37 mm): 40l. Stalin as an orator.

269 Kharalampi Stoyanov **270** Strikers and Train

1950. 30th Anniv of Railway Strike.

770	**269**	4l. brown	50	20
771	**270**	20l. blue	65	30
772	-	60l. olive	1·00	80

DESIGN—VERT: 60l. Two workers and flag.

271 Miner **272** Class 48 Steam Shunting Locomotive

1950

773	**271**	1l. olive	15	10
773a	**271**	1l. violet	30	10
774	**272**	2l. black	1·00	30
774a	**272**	2l. brown	1·00	25
775	-	3l. blue	50	10
776a	-	4l. green	3·25	1·20
777	-	5l. red	65	10
778	-	9l. grey	40	15
779	-	10l. purple	30	10
780	-	15l. red	1·00	30
781	-	20l. blue	1·20	40

DESIGNS—VERT: 3l. Ship under construction; 10l. Power station; 15l., 20l. Woman in factory. HORIZ: 4l. Tractor; 5l., 9l. Threshing machines.

273 Kolarov

1950. Death of Vasil Kolarov (Prime Minister 1949–50). Inscr "1877–1950".

782	**273**	4l. brown	20	15
783	-	20l. blue	85	80

DESIGN—(27½x39½ mm): 20l. Portrait as Type **273**, but different frame.

274 Starislas Dospevski (self-portrait) **274a** *In the Field* (Khristo Storclev)

1950. Painters and paintings.

784	**274**	1l. green	65	15
785	-	4l. orange	2·10	60
786	-	9l. brown	3·25	80
787	**274a**	15l. brown	4·50	1·00
788	**274a**	20l. blue	6·75	3·00
789	-	40l. brown	8·25	4·00
790	-	60l. orange	9·00	6·00

DESIGNS—VERT: 4l. King Kaloyan and Desislava; 9l. Nikolai Pavlovich; 40l. Statue of Debeyanov (Ivan Lazarov); 60l. *Peasant* (Vladimir Dimitrov the Master).

275 Ivan Vazov and Birthplace, Sopot

1950. Birth Centenary of Ivan Vazov (poet).

791	**275**	4l. olive	20	15

276a G. Dimitrov (statesman)

1950. First Death Anniv of Georgi Dimitrov.

792	-	50s. brown (postage)	40	15
793	-	50s. green	40	15
794	**276a**	1l. brown	50	20
795	-	2l. slate	50	20
796	-	4l. purple	1·00	30
797	-	9l. red	1·80	90
798	-	10l. red	2·50	1·20
799	-	15l. grey	2·50	1·20
800	-	20l. blue	4·25	2·00
801	-	40l. brown (air)	8·25	4·00

DESIGNS—HORIZ: 50s. green, Dimitrov and birthplace, Kovachevtsi; 2l. Dimitrov's house, Sofia; 15l. Dimitrov signing new constitution; 20l. Dimitrov; 40l. Mausoleum. VERT: 50s. brown, 4, 9, 10l. Dimitrov in various poses.

277 Runners

1950

802	**277**	4l. green	95	50
803	-	9l. brown (Cycling)	1·00	80
804	-	20l. blue (Putting the shot)	1·30	1·20
805	-	40l. purple (Volleyball)	3·25	2·50

278 Workers and Tractor

1950. Second National Peace Congress.

806	**278**	4l. red	20	15
807	-	20l. blue	95	60

DESIGN—VERT: 20l. Stalin on flag and three heads.

278b

1950. Arms designs.

807a	-	2l. brown	20	15
807b	-	3l. red	20	15
807c	**278b**	5l. red	20	15
807d	-	9l. blue	20	15

Although inscribed "OFFICIAL MAIL", the above were issued as regular postage stamps.

279 Children on Beach

1950. Sunday Delivery.

808	-	1l. green (Sanatorium)	20	15
809	**279**	2l. red	30	15
810	-	5l. orange (Sunbathing)	65	30
811	**279**	10l. blue	1·60	60

280 Molotov, Kolarov, Stalin and Dimitrov **281** Russian and Bulgarian Girls

1950. Second Anniv of Soviet–Bulgarian Treaty of Friendship.

812	**280**	4l. brown	20	15
813	-	9l. red	30	15
814	**281**	20l. blue	65	50
815	-	50l. green	3·25	1·20

DESIGNS—VERT: 9l. Spassky Tower and flags; 50l. Freighter and tractor.

282 Marshal Tolbukhin

1950. Honouring Marshal Tolbukhin.

816	**282**	4l. mauve	30	20
817	-	20l. blue	1·60	80

DESIGN—HORIZ: 20l. Bulgarians greeting Tolbukhin.

284 A. S. Popov

1951. 45th Death Anniv of Aleksandr Popov (radio pioneer).

818	**284**	4l. brown	75	30
819	**284**	20l. blue	1·40	70

286 Georgi Kirkov

1951. Anti-fascist Heroes.

823	-	1l. mauve	40	20
824	-	2l. plum	40	20
825	**286**	4l. red	40	20
826	-	9l. brown	1·20	60
827	-	15l. olive	2·50	1·10
828	-	20l. blue	2·50	1·50
829	-	50l. grey	6·25	2·20

PORTRAITS: 1l. Chankova, Adalbert Antonov-Malchika, Sasho Dimitrov and Lilyana Dimitrova; 2l. Stanke Dimitrov; 9l. Anton Ivanov; 15l. Mikhailov; 20l. Georgi Dimitrov at Leipzig; 50l. Nocho Ivanov and Acram Stoyahov.

285 First Bulgarian Truck

1951. National Occupations. (a) As T 285.

820		1l. violet (Tractor)	20	10
821		2l. green (Steam-roller)	25	10
822	**285**	4l. brown	30	10

289 Embroidery

(b) As T 289.

830	-	1l. brown (Tractor)	30	20
831	-	2l. violet (Steam-roller)	40	30
832	-	4l. brown (Truck)	75	60
833	**289**	9l. violet	1·30	80
834	-	15l. purple (Carpets)	2·30	1·50
835	-	20l. blue (Roses and Tobacco)	5·25	2·20
836	-	40l. green (Fruit)	7·75	3·25

The 9l. and 20l. are vert, the remainder horiz.

290 Turkish Attack

1951. 75th Anniv of April Uprising.

837	**290**	1l. brown	75	35
838	-	4l. green	85	40
839	-	9l. purple	1·30	1·00
840	-	20l. blue	1·90	1·50
841	-	40l. lake	2·50	2·00

DESIGNS—HORIZ: 4l. Proclamation of Uprising; 9l. Cannon and cavalry; 20l. Patriots in 1876 and 1944; 40l. Georgi Benkovsky and Georgi Dimitrov.

291 Dimitur Blagoev as Orator

1951. 60th Anniv of First Bulgarian Social Democratic Party Congress, Buzludzha.

842	**291**	1l. violet	30	20
843	**291**	4l. green	1·00	40
844	**291**	9l. purple	1·80	1·20

292 Babies in Creche

1951. Children's Day.

845	**292**	1l. brown	30	20
846	-	4l. purple	75	30
847	-	9l. green	1·60	60
848	-	20l. blue	3·25	2·00

DESIGNS: 4l. Children building models; 9l. Girl and children's play ground; 20l. Boy bugler and children marching.

293 Workers

1951. Third General Workers' Union Congress.

849	**293**	1l. black	20	15
850	-	4l. brown	30	20

DESIGN inscr "16 XII 1951"; 4l. Georgi Dimitrov and Valdo Chervenkov (Prime minister).

294 Labour medal (Obverse) **295** Labour medal (Reverse)

1952. Order of Labour.

851	**294**	1l. red	20	15
852	**295**	1l. brown	20	15
853	**294**	4l. green	20	15
854	**295**	4l. green	20	15
855	**294**	9l. violet	75	20
856	**295**	9l. blue	75	20

296 Vasil Kolarov Dam

1952

857	**296**	4s. green	20	15
858	**296**	12s. violet	30	15
859	**296**	16s. brown	40	15
860	**296**	44s. red	1·00	20
861	**296**	80s. blue	4·50	50

297 G. Dimitrov and Chemical Works

1952. 70th Birth Anniv of Georgi Dimitrov (statesman). Dated "1882–1952".

862	**297**	16s. brown	95	50
863	-	44s. brown	1·60	1·00
864	-	80s. blue	2·75	1·50

DESIGNS—HORIZ: 44s. Georgi Dimitrov (Prime minister 1946–49) and Prime minister Vulko Chervenkov. VERT: 80s. Full-face portrait of Georgi Dimitrov.

298 Republika Power Station

1952

866	**298**	16s. sepia	65	20
867	**298**	44s. purple	2·10	30

299 N. Vaptsarov (revolutionary)

1952. Tenth Death Anniv of Nikola Vaptsarov (poet and revolutionary).

869	**299**	16s. lake	95	70
870	-	44s. brown	1·90	1·70
871	-	80s. sepia	4·00	1·90

PORTRAITS: 44s. Facing bayonets; 80s. Full-face.

300 Congress Delegates

1952. 40th Anniv of First Workers' Social Democratic Youth League Congress.

872	**300**	2s. lake	20	15
873	-	16s. violet	40	30
874	-	44s. green	1·60	85
875	-	80s. sepia	2·50	1·90

DESIGNS: 16s. Young partisans; 44s. Factory and guards; 80s. Dimitrov addressing young workers.

301 Attack on Winter Palace, St. Petersburg

1952. 35th Anniv of Russian Revolution. Dated "1917 1952".

876	**301**	4s. lake	40	20
877	-	8s. green	50	30
878	-	16s. blue	1·20	40
879	-	44s. sepia	1·50	50
880	-	80s. olive	3·00	2·40

DESIGNS: 8s. Volga–Don canal; 16s. Dove and globe; 44s. Lenin and Stalin; 80s. Lenin, Stalin and Himlay hydro-electric station.

302 **303** Vintagers and Grapes

1952. Wood Carvings depicting National Products.

881		2s. brown	20	15
882		8s. green	20	15
883		12s. brown	40	15
884		16s. purple	80	15
885	**302**	28s. green	1·10	20
886	-	44s. brown	1·50	30
887	**303**	80s. blue	1·70	40
888	**303**	1l. violet	4·00	60
889	**303**	4l. red	4·75	3·50

DESIGNS—VERT: 2s. Numeral in carved frame. HORIZ: 8s. Gift-offering to idol; 12s. Birds and grapes; 16s. Rose-gathering; 44s. "Attar of Roses".

304 V. Levski

1953. 80th Anniv of Execution of Vasil Levski (revolutionary).

890	**304**	16s. brown on cream	20	15
891	-	44s. brown on cream	60	30

DESIGN: 44s. Levski addressing crowd.

305 Russian Army Crossing R. Danube

1953. 75th Anniv of Liberation from Turkey.

892	**305**	8s. blue	30	20
893	-	16s. brown	40	20
894	-	44s. green	95	30
895	-	80s. lake	3·00	1·50
896	-	1l. black	3·50	3·00

DESIGNS—VERT: 16s. Battle of Shipka Pass. HORIZ: 44s. Peasants welcoming Russian soldiers; 80s. Bulgarians and Russians embracing; 1l. Shipka Pass memorial and Dimitrovgrad.

306 Mother and Children

1953. International Women's Day.

897	**306**	16s. blue	30	10
898	**306**	16s. green	30	10

307 Karl Marx

1953. 70th Death Anniv of Karl Marx.

899	**307**	16s. blue	30	20
900	-	44s. brown	70	50

DESIGN—VERT: 44s. Book "Das Kapital".

308 May Day Parade

1953. Labour Day.

901	**308**	16s. red	40	20

309 Stalin

1953. Death of Stalin.

902	**309**	16s. brown	80	30
903	**309**	16s. black	80	30

310 Goce Delcev (Macedonian revolutionary)

1953. 50th Anniv of Ilinden–Preobrazhenie Rising.

904	**310**	16s. brown	20	15
905	-	44s. violet	80	50
906	-	1l. purple	1·10	80

DESIGNS. 44s. Insurgents and flag facing left. HORIZ: 1l. Insurgents and flag facing right.

311 Soldier and Insurgents

1953. Army Day.

907	**311**	16s. red	50	20
908	-	44s. blue	95	30

DESIGN: 44s. Soldier, factories and combine-harvester.

312 Dimitur Blagoev

1953. 50th Anniv of Bulgarian Workers' Social Democratic Party.

909	**312**	16s. brown	50	30
910	-	44s. red	95	30

DESIGN: 44s. Dimitrov and Blagoev.

313 Georgi Dimitrov and Vasil Kolarov

1953. 30th Anniv of September Uprising.

911	**313**	8s. black	30	15
912	-	16s. brown	40	20
913	-	44s. red	1·30	60

DESIGNS: 16s. Insurgent and flag; 44s. Crowd of Insurgents.

314 Railway Viaduct

1953. Bulgarian–Russian Friendship.

914	**314**	8s. blue	20	15
915	-	16s. slate	30	20
916	-	44s. brown	80	40
917	-	80s. orange	95	70

DESIGNS—HORIZ: 16s. Welder and industrial plant; 80s. Combine-harvester. VERT: 44s. Iron foundry.

315 Dog Rose

1953. Medicinal Flowers.

918		2s. blue	20	15
919		4s. orange	20	15
920		8s. turquoise	20	15
921	**315**	12s. green	20	15
922	-	12s. red	20	15
923	-	16s. blue	50	20
924	-	16s. brown	50	20
925	-	20s. red	80	25
926	-	28s. green	85	30
927	-	40s. blue	95	50
928	-	44s. brown	1·50	60
929	-	80s. brown	2·40	1·10
930	-	1l. brown	6·75	1·90
931	-	2l. purple	9·75	4·00

MS931a 161×172 mm. Twelve values as above in green (sold at 6l.) 70·00 70·00

FLOWERS: 2s. Deadly nightshade; 4s. Thorn-apple; 8s. Sage; 16s. Great yellow gentian; 20s. Opium poppy; 28s. Peppermint; 40s. Bear-berry; 44s. Coltsfoot; 80s. Primula; 1l. Dandelion; 2l. Foxglove.

316 Vasil Kolarov Library

1953. 75th Anniv of Kolarov Library, Sofia.

932	**316**	44s. brown	60	40

317 Singer and Musician

1953. Amateur Theatricals.

933	**317**	16s. brown	30	15
934	-	44s. green	70	40

DESIGN: 44s. Folk-dancers.

318 Airplane over Mountains

1954. Air.

935	**318**	8s. green	20	15
936	-	12s. lake	20	15
937	-	16s. brown	20	15
938	-	20s. salmon	20	15
939	-	28s. blue	40	20
940	-	44s. purple	50	20
941	-	60s. brown	85	30
942	-	80s. green	95	40
943	-	1l. green	3·00	85
944	-	4l. blue	5·25	2·40

DESIGNS—VERT: 12s. Exhibition buildings, Plovdiv; 80s. Tirnovo; 4l. Partisans' Monument. HORIZ: 16s. Seaside promenade, Varna; 20s. Combine-harvester in cornfield; 28s. Rila Monastery; 44s. Studena hydro-electric barrage; 60s. Dimitrovgrad; 1l. Sofia University and equestrian statue.

319 Lenin and Stalin

1954. 30th Death Anniv of Lenin.

945	**319**	16s. brown	30	15
946	-	44s. lake	70	20
947	-	80s. blue	95	40
948	-	1l. green	1·90	1·20

DESIGNS—VERT: 44s. Lenin statue; 80s. Lenin–Stalin Mausoleum and Kremlin; 1l. Lenin.

320 Dimitur Blagoev and Crowd

1954. 30th Death Anniv of Blagoev.
949	**320**	16s. brown	20	10
950	-	44s. sepia	80	30

DESIGN: 44s. Blagoev writing at desk.

321 Dimitrov Speaking

1954. Fifth Death Anniv of Dimitrov.
951	**321**	44s. lake	50	30
952	-	80s. brown	95	70

DESIGN—HORIZ: 80s. Dimitrov and blast-furnace.

322 Class 10 Steam Locomotive

1954. Railway Workers' Day.
953	**322**	44s. turquoise	1·70	80
954	**322**	44s. black	1·70	80

323 Miner Operating Machinery

1954. Miners' Day.
955	**323**	44s. green	50	20

324 Marching Soldiers

1954. Tenth Anniv of Fatherland Front Government.
956	**324**	12s. lake	20	15
957	-	16s. red	20	15
958	-	28s. slate	30	20
959	-	44s. brown	60	25
960	-	80s. blue	1·30	50
961	-	1l. green	1·50	60

DESIGNS—VERT: 16s. Soldier and parents; 80s. Girl and boy pioneers; 1l. Dimitrov. HORIZ: 28s. Industrial plant; 44s. Dimitrov and workers.

325 Academy Building

1954. 85th Anniv of Academy of Sciences.
962	**325**	80s. black	1·50	80

326 Gymnast

1954. Sports. Cream paper.
963	**326**	16s. green	1·50	50
964	-	44s. red	1·60	95
965	-	80s. brown	3·50	1·90
966	-	2l. blue	5·25	4·00

DESIGNS—VERT: 44s. Wrestlers; 2l. Ski-jumper. HORIZ: 80s. Horse-jumper.

327 Velingrad Rest Home

1954. 50th Anniv of Trade Union Movement.
967	**327**	16s. green	30	20
968	-	44s. red	50	30

969	-	80s. blue	1·20	95

DESIGNS—VERT: 44s. Foundryman. HORIZ: 80s. Georgi Dimitrov, Dimitur Blagoev and Georgi Kirkov.

328 Geese **329** Communist Party Building

1955
970	**328**	2s. green	20	10
971	-	4s. olive	30	10
972	-	12s. brown	60	20
973	-	16s. brown	95	30
974	-	28s. blue	60	20
975	**329**	44s. red	11·50	3·50
976	-	80s. brown	1·50	50
977	-	1l. green	2·40	95

DESIGNS: 4s. Rooster and hens; 12s. Sow and piglets; 16s. Ewe and lambs; 28s. Telephone exchange; 80s. Flats; 1l. Cellulose factory.

330 Mill Girl

1955. International Women's Day.
978	**330**	12s. brown	10	10
979	-	16s. green	30	15
980	-	44s. blue	1·10	20
981	-	44s. red	1·10	20

DESIGNS—HORIZ: 16s. Girl feeding cattle. VERT: 44s. Mother and baby.

1955. As Nos. 820 and 822 surch **16 CT.**
981a		16s. on 1l. violet	20	10
982	**285**	16s. on 4l. brown	1·90	50

332 Rejoicing Crowds

1955. Labour Day.
983	**332**	16s. red	30	20
984	-	44s. blue	70	30

DESIGN: 44s. Three workers and globe.

333 St. Cyril and St. Methodius

1955. 1100th Anniv of First Bulgarian Literature. On cream paper.
985	**333**	4s. blue	20	15
986	-	8s. olive	20	15
987	-	16s. black	20	15
988	-	28s. red	50	40
989	-	44s. brown	80	50
990	-	80s. red	1·40	95
991	-	2l. black	2·40	2·10

DESIGNS: 8s. Monk writing; 16s. Early printing press; 28s. Khristo Botev (poet); 44s. Ivan Vazov (poet and novelist); 80s. Dimitur Blagoev (writer and editor) and books; 2l. Dimitur Blagoev Polygraphic Complex, Sofia.

334 Sergei Rumyantsev

1955. 30th Death Anniv of Bulgarian Poets. On cream paper.
992	**334**	12s. brown	40	20
993	-	16s. brown	50	30
994	-	44s. green	1·50	95

DESIGNS: 16s. Khristo Yusenov; 44s. Geo Milev.

335 F. Engels and Book

1955. 60th Death Anniv of Engels.
995	**335**	44s. brown on cream	95	80

336 Mother and Children

1955. World Mothers' Congress, Lausanne.
996	**336**	44s. lake on cream	95	80

337 "Youth of the World"

1955. Fifth World Youth Festival, Warsaw.
997	**337**	44s. blue on cream	95	80

338 Main Entrance in 1892

1955. 16th International Fair, Plovdiv.
998	**338**	4s. brown on cream	20	15
999	-	16s. red on cream	25	15
1000	-	44s. green on cream	50	20
1001	-	80s. cream	1·20	40

DESIGNS—VERT: 16s. Sculptured group; 80s. Fair poster. HORIZ: 44s. Fruit.

339 Friedrich Schiller (dramatist) (150th death anniv)

1955. Cultural Annivs. Writers. On cream paper.
1002	**339**	16s. brown	50	20
1003	-	44s. red	1·10	30
1004	-	60s. blue	1·40	40
1005	-	80s. black	1·70	60
1006	-	1l. purple	3·50	1·50
1007	-	2l. olive	4·50	3·00

PORTRAITS: 44s. Adam Mickiewicz (poet, death centenary); 60s. Hans Christian Andersen (150th birth anniv); 80s. Baron de Montesquieu (philosopher, death bicentenary); 1l. Miguel de Cervantes (350th anniv of publication of *Don Quixote*); 2l. Walt Whitman (poet) (centenary of publication of *Leaves of Grass*).

340 Industrial Plant

1955. Bulgarian–Russian Friendship. On cream paper.
1008	**340**	2s. slate	20	15
1009	-	4s. blue	20	15
1010	-	16s. green	60	20
1011	-	44s. brown	80	20
1012	-	80s. green	1·20	30
1013	-	1l. black	1·30	70

DESIGNS—HORIZ: 4s. Dam; 16s. Friendship railway bridge over River Danube between Ruse and Giurgiu (Rumania). VERT: 44s. Monument; 80s. Ivan-Michurin (botanist); 1l. Vladimir Mayakovsky (writer).

341 Emblem

1956. Centenary of Library Reading Rooms. On cream paper.
1014	**341**	12s. red	20	15
1015	-	16s. brown	30	20
1016	-	44s. myrtle	1·20	50

DESIGNS: 16s. K. Pshourka writing; 44s. B. Kiro reading.

342 Quinces

1956. Fruits.
1017	**342**	4s. red	2·10	30
1017a	**342**	4s. green	20	10
1018	-	8s. green (Pears)	95	30
1018a	-	8s. brown (Pears)	20	10
1019	-	16s. dark red (Apples)	1·70	40
1019a	-	16s. red (Apples)	60	20
1020	-	44s. violet (Grapes)	1·90	60
1020a	-	44s. ochre (Grapes)	1·20	30

343 Artillerymen

1956. 80th Anniv of April Uprising.
1021	**343**	16s. brown	40	40
1022	-	44s. green (Cavalry charge)	50	50

344 Blagoev and Birthplace at Zagovichane

1956. Birth Centenary of Dimitur Blagoev (socialist writer).
1023	**344**	44s. turquoise	1·50	95

345 Cherries

1956. Fruits.
1024	**345**	2s. lake	15	10
1025	-	12s. blue (Plums)	20	10
1026	-	28s. buff (Greengages)	40	30
1027	-	80s. red (Strawberries)	1·20	60

346 Football

1956. Olympic Games.
1028	-	4s. blue	60	20
1029	-	12s. red	70	25
1030	-	16s. brown	80	30
1031	**346**	44s. green	1·50	60
1032	-	80s. brown	2·40	1·30
1033	-	1l. lake	3·50	1·50

DESIGNS—VERT: 4s. Gymnastics; 12s. Throwing the discus; 80s. Basketball. HORIZ: 16s. Pole vaulting; 1l. Boxing.

347 Tobacco and Rose

1956. 17th International Fair, Plovdiv.
1034	**347**	44s. red	1·50	60
1035	**347**	44s. green	1·50	60

348 Gliders

1956. Air. 30th Anniv of Gliding Club.
1036	-	44s. blue	40	20
1037	-	60s. violet	50	30
1038	**348**	80s. green	1·50	95

DESIGNS: 44s. Launching glider; 60s. Glider over hangar.

349 National Theatre

1956. Centenary of National Theatre.

1039	**349**	16s. brown	30	20
1040	-	44s. turquoise	70	60

DESIGN: 44s. Dobri Voinikov and Sava Dobroplodni (dramatist).

350 Wolfgang Mozart (composer, birth bicent)

1956. Cultural Anniversaries.

1041		16s. olive	30	20
1042		20s. brown	50	20
1043	**350**	40s. red	70	25
1044	-	44s. brown	80	30
1045	-	60s. slate	95	35
1046	-	80s. brown	1·50	80
1047	-	1l. green	2·40	95
1048	-	2l. green	4·75	3·00

PORTRAITS: 16s. Benjamin Franklin (journalist and statesman, 150th birth anniv); 20s. Rembrandt (artist, 350th birth anniv); 44s. Heinrich Heine (poet, death centenary); 60s. George Bernard Shaw (dramatist, birth centenary); 80s. Fyodor Dostoevsky (novelist, 75th death anniv); 1l. Henrik Ibsen (dramatist, 50th death anniv); 2l. Pierre Curie (physicist, 50th death anniv).

351 Cyclists

1957. Tour of Egypt Cycle Race.

1049	**351**	80s. brown	1·50	70
1050	**351**	80s. turquoise	1·50	70

352 Woman with Microscope

1957. International Women's Day. Inscr as in T **352**.

1051	**352**	12s. blue	10	10
1052	-	16s. brown	30	15
1053	-	44s. green	60	30

DESIGNS: 16s. Woman and children; 44s. Woman feeding poultry.

353 New Times

1957. 60th Anniv of *New Times* (book).

1054	**353**	16s. red	40	20

354 Lisunov Li-2 Airliner

1957. Air. Tenth Anniv of Bulgarian Airways.

1055	**354**	80s. blue	1·50	50

355 St. Cyril and St. Methodius

1957. Centenary of Canonization of Saints Cyril and Methodius (founders of Cyrillic alphabet).

1056	**355**	44s. olive and buff	1·50	60

356 Basketball

1957. Tenth European Basketball Championships.

1057	**356**	44s. green	2·40	70

357 Girl in National Costume

1957. Sixth World Youth Festival, Moscow.

1058	**357**	44s. blue	80	30

358 G. Dimitrov

1957. 75th Birth Anniv of Georgi Dimitrov (statesman).

1059	**358**	44s. red	1·50	50

359 V. Levski

1957. 120th Birth Anniv of Vasil Levski (revolutionary).

1060	**359**	44s. green	95	30

360 View of Turnovo and Ludwig Zamenhof (inventor)

1957. 70th Anniv of Esperanto (invented language) and 50th Anniv of Bulgarian Esperanto Association.

1061	**360**	44s. green	1·50	50

361 Soldiers in Battle

1957. 80th Anniv of Liberation from Turkey.

1062	-	16s. green	20	10
1063	**361**	44s. brown	80	25

DESIGN: 16s. Old and young soldiers.

362 Woman Planting Tree

1957. Reafforestation Campaign.

1064	**362**	2s. green	20	15
1065	-	12s. brown	20	15
1066	-	16s. blue	20	15
1067	-	44s. turquoise	70	30
1068	-	80s. green	1·20	60

DESIGNS—HORIZ: 12s. Red deer in forest; 16s. Dam and trees; 44s. Polikarpov Po-2 biplane over forest; 80s. Trees and cornfield.

363 Two Hemispheres

1957. Fourth World TUC, Leipzig.

1069	**363**	44s. blue	80	30

364 Lenin

1957. 40th Anniv of Russian Revolution. Inscr "1917–1957".

1070	**364**	12s. brown	60	30
1071	-	16s. turquoise	1·30	80
1072	-	44s. blue	2·75	95
1073	-	60s. red	3·00	1·50
1074	-	80s. green	9·75	3·50

DESIGNS: 16s. Cruiser *Aurora*; 44s. Dove of Peace over Europe; 60s. Revolutionaries; 80s. Oil refinery.

365 Youth and Girl

1957. Tenth Anniv of Dimitrov National Youth Movement.

1075	**365**	16s. red	30	20

366 Partisans

1957. 15th Anniv of Fatherland Front.

1076	**366**	16s. brown	30	20

367 Mikhail Glinka (composer, death centenary)

1957. Cultural Celebrities.

1077	**367**	12s. brown	60	20
1078	-	16s. green	70	25
1079	-	40s. blue	1·60	30
1080	-	44s. brown	1·70	40
1081	-	60s. brown	1·90	80
1082	-	80s. purple	3·00	2·75

DESIGNS: 16s. Ion Comenius (educationist) (300th anniv of publication of *Didoetica Opera Omria*); 40s. Carl Linnaeus (botanist, 250th birth anniv); 44s. William Blake (writer, birth bicent); 60s. Carlo Goldoni (dramatist, 250th birth anniv); 80s. Auguste Comte (philosopher, death centenary).

368 Hotel Vasil, Kolarov

1958. Holiday Resorts.

1083		4s. blue	20	15
1084		8s. brown	20	15
1085		12s. green	20	15
1086	**368**	16s. green	20	15
1087	-	44s. turquoise	50	20
1088	-	60s. blue	80	30
1089	-	80s. brown	95	40
1090	-	1l. brown	1·20	50

DESIGNS—HORIZ: 4s. Skis and Pirin Mts; 8s. Old house in Koprivshtita; 12s. Hostel at Yelingrad; 44s. Hotel at Momin-Prokhod; 60s. Seaside hotel and peninsula, Nesebur; 80s. Beach scene, Varna; 1l. Modern hotels, Varna.

369 Brown Hare

1958. Forest Animals.

1091	**369**	2s. deep green & green	70	20
1092	-	12s. brown and green	1·20	30
1093	-	16s. brown and green	1·60	40
1094	-	44s. brown and blue	1·90	60
1095	-	80s. brown and ochre	2·40	80

1096	-	1l. brown and blue	3·00	1·20

DESIGNS—VERT: 12s. Roe doe. HORIZ: 16s. Red deer; 44s. Chamois; 80s. Brown bear; 1l. Wild boar.

370 Marx and Lenin

1958. Seventh Bulgarian Communist Party Congress. Inscr as in T **370**.

1097	**370**	12s. brown	50	20
1098	-	16s. red	80	30
1099	-	44s. blue	1·60	95

DESIGNS: 16s. Workers marching with banners; 44s. Lenin blast furnaces.

371 Wrestlers

1958. Wrestling Championships.

1100	**371**	60s. lake	2·10	1·50
1101	**371**	80s. sepia	2·40	1·90

372 Chessmen and "Oval Chessboard"

1958. Fifth World Students' Team Chess Championship, Varna.

1102	**372**	80s. green	11·50	10·50

373 Russian Pavilion

1958. 18th International Fair, Plovdiv.

1103	**373**	44s. red	95	70

374 Swimmer

1958. Bulgarian Students' Games.

1104	**374**	16s. blue	30	15
1105	-	28s. brown	60	20
1106	-	44s. green	85	50

DESIGNS: 28s. Dancer; 44s. Volleyball players at net.

375 Onions

1958. "Agricultural Propaganda".

1107	**375**	2s. brown	20	15
1108	-	12s. lake (Garlic)	20	15
1109	-	16s. myrtle (Peppers)	30	20
1110	-	44s. red (Tomatoes)	50	25
1111	-	80s. green (Cucumbers)	1·20	40
1112	-	1l. violet (Aubergines)	1·60	50

376 Insurgent with Rifle

1958. 35th Anniv of September Uprising.

1113	**376**	16s. orange	50	30
1114	-	44s. lake	95	70

DESIGN—HORIZ: 44s. Insurgent helping wounded comrade.

377 Conference Emblem

1958. First World Trade Union's Young Workers' Conference, Prague.
1115	**377**	44s. blue	95	70

378 Exhibition Emblem

1958. Brussels International Exhibition.
1116	**378**	1l. blue and black	9·75	9·75

379 Sputnik over Globe

1958. Air. IGY.
1117	**379**	80s. turquoise	6·75	5·75

380 Running

1958. Balkan Games. Inscr "1958".
1118	**380**	16s. brown	85	40
1119	-	44s. olive	95	60
1120	-	60s. blue	1·60	70
1121	-	80s. green	1·90	95
1122	-	4l. lake	11·50	7·25

DESIGNS—HORIZ: 44s. Throwing the javelin; 60s. High-jumping; 80s. Hurdling. VERT: 4l. Putting the shot.

381 Young Gardeners

1958. Fourth Dimitrov National Youth Movement Congress. Inscr as in T 381.
1123	**381**	8s. green	20	15
1124	-	12s. brown	20	15
1125	-	16s. purple	20	15
1126	-	40s. blue	80	20
1127	-	44s. red	1·20	50

DESIGNS—HORIZ: 12s. Farm girl with cattle; 40s. Youth with wheel-barrow. VERT: 16s. Youth with pickaxe and girl with spade; 44s. Communist Party Building.

382 Smirnenski

1958. 60th Birth Anniv of Khristo Smirnenski (poet and revolutionary).
1128	**382**	16s. red	40	20

383 First Cosmic Rockets

1959. Air. Launching of First Cosmic Rocket.
1129	**383**	2l. brown and blue	9·75	9·75

384 Footballers

1959. Youth Football Games, Sofia.
1130	**384**	2l. brown on cream	3·50	2·40

385 UNESCO Headquarters, Paris

1959. Inauguration of UNESCO Headquarters Building.
1131	**385**	2l. purple on cream	3·50	2·40

386 Skier

1959. 40 Years of Skiing in Bulgaria.
1132	**386**	1l. blue on cream	2·40	95

1959. No. 1110 surch **45 CT.**
1133		45s. on 44s. red	1·50	50

388 Military Telegraph Linesman

1959. 80th Anniv of 1st Bulgarian Postage Stamps.
1134	**388**	12s. yellow and green	20	15
1135	-	16s. mauve and purple	50	20
1136	-	60s. yellow and brown	85	40
1137	-	80s. salmon and red	95	40
1138	-	1l. blue	2·40	60
1139	-	2l. brown	4·75	2·40

MS1139a 91×121 mm. 60s. (+4l.40) yellow and black (as 1136). Imperf 75·00 75·00
MS1139b 125×125 mm. Remaining values in different colours (sold at 5l.) Imperf 75·00 75·00

DESIGNS—HORIZ: 16s. 19th-century mail-coach; 80s. Early postal car; 2l. Striking railway workers. VERT: 60s. Bulgarian 1879 stamp; 1l. Radio tower.

389 Great Tits

1959. Birds.
1140	**389**	2s. slate and yellow	40	20
1141	-	8s. green and brown	70	30
1142	-	16s. sepia and brown	80	35
1143	-	45s. myrtle and brown	1·80	70
1144	-	60s. grey and blue	3·50	1·20
1145	-	80s. drab and turquoise	4·75	1·90

DESIGNS—HORIZ: 8s. Hoopoe; 60s. Rock partridge; 80s. European cuckoo. VERT: 16s. Great spotted woodpecker; 45s. Grey partridge.

390 Cotton-picking

1959. Five Year Plan.
1146		2s. brown	20	15
1147		4s. bistre	20	15
1148	**390**	5s. green	20	15
1149	-	10s. brown	20	15
1150	-	12s. brown	20	15
1151	-	15s. mauve	20	15
1152	-	16s. violet	20	15

1153	-	20s. orange	30	20
1154	-	25s. blue	30	20
1155	-	28s. green	40	20
1156	-	40s. blue	50	20
1157	-	45s. brown	50	20
1158	-	60s. red	95	40
1159	-	80s. olive	1·70	30
1160	-	1l. lake	95	50
1161	-	1l.25 blue	3·00	95
1162	-	2l. red	1·80	60

DESIGNS—HORIZ: 2s. Children at play; 10s. Dairymaid milking cow; 16s. Industrial plant; 20s. Combine-harvester; 40s. Hydro-electric barrage; 60s. Furnaceman; 1l.25, Machinist. VERT: 4s. Woman doctor examining child; 12s. Tobacco harvesting; 15s. Machinist; 25s. Power linesman; 28s. Tending sunflowers; 45s. Miner; 80s. Fruit-picker; 1l. Workers with symbols of agriculture and industry; 2l. Worker with banner.

391 Patriots

1959. 300th Anniv of Batak.
1163	**391**	16s. brown	50	20

392 Piper

1959. Spartacist Games. Inscr "1958–1959".
1164	**392**	4s. olive on cream	20	15
1165	-	12s. red on yellow	20	15
1166	-	16s. lake on salmon	30	20
1167	-	20s. blue on blue	50	25
1168	-	80s. green on green	1·50	60
1169	-	1l. brown on orange	1·10	

DESIGNS—VERT: 12s. Gymnastics; 1l. Urn. HORIZ: 16s. Girls exercising with hoops; 20s. Dancers leaping; 80s. Ballet dancers.

393 Soldiers in Lorry

1959. 15th Anniv of Fatherland Front Government.
1170	**393**	12s. blue and red	20	15
1171	-	16s. black and red	20	15
1172	-	45s. blue and red	40	25
1173	-	60s. green and red	50	30
1174	-	80s. brown and red	80	40
1175	-	1l.25 brown and red	1·60	70

DESIGNS—HORIZ: 16s. Partisans meeting Red Army soldiers; 45s. Blast furnaces; 60s. Tanks; 80s. Combine-harvester in cornfield. VERT: 1l.25, Pioneers with banner.

394 Footballer

1959. 50th Anniv of Football in Bulgaria.
1176	**394**	1l.25 green on yellow	7·75	7·75

395 Tupolev Tu-104A Jetliner and Statue of Liberty

1959. Air. Visit of Nikita Khrushchev (Russian Prime Minister) to U.S.A.
1177	**395**	1l. pink and blue	4·00	4·00

396 Globe and Letter

1959. International Correspondence Week.
1178	**396**	45s. black and green	70	20
1179	-	1l.25 red, black & blue	1·30	50

DESIGN: 1l.25, Pigeon and letter.

397 Parachutist

1960. Third Voluntary Defence Congress.
1180	**397**	1l.25 cream & turquoise	3·50	1·60

398 N. Vaptsarov

1960. 50th Birth Anniv of Nikola Vaptsarov (poet and revolutionary).
1181	**398**	80s. brown and green	95	50

399 Dr. L. Zamenhof

1960. Birth Centenary of Dr. Ludwig Zamenhof (inventor of Esperanto).
1182	**399**	1l.25 green & lt green	1·50	95

400

1960. 50th Anniv of State Opera.
1183	**400**	80s. black and green	95	60
1184	-	1l.25 black and red	1·50	85

DESIGN: 1l.25, Lyre.

401 Track of Trajectory of "Lunik 3" around the Moon

1960. Flight of "Lunik 3".
1185	**401**	1l.25 green, yellow & bl	7·25	5·75

402 Skier

1960. Winter Olympic Games.
1186	**402**	2l. brown, blue & black	1·50	1·50

403 Vela Blagoeva

1960. 50th Anniv of International Women's Day. Inscr "1910–1960".
1187	**403**	16s. brown and pink	20	15
1188	-	28s. olive and yellow	20	15
1189	-	45s. green and olive	40	20
1190	-	60s. blue and light blue	50	30
1191	-	80s. brown and red	80	40
1192	-	1l.25 olive and ochre	95	80

PORTRAITS: 28s. Anna Maimunkowa; 45s. Vela Piskova; 60s. Rosa Luxemburg; 80s. Clara Zetkin; 1l.25, Nadezhda Krupskaya.

404 Lenin

1960. 90th Birth Anniv of Lenin.

1193	404	16s. flesh and brown	1·90	80
1194	-	45s. black and pink	3·50	1·60

DESIGN: 45s. "Lenin at Smolny" (writing in chair).

406 Basketball Players

1960. Seventh European Women's Basketball Championships.

1195	406	1l.25 black and yellow	1·90	95

407 Moon Rocket

1960. Air. Landing of Russian Rocket on Moon.

1196	407	1l.25 black, yellow & bl	7·25	5·75

408 Parachutist

1960. World Parachuting Championships, 1960.

1197	408	16s. blue and lilac	60	55
1198	-	1l.25 red and blue	3·00	1·20

DESIGN: 1l.25, Parachutes descending.

409 Gentiana lutea

1960. Flowers.

1199	409	2s. orange, grn & drab	20	15
1200	-	5s. red, green and yellow	80	20
1201	-	25s. orge, grn & salmon	85	25
1202	-	45s. mauve, grn & lilac	95	30
1203	-	60s. red, green and buff	1·50	40
1204	-	80s. blue, green & drab	1·90	1·50

FLOWERS: 5s. *Tulipa rhodopea*; 25s. *Lilium jankae*; 45s. *Rhododendron ponticum*; 60s. *Cypripedium calceolus*; 80s. *Haberlea rhodopenis*.

410 Football

1960. Olympic Games.

1205	410	8s. pink and brown	20	15
1206	-	12s. pink and violet	20	15
1207	-	16s. pink & turquoise	40	20
1208	-	45s. pink and purple	50	25
1209	-	80s. pink and blue	1·10	70
1210	-	2l. pink and green	1·50	95

DESIGNS: 12s. Wrestling; 16s. Weightlifting; 45s. Gymnastics; 80s. Canoeing; 2l. Running.

411 Racing Cyclists

1960. Tour of Bulgaria Cycle Race.

1211	411	1l. black, yellow & red	1·90	1·50

412 Globes

1960. 15th Anniv of WFTU.

1212	412	1l.25 cobalt and blue	95	60

413 Popov

1960. Birth Centenary of Alexsandr Popov (Russian radio pioneer).

1213	413	90s. black and blue	1·50	95

414 Y. Veshin

1960. Birth Centenary of Yavoslav Veshin (painter).

1214	414	1l. olive and yellow	5·75	3·00

415 U.N. Headquarters, New York

1961. 15th Anniv of UNO.

1215	415	1l. cream and brown	2·40	2·40
MS1215a 74×57 mm. **415** 1l. (+1l.) pink and green. Imperf			13·50	13·50

416 Boyana Church

1961. 700th Anniv of Boyana Murals (1959).

1216	416	60s. black, emer & grn	95	40
1217	-	80s. grn, cream & orange	1·50	50
1218	-	1l.25 red, cream & green	1·90	95

DESIGNS (Frescoes of): 80s. Theodor Tiron; 1l.25, Desislava.

417 Cosmic Rocket and Dogs Belda and Strelka

1961. Russian Cosmic Rocket Flight of August, 1960.

1219	417	1l.25 blue and red	6·75	6·75

419 Pleven Costume

1961. Provincial Costumes.

1220	-	12s. yellow, green & orge	20	10
1221	419	16s. brown, buff & lilac	20	10
1222	-	28s. red, black, & green	40	15
1223	-	45s. blue and red	80	20
1224	-	60s. yellow, blue & turq	1·10	30
1225	-	80s. red, green & yellow	1·30	70

COSTUMES: 12s. Kyustendil; 28s. Sliven; 45s. Sofia; 60s. Rhodope; 80c. Karnobat.

420 Clock Tower, Vratsa

1961. Museums and Monuments. Values and star in red.

1226	420	8s. green	20	15
1227	-	12s. violet	20	15
1228	-	16s. brown	20	15
1229	-	20s. blue	20	15
1230	-	28s. turquoise	30	20
1231	-	40s. brown	40	25
1232	-	45s. olive	50	30

1233	-	60s. slate	70	40
1234	-	80s. brown	1·20	50
1235	-	1l. turquoise	1·90	95

DESIGNS—As Type **420**. VERT: 12s. Clock Tower, Bansko; 20s. "Agushev" building, Mogilitsa (Smolensk). HORIZ: 28s. Oslekoff House, Koprivshtitsa; 40s. Pasha's House, Melnik. SQUARE (27×27 mm): 16s. Wine jug; 45s. Lion (bas-relief); 60s. "Horseman of Madara"; 80s. Fresco, Bachkovo Monastery; 1l. Coin of Tsar Konstantin-Asen (13th cent).

421 Dalmatian Pelican

1961. Birds.

1236	-	2s. turquoise, blk & red	25	15
1237	421	4s. orange, blk & grn	30	20
1238	-	16s. orange, brn & grn	40	30
1239	-	80s. yellow, brn & turq	80	1·10
1240	-	1l. yellow, sepia and blue	3·50	1·70
1241	-	2l. yellow, brown & blue	4·75	1·90

DESIGNS: 2s. White capercaillie; 16s. Common pheasant; 80s. Great bustard; 1l. Lammergeier; 2l. Hazel grouse.

422 "Communications and Transport"

1961. 50th Anniv of Transport Workers' Union.

1242	422	80s. green and black	95	50

423 Gagarin and Rocket

1961. World's First Manned Space Flight.

1243	423	4l. turquoise, blk & red	6·75	4·25

424 Shevchenko (Ukrainian poet)

1961. Death Centenary of Taras Shevchenko.

1244	424	1l. brown and green	6·25	4·25

425 Throwing the Discus

1961. World Students' Games. Values and inscr in black.

1245	-	4s. blue	20	15
1246	-	5s. red	20	15
1247	-	16s. olive	30	20
1248	425	45s. blue	50	30
1249	-	1l.25 brown	1·70	50
1250	-	2l. mauve	1·90	1·30

MS1250a 66×66 mm. 5l. blue, yellow and green (Sports Palace and inscriptions). Imperf | 19·00 | 19·00

DESIGNS—VERT: 4s. Water polo; 2l. Basketball. HORIZ: 5s. Tennis; 16s. Fencing; 1l.25, Sports Palace, Sofia.

426 Short-snouted Seahorse

1961. Black Sea Fauna.

1251	-	2s. sepia and green	20	15
1252	-	12s. pink and blue	20	15
1253	-	25s. violet and blue	25	20
1254	426	45s. brown and blue	1·50	95
1255	-	1l. blue and green	4·00	1·50
1256	-	1l.25 brown and blue	4·75	2·40

DESIGNS—HORIZ: 2s. Mediterranean monk seal; 12s. Lung jellyfish; 16s. Common dolphins; 1l. Stellate sturgeons; 1l.25, Thorn-backed ray.

427 "Space" Dogs

1961. Air. Space Exploration.

1257	427	2l. slate and purple	5·75	4·25
1258	-	2l. blue, yellow & orange	10·50	6·75

DESIGN: No. 1258, "Venus" rocket in flight (24×41½ mm).

428 Dimitur Blagoev as Orator

1961. 70th Anniv of First Bulgarian Social Democratic Party Congress, Buzludzha.

1259	428	45s. red and cream	30	20
1260	428	80s. blue and pink	70	50
1261	428	2l. sepia and green	1·50	1·20

429 Hotel

1961. Tourist issue. Inscr in black; designs green. Background colours given.

1262	429	4s. green	10	10
1263	-	12s. blue (Hikers)	10	10
1264	-	16s. green (Tents)	20	15
1265	-	1l.25 bistre (Climber)	1·20	30

Nos. 1263/5 are vert.

430 The Golden Girl

1961. Bulgarian Fables.

1266	430	2s. multicoloured	20	15
1267	-	8s. grey, black & purple	20	15
1268	-	12s. pink, black & green	25	20
1269	-	16s. multicoloured	95	50
1270	-	45s. multicoloured	1·90	80
1271	-	80s. multicoloured	2·40	95

DESIGNS: 8s. Man and woman (*The Living Water*); 12s. Archer and dragon (*The Golden Apple*); 16s. Horseman (*Krali Marko*, national hero); 45s. Female archer on stag (*Samovila-Vila*, fairy); 80s. Tom Thumb and cockerel.

431 Major Titov in Space-suit

1961. Air. Second Russian Manned Space Flight.

1272	431	75s. flesh, blue & olive	4·00	3·00
1273	-	1l.25 pink, bl & violet	4·75	4·00

DESIGN: 1l.25, "Vostok-2" in flight.

432 Amanita caesarea

1961. Mushrooms.

1274	432	2s. red, bistre & black	20	15
1275	-	4s. brown, grn & blk	20	15
1276	-	12s. brown, bistre & blk	20	15
1277	-	16s. brown, mve & blk	20	20
1278	-	45s. multicoloured	30	30
1279	-	80s. orange, sepia & blk	80	60
1280	-	1l.25 lav, brn & blk	1·60	80
1281	-	2l. brown, bistre & black	2·10	1·90

MUSHROOMS: 4s. *Psalliota silvatica*; 12s. *Boletus elegans*; 16s. *Boletus edulis*; 45s. *Lactarius deliciosus*; 80s. *Lepiota procera*; 1l.25, *Pleurotus ostreatus*; 2l. *Armillariella mellea*.

433 Dimitur and
Konstantin
Miladinov (authors)

1961. Publication Centenary of "Bulgarian Popular Songs".
1282	**433**	1l.25 black and olive	1·50	95

1962. Surch. (A) Surch in one line; (B) in two lines.
1283		1s. on 10s. brown (1149)	20	15
1284		1s. on 12s. brown (1150)	20	15
1285		2s. on 15s. mauve (1151)	20	15
1286		2s. on 16s. violet (1152)	20	15
1287		2s. on 20s. orange (1153) (A)	20	15
1288		2s. on 20s. orange (1153) (B)	30	15
1289		3s. on 25s. blue (1154)	20	15
1290		3s. on 28s. green (1155)	20	15
1291		5s. on 44s. green (1087)	30	15
1292		5s. on 44s. red (1110)	30	15
1293		5s. on 45s. brown (1157)	40	20
1294		10s. on 1l. red (1160)	60	30
1295		20s. on 2l. red (1162)	1·20	70
1296		40s. on 4l. red (889)	3·00	1·50

436 Isker River

1962. Air.
1297	**436**	1s. blue and violet	20	15
1298	-	2s. blue and pink	20	15
1299	-	3s. brown and chestnut	20	20
1300	-	10s. black and bistre	60	25
1301	-	40s. black and green	2·30	1·10

DESIGNS: 2s. Yacht at Varna; 3s. Melnik; 10s. Turnovo; 40s. Pirin Mountains.

437 Freighter *Varna*

1962. Bulgarian Merchant Navy.
1302	**437**	1s. green and blue	20	10
1303	-	5s. light blue and green	50	15
1304	-	20s. violet and blue	1·30	50

SHIPS: 5s. Tanker *Komsomols*; 20s. Liner *Georgi Dimitrov*.

438 Rila Mountains

1962. Views.
1305	**438**	1s. turquoise	20	15
1306	-	2s. blue	20	15
1307	-	6s. turquoise	40	20
1308	-	8s. purple	60	30
1309	-	13s. green	1·20	70
1310	-	1l. deep green	6·75	1·90

VIEWS: 2s. Pirin Mts; 6s. Fishing boats, Nesebur; 8s. Danube shipping; 13s. Viden Castle; 1l. Rhodope Mts.

439 Georgi
Dimitrov as
Typesetter

1962. 80th Anniv of State Printing Office.
1311	**439**	2s. red, black & yellow	20	15
1312	-	13s. black, orange & yell	80	40

DESIGN: 13s. Emblem of Printing Office.

440 Pink Roses

1962. Bulgarian Roses. T **440** and similar designs.
1313		1s. pink, green and violet	20	15
1314		2s. red, green and buff	20	15
1315		3s. red, green and blue	40	20
1316		4s. yellow, turquoise & grn	60	25
1317		5s. pink, green and blue	95	30
1318		6s. red, green and turquoise	1·30	70
1319		8s. red, green and yellow	3·00	1·30
1320		13s. yellow, green and blue	5·25	3·75

441 "The World United
against Malaria"

1962. Malaria Eradication.
1321	**441**	5s. yellow, black & brn	60	20
1322	-	20s. yellow, green & blk	1·80	80

DESIGN: 20s. Campaign emblem.

442 Lenin and Front Page of
"Pravda"

1962. 50th Anniv of *Pravda* Newspaper.
1323	**442**	5s. blue, red and black	1·90	1·20

443 Text-book
and Blackboard

1962. Bulgarian Teachers' Congress.
1324	**443**	5s. black, yellow & blue	50	20

444 Footballer

1962. World Football Championship, Chile.
1325	**444**	13s. brown, green & blk	1·90	95

445 Dimitrov

1962. 80th Birth Anniv of Georgi Dimitrov (Prime Minister 1946–49).
1326	**445**	2s. green	50	20
1327	**445**	5s. blue	95	40

446 Bishop

1962. 15th Chess Olympiad, Varna. Inscr "1962". Inscr in black.
1328	**446**	1s. green and grey	20	15
1329	-	2s. bistre and grey	30	20
1330	-	3s. purple and grey	40	25
1331	-	13s. orange and grey	1·90	80
1332	-	20s. blue and grey	2·50	1·50

MS1332a 76×66 mm. 20s. (+30s.) red and green (Chess pieces). Imperf ... 14·50 / 14·50

CHESS PIECES: 2s. Rook; 3s. Queen; 13s. Knight; 20s. Pawn.

XXXV КОНГРЕС
1962

13 =

(447)

1962. 35th Esperanto Congress, Burgas. Surch as T **447**.
1333	**360**	13s. on 44s. green	4·75	3·50

448 Festival Emblem

1962. World Youth Festival, Helsinki. Inscr "1962".
1334	**448**	5s. blue, pink and green	40	20
1335	-	13s. blue, purple & grey	1·10	30

DESIGN: 13s. Girl and emblem.

449 Ilyushin Il-18 Airliner

1962. Air. 13th Anniv of TABSO Airline.
1336	**449**	13s. blue, ultram & blk	1·50	50

450 Apollo

1962. Butterflies and Moths. Multicoloured.
1337		1s. Type **450**	20	15
1338		2s. Eastern festoon	25	15
1339		3s. Meleager's blue	30	15
1340		4s. Camberwell beauty	40	20
1341		5s. Crimson underwing	50	30
1342		6s. Hebe tiger moth	95	40
1343		10s. Danube clouded	3·50	1·30
1344		13s. Cardinal	4·75	2·40

451 K. E. Tsiolkovsky
(scientist)

1962. Air. 13th International Astronautics Congress. Inscr "1962".
1345	**451**	5s. drab and green	4·75	1·90
1346	-	13s. blue and yellow	1·90	95

DESIGN: 13s. Moon rocket.

452 Combine Harvester

1962. Eight Bulgarian Communist Party Congress.
1347	**452**	1s. olive and turquoise	20	15
1348	-	2s. turquoise and blue	25	20
1349	-	3s. brown and red	30	20
1350	-	13s. sepia, red & purple	1·20	60

DESIGNS: 2s. Electric train; 3s. Steel furnace; 13s. Blagoev and Dimitrov.

453 Cover of *History*
of Bulgaria

1962. Bicentenary of Paisii Khilendarski's *History of Bulgaria*.
1351	**453**	2s. black and olive	20	15
1352	-	5s. sepia and brown	50	20

DESIGN—HORIZ: 5s. Father Paisii at work on book.

454 Andrian Nikolaev and
"Vostok 3"

1962. Air. First "Team" Manned Space Flight.
1353	**454**	1s. olive, blue and black	30	20
1354	-	2s. olive, green & black	70	30
1355	-	40s. pink, turquoise & blk	4·00	2·10

DESIGNS: 2s. Pavel Ropovich and "Vostok 4"; 40s. "Vostoks 3" and "4" in flight.

455 Parachutist

1963
1356A		1s. lake	20	10
1357A		1s. brown	20	10
1358A		1s. turquoise	20	10
1359A		1s. green	20	10
1360A	**455**	1s. blue	20	10

DESIGNS—VERT: No. 1356, State crest. HORIZ: No. 1357, Sofia University; 1358, "Vasil Levski" Stadium, Sofia; 1359, "The Camels" (archway), Hisar.

456 Aleko
Konstantinov

1963. Birth Cent of Konstantinov (author).
1361	**456**	5s. green and red	50	30

457 Mars and "Mars 1" Space
Probe

1963. Air. Launching of Soviet Space Station "Mars 1".
1362	**457**	5s. multicoloured	95	50
1363	-	13s. turquoise, red & blk	1·90	95

DESIGN: 13s. Release of probe from rocket.

458 Orpheus
Restaurant, "Sunny
Beach"

1963. Black Sea Coast Resorts.
1364	**458**	1s. blue	20	15
1365a		2s. red	7·25	20
1366		3s. bistre	30	20
1367		5s. purple	50	20
1368		13s. turquoise	1·50	40
1369		20s. green	1·90	50

VIEWS "Sunny Beach": 5s. The Dunes Restaurant; 20s. Hotel. "Golden Sands"; 2s., 3s., 13s. Various hotels.

459 V. Levski

1963. 90th Anniv of Execution of Vasil Levski (revolutionary).
1370	**459**	13s. blue and yellow	1·90	75

460 Dimitrov, Boy
and Girl

1963. Tenth Dimitrov Communist Youth League Congress, Sofia.
1371	**460**	2s. brown, red & black	20	15
1372	-	13s. brown, turq & blk	80	45

DESIGN: 13s. Girl and youth holding book and hammer aloft.

461 Eurasian
Red Squirrel

1963. Woodland Animals.
1373	**461**	1s. brown, red and green on turquoise	20	15
1374	-	2s. blk, red & grn on yell	25	15
1375	-	3s. sep, red & ol on drab	30	20
1376	-	5s. brown, red and blue on violet	95	35

1377	-	13s. black, red and brown on pink	3·50	65
1378	-	20s. sepia, red and blue on blue	4·75	1·10

ANIMALS—HORIZ: 2s. East European hedgehog; 3s. Marbled polecat; 5s. Beech marten; 13s. Eurasian badger. VERT: 20s. European otter.

462 Wrestling

1963. 15th International Open Wrestling Championships, Sofia.

1379	**462**	5s. bistre and black	50	20
1380	-	20s. brown and black	1·50	85

DESIGN—HORIZ: 20s. As Type **462** but different hold.

463 Congress Emblem and Allegory

1963. World Women's Congress, Moscow.

1381	**463**	20s. blue and black	1·50	55

464 Esperanto Star and Sofia Arms

1963. 48th World Esperanto Congress, Sofia.

1382	**464**	13s. multicoloured	1·50	55

465 Rocket, Globe and Moon

1963. Launching of Soviet Moon Rocket "Luna 4". Inscr "2.IV.1963".

1383	**465**	1s. blue	20	10
1384	-	2s. purple	20	10
1385	-	3s. turquoise	20	10

DESIGNS: 2s. Tracking equipment; 3s. Sputniks.

466 Valery Bykovsky in Spacesuit

1963. Air. Second "Team" Manned Space Flights. Inscr "14. VI.1963".

1386	**466**	1s. turquoise and lilac	20	10
1387	-	2s. brown and yellow	30	15
1388	-	5s. red and light red	50	20
1389	-	20s.+10s. grn & lt bl	2·40	1·10

MS1389a 79×68 mm. 50s. purple and brown (Spassk Tower and Globe). Imperf

			4·75	4·25

DESIGNS: 2s. Valentina Tereshkova in spacesuit; 5s. Globe; 20s. Bykovsky and Tereshkova.

1963. Europa Fair, Riccione. Nos. 1314/5 and 1318 (Roses) optd **MOSTRA EUROPEISTICA.1963 RICCIONE** and sailing boat motif or additionally surch.

1390	-	2s. green and buff	50	20
1391	-	5s. on 3s. red, green and blue	70	35
1392	-	13s. on 6s. red, green & turq	1·70	55

468 Relay-racing

1963. Balkan Games. Flags in red, yellow, blue, green and black.

1393	**468**	1s. green	10	10
1394	-	2s. violet	15	10
1395	-	3s. turquoise	20	15
1396	-	5s. red	95	20

1397	-	13s. brown	4·00	3·00

MS1397a 74×69 mm. 50s. black and green (as T **468**). Imperf

			7·00	7·00

DESIGNS: 2s. Throwing the hammer; 3s. Long jumping; 5s. High jumping; 13s. Throwing the discus. Each design includes the flags of the competing countries.

469 Slavonic Scroll

1963. Fifth International Slav Congress, Sofia.

1398	**469**	5s. red, yellow & dp grn	50	20

470 Insurgents

1963. 40th Anniv of September Uprising.

1399	**470**	2s. black and red	30	15

471 *Aquilegia aurea*

1963. Nature Protection. Flowers in natural colours; background colours given.

1400	**471**	1s. turquoise	20	15
1401	-	2s. olive	20	15
1402	-	3s. yellow	20	15
1403	-	5s. blue	40	20
1404	-	6s. purple	50	35
1405	-	8s. light grey	95	45
1406	-	10s. mauve	1·90	85
1407	-	13s. olive	3·50	1·10

FLOWERS: 2s. Edelweiss; 3s. *Primula deorum*; 5s. White water-lily; 6s. Tulip; 8s. *Viola delphinantha*; 10s. Alpine clematis; 13s. *Anemone narcissiflora*.

472 Khristo Smirnenski

1963. 65th Birth Anniv of Smirnenski (poet and revolutionary).

1408	**472**	13s. black and lilac	95	45

473 Chariot Horses (wall-painting)

1963. Thracian Tombs, Kazanlik.

1409	**473**	1s. red, yellow and grey	20	15
1410	-	2s. violet, yellow & grey	20	15
1411	-	3s. turquoise, yell & grey	20	15
1412	-	5s. brown, yellow & grn	40	35
1413	-	13s. black, yellow & grn	1·10	55
1414	-	20s. red, yellow & green	1·90	85

DESIGNS (wall paintings on tombs): 2s. Chariot race; 3s. Flautists; 5s. Tray-bearer; 13s. Funeral feast; 20s. Seated woman.

474 Hemispheres and Centenary Emblem

1964. Centenary of Red Cross.

1415	**474**	1s. yellow, red & black	20	15
1416	-	2s. blue, red and black	20	15
1417	-	3s. multicoloured	20	15
1418	-	5s. turq, red & black	30	20
1419	-	13s. black, red & orange	1·30	55

DESIGNS: 2s. Blood donation; 3s. Bandaging wrist; 5s. Nurse; 13s. Henri Dunant.

475 Speed-skating

1964. Winter Olympic Games, Innsbruck.

1420	**475**	1s. indigo, brown & blue	20	15
1421	-	2s. olive, mauve & black	20	15
1422	-	3s. green, brown & blk	20	15
1423	-	5s. multicoloured	40	20
1424	-	10s. orange, blk & grey	80	45
1425	-	13s. mauve, violet & blk	95	55

MS1425a 64×67 mm. 50s. red, blue and grey (Girl skater). Imperf

			6·50	6·50

DESIGNS: 2s. Figure skating; 3s. Cross-country skiing; 5s. Ski jumping. Ice hockey—10s. Goalkeeper; 13s. Players.

476 Head (2nd cent)

1964. 2500 Years of Bulgarian Art. Borders in grey.

1426	**476**	1s. turquoise and red	20	15
1427	-	2s. sepia and red	20	15
1428	-	3s. bistre and red	20	15
1429	-	5s. blue and red	30	20
1430	-	6s. brown and red	60	25
1431	-	8s. brown and red	85	35
1432	-	10s. olive and red	95	40
1433	-	13s. olive and red	1·20	1·00

DESIGNS: 2s. Horseman (1st to 4th cent); 3s. Jug (19th cent); 5s. Buckle (19th cent); 6s. Pot (19th cent); 8s. Angel (17th cent); 10s. Animals (8th to 10th cent); 13s. Peasant woman (20th cent).

477 The Unborn Maid

1964. Folk Tales. Multicoloured.

1434	**477**	1s. Type **477**	20	15
1435	-	2s. Grandfather's Glove	20	15
1436	-	3s. The Big Turnip	20	15
1437	-	5s. The Wolf and the Seven Kids	30	20
1438	-	8s. Cunning Peter	60	35
1439	-	13s. The Loaf of Corn	1·60	55

478 Turkish Lacewing (*Ascalaphus ottomanus*)

1964. Insects.

1440	**478**	1s. black, yellow & brn	20	15
1441	-	2s. black, ochre & turq	20	15
1442	-	3s. green, black & drab	25	20
1443	-	5s. violet, black & green	90	35
1444	-	13s. brown, black & vio	1·80	55
1445	-	20s. yellow, black & bl	3·00	75

DESIGNS—VERT: 2s. Thread lacewing fly (*Nemoptera coa*); 5s. Alpine longhorn beetle (*Rosalia alpina*); 13s. Cockchafer (*Anisoplia austriaca*). HORIZ: 3s. Cricket (*Saga natalia*); 20s. Hunting wasp (*Scolia flavitrons*).

479 Football

1964. 50th Anniv of Levski Physical Culture Association.

1446	-	2s. Type **479**	20	10
1447	-	13s. Handball	1·20	55

MS1447a 60×60 mm. 60s. green and yellow (Cup and Map of Europe). Imperf

			4·50	4·25

480 Title Page and Petar Beron (author)

1964. 40th Anniv of First Bulgarian Primer.

1448	**480**	20s. black and brown	2·20	2·20

481 Stephenson's *Rocket*, 1829

1964. Railway Transport. Multicoloured.

1449	**481**	1s. Type **481**	20	15
1450	-	2s. Class 05 steam locomotive	20	15
1451	-	3s. German V.320.001 diesel locomotive	20	15
1452	-	5s. Electric locomotive	35	20
1453	-	8s. Class 05 steam locomotive and train on bridge	90	45
1454	-	13s. Class E41 electric train emerging from tunnel	1·30	1·10

482 Alsatian

1964. Dogs. Multicoloured.

1455	**482**	1s. Type **482**	20	15
1456	-	2s. Setter	25	15
1457	-	3s. Poodle	35	20
1458	-	4s. Pomeranian	45	25
1459	-	5s. St. Bernard	60	35
1460	-	8s. Fox terrier	90	55
1461	-	10s. Pointer	3·50	1·60
1462	-	13s. Dachshund	4·50	3·25

(**483**)

1964. Air. International Cosmic Exhibition, Riccione. No. 1386 surch with T **483** and No. 1387 surch as T **483**, but in Italian.

1463	**466**	10s. on 1s. turquoise and lilac	45	45
1464	-	20s. on 2s. brown & yell	1·30	65

484 Partisans and Flag

1964. 20th Anniv of Fatherland. Front Government. Flag in red.

1465	**484**	1s. blue and light blue	20	15
1466	-	2s. olive and bistre	20	15
1467	-	3s. lake and mauve	20	15
1468	-	4s. violet and lavender	20	15
1469	-	5s. brown and orange	20	15
1470	-	6s. blue and light blue	35	20
1471	-	8s. green and light green	70	35
1472	-	13s. brown and salmon	90	55

DESIGNS: 2s. Greeting Soviet troops; 3s. Soviet aid—arrival of goods; 4s. Industrial plant, Kremikovtsi; 5s. Combine-harvester; 6s. "Peace" campaigners; 8s. Soldier of National Guard; 3s. Blagoev and Dimitrov. All with flag as Type **484**.

(**485**)

1964. 21st Int Fair, Plovdiv. Surch with T **485**.

1473	-	20s. on 44s. ochre (No. 1020a)	1·80	75

486 Transport

1964. First National Stamp Exn, Sofia.
1474	**486**	20s. blue	1·60	1·10

487 Gymnastics

1964. Olympic Games, Tokyo. Rings and values in red.
1475	**487**	1s. green and light green	20	15
1476	-	2s. blue and lavender	20	15
1477	-	3s. blue and turquoise	20	15
1478	-	5s. violet and red	35	20
1479	-	13s. blue and light blue	1·20	35
1480	-	20s. green and buff	1·30	75
MS1480a		61×67 mm. 40s.+20s. ochre, red and blue (Rings, tracks etc.). Imperf	5·75	5·50

DESIGNS: 2s. Long-jump; 3s. Swimmer on starting block; 5s. Football; 13s. Volleyball; 20s. Wrestling.

488 Vratsata

1964. Landscapes.
1481	**488**	1s. green	20	15
1482	-	2s. brown	20	15
1483	-	3s. blue	20	15
1484	-	4s. brown	25	15
1485	-	5s. green	45	20
1486	-	6s. violet	70	35

DESIGNS: 2s. The Ritli; 3s. Maliovitsa; 4s. Broken Rocks; 5s. Erkyupria; 6s. Rhodope mountain pass.

489 Paper and Cellulose Factory, Bukovtsi

1964. Air. Industrial Buildings.
1487	**489**	8s. turquoise	45	15
1488	-	10s. purple	60	20
1489	-	13s. violet	70	25
1490	-	20s. blue	1·30	55
1491	-	40s. green	2·20	75

DESIGNS: 10s. Metal works, Plovdiv; 13s. Metallurgical works, Kremikovtzi; 20s. Petrol refinery, Burgas; 40s. Fertiliser factory, Stara-Zagora.

490 Rila Monastery

1964. Philatelic Exn for Franco–Bulgarian Amity.
1492	**490**	5s. black and drab	55	25
1493	-	13s. black and blue	1·30	65

DESIGN: 13s. Notre-Dame, Paris (inscr in French).

491 500-year-old Walnut

1964. Ancient Trees. Values and inscr in black.
1494	**491**	1s. brown	20	15
1495	-	2s. purple	20	15
1496	-	3s. sepia	20	15
1497	-	4s. blue	20	15
1498	-	10s. green	90	35
1499	-	13s. olive	1·30	45

TREES: 2s. Plane (1000 yrs.); 3s. Plane (600 yrs.); 4s. Poplar (800 yrs.); 10s. Oak (800 yrs.); 13s. Fir (1200 yrs.).

492

1964. Eighth Congress of Int Union of Students, Sofia.
1500	**492**	13s. black and blue	90	55

493 Bulgarian Veteran and Soviet Soldier (Sculpture by T. Zlatarev)

1965. 30 Years of Bulgarian–Russian Friendship.
1501	**493**	2s. red and black	45	20

494 "Gold Medal"

1965. Olympic Games, Tokyo (1964).
1502	**494**	20s. black, gold & brown	1·30	75

495 Vladimir Komarov

1965. Flight of "Voskhod 1". Multicoloured.
1503		1s. Type **495**	20	15
1504		2s. Konstantin Feoktistov	20	15
1505		5s. Boris Yegorov	25	20
1506		13s. The three astronauts	1·10	35
1507		20s. "Voskhod I"	1·30	55

496 Corn-cob

1965. Agricultural Products.
1508	**496**	1s. yellow	15	10
1509	-	2s. green	20	10
1510	-	3s. orange	25	10
1511	-	4s. olive	35	15
1512	-	5s. red	40	15
1513	-	10s. blue	45	20
1514	-	13s. bistre	1·30	35

DESIGNS: 2s. Ears of Wheat; 3s. Sunflowers; 4s. Sugar beet; 5s. Clover; 10s. Cotton; 13s. Tobacco.

497 "Victory against Fascism"

1965. 20th Anniv of "Victory of 9 May, 1945".
1515	**497**	5s. black, bistre & grey	20	10
1516	-	13s. blue, black & grey	70	45

DESIGN: 13s. Globes on dove ("Peace").

498 Northern Bullfinch

1965. Song Birds. Multicoloured.
1517		1s. Type **498**	20	15
1518		2s. Golden oriole	25	15
1519		3s. Rock thrush	35	15
1520		5s. Barn swallows	60	20
1521		8s. European roller	70	55
1522		10s. Eurasian goldfinch	2·50	90
1523		13s. Rose-coloured starling	2·75	1·70
1524		20s. Nightingale	3·75	3·50

499 Transport, Globe and Whale

1965. Fourth International Transport Conf, Sofia.
1525	**499**	13s. multicoloured	1·90	1·10

500 ICY Emblem

1965. International Co-operation Year.
1526	**500**	20s. orange, olive & blk	1·40	80

501 ITU Emblem and Symbols

1965. Centenary of ITU.
1527	**501**	20s. yellow, green & bl	1·40	80

502 Pavel Belyaev and Aleksei Leonov

1965. "Voskhod 2" Space Flight.
1528	**502**	2s. purple, grn & drab	45	20
1529	-	20s. multicoloured	3·75	1·50

DESIGN: 20s. Leonov on space.

503 Common Stingray

1965. Fish. Borders in grey.
1530	**503**	1s. gold, black & orange	10	10
1531	-	2s. silver, indigo & blue	20	10
1532	-	3s. gold, black & green	30	15
1533	-	5s. gold, black and red	45	20
1534	-	10s. silver, blue & turq	2·00	1·00
1535	-	13s. gold, black & brown	2·50	1·50

Designs: 2s. Atlantic bonito; 3s. Brown scorpionfish; 5s. Tub gurnard; 10s. Mediterranean horse-mackerel; 13s. Black Sea turbot.

504 Marx and Lenin

1965. Organization of Socialist Countries' Postal Ministers' Conference, Peking.
1536	**504**	13s. brown and red	1·40	90

505 Film and Screen

1965. Balkan Film Festival. Varna.
1537	**505**	13s. black, silver & blue	95	35

506 Quinces

1965. Fruits.
1538	**506**	1s. orange	10	10
1539	-	2s. olive (Grapes)	10	10
1540	-	3s. bistre (Pears)	20	10
1541	-	4s. orange (Plums)	30	10
1542	-	5s. red (Strawberries)	35	20
1543	-	6s. brown (Walnuts)	45	35

507 Ballerina

1965. Ballet Competitions, Varna.
1544	**507**	5s. black and mauve	1·90	1·10

508 Dove, Emblem and Map

1965. "Balkanphila" Stamp Exhibition, Varna.
1545	**508**	1s. silver, blue & yellow	10	10
1546	-	2s. silver, violet & yellow	15	10
1547	-	3s. gold, green & yellow	30	20
1548	-	13s. gold, red & yellow	1·90	1·30
1549	-	20s. brown, blue & silver	1·90	1·70
MS1550		71×62 mm. 40s. gold and blue (T **508**). Imperf	4·25	4·00

DESIGNS: 2s. Yacht emblem; 3s. Stylised fish and flowers; 13s. Stylised sun, planet and rocket. LARGER (45×25½ mm): 20s. Cosmonauts Pavel Belyaev and Aleksei Leonov.

509 Escapers in Boat

1965. 40th Anniv of Political Prisoners' Escape from "Bolshevik Island".
1551	**509**	2s. black and slate	45	20

(510)

1965. National Folklore Competition. No. 1084 surch with T **510**.
1552		2s. on 8s. brown	2·20	2·20

511 Gymnast

1965. Balkan Games.
1553	**511**	1s. black and red	20	15
1554	-	2s. purple and black	20	15
1555	-	3s. purple, black & red	20	15
1556	-	5s. brown, black & red	30	20
1557	-	10s. purple, black & mve	1·00	45
1558	-	13s. purple and black	1·10	55

DESIGNS: 2s. Gymnastics on bars; 3s. Weight-lifting; 5s. Rally car and building; 10s. Basketball; 13s. Rally car and map.

512 Dressage

1965. Horsemanship.
1559	**512**	1s. plum, black & blue	20	15

1560	-	2s. brown, black & ochre		20	15
1561	-	3s. red, black and purple		20	15
1562	-	5s. brown and green		65	20
1563	-	10s. brown, blk & grey		2·75	1·30
1564	-	13s. brown, grn & buff		3·25	1·70

MS1565 80×80 mm. 40s.+20s. plum and grey (as 13s.). Imperf 6·00 5·50

DESIGNS: 5s. Horse-racing. Others, Horse-jumping (various).

513 Young Pioneers

1965. Dimitrov Septembrist Pioneers Organization.

1566	513	1s. green and turquoise	20	15
1567	-	2s. mauve and violet	20	15
1568	-	3s. bistre and olive	20	15
1569	-	5s. ochre and blue	30	20
1570	-	8s. orange and brown	95	45
1571	-	13s. violet and red	1·40	80

DESIGNS: 2s. Admitting recruit; 3s. Camp bugler; 5s. Flying model airplane; 8s. Girls singing; 13s. Young athlete.

514 Junkers Ju 52/3m over Turnovo

1965. Bulgarian Civil Aviation. Multicoloured.

1572		1s. Type 514	20	15
1573	-	2s. Ilyushin Il-14M over Plovdiv	20	15
1574	-	3s. Mil Mi-4 helicopter over Dimitrovgrad	20	15
1575	-	5s. Tupolev Tu-104A over Ruse	35	20
1576	-	13s. Ilyushin Il-18 over Varna	1·10	45
1577	-	20s. Tupolev Tu-114 over Sofia	1·90	80

515 Women of N. and S. Bulgaria

1965. 80th Anniv of Union of North and South Bulgaria.

1578	515	13s. black and green	95	80

516 I.Q.S.Y. Emblem and Earth's Radiation Zones

1965. International Quiet Sun Year.

1579	516	1s. yellow, green & blue	20	15
1580	-	2s. multicoloured	20	15
1581	-	13s. multicoloured	1·20	45

DESIGNS (I.Q.S.Y. emblem and): 2s. Sun and solar flares; 13s. Total eclipse of the Sun.

517 "Spring Greetings"

1966. "Spring". National Folklore.

1582	517	1s. mauve, blue & drab	20	15
1583	-	2s. red, black and drab	20	15
1584	-	3s. violet, red and grey	20	15
1585	-	5s. red, violet and black	30	20
1586	-	8s. purple, brown & mve	20	15
1587	-	13s. mauve, black & bl	1·10	35

DESIGNS: 2s. Drummer; 3s. "Birds" (stylised); 5s. Folk dancer; 8s. Vase of flowers; 13s. Bagpiper.

518 Byala Bridge

1966. Ancient Monuments.

1588	518	1s. turquoise	20	15

1589	-	1s. green	20	15
1590	-	2s. green	20	15
1591	-	2s. purple	20	15
1592	-	8s. brown	55	20
1593	-	13s. blue	95	45

DESIGNS: No. 1589, Svilengrad Bridge; 1590, Fountain, Samokov; 1591, Ruins of Matochina Castle, Khaskovo; 1592, Cherven Castle, Ruse; 1593, Cafe, Bozhentsi, Gabrovo.

519 Christ (from fresco Boyana Church)

1966. "2,500 Years of Culture". Multicoloured.

1594		1s. Type 519	3·75	3·25
1595		2s. Destruction of the Idols (from fresco, Boyana Church) (horiz)	35	35
1596		3s. Bachkovo Monastery	45	40
1597		4s. Zemen Monastery (horiz)	55	45
1598		5s. John the Baptist Church, Nesebur	65	55
1599		13s. Nativity (icon, Aleksandr Nevski Cathedral, Sofia)	95	1·00
1600		20s. Virgin and Child (icon, Archaeological Museum, Sofia)	1·40	1·10

520 The First Gunshot at Koprivshtitsa

1966. 90th Anniv of April Uprising.

1601	520	1s. black, brown & gold	20	15
1602	-	2s. black, red and gold	20	15
1603	-	3s. black, green & gold	20	15
1604	-	5s. black, blue & gold	25	15
1605	-	10s. black, purple & gold	65	20
1606	-	13s. black, violet & gold	75	55

DESIGNS: 2s. Georgi Benkovski and Todor Kableskov; 3s. "Showing the Flag" at Panagyurishte; 5s. Vasil Petleshkov and Tsanko Dyustabanov; 10s. Landing of Khristo Botev's detachment at Kozlodui; 13s. Panyot Volov and Zlarion Dragostinov.

521 Luna reaching for the Moon

1966. Moon Landing of "Luna 9". Sheet 70×50 mm.
MS1607 521 60s. silver, black and red 5·50 5·50

522 W.H.O. Building

1966. Inaug of W.H.O. Headquarters, Geneva.

1608	522	13s. blue and silver	1·10	55

523 Worker

1966. Sixth Trades Union Congress, Sofia.

1609	523	20s. black and pink	1·40	80

524 Indian Elephant

1966. Sofia Zoo Animals. Multicoloured.

1610	524	1s. Type 524	20	15
1611	-	2s. Tiger	20	15
1612	-	3s. Chimpanzee	20	15
1613	-	4s. Ibex	30	20

1614	-	5s. Polar bear	95	35
1615	-	8s. Lion	1·10	55
1616	-	13s. American bison	3·25	1·70
1617	-	20s. Eastern grey kangaroo	4·25	2·20

525 Boy and Girl holding Banners

1966. Third Congress of Bulgarian Sports Federation.

1618	525	13s. blue, orge & cobalt	95	55

526 Radetski and Pioneer

1966. 90th Anniv of Khristo Botev's Seizure of River Paddle-steamer Radetski.

1619	526	2s. multicoloured	30	20

527 Standard-bearer Simov-Kuruto

1966. 90th Death Anniv of Nikola Simov-Kuruto (hero of the Uprising against Turkey).

1620	527	5s. multicoloured	45	20

528 Federation Emblem

1966. Seventh Int Youth Federation Assembly, Sofia.

1621	528	13s. blue and black	95	35

529 UNESCO Emblem

1966. 20th Anniv of UNESCO.

1622	529	20s. ochre, red & black	1·10	55

530 Footballer with Ball

531 Jules Rimet Cup

1966. World Cup Football Championships, London. (a) Showing players in action. Borders in grey.

1623	530	1s. black and brown	20	15
1624	-	2s. black and red	20	15
1625	-	5s. black and bistre	30	20
1626	-	13s. black and blue	85	45
1627	-	20s. black and blue	95	55

(b) Sheet 60×65½ mm. T 531.
MS1628 50s. gold, cerise and grey 4·25 3·75

532 Wrestling

1966. Third Int Wrestling Championships, Sofia.

1629	532	13s. sepia, green & brn	95	55

533 Throwing the Javelin

1966. Third Republican Spartakiade.

1630	533	2s. green, red & yellow	20	15
1631	-	13s. green, red & yellow	75	40

DESIGN: 13s. Running.

534 Map of Balkans, Globe and UNESCO Emblem

1966. Int Balkan Studies Congress, Sofia.

1632	534	13s. green, pink & blue	95	55

535 Children with Construction Toy

1966. Children's Day.

1633	535	1s. black, yellow & red	10	10
1634	-	2s. black, brown & grn	10	10
1635	-	3s. black, yellow & blue	20	15
1636	-	13s. black, mauve & bl	1·50	35

DESIGNS: 2s. Rabbit and Teddy Bear; 3s. Children as astronauts; 13s. Children with gardening equipment.

536 Yuri Gagarin and "Vostok 1"

1966. Russian Space Exploration.

1637	536	1s. slate and grey	10	10
1638	-	2s. purple and grey	10	10
1639	-	3s. brown and grey	10	10
1640	-	5s. lake and grey	20	10
1641	-	8s. blue and grey	35	20
1642	-	13s. turquoise and grey	1·10	35
1643	-	20s.+10s. vio & grey	1·90	65

MS1644 70×62½ mm. 30s.+10s. black, red and grey. Imperf 4·25 3·75

DESIGNS: 2s. German Titov and "Vostok 2"; 3s. Andrian Nikolaev, Povel Popovich and "Vostok 3" and "4"; 5s. Valentina Tereshkova, Vallery Bykovsky and "Vostok 5" and "6"; 8s. Vladimir Komarov, Boris Yegorov, Konstantin Feoktistov and "Voskhod 1"; 13s. Povel Belyaev, Aleksei Leonov and "Voskhod 2"; 20s. Gagarin, Leonov and Tereshkova; 30s. Rocket and globe.

537 St. Clement (14th-cent wood-carving)

1966. 1050th Death Anniv of St. Clement of Ohrid.

1645	537	5s. brown, red & drab	95	55

538 Metodi Shatorov

1966. Anti-fascist Fighters. Frames in gold; value in black.

1646	538	2s. violet and red	10	10
1647	-	3s. brown and mauve	20	10
1648	-	5s. blue and red	30	15
1649	-	10s. brown and orange	65	20
1650	-	13s. brown and red	75	35

PORTRAITS: 3s. Vladno Trichkov; 5s. Vulcho Ivanov; 10s. Rasko Daskalov; 13s. Gen. Vladimir Zaimov.

539 Georgi Dimitrov (statesman)

1966. Ninth Bulgarian Communist Party Congress, Sofia.

| 1651 | **539** | 2s. black and red | 20 | 10 |
| 1652 | - | 20s. black, red and grey | 1·70 | 45 |

DESIGN: 20s. Furnaceman and steelworks.

540 Deer's Head Vessel

1966. The Gold Treasures of Panagyurishte. Multicoloured.

1653	**540**	1s. Type **540**	20	15
1654	-	2s. Amazon	25	15
1655	-	3s. Ram	30	15
1656	-	5s. Plate	35	15
1657	-	6s. Venus	45	20
1658	-	8s. Roe-buck	95	35
1659	-	10s. Amazon (different)	1·10	45
1660	-	13s. Amphora	1·40	55
1661	-	20s. Goat	2·30	1·10

Except for the 5s. and 13s. the designs show vessels with animal heads.

541 Bansko Hotel

1966. Tourist Resorts.

1662	**541**	1s. blue	20	15
1663	-	2s. green (Belogradchik)	20	15
1664	-	2s. lake (Tryavna)	20	15
1665	-	20s. pur (Malovitsa, Rila)	1·10	45

542 Christmas Tree

1966. New Year. Multicoloured.

| 1666 | | 2s. Type **542** | 20 | 15 |
| 1667 | | 13s. Money-box | 85 | 45 |

543 Percho Slaveikov (poet)

1966. Cultural Celebrities.

1668	**543**	1s. bistre, blue & orange	20	15
1669	-	2s. brown, orge & grey	20	15
1670	-	3s. blue, bistre & orange	20	15
1671	-	5s. purple, drab & orge	30	20
1672	-	8s. grey, purple & blue	65	30
1673	-	13s. violet, blue & purple	75	35

CELEBRITIES. Writers (with pen emblem): 2s. Dimcho Debelyanov (poet); 3s. Petko Todorov. Painters (with brush emblem): 5s. Dimitur Dobrovich; 8s. Ivan Murkvichka; 13s. Iliya Beshkov.

544 Dahlias

1966. Flowers. Multicoloured.

1674		1s. Type **544**	15	10
1675		1s. Clematis	20	10
1676		2s. Poet's narcissus	25	10
1677		2s. Foxgloves	30	15
1678		3s. Snowdrops	45	20
1679		5s. Petunias	55	30
1680		13s. Tiger lilies	1·10	35
1681		20s. Canterbury bells	1·40	55

545 Common Pheasant

1967. Hunting. Multicoloured.

1682		1s. Type **545**	30	20
1683		2s. Chukar partridge	30	20
1684		3s. Grey partridge	35	20
1685		5s. Brown hare	95	45
1686		8s. Roe deer	2·50	90
1687		13s. Red deer	2·75	1·60

546 "Philately"

1967. Tenth Bulgarian Philatelic Federation Congress, Sofia.

| 1688 | **546** | 10s. yellow, black & grn | 2·30 | 1·70 |

547 6th-cent B.C. Coin of Thrace

1967. Ancient Bulgarian Coins. Coins in silver on black background except 13s. (gold on black). Frame colours given.

1689	**547**	1s. brown	20	15
1690	-	2s. purple	20	15
1691	-	3s. green	20	15
1692	-	5s. brown	45	35
1693	-	13s. turquoise	1·40	90
1694	-	20s. violet	2·30	1·70

COINS—SQUARE: 2s. 2nd-cent B.C. Macedonian tetradrachm; 3s. 2nd-cent B.C. Odessos (Varna) tetradrachm; 5s. 4th-cent B.C. Macedonian coin of Philip II. HORIZ: (38×25 mm): 13s. Obverse and reverse of 4th cent B.C. coin of King Sevt (Thrace); 20s. Obverse and reverse of 5th-cent B.C. coin of Apollonia (Sozopol).

548 Partisans listening to radio

1967. 25th Anniv of Fatherland Front. Multicoloured.

| 1695 | | 1s. Type **548** | 20 | 15 |
| 1696 | | 20s. Dimitrov speaking at rally | 1·30 | 45 |

549 Nikola Kofardzhiev

1967. Anti-fascist Fighters.

1697	**549**	1s. red, black & blue	20	15
1698	-	2s. green, black & blue	20	15
1699	-	2s. brown, black & blue	20	15
1700	-	10s. blue, black & lilac	65	30
1701	-	20s. purple, black & grey	95	45

PORTRAITS: 2s. Petko Napetov; 5s. Petko Petkov; 10s. Emil Markov; 13s. Traicho Kostov.

550 "Cultural Development"

1967. First Cultural Conference, Sofia.

| 1702 | **550** | 13s. yellow, grn & gold | 95 | 55 |

551 Angora Kitten

1967. Cats. Multicoloured.

1703		1s. Type **551**	20	15
1704		2s. Siamese (horiz)	30	15
1705		3s. Abyssinian	45	20
1706		5s. European black and white	1·50	35
1707		13s. Persian (horiz)	1·90	65
1708		20s. European tabby	2·30	1·70

552 "Golden Sands" Resort

1967. International Tourist Year. Multicoloured.

1709		13s. Type **552**	45	20
1710		20s. Pamporovo	95	45
1711		40s. Old Church, Nesebur	2·30	1·00

553 Scene from Iliev's Opera The Master of Boyana

1967. Third International Young Opera Singers' Competition, Sofia.

| 1712 | **553** | 5s. red, blue and grey | 20 | 15 |
| 1713 | - | 13s. red, blue and grey | 95 | 45 |

DESIGN—VERT: 13s. Vocal Art (song-bird on piano-keys).

554 G. Kirkov

1967. Birth Cent of Georgi Kirkov (patriot).

| 1714 | **554** | 2s. bistre and red | 20 | 15 |

555 Roses and Distillery

1967. Economic Achievements. Multicoloured.

1715	**555**	1s. Type **555**	20	15
1716	-	1s. Chick and incubator	20	15
1717	-	2s. Cucumber and glass-houses	20	15
1718	-	2s. Lamb and farm building	20	15
1719	-	3s. Sunflower and oil-extraction plant	20	15
1720	-	4s. Pigs and piggery	25	15
1721	-	5s. Hops and vines	30	15
1722	-	6s. Grain and irrigation canals	35	15
1723	-	8s. Grapes and "Bulgar" tractor	40	15
1724	-	10s. Apples and tree	45	20
1725	-	13s. Honey bees and honey	95	45
1726	-	20s. Honey bee on flower, and hives	1·20	55

556 DKMS Emblem

1967. 11th Anniv of Dimitrov Communist Youth League.

| 1727 | **556** | 13s. black, red and blue | 95 | 35 |

557 Map and Spassky Tower, Moscow Kremlin

1967. 50th Anniv of October Revolution.

| 1728 | **557** | 1s. multicoloured | 20 | 15 |
| 1729 | - | 2s. olive and purple | 20 | 15 |

1730	-	3s. violet and purple	20	15
1731	-	5s. red and purple	20	15
1732	-	13s. blue and purple	65	35
1733	-	20s. blue and purple	1·40	55

DESIGNS: 2s. Lenin directing revolutionaries; 3s. Revolutionaries; 5s. Marx, Engels and Lenin; 13s. Soviet oil refinery; 20s. "Molniya" satellite and Moon (Soviet space research).

558 Scenic "Fish" and Rod

1967. Seventh World Angling Championships, Varna.

| 1734 | **558** | 10s. multicoloured | 75 | 45 |

559 Cross-country Skiing

1967. Winter Olympic Games, Grenoble (1968).

1735	**559**	1s. black, red & turq	20	15
1736	-	2s. black, bistre & blue	20	15
1737	-	3s. black, blue & purple	20	15
1738	-	5s. black, yellow & grn	30	20
1739	-	13s. black, buff & blue	1·40	45
1740	-	20s.+10s. mult	2·40	90

MS1741 98× 98 mm. (diamond) 40s.+10s. black, ochre and blue. Imperf | 3·75 | 3·25 |

DESIGNS: 2s. Ski jumping; 3s. Biathlon; 5s. Ice hockey; 13, 40s. Ice skating (pairs); 20s. Men's slalom.

560 Bogdan Peak, Sredna Mts

1967. Tourism. Mountain Peaks.

1742	**560**	1s. green and yellow	20	15
1743	-	2s. sepia and blue	20	15
1744	-	3s. indigo and blue	20	15
1745	-	5s. green and blue	30	15
1746	-	10s. brown and blue	40	20
1747	-	13s. black and blue	45	40
1748	-	20s. blue and purple	95	80

DESIGNS—HORIZ: 2s. Cherni Vruh, Vitosha; 5s. Persenk, Rhodopes; 10s. Botev, Stara-Planina; 20s. Vikhren, Pirin. VERT: 3s. Ruen, Osogovska Planina; 13s. Musala, Rila.

561 G. Rakovski

1967. Death Cent of G. Rakovski (revolutionary).

| 1749 | **561** | 13s. black and green | 95 | 55 |

562 Yuri Gagarin, Valentina Tereshkova and Aleksei Leonov

1967. Space Exploration. Multicoloured.

1750		1s. Type **562**	20	15
1751		2s. John Glenn and Edward White	20	15
1752		5s. "Molniya 1"	30	20
1753		10s. "Gemini 6" and "7"	95	35
1754		13s. "Luna 13"	1·00	55
1755		20s. "Gemini 10" docking with "Agena"	1·20	1·10

563 Railway Bridge over Yantra River

1967. Views of Turnovo (ancient capital).

| 1756 | **563** | 1s. black, drab and blue | 20 | 15 |

1757	-	2s. multicoloured	20	15
1758	-	3s. multicoloured	20	15
1759	-	5s. black, slate and red	45	25
1760	-	13s. multicoloured	75	35
1761	-	20s. black, orange & lav	95	55

DESIGNS: 2s. Hadji Nikola's Inn; 3s. Houses on hillside; 5s. Town and river; 13s. "House of the Monkeys"; 20s. Gurko street.

564 The Ruchenitsa (folk dance, from painting by Murkvichka)

1967. Belgian–Bulgarian "Painting and Philately" Exhibition, Brussels.

1762	564	20s. green and gold	1·90	1·70

565 The Shepherd (Zlatko Boyadzhiev)

1967. Paintings in the National Gallery, Sofia. Multicoloured.

1763		1s. Type 565	10	10
1764		2s. The Wedding (Vladimir Dimitrov) (vert)	10	10
1765		3s. The Partisans Ilya Petrov (55×35 mm)	45	20
1766		5s. Anastasia Penchovich (Nikolai Pavlovich) (vert)	95	35
1767		13s. Self-portrait (Zakharii Zograf) (vert)	1·90	1·00
1768		20s. Old Town of Plovdiv (Tsanko Lavrenov)	2·30	1·10
MS1769		65×85 mm. 60s. St. Clement of Ohrid (Anton Mitov)	6·75	6·75

566 Linked Satellites "Cosmos 186" and "188"

1968. "Cosmic Activities". Multicoloured.

1770		20s. Type 566	95	55
1771		40s. "Venus 4" and orbital diagram (horiz)	2·30	1·10

567 Crossing the Danube (Orenburgski)

1968. 90th Anniv of Liberation from Turkey. Paintings. Inscr and frames in black and gold; centre colours below.

1772	567	1s. green	20	15
1773	-	2s. blue	20	15
1774	-	3s. brown	20	15
1775	-	13s. blue	1·10	55
1776	-	20s. turquoise	1·40	65

DESIGNS—VERT: 2s. Flag of Samara (Veschin); 13s. Battle of Orlovo Gnezdo (Popov). HORIZ: 3s. Battle of Pleven (Orenburgski); 20s. Greeting Russian Soldiers (Goudienov).

568 Karl Marx

1968. 150th Birth Anniv of Karl Marx.

1777	568	13s. grey, red & black	95	35

569 Gorky

1968. Birth Cent of Maksim Gorky (writer).

1778	569	13s. green, orange & blk	95	35

570 Dancers

1968. Ninth World Youth and Students' Festival. Sofia. Multicoloured.

1779		2s. Type 570	20	15
1780		5s. Running	20	15
1781		13s. "Doves"	85	35
1782		20s. "Youth" (symbolic design)	95	55
1783		40s. Bulgarian 5c. stamp of 1879 under magnifier and Globe	1·60	1·30

571 Campanula alpina

1968. Wild Flowers. Multicoloured.

1784		1s. Type 571	20	15
1785		2s. Trumpet gentian	20	15
1786		5s. Crocus veluchensis	20	15
1787		5s. Siberian iris	45	20
1788		10s. Dog's-tooth violet	65	20
1789		13s. House leek	1·10	35
1790		20s. Burning bush	1·40	55

572 The Unknown Hero (Ran Bosilek)

1968. Bulgarian-Danish Stamp Exhibition. Fairy Tales. Multicoloured.

1791		13s. Type 572	45	35
1792		20s. "The Witch and the Young Men" (Hans Andersen)	95	80

573 Memorial Temple, Shipka

1968. Bulgarian–West Berlin Stamp Exn.

1793	573	13s. multicoloured	95	55

574 Copper Rolling-mill, Medet

1968. Air.

1794	574	1l. red	3·25	80

575 Lake Smolyan

1968

1795	575	1s. green	20	15
1796	-	2s. myrtle	20	15
1797	-	3s. sepia	20	15
1798	-	8s. green	35	15
1799	-	10s. brown	40	20
1800	-	13s. olive	45	30
1801	-	40s. blue	1·40	35
1802	-	2l. brown	6·50	2·20

DESIGNS: 2s. River Ropotamo; 3s. Lomnitza Gorge, Erma River; 8s. River Isker; 10s. Cruise ship Die Fregatte; 13s. Cape Kaliakra; 40s. Sozopol; 2l. Mountain road, Kamchia River.

576 Gymnastics

1968. Olympic Games, Mexico.

1803	576	1s. black and red	20	15
1804	-	2s. black, brown & grey	20	15
1805	-	3s. black and mauve	20	15
1806	-	10s. black, yell & turq	65	20
1807	-	13s. black, pink & blue	1·40	65
1808	-	20s.+10s. grey, pk & bl	1·90	65
MS1809		74×76 mm. 50s.+10s. black, grey and blue. Imperf	4·75	4·50

DESIGNS: 2s. Horse-jumping; 3s. Fencing; 10s. Boxing; 13s. Throwing the discus; 20s. Rowing; 50s. Stadium and communications satellite.

577 Dimitur on Mt. Buzludzha, 1868

1968. Centenary of Exploits of Khadzhi Dimitur and Stefan Karadzha (revolutionaries).

1810	577	2s. brown and silver	20	10
1811	-	13s. green and gold	75	45

DESIGN: 13s. Dimitur and Karadzha.

578 Human Rights Emblem

1968. Human Rights Year.

1812	578	20s. gold and blue	1·10	55

579 Cinereous Black Vulture

1968. 80th Anniv of Sofia Zoo.

1813	579	1s. black, brown & blue	20	20
1814	-	2s. black, yellow & brn	25	20
1815	-	3s. black and green	30	20
1816	-	5s. black, yellow & red	65	35
1817	-	13s. black, bistre & grn	2·40	1·10
1818	-	20s. black, green & blue	3·25	1·70

DESIGNS: 2s. South African crowned crane; 3s. Common zebra; 5s. Leopard; 13s. Python; 20s. Crocodile.

580 Battle Scene

1968. 280th Anniv of Chiprovtsi Rising.

1819	580	13s. multicoloured	95	20

581 Caterpillar-hunter

1968. Insects.

1820	581	1s. green	30	10
1821	-	1s. brown	30	10
1822	-	1s. blue	30	10
1823	-	1s. blue	30	10
1824	-	1s. purple	30	10

DESIGNS—VERT: No. 1821, Stag beetle (Lucanus cervus); 1822, Procerus scabrosus (ground beetle). HORIZ: No. 1823, European rhinoceros beetle (Oryctes nasicornis); 1824, Perisomena caecigena (moth).

582 Flying Swans

1968. "Co-operation with Scandinavia".

1825		2s. ochre and green	1·90	1·70
1826	582	5s. blue, grey & black	1·90	1·70
1827	-	13s. purple and maroon	1·90	1·70
1828	-	20s. grey and violet	1·90	1·70

DESIGNS: 2s. Wooden flask; 13s. Rose; 20s. "Viking ship".

583 Congress Building and Emblem

1968. International Dental Congress, Varna.

1829	583	20s. gold, green and red	95	35

584 Smirnenski and Verse from Red Squadrons

1968. 70th Birth Anniv of Khristo Smirnenski (poet).

1830	584	13s. black, orange & gold	95	35

585 Dove with Letter

1968. National Stamp Exhibition, Sofia and 75th Anniv of "National Philately".

1831	585	20s. green	1·90	1·70

586 Dalmatian Pelican

1968. Srebirna Wildlife Reservation. Birds. Multicoloured.

1832		1s. Type 586	35	20
1833		2s. Little egret	45	30
1834		3s. Great crested grebe	55	35
1835		5s. Common tern	65	45
1836		13s. White spoonbill	2·00	1·50
1837		20s. Glossy ibis	4·25	2·20

587 Silistra Costume

1968. Provincial Costumes. Multicoloured.

1838		1s. Type 587	20	15
1839		2s. Lovech	20	15
1840		3s. Yambol	20	15
1841		13s. Chirpan	75	35
1842		20s. Razgrad	1·10	65
1843		40s. Ikhtiman	2·40	90

588 *St. Arsenius* (icon)

1968. Rila Monastery. Icons and murals. Multicoloured.
1844	1s. Type **588**	20	15
1845	2s. *Carrying St. Ivan Rilski's Relics* (horiz)	20	15
1846	3s. *St. Michael torments the Rich Man's Soul*	30	20
1847	13s. *St. Ivan Rilski*	1·10	65
1848	20s. *Prophet Joel*	1·70	90
1849	40s. *St. George*	2·75	1·50
MS1850	100×74 mm. 1l. *Arrival of Relics at Rila Monastery*. Imperf	7·50	7·25

589 *Matricaria chamomilla*

1968. Medicinal Plants. Multicoloured.
1851	1s. Type **589**	20	15
1852	1s. "Mespilus oxyacantha"	20	15
1853	2s. Lily of the valley	20	15
1854	3s. Deadly nightshade	20	15
1855	5s. Common mallow	30	15
1856	10s. Yellow peasant's eye	65	20
1857	13s. Common poppy	75	35
1858	20s. Wild thyme	1·10	55

590 Silkworms and Spindles

1969. Silk Industry. Multicoloured.
1859	1s. Type **590**	20	15
1860	2s. Worm, cocoons and pattern	20	15
1861	3s. Cocoons and spinning wheel	20	15
1862	5s. Cocoons and pattern	20	15
1863	13s. Moth, cocoon and spindles	75	20
1864	20s. Moth, eggs and shuttle	1·10	35

591 *Death of Ivan Asen*

1969. Manasses Chronicle (1st series). Multicoloured.
1865	1s. Type **591**	20	15
1866	2s. *Emperor Nicephorus invading Bulgaria*	20	15
1867	3s. *Khan Krum's Feast*	20	15
1868	13s. *Prince Sviatoslav invading Bulgaria*	1·10	45
1869	20s. *The Russian invasion*	1·60	55
1870	40s. *Jesus Christ, Tsar Ivan Alexander and Constantine Manasses*	2·30	1·10

See also Nos. 1911/16.

592 *Saints Cyril and Methodius* (mural, Troyan Monastery)

1969. Saints Cyril and Methodius Commem.
1871	**592** 28s. multicoloured	1·90	1·10

593 Galleon

1969. Air. "SOFIA 1969" International Stamp Exhibition. Transport. Multicoloured.
1872	1s. Type **593**	20	15
1873	2s. Mail coach	20	15
1874	3s. Steam locomotive	20	15
1875	5s. Early motor-car	20	15
1876	10s. Montgolfier's balloon and Henri Giffard's steam-powered dirigible airship	35	20
1877	13s. Early flying machines	65	35
1878	20s. Modern aircraft	1·10	45
1879	40s. Rocket and planets	2·00	1·10
MS1880	57×55 mm. 1l. gold and orange. Imperf	4·75	4·50

DESIGN: 1l. Postal courier.

594 Posthorn Emblem

1969. 90th Anniv of Bulgarian Postal Services.
1881	**594** 2s. yellow and green	20	15
1882	- 13s. multicoloured	65	20
1883	- 20s. blue	1·10	55

DESIGNS: 13s. Bulgarian Stamps of 1879 and 1946; 20s. Post Office workers' strike, 1919.

595 I.L.O. Emblem

1969. 50th Anniv of I.L.O.
1884	**595** 13s. black and green	65	35

596 "Fox" and "Rabbit"

1969. Children's Book Week.
1885	**596** 1s. black, orange & grn	20	15
1886	- 2s. black, blue and red	20	15
1887	- 13s. black, olive & blue	75	35

DESIGNS: 2s. Boy with "hedgehog" and "squirrel"; 13s. *The Singing Lesson.*

597 Hand with Seedling

1969. "10,000,000 Hectares of New Forests".
1888	**597** 2s. black, green & purple	20	10

598 *St. George* (14th Century)

1969. Religious Art. Multicoloured.
1889	1s. Type **598**	20	15
1890	2s. *The Virgin and St. John Bogoslov* (14th century)	20	15
1891	3s. *Archangel Michael* (17th century)	20	15
1892	5s. *Three Saints* (17th century)	30	15
1893	8s. *Jesus Christ* (17th century)	35	15
1894	13s. *St. George and St. Dimitr* (19th century)	75	20
1895	20s. *Christ the Universal* (19th century)	95	45
1896	60s. *The Forty Martyrs* (19th century)	2·75	1·70

1897	80s. *The Transfiguration* (19th century)	3·75	2·20
MS1898	103×165 mm. 40s. ×4, *St. Dimitur* (17th-century)	9·25	9·00

599 Roman Coin

1969. "SOFIA 1969" International Stamp Exhibition. "Sofia Through the Ages".
1899	**599** 1s. silver, blue and gold	10	10
1900	- 2s. silver, green & gold	10	10
1901	- 3s. silver, lake and gold	10	10
1902	- 4s. silver, violet & gold	15	10
1903	- 5s. silver, purple & gold	20	10
1904	- 13s. silver, green & gold	45	15
1905	- 20s. silver, blue & gold	75	35
1906	- 40s. silver, red & gold	1·40	65
MS1907	78×72 mm. 1l. multicoloured. Imperf	6·50	5·50

DESIGNS: 2s. Roman coin showing Temple of Aesculapius; 3s. Church of St. Sophia; 4s. Boyana Church; 5s. Parliament Building; 13s. National Theatre; 20s. Aleksandr Nevski Cathedral; 40s. Sofia University. 44×44 mm. 1l. Arms.

600 St. George and the Dragon

1969. Int Philatelic Federation Congress, Sofia.
1908	**600** 40s. black, orange & sil	2·30	1·10

601 St. Cyril

1969. 1,100th Death Anniv of St. Cyril.
1909	**601** 2s. green & red on silver	20	10
1910	- 28s. blue & red on silver	1·60	65

DESIGN: St. Cyril and procession.

1969. Manasses Chronicle (2nd series). Designs as T **591**, but all horiz. Multicoloured.
1911	1s. *Nebuchadnezzar II and Balthasar of Babylon, Cyrus and Darius of Persia*	10	10
1912	2s. *Cambyses, Gyges and Darius of Persia*	10	10
1913	5s. *Prophet David and Tsar Ivan Alexander*	30	10
1914	13s. *Rout of the Byzantine Army, 811*	95	35
1915	20s. *Christening of Khan Boris*	1·90	45
1916	60s. *Tsar Simeon's attack on Constantinople*	2·75	1·90

602 Partisans

1969. 25th Anniv of Fatherland Front Government.
1917	**602** 1s. lilac, red and black	20	15
1918	- 2s. brown, red & black	20	15
1919	- 3s. green, red and black	20	15
1920	- 5s. brown, red & black	20	15
1921	- 13s. blue, red & black	65	20
1922	- 20s. multicoloured	1·20	55

DESIGNS: 2s. Combine-harvester; 3s. Dam; 5s. Folk singers; 13s. Petroleum refinery; 20s. Lenin, Dimitrov and flags.

603 Gymnastics

1969. Third Republican Spartakiad. Multicoloured.
1923	2s. Type **603**	20	10
1924	20s. Wrestling	95	65

604 "Construction" and soldier

1969. 25th Anniv of Army Engineers.
1925	**604** 6s. black and blue	30	15

605 T. Tserkovski

1969. Birth Cent of Tsanke Tserkovski (poet).
1926	**605** 13s. multicoloured	75	35

606 "Woman" (Roman Statue)

1969. 1,800th Anniv of Silistra.
1927	**606** 2s. grey, blue and silver	20	15
1928	- 13s. brown, grn & silver	1·00	45

DESIGN—HORIZ: 13s. "Wolf" (bronze statue).

607 Skipping-rope Exercise

1969. World Gymnastics Competition, Varna.
1929	**607** 1s. grey, blue and green	20	15
1930	- 2s. grey and blue	20	15
1931	- 3s. grey, green and emerald	20	15
1932	- 5s. grey, purple and red	20	15
1933	- 13s.+5s. grey, bl & red	1·10	55
1934	- 20s.+10s. grey, green and yellow	1·40	65

DESIGNS: 2s. Hoop exercise (pair); 3s. Hoop exercise (solo); 5s. Ball exercise (pair); 13s. Ball exercise (solo); 20s. Solo gymnast.

608 Marin Drinov (founder)

1969. Cent of Bulgarian Academy of Sciences.
1935	**608** 20s. black and red	95	45

609 *Neophit Rilski* (Zakharii Zograf)

1969. Paintings in National Gallery, Sofia. Multicoloured.
1936	1s. Type **609**	10	10
1937	2s. *German's Mother* (Vasil Stoilov)	20	10
1938	3s. *Workers' Family* (Neuko Balkanski) (horiz)	30	10
1939	4s. *Woman Dressing* (Ivan Nenov)	35	10
1940	5s. *Portrait of a Woman* (Nikolai Pavlovich)	45	20
1941	13s. *Krustyn Sarafov as Falstaff* (Dechko Uzunov)	95	30
1942	20s. *Artist's Wife* (N. Mikhailov) (horiz)	1·30	45

| 1943 | 20s. *Worker's Lunch* (Stoyan Sotirov) (horiz) | 1·40 | 55 |
| 1944 | 40s. *Self-portrait* (Tseno Todorov) (horiz) | 1·90 | 80 |

610 Pavel Banya

1969. Sanatoria.

1945	610	2s. blue	20	10
1946	-	5s. blue	20	10
1947	-	6s. green	35	10
1948	-	20s. green	75	35

SANATORIA. 5s. Khisar; 6s. Kotel; 20s. Narechen Polyclinic.

611 Deep-sea Trawler

1969. Ocean Fisheries.

1949	611	1s. grey and blue	20	15
1950	-	1s. green and black	20	15
1951	-	2s. violet and black	20	15
1952	-	3s. blue and black	20	15
1953	-	5s. mauve and black	30	20
1954	-	6s. grey and black	1·50	45
1955	-	13s. flesh, orange & blk	2·30	80
1956	-	20s. brown, ochre & blk	3·00	1·10

DESIGNS: 1s. (No. 1950), Cape hake; 2s. Atlantic horse-mackerel; 3s. South African pilchard; 5s. Large-eyed dentex; 10s. Chub mackerel; 13s. Senegal croaker; 20s. Vadigo.

612 Trapeze Act

1969. Circus. Multicoloured.

1957	612	1s. Type 612	10	10
1958		2s. Acrobats	10	10
1959		3s. Balancing act with hoops	10	10
1960		5s. Juggler, and bear on cycle	20	10
1961		13s. Equestrian act	65	35
1962		20s. Clowns	1·40	55

613 V. Kubasov, Georgi Shonin and "Soyuz 6"

1970. Space Flights of "Soyuz 6, 7 and 8".

1963	613	1s. multicoloured	10	10
1964	-	2s. multicoloured	10	10
1965	-	3s. multicoloured	20	15
1966	-	28s. pink and blue	1·50	55

DESIGNS: 2s. Viktor Gorbacko, Vladislav Volkov, Anatoly Filipchenko and "Soyuz 7"; 3s. Aleksei Elseev, Vladimir Shatalov and "Soyuz 8"; 28s. Three "Soyuz" spacecraft in orbit.

614 Khan Asparerch and "Old-Bulgars" crossing the Danube, 679

1970. History of Bulgaria. Multicoloured.

1967	614	1s. Type 614	20	15
1968		2s. Khan Krum and defeat of Emperor Nicephorus, 811	20	15
1969		3s. Conversion of Khan Boris I to Christianity, 865	20	15
1970		5s. Tsar Simeon and Battle of Akhelo, 917	30	15
1971		8s. Tsar Samuel and defeat of Byzantines, 976	35	15

1972		10s. Tsar Kaloyan and victory over Emperor Baldwin, 1205	55	20
1973		13s. Tsar Ivan Assen II and defeat of Komnine of Epirus, 1230	95	35
1974		20s. Coronation of Tsar Ivailo, 1277	1·40	55

615 Bulgarian Pavilion

1970. "Expo 70" World's Fair, Osaka, Japan (1st issue).

| 1975 | 615 | 20s. silver, yellow & brn | 1·90 | 1·10 |

See Nos. 2009/12.

616 Footballers

1970. World Football Cup, Mexico.

1976	616	1s. multicoloured	10	10
1977	-	2s. multicoloured	10	10
1978	-	3s. multicoloured	10	10
1979	-	5s. multicoloured	20	15
1980	-	20s. multicoloured	1·60	55
1981	-	40s. multicoloured	2·00	75

MS1982 55×99 mm. 80s.+20s. multicoloured. Imperf 4·75 4·50

DESIGNS—HORIZ: 2s. to 40s. Various football scenes. VERT (45×69 mm.) 80s. Football and inscription.

617 Lenin

1970. Birth Cent of Lenin. Multicoloured.

1983	617	2s. Type 617	20	15
1984		13s. Full-face portrait	75	35
1985		20s. Lenin writing	1·60	65

618 *Tephrocactus Alexanderi v. bruchi*

1970. Flowering Cacti. Multicoloured.

1986	618	1s. Type 618	20	15
1987		2s. *Opuntia drummondii*	20	15
1988		3s. *Hatiora cilindrica*	20	15
1989		5s. *Gymnocalycium vatteri*	30	20
1990		8s. *Heliantho cereus grandiflorus*	45	35
1991		10s. *Neochilenia andreaeana*	2·20	80
1992		13s. *Peireskia vargasii v. longispina*	2·30	90
1993		20s. *Neobesseya rosiflora*	2·75	1·10

619 Rose

1970. Bulgarian Roses.

1994	619	1s. multicoloured	20	15
1995	-	2s. multicoloured	20	15
1996	-	3s. multicoloured	30	15
1997	-	4s. multicoloured	40	15
1998	-	5s. multicoloured	45	20
1999	-	13s. multicoloured	95	45
2000	-	20s. multicoloured	1·90	1·10
2001	-	28s. multicoloured	3·25	1·90

DESIGNS: 2s. to 28s. Various roses.

620 Union Badge

1970. 70th Anniv of Agricultural Union.

| 2002 | 620 | 20s. black, gold and red | 1·40 | 45 |

621 Gold Bowl

1970. Gold Treasures of Thrace.

2003	621	1s. black, blue and gold	20	15
2004	-	2s. black, lilac and gold	20	15
2005	-	3s. black, red and gold	20	15
2006	-	5s. black, green & gold	30	20
2007	-	13s. black, orge & gold	1·40	55
2008	-	20s. black, violet & gold	1·90	1·10

DESIGNS: 2s. Three small bowls; 3s. Plain lid; 5s. Pear shaped ornaments; 13s. Large lid with pattern; 20s. Vase.

622 Rose and Woman with Baskets of Produce

1970. "Expo 70" World's Fair, Osaka, Japan (2nd issue). Multicoloured.

2009		1s. Type 622	20	15
2010		2s. Three Dancers	20	15
2011		3s. Girl in National costume	20	15
2012		28s. Dancing couples	1·70	80

MS2013 75×90 mm. 40s. Bulgarian pavilion 1·90 1·90

623 UN Emblem

1970. 25th Anniv of United Nations.

| 2014 | 623 | 20s. gold and blue | 95 | 55 |

624 I. Vasov

1970. 120th Birth Anniv of Ivan Vasov (poet).

| 2015 | 624 | 13s. blue | 85 | 35 |

625 Edelweiss Sanatorium, Borovets

1970. Health Resorts.

2016	625	1s. green	20	15
2017	-	2s. olive	20	15
2018	-	4s. blue	20	15
2019	-	8s. blue	45	15
2020	-	10s. blue	95	20

DESIGNS: 2s. Panorama Hotel, Pamporovo; 4s. Yachts, Albena; 8s. Harbour scene, Rousalka; 10s. Shtastlivetsa Hotel, Mt. Vitosha.

626 Hungarian Retriever

1970. Dogs. Multicoloured.

2021	626	1s. Type 626	20	15
2022		2s. Retriever (vert)	30	15
2023		3s. Great Dane (vert)	35	15

2024		4s. Boxer (vert)	45	20
2025		5s. Cocker spaniel (vert)	55	30
2026		13s. Dobermann pinscher (vert)	1·40	80
2027		20s. Scottish terrier (vert)	2·75	1·20
2028		28s. Russian hound	3·25	1·70

627 Fireman with Hose

1970. Fire Protection.

| 2029 | 627 | 1s. grey, yellow & black | 20 | 10 |
| 2030 | - | 3s. red, grey and black | 30 | 20 |

DESIGN. 3s. Fire-engine.

628 Congress Emblem

1970. Seventh World Sociological Congress, Varna.

| 2031 | 628 | 13s. multicoloured | 75 | 20 |

629 Two Male Players

1970. World Volleyball Championships.

2032	629	2s. black and brown	20	15
2033	-	2s. orange, black & blue	20	15
2034	-	20s. yellow, black & grn	1·20	55
2035	-	20s. multicoloured	1·40	65

DESIGNS: No. 2033, Two female players; 2034, Male player; 2035, Female player.

630 Cyclists

1970. 20th Round-Bulgaria Cycle Race.

| 2036 | 630 | 20s. mauve, yellow & grn | 95 | 55 |

631 Enrico Caruso and Scene from *Il Pagliacci*

1970. Opera Singers. Multicoloured.

2037	631	1s. Type 631	20	15
2038		2s. Khristina Morfova and *The Bartered Bride*	20	15
2039		3s. Petur Raichev and *Tosca*	20	15
2040		10s. Tsvetana Tabakova and *The Flying Dutchman*	35	25
2041		13s. Katya Popova and *The Masters of Nuremberg*	45	15
2042		20s. Fyodor Chaliapin and *Boris Godunov*	2·30	1·30

632 Beethoven

1970. Birth Bicentenary of Ludwig von Beethoven (composer).

| 2043 | 632 | 28s. blue and purple | 2·75 | 2·20 |

633 Ivan Asen II Coin

1970. Bulgarian Coins of the 14th century. Multicoloured.

2044		1s. Type **633**	20	15
2045		2s. Theodor Svetoslav	20	15
2046		3s. Mikhail Shishman	20	15
2047		13s. Ivan Alexander and Mikhail Asen	45	20
2048		20s. Ivan Sratsimir	1·40	45
2049		28s. Ivan Shishman (initials)	1·90	65

634 "Luna 16"

1970. Moon Mission of "Luna 16". Sheet 51×70 mm.

MS2050	**634**	1l. red, silver and blue	7·50	7·25

635 Engels

1970. 150th Birth Anniv of Friedrich Engels.

2051	**635**	13s. brown and red	95	55

636 Snow Crystal

1970. New Year.

2052	**636**	2s. multicoloured	20	10

637 "Lunokhod 1" on Moon

1970. Moon Mission of "Lunokhod 1". Sheet 60×72 mm.

MS2053	**637**	80s. silver, purple and blue	7·25	5·50

638 Girl's Head (Zheko Spiridonov)

1971. Modern Bulgarian Sculpture.

2054	**638**	1s. violet and gold	20	15
2055	-	2s. green and gold	20	15
2056	-	3s. brown and gold	20	15
2057	-	13s. green and gold	65	20
2058	-	20s. red and gold	1·30	45
2059	-	28s. brown and gold	1·90	65
MS2060		61×72 mm. 1l. chestnut and gold	4·75	4·75

SCULPTURES: 2s. *Third Class Carriage* (Ivan Funev); 3s. *Elin Pelin* (Marko Markov); 13s. *Nina* (Andrei Nikolov); 20s. *Kneeling Woman* (Yavorov monument, Ivan Lazarov); 28s. *Engineer* (Ivan Funev). 36½×41 mm. 1l. *Refugees* (Sekul Knimov).

639 Birds and Flowers

1971. Spring.

2061	**639**	1s. multicoloured	10	10
2062	-	2s. multicoloured	10	10
2063	-	3s. multicoloured	10	10
2064	-	5s. multicoloured	10	10
2065	-	13s. multicoloured	45	20
2066	-	20s. multicoloured	1·00	45

DESIGNS: 2s. to 20s. Various designs of birds and flowers similar to Type **639**.

640 *Khan Asparuch crossing Danube* (Boris Angelushev)

1971. Bulgarian History. Paintings. Multicoloured.

2067		2s. Type **640**	20	15
2068		3s. *Ivajlo in Turnovo* (Ilya Petrov)	20	15
2069		5s. *Cavalry Charge, Benkovski* (P. Morosov)	45	20
2070		8s. *Gen. Gzrko entering Sofia, 1878* (D. Gyudzhenov)	95	30
2071		28s. *Greeting Red Army* (Stefan Venev)	3·75	2·00
MS2072		137×131 mm. Nos. 2067/70	1·90	1·70

641 Running

1971. Second European Indoor Track and Field Championships. Multicoloured.

2073		2s. Type **641**	20	15
2074		20s. Putting the shot	1·90	55

642 School Building

1971. Foundation of First Bulgarian Secondary School, Bolgrad.

2075	**642**	2s. green, brown & sil	20	15
2076	-	20s. violet, brown & sil	1·30	45

DESIGN: 20s. Dimitur Mutev, Prince Bogoridi and Sava Radulov (founders).

643 Communards

1971. Centenary of Paris Commune.

2077	**643**	20s. black and red	95	55

644 Georgi Dimitrov challenging Hermann Goering

1971. 20th Anniv of "Federation Internationale des Resistants".

2078	**644**	2s. multicoloured	20	15
2079	**644**	13s. multicoloured	1·40	55

645 Gagarin and Space Scenes

1971. Tenth Anniv of First Manned Space Flight. Sheet 80×53 mm.

MS2080	**645**	40s.+20s. multicoloured	4·75	4·00

646 G. Rakovski

1971. 150th Birth Anniv of Georgi Rakovski (politician and Revolutionary).

2081	**646**	13s. brown, cream & grn	75	20

647 Worker and Banner ("People's Progress")

1971. Tenth Bulgarian Communist Party Congress. Multicoloured.

2082		1s. Type **647**	20	15
2083		2s. Symbols of "Technical Progress" (horiz)	20	15
2084		12s. Men clasping hands ("Bulgarian-Soviet Friendship")	1·40	45

648 Pipkov and Music

1971. Birth Centenary of Panaiot Pipokov.

2085	**648**	13s. black, green & silver	95	55

649 "Three Races"

1971. Racial Equality Year.

2086	**649**	13s. multicoloured	95	55

650 Mammoth

1971. Prehistoric Animals. Multicoloured.

2087		1s. Type **650**	20	20
2088		2s. Bear (vert)	20	20
2089		3s. Hipparion	20	20
2090		13s. Mastodon	1·90	65
2091		20s. Dinotherium (vert)	2·75	1·70
2092		28s. Sabre-toothed tiger	3·25	2·20

651 Facade of Ancient Building

1971. Ancient Buildings of Koprivshitsa.

2093	**651**	1s. green, brown & grn	10	10
2094	-	2s. brown, green & buff	10	10
2095	-	6s. violet, brown & blue	35	15
2096	-	13s. red, blue & orange	95	45

DESIGNS: 1s. to 13s. Different facades.

652 Weights Emblem on Map of Europe

1971. 30th European Weightlifting Championships, Sofia. Multicoloured.

2097		2s. Type **652**	20	15
2098		13s. Figures supporting weights	1·40	45

653 Frontier Guard and Dog

1971. 25th Anniv of Frontier Guards.

2099	**653**	2s. olive, green & turq	20	10

654 Tweezers, Magnifying Glass and "Stamp"

1971. Ninth Congress of Bulgarian Philatelic Federation.

2100	**654**	20s.+10s. brown, black and red	1·90	80

655 Congress Meeting (sculpture)

1971. 80th Anniv of Bulgarian Social Democratic Party Congress, Buzludzha.

2101	**655**	2s. green, cream and red	20	10

656 *Mother* (Ivan Nenov)

1971. Paintings from the National Art Gallery (1st series). Multicoloured.

2102		1s. Type **656**	20	15
2103		2s. *Lazarova* (Stefan Ivanov)	20	15
2104		3s. *Portrait of Yu. Kh.* (Kiril Tsonev)	35	20
2105		13s. *Portrait of a Lady* (Dechko Uzunov)	95	35
2106		30s. *Young Woman from Kalotina* (Vladimir Dimitrov)	1·40	80
2107		40s. *Goryanin* (Stryan Venev)	1·90	1·30

See also Nos. 2145/50.

657 Factory Botevgrad

1971. Industrial Buildings.

2108	**657**	1s. violet	10	10
2109	-	2s. red	10	10
2110	-	10s. violet	35	15
2111	-	13s. red	55	20
2112	-	40s. brown	1·90	45

DESIGNS—VERT: 2s. Petro-chemical plant, Pleven. HORIZ: 10s. Chemical works, Vratsa; 13s. "Maritsa-Istok" plant, Dimitrovgrad; 40s. Electronics factory, Sofia.

658 Free Style Wrestling

1971. European Wrestling Championships, Sofia.

2113	**658**	2s. green, black and blue	10	10
2114	-	13s. black, red and blue	95	45

DESIGN: 13s. Greco-Roman wrestling.

659 Posthorn
Emblem

1971. Organization of Socialist Countries' Postal
Administrations Congress.
2115 **659** 20s. gold and green 95 55

660 Entwined Ribbons

1971. 7th European Biochemical Congress, Varna.
2116 **660** 13s. red, brown & black 95 55

661 "New Republic"
Statue

1971. 25th Anniv of People's Republic.
2117 **661** 2s. red, yellow and gold 10 10
2118 – 13s. green, red and gold 95 45
DESIGN: 13s. Bulgarian flag.

662 Cross-country Skiing

1971. Winter Olympic Games, Sapporo, Japan.
Multicoloured.
2119 **1s.** Type **662** 20 15
2120 2s. Downhill skiing 20 15
2121 3s. Ski jumping 20 15
2122 4s. Figure skating 20 15
2123 13s. Ice hockey 95 65
2124 28s. Slalom skiing 1·90 1·10
MS2125 60×70 mm. 1l. Olympic flame
and stadium 4·75 3·00

663 Brigade
Members

1971. 25th Anniv of Youth Brigades Movement.
2126 **663** 2s. blue 20 10

664 UNESCO Emblem and
Wreath

1971. 25th Anniv of UNESCO.
2127 **664** 20s. multicoloured 95 55

665 The Footballer

1971. Paintings by Kiril Tsonev. Multicoloured.
2128 **1s.** Type **665** 20 15
2129 2s. *Landscape* (horiz) 20 15
2130 3s. *Self-portrait* 30 20
2131 13s. *Lilies* 95 35
2132 20s. *Woodland Scene* (horiz) 1·40 65
2133 40s. *Portrait of a Young Woman* 1·90 90

666 "Salyut" Space-station

1971. Space Flights of "Salyut" and "Soyuz 11".
Multicoloured.
2134 **2s.** Type **666** 20 15
2135 13s. "Soyuz 11" 45 30
2136 40s. "Salyut" and "Soyuz 11"
joined together 2·30 80
MS2137 70×74 mm. 80s. Cosmonauts
G. Dobrovolsky, Vladislav Volkov and
V. Patsaev (victims of "Soyuz 11"
disaster). Imperf 3·25 2·75

667 *Vikhren* (ore carrier)

1972. "One Million Tons of Bulgarian Shipping".
2138 **667** 18s. lilac, red and black 1·40 55

668 Goce Delcev

1972. Birth Centenaries of Macedonian Revolutionaries.
2139 **668** 2s. black and red 10 10
2140 – 5s. black and green 20 10
2141 – 13s. black and yellow 65 35
PATRIOTS: 5s. Jan Sandanski (1972); 13s. Dume Gruev
(1971).

669 Gymnast with Ball

1972. World Gymnastics Championships, Havana (Cuba).
Multicoloured.
2142 13s. Type **669** 95 35
2143 18s. Gymnast with hoop 1·40 65
MS2144 61×74 mm. 70s. Team with
hoops. Imperf 4·75 4·50

1972. Paintings in Bulgarian National Gallery (2nd series).
As T **656** but horiz. Multicoloured.
2145 1s. *Melnik* (Petur Mladenov) 20 15
2146 2s. *Ploughman* (Pencho
Georgiev) 20 15
2147 3s. *By the Death-bed* (Aleksan-
dur Zhendov) 30 20
2148 13s. *Family* (Vladimir Dimitrov) 1·20 35
2149 20s. *Family* (Neuko Balkanski) 1·50 45
2150 40s. *Father Paisii* (Koyu
Denchev) 1·70 55

670 Bulgarian
Worker

1972. Seventh Bulgarian Trade Unions Congress.
2151 **670** 13s. multicoloured 65 20

671 Singing Harvesters

1972. 90th Birth Anniv of Vladimir Dimitrov, the Master
(painter). Multicoloured.
2152 1s. Type **671** 20 15
2153 2s. *Farm Worker* 20 15
2154 3s. *Women Cultivators* (horiz) 30 15
2155 13s. *Peasant Girl* (horiz) 45 20
2156 20s. *My Mother* 1·40 90
2157 40s. *Self-portrait* 1·90 1·30

672 Heart and
Tree Emblem

1972. World Heart Month.
2158 **672** 13s. multicoloured 1·40 80

673 St. Mark's
Cathedral

1972. UNESCO "Save Venice" Campaign.
2159 **673** 2s. green, turquoise & bl 30 20
2160 – 13s. brown, violet & grn 1·20 55
DESIGN: 13s. Doge's Palace.

674 Dimitrov at Typesetting Desk

1972. 90th Birth Anniv of Georgi Dimitrov (statesman).
Multicoloured.
2161 1s. Type **674** 20 15
2162 2s. Dimitrov leading uprising
of 1923 20 15
2163 3s. Dimitrov at Leipzig Trial 20 15
2164 5s. Dimitrov addressing workers 20 15
2165 13s. Dimitrov with Bulgarian
crowd 35 35
2166 18s. Addressing young people 45 45
2167 28s. Dimitrov with children 95 65
2168 40s. Dimitrov's mausoleum 1·90 1·00
2169 80s. Portrait head (green and
gold) 5·50 2·10
MS2170 87×84 mm. As No. 2169, but
centre in red and gold. Imperf 8·25 7·75
2173 80s. As No. 2169 11·00 11·00
No. 2173 has the centre in red and gold, and is imper-
forate.

675 "Lamp of
Learning" and
Quotation

1972. 250th Birth Anniv of Father Paisii Khilendurski
(historian).
2171 **675** 2s. brown, green & gold 20 10
2172 – 13s. brown, grn & gold 1·20 45
DESIGN: 13s. Paisii writing.

676 Canoeing

1972. Olympic Games, Munich. Multicoloured.
2174 1s. Type **676** 20 15
2175 2s. Gymnastics 20 15
2176 3s. Swimming 20 15
2177 13s. Volleyball 45 35
2178 18s. Hurdling 95 55
2179 40s. Wrestling 1·90 1·10
MS2180 64×60 mm. 80s. Running track
and sports. Imperf 4·75 4·50

677 Angel Kunchev

1972. Death Cent of Angel Kunchev (patriot).
2181 **677** 2s. mauve, gold & purple 20 15

678 "Golden Sands"

1972. Black Sea Resorts. Hotels. Multicoloured.
2182 1s. Type **678** 20 15
2183 2s. Druzhba 20 15
2184 3s. "Sunny Beach" 20 15
2185 13s. Primorsko 65 20
2186 28s. Rusalka 1·20 45
2187 40s. Albena 1·40 55

679 Canoeing (Bronze
Medal)

1972. Bulgarian Medal Winners, Olympic Games, Munich.
Multicoloured.
2188 1s. Type **679** 20 15
2189 2s. Long jumping (Silver Medal) 20 15
2190 3s. Boxing (Gold Medal) 20 15
2191 18s. Wrestling (Gold Medal) 1·40 45
2192 40s. Weightlifting (Gold Medal) 1·70 90

680 Subi
Dimitrov

1972. Resistance Heroes. Multicoloured.
2193 1s. Type **680** 10 10
2194 2s. Tsvyatko Radoinov 10 10
2195 3s. Iordan Lyutibrodski 10 10
2196 5s. Mito Ganev 30 15
2197 13s. Nedelcho Nikolov 95 35

681 Commemorative Text

1972. 50th Anniv of U.S.S.R.
2198 **681** 13s. red, yellow & gold 75 35

682 *Lilium
rhodopaeum*

1972. Protected Flowers. Multicoloured.
2199 1s. Type **682** 20 15
2200 2s. Marsh gentian 20 15
2201 3s. Sea lily 20 15
2202 4s. Globe flower 30 20
2203 18s. *Primula frondosa* 95 45
2204 23s. Pale pasque flower 1·40 65
2205 40s. "*Fritillaria stribrnyi*" 1·90 1·00

СВЕТОВЕН ПЪРВЕНЕЦ
(683)

1972. "Bulgaria, World Weightlifting Champions". No.
2192 optd with T **683**.
2206 40s. multicoloured 2·30 1·10

684 Dobri Chintulov

1972. 150th Birth Anniv of Dobri Chintulov (poet).
2207 **684** 2s. multicoloured 35 20

685 Forehead
Ornament
(19th-century)

1972. Antique Ornaments.
2208	**685**	1s. black and brown	20	15
2209	-	2s. black and green	20	15
2210	-	3s. black and blue	20	15
2211	-	8s. black and red	45	20
2212	-	23s. black and brown	1·20	55
2213	-	40s. black and violet	1·90	1·30

DESIGNS: 2s. Belt-buckle (19th-century); 3s. Amulet (18th-century); 8s. Pendant (18th-century); 23s. Earrings (14th-century); 40s. Necklace (18th-century).

686 Divers with Cameras

1973. Underwater Research in the Black Sea.
2214	**686**	1s. black, yellow & blue	20	20
2215	-	2s. black, yellow & blue	20	20
2216	-	18s. black, yellow & blue	95	65
2217	-	40s. black, yellow & blue	1·90	80

MS2218 118×98 mm. 20s. ×4. Designs
as Nos. 2214/17, but background
colours changed (sold at 11l.) 8·75 8·50
DESIGNS—HORIZ: 2s. Divers with underwater research
vessel *Shelf 1*. VERT: 18s. Diver and *NIV 100* diving bell;
40s. Lifting balloon.

687 *The Hanging of
Vasil Levski* (Boris
Angelushev)

1973. Death Cent of Vasil Levski (patriot).
2219	**687**	2s. green and red	20	10
2220	-	20s. brown, cream & grn	1·70	80

DESIGN: 20s. "Vasil Levski" (Georgi Danchov).

688 Elhovo Mask

1973. Kukeris' Festival Masks. Multicoloured.
2221	1a.	Type **688**	20	15
2222	2s.	Breznik	20	15
2223	3s.	Khisar	20	15
2224	13s.	Radomir	65	35
2225	20s.	Karnobat	95	65
2226	40s.	Pernik	4·75	4·25

689
Copernicus

1973. 500th Birth Anniv of Copernicus.
2227	**689**	28s. purple, black & brn	2·30	1·60

1973. "Visit Bulgaria by Air". No. **MS**2072 surch with
various airline emblems and new sheet value.
MS2228 137×131 mm. Nos. 2067/70
surch with new sheet value 1l. 30·00 30·00

690 Vietnamese
"Girl"

1973. Vietnam Peace Treaty.
2229	**690**	18s. multicoloured	75	55

1973. "IBRA 73" Stamp Exhibition, Munich. No. MS1907
optd with **IBRA** and Olympic symbols in green.
MS2230 78×72 mm. 1l. multicoloured £140 £140

691 Common
Poppy

1973. Wild Flowers. Multicoloured.
2231	1s.	Type **691**	20	15
2232	2s.	Ox-eye daisy	20	15
2233	3s.	Peony	20	15
2234	13s.	Cornflower	65	35
2235	18s.	Corn cockle	6·50	4·50
2236	28s.	Meadow buttercup	1·90	1·20

692 C. Botev
(after T. Todorov)

1973. 125th Birth Anniv of Khristo Botev (poet and
revolutionary).
2237	**692**	2s. yellow, brown & grn	20	15
2238	**692**	18s. grn, lt grn & bronze	1·40	1·10

693 Asen Khalachev and Insurgents

1973. 50th Anniv of June Uprising.
2239	**693**	1s. black, red and gold	10	10
2240	-	2s. black, orange & gold	10	10

DESIGN: 2s. *Wounded Worker* (illustration by Boris Angelushev to the poem "September" by Geo Milev).

694 Stamboliiski (from
sculpture by A. Nikolov)

1973. 50th Death Anniv of Aleksandur Stamboliiski
(Prime Minister 1919–23).
2241	**694**	18s. lt brn, brn & orge	65	55
2242	**694**	18s. orange	5·00	4·25

695 Muskrat

1973. Bulgarian Fauna. Multicoloured.
2243	1s.	Type **695**	20	15
2244	2s.	Racoon-dog	20	15
2245	3s.	Mouflon (vert)	20	15
2246	12s.	Fallow deer (vert)	65	45
2247	18s.	European bison	1·90	1·10
2248	40s.	Elk	6·50	4·25

696 Turnovo

1973. Air. Tourism. Views of Bulgarian Towns and Cities.
Multicoloured.
2249	2s.	Type **696**	20	15
2250	13s.	Rusalka	65	25
2251	20s.	Plovdiv	3·75	3·25
2252	28s.	Sofia	95	85

697 Insurgents on the March
(Boris Angelushev)

1973. 50th Anniv of September Uprising.
2253	**697**	2s. multicoloured	20	15
2254	-	5s. violet, pink & red	30	20
2255	-	13s. multicoloured	65	35
2256	-	18s. olive, cream & red	1·40	1·10

DESIGNS—HORIZ: 5s. *Armed Train* (Boris Angelushev).
VERT: 13s. Patriotic poster by N. Mirchev. HORIZ: 18s.
Georgi Dimitrov and Vasil Kolarov.

698 Congress
Emblem

1973. Eight World Trade Union Congress, Varna.
2257	**698**	2s. multicoloured	20	20

699 "Sun" Emblem
and Olympic
Rings

1973. Olympic Congress, Varna. Multicoloured.
2258	13s.	Type **699**	1·90	75
2259	28s.	Lion Emblem of Bulgarian Olympic Committee (vert)	2·30	1·60

MS2260 61×77 mm. 80s. Footballers
(40×25 mm) 6·00 5·50

700 *Prince Kaloyan*

1973. Fresco Portraits, Boyana Church. Multicoloured.
2261	1s.	Type **700**	20	15
2262	2s.	*Desislava*	20	15
2263	3s.	*Saint*	30	20
2264	5s.	*St. Eustratius*	55	25
2265	10s.	*Tsar Constantine-Asen*	95	55
2266	13s.	*Deacon Laurentius*	1·10	65
2267	18s.	*Virgin Mary*	1·30	85
2268	20s.	*St. Ephraim*	1·50	1·10
2269	28s.	*Jesus Christ*	4·75	1·60

MS2270 56×76 mm. 80s. *Scribes*.
Imperf 8·75 8·75

701 Smirnenski and Cavalry Charge

702 Human Rights
Emblem

1973. 75th Birth Anniv of Khristo Smirnenski (poet and
revolutionary).
2271	**701**	1s. blue, red and gold	20	10
2272	**701**	2s. blue, red and gold	45	20

1973. 25th Anniv of Declaration of Human Rights.
2273	**702**	13s. gold, red and blue	65	55

703 Tsar Todor Svetoslav meeting
the Byzantine Embassy, 1307

1973. Bulgarian History. Multicoloured.
2274	1s.	Type **703**	20	15
2275	2s.	Tsar Mikhail Shishman in battle against Byzantines, 1328	20	15
2276	3s.	Battle of Rosokastro, 1332 and Tsar Ivan Aleksandur	20	15
2277	4s.	Defence of Turnovo, 1393 and Patriarch Evtimii	20	15
2278	5s.	Tsar Ivan Shisman's attack on the Turks	30	20
2279	13s.	Momchil attacks Turkish ships at Umur, 1344	65	35
2280	18s.	Meeting of Tsar Ivan Sratsimir and Crusaders, 1396	95	45
2281	28s.	Embassy of Empress Anne of Savoy meets Boyars Balik, Teodor and Dobrotitsa	2·30	1·60

704 "Finn" One-man
Dinghy

1973. Sailing. Various Yachts. Multicoloured.
2282	1s.	Type **704**	20	15
2283	2s.	*Flying Dutchman* two-man dinghy	20	15
2284	3s.	*Soling* yacht	20	15
2285	13s.	*Tempest* dinghy	65	35
2286	20s.	*470* two-man dinghy	95	65
2287	40s.	*Tornado* catamaran	4·75	4·25

705 *Balchik* (Bercho Obreshkov)

1973. 25th Anniv of National Art Gallery, Sofia and
150th Birth Anniv of Stanislav Dospevski (painter).
Multicoloured.
2288	1s.	Type **705**	20	20
2289	2s.	*Mother and Child* (Stryan Venev)	20	20
2290	3s.	*Rest* (Tsenko Boyadzhiev)	20	20
2291	13s.	*Vase with Flowers* (Siruk Skitnik) (vert)	75	35
2292	18s.	*Mary Kuneva* (Iliya Petrov) (vert)	95	45
2293	40s.	*Winter in Plovdiv* (Zlatyn Boyadzhiev) (vert)	4·25	3·75

MS2294 100×95 mm. 50s. *Domnika
Lambreva* (S. Dospevski) (vert); 50s.
Self-portrait (S. Dospevski) (vert) 6·00 4·25

706 Footballers and Emblem

1973. World Cup Football Championship, Munich (1974). Sheet 62×94 mm.
MS2295 **706** 28s. multicoloured (sold at 1l.) ... 6·50 ... 6·50

707 Old Testament Scene (Wood-carving)

1974. Wood-Carvings from Rozhen Monastery.

2296	**707**	1s. dk brn, cream & brn	20	15
2297	-	2s. dk brn, cream & brn	20	15
2298	-	3s. dk brn, cream & brn	20	15
2299	-	5s. olive, cream & green	30	15
2300	-	8s. olive, cream & green	35	20
2301	-	13s. brown, cream and chestnut	55	40
2302	-	28s. brown, cream and chestnut	1·10	65

DESIGNS: Nos. 2296/8, *Passover Table*; 2299/2300, *Abraham and the Angel*; 2301/2, *The Expulsion from Eden*.
Nos. 2296/8, 2299/300 and 2301/2 form three composite designs.

708 *Lenin* (N. Mirchev)

1974. 50th Death Anniv of Lenin. Multicoloured.

2303	2s. Type **708**		20	15
2304	18s. *Lenin with Workers* (W. A. Serov)		95	65

709 *Blagoev addressing Meeting* (G. Kovachev)

1974. 50th Death Anniv of D. Blagoev (founder of Bulgarian Social Democratic Party).

2305	**709**	2s. multicoloured	20	15

710 Sheep

1974. Domestic Animals.

2306	**710**	1s. brown, buff & green	20	15
2307	-	2s. purple, violet & red	20	15
2308	-	3s. brown, pink & green	20	15
2309	-	5s. brown, buff & blue	20	15
2310	-	13s. black, blue and brown	1·10	35
2311	-	20s. brown, pink & blue	3·00	1·80

DESIGNS: 2s. Goat; 3s. Pig; 5s. Cow; 13s. Buffalo; 20s. Horse.

711 Social Economic Integration Emblem

1974. 25th Anniv of Council for Mutual Economic Aid.

2312	**711**	13s. multicoloured	75	55

712 Footballers

1974. World Cup Football Championship.

2313	**712**	1s. multicoloured	20	15
2314	-	2s. multicoloured	20	15
2315	-	3s. multicoloured	20	15
2316	-	13s. multicoloured	55	20
2317	-	28s. multicoloured	95	55
2318	-	40s. multicoloured	2·30	1·60

MS2319 66×78 mm. 1l. multicoloured (55×30 mm) ... 4·75 ... 4·25

DESIGNS: Nos. 2314/19, Various designs similar to Type **712**.

713 Folk-singers

1974. Amateur Arts and Sports Festival. Multicoloured.

2320	1s. Type **713**	20	15
2321	2s. Folk-dancers	20	15
2322	3s. Piper and drummer	20	15
2323	5s. Wrestling	20	15
2324	13s. Athletics	95	85
2325	18s. Gymnastics	1·10	55

714 *Cosmic Research* (Penko Barnbov)

1974. "Mladost '74" Youth Stamp Exhibition, Sofia. Multicoloured.

2326	1s. Type **714**	15	10
2327	2s. *Salt Production* (Mariana Bliznakaa)	20	10
2328	3s. *Fire-dancer* (Detelina Lalova)	55	10
2329	28s. *Friendship Train* (Vanya Boyanova)	2·75	2·40

MS2330 70×70 mm. 60s. *Spring* (Vladimir Kunchev) (40×40 mm) ... 4·25 ... 4·25

715 Motor-cars

1974. World Automobile Federation's Spring Congress, Sofia.

2331	**715**	13s. multicoloured	65	45

716 Period Architecture

1974. UNESCO Executive Council's 94th Session, Varna.

2332	**716**	18s. multicoloured	65	45

717 Chinese Aster

1974. Bulgarian Flowers. Multicoloured.

2333	1s. Type **717**	20	20
2334	2s. Mallow	20	20
2335	3s. Columbine	20	20
2336	18s. Tulip	95	35
2337	20s. Marigold	1·10	45
2338	28s. Pansy	2·75	1·80

MS2339 80×60 mm. 80s. Gaillarde (44×33 mm) ... 3·75 ... 3·25

718 19th Century Post-boy

1974. Centenary of UPU.

2340	**718**	2s. violet & blk on orge	20	15
2341	-	18s. green & blk on orge	95	45

MS2342 80×58 mm. 28s. blue and orange (sold at 80st.) ... 3·25 ... 3·25

DESIGN: 18s. First Bulgarian mail-coach; 20s. UPU emblem.

719 Young Pioneer and Komsomol Girl

1974. 30th Anniv of Dimitrov's Septembrist Pioneers Organization. Multicoloured.

2343	1s. Type **719**	15	10
2344	2s. Pioneer with doves	15	10

MS2345 60×44 mm. 60s. Emblem with portrait of Dimitrov (34×44 mm) ... 2·50 ... 2·20

720 Communist Soldiers with Flag

1974. 30th Anniv of Fatherland Front Government. Multicoloured.

2346	1s. Type **720**	20	15
2347	2s. "Soviet Liberators"	20	15
2348	5s. "Industrialisation"	20	15
2349	13s. "Modern Agriculture"	55	20
2350	18s. "Science and Technology"	1·00	65

721 Stockholm and Emblems

1974. "Stockholm '74" International Stamp Exhibition. Sheet 65×72 mm.
MS2351 **721** 40s. blue, green and yellow ... 7·50 ... 7·50

722 Gymnast on Beam

1974. 18th World Gymnastic Championships, Varna. Multicoloured.

2352	2s. Type **722**	15	10
2353	13s. Gymnast on horse	65	55

723 Doves on Script

1974. European Security and Co-operation Conference. Sheet 97×117 mm containing T **723** and similar vert designs.
MS2354 13s. yellow, blue and chestnut (T **723**); 13s. blue, mauve and chestnut (Map of Europe and script); 13s. green, blue and chestnut (Leaves on script); 13s. multicoloured (Commemorative text) (sold at 60s.) ... 3·50 ... 3·50

724 Envelope with Arrow pointing to Postal Code

1974. Introduction of Postal Coding System (1 January 1975).

2355	**724**	2s. green, orange & blk	20	15

725 "Sourovachka" (twig decorated with coloured ribbons)

1974. New Year.

2356	**725**	2s. multicoloured	20	15

726 Icon of St. Theodor Stratilar

1974. Bulgarian History.

2357	**726**	1s. multicoloured	20	15
2358	-	2s. grey, mauve & black	20	15
2359	-	3s. grey, blue and black	20	15
2360	-	5s. grey, lilac and black	20	15
2361	-	8s. black, buff and brown	30	15
2362	-	13s. grey, green & black	45	20
2363	-	18s. black, gold & red	75	35
2364	-	28s. grey, blue & black	2·20	1·10

DESIGNS: 2s. Bronze medallion; 3s. Carved capital; 5s. Silver bowl of Sivin Jupan; 8s. Clay goblet; 13s. Lioness (torso); 18s. Gold tray; 28s. Double-headed eagle.

727 Apricot

1975. Fruit-tree Blossoms. Multicoloured.

2365	1s. Type **727**	20	15
2366	2s. Apple	20	15
2367	3s. Cherry	20	15
2368	19s. Pear	65	35
2369	28s. Peach	1·60	55

728 Peasant with Flag

1975. 75th Anniv of Bulgarian People's Agrarian Union. Sheet 104×95 mm containing T **728** and similar vert designs.
MS2370 2s. brown, orange and green; 5s. brown, orange and green; 13s. sepia, orange and green; 18s. chestnut, orange and green ... 1·60 ... 1·60

DESIGNS: 5s. Rebels keeping watch during 1923 September uprising; 13s. Dancing; 18s. Woman harvesting fruit.

729 Spanish 6c. Stamp of 1850 and "Espana" Emblem

1975. "Espana 1975" International Stamp Exhibition, Madrid. Sheet 68×100 mm.
MS2371 **729** 40s. multicoloured 8·00 7·50

730 Star and Arrow

1975. 30th Anniv of "Victory in Europe" Day.
2372 **730** 2s. red, black & brown 20 15
2373 - 13s. black, brown & bl 75 35
DESIGNS: 13s. Peace dove and broken sword.

731 "Weights and Measures"

1975. Centenary of Metre Convention.
2374 **731** 13s. violet, black & silver 30 20

732 Tree and open Book

1975. 50th Anniv of Forestry School.
2375 **732** 2s. multicoloured 20 15

733 Michelangelo

1975. 500th Birth Anniv of Michelangelo.
2376 **733** 2s. purple and blue 20 15
2377 - 13s. violet and purple 55 35
2378 - 18s. brown and green 1·10 65
MS2379 70×84 mm. **733** 2s. green and red (sold at 60s.) 2·20 2·20
DESIGNS—HORIZ: Sculptures from Giuliano de Medici's tomb: 13s. *Night*; 18s. *Day*.

734 Festival Emblem

1975. Festival of Humour and Satire, Gabrovo.
2380 **734** 2s. multicoloured 20 15

735 Women's Head and Emblem

1975. International Women's Year.
2381 **735** 13s. multicoloured 45 20

736 Vasil and Sava Kokareshkov

1975. "Young Martyrs to Fascism".
2382 **736** 1s. black, green & gold 10 10
2383 - 2s. black, mauve & gold 10 10
2384 - 5s. black, red and gold 15 10
2385 - 13s. black, blue & gold 55 45
DESIGNS—HORIZ: 2s. Mitko Palauzov and Ivan Vasilev; 5s. Nikola Nakev and Stefcho Kraichev; 13s. Ivanka Pashkolouva and Detelina Mincheva.

737 *Mother feeding Child* (Jean Millet)

1975. World Graphics Exhibition, Sofia. Celebrated Drawings and Engravings. Multicoloured.
2386 1s. Type **737** 20 15
2387 2s. *Mourning a Dead Daughter* (Goya) 20 15
2388 3s. *The Reunion* (Iliya Beshkov) 20 15
2389 13s. *Seated Nude* (Auguste Renoir) 45 20
2390 20s. *Man in a Fur Hat* (Rembrandt) 65 55
2391 40s. *The Dream* (Horore Daumier) (horiz) 2·30 1·20
MS2392 80×95 mm. 1l. *Temptation* (Albrecht Durer) (37×53 mm) 3·75 3·25

738 Gabrovo Costume

1975. Women's Regional Costumes. Multicoloured.
2393 2s. Type **738** 20 15
2394 3s. Trun costume 20 15
2395 5s. Vidin costume 20 15
2396 13s. Goce Delcev costume 75 35
2397 18s. Ruse costume 1·70 55

739 *Bird* (manuscript illumination)

1975. Original Bulgarian Manuscripts. Multicoloured.
2398 1s. Type **739** 20 15
2399 2s. *Head* 20 15
2400 3s. Abstract design 20 15
2401 8s. *Pointing finger* 35 20
2402 13s. *Imaginary creature* 75 35
2403 18s. Abstract design 1·30 45

740 Ivan Vasov

1975. 125th Anniv of Ivan Vasov (writer). Multicoloured.
2404 2s. Type **740** 20 10
2405 13s. Vasov seated 55 20

741 "Soyuz" and Aleksei Leonov

1975. "Apollo"–"Soyuz" Space Link.
2406 **741** 13s. multicoloured 45 20
2407 - 18s. multicoloured 95 35
2408 - 28s. multicoloured 1·90 65
MS2409 76×84 mm. 1l. blue, grey and red 4·25 3·25
DESIGNS: 18s. "Apollo" and Thomas Stafford; 28s. The Link-up; 1l. "Apollo" and "Soyuz" after docking.

742 Ryukyu Sailing Boat, Map and Emblems

1975. International Exposition, Okinawa.
2410 **742** 13s. multicoloured 45 20

743 St. Cyril and St. Methodius

1975. "Balkanphila V" Stamp Exhibition, Sofia.
2411 **743** 2s. brown, lt brn & red 20 10
2412 - 13s. brown, lt brn & grn 55 20
MS2413 90×86 mm. 50s. sepia, brown and orange 2·20 2·20
DESIGNS—VERT: 13s. St. Constantine and St. Helene. HORIZ: 50s. Sophia Church, Sofia (53×43 mm.).

744 Footballer

1975. Eighth Inter-Toto (Football Pools) Congress, Varna.
2414 **744** 2s. multicoloured 20 15

745 Deaths-head Hawk Moth

1975. Hawk Moths. Multicoloured.
2415 1s. Type **745** 20 15
2416 2s. Oleander hawk moth 20 15
2417 3s. Eyed hawk moth 20 15
2418 10s. Mediterranean hawk moth 55 20
2419 13s. Elephant hawk moth 95 45
2420 18s. Broad-bordered bee hawk moth 1·90 75

746 UN Emblem

1975. 30th Anniv of UNO.
2421 **746** 13s. red, brown & black 45 20

747 Map of Europe on Peace Dove

1975. European Security and Co-operation Conference, Helsinki.
2422 **747** 18s. lilac, blue & yellow 85 85

748 D. Khristov

1975. Birth Cent of Dobri Khristov (composer).
2423 **748** 5s. brown, yellow & grn 20 10

749 Constantine's Rebellion against the Turks

1975. Bulgarian History. Multicoloured.
2424 1s. Type **749** 20 15
2425 2s. Vladislav III's campaign 20 15
2426 3s. Battle of Turnovo 20 15
2427 10s. Battle of Chiprovtsi 30 20
2428 13s. 17 th-century partisans 75 35
2429 18s. Return of banished peasants 1·00 55

750 "First Aid"

1975. 90th Anniv of Bulgarian Red Cross.
2430 **750** 2s. brown, black and red 15 10
2431 - 13s. green, black and red 55 20
DESIGN: 13s. "Peace and international Co-operation".

751 Ethnographical Museum, Plovdiv

1975. European Architectural Heritage Year.
2432 **751** 80s. brown, yellow & grn 2·75 2·75

752 Christmas Lanterns

1975. Christmas and New Year. Multicoloured.
2433 2s. Type **752** 20 10
2434 13s. Stylized peace dove 45 35

753 Egyptian Galley

1975. Historic Ships (1st series). Multicoloured.
2435 1s. Type **753** 10 10
2436 2s. Phoenician galley 10 10
2437 3s. Greek trireme 10 10
2438 5s. Roman galley 20 10
2439 13s. *Mora* (Norman ship) 55 35
2440 18s. Venetian galley 1·10 55
See also Nos. 2597/2602, 2864/9, 3286/91 and 3372/7.

754 Modern Articulated Tramcar

1976. 75th Anniv of Sofia Tramways. Multicoloured.

2441	2s. Type **754**	20	10
2442	13s. Early 20th-century tramcar	85	40

755 Skiing

1976. Winter Olympic Games, Innsbruck. Multicoloured.

2443	1s. Type **755**	20	15
2444	2s. Cross-country skiing (vert)	20	15
2445	2s. Ski jumping	20	15
2446	13s. Biathlon (vert)	55	35
2447	18s. Ice hockey (vert)	65	55
2448	18s. Speed skating (vert)	1·90	75
MS2449	70×80 mm. 80s. Ice skating (pairs) (30×55 mm)	3·25	2·75

756 Stylized Bird

1976. 11th Bulgarian Communists Party Congress. Multicoloured.

2450	2s. Type **756**	10	10
2451	5s. "1956–1976, Fulfilment of the Five Year Plans"	20	15
2452	13s. Hammer and Sickle	45	20
MS2453	55×65 mm. 50s. Georgi Dimitrov (Prime Minister and Party secretary-general, 1945–49) (33×43 mm)	1·90	1·60

757 Alexander Graham Bell and early Telephone

1976. Telephone Centenary.

2454	**757** 18s. lt brown, brn & pur	65	35

758 Mute Swan

1976. Waterfowl. Multicoloured.

2455	1s. Type **758**	20	15
2456	2s. Ruddy shelduck	20	15
2457	3s. Common shelduck	30	20
2458	5s. Garganey	1·10	35
2459	13s. Mallard	1·40	85
2460	18s. Red-crested pochard	3·75	2·75

759 Guerillas' Briefing

1976. Cent of April Uprising (1st issue). Multicoloured.

2461	1s. Type **759**	10	10
2462	2s. Peasants' briefing	10	10
2463	5s. Krishina, horse and guard	20	10
2464	13s. Rebels with cannon	55	35

See also Nos. 2529/33.

760 Kozlodui Atomic Energy Centre

1976. Modern Industrial Installations.

2465	**760** 5s. green	20	15
2466	- 8s. red	30	20
2467	- 10s. green	45	25
2468	- 13s. violet	55	30
2469	- 20s. green	75	35

DESIGNS: 8s. Bobaudol plant; 10s. Sviloza chemical works; 13s. Devaya chemical works; 20s. Sestvitro dam.

761 Guard with Patrol-dog

1976. 30th Anniv of Frontier Guards. Multicoloured.

2470	2s. Type **761**	20	15
2471	13s. Mounted guards	45	20

762 Worker with Spade

1976. 30th Anniv of Youth Brigades Movement.

2472	**762** 2s. multicoloured	20	15

763 Botev

1976. Death Cent of Khristo Botev (poet).

2473	**763** 13s. green and brown	65	35

764 "Martyrs of First Congress" (relief)

1976. 85th Anniv of 1st Bulgarian Social Democratic Party Congress, Buzludzha. Multicoloured.

2474	2s. Type **764**	15	10
2475	5s. Modern memorial, Buzludzha Peak	20	10

765 Dimitur Blagoev

1976. 120th Birth Anniv of Dimitur Blagoev (founder of Bulgarian Social Democratic Party).

2476	**765** 13s. black, red and gold	65	20

766 "Thematic Stamps"

1976. 12th Bulgarian Philatelic Federation Congress. Sheet 73×103 mm.

MS2477	**766** 50s. multicoloured	3·25	2·75

767 Children Playing

1976. Child Welfare.

2478	**767** 1s. multicoloured	20	15
2479	- 2s. multicoloured	20	15
2480	- 5s. multicoloured	20	15
2481	- 23s. multicoloured	95	55

DESIGNS: 2s. Girls with pram and boy on rocking horse; 5s. Playing ball; 23s. Dancing.

768 Wrestling

1976. Olympic Games, Montreal. Multicoloured.

2482	1s. Type **768**	20	15
2483	2s. Boxing (vert)	20	15
2484	3s. Weight-lifting (vert)	20	15
2485	13s. Canoeing (vert)	45	20
2486	18s. Gymnastics (vert)	65	35
2487	28s. Diving (vert)	1·00	55
2488	40s. Athletics (vert)	1·40	65
MS2489	70×80 mm. 1l. Weightlifting (vert)	3·25	3·25

769 Belt Buckle, Vidin

1976. Thracian Art (8th–4th Centuries B.C.). Multicoloured.

2490	1s. Type **769**	20	15
2491	2s. Brooch, Durzhanitsa	20	15
2492	3s. Mirror handle, Chukarka	20	15
2493	5s. Helmet cheek guard, Gurlo	20	15
2494	13s. Gold decoration, Orizovo	45	20
2495	18s. Decorated horse-harness, Brezovo	65	30
2496	20s. Greave, Mogilanska Mogila	85	35
2497	28s. Pendant, Bukovtsi	95	55

770 *Partisans at Night* (Petrov)

1976. Paintings by Iliya Petrov and Tsanko Lavrenov from the National Gallery. Multicoloured.

2498	2s. Type **770**	20	15
2499	5s. *Kurshum-Khan* (Lavrenov)	20	15
2500	13s. *Seated Woman* (Petrov)	45	20
2501	18s. *Boy seated in chair* (Petrov) (vert)	95	35
2502	28s. *Old Plovdiv* (Lavrenov) (vert)	1·10	45
MS2503	60×82 mm. 80s. *Self-portrait* (Petrov) (vert)	2·75	2·75

771 Weightlifting

1976. Gold Medal Winners, Montreal Olympic Games. Sheet 98×116 mm containing vert designs as T 771, each with medal in red and gold.

MS2504	25s. yellow (T **771**); 25s. blue (rowing); 25s. green (running); 25s. red (wrestling)	3·25	3·25

772 Fish on line

1976. World Sports Fishing Congress, Varna.

2505	**772** 5s. multicoloured	30	20

773 The Pianist

1976. 75th Birth Anniv of Alex Jhendov (caricaturist).

2506	**773** 2s. dp grn, cream & grn	10	10
2507	- 5s. dp violet, vio & lilac	30	15
2508	- 13s. black, pink & red	45	20

DESIGNS: 5s. *Trick or Treat*; 13s. *The Leader*.

774 St. Theodor

1976. Zemen Monastery. Frescoes. Multicoloured.

2509	2s. Type **774**	20	15
2510	3s. St. Paul and Apostle	20	15
2511	5s. St. Joachim	30	15
2512	13s. Prophet Melchisadek	55	20
2513	19s. St. Porphyrus	75	35
2514	28s. Queen Doya	95	45
MS2515	60×76 mm. 1l. Holy Communion	3·25	3·25

775 Legal Document

1976. 25th Anniv of State Archives.

2516	**775** 5s. multicoloured	30	20

776 Horse Chestnut

1976. Plants. Multicoloured.

2517	1s. Type **776**	20	15
2518	2s. Shrubby cinquefoil	20	15
2519	5s. Holly	20	15
2520	8s. Yew	30	20
2521	13s. *Daphne pontica*	45	35
2522	23s. Judas tree	1·20	55

777 Cloud over Sun

1976. Protection of the Environment. Multicoloured.

2523	2s. Cloud over tree	20	15
2524	18s. Type **777**	65	35

778 Dimitur Polyanov

1976. Birth Cent of Dimitur Polyanov (poet).

2525	**778** 2s. lilac and orange	20	15

779 Congress
Emblem

1976. 33rd Bulgarian People's Agrarian Union Congress.
Multicoloured.

2526	2s. Type **779**		20	10
2527	13s. Flags		55	35

780 Warrior with Horses
(vase painting)

1976. 30th Anniv of United Nations Educational Scientific
and Cultural Organization. Sheet 71×81 mm.

MS2528 **780** 50s. multicoloured			2·75	2·75

781 Khristo Botev (Zlatyu
Boyadzhiev)

1976. Centenary of April Uprising (2nd issue).
Multicoloured.

2529	1s. Type **781**		20	15
2530	2s. Partisan carrying Cherrywood Cannon (Iliya Petrov)		20	15
2531	3s. Necklace of Immortality (Dechko Uzunov)		20	15
2532	13s. April 1876 (Georgi Popov)		45	20
2533	18s. Partisans (Stoyan Venev)		75	45
MS2534 45×82 mm. 60s. The Oath (Svetlin Rusev)			2·20	2·20

782 Tobacco Workers

1976. 70th Birth Anniv of Veselin Staikov (artist).
Multicoloured.

2535	1s. Type **782**		10	10
2536	2s. Melnik		15	10
2537	13s. Boat Builders		55	25

783 "Snowflake"

1976. New Year.

2538	**783**	2s. multicoloured	20	10

784 Zakhari
Stojanov

1976. 125th Birth Anniv of Zakhari Stojanov (writer).

2539	**784**	2s. brown, red and gold	20	10

785 Bronze Coin of Septimus
Severus

1977. Roman Coins struck in Serdica. Multicoloured.

2540	1s. Type **785**		20	15
2541	2s. Bronze coin of Caracalla		20	15
2542	13s. Bronze coin of Caracalla (diff.)		30	20
2543	18s. Bronze coin of Caracalla (diff.)		55	35
2544	23s. Copper coin of Diocletian		95	55

786
Championships
Emblem

1977. World Ski-orienteering Championships.

2545	**786**	13s. blue, red & ultram	55	20

787 Congress
Emblem

1977. Fifth Congress of Bulgarian Tourist Associations.

2546	**787**	2s. multicoloured	20	10

788 "Symphyandra
wanneri"

1977. Mountain Flowers. Multicoloured.

2547	1s. Type **788**		20	15
2548	2s. Petcovia orphanidea		20	15
2549	3s. Campanula lanatre		20	15
2550	13s. Campanula scutellata		55	35
2551	43s. Nettle-leaved bellflower		1·90	75

789 V. Kolarov

1977. Birth Centenary of Vasil Kolarov (Prime Minister
1949–50).

2552	**789**	2s. grey, black & blue	20	10

790 Congress
Emblem

1977. Eighth Bulgarian Trade Unions Congress.

2553	**790**	2s. multicoloured	20	10

791 Joint

1977. World Rheumatism Year.

2554	**791**	23s. multicoloured	95	55

792 Wrestling

1977. World University Games, Sofia. Multicoloured.

2555	2s. Type **792**		20	20
2556	13s. Running		45	25
2557	23s. Handball		85	45
2558	43s. Gymnastics		1·40	85

793 Ivan Vazov
National Theatre

1977. Buildings in Sofia. Pale brown backgrounds.

2559	**793**	12s. red	35	20
2560	-	13s. brown	45	25
2561	-	23s. blue	75	35
2562	-	30s. green	1·10	45
2563	-	80s. violet	1·90	1·20
2564	-	1l. brown	2·40	1·50

DESIGNS: 13s. Party Building; 23s. People's Army Building;
30s. Clement of Ohrid University; 80s. National Art Gal-
lery; 1l. National Assembly Building.

794 Congress
Emblem

1977. 13th Dimitrov Communist Youth League Congress.

2565	**794**	2s. red, green and gold	20	10

795 St. Nicholas Nesebur

1977. Bulgarian Icons. Multicoloured.

2566	1s. Type **795**		20	15
2567	2s. Old Testament Trinity, Sofia		20	15
2568	3s. The Royal Gates, Veliko Turnovo		20	15
2569	5s. Deisis, Nesebur		20	15
2570	13s. St. Nicholas, Elena		45	20
2571	23s. The Presentation of the Blessed Virgin, Rila Monastery		75	35
2572	35s. The Virgin Mary with Infant, Varna		1·10	75
2573	40s. St. Demetrius on Horseback, Provadya		2·40	1·10
MS2574 100×99 mm. 1l. The Twelve Festival Days, Rila Monastery. Imperf			4·25	3·25

796 Wolf

1977. Wild Animals. Multicoloured.

2575	1s. Type **796**		20	15
2576	2s. Red fox		20	15
2577	10s. Weasel		45	20
2578	13s. Wild cat		65	55
2579	23s. Golden jackal		1·90	1·10

797 Congress
Emblem

1977. Third Bulgarian Culture Congress.

2580	**797**	13s. multicoloured	45	20

798 Crafty Peter
riding a Donkey
(drawing by Iliya
Beshkov)

1977. 11th Festival of Humour and Satire, Gabrovo.

2581	**798**	2s. multicoloured	20	10

799 Congress
Emblem

1977. Eighth Congress of the Popular Front, Sofia.

2582	**799**	2s. multicoloured	20	10

800 Newspaper Masthead

1977. Centenary of Bulgarian Daily Press.

2583	**800**	2s. multicoloured	20	10

801 St. Cyril

1977. 1150th Birth Anniv of St. Cyril. Sheet 106×87 mm.

MS2584 **801** 1l. multicoloured			3·75	3·75

802 Conference Emblem

1977. International Writers Conference, Sofia.

2585	**802**	23s. blue, lt blue & grn	1·40	1·10

803 Map of Europe

1977. 21st Congress of European Organization for Quality
Control, Varna.

2586	**803**	23s. multicoloured	95	55

804 Basketball

1977. Women's European Basketball Championships.

2587	**804**	23s. multicoloured	95	55

805 Weightlifter

1977. World Junior Weightlifting Championships.
2588	**805**	13s. multicoloured	45	20

806 Georgi Dimitrov

1977. 95th Birth Anniv of Georgi Dimitrov (statesman).
2589	**806**	13s. brown and red	65	35

807 Tail Section of Tupolev Tu-154

1977. Air. 30th Anniv of Bulgarian Airline "Balkanair".
2590	**807**	35s. multicoloured	1·70	85

808 Games Emblem

1977. World University Games, Sofia (2nd issue). Sheet 84×76 mm.
MS2591	**808**	1l. multicoloured	3·25	2·75

809 T.V. Towers, Berlin and Sofia

1977. "Sozphilex 77" Stamp Exhibition, East Berlin.
2592	**809**	25s. blue and deep blue	95	55

810 Elin Pelin alias Dimitur Stoyanov (writer)

1977. Writers and Painters.
2593	**810**	2s. brown and gold	20	20
2594	-	5s. olive and gold	20	20
2595	-	13s. red and gold	35	25
2596	-	23s. blue and gold	1·10	55

DESIGNS: 5s. Peyu Yavorov (poet); 13s. Boris Angelushev (painter and illustrator); 23s. Iseno Todorov (painter).

1977. Historic Ships (2nd series). As T **753**. Multicoloured.
2597	1s.	Hansa Kogge	20	15
2598	2s.	Santa Maria	20	15
2599	3s.	Drake's Golden Hind	20	15
2600	12s.	Carrack Santa Catherina	40	20
2601	13s.	La Couronne (French galleon)	45	25
2602	43s.	Mediterranean galley	1·90	65

811 Women Canoeists

1977. World Canoe Championships.
2603	**811**	2s. blue and yellow	20	15
2604	-	23s. blue and turquoise	95	45

DESIGN: 23s. Men canoeists.

812 Balloon over Plovdiv

1977. Air. 85th Anniv "Panair". International Aviation Exhibition, Plovdiv.
2605	**812**	25s. orange, yell & brn	95	55

813 Presidents Zhivkov and Brezhnev

1977. Soviet–Bulgarian Friendship.
2606	**813**	18s. brown, red & gold	55	45

814 Conference Building

1977. 64th International Parliamentary Conference, Sofia.
2607	**814**	23s. green, pink and red	95	45

815 Newspaper Mastheads

1977. 50th Anniv of Official Newspaper "Rabotnichesko Delo" (Workers' Press).
2608	**815**	2s. red, green and grey	20	10

816 The Union of Earth and Water

1977. 400th Birth Anniv of Rubens. Multicoloured.
2609	13s.	Type **816**	55	20
2610	23s.	Venus and Adonis (detail)	1·10	1·10
2611	40s.	Amorous Shepherd (detail)	2·20	1·60
MS2612	71×87 mm. 1l. Portrait of a Chambermaid		4·75	3·75

817 Cossack with Bulgarian Child (Angelushev)

1977. Centenary of Liberation from Turkey. (1978). Posters.
2613	**817**	2s. multicoloured	30	15
2614	-	13s. green, blue & red	45	20
2615	-	23s. blue, red & green	85	45
2616	-	25s. multicoloured	95	50

DESIGNS: 13s. Bugler (Cheklarov); 23s. Mars (god of war) and Russian soldiers (Petrov); 25s. Flag of Russian Imperial Army.

818 Albena, Black Sea

1977. Tourism.
2617	**818**	35s. blue, turq & brn	1·30	55
2618	-	43s. yellow, grn & blue	1·40	65

DESIGN: 43s. Rila Monastery.

819 Dr. Nikolai Pirogov (Russian surgeon)

1977. Cent of Dr. Pirogov's Visit to Bulgaria.
2619	**819**	13s. brown, buff & grn	45	35

820 Space walking

1977. Air. 20th Anniv of First Artificial Satellite. Multicoloured.
2620	12s.	Type **820**	45	20
2621	25s.	Space probe over Mars	95	45
2622	35s.	Space probe "Venus-4" over Venus	1·40	55

821 Soviet Emblems and Decree

1977. 60th Anniv of Russian Revolution.
2623	**821**	2s. red, black & stone	30	20
2624	-	13s. red and purple	55	25
2625	-	23s. red and violet	1·00	35

DESIGNS: 13s. Lenin; 23s. "1977" as flame.

822 Diesel Train on Bridge

1977. 50th Anniv of Transport, Bridges and Highways Organization.
2626	**822**	13s. yellow, green & olive	75	55

1977. 150th Birth Anniv of Petko Ratshev Slaveikov (poet). As T **810**.
2627		8s. brown and gold	30	20

824 Decorative Initials of New Year Greeting

1977. New Year. Multicoloured.
2628		2s. Type **824**	20	10
2629		13s. "Fireworks"	45	15

825 Footballer

1978. World Cup Football Championship, Argentina. Multicoloured.
2630		13s. Type **825**	45	35
2631		23s. Shooting the ball	1·40	85
MS2632	77×61 mm. 50s. Tackle for ball		2·50	2·20

826 Baba Vida Fortress, Vidin

1977. Air. "The Danube – European River". Multicoloured.
2633		25s. Type **826**	75	55
2634		35s. Friendship Bridge	1·40	1·20

827 Television Mast, Moscow

1978. 20th Anniv of Organization of Socialist Postal Administrations (O.S.S.).
2635	**827**	13s. multicoloured	45	20

828 Shipka Monument

1978. Centenary of Liberation from Turkey (2nd issue). Sheet 55×73 mm.
MS2636	**828**	50s. multicoloured	1·60	1·60

829 Red Cross in Laurel Wreath

1978. Centenary of Bulgarian Red Cross.
2637	**829**	25s. red, brown & blue	95	55

830 "XXX" formed from Bulgarian and Russian National Colours

1978. 30th Anniv of Bulgarian–Soviet Friendship.
2638	**830**	2s. multicoloured	20	15

831 Leo Tolstoy
(Russian writer)

1978. Famous Personalities.

2639	831	2s. green and yellow	30	15
2640	-	5s. brown and bistre	30	15
2641	-	13s. green and mauve	35	20
2642	-	23s. brown and grey	40	35
2643	-	25s. brown and green	45	40
2644	-	35s. violet and blue	1·40	55

DESIGNS: 5s. Fyodor Dostoevsky (Russian writer); 13s. Ivan Turgenev (Russian writer); 23s. Vassily Vereshchagin (Russian artist); 25s. Giuseppe Garibaldi (Italian patriot); 35s. Victor Hugo (French writer).

832 Nikolai
Roerich (artist)

1978. Nikolai Roerich Exhibition, Sofia.

2645	832	8s. brown, green & red	45	20

833 Bulgarian Flag and Red Star

1978. Communist Party National Conference, Sofia.

2646	833	2s. multicoloured	20	10

834 Goddess

1978. "Philaserdica 79" International Stamp Exhibition (1st issue). Ancient Ceramics. Multicoloured.

2647	834	2s. Type 834	20	15
2648	-	5s. Mask with beard	20	15
2649	-	13s. Decorated vase	45	20
2650	-	23s. Vase with scallop design	75	65
2651	-	35s. Head of Silenus	1·10	1·10
2652	-	53s. Cockerel	4·00	1·60

See also Nos. 2674/9, 2714/18, 2721/5 and 2753/4.

835 "Spirit of Nature"

1978. Birth Cent of Andrei Nikolov (sculptor).

2653	835	13s. blue, mauve & vio	45	20

836 Heart and Arrows

1978. World Hypertension Month.

2654	836	23s. red, orange & grey	95	45

837 "Kor Karoli" and Map of Route

1978. Georgi Georgiev's World Voyage.

2655	837	23s. blue, mauve & grn	1·90	85

838 Doves

1978. 11th World Youth and Students' Festival, Havana.

2656	838	13s. multicoloured	45	20

839 Portrait of a Young Man (Dürer)

1978. Paintings. Multicoloured.

2657	839	13s. Type 839	30	20
2658	-	23s. Bathsheba at the Fountain (Rubens)	45	35
2659	-	25s. Signor de Moret (Hans Holbein the Younger)	55	40
2660	-	35s. Self portrait with Saskia (Rembrandt)	75	45
2661	-	43s. Lady in Mourning (Tintoretto)	95	55
2662	-	60s. Old Man with a Beard (Rembrandt)	1·20	75
2663	-	80s. Man in Armour (Van Dyck)	2·75	1·80

840 Fritillaria stribrnyi

1978. Flowers. Multicoloured.

2664	840	1s. Type 840	20	15
2665	-	2s. Fritillaria drenovskyi	20	15
2666	-	3s. Lilium rhodopaeum	20	15
2667	-	13s. Tulipa urumoffii	45	20
2668	-	23s. Lilium jankae	55	35
2669	-	43s. Tulipa rhodopaea	1·90	1·10

841 Varna

1978. 63rd Esperanto Congress, Varna.

2670	841	13s. orange, red & green	75	45

842 Delcev

1978. 75th Death Anniv of Goce Delcev (Macedonian revolutionary).

2671	842	13s. multicoloured	55	20

843 Freedom Fighters

1978. 75th Anniv of Ilinden-Preobrazhenie Rising.

2672	843	5s. black and red	20	10

844 The Sleeping Venus

1978. World Masters of Art. Sheet 71×71 mm. Imperf.

MS2673	844	1l. multicoloured	2·20	2·20

845 Market (Noiden Petkov)

1978. "Philaserdica 79" International Stamp Exhibition (2nd issue). Paintings of Sofia. Multicoloured.

2674		2s. Type 845	20	20
2675	-	5s. View of Sofia (Euril Stoichev)	20	20
2676	-	13s. View of Sofia (Boris Ivanov)	30	20
2677	-	23s. Tolbukhin Boulevard (Nikola Tanev)	75	35
2678	-	35s. National Theatre (Nikola Petrov)	85	45
2679	-	53s. Market (Anton Mitov)	95	85
MS2679a		186×106 mm. Nos. 2674/9	7·00	7·00

846 Black Woodpecker

1978. Woodpeckers. Multicoloured.

2680		1s. Type 846	20	15
2681	-	2s. Syrian woodpecker	20	15
2682	-	3s. Three-toed woodpecker	20	15
2683	-	13s. Middle-spotted woodpecker	95	55
2684	-	23s. Lesser spotted woodpecker	1·40	75
2685	-	43s. Green woodpecker	3·75	2·40

847 Ivan Vazov National Theatre, Sofia

1978. "Praga 78" and "Philaserdica 79" International Stamp Exhibitions. Sheet 153×110 mm containing T 847 and similar horiz designs. Multicoloured.

MS2686	(a) 40s. Type 847; (b) 40s. Festival Hall, Sofia; (c) 40s. Charles Bridge, Prague; (d) 40s. Belvedere Palace, Prague	3·25	3·25

848 "Elka 55" Computer

1978. Plovdiv International Fair.

2687	848	2s. multicoloured	20	10

849 September 1923 (Boris Angelushev)

1978. 55th Anniv of September Uprising.

2688	849	2s. red and brown	20	10

850 Khristo Danov

1978. 150th Birth Anniv of Khristo Danov (first Bulgarian publisher).

2689	850	2s. orange and lake	20	10

851 The People of Vladaya (Todor Panayotov)

1978. 60th Anniv of Vladaya Mutiny.

2690	851	2s. lilac, brown and red	20	10

852 Hands supporting Rainbow

1978. International Anti-apartheid Year.

2691	852	13s. multicoloured	45	20

853 Pipeline and Flags

1978. Inauguration of Orenburg–U.S.S.R. Natural Gas Pipeline.

2692	853	13s. multicoloured	45	20

854 Acrobats

1978. Third World Sports Acrobatics Championships, Sofia.

2693	854	13s. multicoloured	45	20

855 Salvador Allende

1978. 70th Birth Anniv of Salvador Allende (Chilean politician).

2694	855	13s. brown and red	45	20

856 Human Rights Emblem

1978. 30th Anniv of Declaration of Human Rights.

2695	856	23s. yellow, red & blue	95	55

857 Levski and Matei Mitkaloto (Kalina Taseva)

1978. History of Bulgaria. Paintings. Multicoloured.

2696		1s. Type 857	20	15
2697	-	2s. Give Strength to my Arm (Zlatyu Boyadzhiev)	20	15
2698	-	3s. Rumena Voevoda (Nikola Mirchev) (horiz)	20	15
2699	-	13s. Kolya Ficheto (Elza Goeva)	45	35
2700	-	23s. A Family of the National Revival Period (Naiden Petkov)	1·00	65

858 Tourist Home, Plovdiv

1978. European Architectural Heritage. Multicoloured.
2701		43s. Type **858**	1·50	55
2702		43s. Tower of the Prince, Rila Monastery	1·50	55

859 *Geroi Plevny* and Route Map

1978. Opening of the Varna–Ilichovsk Ferry Service.
2703	**859**	13s. blue, red & green	45	35

860 Mosaic Bird (Santa Sofia Church)

1978. "Bulgaria 78" National Stamp Exhibition, Sofia.
2704	**860**	5s. multicoloured	35	20

861 Monument to St. Clement of Ohrid (university patron) (Lyubemir Dalcher)

1978. 90th Anniv of Sofia University.
2705	**861**	2s. lilac, black & green	20	10

862 Nikola Karastoyanov

1978. Birth Bicentenary of Nikola Karastoyanov (first Bulgarian printer).
2706	**862**	2s. brn, yell & chestnut	35	20

863 Initial from 13th Century Bible Manuscript

1978. Centenary of Cyril and Methodius People's Library. Multicoloured.
2707		2s. Type **863**	20	15
2708		13s. Monk writing (from a 1567 manuscript)	45	20
2709		23s. Decorated page from 16th-century manuscript Bible	85	45
MS2710		63×94 mm. 80s. Seated saint with attendant (from 13th century manuscript Bible)	2·20	2·20

864 Ballet Dancers

1978. 50th Anniv of Bulgarian Ballet.
2711	**864**	13s. green, mauve & lav	45	35

865 Tree of Birds

1978. New Year. Multicoloured.
2712		2s. Type **865**	20	10
2713		13s. Posthorn	30	15

866 1961 Communist Congress Stamp

1978. "Philaserdica 79" International Stamp Exhibition (3rd issue) and Bulgarian Stamp Centenary (1st issue).
2714	-	2s. red and green	20	15
2715	-	13s. claret and blue	20	15
2716	-	23s. green and mauve	30	20
2717	**866**	35s. grey and blue	95	45
2718	-	53s. green and red	1·70	65
MS2719		62×87 mm. 1l. black, yellow and green	2·20	2·20

DESIGNS—HORIZ: 2s. 1901 "Cherrywood Cannon" stamp; 13s. 1946 "New Republic" stamp; 23s. 1957 Canonisation of St. Cyril and St. Methodius stamp; 1l. First Bulgarian stamp. VERT: 53s. 1962 Dimitrov stamp.
See also Nos. 2721/5 and **MS**2755.

867 Council Building, Moscow and Flags

1979. 30th Anniv of Council of Mutual Economic Aid.
2720	**867**	13s. multicoloured	45	20

1979. "Philaserdica 79" Int Stamp Exn (4th issue) and Bulgarian Stamp Cent (2nd issue). As Nos. 2714/18 but inscr "1979" and colours changed.
2721	-	2s. red and blue	20	15
2722	-	13s. claret and green	45	20
2723	-	23s. green, yellow & red	55	35
2724	**866**	35s. grey and red	95	45
2725	-	53s. brown and violet	1·20	65

868 National Bank

1979. Centenary of Bulgarian National Bank.
2726	**868**	2s. grey and yellow	20	10

868a

1979. Coil stamps.
2726a	**868a**	2s. blue	10	10
2726b	**868a**	5s. red	20	10

The 5s. is as T **868a** but different pattern.

869 Stamboliiski

1979. Birth Centenary of Alexandur Stamboliiski (Prime Minister 1919–23).
2727	**869**	2s. brown and yellow	20	10

870 Child's Head as Flower

1979. International Year of the Child.
2728	**870**	23s. multicoloured	95	45

871 Profiles

1979. Eighth World Congress for the Deaf, Varna.
2729	**871**	13s. green and blue	45	20

872 "75" and Emblem

1979. 75th Anniv of Bulgarian Trade Unions.
2730	**872**	2s. green and orange	20	10

873 Soviet War Memorial

1979. Centenary of Sofia as Capital of Bulgaria. Sheet 106×105 mm containing T **873** and similar vert designs. Multicoloured.
MS2731		2s. Type **873**, 5s. Mother and child (sculpture); 13, 23, 25s. Bas-relief from monument to the Liberators of 1876	2·20	2·20

The 13, 23 and 25s. values form a composite design.

874 Rocket

1979. Soviet–Bulgarian Space Flight. Multicoloured.
2732		2s. Georgi Ivanov (horiz)	20	15
2733		12s. Type **874**	35	20
2734		13s. Nikolai Rukavishnikov and Ivanov (horiz)	75	25
2735		25s. Link-up with "Salyut" space station (horiz)	95	45
2736		35s. Capsule descending by parachute	1·10	55
MS2737		67×86 mm. 1l. Globe and orbiting space craft (horiz)	2·75	2·75

875 Carrier Pigeon and Tupolev Tu-154 Jet

1979. Centenary of Bulgarian Post and Telegraph Services. Multicoloured.
2738		2s. Type **875**	20	15
2739		5s. Old and new telephones	20	15
2740		13s. Morse key and teleprinter	45	20
2741		23s. Old radio transmitter and aerials	65	35
2742		35s. T.V. tower and satellite	95	45
MS2743		64×69 mm. 50s. Ground receiving station (38×28 mm)	2·75	2·75

876 Running

1979. Olympic Games. Moscow (1980) (1st issue). Athletics. Multicoloured.
2744		2s. Type **876**	30	25
2745		13s. Pole vault (horiz)	65	55
2746		25s. Discus	1·10	75
2747		35s. Hurdles (horiz)	1·40	1·10
2748		43s. High jump (horiz)	1·90	1·30
2749		1l. Long jump	2·75	2·20
MS2750		90×65 mm. 2l. Shot put	9·75	9·75

See also Nos. 2773/**MS**2779, 2803/**MS**2809, 2816/**MS**2822, 2834/**MS**2840 and 2851/**MS**2857.

877 Thracian Gold Leaf Collar

1979. 48th International Philatelic Federation Congress, Sofia. Sheet 77×86 mm.
MS2751	**877**	1l. multicoloured	4·50	4·50

878 First Bulgarian Stamp and 1975 European Security Conference Stamp

1979. "Philaserdica 79" International Exhibition, Sofia (5th issue). Sheet 63×61 mm.
MS2752	**878**	1l. multicoloured	7·50	7·50

879 Hotel Vitosha-New Otani

1979. "Philaserdica 79" International Stamp Exhibition, Sofia (5th issue) and Bulgaria Day.
2753	**879**	2s. pink and blue	20	10

880 *Good Morning, Little Brother* (illus by Kukuliev of folktale)

1979. "Philaserdica 79" International Stamp Exhibition, Sofia (6th issue) and Bulgarian–Russian Friendship Day.
2754	**880**	2s. multicoloured	20	10

881 First Bulgarian Stamp

1979. Centenary of First Bulgarian Stamp (3rd issue). Sheet 91×121 mm.
MS2755	**881**	5s. multicoloured	60·00	60·00

882 *Man on Donkey* (Boris Angelushev)

1979. 12th Festival of Humour and Satire, Grabovo.
2756	**882**	2s. multicoloured	20	15

883 *Four Women*

1979. 450th Death Anniv of Albrecht Durer (artist). Multicoloured.
2757		13s. Type **883**	20	20
2758		23s. *Three Peasants Talking*	55	35
2759		25s. *The Cook and his Wife*	75	45
2760		35s. *Portrait of Eobanus Hessus*	1·10	65
MS2761 80×81 mm. 80s. *Rhinoceros* (horiz). Imperf			2·20	2·20

884 Clocktower, Byala Cherkva

1979. Air. Clocktowers (1st series). Multicoloured.
2762		13s. Type **884**	35	20
2763		23s. Botevgrad	45	35
2764		25s. Pazardzhik	55	45
2765		35s. Gabrovo	65	65
2766		53s. Tryavna	1·40	1·10

See also Nos. 2891/5.

885 Petko Todorov (birth centenary)

1979. Bulgarian Writers.
2767	**885**	2s. black, brown & yell	25	20
2768	-	2s. green and yellow	25	20
2769	-	2s. red and yellow	25	20

DESIGNS: No. 2768, Dimitur Dimov (70th birth anniv); 2769, Stefan Kostov (birth cent).

886 Congress Emblem

1979. 18th Congress of International Theatrical Institute, Sofia.
2770	**886**	13s. cobalt, blue & black	35	20

887 House of Journalists, Varna

1979. 20th Anniv of House of Journalists (holiday home), Varna.
2771	**887**	8s. orange, black & blue	20	10

888 Children of Different Races

1979. "Banners for Peace" Children's Meeting, Sofia.
2772	**888**	2s. multicoloured	20	10

889 Parallel Bars

1979. Olympic Games, Moscow (1980) (2nd issue). Gymnastics. Multicoloured.
2773		2s. Type **889**	30	25
2774		13s. Horse exercise (horiz)	55	35
2775		25s. Rings exercise	75	55
2776		35s. Beam exercise	95	85
2777		43s. Uneven bars	1·40	1·20
2778		1l. Floor exercise	2·75	2·40
MS2779 65×88 mm. 2l. Horizontal bars			9·75	9·75

890 *Virgin and Child* (Nesebur)

1979. Icons of the Virgin and Child. Multicoloured.
2780		13s. Type **890**	45	20
2781		23s. Nesebur (diff)	55	35
2782		35s. Sozopol	65	45
2783		43s. Sozopol (diff)	75	65
2784		53s. Samokov	1·40	1·10

891 Anton Bezenshek

1979. Centenary of Bulgarian Stenography.
2785	**891**	2s. yellow and grey	20	10

892 Mountaineer

1979. 50th Anniv of Bulgarian Alpine Club.
2786	**892**	2s. multicoloured	20	10

893 Commemorative Inscription

1979. Centenary of Bulgarian Public Health Services.
2787	**893**	2s. black, silver & green	20	20

894 Rocket and Flowers

1979. 35th Anniv of Fatherland Front Government. Multicoloured.
2788		2s. Type **894**	10	10
2789		5s. Russian and Bulgarian flags	15	10
2790		13s. "35" in national colours	35	20

895 "IZOT–0250" Computer

1979. 35th Plovdiv Fair.
2791	**895**	2s. multicoloured	20	10

896 Games Emblem

1979. World University Games, Mexico.
2792	**896**	5s. red, yellow and blue	20	10

897 Footballer

1979. 50th Anniv of DFS Lokomotiv Football Team.
2793	**897**	2s. red and black	20	10

898 Lyuben Karavelov

1979. Death Centenary of Lyuben Karavelov (newspaper editor and President of Bulgarian Revolutionary Committee).
2794	**898**	2s. green and blue	20	10

894 Rocket and Flowers

899 Cross-country Skiing

1979. Winter Olympic Games, Lake Placid (1980).
2795	**899**	2s. red, purple and black	20	15
2796	-	13s. orange, blue & blk	35	20
2797	-	23s. turquoise, blue and black	65	35
2798	-	43s. purple, turq & blk	1·70	55
MS2799 68×77 mm. 1l. green, blue and black. Imperf			3·25	3·25

DESIGNS: 13s. Speed skating; 23s. Skiing; 43s. Luge; 1l. Skiing (different).

900 *Woman from Thrace*

1979. 80th Birth Anniv of Dechko Uzunov (artist). Multicoloured.
2800		12s. *Figure in Red*	35	15
2801		13s. Type **900**	35	20
2802		23s. *Composition II*	1·10	65

901 Canoeing (Canadian pairs)

1979. Olympic Games, Moscow (1980) (3rd issue). Water Sports. Multicoloured.
2803		2s. Type **901**	35	35
2804		13s. Swimming (freestyle)	65	55
2805		25s. Swimming (backstroke) (horiz)	1·10	75
2806		35s. Kayak (horiz)	1·40	1·10
2807		43s. Diving	1·90	1·30
2808		1l. Springboard diving	2·75	2·20
MS2809 64×88 mm. 2l. Water polo			9·75	9·75

902 Nikola Vaptsarov

1979. 70th Birth Anniv of Nikola Vaptsarov (writer).
2810	**902**	2s. pink and red	30	20

903 *Dawn in Plovdiv* (Ioan Leviev)

1979. History of Bulgaria. Paintings. Multicoloured.
2811		2s. *The First Socialists* (Boyan Petrov) (horiz)	20	15
2812		13s. *Dimitur Blagoev as Editor of "Rabotnik"* (Dimitur Gyvdzhenov) (horiz)	35	20
2813		25s. *Workers' Party March* (Stoyan Sotirov) (horiz)	75	45
2814		35s. Type **903**	1·10	85

904 Doves in a Girl's Hair

1979. New Year.
2815	**904**	13s. multicoloured	35	20

905 Shooting

1979. Olympic Games, Moscow (1980) (4th issue). Multicoloured.

2816	2s. Type **905**	35	25
2817	13s. Judo (horiz)	65	55
2818	25s. Wrestling (horiz)	1·10	85
2819	35s. Archery	1·40	1·10
2820	43s. Fencing (horiz)	1·90	1·20
2821	1l. Fencing (different)	2·75	2·20
MS2822	65×89 mm. 2l. Boxing	9·75	9·75

906 Procession with Relics of Saints

1979. Frescoes of Saints Cyril and Methodius in St. Clement's Basilica, Rome. Multicoloured.

2823	2s. Type **906**	20	15
2824	13s. Cyril and Methodius received by Pope Adrian II	30	20
2825	23s. Burial of Cyril the Philosopher	55	35
2826	25s. St. Cyril	75	45
2827	35s. St. Methodius	1·10	65

907 Television Screen showing Emblem

1979. 25th Anniv of Bulgarian Television.

2828	**907**	5s. blue and deep blue	30	20

908 Puppet of Krali Marko (national hero)

1980. 50th Anniv of International Puppet Theatre Organization (UNIMA).

2829	**908**	2s. multicoloured	20	10

909 Thracian Rider (3rd-cent votive tablet)

1980. Centenary of National Archaeological Museum, Sofia.

2830	**909**	2s. brown, gold & purple	20	10
2831	–	13s. brown, gold & grn	35	20

DESIGN: 13s. Grave stele of Deines (5th–6th cent).

910 Meeting of Lenin and Dimitrov (Aleksandur Poplilov)

1980. 110th Birth Anniv of Lenin.

2832	**910**	13s. multicoloured	35	20

911 Diagram of Blood Circulation and Lungs obscured by Smoke

1980. World Health Day. Anti-smoking Campaign.

2833	**911**	5s. multicoloured	20	10

912 Basketball

1980. Olympic Games, Moscow (5th issue). Multicoloured.

2834	2s. Type **912**	35	25
2835	13s. Football	65	55
2836	25s. Hockey	1·10	75
2837	35s. Cycling	1·40	1·10
2838	43s. Handball	1·90	1·30
2839	1l. Volleyball	2·75	2·20
MS2840	66×90 mm. 2s. Weightlifting	9·75	9·75

913 Emblem, Cosmonauts and Space Station

1980. "Intercosmos" Space Programme. Sheet 111×102 mm.

MS2841	**913** 50s. multicoloured	2·20	2·20

914 Penyo Penev

1980. 50th Birth Anniv of Penyo Penev (poet).

2842	**914**	5s. brown, red & turq	30	20

915 Penny Black

1980. "London 1980" International Stamp Exhibition.

2843	**915**	25s. black and red	1·10	75

916 Dimitur Khv. Chorbadzhuski-Chudomir (self-portrait)

1980. 90th Birth Anniv of Dimitur Khv. Chorbadzhusk-Chudomir (artist).

2844	**916**	5s. pink, brown & turq	20	10
2845	–	13s. black, blue & turq	35	35

DESIGN: 13s. "Our People".

917 Nikolai Gyaurov

1980. 50th Birth Anniv of Nikolai Gyaurov (opera singer).

2846	**917**	5s. yellow, brown & grn	30	20

918 Soviet Soldiers raising Flag on Berlin Reichstag

1980. 35th Anniv of "Victory in Europe" Day.

2847	**918**	5s. gold, brown & black	20	10
2848	–	13s. gold, brown & black	35	20

DESIGN: 13s. Soviet Army memorial, Berlin–Treptow.

919 Open Book and Sun

1980. 75th Anniv Bulgarian Teachers' Union.

2849	**919**	5s. purple and yellow	20	10

920 Stars representing Member Countries

1980. 25th Anniv of Warsaw Pact.

2850	**920**	13s. multicoloured	45	20

921 Greek Girl with Olympic Flame

1980. Olympic Games, Moscow (6th issue). Multicoloured.

2851	2s. Type **921**	35	25
2852	13s. Spartacus monument, Sandanski	65	55
2853	25s. Liberation monument, Sofia (detail)	1·10	85
2854	35s. Liberation monument, Plovdiv	1·40	1·00
2855	43s. Liberation monument, Shipka Pass	1·90	1·30
2856	1l. Liberation monument, Ruse	2·75	2·20
MS2857	66×92 mm. 2l. Athlete with Olympic flame, Moscow	9·75	9·75

922 Ballerina

1980. Tenth International Ballet Competition, Varna.

2858	**922**	13s. multicoloured	45	20

923 Europa Hotel, Sofia

1980. Hotels. Multicoloured.

2859	23s. Type **923**	55	35
2860	23s. Bulgaria Hotel, Burgas (vert)	55	35
2861	23s. Plovdiv Hotel, Plovdiv	55	35
2862	23s. Riga Hotel, Ruse (vert)	55	35
2863	23s. Varna Hotel, Prazhba	55	35

1980. Historic Ships (3rd series). As T **753**. Multicoloured.

2864	5s. Hansa kogge *Jesus of Lubeck*	20	15
2865	8s. Roman galley	30	15
2866	13s. Galleon *Eagle*	35	20
2867	23s. *Mayflower*	55	35
2868	35s. Maltese galleon	1·00	45
2869	53s. Galleon *Royal Louis*	1·50	1·10

924 Parachute Descent

1980. 15th World Parachute Championships, Kazanluk. Multicoloured.

2870	13s. Type **924**	35	20
2871	25s. Parachutist in free fall	75	35

925 Clown and Children

1980. First Anniv of "Banners for Peace" Children's Meeting. Multicoloured.

2872	3s. Type **925**	20	15
2873	5s. "Cosmonauts in Spaceship" (vert)	20	15
2874	8s. "Picnic"	20	15
2875	13s. "Children with Ices"	30	20
2876	25s. "Children with Cat" (vert)	45	35
2877	35s. "Crowd"	1·00	45
2878	43s. "Banners for Peace" monument (vert)	1·50	65

926 Assembly Emblem

1980. Assembly of Peoples' Parliament for Peace, Sofia.

2879	**926**	25s. multicoloured	55	45

927 Iordan Iovkov

1980. Birth Centenary of Iordan Iovkov (writer).

2880	**927**	5s. multicoloured	30	25

928 Yakovlev Yak-24 Helicopter, Missile Launcher and Tank

1980. Bulgarian Armed Forces. Multicoloured.

2881	3s. Type **928**		10	10

2882		5s. Mikoyan Gurevich MiG-21 bomber, radar antennae and missile transporter	20	15
2883		8s. Mil Mi-24 helicopter, missile boat and landing ship *Ropucha*	35	20

929 Computer

1980. 36th Plovdiv Fair.

2884	**929**	5s. multicoloured	20	10

930 *Virgin and Child with St. Anne*

1980. Paintings by Leonardo da Vinci. Multicoloured.

2885		5s. Type **930**	20	15
2886		8s. Angel (detail, *The Annunciation*)	20	15
2887		13s. Virgin (detail, *The Annunciation*)	35	20
2888		25s. *Adoration of the Kings* (detail)	65	45
2889		35s. *Woman with Ermine*	1·10	55
MS2890		57×80 mm. 50s. *Mona Lisa*. Imperf	1·60	1·60

1980. Air. Clocktowers (2nd series). As T **884**. Multicoloured.

2891		13s. Byala	35	20
2892		23s. Razgrad	45	35
2893		25s. Karnobat	55	45
2894		35s. Sevlievo	95	55
2895		53s. Berkovitsa	1·90	85

931 *Parodia saint-pieana*

1980. Cacti. Multicoloured.

2896		5s. Type **931**	20	15
2897		13s. *Echinopsis bridgesii*	35	20
2898		25s. *Echinocereus purpureus*	75	45
2899		35s. *Opuntia bispinosa*	1·10	85
2900		53s. *Mamillopsis senilis*	2·30	1·10

932 UN Building and Bulgarian Arms

1980. 25th Anniv of United Nations Membership. Sheet 64×86 mm.

MS2901	**932**	60s. multicoloured	4·25	4·25

933 Wild Horse

1980. Horses. Multicoloured.

2902		3s. Type **933**	20	35
2903		5s. Tarpan	20	35
2904		13s. Arabian	55	55
2905		23s. Anglo-Arabian	1·50	1·10
2906		35s. Draught horse	3·25	2·75

934 Vasil Stoin

1980. Birth Centenary of Vasil Stoin (collector of folk songs).

2907	**934**	5s. violet, yellow & gold	20	10

935 Armorial Lion

1980. New Year. 1300th Anniv of Bulgarian State. Multicoloured.

2908		5s. Type **935**	20	10
2909		13s. Dish and dates "681–1981"	35	15

936 Red Star

1980. 12th Bulgarian Communist Party Congress (1st issue).

2910	**936**	5s. yellow and red	20	10

See also Nos. 2920/2.

937 Cross-country Skier

1981. World Ski-racing Championship, Velingrad.

2911	**937**	43s. orange, blue & blk	1·10	65

938 Midland Hawthorn (*Crataegus oxpacantha*)

1981. Useful Plants. Multicoloured.

2912		3s. Type **938**	20	15
2913		5s. Perforate St. John's wort (*Hypericum perforatum*)	20	15
2914		13s. Elder (*Sambucus nigra*)	45	20
2915		25s. Dewberry (*Rubus caesius*)	85	35
2916		35s. Lime (*Tilia argentea*)	1·00	55
2917		43s. Dog rose (*Rosa canina*)	1·60	1·10

939 Skier

1981. Alpine Skiing World Championships, Borovets.

2918	**939**	43s. yellow, black & blue	1·10	65

940 Nuclear Traces

1981. 25th Anniv of Nuclear Research Institute, Dubna, U.S.S.R.

2919	**940**	13s. black and silver	35	15

941 "XII" formed from Flag

1981. 12th Bulgarian Communist Party Congress (2nd issue).

2920	**941**	5s. multicoloured	20	15
2921	-	13s. red, black and blue	35	20
2922	-	23s. red, black and blue	65	55
MS2923		68×86 mm. 50s. multicoloured	1·60	1·60

DESIGNS: 13s. Stars; 23s. Computer tape; 50s. Georgi Dimitrov and Dimitur Blagoev.

942 Palace of Culture

1981. Opening of Palace of Culture, Sofia.

2924	**942**	5s. dp green, grn & red	20	10

943 *Self-portrait*

1981. 170th Birth Anniv (1980) of Zakharu Zograf (artist). Multicoloured.

2925		5s. Type **943**	20	15
2926		13s. *Portrait of Khristionia Zografska*	45	20
2927		23s. *The Transfiguration* (icon from Preobrazhenie Monastery)	75	35
2928		25s. *Doomsday* (detail) (horiz)	95	55
2929		35s. *Doomsday* (detail – different) (horiz)	1·40	1·10

944 Squacco Heron

1981. Birds. Multicoloured.

2930		5s. Type **944**	20	15
2931		8s. Eurasian bittern	45	20
2932		13s. Cattle egret	65	35
2933		25s. Great egret	1·50	65
2934		53s. Black stork	2·75	1·60

945 Liner *Georgi Dimitrov*

1981. Centenary of Bulgarian Shipbuilding. Multicoloured.

2935		35s. Type **945**	95	35
2936		43s. Freighter *Petimata of RMS*	1·40	55
2937		53s. Tanker *Khan Asparuch*	1·90	85

946 Hofburg Palace, Vienna

1981. "WIPA 1981" International Stamp Exhibition, Vienna.

2938	**946**	35s. crimson, red & green	95	65

947 "XXXIV"

1981. 34th Bulgarian People's Agrarian Union Congress.

2939	**947**	5s. multicoloured	20	15
2940	-	8s. orange, black & blue	30	20
2941	-	13s. multicoloured	55	35

DESIGNS: 8s. Flags; 13s. Bulgarian Communist Party and Agrarian Union flags.

948 Wild Cat

1981. International Hunting Exhibition, Plovdiv.

2942	**948**	5s. stone, black & brown	20	15
2943	-	13s. black, brn & stone	45	20
2944	-	23s. brown, blk & orge	95	45
2945	-	25s. black, brown & mve	1·10	55
2946	-	35s. lt brown, blk & brn	1·50	65
2947	-	53s. brown, blk & grn	2·30	1·10
MS2948		78×103 mm. 1l. brown, black and green (52×42 mm)	3·25	3·25

DESIGNS: 13s. Wild boar; 23s. Mouflon; 25s. Chamois; 35s. Roebuck; 53s. Fallow deer; 1l. Red deer.

949 *Crafty Peter* (sculpture, Georgi Chapkanov)

1981. Festival of Humour and Satire, Gabrovo.

2949	**949**	5s. multicoloured	20	10

950 Bulgarian Arms and UNESCO Emblem

1981. 25th Anniv of UNESCO Membership.

2950	**950**	13s. multicoloured	35	20

951 Deutsche Flugzeugwerke D.F.W. C.V. Biplane

1981. Air. Aircraft. Multicoloured.

2951		5s. Type **951**	20	15
2952		12s. LAS-7 monoplane	30	15
2953		25s. LAS-8 monoplane	75	45
2954		35s. DAR-1 biplane	95	55
2955		45s. DAR-3 biplane	1·10	85
2956		55s. DAR-9 biplane	1·40	1·10

952 "Eye"

1981. Centenary of State Statistical Office.

2957	**952**	5s. multicoloured	20	10

953 Veliko Tirnovo Hotel

1981. Hotels.

2958	**953**	23s. multicoloured	55	35

954 *Flying Figure*

1981. 90th Anniv of First Bulgarian Social Democratic Party Congress, Buzludzha. Sculptures by Velichko Minekov.

2959	**954**	5s. blue and green	20	15
2960	-	13s. brown, blk & orge	35	20

DESIGN: 13s. *Advancing Female*.

955 Animal-shaped Dish

1981. Golden Treasure of Old St. Nicholas. Multicoloured.
2961		5s. Type **955**	20	15
2962		13s. Jug with decorated neck	35	20
2963		23s. Jug with loop pattern	55	45
2964		25s. Jug with bird pattern	75	55
2965		35s. Decorated vase	95	75
2966		53s. Decorated dish	1·90	1·30

956 Badge and Map of Bulgaria

1981. 35th Anniv of Frontier Guards.
2967	**956**	5s. multicoloured	20	10

957 Saints Cyril and Methodius
(9th century)

1981. 1300th Anniv of Bulgarian State.
2968	-	5s. green and grey	20	15
2969	**957**	5s. brown and yellow	20	15
2970	-	8s. violet and lilac	20	15
2971	-	12s. mauve and purple	30	15
2972	-	13s. purple and brown	35	15
2973	-	13s. green and black	35	15
2974	-	16s. green & deep green	45	20
2975	-	23s. black and blue	65	35
2976	-	25s. green and light green	75	45
2977	-	35s. brown and light brown	1·00	55
2978	-	41s. red and pink	1·20	65
2979	-	43s. red and pink	1·20	65
2980	-	53s. dp brown and brown	1·30	70
2981	-	55s. dp green and green	1·40	75

MS2982 Two sheets, each 83×74
mm. (a) 50s. grey and green; (b) 1l.
brown, black and brown 5·00 5·00

DESIGNS: No. 2968, Madara horsemen (8th century);
2970, Plan of Round Church at Veliki Preslav (10th century); 2971, Four Evangelists of King Ivan, 1356; 2972,
Column of Ivan Asen II (13th century); 2973, Manasiev
Chronicle (14th century); 2974, Rising of April 1876; 2975,
Arrival of Russian liberation troops; 2976, Foundation ceremony of Bulgarian Social Democratic Party, 1891; 2977,
Rising of September 1923; 2978, Formation of Fatherland
Front Government, 9 September 1944; 2979, Bulgarian
Communist Party Congress, 1948; 50s. Bas-relief of lion at
Stara Zagora (10th century); 2980, 10th Communist Party
Congress, 1971; 2981, Kremikovski metallurgical combine;
1l. Leonid Brezhnev and Todor Yovkov.

958 Volleyball
Players

1981. European Volleyball Championships.
2983	**958**	13s. red, blue and black	35	20

959 Pegasus
(bronze sculpture)

1981. Day of the Word.
2984	**959**	5s. green	20	10

960 Loaf of Bread

1981. World Food Day.
2985	**960**	13s. brown, black & grn	35	20

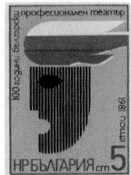

961 Mask

1981. Cent of Bulgarian Professional Theatre.
2986	**961**	5s. multicoloured	20	15

962 Examples of Bulgarian
Art

1981. Cultural Heritage Day.
2987	**962**	13s. green and brown	95	20

963 Footballer

1981. World Cup Football Championship, Spain (1982).
Multicoloured.
2988		5s. Type **963**	20	15
2989		13s. Heading ball	30	20
2990		43s. Saving a goal	95	65
2991		53s. Running with ball	1·10	1·00

964 Dove encircled by
Barbed Wire

1981. Anti-apartheid Campaign.
2992	**964**	5s. red, black and yellow	20	10

1981. 13th Bulgarian Philatelic Federation Congress.
Sheet 51×72 mm containing design as T **962** but
inscr "XIII KONGRES NA SBF SOFIYA" at foot.
MS2993 60s. blue and red 9·25 8·25

965 Mother (Lilyann
Ruseva)

1981. 35th Anniv of UNICEF. Various designs showing
mother and child paintings by named artists.
Multicoloured.
2994		53s. Type **965**	1·70	55
2995		53s. *Bulgarian Madonna* (Vasil Stoilov)	1·70	55
2996		53s. *Village Madonna* (Ivan Milev)	1·70	55
2997		53s. *Mother* (Vladimir Dimitrov)	1·70	55

966 8th Century Ceramic
from Pliska

1981. New Year. Multicoloured.
2998		5s. Armorial lion	20	10
2999		13s. Type **966**	35	15

967 Bagpipes

1982. Musical Instruments. Multicoloured.
3000		13s. Type **967**	30	20
3001		25s. Single and double flutes	55	25
3002		30s. Rebec	65	35
3003		35s. Flute and pipe	75	45
3004		44s. Mandolin	1·50	55

968 Open Book

1982. 125th Anniv of Public Libraries.
3005	**968**	5s. green	20	10

969 *Sofia Plains*

1982. Birth Centenary of Nikola Petrov (artist).
3006		5s. Type **969**	20	15
3007		13s. *Girl Embroidering*	35	20
3008		30s. *Fields of Peshtera*	1·00	55

970 Womans' Head
and Dove

1982. International Decade for Women. Sheet 66×76 mm.
MS3009 **970** 1l. multicoloured 2·75 2·75

971 Peasant Woman

1982. Birth Centenary of Valadimir Dimitrov (artist).
Multicoloured.
3010		5s. Figures in a landscape (horiz)	20	15
3011		8s. Town and harbour (horiz)	20	15
3012		13s. Town scene (horiz)	45	20
3013		25s. *Reapers*	55	35
3014		30s. Woman and child	65	45
3015		35s. Type **971**	95	50

MS3016 65×58 mm. 50s. *Self-portrait*
(horiz) 1·60 1·60

972 Georgi Dimitrov

1982. Ninth Bulgarian Trade Unions Congress, Sofia.
3017	**972**	5s. lt brn, dp brn & brn	10	10
3018	-	5s. brown and blue	20	10

DESIGN: No. 3018, Palace of Culture, Sofia.

973 Summer
Snowflake

1982. Medicinal Plants. Multicoloured.
3019		3s. Type **973**	20	15
3020		5s. Chicory	20	15
3021		8s. Rosebay willowherb	30	15
3022		13s. Solomon's seal	45	20
3023		25s. Sweet violet	85	35
3024		35s. *Ficaria verna*	1·40	55

974 Russian Space Station

1982. 25th Anniv of First Soviet Artificial Satellite.
3025	**974**	13s. multicoloured	35	20

975 Georgi Dimitrov

1982. "Sozphilex '82" Stamp Exhibition, Veliko, Tirnovo.
Sheet 61×82 mm.
MS3026 **975** 50s. red and black 3·25 3·25

976 Dimitrov and Congress
Emblem

1982. 14th Dimitrov Communist Youth League Congress,
Sofia.
3027	**976**	5s. blue, red & yellow	20	10

977 First French and Bulgarian
Stamps

1982. "Philexfrance '82" International Stamp Exhibition,
Paris.
3028	**977**	42s. multicoloured	95	55

978 Abstract with Birds

1982. Alafrangi Frescoes from 19th-century Houses.
3029	**978**	5s. multicoloured	20	15
3030	-	13s. multicoloured	30	20
3031	-	25s. multicoloured	45	35
3032	-	30s. multicoloured	55	45
3033	-	42s. multicoloured	95	55
3034	-	60s. multicoloured	1·90	65

DESIGNS: 13s. to 60s. Various flower and bird patterns.

During 1982 sets were issued for World Cup Football Championship, Spain (5, 13, 30s.), Tenth Anniv of First European Security and Co-operation Conference (5, 13, 25, 30s.), World Cup Results (5, 13, 30s.) and 10th Anniv (1983) of European Security and Co-operation Conference, Helsinki (5, 13, 25, 30s.). Supplies and distribution of these stamps were restricted and it is understood they were not available at face value.

979 Georgi Dimitrov

1982. Birth Centenary of Georgi Dimitrov (statesman). Sheet 76×52 mm.
MS3035 **979** 50s. multicoloured 1·60 1·60

980 Georgi Dimitrov

1982. Ninth Fatherland Front Congress, Sofia.
3036 **980** 5s. multicoloured 20 10

981 Airplane

1982. 35th Anniv of Balkanair (state airline).
3037 **981** 42s. blue, green & red 1·00 65

982 Atomic Bomb Mushroom-cloud

1982. Nuclear Disarmament Campaign.
3038 **982** 13s. multicoloured 45 20

983 Lyudmila Zhivkova

1982. 40th Birth Anniv of Lyudmila Zhivkova (founder of "Banners for Peace" Children's Meetings).
3039 **983** 5s. multicoloured 20 10
3040 **983** 13s. multicoloured 35 15
MS3041 62×67 mm. **983** 1l. multi-
coloured 2·20 2·20

984 Emblem

1982. Tenth Anniv of U.N. Environment Programme.
3042 **984** 13s. green and blue 35 20

985 Wave Pattern

1982. Fifth Bulgarian Painters' Association Congress.
3043 **985** 5s. multicoloured 25 20

986 Child Musicians

1982. Second "Banners for Peace" Children's Meeting (1st issue). Children's Paintings. Multicoloured.
3044 **986** 3s. Type **986** 10 10
3045 5s. Children skating 20 10
3046 8s. Adults, children and flowers 30 15
3047 13s. Children with flags 35 20
MS3048 70×110 mm. 50s. Children in "Sun" balloon (vert) 2·20 2·20
See also Nos. 3057/MS3063.

987 Moscow Park Hotel, Sofia

1982. Hotels. Multicoloured.
3049 32s. Type **987** 85 45
3050 32s. Black Sea Hotel, Varna 85 45

988 Cruiser "Aurora" and Satellite

1982. 65th Anniv of Russian October Revolution.
3051 **988** 13s. red and blue 35 25

989 Hammer and Sickle

1982. 60th Anniv of U.S.S.R.
3052 **989** 13s. red, gold & violet 35 20

990 The Piano

1982. Birth Cent of Pablo Picasso (artist). Multicoloured.
3053 13s. Type **990** 45 25
3054 30s. Portrait of Jacqueline 65 55
3055 42s. Maternity 1·40 85
MS3056 61×79 mm. 1l. Self-portrait 2·75 2·75

991 Boy and Girl

1982. Second "Banners for Peace" Children's Meeting (2nd issue). Multicoloured.
3057 **991** 3s. Type **991** 20 15
3058 5s. Market place 20 15
3059 8s. Children in fancy dress (vert) 20 15
3060 13s. Chickens (vert) 35 20
3061 25s. Interlocking heads 75 35
3062 30s. Lion 85 45
MS3063 70×109 mm. 50s. Boy and girl in garden (vert). Perf or imperf 2·20 2·20

992 Lions

1982. New Year. Multicoloured.
3064 5s. Type **992** 20 10
3065 13s. Decorated letters 35 15

993 Broadcasting Tower

1982. 60th Anniv of Avram Stoyanov Broadcasting Institute.
3066 **993** 5s. blue 20 15

994 Dr. Robert Koch

1982. Cent of Discovery of Tubercle Bacillus.
3067 **994** 25s. brown and green 65 35

995 Simon Bolivar

1982. Birth Anniversaries.
3068 **995** 30s. green and grey 75 45
3069 - 30s. yellow and brown 75 45
DESIGN: No. 3068, Type **995** (bicent); 3069, Rabindranath Tagore (philosopher, 120th anniv).

996 Vasil Levski

1983. 110th Death Anniv of Vasil Levski (revolutionary).
3070 **996** 5s. brown & green 20 10

997 Skier

1983. "Universiade 83" University Games, Sofia.
3071 **997** 30s. multicoloured 75 45

998 Northern Pike

1983. Freshwater Fishes. Multicoloured.
3072 3s. Type **998** 20 15
3073 5s. Beluga sturgeon 20 15
3074 13s. Chub 35 20
3075 25s. Zander 75 35
3076 30s. Wels 85 45
3077 42s. Brown trout 2·40 55

999 Karl Marx

1983. Death Centenary of Karl Marx.
3078 **999** 13s. red, purple & yellow 45 20

1000 Hasek and Illustrations from The Good Soldier Schweik

1983. Birth Centenary of Jaroslav Hasek (Czech writer).
3079 **1000** 13s. brown, grey & grn 35 20

1001 Martin Luther

1983. 500th Birth Anniv of Martin Luther (Protestant reformer).
3080 **1001** 13s. grey, black & brn 45 20

1002 Figures forming Initials

1983. 55th Anniv of Young Workers' Union.
3081 **1002** 5s. red, black & orange 20 15

1003 Khaskovo Costume

1983. Folk Costumes. Multicoloured.
3082 5s. Type **1003** 25 15
3083 8s. Pernik 30 15
3084 13s. Burgas 35 20
3085 25s. Tolbukhin 75 35
3086 30s. Blagoevgrad 85 45
3087 42s. Topolovgrad 2·40 55

1004 Old Man feeding a Chicken

1983. Sixth International Festival of Humour and Satire, Gabrovo.
3088 **1004** 5s. multicoloured 20 10

During 1983 sets were issued for European Security and Co-operation Conference, Budapest (5, 13, 25, 30s.), Olympic Games, Los Angeles (5, 13, 30, 42s.), Winter Olympic Games, Sarajevo (horiz designs, 5, 13, 30, 42s.) and European Security and Co-operation Conference, Madrid (5, 13, 30, 42s.). Supplies and distribution of these stamps were restricted, and it is understood they were not available at face value.

1005 Smirnenski

1983. 85th Birth Anniv of Khristo Smirnenski (poet).
3089 **1005** 5s. red, brown & yellow 20 20

1006 Emblem

1983. 17th Int Geodesy Federation Congress.
3090 **1006** 30s. green, blue & yell 65 45

1007 Stylized Houses

1983. "Interarch 83" World Architecture Biennale, Sofia.
3091 **1007** 30s. multicoloured 75 45

1008 Staunton
Chessmen on Map
of Europe

1983. Eighth European Chess Team Championship,
Plovdiv.
3092 **1008** 13s. multicoloured 45 20

1009 Brazilian and Bulgarian
Football Stamps

1983. "Brasiliana 83" International Stamp Exhibition, Rio
de Janeiro. Sheet 73×103 mm.
MS3093 **1009** 1l. green, brown and
gold 2·75 2·75

1010 Valentina
Tereshkova

1983. Air. 20th Anniv of First Woman in Space. Sheet
121×75 mm containing T **1010** and similar vert
design, each blue and brown.
MS3094 50s. Type **1010**; 50s. Svetlana
Savitskaya, 1982, cosmonaut 3·25 3·25

1011 Television
Mast, Tolbukhin

1983. Air. World Communications Year.
3095 **1011** 5s. blue and red 20 15
3096 – 13s. mauve and red 35 20
3097 – 30s. yellow and red 55 35
DESIGNS: 13s. Postwoman; 30s. Radio tower, Mount
Botev.

1012 Lenin addressing
Congress

1983. 80th Anniv of Second Russian Social Democratic
Workers' Party Congress.
3098 **1012** 5s. pur, dp pur & yell 20 10

1013 Pistol and Dagger on
Book

1983. 80th Anniv of Ilinden-Preobrazhenie Rising.
3099 **1013** 5s. yellow and green 20 10

1014 Crystals and
Hammers within
Gearwheels

1983. 30th Anniv of Mining and Geology Institute, Sofia.
3100 **1014** 5s. grey, purple & blue 20 10

1015 Georgi Dimitrov and
Revolution Scenes

1983. 60th Anniv of September Uprising. Multicoloured.
3101 5s. Type **1015** 20 10
3102 13s. Wreath and revolution
scenes 35 15

1016 Animated
Drawings

1983. Third Animated Film Festival, Varna.
3103 **1016** 5s. multicoloured 20 10

1017 Angora

1983. Cats. Multicoloured.
3104 5s. Type **1017** 25 20
3105 13s. Siamese 45 20
3106 20s. Abyssinian (vert) 65 35
3107 25s. European 95 45
3108 30s. Persian (vert) 1·10 65
3109 42s. Khmer 1·90 1·10

1018 Richard Trevithick's
Locomotive, 1803

1983. Locomotives (1st series). Multicoloured.
3110 5s. Type **1018** 20 10
3111 13s. John Blenkinsop's rack
locomotive *Prince Royal*, 1810 45 35
3112 42s. William Hedley's *Puffing
Billy*, 1813–14 2·00 1·10
3113 60s. Stephenson locomotive
Adler, 1835, Germany 3·25 1·60
See also Nos. 3159/63.

1019 Liberation
Monument, Plovdiv

1983. 90th Anniv of Bulgarian Philatelic Federation and
Fourth National Stamp Exhibition, Plovdiv. Sheet
65×79 mm.
MS3114 **1019** 50s. grey, blue and red 1·60 1·60

1020 Mask and
Laurel as Lyre

1983. 75th Anniv of National Opera, Sofia.
3115 **1020** 5s. red, black & gold 20 10

1021 Ioan
Kukuzel

1983. Bulgarian Composers.
3116 **1021** 5s. yellow, brown & grn 20 15
3117 – 8s. yellow, brown & red 20 15
3118 – 13s. yellow, brown and
green 30 20
3119 – 20s. yellow, brown & bl 35 25
3120 – 25s. yellow, brn & grey 45 35
3121 – 30s. yell, dp brn & brn 55 45
DESIGNS: 8s. Georgi Atanasov; 13s. Petko Stainov; 20s.
Veselin Stoyanov; 25s. Lyubomir Pipkov; 30s. Pancho Vla-
digerov.

1022 Snowflake

1983. New Year.
3122 **1022** 5s. green, blue & gold 20 10

1023 *Angelo Donni*

1983. 500th Birth Anniv of Raphael (artist). Multicoloured.
3123 5s. Type **1023** 20 15
3124 13s. *Portrait of a Cardinal* 35 20
3125 30s. *Baldassare Castiglioni* 45 45
3126 42s. *Woman with a Veil* 95 55
MS3127 59×98 mm. 1l. *Sistine
Madonna* 2·40 2·40

1024 Eurasian Common Shrew

1983. Protected Mammals. Multicoloured.
3128 12s. Type **1024** 45 35
3129 13s. Greater horseshoe bat 65 35
3130 20s. Common long-eared bat 1·00 45
3131 30s. Forest dormouse 1·60 65
3132 42s. Fat dormouse 3·25 1·10

1025 Karavelov

1984. 150th Birth Anniv of Lyuben Karavelov (poet).
3133 **1025** 5s. blue, bistre & brn 20 10

During 1984 sets were issued for European Confi-
dence- and Security-building Measures and Disarma-
ment Conference, Stockholm (5, 13, 30, 42s.) and Winter
Olympic Games, Sarajevo (vert designs, 5, 13, 30, 42s.).
Supplies and distribution of these stamps were restricted
and it is understood that they were not available at face
value.

1026 Mendeleev and
Formulae

1984. 150th Birth Anniv of Dmitry Mendeleev (chemist).
3134 **1026** 13s. multicoloured 35 20

1027 Bulk Carrier *Gen. Vl.
Zaimov*

1984. Ships. Multicoloured.
3135 5s. Type **1027** 20 10
3136 13s. Tanker *Mesta* 35 15
3137 25s. Tanker *Veleka* 65 35
3138 32s. Train ferry *Geroite na Odesa* 80 45
3139 42s. Bulk carrier *Rozhen* 1·40 55

1028 World Cup Stamps

1984. "Espana 84" International Stamp Exhibition, Madrid.
Sheet 89×110 mm.
MS3140 **1028** 2l. multicoloured 8·25 8·25

1029 Pigeon with
Letter over Globe

1984. "Mladost '84" Youth Stamp Exhibition, Pleven (1st
issue).
3141 **1029** 5s. multicoloured 20 10
See also Nos. 3171/2.

1030 Wild Cherries

1984. Fruits. Multicoloured.
3142 5s. Type **1030** 20 15
3143 8s. Wild strawberries 20 15
3144 13s. Dewberries 35 20
3145 20s. Raspberries 55 55
3146 42s. Medlars 1·70 55

1031 Vitosha Conference (K.
Buyukliiski and P. Petrov)

1984. 60th Anniv of Bulgarian Communist Party
Conference, Vitosha.
3147 **1031** 5s. purple, brn & red 20 10

1032 Security Conference 1980

1984. Fifth International Stamp Fair, Essen. Sheet 94×147 mm containing T **1032** and similar horiz design. Multicoloured.

MS3148 1l.50, Type **1032**; 1l.50, Security Conference 35s. stamp 8·75 8·75

1033 Athletes and Doves

1984. Sixth Republican Spartakiad.
3149 **1033** 13s. multicoloured 35 20

1034 Mt. Everest

1984. Bulgarian Expedition to Mt. Everest.
3150 **1034** 5s. multicoloured 20 10

1035 Kogge

1984. Universal Postal Union Congress Philatelic Salon, Hamburg. Sheet 100×107 mm.
MS3151 **1035** 3l. multicoloured 7·50 7·50

1036 Drummer

1984. Sixth Amateur Performers Festival.
3152 **1036** 5s. multicoloured 20 10

1037 Seal

1984. 50 Years of Bulgarian–U.S.S.R. Diplomatic Relations.
3153 **1037** 13s. multicoloured 35 20

1038 Feral Rock Pigeon

1984. Pigeons and Doves. Multicoloured.
3154 **1038** 5s. Type **1038** 20 10
3155 13s. Stock pigeon 35 20
3156 20s. Wood pigeon 55 35
3157 30s. Turtle dove 95 45
3158 42s. Domestic pigeon 1·20 55

1984. Locomotives (2nd series). As T **1018**. Multicoloured.
3159 13s. *Best Friend of Charleston*, 1830, U.S.A. 35 20
3160 25s. *Saxonia*, 1836, Saxony 65 35
3161 30s. *Lafayette*, 1837, U.S.A. 85 45

3162 42s. *Borsig*, 1841, Germany 1·20 60
3163 60s. *Philadelphia*, 1843, U.S.A. 2·00 85

1039 Production Quality Emblem

1984. 40th Anniv of Fatherland Front Government.
3164 **1039** 5s. red, lt green & green 20 15
3165 20s. red and violet 55 25
3166 30s. red and blue 85 45
DESIGNS: 20s. Monument to Soviet Army, Sofia; 30s. Figure nine and star.

1040 *Boy with Harmonica*

1984. Paintings by Nenko Balkanski. Multicoloured.
3167 **1040** 5s. Type **1040** 20 15
3168 30s. *Window in Paris* 85 45
3169 42s. *Portrait of Two Women* (horiz) 1·60 55
MS3170 65×110 mm. 1l. *Self-portrait* 2·75 2·75

1041 Mausoleum of Russian Soldiers

1984. "Mladost '84" Youth Stamp Exhibition, Pleven (2nd issue).
3171 **1041** 5s. multicoloured 20 10
3172 13s. black, grn & red 35 15
DESIGN: 13s. Panorama building.

1042 Pioneers saluting

1984. 40th Anniv of Dimitrov Septembrist Pioneers Organization.
3173 **1042** 5s. multicoloured 20 10

1043 Vaptsarov (after D. Nikolov)

1984. 75th Birth Anniv of Nikola I. Vaptsarov (poet).
3174 **1043** 5s. yellow and red 20 10

1044 Goalkeeper saving Goal

1984. 75th Anniv of Bulgarian Football.
3175 **1044** 42s. multicoloured 95 55

1045 Profiles

1984. "Miadost '84" Youth Stamp Exhibition, Pleven (3rd issue). Sheet 50×76 mm.
MS3176 **1045** 50s. multicoloured 1·60 1·60

1046 Devil's Bridge, R. Arda

1984. Bridges. Multicoloured.
3177 5s. Type **1046** 30 20
3178 13s. Kolo Ficheto Bridge, Byala 55 45
3179 30s. Asparukhov Bridge, Varna 95 85
3180 42s. Bebresh Bridge, Botevgrad 2·00 1·50

1047 Olympic Emblem

1984. 90th Anniv of International Olympic Committee.
3181 **1047** 13s. multicoloured 35 20

1048 Moon and "Luna I", "II" and "III"

1984. 25th Anniv of First Moon Rocket. Sheet 79×57 mm.
MS3182 **1048** 1l. multicoloured 3·25 3·25

1049 Dalmatian Pelican with Chicks

1984. Wildlife Protection. Dalmatian Pelican.
3183 **1049** 5s. multicoloured 45 20
3184 13s. lav, blk & brn 95 45
3185 20s. multicoloured 1·40 1·10
3186 32s. multicoloured 3·25 1·60
DESIGNS: 13s. Two pelicans; 20s. Pelican on water; 32s. Pelican in flight.

1050 Anton Ivanov

1984. Birth Cent of Anton Ivanov (revolutionary).
3187 **1050** 5s. yell, brn & red 20 10

1051 Girl's Profile with Text as Hair

1984. 70th Anniv of Bulgarian Women's Socialist Movement.
3188 **1051** 5s. multicoloured 20 10

1052 Snezhanka Television Tower

1984. Television Towers.
3189 **1052** 5s. blue, green & mve 20 15
3190 1l. brown, mauve & bis 2·30 1·10
DESIGN: 1l. Orelek television tower.

1053 Birds and Posthorns

1984. New Year. Multicoloured.
3191 5s. Type **1053** 20 10
3192 13s. Decorative pattern 35 15

1054 *September Nights*

1984. 80th Birth Anniv of Stoyan Venev (artist). Multicoloured.
3193 5s. Type **1054** 20 15
3194 30s. *Man with Three Orders* 85 45
3195 42s. *The Hero* 1·40 55

1055 Peacock (butterfly)

1984. Butterflies. Multicoloured.
3196 13s. Type **1055** 35 20
3197 25s. Swallowtail 65 35
3198 30s. Great banded grayling 85 45
3199 42s. Orange-tip 1·20 55
3200 60s. Red admiral 2·00 75
MS3201 75×60 mm. 1l. Poplar admiral (*Limenitis populi*) 2·75 2·75

1056 Augusto Sandino

1984. 50th Death Anniv of Augusto Sandino (Nicaraguan revolutionary).
3202 **1056** 13s. black, red & yell 35 20

1057 Tupolev Tu-154 Jetliner

1984. 40th Anniv of ICAO.
3203 **1057** 42s. multicoloured 95 55

1058 *The Three Graces* (detail)

1984. 500th Birth Anniv (1983) of Raphael (artist) (2nd issue). Multicoloured.
3204 5s. Type **1058** 25 20

3205	13s.	Cupid and the Three Graces (detail)	30	25
3206	30s.	Original Sin (detail)	65	45
3207	42s.	La Fornarina	1·30	50
MS3208 106×95 mm. 1l. Galatea (detail)			2·50	2·50

1059 Sofia

1984. Maiden Voyage of Danube Cruise Ship Sofia.

3209	**1059**	13s. dp blue, blue & yell	35	20

1060 Eastern Hog-nosed Skunk

1985. Mammals.

3210	**1060**	13s. black, blue & orge	30	15
3211	-	25s. black, brown & grn	65	35
3212	-	30s. black, brown & yell	75	40
3213	-	42s. multicoloured	1·10	55
3214	-	60s. multicoloured	1·90	85

DESIGNS: 25s. Banded linsang; 30s. Zorilla; 42s. Banded palm civet; 60s. Broad-striped galidia.

1061 Nikolai Liliev

1985. Birth Centenary of Nikolai Liliev (poet).

3215	**1061**	30s. lt brn, brn & gold	65	45

1062 Tsvyatko Radoinov

1985. 90th Birth Anniv of Tsvyatko Radoinov (resistance fighter).

3216	**1062**	5s. brown and red	20	10

1063 Asen Zlatarov

1985. Birth Cent. of Asen Zlatarov (biochemist).

3217	**1063**	5s. purple, yellow & grn	20	10

1064 Research Ship Akademik

1985. 13th General Assembley and 125th Anniv of Intergovernmental Oceanographic Commission. Sheet 90×60 mm.

MS3218 **1064** 80s. multicoloured			2·20	2·20

1065 Lenin Monument, Sofia

1985. 115th Birth Anniv of Lenin. Sheet 55×87 mm.

MS3219 **1065** 50s. multicoloured			1·30	1·30

1066 Olive Branch and Sword Blade

1985. 30th Anniv of Warsaw Pact.

3220	**1066**	13s. multicoloured	30	20

1067 Bach

1985. Composers.

3221	**1067**	42s. blue and red	1·40	65
3222	-	42s. violet and green	1·40	65
3223	-	42s. yellow, brn & orge	1·40	65
3224	-	42s. yellow, brn & red	1·40	65
3225	-	42s. yellow, grn & blue	1·40	65
3226	-	42s. yellow, red & grn	1·40	65

DESIGNS: No. 3222, Mozart; 3223, Tchaikovsky; 3224, Modest Petrovich Musorgsky; 3225, Giuseppe Verdi; 3226, Filip Kutev.

1068 Girl with Birds

1985. Third "Banners for Peace" Children's Meeting, Sofia. Multicoloured.

3227	**1068**	5s. Type **1068**	20	15
3228		8s. Children painting	20	15
3229		13s. Girl among flowers	30	20
3230		20s. Children at market stall	45	25
3231		25s. Circle of children	55	35
3232		30s. Nurse	65	45
MS3233 70×110 mm. 50st. Children dancing (vert). Perf or imperf			2·20	2·20

1069 St. Methodius

1985. 1100th Death Anniv of St. Methodius.

3234	**1069**	13s. multicoloured	65	35

1070 Soldiers and Nazi Flags

1985. 40th Anniv of V.E. ("Victory in Europe") Day. Multicoloured.

3235		5s. Type **1070**	20	15
3236		13s. 11th Infantry parade, Sofia	35	25
3237		30s. Soviet soldier with orphan	75	35
MS3238 90×123 mm. 50s. Soldier raising Soviet flag			1·60	1·60

1071 Woman carrying Child and Man on Donkey

1985. Seventh International Festival of Humour and Satire, Gabrovo.

3239	**1071**	13s. black, yell & red	30	20

1072 Profiles and Flowers

1985. International Youth Year.

3240	**1072**	13s. multicoloured	30	20

1073 Ivan Vazov

1985. 135th Birth Anniv of Ivan Vazov (poet).

3241	**1073**	5s. brown and stone	20	10

1074 Monument to Unknown Soldiers and City Arms

1985. Millenary of Khaskovo.

3242	**1074**	5s. multicoloured	20	10

1075 Festival Emblem

1985. 12th World Youth and Students' Festival, Moscow.

3243	**1075**	13s. multicoloured	30	20

1076 Indira Gandhi

1985. Indira Gandhi (Indian Prime Minister) Commemoration.

3244	**1076**	30s. brown, orge & yell	65	35

1077 Vasil E. Aprilov (founder)

1985. 150th Anniv of New Bulgarian School, Gabrovo.

3245	**1077**	5s. blue, purple & grn	20	10

1078 Congress Emblem

1985. 36th International Shorthand and Typing Federation Congress ("Intersteno"), Sofia.

3246	**1078**	13s. multicoloured	30	20

1079 Alexandr Nevski Cathedral, Sofia

1985. Sixth General Assembly of World Tourism Organization, Sofia.

3247	**1079**	42s. green, blue & orge	95	55

1080 State Arms and UN Flag

1985. 40th Anniv of UNO (3248) and 30th Anniv of Bulgaria's Membership (3249). Multicoloured.

3248		13s. Dove around UN emblem	30	20
3249		13s. Type **1080**	30	20

1081 Rosa "Trakijka"

1985. Roses. Multicoloured.

3250		5s. "Rosa damascena"	20	15
3251		13s. Type **1081**	30	20
3252		20s. "Radiman"	45	25
3253		30s. "Marista"	55	35
3254		42s. "Valentina"	95	45
3255		60s. "Maria"	1·40	55

1082 Peace Dove

1985. Tenth Anniv of European Security and Co-operation Conference, Helsinki.

3256	**1082**	13s. multicoloured	30	20

1083 Water Polo

1985. European Swimming Championships, Sofia. Multicoloured.

3257		5s. Butterfly stroke (horiz)	20	15
3258		13s. Type **1083**	30	20
3259		42s. Diving	1·10	55
3260		60s. Synchronized swimming (horiz)	1·90	75

1084 Edelweiss

1985. 90th Anniv of Bulgarian Tourist Organization.

3261	**1084**	5s. multicoloured	20	10

1085 State Arms

1985. Cent of Union of E. Roumelia and Bulgaria.

3262	**1085**	5s. black, orge & green	20	10

1086 Footballers

1985. World Cup Football Championship, Mexico (1986) (1st issue).

3263	**1086**	5s. multicoloured	20	15
3264	-	13s. multicoloured	30	20
3265	-	30s. multicoloured	65	45
3266	-	42s. multicoloured	1·40	55

MS3267 54×76 mm. 1l. multicoloured (horiz) 2·30 2·30

DESIGNS: 13s. to 1l. Various footballers.
See also Nos. 3346/**MS**3352.

1087 Computer Picture of Boy

1985. International Young Inventors' Exhibition, Plovdiv. Multicoloured.

3268	5s. Type **1087**	20	15	
3269	13s. Computer picture of youth	30	20	
3270	30s. Computer picture of cosmonaut	75	35	

1088 St. John's Church, Nesebur

1985. 40th Anniv of UNESCO. Multicoloured.

3271	**1088**	5s. Type **1088**	20	15
3272		13s. Rila Monastery	30	20
3273		35s. Soldier (fresco, Ivanovo Rock Church)	95	45
3274		42s. Archangel Gabriel (fresco, Boyana Church)	1·10	55
3275		60s. Thracian woman (fresco, Kazanlak tomb)	1·90	75

MS3276 100×83 mm. 1l. Madara horseman (horiz). Imperf 2·20 2·20

1089 Lyudmila Zhivkova Palace of Culture

1985. 23rd United Nations Educational, Scientific and Cultural Organization General Session, Sofia. Sheet 62×95 mm.
MS3277 **1089** 1l. multicoloured 2·20 2·20

1090 Colosseum, Rome

1985. "Italia '85" International Stamp Exhibition, Rome.
3278 **1090** 42s. multicoloured 95 55

1091 "Gladiolus"

1985. Flowers.

3279	**1091**	5s. pink and red	20	15
3280	-	5s. blue and light blue	20	15
3281	-	5s. lt violet & violet	20	15
3282	-	8s. light blue and blue	20	15
3283	-	8s. orange and red	20	15
3284	-	32s. orange and brown	45	55

DESIGNS: No. 3280, Garden iris; 3281, Dwarf morning glory; 3282, Morning glory; 3283, *Anemone coronaria*; 3284, Golden-rayed lily.

1092 St. Methodius

1985. Cultural Congress of European Security and Co-operation Conference, Budapest. Sheet 105×93 mm containing T **1092** and similar vert designs. Multicoloured.
MS3285 50s. St. Cyril; 50s. Map of Europe; 50s. Type **1092** 4·25 4·25

1985. Historic Ships (4th series). As T **753**. Multicoloured.

3286	5s. 17th-century Dutch fly	20	10
3287	12s. *Sovereign of the Seas* (English galleon)	30	15
3288	20s. Mediterranean polacca	45	20
3289	25s. *Prince Royal* (English warship)	55	35
3290	42s. Xebec	1·00	65
3291	60s. 17th-century English warship	1·90	75

1093 Cologne Cathedral

1985. "Philatelia '85" International Stamp Exhibition, Cologne. Sheet 109×56 mm containing T **1093** and similar vert design, each black, blue and red.
MS3292 30s. Type **1093**; 30s. Alexandr Nevski Cathedral, Sofia 1·60 1·60

1094 Bacho Kiro

1985. Revolutionaries.

3293	**1094**	5s. light brown, brown and blue	20	10
3294	-	5s. green, purple & brown	20	10

DESIGN: No. 3294, Georgi S. Rakovski.

1095 Hands, Sword and Bible

1985. 150th Anniv of Turnovo Uprising.
3295 **1095** 13s. brown, blue & pur 30 20

1096 *1185 Revolution* (G. Bogdanov)

1985. 800th Anniv of Liberation from Byzantine Empire. Multicoloured.

3296	5s. Type **1096**	20	15
3297	13s. *1185 Revolution* (Al. Terziev)	35	20
3298	30s. *Battle of Klakotnitsa, 1230* (B. Grigorov and M. Ganovski)	45	35
3299	42s. *Veliko Turnovo* (Ts. Lavrenov)	1·40	55

MS3300 74×80 mm. 1l. Church of St. Dimitrius, Veliko Turnovo (38×28 mm). Imperf 2·20 2·20

1097 Emblem

1985. "Bralkanfila '85" Stamp Exhibition, Vratsa. Sheet 55×80 mm.
MS3301 **1097** 40s. blue, black and deep blue 1·10 1·10

1098 Emblem and Globe

1985. International Development Programme for Posts and Telecommunications.
3302 **1098** 13s. multicoloured 30 20

1099 Popov

1985. 70th Birth Anniv of Anton Popov (revolutionary).
3303 **1099** 5s. red 20 10

1100 Doves around Snowflake

1985. New Year. Multicoloured.

3304	**1100**	5s. Type **1100**	20	10
3305		13s. Circle of stylized doves	30	15

1101 Pointer and Chukar Partridge

1985. Hunting Dogs. Multicoloured.

3306	**1101**	5s. Type **1101**	20	20
3307		8s. Irish setter and common pochard	25	20
3308		13s. English setter and mallard	30	20
3309		20s. Cocker spaniel and Eurasian woodcock	35	25
3310		25s. German pointer and rabbit	55	35
3311		30s. Bulgarian bloodhound and boar	75	40
3312		42s. Dachshund and fox	1·50	55

1102 Person in Wheelchair and Runners

1985. International Year of Disabled Persons (1984).
3313 **1102** 5s. multicoloured 20 10

1103 Georgi Dimitrov (statesman)

1985. 50th Anniv of 7th Communist International Congress, Moscow.
3314 **1103** 13s. red 35 20

1104 Emblem within "40"

1986. 40th Anniv of UNICEF.
3315 **1104** 13s. blue, gold & black 35 20

1105 Blagoev

1986. 130th Birth Anniv of Dimitur Blagoev (founder of Bulgarian Social Democratic Party).
3316 **1105** 5s. purple and orange 20 10

1106 Hands and Dove within Laurel Wreath

1986. International Peace Year.
3317 **1106** 5s. multicoloured 20 10

1107 *Dactylorhiza romana*

1986. Orchids. Multicoloured.

3318	**1107**	5s. Type **1107**	20	15
3319		13s. *Epipactis palustris*	30	20
3320		30s. *Ophrys cornuta*	40	25
3321		32s. *Limodorum abrotivum*	45	35
3322		42s. *Cypripedium calceolus*	85	45
3323		60s. *Orchis papilionacea*	1·40	55

1108 Angora Rabbit

1986. Rabbits.

3324	-	5s. grey, black & brown	20	15
3325	**1108**	25s. red and black	45	20
3326	-	30s. brown, yell & blk	55	25
3327	-	32s. orange and black	65	35
3328	-	42s. red and black	85	45
3329	-	60s. blue and black	1·40	55

DESIGNS: 5s. French grey; 30s. English lop-eared; 32s. Belgian; 42s. English spotted; 60s. Dutch black and white rabbit.

1109 Front Page and Ivan Bogorov

1986. 140th Anniv of *Bulgarian Eagle*.
3330 **1109** 5s. multicoloured 20 10

1110 Neptune and Comet Position, 1980

1986. Appearance of Halley's Comet. Sheet 120×114 mm containing T **1110** and similar horiz designs, each violet, blue and yellow.
MS3331 25s. Type **1110**; 25s. Sun, Earth, Mars, Saturn and comet positions, 1985 and 1910/86; 25s. Uranus and comet positions, 1960, 1926, 1948 and 1970; 25s. Jupiter and comet position, 1911 2·20 2·20

1111 Bashev

1986. 50th Birth Anniv (1985) of Vladimir Bashev (poet).

| 3332 | **1111** | 5s. blue & light blue | 20 | 10 |

1112 Wave Pattern

1986. 13th Bulgarian Communist Party Congress.

3333	**1112**	5s. blue, green and red	10	15
3334	–	8s. blue and red	25	15
3335	–	13s. blue, red & lt blue	30	20
MS3336	60×77 mm. 50s. multicoloured		1·00	1·10

DESIGNS: 8s. Printed circuit as tail of shooting star; 13s. Computer picture of man; 50s. Steel construction tower.

1113 "Vostok I"

1986. 25th Anniv of First Man in Space. Sheet 105×100 mm containing T **1113** and similar horiz design, each deep blue and black.

| MS3337 | 50s. Type **1113**; 50s. Yuri Gagarin | 2·20 | 2·20 |

1114 Monument, Panagyurishte

1986. 110th Anniv of April Uprising.

| 3338 | **1114** | 5s. black, stone and green | 20 | 10 |
| 3339 | – | 13s. black, stone & red | 30 | 15 |

DESIGN: 13s. Statue of Khristo Botev, Vratsa.

1115 Gymnast

1986. 75th Anniv of Levski-Spartak Sports Club. Sheet 81×65 mm. Imperf.

| MS3340 | **1115** | 50s. multicoloured | 1·00 | 1·10 |

1116 Stylized Ear of Wheat

1986. 35th Bulgarian People's Agrarian Union Congress.

3341	**1116**	5s. gold, orange & blk	10	10
3342	–	8s. gold, blue and black	20	10
3343	–	13s. multicoloured	30	15

DESIGNS: 8s. Stylized ear of wheat on globe; 13s. Flags.

1117 Transport Systems

1986. Socialist Countries' Transport Ministers Conference.

| 3344 | **1117** | 13s. multicoloured | 30 | 20 |

1118 Emblem

1986. 17th International Book Fair, Sofia.

| 3345 | **1118** | 13s. grey, red and black | 30 | 20 |

1119 Player with Ball

1986. World Cup Football Championship, Mexico (2nd issue). Multicoloured.

3346	5s. Type **1119**	20	15
3347	13s. Player tackling (horiz)	30	20
3348	20s. Player heading ball (horiz)	35	25
3349	30s. Player kicking ball (horiz)	65	35
3350	42s. Goalkeeper (horiz)	95	45
3351	60s. Player with trophy	1·50	65
MS3352	95×75 mm. 1l. Azteca Stadium (42×31 mm)	2·20	2·20

1120 Square Brooch

1986. Treasures of Preslav. Multicoloured.

3353	5s. Type **1120**	20	15
3354	13s. Pendant (vert)	30	20
3355	20s. Wheel-shaped pendant	35	25
3356	30s. Breast plate decorated with birds and chalice	65	35
3357	42s. Pear-shaped pendant (vert)	95	45
3358	60s. Enamelled cockerel on gold base	1·40	55

1121 Fencers with Sabres

1986. World Fencing Championships, Sofia. Multicoloured.

3359	5s. Type **1121**	20	10
3360	13s. Fencers	30	15
3361	25s. Fencers with rapiers	55	35

1122 Stockholm Town Hall

1986. "Stockholmia 86" International Stamp Exn.

| 3362 | **1122** | 42s. brn, red & dp red | 75 | 65 |

1123 White Stork (Ciconia ciconia)

1986. Nature Protection. Sheet 138×90 mm containing T **1123** and similar vert designs. Multicoloured.

| MS3363 | 30s. Type **1132**; 30s. Yellow water-lily (Nuphar lutea); 30s. Fire salamander (Salamandra salamandra); 30s. White water-lily (Nymphaea alba) | 5·00 | 4·25 |

1124 Arms and Parliament Building, Sofia

1986. 40th Anniv of People's Republic.

| 3364 | **1124** | 5s. green, red & lt grn | 20 | 10 |

1125 Posthorn

1986. 15th Organization of Socialist Countries' Postal Administrations Session, Sofia.

| 3365 | **1125** | 13s. multicoloured | 30 | 20 |

1126 "All Pull Together"

1986. 40th Anniv of Voluntary Brigades.

| 3366 | **1126** | 5s. multicoloured | 20 | 10 |

1127 Dove and Book as Pen Nib

1986. Tenth International Journalists Association Congress, Sofia.

| 3367 | **1127** | 13s. blue & deep blue | 30 | 20 |

1128 Wrestlers

1986. 75th Anniv of Levski-Spartak Sports Club.

| 3368 | **1128** | 5s. multicoloured | 20 | 10 |

1129 Saints Cyril and Methodius with Disciples (fresco)

1986. 1100th Anniv of Arrival in Bulgaria of Pupils of Saints Cyril and Methodius.

| 3369 | **1129** | 13s. brown and buff | 30 | 20 |

1130 Old and Modern Telephones

1986. Centenary of Telephone in Bulgaria.

| 3370 | **1130** | 5s. multicoloured | 20 | 10 |

1131 Weightlifter

1986. World Weightlifting Championships, Sofia.

| 3371 | **1131** | 13s. multicoloured | 30 | 20 |

1986. Historic Ships (5th series). 18th-century ships. As T **753**. Multicoloured.

3372	5s. King of Prussia	10	10
3373	13s. Indiaman	20	15
3374	25s. Xebec	45	25
3375	30s. Sv. Paul	55	35
3376	32s. Topsail schooner	65	45
3377	42s. Victory	1·40	55

1132 (image scaled to 47% of original size)

1986. European Security and Co-operation Conference Review Meeting, Vienna. Sheet 109×86 mm containing T **1132** and similar vert designs.

| MS3378 | 50s. olive, orange and green; 50s. green, orange and blue (Vienna Town Hall); 50s. multicoloured (United Nations Centre, Vienna) | 4·25 | 4·25 |

1133 Silver Jug decorated with Seated Woman

1986. 14th Congress of Bulgarian Philatelic Federation and 60th Anniv of International Philatelic Federation. Repousse work found at Rogozen.

| 3379 | **1133** | 10s. grey, black & bl | 30 | 20 |
| 3380 | – | 10s. green, blk & red | 30 | 20 |

DESIGN: No. 3380, Silver jug decorated with sphinx.

1134 Doves between Pine Branches

1986. New Year.

| 3381 | **1134** | 5s. red, green and blue | 20 | 10 |
| 3382 | – | 13s. mauve, blue & vio | 30 | 20 |

DESIGN: 13s. Fireworks and snowflakes.

1135 Earphones as "60" on Globe

1986. 60th Anniv of Bulgarian Amateur Radio.

| 3383 | **1135** | 13s. multicoloured | 30 | 20 |

1136 The Walnut Tree (Danail Dechev)

1986. 90th Anniv of Sofia Art Academy. Modern Paintings. Sheet 146×102 mm containing T **1136** and similar horiz designs. Multicoloured.

| MS3384 | 25s. Type **1136**; 25s. Resistance Fighters and Soldiers (Iliya Beshkov); 30s. Melnik (Veselin Staikov); 30s. The Olive Grove (Kiril Tsonev) | 3·25 | 3·25 |

1137 Gen. Augusto Sandino and Flag

1988. 25th Anniv of Sandinista National Liberation Front of Nicaragua.

| 3385 | **1137** | 13s. multicoloured | 30 | 20 |

1138 Dimitur and Konstantin Miladinov (authors)

1986. 125th Anniv of "Bulgarian Popular Songs".
3386 **1138** 10s. blue, brn & red 20 10

1139 Pencho Slaveikov (poet)

1986. Writers' Birth Annivs. Multicoloured.
3387 5s. Type **1139** (125th anniv) 20 10
3388 5s. Stoyan Mikhailovski (130th anniv) 20 10
3389 8s. Nikola Atanasov (dramatist) (centenary) 20 10
3390 8s. Ran Bosilek (children's author) (centenary) 20 10

1140 Raiko Daskalov

1986. Birth Cent of Raiko Daskalov (politician).
3391 **1140** 5s. brown 20 10

1141 Girl with Fruit

1986. 500th Birth Anniv of Titian (painter). Multicoloured.
3392 5s. Type **1141** 20 15
3393 13s. Flora 30 15
3394 20s. Lucretia and Tarquin 35 20
3395 30s. Caiphas and Mary Magdalene 50 25
3396 32s. Toilette of Venus (detail) 55 35
3397 42s. Self-portrait 1·10 45
MS3398 105×75 mm. 1l. Danae (32×54 mm) 3·00 2·75

1142 Fiat, 1905

1986. Racing Cars.
3399 **1142** 5s. brown, red & black 20 15
3400 - 10s. red, orange & blk 20 15
3401 - 25s. green, red & black 45 20
3402 - 32s. brown, red & blk 55 35
3403 - 40s. violet, red & black 95 40
3404 - 42s. grey, black and red 1·20 45
DESIGNS: 10s. Bugatti, 1928; 25s. Mercedes, 1936; 32s. Ferrari, 1952; 40s. Lotus, 1985; 42s. Maclaren, 1986.

1143 Steam Locomotive

1987. 120th Anniv of Ruse–Varna Railway.
3405 **1143** 5s. multicoloured 20 20

1144 Debelyanov

1987. Birth Cent of Dimcho Debelyanov (poet).
3406 **1144** 5s. dp blue, yellow & bl 20 10

1145 Lazarus Ludwig Zamenhof (inventor)

1987. Centenary of Esperanto (invented language).
3407 **1145** 13s. blue, yellow & grn 30 20

1146 The Blusher

1987. Edible Fungi. Multicoloured.
3408 5s. Type **1146** 20 15
3409 20s. Royal boletus 30 20
3410 30s. Red-capped scaber stalk 45 35
3411 32s. Shaggy ink cap 65 40
3412 40s. Bare-toothed russula 75 45
3413 60s. Chanterelle 85 55

1147 Worker

1987. Tenth Trade Unions Congress, Sofia.
3414 **1147** 5s. violet and red 20 10

1148 Silver-gilt Plate with Design of Hercules and Auge

1987. Treasure of Rogozen. Multicoloured.
3415 5s. Type **1148** 20 15
3416 8s. Silver-gilt jug with design of lioness attacking stag 20 15
3417 20s. Silver-gilt plate with quatrefoil design 30 20
3418 30s. Silver-gilt jug with design of horse rider 35 25
3419 32s. Silver-gilt pot with palm design 45 30
3420 42s. Silver jug with chariot and horses design 55 35

1149 Ludmila Zhivkova Featival Complex, Varna

1987. Modern Architecture. Sheet 107×100 mm containing T **1149** and similar horiz designs. Multicoloured.
MS3421 30s. Type **1149**; 30s. Ministry of Foreign Affairs building, Sofia; 30s. Interpred building, Sofia; 30s. Hotel, Sandanski 2·20 2·20

1150 Wrestlers

1987. 30th European Freestyle Wrestling Championships, Turnovo.
3422 **1150** 5s. lilac, red and violet 10 10
3423 - 13s. dp blue, red & blue 20 10
DESIGNS: 13st. Wrestlers (different).

1151 Totem Pole

1987. "Capex '87" International Stamp Exhibition, Toronto.
3424 **1151** 42s. multicoloured 75 45

1152 "X" and Flags

1987. Tenth Fatherland Front Congress.
3425 **1152** 5s. green, orange & bl 20 10

1153 Georgi Dimitrov and Profiles

1987. 15th Dimitrov Communist Youth League Congress.
3426 **1153** 5s. purple, green & red 20 10

1154 Mask

1987. Eighth International Festival of Humour and Satire, Gabrovo.
3427 **1154** 13s. multicoloured 30 20

1155 Mastheads

1987. 60th Anniv of Rabotnichesko Delo (newspaper).
3428 **1155** 5s. red and black 20 10

1156 Mariya Gigova

1987. 13th World Rhythmic Gymnastics Championships, Varna.
3429 **1156** 5s. blue and yellow 20 15
3430 - 8s. red and yellow 20 15
3431 - 13s. blue and stone 30 20
3432 - 25s. red and yellow 45 25
3433 - 30s. black and yellow 55 30
3434 - 42s. mauve and yellow 75 35
MS3435 78×87 mm. 1l. violet and ochre 2·20 2·20
DESIGNS: 8s. Iliana Raeva; 13s. Aneliya Ralenkova; 25s. Dilyana Georgieva; 30s. Liliya Ignatova; 42s. Bianka Panova; 1l. Neshka Robeva.

1157 Man breaking Chains around Globe and Kolarov

1158 Stela Blagoeva

1987. Birth Centenary of Stela Blagoeva.
3437 **1158** 5s. brown and pink 20 20

1159 Levski

1987. 150th Birth Anniv of Vasil Levski (revolutionary).
3438 **1159** 5s. brown and green 10 10
3439 - 13s. green and brown 20 10
DESIGN: 13s. Levski and Bulgarian Revolutionary Central Committee emblem.

1160 Roe Deer

1987. Stags. Multicoloured.
3440 5s. Type **1160** 20 15
3441 10s. Elk (horiz) 20 15
3442 32s. Fallow deer 55 25
3443 40s. Sika deer 65 35
3444 42s. Red deer (horiz) 75 45
3445 60s. Reindeer 1·00 55
MS3445a 145×131 mm. Nos. 3340/5. Imperf 3·75 3·75

1161 Barbed Wire as Dove

1987. International Namibia Day.
3446 **1161** 13s. black, red & orge 25 10

1162 Kirkov

1987. 120th Birth Anniv of Georgi Kirkov (pseudonym Maistora) (politician).
3447 **1162** 5s. red and pink 20 10

1163 Phacelia tanacetifolia

1987. Flowers. Multicoloured.
3448 5s. Type **1163** 20 15
3449 10s. Sunflower 20 15
3450 30s. False acacia 50 30
3451 32s. Dutch lavender 55 35
3452 42s. Small-leaved lime 75 45
3453 60s. Onobrychis sativa 1·10 55

1987. 110th Birth Anniv of Vasil Kolarov (Prime Minister 1949–50).
3436 **1157** 5s. multicoloured 20 10

1164 Mil Mi-8 Helicopter, Tupolev Tu-154 and Antonov An-12 Aircraft

1987. 40th Anniv of Balkanair.
3454	**1164**	25s. multicoloured	55	20

1165 1879 5c. Stamp

1987. "Bulgaria '89" International Stamp Exhibition, Sofia (1st issue).
3455	**1165**	13s. multicoloured	20	10

See also Nos. 3569, 3579/82 and 3602/5.

1166 Copenhagen Town Hall

1987. "Hafnia '87" International Stamp Exhibition, Copenhagen.
3456	**1166**	42s. multicoloured	75	55

1167 Portrait of Girl (Stefan Ivanov)

1987. Paintings in Sofia National Gallery. Multicoloured.
3457	**1167**	5s. Type **1167**	20	15
3458		8s. Woman carrying Grapes (Bencho Obreshkov)	20	15
3459		20s. Portrait of a Woman wearing a Straw Hat (David Perez)	35	20
3460		25s. Women listening to Marimba (Kiril Tsonev)	45	30
3461		32s. Boy with Harmonica (Nenko Balkanski)	65	35
3462		60s. Rumyana (Vasil Stoilov)	1·20	55

1168 Battle Scene

1987. 75th Anniv of Balkan War.
3463	**1168**	5s. black, stone and red	20	10

1169 Emblem

1987. 30th Anniv of International Atomic Energy Agency.
3464	**1169**	13s. blue, green and red	35	20

1170 Mastheads

1987. 95th Anniv of Rabotnik, 90th Anniv of Rabotnicheski Vestnik and 60th Anniv of Rabotnichesko Delo (newspapers).
3465	**1170**	5s. red, blue and gold	20	10

1171 Winter Wren

1987. Birds. Multicoloured.
3466		5s. Type **1171**	20	15
3467		13s. Yellowhammer	20	15
3468		20s. Eurasian nuthatch	45	20
3469		30s. Blackbird	65	35
3470		42s. Hawfinch	1·00	45
3471		60s. White-throated dipper	1·40	55

1172 "Vega" Automatic Space Station

1987. 30th Anniv of Soviet Space Exploration. Sheet 98×98 mm containing T **1172** and similar horiz design.
MS3472	50s. blue, orange and purple (Type **1172**); 50s. deep blue, blue and purple ("Soyuz" spacecraft docking with "Mir" space station)	2·75	2·75

1173 Lenin and Revolutionary

1987. 70th Anniv of Russian Revolution.
3473	**1173**	5s. purple and red	10	10
3474	-	13s. blue and red	20	10

DESIGN: 13s. Lenin and cosmonaut.

1174 Biathlon

1987. Winter Olympic Games, Calgary. Multicoloured.
3475		5s. Type **1174**	20	15
3476		13s. Slalom	20	15
3477		30s. Figure skating (women's)	55	35
3478		42s. Four-man bobsleigh	85	55
MS3479	65×87 mm. 1l. Ice hockey		2·20	2·20

1175 "Socfilex" Emblem within Folk-design Ornament

1987. New Year. Multicoloured.
3480		5s. Type **1175**	10	10
3481		13s. Emblem within flower ornament	20	10

1176 Helsinki Conference Centre

1987. European Security and Co-operation Conference Review Meeting, Vienna. Sheet 140×100 mm containing T **1176** and similar vert designs.
MS3482	50s. lavender, brown and red; 50s. multicoloured (Map of Europe); 50s. multicoloured (Vienna Conference Centre)	5·00	5·00

1177 Kabakchiev

1988. 110th Birth Anniv of Khristo Kabakchiev (Communist Party official).
3483	**1177**	5s. multicoloured	20	10

1178 Scilla bythynica

1988. Marsh Flowers. Multicoloured.
3484		5s. Type **1178**	10	10
3485		10s. Geum rhodopaeum	15	10
3486		13s. Caltha polypetala	20	10
3487		25s. Fringed water-lily	45	20
3488		30s. Cortusa matthioli	55	30
3489		42s. Water soldier	65	45

1179 Commander on Horseback

1988. 110th Anniv of Liberation from Turkey. Multicoloured.
3490	**1179**	5s. Type **1179**	10	10
3491		13s. Soldiers	20	10

1180 Emblem

1988. Public Sector Workers' 8th International Congress, Sofia.
3492	**1180**	13s. multicoloured	20	10

1181 Yantra, 1888

1988. Centenary of State Railways. Locomotives. Multicoloured.
3493	**1181**	5s. Type **1181**	15	10
3494		13s. Khristo Botev, 1905	20	15
3495		25s. Steam locomotive No. 807, 1918	55	20
3496		32s. Class 46 steam locomotive, 1943	65	35
3497		42s. Diesel locomotive, 1964	85	45
3498		60s. Electric locomotive, 1979	1·40	55

1182 Ivan Nedyalkov (Shablin)

1988. Post Office Anti-fascist Heroes.
3499	**1182**	5s. light brown and brown	10	10
3500	-	8s. grey and blue	10	10
3501	-	10s. green and olive	15	10
3502	-	13s. pink and red	20	10

DESIGNS: 8s. Delcho Spasov; 10s. Nikola Ganchev (Gudzho); 13s. Ganka Rasheva (Boika).

1183 Traikov

1988. 90th Birth Anniv of Georgi Traikov (politician).
3503	**1183**	5s. orange and brown	20	10

1184 Red Cross, Red Crescent and Globe

1988. 125th Anniv of International Red Cross.
3504	**1184**	13s. multicoloured	20	10

1185 Girl

1988. Fourth "Banners for Peace" Children's Meeting, Sofia. Children's paintings. Multicoloured.
3505		5s. Type **1185**	10	10
3506		8s. Artist at work	20	10
3507		13s. Circus (horiz)	35	15
3508		20s. Kite flying (horiz)	45	20
3509		32s. Accordion player	55	30
3510		42s. Cosmonaut	65	35
MS3511	86×90 mm. 50s. Emblem with film frame (Youth Film Festival) (horiz)		1·10	1·10

1186 Marx

1988. 170th Birth Anniv of Karl Marx.
3512	**1186**	13s. red, black & yellow	20	10

1187 Herring Gull

1988. Birds. Multicoloured.
3513		5s. Type **1187**	20	10
3514		5s. White stork	20	10
3515		8s. Grey heron	40	15
3516		8s. Carrion crow	40	15
3517		10s. Northern goshawk	55	20
3518		42s. Eagle owl	1·60	45

1188 African Elephant

1988. Centenary of Sofia Zoo. Multicoloured.
3519		5s. Type **1188**	10	10
3520		13s. White rhinoceros	20	10
3521		25s. Hunting dog	55	20
3522		30s. Eastern white pelican	65	35
3523		32s. Abyssinian ground hornbill	75	45
3524		42s. Snowy owl	1·00	65

1189 "Soyuz TM" Spacecraft, Flags and Globe

1988. Second Soviet-Bulgarian Space Flight. Multicoloured.
3525		5s. Type **1189**	10	10
3526		13s. Rocket on globe	20	10

1190 Young Inventor

1988. International Young Inventors' Exhibition, Plovdiv.
3527 **1190** 13s. multicoloured 20 10

1191 1856 Handstamp of Russian Duchy of Finland

1988. "Finlandia '88" International Stamp Exhibition, Helsinki.
3528 **1191** 30s. blue and red 45 35

1192 Player taking Corner Kick

1988. Eighth European Football Championship, West Germany. Multicoloured.
3529 5s. Type **1192** 10 10
3530 13s. Goalkeeper and player 20 15
3531 30s. Referee and player 65 35
3532 42s. Player with trophy 85 45
MS3533 90×69 mm. 1l. Stadium (horiz) 2·20 2·20

1193 Portrait of Child

1988. Second Death Anniv of Dechko Uzunov (painter). Multicoloured.
3534 5s. Type **1193** 10 10
3535 13s. Portrait of Mariya Vasileva 35 15
3536 30s. Self-portrait 65 20

1194 Valentina Tereshkova

1988. 25th Anniv of First Woman in Space. Sheet 87×56 mm.
MS3537 **1194** 1l. pink and blue 2·20 2·20

1195 St. John

1988. Icons from Kurdzhali. Multicoloured.
3538 5s. Type **1195** 20 10
3539 8s. St. George and Dragon 20 10

1196 High Jumping

1988. Olympic Games, Seoul. Multicoloured.
3540 5s. Type **1196** 10 10
3541 13s. Weightlifting 20 10
3542 30s. Wrestling 55 30
3543 42s. Gymnastics 85 35
MS3544 115×75 mm. 1l. Volleyball 2·20 2·20

1197 Dimitur and Karadzha

1988. 120th Death Anniv of Khadzhi Dimitur and Stefan Karadzha (revolutionaries).
3545 **1197** 5s. green, black & brn 20 10

1198 Magazines

1988. 30th Anniv of Problems of Peace and Socialism (magazine).
3546 **1198** 13s. multicoloured 20 10

1199 The Dead Tree (Roland Udo)

1988. Paintings in Lyudmila Zhivkova Art Gallery. Multicoloured.
3547 30s. Type **1199** 55 35
3548 30s. Algiers Harbour (Albert Marque) 55 35
3549 30s. Portrait of Hermine David (Jule Pasquin) 55 35
3550 30s. Madonna and Child with two Saints (Giovanni Rosso) 55 35

1200 University Building

1988. Centenary of St. Clement of Ohrid University, Sofia.
3551 **1200** 5s. black, yellow & grn 20 10

1201 Czechoslovakia 1918 Stamp Design

1988. "Praga '88" International Stamp Exhibition, Prague.
3552 **1201** 25s. red and blue 45 35

1202 Korea 1884 5m. Stamp

1988. "Olymphilex '88" Olympic Stamps Exhibition, Seoul.
3553 **1202** 62s. red and green 1·30 1·10

1203 Anniversary Emblem

1988. 25th Anniv of Kremikovtsi Steel Mills.
3554 **1203** 5s. violet, red and blue 20 10

1204 Parliament Building, Sofia, and Map

1988. 80th Interparliamentary Conference, Sofia.
3555 **1204** 13s. blue and red 35 15

1205 Chalice, Glinena

1988. Kurdzhali Culture. Multicoloured.
3556 5s. Type **1205** 20 10
3557 8s. Part of ruined fortifications, Perperikon (vert) 20 10

1206 Soldiers

1988. 300th Anniv of Chiprovtsi Rising.
3558 **1206** 5s. multicoloured 20 10

1207 Brown Bear

1988. Bears. Multicoloured.
3559 5s. Type **1207** 10 10
3560 8s. Polar bear 10 10
3561 13s. Sloth bear 20 10
3562 20s. Sun bear 45 20
3563 32s. Asiatic black bear 65 30
3564 42s. Spectacled bear 1·10 35

1208 Emblem

1988. 80th Council of Mutual Economic Aid Transport Commission Meeting, Sofia.
3565 **1208** 13s. red and black 35 15

1209 Emblem

1988. World Ecoforum.
3566 **1209** 20s. multicoloured 45 20

1210 Amphitheatre, Plovdiv

1988. "Plovdiv '88" National Stamp Exhibition.
3567 **1210** 5s. multicoloured 20 10

1211 Transmission Towers

1988. 25th Anniv of Radio and Television.
3568 **1211** 5s. green, blue & brown 20 10

1212 1879 5c. Stamp

1988. "Bulgaria '89" International Stamp Exhibition (2nd issue).
3569 **1212** 42s. orange, blk & mve 65 55

1213 Ruse (river boat)

1988. 40th Anniv of Danube Commission. Sheet 104×124 mm containing T **1213** and similar horiz design. Multicoloured.
MS3570 1l. Type **1213**; 1l. Al. Stamboli-iski (river cruiser) 4·25 4·50

1214 Children and Cars

1988. Road Safety Campaign.
3571 **1214** 5s. multicoloured 20 10

1215 Rila Hotel, Borovets

1988. Hotels. Multicoloured.
3572 5s. Type **1215** 20 15
3573 8s. Pirin Hotel, Bansko 20 15
3574 13s. Shtastlivetsa Hotel, Vitosha 35 20
3575 30s. Perelik Hotel, Pamporovo 55 30

1216 Tree Decoration

1988. New Year. Multicoloured.
3576 5s. Type **1216** 10 10
3577 13s. "Bulgaria '89" emblem, tree and decorations 20 10

1217 Space Shuttle "Buran"

1988. Energiya--Buran Space Flight. Sheet 102×67 mm.
MS3578 **1217** 1l. blue 2·20 2·00

1218 Mail Coach

1988. "Bulgaria '89" International Stamp Exhibition, Sofia (3rd issue). Mail Transport. Multicoloured.
3579 25s. Type **1218** 55 20
3580 25s. Paddle-steamer 55 20
3581 25s. Lorry 55 20
3582 25s. Biplane 55 20

1219 India 1947 1½a. Independence Stamp

1989. "India 89" International Stamp Exhibition, New Delhi.
3583 **1219** 62s. green and orange 1·10 90

1220 France 1850 10c.
Ceres Stamp

1989. "Philexfrance '89" International Stamp Exhibition, Paris.
| 3584 | **1220** | 42s. brown and blue | 65 | 55 |

1221 Slalom

1989. "Sofia '89" University Winter Games, Sofia. Sheet 84×142 mm containing T **1221** and similar vert designs. Multicoloured. Imperf.
MS3585 25s. Type **1221**; 25s. Ice hockey; 25s. Biathlon; 25s. Speed skating 2·20 2·20

1222 Don Quixote (sculpture, House of Humour and Satire)

1989. International Festival of Humour and Satire, Gabrovo.
| 3586 | **1222** | 13s. multicoloured | 35 | 15 |

1223 *Ramonda serbica*

1989. Flowers. Multicoloured.
3587	**1223**	5s. Type **1223**	10	10
3588		10s. *Paeonia maskula*	20	10
3589		25s. *Viola perinensis*	45	20
3590		30s. *Dracunculus vulgaris*	55	35
3591		42s. *Tulipa splendens*	85	45
3592		60s. *Rindera umbellata*	1·10	55

1224 Common Noctule Bat

1989. Bats. Multicoloured.
3593	**1224**	5s. Type **1224**	20	15
3594		13s. Greater horseshoe bat	35	20
3595		30s. Large mouse-eared bat	1·10	45
3596		42s. Particoloured frosted bat	1·60	1·30

1225 Stamboliiski

1989. 110th Birth Anniv of Aleksandur Stamboliiski (Prime Minister 1919–23).
| 3597 | **1225** | 5s. black and orange | 20 | 10 |

1226 Launch of "Soyuz 33"

1989. Tenth Anniv of Soviet–Bulgarian Space Flight. Sheet 130×90 mm containing T **1226** and similar vert design. Multicoloured.
MS3598 50s. Type **1226**; 50s. Cosmonauts Nicolai Rukavishnikov and Georgi Ivanov 2·20 2·20

1227 Young Inventor

1989. International Young Inventors' Exhibition, Plovdiv.
| 3599 | **1227** | 5s. multicoloured | 20 | 10 |

1228 Stanke Dimitrov-Marek (Party activist)

1989. Birth Centenaries.
| 3600 | **1228** | 5s. red and black | 20 | 10 |
| 3601 | - | 5s. red and black | 20 | 10 |
DESIGN: No. 3601, Petko Yenev (revolutionary).

1229 *John the Baptist* (Toma Vishanov)

1989. "Bulgaria '89" International Stamp Exhibition, Sofia (4th issue). Icons. Multicoloured.
3602		30s. Type **1229**	55	20
3603		30s. *St. Dimitur* (Ivan Terziev)	55	20
3604		30s. *Archangel Michael* (Dimitur Molerov)	55	20
3605		30s. *Madonna and Child* (Toma Vishanov)	55	20

1230 Fax Machine and Woman reading letter

1989. 110th Anniv of Bulgarian Post and Telegraph Services. Multicoloured.
3606	**1230**	5s. Type **1230**	20	15
3607		8s. Telex machine and old telegraph machine	20	15
3608		35s. Modern and old telephones	65	45
3609		42s. Dish aerial and old radio	85	55

1231 *Nike in Quadriga* (relief)

1989. 58th International Philatelic Federation Congress, Sofia. Sheet 87×120 mm.
MS3610 1l. multicoloured 2·20 2·20

1232 A. P. Aleksandrov, A. Ya. Solovov and V. P. Savinikh

1989. Air. "Soyuz TM5" Soviet-Bulgarian Space Flight.
| 3611 | **1232** | 13s. multicoloured | 35 | 20 |

1233 Party Programme

1989. 70th Anniv of First Bulgarian Communist Party Congress, Sofia.
| 3612 | **1233** | 5s. blk, red & dp red | 20 | 10 |

1234 Sofronii Vrachanski (250th anniv)

1989. Writers' Birth Anniversaries.
| 3613 | **1234** | 5s. green, brown & blk | 20 | 10 |
| 3614 | - | 5s. green, brown & blk | 20 | 10 |
DESIGN: No. 3614, Iliya Bluskov (150th anniv).

1235 Birds

1989. Bicentenary of French Revolution. Each black, red and blue.
3615	**1235**	13s. Type **1235**	35	15
3616		30s. Jean-Paul Marat	55	20
3617		42s. Robespierre	75	35

1236 Gymnastics

1989. Seventh Friendly Armies Summer Spartakiad. Multicoloured.
3618	**1236**	5s. Type **1236**	10	10
3619		13s. Show jumping	35	15
3620		30s. Long jumping	55	20
3621		42s. Shooting	75	45

1237 Aprilov

1989. Birth Bicent of Vasil Aprilov (educationist).
| 3622 | **1237** | 8s. lt blue, blue & blk | 20 | 10 |

1238 Zagorchinov

1989. Birth Centenary of Stoyan Zagorchinov (writer).
| 3623 | **1238** | 10s. turq, brown & blk | 20 | 10 |

1239 Woman in Kayak

1989. Canoeing and Kayak Championships, Plovdiv. Multicoloured.
| 3624 | **1239** | 13s. Type **1239** | 35 | 20 |
| 3625 | | 30s. Man in kayak | 75 | 35 |

1240 Felix Nadar taking Photograph from his Balloon *Le Geant* (1863) and Airship *Graf Zeppelin* over Alexsandr Nevski Cathedral, Sofia

1989. 150th Anniv of Photography.
| 3626 | **1240** | 42s. black, stone & yell | 1·10 | 45 |

1241 Lammergeier and Lynx

1989. Centenary of Natural History Museum.
| 3627 | **1241** | 13s. multicoloured | 35 | 30 |

1242 Soldiers

1989. 45th Anniv of Fatherland Front Government. Multicoloured.
3628		5s. Type **1242**	10	10
3629		8s. Welcoming officers	10	10
3630		13s. Crowd of youths	35	15

1243 Lyubomir Dardzhikov

1989. 48th Death Anniversaries of Post Office War Heroes. Multicoloured.
3631		5s. Type **1243**	10	10
3632		8s. Ivan Bankov Dobrev	10	10
3633		13s. Nestor Antonov	35	15

1244 Yasenov

1989. Birth Cent of Khisto Yasenov (writer).
| 3634 | **1244** | 8s. grey, brown & blk | 20 | 10 |

1245 Lorry leaving Weighbridge

1989. 21st Transport Congress, Sofia.
| 3635 | **1245** | 42s. blue & deep blue | 1·10 | 65 |

1246 Nehru

1989. Birth Centenary of Jawaharlal Nehru (Indian statesman).
3636 **1246** 13s. yellow, brn & blk 35 20

1247 Cranes flying

1989. Ecology Congress of European Security and Co-operation Conference, Sofia. Sheet 130×85 mm containing T **1247** and similar vert design. Multicoloured.
MS3637 50s. Type **1247**; 1l. Cranes flying (different) 4·25 4·50

1248 Javelin Sand Boa

1989. Snakes. Multicoloured.
3638 5s. Type **1248** 10 10
3639 10s. Aesculapian snake 20 15
3640 25s. Leopard snake 55 35
3641 30s. Four-lined rat snake 65 45
3642 42s. Cat snake 1·00 55
3643 60s. Whip snake 1·30 65

1249 Tiger and Balloon of Flags

1989. Young Inventors' Exhibition, Plovdiv.
3644 **1249** 13s. multicoloured 35 20

1250 Boy on Skateboard

1989. Children's Games. Sheet 100×120 mm containing T **1250** and similar vert designs. Multicoloured.
MS3645 30s.+15s. Type **1250**; 30s.+15s. Girl with ball and doll; 30s.+15s. Girl jumping over ropes; 30s.+15s. Boy with toy train 3·75 4·00

1251 Goalkeeper saving Ball

1989. World Cup Football Championship, Italy (1990) (1st issue). Multicoloured.
3646 5s. Type **1251** 10 10
3647 13s. Player tackling 20 10
3648 30s. Player heading ball 55 35
3649 42s. Player kicking ball 1·30 55
MS3650 109×54 mm. 50s. Player tackling; 50s. Players 2·20 2·00
See also Nos. 3675/**MS**3679.

1252 Gliders

1989. 82nd International Airsports Federation General Conference, Varna. Aerial Sports. Multicoloured.
3651 5s. Type **1252** 10 10
3652 13s. Hang gliding 35 20
3653 30s. Parachutist landing 75 40
3654 42s. Free falling parachutist 85 45

1253 Children on Road Crossing

1989. Road Safety.
3655 **1253** 5s. multicoloured 20 10

1254 Santa Claus's Sleigh

1989. New Year. Multicoloured.
3656 5s. Type **1254** 20 15
3657 13s. Snowman 35 20

1255 European Shorthair

1989. Cats.
3658 **1255** 5s. black and yellow 20 15
3659 - 5s. black and grey 20 15
3660 - 8s. black and yellow 20 15
3661 - 10s. black & brown 35 20
3662 - 10s. black and blue 35 20
3663 - 13s. black and red 45 25
DESIGNS—HORIZ: No. 3659, Persian; 3660, European shorthair (different); 3662, Persian (different). VERT: No. 3661, Persian (different); 3663, Siamese.

1256 Christopher Columbus and *Santa Maria*

1990. Navigators and their Ships. Multicoloured.
3664 5s. Type **1256** 20 20
3665 8s. Vasco da Gama and *Sao Gabriel* 20 20
3666 13s. Ferdinand Magellan and *Vitoria* 25 20
3667 32s. Francis Drake and *Golden Hind* 65 45
3668 42s. Henry Hudson and *Discoverie* 1·00 55
3669 60s. James Cook and H.M.S. *Endeavour* 1·30 65

1257 Banner

1990. Centenary of Esperanto (invented language) in Bulgaria.
3670 **1257** 10s. stone, green & blk 20 10

1258 *Portrait of Madeleine Rono* (Maurice Brianchon)

1990. Paintings. Multicoloured.
3671 30s. Type **1258** 75 45
3672 30s. *Still Life* (Suzanne Valadon) 75 45
3673 30s. *Portrait of a Woman* (Moise Kisling) 75 45
3674 30s. *Portrait of a Woman* (Giovanni Boltraffio) 75 45

1259 Players

1990. World Cup Football Championship, Italy.
3675 **1259** 5s. multicoloured 20 15
3676 - 13s. multicoloured 35 20
3677 - 30s. multicoloured 65 35
3678 - 42s. multicoloured 1·10 45
MS3679 80×125 mm. 2×50s. multicoloured 2·75 2·50
DESIGNS: 13 to 50s. Various match scenes.

1260 Bavaria 1849 1k. Stamp

1990. "Essen 90" International Stamp Fair.
3680 **1260** 42s. black and red 85 80

1261 Penny Black

1990. "Stamp World London 90" International Stamp Exhibition. Sheet 90×140 mm containing T **1261** and similar horiz design.
MS3681 50s. black and blue (Type **1261**); 50s. black and red (Sir Rowland Hill (instigator of postage stamps)) 2·20 2·10

1262 "100" and Rainbow

1990. Centenary of Co-operative Farming.
3682 **1262** 5s. multicoloured 20 10

1263 *Elderly Couple at Rest*

1990. Birth Centenary of Dimitur Chorbadzhiiski-Chudomir (artist).
3683 **1263** 5s. multicoloured 20 10

1264 Map

1990. Centenary of Labour Day.
3684 **1264** 10s. multicoloured 20 15

1265 Emblem

1990. 125th Anniv of ITU.
3685 **1265** 20s. blue, red & black 55 35

1266 Belgium 1849 10c. "Epaulettes" Stamp

1990. "Belgica 90" International Stamp Exhibition, Brussels.
3686 **1266** 30s. brown and green 65 55

1267 Lamartine and his House

1990. Birth Bicentenary of Alphonse de Lamartine (poet).
3687 **1267** 20s. multicoloured 55 35

1268 Brontosaurus

1990. Prehistoric Animals. Multicoloured.
3688 5s. Type **1268** 20 15
3689 8s. Stegosaurus 20 15
3690 13s. Edaphosaurus 35 20
3691 25s. Rhamphorhynchus 65 45
3692 32s. Protoceratops 85 55
3693 42s. Triceratops 1·30 65

1269 Swimming

1990. Olympic Games, Barcelona (1992) (1st issue). Multicoloured.
3694 5s. Type **1269** 10 10
3695 13s. Handball 35 20
3696 30s. Hurdling 65 40
3697 42s. Cycling 1·10 45
MS3698 77×117 mm. 50s. Tennis player serving; 50s. Tennis player waiting to receive ball 2·75 2·20
See also Nos. 3840/**MS**3844.

1270 Southern Festoon

1990. Butterflies and Moths. Multicoloured.
3699 5s. Type **1270** 20 15
3700 10s. Jersey tiger moth 20 15
3701 20s. Willow-herb hawk moth 45 20
3702 30s. Striped hawk moth 65 45
3703 42s. *Thecla betulae* 75 65
3704 60s. Cynthia's fritillary 1·30 90

1271 Airbus Industrie A310 Jetliner

1990. Aircraft. Multicoloured.
3705 5s. Type **1271** 20 15
3706 10s. Tupolev Tu-204 20 15
3707 25s. Concorde 55 35
3708 30s. Douglas DC-9 60 40
3709 42s. Ilyushin Il-86 75 55

3710	60s. Boeing 747-300/400		1·30	90

No. 3705 is wrongly inscribed Airbus "A300".

1272 Iosif I

1990. 150th Birth Anniv of Exarch Iosif I.
| 3711 | **1272** | 5s. mauve, black & grn | 20 | 10 |

1273 Road and UN Emblem within Triangles

1990. International Road Safety Year.
| 3712 | **1273** | 5s. multicoloured | 20 | 10 |

1274 Putting the Shot

1990. "Olymphilex '90" Olympic Stamps Exhibition, Varna. Multicoloured.
3713	5s. Type **1274**	20	15
3714	13s. Throwing the discus	20	15
3715	42s. Throwing the hammer	75	55
3716	60s. Throwing the javelin	1·10	90

1275 "Sputnik" (first artificial satellite, 1957)

1990. Space Research. Multicoloured.
3717	5s. Type **1275**		10	10
3718	8s. "Vostok" and Yuri Gagarin (first manned flight, 1961)		20	15
3719	10s. Aleksei Leonov spacewalking from "Voskhod 2" (first spacewalk, 1965)		25	20
3720	20s. "Soyuz"–"Apollo" link, 1975		45	35
3721	42s. Space shuttle "Columbia", 1981		1·10	55
3722	60s. Space probe "Galileo"		1·30	90
MS3723	90×71 mm. 1l. Neil Armstrong from "Apollo 11" on lunar surface (first manned moon landing, 1969) (28×53 mm)		2·20	2·20

1276 St. Clement of Ohrid

1990. 1150th Birth Anniv of St. Clement of Ohrid.
| 3724 | **1276** | 5s. brown, black & grn | 20 | 10 |

1277 Tree

1990. Christmas. Multicoloured.
| 3725 | 5s. Type **1277** | 20 | 10 |
| 3726 | 20s. Father Christmas | 45 | 20 |

1278 Skaters

1991. European Figure Skating Championships, Sofia.
| 3727 | **1278** | 15s. multicoloured | 35 | 20 |

1279 Chicken

1991. Farm Animals.
3728	-	20s. brown and black	20	10
3729	-	25s. blue and black	20	10
3730	**1279**	30s. brown and black	20	10
3731	-	40s. brown and black	35	20
3732	-	62s. green and black	55	45
3733	-	86s. red and black	75	45
3734	-	95s. mauve and black	80	50
3735	-	1l. brown and black	85	55
3736	-	2l. green and black	1·60	1·10
3737	-	5l. violet and black	2·75	2·00
3738	-	10l. blue and black	5·00	2·75

DESIGNS: 20s. Sheep; 25s. Goose; 40s. Horse; 62, 95s. Billy goat; 86s. Sow; 1l. Donkey; 2l. Bull; 5l. Common turkey; 10l. Cow.

1280 Death Cap

1991. Fungi. Multicoloured.
3746	5s. Type **1280**	10	10
3747	10s. Amanita verna	25	20
3748	20s. Panther cap	25	20
3749	32s. Fly agaric	35	25
3750	42s. Beefsteak morel	45	35
3751	60s. Satan's mushroom	1·20	50

1281 Good Day (Paul Gauguin)

1991. Paintings. Multicoloured.
3752	20s. Type **1281**	25	20
3753	43s. Madame Dobini (Edgar Degas)	35	25
3754	62s. Peasant Woman (Camille Pissarro)	60	35
3755	67s. Woman with Black hair (Edouard Manet)	70	50
3756	80s. Blue Vase (Paul Cezanne)	1·00	70
3757	2l. Madame Samari (Pierre Auguste Renoir)	2·00	1·10
MS3758	65×90 mm. 3l. Self-portrait (Vincent van Gogh)	3·00	3·00

1282 Map

1991. 700th Anniv of Swiss Confederation.
| 3759 | **1282** | 62s. red and violet | 70 | 50 |

1283 Postman on Bicycle, Envelopes and Paper

1991. 100 Years of Philatelic Publications in Bulgaria.
| 3760 | **1283** | 30s. multicoloured | 35 | 25 |

1284 "Meteosat" Weather Satellite

1991. Europa. Europe in Space. Multicoloured.
| 3761 | 43s. Type **1284** | 1·20 | 60 |
| 3762 | 62s. "Ariane" rocket | 1·70 | 85 |

1285 Przewalski's Horse

1991. Horses. Multicoloured.
3763	5s. Type **1285**	25	20
3764	10s. Tarpan	25	20
3765	25s. Black arab	30	25
3766	35s. White arab	35	30
3767	42s. Shetland pony	45	35
3768	60s. Draught horse	1·20	60

1286 "Expo '91"

1991. "Expo '91" Exhibition, Plovdiv.
| 3769 | **1286** | 30s. multicoloured | 35 | 25 |

1287 Mozart

1991. Death Bicentenary of Wolfgang Amadeus Mozart (composer).
| 3770 | **1287** | 62s. multicoloured | 70 | 50 |

1288 Astronaut and Rear of Space Shuttle "Columbia"

1991. Space Shuttles. Multicoloured.
3771	12s. Type **1288**	15	10
3772	32s. Satellite and "Challenger"	25	20
3773	50s. "Discovery" and satellite	45	25
3774	86s. Satellite and "Atlantis" (vert)	60	35
3775	1l.50 Launch of "Buran" (vert)	1·40	60
3776	2l. Satellite and "Atlantis" (vert)	1·70	60
MS3777	86×74 mm. 3l. Earth, "Atlantis" and Moon	3·00	3·00

1289 Luge

1991. Winter Olympic Games, Albertville (1992). Multicoloured.
3778	30s. Type **1289**	35	25
3779	43s. Skiing	45	30
3780	67s. Ski jumping	70	50
3781	2l. Biathlon	2·30	1·40
MS3782	128×86 mm. 3l. Two-man bobsleigh	3·00	3·00

1290 Sheraton Hotel Balkan, Sofia

1991
| 3783 | **1290** | 62s. multicoloured | 60 | 50 |

1291 Japanese Chin

1991. Dogs. Multicoloured.
3784	30s. Type **1291**	25	25
3785	43s. Chihuahua	35	25
3786	62s. Miniature pinscher	45	30
3787	80s. Yorkshire terrier	60	35
3788	1l. Mexican hairless	80	60
3789	3l. Pug	2·30	1·20

1292 Arms

1991. "Philatelia '91" Stamp Fair, Cologne.
| 3790 | **1292** | 86s. multicoloured | 70 | 60 |

1293 Brandenburg Gate

1991. Bicentenary of Brandenburg Gate, Berlin. Sheet 90×70 mm.
| **MS**3791 | **1293** | 4l. green and blue | 3·00 | 2·75 |

1294 Japan 1871 48mon "Dragon" Stamp

1991. "Phila Nippon '91" International Stamp Exhibition, Tokyo.
| 3792 | **1294** | 62s. black, brown & bl | 45 | 35 |

1295 Early Steam Locomotive and Tender

1991. 125th Anniv of the Railway in Bulgaria. Multicoloured.
| 3793 | 30s. Type **1295** | 35 | 25 |
| 3794 | 30s. Early six-wheeled carriage | 35 | 25 |

1296 Ball ascending to Basket

1991. Centenary of Basketball. Multicoloured.
3795	43s. Type **1296**	35	20
3796	62s. Ball level with basket mouth	45	25
3797	90s. Ball entering basket	60	35
3798	1l. Ball in basket	70	50

1297 *Christ carrying the Cross*

1991. 450th Birth Anniv of El Greco (painter). Multicoloured.
3799	43s. Type **1297**	25	15
3800	50s. Holy Family with St. Anna	30	20
3801	60s. St. John of the Cross and St. John the Evangelist	45	25
3802	62s. St. Andrew and St. Francis	60	30
3803	1l. Holy Family with Magdalene	70	35
3804	2l. Cardinal Fernando Nino de Guevara	1·20	50

MS3805 68×86 mm. 3l. Detail of *Holy Family with St. Anna* (different) (39×50 mm) 2·10 1·40

1298 *Snowman, Moon, Candle, Bell and Heart*

1991. Christmas. Multicoloured.
3806	30s. Type **1298**	25	15
3807	62s. Star, clover, angel, house and Christmas tree	45	25

1299 *Small Pasque Flower*

1991. Medicinal Plants. Multicoloured.
3808	30s.(+15s.) Pale pasque flower	15	10
3809	40s. Type **1299**	25	10
3810	55s. Pulsatilla halleri	30	15
3811	60s. Aquilegia nigricans	35	20
3812	1l. Sea buckthorn	60	25
3813	2l. Blackcurrant	1·20	50

No. 3808 includes a *se-tenant* premium-carrying label for 15s. inscribed "ACTION 2000. For Environment Protection".

1300 *Greenland Seals*

1991. Marine Mammals. Multicoloured.
3814	30s. Type **1300**	15	10
3815	43s. Killer whales	25	15
3816	62s. Walruses	30	20
3817	68s. Bottle-nosed dolphins	35	25
3818	1l. Mediterranean monk seals	60	35
3819	2l. Common porpoises	1·20	50

1301 *Synagogue*

1992. 500th Anniv of Jewish Settlement in Bulgaria.
3820	**1301**	1l. multicoloured	60	25

1302 *Rossini, The Barber of Seville and Figaro*

1992. Birth Bicentenary of Gioacchino Rossini (composer).
3821	**1302**	50s. multicoloured	35	20

1303 *Plan of Fair*

1992. Centenary of Plovdiv Fair.
3822	**1303**	1l. black and stone	60	25

1304 *Volvo "740"*

1992. Motor Cars. Multicoloured.
3823	30s. Type **1304**	25	10
3824	45s. Ford "Escort"	30	15
3825	50s. Fiat "Croma"	35	20
3826	50s. Mercedes Benz "600"	35	20
3827	1l. Peugeot "605"	80	25
3828	2l. B.M.W. "316"	1·40	50

1305 *Amerigo Vespucci*

1992. Explorers. Multicoloured.
3829	50s. Type **1305**	25	20
3830	50s. Francisco de Orellana	25	20
3831	1l. Ferdinand Magellan	70	35
3832	1l. Jimenez de Quesada	70	35
3833	2l. Sir Francis Drake	1·20	55
3834	3l. Pedro de Valdivia	1·70	60

MS3835 121×83 mm. 4l. Christopher Columbus 3·00 2·50

1306 *Granada*

1992. "Granada '92" Int Stamp Exhibition.
3836	**1306**	62s. multicoloured	35	25

1307 *Santa Maria*

1992. Europa. 500th Anniv of Discovery of America by Columbus. Multicoloured.
3837	1l. Type **1307**	1·70	60
3838	2l. Christopher Columbus	3·00	85

Nos. 3837/8 were issued together, *se-tenant*, forming a composite design.

1308 *House*

1992. S.O.S. Children's Village.
3839	**1308**	1l. multicoloured	70	25

1309 *Long Jumping*

1992. Olympic Games, Barcelona (2nd issue). Multicoloured.
3840	50s. Type **1309**	35	20
3841	50s. Swimming	35	20
3842	1l. High jumping	60	35
3843	3l. Gymnastics	1·90	60

MS3844 52×75 mm. 4l. Olympic Torch (vert) 2·30 1·80

1310 *1902 Laurin and Klement Motor Cycle*

1992. Motor Cycles. Multicoloured.
3845	30s. Type **1310**	25	10
3846	50s. 1928 Puch "200 Luxus"	35	15
3847	50s. 1931 Norton "CS 1"	35	15
3848	70s. 1950 Harley Davidson	45	20
3849	1l. 1986 Gilera "SP 01"	70	25
3850	2l. 1990 BMW "K 1"	1·40	50

1311 *Genoa*

1992. "Genova '92" International Thematic Stamp Exhibition.
3851	**1311**	1l. multicoloured	70	25

1312 *Grasshopper*

1992. Insects. Multicoloured.
3852	1l. Four-spotted libellula	10	10
3853	2l. Raphidia notata	35	20
3854	3l. Type **1312**	80	25
3855	4l. Stag beetle	1·20	35
3856	5l. Fire bug	1·40	50
3857	7l. Ant	2·30	1·20
3858	20l. Wasp	5·75	1·80
3859	50l. Praying mantis	14·00	3·50

1313 *Silhouette of Head on Town Plan*

1992. 50th Anniv of Institute of Architecture and Building.
3862	**1313**	1l. red and black	70	25

1314 *Oak*

1992. Trees. Multicoloured.
3863	50s. Type **1314**	20	15
3864	50s. Horse chestnut	20	15
3865	1l. Oak	60	25
3866	1l. Macedonian pine	60	25
3867	2l. Maple	1·40	35
3868	3l. Pear	1·70	60

1315 *Embroidered Flower*

1992. Centenary of Folk Museum, Sofia.
3869	**1315**	1l. multicoloured	70	25

1316 *Bulgaria (freighter)*

1992. Centenary of National Shipping Fleet. Multicoloured.
3870	30s. Type **1316**	10	10
3871	50s. Kastor (tanker)	25	15
3872	1l. Geroite na Sebastopol (train ferry)	70	25
3873	2l. Aleko Konstantinov (tanker)	1·20	50
3874	2l. Bulgaria (tanker)	1·20	50
3875	3l. Varna (container ship)	1·90	70

1317 *Council Emblem*

1992. Admission to Council of Europe.
3876	**1317**	7l. multicoloured	4·75	2·40

1318 *Family exercising on Beach*

1992. Fourth World Sport for All Congress, Varna. Sheet 58×75 mm.
MS3877 **1318** 4l. multicoloured 2·50 2·50

1319 *Santa Claus (Ani Bacheva)*

1992. Christmas. Children's Drawings. Multicoloured.
3878	1l. Type **1319**	60	25
3879	7l. "Madonna and Child" (Georgi Petkov)	3·75	1·60

1320 *Leopard*

1992. Big Cats. Multicoloured.
3880	50s. Type **1320**	35	10
3881	50s. Cheetah	35	10
3882	1l. Jaguar	70	25
3883	2l. Puma	1·40	60
3884	2l. Tiger	1·40	60
3885	3l. Lion	1·70	70

1321 *Cricket*

1992. Sport. Multicoloured.
3886	50s. Type **1321**	35	15
3887	50s. Baseball	35	15
3888	1l. Pony and trap racing	70	25
3889	1l. Polo	70	25
3890	2l. Hockey	1·40	60
3891	3l. American football	1·70	70

1322 *Tengmalm's Owl*

1992. Owls. Multicoloured.
3892	30s. Type **1322**	25	15
3893	50s. Tawny owl (horiz)	35	15
3894	1l. Long-eared owl	70	25
3895	2l. Short-eared owl	1·40	60

| 3896 | 2l. Eurasian scops owl (horiz) | 1·40 | 60 |
| 3897 | 3l. Barn owl | 2·10 | 70 |

1323 *Khan Kubrat (Dimitur Gyudzhenov)*

1992. Historical Paintings. Multicoloured.

3898	50s. Type **1323**	35	15
3899	1l. *Khan Asparukh (Nikolai Pavlovich)*	70	25
3900	2l. *Khan Terval at Tsarigrad (Dimitur Panchev)*	1·20	60
3901	3l. *Prince Boris (Nikolai Pavlovich)*	1·90	95
MS3902	75×90 mm. 4l. *The Warrior (Mito Ganovski)* (vert)	2·50	2·50

1324 Sculpted Head

1993. Centenary of National Archaeological Museum, Sofia.

| 3903 | **1324** 1l. multicoloured | 70 | 25 |

1325 Shooting

1993. "Borovets '93" Biathlon Championship. Multicoloured.

| 3904 | 1l. Type **1325** | 70 | 35 |
| 3905 | 7l. Cross-country skiing | 4·75 | 2·00 |

1326 Rilski

1993. Birth Bicentenary of Neofit Rilski (compiler of Bulgarian grammar and dictionary).

| 3906 | **1326** 1l. bistre and red | 70 | 25 |

1327 *Morning* (sculpture, Georgi Chapkunov)

1993. Europa. Contemporary Art. Multicoloured.

| 3907 | 3l. Type **1327** | 1·70 | 60 |
| 3908 | 8l. *Composition* (D. Buyukliiski) | 3·00 | 1·80 |

1328 Veil-tailed Goldfish

1993. Fish. Multicoloured.

3909	1l. Type **1328**	25	15
3910	2l. Yucatan sail-finned molly	45	20
3911	3l. Two-striped lyretail	70	25
3912	3l. Freshwater angelfish	70	25
3913	4l. Red discus	1·00	35
3914	8l. Pearl gourami	2·10	70

1329 Apple

1993. Fruits. Multicoloured.

3915	1l. Type **1329**	25	10
3916	2l. Peach	45	15
3917	2l. Pear	45	15
3918	3l. Quince	70	25
3919	5l. Pomegranate	1·40	35
3920	7l. Fig	2·10	60

1330 Monteverdi

1993. 350th Death Anniv of Claudio Monteverdi (composer).

| 3921 | **1330** 1l. green, yellow & red | 25 | 15 |

1331 High Jumping

1993. Int Games for the Deaf, Sofia. Multicoloured.

3922	1l. Type **1331**	25	15
3923	2l. Swimming	45	20
3924	3l. Cycling	80	25
3925	4l. Tennis	85	35
MS3926	86×75 mm. 5l. Football	1·20	1·20

1332 Baptism (from Manasses Chronicle)

1993. 1100th Anniv of Preslav and Introduction of Cyrillic Script. Sheet 113×110 mm containing T 1332 and similar horiz designs. Multicoloured.

| MS3927 | 5l. Type **1332**; 5l. Prince Boris I (after Dimitur Gyudzhenov); 5l. Tsar Simeon I (after Dimitur Gyudzhenov); 5l. Cavalry charge (after Manasses Chronicle) | 4·75 | 4·75 |

1333 Prince Alexander

1993. Death Centenary of Prince Alexander I.

| 3928 | **1333** 3l. multicoloured | 70 | 25 |

1334 Tchaikovsky

1993. Death Centenary of Pyotr Tchaikovsky (composer).

| 3929 | **1334** 3l. multicoloured | 70 | 25 |

1335 Crossbow

1993. Weapons. Multicoloured.

3930	1l. Type **1335**	25	15
3931	2l. 18th-century flintlock pistol	45	20
3932	3l. Revolver	70	25
3933	3l. Luger pistol	70	25
3934	5l. Mauser rifle	1·30	40
3935	7l. Kalashnikov assault rifle	1·90	70

1336 Newton

1993. 350th Birth Anniv of Sir Isaac Newton (mathematician).

| 3936 | **1336** 1l. multicoloured | 25 | 15 |

1337 "100" on Stamps and Globe

1993. Centenary of Bulgarian Philately.

| 3937 | **1337** 1l. multicoloured | 25 | 15 |

1338 "Ecology" in Cyrillic Script

1993. Ecology. Multicoloured.

| 3938 | 1l. Type **1338** | 25 | 15 |
| 3939 | 7l. "Ecology" in English | 1·90 | 60 |

1339 Mallard

1993. Hunting. Multicoloured.

3940	1l. Type **1339**	15	10
3941	1l. Common pheasant	15	10
3942	2l. Red fox	35	20
3943	3l. Roe deer	60	25
3944	6l. European brown hare	1·20	50
3945	8l. Wild boar	1·70	70

1340 "Taurus", "Gemini" and "Cancer"

1993. Christmas. Signs of the Zodiac. Multicoloured.

3946	1l. Type **1340**	10	10
3947	1l. "Leo", "Virgo" and "Libra"	10	10
3948	7l. "Aquarius", "Pisces" and "Aries"	1·40	50
3949	7l. "Scorpio", "Sagittarius" and "Capricorn"	1·40	50

Nos. 3946/7 and 3948/9 were each issued together, *se-tenant*; when placed together the four stamps form a composite design.

1341 Sofia Costume

1993. Costumes. Multicoloured.

3950	1l. Type **1341**	25	10
3951	1l. Plovdiv	25	10
3952	2l. Belograd	35	15
3953	3l. Oryakhovo	45	20
3954	3l. Shumen	45	20
3955	8l. Kurdzhali	1·40	60

1342 Freestyle Skiing

1994. Winter Olympic Games, Lillehammer, Norway. Multicoloured.

| 3956 | 1l. Type **1342** | 10 | 10 |
| 3957 | 2l. Speed skating | 35 | 15 |

3958	3l. Two-man luge	60	20
3959	4l. Ice hockey	95	25
MS3960	59×90 mm. 3l. multicoloured	95	95

1343 *Self-portrait* and Tsar Simeon

1994. Death Centenary of Nikolai Pavlovich (artist).

| 3961 | **1343** 3l. multicoloured | 60 | 25 |

1344 Plesiosaurus

1994. Prehistoric Animals. Multicoloured.

3962	2l. Type **1344**	35	10
3963	3l. Archaeopteryx	60	20
3964	3l. Iguanodon	60	20
3965	4l. Edmontonia	80	25
3966	5l. Styracosaurus	95	35
3967	7l. Tyrannosaurus	1·40	50

1345 Players (Chile, 1962)

1994. World Cup Football Championship, U.S.A. Multicoloured.

3968	3l. Type **1345**	60	25
3969	6l. Players (England, 1966)	1·20	35
3970	7l. Goalkeeper making save (Mexico, 1970)	1·30	50
3971	9l. Player kicking (West Germany, 1974)	1·60	70
MS3972	90×123 mm. 5l. Player punching air (Mexico, 1986) (vert); 5l. Player tackling (U.S.A., 1994)	2·50	2·50

1346 Photoelectric Analysis (Georgi Nadzhakov)

1994. Europa. Discoveries. Multicoloured.

| 3973 | 3l. Type **1346** | 1·20 | 60 |
| 3974 | 15l. Cardiogram and heart (Prof. Ivan Mitev) | 4·00 | 1·80 |

1347 Khristov

1994. 80th Birth Anniv of Boris Khristov (actor).

| 3975 | **1347** 3l. multicoloured | 60 | 25 |

1348 Sleeping Hamster

1994. The Common Hamster. Multicoloured.

3976	3l. Type **1348**	60	25
3977	7l. Hamster looking out of burrow	1·00	60
3978	10l. Hamster sitting up in grass	1·70	85
3979	15l. Hamster approaching berry	2·50	1·30

1349 Space Shuttle, Satellite and Dish Aerial

1994. North Atlantic Co-operation Council (North Atlantic Treaty Organization and Warsaw Pact members).

3980	**1349**	3l. multicoloured	60	35

1350 Baron Pierre de Coubertin (founder of modern games)

1994. Cent of International Olympic Committee.

3981	**1350**	3l. multicoloured	60	35

1351 Christ Pantocrator

1994. Icons. Multicoloured.

3982	2l. Type **1351**	25	10	
3983	3l. Raising of Lazarus	45	20	
3984	5l. Passion of Christ	60	25	
3985	7l. Archangel Michael	1·20	50	
3986	8l. Sts. Cyril and Methodius	1·40	60	
3987	15l. Madonna Enthroned	3·00	70	

1352 Vechernik

1994. Christmas. Breads. Multicoloured.

3988	3l. Type **1352**	60	25	
3989	15l. Bogovitsa	3·00	1·60	

1353 "Golden Showers"

1994. Roses. Multicoloured.

3990	2l. Type **1353**	35	10	
3991	3l. "Caen Peace Monument"	60	25	
3992	5l. "Theresa of Lisieux"	95	35	
3993	7l. "Zambra 93"	1·40	60	
3994	10l. "Gustave Courbet"	2·00	65	
3995	15l. "Honore de Balzac"	3·00	1·20	

БЪЛГАРИЯ - С БРОНЗОВИ МЕДАЛИ

(1354)

1994. Bulgaria's Fourth Place in World Cup Football Championship. No. MS3972 overprinted with T **1354** in margin.

MS3996 90×123 mm. 5l. multicoloured; 5l. multicoloured ... 22·00 22·00

1355 "AM/ASES", 1912

1994. Trams. Multicoloured.

3997	1l. Type **1355**	10	10	
3998	2l. "AM/ASES", 1928	35	15	
3999	3l. "M.A.N./AEG", 1931	60	25	
4000	5l. "D.T.O.", 1942	95	35	
4001	8l. Republika, 1951	1·70	70	
4002	10l. Kosmonavt articulated tramcar set, 1961	2·10	85	

1356 Petleshkov and Flag

1995. 150th Birth Anniv of Vasil Petleshkov (leader of 1876 April uprising).

4003	**1356**	3l. multicoloured	60	35

1357 Daisy growing through Cracked Helmet

1995. Europa. Peace and Freedom. Multicoloured.

4004	3l. Type **1357**	1·20	60	
4005	15l. Dove with olive branch on rifle barrel	4·00	1·80	

1358 Player

1995. Centenary of Volleyball. Sheet 92×75 mm containing T **1358** and similar multicoloured design.

MS4006 10l. Type **1358**; 15l. Player hitting ball (vert) ... 4·25 4·25

1359 Sea Lily (Pancratium martimum)

1995. European Nature Conservation Year. Sheet 70×99 mm containing T **1359** and similar horiz design. Multicoloured.

MS4007 10l. Type **1359**; 15l. Imperial Eagle (Aquila heliaca) ... 5·50 5·50

1360 Emperor Penguin

1995. Antarctic Animals. Multicoloured.

4008	1l. Shrimp (horiz)	15	10	
4009	2l. Ice fish (horiz)	35	15	
4010	3l. Sperm whale (horiz)	45	25	
4011	5l. Weddell's seal (horiz)	80	35	
4012	8l. South polar skua (horiz)	1·40	70	
4013	10l. Type **1360**	1·70	85	

1361 Stambolov

1995. Death Cent of Stefan Stambolov (politician).

4014	**1361**	3l. multicoloured	60	35

1362 Pole Vaulting

1995. Olympic Games, Atlanta (1996) (1st issue). Multicoloured.

4015	3l. Type **1362**	45	15	
4016	7l. High jumping	1·20	50	
4017	10l. Long jumping	1·70	60	
4018	15l. Triple jumping	2·50	85	

See also Nos. 4083/6.

1363 Pea

1995. Food Plants. Multicoloured.

4019	2l. Type **1363**	25	15	
4020	3l. Chickpea	45	25	
4021	3l. Soya bean	45	25	
4022	4l. Spinach	70	35	
4023	5l. Peanut	80	50	
4024	15l. Lentil	2·30	85	

1364 "100"

1995. Centenary of Organized Tourism.

4025	**1364**	1l. multicoloured	60	25

1365 Ivan Nikolov-Zograf

1995. Birth Centenary of Vasil Zakhariev (painter).

4026	**1365**	2l. multicoloured	35	15
4027		3l. multicoloured	60	25
4028		5l. black, brown & grn	95	50
4029		10l. multicoloured	1·70	95

DESIGNS: 3l. Rila Monastery; 5l. Self-portrait; 10l. Raspberry Collectors.

1366 "Dove-Hands" holding Globe

1995. 50th Anniv of UNO.

4030	**1366**	3l. multicoloured	60	25

1367 Polikarpov Po-2 Biplane

1995. Aircraft. Multicoloured.

4031	3l. Type **1367**	45	25	
4032	5l. Lisunov Li-2 airliner	80	35	
4033	7l. Junkers Ju 52	1·20	60	
4034	10l. Focke Wulf FW58	1·70	70	

1368 Charlie Chaplin and Mickey Mouse

1995. Centenary of Motion Pictures. Multicoloured.

4035	2l. Type **1368**	35	15	
4036	3l. Marilyn Monroe and Marlene Dietrich	45	25	
4037	5l. Nikolai Cherkasov and Humphrey Bogart	60	30	
4038	8l. Sophia Loren and Liza Minelli	1·50	35	
4039	10l. Gerard Philipe and Toshiro Mifune	1·70	50	
4040	15l. Katya Paskaleva and Nevena Kokanova	2·30	85	

1369 Agate

1995. Minerals. Multicoloured.

4041	1l. Type **1369**	15	10	
4042	2l. Sphalerite	35	15	
4043	5l. Calcite	95	25	
4044	7l. Quartz	1·20	30	
4045	8l. Pyromorphite	1·40	35	
4046	10l. Almandine	1·90	60	

1370 Mary and Joseph

1995. Christmas. Multicoloured.

4047	3l. Type **1370**	60	25	
4048	15l. Three wise men approaching stable	2·30	1·30	

1371 Polynesian Woman with Fruit

1996. Birth Centenary of Kiril Tsonev (painter).

4049	**1371**	3l. multicoloured	60	25

1372 Luther (after Lucas Cranach the elder)

1996. 450th Death Anniv of Martin Luther (Protestant reformer).

4050	**1372**	3l. multicoloured	60	25

1373 Preobrazhenie

1996. Monasteries.

4051	**1373**	3l. green	15	10
4052	-	5l. red	35	20
4053	-	10l. blue	45	25
4054	-	20l. orange	1·20	50
4055	-	25l. brown	1·40	70
4056	-	40l. purple	2·30	1·20

DESIGNS: 5l. Arapov; 10l. Dryanovo; 20l. Bachkov; 25l. Troyan; 40l. Zograf.

1374 Bulgarian National Bank

1996. Fifth Anniv of European Reconstruction and Development Bank.

4063	**1374**	7l. green, red and blue	60	35
4064	-	30l. blue, red & purple	2·30	85

DESIGN: 30l. Palace of Culture, Sofia.

1375 Yew

1996. Conifers. Multicoloured.

4065	5l. Type **1375**	25	10
4066	8l. Silver fir	45	20
4067	10l. Norway spruce	60	25
4068	20l. Scots pine	1·20	35
4069	25l. *Pinus heldreichii*	1·40	50
4070	40l. Juniper	2·30	1·20

1376 Battle Scene and Mourning Women

1996. 120th Anniversaries. Multicoloured.

4071	10l. Type **1376** (April uprising)	60	25
4072	40l. Khristo Botev and script (poet, death anniv) (horiz)	2·30	1·20

1377 Modern Officer's Parade Uniform

1996. Military Uniforms. Multicoloured.

4073	5l. Type **1377**	20	10
4074	8l. Second World War combat uniform	30	15
4075	10l. Balkan War uniform	40	20
4076	20l. Guard officer's ceremonial uniform	95	50
4077	25l. Serbo-Bulgarian War officer's uniform	1·20	60
4078	40l. Russo-Turkish War soldier's uniform	1·70	1·20

1378 Monument

1996. 50th Anniv of the Republic.

4079	**1378**	10l. multicoloured	60	35

1379 Elisaveta Bagryana (poet)

1996. Europa. Famous Women. Multicoloured.

4080	10l. Type **1379**	2·30	1·20
4081	40l. Katya Popova (opera singer)	3·00	1·80

1380 Player

1996. European Football Championship, England. Sheet 71×86 mm containing T 1380 and similar vert design. Multicoloured.

MS4082	10l. Type **1380**; 15l. Player (different)	2·50	2·50

1381 Nikola Stanchev (wrestling, Melbourne 1956)

1996. Olympic Games, Atlanta (2nd issue). Bulgarian Medal Winners. Multicoloured.

4083	5l. Type **1381**	20	10
4084	8l. Boris Georgiev (boxing, Helsinki 1952)	45	20
4085	10l. Ivanka Khristova (putting the shot, Montreal 1976)	70	25
4086	25l. Z. Iordanova and S. Otsetova (double sculls, Montreal 1976)	1·50	60
MS4087	89×68 mm. 15l. Olympic Stadium, Athens, 1896	1·70	1·70

1382 *The Letter* (detail)

1996. 250th Birth Anniv of Francisco Goya (painter). Multicoloured.

4088	5l. Detail of fresco	20	10
4089	8l. Type **1382**	60	35
4090	26l. *3rd of May 1808 in Madrid* (detail)	1·50	70
4091	40l. *Neighbours on a Balcony* (detail)	2·30	1·20
MS4092	99×73 mm. 10l. *Clothed Maja* (50×26 mm); 15l. *Naked Maja* (50×26 mm)	1·70	1·70

1383 Water Flea

1996. Aquatic Life. Multicoloured.

4093	5l. Type **1383**	20	10
4094	10l. Common water louse	45	20
4095	12l. European river crayfish	60	25
4096	25l. Prawn	1·00	35
4097	30l. *Cumella limicola*	1·20	60
4098	40l. Mediterranean shore crab	3·00	1·20

1384 St. Ivan

1996. 1050th Death Anniv of Ivan Rilski (founder of Rila Monastery). Sheet 56×87 mm.

MS4099	**1384**	10l. multicoloured	1·00	1·00

1385 Tryavna

1996. Houses.

4100	**1385**	10l. brown and stone	35	15
4101	-	15l. red and yellow	45	20
4102	-	30l. green and yellow	95	50
4103	-	50l. violet and mauve	1·60	85
4104	-	60l. green and lt green	2·10	1·20
4105	-	100l. ultramarine & bl	3·25	1·80

DESIGNS: 15l. Nesebur; 30l. Tryavna (different); 50l. Koprivshtitsa; 60l. Plovdiv; 100l. Koprivshtitsa (different).

1386 *Philadelphia*, 1836

1996. Steam Locomotives. Multicoloured.

4106	5l. Type **1386**	25	20
4107	10l. *Jenny Lind*, 1847	60	25
4108	12l. *Liverpool*, 1848	70	35
4109	26l. *Anglet*, 1876	1·50	70

1387 Anniversary Emblem and Academy

1996. Centenary of National Arts Academy.

4110	**1387**	15l. black and yellow	95	35

1388 Sword and Miniature from *Chronicle of Ivan Skilitsa*

1996. 1100th Anniv of Tsar Simeon's Victory over the Turks. Multicoloured.

4111	10l. Type **1388**	60	25
4112	40l. Dagger and right-hand detail of miniature	2·30	1·20

Nos. 4111/12 were issued together, *se-tenant*, forming a composite design.

1389 Fishes and Diver (Dilyana Lokmadzhieva)

1996. 50th Anniv of UNICEF. Children's Paintings. Multicoloured.

4113	7l. Type **1389**	45	25
4114	15l. Circus (Velislava Dimitrova)	95	50
4115	20l. Man and artist's pallet (Miglena Nikolova)	1·30	60
4116	60l. Family meal (Darena Dencheva)	3·75	1·90

1390 Christmas Tree

1996. Christmas. Multicoloured.

4117	15l. Type **1390**	80	35
4118	60l. Star over basilica and Christmas tree	3·50	1·80

1391 *Zograf Monastery*

1996. Birth Centenary of Tsanko Lavrenov (painter).

4119	**1391**	15l. multicoloured	80	35

1392 Pointer

1997. Puppies. Multicoloured.

4120	5l. Type **1392**	25	25
4121	7l. Chow chow	35	20
4122	25l. Carakachan dog	1·20	60
4123	50l. Basset hound	2·30	1·20

1393 Bell

1997. 150th Birth Anniv of Alexander Graham Bell (telephone pioneer).

4124	**1393**	30l. multicoloured	95	50

1394 Man drinking

1997. Birth Centenary of Ivan Milev (painter). Murals from Kazaluk. Multicoloured.

4125	5l. Type **1394**	20	15
4126	15l. Woman praying	45	25
4127	30l. Reaper	60	50
4128	60l. Mother and child	1·70	95

1395 Lady March (symbol of spring)

1997. Europa. Tales and Legends. Multicoloured.

4129	120l. Type **1395**	3·00	1·20
4130	600l. St. George (national symbol)	2·30	1·20

1396 Kisimov in Character

1997. Birth Cent of Konstantin Kisimov (actor).

4131	**1396**	120l. multicoloured	25	25

1397 Von Stephan

1997. Death Centenary of Heinrich von Stephan (founder of U.P.U.).

4132	**1397**	60l. multicoloured	25	25

1398 Old Town, Nesebur

1997. Historic Sights.

4133	**1398**	80l. brown and black	10	10
4134	-	200l. violet and black	25	10
4135	-	300l. yellow and black	35	25

4136	–	500l. green and black	60	35
4137	–	600l. yellow and black	80	50
4138	–	1000l. orange and black	1·40	85

DESIGNS: 200l. Sculpture, Ivanovski Church; 300l. Christ (detail of icon), Boyana Church; 500l. Horseman (stone relief), Madara; 600l. Figure of woman (carving from sarcophagus), Sveshary; 1000l. Tomb decoration, Kazanlak.

1399 Gaetano Donizetti

1997. Composers' Anniversaries. Multicoloured.

4139	120l. Type **1399** (birth bicentenary)	45	35
4140	120l. Franz Schubert (birth bicentenary)	45	35
4141	120l. Felix Mendelssohn-Bartholdy (150th death anniv)	45	35
4142	120l. Johannes Brahms (death centenary)	45	35

1400 Trifolium rubens

1997. Flowers in the Red Book. Multicoloured.

4143	80l. Type **1400**	25	10
4144	100l. Tulipa hageri	35	10
4145	120l. Inula spiraeifolia	35	25
4146	200l. Thin-leafed peony	80	35

1401 Anniversary Emblem

1997. 50th Anniv of Civil Aviation.

4147	**1401**	120l. multicoloured	35	25

1402 Georgiev

1997. Death Centenary of Evlogii Georgiev.

4148	**1402**	120l. multicoloured	35	25

1403 Show Jumping and Running

1997. World Modern Pentathlon Championship, Sofia. Multicoloured.

4149	60l. Type **1403**	35	10
4150	80l. Fencing and swimming	35	25
4151	100l. Running and fencing	45	25
4152	120l. Shooting and swimming	60	35
4153	200l. Show jumping and shooting	70	50

1404 St. Basil's Cathedral

1997. 850th Anniv of Moscow and "Moskva '97" International Stamp Exhibition. Sheet 87×96 mm.

MS4154	**1404**	120l. multicoloured	80	60

1405 D 2500 M Boat Engine

1997. Centenary of Diesel Engine. Multicoloured.

4155	80l. Type **1405**	35	10
4156	100l. D 2900 T tractor engine	50	25
4157	120l. D 3900 A truck engine	60	35
4158	200l. D 2500 K fork-lift truck engine	1·00	50

1406 Goddess with Mural Crown

1997. 43rd General Assembly of Atlantic Club, Sofia.

4159	**1406**	120l. mve, bl & ultram	50	35
4160	–	120l. grn, bl & ultram	50	35
4161	–	120l. brn, bl & ultram	50	35
4162	–	120l. vio, bl & ultram	50	35

DESIGNS: No. 4160, Eagle on globe; 4161, Venue; 4162, Venue (different).

1407 Cervantes and Don Quixote with Sancho

1997. 450th Birth Anniv of Miguel de Cervantes (writer).

4163	**1407**	120l. multicoloured	50	25

1408 Raztsvetnikov

1997. Birth Centenary of Asen Raztsvetnikov (writer and translator).

4164	**1408**	120l. multicoloured	50	25

1409 Fragment of Tombstone

1997. Millenary of Coronation of Tsar Samuel. Multicoloured.

4165	120l. Type **1409**	50	25
4166	600l. Tsar Samuel and knights in battle	2·40	1·20

1410 Star and Houses forming Christmas Tree

1997. Christmas. Multicoloured.

4167	120l. Type **1410**	50	25
4168	600l. Stable with Christmas tree roof	2·20	1·20

1411 Speed Skating

1997. Winter Olympic Games, Nagano, Japan (1998). Multicoloured.

4169	60l. Type **1411**	25	10
4170	80l. Skiing	35	20
4171	120l. Shooting (biathlon)	50	25
4172	600l. Ice skating	3·00	1·90

1412 Radiometric System R-400

1997. 25th Anniv of Bulgarian Space Experiments. Sheet 87×68 mm.

MS4173	**1412**	120l. multicoloured	1·20	1·20

1413 State Arms

1997

4174	**1413**	120l. multicoloured	40	25

1414 Botev (after B. Petrov)

1998. 150th Birth and 120th Death (1996) Anniv of Khristo Botev (poet and revolutionary).

4175	**1414**	120l. multicoloured	40	25

1415 Brecht

1998. Birth Cent of Bertolt Brecht (playwright).

4176	**1415**	120l. multicoloured	40	25

1416 Arrows

1998. Cent of Bulgarian Telegraph Agency.

4177	**1416**	120l. multicoloured	40	25

1417 Barn Swallow at Window

1998. 120th Birth Anniv of Aleksandur Bozhinov (children's illustrator). Multicoloured.

4178	120l. Type **1417**	40	15
4179	120l. Blackbird with backpack on branch	40	15
4180	120l. Father Frost and children	40	15
4181	120l. Maiden Rositsa in field holding hands up to rain	40	15

1418 Tsar Alexander II

1998. 120th Anniv of Liberation from Turkey. Multicoloured.

4182	120l. Type **1418**	40	15
4183	600l. Independence monument, Ruse	2·00	95

1419 Christ ascending and Hare pulling Cart of Eggs

1998. Easter.

4184	**1419**	120l. multicoloured	40	25

1420 Torch Bearer

1998. 75th Anniv of Bulgarian Olympic Committee.

4185	**1420**	120l. multicoloured	40	25

1421 Map of Participating Countries

1998. Phare International Programme for Telecommunications and Post.

4186	**1421**	120l. multicoloured	40	25

1422 Girls in Folk Costumes

1998. Europa. National Festivals. Multicoloured.

4187	120l. Type **1422**	1·40	70
4188	600l. Boys wearing dance masks	3·50	2·75

ПЪРВИ
ЗЛАТЕН МЕДАЛ
ЗА БЪЛГАРИЯ

Е. ДАФОВСКА

(1423)

1998. Winning of Gold Medal in 15km Biathlon by Ekaterina Dafovska at Winter Olympic Games, Nagano. No. 4171 optd with T **1423**.

4189	120l. multicoloured	4·00	4·00

1424 Dante and Virgil in Hell

1998. Birth Bicentenary of Eugene Delacroix (artist).

4190	**1424**	120l. multicoloured	40	25

1425 Footballer and Club Badge

1998. 50th Anniv of TsSKA Football Club.

4191	**1425**	120l. multicoloured	40	25

1426 European Tabby

1998. Cats. Multicoloured.

4192	60l. Type **1426**	15	10
4193	80l. Siamese	25	15
4194	120l. Exotic shorthair	40	25
4195	600l. Birman	2·20	1·10

1427 *Oh, You are Jealous!*

1998. 150th Birth Anniv of Paul Gauguin (artist).
4196 **1427** 120l. multicoloured 40 25

1428 Khilendarski-
Bozveli

1998. 150th Death Anniv of Neofit Khilendarski-Bozveli
(priest and writer).
4197 **1428** 120l. multicoloured 40 25

1429 Tackling

1998. World Cup Football Championship, France.
Multicoloured.
4198 60l. Type **1429** 15 10
4199 80l. Players competing for ball 25 15
4200 120l. Players and ball 40 25
4201 600l. Goalkeeper 2·20 1·10
MS4202 68 ×91 mm. 120l. Lion, ball
and Eiffel Tower 1·40 1·40

1430 A. Aleksandrov

1998. Tenth Anniv of Second Soviet–Bulgarian Space
Flight.
4203 **1430** 120l. multicoloured 55 25

1431 Vasco da Gama

1998. "Expo '98" World's Fair, Lisbon. 500th Anniv of
Vasco da Gama's Voyage to India. Multicoloured.
4204 600l. Type **1431** 2·30 70
4205 600l. *Sao Gabriel* (Vasco da
Gama's ship) 2·30 70
 Nos. 4204/5 were issued together, *se-tenant*, forming a
composite design.

1432 Focke Wolf FW 61, 1937

1998. Helicopters. Multicoloured.
4206 80l. Type **1432** 25 10
4207 100l. Sikorsky R-4, 1943 40 15
4208 120l. Mil Mi-V12, 1970 55 25
4209 200l. McDonnell-Douglas MD-
900, 1995 80 40

1433 Mediterranean Monk
Seal (*Monachus monachus*)

1998. International Year of the Ocean. Sheet 67×88 mm.
MS4210 **1433** 120l. multicoloured 4·75 4·75

1434 Talev

1998. Birth Centenary of Dimitur Talev (writer).
4211 **1434** 180l. multicoloured 70 40

1435 Aleksandur
Malinov (Prime
Minister, 1931)

1998. 90th Anniv of Independence.
4212 **1435** 180l. black, blue & yell 70 40

1436 *Limenitis
redukta* and
Ligularia sibirica

1998. Butterflies and Flowers. Multicoloured.
4213 60l. Type **1436** 10 10
4214 180l. Painted lady and *Anthemis
macrantha* 70 25
4215 200l. Red admiral and *Trache-
lium jacquinii* 80 40
4216 600l. *Anthocharis gruneri* and
Geranium tuberosum 2·20 1·20

1437 Smirnenski

1998. Birth Cent of Khristo Smirnenski (writer).
4217 **1437** 180l. multicoloured 70 40

1438 Silhouette of Man

1998. 50th Anniv of Universal Declaration of Human
Rights.
4218 **1438** 180l. multicoloured 70 40

1439 Bruno

1998. 450th Birth Anniv of Giordano Bruno (scholar).
4219 **1439** 180l. multicoloured 70 40

1440 Man diving through
Heart ("I Love You")

1998. Greetings Stamps. Multicoloured.
4220 180l. Type **1440** 70 40
4221 180l. Making wine (holiday)
(vert) 70 40
4222 180l. Man in chalice (birthday)
(vert) 70 40
4223 180l. Waiter serving wine (name
day) (vert) 70 40

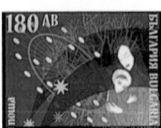

1441 Madonna and Child

1998. Christmas.
4224 **1441** 180l. multicoloured 70 40

1442 Geshov

1999. 150th Birth Anniv of Ivan Evstratiev Geshov
(politician).
4225 **1442** 180l. multicoloured 70 40

1443 National Assembly
Building, Sofia

1999. 120th Anniv of Third Bulgarian State.
Multicoloured.
4226 **1443** 180l. Type **1443** 70 40
4227 180l. Council of Ministers 70 40
4228 180l. Statue of Justice (Supreme
Court of Appeal) 70 40
4229 180l. Coins (National Bank) 70 40
4230 180l. Army 70 40
4231 180l. Lion emblem of Sofia and
lamp post 70 40

1444 Georgi Karakashev (stage
designer) and Set of *Kismet*

1999. Birth Centenaries. Multicoloured.
4232 **1444** 180l. Type **1444** 55 25
4233 200l. Bencho Obreshkov (artist)
and *Lodki* 70 35
4234 300l. Score and Asen Naidenov
(conductor of Sofia Opera) 80 40
4235 600l. Pancho Vladigerov (com-
poser) and score of *Vardar* 1·90 95

1445 Rainbow Lory
(*Trichoglossus
haematodus*)

1999. "Bulgaria '99" European Stamp Exhibition. Parrots.
Sheet 100×110 mm containing T **1445** and similar
vert designs. Multicoloured.
MS4236 600l. Type **1445**; 600l. Eastern
rosella; 600l. Budgerigar; 600l. Green-
winged macaw 12·00 12·00

1446 Sun and Emblem

1999. 50th Anniv of North Atlantic Treaty Organization.
4237 **1446** 180l. multicoloured 55 25

1447 Decorated Eggs

1999. Easter.
4238 **1447** 180l. multicoloured 55 25

1448 Red-crested Pochard and
Ropotamo Reserve

1999. Europa. Parks and Gardens. Multicoloured.
4239 **1448** 180l. Type **1448** 95 40
4240 600l. Central Balkan National
Park 2·40 2·00

1449 Albrecht Durer
(self-portrait) and Nuremberg

1999. "iBRA '99" International Stamp Exhibition,
Nuremberg, Germany.
4241 **1449** 600l. multicoloured 2·00 95

1450 Anniversary Emblem

1999. 50th Anniv of Council of Europe.
4242 **1450** 180l. multicoloured 1·40 70

1451 Honore de Balzac
(novelist)

1999. Birth Anniversaries. Multicoloured.
4243 180l. Type **1451** (bicentenary) 55 15
4244 200l. Johann Wolfgang von
Goethe (poet and play-
wright) (250th anniv) 95 25
4245 300l. Aleksandr Pushkin (poet)
(bicentenary) 1·10 55
4246 600l. Diego de Silva Velazquez
(painter) (400th anniv) 2·00 95

1452 Penny Farthing

1999. Bicycles. Multicoloured.
4247 180l. Type **1452** 55 10
4248 200l. Road racing bicycles 70 15
4249 300l. Track racing bicycles 1·10 40
4250 600l. Mountain bike 2·00 70

1453 St. Cyril and
Methodius

1999. "Bulgaria '99" European Stamp Exhibition, Sofia.
19th-century Icons of Sts. Cyril and Methodius.
Sheet 100×110 mm containing T **1453** and similar
vert designs. Multicoloured.
MS4251 600l. Type **1453**; 600l. St. Cyril
with scroll and staff and St. Metho-
dius; 600l. Sts. Cyril and Methodius
with scrolls; 600l. St. Cyril with
crucifix, St. Methodius and Christ 11·00 11·00

1454 Sopot
Monastery
Fountain

1999. Fountains.
4252 **1454** 1st. light brown 15 10
4254 - 8st. green and black 15 10
4255 - 10st. deep brown 40 10
4257 - 18st. light blue 55 15

4258	-	20st. bright blue	55	25
4260	-	60st. brown and black	1·80	40

DESIGNS: 8st. Peacock Fountain, Karlovo; 10st. Peev Fountain, Kopivshtitsa; 18st. Sandanski Fountain; 20st. Eagle Owl Fountain, Karlovo; 60st. Fountain, Sokolski Monastery.

1455 Oxytropis urumovii

1999. "Bulgaria '99" European Stamp Exhibition, Sofia (2nd issue). Flowers in Pirin National Park. Sheet 109×100 mm containing T **1455** and similar horiz designs. Multicoloured.

MS4265 60st. Type **1455**; Bellflower; 60st. Iris; 60st. Spotted gentian	13·50	13·50

1456 Cracked Green Russula

1999. Fungi. Multicoloured.

4266		10st. Type **1456**	40	10
4267		18st. Field mushroom	55	15
4268		20st. Hygrophorus russula	80	25
4269		60st. Wood blewit	2·20	55

1457 Diagram of path of Eclipse

1999. Solar Eclipse (11 Aug 1999). Sheet 90×90 mm.

MS4270 **1457** 20st. multicoloured	2·00	2·00

1458 Four-leaved Clover

1999. Centenary of Organized Peasant Movement.

4271	**1458**	18st. multicoloured	40	25

1459 1884 25st. Postage Due Stamp

1999. "Bulgaria '99" European Stamp Exhibition, Sofia (3rd issue). 125th Anniv of Universal Postal Union. Sheet 110×102 mm containing T **1459** and similar vert deisgns. Multicoloured.

MS4272 60st. Type **1459**; 60st. Dove and hand with letter; 60st. Globe and left half of messenger; 60st. Right half of messenger with letter and globe	11·00	11·00

1460 Lesser Grey Shrike

1999. Song Birds and their Eggs. Multicoloured.

4273		8st. Type **1460**	25	10
4274		18st. Mistle thrush	55	15
4275		20st. Dunnock	70	25
4276		60st. Ortolan bunting	1·90	80

1461 Greek Tortoise

1999. Reptiles. Multicoloured.

4277		10st. Type **1461**	40	10
4278		18st. Swamp turtle	55	15
4279		30st. Hermann's tortoise	95	40
4280		60st. Caspian turtle	1·90	80

1462 Boxing (16 medals)

1999. Bulgarian Olympic Medal Winning Sports. Multicoloured.

4281		10st. Type **1462**	40	10
4282		20st. High jumping (17 medals)	70	25
4283		30st. Weightlifting (31 medals)	95	40
4284		60st. Wrestling (60 medals)	1·90	80

1463 Police Light and Emblem

1999. Tenth European Police Conference.

4285	**1463**	18st. multicoloured	40	25

1464 Jug

1999. Gold Artefacts from Panagyurishte.

4286	**1464**	2st. brown and green	10	10
4287	-	3st. brown and green	10	10
4288	-	5st. brown and blue	10	10
4289	-	30st. brown and violet	70	25
4290	-	1l. brown and red	2·40	1·40

DESIGNS: 3st. Human figures around top of drinking horn; 5st. Bottom of chamois-shaped drinking horn; 30st. Decorated handle and spout; 1l. Head-shaped jug.

1465 Virgin and Child

1999. Christmas. Religious Icons. Multicoloured.

4291		18st. Type **1465**	40	25
4292		60st. Jesus Christ	1·80	80

1466 Scout beside Fire

1999. Scouts. Multicoloured.

4293		10st. Type **1466**	40	15
4294		18st. Scout helping child	55	25
4295		30st. Scout saluting	80	40
4296		60st. Girl and boy scouts	1·60	80

1467 Emblem

1999. "Expo 2005" World's Fair, Aichi, Japan.

4297	**1467**	18st. multicoloured	55	25

1468 Emblem and Flag

2000. Bulgarian Membership of European Union.

4298	**1468**	18st. multicoloured	1·40	70

1469 White Stork (Ciconia ciconia)

2000. Endangered Species. Sheet 80×60 mm.

MS4299 **1469** 60st. multicoloured	2·75	2·75

1470 Peter Beron and Scientific Instruments

2000. Birth Anniversaries. Multicoloured.

4300		10st. Type **1470** (scientist, bicentenary)	40	15
4301		20st. Zakhari Stoyanov (writer, 150th anniv)	70	25
4302		50st. Kolyo Ficheto (architect, bicentenary)	1·40	55

1471 Madonna and Child with Circuit Board

2000. Europa. Multicoloured.

4303		18st. Type **1471**	1·40	70
4304		60st. Madonna and Child (Leonardo da Vinci) with circuit board	2·75	2·50

1472 Judo

2000. Olympic Games, Sydney. Multicoloured.

4305		10st. Type **1472**	25	10
4306		18st. Tennis	40	15
4307		20st. Pistol shooting	55	25
4308		60st. Long jump	1·60	80

1473 Puss in Boots (Charles Perrault)

2000. Children's Fairytales. Multicoloured.

4309		18st. Type **1473**	55	40
4310		18st. Little Red Riding Hood (Brothers Grimm)	55	40
4311		18st. Thumbelina (Hans Christian Andersen)	55	40

1474 Friends (detail) (Assen Vasiliev)

2000. Artists Birth Centenaries. Art. Multicoloured.

4312		18st. Type **1474**	55	25
4313		18st. All Soul's Day (detail) (Pencho Georgiev)	55	25
4314		18st. Veliko Tunovo (detail) (Ivan Khristov)	55	25
4315		18st. At the Fountain (sculpture) (detail) (Ivan Funev)	55	25

1475 Roman Mosaic (detail), Stara Zagora

2000. "EXPO 2000" World's Fair, Hanover, Germany.

4316	**1475**	60st. multicoloured	1·80	70

1476 Johannes Gutenberg (inventor of printing) and Printed Characters

2000. Anniversaries. Multicoloured.

4317		10st. Type **1476** (600th birth anniv)	25	10
4318		18st. Johann Sebastian Bach (composer, 250th death anniv)	40	15
4319		20st. Guy de Maupassant (writer, 150th birth anniv)	70	25
4320		60st. Antoine de Saint-Exupery (writer and aviator, birth centenary)	2·00	55

1477 La Jeune (Lebardy-Juillot airship) and Eiffel Tower, 1903

2000. Centenary of First Zeppelin Flight. Airship Development. Multicoloured.

4321		10st. Type **1477**	25	10
4322		18st. LZ-13 Hansa (Zeppelin airship) over Cologne	40	15
4323		20st. N-1 Norge over Rome	70	25
4324		60st. Graf Zeppelin over Sofia	2·00	80

1478 Vazov and Text

2000. 150th Birth Anniv of Ivan Vazov (writer).

4325	**1478**	18st. multicoloured	55	25

1479 Letter "e" with Hands

2000. 25th Anniv of Organization for Security and Co-operation in Europe. Helsinki Final Act (establishing governing principles). Sheet 68×72 mm containing T **1479** and similar horiz design. Multicoloured.

MS4326 20st. Type **1479**; 20st. Three "e's"	2·75	2·00

1480 St. Atanasii Church, Startsevo

2000. Churches.

4327	**1480**	22st. black and blue	55	10
4328	-	24st. black and mauve	70	15
4329	-	50st. black and yellow	1·40	40
4330	-	65st. black and green	1·80	70
4331	-	3l. black and orange	6·75	2·75
4332	-	5l. black and rose	11·00	4·75

DESIGNS: 24st. St. Clement of Orhid, Sofia; 50st. Mary of the Ascension, Sofia; 65st. St. Nedelya, Nedelino; 3l. Mary of the Ascension, Sofia (different), Sofia; 5l. Mary of the Ascension, Pamporovo.

1481 Ibex (*Capra ibex*)

2000. Animals. Multicoloured.

4333	10st. Type **1481**	25	10
4334	22st. Argali (*Ovis ammon*)	55	20
4335	30st. European bison (*Bison bonasus*)	70	25
4336	65st. Yak (*Bos grunniens*)	1·90	55

1482 Field Gladiolus (*Gladiolus segetum*)

2000. Spring Flowers. Multicoloured.

4337	10st. Type **1482**	25	10
4338	22st. Liverwort (*Hepatica nobilis*)	55	20
4339	30st. Pheasant's eye (*Adonis vernalis*)	80	25
4340	65st. Peacock anemone (*Anemone pavonina*)	1·90	55

1483 Crowd and Emblem

2000. 50th Anniv of European Convention on Human Rights.

4341	**1483** 65st. multicoloured	2·00	1·40

1484 Order of Gallantry, 1880

2000. Medals. Multicoloured.

4342	12st. Type **1484**	25	10
4343	22st. Order of St. Aleksandu, 1882	70	20
4344	30st. Order of Merit, 1891	80	25
4345	65st. Order of Cyril and Methodius, 1909	2·00	55

1485 Prince Boris-Mihail

2000. Bimillenary of Christianity. Multicoloured.

4346	22st. Type **1485**	70	25
4347	22st. St. Sofroni Vrachanski	70	25
4348	65st. Mary and Child (detail)	2·00	55
4349	65st. Antim I	2·00	55

1486 Seal

2000. 120th Anniv of Supreme Audit Office.

4350	**1486** 22st. multicoloured	70	25

1487 Microchip, Planets and *The Proportions of Man* (Leonardo DaVinci)

2001. New Millennium.

4351	**1487** 22st. multicoloured	70	25

1488 Tram

2001. Centenary of the Electrification of Bulgarian Transport. Multicoloured.

4352	22st. Type **1488**	70	25
4353	65st. Train carriages	2·00	55

1489 Muscat Grapes and Evsinograd Palace

2001. Viticulture. Multicoloured.

4354	12st. Type **1489**	25	10
4355	22st. Gumza grapes and Baba Vida Fortress	70	20
4356	30st. Shiroka Melnishka Loza grapes and Melnik Winery	80	25
4357	65st. Mavrud grapes and Asenova Krepost Fortress	2·00	55

1490 "@" and Microcircuits

2001. Information Technology. Sheet 82×95 mm containing T **1490** and similar horiz design. Multicoloured.

MS4358	Type **1490**; 65st. John Atanasoff (computer pioneer) and ABC	34·00	34·00

1491 Southern Europe and Emblem

2001. Tenth Anniv of the Atlantic Club of Bulgaria. Sheet 87×67 mm.

MS4359	**1491** 65st. multicoloured	5·50	4·00

1492 Eagle and Lakes, Rila

2001. Europa. Water Resources. Multicoloured.

4360	22st. Type **1492**	1·40	1·10
4361	65st. Cave and waterfall, Rhodope	26·00	23·00

1493 Building, Bridge and Kableschkov

2001. 125th Anniv of the April Uprising and 150th Birth Anniv of Todor Kableschkov (revolutionary leader).

4362	**1493** 22st. multicoloured	70	40

1494 Juvenile Egyptian Vulture in Flight

2001. Endangered Species. Egyptian Vulture (*Neophron percnopterus*). Multicoloured.

4363	12st. Type **1494**	40	10
4364	22st. Juvenile landing	70	25
4365	30st. Adult and chick	80	40
4366	65st. Adult and eggs	1·90	55

1495 Georgi (Gundy) Asparuchov (footballer)

2001. Sportsmen. Multicoloured.

4367	22st. Type **1495**	70	40
4368	30st. Dancho (Dan) Kolev (wrestler)	80	50
4369	65st. Gen. Krum Lekarski (equestrian)	1·90	1·10

1496 Rainbow and People

2001. 50th Anniv United Nations High Commissioner for Refugees.

4370	**1496** 65st. multicoloured	1·90	65

1497 Alexander Zhendov

2001. Artists Birth Centenaries. Multicoloured.

4371	22st. Type **1497**	70	40
4372	65st. Ilya Beshkov	2·00	1·20

1498 Court Seal

2001. Tenth Anniv of Constitutional Court.

4373	**1498** 25st. multicoloured	70	40

1499 Flags

2001. North Atlantic Treaty Organization Summit, Sofia. Sheet 116×111 mm containing T **1499** and similar horiz designs.

MS4374	12st. Type **1499**; 24st. Streamer of flags; 25st. Flags in upper right semi-circle; 65st. Flags in upper left semi-circle	3·00	2·00

1500 Children encircling Globe

2001. United Nations Year of Dialogue among Civilizations.

4375	**1500** 65st. multicoloured	1·80	80

1501 Black Sea Turbot (*Scophthalmus maeoticus*)

2001. International Day for the Protection of the Black Sea. Sheet 73×91 mm.

MS4376	**1501** 65st. multicoloured	1·30	1·10

1502 The Nativity

2001. Christmas.

4377	**1502** 25st. multicoloured	70	40

1503 Cape Shabla Lighthouse

2001. Lighthouses.

4378	**1503** 25st. red and green	70	40
4379	– 32st. blue and yellow	80	50

DESIGN: 32st. Kaliakra Cape lighthouse.

1504 Monastery Buildings

2001. Zographu Monastery, Mount Athos. Sheet 85×105 mm containing T **1504** and similar horiz design. Multicoloured.

MS4380	25st. Type **1504**; 65st. Icon	2·75	2·00

1505 Father Christmas (from film by Al. Zahariev)

2001. Bulgarian Animation.

4381	**1505** 25c. multicoloured	80	50

1506 Vincenzo Bellini

2001. Birth Bicentenary of Vincenzo Bellini (composer).

4382	**1506** 25st. multicoloured	80	50

1507 Crowd and Ancient Calendar

2001. Founders of Bulgarian State (1st series). Multicoloured.

4383	10st. Type **1507**	25	10
4384	25st. Khans, Kubrat and Asparuh	80	50
4385	30st. Khans, Krum and Omurtag	95	55
4386	65st. King Boris and Tsar Simeon	2·00	1·20

See also Nos. 4427/7, 4456/9, 4511/14, 4559/62 and 4610/13.

1508 "€" Symbol and Stars

2002. The Euro (European currency).

4387	**1508** 65st. multicoloured	2·00	1·20

1509 Matches

2002. 50th Anniv of United Nations Disarmament Commission.

| 4388 | **1509** | 25st. multicoloured | 80 | 50 |

1510 Limestone Arch

2002. "BALKANMAX '02" International Stamp Exhibition. Sheet 95×87 mm containing T **1510** and similar vert design. Multicoloured.

| MS4389 | 25st. Type **1510**; 65st. Long-legged buzzard (*Buteo rufinus*) | 34·00 | 33·00 |

1511 Figure Skater

2002. Winter Olympic Games, Salt Lake City. Multicoloured.

| 4390 | 25st. Type **1511** | 80 | 50 |
| 4391 | 65st. Speed skater | 2·00 | 1·20 |

1512 Station Building and Bearded Penguins

2002. Tenth National Antarctic Expedition.

| 4392 | **1512** | 25st. multicoloured | 80 | 50 |

1513 Performing Elephant

2002. Europa. Circus. Multicoloured.

| 4393 | 25st. Type **1513** | 95 | 55 |
| 4394 | 65st. Clown | 2·40 | 1·50 |

1514 Veselin Stojano

2002. Birth Centenaries. Multicoloured.

| 4395 | 25st. Type **514** (composer) | 80 | 50 |
| 4396 | 65st. Angel Karaliechev (writer) | 95 | 55 |

1515 *Illustrated Landscape* (Vasil Barakov)

2002. Art. Multicoloured.

4397	10st. Type **1515**	25	10
4398	25st. Book illustration from *Under the Yoke* (novel by Ivan Vazov) (Boris Angulshev) (horiz)	80	50
4399	65st. *The Balcony and Canary* (Ivan Nenov)	2·00	1·20

1516 Stefan Kanchev

2002. First Death Annivs of Stamp Designers. Multicoloured.

| 4400 | 25st. Type **1516** | 80 | 50 |
| 4401 | 65st. Alex Popilov | 2·00 | 1·20 |

1517 Melon (*Cucumis melo*)

2002. Fruits. Multicoloured.

4402	10st. Type **1517**	40	25
4403	25st. Watermelon (*Citrullus lanatus*)	80	50
4404	27st. Pumpkin (*Cucurbita pepo*)	90	55
4405	65st. Calabash (*Lagenaria siceraria*)	2·00	1·20

1518 Cock Bird

2002. Poultry. Multicoloured.

4406	10st. Type **1518**	40	25
4407	20st. Leghorn pair (horiz)	70	40
4408	25st. Two cocks fighting (horiz)	80	50
4409	65st. Plymouth rock pair (inscr "Plimouth Rock")	2·00	1·20

1519 Pope John Paul II and Monument to Cyril & Methodius

2002. Pope John Paul II's Visit to Bulgaria.

| 4410 | **1519** | 65st. multicoloured | 2·00 | 1·20 |

1520 Chess Pieces

2002. Sheet 91×71 mm containing T **1520** and similar vert design.

| MS4411 | 25st. brown, cinnamon and black (Type **1520**); 65st. multicoloured (Hand holding pawn) | 2·75 | 2·00 |

1521 Flag and Stars

2002. Tenth Anniv of Bulgaria's Admission to Council of Europe.

| 4412 | **1521** | 25st. multicoloured | 80 | 50 |

1522 Rabbit

2002. Woodcarvings by Peter Kuschlev.

4413	**1522**	6st. brown and black	15	10
4414	-	12st. orange and black	40	25
4415	-	36st. green and black	1·10	65
4416	-	44st. pink and black	1·40	80

DESIGNS: 12st. Deer; 36st. Bird; 44st. Boar.

1523 *Marie-Luisa* (1st ocean-going liner)

2002. Merchant Ships. Multicoloured.

4417	12st. Type **1523**	40	25
4418	36st. *Persenk* (cargo ship)	1·10	65
4419	49st. *Kaliakra* (sail training ship)	1·60	1·00
4420	65st. *Sofia* (container ship)	2·00	1·20

1524 Father Christmas and Sun

2002. Christmas.

| 4421 | **1524** | 36st. multicoloured | 1·10 | 65 |

1525 Flag and NATO Emblem

2002. Bulgaria's Participation in NATO Conference, Prague. Sheet 85×65 mm.

| MS4422 | **1525** | 65st. multicoloured | 4·00 | 3·00 |

1526 Paper Bird

2002. 30th Anniv of Security and Co-operation in Europe Conference. Sheet 85×60 mm.

| MS4423 | **1526** | 65st. multicoloured | 3·50 | 2·75 |

1527 Tsar Samuil

2002. Founders of Bulgarian State (2nd series). Multicoloured.

4424	18st. Type **1527**	55	35
4425	36st. Tsars Peter II and Assen	1·10	65
4426	49st. Tsar Kaloyan	1·40	80
4427	65st. Tsar Ivan Assen II	1·90	1·10

1528 Exhibition Emblem

2003. Europalia Cultural Exhibition, Belgium.

| 4428 | **1528** | 65st. multicoloured | 2·00 | 1·20 |

1529 *Rose Pickers* (Stoyan Sotirov)

2003. Artists' Birth Centenaries. Multicoloured.

4429	18st. Type **1529**	55	35
4430	36st. *The Blind Fiddler* (Illya Petrov)	1·10	65
4431	65st. *Swineherd* (Zlatyo Boyadjiev)	1·90	1·10

1530 Space Construction surrounding Earth

2003. Space Exploration. Sheet 104×85 mm.

| MS4432 | **1530** | 65st. multicoloured | 2·75 | 2·00 |

1531 Statue of Russian and Bulgarian Soldiers

2003. 125th Anniv of Bulgarian State.

| 4433 | **1531** | 36st. multicoloured | 1·10 | 65 |

1532 Exarch Stefan I, Menorah Candlestick and Dimitar Peshev

2003. 60th Anniv of Rescue of Bulgarian Jews.

| 4434 | **1532** | 36st. multicoloured | 1·10 | 65 |

1533 Silhouettes of Birds and Woman

2003. Europa. Poster Art. Multicoloured.

| 4435 | 36st. Type **1533** | 1·10 | 65 |
| 4436 | 65st. Chicken, legs and farm animals | 1·90 | 1·10 |

1534 *Vase with Fifteen Sunflowers*

2003. 150th Birth Anniv of Vincent van Gogh (artist). Sheet 70×90 mm.

| MS4437 | **1534** | 65st. multicoloured | 1·90 | 1·50 |

1535 Pterodactylus

2003. Dinosaurs. Multicoloured.

4438	30st. Type **1535**	80	50
4439	36st. Gorgosaurus	1·10	65
4440	49st. Mesosaurus	1·50	90
4441	65st. Monoclonius	1·90	1·10

1536 *Nymphoides Peltata*

2003. Water Plants (1st issue). Multicoloured.

| 4442 | **1536** | 36st. multicoloured | 1·10 | 65 |

See also Nos. 4447/50.

1537 Honey Bee (*Apis mellifera*)

2003. Bees. Multicoloured.

4443	20st. Type **1537**	55	35
4444	30st. *Anthidium manicatum*	80	50
4445	36st. Bumble bee (*Bombus subterraneus*)	95	55
4446	65st. Blue carpenter bee (*Xylocopa violacea*)	1·80	1·10

1538 *Butomus umbellatus*

2003. Water Plants (2nd issue). Multicoloured.

4447	20st.	Type **1538**	55	35
4448	36st.	*Sagirraria sagittifolia*	1·10	65
4449	50st.	*Menyanthes trifoliate*	1·50	90
4450	65st.	*Iris pseudoacorus*	1·90	1·10

1539 *Gotze Delchev*

2003. Death Centenary of Gotze Delchev (revolutionary). Centenary of Macedonian Uprising.

4451	**1539**	36st. multicoloured	1·10	65

1540 *Mountains*

2003. International Year of Mountains.

4452	**1540**	65st. multicoloured	6·00	4·50

1541 *Bulgarian and USA Flags as Bowtie*

2003. Centenary of Bulgaria—USA Diplomatic Relations.

4453	**1541**	65st. multicoloured	1·90	1·10

1542 *John Atanasoff*

2003. Birth Centenary of John Atanasoff (computer pioneer).

4454	**1542**	65st. multicoloured	1·90	1·10

1543 *Pawn and Buildings*

2003. European Chess Championship, Plovdiv.

4455	**1543**	65st. multicoloured	1·90	1·10

1544 *Tsar Ivan Alexander*

2003. Founders of Bulgarian State (3rd series). Multicoloured.

4456	30st.	Type **1544**	80	50
4457	45st.	Despot Dobrotitsa	1·20	75
4458	65st.	Tsar Ivan Shishman	1·90	1·10
4459	89st.	Tsar Ivan Sratsimir	2·20	1·30

1545 *Taekwondo*

2003. 80th Anniv of National Olympic Committee. Multicoloured.

4460	20st.	Type **1545**	55	35
4461	36st.	Mountain biking	1·10	65
4462	50st.	Softball	1·50	90
4463	65st.	Canoe slalom	1·90	1·10

1546 *Father Christmas*

2003. Christmas.

4464	**1546**	65st. multicoloured	1·90	1·10

1547 *Carriage and Man wearing Top Hat*

2003. Carriages. Multicoloured.

4465	30st.	Type **1547**	80	50
4466	36st.	Closed carriage with woman passenger	1·10	65
4467	50st.	State coach, woman and dog	1·50	90
4468	65st.	Couple and large carriage	1·90	1·10

1548 *FIFA Centenary Emblem*

2003. Centenary of FIFA (Federation Internationale de Football Association). Multicoloured.

4469	20st.	Type **1548**	55	35
4470	25st.	Early players	70	40
4471	36st.	Early players and rules	1·10	65
4472	50st.	FIFA fair play trophy (vert)	1·40	80
4473	65st.	FIFA world player trophy (vert)	1·90	1·10

1549 *Eye, Square, Compass and Statue*

2003. Tenth Anniv of Re-establishment of Masonic Activity in Bulgaria.

4474	**1549**	80st. multicoloured	2·20	1·30

1550 *Noctua tertia*

2004. Moths. Multicoloured.

4475	40st.	Type **1550**	1·10	65
4476	45st.	*Rethera komarovi*	1·20	75
4477	55st.	*Symtomis marjana*	1·50	90
4478	80st.	*Arctia caja*	2·20	1·30

1551 *Mask*

2004. SERVA, International Masquerade Festival, Pernik.

4479	**1551**	80st. multicoloured	2·20	1·40

1552 *OSCE Emblem and Bridge*

2004. Bulgaria, Chair of Organization for Security and Co-operation in Europe.

4480	**1552**	80st. multicoloured	2·10	1·30

1553 *Theatre Facade*

2004. Centenary of Ivan Vazov National Theatre, Sofia.

4481	**1553**	45st. multicoloured	1·30	80

1554 *Atanas Dalchev*

2004. Birth Centenaries. Multicoloured.

4482	45st.	Type **1554** (poet)	1·30	80
4483	80st.	Lubomir Pipkov (composer)	2·20	1·40

1555 *NATO Emblem and National Colours*

2004. Accession to Full Membership of NATO.

4484	**1555**	80st. multicoloured	2·75	1·80

1556 *Georgi Ivanov*

2004. 25th Anniv of First Bulgarian in Space. Sheet 84×68 mm.

MS4485	**1556**	80st. multicoloured	2·20	1·90

1557 *Cover of Document*

2004. 125th Anniv of Turnovska Constitution and Restoration of Bulgarian State. Sheet 86×67 mm.

MS4486	**1557**	45st. multicoloured	7·00	5·25

1558 *Globe surmounted by Mortar Board*

2004. "Bulgarian Dream" (graduate assistance) Programme.

4487	**1558**	45st. multicoloured	1·30	80

1559 *Salvador Dali (sculpture)*

2004. Birth Centenary of Salvador Dali (artist). Sheet 85×65 mm.

MS4488	**1559**	80st. multicoloured	4·25	3·50

1560 *Luben Dimitrov (sculptor) and Boris Ivanov (cinema director)*

2004. Birth Centenaries. Multicoloured.

4489	45st.	Type **1560**	1·40	90
4490	80st.	Vassil Stoilov and Stoyan Venev (artists)	2·20	1·40

1561 *Mountains and Skiers*

2004. Europa. Holidays. Multicoloured.

4491	45st.	Type **1561**	1·40	90
4492	80st.	Beach scene	2·20	1·40

1562 *Christo Stoychkov*

2004. Bulgarian Footballers. Multicoloured.

4493	45st.	Type **1562**	1·40	90
4494	45st.	Georgi Asparuchov	1·40	90
4495	45st.	Krassimir Balakov	1·40	90
4496	45st.	Nikola Kotkov	1·40	90

1563 *Footballer and Ball*

2004. Euro 2004–European Football Championships, Portugal. Sheet 85×67 mm.

MS4497	**1563**	80st. multicoloured	2·20	1·90

1564 *Seal*

2004. 125th Anniv of Bulgaria—Austria Diplomatic Relations.

4498	**1564**	80st. multicoloured	2·20	1·40

1565 *Lion (statue), Flag and Document*

2004. 125th Anniv of Ministry of Interior.

4499	**1565**	45st. multicoloured	1·40	90

1566a De Dion
Button Post Car
(1905)

2004. 125th Anniv of Postal Service. Sheet 93×80 mm.
MS4500 **1566a** 45st. multicoloured 7·00 5·75
 No. **MS4500** contains a *se-tenant* stamps size label,
which with the stamp forms a composite design.

1567 Red Kite (*Milvus milvus*)

2004. Endangered Species. Preservation of the Black Sea.
Sheet 86×86 mm containing T **1567** and similar
horiz design. Multicoloured.
MS4501 45st. Type **1567**; 80st. *Blennius
 ocellaris* 3·75 3·00

1568 Runner holding Torch and
Olympic Flame (Berlin, 1936)

2004. Olympic Games, Athens 2004. Designs showing
runner and Olympic flame. Multicoloured.
4502 10st. Type **1568** 30 20
4503 20st. Munich, 1972 55 35
4504 45st. Moscow, 1980 1·40 90
4505 80st. Athens, 2004 2·20 1·40

1569 Krum (steamer)

2004. 125th Anniv of Bulgarian Navy. Multicoloured.
4506 10st. Type **1569** 30 20
4507 25st. *Druski* (torpedo boat) 70 45
4508 45st. *Christo Botev* (mine-
 sweeper) 1·40 90
4509 80st. *Smeli* (frigate) 2·20 1·40

1570 Square and Compass

2004. 125th Anniv of Bulgarian Masonic Movement.
4510 **1570** 45st. multicoloured 7·00 5·25

1571 Patriarch Ephtimius
Turnovski

2004. Founders of Bulgarian State (4th series).
Multicoloured.
4511 10st. Type **1571** 30 20
4512 20st. Kniaz Fruzhin and Kniaz
 Constantine 70 45
4513 45st. Georgi Peyachevich and
 Peter Partchevich 1·40 90
4514 80st. Piessii Hilendarski 2·50 1·60

1572 Polyporus squamosus

2004. Fungi. Sheet 125×93 mm containing T **1572** and
similar horiz designs. Multicoloured.
MS4515 10st. Type **1572**; 20st. *Fomes
 fomentarius*; 45st. *Piptoporus betuli-
 nus*; 80st. *Laetiporus sulphurous* 5·00 3·75

1573 Two Sturgeon

2004. Sturgeon (*Huso huso*). Multicoloured.
4516 80st. Type **1573** 2·50 1·60
4517 80st. From below 2·50 1·60
4518 80st. Looking down 2·50 1·60
4519 80st. Eating 2·50 1·60

1574 Father Christmas

2004. Christmas.
4520 **1574** 45st. multicoloured 1·40 90

1575 Hands

2004. 12th Organization for Security and Co-operation in
Europe (OSCE) Council, Sofia. Sheet 84×67 mm.
MS4521 80st. multicoloured 2·10 1·90

1576 Geo Milev

2005. Birth Centenary of Georghi Milev Kassabov (Geo
Milev) (writer and revolutionary).
4522 **1576** 45st. multicoloured 1·50 1·10

1577 Emblem

2005. Centenary of Rotary International (charitable
organization).
4523 **1577** 80st. multicoloured 2·40 1·70

1578 Charlie
Chaplin in *Gold
Rush* (1925)

2005. History of Cinema. Sheet 88×118 mm containing T
1578 and similar vert designs. Multicoloured.
MS4524 10st. Type **1578**; 20st. Scene
 from *Battleship Potemkin* (*Bronenoset
 Potemkin*) (1925); 45st. Marlene
 Dietrich in *Blue Angel* (*Der Blaue
 Engel*) (1930); 80st. Vassil Ghendov
 in *Bulgarian is a Gallant Man* (first
 Bulgarian film) 4·75 4·25

1579 *The Monument*
(lithograph) (Nickolai
Pavlovitch)

2005. 135th Anniv of Exarchate (independent Bulgarian
ecclesiastical organisation). Sheet 68×88 mm.
MS4525 **1579** 45st. multicoloured 2·20 1·80

1580 European Stars
and Bulgarian Flag

2005. Volunteers for Europe (educational campaign).
4526 **1580** 80st. multicoloured 2·40 1·70

1581 Panayot
Hitov and Philip
Totyo

2005. 175th Birth Anniv of Panayot Hitov and Philip
Totyo (revolutionaries).
4527 **1581** 45st. multicoloured 1·50 1·10

1582 Robert Peary

2005. Polar Explorers. Sheet 64×95 mm containing T
1582 and similar horiz design. Multicoloured.
MS4528 45st. Type **1582** (American)
 (North Pole, 1909); 80st. Rual
 Admundsen (Norwegian) (South
 Pole, 1911) 3·75 3·25

1583 Peugeot (1936)

2005. Fire Engines. Sheet 136×77 mm containing T **1583**
and similar horiz design. Multicoloured.
MS4529 10st. Type **1583**; 20st. Mer-
 cedes (1935); 45st. Magirus (1934);
 80st. Renault (1925) 4·75 4·00

1584 Hans Christian
Andersen

2005. Birth Bicentenary of Hans Christian Andersen
(writer). Sheet 87×78 mm.
MS4530 **1584** 80st. multicoloured 2·40 2·00

1585 Hand holding Scroll

2005. Cyrillic Alphabet. Sheet 88×59 mm.
MS4531 **1585** 80st. multicoloured 2·40 2·00

1586 Electric Locomotive 46

2005. Railways. Multicoloured.
4532 45st. Type **1586** 1·50 1·10
4533 80st. Modern locomotive
 DMV 10 7·25 5·50

1587 Radetski (revolutionary
ship) (Georgi Dimov)

2005. Children's Painting.
4534 **1587** 45st. multicoloured 1·50 1·10

1588 Blinis

2005. Europa. Gastronomy. Multicoloured.
4535 45st. Type **1588** 1·50 1·10
4536 80st. Bread, kebab and
 tomatoes 2·40 1·70

1589 Stylized
Figures

2005. 50th Anniv of Europa—CEPT Postage Stamps.
4537 **1589** 45st. violet, green and
 black 1·50 1·10
4538 - 80st. blue, magenta and
 black 2·40 1·70
DESIGNS: 45st. Type **1589**; 80st. Square of figures.

1590 Cordulegaster
bidentata

2005. Dragonflies. Multicoloured.
4539 10st. Type **1590** 30 20
4540 20st. *Erythromma najas* (horiz) 60 45
4541 45st. *Sympetrum pedemonta-
 num* (horiz) 1·30 1·00
4542 80st. *Brachytron pratense* 2·50 1·80

1591 Elias Canetti

2005. Birth Centenary of Elias Canetti (writer).
4543 **1591** 80st. multicoloured 2·50 1·80

1592 Synema
globosum

2005. Spiders. Multicoloured.
4544 45st. Type **1592** 30 20
4545 20st. *Argiope bruennichi* 60 45
4546 45st. *Eresus cinnaberinus* 1·30 1·00
4547 80st. *Araneus diadematus* 2·50 1·80

1593 Flag as Tree Bark

2005. 110th Anniv of Organized Tourism.
4548 **1593** 45st. multicoloured 1·20 90

1594 Map

2005. 120th Anniv of Unification of Bulgaria.
4549 **1594** 45st. multicoloured 1·20 90

1595 Girl wearing Traditional Costume, Sofia

2005. Women's Traditional Costumes. Multicoloured.
4550 20st. Type **1595** 50 40
4551 25st. Pleven 70 55
4552 45st. Sliven 1·20 90
4553 80st. Stara Zagora 2·00 1·60

1596 Stamen Grigoroff (discoverer)

2005. Centenary of Discovery of Lactobacillus bulgaricus Grigoroff (yoghurt bacilli) (1st issue). Sheet 94×81 mm.
MS4554 **1596** 80st. multicoloured 2·20 1·70
See also **MS4557**.

1597 Chess Board and Antoaneta Steffanova (Women's World Chess Champion)

2005. Chess.
4555 **1597** 80st. multicoloured 2·00 1·60

1598 Virgin and Child

2005. Christmas.
4556 **1598** 45st. multicoloured 1·20 90

1599 Stamen Grigoroff (discoverer)

2005. Centenary of Discovery of Lactobacillus bulgaricus Grigoroff (yoghurt bacilli) (2nd issue). Sheet 94×81 mm. Imperf.
MS4557 **1599** 80st. multicoloured 20·00 18·00
 The design of **MS4557** is as Type **1596** with the addition of an owl in the top right corner. The sheets include a perforated number.

1600 Stylized Couple

2005. 50th Anniv of Membership of United Nations. Sheet 86×88 mm.
4558 **1600** 80st. multicoloured 2·20 1·70

1601 Patriarchs Illarion Makariopolski and Antim I

2005. Founders of Bulgarian State (5th series).
4559 **1601** 10st. chocolate and green 35 25
4560 – 20st. brown and green 50 40
4561 – 45st. claret and green 1·20 90
4562 – 80st. purple and green 2·00 1·60
DESIGNS: 10st. Type **1601**; 20st. Georgi Rakovski and Vassil Levski; 45st. Luben Karavelov and Christo Botev; 80st. Panayot Volov and Pavel Bobekov.

1602 Rosa pendulina

2006. Roses. Multicoloured.
4563 54st. Type **1602** 1·40 1·10
4564 1l.50 Rosa gallica 3·75 3·00
4565 2l. Rosa spinosissima 5·00 4·00
4566 10l. Rosa arvensis 24·00 18·00

1603 Mozart

2006. 250th Birth Anniv of Wolfgang Amadeus Mozart.
4567 **1603** 1l. multicoloured 8·50 8·00

1604 Ellin Pellin (writer)

2006. 115th Anniv of National Philatelic Press. Bulgarian Philatelists. Multicoloured.
4568 35st. Type **1604** 85 80
4569 55st. Lazar Dobritch (circus artiste) 1·40 1·20
4570 60st. Boris Christov (opera singer) 1·50 1·30
4571 1l. Bogomil Nonev (writer) 2·50 2·10

1605 Snowboarder

2006. Winter Olympic Games, Turin. Sheet 86×118 mm containing T **1605** and similar vert design. Multicoloured.
MS4572 55st. Type **1605**; 1l. Ice dancers 4·00 3·75

1606 Sextant

2006. Tenth Anniv of Bulgarian Antarctic Cartography. Sheet 86×69 mm.
MS4573 **1606** 1l. multicoloured 2·50 2·20

1607 Ship (15th Century manuscript)

2006. 610th Anniv of Battle at Nikopol.
4574 **1607** 1l.50 multicoloured 3·50 2·75

1608 Martes martes

2006. Ecology. Sheet 86×118 mm containing T **1608** and similar horiz design. Multicoloured.
MS4575 55st. Type **1608**; 1l.50 Ursus arctos 4·75 4·25

1609 Stylized Figure and Stars

2006. Europa. Integration. Multicoloured.
4576 55st. Type **1609** 1·70 1·30
4577 1l. Star as flower 3·50 2·75

1610 Emblem

2006. Meeting of NATO Foreign Ministers, Sofia. Sheet 87×70 mm.
MS4578 **1610** 1l.50 multicoloured 3·50 3·25

1611 Mastheads

2006. 70th Anniv of Trud Newspaper.
4579 **1611** 55st. multicoloured 2·50 2·00

1612 Vesselin Topalov

2006. Vesselin Topalov—World Chess Champion. Sheet 87×71 mm.
MS4580 **1612** 1l.50 multicoloured 3·50 3·25
 No. **MS4580** also exist imperforate.

1613 Building Facade

2006. 25th Anniv of National Palace of Culture.
4581 **1613** 55st. multicoloured 1·70 1·50

1614 Circus aeruginosus

2006. Raptors. Multicoloured.
4582 10st. Type **1614** 35 25
4583 35st. Circus cyaneus 85 65
4584 55st. Circus macrourus 1·20 90
4585 1l. Circus pygargus 2·75 2·10

1615 Building Facade, Ship and Sailor

2006. 125th Anniv of Nikola Vaptsarov Naval Academy, Varna.
4586 **1615** 55st. multicoloured 1·20 90

1616 Players

2006. World Cup Football Championship, Germany. Sheet 87×87 mm.
MS4587 **1616** 1l. multicoloured 2·20 2·00

1617 Emblem

2006. 50th Anniv of Bulgaria in UNESCO.
4588 **1617** 1l. multicoloured 2·20 1·70

1618 Gena Dimitrova

2006. 65th Birth Anniv and First Death Anniv of Gena Dimitrova (opera singer).
4589 **1618** 1l. multicoloured 2·20 1·70

1619 Saponaria strajensis

2006. Flora. Multicoloured.
4590 10st. Type **1619** 35 25
4591 35st. Trachystemon orientalis 85 65
4592 55st. Hypericum calycinum 1·20 90
4593 1l. Rhododendron ponticum 2·75 2·10

1620 Rover Maestro

2006. Bulgaria Automobile Industry. Multicoloured.
4594 10st. Type **1620** 35 25
4595 35st. Moskovitch 85 65
4596 55st. Bulgaralpine 1·20 90
4597 1l. Bulgarrnault 2·75 2·10

1621 *Return of the Prodigal Son*

2006. 400th Birth Anniv of Rembrandt Harmenszoon van Rijn. Sheet 65×84 mm.
MS4598 **1621** 1l. multicoloured 2·75 2·40

1622 *All Soul's Day* (Ivan Murkvitchka)

2006. Art Anniversaries. Multicoloured.
4599 10st. Type **1622** (150th birth anniv) 35 25
4600 35st. *Sozopol—Houses* (Vesselin Statkov) (birth centenary) 1·00 80
4601 55st. *Sofia in Winter* (Nikola Petrov) (90th death anniv) 1·50 1·20
4602 1l. *T. Popova* (John Popov) (birth centenary) 2·75 2·10

1623 *Competitors*

2006. World Sambo Championship, Sofia.
4603 **1623** 55st. multicoloured 1·50 1·20

1624 *Post Van*

2006. Post Europ. Sheet 85×75 mm.
MS4604 **1624** 1l. multicoloured 15·00 14·50

1625 *Angel*

2006. Christmas.
4605 **1625** 55st. multicoloured 1·50 1·20

1626 *Ballot Box and Flags*

2006. Bulgaria and Romania's Membership of European Union. Multicoloured.
4606 55st. Type **1626** 1·50 1·20
4607 1l.50 "EU" 4·00 3·25
MS4608 97×87 mm. Nos. 4606/7 5·75 5·50
Stamps of a similar design were issued by Romania.

1627 *Peter Dimkov*

2006. 120th Birth Anniv of Peter Dimkov (naturopath).
4609 **1627** 55st. multicoloured 1·50 1·20

1628 *Generals Danail Nikolaev and Racho Petrov*

2006. Founders of Bulgarian State (6th series). Multicoloured.
4610 10st. Type **1628** 35 25
4611 35st. Petko Karavelov and Marin Drinov 1·00 80
4612 55st. Konstantin Stoylov and Stephan Stambolov 1·50 1·20
4613 1l. Prince Albert I of Bulgaria 2·75 2·10

1629 *Boeing 737 and Terminal Building*

2006. New Airport Terminal, Sofia. Sheet 87×72 mm.
MS4614 **1629** 55st. multicoloured 1·50 1·30

1631 *Emilian Stanev*

2007. Birth Centenary of Nikola Stoyanov Stanev (Emilian Stanev) (writer).
4616 **1631** 55st. multicoloured 1·40 1·10

1632 *Flags as Stars*

2007. 50th Anniv of Treaty of Rome.
4617 **1632** 1l. multicoloured 2·50 2·00

1633 *Ivan Dimov*

2007. Theatre Personalities. Multicoloured.
4618 10st. Type **1633** 35 25
4619 55st. Sava Ognyanov 1·40 1·10
4620 1l. Krustyo Sarfov 2·50 2·00

1634 *Sputnik*

2007. 50th Anniv of First Manmade Satellite. Sheet 87×56 mm.
MS4621 **1634** 1l. multicoloured 2·50 2·40

1635 *Campfire*

2007. Europa. Centenary of Scouting. Multicoloured. (a) Size 39×28 mm.
4622 55st. Type **1635** 1·40 1·10
4623 1l.50 Route finding 3·75 3·00

(b) Size 31×23 mm.
4624 1l. As Type **1635** 1·40 1·10
4625 1l. As No. 4623 3·75 3·00

1636 *DAR-3 Garvan II (1937)*

2007. Military Aircraft. Multicoloured.
4626 10st. Type **1636** 35 25
4627 35st. DAR-9 Siniger (1939) 85 65

4628 55st. Kaproni Bulgarski KB-6 Papagal (1939) 1·40 1·10
4629 1l. Kaproni Bulgarski KB-11A Fanzan 2·50 2·00

1637 *Boris I*

2007. 1100th Death Anniv of Knyaz (Prince) Boris I (Michael).
4630 **1637** 55st. multicoloured 1·40 1·10

1637a *Basilica and Saint Cyril*

2007. 150th Anniv of Excavation of San Clement Basilica, Rome.
4630a **1637a** 1l. multicoloured 2·75 2·10

1638 *Dimcho Debelyanov*

2007. Birth Anniversaries. Multicoloured.
4631 10st. Type **1638** (poet) (120th) 35 25
4632 35st. Nenko Balkanski (artist) (centenary) 85 65
4633 55st. Vera Lukova (artist) (centenary) 1·20 90
4634 1l. Theodor Trayanov (poet) (125th) 2·75 2·10

1639 *St. Spass Monastery, Lozenski*

2007. Monasteries. Multicoloured.
4635 63st. Type **1639** 1·70 1·30
4636 75st. St. Mina, Obradovski 2·00 1·60
4637 1l.20 St. George the Victor, Kremikovski 3·25 2·50
4638 2l.20 Three Saints, Chepinski 6·00 4·50

1640 *Symbols of Transport*

2007. International Transport Forum, Sofia.
4639 **1640** 1l. multicoloured 2·75 2·10

1641 *Presidents of Bulgaria and Azerbaijan*

2007. 15th Anniv of Bulgaria–Azerbaijan Diplomatic Relations. Sheet 86×64 mm.
MS4640 **1641** 1l. multicoloured 2·75 2·50

1642 *Onosma thracica*

2007. Flora. Multicoloured.
4641 10st. Type **1642** 35 25
4642 45st. *Astracantha aitosensis* 1·20 90
4643 55st. *Veronica krumovii* 1·50 1·20
4644 1l. *Verbascum adrianopolitanum* 2·75 2·10

1643 *Vassal Levski*

2007. 170th Birth Anniv of Vassal Levski (revolutionary leader).
4645 **1643** 55st. multicoloured 1·50 1·20

1644 *Sailor*

2007. Junior World Sailing Championship–Olympian Class 470, Burgas.
4646 **1644** 1l. multicoloured 2·75 2·10

1645 *Lt. Colonel Pavel Kalitin (painting)* and *Battle at Stara Zagora* (Nikola Kozhuharov)

2007. 130th Anniv of Battle at Stara Zagora.
4647 **1645** 55st. multicoloured 1·50 1·20

1646 *Players*

2007. Rugby. 50th (2005) Anniv of Locomotiv Rugby Club, Sofia. World Rugby Championship–2007, France.
4648 **1646** 55st. multicoloured 1·50 1·20

1647 *Lutra lutra* (otter)

2007. Ecology. 15th Anniv of Ropotamo Reserve. Sheet 85×85 mm containing T **1647** and similar horiz design. Multicoloured.
MS4649 55st. Type **1647**; 1l. *Haliaeetus albicilla* (white tailed eagle) 4·25 4·00
The stamps and margins of **MS4549** form a composite design.

1648 *Alcedo atthis* (kingfisher)

2007. Endangered Species. Birds. Sheet 97×130 mm containing T **1648** and similar horiz design. Multicoloured.
MS**4650** 10st. Type **1648**; 35st. *Ticho-droma muraria* (wall creeper); 55st. *Bombycilla garrulous* (waxwing); 1l. *Phoenicopterus ruber* (flamingo) ... 5·50 ... 5·25

1649 Emblem

2007. Tenth Anniv Grand Lodge of the Ancient Freemasons.
4651 **1649** 55st. multicoloured ... 1·50 ... 1·20

1650 Centre Building

2007. Inauguration of Exchange and Sorting Centre, Sofia. Sheet 87×63 mm.
MS**4652 1650** 55st. multicoloured ... 1·50 ... 1·40

1651 Ivan Hadjiski

2007. Birth Centenary of Ivan Hadjiski (social psychologist).
4653 **1651** 55st. multicoloured ... 1·50 ... 1·20

1652 Woman holding Offerings

2007. Christmas.
4654 **1652** 55st. multicoloured ... 1·50 ... 1·20

1653 Rumyana Neykova (European 2000m. skiff rowing champion)

2007. Women Sports Personalities. Multicoloured.
4655 10st. Type **1653** ... 35 ... 25
4656 35st. Stanka Zlateva (World freestyle wrestling champion) ... 85 ... 65
4657 1l. Stefka Kostadinova (World record high jump (30.8.1987)) ... 2·75 ... 2·10

1654 '100' and Soldier

2007. Centenary of Military Reconnaissance.
4658 **1654** 55st. multicoloured ... 1·50 ... 1·20

1655 Hristo Botev

2008. Birth Centenary of Hristo Botev (poet and revolutionary).
4659 **1655** 55st. multicoloured ... 1·50 ... 1·20

1656 Polar Bear

2008. International Polar Year. 20th Anniv of Bulgarian Antarctic Expedition. Sheet 115×85 mm containing T **1656** and similar horiz design. Multicoloured.
MS**4660** 55st. Type **1656**; 1l. Skua stealing penguin chick ... 4·25 ... 4·00
The stamps and margins of MS**4660** form a composite design.

1657 Volleyball Player

2008. Olympic Games, Beijing. Sheet 88×109 mm containing T **1657** and similar vert design. Multicoloured.
MS**4661** 55st. Type **1657**; 1l. Two players ... 4·25 ... 4·00
The stamps of MS**4661** form a composite design of a volley ball match.

1658 Arms of Bulgaria

2008. 130th Anniv of San Stefano Peace Treaty (treaty between Russia and the Ottoman Empire at the end of the Russo-Turkish War (setting up an autonomous self-governing tributary principality of Bulgaria)).
4662 **1658** 55st. multicoloured ... 1·50 ... 1·20

1659 Envelope as Postman

2008. Europa. The Letter. Multicoloured (background colour given).
4663 55st. Type **1659** ... 1·50 ... 1·20
4664 55st. As Type **1659** (purple) ... 1·50 ... 1·20
4665 1l. Envelope as pigeon (blue) ... 2·75 ... 2·10
4666 1l. As No. 4665 (yellow) ... 2·75 ... 2·10

1660 Captain Dimiter Spissarevski

2008. History of Military Aviation. Pilots' Birth Anniversaries. Multicoloured.
4667 55st. Type **1660** (90th birth anniv) ... 1·50 ... 1·20
4668 1l. General Stoyan Stoyanov (95th birth anniv) ... 2·75 ... 2·10
Nos. 4667/8 were issued together, *se-tenant*, forming a composite design.

1661 *Women from the Rhodopes* (Boris Kotsev)

2008. Artists' Birth Centenaries. Multicoloured.
4669 10st. Type **1661** ... 35 ... 25
4670 35st. *Nude* (Eliezer Alsheh) ... 85 ... 65
4671 55st. *Nude* (Vera Nedova) ... 1·50 ... 1·20
4672 1l. *Maritsa* (Assen Peykov) ... 2·75 ... 2·10

1662 Club Members

2008. 60th Anniv of CSKA Central Sports Club. Sheet 90×58 mm.
MS**4673 1662** 55st. multicoloured ... 1·70 ... 1·60

1663 White-headed Marmoset (*Callithrix geoffroyi*)

2008. 120th Anniv of Zoological Gardens, Sofia. Two sheets containing T **1663** and similar vert designs. Multicoloured.
MS**4674** (a) 126×130 mm. 10st. Type **1663**; 20st. Hippopotamus (*Hippopotamus amphibius*); 35st. Bactrian camel (*Camelus bactrianus*); 55st. Meerkat (*Suricata suricatta*); 60st. Blue-and-yellow macaw (*Ara ararauna*); 1l. Eurasian lynx (*Lynx lynx*); (b) 66×85 mm. 55st. Meerkat (*Suricata suricatta*). Imperf ... 7·25 ... 7·25

1664 Alexander Alexandrov

2008. 20th Anniv of Alexander Alexandrov's Flight in Orbital Space Station MIR. Sheet 85×61 mm.
MS**4675 1664** 1l. multicoloured ... 2·75 ... 2·75

1665 BMW R12 Single Carb, 1935

2008. 70th Anniv of Union of Bulgarian Philatelists.
4676 **1665** 60st. multicoloured ... 1·70 ... 1·30
MS**4677** 106×92 mm. 60st. As Type **1665**. Imperf ... 1·90 ... 1·90

1666 *Canis aureus* (golden jackal)

2008. Strandja Nature Park. Sheet 104×79 mm containing T **1666** and similar multicoloured design.
MS**4678** 60st. Type **1666**; 1l.50 *Aquila pomarina* (lesser spotted eagle) (vert) ... 5·50 ... 5·50
The stamps and margins of MS**4678** form a composite design.

1667

2008. 20th Anniv of Bulgaria—European Economic Community.
4679 **1667** 1l. black and yellow ... 2·75 ... 2·10

1668 Wagons Lits (sleeeping car)

2008. 125th Anniv of Orient Express. Multicoloured.
4680 60st. Type **1668** ... 1·70 ... 1·30
4681 1l.50 Steg Wien locomotive No. 5 ... 3·75 ... 3·00
The stamps also show the arms of cities enroute and the emblems of the Orient Express (60st.) or the Bulgarian State Railways (1l.50).

1669 Nikola and Dimitar Petkov

2008. Birth Anniversaries of Dimitar Petkov (Prime Minister 1906–1907) (150th) and Nikola Petkov (politician, son of Dimitar Petkov and leader of Bulgarian Agrarian National Union) (115th).
4682 **1669** 60st. multicoloured ... 1·70 ... 1·30

1670 Tsar Ferdinand

2008. Centenary of Proclamation of Independence. Sheet 48×87 mm.
MS**4683 1670** 60st. multicoloured ... 1·90 ... 1·90

1671 Arms of the Templars

2008. 700th Anniv (2007) of Disbanding of Knights Templar (Order of the Temple) by King Philip IV of France.
4684 **1671** 1l. multicoloured ... 2·75 ... 2·10

1672 Race Car (2008)

2008. Ferrari Racing Cars. Multicoloured.
4685 60st. Type **1672** ... 1·70 ... 1·30
4686 1l. Race car (1952) ... 2·75 ... 2·10
MS**4687** As No. 4685. Imperf ... 1·90 ... 1·90

1673 Arms

2008. 130th Anniv of Bulgarian Red Cross Societies.
4688 **1673** 60st. multicoloured ... 1·70 ... 1·30

1674 Virgin Mary, Rila Monastery (12th–century)

2008. Bulgarian Icons. Multicoloured.
4689		50st. Type **1674**	1·40	1·10
4690		60st. Virgin and Child, Troyan Monastery (18th–century)	1·70	1·30
4691		1l. Virgin and Child, Bachkovo Monastery (14th–century)	2·75	2·10
MS4691a	112×73 mm. As No. 4690. Imperf		1·70	1·70

1675 Virgin and Child

2008. Christmas.
4692	**1675**	60st. multicoloured	1·70	1·30

1676 Saint Clement of Ohrid (St. Kliment Ohridski)

2008. 120th Anniv of Sofia University St. Kliment Ohridski.
4693	**1676**	60st multicoloured	1·70	1·30

1677 Andranik Ozanyan (Armenian general in Balkan Wars of Independence)

2008. Nationalist Liberation Movements of Bulgaria and Armenia. Multicoloured.
4694		60st. Type **1677**	1·70	1·30
4695		1l.50 Peyo Yavorov (Bulgarian poet and revolutionary)	2·75	2·10

1678 Emblem

2009. Bulgaria 2009–European Philatelic Exhibition.
4696	**1678**	60st. multicoloured	1·70	1·30

1679 Abraham Lincoln

2009. Birth Bicentenaries. T **1679** and similar horiz designs. Each green,olive and brown-olive.
4697		10st. Type **1679** (pres of USA)	35	25
4698		50st. Nikolai Gogol (writer)	1·40	1·10
4699		60st. Charles Darwin (naturalist)	1·70	1·30
4700		1l. Edgar Allan Poe (writer)	2·75	2·10
MS4701	55×105mm. 60st. Charles Darwin (different). Imperf		1·70	1·70

1680 *Scolopax rusticola* (Eurasian woodcock)

2009. Ecology–Balkan Mountains. Multicoloured.
4702		60st. Type **1680**	1·70	1·30
4703		1l. *Monticola saxatilis* (rufous-tailed rock thrush)	2·75	2·10
MS4704	106×85 mm. As Nos. 4702/3. Imperf		5·50	5·50

Nos. 4702/3 were printed together, *se-tenant*, forming a composite design.
Stamps of a similar design were issued by Serbia.

1681 Amethyst

2009. 120th Anniv of National Natural Science Museum.
4705	**1681**	60st. multicoloured	1·70	1·30
MS4706	87×61mm. 60st As Type **1681**. Imperf		1·70	1·70

1682 Hagia Sofia Church and St. Alexander Nevsky Cathedral

2009. 130th Anniv of Sofia as Capital of Bulgaria.
4707	**1682**	60st. multicoloured	1·70	1·30

1683 Penguins and Narwhal

2009. Preserve Polar Regions and Glaciers. Sheet 127×63 mm containing T **1683** and similar horiz design. Multicoloured.
MS4708	60st. Type **1683**; 1l.50 Polar bear, elephant seal and white-tailed eagle	5·50	5·50

1684 Flags as '60'

2009. 60th Anniv of NATO (4708). 5th Anniv of Bulgaria's Membership of NATO (4709). Multicoloured.
4709		60st. Type **1684**	1·70	1·30
4710		1l.50 Bulgarian flag as '5'	2·75	2·10

1685 Bicycle

2009. Bicycles. Multicoloured.
4711		10st. Type **1685**	35	25
4712		50st. Purple cycle	1·40	1·10
4713		60st. Penny farthing cycles	1·70	1·30
4714		1l. Early pedal-less cycle	2·75	2·10
MS4715	130×71mm 60st As No. 4714. Imperf 170170		1·70	1·70

Nos. 4711/14 were printed together, *se-tenant*, forming a composite design.

1686 Georgi Ivanov

2009. 30th Anniv of Space Flight of First Bulgarian Cosmonaut. Sheet 93×93 mm.
MS4716	**1686**	60st multicoloured	1·70	1·30

1687 Arms (1879)

2009. 130th Anniv of Restoration of State. Sheet 105×84 mm containing T **1687** and similar horiz design. Multicoloured.
MS4717	60st. Type **1687**; 1l. Arms (1997)	4·50	4·50

1688 *Rathbunia alamosensis*

2009. Cacti. Multicoloured.
4718		10st. Type **1688**	35	25
4719		50st. *Mammillaria pseudoperbella*	1·40	1·10
4720		60st. *Obregonia degenerii*	1·70	1·30
4721		1l.50 Inscr 'Astrophitum mayas'	2·75	2·10
MS4722	71×108 mm. 60t. As No. 4720. Imperf		1·70	1·70

1689 Spiral Galaxy IC 342

2009. Europa. Astronomy. Multicoloured.
4723		60st. Type **1689**	1·70	1·30
4724		1l.50 Andromeda Galaxy (M 31)	2·75	2·10
MS4725	112×90 mm. Size 29×39 mm. 60st.×2, As 4725×2; 1l.50×2, As No. 4726×2		9·00	9·00
4726		60st. As Type **1689**	1·70	1·30
4727		1l.50 As No. 4724 (Andromeda Galaxy (M 31))	2·75	2·10

1690 Members Flags surrounding Euro

2009. Tenth Anniv of Euro Currency.
4728	**1690**	1l. multicoloured	2·75	2·10

1691 *Landscape* (Vassil Ivanov) (birth centenary)

2009. Artists' Anniversaries. Multicoloured.
4729		10st. Type **1691**	35	25
4730		50st. *Three Vases* (Georgi Kolarov) (birth centenary)	1·40	1·10
4731		60st *The Black Sea* (Alexander Mutaffov) (130th birth anniv)	1·70	1·30
4732		1l. *Cast Shadows* (Konstantine Sturkelov) (120th birth anniv)	2·75	2·10

1692 Fan

2009. 80th Anniv of Locomotive Sofia Sports Club.
4733	**1692**	60st. multicoloured	1·70	1·30

1693 *Bubo bubo* (Eurasian eagle owl)

2009. Owls. Multicoloured.
4734		10st. Type **1693**	35	25
4735		50st. *Athene noctua* (Little owl)	1·40	1·10
4736		60st. *Strix uralensis* (Ural owl)	1·70	1·30
4737		1l.50 *Glaucidium passerinum* (Eurasian pygmy owl)	2·75	2·10

1694 Motorcycle and Rider

2009. SuperMoto European Championship. Sheet 96×85 mm.
MS4738	**1694**	60st.multicoloured	1·70	1·70

1695 Petko Voivoda

2009. 165th Birth Anniv of Petko Voivoda (nationalist).
4739	**1695**	60st. multicoloured	1·70	1·30

1696 Todor Burmov (first Minister for Internal Affairs)

2009. 130th Anniv of Ministry of Internal Affairs.
4740	**1696**	60st. multicoloured	1·70	1·30

1697 Airmail Envelope

2009. 130th Anniv of Bulgarian Communications. Sheet 97×117 mm containing T **1697** and similar horiz design. Multicoloured.
MS4741	60st. Type **1697**; 1l. Telephone	4·50	4·50

1698 Neil Armstrong and Lunar Module

2009. 40th Anniv of First Moon Landing. Sheet 101×84 mm.
MS4742	**1698**	60st multicoloured	1·70	1·70

No. **MS**4742 was also issued overprinted for Bulgaria 2009.

1699 Symbols of Science

2009. 140th of National Academy of Science.
4743	**1699**	60st. multicoloured	1·70	1·30

1700 Flags as Pen and Ink

2009. 130th Anniv of Bulgaria–Italy Diplomatic Relations. Sheet 101×71 mm.
MS4744 **1700** 1l. multicoloured 2·75 2·10

1701 Flags and Rose

2009. 130th Anniv of First Bulgarian Diplomatic Relations. Sheet 113×113 mm.
MS4745 **1701** 1l. multicoloured 2·75 2·10

1702 Anniversary Cake enclosed in TV Screen

2009. 50th Anniv of National Television.
4746 **1702** 60st. multicoloured 2·75 2·10

1703 Fokker E. III Monoplane and Marko Parvanov (Bulgarian gunner)

2009. History of Bulgarian Military Aviation. Multicoloured.
4747 60st. Type **1703** 1·70 1·30
4748 1l. Assen Jordanoff (aircraft designer) and Jordanov-1 2·75 2·10
Nos. 4747/8 were printed, *se-tenant*, forming a composite design.

1704 Virgin and Child

2009. Christmas.
4749 **1704** 60st. multicoloured 1·70 1·30

1705 Nikola Vaptsarov

2009. Birth Centenary of Nikola Vaptsarov (poet, communist and revolutionary).
4750 **1705** 60st. multicoloured 1·70 1·30

1706 Dimitar Milandinov

2010. Birth Bicentenary of Dimitar Milandinov (poet and folklorist).
4751 **1706** 60st. multicoloured 1·70 1·30

1707 Headset and Microphone

2010. 75th Anniv of Bulgarian National Radio.
4752 **1707** 60st. multicoloured 1·70 1·30

1708 Luge

2010. Winter Olympic Games, Vancouver. Sheet 98×90 mm containing T **1708** and similar horiz design. Multicoloured.
4753 60st. Type **1708**; 1l. Snow-boarder 4·50 4·50

1709 Frederic Chopin

2010. Birth Bicentenary of Frederic Chopin (composer).
4754 **1709** 1l. multicoloured 2·75 2·10

1710 *Paeonia suffruticosa var. rockii*

2010. Peonies. Sheet 80×86 mm containing T **1710** and similar vert design. Multicoloured.
MS4755 60st×2, Type **1710**; *Paeonia officinalis 'Rubra Plena'* 3·50 3·50

1711 General Georgi Vazov (1860-1934)

2010. 150th Birth Annivs of Bulgarian Commanders. Sheet 113×102 mm containing T **1711** and similar horiz designs. Multicoloured.
MS4756 60st×5, Type **1711**; General Ivan Fichev (1860-1931); General Stilian Kovachev (1860-1939); Colonel Vladimir Serafimov (1860-1934); General Dimitar Geshev (1860-1922) 8·50 8·50

1712 Chess Pieces

2010. World Chess Championship Match 2010 between Viswanathan Anand (winner) and Veselin Topalov. Sheet 69×85 mm.
MS4757 **1712** 1l. ochre, black and light grey 2·75 2·10

1713 House and Hedgehog

2010. Europa. Multicoloured.
4758 60st Type **1713** 1·80 1·40
4759 60st. As Type **1713** (29×39 mm) 1·80 1·40
4760 Hare and fairy carrying lantern 3·00 2·40
4761 1l.50 Hare and fairy carrying lantern 3·00 2·40
MS4762 106×85 mm. 60st. As Type **1713**; 1l.50 As No. 4760 4·75 4·75
The stamps of No. **MS**4762 have no white borders and, with the margins form a composite design.

1714 Dragon and Shanghai Skyline

2010. Expo 2010, Shanghai
4762a **1714** 1l.40 multicoloured 1·80 1·40
MS4763 113×74 mm 1l.40×4, Type **1714**×4 9·50 9·50

1714a Flag

2010. Centenary of Bulgaria–Spain Diplomatic Relations
4764 **1714a** 1l. multicoloured 1·80 1·40

1715 Bird, Mouse and Whale

2010. International Year of Biodiversity
MS4765 78×60 mm. **1715** 1l.50 multicoloured 2·75 2·75

1715a Bulgarian Shepherd Dog

2010. Balkan Dogs
MS4765a **1715a** 60st. multicoloured 1·80 1·40

1716 Emanuil Manolov

2010. Composers Anniversaries. Multicoloured.
4766 1l. Type **1716** (150th birth anniv) 2·75 2·10
4767 1l. Robert Schumann (birth bicentenary) 2·75 2·10

1717 Jules Rimet and Trophies

2010. World Cup Football Championships, South Africa
MS4768 **1717** 79×55 mm. 2l.10 multicoloured 5·50 5·50

1718 St. Procopius

2010. Death Bicentenary of St. Procopius of Varna
4769 **1718** 60st. multicoloured 1·80 1·40

1719 Manoeuvres (1899)

2010. 150th Birth Anniv of Yaroslav Veshin (Czech artist). Multicoloured.
4770 1l. Type **1719** 2·75 2·10
4771 1l. *Return from Market* (1898) 2·75 2·10

1720 Summer and Autumn (Les Saisons (1900))

2010. 150th Birth Anniv of Alphonse (Alfons) Maria Mucha (Czech artist). Multicoloured.
MS4772 1l.×2, Type **1720**; Winter and Spring (*Les Saisons* (1900)) 5·50 5·50

1721 Athletes, Emblem and Book

2010. Youth Olympic Games, Singapore 2010
4773 **1721** 1l.40 multicoloured 3·00 2·40

1722 Entwined Tree Trunks

2010. 125th Anniv of Bulgaria's Reunification
4774 **1722** 60st. multicoloured 1·80 1·40

1723 Magirus Feuerwehrwerke Fire-fighting Appliance

2010. History of the Fire Fighting
MS4775 **1723** 102×71 mm. 65st. multicoloured 1·90 1·90

1724 Giant Panda (*Ailuropoda melanoleuca*)

2010. Pandas. Multicoloured.
MS4776 95x126 mm. 10st. Type **1724**; 60st. Giant panda seated; 1l. Red panda (*Ailurus fulgens*); 1l.50 Red panda, head and shoulders 6·00 6·00

1725 Jak-23

2010. 60th Anniv of Military Jet Aviation. Multicoloured.
4777 50st. Type **1725** 1·60 1·10
4778 65st. Mikoyan-Gurevich type
MiG-15 1·90 1·50
4779 1l. Mikoyan MiG-29 2·75 2·10

1726 Santa wearing
Spectacles

2010. Christmas
4780 **1726** 65st. multicoloured 1·90 1·50

1727 Female
Figures from
Thracian Tomb of
Svestari

2010. Regions. Multicoloured.
MS4781 85x113 mm. 10st. Type **1727**;
50st. Balchik Palace; 65st. Srebarna
Nature Reserve; 1l. Pobiti Kamani
rock formations 4·75 4·75

1728 Self-Portrait

2010. Birth Bicentenary of Zahari Hristovich Dimitrov
(Zahari Zograf) (artist)
MS4782 61x70 mm. **1728** 1l.50
multicoloured 3·00 3·00

1729 San Cristobal Cathedral,
Havana

2010. 50th Anniv of Bulgaria–Cuba Diplomatic Relations.
Multicoloured.
4783 65c. Type **1729** 1·90 1·50
4784 1l.40 St. Alexander Nevsky
Cathedral, Sofia 3·00 2·40
Stamps of a similar design were issued by Cuba

1730 Griffon
Vulture

2010. Balkanfila 2010 International Stamp Exhibition,
Plovdiv
MS4785 88x78 mm. **1730** 65st.
multicoloured 1·90 1·90

1731 *Hydrurga
leptonyx* (leopard seal)

2011. Antarctica
4786 **1731** 58st. black and scarlet-
vermilion 1·80 1·40

1732 Princess Clementine
and Soldiers

2011. 125th Anniv of 9th Plovdiv Infantry Regiment
4787 **1732** 65st. multicoloured 1·90 1·50

1733 Vanga

2011. Birth Centenary of Vangelia Pandeva Dimitrova
(Vanga) (blind mystic, healer and herbalist)
4788 **1733** 65st. multicoloured 1·90 1·50

1734 Space and Haricot Bean

2011. Day of Humor and Joke (April Fool's Day)
4789 **1734** 65st. multicoloured 1·90 1·50
No. 4789 has a *se-tenant* stamp size label attached at
right which, with the stamp forms a composite design of
planets and space.

1735 Politicians

2011. 20th Anniv of Atlantic Club of Bulgaria
MS2790 87x78 mm. **1735** 1l. multi-
coloured 2·75 2·75

1736 Yuri Gagarin

2011. 50th Anniv of First Manned Space Flight.
Multicoloured.
MS4791 83x103 mm. 65st. Type **1736**;
1l.50 *Venera 1* 5·25 5·25

1737 *Capreolus
capreolus* (roe deer)
in Snow

2011. Europa. Forests. Multicoloured.
4792 65st. Type **1737** 2·00 1·60
4793 1l.50 *Scolopax rusticola*
(woodcock) 3·25 2·50
MS4794 106x85 mm. Nos. 4792/3 5·25 5·25

1738 Emperor Galerius

2011. 1700th Anniv of Serdica Edict of Religious
Tolerance, issued by Roman Emperor Galerius. Sheet
102x65 mm
MS4795 **1738** 65st. multicoloured 2·00 2·00

1739 Emblem

2011. 20th Anniv of Commission on Protection of
Competition
4796 **1739** 65st. multicoloured 2·00 1·60

1740 Rabbit as
Newspaper Boy

2011. 120th Anniv of Philatelic Press. Sheet 91x81 mm
MS4797 **1740** 65st. multicoloured 2·00 1·60
MS4797a **1740** 65st. multicoloured 2·00 1·60

1741 Bear and
Woodpecker

2011. Regions. North-Central Bulgaria. Multicoloured.
MS4798 65st Type **1741**; 65st. Coin
and church; 1l. Castle; 1l. Woman
knitting and textiles 10·50 10·50

1742 *Stizostedion lucioperca, Esox
lucius, Hucho hucho* and *Aspius aspius*

2011. Museum of the Danube Fishing, Tutrakan.
Multicoloured.
MS4799 65st. Type **1742**; 65st. *Abramis
brama, Ctenopharyngodon idella,
Cyprinus carpio* and *Carassius caras-
sius*; 1l. *Acipenser ruthenus*; 1l. *Siurus
glanis* and *Loto lota* 10·50 10·00

1743 Mounted Soldiers

2011. 1200th Anniv of Khan Krum Victory at Varbitsa Pass
4800 **1743** 65st. multicoloured 2·00 1·60

1744 *Rhodophyllus sinuatus*

2011. Poisonous Fungi. Multicoloured.
MS4801 65st. Type **1744**; 65st. *Inocybe
patouillardii*; 1l. *Russula emetica*; 1l.
Omphalotus olearius 10·50 10·50

1745 Tall Ship

2011. Tall Ships Regatta, 2011. Sheet 90x66 mm
MS4802 **1745** 1l. multicoloured 2·75 2·10

1746 Fridtjof
Nansen

2011. 150th Birth Anniv of Fridtjof Wedel-Jarlsberg
Nansen (explorer, humanitarian and winner of 1922
Nobel Peace Prize). Sheet 103x77 mm
MS4803 **1746** 1l. multicoloured 2·75 2·75

1747 Franz Liszt

2011. Birth Bicentenary of Franz Liszt
4804 **1747** 1l. multicoloured 2·75 2·10

1748 William Gladstone

2011. 145th Anniv of First Railway in Bulgaria.
Multicoloured.
MS4805 65st. Type **1748**; 1l. Early car-
riage; 1l.50 Early steam locomotive 8·00 8·00

1749 Laika

2011. Dogs in Space. Multicoloured.
MS4806 65st. Type **1749**; 65st.
Belka and Strlka; 1l. Chernushka; 1l.
Zvezdochka 7·50 7·50

1750 Can-AM
Renegade 800

2011. Peter Tsenkov and Todor Hristov, First Bulgarians to
Compete in Dakar Rally
4807 **1750** 1l.50 multicoloured 3·25 2·50

1751 *Scomber
scombrus* (Atlantic
mackerel)

2011. International Day of Black Sea. Multicoloured.
MS4808 1l.×2, Type **1751**; *Mytilus gal-
loprovincialis* (blue mussel) 5·50 5·50

1752 Yosif Tsankov

2011. Birth Centenary of Yosif Tsankov
4809 **1752** 65st. multicoloured 2·00 1·60

1753 '65' as
Snowman

2011. Christmas
4810 **1753** 65st. multicoloured 2·00 1·60

1754 '120', Medical Bag and Building

2011. 120th Anniv of Military Medical Academy, Sofia
4811 **1754** 65st. multicoloured 2·00 1·60

1755 Garden Flowers

2012. Garden Flowers. Multicoloured.
4812 65st. Type **1755** 2·00 1·60
4813 1l. Flowers (different) (vert) 2·75 2·20

1756 Cross

2012. 700th Anniv of disbanding of Order of the Temple
(Knights Templar) by Pope Clement V
4814 **1756** 65st. black and scarlet-
vermilion 2·00 1·60

1757 Anton Mitov

2012. Personalities. Multicoloured.
4815 65st. Type **1757** (artist) (150th
birth anniv) 2·00 1·60
4816 65st. Dimcho Debelyanov
(writer) (125th birth anniv) 2·00 1·60
4817 1l. Petya Dubarova (writer)
(50th birth anniv) 2·75 2·20
4818 1l. Yana Yazova (writer) (birth
centenary) 2·75 2·20

1758 Baldwin
Tower, Tsarevets
Fortress

2012. Europa. Visit Bulgaria. Multicoloured.
4819 65st. Type **1758** 2·00 1·60
4820 1l. Patriarchal Cathedral,
Tsarevets 2·75 2·20
MS4821 85×126 mm. Nos. 4819/20 9·50 9·50

1759 Gentoo Penguins (*Pygoscelis
papua*) and Bulgarian Flag

2012. 20th Bulgarian Antarctic Expedition
4822 1l.40 Type **1759** 3·25 2·50
MS4823 100×87 mm. 65st. Hut, flag
and Gentoo Penguin and chick

1760 *Titanic* at Night

2012. Centenary of *Titanic*. Sheet 100×50 mm
MS4824 **1760** 1l.40 multicoloured 3·25 3·25

1761 Albatros D. II
Aircraft

2012. Centenary of Bulgarian Aviation in Balkan War.
Battle of Edirne
4825 **1761** 65st. multicoloured 2·00 1·60

1762 Parashkev Hadjiev

2012. Birth Centenary of Parashkev Hadjiev (composer)
4826 **1762** 65st. multicoloured 2·00 1·60

1763 Anniversary Emblem

2012. 20th Anniv of Bulgaria's Membership of Council of
Europe
4827 **1763** 1l. multicoloured 2·75 2·20

1764 9th-Century
Stone Lion

2012. Archaeology
4828 **1764** 65st. multicoloured 2·00 1·60

1765 Truck

2012. 50th Anniv of AEBTRI (Association of Bulgarian
Enterprises for International Road Transport and
Roads). Sheet 100×71 mm
MS4829 **1765** 2l.10 multicoloured 9·75 9·75

1766 Football

2012. Euro 2012 – European Footbal Championships,
Poland and Ukraine. Sheet 100×102 mm
MS4830 **1766** 1l. multicoloured 2·75 2·75

1767 Silybum marianum

2012. Flora. Prickly Plants. Multicoloured.
4831 65st. Type **1767** 2·00 1·60
4832 65st. *Cardus acanthoides* 2·00 1·60
4833 1l. *Centauria solstitialis* 2·75 2·20
4834 1l. *Dipsacus laciniatus* 2·75 2·20

1768 Paisius of
Hilendar

2012. 250th Anniv of *Istoriya Slavyanobolgarskaya*
(Slavonic - Bulgarian history) by Paisius of Hilendar
4835 **1768** 65st. multicoloured 2·00 1·60

1769 Rogozen
Treasure

2012. Regions. North-western Bulgaria. Multicoloured.
MS4836 65st Type **1769**; 65st. Cave
paintings in Magura Cave; 1l. Mes-
chite Tower; 1l. Baba Vida Fortress 9·50 7·75

1770 Gymnast

2012. Olympic Games, London
MS4837 **1770** 1l.50 multicoloured 3·25 3·25

1771 Vasil Levski

2012. 175th Birth Anniv of Vasil Levski (revolutionary)
4838 **1771** 65st. multicoloured 2·00 1·60

2012. Moths. Australia 2013 and Thailand 2013
International Stamp Exhibition. Multicoloured.
MS4839 40st. As Type **1550**; 45st. *Re-
thera komoarovi* (As No. 4476); 55st.
Symtomis marjana (As No. 4477);
80st. *Arctia caja* (As No. 4478)

1772 *Impression:
Rising Sun* (Claude
Monet) and Claude
Debussy

2012. Impressionism. 150th Birth Anniv of Claude
Debussy
4840 **1772** 1l. multicoloured 2·75 2·20

1773 Fair Emblem

2012. 120th Anniv of Plovdiv International Fair
4841 **1773** 65st. multicoloured 2·00 2·00

1774 Ivan Stoyanovich

2012. 150th Birth Anniv of Ivan Petrov Stoyanovich
(revolutionary and statesman)
4842 **1774** 65st. multicoloured 2·00 2·00

1775 Monument of
Liberty, Rousse

2012. 150th Birth Anniv of Arnoldo Zocchi (Italian
sculptor)
4843 **1775** 1l. blue 2·75 2·75

1776 *Primula deorum*

2012. Ecology. Parangalitsa Reserve. Multicoloured.
MS4844 65st. Type **1776**; 1l. *Felis silves-
tris silvestris* (European Wild Cat) 5·00 5·00

1777 First Railway Mail Van
and *Rousse-Mid 19th Century*
(Felix Kaniz)

2012. Transport. Railway Post Wagons. Multicoloured.
MS4845 65st. Type **1777**; 65st. Mail
van (1888-1904) and 19th century
postcard showing views of Sofia; 1l.
First Bulgarian State Railways mail
van (1895-1930) and postcard show-
ing folk costumes; 1l. First Bulgarian
State Railways three axle mail van
and 20th century railway map 8·00 8·00

1778 Eurocopter AS532
Cougar Helicopter

2012. Military Helicopters. Sheet 87×67 mm
MS4846 **1778** 65st. multicoloured 2·50 2·50

1779 Andalusian

2012. Horses. Multicoloured.
4847 65st. Type **1779** 2·00 2·00
4848 65st. Irish Cob (Gypsy Vanner) 2·00 2·00
4849 1l. Arab 2·75 2·75
4850 1l. Haflinger Pony 2·75 2·75

1780 Centenary Emblem

2012. Centenary of Ministry of Railways, Posts and
Telegraphs
4851 **1780** 65st. multicoloured 2·00 2·00

1781 Sword Hilt, Lion
and Seal

2012. Centenary of Discovery of Khan Kubrat's Grave and Funerary Hoard (founder of Old Great Bulgaria)
4852 **1781** 1l. multicoloured 2·75 2·75

1782 Stylized Tree

2012. Christmas
4853 **1782** 65st. multicoloured 2·00 2·00

1783 Valley of the Roses (perfume industry) (Vasilena Vasileva)

2012. International Year of Chemistry. Winning Entry (12 - 14 years) in Global Design a Stamp Competition, Chemistry as a Cultural Enterprise
4854 **1783** 65st. multicoloured 2·00 2·00

1784 Thracian Gold Rhyton (4th century B.C.) (Bulgaria)

2012. 20th Anniv of Bulgaria - Kazakhstan Diplomatic Relations. Multicoloured.
4855 65st. Type **1784** 2·00 2·00
4856 1l.40 Two gold deer linked by bird 3·50 3·50

1785 Planets in Orbit

2012. Grand Parade of the Planets 2012. Sheet 102×63 mm
MS4857 **1785** 1l. multicoloured 3·25 3·25

1786 Emblem

2013. Tourism
4858 **1786** 1l. multicoloured 2·75 2·75

1789 Anniversary Emblem

2013. 70th Anniv of Saving Bulgarian Jews
4861 **1789** 1l.40 emerald, scarlet-vermilion and black 3·50 3·50

1790 Bells (as label of No. 4479)

2013. Greetings Stamps
4862 65st. As No. 4221 (making wine) 2·00 2·00
4863 65st. As No. 4394 (clown) (horiz) 2·00 2·00
4864 65st. As T **1740** (rabbit as newspaper boy) 2·00 2·00
4865 1l. Type **1790** 2·75 2·75

1791 Team Members, 1925

2013. Centenary of Cherno More Football Club
4866 **1791** 65st. multicoloured 2·00 2·00

1792 Winning Team Members, 1943

2013. Centenary of Slavia Football Club
4867 **1792** 65st. multicoloured 2·00 2·00

1794 Battle Scene

2013. Centenary of End of First Balkan War. Sheet 120×105 mm
MS4869 65st. Type **1794**; 65st. Triumphal arch; 1l. Surrender of Edirne Fortress; 1l. Tsar Ferdinand on horseback 8·00 8·00

EXPRESS STAMPS

E137 Express Delivery Van

1939
E429 - 5l. blue 1·80 45
E430 **E137** 6l. brown 85 40
E431 - 7l. brown 1·30 40
E432 **E137** 8l. red 1·60 50
E433 - 20l. red 2·50 1·20
DESIGNS—VERT: 5l., 20l. Bicycle messenger; 7l. Motor-cyclist and sidecar.

OFFICIAL STAMPS

O158

1942
O507 **O158** 10s. green 10 10
O508 **O158** 30s. orange 10 10
O509 **O158** 50s. brown 10 10
O510 - 1l. blue 10 10
O511 - 2l. green 15 10
O534 - 2l. red 1·40 50
O512 - 3l. mauve 20 10
O513 - 4l. pink 30 15
O514 - 5l. red 50 20
The 1l. to 5l. are larger (19×23 mm).

O177

1945. Arms designs. Imperf or perf.
O580B 1l. mauve 10 10
O581B **O 177** 2l. green 10 10
O582B - 3l. brown 10 10
O583B - 4l. blue 10 10
O584B - 5l. red 10 10

PARCEL POST STAMPS

P153 Weighing Machine **P154** Loading Motor Lorry

1941
P494 **P153** 1l. green 15 10
P495 A 2l. red 15 10
P496 **P 154** 3l. brown 15 10
P497 B 4l. orange 15 10
P498 **P 153** 5l. blue 15 10
P506 **P 153** 5l. green 20 15
P499 B 6l. purple 15 10
P507 B 6l. brown 20 15
P500 **P 153** 7l. blue 15 10
P508 **P 153** 7l. sepia 20 15
P501 **P 154** 8l. turquoise 20 10
P509 **P 154** 8l. green 20 15
P502 A 9l. olive 30 15
P503 B 10l. orange 40 15
P504 **P 154** 21l. violet 65 20
P505 A 30l. black 1·50 30
DESIGNS—HORIZ: A, Loading mall coach; B, Motor-cycle combination.

P163

1944. Imperf.
P532 **P163** 1l. red 20 15
P533 **P163** 3l. green 20 15
P534 **P163** 5l. green 20 15
P535 **P163** 7l. mauve 20 15
P536 **P163** 10l. blue 20 15
P537 **P163** 20l. brown 20 15
P538 **P163** 30l. purple 40 20
P539 **P163** 50l. orange 75 50
P540 **P163** 100l. blue 1·40 80

POSTAGE DUE STAMPS

D7

1884. Perf.
D75 **D7** 5s. orange 55·00 7·75
D54 **D7** 25s. lake 27·00 7·75
D55 **D7** 50s. blue 27·00 23·00

1886. Imperf.
D50 5s. orange £550 26·00
D51 25s. lake £800 23·00
D52a 50s. blue 33·00 26·00

1893. Surch with bar and 30.
D78d 30s. on 50s. blue (perf) 49·00 16·00
D79 30s. on 50s. blue (imperf) 43·00 16·00

D12

1896. Perf.
D83 **D12** 5s. orange 27·00 4·25
D84 **D12** 10s. violet 16·00 3·75
D85 **D12** 30s. green 13·00 3·25

D16

1901
D124 **D16** 5s. red 1·10 50
D125 **D16** 10s. green 2·20 65
D126 **D16** 20s. blue 16·00 65
D127 **D16** 30s. red 5·50 70
D128 **D16** 50s. orange 14·00 12·50

D37

1915
D200 **D37** 5s. green 55 10
D240 **D37** 10s. violet 20 10
D202 **D37** 20s. red 55 20
D241 **D37** 20s. orange 20 10
D203a **D37** 30s. red 55 20
D242 **D37** 50s. blue 20 10
D243 **D37** 1l. green 55 20
D244 **D37** 2l. red 55 20
D245 **D37** 3l. brown 1·10 40

D110

1932
D326 **D110** 1l. bistre 2·10 1·30
D327 **D110** 2l. red 2·10 1·30
D328 **D110** 6l. purple 4·75 1·50

D111 **D112**

1933
D333 **D111** 20s. sepia 20 10
D334 **D111** 40s. blue 20 10
D335 **D111** 80s. red 20 10
D336 **D 112** 1l. brown 1·00 60
D337 **D 112** 2l. olive 1·00 90
D338 **D 112** 6l. violet 50 40
D339 **D 112** 14l. blue 75 60

1947. As Type D **112**, but larger (18×24 mm).
D646 1l. brown 20 20
D647 2l. red 30 30
D648 8l. orange 20 20
D649 20l. blue 75 30

D293

1951
D849 **D293** 1l. brown 20 15
D850 **D293** 2l. purple 30 15
D851 **D293** 8l. orange 65 50
D852 **D293** 20l. blue 1·70 1·30

Pt. 3

BULGARIAN OCCUPATION OF ROMANIA

100 stotinki = 1 leva.

(DOBRUJA DISTRICT)

(1)

1916. Bulgarian stamps of 1911 optd with T **1**.
1 **23** 1s. grey 25 25
2 - 5s. brown and green 4·75 3·00
3 - 10s. sepia and brown 45 35
4 - 25s. black and blue 45 35

BUNDI

A state of Rajasthan, India. Now uses Indian stamps.

12 pies = 1 anna; 16 annas = 1 rupee.

3 Native Dagger

1894. Imperf.

12	3	½a. grey	7·00	6·00
13	3	1a. red	6·50	6·50
14	3	2a. green	19·00	23·00
8	3	4a. green	95·00	£160
15	3	8a. red	26·00	28·00
16a	3	1r. yellow on blue	25·00	38·00

1898. As T 3, but with dagger point to left.

17a	3	4a. green	27·00	32·00

11 Raja protecting Sacred Cows

1914. Roul or perf.

26	11	¼a. blue	1·90	4·25
38	11	½a. black	3·50	4·75
28	11	1a. red	4·00	16·00
30	11	2½a. yellow	13·00	30·00
31	11	3a. brown	12·00	60·00
32	11	4a. green	4·00	55·00
33a	11	6a. blue	7·00	£140
42	11	8a. orange	9·00	80·00
43	11	10a. olive	17·00	£130
44	11	12a. green	19·00	£130
25	11	1r. lilac	35·00	£140
46	11	2r. brown and black	£100	£250
47	11	3r. blue and brown	£180	£325
48	11	4r. green and red	£350	£425
49	11	5r. red and green	£350	£425

20

1941. Perf.

79	20	3p. blue	3·25	7·00
80	20	6p. blue	7·00	11·00
81	20	1a. red	9·00	13·00
82	20	2a. brown	9·50	24·00
83	20	4a. green	16·00	75·00
84	20	8a. green	21·00	£325
85	20	1r. blue	48·00	£425

21 Maharao Rajah Bahadur Singh

1947.

86	21	¼a. green	2·25	48·00
87	21	½a. violet	2·00	38·00
88	21	1a. green	2·00	40·00
89	-	2a. red	2·00	85·00
90	-	4a. orange	2·50	£100
91	-	8a. blue	3·25	
92	-	1r. brown	19·00	

DESIGNS: 2, 4a. Rajah in Indian dress; 8a., 1r. View of Bundi.

OFFICIAL STAMPS

बूंदी

सरविस

(O1)

1915. Optd as Type O1.

O6A	¼a. blue		1·60
O16Aa	½a. black		75
O8A	1a. red		4·50

O18A	2a. green		11·00
O2A	2½a. yellow		6·00
O3A	3a. brown		5·50
O19A	4a. green		14·00
O11A	6a. blue		15·00
O20A	8a. orange		15·00
O21A	10a. olive		80·00
O22A	12a. green		60·00
O5A	1r. lilac		75·00
O24A	2r. brown and black		£400
O25A	3r. blue and brown		£275
O26A	4r. green and red		£300
O27A	5r. red and green		£325

1915. Optd BUNDI SERVICE.

O6B	11	¼a. blue	2·50
O16B	11	½a. black	3·50
O8Bb	11	1a. red	18·00
O18B	11	2a. green	24·00
O2B	11	2½a. yellow	21·00
O3B	11	3a. brown	23·00
O19B	11	4a. green	95·00
O11B	11	6a. blue	£325
O20B	11	8a. orange	40·00
O21B	11	10a. olive	£120
O22B	11	12a. green	£140
O5B	11	1r. lilac	80·00
O24B	11	2r. brown and black	£200
O25B	11	3r. blue and brown	£225
O26B	11	4r. green and red	£300
O27B	11	5r. red and green	£325

Prices for Nos. O2/27 are for unused examples. Used examples are generally worth a small premium over the prices quoted.

1941. Optd SERVICE.

O53	20	3p. blue	10·00	21·00
O54	20	6p. blue	23·00	21·00
O55	20	1a. red	19·00	19·00
O56	20	2a. brown	28·00	17·00
O57	20	4a. green	80·00	£180
O58	20	8a. green	£300	£850
O59	20	1r. blue	£350	£950

For later issues see **RAJASTHAN**.

BURKINA FASO

A country in W. Africa, formerly known as Upper Volta. The name was changed in August 1984.

100 centimes = 1 franc.

249 *Graphium pylades*

1984. Air. Butterflies. Multicoloured.

738	10f. Type 249		30	10
739	120f. *Hyploimnas misippus*		1·30	55
740	400f. *Danaus chrysippus*		4·25	2·10
741	450f. *Papilio demodocus*		5·00	2·30

250 Soldier with Gun

1984. First Anniv of Captain Thomas Sankara's Presidency. Multicoloured.

742	90f. Type 250		39·00
743	120f. Capt. Sankara and crowd		55·00

1984. Aid for the Sahel. No. 682 of Upper Volta optd BURKINA FASO Aide au Sahel 84.

743a	100f. multicoloured		

1985. Nos. 716/21 of Upper Volta optd BURKINA FASO.

744	25f. Type 246 (postage)		45	20
745	185f. "Pterocarpus lucens"		2·75	1·50
746	200f. "Phlebopus colossus sudanicus"		3·75	1·70
747	250f. "Cosmos sulphureus"		4·50	2·10
748	300f. "Trametes versicolor" (air)		4·75	2·40
749	400f. "Ganoderma lucidum"		6·50	3·25

252 National Flag

1985. National Symbols. Multicoloured.

750	5f. Type 252 (postage)		40	20
751	15f. National arms (vert)		45	25
752	90f. Maps of Africa and Burkina Faso		1·80	90
753	120f. Type 252 (air)		1·60	80
754	150f. As No. 751		2·20	1·00
755	185f. As No. 752		2·50	1·20

253 Footballers and Statue

1985. World Cup Football Championship, Mexico.

756	253	25f. mult (postage)	40	10
757	-	45f. multicoloured	55	20
758	-	90f. multicoloured	1·10	35
759	-	100f. multicoloured (air)	1·20	30
760	-	150f. multicoloured	1·40	55
761	-	200f. mult (horiz)	1·90	85
762	-	250f. mult (horiz)	2·50	1·10
MS763		78×77 mm. 500f. multicoloured (horiz)	5·50	1·30

DESIGNS: 45f. to 500f. Mexican statues and various footballing scenes.

254 Children playing and Boy

1985. Air "Philexafrique" International Stamp Exhibition, Lome, Togo (1st issue). Multicoloured.

764	200f. Type 254		2·00	1·20
765	200f. Solar panels, transmission mast, windmill, dish aerial and tree		2·00	1·20

See also Nos. 839/40.

255 G. A. Long's Steam Tricycle

1985. Centenary of Motor Cycle. Multicoloured.

766	50f. Type 255 (postage)		90	20
767	75f. Pope		1·10	25
768	80f. Manet		1·60	35
769	100f. Ducati (air)		95	30
770	150f. Jawa		1·60	55
771	200f. Honda		2·20	85
772	250f. B.M.W.		2·75	1·10

256 *Chamaeleon dilepis*

1985. Reptiles and Amphibians. Multicoloured.

773	5f. Type 256 (postage)		25	15
774	15f. *Agama stellio*		70	15
775	33f. *Lacerta lepida* (horiz)		1·10	15
776	85f. *Hiperolius marmoratus* (horiz)		1·70	30
777	100f. *Echis leucogaster* (air)		1·40	30
778	150f. *Kinixys erosa* (horiz)		2·10	50
779	250f. *Python regius* (horiz)		3·25	70

257 Benz Victoria, 1893

1985. Motor Cars and Aircraft. Multicoloured.

780	5f. Type 257 (postage)		20	10
781	25f. Peugeot "174", 1927		45	10
782	45f. Bleriot XI airplane		60	10
783	50f. Breguet 14T biplane		60	10
784	500f. Bugatti "Napoleon T41 Royale" (air)		5·25	1·30
785	500f. Airbus Industrie A300		4·25	1·30
786	600f. Mercedes-Benz "540 K", 1938		5·25	1·70
787	600f. Airbus Industrie A300		5·25	1·70
MS788	100×68 mm. 1000f. Louis Bleriot and Bleriot XI, Karl Benz and early Benz motor car		8·50	3·50

258 Wood Duck

1985. Birth Bicentenary of John J. Audubon (ornithologist). Multicoloured.

789	60f. Type 258 (postage)		60	20
790	100f. Northern mockingbird		90	40
791	300f. Northern oriole		3·00	90
792	400f. White-breasted nuthatch		3·50	1·20
793	500f. Common flicker (air)		4·25	1·30
794	600f. Rough-legged buzzard		5·25	1·60
MS795	73×83 mm. 1000f. White-crowned pigeon		9·00	3·50

259 Young Lady Elizabeth Bowes-Lyon on Pony

1985. 85th Birthday of Queen Elizabeth the Queen Mother. Multicoloured.

796	75f. Type 259 (postage)		80	35
797	85f. Marriage of Lady Elizabeth Bowes-Lyon and Albert, Duke of York		80	35
798	500f. Duke and Duchess of York with Princess Elizabeth (air)		4·00	1·30
799	600f. Royal family in Coronation robes		5·25	1·60
MS800	104×64 mm. 1000f. Queen Elizabeth the Queen Mother at christening of Prince William of Wales		8·50	3·50

260 Gaucho on Piebald Horse

1985. "Argentina '85" International Stamp Exhibition, Buenos Aires. Horses. Multicoloured.

801	25f. Type 260 (postage)		45	10
802	45f. Gaucho on horse		75	25
803	90f. Rodeo rider		1·30	40
804	100f. Rider hunting gazelle (air)		1·00	35
805	150f. Horses and gauchos at camp fire		1·50	55
806	200f. Horse and man sitting on steps		2·10	85
807	250f. Riding contest		2·75	1·10
MS808	100×89 mm. 500f. Foal (39×31 mm)		7·50	3·00

261 Electric Locomotive No. 105-30 and Tank Wagon

1985. Trains. Multicoloured.

809	50f. Type 261 (postage)		80	10
810	75f. Diesel shunting locomotive		1·00	25
811	80f. Diesel passenger locomotive		1·30	25
812	100f. Diesel railcar (air)		1·10	10
813	150f. Diesel locomotive No. 6093		1·60	30
814	200f. Diesel railcar No. 105		2·10	40
815	250f. Diesel locomotive pulling passenger train		2·75	55

262 Pot (Tikare)

1985. Handicrafts. Multicoloured.

816	10f. Type **262** (postage)	25	10
817	40f. Pot with lid decorated with birds (P. Bazega)	70	20
818	90f. Bronze statuette of mother with child (Ouagadougou)	1·40	35
819	120f. Bronze statuette of drummer (Ouagadougou) (air)	2·10	50

263 Pholiota mutabilis

1985. Fungi. Multicoloured.

820	15f. Type **263** (postage)	20	10
821	20f. Hypholoma (nematoloma) fasciculare	20	10
822	30f. Ixocomus granulatus	40	20
823	60f. Agaricus campestris	90	15
824	80f. Trachypus scaber	1·40	50
825	250f. Marasmius scorodonius	3·75	1·50
826	150f. Armillaria mellea (air)	2·75	70

264 Virgin and Child

1985. "Italia '85" International Stamp Exhibition, Rome. Paintings by Botticelli. Multicoloured.

827	25f. Type **264** (postage)	50	10
828	45f. Portrait of an Unknown Man	90	20
829	90f. Mars and Venus	1·60	40
830	100f. Birth of Venus (air)	1·20	50
831	150f. Allegory of Calumny	1·40	65
832	200f. Pallas and the Centaur	2·50	85
833	250f. Allegory of Spring	3·25	1·10
MS834	71×91 mm. 500f. Virgin of the Pomegranate (31×39 mm)	5·00	2·00

265 Sikorsky S-55 Helicopter

1985. Red Cross. Multicoloured.

835	40f. Type **265** (postage)	1·70	35
836	85f. Ambulance	3·00	50
837	150f. Henri Dunant (founder) (vert) (air)	2·30	65
838	250f. Nurse attending patient (vert)	3·75	1·10

266 Transport and Communications (development)

1985. Air. "Philexafrique" International Stamp Exhibition, Lome, Togo (2nd issue). Multicoloured.

839	250f. Type **266**	3·50	1·50
840	250f. Youth activities (youth)	3·50	1·50

267 Girls drumming and clapping

1986. Dodo Carnival. Multicoloured.

841	20f. Type **267**	10	10
842	25f. Masked lion dancers	25	10
843	40f. Masked stick dancers and drummers	45	15
844	45f. Stick dancers with elaborate headdresses	55	20
845	90f. Masked elephant dancer	1·20	45
846	90f. Animal dancers	1·20	45

268 Mother breast-feeding Baby

1986. Child Survival Campaign.

847	**268** 90f. multicoloured	1·10	50

269 Couple carrying Rail

1986. Railway Construction. Multicoloured.

848	90f. Type **269** (postage)	85	35
849	120f. Laying tracks	1·00	45
850	185f. Workers waving to passing train	1·50	65
851	500f. Inauguration of First German Railway (Heim) (air)	4·25	2·00
MS852	90×68 mm. 1000f. Experimental inter-city train and diesel locomotive series 290	8·50	3·50

Nos. 851/**MS**852 commemorate the 150th Anniv of German railways.

270 Columbus before King of Portugal, and Nina

1986. 480th Death Anniv of Christopher Columbus (explorer). Multicoloured.

853	250f. Type **270** (postage)	2·50	70
854	300f. Santa Maria and Columbus with astrolabe	2·75	90
855	400f. Columbus imprisoned on Santa Maria	3·75	1·10
856	450f. Landing at San Salvador and Pinta (air)	4·25	1·80
MS857	90×68 mm. 1000f. Fleet leaving Palos	8·50	2·10

271 Village and First Aid Post

1986. "Health For All by Year 2000". Multicoloured.

858	90f. Type **271**	95	35
859	100f. Man receiving first aid (26×36 mm)	95	45
860	120f. People queuing for vaccinations (26×36 mm)	1·30	50

272 "Phryneta aurocinta"

1986. Insects. Multicoloured.

861	15f. Type **272**	25	10
862	20f. Sternocera interrupta	35	10
863	40f. Prosoprocera lactator	80	30
864	45f. Gonimbrasia hecate	90	35
865	85f. Charaxes epijasius	1·40	60

273 Woman feeding Child and Fresh Foods

1986. Gobi Health Strategy. Multicoloured.

866	30f. Type **273**	40	10
867	60f. Ingredients of oral rehydration therapy	70	30
868	90f. Mother holding child for vaccination	1·00	45
869	120f. Doctor weighing child	1·50	55

274 UPU Emblem on Dove

1986. World Post Day.

870	**274** 120f. multicoloured	1·30	55

275 Emblem

1986. International Peace Year.

871	**275** 90f. blue	1·20	55

276 Namende Dancers

1986. National Bobo Culture Week. Multicoloured.

872	10f. Type **276**	25	10
873	25f. Mouhoun dancers	50	10
874	90f. Houet dancer	1·10	45
875	105f. Seno musicians	1·10	50
876	120f. Ganzourgou dancers	1·70	60

277 Warthog

1986. Wildlife. Multicoloured.

877	50f. Type **277**	70	20
878	65f. Spotted hyena	80	30
879	90f. Antelope	1·20	35
880	100f. Red-fronted gazelle	1·20	45
881	120f. Harnessed antelope	1·30	55
882	145f. Hartebeest	1·80	65
883	500f. Kob	5·75	2·20

278 Peul

1986. Traditional Hairstyles. Multicoloured.

884	35f. Type **278**	35	10
885	75f. Dafing	80	35
886	90f. Peul (different)	1·30	45
887	120f. Mossi	1·60	60
888	185f. Peul (different)	2·30	90

279 Charlie Chaplin within Film Frame (10th death anniv)

1987. Tenth Fespaco Film Festival.

889	– 90f. mauve, black & brn	1·10	60
890	– 120f. multicoloured	2·20	85
891	**279** 185f. multicoloured	3·25	1·40

DESIGNS: 90f. Camera on map in film frame; 120f. Cameraman and soundman (60th anniv of first talking film The Jazz Singer).

280 Woman trimming Rug

1987. International Women's Day.

892	**280** 90f. multicoloured	1·00	45

281 Calotripis procera

1987. Flowers. Multicoloured.

893	70f. Type **281**	80	30
894	75f. Acacia seyal	80	30
895	85f. Parkia biglobosa	1·00	50
896	90f. Sterospernum kunthianum	1·00	50
897	100f. Dichrostachys cinerea	1·40	55
898	300f. Combretum paniculatum	3·50	1·30

282 High Jumping

1987. Olympic Games, Seoul (1988). 50th Death Anniv of Pierre de Coubertin (founder of modern Olympic Games). Multicoloured.

899	75f. Type **282**	80	40
900	85f. Tennis (vert)	90	40
901	90f. Ski jumping	95	55
902	100f. Football	1·00	55
903	145f. Running	1·40	70
904	350f. Pierre de Coubertin and tennis game (vert)	3·50	1·70

283 Follereau and Doctor treating Patient

1987. Anti-leprosy Campaign. 10th Death Anniv of Raoul Follereau (pioneer). Multicoloured.

905	90f. Type **283**	1·10	45
906	100f. Laboratory technicians	1·30	45
907	120f. Gerhard Hansen (discoverer of bacillus)	1·50	55
908	300f. Follereau kissing patient	3·50	1·50

284 Woman sweeping

1987. World Environment Day. Multicoloured.

909	90f. Type **284**	1·00	60
910	145f. Emblem	1·50	75

285 Globe in Envelope

1987. World Post Day.

911	**285** 90f. multicoloured	1·00	55

286 Luthuli and Open Book

1987. Anti-Apartheid Campaign. 20th Death Anniv of Albert John Luthuli (anti-apartheid campaigner). Multicoloured.

912	90f. Barbed wire and apartheid victims	1·00	45
913	100f. Type **286**	1·10	45

287 Dagari

1987. Traditional Costumes. Multicoloured.

914	10f. Type **287**	10	10
915	30f. Peul	25	10
916	90f. Mossi (female)	85	45
917	200f. Senoufo	1·60	90
918	500f. Mossi (male)	5·00	2·30

288 Balafon (16 key xylophone)

1987. Traditional Music Instruments. Multicoloured.

919	20f. Type **288**	25	10
920	25f. Kunde en more (3 stringed lute) (vert)	25	20
921	35f. Tiahoun en bwaba (zither)	40	25
922	90f. Jembe en dioula (conical drum)	90	45
923	1000f. Bendre en more (calabash drum) (vert)	9·75	4·50

289 Dwellings

1987. International Year of Shelter for the Homeless.

924	**289** 90f. multicoloured	1·00	45

290 Small Industrial Units

1987. Five Year Plan for Popular Development. Multicoloured.

925	40f. Type **290**	35	10
926	55f. Management of dams	60	25
927	60f. Village community building primary school	60	25
928	90f. Bus (Transport and communications)	1·00	35
929	100f. National education: literacy campaign	1·00	55
930	120f. Intensive cattle farming	1·30	55

291 People with Candles

1988. 40th Anniv of WHO.

931	**291** 120f. multicoloured	1·30	45

292 Exhibition Emblem and Games Mascot

1988. Olympic Games, Seoul, and "Olymphilex '88" Olympic Stamps Exhibition, Rome (932). Multicoloured.

932	30f. Type **292**	30	10
933	160f. Olympic flame (vert)	1·50	60
934	175f. Football	1·70	70
935	235f. Volleyball (vert)	2·30	1·10
936	450f. Basketball (vert)	4·25	2·00

MS937 115×100 mm. 500f. 1500 metres race (36×48 mm) 5·75 5·25

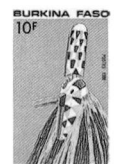

293 Houet "Sparrow Hawk" Mask

1988. Masks. Multicoloured.

938	10f. Type **293**	10	10
939	20f. Ouillo "Young Girls" mask	30	25
940	30f. Houet "Hartebeest" mask	40	25
941	40f. Mouhoun "Blacksmith" mask	45	25
942	120f. Ouri "Nanny" mask	1·30	45
943	175f. Ouri "Bat" mask (horiz)	1·80	75

294 Kieriba Jug

1988. Handicrafts. Multicoloured.

944	5f. Type **294**	10	10
945	15f. Mossi basket (horiz)	10	10
946	25f. Gurunsi chair (horiz)	25	10
947	30f. Bissa basket (horiz)	25	20
948	45f. Ouagadougou hide box (horiz)	45	20
949	85f. Ouagadougou bronze statuette	75	40
950	120f. Ouagadougou hide travelling bag (horiz)	1·10	55

295 Envelopes forming Map

1988. World Post Day.

951	**295** 120f. blue, black & yellow	1·10	45

296 White-collared Kingfisher

1988. Aquatic Wildlife. Multicoloured.

952	70f. Type **296**	60	25
953	100f. Elephantfish	1·00	40
954	120f. Frog	1·40	45
955	160f. White-faced whistling duck	1·60	70

297 Mohammed Ali Jinnah (first Pakistan Governor-General)

1988. Death Anniversaries. Multicoloured.

956	80f. Type **297** (40th anniv) (postage)	75	40
957	120f. Mahatma Gandhi (Indian human rights activist, 40th anniv)	1·10	55
958	160f. John Fitzgerald Kennedy (U.S. President, 25th anniv)	1·70	70
959	235f. Martin Luther King (human rights activist, 20th anniv) (air)	2·10	1·10

298 Shepherds adoring Child

1988. Christmas. Stained Glass Windows. Multicoloured.

960	120f. Type **298**	1·20	40
961	160f. Wise men presenting gifts to Child	1·40	70
962	450f. Virgin and Child	4·00	1·80
963	1000f. Flight into Egypt	8·50	4·50

299 Satellite and Globe

1989. 20th Anniv of FESPACO Film Festival. Multicoloured.

964	75f. Type **299** (postage)	1·70	40
965	500f. Ababacar Samb Makharam (air)	6·25	2·75
966	500f. Jean Michel Tchissoukou	6·25	2·75
967	500f. Paulin Soumanou Vieyra	6·25	2·75

MS968 114×85 mm. As Nos. 965/7 but with anniversary inscriptions and values in gold 21·00 19·00

300 WHO and Aids Emblems

1989. Campaign against AIDS.

969	**300** 120f. multicoloured	1·10	55

301 Oath of the Tennis Court (Jacques Louis David) (½-size illustration)

1989. Air. "Philexfrance 89" International Stamp Exhibition, Paris, and Bicentenary of French Revolution. Multicoloured.

970	150f. Type **301**	1·40	80
971	200f. Storming of the Bastille (Thevenin)	2·00	1·20
972	600f. Rouget de Lisle singing La Marseillaise (Pils)	6·25	3·50

302 Map and Tractor

1989. 30th Anniv of Council of Unity.

973	**302** 75f. multicoloured	75	40

303 Striga generioides

1989. Parasitic Plants. Multicoloured.

974	20f. Type **303**	25	10
975	50f. Striga hermonthica	45	25
976	235f. Striga aspera	2·10	1·10
977	450f. Alectra vogelii	4·00	1·80

304 Sahel Dog

1989. Dogs. Multicoloured.

978	35f. Type **304**	45	25
979	50f. Young dog	55	25
980	60f. Hunting dog	80	35
981	350f. Guard dog	3·50	1·80

305 Statue

1989. Solidarity with Palestinian People.

982	**305** 120f. multicoloured	1·20	45

1989. Nos. 647/9 of Upper Volta optd **BURKINA FASO**.

983	**229** 90f. multicoloured	80	30
984	**229** 120f. multicoloured	1·00	40
985	**229** 170f. multicoloured	1·50	60

307 Pilgrims at Shrine of Our Lady of Yagma

1990. Visit of Pope John Paul II. Multicoloured.

986	120f. Type **307**	1·20	55
987	160f. Pope and crowd	1·70	90

308 Mail Steamer, Globe and Penny Black

1990. 150th Anniv of Penny Black and "Stamp World London 90" International Stamp exhibition. Multicoloured.

988	120f. Type **308**	1·20	55

MS989 70×80 mm. 500f. Penny Black and early mail steamers (vert) 4·25 4·00

309 Goalkeeper catching Ball

1990. World Cup Football Championship, Italy. Multicoloured.

990	30f. Type **309**	35	25
991	150f. Footballers	1·60	70

MS992 72×65 mm. 1000f. Footballers and "1990" 8·50 8·25

310 *Cantharellus cibarius*

1990. Fungi. Multicoloured.

993		10f. Type **310**	20	20
994		15f. *Psalliota bispora*	25	20
995		60f. *Amanita caesarea*	85	60
996		190f. *Boletus badius*	2·75	1·50
MS997 77×108 mm. 75f.×4 As Nos. 993/6			4·75	4·00

311 Open Book

1990. International Literacy Year.

998	**311**	40f. multicoloured	45	20
999	**311**	130f. multicoloured	1·20	55

312 Maps, Emblem and Native Artefacts

1990. Second International Salon of Arts and Crafts, Ouagadougou. Multicoloured.

1000		35f. Type **312**	25	20
1001		45f. Pottery (horiz)	40	20
1002		270f. Cane chair	2·20	1·10

313 De Gaulle

1990. Birth Centenary of Charles de Gaulle (French statesman).

1003	**313**	200f. multicoloured	2·00	90

314 Quartz

1991. Rocks. Multicoloured.

1004		20f. Type **314**	25	10
1005		50f. Granite	70	40
1006		280f. Amphibolite	2·75	1·70

315 Hand Holding Cigarette, Syringe and Tablets

1991. Anti-drugs Campaign.

1007	**315**	130f. multicoloured	1·10	65

316 Film and Landscape

1991. 12th "Fepaco 91" Pan-African Cinema and Television Festival. Multicoloured.

1008		150f. Type **316**	1·70	90
MS1009 77×108 mm. 1000f. *Stallion of Yennenga* (Festival Grand Prix statuette)			12·00	12·00

317 Morse and Key

1991. Birth Bicentenary of Samuel Morse (inventor of signalling system).

1010	**317**	200f. multicoloured	1·80	1·10

318 Traditional Hairstyle

1991

1011	**318**	5f. multicoloured	10	10
1012	**318**	10f. multicoloured	10	10
1013	**318**	25f. multicoloured	10	10
1014	**318**	50f. multicoloured	20	10
1018	**318**	130f. multicoloured	1·10	25
1019	**318**	150f. multicoloured	1·40	60
1020	**318**	200f. multicoloured	1·70	85
1021	**318**	330f. multicoloured	2·20	75

319 *Grewia tenax*

1991. Flowers. Multicoloured.

1025		5f. Type **319**	10	10
1026		15f. *Hymenocardia acide*	10	10
1027		60f. *Cassia sieberiana* (vert)	70	30
1028		100f. *Adenium obesum*	90	55
1029		300f. *Mitragyna inermis*	2·75	1·60

320 Warba

1991. Dance Costumes. Multicoloured.

1030		75f. Type **320**	85	40
1031		130f. Wiskamba	1·20	70
1032		280f. Pa-Zenin	3·00	1·60

321 Pillar Box and Globe

1991. World Post Day.

1033	**321**	130f. multicoloured	1·20	55

322 Cake Tin

1992. Cooking Utensils. Multicoloured.

1034		45f. Type **322**	70	65
1035		130f. Cooking pot (vert)	1·40	70
1036		310f. Pestle and mortar (vert)	2·75	1·40
1037		500f. Ladle and bowl	4·75	2·10

323 Yousouf Fofana

1992. African Nations Cup Football Championship, Senegal. Multicoloured.

1038		50f. Type **323**	50	30
1039		100f. Francois-Jules Bocande	1·00	70
MS1040 98×93 mm. 500f. Stadium and trophy			4·75	4·50

324 Disabled Man at Potter's Wheel

1992. U.N. Decade of the Handicapped.

1041	**324**	100f. multicoloured	90	55

325 Child and Cardiograph

1992. World Health Day. "Health in Rhythm with the Heart".

1042	**325**	330f. multicoloured	3·50	1·80

326 Columbus and *Santa Maria*

1992. "Genova '92" International Thematic Stamp Exhibition and 500th Anniv of Discovery of America by Columbus. Multicoloured.

1043		50f. Type **326**	70	30
1044		150f. Amerindians watching Columbus's fleet off San Salvador	2·10	90
MS1045 129×91 mm. 350f. Route map of first voyage (51×30 mm)			4·75	3·50

327 *Dysdercus voelkeri* (fire bug) on Cotton Boll

1992. Insects. Multicoloured.

1046		20f. Type **327**	25	10
1047		40f. *Rhizopertha dominica* (beetle) on leaf	50	30
1048		85f. *Orthetrum microstigma* (dragonfly) on stem	1·20	50
1049		500f. Honey bee on flower	5·25	2·50

328 Crib

1992. Christmas. Multicoloured.

1050		10f. Type **328**	10	10
1051		130f. Children decorating crib	1·30	65
1052		1000f. Boy with Christmas card	9·50	5·25

329 Film Makers' Monument

1993. 13th "Fespaco" Pan-African Film Festival, Ouagadougou. Multicoloured.

1053		250f. Type **329**	2·50	1·50
1054		750f. Douta Seck (comedian) (horiz)	7·50	4·50

330 Yellow-billed Stork

1993. Birds. Multicoloured.

1055		100f. Type **330**	95	60
1056		200f. Marabou stork	2·00	1·20
1057		500f. Saddle-bill stork	5·00	2·75
MS1058 120×82 mm. Nos. 1046/8 (sold at 1200f.)			14·50	11·00

331 Statue of Liberty, Globe and Ball

1993. World Cup Football Championship, U.S.A. (1994). Multicoloured.

1059		500f. Type **331**	5·00	2·50
1060		1000f. Players, map of world and U.S. flag	9·75	5·50

332 Peterbilt Canadian Hauler and Diesel Locomotive Type BB 852, France

1993. Centenary of Invention of Diesel Engine.

1061	**332**	1000f. multicoloured	9·50	5·25

333 *Saba senegalensis*

1993. Wild Fruits. Multicoloured.

1062		150f. Type **333**	1·60	80
1063		300f. Karite (horiz)	3·00	1·60
1064		600f. Baobab	6·50	3·25

334 Flowers, "Stamps" and Sights of Paris

1993. First European Stamp Salon, Flower Gardens, Paris (1994). Multicoloured.

1065		400f. Type **334**	4·50	2·30
1066		650f. "Stamps", sights of Paris, daffodils and irises	5·75	3·75

335 Peulh Copper Hair Ornament

1993. Jewellery. Multicoloured.

1067		200f. Type **335**	1·80	1·10
1068		250f. Mossi agate necklace (vert)	2·20	1·30
1069		500f. Gourounsi copper bracelet	4·50	2·50

336 Gazelle

1993. The Red-fronted Gazelle. Multicoloured.
1070	30f. Type **336**	1·00	35
1071	40f. Two gazelle	1·00	40
1072	60f. Two gazelle (different)	2·00	75
1073	100f. Gazelle	4·00	1·30
MS1074 110×89 mm. Nos. 1061/4 (sold at 400f.)		6·25	6·00

337 Woodland Kingfisher

1994. Kingfishers. Multicoloured.
1075	600f. Type **337**	4·75	2·75
1076	1200f. Striped kingfisher	9·50	5·50
MS1077 84×72 mm. 2000f. African pygmy kingfisher		15·00	13·50

338 Players

1994. World Cup Football Championship, United States. Multicoloured.
1078	1000f. Type **338**	6·00	2·75
1079	1800f. Goalkeeper saving ball	9·00	4·50
MS1080 84×72 mm. No. 1079 (sold at 2000f.)		9·75	9·25

339 Dog with Puppy

1994. First European Stamp Salon, Flower Gardens, Paris, France.
1081	**339** 1500f. multicoloured	6·75	4·00
MS1082 82×80 mm. No. 1081 (sold at 2000f.)		9·75	9·25

340 Astronaut planting Flag on Moon

1994. 25th Anniv of First Manned Moon Landing. Multicoloured.
1083	750f. Type **340**	3·75	2·10
1084	750f. Landing module on Moon	3·75	2·10

Nos. 1083/4 were issued together, se-tenant, forming a composite design.

341 Guinea Sorrel

1994. Vegetables. Multicoloured.
1085	40f. Type **341**	35	10
1086	45f. Aubergine	35	10
1087	75f. Aubergine	35	20
1088	100f. Okra	60	30

342 Pig

1994. Domestic Animals. Multicoloured.
1089	150f. Type **342**	80	45
1090	1000f. Goat (vert)	4·75	2·75
1091	1500f. Sheep	7·00	3·00

343 Pierre de Coubertin (founder) and Anniversary Emblem

1994. Centenary of Int Olympic Committee.
1092	**343** 320f. multicoloured	1·60	90

344 Donkey Rider

1995. 20th Anniv of World Tourism Organization. Multicoloured.
1093	150f. Type **344**	80	65
1094	350f. Bobo-Dioulasso railway station (horiz)	1·50	90
1095	450f. Great Mosque, Bani (horiz)	2·00	1·20
1096	650f. Roan antelope and map (horiz)	2·75	1·70

345 Crocodile

1995. Multicoloured, colour of frame given.
1097	**345** 10f. brown	10	10
1098	**345** 20f. mauve	10	10
1099	**345** 25f. brown	10	10
1100	**345** 30f. green	10	10
1101	**345** 40f. purple	10	10
1102	**345** 50f. grey	10	10
1103	**345** 75f. purple	25	10
1104	**345** 100f. brown	40	10
1105	**345** 150f. green	55	35
1106	**345** 175f. blue	75	40
1107	**345** 250f. brown	90	60
1108	**345** 400f. green	1·40	1·00

346 *Rabi* (dir. Gaston Kabore)

1995. "Fespaco 95" Pan-African Film Festival and Centenary of Motion Pictures. Multicoloured.
1109	150f. Type **346**	80	50
1110	250f. *Tila* (Idrissa Ouedraogo)	95	65

347 Elvis Presley in "Loving You"

1995. Entertainers. Multicoloured.
1111	300f. Type **347**	1·40	80
1112	400f. Marilyn Monroe	1·80	1·10
1113	500f. Elvis Presley in *Jailhouse Rock*	2·30	1·40
1114	650f. Marilyn Monroe in *Asphalt Jungle*	2·75	1·80
1115	750f. Marilyn Monroe in *Niagara*	3·00	2·10
1116	1000f. Elvis Presley in *Blue Hawaii*	4·50	3·00
MS1117 Two sheets. (a) 123×95 mm. 1500f. Marilyn Monroe in *The Seven Year Itch* (41×48 mm). (b) 137×89 mm. 1500f. Marilyn Monroe and Elvis Presley (60th birth anniv of Presley) (50×41 mm)) Set of 2 sheets		13·00	12·50

348 Common Gonolek

1995. Birds. Multicoloured.
1118	450f. Type **348**	2·00	1·00
1119	600f. Red-cheeked cordon-bleu	3·00	1·50
1120	750f. Golden bishop	3·50	2·10
MS1121 80×120 mm. Nos. 1118/20 (sold at 2000f.)		8·75	8·25

349 Hissing Sand Snake

1995. Reptiles. Multicoloured.
1122	450f. Type **349**	2·50	1·50
1123	500f. Sand python	2·50	1·60
1124	1500f. Tortoise	7·50	4·50

350 Basketball

1995. Olympic Games, Atlanta (1996). Multicoloured.
1125	150f. Type **350**	55	30
1126	250f. Baseball	95	55
1127	650f. Tennis	2·20	1·40
1128	750f. Table tennis	3·25	1·80
MS1129 127×89 mm. 1500f. Dressage (35×50 mm)		6·50	6·25

351 Juan Manuel Fangio (racing driver)

1995. Sportsmen. Multicoloured.
1130	300f. Type **351**	3·75	95
1131	400f. Andre Agassi (tennis player)	1·40	90
1132	500f. Ayrton Senna (racing driver)	2·00	1·10
1133	1000f. Michael Schumacher (racing driver)	3·75	2·10
MS1134 146×112 mm. 1500f. Enzo Ferrari, Formula 1 racing car and Ferrari F40 sports car (56×48 mm)		13·00	8·75

352 Children and Christmas Tree

1995. Christmas. Multicoloured.
1135	150f. Type **352**	75	55
1136	450f. Grotto, Yagma	2·20	1·50
1137	500f. Flight into Egypt	2·50	1·60
1138	1000f. Adoration of the Wise Men	4·50	3·00

353 Headquarters Building, New York

1995. 50th Anniv of United Nations. Multicoloured.
1139	500f. Type **353**	2·20	1·70
1140	1000f. Village council under tree with superimposed U.N. emblem (vert)	4·25	3·00

354 Mossi Type

1995. Traditional Houses. Multicoloured.
1141	70f. Type **354**	25	10
1142	100f. Kassena type	45	25
1143	200f. Roro type	90	35
1144	250f. Peulh type	1·10	55

Nos.1145/8 and Type **355** are left for Christmas, issued on 18 Dec 1995, not yet received.

Nos.1149/50 and Type **356** are left for 50th Anniv of UN, issued on 20 Dec 1995, not yet received.

357 Les Etalons (national team) Emblem

1996. African Cup of Nations Football Championships. Multicoloured.
1151	150f.+25f. Type **357**	80	35
1152	250f.+25f. Player and map of Africa	1·40	65
MS1153 90×84mm. 150f. + 25f. As Type **357**		2·75	1·30

The premium was for the benefit of national sport

358 *Panthera leo* (lions)

1996. Big Cats. Multicoloured.
1154	100f. Type **358**	60	25
1155	150f. *Acinonyx jubatus* (cheetah)	85	30
1156	175f. *Lynx caracal* (caracal)	1·00	40
1157	250f. *Panthera pardus* (leopard)	1·60	70

Nos.1158/9 and Type **359** are left for France–Africa Summit, issued 1996, not yet received.

360 Orchid

1996. Orchids. Multicoloured.
1160	100f. Type **360**	85	45
1161	175f. Yellow orchid	1·30	70
1162	250f. Red and pink orchid	1·90	90
1163	300f. Lime green and dark pink orchid	2·30	1·10

Nos. 1164/5 and Type **361** are left for FESPACO Film Festival, issued 5 February 1997, not yet received.

Nos.1166/9 and Type **362** are left for Fauna, issued 20 March 1997, not yet received.

No. 1170 and Type **363** are left for Death Centenary of H. von Stephan, issued 8 April 1997, not yet received.

Nos.1171/4 and Type **364** are left for Masks, issued 20 May 1997, not yet received.

Nos.1175/8 and Type **365** are left for Ceramics, issued 11 September 1997, not yet received.

Nos. 1179/83 and Type **366** are left for Fish, issued 20 November 1997, not yet received.

Nos.1184/7 and Type **367** are left for African Football, issued 20 January 1998, not yet received.

Nos.1188/91 and Type **368** are left for Traditional Costumes, issued 20 February 1998, not yet received.

Nos. 1192/3 and Type **369** are left for 20th Anniv of Agricultural Development Fund, issued 20 March 1998, not yet received.

Nos. 1194/7 and Type **370** are left for Endangered Species, issued 20 May 1998, not yet received.

Nos. 1198/9 and Type **371** are left for Organization for African Unity Summit, issued 20 May 1998, not yet received.

372 White-winged Triller

1998. Birds. Multicoloured.
1200	5f. Type **372**	15	10

1201		10f. (Arabian) Golden sparrow	15	10
1202		100f. American goldfinch	55	30
1203		170f. Red-legged thrush	95	45
1204		260f. Willow warbler	1·70	85
1205		425f. Blue grosbeak	2·75	1·90
MS1206		106×152 mm. 260f.×9, Bank swallow (sand martin); Kirtland's warbler; Long-tailed minivet; Blue-grey gnatcatcher; Reed bunting; Black-collared apalis; American robin; Cape longclaw; Wood thrush	11·50	3·35
MS1207		106×152 mm. 425f.×9, Song sparrow; Dartford warbler; Eastern bluebird; Rock thrush; Northern mockingbird; Northern cardinal; Eurasian goldfinch; Varied thrush; Northern oriole	17·00	5·75
MS1208		84×110 mm. 1500f. Golden whistler (horiz)	7·25	2·50
MS1209		110×84 mm. 1500f. Swallow	7·25	2·50

Nos.1210 and Type **373** are left for 40th Anniv of Council of Entente, issued 5 May 1999, not yet received.

374 Family of Lions

1999. Lions
1211	374	170f. multicoloured	75	30
1212	374	260f. multicoloured	95	40
1213	374	425f. multicoloured	2·00	85
1214	374	530f. multicoloured	2·30	1·10
1215	374	590f. multicoloured	4·25	2·00

375 Kitten and Butterfly

1999. Pets. Multicoloured.
1216		5f. Type **375**	10	10
1217		10f. Two chinchilla kittens (horiz)	15	10
1218		20f. Yorkshire terriers (horiz)	25	15
1219		25f. Cocker spaniels (horiz)	35	25
MS1220		105×110 mm. Vert: 260f.×6, Afghan hound puppy; Wire fox terrier; Pug; Dalmatian; Boston terrier; Cocker spaniel	5·75	2·30
MS1221		157×88 mm. Horiz: 530f.×6, American wire-haired kitten; Tabby; Burmese blue and frog; Abyssinian; Burmese lilac lying down; Siamese playing with string	13·00	8·00
MS1222		97×79 mm. 1000f. Flowers and two labrador retriever puppies	4·25	2·60
MS1223		105×80 mm. 1000f. Labrador retriever puppy	4·25	2·60
MS1224		110×85 mm. 1000f. Persian tabby (horiz)	4·25	2·60
MS1225		82×110 mm. 1000f. Japanese bobtail kitten	4·25	2·60

376 Gelderlander

1999. Domestic Animals. Multicoloured.
1226		170f. Type **376**	60	25
1227		170f. Trait lourd horse	60	25
1228		170f. Vladimir heavy draft horse	60	25
1229		170f. Percheron horse	60	25
1230		170f. Sumba pony	60	25
1231		170f. Dartmoor pony	60	25
1232		425f. French bulldog	2·10	60
1233		425f. Bernese dog	2·10	60
1234		425f. Griffon dog	2·10	60
1235		425f. King Charles spaniel	2·10	60
1236		425f. Miniature Spitz dog	2·10	60
1237		425f. Yorkshire terrier	2·10	60
1238		590f. American wire-haired cat	3·00	1·20
1239		590f. Japanese bob-tail cats	3·00	1·20
1240		590f. Himalayan cat	3·00	1·20
1241		590f. LaPerm cat	3·00	1·20
1242		590f. Lilac point Siamese cat and kitten	3·00	1·20
1243		590f. Norwegian forest cat	3·00	1·20
MS1244		76×106 mm. 1000f. Shetland pony leaning over stable door (vert)	4·25	3·00
MS1245		106×76 mm. 1000f. Japanese bobtail cat (vert)	4·25	3·00
MS1246		107×77 mm. 1000f. Basset hound (vert)	4·00	3·25

377 Portland

1999. Historic Ships. Multicoloured.
MS1247		135×97 mm. 170f.×3, Type **377**; *Goethe*; *Fulton*	2·25	1·10
MS1248		104×76 mm. 1000f. *Grand Voiler*	4·25	2·00
MS1249		104×76 mm. 1000f. *Batavia*	8·25	4·25

378 Sukhoi Su-24

1999. Aviation. Multicoloured.
MS1250		145×95 mm. 425f.×6, Type **378**; Yakolev Yak-38; Tupolev *Blackjack*; Antonov An-26; Antonov An-22 Antheus (inscr 'Anteus'); Antonov An-124	10·50	6·00
MS1251		76×105 mm. 1000f. Ilyushin Il-76 T (57×42 mm)	4·25	2·75

379 Child holding Food

1999. Millennium 2000
1252		350f. multicoloured	1·40	80

APPENDIX

The following stamps have either been issued in excess of postal needs or have not been available to the public in reasonable quantities at face value. Such stamps may later be given full listing if there is evidence of regular postal use.

1985

85th Birthday of Queen Elizabeth the Queen Mother. 1500f.

1996

Fungi. 150f., 250f., 300f., 400f., 500f., 650f., 1000f.
Fungi. 175f., 250f., 300f., 450f.
Entertainers. 150f., 250f., 300f., 400f., 500f., 650f., 1000f.
Butterflies and Insects. 100f., 150f., 175f., 250f.
Butterflies. 150f., 250f., 450f., 600f.
Insects. 25f., 75f., 300f., 400f.
Andre Agassi Olympic Gold Medal. 400f.
Endangered Birds. 500f., 750f., 1000f., 1500f.

1997

Princess Diana. 260f., 425f.×2, 590f.
Mother Teresa. 260f.

1998

Butterflies. 170f.×9
Christmas. 100f., 170f., 260f., 425f., 530f.
Football World Cup. 50f., 150f., 250f., 450f.

Pt. 1, Pt. 21

BURMA

A territory in the east of India, which was granted independence by the British in 1948. From May 1990 it is now known as Myanmar.

Burma.
1937. 12 pies = 1 anna; 16 annas = 1 rupee.
1953. 100 pyas = 1 kyat.

Japanese Occupation of Burma.
1942. 12 pies = 1 anna; 16 annas = 1 rupee.
1942. 100 cents = 1 rupee.

1937. Stamps of India (King George V) optd **BURMA**.
1	55	3p. grey	2·25	10
3	80	9p. green	1·00	10
2	79	½a. green	1·00	10
4	81	1a. brown	4·50	10
5	59	2a. red	1·00	10
6	61	2½a. orange	75	10
7	62	3a. red	4·50	30
8	83	3½a. blue	7·00	10
9	63	4a. olive	1·00	10
10	64	6a. bistre	1·25	35
11	65	8a. mauve	3·75	10
12	66	12a. red	14·00	3·25
13	67	1r. brown and green	60·00	5·00
14	67	2r. red and orange	45·00	27·00
15	67	5r. blue and violet	55·00	28·00
16	67	10r. green and red	£225	95·00
17	67	15r. blue and olive	£750	£225
18	67	25r. orange and blue	£1300	£500

2 King George VI and "Chinthes" **3** King George VI and "Nagas" **4** "Karaweik" (royal barge)

8 King George VI and Peacock

1938. King George VI.
18b	2	1p. orange	3·25	1·75
19	2	3p. violet	30	3·00
20	2	6p. blue	1·00	10
21	2	9p. green	2·00	1·50
22	3	1a. brown	30	10
23	3	1½a. green	1·50	3·50
24	3	2a. red	3·25	1·00
25	4	2a.6p. red	15·00	3·75
26	-	3a. mauve	16·00	3·75
27	-	3a.6p. blue	4·00	9·50
28	3	4a. blue	3·75	20
29	-	8a. green	4·00	55
30	8	1r. purple and blue	4·00	1·00
31	8	2r. brown and purple	24·00	5·50
32	-	5r. violet and red	75·00	60·00
33	-	10r. brown and green	80·00	90·00

DESIGNS—HORIZ: As Type **4**: 3a. Burma teak; 3a.6p. Burma rice; 8a. River Irrawaddy. VERT: As Type **3**: 5, 10r. King George VI and "Nats".

1940. Cent of First Adhesive Postage Stamp. Surch **COMMEMORATION POSTAGE STAMP 6th MAY 1840 ONE ANNA 1A** and value in native characters.
34	4	1a. on 2a.6p. red	4·25	2·00

For Japanese issues see "Japanese Occupation of Burma".

1945. British Military Administration. Stamps of 1938 optd **MILY ADMN.**
35	2	1p. orange	10	10
36	2	3p. violet	20	2·00
37	2	6p. blue	20	30
38	2	9p. green	30	2·00
39	3	1a. brown	20	10
40	3	1½a. green	20	15
41	3	2a. red	20	15
42	4	2a.6p. red	2·25	3·75
43	-	3a. mauve	1·50	30
44	-	3a.6p. blue	£110	£275
45	3	4a. blue	20	70
46	-	8a. green	20	2·00
47	8	1r. purple and blue	50	50
48	8	2r. brown and purple	50	1·50
49	-	5r. violet and red	50	1·50
50	-	10r. brown and green	50	1·50

1946. British Civil Administration. As 1938, but colours changed.
51	2	3p. brown	15	4·00
52	2	6p. violet	20	30
53	2	9p. green	1·75	7·00
54	3	1a. blue	75	20
55	3	1½a. orange	30	10
56	3	2a. red	30	50
57	4	2a.6p. blue	2·75	8·00
57a	-	3a. blue	6·50	11·00
57b	-	3a.6p. black and blue	3·50	5·50
58	3	4a. purple	70	1·50
59	-	8a. mauve	1·75	7·50
60	8	1r. violet and mauve	3·25	3·75
61	8	2r. brown and orange	9·00	7·50
62	-	5r. green and brown	11·00	30·00
63	-	10r. red and violet	23·00	42·00

14 Burman

1946. Victory.
64	14	9p. green	20	20
65	-	1½a. violet (Burmese woman)	20	10
66	-	2a. red (Chinthe)	20	10
67	-	3a.6p. (Elephant)	50	20

ကြားဖြတ်
အစိုးရ။

(18) Trans. "Interim Government"

1947. Stamps of 1946 opt with T **18** or with larger opt on large stamps.
68	2	3p. brown	1·75	70
69	2	6p. violet	20	30
70	2	9p. green	20	30
71	3	1a. blue	40	30
72	3	1½a. orange	3·00	10
73	3	2a. red	40	15
74	4	2a.6p. blue	1·75	1·00
75	-	3a. blue	2·75	1·75
76	-	3a.6p. black and blue	2·75	3·75
77	3	4a. purple	1·75	30
78	-	8a. mauve	1·75	50
79	8	1r. violet and mauve	9·50	3·50
80	8	2r. brown and orange	9·50	10·00
81	-	5r. green and brown	9·50	8·50
82	-	10r. red and violet	7·00	8·50

20 Gen. Aung San, Chinthe and Map of Burma

1948. Independence Day.
83	20	½a. green	20	10
84	20	1a. pink	25	15
85	20	2a. red	35	20
86	20	3½a. blue	50	35
87	20	8a. brown	75	45

21 Martyrs' Memorial

1948. First Anniv of Murder of Aung San and his Ministers.
88	21	3p. blue	10	10
89	21	6p. green	10	10
90	21	9p. red	15	10
91	21	1a. violet	15	10
92	21	2a. mauve	20	10
93	21	3½a. green	30	15
94	21	4a. brown	40	15
95	21	8a. red	50	20
96	21	12a. purple	65	20
97	21	1r. orange	1·00	35
98	21	2r. blue	1·70	75
99	21	5r. brown	5·00	2·00

22 Playing Cane-ball **25** Bell, Mingun Pagoda

27 Transplanting Rice **28** Lion Throne

1949. First Anniv of Independence.
100	22	3p. blue	1·60	50
120	22	3p. orange	35	25
101	-	6p. green	25	20
121	-	6p. purple	15	20
102	-	9p. green	25	20
122	-	9p. blue	15	20
103	25	1a. red	35	25
123	25	1a. blue	15	20
104	-	2a. orange	35	25
124	-	2a. green	50	30
105	27	2a.6p. mauve	35	25
125	27	2a.6p. green	35	25
106	-	3a. violet	35	25
126	-	3a. red	35	25
107	-	3a.6p. green	55	35
127	-	3a.6p. orange	50	25
108	-	4a. brown	55	35

128	-	4a. red	55	25
109	-	8a. red	70	40
129	-	8a. blue	65	60
110	28	1r. green	1·30	45
130	28	1r. violet	90	90
111	28	2r. blue	2·40	65
131	28	2r. green	1·90	1·20
112	28	5r. brown	5·50	2·10
132	28	5r. green	5·00	2·75
113	28	10r. orange	11·50	3·25
133	28	10r. blue	11·00	7·00

DESIGNS—As Type **22**: 6p. Dancer; 9p. Girl playing saunggaut (string instrument); 2a. Hintha (legendary bird). As Type **25**: 4a. Elephant hauling log. As Type **27**: 3a. Girl weaving; 3a.6p. Royal Palace; 8a. Ploughing paddy field with oxen.

See also Nos. 137/50.

29 UPU Monument, Berne

1949. 75th Anniv of UPU.

114	29	2a. orange	35	35
115	29	3½a. green	40	25
116	29	6a. violet	65	45
117	29	8a. red	90	65
118	29	12½a. blue	1·70	85
119	29	1r. green	2·00	1·30

30 Independence Monument, Rangoon, and Map

1953. Fifth Anniv of Independence.

134	30	14p. green (22×18 mm)	70	25
135	30	20p. red (36½×26½ mm)	90	35
136	30	25p. blue (36½×26½ mm)	1·00	45

1954. New Currency. As 1949 issue but values in pyas and kyats.

137	22	1p. orange	1·20	25
138	-	2p. purple (as 6p.)	40	10
139	-	3p. blue (as 9p.)	40	10
140	25	5p. blue	40	10
141	27	10p. green	40	10
142	-	15p. green (as 2a.)	50	10
143	-	20p. red (as 3a.)	50	10
144	-	25p. orange (as 3a.6p.)	50	25
145	-	30p. red (as 4a.)	50	25
146	-	50p. blue (as 8a.)	60	25
147	28	1k. violet	1·40	60
148	28	2k. green	2·30	90
149	28	5k. blue	6·75	1·30
150	28	10k. blue	14·50	2·20

31 Sangiti Mahapasana Rock Cave in Grounds of Kaba-Aye Pagoda

1954. Sixth Buddhist Council, Rangoon.

151	-	10p. blue	25	10
152	-	15p. purple	35	25
153	31	35p. brown	45	35
154	-	50p. green	75	35
155	-	1k. red	1·50	80
156	-	2k. violet	2·50	1·80

DESIGNS: 10p. Rock caves and Songha of Cambodia; 15p. Buddhist priests and Kuthodaw Pagoda, Mandalay; 50p. Rock cave and Songha of Thailand; 1k. Rock cave and Songha of Ceylon; 2k. Rock cave and Songha of Laos.

32 Fifth Buddhist Council Monuments

1956. Buddha Jayanti.

157	32	20p. green and blue	70	15
158	-	40p. green and blue	1·20	40
159	-	60p. yellow and green	1·40	50
160	-	1k.25 blue and yellow	2·30	1·10

DESIGNS: 40p. Thatbyinnyu Pagoda, Pagan; 60p. Shwedagan Pagoda, Rangoon; 1k.25, Sangiti Mahapasana Rock Cave and Kaba-Aye Pagoda, Rangoon (venue of 6th Buddhist Council).

(33) "Mandalay Town—100 Years/1221–1321"

1959. Centenary of Mandalay. No. 144 surch with T **33** and Nos. 147/8 with two-line opt only.

161	-	15p. on 25p. orange	45	25
162	28	1k. violet	1·60	1·40
163	28	2k. green	3·50	2·10

1961. No. 134 surch as right-hand characters in third line of T **33**.

164	30	15p. on 14p. green	1·80	50

35 Torch-bearer in Rangoon

1961. Second South-East Asia Peninsula Games, Rangoon.

165	35	15p. blue and red	45	25
166	-	25p. green and brown	60	25
167	-	50p. mauve and blue	1·50	40
168	-	1k. yellow and green	2·30	1·10

DESIGNS—VERT: 25p. Contestants; 50p. Women sprinting in Aung San Stadium, Rangoon. HORIZ: 1k. Contestants.

36 Children at Play

1961. 15th Anniv of UNICEF.

169	36	15p. red and pink	80	25

37 Flag and Map

1963. First Anniv of Military Coup by General Ne Win.

170	37	15p. red	60	25

1963. Freedom from Hunger. Nos. 141 and 146 optd **FREEDOM FROM HUNGER.**

171	27	10p. green	1·80	65
172	-	50p. blue	3·50	1·30

(39)

1963. Labour Day. No. 143 optd with T **39**.

173		20p. red	60	25

40 White-browed Fantail

1964. Burmese Birds (1st series).

174	40	1p. black	60	25
175	40	2p. red	70	25
176	40	3p. green	70	25
177	-	5p. blue	80	40
178	-	10p. brown	95	40
179	-	15p. green	1·10	40
180	-	20p. brown and red	1·40	50
181	-	25p. brown and yellow	1·60	50
182	-	50p. blue and red	2·30	75
183	-	1k. blue, yellow & grey	6·50	1·60
184	-	2k. blue, green and red	14·00	4·50
185	-	5k. multicoloured	29·00	12·00

BIRDS—22×26 mm: 5 to 15p. Indian roller. 27×37 mm: 25p. Crested serpent eagle. 50p. Sarus crane. 1k. Indian pied hornbill. 5k. Green peafowl. 35½×25 mm: 20p. Red-whiskered bulbul. 37×27 mm: 2k. Kalij pheasant.

See also Nos. 195/206.

41 ITU Emblem and Symbols

1965. Centenary of ITU.

186	41	20p. mauve	1·40	25
187	41	50p. green (34×24½ mm)	2·75	65

42 ICY Emblem

1965. International Co-operation Year.

188	42	5p. blue	95	15
189	42	10p. brown	1·40	25
190	42	15p. olive	2·10	50

43 Harvesting

1966. Peasants' Day.

191	43	15p. multicoloured	1·20	25

44 Cogwheel and Hammer

1967. May Day.

192	44	15p. yellow, black & blue	1·20	25

45 Aung San and Agricultural Cultivation

1968. 20th Anniv of Independence.

193	45	15p. multicoloured	1·20	25

46 Burma Pearls

1968. Burmese Gems, Jades and Pearls Emporium, Rangoon.

194	46	15p. ultram, blue & yell	1·80	50

1968. Burmese Birds (2nd series). Designs and colours as Nos. 174/85 but formats and sizes changed.

195	40	1p. black	70	40
196	40	2p. red	70	40
197	40	3p. green	75	45
198	-	5p. blue	75	45
199	-	10p. brown	80	65
200	-	15p. yellow	95	75
201	-	20p. brown and red	1·10	75
202	-	25p. brown and yellow	1·20	75
203	-	50p. blue and red	2·50	1·50
204	-	1k. blue, yellow & grey	19·00	1·50
205	-	2k. blue, green and red	16·00	3·75
206	-	5k. multicoloured	33·00	15·00

NEW SIZES—21×17 mm: 1, 2, 3p. 39×21 mm: 20p., 2k. 23×28 mm: 5, 10, 15p. 21×39 mm: 25, 50p., 1, 5k.

47 Spike of Paddy

1969. Peasants' Day.

218	47	15p. yellow, blue & green	1·90	40

48 ILO Emblem

1969. 50th Anniv of ILO.

219	48	15p. gold and green	90	25
220	48	50p. gold and red	1·30	40

49 Football

1969. Fifth South-East Asian Peninsula Games, Rangoon.

221	49	15p. multicoloured	50	20
222	-	25p. multicoloured	90	25
223	-	50p. multicoloured	1·30	30
224	-	1k. black, green & blue	3·00	75

DESIGNS—HORIZ: 25p. Running. VERT: 50p. Weightlifting; 1k. Volleyball.

50 Marchers with Independence, Resistance and Union Flags

1970. 25th Anniv of Burmese Armed Forces.

225	50	15p. multicoloured	1·30	25

51 "Peace and Progress"

1970. 25th Anniv of United Nations.

226	51	15p. multicoloured	1·30	25

52 Boycott Declaration and Marchers

1970. National Day and 50th Anniv of University Boycott. Multicoloured.

227		15p. Type **52**	75	15
228		25p. Students on boycott march	1·00	20
229		50p. Banner and demonstrators	1·80	40

53 Burmese Workers

1971. First Burmese Socialist Programme Party Congress. Multicoloured.

230		5p. Type **53**	1·00	15
231		15p. Burmese races and flags	1·50	20
232		25p. Hands holding scroll	2·00	25
233		50p. Party flag	2·50	50
MS234		179×127 mm. Nos. 230/3. Imperf	25·00	19·00

54 Child drinking Milk

1971. 25th Anniv of UNICEF. Multicoloured.

235		15p. Type **54**	1·00	25
236		50p. Marionettes	1·80	75

55 Aung San and Independence Monument, Panglong

1972. 25th Anniv of Independence. Multicoloured.
237		15p. Type **55**	50	15
238		50p. Aung San and Burmese in national costumes	75	25
239		1k. Flag and map (vert)	1·90	50

56 Burmese and Stars

1972. Tenth Anniv of Revolutionary Council.
240	**56**	15p. multicoloured	1·00	15

57 Human Heart

1972. World Health Day.
241	**57**	15p. red, black & yellow	1·00	25

58 Ethnic Groups

1973. National Census.
242	**58**	15p. multicoloured	1·90	40

59 Casting Vote

1973. National Constitutional Referendum.
243	**59**	5p. red and black	65	15
244	-	10p. multicoloured	75	20
245	-	15p. multicoloured	90	25

DESIGNS—HORIZ: 10p. Voter supporting map. VERT: 15p. Burmese with ballot papers.

60 Open-air Meeting

1974. Opening of 1st Pyithu Hluttaw (People's Assembly). Multicoloured.
246		15p. Burmese flags, 1752–1974 (80×26 mm)	90	25
247		50p. Type **60**	1·40	40
248		1k. Burmese badge	2·10	90

61 UPU Emblem and Carrier Pigeon

1974. Centenary of Universal Postal Union. Multicoloured.
249		15p. Type **61**	75	20
250		20p. Woman reading letter (vert)	1·00	25
251		50p. UPU emblem on "stamps" (vert)	1·40	40
252		1k. Stylized doll (vert)	2·50	65
253		2k. Postman delivering letter to family	5·00	1·30

62 Kachin Couple **63** Bamar Couple

1974. Burmese Costumes. Inscr "SOCIALIST REPUBLIC OF THE UNION OF BURMA".
254	**62**	1p. mauve	40	15
255	**62**	3p. brown and mauve	50	15
256	**62**	5p. violet and mauve	55	15
257	**62**	10p. blue	65	15
258	**62**	15p. green and light green	75	20
259	**63**	20p. black, brown & blue	1·00	20
260	-	50p. violet, brown & ochre	1·50	40
261	-	1k. violet, mauve & black	3·50	1·10
262	-	5k. multicoloured	10·00	3·75

DESIGNS—As Type **62**: 3p. Kayah girl; 5p. Kayin couple and bronze drum; 15p. Chin couple. As Type **63**: 50p. Mon woman; 1k. Rakhine woman; 5k. Musician.

For 15, 50p. and 1k. stamps in these designs, but inscr "UNION OF BURMA", see Nos. 309/11.

64 Woman on Globe and IWY Emblem

1975. International Women's Year.
263	**64**	50p. black and green	70	40
264	-	2k. black and blue	3·50	1·70

DESIGN—VERT: 2k. Globe on flower and IWY emblem.

65 Burmese and Flag

1976. Constitution Day.
265	**65**	20p. black and blue	85	25
266	-	50p. brown and blue	1·10	40
267	-	1k. multicoloured	2·50	95

DESIGNS—As Type **65**: 50p. Burmese with banners and flag. 57×21 mm: 1k. Map of Burma, Burmese and flag.

66 Emblem and Burmese Learning Alphabet

1976. International Literacy Year.
268	**66**	10p. brown and red	40	25
269	-	15p. turquoise, grn & blk	55	40
270	-	50p. blue, orange & black	1·40	65
271	-	1k. multicoloured	2·50	1·30

DESIGNS—HORIZ: 15p. Abacus and open books. 50p. Emblem. VERT: 1k. Emblem, open book and globe.

67 Early Train and Ox-cart

1977. Centenary of Railway.
272		15p. green, black & mauve	9·75	1·60
273	**67**	20p. multicoloured	2·75	55
274	-	25p. multicoloured	4·25	80
275	-	50p. multicoloured	5·50	1·30
276	-	1k. multicoloured	11·00	2·75

DESIGNS—26×17 mm: 15p. Early steam locomotive. As Type **67**—HORIZ: 25p. Diesel locomotive DD1517, steam train and railway station; 50p. Ava railway bridge over River Irrawaddy. VERT: Diesel train emerging from tunnel.

68 Karaweik Hall

1978
277	**68**	50p. brown	1·70	55
278	-	1k. multicoloured	3·25	95

DESIGN—79½×25 mm: 1k. Side view of Karaweik Hall.

69 Jade Naga and Gem

1979. 16th Gem Emporium.
279	**69**	15p. green and turquoise	70	15
280	-	20p. blue, yellow & mauve	95	25
281	-	50p. blue, brown & green	1·50	65
282	-	1k. multicoloured	3·00	1·20

DESIGNS—As T **69**: 20p. Hintha (legendary bird) holding pearl in beak; 50p. Hand holding pearl and amethyst pendant. 55×20 mm: 1k. Gold jewel-studded dragon.

70 "Intelsat IV" Satellite over Burma

1979. Introduction of Satellite Communications System.
283	**70**	25p. multicoloured	70	25

71 IYC Emblem on Map of Burma

1979. International Year of the Child.
284	**71**	25p. orange and blue	1·70	40
285	**71**	50p. red and violet	3·25	65

72 Weather Balloon

1980. World Meteorological Day.
286	**72**	25p. blue, yellow & black	1·40	25
287	-	50p. green, black and red	2·50	65

DESIGN: 50p. Meteorological satellite and WMO emblem.

73 Weightlifting

1980. Olympic Games, Moscow.
288	**73**	20p. green, orange & blk	55	15
289	-	50p. black, orange and red	1·70	40
290	-	1k. black, orange and green	3·25	95

DESIGNS: 50p. Boxing; 1k. Football.

74 ITU and WHO Emblems with Ribbons forming Caduceus

1981. World Telecommunications Day.
291	**74**	25p. orange and black	70	25

75 Livestock and Vegetables

1981. World Food Day. Multicoloured.
292		25p. Type **75**	1·10	25

293		50p. Farm produce and farmer holding wheat	1·40	40
294		1k. Globe and stylized bird	1·90	80

76 Athletes and Person in Wheelchair

1981. International Year of Disabled Persons.
295	**76**	25p. multicoloured	70	40

77 Telephone, Satellite and Antenna

1983. World Communications Year.
296	**77**	15p. blue and black	55	15
297	**77**	25p. mauve and black	70	25
298	**77**	50p. green, black and red	1·40	55
299	**77**	1k. brown, black & green	2·75	1·20

78 Fish and Globe

1983. World Food Day.
300	**78**	15p. yellow, blue & black	70	15
301	**78**	25p. orange, green & black	95	25
302	**78**	50p. green, yellow & black	2·50	1·10
303	**78**	1k. blue, yellow and black	3·50	2·40

79 Globe and Log

1984. World Food Day.
304	**79**	15p. blue, yellow & black	30	15
305	**79**	25p. violet, yellow & black	55	25
306	**79**	50p. green, pink and black	1·40	65
307	**79**	1k. mauve, yellow & black	2·75	1·60

80 Potted Plant

1985. International Youth Year.
308	**80**	15p. multicoloured	70	25

1989. As Nos. 258/9 and 260/1 but inscr "UNION OF BURMA".
309	**62**	15p. dp green & green	40	25
310	-	50p. violet and brown	95	55
311	-	1k. violet, mauve & black	1·50	1·10

Examples of No. 309a, which have been prepared several years earlier but not issued, were inadvertently supplied to Shan State post office in July 1995. Subsequently a limited quantity were sold to philatelists in Yangon.

OFFICIAL STAMPS

1937. Stamps of India (King George V) optd BURMA SERVICE.
O1	55	3p. grey	4·50	10
O3	80	9p. green	5·00	2·25
O2	79	½a. green	19·00	10
O4	81	1a. brown	9·50	10
O5	59	2a. red	20·00	45
O6	61	2½a. orange	9·00	3·75
O7	63	4a. olive	9·50	10
O8	64	6a. bistre	10·00	18·00
O9	65	8a. mauve	9·00	4·00
O10	66	12a. red	9·00	14·00
O11	67	1r. brown and green	25·00	11·00

O12	67	2r. red and orange	50·00	70·00
O13	67	5r. blue and violet	£180	75·00
O14	67	10r. green and red	£450	£250

1939. Stamps of 1938 optd **SERVICE**.

O15	2	3p. violet	20	20
O16	2	6p. blue	20	20
O17	2	9p. green	4·00	7·00
O18	3	1a. brown	20	15
O19	3	1½a. green	3·50	3·75
O20	3	2a. red	1·50	20
O21	4	2a.6p. red	27·00	22·00
O22	3	4a. blue	4·50	2·50
O23	–	8a. green (No. 29)	18·00	4·00
O24	8	1r. purple and blue	16·00	5·50
O25	8	2r. brown and purple	35·00	19·00
O26	–	5r. violet and red (No. 32)	26·00	50·00
O27	–	10r. brown and green (No. 33)	£130	50·00

1946. Stamps of 1946 optd **SERVICE**.

O28	2	3p. brown	3·75	6·50
O29	2	6p. violet	3·00	2·25
O30	2	9p. green	2·25	7·00
O31	3	1a. blue	30	2·00
O32	3	1½a. orange	2·00	20
O33	3	2a. red	40	2·00
O34	4	2a.6p. blue	3·50	13·00
O35	3	4a. purple	1·50	70
O36	–	8a. mauve (No. 59)	5·50	7·50
O37	8	1r. violet and mauve	3·50	11·00
O38	8	2r. brown and orange	8·50	50·00
O39	–	5r. green and brown (No. 62)	21·00	65·00
O40	–	10r. red and violet (No. 63)	21·00	75·00

1947. Interim Government. Nos. O28 etc., optd with T **18** or with large overprint on larger stamps.

O41	2	3p. brown	3·25	40
O42	2	6p. violet	5·00	15
O43	2	9p. green	7·50	90
O44	3	1a. blue	7·50	80
O45	3	1½a. orange	13·00	30
O46	3	2a. red	7·50	15
O47	4	2a.6p. blue	35·00	22·00
O48	3	4a. purple	26·00	40
O49	–	8a. mauve	26·00	4·25
O50	8	1r. violet and mauve	17·00	3·75
O51	8	2r. brown and orange	19·00	21·00
O52	–	5r. green and brown	20·00	23·00
O53	–	10r. brown and green	20·00	35·00

အစိုးရကိစ္စ

(O29) (size of opt varies)

1949. First Anniv of Independence. Nos. 100/4 and 107/113 optd as Type **O29**.

O114	22	3p. blue	55	15
O115	–	6p. green	10	10
O116	–	9p. red	10	10
O117	25	1a. red	10	10
O118	–	2a. orange	20	15
O119	–	3a.6p. green	20	15
O120	–	4a. brown	20	15
O121	–	8a. red	20	15
O122	28	1r. green	55	25
O123	28	2r. blue	90	45
O124	28	5r. brown	2·40	1·70
O125	28	10r. orange	6·00	4·25

1954. Nos. 137/40 and 142/50 optd as Type **O29**.

O151	22	1p. orange	55	15
O152	–	2p. purple	20	15
O153	–	3p. blue	20	15
O154	25	5p. blue	20	15
O155	–	15p. green	20	15
O156	–	20p. red	20	15
O157	–	25p. orange	20	15
O158	–	30p. red	20	15
O159	–	50p. blue	20	15
O160	28	1k. violet	65	15
O161	28	2k. green	1·50	35
O162	28	5k. blue	3·00	95
O163	28	10k. blue	6·50	3·00

1964. No. 139 optd **Service**.

O174		3p. blue	12·00	8·50

1965. Nos. 174/7 and 179/85 optd as Type **O29**.

O196	40	1p. black	15	15
O197	40	2p. red	25	25
O198	40	3p. green	25	25
O199	–	5p. blue	35	25
O200	–	15p. green	35	25
O201	–	20p. brown and red	70	60
O202	–	25p. brown and yellow	80	70
O203	–	50p. blue and red	1·40	85
O204	–	1k. blue, yellow & grey	4·00	1·10
O205	–	2k. blue, green & red	5·25	1·90
O206	–	5k. multicoloured	15·00	13·00

1968. Nos. 195/8 and 200/6 optd as Type **O29**.

O207		1p. black	15	15
O208		2p. red	15	15
O209		3p. green	15	15
O210		5p. blue	25	15
O211		15p. green	25	15
O212		20p. brown and red	25	15
O213		25p. brown and yellow	45	15
O214		50p. blue and red	85	45
O215		1k. blue, yellow and grey	1·30	1·10
O216		2k. blue, green and red	2·75	2·30
O217		5k. multicoloured	6·50	5·75

For later issues see **MYANMAR**.

JAPANESE OCCUPATION OF BURMA

Note.—There are various types of the Peacock overprint. Our prices, as usual in this Catalogue, are for the cheapest type.

 (1) (3)

1942. Postage stamps of Burma of 1937 (India types) optd as T **1**.

J22	55	3p. grey	4·00	23·00
J23	80	9p. green	27·00	70·00
J24	59	2a. red	£130	£225
J2	83	3½a. blue	80·00	

1942. Official stamp of Burma of 1937 (India types) optd as T **1**.

J3	64	6a. bistre	80·00	

1942. Postage stamps of Burma, 1938, optd as T **1** or with T **3** (rupee values).

J25	1	1p. orange	£225	£375
J12	1	3p. violet	21·00	75·00
J27	1	6p. blue	25·00	55·00
J14	1	9p. green	26·00	70·00
J29	3	1a. brown	9·00	42·00
J30	3	1½a. green	23·00	70·00
J16	3	2a. red	27·00	85·00
J17	3	4a. blue	60·00	£120
J18	8	1r. purple and blue	£450	£750
J19	8	2r. brown and purple	£250	£500

1942. Official stamps of Burma of 1939 optd with T **1**.

J7	3	3p. violet	40·00	90·00
J8	3	6p. blue	26·00	65·00
J9	3	1a. brown	27·00	55·00
J35	3	1½a. green	£180	£325
J10	3	2a. red	38·00	£100
J11	3	4a. blue	38·00	80·00

(6a) ("Yon Thon" = "Office Use")

1945. Official stamp of Burma of 1939 optd with T **6a**.

44	–	3a.6p. blue	£110	£275

7

1942. Yano Seal.

J45	7	(1a.) red	50·00	70·00

8 Farmer

1942

J46	8	1a. red	22·00	24·00

1942

(a) Stamps of Japan surch in annas or rupees.

J47	–	¼a. on 1s. brown (No. 314)	48·00	50·00
J48	83	½a. on 2s. red	55·00	50·00
J49	–	¾a. on 3s. green (No. 316)	80·00	80·00
J50	–	1a. on 5s. purple (No. 396)	80·00	70·00
J51	–	3a. on 7s. green (No. 320)	£130	£150

J52	–	4a. on 4s. green (No. 317)	60·00	65·00
J53	–	8a. on 8s. violet (No. 321)	£150	£150
J54	–	1r. on 10s. red (No. 322)	28·00	35·00
J55	–	2r. on 20s. blue (No. 325)	55·00	55·00
J56	–	5r. on 30s. blue (No. 327)	18·00	27·00

(b) No. 386 of Japan commemorating the fall of Singapore, surch in figures.

J56g	–	4a. on 4+2s. green and red	£180	£190

1942. Handstamped **5 C**.

J57	5	5c. on 1a. red (No. J46)	25·00	29·00

1942. Nos. J47/53 with anna surcharges obliterated, and handstamped with new values in figures.

J58	–	1c. on ¼a. on 1s. brown	55·00	55·00
J59	84	2c. on ½a. on 2s. red	55·00	55·00
J60	–	3c. on ¾a. on 3s. green	60·00	60·00
J61	–	3c. on ¾a. on 5s. red	85·00	65·00
J62	–	10c. on 3a. on 7s. green	£170	£140
J63	–	15c. on 4a. on 4s. green	50·00	55·00
J64	–	20c. on 8a. on 8s. violet	£900	£700

1942. Stamps of Japan surch in cents.

J65	–	1c. on 1s. brown (No. 314)	38·00	20·00
J66	83	2c. on 2s. red	60·00	42·00
J67	–	3c. on 3s. green (No. 316)	£100	65·00
J68	–	5c. on 5s. purple (No. 396)	95·00	55·00
J69	–	10c. on 7s. green (No. 320)	£140	80·00
J70	–	15c. on 4s. green (No. 317)	28·00	28·00
J71	–	20c. on 8s. violet (No. 321)	£200	95·00

14 Burma State Crest

1943. Perf or imperf.

J72	14	5c. red	28·00	32·00

15 Farmer

1943

J73a	15	1c. orange	4·25	9·00
J74	15	2c. green	1·25	1·00
J75	15	3c. blue	4·50	1·00
J77	15	5c. red	3·50	7·50
J78	15	10c. brown	9·00	9·00
J79	15	15c. mauve	30	4·25
J80	15	20c. lilac	30	1·00
J81	15	30c. green	1·00	2·75

 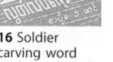

16 Soldier carving word "Independence" **17** Rejoicing Peasant

(18) Boy with National Flag

1943

		Perf or roul		
J85	16	1c. orange	1·25	1·75
J86	17	3c. blue	2·50	3·50
J87	18	5c. red	3·50	4·00

19 Burmese Woman **20** Elephant carrying Log **21** Watch Tower Mandalay

1943

J88	19	1c. orange	20·00	15·00
J89	19	2c. green	50	2·00
J90	19	3c. violet	50	2·25
J91	20	5c. red	75	60
J92	20	10c. blue	2·25	1·10
J93	20	15c. orange	1·00	3·00
J94	20	20c. green	1·00	1·75
J95	20	30c. brown	1·00	2·00
J96	21	1r. orange	30	2·00
J97	21	2r. violet	30	2·25

22 Playing Cane-ball **23** Shan Woman

1943. Shan States issue.

J98	22	1c. brown	42·00	48·00
J99	22	2c. green	48·00	48·00
J100	22	3c. violet	7·00	14·00
J101	22	5c. blue	3·00	8·50
J102	23	10c. blue	16·00	18·00
J103	23	20c. red	45·00	22·00
J104	23	30c. brown	26·00	65·00

ဗမာနိုင်ငံတော်

၂၀ ဆင့်။

(24) "Burma State" and value

1944. Optd with T **24**.

J105	22	1c. brown	4·75	9·00
J106	22	2c. green	60	6·00
J107	22	3c. violet	2·50	7·00
J108	22	5c. blue	2·75	3·50
J109	23	10c. blue	3·25	2·25
J110	23	20c. red	65	1·50
J111	23	30c. brown	1·25	1·75

Pt. 12

BURUNDI

Once part of the Belgian territory, Ruanda-Urundi. Independent on 1 July 1962, when a monarchy was established. After a revolution in 1967 Burundi became a republic.

100 centimes = 1 franc.

1962. Stamps of Ruanda-Urundi optd Royaume du Burundi and bar or surch also. (a) Flowers. (Nos. 178 etc.).

1		25c. multicoloured	25	25
2		40c. multicoloured	25	25
3		60c. multicoloured	55	50
4		1f.25 multicoloured	27·00	25·00
5		1f.50 multicoloured	80	75
6		5f. multicoloured	2·20	1·40
7		7f. multicoloured	3·50	2·50
8		10f. multicoloured	4·75	4·00

(b) Animals (Nos. 203/14).

9		10c. black, red and brown	25	25
10		20c. black and green	25	25
11		40c. black, olive and mauve	25	25
12		50c. brown, yellow & green	25	25
13		1f. black, blue and brown	25	25
14		1f.50 black and orange	25	25
15		2f. black, brown and turq	25	25
16		3f. black, red and brown	25	25
17		3f.50 on 3f. black, red & brn	25	25
18a		4f. on 10f. multicoloured	40	40
19		5f. multicoloured	40	40
20		6f.50 brown, yellow and red	40	40
21		8f. black, mauve and blue	1·40	65
23		10f. multicoloured	4·75	4·00

(c) Animals (Nos. 229/30).

24	25	20f. multicoloured	3·00	1·30
25	–	50f. multicoloured	2·75	2·50

10 King Mwambutsa IV and Royal Drummers

1962. Independence. Inscr "1.7.1962".

No.	Type	Description		
26	10	50c. sepia and lake	15	15
27	A	1f. green, red & deep green	15	15
28	B	2f. sepia and olive	25	15
29	10	3f. sepia and red	25	15
30	A	4f. green, red and blue	25	15
31	B	5f. sepia and violet	35	15
32	10	10f. sepia and green	40	25
33	A	20f. green, red and sepia	95	30
34	A	50f. sepia and mauve	2·75	40

DESIGNS—VERT: A, Burundi flag and arms. HORIZ: B, King and outline map of Burundi.

1962. Dag Hammarskjold Commem. No. 222 of Ruanda-Urundi surch **HOMMAGE A DAG HAMMARSKJOLD ROYAUME DU BURUNDI** and new value. U.N. emblem and wavy pattern at foot. Inscr in French or Flemish.

35		3f.50 on 3f. salmon and blue	25	25
36		6f.50 on 3f. salmon and blue	55	50
37		10f. on 3f. salmon and blue	1·10	90

1962. Malaria Eradication. As Nos. 31 and 34 but colours changed and with campaign emblem superimposed on map.

38		8f. sepia, turquoise & bistre	80	40
39		50f. sepia, turquoise & olive	3·25	1·50

12 Prince Louis Rwagasore

1963. Prince Rwagasore Memorial and Stadium Fund.

40	12	50c.+25c. violet	15	15
41	-	1f.+50c. blue and orange	15	15
42	-	1f.50+75c. vio & bistre	20	20
43	12	3f.50+1f.50 mauve	25	25
44	-	5f.+2f. blue and pink	25	25
45	-	6f.50+3f. violet & olive	35	30

DESIGNS—HORIZ: 1f., 5f. Prince and stadium; 1f.50, 6f.50 Prince and memorial.

13 "Sowing"

1963. Freedom from Hunger.

46	13	4f. purple and olive	20	20
47	13	8f. purple and olive	40	25
48	13	15f. purple and green	55	30

1963. "Peaceful Uses of Outer Space" Nos. 28 and 34 optd **UTILISATIONS PACIFIQUES DE L'ESPACE** around globe encircled by rocket.

49	B	2f. sepia and olive	3·50	3·25
50	B	50f. sepia and mauve	4·75	4·50

1963. First Anniv of Independence. Nos. 30/3 but with colours changed and optd **Premier Anniversaire**.

51	A	4f. green, red and olive	25	15
52	B	8f. sepia and orange	55	25
53	10	10f. sepia and mauve	70	30
54	A	20f. green, red and grey	2·00	50

1963. Nos. 27 and 33 surch.

55	6f.50 on 1f. green, red and deep green	95	25
56	15f. on 20f. grn, red & sepia	1·50	50

17 Globe and Red Cross Flag

1963. Centenary of Red Cross.

57	17	4f. green, red and grey	40	15
58	17	8f. brown, red and grey	55	25
59	17	10f. blue, red and grey	95	40
60	17	20f. violet, red and grey	2·20	50

MS60a 90×140 mm. Nos. 57/60 in new colours, each with **+2f.** surcharge in black. Imperf — 8·00 7·50

IMPERF STAMPS. Many Burundi stamps from No. 61 onwards exist imperf from limited printings and/or miniature sheets.

18 "1962" and UNESCO Emblem

1963. First Anniv of Admission to UNO. Emblems and values in black.

61	18	4f. olive and yellow	25	15
62	-	8f. blue and lilac	40	20
63	-	10f. violet and blue	55	25
64	-	20f. green and yellow	70	40
65	-	50f. brown and ochre	1·40	65

MS65a 111×74 mm. Nos. 64/5 but with emblems changed. Imperf — 8·00 7·50

EMBLEMS: 8f. ITU; 10f. WMO; 20f. UPU, 50f. FAO; **MS65a** 20f. FAO; 50f. WMO.

19 UNESCO Emblem and Scales of Justice

1963. 15th Anniv of Declaration of Human Rights.

66	19	50c. blk, blue and pink	15	15
67	-	1f.50 black, blue & orange	15	15
68	-	3f.50 black, green & brown	25	15
69	-	6f.50 black, green and lilac	40	20
70	-	10f. black, bistre and blue	70	25
71	-	20f. multicoloured	1·40	50

DESIGNS: 3f.50, 6f.50, Scroll; 10f., 20f. Lincoln.

20 Ice-hockey

1964. Winter Olympic Games, Innsbruck.

72	20	50c. black, gold and olive	25	15
73	-	3f.50 black, gold & brown	40	20
74	-	6f.50 black, gold and grey	1·10	25
75	-	10f. black, gold and grey	1·80	50
76	-	20f. black, gold and bistre	2·40	1·30

MS76a 122×85 mm. 10f.+5f. and 20f.+5f. (as Nos. 75/6 but in new colours). Perf or imperf 19·00 18·00

DESIGNS: 3f.50, Figure-skating; 6f.50, Olympic flame; 10f. Speed-skating; 20f. Skiing (slalom).

21 Hippopotamus

1964. Burundi Animals. Multicoloured. (i) Postage. (a) Size as T 21.

77		50c. Impala	15	15
78	21	1f. Type 21	25	15
79		1f.50 Giraffe	35	20
80		2f. African buffalo	40	25
81		3f. Common zebra	55	25
82		3f.50 Waterbuck	60	30

(b) Size 16×42½ mm or 42½×26 mm.

83	4f. Impala	70	40
84	5f. Hippopotamus	80	45
85	6f.50 Common zebra	95	50
86	8f. African buffalo	1·10	55
87	10f. Giraffe	1·40	65
88	15f. Waterbuck	1·60	75

(c) Size 53½×33½ mm.

89	20f. Cheetah	2·75	90
90	50f. African elephant	5·50	1·30
91	100f. Lion	11·00	1·80

(ii) Air. Inscr "POSTE AERIENNE" and optd with gold border. (a) Size 26×42½ mm or 42½×26 mm.

92	6f. Common zebra	95	15
93	8f. African buffalo	1·20	25
94	10f. Impala	1·60	40
95	14f. Hippopotamus	2·40	50
96	15f. Waterbuck	3·00	65

(b) Size 53½×33½ mm.

97	20f. Cheetah	5·50	90
98	50f. African elephant	13·50	1·90

The impala, giraffe and waterbuck stamps are all vert. designs, and the remainder are horiz.

22 Burundi Dancer

1964. World's Fair, New York (1st series). Gold backgrounds.

99	22	50c. multicoloured	15	15
100	-	1f. multicoloured	20	15
101	-	4f. multicoloured	25	15
102	-	6f.50 multicoloured	55	20
103	-	10f. multicoloured	80	25
104	-	15f. multicoloured	1·20	40
105	-	20f. multicoloured	1·60	75

MS105a 120×100 mm. Nos. 103/5. Perf or imperf 8·00 7·50

DESIGNS: 1f. to 20f. Various dancers and drummers as Type **22**.

See also Nos. 175/MS81a.

23 Pope Paul and King Mwambutsa IV

1964. Canonization of 22 African Martyrs. Inscriptions in gold.

106	23	50c. lake and blue	15	15
107	-	1f. blue and purple	20	15
108	-	4f. sepia and mauve	25	15
109	-	8f. brown and red	55	20
110	-	14f. brown and turquoise	1·10	25
111	23	20f. green and red	1·60	65

DESIGNS—VERT: 1f., 8f. Group of martyrs. HORIZ: 4f., 14f., Pope John XXIII and King Mwambutsa IV.

24 Putting the Shot

1964. Olympic Games, Tokyo. Inscr "TOKYO 1964". Multicoloured.

112	24	50c. Type 24	15	15
113		1f. Throwing the discus	15	15
114		3f. Swimming (horiz)	20	15
115		4f. Relay-racing	25	20
116		6f.50 Throwing the javelin	40	25
117		8f. Hurdling (horiz)	70	30
118		10f. Long-jumping (horiz)	80	40
119		14f. High-diving (horiz)	1·10	50
120		18f. High-jumping (horiz)	1·50	75
121		20f. Gymnastics (horiz)	1·60	1·00

MS121a 115×71 mm. 18f.+2f. and 20f.+5f. (as Nos. 120/1). Perf or imperf 7·50 7·00

25 Scientist, Map and Emblem

1965. Anti-T.B. Campaign. Country name, values and Lorraine Cross in red.

122	25	2f.+50c. sepia and drab	15	15
123	25	4f.+1f.50 green & pink	25	20
124	25	5f.+2f.50 violet & buff	55	25
125	25	8f.+3f. blue and grey	70	30
126	25	10f.+5f. red and green	1·10	50

MS126a 100×71 mm. 10f.+10f. sepia and olive. Perf or imperf 2·75 2·50

26 Purple Swamphen

1965. Birds. Multicoloured. (i) Postage. (a) Size as T 26.

127	50c. Type 26	15	15
128	1f. Little bee eater	20	15
129	1f.50 Secretary bird	25	15
130	2f. Painted stork	35	20
131	3f. Congo peafowl	40	20
132	3f.50 African darter	55	25

(b) Size 26×42½ mm.

133	4f. Type 26	70	25
134	5f. Little bee eater	80	30
135	6f.50 Secretary bird	1·10	40
136	8f. Painted stork	1·40	45
137	10f. Congo peafowl	1·60	50
138	15f. African darter	2·75	65

(c) Size 33½×53 mm.

139	20f. Saddle-bill stork	3·50	90
140	50f. Abyssinian ground hornbill	6·75	1·60
141	100f. South African crowned crane	13·50	3·25

(ii) Air. Inscr "POSTE AERIENNE". Optd with gold border. (a) Size 26×42½ mm.

142	6f. Secretary bird	55	15
143	8f. African darter	80	25
144	10f. Congo peafowl	1·10	40
145	14f. Little bee eater	1·80	50
146	15f. Painted stork	2·00	65

(b) Size 33½×53 mm.

147	20f. Saddle-bill stork	3·00	75
148	50f. Abyssinian ground hornbill	6·00	1·30
149	75f. Martial eagle	8·00	1·90
150	130f. Lesser flamingo	11·00	2·50

27 "Relay" Satellite and Telegraph Key

1965. Centenary of ITU. Multicoloured.

151	1f. Type 27	15	15
152	3f. "Telstar 1" and hand telephone	15	15
153	4f. "Lunik 3" and wall telephone	15	15
154	6f.50 Weather satellite and tracking station	20	15
155	8f. "Telstar 2" and headphones	25	20
156	10f. "Sputnik" and radar scanner	40	20
157	14f. "Syncom" and aerial	70	40
158	20f. "Pioneer 5" space probe and radio aerial	1·10	75

MS158a 121×85 mm. Nos. 156 and 158. Perf or imperf 6·00 5·75

28 Arms (reverse of 10f. coin)

1965. First Independence Anniv Gold Coinage Commem. Circular designs on gold foil, backed with multicoloured patterned paper. Imperf. (i) Postage. (a) 10f. coin. Diameter 1½ in.
159	**28**	2f.+50c. red & yellow	40	40
160	-	4f.+50c. blue & red	55	50

(b) 25f. coin. Diameter 1¾ in.
161	**28**	6f.+50c. orange & grey	95	90
162	-	8f.+50c. blue & purple	1·10	1·00

(c) 50f. coin. Diameter 2½ in.
163	**28**	12f.+50c. green & purple	1·80	1·60
164	-	15f.+50c. green & lilac	2·20	2·00

(d) 100f. coin. Diameter 258in.
165	**28**	25f.+50c. blue and flesh	4·00	3·75
166	-	40f.+50c. mauve & brn	5·50	5·00

(ii) Air. (a) 10f. coin. Diameter 1½ in.
167	**28**	3f.+1f. violet & lavender	40	40
168	-	5f.+1f. red & turquoise	55	50

(b) 25f. coin. Diameter 1¾ in.
169	**28**	11f.+1f. purple & yellow	80	75
170	-	14f.+1f. green and red	1·10	1·00

(c) 50f. coin. Diameter 2½ in.
171	**28**	20f.+1f. black and blue	1·40	1·30
172	-	30f.+1f. red and orange	1·90	1·80

(d) 100f. coin. Diameter 2¾ in.
173	**28**	50f.+1f. violet and blue	3·50	3·25
174	-	100f.+1f. purple & mve	6·75	6·25

DESIGNS: The 4, 5, 8, 14, 15, 30, 40 and 100f. each show the obverse side of the coin (King Mwambutsa IV).

1965. Worlds Fair, New York (2nd series). As Nos. 99/105, but with silver backgrounds.
175	**22**	50c. multicoloured	15	15
176	-	1f. multicoloured	20	15
177	-	4f. multicoloured	25	20
178	-	6f.50 multicoloured	55	25
179	-	10f. multicoloured	80	40
180	-	15f. multicoloured	1·10	50
181	-	20f. multicoloured	1·60	75

MS181a 120×100 mm. Nos. 179/81. perf or imperf — 5·50 — 5·00

29 Globe and ICY Emblem

1965. International Co-operation Year. Multicoloured.
182	**29**	1f. Type **29**	15	15
183		4f. Map of Africa and cogwheel emblem of UN Science and Technology Conference	20	15
184		8f. Map of South-East Asia and Colombo Plan emblem	25	20
185		10f. Globe and UN emblem	40	25
186		18f. Map of Americas and "Alliance for Progress" emblem	80	40
187		25f. Map of Europe and CEPT emblems	1·40	65
188		40f. Space map and satellite (UN—"Peaceful Uses of Outer Space")	2·30	1·00

MS188a 100×100 mm. 18f. (Map of Africa and UN emblem); 25f. and 40f. (similar to Nos. 187/8). Perf or imperf — 6·75 — 6·25

30 Prince Rwagasore and Memorial

1966. Prince Rwagasore and Pres. Kennedy Commemoration.
189	**30**	4f.+1f. brown and blue	25	20
190	-	10f.+1f. blue, brn & grn	40	25
191	-	20f.+2f. green and lilac	80	40
192	-	40f.+2f. brown & green	1·90	90

MS193 75×90 mm. 20f.+5f. and 40f.+5f. (as Nos. 189 and 191). Perf or imperf — 6·00 — 5·75

DESIGNS—HORIZ: 10f. Prince Rwagasore and Pres. Kennedy; 20f. Pres. Kennedy and memorial library. VERT: 40f. King Mwambutsa at Pres. Kennedy's grave.

31 Protea

1966. Flowers. Multicoloured. (i) Postage. (a) Size as T **31**.
194		50c. Type **31**	15	15
195		1f. Crossandra	15	15
196		1f.50 Ansellia	20	15
197		2f. Thunbergia	20	15
198		3f. Schizoglossum	25	15
199		3f.50 Dissotis	35	20

(b) Size 41×41 mm.
200		4f. Type **31**	40	20
201		5f. Crossandra	55	25
202		6f.50 Ansellia	70	25
203		8f. Thunbergia	1·40	45
204		10f. Schizoglossum	1·50	50
205		15f. Dissotis	1·80	65

(c) Size 50×50 mm.
206		20f. Type **31**	2·40	1·10
207		50f. Gazania	5·50	1·30
208		100f. Hibiscus	8·00	1·90
209		150f. Markhamia	11·50	2·50

(ii) Air. (a) Size 41×41 mm.
210		6f. Dissotis	40	15
211		8f. Crossandra	55	20
212		10f. Ansellia	70	25
213		14f. Thunbergia	95	30
214		15f. Schizoglossum	1·20	40

(b) Size 50×50 mm.
215		20f. Gazania	1·40	50
216		50f. Type **31**	2·40	75
217		75f. Hibiscus	4·00	1·30
218		130f. Markhamia	7·50	2·50

32 UNESCO

33

1966. 20th Anniv of UNESCO.
MS219 Three sheets, each 201×127 mm, each containing single stamps (Type **32**) with se-tenant label inscribed in English or French and an adjoining block of six stamps (3×2) as Type **33**, forming a composite design of the mural tapestry hanging in the U.N. General Assembly building, New York. (a) Postage: Two sheets 1f.50×7 and 4f.×7. (b) Air. One sheet 14f.×7 multicoloured Set of 3 sheets — 24·00

1967. Fourth Anniv of Independence (1966).
MS220 Four unissued sheets, diamond-shaped, 200×200 mm, each containing eight "Flower" stamps as Type **31** but with values and corresponding designs changed, and centre se-tenant label showing "Flag", "Map", "Arms" or "Flower" emblem. Values: 6, 7, 8, 10, 14, 15, 20 and 50f. Multicoloured. Stamps and sheet margins have the original inscriptions obliterated by the overprint **REPUBLIQUE DU BURUNDI** in black on gold panels Set of 4 sheets — 43·00 — 40·00

1967. Various stamps optd. (i) Nos. 127, etc. (Birds) optd **REPUBLIQUE DU BURUNDI** and bar. (a) Postage.
221		50c. multicoloured	3·50	3·25
222		1f.50 multicoloured	55	50
223		3f.50 multicoloured	70	65
224		5f. multicoloured	95	90
225		6f.50 multicoloured	1·20	1·10
226		8f. multicoloured	1·50	1·40
227		10f. multicoloured	2·00	1·90
228		15f. multicoloured	2·75	2·50
229		20f. multicoloured	5·50	5·00
230		50f. multicoloured	9·50	8·75
231		100f. multicoloured	16·00	15·00

(b) Air.
232		6f. multicoloured	55	50
233		8f. multicoloured	95	65
234		10f. multicoloured	1·40	75
235		14f. multicoloured	2·00	90
236		15f. multicoloured	2·40	1·00
237		20f. multicoloured	4·75	1·90
238		50f. multicoloured	11·50	4·50
239		75f. multicoloured	16·00	5·75
240		130f. multicoloured	24·00	8·25

(ii) Nos. 194, etc. (Flowers) optd as Nos. 221, etc., but with two bars. (a) Postage.
241		50c. multicoloured	15	15
242		1f. multicoloured	15	15
243		1f.50 multicoloured	20	20
244		2f. multicoloured	20	20
245		3f. multicoloured	35	20
246		3f.50 multicoloured	55	25
247		4f. multicoloured	2·40	65
248		5f. multicoloured	25	15
249		6f.50 multicoloured	40	20
250		8f. multicoloured	55	30
251		10f. multicoloured	95	40
252		15f. multicoloured	1·20	50
253		50f. multicoloured	5·50	1·50
254		100f. multicoloured	13·50	3·75
255		150f. multicoloured	16·00	4·50

(b) Air.
256		6f. multicoloured	25	15
257		8f. multicoloured	40	15
258		10f. multicoloured	55	20
259		14f. multicoloured	80	25
260		15f. multicoloured	1·10	40
261		20f. multicoloured	2·30	65
262		50f. multicoloured	5·75	1·50
263		75f. multicoloured	8·00	2·50
264		130f. multicoloured	9·50	3·00

35 Sir Winston Churchill and St. Paul's Cathedral

1967. Churchill Commemoration. Multicoloured.
265		4f.+1f. Type **35** (postage)	55	25
266		15f.+2f. Churchill and Tower of London	80	40
267		20f.+3f. Big Ben and Boadicea Statue, Westminster	1·10	65

MS268 80×80 mm. 50f.+5f. Sir Winston Churchill (57×57 mm). (air). Perf or imperf — 3·50 — 3·25

36 Egyptian Mouthbrooder

1967. Fish. Multicoloured. (a) Postage. (i) Size as T **36**.
269		50c. Type **36**	15	15
270		1f. Spotted climbing-perch	20	15
271		1f.50 Six-banded lyretail	25	15
272		2f. Congo tetra	35	15
273		3f. Jewel cichlid	40	20
274		3f.50 Spotted mouthbrooder	55	20

(ii) Size 53½×27 mm.
275		4f. Type **36**	70	25
276		5f. As 1f.	80	30
277		6f.50. As 1f.50	1·10	40
278		8f. As 2f.	1·40	45
279		10f. As 3f.	2·00	50
280		15f. As 3f.50	3·00	65

(iii) Size 63½×31½ mm.
281		20f. Type **36**	4·00	90
282		50f. Dusky snakehead	8·00	1·30
283		100f. Red-tailed notho	12·00	1·50
284		150f. African tetra	16·00	1·90

(b) Air. (i) Size 50×23 mm.
285		6f. Type **36**	80	15
286		8f. As 1f.	1·20	20
287		10f. As 1f.50	1·60	25
288		14f. As 2f.	2·00	40
289		15f. As 3f.	2·20	50

(ii) Size 59×27 mm.
290		20f. As 3f.50	3·00	65
291		50f. As 50f. (No. 282)	7·50	75
292		75f. As 100f.	11·50	1·30
293		130f. As 150f.	18·00	1·90

37 Baule Ancestral Figures

1967. "African Art". Multicoloured.
294		50c. Type **37** (postage)	15	15
295		1f. "Master of Buli's" carved seat	15	15
296		1f.50 Karumba antelope's head	15	15
297		2f. Bobo buffalo's head	20	15
298		4f. Guma-Goffa funeral figures	25	20
299		10f. Bakoutou "spirit" (carving) (air)	55	25
300		14f. Bamum sultan's throne	70	30
301		17f. Bebin bronze head	95	40
302		24f. Statue of 109th Bakouba king	1·20	50
303		26f. Burundi basketwork and lances	1·90	90

1967. 50th Anniv of Lions International. Nos. 265/**MS**268 optd **1917 1967** and emblem.
304		4f.+1f. multicoloured	1·10	40
305		15f.+2f. multicoloured	1·60	65
306		20f.+3f. multicoloured	1·90	75

MS307 80×80 mm. 50f.+5f. multicoloured (air) Perf or imperf — 5·50 — 5·00

39 Lord Baden-Powell (founder)

1967. 60th Anniv of Scout Movement and World Scout Jamboree, Idaho. Multicoloured.
308		50c. Scouts climbing (postage)	25	15
309		1f. Scouts preparing meal	40	15
310		1f.50 Type **39**	55	20
311		2f. Two scouts	70	20
312		4f. Giving first aid	80	25
313		10f. As 50c. (air)	1·40	25
314		14f. As 1f.	1·60	30
315		17f. Type **39**	1·90	40
316		24f. As 2f.	3·00	50
317		26f. As 4f.	3·25	90

40 The Gleaners (Millet)

1967. World Fair, Montreal. Multicoloured.
318		4f. Type **40**	25	15
319		8f. The Water-carrier of Seville (Velasquez)	55	20
320		14f. The Triumph of Neptune and Amphitrite (Poussin)	95	25
321		18f. Acrobat with a ball (Picasso)	1·10	30
322		25f. Margaret van Eyck (Van Eyck)	1·80	40
323		40f. St. Peter denying Christ (Rembrandt)	2·20	75

MS324 105×105 mm. Nos. 322/3. Perf or imperf — 5·50 — 5·00

41 Boeing 707

1967. Air. Opening of Bujumbura Airport. Aircraft and inscr in black and silver.

325	41	10f. green	55	15
326	-	14f. yellow	95	25
327	-	17f. blue	1·10	40
328	-	26f. purple	2·20	75

AIRCRAFT: 14f. Boeing 727-100 over lakes. 17f. Vickers Super VC-10 over lake. 26f. Boeing 727 over Bujumbura Airport.

42 Pres. Micombero and Flag

1967. First Anniv of Republic. Multicoloured.

329	42	5f. Type 42	25	15
330		14f. Memorial and Arms	80	25
331		20f. View of Bujumbura and Arms	1·20	40
332		30f. "Place de la Revolution" and President Micombero	1·80	65

43 The Adoration of the Shepherds (J. B. Mayno)

1967. Christmas. Religious Paintings. Multicoloured.

333	43	1f. Type 43	25	15
334		4f. The Holy Family (A. van Dyck)	55	25
335		14f. The Nativity (Maitre de Moulins)	1·20	50
336		26f. Madonna and Child (C. Crivelli)	2·00	90
MS337		120×120 mm. Nos. 333/6	6·00	5·75

44 Burundi Scouts

1968. Air. 20th Anniv of Burundi Scouts and 60th Anniv of Scout Movement. Diamond-shaped sheet containing T 44 and similar design. Multicoloured.

MS338	142×142 mm. 24f. and 26f. with two se-tenant labels depicting Lord Baden-Powell and scouting activities	11·00	10·00

DESIGN: 26f. Burundi scouts practising first-aid.

45 Downhill Skiing

1968. Winter Olympic Games, Grenoble. Multicoloured.

339	45	5f. Type 45	25	15
340		10f. Ice-hockey	55	15
341		14f. Figure-skating	95	20
342		17f. Bobsleighing	1·10	25
343		26f. Ski-jumping	1·60	30
344		40f. Speed-skating	2·00	40
345		60f. Olympic torch	2·75	50
MS346		129×82 mm. Nos. 344/5. Perf or imperf	5·50	5·00

46 Portrait of a Young Man (Botticelli)

1968. Famous Paintings. Multicoloured.

347	46	1f.50 Type 46 (postage)	25	15
348		2f. La Maja Vestida (Goya) (horiz)	40	20
349		4f. The Lacemaker (Vermeer)	55	25
350		17f. Woman and Cat (Renoir) (air)	1·10	50
351		24f. "The Jewish Bride (Rembrandt) (horiz)	1·60	65
352		26f. Pope Innocent X (Velasquez)	2·20	1·40

47 Module landing on Moon

1968. Space Exploration. Multicoloured.

353	47	4f. Type 47 (postage)	25	15
354		6f. Russian cosmonaut in Space	40	15
355		8f. Weather satellite	55	20
356		10f. American astronaut in Space	70	25
357		14f. Type 47 (air)	40	30
358		18f. As 6f.	1·10	40
359		25f. As 8f.	1·20	45
360		40f. As 10f.	2·40	1·00
MS361		109×82 mm. 25f. Type 47; 40f. Weather satellite. Perf or imperf	6·00	5·75

48 Salamis aethiops

1968. Butterflies. Multicoloured. (a) Postage. (i) Size 30½×34 mm.

362	48	50c. Type 48	15	15
363		1f. Graphium ridleyanus	15	15
364		1f.50 Cymothoe	25	15
365		2f. Charaxes eupale	40	15
366		3f. Papilio bromius	55	20
367		3f.50 Teracolus annae	70	25

(ii) Size 34×38 mm.

368	48	4f. Type 48	80	25
369		5f. As 1f.	95	30
370		6f.50 As 1f.50	1·10	30
371		8f. As 2f.	1·60	40
372		10f. As 3f.	2·00	45
373		15f. As 3f.50	2·40	50

(iii) Size 41×46 mm.

374	48	20f. Type 48	3·50	75
375		50f. Papilio zenobia	4·00	90
376		100f. Danais chrysippus	8·00	1·30
377		150f. Salamis temora	16·00	1·90

(b) Air. With gold frames. (i) Size 33×37 mm.

378	48	6f. As 3f.50	1·10	25
379		8f. As 1f.	2·00	40
380		10f. As 1f.50	2·40	50
381		14f. As 2f.	3·00	65
382		15f. As 3f.	3·25	75

(ii) Size 39×44 mm.

383	48	20f. As 50f. (No. 375)	4·00	1·00
384		50f. Type 48	8·00	1·30
385		75f. As 100f.	13·50	1·90
386		130f. As 150f.	20·00	2·50

49 Woman by the Manzanares (Goya)

1968. International Letter-writing Week. Multicoloured.

387	49	4f. Type 49 (postage)	55	15
388		7f. Reading a Letter (De Hooch)	70	25
389		11f. Woman reading a Letter (Terborch)	80	40
390		14f. Man writing a Letter (Metsu)	1·10	50
391		17f. The Letter (Fragonard) (air)	1·40	50
392		26f. Young Woman reading Letter (Vermeer)	2·40	55
393		40f. Folding a Letter (Vlgee-Lebruni)	4·00	65
394		50f. Mademoiselle Lavergne (Liotard)	5·50	1·00
MS395		103×120 mm. Nos. 393/4 (without "POSTE AERIENNE" inscr). Perf or imperf	9·50	8·75

50 Football

1968. Olympic Games, Mexico. Multicoloured.

396	50	4f. Type 50 (postage)	15	15
397		7f. Basketball	25	20
398		13f. High jumping	40	25
399		24f. Relay racing	70	40
400		40f. Throwing the javelin	1·50	65
401		10f. Putting the shot (air)	25	15
402		17f. Running	70	25
403		26f. Throwing the hammer	1·40	40
404		50f. Hurdling	2·75	65
405		75f. Long jumping	4·75	90
MS406		95×85 mm. Nos. 404/5 (without "POSTE AERIENNE" inscr). Perf or imperf	7·50	7·00

51 Virgin and Child (Lippi)

1968. Christmas. Paintings. Multicoloured.

407	51	3f. Type 51 (postage)	15	15
408		5f. The Magnificat (Botticelli)	25	15
409		6f. Virgin and Child (Durer)	40	20
410		11f. Virgin and Child (Raphael)	55	25
411		10f. Madonna (Correggio) (air)	55	25
412		14f. The Nativity (Baroccio)	70	30
413		17f. The Holy Family (El Greco)	95	40
414		26f. Adoration of the Magi (Maino)	2·00	75
MS415		Two sheets each 120×120 mm. (a) Nos. 407/10; (b) Nos. 411/14. Perf or imperf	7·50	7·00

52 WHO Emblem and Map

1969. 20th Anniv of World Health Organization Operation in Africa.

416	52	5f. multicoloured	40	15
417	52	6f. multicoloured	55	25
418	52	11f. multicoloured	80	40

53 Hand holding Flame

1969. Air. Human Rights Year.

419	53	10f. multicoloured	55	15
420	53	14f. multicoloured	80	25
421	53	26f. multicoloured	1·40	40

1969. Space Flight of "Apollo 8". Nos. 407/14 optd ***VOL DE NOEL APOLLO 8*** and space module.

422		3f. multicoloured (postage)	15	15
423		5f. multicoloured	40	15
424		6f. multicoloured	55	20
425		11f. multicoloured	80	25
426		10f. multicoloured (air)	70	30
427		14f. multicoloured	95	40
428		17f. multicoloured	1·10	50
429		26f. multicoloured	1·60	75

55 Map showing African Members

1969. Fifth Anniv of Yaounde Agreement between Common Market Countries and African-Malagasy Economic Community. Multicoloured.

430	55	5f. Type 55	15	15
431		14f. Ploughing with tractor	70	20
432		17f. Teacher and pupil	80	25
433		26f. Maps of Africa and Europe (horiz)	1·40	65

56 Resurrection (Isenmann)

1969. Easter. Multicoloured.

434	56	11f. Type 56	70	20
435		14f. Resurrection (Caron)	95	25
436		17f. Noli me Tangere (Schongauer)	1·20	40
437		26f. Resurrection (El Greco)	1·60	75
MS438		102×125 mm. Nos. 434/7. Perf or imperf	4·75	4·50

57 Potter

1969. 50th Anniv of ILO. Multicoloured.

439	57	3f. Type 57	15	15
440		5f. Farm workers	25	20
441		7f. Foundry worker	40	25
442		10f. Harvester	55	40

58 Nurse and Patient

1969. 50th Anniv of League of Red Cross Societies. Multicoloured.

443	58	4f.+1f. Type 58 (postage)	40	15
444		7f.+1f. Stretcher bearers	55	20
445		11f.+1f. Operating theatre	70	25
446		17f.+1f. Blood bank	95	30
447		26f.+3f. Laboratory (air)	1·50	40

448	40f.+3f. Red Cross truck in African village	2·00	65
449	50f.+3f. Nurse and woman patient	2·75	90
MS450	90×97 mm. Nos. 447/9 (without "POSTE AERIENNE" inscr). Perf or imperf	8·75	8·25

59 Steel Works

1969. Fifth Anniv of African Development Bank. Multicoloured.

451	10f. Type **59**	55	50
452	17f. Broadcaster	95	90
453	30f. Language laboratory	1·50	1·40
454	50f. Tractor and harrow	2·50	2·40
MS455	103×125 mm. Nos. 451/4. Perf or imperf	6·00	5·75

60 Pope Paul VI

1969. First Papal Visit to Africa. Multicoloured.

456	3f.+2f. Type **60**	15	15
457	5f.+2f. Pope Paul and map of Africa (horiz)	25	20
458	10f.+2f. Pope Paul and African flags (horiz)	55	25
459	14f.+2f. Pope Paul and the Vatican (horiz)	95	40
460	17f.+2f. Type **60**	1·40	50
461	40f.+2f. Pope Paul and Uganda Martyrs (horiz)	2·20	1·10
462	50f.+2f. Pope Paul enthroned (horiz)	2·75	1·30
MS463	80×103 mm. As Nos. 461/2 but face values 40f.+5f. and 50f.+5f. Perf or imperf	6·00	5·75

61 Girl reading Letter (Vermeer)

1969. International Letter-writing Week. Multicoloured.

464	4f. Type **61**	15	15
465	7f. Graziella (Renoir)	40	20
466	14f. Woman writing a Letter (Terborch)	80	25
467	26f. Galileo (unknown painter)	1·40	50
468	40f. Beethoven (unknown painter)	2·00	90
MS469	133×75 mm. Nos. 467/8. Perf or imperf	6·00	5·75

62 Blast-off

1969. First Man on the Moon. Multicoloured.

470	4f. Type **62** (postage)	40	15
471	6f.50 Rocket in Space	55	20
472	7f. Separation of lunar module	80	25
473	14f. Module landing on Moon	1·20	40
474	17f. Command module in orbit	1·60	50
475	26f. Astronaut descending ladder (air)	2·30	55
476	40f. Astronaut on Moon's surface	3·50	65

| 477 | 50f. Module in sea | 5·50 | 75 |
| **MS**478 | 140×90 mm. 26f. As 14f.; 40f. As 26f.; 50f. As 40f. Perf or imperf | 16·00 | 15·00 |

63 Adoration of the Magi (detail, Rubens)

1969. Christmas. Multicoloured.

479	5f. Type **63** (postage)	1·40	15
480	6f. Virgin and Child with St. John (Romano)	25	20
481	10f. Madonna of the Magnificat (Botticelli)	70	25
482	17f. Virgin and Child (Garofalo) (horiz) (air)	1·10	40
483	26f. Madonna and Child (Ne-gretti) (horiz)	1·60	50
484	50f. Virgin and Child (Barbarelli) (horiz)	3·50	65
MS485	Two sheets (a) 110×85 mm. Nos. 479/81; (b) 85×110 mm. Nos. 482/4. Perf or imperf Set of 2 sheets	8·75	8·25

64 Chelorrhina polyphemus

1970. Beetles. Multicoloured. (a) Postage. (i) Size 39×28 mm.

486	50c. Sternotomis bohemani	15	15
487	1f. Tetralobus flabellicornis	15	15
488	1f.50 Type **64**	20	15
489	2f. Brachytritus hieroglyphicus	25	15
490	3f. Goliathus goliathus	40	20
491	3f.50 Homoderus mellyi	55	20

(ii) Size 46×32 mm.

492	4f. As 50c.	60	25
493	5f. As 1f.	70	25
494	6f.50 Type **64**	80	30
495	8f. As 2f.	1·10	40
496	10f. As 3f.	2·20	50
497	15f. As 3f.50	2·75	65

(iii) Size 62×36 mm.

498	20f. As 50c.	4·00	70
499	50f. Stephanorrhina guttata	8·00	1·00
500	100f. Phyllocnema viridocostata	15·00	1·90
501	150f. Mecynorrhina oberthueri	22·00	2·50

(b) Air. (i) Size 46×32 mm.

502	6f. As 3f.50	80	40
503	8f. As 1f.	1·10	45
504	10f. Type **64**	1·40	50
505	14f. As 2f.	1·60	55
506	15f. As 3f.	1·90	65

(ii) Size 52×36 mm.

507	20f. As 50f. (No. 499)	4·00	75
508	50f. As 50c.	8·00	90
509	75f. As 100f.	12·00	1·00
510	130f. As 150f.	19·00	1·90

65 Jesus Condemned to Death

1970. Easter. The Stations of the Cross (Carredano). Multicoloured.

511	1f. Type **65** (postage)	15	15
512	1f.50 Carrying the Cross	15	15
513	2f. Jesus falls for the First Time	15	15
514	3f. Jesus meets His Mother	20	15
515	3f.50 Simon of Cyrene takes the Cross	25	20
516	4f. Veronica wipes the face of Christ	35	20

517	5f. Jesus falls for the Second Time	40	25
518	8f. The Women of Jerusalem (air)	55	15
519	10f. Jesus falls for the Third Time	70	25
520	14f. Christ stripped	95	30
521	15f. Jesus nailed to the Cross	1·10	40
522	18f. The Crucifixion	1·50	50
523	20f. Descent from the Cross	1·80	65
524	50f. Christ laid in the Tomb	3·50	1·10
MS525	Two sheets each 155×125 mm. (a) Nos. 511/17; (b) Nos. 518/24	15·00	14·00

66 Japanese Parade

1970. World Fair, Osaka, Japan (EXPO '70). Multicoloured.

526	4f. Type **66**	15	15
527	6f.50 Exhibition site from the air	20	15
528	7f. African pavilions	25	20
529	14f. Pagoda	70	25
530	26f. Recording pavilion and pool	1·40	40
531	40f. Tower of the Sun (vert)	1·90	65
532	50f. National flags (vert)	2·20	75
MS533	105×80 mm. As Nos. 531/2 with additional "POSTE AERIENNE" inscr. Perf or imperf	4·75	4·50

67 Burundi Cow

1970. Source of the Nile. Multicoloured.

| 534 | 7f. Any design (postage) | 2·00 | 50 |
| 535 | 14f. Any design (air) | 2·75 | 65 |

Nos. 534 and 535 were each issued in se-tenant sheets of 18 stamps as Type **67**, showing map sections, animals and birds, forming a map of the Nile from Cairo to Burundi.

68 Common Redstart

1970. Birds. Multicoloured. (a) Postage. Size 44×33 mm or 33×44 mm.

536	2f. Great grey shrike (vert)	1·10	15
537	2f. Common starling (vert)	1·10	15
538	2f. Yellow wagtail (vert)	1·10	15
539	2f. Sand martin (vert)	1·10	15
540	3f. Winter wren (vert)	1·40	25
541	3f. Firecrest	1·40	25
542	3f. Eurasian sky lark	1·40	25
543	3f. Crested lark	1·40	25
544	3f.50 Woodchat shrike (vert)	2·00	40
545	3f.50 Rock thrush (vert)	2·00	40
546	3f.50 Black redstarts (vert)	2·00	40
547	3f.50 Ring ousel (vert)	2·00	40
548	4f. Type **68**	2·75	50
549	4f. Dunnock	2·75	50
550	4f. Grey wagtail	2·75	50
551	4f. Meadow pipit	2·75	50
552	5f. Hoopoe (vert)	3·50	65
553	5f. Pied flycatcher (vert)	3·50	65
554	5f. Great reed warbler (vert)	3·50	65
555	5f. River kingfisher (vert)	3·50	65
556	6f.50 House martin	4·00	75
557	6f.50 Sedge warbler	4·00	75
558	6f.50 Fieldfare	4·00	75
559	6f.50 Golden oriole	4·00	75

(b) Air. Size 52×44 mm or 44×52 mm.

560	8f. As No. 536	5·50	90
561	8f. As No. 537	5·50	90
562	8f. As No. 538	5·50	90
563	8f. As No. 539	5·50	90
564	10f. As No. 540	6·75	1·00
565	10f. As No. 541	6·75	1·00
566	10f. As No. 542	6·75	1·00
567	10f. As No. 543	6·75	1·00
568	14f. As No. 544	7·50	1·10
569	14f. As No. 545	7·50	1·10
570	14f. As No. 546	7·50	1·10
571	14f. As No. 547	7·50	1·10
572	20f. Type **68**	8·00	1·30
573	20f. As No. 549	8·00	1·30

574	20f. As No. 550	8·00	1·30
575	20f. As No. 551	8·00	1·30
576	30f. As No. 552	9·50	1·40
577	30f. As No. 553	9·50	1·40
578	30f. As No. 554	9·50	1·40
579	30f. As No. 555	9·50	1·40
580	50f. As No. 556	13·50	1·90
581	50f. As No. 557	13·50	1·90
582	50f. As No. 558	13·50	1·90
583	50f. As No. 559	13·50	1·90

69 Library

1970. International Educational Year. Multicoloured.

584	3f. Type **69**	25	15
585	5f. Examination	40	20
586	7f. Experiments in the labora-tory	70	25
587	10f. Students with electron microscope	1·10	30

70 United Nations Building, New York

1970. Air. 25th Anniv of United Nations. Multicoloured.

588	7f. Type **70**	40	15
589	11f. Security Council in session	70	25
590	26f. Paul VI and U Thant	1·60	40
591	40f. U.N. and National flags	2·20	65
MS592	125×80 mm. As Nos. 590/1 but without "POSTE AERIENNE" inscr. Perf or imperf	6·00	5·75

71 Pres. Micombero and Wife

1970. Fourth Anniv of Republic. Multicoloured

593	4f. Type **71**	25	15
594	7f. Pres. Micombero and flag	55	25
595	11f. Revolution Memorial	80	40
MS596	125×142 mm. Nos. 593/5 (air). Perf or imperf	2·00	1·90

72 King Baudouin and Queen Fabiola

1970. Air. Visit of King and Queen of the Belgians. Each brown, purple and gold.

597	6f. Type **72**	1·40	40
598	20f. Pres. Micombero and King Baudouin	3·50	75
599	40f. Pres. Micombero in evening dress	6·75	1·40
MS600	143×117 mm. As Nos. 597/9 but with "POSTE AERIENNE" inscr omitted. Perf or imperf	13·50	12·50

73 *Adoration of the Magi* (Durer)

1970. Christmas. Multicoloured.

601	6f.50+1f. Type **73** (postage)	1·10	25
602	11f.+1f. *The Virgin of the Eucharist* (Botticelli)	1·40	40
603	20f.+1f. *The Holy Family* (El Greco)	1·60	50
604	14f.+3f. *The Adoration of the Magi* (Velasquez) (air)	1·10	40
605	26f.+1f. *The Holy Family* (Van Cleve)	1·60	65
606	40f.+3f. *Virgin and Child* (Van der Weyden)	2·75	90
MS607	Two sheets each 135×75 mm. (a) Nos. 601/3; (b) Nos. 604/6. Perf or imperf	11·00	10·00

74 *Lenin in Discussion*

1970. Birth Cent of Lenin. Each brown and gold.

608	3f.50 Type **74**	70	20
609	5f. Lenin addressing Soviet	80	25
610	6f.50 Lenin with soldier and sailor	1·10	40
611	15f. Lenin speaking to crowd	1·60	75
612	50f. Lenin	4·00	1·00

75 *Lion*

1971. African Animals (1st series). Multicoloured. (a) Postage. Size 38×38 mm.

613	1f. Type **75**	1·10	25
614	1f. African buffalo	1·10	25
615	1f. Hippopotamus	1·10	25
616	1f. Giraffe	1·10	25
617	2f. Topi	1·40	40
618	2f. Black rhinoceros	1·40	40
619	2f. Common zebra	1·40	40
620	2f. Leopard	1·40	40
621	3f. Grant's gazelle	1·60	50
622	3f. Cheetah	1·60	50
623	3f. African white-backed vultures	1·60	50
624	3f. Okapi	1·60	50
625	5f. Chimpanzee	2·00	65
626	5f. African elephant	2·00	65
627	5f. Spotted hyena	2·00	65
628	5f. Gemsbok	2·00	65
629	6f. Gorilla	2·30	75
630	6f. Blue wildebeest	2·30	75
631	6f. Warthog	2·30	75
632	6f. Hunting dog	2·30	75
633	11f. Sable antelope	3·00	90
634	11f. Caracal	3·00	90
635	11f. Ostriches	3·00	90
636	11f. Bongo	3·00	90

(b) Air. Size 44×44 mm.

637	10f. Type **75**	2·75	80
638	10f. As No. 614	2·75	80
639	10f. As No. 615	2·75	80
640	10f. As No. 616	2·75	80
641	14f. As No. 617	3·50	1·00
642	14f. As No. 618	3·50	1·00
643	14f. As No. 619	3·50	1·00
644	14f. As No. 620	3·50	1·00
645	17f. As No. 621	3·75	1·10
646	17f. As No. 622	3·75	1·10
647	17f. As No. 623	3·75	1·10
648	17f. As No. 624	3·75	1·10
649	24f. As No. 625	4·00	1·30
650	24f. As No. 626	4·00	1·30
651	24f. As No. 627	4·00	1·30

652	24f. As No. 628	4·00	1·30
653	26f. As No. 629	4·25	1·40
654	26f. As No. 630	4·25	1·40
655	26f. As No. 631	4·25	1·40
656	26f. As No. 632	4·25	1·40
657	31f. As No. 633	4·75	1·50
658	31f. As No. 634	4·75	1·50
659	31f. As No. 635	4·75	1·50
660	31f. As No. 635	4·75	1·50

See also Nos. 1028/75, 1178/1225 and 1385/97.

76 *The Resurrection* (Il Sodoma)

1971. Easter. Multicoloured.

661	3f. Type **76** (postage)	25	15
662	6f. *The Resurrection* (Del Castagno)	70	25
663	11f. *Noli Me Tangere* (Correggio)	1·40	40
664	14f. *The Resurrection* (Borrassa) (air)	1·60	25
665	17f. *The Resurrection* (Della Francesca)	2·20	40
666	26f. *The Resurrection* (Pleydenwurff)	4·00	50
MS667	Two sheets each 117×84 mm. (a) Nos. 661/3; (b) Nos. 664/6. Colours changed. Perf or imperf	11·50	10·50

1971. Air. United Nations Campaigns. Nos. 637/48 optd or surch. (a) Optd **LUTTE CONTRE LE RACISME ET LA DISCRIMINATION RACIALE** and Racial Equality Year emblem.

668	10f. multicoloured	1·90	40
669	10f. multicoloured	1·90	40
670	10f. multicoloured	1·90	40
671	10f. multicoloured	1·90	40

(b) Surch **LUTTE CONTRE L'ANALPHABETISME, UNESCO** emblem and premium (Campaign against Illiteracy).

672	14f.+2f. multicoloured	2·50	50
673	14f.+2f. multicoloured	2·50	50
674	14f.+2f. multicoloured	2·50	50
675	14f.+2f. multicoloured	2·50	50

(c) Surch **AIDE INTERNATIONALE AUX REFUGIES**, emblem and premium (Int Help for Refugees).

676	17f.+1f. multicoloured	3·00	65
677	17f.+1f. multicoloured	3·00	65
678	17f.+1f. multicoloured	3·00	65
679	17f.+1f. multicoloured	3·00	65

1971. Air. Olympic Commems. Nos. 653/56 surch. (a) Surch **75eme ANNIVERSAIRE DES JEUX OLYMPIQUES MODERNES (1896–1971)**, Olympic rings and premium.

680	26f.+1f. multicoloured	4·75	1·90
681	26f.+1f. multicoloured	4·75	1·90
682	26f.+1f. multicoloured	4·75	1·90
683	26f.+1f. multicoloured	4·75	1·90

(b) Surch **JEUX PRE-OLYMPIQUES MUNICH 1972**, rings and premium (Olympic Games, Munich (1972)).

684	31f.+1f. multicoloured	6·00	2·30
685	31f.+1f. multicoloured	6·00	2·30
686	31f.+1f. multicoloured	6·00	2·30
687	31f.+1f. multicoloured	6·00	2·30

79 *Venetian Girl*

1971. International Letter-writing Week. Paintings by Durer. Multicoloured.

688	6f. Type **79**	40	40
689	11f. *Jerome Holzschuhers*	55	50
690	14f. *Emperor Maximilian*	70	65
691	17f. *Altar painting, Paumgartner*	1·10	1·00
692	26f. *The Halle Madonna*	1·50	1·40
693	31f. *Self-portrait*	1·90	1·80
MS694	137×80 mm. As Nos. 692/3 (air). Perf or imperf	5·50	5·00

1971. Sixth Congress of International Institute of French Law, Bujumbura. Nos. 668/693 optd **VIeme CONGRES DE L'INSTITUT INTERNATIONAL DE DROIT D'EXPRESSION FRANCAISE.**

695	6f. multicoloured	40	15
696	11f. multicoloured	55	20
697	14f. multicoloured	70	25
698	17f. multicoloured	1·10	30
699	26f. multicoloured	1·50	40
700	31f. multicoloured	1·90	50
MS701	137×80 mm. No. MS**694**. Perf or imperf	4·00	3·75

81 *The Virgin and Child* (Il Perugino)

1971. Christmas. Paintings of Virgin and Child by following artists. Multicoloured.

702	3f. Type **81** (postage)	15	15
703	5f. Del Sarto	40	20
704	6f. Morales	55	25
705	14f. Da Conegliano (air)	1·10	40
706	17f. Lippi	1·60	40
707	31f. Leonardo da Vinci	2·75	90
MS708	Two sheets each 125×80 mm. (a) Nos. 702/4; (b) Nos. 705/7	7·50	7·00

1971. 25th Anniv of UNICEF. Nos. 702/7 surch **UNICEF XXVe ANNIVERSAIRE 1946–1971**, emblem and premium.

709	3f.+1f. mult (postage)	55	25
710	5f.+1f. multicoloured	80	40
711	6f.+1f. multicoloured	95	45
712	14f.+1f. mult (air)	1·10	50
713	17f.+1f. multicoloured	1·60	65
714	31f.+1f. multicoloured	2·40	75
MS715	Two sheets each 125×80 mm. No. MS**708** surch with 2f. premium on each stamp in the sheets	8·00	7·50

83 *Archangel Michael* (icon, St. Mark's)

1971. UNESCO "Save Venice" Campaign. Multicoloured.

716	3f.+1f. Type **83** (postage)	40	15
717	5f.+1f. *La Polenta* (Longhi)	55	25
718	6f.+1f. *Gossip* (Longhi)	70	30
719	11f.+1f. *Diana's Bath* (Pittoni)	1·10	45
720	10f.+1f. *Casa d'Oro* (air)	95	40
721	17f.+1f. *Doge's Palace*	1·60	50
722	24f.+1f. *St. John and St. Paul Church*	2·40	65
723	31f.+1f. *Doge's Palace and Piazzetta* (Canaletto)	3·25	75
MS724	Two sheets each 115×132 mm. (a) Nos. 716/19; (b) Nos. 720/3. Each design in sheet has a 2f. premium. Perf or imperf	13·50	12·50

84 *"Lunar Orbiter"*

1972. Conquest of Space. Multicoloured.

725	6f. Type **84**	25	15
726	11f. "Vostok" spaceship	70	25
727	14f. "Luna 1"	95	40
728	17f. First Man on Moon	1·10	50
729	26f. "Soyuz 11" space flight	1·80	65
730	40f. "Lunar Rover"	2·75	1·30
MS731	135×135 mm. Nos. 725/30 with additional inscr (air)	9·50	8·75

85 *Slalom skiing*

1972. Winter Olympic Games, Sapporo, Japan. Multicoloured.

732	5f. Type **85**	25	15
733	6f. Pair skating	40	15
734	11f. Figure-skating	55	20
735	14f. Ski-jumping	70	25
736	17f. Ice-hockey	80	30
737	24f. Speed skating	1·10	40
738	26f. Ski-bobbing	1·20	45
739	31f. Downhill skiing	1·40	50
740	50f. Bobsleighing	2·40	75
MS741	107×127 mm. As Nos. 738/40. Perf or imperf (air)	9·50	8·75

86 *Ecce Homo* (Metzys)

1972. Easter. Paintings. Multicoloured.

742	3f.50 Type **86**	25	15
743	6f.50 *The Crucifixion* (Rubens)	70	25
744	10f. *The Descent from the Cross* (Portormo)	95	30
745	18f. *Pieta* (Gallegos)	1·90	40
746	27f. *The Trinity* (El Greco)	2·40	65
MS747	111×160 mm. Nos. 742/6. Perf or imperf	8·75	8·25

87 *Gymnastics*

1972. Olympic Games, Munich. Multicoloured.

748	5f. Type **87** (postage)	25	15
749	6f. Throwing the javelin	40	20
750	11f. Fencing	80	25
751	14f. Cycling	1·10	40
752	17f. Pole-vaulting	1·40	50
753	24f. Weightlifting (air)	1·90	65
754	26f. Hurdling	2·00	70
755	31f. Throwing the discus	2·40	80
756	40f. Football	3·25	1·30
MS757	123×75 mm. Nos. 755/6 without "POSTE AERIENNE" inscr	6·00	5·75

88 *Prince Rwagasore, Pres. Micombero and Drummers*

1972. Tenth Anniv of Independence. Multicoloured.

758	5f. Type **88** (postage)	25	15
759	7f. Rwagasore, Micombero and map	40	20
760	13f. Pres. Micombero and Burundi flag	80	25
761	15f. Type **65** (air)	70	40
762	18f. As 7f.	80	50
763	27f. As 13f.	1·40	65
MS764	Two sheets each 147×80 mm. (a) Nos. 758/60; (b) Nos. 761/3	6·00	5·75

1972. Christmas. Madonna and Child paintings by artists given below. Multicoloured.

765	5f. Type **89** (postage)	40	15
766	10f. Raphael	70	25
767	15f. Botticelli	1·10	40

768	18f. S. Mainardi (air)	1·60	50
769	27f. H. Memling	2·00	65
770	40f. Lotto	3·00	1·00
MS771	Two sheets each 128×82 mm. (a) Nos. 765/7; (b) Nos. 768/70	9·50	8·75

90 *Platycoryne crocea*

1972. Orchids. Multicoloured.

772	50c. Type **90** (postage)	40	15
773	1f. *Cattleya trianaei*	55	15
774	2f. *Eulophia cucullata*	70	20
775	3f. *Cymbidium hamsey*	80	20
776	4f. *Thelymitra pauciflora*	95	20
777	5f. *Miltassia*	1·10	25
778	6f. *Miltonia*	1·40	25
779	7f. Type **90**	1·60	25
780	8f. As 1f.	2·00	30
781	9f. As 2f.	2·40	40
782	10f. As 3f.	2·75	45
783	13f. As 4f. (air)	3·00	50
784	14f. As 5f.	3·25	55
785	15f. As 6f.	3·50	65
786	18f. Type **90**	3·75	70
787	20f. As 1f.	4·00	75
788	5f. As 2f.	5·50	1·10
789	36f. As 3f.	6·00	1·50

Nos. 779/89 are size 53×53 mm.

1972. Christmas Charity. Nos. 765/770 surch.

790	5f.+1f. mult (postage)	40	15
791	10f.+1f. multicoloured	80	30
792	15f.+1f. multicoloured	1·20	50
793	18f.+1f. multicoloured (air)	1·60	65
794	27f.+1f. multicoloured	2·50	90
795	40f.+1f. multicoloured	3·50	1·30
MS796	Two sheets as **MS**771 with 2f. premium surch on each stamp	11·50	10·50

92 *H. M. Stanley*

1973. Centenary of Stanley/Livingstone African Exploration. Multicoloured.

797	5f. Type **92** (postage)	55	15
798	7f. Expedition bearers	80	25
799	13f. Stanley directing foray	1·00	40
800	15f. Dr. Livingstone (air)	1·10	50
801	18f. Stanley meets Livingstone	1·40	65
802	27f. Stanley conferring with Livingstone	2·00	90
MS803	100×141 mm. Nos. 800/2. Perf or imperf	5·50	5·00

93 *The Scourging (Caravaggio)*

1973. Easter. Multicoloured.

804	5f. Type **93** (postage)	25	15
805	7f. *Crucifixion* (Van der Weyden)	55	25
806	13f. *The Deposition* (Raphael)	1·10	40
807	15f. *Christ bound to the Pillar* (Guido Reni) (air)	1·60	50
808	18f. *Crucifixion* (M. Grunewald)	1·90	65
809	27f. *The Descent from the Cross* (Caravaggio)	2·75	1·00
MS810	Two sheets each 121×74 mm. (a) Nos. 804/6; (b) Nos. 807/9	11·50	10·50

94 *Interpol Emblem*

1973. 50th Anniv of Interpol. Multicoloured.

811	5f. Type **94** (postage)	25	15
812	10f. Burundi flag	55	15
813	18f. Interpol H.Q., Paris	95	20
814	27f. As 5f. (air)	1·90	35
815	40f. As 10f.	2·40	45

95 *Capricorn, Aquarius and Pisces*

1973. 500th Birth Anniv of Copernicus.

816	**95** 3f. gold, red and black (postage)	40	10
817	– 3f. gold, red and black	40	10
818	– 3f. gold, red and black	40	10
819	– 3f. gold, red and black	40	10
820	– 5f. multicoloured	70	15
821	– 5f. multicoloured	70	15
822	– 5f. multicoloured	70	15
823	– 5f. multicoloured	70	15
824	– 7f. multicoloured	95	20
825	– 7f. multicoloured	95	20
826	– 7f. multicoloured	95	20
827	– 7f. multicoloured	95	20
828	– 13f. multicoloured	1·20	25
829	– 13f. multicoloured	1·20	25
830	– 13f. multicoloured	1·20	25
831	– 13f. multicoloured	1·20	25
832	– 15f. multicoloured (air)	1·40	25
833	– 15f. multicoloured	1·40	25
834	– 15f. multicoloured	1·40	25
835	– 15f. multicoloured	1·40	25
836	– 18f. multicoloured	1·60	30
837	– 18f. multicoloured	1·60	30
838	– 18f. multicoloured	1·60	30
839	– 18f. multicoloured	1·60	30
840	– 27f. multicoloured	2·40	45
841	– 27f. multicoloured	2·40	45
842	– 27f. multicoloured	2·40	45
843	– 27f. multicoloured	2·40	45
844	– 36f. multicoloured	3·25	60
845	– 36f. multicoloured	3·25	60
846	– 36f. multicoloured	3·25	60
847	– 36f. multicoloured	3·25	60
MS848	Two sheets each 137×147 mm. (a) Nos. 816/31; (b) Nos. 832/47	55·00	35·00

DESIGNS: No. 816, Type **95**; 817, Aries, Taurus and Gemini; 818, Cancer, Leo and Virgo; 819, Libra, Scorpio and Sagittarius; 820/23, Greek and Roman Gods; 824/7, Ptolemy and Ptolemaic System; 828/31, Copernicus and Solar System; 823/5, Copernicus, Earth, Pluto and Jupiter; 836/39, Copernicus, Venus, Saturn and Mars; 840/43, Copernicus, Uranus, Neptune and Mercury; 844/7, Earth and spacecraft.

The four designs of each value were issued se-tenant in blocks of four within the sheet, forming composite designs.

96 *Protea cynaroides*

1973. Flora and Butterflies. Multicoloured.

849	1f. Type **96** (postage)	40	10
850	1f. *Precis octavia*	40	10
851	1f. *Epiphora bauhiniae*	40	10
852	1f. *Gazania longiscapa*	40	10
853	2f. *Kniphofia* – "Royal Standard"	80	10
854	2f. *Cymothoe coccinata hew*	80	10
855	2f. *"Nudaurelia zambesina*	80	10
856	2f. *Freesia refracta*	80	10
857	3f. *Calotis eupompe*	1·20	20
858	3f. *Narcissus*	1·20	20
859	3f. *Cineraria hybrida*	1·20	20
860	3f. *Cyrestis camillus*	1·20	20
861	5f. *Iris tingitana*	2·00	30
862	5f. *Papilio demodocus*	2·00	30
863	5f. *Catopsilia avelaneda*	2·00	30
864	5f. *Nerine sarniensis*	2·00	30
865	6f. *Hypolimnas dexithea*	2·40	35
866	6f. *Zantedeschia tropicalis*	2·40	35
867	6f. *Sandersonia aurantiaca*	2·40	35
868	6f. *Drurya antimachus*	2·40	35
869	11f. *Nymphaea capensis*	3·50	50
870	11f. *Pandoriana pandora*	3·50	50
871	11f. *Precis orythia*	3·50	50
872	11f. *Pelargonium domesticum–"Aztec"*	3·50	50

873	10f. Type **96** (air)	3·00	45
874	10f. As No. 850	3·00	45
875	10f. As No. 851	3·00	45
876	10f. As No. 852	3·00	45
877	14f. As No. 853	3·75	55
878	14f. As No. 854	3·75	55
879	14f. As No. 855	3·75	55
880	14f. As No. 856	3·75	55
881	17f. As No. 857	4·25	65
882	17f. As No. 858	4·25	65
883	17f. As No. 859	4·25	65
884	17f. As No. 860	4·25	65
885	24f. As No. 861	4·75	70
886	24f. As No. 862	4·75	70
887	24f. As No. 863	4·75	70
888	24f. As No. 864	4·75	70
889	26f. As No. 865	5·00	75
890	26f. As No. 866	5·00	75
891	26f. As No. 867	5·00	75
892	26f. As No. 868	5·00	75
893	31f. As No. 869	5·75	85
894	31f. As No. 870	5·75	85
895	31f. As No. 871	5·75	85
896	31f. As No. 872	5·75	85

Nos. 849, 852/3, 856, 858/9, 861, 864, 866/7, 869, 872, 876/7, 880, 882/3, 885, 888, 890/1, 893 and 896 depict flora and the remainder butterflies.

The four designs of each value were issued se-tenant in blocks of four within the sheet, forming composite designs.

97 *Virgin and Child (G. Bellini)*

1973. Christmas. Various paintings of the Virgin and Child by artists listed below. Multicoloured.

897	5f. Type **97** (postage)	70	15
898	10f. Van Eyck	1·10	25
899	15f. G. A. Boltraffio	1·60	35
900	18f. Raphael (air)	1·10	25
901	27f. P. Perugino	2·00	45
902	40f. Titian	3·00	65
MS903	Two sheets each 144×78 mm. (a) Nos. 897/9; (b) Nos. 900/2	11·50	5·50

1973. Christmas Charity. Nos. 897/902 surch.

904	**97** 5f.+1f. mult (postage)	1·10	25
905	– 10f.+1f. multicoloured	1·40	30
906	– 15f.+1f. multicoloured	1·60	35
907	– 18f.+1f. mult (air)	1·40	30
908	– 27f.+1f. multicoloured	2·00	45
909	– 40f.+1f. multicoloured	2·75	60
MS910	Two sheets as **MS**903 with 2f. premium surch on each stamp	12·00	5·75

98 *The Pieta (Veronese)*

1974. Easter. Religious Paintings. Multicoloured.

911	5f. Type **98**	40	10
912	10f. *The Virgin and St. John* (Van der Weyden)	55	10
913	18f. *The Crucifixion* (Van der Weyden)	1·50	35
914	27f. *The Entombment* (Titian)	2·30	50
915	40f. *The Pieta* (El Greco)	3·50	75
MS916	145×120 mm. Nos. 911/15	8·75	6·00

99 *Egyptian Mouthbrooder (Haplochromis multicolor)*

1974. Fish. Multicoloured.

917	1f. Type **99** (postage)	1·10	25
918	1f. Spotted mouthbrooder (*Tropheus duboisi*)	1·10	25

919	1f. Freshwater butterfly-fish (*Pantodon buchholzi*)	1·10	25
920	1f. Six-banded distichodus (*Distichodus sexfasciatus*)	1·10	25
921	2f. Rainbow krib (*Pelmatochromis kribensis*)	1·40	30
922	2f. African leaf-fish (*Polycentropsis abbreviata*)	1·40	30
923	2f. Three-lined tetra (*Nannaethiops tritaeniatus*)	1·40	30
924	2f. Jewel cichlid (*Hemichromis bimaculatus*)	1·40	30
925	3f. Spotted climbing-perch (*Ctenopoma acutirostre*)	1·50	35
926	3f. African mouthbrooder (*Tilapia melanopleura*)	1·50	35
927	3f. Angel squeaker (*Synodontis angelicus*)	1·50	35
928	3f. Two-striped lyretail (*Aphyosemion bivittatum*)	1·50	35
929	5f. Diamond fingerfish (*Monodactylus argenteus*)	2·30	50
930	5f. Regal angelfish (*Pygoplites diacanthus*)	2·30	50
931	5f. Moorish idol (*Zanclus canescens*)	2·30	50
932	5f. Peacock hind (*Cephalopholis argus*) and surgeonfish	2·30	50
933	6f. Bigeye (*Priacanthus arenatus*)	2·75	60
934	6f. Rainbow parrotfish (*Scarus guacamaia*) and French angelfish	2·75	60
935	6f. French angelfish (*Pomacanthus arcuatus*)	2·75	60
936	6f. John dory (*Zeus faber*)	2·75	60
937	11f. Scribbled cowfish (*Lactophrys quadricornis*)	5·50	1·20
938	11f. Ocean surgeonfish (*Acanthurus bahianus*)	5·50	1·20
939	11f. Queen triggerfish (*Balistes vetula*)	5·50	1·20
940	11f. Queen angelfish (*Holocanthus ciliaris*)	5·50	1·20
941	10f. Type **99** (air)	2·40	55
942	10f. As No. 918	2·40	55
943	10f. As No. 919	2·40	55
944	10f. As No. 920	2·40	55
945	14f. As No. 921	3·00	65
946	14f. As No. 922	3·00	65
947	14f. As No. 923	3·00	65
948	14f. As No. 924	3·00	65
949	17f. As No. 925	3·50	75
950	17f. As No. 926	3·50	75
951	17f. As No. 927	3·50	75
952	17f. As No. 928	3·50	75
953	24f. As No. 929	4·00	90
954	24f. As No. 930	4·00	90
955	24f. As No. 931	4·00	90
956	24f. As No. 932	4·00	90
957	26f. As No. 933	4·75	1·10
958	26f. As No. 934	4·75	1·10
959	26f. As No. 935	4·75	1·10
960	26f. As No. 936	4·75	1·10
961	31f. As No. 937	6·00	1·40
962	31f. As No. 938	6·00	1·40
963	31f. As No. 939	6·00	1·40
964	31f. As No. 940	6·00	1·40

The four designs of each value are arranged together in se-tenant blocks of four within the sheet, forming composite designs.

100 *Footballers and World Cup Trophy*

1974. World Cup Football Championships.

965	**100** 5f. mult (postage)	40	10
966	– 6f. multicoloured	55	10
967	– 11f. multicoloured	95	20
968	– 14f. multicoloured	1·10	25
969	– 17f. multicoloured	1·40	30
970	– 20f. multicoloured (air)	1·60	35
971	– 26f. multicoloured	2·00	45
972	– 40f. multicoloured	3·00	65
MS973	88×142 mm. As Nos. 970/2 but without airmail inscriptions	7·50	4·50

DESIGNS: Nos. 966/72, Football scenes as Type **100**.

101 *Burundi Flag*

1974. Centenary of UPU. Multicoloured.

974	6f. Type **101** (postage)	70	10
975	6f. Burundi P.T.T. Building	70	10

976	11f. Postmen carrying letters	1·10	15
977	11f. Postmen carrying letters	1·10	15
978	14f. UPU Monument	1·40	20
979	14f. Mail transport	1·40	20
980	17f. Burundi on map	1·80	25
981	17f. Dove and letter	1·80	25
982	24f. Type **101** (air)	2·20	30
983	24f. As No. 975	2·20	30
984	26f. As No. 976	2·40	35
985	26f. As No. 977	2·40	35
986	31f. As No. 978	2·75	40
987	31f. As No. 979	2·75	40
988	40f. As No. 980	4·00	50
989	40f. As No. 981	8·25	1·30
MS990	Two sheets each 96×164 mm.		
	(a) Nos. 974/81; (b) Nos. 982/9	60·00	55·00

The two designs in each denomination were arranged together in *se-tenant* pairs within the sheet, each pair forming a composite design.

102 *St. Ildefonse writing a letter (El Greco)*

1974. International Letter-writing Week. Multicoloured.

991	6f. Type **102**	55	15
992	11f. *Lady sealing a letter* (Chardin)	95	25
993	14f. *Titus at desk* (Rembrandt)	1·10	40
994	17f. *The Love-letter* (Vermeer)	1·40	45
995	26f. *The Merchant G. Gisze* (Holbein)	1·60	60
996	31f. *A. Lenoir* (David)	2·00	70
MS997	95×105 mm. Nos. 955/6	5·50	3·50

103 *Virgin and Child (Van Orley)*

1974. Christmas. Showing Virgin and Child paintings by artists named. Multicoloured.

998	5f. Type **103** (postage)	70	10
999	10f. Hans Memling	1·10	15
1000	15f. Botticelli	1·40	20
1001	18f. Hans Memling (different) (air)	1·60	25
1002	27f. F. Lippi	2·20	30
1003	40f. L. di Gredi	3·25	50
MS1004	Two sheets each 126×89 mm.		
	(a) Nos. 998/1000; (b) Nos. 1001/3	13·50	5·75

1974. Christmas Charity. Nos. 998/1003 surch.

1005	**103** 5f.+1f. mult (postage)	70	10
1006	- 10f.+1f. multicoloured	1·10	15
1007	- 15f.+1f. multicoloured	1·40	20
1008	- 18f.+1f. mult (air)	1·60	25
1009	- 27f.+1f. multicoloured	2·20	30
1010	- 40f.+1f. multicoloured	3·25	50
MS1011	Two sheets as **MS**1004 with 2f. premium on each stamp	13·50	5·75

104 *"Apollo" Spacecraft with Docking Tunnel*

1975. "Apollo–Soyuz" Space Project. Multicoloured.

1012	26f. Type **104** (postage)	1·10	55
1013	26f. Leonov and Kubasov	1·10	55
1014	26f. "Soyuz" Spacecraft	1·10	55
1015	26f. Slayton, Brand and Stafford	1·10	55
1016	31f. "Soyuz" launch	1·50	65
1017	31f. "Apollo" and "Soyuz" spacecraft	1·50	65
1018	31f. "Apollo" third stage separation	1·50	65

1019	31f. Slayton, Brand, Stafford, Leonov and Kubasov	1·50	65
1020	27f. Type **104** (air)	1·10	55
1021	27f. As No. 1012	1·10	55
1022	27f. As No. 1013	1·10	55
1023	27f. As No. 1014	1·10	55
1024	40f. As No. 1015	1·80	70
1025	40f. As No. 1016	1·80	70
1026	40f. As No. 1017	1·80	70
1027	40f. As No. 1018	1·80	70

The four designs in each value were issued together in *se-tenant* blocks of four within the sheet.

105 *Addax*

1975. African Animals (2nd series). Multicoloured.

1028	1f. Type **105** (postage)	55	10
1029	1f. Roan antelope	55	10
1030	1f. Nyala	55	10
1031	1f. White rhinoceros	55	10
1032	2f. Mandrill	80	15
1033	2f. Eland	80	15
1034	2f. Salt's dik-dik	80	15
1035	2f. Thomson's gazelles	80	15
1036	3f. African claw-less otter	1·40	20
1037	3f. Bohar reedbuck	1·40	20
1038	3f. African civet	1·40	20
1039	3f. African buffalo	1·40	20
1040	5f. Black wildebeest	2·00	25
1041	5f. African asses	2·00	25
1042	5f. Angolan black and white colobus	2·00	25
1043	6f. Gerenuk	2·00	25
1044	6f. Addra gazelle	2·20	25
1045	6f. Black-backed jackal	2·20	25
1046	6f. Sitatungas	2·20	25
1047	6f. Banded duiker	2·20	25
1048	11f. Fennec fox	2·75	30
1049	11f. Lesser kudus	2·75	30
1050	11f. Blesbok	2·75	30
1051	11f. Serval	2·75	30
1052	10f. Type **105** (air)	1·80	20
1053	10f. As No. 1029	1·80	20
1054	10f. As No. 1030	1·80	20
1055	10f. As No. 1031	1·80	20
1056	14f. As No. 1032	2·00	25
1057	14f. As No. 1033	2·00	25
1058	14f. As No. 1034	2·00	25
1059	14f. As No. 1035	2·00	25
1060	17f. As No. 1036	2·40	30
1061	17f. As No. 1037	2·40	30
1062	17f. As No. 1038	2·40	30
1063	17f. As No. 1039	2·40	30
1064	24f. As No. 1040	3·25	40
1065	24f. As No. 1041	3·25	40
1066	24f. As No. 1042	3·25	40
1067	24f. As No. 1043	3·25	40
1068	26f. As No. 1044	3·50	45
1069	26f. As No. 1045	3·50	45
1070	26f. As No. 1046	3·50	45
1071	26f. As No. 1047	3·50	45
1072	31f. As No. 1048	4·00	60
1073	31f. As No. 1049	4·00	60
1074	31f. As No. 1050	4·00	60
1075	31f. As No. 1051	4·00	60

The four designs in each value were issued together in horiz. *se-tenant* strips within the sheet, forming composite designs.

1975. Air. International Women's Year. Nos. 1052/9 optd **ANNEE INTERNATIONALE DE LA FEMME**.

1076	**105** 10f. multicoloured	2·00	55
1077	- 10f. multicoloured	2·00	55
1078	- 10f. multicoloured	2·00	55
1079	- 10f. multicoloured	2·00	55
1080	- 14f. multicoloured	2·75	70
1081	- 14f. multicoloured	2·75	70
1082	- 14f. multicoloured	2·75	70
1083	- 14f. multicoloured	2·75	70

1975. Air. 30th Anniv of United Nations. Nos. 1068/75 optd **30eme ANNIVERSAIRE DES NATIONS UNIES**.

1084	26f. multicoloured	3·75	1·40
1085	26f. multicoloured	3·75	1·40
1086	26f. multicoloured	3·75	1·40
1087	26f. multicoloured	3·75	1·40
1088	31f. multicoloured	4·75	1·80
1089	31f. multicoloured	4·75	1·80
1090	31f. multicoloured	4·75	1·80
1091	31f. multicoloured	4·75	1·80

108 *Jonah*

1975. Christmas. 500th Birth Anniv of Michaelangelo. Multicoloured.

1092	5f. Type **108** (postage)	1·10	20
1093	5f. "Libyan Sibyl"	1·10	20
1094	13f. "Daniel"	2·00	35
1095	13f. "Cumaean Sybil"	2·00	35
1096	27f. "Isaiah"	3·50	70
1097	27f. "Delphic Sybil" (different)	3·50	70
1098	18f. "Zachariah" (air)	2·75	35
1099	18f. "Joel"	2·75	35
1100	31f. "Erythraean Sibyl"	3·75	80
1101	31f. "Ezekiel"	3·75	80
1102	40f. "Persian Sybil"	5·50	1·10
1103	40f. "Jeremiah"	5·50	1·10
MS1104	Two sheets each 138×111 mm.		
	(a) Nos. 1092/7; (b) Nos. 1098/1103	38·00	28·00

1975. Christmas Charity. Nos. 1092/1103 surch +1f.

1105	**108** 5f.+1f. mult (postage)	1·10	20
1106	- 5f.+1f. multicoloured	1·10	20
1107	- 13f.+1f. multicoloured	2·00	35
1108	- 13f.+1f. multicoloured	2·00	35
1109	- 27f.+1f. multicoloured	3·50	70
1110	- 27f.+1f. multicoloured	3·50	70
1111	- 18f.+1f. mult (air)	2·75	35
1112	- 18f.+1f. multicoloured	2·75	35
1113	- 31f.+1f. multicoloured	3·75	80
1114	- 31f.+1f. multicoloured	3·75	80
1115	- 40f.+1f. multicoloured	5·50	1·10
1116	- 40f.+1f. multicoloured	5·50	1·10
MS1117	Two sheets as **MS**1104 with 2f. premium on each stamp	38·00	28·00

110 *Speed Skating*

1976. Winter Olympic Games, Innsbruck. Mult.

1118	17f. Type **110** (postage)	1·10	30
1119	24f. Figure-skating	1·50	40
1120	26f. Two-man bobsleigh	1·60	40
1121	31f. Cross-country skiing	2·00	55
1122	18f. Ski-jumping (air)	1·40	35
1123	36f. Skiing (slalom)	2·75	70
1124	50f. Ice-hockey	3·50	90
MS1125	Two sheets (a) 101×101 mm. Nos. 1118/21; (b) 131×131 mm. Nos. 1122/4	16·00	11·50

111 *Basketball*

1976. Olympic Games, Montreal. Multicoloured.

1126	14f. Type **111** (postage)	1·10	40
1127	14f. Pole-vaulting	1·10	40
1128	17f. Running	1·40	50
1129	17f. Football	1·40	50
1130	28f. As No. 1127	1·60	80
1131	28f. As No. 1128	1·60	80
1132	40f. As No. 1129	2·00	1·20
1133	40f. Type **111**	2·00	1·20
1134	27f. Hurdling (air)	1·50	75
1135	27f. High-jumping (horiz)	1·50	75
1136	31f. Gymnastics (horiz)	2·00	1·00
1137	31f. As No. 1134 (horiz)	2·00	1·00
1138	50f. As No. 1135 (horiz)	4·00	1·70
1139	50f. As No. 1136 (horiz)	4·00	1·70
MS1140	Two sheets. (a) 115×120 mm. 14f. Pole vault; 17f. Football; 28f. Basketball; 40f. Running (postage). (b) 99×120 mm. 27f. Gymnastics; 31f. High jump; 50f. Hurdles (air)	27·00	19·00

112 *Battle of Bunker Hill* (detail, John Trumbull)

1976. Air. Bicent of American Revolution. Multicoloured.

1141	18f. Type **112**	1·40	20
1142	18f. As Type **112**	1·40	20
1143	26f. Franklin, Jefferson and John Adams	2·00	35
1144	26f. As No. 1143	2·00	35
1145	36f. *Signing of Declaration of Independence* (Trumbull)	2·75	70
1146	36f. As No. 1145	2·75	70
MS1147	101×148 mm. Nos. 1141/6	13·50	9·75

The two designs of each value form composite pictures. Type **112** is the left-hand portion of the painting.

113 *Virgin and Child (Dirk Bouts)*

1976. Christmas. Multicoloured.

1148	5f. Type **113** (postage)	80	20
1149	13f. *Virgin of the Trees* (Bellini)	1·40	35
1150	27f. *Virgin and Child* (C. Crivelli)	2·40	65
1151	18f. *Virgin and Child* with St. Anne (Leonardo) (air)	2·00	55
1152	31f. *Holy Family with Lamb* (Raphael)	3·00	75
1153	40f. *Virgin with Basket* (Correggio)	4·00	1·10
MS1154	Two sheets each 122×80 mm. (a) Nos. 1148/50; (b) Nos. 1151/3	15·00	11·00

1976. Christmas Charity. Nos. 1148/53 surch +**1F**.

1155	**113** 5f.+1f. mult (postage)	80	20
1156	- 13f.+1f. multicoloured	1·40	35
1157	- 27f.+1f. multicoloured	2·40	65
1158	- 18f.+1f. mult (air)	2·00	55
1159	- 31f.+1f. multicoloured	3·00	75
1160	- 40f.+1f. multicoloured	4·00	1·10
MS1161	Two sheets as **MS**1154 with 2f. premium on each stamp	15·00	11·00

115 *The Ascent of Calvary* (Rubens)

1977. Easter. 400th Birth Anniv of Peter Paul Rubens. Multicoloured.

1162	10f. Type **115**	1·40	50
1163	21f. *Christ Crucified*	3·00	1·00
1164	27f. *The Descent from the Cross*	3·25	1·10
1165	35f. *The Deposition*	4·25	1·40
MS1166	111×85 mm. As Nos. 1162/5 (air)	12·00	9·50

116 *Alexander Graham Bell*

1977. Telephone Centenary and World Telecommunications Day. Multicoloured.

1167	10f. Type **116** (postage)	60	20
1168	10f. Satellite, Globe and telephones	60	20
1169	17f. Switchboard operator and wall telephone	1·30	40
1170	17f. Satellite transmitting to Earth	1·30	40
1171	26f. A. G. Bell and first telephone	1·80	55
1172	26f. Satellites circling Globe, and videophone	1·80	55
1173	18f. Type **116** (air)	1·40	40

1174	18f. As No. 1172	1·40	40
1175	36f. As No. 1169	2·40	70
1176	36f. As No. 1168	2·40	70

MS1177 120×135 mm. 10f. As No. 1171; 17f. Type **116**; 26f. As No. 1168; 18f. As No. 1170; 36f. As No. 1172 9·00 7·00

117 Kobs

1977. African Animals (3rd series). Multicoloured.

1178	2f. Type **117** (postage)	50	15
1179	2f. Marabou storks	50	15
1180	2f. Blue wildebeest	50	15
1181	2f. Bush pig	50	15
1182	5f. Grevy's zebras	85	25
1183	5f. Whale-headed stork	85	25
1184	5f. Striped hyenas	85	25
1185	5f. Pygmy chimpanzee	85	25
1186	8f. Greater flamingoes	1·20	35
1187	8f. Nile crocodiles	1·20	35
1188	8f. Green tree snake	1·20	35
1189	8f. Greater kudus	1·20	35
1190	11f. Large-toothed rock hyrax	1·60	45
1191	11f. Cobra	1·60	45
1192	11f. Golden jackals	1·60	45
1193	11f. Verreaux eagles	1·60	45
1194	21f. Ratel	3·00	90
1195	21f. Bushbuck	3·00	90
1196	21f. Secretary bird	3·00	90
1197	21f. Klipspringer	3·00	90
1198	27f. Bat-eared fox	3·50	1·10
1199	27f. African elephants	3·50	1·10
1200	27f. Vulturine guineafowl	3·50	1·10
1201	27f. Impalas	3·50	1·10
1202	9f. Type **117** (air)	90	25
1203	9f. As No. 1179	90	25
1204	9f. As No. 1180	90	25
1205	9f. As No. 1181	90	25
1206	13f. As No. 1182	1·70	50
1207	13f. As No. 1183	1·70	50
1208	13f. As No. 1184	1·70	50
1209	13f. As No. 1185	1·70	50
1210	30f. As No. 1186	4·00	1·10
1211	30f. As No. 1187	4·00	1·10
1212	30f. As No. 1188	4·00	1·10
1213	30f. As No. 1189	4·00	1·10
1214	35f. As No. 1190	4·25	1·20
1215	35f. As No. 1191	4·25	1·20
1216	35f. As No. 1192	4·25	1·20
1217	35f. As No. 1193	4·25	1·20
1218	54f. As No. 1194	5·50	1·60
1219	54f. As No. 1195	5·50	1·60
1220	54f. As No. 1196	5·50	1·60
1221	54f. As No. 1197	5·50	1·60
1222	70f. As No. 1198	7·75	2·30
1223	70f. As No. 1199	7·75	2·30
1224	70f. As No. 1200	7·75	2·30
1225	70f. As No. 1201	7·75	2·30

The four designs in each value were issued together *se-tenant* in horizontal strips within the sheet, forming composite designs.

118 *The Man of Iron* (Grimm)

1977. Fairy Tales. Multicoloured.

1226	5f. Type **118**	1·80	45
1227	5f. *Snow White and Rose Red* (Grimm)	1·80	45
1228	5f. *The Goose Girl* (Grimm)	1·80	45
1229	5f. *The Two Wanderers* (Grimm)	1·80	45
1230	11f. *The Hermit and the Bear* (Aesop)	3·75	95
1231	11f. *The Fox and the Stork* (Aesop)	3·75	95
1232	11f. *The Litigious Cats* (Aesop)	3·75	95
1233	11f. *The Blind and the Lame* (Aesop)	3·75	95
1234	14f. *The Ice Maiden* (Andersen)	4·25	1·10
1235	14f. *The Old House* (Andersen)	4·25	1·10
1236	14f. *The Princess and the Pea* (Andersen)	4·25	1·10
1237	14f. *The Elder Tree Mother* (Andersen)	4·25	1·10
1238	17f. *Hen with the Golden Egg* (La Fontaine)	4·75	1·20
1239	17f. *The Wolf Turned Shepherd* (La Fontaine)	4·75	1·20
1240	17f. *The Oyster and Litigants* (La Fontaine)	4·75	1·20
1241	17f. *The Wolf and the Lamb* (La Fontaine)	4·75	1·20
1242	26f. *Jack and the Beanstalk* (traditional)	7·25	1·80
1243	26f. *Alice in Wonderland* (Lewis Carroll)	7·25	1·80
1244	26f. *Three Heads in the Well* (traditional)	7·25	1·80
1245	26f. *Tales of Mother Goose* (traditional)	7·25	1·80

119 UN General Assembly and UN 3c. Stamp, 1954

1977. 25th Anniv of United Nations Postal Administration. Multicoloured.

1246	8f. Type **119** (postage)	1·20	30
1247	8f. UN 4c. stamp, 1957	1·20	30
1248	8f. UN 3c. stamp, 1954 (FAO)	1·20	30
1249	8f. UN 1½c. stamp, 1951	1·20	30
1250	10f. Security Council and UN 8c. red, 1954	1·80	45
1251	10f. UN 8c. green, 1956	1·80	45
1252	10f. UN 8c. black, 1955	1·80	45
1253	10f. UN 7c. stamp, 1959	1·80	45
1254	21f. Meeting hall and UN 3c. grey, 1956	3·00	75
1255	21f. UN 8c. stamp, 1956	3·00	75
1256	21f. UN 3c. brown, 1953	3·00	75
1257	21f. UN 3c. green, 1952	3·00	75
1258	24f. Building by night and UN 4c. red, 1957 (air)	3·25	85
1259	24f. UN 8c. brn & grn, 1960	3·25	85
1260	24f. UN 8c. green, 1955	3·25	85
1261	24f. UN 8c. red, 1955	3·25	85
1262	27f. Aerial view of UN 8c. red, 1957	3·50	90
1263	27f. UN 3c. stamp, 1953	3·50	90
1264	27f. UN 8c. green, 1954	3·50	90
1265	27f. UN 8c. brown, 1956	3·50	90
1266	35f. UN Building by day and UN 5c. stamp, 1959	4·75	1·20
1267	35f. UN 3c. stamp, 1962	4·75	1·20
1268	35f. UN 3c. bl & pur, 1951	4·75	1·20
1269	35f. UN 1c. stamp, 1951	4·75	1·20

MS1270 Two sheets each 127×76 mm. (a) 8f. As No. 1253; 10f. As No. 1255; 21f. As No. 1248. (b) 24f. As No. 1263; 27f. As No. 1266; 35f. As No. 1260 22·00 13·50

The four designs in each value were issued together in *se-tenant* blocks of four, each design in the block having the same background.

120 *Virgin and Child* (Jean Lambardos)

1977. Christmas. Paintings of Virgin and Child by artists named. Multicoloured.

1271	5f. Type **120** (postage)	70	30
1272	13f. Melides Toscano	1·30	55
1273	27f. Emmanuel Tzanes	1·90	80
1274	18f. Master of Moulins (air)	1·40	60
1275	31f. Lorenzo di Credi	2·40	1·00
1276	40f. Palma the Elder	3·00	1·30

MS1277 Two sheets each 130×72 mm. (a) Nos. 1271/3. (b) Nos. 1274/6 12·00 10·00

121 Cruiser *Aurora* and Russian 5r. Stamp, 1922

1977. 60th Anniv of Russian Revolution. Multicoloured.

1278	5f. Type **121**	85	35
1279	5f. Russia S.G. 455	85	35
1280	5f. Russia S.G. 1392	85	35
1281	5f. Russia S.G. 199	85	35
1282	8f. Decemberists' Square, Leningrad and Russia S.G. 983	1·30	55
1283	8f. Russia S.G. 2122	1·30	55
1284	8f. Russia S.G. 1041	1·30	55
1285	8f. Russia S.G. 2653	1·30	55
1286	11f. Pokrovski Cathedral, Moscow and Russia S.G. 3929	1·80	75
1287	11f. Russia S.G. 3540	1·80	75
1288	11f. Russia S.G. 3468	1·80	75
1289	11f. Russia S.G. 3921	1·80	75
1290	13f. May Day celebrations, Moscow and Russia S.G. 4518	2·20	90
1291	13f. Russia S.G. 3585	2·20	90
1292	13f. Russia S.G. 3024	2·20	90
1293	13f. Russia S.G. 2471	2·20	90

The four designs in each value were issued in *se-tenant* blocks of four, each design in the block having the same background.

122 Tanker Unloading (Commerce)

1977. 15th Anniv of Independence. Multicoloured.

1294	1f. Type **122**	20	10
1295	5f. Assembling electric armatures (Economy)	35	15
1296	11f. Native dancers (Tourism)	95	40
1297	14f. Picking coffee (Agriculture)	1·40	60
1298	17f. National Palace, Bujumbura	1·90	80

1977. Christmas Charity. Nos. 1271/6 surch **+1F**.

1299	**120**	5f.+1f. mult (postage)	70	30
1300	–	13f.+1f. multicoloured	1·80	75
1301	–	27f.+1f. multicoloured	2·40	1·00
1302	–	18f.+1f. mult (air)	2·00	85
1303	–	31f.+1f. multicoloured	3·00	1·30
1304	–	40f.+1f. multicoloured	3·50	1·50

MS1305 Two sheets as **MS**1277 with 2f. premium on each stamp 17·00 14·00

123 *Madonna and Child* (Solario)

1979. Christmas (1978). Paintings of Virgin and Child by named artists. Multicoloured.

1306	13f. Rubens	1·40	60
1307	17f. Type **123**	1·70	70
1308	27f. Tiepolo	3·00	1·30
1309	31f. Gerard David	3·50	1·50
1310	40f. Bellini	4·75	2·00

MS1311 114×120 mm. Nos. 1306/10 (air) 18·00 15·00

1979. Christmas Charity. Nos. 1306/10 surch **+1F**.

1312	–	13f.+1f. multicoloured	1·40	60
1313	**123**	17f.+1f. multicoloured	1·70	70
1314	–	27f.+1f. multicoloured	3·00	1·30
1315	–	31f.+1f. multicoloured	3·50	1·50
1316	–	40f.+1f. multicoloured	4·75	2·00

MS1317 As **MS**1311 with 2f. premium on each stamp 18·00 15·00

124 Abyssinian Ground Hornbill

1979. Birds. Multicoloured.

1318	1f. Type **124** (postage)	45	35
1319	2f. African darter	60	45
1320	3f. Little bee eater	70	50
1321	5f. Lesser flamingo	90	70
1322	8f. Congo peafowl	1·70	95
1323	10f. Purple swamphen	2·10	1·50
1324	20f. Martial eagle	5·25	3·75
1325	27f. Painted stork	5·75	4·25
1326	50f. Saddle-bill stork	11·50	8·50
1327	6f. Type **124** (air)	90	70
1328	13f. As No. 1319	2·30	1·70
1329	18f. As No. 1320	3·50	2·50
1330	26f. As No. 1321	5·25	3·75

1331	31f. As No. 1322	5·75	4·25
1332	36f. As No. 1323	7·00	5·00
1333	40f. As No. 1324	8·00	6·00
1334	54f. As No. 1325	11·50	8·50
1335	70f. As No. 1326	14·00	10·00

125 Mother and Child

1979. International Year of the Child. Multicoloured.

1336	10f. Type **125**	1·20	85
1337	20f. Baby	2·30	1·70
1338	27f. Child with doll	3·00	2·10
1339	50f. S.O.S. village, Gitega	4·50	3·50

MS1340 131×85 mm. Nos. 1336/9 additionally inscr "+ 2f." 14·00 13·00

126 *Virgin and Child* (Raffaellino Del Garbo)

1979. Christmas. Virgin and Child paintings by named artists. Multicoloured.

1341	20f. Type **126**	2·10	1·50
1342	27f. Giovanni Penni	3·25	2·40
1343	31f. Giulio Romano	4·25	3·00
1344	50f. Detail of *Adoration of the Shepherds* (Jacopo Bassano)	4·50	3·50

MS1345 85×110 mm. Nos. 1341/4 (air) 17·00 16·00

127 Sir Rowland Hill and Penny Black

1979. Death Centenary of Sir Rowland Hill. Multicoloured.

1346	20f. Type **127**	1·40	1·00
1347	27f. German East Africa 25p. stamp and Ruanda-Urundi 5c. stamp	1·80	1·40
1348	31f. Ruanda 1f.25 and 50f. stamps of 1962	2·10	1·50
1349	40f. 4f. (1962) and 14f. (1969) stamps of Burundi	3·50	2·50
1350	60f. Heinrich von Stephan (founder of UPU) and Burundi 14f. UPU stamps of 1974	5·25	3·75

MS1351 110×105 mm. Nos. 1346/50 14·00 13·00

1979. Christmas Charity. Nos. 1341/4 additionally inscr with premium.

1352	20f.+1f. multicoloured	2·10	1·50
1353	27f.+1f. multicoloured	3·25	2·40
1354	31f.+1f. multicoloured	4·25	3·00
1355	50f.+1f. multicoloured	4·50	3·50

MS1356 85×110 mm. As **MS**1345 with 2f. premium on each stamp (air) 17·00 16·00

1980. As Nos. 1318/19 and 1321/3 but new values. (a) With copper frames.

1356a	5f. Abyssinian ground hornbill		
1356b	10f. African darter		
1356c	40f. Lesser flamingo		
1356d	45f. Congo peafowl		
1356e	50f. Purple swamphen		

(b) With grey-green frames.

1356f	5f. As No. 1356a		
1356g	10f. As No. 1356b		
1356h	40f. As No. 1356c		
1356i	45f. As No. 1356d		
1356j	50f. As No. 1356e		

128 Approaching Hurdle (110 m Hurdles, Thomas Munkelt)

1980. Olympic Medal Winners. Multicoloured.

1357	20f. Type **128**	2·50	1·90

1358	20f. Jumping hurdle	2·50	1·90
1359	20f. Completing jump	2·50	1·90
1360	30f. Discus—beginning to throw	4·00	3·00
1361	30f. Continuing throw	4·00	3·00
1362	30f. Releasing discus	4·00	3·00
1363	40f. Football—running for goal (Czechoslovakia)	5·25	3·75
1364	40f. Kicking ball	5·25	3·75
1365	40f. Saving ball	5·25	3·75
MS1366	145×111 mm. As Nos. 1357/65	37·00	34·00

129 The Virgin and Child (Sebastiano Mainardi)

1980. Christmas. Multicoloured.

1367	10f. Type **129**	1·40	1·00
1368	30f. Doni Tondo (Michelangelo)	2·30	1·70
1369	40f. The Virgin and Child (Piero di Cosimo)	5·75	4·25
1370	45f. The Holy Family (Fra Bartolomeo)	8·00	6·00
MS1371	134×103 mm. As Nos. 1367/70 (air)	17·00	16·00

130 Congress Emblem

1980. First National Party Congress, Uprona.

1372	**130**	10f. multicoloured	90	70
1373	**130**	40f. multicoloured	2·50	1·90
1374	**130**	45f. multicoloured	3·00	2·10
MS1375		108×68 mm. As Nos. 1372/4 (air)	6·25	6·00

1981. Christmas Charity. Nos. 1367/70 additionally inscr with premium.

1376	10f.+1f. multicoloured	1·40	1·00
1377	30f.+1f. multicoloured	2·30	1·70
1378	40f.+1f. multicoloured	5·75	4·25
1379	50f.+1f. multicoloured	8·00	6·00
MS1380	134×103 mm. As Nos. 1376/9 but each stamp with 2f. premium (air)	17·00	16·00

131 Kepler and Dish Aerial

1981. 350th Death Anniv of Johannes Kepler (astronomer). First Earth Satellite Station in Burundi. Multicoloured.

1381	10f. Type **131**	2·30	1·70
1382	40f. Satellite and antenna	4·50	3·50
1383	45f. Satellite (different) and antenna	5·75	4·25
MS1384	78×108 mm. Nos. 1381/3	12·50	12·00

132 Giraffes

1982. African Animals (4th series). Multicoloured.

1385	2f. Lion	5·75	4·25
1386	3f. Type **132**	7·00	5·00
1387	5f. Black rhinoceros	9·25	6·75
1388	10f. African buffalo	11·50	8·50
1389	20f. African elephant	46·00	34·00
1390	25f. Hippopotamus	60·00	43·00
1391	30f. Common zebra	65·00	47·00
1392	50f. Warthog	£120	85·00
1393	60f. Eland	£130	95·00
1394	65f. Black-backed jackal	£160	£120
1395	70f. Cheetah	£170	£130
1396	75f. Blue Wildebeest	£180	£140
1397	85f. Spotted hyena	£225	£170

1983. Animal Protection Year. Nos. 1385/97 optd with World Wildlife Fund Emblem.

| 1398 | 2f. Type **131** | 5·75 | 4·25 |

1399	3f. Giraffe	7·00	5·00
1400	5f. Black rhinoceros	9·25	6·75
1401	10f. African buffalo	11·50	8·50
1402	20f. African elephant	46·00	34·00
1403	25f. Hippopotamus	60·00	43·00
1404	30f. Common zebra	65·00	47·00
1405	50f. Warthog	£120	85·00
1406	60f. Eland	£130	95·00
1407	65f. Jackal (Canis mesomelas)	£160	£120
1408	70f. Cheetah	£170	£130
1409	75f. Blue wildebeest	£180	£140
1410	85f. Spotted Hyena	£225	£170

133 Flag and National Party Emblem

1983. 20th Anniv (1982) of Independence. Multicoloured.

1411	10f. Type **133**	90	70
1412	25f. Flag and arms	2·75	2·00
1413	30f. Flag and map of Africa	3·25	2·40
1414	50f. Flag and emblem	4·50	3·50
1415	65f. Flag and President Bagaza	5·75	4·25

134 Virgin and Child (Lucas Signorelli)

1983. Christmas. Multicoloured.

1416	10f. Type **134**	1·80	1·40
1417	25f. E. Murillo	2·75	2·00
1418	30f. Carlo Crivelli	5·75	4·25
1419	50f. Nicolas Poussin	8·00	6·00
MS1420	106×151 mm. As Nos. 1416/19, but with green backgrounds	18·00	17·00

DESIGNS: Virgin and Child paintings by named artists.

1983. Christmas Charity. Nos. 1416/19 additionally inscr with premium.

1421	10f.+1f. multicoloured	1·80	1·40
1422	25f.+1f. multicoloured	2·75	2·00
1423	30f.+1f. multicoloured	5·75	4·25
1424	50f.+1f. multicoloured	8·00	6·00
MS1425	106×151 mm. As MS1420 with 2f. premium on each stamp (air)	18·00	17·00

Nos. 1421/4 have green backgrounds; stamps on MS1425 have carmine backgrounds.

135 Papilio zalmoxis

1984. Butterflies. Multicoloured.

1426	5f. Type **135**	3·50	1·70
1427	5f. Cymothoe coccinata	3·50	1·70
1428	10f. Papilio antimachus	7·00	3·50
1429	10f. Asterope pechueli	7·00	3·50
1430	30f. Bebearia mardania	18·00	7·75
1431	30f. Papilio hesperus	18·00	7·75
1432	35f. Euphaedra perseis	23·00	13·00
1433	35f. Euphaedra neophron	23·00	13·00
1434	65f. Pseudacraea striata	46·00	21·00
1435	65f. Euphaedra imperialis	46·00	21·00

136 Stamps of German East Africa and Belgian Occupation

1984. 19th U.P.U. Congress, Hamburg. Multicoloured.

1436	10f. Type **136**	1·20	90
1437	30f. 1962 Burundi overprinted stamps	4·25	3·25
1438	35f. 1969 14f. Letter-writing Week and 1982 30f. Zebra stamps	5·50	4·00
1439	65f. Heinrich von Stephan (founder of UPU) and 1974 14f. UPU Centenary stamps	7·25	5·50

| MS1440 | 147×84 mm. As Nos. 1436/9 but each 39×31 mm (air) | 19·00 | 18·00 |

137 Jesse Owens (runner)

1984. Olympic Games, Los Angeles. Multicoloured.

1441	10f. Type **137**	1·20	90
1442	30f. Rafer Johnson (discus thrower)	4·25	3·25
1443	35f. Bob Beamon (long jumper)	4·75	3·50
1444	65f. K. Keino (sprinter)	9·00	6·75
MS1445	119×99 mm. As Nos. 1441/4 but some colours changed (air)	20·00	19·00

138 Virgin and Child (Botticelli)

1984. Christmas. Multicoloured.

1446	10f. "Rest on the Flight into Egypt" (Murillo)	1·80	1·40
1447	25f. Virgin and Child (R. del Garbo)	4·25	3·25
1448	30f. Type **138**	4·75	3·50
1449	50f. Adoration of the Shepherds (J. Bassano)	7·25	5·50
MS1450	125×92 mm. As Nos. 1446/9 but some colours changed. Olive border	18·00	17·00

1984. Christmas Charity. As Nos. 1446/49 but with additional premium.

1451	10f.+1f. multicoloured	1·80	1·40
1452	25f.+1f. multicoloured	4·25	3·25
1453	30f.+1f. multicoloured	4·75	3·50
1454	50f.+1f. multicoloured	7·25	5·50
MS1455	125×92 mm. As No. MS1450 with 2f. premium on each stamp (air)	18·00	17·00

139 Thunbergia

1986. Flowers. Multicoloured.

1456	2f. Type **139** (postage)	35	25
1457	3f. African violets	50	35
1458	5f. Clivia	95	70
1459	10f. Cassia	1·90	1·40
1460	20f. Bird of Paradise flower	4·25	3·25
1461	35f. Gloriosa	6·50	5·00
1462	70f. Type **139** (air)	8·50	6·25
1463	75f. As No. 1457	9·50	7·25
1464	80f. As No. 1458	11·00	8·00
1465	85f. As No. 1459	11·50	8·50
1466	100f. As No. 1460	12·00	9·00
1467	150f. As No. 1461	18·00	13·50

140 Bombs as Flats

1987. International Peace Year (1986). Multicoloured.

1468	10f. Type **140**	1·00	70
1469	20f. Molecular diagrams as flower	1·90	1·40
1470	30f. Clasped hands across globe	2·75	2·00
1471	40f. Chicks in split globe	3·75	2·75
MS1472	85×120 mm. Nos. 1468/71	9·50	9·00

141 Map, Airplane and Emblem

1987. Tenth Anniv of Great Lakes Countries Economic Community. Multicoloured.

1473	5f. Type **141**	1·30	90
1474	10f. Map, ear of wheat, cog-wheel and emblem	3·75	2·75
1475	15f. Map, factory and emblem	5·00	3·50
1476	25f. Map, electricity pylons and emblem	7·50	5·50
1477	35f. Map, flags and emblem	12·50	9·00
MS1478	117×114 mm. Nos. 1473/7 plus label	31·00	29·00

142 Leaves and Sticks Shelter

1988. International Year of Shelter for the Homeless (1987). Multicoloured.

1479	10f. Type **142**	65	45
1480	20f. People living in concrete pipes	1·60	1·20
1481	80f. Boys mixing mortar	5·00	3·50
1482	150f. Boys with model house	8·25	5·75
MS1483	124×100 mm. Nos. 1479/82	15·00	14·50

143 Skull between Cigarettes

1989. Anti-smoking Campaign. Multicoloured.

1484	5f. Type **143**	65	45
1485	20f. Cigarettes, lungs and skull	3·25	2·30
1486	80f. Cigarettes piercing skull	11·50	8·00
MS1487	120×80 mm. Nos. 1484/6	15·00	14·50

No. MS1487 also shows World Health Organization 40th Anniv emblem.

1989. Various stamps surch.

1487b	20f. on 3f. mult (No. 1457)
1487c	80f. on 10f. mult (No. 1430)
1487d	80f. on 30f. mult (No. 1431)
1487e	80f. on 35f. mult (No. 1432)
1487f	80f. on 35f. mult (No. 1433)
1487g	85f. on 65f. mult (No. 1435)

144 Pope John Paul II

1990. Papal Visit.

1488	**144**	5f. multicoloured	40	30
1489	**144**	10f. multicoloured	65	50
1490	**144**	20f. multicoloured	1·30	1·00
1491	**144**	30f. multicoloured	2·30	1·80
1492	**144**	50f. multicoloured	3·25	2·50
1493	**144**	80f. multicoloured	5·25	4·00

145 Hippopotamus

1991. Animals. Multicoloured.

1495	5f. Type **145**	55	35
1496	10f. Hen and cockerel	1·10	70
1497	20f. Lion	2·75	1·80
1498	30f. Elephant	4·00	2·50
1499	50f. Helmet guineafowl (Pintade)	5·50	3·50
1500	80f. Crocodile	11·00	7·25
MS1501	109×123 mm. Nos. 1495/1500	25·00	16·00

146 Drummer

1992. Traditional Dancing. Multicoloured.
1502	15f. Type **146**		70	45
1503	30f. Men dancing		1·40	90
1504	115f. Group of drummers (horiz)		5·50	3·50
1505	200f. Men dancing in fields (horiz)		9·00	5·75
MS1506	120×105 mm. Nos. 1502/5		17·00	11·00

147 *Impatiens petersiana*

1992. Flowers. Multicoloured.
1507	15f. Type **147**		1·70	1·10
1508	20f. *Lachenalia aloides* "Nelsonii"		2·50	1·60
1509	30f. Egyptian lotus		3·50	2·30
1510	50f. Kaffir lily		5·50	3·50
MS1511	105×120 mm. Nos. 1507/10		11·00	7·25

148 Pigtail Macaque

1992. Air. Animals. Multicoloured.
1512	100f. Type **148**		2·75	1·80
1513	115f. Grevy's zebra		3·00	2·00
1514	200f. Ox		7·00	4·50
1515	220f. Eastern white pelican		8·50	5·50
MS1516	105×120 mm. Nos. 1512/15		21·00	13·50

149 People holding Hands and Flag

1992. 30th Anniv of Independence. Multicoloured.
1517	30f. Type **149**		70	45
1518	85f. State flag		1·70	1·10
1519	110f. Independence monument (vert)		2·20	1·40
1520	115f. As No. 1518		2·50	1·60
1521	120f. Map (vert)		2·75	1·80
1522	140f. Type **149**		3·00	2·00
1523	200f. As No. 1519		4·25	2·75
1524	250f. As No. 1521		5·25	3·50

150 *Russula ingens*

1992. Fungi. Multicoloured.
1525	10f. Type **150**		30	20
1526	15f. *Russula brunneorigida*		40	25
1527	20f. *Amanita zambiana*		55	35
1528	30f. *Russula subfistulosa*		1·10	70
1529	75f. *Russula meleagris*		2·75	1·80
1530	85f. As No. 1529		3·25	2·20
1531	100f. *Russula immaculata*		3·50	2·30
1532	110f. Type **150**		4·00	2·50
1533	115f. As No. 1526		4·25	2·75
1534	120f. *Russula sejuncta*		5·00	3·25
1535	130f. As No. 1534		5·50	2·75
1536	250f. *Afroboletus luteolus*		11·00	7·25

151 Columbus's Fleet, Treasure and Globes

1992. 500th Anniv of Discovery of America by Columbus. Multicoloured.
1541	200f. Type **151**		5·50	3·50
1542	400f. American produce, globes and Columbus's fleet		11·00	7·25

152 Serval

1992. The Serval. Multicoloured.
1543	30f. Type **152**		85	55
1544	130f. Pair sitting and crouching		5·00	3·25
1545	200f. Pair, one standing over the other		5·50	3·50
1546	220f. Heads of pair		7·00	4·50

153 Running

1992. Olympic Games, Barcelona. Multicoloured.
1547	130f. Type **153**		2·75	1·80
1548	500f. Hurdling		11·00	7·25

154 Emblems

1992. International Nutrition Conference, Rome. Multicoloured.
1549	200f. Type **154**		7·00	4·50
1550	220f. Woman's face made from vegetables (G. Arcimbolo)		8·50	5·50

155 Horsemen

1992. Christmas. Details of *Adoration of the Magi* by Gentile da Fabriano. Multicoloured.
1551	100f. Type **155**		2·10	1·40
1552	130f. Three Kings		2·75	1·80
1553	250f. Holy family		5·00	3·25
MS1554	109×91 mm. Nos. 1551/3 (sold at 580f.)		12·00	7·75

156 Flags of Member Countries and European Community Emblem

1993. European Single Market. Multicoloured.
1555	130f. Type **156**		2·75	1·80
1556	500f. Europe shaking hands with Africa		11·00	7·25

157 Indonongo

1993. Musical Instruments. Multicoloured.
1557	200f. Type **157**		4·00	3·00
1558	220f. Ingoma (drum)		4·25	3·25

1559	250f. Ikembe (xylophone)		4·75	3·75
1560	300f. Umuduri (musical bow)		5·50	4·50

158 Broad Blue-banded Swallowtail

1993. Butterflies. Multicoloured.
1561	130f. Type **158**		3·00	2·40
1562	200f. Green charaxes		4·75	3·75
1563	250f. Migratory glider		6·25	4·75
1564	300f. Red swallowtail		7·00	5·50
MS1565	84×123 mm. Nos. 1561/4 (sold at 980f.)		24·00	19·00

159 Players, Stadium, United States Flag and Statue of Liberty

1993. World Cup Football Championship, U.S.A. (1994). Multicoloured.
1566	130f. Type **159**		4·25	3·25
1567	200f. Players, stadium, United States flag and Golden Gate Bridge		5·50	4·50

160 Cattle

1993. Domestic Animals. Multicoloured.
1568	100f. Type **160**		1·70	1·30
1569	120f. Sheep		2·10	1·70
1570	130f. Pigs		2·50	2·00
1571	250f. Goats		4·25	3·25

161 Woman with Baby and Two Men

1993. Christmas. Each orange and black.
1572	100f. Type **161**		2·10	1·70
1573	130f. Nativity		2·50	2·00
1574	250f. Woman with baby and three men		4·50	3·50
MS1575	127×82 mm. Nos. 1572/4 (sold at 580f.)		10·50	8·25

162 Elvis Presley

1994. Entertainers. Multicoloured.
1576	60f. Type **162**		2·00	1·50
1577	115f. Mick Jagger		4·00	3·00
1578	120f. John Lennon		4·25	3·25
1579	200f. Michael Jackson		7·00	5·50
MS1580	80×114 mm. Nos. 1576/9		17·00	15·00

163 "The Discus Thrower" (statue)

1994. Centenary of International Olympic Committee.
1581	**163**	150f. multicoloured	5·50	4·50

164 Pres. Buyoya handing over Baton of Power to Pres. Ndadaye

1994. First Anniv of First Multi-party Elections in Burundi. Multicoloured.
1582	30f.+10f. Type **164**		85	65
1583	110f.+10f. Pres. Ndadaye (first elected President) giving inauguration speech		2·75	2·10
1584	115f.+10f. Arms on map		3·00	2·40
1585	120f.+10f. Warrior on map		3·25	2·50

165 Madonna, China

1994. Christmas. Multicoloured.
1586	115f. Type **165**		2·50	2·00
1587	120f. Madonna, Japan		2·75	2·10
1588	250f. Black Virgin, Poland		5·50	4·50
MS1589	80×118 mm. No. 1588		7·00	6·50

166 Emblem and Earth

1995. 50th Anniversaries. Multicoloured.
1590	115f. Type **166** (FAO)		2·75	2·20
1591	120f. UNO emblems and dove		3·00	2·30

167 *Cassia didymobotrya*

1995. Flowers. Multicoloured.
1592	15f. Type **167**		30	20
1593	20f. *Mitragyna rubrostipulosa*		40	35
1594	30f. *Phytolacca dodecandra*		55	45
1595	85f. *Acanthus pubescens*		1·70	1·30
1596	100f. *Bulbophyllum comatum*		2·20	1·80
1597	110f. "*Angraecum evrardianum*"		2·50	2·00
1598	115f. *Eulophia burundiensis*		3·00	2·40
1599	120f. *Habenaria adolphii*		3·25	2·75

168 Otraca Bus

1995. Transport. Multicoloured.
1600	30f. Type **168**		55	45
1601	115f. Transintra lorry		2·10	1·70
1602	120f. Lake ferry		2·20	1·80
1603	250f. Air Burundi Beeck King Air		5·00	3·75

169 Boy with Panga

1995. Christmas. Multicoloured.

1604	100f. Type **169**		1·70	1·30
1605	130f. Boy with sheaf of wheat		2·10	1·70
1606	250f. Mother and children		4·25	3·25
MS1607	126×82 mm. Nos. 1604/6 (sold at 580f.)		9·75	8·75

170 Venuste Niyongabo

1996. Olympic Games, Atlanta. Runners. Multicoloured.

1608	130f. Type **170** (5000 m gold medal winner)	2·75	2·20
1609	500f. Arthemon Hatungimana	8·50	6·50

171 Hadada Ibis

1996. Birds. Multicoloured.

1610	15f. Type **171**	40	35
1611	20f. Egyptian goose	55	45
1612	30f. African fish eagle	70	55
1613	120f. Goliath heron	2·10	1·70
1614	165f. South African crowned crane	3·50	2·75
1615	220f. African jacana	5·00	3·75

172 Marlier's Julie

1996. Fish of Lake Tanganyika. Multicoloured.

1616	30f. Type **172**	70	55
1617	115f. *Cyphotilapia frontosa*	2·20	1·80
1618	120f. *Lamprologus brichardi*	2·50	2·00
1619	250f. Stone squeaker	5·00	4·00
MS1620	108×108 mm. Nos. 1616/19 (sold at 615f.)	10·50	9·25

173 Children

1998. 50th Anniv of S.O.S Children's Villages. Multicoloured.

1621	100f. Type **173**	1·50	1·20
1622	250f. Flags, "50" and children waving	3·75	3·00
1623	270f. Children dancing around flag	4·00	3·25

174 Madonna and Child

1999. Christmas (1996–98). Multicoloured.

1624	100f. Type **174** (1996)	1·40	1·10
1625	130f. Madonna and Child (different) (1997)	2·00	1·50
1626	250f. Madonna and Child (different) (1998)	3·75	2·75
MS1627	125×82 mm. Nos. 1624/6 (sold at 580f.)	8·50	7·75

175 Diana, Princess of Wales

1999. Second Death Anniv of Diana, Princess of Wales.

1628	**175**	100f. multicoloured	1·40	1·10
1629	**175**	250f. multicoloured	3·00	2·40
1630	**175**	300f. multicoloured	4·00	3·00

176 Danny Kaye (entertainer) holding African Baby

2000. New Millennium. "A World Free from Hunger".

1631	**176**	350f. multicoloured	2·75	2·20

Pt. 1

BUSHIRE

An Iranian seaport. Stamps issued during the British occupation in the 1914-18 War.

20 chahis = 1 kran, 10 krans = 1 toman

1915. Portrait stamps of Iran (1911) optd BUSHIRE Under British Occupation.

1	57	1ch. orange and green	75·00	80·00
2	57	2ch. brown and red	75·00	70·00
3	57	3ch. green and grey	90·00	90·00
4	57	5ch. red and brown	£500	£450
5	57	6ch. lake and green	75·00	50·00
6	57	9ch. lilac and brown	75·00	90·00
7	57	10ch. brown and red	80·00	85·00
8	57	12ch. blue and green	95·00	90·00
9	57	24ch. green and purple	£180	£100
10	57	1kr. red and blue	£170	65·00
11	57	2kr. red and green	£450	£325
12	57	3kr. black and lilac	£375	£375
13	57	5kr. blue and red	£300	£250
14	57	10kr. red and brown	£275	£225

1915. Coronation issue of Iran optd BUSHIRE Under British Occupation.

15	66	1ch. blue and red	£750	£600
16	66	2ch. red and blue	£12000	£12000
17	66	3ch. green	£850	£850
18	66	5ch. red	£11000	£11000
19	66	6ch. red and green	£9000	£9000
20	66	9ch. violet and brown	£1400	£1100
21	66	10ch. brown and green	£2250	£2250
22	66	12ch. blue	£2500	£2500
23	66	24ch. black and brown	£1000	£750
24	67	1kr. black, brown and silver	£1000	£900
25	67	2kr. red, blue and silver	£950	£950
26	67	3kr. black, lilac and silver	£1100	£1000
27	67	5kr. slate, brown and silver	£1000	£1000
28	-	1t. black, violet and gold	£850	£850
29	-	3t. red, lake and gold	£7000	£6500

Pt. 1

BUSSAHIR (BASHAHR)

A state in the Punjab, India. Now uses Indian stamps.

12 pies = 1 anna; 16 annas = 1 rupee.

1

1895. Various frames. Imperf, perf or roul.

9	1	¼a. pink	£100	£140
10	1	½a. grey	27·00	£170
11	1	1a. red	26·00	£110
12	1	2a. yellow	38·00	£110
13	1	4a. violet	35·00	£110
14	1	8a. brown	26·00	£130
15	1	12a. green	90·00	£150
16	1	1r. blue	60·00	£140

1896. Similar types, but inscriptions on white ground and inscr "POSTAGE" instead of "STAMP".

27	¼a. violet	25·00	25·00
37	¼a. red	5·50	16·00
25	½a. blue	16·00	25·00
26	1a. olive	23·00	55·00
32	1a. red	5·00	19·00
41	2a. yellow	80·00	£100
36	4a. red	80·00	£160

Pt. 1

CAICOS ISLANDS

Separate issues for these islands, part of the Turks and Caicos Islands group, appeared from 1981 to 1985.

100 cents = 1 dollar.

1981. Nos. 514, 518, 520, 523 and 525/7 of Turks and Caicos Islands optd CAICOS ISLANDS.

1	1c. Indigo hamlet	15	30
2	5c. Spanish grunt	20	40
3	8c. Four-eyed butterflyfish	20	40
4	20c. Queen angelfish	35	40
5	50c. Royal gramma ("Fairy Basslet")	40	1·00
6	$1 Fin-spot wrasse	60	1·75
7	$2 Stoplight parrotfish	1·10	3·25

1981. Royal Wedding. Nos. 653/6 of Turks and Caicos Islands optd. (A) Caicos Islands.

8A	35c. Prince Charles and Lady Diana Spencer	20	25
9A	65c. Kensington Palace	30	40
10A	90c. Prince Charles as Colonel of the Welsh Guards	40	50
MS11A	96×82 mm. $2 Glass Coach	1·00	2·00

(B) CAICOS ISLANDS.

8B	35c. Prince Charles and Lady Diana Spencer	30	70
9B	65c. Kensington Palace	40	1·00
10B	90c. Prince Charles as Colonel of the Welsh Guards	50	1·50
MS11B	96×82 mm. $2 Glass Coach	1·00	2·50

1981. Royal Wedding. As Nos. 657/9 of Turks and Caicos Islands, but each inscr "Caicos Islands". Multicoloured. Self-adhesive.

12	20c. Lady Diana Spencer	30	40
13	$1 Prince Charles	80	1·25
14	$2 Prince Charles and Lady Diana Spencer	4·00	5·50

4 Queen or Pink Conch and Lobster Fishing, South Caicos

1983. Multicoloured.

15	8c. Type **4**	2·00	1·00
16	10c. Hawksbill turtle, East Caicos	2·25	1·75
17	20c. Arawak Indians and idol, Middle Caicos	2·25	1·75
18	35c. Boat-building, North Caicos	2·25	2·25
19	50c. Marine biologist at work, Pine Cay	3·25	3·50
20	95c. Boeing 707 airliner at new airport, Providenciales	6·00	3·50
21	$1.10 Columbus's *Pinta*, West Caicos	6·00	3·50
22	$2 Fort George Cay	4·00	5·00
23	$3 Pirates Anne Bonny and Calico Jack at Parrot Cay	6·00	5·00

5 Goofy and Patch

1983. Christmas. Multicoloured.

30	1c. Type **5**	10	30
31	1c. Chip and Dale	10	30
32	2c. Morty	10	30
33	2c. Morty and Ferdie	10	30
34	3c. Goofy and Louie	10	30
35	3c. Donald Duck, Huey, Dewey and Louie	10	30
36	50c. Uncle Scrooge	4·00	3·25
37	70c. Mickey Mouse and Ferdie	4·25	3·75
38	$1.10 Pinocchio, Jiminy Cricket and Figaro	5·00	4·50
MS39	126×101 mm. $2 Morty and Ferdie	3·75	3·50

6 *Leda and the Swan*

1984. 500th Birth Anniv of Raphael. Multicoloured.

40	35c. Type **6**	75	50
41	50c. *Study of Apollo for Parnassus*	1·00	70
42	95c. *Study of two figures for the battle of Ostia*	2·00	1·25
43	$1.10 *Study for the Madonna of the Goldfinch*	2·00	1·50
MS44	71×100 mm. $2.50, *The Garvagh Madonna*	3·00	3·25

7 High Jumping

1984. Olympic Games, Los Angeles.

45	**7**	4c. multicoloured	10	20
46	-	25c. multicoloured	30	20
47	-	65c. black, deep blue and blue	2·25	75
48	-	$1.10 multicoloured	1·25	85
MS49		105×75 mm. $2 multicoloured	3·00	3·00

DESIGNS—VERT: 25c. Archery; 65c. Cycling; $1.10, Football. HORIZ: $2.50, Show jumping.

8 Horace Horsecollar and Clarabelle Cow

1984. Easter. Walt Disney Cartoon Characters. Multicoloured.

50	35c. Type **8**	1·40	60
51	45c. Mickey and Minnie Mouse, and Chip	1·50	75
52	75c. Gyro Gearloose, Chip 'n Dale	1·90	1·25
53	85c. Mickey Mouse, Chip 'n Dale	1·90	1·40
MS54	127×101 mm. $2.20, Donald Duck	5·50	3·75

1984. Universal Postal Union Congress Hamburg. Nos. 20/1 optd UNIVERSAL POSTAL UNION 1874-1984 and emblem.

55	95c. Boeing 707 airliner at new airport, Providenciales	1·00	1·25
56	$1.10 Columbus's "Pinta", West Caicos	1·25	1·50

1984. "Ausipex" International Stamp Exhibition, Melbourne. No. 22 optd AUSIPEX 1984.

57	$2 Fort George Cay	2·40	2·50

11 Seamen sighting American Manatees

1984. 492nd Anniv of Columbus's First Landfall. Multicoloured.

58	10c. Type **11**	1·00	80
59	70c. Columbus's fleet	3·75	3·25
60	$1 First landing in the West Indies	4·25	3·25
MS61	99×69 mm. $2 Fleet of Columbus (different)	2·75	3·00

12 Donald Duck and Mickey Mouse with Father Christmas

1984. Christmas. Walt Disney Cartoon Characters. Multicoloured.

62		20c. Type **12**	1·50	85
63		35c. Donald Duck opening refrigerator	1·75	1·00
64		50c. Mickey Mouse, Donald Duck and toy train	2·50	2·25
65		75c. Donald Duck and parcels	3·00	3·00
66		$1.10 Donald Duck and carol singers	3·25	3·25
MS67		127×102 mm. $2 Donald Duck as Christmas tree	3·75	4·00

13 Thick-billed Vireo

1985. Birth Bicentenary of John J. Audubon (ornithologist). Multicoloured.

68		20c. Type **13**	1·75	50
69		35c. Black-faced grassquit	2·00	95
70		50c. Pearly-eyed thrasher	2·25	1·50
71		$1 Greater Antillean bullfinch	2·75	2·50
MS72		100×70 mm. $2 Striped-headed tanager	3·50	3·50

14 Two Children learning to Read and Write (Education)

1985. International Youth Year. 40th Anniv of United Nations. Multicoloured.

73		16c. Type **14**	20	25
74		35c. Two children on playground swings (Health)	50	55
75		70c. Boy and girl (Love)	1·00	1·10
76		90c. Three children (Peace)	1·25	1·40
MS77		101×71 mm. $2 Child, dove carrying ears of wheat and map of the Americas	2·75	3·75

15 Douglas DC-3 on Ground

1985. 40th Anniv of International Civil Aviation Organization. Multicoloured.

78		35c. Type **15**	3·50	55
79		75c. Convair CV 440 Metropolitan	4·50	1·40
80		90c. Britten Norman Islander	4·50	1·60
MS81		100×70 mm. $2.20, Hand-gliding over the Caicos Islands	3·00	3·25

16 The Queen Mother visiting Foundation for the Disabled, Leatherhead

1985. Life and Times of Queen Elizabeth the Queen Mother. Multicoloured.

82		35c. Type **16**	1·25	55
83		65c. With Princess Anne (horiz)	1·75	95
84		95c. At Epsom, 1961	2·25	1·60
MS85		56×85 mm. $2 Visiting Royal Hospital, Chelsea	5·00	3·00

1985. 150th Birth Anniv of Mark Twain (author). Designs as T **118** of Anguilla, showing Walt Disney cartoon characters in scenes from *Tom Sawyer, Detective*. Multicoloured.

86		8c. Huckleberry Finn (Goofy) and Tom Sawyer (Mickey Mouse) reading reward notice	60	20
87		35c. Huck and Tom meeting Jake Dunlap	1·75	65
88		95c. Huck and Tom spying on Jubiter Dunlap	3·25	2·00
89		$1.10 Huck and Tom with hound (Pluto)	3·25	2·25
MS90		127×101 mm. Tom unmasking Jubiter Dunlap	4·75	4·25

1985. Birth Bicentenaries of Grimm Brothers (folklorists). Designs as T **119** of Anguilla, showing Walt Disney cartoon characters in scenes from *Six Soldiers of Fortune*. Multicoloured.

91		16c. The Soldier (Donald Duck) with his meagre pay	1·70	30
92		25c. The Soldier meeting the Strong Man (Horace Horsecollar)	2·00	45
93		65c. The Soldier meeting the Marksman (Mickey Mouse)	3·00	1·25
94		$1.35 The Fast Runner (Goofy) winning the race against the Princess (Daisy Duck)	3·50	2·25
MS95		126×101 mm. $2 The Soldier and the Strong Man with sack of gold	4·75	4·00

Pt. 21

CAMBODIA

A kingdom in south-east Asia.

From 1887 Cambodia was part of the Union of Indo-China. In 1949 it became an Associated State of the French Union, in 1953 it attained sovereign independence and in 1955 it left the Union.

Following the introduction of a republican constitution in 1970 the name of the country was changed to Khmer Republic and in 1975 to Kampuchea.

In 1989 it reverted to the name of Cambodia. Under a new constitution in 1993 it became a parliamentary monarchy.

1951. 100 cents = 1 piastre.
1955. 100 cents = 1 riel.

1 "Apsara" or Dancing Nymph

2 Throne Room, Phnom-Penh

3 King Norodom Sihanouk

1951

1	1	10c. green and deep green	1·00	4·50
2	1	20c. brown and red	65	1·80
3	1	30c. blue and violet	65	75
4	1	40c. blue and ultramarine	1·40	1·20
5	2	50c. green and deep green	1·20	1·10
6	3	80c. green and blue	2·20	5·50
7	2	1p. violet and blue	1·70	80
8	3	1p.10 red and lake	2·75	5·50
9	1	1p.50 red and lake	2·50	1·80
10	2	1p.50 blue and indigo	2·50	3·00
11	3	1p.50 brown and chocolate	2·50	2·30
12	3	1p.90 blue and indigo	4·50	7·50
13	2	2p. brown and red	3·50	1·00
14	3	3p. brown and red	5·50	3·00
15	1	5p. violet and blue	16·00	8·25
16	2	10p. blue and violet	17·00	13·50
17	3	15p. violet and deep violet	35·00	25·00
MS17a		Three sheets, each 130×90 mm. Nos. 15/17. Price for 3 sheets	£150	†

1952. Students' Aid Fund. Surch **AIDE A L'ETUDIANT** and premium.

18		1p.10+40c. red and lake	5·00	11·00
19		1p.90+60c. blue & indigo	5·00	11·00
20		3p.+1p. brown and red	5·00	11·00
21	1	5p.+2p. violet and blue	5·00	11·00

5 "Kinnari"

1953. Air.

22	5	50c. green	1·50	2·75
23	5	3p. red	2·50	2·30
24	5	3p.30 violet	3·25	6·75
25	5	4p. blue and brown	3·50	1·40
26	5	5p.10 ochre, red and brown	5·00	8·25
27	5	6p.50 purple and brown	4·50	11·00
28	5	9p. green and mauve	6·25	17·00
29	5	11p.50 multicoloured	15·00	23·00
30	5	30p. ochre, brown and green	21·00	33·00
MS30a		Three sheets, each 129×100 mm. Nos. 22, 24, 26 and 30 (sold at 50p.); Nos. 23, 25 and 29 (sold at 25p.); Nos. 27/8 (sold at 20p.) Price for 3 sheets	£225	£225

6 Arms of Cambodia

7 "Postal Transport"

1954

31	-	10c. red	1·80	2·30
32	-	20c. green	2·10	65
33	-	30c. blue	2·10	2·75
34	-	40c. violet	2·30	1·10
35	-	50c. purple	2·10	35
36	-	70c. brown	2·50	4·25
37	-	1p. violet	2·50	2·30
38	-	1p.50 red	2·50	75
39	6	2p. red	2·30	60
40	6	2p.50 green	2·50	75
41	7	2p.50 green	3·25	2·75
42	6	3p. blue	3·25	2·20
43	7	4p. sepia	4·25	3·50
44	6	4p.50 violet	3·50	2·30
45	7	5p. red	4·50	3·25
46	6	6p. brown	4·25	3·25
47	7	10p. violet	5·00	3·50
48	7	15p. blue	6·25	6·25
49	-	20p. blue	14·00	7·00
50	-	30p. green	23·00	12·50
MS50a		Three sheets, each 120×20 mm. Nos. 31/5 (sold at 2p.); Nos. 39/40, 42, 44 and 46 (sold at 20p.); Nos. 41, 43, 45 and 47/8 (sold at 40p.) and one sheet 160×92 mm containing Nos. 36/8 and 49/50 (sold at 60p.) Price for 4 sheets	£225	£225

DESIGNS—VERT: 10c. to 50c. View of Phnom Daun Penah. HORIZ: 70c. 1, 1p.50, 20, 30p. East Gate, Temple of Angkor.

8 King Norodom Suramarit

1955

51		50c. blue	30	25
52	8	50c. violet	45	35
53	8	1r. red	50	35
54	8	2r. blue	90	50
55	-	2r.50 brown	1·40	55
56	-	4r. green	1·80	90
57	-	6r. lake	2·30	1·40
58	8	7r. brown	2·75	1·80
59	-	15r. lilac	3·75	2·75
60	8	20r. green	4·50	4·50

PORTRAIT: Nos. 51, 55/7 and 59, Queen Kossamak.

For stamps as Nos. 58 and 60, but with black border, see Nos. 101/2.

9 King and Queen of Cambodia

1955. Coronation (1st issue).

61	9	1r.50 sepia and brown	1·00	65
62	9	2r. black and blue	1·00	75
63	9	3r. red and orange	1·30	45
64	9	5r. black and green	2·00	90
65	9	10r. purple and violet	3·50	1·00

See Nos. 66/71.

10 King Norodom Suramarit

1956. Coronation (2nd issue).

66	10	2r. red	2·50	2·75
67	-	3r. blue	3·50	3·75
68	-	5r. green	5·00	5·50
69	10	10r. green	10·00	11·00
70	10	30r. violet	24·00	26·00
71	10	50r. purple	46·00	49·00

PORTRAIT—VERT: 3, 5, 50r. Queen of Cambodia.

11 Prince Sihanouk, Flags and Globe

1957. First Anniv of Admission of Cambodia to UNO.

72	11	2r. red, blue and green	2·00	1·50
73	11	4r.50 blue	2·00	1·50
74	11	8r.50 red	2·00	1·50

12

1957. 2,500th Anniv of Buddhism. (a) With premiums.

75	12	1r.50+50c. bis, red & bl	2·00	2·20
76	12	6r.50+1r.50 bis, red & pur	2·75	3·25
77	12	8r.+2r. bistre, red & blue	5·00	5·50

(b) Colours changed and premiums omitted.

78		1r.50 red	1·40	1·20
79		6r.50 violet	1·60	1·40
80		8r. green	1·70	1·60

13 Mythological Bird

1957. Air.

81	13	50c. lake	55	15
82	13	1r. green	1·00	20
83	13	4r. blue	3·00	80
84	13	50r. red	12·00	4·50
85	13	100r. red, green and blue	22·00	8·25
MS85a		160×92 mm. Nos. 81/5 (sold at 160r.)	49·00	49·00

14 King Ang Duong

1958. King Ang Duong Commemoration.

86	14	1r.50 brown and violet	85	75
87	14	5r. bistre and black	1·20	1·10
88	14	10r. sepia and purple	2·40	1·60
MS88a		156×92 mm. Nos. 86/8 (sold at 25r.)	8·25	7·00

15 King Norodom

1958. King Norodom I Commemoration.

89	**15**	2r. brown and blue	1·00	55
90	**15**	6r. green and orange	1·40	85
91	**15**	15r. brown and green	2·75	1·80

MS91a 156×92 mm. Nos. 89/91 (sold at 32r.) | 8·25 | 6·50

16 Children

1959. Children's World Friendship.

92	**16**	20c. purple	45	45
93	**16**	50c. blue	75	75
94	**16**	80c. red	1·50	1·50

1959. Red Cross Fund. Nos. 92/4 surch with red cross and premium.

95	20c.+20c. purple	55	55
96	50c.+30c. blue	1·10	1·10
97	80c.+50c. red	2·20	2·20

18 Prince Sihanouk, Plan of Port and Freighter

1960. Inauguration of Sihanoukville Port.

98	**18**	2r. sepia and red	85	85
99	**18**	5r. brown and blue	85	85
100	**18**	20r. blue and violet	3·25	3·25

1960. King Norodom Suramarit Mourning issue. Nos. 58 and 60 reissued with black border.

101	**8**	7r. brown and black	5·50	6·00
102	**8**	20r. green and black	5·50	6·00

19 Sacred Plough in Procession

1960. Festival of the Sacred Furrow.

103	**19**	1r. purple	1·00	75
104	**19**	2r. brown	1·20	1·10
105	**19**	3r. green	2·00	1·50

20 Child and Book ("Education")

1960. "Works of the Five Year Plan".

106	**20**	2r. brown, blue and green	75	40
107	-	3r. green and brown	90	45
108	-	4r. violet, green and pink	90	65
109	-	6r. brown, orange & green	1·00	75
110	-	10r. blue, green and bistre	2·50	1·60
111	-	25r. red and lake	5·00	3·00

MS111a Two sheets, each 150×100 mm. Nos. 106, 109 and 111 (sold at 42r.); Nos. 107/8 and 110 (sold at 23r.) Price for 2 sheets | 14·50 | 14·50

DESIGNS—HORIZ: 3r. Chhouksar Barrage ("Irrigation"); 6r. Carpenter and huts ("Construction"); 10r. Rice-field ("Agriculture"). VERT: 4r. Industrial scene and books ("National balance-sheet"); 25r. Anointing children ("Child welfare").

21 Flag and Dove of Peace

1961. Peace. Flag in red and blue.

112	**21**	1r.50 green and brown	45	65
113	**21**	5r. red	65	90
114	**21**	7r. blue and green	90	1·40

MS114a 147×93 mm. Nos. 112/14 (sold at 16r.) | 18·00 | 18·00

MS114b as MS114a but stamps in new colours (sold at 20r.) | 14·00 | 14·00

23 Frangipani

1961. Cambodian Flowers.

115	**23**	2r. yellow, green & mauve	75	65
116	-	5r. mauve, green and blue	1·20	1·10
117	-	10r. red, green and blue	3·25	3·00

MS117a 130×100 mm. Nos. 115/17 (sold at 20r.) | 9·25 | 9·25

FLOWERS: 5r. Oleander. 10r. Amaryllis.

24 "Rama" (from temple door, Baphoun)

1961. Cambodian Soldiers Commemoration.

118	**24**	1r. mauve	55	30
118a	**24**	2r. blue	3·75	1·80
119	**24**	3r. green	85	30
120	**24**	6r. orange	1·00	55

MS120a 150×85 mm. Nos. 118/20 (sold at 12r.) | 5·50 | 4·75

25 Prince Norodom Sihanouk and Independence Monument

1961. Independence Monument.

121	**25**	2r. green (postage)	85	35
122	**25**	4r. sepia	90	45
123	**25**	7r. multicoloured (air)	1·10	75
124	**25**	30r. red, blue and green	2·75	2·50
125	**25**	50r. multicoloured	4·25	3·75

MS125a Two sheets, each 150×85 mm. Nos. 121/2 (sold at 10r.); Nos. 123/5 (sold at 100r.). Price for 2 sheets | 18·00 | 16·00

1961. Sixth World Buddhist Conference. Optd **VIe CONFERENCE MONDIALE BOUDDHIQUE 12-11-1961.**

126	**6**	2p.50 (2r.50) green	1·30	75
127	**6**	4p.50 (4r.50) violet	2·00	1·20

27 Power Station (Czech Aid)

1962. Foreign Aid Programme.

128	**27**	2r. lake and red	45	30
129	-	3r. brown, green and blue	45	30
130	-	4r. brown, red and blue	45	40
131	-	5r. purple and green	75	45
132	-	6r. brown and blue	1·40	55

MS132a 150×85 mm. Nos. 128/32 (sold at 25r.) | 9·25 | 7·00

DESIGNS: 3r. Motorway (American Aid); 4r. Textile Factory (Chinese Aid); 5r. Friendship Hospital (Soviet Aid); 6r. Airport (French Aid).

28 Campaign Emblem

1962. Malaria Eradication.

133	**28**	2r. purple and brown	45	35
134	**28**	4r. green and brown	55	45
135	**28**	6r. violet and bistre	70	55

29 Curucmas

1962. Cambodian Fruits (1st issue).

136	**29**	2r. yellow and brown	75	60
137	-	4r. green and turquoise	85	70
138	-	6r. red, green and blue	1·20	1·00

MS138a 150×85 mm. Nos. 136/8 (sold at 15r.) | 7·00 | 5·75

FRUITS: 4r. Lychees. 6r. Mangosteens.

1962. Cambodian Fruits (2nd issue).

139	2r. brown and green	1·00	45
140	5r. green and brown	1·60	75
141	9r. brown and green	1·00	1·00

DESIGNS—VERT: 2r. Pineapples. 5r. Sugar-cane. 9r. "Bread" trees.

1962. Surch.

142	**16**	50c. on 80c. red	75	45
150	-	3r. on 2r.50 brn (No. 55)	1·00	65

1962. Inauguration of Independence Monument. Surch **INAUGURATION DU MONUMENT** and new value.

143	**25**	3r. on 2r. green (postage)	85	50
144	**25**	12r. on 7r. mult (air)	2·10	1·40

32 Campaign Emblem, Corn and Maize

1963. Freedom from Hunger.

145	**32**	3r. chestnut, brown & blue	75	65
146	**32**	6r. chestnut, brown & blue	75	65

33 Temple Preah Vihear

1963. Reunification of Preah Vihear Temple with Cambodia.

147	**33**	3r. brown, purple & green	55	45
148	**33**	6r. green, orange and blue	1·00	75
149	**33**	15r. brown, blue & green	1·60	1·30

35 Kep sur Mer

1963. Cambodian Resorts. Multicoloured.

151	3r. Koh Tonsay (vert)	55	45
152	7r. Popokvil (waterfall) (vert)	90	65
153	20r. Type **35**	3·00	1·30

1963. Red Cross Centenary. Surch **1863 1963 CENTENAIRE DE LA CROIX-ROUGE** and premium.

154	**28**	4r.+40c. green & brown	1·00	90
155	**28**	6r.+60c. violet & bistre	1·50	1·40

37 Scales of Justice

1963. 15th Anniv of Declaration of Human Rights.

156	**37**	1r. green, red and blue	55	55
157	**37**	3r. red, blue and green	1·00	1·00
158	**37**	12r. blue, green and red	1·80	1·80

38 Kouprey

1964. Wild Animal Protection.

159	**38**	50c. brown, green & chest	1·10	50
160	**38**	3r. brown, chestnut & grn	1·70	75
161	**38**	6r. brown, blue and green	2·40	1·60

39 Black-billed Magpie

1964. Birds.

162	**39**	3r. blue, green and indigo	1·30	65
163	-	6r. orange, purple & blue	1·90	1·00
164	-	12r. green and purple	3·50	2·00

BIRDS: 6r. River kingfisher. 12r. Grey heron.

40 "Hanuman"

1964. Air.

165	**40**	5r. mauve, brown & blue	1·10	70
166	**40**	10r. bistre, mauve & green	1·70	80
167	**40**	20r. bistre, violet and blue	2·75	1·70
168	**40**	40r. bistre, blue and red	6·25	3·00
169	**40**	80r. orange, green & purple	10·50	7·50

1964. Air Olympic Games, Tokyo. Surch **JEUX OLYMPIQUES TOKYO-1964**, Olympic rings and value.

170	3r. on 5r. mve, brn and bl	95	55
171	6r. on 10r. bis, mve & grn	1·60	80
172	9r. on 20r. bistre, vio & bl	1·80	1·40
173	12r. on 40r. bis, bl & red	3·75	2·20

42 Airline Emblem

1964. Eighth Anniv of Royal Air Cambodia.

174	**42**	1r.50 red and violet	40	30
175	**42**	3r. red and blue	75	50
176	**42**	7r.50 red and blue	1·50	70

43 Prince Norodom Sihanouk

1964. Tenth Anniv of Foundation of Sangkum (Popular Socialist Community).

177	**43**	2r. violet	75	50
178	**43**	3r. brown	95	60
179	**43**	10r. blue	1·90	1·10

44 Weaving

1965. Native Handicrafts.

180	**44**	1r. violet, brown & bistre	50	50
181	-	3r. brown, green & purple	85	60
182	-	5r. red, purple and green	1·40	1·10

DESIGNS: 3r. Engraving. 5r. Basket-making.

1965. Indo-Chinese People's Conference. Nos. 178/9 optd **CONFERENCE DES PEUPLES INDOCHINOIS.**

183	**43**	3r. brown	75	50
184	**43**	10r. blue	1·00	70

46 ITU Emblem and Symbols

1965. Centenary of ITU.

185	**46**	3r. bistre and green	55	45
186	**46**	4r. blue and red	75	65
187	**46**	10r. purple and violet	1·10	85

47 Cotton

1965. Industrial Plants. Multicoloured.

188		1r.50 Type **47**	75	55
189		3r. Groundnuts	1·20	65
190		7r.50 Coconut palms	1·80	1·20

48 Preah Ko

1966. Cambodian Temples.

191	**48**	3r. green, turquoise & brn	1·40	85
192	-	5r. brown, green & purple	1·60	90
193	-	7r. brown, green & ochre	2·20	1·70
194	-	9r. purple, green and blue	3·75	2·30
195	-	12r. red, green & verm	4·50	3·00

TEMPLES: 5r. Baksei Chamkrong, 7r. Banteay Srei, 9r. Angkor Vat. 12r. Bayon.

49 WHO Building

1966. Inaug of WHO Headquarters, Geneva.

196	**49**	2r. multicoloured	45	35
197	**49**	3r. multicoloured	55	45
198	**49**	5r. multicoloured	1·00	75

50 Tree-planting

1966. Tree Day.

199	**50**	1r. brown, green & dp brn	40	35
200	**50**	3r. brown, green & orange	65	45
201	**50**	7r. brown, green and grey	1·00	55

51 UNESCO Emblem

1966. 20th Anniv of UNESCO.

202	**51**	3r. multicoloured	60	55
203	**51**	7r. multicoloured	80	75

52 Stadium

1966. "Ganefo" Games, Phnom Penh.

204	**52**	3r. blue	45	25
205	-	4r. green	65	45
206	-	7r. red	85	65
207	-	10r. brown	1·30	85

DESIGNS: 4r., 7r., 10r. Various bas-reliefs of ancient sports from Angkor Vat.

53 Wild Boar

1967. Fauna.

208	**53**	3r. black, green and blue	1·40	60
209	-	5r. multicoloured	1·70	95
210	-	7r. multicoloured	2·40	1·40

FAUNA—VERT: 5r. Hog-deer. HORIZ: 7r. Indian elephant.

1967. International Tourist Year. Nos. 191/2, 194/5 and 149 optd **ANNEE INTERNATIONALE DU TOURISME 1967.**

211	**48**	3r. green, turquoise & brn	1·30	80
212	**48**	5r. brown, green & purple	1·40	90
213	-	9r. purple, green and blue	2·20	1·50
214	-	12r. red, green & verm	2·75	1·80
215	**33**	15r. brown, blue & green	3·25	2·00

1967. Millenary of Banteay Srei Temple. No. 193 optd **MILLENAIRE DE BANTEAY SREI 967–1967.**

216		7r. brown, green and ochre	2·20	90

56 Ballet Dancer

1967. Cambodian Royal Ballet. Designs showing ballet dancers.

217	**56**	1r. orange	75	70
218	-	3r. blue	1·50	70
219	-	5r. blue	2·00	1·30
220	-	7r. red	3·00	1·80
221	-	10r. multicoloured	3·75	2·50

1967. Int Literacy Day. Surch **Journee Internationale de l'Alphabetisation 8-9-67** and new value.

222	**37**	6r. on 12r. blue, grn & red	1·20	60
223	**15**	7r. on 15r. brown & green	1·40	95

58 Decade Emblem

1967. International Hydrological Decade.

224	**58**	1r. orange, blue and black	35	25
225	**58**	6r. orange, blue and violet	65	45
226	**58**	10r. orange, lt green & grn	1·00	70

59 Royal University of Kompong-Cham

1968. Cambodian Universities and Institutes.

227	**59**	4r. purple, blue & brown	65	60
228	-	6r. brown, green and blue	85	60
229	-	9r. brown, green and blue	1·20	80

DESIGNS: 6r. "Khmero-Soviet Friendship" Higher Technical Institute; 9r. Sangkum Reaster Niyum University Centre.

60 Doctor tending child

1968. 20th Anniv of WHO.

230	**60**	3r. blue	75	60
231	-	7r. blue	1·10	80

DESIGN: 7r. Man using insecticide.

61 Stadium

1968. Olympic Games, Mexico.

232	**61**	1r. brown, green and red	65	55
233	-	2r. brown, red and blue	75	60
234	-	3r. brown, blue and purple	85	65
235	-	5r. violet	1·00	70
236	-	7r.50 brown, green & red	1·40	80

DESIGNS—HORIZ: 2r. Wrestling; 3r. Cycling. VERT: 5r. Boxing; 7r.50, Runner with torch.

62 Stretcher-party

1968. Cambodian Red Cross Fortnight.

237	**62**	3r. red, green and blue	1·20	60

63 Prince Norodom Sihanouk

1968. 15th Anniv of Independence.

238	**63**	7r. violet, green and blue	65	60
239	-	8r. brown, green and blue	85	80

DESIGN: 8r. Soldiers wading through stream.

64 Human Rights Emblem and Prince Norodom Sihanouk

1968. Human Rights Year.

240	**64**	3r. blue	55	35
241	**64**	5r. purple	1·10	60
242	**64**	7r. black, orange & green	1·50	80

65 ILO Emblem

1969. 50th Anniv of ILO.

243	**65**	3r. blue	45	35
244	**65**	6r. red	65	60
245	**65**	9r. green	1·10	80

66 Red Cross Emblems around Globe

1969. 50th Anniv of League of Red Cross Societies.

246	**66**	1r. multicoloured	55	35
247	**66**	3r. multicoloured	65	60
248	**66**	10r. multicoloured	1·40	80

67 Golden Birdwing

1969. Butterflies.

249	**67**	3r. black, yellow & violet	5·00	1·50
250	-	4r. black, green & verm	6·50	2·30
251	-	8r. black, orange & green	9·25	3·50

DESIGNS: 4r. Tailed jay. 8r. Orange tiger.

68 Diesel Train and Route Map

1969. Opening of Phnom Penh–Sihanoukville Railway.

252	**68**	3r. multicoloured	1·10	90
253	-	6r. brown, black & green	2·20	1·80
254	-	8r. black	3·50	2·75
255	-	9r. blue, turquoise & grn	4·25	2·75

DESIGNS: 6r. Phnom Penh Station; 8r. Diesel locomotive and Kampor Station; 9r. Steam locomotive at Sihanoukville Station.

69 Siamese Tigerfish

1970. Fish. Multicoloured.

256		3r. Type **69**	2·50	1·60
257		7r. Marbled sleeper	5·00	2·75
258		9r. Chevron snakehead	7·00	3·50

70 Vat Tepthidaram

1970. Buddhist Monasteries in Cambodia. Multicoloured.

259		2r. Type **70**	75	60
260		3r. Vat Maniratanaram (horiz)	85	65
261		6r. Vat Patumavati (horiz)	1·60	70
262		8r. Vat Unnalom (horiz)	2·75	80

71 Dish Aerial and Open Book

1970. World Telecommunications Day.

263	**71**	3r. multicoloured	45	25
264	**71**	5r. multicoloured	55	30
265	**71**	9r. multicoloured	1·00	45

72 New Headquarters Building

1970. Opening of New UPU Headquarters Building, Berne.

266	**72**	1r. multicoloured	35	25
267	**72**	3r. multicoloured	55	30
268	**72**	4r. multicoloured	85	35
269	**72**	10r. multicoloured	1·80	60

73 Nelumbium speciosum

1970. Aquatic Plants. Multicoloured.

270		3r. Type **73**	85	35
271		4r. Eichhornia crassipes	1·50	70
272		13r. Nymphea lotus	3·25	1·10

74 "Banteay-srei" (bas-relief)

1970. World Meteorological Day.

273	**74**	3r. red and green	45	30
274	**74**	4r. red, green and blue	75	45
275	**74**	7r. green, blue and black	1·00	95

75 Rocket, Dove and Globe

1970. 25th Anniv of United Nations.

276	**75**	3r. multicoloured	35	25
277	**75**	5r. multicoloured	55	45
278	**75**	10r. multicoloured	1·10	70

76 IEY Emblem

1970. International Education Year.

279	**76**	1r. blue	30	20
280	**76**	3r. purple	35	25
281	**76**	8r. green	80	55

77 Samdech Chuon Nath

1971. Second Death Anniv of Samdech Chuon-Nath (Khmer language scholar).

282	**77**	3r. multicoloured	45	25
283	**77**	8r. multicoloured	1·00	45
284	**77**	9r. multicoloured	1·20	80

For issues between 1971 and 1989 see under KHMER REPUBLIC and KAMPUCHEA in volume 3.

203 17th-century Coach

1989. Coaches. Multicoloured.

1020	2r. Type **203**	25	10
1021	3r. Paris–Lyon coach, 1720	35	15
1022	5r. Mail coach, 1793	45	25
1023	10r. Light mail coach, 1805	1·00	30
1024	15r. Royal mail coach	1·40	45
1025	20r. Russian mail coach	1·70	60
1026	35r. Paris–Lille coupe, 1837 (vert)	3·50	90
MS1027	60×84 mm. 45r. Royal messenger coach, 1815 (31×39 mm)	6·75	1·80

No. **MS**1027 commemorates "Philexfrance '89" International Stamp Exhibition, Paris.

204 *Papilio zagreus*

1989. "Brasiliana 89" International Stamp Exhibition, Rio de Janeiro. Butterflies. Multicoloured.

1028	2r. Type **204**	25	10
1029	3r. *Morpho catenarius*	35	15
1030	5r. *Morpho aega*	45	25
1031	10r. *Callithea sapphira* ("wrongly inscr "saphhira")	1·00	30
1032	15r. *Catagramma sorana*	1·40	45
1033	20r. *Pierella nereis*	1·70	60
1034	35r. *Papilio brasiliensis*	3·50	90
MS1035	100×66 mm. 45r. *Thecla marsyas* (39×31 mm)	7·25	2·30

205 Pirogue

1989. Khmer Culture. Multicoloured.

1036	3r. Type **205**	25	15
1037	12r. Pirogue (two sets of oars)	1·10	60
1038	30r. Pirogue with cabin	3·75	1·80

206 Youth

1989. National Development. Multicoloured.

1039	3r. Type **206**	35	30
1040	12r. Trade unions emblem (horiz)	90	45
1041	30r. National Front emblem (horiz)	2·75	1·50

207 Goalkeeper

1990. World Cup Football Championship, Italy. Multicoloured.

1042	2r. Type **207**	25	10
1043	3r. Dribbling ball	35	15
1044	5r. Controlling ball with thigh	45	25
1045	10r. Running with ball	1·00	30
1046	15r. Shooting	1·40	45
1047	20r. Tackling	1·70	60
1048	35r. Tackling (different)	3·50	90
MS1049	94×75 mm. 45r. Players (31×39 mm)	6·75	1·80

208 Two-horse Postal Van

1990. "Stamp World London 90" International Stamp Exhibition. Royal Mail Horse-drawn Transport. Multicoloured.

1050	2r. Type **208**	25	10
1051	3r. One-horse cart	35	15
1052	5r. Rural post office cart	45	25
1053	10r. Rural post office van	1·00	30
1054	15r. Local post office van	1·40	45
1055	20r. Parcel-post cart	1·70	60
1056	35r. Two-horse wagon	3·50	90
MS1057	69×80 mm. 45r. Rural one-horse van (39×31 mm)	6·75	1·80

209 Rice Grains

1990. Cultivation of Rice. Multicoloured.

1058	3r. Type **209**	25	15
1059	12r. Transporting rice (horiz)	1·10	60
1060	30r. Threshing rice	3·75	1·50

210 Shooting

1990. Olympic Games, Barcelona (1992) (1st issue). Multicoloured.

1061	2r. Type **210**	25	10
1062	3r. Putting the shot	35	15
1063	5r. Weightlifting	45	25
1064	10r. Boxing	1·00	30
1065	15r. Pole vaulting	1·40	45
1066	20r. Basketball	1·70	60
1067	35r. Fencing	3·50	90
MS1068	83×70 mm. 45r. Gymnastics (31×37 mm)	6·75	1·80

See also Nos. 1163/**MS**1170, 1208/**MS**1213 and 1241/**MS**1246.

211 Four-man Bobsleighing

1990. Winter Olympic Games, Albertville (1992) (1st issue). Multicoloured.

1069	2r. Type **211**	25	10
1070	3r. Speed skating	35	15
1071	5r. Figure skating	45	25
1072	10r. Ice hockey	1·00	30
1073	15r. Biathlon	1·40	45
1074	20r. Lugeing	1·70	60

| 1075 | 35r. Ski jumping | 3·50 | 90 |
| **MS**1076 | 64×104 mm. Ice hockey goalkeeper (31×38 mm) | 6·75 | 1·80 |

See also Nos. 1152/**MS**1159.

212 Facade of Banteay Srei

1990. Khmer Culture. Multicoloured.

1077	3r. Type **212**	25	15
1078	12r. Ox-carts (12th-century relief)	1·10	60
1079	30r. Banon ruins (36×21 mm)	3·50	1·50

213 *Zizina oxleyi*

1990. "New Zealand 1990" International Stamp Exhibition, Auckland. Butterflies. Multicoloured.

1080	2r. Type **213**	45	10
1081	3r. *Cupha prosope*	55	15
1082	5r. *Heteronympha merope*	70	25
1083	10r. *Dodonidia helmsi*	1·40	30
1084	15r. *Argirophenga antipodum*	1·90	45
1085	20r. *Tysonotis danis*	2·75	60
1086	35r. *Pyrameis gonnarilla*	4·50	90
MS1087	76×65 mm. 45r. *Pyrameis itea* (39×31 mm)	8·00	2·50

214 "Vostok"

1990. Spacecraft. Multicoloured.

1088	2r. Type **214**	35	10
1089	3r. "Soyuz"	45	15
1090	5r. Satellite	55	25
1091	10r. "Luna 10"	1·00	30
1092	15r. "Mars 1"	1·50	45
1093	20r. "Venus 3"	2·00	60
1094	35r. "Mir" space station	3·75	90
MS1095	92×72 mm. 45r. "Energiya" and space shuttle "Burn" (31×39 mm)	8·00	2·30

215 Poodle

1990. Dogs. Multicoloured.

1096	20c. Type **215**	35	10
1097	80c. Shetland sheepdog	45	10
1098	3r. Samoyede	70	15
1099	6r. Springer spaniel	1·40	20
1100	10r. Wire-haired fox terrier	1·70	30
1101	15r. Afghan hound	2·75	45
1102	25r. Dalmatian	3·50	70
MS1103	95×83 mm. Burmese mountain dog (39×31 mm)	6·75	1·80

216 *Cereus hexagonus*

1990. Cacti. Multicoloured.

1104	20c. Type **216**	25	10
1105	80c. *Arthrocereus rondonianus*	35	10
1106	3r. *Matucana multicolor*	45	15
1107	6r. *Hildewintera aureispina*	90	20
1108	10r. *Opuntia retrosa*	1·10	30
1109	15r. *Erdisia tenuicula*	1·80	45
1110	25r. *Mamillaria yaquensis*	2·50	70

217 Learning to Write

1990. International Literacy Year.

1111	**217**	3r. black and blue	25	15
1112	**217**	12r. black and yellow	1·70	75
1113	**217**	30r. black and pink	5·50	1·80

218 English Nef, 1200

1990. Ships. Multicoloured.

1114	20c. Type **218**	35	10
1115	80c. 16th-century Spanish galleon	45	10
1116	3r. Dutch jacht, 1627	70	15
1117	6r. *La Couronne* (French galleon), 1638	1·40	20
1118	10r. Dumont d'Urville's ship *L'Astrolabe*, 1826	1·70	30
1119	15r. *Louisiane* (steamer), 1864	3·00	45
1120	25r. Clipper, 1900 (vert)	3·50	70
MS1121	97×80 mm. 45r. 19th-century merchant brig (31×39 mm)	7·25	2·30

No. 1118 is wrongly inscribed "d'Uville".

219 Phnom-Penh–Kampong Som Railway

1990. National Development. Multicoloured.

1122	3r. Type **219**	45	30
1123	12r. Port, Kampong Som	2·00	75
1124	30r. Fishing boats, Kampong Som	5·75	1·80

220 Sacre-Coeur de Montmartre and White Bishop

1990. "Paris '90" World Chess Championship, Paris. Multicoloured.

1125	2r. Type **220**	35	15
1126	3r. "The Horse Trainer" (statue) and white knight	45	25
1127	5r. "Victory of Samothrace" (statue) and white queen	70	35
1128	10r. Azay-le-Rideau Chateau and white rook	1·50	40
1129	15r. "The Dance" (statue) and white pawn	2·10	50
1130	20r. Eiffel Tower and white king	3·00	65
1131	35r. Arc de Triomphe and black chessmen	5·00	1·00
MS1132	91×58 mm. 45r. White chessmen (39×31 mm)	8·00	2·50

221 Columbus

1990. 500th Anniv (1992) of Discovery of America by Columbus (1st issue). Multicoloured.

1133	2r. Type **221**	45	15
1134	3r. Queen Isabella's jewel-chest	70	25
1135	5r. Queen Isabella the Catholic	90	35
1136	10r. *Santa Maria* (flagship)	1·50	40
1137	15r. Juan de la Cosa	2·10	50
1138	20r. Monument to Columbus	3·00	65
1139	35r. Devin Pyramid, Yucatan	5·50	1·00

MS1140 79×60 mm. 45r. Christopher
Columbus (31×39 mm) 8·00 2·00
 See also Nos. 1186/MS1193.

222 Tyre Factory

1991. National Festival. Multicoloured.
1141 100r. Type **222** 90 50
1142 300r. Rural hospital 3·25 2·00
1143 500r. Freshwater fishing (27×40
 mm) 5·00 2·75

223 Tackle

1991. World Cup Football Championship, U.S.A. (1994)
(1st issue).
1144 **223** 5r. multicoloured 25 15
1145 - 25r. multicoloured 35 25
1146 - 70r. multicoloured 45 30
1147 - 100r. multicoloured 70 40
1148 - 200r. multicoloured 1·20 45
1149 - 400r. multicoloured 2·50 60
1150 - 1000r. multicoloured 5·75 1·50
MS1151 85×93 mm. 900r. multicol-
oured 8·00 1·80
DESIGNS: 25r. to 1000r. Different footballing scenes.
 See also Nos. 1220/MS1225, 1317/MS1322 and 1381/
MS1386.

224 Speed Skating

1991. Winter Olympic Games, Albertville (1992) (2nd
issue). Multicoloured.
1152 5r. Type **224** 25 15
1153 25r. Slalom skiing 35 25
1154 70r. Ice hockey 45 30
1155 100r. Bobsleighing 70 40
1156 200r. Freestyle skiing 1·20 45
1157 400r. Ice skating 2·50 60
1158 1000r. Downhill skiing 5·75 1·50
MS1159 87×62 mm. 900r. Ski jumping
(31×39 mm) 8·00 1·80

225 Torso of Vishnu
Reclining (11th cent)

1991. Sculpture. Multicoloured.
1160 100r. *Garuda* (Koh Ker, 10th
 century) 45 30
1161 300r. Type **225** 1·80 1·50
1162 500r. *Reclining Nandin* (7th
 century) 2·75 2·00

226 Pole Vaulting

1991. Olympic Games, Barcelona (1992) (2nd issue).
Multicoloured.
1163 5r. Type **226** 25 15
1164 25r. Table tennis 35 25
1165 70r. Running 45 30
1166 100r. Wrestling 70 40
1167 200r. Gymnastics (bars) 1·20 45
1168 400r. Tennis 2·50 60
1169 1000r. Boxing 5·75 1·50
MS1170 78×73 mm. 900r. Gymnastics
(beam) (31×39 mm) 8·00 1·80

227 Douglas DC-10-30

1991. Airplanes. Multicoloured.
1171 5r. Type **227** 25 15
1172 25r. McDonnell Douglas MD-11 35 25
1173 70r. Ilyushin Il-96-300 45 30
1174 100r. Airbus Industrie A310 70 40
1175 200r. Yakovlev Yak-42 1·20 45
1176 400r. Tupolev Tu-154 2·50 60
1177 1000r. Douglas DC-9 5·75 1·50

228 Diaguita
Funerary Urn,
Catamarca

1991. "Espamer '91" Iberia–Latin America Stamp
Exhibition, Buenos Aires. Multicoloured.
1178 5r. Bareales glass pot, Catama-
 rca (horiz) 25 15
1179 25r. Type **228** 35 25
1180 70r. Quiroga urn, Tucuman 45 30
1181 100r. Round glass pot, Santiago
 del Estero (horiz) 70 40
1182 200r. Pitcher, Santiago del
 Estero (horiz) 1·20 45
1183 400r. Diaguita funerary urn,
 Tucuman 2·50 60
1184 1000r. Bareales funerary urn,
 Catamarca (horiz) 5·75 1·50
MS1185 80×65 mm. 900r. Funerary urn,
Catamarce (36×27 mm) 8·00 1·80

229 *Pinta*

1991. 500th Anniv (1992) of Discovery of America by
Columbus (2nd issue). Each brown, stone and black.
1186 5r. Type **229** 25 15
1187 25r. *Nina* 35 25
1188 70r. *Santa Maria* 55 30
1189 100r. Landing at Guanahani,
 1492 (horiz) 70 40
1190 200r. Meeting of two cultures
 (horiz) 1·40 45
1191 400r. La Navidad (first Euro-
 pean settlement in America)
 (horiz) 2·75 60
1192 1000r. Amerindian village
 (horiz) 6·50 1·50
MS1193 84×59 mm. Columbus (39×31
mm) 8·25 1·80

230 *Neptis pryeri*

1991. "Phila Nippon '91" International Stamp Exhibition,
Tokyo. Butterflies. Multicoloured.
1194 5r. Type **230** 25 15
1195 25r. *Papilio xuthus* 35 25
1196 70r. Common map butterfly 45 30
1197 100r. *Argynnis anadiomene* 70 40
1198 200r. *Lethe marginalis* 1·20 45
1199 400r. *Artopoetes pryeri* 2·50 60
1200 1000r. African monarch 5·75 1·50
MS1201 73×57 mm 900r. *Ochlodes
subhyalina* (39×31 mm) 8·00 1·80

231 Coastal Fishing Port

1991. National Development. Food Industry.
Multicoloured.
1202 100r. Type **231** 80 75
1203 300r. Preparing palm sugar
 (29×40 mm) 2·30 1·50
1204 500r. Picking peppers 3·75 2·30

232 Chakdomuk
Costumes

1992. National Festival. Traditional Costumes.
Multicoloured.
1205 150r. Type **232** 80 30
1206 350r. Longvek 2·30 45
1207 1000r. Angkor 3·75 75

233 Wrestling

1992. Olympic Games, Barcelona (3rd issue).
Multicoloured.
1208 5r. Type **233** 25 10
1209 15r. Football 30 15
1210 80r. Weightlifting 35 20
1211 400r. Archery 1·70 45
1212 1500r. Gymnastics 5·50 60
MS1213 79×59 mm. 1000r. show jump-
ing (31×39 mm) 6·25 1·80

234 Neon Tetra

1992. Fish. Multicoloured.
1214 5r. Type **234** 25 10
1215 15r. Siamese fighting fish 30 15
1216 80r. Kaiser tetra 35 20
1217 400r. Dwarf gourami 1·70 45
1218 1500r. Port hoplo 5·50 60
MS1219 80×65 mm. 1000r. Freshwater
angelfish (39×31 mm) 6·25 1·80

235 Germany v.
Columbia

1992. World Cup Football Championship, U.S.A. (1994)
(2nd issue). Multicoloured.
1220 5r. Type **235** 25 10
1221 15r. Netherlands player (horiz) 30 15
1222 80r. Uruguay v. C.I.S. (ex-Soviet
 states) 35 20
1223 400r. Cameroun v. Yugoslavia 1·70 45
1224 1500r. Italy v. Sweden 5·50 60
MS1225 75×51 mm. 1000r. Shot at
goal (39×31 mm) 6·25 1·80

236 Monument

1992. Khmer Culture. 19th-century Architecture.
Multicoloured.
1226 150r. Type **236** 80 75
1227 350r. Stupa 1·90 1·70
1228 1000r. Mandapa library 5·25 4·00

237 Motor Car

1992. 540th Birth Anniv (1992) of Leonardo da Vinci
(artist and inventor). Multicoloured.
1229 5r. Type **237** 30 10
1230 15r. Container ship 35 15
1231 80r. Helicopter 45 20
1232 400r. Scuba diver 2·30 60
1233 1500r. Parachutists (vert) 6·75 90
MS1234 79×59 mm. 1000r. Da Vinci
and drawing of *Flying Man* (31×39
mm) 6·75 2·00

238 Juan de la Cierva and
Autogyro

1992. "Expo '92" World's Fair, Seville. Inventors.
Multicoloured (except MS1240).
1235 5r. Type **238** 25 10
1236 15r. Thomas Edison and electric
 light bulb 30 15
1237 80r. Samuel Morse and Morse
 telegraph 35 20
1238 400r. Narciso Monturiol and
 "Ictineo" (early submarine) 1·70 45
1239 1500r. Alexander Graham Bell
 and early telephone 5·50 60
MS1240 83×62 mm.1000r. pink and
black (Robert Fulton (steamship))
(31×39 mm) 6·25 1·80

239 Weightlifting

1992. Olympic Games, Barcelona (4th issue).
Multicoloured.
1241 5r. Type **239** 30 10
1242 15r. Boxing 35 15
1243 80r. Basketball 45 20
1244 400r. Running 2·30 60
1245 1500r. Water polo 6·75 90
MS1246 71×75 mm. 1000r. Gymnastics
(39×31 mm) 6·75 2·00

240 Palm Trees

1992. Environmental Protection. Multicoloured.
1247 5r. Couple on riverside 30 10
1248 15r. Pagoda 35 15
1249 80r. Type **240** 45 20
1250 400r. Boy riding water buffalo 2·30 60
1251 1500r. Swimming in river 6·75 90
MS1252 100×71 mm. 1000r. Angkor
Wat (39×31 mm) 6·75 2·00

241 Louis de
Bougainville and *La
Boudeuse*

1992. "Genova '92" International Thematic Stamp
Exhibition, Genoa. Multicoloured.
1253 5r. Type **241** 35 10
1254 15r. James Cook and H.M.S.
 Endeavour 45 15
1255 80r. Charles Darwin and H.M.S.
 Beagle 70 20
1256 400r. Jacques Cousteau and
 Calypso 2·30 60

1257	1500r. *Kon Tiki* (replica of balsa raft)	7·25	90
MS1258	80×65 mm. 1000r. Christopher Columbus (28×36 mm)	25	2·00

242 *Albatrellus confluens*

1992. Fungi. Multicoloured.

1259	5r. Type **242**	25	10
1260	15r. Scarlet-stemmed boletus	35	15
1261	80r. Verdigris agaric	45	20
1262	400r. *Telamonia armillata*	2·00	60
1263	1500r. Goaty smell cortinarius	6·00	75

243 Bellanca Pacemaker Seaplane, 1930

1992. Aircraft. Multicoloured.

1264	5r. Type **243**	25	10
1265	15r. Canadair CL-215 fire-fighting amphibian, 1965	30	15
1266	80r. Grumman G-21 Goose amphibian, 1937	35	20
1267	400r. Grumman SA-6 Sealand flying boat, 1947	1·50	45
1268	1500r. Short S.23 Empire "C" Class flying boat, 1936	5·00	60
MS1269	80×60 mm. Grumman G-44 Widgeon, 1940 (31×39 mm)	6·75	1·80

244 Dish Aerial

1992. National Development. Multicoloured.

1270	150r. Type **244**	80	45
1271	350r. Dish aerial, flags and satellite	1·90	60
1272	1000r. Hotel Cambodiana	5·75	90

245 Sociological Institute

1993. National Festival. Multicoloured.

1273	50r. Type **245**	80	45
1274	450r. Motel Cambodiana	1·90	60
1275	1000r. Theatre, Bassac	5·75	90

246 Bottle-nosed Dolphin and Submarine

1993. Wildlife and Technology. Multicoloured.

1276	150r. Type **246**	80	15
1277	200r. Supersonic jet airplane and peregrine falcon	1·00	25
1278	250r. Eurasian beaver and dam	1·10	30
1279	500r. Satellite and natterer's bat	3·00	45
1280	900r. Rufous humming-bird and helicopter	4·50	60

247 *Datura suaveolens*

1993. Wild Flowers. Multicoloured.

1281	150r. Type **247**	80	15
1282	200r. *Convolvulus tricolor*	1·00	25
1283	250r. "Hippeastrum" hybrid	1·10	30
1284	500r. "Camellia" hybrid	3·00	45
1285	900r. *Lilium speciosum*	4·50	60
MS1286	75×50 mm. 1000t. Various flowers (31×39 mm)	6·75	2·10

248 Vihear Temple

1993. Khmer Culture. Multicoloured.

1287	50r. Sculpture of ox	70	45
1288	450r. Type **248**	1·90	1·50
1289	1000r. Offering to Buddha	5·75	3·25

249 Philippine Flying Lemur

1993. Animals. Multicoloured.

1290	150r. Type **249**	70	30
1291	200r. Red giant flying squirrel	90	40
1292	250r. Fringed gecko	1·00	45
1293	500r. Wallace's flying frog	2·30	60
1294	900r. Flying lizard	3·50	1·10

250 *Symbrenthia hypselis*

1993. "Brasiliana '93" International Stamp Exhibition, Rio de Janeiro. Butterflies. Multicoloured.

1295	250r. Type **250**	1·10	30
1296	350r. *Sithon nedymond*	1·90	40
1297	600r. *Geitoneura minyas*	2·75	45
1298	800r. *Argyreus hyperbius*	3·50	60
1299	1000r. *Argyrophenga antipodum*	4·75	1·10
MS1300	82×52 mm. 1500r. *Parage schakra* (39×31 mm)	8·00	2·10

251 Armed Cambodians reporting to U.N. Base

1993. United Nations Transitional Authority in Cambodia Pacification Programme. Each black and blue.

1301	150r. Type **251**	80	15
1302	200r. Military camp	1·00	20
1303	250r. Surrender of arms	1·10	25
1304	500r. Vocational training	2·50	40
1305	900r. Liberation	4·00	45
MS1306	54×84 mm. 1000r. Return to homes (31×39 mm)	6·75	2·10

252 Venetian Felucca

1993. Sailing Ships. Multicoloured.

1307	150r. Type **252**	55	15
1308	200r. Phoenician galley	70	25
1309	250r. Egyptian merchantman	80	30
1310	500r. Genoese merchantman	2·10	40
1311	900r. English merchantman	3·25	45

253 Santos-Dumont, Eiffel Tower and *Ballon No. 6*, 1901

1993. 120th Birth Anniv of Alberto Santos-Dumont (aviator). Multicoloured.

1312	150r. Type **253**	80	15
1313	200r. *14 bis* (biplane), 1906 (horiz)	1·00	25
1314	250r. *Demoiselle* (monoplane), 1909 (horiz)	1·10	30
1315	500r. Embraer EMB-201 A (horiz)	3·00	40
1316	900r. Embraer EMB-111 (horiz)	4·50	45

254 Footballer

1993. World Cup Football Championship, U.S.A. (1994) (3rd issue).

1317	**254**	250r. multicoloured	1·10	15
1318	-	350r. multicoloured	1·90	25
1319	-	600r. multicoloured	2·75	40
1320	-	800r. multicoloured	3·50	40
1321	-	1000r. mult (vert)	4·75	45
MS1322	60×85 mm. 1500r. multicoloured (39×31 mm)		8·50	2·10

DESIGNS: 350r. to 1500r. Various footballing scenes.

255 European Wigeon

1993. "Bangkok 1993" International Stamp Exhibition, Thailand. Ducks. Multicoloured.

1323	250r. Type **255**	1·10	15
1324	350r. Baikal teal	1·90	25
1325	600r. Mandarin	2·75	30
1326	800r. Wood duck	3·50	40
1327	1000r. Harlequin duck	4·75	45
MS1328	63×89 mm. 1500r. Head of mandarin (39×31 mm)	8·50	2·10

256 First Helicopter Model, France, 1784

1993. Vertical Take-off Aircraft. Multicoloured.

1329	150r. Type **256**	80	15
1330	200r. Model of steam helicopter, 1863	1·00	25
1331	250r. New York–Atlanta–Miami autogyro flight, 1927 (horiz)	1·10	30
1332	500r. Sikorsky helicopter, 1943 (horiz)	2·50	40
1333	900r. French vertical take-off jet	4·50	45
MS1334	90×49 mm. 1000r. Juan de la Clerva's C.4, 1923 (first practical autogyro)	6·75	1·80

257 *Cnaphalocrosis medinalis*

1993. National Development. Harmful Insects. Multicoloured.

1335	50r. Type **257**	45	25
1336	450r. Brown leaf-hopper	2·30	30
1337	500r. *Scirpophaga incertulas*	2·50	45
1338	1000r. Stalk-eyed fly	5·25	60

MS1339	89×90 mm. 1000r. *Leptocorisa oratorius* (31×39 mm)	6·25	1·80

258 Ministry of Posts and Telecommunications

1993. 40th Anniv of Independence.

1340	**258**	300r. multicoloured	1·60	60
1341	-	500r. multicoloured	2·50	1·40
1342	-	700r. blue, red & black	3·50	1·80

DESIGNS—VERT: 500r. Independence monument. HORIZ: 700r. National flag.

259 Boy with Pony

1993. Figurines by M. J. Hummel. Multicoloured.

1343	50r. Type **259**	35	10
1344	100r. Girl and pram	80	15
1345	150r. Girl bathing doll	1·10	25
1346	200r. Girl holding doll	1·40	30
1347	250r. Boys playing	1·80	40
1348	300r. Girls pulling boy in cart	2·30	45
1349	350r. Girls playing ring-o-roses	2·50	60
1350	600r. Boys with stick and drum	4·00	90

260 Figure Skating

1994. Winter Olympic Games, Lillehammer, Norway. Multicoloured.

1351	150r. Type **260**	70	15
1352	250r. Two-man luge (horiz)	1·10	25
1353	400r. Skiing (horiz)	1·90	30
1354	700r. Biathlon (horiz)	3·50	40
1355	900r. Speed skating	4·75	45
MS1356	85×60 mm. 1500r. Curling (31×39 mm)	8·50	1·90

261 Opel 4/12 Laubfrosch two-seater, 1924

1994. Motor Cars. Multicoloured.

1357	150r. Type **261**	80	15
1358	200r. Mercedes 35 h.p. four-seater, 1901	1·00	25
1359	250r. Ford Model "T" Tudor sedan, 1927	1·10	30
1360	500r. Rolls Royce 40/50 Silver Ghost tourer, 1907	2·50	40
1361	900r. Hutton racing car, 1908	4·00	45
MS1362	80×60 mm 1000r. Duesenberg model J phaeton, 1931 (31×39 mm)	6·75	1·80

262 Gymnastics

1994. Olympic Games, Atlanta (1996) (1st issue). Multicoloured.

1363	150r. Type **262**	70	10
1364	200r. Football	90	15
1365	250r. Throwing the javelin	1·10	25
1366	300r. Canoeing	1·20	30
1367	600r. Running	2·75	40
1368	1000r. Diving (horiz)	5·00	45
MS1369	79×63 mm. 1500r. Show jumping (31×39 mm)	8·50	1·90

See also Nos. 1437/**MS**1442 and 1495/**MS**1501.

263 Siva and Uma
(10th century,
Banteay Srei)

1994. Khmer Culture. Statues. Multicoloured.
1370	300r. Type **263**		1·60	1·10
1371	500r. Vishnu (6th cent, Tvol Dai-Buon)		2·75	1·80
1372	700r. King Jayavarman VII (12th–13th century, Krol Romeas Angkor)		4·00	2·50

264 Olympic Flag

1994. Centenary of International Olympic Committee. Multicoloured.
1373	100r. Type **264**		45	30
1374	300r. Flag and torch		1·60	90
1375	600r. Flag and Pierre de Coubertin (reviver of modern Olympic Games)		3·50	1·70

265 Mesonyx

1994. Prehistoric Animals. Multicoloured.
1376	150r. Type **265**		70	30
1377	250r. Doedicurus		1·10	45
1378	400r. Mylodon		1·90	70
1379	700r. Uintatherium		3·50	85
1380	1000r. Hyrachyus		4·75	1·30

266 Players

1994. World Cup Football Championship, U.S.A. (4th issue).
1381	**266**	150r. multicoloured	70	15
1382	-	250r. multicoloured	1·10	25
1383	-	400r. multicoloured	1·90	30
1384	-	700r. multicoloured	3·50	40
1385	-	1000r. multicoloured	4·75	45
MS1386	58×78 mm. 1500r. multi-coloured		8·50	1·90

DESIGNS: 250r. to 1500r. Various footballing scenes.

267 "Soldiers in Combat"

1994. Tourism. Statues in Public Gardens. Multicoloured.
1387	300r. "Stag and Hind"		1·90	90
1388	500r. Type **267**		2·75	1·80
1389	700r. "Lions"		4·00	2·75

268 Chlorophanus viridis

1994. Beetles. Multicoloured.
1390	150r. Type **268**		80	15
1391	200r. Chrysochroa fulgidissima		90	30
1392	250r. Lytta vesicatoria		1·10	40
1393	500r. Purpuricenus kaehleri		3·00	75

1394	900r. Herculese beetle		4·25	1·20
MS1395	69×50 mm. Timarcha tenebricosa (31×39 mm)		6·25	1·80

269 Halley's
Diving-bell, 1690

1994. Submarines. Multicoloured.
1396	150r. Type **269**		80	15
1397	200r. Gimnote, 1886 (horiz)		90	30
1398	250r. Peral (Spain), 1888 (horiz)		1·10	40
1399	500r. Nautilus (first nuclear-powered submarine), 1954 (horiz)		3·00	75
1400	900r. Trieste (bathyscaphe), 1953 (horiz)		4·25	1·20
MS1401	80×70 mm. 1000r. Narciso Monturiol's submarine Ictineo, 1885 (39×31 mm)		6·25	1·80

270 Francois-Andre Philidor, 1795

1994. Chess Champions. Multicoloured.
1402	150r. Type **270**		80	15
1403	200r. Mahe de la Bourdonnais, 1821		90	30
1404	250r. Karl Andersser, 1851		1·10	40
1405	500r. Paul Morphy, 1858		3·00	75
1406	900r. Wilhelm Steinitz, 1866		4·25	1·20
MS1407	90×50 mm. 1000r. Emanual Lasker, 1894 (31×38 mm)		6·25	1·80

271 Sikorsky S-42 Flying Boat

1994. Aircraft. Multicoloured.
1408	150r. Type **271**		80	15
1409	200r. Vought-Sikorsky VS-300A helicopter prototype		90	30
1410	250r. Sikorsky S-37 biplane		1·10	40
1411	500r. Sikorsky S-35 biplane		3·00	75
1412	900r. Sikorsky S-43 amphibian		4·25	1·20
MS1413	80×50 mm. 1500r. Sikorsky Ilya Muroments (80th Anniv of first multi-engined airplane) (39×31 mm)		6·25	1·80

272 Penduline Tit

1994. Birds. Multicoloured.
1414	150r. Type **272**		70	15
1415	250r. Bearded reedling		1·10	30
1416	400r. Little bunting		2·00	45
1417	700r. Cirl bunting		3·50	75
1418	1000r. Goldcrest		5·00	1·20
MS1419	60×90 mm. 1500r. African pitta (31×39)		6·75	2·75

273 Postal Service Float

1994. National Independence Festival. Multicoloured.
1420	300r. Type **273**		1·60	90
1421	500r. Soldiers marching		2·30	1·80
1422	700r. Women's army units on parade		3·50	2·75

274 Chruoi Changwar Bridge

1994. National Development. Multicoloured.
1423	300r. Type **274**		1·20	60
1424	500r. Olympique Commercial Centre		2·10	90
1425	700r. Sakyamony Chedei Temple		2·75	1·20

275 Psittacosaurus

1995. Prehistoric Animals. Multicoloured.
1426	100r. Type **275**		25	10
1427	200r. Protoceratops		50	25
1428	300r. Montanoceraptors		75	40
1429	400r. Centrosaurus		1·60	45
1430	700r. Styracosaurus		2·50	60
1431	800r. Triceratops		3·50	90

276 Orange-tip

1995. Butterflies. Multicoloured.
1432	100r. Type **276**		35	10
1433	200r. Scarce swallowtail		90	25
1434	300r. Dark green fritillary		1·40	30
1435	600r. Red admiral		2·00	45
1436	800r. Peacock		3·25	75

277 Swimming

1995. Olympic Games, Atlanta (1996) (2nd issue). Multicoloured.
1437	100r. Type **277**		45	10
1438	200r. Callisthenics (vert)		90	25
1439	400r. Basketball (vert)		1·70	45
1440	800r. Football (vert)		4·00	75
1441	900r. Cycling (vert)		4·75	1·20
MS1442	48×69 mm. 1500r. Running (31×39 mm)		5·50	1·80

278 Death Cap

1995. Fungi. Multicoloured.
1443	100r. Type **278**		45	10
1444	200r. Chanterelle		1·10	30
1445	300r. Honey fungus		1·60	40
1446	600r. Field mushroom		2·75	60
1447	800r. Fly agaric		3·50	70

279 Kneeling
Ascetic

1995. Khmer Culture. Statues. Multicoloured.
1448	300r. Type **279**		1·20	60
1449	500r. Parasurama		2·10	90
1450	700r. Shiva		2·75	1·20

280 Gaur

1995. Protected Animals. Multicoloured.
1451	300r. Type **280**		1·40	45
1452	500r. Kouprey (vert)		2·00	60
1453	700r. Saurus crane (vert)		2·75	90

281 Black-capped
Lory

1995. Parrot Family. Multicoloured.
1454	100r. Type **281**		35	10
1455	200r. Princess parrot		75	25
1456	400r. Eclectus parrot		1·40	30
1457	800r. Scarlet macaw		3·00	60
1458	1000r. Budgerigar		3·75	75
MS1459	52×81 mm. 1500r. Yellow-headed amazon (30×38 mm)		5·00	1·50

282 Bird (sculpture)

1995. Tourism. Public Gardens. Multicoloured.
1460	300r. Type **282**		1·20	60
1461	500r. Water feature		2·10	90
1462	700r. Mythical figures (sculpture)		2·30	1·20

283 Richard Trevithick's
Locomotive, 1804

1995. Steam Locomotives. Multicoloured.
1463	100r. Type **283**		35	10
1464	200r. G. and R. Stephenson's Rocket, 1829		1·10	30
1465	300r. George Stephenson's Locomotion, 1825		1·60	40
1466	600r. Lafayette, 1837		2·50	75
1467	800r. Best Friend of Charleston, 1830		3·25	1·20
MS1468	74×59 mm. 1000r. George Stephenson (inventor of steam locomotive) (31×38 mm)		5·00	2·75

284 Bristol Type
142 Blenheim Mk II
Bomber

1995. Second World War Planes. Multicoloured.
1469	100r. Type **284**		35	10
1470	200r. North American B-25B Mitchell bomber (horiz)		1·10	30
1471	300r. Avro Type 652 Anson Mk I general purpose plane (horiz)		1·60	40
1472	600r. Avro Manchester bomber (horiz)		2·50	75
1473	800r. Consolidated B-24 Liberator bomber (horiz)		3·25	1·20
MS1474	81×49 mm. 1000r. Boeing B-17 Flying Fortress bomber (31×38 mm)		5·00	2·75

285 Gathering Crops

1995. 50th Anniv of FAO. Multicoloured.

1475	300r. Type **285**	1·10	60
1476	500r. Transplanting crops	2·00	90
1477	700r. Paddy field	3·00	1·20

286 Bridge

1995. 50th Anniv of UNO. Preah Kunlorng Bridge. Multicoloured.

1478	300r. Type **286**	1·10	60
1479	500r. People on bridge	2·00	90
1480	700r. Closer view of bridge	3·00	1·20

287 Queen Monineath

1995. National Independence. Multicoloured.

1481	700r. Type **287**	3·25	1·20
1482	800r. King Norodom Sihanouk	4·00	1·50

288 Pennant Coralfish

1995. Fish. Multicoloured.

1483	100r. Type **288**	35	10
1484	200r. Copper-banded butterflyfish	75	30
1485	400r. Crown anemonefish	1·40	40
1486	800r. Palette surgeonfish	3·00	75
1487	1000r. Queen angelfish	3·50	1·20
MS1488	85×50 mm. win-spotted wrasse	5·25	2·30

289 Post Office Building

1995. Cent of Head Post Office, Phnom Penh.

1489	**289** 300r. multicoloured	1·80	70
1490	**289** 500r. multicoloured	2·50	1·20
1491	**289** 700r. multicoloured	3·50	1·50

290 Independence Monument

1995. 40th Anniv of Admission of Cambodia to United Nations Organization. Multicoloured.

1492	300r. Type **290**	1·40	45
1493	400r. Angkor Wat	1·90	90
1494	800r. U.N. emblem and national flag (vert)	3·00	1·20

291 Tennis

1996. Olympic Games, Atlanta (3rd issue). Multicoloured.

1495	100r. Type **291**	25	10
1496	200r. Volleyball	40	15
1497	300r. Football	55	25
1498	500r. Running	1·00	30
1499	900r. Baseball	1·90	60
1500	1000r. Basketball	2·30	90
MS1501	64×94 mm. 1500r. Windsurfing (28×38 mm)	5·25	1·80

292 Kep State Chalet

1996

1502	**292**	50r. blue and black	25	10
1503	-	100r. red and black	30	15
1504	-	200r. yellow and black	65	25
1505	-	500r. blue and black	1·50	30
1506	-	800r. mauve and black	2·30	45
1507	-	1000r. yellow and black	2·50	75
1508	-	1500r. green and black	3·25	1·10

DESIGNS—HORIZ: 100r. Power station; 200r. Wheelchair; 500r. Handicapped basketball team; 1000r. Kep beach; 1500r. Serpent Island. VERT: 800r. Man making crutches.

293 European Wild Cat

1996. Wild Cats. Multicoloured.

1509	100r. *Felis libyca* (vert)	35	10
1510	200r. Type **293**	45	15
1511	300r. Caracal	80	25
1512	500r. Geoffroy's cat	1·40	30
1513	900r. Black-footed cat	2·50	85
1514	1000r. Flat-headed cat	3·00	1·20

294 Player dribbling Ball

1996. World Cup Football Championship, France (1998) (1st issue). Multicoloured.

1515	**294**	100r. multicoloured	45	10
1516	-	200r. multicoloured	70	15
1517	-	300r. multicoloured	1·10	25
1518	-	500r. multicoloured	1·90	40
1519	-	900r. multicoloured	3·50	90
1520	-	1000r. mult (horiz)	4·00	1·40
MS1521		65×79 mm. 1500r. multicoloured (31×38 mm)	6·25	1·80

DESIGNS: 200r. to 1500r. Different players.
See also Nos. 1613/**MS**1619 and 1726/**MS**1732.

295 Tusmukh

1996. Khmer Culture. Multicoloured.

1522	100r. Type **295**	35	25
1523	300r. Ream Iso	1·90	90
1524	900r. Isei	3·25	1·70

296 Pacific Steam Locomotive No. 620, Finland

1996. Railway Locomotives. Multicoloured.

1525	100r. Type **296**	35	10
1526	200r. GNR steam locomotive No. 261, Great Britain	45	15
1527	300r. Steam tank locomotive, 1930	80	25
1528	500r. Steam tank locomotive No. 1362, 1914	1·40	30
1529	900r. LMS Turbomotive No. 6202, 1930, Great Britain	2·50	85
1530	1000r. Locomotive *Snake*, 1884, New Zealand	3·00	1·20
MS1531	80×55 mm. 1500r. Canadian Pacific train with Vistadome observation car (39×31 mm)	6·75	2·30

No. **MS**1531 commemorates "CEPEX '96" International Stamp Exhibition, Toronto.

297 White-rumped Shama

1996. Birds. Multicoloured.

1532	100r. Type **297**	35	10
1533	200r. Pekin robin	45	15
1534	300r. Varied tit	80	25
1535	500r. Black-naped oriole	1·40	30
1536	900r. Japanese bush warbler	2·50	85
1537	1000r. Blue and white flycatcher	3·00	1·20

298 Rhythmic Gymnastics

1996. "Olymphilex '96" Olympic Stamps Exhibition, Atlanta, U.S.A. Multicoloured.

1538	100r. Type **298**	35	10
1539	200r. Judo	45	15
1540	300r. High jumping	80	25
1541	500r. Wrestling	1·40	30
1542	900r. Weightlifting	2·50	85
1543	1000r. Football	3·00	1·20
MS1544	84×55 mm. 1500r. Diving (31×39 mm)	5·75	1·90

299 Douglas M-2, 1926

1996. Biplanes. Multicoloured.

1545	100r. Type **299**	35	10
1546	200r. Pitcairn PS-5 Mailwing, 1926	45	15
1547	300r. Boeing 40-B, 1928	80	25
1548	500r. Potez 25. 1925	1·40	30
1549	900r. Stearman C-3MB, 1927	2·50	85
1550	1000r. de Havilland D.H.4. 1918	3·00	1·20
MS1551	80×60 mm. 1500r. Standar JR-1B, 1918 (39×30 mm)	6·75	2·30

300 Aspara

1996. Tonle Bati Temple Ruins.

1552	**300**	50r. black and yellow	25	10
1553	-	100r. black and blue	35	15
1554	-	200r. black and brown	70	25
1555	-	500r. black and blue	1·10	30
1556	-	800r. black and green	1·60	45
1557	-	1000r. black and green	2·00	75
1558	-	1500r. black and bistre	3·50	1·40

DESIGNS—VERT: 100r. Aspara (different); 200r. Aspara (different); 800r. Taprum Temple; 1000r. Grandmother Peou Temple. HORIZ: 500r. Reliefs on wall; 1500r. Overall view of Tonle Bati.

301 Coelophysis

1996. Prehistoric Animals. Multicoloured.

1559	50r. Type **301**	10	10
1560	100r. Euparkeria	25	10
1561	150r. Plateosaurus	35	15
1562	200r. Herrerasaurus	55	20
1563	250r. Dilophosaurus	60	25
1564	300r. Tuojiangosaurus	80	30
1565	350r. Camarasaurus	1·20	40
1566	400r. Ceratosaurus	1·50	45
1567	550r. Espinosaurio	1·70	55
1568	700r. Ouranosaurus	2·30	75
1569	800r. Avimimus	2·75	90
1570	1200r. Deinonychus	4·00	1·50

Nos. 1559/62, 1563/6 and 1567/70 respectively were issued together, *se-tenant*, each sheetlet containing a composite design of a globe.

302 Jose Raul Capablanca (1921–27)

1996. World Chess Champions. Multicoloured.

1571	100r. Type **302**	35	10
1572	200r. Aleksandr Alekhine (1927–35, 1937–46)	50	15
1573	300r. Vasily Vasilevich Smyslov (1957–58)	85	25
1574	500r. Mikhail Nekhemyevich Tal (1960–61)	1·50	45
1575	900r. Robert Fischer (1972–75)	2·50	75
1576	1000r. Anatoly Karpov (1975–85)	3·00	1·10
MS1577	70×87 mm. 1500r. Garry Kasparov (1985–2000) (31×38 mm)	6·75	1·80

303 Brown Bear

1996. Mammals and their Young. Multicoloured.

1578	100r. Type **303**	35	10
1579	200r. Lion	50	15
1580	300r. Malayan tapir	75	25
1581	500r. Bactrian camel	1·50	45
1582	900r. Ibex (vert)	2·40	60
1583	1000r. Californian sealion (vert)	3·00	1·10

304 Rough Collie

1996. Dogs. Multicoloured.

1584	200r. Type **304**	50	15
1585	300r. Labrador retriever	75	25
1586	500r. Dobermann pinscher	1·50	45
1587	900r. German shepherd	2·40	60
1588	1000r. Boxer	2·75	75

305 Chinese Junk

1996. Ships. Multicoloured.

1589	200r. Type **305**	70	25
1590	300r. Phoenician warship, 1500–1000 B.C.	90	30
1591	500r. Roman war galley, 264–241 B.C.	1·90	55
1592	900r. 19th-century full-rigged ship	3·25	1·10
1593	1000r. *Sirius* (paddle- steamer), 1838	3·50	1·20
MS1594	90×60 mm. 1500r. *Great Eastern* (cable ship and paddle-steamer), 1858 (39×31 mm)	6·75	1·80

306 Silver Pagoda, Phnom Penh

1996. 45th Anniv of Cambodian Membership of Universal Postal Union.

1595	**306** 200r. multicoloured	1·10	45
1596	**306** 400r. multicoloured	1·70	75
1597	**306** 900r. multicoloured	3·50	1·70

307 Environmental Vessel and Helicopter

1996. 25th Anniv of Greenpeace (environmental organization). Multicoloured.

1598	200r. Type **307**	1·10	15
1599	300r. Float-helicopter hovering over motor launch	2·00	45
1600	500r. Helicopter on deck and motor launches	3·00	75
1601	900r. Helicopter with two barrels suspended beneath	5·00	1·10
MS1602 111×90 mm. 10000r. Float-helicopter (31×39 mm)		6·25	1·50

308 Ox

1996. New Year. Year of the Ox. Details of painting by Han Huang. Multicoloured.

1603	500r. Type **308**	90	45
1604	500r. Ox with head turned to right (upright horns)	90	45
1605	500r. Brown and white ox with head up ("handlebar" horns)	90	45
1606	500r. Ox with head in bush ("ram's" horns)	90	45

309 Dam, Phnom Kaun Sat

1996. Tenth International United Nations Volunteers Day. Multicoloured.

1607	100r. Type **309**	45	15
1608	500r. Canal, O Angkrung	2·00	90
1609	900r. Canal, Chrey Krem	3·50	1·70

310 Architect's Model of Reservoir

1996. 43rd Anniv of Independence. Water Management. Multicoloured.

1610	100r. Type **310**	45	15
1611	500r. Reservoir	2·00	90
1612	900r. Reservoir (different)	3·50	1·70

311 Players

1997. World Cup Football Championship, France (1998) (2nd issue).

1613	**311**	100r. multicoloured	45	10
1614	-	200r. multicoloured	70	15
1615	-	300r. multicoloured	1·10	25
1616	-	500r. multicoloured	1·90	40
1617	-	900r. multicoloured	3·50	90
1618	-	1000r. multicoloured	4·00	1·40
MS1619 99×68 mm. 2000r. multicoloured (39×31 mm)			6·75	2·30

DESIGNS: 200r. to 2000r. Different footballing scenes.

312 Two Elephants

1997. The Indian Elephant. Multicoloured.

1620	300r. Type **312**	55	15
1621	500r. Group of three	90	30
1622	900r. Elephants fighting	1·80	70
1623	1000r. Adult and calf	2·10	90

314 Horse-drawn Water Pump, 1731

1997. Fire Engines. Multicoloured.

1630	200r. Type **314**	45	10
1631	500r. Putnam horse-drawn water pump, 1863	70	15
1632	900r. Merryweather horse-drawn engine, 1894	90	25
1633	1000r. Shand Mason Co horse-drawn water pump, 1901	1·20	30
1634	1500r. Maxin Motor Co automatic pump, 1949	1·90	45
1635	4000r. Merryweather exhaust pump, 1950	4·75	1·50
MS1636 106×87 mm. 5400r. Mack Truck Co. mechanical ladder, 1953 (39×31 mm)		6·75	2·30

315 Statue on Plinth

1997. Angkor Wat.

1637	**315**	300r. black and red	45	10
1638	-	300r. black and blue	45	10
1639	-	800r. black and green	90	25
1640	-	1500r. black & brown	1·90	45
1641	-	1700r. black & orange	2·10	55
1642	-	2500r. black and blue	2·75	75
1643	-	3000r. black & green	3·50	1·00

DESIGNS—VERT: No. 1638, Statue in wall recess; 1639, Walled courtyard; 1640, Decorative panel with two figures. HORIZ: No. 1641, Rectangular gateway; 1642, Statues and arched gateway; 1643, Stupa and ruins.

316 Steller's Eider

1997. Aquatic Birds. Multicoloured.

1644	200r. Type **316**	35	10
1645	500r. Egyptian goose	45	10
1646	900r. American wigeon	70	15
1647	1000r. Falcated teal	90	25
1648	1500r. Surf scoter	1·40	40
1649	4000r. Blue-winged teal	3·50	1·00
MS1650 95×75 mm. 5400r. Baikal teal (31×39 mm)		5·75	1·80

317 Von Stephan

1997. Death Centenary of Heinrich von Stephan (founder of UPU).

1651	**317**	500r. blue & dp blue	70	45
1652	**317**	1500r. green and olive	1·90	60
1653	**317**	2000r. yellow & green	2·75	90

318 Main Entrance

1997. Khmer Culture. Banteay Srei Temple. Multicoloured.

1654	500r. Type **318**	70	45
1655	1500r. Main and side entrances	1·90	60
1656	2000r. Courtyard	2·75	90

319 Birman

1997. Cats. Multicoloured.

1657	200r. Type **319**	35	10
1658	500r. Exotic shorthair	50	15
1659	900r. Persian	75	25
1660	1000r. Turkish van	95	30
1661	1500r. American shorthair	1·50	40
1662	4000r. Scottish fold	4·00	1·10
MS1663 90×70 mm. 5400r. Sphinx (31×39 mm)		5·00	1·80

320 No. 488 S.W.R. Loco British Rail No. 30583

1997. Steam Railway Locomotives. Multicoloured.

1664	200r. Type **320**	45	10
1665	500r. *Frederick Smith*	70	25
1666	900r. No. 3131	90	30
1667	1000r. London Transport No. L44, Great Britain	1·20	40
1668	1500r. LNER No. 1711, Great Britain	1·90	60
1669	4000r. No. 60523 *Chateau du Soleil*	5·00	1·80
MS1670 76×60 mm. 5400r. LNER No. 2006, Great Britain		6·25	1·90

321 Shar-pei

1997. Dogs. Multicoloured.

1671	200r. Type **321**	35	10
1672	500r. Chin-chin	50	15
1673	600r. Pekingese	60	25
1674	1000r. Chow-chow (vert)	75	30
1675	1500r. Pug (vert)	1·50	40
1676	4000r. Akita (vert)	4·00	1·10
MS1677 111×88 mm. 5400r. Chinese crested (vert)		5·00	1·80

322 Qunalom Temple

1997. 30th Anniv of Association of South East Asian Nations. Multicoloured.

1678	500r. Type **322**	70	45
1679	1500r. Royal Palace	1·90	60
1680	2000r. National Museum	2·75	90

323 15th-century Caravelle

1997. Sailing Ships. Multicoloured.

1681	200r. Type **323**	45	10
1682	500r. Spanish galleon	55	15
1683	900r. *Great Harry* (British galleon)	80	25
1684	1000r. *La Couronne* (French galleon)	1·00	30
1685	1500r. 18th-century East Indiaman	1·50	40
1686	4000r. 19th-century clipper	4·00	1·10
MS1687 94×68 mm. 5400r. H.M.S. *Victory* (Nelson)		6·25	1·80

324 Public Garden

1997. Public Gardens (Nos. 1688/91) and Tuk Chha Canal (others).

1688	**324**	300r. green and black	45	10
1689	-	300r. red and black	45	10
1690	-	800r. yellow and black	90	30
1691	-	1500r. orange and black	1·90	60
1692	-	1700r. pink and black	2·10	70
1693	-	2500r. blue and black	2·75	90
1694	-	3000r. blue and black	3·50	1·10

DESIGNS—HORIZ: 300r. Statue at intersection of paths; 300r. Hedging in triangular bed; 1500r. Tree and statue of lion; 1700r. View along canal; 2500r. View across canal; 3000r. Closed lock gates. VERT: 800r. Mounted bowl.

325 Satan's Mushroom

1997. Fungi. Multicoloured.

1695	200r. Type **325**	44·00	60·00
1696	500r. *Amanita regalis*	70	15
1697	900r. *Morchella semilibera*	90	30
1698	1000r. *Gomphus clavatus*	1·20	45
1699	1500r. *Hygrophorus hypothejus*	1·90	60
1700	4000r. *Albatrellus confluens*	5·00	1·80
MS1701 110×89 mm. 5400r. Red-cracked boletus		6·75	2·30

326 Peaceful Fightingfish (*Betta imbellis*) and Siamese Fightingfish (*Betta splendens*)

1997. Fish. Multicoloured.

1702	200r. Type **326**	55	10
1703	500r. Banded gourami	80	30
1704	900r. Rosy barbs	1·10	40
1705	1000r. Paradise fish	1·50	55
1706	1500r. *Epalzeorhynchos frenatus*	2·30	75
1707	4000r. *Capoeta tetrazona*	5·00	1·80
MS1708 96×72 mm. 5400r. Harlequin fish		6·75	2·30

327 Kampot Post Office

1997. 44th Anniv of Independence. Multicoloured.

1709	1000r. Type **327**	1·20	75
1710	3000r. Prey Veng Post Office	4·00	1·50

328 *Orchis militaris*

1997. Orchids. Multicoloured.

1711	200r. Type **328**	35	10
1712	500r. *Orchiaceras bivonae*	45	15
1713	900r. *Orchiaceras spuria*	70	25
1714	1000r. *Gymnadenia conopsea*	90	30
1715	1500r. "*Perapias neglecta*"	1·30	20
1716	4000r. "*Pseudorhiza bruniana*"	3·50	1·50
MS1717 70×90 mm. 5400r. *Dactylodenia wintonii*		6·75	2·30

329 In black Jacket

1997. Diana, Princess of Wales Commemoration. Multicoloured.

1718	100r. Type **329**	20	10

1719	200r. In black dress	25	15
1720	300r. In blue jacket	35	20
1721	500r. Close-up of Princess in visor	55	25
1722	1000r. In mine-protection clothing	80	30
1723	1500r. With Elizabeth Dole	1·50	55
1724	2000r. Holding landmine	1·90	70
1725	2500r. With Mother Teresa and Sisters of Charity	2·30	85

330 Player with Ball

1998. World Cup Football Championship, France (3rd issue).

1726	**330**	200r. multicoloured	25	10
1727	-	500r. multicoloured	35	15
1728	-	900r. multicoloured	55	20
1729	-	1000r. multicoloured	70	25
1730	-	1500r. multicoloured	1·00	30
1731	-	4000r. multicoloured	2·75	90
MS1732		110×90 mm. 5400r. multicoloured (39×31 mm)	4·75	1·80

DESIGNS: 500r. to 5400r. Different footballing scenes.

331 Suorprat Gateway

1998. Temple Ruins.

1733	**331**	300r. orange and black	55	20
1734	-	500r. pink and black	80	30
1735	-	1200r. orange and black	1·50	55
1736	-	1800r. orange and black	1·80	60
1737	-	1700r. blue and black	2·10	75
1738	-	2000r. green and black	2·75	90
1739	-	3000r. lilac and black	4·00	1·20

DESIGNS—HORIZ: No. 1734, Kumlung wall; 1735, Bapuon entrance; 1737, Prerup; 1738, Preah Khan. VERT: No. 1736, Palilai; 1739, Bayon.

332 Tiger Cub

1998. New Year. Year of the Tiger. Multicoloured.

1740	200r. Type **332**	35	10
1741	500r. Tiger and cubs	45	15
1742	990r. Tiger on alert	70	25
1743	1000r. Tiger washing itself (horiz)	80	30
1744	1500r. Tiger lying in grass (horiz)	1·10	40
1745	4000r. Tiger snarling (horiz)	3·50	1·40
MS1746	120×90 mm. 5400r. Tiger on rock (31×30 mm)	4·50	1·80

333 Oakland, Antioch and Eastern Electric Locomotive No. 105

1998. Railway Locomotives. Multicoloured.

1747	200r. Type **333**	35	10
1748	500r. New York, Westchester and electric locomotive No. 1	70	25
1749	900r. Spokane and Inland electric locomotive No. MII	80	30
1750	1000r. International Railway electric locomotive	1·10	40
1751	1500r. British Columbia Electric Railway locomotive No. 823	1·60	55
1752	4000r. Southern Pacific electric locomotive No. 200	4·50	1·80
MS1753	88×94 mm. Storage battery locomotive (vert triangle)	5·50	2·00

334 Rottweiler

1998. Dogs. Multicoloured.

1754	200r. Type **334**	25	10
1755	500r. Beauceron	45	15
1756	900r. Boxer	70	25
1757	1000r. Siberian husky	80	30
1758	1500r. Welsh Pembroke corgi	1·10	40
1759	4000r. Basset hound	3·00	1·10
MS1760	110×89 mm. Schnauzer (28×37½ mm)	5·00	1·90

335 Stag Beetle

1998. Beetles. Multicoloured.

1761	200r. Type **335**	25	10
1762	500r. Carabus auronitens (ground beetle)	45	15
1763	900r. Alpine longhorn beetle	70	25
1764	1000r. Geotrupes (dor beetle)	80	30
1765	1500r. Megasoma elephas	1·10	40
1766	4000r. Chalcosoma	3·00	1·10
MS1767	110×90 mm. 5400r. Leptura rubra (longhorn beetle)	5·00	1·90

336 Prerup Temple

1998. Khmer Culture. Multicoloured.

1768	500r. Type **336**	70	45
1769	1500r. Bayon Temple	1·90	60
1770	2000r. Angkor Vat	2·75	90

337 Cutter

1998. Ships. Multicoloured.

1771	200r. Type **337**	35	10
1772	500r. Britannia (mail paddle-steamer, 1840)	70	15
1773	900r. Viking longship, Gokstad	90	25
1774	1000r. Great Britain (steam/sail)	1·10	40
1775	1500r. Medieval coasting nau	1·60	60
1776	4000r. Full-rigged ship (inscr "Fregate")	4·00	1·50
MS1777	110×91 mm. 5400r. Tartane (fishing boat) (39×31 mm)	5·50	2·00

338 Scottish Fold

1998. Domestic Cats. Multicoloured.

1778	200r. Type **338**	35	10
1779	500r. Ragdoll	70	15
1780	900r. Cymric	90	25
1781	1000r. Devon rex	1·10	40
1782	1500r. American curl	1·60	60
1783	4000r. Sphinx	4·00	1·50
MS1784	90×108 mm. 5400r. Japanese bobtail (39×31 mm)	5·50	2·00

339 Petasites japonica

1998. Flowers. Multicoloured.

1785	200r. Type **339**	35	10
1786	500r. Gentiana triflora	70	15
1787	900r. Doronicum cordatum	90	25
1788	1000r. Scabiosa japonica	1·10	40
1789	1500r. Magnolia sieboldii	1·60	60
1790	4000r. Erythronium japonica	4·00	1·50
MS1791	90×101 mm. China aster (30×36 mm)	5·50	2·00

340 Baptism of Christ (Gerard David)

1998. "Italia 98" International Stamp Exhibition, Milan. Paintings. Multicoloured.

1792	200r. Type **340**	35	10
1793	500r. Madonna of Martin van Niuwenhoven (Hans Memling)	70	15
1794	900r. Baptism of Christ (Hendrich Holtzius)	90	25
1795	1000r. Christ with the Cross (Luis de Morales)	1·10	40
1796	1500r. Elias in the Desert (Dirk Bouts)	1·60	60
1797	4000r. The Virgin (Petrus Christus)	4·00	1·50
MS1798	87×107 mm. The Immaculate Conception (Bartolome Murillo) (39×31 mm)	5·50	1·20

There are errors of spelling in some of the inscriptions.

341 Phyciodes tharos

1998. Butterflies. Multicoloured.

1799	200r. Type **341**	35	10
1800	500r. Pararge megera	70	15
1801	900r. Monarch	90	25
1802	1000r. Apollo	1·10	40
1803	1500r. Swallowtail	1·60	60
1804	4000r. Eumenis semele	4·00	1·50
MS1805	91×110 mm. 5400r. Blue morpho (39×31 mm)	5·50	2·00

342 Post Box, 1997

1998. World Post Day. Multicoloured.

1806	1000r. Type **342**	1·70	60
1807	3000r. Wall-mounted post box, 1951	3·50	1·20

343 Big-Headed Turtle

1998. Tortoise and Turtles. Multicoloured.

1808	200r. Type **343**	55	10
1809	500r. Green turtle	70	15
1810	900r. American soft-shelled turtle	1·10	30
1811	1000r. Hawksbill turtle	1·40	45
1812	1500r. Aldabra tortoise	1·90	75
1813	4000r. Leatherback sea turtle	4·50	1·80

MS1814	5400r. Matamata turtle (39×31 mm)	8·00	3·00

344 Bayon Dance

1998. 45th Anniv of Independence. Multicoloured.

1815	500r. Type **344**	80	40
1816	1500r. Bayon dance (different)	1·80	50
1817	2000r. Bayon dance (different)	2·50	80

345 Cheetah

1998. Big Cats. Multicoloured.

1818	200r. Type **345**	25	10
1819	500r. Snow leopard	35	15
1820	900r. Ocelot	70	25
1821	1000r. Leopard	80	30
1822	1500r. Serval	1·10	50
1823	4000r. Jaguar	3·25	1·30
MS1824	90×109 mm. 5400r. Tiger (31×39 mm)	4·50	1·60

346 Rabbit

1999. New Year. Year of the Rabbit. Multicoloured. Showing rabbits.

1825	200r. Type **346**	35	10
1826	500r. Facing left	50	15
1827	900r. Sitting in bush	85	25
1828	1000r. Sitting on rock	95	30
1829	1500r. Sitting upright	1·60	50
1830	4000r. Head looking out from grass (vert)	4·25	1·30
MS1831	110×84 mm. 5400r. Rabbit (39×31 mm)	5·75	1·90

347 Foster and Rastik's Stourbridge Lion, 1829, U.S.A.

1999. Steam Railway Locomotives. Multicoloured.

1832	200r. Type **347**	35	10
1833	500r. Atlantic, 1832	70	15
1834	900r. No. O35, 1934	1·10	25
1835	1000r. Daniel Gooch's Iron Duke, 1847, Great Britain	1·40	30
1836	1500r. 4-6-0	2·10	50
1837	4000r. 4-4-2	5·00	1·60
MS1838	84×109 mm. 5400r. Fire Fly, 1840, Great Britain (39×31 mm)	8·00	1·90

348 Aquamarine

1999. Minerals. Multicoloured.

1839	200r. Type **348**	35	40
1840	500r. Cat's eye	45	50
1841	900r. Malachite	80	90
1842	1000r. Emerald	90	1·00
1843	1500r. Turquoise	1·50	1·70
1844	4000r. Ruby	4·00	4·50
MS1845	107×88 mm. 5400r. Diamond (39×31 mm)	4·75	1·60

349 Alsatian

1999. Dogs. Multicoloured.

1846	200r. Type **349**	35	40
1847	500r. Shih tzu (horiz)	45	50
1848	900r. Tibetan spaniel (horiz)	80	90
1849	1000r. Ainu-ken	90	1·00
1850	1500r. Lhassa apso (horiz)	1·50	1·70
1851	4000r. Tibetan terrier (horiz)	4·00	4·50
MS1852 109×88 mm. 5400r. Tosa inu (31×39 mm)		4·75	1·60

350 La Rapide steam carriage, 1881

1999. Cars. Multicoloured.

1853	200r. Type **350**	25	10
1854	500r. Duryea motor buggy, 1895	35	15
1855	900r. Marius Barbarou voiturette, 1898	55	25
1856	1000r. Panhard and Levassor voiturette, 1898	70	30
1857	1500r. Mercedes-Benz Tonneau, 1901	1·00	50
1858	4000r. Ford model sedan, 1915	2·75	1·30
MS1859 108×86 mm. 5400r. Marcus, 1875 (39×31 mm)		5·50	1·60

351 Ragdoll

1999. Cats. Multicoloured.

1860	200r. Type **351**	35	15
1861	500r. Russian blue	45	20
1862	900r. Bombay	80	25
1863	1000r. Siamese	90	40
1864	1500r. Oriental shorthair	1·50	65
1865	4000r. Somali	4·00	1·60
MS1866 84×109 mm. 5400r. Egyptian mau (31×38 mm)		5·75	1·90

352 Dragon Bridge

1999. Khmer Culture. Multicoloured.

1867	500r. Type **352**	80	25
1868	1500r. Temple of 100 Columns, Kratie	2·00	65
1869	2000r. Krapum Chhouk, Kratie	2·75	1·00

353 Araschnia levana

1999. Butterflies. Multicoloured.

1870	200r. Type **353**	35	10
1871	500r. Painted lady (horiz)	45	15
1872	900r. Clossiana euphrosyne	80	25
1873	1000r. Coenonympha hero	90	30
1874	1500r. Apollo (horiz)	1·50	50
1875	4000r. Plebejus argus	4·00	1·30
MS1876 109×90 mm. 5400r. Purpleedged copper (31×39 mm)		4·50	1·60

354 Saurornitholestes

1999. Prehistoric Animals. Multicoloured.

1877	200r. Type **354**	25	10
1878	500r. Prenocephale	35	15
1879	900r. Wuerhosaurus	55	20
1880	1000r. Muttaburrasaurus	70	25
1881	1500r. Shantungosaurus	1·00	45
1882	4000r. Microceratops	2·75	1·20
MS1883 111×84 mm. 5400r. Daspletosaurus		4·50	1·60

355 Flabellina affinis

1999. Molluscs. Multicoloured.

1884	200r. Type **355**	35	10
1885	500r. Octopus macropus	70	15
1886	900r. Helix hortensis	1·10	25
1887	1000r. Lima hians	1·40	30
1888	1500r. Arion empiricorum	2·10	50
1889	4000r. Swan mussel	5·00	1·30
MS1890 110×84 mm. 5400r. Eledone aldrovandii		8·00	2·50

356 Flowers in a Vase (Henri Fantin-Latour)

1999. "Philexfrance 99" International Stamp Exhibition, Paris. Paintings. Multicoloured.

1891	200r. Type **356**	35	10
1892	500r. Fruit (Paul Cezanne)	70	15
1893	900r. Table and Chairs (Andre Derain)	1·10	25
1894	1000r. Vase on a Table (Henri Matisse)	1·40	30
1895	1500r. Tulips and Marguerites (Othon Friesz)	2·10	50
1896	4000r. Still Life with Tapestry (Matisse)	5·00	1·30
MS1897 107×84 mm. 5400r. Still Life with Tapestry(detail) (Cezanne)		8·00	2·50

357 Prasat Neak Poan

1999. Temples.

1898	**357**	100r. blue and black	25	10
1899	-	300r. red and black	35	15
1900	-	500r. grn & blk (vert)	45	25
1901	-	1400r. green and black	1·20	50
1902	-	1600r. mauve and black	1·40	65
1903	-	1800r. vio & blk (vert)	1·60	70
1904	-	1900r. brown and black	1·80	80

DESIGNS: 300r. Statue, Neak Poan; 500r. Banteay Srey; 1400r. Banteay Samre; 1600r. Banteay Srey; 1800r. Basrelief, Angkor Vat; 1900r. Brasat Takeo.

358 Pagoda, Tongzhou

1999. "China 1999" International Stamp Exhibition, Peking. Multicoloured.

1905	200r. Type **358**	25	10
1906	500r. Pagoda, Tianning Temple	35	15
1907	900r. Pagoda, Summer Palace	85	30
1908	900r. Pagoda, Blue Cloud Temple	85	30
1909	1000r. White pagoda, Bei Hai	90	40
1910	1000r. Pagoda, Scented Hill	90	40
1911	1500r. Pagoda, Yunju Temple	1·50	60
1912	4000r. White pagoda, Miaoying Temple	3·75	1·50

359 Cymbidium insigne

1999. Orchids. Multicoloured.

1913	200r. Type **359**	25	10
1914	500r. Papilionanthe teres	45	15
1915	900r. Panisea uniflora	80	30
1916	1000r. Euanthe sanderiana	90	40
1917	1500r. Dendrobium trigonopus	1·40	50
1918	4000r. Vanda coerulea	4·00	1·50
MS1919 109×80 mm. 5400r. Paphiopedilum callosum (26×36 mm)		5·50	1·80

360 Northern Bullfinch

1999. Birds. Multicoloured.

1920	200r. Type **360**	35	10
1921	500r. Hawfinch	50	15
1922	900r. Western greenfinch	85	35
1923	1000r. Yellow warbler	95	40
1924	1500r. Great grey shrike	1·60	65
1925	4000r. Blue tit	4·25	1·70
MS1926 109×85 mm. 5400r. European robin (39×30 mm)		4·75	1·80

361 Emblem

1999. 46th Anniv of Independence. Multicoloured.

1927	500r. Type **361**	45	35
1928	1500r. People with symbols of transport and industry	1·00	50
1929	2000r. People queueing to vote	1·60	85

362 Tiger Barbs

1999. Fish. Multicoloured.

1930	200r. Type **362**	35	10
1931	500r. Rainbow shark minnow	70	15
1932	900r. Clown rasbora	1·10	35
1933	1000r. Orange-spotted cichlid	1·40	40
1934	1500r. Crescent betta	2·10	65
1935	4000r. Honey gourami	5·00	1·70
MS1936 109×84 mm. Eyespot pufferfish (39×31 mm)		8·00	2·50

363 Harpy Eagle

1999. Birds of Prey. Multicoloured.

1937	200r. Type **363**	35	10
1938	500r. Bateleur (vert)	70	15
1939	900r. Egyptian vulture (vert)	1·10	35
1940	1000r. Peregrine falcon (vert)	1·40	40
1941	1500r. Red-tailed hawk (vert)	2·10	65
1942	4000r. American bald eagle	5·00	1·70
MS1943 109×85 mm. 5400r. Red kite (31×39 mm)		5·00	2·30

364 Mail Carriage and Globe

1999. 125th Anniv of Universal Postal Union.

1944	**364**	1600r. multicoloured	2·30	1·30

365 Giant Panda

1999. Mammals. Multicoloured.

1945	200r. Type **365**	25	10
1946	500r. Yak	35	15
1947	900r. Chinese water deer	60	35
1948	1000r. Eurasian water shrew (horiz)	75	40
1949	1500r. European otter (horiz)	1·10	65
1950	4000r. Tiger (horiz)	3·00	1·50
MS1951 110×81 mm. 5400r. Pere David's deer (39×31 mm)		4·50	2·20

366 Coral Snake

1999. Snakes. Multicoloured.

1952	200r. Type **366**	35	10
1953	500r. Rainbow boa	50	15
1954	900r. Yellow anaconda	85	35
1955	1000r. Southern ring-necked snake	95	40
1956	1500r. Harlequin snake	1·60	65
1957	4000r. Eastern tiger snake	4·25	1·50
MS1958 107×81 mm. 5400r. Green python (36×28 mm)		4·50	2·00

367 Dragon

2000. New Year. Year of the Dragon.

1959	**367**	200r. multicoloured	45	15
1960	-	500r. red, buff and black	70	25
1961	-	900r. multicoloured	1·00	40
1962	-	1000r. multicoloured	1·20	50
1963	-	1500r. multicoloured	2·00	75
1964	-	4000r. multicoloured	4·50	1·70
MS1965 86×110 mm. 4500r. multicoloured			5·00	2·30

DESIGNS: 500r. Dragon enclosed in circle; 900r. Green dragon with red flames; 1000r. Heraldic dragon; 1500r. Red dragon with blue extremities; 4000r. Blue dragon with yellow flames; 4500r. Dragon's head (32×40 mm).

368 Iguanodon

2000. Dinosaurs. Multicoloured.

1966	200r. Type **368**	25	10
1967	500r. Euoplocepalus	35	15
1968	900r. Diplosaurus	60	35
1969	1000r. Diplodocus	75	40
1970	1500r. Stegoceras	1·10	65
1971	4000r. Stegosaurus	3·00	1·50
MS1972 110×85 mm. 4500r. Brachiosaurus (32×40 mm)		4·25	2·00

369 Ground Beetle (Calosoma sycophanta)

2000. Insects. Multicoloured.

1973	200r. Type **369**	35	10
1974	500r. European rhinoceros beetle (Oryctes nasicornis)	50	15
1975	900r. Diochrysa fastuosa	85	35
1976	1000r. Blaps gigas	95	40
1977	1500r. Green tiger beetle (Cincindela campestris)	1·60	65

1978	4000r. *Cissistes cephalotes*		4·25	1·70

MS1979 107×85 mm. 4500r. Scarab beetle (*Scarabaeus aegyptiorum*) (40×32 mm) 4·50 2·20

370 Box Turtle (*Cuora amboinensis*)

2000. "Bangkok 2000" International Stamp Exhibition. Turtles and Tortoise. Multicoloured.

1980	200r. Type **370**		35	10
1981	500r. Yellow box turtle (*Cuora flavomarginata*)		50	15
1982	900r. Black-breasted leaf turtle (*Geoemyda spengleri*) (horiz)		85	35
1983	1000r. Impressed tortoise (*Manouria* (*Geochelone*) *impressa*) (horiz)		95	40
1984	1500r. Reeves' turtle (*Chinemys reevesi*) (horiz)		1·60	65
1985	4000r. Spiny turtle (*Heosemys spinosa*) (horiz)		4·25	1·70

MS1986 111×86 mm. 4500r. Annadal's turtle (*Hieremys annandalei*) (horiz) (40×32 mm) 4·50 2·20

371 Ox-cart carrying Rice

2000. Rice Cultivation.

1987	**371**	100r. green and black	35	10
1988	-	300r. blue and black	45	10
1989	-	500r. mauve and black	70	15
1990	-	1400r. blue and black	1·60	65
1991	-	1600r. brown and black	2·10	85
1992	-	1900r. brown and black	2·50	1·00
1993	-	2200r. red and black	3·00	1·20

DESIGNS: 300r. Harrowing; 500r. Threshing; 1400r. Winnowing; 1600r. Planting; 1900r. Ploughing; 2200r. Binding sheaves.

372 *Jules Petiet* Steam Locomotive

2000. Locomotives. "WIPA 2000" International Stamp Exhibition, Vienna (MS2000). Multicoloured.

1994	200r. Type **372**		45	10
1995	500r. *Longue Chaudiere* steam locomotive, 1891		70	15
1996	900r. *Le Grand Chocolats* steam locomotive		1·10	35
1997	1000r. *Glehn du Busquet* steam locomotive, 1891		1·40	40
1998	1500r. *Le Pendule Francais* diesel locomotive		1·90	65
1999	4000r. TGV 001 locomotive, 1976		5·25	1·70

MS2000 110×86 mm. 4500r. "Le Shuttle" in tunnel (80×32 mm) 6·25 2·50

373 Fly Agaric (*Amanita muscaria*)

2000. Fungi. Multicoloured.

2001	200r. Type **373**		25	10
2002	500r. Panther cap (*Amanita pantherina*)		35	15
2003	900r. *Clitocybe olearia*		60	35
2004	1000r. *Lactarius scrobiculatus*		75	40
2005	1500r. *Scleroderma vulgare*		1·10	65
2006	4000r. *Amanita verna*		3·00	1·70

MS2007 110×86 mm. 4500r. Death cap (*Amanita phalloides*) (32×40 mm) 4·75 2·20

374 *Betta unimaculata* and *Betta pugnax*

2000. Fighting Fish. Multicoloured.

2008	200r. Type **374**		25	10
2009	500r. *Betta macrostoma* and *Betta taeniata*		35	15
2010	900r. *Betta foerschi* and *Betta imbellis*		60	35
2011	1000r. *Betta tessyae* and *Betta picta*		75	40
2012	1500r. *Betta edithae* and *Betta bellica*		1·10	65
2013	4000r. *Betta smaragdina*		3·00	1·70

MS2014 110×85 mm. 4500r. Siamese fighting fish (*Betta splendens*) (40×32 mm) 4·25 2·20

375 Woman in Arched Alcove (stone carving)

2000. Khmer Cultural Heritage. Each brown and black.

2015	500r. Type **375**		55	50
2016	1000r. Woman in flowered head-dress in rectangula bas-relief		1·10	65
2017	2000r. Woman with right arm raised in arche bas-relief		1·70	1·00

376 Galapagos Albatross (*Diomedea irrorata*)

2000. Sea Birds. Multicoloured.

2018	200r. Type **376**		35	10
2019	500r. Kentish plover (*Charadrius alexandrinus*) (vert)		50	15
2020	900r. Blue-footed booby (*Sula nebouxii*)		75	35
2021	1000r. Common tern (*Sterna hirundo*)		95	40
2022	1500r. Herring gull (*Larus argentatus*) (vert)		1·50	65
2023	4000r. Whiskered tern (*Chlidonias hybrida*)		4·00	1·70

MS2024 108×83 mm. 4500r. Gannet (*Sula* (*Morus*) *bassana*) 5·75 3·25

377 *Cypripedium macranthum*

2000. Orchids. Multicoloured.

2025	200r. Type **377**		45	10
2026	500r. *Vandopsis gigantean*		70	15
2027	900r. *Calypso bulbosa*		90	35
2028	1000r. *Vanda luzonica*		1·20	40
2029	1500r. *Paphiopedilum villosum*		1·80	65
2030	4000r. *Vanda merrillii*		4·50	1·70

MS2031 81×107 mm. 4500r. *Paphiopedilum Victoria* 5·00 8·25

378 Rowers in Large Canoe

2000. Tourism. Multicoloured.

2032	500r. Type **378**		80	35
2033	1500r. Front of decorated canoe		2·30	1·00
2034	2000r. Temple, elephant and dancer		3·25	1·30

379 Weightlifting

2000. Sports. Multicoloured.

2035	200r. Type **379**		35	10
2036	500r. Gymnastics		70	15
2037	900r. Baseball		80	35
2038	1000r. Tennis		90	40
2039	1500r. Basketball		1·60	60
2040	4000r. High jump		4·00	1·50

MS2041 110×85 mm. 4500r. Running 4·50 2·00

380 Metz DLK 23-6

2000. Fire Engines. Multicoloured.

2042	200r. Type **380**		35	35
2043	500r. Iveco-Magirus SLF 24/100		70	65
2044	900r. Metz SLF 7000 WS		80	85
2045	1000r. Iveco-Magirus TLF 24/50		90	1·00
2046	1500r. Saval-Konenburg RFF-11.000		1·60	1·50
2047	4000r. Metz TLF 24/50		4·00	3·25

MS2048 110×85 mm. 4500r. Metz TLF 16/25 7·25 6·75

381 Smooth Haired Dachshund

2000. Dachshunds. Multicoloured.

2049	200r. Type **381**		35	10
2050	500r. Wire haired		70	15
2051	900r. Long haired		80	35
2052	1000r. Two smooth haired		90	40
2053	1500r. Mother and pups		1·60	65
2054	4000r. Two puppies		4·00	1·70

MS2055 117×86 mm. 4500r. Head of wire haired (32×40 mm) 5·00 2·20

382 Rover 12 C (1912)

2000. Cars. Espana 2000 International Stamp Exhibition, Madrid. Multicoloured.

2056	200r. Type **382**		35	10
2057	500r. Austin 30 CV (1907)		70	15
2058	900r. Rolls-Royce Silver Ghost (1909)		80	35
2059	1000r. Graham Paige (1929)		80	35
2060	1500r. Austin 12 (1937)		1·60	65
2061	4000r. Mercedes-Benz 300SL (1957)		4·00	1·70

MS2062 110×86 mm. 4500r. MG (1936) (40×32 mm) 4·50 2·20

383 18th-century Korean Painting and Two Kittens

2000. Cats. Multicoloured.

2063	200r. Type **383**		35	10
2064	500r. 18th-century Portuguese tiles and tabby cat		70	15
2065	900r. Satsuma ceramic cat and two cats		80	35
2066	1000r. Goddess Basset (Egyptian) and mother cat and kittens		90	40
2067	1500r. Goddess Freya (engraving) and tortoiseshell cat		1·60	65
2068	4000r. Japanese painting and Manx cat		4·00	1·70

MS2069 110×86 mm. 4500r. Leaping cat (40×32 mm) 5·75 2·50

384 Flowers, Monument and Flag

2000. 47th Anniv of Independence. Multicoloured.

2070	500r. Type **384**		90	35
2071	1500r. Dove, monument and flag		2·50	1·00
2072	2000r. Flag, monument and crowd		3·00	1·30

385 The Courageous Little Tailor

2000. Children's Stories. Multicoloured.

2073	200r. Type **385**		35	10
2074	500r. *Tom Thumb*		70	15
2075	900r. *Thumbelina*		80	35
2076	1000r. *Pinocchio* (horiz)		90	40
2077	1500r. *The Crayfish* (horiz)		1·60	55
2078	4000r. *Peter Pan* (horiz)		4·00	1·70

MS2079 110×85 mm. 4500r. *Pied Piper of Hamelin* (32×40 mm) 4·50 2·20

386 Wattled Starling (*Creatophora cinera*)

2000. Birds. Multicoloured.

2080	200r. Type **386**		35	10
2081	500r. Common starling (*Sturnus vulgaris*)		70	15
2082	900r. Pekin robin (*Leiothrix lutea*)		80	35
2083	1000r. Guianian cock of the rock (*Rupicola rupicola*)		90	40
2084	1500r. Alpine accentor (*Prunella collaris*)		1·60	65
2085	4000r. Bearded reedling (*Panurus biarmicus*) (inscr "biarnicus")		4·00	1·70

MS2086 85×110 mm. 4500r. Inscr *Muscicapula pallipes* (32×40 mm) 4·50 2·20

387 Johannes Gutenberg (invention of printing press)

2001. Millennium. Multicoloured.

2087	200r. Type **387**		35	10
2088	500r. Michael Faraday (discovery of electricity)		70	15
2089	900r. Samuel Morse (invention of Morse code)		80	35
2090	1000r. Alexander Bell (invention of telephone)		90	40
2091	1500r. Enrico Fermi (discovery of nuclear fission)		1·60	65
2092	4000r. Edward Roberts (invention of personal computer)		4·00	1·70

MS2093 86×112 mm. 5400r. Christopher Columbus (discovery of America) (40×32 mm); 5400r. Neil Armstrong (first moon walk) (40×32 mm) 10·00 5·00

388 Snake Head

2001. Year of the Snake. Multicoloured.

2094	200r. Type **388**		35	10
2095	500r. Two snakes entwined		70	15

2096	900r. Snake entwined with moon	80	35
2097	1000r. Entwined snakes (different)	90	40
2098	1500r. Snake encircling moon	1·60	65
2099	4000r. Three snakes' heads	4·00	1·70
MS2100	110×86 mm. 5400r. Snake head (different) (40×32 mm)	5·75	2·50

389 Sandou Ladder Transport (1910)

2001. Fire Engines. Multicoloured.
2101	200r. Type **389**	35	10
2102	500r. Gallo ladder transport (1899)	70	15
2103	900r. Merry Weather appliance (1950)	80	35
2104	1000r. Merry Weather ambulance (1940)	90	40
2105	1500r. Man-Metz appliance (1972)	1·60	65
2106	4000r. Roman diesel appliance (1970)	4·00	1·70
MS2107	111×87 mm. 5400r. Metropolitan steam engine (1898) (40×32 mm).	5·75	2·50

390 Puff Ball (*Lycoperdon perlatum*)

2001. Fungi. Multicoloured.
2108	200r. Type **390**	35	10
2109	500r. Trametes versicolor	70	15
2110	900r. Hypholoma sublaterium (inscr "Hipholoma")	80	35
2111	1000r. Fly agaric (Amanita muscaria)	90	40
2112	1500r. Lycoperdon umbrinum	1·60	65
2113	4000r. Cortinarius orellanus	4·00	1·70
MS2114	111×84 mm. 5400r. Death cap (Amanita phalloides) (32×40 mm)	5·75	2·50

391 Preah Vihear

2001. Temples.
2115	**391**	200r. blue and black	45	10
2116	-	300r. red and black	55	10
2117	-	600r. green and black	80	15
2118	-	1000r. orange and black	1·20	40
2119	-	1500r. green and black	1·80	65
2120	-	1700r. violet and black	2·10	85
2121	-	2200r. brown and black	2·50	1·00

DESIGNS: 300r. Thonmanom; 600r. Tasom; 1000r. Kravan; 1500r. Takeo; 1700r. Mebon; 2200r. Banteay Kdei.

392 Angkor Wat

2001. Third Anniv of Day of Khmer Culture. Showing basreliefs. Multicoloured.
2122	500r. Type **392**	80	35
2123	1500r. Bayon Temple	2·00	1·00
2124	2000r. Bayon Temple (different)	2·30	1·30

393 Large Tortoiseshell (*Nymphalis polychloros*)

2001. Butterflies. Belgica 2001 International Stamp Exhibition, Brussels. Multicoloured.
2125	200r. Type **393**	35	10
2126	500r. Cethosia hypsea	70	15
2127	900r. Papilio palinurus	80	35
2128	1000r. Lesser purple emperor (Apatua ilia)	90	40
2129	1500r. Clipper (Parthenos Sylvia)	1·60	65
2130	4000r. Morpho grandensas	4·00	1·70

| **MS**2131 | 111×85 mm. 5400r. Heliconius melpomene (40×32 mm) | 5·75 | 2·50 |

394 Gary Cooper

2001. Cinema Actors. Multicoloured.
2132	200r. Type **394**	35	10
2133	500r. Marlene Dietrich	70	15
2134	900r. Walt Disney	80	35
2135	1000r. Clark Gable	90	40
2136	1500r. Jeanette Macdonald	1·60	65
2137	4000r. Melvyn Douglas	4·00	1·70
MS2138	86×111 mm. 5400r. Rudolf Valentino (32×40 mm); 5400r. Marilyn Monroe (32×40 mm)	10·00	4·50

395 TVR M series (1972)

2001. Cars. Multicoloured.
2139	200r. Type **395**	40	10
2140	500r. Ferrari 410 (1956)	75	15
2141	900r. Peugeot 405 (1995)	1·10	35
2142	1000r. Fiat 8VZ (1953)	1·30	40
2143	1500r. Citroen Xsara (1997)	1·70	65
2144	4000r. Renault Espace (1997)	3·75	1·50
MS2145	111×85 mm. 5400r. Ferrari 250 GT (1963) (40×32 mm)	5·75	2·30

396 Bayon Temple

2001. Tourism. Bayon Temple. Multicoloured.
2146	500r. Type **396**	65	35
2147	1500r. Faces and monument	1·80	1·10
2148	2000r. Face and trees	2·40	1·50

397 Steam Locomotive 4-6-0

2001. Trains. Philanippon '01 International Stamp Exhibition, Tokyo. Multicoloured.
2149	200r. Type **397**	35	20
2150	500r. Steam locomotive 4-6-4	65	45
2151	900r. Steam locomotive 4-4-0	75	55
2152	1000r. Steam locomotive 4-6-4	1·00	65
2153	1500r. Locomotive 4-6-2	1·50	1·10
2154	4000r. Locomotive 4-8-2	3·75	2·75
MS2155	110×84 mm. 5400r. Steam locomotive 2-8-2 (40×32 mm).	6·50	4·50

398 Emperor Penguin (*Aptenodytes forsteri*)

2001. Penguins. Multicoloured.
2156	200r. Type **398**	35	20
2157	500r. Jackass penguin (Spheniscus demersus)	65	45
2158	900r. Humboldt penguin (Spheniscus humboldti)	75	55
2159	1000r. Rockhopper penguin (Eudypes crestatus) (inscr "cristatus")	1·00	65
2160	1500r. King penguin (Aptenodytes patagonica)	1·50	1·10
2161	4000r. Bearded penguin (Pygocelis Antarctica)	3·75	2·75
MS2162	108×83 mm. 5400r. Gentoo penguin (Pygoscelis papua) (40×32 mm)	6·50	4·50

399 Singapura

2001. Cats. Multicoloured.
2163	200r. Type **399**	35	20
2164	500r. Cymric	65	45
2165	900r. Exotic short haired (inscr "shirthair")	75	55
2166	1000r. Ragdoll	1·00	65
2167	1500r. Manx	1·50	1·10
2168	4000r. Somali	3·75	2·75
MS2169	110×85 mm. 5400r. Egyptian mau (40×32 mm)	6·50	4·50

400 Khleng Chak

2001. Traditional Kites. Multicoloured.
2170	300r. Type **400**	45	20
2171	500r. Khleng Kanton	75	35
2172	1000r. Khleng Phnong	1·25	1·10
2173	1500r. Khleng KaunMorn	1·70	1·10
2174	3000r. Khleng Me Ambao	3·50	2·20

401 Parodia cintiensis

2001. Cacti. Multicoloured.
2175	200r. Type **401**	35	20
2176	500r. Astrophytum asterias	65	45
2177	900r. Parodia faustiana	75	55
2178	1000r. Coryphantha sulcolanata	1·00	65
2179	1500r. Neochilenia hankena	1·50	1·10
2180	4000r. Mammillaria boolii (inscr "Mamillaria")	3·75	2·75
MS2181	110×85 mm. 5400r. Mammillaria inscr "Mamilleria swinglei" (32×40 mm)	5·50	4·50

402 Fishing Dance

2001. Dances. Multicoloured.
2182	500r. Type **402**	45	35
2183	1500r. Red fish dance	1·80	1·30
2184	2000r. Dance of Apsara	2·20	1·80

403 Timber Wolf (*Canis occidentalis*)

2001. Wolves and Foxes. Multicoloured.
2185	200r. Type **403**	35	20
2186	500r. Alaska tundra wolf (Canis tundrorum)	65	45
2187	900r. Fox (inscr "Vulpes fulvas")	75	55
2188	1000r. Coyote (Canis latrans)	1·00	65
2189	1500r. Fennec fox (Vulpes zerda)	1·50	1·10
2190	4000r. Arctic fox (Alopex lagopus)	3·75	2·75
MS2191	112×87 mm. 5400r. Iberian wolf (Canis signatus) (40×32 mm)	5·50	4·50

404 Australopithecus anamensis

2001. Prehistoric Man. Multicoloured.
2192	100r. Type **404**	35	20
2193	200r. Australopithecus afarensis	45	35
2194	300r. Australopithecus africanus	55	40

2195	500r. Australopithecus rudolfensis	65	45
2196	500r. Australopithecus boisei	65	45
2197	1000r. Homo habilis	1·10	65
2198	1500r. Homo erectus	1·60	1·00
2199	4000r. Homo sapiens neanderthalensis (inscr "nesnderthalensis")	4·25	2·00
MS2200	110×85 mm. 5400r. Homo sapiens sapiens (40×32 mm)	6·00	4·50

404a World Cup Champions (1934)

2001. Italian Football. Multicoloured.
2200a	200r. Type **404a**	35	20
2200b	500r. World Cup champions (1938)	55	45
2200c	900r. European Cup champions (1968)	1·00	65
2200d	1000r. World Cup champions (1982)	1·10	85
2200e	1500r. World Cup qualifying team (2002)	1·70	1·30
2200f	4000r. Federazione Italiana Giuoco Calcio emblem	4·50	3·25

404b Castle (18th-century)

2001. Chess. Multicoloured.
2200g	200r. Type **404b**	35	20
2200h	500r. Pawn (19th-century)	55	45
2200i	900r. King (19th-century)	1·00	65
2200j	1000r. Bishop (17th-century)	1·10	85
2200k	1500r. Queen (17th-century)	1·70	1·30
2200l	4000r. Knight (20th-century) 2.74	4·50	3·25
MS2200m	112×87 mm. 5400r. King (16th-century) (40×32 mm)	5·75	3·75

405 Preah Vihear Temple

2002. Tenth Anniv of ASEAN (Association of South East Asian Nations) Post. Temples. Multicoloured.
2201	500r. Type **405**	80	55
2202	900r. Preah Ko	1·50	1·10
2203	1500r. Banteay Srei	2·30	1·60
2204	2500r. Bayon	3·50	2·50
2205	3500r. Ankor Wat	4·50	3·75

406 Bridge No. 26, Route 6A

2003. Japanese Grant Aid. Multicoloured.
2206	100r. Type **406**	25	10
2207	200r. Bridge No. 25, Route 6A	45	20
2208	400r. Chroy Changvar bridge	70	35
2209	800r. Kazuna bridge	1·10	55
2210	3500r. Monument	5·75	2·75

407 Ox Cart carrying supplies

2003. 140th Anniv of Red Cross and Red Crescent. Multicoloured.
2211	100r. Type **407**	25	15
2212	200r. Red Cross worker (vert)	35	25
2213	300r. Queen Norodom Monineath Sihanouk and young men	40	30
2214	400r. Queen greeting young woman in crowd	45	35
2215	500r. Queen and man	55	40
2216	700r. Queen greeting older woman in crowd	80	60

2217	800r. Queen presenting cloth	90	65
2218	1000r. Woman with shaved head and Queen	1·10	85
2219	1900r. Queen and M. Bun Rany Hun Sen (pres. of Cambodian Red Cross) (vert)	2·10	1·60
2220	2100r. M. Bun Rany Hun Sen and Red Cross worker (vert)	2·30	1·70
2221	4000r. Queen and M. Bun Rany Hun Sen holding baby	4·50	3·25

408 Sugar Palm Tree

2003. Sugar Palm. Multicoloured.

2222	300r. Type **408**	80	60
2223	500r. Female flower	1·20	90
2224	700r. Male flower	1·90	1·40
2225	1500r. Fruit	4·00	3·00

409 Ankor Wat, Cambodia

2003. 50th Anniv of China–Cambodia Diplomatic Relations. Multicoloured.

2226	2000r. Type **409**	2·75	2·10
2227	2000r. Great Wall, China	2·75	2·10

410 Conference Emblem

2003. 36th ASEAN Ministerial Meeting and Tenth ASEAN Regional Forum, Phnom Penh. Multicoloured.

2228	400r. Type **410**	90	65
2229	500r. Dancer (Apsara dance)	1·00	75
2230	600r. Seated dancer	1·10	85
2231	1600r. Two seated dancers	2·75	2·00
2232	1900r. Two dancers (Temonorom dance)	3·25	2·40

411 King Norodom Sihanouk and Map

2003. 50th Anniv of Independence. King Norodom Sihanouk. Multicoloured.

2233	200r. Type **411**	35	25
2234	400r. With soldiers (vert)	45	35
2235	500r. Seated (vert)	55	40
2236	800r. With arm extended (vert)	90	65
2237	1000r. Saluting (vert)	1·10	85
2238	2000r. Independence monument and King Norodom Sihanouk (vert)	2·30	1·70
2239	5000r. Wearing suit	5·75	4·25

413 Bayon Sculpture

2004. Day of Khmer Culture. Multicoloured.

2240	100r. Type **413**	45	35
2241	200r. Banteay Srei sculpture	55	40
2242	400r. Banteay Srei sculpture (detail)	70	50
2243	800r. Bayon sculpture (different) (vert)	90	65
2244	3500r. Banteay Srei sculpture (detail) (different) (vert)	3·00	2·30
MS2245	110×85 mm. 2000r. As No. 2250 with design enlarged (vert)	3·50	2·50

414 Waterwheel

2004. Tourism. Landscapes. Multicoloured.

2246	600r. Type **414**	1·10	85
2247	900r. Paddy fields	1·70	1·30
2248	2000r. River and palms	3·50	2·50
MS2249	110×85 mm. 2000r. Ox cart	3·75	2·75

415 Two Dancers

2004. Tepmonorum Dance. Multicoloured.

2250	400r. Type **415**	80	60
2251	1000r. Two dancers wearing blue outfits	1·70	1·10
2252	2100r. Two female dancers	3·75	2·75
MS2253	110×85 mm. 2000r. As No. 2259 with design enlarged	3·75	2·75

416 Cassia fistula

2004. Flowers. Multicoloured.

2254	600r. Type **416**	80	60
2255	700r. *Butea monosperma*	90	65
2256	900r. *Couroupita quianensis*	1·00	75
2257	1000r. *Delonix regia* (horiz)	1·20	90
2258	1800r. *Lagerstroemia floribunda*	2·30	1·70
MS2259	110×85 mm. 2000r. *Lagerstroemia floribunda* (horiz)	3·75	2·75

417 Preah Khan

2004. Tourism. Temples. Multicoloured.

2260	200r. Type **417**	45	35
2261	500r. Pre Rup	55	40
2262	600r. Banteay Samre	70	50
2263	1600r. Bayon	1·60	1·20
2264	1900r. Ankor Wat	1·80	1·30
MS2265	110×85 mm. 2000r. Stone head, Bayon (vert)	3·75	2·75

418 King Norodom Sihamoni

2004. Coronation of King Norodom Sihamoni. Multicoloured.

2266	100r. Type **418**	25	15
2267	400r. With monks	35	25
2268	500r. Planting tree	45	35
2269	600r. King Norodom Sihamoni (portrait)	50	40
2270	700r. With crowd, greeting child (horiz)	55	40
2271	900r. Greeting men in uniform (horiz)	70	50
2272	2100r. Releasing dove (horiz)	1·50	1·10
2273	2200r. With young men (horiz)	1·60	1·20
2274	4000r. King Norodom Sihamoni and temple (horiz)	2·75	2·10

412 Scoop-shaped Fishing Basket

2004. Fishing Tools. Multicoloured.

2275	100r. Type **412**	45	35
2276	200r. Narrow basket	55	40
2277	800r. Cylindrical basket	90	65
2278	1700r. Goblet-shaped basket (vert)	1·50	1·25
2279	2200r. Cylindrical basket with baffles (vert)	2·00	1·50
MS2280	85×110 mm. 2000r. Child and basket (vert)	4·50	3·25

419 Anniversary Emblem

2005. 50th Anniv of Cambodian Red Cross Society. Multicoloured.

2281	400r. Type **419**	45	35
2282	700r. Signing book (horiz)	55	40
2283	800r. Lok Chumteav Bun Rany Hun Sen (president) dispensing aid (horiz)	80	60
2284	1900r. Queen Mother Norodom Monineath Sihanouk dispensing aid (horiz)	1·70	1·30
2285	2100r. Lok Chumteav Bun Rany Hun Sen presenting certificate to volunteer (horiz)	1·90	1·40
2286	2200r. King Norodom Sihamoni and Queen Mother Norodom Monineath Sihanouk on dais (horiz)	2·00	1·50

420 Aspara Dance

2005. Traditional Dance. Aspara Dance. Multicoloured.

2287	800r. Type **420**	55	40
2288	900r. Gold skirt, facing right	70	50
2289	1400r. Blue skirt, facing left	1·00	75
2290	1600r. Cream skirt, leg raised	1·90	1·40
2291	2000r. Chequered skirt, facing left	2·00	1·50

421 Banteay Kdei

2005. Cultural Heritage. Multicoloured.

2292	500r. Type **421**	55	40
2293	700r. Elephant terrace, Angkor Thom	70	50
2294	1000r. Thommanon temple, Angkor	1·00	75
2295	2000r. Ta Prohm temple, Angkor	1·80	1·30
2296	2500r. Angkor Wat	2·10	1·60

422 Nymphaea

2005. Flowers. *Nymphaea*. Multicoloured.

2297	100r. Type **422**	45	35
2298	500r. Cream flower	55	40
2299	1200r. Blue flower	1·10	85
2300	2000r. Yellow flower	1·60	1·20

2301	2500r. Pink flower	1·90	1·40
MS2302	110×85 mm. 4000r. Basket of deep pink flowers (horiz)	4·50	3·25

Nos. 2303/8 and Type **423** are left for Fish issued on 5 September 2005, not yet received.

424 King Norodom Sihamoni

2005. First Anniv of Coronation of Preah Karuna Preah Bat Sâmdech Preah Bâromneath Norodom Sihamoni, King of Cambodia

2309	**424**	500r. multicoloured	55	40
2310	**424**	1500r. multicoloured	1·10	85
2311	**424**	2200r. multicoloured	1·70	1·30

425 Woman holding Scoop

2006. Khmer Cultural Heritage. Weaving. Multicoloured.

2312	100r. Type **425**	35	25
2313	800r. Dye pots	60	40
2314	1500r. Woman seated at frame	1·10	75
2315	2200r. Woman winding yarn	1·50	1·10
2316	3500r. Woman weaving cloth	2·30	1·70
MS2317	110×85 mm. 5400r. Woman seated at loom weaving pink cloth (horiz)	4·00	3·25

426 Sousa chinensis (Chinese white dolphin)

2006. Aquatic Mammals. Multicoloured.

2318	500r. Type **426**	45	25
2319	900r. *Neophocaena phocaenoides* (finless porpoise)	60	40
2320	1400r. *Delphinus capensis tropicalis* (Arabian long-beaked common dolphin) (insc 'Dolphinus')	1·10	60
2321	2100r. *Stenella longirrostris roseinventris* (dwarf spinner dolphin)	1·40	1·00
2322	3500r. *Tusiops aduncus* (Indo-Pacific bottlenose dolphin)	2·20	1·60

Nos. 2324/8 are vacant.

427 Hanuman and Mermaid, Princess Sovanna Maccha

2006. *The Reamker* (Cambodian epic poem). Khmer Dance Theatre

MS2329	110×85 mm. 5400r. Type **427**	4·50	3·25

Nos. 2330/5 and Type **428** are vacant.

429 Chhai Yaim

2006. Dance. Multicoloured.

2336	600r. Type **429**	60	40
2337	1900r. Buffalo sacrifice	1·30	90
2338	2200r. inscr 'Mouth Organ Dance'	1·50	1·10
2339	3500r. Rice harvest	2·30	1·70

Nos. 2340/5 and Type **430** are vacant.

431 Couple and No. 1 Emblem

2006. HIV/AIDS Prevention. '100% Condom Use' (Population Services International (PSI) Number One, condom social marketing programme). Multicoloured.

2346		300r. Type **431**	35	25
2347		500r. Rickshaw (cyclo) driver	45	35
2348		2200r. Water Festival	1·40	1·00

Nos. 2349/59 and Types **432/433** are vacant.

434 Temple and Anniversary Emblem

2007. 25th Anniv of Handicap International

2360	**434**	1000r. multicoloured	80	60
2361	**434**	1500r. multicoloured	1·20	85

Nos. 2362/6 and Type **435** are vacant.

436 Secretariat Building, Bandar Seri Begawan, Brunei Darussalam

2007. Architecture. 40th Anniv of ASEAN (Association of South-East Asian Nations). Multicoloured.

2367	1000r. Type **436**	80	60
2368	1000r. National Museum, Cambodia	80	60
2369	1000r. Fatahillah Museum, Jakarta	80	60
2370	1000r. Traditional house, Laos	80	60
2371	1000r. Railway Headquarters Building, Malaysia	80	60
2372	1000r. Yangon Post Office, Union of Myanmar	80	60
2373	1000r. Malacanang Palace, Manila	80	60
2374	1000r. National Museum, Singapore	80	60
2375	1000r. Vimanmek Mansion, Bangkok, Thailand	80	60
2376	1000r. Presidential Palace, Hanoi, Vietnam	80	60

Nos. 2377/82 and Type **437** are vacant.

438 Tian'anmen (Gate of Heavenly Peace), Beijing, China (inscr 'Tian An Men Rostrum')

2008. 50th Anniv of Cambodia - China Friendship. Multicoloured.

2383	2000r. Type **438**	2·30	1·70
2384	2000r. Royal Palace, Phnom Penh, Cambodia	2·30	1·70

439 Dancer

2008. Dances. Robam Jun Por (best wishes/blessings). Multicoloured.

2385	600r. Type **439**	70	50
2386	1000r. Dancer facing left, right hand raised (mauve)	1·20	85
2387	1700r. Dancer holding cup in right hand (light green)	2·00	1·40
2388	1800r. Dancer right leg and left arm raised (new blue)	2·10	1·50
2389	1900r. Dancer kneeling with cup in left hand (new blue)	2·20	1·60
MS2390	98×75 mm. 6000r. Dancer with Angkor Wat in background	7·00	5·25

440 Temple Walls

2008. Cultural Heritage. Temple of Preah Vihear (1st series). Multicoloured.

2391	600r. Type **440**	70	50
2392	700r. Steps, rocks, tree and temple walls	80	60
2393	1000r. Entrance gate	1·20	85
2394	2000r. Trees and walls with pediments	2·30	1·70
2395	3000r. Ruins against the sky and flag	3·50	2·50

441 Woman decorating Pot

2008. Khmer Cultural Heritage. Pottery. Multicoloured.

2396	100r. Type **441**	10	10
2397	700r. Woman building large pot by hand	80	60
2398	1900r. Woman seated decorating inscised pot	2·20	1·60
2399	2000r. Woman holding wooden implement to impress design on pot	2·30	1·70
2400	2200r. Woman raising pot on wheel	2·50	1·80
MS2401	110×85 mm. 6000r. Ox cart carrying pots	7·00	5·25

442 Children in Class and playing Football

2009. 30th Anniv of Victory Day. Multicoloured.

2402	100r. Type **442**	10	10
2403	200r. Ox cart and agricultural scenes	25	15
2404	1500r. Factory workers, power lines, refinery and dam	1·80	1·30
2405	2200r. Symbols of communication	2·50	1·80
2406	2500r. Symbols of transport	3·00	2·10
2407	2800r. Symbols of cultural heritage	3·25	2·30
2408	3000r. Flag and anniversary emblem (vert)	3·50	2·50

443 Temple

2009. Cultural Heritage. Temple of Preah Vihear (2nd series). Multicoloured.

2409	300r. Type **443**	35	25
2410	800r. Walls, entrances with pediments	95	65
2411	1600r. Multi-headed serpents	1·90	1·30
2412	1800r. Ruins against the sky	2·10	1·50
2413	2800r. Aerial view of Preah Vihear	3·25	2·30
MS2414	111×75 mm. 6000r. Temple of Preah Vihear	7·25	5·50

444 Plough

2010. Ancient Agricultural Tools. Multicoloured.

2415	300r. Type **444**	35	25
2416	1200r. Rake-shaped harrow	1·40	1·00
2417	1700r. Roller	2·00	1·40
2418	1800r. Pedal-driven chain pump	2·10	1·50
2419	2800r. Cart	3·25	2·30
MS2420	90×70 mm. 6000r. Woman working pedal-driven chain pump (vert)	7·25	5·50

446 Globe as Face and Rubbish

2010. Combat Climate Change. Multicoloured.

2421	200r. Type **446**	25	15
2422	800r. Watering can, hand enclosing globe and cars under water	95	65
2423	1400r. Globe opened to reveal green field and tree	1·60	1·20
2424	1700r. Egg timer enclosing icebergs draining into factory	2·00	1·40
2425	3000r. Forest and hands enclosing tree	3·50	2·50
MS2426	110×70 mm. 6000r. Cars under water (as detail of No. 2423)	7·25	5·50

447 Anniversary Emblem

2010. 60th Anniv of Cambodia - USA Diplomatic Relations

2427	**447**	2800r. multicoloured	3·25	2·30

448 Condoms

2011. 30th Anniv of Discovery of AIDS. Multicoloured.

2428	1000r. Type **448**	1·20	85
2429	1500r. Couple and child	1·80	1·30
2430	2800r. Young people in club	3·50	2·50
2431	4000r. Pair of green doves	5·25	3·75

EXPRESS MAIL STAMPS

E313 Bohemian Waxwing

1997. Birds. Multicoloured.

E1624	600r. Type E **313**	1·10	45
E1625	700r. Great grey shrike	1·30	65
E1626	1000r. Eurasian tree sparrow	1·80	75
E1627	2000r. Black redstart	3·50	1·70
E1628	2500r. Reed bunting	4·75	2·00
E1629	3000r. Ortolan bunting	5·25	2·50

POSTAGE DUE STAMPS

D13

1957

D81	**D13**	10c. red, blue & black	35	35
D82	**D13**	50c. red, blue & black	75	60
D83	**D13**	1r. red, blue & black	1·20	90
D84	**D13**	3r. red, blue & black	1·50	1·40
D85	**D13**	5r. red, blue & black	2·50	2·10

Pt. 1

CAMEROON

Former German colony occupied by British and French troops during 1914–16. The territory was divided between them and the two areas were administered under League of Nations mandates from 1922, converted into United Nations trusteeships in 1946.

The British section was administered as part of Nigeria until 1960, when a plebiscite was held. The northern area voted to join Nigeria and the southern part joined the newly-independent Cameroun Republic (formerly the French trust territory). In November 1995 this republic joined the Commonwealth.

12 pence = 1 shilling;
20 shillings = 1 pound.

I. CAMEROONS EXPEDITIONARY FORCE

1915. "Yacht" key-types of German Kamerun surch C.E.F. and value in English currency.

B1	N	½d. on 3pf. brown	13·00	55·00
B2	N	½d. on 5pf. green	6·00	10·00
B3	N	1d. on 10pf. red	1·25	9·50
B4	N	2d. on 20pf. blue	3·50	22·00
B5	N	2½d. on 25pf. black and red on yellow	16·00	55·00
B6	N	3d. on 30pf. black and orange on buff	13·00	60·00
B7	N	4d. on 40pf. black and red	13·00	60·00
B8	N	6d. on 50pf. black and purple on buff	13·00	60·00
B9	N	8d. on 80pf. black and red on rose	13·00	60·00
B10	O	1s. on 1m. red	£200	£900
B11	O	2s. on 2m. blue	£225	£950
B12	O	3s. on 3m. black	£225	£950
B13	O	5s. on 5m. red and black	£275	£1000

II. CAMEROONS TRUST TERRITORY

Issue used in the British trusteeship from October 1960 to June 1961 in the northern are and until Spetember 1961 in the southern area, when they joined with Nigeria nad the Cameroun Republic respectively.

1960. Stamps of Nigeria of 1953 optd CAMEROONS U.K.T.T.

T1	18	½d. black and orange	10	2·25
T2	-	1d. black and green	10	70
T3	-	1½d. green	10	20
T4	-	2d. grey	60	3·25
T5	-	3d. black and lilac	15	10
T6	-	4d. black and blue	10	2·75
T7	-	6d. brown and black	30	20
T8	-	1s. black and purple	30	10
T9	26	2s.6d. black and green	1·50	1·00
T10	-	5s. black and orange	2·00	3·50
T11	-	10s. black and brown	3·00	7·00
T12	29	£1 black and violet	16·00	32·00

III. REPUBLIC OF CAMEROON

The Republic of Cameroon joined the Commonwealth on 1 November 1995 and issues from that date will be listed below, when examples and information have been received.

PRICES: Prices shown for used stamps of Cameroon are somewhat tentative, but have been compiled with the assistance of collectors of these issues. Unused stamps for this period are scarce to rare and, when offered, can command very high prices. Under the cirumstances it has been decided not to quote unused prices at the present time, but we hope to be able to add these in a future edition of this catalogue.

418 Athlete holding Olympic Rings ('Records du monde')

1996. Olympic Games, Atlanta. Multicoloured.

1186	125f. Type **418**	10·00	65
1187	250f. As No. 1186 but inscr 'Records olympiques' (vert)	10·00	1·40

419 Conference Emblem

1996. 32nd Conference of Heads of State of Organisation of African Unity, Yaounde.

1188	**419**	125f. multicoloured		1·25
1189	**419**	200f. multicoloured (1997)		1·10
1190	**419**	250f. multicoloured (1997)	5·00	1·40
1191	-	410f. multicoloured (vert)	5·00	1·90

Imprint dates: '1996' Nos. 1188, 1191; '1997' Nos. 1188a, 1189, 1190.

420 Emblem

1997
1192	**420**	500f. multicoloured	15·00	15·00

No. 1192 was originally produced to pay fees for opening a Cameroon Postal Savings Bank account, but has been found used on mail.

421 Pineapple

1998. Tourism. Multicoloured.
1193	100f. Type **421**		15·00	2·50
1194	125f. Type **421**		50·00	2·50
1195	150f. Coffee		15·00	3·00
1196	175f. Crowned crane		8·00	6·00
1197	200f. Mandrill		7·00	1·10
1198	250f. As No. 1195		5·00	1·40
1199	410f. As No. 1196		5·00	1·90

422 *Lanius* sp. (bird)

1998
1200	**422**	125f. multicoloured	2·00	65

423 World Cup Trophy, Emblem and Cameroon Flag

1998. Fourth Participation of Cameroon in World Cup Football, France. Multicoloured.
1201	125f. Type **423**		£100	5·00
1202	250f. Football and map containing national colours (horiz)		5·00	2·75

424 Emblem

1998. 50th Anniv of Declaration of Human Rights.
1203	**424**	370f. multicoloured	3·50	3·50

425 Flags and Africa on Globe

1999. CEMAC Conference, Yaounde. Multicoloured.
1204	125f. Flags (different) and Africa on globe		£100	8·00
1205	225f. Type **425**		15·00	2·50

426 National Symbols

2000. National Symbols. Multicoloured.
1206	125f. Type **426**		1·00	65
1207	200f. Outline map enclosing Cameroon scenes (vert)		1·50	1·10
1208	250f. Airplane over landscape with wild animals (vert)		2·50	1·40

427 Congress Centre, Yaounde

2001. 30th Anniv of Co-operation between Cameroon and People's Republic of China.
1209	**427**	125f. multicoloured	5·00	1·25

428 Chantal Biya with Baby

2001. Chantal Biya Foundation. Multicoloured.
1210	125f. Type **428**		4·00	2·50
1211	250f. Baby in uterus and emblems		6·00	1·25

MS1212 110×90 mm. Nos. 1210/11

429 Lion, National Flags and Football

2002. World Cup Football, Japan and South Korea. Multicoloured.
1213	125f. Type **429**		2·00	1·25
1214	250f. Pres. Paul Biya, lion and Africa Cup (horiz)		5·00	2·75

MS1215 Circular 96×96 mm. No. 1213; As No. 1214 but square

430 Emblem

2002. 71st General Assembly of Interpol, Yaounde.
1216	**430**	125f. multicoloured	2·00	1·25

MS1217 91×120 mm. No. 1216

431 Pres. Biya, Japanese Prime Minister Koizumi and Primary School Mfandena 2, Yaoundé)

2005. Co-operation between Cameroon and Japan.
1218	**431**	100f. multicoloured	1·25	1·25
1219	**431**	125f. multicoloured		1·25
1220	**431**	200f. multicoloured	2·25	2·25
1221	**431**	250f. multicoloured	2·75	2·75
1222	**431**	370f. multicoloured	3·50	3·50
1223	**431**	410f. multicoloured	3·75	3·75
1224	**431**	500f. multicoloured	4·50	4·50
1225	**431**	1000f. multicoloured	7·50	7·50

432 Pope Benedict XVI and Pres. Biya

2009. Papal Visit.
1226	**432**	200f. multicoloured	2·00	2·00
1227	**432**	250f. multicoloured	2·50	2·50

433 Cameroon Flag

2010. 50th Anniv of Independence of French Cameroon and Reunification with British Cameroon. Multicoloured (except 500f.).
1228	125f. Type **433**		1·25	1·25
1229	200f. 50th anniversary medallion		2·00	2·00
1230	250f. Arms of Cameroon		2·50	2·50
1231	500f. Pres. Paul Biya (black)		5·00	5·00

MS1232 85×112 mm. 1000f. Pres. Paul Biya (colour photo)

434 'AFRICA 21' and Emblem

2010. Africa 21 International Conference, Yaoundé
1233	**434**	125f. black and grey	1·25	1·25
1234	**434**	250f. multicoloured	2·50	2·50

435 Camair Boeing 767

2011. First Flight of Camair Co (Cameroons Airline Corporation). Multicoloured.
1235	250f. Type **435**		2·00	2·00
1236	500f. As Type **435** but green, red and yellow background		4·00	4·00

MS1237 212×95 mm. Nos. 1235/6

436 Laying Optical Fibre

2011. 40th Anniv of Co-operation between China and Cameroon. Multicoloured.
1238	125f. Type **436**		1·00	1·00
1239	200f. Gynaco-Obstetric and Paediatric Hospital, Yaoundé		1·50	1·50
1240	250f. Multipurpose Sports Complex, Yaoundé		2·00	2·00
1241	500f. Pres. Paul Biya of Cameroon and Chinese President Hu Jintao		4·00	4·00

MS1242 130×90 mm. Nos. 1238/40
MS1243 130×90 mm. 500f. As No. 1241 but 60×40 mm

437 Emblem

2011. 30th Anniv of Discovery of AIDS. Multicoloured.
1244	100f. Type **437**		60	60
1245	250f. AIDS ribbon and Africa on globe		1·50	1·50
1246	500f. Chantal Biya (first lady of Cameroon and founder of African Synergy against AIDS and Suffering)		3·00	3·00

Pt. 6, Pt. 7, Pt. 12

CAMEROUN

Territory in western Africa which became a German Protectorate in 1884. During 1914-16 it was occupied by Allied troops and in 1922 Britain and France were granted separate United Nations mandates.

In 1960 the French trust territory became an independent republic and, following a plebiscite, in September 1961 the southern part of the area under British control joined the Cameroon Republic. In November 1995 the republic joined the Commonwealth.

A. German Colony of Kamerun.
100 pfennig = 1 mark.

B. French Administration of Cameroon.
100 centimes = 1 franc.

A. GERMAN COLONY OF KAMERUN

1897. Stamps of Germany optd Kamerun.
K1a	**8**	3pf. brown	13·50	23·00
K2	**8**	5pf. green	8·00	11·50
K3	**9**	10pf. red	5·75	6·00
K4	**9**	20pf. blue	5·75	10·00
K5	**9**	25pf. orange	25·00	55·00
K6a	**9**	50pf. brown	19·00	36·00

1900. "Yacht" key-types inscr "KAMERUN".
K7	**N**	3pf. brown	1·80	2·30
K21	**N**	5pf. green	1·10	2·30
K22	**N**	10pf. red	3·50	2·30
K10	**N**	20pf. blue	32·00	3·25
K11	**N**	25pf. black & red on yell	2·00	7·50
K12	**N**	30pf. black & orge on buff	2·75	6·25
K13	**N**	40pf. black and red	2·75	5·75
K14	**N**	50pf. black & pur on buff	2·75	8·50
K15	**N**	80pf. black & red on rose	3·50	15·00
K16	**O**	1m. red	90·00	£100
K17	**O**	2m. blue	7·50	£100
K18	**O**	3m. black	7·50	£160
K19	**O**	5m. red and black	£225	£700

B. FRENCH ADMINISTRATION OF CAMEROON

1915. Stamps of Gabon with inscription "AFRIQUE EQUATORIALE-GABON" optd Corps Expeditionnaire Franco-Anglais CAMEROUN.
1	**7**	1c. brown and orange	£100	60·00
2	**7**	2c. black and brown	£170	£170
3	**7**	4c. violet and blue	£170	£170
4	**7**	5c. olive and green	37·00	33·00
5	**7**	10c. red and lake (on No. 37 of Gabon)	39·00	22·00
6	**7**	20c. brown and violet	£170	£190
7	**8**	25c. brown and blue	70·00	60·00
8	**8**	30c. red and grey	£170	£190
9	**8**	35c. green and violet	70·00	55·00
10	**8**	40c. blue and brown	£170	£190
11	**8**	45c. violet and red	£170	£190
12	**8**	50c. grey and green	£170	£190
13	**8**	75c. brown and orange	£180	£200
14	**9**	1f. yellow and brown	£190	£200
15	**9**	2f. brown and red	£200	£225

1916. Optd Occupation Francaise du Cameroun. (a) On stamps of Middle Congo
16	**1**	1c. olive and brown	£100	£110
17	**1**	2c. violet and brown	£100	£110
18	**1**	4c. blue and brown	£100	£110
19	**1**	5c. green and blue	50·00	50·00
20	**2**	35c. brown and blue	£120	90·00
21	**2**	45c. violet and orange	£100	£100

(b) On stamps of French Congo
22	**6**	15c. violet and green	£110	£110
23	**8**	20c. green and red	£120	£110
24	**8**	30c. red and yellow	£100	90·00
25	**8**	40c. brown and green	70·00	£100
26	**8**	50c. violet and lilac	£110	£100
27	**8**	75c. purple and orange	£100	80·00
28	**-**	1f. drab and grey (48)	£120	£120
29	**-**	2f. red and brown (49)	£120	£120

1916. Stamps of Middle Congo optd CAMEROUN Occupation Francaise.
30	**1**	1c. olive and brown	35	3·25
31	**1**	2c. violet and brown	65	3·25
32	**1**	4c. blue and brown	75	3·25
33	**1**	5c. green and blue	90	2·40
34	**1**	10c. red and blue	1·20	2·75
34a	**1**	15c. purple and red	3·00	4·50
35	**1**	20c. brown and blue	1·70	3·50
36	**2**	25c. blue and green	1·00	1·30
37	**2**	30c. pink and green	2·00	2·75
38	**2**	35c. brown and blue	1·70	3·50
39	**2**	40c. green and brown	2·00	4·75
40	**2**	45c. violet and orange	2·75	5·50
41	**2**	50c. green and orange	2·75	4·50
42	**2**	75c. brown and blue	2·50	6·00
43	**3**	1f. green and violet	2·30	3·50
44	**3**	2f. violet and green	8·75	16·00
45	**3**	5f. blue and pink	13·00	33·00

1921. Stamps of Middle Congo (colours changed) optd CAMEROUN.
46	**1**	1c. orange and green	20	5·50
47	**1**	2c. red and brown	20	5·75
48	**1**	4c. green and grey	45	6·25
49	**1**	5c. orange and red	45	3·25
50	**1**	10c. light green and green	90	3·75
51	**1**	15c. orange and blue	1·50	6·25
52	**1**	20c. grey and purple	2·00	5·00
53	**2**	25c. orange and green	1·90	2·00
54	**2**	30c. red and carmine	1·50	5·50
55	**2**	35c. blue and green	2·00	5·50
56	**2**	40c. orange and green	1·90	5·50
57	**2**	45c. red and brown	1·30	5·00
58	**2**	50c. ultramarine and blue	1·10	3·50
59	**2**	75c. green and purple	1·30	6·00
60	**3**	1f. orange and grey	3·25	6·50
61	**3**	2f. red and green	7·75	18·00
62	**3**	5f. grey and red	8·75	33·00

1924. Stamps of 1921 surch.
63	**1**	25c. on 15c. orange & blue	1·20	7·75
64	**3**	25c. on 2f. red and green	1·80	7·75
65	**3**	25c. on 5f. grey and red	1·50	8·25

66	2	"65" on 45c. red and brown	2·20	8·75
67	2	"85" on 75c. green & red	3·25	9·00

5 Cattle fording River

1925

68	5	1c. mauve and olive	20	3·75
69	5	2c. green & red on green	35	2·50
70	5	4c. black and blue	45	3·25
71	5	5c. mauve and yellow	40	40
72	5	10c. orange & pur on yell	1·30	90
73	5	15c. green	2·75	5·50
88	5	15c. red and lilac	1·00	3·00
74	A	20c. brown and olive	1·70	5·75
89	A	20c. green	1·10	3·25
90	A	20c. brown and red	65	25
75	A	25c. black and green	1·40	55
76	A	30c. red and green	1·30	1·20
91	A	30c. green and olive	1·10	1·30
77	A	35c. black and brown	1·80	7·00
91a	A	35c. green	4·50	5·75
78	A	40c. violet and orange	4·00	3·25
79	A	45c. red	1·00	5·50
92	A	45c. brown and mauve	3·25	3·50
80	A	50c. red and green	3·00	45
93	A	55c. red and blue	5·00	8·25
81	A	60c. black and mauve	2·50	5·25
94	A	60c. red	1·30	6·00
82	A	65c. brown and blue	3·00	90
83	A	75c. blue	1·70	3·00
95	A	75c. mauve and brown	1·30	1·40
95a	A	80c. brown and red	2·00	7·75
84	A	85c. blue and red	1·40	3·25
96	A	90c. red	3·50	3·50
85	B	1f. brown and blue	2·20	6·50
97	B	1f. blue	1·70	1·40
98	B	1f. mauve and brown	2·00	2·75
99	B	1f. brown and green	4·00	2·00
100	B	1f.10 brown and red	4·50	11·50
100a	B	1f.25 blue and brown	12·00	11·50
101	B	1f.50 blue	3·00	95
101a	B	1f.75 red and brown	2·30	1·90
101b	B	1f.75 blue	11·50	16·00
86	B	2f. orange and olive	4·50	1·10
102	B	3f. mauve and brown	5·00	2·50
87	B	5f. black & brown on bl	5·25	1·50
103	B	10f. mauve and orange	12·00	9·00
104	B	20f. green and red	30·00	21·00

DESIGNS—VERT: A, Tapping rubber-trees. HORIZ: B, Liana suspension bridge.

1926. Surch with new value.

105		1f.25 on 1f. blue	1·80	6·00

1931. "Colonial Exhibition" key-types inscribed "CAMEROUN".

106	E	40c. green	5·25	9·25
107	F	50c. mauve	5·50	9·00
108	G	90c. orange	6·25	8·75
109	H	1f.50 blue	6·25	6·75

14 Sailing Ships

1937. Paris International Exhibition. Inscr "EXPOSITION INTERNATIONALE PARIS 1937".

110	-	20c. violet	2·30	6·75
111	14	30c. green	2·50	6·50
112	-	40c. red	1·80	6·25
113	-	50c. brown & deep brown	2·30	3·50
114	-	90c. red	2·10	5·50
115	-	1f.50 blue	2·00	6·25

MS115a 120×100 mm. 163f. red and agate | 10·50 | 31·00

DESIGNS—VERT: 20c. Allegory of Commerce; 50c. Allegory of Agriculture. HORIZ: 40c. Berber, Negress and Annamite; 90c. France extends torch of Civilization; 1f.50, Diane de Poitiers.

19 Pierre and Marie Curie

1938. International Anti-cancer Fund.

116	19	1f.75+50c. blue	10·50	33·00

20

1939. New York World's Fair.

117	20	1f.25 red	2·30	6·75
118	20	2f.25 blue	2·75	6·75

21 Lamido Woman

1939

119	21	2c. black	30	5·25
120	21	3c. mauve	40	5·25
121	21	4c. blue	75	5·25
122	21	5c. brown	60	5·25
123	21	10c. green	65	4·75
124	21	15c. red	90	6·50
125	21	20c. purple	95	6·50
126	A	25c. black	1·40	4·75
127	A	30c. orange	85	6·50
128	A	40c. blue	85	5·25
129	A	45c. green	2·10	8·50
130	A	50c. brown	1·10	4·00
131	A	60c. blue	90	7·25
132	A	70c. purple	3·00	8·75
133	B	80c. blue	3·50	10·50
134	B	90c. blue	2·10	2·30
135	B	1f. red	3·25	4·25
135a	B	1f. brown	1·90	3·25
136	B	1f.25 red	4·50	16·00
137	B	1f.40 orange	2·75	8·00
138	B	1f.50 brown	1·70	3·00
139	B	1f.60 brown	2·75	8·25
140	B	1f.75 blue	2·20	4·00
141	B	2f. green	1·90	2·30
142	B	2f.25 blue	2·50	4·75
143	B	2f.50 purple	3·25	4·00
144	B	3f. violet	1·70	2·50
145	C	5f. brown	2·40	2·75
146	C	10f. purple	2·40	5·75
147	C	20f. green	4·00	6·50

DESIGNS—VERT: A, Banyo Waterfall; C, African boatman. HORIZ: B, African elephants.

25 Storming the Bastille

1939. 150th Anniv of Revolution.

148	25	45c.+25c. green	10·00	22·00
149	25	70c.+30c. brown	10·00	22·00
150	25	90c.+35c. orange	10·00	27·00
151	25	1f.25+1f. red	10·00	28·00
152	25	2f.25+2f. blue	12·00	33·00

1940. Adherence to General de Gaulle. Optd **CAMEROUN FRANCAIS 27-8-40**.

153	21	2c. black	90	1·60
154	21	3c. mauve	90	3·25
155	21	4c. blue	55	1·70
156	21	5c. brown	7·75	7·50
157	21	10c. green	75	1·60
158	21	15c. red	1·40	5·50
159	21	20c. purple	26·00	23·00
160	A	25c. black	1·10	95
161	A	30c. orange	22·00	23·00
162	A	40c. blue	6·00	4·75
163	A	45c. green	1·80	2·00
164	-	50c. red & green (No. 80)	90	1·20
165	A	60c. blue	6·75	9·75
166	A	70c. purple	1·80	1·90
167	B	80c. blue	7·25	4·00
168	B	90c. blue	55	80
169	20	1f.25 red	4·50	5·00
170	B	1f.25 red	85	90
171	B	1f.40 orange	1·40	2·20
172	B	1f.50 brown	70	1·00
173	B	1f.60 brown	1·00	1·40
174	B	1f.75 blue	85	1·30
175	20	2f.25 blue	3·50	3·50
176	B	2f.25 blue	70	1·10
177	B	2f.50 purple	70	55
178	-	5f. black and brown on blue (No. 87)	19·00	6·50
179	C	5f. brown	24·00	5·50

180	-	10f. mve & orge (No. 103)	28·00	7·75
181	C	10f. purple	80·00	75·00
182	-	20f. green & red (No. 104)	65·00	11·00
183	C	20f. green	£160	£200

1940. War Relief Fund. Nos. 100a, 101a and 86 surch **OEUVRES DE GUERRE** and premium.

184		1f.25+2f. blue and brown	37·00	46·00
185		1f.75+3f. red and brown	37·00	46·00
186		2f.+5f. orange and olive	27·00	30·00

1940. Spitfire Fund. Nos. 126, 129, 131/2 surch +5 **Frs. SPITFIRE**.

187	A	25c.+5f. black	£120	£120
188	A	45c.+5f. green	£120	£120
189	A	60c.+5f. blue	£130	£130
190	A	70c.+5f. purple	£130	£130

1941. Spitfire Fund. Surch **SPITFIRE+10 fr.** General de **GAULLE**.

190a	20	1f.25+10f. red	£120	£130
190b	20	2f.25+10f. blue	£120	£130

29b Sikorsky S-43 over Map **29c** Sikorsky S-43 Amphibian

1941. Air.

190c	29b	25c. red	1·00	7·00
190d	29b	50c. green	75	7·00
190e	29b	1f. green	2·50	7·00
190f	29c	2f. olive	1·50	4·75
190g	29c	3f. brown	1·70	5·00
190h	29c	4f. blue	1·30	5·00
190i	29c	6f. myrtle	1·50	4·25
190j	29c	7f. purple	1·40	4·25
190k	29c	12f. orange	7·25	16·00
190l	29c	20f. red	4·50	8·50
190m		50f. blue	4·75	8·50

DESIGN: 50f. Latecoere 631 flying boat over harbour.

1941. Laquintinie Hospital Fund. Surch **+10 Frs. AMBULANCE LAQUINTINIE**.

191	20	1f.25+10f. red	41·00	47·00
192	20	2f.25+10f. blue	50·00	47·00

31 Cross of Lorraine, Sword and Shield **32** Fairey FC-1

1942. Free French Issue.

193	31	5c. brown (postage)	15	1·90
194	31	10c. blue	15	60
195	31	25c. green	15	70
196	31	30c. red	40	70
197	31	40c. green	50	60
198	31	80c. purple	60	95
199	31	1f. mauve	90	55
200	31	1f.50 red	80	45
201	31	2f. black	85	55
202	31	2f.50 blue	60	70
203	31	4f. violet	60	1·20
204	31	5f. yellow	90	1·40
205	31	10f. brown	65	45
206	31	20f. green	95	1·20
207	32	1f. orange (air)	1·30	5·50
208	32	1f.50 red	2·00	6·25
209	32	5f. purple	1·20	6·25
210	32	10f. black	1·40	6·75
211	32	25f. blue	2·00	6·75
212	32	50f. green	2·75	4·00
213	32	100f. red	2·30	4·25

1943. Surch **Valmy+100 frs.**

213a	-	1f.25+100f. blue and brown (No. 100a)	13·00	65·00
213b	20	1f.25+100f. red	10·50	65·00
213c	-	1f.25+100f. red (No. 136)	33·00	65·00
213d	-	1f.50+100f. brown (No. 138)	20·00	65·00
213e	20	2f.25+100f. blue	18·00	65·00

33

1944. Mutual Aid and Red Cross Funds.

214	33	5f.+20f. red	85	11·00

1945. Surch.

215	31	50c. on 5c. brown	1·30	7·00
216	31	60c. on 5c. brown	55	7·00
217	31	70c. on 5c. brown	65	7·25
218	31	1f.20 on 5c. brown	1·00	7·25
219	31	2f.40 on 25c. green	1·00	2·75
220	31	3f. on 25c. green	1·10	3·25
221	31	4f.50 on 25c. green	1·70	8·75
222	31	15f. on 2f.50 blue	1·40	8·25

34 Felix Eboue

1945

223	34	2f. black	45	2·30
224	34	25f. green	90	5·50

35 "Victory"

1946. Air. Victory.

225	35	8f. purple	70	2·30

36 Chad

1946. Air. From Chad to the Rhine. Inscr "DU TCHAD AU RHIN".

226	36	5f. blue	2·50	8·25
227	-	10f. purple	1·70	8·25
228	-	15f. red	2·00	8·25
229	-	20f. blue	2·10	8·25
230	-	25f. brown	3·00	8·25
231	-	50f. black	2·75	8·50

DESIGNS: 10f. Koufra; 15f. Mareth; 20f. Normandy; 25f. Paris; 50f. Strasbourg.

37 Zebu and Herdsman **45** Aeroplane, African and Mask

1946

232	37	10c. green (postage)	25	2·10
233	37	30c. orange	25	4·00
234	37	40c. blue	25	5·75
235	-	50c. sepia	70	1·40
236	-	60c. purple	90	5·50
237	-	80c. brown	90	6·00
238	-	1f. orange	1·10	30
239	-	1f.20 green	1·50	6·50
240	-	1f.50 red	2·75	3·25
241	-	2f. black	90	30
242	-	3f. red	2·40	35
243	-	3f.60 red	2·30	6·75
244	-	4f. blue	1·10	30
245	-	5f. red	2·20	70
246	-	6f. blue	2·20	15
247	-	10f. green	1·60	30
248	-	15f. blue	2·75	85
249	-	20f. green	3·25	1·00
250	-	25f. black	2·75	1·80
251	-	50f. green (air)	2·75	1·30
252	-	100f. brown	3·50	2·50
253	45	200f. olive	6·25	5·00

DESIGNS—VERT: 50c. to 80c. Tikar women; 1f. to 1f.50, Africans carrying bananas; 2f. to 4f. Bowman; 5f. to 10f. Lamido horsemen; 15f. to 25f. Native head. HORIZ: 50f. Birds over mountains; 100f. African horsemen and Dewoitine D-333 trimotor airplane.

46 People of Five Races, Lockheed
Constellation Airplane and Globe

1949. Air. 75th Anniv of UPU.
254 **46** 25f. multicoloured 4·00 7·50

47 Doctor and Patient

1950. Colonial Welfare Fund.
255 **47** 10f.+2f. green & turq 5·25 15·00

48 Military
Medal

1952. Military Medal Centenary.
256 **48** 15f. red, yellow and
green 5·50 5·00

49 Porters **50** Transporting Logs
Carrying
Bananas

1953
257 **49** 8f. violet, orange and
purple (postage) 65 25
258 **49** 15f. brown, yellow & red 2·50 55
259 - 40f. brown, pink & choc 2·00 70
260 **50** 50f. ol, brn & sep (air) 5·00 90
261 - 100f. sepia, brown & turq 13·00 1·80
262 - 200f. brown, blue & grn 15·00 7·00
262a - 500f. indigo, blue and
lilac 28·00 17·00

DESIGNS—As Type **49**: 40f. Woman gathering coffee. As
Type **50**: 100f. Airplane over giraffes; 200f. Freight-
ers, Douala Port. VERT: 500f. Sud Ouest Corse II over Piton
d'Humsiki.

51 Edea Barrage

1953. Air. Opening of Edea Barrage.
263 **51** 15f. blue, lake and
brown 2·75 1·00

52 "D-Day"

1954. Air. Tenth Anniv of Liberation.
264 **52** 15f. green and turquoise 7·75 6·50

53 Dr. Jamot and Students

1954. Air. 75th Birthday of Dr. Jamot (physician).
265 **53** 15f. brown, blue & green 5·25 7·25

54 Native Cattle

1956. Economic and Social Development Fund. Inscr
"F.I.D.E.S.".
266 **54** 5f. brown and sepia 55 30
267 - 15f. turq, blue & black 1·40 45
268 - 20f. turquoise and blue 1·20 75
269 - 25f. blue 1·80 90
DESIGNS: 15f. R. Wouri bridge; 20f. Technical education;
25f. Mobile medical unit.

55 Coffee

1956
270 **55** 15f. vermilion and red 50 30

56 Woman, Child and
Flag

1958. First Anniv of First Cameroun Govt.
271 **56** 20f. multicoloured 55 35

57 "Human
Rights"

1958. 30th Anniv of Declaration of Human Rights.
272 **57** 20f. brown and red 1·20 2·50

58 "Randia
malleifera

1958. Tropical Flora.
273 **58** 20f. multicoloured 1·10 55

59 Loading Bananas on
Ship at Douala

1959
274 **59** 20f. multicoloured 1·00 35
275 - 25f. green, brn & pur 1·20 90
DESIGN—VERT: 25f. Bunch of bananas and native bearers
in jungle path.

C. INDEPENDENT REPUBLIC

60 Prime Minister
A. Ahidjo

1960. Proclamation of Independence. Inscr "1 ER JANVIER
1960".
276 20f. multicoloured 80 25
277 **60** 25f. green, bistre & black 80 25
DESIGN: 20f. Cameroun flag and map.

61 "Uprooted Tree"

1960. World Refugee Year.
278 **61** 30f. green, blue and
brown 1·10 55

62 CCTA
Emblem

1960. Tenth Anniv of African Technical Co-operation
Commission.
279 **62** 50f. black and purple 1·60 80

63 Map and Flag

1961. Red Cross Fund. Flag in green, red and yellow;
cross in red; background colours given.
280 **63** 20f.+5f. green and red 1·20 95
281 **63** 25f.+10f. red and green 1·50 1·20
282 **63** 30f.+15f. red and green 2·10 1·60

64 U.N. Headquarters,
Emblem and Cameroun
Flag

1961. Admission to UNO. Flag in green, red and yellow;
emblem in blue, buildings and inscr in colours
given.
283 **64** 15f. brown and green 50 30
284 **64** 25f. green and blue 75 40
285 **64** 85f. purple, blue and red 2·30 1·40

1961. Surch **REPUBLIQUE FEDERALE** and value in
Sterling currency.
286 - ½d. on 1f. orange (238)
(postage) 45 25
287 - 1d. on 2f. black (241) 45 40
288 **54** 1½d. on 5f. brown &
sepia 55 45
289 - 2d. on 10f. green (247) 1·00 70
290 - 3d. on 15f. turquoise,
indigo and black (267) 1·30 70
291 - 4d. on 15f. vermilion and
red (270) 1·50 90
292 - 6d. on 20f. mult (274) 2·10 1·30
293 **60** 1s. on 25f. grn, bis & blk 3·00 2·20
294a **61** 2s.6d. on 30f. green, blue
and brown 5·50 5·00
295a - 5s. on 100r. sepia,
brown and turquoise
(264) (air) 10·00 9·50
296a - 10s. on 200f. brown,
blue and green (265) 20·00 19·00
297a - £1 on 500f. indigo, blue
and lilac (253a) 34·00 32·00

The above were for use in the former British Cameroon
Trust Territory pending the introduction of the Cameroun
franc.

66 Pres. Ahidjo and Prime
Minister Foncha

1962. Reunification. (a) T **66**.
298 20f. brown and violet
299 25f. brown and green
300 60f. green and red

(b) T **66** surch in Sterling currency.
301 3d. on 20f. brown & violet
302 6d. on 25f. brown and green
303 2s.6d. on 60f. green and red

68 Lions International
Badge, Doctor and Leper

1962. World Leprosy Day. Lions International Relief Fund.
304 **68** 20f.+5f. purple & brown 75 70
305 **68** 25f.+10f. purple & blue 95 90
306 **68** 50f.+15f. purple & green 1·80 1·60

69 European, African and Boeing
707 Airliners

1962. Air. Foundation of "Air Afrique" Airline.
307 **69** 25f. purple, violet & grn 1·00 50

70 Campaign
Emblem

1962. Malaria Eradication.
308 **70** 25f.+5f. mauve 1·00 80

71 Giraffes and
Waza Camp

1962. (a) Postage. Animals.
309 A 50c. sepia, blue &
turquoise 10 10
310 B 1f. black, turquoise
& orge 10 10
311 C 1f.50 brown, sage & blk 20 10
312 D 2f. black, blue and green 20 20
313 C 3f. brown, orange &
purple 20 20
314 B 4f. sepia, green & turq 25 20
315 D 5f. purple, green &
brown 35 20
316 A 6f. sepia, blue and
lemon 45 25
317 E 8f. blue, red and green 95 70
318 F 10f. black, orange & blue 75 25
319 A 15f. brown, blue & turq 1·40 45
320 F 20f. brown and grey 95 45
321 F 25f. brown, yellow & grn 2·75 1·00
322 E 30f. black, blue & brown 3·00 1·10
323 **71** 40f. lake and green 6·50 2·10

(b) Air.
324 50f. brown, myrtle & blue 95 70
325 100f. multicoloured 4·75 1·50
326 200f. black, brn & turq 8·00 2·40
327 500f. buff, purple and blue 11·00 3·75
DESIGNS—HORIZ: As Type **71**: A, Moustached monkey; B,
African elephant and Ntem Falls; C, Kob, Dschang; D, Hip-
popotamus, Hippo Camp; E, African manatee, Lake Ossa;
F, Buffalo, Batoun Region. (48×27 mm): 50f. Cocotiers
Hotel, Douala; 100f. *Cymothoe sangaris* (butterfly); 200f.
Ostriches; 500f. Kapsikis, Mokolo (landscape).

72 Union Flag

1962. First Anniv of Union of African and Malagasy
States. Flag in green, red and gold.
328 **72** 30f. brown 2·00 90

73 Map and View

1962. First Anniv of Reunification.
329 **73** 9f. bistre, violet & brown 35 25
330 **73** 18f. red, green and blue 45 40
331 - 20f. bistre, blue and
purple 60 40
332 - 25f. orange, sepia & blue 60 45
333 - 50f. blue, sepia and red 1·50 90
DESIGNS: 20f., 25f. Sunrise over Cameroun; 50f. Com-
memorative scroll.

74 "The School Under the Tree"

1962. Literacy and Popular Education Plan.
| 334 | 74 | 20f. red, yellow and green | 1·00 | 50 |

75 Globe and "Telstar"

1963. First Trans-Atlantic Television Satellite Link.
335	75	1f. ol, vio & blue (postage)	20	10
336	75	2f. lake, green and blue	30	25
337	75	3f. olive, purple and green	30	25
338	75	25f. blue and green	1·00	1·00
339	75	100f. brown and green (air) (48×27 mm)	2·30	1·40

76 Globe and Emblem

1963. Freedom from Hunger.
| 340 | 76 | 18f.+5f. blue, brn & grn | 90 | 50 |
| 341 | 76 | 25f.+5f. green & brown | 1·30 | 60 |

77 VHF Station, Mt. Bankolo, Yaounde

1963. Inauguration of Doala–Yaounde VHF Radio Service.
342	77	15f. mult (postage)	45	30
343	-	20f. multicoloured	60	45
344	-	100f. multicoloured (air)	2·30	1·40
DESIGNS: 20f. Aerials and control panel; 100f. Edea relay station (26×44 mm).

78 "Centre regional ..."

1963. Inauguration of UNESCO Regional Schoolbooks Production Centre, Yaounde.
345	78	20f. black and green	45	25
346	78	25f. red, black and orange	55	25
347	78	100f. red, black and gold	2·00	1·10

1963. Air. African and Malagasian Posts and Telecommunications Union. As T **18** of Central African Republic.
| 348 | | 85f. multicoloured | 2·20 | 1·50 |

80 Pres. Ahidjo

1963. Second Anniv of Reunification. Multicoloured.
349	80	9f. Type **80**	40	30
350		18f. Map and flag	60	30
351		20f. Type **80**	75	40

1963. Air. Inauguration of "DC-8" Service. As T **11** of Congo Republic.
| 352 | | 50f. multicoloured | 1·30 | 60 |

82 Globe and Scales of Justice

1963. 15th Anniv of Declaration of Human Rights.
353	82	9f. brown, black and blue	40	25
354	82	18f. red, black and green	55	25
355	82	25f. green, black & red	75	35
356	82	75f. blue, black & yellow	1·80	95

83 Lion

1964. Waza National Park.
| 357 | 83 | 10f. bistre green & brown | 1·40 | 45 |
| 358 | 83 | 25f. bistre and green | 2·00 | 85 |

84 Football Stadium, Yaounde

1964. Tropics Cup. Inscr as in T **84**.
359	84	10f. brown, turquoise & grn	45	25
360	-	18f. green, red and violet	60	40
361	-	30f. blue, brown and black	1·00	60
DESIGNS: 18f. Sports Equipment; 30f. Stadium Entrance. Yaounde.

85 Palace of Justice, Yaounde

1964. First Anniv of European–African Economic Convention. Multicoloured.
| 362 | 85 | 15f. Type **85** | 1·20 | 70 |
| 363 | | 40f. Sun, moon and economic emblems (vert) | 2·30 | 1·40 |

86 Olympic Flame and Hurdling

1964. Olympic Games, Toyko.
364	86	9f. red, blk & grn (postage)	1·70	1·40
365		10f. brown, violet and red	2·20	1·40
366		300f. turquoise, brown and red (air)	8·25	4·75
MS366a	168×100 mm. Nos. 364/66		14·50	14·50
DESIGNS—VERT: 10f. Running. HORIZ: 300f. Wrestling.

87 Ntem Falls

1964. Folklore and Tourism.
367		9f. red, blue & grn (postage)	55	25
368		18f. blue, brown and red	75	45
369	87	20f. drab, green and red	90	45
370	-	25f. red, brown & orange	1·40	75
371	-	50f. brown, grn & bl (air)	2·20	70
372	-	250f. sepia, grn & brn	11·00	3·75
DESIGNS—As Type **87**. VERT: 9f. Bamileke dance costume; 18f. Bamenda dance mask. HORIZ: 25f. Fulani horseman. LARGER (43×27½ mm): 50f. View of Kribi and Longji; 250f. Black rhinoceros.

88 Co-operation

1964. French, African and Malagasy Co-operation.
| 373 | 88 | 18f. brown, green and blue | 95 | 40 |
| 374 | 88 | 30f. brown, turq & brn | 1·40 | 55 |

89 Pres. Kennedy

1964. Air. Pres. Kennedy Commem.
| 375 | 89 | 100f. sepia, grn & apple | 2·30 | 2·20 |
| MS375a | 89 | 129×90 mm. Block of four | 9·00 | 9·00 |

90 Inscription recording laying of First Rail

1965. Opening of Mbanga–Kumba Railway.
| 376 | 90 | 12f. indigo, green and blue | 95 | 50 |
| 377 | - | 20f. yellow, green and red | 2·50 | 1·00 |
DESIGN—HORIZ: (36×22 mm): 20f. Series BB500 diesel locomotive.

91 Abraham Lincoln

1965. Air. Death Centenary of Abraham Lincoln.
| 378 | 91 | 100f. multicoloured | 2·30 | 1·60 |

92 Ambulance and First Aid Post

1965. Cameroun Red Cross.
| 379 | 92 | 25f. yellow, green and red | 75 | 30 |
| 380 | - | 50f. brown, red and grey | 1·50 | 55 |
DESIGN—VERT: 50f. Nurse and child.

93 "Syncom" and ITU Emblem

1965. Air. Centenary of ITU.
| 381 | 93 | 70f. black, blue and red | 1·60 | 85 |

94 Churchill giving "V" Sign

1965. Air. Churchill Commem. Multicoloured.
| 382 | 94 | 12f. Type **94** | 1·20 | 70 |
| 383 | | 18f. Churchill, oak spray and cruiser "De Grasse" | 1·20 | 70 |

95 "Map" Savings Bank

1965. Federal Postal Savings Bank.
384	95	9f. yellow, red and green	40	25
385	-	15f. brown, green & blue	55	25
386	-	20f. brown, chest & turq	60	40
DESIGNS—HORIZ: (48×27 mm): 15f. Savings Bank building. VERT: (27×48 mm): 20f. "Cocoa-bean" savings bank.

96 Africa Cup and Players

1965. Winning of Africa Cup by Oryx Football Club.
| 387 | 96 | 9f. brown, yellow and red | 75 | 35 |
| 388 | 96 | 20f. blue, yellow and red | 1·50 | 55 |

97 Map of Europe and Africa

1965. "Europafrique".
| 389 | 97 | 5f. red, lilac and black | 30 | 25 |
| 390 | - | 40f. multicoloured | 1·30 | 80 |
DESIGN: 40f. Yaounde Conference.

98 UPU Monument, Berne and Doves

1965. Fifth Anniv of Admission to UPU.
| 391 | 98 | 30f. purple and red | 80 | 60 |

99 ICY Emblem

1965. International Co-operation Year.
| 392 | 99 | 10f. red & blue (postage) | 45 | 35 |
| 393 | 99 | 100f. blue and red (air) | 2·30 | 1·00 |

100 Pres. Ahidjo and Government House

1965. Re-election of Pres. Ahidjo. Multicoloured.
394		9f. Pres. Ahidjo wearing hat, and Government House (vert)	30	10
395		18f. Type **100**	45	20
396		20f. As 9f.	55	25
397		25f. Type **100**	85	45

101 Musgum Huts, Pouss

1965. Folklore and Tourism.
398	101	9f. green, brown and red (postage)	40	25
399	-	18f. brown, green & blue	45	25
400	-	20f. brown and blue	95	40
401	-	25f. grey, lake and green	95	40
402	-	50f. brown, blue and green (48×27 mm) (air)	2·20	80

DESIGNS—HORIZ: 18f. Great Calao's dance (N. Cameroons); 25f. National Tourist office, Yaounde; 50f. Racing pirogue on Sanaga River, Edea. VERT: 20f. Sultan's palace gate Foumban.

102 "Vostok 6"

1966. Air. Spacecraft.

403	102	50f. green and red	95	55
404	-	100f. blue and purple	2·10	90
405	-	200f. violet and blue	3·75	2·20
406	-	500f. blue and indigo	8·75	4·50

DESIGNS: 100f. "Gemini 4", and White in space; 200f. "Gemini 5"; 500f. "Gemini 6" and "Gemini 7" making rendezvous.

103 Mountain's Hotel, Buea

1966. Cameroun Hotels.

407	103	9f. bistre, green and red (postage)	35	25
408	-	20f. black, green & blue	45	25
409	-	35f. red, brown & green	95	55
410	103	18f. black, grn & bl (air)	45	25
411	-	25f. indigo, red and blue	65	45
412	-	50f. brown, orange & grn	2·40	1·10
413	-	60f. brown, green & blue	1·40	75
414	-	85f. blue, red and green	1·80	85
415	-	100f. purple, blue & grn	2·75	1·20
416	-	150f. orange, brn & blue	3·50	1·60

HOTELS—HORIZ: 20f. Deputies, Yaounde. 25f. Akwa Palace, Douala. 35f. Dschang. 50f. Terminus, Yaounde. 60f. Imperial, Yaounde. 85f. Independence, Yaounde. 150f. Huts, Waza Camp. VERT: 100f. Hunting Lodge, Mora.

104 Foumban Bas-relief

1966. World Festival of Negro Arts, Dakar.

417	104	9f. black and red	75	25
418	-	18f. purple, brn and grn	75	30
419	-	20f. brown, blue & violet	1·00	40
420	-	25f. brown and plum	1·20	40

DESIGNS—VERT: 18f. Ekoi mask; 20f. Bamileke statue. HORIZ: 25f. Bamoun stool.

105 WHO Headquarters, Geneva

1966. U.N. Agency Buildings.

421	105	50f. lake, blue and yellow	1·20	70
422	-	50f. yellow, blue & green	55	25

DESIGN: No. 422, ITU Headquarters, Geneva.

106 Phaeomeria magnifica

1966. Flowers. Multicoloured. (a) Postage. Size as T **106**.

423	9f. Type **106**	60	25
424	15f. Strelitzia reginae	95	25
425	18f. Hibiscus schizopetalus x rosa-sinensis	75	25
426	20f. Antigonon leptopus	75	25

(b) Air. Size 26×45½ mm.

427	25f. Hibiscus mutabilis ("Caprice des dames")	75	25
428	50f. Delonix regia	1·50	30
429	100f. Bougainvillea glabra	3·00	60
430	200f. Thevetia peruviana	4·50	1·60
431	250f. Hippeastrum equestre	5·50	2·10

For stamps as Type **106** but showing fruits, see Nos. 463/71.

107 Mobile Gendarmerie

1966. Air. Cameroun Armed Forces.

432	107	20f. blue, brown & plum	55	25
433	-	25f. green, violet & brown	55	25
434	-	60f. indigo, green & blue	1·80	80
435	-	100f. blue, red & purple	2·75	1·20

DESIGNS: 25f. Paratrooper; 60f. Gunboat Vigilant; 100f. Dassault MD-315 Flamant airplane.

108 Wembley Stadium

1966. Air. World Cup Football Championship.

436	108	50f. green, blue and red	1·40	55
437	-	200f. red, blue and green	4·50	2·20

DESIGN: 200f. Footballers.

109 Douglas DC-8F Jet Trader and "Air Afrique" Emblem

1966. Air. Inauguration of DC-8 Air Service.

438	109	25f. grey, black & purple	80	45

110 U.N. General Assembly

1966. Sixth Anniv of Admission to U.N.

439	110	50f. purple, green & blue	90	25
440	-	100f. blue, brown & green	1·90	85

DESIGN—VERT: 100f. Africans encircling U.N. emblem within figure "6".

111 1st Minister's Residency, Buea (side view)

1966. Fifth Anniv of Cameroun's Reunification. Multicoloured.

441	111	9f. Type **111**	40	25
442	-	18f. Prime Minister's Residency, Yaounde (front view)	50	25
443	-	20f. As 18f. but side view	55	45
444	-	25f. As Type **111** but front view	85	45

112 Learning to Write

1966. 20th Anniv of UNESCO and UNICEF.

445	112	50f. brown, purple & blue	1·30	60
446	-	50f. black, blue & purple	1·30	60

DESIGN: No. 446. Cameroun children.

113 Buea Cathedral

1966. Air. Religious Buildings.

447	113	18f. purple, blue & green	45	25
448	-	25f. violet, brown & green	55	25
449	-	30f. lake, green & purple	75	40
450	-	60f. green, red & turquoise	1·40	70

BUILDINGS: 25f. Yaounde Cathedral. 30f. Orthodox Church, Yaounde. 60f. Garoua Mosque.

114 Proclamation

1967. Seventh Anniv of Independence.

451	114	20f. red, green & yellow	2·00	1·10

115 Map of Africa, Railway Lines and Signals

1967. Fifth African and Malagasy Railway Technicians Conference, Yaounde. Multicoloured.

452	115	20f. Type **115**	2·30	1·00
453	-	20f. Map of Africa and diesel train	3·25	1·40

116 Lions Emblem and Jungle

1967. 50th Anniv of Lions International. Multicoloured.

454	116	50f. Type **116**	95	55
455	-	100f. Lions emblem and palms	2·00	1·20

117 Aircraft and ICAO Emblem

1967. International Civil Aviation Organization.

456	117	50f. multicoloured	1·30	60

118 Dove and IAEA Emblem

1967. International Atomic Energy Agency.

457	118	50f. blue and green	1·30	60

119 Rotary Banner and Emblem

1967. Tenth Anniv of Cameroun Branch, Rotary Int.

458	119	25f. red, gold and blue	1·20	55

120 "Pioneer A"

1967. Air. "Conquest of the Moon".

459	120	25f. green, brown & blue	45	25
460	-	50f. violet, purple & grn	90	40
461	-	100f. purple, brown & bl	2·30	90
462	-	250f. purple, grey and brown	5·00	2·75

DESIGNS: 50f. "Ranger 6"; 100f. "Luna 9"; 250f. "Luna 10".

121 Grapefruit

1967. Fruits. Multicoloured.

463	121	1f. Type **121**	10	10
464	-	2f. Papaw	10	10
465	-	3f. Custard-apple	25	25
466	-	4f. Breadfruit	25	25
468	-	5f. Coconut	35	25
468	-	6f. Mango	45	25
469	-	8f. Avocado	95	30
470	-	10f. Pineapple	1·50	45
471	-	30f. Bananas	3·50	1·50

122 Sanaga Waterfalls

1967. International Tourist Year.

472	122	30f. multicoloured	80	35

123 Map, Letters and Pylons

1967. Air. Fifth Anniv of African and Malagasy Posts and Telecommunications Union (UAMPT).

473	123	100f. pur, lake & turq	2·20	95

124 Harvesting Coconuts (carved box)

1967. Cameroun Art.

474	124	10f. brown, red and blue	35	25
475	-	20f. brown, green & yell	50	30
476	-	30f. brown, red & green	90	45
477	-	100f. brown, red & grn	2·30	95

DESIGNS (Carved boxes): 20f. Lion-hunting; 30f. Harvesting coconuts (different); 100f. Carved chest.

125 Crossed Skis

1967. Air. Winter Olympic Games, Grenoble.

478	125	30f. brown and blue	1·50	85

126 Cameroun Exhibit

1967. Air. World Fair, Montreal.

479	126	50f. brown, chest & pur	95	40
480	-	100f. brown, purple & grn	3·00	1·10
481	-	200f. green, purple & brn	4·25	2·20

DESIGNS: 100f. Totem poles; 200f. African pavilion.

For No. 481 optd **PREMIER HOMME SUR LA LUNE 20 JUILLET 1969/FIRST MAN LANDING ON MOON 20 JULY 1969** see note below Nos. 512/17.

127 Chancellor Adenauer and Cologne Cathedral

1967. Air. Adenauer Commem. Multicoloured.
482	30f. Type **127**	95	40
483	70f. Adenauer and Chancellor's residence, Bonn	2·00	70

128 Arms of the Republic

1968. Eighth Anniv of Independence.
484	**128**	30f. multicoloured	1·00	50

129 Pres. Ahidjo and King Faisal of Saudi Arabia

1968. Air. Pres. Ahidjo's Pilgrimage to Mecca and Visit to the Vatican. Multicoloured.
485	30f. Type **129**	85	45
486	60f. Pope Paul VI greeting Pres. Ahidjo	2·10	70

130 "Explorer VI" (televised picture of Earth)

1968. Air. Telecommunications Satellites.
487	**130**	20f. grey, red and blue	50	25
488	-	30f. blue, indigo and red	80	45
489	-	40f. green, red & plum	1·10	50

DESIGNS: 30f. "Molnya"; 40f. "Molnya" (televised picture of Earth).

131 Douala Port

1968. Air. Five-year Development Plan.
490		20f. blue, red and green	55	30
491		30f. blue, green & brown	4·50	1·80
492		30f. blue, brown & green	1·00	50
493		40f. brown, green & turq	1·00	40
494	**131**	60f. purple, indigo & blue	2·50	1·00

DESIGNS—VERT: 20f. Steel forge; 30f. (No. 491), "Transcamerounais" express train leaving tunnel; 30f. (No. 492), Tea-harvesting; 40f. Rubber-tapping.

132 Spiny Lobster

1968. Fish and Crustaceans.
495	**132**	5f. green, brown & violet	20	20
496	-	10f. slate, brown & blue	30	20
497	-	15f. brown, chest & pur	65	20
498	-	20f. brown and blue	75	20
499	-	25f. blue, brown and green	1·10	55
500	-	30f. brown, blue and red	1·50	55

501	-	40f. blue, brown & orge	1·70	70
502	-	50f. red, slate and green	2·50	85
503	-	55f. purple, brown & blue	3·25	1·20
504	-	60f. blue, purple & green	5·25	1·60

DESIGNS—HORIZ: 10f. Freshwater crayfish; 15f. Nile mouthbrooder; 20f. Sole. 25f. Northern pike; 30f. Swimming crab; 55f. Dusky snakehead; 60f. Capitaine threadfin. VERT: 40f. African spadefish; 50f. Prawn.

133 Refinery and Tanker

1968. Inauguration of Petroleum Refinery, Port Gentil, Gabon.
505	**133**	30f. multicoloured	1·20	45

134 Boxing

1968. Air. Olympic Games, Mexico.
506	**134**	30f. brown, green & emer	75	35
507	-	50f. brown, red & green	1·30	60
508	-	60f. brown, blue & green	1·50	70
MS509	131×101 mm. Nos. 506/8		4·50	4·50

DESIGNS: 50f. Long-jumping; 60f. Gymnastics.

135 Human Rights Emblem

1968. Human Rights Year.
510	**135**	15f. blue & orge (postage)	60	25
511	**135**	30f. green & purple (air)	75	40

136 Mahatma Gandhi and Map of India

1968. Air. "Apostles of Peace".
512	**136**	30f. black, yellow & blue	55	45
513	-	30f. black and blue	55	45
514	-	40f. black and pink	95	75
515	-	60f. black and lilac	1·20	75
516	-	70f. black, blue & buff	1·30	90
517	-	70f. black and green	1·30	90
MS518	122×162 mm. Nos. 512, 514/15 and 517		7·50	7·50

PORTRAITS: No. 513, Martin Luther King. No. 514, J. F. Kennedy. No. 515, R. F. Kennedy. No. 516, Gandhi (full-face). No. 517, Martin Luther King (half-length).

During 1969, Nos. 481 and 512/17 were issued optd **PREMIER HOMME SUR LA LUNE 20 JUILLET 1969/ FIRST MAN LANDING ON MOON 20 JULY 1969** in very limited quantities.

137 The Letter (A. Cambon)

1968. Air. "Philexafrique" Stamp Exhibition, Abidjan (in 1969). (1st issue).
519	**137**	100f. multicoloured	3·25	2·50

138 Wouri Bridge and 1f. stamp of 1925

1969. Air. "Philexafrique" Stamp Exhibition, Abidjan, Ivory Coast (2nd issue).
520	**138**	50f. blue, olive and green	3·25	2·10

139 President Ahidjo

1969. Ninth Anniv of Independence.
521	**139**	30f. multicoloured	80	30

140 Vat of Chocolate

1969. Chocolate Industry Development.
522	**140**	15f. blue, brown and red	45	25
523	-	30f. brown, choc & grn	75	40
524	-	50f. red, green & bistre	1·00	55

DESIGNS—HORIZ: 30f. Chocolate factory. VERT: 50f. Making confectionery.

141 Caladium bicolor

1969. Air. Third Int Flower Show, Paris. Multicoloured.
525	**141**	30f. Type **141**	80	55
526	-	50f. Aristolochia elegans	1·70	80
527	-	100f. Gloriosa simplex	3·50	1·50

142 Reproduction Symbol

1969. Abbia Arts and Folklore.
528	**142**	5f. purple, turq & blue	30	20
529	-	10f. orange, olive & blue	45	20
530	-	15f. indigo, red & blue	45	25
531	-	30f. green, brown & blue	95	40
532	-	70f. red, green and blue	1·90	85

DESIGNS—HORIZ: 10f. "Two Toucans"; 30f. "Vulture attacking Monkey". VERT: 15f. Forest Symbol; 70f. Oliphant-player.

143 Post Office, Douala

1969. Air. New Post Office Buildings.
533	**143**	30f. brown, blue & green	55	25
534	-	50f. red, slate & turquoise	95	45
535	-	100f. brown and turquoise	1·80	85

DESIGNS: 50f. G.P.O., Buea; 100f. G.P.O., Bafoussam.

144 Coronation of Napoleon (David)

1969. Air. Birth Bicent of Napoleon Bonaparte.
536	**144**	30f. multicoloured	1·20	70
537	-	1,000f. gold	42·00	40·00

DESIGN: 1,000f. Napoleon crossing the Alps. No. 537 is embossed on gold foil.

145 Kumba Station

1969. Opening of Mbanga–Kumba Railway. Multicoloured.
538	30f. Type **145**	1·10	55
539	50f. Diesel train on bridge over River Mungo (vert)	2·75	1·00

146 Bank Emblem

1969. Fifth Anniv of African Development Bank.
540	**146**	30f. brown, green & vio	80	40

1969. Air. Negro Writers. Portrait designs as T **136**.
541	15f. brown and blue	45	25
542	30f. brown and purple	75	25
543	30f. brown and yellow	75	25
544	50f. brown and green	95	45
545	50f. brown and agate	95	45
546	100f. brown and yellow	1·90	1·10
MS547	115×125 mm. Nos. 541/6	7·25	7·25

DESIGNS—VERT: No. 541, Dr. P. Mars (Haiti); No. 542, W. Dubois (U.S.A.); No. 543, A. Cesaire (Martinique); No. 544, M. Garvey (Jamaica); No. 545, L. Hughes (U.S.A.); No. 546, R. Maran (Martinique).

148 I.L.O. Emblem

1969. Air. 50th Anniv of I.L.O.
548	**148**	30f. black and turquoise	70	40
549	**148**	50f. black and mauve	1·30	60

149 Astronauts and "Apollo 11" in Sea

1969. Air. First Man on the Moon. Multicoloured.
550	**200f.** Type **149**		4·75	2·20
551	500f. Astronaut and module on Moon		11·50	4·50

150 Airplane, Map and Airport

1969. Tenth Anniv of Aerial Navigation Security Agency for Africa and Madagascar (ASECNA).
552	**150**	100f. green	1·80	85

151 President Ahidjo, Arms and Map

1970. Air. Tenth Anniv of Independence.

553	151	1,000f. gold & mult	25·00	23·00

No. 553 is embossed on gold foil.

152 Mont Febe Hotel, Yaounde

1970. Air. Tourism.

554	152	30f. grey, green & brn	80	30

153 Lenin

1970. Air. Birth Centenary of Lenin.

555	153	50f. brown and yellow	1·90	75

154 Lantana camara

1970. African Climbing Plants. Multicoloured.

556		15f. Type 154 (postage)	45	25
557		30f. Passiflora quadrangularis	1·00	40
558		50f. Cleome speciosa (air)	1·50	70
559		100f. Mussaenda erythrophylla	3·00	1·40

155 Lions' Emblem and Map of Africa

1970. Air. 13th Congress of Lions International District 403, Yaounde.

560	155	100f. multicoloured	2·20	95

156 New UPU HQ.

1970. New UPU Headquarters Building, Berne.

561	156	30f. green, violet & blue	90	25
562	156	50f. blue, red and grey	1·30	40

157 U.N. Emblem and Stylized Doves

1970. Air. 25th Anniv of United Nations.

563	157	30f. brown and orange	90	45
564	-	50f. indigo and blue	1·30	65

DESIGN—VERT: 50f. U.N. emblem and stylized dove.

158 Fermenting Vats

1970. Brewing Industry.

565	158	15f. brown, green & grey	45	25
566	-	30f. red, brown and blue	90	40

DESIGN: 30f. Storage tanks.

159 Japanese Pavilion

1970. Air. Expo 70.

567	159	50f. blue, red and green	95	55
568	-	100f. red, blue and green	2·00	90
569	-	150f. brown, slate & blue	3·50	1·60

DESIGNS—VERT: 100f. Expo Emblem and Map of Japan. HORIZ: 150f. Australian Pavilion.

160 Gen. De Gaulle in Tropical Kit

1970. Air. "Homage to General De Gaulle".

570	160	100f. brown, blue & grn	3·00	1·60
571	-	200f. blue, green & brn	5·50	2·50

DESIGN: 200f. Gen. De Gaulle in military uniform.

Nos. 570/1 were issued together as a triptych, separated by a stamp-size label showing maps of France and Cameroun.

161 Aztec Stadium, Mexico City

1970. Air. World Cup Football Championship, Mexico. Multicoloured.

572	161	50f. Type 161	95	55
573		100f. Mexican team	2·00	1·10
574		200f. Pele and Brazilian team with World Cup (vert)	3·50	1·90

162 Dancers

1970. Ozila Dancers.

575	162	30f. red, orange & grn	1·20	45
576	162	50f. red, brown & scar	2·40	95

163 Doll in National Costume

1970. Cameroun Dolls.

577	163	10f. green, black & red	65	45
578	163	15f. red, green & yellow	75	55
579	163	30f. brown, green & blk	1·60	70

164 Beethoven (after Stieler)

1970. Air. Birth Bicent of Beethoven.

580	164	250f. multicoloured	5·25	2·75

1970. Air. Rembrandt Paintings. As T **144**. Multicoloured.

581		70f. Christ at Emmaus	1·50	60
582		150f. The Anatomy Lesson	2·50	1·30

166 "Industry and Agriculture"

1970. "Europafrique" Economic Community.

583	166	30f. multicoloured	80	40

167 Bust of Dickens

1970. Air. Death Centenary of Charles Dickens.

584	167	40f. brown and red	95	35
585	-	50f. multicoloured	1·10	55
586	-	100f. multicoloured	1·90	1·10

DESIGNS: 50f. Characters from David Copperfield; 100f. Dickens writing.

1971. Air. De Gaulle Memorial Issue. Nos. 570/1 optd IN MEMORIAM 1890-1970.

587	160	100f. brown, blue & grn	3·00	1·40
588	-	200f. blue, green & brn	5·50	2·30

169 University Buildings

1971. Inauguration of Federal University, Yaounde.

589	169	50f. green, blue & brown	1·00	45

170 Presidents Ahidjo and Pompidou

1971. Visit of Pres. Pompidou of France.

590	170	30f. multicoloured	1·50	70

171 "Cameroun Youth"

1971. Fifth National Youth Festival.

591	171	30f. multicoloured	80	45

172 Timber Yard, Douala

1971. Air. Industrial Expansion.

592	172	40f. brown, green & red	55	25
593	-	70f. brown, green and blue	1·20	50
594	-	100f. red, blue & green	1·60	70

DESIGNS—VERT: 70f. "Alucam" aluminium plant, Edea. HORIZ: 100f. Mbakaou Dam.

173 Gerbera hybrida

1971. Flowers. Multicoloured.

595		20f. Type 173	65	40
596		40f. Opuntia polyantha	1·50	55
597		50f. Hemerocallis hybrida	1·90	70

For similar designs inscr "United Republic of Cameroon" etc., see Nos. 648/52.

174 "World Races"

1971. Racial Equality Year. Multicoloured.

598	174	20f. Type 174	50	25
599		30f. Hands of four races clasping globe	75	25

175 Crowned Cranes, Camp de Waza

1971. Landscapes.

600	175	10f. blue, red and green	1·70	45
601	-	20f. red, brown & green	1·10	45
602	-	30f. green, blue & brown	1·10	45

DESIGNS: 20f. African pirogue; 30f. Sanaga River.

176 Relay-racing

1971. Air. 75th Anniv of Modern Olympic Games.

603	176	30f. blue, red and brown	60	30
604	-	50f. purple and blue	85	40
605	-	100f. black, green & red	1·70	70

DESIGNS—VERT: 50f. Olympic runner with torch. HORIZ: 100f. Throwing the discus.

177 Villalba (deep-sea trawler)

1971. Air. Fishing Industry.

606	177	30f. brown, green & blue	95	50
607	-	40f. purple, blue & green	1·00	70
608	-	70f. brown, red and blue	1·90	90
609	-	150f. multicoloured	4·75	1·90

DESIGNS: 40f. Traditional fishing method, Northern Cameroun; 70f. Fish quay, Douala; 150f. Shrimp-boats, Douala.

178 Peace Palace, The Hague

1971. 25th Anniv of International Court of Justice, The Hague.

610	178	50f. brown, blue & green	90	35

179 1916 French Occupation 20c. and 1914-18 War Memorial, Yaounde

1971. Air. "Philatecam 71" Stamp Exhibition, Yaounde (1st issue).

611	179	20f. brown, ochre & grn	50	25
612	-	25f. brown, green & blue	60	25
613	-	40f. green, grey & brown	95	25
614	-	50f. multicoloured	1·10	45
615	-	100f. green, brown & orge	2·10	85

DESIGNS: 25f. 1954 15f. Jamot stamp and memorial; 40f. 1965 25f. Tourist Office stamp and public buildings, Yaounde; 50f. German stamp and Imperial German postal emblem; 100f. 1915 Expeditionary Force optd, error, and Expeditionary Force memorial.

See also No. 620.

180 Rope Bridge

1971. "Rural Life". Multicoloured.

616		40f. Type **180**	1·40	45
617		45f. Local market (horiz)	1·40	45

181 Bamoun Horseman (carving)

1971. Cameroun Carving.

618	**181**	10f. brown and yellow	45	20
619	-	15f. brown and yellow	45	25

DESIGN: 15f. Fetish statuette.

182 Pres. Ahidjo, Flag and "Reunification" Road

1971. Air. "Philatecam 71" Stamp Exhibition, Yaounde (2nd issue).

620	**182**	250f. multicoloured	6·00	4·25

183 Satellite and Globe

1971. Pan-African Telecommunications Network.

621	**183**	40f. multicoloured	80	50

184 UAMPT Headquarters, Brazzaville and Carved Stool

1971. Air. Tenth Anniv of African and Malagasy Posts and Telecommunications Union.

622	**184**	100f. multicoloured	1·90	85

185 Children acclaiming Emblem

1971. 25th Anniv of UNICEF.

623	**185**	40f. purple, blue & slate	85	25
624	-	50f. red, green and blue	1·00	50

DESIGN—VERT: 50f. Ear of Wheat and Emblem.

186 The Annunciation (Fra Angelico)

1971. Air. Christmas. Paintings. Multicoloured.

625		40f. Type **186**	55	25
626		45f. Virgin and Child (Del Sarto)	80	45
627		150f. The Holy Family with the Lamb (detail Raphael) (vert)	3·25	1·20

187 Cabin, South-Central Region

1972. Traditional Cameroun Houses. Multicoloured.

628		10f. Type **187**	30	25
629		15f. Adamaoua round house	50	25

188 Airline Emblem

1972. Air. Cameroun Airlines' Inaugural Flight.

630	**188**	50f. multicoloured	80	25

189 Giraffe and Palm Tree

1972. Festival of Youth. Multicoloured.

631		2f. Type **189**	30	10
632		5f. Domestic scene	30	10
633		10f. Blacksmith (horiz)	30	20
634		15f. Women	30	20

190 Africa Cup

1972. African Football Cup Championship. Multicoloured.

635		20f. Type **190**	65	25
636		40f. Players with ball (horiz)	85	40
637		45f. Team captains	1·40	55

191 St. Mark's Square and Doge's Palace (detail-Caffi)

1972. Air. UNESCO "Save Venice" Campaign. Multicoloured.

638		40f. Type **191**	75	40
639		100f. Regatta on the Grand Canal (detail – Canaletto)	2·00	70
640		200f. Regatta on the Grand Canal (detail – Canaletto) (different)	4·00	1·40

192 Assembly Building, Yaounde

1972. 110th Session of Inter-Parliamentary Council, Yaounde.

641	**192**	40f. multicoloured	80	40

193 Horseman, North Cameroun

1972. Traditional Life and Folklore. Multicoloured.

642		15f. Type **193**	40	20
643		20f. Bororo woman (vert)	50	20
644		40f. Wouri River and Mt. Cameroun	1·80	55

194 Pataiev, Dobrovolsky and Volkov

1972. Air. "Soyuz 11" Cosmonauts. Memorial Issue.

645	**194**	50f. multicoloured	90	50

195 U.N. Building, New York, Gate of Heavenly Peace, Peking and Chinese Flag

1972. Air. Admission of Chinese People's Republic to U.N.

646	**195**	50f. multicoloured	2·75	70

196 Chemistry Laboratory, Federal University

1972. Pres. Ahidjo Prize.

647	**196**	40f. red, green & purple	80	50

1972. Flowers. As T 173, but inscr "UNITED REPUBLIC OF CAMEROON", etc. Multicoloured.

648		40f. "Solanum macranthum"	85	30
649		40f. Solanum macranthum	1·00	25
650		45f. Hoya carnosa	1·00	50
651		45f. Cassia alata	1·20	30
652		50f. Crinum sanderianum	1·50	40

197 Swimming

1972. Air. Olympic Games, Munich.

653	**197**	50f. green, brown & lake	95	45
654	-	50f. brown, blue and sepia	95	45
655	-	200f. lake, grey & purple	3·75	1·70

MS656 140×100 mm. As Nos. 653/5 but colours changed; 50f. brown, violet and blue; 50f. brown, blue and purple; 200f. brown and blue 6·50 6·50
DESIGNS—HORIZ: No. 655, Horse-jumping. VERT: No. 654, Boxing.

198 Charaxes ameliae

1972. Butterflies. Multicoloured.

657		40f. Type **198**	3·00	90
658		45f. Papiliotynderaeus	4·25	1·30

1972. No. 471 surch.

659		40f. on 30f. multicoloured	1·00	50

1972. Air. Olympic Gold Medal Winners. Nos. 653/5 optd as listed below.

660	50f. green, brown and red	95	45
661	50f. brown, blue and sepia	95	45
662	200f. lake, grey and purple	3·75	1·70

OVERPRINTS: No. 660, **NATATION MARK SPITZ 7 MEDAILLES D'OR**. No. 661, **SUPER-WELTER KOTTYSCH MEDAILLE D'OR**. No. 662, **CONCOURS COMPLET MEADE MEDAILLE D'OR**.

201 Great Blue Turacos

1972. Birds. Multicoloured.

663		10f. Type **201**	1·20	45
664		45f. Red-faced lovebirds (horiz)	2·75	1·10

202 The Virgin with Angels (Cimabue)

1972. Air. Christmas. Multicoloured.

665		45f. Type **202**	1·00	45
666		140f. The Madonna of the Rose Arbour (S. Lochner)	2·75	1·60

203 St. Theresa

1973. Air. Birth Centenary of St. Theresa of Lisieux.

667	**203**	45f. blue, brown & violet	75	25
668	-	100f. mauve, brown, & bl	1·70	70

DESIGN: 100f. Lisieux Basilica.

204 Emperor Haile Selassie and "Africa Hall", Addis Ababa

1973. Air. 80th Birthday of Emperor Haile Selassie of Ethiopia.

669	**204**	45f. multicoloured	90	50

205 Cotton Cultivation, North Cameroun

1973. Third Five Year Plan. Multicoloured.

670		5f. Type **205**	20	10
671		10f. Cacao pods, South-central region	30	10
672		15f. Forestry, South-eastern area	50	20
673		20f. Coffee plant, West Cameroun	1·00	25
674		45f. Tea-picking, West Cameroun	2·20	40

206 "Food for All"

1973. Air. Tenth Anniv of World Food Programme.

675	**206**	45f. multicoloured	80	45

207 Human Hearts

1973. Air. 25th Anniv of W.H.O.

676	**207**	50f. red and blue	90	45

208 Pres. Ahidjo, Map, Flag and Cameroun Stamp

1973. First Anniv of United Republic. Multicoloured.

677		10f. Type **208** (postage)	65	25
678		20f. Pres. Ahidjo, proclamation and stamp	1·00	50
679		45f. Pres. Ahidjo, map of Cameroun rivers and stamp (air)	85	25
680		70f. Significant dates on Cameroun flag	1·10	65

209 Mask

1973. Bamoun Masks.

681	**209**	5f. black, brown & green	10	10
682	-	10f. brown, black & purple	30	10
683	-	45f. brown, black & red	75	40
684	-	100f. brown, black & blue	1·90	70

DESIGNS: 10f., 45f., 100f., as Type **209**, but different masks.

210 Dr. G. A. Hansen

1973. Centenary of Hansen's Identification of Leprosy Bacillus.

685	**210**	45f. blue, lt blue & brown	1·70	70

211 Scout Emblem and Flags

1973. Air. Admission of Cameroun to 24th World Scout Conference.

686	**211**	40f. multicoloured	85	35
687	**211**	45f. multicoloured	1·20	50
688	**211**	100f. multicoloured	2·50	80

1973. African Solidarity "Drought Relief". No. 670 surch **100F. SECHERESSE SOLIDARITE AFRICAINE.**

689	**205**	100f. on 5f. multicoloured	1·70	1·20

213 Folk-dancers

1973. Folklore Dances of South-west Cameroun. Multicoloured.

690		10f. Type **213**	20	10
691		25f. Dancer in plumed hat	55	20
692		45f. Dancers with "totem"	1·10	30

214 WMO Emblem

1973. Centenary of WMO.

693	**214**	45f. blue and green	1·50	40

215 Garoua Party H.Q. Building

1973. Seventh Anniv of Cameroun National Union.

694	**215**	40f. multicoloured	80	45

216 Crane with Letter and Telecommunications Emblem

1973. 12th Anniv of UAMPT.

695	**216**	100f. blue, lt blue & green	1·70	75

217 African Mask and Old Town Hall, Brussels

1973. Air. African Fortnight, Brussels.

696	**217**	40f. brown and purple	80	45

218 Avocado

1973. Cameroun Fruits. Multicoloured.

697		10f. Type **218**	60	25
698		20f. Mango	75	30
699		45f. Plum	1·70	65
700		50f. Custard-apple	2·10	80

219 Map of Africa

1973. Air. Aid for Handicapped Children.

701	**219**	40f. red, brown & green	80	50

220 Kirdi Village

1973. Cameroun Villages.

702	**220**	15f. black, green & brown	35	20
703	-	45f. brown, red & orange	85	45
704	-	50f. black, green & orange	1·00	55

DESIGNS: 45f. Mabas village. 50f. Fishing village.

221 Earth Station

1973. Air. Inauguration of Satellite Earth Station, Zamengoe.

705	**221**	100f. brown, blue & grn	1·40	75

222 *The Madonna with Chancellor Rolin* (Van Eyck)

1973. Air. Christmas. Multicoloured.

706		45f. Type **222**	1·00	55
707		140f. *The Nativity* (Federico Fiori–Il Barocci)	2·75	1·70

223 Handclasp on Map of Africa

1974. Tenth Anniv of Organization of African Unity.

708	**223**	40f. blue, red and green	55	25
709	**223**	45f. green, blue and red	65	25

224 Mill-worker

1974. C.I.C.A.M. Industrial Complex.

710	**224**	45f. brown, green & red	80	25

225 Bilinga Carved Panel (detail)

1974. Cameroun Art.

711	**225**	10f. brown and green	30	25
712	-	40f. brown and red	85	25
713	-	45f. red and blue	1·05	60

DESIGNS: 40f. Tubinga carving (detail); 45f. Acajou Ngollon carved panel (detail).

1974. No. 469 surch.

714		40f. on 8f. multicoloured	80	35

227 Cameroun Cow

1974. Cattle-raising in North Cameroun. Multicoloured.

715		40f. Type **227** (postage)	1·20	50
716		45f. Cattle in pen (air)	1·20	50

228 Route-map and Track

1974. Trans-Cameroun Railway. Inauguration of Yaounde–Ngaoundere Line.

717	**228**	5f. brown, blue & green	45	25
718	-	20f. brown, blue & violet	95	40
719	-	40f. red, blue & green	1·80	80
720	-	100f. green, blue & brown	3·00	1·40

DESIGNS—HORIZ. 20f. Laying track; 100f. Railway bridge over Djerem River. VERT. 40f. Welding rails.

229 Sir Winston Churchill

1974. Air. Birth Cent of Sir Winston Churchill.

721	**229**	100f. black, red & blue	1·60	75

230 Footballer and City Crests

1974. Air. World Cup Football Championship.

722	**230**	45f. orange, slate & grey	80	25
723		100f. orange, slate & grey	1·40	70
724		200f. blue, orange & blk	3·00	1·70

DESIGNS: 100f. Goalkeeper and city crests; 200f. World Cup.

1974. Air. West Germany's Victory in World Cup Football Championship. Nos. 722/4 optd **7th JULY 1974 R.F.A. 2 HOLLANDE 1 7 JUILLET 1974.**

725	**230**	45f. orange, slate & grey	75	25
726	-	100f. orange, slate & grey	1·30	70
727	-	200f. blue, orange & blk	2·75	1·70

232 UPU Emblem and Hands with Letters

1974. Centenary of Universal Postal Union.

728	**232**	40f. red, blue and green (postage)	90	45
729	-	100f. green, vio & bl (air)	1·70	85
730	-	200f. green, red and blue	2·75	1·70

DESIGNS: 100f. Cameroun UPU headquarters stamps of 1970; 200f. Cameroun UPU 75th anniv stamps of 1949.

233 Copernicus and Solar System

1974. Air. 500th Birth Anniv (1973) of Copernicus.

731	**233**	250f. blue, red & brown	4·00	2·30

234 Modern Chess Pieces

1974. Air. Chess Olympics, Nice.

732	**234**	100f. multicoloured	4·00	1·60

235 African Mask and "Arphila" Emblem

1974. Air. "Arphila 75" Stamp Exhibition, Paris.

733	**235**	50f. brown and red	60	45

236 African Leaders, UDEAC HQ and Flags

1974. Tenth Anniv of Central African Customs and Economics Union.

734	**236**	40f. mult (postage)	1·40	70
735	-	100f. multicoloured (air)	1·80	75

DESIGN: 100f. Similar to Type **236**.

1974. No. 717 surch **100F 10 DECEMBRE 1974.**

736	**228**	100f. on 5f. brn, bl & grn	1·90	1·10

238 "Apollo" Emblem, Astronaut, Module and Astronaut's Boots

1974. Air. Fifth Anniv of 1st Landing on Moon.

737	**238**	200f. brown, red & blue	3·25	1·70

1974. Christmas. As T **222**. Multicoloured.

738		40f. *Virgin of Autumn* (15th-century sculpture)	95	45
739		45f. *Virgin and Child* (Luis de Morales)	1·20	60

239 De Gaulle and Eboue

1975. Air. 30th Anniv of Felix Eboue ("Free French" leader).
740	**239**	45f. multicoloured	1·70	70
741	**239**	200f. multicoloured	6·00	2·75

240 Celosia cristata

1975. Flowers of North Cameroun. Multicoloured.
742	**240**	5f. Type **240**	20	20
743		40f. Costus spectabilis	1·20	40
744		45f. Mussaenda erythrophylla	1·40	50

241 Fish and Fishing-boat

1975. Offshore Fishing.
745	**241**	40f. brown, blue & choc	1·90	70
746	-	45f. brown, bistre & blue	1·90	70

DESIGN: 45f. Fishing-boat and fish in net.

242 Afo Akom Statue

1975
747	**242**	40f. multicoloured	50	25
748	**242**	45f. multicoloured	75	45
749	**242**	200f. multicoloured	2·50	1·60

243 Polypore (fungus)

1975. Natural History. Multicoloured.
750	**243**	15f. Type **243**	75·00	2·10
751		40f. Nymphalis Chrysalis	45·00	95

244 View of Building

1975. Inaug of New Ministry of Posts Building.
752	**244**	40f. blue, green & brown	65	25
753	**244**	45f. brown, green & blue	90	50

245 Presbyterian Church, Elat

1975. Churches and Mosque.
754	**245**	40f. brown, blue & black	45	25
755	-	40f. brown, blue & slate	45	25
756	-	45f. brown, green & blk	55	25

DESIGNS: No. 755, Foumban Mosque; No. 756, Catholic Church, Ngaoundere.

246 Marquis de Lafayette (after Chappel) and Naval Battle

1975. Air. Bicent (1976) of American Revolution.
757	**246**	100f. blue, turq & brn	2·10	1·10
758	-	140f. blue, brown & green	2·30	1·10
759	-	500f. green, brown & blue	7·25	2·50

DESIGNS: 140f. George Washington (after Stuart) and Continental Infantry (after Ogden); 500f. Benjamin Franklin (after Peale and Nee) and Boston.

247 Harvesting Maize

1975. "Green Revolution". Multicoloured.
760	**247**	40f. Type **247**	75	25
761		40f. Ploughing with oxen (horiz)	75	25

248 The Burning Bush (N. Froment)

1975. Air. Christmas. Multicoloured.
762	**248**	50f. Type **248**	85	50
763		500f. Adoration of the Magi (Gentile da Fabriano) (horiz)	7·25	5·25

249 Tracking Aerial

1976. Inauguration of Satellite Monitoring Station, Zamengoe. Multicoloured.
764	**249**	40f. Type **249**	50	25
765		100f. Close-up of tracking aerial (vert)	1·20	50

250 Porcelain Rose

1976. Flowers. Multicoloured.
766	**250**	40f. Type **250**	90	25
767		50f. Flower of North Cameroun	1·40	35

251 Concorde

1976. Air. Concorde's First Commercial Flight, Paris to Rio de Janeiro.
768	**251**	500f. multicoloured	5·25	2·75
MS769	130×93 mm. No. 768		7·75	7·75

252 Masked Dancer

1976. Cameroun Dances. Multicoloured.
770	**252**	40f. Type **252** (postage)	80	50
771		50f. Drummers and two dancers (air)	60	25
772		100f. Female dancer	1·20	50

253 Telephone Exchange

1976. Air. Telephone Centenary.
773	**253**	50f. multicoloured	85	55

254 Young Men Building House

1976. Tenth Anniv of National Youth Day. Multicoloured.
774	**254**	40f. Type **254**	45	25
775		45f. Gathering palm leaves	50	25

255 Dr. Adenauer and Cologne Cathedral

1976. Birth Centenary of Dr. Konrad Adenauer (Statesman).
776	**255**	100f. multicoloured	95	45

256 Adoration of the Shepherds (Charles Le Brun)

1976. Air. Christmas.. Multicoloured.
777	**256**	30f. Type **256**	80	35
778		60f. Adoration of the Magi (Rubens)	1·00	45
779		70f. Virgin and Child (Bellini)	1·30	60
780		500f. The New-born (G. de la Tour)	8·50	4·75
MS781	149×119 mm. Nos. 777/80		12·50	12·50

257 Pres. Ahidjo and Douala Party H.Q.

1976. Tenth Anniv of Cameroun National Union. Multicoloured.
782	**257**	50f. Type **257**	45	20
783		50f. Pres. Ahidjo and Yaounde Party H.Q.	45	20

258 Bamoun Copper Pipe

1977. Second World Festival of Negro Arts, Nigeria. Multicoloured.
784	**258**	50f. Type **258** (postage)	75	30
785		60f. Traditional chief on throne (sculpture) (air)	1·10	45

259 Crowned Cranes ("Crown-Cranes")

1977. Cameroun Birds. Multicoloured.
786		30f. Ostrich	2·50	70
787		50f. Type **259**	2·75	80

260 Christ on the Cross (Issenheim Altarpiece, Mathias Grunewald)

1977. Air. Easter. Multicoloured.
788		50f. Type **260**	95	30
789		125f. Christ on the Cross (Veslasquez) (vert)	1·50	75
790		150f. The Entombment (Titian)	2·50	1·10
MS791	210×115 mm. Nos. 788/90		7·00	7·00

261 Lions Club Emblem

1977. Air. 19th Congress of Douala Lions Club.
792	**261**	250f. multicoloured	3·50	2·10

262 Rotary Club Emblem, Mountain and Road

1977. Air. 20th Anniv of Douala Rotary Club.
793	**262**	60f. red and blue	75	45

263 Jean Mermoz and Seaplane "Comte de la Vaulx"

1977. Air. History of Aviation.
794	**263**	50f. blue, orange & brown	95	40
795	-	60f. purple and orange	95	55
796	-	80f. lake and blue	1·20	55
797	-	100f. green and yellow	1·60	80
798	-	300f. blue, red & purple	5·25	2·50

799	-	500f. purple, grn & plum	7·75	4·50

MS800 Two sheets (a) 170×100 mm. Nos. 794/6; (b) 190×100 mm. Nos. 797/9. 20·00 20·00

DESIGNS—VERT: 60f. Antoine de Saint-Exupery and Latecoere 2b. HORIZ: 80f. Maryse Bastie and Caudron C-635 Simoun; 100f. Sikorski S-43 amphibian (1st airmail, Marignane-Douala, 1937); 300f. Concorde; 500f. Charles Lindbergh and *Spirit of St. Louis*.

1977. Air. Tenth Anniv of International French Language Council. As T **204** of Benin.

801	70f. multicoloured	1·40	1·10

264 Cameroun 40f. and Basle 2½r. Stamps

1977. "Jufilex" Stamp Exhibition, Berne.

802	**264**	50f. multicoloured	95	45
803	-	70f. green, black & brown	1·30	60
804	-	100f. multicoloured	2·10	95

DESIGNS: 70f. Zurich 4r. and Kamerun 1m. stamps; 100f. Geneva 5+5c. and Cameroun 20f. stamps.

265 Stafford and "Apollo" Rocket

1977. U.S.A.–U.S.S.R. Space Co-operation. Multicoloured.

805	40f. Type **265** (postage)	45	25
806	60f. Leonov and "Soyuz" rocket	65	25
807	100f. Brand and "Apollo" space vehicle (air)	95	45
808	250f. "Apollo–Soyuz" link-up	2·30	1·10
809	350f. Kubasov and "Soyuz" vehicle	3·25	1·50

MS810 120×81 mm. 500f. Slayton and space handshake 5·00 5·00

266 Luge Sledging

1977. Winter Olympics, Innsbruck. Multicoloured.

811	40f. Type **266** (postage)	1·10	45
812	50f. Ski-jumping	1·70	45
813	140f. Ski-marathon (air)	1·20	60
814	200f. Ice-hockey	1·80	85
815	350f. Figure-skating	3·25	1·50

MS816 116×77 mm. 500f. Slalom 5·00 5·00

1977. Palestinian Welfare. No. 765 optd **Au bien-etre des familles des martyrs et des combattants pour la liberte de la Palestine.** To the Welfare of the families of martyrs and freedom fighters of Palestine.

817	100f. multicoloured	95	55

268 Mao Tse-tung and Great Wall of China

1977. First Death Anniv of Mao Tse-tung.

818	**268**	100f. brown and green	2·75	90

269 Knee Joint

1977. Air. World Rheumatism Year.

819	**269**	70f. brown, red & blue	75	30

1977. Air. First Paris–New York Commercial Flight of Concorde. Nos. 798 and 768 optd **PREMIER VOL PARIS–NEW YORK FIRST FLIGHT PARIS–NEW YORK 22 nov. 1977 — 22nd Nov. 1977.**

820	-	300f. blue, red & purple	3·25	1·60
821	**251**	500f. multicoloured	5·00	2·50

271 The Nativity (Albrecht Altdorfer)

1977. Christmas. Multicoloured.

822	30f. Type **271** (postage)	55	25
823	50f. *Madonna of the Grand Duke* (Raphael)	1·10	40
824	60f. *Virgin and Child with Four Saints* (Bellini) (horiz) (air)	1·00	45
825	400f. *Adoration of the Shepherds* (G. de la Tour) (horiz)	5·00	2·50

272 Club Flag and Rotary Emblem

1978. 20th Anniv of Yaounde Rotary Club.

826	**272**	50f. multicoloured	75	30

273 Pres. Ahidjo, Flag and Map

1978. New Cameroun Flag. Multicoloured.

827	50f. Type **273** (postage)	90	30
828	60f. President, Flag and arms (air)	75	30

274 Cardioglossa escalerae

1978. Cameroun Frogs. Multicoloured.

829	50f. Type **274** (postage)	1·40	55
830	60f. *Cardioglossa elegans*	2·10	80
831	100f. *Cardioglossa trifasciata* (air)	3·00	1·20

275 *L'Arlesienne* (Van Gogh)

1978. Air. Paintings. Multicoloured.

832	200f. Type **275**	4·50	1·80
833	200f. *Deposition of Christ* (Durer)	3·50	1·10

276 Raoul Follereau and Leprosy Distribution Map

1978. Air. World Leprosy Day.

834	**276**	100f. multicoloured	1·20	55

277 Capt. Cook and the Siege of Quebec

1978. Air. 250th Birth Anniv of Capt. James Cook.

835	**277**	100f. green, blue & lilac	2·10	90
836	-	250f. brown, red and lilac	4·75	2·00

DESIGN: 250f. Capt. Cook, H.M.S. *Adventure* and H.M.S. *Resolution*.

278 Footballers

1978. Air. World Cup Football Championship, Argentina. Multicoloured.

837	100f. Argentinian Team (horiz)	1·00	45
838	200f. Type **278**	2·00	95
839	1000f. Football illuminating globe	10·00	5·50

279 Jules Verne and scene from *From the Earth to the Moon*

1978. 150th Birth Anniv of Jules Verne (novelist). Multicoloured.

840	250f. Type **279** (postage)	2·30	80
841	400f. Portrait and *20,000 Leagues under the Sea* (horiz) (air)	4·00	1·60

280 *Hypolimnas salmacis*

1978. Butterflies. Multicoloured.

842	50f. Type **280**	1·40	65
843	25f. *Euxanthe trajanus*	1·80	65
844	30f. *Euphaedra cyparissa*	2·50	65

281 Planting Trees

1978. Protection against Saharan Encroachment.

845	**281**	10f. multicoloured	30	10
846	**281**	15f. multicoloured	35	10

282 Carved Bamoun Drum

1978. Musical Instruments. Multicoloured.

847	50f. Type **282**	45	25
848	60f. Gueguerou (horiz)	80	40
849	100f. Mvet Zither (air)	1·20	50

283 Presidents of Cameroon and France with Independence Monument, Douala

1978. Visit of President Giscard d'Estaing.

850	**283**	60f. multicoloured	1·40	80

284 African, Human Rights Charter and Emblem

1979. 30th Anniv of Declaration of Human Rights.

851	**284**	5f. mult (postage)	30	10
852	**284**	500f. multicoloured (air)	6·00	2·75

See also No. 1070.

285 Lions Emblem and Map of Cameroun

1979. Air. Lions International Congress.

853	**285**	60f. multicoloured	75	40

286 Globe, Emblem and Waving Children

1979. International Year of the Child.

854	**286**	50f. multicoloured	75	25

287 Penny Black, Rowland Hill and German Cameroun 10pf. Stamp

1979. Air. Death Cent of Sir Rowland Hill.

855	**287**	100f. black, red & turq	1·20	60

288 Black Rhinoceros

1979. Endangered Animals (1st series). Multicoloured.

856	50f. Type **288**	1·30	35
857	60f. Giraffe (vert)	1·70	45
858	60f. Gorilla	1·70	45
859	100f. African elephant (vert)	2·75	65
860	100f. Leopard	2·75	65

See also Nos. 891/2, 904/6, 975/7, 939/40 and 1007/8.

289 "Telecom 79"

1979. Air. Third World Telecommunications Exhibition, Geneva.

861	**289**	100f. orange, blue & grey	1·20	60

290 Pope John
Paul II

1979. Air. Popes.
862	**290**	100f. blue, violet & grn	2·30	80
863	-	100f. brown, red & green	2·30	80
864	-	100f. chestnut, olive & grn	2·30	80

DESIGNS: No. 863, Pope John Paul I. No. 864, Pope Paul VI.

291 Dr. Jamot, Map and
Glossina palpalis

1979. Birth Centenary of Dr. Eugene Jamot (discoverer of sleeping sickness cure).
865	**291**	50f. brown, blue and red	2·75	70

292 *The Annunciation* (Fra
Filippo Lippi)

1979. Christmas. Multicoloured.
866	10f. Type **292**		10	10
867	50f. *Rest during the Flight into Egypt* (Antwerp Master)		45	10
868	60f. *The Nativity* (Kalkar)		80	25
869	60f. *The Flight into Egypt* (Kalkar)		80	25
870	100f. *The Nativity* (Boticelli)		1·60	45

293 "Double Eagle II" and
Balloonists

1979. Air. First Atlantic Crossing by Balloon. Multicoloured.
871	500f. Type **293**		5·25	2·00
872	500f. *Double Eagle II* over Atlantic and balloonists in basket		5·25	2·00

294 *Piper capense*

1979. Medicinal Plants. Multicoloured.
873	50f. Type **294**		1·10	25
874	60f. *Pteridium aquilinum*		1·30	25

295 Pres. Ahidjo, Map,
Independence Stamp and
Arms

1980. 20th Anniv of Independence.
875	**295**	50f. multicoloured	60	25

296 Congress Building

1980. Third Ordinary Congress of Cameroun National Union, Bafoussam.
876	**296**	50f. multicoloured	60	25

297 Globe

1980. 75th Anniv of Rotary International. Multicoloured.
877	200f. Type **297**		2·20	90
878	200f. Map of Cameroun		2·20	90
MS879 179×140 mm. Nos. 877/8 plus 8 labels			5·00	5·00

298 Voacanga Fruit and
Seeds

1980. Medicinal Plants. Multicoloured.
880	50f. Type **298**		65	10
881	60f. Voacanga tree		75	10
882	100f. Voacanga flowers		1·10	25

299 *Dissotis
perkinsiae*

1980. Flowers. Multicoloured.
883	50f. Type **299**		70	10
884	60f. *Brillantaisia* sp.		1·00	20
885	100f. *Clerodendron splendens*		1·70	45

300 Ka'aba, Mecca

1980. 1350th Anniv of Mohammed's Occupation of Mecca.
886	**300**	50f. multicoloured	95	40

301 Ice Skating

1980. Air. Olympic Games, Moscow and Lake Placid.
887	-	100f. brown and ochre	95	45
888	**301**	150f. brown and blue	1·30	60
889	-	200f. brown and green	2·00	75
890	-	300f. brown and red	2·50	1·30

DESIGNS: 100f. Running; 200f. Throwing the Javelin; 300f. Wrestling.

302 Crocodile

1980. Endangered Animals (2nd series). Multicoloured.
891	200f. Type **302**		3·00	80
892	300f. Kob		4·00	1·30

303 Bororo Girls and Roumsiki
Peak

1980. Tourism. Multicoloured.
893	50f. Type **303**		55	25
894	60f. Dschang tourist centre		55	25

304 Banana Trees

1981. Bertona Agricultural Research Station. Multicoloured.
895	50f. Type **304**		65	10
896	60f. Cattle in watering hole		85	25

305 Girl on
Crutches

1981. Int Year of Disabled People. Multicoloured.
897	60f. Type **305**		55	25
898	150f. Boy in wheelchair		1·40	65

306 Camair Headquarters, Douala

1981. Tenth Anniv of Cameroun Airlines. Multiicoloured.
899	100f. Type **306**		95	35
900	200f. Boeing 747 "Mount Cameroun"		2·00	75
901	300f. Douala International Airport		3·00	1·10

307
Presentation
African Club
Champions Cup

1981. Football Victories of Cameroun Clubs. Multicoloured.
902	60f. Type **307**		95	45
903	60f. Cup presentation (African Cup Winner's Cup)		95	45

308 African Buffalo

1981. Endangered Animals (3rd series). Multicoloured.
904	50f. Type **308**		1·50	45
905	50f. Cameroun tortoise		1·50	45
906	100f. Long-tailed pangolin		3·00	50

309 Prince Charles,
Lady Diana Spencer
and St. Paul's
Cathedral

1981. Wedding of Prince of Wales. Multicoloured.
907	500f. Type **309**		4·50	1·90
908	500f. Prince Charles, Lady Diana and Royal Coach		4·50	1·90
MS909 145×94 mm. Nos. 907/8			10·00	10·00

310 Bafoussam–Bamenda
Road

1981. Tourism.
910	**310**	50f. multicoloured	55	25

311 Yuri Gagarin and "Vostok 1"

1981. 20th Anniv of First Men in Space. Multicoloured.
911	500f. Type **311**		5·00	1·70
912	500f. Alan Shepard and "Freedom 7"		5·00	1·70

312 Cam Iroko (freighter)
in Harbour

1981. Cameroun Shipping Lines.
913	**312**	60f. multicoloured	95	40

313 Scout Salute
and Badge within
Knotted Rope, and
National Flag

1981. Air. Fourth African Scouting Conference, Abidjan. Multicoloured.
914	100f. Type **313**		95	40
915	500f. Saluting Girl Guide		4·50	1·80

314 Unity Monument

1981. 20th Anniv of Reunification.
916	**314**	50f. multicoloured	60	25

315 *L'Estaque* (Cezanne)

1981. Air. Paintings. Multicoloured.
917	500f. Type **315**	6·00	1·80
918	500f. *Guernica* (detail) (Picasso)	6·00	1·80

316 *Virgin and Child* (detail of San Zeno altarpiece, Mantegna)

1981. Air. Christmas. Paintings. Multicoloured.
919	50f. "Virgin and Child" (detail, *The Burning Bush*) (Nicholas Froment)	45	10
920	60f. Type **316**	60	25
921	400f. *The Flight into Egypt* (Giotto) (horiz)	3·50	1·30
MS922	190×111 mm. Nos. 919/21	7·75	7·75

317 *Voacanga thouarsii*

1981. Medicinal Plants. Multicoloured.
923	60f. Type **317**	1·00	35
924	70f. *Cassia alata*	1·30	50

318 *Descent from the Cross* (detail, Giotto)

1982. Easter. Paintings. Multicoloured.
925	100f. *Christ in the Garden of Olives* (Eugene Delacroix)	1·00	30
926	200f. Type **318**	1·90	70
927	250f. *Pieta in the Countryside* (Bellini)	2·30	80

319 Carving, Giraffes and Map

1982. "Philexfrance 82" International Stamp Exhibition, Paris.
928	**319** 90f. multicoloured	1·50	35

320 Clay Water Jug

1982. Local Handicrafts. Multicoloured.
929	60f. Python-skin handbag	60	25
930	70f. Type **320**	80	25

321 Pres. Ahidjo, Map and Arms

1982. Tenth Anniv of United Republic.
931	**321** 500f. multicoloured	5·25	1·70

322 Douala Town Hall

1982. Town Halls. Multicoloured.
932	40f. Type **322**	45	10
933	60f. Yaounde town hall	60	25

See also No. 1139.

323 Cameroun Football Team

1982. World Cup Football Championship, Spain. Multicoloured.
934	100f. Type **323**	1·50	45
935	200f. Cameroun and Algerian teams	3·00	75
936	300f. Nkono Thomas, Cameroun goalkeeper	4·50	1·00
937	400f. Cameroun team (different)	6·00	1·50
MS938	216×95 mm. No. 937×2	15·00	15·00

324 Bongo

1982. Endangered Animals (4th series). Multicoloured.
939	200f. Type **324**	3·00	80
940	300f. Black colobus	4·25	1·30

325 Cameroun Mountain Francolin ("Perdrix")

1982. Birds. Multicoloured.
941	10f. Type **325**	1·80	35
942	15f. Red-eyed dove ("Tourterelle")	2·10	60
943	20f. Barn swallow ("Hirondelle")	3·00	80

See also No. 1071.

326 Scouts round Campfire

1982. 75th Anniv of Boy Scout Movement. Multicoloured.
944	200f. Type **326**	2·30	80
945	400f. Lord Baden-Powell	4·00	1·60

327 ITU Emblem

1982. ITU Delegates' Conference, Nairobi.
946	**327** 70f. multicoloured	75	25

328 Nyasoso Chapel

1982. 25th Anniv of Presbyterian Church. Multicoloured.
947	45f. Buea Chapel	50	25
948	60f. Type **328**	75	25

329 World Cup, Footballers and Globe

1982. World Cup Football Championship Result.
949	**329** 500f. multicoloured	5·25	2·20
950	**329** 1000f. multicoloured	10·50	3·50

330 *Olympia* (Edouard Manet)

1982. Air. Artists' Anniversaries. Multicoloured.
951	500f. Type **330** (150th birth anniv)	5·50	2·10
952	500f. *Still-life* (Georges Braque, birth centenary)	5·50	2·10

331 Council Headquarters, Brussels

1983. 30th Anniv of Customs Co-operation Council. Multicoloured.
953	250f. Type **331**	2·30	1·10
954	250f. Council emblem	2·30	1·10

332 Yaounde University Hospital

1983. Second Yaounde Medical Days.
955	**332** 60f. multicoloured	75	25
956	**332** 70f. multicoloured	95	25

333 Pres. Kennedy

1983. Air. 20th Death Anniv of John F. Kennedy (U.S. President).
957	**333** 500f. multicoloured	5·00	2·20

334 Woman Doctor

1983. Cameroun Women. Multicoloured.
958	60f. Type **334**	75	25
959	70f. Woman lawyer	75	25

335 Lions Emblem and Map

1983. Air. District 403 of Lions International Convention, Douala.
960	**335** 70f. multicoloured	65	25
961	**335** 150f. multicoloured	1·10	65

336 Bafoussam Town Hall

1983. Town Halls. Multicoloured.
962	60f. Type **336**	65	25
963	70f. Garoua town hall	75	25

337 President Biya and National Flag

1983. 11th Anniv of United Republic. Multicoloured.
964	60f. Type **337**	55	20
965	70f. Pres. Biya and national arms	75	25

338 Container Ship and Buoy

1983. 25th Anniv of IMO.
966	**338** 500f. multicoloured	5·00	2·10

339 Martial Eagle ("L'Aigle Martial")

1983. Birds. Multicoloured.
967	25f. Type **339**	1·10	45
968	30f. Rufous-breasted sparrow hawk ("L'Epervier")	1·50	60
969	50f. Purple heron ("Le Heron Pourpre")	2·75	80

See also Nos. 1157 and 1169.

340 Bread Mask ("Wery-Nwen-Nto")

1983. Cameroun Artists. Multicoloured.
970	60f. Type **340**	75	20
971	70f. Basket with lid ("Chechia Bamoun")	95	25

341 Mobile Rural Post Office

1983. World Communications Year. Multicoloured.
972	90f.	Type **341**	95	30
973	150f.	Radio operator with morse key	1·50	50
974	250f.	Tom-tom drums	2·75	85

342 African Civet

1983. Endangered Animals (5th series). Multicoloued.
975	200f.	Type **342**	2·75	75
976	200f.	Gorilla	2·75	75
977	350f.	Guinea-pig (vert)	4·50	1·50

See also No. 1170.

343 Jeanne d'Aragon (Raphael)

1983. Air. Paintings. Multicoloured.
978	500f.	Type **343**	5·50	1·90
979	500f.	*Massacre of Scio* (Delacroix)	5·50	1·90

344 Lake Tizon

1983. Landscapes. Multicoloured.
980	60f.	Type **344**	55	20
981	70f.	Mount Cameroun in eruption	75	25

345 Boy and Girl holding Hands

1983. 35th Anniv of Declaration of Human Rights.
982	**345**	60f. multicoloured	55	20
983	**345**	70f. multicoloured	75	20

346 Christmas Tree

1983. Christmas. Multicoloured.
984	60f.	Type **346**	50	20
985	200f.	Stained-glass window, Yaounde Cathedral	1·80	75
986	500f.	Statue of angel, Reims Cathedral	4·75	1·70
987	500f.	*The Rest on the Flight into Egypt* (Philipp Otto Runge) (horiz)	4·75	1·70
MS988	140×89 mm. Nos. 985/7		12·00	12·00

348 *Pieta* (G. Hernandez)

1984. Air. Easter. Multicoloured.
992	200f.	Type **348**	2·00	75
993	500f.	*Martyrdom of St. John the Evangelist* (C. le Brun)	5·00	2·20
MS994	160×104 mm. Nos. 992/3		8·25	8·25

349 Urban Council Building, Bamenda

1984. Town Halls. Multicoloured.
995	60f.	Type **349**	60	25
996	70f.	Mbalmayo	75	35

350 High Jump

1984. Air. Olympic Games, Los Angeles. Multicoloured.
997	100f.	Type **350**	95	40
998	150f.	Volleyball	1·40	60
999	250f.	Basketball	2·30	90
1000	500f.	Cycling	4·50	1·80

351 Running with Ball

1984. Air. European Football Championship. Multicoloured.
1001	250f.	Type **351**	2·30	90
1002	250f.	Heading ball	2·30	45
1003	500f.	Tackle	4·50	1·80
MS1004	130×85 mm. As Nos. 1001/3, but with the background colours different		11·00	11·00

352 Catholic Church, Zoetele

1984. Churches. Multicoloured.
1005	60f.	Type **352**	55	25
1006	70f.	Marie Gocker Protestant Church, Yaounde	75	40

353 Antelope

1984. Endangered Animals (6th series). Multicoloured.
1007	250f.	Type **353**	3·50	1·10
1008	250f.	Wild boar	3·50	1·10

354 Pres. Biya and Arms

1984. Air. President's Oath-taking Ceremony. (a) Inscr in French.
1009	**354**	60f. multicoloured	45	25
1010	**354**	70f. multicoloured	55	25
1011	**354**	200f. multicoloured	2·00	70

(b) Inscr in English.
1012	60f. multicoloured	50	25
1013	70f. multicoloured	75	25
1014	200f. multicoloured	2·00	70

355 *Diana Bathing* (Watteau)

1984. Air. Anniversaries. Multicoloured.
1015	500f.	Type **355** (300th birth anniv) (wrongly inscr "1624")	5·75	1·90
1016	500f.	Diderot (encyclopaedist, death bicentenary)	5·75	1·90

1984. Air. Olympic Games Medal Winners. Nos. 997/1000 optd.
1017	100f.	MOEGENBURG (R.F.A.) 11-08-84	95	50
1018	150f.	U.S.A. 11-08-84	1·40	70
1019	250f.	YOUGOSLAVIE 9-08-84	2·30	1·10
1020	500f.	GORSKI (U.S.A.) 3-08-84	4·50	2·20

357 Nightingale ("Le Rossignol")

1984. Birds. Multicoloured.
1021	60f.	Type **357**	3·00	80
1022	60f.	Ruppell's griffon ("Le Vautour")	3·00	80

See also No. 1158.

358 Neil Armstrong

1984. Air. 15th Anniv of First Man on the Moon. Multicoloured.
1023	500f.	Type **358**	5·00	1·90
1024	500f.	Launching of "Apollo 12"	5·00	1·90

359 Maize and Young Plants

1984. Agro-pastoral Fair. Bamenda. Multicoloured.
1025	60f.	Type **359**	65	25
1026	70f.	Zebus	75	30
1027	300f.	Potatoes	3·50	1·30

360 Anniversary Emblem

1984. 40th Anniv of ICAO.
1028	-	200f. multicoloured	1·90	90
1029	**360**	200f. blue & deep blue	1·90	90
1030	-	300f. multicoloured	2·75	1·40
1031	-	300f. multicoloured	3·50	1·50

DESIGNS: No. 1028, "Icarus" (Hans Herni); 1030, Cameroun Airlines Boeing 737; 1031, "Solar Princess" (Sadiou Diouf).

361 Wrestling

1985. "Olymphilex '85" International Thematic Stamps Exhibition, Lausanne.
1032	**361**	150f. multicoloured	1·50	70

362 Balafons (xylophone)

1985. Musical Instruments. Multicoloured.
1033	60f.	Type **362**	65	20
1034	70f.	Mvet (stringed instrument)	85	30
1035	100f.	Flute	1·40	40

363 Intelcam Headquarters, Yaounde

1985. 20th Anniv of Int Telecommunications Satellite Consortium.
1036	-	125f. black, orange & bl	1·70	60
1037	**363**	200f. multicoloured	2·20	90

DESIGN: 125f. "Intelsat V" satellite.

365 U.N. Emblem and Headquarters

1985. 40th Anniv of UNO.
1038	**365**	250f. multicoloured	2·50	1·00
1039	**365**	500f. multicoloured	5·00	2·00

366 French and Cameroun Flags and Presidents

1985. President Mitterrand of France's Visit to Cameroun. (a) Inscr "Mitterand" in error.
1040	**366**	60f. multicoloured	
1041	**366**	70f. multicoloured	

(b) Inscr corrected to "Mitterrand".

1041a	60f. multicoloured	1·40 45
1041b	70f. multicoloured	1·40 45

367 UNICEF Emblem

1985. Child Survival Campaign.

1042	367	60f. black, blue & yell	65 25
1043	-	300f. multicoloured	3·00 1·30

DESIGN: Doctor inoculating babies.

368 Lake Barumbi, Kumba

1985. Landscapes. Multicoloured.

1044	60f. Type 368	80 25
1045	70f. Pygmy village, Bonando	80 30
1046	150f. River Cameroun	1·60 65

369 Ebolowa Town Hall

1985. Town Halls. Multicoloured.

1047	60f. Type 369	55 25
1048	60f. Ngaoundere town hall	55 25

370 Pope John Paul II

1985. Papal Visit to Cameroon. Multicoloured.

1049	60f. Type 370	1·00 40
1050	70f. Pope John Paul II holding crucifix	1·30 70
1051	200f. Pres. Biya and Pope John Paul II	3·50 1·70
MS1052	137×100 mm. Nos. 1049/51	6·75 6·75

371 Porcupine

1985. Animals. Multicoloured.

1053	125f. Type 371	1·40 55
1054	200f. Squirrel	2·20 90
1055	350f. Greater cane rat	3·75 1·60

372 Wooden Mask

1985. Cameroun Art (1st series). Multicoloured.

1056	60f. Type 372	65 20
1057	70f. Wooden mask (different)	80 30
1058	100f. Men using pestle and mortar (wooden bas-relief)	1·40 75

See also Nos. 1081/3.

373 Tomb of Henri Claude d'Harcourt (detail)

1985. Air. Death Anniversaries. Multicoloured.

1059	500f. Type 373 (bicentenary Jean Baptiste Pigalle (sculptor))	5·75 2·30
1060	500f. Louis Pasteur (bacteriologist, 90th anniv) (after Edelfelt)	5·75 2·30

374 Yellow-casqued Hornbill ("Le Toucan")

1985. Birds. Multicoloured.

1061	140f. Type 374	2·00 70
1062	150f. Cock	2·10 70
1063	200f. European robins ("Le Rouge-gorge")	3·00 1·10

See also No. 1156.

375 Child's Toys

1985. Air. Christmas. Multicoloured.

1064	250f. Type 375	2·30 1·00
1065	300f. Akono church	2·75 1·30
1066	400f. Christmas crib	3·25 1·70
1067	500f. The Virgin of the Blue Diadem (Raphael)	5·00 2·30

376 Emblem, Flag and Volunteers

1986. 25th Anniv of American Peace Corps in Cameroun.

1068	376	70f. multicoloured	75 30
1069	376	100f. multicoloured	1·00 45

1986. As Nos. 851 and 941 but inscr "Republique du Cameroun/Republic of Cameroon".

1070	284	5f. multicoloured	25 10
1071	325	10f. multicoloured	45 10

377 Virgin Mary (Pierre Prud'hon)

1986. Easter. Multicoloured.

1072	210f. Type 377	2·00 95
1073	350f. Stoning of St. Stephen (Van Scorel)	3·00 1·50

378 "Anax sp."

1986. Insects. Multicoloured.

1074	70f. Type 378	1·20 45
1075	70f. Bee on flower (vert)	1·30 50
1076	100f. Grasshopper	1·90 70

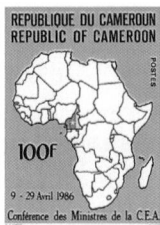

379 Map of Africa

1986. Economic Commission for Africa Ministers' Conference. Multicoloured.

1077	100f. Type 379	1·00 55
1078	175f. Members' flags	2·10 85

380 Azteca Stadium

1986. Air. World Cup Football Championship, Mexico. Multicoloured.

1079	300f. Type 380	2·75 1·40
1080	400f. Mexico team	3·75 1·70

1986. Cameroun Art (2nd series). As T 372. Multicoloured.

1081	70f. Copper Statuette	65 30
1082	100f. Wooden ash-tray	95 35
1083	130f. Wooden horseman	1·70 55

381 Queen Elizabeth

1986. 60th Birthday of Queen Elizabeth II. Multicoloured.

1084	100f. Type 381	1·10 50
1085	175f. Queen and President Biya	1·60 80
1086	210f. Queen Elizabeth (different)	2·10 1·00

382 President Biya

1986. First Anniv of Cameroun Republic Democratic Party. Multicoloured.

1087	70f. Type 382	80 30
1088	70f. Bamenda Party headquarters (horiz)	80 30
1089	100f. President Biya making speech	1·00 40

383 Argentine Team

1986. Air. World Cup Football Championship Winners.

1090	383	250f. multicoloured	3·00 1·40

384 Mask Dancer with Sword

1986. Traditional Dances of North-west Kwem. Multicoloured.

1091	100f. Type 384	1·00 55
1092	130f. Mask dancer with rattle	1·40 70

385 Cheetah

1986. Endangered Animals (7th series). Multicoloured.

1093	300f. Type 385	3·25 1·50
1094	300f. Varan	3·25 1·50

386 Bishop Desmond Tutu (Nobel Peace Prize Winner)

1986. International Peace Year. Multicoloured.

1095	175f. Type 386	1·90 80
1096	200f. Type 386	2·10 95
1097	250f. I.P.Y. and U.N. emblems	2·40 1·20

387 Pierre Curie (physicist)

1986. Air. Death Anniversaries. Multicoloured.

1098	500f. Type 387 (80th anniv)	6·75 2·50
1099	500f. Jean Mermoz and Arc en Ciel (aviation pioneer, 50th anniv)	6·75 2·50

388 Emblem

1986. National Federation of Cameroun Handicapped Associations.

1100	388	70f. yellow and red	70 25

389 Man holding Syringe and National Flag "Umbrella" over Woman and Child

1986. African Vaccination Year.

1101	70f. Type 389	85 30
1102	100f. Flag behind woman holding child being immunised	1·00 45

390 Trees on Map

1986. National Tree Day.

1103	70f. Type 390	85 30
1104	100f. Hands holding clump of earth and seedling	1·00 45

391 Loading Palm Nuts onto Trailer at Dibombari

1986. Agricultural Development. Multicoloured.

1105	70f. Type 391	85 30

1106	70f. Payment for produce harvested	85	30
1107	200f. Pineapple plantation	1·90	90

392 *Antestiopsis lineaticollis intricata*

1987. Harmful Insects. Multicoloured.

1108	70f. Type **392**	1·10	45
1109	100f. "Distantiella theobroma"	1·60	65

393 Millet

1987. Agricultural Show, Maroua. Multicoloured.

1110	70f. Type **393**	85	30
1111	100f. Cotton	1·00	45
1112	150f. Cattle	1·50	80

394 Shot-putting

1987. Fourth All-Africa Games, Kenya. Multicoloured.

1113	100f. Type **394**	95	40
1114	140f. Pole-vaulting	1·40	60

395 Drill Baboon

1988. Endangered Mammals. Drill Baboon. Multicoloured.

1115	30f. Type **395**	1·80	80
1116	40f. Adult baboons	2·00	90
1117	70f. Young baboon	2·50	1·50
1118	100f. Mother with baby	4·75	2·10

396 National Assembly Building

1989. Centenary of Interparliamentary Union.

1119	**396** 50f. multicoloured	55	15

397 Cameroun and Argentine Players

1990. World Cup Football Championship, Italy. Multicoloured.

1120	200f. Type **397**	1·80	75
1121	250f. Cameroun player and match scene	2·20	1·10
1122	250f. Cameroun winning goal	2·20	1·10
1123	300f. Cameroun first eleven	2·75	1·40
MS1124	108×77 mm. Nos. 1120/3	10·00	10·00

1990. Nos. 1062 and 1093 surch.

1125	— 20f. on 150f. multicoloured	1·90	20
1126	**385** 70f. on 300f. multicoloured	6·25	35

399 Milla and Match Scene

1990. Roger Milla, 4th Best Player in World Cup.

1127	**399** 500f. multicoloured	5·25	2·75
MS1128	108×76 mm. No. 1125	8·50	8·50

400 Anniversary Emblem

1990. 40th Anniv of United Nations Development Programme.

1129	**400** 50f. multicoloured	55	25

401 UNESCO and ILY Emblems

1990. International Literacy Year.

1130	**401** 200f. black, lt blue & bl	1·90	80

402 Arms and Pres. Paul Biya

1991. 30th Anniv (1990) of Independence. Multicoloured.

1131	150f. Type **402**	1·60	70
1132	1000f. Flag, city and 1960 20f. Independence stamp	9·75	4·50
MS1133	164×99 mm. Nos. 1131/2	12·00	12·00

403 Treating Cacao Plantation

1991. Unissued stamps (for Ebolowa Agricultural Show) with bars over inscr and surch **125F**. Multicoloured.

1134	125f. on 70f. Type **403**	95	45
1135	125f. on 100f. Sheep	1·30	75

The stamps without surcharge were sold only by the Paris agency.

405 Snake on National Colours and Map

1991. Anti-AIDS Campaign. Multicoloured.

1137	15f. Type **405**	10	10
1138	25f. Youth pushing back "AIDS" in French and English (horiz)	40	10

See also Nos. 1171/2.

1991. As No. 932 but inscr "Republic du Cameroun / Republic of Cameroun".

1139	**322** 40f. multicoloured	45	10

406 Oribi

1991. Sovereign Military Order of Malta Child Survival Project. Antelopes. Multicoloured.

1140	125f.+10f. Type **406**	1·00	1·10
1141	250f.+20f. Waterbucks	2·75	2·20
MS1142	144×90 mm. Nos. 1140/1	6·25	6·25

407 Serle's Bush Shrike ("La Pie Grieche du Mont-kupe")

1991. Birds. Multicoloured.

1143	70f. Type **407**	75	45
1144	70f. Grey-necked bald crow ("Le Picathartes Chauve ") (horiz)	75	45
1145	300f. As No. 1144	2·75	1·60
1146	350f. Type **407**	3·50	1·60
MS1147	108×80 mm. Nos. 144/5	7·75	7·75

408 African Elephant

1991. Animals. Multicoloured.

1148	125f. Type **408**	1·50	70
1149	250f. Buffalo	2·75	1·60
MS1150	120×80 mm. Nos. 1148/9	6·25	6·25

409 Mvolye Church

1991. Centenary (1990) of Catholic Church in Cameroun. Multicoloured.

1151	125f. Type **409**	1·40	70
1152	250f. Akono church	2·40	1·50
MS1153	108×80 mm. Nos. 1151/2	4·00	4·00

410 Emblems

1991. Seventh African Group Meeting of Int Savings Banks Institute, Yaounde.

1154	**410** 250f. multicoloured	2·40	1·20
MS1155	107×80 mm. No. 1154	2·75	2·75

1992. Birds. As previous designs but with values changed. Multicoloured.

1156	125f. As No. 1063	1·40	50
1157	200f. As No. 968	2·00	85
1158	350f. Type **357**	3·50	1·50

411 Columbus's Fleet

1992. 500th Anniv of Discovery of America by Columbus. Multicoloured.

1159	125f. Type **411**	1·40	70
1160	250f. Columbus kneeling on beach	2·50	1·40
1161	400f. Meeting Amerindians	3·75	2·10
1162	500f. Fleet crossing the Atlantic	5·25	3·00

412 Mbappe Lepe (footballer)

1992. Cameroun Football. Multicoloured.

1163	125f. Type **412**	1·30	70
1164	250f. League emblem	2·50	1·50
1165	400f. National Football Federation emblem (horiz)	3·75	2·10
1166	500f. Ahmadou Ahidjo Stadium, Yaounde (horiz)	5·50	3·00

See also Nos. 1173/5.

413 Crocodile

1993. Endangered Animals. Mult. Self-adhesive.

1167	125f. Type **413**	1·40	70
1168	250f. Kob (vert)	2·40	1·40

1993. As Nos. 967 and 975 but inscr "REPUBLIQUE DU CAMEROUN REPUBLIC OF CAMEROON" and values changed.

1169	**339** 370f. multicoloured	3·50	1·80
1170	**342** 410f. multicoloured	4·25	2·10

1993. Anti-AIDS Campaign. As Nos. 1137/8 but values changed. Multicoloured.

1171	100f. Type **405**	1·00	60
1172	175f. As No. 1138	1·90	1·00

1993. As Nos. 1163/5 but values changed.

1173	10f. As No. 1165		
1174	25f. As No. 1164		
1175	50f. Type **412**		

414 President Biya holding Football and Lion (national team mascot)

1994. World Cup Football Championship, United States. Multicoloured.

1176	125f. Type **414**	85	45
1177	250f. Emblem, lion, player and map of Cameroun	1·40	75
1178	450f. Players, ball showing world map, national flag and trophy	2·50	1·50
1179	500f. Eagle and lion supporting ball	3·00	1·70
MS1180	120×100 mm. Nos. 1176/9	13·00	13·00

415 Grey Parrot

1995

1181	**415** 125f. multicoloured	1·30	45

416 Chi-rho, Cross and Pope John Paul II

1995. Second Papal Visit.

1182	**416** 55f. black, pink & yell	35	25
1183	— 125f. multicoloured	85	35

DESIGN: 125f. Pope and open book.

417 Anniversary Emblem and Dove carrying Branch

1995. 50th Anniv of UNO Multicoloured.

1184	200f. Type **417**	1·20	55
1185	250f. Anniversary emblem and figures joining hands	1·50	75

MILITARY FRANK STAMP

Cameroon joined the Commonwealth on 1 November 1995.

M78 Arms and Crossed Swords

1963. No value indicated.

M1	**M78** (–) lake	3·00	3·25

POSTAGE DUE STAMPS

D8 Felling Mahogany Tree

1925

D88	**D8**	2c. black and blue	40	3·75
D89	**D8**	4c. purple and olive	40	3·00
D90	**D8**	5c. black and lilac	80	3·75
D91	**D8**	10c. black and red	80	4·50
D92	**D8**	15c. black and grey	1·00	4·25
D93	**D8**	20c. black and olive	1·70	4·75
D94	**D8**	25c. black and yellow	1·60	5·75

D95	D8	30c. orange and blue	1·60	5·75
D96	D8	50c. black and brown	1·90	5·00
D97	D8	60c. red and green	2·00	6·50
D98	D8	1f. green & red on grn	2·30	1·70
D99	D8	2f. mauve and red	4·00	8·25
D100	D8	3f. blue and brown	7·25	10·50

D25 African Idols

1939

D148	D25	5c. purple	45	4·50
D149	D25	10c. blue	55	5·00
D150	D25	15c. red	35	4·50
D151	D25	20c. brown	35	4·50
D152	D25	30c. blue	35	3·25
D153	D25	50c. green	40	4·50
D154	D25	60c. purple	55	4·50
D155	D25	1f. violet	90	3·25
D156	D25	2f. orange	1·00	5·00
D157	D25	3f. blue	1·10	6·00

D46

1947

D254	D46	10c. red	25	4·50
D255	D46	30c. orange	25	4·75
D256	D46	50c. black	25	4·75
D257	D46	1f. red	70	4·50
D258	D46	2f. green	2·10	5·00
D259	D46	3f. mauve	2·10	5·25
D260	D46	4f. blue	1·80	4·75
D261	D46	5f. brown	1·70	4·75
D262	D46	10f. blue	2·10	3·00
D263	D46	20f. sepia	2·75	4·50

D77 Hibiscus rosa sinensis

1963. Flowers. Multicoloured.

D342	50c. Type D 77	10	50
D343	50c. Erythrine	10	50
D344	1f. Plumeria lutea	10	50
D345	1f. Ipomoea sp.	10	50
D346	1f.50 Grinum sp.	10	50
D347	1f.50 Hoodia gordonii	10	50
D348	2f. Ochna	20	60
D349	2f. Gloriosa	20	60
D350	5f. Costus spectabilis	20	60
D351	5f. Bougainvillea spectabilis	20	60
D352	10f. Delonix regia	55	55
D353	10f. Haemanthus	55	55
D354	20f. Titanopsis	1·30	1·20
D355	20f. Ophthalmophyllum	1·30	1·20
D356	40f. Zingiberaceae	2·00	1·80
D357	40f. Amorphophalus	2·00	1·80

No post 1995 issues, see West Africa catalogue.

Cameroun joined the Commonwealth on 1 November 1995.

Pt. 1

CANADA

A British dominion consisting of the former province of Canada with British Columbia, New Brunswick, Newfoundland, Nova Scotia and Prince Edward Island.

1851. 12 pence = 1 shilling (Canadian).
1859. 100 cents = 1 dollar.

COLONY OF CANADA

1 Beaver 2 Prince Albert 3

4 5 6 Jacques Cartier

1851. Imperf

17	4	½d. red	£1000	£600
5	1	3d. red	£2500	£225
9	2	6d. purple	£40000	£1100
12	5	7½d. green	£12000	£2500
14	6	10d. blue	£13000	£1700
4	3	12d. black	£180000	£100000

1858. Perf

25		½d. red	£4500	£950
26	1	3d. red	£12000	£375
27a	2	6d. purple	£16000	£3750

1859. Values in cents. Perf

29	4	1c. red	£400	50·00
44	4	2c. red	£600	£170
31	1	5c. red	£425	18·00
36	2	10c. brown	£1300	80·00
38	2	10c. purple	£1400	80·00
40	5	12½c. green	£1100	70·00
42	6	17c. blue	£1500	95·00

DOMINION OF CANADA

13 14

1868. Various frames.

54	13	½c. black	80·00	65·00
55	14	1c. brown	£550	65·00
56a	14	1c. yellow	£1100	£100
57	14	2c. green	£750	50·00
49	14	3c. red	£1500	35·00
63	14	5c. green	£850	85·00
59b	14	6c. brown	£1300	65·00
60	14	12½c. blue	£950	60·00
69	14	15c. blue	£170	35·00
70	14	15c. purple	75·00	20·00

21 27

1870. Various frames.

101	27	½c. black	20·00	11·00
75	21	1c. yellow	42·00	2·25
104	21	2c. green	60·00	3·50
105	21	3c. red	55·00	1·50
106	21	5c. grey	£110	1·75
107	21	6c. brown	50·00	16·00
117	-	8c. grey	£180	8·50
120	-	8c. purple	£110	8·50
111	21	10c. pink	£250	38·00

On 8c. head is to left.

28

1893

115	28	20c. red	£250	65·00
116	28	50c. blue	£275	45·00

30

1897. Jubilee.

121	30	½c. black	75·00	75·00
122	30	1c. orange	12·00	6·00
124	30	2c. green	22·00	9·50
126	30	3c. red	12·00	2·25
128	30	5c. blue	50·00	16·00
129	30	6c. brown	£130	£130
130	30	8c. violet	50·00	38·00
131	30	10c. purple	85·00	70·00
132	30	15c. slate	£140	£120
133	30	20c. red	£140	£100
134	30	50c. blue	£190	£110
136	30	$1 lake	£550	£550
137	30	$2 violet	£1000	£425
138	30	$3 bistre	£1400	£800
139	30	$4 violet	£1300	£700
140	30	$5 green	£1300	£700

31

1897. Maple-leaves in four corners.

141	31	½c. black	16·00	7·50
143	31	1c. green	27·00	90
144	31	2c. violet	24·00	1·50
145	31	3c. red	48·00	2·25
146	31	5c. blue	70·00	2·75
147	31	6c. brown	60·00	32·00
148	31	8c. orange	85·00	9·00
149	31	10c. purple	£140	55·00

1898. As T 31 but figures in lower corners.

150	½c. black	7·50	1·10
151	1c. green	30·00	1·00
154	2c. purple	28·00	30
155	2c. red	38·00	30
156	3c. red	80·00	1·00
157	5c. blue	£110	4·00
159	6c. brown	£100	65·00
160	7c. yellow	70·00	24·00
162	8c. orange	£120	45·00
163	10c. purple	£170	14·00
165	20c. green	£300	50·00

33

1898. Imperial Penny Postage.

166	33	2c. black, red and lavender	30·00	6·50

1899. Surch 2 CENTS.

171	2c. on 3c. red (No. 145)	22·00	8·00
172	2c. on 3c. red (No. 156)	19·00	4·25

35 King Edward VII

1903

175	35	1c. green	30·00	50
176	35	2c. red	20·00	50
178	35	5c. blue	90·00	2·75
180	35	7c. olive	85·00	2·75
182	35	10c. purple	£160	23·00
185	35	20c. olive	£300	32·00
187	35	50c. violet	£450	£120

36 King George V and Queen Mary, when Prince and Princess of Wales

1908. Tercentenary of Quebec. Dated "1608 1908".

188	36	½c. brown	5·00	3·50
189	-	1c. green	29·00	3·00
190	-	2c. red	26·00	1·00
191	-	5c. blue	65·00	35·00
192	-	7c. olive	90·00	65·00
193	-	10c. violet	£100	85·00
194	-	15c. orange	£120	95·00
195	-	20c. brown	£160	£130

DESIGNS: 1c. Cartier and Champlain; 2c. King Edward VII and Queen Alexandra; 5c. Champlain's House in Quebec; 7c. Generals Montcalm and Wolfe; 10c. Quebec in 1700; 15c. Champlain's departure for the West; 20c. Cartier's arrival before Quebec.

44

1912

196	44	1c. green	11·00	50
200	44	2c. red	9·00	50
205	44	3c. brown	6·50	50
205b	44	5c. blue	70·00	75
209	44	7c. yellow	25·00	3·25
210	44	10c. purple	£100	2·75
212	44	20c. olive	45·00	1·50
215	44	50c. sepia	50·00	3·75

See also Nos. 246/55.

1915. Optd WAR TAX diagonally.

225	5c. blue	£120	£200
226	20c. olive	60·00	£100
227	50c. sepia	£130	£170

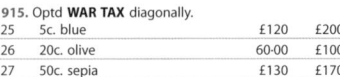

46

1915

228	46	1c. green	7·00	50
229	46	2c. red	26·00	2·50

47

1916

233	47	2c. +1c. red	55·00	2·25
239	47	2c. +1c. brown	6·50	50

48 Quebec Conference, 1864, from painting The Fathers of the Confederation by Robert Harris

1917. 50th Anniv of Confederation.

244	48	3c. brown	22·00	3·25

1922

246	44	1c. yellow	3·25	60
247	44	2c. green	2·25	10
248	44	3c. red	3·75	10
249	44	4c. yellow	8·00	3·50
250	44	5c. violet	5·00	1·75
251	44	7c. brown	12·00	9·00
252	44	8c. blue	23·00	11·00
253	44	10c. blue	15·00	3·25
254	44	10c. brown	26·00	4·00
255	44	$1 orange	55·00	9·50

1926. Surch 2 CENTS

(a) In one line

264	2c. on 3c. red	50·00	60·00

(b) In two lines

265	2c. on 3c. red	18·00	27·00

51 Sir J. A. Macdonald 52 "The Fathers of the Confederation"

1927. 60th Anniv of Confederation

I. Commemoration Issue. Dated "1867–1927".

266	51	1c. orange	2·50	1·50
267	52	2c. green	2·25	30
268	-	3c. red	10·00	5·00
269	-	5c. violet	6·00	4·25
270	-	12c. blue	30·00	7·00

DESIGNS—HORIZ: As Type 52: 3c. Parliament Buildings, Ottawa; 12c. Map of Canada, 1867–1927. VERT: As Type 51: 5c. Sir W. Laurier.

56 Darcy McGee 57 Sir W. Laurier and Sir J. A. Macdonald

II. Historical Issue.

271	56	5c. violet	3·00	2·50
272	57	12c. green	17·00	4·50
273	-	20c. red	17·00	13·00

DESIGN—As Type 57: 20c. R. Baldwin and L. H. Lafontaine.

59

1928. Air.

274	59	5c. brown	8·00	5·00

60 King George V　　**61** Mount Hurd and Indian Totem Poles

1928

275	60	1c. orange	2·75	2·75
276	60	2c. green	1·25	20
277	60	3c. lake	19·00	22·00
278	60	4c. bistre	13·00	11·00
279	60	5c. violet	6·50	7·50
280	60	5c. blue	7·50	7·50
281	61	10c. green	8·50	2·25
282	-	12c. black	26·00	18·00
283	-	20c. lake	38·00	18·00
284	-	50c. blue	£150	50·00
285	-	$1 olive	£150	80·00

DESIGNS—HORIZ: 12c. Quebec Bridge; 20c. Harvesting with horses; 50c. *Bluenose* (fishing schooner); $1 Parliament Buildings, Ottawa.

66　　**67** Parliamentary Library, Ottawa

68 The Old Citadel, Quebec

1930

288	66	1c. orange	1·75	1·25
289	66	1c. green	2·75	10
290	66	2c. green	1·75	10
291	66	2c. red	2·50	3·00
292b	66	2c. brown	1·50	10
293	66	3c. red	2·00	10
294	66	4c. yellow	11·00	4·50
295	66	5c. violet	2·75	7·00
296	66	5c. blue	5·50	20
297	66	8c. blue	11·00	16·00
298	66	8c. orange	7·50	5·50
299	67	10c. olive	22·00	1·50
300	68	12c. black	14·00	5·50
301	-	20c. red	22·00	2·00
302	-	50c. blue	90·00	17·00
303	-	$1 olive	£130	35·00

DESIGNS—HORIZ: 20c. Harvesting with tractor; 50c. Acadian Memorial Church, Grand Pre, Nova Scotia; $1 Mount Edith Cavell.

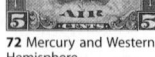

72 Mercury and Western Hemisphere

1930. Air.

310	72	5c. brown	26·00	25·00

73 Sir Georges Etienne Cartier

1931

312	73	10c. green	13·00	20

1932. Air. Surch 6 and bars.

313	59	6c. on 5c. brown	3·00	2·50

1932. Surch 3 between bars.

314a	66	3c. on 2c. red	1·00	60

76 King George V　　**77** Duke of Windsor when Prince of Wales　　**78** Allegory of British Empire

1932. Ottawa Conference

(a) Postage

315	76	3c. red	70	80
316	77	5c. blue	13·00	5·50
317	78	13c. green	13·00	6·00

(b) Air. **Surch 6 6 OTTAWA CONFERENCE 1932.**

318	72	6c. on 5c. brown	14·00	22·00

80 King George V

1932. King George V

319	80	1c. green	60	10
320	80	2c. brown	70	10
321b	80	3c. red	85	10
322	80	4c. brown	48·00	13·00
323	80	5c. blue	12·00	10
324	80	8c. orange	38·00	4·25

81 Parliament Buildings, Ottawa

1933. UPU Congress (Preliminary Meeting).

329	81	5c. blue	11·00	3·00

1933. Optd **WORLD'S GRAIN EXHIBITION & CONFERENCE REGINA 1933.**

330		20c. red (No. 295)	19·00	10·00

83 S.S. *Royal William* (after S. Skillett)

1933. Cent of First Transatlantic Steamboat Crossing.

331	83	5c. blue	20·00	4·25

84 Jacques Cartier approaching Land

1934. Fourth-century of Discovery of Canada.

332	84	3c. blue	7·00	1·50

85 U.E.L. Statue, Hamilton

1934. 150th Anniv of Arrival of United Empire Loyalists.

333	85	10c. olive	13·00	8·50

86 Seal of New Brunswick

1934. 150th Anniv of New Brunswick.

334	86	2c. brown	1·50	3·50

87 Queen Elizabeth II when Princess　　**88** King George VI when Duke of York　　**89** King George V and Queen Mary

1935. Silver Jubilee. Dated "1910–1935".

335	87	1c. green	80	80
336	88	2c. brown	70	80
337	89	3c. red	3·50	1·75
338	-	5c. blue	5·50	9·00
339	-	10c. green	11·00	9·50
340	-	13c. blue	12·00	9·50

DESIGNS—VERT: 5c. Duke of Windsor when Prince of Wales. HORIZ: 10c. Windsor Castle; 13c. Royal Yacht *Britannia*.

93 King George V　　**94** Royal Canadian Mounted Policeman

99 Daedalus

1935

(a) Postage

341	93	1c. green	1·75	10
342	93	2c. brown	1·75	10
343	93	3c. red	1·75	10
344	93	4c. yellow	3·50	2·75
345	93	5c. blue	3·50	10
346	93	8c. orange	4·25	5·00
347	94	10c. red	6·50	50
348	-	13c. purple	7·50	65
349	-	20c. green	25·00	1·50
350	-	50c. violet	25·00	7·00
351	-	$1 blue	42·00	11·00

(b) Air

355	99	6c. brown	3·50	1·00

100 King George VI and Queen Elizabeth

1937. Coronation.

356	100	3c. red	1·75	1·50

101 King George VI　　**102** Memorial Chamber Parliament Buildings, Ottawa

104 Fort Garry Gate, Winnipeg　　**107** Fairchild 45-80 Sekani Seaplane over *Distributor* on Mackenzie River

1937

(a) Postage

357	101	1c. green	2·25	10
358	101	2c. brown	3·00	10
359	101	3c. red	1·75	10
360	101	4c. yellow	5·50	1·75
361	101	5c. blue	6·50	10
362	101	8c. orange	6·50	3·75
363	102	10c. red	5·00	60
364	-	13c. blue	32·00	2·75
365	104	20c. brown	25·00	2·75
366	-	50c. green	50·00	16·00
367	-	$1 violet	65·00	16·00

DESIGNS—HORIZ: 13c. Halifax Harbour; 50c. Vancouver Harbour; $1 Chateau de Ramezay, Montreal.

(b) Air

371	107	6c. blue	19·00	2·25

108 Queen Elizabeth II when Princess and Princess Margaret

1939. Royal Visit.

372	108	1c. black and green	2·50	25
373	-	2c. black and brown	3·00	2·00
374	-	3c. black and red	2·00	25

DESIGNS—HORIZ: 3c. King George VI and Queen Elizabeth. VERT: 2c. National War Memorial, Ottawa.

111 King George VI in Naval Uniform　　**112** King George VI in Military Uniform　　**114** Grain Elevator

115 Farm Scene　　**121** Air Training Camp

1942. War Effort.

(a) Postage

375	111	1c. green (postage)	1·50	10
376	112	2c. brown	1·75	10
377	-	3c. red	1·25	60
378	-	3c. purple	1·50	10
379	114	4c. grey	5·50	3·00
380	112	4c. red	70	10
381	111	5c. blue	3·25	10
382	115	8c. brown	5·50	1·00
383	-	10c. brown	13·00	10
384	-	13c. green	10·00	10·00
385	-	14c. green	28·00	1·00
386	-	20c. brown	21·00	45
387	-	50c. violet	26·00	7·00
388	-	$1 blue	50·00	12·00

(b) Air

399	121	6c. blue (air)	32·00	13·00
400	121	7c. blue	5·00	50

DESIGNS—As Type 112: 3c. King George VI. As Type 121. VERT: 10c. Parliament Buildings. HORIZ: 13, 14c. Ram tank; 20c. Corvette; 50c. Munitions factory; $1 H.M.S. *Cossack* (destroyer).

122 Ontario Farm Scene

1946. Re-conversion to Peace.

(a) Postage

401	122	8c. brown (postage)	2·75	2·75
402	-	10c. green	2·75	10
403	-	14c. sepia	6·50	3·25
404	-	20c. grey	3·75	10
405	-	50c. green	16·00	6·50
406	-	$1 purple	27·00	6·50

(b) Air

407	-	7c. blue (air)	6·00	40

DESIGNS: 10c. Great Bear Lake; 14c. St. Maurice River power station; 20c. Combine harvester; 50c. Lumbering in British Columbia; $1 *Abegweit* (train ferry); 7c. Canada geese in flight.

129 Alexander Graham Bell and "Fame"

1947. Birth Centenary of Alexander Graham Bell (inventor of the telephone).

408	129	4c. blue	15	50

130 "Canadian Citizenship"

1947. Advent of Canadian Citizenship and 80th Anniv of Confederation.

409	130	4c. blue	10	40

131 Queen Elizabeth II when Princess

1948. Princess Elizabeth's Wedding.
410 **131** 4c. blue 15 15

132 Queen Victoria, Parliament Building, Ottawa, and King George VI

1948. Centenary of Responsible Government.
411 **132** 4c. grey 10 10

133 Cabot's Ship *Matthew*

1949. Entry of Newfoundland into Canadian Confederation.
412 **133** 4c. green 30 10

134 *Founding of Halifax, 1749* (after C. W. Jeffries)

1949. Halifax Bicentenary.
413 **134** 4c. violet 45 10

135 King George VI

1949. Portraits of King George VI.

414	**135**	1c. green	50	10
415	-	2c. sepia	2·25	45
415a	-	2c. green	2·50	10
416	-	3c. purple	30	10
417	-	4c. red	20	10
418	-	5c. blue	2·50	60

1950. As Nos. 414 and 416/18 but without "POSTES POSTAGE".

424	1c. green	70	1·00
425	2c. sepia	70	4·50
426	3c. purple	70	65
427	4c. red	70	20
428	5c. blue	70	2·50

141 Oil Wells in Alberta **142** Drying Furs

1950

432	**142**	10c. purple	5·00	
441	-	20c. grey	2·75	10
431	**141**	50c. green	6·00	1·00
433	-	$1 blue	45·00	6·00

DESIGNS: 20c. Forestry products; $1 Fisherman.

145 Mackenzie King

1951. Canadian Prime Ministers.

434		3c. green (Borden)	20	1·50
444	-	3c. purple (Abbott)	35	75
435	**145**	4c. red	60	15
445	-	4c. red (A. Mackenzie)	25	35
475	-	4c. violet (Thompson)	20	75
483	-	4c. violet (Bennett)	25	60
476	-	5c. blue (Bowell)	20	50
484	-	5c. blue (Tupper)	25	10

146 Mail Trains, 1851 and 1951 **149** Reproduction of 3d., 1851

1951. Centenary of First Canadian Postage Stamp. Dated "1851 1951".

436	**146**	4c. black	75	10
437	-	5c. violet	2·00	3·00
438	-	7c. blue	75	1·75
439	**149**	15c. red	1·60	10

DESIGNS—As Type **146**: 5c. *City of Toronto* and S.S. *Prince George*; 7c. Mail coach and Canadair DC-4M North Star airplane.

150 Queen Elizabeth II when Princess and Duke of Edinburgh

1951. Royal Visit.
440 **150** 4c. violet 20 30

152 Red Cross Emblem

1952. 18th Int Red Cross Conf, Toronto.
442 **152** 4c. red and blue 15 10

153 Canada Goose

1952
443 **153** 7c. blue 1·25 10

154 Pacific Coast Indian House and Totem Pole **160** Textile Industry

164 Northern Gannet **165** Eskimo Hunter

1953

477	**165**	10c. brown	1·25	10
474	**164**	15c. black	1·50	10
488	-	20c. green	75	10
489	-	25c. red	75	10
462	**160**	50c. green	1·75	10
446	**154**	$1 black	3·25	20

DESIGNS (As Type **160**)—HORIZ: 20c. Pulp and paper industry. VERT: 25c. Chemical industry.

155 Polar Bear

1953. National Wild Life Week.

447	**155**	2c. blue	15	10
448	-	3c. sepia (Elk)	15	70
449	-	4c. slate (American bighorn)	15	10

158 Queen Elizabeth II

1953

450	**158**	1c. brown	10	10
451	**158**	2c. green	15	10
452	**158**	3c. red	15	15
453	**158**	4c. violet	20	10
454	**158**	5c. blue	25	10

159 Queen Elizabeth II

1953. Coronation.
461 **159** 4c. violet 10 10

161

1954

463	**161**	1c. brown	10	10
464	**161**	2c. green	20	10
465	**161**	3c. red	1·00	10
466	**161**	4c. violet	30	10
467	**161**	5c. blue	30	10
468	**161**	6c. orange	1·75	55

1954. National Wild Life Week. As T **155**.

472	4c. slate (Walrus)	45	20
473	5c. blue (American beaver)	35	10

166 Musk-ox **167** Whooping Cranes

1955. National Wild Life Week.

478	**166**	4c. violet	30	10
479	**167**	5c. blue	1·00	20

168 Dove and Torch

1955. Tenth Anniv of ICAO.
480 **168** 5c. blue 35 20

169 Pioneer Settlers

1955. 50th Anniv of Alberta and Saskatchewan Provinces.
481 **169** 5c. blue 20 25

170 Scout Badge and Globe

1955. Eighth World Scout Jamboree.
482 **170** 5c. brown and green 30 10

173 Ice-hockey Players

1956. Ice-hockey Commemoration.
485 **173** 5c. blue 20 20

1956. National Wild Life Week. As T **155**.

486	4c. violet (Reindeer)	20	15
487	5c. blue (Mountain goat)	20	10

178

1956. Fire Prevention Week.
490 **178** 5c. red and black 30 10

179 Fishing

1957. Outdoor Recreation.

491	**179**	5c. blue	40	10
492	-	5c. blue	40	10
493	-	5c. blue	40	10
494	-	5c. blue	40	10

DESIGNS: No. 492, Swimming; 493, Hunting; 494, Skiing.

183 White-billed Diver

1957. National Wild Life Week.
495 **183** 5c. black 50 20

184 Thompson with Sextant, and North American Map

1957. Death Cent of David Thompson (explorer).
496 **184** 5c. blue 45 30

185 Parliament Buildings, Ottawa

1957. 14th UPU Congress, Ottawa.

497	**185**	5c. slate	15	10
498	-	15c. slate	55	1·75

DESIGNS—HORIZ (33½×22 mm): 15c. Globe within post-horn.

187 Miner

1957. Mining Industry.
499 **187** 5c. black 35 20

188 Queen Elizabeth II and Duke of Edinburgh

1957. Royal Visit.
500 **188** 5c. black 30 10

189 "A Free Press"

1958. The Canadian Press.
501 **189** 5c. black 20 70

190 Microscope

1958. International Geophysical Year.
502 **190** 5c. blue 20 10

191 Miner panning for Gold

1958. Centenary of British Columbia.
503 **191** 5c. turquoise 20 10

192 La Verendrye statue

1958. La Verendrye (explorer) Commemoration.
504 **192** 5c. blue 20 10

193 Samuel de Champlain and Heights of Quebec

1958. 350th Anniv of Founding of Quebec by Samuel de Champlain.
505 **193** 5c. brown and green 30 10

194 Nurse

1958. National Health.
506 **194** 5c. purple 30 10

195 "Petroleum 1858–1958"

1958. Centenary of Canadian Oil Industry.
507 **195** 5c. red and olive 30 10

196 Speaker's Chair and Mace

1958. Bicentenary of First Elected Assembly.
508 **196** 5c. slate 30 10

197 John McCurdy's Biplane *Silver Dart*

1959. 50th Anniv of First Flight of the *Silver Dart* in Canada.
509 **197** 5c. black and blue 30 10

198 Globe showing NATO Countries

1959. Tenth Anniv of NATO.
510 **198** 5c. blue 40 10

199

1959. "Associated Country Women of the World" Commemoration.
511 **199** 5c. black and olive 15 10

200 Queen Elizabeth II

1959. Royal Visit.
512 **200** 5c. red 30 10

201 Maple Leaf linked with American Eagle

1959. Opening of St. Lawrence Seaway.
513 **201** 5c. blue and red 20 10

202 Maple Leaves

1959. Bicentenary of Battle of Quebec.
514 **202** 5c. green and red 30 10

203 Girl Guides Badge

1960. Golden Jubilee of Canadian Girl Guides Movement.
515 **203** 5c. blue and brown 20 10

204 Dollard des Ormeaux

1960. Tercent of Battle of Long Sault.
516 **204** 5c. blue and brown 20 10

205 Surveyor, Bulldozer and Compass Rose

1961. Northern Development.
517 **205** 5c. green and red 15 10

206 E. Pauline Johnson

1961. Birth Centenary of E. Pauline Johnson (Mohawk poetess).
518 **206** 5c. green and red 15 10

207 Arthur Meighen (statesman)

1961. Arthur Meighen Commemoration.
519 **207** 5c. blue 15 10

208 Engineers and Dam

1961. Colombo Plan.
520 **208** 5c. brown and blue 30 10

209 "Resources for Tomorrow"

1961. Natural Resources.
521 **209** 5c. green and brown 15 10

210 "Education"

1962. Education Year.
522 **210** 5c. black and brown 15 10

211 Lord Selkirk and Farmer

1962. 150th Anniv of Red River Settlement.
523 **211** 5c. brown and green 20 10

212 Talon bestowing Gifts on Married Couple

1962. Jean Talon Commemoration.
524 **212** 5c. blue 20 10

213 British Columbia and Vancouver Island 2½d. Stamp of 1860, and Parliament Buildings, B.C.

1962. Centenary of Victoria, B.C.
525 **213** 5c. red and black 30 10

214 Highway (map version) and Provincial Arms

1962. Opening of Trans-Canada Highway.
526 **214** 5c. black and brown 15 20

215 Queen Elizabeth II and Wheat (agriculture) Symbol

1962. Different symbols in top left corner.

527 **215** 1c. brown 10 10
528 - 2c. green 15 20
529 - 3c. violet 15 10
530 - 4c. red 20 10
531 - 5c. blue 50 10

SYMBOLS: 1c. Crystals (Mining); 2c. Tree (Forestry); 3c. Fish (Fisheries); 4c. Electricity pylon (Industrial power); 5c. Wheat (Agriculture).

216 Sir Casimir Gzowski

1963. 150th Birth Anniv of Sir Casimir Gzowski (engineer).
535 **216** 5c. purple 15 10

217 "Export Trade"

1963
536 **217** $1 red 4·75 2·00

218 Frobisher and barque "Gabriel"

1963. Sir Martin Frobisher Commemoration.
537 **218** 5c. blue 30 10

219 Horseman and Map

1963. Bicent of Quebec–Trois-Rivieres–Montreal Postal Service.
538 **219** 5c. brown and green 20 25

220 Canada Geese

1963
539 **220** 15c. blue 1·00 10

221 Douglas DC-9 Airliner and Uplands Airport, Ottawa

1964
540 **221** 7c. blue 35 70
540a **221** 8c. blue 50 50

222 "Peace on Earth"

1964. "Peace".
541 **222** 5c. ochre, blue & turq 15 10

223 Maple Leaves

1964. "Canadian Unity".
542 **223** 5c. lake and blue 10 10

224 White Trillium and Arms of Ontario

1964. Provincial Badges.
543 **224** 5c. green, brown and orange 40 20
544 - 5c. green, brown and yellow 40 20
545 - 5c. red, green and violet 30 20
546 - 5c. blue, red and green 30 20
547 - 5c. purple, green and brown 30 20
548 - 5c. brown, green and mauve 30 20
549 - 5c. lilac, green and purple 50 20
550 - 5c. green, yellow and red 30 20
551 - 5c. sepia, orange and green 30 20
552 - 5c. black, red and green 30 20
553 - 5c. drab, green and yellow 30 20
554 - 5c. blue, green and red 30 20
555 - 5c. red and blue 30 20

FLOWERS AND ARMS OF: No. 544, Madonna Lily, Quebec; 545, Purple Violet, New Brunswick; 546, Mayflower, Nova Scotia; 547, Dogwood, British Columbia; 548, Prairie Crocus, Manitoba; 549, Lady's Slipper, Prince Edward Island; 550, Wild Rose, Alberta; 551, Prairie Lily, Saskatchewan; 552, Pitcher Plant, Newfoundland; 553, Mountain Avens, Northwest Territories; 554, Fireweed, Yukon Territory; 555, Maple Leaf, Canada.

1964. Surch **8**.
556 **221** 8c. on 7c. blue 15 15

238 Fathers of the Confederation Memorial, Charlottetown

1964. Centenary of Charlottetown Conference.
557 238 5c. black 10 10

239 Maple Leaf and Hand with Quill Pen

1964. Centenary of Quebec Conference.
558 239 5c. red and brown 15 10

240 Queen Elizabeth II

1964. Royal Visit.
559 240 5c. purple 15 10

241 "Canadian Family"

1964. Christmas.
560 241 3c. red 10 10
561 241 5c. blue 10 10

242 "Co-operation"

1965. International Co-operation Year.
562 242 5c. green 35 10

243 Sir W. Grenfell

1965. Birth Centenary of Sir Wilfred Grenfell (missionary).
563 243 5c. green 20 10

244 National Flag

1965. Inauguration of National Flag.
564 244 5c. red and blue 15 10

245 Sir Winston Churchill

1965. Churchill Commemoration.
565 245 5c. brown 15 10

246 Peace Tower, Parliament Buildings, Ottawa

1965. Inter-Parliamentary Union Conference, Ottawa.
566 246 5c. green 10 10

247 Parliament Buildings, Ottawa, 1865

1965. Centenary of Proclamation of Ottawa as Capital.
567 247 5c. brown 10 10

248 "Gold, Frankincense and Myrrh"

1965. Christmas.
568 248 3c. green 10 10
569 248 5c. blue 10 10

249 "Alouette 2" over Canada

1966. Launching of Canadian Satellite, "Alouette 2".
570 249 5c. blue 15 10

250 La Salle

1966. 300th Anniv of La Salle's Arrival in Canada.
571 250 5c. green 15 10

251 Road Signs

1966. Highway Safety.
572 251 5c. yellow, blue and black 15 10

252 Canadian Delegation and Houses of Parliament

1966. Centenary of London Conference.
573 252 5c. brown 10 10

253 Douglas Point Nuclear Power Station

1966. Peaceful Uses of Atomic Energy.
574 253 5c. blue 10 10

254 Parliamentary Library, Ottawa

1966. Commonwealth Parliamentary Association Conference, Ottawa.
575 254 5c. purple 10 10

255 Praying Hands, after Durer

1966. Christmas.
576 255 3c. red 10 10
577 255 5c. orange 10 10

256 Flags and Canada on Globe

1967. Canadian Centennial.
578 256 5c. red and blue 10 10

257 Queen Elizabeth, Northern Lights and Dog-team
262 "Alaska Highway" (A. Y. Jackson)

1967
579 257 1c. brown 10 10
580 - 2c. green 10 20
581 - 3c. purple 30 50
582 - 4c. red 20 10
583 - 5c. blue 20 10
601 - 6c. red 45 10
607 - 6c. black 30 10
609 - 7c. green 30 70
584 262 8c. purple 25 1·00
610 - 8c. black 30 10
585 - 10c. olive 25 10
586 - 15c. purple 30 10
587 - 20c. blue 1·75 10
588 - 25c. green 1·75 10
589 - 50c. brown 1·50 10
590 - $1 red 1·50 1·25

DESIGNS—As Type 257: 2c. Totem pole; 3c. Combine-harvester and oil derrick; 4c. Ship in lock; 5c., Harbour scene; 6c., 7c. "Transport"; 8c. (No. 610), Library of Parliament. As Type 262: 10c. *The Jack Pine* (T. Thomson); 15c. *Bylot Island* (L. Harris); 20c. *Quebec Ferry* (J. W. Morrice); 25c. *The Solemn Land* (J. E. H. MacDonald); 50c. *Summer's Stores* (Grain elevators, J. Ensor); $1 *Oilfield* (near Edmonton, H. G. Glyde).

269 Canadian Pavilion

1967. World Fair, Montreal.
611 269 5c. blue and red 10 10

270 Allegory of "Womanhood" on Ballot-box

1967. 50th Anniv of Women's Franchise.
612 270 5c. purple and black 10 10

271 Queen Elizabeth II and Centennial Emblem

1967. Royal Visit.
613 271 5c. plum and brown 15 10

272 Athlete

1967. Pan-American Games, Winnipeg.
614 272 5c. red 10 10

273 "World News"

1967. 50th Anniv of Canadian Press.
615 273 5c. blue 10 10

274 Governor-General Vanier

1967. Vanier Commemoration.
616 274 5c. black 10 10

275 People of 1867, and Toronto, 1967

1967. Cent of Toronto as Capital City of Ontario.
617 275 5c. green and red 10 10

276 Carol Singers

1967. Christmas.
618 276 3c. red 10 10
619 276 5c. green 10 10

277 Grey Jays

1968. Wild Life.
620 277 5c. multicoloured 30 10
See also Nos. 638/40.

278 Weather Map and Instruments

1968. 20th Anniv of First Meteorological Readings.
621 278 5c. multicoloured 15 10

279 Narwhal

1968. Wild Life.
622 279 5c. multicoloured 15 10

280 Globe, Maple Leaf and Rain Gauge

1968. International Hydrological Decade.
623 280 5c. multicoloured 15 10

281 The Nonsuch

1968. 300th Anniv of Voyage of the *Nonsuch*.
624 281 5c. multicoloured 20 10

282 Lacrosse Players

1968. Lacrosse.
625 282 5c. multicoloured 15 10

283 Front Page of *The Globe*, George Brown and Legislative Building

1968. 150th Birth Anniv of George Brown (politician and journalist).
626 283 5c. multicoloured 10 10

284 H.
Bourassa
(politician and
journalist)

1968. Birth Centenary of Henri Bourassa.
627 **284** 5c. black, red and cream 10 10

285 John McCrae,
Battlefield and First Lines of
In Flanders Fields

1968. 50th Death Anniv of John McCrae (soldier and
poet).
628 **285** 5c. multicoloured 10 10

286 Armistice
Monument,
Vimy

1968. 50th Anniv of 1918 Armistice.
629 **286** 15c. black 30 40

287 Eskimo
Family (carving)

1968. Christmas.
630 **287** 5c. black and blue 10 10
631 – 6c. black and ochre 10 10
DESIGN: 6c. *Mother and Child* (carving).

289 Curling

1969. Curling.
632 **289** 6c. black, blue and red 15 25

290 Vincent
Massey

1969. Vincent Massey, First Canadian-born Governor-
General.
633 **290** 6c. sepia and ochre 10 10

291 *Return from the Harvest
Field* (Suzor-Cote)

1969. Birth Centenary of Marc Aurele de Foy Suzor-Cote
(painter).
634 **291** 50c. multicoloured 1·50 2·75

292 Globe and
Tools

1969. 50th Anniv of I.L.O.
635 **292** 6c. green 10 10

293 Vickers Vimy Aircraft
over Atlantic Ocean

1969. 50th Anniv of 1st Non-stop Transatlantic Flight.
636 **293** 15c. brown, green and
blue 40 55

294 *Sir William
Osler* (J. S.
Sargent)

1969. 50th Death Anniv of Sir William Osler (physician).
637 **294** 6c. blue and brown 20 10

295
White-throated
Sparrow

1969. Birds. Multicoloured.
638 6c. Type **295** 25 10
639 10c. Savannah sparrow ("Ips-
wich Sparrow") (horiz) 35 1·10
640 25c. Hermit thrush (horiz) 1·10 3·75

298 Flags of
Winter and
Summer Games

1969. Canadian Games.
641 **298** 6c. green, red and blue 10 10

299 Outline of Prince
Edward Island showing
Charlottetown

1969. Bicentenary of Charlottetown as Capital of Prince
Edward Island.
642 **299** 6c. brown, black and
blue 20 20

300 Sir Isaac
Brock and
Memorial
Column

1969. Birth Bicentenary of Sir Isaac Brock.
643 **300** 6c. orange, bistre and
brown 10 10

301 Children
of the World in
Prayer

1969. Christmas.
644 **301** 5c. multicoloured 10 10
645 **301** 6c. multicoloured 10 10

302 Stephen Butler
Leacock, Mask and
"Mariposa"

1969. Birth Centenary of Stephen Butler Leacock
(humorist).
646 **302** 6c. multicoloured 10 10

303 Symbolic Cross-roads

1970. Centenary of Manitoba.
647 **303** 6c. blue, yellow and red 15 10

304 "Enchanted
Owl" (Kenojuak)

1970. Centenary of Northwest Territories.
648 **304** 6c. red and black 10 10

305 Microscopic View of
Inside of Leaf

1970. International Biological Programme.
649 **305** 6c. green, yellow and
blue 15 10

306 Expo 67 Emblem and
stylized Cherry Blossom

1970. World Fair, Osaka. Multicoloured.
650 25c. Type **306** (red) 1·50 2·25
651 25c. Dogwood (violet) 1·50 2·25
652 25c. White trillium (green) 1·50 2·25
653 25c. White garden lily (blue) 1·50 2·25
NOTE: Each stamp shows a stylized cherry blossom, in a
different colour, given above in brackets.

310 Henry Kelsey

1970. 300th Birth Anniv of Henry Kelsey (explorer).
654 **310** 6c. multicoloured 10 10

311 "Towards Unification"

1970. 25th Anniv of UNO.
655 **311** 10c. blue 75 1·50
656 **311** 15c. mauve and lilac 75 50

312 Louis Riel
(Metis leader)

1970. Louis Riel Commemoration.
657 **312** 6c. blue and red 10 10

313
Mackenzie's
Inscription,
Dean Channel

1970. Sir Alexander Mackenzie (explorer).
658 **313** 6c. brown 15 10

314 Sir Oliver Mowat
(statesman)

1970. Sir Oliver Mowat Commemoration.
659 **314** 6c. red and black 10 10

315 *Isles of Spruce* (A.
Lismer)

1970. 50th Anniv of "Group of Seven" (artists).
660 **315** 6c. multicoloured 10 10

316 *Horse-drawn
Sleigh* (D. Niskala)

1970. Christmas. Children's Drawings. Multicoloured.
661 5c. Type **316** 30 20
662 5c. *Stable and Star of Bethlehem*
(L. Wilson) 30 20
663 5c. *Snowmen* (M. Lecompte) 30 20
664 5c. *Skiing* (D. Durham) 30 20
665 5c. *Santa Claus* (A. Martin) 30 20
666 6c. *Santa Claus* (E. Bhat-
tacharya) 30 20
667 6c. *Christ in Manger* (J. McKin-
ney) 30 20
668 6c. *Toy Shop* (N. Whateley) 30 20
669 6c. *Christmas Tree* (J. Pom-
perleau) 30 20
670 6c. *Church* (J. McMillan) 30 20
671 10c. *Christ in Manger* (C. Fortier)
(37×20 mm) 25 30
672 15c. *Trees and Sledge* (J. Dojcak)
(37×20 mm) 35 60

328 Sir Donald
A. Smith

1970. 150th Birth Anniv of Sir Donald Alexander Smith.
673 **328** 6c. yellow, brown and
green 15 10

329 *Big Raven* (E.
Carr)

1971. Birth Centenary of Emily Carr (painter).
674 **329** 6c. multicoloured 20 30

330 Laboratory
Equipment

1971. 50th Anniv of Discovery of Insulin.
675 **330** 6c. multicoloured 30 30

331 "The Atom"

1971. Birth Centenary of Lord Rutherford (scientist).
676 **331** 6c. yellow, red and
brown 20 20

332 Maple "Keys"

1971. "The Maple Leaf in Four Seasons". Multicoloured.
677	6c. Type **332** (spring)	20	20
678	6c. Green leaves (summer)	20	20
679	7c. Autumn leaves	20	20
680	7c. Withered leaves and snow (winter)	20	20

333 Louis Papineau

1971. Death Centenary of Louis-Joseph Papineau (politician).
681	**333**	6c. multicoloured	15	25

334 Chart of Coppermine River

1971. Bicentenary of Samuel Hearne's Expedition to the Coppermine River.
682	**334**	6c. red, brown and buff	40	40

335 "People" and Computer Tapes

1971. Centenary of first Canadian Census.
683	**335**	6c. blue, red and black	30	20

336 Maple Leaves

1971. Radio Canada International.
684	**336**	15c. red, yellow and black	50	1·50

337 "B. C."

1971. Centenary of British Columbia's Entry into the Confederation.
685	**337**	7c. multicoloured	15	10

338 Indian Encampment on Lake Huron (Kane)

1971. Death Centenary of Paul Kane (painter).
686	**338**	7c. multicoloured	20	10

339 "Snowflake"

1971. Christmas.
687	**339**	6c. blue	10	10
688	**339**	7c. green	15	10
689	-	10c. silver and red	50	1·25
690	-	15c. silver, purple and lavender	65	2·00

DESIGN: 10c., 15c. "Snowflake" design similar to Type **339** but square (26×26 mm).

340 Pierre Laporte (Quebec Cabinet Minister)

1971. First Anniv of Assassination of Pierre Laporte.
691	**340**	7c. black on buff	15	10

341 Skaters

1972. World Figure Skating Championships, Calgary.
692	**341**	8c. purple	15	20

342 J. A. MacDonald

343 Forest, Central Canada

344 Vancouver

1972
693	**342**	1c. orange	10	30
694	-	2c. green	10	10
695	-	3c. brown	10	50
696	-	4c. black	10	50
697	-	5c. mauve	10	10
698	-	6c. red	10	50
699	-	7c. brown	40	50
700	-	8c. blue	15	10
701	-	10c. red	75	10
702a	**343**	10c. green, turquoise and orange	40	15
703b	-	15c. blue and brown	1·25	10
704a	-	20c. orange, violet and blue	1·50	10
705b	-	25c. ultramarine and blue	1·00	10
706	-	50c. green, blue and brown	1·00	30
709a	**344**	$1 multicoloured	85	70
708	-	$2 multicoloured	1·50	2·00

DESIGNS—As Type **342** (1 to 7c. show Canadian Prime Ministers): 2c. W. Laurier; 3c. R. Borden; 4c. W. L. Mackenzie King; 5c. R. B. Bennett; 6c. L. B. Pearson; 7c. Louis St. Laurent; 8, 10c. Queen Elizabeth II. As Type **343**: 15c. American bighorn; 20c. Prairie landscape from the air; 25c. Polar bears; 50c. Seashore, Eastern Canada. As Type **344**: $2 Quebec.

345 Heart

1972. World Health Day.
719	**345**	8c. red	30	10

346 Frontenac and Fort Saint-Louis, Quebec

1972. 300th Anniv of Governor Frontenac's Appointment to New France.
720	**346**	8c. red, brown and blue	15	15

347 Plains Indians' Artefacts **347a** Buffalo Chase

1972. Canadian Indians

(a) Horiz designs showing Artefacts as T **347** or Scenes from Indian Life as T **347a**.
721	**347**	8c. multicoloured	40	10
722	**347a**	8c. brown, yellow & blk	40	10
723	-	8c. multicoloured	40	10
724	-	8c. multicoloured	40	10
725	-	8c. multicoloured	40	10
726	-	8c. brown, yellow & blk	40	10
727	-	8c. multicoloured	40	10
728	-	8c. multicoloured	40	10
729	-	10c. multicoloured	40	20
730	-	10c. red, brown and black	40	20

TRIBES: Nos. 721/2, Plains Indians; Nos. 723/4, Algonkians; Nos. 725/6, Pacific Coast Indians; Nos. 727/8, Subarctic Indians; Nos. 729/30, Iroquoians.

348 Thunderbird and Tribal Pattern **348a** Dancer in Ceremonial Costume

(b) Vert designs showing Thunderbird and pattern as T **348** or Costumes as T **348a**.
731	**348**	8c. orange, red and black	40	15
732	**348a**	8c. multicoloured	40	15
733	-	8c. red, violet and black	40	10
734	-	8c. green, brown and black	40	10
735	-	8c. red and black	40	10
736	-	8c. multicoloured	40	10
737	-	8c. green, brown and black	40	10
738	-	8c. multicoloured	40	10
739	-	10c. brown, orange & blk	40	20
740	-	10c. multicoloured	40	20

TRIBES: Nos. 731/2, Plains Indians; Nos. 733/4, Algonkians; Nos. 735/6, Pacific Coast Indians; Nos. 737/8, Subarctic Indians; Nos. 739/40, Iroquoians.

349 Earth's Crust

1972. Earth Sciences.
741	-	15c. multicoloured	1·10	1·90
742	-	15c. grey, blue and black	1·10	1·90
743	**349**	15c. multicoloured	1·10	1·90
744	-	15c. green, orange and black	1·10	1·90

DESIGNS AND EVENTS: No. 741 Photogrammetric surveying (12th Congress of International Society of Photogrammetry); No. 742 "Siegfried" lines (6th Conference of Int Cartographic Association); No. 743 (24th International Geological Congress); No. 744 Diagram of village at road-intersection (22nd Int Geographical Congress).

350 Candles

1972. Christmas. Multicoloured.
745	6c. Type **350**	15	10
746	8c. Type **350**	15	10
747	10c. Candles with fruits and pine boughs (horiz)	50	1·25
748	15c. Candles with prayer-book, caskets and vase (horiz)	60	2·00

Nos. 747/8 are size 36×20 mm.

351 The Blacksmith's Shop (Krieghoff)

1972. Death Centenary of Cornelius Krieghoff (painter).
749	**351**	8c. multicoloured	30	15

352 F. de Montmorency-Laval

1973. 350th Birth Anniv of Monsignor de Laval (1st Bishop of Quebec).
750	**352**	8c. blue, gold and silver	20	40

353 Commissioner French and Route of the March West

1973. Centenary of Royal Canadian Mounted Police.
751	**353**	8c. brown, orange and red	35	20
752	-	10c. multicoloured	1·00	1·25
753	-	15c. multicoloured	2·25	2·00

DESIGNS: 10c. Spectrograph; 15c. Mounted policeman.

354 Jeanne Mance

1973. 300th Death Anniv of Jeanne Mance (nurse).
754	**354**	8c. multicoloured	20	40

355 Joseph Howe

1973. Death Centenary of Joseph Howe (Nova Scotian politician).
755	**355**	8c. gold and black	20	40

356 Mist Fantasy (MacDonald)

1973. Birth Cent of J. E. H. MacDonald (artist).
756	**356**	15c. multicoloured	30	55

357 Oaks and Harbour

1973. Centenary of Prince Edward Island's Entry into the Confederation.
757	**357**	8c. orange and red	20	30

358 Scottish Settlers

1973. Bicentenary of Arrival of Scottish Settlers at Pictou, Nova Scotia.
758	**358**	8c. multicoloured	25	20

359 Queen Elizabeth II

1973. Royal Visit and Commonwealth Heads of Government Meeting, Ottawa.

| 759 | **359** | 8c. multicoloured | 25 | 20 |
| 760 | **359** | 15c. multicoloured | 80 | 1·50 |

360 Nellie McClung

1973. Birth Centenary of Nellie McClung (feminist).

| 761 | **360** | 8c. multicoloured | 20 | 50 |

361 Emblem of 1976 Olympics

1973. 1976 Olympic Games, Montreal (1st issue).

| 762 | **361** | 8c. multicoloured | 25 | 15 |
| 763 | **361** | 15c. multicoloured | 45 | 1·25 |

See also Nos. 768/71, 772/4, 786/9, 798/802, 809/11, 814/16, 829/32, 833/7 and 842/4.

362 Ice-skate

1973. Christmas. Multicoloured.

764		6c. Type **362**	15	10
765		8c. Bird decoration	15	10
766		10c. Santa Claus (20×36 mm)	50	1·10
767		15c. Shepherd (20×36 mm)	60	1·50

363 Diving

1974. 1976 Olympic Games, Montreal. (2nd issue). "Summer Activities". Each blue.

768		8c. Type **363**	30	50
769		8c. "Jogging"	30	50
770		8c. Cycling	30	50
771		8c. Hiking	30	50

1974. 1976 Olympic Games, Montreal. (3rd issue). As T **361** but smaller (20×36½ mm).

772	**361**	8c. multicoloured	25	45
773		10c. +5c. multicoloured	40	1·00
774		15c. +5c. multicoloured	45	1·40

364 Winnipeg Signpost, 1872

1974. Winnipeg Centennial.

| 775 | **364** | 8c. multicoloured | 20 | 15 |

365 Postmaster and Customer

1974. Centenary of Canadian Letter Carrier Delivery Service. Multicoloured.

776		8c. Type **365**	50	80
777		8c. Postman collecting mail	50	80
778		8c. Mail handler	50	80
779		8c. Mail sorters	50	80
780		8c. Postman making delivery	50	80
781		8c. Rural delivery by car	50	80

366 "Canada's Contribution to Agriculture"

1974. Centenary of "Agricultural Education". Ontario Agricultural College.

| 782 | **366** | 8c. multicoloured | 20 | 20 |

367 Telephone Development

1974. Centenary of Invention of Telephone by Alexander Graham Bell.

| 783 | **367** | 8c. multicoloured | 20 | 20 |

368 Bicycle Wheel

1974. World Cycling Championships, Montreal.

| 784 | **368** | 8c. black, red and silver | 20 | 30 |

369 Mennonite Settlers

1974. Centenary of Arrival of Mennonites in Manitoba.

| 785 | **369** | 8c. multicoloured | 20 | 20 |

1974. 1976 Olympic Games, Montreal (4th issue). "Winter Activities". As T **363**. Each red.

786		8c. Snow-shoeing	55	60
787		8c. Skiing	55	60
788		8c. Skating	55	60
789		8c. Curling	55	60

370 Mercury, Winged Horses and UPU Emblem

1974. Centenary of UPU.

| 790 | **370** | 8c. violet, red and blue | 15 | 15 |
| 791 | **370** | 15c. red, violet and blue | 50 | 1·50 |

371 The Nativity (J. P. Lemieux)

1974. Christmas. Multicoloured.

792		6c. Type **371**	10	10
793		8c. Skaters in Hull (H. Masson) (34×31 mm)	10	10
794		10c. The Ice Cone, Montmorency Falls (R. C. Todd)	30	75
795		15c. Village in the Laurentian Mountains (C. A. Gagnon)	35	1·10

372 Marconi and St. John's Harbour, Newfoundland

1974. Birth Centenary of Guglielmo Marconi (radio pioneer).

| 796 | **372** | 8c. multicoloured | 20 | 20 |

373 Merritt and Welland Canal

1974. William Merritt Commemoration.

| 797 | **373** | 8c. multicoloured | 20 | 30 |

374 Swimming

1975. 1976 Olympic Games, Montreal (5th issue). Multicoloured.

798		8c.+2c. +2c. Type **374**	45	65
799		10c.+5c. +5c. Rowing	60	1·25
800		15c.+5c. +5c. Sailing	70	1·40

375 "The Sprinter"

1975. 1976 Olympic Games, Montreal (6th issue). Multicoloured.

| 801 | | $1 Type **375** | 1·25 | 2·00 |
| 802 | | $2 "The Diver" (vert) | 1·75 | 3·50 |

376 Anne of Green Gables (Lucy Maud Montgomery)

1975. Canadian Writers (1st series). Multicoloured.

| 803 | | 8c. Type **376** | 30 | 10 |
| 804 | | 8c. Maria Chapdelaine (Louis Hemon) | 30 | 10 |

See also Nos. 846/7, 940/1 and 1085/6.

377 Marguerite Bourgeoys (founder of the Order of Notre Dame)

378 S. D. Chown (founder of United Church of Canada)

1975. Canadian Celebrities.

*(a) As T **377***

| 805 | **377** | 8c. multicoloured | 60 | 40 |
| 806 | – | 8c. multicoloured | 60 | 40 |

*(b) As T **378***

| 807 | **378** | 8c. multicoloured | 30 | 75 |
| 808 | – | 8c. multicoloured | 30 | 75 |

DESIGNS—As Type **377**: No. 806, Alphonse Desjardins (leader of Credit Union movement). As Type **378**: No. 808, Dr. J. Cook (first moderator of Presbyterian Church in Canada).

379 Pole-vaulting

1975. 1976 Olympics (7th issue). Multicoloured.

809		20c. Type **379**	40	50
810		25c. Marathon-running	55	80
811		50c. Hurdling	70	1·25

380 Untamed (photo by Walt Petrigo)

1975. Centenary of Calgary.

| 812 | **380** | 8c. multicoloured | 30 | 30 |

381 I. W. Y. Symbol

1975. International Women's Year.

| 813 | **381** | 8c. grey, brown and black | 30 | 30 |

382 Fencing

1975. Olympic Games, Montreal (1976) (8th issue). Multicoloured.

814		8c.+2c. +2c. Type **382**	35	75
815		10c.+5c. +5c. Boxing	45	1·50
816		15c.+5c. +5c. Judo	55	1·75

383 "Justice-Justitia" (statue by W. S. Allward)

1975. Centenary of Canadian Supreme Court.

| 817 | **383** | 8c. multicoloured | 20 | 30 |

384 William D. Lawrence (full-rigged ship)

1975. Canadian Ships (1st series). Coastal Vessels.

818	**384**	8c. brown and black	70	75
819	–	8c. green and black	70	75
820	–	8c. green and black	70	75
821	–	8c. brown and black	70	75

DESIGNS: No. 819, *Neptune* (steamer); 820, *Beaver* (paddle-steamer); 821, *Quadra* (steamer).
See also Nos. 851/4, 902/5 and 931/4.

385 Santa Claus (G. Kelly)

1975. Christmas. Multicoloured.

822		6c. Type **385**	15	10
823		8c. "Skater" (B. Cawsey)	15	10
824		8c. "Child" (D. Hebert)	15	10
825		8c. "Family" (L. Caldwell)	15	10
826		10c. "Gift" (D. Lovely)	30	50
827		15c. "Trees" (R. Kowalski) (horiz)	40	75

386 Text, Badge and Bugle

1975. 50th Anniv of Royal Canadian Legion.

| 828 | **386** | 8c. multicoloured | 20 | 20 |

387 Basketball

1976. Olympic Games, Montreal (9th issue). Multicoloured.

829		8c.+2c. +2c. Type **387**	1·50	1·00
830		10c.+5c. +5c. Gymnastics	60	1·40
831		20c.+5c. +5c. Soccer	70	1·60

388 Games
Symbol and
Snow Crystal

1976. 12th Winter Olympic Games, Innsbruck.
832 **388** 20c. multicoloured 20 40

389
"Communications
Arts"

1976. Olympic Games, Montreal (10th issue).
Multicoloured.
833 20c. Type **389** 40 25
834 25c. Handicrafts 65 75
835 50c. Performing Arts 95 1·60

390 Place Ville Marie and Notre-Dame
Church

1976. Olympic Games, Montreal (11th issue).
Multicoloured.
836 $1 Type **390** 2·25 4·50
837 $2 Olympic stadium and flags 2·75 5·50

391 Flower and Urban
Sprawl

1976. HABITAT. U.N. Conference on Human Settlements,
Vancouver.
838 **391** 20c. multicoloured 20 30

392 Benjamin Franklin and
Map

1976. Bicentenary of American Revolution.
839 **392** 10c. multicoloured 20 35

393 Wing Parade
before Mackenzie
Building

1976. Centenary of Royal Military College. Multicoloured.
840 8c. Colour party and Memo-
rial Arch 25 30
841 8c. Type **393** 25 30

394 Transfer of Olympic
Flame by Satellite

1976. Olympic Games, Montreal (12th issue).
Multicoloured.
842 8c. Type **394** 20 10
843 20c. Carrying the Olympic flag 45 60
844 25c. Athletes with medals 45 85

395 Archer

1976. Disabled Olympics.
845 **395** 20c. multicoloured 20 30

396 Sam McGee
(Robert W. Service)

1976. Canadian Writers (2nd series). Multicoloured.
846 8c. Type **396** 15 40
847 8c. Le Survenant (Germaine
Guevremont) 15 40

397 Nativity (F.
Mayer)

1976. Christmas. Stained-glass Windows. Multicoloured.
848 8c. Type **397** 10 10
849 10c. Nativity (G. Maile & Son) 10 10
850 20c. Nativity (Yvonne Williams) 20 60

398 Northcote
(paddle-steamer)

1976. Canadian Ships (2nd series). Inland Vessels.
851 **398** 10c. lt brown, brn & blk 45 60
852 - 10c. blue and black 45 60
853 - 10c. blue and black 45 60
854 - 10c. lt green, green
& blk 45 60

DESIGNS: No. 852, Passport (paddle-steamer); 853, Chicora
(paddle-steamer); 854, Athabasca (steamer).

399 Queen
Elizabeth II

1977. Silver Jubilee.
855 **399** 25c. multicoloured 30 50

400 Bottle
Gentian

401 Queen
Elizabeth II
(bas-relief
by J. Huta)

402 Houses
of
Parliament

403 Trembling
Aspen

404 Prairie Town Main
Street

405 Fundy National Park

1977
856 **400** 1c. multicoloured 10 20
870 **402** 1c. blue 1·25 3·25
857 - 2c. multicoloured 10 10
858 - 3c. multicoloured 10 10
859 - 4c. multicoloured 10 10
860 - 5c. multicoloured 10 10
871 **402** 5c. lilac 50 1·25

861 - 10c. multicoloured 15 10
866 - 12c. multicoloured 15 60
867 **401** 12c. blue, grey and black 15 10
872 **402** 12c. blue 70 30
868 **401** 14c. red, grey and black 20 10
873 **402** 14c. red 15 10
866a - 15c. multicoloured 15 15
875 **403** 15c. multicoloured 15 10
869 **401** 17c. black, grey and
green 50 10
874 **402** 17c. green 30 10
876 - 20c. multicoloured 15 10
877 - 25c. multicoloured 15 10
869b **401** 30c. dp pur, grey & pur 70 1·25
878 - 30c. multicoloured 20 10
869c **401** 32c. black, grey and blue 50 1·25
879 - 35c. multicoloured 25 10
883 **404** 50c. multicoloured 85 1·00
883b - 60c. multicoloured 65 80
881 - 75c. multicoloured 1·00 1·50
882 - 80c. multicoloured 85 1·25
884 **405** $1 multicoloured 70 50
884b - $1 multicoloured 85 45
884c - $1.50 multicoloured 1·75 2·75
885 - $2 multicoloured 1·00 45
885c - $2 multicoloured 4·75 2·00
885d - $5 multicoloured 3·00 3·00
885e - $5 multicoloured 8·00 4·50

DESIGN—As Type **400**: 2c. Red columbine; 3c. Canada lily;
4c. Hepatica; 5c. Shooting star; 10c. Franklin's lady's slip-
per orchid. 12c. Jewel-weed; 15c. (No. 866a) Canada vio-
let. As Type **403**: 20c. Douglas fir; 25c. Sugar maple; 30c.
Red oak; 35c. White pine. As Type **404**: 60c. Ontario City
street; 75c. Eastern City street; 80c. Maritimes street. As
Type **405**: $1 Glacier; $1.50, Waterton Lakes; $2 (No. 885)
Kluane; $2 (No. 885c) Banff; $5 (No. 885d) Point Pelee; $5
(No. 885e) La Maurice.

406 Puma

1977. Endangered Wildlife (1st series).
886 **406** 12c. multicoloured 20 20
See also Nos. 906, 936/7, 976/7 and 1006/7.

407 "April in
Algonquin Park"

1977. Birth Centenary of Tom Thomson (painter).
Multicoloured.
887 12c. Type **407** 15 20
888 12c. Autumn Birches 15 20

408 Crown and Lion

1977. Anniversaries. Multicoloured.
889 12c. Type **408** 15 25
890 12c. Order of Canada 15 25
EVENTS: No. 889, 25th anniv of First Canadian-born Gover-
nor-General; No. 890, 10th anniv of Order of Canada.

409 Peace Bridge, Niagara
River

1977. 50th Anniv of Opening of Peace Bridge.
891 **409** 12c. multicoloured 15 15

410 Sir Sandford Fleming
(engineer)

1977. Famous Canadians.
892 **410** 12c. blue 30 30
893 - 12c. brown 30 30
DESIGN: No. 893, Joseph E. Bernier (explorer) and Arctic
(survey ship).

411 Peace Tower,
Parliament Buildings,
Ottawa

1977. 23rd Commonwealth Parliamentary Conference.
894 **411** 25c. multicoloured 20 30

412 Hunter Braves
following Star

1977. Christmas. Canada's first carol Jesous Ahatonhia.
Multicoloured.
895 10c. Type **412** 10 10
896 12c. Angelic choir 10 10
897 25c. Christ Child and Chiefs
from afar 20 45

413 Seal Hunter
(soapstone sculpture)

1977. Canadian Eskimos ("Inuits") (1st series). Hunting.
Multicoloured.
898 12c. Type **413** 35 35
899 12c. Fishing with spear 35 35
900 12c. Disguised archer 35 35
901 12c. Walrus hunting 35 35
See also Nos. 924/7, 958/61 and 989/92.

414 Pinky (fishing boat)

1977. Canadian Ships (3rd series). Sailing Craft.
Multicoloured.
902 12c. Type **414** 20 35
903 12c. Malahat (schooner) 20 35
904 12c. Tern schooner 20 35
905 12c. Mackinaw boat 20 35

415 Peregrine Falcon

1978. Endangered Wildlife (2nd series).
906 **415** 12c. multicoloured 30 20

416 Pair of 1851 12d.
Black Stamps

1978. "CAPEX '78" International Philatelic Exhibition,
Toronto.
907 **416** 12c. black and sepia 10 10
914 - 14c. blue, lt grey & grey 15 10
915 - 30c. red, lt grey and grey 25 40
916 - $1.25 violet, lt grey
& grey 70 1·50
MS917 101×96 mm. Nos. 914/16 1·25 2·50
DESIGNS: 14c. Pair of 1855 10d. Cartier stamps; 30c. Pair
of 1857 ½d. red stamps; $1.25, Pair of 1851 6d. Prince Al-
bert stamps.

417 Games Emblem

1978. 11th Commonwealth Games, Edmonton (1st issue).
Multicoloured.
908 14c. Type **417** 10 10
909 30c. Badminton 20 60
See also Nos. 918/21.

418 *Captain Cook*
(Nathaniel Dance)

1978. Bicentenary of Cook's Third Voyage. Multicoloured.

910	14c. Type **418**		20	20
911	14c. *Nootka Sound* (J. Webber)		20	20

419 Hardrock Silver Mine,
Cobalt, Ontario

1978. Resources Development. Multicoloured.

912	14c. Type **419**		15	20
913	14c. Giant excavators, Atha-basca Tar Sands		15	20

1978. 11th Commonwealth Games, Edmonton (2nd issue). As T **417**. Multicoloured.

918	14c. Games stadium		20	20
919	14c. Running		20	20
920	30c. Alberta legislature building		50	50
921	30c. Bowls		50	50

420 Princes' Gate
(Exhibition entrance)

1978. Centenary of National Exhibition.

922	**420**	14c. multicoloured	15	30

421 Marguerite
d'Youville

1978. Marguerite d'Youville (founder of Grey Nuns) Commemoration.

923	**421**	14c. multicoloured	15	30

1978. Canadian Eskimos ("Inuits") (2nd series). Travel. As T **413**. Multicoloured.

924	14c. *Woman on foot* (painting by Pitseolak)		30	40
925	14c. *Migration* (soapstone sculpture of sailing umiak by Joe Talurinili)		30	40
926	14c. *Aeroplane* (stonecut and stencil print by Pudlo)		30	40
927	14c. *Dogteam and dogsled* (ivory sculpture by Abraham Kingmeatook)		30	40

422 *Madonna
of the Flowering
Pea* (Cologne
School)

1978. Christmas. Paintings. Multicoloured.

928	12c. Type **422**		10	10
929	14c. *The Virgin and Child with St. Anthony and Donor* (detail, Hans Memling)		10	10
930	30c. *The Virgin and Child* (Jacopo di Cione)		25	90

423 *Chief Justice Robinson*
(paddle-steamer)

1978. Canadian Ships (4th series). Ice Vessels. Multicoloured.

931	14c. Type **423**		45	65
932	14c. *St. Roch* (steamer)		45	65
933	14c. *Northern Light* (steamer)		45	65
934	14c. *Labrador* (steamer)		45	65

424 Carnival
Revellers

1978. Quebec Carnival.

935	**424**	14c. multicoloured	20	20

425 Eastern Spiny
Soft-shelled Turtle

1979. Endangered Wildlife (3rd series). Multicoloured.

936	17c. Type **425**		20	10
937	35c. Bowhead whale		90	90

426 Knotted Ribbon
round Woman's
Finger

1979. Postal Code Publicity. Multicoloured.

938	17c. Type **426**		20	15
939	17c. Knotted string around man's finger		20	15

427 Scene from *Fruits of
the Earth* by Frederick
Philip Grove

1979. Canadian Writers (3rd series). Multicoloured.

940	17c. Type **427**		15	15
941	17c. Scene from *Le Vaisseau d'Or* by Emile Nelligan		15	15

428 Charles-Michel
de Salaberry
(military hero)

1979. Famous Canadians. Multicoloured.

942	17c. Type **428**		25	15
943	17c. John By (engineer)		25	15

429 Ontario

1979. Canada Day. Flags. Multicoloured.

944a	17c. Type **429**		25	40
944b	17c. Quebec		25	40
944c	17c. Nova Scotia		25	40
944d	17c. New Brunswick		25	40
944e	17c. Manitoba		25	40
944f	17c. British Columbia		25	40
944g	17c. Prince Edward Island		25	40
944h	17c. Saskatchewan		25	40
944i	17c. Alberta		25	40
944j	17c. Newfoundland		25	40
944k	17c. Northwest Territories		25	40
944l	17c. Yukon Territory		25	40

430 Paddling Kayak

1979. Canoe-Kayak Championships.

956	**430**	17c. multicoloured	15	30

431 Hockey Players

1979. Women's Field Hockey Championships, Vancouver.

957	**431**	17c. black, yellow and green	15	30

1979. Canadian Eskimos (3rd series). Shelter and the Community. As T **413**. Multicoloured.

958	17c. *Summer Tent* (print by Kiakshuk)		15	40
959	17c. *Five Eskimos building an Igloo* (soapstone sculpture by Abraham)		15	40
960	17c. *The Dance* (print by Kalvak)		15	40
961	17c. *Inuit drum dance* (soapstone sculptures by Madeleine Isserkut and Jean Mapsalak)		15	40

432 Toy Train

1979. Christmas. Multicoloured.

962	15c. Type **432**		10	10
963	17c. Hobby-horse		10	10
964	35c. Rag doll (vert)		25	1·00

433 *Child watering
Tree of Life* (painting
by Marie-Annick
Viatour)

1979. International Year of the Child.

965	**433**	17c. multicoloured	15	30

434 Canadair CL-215

1979. Canadian Aircraft (1st series). Flying Boats. Multicoloured.

966	17c. Type **434**		25	20
967	17c. Curtiss HS-2L		25	20
968	35c. Vickers Vedette		65	65
969	35c. Consolidated Canso		65	65

See also Nos. 996/9, 1026/9 and 1050/3.

435 Map of Arctic
Islands

1980. Centenary of Arctic Islands Acquisition.

970	**435**	17c. multicoloured	15	30

436 Skier

1980. Winter Olympic Games, Lake Placid.

971	**436**	35c. multicoloured	55	85

437 *A Meeting of the
School Trustees* (Robert
Harris)

1980. Centenary of Royal Canadian Academy of Arts. Multicoloured.

972	17c. Type **437**		25	20
973	17c. *Inspiration* (Philippe Hebert)		25	20
974	35c. *Sunrise on the Saguenay* (Lucius O'Brien)		50	55
975	35c. Thomas Fuller's design sketch for the original Parliament Buildings		50	55

438 Canadian Whitefish

1980. Endangered Wildlife (4th series). Multicoloured.

976	17c. Type **438**		30	15
977	17c. Prairie chicken		30	15

439 Garden Flowers

1980. International Flower Show, Montreal.

978	**439**	17c. multicoloured	15	20

440 "Helping
Hand"

1980. Rehabilitation.

979	**440**	17c. gold and blue	15	20

441 Opening Bars of *O
Canada*

1980. Centenary of *O Canada* (national song). Multicoloured.

980	17c. Type **441**		15	15
981	17c. Calixa Lavallee (composer), Adolphe-Basile Routhier (original writer) and Robert Stanley Weir (writer of English version)		15	15

442 John G.
Diefenbaker
(statesman)

1980. John G. Diefenbaker Commemoration.

982	**442**	17c. blue	15	20

443 Emma Albani
(singer)

1980. Famous Canadians. Multicoloured.

983	17c. Type **443**		15	25
984	17c. Healey Willan (composer)		15	25
985	17c. Ned Hanlan (oarsman) (horiz)		15	15

444 Alberta

1980. 75th Anniv of Alberta and Saskatchewan Provinces. Multicoloured.

986	17c. Type **444**		15	15
987	17c. Saskatchewan		15	15

445 Uraninite Molecular
Structure

1980. Uranium Resources.
988 **445** 35c. multicoloured 30 30

1980. Canadian Eskimos ("Inuits") (4th series). Spirits. As T 413. Multicoloured.
989 17c. *Return of the Sun* (print, Kenojouak) 20 15
990 17c. *Sedna* (sculpture, Ashoona Kiawak) 20 15
991 35c. *Shaman* (print, Simon Tookoome) 35 55
992 35c. *Bird Spirit* (sculpture, Doris Hagiolok) 35 55

446 *Christmas Morning* (J. S. Hallam)

1980. Christmas. Multicoloured.
993 15c. Type **446** 10 10
994 17c. *Sleigh Ride* (Frank Hennessy) 15 10
995 35c. *McGill Cab Stand* (Kathleen Morris) 30 1·40

447 Avro (Canada) CF-100 Canuck Mk 5

1980. Canadian Aircraft (2nd series). Multicoloured.
996 17c. Type **447** 40 20
997 17c. Avro Type 683 Lancaster 40 20
998 35c. Curtiss JN-4 Canuck biplane 60 65
999 35c. Hawker Hurricane Mk I 60 65

448 Emmanuel-Persillier Lachapelle

1980. Dr. E.-P. Lachapelle (founder, Notre-Dame Hospital, Montreal) Commemoration.
1000 **448** 17c. brown, deep brown and blue 15 15

449 Mandora (18th century)

1981. "The Look of Music" Exhibition, Vancouver.
1001 **449** 17c. multicoloured 15 15

450 Henrietta Edwards

1981. Feminists. Multicoloured.
1002 17c. Type **450** 30 30
1003 17c. Louise McKinney 30 30
1004 17c. Idola Saint-Jean 30 30
1005 17c. Emily Stowe 30 30

451 Vancouver Marmot

1981. Endangered Wildlife (5th series). Multicoloured.
1006 17c. Type **451** 15 10
1007 35c. American bison 35 30

452 Kateri Tekakwitha

1981. 17th-century Canadian Women. Statues by Emile Brunet.
1008 **452** 17c. brown and green 15 20
1009 - 17c. deep blue and blue 15 20
DESIGN: No. 1009, Marie de l'Incarnation.

453 *Self Portrait* (Frederick H. Varley)

1981. Canadian Paintings. Multicoloured.
1010 17c. Type **453** 20 10
1011 17c. *At Baie Saint-Paul* (Marc-Aurele Fortin) (horiz) 20 10
1012 35c. *Untitled No 6* (Paul-Emile Borduas) 40 45

454 Canada in 1867

1981. Canada Day. Maps showing evolution of Canada from Confederation to present day. Multicoloured.
1013 17c. Type **454** 15 20
1014 17c. Canada in 1873 15 20
1015 17c. Canada in 1905 15 20
1016 17c. Canada since 1949 15 20

455 Frere Marie-Victorin

1981. Canadian Botanists. Multicoloured.
1017 17c. Type **455** 20 30
1018 17c. John Macoun 20 30

456 *The Montreal Rose*

1981. Montreal Flower Show.
1019 **456** 17c. multicoloured 15 20

457 Drawing of Niagara-on-the-Lake

1981. Bicentenary of Niagara-on-the-Lake (town).
1020 **457** 17c. multicoloured 15 20

458 Acadian Community

1981. Centenary of First Acadia (community) Convention.
1021 **458** 17c. multicoloured 15 20

459 Aaron R. Mosher

1981. Birth Centenary of Aaron R. Mosher (founder of Canadian Labour Congress).
1022 **459** 17c. multicoloured 15 20

460 Christmas Tree, 1781

1981. Christmas. Bicentenary of First Illuminated Christmas Tree in Canada.
1023 15c. Type **460** 20 15
1024 15c. Christmas Tree, 1881 20 15
1025 15c. Christmas Tree, 1981 20 15

461 de Havilland Tiger Moth

1981. Canadian Aircraft (3rd series). Multicoloured.
1026 17c. Type **461** 25 15
1027 17c. Canadair CL-41 Tutor jet trainer 25 15
1028 35c. Avro (Canada) CF-102 jet airliner 45 40
1029 35c. de Havilland DHC-7 Dash 7 45 40

462 Canadian Maple Leaf Emblem

1981
1030a **462** A (30c.) red 20 45
No. 1030a was printed before a new first class domestic letter rate had been agreed, "A" representing the face value of the stamp, later decided to be 30c.

1982. As T **462** but including face values.
1033 5c. purple 10 20
1033d 8c. blue 1·75 2·50
1034 10c. green 1·50 2·25
1032 30c. red, grey and blue 30 60
1036 30c. red 35 40
1032b 32c. red, brown and stone 45 45
1036b 32c. red 1·50 2·50

463 1851 3d. Stamp

1982. "Canada 82" International Philatelic Youth Exhibition, Toronto. Stamps on Stamps. Mult.
1037 30c. Type **463** 30 30
1038 30c. 1908 Centenary of Quebec 15c. commemorative 30 30
1039 35c. 1935 10c. R.C.M.P 30 50
1040 35c. 1928 10c. 30 50
1041 60c. 1929 50c. 60 1·00
MS1042 159×108 mm. Nos. 1037/41 2·25 3·75

464 Jules Leger

1982. Jules Leger (politician) Commemoration.
1043 **464** 30c. multicoloured 20 20

465 Stylized drawing of Terry Fox

1982. Cancer victim Terry Fox's "Marathon of Hope" (Trans-Canada fund-raising run) Commemoration.
1044 **465** 30c. multicoloured 20 20

466 Stylized Open Book

1982. Patriation of Constitution.
1045 **466** 30c. multicoloured 20 20

467 Male and Female Salvationists with Street Scene

1982. Centenary of Salvation Army in Canada.
1046 **467** 30c. multicoloured 20 20

468 *The Highway near Kluane Lake* (Yukon Territory) (Jackson)

1982. Canada Day. Paintings of Canadian Landscapes. Multicoloured.
1047a 30c. Type **468** 35 40
1047b 30c. *Street Scene, Montreal* (Quebec) (Hebert) 35 40
1047c 30c. *Breakwater* (Newfoundland) (Pratt) 35 40
1047d 30c. *Along Great Slave Lake* (Northwest Territories) (Richard) 35 40
1047e 30c. *Till Hill* (Prince Edward Island) (Lamb) 35 40
1047f 30c. *Family and Rainstorm* (Nova Scotia) (Colville) 35 40
1047g 30c. *Brown Shadows* (Saskatchewan) (Knowles) 35 40
1047h 30c. *The Red Brick House* (Ontario) (Milne) 35 40
1047i 30c. *Campus Gates* (New Brunswick) (Bobak) 35 40
1047j 30c. *Prairie Town—Early Morning* (Alberta) (Kerr) 35 40
1047k 30c. *Totems at Ninstints* (British Columbia) (Plaskett) 35 40
1047l 30c. *Doc Snider's House* (Manitoba) (Fitzgerald) 35 40

469 Regina Legislative Building

1982. Centenary of Regina.
1048 **469** 30c. multicoloured 20 20

470 Finish of Race

1982. Centenary of Royal Canadian Henley Regatta.
1049 **470** 30c. multicoloured 20 25

471 Fairchild FC-2W1

1982. Canadian Aircraft (4th series). Bush Aircraft. Multicoloured.
1050 30c. Type **471** 35 20
1051 30c. de Havilland DHC-2 Beaver 35 20
1052 60c. Fokker Super Universal 65 85
1053 60c. Noorduyn Norseman 65 85

472 Decoy

1982. Heritage Artefacts.
1054 **472** 1c. black, lt brn and brn 10 10
1055 - 2c. black, blue and green 10 10

1056	-	3c. black and deep blue	10	10
1057	-	5c. black, pink and brown	10	10
1058	-	10c. black, blue & turq	10	10
1059	-	20c. black, lt brn & brn	20	10
1060	-	25c. multicoloured	1·25	10
1061	-	37c. black, grn & dp grn	45	70
1062	-	39c. black, grey and violet	1·75	2·00
1063	-	42c. multicoloured	2·25	1·00
1064	-	48c. dp brn, brn & pink	50	40
1065	-	50c. black, lt blue & blue	1·75	20
1066	-	55c. multicoloured	2·00	30
1067	-	64c. dp grey, blk & grey	60	35
1068	-	68c. black, lt brn & brn	1·75	50
1069	-	72c. multicoloured	2·00	35

DESIGNS—VERT: 2c. Fishing spear; 3c. Stable lantern; 5c. Bucket; 10c. Weathercock; 20c. Skates; 25c. Butter stamp. HORIZ: 37c. Plough; 39c. Settle-bed; 42c. Linen chest; 48c. Cradle; 50c. Sleigh; 55c. Iron kettle; 64c. Kitchen stove; 68c. Spinning wheel; 72c. Hand-drawn cart.

475 Mary, Joseph and Baby Jesus

1982. Christmas. Nativity Scenes.

1080	30c. Type 475	20	10
1081	35c. The Shepherds	25	60
1082	60c. The Three Wise Men	45	1·50

476 Globes forming Symbolic Designs

1983. World Communications Year.

1083	**476**	32c. multicoloured	30	30

477 Map of World showing Canada

1983. Commonwealth Day.

1084	**477**	$2 multicoloured	2·00	3·25

478 Scene from Novel *Angeline de Montbrun* by *Laure Conan* (Felicite Angers)

1983. Canadian Writers (4th series).

1085	32c. Type 478	40	90
1086	32c. Woodcut illustrating *Sea-gulls* (poem by E. J. Pratt)	40	90

479 St. John Ambulance Badge and "100"

1983. Centenary of St. John Ambulance in Canada.

1087	**479**	32c. red, yellow and brown	30	30

480 Victory Pictogram

1983. "Universiade 83" World University Games, Edmonton.

1088	**480**	32c. multicoloured	25	15
1089	**480**	64c. multicoloured	50	70

481 Fort William, Ontario

1983. Canada Day. Forts (1st series). Multicoloured.

1090	32c. Fort Henry, Ontario (44×22 mm)	55	80
1091	32c. Type 481	55	80
1092	32c. Fort Rodd Hill, British Columbia	55	80
1093	32c. Fort Wellington, Ontario (28×22 mm)	55	80
1094	32c. Fort Prince of Wales, Manitoba (28×22 mm)	55	80
1095	32c. Halifax Citadel, Nova Scotia (44×22 mm)	55	80
1096	32c. Fort Chambly, Quebec	55	80
1097	32c. Fort No. 1, Point Levis, Quebec	55	80
1098	32c. Coteau-du-Lac Fort, Quebec (28×22 mm)	55	80
1099	32c. Fort Beausejour, New Brunswick (28×22 mm)	55	80

See also Nos. 1163/72.

482 Scouting Poster by Marc Fournier (aged 21)

1983. Scouting in Canada (75th Anniv) and 15th World Scout Jamboree, Alberta.

1100	**482**	32c. multicoloured	30	30

483 Cross Symbol

1983. Sixth Assembly of the World Council of Churches, Vancouver.

1101	**483**	32c. green and lilac	30	20

484 Sir Humphrey Gilbert (founder)

1983. 400th Anniv of Newfoundland.

1102	**484**	32c. multicoloured	30	30

485 "NICKEL" Deposits

1983. Cent of Discovery of Sudbury Nickel Deposits.

1103	**485**	32c. multicoloured	30	30

486 Josiah Henson and Escaping Slaves

1983. 19th-century Social Reformers. Multicoloured.

1104	32c. Type 486	35	50
1105	32c. Father Antoine Labelle and rural village (32×26 mm)	35	50

487 Robert Stephenson's Locomotive *Dorchester*, 1836

1983. Railway Locomotives (1st series). Multicoloured.

1106	32c. Type 487	1·00	1·00
1107	32c. Locomotive *Toronto*, 1853	1·00	1·00
1108	37c. Timothy Hackworth's locomotive *Samson*, 1838	1·00	1·00
1109	64c. Western Canadian Railway locomotive *Adam Brown*, 1855	1·60	2·50

See also Nos. 1132/5, 1185/8 and 1223/6.

488 School Coat of Arms

1983. Centenary of Dalhousie Law School.

1110	**488**	32c. multicoloured	30	40

489 City Church

1983. Christmas. Churches. Multicoloured.

1111	32c. Type 489	30	10
1112	37c. Family walking to church	40	90
1113	64c. Country chapel	1·00	2·00

490 Royal Canadian Regiment and British Columbia Regiment

1983. Canadian Army Regiments. Multicoloured.

1114	32c. Type 490	75	1·25
1115	32c. Royal Winnipeg Rifles and Royal Canadian Dragoons	75	1·25

491 Gold Mine in Prospecting Pan

1984. 50th Anniv of Yellowknife.

1116	**491**	32c. multicoloured	30	30

492 Montreal Symphony Orchestra

1983. 50th Anniv of Montreal Symphony Orchestra.

1117	**492**	32c. multicoloured	35	30

493 Jacques Cartier

1984. 450th Anniv of Jacques Cartier's Voyage to Canada.

1118	**493**	32c. multicoloured	40	30

494 U.S.C.S. *Eagle*

1984. Tall Ships Visit.

1119	**494**	32c. multicoloured	35	30

495 Service Medal

1984. 75th Anniv of Canadian Red Cross Society.

1120	**495**	32c. multicoloured	35	40

496 Oared Galleys

1984. Bicentenary of New Brunswick.

1121	**496**	32c. multicoloured	35	30

497 St. Lawrence Seaway

1984. 25th Anniv of St. Lawrence Seaway.

1122	**497**	32c. multicoloured	45	30

498 *New Brunswick*

1984. Canada Day. Paintings by Jean Paul Lemieux. Multicoloured.

1123a	32c. Type **498**	50	60
1123b	32c. *British Columbia*	50	60
1123c	32c. *Northwest Territories*	50	60
1123d	32c. *Quebec*	50	60
1123e	32c. *Manitoba*	50	60
1123f	32c. *Alberta*	50	60
1123g	32c. *Prince Edward Island*	50	60
1123h	32c. *Saskatchewan*	50	60
1123i	32c. *Nova Scotia* (vert)	50	60
1123j	32c. *Yukon Territory*	50	60
1123k	32c. *Newfoundland*	50	60
1123l	32c. *Ontario* (vert)	50	60

The captions on the Northwest Territories and Yukon Territory paintings were transposed at the design stage.

499 Loyalists of 1784

1984. Bicentenary of Arrival of United Empire Loyalists.

1124	**499**	32c. multicoloured	30	30

500 St. John's Basilica

1984. Bicentenary of Roman Catholic Church in Newfoundland.

1125	**500**	32c. multicoloured	30	25

501 Coat of Arms of Pope John Paul II

1984. Papal Visit.

1126	**501**	32c. multicoloured	40	20
1127	**501**	64c. multicoloured	85	1·10

502 Louisbourg Lighthouse, 1734

1984. Canadian Lighthouse (1st series). Multicoloured.

1128	32c. Type **502**	1·75	1·75
1129	32c. Fisgard Lighthouse, 1860	1·75	1·75
1130	32c. Ile Verte Lighthouse, 1809	1·75	1·75
1131	32c. Gibraltar Point Lighthouse, 1808	1·75	1·75

See also Nos. 1176/9.

503 Great Western Railway Locomotive *Scotia*, 1860

1984. Railway Locomotives (2nd series). Multicoloured.

1132	32c. Type **503**		1·40	1·40
1133	32c. Northern Pacific Railroad locomotive *Countess of Dufferin*, 1872		1·40	1·40
1134	37c. Grand Trunk Railway Class E3 locomotive, 1886		1·40	1·60
1135	64c. Canadian Pacific Class D10a steam locomotive		2·00	2·75
MS1136	153×104 mm. As Nos. 1132/5, but with background colour changed from green to blue		5·50	6·50

No. **MS**1136 commemorates "CANADA '84" National Stamp Exhibition, Montreal.
See also Nos. 1185/8 and 1223/6.

504 *The Annunciation* (Jean Dallaire)

1984. Christmas. Religious Paintings. Multicoloured.

1137	32c. Type **504**		40	10
1138	37c. *The Three Kings* (Simone Bouchard)		70	1·00
1139	64c. *Snow in Bethlehem* (David Milne)		90	1·75

505 Pilots of 1914–18, 1939–45 and 1984

1984. 60th Anniv of Royal Canadian Air Force.

1140	**505**	32c. multicoloured	35	30

506 Treffle Berthiaume (editor)

1984. Centenary of *La Presse* (newspaper).

1141	**506**	32c. brown, red & lt brn	35	30

507 Heart and Arrow

1985. International Youth Year.

1142	**507**	32c. multicoloured	30	30

508 Astronaut in Space, and Planet Earth

1985. Canadian Space Programme.

1143	**508**	32c. multicoloured	40	30

509 Emily Murphy

1985. Women's Rights Activists. Multicoloured.

1144	32c. Type **509**		40	90
1145	32c. Therese Casgrain		40	90

510 Gabriel Dumont (Metis leader) and Battle of Batoche, 1885

1985. Centenary of the North-West Rebellion.

1146	**510**	32c. blue, red and grey	30	30

511 Rear View, Parliament Building, Ottawa

512 Queen Elizabeth II

512a Queen Elizabeth II in 1984 (from photo by Karsh)

1985

1147b	-	1c. green	1·00	80
1148	-	2c. green	25	1·50
1149	-	5c. brown	75	1·75
1150a	-	6c. brown	70	50
1150b	-	6c. purple	2·50	1·00
1151	**511**	34c. black	2·25	2·75
1155	**511**	34c. multicoloured	60	10
1158	**511**	34c. brown	2·25	3·00
1161	**512**	34c. black and blue	1·40	30
1152	**511**	36c. purple	4·00	5·00
1156a	**511**	36c. multicoloured	30	45
1159	**511**	36c. red	2·25	55
1162	**512**	36c. purple	2·75	1·10
1153	**511**	37c. blue	1·75	30
1157	-	37c. multicoloured	85	10
1162a	**512a**	37c. multicoloured	3·50	10
1154	**511**	38c. blue	2·75	1·25
1157c	-	38c. multicoloured	65	10
1160b	**511**	38c. green	50	30
1162b	**512a**	38c. multicoloured	1·50	20
1162c	**512a**	39c. multicoloured	1·00	20
1162d	**512a**	40c. multicoloured	1·00	20
1162e	**512a**	42c. multicoloured	1·00	40
1162f	**512a**	43c. multicoloured	1·25	80
1162g	**512a**	45c. multicoloured	2·50	80
1162h	**512a**	46c. multicoloured	1·00	45
1162i	**512a**	47c. multicoloured	1·00	60

DESIGNS: 1, 5, 6c. (1150b) East Block, Parliament Building; 2, 6c. (1150a) West Block, Parliament Building; 37c. (1157) Front view, Parliament Building; 38c. (1157c) Side view, Parliament Building.

1985. Canada Day. Forts (2nd series). As T **481**. Multicoloured.

1163	34c. Lower Fort Garry, Manitoba		50	60
1164	34c. Fort Anne, Nova Scotia		50	60
1165	34c. Fort York, Ontario		50	60
1166	34c. Castle Hill, Newfoundland		50	60
1167	34c. Fort Whoop Up, Alberta		50	60
1168	34c. Fort Erie, Ontario		50	60
1169	34c. Fort Walsh, Saskatchewan		50	60
1170	34c. Fort Lennox, Quebec		50	60
1171	34c. York Redoubt, Nova Scotia		50	60
1172	34c. Fort Frederick, Ontario		50	60

Nos. 1163 and 1168 measure 44×22 mm and Nos. 1166/7 and 1171/2 28×22 mm.

513 Louis Hebert (apothecary)

1985. 45th International Pharmaceutical Sciences Congress of Pharmaceutical Federation, Montreal.

1173	**513**	34c. multicoloured	45	45

514 Parliament Buildings and Map of World

1985. 74th Conference of Inter-Parliamentary Union, Ottawa.

1174	**514**	34c. multicoloured	45	45

515 Guide and Brownie Saluting

1985. 75th Anniv of Girl Guide Movement.

1175	**515**	34c. multicoloured	45	35

516 Sisters Islets Lighthouse

1985. Canadian Lighthouses (2nd series). Multicoloured.

1176	34c. Type **516**		2·00	2·00
1177	34c. Pelee Passage Lighthouse		2·00	2·00
1178	34c. Haut-fond Prince Lighthouse		2·00	2·00
1179	34c. Rose Blanche Lighthouse, Cains Island		2·00	2·00
MS1180	190×90 mm. Nos. 1176/9		7·50	8·00

No. **MS**1180 publicises "Capex 87" International Stamp Exhibition, Toronto.

517 Santa Claus in Reindeer-drawn Sleigh

1985. Christmas. Santa Claus Parade. Multicoloured.

1181	32c. Canada Post's parade float		60	85
1182	34c. Type **517**		70	20
1183	39c. Acrobats and horse-drawn carriage		1·00	1·25
1184	68c. Christmas tree, pudding and goose on float		1·90	2·50

1985. Steam Railway Locomotives (3rd series). As T **503**. Multicoloured.

1185	34c. Grand Trunk Railway Class K2		1·25	1·75
1186	34c. Canadian Pacific Class P2a		1·25	1·75
1187	39c. Canadian Northern Class O10a		1·25	1·50
1188	68c. Canadian Govt Railway Class H4D		2·00	2·75

518 Naval Personnel of 1910, 1939–45 and 1985

1985. 75th Anniv of Royal Canadian Navy.

1189	**518**	34c. multicoloured	65	65

519 *The Old Holton House, Montreal* (James Wilson Morrice)

1985. 125th Anniv of Montreal Museum of Fine Arts.

1190	**519**	34c. multicoloured	40	50

520 Map of Alberta showing Olympic Sites

1986. Winter Olympic Games, Calgary (1988) (1st issue).

1191	**520**	34c. multicoloured	40	50

See also Nos. 1216/17, 1236/7, 1258/9 and 1281/4.

521 Canada Pavilion

1986. "Expo '86" World Fair, Vancouver (1st issue). Multicoloured.

1192	34p. Type **521**		1·25	50
1193	39p. Early telephone, dish aerial and satellite		2·00	3·25

See also Nos. 1196/7.

522 Molly Brant

1986. 250th Birth Anniv of Molly Brant (Iroquois leader).

1194	**522**	34c. multicoloured	40	50

523 Aubert de Gaspe and Scene from *Les Anciens Canadiens*

1986. Birth Bicentenary of Philippe Aubert de Gaspe (author).

1195	**523**	34c. multicoloured	40	50

1986. "Expo '86" World Fair, Vancouver (2nd issue). As T **521**. Multicoloured.

1196	34c. Expo Centre, Vancouver (vert)		70	50
1197	68c. Early and modern trains		1·40	3·25

524 Canadian Field Post Office and Cancellation, 1944

1986. 75th Anniv of Canadian Forces Postal Service.

1198	**524**	34c. multicoloured	60	60

525 Great Blue Heron

1986. Birds of Canada. Multicoloured.

1199	34c. Type **525**		1·75	2·25
1200	34c. Snow goose		1·75	2·25
1201	34c. Great horned owl		1·75	2·25
1202	34c. Spruce grouse		1·75	2·25

526 Railway Rotary Snowplough

1986. Canada Day. Science and Technology. Canadian Inventions (1st series). Multicoloured.

1203	34c. Type **526**		1·75	2·25
1204	34c. Space shuttle "Challenger" launching satellite with Canadarm		1·75	2·25
1205	34c. Pilot wearing anti-gravity flight suit and Supermarine Spitfire		1·75	2·25
1206	34c. Variable-pitch propeller and Avro 504 airplane		1·75	2·25

See also Nos. 1241/4 and 1292/5.

527 C.B.C. Logos over Map of Canada

1986. 50th Anniv of Canadian Broadcasting Corporation.
1207	**527**	34c. multicoloured	40	50

528 Ice Age Artefacts, Tools and Settlement

1986. Exploration of Canada (1st series). Discoverers. Multicoloured.
1208		34c. Type **528**	1·50	2·00
1209		34c. Viking ships	1·50	2·00
1210		34c. John Cabot's *Matthew*, 1497, compass and Arctic char (fish)	1·50	2·00
1211		34c. Henry Hudson cast adrift, 1611	1·50	2·00
MS1212	119×84 mm. Nos. 1208/11		5·50	7·50

No. **MS**1212 publicises "Capex '87" International Stamp Exhibition, Toronto. See also Nos. 1232/5, 1285/8 and 1319/22.

529 Crowfoot (Blackfoot Chief) and Indian Village

1986. Founders of the Canadian West. Multicoloured.
1213		34c. Type **529**	80	1·00
1214		34c. James Macleod of the North West Mounted Police and Fort Macleod	80	1·00

530 Peace Dove and Globe

1986. International Peace Year.
1215	**530**	34c. multicoloured	60	60

531 Ice Hockey

1986. Winter Olympic Games, Calgary (1988) (2nd issue). Multicoloured.
1216		34c. Type **531**	1·75	1·75
1217		34c. Biathlon	1·75	1·75

532 Angel with Crown

1986. Christmas. Multicoloured.
1218		29c. Angel singing carol (36×22 mm)	65	35
1219		34c. Type **532**	60	25
1220		39c. Angel playing lute	1·00	1·60
1221		68c. Angel with ribbon	1·75	3·00

533 John Molson with Theatre Royal, Montreal, *Accomodation* (paddle-steamer) and Railway Train

1986. 150th Death Anniv of John Molson (businessman).
1222	**533**	34c. multicoloured	1·25	75

1986. Railway Locomotives (4th series). As T **503** but size 60×22 mm. Multicoloured.
1223		34c. Canadian National Class V-1-a diesel locomotive No. 9000	1·90	1·90
1224		34c. Canadian Pacific Class T1a steam locomotive No. 9000	1·90	1·90
1225		39c. Canadian National Class U-2-a steam locomotive	1·90	1·00
1226		68c. Canadian Pacific Class H1c steam locomotive No. 2850	2·50	3·50

534 Toronto's First Post Office

1987. "Capex '87" International Stamp Exhibition, Toronto. Post Offices.
1227		34c. Type **534**	60	20
1228		36c. Nelson-Miramichi, New Brunswick	65	45
1229		42c. Saint-Ours, Quebec	70	65
1230		72c. Battleford, Saskatchewan	1·00	1·25
MS1231	155×92 mm. 36c. As No. 1227 and Nos. 1228/30, but main inscr in green		3·25	2·75

535 Etienne Brule exploring Lake Superior

1987. Exploration of Canada (2nd series). Pioneers of New France. Multicoloured.
1232		34c. Type **535**	1·75	2·00
1233		34c. Radisson and Des Groseilliers with British and French flags	1·75	2·00
1234		34c. Jolliet and Father Marquette on the Mississippi	1·75	2·00
1235		34c. Jesuit missionary preaching to Indians	1·75	2·00

1987. Winter Olympic Games, Calgary (1988) (3rd issue). As T **531**. Multicoloured.
1236		36c. Speed skating	50	40
1237		42c. Bobsleighing	75	60

536 Volunteer Activities

1987. National Volunteer Week.
1238	**536**	36c. multicoloured	30	35

537 Canadian Coat of Arms

1987. Fifth Anniv of Canadian Charter of Rights and Freedoms.
1239	**537**	36c. multicoloured	75	35

538 Steel Girder, Gear Wheel and Microchip

1987. Centenary of Engineering Institute of Canada.
1240	**538**	36c. multicoloured	75	40

539 R. A. Fessenden (AM Radio)

1987. Canada Day. Science and Technology. Canadian Inventors (2nd series). Multicoloured.
1241		36c. Type **539**	1·25	1·75
1242		36c. C. Fenerty (newsprint pulp)	1·25	1·75
1243		36c. G.-E. Desbarats and W. Leggo (half-tone engraving)	1·25	1·75
1244		36c. F. N. Gisborne (first North American undersea telegraph)	1·25	1·75

540 *Segwun*

1987. Canadian Steamships. Multicoloured.
1245		36c. Type **540**	1·75	2·50
1246		36c. *Princess Marguerite* (52×22 mm)	1·75	2·50

541 Figurehead from *Hamilton*, 1813

1987. Historic Shipwrecks. Multicoloured.
1247		36c. Type **541**	1·50	2·00
1248		36c. Hull of *San Juan*, 1565	1·50	2·00
1249		36c. Wheel from *Breadalbane*, 1853	1·50	2·00
1250		36c. Bell from *Ericsson*, 1892	1·50	2·00

542 Air Canada Boeing 767-200 and Globe

1987. 50th Anniv of Air Canada.
1251	**542**	36c. multicoloured	1·00	35

543 Summit Symbol

1987. Second Int Francophone Summit, Quebec.
1252	**543**	36c. multicoloured	30	35

544 Commonwealth Symbol

1987. Commonwealth Heads of Government Meeting, Vancouver.
1253	**544**	36c. multicoloured	35	40

545 Poinsettia

1987. Christmas. Christmas Plants. Multicoloured.
1254		31c. Decorated Christmas tree and presents (36×20 mm)	90	50
1255		36c. Type **545**	40	20
1256		42c. Holly wreath	1·25	50
1257		72c. Mistletoe and decorated tree	1·75	80

1987. Winter Olympic Games, Calgary (1988) (4th issue). As T **531**. Multicoloured.
1258		36c. Cross-country skiing	90	75
1259		36c. Ski-jumping	90	75

546 Football, Grey Cup and Spectators

1987. 75th Grey Cup Final (Canadian football championship), Vancouver.
1260	**546**	36c. multicoloured	35	40

547 Flying Squirrel　　**548** Lynx

1988. Canadian Mammals and Architecture. Multicoloured.

(a) As T **547**
1261		1c. Type **547**	10	10
1262		2c. Porcupine	10	10
1263		3c. Muskrat	10	10
1264		5c. Varying hare	10	10
1265		6c. Red fox	10	10
1266		10c. Striped skunk	10	10
1267		25c. American beaver	30	15

(b) As T **548**
1268		43c. Lynx (26×20 mm)	1·40	1·25
1269		44c. Walrus (27×21 mm)	1·40	20
1270		45c. Pronghorn (27×21 mm)	50	40
1270c		46c. Wolverine (27×21 mm)	1·50	1·50
1271		57c. Killer whale (26×20 mm)	2·00	55
1272		59c. Musk ox (27×21 mm)	3·50	2·75
1273		61c. Wolf (27×21 mm)	70	1·25
1273b		63c. Harbour porpoise (27×21 mm)	2·00	2·50
1274		74c. Wapiti (26×20 mm)	1·60	50
1275		76c. Brown bear (27×21 mm)	2·50	50
1276		78c. White whale (27×21 mm)	1·00	55
1276c		80c. Peary caribou (27×21 mm)	1·00	60

548a Runnymede Library, Toronto

(c) As T **548a**.
1277		$1 Type **548a**	1·50	30
1278		$2 McAdam Railway Station, New Brunswick	2·25	50
1279		$5 Bonsecours Market, Montreal	4·75	4·00

1988. Winter Olympic Games, Calgary (5th issue). As T **531**. Multicoloured.
1281		37c. Slalom skiing	85	50
1282		37c. Curling	85	50
1283		43c. Figure skating	85	45
1284		74c. Luge	1·40	80

549 Trade Goods, Blackfoot Encampment and Page from Anthony Henday's Journal

1988. Exploration of Canada (3rd series). Explorers of the West. Multicoloured.
1285		37c. Type **549**	1·00	70
1286		37c. Discovery and map of George Vancouver's voyage	1·00	70
1287		37c. Simon Fraser's expedition portaging canoes	1·00	70
1288		37c. John Palliser's surveying equipment and view of prairie	1·00	70

550 *The Young Reader* (Ozias Leduc)

1988. Canadian Art (1st series).
1289	**550**	50c. multicoloured	70	70

See also Nos. 1327, 1384, 1421, 1504, 1539, 1589, 1629, 1681, 1721, 1825, 1912, 2011, 2097 and 2133.

551 Mallard landing on Marsh

1988. Wildlife and Habitat Conservation. Multicoloured.

1290	37c. Type **551**	1·00	50
1291	37c. Moose feeding in marsh	1·00	50

552 Kerosene Lamp and Diagram of Distillation Plant

1988. Canada Day. Science and Technology. Canadian Inventions (3rd series). Multicoloured.

1292	37c. Type **552**	1·00	1·00
1293	37c. Ears of Marquis wheat	1·00	1·00
1294	37c. Electron microscope and magnified image	1·00	1·00
1295	37c. Patient under "Cobalt 60" cancer therapy	1·00	1·00

553 *Papilio brevicauda*

1988. Canadian Butterflies. Multicoloured.

1296	37c. Type **553**	80	1·00
1297	37c. *Lycaeides idas*	80	1·00
1298	37c. *Oeneis macounii*	80	1·00
1299	37c. *Papilio glaucus*	80	1·00

554 St. John's Harbour Entrance and Skyline

1988. Centenary of Incorporation of St. John's, Newfoundland.

1300	**554** 37c. multicoloured	35	40

555 Club Members working on Forestry Project and Rural Scene

1988. 75th Anniv of 4-H Clubs.

1301	**555** 37c. multicoloured	35	40

556 Saint-Maurice Ironworks

1988. 250th Anniv of Saint-Maurice Ironworks, Quebec.

1302	**556** 37c. black, orange & brn	40	40

557 Tahltan Bear Dog

1988. Canadian Dogs. Multicoloured.

1303	37c. Type **557**	1·25	1·40
1304	37c. Nova Scotia duck tolling retriever	1·25	1·40
1305	37c. Canadian eskimo dog	1·25	1·40
1306	37c. Newfoundland	1·25	1·40

558 Baseball, Glove and Pitch

1988. 150th Anniv of Baseball in Canada. Multicoloured.

1307	**558** 37c. multicoloured	35	40

559 Virgin with Inset of Holy Child

1988. Christmas. Icons. Multicoloured.

1308	32c. Holy Family (36×21 mm)	45	55
1309	37c. Type **559**	45	20
1310	43c. Virgin and Child	50	45
1311	74c. Virgin and Child (different)	90	75

On No. 1308 the left-hand third of the design area is taken up by the bar code.

No. 1309 also commemorates the millennium of Ukrainian Christianity.

560 Bishop Inglis and Nova Scotia Church

1988. Bicentenary of Consecration of Charles Inglis (first Canadian Anglican bishop) (1987).

1312	**560** 37c. multicoloured	35	40

561 Frances Ann Hopkins and *Canoe manned by Voyageurs*

1988. 150th Birth Anniv of Frances Anne Hopkins (artist).

1313	**561** 37c. multicoloured	35	40

562 Angus Walters and *Bluenose* (yacht)

1988. 20th Death Anniv of Angus Walters (yachtsman).

1314	**562** 37c. multicoloured	40	40

563 Chipewyan Canoe

1989. Small Craft of Canada (1st series). Native Canoes. Multicoloured.

1315	38c. Type **563**	90	70
1316	38c. Haida canoe	90	70
1317	38c. Inuit kayak	90	70
1318	38c. Micmac canoe	90	70

See also Nos. 1377/80 and 1428/31.

564 Matonabbee and Hearne's Expedition

1989. Exploration of Canada (4th issue). Explorers of the North. Multicoloured.

1319	38c. Type **564**	1·25	75
1320	38c. Relics of Franklin's expedition and White Ensign	1·25	75
1321	38c. Joseph Tyrell's compass, hammer and fossil	1·25	75
1322	38c. Vilhjalmur Stefansson, camera on tripod and sledge dog team	1·25	75

565 Construction of Victoria Bridge, Montreal and William Notman

1989. Canada Day. "150 Years of Canadian Photography". Designs showing early photographs and photographers. Multicoloured.

1323	38c. Type **565**	85	85
1324	38c. Plains Indian village and W. Hanson Boorne	85	85
1325	38c. Horse-drawn sleigh and Alexander Henderson	85	85
1326	38c. Quebec street scene and Jules-Ernest Livernois	85	85

566 Tsimshian Ceremonial Frontlet, c. 1900

1989. Canadian Art (2nd series).

1327	**566** 50c. multicoloured	1·00	60

567 Canadian Flag and Forest

1989. Self-adhesive. Multicoloured.

1328	38c. Type **567**	1·50	2·75
1328b	39c. Canadian flag and prairie	1·50	2·75
1328c	40c. Canadian flag and sea	1·75	1·75
1328d	42c. Canadian flag over mountains	2·00	3·00
1328e	43c. Canadian flag over lake	1·75	2·50

568 Archibald Lampman

1989. Canadian Poets. Multicoloured.

1329	38c. Type **568**	1·25	1·40
1330	38c. Louis-Honore Frechette	1·25	1·40

569 *Clavulinopsis fusiformis*

1989. Mushrooms. Multicoloured.

1331	38c. Type **569**	70	1·00
1332	38c. *Boletus mirabilis*	70	1·00
1333	38c. *Cantharellus cinnabarinus*	70	1·00
1334	38c. *Morchella esculenta*	70	1·00

570 Night Patrol, Korea

1989. 75th Anniv of Canadian Regiments. Multicoloured.

1335	38c. Type **570** (Princess Patricia's Canadian Light Infantry)	1·75	1·75
1336	38c. Trench raid, France, 1914–18 (Royal 22e Regiment)	1·75	1·75

571 Globe in Box

1989. Canada Export Trade Month.

1337	**571** 38c. multicoloured	40	45

572 Film Director

1989. Arts and Entertainment.

1338	**572** 38c. brown, dp brn & vio	1·00	1·25
1339	- 38c. brown, dp brn & grn	1·00	1·25
1340	- 38c. brown, dp brn & mve	1·00	1·25
1341	- 38c. brown, dp brn & bl	1·00	1·25

DESIGNS: No. 1339, Actors; No. 1340, Dancers; No. 1341, Musicians.

573 *"now II"* (Lawren S. Harris)

1989. Christmas. Paintings of Winter Landscapes. Multicoloured.

1342	33c. *Champ-de-Mars, Winter* (William Brymner) (35×21 mm)	1·00	65
1343	38c. *Bend in the Gosselin River* (Marc-Aurele Suzor-Cote) (21×35 mm)	40	25
1344	44c. Type **573**	65	50
1345	76c. *Ste. Agnes* (A. H. Robinson)	1·40	85

On No. 1342 the left-hand third of the design area is taken up by a bar code.

574 Canadians listening to Declaration of War, 1939

1989. 50th Anniv of Outbreak of Second World War (1st issue).

1346	**574** 38c. black, silver & pur	1·10	1·25
1347	- 38c. black, silver and grey	1·10	1·25
1348	- 38c. black, silver and green	1·10	1·25
1349	- 38c. black, silver and blue	1·10	1·25

DESIGNS: No. 1347, Army mobilization; No. 1348, British Commonwealth air crew training; No. 1349, North Atlantic convoy.

See also Nos. 1409/12, 1456/9, 1521/4, 1576/9, 1621/4, and 1625/8.

575 Canadian Flag **576**

1989

1350	**575** 1c. multicoloured	20	1·00
1351	- 5c. multicoloured	40	30
1352	- 39c. multicoloured	1·40	2·25
1354	**576** 39c. multicoloured	70	10
1360	- 39c. purple	60	75
1353	- 40c. multicoloured	2·00	2·75
1355	- 40c. multicoloured	80	10
1361	- 40c. blue	40	60
1356	- 42c. multicoloured	1·00	15
1362	- 42c. red	40	60
1357	- 43c. multicoloured	1·00	1·50
1363	- 43c. green	1·50	2·25
1358d	- 45c. multicoloured	1·00	1·00
1364	- 45c. green	65	1·50
1359	- 46c. multicoloured	1·10	65
1365	- 46c. red	60	1·25
1367	- 47c. multicoloured	1·00	75
1368	- 48c. multicoloured	80	1·50
1369	- 49c. multicoloured	1·10	1·50
1370	- 50c. multicoloured	1·10	1·25
1371	- 50c. multicoloured	1·10	1·25
1372	- 50c. multicoloured	1·10	1·25
1373	- 50c. multicoloured	1·10	1·25
1374	- 50c. multicoloured	1·10	1·25
1374a	- 51c. multicoloured	1·00	1·25
1374b	- 51c. multicoloured	1·00	1·25
1374c	- 51c. multicoloured	1·00	1·25
1374d	- 51c. multicoloured	1·00	1·25
1374e	- 51c. multicoloured	65	70

DESIGNS: Nos. 1351/3, 1360/5, As T **575** but different folds in flag. As T **576**: No. 1355, Flag over forest; 1356, Flag over mountains; 1357, Flag over prairie; 1358d, Flag and skyscraper; 1359, Flag and iceberg; 1367, Flag and inukshuk (Inuit cairn); 1368, Flag in front of Canada Post Headquarters, Ottawa, Flag and Edmonton; 1370, Broadway Bridge, Saskatoon; 1371, Durrell, South Twillingate Island; 1372, Shannon Falls, Squamish; 1373, Church of Saint-Hilaire, Quebec; 1374, Cruise boat and skyline, Toronto; 1374a, Winter scene near New Glasgow, Prince Edward Island; 1374b, Bridge, Bouctouche, New Brunswick; 1374c, Wind turbines, Pincher Creek, Alberta; 1374d, Southwest bastion, Lower Fort Garry National Historic Site, Manitoba; 1374e, Dogsled, St. Elias Mountains, Yukon.

No. 1359 comes with ordinary or self-adhesive gum and 1367/9 and 1370/4e are self-adhesive.

577 Norman Bethune in 1937 and performing Operation, Montreal

1990. Birth Centenary of Dr. Norman Bethune (surgeon). Multicoloured.
1375	39c. Type **577**		1·75	2·25
1376	39c. Bethune in 1939, and treating wounded Chinese soldiers		1·75	2·25

1990. Small Craft of Canada (2nd series). Early Work Boats. As T **563.** Multicoloured.
1377	39c. Fishing dory	1·10	1·50
1378	39c. Logging pointer	1·10	1·50
1379	39c. York boat	1·10	1·50
1380	39c. North canoe	1·10	1·50

578 Maple Leaf Mosaic

1990. Multiculturalism.
1381	**578**	39c. multicoloured	35	40

579 Mail Van (facing left)

1990. "Moving the Mail". Multicoloured.
1382	Type **579**	39c.	75	75
1383		39c. Mail van (facing right)	75	75

1990. Canadian Art (3rd series). As T **550.** Multicoloured.
1384	50c. The West Wind (Tom Thomson)	1·00	1·00

580 Amerindian and Inuit Dolls

1990. Dolls. Multicoloured.
1385	39c. Type **580**	1·25	1·50
1386	39c. 19th-century settlers' dolls	1·25	1·50
1387	39c. Commerical dolls, 1917–36	1·25	1·50
1388	39c. Commercial dolls, 1940–60	1·25	1·50

581 Canadian Flag and Fireworks

1990. Canada Day.
1389	**581**	39c. multicoloured	50	50

582 Stromatolites (fossil algae)

1990. Prehistoric Canada (1st series). Primitive Life. Multicoloured.
1390	39c. Type **582**	1·25	1·50
1391	39c. Opabinia regalis (soft invertebrate)	1·25	1·50

1392	39c. Paradoxides davidis (trilobite)	1·25	1·50
1393	39c. Eurypterus remipes (sea scorpion)	1·25	1·50
See also Nos. 1417/20, 1568/71 and 1613/16.

583 Acadian Forest

1990. Canadian Forests. Multicoloured.
1394	39c. Type **583**	80	70
1395	39c. Great Lakes–St. Lawrence forest	80	70
1396	39c. Pacific Coast forest	80	70
1397	39c. Boreal forest	80	70

584 Clouds and Rainbow

1990. 150th Anniv of Weather Observing in Canada.
1398	**584**	39c. multicoloured	60	50

585 "Alphabet" Bird

1990. International Literacy Year.
1399	**585**	39c. multicoloured	40	50

586 Sasquatch

1990. Legendary Creatures. Multicoloured.
1400	39c. Type **586**	1·25	1·50
1401	39c. Kraken	1·25	1·50
1402	39c. Werewolf	1·25	1·50
1403	39c. Ogopogo	1·25	1·50

587 Agnes Macphail

1990. Birth Centenary of Agnes Macphail (first woman elected to Parliament).
1404	**587**	39c. multicoloured	40	50

588 Virgin Mary with Christ Child and St. John the Baptist (Norval Morrisseau)

1990. Christmas. Native Art.
1405	-	34c. multicoloured	65	55
1406	**588**	39c. multicoloured	30	20
1407	-	45c. multicoloured	35	45
1408	-	78c. black, red and grey	70	75
DESIGNS—35×21 mm: 34c. Rebirth (Jackson Beardy). As T **588**; 45c. Mother and Child (Inuit sculpture, Cape Dorset); 78c. Children of the Raven (Bill Reid).
No. 1405 includes a bar code in the design.

1990. 50th Anniv of Second World War (2nd issue). As T **574.**
1409	39c. black, silver and green	2·00	2·00
1410	39c. black, silver and brown	2·00	2·00
1411	39c. black, silver and brown	2·00	2·00
1412	39c. black, silver and mauve	2·00	2·00
DESIGNS: No. 1409, Canadian family at home, 1940; 1410, Packing parcels for the troops; 1411, Harvesting; 1412, Testing anti-gravity flying suit.

589 Jennie Trout (first woman physician) and Women's Medical College, Kingston

1991. Medical Pioneers. Multicoloured.
1413	40c. Type **589**	1·10	90
1414	40c. Wilder Penfield (neurosurgeon) and Montreal Neurological Institute	1·10	90
1415	40c. Frederick Banting (discoverer of insulin) and University of Toronto medical faculty	1·10	90
1416	40c. Harold Griffith (anesthesiologist) and Queen Elizabeth Hospital, Montreal	1·10	90

1991. Prehistoric Canada (2nd series). Primitive Vertebrates. As T **582.** Multicoloured.
1417	40c. Foord's crossopt (Eusthenopteron foordi) (fish fossil)	2·25	2·50
1418	40c. Hylonomus lyelli (land reptile)	2·25	2·50
1419	40c. Fossil conodonts (fossil teeth)	2·25	2·50
1420	40c. Archaeopteris halliana (early tree)	2·25	2·50

1991. Canadian Art (4th series). As T **550.** Multicoloured.
1421	50c. Forest, British Columbia (Emily Carr)	1·25	1·75

590 Blue Poppies and Butchart Gardens, Victoria

1991. Public Gardens. Multicoloured.
1422	40c. Type **590**	70	70
1423	40c. Marigolds and International Peace Garden, Boissevain	70	70
1424	40c. Lilac and Royal Botanical Gardens, Hamilton	70	70
1425	40c. Roses and Montreal Botanical Gardens	70	70
1426	40c. Rhododendrons and Halifax Public Gardens	70	70

591 Maple Leaf

1991. Canada Day.
1427	**591**	40c. multicoloured	50	60

1991. Small Craft of Canada (3rd series). As T **563.** Multicoloured.
1428	40c. Verchere rowboat	1·40	1·40
1429	40c. Touring kayak	1·40	1·40
1430	40c. Sailing dinghy	1·40	1·40
1431	40c. Cedar strip canoe	1·40	1·40

592 South Nahanni River

1991. Canadian Rivers (1st series). Multicoloured.
1432	40c. Type **592**	1·00	1·40
1433	40c. Athabasca River	1·00	1·40
1434	40c. Boundary Waters, Voyageur Waterway	1·00	1·40
1435	40c. Jacques-Cartier River	1·00	1·40
1436	40c. Main River	1·00	1·40
See also Nos. 1492/6, 1558/62 and 1584/8.

593 Leaving Europe

1991. Centenary of Ukrainian Immigration. Panels from The Ukrainian Pioneer by William Kurelek. Multicoloured.
1437	40c. Type **593**	80	85
1438	40c. Canadian Winter	80	85
1439	40c. Clearing the Land	80	85
1440	40c. Harvest	80	85

594 Ski Patrol rescuing Climber

1991. Emergency Services. Multicoloured.
1441	40c. Type **594**	2·25	2·25
1442	40c. Police at road traffic accident	2·25	2·25
1443	40c. Firemen on extending ladder	2·25	2·25
1444	40c. Boeing-Vertol Chinook rescue helicopter and Spindrift (lifeboat)	2·25	2·25

595 The Witched Canoe

1991. Canadian Folktales. Multicoloured.
1445	40c. Type **595**	1·40	95
1446	40c. The Orphan Boy	1·40	95
1447	40c. Chinook	1·40	95
1448	40c. Buried Treasure	1·40	95

596 Grant Hall Tower

1991. 150th Anniv of Queen's University, Kingston.
1449	**596**	40c. multicoloured	1·10	1·00

597 North American Santa Claus

1991. Christmas. Multicoloured.
1450	35c. British Father Christmas (35×21 mm)	1·00	1·00
1451	40c. Type **597**	1·00	20
1452	46c. French Bonhomme Noel	1·25	1·60
1453	80c. Dutch Sinterklaas	2·00	3·75

598 Players jumping for Ball

1991. Basketball Centenary. Multicoloured.
1454	40c. Type **598**	1·50	75
MS1455	155×90 mm. 40c. Type **598**, but with shorter inscr below face value; 46c. Player taking shot; 80c. Player challenging opponent	6·50	6·00

1991. 50th Anniv of Second World War (3rd issue). As T **574.**

1456	40c. black, silver and blue	2·00	2·00
1457	40c. black, silver and brown	2·00	2·00
1458	40c. black, silver and lilac	2·00	2·00
1459	40c. black, silver and brown	2·00	2·00

DESIGNS: No. 1456, Women's services, 1941; 1457, Armament factory; 1458, Cadets and veterans, 1459, Defence of Hong Kong.

599 Blueberry

600 McIntosh Apple

600a Court House, Yorktown

1991. Multicoloured

(a) Edible Berries. As T 599

1460	1c. Type **599**	10	10
1461	2c. Wild strawberry	10	10
1462	3c. Black crowberry	50	10
1463	5c. Rose hip	10	10
1464	6c. Black raspberry	10	10
1465	10c. Kinnikinnick	10	10
1466	25c. Saskatoon berry	25	25

(b) Fruit and Nut Trees. As T 600.

1467	48c. Type **600**	50	35
1468	49c. Delicious apple	2·50	1·00
1469	50c. Snow apple	1·50	1·00
1470	52c. Grauenstein apple	1·60	50
1471	65c. Black walnut	1·75	50
1472	67c. Beaked hazelnut	1·75	1·25
1473	69c. Shagbark hickory	2·75	1·25
1474	71c. American chestnut	3·00	1·00
1475	84c. Stanley plum	1·00	75
1476	86c. Bartlett pear	2·75	1·00
1477	88c. Westcot apricot	1·75	1·60
1478	90c. Elberta peach	1·60	1·00

(c) Architecture. As T 600a.

1479b	$1 Type **600a**	2·75	1·00
1480b	$2 Provincial Normal School, Truro	3·50	1·60
1481	$5 Public Library, Victoria	6·00	4·75

601 Ski Jumping

1992. Winter Olympic Games, Albertville. Mulicoloured.

1482	42c. Type **601**	1·25	1·25
1483	42c. Figure skating	1·25	1·25
1484	42c. Ice hockey	1·25	1·25
1485	42c. Bobsleighing	1·25	1·25
1486	42c. Alpine skiing	1·25	1·25

602 Ville-Marie in 17th Century

1992. "CANADA 92" International Youth Stamp Exhibition, Montreal. Multicoloured.

1487	42c. Type **602**	1·50	1·50
1488	42c. Modern Montreal	1·50	1·50
1489	48c. Compass rose, snow shoe and crow's nest of Cartier's ship *Grande Hermine*	2·25	1·25
1490	84c. Atlantic map, Aztec "calendar stone" and navigational instrument	3·50	4·50
MS1491	181×120 mm. Nos. 1487/90	8·00	8·00

1992. Canadian Rivers (2nd series). As T **592** but horiz. Multicoloured.

1492	42c. Margaree River	1·50	1·50
1493	42c. West (Eliot) River	1·50	1·50
1494	42c. Ottawa River	1·50	1·50
1495	42c. Niagara River	1·50	1·50
1496	42c. South Saskatchewan River	1·50	1·50

603 Road Bed Construction and Route Map

1992. 50th Anniv of Alaska Highway.

1497	**603**	42c. multicoloured	1·50	70

1992. Olympic Games, Barcelona. As T **601.** Multicoloured.

1498	42c. Gymnastics	1·10	1·25
1499	42c. Athletics	1·10	1·25
1500	42c. Diving	1·10	1·25
1501	42c. Cycling	1·10	1·25
1502	42c. Swimming	1·10	1·25

604 *Quebec, Patrimoine Mondial* (A. Dumas)

1992. Canada Day. Paintings. Multicoloured.

1503a	42c. Type **604**	1·50	1·75
1503b	42c. *Christie Passage, Hurst Island, British Columbia* (E. J. Hughes)	1·50	1·75
1503c	42c. *Toronto, Landmarks of Time* (Ontario) (V. McIndoe)	1·50	1·75
1503d	42c. *Near the Forks* (Manitoba) (S. Gouthro)	1·50	1·75
1503e	42c. *Off Cape St. Francis* (Newfoundland) (R. Shepherd)	1·50	1·75
1503f	42c. *Crowd at City Hall* (New Brunswick) (Molly Bobak)	1·50	1·75
1503g	42c. *Across the Tracks to Shop* (Alberta) (Janet Mitchell)	1·50	1·75
1503h	42c. *Cove Scene* (Nova Scotia) (J. Norris)	1·50	1·75
1503i	42c. *Untitled* (Saskatchewan) (D. Thauberger)	1·50	1·75
1503j	42c. *Town Life* (Yukon) (T. Harrison)	1·50	1·75
1503k	42c. *Country Scene* (Prince Edward Island) (Erica Rutherford)	1·50	1·75
1503l	42c. *Playing on an Igloo* (Northwest Territories) (Agnes Nanogak)	1·50	1·75

1992. Canadian Art (5th series). As T **550.** Multicoloured.

1504	50c. *Red Nasturtiums* (David Milne)	1·25	1·40

605 Jerry Potts (scout)

1992. Folk Heroes. Multicoloured.

1505	42c. Type **605**	1·25	1·50
1506	42c. Capt. William Jackman and wreck of *Sea Clipper*, 1867	1·25	1·50
1507	42c. Laura Secord (messenger)	1·25	1·50
1508	42c. Jos Montferrand (lumberjack)	1·25	1·50

606 Copper

1992. 150th Anniv of Geological Survey of Canada. Minerals. Multicoloured.

1509	42c. Type **606**	1·75	2·00
1510	42c. Sodalite	1·75	2·00
1511	42c. Gold	1·75	2·00
1512	42c. Galena	1·75	2·00
1513	42c. Grossular	1·75	2·00

607 Satellite and Photographs from Space

1992. Canadian Space Programme. Multicoloured.

1514	42c. Type **607**	1·25	1·75
1515	42c. Space shuttle over Canada (hologram) (32×26 mm)	1·25	1·75

608 Babe Siebert, Skates and Stick

1992. 75th Anniv of National Ice Hockey League. Multicoloured.

1516	42c. Type **608**	1·60	1·75
1517	42c. Claude Provost, Terry Sawchuck and team badges	1·60	1·75
1518	42c. Hockey mask, gloves and modern player	1·60	1·75

609 Companion of the Order of Canada Insignia

1992. 25th Anniv of the Order of Canada and Daniel Roland Michener (former Governor-General) Commermoration. Multicoloured.

1519	42c. Type **609**	1·40	1·75
1520	42c. Daniel Roland Michener	1·40	1·75

1992. 50th Anniv of Second World War (4th issue). As T **574.**

1521	42c. black, silver & brown	2·25	2·50
1522	42c. black, silver & green	2·25	2·50
1523	42c. black, silver & brown	2·25	2·50
1524	42c. black, silver and blue	2·25	2·50

DESIGNS: No. 1521, Reporters and soldier, 1942; 1522, Consolidated Liberator bombers over Newfoundland; 1523 Dieppe raid; 1524, U-boat sinking merchant ship.

610 Estonian Jõuluvana

1992. Christmas. Multicoloured.

1525	37c. North American Santa Claus (35×21 mm)	1·10	80
1526	42c. Type **610**	40	20
1527	48c. Italian La Befana	1·50	2·25
1528	84c. German Weihnachtsmann	2·25	3·25

611 Adelaide Hoodless (women's movement pioneer)

1993. Prominent Canadian Women. Multicoloured.

1529	43c. Type **611**	1·10	1·50
1530	43c. Marie-Josephine Gerin-Lajoie (social reformer)	1·10	1·50
1531	43c. Pitseolak Ashoona (Inuit artist)	1·10	1·50
1532	43c. Helen Kinnear (lawyer)	1·10	1·50

612 Ice Hockey Players with Cup

1993. Centenary of Stanley Cup.

1533	**612**	43c. multicoloured	1·00	60

613 Coverlet, New Brunswick

1993. Hand-crafted Textiles. Multicoloured.

1534	43c. Type **613**	1·50	2·00
1535	43c. Pieced quilt, Ontario	1·50	2·00
1536	43c. Doukhobor bedcover, Saskatchewan	1·50	2·00
1537	43c. Ceremonial robe, Kwakwaka'wakw	1·50	2·00
1538	43c. Boutonne coverlet, Quebec	1·50	2·00

1993. Canadian Art (6th series). As T **550.** Multicoloured.

1539	86c. *The Owl* (Kenojuak Ashevak)	2·25	3·25

614 Empress Hotel, Victoria

1993. Historic Hotels. Multicoloured.

1540	43c. Type **614**	60	1·10
1541	43c. Banff Springs Hotel	60	1·10
1542	43c. Royal York Hotel, Toronto	60	1·10
1543	43c. Le Chateau Frontenac, Quebec	60	1·10
1544	43c. Algonquin Hotel, St. Andrews	60	1·10

615 Algonquin Park, Ontario

1993. Canada Day. Provincial and Territorial Parks. Multicoloured.

1545	43c. Type **615**	70	80
1546	43c. De La Gaspesie Park, Quebec	70	80
1547	43c. Cedar Dunes Park, Prince Edward Island	70	80
1548	43c. Cape St. Mary's Seabird Reserve, Newfoundland	70	80
1549	43c. Mount Robson Park, British Columbia	70	80
1550	43c. Writing-on-Stone Park, Alberta	70	80
1551	43c. Spruce Woods Park, Manitoba	70	80
1552	43c. Herschel Island Park, Yukon	70	80
1553	43c. Cypress Hills Park, Saskatchewan	70	80
1554	43c. The Rocks Park, New Brunswick	70	80
1555	43c. Blomidon Park, Nova Scotia	70	80
1556	43c. Katannilik Park, Northwest Territories	70	80

616 Toronto Skyscrapers

1993. Bicentenary of Toronto.

1557	**616**	43c. multicoloured	1·00	70

1993. Canadian Rivers (3rd series). As T **592.** Multicoloured.

1558	43c. Fraser River	80	1·10
1559	43c. Yukon River	80	1·10
1560	43c. Red River	80	1·10
1561	43c. St. Lawrence River	80	1·10
1562	43c. St. John River	80	1·10

617 Taylor's Steam Buggy, 1867

1993. Historic Automobiles (1st issue). Sheet 177×125 mm, containing T **617** and similar horiz designs. Multicoloured.
MS1563 43c. Type **617**; 43c. Russel Model L touring car, 1908; 49c. Ford Model T touring car, 1914 (43×22 mm); 49c. Studebaker Champion Deluxe Starlight coupe, 1950 (43×22 mm); 86c. McLaughlin-Buick 28–496 special, 1928 (43×22 mm); 86c. Gray-Dort 25 SM luxury sedan, 1923 (43×22 mm) ... 7·50 ... 8·00

See also Nos. **MS**1611, **MS**1636 and **MS**1683/4.

618 *The Alberta Homesteader*

1993. Folk Songs. Multicoloured.
1564	43c. Type **618**	70	1·00
1565	43c. *Les Raftmans* (Quebec)	70	1·00
1566	43c. *I'se the B'y that Builds the Boat* (Newfoundland)	70	1·00
1567	43c. *Onkwa:ri Tenhanonniahkwe* (Mohawk Indian)	70	1·00

1993. Prehistoric Canada (3rd series). Dinosaurs. As T **582** but 40×28 mm. Multicoloured.
1568	43c. Massospondylus	80	80
1569	43c. Stryacosaurus	80	80
1570	43c. Albertosaurus	80	80
1571	43c. Platecarpus	80	80

619 Polish Swiety Mikolaj

1993. Christmas. Multicoloured.
1572	38c. North American Santa Claus (35×22 mm)	90	90
1573	43c. Type **619**	55	20
1574	49c. Russian Ded Moroz	1·10	1·40
1575	86c. Australian Father Christmas	1·90	2·75

1993. 50th Anniv of Second World War (5th issue). As T **574**.
1576	43c. black, silver and green	2·25	2·25
1577	43c. black, silver and blue	2·25	2·25
1578	43c. black, silver and blue	2·25	2·25
1579	43c. black, silver and brown	2·25	2·25

DESIGNS: No. 1576, Loading munitions for Russia, 1943; No. 1577, Loading bombs on Avro Lancaster; No. 1578, Escorts attacking U-boat; No. 1579, Infantry advancing, Italy.

620 (face value at right)

1994. Self-adhesive Greetings stamps. Mult.
1580	43c. Type **620**	1·00	1·00
1581	43c. As Type **620** but face value at left	1·00	1·00

It was intended that the sender should insert an appropriate greetings label into the circular space on each stamp before use.
For 45c. values in this design see Nos. 1654/5.

621 Jeanne Sauve

1994. Jeanne Sauve (former Governor-General) Commemoration.
1582	**621**	43c. multicoloured	60	60

622 Timothy Eaton, Toronto Store of 1869 and Merchandise

1994. 125th Anniv of T. Eaton Company Ltd (department store group).
1583	**622**	43c. multicoloured	55	75

1994. Canadian Rivers (4th series). As T **592**, but horiz. Multicoloured.
1584	43c. Saguenay River	80	90
1585	43c. French River	80	90
1586	43c. Mackenzie River	80	90
1587	43c. Churchill River	80	90
1588	43c. Columbia River	80	90

1994. Canadian Art (7th series). As T **550**. Multicoloured.
1589	88c. *Vera* (detail) (Frederick Varley)	1·50	2·00

623 Lawn Bowls

1994. 15th Commonwealth Games, Victoria. Multicoloured.
1590	43c. Type **623**	50	70
1591	43c. Lacrosse	50	70
1592	43c. Wheelchair race	50	70
1593	43c. High jumping	50	70
1594	50c. Diving	50	55
1595	88c. Cycling	2·25	2·00

624 Mother and Baby

1994. International Year of the Family. Sheet 178×134 mm, containing T **624** and similar vert designs. Multicoloured.
MS1596 43c. Type **624**; 43c. Family outing; 43c. Grandmother and granddaughter; 43c. Computer class; 43c. Play group, nurse with patient and female lawyer ... 3·00 ... 3·50

625 Big Leaf Maple Tree

1994. Canada Day. Maple Trees. Multicoloured.
1597	43c. Type **625**	80	90
1598	43c. Sugar maple	80	90
1599	43c. Silver maple	80	90
1600	43c. Striped maple	80	90
1601	43c. Norway maple	80	90
1602	43c. Manitoba maple	80	90
1603	43c. Black maple	80	90
1604	43c. Douglas maple	80	90
1605	43c. Mountain maple	80	90
1606	43c. Vine maple	80	90
1607	43c. Hedge maple	80	90
1608	43c. Red maple	80	90

626 Billy Bishop (fighter ace) and Nieuport 17

1994. Birth Centenaries. Multicoloured.
1609	43c. Type **626**	1·00	1·25
1610	43c. Mary Travers ("La Bolduc") (singer) and musicians	1·00	1·25

1994. Historic Automobiles (2nd issue). Sheet 177×125 mm, containing horiz designs as T **617**. Multicoloured.
MS1611 43c. Ford Model F60L-AMB military ambulance, 1942–43; 43c. Winnipeg police wagon, 1925; 50c. Sicard snowblower, 1927 (43×22 mm); 50c. Bickle Chieftain fire engine, 1936 (43×22 mm); 88c. St. John Railway Company tramcar No. 40, 1894 (51×22 mm); 88c. Motor Coach Industries Courier 50 Skyview coach, 1950 (51×22 mm) ... 10·00 ... 10·00

No. **MS**1611 was sold in a protective pack.

627 Symbolic Aircraft, Radar Screen and Clouds

1994. 50th Anniv of ICAO.
1612	**627**	43c. multicoloured	1·00	70

1994. Prehistoric Canada (4th series). Mammals. As T **582**, but 40×28 mm. Multicoloured.
1613	43c. Coryphodon	2·00	2·00
1614	43c. Megacerops	2·00	2·00
1615	43c. Arctodus simus (bear)	2·00	2·00
1616	43c. Mammuthus primigenius (mammoth)	2·00	2·00

628 Carol Singing around Christmas Tree

1994. Christmas. Multicoloured.
1617	(–)c. Carol singer (35×21 mm)	65	75
1618	43c. Type **628**	50	20
1619	50c. Choir (vert)	1·00	1·40
1620	88c. Couple carol singing in snow (vert)	2·25	3·25

No. 1617 is without face value, but was intended for use as a 38c. on internal greetings cards posted before 31 January 1995. The design shows a barcode at left.

1994. 50th Anniv of Second World War (6th issue). As T **574**.
1621	43c. black, silver and green	2·25	2·25
1622	43c. black, silver and red	2·25	2·25
1623	43c. black, silver and blue	2·25	2·25
1624	43c. black, silver and grey	2·25	2·25

DESIGNS: No. 1621, D-Day landings, Normandy; No. 1622, Canadian artillery, Normandy; No. 1623, Hawker Typhoons on patrol; No. 1624, Canadian infantry and disabled German self-propelled gun, Walcheren.

1995. 50th Anniv of Second World War (7th issue). As T **574**.
1625	43c. black, silver and purple	2·25	2·25
1626	43c. black, silver and brown	2·25	2·25
1627	43c. black, silver and green	2·25	2·25
1628	43c. black, silver and blue	2·25	2·25

DESIGNS: No. 1625, Returning troop ship; 1626, Canadian P.O.W.s celebrating freedom; 1627, Canadian tank liberating Dutch town; 1628, Parachute drop in support of Rhine Crossing.

1995. Canadian Art (8th series). As T **550**. Multicoloured.
1629	88c. *Floraison* (Alfred Pellan)	1·50	2·25

629 Flag and Lake

1995. 30th Anniv of National Flag. No face value.
1630	**629**	(43c.) multicoloured	1·00	50

630 Louisbourg Harbour

1995. 275th Anniv of Fortress of Louisbourg. Multicoloured.
1631	(43c.) Type **630**	70	80
1632	(43c.) Barracks (32×29 mm)	70	80
1633	(43c.) King's Bastion (40×29 mm)	70	80

1634	(43c.) Site of King's Garden, convent and hospital (56×29 mm)	70	80
1635	(43c.) Site of coastal fortifications	70	80

1995. Historic Automobiles (3rd issue). Sheet 177×125 mm, containing horiz designs as T **617**. Multicoloured.
MS1636 43c. Cockshutt "30" farm tractor, 1950; 43c. Bombadier "Ski-Doo Olympique 335" snowmobile, 1970; 50c. Bombadier "B-12 CS" multi-passenger snowmobile, 1948 (43×22 mm); 50c. Gotfredson "Model 20" farm truck, 1924 (43×22 mm); 88c. Robin-Nodwell "RN 110" tracked carrier, 1962 (43×22 mm); 88c. Massey-Harris "No. 21" self-propelled combine-harvester, 1942 (43×22 mm) ... 7·00 ... 7·50

No. **MS**1636 was sold in a protective pack.

631 Banff Springs Golf Club, Alberta

1995. Centenaries of Canadian Amateur Golf Championship and of the Royal Canadian Golf Association. Multicoloured.
1637	43c. Type **631**	80	80
1638	43c. Riverside Country Club, New Brunswick	80	80
1639	43c. Glen Abbey Golf Club, Ontario	80	80
1640	43c. Victoria Golf Club, British Columbia	80	80
1641	43c. Royal Montreal Golf Club, Quebec	80	80

632 *October Gold* (Franklin Carmichael)

1995. Canada Day. 75th Anniv of Group of Seven (artists). Miniature sheets, each 180×80 mm, containing square designs as T **632**. Multicoloured.
MS1642a 43c. Type **632**; 43c. *From the North Shore, Lake Superior* (Lawren Harris); 43c. *Evening, Les Eboulements* (A. Jackson) ... 3·00 ... 3·50
MS1642b 43c. *Serenity, Lake of the Woods* (Frank Johnston); 43c. *A September Gale, Georgian Bay* (Arthur Lismer); 43c. *Falls, Montreal River* (J. E. H. MacDonald); 43c. *Open Window* (Frederick Varley) ... 3·00 ... 3·50
MS1642c 43c. *Mill Houses* (Alfred Casson); 43c. *Pembina Valley* (Lionel FitzGerald); 43c. *The Lumberjack* (Edwin Holgate) ... 3·00 ... 3·50

The three sheets were sold together in an envelope which also includes a small descriptive booklet.

633 Academy Building and Ship Plan

1995. Centenary of Lunenburg Academy.
1643	**633**	43c. multicoloured	50	45

634 Aspects of Manitoba

1995. 125th Anniv of Manitoba as Canadian Province.
1644	**634**	43c. multicoloured	50	45

635 Monarch Butterfly

1995. Migratory Wildlife. Multicoloured.

1645	45c. Type **635**	1·10	1·40
1646	45c. Belted kingfisher*	1·10	1·40
1647	45c. Belted kingfisher*	1·10	1·40
1648	45c. Pintail	1·10	1·40
1649	45c. Hoary bat	1·10	1·40

*No. 1646: Inscr "aune migratrice" in error. No. 1647: Inscr corrected to "faune migratrice".

636 Quebec Railway Bridge

1995. 20th World Road Congress, Montreal. Bridges. Multicoloured.

1650	45c. Type **636**	2·25	2·25
1651	45c. 401-403-410 Interchange, Mississauga	2·25	2·25
1652	45c. Hartland Bridge, New Brunswick	2·25	2·25
1653	45c. Alex Fraser Bridge, British Columbia	2·25	2·25

1995. Self-adhesive Greetings stamps. As T **620**. Multicoloured. Imperf.

1654	45c. Face value at right	60	75
1655	45c. Face value at left	60	75

It is intended the sender should insert an appropriate greetings label into the circular space on each stamp before use.

637 Mountain, Baffin Island, Polar Bear and Caribou

1995. 50th Anniv of Arctic Institute of North America. Multicoloured.

1656	45c. Type **637**	1·00	1·25
1657	45c. Arctic poppy, Auyuittuq National Park and cargo canoe	1·00	1·25
1658	45c. Inuk man and igloo	1·00	1·25
1659	45c. Ogilvie Mountains, dog team and ski-equipped airplane	1·00	1·25
1660	45c. Inuit children	1·00	1·25

638 Superman

1995. Comic Book Superheroes. Multicoloured.

1661	45c. Type **638**	80	90
1662	45c. Johnny Canuck	80	90
1663	45c. Nelvana	80	90
1664	45c. Captain Canuck	80	90
1665	45c. Fleur de Lys	80	90

639 Prime Minister MacKenzie King signing U.N. Charter, 1945

1995. 50th Anniv of United Nations.

1666	**639**	45c. multicoloured	75	50

640 *The Nativity*

1995. Christmas. Sculptured Capitals from Ste.-Anne-de-Beaupre Basilica designed by Emile Brunet (Nos. 1668/70). Multicoloured.

1667	40c. Sprig of holly (35×22 mm)	85	70
1668	45c. Type **640**	50	20
1669	52c. *The Annunciation*	1·60	1·60
1670	90c. *The Flight to Egypt*	2·25	2·75

641 World Map and Emblem

1995. 25th Anniv of La Francophonie and The Agency for Cultural and Technical Co-operation.

1671	**641**	45c. multicoloured	60	50

642 Concentration Camp Victims, Uniform and Identity Card

1995. 50th Anniv of the End of The Holocaust.

1672	**642**	45c. multicoloured	70	50

643 American Kestrel

1996. Birds (1st series). Multicoloured.

1673	45c. Type **643**	1·90	1·75
1674	45c. Atlantic puffin	1·90	1·75
1675	45c. Pileated woodpecker	1·90	1·75
1676	45c. Ruby-throated hummingbird	1·90	1·75

See also Nos. 1717/20, 1779/82, 1865/8, 1974/7 and 2058/61.

644 *Louis R. Desmarais* (tanker), Three-dimensional Map and Radar Screen

1996. High Technology Industries. Multicoloured.

1677	45c. Type **644**	65	1·00
1678	45c. Canadair Challenger 601-3R, jet engine and navigational aid	65	1·00
1679	45c. Map of North America and eye	65	1·00
1680	45c. Genetic engineering experiment and Canola (plant)	65	1·00

1996. Canadian Art (9th series). As T **550**. Multicoloured.

1681	90c. *The Spirit of Haida Gwaii* (sculpture) (Bill Reid)	1·40	2·25

645 *One World, One Hope* (Joe Average)

1996. 11th International Conference on AIDS, Vancouver.

1682	**645**	45c. multicoloured	70	70

1996. Historic Automobiles (4th issue). Sheet 177×125 mm, containing horiz designs as T **617**. Multicoloured.

MS1683 45c. Still Motor Co electric van, 1899; 45c. Waterous Engine Works steam roller, 1914; 52c. International D.35 delivery truck, 1938; 52c. Champion road grader, 1936; 90c. White Model WA 122 articulated lorry, 1947 (51×22 mm); 90c. Hayes HDX 45-115 logging truck, 1975 (51×22 mm) — 7·50 8·00

No. MS1683 also includes the "CAPEX '96" International Stamp Exhibition logo on the sheet margin and was sold in a protective pack.

1996. "CAPEX '96" International Stamp Exhibitiion, Toronto. Sheet 368×182 mm, containing horiz designs as Nos. MS1563, MS1611, MS1636 and MS1683, but with different face values, and one new design (45c.).

MS1684 5c. Bombadier "Ski–Doo Olympique 335" snowmobile, 1970; 5c. Cockshutt "30" farm tractor, 1950; 5c. Type **617**; 5c. Ford "Model F160L-AMB" military ambulance, 1942; 5c. Still Motor Co electric van, 1895; 5c. International "D.35" delivery truck, 1936; 5c. Russel "Model L" touring car, 1908; 5c. Winnipeg police wagon, 1925; 5c. Waterous Engine Works steam roller, 1914; 5c. Champion road grader, 1936; 10c. White "Model WA 122" articulated lorry, 1947 (51×22 mm); 10c. St. John Railway Company tramcar, 1894 (51×22 mm); 10c. Hayes "HDX 45-115" logging truck, 1975 (51×22 mm); 10c. Motor Couch Industries "Courier 50 Skyview" coach, 1950 (51×22 mm); 20c. Ford "Model T" touring car, 1914 (43×22 mm); 20c. McLaughlin-Buick "28-496 special", 1928 (43×22 mm); 20c. Bombadier "B-12 CS" multi-passenger snowmobile, 1948 (43×22 mm); 20c. Robin-Nodwell "RN 110" tracked carrier, 1962 (43×22 mm); 20c. Studebaker "Champion Deluxe Starlight" coupe, 1950 (43×22 mm); 20c. Gray-Dort "25 SM" luxury sedan, 1923 (43×22 mm); 20c. Gotfredson "Model 20" farm truck, 1924 (43×22 mm); 20c. Massey-Harris "No. 21" self-propelled combine-harvester, 1942 (43×22 mm); 20c. Bickle "Chieftain" fire engine, 1936 (43×22 mm); 20c. Sicard snowblower, 1927 (43×22 mm); 45c. Bricklin "SV-1" sports car, 1975 (51×22 mm) — 8·00 9·00

The price quoted for No. **MS1684** is for a folded example.

646 Skookum Jim Mason and Bonanza Creek

1996. Centenary of Yukon Gold Rush. Multicoloured.

1685	45c. Type **646**	80	1·00
1686	45c. Prospector and boats on Lake Laberge	80	1·00
1687	45c. Superintendent Sam Steele (N.W.M.P.) and U.S.A.–Canada border	80	1·00
1688	45c. Dawson saloon	80	1·00
1689	45c. Miner with rocker box and sluice	80	1·00

647 Patchwork Quilt Maple Leaf

1996. Canada Day. Self-adhesive. Imperf.

1690	**647**	45c. multicoloured	1·00	60

648 Ethel Catherwood (high jump), 1928

1996. Canadian Olympic Gold Medal Winners. Multicoloured.

1691	45c. Type **648**	70	85
1692	45c. Etienne Desmarteau (56lb weight throw), 1904	70	85
1693	45c. Fanny Rosenfeld (400 m relay), 1928	70	85
1694	45c. Gerald Ouellette (small bore rifle, prone), 1956	70	85
1695	45c. Percy Williams (100 and 200 m), 1928	70	85

649 Indian Totems, City Skyline, Forest and Mountains

1996. 125th Anniv of British Columbia.

1696	**649**	45c. multicoloured	50	50

650 Canadian Heraldic Symbols

1996. 22nd International Congress of Genealogical and Heraldic Sciences, Ottawa.

1697	**650**	45c. multicoloured	50	50

651 *L'Arivee d'un Train en Gare* (1896)

1996. Centenary of Cinema. Two sheets, each 180×100 mm, containing T **651** and similar vert designs. Multicoloured. Self-adhesive.

MS1698a 45c. Type **651**; 45c. *God's Country* (1919); 45c. *"Hen Hop"* (1942); 45c. *Pour la Suite du Monde* (1963); 45c. *Goin' Down the Road* (1970). — 4·25 4·75

MS1698b 45c. *"Mon Oncle Antoine"* (1971); 45c. *The Apprenticeship of Duddy Kravitz* (1974); 45c. *Les Ordres* (1974); 45c. *Les Bons Debarras* (1980); 45c. *The Grey Fox* (1982) — 4·25 4·75

The two sheets were sold together in an envelope with a descriptive booklet.

652 Interlocking Jigsaw Pieces and Hands

1996. Literacy Campaign.

1699	**652**	45c. +5c. mult	85	1·00

653 Edouard Montpetit and Montreal University

1996. Edouard Montpetit (academic) Commem.

1700	**653**	45c. multicoloured	50	50

654 Winnie and Lt. Colebourn, 1914

1996. Stamp Collecting Month. *Winnie the Pooh.* Multicoloured.

1701	45c. Type **654**	1·75	1·50
1702	45c. Christopher Robin Milne and teddy bear, 1925	1·75	1·50
1703	45c. Illustration from *Winnie the Pooh*, 1926	1·75	1·50
1704	45c. Winnie the Pooh at Walt Disney World, 1996	1·75	1·50
MS1705	152×112 mm. Nos 1701/4	6·25	6·50

655 Margaret Laurence

1996. Canadian Authors.

1706	**655**	45c. multicoloured	80	1·40
1707	-	45c. black, grey and red	80	1·40

1708	-	45c. multicoloured	80	1·40
1709	-	45c. multicoloured	80	1·40
1710	-	45c. multicoloured	80	1·40

DESIGNS: No. 1707, Donald G. Creighton; 1708, Gabrielle Roy; 1709, Felix-Antoine Savard; 1710, Thomas C. Haliburton.

656 Children tobogganing

1996. Christmas. 50th Anniv of UNICEF. Multicoloured.

1711	45c. Type **656**	50	20
1712	52c. Father Christmas skiing	70	1·00
1713a	90c. Couple ice-skating	1·25	2·00

657 Head of Ox

1997. Chinese New Year ("Year of the Ox").

1714	**657**	45c. multicoloured	85	90
MS1715 155×75 mm. No. 1714×2			2·00	2·50

No. **MS**1715 is an extended fan shape with overall measurements as quoted.

1997. "HONG KONG '97" International Stamp Exhibition. As No. **MS**1715, but with exhibition logo added to the sheet margin in gold.

MS1716 155×75 mm. No. 1714×2	6·50	7·50

1997. Birds (2nd series). As T **643**. Multicoloured.

1717	45c. Mountain bluebird	1·25	1·40
1718	45c. Western grebe	1·25	1·40
1719	45c. Northern gannet	1·25	1·40
1720	45c. Scarlet tanager	1·25	1·40

1997. Canadian Art (10th series). As T **550**. Multicoloured.

1721	90c. *York Boat on Lake Winnipeg, 1930* (Walter Phillips)	1·50	2·25

658 Man and Boy with Bike, and A. J. and J. W. Billes (company founders)

1997. 75th Anniv of the Canadian Tire Corporation.

1722	**658**	45c. multicoloured	80	70

659 Abbe Charles-Emile Gadbois

1997. Abbe Charles-Emile Gadbois (musicologist) Commemoration.

1723	**659**	45c. multicoloured	60	50

660 Blue Poppy

1997. "Quebec in Bloom" International Floral Festival.

1724	**660**	45c. multicoloured	75	55

661 Nurse attending Patient

1997. Centenary of Victorian Order of Nurses.

1725	**661**	45c. multicoloured	1·25	50

662 Osgoode Hall and Seal of Law School

1997. Bicentenary of Law Society of Upper Canada.

1726	**662**	45c. multicoloured	75	50

663 Great White Shark

1997. Ocean Fishes. Multicoloured.

1727	45c. Type **663**	1·00	1·25
1728	45c. Pacific halibut	1·00	1·25
1729	45c. Common sturgeon	1·00	1·25
1730	45c. Blue-finned tuna	1·00	1·25

664 Lighthouse and Confederation Bridge

1997. Opening of Confederation Bridge, Northumberland Strait. Multicoloured.

1731	45c. Type **664**	1·40	1·00
1732	45c. Confederation Bridge and great blue heron	1·40	1·00

665 Gilles Villeneuve in Ferrari T-3

1997. 15th Death Anniv of Gilles Villeneuve (racing car driver). Multicoloured.

1733	45c. Type **665**	1·00	60
1734	90c. Villeneuve in Ferrari T-4	2·00	2·25
MS1735 203×115 mm. Nos. 1733/4 each × 4		8·00	8·00

666 Globe and the *Matthew*

1997. 500th Anniv of John Cabot's Discovery of North America.

1736	**666**	45c. multicoloured	1·00	55

667 Sea to Sky Highway, British Columbia, and Skier

1997. Scenic Highways (1st series). Multicoloured.

1737	45c. Type **667**	1·25	1·40
1738	45c. Cabot Trail, Nova Scotia, and rug-making	1·25	1·40
1739	45c. Wine route, Ontario, and glasses of wine	1·25	1·40
1740	45c. Highway 34, Saskatchewan, and cowboy	1·25	1·40

See also Nos. 1810/13 and 1876/9.

668 Kettle, Ski-bike, Lounger and Plastic Cases

1997. 20th Congress of International Council of Societies for Industrial Design.

1741	**668**	45c. multicoloured	60	50

669 Caber Thrower, Bagpiper, Drummer and Highland Dancer

1997. 50th Anniv of Glengarry Highland Games, Ontario.

1742	**669**	45c. multicoloured	1·00	50

670 Knights of Columbus Emblem

1997. Centenary of Knights of Columbus (welfare charity) in Canada.

1743	**670**	45c. multicoloured	50	50

671 Postal and Telephone Workers with PTTI Emblem

1997. 28th World Congress of Postal, Telegraph and Telephone International Staff Federation, Montreal.

1744	**671**	45c. multicoloured	50	50

672 CYAP Logo

1997. Canada's Year of Asia Pacific.

1745	**672**	45c. multicoloured	1·00	50

673 Paul Henderson celebrating Goal

1997. 25th Anniv of Canada–U.S.S.R. Ice Hockey Series. Multicoloured.

1746	45c. Type **673**	1·25	1·25
1747	45c. Canadian team celebrating	1·25	1·25

674 Martha Black

1997. Federal Politicians. Multicoloured.

1748	45c. Type **674**	70	1·00
1749	45c. Lionel Chevrier	70	1·00
1750	45c. Judy LaMarsh	70	1·00
1751	45c. Real Caouette	70	1·00

675 Vampire and Bat

1997. The Supernatural. Centenary of Publication of Bram Stoker's *Dracula*. Multicoloured.

1752	45c. Type **675**	65	85
1753	45c. Werewolf	65	85
1754	45c. Ghost	65	85
1755	45c. Goblin	65	85

676 Grizzly Bear

1997. Fauna. Multicoloured.

1756	$1 Great northern diver ("Loon") (47×39 mm) (27.10.98)	1·00	90
1757	$1 White-tailed deer (47×39 mm) (20.10.05)	1·50	1·50
1758	$1 Atlantic walrus (47×39 mm) (20.10.05)	1·50	1·50
1759	$2 Polar bear (47×39 mm) (27.10.98)	2·25	1·75
1760	$2 Peregrine falcon (47×39 mm) (19.12.05)	2·25	2·50
1761	$2 Sable Island horse (mare and foal) (47×39 mm) (19.12.05)	2·25	2·50
1762	$5 Moose (19.12.03)	8·00	7·00
1762b	$8 Type **676**	9·00	9·00
1762c	$10 Blue whale (128×49 mm) (4.10.2010)	9·00	9·00
MS1762d Two sheets, each 155×130 mm. (a) Nos. 1757/8, each ×2. (b) Nos. 1760/1, each ×2		10·00	10·50

677 *Our Lady of the Rosary* (detail, Holy Rosary Cathedral, Vancouver)

1997. Christmas. Stained Glass Windows. Multicoloured.

1763a	45c. Type **677**	50	40
1764	52c. *Nativity* (detail, Leith United Church, Ontario)	60	65
1765	90c. *Life of the Blessed Virgin* (detail, St. Stephen's Ukrainian Catholic Church, Calgary)	1·00	1·40

678 Livestock and Produce

1997. 75th Anniv of Royal Agricultural Winter Fair, Toronto.

1766	**678**	45c. multicoloured	1·50	55

679 Tiger

1998. Chinese New Year ("Year of the Tiger").

1767	**679**	45c. multicoloured	60	50
MS1768 130×110 mm. As No. 1767×2			1·25	1·50

No. **MS**1768 is diamond-shaped with overall measurements as quoted.

680 John Robarts (Ontario, 1961–71)

1998. Canadian Provincial Premiers. Multicoloured.

1769	45c. Type **680**	65	75
1770	45c. Jean Lesage (Quebec, 1960–66)	65	75
1771	45c. John McNair (New Brunswick, 1940–52)	65	75
1772	45c. Tommy Douglas (Saskatchewan, 1944–61)	65	75
1773	45c. Joseph Smallwood (Newfoundland, 1949–72)	65	75
1774	45c. Angus MacDonald (Nova Scotia, 1933–40, 1945–54)	65	75
1775	45c. W. A. C. Bennett (British Columbia, 1960–66)	65	75
1776	45c. Ernest Manning (Alberta, 1943–68)	65	75
1777	45c. John Bracken (Manitoba, 1922–43)	65	75
1778	45c. J. Walter Jones (Prince Edward Island, 1943–53)	65	75

1998. Birds (3rd series). As T 643. Multicoloured.

1779		45c. Hairy woodpecker	1·40	1·25
1780		45c. Great crested flycatcher	1·40	1·25
1781		45c. Eastern screech owl	1·40	1·25
1782		45c. Rosy finch ("Gray-crowned Rosy-finch")	1·40	1·25

681 Maple Leaf

1998. Self-adhesive Automatic Cash Machine Stamps. Imperf.

1783	681	45c. multicoloured	45	40

For stamps in this design, but without "POSTAGE POSTES" at top left see Nos. 1836/40.

682 Coquihalla Orange Fly

1998. Fishing Flies. Multicoloured.

1784	45c. Type **682**	90	90
1785	45c. Steelhead Bee	90	90
1786	45c. Dark Montreal	90	90
1787	45c. Lady Amherst	90	90
1788	45c. Coho Blue	90	90
1789	45c. Cosseboom Special	90	90

683 Mineral Excavation, Oil Rig and Pickaxe

1998. Centenary of Canadian Institute of Mining, Metallurgy and Petroleum.

1790	683	45c. multicoloured	70	50

684 1898 2c. Imperial Penny Postage Stamp and Postmaster General Sir William Mulock

1998. Centenary of Imperial Penny Postage.

1791	684	45c. multicoloured	1·00	55

685 Two Sumo Wrestlers

1998. First Canadian Sumo Basho (tournament), Vancouver. Multicoloured.

1792	45c. Type **685**	65	75
1793	45c. Sumo wrestler in ceremonial ritual	65	75
MS1794	84×152 mm. Nos. 1792/3	1·25	1·50

686 St. Peters Canal, Nova Scotia

1998. Canadian Canals. Multicoloured.

1795	45c. Type **686**	1·10	1·25
1796	45c. St. Ours Canal, Quebec	1·10	1·25
1797	45c. Port Carling Lock, Ontario	1·10	1·25
1798	45c. Lock on Rideau Canal, Ontario	1·10	1·25
1799	45c. Towers and platform of Peterborough Lift Lock, Trent–Severn Waterway, Ontario	1·10	1·25
1800	45c. Chambly Canal, Quebec	1·10	1·25
1801	45c. Lachine Canal, Quebec	1·10	1·25
1802	45c. Rideau Canal in winter, Ontario	1·10	1·25
1803	45c. Boat on Big Chute incline railway, Trent–Severn Waterway, Ontario	1·10	1·25
1804	45c. Sault Ste. Marie Canal, Ontario	1·10	1·25

687 Staff of Aesculapius and Cross

1998. Canadian Health Professionals.

1805	687	45c. multicoloured	1·00	55

688 Policeman of 1873 and Visit to Indian Village

1998. 125th Anniv of Royal Canadian Mounted Police. Multicoloured.

1806	45c. Type **688**	90	75
1807	45c. Policewoman of 1998 and aspects of modern law enforcement	90	75
MS1808	160×102 mm. Nos. 1806/7	1·75	1·90

689 William J. Roue (designer) and *Bluenose* (schooner)

1998. William James Roue (naval architect) Commemoration.

1809	689	45c. multicoloured	70	50

1998. Scenic Highways (2nd series). As T 667. Multicoloured.

1810	45c. Dempster Highway, Yukon, and caribou	65	75
1811	45c. Dinosaur Trail, Alberta, and skeleton	65	75
1812	45c. River Valley Drive, New Brunswick, and fern	65	75
1813	45c. Blue Heron Route, Prince Edward Island, and lobster	65	75

690 *Painting* (Jean-Paul Riopelle)

1998. 50th Anniv of *Refus Global* (manifesto of The Automatistes group of artists). Multicoloured. Self-adhesive. Imperf.

1814	45c. Type **690**	1·10	1·10
1815	45c. *La derniere campagne de Napoleon* (Fernand Leduc) (37×31½ mm)	1·10	1·10
1816	45c. *Jet fuligineux sur noir torture* (Jean-Paul Mousseau)	1·10	1·10
1817	45c. *Le fond du garde-robe* (Pierre Gauvreau) (29½×42 mm)	1·10	1·10
1818	45c. *Joie lacustre* (Paul-Emile Borduas)	1·10	1·10
1819	45c. *Seafarers Union* (Marcelle Ferron) (36×34 mm)	1·10	1·10
1820	45c. *Le tumulte a la machoire crispee* (Marcel Barbeau) (36×34 mm)	1·10	1·10

691 Napoleon-Alexandre Comeau (naturalist)

1998. Legendary Canadians. Multicoloured.

1821	45c. Type **691**	55	75
1822	45c. Phyllis Munday (mountaineer)	55	75
1823	45c. Bill Mason (film-maker)	55	75
1824	45c. Harry Red Foster (sports commentator)	55	75

1998. Canadian Art (11th series). As T 550. Multicoloured.

1825	90c. *The Farmer's Family* (Bruno Bobak)	1·00	1·60

692 Indian Wigwam

1998. Canadian Houses. Multicoloured.

1826	45c. Type **692**	50	70
1827	45c. Settler sod hut	50	70
1828	45c. Maison Saint-Gabriel (17th-century farmhouse), Quebec	50	70
1829	45c. Queen Anne style brick house, Ontario	50	70
1830	45c. Terrace of town houses	50	70
1831	45c. Prefabricated house	50	70
1832	45c. Veterans' houses	50	70
1833	45c. Modern bungalow	50	70
1834	45c. Healthy House, Toronto	50	70

693 University of Ottawa

1998. 150th Anniv of University of Ottawa.

1835	693	45c. multicoloured	50	50

1998. As T **681**, but without "POSTAGE POSTES" at top left. Self-adhesive gum, imperf (46c.) or ordinary gum, perf (others).

1839	681	45c. multicoloured	1·25	1·25
1840	681	46c. multicoloured	1·00	1·25
1836	681	55c. multicoloured	1·75	1·75
1837	681	73c. multicoloured	1·25	1·40
1838	681	95c. multicoloured	2·25	2·25

694 Performing Animals

1998. Canadian Circus. Multicoloured.

1851	45c. Type **694**	1·25	1·25
1852	45c. Flying trapeze and acrobat on horseback	1·25	1·25
1853	45c. Lion tamer	1·25	1·25
1854	45c. Acrobats and trapeze artists	1·25	1·25
MS1855	133×133 mm. Nos. 1851/4	4·00	4·50

695 John Peters Humphrey (author of original Declaration draft)

1998. 50th Anniv of Universal Declaration of Human Rights.

1856	695	45c. multicoloured	50	50

696 H.M.C.S. *Sackville* (corvette)

1998. 75th Anniv of Canadian Naval Reserve. Multicoloured.

1857	45c. Type **696**	80	90
1858	45c. H.M.C.S. *Shawinigan* (coastal defence vessel)	80	90

697 Angel blowing Trumpet

1998. Christmas. Statues of Angels. Multicoloured.

1859	45c. Type **697**	50	20
1860b	52c. Adoring Angel	85	75
1861b	90c. Angel at prayer	1·60	2·00

698 Rabbit

1999. Chinese New Year ("Year of the Rabbit").

1862	698	46c. multicoloured	50	50
MS1863		Circular 100 mm dia. **698** 95c. mult (40×40 mm)	1·75	2·25

No. **MS**1863 also exists with the "CHINA '99" World Stamp Exhibition, Beijing, logo overprinted in gold on the top of the margin.

699 Stylized Mask and Curtain

1999. 50th Anniv of Le Theatre du Rideau Vert.

1864	699	46c. multicoloured	50	50

1999. Birds (4th series). As T 643. Multicoloured.

(a) Ordinary gum

1865	46c. Northern goshawk	85	85
1866	46c. Red-winged blackbird	85	85
1867	46c. American goldfinch	85	85
1868	46c. Sandhill crane	85	85

(b) Self-adhesive

1869	46c. Northern Goshawk	85	85
1870	46c. Red-winged Blackbird	85	85
1871	46c. American Goldfinch	85	85
1872	46c. Sandhill Crane	85	85

700 "The Raven and the First Men" (B. Reid) and The Great Hall

1999. 50th Anniv of University of British Columbia Museum of Anthropology.

1873	700	46c. multicoloured	50	50

701 *Marco Polo* (full-rigged ship)

1999. Canada–Australia Joint Issue. *Marco Polo* (emigrant ship).

1874	701	46c. multicoloured	50	50
MS1875		160×95 mm. 85c. As No. 1728 of Australia. 46c. Type **701**. (No. **MS**1875 was sold at $1.25 in Canada)	1·75	2·00

No. **MS**1875 includes the "Australia '99" emblem on the sheet margin and was postally valid in Canada to the value of 46c.

The same miniature sheet was also available in Australia.

1999. Scenic Highways (3rd series). As T 667. Multicoloured.

1876	46c. Route 132, Quebec, and hang-glider	75	85
1877	46c. Yellowhead Highway, Manitoba, and bison	75	85
1878	46c. Dempster Highway, Northwest Territories, and Indian village elder	75	85

| 1879 | 46c. The Discovery Trail, New-foundland, and whale's tailfin | 75 | 85 |

702 Inuit Children and Landscape

1999. Creation of Nunavut Territory.

| 1880 | **702** | 46c. multicoloured | 50 | 50 |

703 Elderly Couple on Country Path

1999. International Year of Older Persons.

| 1881 | **703** | 46c. multicoloured | 50 | 50 |

704 Khanda (Sikh symbol)

1999. Centenary of Sikhs in Canada.

| 1882 | **704** | 46c. multicoloured | 50 | 50 |

705 *Arethusa bulbosa* (orchid)

1999. 16th World Orchid Conference, Vancouver. Multicoloured.

1883	**705**	46c. Type **705**	75	75
1884		46c. *Amerorchis rotundifolia*	75	75
1885		46c. *Cypripedium pubescens*	75	75
1886		46c. *Platanthera psycodes*	75	75

706 Bookbinding

1999. Traditional Trades. Multicoloured.

1887	1c. Type **706**	10	10
1888	2c. Decorative ironwork	10	10
1889	3c. Glass-blowing	10	10
1890	4c. Oyster farming	10	10
1891	5c. Weaving	10	10
1892	9c. Quilting	10	10
1893	10c. Wood carving	10	15
1894	25c. Leatherworking	20	25

(b) Self-adhesive.

1895	65c. Jewellery making (horiz)	50	55
1896	77c. Basket weaving (horiz)	1·50	1·50
1897	$1.25 Wood-carving (horiz)	1·00	1·10

707 Northern Dancer (racehorse)

1999. Canadian Horses. Multicoloured. Ordinary or self-adhesive gum.

(a) Ordinary gum or self-adhesive gum

1903	46c. Type **707**	80	80
1904	46c. *Kingsway Skoal* (rodeo horse)	80	80
1905	46c. *Big Ben* (show jumper)	80	80
1906	46c. *Armbro Flight* (trotter)	80	80

708 Logo engraved on Limestone

1999. 150th Anniv of Barreau du Quebec (Quebec lawyers' association).

| 1911 | **708** | 46c. multicoloured | 50 | 50 |

1999. Canadian Art (12th series). As T **550**. Multicoloured.

| 1912 | 95c. *Coq licorne* (Jean Dallaire) | 1·25 | 1·75 |

709 Athletics

1999. 13th Pan-American Games, Winnipeg. Multicoloured.

1913	46c. Type **709**	85	90
1914	46c. Cycling	85	90
1915	46c. Swimming	85	90
1916	46c. Football	85	90

1999. "China '99" International Stamp Exhibition, Beijing. Sheet 78×133 mm, containing Nos. 1883/6. Multicoloured.

| MS1917 | 46c. Type **705**; 46c. *Amerorchis rotundifolia*; 46c. *Cypripedium pubescens*; 46c. *Platanthera psycodes* | 2·25 | 2·75 |

710 Female Rower

1999. 23rd World Rowing Championships, St. Catharines.

| 1918 | **710** | 46c. multicoloured | 50 | 50 |

711 UPU Emblem and World Map

1999. 125th Anniv of Universal Postal Union.

| 1919 | **711** | 46c. multicoloured | 75 | 50 |

712 de Havilland Mosquito F.B. VI

1999. 75th Anniv of Canadian Air Force. Multicoloured.

1920	46c. Type **712**	75	85
1921	46c. Sopwith F.1 Camel	75	85
1922	46c. de Havilland Canada DHC-3 Otter	75	85
1923	46c. de Havilland Canada CC-108 Caribou	75	85
1924	46c. Canadair CL-28 Argus Mk 2	75	85
1925	46c. Canadair (North American) F-86 Sabre 6	75	85
1926	46c. McDonnell Douglas CF-18	75	85
1927	46c. Sopwith 5.F.1 Dolphin	75	85
1928	46c. Armstrong Whitworth Siskin IIIA	75	85
1929	46c. Canadian Vickers (Northrop) Delta II	75	85
1930	46c. Sikorsky CH-124A Sea King helicopter	75	85
1931	46c. Vickers-Armstrong Wellington Mk II	75	85
1932	46c. Avro Anson Mk I	75	85
1933	46c. Canadair (Lockheed) CF-104G Starfighter	75	85
1934	46c. Burgess-Dunne	75	85
1935	46c. Avro 504K	75	85

713 Fokker DR-1

1999. 50th Anniv of Canadian International Air Show. Multicoloured.

1936	46c. Type **713**	85	90
1937	46c. H101 Salto glider	85	90
1938	46c. de Havilland DH100 Vampire Mk III	85	90
1939	46c. Wing walker on Stearman A-75	85	90

Nos. 1936/9 were printed together, se-tenant, forming a composite design which includes a nine-plane Snowbird formation of Canadair CT114 Tutor in the background.

714 NATO Emblem and National Flags

1999. 50th Anniv of North Atlantic Treaty Organization.

| 1940 | **714** | 46c. multicoloured | 1·00 | 50 |

715 Man ploughing on Book

1999. Centenary of Frontier College (workers' education organization).

| 1941 | **715** | 46c. multicoloured | 50 | 50 |

716 Master Control Sports Kite

1999. Stamp Collecting Month. Kites. Multicoloured.

1942	46c. Type **716**	55	65
1943	46c. Indian Garden Flying Carpet (irregular rectangle, 35½×32 mm)	55	65
1944	46c. Gibson Girl box kite (horiz, 38½×25 mm)	55	65
1945	46c. Dragon Centipede (oval, 39×29 mm)	55	65

717 Boy holding Dove

1999. New Millennium. Three sheets, each 108×108 mm, containing T **717** and similar square designs in blocks of 4. Self-adhesive.

MS1946	– 46c.×4 multicoloured	2·00	2·50
MS1947	717 55c.×4 multicoloured	4·50	4·75
MS1948	– 95c.×4 brown	3·75	4·50

DESIGNS: 46c. Holographic image of dove in flight; 95c. Dove with olive branch.

718 Angel playing Drum

1999. Christmas. Victorian Angels. Multicoloured.

1949	46c. Type **718**	60	20
1950	55c. Angel with toys	80	50
1951	95c. Angel with star	1·40	2·25

719 Portia White (singer)

1999. Millennium Collection (1st series). Entertainment and Arts. Miniature sheets, each 108×112 mm, containing T **719** and similar vert designs. Multicoloured.

MS1952	46c. Type **719**; 46c. Glenn Gould (pianist); 46c. Guy Lombardo (conductor of *Royal Canadians*); 46c. Félix Leclerc (musician, playwright and actor)	2·25	2·75
MS1953	46c. Artists looking at painting (Royal Canadian Academy of Arts); 46c. Cloud, stave and pencil marks (The Canada Council); 46c. Man with video camera (National Film Board of Canada); 46c. Newsreader (Canadian Broadcasting Corporation)	2·25	2·75
MS1954	46c. Calgary Stampede; 46c. Circus performers; 46c. Ice hockey (Hockey Night); 46c. Goalkeeper (Ice hockey live from The Forum)	2·25	2·75
MS1955	46c. IMAX cinema; 46c. Computer image (Softimage); 46c. Ted Rogers Sr (*Plugging in the Radio*); 46c. Sir William Stephenson (inventor of radio facsimile system)	2·25	2·75

See also Nos. **MS**1959/62, **MS**1969/73 and **MS**1982/5.

720 Millennium Partnership Programme Logo

2000. Canada Millennium Partnership Programme.

| 1956 | **720** | 46c. red, green and blue | 50 | 50 |

721 Chinese Dragon

2000. Chinese New Year ("Year of the Dragon").

| 1957 | **721** | 46c. multicoloured | 50 | 50 |
| MS1958 | 150×85 mm. **721** 90c. multicoloured | 1·25 | 1·50 |

2000. Millennium Collection (2nd series). Charities, Medical Pioneers, Peacekeepers and Social Reforms. Miniature sheets, each 108×112 mm, containing vert designs as T **719**. Multicoloured.

MS1959	46c. Providing equipment (Canadian International Development Agency); 46c. Dr. Lucille Teasdale (medical missionary); 46c. Terry Fox (Marathon of Hope); 46c. Delivering meal (Meals on Wheels)	2·25	2·50
MS1960	46c. Sir Frederick Banting (discovery of insulin); 46c. Armand Frappier (developer of BCG vaccine); 46c. Dr. Hans Selye (research into stress); 46c. *Dr. Maude Abbott* (pathologist) (M. Bell Eastlake)	2·25	2·50
MS1961	46c. Senator Raoul Dandurand (diplomat); 46c. Pauline Vanier and Elizabeth Smellie (nursing pioneers); 46c. Lester B. Pearson (diplomat); 46c. One-legged man (Ottawa Convention on Banning Landmines)	2·25	2·50
MS1962	46c. Nun and surgeon (medical care); 46c. *Women are persons* (sculpture by Barbara Paterson) (Appointment of women senators); 46c. Alphonse and Dorimène Desjardins (People's bank movement); 46c. Father Moses Coady (Adult education pioneer)	2·25	2·50

722 Wayne Gretzky (ice-hockey player)

2000. 50th National Hockey League All-Star Game. Multicoloured.

1963	46c. Type **722**	80	80
1964	46c. Gordie Howe (No. 9 in white jersey)	80	80
1965	46c. Maurice Richard (No. 9 in blue and red jersey)	80	80
1966	46c. Doug Harvey (No. 2)	80	80
1967	46c. Bobby Orr (No. 4)	80	80
1968	46c. Jacques Plante (No. 1)	80	80

See also Nos. 2052/7, 2118/23, 2178/3, 2250/5 and 2316/27.

2000. Millennium Collection (3rd series). First Inhabitants, Great Thinkers, Culture and Literary Legends, and Charitable Foundations. Miniature sheets, each 108×112 mm, containing vert designs as T **719**. Multicoloured.

MS1969	46c. Pontiac (Ottawa chief); 46c. Tom Longboat (long-distance runner); 46c. *Inuit Shaman* (sculpture by Paul Toolooktook); 46c. Shaman and patient (Indian medicine)	2·25	2·50
MS1970	46c. Prof. Marshall McLuhan (media philosopher); 46c. Northrop Frye (literary critic); 46c. Roger Lemelin (novelist); 46c. Prof. Hilda Marion Neatby (educator)	2·25	2·50
MS1971	46c. Bow of Viking longship (L'Anse aux Meadows World Heritage Site); 46c. Immigrant family (Pier 21 monument); 46c. Neptune mask (Neptune Theatre, Halifax); 46c. Auditorium and actor (The Stratford Festival)	2·25	2·50
MS1972	46c. W. O. Mitchell (writer); 46c. Gratien Gélinas (actor, producer and playwright); 46c. Text and fountain pen (Cercle du Livre de France); 46c. Harlequin and roses (Harlequin Books)	2·25	2·50
MS1973	46c. Hart Massey (Massey Foundation); 46c. Izaak Walton Killam and Dorothy Killam; 46f. Eric Lafferty Harvie (Glenbow Foundation); 46c. Macdonald Stewart Foundation	2·25	2·50

2000. Birds (5th series). As T **643**. Multicoloured

(a) Ordinary or self-adhesive gum

1974	46c. Canadian warbler	85	90
1975	46c. Osprey	85	90
1976	46c. Pacific diver ("Pacific Loon")	85	90
1977	46c. Blue jay	85	90

2000. Millennium Collection (4th series). Canadian Agriculture, Commerce and Technology. Miniature sheets, each 108×112 mm, containing vert designs as T **719**. Multicoloured.

MS1982	46c. Sir Charles Saunders (developer of Marquis wheat); 46c. Baby (Pablum baby food); 46c. Dr. Archibald Gowanlock Huntsman (frozen fish pioneer); 46c. Oven chips and field of potatoes (McCain Frozen Foods)	2·25	2·50
MS1983	46c. Early trader and Indian (Hudson's Bay Company); 46c. Satellite over earth (Bell Canada Enterprises); 46c. Jos. Louis biscuits and Vachon family (Vachon Family Bakery); 46c. Bread and eggs (George Weston Limited)	2·25	2·50
MS1984	46c. George Klein and cog wheels (inventor of electric wheelchair and micro-surgical staple gun); 46c. Abraham Gesner (developer of kerosene); 46c. Alexander Graham Bell (inventor of telephone); 46c. Joseph-Armand Bombadier (inventor of snowmobile)	2·25	2·50
MS1985	46c. Workers and steam locomotive (Rogers Pass rail tunnel); 46c. Manic 5 dam (Manicouagan River hydro-electric project); 46c. Mobile Servicing System for International Space Station (Canadian Space Program); 46c. CN Tower (World's tallest building)	2·25	2·50

723 Judges and Supreme Court Building

2000. 125th Anniv of Supreme Court of Canada.

1986	**723**	46c. multicoloured	50	50

724 Lethbridge Bridge, Synthetic Rubber Plant, X-ray of Heart Pacemaker and Microwave Radio System

2000. 75th Anniv of Ceremony for Calling of an Engineer.

1987	**724**	46c. multicoloured	50	50

Each vertical pair completes the engineer's ring as shown on Type **274**.

725

2000. "Picture Postage" Greetings Stamps. Self-adhesive.

1988	**725**	46c. multicoloured	50	50

No. 1988 was issued to include appropriate greetings labels which could be inserted into the rectangular space on each stamp.
See also Nos. 2045 and 2099.

726 Coastal-style Mailboxes in Autumn

2000. Traditional Rural Mailboxes. Multicoloured.

1989	46c. Type **726**	75	75
1990	46c. House and cow-shaped mailboxes in springtime	75	75
1991	46c. Tractor-shaped mailbox in summertime	75	75
1992	46c. Barn and duck-shaped mailboxes in winter	75	75

727 Gorge and Fir Tree

2000. Canadian Rivers and Lakes. Multicoloured. Self-adhesive.

1993	55c. Type **727**	60	65
1994	55c. Lake and water lilies	60	65
1995	55c. Glacier and reflected mountains	60	65
1996	55c. Estuary and aerial view	60	65
1997	55c. Waterfall and forest edge	60	65
1998	95c. Iceberg and mountain river	95	1·10
1999	95c. Rapids and waterfall	95	1·10
2000	95c. Moraine and river	95	1·10
2001	95c. Shallows and waves on lake	95	1·10
2002	95c. Forest sloping to waters edge and tree	95	1·10

728 Queen Elizabeth the Queen Mother with Roses

2000. Queen Elizabeth the Queen Mother's 100th Birthday.

2003	**728**	95c. multicoloured	1·40	1·40

729 Teenager with Two Children

2000. Centenary of Boys and Girls Clubs of Canada.

2004	**729**	46c. multicoloured	50	50

730 Clouds over Rockies and Symbol

2000. 57th General Conference Session of Seventh-day Adventist Church, Toronto.

2005	**730**	46c. multicoloured	50	50

731 Space Travellers and Canadian Flag (Rosalie Anne Nardelli)

2000. "Stampin' the Future" (children's stamp design competition). Multicoloured.

2006	46c. Type **731**	60	70
2007	46c. *Travelling to the Moon* (Sarah Lutgen)	60	70
2008	46c. *Astronauts in shuttle* (Andrew Wright)	60	70
2009	46c. *Children completing Canada as jigsaw* (Christine Weera)	60	70
MS2010	114×90 mm. Nos. 2006/9	2·40	3·00

732 Tall Ships, Halifax Harbour

2000. Canadian Art (13th series). As T **550**. Mult.

2011	95c. *The Artist at Niagara, 1858* (Cornelius Krieghoff)	1·25	1·75

2000. Tall Ships Race. Multicoloured. Self-adhesive.

2012	46c. Type **732**	75	85
2013	46c. Tall ships, Halifax Harbour (face value top right)	75	85

Nos. 2012/13 are arranged as five *se-tenant* pairs on a background photograph of Halifax Harbour.

733 Workers, Factory and Transport

2000. Centenary of Department of Labour.

2014	**733**	46c. multicoloured	50	50

734 Petro-Canada Sign, Oil Rig and Consumers

2000. 25th Anniv of Petro-Canada (oil company). Self-adhesive.

2015	**734**	46c. multicoloured	75	50

735 Narwhal

2000. Whales. Multicoloured.

2016	46c. Type **735**	1·40	1·40
2017	46c. Blue whale (*Balaenoptera musculus*)	1·40	1·40
2018	46c. Bowhead whale (*Balaena mysticetus*)	1·40	1·40
2019	46c. White whales (*Delphinapterus leucas*)	1·40	1·40

Nos. 2016/19 were printed together, *se-tenant*, with the backgrounds forming an overall composite design.

736

2000. "Picture Postage" Christmas Greetings. Self-adhesive.

2020	**736**	46c. multicoloured	50	50

See also Nos. 2045/9 and 2099/103.

737 *The Nativity* (Susie Matthias)

2000. Christmas. Religious Paintings by Mouth and Foot Artists. Multicoloured.

2021	46c. Type **737**	50	20
2022	55c. *The Nativity and Christmas Star* (Michael Guillemette)	65	60
2023	95c. *Mary and Joseph journeying to Bethlehem* (David Allan Carter)	1·25	1·90

738 Lieut.-Col. Sam Steele, Lord Strathcona's Horse

2000. Canadian Regiments. Multicoloured.

2024	46c. Type **738**		75	75
2025	46c. Drummer, Voltigeurs de Quebec		75	75

739 Red Fox

2000. Wildlife. Multicoloured.

2026	60c. Type **739**	65	75
2027	75c. Grey wolf	1·25	1·25
2028	$1.05 White-tailed deer	1·10	1·25

740 Maple Leaves **740a** Maple Leaves and Key **740b** Red Maple Leaf and Stem

2000. Self-adhesive.

(a) Coil stamps

2029	**740**	47c. multicoloured	1·00	1·00
2030	**740**	48c. multicoloured	1·00	1·00
2031	**740a**	49c. multicoloured	1·00	1·00
2032	**740b**	80c. multicoloured	1·10	1·10

(b) Booklet stamp

2036	**740b**	$1.40 multicoloured (green leaf)	1·90	1·90

2000. "Picture Postage" Greetings Stamps. As T **725** and **736**. Multicoloured. Self-adhesive.

2045	47c. Type **725**	55	60
2046	47c. Type **736**	55	60
2047	47c. Roses frame	55	60
2048	47c. Mahogany frame	55	60
2049	47c. Silver frame	55	60

741 Green Jade Snake

2001. Chinese New Year. ("Year of the Snake").

2050	**741**	47c. multicoloured	50	50
MS2051	112×75 mm. $1.05, Brown jade snake		1·25	1·60

2001. National Hockey League. All-Star Game Players (2nd series). As T **722**. Multicoloured.

2052	47c. Jean Beliveau (wearing No. 4)	75	75
2053	47c. Terry Sawchuk (on one knee)	75	75
2054	47c. Eddie Shore (wearing No. 2)	75	75
2055	47c. Denis Potvin (wearing No. 5)	75	75
2056	47c. Bobby Hull (wearing No. 9)	75	75
2057	47c. Syl Apps (in Toronto jersey)	75	75

See also Nos. 2118/23 and 2178/83.

2001. Birds (6th series). As T **643**. Multicoloured.

Ordinary or self-adhesive gum

2058	47c. Golden eagle	75	75
2059	47c. Arctic tern	75	75
2060	47c. Rock ptarmigan	75	75
2061	47c. Lapland bunting ("Lapland Longspur")	75	75

742 Highjumping

2001. Fourth Francophonie Games. Multicoloured.

2066	47c. Type **742**	70	70
2067	47c. Folk dancing	70	70

743 Ice Dancing

2001. World Figure Skating Championships, Vancouver. Multicoloured.

2068	47c. Type **743**	80	80
2069	47c. Pairs	80	80

2070	47c. Men's singles	80	80
2071	47c. Women's singles	80	80

744 3d. Beaver Stamp of 1851

2001. 150th Anniv of the Canadian Postal Service.

2072	**744**	47c. multicoloured	1·00	1·00

745 Toronto Blue Jay Emblem, Maple Leaf and Baseball

2001. 25th Season of the Toronto Blue Jays (baseball team). Self-adhesive.

2073	**745**	47c. multicoloured	60	70

746 North and South America on Globe

2001. Summit of the Americas, Quebec.

2074	**746**	47c. multicoloured	1·00	50

747 Butchart Gardens, British Columbia

2001. Tourist Attractions (1st series). Multicoloured. Self-adhesive.

2075	60c. Type **747**	95	1·10
2076	60c. Apple Blossom Festival, Nova Scotia	95	1·10
2077	60c. White Pass and Yukon Route	95	1·10
2078	60c. Sugar Bushes, Quebec	95	1·10
2079	60c. Court House, Niagra-on-the-Lake, Ontario	95	1·10
2080	$1.05 The Forks, Winnipeg, Manitoba	1·40	1·60
2081	$1.05 Barkerville, British Colombia	1·40	1·60
2082	$1.05 Canadian Tulip Festival, Ontario	1·40	1·60
2083	$1.05 Auyuittuq National Park, Nunavut	1·40	1·60
2084	$1.05 Signal Hill, St. John's, Newfoundland	1·40	1·60

See also Nos. 2143/52, 2205/14 and 2257/61.

748 Christ on Palm Sunday and Khachkar (stone cross)

2001. 1700th Anniv of Armenian Church.

2085	**748**	47c. multicoloured	60	70

749 Cadets, Mackenzie Building and Military Equipment

2001. 125th Anniv of Royal Military College of Canada.

2086	**749**	47c. multicoloured	70	45

750 Pole-vaulting

2001. Eighth International Amateur Athletic Federation World Championships, Edmonton. Multicoloured.

2087	47c. Type **750**	80	1·00
2088	47c. Sprinting	80	1·00

751 *Pierre Trudeau* (Myfanwy Pavelic)

2001. Pierre Trudeau (former Prime Minister) Commemoration.

2089	**751**	47c. multicoloured	60	45
MS2090	128×155 mm. No. 2090×4		2·00	2·25

752 *Morden Centennial* Rose

2001. Canadian Roses. Multicoloured.

(a) Self-adhesive

2091	47c. Type **752**	1·00	1·10
2092	47c. *Agnes*	1·00	1·10
2093	47c. *Champlain*	1·00	1·10
2094	47c. *Canadian White Star*	1·00	1·10

(b) PVA gum

MS2095	145×90 mm. Nos. 2091/4	3·50	4·00

753 Ottawa Chief Hassaki addressing Peace Delegates

2001. 300th Anniv of Great Peace Treaty of Montreal between American Indians and New France.

2096	**753**	47c. multicoloured	60	70

2001. Canadian Art (14th series). As T **550**. Multicoloured.

2097	$1.05 *The Space Between Columns 21* (Italian) (Jack Shadbolt)	1·40	1·75

754 Clown juggling with Crutches and Handicapped Boy

2001. The Shriners (charitable organization) Commemoration.

2098	**754**	47c. multicoloured	60	45

755 Toys and Flowers

2001. "Picture Postage" Greetings Stamps. Frames as Nos. 2045/7 and 2049, but each inscr "Domestic Lettermail Postes-lettres du regime interieur". Multicoloured. Self-adhesive.

2099	As Type **725**	60	60
2100	As Type **736**	60	60
2101	Type **755**	60	60
2102	Roses frame	60	60
2103	Silver frame	60	60

756 Jean Gascon and Jean-Louis Roux (founders of Theatre du Nouveau Monde, Montreal)

2001. Theatre Anniversaries. Multicoloured.

2104	47c. Type **756** (50th anniv)	65	80
2105	47c. Ambrose Small (founder of Grand Theatre, London, Ontario) (centenary)	65	80

757 Hot Air Balloons

2001. Stamp Collecting Month. Hot Air Balloons. Multicoloured, background colours given below. Self-adhesive.

2106	47c. Type **757** (green background)	80	90
2107	47c. Balloons with lavender background	80	90
2108	47c. Balloons with mauve background	80	90
2109	47c. Balloons with bistre background	80	90

758 Horse-drawn Sleigh and Christmas Lights

2001. Christmas. Festive Lights. Multicoloured.

2110	47c. Type **758**	70	20
2111	60c. Ice skaters and Christmas lights	1·00	1·00
2112	$1.05 Children with snowman and Christmas lights	1·40	1·90

759 Pattern of Ys Logo

2001. 150th Anniv of YMCA in Canada.

2113	**759**	47c. multicoloured	70	45

760 Statues from Canadian War Memorial, Ottawa and Badge

2001. 75th Anniv of Royal Canadian Legion.

2114	**760**	47c. multicoloured	70	45

761 Queen Elizabeth II and Maple Leaf

2002. Golden Jubilee.

2115	**761**	48c. multicoloured	70	45

762 Horse and Bamboo Leaves

2002. Chinese New Year ("Year of the Horse"). Multicoloured.

2116	**762**	48c. multicoloured	60	45
MS2117	102×102 mm. $1.25, Horse and peach blossom		1·40	1·75

2002. National Hockey League. All-Star Game Players (3rd series). As T **722**. Multicoloured.

2118	48c. Tim Horton (wearing Maple Leaf No. 7 jersey)	1·00	1·00
2119	48c. Guy Lafleur (wearing Canadiens No. 10 jersey)	1·00	1·00
2120	48c. Howie Morenz (wearing Canadiens jersey and brown gloves)	1·00	1·00
2121	48c. Glenn Hall (wearing Chicago Blackhawks jersey)	1·00	1·00
2122	48c. Red Kelly (wearing Maple Leaf No. 4 jersey)	1·00	1·00
2123	48c. Phil Esposito (wearing Boston Bruins No. 7 jersey)	1·00	1·00

763 Speed Skating

2002. Winter Olympic Games, Salt Lake City. Multicoloured.

2124	48c. Type **763**	75	85
2125	48c. Curling	75	85
2126	48c. Aerial skiing	75	85
2127	48c. Women's ice hockey	75	85

764 Lion Symbol of Governor General and Rideau Hall, Ottawa

2002. 50th Anniv of First Canadian Governor-General.

2128	**764**	48c. multicoloured	60	45

765 University of Manitoba (125th Anniv)

2002. Canadian Universities' Anniversaries (1st issue). Multicoloured.

2129	48c. Type **765**	85	85
2130	48c. Universite Laval, Quebec (150th anniv of charter)	85	85
2131	48c. Trinity College, Toronto (150th anniv of foundation)	85	85
2132	48c. Saint Mary's University, Halifax (bicent)	85	85

See also Nos. 2190/1, 2271/2, 2333/7, 2419, 2487 and 2544/5.

2002. Canadian Art (15th series). As T **550**. Multicoloured.

2133	$1.25 *Church and Horse* (Alex Colville)	1·40	1·60

766 *City of Vancouver* Tulip and Vancouver Skyline

2002. 50th Canadian Tulip Festival, Ottawa. Tulips. Multicoloured. Self-adhesive.

2134	48c. Type **766**	70	85
2135	48c. *Monte Carlo* and Dows Lake tulip beds	70	85
2136	48c. *Ottawa* and National War Memorial	70	85
2137	48c. *The Bishop* and Ottawa Hospital	70	85

767 *Dendronepthea gigantea* and *Dendronepthea* (coral)

2002. Canada–Hong Kong Joint Issue. Corals. Multicoloured.

2138	48c. Type **767**	70	85

2139	48c. *Tubastrea, Echinogorgia* and island	70	85
2140	48c. North Atlantic pink tree coral, Pacific orange cup and North Pacific horn coral	70	85
2141	48c. North Atlantic giant orange tree coral and black coral	70	85
MS2142	161×87 mm. Nos. 2138/41	2·25	3·00

2002. Tourist Attractions (2nd series). As T **747**. Multicoloured. Self-adhesive.

2143	65c. Yukon Quest Sled Dog Race	1·00	1·10
2144	65c. Icefields Parkway, Alberta	1·00	1·10
2145	65c. Train in Agawa Canyon, Northern Ontario	1·00	1·10
2146	65c. Old Port, Montreal	1·00	1·10
2147	65c. Saw mill, Kings Landing, New Brunswick	1·00	1·10
2148	$1.25 Northern Lights, North-west Territories	1·75	2·00
2149	$1.25 Stanley Park, British Columbia	1·75	2·00
2150	$1.25 Head-Smashed-In Buffalo Jump, Alberta	1·75	2·00
2151	$1.25 Saguenay Fjord, Quebec	1·75	2·00
2152	$1.25 Lighthouse, Peggy's Cove, Nova Scotia	1·75	2·00

768 *Embacle* (Charles Daudelin)

2002. Sculptures. Multicoloured.

| 2153 | 48c. Type **768** | 60 | 70 |
| 2154 | 48c. *Lumberjacks* (Leo Mol) | 60 | 70 |

769 1899 Queen Victoria 2c. Stamp, Stonewall Post Office and Postmark

2002. Centenary of Canadian Postmasters and Assistants Association.

| 2155 | **769** | 48c. multicoloured | 60 | 70 |

770 World Youth Day Logo

2002. 17th World Youth Day, Toronto. Self-adhesive.

| 2156 | **770** | 48c. multicoloured | 60 | 70 |

2002. "Amphilex 2002" International Stamp Exhibition, Amsterdam. Ordinary gum.

| **MS**2157 | 160×97 mm. As Nos. 2134/7 | 2·25 | 2·75 |

771 Hands gripping Rope and P.S.I. Logo

2002. Public Services International World Congress, Ottawa.

| 2158 | **771** | 48c. multicoloured | 60 | 45 |

772 Tree in Four Seasons

2002. 75th Anniv of Public Pensions.

| 2159 | **772** | 48c. multicoloured | 60 | 45 |

773 Mount Elbrus, Russia

2002. International Year of Mountains. Multicoloured. Self-adhesive.

2160	48c. Type **773**	70	85
2161	48c. Puncak Jaya, Indonesia	70	85
2162	48c. Mount Everest, Nepal	70	85
2163	48c. Mount Kilimanjaro, Tanzania	70	85
2164	48c. Vinson Massif, Antarctica	70	85
2165	48c. Mount Aconcagua, Argentina	70	85
2166	48c. Mount McKinley, U.S.A.	70	85
2167	48c. Mount Logan, Canada	70	85

774 Teacher writing on Board

2002. World Teachers' Day.

| 2168 | **774** | 48c. multicoloured | 60 | 45 |

775 Frieze from Toronto Stock Exchange and Globe

2002. 150th Anniv of Toronto Stock Exchange.

| 2169 | **775** | 48c. multicoloured | 60 | 45 |

776 Sir Sandford Fleming, Map of Canada and *Iris* (cable ship)

2002. Communications Centenaries. Multicoloured.

| 2170 | 48c. Type **776** (opening of Pacific Cable) | 65 | 75 |
| 2171 | 48c. Guglielmo Marconi, Map of Canada and wireless equipment (first Transatlantic radio message) | 65 | 75 |

777 *Genesis* (painting by Daphne Odjig)

2002. Christmas. Aboriginal Art. Multicoloured.

2172	48c. Type **777**	55	20
2173	65c. *Winter Travel* (painting by Cecil Youngfox)	70	70
2174	$1.25 *Mary and Child* (sculpture by Irene Katak Angutitaq)	1·25	1·75

778 Conductor's Hands and Original Orchestra

2002. Centenary of Quebec Symphony Orchestra.

| 2175 | **778** | 48c. multicoloured | 1·00 | 45 |

779 Sculpture of Ram's Head

2003. Chinese New Year ("Year of the Ram"). Multicoloured.

| 2176 | 48c. Type **779** | 60 | 45 |
| **MS**2177 | 125×103 mm. $1.25 Sculpture of goat's head (33×57 mm) | 1·25 | 1·50 |

2003. National Hockey League. All-Star Game Players (4th series). As T **722**. Multicoloured

(a) Ordinary gum

2178	48c. Frank Mahovlich (wearing Maple Leaf No. 27 jersey)	80	90
2179	48c. Raymond Bourque (wearing Boston Bruins No. 77 jersey)	80	90
2180	48c. Serge Savard (wearing Canadiens No. 18 jersey)	80	90
2181	48c. Stan Mikita (wearing Chicago Blackhawks No. 21 jersey)	80	90
2182	48c. Mike Bossy (wearing New York Islanders No. 22 jersey)	80	90
2183	48c. Bill Durnan (wearing Canadiens jersey and brown gloves)	80	90

(b) Self-adhesive

2184	48c. Frank Mahovlich (wearing Maple Leaf No. 27 jersey)	75	90
2185	48c. Raymond Bourque (wearing Boston Bruins No. 77 jersey)	75	90
2186	48c. Serge Savard (wearing Canadiens No. 18 jersey)	75	90
2187	48c. Stan Mikita (wearing Chicago Blackhawks No. 21 jersey)	75	90
2188	48c. Mike Bossy (wearing New York Islanders No. 22 jersey)	75	90
2189	48c. Bill Durnan (wearing Canadiens jersey and brown gloves)	75	90

779a Bishop's University, Quebec (150th anniv of university status)

2003. Canadian Universities' Anniversaries (2nd issue). Multicoloured.

2190	48c. Bishop's University, Quebec (150th anniv of university status)	70	75
2191	48c. University of Western Ontario, London (125th anniv)	70	75
2192	48c. St. Francis Xavier University, Nova Scotia (150th Anniv)	70	75
2193	48c. Macdonald Institute, University of Guelph, Ontana (centenary)	70	75
2194	48c. Universite de Montreal (125th anniv)	70	75

780 Leach's Storm Petrel

2003. Bird Paintings by John Audubon (1st series). Multicoloured

(a) Ordinary gum

2195	48c. Type **780**	85	85
2196	48c. Brent goose ("Brant")	85	85
2197	48c. Great cormorant	85	85
2198	48c. Common murre	85	85

(b) Self-adhesive

| 2199 | 65c. Gyrfalcon (vert) | 2·00 | 2·50 |

See also Nos. 2274/8 and 2340/4.

781 Ranger looking through Binoculars

2003. 60th Anniv of Canadian Rangers.

| 2200 | **781** | 48c. multicoloured | 70 | 45 |

782 Greek Figure with Dove

2003. 75th Anniv of American Hellenic Educational Progressive Association in Canada.

| 2201 | **782** | 48c. multicoloured | 70 | 45 |

783 Firefighter carrying Boy and Burning Buildings

2003. Volunteer Firefighters.

| 2202 | **783** | 48c. multicoloured | 1·25 | 65 |

784 Queen Elizabeth II

2003. 50th Anniv of Coronation.

| 2203 | **784** | 48c. multicoloured | 1·00 | 55 |

785 Quebec City (c. 1703) Seal and Excerpt from Letter

2003. Pedro da Silva (first official courier of New France).

| 2204 | **785** | 48c. multicoloured | 70 | 55 |

2003. Tourist Attractions (3rd series). As T **747**. Multicoloured. Self-adhesive.

2205	65c. Wilberforce Falls, Nunavut	1·10	1·40
2206	65c. Inside Passage, British Columbia	1·10	1·40
2207	65c. Royal Canadian Mounted Police Depot Division, Regina, Saskatchewan	1·10	1·40
2208	65c. Casa Loma, Toronto	1·10	1·40
2209	65c. Gatineau Park, Quebec	1·10	1·40
2210	$1.25 Dragon boat race, Vancouver	1·75	1·90
2211	$1.25 Polar bear, Churchill, Manitoba	1·75	1·90
2212	$1.25 Niagara Falls, Ontario	1·75	1·90
2213	$1.25 Magdalen Islands, Quebec	1·75	1·90
2214	$1.25 Province House, Charlottetown, Prince Edward Island	1·75	1·90

2003. Vancouver's Successful Bid for Winter Olympic Games, 2010. No. 1368 (Canadian flag definitive) optd **VANCOUVER 2010**.

| 2215 | 48c. multicoloured | 80 | 80 |

787 Mountains and Sea

2003. Canada–Alaska Cruise "Picture Postage". Multicoloured. Self-adhesive.

| 2216 | (–) Type **787** | 3·75 | 4·50 |
| 2217 | (–) Tail fin of whale, mountains and sea | 3·75 | 4·50 |

788 Assembly Logo

2003. Tenth Lutheran World Federation Assembly, Winnipeg.

| 2218 | **788** | 48c. multicoloured | 70 | 55 |

789 Canadian F-86 Sabre Fighter Plane, Sailors and Infantrymen

2003. 50th Anniv of Signing of Korea Armistice.

| 2219 | **789** | 48c. multicoloured | 70 | 55 |

790 Anne Hebert

2003. 50th Anniv of National Library of Canada. Showing authors and portions of their handwritten text. Multicoloured.

2220	48c. Type **790**	80	85
2221	48c. Hector de Saint-Denys Garneau	80	85
2222	48c. Morley Callaghan	80	85
2223	48c. Susanna Moodie and Catharine Parr Traill	80	85

791 Cyclists in Road Race

2003. World Road Cycling Championships, Hamilton, Ontario.

2224	**791** 48c. multicoloured	1·10	70

792 Marc Garneau

2003. Stamp Collecting Month. Canadian Astronauts. Multicoloured. Self-adhesive.

2225	48c. Type **792**	85	1·00
2226	48c. Roberta Bondar	85	1·00
2227	48c. Steve MacLean	85	1·00
2228	48c. Chris Hadfield	85	1·00
2229	48c. Robert Thirsk	85	1·00
2230	48c. Bjarni Tryggvason	85	1·00
2231	48c. Dave Williams	85	1·00
2232	48c. Julie Payette	85	1·00

793 Maple Leaves, Canada

2003. National Emblems. Multicoloured.

2233	48c. Type **793**	1·00	1·00
2234	48c. Cassis fistula flowers, Thailand	1·00	1·00
MS2235	120×96 mm. Nos. 2233/4	2·00	2·25

No. **MS**2235 commemorates Bangkok 2003 International Stamp Exhibition, Thailand.

Stamps of the same designs were issued by Thailand.

794 White Birds

2003. 80th Birth Anniv of Jean-Paul Riopelle (painter and sculptor). T **794** and similar horiz designs showing details from fresco *L'Hommage a Rosa Luxemburg*. Multicoloured.

MS2236	178×244 mm. 48c. Type **794**; 48c. Two white herons and white birds; 48c. Flying bird, flower and three white birds in cameo; 48c. Grouse on moor, white bird and sun; 48c. Two flying white birds in cameo and silhouette of falcon; 48c. Two white birds and cameo of flying duck	4·00	5·00
MS2237	159×95 mm. $1.25 Eggs and bird silhouette	2·00	2·50

795 Ice Skates and Wrapped Presents

2003. Christmas. Multicoloured.

2238	48c. Type **795**	70	55
2239	65c. Teddy bear and wrapped presents	1·25	1·50
2240	$1.25 Toy duck on wheels and wrapped presents	1·90	2·50

796 Queen Elizabeth II, 2002

2003. Self-adhesive.

2241	**796** 49c. black, mauve and scarlet	1·10	80
2242	**796** 50c. multicoloured	70	80

797 Monkey King on Cloud

2004. Chinese New Year ("Year of the Monkey"). Showing scenes from *Journey to the West* by Wu Ch'eng-en. Multicoloured.

2247	49c. Type **797**	1·00	70
MS2248	115×82 mm. $1.40 Monkey on road to India	1·90	2·25

2004. Hong Kong 2004 International Stamp Exhibition. No. **MS**2248 optd Hong Kong Stamp Expo 2004 and exhibition emblem in gold on sheet margin.

MS2249	115×82 mm. $1.40 Monkey on road to India	1·90	2·25

2004. National Hockey League. All-Star Players (5th series). As T **722**. Multicoloured. Ordinary or self-adhesive gum.

(a) Ordinary gum

2250	49c. Larry Robinson (wearing Canadiens jersey)	1·40	1·40
2251	49c. Marcel Dionne (wearing Los Angeles Kings jersey)	1·40	1·40
2252	49c. Ted Lindsay (wearing Detroit Red Wings jersey)	1·40	1·40
2253	49c. Johnny Bower (wearing Toronto Maple Leafs goal keeper kit)	1·40	1·40
2254	49c. Brad Park (wearing New York Rangers jersey)	1·40	1·40
2255	49c. Milt Schmidt (wearing Boston Bruins jersey)	1·40	1·40

(b) Self-adhesive

2256	49c. Larry Robinson (wearing Canadiens jersey)	1·00	1·25
2256b	49c. Marcel Dionne (wearing Los Angeles Kings jersey)	1·00	1·25
2256c	49c. Ted Lindsay (wearing Detroit Red Wings jersey)	1·00	1·25
2256d	49c. Johnny Bower (wearing Toronto Maple Leafs goal keeper kit)	1·00	1·25
2256e	49c. Brad Park (wearing New York Rangers jersey)	1·00	1·25
2256f	49c. Milt Schmidt (wearing Boston Bruins jersey)	1·00	1·25

798 Bonhomme (Snowman), Quebec Winter Carnival

2004. Tourist Attractions (4th series). Multicoloured. Self-adhesive. Imperf.

2257	49c. Type **798**	1·25	1·40
2258	49c. St. Joseph's Oratory	1·25	1·40
2259	49c. Audience at International Jazz Festival, Montreal	1·25	1·40
2260	49c. People watching Traversee Internationale du Lac St-Jean	1·25	1·40
2261	49c. People at Canadian National Exhibition and Prince's Gate	1·25	1·40

799 Governor General Ramon Hnatyshyn

2004. 70th Birth Anniv of Governor General Ramon Hnatyshyn.

2262	**799** 49c. multicoloured	70	70

800 *Fram* (polar research ship)

2004. 150th Birth Anniv of Otto Sverdrup (polar explorer). Each purple and buff.

2263	49c. Type **800**	1·50	70
MS2264	166×60 mm. $1.40 As No. 2263 plus two labels	2·25	2·50

Stamps of similar designs were issued by Greenland and Norway.

801 Silhouettes of Cadets

2004. 125th Anniv of Royal Canadian Army Cadets. Self-adhesive. Imperf.

2265	**801** 49c. multicoloured	1·25	1·00

802 Subway Train, Toronto

2004. Light Rail Urban Transit. Multicoloured.

2266	49c. Type **802**	1·50	1·50
2267	49c. TransLink SkyTrain, Vancouver	1·50	1·50
2268	49c. Metro train, Montreal	1·50	1·50
2269	49c. CTrain, Calgary	1·50	1·50

803 Canadian Map and Employee

2004. 40th Anniv of Home Hardware (co-operative business). Self-adhesive.

2270	**803** 49c. multicoloured	90	90

2004. Canadian Universities Anniversaries (3rd series). As T **779a**. Multicoloured.

2271	49c. University of Sherbrooke (50th anniv)	90	90
2272	49c. University of Prince Edward Island (bicent)	90	90

804 Teddy Bears

2004. Centenary of Montreal Children's Hospital. Self-adhesive.

2273	**804** 49c. multicoloured	90	90

805 Ruby-crowned kinglet

2004. Bird Paintings by John Audubon (2nd series). Multicoloured.

(a) Ordinary gum

2274	49c. Type **805**	85	85
2275	49c. White-winged crossbill	85	85
2276	49c. Bohemian waxwing	85	85
2277	49c. Boreal chickadee	85	85

(b) Self-adhesive. Imperf.

2278	80c. Lincoln's sparrow	2·00	2·25

806 Sir Samuel Cunard

2004. Sir Samuel Cunard and Sir Hugh Allan (founders of transatlantic mail service) Commemorations. Multicoloured. Self-adhesive.

2279	49c. Type **806**	80	1·00
2280	49c. Sir Hugh Allan	80	1·00

Nos. 2279/80 were printed together, *se-tenant*, forming a composite design.

806a Butterfly on Flower

2004. "Write me...Ring me" Greetings Stamps. Multicoloured.

2280a	(49c.) Type **806a**	2·00	2·00
2280b	(49c.) Two young children at beach	2·00	2·00
2280c	(49c.) Red rose	2·00	2·00
2280d	(49c.) Pug (dog)	2·00	2·00

Nos. 2280a/d are inscribed "Domestic Lettermail" (initial value was 49c.).

807 Soldiers storming Juno Beach, Normandy

2004. 60th Anniv of D-Day Landings.

2281	**807** 49c. multicoloured	1·25	80

808 Pierre Dugua de Mons

2004. 400th Anniv of First French Settlement in Acadia, St. Croix Island (1st issue).

2282	**808** 49c. ochre, blue and orange	80	70

See also No. 2361, 2400 and 2508.

809 Spyros Louis (Greek athlete) and Marathon Runner

2004. Olympic Games, Athens, Greece. Multicoloured.

2283	49c. Type **809**	1·50	1·50
2284	49c. Girls playing football	1·50	1·50

810 Golfer and Trophy from Early Tournament

2004. Canadian Open Golf Championship. Multicoloured. Self-adhesive.

2285	49c. Type **810**	1·00	1·25
2286	49c. Golfer and trophy from modern tournament	1·00	1·25

811 Segmented Heart

2004. 50th Anniv of Montreal Heart Institute. Self-adhesive.

| 2287 | **811** | 49c. multicoloured | 80 | 1·00 |

812 Goldfish in Bowl

2004. Pets. Multicoloured. Self-adhesive. Imperf.

2288		(49c.) Type **812**	1·10	1·25
2289		49c. Two cats on chair	1·10	1·25
2290		49c. Child with rabbit	1·10	1·25
2291		49c. Child with dog	1·10	1·25

813 Gerhard Herzberg (Chemistry, 1971)

2004. Nobel Chemistry Prize Winners. Multicoloured.

| 2292 | | 49c. Type **813** | 90 | 1·00 |
| 2293 | | 49c. Michael Smith (Chemistry, 1993) | 90 | 1·00 |

814 Maple Leaf in Photo Album Frame

2004. Picture Postage. Multicoloured. Self-adhesive.

| 2294 | | (49c.) Type **814** | 90 | 1·00 |
| 2295 | | (49c.) Maple leaf in silver frame | 90 | 1·00 |

Nos. 2294/2295 were both inscribed "Domestic Postage Paid" and sold for 49c.

815 Victoria Cross (embossed)

2004. 150th Anniv of First Canadian Recipient of the Victoria Cross. Multicoloured.

| 2296 | | 49c. Type **815** | 1·10 | 1·25 |
| 2297 | | 49c. Victoria Cross and signature of Queen Elizabeth II | 1·10 | 1·25 |

Nos. 2296/7 were printed together as sheetlets of 16 around a central illustration and the names of 94 Canadians who have received the Victoria Cross.

816 Self-portrait, 1974

2004. "Art Canada". Birth Centenary of Jean Paul Lemieux (artist). Multicoloured.

| 2298 | | 49c. Type **816** | 1·00 | 85 |

MS2299 150×86 mm. 49c. Type **815**; 80c. *A June Wedding*, 1972 (53×34 mm); $1.40 *Summer*, 1959 (64×31 mm) | 4·50 | 5·00 |

817 Santa in his Sleigh and Reindeer

2004. Christmas. Multicoloured. Self-adhesive.

2300		49c. Type **817**	1·00	45
2301		80c. Santa sitting in a Cadillac and towing a house	1·60	2·00
2302		$1.40 Santa driving a train	2·50	3·00

818 Red Calla Lily

2004. Flowers. Multicoloured. (1st series)

Self-adhesive

2303		50c. Type **818**	70	80
2304		51c. Red bergamot	70	55
2305		85c. Yellow calla lily	1·00	1·00
2306		89c. Lady's slipper orchids	1·25	1·25
2307		$1.05 Pink fairy slipper orchids	1·50	1·60
2308		$1.45 purple Dutch iris	1·90	2·00
2309		$1.49 Himalayan blue poppies	1·90	2·00

Nos. 2305/9 come imperf.
See also Nos. 2470/**MS**2477 and 2530/**MS**2537.

819 Rooster facing East (right)

2005. Chinese New Year ("Year of the Rooster"). 35th Anniv of Diplomatic Relations with China (**MS**2315b). T **819** and similar multicoloured designs.

| 2314 | | 50c. Type **819** | 1·00 | 60 |

MS2315 Two sheets, each 105×82 mm. (a) $1.45 Rooster facing west (left) (40×41 mm). (b) $1.45 As No. **MS**2315a. | 2·50 | 3·00 |

Nos. **MS**2315a/b both have a barcode tab attached at foot.

2004. National Hockey League. All-Star Game Players (6th series). As T **722**. Multicoloured.

(a) Ordinary gum

2316		50c. Henri Richard (wearing Habs jersey)	1·40	1·40
2317		50c. Grant Fuhr (wearing Oilers goal keeper kit)	1·40	1·40
2318		50c. Allan Stanley (wearing Toronto Maple Leafs jersey)	1·40	1·40
2319		50c. Pierre Pilote (wearing Chicago Black Hawks jersey)	1·40	1·40
2320		50c. Bryan Trottier (wearing New York Islanders jersey)	1·40	1·40
2321		50c. John Bucyk (wearing Boston Bruins jersey)	1·40	1·40

(b) Self-adhesive

820 Alevin Fishing Fly

2005. Fishing Flies. Multicoloured.

(a) Ordinary gum

MS2328 190×112 mm. 50c.×4 Type **820**; Jock Scott; P.E.I. Fly; Mickey Finn | 3·00 | 3·25 |

(b) Self-adhesive.

2329		50c. Type **820**	1·25	1·25
2330		50c. Jock Scott	1·25	1·25
2331		50c. Mickey Finn	1·25	1·25
2332		50c. P.E.I. Fly	1·25	1·25

2005. Canadian Universities Anniversaries (4th series). As T **779a** (No. 2190). Multicoloured.

| 2333 | | 50c. Nova Scotia Agricultural College | 80 | 75 |

821 Inukshuk of Five Rocks

2005. Expo 2005 International Exhibition, Aichi, Japan.

| 2335 | **821** | 50c. multicoloured | 70 | 50 |

822 Yellow Daffodils

2005. Daffodils. Multicoloured

(a) Self-adhesive

| 2336 | | 50c. Type **822** | 90 | 90 |
| 2337 | | 50c. White daffodils with yellow trumpets | 90 | 90 |

(b) Ordinary gum.

MS2338 120×80 mm. Nos. 2336/7 | 1·25 | 1·60 |

No. **MS**2338 also commemorates Pacific Explorer 2005 World Stamp Expo Exhibition, Sydney, Australia.

823 TD Bank Building of c.1900, Cashier and TD Tower, Toronto

2005. 150th Anniv of TD Bank Financial Group. Self-adhesive.

| 2339 | **823** | 50c. multicoloured | 80 | 80 |

824 Horned Lark

2005. Bird Paintings by John Audubon (3rd series). Multicoloured

(a) Ordinary gum

2340		50c. Type **824**	1·25	1·25
2341		50c. Piping plover	1·25	1·25
2342		50c. Stilt sandpiper	1·25	1·25
2343		50c. Willow ptarmigan	1·25	1·25

(b) Self-adhesive. Size 45×35 mm

| 2344 | | 85c. Double-crested cormorant | 1·90 | 2·25 |

825 Jacques Cartier Bridge, Montreal, Quebec

2005. Bridges. Multicoloured. Self-adhesive.

2345		50c. Type **825**	75	1·00
2346		50c. Souris Swinging Bridge, Manitoba	75	1·00
2347		50c. Angus L. Macdonald Bridge, Halifax, Nova Scotia	75	1·00
2348		50c. Canso Causeway, Nova Scotia	75	1·00

826 Magazine Covers of 1911, 1954, 1962 and 1917

2005. Centenary of Maclean's Magazine.

| 2349 | **826** | 50c. multicoloured | 60 | 50 |

827 Saskatoon Berries and Osprey, Waterton Lakes National Park, Alberta, Canada

2005. Biosphere Reserves. Multicoloured.

| 2350 | | 50c. Type **827** | 1·10 | 1·10 |
| 2351 | | 50c. Red Deer stags, Killarney National Park, Ireland | 1·10 | 1·10 |

MS2352 120×70 mm. Nos. 2350/1 | 2·10 | 2·40 |

Stamps in similar designs were issued by Ireland.

828 Sailor Lookout, Canadian Navy Corvette and Survivors in Lifeboat

2005. 60th Anniv of Battle of the Atlantic.

| 2353 | **828** | 50c. multicoloured | 1·00 | 60 |

829 Candle, Silhouettes, Memorial Cross GRV and New Museum Building

2005. Opening of New Canadian War Museum Building, Ottawa. Self-adhesive.

| 2354 | **829** | 50c. multicoloured | 70 | 70 |

830 *Down in the Laurentides*

2005. "Art Canada". 150th Birth Anniv of Homer Watson (artist). Paintings. Multicoloured.

| 2355 | | 50c. Type **830** | 70 | 50 |

MS2356 150×87 mm. 50c. Type **830**; 85c. *The Flood Gate* (53×39 mm) | 1·10 | 1·40 |

No. **MS**2356 also commemorates the 125th anniversary of the National Gallery of Canada.

831 Volunteer with Search Dog, Crashed Aircraft and Satellite

2005. Search and Rescue. Sheet 260×170 mm containing T **831** and similar vert designs. Multicoloured.

MS2357 50c.×2 Type **831**; 50c.×2 Rescuers, crew in life raft and sinking ship; 50c.×2 Seaman winched into helicopter and float plane; 50c.×2 Mountain rescue team with stretcher and satellite | 6·50 | 6·50 |

832 Ellen Fairclough and Parliament Buildings, Ottawa

2005. Birth Centenary of Ellen Fairclough (first woman federal cabinet minister).

| 2358 | **832** | 50c. multicoloured | 70 | 50 |

833 Diver spinning in mid-air

2005. 11th FINA (Federation Internationale de Natation) World Championships, Montreal. Multicoloured.

| 2359 | | 50c. Type **833** | 75 | 90 |
| 2360 | | 50c. Swimmer in butterfly stroke | 75 | 90 |

834 Port-Royal, 1605 (from drawing by Samuel de Champlain)

2005. French Settlement in North America (2nd issue). 400th Anniv of Founding of Port-Royal, Nova Scotia.

2361	**834**	50c. multicoloured	70	55

835 Chemicals Plant, Calgary Skyline, Mount Grassi and Railway Line

2005. Centenary of Alberta Province. Self-adhesive.

2362	**835**	50c. multicoloured	70	55

The backing paper is illustrated with four different scenes, each running across two stamps: Calgary Stampede; Jasper Avenue, Edmonton, 1963; Lake Minnewanka, Banff; and oil refinery of c. 1912.

836 Woman with Arms outstretched, Sunflowers and Legislature Building, Regina

2005. Centenary of Saskatchewan.

2363	**836**	50c. multicoloured	70	55

837 1930 50c. Acadian Memorial Church Stamp and Acadian Flag

2005. 250th Anniv of Deportation of French Settlers from Acadia (Nova Scotia) to British Colonies of North America.

2364	**837**	50c. multicoloured	80	60

838 Oscar Peterson

2005. 80th Birthday of Oscar Peterson (jazz composer and musician).

2365	**838**	50c. multicoloured	1·00	50
MS2366 112×116 mm. No. 2365×4			3·50	4·25

839 Children playing and discarded Leg Braces

2005. 50th Anniv of Mass Polio Vaccination in Canada.

2367	**839**	50c. multicoloured	70	50

840 Wall climbing

2005. Youth Sports. Multicoloured. Self-adhesive.

2368	50c. Type **840**		60	70
2369	50c. Skateboarding		60	70
2370	50c. Mountain biking		60	70
2371	50c. Snowboarding		60	70

841 *Puma concolor* (cougar)

2005. 35th Anniv of Canada—China Diplomatic Relations. Carnivores. Multicoloured.

2372	50c. Type **841**		60	70
2373	50c. *Panthera pardus orientalis* (Amur leopard)		60	70
MS2374 108×58 mm. Nos. 2372/3			1·25	1·60

Stamps of the same design were issued by China (People's Republic).

842 Snowman

2005. Christmas (1st issue). Self-adhesive.

2375	**842**	50c. multicoloured	70	50

843 Creche by Michel Forest

2005. Christmas (2nd issue). Showing Christmas creches. Multicoloured. Self-adhesive.

2376	50c. Type **843**		70	50
2377	85c. Creche with aboriginal figures by Keena (31×39 mm)		1·40	2·00
2378	$1.45 Creche by Sylvia Daoust (27×40 mm)		2·25	3·00

844 Chow

2006. Chinese New Year ("Year of the Dog"). Multicoloured.

2379	51c. Type **844**		60	60
MS2380 129×106 mm. $1.49 Chow with puppy			2·50	3·00

845 Queen Elizabeth II, Ottawa, 2002

2006. 80th Birthday of Queen Elizabeth II (1st issue). Self-adhesive.

2381	**845**	51c. multicoloured	70	70

See also No. **MS**2392.

846 Team Pursuit Speed Skating

2006. Winter Olympic Games, Turin, Italy. Multicoloured.

2382	51c. Type **846**		75	75
2383	51c. Skeleton (sled)		75	75

847 Trilliums and Black-throated Blue Warbler (Shade Garden)

2006. Gardens. Multicoloured. Self-adhesive.

2384	51c. Type **847**		1·25	1·25
2385	51c. Purple coneflowers and American painted lady butterfly (flower garden)		1·25	1·25
2386	51c. Water lilies and green darner dragonfly		1·25	1·25
2387	51c. Rock garden and blue-spotted salamander		1·25	1·25

848 Balloons

2006. Greetings Stamp. Self-adhesive.

2388	**848**	51c. multicoloured	75	75

849 *The Field of Rapeseed*

2006. "Art Canada". Paintings by Dorothy Knowles. Multicoloured.

2389	51c. Type **849**		75	50
MS2390 150×87 mm. 51c. Type **849**; 89c. *North Saskatchewan River* (42×51 mm)			2·25	2·75

850 Hands enclosing Globe

2006. 50th Anniv of Canadian Labour Congress.

2391	**850**	51c. multicoloured	70	50

2006. 80th Birthday of Queen Elizabeth II (2nd issue). Sheet 125×75 mm. Multicoloured.

MS2392 $1.49×2 As Type **845** but 39×31 mm			4·75	5·50

851 Colophon emerging from Book

2006. Centenary of McClelland & Stewart (publishing house). Self-adhesive.

2393	**851**	51c. blue and silver	1·40	1·25

852 Mid 19th-Century Transformation Mask and Other Exhibits

2006. 150th Anniv of Canadian Museum of Civilization, Gatineau, Quebec. Self-adhesive.

2394	**852**	89c. multicoloured	1·75	2·25

853 Lorne Greene

2006. Canadians in Hollywood. Multicoloured

(a) Self-adhesive

2395	51c. Type **853**		75	85
2396	51c. Fay Wray		75	85
2397	51c. Mary Pickford		75	85
2398	51c. John Candy		75	85

(b) Ordinary gum

MS2399 180×63 mm. As Nos. 2395/8			3·25	3·75

854 Champlain's Ship

2006. French Settlement in North America (3rd issue). 400th Anniv of Samuel de Champlain's Survey of East Coast of North America.

2400	51c. ×2 Type **854**		70	50
MS2401 204×146 mm. 51c. Type **854**; 39c.×2, As Type **2879** of USA			1·00	1·25

No. **MS**2401 also commemorates Washington 2006 International Stamp Exhibition.

A self-adhesive stamp in the same design and an identical miniature sheet were also issued by the United States.

855 Girl watching Beluga Whale

2006. 50th Anniv of Vancouver Aquarium. Self-adhesive.

2402	**855**	51c. multicoloured	70	60

856 Pilot and Snowbirds

2006. 35th Anniv of Snowbirds Demonstration Team (431 Squadron). Multicoloured.

2403	51c. Type **856**		1·25	1·25
2404	51c. Snowbirds and emblem		1·25	1·25
MS2405 130×65 mm. Nos. 2403/4			2·50	2·50

857 James White (Chief Geographer), Proportional Dividers and Modern Map

2006. Centenary of *The Atlas of Canada*.

2406	**857**	51c. multicoloured	1·25	1·00

858 Player and Event Tickets

2006. World Lacrosse Championships, London, Ontario. Self-adhesive.

2407	**858**	51c. multicoloured	70	70

859 Early and Modern Climbers

2006. Centenary of the Alpine Club of Canada. Self-adhesive.

| 2408 | **859** | 51c. multicoloured | 1·00 | 85 |

860 Barrow's Goldeneye

2006. Duck Decoys. Multicoloured.

2409	51c. Type **860**		1·10	1·10
2410	51c. Mallard (decoy with white ring around neck)		1·10	1·10
2411	51c. Black duck (plain brown decoy)		1·10	1·10
2412	51c. Red-breasted merganser (black and white decoy with red bill)		1·10	1·10
MS2413	130×145 mm. Nos. 2409/12		4·00	4·25

861 "g" as Beaver enclosing "50"

2006. 50th Anniv of the Society of Graphic Designers of Canada.

| 2414 | **861** | 51c. multicoloured | 70 | 50 |

862 Glasses of Wine

2006. Canadian Wine and Cheese. Multicoloured. Self-adhesive.

2415	51c. Type **862**		80	90
2416	51c. Wine taster (horiz as Type **862**)		80	90
2417	51c. Canadian cheeses (wedge-shaped, 36×38 mm)		80	90
2418	51c. Serving cheese platter at fromagerie (wedge-shaped, 36×38 mm)		80	90

2006. Canadian Universities Anniversaries (5th series). Vert design as T **779a** (No. 2190). Multicoloured.

| 2419 | 51c. Macdonald College, Sainte-Anne-de-Bellevue, Quebec (centenary) | | 1·00 | 85 |

863 Newfoundland Marten

2006. Endangered Species (1st series). Multicoloured

(a) Self-adhesive

2420	51c. Type **863**		1·10	1·10
2421	51c. Blotched tiger salamander		1·10	1·10
2422	51c. Blue racer		1·10	1·10
2423	51c. Swift fox		1·10	1·10

(b) Ordinary gum. Size 48×24 mm.

| **MS**2424 | 160×74 mm. Nos. 2420/3 | | 4·00 | 4·50 |

See also Nos. 2511/**MS**2515.

864 Maureen Forrester and Place des Arts, Montréal

2006. Canadian Opera Singers. Multicoloured.

2425	51c. Type **864**		1·10	1·10
2426	51c. Raoul Jobin and Palais Garnier, Paris		1·10	1·10
2427	51c. Leopold Simoneau, Pierrette Alarie and Opera-Comique, France		1·10	1·10
2428	51c. Jon Vickers and La Scala, Milan		1·10	1·10

| 2429 | 51c. Edward Johnson and Metropolitan Opera Company, New York | | 1·10 | 1·10 |

865 Madonna and Child (detail) (Antoine-Sebastien Falardeau)

2006. Christmas (1st issue). Self-adhesive.

| 2430 | **865** | 51c. multicoloured | 85 | 55 |

866 Snowman (Yvonne McKague Housser)

2006. Christmas (2nd issue). Showing Christmas cards from 1931 *Painters of Canada* series. Multicoloured. Self-adhesive.

2431	51c. Type **866**		85	55
2432	89c. Winter Joys (J. E. Sampson)		1·75	2·25
2433	$1.49 Contemplation (Edwin Holgate)		2·25	3·25

867 Ice Fields and Fjord, Sirmilik National Park, Nunavut

2006

(a) Self-adhesive stamps inscr "P" instead of face value. Each showing Canadian flag. Multicoloured.

2434	(51c.) Type **867**		1·10	1·25
2435	(51c.) Coast and ancient trees, Chemainus, British Columbia		1·10	1·25
2436	(51c.) Polar bears, Churchill, Manitoba		1·10	1·25
2437	(51c.) Lighthouse at Bras d'Or Lake, Nova Scotia		1·10	1·25
2438	(51c.) Tuktut Nogait National Park, Northwest Territories		1·10	1·25
2439	(52c.) Sambra Island lighthouse, Nove Scotia (red and white striped)		1·40	1·40
2440	(52c.) Point Clark lighthouse, (trees at left)(above cliff) Ontario		1·40	1·40
2441	(52c.) Cap-des-Rosiers lighthouse, Quebec		1·40	1·40
2442	(52c.) Warren Landing lighthouse, Manitoba (in sandunes)		1·40	1·40
2443	(52c.) Pachena Point lighthouse, and keepers house, British Coloumbia		1·40	1·40
2444	(52c.) Pachena Point Lighthouse and part of keeper's house (at right)		1·40	1·40
2445	(57c.) Watson's Mill (three storey stone building), Manotick, Ontario		1·40	1·40
2446	(57c.) Keremeos Grist Mill (wooden building with waterwheel at left), British Columbia		1·40	1·40
2447	(57c.) Old stone Mill National Historic Site (four storey stone building with red doors), Delta, Ontario		1·40	1·40
2448	(57c.) Riordon Grist Mill (two storey stone building), Caraquet, New Brunswick		1·40	1·40
2449	(57c.) Cornell Mill (weir at right), Stanbridge East, Quebec		1·40	1·40

(b) Ordinary gum

| **MS**2450 | 130x70 mm. As Nos. 2445/9 (ordinary gum) | | 6·25 | 7·00 |

Nos. 2434/8 were inscribed "P" and initially sold for 51c. each and Nos. 2439/43 were inscribed 'P' and initially sold for 52c. each and nos 2445/9 were all inscribed 'P' and initially sold for 57c.

868 Queen Elizabeth II, 2005

2006. Self-adhesive booklet stamps. Multicoloured.

2464	(51c.) Type **868**		90	90
2465	(52c.) Queen Elizabeth II, Saskatoon, 2005 (27.12.07)		1·00	1·00
2466	(54c.) Queen Elizabeth in Canada, 19 May 2005 (red background) (12.1.09)		1·25	1·25
2467	(57c.) Queen Elizabeth II (wearing deep blue jacket and hat) (11.1.10)		1·40	1·40
2468	(63c.) Queen Elizabeth II (wearing cream hat with yellow ribbon) at Mi'kmaq Cultural Village, June 28 2010 (14.1.13)		1·40	1·40

No. 2464/8 were all inscribed "P" and were initially sold for 51c. (2464), 52c. (2465), 54c. (2466), 57c. (2467) or 63c. (2468).

No. 2469 is left for possible additions to these definitive stamps.

869 Spotted coralroot

2006. Flowers (2nd series). Multicoloured

(a) Self-adhesive coil stamps

2470	**869**	(51c.) Spotted coralroot	60	35
2471	**869**	93c. Flat-leaved bladderwort	1·10	1·25
2472	**869**	$1.10 Marsh skullcap	1·25	1·50
2473	**869**	$1.55 Little larkspur	1·75	2·25

(b) Self-adhesive booklet stamps

2474	93c. Flat-leaved bladderwort		1·10	1·25
2475	$1.10 Marsh skullcap		1·25	1·50
2476	$1.55 Little larkspur		1·75	2·25

(c) Ordinary gum.

| **MS**2477 | 120×72 mm. As Nos. 2470/3 | | 6·00 | 7·00 |

No. 2470 was inscribed "P" and initially sold for 51c. each.

870 Pig

2007. Chinese New Year ("Year of the Pig"). Multicoloured.

| 2478 | 52c. Type **870** | | 1·25 | 60 |
| **MS**2479 | 98×97 mm. $1.55 Pig (running to right) | | 2·25 | 2·75 |

No. 2479 is cut in a lantern shape.

871 Ribbons and Confetti

2007. Greetings Stamp. Self-adhesive.

| 2480 | **871** | 52c. multicoloured | 85 | 1·00 |

872 King Eider (*Somateria spectabilis*)

2007. International Polar Year. Multicoloured.

2481	52c. Type **872**		1·50	1·50
2482	52c. *Crossota millsaeare* (deep-sea jellyfish)		1·50	1·50
MS2483	105×70 mm. Nos. 2481/2		3·00	3·00

873 *Syringa vulgaris* "Princess Alexandra"

2007. Lilacs. Multicoloured.

(a) Self-adhesive.

| 2484 | 52c. Type **873** | | 90 | 90 |
| 2485 | 52c. *Syringa×prestoniae* "Isabella" | | 90 | 90 |

(b) Ordinary gum.

| **MS**2486 | 128×80 mm. As Nos. 2484/5 | | 1·75 | 2·00 |

2007. Canadian Universities' Anniversaries (6th issue). As T **779a** (No. 2190). Multicoloured. Self-adhesive.

| 2487 | 52c. HEC (Ecole des hautes etudes commerciales), Montreal (centenary) | | 85 | 85 |
| 2488 | 52c. University of Saskatchewan | | 85 | 85 |

874 Jelly Shelf

2007. "Art Canada". Paintings by Mary Pratt. Multicoloured.

| 2489 | 52c. Type **874** | | 75 | 50 |
| **MS**2490 | 150×87 mm. 52c. Type **874**; $1.55 Iceberg in the North Atlantic (62×40 mm) | | 3·00 | 3·50 |

875 Parliament Buildings, Ottawa, 2007 and Lumberers Regatta, 1860

2007. 150th Anniv of Ottawa as Capital of Canada

(a) Self-adhesive

| 2491 | **875** | 52c. multicoloured | 1·00 | 85 |

(b) Ordinary gum.

| **MS**2492 | 102×102 mm. 52c. As No. 2491; $1.55 As No. 2491 | | 3·50 | 3·75 |

876 University of Lethbridge (Arthur Erickson), 1971

2007. Centenary of Royal Architectural Institute of Canada. Multicoloured.

2493	52c. Type **876**		1·00	1·00
2494	52c. St. Mary's Church (Douglas Cardinal), 1969		1·00	1·00
2495	52c. Ontario Science Centre (Raymond Moriyama), 1969		1·00	1·00
2496	52c. National Gallery of Canada (Moshe Safdie), 1988		1·00	1·00

877 Capt. George Vancouver

2007. 250th Birth Anniv of Captain George Vancouver (explorer of west coast of North America).

| 2497 | **877** | $1.55 multicoloured | 2·50 | 2·50 |
| **MS**2498 | 70×120 mm. **877** $1.55 multicoloured | | 2·50 | 3·00 |

878 Official U-20 World Cup Football and Canadian Team in Action

2007. FIFA U-20 World Cup, Canada.

| 2499 | **878** | 52c. multicoloured | 1·00 | 85 |

879 Gordon Lightfoot

2007. Canadian Recording Artists (1st series). Multicoloured

(a) Self-adhesive

2500	52c. Type **879**		1·00	1·10
2501	52c. Joni Mitchell		1·00	1·10
2502	52c. Anne Murray		1·00	1·10
2503	52c. Paul Anka		1·00	1·10

(b) Ordinary gum.

| **MS**2504 | Circular 105×105 mm. As Nos. 2500/3 | | 3·25 | 4·00 |

880 Sunrise over Alexander Bay,
Terra Nova National Park,
Newfoundland

2007. 50th Anniv of Terra Nova National Park,
Newfoundland. Self-adhesive.

2505	**880**	52c. multicoloured	1·00	1·00

881 Jasper National Park

2007. Centenary of Jasper National Park, Alberta. Self-
adhesive.

2506	**881**	52c. multicoloured	1·00	1·00

882 Scouts forming
Emblem

2007. Centenary of Scouting. Self-adhesive.

2507	**882**	52c. multicoloured	1·25	1·00

883 Membertou (Grand
Chief of the Mi'kmaq) and
French Settlement, Port
Royal

2007. French Settlement in North America (4th issue).
Chief Membertou.

2508	**883**	52c. multicoloured	1·00	85

884 Founding Members
and Registry Roll

2007. Centenary of the Law Society of Saskatchewan.

2509	**884**	52c. multicoloured	1·00	1·00

885 Books, Photograph of
James Muir Gavel (first
President)

2007. Centenary of the Law Society of Alberta.

2510	**885**	52c. multicoloured	1·00	85

2007. Endangered Species (2nd series). As T **863**.
Multicoloured

(a) Self-adhesive.

2511	52c. North Atlantic right whale	1·40	1·40
2512	52c. Northern cricket frog	1·40	1·40
2513	52c. White sturgeon	1·40	1·40
2514	52c. Leatherback turtle	1·40	1·40

(b) Ordinary gum. Size 48×24 mm.

MS2515	160×75 mm. As Nos. 2511/14	5·00	5·00

886 *Hippodamia
convergens*
(convergent
lady beetle)

2007. Beneficial Insects. . Multicoloured.

2516	1c. Type **886**		10	10
2517	2c. *Danaus plexippus* (Monarch Butterfly Caterpillar)		10	10
2518	3c. *Chrysopa oculata* (Golden-eyed Lacewing)		10	10
2518a	4c. *Polistes fuscatus* (Paper Wasp) (19.10.10)		10	10

2519	5c. *Bombus polaris* (Northern Bumblebee)		10	10
2519a	6c. *Zelus luridus* (Assassin Bug) (19.10.10)		15	10
2519b	7c. *Oncopeltus fasciatus* (Large Milkweed Bug) (19.10.10)		20	15
2519c	8c. *Chauliognathus marginatus* (Margined Leatherwing) (19.10.10)		25	20
2519d	9c. *Chrysochus auratus* (Dog-bane Beetle) (19.10.10)		25	20
2520	10c. *Aeshna canadensis* (Canada Darner Dragonfly)		25	20
2521	25c. *Hyalophora cecropia* (Cecropia Moth)		50	40
MS2522	133×58 mm. Nos. 2516/18, 2519 and 2520/1		1·00	1·25
MS2523	133×58 mm. Nos. 2518a and 2519a/d (19.10.10)		1·00	1·25

No. **MS**2524 is inscr with emblem and 'The Royal Phila-
telic Society of Canada 1887-2012' on the left margin.

887 Reindeer

2007. Christmas (1st issue). Self-adhesive.

2526	**887**	(52c.) multicoloured	1·00	85

No. 2526 was inscribed 'P' and initially sold for 52c.

888 Nativity
('HOPE')

2007. Christmas (2nd issue). Multicoloured. Self-adhesive.

2527		(52c.) Type **888**	1·00	85
2528		93c. Angel playing trumpet ('JOY')	2·00	2·50
2529		$1.55 Dove ('PEACE')	2·75	3·25

No. 2527 was inscribed 'P' and initially sold for 52c.

889 *Odontioda*
Island Red

2007. Flowers (3rd series). Canadian Hybrid Orchids.
Multicoloured. (a) Self-adhesive.

(a) Coil stamps

2530	(52c.) Type **889**	1·00	85
2531	96c. *Potinara* Janet Elizabeth 'Fire Dancer'	1·75	1·75
2532	$1.15 *Laeliocattleya* Memoria Evelyn Light	1·90	1·90
2533	$1.60 *Masdevallia* Kaleidoscope 'Conni'	2·75	3·00

(b) Stamps from self-adhesive panes

2534	96c. As No. 2531	1·75	2·00
2535	$1.15 As No. 2532	2·25	2·75
2536	$1.60 As No. 2533	2·75	3·25

(c) Ordinary gum

MS2537	120×72 mm. As Nos. 2530/3	7·50	8·50

No. 2530 was inscribed 'P' and sold for 52c.

890 Rat Bride

2008. Chinese New Year ('Year of the Rat'). Multicoloured.

2538	52c. Type **890**	1·25	1·00
MS2539	130×100 mm. $1.60 Rat groom	2·75	3·25

891 Fireworks

2008. Greetings Stamp. Self-adhesive.

2540	**891**	(52c.) multicoloured	1·25	1·25

No. 2540 was inscribed 'P' and initially sold for 52c.

892 *Paeonia lactiflora*
'Elgin'

2008. Peonies. Multicoloured

(a) Self-adhesive

2541	52c. Type **892**	1·00	1·00
2542	52c. *Paeonia lactiflora* 'Coral 'n Gold'	1·00	1·00

(b) Ordinary gum.

MS2543	120×84 mm. As Nos. 2541/2	2·00	2·25

893 Dentistry
Building, University
of Alberta
(centenary)

2008. Canadian Universities' Anniversaries (7th issue).
Multicoloured. Self-adhesive.

2544	52c. Type **893**	1·00	1·00
2545	52c. Walter C. Koerner Library, University of British Colum-bia (centenary)	1·00	1·00

894 Ice Hockey Players

2008. International Ice Hockey Federation World
Championship, Halifax and Quebec. Self-adhesive.

2546	**894**	52c. multicoloured	1·00	1·00

895 Guide Dog at Work

2008. Guide Dogs. Self-adhesive.

2547	**895**	52c. multicoloured	1·40	1·40

No. 2547 also has the face value in Braille.

896 Welder working on Pipeline

2008. Oil and Gas Industry. Multicoloured. Self-adhesive.

2548	52c. Type **896**	1·10	1·10
2549	52c. James Miller Williams (drilled first Canadian oil well, 1858) and Charles Tripp (developed bitumen deposits of southwest Ontario, 1850s)	1·10	1·10

897 Samuel de Champlain's
Ship, Native Canoe and
New Settlement of Quebec,
1608

2008. French Settlement in North America (5th issue).
400th Anniv of City of Quebec. Fluorescent frame.

2550	**897**	52c. multicoloured	1·00	90

A stamp in a similar design was issued by France.

898 Self-portrait

2008. Art Canada. Birth Centenary of Yousuf Karsh
(portrait photographer). Multicoloured

(a) Ordinary gum

2551	52c. Type **898**	1·00	90
MS2552	150×87 mm. 52c. Type **898**; 96c. Audrey Hepburn; $1.60 Winston Churchill	5·25	6·00

(b) Self-adhesive.

2553	96c. Audrey Hepburn	2·00	2·50
2554	$1.60 Winston Churchill	3·50	4·00

899 50 Cent Coin, 1908

2008. Centenary of the Royal Canadian Mint.

2555	**899**	52c. multicoloured	1·00	90

900 Nurse

2008. Centenary of Canadian Nurses Association. Self-
adhesive.

2556	**900**	52c. multicoloured	1·10	1·10

901 Anne

2008. Centenary of Publication of *Anne of Green Gables*
by Lucy Maud Montgomery. Multicoloured

(a) Self-adhesive.

2557	52c. Type **901**	1·00	1·00
2558	52c. Green Gables (house), Cavendish, Prince Edward Island	1·00	1·00

(b) Ordinary gum.

MS2559	124×72 mm. As Nos. 2557/8	1·75	2·00

2008. Canadians in Hollywood (2nd series). As T **853**.
Multicoloured

(a) Self-adhesive

2560	52c. Norma Shearer	1·25	1·25
2561	52c. Chief Dan George	1·25	1·25
2562	52c. Marie Dressler	1·25	1·25
2563	52c. Raymond Burr	1·25	1·25

(b) Ordinary gum.

MS2564	136×77 mm. As Nos. 2560/3	4·00	4·50

902 Athlete and
Canadian Flag

2008. Olympic Games, Beijing. Self-adhesive.

2565	**902**	52c. multicoloured	1·40	1·40

903 Lifeguard and Water
Rescue

2008. Centenary of Lifesaving Society. Self-adhesive.

2566	**903**	52c. multicoloured	1·00	1·00

904 Panning for Gold

2008. 150th Anniv of British Columbia.

2567	**904**	52c. multicoloured	1·40	1·00

905 McLaughlin Buick, c. 1912
and Sam McLaughlin

2008. Sam McLaughlin (founder of McLaughlin Motor Car Company and philanthropist) Commemoration.

| 2568 | **905** | 52c. multicoloured | 1·00 | 85 |

2008. Endangered Species (3rd series). As T **863**. Multicoloured

(a) Self-adhesive

2569	52c. Prothonotary warbler	1·40	1·40
2570	52c. Taylor's checkerspot (butterfly)	1·40	1·40
2571	52c. Roseate tern	1·40	1·40
2572	52c. Burrowing owl	1·40	1·40

(b) Ordinary gum. Size 48×24 mm.

| MS2573 | 160×75 mm. As Nos. 2569/72 | 5·00 | 5·50 |

906 Woman with Megaphone

2008. Mental Health. Self-adhesive.

| 2574 | **906** | (52c.)+10c. +10c. multicoloured | 1·25 | 1·40 |

No. 2574 was inscribed 'P+10' and initially sold for 52c. plus a 10c. surcharge for the Canada Post Foundation for Mental Health.

907 Québec City Skyline

2008. 12th Francophone Summit, Quebec.

| 2575 | **907** | 52c. multicoloured | 1·00 | 85 |

908 Infant Jesus (creche figure by Antonio Caruso)

2008. Christmas (1st issue). Self-adhesive.

| 2576 | **908** | (52c.) multicoloured | 1·10 | 85 |

No. 2576 was inscribed 'P' and was initially sold for 52c.

909 Child making Snow Angels

2008. Christmas (2nd issue). Winter Fun. Showing children

(a) Self-adhesive

2577	(52c.) Type **909**	1·10	85
2578	96c. Child skiing	1·90	2·25
2579	$1.60 Child tobogganing	3·00	3·50

(b) Ordinary gum.

| MS2580 | 102×72 mm. As Nos. 2577/9 | 5·50 | 6·50 |

No. 2577 was inscribed 'P' and was initially sold for 52c.

910 Ox

2009. Chinese New Year. Year of the Ox. Multicoloured.

| 2581 | (54c.) Type **910** | 1·40 | 1·00 |

| MS2582 | 40×140 mm. $1.65 Earthenware cooking pot by Shu-Hwei Kao | 3·25 | 3·75 |

No. 2581 was inscribed 'P' and initially sold for 54c. It has a background flower pattern which extends over the stamps and sheet margins.

2009. China 2009 World Stamp Exhibition. No. MS2582 optd with **CHINA 2009** logo in gold on the sheet margin.

| MS2583 | 40×140 mm. $1.65 Earthenware cooking pot by Shu-Hwei Kao | 3·25 | 3·75 |

911 Freestyle Skiing

2009. Winter Olympic Games, Vancouver, 2010 (1st issue). Olympic Sports. Multicoloured

(a) Self-adhesive

2584	(54c.) Type **911**	1·40	1·40
2585	(54c.) Snowboarding	1·40	1·40
2586	(54c.) Ice sledge hockey	1·40	1·40
2587	(54c.) Bobsleigh	1·40	1·40
2588	(54c.) Curling	1·40	1·40

(b) Ordinary gum.

| MS2589 | 140×82 mm. As Nos. 2584/8 | 5·75 | 6·25 |

Nos. 2584/8 and stamps from **MS2589** were all inscribed 'P' and initially sold for 54c. each.

912 Vancouver 2010 Winter Olympic Games Emblem

2009. Winter Olympic Games, Vancouver, 2010 (2nd issue). Mascots and Emblems. Multicoloured

(a) Ordinary gum.

2590	(54c.) Type **912**	1·00	1·25
2591	(54c.) Vancouver 2010 Paralympic Games emblem	1·00	1·25
2592	98c. Miga skiing	2·00	2·25
2593	$1.18 Sumi curling (12 Feb)	2·25	2·75
2594	$1.65 Quatchi playing ice hockey	3·25	3·75

(b) Self-adhesive stamps from panes of six

2595	98c. As No. 2592	2·25	2·50
2596	$1.18 As No. 2593	2·50	3·00
2597	As No. 2594	3·50	4·00

(c) Ordinary gum

| MS2598 | 140×82 mm. As Nos. 2590/4 | 9·00 | 10·00 |

Nos. 2590/1 were initially sold for 54c. each.

913 Stylized Ribbons, Fireworks and Confetti bursting from Envelope

2009. Greetings Stamp. 'Celebrate'. Self-adhesive.

| 2599 | **913** | (54c.) multicoloured | 1·10 | 1·00 |

No. 2599, inscribed 'P', was initially sold for 54c.

914 Rosemary Brown (civil rights campaigner) and BC Legislative Building

2009. Black History Month. Multicoloured.

| 2600 | 54c. Type **914** | 1·00 | 1·25 |
| 2601 | 54c. Abraham Doras Shadd (holding lantern) and runaway slaves | 1·00 | 1·25 |

915 Flight of *Silver Dart*, Bras d'Or Lake, Nova Scotia, 23 February 1909

2009. Centenary of First Powered Flight in Canada. Self-adhesive.

| 2602 | **915** | (54c.) multicoloured | 1·50 | 1·00 |

916 White Rhododendron with Pink Buds

2009. Rhododendrons. Multicoloured

(a) Self-adhesive

| 2603 | 54c. Type **916** | 1·10 | 1·25 |
| 2604 | 54c. Deep pink rhododendron | 1·10 | 1·25 |

(b) Ordinary gum.

| MS2605 | 120×74 mm. As Nos. 2603/4 | 2·00 | 2·50 |

917 *Striped Column* (Jack Bush), 1964

2009. Art Canada. Birth Centenary of Jack Bush (artist). Design showing paintings. Multicoloured.

| 2606 | 54c. Type **917** | 1·00 | 85 |

| MS2607 | 150×87 mm. No. 2606; Chopsticks, 1977 (57×23 mm) | 4·00 | 4·50 |

918 Horsehead Nebula and Dominion Astrophysical Observatory, Saanich, BC

2009. International Year of Astronomy. Multicoloured

(a) Self-adhesive

| 2608 | 54c. Type **918** | 1·10 | 1·25 |
| 2609 | 54c. Eagle Nebula and Canada-France-Hawaii Telescope, Mauna Kea, Hawaii | 1·10 | 1·25 |

(b) Ordinary gum.

| MS2610 | 101×90 mm. As Nos. 2608/9 but 30×40 mm | 2·00 | 2·50 |

919 Polar Bear

2009. Preserve the Polar Regions and Glaciers. Multicoloured.

| 2611 | 54c. Type **919** | 1·25 | 1·25 |
| 2612 | 54c. Arctic tern | 1·25 | 1·25 |

| MS2613 | 120×80 mm. Nos. 2611/12 | 2·50 | 2·50 |

920 Canadian Horse

2009. Canadian Horse and Newfoundland Pony. Multicoloured. Self-adhesive.

| 2614 | 54c. Type **920** | 1·40 | 1·40 |
| 2615 | 54c. Newfoundland Pony | 1·40 | 1·40 |

Nos. 2614/2615 form a composite background design.

921 Canadian Flag and Globe

2009. Centenary of Department of Foreign Affairs and International Trade.

| 2616 | **921** | 54c. multicoloured | 1·25 | 1·00 |

922 Niagara Falls in 1909 and 2009

2009. Centenary of the Boundary Waters Treaty.

| 2617 | **922** | 54c. multicoloured | 1·00 | 85 |

923 Robert Charlebois

2009. Canadian Recording Artists (2nd series). Multicoloured

(a) Self-adhesive

2618	54c. Type **923**	80	90
2619	54c. Edith Butler	80	90
2620	54c. Stompin' Tom Connors	80	90
2621	54c. Bryan Adams	80	90

(b) Ordinary gum.

| MS2622 | Circular 105×105 mm. As Nos. 2618/21 | 4·00 | 4·50 |

924 Mr. PG, Prince George, British Columbia

2009. Roadside Attractions. Multicoloured.

(a) Self-adhesive

2623	54c. Type **924**	1·40	1·50
2624	54c. Sign Post Forest, Watson Lake, Yukon	1·40	1·50
2625	54c. Inukshuk (stone giant), Hay River, Northwest Territories	1·40	1·50
2626	54c. Pysanka (giant Easter egg), Vegreville, Alberta	1·40	1·50

(b) Ordinary gum.

| MS2627 | 98×109 mm. As Nos. 2623/6 | 4·00 | 5·00 |

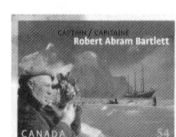

925 Captain Bartlett with Sextant and *Roosevelt* in the Canadian Arctic

2009. Captain Robert Abram 'Bob' Bartlett (Arctic explorer, ice captain and scientist) Commemoration.

| 2628 | **925** | 54c. multicoloured | 1·25 | 85 |

No. 2628 commemorates the centenary of Capt. Bartlett's attempt to reach the North Pole.

926 Five-pin Bowling

2009. Canadian Inventions. Sports. Multicoloured. Self-adhesive.

2629	54c. Type **926**	1·25	1·40
2630	54c. Ringette	1·25	1·40
2631	54c. Lacrosse	1·25	1·40
2632	54c. Basketball	1·25	1·40

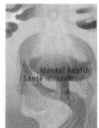

927 Tree and River inside Human Head and Sun breaking through Clouds

2009. Mental Health. Self-adhesive.

| 2633 | **927** | (54c.) +10c. multicoloured | 1·25 | 1·40 |

No. 2633 was inscr 'P+10' and was initially valid for 54c. plus a 10c. surcharge for the Canada Post Foundation for Mental Health.

928 Detail from Maurice Richard's Hockey Sweater

929 Maurice Richard, 19 October 1957

2009. Centenary of Montreal Canadiens (ice hockey team). Multicoloured. Self-adhesive

(a)

| 2634 | **928** | (54c.) multicoloured | 1·25 | 1·25 |

(b) Sheet 130×100 mm containing T **929** and similar horiz designs showing 500th goals of famous players.

| MS2635 | $3 Type **929**; Jean Beliveau, 11 February 1971; Guy Lafleur, 20 December 1983 | 18·00 | 20·00 |

No. 2634 was inscribed 'P' and originally sold for 54c. The stamps within No. MS2635 are based on digital clips and use Motionstamp technology to show action replays of goals.

930 Two Soldiers (detail from National War Memorial, Ottawa)

2009. 'Lest We Forget'

(a) Self-adhesive

| 2636 | **930** | (54c.) multicoloured | 1·10 | 1·10 |

(b) Ordinary gum.

| MS2637 | 108×60 mm. As Type **930**×2 | 2·50 | 3·00 |

No. 2636 and the stamps within MS2637 were all inscr 'P' and were originally sold for 54c.
MS2637 was originally sold for $1.08.

931 Madonna and Infant Jesus

2009. Christmas (1st issue). Showing creche figures by Antonio Caruso. Multicoloured

(a) Self-adhesive

2638	(54c.) Type **931**		1·25	95
2639	98c. Magi with gift		2·00	2·50
2640	$1.65 Shepherd carrying lamb		3·25	4·00

(b) Ordinary gum.

| MS2641 | 150×100 mm. As Nos. 2576 and 2638/40 | 7·00 | 8·00 |

No. 2638 was inscr 'P' and was originally sold for 54c.

932 Christmas Tree

2009. Christmas (2nd issue). Self-adhesive.

| 2642 | **932** | (54c.) multicoloured | 1·10 | 85 |

No. 2642 was inscribed 'P' and was initially valid for 54c.

933 Tiger Seal

2010. Chinese New Year (Year of the Tiger)

| 2643 | (54c.) Type **933** | | 1·25 | 1·00 |
| MS2644 | 40×140 mm. 170c. Tiger's head seal | | 3·50 | 4·00 |

934 Striped Coralroot (*Corallorhiza striata*)

2010. Flowers (4th series). Wild Orchids. Multicoloured

(a) Self-adhesive stamps from vert coils

2645	(57c.) Type **934**		1·10	95
2646	$1 Giant helleborine (*Epipactis gigantea*)		2·25	2·00
2647	$1.22 Rose pogonia (*Pogonia ophioglossoides*)		2·40	2·75
2648	$1.70 Grass pink (*Calopogon tuberosus*)		3·50	3·75

(b) Self-adhesive stamps from horiz coils

| 2648a | (57c.) Type **934** | | 1·10 | 95 |

(c) Self-adhesive

2649	$1 As No. 2646		2·50	2·75
2650	$1.22 As No. 2647		2·75	3·25
2651	$1.70 As No. 2648		4·00	4·50

(d) Ordinary gum.

| MS2652 | 120×72 mm. As Nos. 2645/8 | 9·25 | 9·75 |

No. 2645 was inscribed 'P' and originally sold for 57c.

935 Whistler, British Columbia

2010. Olympic Winter Games, Vancouver (3rd issue). Multicoloured

(a) Self-adhesive

| 2653 | 57c. Type **935** | | 1·40 | 1·40 |
| 2654 | 57c. Vancouver | | 1·40 | 1·40 |

(b) Ordinary gum.

| MS2655 | 141×83 mm. As Nos. 2653/4 | 2·75 | 3·25 |

936 William Hall, V.C. in 1900 and HMS *Shannon*

2010. Black History Month.

| 2656 | **936** | 57c. multicoloured | 1·50 | 1·10 |

937 *Romeo LeBlanc* (Christan Nicholson)

2010. Romeo LeBlanc (former Minister of Fisheries and Governor General of Canada 1995–9) Commemoration.

| 2657 | **937** | 57c. multicoloured | 1·25 | 1·10 |

938 Vancouver 2010 Olympic Gold Medal

2010. Olympic Winter Games, Vancouver (4th issue). Canada's First Olympic Gold on Canadian Soil

(a) Self-adhesive

| 2658 | **938** | 57c. multicoloured | 1·40 | 1·25 |

(b) Ordinary gum.

| MS2659 | 150×60 mm. As Type **938**×2 | 2·50 | 2·75 |

939 Child with Painted Face, Bobsleigh and Speed Skaters

2010. Olympic Winter Games, Vancouver (5th issue). Multicoloured

(a) Self-adhesive

| 2660 | 57c. Type **939** | | 1·40 | 1·40 |

| 2661 | 57c. Child with painted face, Chandra Crawford with gold medal (Turin 2006) and skiers | | 1·40 | 1·40 |

(b) Ordinary gum.

| MS2662 | 134×60 mm. As Nos. 2660/1 | 2·50 | 2·75 |

940 African Violet 'Decelles' Avalanche'

2010. African Violets. Multicoloured

(a) Self-adhesive

| 2663 | (57c.) Type **940** | | 1·40 | 1·40 |
| 2664 | (57c.) African violet 'Picasso' (violet and white flowers) | | 1·40 | 1·40 |

(b) Ordinary gum.

| MS2665 | 120×82 mm. As Nos. 2663/4 | 2·50 | 2·75 |

Nos. 2663/4 and the stamps within MS2665 were all inscr 'P' and were originally sold for $1.14.
MS2665 was originally sold for $1.14.

941 Figures forming Maple Leaf and Star of David

2010. Canada–Israel, 60 Years of Friendship. Self-adhesive.

| 2666 | **941** | $1.70 rosine, new blue and brownish grey | 4·25 | 4·50 |

A similar design was issued by Israel,

942 Tee Yee Neen Ho Ga Row

2010. Four Indian Kings paintings by John Verelst. Multicoloured.

2667	57c. Type **942**		1·60	1·60
2668	57c. *Sa Ga Yeath Qua Pieth Tow*		1·60	1·60
2669	57c. *Ho Nee Yeath Taw No Row*		1·60	1·60
2670	57c. *Etow Oh Koam*		1·60	1·60
MS2671	168×75 mm. Nos. 2667/70		5·75	5·75

The portraits show representatives of the Iroquois and Algonquin nations who travelled to London in 1710 for an audience with Queen Anne.

2010. London 2010 Festival of Stamps. No. MS2671 optd with **LONDON 2010 FESTIVAL OF STAMPS** logo on the sheet margin.

| MS2672 | 168×75 mm. Nos. 2667/70 | 5·00 | 5·50 |

943 HMCS *Niobe* and Sailor, c. 1910

2010. Centenary of the Canadian Navy. Multicoloured

(a) Self-adhesive

| 2673 | 57c. Type **943** | | 1·40 | 1·40 |
| 2674 | 57c. HMCS *Halifax* (modern frigate) and Wren | | 1·40 | 1·40 |

(b) Ordinary gum.

| MS2675 | 108×64 mm. As Nos. 2673/4 | 2·75 | 3·00 |

944 Harbour Porpoise (*Phocoena phocoena*)

2010. . Each black, dull ultramarine and turquoise-blue.

2676	57c. Type **944**		1·40	1·40
2677	57c. Sea otter (*Enhydra lutris*)		1·40	1·40
MS2678	105×69 mm. As Nos. 2676/7		2·50	2·75

Stamps of a similar design were issued by Sweden.

945 *Selasphorus rufus* (hummingbird) (Wing Yan Tam)

2010. Canadian Geographic's Wildlife Photography of the Year

(a) Self-adhesive

2679	57c. Type **945**		1·40	1·40
2680	57c. *Tachycineta bicolor* (tree swallows) (Mark Bradley)		1·40	1·40
2681	57c. *Tettigoniidae* (katydid) (Julie Bazinet) (vert)		1·40	1·40
2682	57c. *Ardea herodias* (great blue heron) (Martin Cooper) (vert)		1·40	1·40
2683	57c. *Vulpes vulpes* (red fox) (Ben Boulter) (vert)		1·40	1·40

(b) Ordinary gum

| 2684 | 150×100 mm. As Nos. 2679/83 | | 6·25 | 6·75 |

946 Man wearing Rotary Vest

2010. Centenary of Rotary International

| 2685 | **946** | 57c. multicoloured | 1·40 | 1·40 |

947 *Rollande*, 1929

2010. Art Canada. Multicoloured.

| 2686 | 57c. Type **947** | | 1·25 | 1·10 |
| MS2687 | 150×87 mm. 57c. Type **947**; $1.70 *At the Theatre*, 1928 (42×40 mm) | | 5·50 | 6·00 |

2010. Roadside Attractions (2nd series)

(a) Self-adhesive

2688	(57c.) The Coffee Pot, Davidson, SK		1·40	1·40
2689	(57c.) Happy Rock, Gladstone, Manitoba		1·40	1·40
2690	(57c.) Goose, Wawa, Ontario		1·40	1·40
2691	(57c.) Puffin, Longue-Pointe-de-Mingan, Quebec		1·40	1·40

(b) Ordinary gum

| MS2692 | 99×109 mm. As Nos. 2688/91 | | 5·00 | 5·00 |

Nos. 2688/91 and the stamps within MS2692 were all inscr 'P' and were originally sold for 57c.

948 Guides

2010. Centenary of Girl Guides of Canada

| 2693 | **948** | (57c.) multicoloured | 1·40 | 1·40 |

No. 2693 was inscr 'P' and was originally sold for 57c.

949 Coins, Glass and Amber Trading Beads and 17th-century Map of Avalon Peninsula, Newfoundland

2010. 400th Anniv of Cupids, Newfoundland (first English settlement in Canada)

| 2694 | **949** | 57c. multicoloured | 1·25 | 1·10 |

950 Immigrant Boy, Boy ploughing and SS *Sardinian*

2010. 'Home Children' (British orphaned and abandoned children sent to Canada)
2695	**950**	57c. multicoloured	1·25	1·10

951 Mental Health Patient on Road to Recovery

2010. Mental Health
2696	**951**	(57c.)+10c. +10c. multi-coloured	1·40	1·40

No. 2696 was inscr 'P+10' and was initially valid for 57c. plus a 10c. surcharge for the Canada Post Foundation for Mental Health.

952 Our Lady of the Night (sculpture by Antonio Caruso)

2010. Christmas (1st issue)
2697	**952**	(57c.) multicoloured	1·25	1·10

953 Red Baubles

2010. Christmas (2nd issue). Multicoloured.

(a) Self-adhesive
2698	(57c.) Type **953**	1·25	1·10
2699	$1 Blue baubles	2·40	2·25
2700	$1.70 Pink baubles	3·75	3·50

(b) Ordinary gum
MS2701 116×60 mm. As Nos. 2698/700		7·50	7·75

954 Rabbit

2011. Chinese New Year (Year of the Rabbit). Multicoloured.
2702	**954**	(59c.) Type **954**	1·25	1·10
MS2703 140x40mm. $1.75 Two rabbits (on medallion)			3·75	3·50

955 Arctic Hares

2011. Young Wildlife. Multicoloured.

(a) Self-adhesive coil stamps
2704	(59c.) Type **955**	1·25	1·10
2705	(61c.) Three young raccoons (16.1.12)	1·50	1·40
2706	(63c.) Four baby woodchucks (14.1.13)	1·40	1·25
2707	$1.03 Red fox cub	2·25	2·10
2708	$1.05 Two caribou calves (16.1.12)	2·25	2·10
2709	$1.10 Young porcupine (14.1.13)	2·25	2·10
2710	$1.25 Two Canada geese goslings	2·75	2·50
2711	$1.29 Loon and two chicks (16.1.12)	2·75	2·50
2712	$1.34 Deer fawn (14.1.13)	2·50	2·25
2713	$1.75 Polar bear cub	3·75	3·50
2714	$1.80 Two young moose (16.1.12)	3·75	3·50
2715	$1.85 Black Bear cub (14.1.13)	2·75	2·75

(b) Self-adhesive stamps from panes of six
2716	$1.03 As No. 2707	2·25	2·10
2717	$1.05 As No. 2708 (16.1.12)	2·25	2·10
2718	$1.10 As No. 2709 (14.1.13)	2·25	2·10
2719	$1.25 As No. 2710	2·75	2·50
2720	$1.29 As No. 2711 (16.1.12)	2·75	2·50
2721	$1.34 As No. 2712 (14.1.13)	2·50	2·25
2722	$1.75 As No. 2713	3·75	3·50

2723	$1.80 As No. 2714 (16.1.12)	2·75	2·50
2724	$1.85 As No. 2715 (14.1.13)	2·75	2·75

(c) Ordinary gum
MS2725 120×72 mm. As Nos. 2704, 2707, 2710 and 2713		10·00	9·50
MS2726 120×72 mm. As Nos. 2705, 2708, 2711 and 2714 (16.1.12)		10·25	9·75
MS2727 120×72 mm. As Nos. 2706, 2709, 2712 and 2715 (14.1.13)		9·00	8·50

Nos. 2704/6 were inscribed 'P' and originally sold for 59c. (2704), 61c. (2705) or 63c. (2706).

956 Canadian Flag on Soldier's Uniform and Helicopter lifting Supplies

956a CCGS *Louis S. St. Laurent* (icebreaker and Coast Guard flagship)

956b Muskoka Chairs with Maple Leaf Design on Lakeside Jetty

2011. 'Canadian Pride'. Multicoloured.

(a) Self-adhesive booklet stamps
2728	(59c.) Type **956**	1·25	1·10
2729	(59c.) Canadian flag on hot air balloon	1·25	1·10
2730	(59c.) Canadian flag on search and rescue uniform and ship	1·25	1·10
2731	(59c.) Canadian flag on Canadarm	1·25	1·10
2732	(59c.) Canadian flag on back-pack and Colosseum, Rome	1·25	1·10
2733	(61c.) Type **956a** (16.1.12)	1·50	1·40
2734	(61c.) Vintage van with Canadian flag in rear window (16.1.12)	1·50	1·40
2735	(61c.) Nicolas Gill carrying Ca-nadian flag, Olympic Games, Athens, 2004 (16.1.12)	1·40	1·50
2736	(61c.) Pierre Leuders in bobsled with Canadian flag (16.1.12)	1·50	1·40
2737	(61c.) Young Inuit child waving Canadian flag (16.1.12)	1·40	1·50
2738	(63c.) Type **936b** (14.1.13)	1·40	1·25
2739	(63c.) Maple leaf on hay bale (14.1.13)	1·40	1·25
2740	(63c.) Maple leaf on yacht spin-naker (14.1.13)	1·40	1·25
2741	(63c.) Canadian people forming maple leaf flag, Canada Day, Winnipeg (14.1.13)	1·40	1·25
2742	(63c.) Maple leaf on fishing hut on frozen Lake Scugog, Ontario (14.1.13)	1·40	1·25

(b) Ordinary gum
MS2749 148×70 mm. As Nos. 2728/32		6·25	6·00
MS2749a 130×71 mm. As Nos. 2733/7		7·50	7·00
MS2749b 130×71 mm. As Nos. 2738/42		7·00	6·25

Nos. 2728/42 and the stamps within **MS**2749/*b* were all inscr 'P' and were originally sold for 59c. (2728/32, **MS**2749), 61c. (2733/7, **MS**2749*a*) or 63c. (2738/42, **MS**2749*b*) each.

Nos. 2743/9 are left for additions to this definitive series.

957 Carrie Best (journalist and civil rights campaigner)

2011. Black History Month. Multicoloured.
2750	59c. Type **957**	1·25	1·10
2751	59c. Fergie (Ferguson) Jenkins (baseball pitcher)	1·25	1·10

958 Wrapped Gift

2011. Greetings Stamp. 'Celebration'
2752	**958**	(59c.) multicoloured	1·25	1·10

No. 2752, inscribed 'P', was initially sold for 59c.

959 Pow-wow Dancer, 1978

2011. Art Canada. Paintings by Daphne Odjig

(a) Ordinary gum
2753	59c. Type **959**	1·25	1·10
MS2754 150×87 mm. 59c. Type **959**; $1.03 *Pow-wow*, 1969 (32×39 mm); $1.75 *Spiritual Renewal*, 1984 (55×39 mm)		7·50	7·25

(b) Self-adhesive
2755	$1.03 *Pow-wow*, 1969 (32×39 mm)	2·25	2·10
2756	$1.75 *Spiritual Renewal*, 1984 (55×39 mm)	3·75	3·50

960 Sunflower 'Prado Red' **961** Sunflower 'Sunbright'

2011. Sunflowers (*Helianthus annuus*)

(a) Coil stamps. Horiz designs as T **960**. Self-adhesive.
2757	(59c.) Type **960**	1·40	1·25
2758	(59c.) Sunflower 'Sunbright'	1·40	1·25

(b) Booklet stamps. Vert designs as T **961**. Self-adhesive.
2759	(59c.) Sunflower 'Prado Red'	1·40	1·25
2760	(59c.) Type **961**	1·40	1·25

(c) Ordinary gum. Sheet 120×84 mm containing T **961** and similar vert design
MS2761 (59c.) Sunflower 'Prado Red'; (59c.) As Type **961**		2·50	2·25

Nos. 2757/60 and the stamps within **MS**2761 were all inscr 'P' and were originally valid for 59c.

962 Ram's Head

2011. Signs of the Zodiac. Multicoloured.

(a) Self-adhesive
2762	(59c.) Type **962**	1·40	1·25
2763	(59c.) Taurus (21.4.11)	1·40	1·25
2764	(59c.) Gemini (20.5.11)	1·40	1·25
2765	(59c.) Cancer (22.6.11)	1·40	1·25
2766	(61c.) Leo (23.7.12)	1·40	1·25
2767	(61c.) Virgo (23.7.12)	1·40	1·25
2768	(61c.) Libra (23.7.12)	1·40	1·25
2769	(61c.) Scorpio (23.7.12)	1·40	1·25
2770	(63c.) Sagittarius (20.2.13)	1·40	1·25
2771	(63c.) Capricorn (20.2.13)	1·40	1·25
2772	(63c.) Aquarius (20.2.13)	1·40	1·25
2773	(63c.) Pisces (20.2.13)	1·40	1·25

(b) Ordinary gum
MS2774 128×128 mm. As Nos. 2762/5 (22.6.11)		5·50	5·00
MS2775 128×128 mm. As Nos. 2766/9 (23.7.12)		5·50	5·50
MS2776 128×128 mm. As Nos. 2770/3 (20.2.13)		5·50	5·00
MS2776a 156×188 mm. As Nos. 2762/73 (20.2.13)		5·50	5·00

Nos. 2762/73 and the stamps within **MS**2774/6*a* were all inscr 'P' and were originally valid for 59c. (2762/5, **MS**2774), 61c. (2766/9, **MS**2775) or 63c. (2770/3, **MS**2776/*a*).

963 Tree

2011. International Year of Forests. Multicoloured.

(a) Self-adhesive
2777	(59c.) Type **963**	1·25	1·10
2778	(59c.) Forest floor with fungi	1·25	1·10

(b) Ordinary gum
MS2779 70×125 mm. As Nos. 2777/8		2·50	2·25

Nos. 2777/8 and the stamps within **MS**2779 form a composite design showing forest trees and undergrowth.

Nos. 2777/8 and the stamps within **MS**2779 were all inscr 'P' and were originally valid for 59c.

964 Prince William and Miss Catherine Middleton, November 2010

2011. Royal Wedding (1st issue). Multicoloured.

(a) Ordinary paper
2780	(59c.) Type **964**	1·25	1·10
2781	$1.75 Prince William and Miss Catherine Middleton embrac-ing, November 2010	3·75	3·50
MS2782 120×83 mm. Nos. 2780/1		5·00	4·75
MS2783 As No. **MS**2782 but with gold crown on upper left sheet margin		5·00	4·75

(b) Self-adhesive
2784	(59c.) As Type **964**	1·40	1·25
2785	$1.75 As No. 2768	4·00	3·75

Nos. 2780 and 2784 were both inscr 'P' and originally valid for 59c.

965 Mail Barrel rigged with Sail and Rudder, Magdalen Islands, 1910

2011. Methods of Mail Delivery. Multicoloured.
2786	59c. Type **965**	1·25	1·10
2787	59c. Dog sled carrying mail in winter, northern Canada	1·25	1·10

Nos. 2786/7 were printed together, *se-tenant*, each pair forming a composite design.

966 Hiker, Moose and Eagle in Mountain Landscape

2011. Centenary of Parks Canada
2788	**966**	59c. multicoloured	1·40	1·25

967 Concrete Tower of Burrard Bridge, Vancouver

2011. Art Déco. Multicoloured.

(a) Self-adhesive
2789	(59c.) Type **967**	1·40	1·25
2790	(59c.) Wall of Cormier House with stone carving, Montreal	1·40	1·25
2791	(59c.) R. C. Harris Water Treat-ment Plant, Toronto	1·40	1·25
2792	(59c.) Detail from Supreme Court of Canada, Ottawa	1·40	1·25
2793	(59c.) Dominion Building, Regina	1·40	1·25

(b) Ordinary gum
MS2794 127×84 mm. As Nos. 2789/93		6·50	6·25

Nos. 2789/93 and the stamps within **MS**2794 were all inscr 'P' and were originally valid for 59c.

968 Duke and Duchess of Cambridge in State Landau

2011. Royal Wedding (2nd issue)

(a) Self-adhesive
2795	**968**	(59c.) multicoloured	1·40	1·25

(b) Ordinary gum

MS2796 120×84 mm. As Type **968**×2 (sheet margin showing Westminster Abbey) 3·00 2·75

MS2797 120×84 mm. As Type **968**×2 (sheet margin showing Parliament Buildings, Canada and optd with gold maple leaf and 'Royal Tour 2011 From June 30 to July 8' in English and French) 3·00 2·75

No. 2795 and the stamps within **MS**2796/7 were inscr 'P' and were originally valid for 59c.

969 Ginette Reno

2011. Canadian Recording Artists (3rd series). Multicoloured.

(a) Self-adhesive

2798	(59c.) Type **969**	1·40	1·25
2799	(59c.) Bruce Cockburn	1·40	1·25
2800	(59c.) Robbie Robertson	1·40	1·25
2801	(59c.) Kate and Anna McGarrigle	1·40	1·25

(b) Ordinary gum

2802	(59c.) As Type **969**	1·40	1·25
2803	(59c.) As No. 2799	1·40	1·25
2804	(59c.) As No. 2800	1·40	1·25
2805	(59c.) As No. 2801	1·40	1·25

MS2806 Circular 105×105 mm. As Nos. 2798/801 10·00 9·50

Nos. 2798/5 and the stamps within **MS**2806 were all inscr 'P' and were originally valid for 59c.

2011. Roadside Attractions (3rd series). Multicoloured.

(a) Self-adhesive

2807	(59c.) The World's Largest Lobster, Shediac, New Brunswick	1·40	1·25
2808	(59c.) The Wild Blueberry, Oxford, Nova Scotia	1·40	1·25
2809	(59c.) The Big Potato, O'Leary, Prince Edward Island	1·40	1·25
2810	(59c.) The Giant Squid, Glover's Harbour, Newfoundland	1·40	1·25

(b) Ordinary gum

MS2811 98×109 mm. As Nos. 2807/10 6·50 6·25

Nos. 2807/10 and the stamps within **MS**2811 were all inscr 'P' and were originally valid for 59c.

970 *Miss Supertest III*

2011. *Miss Supertest III* (hydroplane, winner of Harmsworth Trophy 1959, 1960 and 1961). Multicoloured.

(a) Self-adhesive

2812	(59c.) Type **970**	1·40	1·25

(b) Ordinary paper

MS2813 132×70 mm. As Type **970**; $1·75 *Miss Supertest III* in race 5·00 5·25

No. 2812 and the left-hand stamp within **MS**2813 were inscr 'P' and were originally valid for 59c.

971 *Cardiac Pacemaker*

2011. Canadian Innovations. Multicoloured.

2814	59c. Type **971**	1·40	1·25
2815	59c. BlackBerry	1·40	1·25
2816	59c. Electric oven	1·40	1·25
2817	59c. Electric wheelchair	1·40	1·24

972 *The Puzzle* (Miriane Majeau)

2011. Mental Health. Multicoloured.

(a) Self-adhesive

2818	(59c.) +10c. Type **972**	1·50	1·40

(b) Ordinary gum

MS2819 118×100 mm. As Type **972**×2 3·25 3·00

No. 2818 and the stamps within **MS**2819 were inscr 'P+10' and were initially valid for 59c. plus a 10c. surcharge for the Canada Foundation for Mental Health.

973 Dr. John Charles Polanyi (Nobel Prize for Chemistry, 1986)

2011. International Year of Chemistry

2820	**973**	(59c.) multicoloured	1·25	1·10

No. 2820 was inscr 'P' and was originally valid for 59c.

974 *Angel appearing to Joseph*

2011. Christmas (1st issue). Stained-glass Windows from the Cathedral of the Immaculate Conception, Kingston, Ontario. Multicoloured.

(a) Self-adhesive

2821	(59c.) Type **974**	1·25	1·10
2822	$1·03 Nativity	2·25	2·10
2823	$1·75 Epiphany	3·75	3·50

(b) Ordinary gum

MS2824 105×60 mm. As Nos. 2821/3 7·25 7·50

975 *Holly*

2011. Christmas (2nd issue)

2825	**975**	(59c.) multicoloured	1·25	1·10

No. 2825 was inscr 'P' and was originally valid for 59c.

976 Dragon **977** Dragon's Head

2012. Chinese New Year (Year of the Dragon)

(a) Ordinary paper

2826	(61c.) Type **976**	1·50	1·40

MS2827 118×90 mm. $1·75 Two white rabbits (Year of the Rabbit); $1·80 Type **977** (transition to Year of the Dragon) 7·25 7·00

MS2828 140×41 mm. $1·80 Type **977** 22·00 21·00

(b) Self-adhesive

2829	$1·80 Type **977**	

978 Queen Elizabeth II

2012. Diamond Jubilee (1st issue)

2830	**2829**	(61c.) multicoloured	15·00	14·00

979 1953 Coronation Stamp (as Type **159**)

2012. Diamond Jubilee (2nd issue). Multicoloured.

MS2831 (61c.) Type **979**×4 6·00 5·75

MS2832 (61c.) 1967 Royal Visit 5c. stamp (as Type **271**)×4 6·00 5·75

MS2833 (61c.) 1977 Silver Jubilee 25c. stamp (as Type **399**)×4 6·00 5·75

MS2834 (61c.) 1990 Queen Elizabeth II 40c. definitive stamp (No. 1162d)×4 6·00 5·75

MS2835 (61c.) 2002 Golden Jubilee 48c. stamp (as Type **761**)×4 6·00 5·75

MS2836 (61c.) As Type **978** (32×40 mm)×4 6·00 5·75

980 John Ware

2012. Black History Month. John Ware (cowboy and rancher) and Viola Desmond (civil rights campaigner)

2837	(61c.) Type **980**	1·50	1·40
2838	(61c.) Viola Desmond	1·50	1·40

Nos. 2836/7 were inscr 'P' and were initially sold for 61c. each.

981 *Smoothly She Shifted*

2012. Art Canada. Sculptures by Joe Fafard

(a) Ordinary gum

2839	(61c.) Type **981**	2·25	2·10

MS2840 150×87 mm. (61c.) Type **981**; $1·05 *Dear Vincent* (Van Gogh seated in chair) (32×39 mm); $1·80 *Capillery* (three lasercut steel and bronze horses) (65×32 mm) 7·50 7·00

(b) Self-adhesive

2841	$1·05 *Dear Vincent* (Van Gogh seated in chair) (32×39 mm)	2·25	2·10
2842	$1·80 *Capillery* (three lasercut steel and bronze horses) (65×32 mm)	3·75	3·50

982 *Daylily 'Louis Lorrain'*

2012. Daylilies. Multicoloured.

(a) Coil stamp

2843	(61c.) Type **982**	1·50	1·40
2844	(61c.) Common orange daylily (*Hemerocallis fulva*)	1·50	1·40

(b) Booklet stamps. Size 32×25 mm

2845	(61c.) Common orange daylily (*Hemerocallis fulva*)	1·50	1·40
2846	(61c.) Type **982**	1·50	1·40

(c) Ordinary gum. Sheet 120×84 mm.

MS2847 120×84 mm. As Nos. 2845/6 1·50 1·40

Nos. 2842/5 and the stamps within **MS**2846 were all inscr 'P' and were originally valid for 61c.

983 Bow of *Titanic* (left portion) and Map showing Halifax

2012. Centenary of the Sinking of the *Titanic*

(a) Ordinary gum

2848	(61c.) Type **983**	1·40	1·25
2849	(61c.) Bow of *Titanic* (right portion) and map showing Southampton	1·40	1·25
2850	(61c.) Stern of *Titanic* (left portion) and propeller	1·40	1·25
2851	(61c.) Stern of *Titanic* (right portion) and propeller	1·40	1·25

MS2852 114×72 mm. $1·80 *Titanic* (84×36 mm) 2·75 2·50

(b) Self-adhesive

2853	(61c.) As Type **983**	1·40	1·25
2854	(61c.) As No. 2849	1·40	1·25
2855	$1·80 *Titanic* (84×36 mm) (as stamp within **MS**2852)	2·75	2·50

984 Thomas Douglas, 5th Earl of Selkirk (settlement founder), Settlers, Local Trapper and Métis (oil painting by Mark Heine)

2012. Bicentenary of the Red River Settlement

2856	**984**	(61c.) multicoloured	1·40	1·25

985 Queen Elizabeth II in 1953 and 2012

2012. Diamond Jubilee (3rd issue)

2857	**985**	$2 deep lilac	4·25	1·25

MS2858 124×136 mm. No. 2857 4·25 4·00

986 Franklin and Beaver

2012. Children's Literature. Franklin the Turtle (character from books by Paulette Bourgeois). Illlustrations by Brenda Clark

(a) Self-adhesive

2859	(61c.) Type **986**	1·40	1·25
2860	(61c.) Franklin with young sister Harriet	1·40	1·25
2861	(61c.) Franklin and Snail	1·40	1·25
2862	(61c.) Franklin, Bear and goldfish in bowl	1·40	1·25

(b) Ordinary gum

MS2863 150×100 mm. As Nos. 2859/62 5·50 5·00

987 Saddled Horse

2012. Centenary of the Calgary Stampede

(a) Self-adhesive

2864	(61c.) Type **987**	1·40	1·25
2865	$1·05 Centenary belt buckle	2·25	2·10

(b) Ordinary gum

MS2866 117×70 mm. As Nos. 2864/5 3·75 3·50

988 Louise Arbour

2012. Difference Makers

(a) Self-adhesive

2867	(61c.) bright reddish violet, silver and vermilion	1·40	1·25
2868	(61c.) new blue, silver and vermilion	1·40	1·25
2869	(61c.) turquoise-green, silver and vermilion	1·40	1·25
2870	(61c.) bright green, silver and vermilion	1·40	1·25

(b) Ordinary gum

MS2871 96×96 mm. As Nos. 2867/70 5·50 5·00

989 Major-General Sir Isaac Brock (leader of British Forces in Canada)

2012. Bicentenary of War of 1812 between United States and Britain. Multicoloured.

2872	(P) (61c.) Type **989**	1·40	1·25
2873	(P) (61c.) Shawnee War Chief Tecumseh (leader of Ohio Native Nations Confederation)	1·40	1·15

990 Rowers in Double-Scull Boat and Maple Leaf

2012. Olympic Games, London
2874	**990**	(61c.) multicoloured	1·40	1·25

991 BC Lions Logo

2012. CFL (Canadian Football League) Team Logos

(a) Self-adhesive coil stamps
2875	(61c.) black and orange-red	1·40	1·25
2876	(61c.) bottle-green, orange-yellow and black	1·40	1·25
2877	(61c.) black and rosine	1·40	1·25
2878	(61c.) black, pale green and deep emerald	1·40	1·25
2879	(61c.) deep ultramarine, gold and black	1·40	1·25
2880	(61c.) black, orange-yellow and bright scarlet	1·40	1·25
2881	(61c.) deep violet-blue, cobalt and black	1·40	1·25
2882	(61c.) multicoloured	1·40	1·25

(b Ordinary gum
MS2883	130×69 mm. As Nos. 2875/82	11·00	11·00

992 Tommy Douglas

2012. Tommy Douglas (politician and founder of Medicare) Commemoration
2884	**992**	(61c.) multicoloured	1·40	1·25

No. 2884 was inscr 'P' and originally sold for 61c.

993 BC Lions

2012. 100th Grey Cup Game. Multicoloured.

(a) Self-adhesive
2885		(61c.) Grey Cup and two players	1·40	1·25
2886		(61c.) Type **993**	1·40	1·25
2887		(61c.) Edmonton Eskimos	1·40	1·25
2888		(61c.) Calgary Stampeders	1·40	1·25
2889		(61c.) Saskatchewan Roughriders	1·40	1·25
2890		(61c.) Winnipeg Blue Bombers	1·40	1·25
2891		(61c.) Hamilton Tiger-Cats	1·40	1·25
2892		(61c.) Toronto Argonauts	1·40	1·25
2893		(61c.) Alouettes de Montréal	1·40	1·25

(b) Ordinary gum
MS2894	137×225 mm. As Nos. 2885/93	12·50	12·50

Nos. 2885/93 were all inscr 'P' and were originally valid for 61c.

994 Heart and Circle of Children's Handprints

2012. Canada Post Community Foundation
2895	**994**	(61c.) +10c. multicoloured	1·40	1·25

No. 2895 was inscr 'P+10' and was initially valid for 61c. plus a 10c. surcharge for the Canada Post Community Foundation.

995 The Black Watch of Canada

2012. 150th Anniv of the Black Watch of Canada, the Royal Hamilton Light Infantry and the Royal Regiment of Canada. Multicoloured.

(a) Self-adhesive
2896	(61c.) The Black Watch (RHR) of Canada	1·40	1·25
2897	(61c.) The Royal Hamilton Light Infantry (Wentworth Regiment)	1·40	1·25
2898	(61c.) The Royal Regiment of Canada	1·40	1·25

(b) Ordinary gum
MS2899	160×75 mm. As Nos. 2896/8	4·25	4·00

996 Madonna and Child (stained-glass window, St. Mary's Cathedral, Kingston, Ontario)

2012. Christmas (1st issue)
2900	**996**	(61c.) multicoloured	1·40	1·25

No. 2900 was inscr 'P' and was initially valid for 61c.

997 Gingerbread Man and Woman

2012. Christmas (2nd issue). Gingerbread Cookies. Multicoloured.

(a) Self-adhesive
2901	(61c.) Type **997**	1·40	1·25
2902	$1.05 Gingerbread stars	2·25	2·10
2903	$1.80 Gingerbread snowflake	2·75	2·75

(b) Ordinary gum
MS2904	85×54 mm. As Nos. 2901/3	6·50	6·50

No. 2901 was inscr 'P' and was originally valid for 61c.

2012. 125th Anniv of the Royal Philatelic Society of Canada. Sheet 133×58 mm containing designs as Nos. 2518/a and 2519c
MS2905	3c. *Chrysopa oculata* (golden-eyed lacewing); 4c. *Polistes fuscatus* (paper wasp); 8c. *Chauliognathus marginatus* (margined leatherwing)	1·00	1·25

998 Water Snake

2013. Chinese New Year (Year of the Snake)

(a) Ordinary gum
2906	(61c.) Type **999**	1·40	1·25
MS2907	90×117 mm. $1.80 Dragon's head; $1.85 Jade snake (transition to Year of the Snake)	5·50	5·50
MS2908	40×140 mm. $1.85 Jade snake	2·75	2·75

(b) Self-adhesive
2909	$1.85 Jade snake	2·75	2·75

No. 2906 was inscr 'P' and originally sold for 61c.

999 Raoul Wallenberg in 1944, Hungarian Jews and Schutz Pass

2013. Raoul Wallenberg (Second World War rescuer of Jews) Commemoration
2910	**999**	$1.85 multicoloured	2·75	2·75

1000 Joe Fortes

2013. Black History Month. Joe Fortes
2911	**1000**	(63c.) multicoloured	1·40	1·25

No. 2911 was inscr 'P' and was originally valid for 63c.

1001 Oliver Jones

2013. Black History Month. Oliver Jones (jazz musician)
2912	**1001**	(63c.) multicoloured	1·40	1·25

No. 2912 was inscr 'P' and was originally valid for 63c.

1002 Magnolia 'Eskimo'

2013. Magnolias. Multicoloured.

(a) Self-adhesive coil stamps. Size 24×20 mm
2913	(63c.) Type **1002**	1·40	1·25
2914	(63c.) Magnolia 'Yellow Bird'	1·40	1·25

(b) Self-adhesive booklet stamps. Size 32×26 mm
2915	(63c.) Magnolia 'Yellow Bird'	1·40	1·25
2916	(63c.) As Type **1002**	1·40	1·25

(c) Ordinary gum. Sheet 120×84 mm
MS2917	As Nos. 2915/16	2·75	2·50

Nos. 2913/16 and the stamps within MS2917 were all inscr 'P' and originally sold for 63c.

1003 *Hot Properties #1* (Jim Breukelman), 1987

2013. 150 Years of Photography

(a) Self-adhesive
2918	(63c.) Type **1003**	1·40	1·25
2919	(63c.) *Louis-Joseph Papineau* (Thomas Coffin Doane), 1852	1·40	1·25
2920	(63c.) *The Kitchen Sink* (Margaret Watkins), 1919	1·40	1·25
2921	(63c.) *Andor Pasztor* (Gabor Szilasi), 1978	1·40	1·25
2922	(63c.) *Koo-tuck-tuck* (Geraldine Moodie), 1903-5	1·40	1·25
2923	$1.10 *Small Basement Camera Shop, circa 1937* (Rodney Graham), 2011	2·25	2·10
2924	$1.85 *Yousuf Karsh, from the series 48 Views* (Arnaud Maggs), 1981 (shows 12 views)	2·75	2·75

(b) Ordinary gum
MS2925	150×75 mm. As Nos. 2919/20 and 2922	4·00	4·00
MS2926	150×75 mm. As Nos. 2918, 2921 and 2923/4	7·50	7·50

Nos. 2918/22 were inscr 'P' and were originally valid for 63c.

1004 Soldiers from 1890, First World War, Second World War and 2013

2013. 150th Anniv of the Princess of Wales' Own Regiment
2927	**1004**	(63c.) multicoloured	1·40	1·25

No. 2927 was inscr 'P' and was originally valid for 63c.

1005 'Punky' (one year old cat)

2013. 'Adopt a Pet'. Animals from Toronto Humane Society Shelter and Toronto Parrot Sanctuary

(a) Self-adhesive
2928	(63c.) Type **1005**	1·40	1·25
2929	(63c.) 'Buddy' (parrot) (24×24 mm)	1·40	1·25
2930	(63c.) 'Captain' (80% pug cross-breed dog)	1·40	1·25
2931	(63c.) 'Wrinkles' (dog) (40×40 mm)	1·40	1·25
2932	(63c.) 'Mickey' (black cat)	1·40	1·25

(b) Ordinary gum
MS2933	152×100 mm. As Nos. 2928/32	6·50	6·50

Nos. 2928/32 and the stamps within MS9233 were all inscr 'P' and were originally valid for 63c.

1006 Zhong Hua Men Archway, Chinatown East, Toronto

2013. Chinatown Gates. Multicoloured.

(a) Self-adhesive
2934	(63c.) Type **1006**	1·40	1·25
2935	(63c.) North Gate, Montréal, 1999	1·40	1·25
2936	(63c.) Chinatown Gate (pedestrian overpass linking Dynasty and Mandarin buildings), Winnipeg, 1987	1·40	1·25
2937	(63c.) Millennium Gate, Vancouver, 2002	1·40	1·25
2938	(63c.) Chinese Gate, Edmonton, 1987	1·40	1·25
2939	(63c.) Chinatown Gateway, Ottawa, 2010	1·40	1·25
2940	(63c.) Timber gate at entrance to Missisauga Chinese Centre	1·40	1·25
2941	(63c.) Gate of Harmonious Interest, Victoria, 1981	1·40	1·25

(b) Ordinary gum
MS2942	Circular 150 mm diameter. As Nos. 2934/41	10·50	10·50

OFFICIAL STAMPS

1949. Optd **O.H.M.S.**
O162	111	1c. green (postage)	5·00	7·00
O163	112	2c. brown	12·00	12·00
O164	-	3c. purple (No. 378)	4·25	4·75
O165	112	4c. red	5·00	4·50
O171	-	7c. blue (No. 407) (air)	24·00	12·00
O166	-	10c. green (No. 402)	7·50	15
O167	-	14c. sepia (No. 403)	13·00	7·50
O168	-	20c. grey (No. 404)	12·00	1·00
O169	-	50c. green (No. 405)	£180	£150
O170	-	$1 purple (No. 406)	45·00	65·00

1949. Optd **O.H.M.S.**
O172	135	1c. green	4·75	3·25
O173	-	2c. sepia (No. 415)	3·50	4·00
O174	-	3c. purple (No. 416)	2·75	3·25
O175	-	4c. red (No. 417)	2·75	35
O176	-	5c. blue (No. 418)	8·00	3·00
O177	141	50c. green	45·00	48·00

1950. Optd **G.**
O178	135	1c. green (postage)	1·50	10
O179	-	2c. sepia (No. 415)	5·50	6·00
O180	-	2c. green (No. 415a)	1·75	10
O181	-	3c. purple (No. 416)	2·25	10
O183	-	4c. red (No. 417)	3·00	60
O184	-	5c. blue (No. 418)	6·50	2·50
O190	-	7c. blue (No. 407) (air)	24·00	15·00
O193	153	7c. blue	2·00	3·50
O185	-	10c. green (No. 402)	3·00	10
O191	142	10c. purple	4·00	1·00
O186	-	14c. sepia (No. 403)	23·00	12·00
O187	-	20c. grey (No. 404)	55·00	1·25
O194	-	20c. grey (No. 441)	2·50	20
O188	141	50c. green	17·00	24·00
O189	-	$1 purple (No. 406)	80·00	80·00
O192	-	$1 blue (No. 433)	80·00	90·00

1953. First Queen Elizabeth II stamps optd **G.**
O196	158	1c. brown	15	10
O197	158	2c. green	20	10
O198	158	3c. red	20	10
O199	158	4c. violet	30	10
O200	158	5c. blue	30	10
O201	160	50c. green	3·25	4·50

1953. Pictorial stamps optd **G.**
O206	165	10c. brown	70	80
O207	-	20c. green (No. 488)	3·50	30
O201	160	50c. green	3·25	4·50
O195	154	$1 black	8·00	15·00

1955. Second Queen Elizabeth II stamps optd **G**.

O202	**161**	1c. brown	65	20
O203	**161**	2c. green	15	20
O204	**161**	4c. violet	40	1·00
O205	**161**	5c. blue	15	10

1963. Third Queen Elizabeth II stamps optd **G**.

O208	**215**	1c. brown	50	6·00
O209	**215**	2c. green	1·00	6·00
O210	**215**	4c. red	60	2·25
O211	**215**	5c. red	50	2·50

OFFICIAL SPECIAL DELIVERY STAMPS

1950. Optd **O.H.M.S.**

OS20	10c. green (No. S15)	17·00	35·00

1950. Optd **G**.

OS21	10c. green (No. S15)	26·00	30·00

POSTAGE DUE STAMPS

D1

1906

D1	**D1**	1c. violet	10·00	2·75
D3	**D1**	2c. violet	32·00	1·00
D5	**D1**	4c. violet	48·00	60·00
D7	**D1**	5c. violet	45·00	4·75
D8	**D1**	10c. violet	32·00	25·00

D2

1930

D9	**D2**	1c. violet	8·50	11·00
D10	**D2**	2c. violet	7·50	2·25
D11	**D2**	4c. violet	15·00	6·50
D12	**D2**	5c. violet	16·00	40·00
D13	**D2**	10c. violet	65·00	40·00

D3

1933

D14	**D3**	1c. violet	13·00	18·00
D15	**D3**	2c. violet	9·00	5·00
D16	**D3**	4c. violet	17·00	15·00
D17	**D3**	10c. violet	29·00	45·00

D4

1935

D18	**D4**	1c. violet	80	10
D19	**D4**	2c. violet	3·75	10
D20	**D4**	3c. violet	6·00	5·00
D21	**D4**	4c. violet	1·50	10
D22	**D4**	5c. violet	6·00	5·50
D23	**D4**	6c. violet	2·00	2·25
D24	**D4**	10c. violet	70	10

D5

1967

(a) Size 21×17½ mm.

D25	**D5**	1c. red	2·00	4·75
D26	**D5**	2c. red	1·25	1·00
D27	**D5**	3c. red	2·25	6·00
D28	**D5**	4c. red	2·75	1·25
D29	**D5**	5c. red	4·25	6·50
D30	**D5**	6c. red	1·60	3·75
D31	**D5**	10c. red	2·00	2·50

(b) Size 19½×16 mm.

D32	1c. red	1·50	75
D33	2c. red	1·00	3·00
D34	3c. red	3·50	5·50
D35	4c. red	1·25	60
D36a	5c. red	30	2·00
D37	6c. red	2·75	3·75
D38	8c. red	30	45
D39	10c. red	1·00	45
D40	12c. red	30	50
D41	16c. red	5·00	6·00
D42	20c. red	30	1·25
D43	24c. red	30	1·50
D44	50c. red	40	2·00

REGISTRATION STAMPS

R1

1875

R1	**R1**	2c. orange	65·00	1·00
R6	**R1**	5c. green	90·00	1·25
R9	**R1**	8c. blue	£425	£275

SPECIAL DELIVERY STAMPS

S1

1898

S2	**S1**	10c. green	60·00	14·00

S2

1922

S4	**S2**	20c. red	40·00	6·50

S3 Mail-carrying, 1867 and 1927

1927. 60th Anniv of Confederation.

S5	**S3**	20c. orange	12·00	15·00

S4

1930

S6	**S4**	20c. red	42·00	7·50

1932. As Type **S4**, but inscr "CENTS" instead of "TWENTY CENTS".

S7	20c. red	45·00	18·00

S5 Allegory of Progress

1935

S8	**S5**	20c. red	4·75	5·00

S6 Canadian Coat of Arms

1938

S9	**S6**	10c. green	22·00	4·00
S10	**S6**	20c. green	42·00	28·00

1939. Surch 10 10 and bars.

S11	10c. on 20c. red	10·00	19·00

S8 Coat of Arms and Flags

S9 Lockheed L.18 Lodestar

1942

(a) Postage

S12	**S8**	10c. green (postage)	11·00	30

(b) Air

S13	**S9**	16c. blue (air)	6·00	45
S14	**S9**	17c. blue	4·50	55

1946

(a) Postage

S15	10c. green (postage)	9·50	1·00

(b) Air

S16	17c. blue (air)	4·50	8·50

DESIGNS: 10c. As Type S **8** but with wreath of leaves; 17c. As Type S **9** but with Canadair DC-4M North Star airplane.

Pt. 22

CANAL ZONE

Territory adjacent to the Panama Canal leased by the U.S.A. from the Republic of Panama. The U.S. Canal Zone postal service closed on 30 September 1979.

1904. 100 centavos = 1 peso.
1906. 100 centesimos = 1 balboa.
1924. 100 cents = 1 dollar (U.S.).

1904. Stamps of Panama (with PANAMA optd twice) optd **CANAL ZONE** horiz in one line.

1	**5**	2c. red (No. 54)	£450	£350
2	**5**	5c. blue (No. 55)	£275	£180
3	**5**	10c. orange (No. 56)	£375	£225

1904. Stamps of the United States of 1902 optd **CANAL ZONE PANAMA**.

4	**103**	1c. green	36·00	20·00
5	**117**	2c. red	27·00	25·00
6	**107**	5c. blue	£100	60·00
7	**109**	8c. violet	£160	95·00
8	**110**	10c. brown	£140	80·00

1904. 1905 stamps optd **CANAL ZONE** in two lines.

9	**38**	1c. green	3·25	2·30
10	**38**	2c. red	5·00	3·00

1904. Stamps with PANAMA optd twice, optd **CANAL ZONE** in two lines or surch also.

11	**5**	2c. red (No. 54)	7·75	5·50
12	**5**	5c. blue (No. 55)	8·75	4·00
14	**5**	8c. on 50c. brown (No. 65)	35·00	25·00
13	**5**	10c. orange (No. 56)	23·00	13·50

1906. 1892 stamps surch PANAMA on both sides and **CANAL ZONE** and new value in centre between bars.

19	1c. on 20c. violet (No. 64)	2·20	1·70
22	2c. on 1p. red (No. 66)	3·00	3·00

1906. 1906 stamps optd **CANAL ZONE** vert.

26	**42**	1c. black and green	2·75	1·20
27	**43**	2c. black and red	3·50	1·50
28	**45**	5c. black and blue	6·50	2·50
29	**46**	8c. black and purple	23·00	8·75
30	**47**	10c. black and violet	22·00	8·75

1909. 1909 stamps optd **CANAL ZONE** vert.

35	**48**	1c. black and green	4·25	1·40
36	**49**	2c. black and red	5·00	1·50
37	**51**	5c. black and blue	19·00	4·25
38	**52**	8c. black and purple	13·00	6·50
43	**53**	10c. black and purple	55·00	9·25

1911. Surch **CANAL ZONE 10 cts.**

53	**38**	10c. on 13c. grey	6·50	2·50

1914. Optd **CANAL ZONE** vert.

54	10c. grey	55·00	13·50

1915. 1915 and 1918 stamps optd **CANAL ZONE** vert.

55	1c. black and green (No. 162)	11·00	7·00
56	2c. black and red (No. 163)	13·00	4·75
57	5c. black and blue (No. 166)	12·00	6·25
58	10c. black & orange (No. 167)	25·00	12·00
59	12c. black & violet (No. 178)	19·00	5·50
60	15c. black & blue (No. 179)	55·00	27·00
61	24c. black & brown (No. 180)	46·00	15·00
62	50c. black & orange (No. 181)	£300	£170
63	1b. black & violet (No. 182)	£190	70·00

1921. 1921 stamps optd **CANAL ZONE** vert.

64	**65**	1c. green	4·25	1·60
65	-	2c. red (No. 186)	3·25	1·40
66	**68**	5c. blue	12·00	3·75
67	-	10c. violet (No. 191)	20·00	8·25
68	-	15c. blue (No. 192)	55·00	19·00
69	-	24c. sepia (No. 194)	75·00	25·00
70	-	50c. black (No. 195)	£160	£100

1924. 1924 stamps optd **CANAL ZONE** vert.

72	**72**	1c. green	11·00	5·00
73	**72**	2c. red	8·25	3·00

1924. Stamps of the United States of 1922 optd **CANAL ZONE** horiz.

74	½c. sepia (No. 559)	1·90	80

75		1c. green (No. 602)	2·00	1·10
76		1½c. brown (No. 603)	2·75	1·90
103		2c. red (No. 604)	2·75	1·40
87		3c. violet (No. 638a)	4·00	3·50
88		5c. blue (No. 640)	5·00	3·25
106		10c. orange (No. 645)	19·00	11·00
90		12c. purple (No. 693)	25·00	15·00
141		14c. blue (No. 695)	5·00	3·75
92		15c. grey (No. 696)	8·25	5·00
93		17c. black (No. 697)	5·00	3·25
94		20c. red (No. 698)	8·00	3·50
95		30c. sepia (No. 700)	6·25	4·00
84		50c. mauve (No. 701)	85·00	49·00
97		$1 brown (No. 579)	£150	60·00

1926. Liberty Bell stamp of United States optd **CANAL ZONE**.

101	**177**	2c. red	5·50	4·25

22 Gen. Gorgas **24** Panama Canal under Construction

1928

107	**22**	1c. green	25	10
108	-	2c. red	25	10
109	**24**	5c. blue	1·10	45
110	-	10c. orange	25	20
111	-	12c. purple	80	65
112	-	14c. blue	95	75
113	-	15c. grey	45	35
114	-	20c. brown	65	20
115	-	30c. black	95	75
116	-	50c. mauve	1·60	70

PORTRAITS: 2c. Gen. Goethals. 10c. H. F. Hodges. 12c. Col. Gaillard. 14c. Gen. Sibert. 15c. Jackson Smith. 20c. Admiral Rousseau. 30c. Col. S. B. Williamson. 50c. Governor Blackburn.

1929. Air. Stamps of 1928 surch **AIR MAIL** and value.

124	-	10c. on 50c. mauve	9·25	6·50
117	**22**	15c. on 1c. green	8·75	6·00
125	-	20c. on 2c. red	5·25	1·60
119	-	25c. on 2c. red	3·75	2·20

36 Steamer, Panama Canal

1931. Air.

126	**36**	4c. purple	80	70
127	**36**	5c. green	65	35
128	**36**	6c. brown	80	40
129	**36**	10c. orange	1·10	40
130	**36**	15c. blue	1·40	40
131	**36**	20c. violet	2·20	40
132	**36**	30c. red	5·00	1·10
133	**36**	40c. yellow	3·75	1·20
134	**36**	$1 black	9·75	1·70

1933. No. 720 of United States optd **CANAL ZONE**.

140	3c. violet	3·00	35

38 Gen. Goethals

1934. 20th Anniv of Opening of Panama Canal.

142	**38**	3c. violet	25	20

45 Balboa (before construction)

1939. 25th Anniv of Opening of Panama Canal and 10th Anniv of Canal Zone Airmail Service. (a) Postage. As T **45**. Inscr "25TH ANNIVERSARY 1939 OPENING PANAMA CANAL 1914".

149	**45**	1c. green	70	35
150	-	2c. red	75	40
151	-	3c. violet	75	25
152	-	5c. blue	1·70	1·40
153	-	6c. orange	3·25	3·25
154	-	7c. black	3·50	3·25
155	-	8c. green	5·50	3·75
156	-	10c. blue	3·75	5·50
157	-	11c. green	8·75	8·75
158	-	12c. purple	9·25	8·25
159	-	14c. violet	9·25	8·25
160	-	15c. olive	13·00	6·50

161	-	18c. red	11·00	9·25
162	-	20c. brown	16·00	8·25
163	-	25c. orange	20·00	19·00
164	-	50c. purple	31·00	6·50

DESIGNS: 2c. Balboa (after construction); 3c., 5c. Gaillard Cut; 6c., 7c. Bas Obispo; 8c., 10c. Gatun Locks; 11c., 12c. Canal Channel; 14c., 15c. Gamboa; 18c., 20c. Pedro Miguel Locks; 25c.50c. Gatun Spillway.

(b) Air. Inscr "TENTH ANNIVERSARY AIR MAIL" and "25TH ANNIVERSARY OPENING PANAMA CANAL".

143	5c. black	4·25	2·50
144	10c. violet	3·75	3·25
145	15c. brown	5·50	1·10
146	25c. blue	14·00	8·75
147	30c. red	15·00	8·50
148	$1 green	38·00	30·00

DESIGNS—HORIZ: As Type **45**: 5c. Douglas DC-3 airplane over Sosa Hill; 10c. Douglas DC-3 airplane, Sikorsky S-42A flying boat and map of Central America; 15c. Sikorsky S-42A and Fort Amador; 25c. Sikorsky S-42A at Cristobal Harbour, Manzanillo Island; 30c. Sikorsky S-42A over Culebra Cut. $1 Sikorsky S-42A and palm trees.

1939. Stamps of United States (1938) optd **CANAL ZONE**.

165	**276**	½c. orange	20	10
166	-	1½c. brown (No. 801)	20	10

67 John F. Stevens

1946. Portraits.

188		½c. red (Davis)	45	25
189		1½c. brown (Magoon)	45	25
190		2c. red (Theodore Roosevelt)	20	20
191	**67**	5c. blue	40	20
192	-	25c. green (Wallace)	95	60

69 Northern Coati and Barro Colorado Island

1948. 25th Anniv of Establishment of Canal Zone Biological Area.

194	**69**	10c. black	1·90	85

70 *Arriving at Chagres on the Atlantic Side*

1949. Centenary of the Gold Rush.

195	**70**	3c. blue	70	25
196	-	6c. violet	70	35
197	-	12c. green	1·90	1·00
198	-	18c. mauve	2·20	1·60

DESIGNS: 6c. *Up the Chagres River to Las Cruces*"; 12c. *Las Cruces Trail to Panama*; 18c. *Leaving Panama for San Francisco*.

74 Western Hemisphere

1951. Air.

199	**74**	4c. purple	80	40
200	**74**	5c. green	1·10	65
201	**74**	6c. brown	55	25
202	**74**	7c. olive	1·10	50
210	**74**	8c. red	80	35
203	**74**	10c. orange	1·00	40
204	**74**	15c. purple	5·50	3·00
205	**74**	21c. blue	8·25	4·25
206	**74**	25c. yellow	13·00	3·00
207	**74**	31c. red	8·25	4·00
208	**74**	35c. blue	8·75	3·00
209	**74**	80c. black	5·00	1·60

75 Labourers in Gaillard Cut

1951. West Indian Panama Canal Labourers.

211	**75**	10c. red	3·25	1·60

76 Locomotive *Nueva Granada*, 1852

1955. Centenary of Panama Railway.

212	**76**	3c. violet	1·10	65

77 Gorgas Hospital

1957. 75th Anniv of Gorgas Hospital.

213	**77**	3c. black on green	50	40

78 *Ancon II* (liner)

1958

214	**78**	4c. turquoise	45	35

79 Roosevelt Medal and Map of Canal Zone

1958. Birth Centenary of Theodore Roosevelt.

215	**79**	4c. brown	65	35

80 "First Class" Scout Badge

1960. 50th Anniv of American Boy Scout Movement.

216	**80**	4c. ochre, red and blue	60	45

81 Administration Building, Balboa

1960

217	**81**	4c. purple	20	20

82 U.S. Army Caribbean School Crest

1961. Air.

221	**82**	15c. blue and red	1·90	80

83 Girl Scout Badge and Camp on Lake Gatun

1962. 50th Anniv of U.S. Girl Scout Movement.

222	**83**	4c. ochre, green and blue	45	35

84 Campaign Emblem and Mosquito

1962. Air. Malaria Eradication.

223	**84**	7c. black on yellow	55	45

85 Thatcher Ferry Bridge

1962. Opening of Thatcher Ferry Bridge.

224	**85**	4c. black and silver	40	25

86 Torch of Progress

1963. Air. "Alliance for Progress".

225	**86**	15c. blue, green and black	1·60	95

87 Cristobal

1964. Air. 50th Anniv of Panama Canal.

226	**87**	6c. black and green	65	40
227	-	8c. black and red	65	40
228	-	15c. black and blue	1·40	80
229	-	20c. black and purple	1·70	1·10
230	-	30c. black and brown	3·00	2·50
231	-	80c. black and bistre	4·75	3·25

DESIGNS: 8c. Gatun Locks; 15c. Madden Dam; 20c. Gaillard Cut; 30c. Miraflores Locks; 80c. Balboa.

93 Seal and Jetliner

1965. Air.

232	**93**	6c. black and green	55	35
233	**93**	8c. black and red	50	20
234	**93**	10c. black and orange	40	20
235	**93**	11c. black and green	40	20
236	**93**	13c. black and green	95	25
237	**93**	15c. black and blue	80	20
238	**93**	20c. black and violet	85	35
239	**93**	22c. black and violet	1·20	2·20
240	**93**	25c. black and green	85	75
241	**93**	30c. black and brown	1·20	35
242	**93**	35c. black and red	1·40	2·20
243	**93**	80c. black and ochre	2·75	80

94 Goethal's Memorial, Balboa

1968

244	**94**	6c. blue and green	35	35
245	-	8c. multicoloured	40	20

DESIGN: 8c. Fort San Lorenzo.

96 Dredger *Cascadas*

1976

249	**96**	13c. black, green & blue	40	20

97 Electric Towing Locomotive

1978

251	**97**	15c. green and deep green	45	20

OFFICIAL STAMPS

1941. Air. Optd **OFFICIAL PANAMA CANAL**.

O167	**36**	5c. green	6·00	1·60
O168	**36**	6c. brown	13·00	5·50
O169	**36**	10c. orange	9·25	3·75
O170	**36**	15c. blue	12·00	4·25
O171	**36**	20c. violet	14·00	7·75
O172	**36**	30c. red	20·00	9·75
O173	**36**	40c. yellow	19·00	8·75
O174	**36**	$1 black	22·00	13·00

1941. Optd **OFFICIAL PANAMA CANAL**.

O180	**22**	1c. green	2·20	45
O181	**38**	3c. violet	4·00	80
O182	**24**	5c. blue	£1100	55·00
O183	-	10c. orange	8·25	2·20
O184	-	15c. grey (No. 113)	14·00	3·25
O185	-	20c. brown (No. 114)	16·00	3·75
O186	-	50c. mauve (No. 116)	41·00	9·75

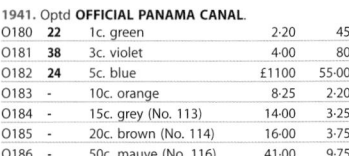

67 John F. Stevens

1947. No. 192 optd **OFFICIAL PANAMA CANAL**.

O193	**67**	5c. blue	9·75	3·25

POSTAGE DUE STAMPS

1914. Postage Due stamps of United States of 1894 optd **CANAL ZONE** diag.

D55	**D87**	1c. red	95·00	22·00
D56	**D87**	2c. red	£275	47·00
D57	**D87**	10c. red	£1100	44·00

1915. Postage Due stamps of Panama of 1915 optd **CANAL ZONE** vert.

D59	**D58**	1c. brown	13·50	5·50
D60	-	2c. brown	£250	19·00
D61	-	10c. brown	55·00	11·00

1915. Postage Due stamps of Panama of 1915 surch **CANAL ZONE** vert and value in figures.

D62	**D58**	1c. on 1c. brown	£120	16·00
D63	-	2c. on 2c. brown	27·00	8·25
D66	-	4c. on 4c. brown	38·00	16·00
D64	-	10c. on 10c. brown	25·00	5·50

1925. Postage Due stamps of United States of 1894 optd **CANAL ZONE** horiz in two lines.

D92	**D87**	1c. red	8·75	3·25
D93	**D87**	2c. red	16·00	4·25
D94	**D87**	10c. red	£160	22·00

1925. Stamps of Canal Zone of 1924 optd **POSTAGE DUE**.

D89		1c. green (No. 75)	£100	16·00
D90		2c. red (No. 103)	25·00	7·75
D91		10c. orange (No. 106)	55·00	12·00

1929. No. 109 surch **POSTAGE DUE** and value and bars.

D120	**24**	1c. on 1c. blue	5·00	2·50
D121	**24**	2c. on 5c. blue	8·75	3·50
D122	**24**	5c. on 5c. blue	8·75	3·50
D123	**24**	10c. on 5c. blue	8·75	3·50

D37 Canal Zone Shield

1932

D135	**D37**	1c. red	20	20
D136	**D37**	2c. red	20	20
D137	**D37**	5c. red	40	20
D138	**D37**	10c. red	1·50	1·60
D139	**D37**	15c. red	1·20	1·10

Pt. 17

CANTON

A treaty port in S. China. Stamps issued at the French Indo-Chinese P.O., which was closed in 1922.

1901. 100 centimes = 1 franc.
1919. 100 cents = 1 piastre.

Stamps of Indo-China overprinted or surcharged.

CANTON
州 廣
(1)

1901. "Tablet" key-type, optd with T **1**. The Chinese characters represent "Canton" and are therefore the same on every value.

1	**D**	1c. black and blue	1·50	2·00
2	**D**	2c. brown on yellow	2·00	2·75
3	**D**	4c. brown on grey	3·50	3·00
4	**D**	5c. green	1·80	2·00
6	**D**	10c. black on lilac	5·50	9·25
7	**D**	15c. blue	3·75	4·50
8	**D**	15c. grey	7·50	5·00
9	**D**	20c. red on green	18·00	25·00
10	**D**	25c. black on pink	14·00	10·00
11	**D**	30c. brown on drab	28·00	60·00
12	**D**	40c. red on yellow	55·00	65·00
13	**D**	50c. red on rose	38·00	65·00
14	**D**	75c. brown on orange	50·00	95·00
15	**D**	1f. green	70·00	75·00
16	**D**	5f. mauve on lilac	£250	£250

1903. "Tablet" key-type, surch. as T **1**. The Chinese characters indicate the value and therefore differ for each value.

17		1c. black on blue	3·00	8·25
18		2c. brown on yellow	6·00	8·00
19		4c. brown on grey	4·00	9·25
20		5c. green	3·00	9·25
21		10c. red	3·00	8·75
22		15c. grey	3·50	4·00
23		20c. red on green	15·00	34·00
24		25c. blue	7·50	14·00
25		25c. black on pink	13·00	14·50
26		30c. brown on drab	50·00	55·00
27		40c. red on yellow	75·00	80·00
28		50c. red on rose	£350	£325
29		50c. brown on blue	85·00	95·00
30		75c. brown on orange	£110	95·00
31		1f. green	80·00	90·00
32		5f. mauve on lilac	£100	95·00

1906. Surch **CANTON** (letters without serifs) and value in Chinese.

33	**8**	1c. green	2·00	4·75
34	**8**	2c. purple on yellow	1·60	2·75
35	**8**	4c. mauve on blue	1·50	2·50
36	**8**	5c. green	1·80	2·50
37	**8**	10c. red	4·50	4·75
38	**8**	15c. brown on blue	5·00	8·50
39	**8**	20c. red on green	3·50	6·50
40	**8**	25c. blue	3·75	3·00
41	**8**	30c. brown on cream	5·50	14·00
42	**8**	35c. black on yellow	2·75	6·50
43	**8**	40c. black on grey	7·00	16·00
44	**8**	50c. brown on cream	9·25	18·00
45	**D**	75c. brown on orange	75·00	95·00
46	**8**	1f. green	16·00	36·00
47	**8**	2f. brown on yellow	38·00	75·00
48	**D**	5f. mauve on lilac	£100	£120
49	**8**	10f. red on green	75·00	£120

1908. 1907 stamps surch **CANTON** and value in Chinese.

50	**10**	1c. black and brown	1·00	50
51	**10**	2c. black and brown	80	75
52	**10**	4c. black and blue	1·20	1·80
53	**10**	5c. black and green	1·40	90
54	**10**	10c. black and red	2·50	1·00
55	**10**	15c. black and violet	4·00	3·00
56	**10**	20c. black and violet	4·75	5·00
57	**11**	25c. black and blue	7·25	1·00
58	**11**	30c. black and brown	9·00	7·25
59	**11**	35c. black and green	10·00	7·50
60	**11**	40c. black and brown	20·00	7·75
61	**11**	50c. black and red	21·00	5·00
62	**12**	75c. black and orange	19·00	9·50
63	**-**	1f. black and red	40·00	22·00
64	**-**	2f. black and green	60·00	70·00
65	**-**	5f. black and blue	75·00	70·00
66	**-**	10f. black and violet	£120	£120

1919. As last, but additionally surch.

67	**10**	⅔c. on 1c. black and brown	90	4·50
68	**10**	⅗c. on 2c. black and brown	75	1·90
69	**10**	1⅓c. on 4c. black and blue	1·30	2·75
70	**10**	2c. on 5c. black and green	2·00	85
71	**10**	4c. on 10c. black and red	1·80	1·40
72	**10**	6c. on 15c. black & violet	2·75	2·50
73	**11**	8c. on 20c. black & violet	2·75	2·50
74	**11**	10c. on 25c. black & blue	6·50	45
75	**11**	12c. on 30c. black & brown	3·75	1·80
76	**11**	14c. on 35c. black & green	90	75
77	**11**	16c. on 40c. black & brown	2·00	1·80
78	**11**	20c. on 50c. black and red	4·50	45
79	**12**	30c. on 75c. black & orange	4·00	75
80	**-**	40c. on 1f. black and red	21·00	10·00
81	**-**	80c. on 2f. black and green	28·00	21·00
82	**-**	2p. on 5f. black and blue	16·00	40·00
83	**-**	4p. on 10f. black & violet	12·00	46·00

Pt. 9

CAPE JUBY

Former Spanish possession on the N.W. coast of Africa, ceded to Morocco in 1958.

100 centimos = 1 peseta.

1916. Stamps of Rio de Oro surch **CABO JUBI** and value.

1	**12**	5c. on 4p. red	£250	27·00
2	**12**	10c. on 10p. violet	55·00	27·00
3	**12**	15c. on 50c. brown	55·00	27·00
4	**12**	40c. on 1p. lilac	90·00	37·00

1919. Stamps of Spain optd **CABO JUBY**.

5	**38a**	¼c. green	20	20
18	**66**	1c. green (imperf)	28·00	18·00
6	**64**	2c. brown	20	20
7	**64**	5c. green	70	45
8	**64**	10c. red	90	65
9	**64**	15c. yellow	3·75	3·50
10	**64**	20c. green	24·00	23·00
11	**64**	20c. violet	£140	47·00
12	**64**	25c. blue	3·50	1·80
13	**64**	30c. green	3·50	1·80
14	**64**	40c. orange	3·50	1·40
15	**64**	50c. blue	4·50	3·50
16	**64**	1p. red	12·00	11·00
17	**64**	4p. purple	50·00	50·00
18	**64**	10p. orange	70·00	70·00

1925. Stamps of Spain optd **CABO JUBY**.

19a	**68**	2c. green		£375
20	**68**	5c. purple	5·50	4·25
21	**68**	10c. green	16·00	4·25
22	**68**	20c. violet	32·00	14·50

1926. As Red Cross stamps of Spain of 1926 optd **CABO-JUBY**.

23	**70**	1c. orange	17·00	17·00
24	**-**	2c. red	17·00	17·00
25	**-**	5c. brown	4·25	4·25
26	**-**	10c. green	2·10	2·10
27	**70**	15c. violet	1·50	1·50
28	**-**	20c. purple	1·50	1·50
29	**71**	25c. red	1·50	1·50
30	**70**	30c. green	1·50	1·50
31	**-**	40c. blue	50	50
32	**-**	50c. red	50	50
33	**-**	1p. red	50	50
34	**-**	4p. bistre	1·90	1·90
35	**71**	10p. violet	4·50	4·50

1929. Seville and Barcelona Exhibition stamps of Spain (Nos. 504/14) optd **CABO JUBY**.

36	**-**	5c. red	50	70
37	**-**	10c. green	50	70
38	**83**	15c. blue	50	70
39	**84**	20c. violet	50	70
40	**83**	25c. red	50	70
41	**-**	30c. brown	50	70
42	**-**	40c. blue	50	70
43	**84**	50c. orange	60	90
44	**-**	1p. grey	24·00	34·00
45	**-**	4p. red	35·00	55·00
46	**-**	10p. brown	35·00	55·00

1934. Stamps of Spanish Morocco optd **Cabo Juby**. (a) Stamps of 1928.

47	**11**	1c. red	1·90	1·40
48	**11**	2c. violet	4·25	2·75
49	**11**	5c. blue	4·25	2·75
50	**11**	10c. green	10·50	8·25
51	**11**	15c. brown	25·00	18·00
52	**12**	25c. red	4·25	2·75
53	**-**	1p. green	42·00	33·00
54	**-**	2p.50 purple	£100	70·00
55	**-**	4p. blue	£120	95·00

(b) Stamps of 1933.

56	**14**	1c. red	45	35
57	**-**	10c. green	2·75	2·10
58	**14**	20c. black	9·50	6·25
59	**-**	30c. red	9·50	6·25
60	**15**	40c. blue	31·00	25·00
61	**15**	50c. orange	60·00	47·00

1935. Stamps of Spanish Morocco of 1933 optd **CABO JUBY**.

62	**14**	1c. red	20	10
63	**-**	2c. green	60	50
64	**-**	5c. mauve	2·40	1·70
65	**-**	10c. green	16·00	11·00
66	**-**	15c. yellow	5·50	4·25
67	**14**	20c. black	5·50	4·25
68	**-**	25c. red	70·00	47·00
73	**-**	25c. violet	5·25	5·25
74	**-**	30c. red	5·25	5·25
75	**-**	40c. orange	7·50	7·50
76	**-**	50c. blue	15·00	15·00
77	**-**	60c. green	20·00	20·00
69	**-**	1p. grey	10·50	7·00
78	**-**	2p. brown	£110	£110
70	**-**	2p.50 brown	37·00	27·00
71	**-**	4p. green	60·00	45·00
72	**-**	5p. black	50·00	36·00

1937. First Anniv of Civil War. Nos. 184/99 of Spanish Morocco optd **CABO JUBY**.

79		1c. blue	50	50
80		2c. brown	50	50
81		5c. mauve	50	50
82		10c. green	50	50
83		15c. blue	50	50
84		20c. purple	50	50
85		25c. mauve	50	50
86		30c. red	50	50
87		40c. orange	1·50	1·50
88		50c. blue	1·50	1·50

89		60c. green	1·50	1·50
90		1p. violet	1·50	1·50
91		2p. blue	£110	£110
92		2p.50 black	£110	£110
93		4p. brown	£110	£110
94		10p. black	£110	£110

1938. Air. Nos. 203/12 of Spanish Morocco optd **CABO JUBY**.

95		5c. brown	20	20
96		10c. green	20	20
97		20c. red	20	20
98		40c. blue	3·75	3·75
99		50c. mauve	20	20
100		75c. blue	20	20
101		1p. brown	20	20
102		1p.50 violet	2·50	2·50
103		2p. red	5·50	5·50
104		3p. black	15·00	15·00

1939. As Nos. 213/16 of Spanish Morocco optd **CABO JUBY**.

105		5c. red	55	55
106		10c. green	55	55
107		15c. purple	55	55
108		20c. blue	55	55

1940. Nos. 217/32 of Spanish Morocco, but without "ZONA" on back, optd **CABO JUBY**.

109		1c. brown	15	15
110		2c. green	15	15
111		5c. blue	15	15
112		10c. mauve	15	15
113		15c. green	15	15
114		20c. violet	15	15
115		25c. brown	15	15
116		30c. green	15	15
117		40c. green	60	60
118		45c. red	60	60
119		50c. brown	60	60
120		75c. blue	2·00	2·00
121		1p. brown and blue	4·25	4·25
122		2p.50 green and brown	12·50	12·50
123		5p. brown and purple	12·50	12·50
124		10p. brown & deep brown	35·00	35·00

1942. Air. Nos. 258/62 of Spanish Morocco, but without "Z" opt and inscr **CABO JUBY**.

125		5c. blue	15	15
126		10c. red	15	15
127		15c. green	15	15
128		90c. pink	55	55
129		5p. black	1·80	1·80

1944. Nos. 269/82 (agricultural scenes) of Spanish Morocco optd **CABO JUBY**.

130	**-**	1c. blue and brown	15	15
131	**-**	2c. light green & green	15	15
132	**26**	5c. green and brown	15	15
133	**-**	10c. orange and blue	15	15
134	**-**	15c. light green & green	15	15
135	**-**	20c. black and purple	15	15
136	**-**	25c. brown and blue	15	15
137	**-**	30c. blue and green	15	15
138	**-**	40c. purple and brown	15	15
139	**26**	50c. brown and blue	15	15
140	**-**	75c. blue and green	1·40	1·40
141	**-**	1p. brown and blue	1·40	1·40
142	**-**	2p.50 blue and black	4·00	4·00
143	**-**	10p. black and orange	27·00	27·00

1946. Nos. 285/94 (craftsmen) of Spanish Morocco optd **CABO JUBY**.

144	**-**	1c. brown and purple	25	25
145	**27**	2c. violet and green	25	25
146	**-**	10c. blue and orange	25	25
147	**27**	15c. green and blue	25	25
148	**-**	25c. blue and green	25	25
149	**-**	40c. brown and blue	25	25
150	**27**	45c. red and black	30	30
151	**-**	1p. blue and green	2·20	2·20
152	**-**	2p.50 green and orange	6·50	6·50
153	**-**	10p. grey and blue	20·00	20·00

1948. Nos. 307/17 (transport and commerce) of Spanish Morocco, but without "Z" on back, optd **CABO JUBY**.

154	**30**	2c. brown and violet	25	25
155	**-**	5c. violet and purple	25	25
156	**-**	15c. green and blue	25	25
157	**-**	25c. green and black	25	25
158	**-**	35c. black and blue	25	25
159	**-**	50c. violet and red	25	25
160	**-**	70c. blue and black	25	25
161	**-**	90c. green and mauve	25	25
162	**-**	1p. violet and blue	35	35
163	**30**	2p.50 green and purple	2·00	2·00
164	**-**	10p. blue and black	6·00	6·00

EXPRESS LETTER STAMPS

1919. Express letter stamp of Spain optd **CABO JUBY**.

E18	**E53**	20c. red	3·50	3·50

1926. Red Cross stamp. As Express letter stamp of Spain optd **CABO-JUBY**.

E36	**E77**	20c. black and blue	4·50	4·50

1934. Stamp of Spanish Morocco optd **Cabo Juby**.

E62	**E12**	20c. black	10·50	10·50

1935. Stamp of Spanish Morocco optd **CABO JUBY**.

E79	**E16**	20c. red	5·25	5·25

1937. No. E200 of Spanish Morocco optd **CABO JUBY**.

E95	**E19**	20c. red	1·50	1·50

1940. No. E233 of Spanish Morocco optd **CABO JUBY**.

E125	**E21**	25c. red	55	55

Pt. 1

CAPE OF GOOD HOPE

Formerly a British Colony, later the southern-most province of the Union of South Africa.

12 pence = 1 shilling;
20 shillings = 1 pound.

1 'Hope'

1853. Imperf.

18	**1**	1d. red	£275	£300
19	**1**	4d. blue	£250	£110
20	**1**	6d. lilac	£375	£500
8b	**1**	1s. green	£425	£550

3

1861. Imperf.

13	**3**	1d. red	£17000	£2750
14	**3**	4d. blue	£25000	£1900

4 'Hope' seated with vine and ram (with outer frame)

1864. With outer frame line. Perf.

23a	**4**	1d. red	£120	35·00
24	**4**	4d. blue	£180	4·50
52a	**4**	6d. purple	19·00	20
53a	**4**	1s. green	£160	1·00

6 (no outer frame line)

1868. Surch.

32		1d. on 6d. violet	£750	£140
33		1d. on 1s. green	£130	70·00
34	**6**	3d. on 4d. blue	£160	2·00
27		4d. on 6d. violet	£500	18·00

1880. No outer frame line.

48		½d. black	10·00	10
49		1d. red	13·00	10
36		3d. pink	£325	38·00
43		3d. purple	11·00	1·75
51		4d. blue	23·00	50
54		5s. orange	£170	9·00

1880. Surch **THREEPENCE**.

35		3d. on 4d. pink	£110	3·25

1880. Surch **3**.

37		"3" on 3d. pink	£120	2·00

1882. Surch **One Half-penny**.

47		½d. on 3d. purple	55·00	7·00

1882

61		½d. green	1·50	50
62		2d. brown	3·25	3·25
56		2½d. olive	23·00	10
63a		2½d. blue	11·00	10
64		3d. mauve	17·00	1·25
65		4d. olive	10·00	4·00
66		1s. green	£100	8·00
67		1s. yellow	17·00	3·25

On the 2½d. stamps the value is in a white square at upper right-hand corner as well as at foot.

1891. Surch 2½d.

55a		2½d. on 3d. mauve	7·50	20

1893. Surch ONE PENNY.

57a		1d. on 2d. brown	5·50	50

17 'Hope' standing. Table Bay in background

1893

58	17	½d. green	8·50	20
59a	17	1d. red	3·50	10
60	17	3d. mauve	7·00	3·00

18 Table Mountain and Bay and Arms of the colony

1900

69	18	1d. red	7·50	10

19

1902. Various frames.

70	19	½d. green	3·00	10
71	19	1d. red	2·75	10
72	19	2d. brown	22·00	80
73	19	2½d. blue	4·50	11·00
74	19	3d. purple	15·00	1·25
75	19	4d. green	18·00	65
76	19	6d. mauve	27·00	30
77	19	1s. yellow	18·00	1·25
78	19	5s. orange	£160	26·00

Pt. 9, Pt. 12

CAPE VERDE ISLANDS

Islands in the Atlantic. Formerly Portuguese; became independent on 5 July 1975.

1877. 1000 reis = 1 milreis.
1913. 100 centavos = 1 escudo.

1877. "Crown" key-type inscr "CABO VERDE".

1	P	5r. black	3·50	2·30
2a	P	10r. yellow	20·00	11·00
18	P	10r. green	3·00	2·30
3	P	20r. bistre	2·40	1·40
19	P	20r. red	5·75	4·00
4	P	25r. pink	2·40	1·60
20	P	25r. lilac	4·25	3·25
5	P	40r. blue	95·00	60·00
21	P	40r. yellow	4·25	2·25
15	P	50r. green	£300	£140
22	P	50r. blue	8·25	6·25
7b	P	100r. lilac	6·75	3·50
8	P	200r. orange	5·25	4·00
9b	P	300r. brown	6·25	5·25

1886. "Embossed" key-type inscr "PROVINCIA DE CABO-VERDE".

33	Q	5r. black	4·75	3·25
34	Q	10r. green	4·75	3·50
35	Q	20r. red	8·75	5·50
26	Q	25r. mauve	8·75	5·75
27	Q	40r. brown	8·75	3·50
28	Q	50r. blue	8·75	3·50
29	Q	100r. brown	8·75	5·00
30	Q	200r. lilac	19·00	11·00
31	Q	300r. orange	22·00	4·50

1894. "Figures" key-type inscr "CABO-VERDE".

37	R	5r. orange	1·70	1·40
38	R	10r. mauve	1·70	1·40
39	R	15r. brown	4·00	2·75
40	R	20r. lilac	4·00	2·75
41	R	25r. green	3·50	2·30
42	R	50r. blue	3·50	2·30
51	R	75r. red	12·00	6·25
43	R	80r. green	34·00	27·00
44	R	100r. brown on buff	9·75	5·50
58	R	150r. red on rose	34·00	29·00
59	R	200r. blue on blue	34·00	29·00
46	R	300r. blue on buff	39·00	18·00

1898. "King Carlos" key-type inscr "CABO VERDE".

60	S	2½r. grey	40	35
61	S	5r. orange	55	35
62	S	10r. green	55	35
63	S	15r. brown	5·72	2·10
111	S	15r. green	2·20	1·50
64	S	20r. lilac	1·70	95
65	S	25r. green	3·50	1·30
112	S	25r. red	1·20	25
66	S	50r. blue	3·50	1·60
113	S	50r. brown	4·50	3·00
114	S	65r. blue	29·00	18·00
67	S	75r. red	9·00	3·50
115	S	75r. purple	4·00	2·75
68	S	80r. mauve	9·00	3·50
69	S	100r. blue on blue	3·50	1·90
116	S	115r. brown on pink	18·00	12·00
117	S	130r. brown on yellow	19·00	12·00
70	S	150r. brown on yellow	9·00	5·25
71	S	200r. purple on pink	4·25	3·00
72	S	300r. blue on pink	10·50	5·25
118	S	400r. blue on yellow	20·00	12·50
73	S	500r. black on blue	10·50	5·25
74	S	700r. mauve on yellow	30·00	19·00

1902. Key-types of Cape Verde Is. surch.

119	S	50r. on 65r. blue	4·75	3·75
75	Q	65r. on 5r. black	5·75	4·00
78	R	65r. on 10r. mauve	7·25	4·00
79	R	65r. on 20r. lilac	7·25	4·00
80	R	65r. on 100r. brn on buff	9·25	5·50
76	Q	65r. on 200r. lilac	5·75	4·00
77	Q	65r. on 300r. orange	5·75	4·00
85	R	115r. on 5r. orange	4·25	3·25
82	Q	115r. on 10r. green	5·75	4·00
83	Q	115r. on 20r. red	5·75	4·00
87	R	115r. on 25r. green	3·00	2·30
88	R	115r. on 150r. red on rose	8·75	6·75
90	Q	130r. on 50r. blue	5·75	4·00
93	R	130r. on 75r. red	4·25	3·25
96	R	130r. on 80r. green	3·50	2·20
92	Q	130r. on 100r. brown	5·75	4·00
97	R	130r. on 200r. blue on blue	3·75	2·75
106	V	400r. on 2½r. brown	1·70	1·60
98	Q	400r. on 25r. mauve	3·00	2·75
99	Q	400r. on 40r. brown	5·75	5·00
101	R	400r. on 50r. blue	5·75	3·25
103	R	400r. on 300r. blue on buff	2·75	1·80

1902. "King Carlos" key-type of Cape Verde Is. optd PROVISORIO.

107		15r. brown	1·90	1·30
108		25r. green	1·90	1·30
109		50r. blue	1·90	1·30
110		75r. red	3·75	2·75

1911. "King Carlos" key-type of Cape Verde Is. optd REPUBLICA.

120		2½r. grey	35	30
121		5r. orange	35	30
122		10r. green	1·20	95
123		15r. green	1·00	50
124		20r. lilac	1·70	95
125		25r. red	1·00	50
126		50r. brown	10·50	7·25
127		75r. purple	1·60	95
128		100r. blue on blue	1·60	95
129		115r. brown on pink	1·60	95
130		130r. brown on yellow	1·60	95
131		200r. purple on pink	8·00	4·75
132		400r. blue on yellow	4·00	1·40
133		500r. black on blue	4·00	1·40
134		700r. mauve on yellow	4·00	1·40

1912. "King Manoel" key-type inscr "CABO VERDE" and optd REPUBLICA.

135	T	2½r. lilac	25	25
136	T	5r. black	25	25
137	T	10r. green	50	45
138	T	20r. red	3·00	1·60
139	T	25r. brown	50	25
140	T	50r. blue	5·75	4·00
141	T	75r. brown	1·30	1·20
142	T	100r. brown on green	1·30	1·20
143	T	200r. green on pink	2·10	1·20
144	T	300r. black on blue	2·10	1·20
145	T	400r. blue and black	4·50	3·50
146	T	500r. brown and olive	4·50	3·50

1913. Surch. REPUBLICA CABO VERDE and new value on "Vasco da Gama" issues of (a) Portuguese Colonies.

147		¼c. on 2½r. green	1·60	80
148		½c. on 5r. red	1·60	80
149		1c. on 10r. purple	1·60	80
150		2½c. on 25r. green	1·10	50
151		5c. on 50r. blue	2·20	1·80
152		7½c. on 75r. brown	4·50	3·50
153		10c. on 100r. brown	2·20	2·20
154		15c. on 150r. bistre	3·00	3·00

(b) Macao.

155		¼c. on ½a. green	1·60	1·00
156		½c. on 1a. red	1·60	1·00
157		1c. on 2a. purple	1·60	1·00
158		2½c. on 4a. green	1·60	1·00
159		5c. on 8a. blue	8·50	7·50
160		7½c. on 12a. brown	6·75	3·00
161		10c. on 16a. brown	2·75	2·00
162		15c. on 24a. bistre	7·25	4·00

(c) Timor.

163		¼c. on ½a. green	1·60	1·00
164		½c. on 1a. red	1·60	1·00
165		1c. on 2a. purple	1·60	1·00
166		2½c. on 4a. green	1·60	1·00
167		5c. on 8a. blue	7·25	7·00
168		7½c. on 12a. brown	6·75	3·75
169		10c. on 16a. brown	2·75	2·00
170		15c. on 24a. bistre	5·50	4·00

1913. Stamps of 1902 optd REPUBLICA.

171	S	75r. red (No. 110)	6·75	4·75
192	R	115r. on 5r. (No. 85)	1·70	95
193	Q	115r. on 10r. (No. 82)	3·00	1·90
195	Q	115r. on 20r. (No. 83)	3·25	2·10
198	R	115r. on 25r. (No. 87)	3·00	1·90
200	R	115r. on 150r. (No. 88)	1·00	95
201	Q	130r. on 50r. (No. 90)	3·00	1·60
202	R	130r. on 75r. (No. 93)	3·00	1·20
204	R	130r. on 80r. (No. 96)	3·00	1·20
206	Q	130r. on 100r. (No. 92)	2·00	1·20
208	R	130r. on 200r. (No. 97)	2·00	1·20

1914. "Ceres" key-type inscr "CABO VERDE". Name and value in black.

219	U	¼c. green	35	30
220	U	½c. black	35	30
221	U	1c. green	35	30
222	U	1½c. brown	35	30
223	U	2c. red	35	30
224	U	2c. grey	40	30
180	U	2½c. violet	75	65
214	U	2½c. mauve	35	30
215	U	3c. orange	30	25
216	U	4c. red	30	25
228	U	4½c. grey	40	40
229	U	5c. blue	45	40
230	U	6c. mauve	40	40
231	U	7c. blue	40	40
232	U	7½c. brown	40	40
233	U	8c. grey	75	55
234	U	10c. red	40	40
235	U	12c. green	70	65
236	U	15c. pink	40	40
237	U	20c. green	40	40
238	U	24c. blue	1·20	95
239	U	25c. brown	1·20	95
188	U	30c. brown on green	5·75	3·75
240	U	30c. green	55	50
189	U	40c. brown on pink	3·25	2·75
241	U	40c. turquoise	55	50
190	U	50c. orange on orange	4·00	2·75
242	U	50c. mauve	1·00	80
243	U	60c. blue	1·40	1·00
244	U	60c. red	1·60	95
245	U	80c. red	5·00	1·40
191	U	1e. green on blue	4·00	3·00
246	U	1e. pink	5·75	3·00
247	U	1e. blue	6·25	3·75
248	U	2e. purple	5·75	3·00
249	U	5e. brown	10·50	7·25
250	U	10e. pink	24·00	14·50
251	U	20e. green	65·00	49·00

1921. Nos. 153/4 surch.

252		2c. on 15c. on 150r. brown	2·75	1·90
253		4c. on 10c. on 100r. brown	3·25	3·00

1921. No. 69 surch 6 c. REPUBLICA.

254	S	6c. on 100r. blue on blue	3·25	2·50

1921. Charity Tax stamp of Portuguese Colonies (General issues) optd CABO VERDE CORREIOS or surch also.

255		¼ on 1c. green	60	40
256		½c. on 1c. green	75	55
257		1c. green	1·10	85

1922. Provisionals of 1913 surch $04.

260	R	4c. on 130r. on 75r. red (No. 202)	80	60
262	R	4c. on 130r. on 80r. green (No. 204)	1·10	85
265	R	4c. on 130r. on 200r. blue (No. 208)	1·10	90

1925. Provisional stamps of 1902 surch Republica 40 C.

267	V	40c. on 400r. on 2½r. brown (No. 106)	1·10	90
268	R	40c. on 400r. on 300r. blue on buff (No. 103)	1·10	90

1931. No. 245 surch 70 C.

269	U	70c. on 80c. red	29·00	11·00

1934. As T 17 of Angola (new "Ceres" type).

270	17	1c. brown	20	15
271	17	5c. sepia	20	15
272	17	10c. mauve	20	15
273	17	15c. black	30	25
274	17	20c. grey	30	25
275	17	30c. green	30	25
276	17	40c. red	30	25
277	17	45c. blue	1·20	95
278	17	50c. brown	1·00	65
279	17	60c. olive	1·00	65
280	17	70c. brown	1·00	65
281	17	80c. green	1·00	65
282	17	85c. red	4·50	3·00
283	17	1e. red	3·00	50
284	17	1e.40 blue	4·00	3·00
285	17	2e. mauve	5·25	3·00
286	17	5e. green	23·00	5·75
287	17	10e. brown	36·00	21·00
288	17	20e. orange	70·00	28·00

1938. As Nos. 383/409 of Angola.

289		1c. olive (postage)	25	20
290		5c. brown	25	20
291		10c. red	25	20
292		15c. purple	1·10	95
293		20c. slate	50	30
294		30c. purple	50	20
295		35c. green	50	30
296		40c. brown	50	30
297		50c. mauve	50	30
298		60c. black	50	30
299		70c. violet	50	30
300		80c. orange	50	30
301		1e. red	80	30
302		1e.75 blue	2·10	80
303		2e. green	4·00	3·00
304		5e. olive	9·25	2·30
305		10e. blue	14·50	3·00
306		20e. brown	49·00	6·00
307		10c. red (air)	85	70
308		20c. violet	85	70
309		50c. orange	85	70
310		1e. blue	85	70
311		2e. red	2·00	1·10
312		3e. green	2·75	1·90
313		5e. brown	8·00	2·75
314		9e. red	13·00	4·75
315		10e. mauve	14·50	6·25

14 Route of President's Tour

1939. Pres. Carmona's 2nd Colonial Tour.

316	14	80c. violet on mauve	4·50	3·00
317	14	1e.75 blue on blue	37·00	27·00
318	14	20e. brown on cream	75·00	25·00

1948. Nos. 276 and 294 surch.

319		10c. on 30c. purple	1·80	1·00
320		25c. on 40c. red	1·90	1·00

16 Machado Point, Sao Vicente **17** Ribeira Brava, Sao Nicolau

1948

321	16	5c. purple and bistre	50	40
322	-	10c. green and light green	50	40
323	17	50c. purple and lilac	1·00	40
324	-	1e. purple	3·75	1·70
325	-	1e.75 blue and green	4·50	2·40
326	-	2e. brown and ochre	10·50	3·00
327	-	5e. green and yellow	21·00	5·75
328	-	10e. red and orange	34·00	19·00
329	-	20e. violet and buff	85·00	36·00

DESIGNS:—VERT: 10c. Ribeira Grande. HORIZ: 1e. Porto Grande, Sao Vicente; 1e.75, 5e. Mindelo, Sao Vicente; 2e. Joao de Evora beach, Sao Vicente; 10e. Volcano, Fogo; 20e. Paul.

1948. Honouring the Statue of Our Lady of Fatima. As T 33 of Angola.

330		50c. blue	13·00	8·50

1949. 75th Anniv of U.P.U. As T **39** of Angola.
331	1e. mauve	10·50	5·00

1950. Holy Year. As T **41/2** of Angola.
| 332 | 1e. brown | 1·20 | 65 |
| 333 | 2e. blue | 4·75 | 2·75 |

1951. Surch with figures and bars over old value.
334	10c. on 35c. (No. 295)	65	55
335	20c. on 70c. (No. 299)	85	65
336	40c. on 70c. (No. 299)	1·00	65
337	50c. on 80c. (No. 300)	1·00	65
338	1e. on 1e.75 (No. 302)	1·10	65
339	2e. on 10e. (No. 305)	5·25	2·10

1951. Termination of Holy Year. As T **44** of Angola.
340	2e. violet and mauve	1·50	1·00

1952. No. 302 surch with figures and cross over old values.
341	10c. on 1e.75 blue	1·30	1·20
342	20c. on 1e.75 blue	1·30	1·20
343	50c. on 1e.75 blue	6·25	6·00
344	1e. on 1e.75 blue	75	20
345	1e.50 on 1e.75 blue	75	20

20 Map, c. 1471 **21** V. Dias and G. de Cintra

1952. Portuguese Navigators as T **20/21**. Multicoloured.
346	5c. Type **20**	20	20
347	10c. Type **21**	20	20
348	30c. D. Afonso and A. Fernandes	20	20
349	50c. Lancarote and S. da Costa	20	20
350	1e. D. Gomes and A. da Nola	20	20
351	2e. Princes Fernando and Henry the Navigator	1·40	20
352	3e. A. Goncalves and D. Dias	12·00	1·90
353	5e. A. Goncalves Baldaia and J. Fernandes	4·00	95
354	10e. D. Eanes da Gra and A. de Freitas	8·00	2·30
355	20e. Map, 1502	14·50	2·75

22 Doctor giving Injection

1952. First Tropical Medicine Congress, Lisbon.
356	**22**	20c. black and green	75	55

23 Facade of Monastery

1953. Missionary Art Exhibition.
357	**23**	10c. brown and olive	20	20
358	**23**	50c. violet and salmon	95	45
359	**23**	1e. green and orange	2·30	1·40

1953. Portuguese Stamp Centenary. As T **48** of Angola.
360	50c. multicoloured	1·90	1·30

1954. Fourth Cent of Sao Paulo. As T **49** of Angola.
361	1e. black, green and buff	85	65

24 Arms of Cape Verde Is. and Portuguese Guinea

1955. Presidential Visit.
362	**24**	1e. multicoloured	55	40
363	**24**	1e.60c. multicoloured	1·30	1·10

25 Arms of Praia

1958. Centenary of City of Praia. Multicoloured.
364	**25**	1e. on yellow	65	55
365	**25**	2e.50 on salmon	1·30	1·10

1958. Brussels International Exn. As T **55** of Angola.
366	2e. multicoloured	95	45

1958. Sixth International Congress of Tropical Medicine. As T **56** of Angola. Multicoloured.
367	3c. "Aloe vera" (plant)	5·75	2·75

26 Prince Henry the Navigator

1960. 500th Death Anniv of Prince Henry the Navigator.
368	**26**	2e. multicoloured	1·40	1·40

27 Antonio da Nola

1960. 500th Anniv of Colonization of Cape Verde Islands. Multicoloured.
369	1e. Type **27**	95	55
370	2e.50 Diogo Gomes	2·30	1·20

28 "Education"

1960. Tenth Anniv of African Technical Co-operation Commission.
371	**28**	2e.50 multicoloured	1·40	85

29 Arms of Praia

1961. Urban Arms. As T **29**. Arms multicoloured; inscriptions in red and green; background colours given.
372	5c. buff	30	20
373	15c. blue	30	20
374	20c. yellow	30	20
375	30c. lilac	30	20
376	1e. green	75	20
377	2e. lemon	75	20
378	2e.50 pink	1·10	50
379	3e. brown	1·80	65
380	5e. blue	1·80	65
381	7e.50 olive	1·90	1·10
382	15e. mauve	2·75	1·10
383	30e. yellow	7·25	3·00

ARMS: 15c. Nova Sintra. 20c. Ribeira Brava. 30c. Assomada. 1e. Maio. 2e. Mindelo. 2e.50 Santa Maria. 3e. Pombas. 5e. Sal-Rei. 7e.50. Tarrafal. 15e. Maria Pia. 30e. San Felipe.

1962. Sports. As T **62** of Angola. Multicoloured.
384	50c. Throwing the javelin	40	30
385	1e. Discus thrower	1·10	40
386	1e.50 Batsman (cricket)	75	45
387	2e.50 Boxing	1·10	55
388	4e.50 Hurdler	1·90	1·30
389	12e.50 Golfers	3·50	2·75

1962. Malaria Eradication. Mosquito design as T **63** of Angola. Multicoloured.
390	2e.50 *Anopheles pretoriensis*	1·50	1·20

1963. Tenth Anniv of T.A.P. Airline. As T **69** of Angola.
391	2e.50 multicoloured	1·10	85

1964. Centenary of National Overseas Bank. As T **71** of Angola but portrait of J. da S. M. Leal.
392	1e.50 multicoloured	1·10	85

1965. Centenary of I.T.U. As T **73** of Angola.
393	2e.50 multicoloured	2·30	1·70

30 Militia Regiment Drummer, 1806

1965. Portuguese Military Uniforms. Multicoloured.
394	50c. Type **30**	40	30
395	1e. Militiaman, 1806	55	30
396	1e.50 Infantry Grenadiers officers, 1833	70	55
397	2e.50 Infantry grenadier, 1833	1·40	45
398	3e. Cavalry officer, 1834	2·75	65
399	4e. Infantry grenadier, 1835	1·30	65
400	5e. Artillery officer, 1848	1·40	65
401	10e. Infantry drum-major, 1856	3·25	2·10

1966. 40th Anniv of National Revolution. As T **77** of Angola, but showing different building. Multicoloured.
402	1e. Dr A. Moreira's Academy and Public Assistance Building	65	55

1967. Centenary of Military Naval Association. As T **79** of Angola. Multicoloured.
403	1e. F. da Costa and gunboat *Mandovy*	85	65
404	1e. 50 C. Araujo and minesweeper *Augusto Castilho*	1·30	1·00

1967. 50th Anniv of Fatima Apparitions. As T **80** of Angola. Multicoloured.
405	1e. Image of Virgin Mary	40	30

33 President Tomas

1968. Visit of President Tomas of Portugal.
406	**33**	1e. multicoloured	40	30

1968. 500th Birth Anniv of Pedro Cabral (explorer). As T **84** of Angola. Multicoloured.
407	1e. Cantino's map, 1502	95	85
408	1e.50 Pedro Alvares Cabral (vert)	1·50	95

34 Port of Sao Vicente

1968. "Produce of Cape Verde Islands". Multicoloured.
409	50c. Type **34**	30	20
410	1e. Purgueira (*Tatrophus curcus*) (vert)	45	25
411	1e.50 Groundnuts (vert)	45	25
412	2e.50 Castor-oil plant (vert)	45	25
413	3e.50 Inhame (*Dioscorea alata*) (vert)	45	25
414	4e. Date palm (vert)	45	25
415	4e.50 Goiabeira (*Psidium guajava*) (vert)	75	30
416	5e. Tamarind (vert)	1·10	40
417	10e. Manioc (vert)	1·50	75
418	30e. Girl of Cape Verde (vert)	3·50	2·75

1969. Birth Centenary of Admiral Gago Coutinho. As T **86** of Angola. Multicoloured.
419	30c. Fairey IIID seaplane *Lusitania* and map of Lisbon-Rio flight (vert)	30	20

1969. 500th Birth Anniv of Vasco da Gama (explorer). Multicoloured. As T **87** of Angola.
420	1e.50 Vasco da Gama (vert)	40	30

1969. Centenary of Overseas Administrative Reforms. As T **88** of Angola.
421	2e. multicoloured	40	30

1969. 500th Birth Anniv of King Manoel I. As T **89** of Angola. Multicoloured.
422	3e. Manoel I	55	40

1970. Birth Centenary of Marshal Carmona. As T **91** of Angola. Multicoloured.
423	2e.50 Half-length portrait	55	40

35 Desalination Installation

1971. Inauguration of Desalination Plant, Mindelo.
424	**35**	4e. multicoloured	1·30	1·00

1972. 400th Anniv of Camoens' *Lusiad* (epic poem). As T **96** of Angola. Multicoloured.
425	5e. Galleons at Cape Verde	65	30

1972. Olympic Games, Munich. As T **97** of Angola. Multicoloured.
426	4e. Basketball and boxing	65	30

1972. 50th Anniv of First Flight Lisbon–Rio de Janeiro. As T **98** of Angola. Multicoloured.
427	3e.50 Fairey IIID seaplane *Lusitania* near Sao Vicente	65	30

1973. Centenary of I.M.O./W.M.O. As Type **99** of Angola.
428	2e.50 multicoloured	65	30

1975. Independence. No. 407 optd **INDEPENDENCIA 5-Julho-75.**
430	1e. multicoloured	1·00	60

37 Cabral, Flag and People

1975. Third Anniv of Amilcar Cabral's Assassination.
431	**37**	5e. multicoloured	1·25	75

38 Islanders with Broken Shackles

1976. First Anniv of Independence.
432	**38**	50c. multicoloured	40	25
433	**38**	3e. multicoloured	15	10
434	**38**	15e. multicoloured	40	20
435	**38**	50e. multicoloured	1·25	65
MS436	150×110 mm. Nos. 432/5	10·00	7·50	

1976. Nos. 428, 424 and 415 optd **REPUBLICA DE.**
437	**38**	2e.50 multicoloured (No. 428)	1·00	50
438	**38**	4e. multicoloured (No. 424)	30·00	10·00
439	**38**	4e.50 multicoloured (No. 415)	4·50	2·75

40 Cabral and Map

1976. 20th Anniv of PAIGC (Revolutionary Party).
440	**40**	1e. multicoloured	75	40

41 Map of Islands

1977. Red Cross.
441	**41**	50c. multicoloured	1·00	60

42 Printed Circuit

1977. International Telecommunications Day.
442	**42**	5e.50 orange, brown and black	40	25

43 Ashtray on Stand

1977. Craftsmanship in Coconut. Multicoloured.
443	20c. Type **43**	10	10
444	30c. Ornamental bell	10	10
445	50c. Lamp	10	10
446	1e. Nativity	10	10
447	1e.50 Desk lamp	15	10
448	5e. Storage jar	50	25

449		10e. Container with hinged lid	1·00	50
450		20e. Tobacco jar	2·00	1·00
451		30e. Stringed instrument	3·00	1·50

44 5r. Stamp, 1877

1977. Centenary of First Cape Verde Stamps.
452	**44**	4e. multicoloured	1·00	60
453	**44**	8e. multicoloured	2·00	1·20

45 Congress Emblem

1977. Third PAIGC Congress, Bissau.
454	**45**	3e.50 multicoloured	2·00	1·20

1978. No. 419 surch **3$00**.
455		3e. on 30c. multicoloured	4·00	2·00

47 Microwave Antenna

1978. Tenth World Telecommunications Day.
456	**47**	3e.50 multicoloured	40	20

48 Textile Pattern

1978. Handicrafts. Multicoloured.
457	50c. Type **48**		10	10
458	1e.50 Carpet runner and map of Islands		30	15
459	2e. Woven ribbon and map of Islands		40	20
460	3e. Shoulder bag and map of Islands		55	30
461	10e. Woven Cushions (vert)		1·80	1·00

49 Map of Africa

1978. International Anti-Apartheid Year.
462	**49**	4e.50 multicoloured	1·20	75

50 Freighter *Cabo Verde*

1978. First Cape Verde Merchant Ship.
463	**50**	1e. multicoloured	80	30

51 Human Rights Emblem

1978. 30th Anniv of Declaration of Human Rights.
464	**51**	1e.50 multicoloured	60	40
465	**51**	2e. multicoloured	80	50

52 Children with Flowers

1979. International Year of the Child. Multicoloured.
466	1e.50 Children with balloons and flags		60	30
467	3e.50 Type **52**		1·20	1·40

53 Monument

1979. 20th Anniv of Pindjiguiti Massacre.
468	**53**	4e.50 multicoloured	15	10

54 Poster

1979. First National Youth Week.
469	**54**	3e.50 multicoloured	80	35

55 Mindelo

1980. Centenary of Mindelo City.
470	**55**	4e. multicoloured	55	15

56 Family, Graph and Map

1980. First Population and Housing Census.
471	**56**	3e.50 multicoloured	65	35
472	**56**	4e.50 multicoloured	80	45

57 National Flag

1980. Fifth Anniv of Independence (1st issue).
473	**57**	4e. multicoloured	75	40

See also Nos. 481/3.

58 Running

1980. Olympic Games, Moscow. Multicoloured.
474	1e. Type **58**		10	10
475	2e.50 Boxing		10	10
476	3e. Basketball		10	10
477	4e. Volleyball		30	15
478	20e. Swimming		50	90
479	50e. Tennis		3·75	2·30
MS480	98×67 mm. 30e. Football (horiz)		10·00	7·50

59 Stylized Bird

1980. Fifth Anniv of Independence (2nd issue).
481	**59**	4e. multicoloured	40	25
482	**59**	7e. multicoloured	75	45
483	**59**	11e. multicoloured	1·20	80

60 Cigarette, Cigar, Pipe and Diseased Heart

1980. World Health Day. Anti-smoking Campaign. Multicoloured.
484	4e. Type **60**		1·00	45
485	7e. Healthy lungs plus smoking equals diseased lungs		1·50	75

61 Albacore

1980. Marine Life. Multicoloured.
486	50c. Type **61**		10	10
487	4e.50 Atlantic horse-mackerel		30	15
488	8e. Mediterranean moray		50	45
489	10e. Brown meagre		70	35
490	12e. Skipjack tuna		80	40
491	50e. Blue shark		3·25	1·80

62 *Area Verdel*

1980. Freighters. Multicoloured.
492	3e. Type **62**		30	20
493	5e.50 *Ilha do Maio*		60	20
494	7e.50 *Ilha de Komo*		80	40
495	9e. *Boa Vista*		1·00	50
496	12e. *Santo Antao*		1·40	65
497	30e. *Santiago*		3·25	1·80

63 *Lochnera rosea*

1980. Flowers. Multicoloured.
498	50c. Type **63**		10	10
499	4e.50 *Poinciana regia Bojer*		40	20
500	8e. *Mirabilis jalapa*		85	45
501	10e. *Nerium oleander*		25	10
502	12e. *Bougainvillea litoralis*		1·00	55
503	30e. *Hibiscus rosa sinensis*		2·50	1·25

64 Desert Scene and Hands holding plant

1981. Desert Erosion Prevention. Multicoloured.
504	4e.50 Type **64**		70	35
505	10e.50 Hands caring for plant and river scene		1·60	80

65 Map, Flag, and "Official Bulletin" announcing Constitution

1981. Sixth Anniv of Constitution.
506	**65**	4e.50 multicoloured	1·50	70

66 Austrian Winter Olympics Stamps of 1975

1981. WIPA 1981 International Stamp Exhibition, Vienna. Sheet 107×62 mm.
MS507	**66**	50e. multicoloured	3·75	3·75

67 Antenna

1981. Telecommunications. Multicoloured.
508	4e.50 Type **67**		40	20
509	8e. Dish antenna		75	35
510	20e. Dish antenna and satellite		1·80	90

68 Disabled Person in Wheelchair and IYDP Emblem

1981. International Year of Disabled Persons.
511	**68**	4e.50 multicoloured	75	30

69 Moorhens

1981. Birds. Multicoloured.
512	1e. Little egret (vert)		20	15
513	4e.50 Barn owl (vert)		40	20
514	8e. Grey-headed kingfisher (vert)		90	30
515	10e. Type **69**		2·30	1·10
516	12e. Helmet guineafowls		2·50	1·30
MS517	79×54 mm. 50e. Raza Island lark (*Alauda razae*) (vert)		9·00	5·00

70 Map showing Member States

1982. CILSS Congress, Praia.
518	**70**	11e.50 multicoloured	55	50

71 Tackle

1982. "Amilcar Cabral" Football Cup Competition. Multicoloured.
519	4e.50 Type **71**		55	15

520		7e.50 Running with ball	95	35
521		11e.50 Goalmouth scene	1·40	65

72 Militiawomen

1982. First Anniv of Cape Verde Women's Organization. Multicoloured.

522		4e.50 Type **72**	30	15
523		8e. Women farmers	94	40
524		12e. Nursery teacher	1·30	70

73 Footballers

1982. World Cup Football Championship, Spain.

525	**73**	1e.50 multicoloured	15	10
526	–	4e.50 multicoloured	40	25
527	–	8e. multicoloured	80	40
528	–	10e.50 multicoloured	1·00	60
529	–	12e. multicoloured	1·20	65
530	–	20e. multicoloured	2·00	1·10
MS531		82×96 mm. 50e. multicoloured (29×37 mm)	4·75	2·75

DESIGNS: 4e.50 to 50e. Various footballing scenes.

74 Morrissey-Ernestina

1982. Return of Schooner Morrissey-Ernestina.

532	**74**	12e. multicoloured	2·50	1·50

75 San Vicente Shipyard

1982. Seventh Anniv of Independence.

533	**75**	10e.50 multicoloured	2·00	1·00

76 Hypolimnas misippus

1982. Butterflies. Multicoloured.

534		2e. Type **76**	30	15
535		4e.50 Melanitis lede	70	30
536		8e. Catopsilia florella	1·30	60
537		10e.50 Colias electo	1·60	75
538		11e.50 Danaus chrysippus	1·80	80
539		12e. Papilio demodecus	2·00	85

77 Amilcar Cabral

1983. Amilcar Cabral Symposium.

540	**77**	7e. multicoloured	80	65
541	**77**	10e.50 multicoloured	1·30	1·00

78 Francisco Xavier de Cruz (composer)

1983. Composers and Poets. Multicoloured.

543		7e. Type **78**	1·00	60
544		14e. Eugenio Tavares (poet)	2·00	1·30

79 "World Communications Network"

1983. World Communications Year.

545	**79**	13e. multicoloured	1·50	75

80 Cape Verde Cone

1983. Shells. Multicoloured.

546		50c. Type **80**	10	10
547		1e. Conus decoratus	15	15
548		3e. Conus salreiensis	40	25
549		10e. Conus verdensis	1·40	1·40
550		50e. Conus cuneolus	6·50	3·50

81 Arch and Cross

1983. 450th Anniv of Christianity in Cape Verde Islands.

551	**81**	7e. multicoloured	1·40	1·30

82 Auster D5/160 Husky

1984. 40th Anniv of ICAO. Multicoloured.

552		50c. Type **82**	25	10
553		2e. de Havilland Dove	30	15
554		10e. Hawker Siddeley HS748	90	60
555		13e. de Havilland Dragon Rapide	1·20	95
556		20e. de Havilland Twin Otter	1·80	1·50
557		50e. Britten-Norman Islander	4·75	3·50

83 Families, Houses and Emblems as Balloons

1984. National Solidarity Campaign.

558	**83**	6e.50 multicoloured	1·20	50
559	**83**	13e.50 multicoloured	2·30	1·20

84 Figure rising from Nautilus Shell

1985. Second Cape Verde Womens' Organization Conference.

560	**84**	8e. multicoloured	1·30	1·00

85 Emblem

1985. Tenth Anniv of Independence.

561	**85**	8e. multicoloured	1·40	95
562	**85**	12e. multicoloured	2·00	1·40

87 "Steamer"

1985.

564	**87**	30e. on 10c. multicoloured	22·00	22·00
MS565		Three sheets, each 190×260 mm. (a) 50e. As No. 564 but ship upper structure red×4; (b) 50e. As No. 564 but ship upper structure yellow×4; (c) 50e. As No. 564 but ship upper structure green×4	£375	

88 Mabuya vaillanti

1986. Endangered Reptiles. Multicoloured.

566		8e. Type **88**	4·50	2·50
567		10e. Tarentola gigas brancoensis	5·50	3·25
568		15e. Tarentola gigas gigas	8·00	4·75
569		30e. Hemidactylus bouvieri	16·00	10·00
MS570		130×60 mm. 50e. Type **88**; 50e. As No. 569	25·00	20·00

89 Food in Pot over Fire

1986. World Food Day. Multicoloured.

571		8e. Type **89**	45	35
572		12e. Women pounding food in mortar	70	55
573		15e. Woman rolling flat bread with stone	1·00	70

90 Dove and Olive Branch

1986. International Peace Year.

574	**90**	12e. multicoloured	65	35
575	**90**	30e. multicoloured	1·70	85

91 Family Planning and Child Health Centre, Praia, and Woman breast-feeding Baby

1987. Child Survival Campaign. Multicoloured.

576		8e. Type **91**	40	30
577		10e. Assomada SOS children's village	50	35
578		12e. Family planning clinic, Mindelo, and nurse with child	60	45
579		16e. Children's home, Mindelo, and nurse with baby	80	55
580		100e. Calouste Gulbenkian kindergarten, Praia, and child writing	4·75	3·50

92 Mindelo City

1987. Tourism. Multicoloured.

581		1e. Type **92**	20	10
582		2e.50 Santo Antao island	25	15
583		5e. Fogo island	30	20
584		8e. Pillory, Velha City	50	25
585		10e. Boa Entrada valley, Santiago island	60	30
586		12e. Fishing boats, Santiago	75	40
587		100e. Furna harbour, Brava island	6·00	3·00

93 Carvalho (schooner)

1987. Sailing Ships. Multicoloured.

588	**93**	12e. black, mauve & blue	80	50
589	–	16e. black, blue & mauve	1·00	85
590	–	50e. black, blue & dp blue	3·00	2·50
MS591		105×105 mm 60e.×2, black, brown and violet	7·25	6·25

DESIGNS: 16e. Nauta; 50e. Maria Sony; 60e. Madalan.

94 Emblem

1987. Second National Development Plan.

592	**94**	8e. multicoloured	1·00	50

95 Moths on Stem

1988. Crop Protection. Multicoloured.

593		50c. Type **95**	10	10
594		2e. Caterpillars on plant treated with bio-insecticides	20	15
595		9e. Use of imported predators	75	45
596		13e. Use of imported predatorial insects	1·10	60
597		16e. Locust on stem	1·40	80
598		19e. Damaged wood	1·60	90
MS599		115×70 mm. 50e. Agricultural Research Institute (41×30 mm)	4·00	4·50

96 17th-century Dutch Map

1988. Antique Maps of Cape Verde Islands. Multicoloured.

600		1e. Type **96**	55	30
601		2e.50 18th-cent Belgian map	90	50
602		4e.50 18th-cent French map	1·10	65
603		9e.50 18th-cent English map	1·30	80
604		19e.50 19th-cent English map	1·60	1·00
605		20e. 18th-cent French map (vert)	2·30	1·30

97 Church of the Abbot of the Holy Shelter, Tarrafal, Santiago

1988. Churches. Multicoloured.

606		5e. Type **97**	30	20
607		8e. Church of Our Lady of Light, Maio	50	30
608		10e. Church of the Nazarene, Praia, Santiago	65	35
609		12e. Church of Our Lady of the Rosary, Sao Nicolau	80	40
610		15e. Church of the Nazarene, Mindelo, Sao Vicente	1·10	50
611		20e. Church of Our Lady of Grace, Praia, Santiago	1·40	1·30

98 Boy filling Tin with Water

1988. Water Economy Campaign.

| 612 | 98 | 12e. multicoloured | 80 | 50 |

99 Red Cross Workers

1988. 125th Anniv of Red Cross Movement.

| 613 | 99 | 7e. multicoloured | 75 | 40 |

100 Group of Youths and Pres. Pereira

1988. Third Congress of African Party for the Independence of Cape Verde. Multicoloured.

614	7e. Type **100**	30	20
615	10e.50 Pres. Pereira and Perez de Cuellar (U.N. Secretary-General)	50	30
616	30e. Emblem and Pres. Pereira	1·40	80
MS617 130×90 mm. 100e. As No. 616		4·75	4·00

101 Handball

1988. Olympic Games, Seoul. Multicoloured.

618	12e. Type **101**	85	60
619	15e. Tennis	1·10	80
620	20e. Football	1·50	1·10
621	30e. Boxing	2·00	1·70
MS622 130×90 mm. 50e. Long jump		3·00	3·00

102 Hot-air Balloon *Pro Juventute*

1989. Second Pro Juventute Congress.

| 623 | **102** | 30e. multicoloured | 1·50 | 75 |

103 Silva

1989. Death Centenary of Roberto Duarte Silva (chemist).

| 624 | **103** | 12e.50 multicoloured | 1·50 | 75 |

104 *Liberty guiding the People* (Eugene Delacroix)

1989. Bicentenary of French Revolution.

625	**104**	20e. multicoloured	90	50
626	**104**	24e. multicoloured	1·20	60
627	**104**	25e. multicoloured	1·20	65
MS628 120×76 mm. 100e. multicoloured			4·75	4·00

DESIGNS: 29×37 mm. 100e. Detail of Arc de Triomphe, Paris.

No. **MS**628 also commemorates "Philexfrance 89" International Stamp Exhibition.

105 Anniversary Emblem

1989. Centenary of Interparliamentary Union. Multicoloured.

| 629 | 2e. Type **105** | 20 | 10 |
| 630 | 4e. Dove | 30 | 20 |

| 631 | 13e. National Assembly building | 90 | 65 |

106 Fonte Lima Women firing Pots

1989. Traditional Pottery. Multicoloured.

632	13e. Type **106**	50	35
633	20e. Terra di Monti women and children arranging pots to bake in sun (vert)	85	55
634	24e. Terra di Monti woman shaping pot	1·00	65
635	25e. Fonte Lima women kneading clay (vert)	1·10	70

107 Boy and Truck

1989. Christmas. Home-made Toys. Multicoloured.

636	1e. Type **107**	25	25
637	6e. Boy with car on waste ground	35	30
638	8e. Boy with truck on pavement	50	35
639	11e.50 Boys with various vehicles	1·00	50
640	18e. Boys and sit-on scooter	1·50	90
641	100e. Boy with boat	5·00	4·50

108 Pope John Paul II

1990. Papal Visit.

642	**108**	13e. multicoloured	1·00	50
643	**108**	20e. multicoloured	1·00	50
MS644 110 mm. 200e. multicoloured			6·50	6·00

DESIGN: 200e. Pope wearing mitre.

109 Green Turtles

1990. Turtles. Multicoloured.

645	50c. Type **109**	15	10
646	1e. Leatherback turtles	20	10
647	5e. Olive ridley turtles	45	25
648	10e. Loggerhead turtles	90	60
649	42e. Hawksbill turtles	3·50	2·50

110 Footballers

1990. World Cup Football Championship, Italy.

650	**110**	4e. multicoloured	15	10
651	-	7e.50 multicoloured	20	10
652	-	8e. multicoloured	25	10
653	-	100e. multicoloured	3·00	2·00
MS654 87×54 mm. 100e. multicoloured			4·00	2·50

DESIGNS: 7e.50 to 100e. Different footballing scenes.

111 Face

1990. First Congress of Cape Verde Women's Movement.

| 655 | **111** | 9e. multicoloured | 50 | 30 |

112 Teacher helping Boy to Read

1990. International Literacy Year. Multicoloured.

656	2e. Type **112**	20	10
657	3e. Teacher with adult class	25	15
658	15e. Teacher with flash-card	80	50
659	19e. Adult student pointing to letters on blackboard	1·10	70

113 Diphtheria Treatment and Emile Roux (pioneer of antitoxic method)

1990. Vaccination Campaign. Multicoloured.

660	5e. Type **113**	75	30
661	13e. Tuberculosis vaccination and Robert Koch (discoverer of tubercle bacillus)	1·40	75
662	20e. Tetanus vaccination and Gaston Ramon	2·30	1·30
663	24e. Poliomyelitis oral vaccination and Jonas Edward Salk (discoverer of vaccine)	2·50	1·50

114 Musician on Bull's Back

1990. Traditional Stories. Multicoloured.

664	50c. Type **114**	10	10
665	2e.50 Fisherman and mermaid ("Joao Piquinote")	20	15
666	12e. Girl and snake	90	50
667	25e. Couple and eggs ("Ti Lobo, Ti Lobo")	1·80	1·00

115 World Map and Beam destroying AIDS Virus

1991. Anti-AIDS Campaign. Multicoloured.

| 668 | 13e. Type **115** | 2·40 | 1·80 |
| 669 | 24e. Beam, AIDS virus and "SIDA" | 4·50 | 3·35 |

116 Fishing Boat at Sea and Fishermen on Shore

1991. Fishing Industry. Multicoloured.

670	10e. Type **116**	60	45
671	24e. Fisherman removing hook from fish	1·50	1·20
672	25e. Fishing boats	1·60	1·20
673	50e. Fishermen taking in lines	3·25	2·30

117 Our Lady of the Rosary Church

1991. Tourism. Ruins of Ribeira Grande, Santiago Island. Multicoloured.

674	12e.50 Type **117**	75	50
675	15e. Se Cathedral	90	75
676	20e. Sao Filipe fortress	1·30	1·00
677	30e. St. Francis's Convent	1·80	1·50
MS678 81×79 mm. 100e. Pillory (vert)		5·25	5·25

118 *Lavandula rotundifolia*

1991. Medicinal Plants. Multicoloured.

679	10e. Type **118**	45	30
680	15e. *Micromeria forbesii*	70	50
681	21e. *Sarcostemma daltonii*	90	70
682	24e. *Periploca chevalieri*	1·10	80
683	30e. *Echium hypertropicum*	1·30	1·10
684	35e. *Erysimum caboverdeanum*	1·50	1·20

119 Guitar

1991. Musical Instruments. Multicoloured.

685	10e. Type **119**	50	40
686	20e. Violin	1·00	80
687	29e. Guitar with five double strings	1·40	1·20
688	47e. Cimboa	2·30	1·90
MS689 97×82 mm. (a) 60e. Accordian (horiz)		3·50	2·50

120 Crib (Tito Livio Goncalves)

1991. Christmas. Multicoloured.

| 690 | 31e. Type **120** | 1·00 | 90 |
| 691 | 50e. Fonte-Lima crib | 1·60 | 1·50 |

121 Rose Apples

1992. Tropical Fruits. Multicoloured.

692	16e. Type **121**	80	60
693	25e. Mangoes	1·30	1·10
694	31e. Cashews	1·50	1·40
695	32e. Avocados	1·60	1·50

122 Ships anchored in Bay

1992. 500th Anniv of Discovery of America by Columbus. Columbus's Landings in Cape Verde Islands. Multicoloured.

696	40e. Type **122**	2·50	2·00
697	40e. Caravel	2·50	2·00
MS698 130×63 mm. Nos. 696/7 (sold at 150e.)		9·50	7·50

123 Alhambra, Granada

1992. Granada 92 International Stamp Exhibition, Spain. Sheet 135×95 mm.

| **MS**699 **123** 50e. multicoloured (sold at 150e.) | | 8·00 | 8·00 |

124 Throwing the Javelin

1992. Olympic Games, Barcelona. Multicoloured.

700	16e. Type **124**	60	40
701	20e. Weightlifting	80	65
702	32e. Pole vaulting	1·30	1·00
703	40e. Putting the shot	1·50	1·30
MS704 98×71 mm. 100e. Gymnastics (26×32 m)		3·75	3·75

125 Oxen and Sugar Cane

1992. Production of Molasses. Multicoloured.

705	19e. Type **125**		85	45
706	20e. Crushing cane		90	75
707	37e. Feeding cane into mill		1·70	1·60
708	38e. Cooking molasses		1·80	1·70

126 Cat

1992. Domestic Animals. Multicoloured.

709	16e. Type **126**		75	25
710	31e. Chickens		1·50	1·30
711	32e. Dog (vert)		1·50	1·40
712	50e. Horse		2·30	2·00

127 Tubastrea aurea

1993. Corals. Multicoloured.

713	5e. Type **127**		20	15
714	31e. Corallium rubrum		1·20	1·00
715	37e. Porites porites		1·80	1·60
716	50e. Millepora alcicornis		£180	1·60

128 Praia Harbour, Santiago Island, 1806

1993. Brasilliana 93 International Stamp Exhibition, Rio de Janeiro, and union of Portuguese-speaking Capital Cities. Sheet 118×75 mm.

MS717	**128** 100e. multicoloured		5·50	4·50

129 King Ferdinand and Queen Isabella of Spain and Pope Alexander VI

1993. 500th Anniv of Pope Alexander VI's Bulls (on Portuguese and Spanish spheres of influence) and of Treaty of Tordesillas. Multicoloured.

718	37e. Type **129**		1·10	95
719	37e. King Joao II of Portugal and Pope Julius II		1·10	95
720	38e. Astrolabe, quill and left-half of globe		1·20	1·00
721	38e. Map of Iberian Peninsula and right-half of globe with Cape Verde Islands high-lighted		1·20	1·00

Stamps of the same value were issued together in se-tenant pairs, each pair forming a composite design.

130 Palinurus charlestoni

1993. Lobsters. Multicoloured.

722	2e. Type **130**		25	20
723	10e. Brown lobster		60	50
724	17e. Royal lobster		1·00	90
725	38e. Stone lobster		2·30	2·00
MS726	110×70 mm.100e. Royal lobster on seabed (51×36 mm)		5·75	5·75

131 Cory's Shearwater

1993. Nature Reserves. Multicoloured.

727	10e. Type **131** (Branco and Raso Islets)		80	70
728	30e. Brown booby (De Cima and Raso Islets)		2·50	2·00
729	40e. Magnificent frigate bird (Curral Velho and Baluarte Islets)		3·50	2·50
730	41e. Red-billed tropic bird (Raso and De Cima Islets)		3·75	2·75

132 Rose

1993. Flowers. Multicoloured.

731	5e. Type **132**		25	20
732	30e. Bird of Paradise flower		1·30	1·10
733	37e. Sweet William		1·60	1·40
734	50e. Cactus dahlia		1·90	1·80

1994. Hong Kong 94 International Stamp Exhibition,. Sheet 110×70 mm. Multicoloured.

MS735	No. 729 (sold at 150e.)		9·00	9·00

133 Map and Prince Henry

1994. 600th Birth Anniv of Prince Henry the Navigator.

736	**133** 37e. multicoloured		2·75	2·00

134 Players and Giants Stadium, New York

1994. World Cup Football Championship, U.S.A. Multicoloured.

737	1e. Type **134**		40	10
738	20e. Referee showing red card and Rose Bowl, Los Angeles		80	55
739	37e. Scoring goal and Foxboro Stadium, Boston		1·50	1·00
740	38e. Linesman raising flag and Silverdome, Detroit		1·60	1·10
MS741	110×70 mm. 100e. Tackle and RFK Stadium, Washington D.C		4·50	3·00

135 Sand Tiger

1994. Sharks. Multicoloured.

742	21e. Type **135**		1·30	1·20
743	27e. Black-tipped shark		1·60	1·50
744	37e. Whale shark		2·30	2·10
745	38e. Velvet belly		2·50	2·20

136 "Prata" Bananas

1994. Bananas. Multicoloured.

746	12e. Type **136**		70	40
747	16e. "Pao" bananas (horiz)		90	55
748	30e. "Ana roberta" bananas		1·60	1·00
749	40e. "Roxa" bananas		2·30	1·30
MS750	64×82 mm. 100e. "Prata" bananas on tree (27×40 mm) (sold at 150e.)		8·00	5·00

No. **MS**750 commemorates Philakorea 1994 Interna-tional and Singpex 94 stamp exhibitions.

137 Fontes Pereira de Melo

1994. Lighthouses. Multicoloured.

751	2e. Type **137**		50	40
752	37e. Morro Negro		2·50	2·30

753	38e. D. Amelia (vert)		2·75	2·50
754	50e. D. Maria Pia (vert)		8·50	3·00

138 X-Ray Tube and Dates

1995. Centenary of Discovery of X-Rays by Wilhelm Rontgen.

755	**138** 20e. multicoloured		1·50	1·30
756	**138** 37e. multicoloured		2·75	2·50
MS757	Sheet 142×95 mm. Nos. 755/6 (sold at 100e.)		7·00	7·00

139 Child with Tuna

1995. 50th Anniv of FAO. Multicoloured.

758	37e. Type **139**		2·20	2·20
759	38e. Globe and wheat ear		2·40	2·40

140 Wire-haired Fox Terrier and Two Foxhounds and Fox Terrier (John Emms)

1995. Dogs. Heads of dogs and paintings. Multicoloured.

760	1e. Type **140**		20	20
761	10e. Cavalier King Charles and Shooting Over Dogs (Richard Ansdell)		15	10
762	40e. German shepherd and rough collies		2·30	1·60
763	50e. Bearded collie and Hounds at Full Cry (Thomas Blinks)		2·75	2·00

141 Communications

1995. 20th Anniv of Independence.

764	**141** 37e. multicoloured		1·30	1·00

142 Sweet William (Dianthus barbatus)

1995. Singapore 95 International Stamp Exhibition. Sheet 110×70 mm.

MS765	**142** 37e. multicoloured (sold at 150e.)		7·00	7·00

143 Horse Race

1995. St. Philip's Flag Festival, Fogo. Multicoloured.

766	2e. Type **143**		20	20
767	10e. Preparing for horse race		25	25
768	37e. Preparing food and clap-ping to music		95	85
769	40e. Crowd watching final horse race		1·10	95

144 Grasshopper playing Guitar

1995. Childrens' Stories. 300th Death Anniv of Jean de La Fontaine (writer). Scenes from The Ant and the Grasshopper. Multicoloured.

770	10e. Type **144**		25	20
771	25e. Grasshopper in snowstorm looking through ants' window		60	55
772	38e. Ant laying-in supplies for winter		90	80
773	45e. Ants welcoming grasshop-per into their home		1·10	1·00

145 Sonchus daltonii

1996. Endangered Flowers. Multicoloured.

774	20e. Type **145**		65	60
775	37e. Echium vulcanorum		1·20	1·00
776	38e. Nauplius smithii		1·30	1·10
777	50e. Campanula jacobaea		1·60	1·40

146 Table Tennis

1996. Olympic Games, Atlanta. Multicoloured.

778	1e. Type **146**		25	40
779	37e. Gymnastics		1·40	1·40
780	100e. Athletics		1·50	75

147 Student (Education of Girls)

1996. 50th Anniv of UNICEF. Multicoloured.

781	20e. Type **147**		1·50	75
782	40e. Mother kissing child (Right to Love)		80	75

148 Deep Sea Fishing

1996. Water Sports. Multicoloured.

783	2e.50 Type **148**		50	25
784	10e. Sailboard		5·00	45
785	22e.50 Jet skiing		1·10	1·00
786	100e. Surfing (horiz)		4·75	4·50
MS787	155×110 mm. 100e. Fish (scuba diving) (78×60 mm)		5·25	5·00

1997. Nos. 582 and 650/1 surch.

788	3e. on 2e.50 multicoloured		50	50
789	37e. on 4e. multicoloured		5·00	5·00
790	38e. on 7e.50 multicoloured		5·00	5·00

150 State Arms

1997. National Symbols. Multicoloured.

791	20e. Type **150**		80	70
792	37e. National anthem		1·20	1·00
793	50e. State flag		1·50	1·30

151 Small-toothed Sawfish

1997. The Small-toothed Sawfish. Multicoloured.

794	15e. Type **151**		70	70
795	15e. Underside of sawfish		70	70

796	15e. Sawfish and school of fishes		70	70
797	15e. Two sawfishes		20	10

152 Fish and Dolphins

1997. Oceans. Multicoloured.

798	45e. Type **152**		1·50	1·50
799	45e. Mermaid and merman		1·50	1·50
800	45e. Fishes, eel, coral and sunken gate		1·50	1·50

Nos. 798/800 were issued together, *se-tenant*, forming a composite design.

153 Yellow-finned Tuna

1997. Tuna. Multicoloured.

801	13e. Type **153**		50	45
802	21e. Big-eyed tuna		80	75
803	41e. Little tuna		1·60	1·50
804	45e. Skipjack tuna		1·80	1·60

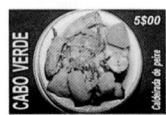

154 Players chasing Ball

1998. World Cup Football Championship, France. Multicoloured.

805	10e. Type **154**		40	20
806	30e. Ball in net (vert)		1·10	80
807	45e. Player with ball (vert)		1·60	1·10
808	50e. Globe, football and trophy		1·80	1·30

155 Fish Dish

1998. Local Cuisine.

809	**155**	5e. multicoloured	30	30
810	-	25e. multicoloured	1·30	1·30
811	-	35e. multicoloured	1·80	1·80
812	-	40e. multicoloured	2·00	2·00

DESIGNS: 25e. to 40e. Different food dishes.

156 Navigators reading Books and Banana Tree

1998. 500th Anniv (1997) of Vasco da Gama's Expedition to India. Multicoloured.

813	50e. Type **156**		1·80	1·80
814	50e. Seaman with sword and couple		1·80	1·80
815	50e. Compass rose and Portuguese galleon in harbour		1·80	1·80

Nos. 813/15 were issued together, *se-tenant*, forming a composite design.

157 Brava Island Costume

1998. Local Women's Costumes. Multicoloured.

816	10e. Type **157**		25	25
817	18e. Fogo Island		75	60
818	30e. Boa Vista Island		1·30	1·20
819	50e. Santiago Island		2·00	1·90

158 *Byblia ilithyia*

1999. Butterflies and Moths. Multicoloured.

820	5e. Type **158**		25	25
821	10e. *Aganais speciosa*		30	30
822	20e. Crimson-speckled moth		80	75
823	30e. Painted lady		35	15
824	50e. Cabbage looper		1·90	1·80
825	100e. *Grammodes congenita*		3·75	3·50
MS826	114×68 mm. No. 822/3		3·75	3·75

159 Concorde in Flight

1999. 30th Anniv of Concorde (supersonic airplane). Multicoloured.

827	30e. Type **159**		2·75	2·75
828	50e. Concorde on airport apron		4·50	4·50

160 Alain Gerbault (solo yachtsman) and Mindelo Harbour

1999. "Philexfrance 99" International Stamp Exhibition, Paris, France. Multicoloured.

829	30e. Type **160**		3·00	3·00
830	50e. Roberto Duarte Silva (chemist) and Eiffel Tower, Paris		3·00	3·00
MS831	155×79 mm. Nos. 829/30 (sold at 100e.)		7·00	7·00

161 Globe in Envelope and UPU Emblem

1999. 125th Anniv of Universal Postal Union. Multicoloured.

832	30e. Type **161**		2·30	22·30
833	50e. Paper airplanes		3·50	3·50

Nos. 832/3 are not inscribed with the country name.

162 Cola Sanjon Dance

1999. Local Dances. Multicoloured.

834	10e. Type **162**		35	35
835	30e. Contradanca		1·00	1·00
836	50e. Desfile de Tabanca (horiz)		1·80	1·70
837	100e. Batuque (horiz)		3·50	3·25

163 Globe, Open Book and Hourglass

2000. New Millennium. Multicoloured.

838	40e. Type **163**		2·30	2·30
839	50e. "2000" (horiz)		2·50	2·50

164 Baby

2000. 50th Anniv (1999) of S.O.S. Children's Villages. Multicoloured.

840	50e. Type **164**		1·80	1·60
841	100e. Child and emblem (horiz)		3·50	3·25

165 "25" and Emblem

2000. 25th Anniv of Independence.

842	**165**	50e. multicoloured	1·50	1·50

166 Gymnastics

2000. Olympic Games, Sydney. Multicoloured.

843	10e. Type **166**		35	30
844	40e. Taekwondo		1·00	90
845	50e. Athletics		1·50	1·40
MS846	70×120 mm. Nos. 843/5		3·00	3·00

167 Dragon Tree

2000. Dragon Tree.

847	**167**	5e. green	25	25
848	**167**	40e. red	1·30	80
849	**167**	60e. brown	2·00	1·30

168 Students (left-hand detail)

2000. 134th Anniv of the Liceu de Sao Nicolau Seminary. Multicoloured.

850	60e. Type **168**		2·00	1·90
851	60e. Students (right-hand detail)		2·00	1·90
852	60e. Jose Alves Feio, Jose Julio Dias (co-founders) and Antonio Jose de Oliveira Boucas (Principal) (56×26 mm)		70	35

Nos. 850/2 were issued together, *se-tenant*, forming a composite design.

169 White Sea Bream (*Diplodus sargus*)

2001. Fish. Multicoloured.

853	10e. Type **169**		50	50
854	22e. *Diplodus prayensis*		1·10	1·00
855	28e. Marmora sea bream (*Lithognathus mormyrus*)		1·40	1·30
856	48e. *Diplodus fasciatus*		2·30	2·10
857	60e. *Diplodus puntazzo*		2·75	2·50

170 *Thomisus onustus*

2001. Spiders. Multicoloured.

858	13e. Type **170**		65	65
859	16e. *Scytodes velutina*		75	70
860	40e. *Hersiliola simony*		2·00	1·80
861	100e. *Loxosceles rufescens*		4·75	4·50

171 *Acacia albida*

2001. Trees. Multicoloured.

862	50e. Type **171**		2·10	2·00
863	60e. *Ficus sycomorus*		2·50	2·30

172 Grand Place, Brussels and Fountain

2001. "Belgica 2001" International Stamp Exhibition, Brussels. Sheet 116×86 mm.

MS864	**172**	100e. multicoloured	4·00	4·00

173 *Artemisia gorgonum* (inscr "Artimisia")

2001. Plants (1st series). Multicoloured.

865	20e. Type **173**		70	65
866	27e. *Globularia amygdalifolia*		90	85
867	47e.50 *Sidereoxylon marginata* (horiz)		1·60	1·50
868	50e. *Umbilicus schmidtii* (horiz)		1·70	1·70
869	60e. *Verbascum cystolithicum*		2·10	1·90
870	100e. *Limonium lobinii*		3·50	3·25

See also Nos. 873/6.

174 Children encircling Globe

2001. United Nations Year of Dialogue among Civilizations.

871	**174**	60e. multicoloured	2·00	2·00

175 Antonio Goncalves

2001. Birth Centenary of Antonio Aurelio Goncalves (writer).

872	**175**	100e. multicoloured	3·25	3·00

2002. Plants (2nd series). As T **173** . Multicoloured.

873	10e. *Euphorbia tuckeyana* (inscr "tuckeyna") (horiz)		35	35
874	50e. *Limonium*		1·80	1·60
875	60e. *Aeonium gorgoneum*		2·00	1·90
876	100e. *Polycarpaea gayi*		3·50	3·25

176 Player heading Ball into Goal

2002. World Cup Football Championship, Japan and South Korea. Multicoloured.

877	60e. Type **176**		2·00	1·80
878	100e. Player kicking ball towards goal		3·25	3·00

177 Two Adult Turtles

2002. Marine Turtles (*Caretta caretta*). Multicoloured.

879	10e. Type **177**		45	40
880	20e. Laying eggs		80	70
881	30e. Young emerging from sand		1·30	1·20
882	60e. Young crawling towards sea		2·60	2·50
883	100e. Adult swimming		4·25	4·00
MS884	150×110 mm. 100e. Adult on beach (80×61 mm)		4·25	4·25

178 Basket from St.
Nicholas Island

2002. Traditional Baskets. Multicoloured.
885	20e. Type **178**	70	65
886	33e. From St. Anthony Island	1·20	1·10
887	60e. From Santiago Island	2·10	2·00
888	100e. From Boa Vista Island	3·50	3·25

179 Carlos Alberto Silva
Martins (Katchass)
(musician)

2003. Poets and Musicians. Multicoloured.
889	12e. Type **179**	50	45
890	20e. Jorge Monteiro (Jota-monte) (composer)	75	70
891	32e. Luís Rendall (composer)	1·20	1·00
892	47e.50 Jorge Barbosa (poet)	1·80	1·70
893	60e. Januario Leite (poet)	2·20	2·10
894	100e. Jose Lopes (poet)	3·75	3·50

180 Cesaria Evora

2003. Cesaria Evora (singer) Commemoration.
Multicoloured.
895	60e. Type **180**	2·30	2·00
896	100e. Cesaria Evora (different)	3·75	3·50
MS897	85×115 mm. 200e. Cesaria Evora's legs (51×38 mm)	7·75	7·25

MS897 forms a composite design of Cesaria Evora singing.

181 Purple Heron
(*Ardea purpurea boumei*)

2003. Herons and Egrets. Multicoloured.
898	10e. Type **181**	80	70
899	27e. Grey heron (*Ardea cinerea*)	1·10	1·00
900	42e. Cattle egret (*Bubulcus ibis*)	1·80	1·60
901	60e. Little egret (*Egretta garzeta*)	2·50	2·25

182 Scout

2003. Scouting. Multicoloured.
902	60e. Type **182** (13th anniv of Scouts Association)	2·30	2·00
903	100e. Scout with raised hand (3rd anniv of Catholic Scouts Corps)	3·50	3·25

183 Blue Whale
(*Balaenoptera musculus*)

2003. Marine Mammals. Multicoloured.
904	10e. Type **183**	65	60
905	20e. Sperm whale (*Physeter macrocephalus*)	1·30	1·30
906	50e. Humpback whale (*Megaptera novaeangliae*)	3·25	3·00
907	60e. Pilot whale (*Globicephala macrorhynchus*)	4·00	3·75

184 CAMS 51-F (biplane flying boat)
at Calheta de Sao Martinho

2003. 75th Anniv of First Postal Hydroplane Base, Calheta
de Sao Martinho. Multicoloured.
908	10e. Type **184**	65	60
909	42e. Paulin Paris (1st pilot) and route	2·75	2·50
910	60e. Route and CAMS 51-F	3·75	3·50
MS911	100×54 mm. 100e. As No. 908 but with design enlarged (57×33 mm)	4·75	4·50

185 Pope John
Paul II and Child

2003. 25th Anniv of the Pontificate of Pope John Paul II.
Multicoloured.
912	30e. Type **185**	1·90	1·50
913	60e. Pope John Paul II and ships (horiz)	3·50	3·50
MS914	83×64 mm. 100e. Pope John Paul II blessing crucifix	6·00	6·00

186 Mahogany
(*Khaya senegalensis*)

2004. Trees. Multicoloured.
915	20e. Type **186**	90	80
916	27e. Black thorn (*Acacia nilotica*)	1·30	1·10
917	60e. Ceiba (*Ceiba pentandra*)	2·50	2·40
918	100e. Palm (*Phoenix atlantica*)	4·25	4·00

187 Windmill

2004. Ecological Energy Production.
919	**187** 20e. blue	80	70
920	**187** 60e. magenta	2·50	2·20
921	**187** 100e. green	4·00	3·75

188 Taekwondo

2004. Olympic Games, Athens. Multicoloured.
922	10e. Type **188**	60	50
923	60e. Gymnastics	2·50	2·30
924	100e. Boxing (horiz)	4·00	3·75

189 Ponta Barril,
Sao Nicolau

2004. Lighthouses. Multicoloured.
925	10e. Type **189**	60	50
926	30e. Ponta Jalunga, Brava	1·80	1·50
927	40e. Dom Luis, Sao Vicente (horiz)	2·25	2·00
928	50e. Ponta Preta, Santiago (horiz)	3·00	2·75

190 House with Veranda

2004. Fogo Island's Historic Houses. Multicoloured.
929	20e. Type **190**	80	75
930	40e. House with veranda, bay window and wall with gate	2·00	1·75
931	50e. Three storied house	2·50	2·25
932	60e. Pink house	3·25	3·73

191 Wall-mounted
Telephone

2004. Twentieth-century Telephones. Multicoloured.
933	10e. Type **191**	1·00	75
934	40e. Early windup handset	1·50	1·50
935	60e. Candlestick telephone	2·30	2·00
936	100e. Bakelite telephone	3·75	3·00

192 storia storia

2005. Stories. Multicoloured.
937	10e. Type **192**	75	35
938	20e. era um vez!	1·30	60
939	30e. sapatinha ribera baxu	1·50	1·00
940	60e. Quem ki sabi mas conta midjor	75	45

193 Amilcar Cabral (freedom fighter)

2005. 30th Anniv of Independence.
941	**193** 60e. multicoloured	3·50	3·00

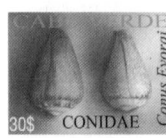

194 Conus evorai

2005. Shells. Multicoloured.
942	30e. Type **194**	1·30	90
943	40e. Harpa doris	2·00	1·80
944	50e. Strombus lotus	2·50	2·25
945	60e. Phyllonotus duplex	3·00	2·75

195 Passer
iagoensis

2005. Birds. Multicoloured.
946	19e. Type **195**	1·40	1·00
947	42e. Estrilda astrild	1·80	1·50
948	44e. Passer domesticus	2·00	1·80
949	55e. Acrocephalus brevipennis	2·50	2·25

196 Emblem

2005. World Information Society Summit, Tunis.
950	**196** 60e. multicoloured	4·00	3·50

197 Tobacco Pipes

2005. Artefacts. Multicoloured.
951	5e. Type **197**	50	50
952	10e. Spy glass, ornate stand and decorated box	75	75
953	30e. Cannon	2·75	2·50
954	60e. Astrolabe	5·50	2·25
MS955	115×85 mm. 100e. Shackles (80×60 mm)	7·50	7·50

CHARITY TAX STAMPS

Used on certain days of the year as an additional postal tax on internal letters. Other values in some of the types were for use on telegrams only. The proceeds were devoted to public charities. If one was not affixed in addition to the ordinary postage, postage due stamps were used to collect the deficiency and the fine.

1925. As Marquis de Pombal issue of Portugal but inscr "CABO VERDE".
C266	**C73**	15c. violet	1·40	1·40
C267	-	15c. violet	1·40	1·40
C268	**C75**	15c. violet	1·40	1·40

C16 St. Isabel

1948.
C321	**C16**	50c. green	4·75	3·00
C322	**C16**	1e. red	9·25	3·75

1959. Surch.
C368	50c. on 1e. red	55	30

1959. Colours changed.
C369	50c. mauve	2·40	1·40
C370	1e. blue	2·40	1·40

C31

1967.
C406	**C31**	30c. multicoloured	40	40
C407	**C31**	50c. mult (purple panel)	85	85
C408	**C31**	50c. mult (red panel)	65	65
C409	**C31**	1e. mult (brown panel)	95	95
C410	**C31**	1e. mult (purple panel)	95	95

C32

1968. Pharmaceutical Tax stamps surch as in Type **C32**.
C411a	**C32**	50c. on 1c. black, orange and green	1·50	1·10
C412c	**C32**	50c. on 2c. black, orange and green	70	40
C413	**C32**	50c. on 3c. black, orange and green	1·20	65
C414	**C32**	50c. on 5c. black, orange and green	1·20	65
C415	**C32**	50c. on 10c. black, orange and green	1·40	1·10
C416	**C32**	1e. on 1c. black, orange and green	3·00	2·20
C417a	**C32**	1e. on 2c. black, orange and green	2·10	1·70

NEWSPAPER STAMP

1893. "Newspaper" key-type inscr "CABO VERDE".
N37	**V**	2½r. brown	1·70	80

POSTAGE DUE STAMPS

1904. "Due" key-type inscr "CABO VERDE".
D119	**W**	5r. green	65	40
D120	**W**	10r. grey	65	40
D121	**W**	20r. brown	80	50
D122	**W**	30r. orange	2·00	50
D123	**W**	50r. brown	80	45
D124	**W**	60r. brown	15·00	5·25
D125	**W**	100r. mauve	3·00	1·60
D126	**W**	130r. blue	3·00	1·30

D127	W	200r. red	2·75	2·40
D128	W	500r. lilac	8·00	4·00

1911. Nos. D119/28 optd REPUBLICA.

D135	5r. green	45	30
D136	10r. grey	45	35
D137	20r. brown	55	35
D138	30r. orange	55	35
D139	50r. brown	1·00	60
D140	60r. brown	1·00	60
D141	100r. mauve	1·00	60
D142	130r. blue	1·20	95
D143	200r. red	3·25	2·20
D144	500r. lilac	4·00	3·50

1921. "Due" key-type inscr "CABO VERDE" with currency in centavos.

D252	½c. green	40	30
D253	1c. slate	40	30
D254	2c. brown	40	30
D255	3c. orange	40	30
D256	5c. brown	40	30
D257	6c. brown	40	30
D258	10c. mauve	40	30
D259	13c. blue	80	70
D260	20c. red	90	80
D261	50c. grey	2·50	1·80

1925. As Nos. C266/8, optd MULTA.

D266	C73	30c. violet	96	85
D267	-	30c. violet	95	85
D268	C75	30c. violet	95	85

1952. As Type D45 of Angola, but inscr "CABO VERDE". Numerals in red; name in black.

D356	10c. brown and grey	30	30
D357	30c. black, blue & mauve	30	30
D358	50c. blue, green & yellow	30	30
D359	1e. blue and pale blue	30	30
D360	2e. brown and orange	40	40
D361	5e. green and grey	1·20	1·20

Pt. 4
CARABISCH NEDERLAND (CARIBBEAN NETHERLANDS)

A Netherlands colony consisting of two groups of islands in the Caribbean Sea, N. of Venezuela. Later part of Netherlands Antilles. On 10th October 2010 Bonaire, Saba and Sint Eustatius, as Caribbean Netherlands, became special municipalities of the Netherlands

100 cents = 1 gulden.

1 Saba, Bonaire and Sint Eustatius islands, Arms and Queen Beatrix of Netherlands

2010. Constitutional Reform

1	1	111c. multicoloured	3·50	3·50

Pt. 7
CAROLINE ISLANDS

A group of islands in the Pacific Ocean, formerly a German protectorate; under Japanese mandate after 1918. Now under United States trusteeship.

100 pfennig = 1 mark.

1899. Stamps of Germany optd Karolinen.

7	8	3pf. brown	15·00	18·00
8	8	5pf. green	22·00	22·00
9	9	10pf. red	22·00	24·00
10	9	20pf. blue	29·00	35·00
11	9	25pf. orange	65·00	75·00
12	9	50pf. brown	65·00	75·00

1901. "Yacht" key-types inscr "KAROLINEN".

13	N	3pf. brown	1·30	2·20
14	N	5pf. green	1·30	2·75
15	N	10pf. red	1·30	6·00
16	N	20pf. blue	1·50	11·00
17	N	25pf. black & red on yellow	1·90	18·00
18	N	30pf. black & orge on buff	1·90	18·00
19	N	40pf. black and red	1·90	20·00
20	N	50pf. black & pur on buff	2·40	27·00
21	N	80pf. black & red on rose	3·75	31·00
22	O	1m. red	5·50	75·00
23	O	2m. blue	8·75	£110
24	O	3m. black	13·00	£190
25	O	5m. red and black	£200	£650

1910. No. 13 surch 5 Pf.

26	N	5pf. on 3pf. brown	†	£7500

Pt. 3
CASTELROSSO

One of the Aegean Is. Occupied by the French Navy on 27 December 1915. The French withdrew in August 1921 and, after a period of Italian Naval administration, the island was included in the Dodecanese territory.

A. French Occupation.
100 centimes = 1 franc = 4 piastres.

B. Italian Occupation.
100 centesimi = 1 lira.

A. FRENCH OCCUPATION

1920. Stamps of 1902–20 of French Post Offices in Turkish Empire optd B. N. F. CASTELLORIZO.

F1	A	1c. grey	60·00	60·00
F2	A	2c. purple	60·00	60·00
F3	A	3c. red	60·00	60·00
F4	A	5c. green	75·00	70·00
F5	B	10c. red	75·00	70·00
F6	B	15c. red	£110	£100
F7	B	20c. brown	£120	£120
F9	B	30c. lilac	£130	£130
F10	C	40c. red and blue	£225	£225
F8	C	1pi. on 20c. blue	£120	£120
F11	C	2pi. on 50c. brown & lilac	£250	£250
F12	C	4pi. on 1f. red & green	£325	£325
F13	C	20pi. on 5f. blue & brown	£900	£850

1920. Optd O. N. F. Castellorizo. (a) On stamps of 1902–20 of French Post Offices in Turkish Empire.

F14	A	1c. grey	50·00	50·00
F15	A	2c. purple	50·00	50·00
F16	A	3c. red	50·00	50·00
F17	A	5c. green	50·00	50·00
F18	B	10c. red	55·00	55·00
F19	B	15c. red	65·00	65·00
F20	B	20c. brown	£130	£130
F22	B	30c. lilac	£120	£120
F23	C	40c. red and blue	£120	£120
F21	C	1pi. on 25c. blue	£130	£120
F24	C	2pi. on 50c. brown & lilac	£120	£120
F25	C	4pi. on 1f. red and green	£150	£150
F26	C	20pi. on 5f. blue & brown	£550	£500

(b) On Nos. 334 and 341 of France.

F27	18	10c. red	55·00	32·00
F28	18	25c. blue	55·00	32·00

1920. Stamps of France optd O F CASTELLORISO.

F29		5c. green	£300	£275
F30		10c. red	£300	£275
F31		20c. red	£300	£275
F32		25c. blue	£300	£275
F33	13	50c. brown and lilac	£1600	£1600
F34	13	1f. red and green	£1600	£1600

B. ITALIAN OCCUPATION

1922. Stamps of Italy optd CASTELROSSO.

15	37	5c. green	2·20	27·00
16	37	10c. red	2·20	27·00
17	37	15c. grey	2·20	38·00
18	41	20c. orange	2·20	38·00
19	39	25c. blue	2·20	30·00
20	39	40c. brown	2·20	30·00
21	39	50c. violet	2·20	38·00
22	39	60c. red	2·20	43·00
23	39	85c. brown	2·75	55·00
24	34	1l. brown and green	2·75	55·00

2

1923

10	2	5c. green	4·00	18·00
11	2	10c. red	4·00	18·00
12	2	25c. blue	4·00	18·00
13	2	50c. purple	4·00	18·00
14	2	1l. brown	4·00	18·00

1930. Ferrucci stamps of Italy optd CASTELROSSO.

25	114	20c. violet	8·50	7·50
26	-	25c. green (No. 283)	8·50	13·00
27	-	50c. black (as No. 284)	8·50	7·50
28	-	1l.25 blue (No. 285)	8·50	15·00
29	-	5l.+2l. red (as No. 286)	39·00	75·00

1932. Garibaldi stamps of Italy optd CASTELROSSO.

30		10c. brown	34·00	55·00
31	128	20c. brown	34·00	55·00
32	-	25c. green	34·00	55·00
33	128	30c. blue	34·00	55·00
34	-	50c. purple	34·00	55·00
35	-	75c. red	34·00	55·00
36	-	1l.25 blue	34·00	55·00
37	-	1l.75+25c. brown	34·00	55·00
38	-	2l.55+50c. red	34·00	55·00
39	-	5l.+1l. violet	34·00	55·00

Pt. 20
CAUCA

A State of Colombia, reduced to a Department in 1886, now uses Colombian stamps.

100 centavos = 1 peso.

2

1902. Imperf.

2	2	10c. black on red	6·00	5·75
3	2	20c. black on orange	4·00	3·75

Pt. 16
CAVALLA (KAVALLA)

French P.O. in a former Turkish port, now closed.

100 centimes = 1 franc.
40 paras = 1 piastre.

1893. Stamps of France optd Cavalle or surch also in figures and words.

41	10	5c. green	19·00	36·00
43	10	10c. black on lilac	12·00	13·00
45	10	15c. blue	50·00	28·00
46	10	1pi. on 25c. black on pink	21·00	4·50
47	10	2pi. on 50c. red	80·00	46·00
48	10	4pi. on 1f. green	£110	70·00
49	10	8pi. on 2f. brown on blue	£120	£130

1902. "Blanc", "Mouchon" and "Merson" key-types inscr "CAVALLE". The four higher values surch also.

50	A	5c. green	2·75	2·30
51	B	10c. red	3·75	2·75
52	B	15c. red	13·00	12·00
53	B	15c. orange	4·50	2·75
54	B	1pi. on 25c. blue	4·25	2·50
55	C	2pi. on 50c. brown & lilac	6·00	4·00
56	C	4pi. on 1f. red and green	7·25	5·50
57	C	8pi. on 2f. lilac and brown	22·00	13·00

Pt. 1
CAYES OF BELIZE

A chain of several hundred islands, coral atolls, reefs and sandbanks stretching along the eastern seaboard of Belize. The following issues for the Cayes of Belize fall outside the criteria for full listing as detailed on page viii.

100 cents = 1 dollar

APPENDIX

1984

Marine Life, Map and Views, 1, 2, 5, 10, 15, 25, 75c., $3, $5.
250th Anniv of *Lloyd's List* (newspaper). 25, 75c., $1, $2.
Olympic Games, Los Angeles. 10, 15, 75c., $2.
90th Anniv of "Caye Service" Local Stamps. 10, 15, 75c., $2.

1985

Birth Bicent of John J. Audubon (ornithologist). 25, 75c., $1, $3.
Shipwrecks. $1×4.

Pt. 1
CAYMAN ISLANDS

A group of islands in the British West Indies. A dependency of Jamaica until August 1962, when it became a Crown Colony.

1900. 12 pence = 1 shilling; 20 shillings = 1 pound.
1969. 100 cents = 1 Jamaican dollar.

1

1900

1a	1	½d. green	13·00	22·00
2	1	1d. red	14·00	3·75

2

1902

8	2	½d. green	10·00	14·00
4	2	1d. red	10·00	10·00
10	2	2½d. blue	10·00	4·75
13	2	4d. brown and blue	35·00	60·00
11	2	6d. brown	18·00	38·00
14	2	6d. olive and red	40·00	75·00
12	2	1s. orange	29·00	48·00
15	2	1s. violet and green	60·00	85·00
16	2	5s. orange and green	£200	£325

1907. Surch One Halfpenny.

17	½d. on 1d. red	55·00	85·00

1907. Surch.

18	½d. on 5s. orange and green	£300	£450
19	1d. on 5s. orange and green	£275	£400
35	2½d. on 4d. brown and blue	£1800	£3500

11 8

1907

38	11	¼d. brown	4·25	50
25	8	½d. green	4·25	4·00
26	8	1d. red	1·75	75
27	8	2½d. blue	5·50	2·50
28	8	3d. purple on yellow	3·25	2·75
29	8	4d. black and red on yellow	60·00	80·00
30	8	6d. purple	23·00	35·00
31	8	1s. black on green	9·00	22·00
32	8	5s. green and red on yellow	38·00	75·00
34	8	10s. green and red on green	£180	£250

12

1912

40	12	¼d. brown	1·00	40
41	12	½d. green	2·75	5·00
42	12	1d. red	3·25	2·50
43	12	2d. grey	1·00	10·00
44	12	2½d. blue	6·00	8·50
45a	12	3d. purple on yellow	3·50	8·00
46	12	4d. black and red on yellow	1·00	10·00
47	12	6d. purple	3·75	7·50
48b	12	1s. black on green	3·50	3·50
49	12	2s. purple and blue on blue	12·00	65·00
50	12	3s. green and violet	19·00	75·00
51	12	5s. green and red on yellow	80·00	£170
52b	12	10s. green and red on green	£120	£180

1917. Surch 1½d with WAR STAMP. in two lines.

54	1½d. on 2½d. blue	1·75	6·00

1917. Optd or surch as last, but with WAR STAMP in one line and without full point.

57	½d. green	60	2·50
58	1½d. on 2d. grey	4·50	7·50
56	1½d. on 2½d. blue	30	60
59	1½d. on 2½d. orange	80	1·25

19

1921

69	19	¼d. brown	50	1·50
70	19	½d. green	50	30
71	19	1d. red	1·40	85
72	19	1½d. brown	1·75	30
73	19	2d. grey	1·75	4·00
74	19	2½d. blue	50	50
75	19	3d. purple on yellow	2·50	4·00
62	19	4d. red on yellow	1·00	4·50
76	19	4½d. green	3·50	3·00
77	19	6d. red	5·50	5·00
63	19	1s. black on green	1·25	9·50
80	19	2s. violet on blue	14·00	29·00
81	19	3s. violet	23·00	16·00

82	19	5s. green on yellow	26·00	55·00
83	19	10s. red on green	70·00	£100

20 Kings William IV and George V

1932. Centenary of "Assembly of Justices and Vestry".

84	20	¼d. brown	1·50	1·00
85	20	½d. green	2·75	9·50
86	20	1d. red	2·75	14·00
87	20	1½d. orange	2·75	2·75
88	20	2d. grey	2·75	3·50
89	20	2½d. blue	2·75	1·50
90	20	3d. green	7·50	6·00
91	20	6d. purple	11·00	23·00
92	20	1s. black and brown	17·00	32·00
93	20	2s. black and blue	50·00	85·00
94	20	5s. black and green	£100	£160
95	20	10s. black and red	£350	£450

21 Cayman Islands

1935

96	21	¼d. black and brown	50	1·00
97	-	½d. blue and green	1·00	1·00
98	-	1d. blue and red	4·00	2·25
99	-	1½d. black and orange	1·50	1·75
100	-	2d. blue and purple	3·75	1·10
101	-	2½d. blue and black	3·25	1·25
102	21	3d. black and green	2·50	3·00
103	-	6d. purple and black	8·50	4·00
104	-	1s. blue and orange	6·00	6·50
105	-	2s. blue and black	48·00	35·00
106	-	5s. green and black	65·00	65·00
107	-	10s. black and red	£100	£150

DESIGNS—HORIZ: ½, 2d., 1s. Cat boat; 1d., 2s. Red-footed boobys ("Booby-birds"); 2½, 6d., 5s. Hawksbill turtles. VERT: 1½d., 10s. Queen or pink conch shells and coconut palms.

1935. Silver Jubilee. As T **13** of Antigua.

108	-	½d. black and green	15	1·00
109	-	2½d. brown and blue	6·00	1·00
110	-	6d. blue and olive	1·50	7·00
111	-	1s. grey and purple	12·00	10·00

1937. Coronation. As T **2** of Aden.

112	-	½d. green	30	1·90
113	-	1d. red	50	20
114	-	2½d. blue	95	40

26 Beach View **29** Hawksbill Turtles

1938

115a	26	¼d. orange	10	65
116	-	½d. green	1·00	55
117	-	1d. red	30	75
118	26	1½d. black	30	10
119a	29	2d. violet	60	30
120	-	2½d. blue	40	20
120a	-	2½d. orange	3·50	50
121	-	3d. orange	40	15
121a	-	3d. blue	3·00	30
122a	29	6d. olive	3·25	1·25
123	-	1s. brown	6·50	10
124a	26	2s. green	25·00	9·00
125	-	5s. red	40·00	15·00
126	29	10s. brown	32·00	9·00

DESIGNS—HORIZ: ½d., 1s. Caribbean dolphin; 1d., 3d. Map of Islands; 2½d., 5s. *Rembro* (schooner).

1946. Victory. As T **9** of Aden.

127	-	1½d. black	50	40
128	-	3d. yellow	50	40

1948. Silver Wedding. As T **10/11** of Aden.

129	-	½d. green	10	1·00
130	-	10s. blue	24·00	30·00

1949. U.P.U. As T **20/25** of Antigua.

131	-	2½d. orange	30	1·00
132	-	3d. blue	1·50	2·25
133	-	6d. olive	60	2·25
134	-	1s. brown	60	50

31 Cat Boat

1950

135	31	¼d. blue and red	15	60
136	-	½d. violet and green	15	1·25
137	-	1d. olive and blue	60	75
138	-	1½d. green and brown	40	75
139	-	2d. violet and red	1·25	1·50
140	-	2½d. blue and black	1·25	60
141	-	3d. green and blue	1·40	1·50
142	-	6d. brown and blue	2·00	1·25
143	-	9d. red and green	13·00	2·00
144	-	1s. brown and orange	3·25	2·75
145	-	2s. violet and purple	14·00	11·00
146	-	5s. olive and violet	24·00	7·00
147	-	10s. black and red	29·00	23·00

DESIGNS: ½d. Coconut grove, Cayman Brac; 1d. Green turtle; 1½d. Making thatch rope; 2d. Cayman seamen; 2½d. Map; 3d. Parrotfish; 6d. Bluff, Cayman Brac; 9d. Georgetown Harbour. 1s. Turtle in "crawl"; 2s. *Ziroma* (schooner); 5s. Boat-building; 10s. Government offices, Grand Cayman.

44 South Sound Lighthouse, Grand Cayman

1953. As 1950 issue but with portrait of Queen Elizabeth II as in T **44**.

148	-	¼d. blue and red	1·00	50
149	-	½d. violet and green	75	50
150	-	1d. olive and blue	70	40
151	-	1½d. green and brown	60	20
152	-	2d. violet and red	3·00	85
153	-	2½d. blue and black	3·50	80
154	-	3d. green and blue	4·00	60
155	-	4d. black and blue	2·00	40
156	-	6d. brown and blue	1·75	30
157	-	9d. red and green	7·50	30
158	-	1s. brown and orange	3·75	20
159	-	2s. violet and purple	13·00	9·00
160	-	5s. olive and violet	15·00	8·00
161	-	10s. black and red	23·00	8·00
161a	-	£1 blue	45·00	13·00

Portrait faces right on ¼d., 2d., 2½d., 4d., 1s. and 10s. values and left on others. The £1 shows a larger portrait of the Queen (vert).

1953. Coronation. As T **13** of Aden.

162	-	1d. black and green	30	2·00

46 Arms of the Cayman Islands

1959. New Constitution.

163	46	2½d. black and blue	45	2·50
164	46	1s. black and orange	55	50

48 Cat Boat

1962. Portraits as in T **48**.

165	-	¼d. green and red	55	1·00
166	48	1d. black and olive	80	20
167	-	1½d. yellow and purple	2·75	80
168	-	2d. blue and brown	1·50	30
169	-	2½d. violet and turquoise	85	1·00
170	-	3d. blue and red	30	10
171	-	4d. green and purple	3·75	60
172	-	6d. turquoise and sepia	3·25	30
173	48	9d. blue and purple	4·00	40
174	-	1s. sepia and red	1·50	10
175	-	1s.3d. turquoise and brown	6·50	2·25
176	-	1s.9d. turquoise and violet	20·00	1·25
177	-	5s. plum and green	13·00	15·00
178	-	10s. olive and blue	22·00	15·00
179	-	£1 red and black	22·00	28·00

DESIGNS—VERT: ¼d. Cuban amazon ("Cayman Parrot"); 9d. Angler with king mackerel; 10s. Arms; £1 Queen Elizabeth II. HORIZ: 1½d. *Schomburgkia thomsoniana* (orchid); 2d. Cayman Islands map; 2½d. Fisherman casting net; 3d. West Bay Beach; 4d. Green turtle; 6d. *Lydia E. Wilson* (schooner), 1s Iguana; 1s.3d. Swimming pool, Cayman Brac; 1s.9d. Water sports; 5s. Fort George.

1963. Freedom from Hunger. As T **28** of Aden.

180	-	1s.9d. red	30	15

1963. Centenary of Red Cross. As T **33** of Antigua.

181	-	1d. red and black	30	1·00
182	-	1s.9d. red and blue	70	1·75

1964. 400th Birth Anniv of Shakespeare. As T **34** of Antigua.

183	-	6d. purple	20	10

1965. Centenary of ITU. As T **36** of Antigua.

184	-	1d. blue and purple	15	10
185	-	1s.3d. purple and green	55	45

1965. ICY. As T **37** of Antigua.

186	-	1d. purple and turquoise	20	10
187	-	1s. green and lavender	80	25

1966. Churchill Commemoration. As T **38** of Antigua.

188	-	¼d. blue	10	2·25
189	-	1d. green	60	15
190	-	1s. brown	1·50	15
191	-	1s.9d. violet	1·60	75

1966. Royal Visit. As T **39** of Antigua.

192	-	1d. black and blue	75	35
193	-	1s.9d. black and mauve	2·75	1·50

1966. World Cup Football Championship. As T **40** of Antigua.

194	-	1½d. multicoloured	25	10
195	-	1s.9d. multicoloured	75	25

1966. Inauguration of WHO Headquarters, Geneva. As T **41** of Antigua.

196	-	2d. black, green and blue	65	15
197	-	1s.3d. black, purple and ochre	1·60	60

62 Telephone and Map

1966. International Telephone Links.

198	62	4d. multicoloured	20	20
199	62	9d. multicoloured	20	30

1966. 20th Anniv of UNESCO. As T **54/6** of Antigua.

200	-	1d. multicoloured	15	10
201	-	1s.9d. yellow, violet and olive	60	10
202	-	5s. black, purple and orange	1·50	70

63 B.A.C One Eleven 200/400 Airliner over *Ziroma* (Cayman schooner)

1966. Opening of Cayman Jet Service.

203	63	1s. black, blue and green	35	30
204	63	1s.9d. purple, blue and green	40	35

64 Water-skiing

1967. International Tourist Year. Multicoloured.

205	-	4d. Type **64**	35	10
206	-	6d. Skin diving	35	30
207	-	1s. Sport fishing	35	30
208	-	1s.9d. Sailing	40	75

68 Former Slaves and Emblem

1968. Human Rights Year.

209	68	3d. green, black and gold	10	10
210	68	9d. brown, gold and green	10	10
211	68	5s. ultram, gold and green	30	90

69 Long-jumping

1968. Olympic Games, Mexico. Multicoloured.

212	-	1s. Type **69**	15	10
213	-	1s.3d. High-jumping	20	25
214	-	2s. Pole-vaulting	20	75

72 The Adoration of the Shepherds (Fabritius)

1968. Christmas. Multicoloured.

215	-	¼d. Type **72***	10	20
221	-	¼d. Type **72***	10	20
216	-	1d. *The Adoration of the Shepherds* (Rembrandt)	10	10
217	-	6d. Type **72**	15	10
218	-	8d. As 1d.	15	15
219	-	1s.3d. Type **72**	20	25
220	-	2s. As 1d.	25	35

*No. 215 has a brown background and No. 221 a bright purple one.

74 Grand Cayman Thrush ("Cayman Thrush")

1969. Multicoloured.

222	-	¼d. Type **74**	10	75
223	-	1d. Brahmin cattle	10	10
224	-	2d. Blowholes on the coast	10	10
225	-	2½d. Map of Grand Cayman	15	10
226	-	3d. Georgetown scene	10	10
227	-	4d. Royal Poinciana	15	10
228	-	6d. Cayman Brac and Little Cayman on chart	20	10
229	-	8d. Motor vessels at berth	25	10
230	-	1s. Basket-making	15	10
231	-	1s.3d. Beach scene	35	1·00
232	-	1s.6d. Straw-rope making	35	1·00
233	-	2s. Great barracuda	1·25	80
234	-	4s. Government House	35	80
235	-	10s. Arms of the Cayman Islands (vert)	1·00	1·50
236	-	£1 black, ochre and red (Queen Elizabeth II) (vert)	1·25	2·00

1969. Decimal Currency. Nos. 222/36 surch **C-DAY 8th September 1969**. Multicoloured.

238	74	¼c. on ¼d.	10	75
239	-	1c. on 1d.	10	10
240	-	2c. on 2d.	10	10
241	-	3c. on 4d.	10	10
242	-	4c. on 2½d.	10	10
243	-	5c. on 6d.	10	10
244	-	7c. on 8d.	10	10
245	-	8c. on 3d.	15	10
246	-	10c. on 1s.	25	10
247	-	12c. on 1s.3d.	35	1·75
248	-	15c. on 1s.6d.	45	1·50
249	-	20c. on 2s.	1·25	1·75
250	-	40c. on 4s.	45	85
251	-	$1 on 10s.	1·00	2·50
252	-	$2 on £1	1·50	3·25

90 *Madonna and Child* (Vivarini)

1969. Christmas. Multicoloured. Background colours given.

253	90	¼c. red	10	10
254	90	¼c. mauve	10	10
255	90	¼c. green	10	10
256	90	¼c. blue	10	10
257	-	1c. red	10	10
258	90	5c. red	10	10
259	-	7c. green	10	10
260	90	12c. green	15	15
261	-	20c. purple	20	25

DESIGNS: 1c., 7c., 20c. *The Adoration of the Kings* (Gossaert).

92 *Noli me tangere* (Titian)

1970. Easter. Multicoloured; frame colours given.

262	92	¼c. red	10	10
263	92	¼c. green	10	10
264	92	¼c. brown	10	10
265	92	¼c. violet	10	10
266	92	10c. blue	35	10
267	92	12c. brown	40	10
268	92	40c. plum	55	60

93 Barnaby (*Barnaby Rudge*)

1970. Death Centenary of Charles Dickens.

269	93	1c. black, green and yellow	10	10
270	-	12c. black, brown and red	35	10
271	-	20c. black, brown and gold	40	10
272	-	40c. black, ultram & blue	45	25

DESIGNS: 12c. Sairey Gamp (*Martin Chuzzlewit*); 20c. Mr. Micawber and David (*David Copperfield*); 40c. The "Marchioness" (*The Old Curiosity Shop*).

97 Grand Cayman Thrush ("Cayman Thrush")

1970. Decimal Currency. Designs as Nos. 222/36, but with values inscribed in decimal currency as in T **97**.

273		¼c. multicoloured	65	30
274		1c. multicoloured	10	10
275		2c. multicoloured	10	10
276		3c. multicoloured	20	10
277		4c. multicoloured	20	10
278		5c. multicoloured	35	10
279		7c. multicoloured	30	10
280		8c. multicoloured	30	10
281		10c. multicoloured	30	10
282		12c. multicoloured	90	1·00
283		15c. multicoloured	1·25	4·00
284		20c. multicoloured	3·25	1·25
285		40c. multicoloured	85	75
286		$1 multicoloured	1·25	4·75
287		$2 black, ochre and red	2·00	4·75

98 The Three Wise Men

1970. Christmas.

288	98	¼c. green, grey and emerald	10	10
289	-	1c. black, yellow and green	10	10
290	98	5c. grey, orange and red	10	10
291	-	10c. black, yellow and red	10	10
292	98	12c. grey, green and blue	15	10
293	-	20c. black, yellow and green	20	15

DESIGN: 1, 10, 20c. Nativity scene and Globe.

100 Grand Cayman Terrapin

1971. Turtles. Multicoloured.

294		5c. Type **100**	30	25
295		7c. Green turtle	35	25
296		12c. Hawksbill turtle	55	30
297		20c. Turtle farm	1·00	1·40

101 *Dendrophylax fawcettii*

1971. Orchids. Multicoloured.

298		¼c. Type **101**	10	1·25
299		2c. *Schomburgkia thomsoniana*	60	90
300		10c. *Vanilla claviculata*	2·25	50
301		40c. *Oncidium variegatum*	4·50	3·50

102 *Adoration of the Kings* (French 15th century)

1971. Christmas. Multicoloured.

302		¼c. Type **102**	10	10
303		1c. *The Nativity* (Parisian, 14th century)	10	10
304		5c. *Adoration of the Magi* (Burgundian, 15th century)	10	10
305		12c. Type **102**	20	15
306		15c. As 1c.	20	25
307		20c. As 5c.	25	35
MS308		113×115 mm. Nos. 302/7	1·25	2·25

103 Turtle and Telephone Cable

1972. Co-axial Telephone Cable.

309	103	2c. multicoloured	10	10
310	103	10c. multicoloured	15	10
311	103	40c. multicoloured	30	40

104 Court House Building

1972. New Government Buildings. Multicoloured.

312		5c. Type **104**	10	10
313		15c. Legislative Assembly Building	10	10
314		25c. Type **104**	15	15
315		40c. As 15c.	20	30
MS316		121×108 mm. Nos. 312/15	50	2·00

1972. Royal Silver Wedding. As T **52** of Ascension but with Hawksbill Turtle and Queen or Pink Conch in background.

317		12c. violet	15	10
318		30c. green	15	20

106 $1 Coin and Note

1972. First Issue of Currency. Multicoloured.

319		3c. Type **106**	20	10

320		6c. $5 Coin and note	20	70
321		15c. $10 Coin and note	60	30
322		25c. $25 Coin and note	80	45
MS323		128×107 mm. Nos. 319/22	3·50	3·25

107 *The Way of Sorrow*

1973. Easter. Stained-glass Windows. Multicoloured.

324		10c. Type **107**	15	10
325		12c. *Christ Resurrected*	20	10
326		20c. *The Last Supper* (horiz)	25	15
327		30c. *Christ on the Cross* (horiz)	30	25
MS328		122×105 mm. Nos. 324/7 (imperf)	1·00	1·60

108 *The Nativity* (Sforza Book of Hours)

1973. Christmas.

329	108	3c. multicoloured	10	10
330	-	5c. multicoloured	10	10
331	108	9c. multicoloured	15	10
332	-	12c. multicoloured	15	10
333	108	15c. multicoloured	15	15
334	-	25c. multicoloured	20	25

DESIGN: 5, 12, 25c. *The Adoration of the Magi* (Breviary of Queen Isabella).

1973. Royal Wedding. As T **47** of Anguilla. Background colour given. Multicoloured.

335		10c. green	10	10
336		30c. mauve	15	10

109 White-winged Dove

1974. Birds (1st series). Multicoloured.

337		3c. Type **109**	2·00	30
338		10c. Vitelline warbler	2·75	30
339		12c. Antillean grackle ("Greater Antilliean Grackle")	2·75	30
340		20c. Great red-bellied woodpecker ("West Indian Red-bellied Woodpecker")	4·25	80
341		30c. Stripe-headed tanager	5·50	1·50
342		50c. Yucatan vireo	7·00	5·50

See also Nos. 383/8.

110 Old School Building

1974. 25th Anniv of University of West Indies. Multicoloured.

343		12c. Type **110**	10	10
344		20c. New Comprehensive School	15	20
345		30c. Creative Arts Centre, Mona	15	60

111 Hermit Crab and Staghorn Coral

1974. Size 41½×27 mm or 27×41½ mm. Multicoloured.

346		1c. Type **111**	3·50	1·25
347		3c. Treasure-chest and lion's paw	3·50	75

348		4c. Treasure and spotted scorpionfish	50	70
349		5c. Flintlock pistol and brain coral	3·00	75
350		6c. Blackbeard and green turtle	35	2·25
366		8c. As 9c.	2·50	8·50
351		9c. Jewelled pomander and porkfish	4·00	11·00
352		10c. Spiny lobster and treasure	4·50	80
353		12c. Jewelled sword and dagger and sea-fan	35	2·00
354		15c. Cabrit's murex and treasure	45	1·25
417		20c. Queen or pink conch and treasure	3·50	3·00
356		25c. Hogfish and treasure	45	70
357		40c. Gold chalice and seawhip	4·00	1·25
358		$1 Coat of arms (vert)	2·75	3·25
419		$2 Queen Elizabeth II (vert)	8·50	6·50

For smaller designs see Nos. 445/52.

112 Sea Captain and Ship (Shipbuilding)

1974. Local Industries. Multicoloured.

360		8c. Type **112**	30	10
361		12c. Thatcher and cottage	25	10
362		20c. Farmer and plantation	25	20
MS363		92×132 mm. Nos. 360/2	1·50	3·25

113 Arms of Cinque Ports and Lord Warden's Flag

1974. Birth Centenary of Sir Winston Churchill. Multicoloured.

380		12c. Type **113**	15	10
381		50c. Churchill's coat of arms	45	70
MS382		98×86 mm. Nos. 380/1	60	1·60

1975. Birds (2nd series). As T **109**. Multicoloured.

383		3c. Common flicker ("Yellow-shafted Flicker")	70	50
384		10c. Black-billed whistling duck ("West Indian Tree Duck")	1·25	50
385		12c. Yellow warbler	1·40	65
386		20c. White-bellied dove	2·00	2·00
387		30c. Magnificent frigate bird	3·25	4·25
388		50c. Cuban amazon ("Cayman Amazon")	3·75	12·00

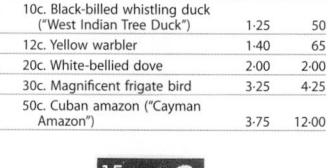

114 "The Crucifixion"

1975. Easter. French Pastoral Staffs.

389	114	15c. multicoloured	10	20
390	-	35c. multicoloured	20	45
MS391		128×98 mm. Nos. 389/90	65	2·75

DESIGN: 35c. Pastoral staff similar to Type **114**.

115 Israel Hands

1975. Pirates. Multicoloured.

392		10c. Type **115**	35	15
393		12c. John Fenn	35	30
394		20c. Thomas Antis	60	50
395		30c. Edward Low	65	1·50

1975. Christmas. *Virgin and Child with Angels*. As T **114**.

396		12c. multicoloured	10	10
397		50c. multicoloured	30	30
MS398		113×85 mm. Nos. 396/7	1·00	3·00

116 Registered Cover,
Government House and Sub-Post
Office

1975. 75th Anniv of First Cayman Islands Postage Stamp.
Multicoloured.

399	10c. Type **116**	15	10
400	20c. ½d. stamp and 1890–94 postmark	20	15
401	30c. 1d. stamp and 1908 surcharge	30	25
402	50c. ½d. and 1d. stamps	45	65
MS403	117×147 mm. Nos. 399/402	2·50	3·00

117 Seals of Georgia, Delaware and New Hampshire

1976. Bicentenary of American Revolution. Mulicoloured.

404	10c. Type **117**	40	15
405	15c. Carolina, New Jersey and Maryland seals	55	20
406	20c. Virginia, Rhode Island and Massachusetts seals	65	25
407	25c. New York, Connecticut and North Carolina seals	65	35
408	30c. Pennsylvania seal, Liberty Bell and U.S. Great Seal	70	40
MS409	166×124 mm. Nos. 404/8	4·00	8·50

118 "470" Dinghies

1976. Olympic Games, Montreal. Multicoloured.

410	20c. Type **118**	40	10
411	50c. Racing dinghy	70	50

119 Queen Elizabeth II and Westminster Abbey

1977. Silver Jubilee. Multicoloured.

427	8c. The Prince of Wales' visit, 1973	10	20
428	30c. Type **119**	15	40
429	50c. Preparation for the Anointing (horiz)	30	75

120 Scuba Diving

1977. Tourism. Multicoloured.

430	5c. Type **120**	15	10
431	10c. Exploring a wreck	20	10
432	20c. Royal gramma ("Fairy basslet") (fish)	55	20
433	25c. Sergeant major (fish)	65	35
MS434	146×89 mm. Nos. 430/3	2·00	4·50

121 Composia fidelissima (moth)

1977. Butterflies and Moth. Multicoloured.

435	5c. Type **121**	75	20
436	8c. Heliconius charithonia	85	20
437	10c. Danaus gilippus	85	20
438	15c. Agraulis vanillae	1·25	45

439	20c. Junonia evarete	1·25	45
440	30c. Anartia jatrophae	1·50	70

122 Cruise Liner
Southward

1978. New Harbour and Cruise Ships. Multicoloured.

441	3c. Type **122**	40	10
442	5c. Cruise liner Renaissance	40	10
443	30c. New harbour (vert)	90	25
444	50c. Cruise liner Daphne (vert)	1·25	65

1978. As Nos. 346/7, 349, 352, 417, 357/8 and 419, but
designs smaller, 40×26 mm or 26×40 mm.

445	1c. Type **111**	1·00	1·25
446	3c. Treasure chest and lion's paw	80	50
447	5c. Flintlock pistol and brain coral	1·50	2·00
448	10c. Spiny lobster and treasure	1·25	60
449	20c. Queen or pink conch and treasure	2·25	1·00
450	40c. Gold chalice and seawhip	13·00	18·00
451	$1 Coat of arms	20·00	5·50
452	$2 Queen Elizabeth II (vert)	4·00	20·00

123 The Crucifixion
(Durer)

1978. Easter and 450th Death Anniv of Durer.

459	**123**	10c. mauve and black	30	10
460	-	15c. yellow and black	40	15
461	-	20c. turquoise and black	50	20
462	-	30c. lilac and black	60	35
MS463	120×108 mm. Nos. 459/62		4·25	6·50

DESIGNS: 15c. Christ at Emmaus; 20c. The Entry into Jerusalem; 30c. Christ washing Peter's Feet.

124 "Explorers"
Singing Game

1978. Third International Council Meeting of Girls'
Brigade. Multicoloured.

464	3c. Type **124**	20	10
465	10c. Colour party	25	10
466	20c. Girls and Duke of Edinburgh Award interests	40	20
467	50c. Girls using domestic skills	70	80

125 Yale of
Beaufort

1978. 25th Anniv of Coronation.

468	**125**	30c. green, mauve and silver	20	25
469	-	30c. multicoloured	20	25
470	-	30c. green, mauve and silver	20	25

DESIGNS: No. 469, Queen Elizabeth II; 470, Barn owl.

126 Four-eyed Butterflyfish

1978. Fish (1st series). Multicoloured.

471	3c. Type **126**	25	10
472	5c. Grey angelfish	30	10
473	10c. Squirrelfish	45	10

474	15c. Queen parrotfish	60	30
475	20c. Spanish hogfish	70	35
476	30c. Queen angelfish	80	50

127 Lockheed L.18 Lodestar

1979. 25th Anniv of Owen Roberts Airfield.
Multicoloured.

477	3c. Type **127**	30	15
478	5c. Consolidated PBY-5A Catalina amphibian	30	15
479	10c. Vickers Viking 1B	35	15
480	15c. B.A.C. One Eleven 455 on tarmac	65	25
481	20c. Piper PA-31 Cheyenne II, Bell 47G Trooper helicopter and Hawker Siddeley H.S.125	75	35
482	30c. B.A.C. One Eleven 475 over airfield	1·00	50

128 Trumpetfish

1979. Fish (2nd series). Multicoloured.

483	1c. Type **128**	10	10
484	3c. Nassau grouper	25	10
485	5c. French angelfish	25	10
486	10c. Schoolmaster snapper	35	10
487	20c. Banded butterflyfish	55	25
488	50c. Black-barred soldierfish	1·00	70

129 1900 1d. Stamp

1979. Death Centenary of Sir Rowland Hill.

489	**129**	5c. black, carmine and blue	10	10
490	-	10c. multicoloured	15	10
491	-	20c. multicoloured	20	25
MS492	138×90 mm. 50c. mult		55	65

DESIGNS: 10c. Great Britain 1902 3d. purple on lemon;
20c. 1955 £1 blue.

130 The Holy Family and Angels

1979. Christmas. Multicoloured.

493	10c. Type **130**	15	10
494	20c. Angels appearing to Shepherds	25	10
495	30c. Nativity	30	20
496	40c. The Magi	40	30

131 Local Rotary Project

1980. 75th Anniv of Rotary International.

497	**131**	20c. blue, black and yellow	20	15
498	-	30c. blue, black and yellow	25	20
499	-	50c. blue, yellow and black	35	30

DESIGNS—VERT: 30c. Paul P. Harris (founder); 50c. Rotary
anniversary emblem.

132 Walking Mail Carrier

1980. "London 1980" International Stamp Exhibition.
Multicoloured.

500	5c. Type **132**	10	10
501	10c. Delivering mail by cat boat	15	10
502	15c. Mounted mail carrier	20	10

503	30c. Horse-drawn wagonette	25	15
504	40c. Postman on bicycle	35	15
505	$1 Motor transport	45	55

133 Queen Elizabeth the
Queen Mother at the Derby,
1976

1980. 80th Birthday of the Queen Mother.

506	**133**	20c. multicoloured	20	25

134 American Thorny
Oyster

1980. Shells (1st series). Multicoloured.

507	5c. Type **134**	25	10
508	10c. West Indian murex	30	10
509	30c. Angular triton	45	40
510	50c. Caribbean vase	70	80

See also Nos. 565/8 and 582/5.

135 Lantana camara

1980. Flowers (1st series). Multicoloured.

511	5c. Type **135**	15	10
512	15c. Bauhinia variegata	20	10
513	30c. Hibiscus hybrid	25	10
514	$1 Crinum amabile ("Milk and Wine Lily")	50	90

See also Nos. 541/4.

136 Juvenile
Tarpon and Fire
Sponge

1980. Multicoloured

515A	3c. Type **136**	1·00	2·50
516B	5c. Flat tree or mangrove-root oyster	1·25	80
517A	10c. Mangrove crab	50	1·50
518A	15c. Lizard and Phyciodes phaon (butterfly)	1·00	1·75
519A	20c. Louisiana heron (Tricoloured Heron)	1·50	2·25
520A	30c. Red mangrove flower	70	1·00
521A	40c. Red mangrove seeds	75	1·00
522A	50c. Waterhouse's leaf-nosed bat	1·25	1·50
523A	$1 Black-crowned night heron	4·50	5·00
524A	$2 Coat of arms	1·25	3·75
525A	$4 Queen Elizabeth II	2·00	4·25

137 Eucharist

1981. Easter. Multicoloured.

526	3c. Type **137**	10	10
527	10c. Crown of thorns	10	10
528	20c. Crucifix	15	10
529	$1 Lord Jesus Christ	50	60

138 Wood Slave

1981. Reptiles and Amphibians. Multicoloured.

530	20c. Type **138**	25	20
531	30c. Cayman iguana	30	35
532	40c. Lion lizard	40	45
533	50c. Terrapin ("Hickatee")	45	55

139 Prince Charles

1981. Royal Wedding. Multicoloured.

534	20c. Wedding bouquet from Cayman Islands	15	10
535	30c. Type **139**	20	10
536	$1 Prince Charles and Lady Diana Spencer	50	75

140 Disabled Scuba Divers

1981. Int Year for Disabled Persons. Multicoloured.

537	5c. Type **140**	10	10
538	15c. Old school for the handicapped	25	20
539	20c. New school for the handicapped	30	25
540	$1 Disabled people in wheelchairs by the sea	1·25	85

1981. Flowers (2nd series). As T 135. Multicoloured.

541	3c. *Bougainvillea spectabilis*	10	10
542	10c. Morning Glory	15	10
543	20c. *Hippeastrum equestre* (Wild amaryllis)	25	25
544	$1 *Cordia sebestena*	1·00	1·75

141 Dr. Robert Koch and Microscope

1982. Centenary of Robert Koch's Discovery of Tubercle Bacillus. Multicoloured.

545	15c. Type **141**	25	25
546	30c. Koch looking through microscope (vert)	45	45
547	40c. Microscope (vert)	70	70
548	50c. Dr. Robert Koch (vert)	80	80

142 Bride and Groom walking down Aisle

1982. 21st Birthday of Princess of Wales. Multicoloured.

549	20c. Cayman Islands coat of arms	20	25
550	30c. Lady Diana Spencer in London, June, 1981	60	45
551	40c. Type **142**	60	65
552	50c. Formal portrait	2·25	1·00

CAYMAN ISLANDS

143 Pitching Tent

1982. 75th Anniv of Boy Scout Movement. Multicoloured.

553	3c. Type **143**	15	10
554	20c. Scouts camping	40	40
555	30c. Cub Scouts and Leaders	60	55
556	50c. Boating skills	80	85

CAYMAN ISLANDS

144 *Madonna and Child with the Infant Baptist*

1982. Christmas. Raphael Paintings. Multicoloured.

557	3c. Type **144**	10	10
558	10c. *Madonna of the Tower*	20	20
559	20c. *Ansidei Madonna*	35	35
560	30c. *Madonna and Child*	50	50

145 Mace

1982. 150th Anniv of Representative Government. Multicoloured.

561	3c. Type **145**	10	20
562	10c. Old Courthouse	20	20
563	20c. Commonwealth Parliamentary Association coat of arms	35	45
564	30c. Legislative Assembly building	50	90

1983. Shells (2nd series). As T 134. Multicoloured.

565	5c. Colourful Atlantic moon	15	30
566	10c. King helmet	25	30
567	20c. Rooster-tail conch	30	40
568	$1 Reticulated cowrie-helmet	50	4·00

146 Legislative Building, Cayman Brac

1983. Royal Visit. Multicoloured.

569	20c. Type **146**	45	35
570	30c. Legislative Building, Grand Cayman	60	50
571	50c. Duke of Edinburgh (vert)	1·25	90
572	$1 Queen Elizabeth II (vert)	2·00	2·00
MS573	113×94 mm. Nos. 569/72	6·50	4·25

147 Satellite View of Earth

1983. Commonwealth Day. Multicoloured.

574	3c. Type **147**	20	15
575	15c. Cayman Islands and Commonwealth flags	50	40
576	20c. Fishing	50	40
577	40c. Portrait of Queen Elizabeth II	75	80

148 MRCU Cessna Ag Wagon

1983. Bicentenary of Manned Flight. Multicoloured.

578	3c. Type **148**	60	50
579	10c. Consolidated PBY-5A Catalina amphibian	65	50
580	20c. Boeing 727-200	1·25	1·50
581	40c. Hawker Siddeley H.S.748	1·75	3·75

1984. Shells (3rd series). As T 134. Multicoloured.

582	3c. Florida moon	70	40
583	10c. Austin's cone	80	40
584	30c. Leaning dwarf triton	2·25	2·75
585	50c. Filose or threaded turban	2·50	4·25

149 *Song of Norway* (cruise liner)

1984. 250th Anniv of *Lloyd's List* (newspaper). Multicoloured.

586	5c. Type **149**	55	20
587	10c. View of old harbour	55	25
588	25c. Wreck of *Ridgefield* (freighter)	1·10	1·00
589	50c. *Goldfield* (schooner)	2·00	2·75
MS590	105×75 mm. $1 *Goldfield* (schooner) (different)	2·10	2·25

1984. Universal Postal Union Congress, Hamburg. No. 589 optd UPU CONGRESS HAMBURG 1984.

591	50c. Schooner *Goldfield*	1·50	2·00

151 Snowy Egret

1984. Birds of the Cayman Islands (1st series). Multicoloured.

592	5c. Type **151**	1·00	75
593	10c. Bananaquit	1·00	75
594	35c. Belted kingfisher ("Kingfisher")	3·25	2·50
595	$1 Brown booby	6·00	11·00

See also Nos. 627/30.

152 Couple on Beach at Sunset

1984. Christmas. Local Festivities. Multicoloured.

596	5c. Type **152**	85	1·50
597	5c. Family and schooner	85	1·50
598	5c. Carol singers	85	1·50
599	5c. East End bonfire	85	1·50
600	25c. Yachts	1·25	1·50
601	25c. Father Christmas in power-boat	1·25	1·50
602	25c. Children on beach	1·25	1·50
603	25c. Beach party	1·25	1·50
MS604	59×79 mm. $1 As No. 599, but larger 27×41 mm	4·00	4·50

Nos. 596/9 and 600/3 were each printed together, *se-tenant*, the four designs of each value forming a composite picture of a beach scene at night (5c.) or in the daytime (25c.).

153 *Schomburgkia thomsoniana* (var. minor)

1985. Orchids. Multicoloured.

605	5c. Type **153**	1·00	30
606	10c. *Schomburgkia thomsoniana*	1·00	30
607	25c. *Encyclia plicata*	2·50	1·00
608	50c. *Dendrophylax fawcettii*	3·75	3·00

154 Freighter Aground

1985. Shipwrecks. Multicoloured.

609	5c. Type **154**	90	50
610	25c. Submerged sailing ship	2·75	1·25
611	35c. Wrecked trawler	3·00	2·50
612	40c. Submerged wreck on its side	3·25	3·50

155 Athletics

1985. International Youth Year. Multicoloured.

613	5c. Type **155**	25	25
614	15c. Students in library	40	30
615	25c. Football (vert)	75	55
616	50c. Netball (vert)	1·75	2·50

156 Morse Key (1935)

1985. 50th Anniv of Telecommunications System. Multicoloured.

617	5c. Type **156**	45	70
618	10c. Hand cranked telephone	50	70
619	25c. Tropospheric scatter dish (1966)	1·50	80
620	50c. Earth station dish aerial (1979)	2·50	5·00

1986. 60th Birthday of Queen Elizabeth II. As T 110 of Ascension. Multicoloured.

621	5c. Princess Elizabeth at wedding of Lady May Cambridge, 1931	10	30
622	10c. In Norway, 1955	15	30
623	25c. Queen inspecting Royal Cayman Islands Police, 1983	1·50	75
624	50c. During Gulf tour, 1979	75	2·00
625	$1 At Crown Agents Head Office, London, 1983	1·10	2·75

157 Magnificent Frigate Bird

1986. Birds of the Cayman Islands (2nd series). Multicoloured.

627	10c. Type **157**	1·75	1·00
628	25c. Black-billed whistling duck ("West Indian Whistling Duck") (vert)	2·25	1·40
629	35c. La Sagra's flycatcher (vert)	2·50	2·50
630	40c. Yellow-faced grassquit	3·00	5·00

1986. Royal Wedding. As T 112 of Ascension. Multicoloured.

633	5c. Prince Andrew and Miss Sarah Ferguson	40	25
634	50c. Prince Andrew aboard H.M.S. *Brazen*	1·60	2·25

158 Red Coral Shrimp

1986. Marine Life. Multicoloured.

635	5c. Type **158**	40	1·00
636	10c. Yellow crinoid	40	50
637	15c. Hermit crab	35	60
638	20c. Tube dwelling anemone	35	1·75
639	25c. Christmas tree worm	45	2·50
640	35c. Porcupinefish	70	2·75
641	50c. Orangeball anenome	80	4·50
642	60c. Basket starfish	3·50	9·00
643	75c. Flamingo tongue	10·00	11·00
644	$1 Sea anemone	1·10	2·50
645	$2 Diamond blenny	1·25	4·75
646	$4 Rough file shell	2·00	6·50

159 Golf

1987. Tourism. Multicoloured.

647	5c. Type **159**	2·50	1·25
648	15c. Sailing	2·50	1·25
649	25c. Snorkelling	2·50	1·25
650	35c. Paragliding	2·75	2·00
651	$1 Game fishing	5·50	11·00

160 Ackee

1987. Cayman Islands Fruits. Multicoloured.

652	5c. Type **160**	75	1·25
653	25c. Breadfruit	2·00	55
654	35c. Pawpaw	2·00	70
655	$1 Soursop	4·50	8·00

161 Lion Lizard

1987. Lizards. Multicoloured.

656	10c. Type **161**	2·25	65
657	50c. Iguana	4·50	3·50
658	$1 Anole	5·50	7·00

162 Poinsettia

1987. Flowers. Multicoloured.

659	5c. Type **162**	65	45
660	25c. Periwinkle	1·75	75
661	35c. Yellow allamanda	1·90	1·10
662	75c. Blood lily	3·50	4·50

163 *Hemiargus ammon*
and *Strymon martialis*

1988. Butterflies. Multicoloured.

663	5c. Type **163**	1·25	65
664	25c. *Phocides pigmalion*	2·50	85
665	50c. *Anaea troglodyta*	4·00	3·75
666	$1 *Papilio andraemon*	5·00	5·00

164 Green-backed
Heron

1988. Herons. Multicoloured.

667	5c. Type **164**	1·25	65
668	25c. Louisiana heron	2·25	85
669	50c. Yellow-crowned night heron	3·00	3·00
670	$1 Little blue heron	3·50	4·25

165 Cycling

1988. Olympic Games, Seoul. Multicoloured.

671	10c. Type **165**	3·00	1·00
672	50c. Cayman Airways Boeing 727 airliner and national team	4·00	3·25
673	$1 "470" dinghy	4·00	4·25
MS674	53×60 mm. $1 Tennis	4·00	3·00

166 Princess
Alexandra

1988. Visit of Princess Alexandra. Multicoloured.

| 675 | 5c. Type **166** | 1·75 | 1·00 |
| 676 | $1 Princess Alexandra in evening dress | 7·50 | 6·50 |

167 George Town Post
Office, and Cayman
Postmark on Jamaica 1d.,
1889

1989. Centenary of Cayman Islands Postal Service. Multicoloured.

677	**167**	5c. multicoloured	85	1·00
678	–	25c. green, black and blue	2·00	1·00
679	–	35c. multicoloured	2·00	1·25
680	–	$1 multicoloured	8·00	9·50

DESIGNS: 25c. *Orinoco* (mail steamer) and 1900 ½d. stamp; 35c. G.P.O., Grand Cayman and "London 1980" $1 stamp; $1 Cayman Airways B.A.C. One Eleven 200/400 airplane and 1966 1s. Jet Service stamp.

168 Captain Bligh
ashore in West
Indies

1989. Captain Bligh's Second Breadfruit Voyage, 1791–93. Multicoloured.

681	50c. Type **168**	5·00	5·00
682	50c. H.M.S. *Providence* (sloop) at anchor	5·00	5·00
683	50c. Breadfruit in tubs and H.M.S. *Assistant* (transport)	5·00	5·00
684	50c. Sailors moving tubs of breadfruit	5·00	5·00
685	50c. Midshipman and stores	5·00	5·00

Nos. 681/5 were printed together, *se-tenant*, forming a composite design.

169 Panton House

1989. Architecture. Designs showing George Town buildings. Multicoloured.

686	5c. Type **169**	75	1·00
687	10c. Town hall and clock tower	75	1·00
688	25c. Old Court House	1·40	60
689	35c. Elmslie Memorial Church	1·60	75
690	$1 Post Office	3·50	6·50

170 Map of Grand
Cayman, 1773, and
Surveying Instruments

1989. Island Maps and Survey Ships. Multicoloured.

691	5c. Type **170**	2·00	1·50
692	25c. Map of Cayman Islands, 1956, and surveying instruments	4·25	1·25
693	50c. H.M.S. *Mutine*, 1914	6·00	5·50
694	$1 H.M.S. *Vidal*, 1956	9·00	11·00

171 French Angelfish

1990. Angelfishes. Multicoloured.

707	10c. Type **171**	1·25	70
708	25c. Grey angelfish	2·25	90
709	50c. Queen angelfish	3·50	4·25
710	$1 Rock beauty	5·50	8·00

1990. 90th Birthday of Queen Elizabeth the Queen Mother. As T **134** of Ascension.

| 711 | 50c. multicoloured | 1·25 | 2·25 |
| 712 | $1 black and blue | 2·75 | 4·00 |

DESIGNS—21×36 mm: 50c. Silver Wedding photograph, 1948. 29×37 mm: $1 King George VI and Queen Elizabeth with Winston Churchill, 1940.

172 *Danaus eresimus*

1990. "Expo 90" International Garden and Greenery Exhibition, Osaka. Butterflies. Multicoloured.

713	5c. Type **172**	65	60
714	25c. *Brephidium exilis*	1·50	1·10
715	35c. *Phyciodes phaon*	1·75	1·25
716	$1 *Agraulis vanillae*	4·00	6·50

173 Goes Weather Satellite

1991. International Decade for Natural Disaster Reduction. Multicoloured.

717	5c. Type **173**	80	70
718	30c. Meteorologist tracking hurricane	2·00	1·10
719	40c. Damaged buildings	2·25	1·25
720	$1 U.S. Dept of Commerce weather reconnaisance Lockheed WP-3D Orion	5·00	8·00

174 Angels and *Datura
candida*

1991. Christmas. Multicoloured.

721	5c. Type **174**	80	80
722	30c. Mary and Joseph going to Bethlehem and *Allamanda cathartica*	2·00	60
723	40c. Adoration of the Kings and *Euphorbia pulcherrima*	2·25	1·10
724	60c. Holy Family and *Guaiacum officinale*	3·25	6·00

175 Coconut Palm

1991. Island Scenes. Multicoloured.

725	5c. Type **175**	50	50
726	15c. Beach scene (horiz)	1·75	50
727	20c. Poincianas in bloom (horiz)	70	35
728	30c. Blowholes (horiz)	1·75	50
729	40c. Police band (horiz)	2·50	1·40
730	50c. *Song of Norway* (liner) at George Town	2·00	1·40
731	60c. The Bluff, Cayman Brac (horiz)	1·75	2·25
732	80c. Coat of arms	1·50	2·50
733	90c. View of Hell (horiz)	1·60	2·50
734	$1 Game fishing (horiz)	3·25	2·50
735	$2 *Nieuw Amsterdam* (1983) and *Holiday* (liners) in harbour	8·00	7·50
736	$8 Queen Elizabeth II	16·00	19·00

1992. 40th Anniv of Queen Elizabeth II's Accession. As T **143** of Ascension. Multicoloured.

737	5c. Caymans' house	30	30
738	20c. Sunset over islands	1·00	50
739	30c. Beach	1·10	65
740	40c. Three portraits of Queen Elizabeth	1·10	1·00
741	$1 Queen Elizabeth II	2·00	3·50

176 Single Cyclist

1992. Olympic Games, Barcelona. Cycling. Multicoloured.

742	15c. Type **176**	1·75	65
743	40c. Two cyclists	2·50	1·50
744	60c. Cyclist's legs	3·00	3·25
745	$1 Two pursuit cyclists	3·75	4·50

177 Woman and
Donkey with
Panniers

1992. Island Heritage. Multicoloured.

746	5c. Type **177**	50	50
747	30c. Fisherman weaving net	1·25	85
748	40c. Maypole dancing	1·50	1·10
749	60c. Basket making	2·50	3·50
750	$1 Cooking on caboose	3·00	4·50

178 Yellow Stingray

1993. Rays. Multicoloured.

751	5c. Type **178**	70	60
752	30c. Southern stingray	1·75	1·25
753	40c. Spotted eagle-ray	2·00	1·50
754	$1 Manta	4·25	5·50

179 Turtle and
Sailing Dinghies

1993. Tourism. Multicoloured.

755	15c. Type **179**	1·50	1·75
756	15c. Tourist boat, fishing launch and scuba diver	1·50	1·75
757	15c. Golf	1·50	1·75
758	15c. Tennis	1·50	1·75
759	15c. Pirates and ship	1·50	1·75
760	30c. Liner, tourist launch and yacht	1·75	1·90
761	30c. George Town street	1·75	1·90
762	30c. Tourist submarine	1·75	1·90
763	30c. Motor scooter riders and cyclist	1·75	1·90
764	30c. Cayman Airways Boeing 737 airliners	1·75	1·90

180 Cuban Amazon
with Wings spread

1993. Endangered Species. Cuban Amazon ("Grand Cayman Parrot"). Multicoloured.

765	5c. Type **180**	85	1·50
766	5c. On branch with wings folded	85	1·50
767	30c. Head of parrot	2·25	2·50
768	30c. Pair of parrots	2·25	2·50

181 *Ionopsis utricularioides*
and Manger

1993. Christmas. Orchids. Multicoloured.

769	5c. Type **181**	1·25	75
770	40c. *Encyclia cochleata* and shepherd	2·75	85
771	60c. *Vanilla pompona* and wise men	3·75	4·00
772	$1 *Oncidium caymanense* and Virgin Mary	4·75	7·00

182 Queen
Angelfish

1994. "Hong Kong '94" International Stamp Exhibition. Reef Life. Sheet 121×85 mm, containing T **182** and similar vert designs. Multicoloured.
MS773	60c. Type **182**; 60c. Diver with porkfish and short-finned hogfish; 60c. Rock beauty and Royal gramma; 60c. French angelfish and Banded butterflyfish	8·50	·9·50

183 Flags of Great
Britain and Cayman
Islands

1994. Royal Visit. Multicoloured.
774	5c. Type **183**	2·00	1·25
775	15c. Royal Yacht *Britannia*	3·00	1·00
776	30c. Queen Elizabeth II	3·00	1·25
777	$2 Queen Elizabeth and Prince Philip disembarking	9·00	12·00

184 Black-billed
Whistling Duck

1994. Black-billed Whistling Duck ("West Indian Whistling Duck"). Multicoloured.
778	5c. Type **184**	1·50	1·00
779	15c. Duck landing on water (horiz)	2·25	75
780	20c. Duck preening (horiz)	2·25	80
781	80c. Duck flapping wings	4·50	5·50
782	$1 Adult and duckling	5·00	6·50
MS783	71×45 mm. $1 As No. 782, but including Cayman Islands National Trust symbol	7·00	8·00

185 Electrostrymon
angelia

1994. Butterflies. Multicoloured.
784	10c. Type **185**	1·00	1·50
785	10c. *Eumaeus atala*	1·00	1·50
786	$1 *Eurema daira*	4·75	5·00
787	$1 *Urbanus dorantes*	4·75	5·00

186 H.M.S. *Convert*
(frigate)

1994. Bicentenary of Wreck of Ten Sail off Grand Cayman. Multicoloured.
788	10c. Type **186**	55	55
789	10c. Merchant brig and full-rigged ship	55	55
790	15c. Full-rigged ship near rock	75	50
791	20c. Long boat leaving full-rigged ship	85	55
792	$2 Merchant brig	4·50	7·50

187 Young Green Turtles

1995. Sea Turtles. Multicoloured.
793	10c. Type **187**	55	45
794	20c. Kemp's ridley turtle	80	55
795	25c. Hawksbill turtle	90	60
796	30c. Leatherback turtle	95	70
797	$1.30 Loggerhead turtle	3·50	4·75
798	$2 Pacific ridley turtles	4·50	6·00
MS799	167×94 mm. Nos. 793/8	10·00	11·50

188 Running

1995. CARIFTA and IAAF Games, George Town. Multicoloured.
800	10c. Type **188**	60	40
801	20c. High jumping	90	70
802	30c. Javelin throwing	1·25	80
803	$1.30 Yachting	4·25	6·00
MS804	100×70 mm. $2 Athletes with medals	6·50	7·50

1995. 50th Anniv of End of Second World War. As T **161** of Ascension. Multicoloured.
805	10c. Members of Cayman Home Guard	70	55
806	25c. *Comayagua* (freighter)	1·75	85
807	40c. U-boat *U125*	2·00	1·50
808	$1 U.S. Navy L-3 airship	3·75	6·00
MS809	75×85 mm. $1.30, Reverse of 1939–45 War Medal (vert)	2·50	3·00

189 Queen
Elizabeth the Queen
Mother

1995. 95th Birthday of Queen Elizabeth the Queen Mother. Sheet 70×90 mm.
MS810	**189** $4 multicoloured	8·50	9·50

190 Ox and Christ
Child

1995. Christmas. Nativity Animals. Multicoloured.
811	10c. Type **190**	70	30
812	20c. Sheep and lamb	1·25	45
813	30c. Donkey	2·00	60
814	$2 Camels	8·00	10·00
MS815	160×75 mm. Nos. 811/14	11·00	11·00

191 Sea Grape

1996. Wild Fruit. Multicoloured.
816	10c. Type **191**	50	40
817	25c. Guava	1·00	50
818	40c. West Indian cherry	1·50	80
819	$1 Tamarind	2·75	4·50

192 "Laser" Dinghy

1996. Centenary of Modern Olympic Games. Multicoloured.
820	10c. Type **192**	55	40
821	20c. Sailboarding	85	60
822	30c. "Finn" dinghy	1·00	80
823	$2 Running	4·25	7·00

193 Guitar and Score
of National Song

1996. National Identity. Multicoloured.
824	10c. Type **193**	35	40
825	20c. Cayman Airways Boeing 737-200	1·25	40
826	25c. Queen Elizabeth opening Legislative Assembly	75	50
827	30c. Seven Mile Beach	75	55
828	40c. Scuba diver and stingrays	1·00	75
829	60c. Children at turtle farm	2·00	1·10
830	80c. Cuban amazon ("Cayman Parrot") (national bird)	3·00	2·25
831	90c. Silver thatch palm (national tree)	1·75	2·25
832	$1 Cayman Islands flag	3·75	2·50
833	$2 Wild Banana Orchid (national flower)	5·50	5·50
834	$4 Cayman Islands coat of arms	9·00	13·00
835	$6 Cayman Islands currency	11·00	15·00

194 Christmas Time
on *North Church Street*
(Joanne Sibley)

1996. Christmas. Paintings. Multicoloured.
836	10c. Type **194**	40	30
837	25c. *Gone Fishing* (Lois Brezinsky)	70	50
838	30c. *Claus Encounters* (John Doak)	80	70
839	$2 *A Caymanian Christmas* (Debbie van der Bol)	4·00	6·50

1997. "HONG KONG '97" International Stamp Exhibition. Sheet 130×90 mm, containing design as No. 830 with "1997" imprint date. Multicoloured.
MS840	80c. Cuban amazon ("Cayman Parrot")	1·75	2·00

1997. Golden Wedding of Queen Elizabeth and Prince Philip. As T **173** of Ascension. Multicoloured.
841	10c. Queen Elizabeth	1·10	1·40
842	10c. Prince Philip and Prince Charles at Trooping the Colour	1·10	1·40
843	30c. Prince William horse riding, 1989	1·75	1·90
844	30c. Queen Elizabeth and Prince Philip at Royal Ascot	1·75	1·90
845	40c. Prince Philip at the Brighton Driving Trials	1·90	2·00
846	40c. Queen Elizabeth at Windsor Horse Show, 1993	1·90	2·00
MS847	110×70 mm. $1 Queen Elizabeth and Prince Philip in landau (horiz)	5·50	5·50

195 Children accessing
Internet

1997. Telecommunications. Multicoloured.
848	10c. Type **195**	35	25
849	25c. Cable & Wireless cable ship	70	45
850	30c. New area code "345" on children's T-shirts	75	60
851	60c. Satellite dish	1·50	2·50

196 Santa in
Hammock

1997. Christmas. Multicoloured.
852	10c. Type **196**	35	25
853	30c. Santa with children on the Bluff	65	45
854	40c. Santa playing golf	1·50	80
855	$1 Santa scuba diving	2·00	3·50

1998. Diana, Princess of Wales Commemoration. As T **177** of Ascension. Multicoloured.
856	10c. Wearing gold earrings, 1997	40	30
857	20c. Wearing black hat	70	90
MS858	145×70 mm. 10c. As No. 856; 20c. As No. 857; 40c. With bouquet, 1995; $1 Wearing black and white blouse, 1983 (sold at $1.70 + 30c. charity premium)	2·75	4·00

1998. 80th Anniv of the Royal Air Force. As T **178** of Ascension. Multicoloured.
859	10c. Hawker Horsley	60	70
860	20c. Fairey Hendon	75	80
861	25c. Hawker Siddeley Gnat	85	90
862	30c. Hawker Siddeley Dominie	95	1·00
MS863	110×77 mm. 40c. Airco D.H.9; 60c. Spad 13 Scout; 80c. Airspeed Oxford; $1 Martin Baltimore	5·50	6·50

197 Black-billed
Whistling Duck
("West Indian
Whistling Duck")

1998. Birds. Multicoloured.
864	10c. Type **197**	1·25	60
865	20c. Magnificent frigate bird ("Magnificant Frigatbird")	1·75	60
866	60c. Red-footed booby	2·75	3·00
867	$1 Cuban amazon ("Grand Cayman Parrot")	3·50	4·25

198 Santa at the
Blowholes

1998. Christmas. Multicoloured.
868	10c. Type **198**	30	30
869	30c. Santa diving on wreck of *Capt. Keith Tibbetts*	75	60
870	40c. Santa at Pedro Castle	90	75
871	60c. Santa arriving on Little Cayman	1·75	2·50

199 *They Rolled the
Stone Away* (Miss Lassie)

1999. Easter. Paintings by Miss Lassie (Gladwyn Bush). Multicoloured.
884	10c. Type **199**	30	35
885	20c. *Ascension* (vert)	60	70
886	30c. *The World Praying for Peace*	75	85
887	40c. *Calvary* (vert)	95	1·10

200 *Cayman House* (Jessica
Cranston)

1999. Vision 2008 Project. Children's Paintings. Multicoloured.
888	10c. Type **200**	40	20
889	30c. *Coral Reef* (Sarah Hetley)	1·00	55
890	40c. *Fisherman on North Sound* (Sarah Cuff)	1·10	70
891	$2 *Three Fish and a Turtle* (Ryan Martinez)	4·25	6·50

1999. Royal Wedding. As T **185** of Ascension. Multicoloured.
892	10c. Photographs of Prince Edward and Miss Sophie Rhys-Jones	50	30
893	$2 Engagement photograph	3·75	4·75

1999. 30th Anniv of First Manned Landing on Moon. As T **186** of Ascension. Multicoloured.
894	10c. Coastguard cutter on patrol during launch	45	35
895	25c. Firing of third stage rockets	80	60
896	30c. Buzz Aldrin descending to Moon's surface	85	65

| 897 | 60c. Jettisoning of lunar module | 1·40 | 2·25 |
| MS898 | 90×80 mm. $1.50, Earth as seen from Moon (circular, 40 mm diam) | 3·25 | 3·50 |

1999. "Queen Elizabeth the Queen Mother's Century". As T **187** of Ascension. Multicoloured.

899	10c. Visiting anti-aircraft battery, London, 1940	45	40
900	20c. With children on her 94th birthday, 1994	65	65
901	30c. With Prince Charles and Prince William, 1997	80	90
902	40c. Reviewing Chelsea Pensioners, 1986	90	1·00
MS903	145×70 mm. $1.50, Duchess of York with Princess Elizabeth, 1926, and Royal Wedding, 1923	2·50	3·00

201 1969 Christmas ¼c. Stamp

1999. Christmas. Designs showing previous Christmas stamps. Multicoloured.

904	10c. Type **201**	40	25
905	30c. 1984 Christmas 5c.	70	50
906	40c. 1997 Christmas 10c.	85	65
907	$1 1979 Christmas 20c. (horiz)	1·90	2·50
MS908	111×100 mm. Nos. 904/7	3·50	3·50

2000. "Stamp Show 2000" International Stamp Exhibition, London. Kings and Queens of England. As T **223** of British Virgin Islands. Multicoloured.

909	10c. King Henry VII	60	70
910	10c. King Henry VIII	1·40	1·75
911	40c. Queen Mary I	1·40	1·75
912	40c. King Charles II	1·40	1·75
913	40c. Queen Anne	1·40	1·75
914	40c. King George IV	1·40	1·75
915	40c. King George V	1·40	1·75

202 Ernie fishing from Rubber Ring

2000. "Sesame Street" (children's T.V. programme). Multicoloured.

916	10c. Type **202**	25	35
917	20c. Grover flying	40	50
918	20c. Zoe in airplane	40	50
919	20c. Oscar the Grouch in balloon	40	50
920	20c. The Count on motorbike	40	50
921	20c. Big Bird rollerskating	40	50
922	20c. Cookie Monster heading for Cookie Factory	40	50
923	20c. Type **202**	40	50
924	20c. Bert in rowing boat	40	50
925	30c. Elmo snorkeling	40	50
926	30c. As No. 920	55	55
MS927	139×86 mm. 20c. Elmo with stamps	1·00	1·00

Nos. 917/25 were printed together, *se-tenant*, with the backgrounds forming a composite design.

2000. 18th Birthday of Prince William. As T **191** of Ascension. Multicoloured.

928	10c. Prince William in 1999 (horiz)	50	40
929	20c. In evening dress, 1997 (horiz)	75	60
930	30c. At Muick Falls, 1997	90	80
931	40c. In uniform of Parachute Regiment, 1986	1·25	1·25
MS932	175×95 mm. $1 As baby with toy mouse (horiz) and Nos. 928/31	7·50	7·50

203 Green Turtle

2000. Marine Life. Multicoloured.

| 933 | 10c. Type **203** | 55 | 45 |
| 934 | 20c. Queen angel fish | 80 | 50 |

| 935 | 30c. Sleeping parrotfish | 1·10 | 65 |
| 936 | $1 Green moray eel | 3·50 | 4·50 |

204 Boy thinking about Drugs and Fitness

2000. National Drugs Council. Multicoloured.

937	10c. Type **204**	60	35
938	15c. Rainbow, sun, clouds and "ez2B Drug Free"	85	35
939	30c. Musicians dancing	1·40	65
940	$2 Hammock between two palm trees	5·00	8·00

205 Children on Beach ("Backing Sand")

2000. Christmas. Traditional Customs. Multicoloured.

941	10c. Type **205**	85	50
942	30c. Christmas dinner	2·00	80
943	40c. Yard dance	2·25	85
944	60c. Conch shell borders	2·75	3·25

206 Woman on Beach

2001. United Nations Women's Human Rights Campaign.

| 945 | **206** 10c. multicoloured | 60 | 60 |

207 Red Mangrove Cay

2001. Cayman Brac Tourism Project. Multicoloured.

946	15c. Type **207**	1·10	75
947	20c. Peter's Cave (vert)	1·25	80
948	25c. Bight Road steps (vert)	1·40	90
949	30c. Westerly Ponds	1·50	1·00
950	40c. Aerial view of Spot Bay	1·75	1·40
951	60c. The Marshes	2·75	3·50

208 Work of National Council of Voluntary Organizations

2001. Non-Profit Organizations. Multicoloured.

952	15c. Type **208**	80	65
953	20c. Pet welfare (Cayman Humane Society)	1·75	1·00
954	25c. Stick figures (Red Cross and Red Crescent)	1·75	1·50
955	30c. Pink flowers (Cayman Islands Cancer Society) (vert)	1·75	1·50
956	40c. Women's silhouettes and insignia (Lions Club Breast Cancer Awareness Campaign) (vert)	1·90	1·75
MS957	145×95 mm. Nos. 952/6 (sold at $1.80)	7·50	8·00

No. MS957 was sold at $1.80 which included a 50c. donation to the featured organisations.

209 Children walking Home

2001. Transportation. Multicoloured.

| 958 | 15c. Type **209** | 70 | 60 |
| 959 | 15c. Boy on donkey | 70 | 60 |

960	20c. Bananas by canoe	70	45
961	25c. Horse and buggy	1·00	55
962	30c. Catboats fishing	1·00	55
963	40c. Schooner	1·25	65
964	60c. Police cyclist (vert)	2·50	1·50
965	80c. Lady drivers	2·00	1·75
966	90c. Launching *Cimboco* (motor coaster) (vert)	2·50	2·00
967	$1 Amphibian aircraft	2·75	2·25
968	$4 Container ship	8·50	9·00
969	$10 Boeing 767 airliner	18·00	20·00

210 Father Christmas on Scooter with Children, Cayman Brac

2001. Christmas. Multicoloured.

970	15c. Type **210**	1·00	55
971	30c. Father Christmas on eagle ray, Little Cayman	1·40	80
972	40c. Father Christmas in catboat, Grand Cayman	1·60	1·10
973	60c. Father Christmas parasailing over Grand Cayman	2·40	3·00

211 Statue of Liberty, U.S. and Cayman Flags

2002. In Remembrance. Victims of Terrorist Attacks on U.S.A. (11 September 2001).

| 974 | **211** $1 multicoloured | 3·00 | 3·50 |

2002. Golden Jubilee. As T **200** of Ascension.

975	15c. grey, blue and gold	50	40
976	20c. multicoloured	65	40
977	30c. black, blue and gold	80	60
978	80c. multicoloured	2·00	2·25
MS979	162×95 mm. Nos. 975/8 and $1 multicoloured	7·00	7·00

DESIGNS—HORIZ: 15c. Princess Elizabeth as young child; 20c. Queen Elizabeth in evening dress, 1976; 30c. Princess Elizabeth and Princess Margaret as Girl Guides, 1942; 80c. Queen Elizabeth at Newbury, 1996. VERT (38×51 mm)—$1 Queen Elizabeth after Annigoni.

Designs as Nos. 975/8 in No. MS979 omit the gold frame around each stamp and the "Golden Jubilee 1952–2002" inscription.

212 Snoopy painting Woodstock at Cayman Brac Bluff

2002. "A Cayman Vacation". Peanuts (cartoon characters by Charles Schulz). Multicoloured.

980	15c. Type **212**	75	65
981	20c. Charlie Brown and Sally at Hell Post Office, Grand Cayman	80	65
982	25c. Peppermint Patty and Marcie on beach, Little Cayman	85	75
983	30c. Snoopy as Red Baron and Boeing 737-200 over Grand Cayman	1·10	85
984	40c. Linus and Snoopy at Point of Sand, Little Cayman	1·40	1·10
985	60c. Charlie Brown playing golf at The Links, Grand Cayman	2·25	3·00
MS986	230×160 mm. Nos. 980/5	6·50	7·00

No. MS986 is die-cut in the shape of a suitcase.

213 Cayman Islands Footballers

2002. World Cup Football Championship, Japan and Korea and 35th Anniv of Cayman Islands Football Association.

| 987 | **213** 30c. multicoloured | 1·50 | 1·25 |
| 988 | **213** 40c. multicoloured | 1·50 | 1·25 |

2002. Queen Elizabeth the Queen Mother Commemoration. As T **202** of Ascension.

| 989 | 15c. black, gold and purple | 80 | 30 |
| 990 | 30c. multicoloured | 1·25 | 60 |

991	40c. black, gold and purple	1·50	1·00
992	$1 multicoloured	2·75	3·75
MS993	145×70 mm. Nos. 991/2	5·00	6·00

DESIGNS: 15c. Queen Elizabeth at Red Corss and St. John's summer fair, London, 1943; 30c. Queen Mother at Royal Caledonian School, Bushey; 40c. Duchess of York in 1936; $1 Queen Mother at film premiere in 1989.

Designs in No. MS993 omit the "1900–2002" inscription and the coloured frame.

214 Angel Gabriel appearing to Virgin Mary

2002. Christmas. Multicoloured.

994	15c. Type **214**	60	55
995	20c. Mary and Joseph travelling to Bethlehem	70	55
996	30c. The Holy Family	85	60
997	40c. Angel appearing to shepherds	1·00	90
998	60c. Three Wise Men	1·60	2·50
MS999	234×195 mm. Nos. 994/8	4·25	5·00

215 Catalina Flying Boat, North Sound, Grand Cayman

2002. 50th Anniv of Cayman Islands. Aviation. Multicoloured.

1000	15c. Type **215**	1·10	75
1001	20c. Grand Cayman Airport, 1952	1·25	75
1002	25c. Cayman Brac Airways AC 50	1·25	80
1003	30c. Cayman Airways Boeing 737	1·40	85
1004	40c. British Airways Concorde at Grand Cayman, 1984	2·00	1·50
1005	$1.30 Island Air DHC 6 Twin Otter on Little Cayman	4·50	5·50

216 Skipping

2003. Children's Games. Multicoloured.

1006	15c. Type **216**	80	60
1007	20c. Maypole dancing	90	60
1008	25c. Gig	1·00	70
1009	30c. Hopscotch	1·10	70
1010	$1 Marbles	3·00	4·00

2003. 50th Anniv of Coronation. As T **206** of Ascension. Multicoloured.

1011	15c. Queen Elizabeth II wearing Imperial State Crown	75	35
1012	$2 Newly crowned Queen flanked by Bishops of Durham and Bath & Wells	4·25	5·00
MS1013	95×115 mm. 20c. As 15c.; $4 As $2	9·00	10·00

Nos. 1011/12 have red frames; stamps from MS1013 have no frame and country name in mauve panel.

2003. As T **207** of Ascension.

| 1014 | $4 black, red and violet | 8·00 | 8·50 |

2003. 21st Birthday of Prince William of Wales. As T **208** of Ascension. Multicoloured.

1015	15c. Prince William at Tidworth Polo Club, 2002 and on Raleigh International Expedition, 2000	70	35
1016	40c. At Golden Jubilee church service, 2002 and Queen Mother's 101st birthday, 2001	1·25	
1017	80c. At Queen Mother's 101st birthday and at Holyrood House, 2001	2·25	3·00
1018	$1 At Eton College and at Christmas Day church service in 2000	2·25	3·00

217 Turtles hatching

2003. 500th Anniv of Discovery of Cayman Islands. Multicoloured.

| 1019 | 15c. Type **217** | 80 | 65 |

1020	20c. Old waterfront, George Town, 1975	1·00	75
1021	20c. *Santa Maria* (Columbus) and turtle	1·25	80
1022	25c. Nassau grouper (fish) and corals	1·25	80
1023	30c. *Kirk-B* (Cayman Brac schooner)	1·40	80
1024	40c. George Town harbour	1·40	85
1025	60c. Musical instruments	1·50	1·40
1026	80c. Smokewood tree and ghost orchids	2·25	2·25
1027	90c. Little Cayman Baptist Church	2·25	2·50
1028	$1 Loading thatch rope onto *Caymania*	2·75	3·00
1029	$1.30 Children's dance troupe	3·25	4·50
1030	$2 Cayman Parliament in session	4·25	6·00
MS1031	216×151 mm. Nos. 1019/30	21·00	23·00

218 Bell and "Merry Christmas"

2003. Christmas. Multicoloured.

1032	15c. Type **218**	85	55
1033	20c. Christmas wreath and "Celebrate with Family"	95	55
1034	30c. Gold star, angel and "Happy New Year"	1·25	60
1035	40c. Christmas lights and "Happy Holidays"	1·50	70
1036	60c. Poinsettias and "Seasons Greetings"	2·00	2·75

219 Female and Calf

2003. Endangered Species. Short-finned Pilot Whale. Multicoloured.

1037	15c. Type **219**	1·40	75
1038	20c. Four pilot whales	1·50	90
1039	30c. Two pilot whales at surface	1·75	1·10
1040	40c. Short-finned pilot whale	2·50	1·90

220 *Lady Slater*

2004. Centenary of Shipping Registry. Multicoloured.

1041	15c. Type **220**	85	55
1042	20c. *Seanostrum*	95	70
1043	30c. *Kirk Pride*	1·40	1·00
1044	$1 *Boadicea*	4·25	5·50

221 *Jesus carrying His Cross* (Carole Mayer)

2004. Easter. Multicoloured.

1045	15c. Type **221**	75	40
1046	30c. *The Ascension* (Natasha Claire Kozaily)	1·25	1·00

222 Swimming

2004. Olympic Games, Athens, Greece. Multicoloured.

1047	15c. Type **222**	75	40
1048	40c. Sprinting	1·25	75
1049	60c. Long jump	1·90	1·60
1050	80c. Two Cayman Islands swimmers	2·40	3·00

223 Blue Iguana

2004. Blue Iguana. Multicoloured.

1051	15c. Type **223**	75	60
1052	20c. Baby iguana hatching from egg	85	60
1053	25c. Four iguanas	95	70
1054	30c. Baby iguana on finger	1·10	70
1055	40c. Iguana with open mouth	1·25	80
1056	90c. Eye of iguana	2·75	3·50
MS1057	104×58 mm. 60c. Iguana on rock facing right; 80c. Iguana on rock facing left	4·50	5·00

2005. Bicentenary of Battle of Trafalgar. As T **216** of Ascension. Multicoloured.

1058	15c. HMS *Victory* (horiz)	1·00	70
1059	20c. HMS *Tonnant* tangling into bow of *Algesiras* (horiz)	1·10	70
1060	25c. Flint cannon lock and linstock (horiz)	1·10	80
1061	60c. Boatswain's Mate RN (horiz)	1·75	1·25
1062	$1 Portrait of Admiral Nelson	2·75	3·00
1063	$2 HMS *Orion* in action against *Intrepide* (horiz)	5·00	6·00
MS1064	120×79 mm. 60c. *Pluton*; $2 HMS *Tonnant*	6·00	7·00

No. 1058 contains traces of powdered wood from HMS *Victory*.

224 Rotary Emblem

2005. Centenary of Rotary International.

1065	**224** 15c. multicoloured	70	60
1066	– 30c. ultramarine, black and grey	1·10	1·00

DESIGN: 30c. Polio Plus and Rotary emblems.

225 *Myrmecophila purpurea*

2005. Orchids. Multicoloured.

1067	15c. Type **225**	75	55
1068	20c. *Prosthechea boothiana*	80	55
1069	30c. *Tolumnia calochila* (vert)	90	60
1070	40c. *Encyclia phoenicia*	1·10	80
1071	80c. *Prosthechea cochleata* (vert)	2·00	2·50
MS1072	80×52 mm. $1.50 *Encyclia kingsii*	4·00	4·50

2005. Pope John Paul II Commemoration. As T **219** of Ascension.

1073	30c. multicoloured	1·75	1·25

226 The Queen (butterfly)

2005. Butterflies. Multicoloured. (a) Ordinary gum.

1074	15c. Type **226**	70	60
1075	20c. Mexican fritillary	75	65
1076	25c. Malachite	80	70
1077	30c. Cayman crescent spot	85	70
1078	40c. Cloudless sulphur	1·10	80
1079	90c. Swallowtail	2·25	3·00

(b) Self-adhesive. Size 29×24 mm.

1080	15c. Type **226**	70	80
1081	20c. Mexican fritillary	75	85
1082	30c. Cayman crescent spot	90	1·10

227 Angels

2005. Christmas. Multicoloured.

1083	15c. Type **227**	60	40
1084	30c. Three Wise Men (horiz)	80	50
1085	40c. Holy Family	1·00	75
1086	60c. Shepherds (horiz)	1·40	1·75
MS1087	156×106 mm. Nos. 1083/6	3·50	3·50

228 Wash Wood (*Jacquinia keyensis*)

2006. Trees. Multicoloured.

1088	15c. Type **228**	70	50
1089	20c. Red mangrove (*Rhizophora mangle*)	80	60
1090	30c. Ironwood (*Chionanthus caymanensis*)	90	60
1091	60c. West Indian cedar (*Cedrela odorata*)	1·75	1·40
1092	$2 Spanish elm (*Cordia gerascanthus*)	4·50	5·50

2006. 80th Birthday of Queen Elizabeth II. As T **223** of Ascension. Multicoloured.

1093	15c. Princess Elizabeth as young child	80	50
1094	40c. Queen Elizabeth in uniform, c. 1952	1·50	80
1095	$1 Wearing tiara	2·25	2·50
1096	$2 Wearing white blouse	4·25	4·75
MS1097	144×75 mm. As Nos. 1094/5, but without white borders	8·00	8·50

229 Hawksbill Turtle

2006. Cayman's Aquatic Treasures. Multicoloured. (a) Ordinary gum.

1098	25c. Type **229**	1·00	90
1099	25c. Grey angelfish	1·00	90
1100	60c. Queen angelfish (vert)	2·00	1·75
1101	75c. Diamond blenny	2·25	2·50
1102	$1 Spotted drum (juvenile) (vert)	3·00	3·50
MS1103	145×95 mm. As Nos. 1098/102	8·00	8·50

(b) Size 29×24 mm. Self-adhesive.

1104	25c. As Type **229**	90	1·10
1105	25c. As No. 1099	90	1·10
1106	60c. As No. 1100	1·75	2·00
1107	75c. As No. 1101	1·90	2·50

Stamps from **MS**1103 do not have white borders.

230 Bananaquit

2006. Birds (1st series). Multicoloured.

1108	25c. Type **230**	75	15
1109	50c. Vitelline warbler	1·40	90
1110	75c. Cuban Amazon ("Grand Cayman Parrot")	1·75	1·25
1111	80c. White-bellied dove ("Caribbean Dove")	1·75	1·25
1112	$1 Caribbean elaenia	2·00	1·75
1113	$1.50 Great red-bellied woodpecker ("West Indian Woodpecker")	3·00	3·00
1114	$1.60 Thick-billed vireo	3·25	3·25
1115	$2 Common flicker ("Northern Flicker")	4·00	4·25
1116	$4 Cuban bullfinch	8·00	8·50
1117	$5 Stripe-headed tanager ("Western spindalis")	9·00	9·50
1118	$10 Loggerhead kingbird	17·00	18·00
1119	$20 Red-legged thrush	30·00	32·00

See also Nos. 1124/6.

231 "Faith" and the Three Magi

2006. Christmas. Multicoloured.

1120	25c. Type **231**	75	30
1121	75c. "Hope" and prophet speaking of the Messiah	1·90	1·75
1122	80c. "Joy" and angel	1·90	1·75
1123	$1 "Love" and Mary with baby Jesus	2·00	2·50

232 Bananaquit

2007. Birds (2nd series). Designs as Nos. 1108, and 1110/11 but each 30×25 mm with redrawn inscriptions. Self-adhesive.

1124	25c. Type **232**	1·10	1·40
1125	75c. Cuban amazon ('GRAND CAYMAN PARROT')	2·25	2·75
1126	80c. White-bellied dove ('CARIBBEAN DOVE')	2·25	2·75

233 Brac Reef Dock

2007. Cayman Islands Scenes. Multicoloured.

1127	20c. Type **233**	70	50
1128	25c. Waterfront, Hog Sty Bay, George Town, Grand Cayman	75	60
1129	30c. East End blowholes, Grand Cayman Island (vert)	80	60
1130	40c. Man lying in hammock on beach at sunset (vert)	1·10	75
1131	75c. Poinciana flowers	2·00	2·50
1132	$1 Driftwood on shore, Little Cayman Island	2·25	2·75

2007. Centenary of Scouting. As T **281** of Bahamas. Multicoloured.

1133	25c. Early Wolf Cubs with their flag	75	50
1134	75c. Modern Cub Scouts after Remembrance Day Parade, 2006	2·00	2·00
1135	80c. Scouts camping	2·00	2·00
1136	$1 Drill team, Remembrance Day Parade, 2005	2·25	2·50
MS1137	90×65 mm. 50c. Cayman Islands scouts in opening ceremony of 13th Caribbean Scout Jamboree, Jamaica, 2006 (vert); $1.50 Lord Baden-Powell (vert)	3·75	4·00

2007. Diamond Wedding of Queen Elizabeth II and Duke of Edinburgh. As T **58** of British Indian Ocean Territory. Multicoloured.

1138	50c. Princess Elizabeth alighting from car and Lt. Philip Mountbatten, c. 1949	1·40	1·10
1139	75c. Princess Elizabeth wearing tiara and wedding veil, 1949	2·00	2·00
1140	80c. Queen Elizabeth the Queen Mother and Princesses Elizabeth and Margaret	2·00	2·00
1141	$1 Princess Elizabeth and Duke of Edinburgh in procession down Westminster Abbey aisle on wedding day, 1949	2·25	2·50
MS1142	125×85 mm. $2 Princess Elizabeth and Lt. Philip Mountbatten, c. 1949 (42×56 mm)	4·25	4·75

234 Nativity

2007. Christmas. Stained glass windows. Multicoloured.

1143	25c. Type **234**	75	50
1144	50c. Jesus Christ	1·40	1·00
1145	75c. Jesus with disciples	1·75	1·40
1146	80c. Peace dove	1·75	1·75
1147	$1 The Cross	2·25	2·25
1148	$1.50 Shepherd with lamb	3·25	4·00

235 Beach at Sunset and Turtles ('Hello')

2008. Greetings Stamps. Multicoloured. (a) Ordinary gum.

1149	20c. Type **235**	60	65
1150	20c. Crossed fingers and horse-shoes ('Good Luck')	60	65
1151	20c. Balloons and stars ('Congratulations')	60	65
1152	20c. Invitation and fireworks ('You're Invited')	60	65
1153	20c. Fountain pen and flowers ('Best Wishes')	60	65
1154	20c. Cupid and hearts ('Love')	60	65
1155	25c. Type **235**	60	65
1156	25c. As No. 1150	60	65
1157	25c. As No. 1151	60	65
1158	25c. As No. 1152	60	65
1159	25c. As No. 1153	60	65
1160	25c. As No. 1154	60	65
1161	50c. Type **235**	1·00	1·25
1162	50c. As No. 1150	1·00	1·25
1163	50c. As No. 1151	1·00	1·25
1164	50c. As No. 1152	1·00	1·25
1165	50c. As No. 1153	1·00	1·25
1166	50c. As No. 1154	1·00	1·25
1167	75c. Type **235**	1·50	1·60
1168	75c. As No. 1150	1·50	1·60
1169	75c. As No. 1151	1·50	1·60
1170	75c. As No. 1152	1·50	1·60
1171	75c. As No. 1153	1·50	1·60
1172	75c. As No. 1154	1·50	1·60
1173	80c. Type **235**	1·60	1·75
1174	80c. As No. 1150	1·60	1·75
1175	80c. As No. 1151	1·60	1·75
1176	80c. As No. 1152	1·60	1·75
1177	80c. As No. 1153	1·60	1·75
1178	80c. As No. 1154	1·60	1·75
1179	$1 Type **235**	1·75	1·90
1180	$1 As No. 1150	1·75	1·90
1181	$1 As No. 1151	1·75	1·90
1182	$1 As No. 1152	1·75	1·90
1183	$1 As No. 1153	1·75	1·90
1184	$1 As No. 1154	1·75	1·90

(b) Self-adhesive. Size 30×25 mm.

1185	20c. As Type **235**	55	65
1186	25c. As No. 1151	55	65
1187	25c. As No. 1152	55	65
1188	25c. As No. 1154	55	65

236 Land Crab

2008. Darwin Initiative. Indigenous Creatures. Multicoloured.

1189	20c. Type **236**	70	50
1190	25c. Dragonfly ("Needlecase")	75	55
1191	75c. Little Cayman green anole	2·00	2·00
1192	80c. Cayman Brac ground boa	2·00	2·00
1193	$1 White-shouldered bat	2·25	2·50
MS1194	110×78 mm. $2 Caribbean reef squid	4·25	4·75

2008. Olympic Games, Beijing. As T **287** of Bahamas. Multicoloured.

1195	20c. Swimming – backstroke	70	55
1196	25c. Swimming – butterfly	75	60
1197	50c. Running	1·50	1·50
1198	75c. Hurdling	2·00	2·50

238 Father Christmas on board Sailing Ship

2008. Christmas. Unique Transportation. Multicoloured.

1202	25c. Type **238**	75	60
1203	75c. Father Christmas with horse and carriage laden with presents	2·25	2·00
1204	80c. Father Christmas in helicopter dropping presents by parachute	2·25	2·00
1205	$1 Father Christmas with racing car	2·75	2·75

239 Silver Thatch Palm

2009. Silver Thatch Palm. Multicoloured.

1206	25c. Type **239**	90	95
1207	25c. Rope strands	90	95
1208	25c. Twisting the three strands into rope ('Cobbing rope')	90	95
1209	25c. Basketware ('Thatch products')	90	95
1210	25c. Traditional home with silver thatch roof	90	95

Nos. 1206/10 were printed together, *se-tenant*, forming a composite design.

240 Hammock at Sunset

2009. Cayman Islands Scenes (2nd series). Multicoloured.

1211	20c. Type **240**	45	55
1212	25c. Cayman Islands houses	55	60
1213	75c. Palm trees on beach (vert)	2·00	2·00
1214	80c. Cruise ships off Cayman Islands	2·00	2·00
1215	$1 Street with signpost (vert)	2·25	2·50
1216	$1.50 Inland landscape of rocks and scrub	4·25	4·50
MS1217	80×65 mm. $2 Iguana in road, Little Cayman	5·25	5·25

(b) Self-adhesive. Size 30×25 mm.

1218	20c. As Type **240**	55	60
1219	25c. As No. 1212	65	70

2009. International Year of Astronomy. 40th Anniv of First Moon Landing. A T **214** of Bermuda. Multicoloured.

1220	20c. Mars Rover, 2004	45	50
1221	25c. Space Transportation System 71 launch, 1995	50	55
1222	75c. Hubble Telescope	1·50	1·75
1223	$1 Apollo 11, 1969	2·25	2·50
1224	$1.50 International Space Station	3·25	3·50
MS1225	100×80 mm. $2 *Hadley Rille* (astronaut Jim Irwin and Lunar Rover) (Alan Bean) (39×59 mm). Wmk upright	3·75	4·00

241 Women's Hands signing Petition

2009. 'Equality through Democracy'. 50th Anniv of the Constitution and Women's Suffrage. Multicoloured.

1226	25c. Type **241**	60	60
1227	25c. Town Hall, George Town	60	60
1228	50c. Woman casting vote	1·25	1·25
MS1229	135×86 mm. Nos. 1226/8	2·50	2·50

242 10c. Santa in Hammock Stamp

2009. Christmas. Showing 1997 Christmas stamps. Multicoloured.

1230	25c. Type **242**	60	60
1231	75c. 30c. Santa with children on the Bluff stamp	1·50	1·75
1232	80c. 40c. Santa playing golf	1·60	2·00
1233	$1 Santa scuba diving stamp	2·25	2·50

243 Hawk-wing Conch (*Strombus raninus*)

2010. Shells

(a) Ordinary gum

1234	20c. Type **243**	60	65
1235	25c. Ornate scallop (*Chlamys ornata*)	80	85
1236	60c. Chestnut turban (*Turbo castanea*)	1·50	1·60
1237	75c. Beautiful mitre (*Vexillum pulchellum*)	1·90	2·00
1238	80c. Four-toothed nerite (*Nerita versicolor gmelin*)	2·00	2·10
1239	$1.60 White-spotted marginella (*Marginella guttata*)	4·25	4·50
MS1240	94×64 mm. $3 Queen conch (*Strombus gigas*)	7·75	8·00

(b) Self-adhesive

1241	25c. As No. 1235	80	85
1242	75c. As No. 1237	1·90	2·00

244 Brownie, Rainbow and Guide Uniforms

2010. Centenary of Girlguiding. Multicoloured.

1243	20c. Type **244**	55	60
1244	25c. Camping	65	70
1245	50c. Parade of guides, 1930s	1·20	1·40
1246	80c. Badges of rainbows, brownies and guides	2·00	2·10

2011. Royal Wedding. Multicoloured.

1247	25c. Duke and Duchess of Cambridge kissing on Buckingham Palace balcony (vert)	80	85
1248	75c. Duke and Duchess of Cambridge waving from State Landau	1·90	2·00
1249	80c. Duke and Duchess of Cambridge at Westminster Abbey after wedding ceremony (vert)	2·00	2·10
1250	$2 Prince William, Miss Catherine Middleton and her father	4·50	5·00

245 Catching Turtles

2011. Catboats. Multicoloured.

(a) Ordinary paper

1251	20c. Type **245**	60	65
1252	25c. Building catboat	80	85
1253	25c. Sailing catboat around Cayman Brac's Bluff	80	85
1254	50c. Catboats racing regatta style	1·20	1·40
1255	$1.60 Unloading cargo from catboats	4·25	4·50
1256	$2 Sewing the sail	4·75	5·00

(b) Self-adhesive. Size 30×25 mm

1257	25c. As No. 1252	80	85

246 King James Bible

2011. Christmas. 400th Anniv of the King James Bible. Multicoloured.

1258	25c. Type **246**	90	95
1259	75c. King James I of Scotland (1566-1625) and VI of England (1603-25)	1·90	2·00
1260	80c. William Tyndale (translator)	2·10	2·25
1261	$1 Printing the King James Bible	2·50	2·75
1262	$1.60 Translators in the Jerusalem Chamber of Westminster Abbey for final editing	3·75	4·00

247 Almeria L. McLaughlin Tomlinson (1882-1974) (midwife)

2011. Pioneers. Multicoloured.

1263	20c. Type **247**	60	65
1264	25c. Captain Rayal B. Bodden (1885-1976) (shipwright and builder)	1·00	1·10
1265	75c. Irksie Leila Yates (1899-1996) (maternity nurse)	2·10	2·25
1266	$1.50 Major Joseph R. Walter (1890-1965) (Inspector of Police)	3·00	3·25

248 Queen Elizabeth II

2012. Diamond Jubilee. Multicoloured.

(a) Ordinary paper

1267	25c. Type **248**	65	70
1268	80c. Queen Elizabeth II wearing pink hat, c. 1970	2·00	2·10
1269	$1 Queen Elizabeth II on walkabout through crowd, c. 2000	2·50	2·75
1270	$1.50 Coronation of Queen Elizabeth II, 1953	3·75	4·00

(b) Self-adhesive. Size 30×25 mm

1271	25c. As Type **248**	65	70

No. 1271 is as Type **248** but with the face value at bottom right and the inscription 'Diamond Jubilee 1952 - 2012' at centre right.

249 Athlete

2012. Olympic Games, London. Multicoloured.

1272	25c. Type **249**	65	70
1273	50c. Hurdler	1·25	1·50
1274	75c. Swimmer (butterfly)	1·90	2·00
1275	80c. Two athletes sprinting at finish	2·00	2·10
1276	$1.60 Swimming (front crawl)	4·00	4·25

250 Patrol Boats

2012. Emergency Services. Multicoloured.

(a) Ordinary gum

1277	20c. Type **250**	50	55
1278	25c. Ambulance Service	65	70
1279	75c. Fire Department	1·90	2·00
1280	$1.50 9-1-1 Public Safety Communications	3·75	4·00
1281	$2 Police Helicopter	5·00	5·25

(b) Self-adhesive. Size 30×25 mm

1282	25c. As No. 1278	65	70
1283	75c. As No. 1279	1·90	2·00

No. 1278 has the inscription 'Ambulance Service' along the right-hand edge of the stamp reading downwards, but No. 1282 has it reading upwards.

No. 1283 has the inscription 'Fire Department' along the left-hand edge of the stamp starting at the bottom left corner instead of above the face value.

251 Stoplight Parrotfish (*Sparisoma viride*)

2012. Marine Life. Multicoloured.

(a) Ordinary paper

1284	25c. Type **251**	35	40
1285	50c. Green Sea Turtle (*Chelonia mydas*)	75	80
1286	75c. Common Sea Fan (*Gorgonia ventalina*) and Yellow Tube Sponge (*Aplysina fistularis*)	1·10	1·25
1287	80c. Upside-down Jellyfish (*Cassiopea xamachana*)	1·25	1·40
1288	$1 Yellowtail Damselfish (*Microspathodon chrysurus*)	1·50	1·60
1289	$1.50 Spotted Trunkfish (*Lactophrys bicaudalis*)	2·25	2·40
1290	$1.60 Caribbean Spiny Lobster (*Panulirus argus*)	2·40	2·50

1291		$2 Giant Barrel Sponge (Xest-ospongia muta)	3·00	3·25
1292		$4 Caribbean Reef Shark (Carcharhinus perezii)	6·00	6·25
1293		$5 Great Barracuda (Sphyraena barracuda)	7·25	7·50
1294		$10 Southern Stingray (Dasyatis americana)	14·50	15·00
1295		$20 West Indian Spider Crab (Mithrax spinosissimus)	29·00	30·00
MS1296		No. 1288×4	10·00	10·00

(b) Self-adhesive. Size 30x25 mm

1297		25c. As Type 251	35	40
1298		75c. As No. 1286	1·10	1·25
1299		80c. As No. 1287	1·25	1·40

252 Mary and Jesus

2012. Christmas. Paintings by Gladwyn K. Bush (Miss Lassie). Multicoloured.

1300		25c. Type 252	65	70
1301		75c. His Name is Jesus	1·90	2·00
1302		80c. Every Knee shall Bow	2·00	2·10
1303		$1 Nativity	2·50	2·50

Pt. 12

CENTRAL AFRICAN EMPIRE

Central African Republic was renamed Central African Empire on 4 December 1976, when Pres. Bokassa became Emperor.

The country reverted to Central African Republic on his overthrow in 1979.

100 centimes = 1 franc.

1977. Various stamps of Central African Republic optd **EMPIRE CENTRAFRICAIN**.

439	150	3f. mult (postage)	55	50
444	167	10f. multicoloured	30	25
457	–	10f. red and blue (386)	30	25
459	172	10f. multicoloured	45	40
460	–	15f. multicoloured (391)	75	75
465	–	15f. brown, grn & bl (397)	30	25
445	–	20f. multicoloured (366)	45	40
461	–	20f. multicoloured (392)	55	55
446	–	25f. multicoloured (367)	35	30
451	–	25f. multicoloured (376)	35	30
449	168	30f. multicoloured	30	25
452	–	30f. multicoloured (377)	55	55
462	–	30f. multicoloured (393)	30	25
447	–	40f. multicoloured (370)	45	40
450	–	40f. multicoloured (373)	45	40
453	–	40f. multicoloured (378)	45	40
454	–	40f. multicoloured (380)	55	55
455	170	40f. multicoloured	45	40
456	–	40f. multicoloured (384)	75	75
458	–	40f. multicoloured (389)	75	75
482	–	40f. multicoloured (423)	40	25
466	–	50f. blue, brn & grn (398)	75	75
483	–	50f. mult (424) (air)	45	25
440	163	100f. multicoloured	1·70	1·60
441	164	100f. grn, red & brn	1·80	1·80
442	165	100f. brn, grn & blue	1·70	1·60
448	–	100f. multicoloured (371)	95	90
463	173	100f. red and blue	95	90
467	178	100f. multicoloured	95	90
468	179	100f. black and yellow	1·70	1·60
469	180	100f. purple, blue & grn	1·80	1·90
484	–	100f. multicoloured (425)	95	90
491	185	100f. multicoloured	1·80	1·90
464	174	200f. multicoloured	4·25	2·10
443	166	500f. red, green & brown	8·50	8·25

1977. "Apollo–Soyuz" Space Link. Nos. 410/MS415 of Central African Republic optd **EMPIRE CENTRAFRICAIN**.

470	181	40f. mult (postage)	50	25
471	–	50f. multicoloured	75	40
472	–	100f. multicoloured (air)	95	55
473	–	200f. multicoloured	1·90	90
474	–	300f. multicoloured	3·00	1·30
MS475		103×78 mm. 500f. multicoloured	5·25	3·50

1977. Air. Bicentenary of American Revolution. Nos. 416/MS421 of Central African Republic optd **EMPIRE CENTRAFRICAIN**.

476	182	100f. multicoloured	1·00	70
477	–	125f. multicoloured	1·40	1·10
478	–	150f. multicoloured	1·60	1·30
479	–	200f. multicoloured	2·30	1·80
480	–	250f. multicoloured	2·50	2·00
MS481		119×81 mm. 450f. multicoloured	5·25	5·25

1977. Winners of Winter Olympic Games, Innsbruck. Nos. 426/MS430 of Central African Republic optd **EMPIRE CENTRAFRICAIN**.

485		40f. mult (postage)	55	50
486		60f. multicoloured	75	65
487	184	100f. multicoloured (air)	1·00	80
488	–	200f. multicoloured	2·20	1·70
489	–	300f. multicoloured	3·25	2·40
MS490		103×78 mm. 500f. multicoloured	5·25	5·00

1977. "Viking" Space Mission. Nos. 433/MS438 of Central African Republic optd **EMPIRE CENTRAFRICAIN**.

492	186	40f. mult (postage)	55	50
493	–	60f. multicoloured	75	65
494	–	100f. multicoloured (air)	1·00	90
495	–	200f. multicoloured	2·30	2·20
496	–	300f. multicoloured	3·50	3·50
MS497		102×78 mm. 500f. multicoloured	5·25	5·00

189 Pierre and Marie Curie (Physics, 1903)

1977. Nobel Prize-winners. Multicoloured.

503		40f. Type 189 (postage)	1·00	40
504		60f. W. C. Rontgen (Physics, 1901)	90	45
505		100f. Rudyard Kipling (Literature, 1907) (air)	1·80	50
506		200f. Ernest Hemingway (Literature, 1954)	3·50	85
507		300f. L. Pirandello (Literature, 1934)	3·50	1·00
MS508		118×80 mm. 500f. Rabindranath Tagore (Literature, 1913)	5·25	1·90

190 Roman Temple and Italy 1933 3l. stamp

1977. Graf Zeppelin Flights. Multicoloured.

509		40f. Type 190 (postage)	85	25
510		60f. St. Basil's Cathedral, Moscow, and Russia 1930 40k. stamp	1·00	45
511		100f. North Pole and Germany 1931 "Polarfahrt" stamp (air)	1·40	45
512		200f. Museum of Science and Industry, Chicago, and Germany 1933 "Chicagofahrt" stamp	2·50	75
513		300f. Brandenburg Gate, Berlin, and German 1931 stamp	3·75	1·00
MS514		129×90 mm. 500f. Capitol, Washington, and US $1.30 stamp, 1930	5·50	2·20

191 Charles Lindbergh and Spirit of St. Louis

1977. History of Aviation. Multicoloured.

515		50f. Type 191	50	25
516		60f. Alberto Santos-Dumont and 14 bis biplane	75	25
517		100f. Louis Bleriot and Bleriot XI	1·40	45
518		200f. Roald Amundsen and Dornier Wal flying boat	2·10	60
519		300f. Concorde	4·00	1·40
MS520		117×91 mm. 500f. Lindbergh and his arrival in Paris	5·00	1·80

192 Lily

1977. Flowers. Multicoloured.

521		5f. Type 192	45	30
522		10f. Hibiscus	90	70

193 Group of Africans and Rotary Emblem

1977. 20th Anniv of Bangui Rotary Club.

523	193	60f. multicoloured	3·50	1·80

194 Africans queueing beside Bible

1977. Bible Week.

524	194	40f. multicoloured	5·75	1·40

195 Printed Circuit

1977. World Telecommunications Day.

525	195	100f. orange, brown & blk	3·00	2·10

196 Doctor inoculating Child

1977. Air. World Health Day.

526	196	150f. multicoloured	3·50	1·80

197 Goalkeeper

1977. World Cup Football Championship (1978). Multicoloured.

527	197	50f. Type 197	50	25
528		60f. Goalmouth melee	60	25
529		100f. Mid-field play	1·00	30
530		200f. World Cup poster	2·10	60
531		300f. Mario Jorge Lobo Zagalo (Argentine team) and Buenos Aires stadium	3·75	1·30
MS532		120×81 mm. 500f. Ferenc Puskas (Hungarian player)	6·25	2·20

198 Emperor Bokassa I

1977. Coronation of Emperor Bokassa.

533	198	40f. mult (postage)	35	15
534	198	60f. multicoloured	50	25
535	198	100f. multicoloured	1·00	55
536	198	150f. multicoloured	1·40	70
537	198	200f. mult (air)	1·90	85
538	198	300f. multicoloured	2·50	1·40
MS539		102×80 mm. 500f. Emperor Bokassa, inscription and furled flag (48×39 mm)	5·25	2·50

199 Bangui Telephone Exchange

1978. Opening of Automatic Telephone Exchange, Bangui. Multicoloured.

541	199	40f. Type 199	45	25
542		60f. Bangui Telephone Exchange (different)	60	35

200 Bokassa Sports Palace

1978. Bokassa Sports Palace. Multicoloured.

543		40f. Type 200	45	25
544		60f. Sports Palace (different)	60	35

201 The Holy Family

1978. 400th Birth Anniv of Rubens. Multicoloured.

545		60f. Type 201	75	25
546		150f. Marie de Medici	1·30	45
547		200f. The Artist's Sons	2·00	65
548		300f. Neptune (horiz)	3·25	85
MS549		90×116 mm. 500f. Marie de Medici (different) (37×49 mm)	5·75	2·00

202 Black Rhinoceros

1978. Endangered Animals. Multicoloured.

550		40f. Type 202	1·10	25
551		50f. Crocodile	1·70	30
552		60f. Leopard (vert)	1·90	45
553		100f. Giraffe (vert)	3·00	65
554		200f. African elephant	7·75	90
555		300f. Gorilla (vert)	9·25	1·50

203 Mail Coach and Satellite

1978. 100 Years of Progress in Posts and Telecommunications. Multicoloured.

556		40f. Type 203 (postage)	45	25
557		50f. Steam locomotive and space communications	1·80	85
558		60f. Paddle-steamer and ship-to-shore communications	55	25
559		80f. Renault car and "Pioneer" satellite	75	25
560		100f. Mail balloon and "Apollo"–"Soyuz" link-up (air)	1·00	40
561		200f. Seaplane Comte da la Vaulx and Concorde	1·80	70
MS562		104×70 mm. 500f. Tom-toms and Zeppelin (53×35 mm)	6·75	1·90

205 H.M.S. Endeavour under Repair (after W. Byrne)

1978. 250th Birth Anniv of Captain Cook. Multicoloured.

578		60f. Type 205	75	25
579		80f. Cook on board Endeavour (vert)	1·00	40
580		200f. Landing party in New Hebrides	2·75	75
581		350f. Masked paddlers in canoe (after Webber)	4·50	1·50

206 Ife Bronze Head

1978. Second World Festival of Negro Arts, Lagos.

582	206	20f. black and yellow	30	25

583	-	30f. black and blue	30	25
584	-	60f. multicoloured	70	40
585	-	100f. multicoloured	1·20	70

DESIGNS—VERT: 30f. Carved mask. HORIZ: 60f. Dancers; 100f. Dancers with musical instruments.

207 Clement Ader and *Avion III*

1978. Air. Aviation Pioneers. Multicoloured.

586	40f. Type **207**	50	25
587	50f. Wright Brothers and glider No. III	50	25
588	60f. Alcock, Brown and Vickers Vimy	60	40
589	100f. Sir Alan Cobham and De Havilland D.H.50	1·20	40
590	150f. Dr. Claude Dornier and Dornier Gs1 flying boat	1·80	70
MS591	117×80 mm. 500f. Wright Brothers and *Flyer*	5·50	1·80

208 *Self-portrait*

1978. 450th Death Anniv of Albrecht Durer (artist). Multicoloured.

592	60f. Type **208**	60	25
593	80f. *The Four Apostles*	1·00	25
594	200f. *The Virgin and Child*	2·40	90
595	350f. *The Emperor Maximilian I*	4·00	1·50

1978. Air. "Philexafrique" Stamp Exhibition, Gabon (1st issue) and International Stamp Fair, Essen. As T **237** of Benin. Multicoloured.

| 596 | 100f. Red crossbills and Mecklenberg-Schwerin 1856 ¼s. stamp | 2·20 | 1·40 |
| 597 | 100f. Crocodile and Central African Republic 1960 500f. stamp | 2·20 | 1·40 |

See also Nos. 647/8.

209 Third Mummiform Coffin

1978. Treasures of Tutankhamun. Multicoloured.

598	40f. Type **209**	70	30
599	60f. Tutankhamun and Ankhesenamun (back of gilt throne)	95	35
600	80f. Ecclesiastical throne	1·40	50
601	100f. Head of Tutankhamun (wooden statuette)	1·50	50
602	120f. Lion's head (funerary bedhead)	2·00	65
603	150f. Life-size statue of Tut- ankhamun	2·50	70
604	180f. Gilt throne	3·25	85
605	250f. Canopic coffin	4·00	1·10

210 Lenin speaking at the Smolny Institute

1978. 60th Anniv of Russian Revolution.

606	**210**	40f. multicoloured	50	30
607	-	60f. multicoloured	60	45
608	-	100f. black, grey and gold	1·00	50
609	-	150f. red, black and gold	1·90	80

610	-	200f. multicoloured	2·50	1·00
611	-	300f. multicoloured	3·25	1·50
MS612	78×110 mm. 500f. multicol- oured		5·25	4·00

DESIGNS—VERT: 60f. Lenin addressing crowd in Red Square; 200f. Lenin in Smolny Institute; 300f. Lenin and banner; 500f. Cruiser *Aurora* and Order of Lenin. HORIZ: 100f. Lenin, Kurpskaya and family; 150f. Lenin, cruiser *Aurora*, banner and revolutionaries.

211 Catherine Bokassa

1978. First Anniv of Emperor Bokassa's Coronation. Multicoloured.

613	40f. Type **211** (postage)	50	25
614	60f. Emperor Bokassa	70	30
615	150f. The Emperor and Empress (horiz) (air)	1·70	75
MS616	Two sheets. (a) 101×82 mm. 250f. Coronation ceremony (horiz); (b) 76×100 mm. 1000f. Emperor and eagle	12·00	5·50

212 Rowland Hill, Letter-weighing Scale and Penny Black

1978. Death Centenary of Sir Rowland Hill (1st issue). Multicoloured.

617	40f. Type **212** (postage)	55	25
618	50f. Postman on bicycle and U.S. 5c. stamp, 1847	55	25
619	60f. Danish postman and Austrian newspaper stamp, 1856	80	35
620	80f. Postilion, mail coach and Geneva 5+5c. stamp, 1843	95	45
621	100f. Postman, mail train and Tuscan 3l. stamp, 1860 (air)	2·40	1·00
622	200f. Mail balloon and French 10c. stamp, 1850	1·70	70
MS623	81×85 mm. 500f. First Central African Republic stamps, 1959 (37×38 mm)	5·50	1·80

See also Nos. 671/MS675.

1978. Argentina's Victory in World Cup Football Championship. Nos. 527/31 optd **VAINQUEUR ARGENTINE.**

625	50f. Type **197**	55	35
626	60f. Goalmouth melee	60	40
627	100f. Midfield play	95	60
628	200f. World Cup poster	2·00	1·10
629	300f. Mario Jorge Lobo Zagalo and Buenos Aires Stadium	3·00	1·40
MS630	120×81 mm. 500f. multicol- oured, optd **ARGENTINE-PAYS BAS 3-1/25 juin 1978**	5·25	5·25

214 Children painting and Dutch Master

1979. International Year of the Child (1st issue). Multicoloured.

631	40f. Type **214** (postage)	50	10
632	50f. Eskimo children and skier	65	20
633	60f. Benz automobile and children with toy car	85	25
634	80f. Satellite and children launching rocket	1·20	25
635	100f. Dornier Do-X flying boat and Chinese child flying kite (air)	1·30	45
636	200f. Hurdler and children play- ing leap-frog	2·50	70
MS637	109×79 mm. 500f. Albert Einstein and child with abacus (55×32 mm)	5·50	1·80

See also Nos. 666/70.

215 High Jump

1979. Pre-Olympic Year (1st issue). Multicoloured.

639	40f. Type **215** (postage)	50	10
640	50f. Cycling	55	20
641	60f. Weightlifting	65	25
642	80f. Judo	90	30
643	100f. Hurdles (air)	1·00	40
644	200f. Long jump	1·90	70
MS645	110×79 mm. 500f. Pole vault (55×37 mm)	5·00	1·70

See also Nos. 676/80 and 700/MS706.

216 Co-operation Monument, *Aurivillius arata* and Hibiscus

1979. "Philexafrique" Exhibition (2nd issue). Multicoloured.

| 647 | 60f. Type **216** | 2·40 | 1·20 |
| 648 | 150f. Envelopes, van, canoeist and UPU emblem | 4·25 | 2·30 |

217 School Teacher

1979. 50th Anniv of International Bureau of Education.

| 649 | **217** | 70f. multicoloured | 85 | 45 |

218 "Madonna seated on a Bench" (woodcut)

1979. 450th Death Anniv (1978) of Albrecht Durer (artist) (2nd issue). Sheet 90×115 mm.

| MS650 | **218** | 500f. green and lake | 5·50 | 1·80 |

219 Chicken

1979. National Association of Farmers. Multicoloured.

651	10f. Type **219** (postage)	1·80	1·10
652	20f. Bullock	1·80	1·10
653	40f. Sheep	3·75	2·20
654	60f. Horse (air)	5·50	2·10

OFFICIAL STAMPS

1977. Official stamps of Central African Republic optd **EMPIRE CENTRAFRICAIN.**

O498	**O109**	5f. multicoloured	25	10
O499	**O109**	40f. multicoloured	45	25
O500	**O109**	100f. multicoloured	1·20	40
O501	**O109**	140f. multicoloured	1·50	80
O502	**O109**	200f. multicoloured	2·50	1·10

O204 Coat of Arms

1978

O564	**O204**	1f. multicoloured	10	10
O565	**O204**	2f. multicoloured	10	10
O566	**O204**	5f. multicoloured	10	10
O567	**O204**	10f. multicoloured	25	10
O568	**O204**	15f. multicoloured	25	10
O569	**O204**	20f. multicoloured	25	10
O570	**O204**	30f. multicoloured	45	25
O571	**O204**	40f. multicoloured	45	25
O572	**O204**	50f. multicoloured	70	55
O673	**O204**	60f. multicoloured	65	45
O574	**O204**	100f. multicoloured	1·10	90
O575	**O204**	130f. multicoloured	1·40	1·50
O576	**O204**	140f. multicoloured	1·70	1·30
O577	**O204**	200f. multicoloured	3·25	1·60

Pt. 12

CENTRAL AFRICAN REPUBLIC

Formerly Ubangi-Shari. An independent republic within the French Community.

100 centimes = 1 franc.

1 President Boganda

1959. Republic. First Anniv. Centres multicoloured. Frame colours given.

1	**1**	15f. blue	55	25
2	-	25f. red	55	25

DESIGN—HORIZ. 25f. As Type **1** but flag behind portrait.

1960. Tenth Anniv of African Technical Co-operation Commission. As T **62** of Cameroun.

3	50f. blue and green	1·80	95

3 *Dactyloceras widenmanni*

4 Abyssinian Roller

1960.

4	-	50c. brn, red & turq (postage)	10	10
5	-	1f. myrtle, brown & violet	10	10
6	-	2f. myrtle, brown and green	10	20
7	-	3f. brown, red and olive	45	20
8	**3**	5f. brown and green	45	25
9	-	10f. blue, black and green	95	55
10	-	20f. red, black and green	2·30	80
12	-	50f. turq, red & green (air)	1·90	60
11	-	85f. red, black and green	7·25	1·70
13	**4**	100f. violet, brown & green	2·40	90
14	-	200f. multicoloured	4·50	2·20
15	-	250f. multicoloured	6·75	2·50
16	-	500f. brown, blue and green	13·00	5·25

BUTTERFLIES—As Type **3**: 50c., 3f. *Cymothoe sangaris*; 1f., 2f. *Charaxe mobilis*; 10f. *Charaxes ameliae*; 20f. *Charaxes zingha*; 85f. *Drurya antimachus*. BIRDS—As Type **4**: 50f. Great blue turaco; 200f. Green turaco; 250f. Red-faced lovebirds; 500f. African fish eagle.
 See also Nos. 42/5.

1960. National Festival. No. 2 optd **FETE NATIONALE 1-12-1960**.

17	25f. multicoloured	1·40	1·30

1960. Air. Olympic Games. No. 276 of French Equatorial Africa optd with Olympic rings, **XVIIe OLYMPIADE 1960 REPUBLIQUE CENTRAFRICAINE** and surch 250F and bars.

18	250f. on 500f. blue, blk & grn	8·75	8·25

7 Pasteur Institute, Bangui

1961. Opening of Pasteur Institute, Bangui.

19	**7**	20f. multicoloured	1·00	80

8 U.N. Emblem, Map and Flag

1961. Admission into UNO.

20	**8**	15f. multicoloured	40	30
21	**8**	25f. multicoloured	50	30
22	**8**	85f. multicoloured	1·50	1·00

1961. National Festival. Optd with star and **FETE NATIONALE 1-12-01**.

23	25f. multicoloured	2·00	1·90

1962. Air. "Air Afrique" Airline. As T **69** of Cameroun.

24	50f. violet, brown and green	95	70

1962. Union of African States and Madagascar Conference, Bangui. Surch **U.A.M. CONFERENCE DE BANGUI 25-27 MARS 1962 50F.**

25	50f. on 85f. multicoloured	1·70	1·60

1962. Malaria Eradication. As T **70** of Cameroun.

26	25f.+5f. slate	1·10	1·10

12 Hurdling

1962. Sports.

27	**12**	20f. sep, yell & grn (postage)	45	30
28	-	50f. sepia, yellow and green	1·30	80
29	-	100f. sep, yell & grn (air)	2·20	1·50

DESIGNS—As Type **12**: 50f. Cycling. VERT: (26×47 mm): 100f. Pole-vaulting.

13 Pres. Dacko

1962.

30	**13**	20f. multicoloured	35	20
31	**13**	25f. multicoloured	45	25

1962. First Anniv of Union of African and Malagasy States. As T **72** of Cameroun.

32	30f. green	1·20	95

15 Athlete

1962. Air. "Coupe des Tropiques" Games, Bangui.

33	**15**	100f. brown, turquoise & red	2·40	1·60

1963. Freedom from Hunger. As T **76** of Cameroun.

34	25f.+5f. turquoise, brn & bis	1·00	1·00

17 "National Army"

1963. Third Anniv of Proclamation of Republic.

35	**17**	20f. multicoloured	65	45

18 "Posts and Telecommunications"

1963. Air. African and Malagasy Posts and Telecommunications Union.

36	**18**	85f. multicoloured	1·80	90

19 "Telecommunications"

1963. Space Telecommunications.

37	**19**	25f. green and purple	75	60
38	-	100f. green, orange & blue	1·80	1·60

DESIGN: 100f. Radio waves and globe.

20 "Young Pioneers"

1963. Young Pioneers.

39	**20**	30f. brown, blue & turquoise	85	50

21 Boali Falls

1963.

40	**21**	30f. purple, green and blue	85	50

22 Map of Africa and Sun

1963. Air. "African Unity".

41	**22**	25f. ultramarine, yellow & bl	65	45

23 *Colotis evippe*

1963. Butterflies. Multicoloured.

42	1f. Type **23**		20	20
43	3f. *Papilio dardanus*		55	25
44	4f. *Papilio lormieri*		80	35
45	60f. *Papilio zalmoxis*		5·00	3·00

24 "Europafrique"

1963. Air. European–African Economic Convention.

46	**24**	50f. multicoloured	2·75	2·10

25 ABJ-6 Diesel Railcar

1963. Air. Bangui–Douala Railway Project.

47	-	20f. green, purple & brown	65	50
48	**25**	25f. chocolate, blue & brn	95	60
49	-	50f. violet, purple & brown	2·50	1·90
50	-	100f. purple, turquoise and brown	3·75	2·75
MS50a	190×98 mm. Nos. 47/50		8·00	8·00

DESIGNS: (Diesel rolling stock)—HORIZ. 20f. ABJ-6 railcar; 100f. Diesel locomotive. VERT: 50f. Series BB500 diesel shunter.

26 UNESCO Emblem, Scales of Justice and Tree

1963. 15th Anniv of Declaration of Human Rights.

51	**26**	25f. bistre, green and brown	85	60

27 Bangui Cathedral

1964. Air.

52	**27**	100f. brown, green & blue	2·00	1·10

28 Cleopatra, Temple of Kalabsha

1964. Air. Nubian Monuments Preservation.

53	**28**	25f.+10f. mauve, bl & grn	1·30	1·20
54	**28**	50f.+10f. brn, grn & turq	2·20	2·10
55	**28**	100f.+10f. pur, vio & grn	3·50	3·25

29 Radar Scanner

1964. Air. World Meteorological Day.

56	**29**	50f. violet, brown and blue	1·00	1·00

30 "Tree" and Sun Emblem

1964. International Quiet Sun Years.

57	**30**	25f. orange, ochre & turq	1·30	85

31 Map and African Heads of State

1964. Air. 5th Anniv of Equatorial African Heads of State Conference.

58	**31**	100f. multicoloured	1·80	90

32 Throwing the Javelin

1964. Air. Olympic Games, Tokyo.

59	**32**	25f. brown, green and blue	45	30
60	-	50f. red, black and green	95	55
61	-	100f. brown, blue and green	2·20	1·30
62	-	250f. black, green and red	6·50	3·00
MS62a	130×100 mm. Nos. 59/62		16·00	15·00

DESIGNS: 50f. Basketball; 100f. Running; 250f. Diving and swimming.

33 Pres. Kennedy

1964. Air. Pres. Kennedy Memorial Issue.

63	**33**	100f. brown, black & violet	2·40	1·70
MS63a 90×130 mm. No. 63 in block of four			10·50	10·00

34 African Child

1964. Child Welfare. Different portraits of children. As T 34.

64	**34**	20f. brown, green & purple	45	25
65	-	25f. brown, blue and red	45	30
66	-	40f. brown, purple & green	60	45
67	-	50f. brown, green and red	80	60
MS67a 144×100 mm. Nos. 64/7			3·25	3·00

1964. French, African and Malagasy Co-operation. As T 88 of Cameroun.

68		25f. brown, red and green	85	50

35 Silhouettes of European and African

1964. National Unity.

69	**35**	25f. multicoloured	85	50

36 "Economic Co-operation"

1964. Air. "Europafrique".

70	**36**	50f. green, red and yellow	1·20	85

37 Handclasp

1965. Air. International Co-operation Year.

71	**37**	100f. multicoloured	1·80	90

38 Weather Satellite

1965. Air. World Meteorological Day.

72	**38**	100f. blue and brown	1·80	90

39 Abraham Lincoln

1965. Air. Death Centenary of Abraham Lincoln.

73	**39**	100f. flesh, blue & green	1·80	90

40 Team of Oxen

1965. Harnessed Animals in Agriculture.

74	**40**	25f. red, brown and green	50	30
75	-	50f. purple, green and blue	95	55
76	-	85f. brown, green and blue	1·30	80
77	-	100f. multicoloured	1·70	90

DESIGNS: 50f. Ploughing with bullock; 85f. Ploughing with oxen; 100f. Oxen with hay cart.

41 Pouget-Maisonneuve Telegraph Instrument

1965. Centenary of ITU.

78	**41**	25f. blue, red & grn (post)	55	45
79	-	30f. lake and green	60	55
80	-	50f. red and violet	1·00	70
81	-	85f. blue and purple	1·80	1·20
82	-	100f. brown, blue & green (48½×27 mm) (air)	2·00	1·20

DESIGNS—VERT: 30f. Chappe's telegraph instrument; 50f. Doignon regulator for Hughes telegraph. HORIZ: 85f. Pouillet's telegraph apparatus; 100f. "Relay" satellite and ITU emblem.

42 Women and Loom ("To Clothe")

1965. "MESAN" Welfare Campaign. Designs depicting "Five Aims".

83	**42**	25f. green, brown and blue (postage)	45	30
84	-	50f. brown, blue and green	80	55
85	-	60f. brown, blue and green	1·00	65
86	-	85f. multicoloured	1·40	70
87	-	100f. blue, brown and green (48×27 mm) (air)	1·80	1·10

DESIGNS: 50f. Doctor examining child, and hospital ("To care for"); 60f. Student and school ("To instruct"); 85f. Women and child, and harvesting scene ("To nourish"); 100f. Village houses ("To house"). "MESAN—Mouvement Evolution Social Afrique Noire".

43 Coffee Plant, Hammer Grubs and *Epicampoptera strandi*

1965. Plant Protection.

88	**43**	2f. purple, red and green	30	10
89	-	3f. red, green and black	75	20
90	-	30f. purple, green and red	4·50	90

DESIGNS—HORIZ: 3f. Coffee plant, caterpillar and hawk-moth. VERT: 30f. Cotton plant caterpillar and rose-moth.

1965. Surch.

91		2f. on 3f. (No. 43)	4·25	4·00
92	**1**	5f. on 15f.	3·75	3·00
93	-	5f. on 85f. (No. 76)	35	30
94	**13**	10f. on 20f.	4·50	4·25
95	-	10f. on 100f. (No. 77)	55	55

45 Camp Fire

1965. Scouting.

96	**45**	25f. red, purple and blue	75	25
97	-	50f. brown and blue (Boy Scout)	1·30	65

46 U.N. and Campaign Emblems

1965. Freedom from Hunger.

98	**46**	50f. brown, blue and green	1·10	75

47 "Industry and Agriculture"

1965. Air. "Europafrique".

99	**47**	50f. multicoloured	1·00	75

48 Mercury (statue after Coysevox)

1965. Air. Fifth Anniv of Admission to UPU.

100	**48**	100f. black, blue & red	2·30	1·30

49 Father and Child

1965. Air. Red Cross.

101	**49**	50f. black, blue and red	1·20	55
102	-	100f. brown, green and red (Mother and Child)	2·50	1·20

50 Grading Diamonds

1966. National Diamond Industry.

103	**50**	25f. brown, violet and red	1·00	50

51 Mbaka Porter

1966. World Festival of Negro Arts, Dakar.

104	**51**	25f. multicoloured	85	50

52 WHO Building

1966. WHO Headquarters, Geneva. Inaug.

105	**52**	25f. violet, blue & yellow	85	50

53 Eulophia cucullata

1966. Flowers. Multicoloured.

106		2f. Type **53**	25	10
107		5f. *Lissochilus horsfalii*	45	10
108		10f. *Tridactyle bicaudata*	45	25
109		15f. *Polystachya*	95	50
110		20f. *Eulophia alta*	1·40	60
111		25f. *Microcelia macrorrhynchium*	2·00	95

54 Douglas DC-8F Aircraft and "Air Afrique" Emblem

1966. Air. Inaug of "DC-8" Air Services.

112	**54**	25f. multicoloured	85	45

55 Congo Forest Mouse

1966. Rodents. Multicoloured.

113		5f. Type **55**	55	30
114		10f. Black-striped mouse	1·00	50
115		20f. Dollman's tree mouse	1·70	80

56 "Luna 9"

1966. Air. "Conquest of the Moon". Multicoloured.

116		130f. Type **56**	1·70	1·00
117		130f. "Surveyor"	1·70	1·00
118		200f. *From the Earth to the Moon* (Jules Verne)	3·25	1·80
MS119 132×160 mm. Nos. 116/18			8·25	7·75

57 Cernan

1966. Air. Astronauts. Multicoloured.

120	**57**	50f. Type **57**	1·10	60
121		50f. Popovich	1·10	60

58 Satellite "D 1" and Rocket "Diamant"

1966. Air. Launching of Satellite "D 1".

122	**58**	100f. purple and brown	1·80	95

59 UNESCO Emblem

1966. 20th Anniv of UNESCO.

123	**59**	30f. multicoloured	60	45

60 Symbols of Industry and Agriculture

1966. Air. Europafrique.

124	**60**	50f. multicoloured	1·20	95

61 Pres. Bokassa

1967

125	61	30f. black, ochre & green	60	35

1967. Provisional Stamps. (a) Postage. No. 111 surch XX and value.

126		10f. on 25f. multicoloured	50	25

(b) Air. No. 112 with face value altered by obliteration of figure "2" in "25".

127	54	5f. multicoloured	45	25

63 Douglas DC-8 over Bangui M'Poko Airport

1967. Air.

128	63	100f. blue, green & brown	2·30	1·10

64 Aerial View of Fair

1967. Air. World Fair, Montreal.

129	64	100f. brown, ultram & bl	2·00	80

65 Central Market, Bangui

1967. Multicoloured.. Multicoloured..

130		30f. Type 65	85	45
131		30f. Safari Hotel, Bangui	85	35

66 Map, Letters and Pylons

1967. Air. Fifth Anniv of African and Malagasy Posts and Telecommunications Union (UAMPT).

132	66	100f. purple, grn & red	2·00	85

67
Leucocoprinus africanus

1967. Mushrooms. Multicoloured.

133		5f. Type 67	5·25	60
134		10f. *Synpodia arborescens*	8·25	1·00
135		15f. *Phlebopus sudanicus*	9·25	1·30
136		30f. *Termitomyces schimperi*	26·00	3·25
137		50f. *Psalliota sebedulis*	42·00	5·00

68 Projector, Africans and Map

1967. "Radiovision" Service.

138	68	30f. blue, green and brown	85	50

69 Coiffure

1967. Female Coiffures. Showing different hairstyles.

139	69	5f. brown and blue	30	15
140	-	10f. brown, choc & red	45	25
141	-	15f. brown, choc & grn	75	45
142	-	20f. brown, choc & orge	95	55
143	-	30f. brown, choc & purple	1·30	70

70 Inoculation Session

1967. Vaccination Programme, 1967–70.

144	70	30f. brown, green & red	85	60

71 Douglas DC-3

1967. Aircraft.

145	71	1f. grey, grn & brn (post)	10	10
146	-	2f. black, blue and purple	10	10
147	-	5f. black, green and blue	30	10
148	-	100f. brown, grn & bl (air)	2·00	85
149	-	200f. blue, brown and green	4·75	1·80
150	-	500f. slate, red and blue	12·50	4·75

DESIGNS—As T **71**: 2f. Beechcraft Baron; 5f. Douglas DC-4. 48×27 mm: 100f. Potez 25-TOE; 200f. Junkers 52/3m; 500f. Sud Aviation Caravelle.

72 Presidents Boganda and Bokassa

1967. Air. Ninth Anniv of Republic.

151	72	130f. multicoloured	2·00	1·30

73 Primitive Shelter, Toulou

1967. Sixth Pan-African Prehistory Congress, Dakar.

152	73	30f. blue, purple and red	75	40
153	-	50f. bistre, ochre & green	1·50	80
154	-	100f. purple, brown & blue	2·75	1·10
155	-	130f. red, green & brown	3·00	1·10

DESIGNS—VERT: 50f. Kwe perforated stone; 100f. Megaliths, Bouar. HORIZ: 130f. Rock drawings, Toulou.

74 Pres. Bokassa

1968. Air.

156	74	30f. multicoloured	85	50

75 Human Rights Emblem, Human Figures and Globe

1968. Air. Human Rights Year.

157	75	200f. red, green and violet	3·50	1·70

76 Human Figure and WHO Emblem

1968. Air. 20th Anniv of WHO.

158	76	200f. red, blue & brown	3·75	2·10

77 Alpine Skiing

1968. Air. Olympic Games, Grenoble and Mexico.

159	77	200f. brown, blue and red	5·00	3·25
160	-	200f. brown, blue and red	5·00	3·25

DESIGN: No. 160, Throwing the javelin.

78 Parachute-landing on Venus

1968. Air. "Venus 4". Exploration of planet Venus.

161	78	100f. blue, turquoise & green	1·80	95

79 Marie Curie and impaled Crab (of Cancer)

1968. Air. Marie Curie Commem.

162	79	100f. brown, violet & blue	2·40	1·20

80 Refinery and Tanker

1968. Inauguration of Petroleum Refinery, Port Gentil, Gabon.

163	80	30f. multicoloured	85	40

1968. Air. Surch. Nos. 165/6 are obliterated with digit.

164	56	5f. on 130f. (No. 116)	10	10
165	-	10f. (100f. No. 148)	30	10
166	-	20f. (200f. No. 149)	45	30
167	-	50f. on 130f. (No. 117)	1·00	60

82 "CD-8" Bulldozer

1968. Bokassa Project.

168	82	5f. brown, black & green	35	15
169	-	10f. black, brown & green	65	30
170	-	20f. green, yellow & brown	75	40
171	-	30f. blue, drab and brown	1·20	55
172	-	30f. red, blue and green	1·20	60

DESIGNS: 10f. Baoule cattle; 20f. Spinning-machine; 30f. (No. 171) Automatic looms; 30f. (No. 172), "D4-C" bulldozer.

83 Bangui Mosque

1968. Second Anniv of Bangui Mosque.

173	83	30f. flesh, green and blue	80	45

84 Za Throwing-knife

1968. Hunting Weapons.

174	84	10f. blue and bistre	45	25
175	-	20f. green, brown & blue	60	40
176	-	30f. green, orange & blue	95	45

DESIGNS: 20f. Kpinga-Gbengue throwing-knife; 30f. Mbano cross-bow.

85 *Ville de Bangui* (1958)

1968. River Craft.

177	85	10f. blue, green and purple (postage)	60	40
178	-	30f. brown, blue & green	1·10	55
179	-	50f. black, brown & grn	1·90	90
180	-	100f. brown, grn & bl (air)	2·40	1·10
181	-	130f. blue, green & purple	2·75	1·40

DESIGNS: 30f. *J. B. Gouandjia* (1968); 50f. *Lamblin* (1944). LARGER (48×27 mm): 100f. *Pie X* (Bangui, 1894); 130f. *Ballay* (Bangui, 1891).

86 *Madame de Sevigne* (French School, 17th century)

1968. Air. "Philexafrique" Stamp Exhibition, Abidjan, Ivory Coast (1969) (1st issue).

182	86	100f. multicoloured	3·00	2·50

87 President Bokassa, Cotton Plantation, and Ubangui Chari stamp of 1930

1969. Air. "Philexafrique" Stamp Exhibition, Abidjan, Ivory Coast (2nd issue).

183	87	50f. black, green & brown	1·80	1·70

88 "Holocerina angulata"

1969. Air. Butterflies. Multicoloured.

184	88	10f. Type 88	75	30
185	-	20f. *Nudaurelia dione*	1·20	55
186	-	30f. *Eustera troglophylla* (vert)	2·75	85
187	-	50f. *Aurivillius aratus*	4·50	2·20
188	-	100f. *Epiphora albida*	7·50	3·50

89 Throwing the Javelin

1969. Sports. Multicoloured.

189	89	5f. Type 89 (postage)	20	10
190	-	10f. Start of race	30	15
191	-	15f. Football	45	20
192	-	50f. Boxing (air)	1·00	40

193		100f. Basketball	2·10	70

Nos. 192/3 are 48×28 mm.

90 Miner and Emblems

1969. 50th Anniv of I.L.O.
194	90	30f. multicoloured	90	40
195	90	50f. multicoloured	1·40	65

91 "Apollo 8" over Moon's Surface

1969. Air. Flight of "Apollo 8" Around Moon.
196	91	200f. multicoloured	3·50	1·80

92 Nuremberg Spire and Toys

1969. Air. International Toy Fair, Nuremberg.
197	92	100f. black, purple & grn	1·90	1·10

1969. Air. Birth Bicentenary of Napoleon Bonaparte. As T **144** of Cameroun. Multicoloured.
198		100f. *Napoleon as First Consul (Girodet-Trioson)* (vert)	2·30	1·40
199		130f. *Meeting of Napoleon and Francis II of Austria (Gros)*	3·25	1·60
200		200f. *Marriage of Napoleon and Marie-Louise (Rouget)*	4·75	3·00

93 President Bokassa in Military Uniform

1969
201	93	30f. multicoloured	60	30

1969. Tenth Anniv of ASECNA. As T **151** of Cameroun.
202		100f. blue	1·80	85

94 Pres. Bokassa, Flag and Map

1970. Air. Die-stamped on gold foil.
203	94	2000f. gold	37·00	35·00

95 Garayah

1970. Musical Instruments.
204	95	10f. brown, sepia & green	60	25
205	-	15f. brown and green	65	25
206	-	30f. brown, lake & yellow	1·00	50
207	-	50f. blue and red	1·50	55
208	-	130f. brown, olive & blue	5·00	1·30

DESIGNS—VERT: 130f. Gatta and Babylon. HORIZ: 15f. Ngombi; 30f. Xylophone; 50f. Nadla.

96 Flour Storage Depot

1970. Societie Industrielle Centrafricaine des Produits Alimentaires et Derives (SICPAD) Project. Multicoloured.
209		25f. Type **96**	11·50	80
210		50f. Mill machinery	24·00	1·60
211		100f. View of flour mill	36·00	2·50

97 F. D. Roosevelt (25th Death Anniv)

1970. Air. World Leaders. Multicoloured.
212		100f. Lenin (birth centenary)	3·50	1·50
213		100f. Type **97**	1·90	1·00

1970. New UPU Headquarters Building, Berne. As T **156** of Cameroun.
214		100f. vermilion, red and blue	1·70	75

1970. Air. Moon Landing of "Apollo 12". No. 196 optd **ATTERRISSAGE d'APOLLO 12 19 novembre 1969.**
215	91	200f. multicoloured	15·00	10·50

99 Pres. Bokassa

1970
216	99	30f. multicoloured	7·25	4·50
217	99	40f. multicoloured	8·25	4·75

100 Cheese Factory, Sarki **101** Silkworm

1970. "Operation Bokassa" Development Projects. Multicoloured.
218		5f. Type **100** (postage)	45	25
219		10f. M'Bali Ranch	5·50	4·00
220		20f. Zebu bull and herdsman (vert)	75	40
221		40f. Type **101**	2·20	70
222		140f. Type **101** (air)	2·20	90

102 African Dancer

1970. Air. "Knokphila 70" Stamp Exhibition, Knokke, Belgium. Multicoloured.
223		100f. Type **102**	1·80	60
224		100f. African produce	2·00	60

103 Footballer

1970. Air. World Cup Football Championship, Mexico.
225	103	200f. multicoloured	3·75	1·70

104 Central African Republic's Pavilion

1970. Air. "EXPO 70", Osaka, Japan.
226	104	200f. multicoloured	4·00	1·90

105 Dove and Cogwheel

1970. Air. 25th Anniv of UNO.
227	105	200f. black, yellow & bl	3·75	1·70

106 Presidents Mobutu, Bokassa and Tombalbaye

1970. Air. Reconciliation with Chad and Zaire.
228	106	140f. multicoloured	2·75	1·10

107 Scaly Francolin and Helmeted Guineafowl

1971. Wildlife. Multicoloured.
229		5f.+5f. Type **107**	4·75	2·20
230		10f.+5f. Common duiker and true achatina (snail)	6·25	3·00
231		20f.+5f. Hippopotamus, African elephant and tortoise in tug-of-war	7·75	3·25
232		30f.+10f. Tortoise and Senegal coucal	10·50	7·75
233		50f.+20f. Monkey and leopard	18·00	12·50

108 Lengue Dancer

1971. Traditional Dances. Multicoloured.
234		20f.+5f. Type **108**	55	25
235		40f.+10f. Lengue (diff)	95	45
236		100f.+40f. Teke	2·75	1·30
237		140f.+40f. Englabolo	3·25	1·60

110 Monteir's Mormyrid

1971. Fish. Multicoloured.
244		10f. Type **110**	35	25
245		20f. Trunk-nosed mormyrid	75	30
246		30f. Wilverth's mormyrid	1·20	65
247		40f. Elephant-nosed mormyrid	2·30	75
248		50f. Curve-nosed mormyrid	3·00	1·30

111 Satellite and Globe

1971. Air. World Telecommunications Day.
249	111	100f. multicoloured	1·90	90

112 Berberati Cathedral

1971. Consecration of Roman Catholic Cathedral, Berberati.
250	112	5f. multicoloured	45	20

113 Gen. De Gaulle

1971. First Death Anniv of De Gaulle.
251	113	100f. multicoloured	3·50	2·10

114 Lesser Bushbaby

1971. Animals: Primates. Multicoloured.
252		30f. Type **114**	85	65
253		40f. Western needle-clawed bushbaby	1·20	75
254		100f. Angwantibo (horiz)	2·75	1·70
255		150f. Potto (horiz)	4·75	2·50
256		200f. Red colobus (horiz)	6·50	3·75

1971. Air. Tenth Anniv of African and Malagasy Posts and Telecommunications Union. Similar to T **184** of Cameroun. Multicoloured.
257		100f. Headquarters and carved head	1·90	90

115 Shepard in Capsule

1971. Space Achievements. Multicoloured.
258		40f. Type **115**	55	40
259		40f. Gagarin in helmet	55	40
260		100f. Aldrin in Space	1·40	55
261		100f. Leonov in Space	1·40	55
262		200f. Armstrong on Moon	2·50	1·20
263		200f. "Lunokhod 1" on Moon	2·50	1·20

116 Crab Emblem

1971. Air. Anti-cancer Campaign.
264	116	100f. multicoloured	2·40	1·20

117 "Operation Bokassa"

1971. 12th Year of Independence.
265 **117** 40f. multicoloured 80 50

118 Racial Equality Year Emblem

1971. Racial Equality Year.
266 **118** 50f. multicoloured 80 50

119 IEY Emblem and Child with Toy Bricks

1971. Air. 25th Anniv of UNESCO.
267 **119** 140f. multicoloured 1·90 85

120 African Children

1971. Air. 25th Anniv of UNICEF.
268 **120** 140f.+50f. multicoloured 3·00 1·80

121 Arms and Parade

1972. Bokassa Military School.
269 **121** 30f. multicoloured 80 50

122 Pres. G. Nasser

1972. Air. Nasser Commemoration.
270 **122** 100f. ochre, brown & red 2·10 95

123 Book Year Emblem

1972. International Book Year.
271 **123** 100f. gold, yellow & brn 3·00 1·30

124 Heart Emblem

1972. World Heart Month.
272 **124** 100f. red, black & yellow 1·80 95

125 First-Aid Post

1972. Red Cross Day.
273 **125** 150f. multicoloured 3·25 1·60

126 Global Emblem

1972. World Telecommunications Day.
274 **126** 50f. black, yellow & red 95 60

127 Boxing

1972. Air. Olympic Games, Munich.
275 **127** 100f. bistre and brown 1·70 1·10
276 - 100f. violet and green 1·70 1·10
MS277 130×100 mm. Designs as Nos. 275/6, but colours changed: 100f. emerald and purple; 100f. purple and brown 4·50 4·25
DESIGN—VERT: No. 276 Long jump.

128 Pres. Bokassa and Family

1972. Mothers' Day.
278 **128** 30f. multicoloured 60 40

129 Pres. Bokassa planting Cotton Bush

1972. "Operation Bokassa" Cotton Development.
279 **129** 40f. multicoloured 95 45

130 Savings Bank Building

1972. Opening of New Postal Cheques and Savings Bank Building.
280 **130** 30f. multicoloured 95 45

131 "Le Pacifique" Hotel

1972. "Operation Bokassa" Completion of "Le Pacifique" Hotel.
281 **131** 30f. blue, red and green 55 25

132 Giraffe and Monkeys

1972. Clock-faces from Central African HORCEN Factory. Multicoloured.
282 5f. Rhinoceros chasing African 30 25
283 10f. Camp fire and Native warriors 45 25
284 20f. Fishermen 45 30
285 30f. Type **132** 75 55
286 40f. Warriors fighting 1·20 70

133 Postal Runner **134** Tiling's Postal Rocket, 1931

1972. "CENTRAPHILEX" Stamp Exhibition, Bangui.
287 **133** 10f. mult (postage) 30 20
288 - 20f. multicoloured 45 25
289 **134** 40f. orange, blue and slate (air) 70 45
290 - 50f. blue, slate & orange 80 70
291 - 150f. grey, orange & brn 2·30 1·50
292 - 200f. blue, orange & brn 3·25 2·30
MS293 201×100 mm. Nos. 289/92 8·75 8·50
DESIGNS—AS Type **133**: HORIZ: Protestant Youth Centre. As Type **134**: VERT: 50f. Douglas DC-3 and camel postman; 150f. "Sirio" satellite and rocket. HORIZ: 200f. "Intelsat 4" satellite and rocket.

135 University Buildings

1972. Inauguration of Bokassa University.
294 **135** 40f. grey, blue and red 80 45

136 Mail Van

1972. World UPU Day.
295 **136** 100f. multicoloured 2·00 80

137 Paddy Field

1972. Bokassa Plan. State Farms. Multicoloured.
296 5f. Type **137** 65 20
297 25f. Rice cultivation 1·30 25

138 Four Linked Arrows

1972. Air. "Europafrique".
298 **138** 100f. multicoloured 1·60 85

1972. Air. Munich Olympic Gold Medal Winners. Nos. 275/6 optd as listed below.
299 **127** 100f. bistre and brown 1·60 95
300 - 100f. violet and green 1·60 95
MS301 130×100 mm. MS277 with opts as Nos. 299/300 3·75 3·50
OVERPRINTS: No. 299, **POIDS-MOYEN LEMECHEV MEDAILLE D'OR.** No. 300, **LONGUEUR WILLIAMS MEDAILLE D'OR.**

140 Hotel Swimming Pool

1972. Opening of Hotel St. Sylvestre.
302 **140** 30f. brown, turq & grn 45 30
303 - 40f. purple, green & blue 50 35

DESIGN: 40f. Facade of Hotel.

141 Landing Module and Lunar Rover on Moon

1972. Air. Moon Flight of "Apollo 16".
304 **141** 100f. green, blue & grey 1·60 80

142 Virgin and Child (F. Pesellino)

1972. Air. Christmas. Multicoloured.
305 100f. Type **142** 1·80 1·10
306 150f. Adoration of the Child (F. Lippi) 2·75 1·50

143 Learning to Write

1972. "Central African Mothers". Multicoloured.
307 5f. Type **143** 10 10
308 10f. Baby-care 30 10
309 15f. Dressing hair 40 25
310 20f. Learning to read 45 25
311 180f. Suckling baby 2·50 1·30
312 190f. Learning to walk 2·50 1·50

144 Louys (marathon), Athens, 1896

1972. Air. 75th Anniv of Revival of Olympic Games.
313 **144** 30f. purple, brown & grn 35 25
314 - 40f. green, blue & brown 45 25
315 - 50f. violet, blue and red 55 45
316 - 100f. purple, brn & grey 1·20 55
317 - 150f. black, blue & purple 1·70 1·30
DESIGNS: 40f. Barrelet (sculling), Paris, 1900; 50f. Prinstein (triple-jump), St. Louis, U.S.A., 1904; 100f. Taylor (400 m freestyle swimming), London, 1908; 150f. Johansson (Greco-Roman wrestling), Stockholm, 1912.

145 WHO Emblem, Doctor and Nurse

1973. Air. 25th Anniv of WHO.
318 **145** 100f. multicoloured 1·60 85

146 "Telecommunications"

1973. World Telecommunications Day.
319 **146** 200f. orange, blue & black 2·40 1·20

147 Harvesting

1973. Tenth Anniv of World Food Programme.
| 320 | 147 | 50f. multicoloured | 80 | 50 |

148 *Garcinia punctata*

1973. "Flora". Multicoloured.
321		10f. Type **148**	45	20
322		20f. *Bertiera racemosa*	65	25
323		30f. *Coryanthe pachyceras*	90	50
324		40f. *Combretodendron africanum*	1·30	60
325		50f. *Xylopia villosa*	1·70	25

149 Pygmy Chameleon

1973
| 326 | 149 | 15f. multicoloured | 1·50 | 40 |

150 *Mboyo Ndili*

1973. Caterpillars. Multicoloured.
327		3f. Type **150**	75	25
328		5f. *Piwili*	1·20	45
329		25f. *Loulia Konga*	2·50	65

1973. African Solidarity "Drought Relief". No. 321 surch **SECHERESSE SOLIDARITE AFRICAINE** and value.
| 330 | 148 | 100f. on 10f. mult | 1·60 | 1·10 |

1973. UAMPT. As Type **216** of Cameroun.
| 331 | | 100f. red, brown and olive | 1·10 | 70 |

1973. Air. African Fortnight, Brussels. As T **217** of Cameroun.
| 332 | | 100f. brown and violet | 1·30 | 75 |

152 African and Symbolic Map

1973. Air. Europafrique.
| 333 | 152 | 100f. red, green & brown | 1·60 | 85 |

153 Bird with Letter

1973. Air. World UPU Day.
| 334 | 153 | 200f. multicoloured | 2·30 | 1·40 |

154 Weather Map

1973. Air. Centenary of IMO/WMO.
| 335 | 154 | 150f. multicoloured | 2·40 | 1·00 |

155 Copernicus

1973. Air. 500th Birth Anniv of Copernicus.
| 336 | 155 | 100f. multicoloured | 2·75 | 1·80 |

156 Pres. Bokassa

1973
337	156	1f. mult (postage)	10	10
338	156	2f. multicoloured	10	10
339	156	3f. multicoloured	10	10
340	156	5f. multicoloured	10	10
341	156	10f. multicoloured	35	10
342	156	15f. multicoloured	35	20
343	156	20f. multicoloured	45	25
344	156	30f. multicoloured	45	30
345	156	40f. multicoloured	60	35
346	-	50f. multicoloured (air)	65	35
347	-	100f. multicoloured	1·30	70

DESIGNS—SQUARE (35×35 mm): 50f. Pres. Bokassa facing left. VERT (26×47 mm): 100f. Pres. Bokassa in military uniform.

158 Launch

1973. Air. Moon Flight of "Apollo 17".
348	158	50f. red, green & brown	55	30
349	-	65f. green, red & purple	75	45
350	-	100f. blue, brown & red	1·20	70
351	-	150f. green, brown & red	1·70	85
352	-	200f. green, red and blue	2·20	1·30

DESIGNS—HORIZ: 65f. Surveying lunar surfaces; 100f. Descent on Moon. VERT: 150f. Astronauts on Moon's surface; 200f. Splashdown.

159 Interpol Emblem within "Eye"

1973. 50th Anniv of Interpol.
| 353 | 159 | 50f. multicoloured | 80 | 55 |

160 St. Theresa

1973. Air. Birth Centenary of St. Theresa of Lisieux.
| 354 | 160 | 500f. blue and light blue | 6·25 | 4·00 |

161 Main Entrance

1974. Opening of "Catherine Bokassa" Mother-and-Child Centre.
| 355 | 161 | 30f. brown, red and blue | 35 | 25 |
| 356 | - | 40f. brown, blue and red | 45 | 40 |

DESIGN: 40f. General view of Centre.

162 Cigarette-packing Machine

1974. "Centra" Cigarette Factory.
357	162	5f. purple, green & red	10	10
358	-	10f. blue, green & brown	35	20
359	-	30f. green, blue and red	45	25

DESIGNS: 10f. Administration block and factory building; 30f. Tobacco warehouse.

163 "Telecommunications"

1974. World Telecommunications Day.
| 360 | 163 | 100f. multicoloured | 1·50 | 85 |

164 "Peoples of the World"

1974. World Population Year.
| 361 | 164 | 100f. green, red & brown | 1·20 | 70 |

165 Mother and Baby

1974. 26th Anniv of WHO.
| 362 | 165 | 100f. brown, blue & grn | 1·70 | 75 |

166 Letter and UPU Emblem

1974. Centenary of UPU.
| 363 | 166 | 500f. red, green & brown | 7·00 | 4·25 |

167 Battle Scene

1974. "Activities of Forces' Veterans". Multicoloured.
364		10f. Type **167**	10	10
365		15f. "Today" (Peace-time activities)	20	10
366		20f. Planting rice	30	10
367		25f. Cattle-shed	35	20
368		30f. Workers hoeing	35	25
369		40f. Veterans' houses	55	25

1974. Tenth Anniv of Central African Customs and Economics Union. As Nos. 734/5 of Cameroun.
| 370 | | 40f. multicoloured (postage) | 60 | 35 |
| 371 | | 100f. multicoloured (air) | 1·30 | 80 |

168 Modern Building

1975. "OCAM City" Project.
372	168	30f. multicoloured	35	10
373	-	40f. multicoloured	45	25
374	-	50f. multicoloured	55	40
375	-	100f. multicoloured	1·00	55

DESIGNS: Nos. 373/5, Various views similar to Type **150**.

1975. "J. B. Bokassa Pilot Village Project". As T **168**, but inscr "VILLAGE PILOTE J. B. BOKASSA".
376		25f. multicoloured	30	10
377		30f. multicoloured	35	25
378		40f. multicoloured	45	30

DESIGNS: Nos. 376/8, Various views similar to Type **168**.

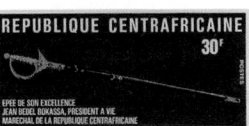

169 President Bokassa's Sword

1975. "Homage to President Bokassa". Multicoloured.
379		30f. Type **169** (postage)	45	30
380		40f. President Bokassa's baton	55	25
381		50f. Pres. Bokassa in uniform (vert, 36×49 mm) (air)	60	35
382		100f. Pres. Bokassa in cap and cape (vert, 36×49 mm)	1·30	55

170 Foreign Minister and Ministry

1975. Government Buildings. Multicoloured.
| 383 | | 40f. Type **170** | 55 | 35 |
| 384 | | 40f. Television Centre (36×23 mm) | 55 | 35 |

171 "No Entry"

1975. Road Signs.
385	171	5f. red and blue	10	10
386	-	10f. red and blue	10	10
387	-	20f. red and blue	30	10
388	-	30f. multicoloured	45	25
389	-	40f. multicoloured	75	30

SIGNS: 10f. "Stop"; 20f. "No stopping"; 30f. "School"; 40f. "Crossroads".

172 Kob

1975. Wild Animals. Multicoloured.
390		10f. Type **172**	45	10
391		15f. Warthog	90	25
392		20f. Waterbuck	1·20	25
393		30f. Lion	1·30	40

173 Carved Wooden Mask

1975. Air. "Arphila" International Stamp Exhibition. Paris.
| 394 | 173 | 100f. red, rose and blue | 1·30 | 70 |

174 Dr. Schweitzer and Dug-out Canoe

1975. Air. Birth Centenary of Dr. Albert Schweitzer.
| 395 | 174 | 200f. black, blue & brown | 3·75 | 2·00 |

175 Forest
Scene

1975. Central African Woods.
396	**175**	10f. brown, green & red	10	10
397	-	15f. brown, green & blue	30	10
398	-	50f. blue, brown & green	55	25
399	-	100f. brown, blue & grn	1·20	60
400	-	150f. blue, brown & grn	1·60	1·00
401	-	200f. brown, red & green	2·10	1·40

DESIGNS—VERT: 15f. Cutting sapeles. HORIZ: 50f. Mobile crane; 100f. Log stack; 150f. Floating logs; 200f. Timber-sorting yard.

176 Women's Heads and Women Working

1975. International Women's Year.
402	**176**	40f. multicoloured	45	25
403	**176**	100f. multicoloured	1·30	65

177 River Vessel *Jean Bedel Bokassa*

1976. Air. Multicoloured.
404	**177**	30f. Type **177**	60	30
405		40f. Frontal view of *Jean Bedel Bokassa*	85	50

178 Co-operation Monument

1976. Air. Central African–French Co-operation and Visit of President Giscard d'Estaing. Multicoloured.
406	**178**	100f. Type **178**	1·30	85
407		200f. Flags and Presidents Giscard d'Estaing and Bokassa	2·75	1·40

179 Alexander Graham Bell

1976. Telephone Centenary.
408	**179**	100f. black and yellow	1·70	1·00

180 Telecommunications Satellite

1976. World Telecommunications Day.
409	**180**	100f. purple, blue & grn	1·70	1·10

181 Rocket on Launch-pad

1976. Apollo–Soyuz Space Link. Multicoloured.
410		40f. Type **181** (postage)	60	30
411		50f. Blast-off	75	40
412		100f. "Soyuz" in flight (air)	1·00	25
413		190f. "Apollo" in flight	1·90	65
414		300f. Crew meeting in space	3·00	1·00
MS415	103×78 mm. 500f. Space link		5·00	1·90

182 French Hussar

1976. Air. American Revolution Bicent. Multicoloured.
416		100f. Type **182**	85	40
417		125f. Black Watch soldier	1·20	50
418		150f. German Dragoons' officer	1·20	55
419		200f. British Grenadiers' officer	2·20	60
420		250f. American Ranger	2·50	95
MS421	119×81 mm. 450f. American dragoon		7·25	2·10

183 *Drurya antimachus*

1976. Butterflies. Multicoloured.
422		30f. Type **183** (postage)	5·25	1·10
423		40f. *Argema mittrei* (vert)	7·50	1·10
424		50f. *Acherontia atropos* and *Saturnia pyri* (air)	4·75	1·10
425		100f. *Papilio nireus* and *Heniocha marnois*	9·50	1·60

184 Dorothy Hamill of U.S.A. (figure skating)

1976. Medal Winners, Winter Olympic Games, Innsbruck. Multicoloured.
426		40f. Piero Gros of Italy (slalom) (horiz) (postage)	50	25
427		60f. Karl Schnabl and Toni Innauer of Austria (ski-jumping) (horiz)	75	40
428		100f. Type **184** (air)	95	45
429		200f. Alexandre Gorshkov and Ludmilla Pakhomova (figure-skating, pairs) (horiz)	1·90	75
430		300f. John Curry of Great Britain (figure-skating)	3·00	1·10
MS431	103×78 mm. 500f. Rosi Mittermaier of West Germany (skiing)		6·00	1·90

185 UPU Emblem, Letters, and Types of Mail Transport

1976. World UPU Day.
432	**185**	100f. multicoloured	1·60	90

186 Assembly of "Viking"

1976. "Viking" Space Mission to Mars. Multicoloured.
433		40f. Type **186** (postage)	50	25
434		60f. Launch of "Viking"	75	40
435		100f. Parachute descent on Mars (air)	95	45
436		200f. "Viking" on Mars (horiz)	1·90	70
437		300f. "Viking" operating gravel scoop	3·00	1·00
MS438	102×78 mm. 500f. "Viking" in flight (horiz)		5·00	1·90

220 Ski Jump

1979. Air. Winter Olympic Games, Lake Placid (1980). Multicoloured.
655		60f. Type **220**	60	25
656		100f. Downhill skiing	1·00	45
657		200f. Ice hockey	2·10	90
658		300f. Skiing (slalom)	3·00	1·40
MS659	103×77 mm. 500f. Two-man bobsleigh		5·50	1·80

Issues between 1977 and 1979 are listed under **CENTRAL AFRICAN EMPIRE**.

1979. "Apollo 11" Moon Landing. Tenth Anniv. Nos. 433/7 optd **ALUNISSAGE APOLLO XI JUILLET 1969** and lunar module.
660	**186**	40f. mult (postage)	50	30
661	-	60f. multicoloured	65	45
662	-	100f. multicoloured (air)	95	60
663	-	200f. multicoloured	1·80	95
664	-	300f. multicoloured	2·75	1·40
MS665	102×78 mm. 500f. multicoloured		5·50	5·00

222 Thumbelina (Andersen)

1979. International Year of the Child (2nd issue). Multicoloured.
666		30f. Type **222**	30	10
667		40f. *Sleeping Beauty* (horiz)	40	10
668		60f. *Hansel and Gretel*	55	25
669		200f. *The Match Girl* (horiz)	2·10	75
670		250f. *The Little Mermaid*	2·50	85

223 Steam Locomotive, U.S.A. Stamp and Hill

1979. Death Centenary of Sir Rowland Hill (2nd issue). Multicoloured.
671		60f. Type **223**	55	25
672		100f. Locomotive *Champion* (1882, U.S.A.), French stamp and Hill	1·00	35
673		150f. Steam locomotive, German stamp and Hill	1·70	55
674		250f. Steam locomotive, British stamp and Hill	2·75	1·10
MS675	115×78 mm. 500f. Locomotive, Central African Republic stamps and Hill		6·00	2·10

224 Basketball

1979. Olympic Games, Moscow (2nd issue). Basketball.
676	**224**	50f. multicoloured	45	10
677	-	125f. multicoloured	1·20	45
678	-	200f. multicoloured	2·00	60
679	-	300f. multicoloured	3·00	95
680	-	500f. multicoloured	4·50	1·50

DESIGNS: 125f. to 500f. Views of different basketball matches.

1980. Various stamps, including one unissued, of Central African Empire optd **REPUBLIQUE CENTRAFRICAINE**.
681	**192**	5f. multicoloured	20	20
682	-	10f. mult (No. 522)	20	25
683	-	20f. multicoloured (Balambo (stand))	20	10
684	**206**	20f. black and yellow	20	10
685	-	30f. black and blue (No. 583)	40	20

226 "Viking"

1980. Space Exploration. Multicoloured.
686		40f. Type **226** (postage)	45	10
687		50f. "Apollo"–"Soyuz" link	55	15
688		60f. "Voyager"	65	20
689		100f. European Space Agency	1·10	30
690		150f. Early satellites (air)	1·50	40
691		200f. Space shuttle	2·00	55
MS692	85×58 mm. 500f. Neil Armstrong (50×41 mm)		5·25	1·60

1980. Air. Winter Olympic Medal Winners. Nos. 655/8 optd as listed below.
693	**220**	60f. multicoloured	55	25
694	-	100f. multicoloured	95	45
695	-	200f. multicoloured	1·80	90
696	-	300f. multicoloured	2·75	1·40
MS697	103×77 mm. 500f. multicoloured		5·50	3·25

DESIGNS: 60f. **VAINQUEUR INNAVER AUTRICHE**; 100f. **VAINQUEUR MOSER-PROELL AUTRICHE**; 200f. **VAINQUEUR ETATS-UNIS**; 300f. **VAINQUEUR STENMARK SUEDE**; 500f. **VAINQUEURS / SCHAERER-BENZ / SUISSE**.

228 Telephone and Sun

1980. World Telecommunications Day. Multicoloured.
698		100f. Type **228**	1·00	60
699		150f. Telephone and sun (different)	1·50	85

229 Walking

1980. Olympic Games, Moscow (3rd issue). Multicoloured.
700		30f. Type **229** (postage)	40	10
701		40f. Women's relay	50	10
702		70f. Running	75	25
703		80f. Women's high jump	75	25
704		100f. Boxing (air)	95	25
705		150f. Hurdles	1·50	45
MS706	87×84 mm. 250f. Long jump (39×36 mm)		5·25	1·60

229a Fruit

1980
706a	**229a**	40f. multicoloured	

230 Agriculture

1980. European-African Co-operation. Multicoloured.
707		30f. Type **230** (postage)	35	10
708		40f. Industry	45	10
709		70f. Communications	80	25
710		100f. Building construction and rocket	1·40	40
711		150f. Meteorological satellite (air)	1·50	50
712		200f. Space shuttle	1·80	65
MS713	89×64 mm. 500f. Concorde (41×29 mm)		5·25	1·70

1980. Olympic Medal Winners. Nos. 676/80 optd.

717	50f. **MEDAILLE OR YOUGO-SLAVIE**	50	25
718	125f. **MEDAILLE OR URSS**	1·20	45
719	200f. **MEDAILLE OR URSS**	1·80	70
720	300f. **MEDAILLE ARGEN TITALIE**	3·00	1·10
721	500f. **MEDAILLE BRONZE URSS**	4·50	1·70

232 *Foligne Madonna (detail)*

1980. Christmas. Multicoloured.

722	60f. Type **232**	60	25
723	150f. *Virgin and Saints*	1·50	65
724	250f. *Conestabile Madonna*	2·75	1·10

1980. Fifth Anniv of African Posts and Telecommunications Union. As T **269** of Benin.

725	70f. multicoloured	75	40

233 *Peruvian Football Team*

1981. World Cup Football Championship, Spain (1982). Multicoloured.

726	10f. Type **233** (postage)	10	10
727	15f. Scottish team	20	10
728	20f. Mexican team	30	10
729	25f. Swedish team	30	10
730	30f. Austrian team	45	10
731	40f. Polish team	45	25
732	70f. French team	75	25
733	60f. Italian team	75	25
734	70f. West German team	95	35
735	80f. Brazilian team	95	40
736	100f. Dutch team (air)	95	25
737	200f. Spanish team	1·80	45
MS738	119×87 mm. 500f. Argentina team	6·00	1·70

234 *Fight between Jacob and the Angel*

1981. Air. 375th Birth Anniv of Rembrandt. Multicoloured.

739	60f. Type **234**	55	25
740	90f. *Christ in the Tempest*	95	25
741	150f. *Jeremiah mourning the Destruction of Jerusalem*	1·70	70
742	250f. *Anna accused by Tobit of Theft of a Goat*	2·75	80
MS743	104×80 mm. 500f. *Belshazzar's Feast* (horiz)	5·50	1·80

1981. Olympic Games Medal Winners. Nos. 700/**MS**706 optd.

744	30f. **50 K.M. MARCHE HARTWIG GAUDER–G.D.R.** (postage)	30	10
745	40f. **4×400 M. DAMES–U.R.S.S**	45	25
746	70f. **100 M. COURSE HOMMES ALAN WELLS–G.B.R**	75	30
747	80f. **SAUT EN HAUTEUR DAMES SARA SIMEONI– ITALIE**	75	45
748	100f. **BOXE–71 KG ARMANDO MARTINEZ–CUBA** (air)	1·00	35
749	150f. **110 M. HAIES HOMMES THOMAS MUNKELT–G.D.R**	1·50	65
MS750	87×84 mm. 250f. **SAUT LONGUEUR / LUTZ DOMBROWSKI– G.D.R**	5·50	5·00

236 ITU and WHO Emblems and Ribbons forming Caduceus

1981. World Telecommunications Day.

751	**236** 150f. multicoloured	1·40	75

237 Boeing 747 carrying Space Shuttle "Enterprise"

1981. Conquest of Space. Multicoloured.

752	100f. "Apollo 15" and jeep on the Moon	95	40
753	150f. Type **237**	1·40	45
754	200f. Space Shuttle launch	1·80	65
755	300f. Space Shuttle performing experiment in space	3·00	1·00
MS756	103×78 mm. 500f. Space shuttle approaching landing strip	6·00	1·70

238 *Family of Acrobats with a Monkey*

1981. Birth Bicentenary of Pablo Picasso. Multicoloured.

757	40f. Type **238** (postage)	45	10
758	50f. *The Balcony*	75	25
759	80f. *The Artist's Son as Pierrot*	1·20	40
760	100f. *The Three Dancers*	1·70	45
761	150f. *Woman and Mirror with Self-portrait* (air)	2·10	50
762	200f. *Sleeping Woman, the Dream*	5·00	1·40
MS763	78×113 mm. 500f. *Portrait of Maria* (40×50 mm)	5·50	1·60

239 Tractor and Plough breaking Chain

1981. First Anniv of Zimbabwe's Independence.

764	**239** 100f. multicoloured	1·00	45
765	**239** 150f. multicoloured	1·40	60
766	**239** 200f. multicoloured	2·00	80

240 Prince Charles

1981. Royal Wedding (1st issue). Multicoloured.

767	75f. Type **240**	55	25
768	100f. Lady Diana Spencer	95	30
769	150f. St. Paul's Cathedral	1·40	65
770	175f. Couple and Prince's personal Standard	1·80	65
MS771	99×91 mm. 500f. Prince and Lady Diana	7·75	1·80

See also Nos. 772/**MS**778.

241 Lady Diana Spencer with Children

1981. Royal Wedding (2nd issue). Multicoloured.

772	40f. Type **241** (postage)	45	10
773	50f. Investiture of the Prince of Wales	55	25
774	80f. Lady Diana Spencer at Althorp House	75	25
775	100f. Prince Charles in naval uniform	1·20	40
776	150f. Prince of Wales's feathers (air)	2·30	55
777	200f. Highgrove House	3·50	1·00
MS778	120×70 mm. 500f. St. Paul's Cathedral (57×33 mm)	5·25	1·80

242 C. V. Rietschoten

1981. Navigators. Multicoloured.

779	40f. Type **242** (postage)	45	25
780	50f. M. Pajot	45	30
781	60f. L. Jaworski	65	45
782	80f. M. Birch	85	55
783	100f. O. Kersauson (air)	1·20	60
784	200f. Sir Francis Chichester	2·20	1·10
MS785	100×80 mm. 500f. A. Colas	6·00	1·60

243 Renault, 1906

1981. 75th Anniv of French Grand Prix Motor Race. Multicoloured.

786	20f. Type **243**	45	10
787	40f. Mercedes-Benz, 1937	45	10
788	50f. Matra-Ford, 1969	65	25
789	110f. Tazio Nuvolari	1·40	45
790	150f. Jackie Stewart	2·00	70
MS791	104×80 mm. 450f. Racing car, 1914	7·75	4·00

244 Emperor's Crown pierced by Bayonet

1981. Overthrow of the Empire. Multicoloured.

792	5f. Type **244**	10	10
793	10f. Type **244**	25	10
794	25f. Axe splitting crown, and angel holding map	30	10
795	60f. As 25f.	65	25
796	90f. Emperor Bokassa's statue being toppled and map of Republic	1·00	45
797	500f. As 90f.	4·50	2·00

245 FAO Emblem

1981. World Food Day.

798	**245** 90f. green, brown & yell	95	30
799	**245** 110f. green, brown & bl	1·10	45

246 Lizard

1981. Air. Reptiles. Multicoloured.

800	30f. Type **246**	80	20
801	60f. Snake	1·00	30
802	110f. Crocodile	1·80	50

247 Plumed Guineafowl ("Komba")

1981. Birds. Multicoloured.

803	50f. Type **247**	65	25
804	90f. Schlegel's francolin ("Dodoro")	1·30	25
805	140f. Black-headed bunting and ortolan bunting ("Kaya")	2·10	40

248 Bank Building

1981. Central African States' Bank.

806	**248** 90f. multicoloured	95	30
807	**248** 110f. multicoloured	1·10	45

249 *Madonna and Child (Fra Angelico)*

1981. Christmas. Various paintings showing Virgin and Child by named artists. Multicoloured.

808	50f. Type **249** (postage)	65	25
809	60f. Cosme-Tura	85	35
810	90f. Bramantino	1·30	50
811	110f. Memling	1·70	70
812	140f. Correge (air)	1·80	45
813	200f. Gentileschi	3·00	70
MS814	81×98 mm. 500f. *The Holy Family* (Cranach) (41×50 mm)	6·25	1·90

250 Scouts with Packs

1982. 75th Anniv of Boy Scout Movement. Multicoloured.

815	100f. Type **250**	1·10	45
816	150f. Three scouts (horiz)	1·60	60
817	200f. Scouts admiring mountain view (horiz)	2·30	85
818	300f. Scouts taking oath	3·25	1·40
MS819	84×113 mm. 500f. Lord Baden-Powell, scout and totem	5·75	1·70

251 African Elephant

1982. Animals. Multicoloured.

820	60f. Type **251** (postage)	70	10

821	90f. Giraffe		1·00	30
822	100f. Addax		1·20	40
823	110f. Okapi		1·40	55
824	300f. Mandrill (air)		3·00	70
825	500f. Lion		5·00	1·50
MS826	100×80 mm. 600f. Nile croco- dile (47×38 mm)		6·50	1·80

252 *Grandfather Snowman*

1982. Norman Rockwell Illustrations. Multicoloured.

827	30f. Type **252**	30	10
828	60f. *Croquet Players*	80	25
829	110f. *Women talking*	1·20	45
830	150f. *Searching*	1·70	60

253 *Vickers Valentia biplane, 1928*

1982. Transport. Multicoloured.

831	5f. Astra Torres AT-16 airship, 1919 (postage)	10	10
832	10f. Beyer-Garrat 1 locomotive	10	10
833	20f. Bugatti *Royale* car, 1926	30	25
834	110f. Type **253**	1·30	45
835	300f. Nuclear-powered freighter *Savannah* (air)	3·75	70
836	500f. Space shuttle	5·25	1·50
MS837	100×81 mm. 600f. Man with winged horse (38×48 mm)	5·25	1·60

254 George Washington

1982. Anniversaries. Multicoloured.

838	200f. *Le Jardin de Bellevue* (E. Manet) (150th birth anniv) (horiz)	3·00	90
839	300f. Type **254** (250th birth anniv)	2·75	1·00
840	400f. Goethe (150th death anniv)	3·75	1·50
841	500f. Princess of Wales (21st Birthday)	4·50	2·30
MS842	80×104 mm. 500f. Princess of Wales (different)	5·25	1·60

255 Edward VII and Lady Diana Spencer with her Brother

1982. 21st Birthday of Princess of Wales. Multicoloured.

843	5f. George II and portrait of Lady Diana as child (postage)	10	10
844	10f. Type **255**	10	10
845	20f. Charles I and Lady Diana with guinea pig	30	10
846	110f. George V and Lady Diana as student in Switzerland	1·20	25
847	300f. Charles II and Lady Diana in skiing clothes (air)	3·00	70
848	500f. George IV and Lady Diana as nursery teacher	4·75	1·50
MS849	120×74 mm. 600f. Prince and Princess of Wales on wedding day (56×33 mm)	5·75	1·60

256 Football

1982. Olympic Games, Los Angeles. (1984). Multicoloured.

850	5f. Type **256** (postage)	10	10
851	10f. Boxing	10	10
852	20f. Running	30	10
853	110f. Hurdling	1·00	25
854	300f. Diving (air)	2·75	70
855	500f. Show jumping	4·50	1·50
MS856	80×108 mm. 600f. Basketball (38×56 mm)	5·50	1·70

257 Weather Satellite

1982. Space Resources. Multicoloured.

857	5f. Space shuttle and scientist (Food resources) (postage)	10	10
858	10f. Type **257**	10	10
859	20f. Space laboratory (Industrial use)	30	10
860	110f. Astronaut on Moon (Lunar resources)	1·00	25
861	300f. Satellite and energy map (Planetary energy) (air)	2·75	75
862	500f. Satellite and solar panels (Solar energy)	4·50	1·50
MS863	104×67 mm. 600f. Kohoutek, Halley's comet and satellites (Energy from comets)	5·50	1·60

1982. Birth of Prince William of Wales. Nos. 767/70 optd **NAISSANCE ROYALE 1982**.

864	**240** 75f. multicoloured	55	25
865	– 100f. multicoloured	75	45
866	– 150f. multicoloured	1·30	60
867	– 175f. multicoloured	1·90	85
MS868	69×91 mm. 500f. multicoloured	4·75	3·75

259 Pestle and Mortar, Chopping Board and Dish

1982. Utensils. Multicoloured.

869	5f. Basket of vegetables (horiz)	10	10
870	10f. As No. 869	10	10
871	25f. Flagon made from deco-rated gourd	30	10
872	60f. As No. 871	75	25
873	120f. Clay jars (horiz)	1·40	45
874	175f. Decorated bowls (horiz)	1·80	65
875	300f. Type **259**	3·75	1·30

260 Footballers

1982. World Cup Football Championship Results. Unissued stamps optd as T **260**. Multicoloured.

876	60f. **ITALIE 1er ALLEMAGNE 2e (R.F.A.)**	80	25
877	150f. **POLOGNE 3e**	1·60	60
878	300f. **FRANCE 4e**	3·25	1·30
MS879	104×81 mm. 500f. **ITALIE 1er**	5·25	1·60

261 Jean Tubind

1982. Painters. Multicoloured.

880	40f. Type **261**	55	25
881	70f. Pierre Ndarata and 10f. stamp	85	35
882	90f. As No. 881	1·10	45
883	140f. Type **261**	1·70	75

262 Globe and UPU Emblem

1982. UPU Day.

884	**262** 60f. violet, blue and red	55	25
885	**262** 120f. violet, yellow & red	1·20	50

263 Hairpins and Comb

1983. Hair Accessories.

886	**263** 20f. multicoloured	10	10
887	**263** 30f. multicoloured	35	20
888	**263** 70f. multicoloured	65	30
889	**263** 80f. multicoloured	95	45
890	**263** 120f. multicoloured	1·30	50

264 Koch and Microscope

1982. Centenary of Discovery of Tubercle Bacillus by Dr. Robert Koch.

891	**264** 100f. mauve and black	1·20	30
892	**264** 120f. red and black	1·50	50
893	**264** 175f. blue and black	2·00	80

265 Emblem

1982. Tenth Anniv of United Nations Environment Programme.

894	**265** 120f. blue, orange & blk	1·20	35
895	**265** 150f. blue, yellow & blk	1·30	55
896	**265** 300f. blue, green & black	2·75	1·10

266 Granary

1982.

897	**266** 60f. multicoloured	55	25
898	**266** 80f. multicoloured	95	40
899	**266** 120f. multicoloured	1·30	60
900	**266** 200f. multicoloured	2·20	1·10

267 The Beautiful Gardener

1982. Air. Christmas. Paintings by Raphael. Multicoloured.

901	150f. Type **267**	2·00	45
902	500f. *The Holy Family*	5·00	1·50

268 Stylized Transmitter

1983. I.T.U. Delegates' Conference, Nairobi (1982).

903	**268** 100f. multicoloured	95	40
904	**268** 120f. multicoloured	1·30	55

269 Steinitz

1983. Chess Masters. Multicoloured.

905	5f. Type **269** (postage)	10	10
906	10f. Aaron Niemsovich	10	10
907	20f. Aleksandr Alekhine	30	10
908	110f. Botvinnik	1·40	25
909	300f. Boris Spassky (air)	3·50	80
910	500f. Bobby Fischer	5·00	1·40
MS911	116×72 mm. 600f. Korchnoi and Karpov (55×52 mm)	6·75	2·10

270 George Washington

1983. Celebrities. Multicoloured.

912	20f. Type **270** (postage)	10	10
913	110f. Pres. Tito of Yugoslavia	1·10	30
914	500f. Princess of Wales with Prince William (air)	5·00	1·60
MS915	120×70 mm. 600f. Prince and Princess of Wales with Prince William	5·00	3·00

271 Telephone, Satellite and Globe

1983. U.N. Decade for African Transport and Communications. Multicoloured.

916	5f. Type **271**	10	10
917	60f. Type **271**	75	25
918	120f. Radar screen and map of Africa	1·20	45
919	175f. As No. 918	1·70	60

272 Billy Hamilton and Bruno Pezzey

1983. World Cup Football Championship, Spain. Multicoloured.

920	5f. Type **272** (postage)	10	10
921	10f. Sergeij Borovski and Zbigniew Boniek	10	10
922	20f. Pierre Littbarski and Jesus Maria Zamora	35	25
923	110f. Zico and Alberto Pajsarella	1·30	30
924	300f. Paolo Rossi and Smolarek (air)	2·75	75
925	500f. Rummenigge and Alain Giresse	5·00	1·30
MS926	101×81 mm. 600f. Paolo Rossi and Karl Heinz Rummenigge	5·50	3·00

273 *Entombment*

1983. Easter. Paintings by Rembrandt. Multicoloured.
927	100f. Type **273**	95	45
928	300f. *Christ on the Cross*	2·75	1·30
929	400f. *Descent from the Cross*	3·75	1·80

274 J. and L. Robert and Colin Hullin's Balloon, 1784

1983. Air. Bicentenary of Manned Flight. Multicoloured.
930	65f. Type **274**	85	25
931	130f. John Wise and *Atlantic*, 1859	1·40	35
932	350f. *Ville d'Orleans*, Paris, 1870	3·75	1·10
933	400f. Modern advertising balloon	4·25	1·40
MS934	116×91 mm. 500f. Montgolfier balloon, 1783	6·00	1·60

275 Emile Levassor, Rene Panhard and Panhard-Levassor Car, 1895

1983. Car Manufacturers. Multicoloured.
935	10f. Type **275** (postage)	10	10
936	20f. Henry Ford and first Ford car, 1896	10	10
937	30f. Louis Renault and first Renault car, 1899	30	25
938	80f. Ettore Bugatti and Bugatti "Type 37", 1925	95	30
939	400f. Enzo Ferrari and Ferrari "815 Sport", 1940 (air)	4·25	1·00
940	500f. Ferdinand Porsche and Porsche "356 Coupe", 1951	4·75	1·20
MS941	77×88 mm. 600f. Karl Benz and first petrol-driven car, 1886	5·75	1·60

276 IMO Emblem

1983. 25th Anniv of Int Maritime Organization.
942	**276**	40f. blue, lt blue & turq	45	10
943	**276**	100f. multicoloured	95	45

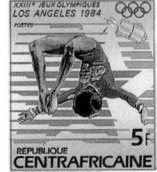

277 Gymnastics

1983. Olympic Games, Los Angeles. Multicoloured.
944	5f. Type **277** (postage)	10	10
945	40f. Javelin	45	10
946	60f. High jump	60	25
947	120f. Fencing	1·50	30
948	200f. Cycling (air)	2·00	45
949	300f. Sailing	3·00	75
MS950	108×80 mm. 600f. Ball games (horiz 50×41 mm)	5·50	1·60

278 WCY Emblem and Satellite

1983. World Communications Year. Multicoloured.
951	50f. Type **278**	40	25
952	130f. WCY emblem and satellite (different)	1·30	50

279 Horse Jumping

1983. Air. Pre-Olympic Year. Multicoloured.
953	100f. Type **279**	95	40
954	200f. Dressage	2·00	80
955	300f. Jumping double jump	3·00	90
956	400f. Trotting	4·00	1·30
MS957	104×79 mm. 500f. Horse jumping (different)	5·75	1·60

280 Andre Kolingba

1983. Second Anniv of Military Committee for National Recovery.
958	**280**	65f. multicoloured	55	25
959	**280**	130f. multicoloured	1·40	40

281 Antenna, Bangui M'Poko Earth Station

1983. Bangui M'Poko Earth Station.
960	**281**	130f. multicoloured	1·40	60

282 Flower and Broken Chain on Map of Africa

1983. Namibia Day.
961	**282**	100f. green, lt grn & red	1·30	45
962	**282**	200f. multicoloured	1·80	85

283 J. Montgolfier and Balloon

1983. Bicentenary of Manned Flight. Multicoloured.
963	50f. Type **283** (postage)	45	10
964	100f. J. Blanchard and Channel crossing, 1785	1·00	25
965	200f. Joseph Gay-Lussac and ascent to 4000 m, 1804	2·20	65
966	300f. Henri Giffard and steam-powered dirigible airship, 1852	3·00	1·00
967	400f. Santos-Dumont and airship *Ballon No. 6*, Paris, 1901 (air)	4·00	1·30
968	500f. A. Laquot and captive observation balloon, 1914	5·00	1·70

MS969 79×85 mm. 600f. J. Charles and hydrogen balloon and G. Tissandier and dirigible 6·00 1·60

284 "Global Communications"

1983. World Communications Year. UPU Day.
970	**284**	205f. multicoloured	2·00	1·00

285 Black Rhinoceros

1983. Endangered Animals. Multicoloured.
971	10f. Type **285** (postage)	40	10
972	40f. Two rhinoceros	1·10	20
973	70f. Black rhinoceros (different)	1·80	35
974	180f. Black rhinoceros and young	5·00	65
975	400f. Rangers attending sick rhinoceros (air)	5·25	1·20
976	500f. Wild animals and flag	6·50	1·40
MS977	111×75 mm. 600f. Cheetah (47×32 mm)	5·75	1·70

286 Handicapped Person and Old Man

1983. National Day of the Handicapped and Old.
978	**286**	65f. orange and mauve	55	30
979	**286**	130f. orange and blue	1·20	55
980	**286**	250f. orange and green	1·80	85

287 Fish Pond

1983. Fishery Resources. Multicoloured.
981	25f. Type **287**	20	10
982	65f. Net fishing	80	25
983	100f. Traditional fishing	1·00	45
984	130f. Butter catfish, eel and cichlids on plate	2·00	70
985	205f. Weir basket	2·40	75

288 *The Annunciation* (Leonardo da Vinci)

1984. Air. Christmas. Multicoloured.
986	130f. Type **288**	1·20	40
987	205f. *The Virgin of the Rocks* (Leonardo da Vinci)	2·00	55
988	350f. *Adoration of the Shepherds* (Rubens)	3·50	1·10
989	500f. *A. Goubeau before the Virgin* (Rubens)	4·75	1·40

289 Bush Fire

1984. Nature Protection. Multicoloured.
990	30f. Type **289**	2·10	40
991	130f. Soldiers protecting wildlife from hunters	3·00	1·00

290 Goethe and Scene from "Faust"

1984. Celebrities. Multicoloured.
992	50f. Type **290** (postage)	45	10
993	100f. Henri Dunant and battle scene	95	10
994	200f. Alfred Nobel	1·60	40
995	300f. Lord Baden-Powell and scout camp	2·50	70
996	400f. President Kennedy and first foot-print on Moon (air)	4·25	1·10
997	500f. Prince and Princess of Wales	4·75	1·30
MS998	101×72 mm. 600f. Prince and Princess of Wales	5·25	1·60

291 Fixed Bar

1984. Air. Olympic Games, Los Angeles. Gymnastics. Multicoloured.
999	65f. Type **291**	55	25
1000	100f. Parallel bars	1·00	25
1001	130f. Ribbon (horiz)	1·40	40
1002	205f. Cord	2·20	70
1003	350f. Hoop	3·75	1·10
MS1004	102×78 mm. 500f. Rhythmic team gymnastics (horiz)	5·25	1·60

292 *Madonna and Child* (Raphael)

1984. Paintings. Multicoloured.
1005	50f. Type **292** (postage)	50	10
1006	100f. *The Madonna of the Pear* (Durer)	1·00	20
1007	200f. *Aldobrandini Madonna* (Raphael)	2·20	50
1008	300f. *Madonna of the Pink* (Durer)	3·00	85
1009	400f. *Virgin and Child* (Correggio) (air)	4·00	1·60
1010	500f. *The Bohemian* (Modigliani)	5·50	2·10
MS1011	80×111 mm. 600f. *Madonna and Child on the Throne* (Raphael) (vert 29×58 mm)	6·00	1·60

293 *Le Pericles* (mail ship)

1984. Transport. Multicoloured. (a) Ships.
1012	65f. Type **293**	80	30
1013	120f. *Pereire* (steamer)	1·30	55
1014	250f. *Admella* (passenger steamer)	2·50	1·10
1015	400f. *Royal William* (paddle-steamer)	4·50	1·90
1016	500f. *Great Britain* (steam/sail)	5·50	2·50

(b) Locomotives.
1017	110f. CC-1500 ch	1·20	45
1018	240f. Series 210, 1968	2·50	95
1019	350f. 231-726, 1937	3·75	1·30
1020	440f. Pacific Series S3/6, 1908	5·00	1·50
1021	500f. Henschel 151 Series 45, 1937	5·75	3·25

Nos. 1017/21 each include an inset portrait of George Stephenson in the design.

294 Forest

1984. Forest Resources. Multicoloured.

| 1022 | 70f. Type **294** | 85 | 30 |
| 1023 | 130f. Log cabin and timber | 1·70 | 65 |

295 Weighing
Baby and Emblem

1984. Infant Survival Campaign. Multicoloured.

1024	10f. Type **295**	10	10
1025	30f. Vaccinating baby	45	25
1026	65f. Feeding dehydrated baby	55	40
1027	100f. Mother, healthy baby and foodstuffs	1·10	60

296 Bangui-Kette Conical
Trap

1984. Fish Traps. Multicoloured.

1028	50f. Type **296**	75	30
1029	80f. Mbres fish trap	1·00	60
1030	150f. Bangui-Kette round fish trap	2·20	80

297 Galileo and
"Ariane" Rocket

1984. Space Technology. Multicoloured.

1031	20f. Type **297** (postage)	30	10
1032	70f. Auguste Piccard and strato-sphere balloon *F.N.R.S.*	70	25
1033	150f. Hermann Oberth and satellite	1·50	50
1034	205f. Albert Einstein and "Giotto" satellite	2·00	65
1035	300f. Marie Curie and "Viking I" and "II" (air)	3·50	90
1036	500f. Dr. U. Merbold and "Navette" space laboratory	4·50	1·10
MS1037	75×59 mm. 600f. Neil Arm-strong and "Apollo II" (41×34 mm)	5·25	1·60

298 *Leptoporus lignosus*

1984. Fungi. Multicoloured.

1038	5f. Type **298**	10	10
1039	10f. *Phlebopus sudanicus*	10	10
1040	40f. *Termitomyces letestui*	60	25
1041	130f. *Lepiota esculenta*	1·50	30
1042	300f. *Termitomyces aurantiacus* (air)	3·25	85
1043	500f. *Termitomyces robustus*	6·00	1·30
MS1044	68×90 mm. 600f. *Tricholoma lobayensis* (34×40 mm)	6·00	1·80

299 Hibiscus

1984. Flowers. Multicoloured.

1045	65f. Type **299**	90	45
1046	130f. Canna	1·60	75
1047	205f. Water Hyacinth	2·50	1·00

300 G. Boucher (speed skating)

1984. Winter Olympic Gold Medallists. Multicoloured.

1048	30f. Type **300** (postage)	30	10
1049	90f. W. Hoppe, R. Wetzig, D. Schauerhammer and A. Kirchner (bobsleigh)	95	30
1050	140f. P. Magoni (ladies' slalom)	1·40	45
1051	200f. J. Torvill and C. Dean (ice skating)	2·00	60
1052	400f. M. Nykanen (90 m ski jump) (air)	4·00	1·00
1053	400f. Russia (ice hockey)	4·75	1·30
MS1054	79×58 mm. 600f. W.D. Johnson (men's downhill skiing)	5·50	1·60

301 Workers sowing Cotton
Seeds

1984. Economic Campaign. Multicoloured.

1055	25f. Type **301**	35	20
1056	40f. Selling cotton	55	45
1057	130f. Cotton market	1·60	65

302 Woman picking corn

1984. World Food Day.

| 1058 | **302** | 205f. multicoloured | 2·50 | 1·00 |

303 Abraham Lincoln

1984. Celebrities. Multicoloured.

1059	50f. Type **303** (postage)	50	90
1060	90f. Auguste Piccard (undersea explorer)	95	30
1061	120f. Gottlieb Daimler (automo-bile designer)	1·50	45
1062	200f. Louis Bleriot (pilot)	2·30	60
1063	350f. A. Karpov (chess cham-pion) (air)	3·75	90
1064	400f. Henri Dunant (founder of Red Cross)	4·25	1·10
MS1065	79×114 mm. 600f. Queen Elizabeth, the Queen Mother (85th birthday, 1985) (35×50 mm)	5·25	1·60

304 Profile, Water and
Emblem

1984. Bangui Rotary Club and Water.

| 1066 | **304** | 130f. multicoloured | 1·70 | 50 |
| 1067 | **304** | 205f. multicoloured | 2·50 | 80 |

305 United States (4×400
m relay)

1985. Air Olympic Games Gold Medallists. Multicoloured.

1068	60f. Type **305**	55	20
1069	140f. E. Moses (400 m hurdles)	1·60	45
1070	300f. S. Aouita (5000 m)	3·50	90

| 1071 | 440f. D. Thompson (decathlon) | 4·25 | 1·20 |
| **MS**1072 | 102×76 mm. 500f. J. Cruz (800 metres) (horiz) | 5·50 | 3·00 |

306 *Virgin and Infant Jesus* (Titian)

1985. Air Christmas (1984). Multicoloured.

1073	130f. Type **306**	1·20	60
1074	350f. *Virgin with Rabbit* (Titian)	3·25	1·30
1075	400f. *Virgin and Child* (Titian)	3·75	1·50

307 Eastern Screech Owls

1985. Air. Birth Bicentenary of John J. Audubon (ornithologist) (1st issue). Multicoloured.

1076	60f. Type **307**	60	20
1077	110f. Mangrove cuckoo (vert)	1·20	50
1078	200f. Mourning doves (vert)	2·00	1·00
1079	500f. Wood ducks	5·25	2·20

See also Nos. 1099/1104.

1985. International Exhibitions. Nos. 1014/15, 1019/20 and **MS**1004 optd.

1083	250f. multicoloured (postage)	2·40	1·50
1084	350f. multicoloured	3·50	1·80
1085	400f. multicoloured	4·25	2·30
1086	440f. multicoloured	5·25	2·75
MS1087	102×78 mm. 500f. multicol-oured (air)	4·75	4·50

DESIGNS: 250f. **ARGENTINA '85 BUENOS AIRES**; 350f. **TSUKUBA EXPO '85**; 400f. **Italia '85 ROME** and emblem; 440f. **MOPHILA '85 HAMBOURG**; 500f. **OLYMPICPHILEX '85 LUSANNE** and emblem.

310 *Chelorrhina
polyphemus*

1985. Beetles. Multicoloured.

1088	15f. Type **310**	1·70	25
1089	20f. *Fornasinius russus*	2·10	35
1090	25f. *Goliathus giganteus*	2·50	45
1091	65f. *Goliathus meleagris*	6·25	75

311 Olympic Games Poster and
Stockholm

1985. "Olymphilex '85" Olympic Stamps Exhibition, Lausanne. Multicoloured.

1092	5f. Type **311** (postage)	15	10
1093	10f. Olympic Games poster and Paris	15	10
1094	20f. Olympic Games poster and London	30	15
1095	100f. Olympic Games poster and Tokyo	3·00	75
1096	400f. Olympic Games poster and Mexico (air)	4·00	90
1097	500f. Olympic Games poster and Munich	4·50	1·10
MS1098	107×68 mm. 600f. Baron Pierre de Coubertin (55×25 mm)	5·50	1·60

312 Blue Jay

1985. Birth Bicentenary of John J. Audubon (ornithologist) (2nd issue). Multicoloured.

1099	40f. Type **312** (postage)	65	15
1100	80f. Chuck Will's widow	1·00	20
1101	130f. Ivory-billed woodpecker	1·70	40
1102	250f. Collie's magpie-jay	2·75	60
1103	300f. Mangrove cuckoo (horiz) (air)	3·00	70
1104	500f. Barn swallow (horiz)	5·25	1·30
MS1105	69×103 mm. 600f. Pileated woodpeckers	6·25	1·70

313 Delivering Post by Van

1985. "Philexafrique" Stamp Exhibition, Lome, Togo (1st issue). Multicoloured.

| 1106 | 200f. Type **313** | 2·30 | 1·10 |
| 1107 | 200f. Scouts and flag | 2·30 | 1·10 |

See also Nos. 1154/5.

314 Tiger and Rudyard
Kipling

1985. Int Youth Year (1st issue). Multicoloured.

1108	100f. Type **314**	1·20	40
1109	200f. Men on horseback and Joseph Kessel	2·20	80
1110	300f. Submarine gripped by octopus and Jules Verne	2·75	1·20
1111	400f. Mississippi stern-wheeler, Huckleberry Finn and Mark Twain	3·75	1·70

See also Nos. 1163/**MS**1169.

315 Louis Pasteur

1985. Anniversaries. Multicoloured.

1112	150f. Type **315** (centenary of discovery of anti-rabies vac-cine) (postage)	2·20	60
1113	200f. Henri Dunant (founder of Red Cross) and 125th anniv of Battle of Solferino (horiz)	2·50	80
1114	300f. Girl guides (75th anniv of Girl Guide Movement) (air)	2·20	1·20
1115	450f. Queen Elizabeth the Queen Mother (85th birthday)	4·00	2·00
1116	500f. Statue of Liberty (cent)	5·00	2·40

316 Pele and Footballers

1985. World Cup Football Championship, Mexico. Multicoloured.

1117	5f. Type **316** (postage)	10	10
1118	10f. Harald "Tony" Schumacher	10	10
1119	20f. Paolo Rossi	10	15
1120	350f. Kevin Keegan (wrongly inscr "Kervin")	3·25	1·00
1121	400f. Michel Platini (air)	4·00	1·00
1122	500f. Karl Heinz Rummenigge	4·50	1·20
MS1123	94×64 mm. 600f. Diego Armando Maradona	5·25	1·50

317 La Kotto Waterfalls

1985
1124	**317**	65f. multicoloured	95	35
1125	**317**	90f. multicoloured	1·10	45
1126	**317**	130f. multicoloured	1·70	75

318 Pope with Hand raised in Blessing

1985. Papal Visit. Multicoloured.
1127	65f. Type **318**	1·00	35
1128	130f. Pope John Paul II in Communion robes	1·90	75

319 Soldier using Ox-drawn Plough

1985. Economic Campaign. Multicoloured.
1129	5f. Type **319**	15	10
1130	60f. Soldier sowing cotton	60	30
1131	130f. Soldier sowing cotton (different)	1·30	50

320 As Young Girl with her Brother

1985. 85th Birthday of Queen Elizabeth the Queen Mother. Multicoloured.
1132	100f. Type **320** (postage)	80	25
1133	200f. Queen Mary with Duke and Duchess of York	1·90	45
1134	300f. Duchess of York inspecting Irish Guards	3·00	85
1135	350f. Duke and Duchess of York with the young Princesses	3·25	95
1136	400f. In the Golden State Coach at Coronation of King George VI (air)	4·00	1·00
1137	500f. At the service for her Silver Wedding	5·00	1·30
MS1138 75×87 mm. 600f. Holding Prince Charles at his christening		5·25	1·50

321 Dr. Labusquiere and Map of Republic

1985. Eighth Death Anniv of General Doctor Labusquiere.
1139	**321**	10f. multicoloured	15	10
1140	**321**	45f. multicoloured	45	25
1141	**321**	110f. multicoloured	95	50

322 Mail Van delivering Parcels to Local Post Office

1985. Postal Service. Multicoloured.
1142	15f. Type **322**	15	10
1143	60f. Van collecting mail from local post office	60	25
1144	150f. Vans at main post office	1·50	75

323 Gagarin, Korolev and Space Station Complex

1985. Space Research. Multicoloured.
1145	40f. Type **323** (postage)	30	10
1146	110f. Copernicus and "Cassini" space probe	1·00	40
1147	240f. Galileo and "Viking" orbiter	2·20	70
1148	300f. T. von Karman and astronaut recovering satellite	2·75	80
1149	450f. Percival Lowell and "Viking" space probe (air)	4·75	1·00
1150	500f. Dr. U. Merbold and "Columbus" space station	5·00	1·20
MS1151 96×68 mm. 600f. "Apollo II" capsule and astronaut		5·50	1·50

324 Damara Solar Energy Plant

1985
1152	**324**	65f. multicoloured	80	30
1153	**324**	130f. multicoloured	1·40	65

325 Ouaka Sugar Refinery

1985. "Philexafrique" Stamp Exhibition, Lome, Togo (2nd issue). Multicoloured.
1154	250f. Nature studies	3·50	1·60
1155	250f. Type **325**	3·50	1·60

326 Pres. Mitterrand, Gen. Kolingba and Flags

1985. Visit of President Mitterrand of France.
1156	**326**	65f. multicoloured	65	25
1157	**326**	130f. multicoloured	1·30	50
1158	**326**	160f. multicoloured	1·90	80

327 Map and U.N. Emblem

1985. 40th Anniv of UNO and 25th Anniv of Central African Republic Membership.
1159	**327**	140f. multicoloured	1·30	60

328 Virgin and Angels (Master of Burgo de Osma)

1985. Air. Christmas. Multicoloured.
1160	100f. Type **328**	1·00	35
1161	200f. Nativity (Louis Le Nain)	2·20	85
1162	400f. Virgin and Child with Dove (Piero di Cosimo)	4·00	1·60

329 Leonardo da Vinci and Madonna of the Eyelet

1985. Int Youth Year (2nd issue). Multicoloured.
1163	40f. Type **329** (postage)	55	10
1164	80f. Johann Sebastian Bach	95	25
1165	100f. Diego Velasquez and St. John of Patmos	1·20	40
1166	250f. Franz Schubert and illustration of King of Aulnes	2·50	60
1167	400f. Francisco Goya and Vicente Osario de Moscoso (air)	4·25	1·00
1168	500f. Wolfang Amadeus Mozart	4·75	1·20
MS1169 79×79 mm. 600f. Pablo Picasso and Woman in Plumed Hat		6·50	1·80

330 Halley and "Comet"

1985. Appearance of Halley's Comet (1st issue). Multicoloured.
1170	100f. Type **330** (postage)	75	25
1171	200f. Newton's telescope	1·80	45
1172	300f. Halley and Newton observing comet	2·75	80
1173	350f. American space probe and comet	3·25	1·00
1174	400f. Sun, Russian space probe and diagram of comet trajectory (air)	3·75	95
1175	400f. Infra-red picture of comet	4·75	1·20
MS1176 70×100 mm. 600f. American space probe, Earth, sun and comet		5·50	1·60
See also No. 1184/8.			

331 Columbus with Globe

1986. 480th Death Anniv of Christopher Columbus (explorer). Multicoloured.
1177	90f. Type **331** (postage)	95	25
1178	110f. Receiving blessing	1·20	40
1179	240f. Crew going ashore in rowing boat	2·40	1·00
1180	300f. Columbus with American Indians	3·00	80
1181	400f. Ships at sea in storm (air)	4·25	1·60
1182	500f. Sun breaking through clouds over fleet	5·00	1·90
MS1183 71×100 mm. 600f. Columbus		5·25	1·50

332 Halley and Comet

1986. Air. Appearance of Halley's Comet (2nd issue). Multicoloured.
1184	110f. Type **332**	95	25
1185	130f. "Giotto" space probe	1·30	25
1186	200f. Comet and globe	2·00	55
1187	300f. "Vega" space probe	2·75	75
1188	400f. Space shuttle	4·00	1·00

1986. Nos. 874/5 surch.
1188a	30f. on 175f. multicoloured		
1188b	**259**	65f. on 300f. multicoloured	

333 Spiky Hair Style

1986. Traditional Hair Styles. Multicoloured.
1189	20f. Type **333**	35	10
1190	30f. Braids around head	40	20
1191	65f. Plaits	55	35
1192	160f. Braids from front to back of head	2·20	70

334 Communications

1986. Franco-Central African Week. Multicoloured.
1193	40f. Type **334**	45	15
1194	60f. Youth	55	25
1195	100f. Basket weaver (craft)	1·20	45
1196	130f. Cyclists (sport)	1·70	60

335 Allamanda neriifolia

1986. Flora and Fauna. Multicoloured.
1197	25f. Type **335** (postage)	30	15
1198	65f. Bongo (horiz)	85	25
1199	160f. Plumieria acuminata	1·80	40
1200	300f. Cheetah (horiz)	3·50	85
1201	400f. Eulophia erthoplata (air)	4·00	1·00
1202	500f. Leopard (horiz)	5·25	1·20
MS1203 100×69 mm. 600f. Giant eland and Eulophia cucllata (50×29)		5·50	1·70

336 Palm Tree and Bossongo Oil Refinery

1986. Centrapalm. Multicoloured.
1204	25f. Type **336**	30	20
1205	65f. Type **336**	75	45
1206	120f. Palm tree and Bossongo agro-industrial complex	1·30	75
1207	160f. As No. 1206	1·70	90

337 Pointer

1986. Dogs and Cats. Multicoloured.
1208	10f. Type **337** (postage)	20	15
1209	20f. Egyptian mau	45	25
1210	200f. Newfoundland	2·50	70
1211	300f. Borzoi (air)	3·25	70
1212	400f. Persian red	4·75	1·10
MS1213 95×60 mm. 500f. Spaniel and Burmese		5·50	1·60

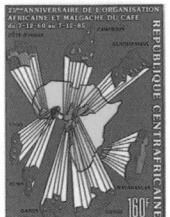

338 Map of Africa showing Member Countries

1986. 25th Anniv of African and Malagasy Coffee Producers Organization. Multicoloured.
| 1214 | **338** | 160f. multicoloured | 1·70 | 70 |

339 Trophy, Brazilian flag, L.-A. Muller and Socrates

1986. World Cup Football Championship, Mexico. Multicoloured.
1215	30f. Type **339** (postage)	30	15
1216	110f. Trophy, Belgian flag, V. Scifo and F. Ceulemans	1·00	45
1217	160f. Trophy, French flag, Y. Stopyra and M. Platini	1·50	55
1218	350f. Trophy, West German flag, A. Brehme and H. Schumacher	3·25	90
1219	450f. Trophy, Argentinian flag and Diego Maradona (air)	4·25	1·20
MS1220	110×68 mm. 500f. Hands holding trophy, H. Schumacher and J. L. Burruehaga (50×35 mm)	5·25	1·70

340 Judith Resnik and Astronaut

1986. Anniversaries and "Challenger" Astronauts Commemoration. Multicoloured.
MS1227	86×86 mm. 500f. "Challenger" crew (50×41 mm)	4·50	1·50
1221	15f. Type **340** (postage)	20	10
1222	25f. Frederic Bartholdi and torch (centenary of Statue of Liberty)	35	10
1223	70f. Elvis Presley (9th death anniv)	1·30	25
1224	300f. Ronald MacNair and man watching astronaut on screen	3·00	80
1226	450f. Christa McAulife and Shuttle lifting off (air)	4·25	1·50
1225	485f. on 70f. No. 1223	6·75	1·40

341 People around Globe within Emblem

1986. International Peace Year.
| 1228 | **341** | 160f. multicoloured | 1·60 | 65 |

342 Globe, Douglas DC-10 and "25"

1986. 25th Anniv of Air Afrique.
| 1229 | **342** | 200f. multicoloured | 1·80 | 85 |

343 Emblem and Flag as Map

1986. UNICEF Child Survival Campaign. Multicoloured.
1230	15f. Type **343**	10	10
1231	130f. Doctor vaccinating child	1·30	60
1232	160f. Basket of fruit and boy holding fish on map	1·50	75

344 Nativity (detail, Giotto)

1986. Air. Christmas. Multicoloured.
1233	250f. Type **344**	2·30	1·10
1234	440f. Adoration of the Magi (detail, Sandro Botticelli) (vert)	4·25	1·60
1235	500f. Nativity (detail, Giotto) (different)	5·00	2·00

345 Transmission Mast, People with Radios and Baskets of Produce

1986. African Telecommunications Day. Telecommunications and Agriculture. Mult.
| 1236 | 170f. Type **345** (Rural Radio Agriculture Project) | 1·90 | 95 |
| 1237 | 265f. Lorry, satellite, men using telephones and sacks of produce | 2·75 | 1·40 |

346 Steam Locomotive Class DH 2 Green Elephant and Alfred de Glehn

1986. 150th Anniv of German Railways. Multicoloured.
1238	40f. Type **346** (postage)	50	10
1239	70f. Rudolf Diesel (engineer) and steam locomotive No. 1829 Rheingold	75	45
1240	160f. Electric locomotive Type 103 Rapide and Carl Golsdorf	1·90	55
1241	300f. Wilhelm Schmidt and Beyer-Garratt type steam locomotive	3·25	90
1242	400f. De Bousquet and compound locomotive Class 3500 (air)	4·00	1·20
MS1243	83×67 mm. 500f. Werner von Siemens (electrical engineer) and electric locomotive	5·00	1·50

347 Player returning Ball

1986. Air. Olympic Games, Seoul (1988) (1st issue). Tennis. Multicoloured.
1244	150f. Type **347**	1·70	55
1245	250f. Player serving (vert)	2·75	75
1246	440f. Right-handed player returning to left-handed player (vert)	4·25	1·40
1247	600f. Left-handed player returning to right-handed player	6·00	1·60
See also Nos. 1261/4, 1310/13 and 1315/18.

348 "Miranda" Satellite, Uranus, "Mariner II' and William Herschel (astronomer)

1987. Space Research. Multicoloured.
1248	25f. Type **348** (postage)	30	10
1249	65f. Mars Rover vehicle and Werner von Braun (rocket pioneer)	70	20
1250	160f. "Mariner II", Titan and Rudolf Hanel	1·50	40
1251	300f. Space ship "Hermes", space platform "Eureka" and Patrick Baudry	2·75	80

1987. Air. Halley's Comet.
| 1252 | 400f. Halley's Comet, "Giotto" space probe and Dr. U. Keller (air) | 3·50 | 1·10 |
| 1253 | 500f. European space station "Columbus", Wubbo Ockels and Ulf Merbold | 4·50 | 1·20 |

349 Footballer and "Woman with Umbrella" Fountain

1987. Olympic Games, Barcelona (1992). Multicoloured.
1255	30f. Type **349** (postage)	35	15
1256	150f. Judo competitors and Barcelona Cathedral	1·30	50
1257	265f. Cyclist and Church of the Holy Family	2·50	80
1258	350f. Diver and Christopher Columbus's tomb (air)	3·25	1·00
1259	495f. Runner and human tower	4·75	1·50

350 Triple Jumping

1987. Air. Olympic Games, Seoul (1988) (2nd issue). Multicoloured.
1261	100f. Type **350**	95	35
1262	200f. High jumping (horiz)	1·80	75
1263	300f. Long jumping (horiz)	2·75	1·10
1264	400f. Pole vaulting	3·50	1·50
MS1265	104×86 mm. 500f. High jumping (different) (horiz)	4·50	2·50

351 Two-man Luge

1987. Winter Olympic Games, Calgary (1988) (1st issue). Multicoloured.
1266	20f. Type **351** (postage)	30	10
1267	140f. Cross-country skiing	1·40	55
1268	250f. Figure skating	2·30	70
1269	300f. Ice hockey (air)	2·75	90
1270	400f. Slalom	3·75	1·20
MS1271	130×77 mm. 500f. Downhill skiing	4·50	1·50
See also Nos. 1320/MS1324.

352 Peace Medal

1987. International Peace Year (1986).
| 1272 | **352** | 50f. brown, blue & blk | 45 | 25 |
| 1273 | **352** | 160f. brown, grn & blk | 1·50 | 1·30 |

1987. Tenth Death Anniv of Elvis Presley (singer). Nos. 1223 and 1225 optd **Elvis Presley 1977–1987.**
| 1274 | 70f. multicoloured | 95 | 25 |
| 1275 | 485f. on 70f. multicoloured | 5·75 | 1·70 |

354 Woman at Village Pump

1987. International Decade of Drinkable Water. Multicoloured.
1276	5f. Type **354**	33·00	
1277	10f. Woman at village pump (different)	33·00	
1278	200f. Three women at village pump	38·00	

355 Charaxes candiope

1987. Butterflies. Multicoloured.
1279	100f. Type **355**	1·50	65
1280	120f. Graphium leonidas	2·00	75
1281	130f. Charaxes brutus	2·20	80
1282	160f. Salamis aetiops	2·50	1·00

356 Nola Football Team

1987. Campaign for Integration of Pygmies.
| 1283 | 356 | 90f. multicoloured | 1·50 | 80 |
| 1284 | 356 | 160f. multicoloured | 2·00 | 1·20 |

357 James Madison (U.S. President, 1809–17)

1987. Anniversaries and Celebrities. Multicoloured.
1285	40f. Type **357** (bicent of U.S. constitution) (postage)	45	15
1286	160f. Queen Elizabeth II and Prince Philip (40th wedding anniv)	1·50	25
1287	200f. Steffi Graf (tennis player)	2·00	55
1288	300f. Gary Kasparov (chess champion) and The Chess Players (after Honore Daumier) (air)	3·00	85
1289	400f. Boris Becker (tennis player)	3·75	1·30
MS1290	86×86 mm. 500f. Scene from Orpheus (opera) and Christoph Wilibald Gluck (composer, death bicent) (50×35 mm)	5·50	1·50

358 Brontosaurus

1988. Prehistoric Animals. Multicoloured.
1291	50f. Type **358**	50	15
1292	65f. Triceratops	65	20
1293	100f. Ankylosaurus	1·00	35
1294	160f. Stegosaurus	1·60	55
1295	200f. Tyrannosaurus rex (vert)	2·00	75
1296	240f. Corythosaurus (vert)	2·40	85
1297	300f. Allosaurus (vert)	3·00	1·10
1298	350f. Brachiosaurus (vert)	3·75	1·40

359 Pres. Kolingba vaccinating Baby

1988. 40th Anniv of WHO.
| 1299 | 359 | 70f. multicoloured | 75 | 45 |
| 1300 | 359 | 120f. multicoloured | 1·20 | 65 |

360 Carmine Bee Eater

1988. Scouts and Birds. Multicoloured.

1301	25f. Type **360** (postage)	30	15
1302	170f. Red-crowned bishop	1·50	60
1303	300f. Lesser pied kingfisher	3·00	1·40
1304	400f. Red-cheeked cordon-bleu (air)	2·75	1·60
1305	450f. Lizard buzzard	3·25	2·10
MS1306	90×70 mm. 500f. Splendid glossy starling	5·25	1·70

361 Schools replanting Campaign

1988. National Tree Day. Multicoloured.

1307	50f. Type **361**	45	25
1308	100f. Type **361**	95	60
1309	130f. Felling tree and planting saplings	1·50	75

362 1972 100f. Stamp and Beam Exercise

1988. Air. Olympic Games, Seoul (3rd issue). Gymnastics. Multicoloured.

1310	90f. Type **362**	95	35
1311	200f. 1964 50f. stamp and beam exercise (horiz)	1·80	65
1312	300f. 1964 100f. stamp and vault exercise (horiz)	2·75	1·10
1313	400f. 1964 250f. stamp and parallel bars exercise (horiz)	3·50	1·50
MS1314	105×85 mm. 500f. 1972 100f. stamp and ring exercise (horiz)	4·50	2·30

363 Running

1988. Olympic Games, Seoul (4th issue). Multicoloured.

1315	150f. Type **363** (postage)	1·50	25
1316	300f. Judo	2·75	80
1317	400f. Football (air)	3·00	1·00
1318	450f. Tennis	4·50	1·40
MS1319	70×100 mm. 500f. Boxing (horiz)	4·50	1·50

364 Cross-country Skiing

1988. Winter Olympic Games, Calgary (2nd issue). Multicoloured.

1320	170f. Type **364** (postage)	1·50	45
1321	350f. Ice hockey	3·00	80
1322	400f. Downhill skiing (air)	2·75	80
1323	450f. Slalom	3·75	1·20
MS1324	122×85 mm. 500f. Slalom (horiz)	4·50	1·40

1988. Nos. 1302/5 surch.

1325	30f. on 170f. mult (postage)	40	20
1326	70f. on 300f. mult	1·10	65
1327	160f. on 400f. mult (air)	1·90	1·00
1328	200f. on 450f. mult	2·75	1·40

366 Hospital and Grounds

1988. First Anniv of L'Amitie Hospital. Multicoloured.

1329	5f. Type **366**	45	25
1330	60f. Aerial view of hospital complex	95	55
1331	160f. Hospital entrance	1·50	80

367 Buildings Complex

1988. 30th Anniv of Republic. Multicoloured.

| 1332 | 65f. Family on map, flags and dove | 50·00 | |
| 1334 | 240f. Type **367** | 50·00 | |

368 Kristine Otto (East Germany)

1989. Olympic Games, Seoul, Gold Medal Winners. Multicoloured.

1335	150f. Type **368** (100 m butterfly and 100 m backstroke) (postage)	1·80	55
1336	240f. Matt Biondi (100 m freestyle)	2·75	80
1337	300f. Florence Griffith-Joyner (U.S.A.) (100 and 200 m sprints)	3·50	90
1338	450f. Pierre Durand (France) (show jumping) (air)	5·50	1·30
MS1339	98×68 mm. 600f. Carl Lewis (USA) (100m., 200m., long jump relay)	6·25	1·80

369 Hebmuller and Volkswagen Cabriolet, 1953

1989. Transport. Multicoloured.

1340	20f. Type **369** (postage)	30	10
1341	205f. Werner von Siemens and his first electric locomotive, 1879	2·00	70
1342	300f. Dennis Conner and *Stars and Stripes* (winner of Americas Cup yacht races)	2·75	80
1343	400f. Andre Citroen and "16 Six" car, 1955	3·75	1·40
1344	450f. Mare Seguin and Decauville Mallet locomotive, 1895 (air)	4·00	1·40
MS1345	80×75 mm. 750f. Duesenberg brothers and "J" Phaeton, 1929 (41×29 mm)	6·75	2·10

370 Allegory in Honour of Liberty

1989. Bicentenary of French Revolution and "Philexfrance 89" International Stamp Exhibition, Paris (1st issue). Multicoloured.

| 1346 | 200f. Type **370** | 2·50 | 80 |

| 1347 | 300f. Declaration of Rights of Man | 3·00 | 1·50 |
| **MS**1348 | 113×80 mm. 500f. Demolition of the Bastille (51×40 mm) | 5·00 | 3·25 |

See also Nos. 1366/**MS**1370.

371 Statue of Liberty at Night

1989. Centenary of Statue of Liberty. Multicoloured.

1349	150f. Type **371**	1·50	70
1350	150f. Maintenance worker	1·50	70
1351	150f. Close-up of face	1·50	80
1352	200f. Maintenance worker (different)	1·80	1·10
1353	200f. Colour party in front of statue	1·80	1·10
1354	200f. Close-up of head at night	1·80	1·10

373 "Apollo 11" Astronaut on Moon

1989. Air. 20th Anniv of First Manned Landing on Moon. Multicoloured.

1355	40f. Type **373**	35	20
1356	80f. "Apollo 15" astronaut and moon buggy	75	30
1357	130f. "Apollo 16" module landing in sea	1·50	55
1358	1000f. "Apollo 17" astronaut on Moon	9·00	2·75

374 Champagnat, Map and "Madonna and Child"

1989. Birth Bicentenary of Marcelino Champagnat (founder of Marist Brothers). Multicoloured.

1359	15f. Type **374**	10	10
1360	50f. Champagnat, cross, globe and emblem	45	25
1361	160f. Champagnat and flags (horiz)	1·60	1·20

375 Food Products

1989. Bambari Harvest Festival. Multicoloured.

| 1362 | 100f. Type **375** | 1·00 | 60 |
| 1363 | 160f. Ploughing with oxen | 1·60 | 75 |

376 Raising of Livestock

1989. World Food Day. Multicoloured.

| 1364 | 60f. Type **376** | 55 | 40 |
| 1365 | 240f. Soldiers catching poachers | 2·40 | 1·20 |

377 Gen. Kellermann and Battle of Valmy

1989. Bicentenary of French Revolution and "Philexfrance 89" International Stamp Exhibition, Paris (2nd issue). Multicoloured.

1366	160f. Type **377**	1·80	40
1367	200f. Gen. Dumouriez and Battle of Jemappes (wrongly inscr "JEMMAPES")	2·40	60
1368	500f. Gen. Pichegru and capture of Dutch fleet (air)	5·50	1·30
1369	600f. Gen. Hoche and Royalist landing at Quiberon	6·50	1·20
MS1370	160×107 mm. 1000f. Napoleon Bonaparte and Battle of Rivoli (60×50 mm)	14·50	3·75

378 Players and Trophy

1989. Victory in 1987 African Basketball Championships, Tunis (1st issue). Multicoloured.

1371	160f. Type **378**	1·50	70
1372	240f. National team with medals and trophy (horiz)	2·00	95
1373	500f. Type **378**	5·00	2·10

See also Nos. 1383/4.

379 Governor's Palace, 1906

1989. Centenary of Bangui. Multicoloured.

1374	100f. Type **379**	1·00	45
1375	160f. Bangui post office	1·70	95
1376	200f. A. Dosilie (founder of Bangui post office) (vert)	2·10	1·00
1377	1000f. Michel Dolisie and Chief Gbembo agreeing peace pact (vert)	9·75	4·50

380 Footballer and Palermo Cathedral Belltower

1989. World Cup Football Championship, Italy (1990) (1st issue). Multicoloured.

1378	20f. Type **380** (postage)	15	20
1379	160f. Footballer and St. Francis's church, Bologna	1·50	45
1380	200f. Footballer and Old Palace, Florence	2·00	70
1381	120f. Footballer and Church of Trinita dei Monti, Rome (air)	1·20	55
MS1382	83×84 mm. 1000f. Footballer and Milan cathedral (30×42 mm)	10·00	2·30

See also Nos. 1405/8.

381 Trophy and Map of Africa

1990. Victory in 1987 African Basketball Championships, Tunis (2nd issue).

| 1383 | **381** 100f. multicoloured | 95 | 45 |
| 1384 | **381** 130f. multicoloured | 1·30 | 70 |

382 Tree with Map as Foliage

1990. Inauguration (1989) of Forest Conservation Organization.

1385	**382**	160f. multicoloured	1·70	70

383 Speed Skating

1990. Winter Olympic Games, Albertville (1992). Multicoloured.

1386	10f. Type **383** (postage)	15	15	
1387	60f. Cross-country skiing	55	40	
1388	500f. Slalom skiing (air)	4·50	1·10	
1389	750f. Ice dancing	6·75	1·60	
MS1390	105×71 mm. 1000f. Skiing	8·75	2·10	

384 *Euphaera eusemoides*

1990. Scouts and Butterflies. Multicoloured.

1391	25f. Type **384**	30	15	
1392	65f. Becker's glider	55	25	
1393	160f. *Pseudacraea clarki*	1·50	40	
1394	250f. Giant charaxes	2·40	70	
1395	300f. *Euphaedra gausape*	2·75	75	
1396	500f. Red swallowtail	4·50	1·10	
MS1397	131×103 mm. 1000f. *Euphaedra edwardsi*	9·50	2·20	

385 Throwing the Javelin

1990. Olympic Games, Barcelona (1992). Multicoloured.

1398	10f. Type **385** (postage)	15	15	
1399	40f. Running	40	25	
1400	130f. Tennis	1·20	40	
1401	240f. Hurdling (horiz)	2·20	55	
1402	400f. Yachting (horiz) (air)	3·75	1·00	
1403	500f. Football (horiz)	4·75	1·30	
MS1404	95×68 mm. 1000f. Boxing (38×27 mm)	8·75	2·10	

386 Footballers and Globe

1990. Air. World Cup Football Championship, Italy (2nd issue).

1405	**386**	5f. multicoloured	20	10
1406	-	30f. multicoloured	30	15
1407	-	500f. multicoloured	5·00	1·10
1408	-	1000f. multicoloured	8·75	2·10

DESIGNS: 30 to 1000f. Various footballing scenes.

387 Pres. Gorbachev of U.S.S.R., Map of Malta and Pres. Bush of U.S.A.

1990. Anniversaries and Events. Multicoloured.

1409	120f. Type **387** (summit conference, Malta) (postage)	95	25
1410	130f. Sir Rowland Hill and Penny Black (150th anniv of first postage stamps)	1·20	25
1411	160f. Galileo space probe and planet Jupiter	1·30	25
1412	200f. Pres. Gorbachev meeting Pope John Paul II, statue of Saturn and dove	1·80	40
1413	240f. Neil Armstrong and eagle (21st anniv of first manned landing on Moon)	2·20	55
1414	250f. Concorde, German experimental Maglev train and Rotary International emblem	2·40	70
1415	300f. Don Mattingly (baseball player) and New York Yankees club badge (air)	2·75	70
1416	500f. Charles de Gaulle (French statesman, birth centenary)	4·75	1·10
MS1417	82×112 mm. 1000f. Astronauts and rocket (35×50 mm)	8·75	2·10

388 AIDS Information on Radio, Television and Leaflets

1991. Anti-AIDS Campaign. Multicoloured.

1418	5f. Type **388**	25	10
1419	70f. Type **388**	1·00	50
1420	120f. Lecture on AIDS (vert)	1·50	75

389 Demonstrators

1991. Protection of Animals. Multicoloured.

1421	15f. Type **389**	40	10
1422	60f. Type **389**	1·50	35
1423	100f. Decrease in elephant population, 1945–2045 (vert)	2·20	50

390 Butter Catfish

1991. Fishes. Multicoloured.

1424	50f. Type **390**	85	25
1425	160f. Type **390**	2·00	80
1426	240f. Distichodus	3·00	1·40

391 President Kolingba

1992. Tenth Anniv (1991) of Assumption of Power by Military Committee under Andre Kolingba.

1427	**391**	160f. multicoloured	1·50	65

392 Count Ferdinand von Zeppelin (airship pioneer)

1992. Celebrities, Anniversaries and Events. Multicoloured.

1428	80f. Type **392** (75th death anniv) (postage)	80	20
1429	140f. Henri Dunant (founder of Red Cross)	1·50	45
1430	160f. Michael Schumacher (racing driver)	1·80	70
1431	350f. Brandenburg Gate (bicent) and Konrad Adenauer (German Federal Republic Chancellor) signing 1949 constitution	4·25	1·20
1432	500f. Pope John Paul II (tour of West Africa) (air)	5·50	1·20
1433	600f. Wolfgang Amadeus Mozart (composer, death bicent (1991))	6·50	1·40
MS1434	81×105 mm. 1000f. Christopher Columbus, *Santa Maria* and 15th-cent view of La Cartuja de las Cuevas (Expo' 92 World's Fair, Seville)	9·50	2·10

393 Dam

1993. River M'Bali Dam. Multicoloured.

1435	160f. Type **393**	1·50	70
1436	200f. People fishing near dam (self-sufficiency in food)	2·00	90

394 Compass Rose and Organization Emblem

1993. International Customs Day and 40th Anniv of Customs Co-operation Council.

1437	**394**	240f. multicoloured	2·30	1·40

395 Breastfeeding

1993. International Nutrition Conference, Rome (1992). Multicoloured.

1438	90f. Type **395**	75	40
1439	140f. Foodstuffs	1·30	70

396 Bangui University

1993

1440	**396**	100f. multicoloured	95	40

397 Masako Owada as Baby

1993. Wedding of Crown Prince Naruhito of Japan and Masako Owada. Multicoloured.

1441	50f. Type **397** (postage)	40	25
1442	65f. Prince Naruhito as child with parents	60	25
1443	160f. Masako Owada at Harvard University, U.S.A.	1·60	55
1444	450f. Prince Naruhito at Oxford University (air)	4·25	1·20
MS1445	184×83 mm. 750f. Prince Naruhito and Masako Owada	6·75	1·80

398 Presley singing *Heartbreak Hotel* (1956)

1993. 16th Death Anniv of Elvis Presley (entertainer). Multicoloured.

1446	200f. Type **398**	2·10	55
1447	300f. *Love Me Tender*, 1957	3·00	80
1448	400f. *Jailhouse Rock*, 1957	3·75	1·40
1449	600f. *Harum Scarum*, 1965 (air)	5·50	1·40
MS1450	98×69 mm. 1000f. Elvis performing (35×50 mm)	8·75	2·30

399 First World Cup Final, 1928, and Uruguay v. Argentina, 1930

1993. World Cup Football Championship, U.S.A. (1994). History of the World Cup. Multicoloured.

1451	40f. Type **399**	35	10
1452	50f. Italy v. Czechoslovakia, 1934, and Italy v. Hungary, 1938	45	10
1453	60f. Uruguay v. Brazil, 1950, and Germany v. Hungary, 1954	55	25
1454	80f. Brazil v. Sweden, 1958, and Brazil v. Czechoslovakia, 1962	75	25
1455	160f. England v. West Germany, 1966, and Brazil v. Italy, 1970	1·50	25
1456	200f. West Germany v. The Netherlands, 1974, and Argentina v. The Netherlands, 1978	1·80	40
1457	400f. Italy v. West Germany, 1982, and Argentina v. West Germany, 1986	3·50	70
1458	500f. West Germany v. Argentina, 1990, and 1994 Championship emblem and player	4·50	1·20
MS1459	101×85 mm. 1000f. West Germany and Argentina teams (59×29 mm)	8·75	2·10

400 Baron Pierre de Coubertin (founder of modern games)

1993. Centenary (1996) of Modern Olympic Games. Multicoloured.

1460	90f. Ancient Greek athlete	75	30
1461	90f. Type **400**	75	30
1462	90f. Charles Bennett (running), Paris, 1900	75	30
1463	90f. Etienne Desmarteau (stone throwing), St. Louis, 1904	75	30
1464	90f. Harry Porter (high jump), London, 1908	75	30
1465	90f. Patrick MacDonald (putting the shot), Stockholm, 1912	75	30
1466	90f. Coloured and black Olympic rings (1916)	75	30
1467	90f. Frank Loomis (400 m hurdles), Antwerp, 1920	75	30
1468	90f. Albert White (diving), Paris, 1924	95	35
1469	100f. El Ouafi (marathon), Amsterdam, 1928	95	35
1470	100f. Eddie Tolan (100 m), Los Angeles, 1932	95	35
1471	100f. Jesse Owens (100 m, long jump and 200 m hurdles), Berlin, 1936	95	35
1472	100f. Coloured and black Olympic rings (1940)	95	35
1473	100f. Coloured and black Olympic rings (1944)	95	35
1474	100f. Tapio Rautavaara (throwing the javelin), London, 1948	95	35
1475	100f. Jean Boiteux (400 m freestyle swimming), Helsinki, 1952	95	35
1476	100f. Petrus Kasterman (three-day equestrian event), Melbourne, 1956	95	35

1477	100f. Sante Gaiardoni (cycling), Rome, 1960	95	35
1478	160f. Anton Geesink (judo), Tokyo, 1964	1·50	45
1479	160f. Bob Beamon (long jump), Mexico, 1968	1·50	45
1480	160f. Mark Spitz (swimming), Munich, 1972	1·50	45
1481	160f. Nadia Comaneci (gymnastics (beam)), Montreal, 1976	1·50	45
1482	160f. Aleksandre Ditjatin (gymnastics (rings) and dressage), Moscow, 1980	1·50	45
1483	160f. J. F. Lamour (sabre), Los Angeles, 1984	1·50	45
1484	160f. Pierre Durand (show jumping, Seoul, 1988	1·50	45
1485	160f. Michael Jordan (basketball), Barcelona, 1992	1·50	45
1486	160f. Footballer and Games emblem, Atlanta, 1996	1·50	45

401 Man planting Sapling, and Animals

1993. Biodiversity. Multicoloured.

1487	100f. Type **401**	1·50	70
1488	130f. Man amongst flora and fauna (vert)	2·10	90

402 Woman selling Foodstuffs

1993. The Environment and Sustainable Development. Multicoloured.

1489	160f. Type **402**	1·50	70
1490	240f. Woman tending cooking pot	2·50	1·40

403 Saltoposuchus

1993. Prehistoric Animals. Multicoloured.

1491	25f. Type **403**	35	10
1492	25f. Rhamphorhynchus	35	10
1493	25f. Dimorphodon	35	10
1494	25f. Archaeopteryx	35	10
1495	30f. "Compsognathos longipes"	35	10
1496	30f. "Cryptocleidus oxoniensis"	35	10
1497	30f. Stegosaurus	35	10
1498	30f. Cetiosaurus	35	10
1499	50f. Brontosaurus	45	20
1500	50f. "Corythosaurus casuarius"	45	20
1501	50f. Styracosaurus	45	20
1502	50f. Gorgosaurus	45	20
1503	500f. Scolosaurus	4·75	1·00
1504	500f. Trachodon	4·75	1·00
1505	500f. Struthiomimus	4·75	1·00
1506	500f. "Tarbosaurus bataar"	4·75	1·00
MS1507	120×170 mm. 1000f. Tylosaur (50×59 mm) (air)	10·00	2·30

Nos. 1491/1506 were issued together, *se-tenant*, forming a composite design of a volcanic landscape.

404 Th. Haug (combined skiing, Chamonix, 1924)

1994. Winter Olympic Games, Lillehammer, Norway. Previous Medal Winners. Multicoloured.

1508	100f. Type **404**	1·00	25
1509	100f. J. Heaton (luge, St. Moritz, 1928)	1·00	25

1510	100f. B. Ruud (ski jumping, Lake Placid, 1932)	1·00	25
1511	100f. I. Ballangrud (speed skating, Garmisch-Partenkirchen, 1936)	1·00	25
1512	100f. G. Fraser (slalom, St. Moritz, 1948)	1·00	25
1513	100f. West German 4-man bobsleigh team (Oslo, 1952)	1·00	25
1514	100f. U.S.S.R. ice hockey team (Cortina d'Ampezzo, 1956)	1·00	25
1515	100f. J. Vuarnet (downhill skiing, Squaw Valley, 1960)	1·00	25
1516	200f. M. Goitschel (giant slalom, Innsbruck, 1964)	1·70	45
1517	200f. Jean-Claud Killy (special slalom, Grenoble, 1968)	1·70	45
1518	200f. U. Wehling (cross-country skiing, Sapporo, 1972)	1·70	45
1519	200f. Irina Rodnina and Aleksandr Zaitsev (figure skating, Innsbruck, 1976)	1·70	45
1520	200f. E. Heiden (speed skating, Lake Placid, 1980)	1·70	45
1521	200f. Katarina Witt (figure skating, Sarajevo, 1984)	1·70	45
1522	200f. J. Mueller (single luge, Calgary, 1988)	1·70	45
1523	200f. E. Grospiron (acrobatic skiing, Albertville, 1992)	1·70	45
1524	200f. Speed skiing, Lillehammer, 1994	1·70	45

405 Ansellia africa

1994. Flowers, Vegetables, Fruit and Fungi. Multicoloured.

1525	25f. Type **405**	10	10
1526	30f. Yams	30	10
1527	40f. Oranges	30	10
1528	50f. Termite mushroom	40	10
1529	60f. *Polystachia bella* (flower)	45	10
1530	65f. Manioc	55	10
1531	70f. Banana	55	10
1532	80f. *Synpodia arborescens* (wrongly inscr "Sympodia") (fungi)	75	10
1533	90f. *Aerangis rhodosticta* (flower)	75	10
1534	100f. Maize	85	10
1535	160f. Mango	1·40	25
1536	200f. *Phlebopus sudanicus* (fungi)	1·70	25
1537	300f. Coffee beans	2·75	45
1538	400f. Sweet potato	3·75	55
1539	500f. *Angraecum eburneum* (flower)	4·50	75
1540	600f. *Leucocoprinus africanus* (fungi)	5·25	90

Nos. 1525/40 were issued together, *se-tenant*, the backgrounds forming a composite design.

MILITARY FRANK STAMPS

1963. Optd FM. No. M1 also has the value obliterated with two bars. Centre multicoloured; frame colour given.

M35	1	(–) on 15f. blue	14·50
M36	1	15f. blue	15·00

OFFICIAL STAMPS

O41 Arms

1965

O78	**O41**	1f. multicoloured	10	10
O79	**O41**	2f. multicoloured	10	10
O80	**O41**	5f. multicoloured	10	10
O81	**O41**	10f. multicoloured	30	10
O82	**O41**	20f. multicoloured	50	25
O83	**O41**	30f. multicoloured	90	55
O84	**O41**	50f. multicoloured	1·00	80
O85	**O41**	100f. multicoloured	2·50	1·20
O86	**O41**	130f. multicoloured	4·00	2·30
O87	**O41**	200f. multicoloured	6·00	3·00

O109 Arms

1971

O238	**O109**	5f. multicoloured	10	10
O239	**O109**	30f. multicoloured	50	25
O240	**O109**	40f. multicoloured	85	25
O241	**O109**	100f. multicoloured	1·50	55
O242	**O109**	140f. multicoloured	2·20	80
O243	**O109**	200f. multicoloured	3·50	1·40

POSTAGE DUE STAMPS

D15 *Sternotomis gama* (Beetle)

1962. Beetles.

D33	50c. brown and turquoise	10	10
D34	50c. turquoise and brown	10	10
D35	1f. brown and green	20	20
D36	1f. green and brown	20	20
D37	2f. pink and black	25	25
D38	2f. green, black and pink	25	25
D39	5f. green and brown	45	40
D40	5f. green and brown	45	40
D41	10f. green, black and drab	75	75
D42	10f. drab, black and green	75	75
D43	25f. brown, black and green	2·00	1·90
D44	25f. brown, green and black	2·00	1·90

DESIGNS: No. D33, Type D **15**; D34, *Sternotomis virescens*; D35, *Augosoma centaurus*; D36, *Phosphorus virescens* and *Ceroplesis carabarica*; D37, *Ceroplesis S.P.*; D38, *Cetoine scaraboidae*; D39, *Cetoine scaraboidae*; D40, *Macrorhina S.P.*; D41, *Taurina longiceps*; D42, *Phryneta leprosa*; D43, *Monohamus griseoplagiatus*; D44, *Jambonus trifasciatus*.

D308 Giant Pangolin (*Manis gigantea*)

1985

D1080	**D308**	5f. multicoloured	40	35
D1081	**D308**	20f. multicoloured	70	70
D1082	**D308**	30f. multicoloured	80	80

APPENDIX

The following stamps have either been issued in excess of postal needs or have not been availble to the public in reasonable quantities at face value. Such stamps may later be given full listing if there is evidence of regular postal use.

All the stamps listed below are embossed on gold foil.

1977

Coronation of Emperor Bokassa. Air 2500f.

1978

100 Years of Progress in Posts and Telecommunications. Air 1500f.
Death Centenary of Sir Rowland Hill. Air 1500f.

1979

International Year of the Child. Air 1500f.
Olympic Games, Moscow. Air 1500f. ("The Discus-thrower")
Space Exploration. Air 1500f.

1980

Olympic Games, Moscow. Air 1500f. (Relay)
European-African Co-operation. Air 1500f.
World Cup Football Championship, Spain. Air 1500f.

1981

Olympic Games Medal Winners. 1980 Olympic Games issue optd. Air 1500f.
Birth Centenary of Pablo Picasso. Air 1500f.
Wedding of Prince of Wales. Air 1500f.
Navigators. Air 1500f.
Christmas. Air 1500f.

1982

Animals and Rotary International. Air 1500f.
Transport. Air 1500f.
21st Birthday of Princess of Wales. Air 1500f.
Olympic Games, Los Angeles. Air 1500f. (horiz)
Space Resources. Air 1500f.

1983

Chess Masters. Air 1500f.
World Cup Football Championship, Spain. Air 1500f.
Car Manufacturers. Air 1500f.
Olympic Games, Los Angeles. Air 1500f.
Olympic Games, Los Angeles. Air 1500f. (vert)
Bicentenary of manned flight. Air 1500f.

1984

Winter Olympic Gold Medalists. Air 1500f.
Celebrities. Air 1500f.

1985

85th Birthday of Queen Elizabeth the Queen Mother. Air 1500f.
Appearence of Halley's Comet. Air 1500f.
480th Death Anniv of Christopher Columbus. Air 1500f.

1988

Olympic Games, Seoul. Air 1500f.
Scouts and Birds. Air 1500f.

1989

Olympic Games, Seoul, Gold Medal Winner. Air 1500f.
Bicentenary of French Revolution. Air 1500f.
World Cup Football Championship, Italy. Air 1500f.

1990

Winter Olympic Games, Albertville (1992). Air 1500f.
Scouts and Butterflies. Air 1500f.
Birth Centenary of Charles de Gaulle. Air 1500f.

1993

Wedding of Crown Prince Naruhito of Japan and Masako Owada. Air 1500f.
16th Death Anniv of Elvis Presley. Air 1500f.
World Cup Football Championship, U.S.A. (1994). Air 1500f.
Visit of Pope John Paul II to Africa. Air 1500f.

1994

Winter Olympic Games, Lillehammer. Air 1500f.

Pt. 10

CENTRAL LITHUANIA

Became temporarily independent in 1918 and was subsequently absorbed by Poland.

100 fenigi = 1 mark.

POLISH OCCUPATION

1

1920. Imperf or perf.

1	1	25f. red	10	10
20	1	25f. green	20	30
2	1	1m. blue	10	10
21	1	1m. brown	20	30
3	1	2m. violet	15	15
22	1	2m. yellow	20	30

1920. Stamps of Lithuania of 1919 surch **SRODKOWA LITWA POCZTA**, new value and Arms of Poland and Lithuania. Perf.

4	5	4m. on 15s. violet	6·50	8·00
5	5	4m. on 10s. red	4·00	5·00
6	5	4m. on 20s. blue	6·00	8·00
7	5	4m. on 30s. orange	5·00	6·00
8	6	6m. on 50s. green	6·00	7·00
9	6	6m. on 60s. red and violet	6·00	8·00
10	6	6m. on 75s. red & yellow	6·00	8·00
11	7	10m. on 1a. red & grey	12·00	14·00
12	7	10m. on 3a. red & brown	£450	£550
13	7	10m. on 5a. red and green	£450	£550

3 Girl

1920. Imperf or perf. Inscr "LITWA SRODKOWA".

14	3	25f. grey	15	15
15	-	1m. orange	20	15
16	-	2m. red	40	50
17	-	4m. olive and yellow	60	75
18	-	6m. grey and red	1·00	1·25
19	-	10m. yellow and brown	1·50	2·00

DESIGNS: 1m. Warrior; 2m. Ostrabrama Gate, Vilnius; 4m. St. Stanislaus Cathedral and Tower, Vilnius; 6m. Rector's insignia; 10m. Gen. Zeligowski.

1921. Fund for Polish Participation in Plebiscite for Upper Silesia. Surch **NA SLASK** and new value. Imperf or perf.

23	1	25f.+2m. red	50	60
24	1	25f.+2m. green	50	60
25	1	1m.+2m. blue	60	80
26	1	1m.+2m. brown	60	80
27	1	2m.+2m. violet	70	1·10
28	1	2m.+2m. yellow	70	1·10

1921. Red Cross Fund. Nos. 16/17 surch with cross and value. Imperf or perf.

29		2m.+1m. red	50	65
30		4m.+1m. green and yellow	50	65

1921. White Cross Fund. As Nos. 16, 17 and 19, but with cross and value in white added. Imperf or perf.

31		2m.+1m. purple	30	30
32		4m.+1m. green and buff	30	30
33		10m.+2m. yellow and brown	30	30

13 St. Nicholas Cathedral **14** St. Stanislaus Cathedral

1921. Imperf or perf.

34	13	1m. yellow and slate	30	40
35	14	2m. green and red	30	40
36	–	3m. green	40	50
37	–	4m. brown	40	60
38	–	5m. brown	40	60
39	–	6m. buff and green	40	60
40	–	10m. buff and purple	60	80
41	–	20m. buff and brown	60	90

DESIGNS—HORIZ: 4m. Queen Jadwiga and King Wladislaw Jagiello; 6m. Poczobut Observatory, Vilnius University; 10m. Union of Lithuania and Poland, 1569; 20m. Kosciuszko and Mickiewicz. VERT: 3m. Arms (Eagle); 5m. Arms (Shield).

21 Entry into Vilnius **22** General Zeligowski

1921. First Anniv of Entry of Gen. Zeligowski into Vilnius. Imperf or perf.

42	21	100m. blue and bistre	1·75	1·75
43	22	150m. green and brown	2·25	2·25

24 Arms

1922. Opening of National Parliament. Inscr "SEJM—WILNIE". Imperf or perf.

44		10m. brown	1·50	1·75
45	24	25m. red and buff	1·75	1·90
46	–	50m. blue	2·75	3·00
47	–	75m. lilac	4·00	4·50

DESIGNS—HORIZ: 50m. National Assembly, Vilnius. VERT: 10m. Agriculture; 75m. Industry.

POSTAGE DUE STAMPS

D9 Government Offices

1921. Inscr "DOPLATA". Imperf or perf.

D23	D9	50f. red	50	60
D24	–	1m. green	50	60
D25	–	2m. purple	50	60
D26	–	3m. purple	75	90
D27	–	5m. purple	75	90
D28	–	20m. red	1·00	1·00

DESIGNS—HORIZ: 2m. Castle on Troki Island. VERT: 1m. Castle Hill, Vilnius; 3m. Ostrabrama Gate, Vilnius; 5m. St. Stanislaus Cathedral; 20m. (larger) St. Nicholas Cathedral.

`Pt. 1`

CEYLON

An island to the south of India formerly under British administration, then a self-governing Dominion. The island became a Republic within the Commonwealth on 22 May 1972 and was renamed Sri Lanka (q.v.).

1857. 12 pence = 1 shilling; 20 shillings = 1 pound.
1872. 100 cents = 1 rupee.

1 **2** **4**

1857. Imperf.

17	4	½d. lilac	£190	£250
2	1	1d. blue	£1100	45·00

3	1	2d. green	£200	65·00
4	2	4d. red	£70000	£4500
5	1	5d. brown	£1600	£150
6	1	6d. brown	£2750	£140
7	2	8d. brown	£28000	£1500
8	2	9d. brown	£60000	£900
9	1	10d. orange	£900	£325
10	1	1s. violet	£5500	£200
11	2	1s.9d. green	£800	£800
12	2	2s. blue	£6500	£1300

The prices of these imperf stamps vary greatly according to condition. The above prices are for fine copies with four margins. Poor to medium specimens are worth much less.

1861. Perf.

48c	4	½d. lilac	55·00	55·00
49	1	1d. blue	£180	8·50
50	1	2d. green	£100	14·00
64b	1	2d. yellow	90·00	9·00
65b	2	4d. red	80·00	20·00
22	1	5d. brown	£120	8·00
66c	1	5d. green	60·00	55·00
67	1	6d. brown	£130	10·00
56	2	8d. brown	£130	70·00
69b	2	9d. brown	70·00	6·00
70b	1	10d. orange	85·00	17·00
71b	1	1s. violet	£140	11·00
72b	2	2s. blue	£150	15·00

8

1866. The 3d. has portrait in circle

61	8	1d. blue	25·00	11·00
62	–	3d. red	90·00	50·00

9 **10** **30**

1872. Various frames.

147	9	2c. green	3·00	15
256	9	2c. brown	5·00	30
122	10	4c. grey	48·00	1·50
148	10	4c. purple	6·00	30
149	10	4c. red	7·00	13·00
258	10	4c. yellow	4·00	3·50
150a	–	8c. yellow	5·00	11·00
126	–	16c. violet	£130	2·75
127	–	24c. green	75·00	2·25
128	–	32c. grey	£180	15·00
129	–	36c. blue	£200	29·00
130	–	48c. red	95·00	9·00
131	–	64c. brown	£300	75·00
132	–	96c. grey	£275	29·00
201	30	1r.12 red	29·00	29·00
138	30	2r.50 red	£800	£425
249	30	2r.50 purple on red	40·00	60·00

1882. Nos. 127 and 131 surch in words and figures.

142	30	16c. on 24c. green	40·00	9·00
143	30	20c. on 64c. brown	13·00	9·00

1885. As Nos. 148/132 surch Postage & Revenue and value in words.

178		5c. on 4c. red	26·00	5·00
179		5c. on 8c. yellow	90·00	11·00
180		5c. on 16c. violet	£170	17·00
154		5c. on 24c. green	£6000	£110
182		5c. on 24c. purple	—	£500
155		5c. on 32c. grey	65·00	15·00
156		5c. on 36c. blue	£300	13·00
157		5c. on 48c. red	£2500	65·00
158		5c. on 64c. brown	£130	12·00
159		5c. on 96c. grey	£550	70·00

1885. As Nos. 126/249 surch with new value in words.

184		10c. on 16c. violet	£13000	£1700
162		10c. on 24c. green	£500	£130
185		10c. on 24c. purple	17·00	10·00
163		10c. on 36c. blue	£450	£250
174		10c. on 64c. brown	90·00	£160
186		15c. on 16c. violet	14·00	11·00
165		20c. on 24c. green	75·00	27·00
166		20c. on 32c. grey	85·00	70·00
167		25c. on 32c. grey	25·00	7·50
168		28c. on 48c. red	40·00	10·00
169x		30c. on 36c. blue	15·00	10·00
170		56c. on 96c. grey	32·00	25·00
176		1r.12 on 2r.50 red	£110	48·00

1885. Surch **REVENUE AND POSTAGE 5 CENTS**

187		5c. on 8c. lilac (as No. 150a)	26·00	1·50

1885. As Nos. 126/32 surch in words and figures.

188		10c. on 24c. on 24c. purple	13·00	8·50
189		15c. on 16c. on 16c. yellow	60·00	15·00
190		28c. on 32c. on 32c. grey	28·00	2·50
191		30c. on 36c. on 36c. olive	29·00	16·00
192		56c. on 96c. on 96c. grey	50·00	17·00

1885. Surch **1 R. 12 C.**

193		1r.12 on 2r.50 on 2r.50 red	60·00	£140

1886

245	39	3c. brown and green	6·50	45
257	39	3c. green	5·00	55
195	28	5c. purple	3·75	10
259	39	6c. red and black	3·00	45
260	39	12c. olive and red	5·50	9·50
196	39	15c. olive	9·00	2·25
261	39	15c. blue	8·50	1·25
198	39	25c. brown	6·00	1·75
199	39	28c. grey	25·00	1·40
247	39	30c. mauve and brown	4·75	3·25
262	39	75c. black and brown	10·00	9·50
263	43	1r.50 red	32·00	55·00
264	43	2r.25 blue	35·00	55·00

1887. Nos. 148/9 surch

A. Surch TWO CENTS

202	10	2c. on 4c. purple	1·40	80
203	10	2c. on 4c. red	2·50	30

B. Surch TWO.

204		2(c). on 4c. purple	1·00	30
205		2(c). on 4c. red	8·50	20

C. Surch 2 Cents and bar.

206		2c. on 4c. purple	80·00	32·00
207		2c. on 4c. red	4·25	75

D. Surch Two Cents and bar.

208		2c. on 4c. purple	65·00	28·00
209		2c. on 4c. red	2·50	1·10

E. Surch 2 Cents without bar.

210		2c. on 4c. purple	65·00	38·00
211		2c. on 4c. red	15·00	1·00

1890. Surch **POSTAGE Five Cents REVENUE**.

233	39	5c. on 15c. olive	4·00	2·50

1891. Surch **FIFTEEN CENTS**.

239		15c. on 25c. brown	19·00	19·00
240		15c. on 28c. grey	20·00	9·00

1892. Surch **3 Cents** and bar.

241	10	3c. on 4c. purple	1·00	3·25
242	10	3c. on 4c. red	8·50	12·00
243	39	3c. on 28c. grey	6·50	6·00

1898

(a) Surch Six Cents.

250		6c. on 15c. green	1·25	75

(b) Surch with new value

254	30	1r.50 on 2r.50 grey	21·00	55·00
255	30	2r.25 on 2r.50 yellow	48·00	85·00

44 **45**

1903. Various frames.

277	44	2c. brown	2·00	10
278	45	3c. green (A)	1·50	15
293	45	3c. green (B)	1·00	75
279	45	4c. orange and blue	2·75	1·50
268	–	5c. purple	2·50	60
289	–	5c. purple	6·50	10
281	–	6c. red	4·50	15
291	–	6c. red	2·50	10
294	45	10c. olive and red	2·50	3·50
282	45	12c. olive and red	1·50	1·75
283	45	15c. blue	3·50	60
284	45	25c. brown	6·00	3·75
295	45	25c. grey	2·50	2·75
285	45	30c. violet and green	2·50	3·00
296	45	50c. brown	4·00	7·50
286	45	75c. blue and orange	5·25	8·00
297	45	1r. purple on yellow	8·00	12·00
287	45	1r.50 grey	29·00	11·00
298	45	2r. red on yellow	15·00	29·00
288	45	2r.25 brown and green	22·00	32·00
299	45	5r. black on green	45·00	95·00
300	45	10r. black on red	£130	£275

(A) has value in shaded tablet; (B) in white tablet as in Type **45**.

Nos. 268 and 281 have the value in words; Nos. 289 and 291 in figures.

52

1912

301	52	1c. brown	1·00	10
307a	52	2c. orange	30	20
339	52	3c. brown	5·50	75
340	52	3c. grey	75	20
341	52	5c. purple	60	15
342	52	6c. red	3·00	75
343	52	6c. violet	2·25	15
345	52	9c. red on yellow	2·75	30
346	52	10c. olive	1·40	40
311a	52	15c. blue	1·75	15
349a	52	15c. green on yellow	4·75	1·00
350b	52	20c. blue	3·50	45
351	52	25c. yellow and blue	3·00	1·90
352	52	30c. green and violet	1·60	5·00
353	52	50c. black and red	2·00	80
315	52	1r. purple on yellow	5·50	4·50
355	52	2r. black and red on yellow	7·00	13·00
317	52	5r. black on green	20·00	42·00
318	52	10r. purple & blk on red	70·00	90·00
319	52	20r. black and red on blue	£150	£160

1912. Large type, As Bermuda T **15**

358		50r. purple	£700	£1200
359		100r. black	£2750	
360		100r. purple and blue	£1900	

1918. Optd **WAR STAMP**, No. 335 surch **ONE CENT** and bar also.

335		1c. on 5c. on 5c. purple	50	40
330		2c. orange	20	40
332		3c. green	20	50
333		5c. purple	50	30

1918. Surch **ONE CENT** and bar.

337		1c. on 5c. on 5c. purple	15	25

1926. Surch with new value and bar.

361		2c. on 3c. on 3c. grey	2·75	1·00
362		5c. on 6c. on 6c. violet	75	40

57

1927

363	57	1r. purple	2·50	1·25
364	57	2r. green and red	3·75	2·75
365	57	5r. green and purple	17·00	26·00
366	57	10r. green and orange	60·00	£130
367	57	20r. purple and blue	£225	£375

59 Adam's Peak

1935. King George V.

368	–	2c. black and red	30	40
369	59	3c. black and green	35	40
370	–	6c. black and blue	30	30
371	–	9c. green and orange	1·00	65
372	–	10c. black and purple	1·25	3·00
373	–	15c. brown and green	1·50	50
374	–	20c. black and blue	2·75	3·25
375	–	25c. blue and brown	1·40	1·25
376	–	30c. red and green	2·25	3·50
377	–	50c. black and violet	15·00	1·75
378	–	1r. violet and brown	35·00	26·00

DESIGNS—VERT: 2c. Tapping rubber; 6c. Colombo Harbour; 9c. Plucking tea; 20c. Coconut palms. HORIZ: 10c. Hill paddy (rice); 15c. River scene; 25c. Temple of the Tooth, Kandy; 30c. Ancient irrigation tank; 50c. Indian elephants; 1r. Trincomalee.

1935. Silver Jubilee. As T **13** of Antigua.

379		6c. blue and grey	75	30
380		9c. green and blue	75	2·75
381		20c. brown and blue	4·25	2·75
382		50c. grey and purple	5·25	16·00

1937. Coronation. As T **2** of Aden.

383		6c. red	65	1·00
384		9c. green	2·50	4·50
385		20c. blue	3·50	4·00

70 Sigiriya (Lion Rock)

1938. As 1935 issue but with portrait of King George VI, and "POSTAGE & REVENUE" omitted (Nos. 386b/396b) or as T **57**, but head of King George VI to right (No. 397a)

386b	-	2c. black and red	2·75	10
387d	**59**	3c. black and green	1·00	10
387f	-	5c. green and orange	30	10
388	-	6c. black and blue	30	10
389	**70**	10c. black and blue	3·25	20
390	-	15c. green and brown	2·00	20
391	-	20c. black and brown	3·25	20
392a	-	25c. blue and brown	4·25	20
393	-	30c. red and green	12·00	3·50
394e	-	50c. black and violet	7·00	20
395	-	1r. blue and brown	19·00	1·50
396	-	2r. black and red	16·00	4·25
396b	-	2r. black and violet	3·50	3·00
397a	-	2r. black and violet	35·00	13·00

DESIGNS—VERT: 5c. Coconut palms; 20c. Plucking tea; 2r. Ancient guard-stone, Anuradhapura. Others, same as for corresponding values of 1935 issue.

1940. Surch with new value and bars.

398		3c. on 6c. on 6c. blk & bl (No. 388)	65	10
399		3c. on 20c. on 20c. blk & bl (No. 391)	5·50	3·25

1946. Victory. As T **9** of Aden.

400		6c. blue	30	35
401		15c. brown	30	1·75

75 Parliament Building

1947. New Constitution.

402	**75**	6c. black and blue	20	15
403	-	10c. black, orange and red	30	40
404	-	15c. green and purple	30	80
405	-	25c. yellow and green	30	1·75

DESIGNS—VERT: 10c. Adam's Peak; 25c. Anuradhapura. HORIZ: 15c. Temple of the Tooth.

79 Lion Flag of Dominion
80 D. S. Senanayake

1949. First Anniv of Independence.

406	**79**	4c. red, yellow and brown	20	20
407	**80**	5c. brown and green	10	10
408	**79**	15c. red, yellow and orange	1·00	40
409	**80**	25c. brown and blue	15	1·00

No. 408 is larger, 28×22 mm.

82 Globe and Forms of Transport

1949. 75th Anniv of UPU. Inscr as in T **82**. Designs showing globe.

410	**82**	5c. brown and green	75	10
411	-	15c. black and red (horiz)	1·10	2·75
412	-	25c. black and blue (vert)	1·10	1·10

85 Kandyan Dancer
88 Sigiriya (Lion Rock)

90 Ruins at Madirigiriya

1950

413	**85**	4c. purple and red	15	10
414	-	5c. green	15	10
415	-	15c. green and violet	2·50	50
416	**88**	30c. red and yellow	30	70
417	-	75c. blue and orange	8·50	20

418	**90**	1r. blue and brown	1·75	30

DESIGNS—VERT (As Types **85** and **88**): 5c. Kiri Vehera, Polonnaruwa; 15c. Vesak orchid. (As Type **90**): 75c. Octagon Library, Temple of the Tooth.

94 Coconut Trees
99 Tea Plantation

1951

419	-	2c. brown and turquoise	10	1·25
420	-	3c. black and violet	10	1·00
421	-	6c. sepia and green	15	30
422	**94**	10c. green and grey	1·00	65
423	-	25c. orange and blue	20	20
424	-	35c. red and green	1·50	1·50
425	-	40c. brown	5·00	1·00
426	-	50c. slate	30	10
427	**99**	85c. black and turquoise	1·50	30
428	-	2r. blue and brown	10·00	1·25
429	-	5r. brown and orange	12·00	1·40
430	-	10r. brown and buff	60·00	24·00

DESIGNS—VERT (As Type **94**): 2c. Sambars, Ruhuna National Park; 3c. Ancient guardstone, Anuradhapura; 6c. Harvesting rice; 25c. Sigiriya fresco; 35c. Star orchid. (As Type **99**): 5r. Bas-relief, Anuradhapura; 10r. Harvesting rice. HORIZ (As Type **94**): 40c. Rubber plantation; 50c. Outrigger canoe. (As Type **99**): 2r. River Gal Dam.

103 Ceylon, Mace and Symbols of Progress

1952. Colombo Plan Exhibition.

431	**103**	5c. green	30	10
432	**103**	15c. blue	30	60

104 Queen Elizabeth II

1953. Coronation.

433	**104**	5c. green	1·50	10

105 Ceremonial Procession

1954. Royal Visit.

434	**105**	10c. blue	1·25	10

106 King Coconuts

1954

435	**106**	10c. orange, brown and buff	10	10

107 Farm Produce

1955. Royal Agricultural and Food Exhibition.

436	**107**	10c. brown and orange	10	10

108 Sir John Kotelawala and House of Representatives

1956. Prime Minister's 25 Years of Public Service.

437	**108**	10c. green	10	10

109 Arrival of Vijaya in Ceylon
110 Lampstand and Dharmachakra

1956. Buddha Jayanti. Inscr "2500".

438	**109**	3c. blue and grey	15	15
439	**110**	4c.+2c. +2c. yellow and blue	20	75
440	-	10c.+5c. +5c. red, yell & grey	20	1·00
441	-	15c. blue	20	10

DESIGNS—VERT: 10c. Hand of Peace and Dharmachakra. HORIZ: 15c. Dharmachakra encircling the globe.

113 Mail Transport
114 Stamp of 1857

1957. Stamp Centenary.

442	**113**	4c. red and turquoise	75	50
443	**113**	10c. red and blue	75	10
444	**114**	35c. brown, yellow and blue	30	50
445	**114**	85c. brown, yellow & grn	80	1·60

1958. Nos. 439/40 with premium obliterated with bars.

446	**110**	4c. yellow and blue	10	10
447	-	10c. red, yellow and grey	10	10

117 Kandyan Dancer

1958. As Nos. 413 and 419 etc, and 435, but with inscriptions changed as in T **117**.

448		2c. brown and turquoise	10	50
449		3c. black and violet	10	70
450		4c. purple and red	10	10
451		5c. green	10	1·60
452		6c. sepia and green	10	1·00
453		10c. orange, brown and buff	10	10
454		15c. green and violet	3·50	1·00
455		25c. orange and blue	25	10
456		30c. red and yellow	25	1·40
457		35c. red and green	3·25	30
459		50c. slate	30	10
460a		75c. blue and orange	10·00	3·25
461		85c. black and turquoise	3·75	11·00
462		1r. blue and brown	60	10
463		2r. blue and brown	3·75	30
464		5r. brown and orange	15·00	30
465		10r. brown and buff	15·00	1·00

118 "Human Rights"

1958. Tenth Anniv of Declaration of Human Rights.

466	**118**	10c. red, brown and purple	10	10
467	**118**	85c. red, turq & grn	30	1·00

119 Portraits of Founders and University Buildings

1959. Institution of Pirivena Universities.

468	**119**	10c. orange and blue	10	10

120 "Uprooted Tree"

1960. World Refugee Year.

469	**120**	4c. brown and gold	10	85
470	**120**	25c. violet and gold	10	15

121 S. W. R. D. Bandaranaike

1961. Prime Minister Bandaranaike Commemoration.

471	**121**	10c. blue and turquoise	10	10

See also Nos. 479 and 481.

122 Ceylon Scout Badge

1962. Golden Jubilee of Ceylon Boy Scouts Association.

472	**122**	35c. buff and blue	15	10

123 Campaign Emblem

1962. Malaria Eradication.

473	**123**	25c. red and drab	10	10

124 De Havilland Leopard Moth and Hawker Siddeley Comet 4

1963. 25th Anniv of Airmail Services.

474	**124**	50c. black and blue	50	50

125 "Produce" and Campaign Emblem

1963. Freedom from Hunger.

475	**125**	5c. red and blue	75	2·00
476	**125**	25c. brown and olive	3·00	30

(126)

1963. No. 450 surch with T **126**.

477		2c. on 4c. on 4c. purple and red	10	10

127 "Rural Life"

1963. Golden Jubilee of Ceylon Co-operative Movement (1962).

478	**127**	60c. red and black	2·00	50

1963. Design as T **121**, but smaller (21×26 mm) and with inscription rearranged at top.

479		10c. blue	10	10
481		10c. violet and grey	10	10

No. 481 has a decorative pattern at foot instead of the inscription.

129 Terrain, Indian Elephant and Tree

1963. National Conservation Week.
480 129 5c. sepia and blue 60 40

131 Anagarika Dharmapala (Buddhist missionary)

1964. Birth Centenary of A. Dharmapala (founder of Maha Bodhi Society).
482 131 25c. sepia and yellow 10 10

135 D. S. Senanayake
143 Ceylon Jungle Fowl

138 Ruins at Madirigiriya

1964
485 - 5c. multicoloured 2·00 1·00
486 135 10c. green 80 10
487 - 10c. green 10 10
488 - 15c. multicoloured 4·25 30
489 138 20c. purple and buff 20 25
494 143 60c. multicoloured 4·75 1·25
495 - 75c. multicoloured 3·00 70
497 - 1r. brown and green 1·00 30
499 - 5r. multicoloured 10·00 10·00
500 - 10r. multicoloured 26·00 3·00
MS500a 148×174 mm. As Nos. 485, 488, 494 and 495 (imperf) 7·00 14·00

DESIGNS—HORIZ (As Type **143**): 5c. Southern grackle ("Grackle"); 15c. Common peafowl ("Peacock"); 75c. Asian black-headed oriole ("Oriole"). (As Type **138**): 5r. Girls transplanting rice. VERT (As Type **135**): 10c. (No. 487) Similar portrait, but large head and smaller inscriptions. (21×35 mm): 1r. Tea plantation. (23×36 mm): 10r. Map of Ceylon.

150 Exhibition Buildings and Cogwheels

1964. Industrial Exhibition.
501 - 5c. multicoloured 10 75
502 150 5c. multicoloured 10 75

No. 501 is inscribed "INDUSTRIAL EXHIBITION" in Sinhala and Tamil, No. 502 in Sinhala and English.

151 Trains of 1864 and 1964

1964. Centenary of Ceylon Railways.
503 - 60c. blue, purple and green 2·75 40
504 151 60c. blue, purple and green 2·75 40

No. 503 is inscribed "RAILWAY CENTENARY" in Sinhala and Tamil, No. 504 in Sinhala and English.

152 ITU Emblem and Symbols

1965. Centenary of ITU.
505 152 2c. blue and red 1·00 1·10
506 152 30c. brown and red 3·25 45

153 ICY Emblem

1965. International Co-operation Year.
507 153 3c. blue and red 1·25 1·00
508 153 50c. black, red and gold 3·25 50

154 Town Hall, Colombo

1965. Centenary of Colombo Municipal Council.
509 154 25c. green and sepia 20 20

1965. No. 481 surch **5**.
510 5c. on 10c. violet and grey 10 2·00

157 Kandy and Council Crest

1966. Centenary of Kandy Municipal Council.
512 157 25c. multicoloured 20 20

158 WHO Building

1966. Inauguration of WHO Headquarters, Geneva.
513 158 4c. multicoloured 3·00 3·00
514 158 1r. multicoloured 7·50 1·50

159 Rice Paddy and Map of Ceylon

1966. International Rice Year. Multicoloured.
515 6c. Type **159** 20 75
516 30c. Rice paddy and globe 30 15

161 UNESCO Emblem

1966. 20th Anniv of UNESCO.
517 161 3c. multicoloured 2·75 3·75
518 161 50c. multicoloured 8·00 50

162 Water-resources Map

1966. International Hydrological Decade.
519 162 2c. brown, yellow and blue 30 85
520 162 2r. multicoloured 2·00 2·25

163 Devotees at Buddhist Temple

1967. Poya Holiday System. Multicoloured.
521 5c. Type **163** 15 60
522 20c. Mihintale 15 10
523 35c. Sacred Bo-tree, Anuradhapura 15 15
524 60c. Adam's Peak 15 10

167 Galle Fort and Clock Tower

1967. Centenary of Galle Municipal Council.
525 167 25c. multicoloured 70 20

168 Field Research

1967. Centenary of Ceylon Tea Industry. Multicoloured.
526 4c. Type **168** 60 80
527 40c. Tea-tasting equipment 1·75 1·50
528 50c. Leaves and bud 1·75 20
529 1r. Shipping tea 1·75 10

169 Elephant Ride

1967. International Tourist Year.
530 169 45c. multicoloured 2·25 80

1967. First National Stamp Exhibition. No. **MS**500a optd **FIRST NATIONAL STAMP EXHIBITION 1967.**
MS531 148×174 mm. Nos. 485, 488, 494/5. Imperf 7·00 9·00

170 Ranger, Jubilee Emblem and Flag

1967. Golden Jubilee of Ceylon Girl Guides' Association.
532 170 3c. multicoloured 50 20
533 170 25c. multicoloured 75 10

171 Colonel Olcott and Buddhist Flag

1967. 60th Death Anniv of Colonel Olcott (theosophist).
534 171 15c. multicoloured 30 20

172 Independence Hall

1968. 20th Anniv of Independence. Multicoloured.
535 5c. Type **172** 10 55
536 1r. Lion flag and sceptre 50 10

174 Sir D. B. Jayatilleke

1968. Birth Centenary of Sir Baron Jayatilleke (scholar and statesman).
537 174 25c. brown 10 10

175 Institute of Hygiene

1968. 20th Anniv of World Health Organization.
538 175 50c. multicoloured 10 10

176 Vickers Super VC-10 over Terminal Building

1968. Opening of Colombo Airport.
539 176 60c. multicoloured 1·00 10

177 Open Koran and "1400"

1968. 1400th Anniv of Koran.
541 177 25c. multicoloured 10 10

178 Human Rights Emblem

1968. Human Rights Year.
542 178 2c. multicoloured 10 30
543 178 20c. multicoloured 10 10
544 178 40c. multicoloured 10 10
545 178 2r. multicoloured 80 4·75

179 All-Ceylon Buddhist Congress Headquarters

1968. Golden Jubilee of All-Ceylon Buddhist Congress.
546 179 5c. multicoloured 10 50

180 E. W. Perera (patriot)

1969. Perera Commemoration.
547 180 60c. brown 10 30

181 Symbols of Strength in Savings

1969. Silver Jubilee of National Savings Movement.
548 181 3c. multicoloured 10 30

182 Seat of Enlightenment under Sacred Bodhi Tree

1969. Vesak Day. Inscr "Wesak".
549 182 4c. multicoloured 10 50
550 182 6c. multicoloured 10 50
551 182 35c. multicoloured 10 10
DESIGN: 6c. Buduresmala (six-fold Buddha-rays).

184 A. E. Goonesinghe

1969. Goonesinghe Commemoration.
552 184 15c. multicoloured 10 10

185 ILO Emblem

1969. 50th Anniv of ILO.
553 185 5c. black and blue 10 10
554 185 25c. black and red 10 10

186 Convocation Hall, University of Ceylon

1969. Educational Centenary. Multicoloured.
555 4c. Type **186** ... 10 80
556 35c. Lamp of learning, globe and flags (horiz) ... 20 10
557 50c. Uranium atom ... 20 10
558 60c. Symbols of scientific education ... 30 10

188 Ath Pana (Elephant Lamp)

1969. Archaeological Centenary. Multicoloured.
559 6c. Type **188** ... 25 1·50
560 1r. Rock fortress of Sigiriya ... 25 10

190 Leopard

1970. Wild Life Conservation. Multicoloured.
561 5c. Water buffalo ... 1·25 1·25
562 15c. Slender loris ... 2·00 1·25
563 50c. Spotted deer ... 1·40 1·25
564 1r. Type **190** ... 1·40 1·75

191 Emblem and Symbols

1970. Asian Productivity Year.
565 **191** 60c. multicoloured ... 10 10

192 New UPU HQ Building

1970. New UPU Headquarters Building.
566 **192** 50c. orange, black and blue ... 50 10
567 **192** 1r.10 red, black and blue ... 4·50 40

193 Oil Lamp and Caduceus

1970. Centenary of Colombo Medical School.
568 **193** 5c. multicoloured ... 1·25 80
569 **193** 45c. multicoloured ... 1·50 60

194 Victory March and S. W. R. D. Bandaranaike

1970. Establishment of United Front Government.
570 **194** 10c. multicoloured ... 10 10

195 U.N. Emblem and Dove of Peace

1970. 25th Anniv of United Nations.
571 **195** 2r. multicoloured ... 2·00 4·00

196 Keppetipola Dissawa

1970. 152nd Death Anniv of Keppetipola Dissawa (Kandyan patriot).
572 **196** 25c. multicoloured ... 10 10

197 Ola Leaf Manuscript

1970. International Education Year.
573 **197** 15c. multicoloured ... 2·75 1·25

198 C. H. de Soysa

1971. 135th Birth Anniv of C. H. de Soysa (philanthropist).
574 **198** 20c. multicoloured ... 15 50

199 D. E. H. Pedris (patriot)

1971. D. E. H. Pedris Commemoration.
575 **199** 25c. multicoloured ... 15 50

200 Lenin

1971. Lenin Commemoration.
576 **200** 40c. multicoloured ... 25 50

201 Ananda Rajakaruna

1971. Poets and Philosophers.
577 **201** 5c. blue ... 10 15
578 - 5c. brown ... 10 15
579 - 5c. orange ... 10 15
580 - 5c. blue ... 10 15
581 - 5c. brown ... 10 15

PORTRAITS: No. 578, Arumuga Navalar; 579, Rev. S. Mahinda; 580, Ananda Coomaraswamy; 581, Cumaratunga Munidasa.

1971. Surch in figures.
582 **182** 5c. on 4c. multicoloured ... 7·00 1·75
583 **186** 5c. on 10c. multicoloured ... 10 1·25
584 **194** 15c. on 10c. multicoloured ... 10 30
585 - 25c. on 6c. mult (No. 550) ... 30 60
586 **188** 25c. on 6c. multicoloured ... 30 2·25

203 Colombo Plan Emblem and Ceylon

1971. 20th Anniv of Colombo Plan.
587 **203** 20c. multicoloured ... 20 30

204 Globe and CARE Package

1971. 20th Anniv of Co-operative for American Relief Everywhere.
588 **204** 50c. blue, violet and lilac ... 35 30

205 WHO Emblem and Heart

1972. World Health Day.
589 **205** 25c. multicoloured ... 2·50 60

206 Map of Asia and U.N. Emblem

1972. 25th Anniv of ECAFE.
590 **206** 85c. multicoloured ... 4·75 2·75

OFFICIAL STAMPS

1895. Stamps of Queen Victoria optd **On Service**.
O11 9 2c. green ... 18·00 70
O18 9 2c. brown ... 11·00 60
O12 39 3c. brown and green ... 11·00 2·75
O19 39 3c. green ... 12·00 4·75
O13 28 5c. purple ... 5·50 30
O14 39 15c. olive ... 22·00 65
O20 39 15c. blue ... 26·00 60
O15 39 25c. brown ... 13·00 3·25
O16 39 30c. mauve and brown ... 13·00 60
O21 39 75c. black and brown ... 8·50 9·00
O17 30 1r.12 red ... 95·00 65·00

1903. Stamps of King Edward VII optd **On Service**.
O22 44 2c. brown ... 21·00 1·00
O23 45 3c. green ... 15·00 2·00
O24 - 5c. purple (No. 268) ... 30·00 9·00
O25 45 15c. blue ... 40·00 2·50
O26 45 25c. brown ... 35·00 18·00
O27 45 30c. violet and green ... 20·00 1·50

For later issues see **SRI LANKA**.

Pt. 6, Pt. 12

CHAD

Formerly a dependency of Ubangi-Shari. Became one of the separate colonies of Fr. Equatorial Africa in 1937. In 1958 became a republic within the French Community.

100 centimes = 1 franc.

1922. Stamps of Middle Congo, colours changed, optd **TCHAD**.
1 1 1c. pink and violet ... 60 6·75
2 1 2c. brown and pink ... 1·50 6·75
3 1 4c. blue and violet ... 2·10 7·25
4 1 5c. brown and green ... 3·00 7·75
5 1 10c. green and turquoise ... 5·25 8·50
6 1 15c. violet and pink ... 4·50 9·00
7 1 20c. green and violet ... 8·75 18·00
8 2 25c. brown and chocolate ... 10·50 34·00
9 2 30c. red ... 3·25 8·25
10 2 35c. blue and pink ... 3·75 11·00
11 2 40c. brown and green ... 3·75 11·50
12 2 45c. violet and green ... 3·75 11·00
13 2 50c. blue and light blue ... 3·00 11·00
14 2 60 on 75c. violet on pink ... 5·00 16·00
15 2 75c. pink and violet ... 4·00 10·50
16 3 1f. blue and pink ... 19·00 37·00
17 3 2f. blue and violet ... 24·00 60·00
18 3 5f. blue and brown ... 20·00 55·00

1924. Stamps of 1922 and similar stamps further optd **AFRIQUE EQUATORIALE FRANCAISE**.
19 1 1c. pink and violet ... 35 6·00
20 1 2c. brown and pink ... 25 6·25
21 1 4c. blue and violet ... 70 6·50
22 1 5c. brown and green ... 75 6·25
23 1 10c. green and turquoise ... 2·50 7·75
24 1 10c. red and grey ... 1·10 6·25
25 1 15c. violet and red ... 1·10 6·50
26 1 20c. green and violet ... 2·10 6·75
27 2 25c. brown and chocolate ... 2·10 6·75
28 2 30c. red ... 1·40 6·75
29 2 30c. grey and blue ... 95 6·25
30 2 30c. olive and green ... 2·10 8·25
31 2 35c. blue and pink ... 1·10 7·00
32 2 40c. brown and green ... 2·10 6·75
33 2 45c. violet and green ... 1·90 7·75
34 2 50c. blue and light blue ... 1·20 7·00
35 2 50c. green and purple ... 2·40 2·30
36 2 60 on 75c. violet on pink ... 85 7·25
37 2 65c. brown and blue ... 3·50 10·00
38 2 75c. pink and violet ... 1·40 5·50
39 2 75c. blue and light blue ... 2·20 5·75
40 2 75c. purple and brown ... 3·75 9·75
41 2 90c. carmine and red ... 6·25 25·00
42 3 1f. blue and pink ... 3·00 4·75
43 3 1f.10 green and blue ... 3·75 11·50
44 3 1f.25 brown and blue ... 13·50 28·00
45 3 1f.50 ultramarine and blue ... 6·00 28·00
46 3 1f.75 brown and mauve ... 55·00 95·00
47 3 2f. blue and violet ... 3·25 5·50
48 3 3f. mauve on pink ... 8·75 39·00
49 3 5f. blue and brown ... 3·75 7·25

1925. Stamps of Middle Congo optd **TCHAD** and **AFRIQUE EQUATORIALE FRANCAISE** and surch also.
50 65 on 1f. brown and green ... 2·75 8·50
51 85 on 1f. brown and green ... 2·75 8·50
52 2 90 on 75c. red and pink ... 2·30 8·75
53 3 1f.25 on 1f. blue & ultram ... 1·40 6·25
54 3 1f.50 on 1f. blue & ultram ... 3·00 8·75
55 3 3f. on 5f. brown and red ... 5·25 14·50
56 3 10f. on 5f. green and red ... 15·00 34·00
57a 3 20f. on 5f. violet & ultram ... 24·00 43·00

1931. "Colonial Exhibition" key-types inscr "TCHAD".
58 E 40c. green ... 5·00 15·00
59 F 50c. mauve ... 5·00 15·00
60 G 90c. red ... 5·00 15·00
61 H 1f.50 blue ... 5·00 15·00

2 "Birth of the Republic"

1959. First Anniv of Republic.
62 2 15f. multicoloured ... 3·50 3·25
63 25f. lake and myrtle ... 75 50
DESIGN: 25f. Map and birds.

1960. Tenth African Technical Co-operation Commission. As T **62** of Cameroun.
64 50f. violet and purple ... 2·75 4·75

1960. Air. Olympic Games. No. 276 of French Equatorial Africa surch with Olympic rings and **XVIIe OLYMPIADE 1960 REPUBLIQUE DU TCHAD 250F.**
65 250f. on 500f. blue, black & grn ... 13·50 13·00

3 Flag, Map and U.N. Emblem

1961. Admission into U.N.
66 3 15f. multicoloured ... 65 25
67 3 25f. multicoloured ... 80 40
68 3 85f. multicoloured ... 2·40 1·10

4 Shari Bridge and Hippopotamus

1961
69 - 50c. green and black ... 10 10
70 - 1f. green and black ... 10 10
71 - 2f. brown and black ... 10 10
72 - 3f. orange and green ... 10 10
73 - 4f. red and black ... 20 10
74 4 5f. lemon and black ... 20 20
75 - 10f. pink and black ... 40 25
76 - 15f. violet and black ... 80 30
77 - 20f. red and black ... 90 45
78 - 25f. blue and black ... 1·00 50
79 - 30f. blue and black ... 1·20 65
80 - 60f. yellow and black ... 2·30 1·00
81 - 85f. orange and black ... 2·00 1·20

DESIGNS (with animal silhouettes)—VERT: 50c. Biltine and Dorcas gazelle; 1f. Logone and elephant; 2f. Batha and lion; 3f. Salamat and buffalo; 4f. Ouaddai and greater kudu; 10f. Abtouyour and bullock; 15f. Bessada and Derby's eland; 20f. Tibesti and moufflon; 25f. Tikem Rocks and hartebeest; 30f. Kanem and cheetah; 60f. Borkou and oryx; 85f. Guelta D'Archei and addax.

5 Red Bishops

1961. Air.
82	**5**	50f. black, red and green	1·50	55
83	-	100f. multicoloured	4·50	1·30
84	-	200f. multicoloured	4·75	2·40
85	-	250f. blue, orange and green	10·00	4·25
86	-	500f. multicoloured	22·00	13·00

BIRDS: 100f. Scarlet-chested sunbird; 200f. African paradise flycatcher; 250f. Malachite kingfisher; 500f. Carmine bee eater.

1962. Air. "Air Afrique" Airline. As T **69** of Cameroun.
87		25f. blue, brown and black	1·00	40

1962. Malaria Eradication. As T **70** of Cameroun.
88		25f.+5f. orange	1·30	1·10

1962. Sports. As T **12** of Central African Republic. Multicoloured.
89		20f. Relay-racing (horiz) (postage)	75	60
90		50f. High-jumping (horiz)	1·80	95
91		100f. Throwing the discus (air)	3·75	1·90

The 100f. is 26×47 mm.

1962. First Anniv of Union of African and Malagasy States. As No. 328 of Cameroun.
92	**72**	30f. blue	1·30	70

1963. Freedom from Hunger. As T **76** of Cameroun.
93		25f.+5f. blue, brown & green	1·30	1·10

6 Pres. Tombalbaye

1963
94	**6**	20f. multicoloured	65	30
95	**6**	85f. multicoloured	1·70	80

1963. Air. African and Malagasy Posts and Telecommunications Union. As T **11** of Central African Republic.
96		85f. multicoloured	2·20	1·10

1963. Space Telecommunications, As Nos. 37/8 of Central African Republic.
97		25f. violet, emerald and green	85	55
98		100f. blue and pink	3·25	1·60

1963. Air. First Anniv of "Air Afrique" and Inauguration of "DC-8" Service. As T **11** of Congo Republic.
99		50f. multicoloured	2·40	1·10

1963. Air. European–African Economic Convention. As T **24** of Central African Republic.
100		50f. multicoloured	1·70	95

7 Carved Thread-weight

1963. Sao Art.
101	**7**	5f. orange and turquoise	20	10
102	-	15f. purple, slate and red	50	25
103	-	25f. brown and blue	1·00	70
104	-	60f. bronze and brown	2·50	1·00
105	-	80f. bronze and brown	3·00	1·30

DESIGNS: 15f. Ancestral mask; 25f. Ancestral statuette; 60f. Gazelle's-head pendant; 80f. Pectoral.

1963. 15th Anniv of Declaration of Human Rights. As Central African Republic T **26**.
106		25f. purple and green	1·00	55

8 Broussard Monoplane

1963. Air.
107	**8**	100f. blue, green & brown	3·75	1·80

9 Pottery

1964. Sao Handicrafts.
108	**9**	10f. black, orange & blue	40	25
109	-	30f. red, black and yellow	95	50
110	-	50f. black, red and green	1·50	75
111	-	85f. black, yellow & purple	2·30	1·10

DESIGNS: 30f. Canoe-building; 50f. Carpet-weaving; 85f. Blacksmith working iron.

10 Rameses II in War Chariot, Abu Simbel

1964. Air. Nubian Monuments Preservation Fund.
112	**10**	10f.+5f. violet, grn & red	90	55
113	**10**	25f.+5f. purple, grn & red	1·50	85
114	**10**	50f.+5f. turq, grn & red	3·00	1·90

1964. World Meteorological Day. As T **14** of Congo Republic.
115		50f. violet, blue and purple	1·30	75

11 Cotton

1964. Multicoloured.
116	20f. Type **11**		1·70	70
117	25f. Flamboyant tree		1·80	85

1964. Air. Fifth Anniv of Equatorial African Heads of State Conf. As T **31** of Central African Republic.
118		100f. multicoloured	2·40	1·10

12 Globe, Chimneys and Ears of Wheat

1964. Air. Europafrique.
119	**12**	50f. orange, purple & brn	1·70	85

13 Football

1964. Air. Olympic Games. Tokyo.
120	**13**	25f. green, lt green & brn	1·00	60
121	-	50f. brown, indigo & blue	1·80	1·00
122	-	100f. black, green and red	3·50	1·90
123	-	200f. black, bistre and red	6·25	3·50
MS123a	191×100 mm. Nos. 120/3		17·00	13·50

DESIGNS—VERT: 50f. Throwing the javelin; 100f. High-jumping. HORIZ: 200f. Running.

1964. Air. Pan-African and Malagasy Post and Telecommunications Congress, Cairo. As T **23** of Congo Republic.
124		25f. sepia, red and mauve	1·00	40

1964. French, African and Malagasy Co-operation. As T **88** of Cameroun.
125		25f. brown, blue and red	1·50	80

14 Pres. Kennedy

1964. Air. Pres. Kennedy Commem.
126	**14**	100f. multicoloured	2·50	1·80
MS126a	90×129 mm. No. 126 (×4)		12·00	9·75

15 National Guard

1964. Chad Army. Multicoloured.
127	20f. Type **15**		80	40
128	25f. Standard-bearer and troops of Land Forces		1·10	40

16 Barbary Sheep

1964. Fauna. Protection. Multicoloured.
129	5f. Type **16**		40	10
130	10f. Addax		70	30
131	20f. Scimitar oryx		1·30	45
132	25f. Giant eland (vert)		1·70	60
133	30f. Giraffe, African buffalo and lion (Zakouma Park)(vert)		2·30	75
134	85f. Greater kudu (vert)		5·00	1·50

17 Perforator of Olsen's Telegraph Apparatus

1965. I.T.U. Centenary.
135	**17**	30f. brown, red and green	90	40
136	-	60f. green, red and brown	1·50	75
137	-	100f. green, brown & red	2·40	1·10

DESIGNS—VERT: 60f. Milde's telephone. HORIZ: 100f. Distributor of Baudot's telegraph apparatus.

18 Badge and Mobile Gendarmes

1965. National Gendarmerie.
138	**18**	25f. multicoloured	90	50

19 ICY Emblem

1965. Air. International Co-operation Year.
139	**19**	100f. multicoloured	1·80	1·10

20 Abraham Lincoln

1965. Air. Death Centenary of Abraham Lincoln.
140	**20**	100f. multicoloured	2·50	1·30

21 Guitar

1965. Native Musical Instruments.
141	-	1f. brown & grn (postage)	10	10
142	**21**	2f. brown, purple and red	10	10
143	-	3f. lake, black and brown	10	10
144	-	15f. green, orange and red	1·00	30
145	-	60f. green and lake	2·00	1·40
146	-	100f. ultram, brn & bl (48½×27 mm) (air)	3·00	1·90

DESIGNS—VERT: 1f. Drum and seat; 3f. Shoulder drum; 60f. Harp. HORIZ: 15f. Viol; 100f. Xylophone.

22 Sir Winston Churchill

1965. Air. Churchill Commemoration.
147	**22**	50f. black and green	1·50	85

23 Dr. Albert Schweitzer (philosopher and missionary) and "Appealing Hands"

1966. Air. Schweitzer Commemoration.
148	**23**	100f. multicoloured	3·00	1·50

24 Mask in Mortar

1966. World Festival of Negro Arts, Dakar.
149	**24**	15f. purple, bistre & blue	50	20
150	-	20f. brown, red and green	80	40
151	-	60f. purple, blue and red	1·90	90
152	-	80f. green, brown & violet	3·00	1·20

DESIGNS—Sao Art: 20f. Mask; 60f. Mask (different) (All from J. Courtin's excavations at Bouta Kebira); 80f. Armband (from INTSH excavations, Gawi).

1966. No. 94 surch.
153	**6**	25f. on 20f. multicoloured	90	55

26 WHO Building

1966. Inaug of WHO Headquarters, Geneva.
154	**26**	25f. blue, yellow and red	65	30
155	**26**	32f. blue, yellow & green	85	40

27 Caduceus and Map of Africa

1966. Central African Customs and Economic Union.
156	**27**	30f. multicoloured	90	50

28 Footballer

1966. World Cup Football Championship.
157	**28**	30f. red, green and emerald	80	40
158	-	60f. red, black and blue	1·60	75

DESIGN—VERT: 60f. Footballer (different).

29 Youths, Flag and Arms

1966. Youth Movement.
159 **29** 25f. multicoloured 90 50

30 Columns

1966. 20th Anniv of UNESCO.
160 **30** 32f. blue, violet and red 90 50

1966. Air. Inauguration of "DC-8" Air Services. As T **54** of Central African Republic.
161 30f. grey, black and green 90 40

31 Skull of Lake Chad Man ("*Tchadanthropus uxoris*")

1966. Archaeological Excavation.
162 **31** 30f. slate, yellow and red 2·40 1·10

32 White-throated Bee Eater

1966. Air. Birds. Multicoloured.
163 50f. Greater blue-eared glossy
 starling 1·60 70
164 100f. Type **32** 3·50 1·70
165 200f. African pigmy kingfisher 6·00 2·75
166 250f. Red-throated bee eater 7·75 3·00
167 500f. Little green bee eater 14·00 6·00

33 Battle-axe

1966. Prehistoric Implements.
168 **33** 25f. brown, blue and red 75 30
169 - 30f. black, brown & blue 1·00 50
170 - 85f. brown, red and blue 2·75 95
171 - 100f. brown, turq & sepia 3·25 1·40
MS172 129×99 mm. Nos. 168/71 13·00 9·25
DESIGNS: 30f. Arrowhead; 85f. Harpoon; 100f. Sandstone grindstone and pounder. From Tchad National Museum.

34 Congress Palace

1967. Air.
173 **34** 25f. multicoloured 90 40

35 Sportsmen and Dais on Map

1967. Sports Day.
174 **35** 25f. multicoloured 90 55

36 *Colotis protomedia klug*

1967. Butterflies. Multicoloured.
175 Type **36** 5f. 1·40 40
176 10f. *Charaxes jasius epijasius* L 2·75 95
177 20f. *Junonia cebrene trim* 6·00 2·00
178 130f. *Danaida petiverana* H.D. 13·00 3·50

37 Lions Emblem

1967. Air. 50th Anniv of Lions International.
179 **37** 50f.+10f. multicoloured 1·80 95

38 Dagnaux's Breguet "19" Aircraft

1967. Air. First Anniv of Air Chad Airline.
180 **38** 25f. green, blue & brown 90 40
181 - 30f. indigo, green and
 blue 1·10 55
182 - 50f. brown, green & blue 2·10 1·20
183 - 100f. red, blue and green 3·75 1·60
DESIGNS: 30f. Latecoere "631" flying-boat; 50f. Douglas "DC-3"; 100f. Piper Cherokee "6".

1967. Air. Fifth Anniv of UAMPT. As T **66** of Central African Republic.
184 100f. brown, bistre & mve 2·40 1·10

39 H.Q. Building

1967. Opening of WHO Regional Headquarters, Brazzaville.
185 **39** 30f. multicoloured 90 50

40 Scouts and Jamboree Emblem

1967. World Scout Jamboree, Idaho. Multicoloured.
186 Type **40** 25f. 80 30
187 32f. Scout and Jamboree
 emblem 1·10 40

41 Flour Mills

1967. Economic Development.
188 **41** 25f. slate, brown and
 blue 70 30
189 - 30f. blue, brown & green 90 50
DESIGN: 30f. Land reclamation, Lake Bol.

42 Woman and Harpist

1967. Bailloud Mission in the Ennedi. Rock paintings.
190 2f. choc, brn & red (post) 50 15
191 10f. red, brown and
 violet 1·20 40
192 **42** 15f. lake, brown and
 blue 1·60 40
193 - 20f. red, brown and
 green 3·00 1·10
194 - 25f. red, brown and blue 3·25 1·20
195 - 30f. lake, brown and
 blue 1·50 75
196 - 50f. lake, brown and
 green 2·40 1·20
197 - 75f. red, brn & grn (air) 6·75 2·10
198 - 125f. lake, brown & blue 8·00 3·00
DESIGNS: 2f. Archers; 10f. Male and female costumes; 20f. Funeral vigil; 25f. *Dispute*; 30f. Giraffes; 50f. Cameleer pursuing ostrich. (48×27 mm); 100f. Masked dancers; 125f. Hunters and hare.

43 Emblem of Rotary International

1968. Tenth Anniv of Rotary Club, Fort Lamy.
199 **43** 50f. multicoloured 1·30 75

44 Downhill Skiing

1968. Air. Winter Olympic Games, Grenoble.
200 **44** 30f. brown, green &
 purple 1·20 60
201 - 100f. blue, green & turq 3·75 1·60
DESIGN—VERT: 100f. Ski-jumping.

45 Chancellor Adenauer

1968. Air. Adenauer Commemoration.
202 **45** 52f. brown, lilac and
 green 1·50 75
MS203 120×170 mm. No. 202×4 6·50 6·00

46 "Health Services"

1968. Air. Anniv of WHO.
204 **46** 25f. multicoloured 70 45
205 **46** 32f. multicoloured 90 45

47 Allegory of Irrigation

1968. International Hydrological Decade.
206 **47** 50f. blue, brown & green 1·20 50

48 *The Snake-charmer*

1968. Air. Paintings by Henri Rousseau. Multicoloured.
207 100f. Type **48** 3·75 2·10
208 130f. *The War* (49×35 mm) 5·75 3·00

49 College Building, Student and Emblem

1968. National College of Administration.
209 **49** 25f. purple, blue and red 75 30

50 Child writing and Blackboard

1968. Literacy Day.
210 **50** 60f. black, blue & brown 1·20 55

51 Harvesting Cotton

1968. Cotton Industry.
211 **51** 25f. purple, green & blue 80 30
212 - 30f. brown, blue & green 85 40
DESIGN—VERT: 30f. Loom, Fort Archambault Mill.

52 *Utetheisa pulchella*

1968. Butterflies and Moths. Multicoloured.
213 25f. Type **52** 4·00 90
214 30f. *Ophideres materna* 4·75 1·00
215 50f. *Gynanisa maja* 7·75 1·20
216 100f. *Epiphora bauhiniae* 9·50 2·40

53 Hurdling

1968. Air. Olympic Games, Mexico.
217 **53** 32f. chocolate, grn & brn 1·20 75
218 - 80f. purple, blue and red 3·00 1·40
DESIGN: 80f. Relay-racing.

54 Human Rights Emblem within Man

1968. Human Rights Year.
219 **54** 32f. red, green and blue 90 40

1969. Air. "Philexafrique" Stamp Exn, Abidjan, Ivory Coast (1st issue). As T **137** of Cameroun. Multicoloured.
220 100f. *The actor Wolf, called Bernard* (J. L. David) 4·25 3·75

1969. Air. "Philexafrique" Stamp Exn, Abidjan, Ivory Coast (2nd issue). As T **138** of Cameroun. Multicoloured.
221 50f. Moundangs dancers and
 Chad postage due stamp
 of 1930 2·75 2·50

55 G. Nachtigal and Tibesti landscape, 1869

1969. Air. Chad Explorers.
222 - 100f. violet, green & blue 2·75 1·10
223 **55** 100f. purple, blue &
 brown 2·75 1·10
DESIGN: No. 222, H. Barth (portrait) and aboard canoe, Lake Region, 1851.

56 "Apollo 8" circling Moon

1969. Air. Flight of "Apollo 8" around the Moon.
224 **56** 100f. black, blue &
 orange 2·40 1·10

57 St. Bartholomew

1969. Jubilee Year of Catholic Church. Multicoloured.
225	50c.	St. Paul	10	10
226	1f.	St. Peter	10	10
227	2f.	St. Thomas	10	10
228	5f.	St. John the Evangelist	10	10
229	10f.	Type **57**	15	10
230	20f.	St. Matthew	35	15
231	25f.	St. James the Less	40	20
232	30f.	St. Andrew	55	30
233	40f.	St. Jude	60	40
234	50f.	St. James the Greater	75	40
235	85f.	St. Philip	1·20	70
236	100f.	St. Simon	1·20	80

58 Mahatma Gandhi

1969. Air. "Apostles of Peace".
237	**58**	50f. brown and green	1·50	75
238	-	50f. sepia and agate	1·50	75
239	-	50f. brown and pink	1·50	75
240	-	50f. brown and blue	1·50	75
MS241	120×160 mm. Nos. 237/40		6·75	6·50

DESIGNS: No. 238, President Kennedy; No. 239, Martin Luther King; No. 240, Robert F. Kennedy.

59 Motor Vehicles and ILO Emblem

1969. 50th Anniv of ILO.
242	**59**	32f. blue, purple & green	90	50

60 Cipolla, Baran and Sambo (pair with cox) **61** "African Woman" (Bezombes)

1969. "World Solidarity". Multicoloured. (a) Gold Medal Winners, Mexico Olympics.
243	1f.	Type **60**	50	45
244	1f.	R. Beamon (long-jump)	40	40
245	1f.	I. Becker (women's pentathlon)	40	40
246	1f.	C. Besson (women's 400 m)	40	40
247	1f.	W. Davenport (110 m hurdles)	40	40
248	1f.	K. Dibiasi (diving)	40	40
249	1f.	R. Fosbury (high-jump)	40	40
250	1f.	M. Gamoudi (5000 m)	40	40
251	1f.	Great Britain (sailing)	40	40
252	1f.	J. Guyon (cross-country riding)	40	40
253	1f.	D. Hemery (400 m hurdles)	40	40
254	1f.	S. Kato (gymnastics)	40	40
255	1f.	B. Klinger (small bore rifle shooting)	40	40
256	1f.	R. Matson (shot put)	40	40
257	1f.	R. Matthes (100 m backstroke)	40	40
258	1f.	D. Meyer (women's 200 m freestyle)	40	40
259	1f.	Morelon and Trentin (tandem cycle)	40	40
260	1f.	D. Rebillard (4000 m cycle pursuit)	40	40
261	1f.	T. Smith (200 m)	40	40
262	1f.	P. Trentin (1000 m cycle)	40	40

263	1f.	F. Vianelli (196 km cycle race)	40	40
264	1f.	West Germany (dressage)	40	40
265	1f.	M. Wolke (welterweight boxing)	40	40
266	1f.	Zimmermann and Esser (women's kayak pair)	40	40

(b) Paintings.
267	1f.	Type **61**	40	40
268	1f.	"Mother and Child" (Gauguin)	40	40
269	1f.	"Holy Family" (Murillo) (horiz)	40	40
270	1f.	"Adoration of the Kings" (Rubens)	40	40
271	1f.	"Three Negroes" (Rubens)	40	40
272	1f.	"Woman with Flowers" (Veneto)	40	40

62 Presidents Tombalbaye and Mobutu

1969. Air. First Anniv of Central African States Union.
273	**62**	1000f. gold, red and blue	30·00	29·00

This stamp is embossed in gold foil; colours of flags enamelled.

63 "Cochlospermum tinctorium"

1969. Flowers. Multicoloured.
274	1f.	Type **63**	40	10
275	4f.	*Parkia biglobosa*	65	20
276	10f.	*Pancratium trianthum*	90	40
277	15f.	*Ipomoea aquatica*	1·50	50

1969. Air. Birth Bicentenary of Napoleon Bonaparte. Multicoloured. As T **144** of Cameroun.
278	30f.	*Napoleon visiting the Hotel des Invalides* (Veron-Bellecourt)	1·50	1·10
279	85f.	*The Battle of Wagram* (H. Vernet)	3·00	1·50
280	130f.	*The Battle of Austerlitz* (Gerard)	5·00	2·50

64 Frozen Carcases

1969. Frozen Meat Industry.
281	**64**	25f. red, green and orange	60	30
282	-	30f. brown, slate & green	75	40

DESIGN: 30f. Cattle and refrigerated abattoir, Farcha.

1969. Fifth Anniv of African Development Bank. As T **146** of Cameroun.
283	30f.	brown, green and red	75	40

66 Astronaut and Lunar Module

1969. Air. First Man on the Moon. Embossed on gold foil.
289	**66**	1000f. gold	30·00	29·00

67 Nile Mouthbrooder

1969. Fishes.
290	**67**	2f. purple, grey and green	50	15
291	-	3f. grey, red and blue	75	25
292	-	5f. blue, yellow and ochre	1·10	35
293	-	20f. blue, green and red	3·50	90

FISHES: 3f. Deep-sided citharinid; 5f. Nile pufferfish; 20f. Lesser tigerfish.

1969. Tenth Anniv of ASECNA. As T **150** of Cameroun.
294	30f.	orange	90	50

68 President Tombalbaye

1970. President Tombalbaye.
295	**68**	25f. multicoloured	75	30

69 *Village Life* (G. Narcisse)

1970. Air. African Paintings. Multicoloured.
296	100f.	Type **69**	3·50	1·50
297	250f.	*Market Woman* (I. N'Diaye)	5·50	2·20
298	250f.	*Flower-seller* (I. N'Diaye) (vert)	5·50	2·20

70 Lenin

1970. Birth Centenary of Lenin.
299	**70**	150f. black, cream & gold	4·25	1·90

1970. New U.P.U. Headquarters Building, Berne, As T **156** of Cameroun.
300	30f.	brown, violet and red	90	50

71 Class and Torchbearers

1970. International Education Year.
301	**71**	100f. multicoloured	2·10	1·20

72 Osaka Print

1970. Air. World Fair "EXPO 70", Osaka, Japan.
302	**72**	50f. green, blue and red	90	55
303	-	100f. blue, green and red	1·50	75
304	-	125f. slate. brown & red	2·20	1·10

DESIGNS: 100f. Tower of the Sun; 125f. Osaka print (different).

1970. Air. "Apollo" Moon Flights. Nos. 164/6 surch with new value, and optd with various inscriptions and diagrams concerning space flights.
305	**32**	50f. on 100f. mult ("Apollo 11")	1·50	55
306	-	100f. on 200f. mult ("Apollo 12")	3·00	90
307	-	125f. on 250f. mult ("Apollo 13")	3·75	1·10

74 Meteorological Equipment and "Agriculture"

1970. World Meteorological Day.
308	**74**	50f. grey, green & orange	1·10	45

75 "DC-8-63" over Airport

1970. Air. "Air Afrique" DC-8 "Fort Lamy".
309	**75**	30f. multicoloured	1·20	60

76 Ahmed Mangue (Minister of Education)

1970. Ahmed Mangue (air crash victim) Commem.
310	**76**	100f. black, red and gold	1·80	75

77 Tanning

1970. Trades and Handicrafts.
311	**77**	1f. bistre, brown and blue	15	10
312	-	2f. brown, blue and green	20	10
313	-	3f. violet, brown & mauve	35	15
314	-	4f. brown, bistre & green	40	15
315	-	5f. brown, green and red	80	50

DESIGNS—VERT: 2f. Dyeing; 4f. Water-carrying. HORIZ: 3f. Milling palm-nuts for oil; 5f. Copper-founding.

78 U.N. Emblem and Dove

1970. 25th Anniv of United Nations.
316	**78**	32f. multicoloured	90	55

79 *The Visitation* (Venetian School, 15th cent)

1970. Air. Christmas. Multicoloured.
317	20f.	Type **79**	80	50
318	25f.	*The Nativity* (Venetian School, 15th cent)	1·20	55
319	30f.	*Virgin and Child* (Veneziano)	1·40	75

80 Map and OCAM Building

1971. OCAM (Organization Commune Africaine et Malgache) Conference, Fort Lamy.
320	**80**	30f. multicoloured	90	50

81 Maritius "Post Office"
2d. of 1847

1971. Air. "PHILEXOCAM" Stamp Exhibition, Fort-Lamy.

321	**81**	10f. slate, brown & turq	55	30
322	-	20f. brown, black & turq	55	30
323	-	30f. brown, black and red	75	50
324	-	60f. black, brown & purple	1·20	60
325	-	80f. slate, brown and blue	1·80	1·10
326	-	100f. brown, slate & blue	2·20	1·50
MS327		160×130 mm. Nos. 321/6	8·75	8·25

DESIGNS—20f. Tuscany 3 lire of 1860; 30f. France 1f. of 1849; 30f., 60f. U.S.A. 10c. of 1847; 80f. Japan 5 sen of 1872; 100f. Saxony 3pf. of 1850.

82 Pres. Nasser

1971. Air. First Death Anniv of Gamal Abdel Nasser (Egypt).

328	**82**	75f. multicoloured	1·20	55

83 "Racial Harmony" Tree

1971. Racial Equality Year.

329	**83**	40f. red, green and blue	1·10	60

1971. Air. Reconciliation with Central African Republic and Zaire. As T **106** of Central African Republic.

330		100f. multicoloured	2·10	1·10

84 Map and Dish Aerial

1971. World Telecommunications Day.

331	**84**	5f. orge, red & bl (postage)	35	10
332	-	40f. green, brown & pur	95	40
333	-	50f. black, brown & red	1·10	60
334	-	125f. red, green & blue (air)	2·75	1·40

DESIGNS: 40f. Map and communications tower; 50f. Map and satellite. (48×27 mm); 125f. Map and telecommunications symbols.

85 Scouts by Camp-fire

1971. Air. World Scout Jamboree, Asagiri, Japan.

335	**85**	250f. multicoloured	5·75	2·75

86 Great Egret

1971. Air.

336	**86**	1000f. multicoloured	60·00	22·00

87 Ancient Marathon Race

1971. Air. 75th Anniv of Modern Olympic Games. Multicoloured.

337	**87**	40f. Type **87**	95	50
338	-	45f. Ancient stadium, Olympia	1·30	50
339	-	75f. Ancient wrestling	1·60	75
340	-	130f. Athens Stadium, 1896 Games	2·50	1·10

88 Sidney Bechet

1971. Air. Famous American Black Musicians. Multicoloured.

341	**88**	50f. Type **88**	2·00	85
342	-	75f. Duke Ellington	3·00	1·20
343	-	100f. Louis Armstrong	4·75	1·70

89 Gen. de Gaulle

1971. Air. First Death Anniv of De Gaulle.

344	-	200f. gold, blue and light blue	9·00	8·75
345	**89**	200f. gold, green & yellow	8·75	8·25
MS346		110×70 mm. Nos. 344/5 and central stamp-sized label with inscr	22·00	22·00

DESIGN: No. 344, Governor-General Felix Eboue.

1971. Air. Tenth Anniv of African and Malagasy Posts and Telecommunications Union. As T **184** of Cameroun. Multicoloured.

347		100f. Headquarters building and Sao carved animal head	1·80	1·10

90 Children's Heads

1971. 25th Anniv of UNICEF.

348	**90**	50f. blue, green & purple	1·20	55

On the above stamp, "24e" has been obliterated and "25e" inserted in the commemorative inscription.

91 Gorane Nangara Dancers

1971. Chad Dancers. Multicoloured.

349		10f. Type **91**	75	30
350		15f. Yondo initiates	1·10	45
351		30f. M'Boum (vert)	1·60	65
352		40f. Sara Kaba (vert)	2·40	90

93 Presidents Pompidou and Tombalbaye

1972. Visit of French President.

354	**93**	40f. multicoloured	1·90	85

94 Bobsleighing

1972. Air. Winter Olympic Games, Sapporo, Japan.

355	**94**	50f. red and blue	1·10	70
356	-	100f. green and purple	2·20	95

DESIGN: 100f. Slalom.

95 Human Heart

1972. World Heart Month.

357	**95**	100f. red, blue and violet	2·10	1·10

96 *Gorrizia dubiosa*

1972. Insects. Multicoloured.

358	**96**	1f. Type **96**	85	25
359		2f. *Argiope sector*	1·40	30
360		3f. *Nephila senegalense*	1·60	40
361		4f. *Oryctes boas*	2·75	55
362		5f. *Hemistigma albipunctata*	3·50	55
363		25f. *Dinothrombium tinctorium*	1·10	40
364		30f. *Bupreste sternocera* H.	1·70	45
365		40f. *Hyperechia bomboides*	2·10	50
366		50f. *Chrysis* (Hymenoptere)	2·50	70
367		100f. *Tithoes confinis* (Longicore)	4·25	1·20
368		130f. *Galeodes araba* (Solifuge)	7·00	1·90

1972. Air. UNESCO "Save Venice" Campaign. As T **191** of Cameroun. Multicoloured.

369		40f. "Harbour Panorama" (detail, Caffi)	1·80	70
370		45f. *Venice Panorama* (detail, Caffi) (horiz)	2·40	1·10
371		140f. *Grand Canal* (detail, Caffi)	4·75	2·10

97 Hurdling

1972. Olympic Games, Munich. Multicoloured.

372	**97**	50f. Type **97**	90	45
373		130f. Gymnastics	2·20	1·10
374		150f. Swimming	3·00	1·40
MS375		102×86 mm. 300f. Cycling	7·75	3·25

98 Alphonse Daudet and Scene from *Tartarin de Tarascon*

1972. Air. International Book Year.

376	**98**	100f. brown, red & purple	2·20	1·10

99 Dromedary

1972. Domestic Animals.

377	**99**	25f. brown and violet	1·30	30
378	-	30f. blue and mauve	1·70	40
379	-	40f. brown and green	2·40	55
380	-	45f. brown and blue	2·75	60

DESIGNS: 30f. Horse; 40f. Saluki hound; 45f. Goat.

100 "Luna XVI" and Moon Probe

1972. Air. Russian Moon Exploration.

381	**100**	100f. violet, brown & blue	2·20	95
382	-	150f. brown, blue & violet	3·00	1·50

DESIGN—HORIZ: 150f. "Lunokhod 1" Moon vehicle.

101 Tobacco Production

1972. Economic Development.

383	**101**	40f. green, red & brown	80	40
384	-	50f. brown, green & blue	1·20	55

DESIGN: 50f. Ploughing with oxen.

102 Microscope, Cattle and Laboratory

1972. Air. 20th Anniv of Farcha Veterinary Laboratory.

385	**102**	75f. multicoloured	1·50	60

103 Massa Warrior

1972. Chad Warriors. Multicoloured.

386	**103**	15f. Type **103**	85	30
387		20f. Moudang archer	1·00	55

104 King Faisal and Pres. Tombalbaye

1972. Visit of King Faisal of Saudi Arabia. Multicoloured.

389		75f. King Faisal and Ka'aba, Mecca (air)	1·50	75
388		100f. Type **104** (postage)	2·75	1·30

105 Gen. Gowon, Pres. Tombalbaye and Map

1972. Visit of Gen. Gowon, Nigerian Head-of-State.

390	**105**	70f. multicoloured	1·10	50

106 *Madonna and Child* (G. Bellini)

1972. Air. Christmas. Paintings. Multicoloured.

391		40f. Type **106**	90	40

392		75f. *Virgin and Child* (bas-relief, Da Santivo, Dall' Occhio)	1·40	65
393		80f. *Nativity* (B. Angelico) (horiz)	2·10	80
394		90f. *Adoration of the Magi* (P. Perugino)	2·40	1·40

107 Commemorative Scroll

1972. 50th Anniv of U.S.S.R.

| 395 | 107 | 150f. multicoloured | 2·20 | 85 |

108 High-jumping

1973. Second African Games, Lagos. Multicoloured.

396		Type **108**	1·10	55
397		125f. Running	1·90	80
398		200f. Putting the shot	3·00	1·40
MS399		103×86 mm. 250f. Throwing the discus	4·25	2·75

109 Copernicus and Planetary System Diagram

1973. Air. 500th Birth Anniv of Nicholas Copernicus.

| 400 | 109 | 250f. grey, brown & mve | 6·00 | 2·50 |

1973. African Solidarity. "Drought Relief". No. 377 surch **SECHERESSE SOLIDARITE AFRICAINE 100F.**

| 401 | 99 | 100f. on 25f. brown & vio | 2·40 | 1·10 |

1973. UAMPT. As Type **216** of Cameroun.

| 402 | | 100f. green, red & brown | 2·10 | 95 |

111 "Skylab" over Globe

1974. Air. "Skylab" Exploits.

| 403 | 111 | 100f. brown, red & blue | 1·80 | 80 |
| 404 | - | 150f. turquoise, blue & brn | 3·00 | 1·20 |

DESIGN: 150f. Close-up of "Skylab".

112 Chad Mother and Children

1974. First Anniv of Chad Red Cross.

| 405 | 112 | 30f.+10f. multicoloured | 1·00 | 85 |

113 Football Players

1974. Air. World Cup Football Championship, West Germany.

406	113	50f. brown and red	75	60
407	-	125f. green and red (vert)	2·10	95
408	-	150f. red and green	2·75	1·50

DESIGNS: Nos. 407/8, Footballers in action similar to Type **113**.

114 Chad Family

1974. Air. World Population Year.

| 409 | 114 | 250f. brown, green & bl | 4·50 | 2·40 |

115 U.P.C. Emblem and Mail Canoe

1974. Air. Centenary of U.P.U.

410	115	30f. brown, red & green	75	30
411	-	40f. black and blue	1·10	50
412	-	100f. blue, brown & blk	2·20	75
413	-	150f. violet, green & turq	3·00	1·10

DESIGNS—U.P.U. Emblem and: 40f. Electric train; 100f. Jet airliner; 150f. Satellite.

116 Rotary Emblem

1975. 70th Anniv of Rotary International.

| 414 | 116 | 50f. multicoloured | 1·10 | 55 |

117 Heads of Women of Four Races

1975. Air. International Women's Year.

| 415 | 117 | 250f. multicoloured | 5·25 | 2·50 |

118 "Apollo" and "Soyuz" Spacecraft about to dock

1975. Air. "Apollo–Soyuz" Test Project.

| 416 | 118 | 100f. brown, blue & green | 1·60 | 75 |
| 417 | - | 130f. brown, blue & green | 2·10 | 1·00 |

DESIGN: 130f. "Apollo" and "Soyuz" spacecraft docked.

119 *Craterostigma plantagineum*

1975. Flowers. Multicoloured.

418		5f. Type **119**	30	10
419		10f. *Tapinanthus globiferus*	50	15
420		15f. *Commelina forsalaei* (vert)	75	20
421		20f. *Adenium obasum*	90	25
422		25f. *Hibiscus esulenus*	1·50	30
423		30f. *Hibiscus sabdariffa*	1·70	50
424		40f. *Kigelia africana*	2·40	75

120 Football

1975. Air. Olympic Games, Montreal (1976).

425	120	75f. green and red	1·10	55
426	-	100f. brown, blue & red	1·80	80
427	-	125f. blue and brown	2·10	1·20

DESIGNS: 100f. Throwing the discus; 125f. Running.

1975. Air. Successful Rendezvous of "Apollo–Soyuz" Mission. Optd **JONCTION 17 JUILLET 1975.**

| 428 | 118 | 100f. brown, blue & grn | 1·70 | 95 |
| 429 | - | 130f. brown, blue & grn | 2·30 | 1·50 |

122 Stylized British and American Flags

1975. Air. Bicentenary of American Revolution.

| 430 | 122 | 150f. blue, red & brown | 2·75 | 1·20 |

123 *Adoration of the Shepherds* (Murillo)

1975. Air. Christmas. Religious Paintings. Multicoloured.

431		40f. Type **123**	85	55
432		75f. *Adoration of the Shepherds* (G. de la Tour)	1·60	80
433		80f. *Virgin of the Bible* (R. van der Weyden) (vert)	1·80	80
434		100f. *Holy Family with the Lamb* (attrib. Raphael) (vert)	2·75	1·40

124 Alexander Graham Bell and Satellite

1976. Telephone Centenary.

| 435 | 124 | 100f. multicoloured | 1·70 | 75 |
| 436 | 124 | 125f. multicoloured | 2·50 | 1·10 |

125 U.S.S.R. (ice hockey)

1976. Winter Olympics. Medal-winners, Innsbruck. Multicoloured.

437		60f. Type **125** (postage)	95	50
438		90f. Ski-jumping (K. Schnabl, Austria)	1·40	50
439		250f. Bobsleighing (West Germany) (air)	3·25	1·10
440		300f. Speed-skating (J. E. Storholt, Norway)	4·00	1·50
MS441		103×78 mm. 500f. F. Klammer of Austria (downhill skiing)	6·50	2·75

These stamps were not issued without overprints.

126 Paul Revere (after Copley) and his Night Ride

1976. Air. Bicentenary of American Revolution.. Multicoloured.

442		100f. Type **126**	1·20	30
443		125f. Washington (after Stuart) and *Washington crossing the Delaware* (detail, Leutze)	1·50	50
444		150f. Lafayette offering his serv- ices to America	2·10	65
445		200f. Rochambeau and detail *Siege of Yorktown* (Couder)	2·40	95
446		250f. Franklin (after Duplessis) and *Declaration of Independ- ence* (detail, Trumball)	3·75	1·10

127 Hurdles

1976. Olympic Games, Montreal. Multicoloured.

448		45f. Type **127** (postage)	90	30
449		100f. Boxing (air)	1·50	60
450		200f. Pole vaulting	2·75	90
451		300f. Putting the shot	3·75	1·20
MS452		103×77 mm. 500f. Sprint	6·50	2·75

MS447 103×78 mm. 400f. De Grasse (after Mauzaisse) and Battle of *Virginia Capes* (detail, Zveg) 6·50 2·75

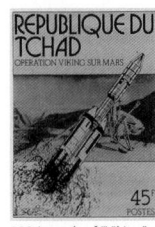

128 Launch of "Viking"

1976. "Viking" landing on Mars. Multicoloured.

453		45f. Type **128** (postage)	60	30
454		90f. Trajectory of flight	1·50	50
455		100f. Descent to Mars (air)	1·10	45
456		200f. "Viking" in flight	2·40	65
457		250f. "Viking" on landing approach	3·00	1·10
MS458		114×89 mm. 450f. "Viking" on Mars	5·00	1·90

129 Flag and Clasped Hands on Map of Chad

1976. National Reconciliation. Multicoloured.

459		30f. Type **129**	65	30
460		60f. Type **129**	1·20	60
461		120f. Map, people and various occupations	2·75	1·20

130 Release of Political Prisoners

1976. First Anniv of April 1st Revolution. Multicoloured.

462		30f. Type **130**	35	20
463		60f. Officer-cadets on parade	85	55
464		120f. Type **130**	1·80	85

131 Concorde

1976. Air. Concorde's First Commercial Flight.

| 465 | 131 | 250f. blue, red & black | 6·50 | 3·75 |

132 Gourd and Ladle

1976. Pyrogravated Gourds.

466	132	30f. multicoloured	60	30
467	-	60f. multicoloured	95	45
468	-	120f. multicoloured	1·90	95

DESIGNS: 60f., 120f. Gourds with different decorations.

1976. Nobel Prizewinners. As T **189** of Central African Empire. Multicoloured.

469	45f. Robert Koch (Medicine, 1905)	1·50	55
470	90f. Anatole France (Literature, 1921)	1·80	80
471	100f. Albert Einstein (Physics, 1921) (air)	2·20	55
472	200f. Dag Hammarskjold (Peace, 1961)	2·75	80
473	300f. Dr. S. Tomonaga (Physics, 1965)	4·25	1·10
MS474	116×79 mm. 500f. Alexander Fleming (Medicine, 1945)	9·00	3·00

133 *The Nativity* (Hans Holbein)

1976. Air. Christmas. Multicoloured.

475	30f. *The Nativity* (Altdorfer)	60	30
476	60f. Type **133**	90	50
477	120f. *Adoration of the Shepherds* (Honthorst) (horiz)	1·60	95
478	150f. *Adoration of the Magi* (David) (horiz)	2·40	1·40

134 *Lesdiguieres Bridge*

1976. Air. Centenary of Impressionism. Paintings by Johan Bathold Jongkind. Multicoloured.

| 479 | 100f. Type **134** | 1·90 | 1·10 |
| 480 | 120f. *Warship* | 2·20 | 1·10 |

1977. Zeppelin Flights. As T **190** of Central African Empire. Multicoloured.

481	100f. Friedrichshafen and German 50pf. stamp, 1936 (postage)	2·10	1·70
482	125f. Polar scene and German 1m. stamp, 1931 (air)	2·00	60
483	150f. Chicago store and German 4m. stamp, 1933	3·25	75
484	175f. New York, London and German 2m. stamp, 1928	3·75	90
485	200f. New York and U.S. $2.60 stamp, 1930	4·00	1·40
MS486	130×92 mm. 500f. As No. 485	8·75	2·75

1977. Air. Tenth Anniv of International French Language Council. As T **204** of Benin.

| 487 | 100f. multicoloured | 1·10 | 65 |

135 *Simon Bolivar*

1977. Great Personalities. Multicoloured.

488	150f. Type **135**	1·70	65
489	175f. Joseph J. Roberts	2·30	80
490	200f. Queen Wilhelmina	3·00	1·10
491	200f. General de Gaulle	3·50	1·30
493	250f. Coronation of Queen Elizabeth II (horiz)	3·75	1·50
492	325f. King Baudouin and Queen Fabiola	4·25	1·60

136 *Queen Elizabeth II*

1977. 25th Anniv of Queen Elizabeth II's Accession to Throne Multicoloured.

| 493a | 250f. Type **136** | 2·50 | 90 |

| MS494 | 110×91 mm. 450f. Queen Elizabeth and Prince Philip | 6·50 | 2·40 |

137 *Lafayette and Arrival in America*

1977. Air. Bicentenary of American Independence. Multicoloured.

495	100f. Type **137**	1·50	65
496	120f. Abraham Lincoln	1·90	80
497	150f. F. J. Madison	2·50	1·10

138 *Radio Aerial, Sound Waves and Map*

1977. Posts and Telecommunications Emblems.

498	30f. black and yellow	60	30
499	**138** 60f. multicoloured	90	40
500	– 120f. multicoloured	1·70	95

DESIGNS—HORIZ (47×26 mm): 30f. Posthorn and initials "ONPT". VERT (26×36 mm): 120f. Telecommunications skyline and initials "TIT".

139 *Concorde*

1977. Air. "North Atlantic"—Concorde and Lindbergh Commemorations.

501	**139** 100f. blue, red & lt blue	2·30	1·20
502	– 120f. brown, blue & grn	1·40	75
503	– 150f. violet, red & green	1·80	1·10
504	– 200f. orange, pur & brn	2·40	1·20
505	– 300f. blue, purple & blk	3·50	1·80

DESIGNS: 120f. to 300f. Various portraits of Lindbergh with *Spirit of St. Louis* against different backgrounds.

140 *"Mariner 10"*

1977. Air. Space Research.

506	**140** 100f. blue, olive & green	1·20	85
507	– 200f. brown, green & red	2·40	1·40
508	– 300f. brown, grn & bistre	3·50	1·80

DESIGNS: 200f. "Luna 21"; 300f. "Viking".

141 *Running*

1977. Air. Sports.

509	**141** 30f. brown, red & blue	40	25
510	– 60f. brown, blue & orge	90	50
511	– 120f. multicoloured	1·50	80
512	– 125f. mauve, violet & grn	2·10	1·00

DESIGNS: 60f. Volleyball; 120f. Football; 125f. Basketball.

142 *"Back Pain"*

1977. World Rheumatism Year.

513	**142** 30f. red, green and violet	60	30
514	– 60f. red, violet and green	1·00	50
515	– 120f. blue, red & lt blue	1·70	1·00

DESIGNS—HORIZ: 60f. "Neck pain". VERT: 120f. "Knee pain".

1977. Air. First Commercial Paris–New York Flight of Concorde. Optd **PARIS NEW-YORK 22.11.77.**

| 516 | **139** 100f. blue, red & lt blue | 3·50 | 1·80 |

144 *Saving a Goal*

1977. World Football Cup Championship. Multicoloured.

517	40f. Type **144**	55	15
518	60f. Heading the ball	80	30
519	100f. Referee	1·50	50
520	200f. Foot kicking ball	3·00	95
521	300f. Pele (Brazilian player)	4·50	1·30
MS522	118×80 mm. 500f. Helmut Schoen and stadium	6·50	2·75

145 *Christ in the Manger* (detail)

1977. Air. Christmas. Paintings by Rubens. Multocoloured.

523	30f. Type **145**	75	35
524	60f. Virgin and Child with Two Donors	1·50	60
525	100f. The Adoration of the Shepherds	2·10	85
526	125f. The Adoration of the Magi (detail)	2·30	1·20

1978. Coronation of Queen Elizabeth II. No. 493 **MS494** optd **ANNIVERSAIRE DU COURONNEMENT 1953–1978.**

| 527 | 250f. multicoloured | 3·25 | 1·90 |
| MS528 | 111×92 mm. 450f. multicoloured | 6·75 | 4·00 |

147 *Antoine de Saint-Exupery*

1978. Air. History of Aviation. Multicoloured.

529	40f. Type **147**	75	30
530	50f. Wright Brothers and aircraft in flight	90	50
531	80f. Hugo Junkers	1·20	65
532	100f. Italo Balbo	1·70	85
533	120f. "Concorde"	2·00	1·00
MS534	104×98 mm. 500f. Wright Brothers and aircraft on ground	7·50	2·75

1978. Air. "Philexafrique" Stamp Exhibition, Gabon (1st issue), and International Stamp Fair, Essen. As T **237** of Benin. Multicoloured.

| 535 | 100f. Grey heron and Mecklenburg-Strelitz, ¼sgr. stamp, 1864 | 3·75 | 2·40 |
| 536 | 100f. Black rhinoceros and Chad 500f. stamp, 1961 | 3·75 | 2·40 |

148 *Portrait*

1978. 450th Death Anniv of Albrecht Durer (artist). Multicoloured.

537	60f. Type **148**	65	20
538	150f. *Jacob Muffel*	2·10	50
539	250f. *Young Girl*	3·25	95
540	350f. *Oswolt Krel*	5·00	1·20

149 *Helene Fourment*

1978. 400th Birth Anniv of Peter Paul Rubens (artist). Multicoloured.

541	60f. *Abraham and Melchisedek* (horiz)	95	20
542	120f. Type **149**	2·00	40
543	200f. *David and the Elders of Israel* (horiz)	3·00	95
544	300f. *Anne of Austria*	5·25	1·20
MS545	78×104 mm. 500f. *Marie de Medici*	7·25	2·75

150 *Head and Unhealthy and Healthy Villages*

1978. National Health Day.

| 546 | **150** 60f. multicoloured | 1·10 | 55 |

1978. World Cup Football Championship Finalists. Nos. 517/21 optd with teams and scores of past finals.

547	**144** 40f. multicoloured	55	30
548	– 60f. multicoloured	80	45
549	– 100f. multicoloured	1·60	75
550	– 200f. multicoloured	3·00	1·40
551	– 300f. multicoloured	4·50	2·20
MS552	118×80 mm. 500f. multicoloured	6·50	6·00

OPTS: 40f. **1962 BRESIL-TCHECOSLOVAQUE 3-1**; 60f. **1966 GRANDE BRETAGNE ALLEMAGNE (RFA) 4-2**; 100f. **1970 BRESIL-ITALIE 4-1**; 200f. **1974 ALLEMAGNE (RFA)-PAYS BAS 2-1**; 300f. **1978 ARGENTINE-PAYS BAS 3-1**; 500f. **ARGENTINE-PAYS BAS 3-1.**

152 *Camel Riders, Satellites and UPU Emblem*

1978. "Philexafrique 2" Exhibition, Libreville, Gabon (2nd issue).

| 553 | **152** 60f. red, mauve & blue | 3·00 | 1·70 |
| 554 | – 150f. multicoloured | 5·00 | 3·00 |

DESIGN: 150f. Mother and child, native village and hibiscus.

153 *Sand Gazelle*

1979. Endangered Animals. Multicoloured.

555	40f. Type **153**	1·40	25
556	50f. Addax	1·50	45
557	60f. Scimitar oryx	1·80	70
558	100f. Cheetah	3·00	1·20
559	150f. African ass	4·50	1·60
560	300f. Black rhinoceros	8·75	2·00

154 *African Boy and Wall Painting*

1979. International Year of the Child. Multicoloured.

561	65f. Type **154**	75	20
562	75f. Asian girl	90	40
563	100f. European child and doves	1·10	50
564	150f. African boys and drawing of boats	1·80	75
MS565	103×77 mm. 250f. Pencil and drawing of hands	3·50	1·70

155 The Holy Family with There Hares (woodcut)

1979. 450th Death Anniv (1978) of Albrecht Durer (artist). Sheet 90×115 mm.
MS566 **155** 500f. lake and brown — 7·75 / 2·40

1979. Tenth Anniv of "Apollo 11" Moon Landing. Nos. 453/7 optd with lunar module and **ALUNISSAGE APOLLO XI JUILLET 1969.**

No.		Description		
567		45f. Type **128** (postage)	65	30
568		90f. Trajectory of flight	1·20	50
569		100f. Descent on Mars (air)	1·20	70
570		200f. "Viking" in flight	2·30	1·20
571		250f. "Viking" on landing approach	3·00	1·60
MS572		114×89 mm. 450f. multicoloured	5·50	5·25

157 Hurdles

1979. Air. Olympic Games, Moscow 1980. Multicoloured.

573	15f. Type **157**	15	10
574	30f. Hockey	35	25
575	250f. Swimming	2·75	95
576	350f. Running	3·75	1·20
MS577	117×80 mm. 500f. Yachting	6·75	2·75

158 Reed Canoe and Austrian 10k. stamp, 1910

1979. Air. Death Centenary of Sir Rowland Hill. Multicoloured.

578	65f. Type **158**	90	10
579	100f. Sailing canoe and U.S. $1 stamp of 1894	1·50	50
580	200f. *Curacao* (paddle-steamer) and French 1f. stamp of 1853	2·75	85
581	300f. *Calypso* (liner) and Holstein 1¼s. stamp of 1864	3·25	1·10
MS582	103×91 mm. 500f. Liner and Chad 10c. Postage Due stamps of 1930	7·25	2·75

159 Slalom

1979. Winter Olympic Games, Lake Placid (1980). Multicoloured.

583	20f. Type **159**	35	10
584	40f. Biathlon	60	10
585	60f. Ski jump (horiz)	90	20
586	150f. Women's giant slalom	1·80	50
587	350f. Cross-country skiing (horiz)	3·50	1·20
588	500f. Downhill skiing (horiz)	5·25	1·80

160 Concorde and Map of Africa

1980. 20th Anniv of African Air Safety Organization (ASECNA).

589	**160**	15f. multicoloured	15	10
590	**160**	30f. multicoloured	35	15
591	**160**	60f. multicoloured	65	30

1981. Various stamps optd **POSTES 1981** or surch also.

592	**157**	30f. on 15f. multicoloured	1·30	85
593	–	30f. mult (No. 574)	1·30	85
594	**158**	60f. on 65f. multicoloured	2·40	1·60
595	–	60f. on 100f. mult (No. 579)	2·40	1·60

162 Footballer

1982. World Cup Football Championship, Spain. Multicoloured.

596	30f. Hungary (postage)	35	10
597	40f. Type **162**	55	10
598	50f. Algeria	55	30
599	60f. Argentina	65	40
600	80f. Brazil (air)	1·00	45
601	300f. West Germany	3·50	1·00
MS602	77×100 mm. 500f. Spain (38×48 mm)	6·50	2·20

DESIGNS: As T **162** but each value showing different team's footballer.

163 Lady Diana and her Brother (1967)

1982. 21st Birthday of Princess of Wales. Multicoloured.

603	30f. Lady Diana in christening robe (1961) (postage)	45	10
604	40f. Portrait of Lady Diana (1965)	50	15
605	50f. Type **163**	75	30
606	60f. Lady Diana and her pony (1975)	80	40
607	80f. Lady Diana in Switzerland (1977) (air)	1·00	40
608	300f. Lady Diana as nursery teacher (1980)	3·50	1·10
MS609	78×75 mm. 500f. Princess of Wales (39×36 mm)	6·00	1·90

164 West German Scouts

1982. 75th Anniv of Scout Movement. Multicoloured.

610	30f. Type **164** (postage)	55	10
611	40f. Upper Volta scouts	55	15
612	50f. Mali scouts and African dancers	75	30
613	60f. Scottish scout, piper and dancer	80	40
614	80f. Kuwait scouts (air)	1·00	40
615	300f. Chad cub scout	3·50	1·10
MS616	110×74 mm. 500f. Chad scouts (53×35 mm)	5·50	1·90

165 Judo

1982. Olympic Games, Los Angeles (1984) (1st issue). Multicoloured.

617	30f. Gymnastics (horse exercise) (postage)	35	10
618	40f. Show jumping	55	15
619	50f. Type **165**	55	30
620	60f. High jumping	65	40
621	80f. Hurdling (air)	1·00	40
622	300f. Gymnastics (floor exercise)	3·50	1·10
MS623	110×82 mm. 500f. Relay (56×38 mm)	5·50	1·90

See also Nos. 678/MS684 and 735/MS739.

1982. Birth of Prince William of Wales. Nos. 603/8 optd **21 JUIN 1982 WILLIAM ARTHUR PHILIP LOUIS PRINCE DE GALLES.**

624	30f. Type **163** (postage)	55	10
625	40f. Portrait of Lady Diana as a young girl	55	10
626	50f. Lady Diana and her brother	75	30
627	60f. Lady Diana with her pony	80	30
628	80f. Lady Diana in Switzerland (air)	90	30
629	300f. Lady Diana with children	3·50	1·30
MS630	78×75 mm. 500f. Portrait (39×36 mm)	5·50	2·75

167 Marco Tardelli (Italy) and Passarella (Argentine)

1983. World Cup Football Championship Results. Multicoloured.

631	30f. Type **167** (postage)	55	10
632	40f. Paolo Rossi (Italy) and Zico (Brazil)	55	15
633	50f. Pierre Littbarski (West Germany) and Platini (France)	75	30
634	60f. Gabriele Oriali (Italy) and Smolarek (Poland)	80	40
635	70f. Boniek (Poland) and Alain Giresse (France) (air)	90	40
636	300f. Bruno Conti (Italy) and Paul Breitner (West Germany)	3·25	1·10
MS637	110×79 mm. 500f. Rummenigge (West Germany) and Paolo Rossi (Italy) (56×32 mm)	6·25	2·30

168 Philidor and 19th-century European Rook

1982. Chess Grand Masters. Multicoloured.

638	30f. Type **168** (postage)	85	10
639	40f. Paul Morphy and 19th-century Chinese knight	1·00	15
640	50f. Howard Staunton and Lewis knight	1·30	30
641	60f. Jean-Paul Capablanca and African knight	1·40	40
642	80f. Boris Spassky and Staunton knight (air)	2·10	55
643	300f. Anatoly Karpov and 19th-century Chinese knight	4·25	1·10
MS644	98×80 mm. 500f. Victor Kortschnoi and modern chess pieces (53×35 mm)	9·50	2·75

169 K. E. Tsiolkovski and "Soyuz"

1983. Exploitation of Space. Multicoloured.

645	30f. Type **169** (postage)	55	10
646	40f. R. H. Goddard and space telescope	55	15
647	50f. Korolev and ultra-violet telescope	75	30
648	60f. Von Braun and Space Shuttle	60	30
649	80f. Esnault Pelterie and "Ariane" rocket and "Symphonie" satellite (air)	1·00	40
650	300f. H. Oberth and construction of orbiting space station	3·50	1·10
MS651	85×85 mm. 500f. J.F.Kennedy and first man on the Moon (vert 41×50 mm)	6·25	2·30

170 Charles and Robert Balloon, 1783

1983. Air. Balloons. Multicoloured.

652	100f. Type **170**	85	25
653	200f. Blanchard balloon, Berlin, 1788	1·80	50
654	300f. Charles Green balloon, London, 1837 (horiz)	2·40	80
655	400f. Modern advertising airship (horiz)	3·00	1·00
MS656	79×98 mm. 500f. Montgolfiere balloon, 1783	6·50	2·30

171 Bobsleigh

1983. Winter Olympic Games, Sarajevo. Multicoloured.

657	30f. Type **171** (postage)	55	10
658	40f. Speed skating	55	15
659	50f. Cross-country skiing	75	30
660	60f. Ice hockey	80	40
661	80f. Ski jump (air)	1·00	40
662	300f. Downhill skiing	3·50	1·10
MS663	100×80 mm. 500f. Ice dancing	5·50	2·20

172 Montgolfier Brothers and *Le Martia* Balloon, 1783

1983. Bicentenary of Manned Flight. Multicoloured.

664	25f. Type **172** (postage)	35	10
665	45f. Pilatre de Rozier and first manned flight, 1783	75	25
666	50f. Jacques Garnerin and balloon (first parachute descent, 1797)	75	30
667	60f. J. P. Blanchard and balloon at Chelsea, 1784	85	70
668	80f. H. Giffard and steam-powered dirigible, 1852 (air)	1·10	40
669	250f. Zeppelin and airship **L 21**, 1900	3·25	1·10
MS670	57×95 mm. 300f. Montgolfier Brothers and ascent of La Flesselles (41×38 mm)	6·25	1·90

173 Gottlieb Daimler, Karl Benz and Mercedes "Type S," 1927

1983. Car Manufacturers. Multicoloured.

671	25f. Type **173** (postage)	40	10
672	35f. Friedrich von Martini and Torpedo, Martini "Type GC 32", 1913	75	15
673	50f. Walter P. Chrysler and Chrysler "70", 1924	75	30
674	60f. Nicola Romeo and Alfa Romeo "6 C 1750 Grand Sport", 1929	85	40
675	80f. Stewart Rolls, Henry Royce and "Phantom II Continental", 1934 (air)	1·50	40
676	250f. Lord Shrewsbury and Talbot-Lago "Record", 1948	3·75	1·10
MS677	109×68 mm. 300f. Ettore Bugatti and Royale Coupe de Ville "41", 1926–33	4·25	1·60

174 Kayak

1983. Olympic Games, Los Angeles (2nd issue). Multicoloured.

678	25f. Type **174** (postage)	35	10
679	45f. Long jumping	75	15
680	50f. Boxing	75	30
681	60f. Discus-throwing	85	40
682	80f. Relay race (air)	1·10	40
683	350f. Horse jumping	3·75	1·10
MS684	90×93 mm. 500f. Gymnastics (horiz 50×41 mm)	5·00	1·60

175 Dove on Map

1983. Peace and Reconciliation. Multicoloured.

685	50f. Type **175** (postage)	60	15
686	50f. Foodstuffs on map	60	15
687	50f. President Habre	80	20
688	60f. As No. 687	75	15
689	80f. Type **175**	85	30
690	80f. As No. 686	90	30
691	80f. As No. 687	1·20	30
692	100f. As No. 687	1·00	30
693	150f. Type **175** (air)	1·80	55
694	150f. As No. 686	1·80	55
695	200f. Type **175**	2·50	80
696	200f. As No. 686	2·50	80

1983. 15th World Scout Jamboree, Canada. Nos. 610/15 optd **XV WORLD JAMBOREE MONDIAL ALBERTA CANADA 1983**.

697	30f. multicoloured (postage)	35	10
698	40f. multicoloured	45	10
699	50f. multicoloured	55	20
700	60f. multicoloured	65	20
701	80f. multicoloured (air)	80	45
702	300f. multicoloured	3·25	1·60

1983. 60th Anniv of Int Chess Federation. Nos. 638/43 optd **60e ANNIVERSAIRE FEDERATION MONDIAL D'ECHECS 1924–1984**.

704	30f. multicoloured (postage)	1·00	10
705	40f. multicoloured	1·30	20
706	50f. multicoloured	1·70	30
707	60f. multicoloured	2·00	45
708	80f. multicoloured (air)	2·50	65
709	500f. multicoloured	5·00	2·20
MS710	98×80 mm. 500f. multicoloured	9·00	4·00

178 Chad Martyrs

1984. Celebrities. Multicoloured.

711	50f. Type **178** (postage)	60	15
712	200f. P. Harris and Rotary Headquarters, U.S.A.	2·20	50
713	300f. Alfred Nobel and will	3·75	90
714	350f. Raphael and *Virgin with the Infant and St. John the Baptist*	5·25	1·10
715	400f. Rembrandt and *The Holy Family* (air)	5·25	1·10
716	500f. Goethe and Scenes from *Faust*	6·50	1·40
MS717	78×86 mm. 600f. Rubens and *Helene Fourment and two of her Children*	7·75	2·40

179 Martyrs Memorial

1984. Martyrs Memorial.

718	**179**	50f. mult (postage)	60	10
719	**179**	80f. multicoloured	90	25
720	**179**	120f. multicoloured	1·20	40
721	**179**	200f. multicoloured (air)	2·40	75
722	**179**	250f. multicoloured	3·00	1·00

180 Durer and Painting

1984. Celebrities and Events. Multicoloured.

723	50f. Type **180** (postage)	1·10	10
724	200f. Henri Dunant and battle scene	2·40	50
725	300f. Early telephone and satellite receiving station, Goonhilly Downs	3·25	80
726	350f. President Kennedy and first foot-print on Moon	4·00	95
727	400f. Infra-red satellite picture (Europe–Africa co-operation) (air)	4·75	1·10
728	500f. Prince and Princess of Wales	5·50	1·40
MS729	60×110 mm. 600f. Wedding of Prince and Princess of Wales	6·50	1·90

181 "Communications"

1984. World Communications Year.

730	**181**	50f. mult (postage)	55	10
731	**181**	60f. multicoloured	75	15
732	**181**	70f. multicoloured	90	30
733	**181**	125f. multicoloured (air)	1·50	35
734	**181**	250f. multicoloured	2·75	1·10

182 Two-man Kayak

1984. Air. Olympic Games, Los Angeles (3rd issue). Multicoloured.

735	100f. Type **182**	1·10	45
736	200f. Kayaks (close-up)	2·20	85
737	300f. One-man kayak	2·75	1·30
738	400f. Coxed fours	3·75	1·70
MS739	104×80 mm. 500f. Coxless four	5·25	2·75

183 Class 13 Kitson Steam Locomotive

1984. Historic Transport. Multicoloured.

740	50f. Type **183** (postage)	95	25
741	200f. Sailing boat on Lake Chad	2·50	90
742	300f. Graf Zeppelin (airship)	4·75	1·40
743	350f. Six-wheel Renault automobile, 1930	4·50	1·70
744	400f. Bloch "120" airplane (air)	4·75	1·90
745	500f. Douglas "DC-8" airplane	5·75	2·30
MS746	84×109 mm. 600f. Ariane space rocket and "Intelsat V" communications satellite	6·75	4·00

184 African with broken Manacles

1984. Second Anniv of Entrance of Government Forces in N'Djamena.

747	**184**	50f. multicoloured	75	40

185 Pres. Hissein Habre

1984

748	**185**	125f. black, blue & yellow	1·80	75

186 British East Indiaman

1984. Transport. Multicoloured. (a) Ships.

749	90f. Type **186**	1·20	50
750	125f. *Vera Cruz* (steamer)	1·90	75
751	200f. *Carlisle Castle* (sail merchantman)	3·25	1·20
752	300f. *Britannia* (steamer)	4·50	1·60

(b) Locomotives.

753	100f. Series 701, 1885, France	1·60	45
754	150f. *Columbia*, 1888, Belgium	1·90	75
755	250f. Mediterranean locomotive, 1900, Italy	3·25	1·10
756	350f. MAV 114	4·50	1·70

187 Virgin and Child

1984. Christmas.

757	**187**	50f. brown and blue	60	20
758	**187**	60f. brown and orange	70	30
759	**187**	80f. brown and green	90	45
760	**187**	85f. brown and purple	60	40
761	**187**	100f. brown and orange	1·50	55
762	**187**	135f. brown and blue	1·60	85

188 Guitars

1985. European Music Year. Multicoloured.

763	20f. Type **188**	30	10
764	25f. Harps	35	10
765	30f. Xylophones	40	20
766	50f. Drums	55	40
767	70f. As No. 766	90	45
768	80f. As No. 764	1·10	50
769	100f. Type **188**	1·50	70
770	250f. As No. 765	3·00	1·40

189 *Chlorophyllum molybdites*

1985. Fungi. Multicoloured.

771	25f. Type **189**	50	10
772	30f. *Tulostoma volvulatum*	70	10
773	50f. *Lentinus tuberregium*	90	40
774	70f. As No. 773	1·30	50
775	80f. *Podaxis pistillaris*	1·50	55
776	100f. Type **189**	2·20	85

190 Stylized Tree and Scout

1985. Air. "Philexafrique" Stamp Exhibition, Lome, Togo (1st issue). Multicoloured.

777	200f. Type **190**	3·00	2·30
778	200f. Fokker "27" airplane	3·00	2·30

See also Nos. 808/9.

191 Abraham Lincoln

1985. Celebrities. Multicoloured.

779	25f. Type **191** (postage)	35	10
780	45f. Henri Dunant (founder of Red Cross)	80	10
781	50f. Gottlieb Daimler (automobile designer)	85	20
782	60f. Louis Bleriot (pilot) (air)	1·00	30
783	80f. Paul Harris (founder of Rotary International)	1·10	50
784	350f. Auguste Piccard (undersea explorer)	5·00	1·70
MS785	78×75 mm. 600f. Anatoly Karpov (chess champion)	7·75	4·25

192 Figures within Geometric Pattern

1985. International Youth Year. Multicoloured.

786	70f. Type **192**	80	35
787	200f. Figures on ribbon around globe	2·00	1·20

193 Sun and Hands breaking through Darkness

1985. Third Anniv of Entrance of Government Forces in N'DJamena. Multicoloured.

788	70f. Type **193**	85	40
789	70f. Claw attacking hand	85	40
790	70f. Pres. Hissein Habre (36×48 mm)	85	40
791	110f. Type **193**	1·50	85
792	110f. As No. 789	1·50	85
793	110f. As No. 790	1·50	85

194 Saddle-bill Stork ("Jabiru")

1985. Birth Bicentenary of John J. Audubon (ornithologist).

794	**194**	70f. black, blue & brown	1·20	60
795	—	110f. olive, green & brown	1·70	85
796	—	150f. blue, red and olive	2·40	1·20